The Concise Columbia Encyclopedia

THIRD EDITION

The Concise Columbia ENCYCLOPEDIA

THIRD EDITION

COLUMBIA UNIVERSITY PRESS

Sold and Distributed by

HOUGHTON MIFFLIN COMPANY

Columbia University Press
New York

Printed in the United States of America

Casebound editions of Columbia University Press books are printed on permanent and durable acid-free paper.

Library of Congress Cataloging-in-Publication Data

The concise Columbia encyclopedia.—3rd ed.
p. cm.
ISBN 0–395–62439–8 (alk. paper)
1. Encyclopedias and dictionaries.
AG5.C737 1994
031—dc20 94–16721
CIP

A World of Knowledge at Your Fingertips

Depend upon it, there comes a time when for every addition of knowledge you forget something that you knew before. It is of the highest importance, therefore, not to have useless facts elbowing out the useful ones.

—Sherlock Holmes, in Sir Arthur Conan's Doyle's *Study in Scarlet*, ch. 2

Mixing one's wines may be a mistake, but old and new wisdom mix admirably.

—The Singer, in the Prologue of Bertolt Brecht's *The Caucasian Chalk Circle*

This third edition of *The Concise Columbia Encyclopedia* places an extraordinary amount of information about the world in handy form at your fingertips. Thousands of facts, old and new, have been assembled to provide useful information on the topics we believe you are most likely to ask as you sit at your desk at home, at school, or in the office. For how long did the lives of Sir Arthur Conan Doyle and Bertolt Brecht overlap? Where is the Caucasus? What is ASCII? What is NAFTA? MRI? To search for and find answers to such questions is to gain knowledge, to advance a step further each time on the road to wisdom. We have tried to make your seeking and finding as easy and pleasurable as possible.

Coverage

The world of knowledge we are putting in your hands encompasses the areas and countries of our planet, the significant events from prehistory to the present, the people who have made history or are making it today. But its boundaries also include our knowledge of the universe as revealed by the most searching telescopes and microscopes, a myriad of life forms besides humanity, works created by nature as well as by people, and of course the abstract worlds of imagination and theory.

Versatility

We have made *The Concise Columbia Encyclopedia* versatile. Its entries are short, so you can check facts fast. But you can also pursue a train of thought in several articles by means of its system of cross-references. When a term within an article is spelled in small capitals, it has a separate article of its own. That article may itself contain terms in small capitals, pointing you to further lines of research you may wish to pursue. This system allows us to present a great quantity of information without duplication. We convey the information about each object, person, place, event, or idea in full sentences as simply and elegantly as possible. We have written the book not only to be dipped into, but settled into.

Currency

Knowledge is not static and neither is the world. Among all the events that have occurred since the publication of the second edition of *The Concise Columbia Encyclopedia,* surely nothing can compare, in its effect on a many-articled, closely interrelated work such as this, with the collapse of Communism in many parts of the world. But thousands of other articles have also been changed for this third edition to take account of all the new leaders, new population figures, new awards, new world records, new events, all those topics that have come to the front of our minds in the mid-1990s.

Authority

To help us ensure the accuracy of our information, we enlisted the help of academic consultants and advisers. At Columbia University and elsewhere we consulted authorities with specialized knowledge of anthropology, architecture, art, astronomy, bioethics, biology, botany, business, chemistry, computer science, dance, economics, education, geography, history, language and linguistics, literature, medicine, music, mythology, philosophy, physics, politics and political science, psychology, religion, sociology, sports, technology, theater and motion pictures, and many more subjects. Our thanks to these consultants and advisers can be found immediately after this preface.

The Articles

In order to convey so much information in a book that is as easy to use at your desk as a telephone or a calculator, we have followed some necessary principles. Our articles always go beyond the mere definitions you would find in a dictionary. We provide context. On the other hand, we do not summarize the very broadest topics, such as "literature." And our entries in "modern art" and "education" point you to the separate articles that are more likely to be the objects of your search. We have used the Pinyin system for the transliteration of Chinese names selectively, keeping traditional transliterations where they would be expected. We have given pronunciation for proper names that may be difficult to pronounce and for languages and language families. The key to pronunciation is on page xiii. We give metric equivalents for measurements in English standard units, and provide a list of abbreviations on page xiv.

The Maps, Photographs, Drawings, and Tables

The most notable change between the second and third editions of *The Concise Columbia Encyclopedia* is that the book is now more heavily illustrated. Maps now accompany the articles on the continents and countries—visually locating every single country in its immediate geographical environment. Photographs bring people to life before you, exemplify styles mentioned in articles, or present works of art discussed. Drawings help you understand some subjects more easily than words can, and tables collect related facts that would otherwise be scattered throughout the book. We hope that you will derive as much use from *The Concise Columbia Encyclopedia*'s third edition as we have had pleasure in trying to make it useful.

James Raimes

Staff

Editor	Paul G. Lagassé
Assistant Editors	Lora Goldman, Bonny R. Hart, Alan D. Levy
Publisher	John D. Moore
Project Director	James Raimes
Director of Design and Production	Audrey Smith
Art Director	Teresa Bonner
Designer	Ann Gold
Cartographer	Christopher L. Brest
Photo Researcher	Patricia Burns
Art Supervisor	Heather Saunders
Copy Chief	Jonathan Director
Copy checkers	William Bramlette, Suzanne Cogan, Emulsion-Down Typographers, Lynne Glasner, Andrew G. Lawrence, Jane Dickler Lebow, Katherine A. Lebow, Leah Schanzer

Acknowledgments

The information in this third edition of *The Concise Columbia Encyclopedia* derives not only from the information in the first and second editions, but also from the information in the fifth edition of *The Columbia Encyclopedia*, the closely related work published in 1993. We would therefore like to acknowledge the work of the editors of these books. Judith S. Levey and Agnes Greenhall were the editors of the first edition of *The Concise Columbia Encyclopedia*, and Barbara A. Chernow and George A. Vallasi were the editors of the second edition. Barbara A. Chernow and George A. Vallasi were also the editors of the fifth edition of *The Columbia Encyclopedia*. We thank them again here for their excellent work managing the large team of researchers and writers whose names appear in that work. We thank Robert Rosenbaum for his help updating *The Concise Columbia Encyclopedia* in 1990.

We would also like to thank the following academic specialists who worked on this edition of *The Concise Columbia Encyclopedia* or on the fifth edition of *The Columbia Encyclopedia*.

Consultants for the latter were: in the Humanities, Peter J. Awn; in History, Richard Bulliet; in Geography, Saul B. Cohen; in the Social Sciences, Kelvin J. Lancaster; in the Life Sciences, Don Melnick; in the Physical Sciences, Erick J. Weinberg.

Advisers on areas in the humanities were: African Literature, Susan Hall; American Art, Jonathan K. Crary; American Literature, Andrew Delbanco; Ancient Religion, Holland Hendrix; Architecture, Adolf K. Placzek; the Bible, Richard A. Norris; British Literature up to Dickens, David Scott Kastan; British Literature since Dickens, Michael Seidel; Dance, Irish M. Fanger; East Asian Literature, Marsha L. Wagner; Eastern and Primitive (and other) Art, Vidya Dehejia; Eastern Religion, Paul B. Watt; European Art up to 1600, John Malcolm Russell; European Art since 1600, Janis Thomlinson; Film and Drama, Maurice Charney; French Literature, Antoine Compagnon; German, Dutch, and Yiddish Literature, Inge D. Halpert; Islam, Ali Asani; Italian Literature, Luigi Fontanella and Maristella Lorch; Judaism, Jay harris; Latin and Greek Literature, Holland Hendrix; Minority Religion, Robert Ellwood; Music, Ian Bent, Tom Baker, and James T. Walsh; Philosophy, Charles Larmore; Popular Music, Monica Berger; Print and Broadcast Journalism, Osborn Elliott; Protestantism, Pamela Biel; Roman Catholicism, Robert Somerville; Russian and Slavic Literature, William E. Harkins; Spanish-American Literature, Diane Marting; Spanish, Portuguese, and Brazilian Literature, Irwin Stern.

Advisers on areas in the Social Sciences were: Anthropology and Archaeology, Robert Carneiro; Business, Economics, and Labor, Donald Dewey; Education, Lawrence Cremin and Ellen Condliffe Lagemann; Language, William Labov and Deborah Mandelbaum; Law, Vincent Blasi; Political Science and Government, Robert Jervis; Sociology, Sigmund Diamond; Sports and Games, Benjamin Rader.

Advisers in History were: Africa, Graham Irwin and David Northrup; Ancient History, W.V. Harris; China, Japan, and Korea up to 1900, Gari Ledyard and Robert Hymes; China, Japan, and Korea since 1900, Madeleine Zelin; France, Belgium, and Luxembourg since 1500, Isser Woloch; Germany, Austria, Switzerland, Holland, and Scandinavia since 1600, Willem Smit; Great Britain, Ireland, Australia, and New Zealand up to 1837, Karl Bottigheimer; Great Britain, Ireland, Australia, and New Zealand since 1837, David Cannadine; India and South East Asia, Ainslie T. Embree; Japan and the Pacific Rim since 1900, Carol Gluck and Daniel A. Metraux; Latin America, Robert M. Levine; Medieval Europe, Caroline Walker Bynum; Middle East, North Africa, and Central Asia, Reeva S. Simon; Military History, Alex Roland; Russia and East Europe, Mark Von Hagen; Spain, Portugal, Italy, and Greece since 1500, Edward Malefakis; U.S. History up to 1860; Martin Torodash; U.S. and Canadian History, 1860–1939, James P. Shenton; U.S. and Canadian History since 1939, Mark Carnes.

Advisers in the Life Sciences were: Agriculture, Kenneth Robinson and William C. Kennard; Anatomy and Physiology, Jeffrey T. Laitman and Ermelinda Bonaccio; Botany, Douglas C. Daly; Cell Biology, Biochemistry, and Genetics, Eric Holtzman; Environmental Studies and Conservation, Mary C. Pearl; Food and Nutrition, Ellen C. Dierenfeld and Sharon Akabas; Invertebrate Zoology, Judith E. Winston; Medicine, John D. Frame; Pathology, Stephen M. Factor; Psychology and Psychiatry, Irving I. Gottesman; Vertebrate Zoology, John L. Gittleman.

Advisers in Geography were: Africa, James L. Newman; Australia, Janice Monk; Canada, Victor Konrad; China, Clifton W. Pannell; East Europe, William Berentsen; Former Soviet Union, Baltic Nations, and Italy, Allan Rodgers; France, Julian V. Minghi; Germany, Austria, and Switzerland, Robert Sinclair; Great Britain and Ireland, Neil Reid; Japan and Korea, Kenneth E. Corey; Low Countries, Robert Aangenbrug; Mexico, Central America, and the Caribbean, Thomas D. Boswell; Middle East, Rowland Illick; New Zealand, Gordon R. Lewthwaite; Pacific Islands, Tom McKnight; Polar Regions, Charles R. Bentley; Scandinavia, Robert Ostergren; South America, David J. Robinson; South Asia, John E. Brush; South East Asia, Richard Ulack; Spain and Portugal, Daniel W. Gade; Turkey, Greece, Cyprus, and Malta, Ian R. Manners; United States, Peter O. Muller.

Advisers in the Physical Sciences were: Astronomy, David Helfand and Edwin G. Abel; Earth Sciences, John Mutter; Electrical Engineering, Computers, Chemical Engineering, and Mining, H.E. Meadows, Edwin G. Abel, and Keith Barker; General and Organic Chemistry, Robert M. Kennedy and Edwin G. Abel; Inorganic Chemistry, Metallurgy, and Crystallography, Gerard Parkin; Mathematics, Hyman Bass; Mechanical Engineering, Civil Engineering, and Aerospace, C.K. Chu and Robert A. Gross; Physics, Gerald Feinberg and Erick J. Weinberg.

Photo Credits

We are grateful to the following copyright owners for permission to reproduce photographs found at the articles listed.

Alinari/Art Resource, NY: Baroque; Brunelleschi, Filippo; Egyptian architecture; Parthenon Art Resource, NY: Bison; Escher, M.C.; Pisa; Schiele, Egon

Bettmann Archives: Bergman, Ingrid; Brady, Matthew; Cactus; Chaplin, Charlie; Concentration camp; Dewey, John; Douglass, Frederick; Engels, Friedrich; Gates, Bill; Graham, Martha; Johns, Jasper; Kitchener, Horatio; Lange, Dorothea; Lenin, Vladimir; Nast, Thomas; Perelman, S.J.; Taylor, Elizabeth; Thomas, Dylan; Wagner, Richard; Yalta Conference

Bridgeman/Art Resource, NY: Raeburn, Sir Henry

The British Tourist Authority: Hampton; Stonehenge

Foto Marburg/Art Resource, NY: Amiens; Corot, Jean-Baptiste; Courbet, Gustave; Gropius, Walter; Tutankhamen

German Informational Center, NY: Berlin

Giraudon/Art Resource, NY: Commedia dell'arte; Indus Valley civilization; Merovingian art; Whistler, James

The Metropolitan Museum of Art, Sansbury-Mills Fund, 1952: Blake engraving; Chippendale, Thomas; Hokusai; Japanese art; Silhouette; Stieglitz, Alfred

NASA: Hubble, Edwin

National Baseball Library and Archive, Cooperstown, NY: Cobb, Ty; Koufax, Sandy

Photofest: Charles, Ray; Coleman, Ornette; Franklin, Aretha; Gillespie, Dizzy; Hepburn, Katharine; Hitchcock, Alfred; Karloff, Boris; Markova, Dame Alicia; Monk, Thelonius; Pickford, Mary; Pryor, Richard; Ray, Satyajit; Shepard, Sam; Welles, Orson

Rakoczky/Art Resource, NY: Machu Picchu

Reuters/Bettmann Archive: Davis, Miles; Diana, Princess

Scala/Art Resource, NY: Lorenzetti; Norman architecture

Springer/Bettmann Film Archive: Fellini, Federico; Hemingway, Ernest; LaGuardia, Fiorello

Tate Gallery, London/Art Resource, NY: Moore, Henry

UPI/Bettmann Archive: Begin, Menachem; Boa; Brooks, Gwendolyn; Connors, Jimmy; Friedan, Betty: Gonzales, Pancho; Lombardi, Vince; Mandela, Nelson; Marathon race; Mboya, Thomas; Mencken, H.L.; Nureyev, Rudolf; Oppenheimer, Robert; Orr, Bobby; Ride, Sally; Roosevelt, Eleanor and Franklin Delano; Schweitzer, Albert; Shaw, George Bernard; Stein, Gertrude; Warhol, Andy; Williams, Ted

Vanni/Art Resource, NY: Beaubourg; Pei, I.M.

Victoria and Albert Museum/Art Resource, NY: Rietveld, Gerrit

Werner Forman/Art Resource, NY: Canyon de Chelly; Luoyang

Photo Jerry Thompson, courtesy Whitney Museum of American Art: Whitney Museum

How to Use the Concise Columbia Encyclopedia

The Concise Columbia Encyclopedia is easy to use. All articles are arranged alphabetically, with article heads in **boldface.** The headings of biographical articles are inverted and alphabetized by the subject's name, e.g., the American composer Stephen Foster appears as **Foster, Stephen Collins.** Exceptions to this rule are made for some figures from history and folklore, e.g., the African-American folk hero John Henry is listed as **John Henry.**

Generally, articles with the same heading are alphabetized in order of persons, places, and things, so that **Washington, George** comes before **Washington** (state), which in turn comes before **Washington, Treaty of.** The order of alphabetization for persons is determined by rank: saints, popes, emperors, monarchs, followed by titled nobility. Monarchs of the same name are listed alphabetically by country and numerically within the country; thus all kings Charles of France appear before any kings Charles of Spain.

The method of alphabetization disregards word breaks. **Capetians,** for example, appears before **Cape Town,** and **artillery** before **art nouveau.** The following special cases of alphabetization should also be noted: (1) Names with **von, de,** and similar prefixes, are alphabetized using the most common form of the name: **Van Gogh, Vincent,** but **Bismarck, Otto von.** (2) Names beginning with **Mc** and **Mac** are treated as though they begin with **Mac;** thus **McGuffey, William Holmes** appears before **Mach, Ernst.** (3) Abbreviations in article headings are treated as though they were spelled out: **St. Clair, Arthur** appears before **Saint Clair, Lake.** (4) Japanese and Chinese names are listed in the traditional order, surname first, without a comma, e.g., **Hosokawa Morihiro;** Americans of Japanese descent are listed in the Western style, e.g., **Noguchi, Isamu.**

Family Articles. In an effort to save space, we have combined similarly named rulers of certain empires and nations into a single article; thus all 18 kings of France named Louis appear as easily recognizable entries under the heading "**Louis,** Frankish kings and kings of France." Likewise, members of the same family are sometimes grouped together: for example, the Rockefellers appear under the heading "**Rockefeller,** family of American industrialists, bankers, and philanthropists." When a family member has been particularly prominent outside the family tradition, however, he or she has a separate entry, as does former U.S. Vice President Nelson Rockefeller.

Some related subjects have also been covered under a single article: for example, air and water pollution have been included in the article **pollution,** and a discussion of the Bill of Rights can be found under the entry **Constitution of the United States.**

Titles of Foreign Works. The titles of works of literature, art, music, and dance are given in English unless the work is well known under the original foreign title. The dates accompanying such works are the dates of original publication, exhibition, or performance.

Cross-references. To utilize space efficiently, whenever possible, information included in one article is not repeated in another. Instead, cross-references are used extensively to lead the reader to articles containing additional material relevant to the entry he or she is consulting. These articles may expand upon the subject at hand, provide background (including important people), or supply clues to other aspects of the subject and to related topics. Because it provides immediate access to pertinent information, this network of cross-references also replaces an index. All cross-references appear in SMALL CAPITALS.

Basically there are four types of cross-references. The first type comprises those found within the text of an article, as at the beginning of the article **solar energy:**

> . . . any form of ENERGY radiated by the SUN, including light, radio waves, and X rays. Solar energy is needed by green plants for the process of PHOTOSYNTHESIS, which is the ultimate source of all food. The energy in fossil fuels (e.g., COAL and PETROLEUM) and other or-

ganic fuels (e.g., WOOD) is derived from solar energy. . . .

The second type of cross-reference consists of those found at the end of an article, referring the reader to related subjects, including biographies. For example:

computer . . . See also ANALOG-TO-DIGITAL CONVERSION; ARTIFICIAL INTELLIGENCE; BAUD; BOOLEAN ALGEBRA; DIGITAL-TO-ANALOG CONVERSION; PROGRAMMING LANGUAGE; VIDEOTEX.

philosophy . . . The many rigorous systems of Eastern philosophy are founded in religion (see BUDDHISM; CONFUCIANISM; HINDUISM; ISLAM; JAINISM; SHINTO; TAOISM; VEDANTA). See also names of individual philosophers, e.g., NIETZSCHE, FRIEDRICH; SCHOPENHAUER, ARTHUR; TEILHARD DE CHARDIN, PIERRE.

Cross-references also refer the reader to tables that combine a variety of facts directly relevant to the article being consulted. For example, at the end of the article on the element **argon,** the following cross-references appear: See ELEMENT (table); PERIODIC TABLE.

The third type of cross-reference appears as a boldface entry within the alphabetical sequence. It may be an acronym (**COBOL:** see PROGRAMMING LANGUAGE); an alternate spelling (**Chou En-lai:** see ZHOU ENLAI) or name (**infantile paralysis:** see POLIOMYELITIS); a real name when a person is known under a pseudonym (**Clemens, Samuel Langhorne:** see TWAIN, MARK); a topic discussed under an entry other than its own name (**alto:** see VOICE); or it may direct the reader to a number of related articles (**firearm:** see ARTILLERY; GUN; SMALL ARMS).

A special category of cross-reference, somewhat different from the three previously mentioned, consists of those referring to a boldface subentry under a main heading. Such cross-references can occur within an article or as a separate entry; often, for clarity, the words "see under" are used. An example of such a cross-reference in the text of an article is that to John Wilkes Booth in the article **Lincoln, Abraham**: ". . . he was shot by the actor John Wilkes Booth (see under BOOTH, JUNIUS BRUTUS)." Two examples of these cross-references as separate entries are: **Richard Lion-Heart:** see Richard I under RICHARD, kings of England; and **Passover:** see under JEWISH HOLIDAYS.

Abbreviations. Although abbreviations have been kept to a minimum, some have been adopted to save space. They usually appear in special constructions designed to convey important information at a glance—as can be seen, for example, in the first sentence of the article on the Churchill River: "**Churchill,** river, NE Canada, called the Hamilton R. until renamed (1965) for Sir Winston Churchill." Common abbreviations include those for compass points, the months of the year, the states of the United States, and such words as Corporation (Corp.) and graduated (grad.). Other, less familiar abbreviations appear in the list entitled "Abbreviations."

Key to Pronunciation

ə sof*a* (sō'fə), it*e*m (ī'təm), eas*i*ly (ē'zəlē), cann*o*n (kăn'ən), circ*u*s (sûr'kəs)
ă *a*ct (ăkt), b*a*t (băt)
ā *a*pe (āp), f*ai*l (fāl), d*a*y (dā)
â *ai*r (âr), c*a*re (kâr)
ä *a*rt (ärt), f*a*ther (fä'~~th~~ər)
b *b*ack (băk), la*b*or (lā'bər), ca*b* (kăb)
ch *ch*in (chĭn), ha*tch*et (hăch'ət), ri*ch* (rĭch)
d *d*ock (dŏk), la*d*y (lā'dē), sa*d* (săd)
ĕ *e*nd (ĕnd), st*ea*dy (stĕd'ē), m*e*t (mĕt)
ē *e*ve (ēv), cl*ea*r (klēr), s*ee* (sē)
f *f*at (făt), *ph*ase (fāz), cou*gh* (kôf)
g *g*et (gĕt), bi*gg*er (bĭg'ər), ta*g* (tăg)
h *h*and (hănd), a*h*ead (əhĕd')
hw *wh*eel (hwēl), *wh*ich (hwĭch)
ĭ *i*t (ĭt), p*i*ll (pĭl), m*i*rror (mĭr'ər)
ī *i*ron (ī'ərn), *eye* (ī), b*uy*er (bī'ər)
j *j*am (jăm), *g*inger (jĭn'jər), e*dg*e (ĕj)
k *k*it (kĭt), ta*ck*le (tak'əl), *c*oo*k* (ko͝ok)
l *l*itt*l*e (lĭt'əl), ho*ll*y (hŏl'ē), pu*ll* (po͝ol)
m *m*an (măn), ha*mm*er (hăm'ər), cli*mb* (klīm)
n *n*ew (no͝o), *kn*ow*n* (nōn), wi*nn*er (wĭn'ər)
ng si*ng*i*ng* (sĭng'ĭng), fi*n*ger (fĭng'gər), sa*ng* (săng), sa*n*k (săngk)
ŏ h*o*t (hŏt), b*o*dy (bŏd'ē)
ō *o*ver (ō'vər), h*o*pe (hōp), gr*ow* (grō)
ô *o*rbit (ôr'bit), f*a*ll (fôl), s*aw* (sô)
o͝o f*oo*t (fo͝ot), w*o*lf (wo͝olf), p*u*t (po͝ot), p*u*re (pyo͝or)
o͞o b*oo*t (bo͞ot), l*o*se (lo͞oz), dr*ew* (dro͞o), tr*ue* (tro͞o)
oi *oi*l (oil), r*oy*al (roi'əl), b*oy* (boi)
ou *ou*t (out), cr*ow*d (kroud), h*ow* (hou)
p *p*i*p*e (pīp), ha*pp*y (hăp'ē)
r *r*oad (rōd), appea*r*ed (əpērd'), ca*r*pente*r* (kr̆'pəntər)
s *s*o (sō), *c*ite (sīt), ba*s*te (bāst)
sh *sh*all (shăl), *s*ure (sho͝or), na*t*ion (nā'shən)
t *t*ight (tīt), be*tt*er (bĕt'ər), *t*alke*d* (tôkt)
th *th*in (thĭn), ba*th* (băth)
~~th~~ *th*en (~~th~~ĕn), fa*th*er (fä'~~th~~ər), ba*th*e (bā~~th~~)
ŭ b*u*t (bŭt), fl*oo*d (flŭd), s*o*me (sŭm)
û c*u*rl (kûrl), g*i*rl (gûrl), f*e*rn (fûrn), w*o*rm (wûrm)
v *v*est (vĕst), tri*v*ial (trĭv'ēəl), e*v*e (ēv)
w *w*ax (wăks), t*w*ins (twĭnz), co*w*ard (kou'ərd)
y *y*ou (yo͞o), on*i*on (ŭn'yən)
z *z*ipper (zĭp'ər), ea*s*e (ēz), tread*s* (trĕdz)
zh plea*s*ure (plĕzh'ər), rou*g*e (ro͞ozh)

Foreign Sounds
ö as in French p*eu* (pö), German G*oe*the (gö'tə)
ü as in French Cl*u*ny (klünē')
kh as in German a*ch* (äkh), i*ch* (ĭkh); Scottish lo*ch* (lŏkh)
N this symbol indicates that the preceding vowel is nasal as in French c*in*q (săNk), *un* (öN), s*an*s (säN), t*om*be (tôNb), *en* (äN)

Accents and Hyphens
' primary accent, written after accented vowel or syllable: Nebraska (nəbrăs'kə), James Buchanan (byo͞okă'nən)
" secondary accent: Mississippi (mĭs"əs-sĭp'ē)
– dash, replacing obvious portion of pronunciation: hegemony (hĭjĕm'ənē, hē–, hēj'əmō"nē, hĕg'ə–)
\- hyphen, to prevent ambiguity in syllabification: Erlanger (ûr'lăng-ər), dishearten (dĭs-här'tən)

Abbreviations

Å = angstrom
abbr. = abbreviation(s), abbreviated
A.D. = *anno Domini* [in the year of the Lord]
Adm. = Admiral
Afrik. = Afrikaans
alt. = altitude
Alta. = Alberta
Arab. = Arabic
AU = astronomical unit(s)
AV = Authorized Version (King James Version)
b. = born, born in
B.C. = Before Christ
B.C. = British Columbia
Brig. Gen. = Brigadier General
Bulg. = Bulgarian
C = Celsius (centigrade)
c. = *circa* [about]
cal = calorie(s)
cant. = Canticles (Song of Solomon)
Capt. = Captain
cc = cubic centimeter(s)
Cent. = century, centuries
Chin. = Chinese
Chron. = Chronicles
cm = centimeter(s)
cm/sec^2 = centimeter(s) per second per second
Co. = Company; County
Col. = Colonel, Colossians
Coll. = Collection
Comdr. = Commander
Cor. = Corinthians
Cpl. = Corporal
cu = cubic
d. = died, died in
Dan. = Daniel; Danish
Deut. = Deuteronomy
dist. = district
Du. = Dutch
E = east, eastern
Eccles. = Ecclesiastes
Ecclus. = Ecclesiasticus
e.g. = *exempli gratia* [for example]
Eng. = English
Eph. = Ephesians
est. = established; estimated
eV = electron volts
Ex. = Exodus
Ezek. = Ezekiel
F = Fahrenheit; farad
Finn. = Finnish
fl. = *floruit* [flourished]
Fr. = French
ft = foot, feet
ft/sec^2 = feet per second per second
G = gram
Gal. = Galatians
gal. = gallon(s)
Gall. = Gallery
Gen. = General, Genesis
Ger. = German
Gov. = Governor
Gr. = Greek
^{h} = hour(s)
Hab. = Habakkuk
Hag. = Haggai
Heb. = Hebrew; Hebrews (New Testament)
H.M.S. = His (Her) Majesty's Ship; His (Her) Majesty's Service
Hon. = the Honorable
hr = hour(s)
Hung. = Hungarian
Hz = hertz or cycle(s) per second
Icel. = Icelandic
i.e. = *id est* [that is]
in. = inch(es)
inc. = incorporated
Isa. = Isaiah
Ital. = Italian
j = joule(s)
Jap. = Japanese
Jer. = Jeremiah
K = Kelvin
kg = kilogram(s)
km = kilometer(s)
kw = kilowatt(s)
Lam. = Lamentations
Lat. = Latin
lat. = latitude
Lev. = Leviticus
Lib. = Library
lim = limit
Lith. = Lithuanian
long. = longitude
Lt. = Lieutenant
m = meter(s)
^{m} = minute(s)
m/sec^2 = meters per second per second
Mac. = Maccabees
Mal. = Malachi
Man. = Manitoba
Mat. = Matthew
MeV = million electron volts
Mex. = Mexican
mg = milligram(s)
mi = mile(s)
min = minute(s)
mm = milimeter(s)
Mod. = Modern
mph = miles per hour
Msgr = Monsignor
Mus. = Museum
Mw = megawatt(s)
N = north; northern
N.B. = New Brunswick
Neh. = Nehemiah
N.F. = Newfoundland
Nor. = Norwegian
N.S. = New Style; Nova Scotia
Num. = Numbers
N.Y.C. = New York City
Obad. = Obadiah
O.E. = Old English
O.N. = Old Norse
Ont. = Ontario
O.S. = Old Style
oz = ounce(s)
P.E.I. = Prince Edward Island
Pers. = Persian
Philip. = Philippians
pl. = plural
Pol. = Polish
pop. = population
Port. = Portuguese
Pres. = President
Prime Min. = Prime Minister
Prov. = Proverbs
prov(s). = province(s)
pseud. = pseudonym
Pss. = Psalms
pt = pint(s)
pt. = part(s)
pub. = published
qt = quart(s)
Que. = Quebec
R = river
r. = reigned
Rep. = Representative
Rev. = Revelation; the Reverend
Rom. = Romans
rpm = revolution(s) per minute
RSV = Revised Standard Version
Rum. = Rumanian
Rus. = Russian
RV = Revised Version
S = south, southern
^{s} = second(s)
Sam. = Samuel
Sask. = Saskatchewan
Secy. = Secretary
Sen. = Senator
Sgt. = Sergeant
Skt. = Sanskrit
Song = Song of Solomon
Span. = Spanish
sq = square
S.S. = Steamship
SSR = Soviet Socialist Republic
Swed. = Swedish
Thess. = Thessalonians
Tim. = Timothy
tr. = translation
Turk. = Turkish
Ukr. = Ukrainian
UN = United Nations
uninc. = unincorporated
U.S. = United States
U.S.S. = United States Ship
USSR = Union of Soviet Socialist Republics
v. = versus
V = volt(s)
var. = variety (in botany)
Vice Pres. = Vice President
vol. = volume(s)
W = west; western; watt(s)
wt. = weight
yd = yard(s)
Zech. = Zechariah
Zeph. = Zephaniah

The Concise Columbia Encyclopedia

THIRD EDITION

A

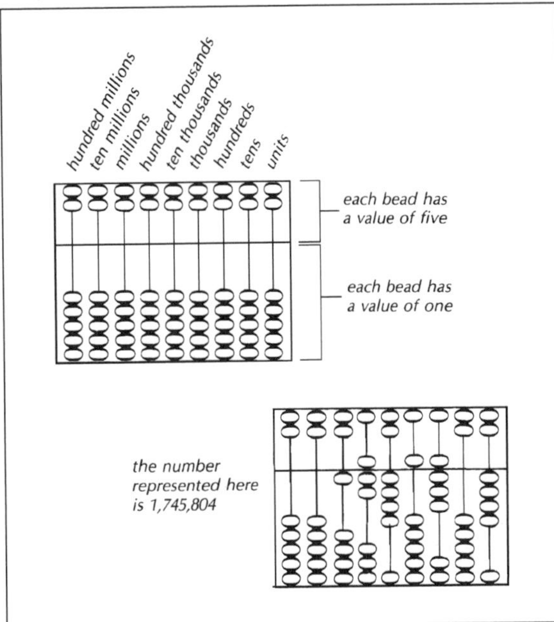

Chinese abacus: Numbers are represented by moving beads to the central crossbar

Aachen [ä'khən] or **Aix-la-Chapelle,** city (1989 est. pop. 233,000), North Rhine–Westphalia, W Germany. It is an industrial center producing textiles, machinery, and other manufactures. Its mineral baths have been famous since Roman times. CHARLEMAGNE made it his northern capital, building a palace and cathedral there, and the city was (936–1531) the coronation place of German kings. Later it was taken by France (1801) and then by Prussia (1815). After WORLD WAR I Aachen was occupied by the Allies, and two thirds of it was destroyed during WORLD WAR II.

Aalto, Alvar [äl'tō], 1896–1976, Finnish architect. He adapted Finnish building traditions to modern technology. Among his buildings are the Maison Carré in Paris and Baker House in Cambridge, Mass. (1947–48). He was also famous for his designs for laminated-wood furniture.

aardvark, nocturnal MAMMAL (genus *Orycteropus*) found in Africa. About 6 ft (180 cm) long, it has a long snout, large, erect ears, a body almost devoid of hair, and a long tail. It claws open ant and termite nests with its forefeet and uses its long, sticky tongue to capture insects.

Aaron, in the BIBLE, the first high priest, the brother of MOSES, and his spokesman. Through him Jehovah performed miracles, although Aaron had made the GOLDEN CALF and allowed its worship. His descendants became temple priests.

Aaron, Hank (Henry Louis Aaron), 1934–, American baseball player; b. Mobile, Ala. A right-handed batter, he played with the Braves (1954–74) in Milwaukee and Atlanta and with the Milwaukee Brewers (1975–76). In 1974 he broke Babe RUTH's career record for home runs, finishing with 755. He also holds records for runs batted in (2,297) and extra-base hits (1,477).

abacus, an ancient computing device using movable beads strung on a number of parallel wires within a frame. Each wire represents a decimal place: ones, tens, hundreds, and so on. The beads are grouped to form numbers and shifted in specified patterns to add, subtract, multiply, or divide.

Abadan, city (1976 pop. 296,081), Khuzestan prov., SW Iran, on Abadan Island, in the SHATT AL ARAB delta, at the head of the PERSIAN GULF. After oil was discovered (1908) nearby, Abadan became the terminus of oil pipelines and an oil-refining and shipping center. Iraqi forces damaged Abadan's oil refinery in their invasion of Khuzestan in 1980.

abalone, marine GASTROPOD mollusk (genus *Haliotis*), covered by a single ear-shaped shell perforated with respiratory holes on one side. The abalone is hunted for its large, edible muscular foot and the iridescent MOTHER-OF-PEARL lining of its shell, used for buttons. It feeds by scraping the substrate with its rasping tongue (radula).

Abbas I (Abbas the Great), 1557–1629, shah of PERSIA (1587–1628), of the Safavid dynasty. He broke the power of the tribal chiefs, ended the Uzbek threat, and extended his domain at the expense of the Turks and Portuguese.

Abbasid or **Abbaside,** Arabic family descended from **Abbas,** d. 653, the uncle of MUHAMMAD. They rose to power by massacring the ruling Umayyad family and held the CALIPHATE from 749 to 1258. Prominent Abbasid caliphs include al-MANSUR and HARUN AR-RASHID, under whom the caliphate reached its greatest power. The long Abbasid decline ended with their overthrow (13th cent.) by the Seljuk Turks.

Abbott, George, 1889–, American theatrical director and playwright; b. Forestville, N.Y. He was a master of FARCE and MUSICALS. His hits include *Three Men on a Horse* (1935), *Damn Yankees* (1955), and *Fiorello!* (1960; Pulitzer).

Abbott and Costello, American comedy team. Its members were William "Bud" Abbott, 1895–1974, and Lou (Cristillo) Costello, 1906–59. They performed (1931–57) routines ("Who's on First") on the stage, radio, and television and in a series of successful films, including *Buck Privates* (1941).

Abd al-Hamid, sultans of the OTTOMAN EMPIRE (Turkey). **Abd al-Hamid I,** 1725–89 (r.1774–89), witnessed the decline of Turkey and the rise of Russia as the foremost power in the area. **Abd al-Hamid II,** 1842–1918 (r.1876–1909), suspended (1876) the constitution and ruled as an absolute monarch. The last RUSSO-TURKISH WAR was a disaster, resulting in a great loss of Turkish lands. He was eventually deposed by the Young Turks.

Abd ar-Rahman, Muslim rulers of Spain. **Abd ar-Rahman,** d. 732, governor of Spain (721–32), fought the Franks and was defeated by CHARLES MARTEL. **Abd ar-Rahman I,** d. 788, first Umayyad emir of Córdoba (756–88), escaped to Spain after his family's massacre by the Abbasid. There he defeated (756) the emir of Córdoba and established himself in power. **Abd ar-Rahman III** (891–961), Umayyad emir and first caliph (929–61) of Córdoba, regained lands lost by his predecessors, maintained a powerful military force, and made Córdoba one of the greatest cities in the West.

Abdias: see OBADIAH.

abdomen, in vertebrates, portion of the trunk between the diaphragm and lower pelvis. In humans the abdominal cavity is lined with a thin membrane, the peritoneum, which encloses the STOMACH, intestines, LIVER, and GALL BLADDER. The PANCREAS, KIDNEYS, urinary bladder, and, in the female, reproductive organs are also located within the abdominal cavity. In insects and some other invertebrates the term *abdomen* refers to the rear portion of the body.

Abdul-Jabbar, Kareem, 1947–, American basketball player; b. N.Y.C. as Ferdinand Lewis ("Lew") Alcindor, Jr. He led the Univ. of California, Los Angeles, to three national titles (1967–69) and played center for the Milwaukee Bucks (1969–75) and Los Angeles Lakers (1975–89). The 7 ft 2 in. (218 cm) Abdul-Jabbar was rookie of the year in 1970, won most-valuable-player honors six times, played a record 1,560 NBA games, and scored a record 38,387 points.

Abdullah, 1882–1951, emir of Transjordan (1921–46) and king of JORDAN (1946–51). In the first ARAB-ISRAELI WAR he commanded the

Arab Legion and annexed those portions of Palestine not assigned to Israel.

à Becket, Thomas: see THOMAS À BECKET, SAINT.

Abe Kōbō, 1924–93, Japanese novelist and dramatist. Often compared to KAFKA, he wrote of the human predicament in the 20th cent. in a realistic yet symbolic style. His minute descriptions of surrealistic situations often lend his works a nightmarish quality. Among Abe's novels are *Woman in the Dunes* (tr. 1964) and *Secret Rendezvous* (tr. 1979). His plays include *Friends* (tr. 1969).

Abel, in the BIBLE, son of ADAM and EVE. A shepherd, he was killed by his brother CAIN.

Abel, I(orwith) W(ilbur), 1908–87, American labor leader; b. Magnolia, Ohio. He worked in a Canton rolling mill at 17 and was appointed (1937) staff representative of the organization that became the United Steelworkers of America. He was an Ohio district director of the union (1942–52), became (1953) secretary-treasurer, and served (1965–77) as president.

Abel, Niels Henrik, 1802–29, Norwegian mathematician. One of the greatest mathematicians of the 19th cent., he pioneered in the theory of elliptic functions, investigated generalizations of the binomial theorem, and proved the impossibility of representing a solution of a general equation of fifth degree or higher by a radical expression.

Abelard, Peter [ăb'əlärd], 1079–1142, French philosopher. Because his fame as a dialectician drew so many students, he is regarded as the founder of the Univ. of Paris. His secret marriage to a pupil, Heloïse, ended when her uncle, Canon Fulbert of Notre Dame, hired ruffians to emasculate him. Becoming a monk, he built a hermitage and monastery, the Paraclete, which he later presented to Heloïse, who had become an abbess. Abelard's first theological work had been burned (1121) as heretical; in 1140 the mystic St. BERNARD OF CLAIRVAUX secured his condemnation by the council of Sens, and he retired in submission to Cluny. Following PLATO in theology, Abelard espoused the method of ARISTOTLE's dialectic, holding that the system of LOGIC could be applied to the truths of faith. His view of universals anticipated the conceptualism of St. THOMAS AQUINAS. His most influential and controversial work, *Sic et non,* collected contradictory writings of the Church fathers.

Aberdeen, George Hamilton-Gordon, 4th **earl of,** 1784–1860, British statesman. He served in the cabinets of WELLINGTON and PEEL as foreign secretary (1828–30; 1841–46). In 1842 he settled the Northeast Boundary Dispute with the U.S. by the WEBSTER-ASHBURTON TREATY. As prime minister (1852–55) he was quite successful in home affairs, but he resigned after failing to prevent British involvement in the unpopular CRIMEAN WAR.

Aberhart, William, 1878–1943, premier of ALBERTA (1935–43). He helped to organize (c.1932) the SOCIAL CREDIT movement to make direct payments to all citizens and headed the first Social Credit government.

Abernathy, Ralph, 1926–90, American civil-rights leader; b. Linden, Ala. A Baptist minister, he helped organize the Montgomery bus boycott (1955). He was treasurer, vice president, and, after the assassination of Martin Luther KING, Jr., president of the Southern Christian Leadership Conference (SCLC). An advocate of nonviolence as a means to social change, he led the Poor People's Campaign on Washington, D.C., after King's death. He resigned from the SCLC in 1977.

aberration, in optics, condition that causes a blurring and loss of clearness in the images produced by lenses or mirrors. Spherical aberration is the failure of a LENS or MIRROR of spherical section to bring parallel rays of light to a single focus; it can be prevented by using a more complex parabolic section. Chromatic aberration, the blurred coloring at the edge of an image, arises because some colors of light are bent, or refracted, more than others after passing through a lens; it can be cured by using a corrective lens.

aberration of starlight, angular displacement, caused by the earth's orbital motion, of the apparent path of light from a star, resulting in a displacement of its apparent position from its true position.

Abidjan, city (1986 est. pop. 2,534,000), former capital of Côte d'Ivoire, on the Gulf of Guinea. It is the largest city and administrative center of Côte d'Ivoire. Its port is on an island connected with the rest of the city by two bridges. Coffee, cocoa, timber, pineapples, and plantains are the chief exports. Processed food, textiles, automobiles, and chemicals are among the manufactures. One of Africa's most modern cities, it has an international airport nearby and growing tourism. Abidjan became the capital of France's Côte d'Ivoire colony in 1934. In 1983 YAMOUSSOUKRO was designated as the capital, but most government offices and foreign embassies are still in Abidjan.

Abilene, city (1990 pop. 106,654), seat of Taylor co., W central Texas; inc. 1882. First settled (1881) by buffalo hunters, it grew as a cattle-shipping point. It is a center of industry (e.g., petroleum, aircraft, electronics) and agriculture (e.g., cattle, cotton, sorghum) and serves as headquarters for regional oil interests. It is the site of Abilene Christian Univ., Hardin-Simmons Univ., and McMurry College.

ABM (antiballistic missile): see MISSILE, GUIDED.

abolitionists, in U.S. history, especially from 1830 to 1860, advocates of the compulsory emancipation of African-American slaves. Abolitionists are to be distinguished from free-soilers, who opposed the extension of SLAVERY. The active campaign had its mainspring in the revival (1820s) in the North of evangelical religion, with its moral urgency to end sinful practices. It reached crusading stage in the 1830s, led by Theodore D. Weld, the brothers Arthur and Lewis Tappan, and William Lloyd GARRISON. The American Anti-Slavery Society, established in 1833, flooded the slave states with abolitionist literature and lobbied in Washington, D.C. Writers like J.G. WHITTIER and orators such as Wendell PHILLIPS lent strength to the cause. Despite unanimity on their goal, abolitionists were divided over the method of achieving it, Garrison advocating moral suasion, others direct political action. *Uncle Tom's Cabin,* by Harriet B. STOWE, became an effective piece of abolitionist propaganda, and the KANSAS question aroused both North and South. The culminating act of abolitionism was John BROWN's raid on Harpers Ferry. Abolitionist demands for immediate freeing of the slaves after the outbreak of the CIVIL WAR resulted in Pres. Lincoln's *Emancipation Proclamation.* The abolitionist movement was one of high moral purpose and courage; its uncompromising temper hastened the demise of slavery in the U.S.

abominable snowman or **yeti,** manlike creature associated with the Himalayas. Known through tracks ascribed to it and alleged encounters, it is supposedly 6 to 7 ft (1.8 to 2.1 m) tall and covered with long hair. While many scholars dismiss it as a myth, others claim it may be a kind of ape.

aborigines: see AUSTRALIAN ABORIGINES.

abortion, expulsion of the embryo or fetus before it is viable outside the uterus, i.e., before the 24th week or so after conception, in humans (see REPRODUCTION). Spontaneous abortion, or miscarriage, may be caused by death of the fetus due to abnormality or disease or by trauma to the expectant mother. Abortion may also be induced, the fetus removed from the uterus by such methods as vacuum suction, dilation and curettage, intrauterine saline injection, the "abortion pill" (the drug mifepristone [RU486] in combination with another drug), and hysterotomy (surgical incision of the uterus). Abortion was long practiced as a form of BIRTH CONTROL until pressure from the Roman Catholic Church and changing opinion led in the 19th cent. to the passage of strict antiabortion laws. Attitudes toward abortion have become more liberal in the 20th cent. By the 1970s, abortion had been legalized in most European countries and Japan; in the U.S., according to a 1973 Supreme Court ruling (see ROE V. WADE), abortions are permitted during the first six months of pregnancy. Abortion remains a controversial issue in the U.S., however, and in 1977 Congress barred the use of Medicaid funds for abortion except for therapeutic reasons and in certain other specified instances. Several state legislatures passed restrictive abortion laws in hope that the more conservative Rehnquist Court would overturn Roe v. Wade, but in 1992 the Court reaffirmed the basic principles of the 1973 decision, although it permitted restrictions that do not pose an "undue burden" on women seeking abortions.

Abraham or **Abram,** progenitor of the Hebrews. He is an example of the person devoted to God, as in his willingness to sacrifice his son ISAAC. Revered by several religions, he is principally important as the founder of JUDAISM. He received the promise of CANAAN for his people, who are descended from Isaac. Gen. 11–25. Through another son, ISHMAEL, he is considered by Muslims an ancestor of the Arabs.

Abram: see ABRAHAM.

Abrams, Creighton Williams, 1914–74, U.S. military officer; b. Springfield, Mass. He served with distinction in World War II, in Korea (1953–54), and in West Germany (1960–62). In 1964 he was promoted to general. After serving as deputy commander of the U.S. forces in the VIETNAM WAR under Gen. William C. WESTMORELAND, he was commanding general (1968–72). He was also U.S. army chief of staff (1972–74).

abrasive, material used to grind, smooth, cut, or polish another substance. Natural abrasives include SAND, PUMICE, CORUNDUM, and ground QUARTZ. Carborundum (SILICON CARBIDE) and ALUMINA (aluminum oxide) are major synthetic abrasives. The hardest abrasives are natural or synthetic DIAMONDS, used in the form of dust or minuscule stones.

Abravanel or **Abarbanel, Judah,** c.1460–c.1523, Jewish philosopher, also known as Leone Ebreo; b. Lisbon. He was influenced by the scholars of the Platonic Academy of Florence and by MAIMONIDES and IBN GABIROL. His *Philosophy of Love* (pub. posthumously, 1535), a classic exposition of platonic love, had a profound effect on philosophers of the 16th and 17th cent., notably BRUNO and SPINOZA.

Absalom [ăb'səlŏm], beloved son of DAVID. He murdered his brother AMNON and fled. After being forgiven by David, Absalom stirred up a rebellion, in which he died.

Abscam, U.S. scandal resulting from an investigation begun in 1978 by the Federal Bureau of Investigation. The FBI created a front (Abdul Enterprises, Ltd., hence, Abscam) for its agents, who, posing as associates of an Arab sheik, offered selected public officials money or other considerations in exchange for special favors. The videotaped meetings resulted in the indictments (1980) and convictions of one senator and four congressmen on charges including bribery and conspiracy; another congressman was convicted on lesser charges. The FBI's tactics raised questions about entrapment, and the conviction of Florida Rep. Richard Kelly was overturned (1982).

abscess, accumulation of pus in tissues as a result of infection. Characterized by inflammation and painful swelling, it may occur in various parts of the body, e.g., skin, gum, eyelid, and middle ear. Many abscesses respond to treatment with ANTIBIOTICS; others require surgical drainage.

absolute value, magnitude of a mathematical expression, disregarding its sign; thus the absolute value is always positive. In symbols, if $|a|$ denotes the absolute value of a number a, then $|a| = a$ for $a > 0$ and $|a| = -a$ for $a < 0$.

absolute zero, the zero point of the ideal gas temperature scale, denoted by 0 degrees on the KELVIN and Rankine temperature scales (−273.15°C; −459.67°F). At this point, the volume of an ideal gas would be zero and, theoretically, all molecular motion would cease. In actuality, all gases condense well above this point. See also TEMPERATURE.

absorption, taking of molecules of one substance directly into another substance. Absorption may be either a physical or a chemical process. Physical absorption depends on the solubility of the substance absorbed, and chemical absorption involves chemical reactions between the absorbed substance and the absorbing medium. See also ADSORPTION.

abstract expressionism, movement in painting that emerged in New York City in the mid-1940s and attained prominence in American art in the following decade; also called action painting and the New York School. Given impetus by the work of Arshile GORKY, abstract expressionism is marked by an attention to surface qualities, i.e., brushstroke and texture; the use of huge canvases; the harnessing of accidents that occur while painting; and the glorification of the act of painting itself. The first important school in American painting to declare independence from European styles and to influence art abroad, abstract expressionism enormously affected the kinds of art that followed it, especially in the use of color and material. Major artists in the movement include Jackson POLLOCK, Willem DE KOONING, Hans HOFMANN, Robert MOTHERWELL, Franz KLINE, and Mark ROTHKO.

Abu al-Ala al-Maari, 973–1057, Arabic poet. He was blind from childhood. Brilliantly original, he discarded classicism for intellectual urbanity. Later he favored ascetic purity and wrote more stereotypical poetry.

Abu al-Faraj Ali of Esfahan, 897–967, Arabic scholar. He is mainly known for his poetic anthology *Kitab al-Aghani* [book of songs], an important source for information on medieval Islamic society.

Abu Bakr, 573–634, 1st caliph, father-in-law and successor of MUHAMMAD. He was probably the Prophet's first convert. During his critical two-year caliphate (632–34), ISLAM began the phenomenal growth that was to make it a world religion.

Abu Dhabi, city (1991 est. pop. 798,000), capital of the UNITED ARAB EMIRATES.

Abu Hanifa, c.699–767, Muslim theologian. A wealthy merchant from Kufa, Iraq, he founded Hanifi, the first of Islam's four orthodox schools of law. His thinking reflects a concern for the solidarity of the Muslim community. Accorded official status in many countries formerly under Ottoman administration, Hanifi is the most widespread of Islamic legal systems.

Abuja, city and federal capital territory (1991 pop. 378,671), Nigeria. Plans to move the capital from LAGOS were approved in 1976, and a 3,000-sq mi (7,770-sq km) capital territory was created near the old town of Abuja (renamed Suleja). The site, near the center of the country, has a good climate and is not associated with any particular ethnic group. Abuja officially became Nigeria's capital in 1991.

Abu Nuwas, d. c.810, Arabic poet. A favorite of the caliphs HARUN AR-RASHID and Amin, he spent much time in Baghdad. His exquisite poetry echoes the extravagance of court life.

Abu Said ibn Abi al-Khair, 967–1049, Persian poet, a Sufi and a DERVISH. He was the first to write rubaiyat (quatrains) in the Sufistic strain that OMAR KHAYYAM made famous.

Abu Simbel or **Ipsambul,** village, S Egypt, on the NILE R. Its two temples, hewn (c.1250 B.C.) out of rock cliffs in the reign of RAMSES II, were dismantled and raised over 200 ft (61 m) to avoid waters rising behind the ASWAN HIGH DAM. The project was completed (1966) with UNESCO aid.

Abu Tammam Habib ibn Aus, c.805–c.845, Arabic poet, compiler of the Hamasa. Often describing historical events, his poems of valor are important as source material.

Abyssinian cat: see under CAT.

Ac, chemical symbol of the element ACTINIUM.

AC: see ELECTRICITY; GENERATOR; MOTOR, ELECTRIC.

acacia, plant (genus *Acacia*) of the PULSE family, mostly tropical and subtropical thorny shrubs and trees. Some have a feathery foliage composed of leaflets; others have no leaves but have flattened leaflike stems containing chlorophyll. Various species yield lac (for shellac), catechu (a dye), gum arabic, essential oils, tannins, and hardwood timber.

Acadia [əkā'dēə], region and former French colony, centered on NOVA SCOTIA, but including also PRINCE EDWARD ISLAND and much of the mainland coast from Quebec to Maine. In 1605 the French founded Port Royal (now ANNAPOLIS ROYAL), the first and chief town. During the FRENCH AND INDIAN WARS, the Peace of Utrecht (1713) gave Britain possession of the Nova Scotian peninsula, and, by the Treaty of PARIS (1763), all of Acadia fell to Britain. Doubting the loyalty of the French inhabitants (called Acadians), the British expelled many of them in 1755 and 1758. Most were scattered among the British colonies to the south, many of them later returning to the area. Other exiles found havens elsewhere, notably the Cajuns of S Louisiana, who still preserve a separate folk culture. The sufferings of the expulsion are depicted in LONGFELLOW's poem *Evangeline*.

Acadia National Park: see NATIONAL PARKS (table).

acanthus, common name for the Acanthaceae, a family of chiefly perennial herbs and shrubs, mostly tropical. Many members have decorative spiny leaves and are cultivated as ornamentals, e.g., bear's breech, whose ornate leaves provided a motif often used in Greek and Roman art and architecture. In Christian art, the acanthus symbolizes heaven.

Acapulco, city (1990 pop. 592,187), winter resort on the tropical Pacific coast of S Mexico, known for its fine beaches, luxury hotels and villas, and deep-sea fishing. Founded (1550) on a natural harbor, it was a base for Spanish explorers and was important in trade with the Philippines. It became a favored haunt of wealthy vacationers in the 1920s.

acceleration: see MOTION.

accelerator: see PARTICLE ACCELERATOR.

accounting, classification, analysis, and interpretation of the financial, or bookkeeping, records of an enterprise, used to evaluate the progress or failures of a business and to recognize the factors that determine its true condition. In the U.S. accountants who pass a required examination are granted the title Certified Public Accountant (CPA). A branch of accounting is **auditing,** the examination of accounts by persons who have had no part in their preparation. Annual audits are required for all publicly held businesses.

Accra, city (1984 pop. 867,459), capital of Ghana, on the Gulf of Guinea. The nation's largest city and its administrative and economic center, Accra is linked by road and rail with KUMASI, in the interior, and with the seaport of Tema. Manufactures include processed food, wood products, and textiles. The city became (1876) the capital of the British Gold Coast colony and grew economically after completion (1923) of a railroad to the interior. Riots in the city (1948) accelerated the movement for Ghana's independence. Today Accra is a sprawling, modern city with wide avenues; points of interest include a 17th-cent. Danish castle.

acculturation, the more or less continuous interaction between social groups brought about by accommodation and resulting in the intermixture of shared, learned behavior patterns. It may result in almost complete absorption of the culture of one of the groups or a relatively equal merging of traits and patterns from both cultures. Syncretism occurs when a subordinate group molds elements of a dominant culture to fit its own traditions.

acetaminophen, an ANALGESIC and fever-reducing medicine similar in effect to ASPIRIN. It is less irritating to the stomach than aspirin but lacks aspirin's anti-inflammatory effect.

ACE inhibitor or **angiotensin-converting enzyme inhibitor,** drug used to reduce elevated blood pressure (see HYPERTENSION), treat congestive heart failure (see HEART DISEASE), and alleviate strain on hearts damaged by heart attack. ACE inhibitors block production of an enzyme that helps make blood vessels constrict, thus widening the vessels and making it easier for the heart to pump blood through the body. Captopril is a commonly used ACE inhibitor.

acetone, dimethyl ketone, or **2-propanone** (CH_3COCH_3), colorless, flammable liquid. Acetone is widely used in industry as a solvent for many organic substances and is a component of most paint and varnish removers. It is used in making synthetic RESINS and fillers, smokeless powders, and many other organic compounds.

acetylcholine, organic compound containing carbon, hydrogen, oxygen, and nitrogen, essential for the conduction of nerve impulses in animals. It is found in highest concentrations at nerve terminals and is liberated at these nerve cell endings. There is strong evidence that acetylcholine is the transmitter substance that conducts impulses from one cell to another in the parasympathetic nervous system, and from nerve cells to smooth muscle, skeletal muscle, and exocrine glands.

acetylene or **ethyne** ($HC{\equiv}CH$), a colorless gas and the simplest alkyne (see HYDROCARBON). Explosive on contact with air, it is stored dissolved under pressure in ACETONE. It is used to make neoprene RUBBER, PLASTICS, and RESINS. The oxyacetylene torch mixes and burns oxygen and acetylene to produce a very hot flame—as high as 6300°F (3480°C)—that can cut steel and weld iron and other metals.

Achaea [əkē'ə], region of ancient GREECE, in the N Peloponnesus on the Gulf of Corinth, home of the **Achaeans**, the ruling class in the PELOPONNESUS from c.1250 B.C. Before the 5th cent. B.C. the Achaean cities joined in the First **Achaean League**, which was dissolved after it opposed (338 B.C.) PHILIP II of Macedon. The Second Achaean League, formed in 280 B.C., almost drove MACEDON from Achaea but was stopped by SPARTA. In 198 B.C., with Roman aid, the league won power. Later, suspecting pro-Macedonian sympathies, Rome deported many Achaeans (168 B.C.) to Italy. In 146 B.C. Achaea waged a suicidal war against Rome, which easily won, dissolved the league, and ended Greek liberty.

Achaemenids [ăk"əmĕn'ĭdz], dynasty of ancient PERSIA. The Achaemenid rulers (c.550–330 B.C.) included CYRUS THE GREAT, Cambyses, DARIUS I, Xerxes I, and ARTAXERXES I. The dynasty ended with DARIUS III.

Achebe, Chinua, 1930–, Nigerian novelist. His novels, written in English, depict Ibo society and the impact of colonialism, e.g., *Things Fall Apart* (1958) and *A Man of the People* (1966). A former broadcaster and diplomat for Biafra, he has also published poetry, e.g., *Christmas in Biafra* (1973). A later novel is *Anthills of the Savannah* (1987).

Acheson, Dean Gooderham, 1893–1971, U.S. secretary of state (1949–53); b. Middletown, Conn. Serving Pres. TRUMAN, he established the policy of containment of Communist expansion. He also helped to establish the NORTH ATLANTIC TREATY ORGANIZATION.

Achilles, in Greek mythology, foremost hero of the TROJAN WAR; son of Peleus and Thetis. Thetis attempted to make him immortal by bathing him in the river STYX, but the heel she held remained vulnerable. Knowing Achilles was fated to die at Troy, Thetis disguised him as a girl and hid him at Skyros. He was found by ODYSSEUS, who persuaded him to go to war. At Troy he quarreled with AGAMEMNON and sulked in his tent until his friend Patroclus was killed by HECTOR. Filled with grief and rage, Achilles slew Hector and dragged his body to the Greek camp. He was later killed by PARIS, who wounded him in his heel.

acidophilus milk: see FERMENTED MILK.

acid rain, form of precipitation (rain, snow, sleet, or hail) containing high levels of sulfuric or nitric acids (pH below 5.5–5.6). Produced when sulfur dioxide and various nitrogen oxides combine with atmospheric moisture, acid rain can contaminate drinking water, damage vegetation and aquatic life, and erode buildings and monuments. It has been an increasingly serious problem since the 1950s, particularly in the NE U.S., Canada, and W Europe, especially Scandinavia. Automobile exhausts and the burning of high-sulfur industrial fuels are thought to be the main causes, but natural sources, e.g., volcanic gases and forest fires, may also be significant. The U.S. Clean Air Act (1970) and its amendments have significantly reduced sulfur dioxide (but not nitrogen oxide) emissions. See also ECOLOGY; POLLUTION; WASTE DISPOSAL.

acids and bases, two related classes of chemicals; the members of each class have a number of common properties when dissolved in a solvent, usually water. Acids in water solutions exhibit the following common properties: they taste sour; turn LITMUS paper red; and react with certain metals, such as zinc, to yield hydrogen gas. Bases in water solutions exhibit these common properties: they taste bitter; turn litmus paper blue; and feel slippery. When a water solution of acid is mixed with a water solution of base, a SALT and water are formed; this process, called neutralization, is complete only if the resulting solution has neither acidic nor basic properties. When an acid or base dissolves in water, a certain percentage of the acid or base particles will break up, or dissociate, into oppositely charged ions. The Arrhenius theory of acids and bases defines an acid as a compound that can dissociate in water to yield hydrogen ions (H^+) and a base as a compound that can dissociate in water to yield hydroxyl ions (OH^-). The Brönsted-Lowry theory defines an acid as a proton donor and a base as a proton acceptor. The Lewis theory defines an acid as a compound that can accept a pair of electrons and a base as a compound that can donate a pair of electrons. Each of the three theories has its own advantages and disadvantages; each is useful under certain conditions. Strong acids, such as HYDROCHLORIC ACID, and strong bases, such as potassium hydroxide, have a great tendency to dissociate in water and are completely ionized in solution. Weak acids, such as acetic acid, and weak bases, such as AMMONIA, are reluctant to dissociate in water and are only partially ionized in solution. Strong acids and strong bases make very good ELECTROLYTES (see ELECTROLYSIS), i.e., their solutions readily conduct electricity. Weak acids and weak bases make poor electrolytes. See also AMPHOTERISM; BUFFER; CATALYST; INDICATORS, ACID-BASE; TITRATION; article on pH.

ACLU: see AMERICAN CIVIL LIBERTIES UNION.

Acmeists, school of Russian poets that arose in 1912 in reaction to the SYMBOLISTS; it emphasized concreteness of imagery and clarity of expression. The leading Acmeists were Nikolai Gumilev, Anna AKHMATOVA, and Osip MANDELSTAM.

acne, inflammatory disease of the sebaceous glands, characterized by blackheads, cysts, and pimples. The lesions appear on the face, neck, chest, back, and arms, and may be mild to severe. Most prevalent during adolescence, acne may appear in adulthood. Its cause is unknown, but contributing factors include genetic predisposition and hormonal changes during puberty. Treatment includes use of cleansers, ANTIBIOTICS, surgical drainage of lesions, and, for severe cases, retinoic acid derivatives.

Acoma or **Ácoma,** pueblo (1990 pop. 2590), W central N. Mex., situated atop a steep-sided 357-ft (109-m) MESA. Founded c.1100–1250, it is considered the oldest continuously inhabited community in the U.S. The resident PUEBLO retain aspects of their 700-year-old culture; the men are weavers, the women highly skilled and renowned potters.

Aconcagua, mountain 22,835 ft (6,960 m) high, in the ANDES of Argentina. It is the highest peak in the Americas.

acorn: see OAK.

acoustics, the science of SOUND, including its production, propagation, and effects. An important practical application of acoustics is in the designing of auditoriums, which requires a knowledge of the characteristics of sound WAVES. Reflection of sound can cause an ECHO, and repeated reflections in an enclosed space can cause reverberation, the persistence of sound. Some reverberation in auditoriums is desirable to avoid deadening the sound of music. Reflection can be reduced through the proper configuration and texture of walls, and by the use of sound-absorbent materials. Another acoustical problem is INTERFERENCE, which can create "dead spots" in auditoriums for certain frequencies.

acquired characteristics, modifications produced in an individual plant or animal as a result of mutilation, disease, use and disuse, or any distinctly environmental influence. Belief in the inheritability of acquired characteristics was accepted by LAMARCK but ultimately rejected by modern geneticists, who have affirmed that inheritance is determined solely by reproductive cells and unaffected by somatic (body) cells.

acquired immunodeficiency syndrome: see AIDS.

acropolis, elevated, fortified section of ancient Greek cities. The Acropolis of Athens was adorned in the 5th cent. B.C. with some of the world's greatest architectural monuments. The remains of the PARTHENON, ERECHTHEUM, and Propylaea still stand.

acrylic. 1 Also called **acrylic fiber,** any of a group of SYNTHETIC TEXTILE FIBERS, such as Arilan and Orlon, that are polymers primarily composed of the acrylonitrile monomer CH_2=CHCN. **2** Also called **acrylic resin,** any of a group of thermoplastic resins that are polymers produced from esters of acrylic acid ($C_3H_4O_2$) or methacrylic acid ($C_3H_6O_2$). They are used in paints (e.g., Lucite) and plastics (e.g., Plexiglas).

Actaeon [ăktē'ən], in Greek mythology, a hunter. Because he saw ARTEMIS bathing naked, she changed him into a stag, and he was killed by his own dogs.

actinide series, the radioactive metals, with atomic numbers 89 through 103, in group IIIb of the PERIODIC TABLE. They are ACTINIUM, THORIUM, PROTACTINIUM, URANIUM, NEPTUNIUM, PLUTONIUM, AMERICIUM, CURIUM, BERKELIUM, CALIFORNIUM, EINSTEINIUM, FERMIUM, MENDELEVIUM, NOBELIUM, and LAWRENCIUM. All members of the series have chemical properties similar to actinium. Those elements with atomic numbers greater than 92 are called TRANSURANIUM ELEMENTS.

actinium (Ac), radioactive element; discovered in 1899 by André Debierne in uranium residues from pitchblende. Actinium, a silver-white metal, is the first member of the ACTINIDE SERIES. The most stable isotope has a half-life of 21.6 years. See ELEMENT (table); PERIODIC TABLE.

action painting: see ABSTRACT EXPRESSIONISM.

activation energy: see CATALYST.

Acts of the Apostles, fifth book of the NEW TESTAMENT, between the GOSPELS and the EPISTLES. The only contemporary historical account of CHRISTIANITY's early expansion, it was written between A.D. 60 and 80 as a sequel to the Gospel of St. LUKE, who is its traditional author. The Acts chiefly deal with the work of St. PETER (1–12) and St. PAUL (13–21).

acupuncture, technique of medical treatment, based on traditional Chinese medicine, in which a number of very fine metal needles are inserted into the skin at any of some 800 specially designated points. In China it has long been used for pain relief and treatment of such ailments as ARTHRITIS, HYPERTENSION, and ULCERS. It is also now used as ANESTHESIA for childbirth and some surgery. (Unlike conventional anesthesia, it does not lower blood pressure or depress breathing.) Acupuncture is said to work by manipulating the body's electrical energy flow, allowing the body to balance and heal itself, e.g., by stimulating the production of ENDORPHINS in cases of chronic pain. U.S. research has focused on the use of acupuncture in pain relief and anesthesia, to counteract the side effects of CHEMOTHERAPY, and as an aid in reducing the cravings of former smokers and drug addicts.

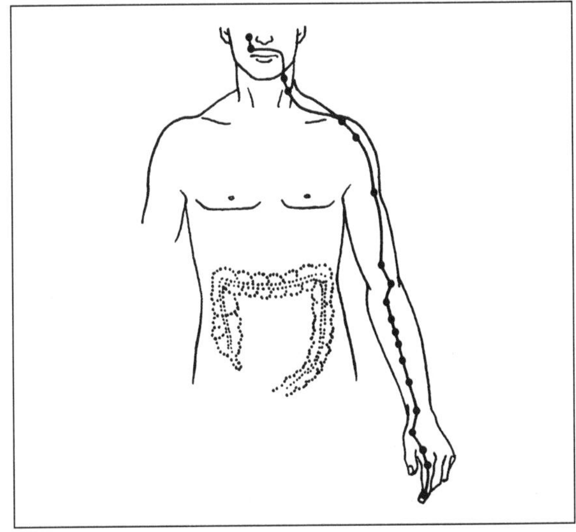

Acupuncture points for treating diseases of the large intestine

ADA: see PROGRAMMING LANGUAGE.

Adam [Heb., = man], in the BIBLE, the first person. His story, from his creation to his expulsion (with EVE, his wife) from the Garden of EDEN, is told in Genesis. To St. PAUL, Adam represented the physical aspect of humanity.

Adam, Adolphe Charles [ädäN'], 1803–56, French composer. His more than 50 stage works include the ballet *Giselle* (1841). He also wrote the popular song *Cantique de Noël*.

Adam, Robert, 1728–92, and **James Adam,** 1730–94, Scottish architects, brothers. Robert possessed the great creative talents. They designed public and private buildings in England and Scotland, and numerous interiors, pieces of furniture, and decorative objects. Robert's light, elegant style was a personal reconstitution of Palladian, Renaissance, and antique elements. The Adam manner grew vastly popular and has never disappeared. Interesting examples of Adam planning and decoration are at Osterly Park (1761–80) and Syon House (1762–69), both near London.

Adams, family of distinguished Americans from Massachusetts. **John Adams** was president of the U.S. (see separate article). He and his wife, Abigail (Smith) Adams, were the parents of **John Quincy Adams,** who was also president of the U.S. (see separate article). His son, **Charles Francis Adams,** 1807–86, b. Boston, was U.S. minister to Great Britain (1861–68). He maintained the Northern cause with a wisdom and dignity that won British respect, and he is credited with preventing British recognition of the CONFEDERACY. Later he represented the U.S. in the settlement of the ALABAMA CLAIMS. His son **Charles Francis Adams,** 1835–1915, b. Boston, was an economist and historian. An expert on railroad financing, he was president of the Union Pacific RR (1884–90). His works include *Three Episodes of Massachusetts History* (1892). His brother **Brooks Adams,** 1848–1927, b. Quincy, Mass., was a historian. His belief that civilizations rose and fell according to the growth and decline of commerce was first developed in *The Law* *of Civilization and Decay* (1895). Among his other important works are *America's Economic Supremacy* (1900) and *Theory of Social Revolutions* (1913). His ideas influenced another brother, **Henry Adams,** 1838–1918, b. Boston, who was also a writer and historian. In developing a philosophy of history he found a unifying principle in force, or energy, and applied it in two books, *Mont-Saint-Michel and Chartres* (1913) and *The Education of Henry Adams* (1918). He also wrote *History of the United States of America* (9 vol., 1889–91).

Adams, Ansel, 1902–84, American photographer; b. San Francisco. Working against the aesthetic of the 1930s, he produced superb regional landscapes, notably of the American Southwest. He also wrote technical manuals and helped to found the first museum and college photography departments.

Adams, James Truslow, 1878–1949, American historian; b. Brooklyn, N.Y. His works include *The Founding of New England* (1921; Pulitzer), *The Adams Family* (1930), and *The Epic of America* (1931). He was editor of the *Dictionary of American History* (6 vol., 1940).

Adams, John, 1735–1826, 2d president of the U.S. (1797–1801); b. Quincy (then in Braintree), Mass.; father of John Quincy ADAMS. He graduated from Harvard Univ. in 1755 and became a lawyer. As a moderate but forceful leader of the group who opposed British measures leading to the AMERICAN REVOLUTION, he later served in both CONTINENTAL CONGRESSES and argued eloquently for the DECLARATION OF INDEPENDENCE, which he signed. Adams served the new nation as a diplomat, negotiating the Treaty of PARIS (1783) to end the Revolution and serving (1785–88) as envoy to Great Britain. He became Pres. WASHINGTON's vice president (1789–97) and in 1797 succeeded him as president. Adams's administration as president revealed his honest and stubborn integrity. Although allied with Alexander HAMILTON and the conservative, property-respecting Federalists, he was not dominated by them in their struggle with the Jeffersonians (see JEFFERSON, THOMAS). By conciliation he prevented war with France (see XYZ AFFAIR). He did not wholly support the ALIEN AND SEDITION ACTS. After 1801 he lived in retirement in Quincy. His wife, **Abigail (Smith) Adams,** 1744–1818, b. Weymouth, Mass., was the chief figure in the social life of her husband's administration. Lively and intelligent, she was one of the most distinguished and influential of American first ladies.

Adams, John Couch, 1819–92, English astronomer. By mathematical calculation based on irregularities in the motion of the planet Uranus, he and U.J.J. LEVERRIER independently and accurately predicted (1845–46) the position of the then unknown planet NEPTUNE. Adams also made valuable studies of the moon's motions, of the great meteor shower of 1866, and of terrestrial magnetism.

Adams, John Quincy, 1767–1848, 6th president of the U.S. (1825–29); b. Quincy (then in Braintree), Mass; son of John and Abigail ADAMS; father of Charles Francis Adams (see ADAMS, family). As U.S. senator from Massachusetts (1803–8), he angered his fellow Federalists by supporting Jeffersonian policies (see JEFFERSON, THOMAS). He gained fame as secretary of state (1817–25) for Pres. James MONROE, his greatest achievement being the MONROE DOCTRINE. Elected president (1825) in the House of Representatives through the support of Henry CLAY, Adams had an unhappy, ineffective administration, despite his attempts to institute a program of internal improvements. He won new respect as a U.S. representative from Massachusetts (1831–48), eloquently attacking all measures that would extend SLAVERY.

Adams, Samuel, 1722–1803, American Revolutionary patriot; b. Boston. His speeches and writings helped to spark the AMERICAN REVOLUTION. He signed the DECLARATION OF INDEPENDENCE, was a member (1774–81) of the CONTINENTAL CONGRESS, and was governor (1794–97) of Massachusetts.

Adana, city (1990 pop. 931,555), capital of Adana prov., S Turkey, on the Seyhan R. Turkey's fourth largest city, it is the commercial center of a farming region where cotton, grains, and other crops are grown. The city's manufactures include processed food and textiles. An ancient city probably founded by the HITTITES, it prospered from 66 B.C. as a Roman colony. It later declined but was revived (A.D. c.782) by HARUN AR-RASHID. In the 16th cent. it passed to the Ottoman Turks. Near Adana is a Hittite archaeological site.

adaptation, in biology, the adjustment of living matter to environmental conditions, including other living things. Animals and plants are adapted for securing food and surviving even in conditions of drought, great heat, or extreme cold. Adaptations are believed to arise when genetic variations that increase an organism's chances of survival are passed on to succeeding generations. See also ECOLOGY; EVOLUTION; GENETICS.

adaptive radiation, in biology, the evolution of an ancestral species adapted to a particular way of life into several species, each adapted to a different habitat. Illustrating the principle are the 14 species of DARWIN's finches, small land birds of the Galapagos Islands: 3 are ground-dwelling seedeaters, 3 live on cactus plants and are seedeaters, 1 is a tree-dwelling seedeater, 7 are tree-dwelling insect eaters, but all derive from a single species of ground-dwelling, seedeating finch that probably emigrated from the South American mainland.

Addams, Charles Samuel, 1912–88, American cartoonist; b. Westfield, N.J. His work, best known from *The New Yorker* magazine, is famed for its wit, fantasy, and sense of the macabre.

Addams, Jane, 1860–1935, American social worker; b. Cedarville, Ill. In 1889 she and Ellen Gates Starr founded Hull House, a Chicago settlement house that served the neighborhood poor and became a center for social reform activities. A leader of the WOMAN SUFFRAGE and pacifist movements, Addams shared the 1931 Nobel Peace Prize. She wrote several books on social issues and two autobiographical volumes.

addax: see ANTELOPE.

adder: see VIPER.

addiction: see DRUG ADDICTION AND DRUG ABUSE.

Addis Ababa, city (1988 est. pop. 1,686,000), capital of Ethiopia. Addis Ababa is Ethiopia's largest city, its administrative and communications center, and the main trade center for coffee (Ethiopia's chief export), tobacco, grains, and hides; much of its commerce is shipped by rail to the port of DJIBOUTI. Addis Ababa became (1889) Ethiopia's capital and was captured (1936) by the Italians and made the capital of ITALIAN EAST AFRICA. It was retaken by the Allies in 1941 and returned to Ethiopian rule. A modern city, it has been the site of many international conferences and organizations, including the ORGANIZATION OF AFRICAN UNITY. Notable buildings include Coptic and Roman Catholic cathedrals.

Addison, Joseph, 1672–1719, English essayist, poet, and statesman. His *Remarks on Italy* (1705) recorded early travels. The prominence he attained with the epic *Campaign* (1704) on MARLBOROUGH's victory at Blenheim led to political appointments, and he served in Parliament (1708–19). Addison contributed to his friend Richard STEELE's periodical the *Tatler* after 1710. There, and in the *Spectator* and *Guardian,* he raised the English essay to an unequaled height. In prose marked by simplicity, order, and precision, Addison advocated reason and moderation in life.

Addison's disease, progressive disease brought about by atrophy of the outer layer (cortex) of the adrenal gland; also called chronic adrenocortical insufficiency. The deterioration of this tissue causes a decrease in the secretion of vital steroid hormones, producing such symptoms as ANEMIA, weakness, abnormal skin pigmentation, and weight loss. The cause of the disease is unknown. Once thought inevitably fatal, the disease is now treated with adrenocortical hormones.

Adelaide, city (1991 pop. 1,023,617), capital and chief port of South Australia, at the mouth of the Torrens R., on Gulf St. Vincent. It has automotive, textile, and service industries, and exports grains, wool, dairy products, and fruit. Founded in 1836, it was named for William IV's consort. The biennial Adelaide Festival of the Arts, begun in 1960, is held in the Adelaide Festival Centre (opened 1977). It is also known for its parks.

Aden, city (1987 est. pop. 417,000), chief port of Yemen, on the Gulf of Aden near the southern entrance to the Red Sea. The city is built on two peninsulas, each with a high volcanic headland. Most of the population lives on Aden peninsula; Little Aden peninsula has an oil refinery and other industries. Aden has been the chief trade center of S ARABIA since ancient times. It declined with the discovery (15th cent.) of an all-water route around Africa to India, but revived when the SUEZ CANAL opened in 1869. The region was held by Muslim Arabs (7th–16th cent.) and by the Ottoman Turks (from 1538). The British captured Aden in 1839 and made it a crown colony in 1935. The capital of independent Southern Yemen (see YEMEN) from 1970 to 1990, Aden was designated the economic capital of united Yemen in 1990 and a free-trade zone is planned.

Aden, Gulf of, western arm of the Arabian Sea, 550 mi (885 km) long, between E Africa and SW Asia. It is connected with the RED SEA by the BAB EL MANDEB and is an important link in the MEDITERRANEAN SEA–SUEZ CANAL–INDIAN OCEAN sealane.

Adenauer, Konrad, 1876–1967, West German chancellor (1949–63). He was a member of the Catholic Center party until 1933, when he was imprisoned by the NAZIS. After World War II he was a founder and president of the Christian Democratic Union. As chancellor, he presided over the spectacular rebirth of West GERMANY's economy, and guided that nation's reentry into the European community and recovery in 1955 of its full sovereignty.

adenoids: see TONSILS.

adenosine triphosphate (ATP), organic compound composed of adenine, ribose, and three phosphate units. ATP serves as the major energy source within cells, driving such biological processes as photosynthesis, muscle contraction, and protein synthesis. It is broken down by hydrolysis (reaction with water) to yield adenosine diphosphate (ADP), inorganic phosphate, and energy. ADP can be further broken down by hydrolysis to yield adenosine monophosphate (AMP), inorganic phosphate, and energy. Excess phosphate yielded from these and subsequent reactions is used to produce new ATP from AMP.

adhesion and cohesion, attractive forces between material bodies. Adhesive forces act between different substances, whereas cohesive forces act within a single substance, holding its atoms, ions, or molecules together. Without these forces, solids and liquids would act as gases. SURFACE TENSION in liquids results from cohesion, and CAPILLARITY results from a combination of adhesion and cohesion. FRICTION between two solid bodies depends in part on adhesion.

Adirondack Mountains, forested mountain wilderness area, NE New York, with many scenic gorges, waterfalls, and lakes. The Adirondacks rise to a high point of 5,344 ft (1,629 m) at Mt. Marcy and are geologically a southern extension of the CANADIAN SHIELD. Lake Placid and Lake George are important area resorts. The **Adirondack Park,** a state park encompassing the area (est. 1892), is the largest park in the U.S. outside Alaska, but less than half its land is state-owned preserve.

Adler, Alfred, 1870–1937, Austrian psychiatrist, early associate of Sigmund FREUD and founder of the school of individual psychology. Rejecting Freud's emphasis on sex, Adler maintained that personality difficulties are rooted in a feeling of inferiority (see COMPLEX) deriving from restrictions on the individual's need for self-assertion. His best-known work is *The Practice and Theory of Individual Psychology* (1923).

Adler, Cyrus, 1863–1940, American Jewish educator; b. Van Buren, Ark. Founder of the American Jewish Historical Society, American Jewish Committee, and Jewish Welfare Board, he was president of Dropsie College (1908–40) and the Jewish Theological Seminary (1924–40). He was an editor of the *Jewish Encyclopedia*, and wrote articles and books.

Adler, Felix, 1851–1933, American educator and leader in social welfare; b. Germany. Founder of the ETHICAL CULTURE MOVEMENT (1876) and Society, he also organized the Workingmen's Lyceum, the Workingmen's School, and the Manhattan Trade School for Girls. He was for many years chairman of the National Child Labor Committee, and wrote *Creed and Deed* (1877) and *An Ethical Philosophy of Life* (1918), among other books.

Adler, Larry, 1914–, American harmonica player; b. Baltimore. He played with the world's major symphony orchestras and is generally credited with elevating the harmonica to concert status in the classical music world.

Adonis, in Greek mythology, beautiful youth loved by APHRODITE and PERSEPHONE. When he was killed by a boar, both goddesses claimed him. ZEUS decreed that he spend half the year above the ground with Aphrodite, the other half in the underworld with Persephone. His death and resurrection, symbolic of the seasonal cycle, were celebrated at the festival Adonia.

adoption, act creating the legal relation of parent and child. It was known in antiquity but was not part of the English COMMON LAW. In the U.S. it is governed by statute. Adoption's historical roots include the need to continue a family line where there is no natural heir. Today the usual focus is the child's welfare. A hearing before a judge is generally required, as is consent of the natural parent or guardian and that of the child if he or she is above a certain age. The natural parents generally lose their rights and duties toward the child; the adoptive parents assume them. Many states now permit adoption by unmarried adults; some allow adoption by homosexual couples. Adoption by relatives is most common; in adoption by unrelated adults, the courts have traditionally attempted to ease adjustment to the adoptive family by maintaining secrecy regarding the child's origin. Since the 1970s, however, a growing number of adopted children have attempted to identify their natural parents, and "open adoption," in which adoptive and birth parents maintain a relationship, has become more popular. See also FOSTER CARE.

Adorno, Theodor Wiesengrund, 1903–69, German philosopher, sociologist, and music critic. From 1928, he was closely associated with the Frankfurt Institute for Social Research. When the Nazis came to power, he emigrated to Britain (1934) and then the U.S. (1938), where with Max Horkheimer he wrote the *Dialectic of Enlightenment* (1947) and collaborated on *The Authoritarian Personality* (1950), a study of fascism. He returned to Frankfurt (1949) and was director (1958–69) of the institute.

adrenal glands, pair of small endocrine glands (see ENDOCRINE SYSTEM) situated atop the kidneys. The outer yellowish layer (cortex) secretes about 30 steroid hormones, most importantly aldosterone, which regulates water and salt balance in the body, and cortisol, which controls carbohydrate, fat, and protein metabolism. The inner reddish portion (medulla) of the adrenals secretes the emergency-response hormones EPINEPHRINE (adrenaline) and norepinephrine.

adrenaline: see EPINEPHRINE.

Adrian I, d. 795, pope (772–95). A Roman, he successfully urged CHARLEMAGNE to defeat the LOMBARDS and acquired from him additional lands for the PAPAL STATES. He supported the Byzantine empress Irene in her struggle against ICONOCLASM.

Adrian IV, d. 1159, pope (1154–59). The only Englishman to become pope, he was originally named Nicholas Breakspear. In 1155 he defeated the opposition of Arnold of Brescia and crowned Holy Roman Emperor FREDERICK I. He later quarreled with Frederick and William I of Sicily. His donation of Ireland as a fief to Henry II of England is disputed.

Adrian, Roman emperor: see HADRIAN.

Adriatic Sea, arm of the MEDITERRANEAN SEA, c.500 mi (800 km) long, between Italy (W) and Slovenia, Croatia, Yugoslavia and Albania (E). It is 58–140 mi (93–225 km) wide, with a maximum depth of c.4,100 ft (1,250 m). VENICE is the chief port.

adsorption, the adhesion of molecules to the surfaces of solids, as opposed to ABSORPTION, in which the molecules actually enter the absorbing medium. Charcoal, for example, which has a great surface area because of its porous nature, can adsorb large volumes of gases, including most of the poisonous ones, and thus is used in gas masks and filters.

Advanced Research Projects Agency, U.S. government agency (est. 1958) administered by the Defense Dept. It has been crucial in developing several important technologies, especially military computers. It funds much of the U.S.'s ARTIFICIAL INTELLIGENCE research, as well as microelectronics, materials science, and behavioral science projects.

Advent, Christian penitential season, lasting in the West from the Sunday nearest Nov. 30 until Christmas. It is the first season of the church calendar.

Advent Christian Church: see ADVENTISTS.

Adventists, members of a group of religious denominations whose distinctive doctrine centers in their belief concerning the imminent second coming of Jesus. Adventism is specifically applied to the teachings of William Miller. The largest group, the Seventh-Day Adventists, were formally organized in 1863 and are fundamentally evangelical. In 1990 there were 717,446 Seventh-Day Adventists in the U.S. Other Adventist groups are the Church of God, the Advent Christian Church, and the Primitive Advent Christian Church.

A.E.: see RUSSELL, GEORGE WILLIAM.

Aegean civilization [ējē'ən], cultures of pre-Hellenic GREECE. MINOAN CIVILIZATION flourished on Crete and MYCENAEAN CIVILIZATION on the Greek mainland. Sites of other cultures have been found at TROY and in the Cyclades.

Aegean Sea, arm of the MEDITERRANEAN SEA, off SE Europe, between Greece and Turkey, center of the classical Greek world. The island-studded sea is c.400 mi (640 km) long, 200 mi (320 km) wide, and more than 6,600 ft (2,010 m) deep off N CRETE at its southern limit. Major islands include ÉVVOIA, the Sporades, the CYCLADES, SÁMOS, KHÍOS, LESBOS, Thásos, and the DODECANESE. Sardines and sponges are taken from the sea, and some oil and natural gas has been discovered.

Aegisthus, in Greek mythology, son of Thyestes. Aegisthus revenged his brothers' murder by killing his uncle ATREUS. He was later CLYTEMNESTRA's lover, helped her to slay AGAMEMNON, and was himself killed by ORESTES.

Aeken, Jerom van: see BOSCH, HIERONYMUS.

Aeneas [ĭnē'əs], in classical legend, a Trojan; son of Anchises and VENUS. After Troy's fall he escaped, tarried with DIDO at CARTHAGE, then went to Italy, where his descendants founded Rome. His deeds are celebrated in VERGIL's *Aeneid*.

Aeolians: see GREECE.

aerial: see ANTENNA.

aerobics [Gr., = with oxygen], endurance exercises in which the volume of breathing is increased and the heart is forced to beat faster than usual for a prolonged period of time, thereby pumping an increased amount of oxygen-rich blood to the muscles being used. Such aerobic activities as running, swimming, and cycling can strengthen the cardiovascular system, improving the body's use of oxygen and allowing the heart to work less strenuously.

aerodynamics, study of gases in motion. Because the principal application of aerodynamics is the design of AIRPLANES, air is the principal gas with which this science is concerned. Bernoulli's principle, which states that the pressure of a moving gas decreases as its velocity increases, has been used to explain the lift produced by a wing having a curved upper surface and a flat lower surface (see AIRFOIL). Because the flow is faster across the curved surface than across the flat one, a greater pressure is exerted in the upward direction. Aerodynamics is also concerned with the drag caused by air friction, which is reduced by making the surface area of the craft as small as possible. At speeds close to the speed of sound, or Mach 1 (see MACH NUMBER), there is also a large, sudden increase of drag, which has been called the sonic, or sound, barrier. Aerodynamics is also used in designing automobile bodies and trains for minimum drag and in computing wind stresses on bridges, buildings, and the like. The WIND TUNNEL is one of the basic experimental tools of the aerodynamicist. See SHOCK WAVE; SONIC BOOM.

aerogel, any of a group of extremely light and porous solid materials; the lightest is less than four times as dense as dry air. Aerogels are produced from certain gels (see COLLOID) by heating the gel under pressure, which causes the liquid in the gel to become supercritical (in a state between a liquid and a gas) and lose its surface tension. In this state, the liquid may be removed from the gel by applying additional heat, without disrupting the porous network formed by the gel's solid component. Silica-, melamine-, and carbon-based aerogels have been produced. Silica-based aerogels are among the lightest, and some, nicknamed "solid smoke" or "frozen smoke," are nearly transparent. Heavier aerogels were first developed in 1931 and have been used to detect high-energy particles emitted by PARTICLE ACCELERATORS. Newer, lighter aerogels with relatively high insulating properties are being tested as substitutes for the CHLOROFLUOROCARBON foams used as refrigerator insulation and as replacements for the air between the panes of double-glazed windows.

aeronautics: see AERODYNAMICS; AIRPLANE; AVIATION.

aerosol, a COLLOID in which small solid or liquid particles are suspended in a gas. Natural aerosols such as fog or smoke occur throughout the ATMOSPHERE, which is itself an aerosol. The term is also used to describe a container of paint, insecticide, or other substance held under pressure by a propellant, which releases the substance in the form of a fine spray or foam. The particles produced by an aerosol container, however, are larger than those in a true aerosol. FREON was the most common aerosol propellant, but its use has been banned because Freon is thought to destroy the OZONE LAYER of the stratosphere.

Aeschines, c.390–314? B.C., Athenian orator. He became politically powerful through his oratorical gifts. Opposing resistance to PHILIP II of Macedon, he was the bitter rival of DEMOSTHENES.

Aeschylus [ĕs'kĭləs, ēs'–], 525–456 B.C., Athenian tragic poet. First of the three great Greek tragedians, he preceded SOPHOCLES and EURIPIDES. He wrote perhaps 90 plays, of which seven survive intact. Often credited with inventing TRAGEDY, he added an actor to what had been a dialogue, thus increasing its possibilities. His choral lyrics rank with those of PINDAR. Among his best-known plays are *The Seven against Thebes* and *Prometheus Bound*. His only extant trilogy, the *Oresteia*, a history of the house of ATREUS, is considered by many the greatest Attic tragedy.

Aesop, semilegendary ancient Greek fabulist, supposedly a slave. The fables called Aesop's were preserved by various writers and include "The Fox and the Grapes" and "The Tortoise and the Hare."

aesthetics, branch of philosophy dealing with the nature of art and the criteria of artistic judgment. The conception of art as imitation of nature was formulated by PLATO and developed by ARISTOTLE, both of whom held that beauty inheres in the object itself and may be judged objectively. KANT held that the subject may have universal validity, while other thinkers, e.g., HUME, identified beauty with that which pleases the observer. Modern philosophers especially concerned with aesthetic questions have included CROCE, CASSIRER, John DEWEY, and SANTAYANA.

Æthelbert [ĕ'thəlbərt, ă–], d. 616, king of Kent (560?–616). Although he was defeated (568) by the West Saxons, he later became the strongest ruler in S England. In 597 he was converted to Christianity by St. AUGUSTINE OF CANTERBURY and became the first Christian king of Anglo-Saxon England.

Æthelbert, d. 865, king of WESSEX (860–65), son of ÆTHELWULF. After his father's death in 858, he ruled KENT, Surrey, SUSSEX, and ESSEX, reuniting them with Wessex when in 860 he succeeded his brother Æthelbald in that kingdom.

Æthelflæd [ĕ'thəlflĕd] or **Ethelfleda** [–flē'də], d. 918, daughter of ALFRED and wife of Æthelred, ealdorman of MERCIA. After her husband's death in 911, she ruled the semi-independent Mercia alone and was known as the Lady of the Mercians.

Æthelred [ĕ'thəlrĕd, ă–], 965–1016, king of England (978–1016), called Æthelred the Unready [Old Eng., = without counsel]. He was the son of EDGAR, and the half brother and successor of Edward the Martyr. A weak king, he reigned at the height of Danish power. Although he began paying tribute through the DANEGELD to the Danes in 991, they returned in 997 to plunder his realm, staying until 1000. In 1002 Æthelred married Emma, sister of the duke of Normandy, possibly hoping to gain an ally. Although by 1009 a navy existed, the treason of its commanders rendered it useless. In 1013 the Danish king SWEYN returned to conquer; he was well received in the DANELAW and London capitulated. Æthelred fled to Normandy but was restored in 1014 on Sweyn's death. In 1016 Æthelred's son EDMUND IRONSIDE succeeded him, made a treaty with CANUTE, son of Sweyn, and died. Canute succeeded him and married Æthelred's widow.

Æthelstan: see ATHELSTAN.

Æthelwulf [ĕ'thəlwŏŏlf, ă–], d. 858, king of WESSEX (839–56), son of EGBERT and father of ÆTHELBERT and ALFRED. With his son Æthelbald, he won a notable victory over the Danes at Aclea (851). He married Judith of France in 856. A man of great piety, he learned while on a pilgrimage in Rome that Æthelbald would resist his return. He left his son as king in Wessex and ruled in Kent and its dependencies.

aether: see ETHER, in physics.

Aetna: see ETNA.

Aetolia [ētō l'yə], region of ancient GREECE, N of the gulfs of Corinth and Calydon, E of the Achelous R. It was the center of the **Aetolian League**, formed in the 4th cent. B.C. to oppose the Achaean League (see under ACHAEA) and the Macedonians. With Rome it defeated PHILIP V of Macedon (197 B.C.), but then it allied itself against Rome with ANTIOCHUS III of Syria. His defeat (189 B.C.) marked the end of the league's power.

affirmative action, U.S. program to overcome the effects of past discrimination by giving some form of preferential treatment to ethnic minorities and women. The term is usually applied to those plans that set forth goals and time tables, required since the early 1970s of government contractors and universities receiving public funds. The Equal Employment Opportunities Act (1972) set up a commission to enforce such plans. The establishment of racial quotas in the name of affirmative action brought charges of so-called reverse discrimination in the late 1970s. The U.S. Supreme Court accepted such an argument in 1978 in the UNIVERSITY OF CALIFORNIA REGENTS V. BAKKE, but in 1979 the Court approved the use of quotas in a case involving voluntary affirmative-action programs in unions and private businesses. In the 1980s, under the Reagan administration and as a result of several Supreme Court decisions, the federal government's role in affirmative action was considerably diluted. The 1991 Civil Rights Act, however, restored some of the protections of the earlier laws.

Afghan hound, tall, swift HOUND; shoulder height, 24–28 in. (61–71.1 cm); weight, 50–60 lb (22.7–27.2 kg). Its long, silky coat may be any color. The breed originated in Egypt c.5,000 years ago, was perfected in Afghanistan, and was brought to England after World War I.

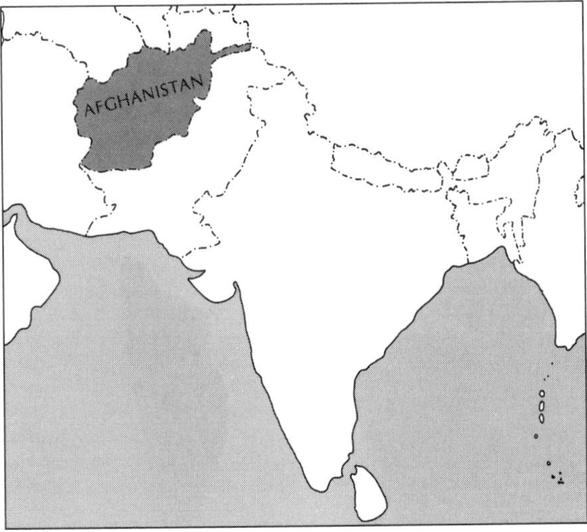

Afghanistan, officially Islamic State of Afghanistan, republic (1992 est. pop. 16,096,000), 249,999 sq mi (647,497 sq km), S central Asia, bordered by Iran (W), Pakistan (E and S), Turkmenistan, Uzbekistan, and Tajikistan (N), and China (NE). Principal cities include KABUL (the capital), KANDAHAR, and HERAT. Most of Afghanistan is mountainous, and the towering ranges of the HINDU KUSH reach a height of more than 24,000 ft (7,315 m); fertile valleys and plains, home of most of the population, nestle in the mountains. The land is mainly dry, and the rivers (unnavigable for the most part) are used for irrigation. Agriculture is the mainstay of the economy, although less than 10% of the land is cultivated and much arable land was damaged by warfare in the 1980s; corn, barley, rice, and fruit are grown, and sheep are raised for skins, wool, and meat. Industry and the development of minerals (except for natural gas, which is exported) are still in the beginning stages. Imports (mostly manufactured goods) greatly exceed exports (wool, hides, fruit). The population is diverse, including Afghans and Pathans, Tajiks, Hazaras, Uzbeks, and nomadic Turkmen. The vast majority are Sunni Muslims, but there is a sizable Shiite minority. Pushtu (Afghan), Dari (Persian), Tajik, and Uzbek are the principal languages.

History. Afghanistan, astride the land route to India (through the famed KHYBER PASS), has fallen to many conquerors through the ages, e.g., DARIUS I (c.500 B.C.); ALEXANDER THE GREAT (329–327 B.C.); and numerous Arab invaders (from the 7th cent. A.D.), who established Islam as the dominant culture. Mahmud of Ghazni, who conquered (11th cent.) an empire stretching from Iran to India, was the greatest of Afghanistan's rulers. The country was later conquered by JENGHIZ KHAN (c.1220) and TIMUR (14th cent.). Afghanistan became a united state (1747) under Ahmad Shah, who founded the Durani dynasty. During the 19th cent. Britain, to protect its Indian empire from Russia, tried to establish authority in neighboring Afghanistan; the result was two British-Afghan Wars (1838–42, 1878–80). An agreement (1907) gave Britain control over Afghanistan's foreign affairs, but the emir Amanullah engaged Britain in a third Afghan War (1919), which gave Afghanistan full independence. Amanullah embarked on a modernization program, and in 1926 proclaimed a monarchy to replace the emirate. The last king, Muhammad Zahir Shah, was overthrown in 1973 in a military coup led by Lt. Gen. Muhammad Daoud Khan, who proclaimed a republic. Daoud was killed in a coup (1978) that brought a pro-Soviet regime to power, and in 1979 a coup supported by Soviet troops installed Babrak Karmal as president. Over 5 million Afghans eventually fled to Iran and Pakistan. Losses inflicted by U.S.-supported rebels (mujahedin) eventually led to a Soviet troop withdrawal (1989), but the USSR continued to aid the regime, now headed by Pres. Najibullah. In 1991 the U.S. and USSR agreed to stop arming all sides, and in 1992 Najibullah was ousted and Kabul fell. An interim government, headed by Pres. Burhanuddin Rabbani, was appointed, but fighting broke out among rival rebel factions, and various factions controlled parts of the country. An agreement (1993) that called for power-sharing in the interim government and eventual elections failed to end the bloodshed.

aflatoxins, TOXINS produced by a mold (*Aspergillus*) that grows on stored grains, peanuts, and other food products. Potent CARCINOGENS, aflatoxins are most commonly produced when such foods are improperly stored and often cause disease in farm animals that eat contaminated feed. They can also be produced in the field, particularly if severe climatic changes occur or the plants are attacked by insects.

AFL-CIO: see AMERICAN FEDERATION OF LABOR AND CONGRESS OF INDUSTRIAL ORGANIZATIONS.

Africa, second largest continent, c.11,677,240 sq mi (30,244,050 sq km) including Madagascar and smaller offshore islands. It is connected to Asia by the narrow Isthmus of Suez. Mt. Kibo (19,340 ft/5,895 m), a peak of KILIMANJARO, in Tanzania, is the highest point; the lowest point, 436 ft (133 m) below sea level, is the Qattarah Depression, in Egypt. E Africa's lake-filled GREAT RIFT VALLEY is the continent's most spectacular feature. Mountain ranges include the ATLAS MTS. (N), the Ethiopian Highlands and Ruwenzori Mts. (E), and the Drakensberg Mts. (S). Chief rivers are the NILE, CONGO (Zaïre), NIGER, and ZAMBEZI. Climatic conditions range from hot and rainy all year near the equator, through tropical savanna with alternating wet and dry seasons immediately north and south of the equatorial region, to hot and dry in the great SAHARA desert, in the north, and the smaller KALAHARI desert, in the south. At its north and south extremities the continent has a Mediterranean-type climate. The countries of Africa are Algeria, Angola, Benin, Botswana, Burkina Faso, Burundi, Cameroon, Cape Verde, the Central African Republic, Chad, the Comoros, Congo, Côte d'Ivoire, Djibouti, Egypt, Equatorial Guinea, Eritrea, Ethiopia, Gabon, Gambia, Ghana, Guinea, Guinea-Bissau, Kenya, Lesotho, Liberia, Libya, Madagascar, Malawi, Mali, Mauritania, Mauritius, Morocco, Mozambique, Namibia, Niger, Nigeria, Rwanda, São Tomé and Principe, Senegal, the Seychelles, Sierra Leone, Somalia, South Africa, Sudan, Swaziland, Tanzania, Togo, Tunisia, Uganda, Zaïre, Zambia, and Zimbabwe; Western Sahara is occupied by Morocco (see separate articles). African peoples, who make up about 10% of the world's population, are divided into more than 50 nations and are further fragmented into numerous ethnic and linguistic groups (see AFRICAN LANGUAGES).

African art, traditional art created by peoples S of the Sahara. The predominant art forms are masks and figures, which were generally used in religious ceremonies. The decorative arts, especially in textiles and in the ornamentation of everyday tools, were a vital art in nearly all African cultures. Established forms evolved long before the arrival (15th cent.) of the Portuguese in Africa, but most works older than 150 years have perished. Their creators valued them for ritual use rather than aesthetic accomplishment. Wood—

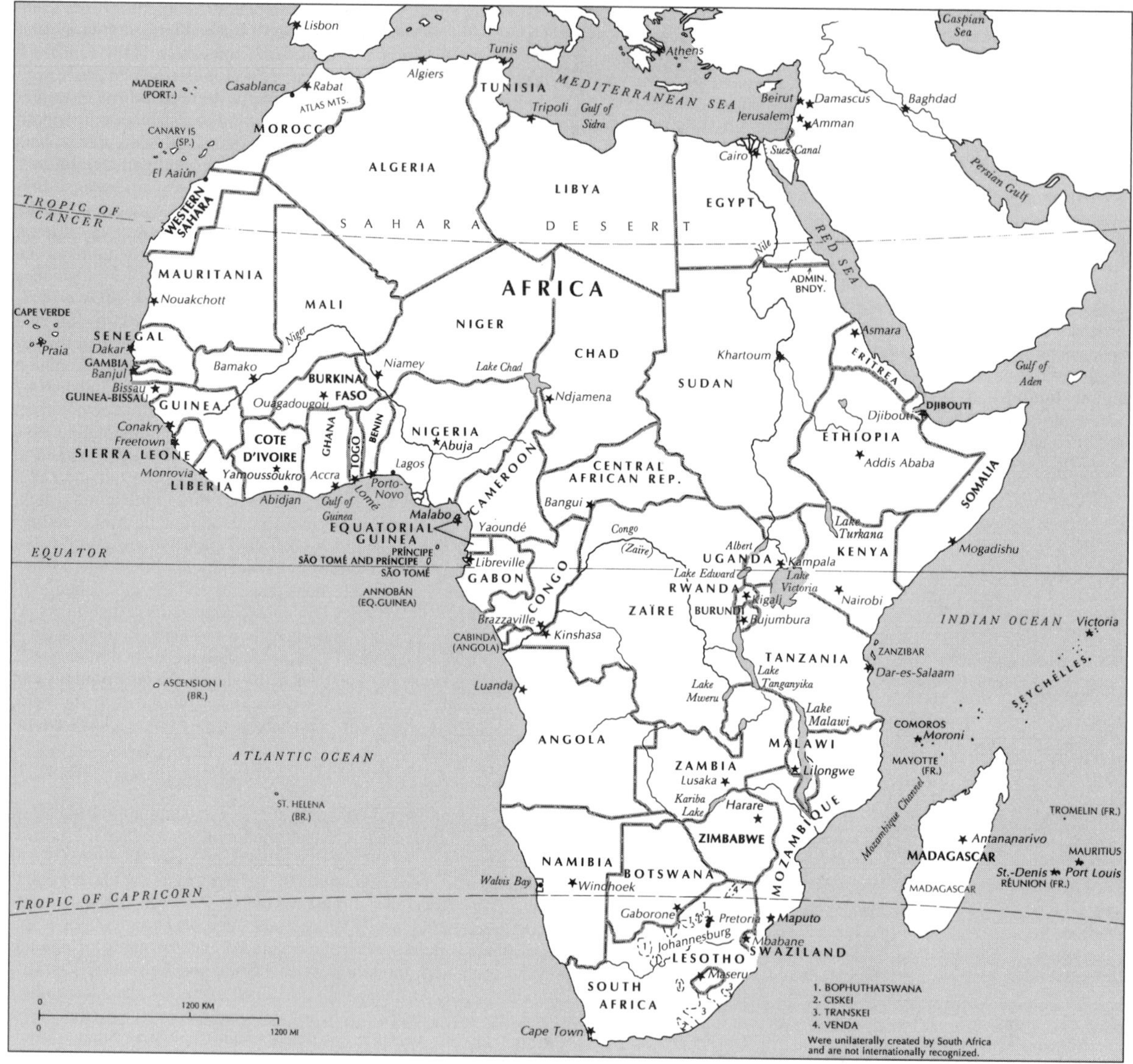

often embellished with clay, shells, beads, ivory, metal, feathers, and shredded raffia—was the dominant material. In Sudan and on the Guinea coast the wood-carving style was highly abstract. Distortion often emphasized features of cultic significance. The Bambara of W Mali are famous for their striking wooden headdresses in the form of antelope heads. In NW Guinea the Baga made snake carvings, drums supported by small standing figures, and spectacular masks. The southern groups of Senufu in Côte d'Ivoire made masks representing human features with geometric projections and legs jutting out of each side of the face. During the 18th and 19th cent. the ASHANTI kingdom of Ghana used a system of brass weights to weigh gold dust; these weights were small figures cast by CIRE PERDUE. Among Africa's most remarkable cire perdue bronzes are figures and portraits from Nigeria's BENIN culture, executed from the 12th–19th cent., which exhibit technical sophistication, superb modeling, and naturalistic detail. The Benin people also worked in terra cotta, iron, and ivory. From N Nigeria, the remarkable Nok terra-cotta heads are the earliest African sculpture yet found (c.500–200 B.C.). The art of the Yoruba of S Nigeria is often brilliantly polychromed. On the banks of the Middle Cross R. are about 300 monolithic carvings, supposedly Ekoi ancestor figures from between 1600 and 1900. The small tribes of Cameroon did woodcarvings and sculptures that include large house posts and ritual objects. Among the Fang tribes of Gabon, decorative motifs on stringed musical instruments emphasized the human figure. The Bapende of W Congo made ivory pendants portraying human faces, while the Baluba of SE Congo produced bowls and stools supported by slender figures. The dynamic and expressive free-standing figures of the Badjokwe of S Congo and Angola are particularly outstanding. African art came to European notice c.1905, and modern art, particularly CUBISM, as well as such artists as PICASSO and MODIGLIANI were strongly influenced by it. The Museum of Primitive Art (N.Y.C.) and the Field Museum of Natural History (Chicago) have fine collections of African art.

African languages, geographic rather than linguistic classification of languages spoken on the African continent. These languages do not belong to a single family but are divided among several distinct linguistic stocks having no common origin. The principal linguistic families of Africa are now generally said to be Hamito-Semitic; Niger-Kordofanian (including Niger-Congo); Nilo-Saharan; and Khoisan, or Click. Two other stocks, Indo-European and Malayo-Polynesian, are also represented. For a more detailed categorization of the languages of Africa, see the table accompanying this article.

African literature. Although ancient African Muslim books in Swahili and Arabic exist, African literature before the 19th cent. is almost entirely an oral tradition. The continent's seemingly inexhaustible supply of myths, tales, legends, riddles, and proverbs

MAJOR AFRICAN LANGUAGES (**Asterisk indicates a dead language*)

Hamito-Semitic or **Aafroasiatic Languages** (*for Hamito-Semitic languages that were or are spoken in W Asia, see the Hamito-Semitic classification in the table "Major Languages of Europe, Asia, and Some Islands of the Pacific and Indian Oceans" accompanying the* LANGUAGE *article*)	
SEMITIC (spoken in North Africa, Ethiopia, and Eritrea)	
Arabic	Egyptian Arabic, Western Arabic
Ethiopic	Amharic (or Abyssinian), Geez (Classical Ethiopic),* Tigré, Tigrinya
HAMITIC	
Egyptian (was spoken in Egypt)	Ancient Egyptian,* Coptic*
Berber (spoken throughout North Africa except Egypt)	Kabyle, Modern Berber, Rif, Siwi, Tamachek, Tuareg, Zanaga
Cushitic (spoken near Ethiopia and adjoining regions)	Agau, Beja, Burji, Geleba, Gimira, Janjaro, Kaffa, Konso, Maji, Oromo, Saho-Afar, Sidamo, Somali
CHAD (spoken near Lake Chad, central Africa, and in W Africa)	Angas, Bolewa, Gwandara, Hausa, Hiji, Kuseri, Mandara, Ngala, Ron, Shirawa, Sokoro

Indo-European Languages (*for a full presentation of the Indo-European language family, see table accompanying the* LANGUAGE *article*)	
GERMANIC	
West Germanic	
Low German	Afrikaans (spoken in South Africa), English (spoken in South Africa, Zimbabwe, and other African countries)
ITALIC	
Romance (spoken in a number of African countries)	French, Italian, Portuguese, Spanish

Khoisan or **Click Languages** (*spoken in S and E Africa*)	
	Hatsa (or Hadzapi)
	Sandawe
SOUTH AFRICAN KHOISAN	San, Khoikhoi

Malayo-Polynesian languages (*spoken in Madagascar; for a full presentation of the Malayo-Polynesian language family, see table accompanying the* LANGUAGE *article*)	
WESTERN	Malagasy

Niger-Kordofanian Languages	
NIGER-CONGO (spoken in S and central Africa and sub-Saharan W Africa)	
West Atlantic	Dyola, Fulani, Gola, Kissi, Temne, Wolof
Mande	Dyula, Malinke, Mende
Gur (or Voltaic)	Dagomba, Mamprusi, Mossi
Kwa	Akan, Ashanti, Bini, Ewe, Ibo, Ijo, Nupe, Yoruba
Benue-Congo	
Bantu	Bemba, Ganda, Kikuyu, Kongo, Lingala, Luba, Makua, Mbundu, Ruanda, Rundi, Shona, Sesotho, Swahili, Thonga, Xhosa, Zulu
Non-Bantu	Efik, Jukun, Tiv
Adamawa-Eastern	Azande, Banda, Sango
KORDOFANIAN (spoken in Sudan)	
Katla	Katla
Koalib	Koalib
Talodi	Talodi
Tegali	Tegali
Tumtum	Tumtum

Nilo-Saharan Languages	
SONGHAI (spoken in Mali)	Songhai
SAHARAN (spoken near Lake Chad and in the central Sahara)	Daza, Kanuri, Teda, Zaghawa
MABAN (spoken east of Lake Chad)	Maba
PURIAN (spoken in Sudan)	Fur
KOMAN (spoken in Ethiopia and Sudan)	Ganza, Gule, Gumuz, Koma Mao, Uduk
CHARI-NILE (spoken in Sudan, Zaire, Uganda, Cameroon, Chad, Central African Republic, mainland Tanzania, and Ethiopia)	
Eastern Sudanic	
Nubian	Birked, Midobi
Nilotic	Dinka, Masai, Nandi, Nuer, Shilluk, Suk, Turkana
Central Sudanic	Bongo-Bagirmi, Efe, Mangebetu Berta, Kunama

continues to enrich African writing, which appears in native, especially Bantu, languages, and in French, English, and Portuguese. The African writer best known before the 1930s was the South African Thomas Mofolo, whose novels (in Sesotho) included *Chaka* (tr. 1931). French-African writers in Paris in the 1930s, led by the poet-statesman Léopold Sédar SENGHOR, espoused *négritude,* a rejection of French assimilationist policy. After World War II, writers focused on decaying colonialism and on the "new" Africa. National literatures began to appear, notably in Nigeria with the work of Chinua ACHEBE, Wole SOYINKA, Amos TUTUOLA, and others, and in Senegal and Cameroon. Major African writers in English include Ezekiel Mphahlele and Oswald Mtshali (South Africa), Bessie Head (Botswana), Ayi Kwei Armah (Ghana), and Ngugi wa Thiong'o and Okot p'Bitek (Kenya). Among leading writers in French are Mongo Beti (Cameroon); Camara Laye (Guinea); Birago Diop, Sembene Ousmane, and Mariama Ba (Senegal); David Diop (born in France); and Tchicaya U Tamsi (Congo). One of the best-known writers in Portuguese was Agostinho Neto (1922–79), president of Angola (1975–79).

African Methodist Episcopal Church, a leading African-American denomination of METHODISM, founded (1816) by Richard Allen. The church has over 3,000,000 American members.

African Methodist Episcopal Zion Church, one of the largest African Methodist bodies, founded (1796) by African-American Methodists. The church had a U.S. membership of 1,200,000 in 1991.

African National Congress (ANC), the oldest black (now multiracial) political organization in South Africa; founded in 1912. Prominent in its opposition to APARTHEID, the organization was banned in 1960 and initiated guerrilla attacks in 1961. In 1964 its leader, Nelson MANDELA, was sentenced to life in prison, and the leadership was forced into exile. Although outlawed, the ANC became the popularly acknowledged vehicle of mass resistance to apartheid in the late 1970s and the 1980s. Following the end of the ban on the ANC and the release of Mandela in 1990, many of its leaders returned from exile, and the ANC negotiated with the government for black enfranchisement and an end to apartheid. In the early 1990s there were violent clashes between supporters of the ANC and Inkatha (see BUTHELEZI, MANGOSUTHU GATSHA). The ANC became a registered political party in 1994 in advance of the first South African elections open to citizens of all races, which they won.

African violet, common name for plants (mostly hybrids of *Saintpaulia ionantha*) of the GESNERIA family, grown chiefly as houseplants for their colorful flowers and fuzzy foliage.

Afrikaans [ăf″rəkäns′], one of the official languages of South Africa. It is a Germanic language of the Indo-European family. See AFRICAN LANGUAGES (table).

Ag, chemical symbol of the element SILVER.

Aga Khan III, 1877–1957, Muslim leader. As hereditary ruler of the Muslim Ismaili sect he was born to great power and wealth. He supported the British in India, founded (1906) the All-India Muslim League, and represented India in various international bodies.

Agamemnon, in Greek mythology, leader of the Greeks in the TROJAN WAR; brother of MENELAUS; son of ATREUS. His children by CLYTEMNESTRA were IPHIGENIA, ELECTRA, and ORESTES. To obtain favorable winds for the fleet against Troy, he sacrificed Iphigenia to ARTEMIS, incurring Clytemnestra's hatred. At Troy he quarreled with ACHILLES; that dispute forms a main theme of HOMER's *Iliad.* He withdrew from the war and returned to Mycenae, where he was murdered by Clytemnestra and her lover, AEGISTHUS. To avenge his death, Orestes and Electra killed Aegisthus and their mother.

Aga Muhammad Khan or **Agha Muhammad Khan,** 1742–97, shah of PERSIA (1796–97), founder of the Kajar, or Qajar, dynasty. In 1794 he killed the last ruler of the Zand dynasty and climaxed his campaign for the throne with a wholesale massacre. Hated by his subjects for his brutality, he was assassinated.

Agana or **Agaña,** city (1990 pop. 4,785), capital of GUAM, W Pacific. It is the adminstrative center of Guam; much of the city's economic activity is related to providing goods and services to the U.S. military bases on Guam. Tourism is also important. Agana was completely destroyed in World War II.

agar, product consisting of the sugar galactose, obtained from some red ALGAE species (see SEAWEED). Dissolved in boiling water and cooled, agar becomes gelatinous; it is used as a culture medium (especially for BACTERIA), a laxative, and a food thickener.

Agassiz, Louis (Jean Louis Rodolphe Agassiz) [ăg′əsē], 1807–73, Swiss-American zoologist and geologist. In 1832 he became professor of natural history at the Univ. of Neuchâtel, which he made a center for scientific study. He also examined glacial movements and deposits before coming to the U.S. in 1846, where he taught at Harvard (from 1848) and strongly influenced a generation of scientists. His writings include *Research on Fossil Fish* (5 vol., 1833–44) and *Contributions to the Natural History of the United States* (4 vol., 1857–62).

agate, extremely fine-grained variety of CHALCEDONY, banded in two or more colors. The banding occurs because agates are formed by the slow deposition of silica from solution into cavities of older rocks. Agates are found primarily in Brazil, Uruguay, India, Mexico, and the U.S. They are valued as semiprecious gems and are used in the manufacture of grinding equipment.

agave: see AMARYLLIS.

Agee, James, 1909–55, American writer; b. Knoxville, Tenn. His works include *Let Us Now Praise Famous Men* (1941), a telling commentary on Depression-era tenant farmers, and *A Death in the Family* (1957; Pulitzer), a poetic novel. His movie criticism and scripts are collected in *Agee on Film* (2 vol., 1958–60).

Agent Orange: see HERBICIDE.

Aggeus [ăgē′əs], Vulgate form of HAGGAI.

aggression, form of behavior characterized by verbal or physical attack. It may be either appropriate and self-protective or destructive. When aggression in adults is not a response to a clear threat, it is often considered a symptom of mental disorder. It may be directed outward, against others, as in explosive personality disorders, or inward, against oneself, leading to self-damaging acts. Some investigators of human behavior, such as Sigmund FREUD and Konrad LORENZ, have argued that aggressive behavior is innate, but others have proposed that it is learned. Brain abnormalities plus hormonal, genetic, and social factors (including poverty and violence in the media) are all being studied for their influence on aggressive behavior.

Agincourt [ăzhăNkōōr′], village, N France, where in 1415 Henry V of England defeated an army of French knights in the HUNDRED YEARS WAR. The victory of Henry's longbow men made obsolete the warfare methods of the age of chivalry and enabled England to conquer much of France.

aging: see GERONTOLOGY.

Agnew, Spiro Theodore, 1918–, 39th vice president of the U.S.; b. Baltimore, Md. Governor of Maryland (1967–69), he was vice president (1969–73) in the administration of Pres. Richard M. NIXON. A critic of liberals and VIETNAM WAR protestors, he resigned (Oct. 10, 1973) after evidence revealed political corruption during his years in Maryland politics. He pleaded no contest to the charge of evading income tax, was sentenced to probation, and fined. In 1981 a state court ordered Agnew to repay Maryland over $248,000, for bribes he took while in state office.

Agnon, S(hmuel) Y(osef) [ägnōn′], 1888–1970, Israeli writer; b. Poland as Samuel Josef Czaczkes. Regarded as the greatest modern writer of fiction in Hebrew, he shared the 1966 Nobel Prize in literature. His novels and stories explore Jewish life; they include the novels *The Bridal Canopy* (1919) and *The Day Before Yesterday* (1945).

agnosticism, form of skepticism that holds that the existence of God cannot be logically proved or disproved. Agnosticism is not to be confused with ATHEISM, which denies the existence of God. KANT and Herbert SPENCER considered themselves agnostics.

Agra, former province, N central India. The presidency, or province, of Agra was created in 1833 by the British. In 1902 it became part of the United Provinces of Agra and Oudh. The city of **Agra** (1991 pop. 891,790), Uttar Pradesh state, is on the Jumna R. A district administrative headquarters, it produces shoes, glassware, carpets, and other goods. AKBAR founded Agra, and it was a MOGUL capital until 1658. The British annexed it in 1836. It is noted for its architecture, especially the TAJ MAHAL.

agriculture, science of producing crops and livestock; it aims to increase production and protect the land from deterioration. Branches include AGRONOMY, HORTICULTURE, ENTOMOLOGY, animal husbandry, and DAIRYING. Historically, agriculture has been linked with social, economic, and political organization. Its development among early peoples encouraged stable settlements, and it later became associated with landholding, SLAVERY, and FEUDALISM. During the agricultural revolution (16th and 17th cent.), horticultural knowledge expanded, and crops and farming methods were exchanged internationally. The invention of machines such as McCormick's reaper (1831) and the general-purpose tractor (c.1924) led to mechanized, large-scale farming. Modern Western agriculture also depends on breeding programs; FERTILIZERS and PESTICIDES or INTEGRATED PEST MANAGEMENT; food processing techniques, e.g., REFRIGERATION; efficient marketing; agricultural colleges and research centers; and, in many nations, government subsidies. See also GREEN REVOLUTION; ORGANIC FARMING.

Agriculture, United States Department of, federal executive department established (1862) to administer all federal programs related to food production and rural life. It assists farmers through its research, planning, and service agencies, and aids consumers by inspecting and grading many products; it also administers the Food Stamp Program and issues a wide range of publications on farming and horticulture. The Forest Service and the Soil Conservation Service are part of the department.

agronomy, branch of AGRICULTURE concerned with soil management and with the breeding, physiology, and production of major field crops. It deals mainly with large-scale crops (e.g., cotton, soybeans, and wheat), while HORTICULTURE concerns fruits, vegetables, and ornamentals.

Aguinaldo, Emilio [ägēnäl′dō], 1869–1964, Philippine leader. After leading (1896) a rebellion against Spanish rule, he cooperated with

U.S. forces in the SPANISH-AMERICAN WAR. He later rebelled (1899–1901) against U.S. rule.

Ahab [ā'hăb], d. c.853 B.C., king of Israel (c.874–c.853 B.C.), son and successor of Omri. One of the greatest kings of the northern kingdom, he was killed in a war against Damascus. The biblical account of Ahab's reign is mostly concerned with its religious aspects, especially his marriage to Jezebel, a willful woman of Tyre who was attached to foreign cults and behavior. To the devout she represented evil, and she met her match in ELIJAH.

Ahad Ha-Am [äkhäd'hä-äm'] [Heb., = one of the people], 1856–1927, pseud. of Asher Ginsberg, Jewish thinker and Zionist leader; b. Russia. A critic of those who sought immediate settlement in Palestine, he saw Palestine as a "spiritual center" giving strength and direction to Jews in the Diaspora. Some of his essays appear in *Selected Essays of Ahad Ha-Am* (tr. 1912).

Ahasuerus: see ESTHER.

Ahaz [ā'hăz], d. c.727 B.C., king of Judah (c.731–727 B.C.). His reign marked the end of the real independence of Judah. In the BIBLE he is opposed by ISAIAH for his alliance with Assyria against Israel and Syria, and denounced for having heathen abominations and for using the Temple gold to pay tribute to Assyria.

Ahmadabad or **Ahmedabad,** city (1991 pop. 2,873,000), capital of Gujarat state, NW India, on the Sabarmati R. It is an industrial center noted for its cotton mills. Founded in 1412 by the Sultan Ahmad Shah, it fell to AKBAR in 1573 and prospered under the MOGULS, who controlled the city until 1758 when it came under the MAHRATTAS. It has many mosques, tombs, and temples. It came under British control in 1818.

Ahmed, sultans of the OTTOMAN EMPIRE (Turkey). **Ahmed I,** 1589–1617 (r.1603–17), made peace (1606) with Austria, agreeing to Transylvania's independence and recognizing other European rulers as his equals for the first time. **Ahmed II,** 1642–95 (r.1691–95), saw the beginning of the Turks' forced retreat from Hungary. **Ahmed III,** 1673–1736 (r.1703–30), seized (1715) the Peloponnesus and the Ionian Isles (except Corfu) from Venice, but he lost important Balkan territories to Austria. He was overthrown by the JANISSARIES and died in prison.

Ahvenanmaa Islands or **Åland Islands,** Finland, strategically important group of c.7,000 islands (less than 100 inhabited) at the entrance to the Gulf of Bothnia in the Baltic Sea. Originally colonized as part of Sweden, the islands were ceded (1809) to Russia, demilitarized (1856) by international agreement, and confirmed (1921) as part of Finland by the League of Nations. Finland renounced the League's guarantee of autonomy in 1951, but accorded rights of self-government to the islanders, who are largely Swedish.

AIDS or **acquired immunodeficiency syndrome,** disease caused by strains of a virus, known as HIV (human immunodeficiency virus), that attacks certain white blood cells called T4, or CD4, cells. The virus is spread through the exchange of body fluids (primarily semen, blood, and blood products) and can persist in the body for a decade or more without any apparent symptoms. The disease weakens the body's immune system, allowing other diseases, including Kaposi's sarcoma (otherwise a relatively uncommon form of cancer), *Pneumocystis carinii* PNEUMONIA, pulmonary tuberculosis, invasive cervical cancer, and encephalitis, to overwhelm the individual. The drugs AZT, ddI, and ddC, which interfere with HIV's ability to reproduce itself, are used to treat patients with HIV infection and AIDS. Studies are ongoing for an effective vaccine and other treatments. Although AIDS has largely affected male homosexuals, drug abusers, prostitutes, and hemophiliacs in the U.S., heterosexually transmitted infection has increased in the U.S. and reached epidemic proportions in several African and Asian nations.

aids, in FEUDALISM, a type of due paid by a vassal to his lord. Aids varied with time and place, although in England the aids specified in the MAGNA CARTA (1215) were due only on the knighting of the lord's eldest son and the marriage of his eldest daughter, or for ransoming the lord from captivity. Aids were similar to SCUTAGE and TALLAGE. In France, aids continued as a royal tax until the French Revolution (1789).

Aiken, Conrad, 1889–1973, American writer; b. Savannah, Ga. Often concerned with the quest for self-knowledge, he is best known for his richly musical verse, e.g., *Selected Poems* (1929, Pulitzer), *A Letter from Li Po* (1955). His other works include the novels *Blue Voyage* (1927) and *Great Circle* (1933), short stories, critical essays, and an autobiography (1952).

ailanthus, tree (genus *Ailanthus*) of the family Simarubaceae. Ailanthus is native to warm regions of Asia and Australia. Its wood is used in cabinetmaking and for charcoal manufacture. The bark and leaves are used medicinally, and the leaves provide food for silkworms. Females of a species called tree of heaven are cultivated for their attractive foliage and their resistance to smoke and soot; the flowers of the male plant, however, have a disagreeable odor.

Ailey, Alvin, 1931–89, American modern dancer and choreographer; b. Rogers, Tex. He studied with Lester Horton. In the late 1950s, he formed his own company, Alvin Ailey's American Dance Theater, which became noted for its use of African motifs. His best-known works include *Creation of the World* (1954) and *Revelations* (1960).

Ainu, aborigines of Japan, possibly of Caucasoid descent, having both European and Asian physical traits. Invaders from Asia forced the Ainu to the N Japanese island of HOKKAIDO and to Sakhalin and the Kuril Islands, in Russia. Their animistic religion centers on a bear cult. They live by hunting, fishing, farming, and selling crafts to tourists.

air, law of the, law connected with the use of the air (including radio and telegraph communication); more commonly, body of laws governing civil aviation. Spurred by the growth of air transport, the victorious nations of World War I, meeting in Paris in 1919, drew up the International Convention for Air Navigation, commonly called the Paris Convention; this agreement recognized national claims to air space and established rules for aircraft registration and operating safety. U.S. air laws are modeled on the Convention, and are administered by the FEDERAL AVIATION ADMINISTRATION. There are also many general conventions and bilateral agreements between nations. In 1944 a conference of 52 nations established the International Civil Aviation Organization (see UNITED NATIONS, table 3), to ensure the orderly growth of international aviation. The successful launching of SATELLITES necessitated the development of SPACE LAW.

air conditioning, mechanical process for controlling the temperature, humidity, cleanliness, and circulation of air in buildings and rooms. Most air conditioners operate by ducting air across the colder, heat-absorbing side of a REFRIGERATION apparatus, and directing the cooled air back into the air-conditioned space. Small window conditioners vent heat outdoors. Larger systems use circulating water to remove heat. Air conditioning provides the heat, humidity, and contamination controls essential in the manufacture of such products as chemicals and pharmaceuticals.

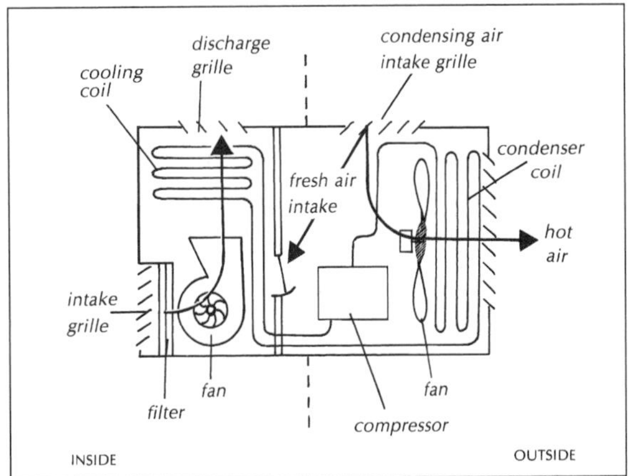

Cross-section of air conditioning unit

aircraft carrier, ship designed to carry aircraft and to permit takeoff and landing of planes. Its distinctive features are a flat upper deck (flight deck) that functions as a takeoff and landing field, and a main deck (hangar deck) beneath the flight deck for storing and servicing the aircraft. The aircraft carrier remained an experimental and untested war vessel until WORLD WAR II, when the Japanese wreaked havoc on the British, Dutch, and U.S. navies with carrier-borne aircraft. By 1942 the aircraft carrier had replaced the battleship as the major unit in a modern fleet, and during the war it was indispensable in naval operations against a sea- or shore-based enemy, with two major battles (Coral Sea and Midway, 1942) being fought entirely by aircraft, and the opposing fleets never coming within gunshot range of each other. U.S. carriers of the *Essex* class spearheaded the island-hopping campaign in the Pacific. A new era in carrier design opened when the U.S. launched (1960) the nuclear-powered *Enterprise,* a vessel capable of lengthy voyages without refueling. A nuclear-powered successor, the *Nimitz*, was the largest ship afloat when launched in 1972. Amphibious assault ships are carrierlike ships that use helicopters and VTOL aircraft, such as Harriers, to land and support marines.

air-cushion vehicle (ACV), **ground-effect machine,** or **Hovercraft,** vehicle designed to travel at a short distance above ground or water, moving on a cushion of air that is held in a chamber beneath the vehicle. ACVs offer the potential for very high speeds. The maximum size of ACVs is now over 100 tons and some of those travel at over 100 mph (160 kph). Small ACVs, usually called flarecraft, can carry one to eight people at 150 mi (240 km) per hr.

airedale terrier, largest of the TERRIER group; shoulder height, c.23 in. (58.4 cm); weight, 40–50 lb (18.1–22.7 kg). Its dense, wiry, close-lying coat is a mixture of tan, black, and grizzle. The breed was probably produced from crosses of the extinct black-and-tan terrier and the otterhound.

airfoil, surface designed to develop a desired force by reaction with a fluid, especially air, that is flowing across the surface. Examples of airfoils are the fixed wings of AIRPLANES, which produce lift (see AERODYNAMICS), and control surfaces, such as ailerons, elevators, rudders, and flaps, that are manipulated to produce variable forces. Other airfoils include spoilers, propeller blades, and the blades utilized in turbojet engines.

air force, national military organization for air warfare. Although balloons were used by French forces in Italy in 1859 and by the Union in the U.S. Civil War, air forces in the modern sense date from WORLD WAR I, when the offensive capabilities of the AIRPLANE were first demonstrated. Airplanes were first controlled by national armies and used for reconnaissance and support of ground forces, but as their effectiveness as tactical weapons increased, independent air forces were called for. Arguing that future wars would be won by strategic bombing of an enemy's industrial centers, military leaders, including Italian Gen. Giulio Douhet, U.S. Gen. William MITCHELL, and British Air Chief Marshal Sir Hugh Trenchard urged intensive development of air power. By WORLD WAR II, control of the air over both land and sea proved crucial in most major engagements, and the air force became a separate branch of the armed services in many countries. The first great air battle in history was the Battle of Britain (1940), in which the British Royal Air Force stood off the German Luftwaffe over England. The effect of air power in revolutionizing naval warfare was demonstrated in the 1941 surprise attack by Japanese aircraft, launched from AIRCRAFT CARRIERS, on PEARL HARBOR. Air forces on both sides engaged in strategic and tactical bombing, attacks on naval and merchant ships, transportation of personnel and cargo, mining of harbors and shipping lanes, antisubmarine patrols, and photo reconnaissance, as well as support of ground, naval, and amphibious operations. After World War II, the airplane was largely superseded by the ballistic missile as a strategic weapon, but with helicopters joining the traditional fighter planes, bombers, and cargo planes of the modern air force, air power continued to be of primary importance in tactical operations, particularly in "limited" wars such as those in Southeast Asia and the Middle East. The PERSIAN GULF WAR, which saw the introduction of stealth fighter planes (see STEALTH TECHNOLOGY), produced the first unambiguously decisive air-power victory in warfare.

air navigation, science and technology of determining the position of an aircraft with respect to the surface of the earth and accurately maintaining a desired course (see NAVIGATION). The two most common methods are governed by visual flight regulations (VFR) and instrument flight regulations (IFR). Small airborne computer systems can now give the pilot the plane's position—the Global Positioning System (see NAVIGATION SATELLITE) permits determination of a plane's position to within a few hundred feet—and can carry out dead reckoning by monitoring all course and speed changes. The automatic pilot also interprets data on direction, speed, and altitude to maintain an aircraft in straight, level flight. For landing, the pilot is often guided by radio communication from a controller observing the plane via ground-based radar. Some systems actually land the plane automatically, although the pilot always has the option of overriding manually.

airplane, aeroplane, or **aircraft,** heavier-than-air vehicle, mechanically driven and fitted with fixed wings that support it in flight through the dynamic action of the air. On Dec. 17, 1903, Americans Orville and Wilbur WRIGHT flew the first airplane near Kitty Hawk, N.C. The machine was a biplane with two propellers chain-driven by a gasoline motor. Modern airplanes are monoplanes (airplanes with one set of wings). Airplanes may further be classified as driven by propeller, JET PROPULSION, or ROCKET. The airplane has six main parts: fuselage, wings, stabilizer (or tail plane), rudder, one or more engines, and landing gear. The fuselage is the main body, usually streamlined in form. The wings are the main supporting surfaces. The airplane's lift, or force supporting it in flight, is basically the result of the direct action of air against the surfaces of the wings (see AERODYNAMICS). With the use of jet engines and the resulting higher speeds, airplanes have become less dependent on large values of lift from the wings. Consequently wings have been shortened and swept back so as to produce less drag, especially at supersonic speeds. At the trailing edge of the wings are attached movable surfaces, called ailerons (see AIRFOIL) that are used to gain lateral control and to turn the plane. Directional stability is provided by the tail fin, a fixed vertical airfoil at the rear of the airplane. The stabilizer is a fixed horizontal airfoil at the rear of the airplane used to suppress undesired pitching motion. The elevators, which are movable auxiliary surfaces attached to the stabilizers, are used to produce controlled pitching. The rudder, generally at the rear of the tail fin, is a movable auxiliary airfoil that gives the craft a yawing movement in normal flight. The landing gear is the understructure that supports the weight of the craft when on the ground or on the water and that reduces the shock on landing. Modern fly-by-wire control systems rely on computers and electronics rather than cables to operate aircraft control surfaces. See AVIATION; SEAPLANE; SHORT TAKEOFF AND LANDING AIRCRAFT; VERTICAL TAKEOFF AND LANDING AIRCRAFT.

air plant: see EPIPHYTE.

air pollution: see POLLUTION.

airship or **dirigible,** aircraft consisting of a cigar-shaped balloon that carries a propulsion system (propellers), a steering mechanism, and accommodations for passengers, crew, and cargo. The balloon section is filled with a lighter-than-air gas—either helium, which is nonflammable, or hydrogen—to give the airship its lift. The balloon maintains its form by the internal gas pressure in the nonrigid (blimp) and semirigid types of airships; the latter in addition has a rigid keel. The rigid type maintains its form by having a metal framework that holds its shape regardless of the internal gas pressure; inside the hull are a number of small gas-filled balloons. The first successful power-driven airship was built by the French inventor Henri Giffard in 1852. Count Ferdinand von ZEPPELIN of Germany invented the first rigid airship, which was completed in 1900. The German airship *Hindenburg* burned at its mooring mast at Lakehurst, N.J., in 1937. No rigid airship survived World War II. Modern blimps are used in antisubmarine warfare, television photography, and advertising.

air traffic control, system by which aircraft are safely routed into and out of major airports. In the U.S., it is centered on 22 regional control centers that route air traffic to and from control centers at airports. Transponders in every commercial, and many private, aircraft and ground-based radar provide information on location, altitude, and speed to the controllers, who are responsible for maintaining safe distances between the aircraft. See also AIR NAVIGATION.

Aix-la-Chapelle: see AACHEN, Germany.

Aix-la-Chapelle, Treaty of: see AUSTRIAN SUCCESSION, WAR OF THE.

Ajax, in Greek mythology. **1** The Telamonian Ajax, hero of the TROJAN WAR. In the *Iliad* he is a huge man, slow of thought and speech, but very courageous. He and ODYSSEUS rescued the corpse of ACHILLES. When Odysseus was awarded Achilles' armor the disappointed Ajax went mad and committed suicide. **2** The Locrian Ajax, who raped CASSANDRA in the sack of Troy. Shipwrecked by ATHENA, he was saved by POSEIDON, but struck dead by lightning for his defiance.

Akbar, 1542–1605, Mogul emperor of INDIA (1556–1605). An outstanding general, Akbar added AFGHANISTAN, Baluchistan, and N India to his domains. His reign was marked by administrative reform, religious toleration, and the flowering of art and literature.

Akhenaton: see IKHNATON.

Akhmatova, Anna [əkhmä'təvə], pseud. of **Anna Andreyevna Gorenko,** 1889–1966, Russian poet of the ACMEIST school. Her brief, highly emotional lyrics are simply and musically written. Among her most important volumes are *The Rosary* (1914) and *The Course of Time* (1966).

Akiba ben Joseph [əkē'bə], A.D. c.50–c.135, Palestinian rabbi. He compiled a collection of Hebrew Oral Law, *Mishna of Rabbi Akiba* (see MISHNA). After siding with BAR KOKBA in his revolt against Rome, Akiba was imprisoned and, it is said, tortured to death by the Romans.

Akihito [äkē'hētō], 1933–, emperor of Japan (1989–). The son and successor of HIROHITO, he was the first member of the royal family to marry (1959) a commoner, Shoda Michiko.

Akkad [ă'kăd, ä'käd], northern part of later BABYLONIA, in Mesopotamia; the southern part was SUMER. In the 4th millennium B.C. a Semitic city-state appeared, and under Sargon (c.2340 B.C.) Akkad became an imperial power. Akkad and Sumer were united as Babylonia by HAMMURABI. The name Akkad also appears as Accad.

Akkadian [əkā'dēən], language belonging to the Semitic subfamily of the Hamito-Semitic family of languages. Also called Assyro-Babylonian, Akkadian was current in ancient MESOPOTAMIA (now IRAQ) from about 3000 B.C. until the time of Jesus. See LANGUAGE (table).

Akron, city (1990 pop. 223,019), seat of Summit co., NE Ohio, on the Little Cuyahoga R. and the Ohio and Erie Canal; settled 1825; inc. as a city 1865. It is a port of entry and an important industrial and transportation center. With the opening of the first plant in 1870, Akron became the rubber capital of the U.S. Despite the closing of the plants, headquarters of rubber producers are still located there. Heavy machinery, aerospace industries, and polymer research are important. Akron's Art Institute is well known.

Akte: see ATHOS.

Akutagawa Ryunosuke, 1892–1927, Japanese author. One of Japan's finest short-story writers, he derived many of his tales from historical Japanese sources, but told them with psychological insights in an individualistic style. "Rashomon" (1915) and "In a Grove" (1921) were made into the classic 1950 film *Rashomon*, directed by KUROSAWA AKIRA.

al-. For most Arabic names beginning thus, see the second part of the name, e.g., SADAT, ANWAR AL-.

Al, chemical symbol of the element ALUMINUM.

Alabama, state in the SE U.S.; bordered by Tennessee (N), Georgia (E), Florida and the Gulf of Mexico (S), and Mississippi (W).

Area, 51,609 sq mi (133,677 sq km). *Pop.* (1990) 4,040,587, a 3.9% increase over 1980 pop. *Capital,* Montgomery. *Statehood,* Dec. 14, 1819 (22d state). *Highest pt.,* Cheaha Mt., 2,407 ft (734 m); *lowest pt.,* sea level. *Nickname,* Heart of Dixie. *Motto,* We Dare Defend Our Rights. *State bird,* yellowhammer. *State flower,* camellia. *State tree,* Southern (longleaf) pine. *Abbr.,* Ala.; AL.

Land and People. Except for the southern edge of the APPALACHIAN MOUNTAINS, in the northeast, Alabama consists mostly of rolling plains drained by the Alabama and Tombigbee rivers. The fertile Black Belt is located in central Alabama. The climate is subtropical and humid. More than 60% of the population lives in urban areas, principally in BIRMINGHAM, a steel center; MOBILE, a major U.S. port; MONTGOMERY, the capital; and HUNTSVILLE, an aerospace center. The population in 1990 was 73.6% white and 25.3% African American, with the remainder in other groups.

Economy. Cotton remains one of the chief crops; others include peanuts and soybeans. Cattle, poultry, and catfish are raised. Dams on the TENNESSEE R., in the north, provide power for the state's industries, whose leading products are iron and steel, paper and wood products, chemicals, electronics, textiles, and processed foods. Oil is produced in the south, and fishing is important along the coast. Lumbering is a major industry throughout Alabama.

Government. According to the constitution of 1901, the government is headed by a governor elected to a four-year term. The legislature is composed of a 35-member senate and 105-member house of representatives elected to four-year terms. Alabama sends seven representatives and two senators to the U.S. Congress and has nine electoral votes.

History. When Spanish explorers, including Hernando DE SOTO, visited the region during the 16th cent., they found the CREEK, CHEROKEE, CHOCTAW, and CHICKASAW tribes. In 1702 the French established the first white settlement. Andrew JACKSON defeated (1814) the Creek Confederacy at Horseshoe Bend, ushering in a period of rapid settlement. Subsequently, huge plantations utilizing slave labor were established to cultivate cotton. Alabama seceded from the Union in 1861. Following the CIVIL WAR the defeated state was placed under military rule; it was readmitted to the Union in 1868. Alabama slowly recovered from the war and the corruption of RECONSTRUCTION, a process made easier by the beginning of industrialization. Agricultural diversification began after the boll weevil infested the cotton fields during the early 20th cent. The 1954 Supreme Court decision outlawing school segregation ushered in a painful period of INTEGRATION and the growth of the CIVIL-RIGHTS movement. Despite opposition by Gov. George WALLACE and acts of racial violence in the state, most public schools in Alabama had been successfully desegregated by the early 1970s. From the late 1970s to early 90s public attention largely shifted to economic issues, and major efforts were made to assure the state's growth by encouraging further diversification of manufacturing industries.

Alabama claims, claims by the U.S. against Great Britain after the U.S. CIVIL WAR for damage to merchant ships caused by British-built Confederate cruisers. A tribunal (1871–72) at Geneva awarded the U.S. $15.5 million for damage caused by the Confederate ships *Alabama, Florida,* and *Shenandoah.*

alabaster, fine-grained, translucent variety of the mineral GYPSUM, pure white or streaked with reddish brown. Its softness makes it easily carved but also easily broken, soiled, and weathered. Quarried in England and Italy, it is used to make statuary and other decorative objects. The Oriental alabaster of ancient Egyptian and Roman tombs is actually MARBLE, a calcium carbonate, whereas gypsum is a calcium sulfate.

Alain-Fournier [älăN-fo͞ornyā'], 1886–1914, French novelist; b. Henri Alban Fournier. His single full-length work, *The Wanderer* (1913), about a youthful search for the ideal, is a delicate blend of symbolism and realism.

Alamein, El [ĕl ăləmān'], or **Al Alamayn** [äl älămān'], town, N Egypt, on the Mediterranean Sea. During WORLD WAR II it was the site of a decisive British victory (1942) against the Germans. The victory saved Egypt for the Allies and led to the defeat (1943) of the Axis powers in North Africa.

Alamo, the [Span., = cottonwood], chapel-fort in San Antonio, Tex., built c.1744. It was held by Davy CROCKETT, Jim Bowie, W. TRAVIS, and about 180 other Texans against a siege by an army of several thousand Mexicans under Gen. SANTA ANNA (Feb. 24–Mar. 6, 1836) during the Texas Revolution. While the defenders died, their resistance rallied others who defeated the Mexicans six weeks later, crying "Remember the Alamo!"

Åland Islands: see AHVENANMAA ISLANDS.

Alarcón, Pedro Antonio de [älärkōn'], 1833–91, Spanish writer and diplomat. His novels, witty and often realistic, include *The Three-Cornered Hat* (1874), on which FALLA based a ballet, and *Captain Venom* (1881).

Alarcón y Mendoza, Juan Ruiz de [ē mändō'thä], 1581?–1639, Spanish dramatic poet; b. Mexico. His brilliant and lively comedies (2 vol., 1628–34) make him a major literary figure of Spain's GOLDEN AGE. The most famous, *The Suspicious Truth,* was the model for *The Liar* by CORNEILLE.

Alaric I, c.370–410, Visigothic king. After the death of Roman Emperor THEODOSIUS I he ravaged the Balkans until stopped by STILICHO, invaded Italy, and sacked Rome (410).

Alas, Leopoldo [ä'läs], pseud. **Clarín,** 1852–1901, Spanish writer. He was a professor of law at the Univ. of Oviedo. His masterpiece is the naturalistic novel *The Regent's Wife* (1885), a detailed analysis of provincial life.

Alaska, largest state in area of the U.S. but second smallest by population (only Wyoming has fewer people), occupying the northwest extremity of the North American continent, separated from the coterminous U.S. by NW Canada. It is bordered by British Columbia and Yukon Territory (E), the Pacific Ocean (S), the Bering Sea (W), and the Arctic Ocean (N).

Area, 586,412 sq mi (1,518,800 sq km). *Pop.* (1990) 550,043, a 37.3% increase over 1980 pop. *Capital,* Juneau. *Statehood,* Jan. 3, 1959 (49th state). *Highest pt.,* Mt. McKinley, 20,320 ft (6,198 m); *lowest pt.,* sea level. *Motto,* North to the Future. *State bird,* willow ptarmigan. *State flower,* forget-me-not. *State tree,* Sitka spruce. *Abbr.,* AK.

Land and People. Along the heavily indented coast are two peninsulas, the Seward Peninsula to the west, and, farther south, the Alaska Peninsula, from which the ALEUTIAN ISLANDS extend. The interior is dominated by rugged mountains, including the Alaska Range, where Denali, or Mount MCKINLEY (20,320 ft/6,198 m), the highest point in North America, is located. Many tourists are attracted by the state's dramatic scenery, some of the most spectacular located in its eight NATIONAL PARKS (see table). Winters in the interiors are very cold; summers are brief but hot. The COAST RANGES dominate the more temperate panhandle region, in the southeast, where the Inside Passage traverses the Alexander Archipelago, located just offshore. Principal lowlands are in the central region—drained by the YUKON R.—and, in the far north, the North Slope, along the Arctic coast. Over 65% of the land is controlled by the federal government. The largest city is ANCHORAGE, followed by FAIRBANKS and JUNEAU; more than 67% of the population lives in urban areas. In 1990 the population was 75% white, 15% ESKIMO and ALEUTS, and the remainder largely African American and Asian American.

Economy. The economy has been transformed since the discovery (1968) of North Slope oil and natural gas deposits, and their exploitation dominates the economy. The Alaska pipeline (built 1974–77) carries oil from PRUDHOE BAY to the port of Valdez, in the south. Coal, platinum, copper, gold, and uranium are among other minerals mined. Alaska has the largest fishing industry in the U.S.; the small manufacturing sector is dominated by the processing of fish and lumber. Fur export is important. Because of the harsh climate and terrain there is little agriculture.

Government. The constitution (adopted 1956) provides for a governor elected to a four-year term. The state legislature is composed of a senate whose 20 members serve four-year terms and a house whose 40 members serve two-year terms. Alaska sends two senators and one representative to the U.S. Congress and has three electoral votes.

History. The first white settlers were Russians who crossed the BERING STRAIT in search of furs and established (1784) the first permanent settlement on Kodiak Island. In 1867 Russia sold Alaska to the U.S. for $7.2 million. The first influx of Americans came in the gold rush of the 1890s and the 1900s. During WORLD WAR II the Japanese occupied (1942) Attu, Agattu, and Kiska, in the Aleutian Islands, but were driven out (1943) by U.S. forces. The war contributed to Alaska's economic development through construction of the Alaska Highway and of defense installations. The state's greatest economic boom occurred after the extensive oil discoveries of 1968, and huge off-shore deposits found in 1980 promised future development. Against strong opposition by state residents favoring private control of resources, the U.S. Congress approved (1980) the Alaska lands bill, which designated more than 104 million acres (42 million hectares) of national parks, wildlife refuges, and wilderness areas. In 1989 an oil tanker bringing oil from PRUDHOE BAY spilled 10 million gallons of oil near the port of Valdez causing severe economic and environmental damage.

Alaskan malamute, strong, compact WORKING DOG; shoulder height, c.23 in. (58.2 cm); weight, 70–85 lb (31.75–38.5 kg). Its coarse coat, composed of oily, woolly underhairs and a thick cover coat, may be any shade of gray or black, with white markings. The malamute has been raised for centuries as a sled dog.

Alba or **Alva, Fernando Álvarez de Toledo, duque de** [ăl'bə, ăl'və], 1507?–82, Spanish governor general and regent of the NETHERLANDS (1567–73). A ruthless absolutist, he crushed the rebellious provinces, executing some 18,000 Netherlanders, and defeated (1572) the invading army of WILLIAM THE SILENT. Recalled to Spain, he completed the conquest (1580) of PORTUGAL by capturing Lisbon.

albacore: see TUNA.

Albania, Albanian *Shqipnija* or *Shqiperia,* officially Republic of Albania, republic (1992 est. pop. 3,285,000), 11,101 sq mi (28,752 sq km), SE Europe, on the Adriatic coast of the Balkan Peninsula; bordered by Yugoslavia (N), Macedonia (E), and Greece (S). TIRANË is the capital. Except for the fertile ADRIATIC coast, Albania is mountainous, rising to 9,066 ft (2,763 m) at Mt. Korab, on the Macedonian border. Albania is rich in mineral resources—notably oil and natural gas, lignite, copper, chromium, and limestone—and mining was the largest source of income. The leading industries included food processing, textiles, cement and building materials, petroleum products, and footwear. With the end of Communist rule, however, the mining and industry have largely collapsed, and many Albanians have illegally emigrated to Greece in search of work. About one fifth of the land is cultivated, largely as small, inefficient farms. Olives, grapes, grains, cotton, tobacco, and livestock are the main agricultural products. More than 95% of the population is ethnically Albanian; the Albanian language is an Indo-European tongue with two dialects. The population is predominantly Muslim, with Roman Catholic and Greek Orthodox minorities.

History. Albania was settled in ancient times by Illyrians and Thracians; the area then comprised parts of ILLYRIA and EPIRUS. The Greeks colonized the coast, and the entire region came under Roman and Byzantine rule. SCANDERBEG (d. 1468), Albania's national hero, delayed but did not stop the OTTOMAN EMPIRE's conquest of the area, which was complete by 1478. More than four centuries of Turkish Islamic rule followed, and national aspirations were suppressed until, during the First BALKAN WAR, Albania proclaimed independence (1912). In 1913 an international commission assigned large areas claimed by Albania to MONTENEGRO, SERBIA, and GREECE. The scene of political chaos and a battleground for contending European and Balkan forces after WORLD WAR I, the country came (1925) under the rule of Ahmed Zogu, who proclaimed himself (1928) King ZOG. Italy invaded Albania in 1939, setting up a puppet government that fought with the Axis powers in WORLD WAR II. After 1944, power passed to guerrilla leader Enver HOXHA, a Communist, who proclaimed a republic in 1946. Opposed to de-Stalinization, Albania broke with the USSR in 1961. It became a close ally of China, but that friendship ended in 1978. Albania remained extremely undeveloped economically as a result of its isolation and tight government control. Hoxha died in 1985 and

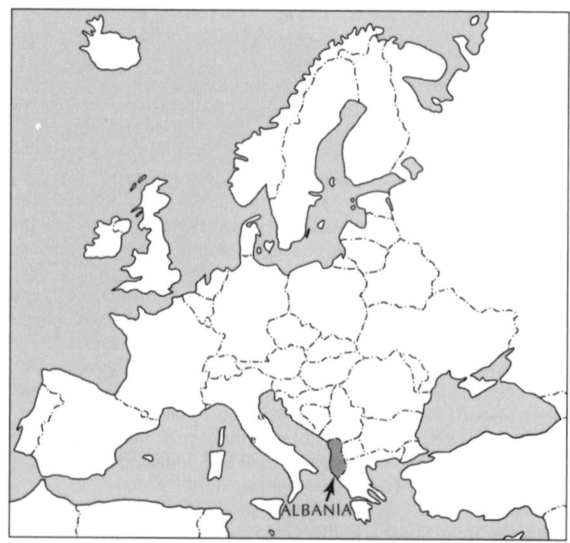

was succeeded by Ramiz Alia, who slowly eased Albania's authoritarian policies and self-imposed isolation. Limited tourism was encouraged, and diplomatic relations were restored with the USSR (1990) and U.S. (1991). The Communists won (1991) in free parliamentary elections, but a deteriorating economy and social unrest forced them to form a coalition government. In new elections (1992) the Socialists (Communists) lost to the opposition Democrats. Alia resigned, and Democratic party leader Sali Berisha became president. Albania's economic problems remain severe, and there is widespread poverty.

Albany, Alexander Stuart or **Stewart, duke of:** see STUART, ALEXANDER, DUKE OF ALBANY.

Albany, city (1990 pop. 101,082), state capital and seat of Albany co., E N.Y., on the Hudson R.; settled 1624, inc. 1686. A deepwater port and trading center for a farm and resort area, it has diversified manufactures, including textiles, paper, chemicals, and automotive parts. The Dutch built (1613) a fur trading post there; the English took control and named the city in 1664. State capital from 1797, it grew with the opening of the Erie and Champlain canals (1820s). The state capitol (1867–98), many old houses, and new state office buildings are prominent in the city, which was redeveloped in the 1960s.

Albany Congress, 1754, a meeting of British colonial representatives in Albany, N.Y. Because of the impending war with France, a treaty was made between seven British colonies and the Iroquois. Benjamin FRANKLIN's Plan of Union for the colonies was also approved, but was later rejected by the colonial legislatures and by the crown.

albatross, sea BIRD (family Diomedeidae) with tapered wings that enable it to excel at gliding and flying. Most are found in the South Pacific, although a few, e.g., the black-footed albatross (*Diomedea nigripes*), frequent the north Pacific. The wandering albatross (*D. exulans*), with a wingspan of 10 to 12 ft (305 to 366 cm), was made famous by COLERIDGE's *Rime of the Ancient Mariner.*

Albee, Edward, 1928–, American playwright; b. Washington, D.C. His clever, often satiric plays include the one-act *The Zoo Story* (1959), and the full-length *Who's Afraid of Virginia Woolf?* (1962), widely regarded as his finest work; *A Delicate Balance* (1967; Pulitzer); *Seascape* (1975; Pulitzer); and *Three Tall Women* (1991; Pulitzer).

Albemarle, George Monck or **Monk,** 1st **duke of:** see MONCK, GEORGE, 1ST DUKE OF ALBEMARLE.

Albéniz, Isaac, 1860–1909, Spanish pianist and composer. Influenced by LISZT and DEBUSSY, he is best remembered for his later piano works, especially *Iberia* (1906–9), which combine Spanish folk material with brilliant pianistic idiom.

Albers, Josef, 1888–1976, German-American artist, designer, and teacher; b. Germany. After working at the BAUHAUS (1920–23), he came to the U.S. As director of the Yale School of Art (1950–58), he was a major figure in American art education. He is best-known for a series of paintings, *Homage to the Square,* which portrays colors in quasi-concentric squares.

Albert, kings of the Belgians. **Albert I,** 1875–1934 (r.1909–34), was the nephew and successor of LEOPOLD II. During WORLD WAR I he led his country in resisting the German invasion (1914). He also improved social conditions in Belgium and the Belgian Congo (see ZAÏRE). His son, LEOPOLD III, succeeded him. **Albert II,** 1934– (r.1993–), is the younger son of Leopold III. He became king when BAUDOUIN I, his brother, died childless.

Albert, 1819–61, prince consort of VICTORIA of Great Britain; son of Ernest I, duke of Saxe-Coburg-Gotha. His initial unpopularity as an alien prince was modified by his devotion to the queen and his concern with public affairs, particularly diplomacy. His insistence on a moderate approach to the TRENT AFFAIR may have avoided war with the U.S.

Alberta, province (1991 pop. 2,545,553), 255,284 sq mi (661,185 sq km), W Canada, bordered by Saskatchewan (E), the Northwest Territories (N), British Columbia (W), and Montana (S). Alberta is a high plateau, rising in the west to the ROCKY MOUNTAINS and the CONTINENTAL DIVIDE. Although it is one of the Prairie Provinces, only about 25% of Alberta's area, chiefly in the south, is treeless. Central Alberta is partly wooded, and the north is principally timberland. The province is drained by the Athabasca, the Saskatchewan, the Red Deer, and other rivers. The population is centered in S and central Alberta, and the principal cities are EDMONTON, the capital, and CALGARY. Until the mid–20th cent., agriculture was Alberta's basic industry. Grain, especially wheat, is the dominant crop, and livestock raising, dairying, lumbering, manufacturing (principally petroleum products and processed food), and service industries are also important. Since the early 1960s, however, mineral exploitation has been the major industry. Alberta is believed to have some of the richest oil deposits in the world—notably the tar beds of the Athabasca River—and has abundant natural gas. Its coal beds contain about one half of Canada's known reserves. Tourists are attracted to the province's outstanding national parks—Jasper, Banff, Waterton Lakes, and Wood Buffalo.

History. Alberta was part of the territory granted (1670) to the HUDSON'S BAY COMPANY and was dominated by the fur trade. In 1870 the company sold the area to the newly created confederation of Canada and in 1872 the mounted police established Fort Macleod in S Alberta. In 1882 the region became an administrative division, and the Canadian Pacific Railway opened the area to settlement. Alberta became a province in 1905. Oil was discovered in 1914, but only when a find was made near Edmonton in 1947 did Alberta's economy begin to change. By the early 1990s Alberta was producing over 80% of Canada's petroleum and some 85% of its natural gas. Politically, Albertans turned to William ABERHART and the SOCIAL CREDIT party in 1935. In 1971 the Progressive Conservatives gained control of the Provincial Assembly. Alberta sends 6 senators (appointed) and 26 representatives (elected) to the national parliament.

Alberti, Leone Battista, 1404–72, Italian architect, musician, painter, and humanist. His treatise *De re aedificatoria* (c.1450), though dependent on the Roman architect Vitruvius, was the first modern work on architecture, and influenced the development of RENAISSANCE architectural style. Among the notable buildings erected from his designs is the Palazzo Rucellai, Florence. Alberti's treatises on painting (1436) and sculpture (c.1464) were also influential.

Albertus Magnus, Saint, or **Saint Albert the Great,** b. 1193 or 1206, d. 1280, scholastic philosopher, Doctor of the Church, called the Universal Doctor. A DOMINICAN, he attempted in his *Summa theologiae* to reconcile Aristotelianism with Christian thought. St. THOMAS AQUINAS was his pupil. Albertus was also deeply interested in natural science and was the first to produce arsenic in a free form. Feast: Nov. 15. See also ARISTOTLE; SCHOLASTICISM.

Albertville, town (1991 est. pop. 18,000), Savoie dept., SE France. Located in the French ALPS on the Arly R. just above its influx into the Isère R., Albertville is a transportation and commercial center in a winter sports region. The 1992 winter Olympic games were based there.

Albigenses, religious sect of S France (12th–13th cent.), whose beliefs were similar in many ways to MANICHAEISM. They were Christian heretics who believed in the coexistence of good and evil. They held that matter was evil and that Jesus only seemed to have a body. Ascetic and enthusiastic, they persisted despite papal opposition. The murder of a papal legate led INNOCENT III to declare (1208) the Albigensian Crusade, which was soon redirected toward political ends. In 1233 the INQUISITION was formed to halt Albigensianism, and slowly over 100 years the movement died.

albino, animal or plant lacking normal pigmentation. The albino body covering (skin, hair, and feathers) and eyes lack pigment. In humans and other animals albinism is inherited as a recessive trait. Breeding has established albino races in some domestic animals.

Albinus: see ALCUIN.

albumin, member of a class of water-soluble, heat-coagulating PROTEINS. Albumins are widely distributed in plant and animal tissues, e.g., ovalbumin of egg, lactalbumin of milk, and leucosin of wheat. Some contain carbohydrates. Normally constituting about 55% of the plasma proteins, albumins adhere chemically to various substances in the blood, e.g., AMINO ACIDS, and thus play a role in their transport. Albumins and other blood proteins aid in regulating the distribution of water in the body. Albumins are also used in textile printing, the fixation of dyes, sugar refining, and other important processes.

Albuquerque, Afonso de, 1453–1515, Portuguese admiral, founder of the Portuguese empire in the East. He captured Goa (1510), Malacca (1511), and Hormuz (1513), built a series of forts in INDIA, and established shipbuilding and other industries. Control of the spice trade and of trade routes were nearly accomplished during his tenure.

Albuquerque, city (1990 pop. 384,736), seat of Bernalillo co., W central N. Mex., on the upper Rio Grande; inc. 1890. It is the largest city in the state, and the industrial and commercial center of a timber and farm area. Its diverse industries include electronics, truck trailer manufacturing, and federal nuclear research and weapons development. The city's downtown was the site of a 1980s urban renewal project. Albuquerque is also noted as a health resort and medical center. The city was founded by the Spanish in 1706 and grew with the arrival (1880) of the railroad.

Alcaeus [ălsē'əs], d. c.580 B.C., Greek poet, early personal lyric writer. Traditionally an associate of SAPPHO, he wrote both light and political verse. The Alcaic strophe was admired and adapted by HORACE.

Alcalá Zamora, Niceto [älkälä' thämō'rä], 1877–1949, president of Spain (1931–36). He helped to lead the republican revolution of 1931 and became the first president of the second Spanish republic. He was deposed (1936) by the CORTES on a Socialist motion and went into exile.

Alcatraz, island in San Francisco Bay, W Calif. Discovered (1769) and fortified by the Spanish, it was (1859–1933) the site of a U.S. military prison and then (1933–63) federal maximum security prison, called "The Rock." It became part of the Golden Gate National Recreational Area in 1972.

Alcestis, in Greek mythology, the devoted wife of a Thessalian king, Admetus. She willingly died in his place, to ensure his immortality. In some myths HERCULES rescued her from the dead; in others PERSEPHONE reunited husband and wife. EURIPIDES dramatized the legend in his *Alcestis*.

alchemy, ancient art or pseudoscience that sought to turn base metals into gold or silver through the agency of a secret substance known by various names (philosopher's stone, elixir, grand magistry). Emerging in China and Egypt by the 3d cent. B.C., alchemy was cloaked in mysticism and allegory, and in time degenerated into superstition. Revived (8th cent.) in Alexandria by the Arabs, it reached W Europe by the Middle Ages. In the 15th–17th cent. experimentation again fell into disrepute, but the base had been laid for modern CHEMISTRY.

Alcibiades [ălsĭbī'ədēz], c.450–404 B.C., Athenian statesman and general. A leader against SPARTA in the PELOPONNESIAN WAR, he was defeated at Mantinea (418 B.C.). He promoted the Sicilian campaign (415) but was accused (probably falsely) of sacrilege. Called home for trial, he fled to Sparta, where he aided Agis I, and then to Persia (413). Recalled to ATHENS, he won a brilliant naval victory (410) and recovered Byzantium (408). Blamed unjustly for the defeat of the Athenian fleet at Notium (c.406), he was sent into exile, and LYSANDER had him murdered.

Alcindor, Lew: see ABDUL-JABBAR, KAREEM.

alcohol, any of a class of organic compounds with the general formula R–OH, where R is an alkyl group made up of carbon and hydrogen and –OH is one or more hydroxyl groups, each made up of one atom of oxygen and one of hydrogen. Although the term *alcohol* ordinarily refers to ETHANOL, the alcohol in alcoholic beverages, the class of alcohols also includes methanol and the amyl, butyl, and propyl alcohols, all with one hydroxyl group; the glycols, with two hydroxyl groups; and glycerol, with three. Many of the characteristic properties and reactions of alcohols are due to the polarity, or unequal distribution of electric charges, in the C–O–H portion of the molecule.

Alcoholics Anonymous (AA), worldwide organization dedicated to the recovery of alcoholics; est. 1935 by two alcoholics. The organization, which functions through local, anonymous self-help groups, is based on a philosophy of life that has enabled countless numbers of people to recover from ALCOHOLISM. In 1992 there were over 2 million members worldwide. **Al-Anon,** for spouses, relatives, and friends of alcoholics, and **Al-Ateen,** for their adolescent children, function similarly.

alcoholism, chronic illness characterized by the habitual consumption of alcohol to a degree that interferes with physical or mental health, or with normal social or occupational behavior. A widespread health problem, it produces both physical and psychological addiction (see DRUG ADDICTION AND DRUG ABUSE). Alcohol is a central nervous system DEPRESSANT that reduces anxiety, inhibition, and feelings of guilt; lowers alertness; impairs perception, judgment, and muscular coordination; and, in high doses, can cause unconsciousness and even death. Long-term alcoholism damages the brain, liver (see CIRRHOSIS), heart, and other organs. Symptoms of alcohol withdrawal can range from a simple hangover to severe delirium tremens (a condition characterized by deliriousness, violent trembling, hallucinations, and seizures). Treatment includes use of disulfiram (Antabuse), a drug that produces discomfort if alcohol is consumed; anti-anxiety drugs to suppress withdrawal symptoms; psychological counseling; and support from groups such as ALCOHOLICS ANONYMOUS.

Alcott, (Amos) Bronson, 1799–1888, American educational and social reformer; b. near Wolcott, Conn. Despite his meager formal education, he became a teacher and founded Temple School in Boston. A leading exponent of TRANSCENDENTALISM, he was (1843) one of the founders of a cooperative vegetarian community, "Fruitlands," and then, as superintendent, reformed the Concord public schools. The poverty that plagued his life was eventually alleviated by the writings of his daughter Louisa May ALCOTT.

Alcott, Louisa May, 1832–88, American writer; b. Germantown, Pa.; daughter of Bronson ALCOTT. Educated by her father, she was also influenced by her friends EMERSON and THOREAU. Alcott received notice for *Hospital Sketches* (1863), a collection of letters written while she was a Civil War nurse. She achieved fame with *Little Women* (1868–69), a largely autobiographical novel for young people that portrays Victorian American family life. Its sequels are *Little Men* (1871) and *Jo's Boys* (1886).

Alcuin or **Albinus,** 735?–804, English churchman and educator. Invited (781?) to CHARLEMAGNE's court at Aachen, he was the moving spirit of the CAROLINGIAN renaissance. Alcuin established the study of the seven liberal arts, which became the curriculum for medieval Europe, and encouraged the preservation of ancient texts. His letters are extant.

Aldanov, Mark [əldä'nəf], pseud. of **Mark Aleksandrovich Landau,** 1886–1957, Russian novelist. Aldanov emigrated to France in 1919 and to the U.S. in 1941. His works include *The Thinker* (1923–27), about the era from 1793 to 1821 in France; *The Tenth Symphony* (1931), set in the Vienna of BEETHOVEN's time; and *The Fifth Seal* (1939), which portrays the decay of revolutionary idealism during the SPANISH CIVIL WAR.

alder, deciduous tree or shrub (genus *Alnus*) of the BIRCH family, widely distributed, especially in mountainous, moist areas of the north temperate zone and in the Andes. The bark of the black alder (*A. glutinosa*), once used medicinally, is still used for dyes and tanning. Red alder (*A. rubra*) is the most important hardwood on the Pacific coast of North America.

Aldington, Richard, 1892–1962, English poet and novelist. A leading IMAGIST, he was married to Hilda DOOLITTLE. His poetry, e.g., *Images* (1915), is remarkable for verbal precision; his novels, e.g., *Death of a Hero* (1929) are bitter satires.

Aldrich, Nelson Wilmarth, 1841–1915, U.S. senator from Rhode Island (1881–1911); b. Foster, R.I. A Republican spokesman for big business, he co-authored the PAYNE-ALDRICH TARIFF ACT (1909) and helped shape monetary policy.

Aldrich, Thomas Bailey, 1836–1907, American author; b. Portsmouth, N.H. He is most widely known for his autobiographical *The Story of a Bad Boy* (1870). A skillful writer of light verse, he also served (1881–90) as editor of the *Atlantic Monthly*.

Aldrin, Buzz (Edwin Eugene Aldrin, Jr.), 1930–, American astronaut; b. Montclair, N.J. During the *Apollo 11* lunar-landing mission (July 16–24, 1969), Neil ARMSTRONG (the commander) and Aldrin (the lunar-module pilot) became the first and second persons, respectively, to walk on the moon (see SPACE EXPLORATION, table). Aldrin was pilot of *Gemini 12* (Nov. 11–15, 1966) and, after retiring from NASA, served (1971–72) as commandant of the Aerospace Research Pilots' School at Edwards Air Force Base, Calif.

ale: see BEER.

Aleichem, Sholom: see SHOLOM ALEICHEM.

Aleixandre, Vicente [älähän'drā], 1898–1984, Spanish poet. His verse includes the surrealist *Destruction of Love* (1935) and *A Longing for the Light* (tr. 1979). He was awarded the 1977 Nobel Prize in literature.

Aleksey II, 1929–, Russian Orthodox clergyman; b. Estonia, as Aleksey M. Ridiger. He became bishop of Tallinn and Estonia in 1961 and was (1988–90) metropolitan of Leningrad (now St. Petersburg) and Novgorod. In 1990 he was elected patriarch (head) of the Russian church.

Alemán Valdés, Miguel, 1902–83, president of MEXICO (1946–52). The first civilian president after MADERO, he initiated a vigorous program of modernization.

Alembert, Jean le Rond d' [däläNbĕr'], 1717–83, French mathematician and philosopher, a leading figure of the ENLIGHTENMENT. His treatise on DYNAMICS (1743) enunciated d'Alembert's principle, which permitted the reduction of a problem in dynamics to one in STATICS. He did important work on the mechanics of rigid bodies, the motions of fluids and vibrating strings, and the three-body problem in CELESTIAL MECHANICS. DIDEROT made him coeditor of the ENCYCLOPÉDIE, for which he wrote the "preliminary discourse" (1751) and mathematical, philosophical, and literary articles.

Alepoudelis, Odysseus: see ELYTIS, ODYSSEUS.

Aleppo or **Alep,** city (1985 est. pop. 1,200,000), NW Syria. Located in a semidesert region where grains, cotton, and fruit are grown, the city produces silk and wool, dried fruits and nuts, hides, and other goods. It was settled perhaps as early as the 6th millennium B.C. and passed to the Assyrians, Persians, and Seleucids. By the 4th cent. A.D. it was a center of Christianity in the Byzantine Empire. The Arabs, Seljuk Turks, and others later held it. Aleppo prospered under the Ottoman Turks (from 1517) and the French (from 1918), and as part of independent Syria (from 1941). Historic structures include the Great Mosque (715) and the Byzantine citadel (12th cent.).

Aleutian Islands, strategically important chain of rugged, volcanic islands, W Alaska, curving westward c.1,200 mi (1,900 km) between the Bering Sea and the Pacific Ocean. Unalaska, the most populous island, is part of the easternmost group, the Fox Islands. Extending west to a point near Russia are the Andreanof, Rat, Near, and Semichi island groups. The Aleutians were discovered in 1741 by Vitus BERING and bought by the U.S. from Russia in 1867 as part of the Alaska purchase. Three western islands—Attu, Agattu, and Kiska—were occupied (1942–43) by Japan.

Aleuts, native inhabitants of the ALEUTIAN ISLANDS and W Alaska. They speak an Eskimo-Aleut language (see NATIVE AMERICAN LANGUAGES) and, like the ESKIMO, resemble Siberian peoples. Their skill in hunting sea mammals was exploited by Russian fur traders, and wars with mainland tribes helped to reduce their numbers from an estimated 20,000 when Vitus BERING encountered them in 1741 to around 3,000 a century later. There were 23,797 Aleuts in 1990.

Alexander III, d. 1181, pope (1159–81), a Sienese born Orlando Bandinelli. His rule was contested by antipopes until 1178. He backed the LOMBARD LEAGUE in opposing Holy Roman Emperor FREDERICK I, who exiled him to France until 1176. A learned canon lawyer, he issued many rules for governing the church. In 1179 he convened the Third Lateran Council.

Alexander VI, 1431?–1503, pope (1492–1503), a Spaniard named Rodrigo de Borja (Ital., Borgia). Notorious in later centuries as a corrupt and worldly pope, he showered his illegitimate children, Cesare and Lucretia BORGIA, with money and favors. Girolamo SAVONAROLA was his outspoken critic. Alexander opposed CHARLES VIII of France and proclaimed (1494) the line of demarcation between Spanish and Portuguese colonial possessions.

Alexander, czars of Russia. **Alexander I,** 1777–1825 (r.1801–25), was the son of PAUL I. He began his reign by relaxing political repression to a degree. In 1805 he joined the coalition against NAPOLEON I, but after Russian defeats he made a tenuous alliance with France by signing the Treaty of Tilsit (1807). After the French invasion of Russia (1812) was repulsed he created the HOLY ALLIANCE, joining with METTERNICH to suppress national and liberal movements. His reactionary domestic policies led to opposition, and when his brother NICHOLAS I succeeded him in 1825 a revolt took place (see DECEMBRISTS). **Alexander II,** 1818–81 (r.1855–81), son of Nicholas I, negotiated an end to the CRIMEAN WAR (1853–56; see PARIS, TREATY OF) and adopted important reforms, principally the emancipation of the serfs (1861; see EMANCIPATION, EDICT OF) and the introduction of limited local self-government (see ZEMSTVO). His foreign policy included the suppression of the Polish uprising of 1863; the annexation of Central Asia (1865–76); and the RUSSO-TURKISH WARS (1877–78). His domestic reforms were seen as insufficient by the intelligentsia, some of whom formed populist groups. Increasing repression led to terrorism, and in 1881 Alexander was assassinated. **Alexander III,** 1845–94 (r.1881–94), was the son of Alexander II. Surrounded by reactionary advisors, he increased police power and censorship; weakened the *zemstvos;* imposed controls on the peasantry; forced Russification on national minorities; and persecuted the Jews. His foreign policy culminated in the TRIPLE ALLIANCE AND TRIPLE ENTENTE. His son NICHOLAS II succeeded him.

Alexander, 1893–1920, king (1917–20) of the Hellenes (Greece). He became Greek king when his father, CONSTANTINE I, was forced by the Allies to abdicate because of his pro-German sympathies. After Alexander's death, his father was restored to the throne.

Alexander III, king of Macedon: see ALEXANDER THE GREAT.

Alexander, kings of Scotland. **Alexander I,** 1078?–1124 (r.1107–24), was the son of MALCOLM III. He opposed English efforts to rule the church in Scotland and established abbeys at Inchcolm and Scone. **Alexander II,** 1198–1249 (r.1214–49), joined the English barons in their revolt against King JOHN but made a tenuous peace with HENRY III. **Alexander III,** 1241–86 (r.1249–86), acquired for Scotland the HEBRIDES and also the Isle of MAN, already claimed from Norway by his father.

Alexander, rulers of SERBIA and YUGOSLAVIA. **Alexander** (Alexander Karadjordjević), 1806–85, prince of Serbia (1842–58), was the son of KARAGEORGE. An ineffectual ruler, he was deposed in favor of Miloš Obrenović. **Alexander** (Alexander Obrenović), 1876–1903, king of Serbia (1889–1903), instituted a conservative regime but, after accepting a somewhat liberal constitution, was assassinated by a clique of army officers. **Alexander,** 1888–1934, king of Yugoslavia (1921–34), the son and successor of PETER I, became (1918) regent of the kingdom of Serbs, Croats, and Slovenes, which he renamed (1929) Yugoslavia. He was assassinated by a Yugoslav terrorist.

Alexander, Harold Rupert Leofric George, 1st **Earl Alexander of Tunis,** 1891–1969, British field marshal. In WORLD WAR II, he commanded the retreats at Dunkirk (1940) and in Myanmar (1942) and the triumphs in N Africa and Sicily (1943). Later he was governor general of Canada (1946–52) and minister of defense (1952–54) in Winston CHURCHILL's cabinet.

Alexander Nevsky, 1220–63, Russian hero. As prince of Novgorod (1236–52) he earned his surname by his victory (1240) over the Swedes on the Neva R. He later defeated the Livonian Knights, invading from Germany (1242), and the Lithuanians (1245). When the TATARS occupied Russia he was made grand duke of Vladimir-Suzdal (1252).

Alexander the Great or **Alexander III,** 356–323 B.C., king of MACEDON. The son of PHILIP II, he was tutored by ARISTOTLE. Upon succeeding to the throne in 336 B.C. he won ascendancy over all of GREECE by putting down uprisings in THRACE and ILLYRIA, and by sacking THEBES. As head of an allied Greek army, viewing himself as the champion of pan-HELLENISM, he started east (334) on what was to be the greatest conquest of ancient times. He defeated the Persians at the battles of Granicus (334) and Issus (333). Tyre and Gaza fell after a year's struggle, and he entered Egypt (332), where he founded ALEXANDRIA. Moving to Mesopotamia, he overthrew the Persian Empire of DARIUS III at the battle of Gaugamela (331). Pushing on through eastern PERSIA (330–327), he invaded northern INDIA (326), but there his forces would go no further. The fleet was sent back to the head of the Persian Gulf, and Alexander himself led his soldiers through the desert, reaching Susa in 324 B.C. He died of a fever a year later, at age 33. He was incontestably one of the greatest generals of all time and one of the most powerful personalities of antiquity.

Alexandra, 1844–1925, queen consort of EDWARD VII of Great Britain, whom she married in 1863. She was the daughter of CHRISTIAN IX of Denmark.

Alexandra Feodorovna, 1872–1918, czarina of Russia, consort of

NICHOLAS II. A granddaughter of Queen VICTORIA and princess of Hesse, she encouraged the czar's reactionary policies under the influence of RASPUTIN. With her family she was shot by the Bolsheviks (see BOLSHEVISM).

Alexandria, city (1986 pop. 2,917,327), N Egypt, on the Mediterranean Sea, W of the Nile R. delta. The city is Egypt's leading port, a commercial and transportation center, and the heart of a major industrial area with such manufactures as refined petroleum, textiles, processed food, paper, and plastics. Founded in 332 B.C. by ALEXANDER THE GREAT, Alexandria was (304 B.C.–30 B.C.) the capital of the PTOLEMIES. The city was the greatest center of Hellenistic and Jewish culture. It had a great university and two celebrated royal libraries, but their valuable collections have not survived. Alexandria became part of the empire of ROME in 30 B.C. and later of the BYZANTINE EMPIRE. The Muslim Arabs took the city in 642 A.D. After Cairo became (969) Egypt's capital, Alexandria declined. It fell to NAPOLEON I in 1798 and to the British in 1801. During WORLD WAR II the city was the chief Allied naval base in the E Mediterranean. At a 1944 meeting in Alexandria, plans for the ARAB LEAGUE were drawn up. A few of Alexandria's ancient monuments are still visible. The Greco-Roman Museum houses a vast collection of Coptic, Roman, and Greek art.

Alexandria, city (1990 pop. 111,183), N Va., on the Potomac R.; inc. 1779. A residential suburb of WASHINGTON, D.C., it also has railroad yards, varied industries, government buildings, office complexes, and research firms. Portions of the city were part of the DISTRICT OF COLUMBIA from 1790 to 1847. Nearby is MOUNT VERNON; in the city are many sites associated with George Washington.

Alexius, Byzantine emperors. **Alexius I** (Comnenus), 1048–1118 (r.1081–1118), nephew of ISAAC I, obtained the crown by overthrowing Nicephorus III. He withstood the Normans under ROBERT GUISCARD and BOHEMOND I, and defeated the Pechenegs (1091) and CUMANS (1095). During the First CRUSADE he persuaded the leaders to pledge to him their Byzantine conquests. In 1108 he forced Bohemond, who had seized Antioch, to acknowledge his suzerainty. In his last years his daughter, Anna Comnena, intrigued against his son, JOHN II. Alexius restored Byzantine power but drained the empire's resources. **Alexius II** (Comnenus), 1168–83 (r.1180–83), son of MANUEL I, ruled under the regency of his mother, Mary of Antioch. His cousin procured the deaths of Mary and Alexius and became Andronicus I. **Alexius III** (Angelus), d. after 1210 (r.1195–1203), deposed his brother ISAAC II, but the act served as pretext for the leaders of the Fourth Crusade to attack (1203) Constantinople and to restore Isaac, with his son **Alexius IV,** d. 1204, as coemperor. **Alexius V** (Ducas Mourtzouphlos), d. 1204, son-in-law of Alexius III, overthrew Isaac and Alexius IV but was killed soon afterward by the Crusaders, who set up the Latin empire of Constantinople.

alfalfa or **lucern,** perennial plant (*Medicago sativa*) of the PULSE family, probably native to Persia and now widely cultivated. It is an important pasture and hay plant. Alfalfa is valued for its high yield of protein, its effectiveness in weed control, its role in crop rotation and nitrogen fixation, and as a source of chlorophyll and carotene.

Al Fatah: see ARAFAT, YASIR; PALESTINE LIBERATION ORGANIZATION.

Alfieri, Vittorio, Conte [älfyĕ'rē], 1749–1803, Italian tragic poet. A Piedmontese, he traveled widely and returned to Italy with a desire to revive national spirit. He wrote 19 tragedies, among them *Philip the Second, Saul,* and *Antigone,* all in the French classical tradition; comedies; satire; and an autobiography. His collected works, published (1805–15) by his friend the countess of Albany, contributed greatly to the rise of Italian nationalism.

Alfonso, kings of ARAGÓN. **Alfonso I,** d. 1134, king of Aragón and Navarre (1104–34), captured many towns from the Moors. **Alfonso II,** 1152–96, king of Aragón (1162–96), inherited Provence and conquered (1171) Teruel. **Alfonso V** (the Magnanimous), 1396–1458, king of Aragón and Sicily (1416–58), conquered NAPLES and was recognized by the pope as its king (1443–58). He maintained a splendid court there and tried to introduce Spanish institutions.

Alfonso, kings of Portugal. **Alfonso I,** 1109?–85, the first king (r.1139–85), extended his territories by defeating (1139) the MOORS and, with the help of allies, captured (1147) Lisbon. His grandson, **Alfonso II** (the Fat), 1185–1223 (r.1211–23), tried to confiscate Roman Catholic Church holdings and was excommunicated (1219). His army won major victories (1212, 1217) over the Moors. His son, **Alfonso III,** 1210–79 (r.1248–79), completed (1249) the reconquest of Portugal from the Moors, instituted many reforms, and encouraged commerce and the development of towns. **Alfonso IV,** 1291–1357 (r.1325–57), warred fruitlessly against CASTILE before both kingdoms combined forces to defeat (1340) the Moors. He countenanced the murder of Inés de CASTRO. **Alfonso V,** 1432–81 (r.1438–81), put down a civil war (1449), invaded Morocco to capture Tangier (1471), and lost a war (1476–79) with Castile. **Alfonso VI,** 1643–83 (r.1656–83), slightly paralyzed and mentally defective, ousted (1662) his mother as regent and appointed as her successor the count of Castelho Melhor, who won the war (1663–65) that secured Spain's recognition (1668) of Portugal's independence. Alfonso's wife and his brother (later PETER II) forced Castelho Melhor from power in 1667, and Alfonso made his brother regent.

Alfonso, Spanish kings. **Alfonso I** (the Catholic), 693?–757, Spanish king of ASTURIAS (739–57), extended its territory with the help of the BERBERS' revolt (740–41) against the MOORS. His grandson, **Alfonso II** (the Chaste), 759–842, king of Asturias (791–842), established his capital at Oviedo and continued the struggle against the Moors. **Alfonso III** (the Great), 838?–911?, king of Asturias (866–911?) recovered LEÓN from the Moors, but after his forced abdication it was divided among his sons. **Alfonso V** (the Noble), 994?–1027, king of León (999–1027), chartered (1020) the city of León, but he was killed in the siege of Viseu. **Alfonso VI,** 1030–1109, king of León (1065–1109) and CASTILE (1072–1109), took Galicia (1073) and became the most powerful Christian ruler in Spain. He conquered (1085) Toledo and other cities, but was defeated twice (1086, 1108) by Muslim armies. **Alfonso VII** (the Emperor), 1104–57, king of Castile and León (1126–57), gained supremacy over other Christian states and had himself crowned emperor (1135). But his conquests of CÓRDOBA (1146) and Almería (1147) from the Moors were soon lost. **Alfonso VIII** (the Noble), 1155–1214, king of Castile (1158–1214), restored order in his kingdom and won a great victory (1212) over the Moors. **Alfonso X** (the Wise), 1221–84, king of Castile and León (1252–84), took CÁDIZ from the Moors (1262). His subjection of the nobles led to a revolt, and a civil war broke out over the succession during his last years. He was a great patron of science and the arts. The Alfonsine Tables of astronomical data were published under his aegis. **Alfonso XI,** 1311–50, king of Castile and León (1312–50), lost Gibraltar to the Moors (1333) but won the great victory of Tarifa (1340) and conquered Algeciras (1344). **Alfonso XII,** 1857–85, king of Spain (1874–85), was a popular monarch who consolidated the monarchy, suppressed republican agitation, and restored order. **Alfonso XIII,** 1886–1941, king of Spain (1886–1931), supported the military dictatorship (1923–30) of Miguel PRIMO DE RIVERA, but social unrest and a republican election victory led to his deposition and exile (1931).

Alfred, 849–99, king of WESSEX (871–99), sometimes called Alfred the Great. The son of ÆTHELWULF, he shared his father's piety. When his brother ÆTHELRED took the Wessex throne (865), Alfred aided him in battles against the Danes, who threatened to overrun England. Unable to establish a clear victory, Alfred rid Wessex of the Danes by paying the DANEGELD when he became king in 871. In 878, however, the Danes returned, and Alfred's flight to Somerset at that time is the basis for the legend about the king and a peasant woman's burned cakes. In May 878, Alfred triumphed over the Danes at Edington. This victory produced relative security, and Alfred began to institute reforms, including a code of laws combining Christian doctrine with a strong, centralized monarchy. His greatest achievements were the creation of a navy, the revival of learning among the clergy, the education of youths and nobles at court, the establishment of Old English literary prose, his own English translation of Latin works, and his influence on the extant form of the ANGLO-SAXON CHRONICLE.

algae, primitive organisms that contain CHLOROPHYLL and carry on PHOTOSYNTHESIS but lack true roots, stems, and leaves. While historically considered plants, many algae are now classified in the kingdoms Monera and Protista. They are abundant both in the sea and freshwater; nearly all SEAWEEDS are marine algae. Algae occur as microscopic single cells (e.g., DIATOMS) and more complex forms of many cells grouped in spherical colonies (e.g., *Volvox*), in ribbonlike filaments (e.g., *Spirogyra*), and in giant forms (e.g., the marine kelps). The cells of colonies are generally similar, but some are specialized for reproduction and other functions. The BLUE-GREEN ALGAE (cyanobacteria) and green algae include most of the freshwater forms, such as pond scum, a green slime found in stagnant water. Brown and red algae are more complex, chiefly marine forms whose green chlorophyll is masked by the presence of other pigments. Algae are primary food producers in the food chain and also provide oxygen for aquatic life. Algae that thrive in polluted water can over-multiply, resulting in an algal bloom and seriously unbalancing their ecosystem.

algebra, branch of MATHEMATICS concerned with operations on sets of numbers or other elements that are often represented by symbols. In elementary algebra, letters are used to stand for numbers, e.g., in the POLYNOMIAL equation $ax^2 + bx + c = 0$, the letters a, b, and c are called the coefficients of the EQUATION and stand for fixed numbers, or constants. The letter x stands for an unknown number, or variable, whose value depends on the values of a, b, and c and may be determined by solving the equation. Much of classical algebra is concerned with finding solutions to equations or systems of equations, i.e., finding the roots, or values of the unknowns, that upon substitution into the original equation will make it a numerical identity. Algebra is a generalization of ARITHMETIC and gains much of its power from dealing symbolically with elements and operations (chiefly addition and multiplication) and relationships (such as equality) connecting the elements. Thus $a + a = 2a$ and $a + b = b + a$ no matter what numbers a and b represent.

Alger, Horatio, 1834–99, American writer of boys' stories; b. Revere, Mass. The heroes of his over 100 books, e.g., *Ragged Dick* (1867), gain success by leading exemplary lives and struggling valiantly against poverty and adversity.

Algeria, Arab. *Al Djazair,* Fr. *Algérie,* officially Democratic and Popular Republic of Algeria, republic (1992 est. pop. 26,667,000), 919,590 sq mi (2,381,741 sq km), NW Africa, bordered by Mauritania, Morocco, and Western Sahara (W), the Mediterranean Sea (N), Tunisia and Libya (E), and Niger and Mali (S). The principal cities are ALGIERS (the capital) and ORAN. The ATLAS MTS. divide northern Algeria into a coastal lowland strip (the Tell) and a semiarid plateau. In the south is the much larger, but arid and sparsely populated, Saharan region; Algeria's highest point, Mt. Tahat (9,541 ft/2,908 m), in the Ahaggar Mts., is located here. About a quarter of Algeria's work force are farmers, producing cereals, wine, citrus fruits, and cork. Mining and manufacturing, developed since the 1960s, contribute the bulk of the national income. Petroleum is the leading export, and much natural gas is produced, with proven reserves that are among the world's largest. The state plays a leading role in planning the economy and owns many important industrial concerns. The great majority of the population are Sunni Muslims of Arab-Berber descent; Europeans, who before independence accounted for 10% of the total, now are only 1% of the population. Arabic is the official language, but French is widely spoken, and a sizable minority speaks a Berber language.

History. The earliest known inhabitants of the region that is now Algeria were Berber-speaking nomads who were settled there by the 2d millennium B.C. As NUMIDIA, it became (9th cent. B.C.) a province of Carthage and then (106 B.C.) of Rome; during the Christian era, St. AUGUSTINE (354–430) was bishop at Hippo (now Annaba). With Rome's decline in the 5th cent. A.D., Algeria was conquered by the Vandals (430–31), the Byzantine Empire (6th cent.), and finally, in the late 7th and early 8th cent., by the Arabs, whose introduction of Islam profoundly altered the character of the area. Spain captured the coastal cities in the 15th cent. but was expelled (mid-16th cent.) with the help of the Ottoman Turks, who assumed control. During this period the Algerian coast was a stronghold of pirates and a center of the slave trade. France invaded Algeria in 1830 and declared it a colony in 1848. Europeans began to arrive in large numbers, dominating the government and the economy, and leaving the native Muslim population with scant political or economic power. A nationalist movement began to develop after World War I, and a war for independence, led by the National Liberation Front (FLN), broke out in 1954. After more than seven years of bitter fighting, in which at least 100,000 Muslim and 10,000 French soldiers were killed, Algeria became independent on July 3, 1962. Since independence, Algeria has been a prominent nonaligned state and a champion of the movements against white minority rule in Africa. It also has supported the protracted struggle of the Polisario Front for the independence of WESTERN SAHARA (formerly Spanish Sahara) from Morocco. Ahmed Ben Bella, prime minister and then president of Algeria after independence, was deposed by Houari Boumedienne in 1965. After Boumedienne's death (1978), Chadli Benjedid succeeded (1979) him as president. Riots in 1988 led Pres. Benjedid to reduce the role of the state economically and of the FLN politically. After Islamic fundamentalists won 42% of the seats in the first round of parliamentary elections in Dec. 1991, the army forced Benjedid to resign (1992) and cancelled the election. A civilian-led state council was installed, but real power resided with the army. The fundamentalist party was banned and its leaders arrested. Fundamentalists launched a guerrilla insurrection, and Algeria was torn by violence from both sides. In 1994 Gen. Liamine Zeroual, the defense minister, was appointed president, replacing the state council.

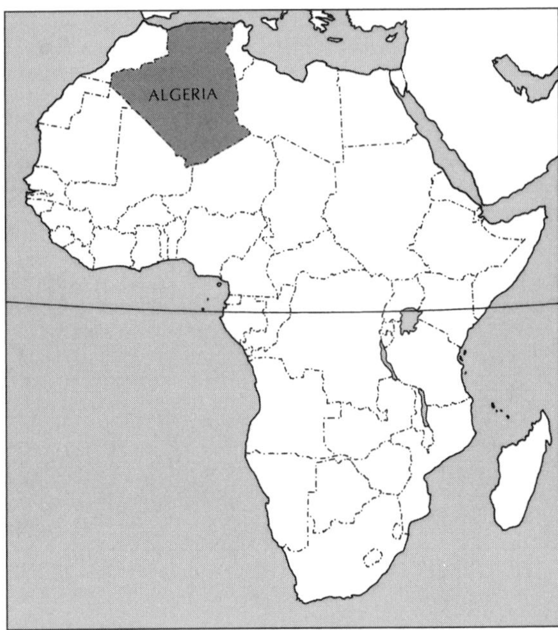

Algiers, city (1987 pop. 1,507,241), capital of Algeria, N Algeria, on the Bay of Algiers of the Mediterranean Sea. It is a major North African port, a winter resort, and a commercial center. Industries include metallurgy, oil refining, and automotive construction. Founded by the Phoenicians, the city disappeared after the fall of the Roman Empire and was reestablished in the late 10th cent. by the Muslims. The French captured the port in 1830. During WORLD WAR II Algiers was Allied headquarters in North Africa. The city played an important role in the Algerian independence struggle (1954–62). Algiers is divided into the newer, French-built sector and the original Muslim quarter, with its 16th-cent. casbah fortress.

ALGOL: see PROGRAMMING LANGUAGE.

Algonquian [ălgŏng'kwĭn], branch of the Algonquian-Wakashan linguistic family of North America. See NATIVE AMERICAN LANGUAGES (table).

Alhazen: see IBN AL-HAYTHAM.

Ali, Muhammad, 1942–, American boxer; b. Louisville, Ky., as Cassius Marcellus Clay, Jr. He changed (1964) his name when he became a BLACK MUSLIM. After winning (1960) an Olympic gold medal, he defeated (1964) Sonny Liston for the heavyweight crown, but was stripped of the title in 1967 when he refused induction into the U.S. armed forces on religious grounds. In 1971 the U.S. Supreme Court upheld his draft appeal. Ali regained the title in 1974 by defeating George Foreman, lost it to Leon Spinks in 1978, but won it a third time (from Spinks) later that year. Ali lost to Larry Holmes in 1980.

Alice Springs, town (1986 pop. 22,759), Northern Territory, central Australia. It is the center of an area with cattle ranches and aborigine reservations. Tourism is important, and gold and other minerals are mined nearby. The town was called Stuart until 1933.

alien, in law, a resident of a state who is not a national or citizen of that state. A country may exclude individuals or groups it deems undesirable; most, for example, bar criminals, paupers, and the diseased. With some exceptions, e.g., diplomats, aliens are subject to the laws of the country in which they reside. Permanent residents may be liable to taxation and military conscription. In the U.S., aliens are required to register each year; an alien may acquire citizenship by a legal procedure known as naturalization. **Illegal aliens** are citizens of foreign countries who lack legal status in the country in which they are living. In the U.S., most recent illegal aliens have come from Latin America. A 1986 law to stop the flow and end the underground lives of these aliens made it illegal for employers to hire them and granted legal status to those who could prove continuous residence in the U.S. since before Jan. 1, 1982. Special allowances were made for seasonal farm workers. Although an estimated 3.9 million aliens were eligible, only about half applied before the May 1988 deadline.

Alien and Sedition Acts, 1798, four laws passed by the Federalist-controlled U.S. Congress in response to the threat of war with France (see XYZ AFFAIR). Designed to destroy the Jeffersonian Republicans who expressed sympathy for France, the laws lengthened the residency requirement for citizenship, empowered the president to expel "dangerous" aliens, and proscribed spoken or written criticism of the government. The Acts provoked the KENTUCKY AND VIRGINIA RESOLUTIONS.

Ali ibn Abu Talib, d. 661, cousin and son-in-law of MUHAMMAD, fourth caliph of the Islamic community, and martyred hero and first imam of the SHIITE movement in Islam. As a child, he became one of Muhammad's first converts. He married Muhammad's youngest daughter, Fatima, and twice commanded the Prophet's armies. During the civil war that broke out (656) between various factions of the early Muslim community, he was elevated to the caliphate. His murder at Kufa, Iraq, inspired the Shiite movement (shi'ah = "party," i.e., of Ali), which regards Ali as Muhammad's chosen successor.

Ali Pasha, 1744?–1822, Turkish governor of Yannina (1787–1820), a Greek province of the OTTOMAN EMPIRE. He ruled as a quasi-independent despot over most of Albania and Epirus. He resisted (1820) Turkish military efforts to depose him, tying up troops needed against the rebels in the Greek War of Independence. He was assassinated.

alkali, HYDROXIDE of an ALKALI METAL. Alkalies are soluble in water and form strongly basic solutions. They neutralize acids, forming salts and water. Strong alkalies (e.g., those of sodium or potassium) are called caustic alkalies. The term *alkali* is sometimes applied to sodium or potassium carbonate or to the hydroxide of an ALKALINE-EARTH METAL.

alkali metals, elements in group Ia of the PERIODIC TABLE. In order of increasing atomic number, they are LITHIUM, SODIUM, POTASSIUM, RUBIDIUM, CESIUM, and FRANCIUM. They are softer than other metals, and have lower melting points and densities. All react violently with water, releasing hydrogen and forming hydroxides. They tarnish rapidly, even in dry air. They never occur uncombined in nature.

alkaline-earth metals, elements in group IIa of the PERIODIC TABLE. In order of increasing atomic number, they are BERYLLIUM, MAGNESIUM, CALCIUM, STRONTIUM, BARIUM, and RADIUM. They are softer than most other metals and react readily with water. Their properties are exceeded by the corresponding ALKALI METAL.

alkaline earths, oxides of the ALKALINE-EARTH METALS. They are not readily soluble in water and form solutions less basic than those of ALKALIES.

alkaloid, any of a class of organic compounds composed of carbon, hydrogen, nitrogen, and usually oxygen, that are often derived from plants. The name means alkalilike, but some alkaloids do not exhibit alkaline properties. Many alkaloids, though poisons, have physiological effects that render them valuable as medicines. For example, curarine, found in the deadly extract CURARE, is a powerful muscle relaxant; atropine is used to dilate the pupils of the eye; and physostigmine is a specific for certain muscular diseases. Narcotic alkaloids used in medicine include MORPHINE and CODEINE for pain relief and COCAINE as a local anesthetic. Other common alkaloids include CAFFEINE, LSD, QUININE, SEROTONIN, STRYCHNINE, and nicotine.

alkane, alkene, and **alkyne:** see HYDROCARBON.

Allah: see ISLAM.

Allen, Ethan, 1738–89, American Revolutionary hero; b. Litchfield (?), Conn. In 1775 he led the GREEN MOUNTAIN BOYS at the capture of Fort TICONDEROGA and was captured by the British in an expedition against Canada. Exchanged in 1778, he promoted independence and statehood for Vermont. His brother, **Ira Allen,** 1751–1814, was a political leader in Vermont.

Allen, Gracie: see BURNS, GEORGE.

Allen, Woody, 1935–, American film director, writer, and actor; b. Brooklyn, N.Y., as Allen Stewart Konigsberg. His films, mainly comedies that depict neurotic urban characters preoccupied with sex, death, and psychiatry, include *Sleeper* (1973), *Annie Hall* (1977; Academy Award), *Broadway Danny Rose* (1984), *Hannah and Her Sisters* (1987), *Alice* (1990), and *Manhattan Murder Mystery* (1993). In 1992, in a bitter public dispute, Allen sued actress Mia Farrow for custody of their children and lost (1993).

Allenby, Edmund Henry Hynman Allenby, 1st **Viscount,** 1861–1936, British field marshal. In WORLD WAR I, he invaded Palestine and ended Turkish resistance (1918). He later served as British high commissioner for Egypt and the Sudan (1919–25).

Allende, Isabel, 1942–, Chilean novelist. Living abroad since the 1973 coup in which her uncle, Pres. Salvadore ALLENDE, died, she is among the most notable contemporary Latin American writers. Her vivid fiction, which fuses realism with political, often feminist concerns, includes *The House of Spirits* (1982), *Eva Luna* (1987), and *The Infinite Plan* (1993).

Allende Gossens, Salvador [äyän'dā gō'säns], 1908–73, president of CHILE (1970–73). A founder of the Chilean Socialist party (1933), he was elected president of Chile by a narrow plurality (1970)—the first freely elected Marxist leader in the Americas. His socialist program disrupted the economy and led to inflation and widespread strikes. During the army coup that overthrew (1973) his regime, he either was murdered or committed suicide.

Allentown, city (1990 pop. 105,090), seat of Lehigh co., E Pa., on the Lehigh R.; founded 1762, inc. as a city 1867. It is a commercial and industrial center in the agricultural Lehigh Valley, producing varied electronic and mechanical manufactures. Iron, cement, and mining are the mainstays. The city was settled by members of various German religious groups. Muhlenberg is one of several colleges located there.

allergy, adverse physical reaction of some people to substances that are not toxic per se and are innocuous to other people. Allergens, or allergy-producing substances, cause the release of histamine, an organic compound responsible for allergic symptoms. There are various types of allergens: airborne (e.g., pollen), which may cause sneezing, as with hay fever, or asthma; contactants (e.g., poison ivy and dyes), which often cause rashes; food (e.g., chocolate or fish), which may cause a rash, such as eczema or hives, or a respiratory reaction; or drugs (e.g., sulfa drugs), which in the allergic person can cause a violent reaction. Treatment includes desensitization (injections), antihistamine drugs, and avoidance of allergens.

Alleyn, Edward, 1566–1626, English actor. The only rival of Richard BURBAGE, he played the title roles in Christopher MARLOWE's *Tamburlaine, Jew of Malta,* and *Faustus.*

Alliance for Progress: see ORGANIZATION OF AMERICAN STATES.

alligator, aquatic REPTILE (genus *Alligator*) in the same order as the CROCODILE. The American alligator (*A. mississipiensis*) is found in swamps and streams from North Carolina to Florida and along the Gulf Coast. The young are brown or black with yellow bands; adults are solid black. Males commonly reach a length of 9 ft (2.7 m) and a weight of 250 lb (110 kg). The alligator is protected by law.

Alliluyeva, Svetlana [äl-lĕlo͞o'yəvə], 1926–, only daughter of Soviet leader Joseph STALIN. In 1966 she defected to the West, becoming a U.S. citizen. She has written *Twenty Letters to a Friend* (1967) and *Only One Year* (1969). She returned to the USSR from 1984 to 1986.

allotropy, the occurrence of certain chemical elements in two or more forms; the forms are called allotropes. Allotropes generally differ in physical properties, such as color and hardness; they may also differ in molecular structure or in chemical activity but are usually alike in most chemical properties. DIAMOND and GRAPHITE are two allotropes of the element CARBON.

alloy, substance with metallic properties consisting of a METAL fused with one or more metals or nonmetals. An alloy may be a homogeneous solid solution, a heterogeneous mixture of tiny crystals, a true chemical compound, or a mixture of these. Alloys generally have properties different from those of their constituent elements and are used more extensively than pure metals. Alloys of IRON and CARBON are among the most widely used and include CAST IRON and STEEL. BRASS and BRONZE are important alloys of COPPER. Because pure GOLD and SILVER are too soft for many uses, they are often alloyed, either with each other or with other metals, e.g., copper or PLATINUM. Amalgams are alloys that contain MERCURY. Other alloys include BRITANNIA METAL, DURALUMIN, and SOLDER.

All Saints' Day, Nov. 1, feast of the Roman Catholic and Anglican churches, the day God is glorified for all his saints, known and unknown. Roman Catholics are obliged to hear Mass on this day. In medieval England it was called All Hallows; hence the name Halloween (Hallows' eve) for the preceding day (Oct. 31).

allspice: see PIMENTO.

Allston, Washington, 1779–1843, American painter; b. Georgetown co., S.C. Allston traveled to London, where he studied with Benjamin WEST. Many of his greatest works, marked by a controlled romanticism, were done in England (1810–18). Allston's finest paintings are lyrical landscapes, e.g., *Moonlit Landscape* (1819; Mus. Fine Arts, Boston).

Alma-Ata: see ALMATY.

Almagest: see PTOLEMY (Claudius Ptolemaeus).

Al Manamah, city (1988 est. pop. 155,000), capital of Bahrain, on the PERSIAN GULF. It has oil refineries and light industries and is a free port.

Almaty, formerly **Alma-Ata,** city (1989 pop. 1,128,000), capital of Kazakhstan, central Asia, in the foothills of the Trans-Ili Ala-Tau. Almaty is the industrial and cultural center of Kazakhstan. Leading industries include food and tobacco processing and railroad equipment repair. Originally called Verny, the city was founded in 1854 as a Russian fort and trade center.

Almeida, Francisco de [älmā'də], c.1450–1510, Portuguese admiral, first viceroy of Portuguese India (1505–9). He developed Portugal's trade with India by making alliances with Indian rulers and other tactics. He thwarted Egypt's commercial challenge by winning a great sea battle.

Almohads [ăl'məhădz], Berber Muslim dynasty that ruled Morocco and Spain in the 12th and 13th cent. It had its origins in the puritanical sect founded c.1120 by ibn Tumart. By 1174 the Almohads had completely displaced the ruling ALMORAVIDS. The Almohads, in turn, were defeated in Spain by the Spanish and Portuguese in 1212, and in Morocco by the Merenid dynasty in 1269.

almond, name for a small tree *(Prunus amygdalus)* of the ROSE family and for the nutlike edible seed of its drupe fruit. Almonds are now cultivated mainly in E Asia, Italy, Spain, and California. Almond fruit is fleshless; otherwise, the tree closely resembles the peach tree. Almond oil, pressed from the nut, is used for flavoring and in soaps and cosmetics.

Almoravids [ălmôr'əvĭdz], Berber Muslim dynasty that ruled Morocco and Muslim Spain in the 11th and 12th cent. They founded MARRAKESH as the capital of their powerful empire. Called on for help by the Moors in Spain, they defeated (1086) ALFONSO VI of Castile and displaced the local Moorish rulers. Never entirely stable, the dynasty was overthrown by the ALMOHADS in 1174.

aloe, succulent perennials (genus *Aloe*) of the LILY family, native chiefly to Africa, but cultivated elsewhere. The leaves contain aloin, a purgative. Various drug-yielding species are used medicinally, as well as for X-ray-burn treatment, insect repellent, and transparent pigment. Biblical aloes is unrelated. American and false aloe are agaves of the AMARYLLIS family.

Alonso, Alicia [älōn'sō], 1921–, Cuban ballerina and choreographer. She danced on Broadway before soloing with several companies. She had a huge repertoire that ranged from classical to MODERN DANCE. Her own works, e.g., *La Tinaja* (1942), were created for her Cuban company, founded in 1948, which is now the National Ballet.

alpaca, partially domesticated South American hoofed MAMMAL. The highland tribes of Bolivia, Chile, and Peru breed the alpaca for its wool, which is shaded from black through brown to white and has been exported since 1836. Alpacas feed on grasses and require a pure water supply. Like the LLAMA, the alpaca belongs to the CAMEL family.

Alp Arslan, 1029–72, Seljuk sultan of PERSIA (1063–72). He won great victories over the Byzantine Christians, especially at Manzikert (1071), and conquered Syria. He was murdered by one of his prisoners of war.

alphabet, system of WRITING, theoretically having a one-for-one relation between character (or letter) and phoneme (see PHONETICS). Few alphabets have achieved an ideal exactness. A system of writing is called a syllabary when one character represents a syllable rather than a phoneme, e.g., the kana used in Japanese. The precursors of the alphabet were the iconographic and ideographic writing of ancient peoples, such as CUNEIFORM and the HIEROGLYPHIC writing of the Egyptians. The alphabet of modern Western Europe is the Roman alphabet. Russian, Serbian, Bulgarian, and many languages of the former Soviet republics are written in the Cyrillic alphabet, an augmented Greek alphabet. Greek, Hebrew, and Arabic all have their own alphabets. The most important writing of India is the Devanagari, an alphabet with syllabic features. The Roman alphabet is derived from the Greeks, who had imitated the Phoenician alphabet. The exact steps are unknown, but the Phoenician, Hebrew, Arabic, and Devanagari systems are based ultimately on signs of Egyptian hieroglyphic writing. Two European alphabets of the late Roman era were the RUNES and the ogham. An exotic modern system is the Cherokee syllabary of SEQUOYAH.

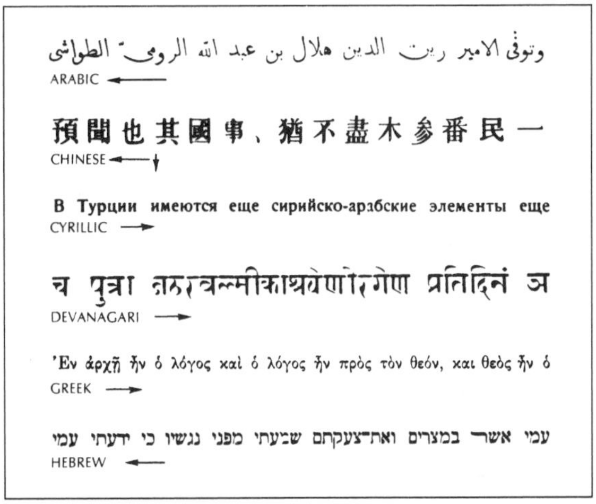

ARABIC ←

預聞也其國事、猶不盡木參番民一

CHINESE ←

В Турции имеются еще сирийско-арабские элементы еще

CYRILLIC →

DEVANAGARI →

Ἐν ἀρχῇ ἦν ὁ λόγος καὶ ὁ λόγος ἦν πρὸς τὸν θεόν, καὶ θεὸς ἦν ὁ

GREEK →

HEBREW ←

Alphabet: Examples of letters in various alphabets (arrows indicate the direction of reading)

alpha particle, one of the three types of radiation resulting from natural RADIOACTIVITY. An alpha particle is an ordinary helium nucleus, which consists of two protons and two neutrons.

Alps, great mountain system of S central Europe, c.500 mi (800 km) long and c.100 mi (160 km) wide, curving in a great arc through parts of France, Italy, Switzerland, Germany, and Austria. The mountains are known for their towering, snowcapped peaks, deep U-shaped glacial valleys, modern glaciers, and many fine lakes such as Geneva, Lucerne, Como, Garda, and Maggiore. Famous winter sports centers in the Alps include Chamonix, SAINT MORITZ,

Kitzbühel, Cortina d'Ampezzo, and INNSBRUCK. The principal peaks include MONT BLANC (15,771 ft/4,807 m), the highest; Gran Paradiso; MATTERHORN; Jungfrau; and Grossglockner. The Alps are crossed by three of the world's longest tunnels—the Simplon, St. Gotthard, and Mont Cénis—and by many routes such as the BRENNER PASS and the Great and Little St. Bernard passes.

Alsace-Lorraine, region of NE France, bounded by Belgium, Luxembourg, and Germany (N and E). Alsace lies to the east of Lorraine. Hops are grown, and vineyards are numerous. Potassium, iron, and coal deposits are exploited. STRASBOURG is Alsace's leading industrial center. Most of the population speaks French, but German is also spoken, especially around Metz. Both Alsace and Lorraine were included in the HOLY ROMAN EMPIRE. Lorraine emerged as a duchy, and Alsace was divided into many fiefs and free cities by the 13th cent. France gradually acquired both regions in the 17th and 18th cent. As a result of the FRANCO-PRUSSIAN WAR (1870–71) much of the area was annexed to Germany and formed the "imperial land" of Alsace-Lorraine. After WORLD WAR I Alsace-Lorraine was returned to France, but it was again annexed (1940–45) to Germany during WORLD WAR II.

Altaic, subfamily of the URALIC AND ALTAIC family of languages. See LANGUAGE (table).

Altamira: see PALEOLITHIC ART.

Altdorfer, Albrecht [ältdôr′fər], 1480–1538, German painter and engraver. His romantic allegorical and biblical works, e.g., *Susannah at the Bath* (1526; Alte Pinakothek, Munich), vibrate with intense movement. He was perhaps the first German to paint pure landscape.

alternating current: see ELECTRICITY; GENERATOR; MOTOR, ELECTRIC.

alternative medicine, techniques for treating and preventing disease that are regarded by modern Western medicine as scientifically unproven or unorthodox. The term *alternative medicine* can encompass a wide range of therapies, including CHIROPRACTIC, homeopathy, ACUPUNCTURE, HERBAL MEDICINE, MEDITATION, BIOFEEDBACK, massage therapy, and various "new-age" therapies such as guided imagery and naturopathy. Although many alternative therapies have long been widely employed in the treatment of disease, the scientifically oriented modern medical establishment has typically been skeptical about, and sometimes strongly opposed to, their use. In 1993 the U.S. National Institutes of Health established the Office of Alternative Medicine to examine the merits of such techniques. See also HOLISTIC MEDICINE.

alternator: see GENERATOR.

Altgeld, John Peter, 1847–1902, American politician, governor (1892–96) of Illinois; b. Germany. A Democrat and a staunch defender of human rights, he pardoned three men convicted for the HAYMARKET SQUARE RIOT of 1886, and protested the sending of federal troops to end the Pullman strike (1894). His liberal actions lost him reelection (1896).

Althing, parliament of ICELAND. The oldest assembly in Europe, first convened in 930, it voted Iceland's independence from Denmark in 1944. It is now a 63-member unicameral body, but until 1991 it comprised a lower house (two thirds of members) and an upper house (one third). Members are elected by a system of proportional representation.

altimeter, device for measuring altitude. The most common type, used in airplanes and balloons and by mountain climbers, consists of an aneroid BAROMETER, calibrated so that the drop in atmospheric pressure indicates the elevation above sea level. The radio altimeter indicates the actual altitude over the earth's surface by measuring the time it takes for a radio signal to travel to earth and back.

altiplano, densely populated upland plateau (alt. c.12,000 ft/3,660 m) in the ANDES of Bolivia and Peru. It has a cool climate and bleak aspect. Corn, wheat, and potatoes are the chief crops; mining is the principal industry. LA PAZ and Oruro, in Bolivia, are the largest cities.

altitude, vertical distance of an object above sea level or another reference point on the earth's or another astronomical body's surface. On earth it is usually measured by the reduction in atmospheric pressure with height, as shown on a BAROMETER or ALTIMETER. Vertical distances on other planets can be determined by means of radar and optical imaging. In surveying and astronomy, altitude is the vertical angle of an observed point, such as a star or planet, above the horizon plane (see ASTRONOMICAL COORDINATE SYSTEMS).

alto: see VOICE.

alumina or **aluminum oxide,** chemical compound (Al_2O_3) that is widely distributed in nature and occurs combined with silica and other minerals in clays, feldspars, and micas, and in almost pure form in CORUNDUM. It is the major component of BAUXITE and is used in the production of ALUMINUM metal. Alumina is also used as an ABRASIVE, in ceramics, in pigments, and in the manufacture of chemicals.

aluminum or **aluminium** (Al), metallic element, used in antiquity but first isolated by Friedrich WÖHLER in 1827. The silver-white metal is ductile and malleable, and conducts heat and electricity. Although very reactive chemically, aluminum resists corrosion by forming a protective oxide (alumina) coating. The most abundant metal in the earth's crust (about 8% by weight), it occurs combined with other elements in such minerals as alum, BAUXITE, CORUNDUM, CRYOLITE, FELDSPAR, and MICA. Aluminum and its compounds are used in paints, foil, jewelry, and welding. Aluminum wire, cheaper and lighter than copper wire, is used in high-tension power transmission. The strong, hard alloy DURALUMIN is used in aircraft. See ELEMENT (table); PERIODIC TABLE.

aluminum oxide: see ALUMINA.

Alvarado, Pedro de [älvärä′thō], 1486–1541, Spanish CONQUISTADOR. A chief lieutenant of Hernán CORTÉS during the conquest of MEXICO, Alvarado conquered GUATEMALA in 1523 and served as governor until his death. Exercising absolute control, he founded many cities and developed the colony while searching for the fabled Seven Cities of Cibola. He was killed quelling a rebellion of indigenous peoples in W Mexico.

Alvarez, Luis Walter, 1911–88, American physicist; b. San Francisco. He was awarded the 1968 Nobel Prize in physics for the development of the liquid-hydrogen bubble chamber (see PARTICLE DETECTOR). He also helped develop the ground-control approach system for aircraft in the 1940s and played an important part in the MANHATTAN PROJECT. He; his son, the geologist **Walter Alvarez,** 1940–, b. Berkeley, Calif.; and others proposed that unusually high levels of iridium at the boundary between Cretaceous and Tertiary rocks indicated a major meteor impact and that this might be the cause of the MASS EXTINCTION of the DINOSAURS.

alyssum, chiefly annual and perennial herb (genus *Alyssum*) of the MUSTARD family, native to the Mediterranean. Some species, with masses of yellow or white flowers, are cultivated as rock-garden and border ornamentals. The annual sweet alyssum has fragrant white or lilac blossoms. Once called madwort or healbite, alyssum was thought to cure rabies.

Alzheimer's disease, degenerative disease of the brain cells producing loss of memory and general intellectual impairment. It usually affects people over age 65, although it can appear earlier, especially in some familial forms of the disease. As the disease progresses, a variety of symptoms may become apparent, including confusion, irritability, and restlessness, as well as disorientation and impaired judgment and concentration. The cause is unknown, although there appears to be a genetic component; the excessive beta amyloid proteins and the traces of aluminum found in the brains of victims are being studied as possible contributors. There is no cure, but the drug tacrine provides temporary improvement for some patients.

Am, chemical symbol of the element AMERICIUM.

AM: see MODULATION.

Amadeus VIII, 1383–1451, duke (from 1416) of Savoy and antipope (1439–49) with the name Felix V. The last of the antipopes, he was elected at the Council of BASEL, but had few supporters. He yielded his claim when Nicholas V became pope.

Amado, Jorge [əmä′do͞o], 1912–, Brazilian novelist. His vibrant novels of the lives of ordinary Brazilians include *The Violent Land* (1942), *Gabriela, Clove and Cinnamon* (1958), the ebullient *Doña Flor and Her Two Husbands* (1966), and *The War of the Saints* (tr. 1993).

Amalekites [ăm′ələkīts], aboriginal people of CANAAN and the Sinai peninsula. They waged war against the Hebrews, until dispersed by SAUL and DAVID.

amalgam: see ALLOY.

Amalric or **Amaury,** Latin kings of Jerusalem. **Amalric I,** c.1137–1174 (r.1162–74), lost the suzerainty of Egypt to the Turkish sultan Nur ad-Din and eventually to SALADIN. **Amalric II,** c.1155–1205 (r.1197–1205), married the daughter of Amalric I. He was also king of Cyprus (1194–1205).

Amalthea, in astronomy, natural satellite of JUPITER.

amaranth, common name for the family Amaranthaceae (also called the pigweed family), herbs, trees, and vines found mainly in warm regions of the Americas and Africa. The genus *Amaranthus* includes several species called amaranth, characterized by a lasting red pigment in the stems and leaves; common weeds, e.g., the green amaranth (*A. retroflexus*); and various plants known as TUMBLEWEED and pigweed. Some species have long been used as potherbs and cereals in the Old and New World. The globe amaranth, or BACHELOR'S BUTTON (genus *Gomphrenia*), and the cockscomb (genus *Celosia*) are tropical annuals that are dried and used in everlasting bouquets.

Amarillo, city (1990 pop. 157,615), seat of Potter co., N Tex.; inc. 1899. A plains city, it is the commercial and industrial center of the Texas Panhandle. Oil, gas, helium, and zinc are produced, along with various manufactures. The city handles grains and livestock raised in the area. It grew with the coming (1887) of the railroad and became an industrial city after the discovery of gas (1918) and oil (1921).

amaryllis, common name for some members of the Amaryllidaceae, a family of mostly perennial plants with flat, narrow leaves and lilylike flowers borne on separate, leafless stalks. Widely distributed, they are found especially in tropical and subtropical lowlands. Ornamentals of the family are mistaken for plants of the LILY family, which differ in the position of the ovary (see FLOWER). The best-known member of the family is the extensively hybridized amaryllis (genus *Hippeastrum*) of commerce, grown as a houseplant (or outside in the South) for its large, showy, variously colored flowers. The family also includes the showy-blossomed true amaryllis, or belladonna lily (*Amaryllis belladonna*); NARCISSUS; and the snowdrops (genus *Galanthus*), whose small, early-blooming flowers are symbolic of consolation and promise. The genus *Agave*, the tropical American counterpart of the African genus ALOE, contains the most economically important plants in the family. Different agaves provide soap, food, beverages, and fiber (see SISAL HEMP).

Amaury. For persons thus named, see AMALRIC.

Amazon, world's second longest river, flowing c.3,900 mi (6,280 km) east across N South America to enter the Atlantic Ocean through a wide delta in N Brazil. It is formed by the junction in N Peru of the Ucayili and Marañón rivers. It has more than 500 tributaries, drains c.40% of the continent, and carries more water than any other river in the world. The Amazon traverses the world's largest rain forest (selva); since the 1960s the population and development in the area have steadily increased. There are no waterfalls or other obstructions along its course, and ships of 14-ft (4-m) draft can travel very nearly its full length (to Iquitos, Peru). Belém and Manaus in Brazil are other ports.

Amazon, in Greek mythology, one of a tribe of warlike women from Asia Minor. The Amazons had a matriarchal society, in which women governed and fought while men performed the household tasks. Several Greek heroes proved their mettle against Amazons, e.g., HERCULES and THESEUS.

amber, yellow to brown fossil RESIN exuded by coniferous trees now extinct; the best amber is transparent. Highly polished amber is used to make small decorative objects, e.g., beads and amulets. When rubbed with a cloth, amber becomes charged with static electricity. Bubbles of air, leaves, bits of wood, or insects, sometimes of extinct species, are often found trapped in amber. The chief source of the world's amber is the Baltic coast of Germany.

ambergris, a waxlike substance that is formed in the intestine of the sperm whale. It is found floating on tropical seas or cast up on the shore in yellow, gray, black, or variegated masses. Greatly valued from earliest times, ambergris is now used as a fixative in perfumes.

Ambler, Eric, 1909–, English novelist. He is the author of popular suspense stories, usually involving international intrigue, e.g., *A Coffin for Dimitrios* (1939), *To Catch a Spy* (1964), and *The Care of Time* (1981).

Amboise, Jacques d': see D'AMBOISE, JACQUES.

Ambrose, Saint, 340?–397, bishop of MILAN, Doctor of the Church. A popular governor in Milan, Ambrose was made (374) bishop by popular demand. He opposed ARIANISM and was an adviser to Emperor Gratian, whom he persuaded to outlaw (379) heresy in the West. His preaching helped to convert St. AUGUSTINE. Ambrose wrote many theological works and is associated with the type of PLAINSONG called Ambrosian chant. Feast: Dec. 7.

ameba or **amoeba,** one-celled PROTOZOAN in the phylum Sarcodina. Amebas constantly change their body shape as they form temporary extensions called pseudopods, or false feet, used for feeding and locomotion. Most amebas range from 5 to 20 microns in diameter. They engulf their prey (diatoms, algae, or bacteria) with their pseudopods, forming vacuoles in which food is digested by ENZYMES. Reproduction is usually by binary fission (splitting) to produce two daughter amebas, the nucleus dividing by MITOSIS; some also reproduce sexually. Amebas live in fresh and marine waters and the upper layers of soil. Many are PARASITES of aquatic and terrestrial animals, and some cause disease, e.g., amebic dysentery.

Ameling, Elly, 1938–, Dutch soprano. Although she has sung opera, she is noted for her sensitive interpretations of French and German art songs, particularly the LIEDER of Schubert. She made her U.S. debut in New York City in 1968.

Amen: see AMON.

Amenemhet I [ä″mĕnĕm′hĕt, ā″–], d. 1970 B.C., king of EGYPT founder of the XII dynasty that initiated the Middle Kingdom. He centralized the government in a virtually feudal form. The dynasty enabled the arts and science to flourish.

Amenhotep I [ä″mĕnhō′tĕp, ā–] or **Amenophis I,** fl. 1570 B.C., king of EGYPT of the XVIII dynasty. A great military leader, he extended Egypt's power E to the Euphrates and S to the second cataract of the NILE. THUTMOSE I succeeded him.

amenorrhea, cessation of MENSTRUATION. Primary amenorrhea is a delay in or a failure to start menstruation; secondary amenorrhea is a cessation in the menstrual cycle. It can be caused by dysfunctioning of the pituitary gland, ovaries, uterus, or hypothalamus, by surgical removal of the ovaries or uterus, by stress or other emotional factors, or by inadequate nutrition. Women with anorexia and female athletes have an increased incidence of amenorrhea.

American Association for the Advancement of Science (AAAS), est. 1848 to foster scientific freedom, improve the effective application of science for human needs, and increase public understanding of science. Headquartered in Washington, D.C., it has over 135,000 members in all fields and 296 affiliated groups. Among its publications is the weekly newsmagazine and journal *Science*.

American Ballet Theatre (ABT), a foremost international dance company of the 20th cent. It was founded as the Mordkin Ballet (1937–40) and was known (1940–56) as the Ballet Theater. It presents newly staged classics and dances with American themes. Choreographers have included George BALANCHINE, Agnes DE MILLE, Jerome ROBBINS, and Antony TUDOR; dancers have included Alicia ALONSO, Erik BRUHN, Maria Tallchief, and Igor YOUSKEVITCH.

American Bar Association (ABA), organization of lawyers admitted to any state bar; est. 1878. It promotes professional activities as well as uniformity of U.S. laws, high professional standards, and improved judicial administration. ABA committees address such topics as legal education, professional ethics, and legal aid for the poor. In 1991 the organization had more than 383,000 members.

American Civil Liberties Union (ACLU), nonpartisan organization devoted to protecting basic rights set forth in the U.S. CONSTITUTION; est. 1920 by Jane ADDAMS, Roger BALDWIN, Norman THOMAS, and others. Its special concerns are expression of opinion, equality before the law, and due process. The ACLU has argued or supported nearly every major U.S. civil liberties court case since its founding and, since the early 1980s, it has emphasized the passage of protective laws as well. The ACLU has some 275,000 members.

American Colonization Society, organized (Dec. 1816–Jan. 1817) to transport free African Americans from the U.S. and settle them in Africa. Land purchases (1821) in Africa by the society led to the foundation of LIBERIA, and more than 11,000 African Americans were sent there before 1860. The colonization movement was attacked by ABOLITIONISTS and was unpopular with many African Americans; it declined after 1840.

American Federation of Labor and Congress of Industrial Organizations (AFL-CIO), a federation of autonomous trade unions in the U.S., Canada, Mexico, Panama, and U.S. territories. It was formed in 1955 by the merger of the AFL and the CIO. Although it does not participate directly in COLLECTIVE BARGAINING, the AFL-CIO serves as the leading voice of American trade unionism, actively lobbying on the national and state levels and supporting political candidates. From its founding in 1886, the AFL emphasized organization of skilled workers on a craft rather than an industrial basis. Under the successive leadership of Samuel GOMPERS, William GREEN, and George MEANY, the AFL secured higher wages, shorter hours, workers' compensation, child labor laws, and exemption of labor from antitrust legislation. In the early 1930s a strong minority faction within the AFL advocated the organization of workers in basic industries (such as steel, autos, and rubber) on an industry-wide basis. John L. LEWIS led this militant group in forming a Committee for Industrial Organization, which, after expulsion from the parent body in 1938, changed its name to the Congress of Industrial Organizations. The CIO, under the presidency of Lewis and later of Philip MURRAY, enjoyed considerable success. In 1955, however, at a time of growing labor concern over the perceived anti-union policies of the Eisenhower administration, the two organizations merged, with Meany as president, and adopted the present name. Lane KIRKLAND succeeded Meany as president in 1979. Ultimate authority in the AFL-CIO is vested in a biennial convention; the executive council governs between conventions. In 1992 the federation included 88 international unions, with a U.S. membership of about 14.1 million. See also UNION, LABOR.

American foxhound: see FOXHOUND.

American Fur Company, chartered (1808) by John Jacob ASTOR to rival Canadian fur companies. The company gained a virtual monopoly of the Great Lakes trade and expanded W into the Missouri valley and Rocky Mountain areas.

American Indian languages: see NATIVE AMERICAN LANGUAGES.

American Indian Movement (AIM), activist organization of the Native American civil-rights movement, est. 1968. After briefly occupying (Nov. 1972) the Bureau of INDIAN AFFAIRS to protest programs controlling tribal development, AIM members led (1973) 200 SIOUX in a 71-day takeover of WOUNDED KNEE, S.Dak., to demand a review of 300 treaties with the U.S. government. AIM also sponsored talks resulting in the 1977 International Treaty Conference with the UN in Geneva, Switzerland.

American Indians: see MIDDLE AMERICA, INDIGENOUS PEOPLES OF; NORTH AMERICA, INDIGENOUS PEOPLES OF; SOUTH AMERICA, INDIGENOUS PEOPLES OF; and individual peoples. See also AMERICAS, PREHISTORY OF THE; NATIVE AMERICAN LANGUAGES.

American Museum of Natural History, New York City, inc. 1869; est. to promote the study of natural science and related subjects. Buildings on its present site were opened in 1877. The Hayden Planetarium was added in 1935 and the Roosevelt Memorial building in 1936. The museum's explorations and research programs have provided it with specimens and data of great value; it maintains exhibitions in all branches of natural history.

American party: see KNOW-NOTHING MOVEMENT.

American Revolution, 1775–83, struggle by which the THIRTEEN COLONIES that were to become the United States won independence from Britain. By the middle of the 18th cent., differences in life, thought, and economic interests had formed between the colonies and the mother country. The British government, favoring a policy of MERCANTILISM, tried to regulate colonial commerce in the British interest, and provoked colonial opposition. The STAMP ACT passed by Parliament in 1765 roused a violent colonial outcry as an act of taxation without representation. The TOWNSHEND ACTS (1767) led to such acts of violence as the BOSTON MASSACRE (1770), the burning of the H.M.S. *Gaspee* (1772), and the BOSTON TEA PARTY (1773). In 1774 Britain responded with the coercive INTOLERABLE ACTS. The colonists convened the CONTINENTAL CONGRESS and petitioned the king for redress of their grievances. Fighting erupted on Apr. 19, 1775, at LEXINGTON AND CONCORD, and was followed by the capture of Fort Ticonderoga from the British, the battle of BUNKER HILL, and the unsuccessful colonial assault on Quebec (1775–76). The Continental Congress appointed (1775) George WASHINGTON to command the Continental army and, on July 4, 1776, adopted the DECLARATION OF INDEPENDENCE. Many colonists, however, remained pro-British Loyalists. The colonial victory in the SARATOGA CAMPAIGN (1777) helped forge a French-American alliance (1778), bringing vital aid to the colonists. Following the terrible ordeal of Washingon's army at VALLEY FORGE and the indecisive battle of MONMOUTH (1778), the war shifted to the South during the Carolina campaign (1780–81). The surrender (Oct. 1781) of Gen. CORNWALLIS at the close of the YORKTOWN CAMPAIGN ended the fighting, and the Treaty of Paris (1783) recognized the U.S. as a nation.

American Samoa, unincorporated territory of the U.S. (1990 pop. 46,773), 76 sq mi (197 sq km), comprising the eastern half of the Samoa island chain in the South Pacific. The major islands are Tutuila, the Manu'a group, Rose and Sand, and Swains. Pago Pago, the capital, is on Tutuila. The islands are mountainous and wooded; agriculture, fish canning, and some light industry are conducted. The Polynesian natives, considered U.S. nationals, elect a governor and legislature, and send a nonvoting delegate to Congress. American Samoa, defined by treaty in 1899, was administered by the U.S. Dept. of the Navy until 1951, when it passed to Dept. of the Interior jurisdiction.

American Samoa, The National Park of: see NATIONAL PARKS (table).

American Society for the Prevention of Cruelty to Animals (ASPCA), founded (1866) in the U.S. to shelter homeless animals, assist in livestock care, and help to enforce game laws. It is modeled on England's Royal Society for the Prevention of Cruelty to Animals (founded 1824).

American Standard Code for Information Interchange: see ASCII.

Americans with Disabilities Act (1990), U.S. civil-rights law that forbids discrimination against otherwise qualified individuals on the basis of a physical or mental handicap. The act is also designed to end most physical barriers to disabled persons in employment and in the use of accommodations, transportation, and telecommunications. The law also protects people with AIDS and alcoholics and drug abusers who are in treatment.

Americas, prehistory of the. It is generally agreed that the first people to inhabit the Americas crossed the BERING STRAIT from NE Asia in migration waves perhaps beginning before 30,000 B.C. The earliest evidence of human occupation in North America has been dated at c.19,000 B.C. and in South America at c.30,000 B.C., but there have been questions about the dating of these finds. The CLOVIS CULTURE of North America definitively dates from c.10,000 B.C., and by 8000 B.C. it is clear that peoples had spread throughout the Americas. Between 5000 B.C. and 1000 B.C., agriculture, pottery, and complex social systems throughout the Americas marked the end of the STONE AGE and the rise of the high civilizations. See MIDDLE AMERICA, INDIGENOUS PEOPLES OF; NORTH AMERICA, INDIGENOUS PEOPLES OF; SOUTH AMERICA, INDIGENOUS PEOPLES OF; and articles on individual peoples.

americium (Am), synthetic radioactive element, discovered by Glenn SEABORG and colleagues in 1944 by neutron bombardment of plutonium. The silver-white metal is in the ACTINIDE SERIES. Half-lives of the many isotopes range from 1.3 hr to over 7,000 years. Americium is used in many home smoke detectors. See ELEMENT (table); PERIODIC TABLE.

amethyst, most highly valued variety of QUARTZ, violet to purple in color, used as a gem. Amethyst is found in Brazil, Uruguay, Sri Lanka, Siberia, and North America. It has superstitious associations, being regarded as a love charm, a sleeping aid, and a guard against thieves and drunkenness.

Amharic [ămhâr'ĭk], language of ETHIOPIA. It belongs to the Ethiopic group of Hamito-Semitic languages. See AFRICAN LANGUAGES (table).

Amherst, Jeffrey Amherst, Baron, 1717–97, British army officer. During the last of the FRENCH AND INDIAN WARS, he commanded British forces at the capture of Louisbourg, N.S. (1758), TICONDEROGA (1759), and Montreal (1760). Amherst, Mass., and Amherst College are named for him.

Amiens [ämyăN'], city (1990 pop. 131,872), capital of Somme dept.,

N France. A textile and farm-market center, it has been occupied by many invaders; after being devastated in both world wars the city was rebuilt. Its Cathedral of Notre Dame (begun c.1220) is France's largest Gothic cathedral.

Amiens Cathedral

Amiens, Treaty of: see FRENCH REVOLUTIONARY WARS.

Amin, Idi, c.1925–, president of UGANDA (1971–79). Seizing control of the government from Milton OBOTE in 1971, he instituted a harsh and brutal regime and expelled Uganda's Asian population. He was driven into exile in 1979.

amino acid, any of a class of organic compounds having a carboxyl group (COOH) and an amino group (NH_2). Some 22 amino acids are commonly found in animals and more than 100 less common forms are found in nature, chiefly in plants. When the carboxyl carbon atom of one amino acid binds to the nitrogen of another with the release of a water molecule, a linkage called a peptide bond is formed. Chains of amino acids, joined head-to-tail in this manner, are synthesized by living systems and are called polypeptides (up to about 50 amino acids) and PROTEINS (over 50 amino acids). Many of the amino acids necessary in metabolism can be synthesized in the human or animal body when needed; these are called nonessential. Others cannot be synthesized in sufficient quantities; these are termed essential and must be provided in the diet.

Amis, Kingsley, 1922–, English novelist. He is best known for *Lucky Jim* (1953), a brilliant satire on academic life. Later novels include *That Certain Feeling* (1955), *Jake's Thing* (1979), *Stanley and the Women* (1985), and *Difficulties with Girls* (1989). Amis also writes espionage novels, poetry, and nonfiction. His son, **Martin Amis,** 1949–, is also a novelist. His bitterly satirical fiction exposes the dark side of contemporary English society. His novels include *Dead Babies* (1975) and *Time's Arrow* (1991).

Amman, city (1990 est. pop. 1,000,000), capital of Jordan, N central Jordan, on the Jabbok R. Jordan's largest city and industrial and commercial heart, Amman is a transportation hub, especially for pilgrims en route to MECCA. It is noted for its colored marble; textiles, leather goods, cement, and other manufactures are produced. Amman is the biblical Rabbah, the Ammonite capital. It fell to King David, Assyria, Rome, and other conquerors. After the Arab conquest (635) it declined, reviving as the capital of Trans-Jordan after 1921. Palestinian refugees swelled the population after the Arab-Israeli Wars of 1948 and 1967. The city's historic structures include a Roman amphitheater.

ammeter, instrument used to measure, in AMPERES, the magnitude of an electric current. An ammeter is usually combined with a VOLTMETER and an OHMMETER in a multipurpose instrument. Although most ammeters are based on the d'Arsonval GALVANOMETER and are of the analog type, digital ammeters are becoming increasingly common.

Ammon: see AMON.

ammonia, chemical compound (NH_3), colorless gas with a characteristic pungent, penetrating odor. It is extremely soluble in water. Ammonia and ammonia vapors are irritating—prolonged exposure and inhalation cause serious injury and may be fatal. The major use of ammonia and its compounds is as FERTILIZERS. Ammonia solutions are used to clean, bleach, and deodorize; to etch aluminum; to saponify oils and fats; and in chemical manufacture. Ammonia is usually produced by direct combination of nitrogen with hydrogen at high temperature and pressure in the presence of a catalyst.

amnesia, condition characterized by loss of memory for long or short intervals. It may be caused by physical injury, shock, senility, or severe illness. In other cases, a painful experience and everything remindful of it, including the individual's identity, is unconsciously repressed (see DEFENSE MECHANISM). Attempts to cure this type of amnesia include efforts to establish associations with the past through suggestion and HYPNOSIS.

amnesty, in law, exemption from prosecution for some criminal action. It is distinguished from a pardon, which is an act of forgiveness following conviction. Amnesties are usually extended to groups of persons involved in disorders or insurrections; after the Civil War the U.S. granted a qualified amnesty to the Confederate forces.

Amnesty International (AI), organization (est. 1961) that campaigns against the detention of political prisoners and against other HUMAN RIGHTS violations throughout the world. It was awarded the Nobel Peace Prize in 1977 after effecting the release of more than 10,000 prisoners. In 1993 the organization had 1.2 million members worldwide.

amniocentesis, diagnostic procedure in which a sample of the amniotic fluid surrounding the fetus is removed from the uterus with a fine needle inserted through the abdomen of the pregnant woman (see PREGNANCY). Fetal cells in the fluid can be grown in the laboratory and studied to detect the presence of certain genetic disorders (e.g., DOWN'S SYNDROME, TAY-SACHS DISEASE) or physical abnormalities. Generally recommended when there is a family history of genetic disorders or when the woman is over age 35, the procedure is usually carried out around the 14th or 15th week of pregnancy, when there is sufficient amniotic fluid and ABORTION is still an option. See also BIRTH DEFECTS; CHORIONIC VILLUS SAMPLING.

Amnon, DAVID's eldest son. He raped his half sister Tamar and was killed for it by her brother ABSALOM.

amoeba: see AMEBA.

Amon [ā'mən, ä'–], **Ammon** [ă'mən], or **Amen** [ä'mĕn], ancient Egyptian deity. Originally the chief god of Thebes, Amon grew increasingly important in Egypt, and eventually, as Amon Ra, he was identified with RA as the supreme deity. He was also identified with the Greek ZEUS (the Roman JUPITER).

Amos, book of the OLD TESTAMENT, 30th in order in the Authorized Version, third of the Minor PROPHETS. The shepherd-prophet preached in the northern kingdom of Israel under Jeroboam II (r. c.793–753 B.C.). The book falls into three parts: God's judgment on Gentile nations, finally on Israel; three sermons on the doom of Israel; five visions of destruction, the last promising redemption.

Amoy: see XIAMEN.

Ampère, André Marie, 1775–1836, French physicist, mathematician, and natural philosopher. He extended the work of Hans OERSTED on the relationship of electricity and magnetism, formulated Ampère's law describing the contribution of a current element to magnetic induction, and invented the astatic needle. The basic unit of electric current, the AMPERE, is named for him.

ampere (amp or A), basic unit of electric current and the fundamental electrical unit used with the mks system of units of the METRIC SYSTEM. The ampere is officially defined as the current in a pair of equally long, parallel, straight wires 1 meter apart that produces a force of 0.0000002 newton between the wires for each meter of their length.

amphetamine, any of a class of powerful drugs that act as stimulants (see DRUG) on the central nervous system. Popularly known as "bennies," "speed," or "uppers," amphetamines enhance mental alertness and the ability to concentrate; cause wakefulness, talkativeness, and euphoria; and temporarily reverse the effects of fatigue. They have been used to treat obesity, narcolepsy and minimal brain dysfunction. Amphetamines can produce insomnia, hyperactivity, and irritability, as well as such severe systemic disorders as cardiac irregularities, elevated blood pressure, and gastric disturbances. The drugs are addictive and easily abused; addiction can result in psychosis or death from overexhaustion or cardiac arrest (see DRUG ADDICTION AND DRUG ABUSE).

amphibian, cold-blooded animal of the class Amphibia, the most primitive of terrestrial VERTEBRATES. Unlike REPTILES, the amphibians, which include FROGS and TOADS, SALAMANDERS and newts, and the limbless CAECILIANS, have moist skins without scales or with small, hidden scales. Most amphibians deposit their eggs in water or a moist, protected place. The young undergo METAMORPHOSIS from aquatic, water-breathing, limbless TADPOLES to terrestrial or partly terrestrial, air-breathing, four-legged adults.

amphitheater, open structure for the exhibition of gladiatorial contests and spectacles, built in cities throughout the Roman Empire, e.g., at Rome (see COLOSSEUM), Arles (France), and Cirencester (England). The typical amphitheater was elliptical, with seats rising around a central arena; quarters for the gladiators and animals were under the arena. The word is now used for various quite unrelated structures.

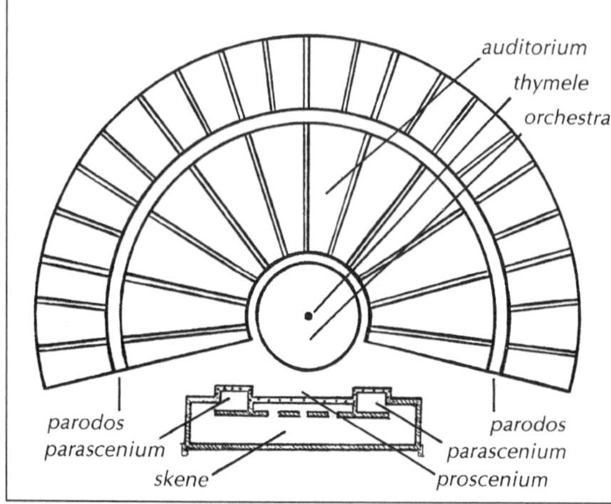

Amphitheater

amphoterism, in chemistry, the property of certain compounds of acting either as acids or as bases (see ACIDS AND BASES), depending on the reaction in which they are involved. Many hydroxide compounds and organic molecules that contain both acidic (e.g., carboxyl) and basic (e.g., amino) FUNCTIONAL GROUPS are usually amphoteric.

amplifier, device in which a varying input signal controls a flow of energy to produce an output signal that varies in the same way but has a larger amplitude; the input signal may be a current, a voltage, a mechanical motion, or any other signal, and the output signal is usually of the same nature. The ratio of the output voltage to the input voltage is called the voltage gain. The most common types of amplifiers are electronic and use a series of TRANSISTORS as their principal components. In most cases, the transistors are incorporated into INTEGRATED-CIRCUIT chips. Transistor amplifiers are used in RADIO and TELEVISION transmitters and receivers, stereophonic sound reproduction systems, and intercoms.

amplitude modulation: see MODULATION.

Amru al-Kais, fl. 6th cent., Arabic poet, long esteemed by Arabs as the model for erotic poetry. Like much pre-Islamic poetry, his verse is subjective and stylistically perfect.

Amsterdam, constitutional capital and largest city (1991 est. pop. 700,000) of the Netherlands, on the Ij and Amstel rivers. It is a major port joined with the North Sea and the Rhine by canals. One of Europe's great commercial, intellectual, and artistic capitals, it has a major stock exchange and is a diamond-cutting center. It is built on piles and is cut by some 40 canals crossed by about 400 bridges. Chartered c.1300, it joined the HANSEATIC LEAGUE in 1369 and the anti-Spanish Netherland provinces in 1578. An influx of refugees contributed to its growth, and the city reached its apex in the 17th cent. After French rule (1795–1814) it became the Dutch capital. Amsterdam suffered greatly under German occupation (1940–45) during WORLD WAR II. Points of interest include the city hall (16th cent.); the university (est. 1632); the Rijks Museum, with its Rembrandts and other Dutch master paintings; and the municipal museum, with its Van Gogh collection.

Amu Darya, river, E central Asia, known to the ancient Greeks and Persians as the Oxus. It is c.1,600 mi (2,580 km) long and flows generally northwest from sources in the snow-capped Pamirs along the border of Afghanistan and Tajikstan, Uzbekistan, and Turkmenistan through the Kara Kum desert in E Turkmenistan to a large delta on the ARAL SEA in NW Uzbekistan. The waters of the river are used for irrigation in Turkmenistan and Uzbekistan.

Amundsen, Roald [ä'mo͝onsən], 1872–1928, Norwegian explorer. He commanded the first single ship to sail through the NORTHWEST PASSAGE (1903–6) and was the first person to reach the South Pole (1911). In 1926, with the aviator Umberto Nobile and the financier Lincoln ELLSWORTH, Amundsen took part in the first airplane flight over the North Pole. When Nobile crashed in the Arctic in 1928, Amundsen was killed in the rescue attempt. His works, which include *The South Pole* (1913), have added much to knowledge of the polar regions.

Amur, river, c.1,800 mi (2,900 km) long, NE Asia. It flows generally southeast, forming for more than 1,000 mi (1,610 km) the border between Russia and China, then northeast through the Russian Far East, entering the Tartar Strait opposite SAKHALIN Island. Its chief tributaries are the USSURI and SUNGARI. The river is navigable by small craft for its entire length during the ice-free season (May–Nov.)

Amurath. For Ottoman sultans thus named, see MURAD.

amyotrophic lateral sclerosis (ALS), degenerative disease that affects nerve cells in the brain and spinal cord, preventing them from sending impulses to the muscles. The muscles atrophy quickly, causing weakness, paralysis, and eventual death. About half of the inherited cases are caused by a gene mutation on chromosome 21. Lou GEHRIG died of the disease in 1941, bringing it national attention.

Anabaptists, name applied, originally in scorn, to certain Christian sects holding that infant baptism is not authorized in Scripture, but that baptism should be administered only to believers. Prominent in Europe during the 16th cent., they were persecuted everywhere. Their chief leaders were Thomas MÜNZER and JOHN OF LEIDEN. MENNONITES and Hutterites are descended from them.

Anabasis: see XENOPHON.

anabolic steroid or **androgenic steroid,** any of a group of synthetic derivatives of TESTOSTERONE that promote muscle and bone growth. Used therapeutically to treat chronic debilitating diseases, anabolic steroids have also been used by bodybuilders and athletes seeking increased muscle mass and enhanced strength and stamina. Such use is banned by the International Olympic Committee and other governing bodies in sports, and in 1988 a federal law was enacted that made it illegal to distribute anabolic steroids for nontherapeutic uses. Abuse of anabolic steroids may lead to increased aggressiveness, irritability, and other disruptive behavioral effects, including symptoms characteristic of drug addiction; long term effects are not known.

anaconda: see BOA.

Anacreon, fl. c.521 B.C., Greek LYRIC poet, celebrator of love and wine. The Anacreontics, in his style, were written from Hellenistic to late Byzantine times.

anae-. For words beginning thus, see ANE-.

Anaheim, city (1990 pop. 266,406), Orange co., S Calif., SE of LOS ANGELES; founded 1857, inc. 1876. A major tourist center, Anaheim contains the Disneyland theme park (opened 1955); Anaheim Stadium, home of the California Angels baseball and Los Angeles Rams football teams; and the Anaheim Convention Center. It is also the site of a large electronic equipment industry.

analgesic, any agent used to relieve pain. Analgesic drugs include nonnarcotics, such as ASPIRIN and other salicylates, IBUPROFEN, and ACETAMINOPHEN; NARCOTICS, such as MORPHINE and CODEINE; and synthetic narcotics with morphinelike action, such as propoxyphene

(Darvon) and meperidine (Demerol). Techniques that provide analgesia include ACUPUNCTURE, HYPNOSIS, and BIOFEEDBACK.

analog circuit, ELECTRIC CIRCUIT in which the output voltage and current values are considered significant over a continuum. Analog circuits may be used for such purposes as amplifying signals corresponding to sound waves. See also DIGITAL CIRCUITS.

analog computer: see COMPUTER.

analog-to-digital conversion, the process of changing continuously varying data into digital quantities that represent the magnitude of the data at the moment the conversion is made. The most common use is to change analog signals into a form that can be manipulated by digital COMPUTER, as in data communications. See also DIGITAL-TO-ANALOG CONVERSION.

analysis, branch of MATHEMATICS that uses the concepts and methods of the CALCULUS. It includes basic calculus; advanced calculus, in which such underlying concepts as that of a limit are subjected to rigorous examination; differential and integral equations, in which the unknowns are FUNCTIONS rather than numbers; VECTOR and tensor analysis; differential geometry; and many other fields.

analytical chemistry: see CHEMISTRY.

analytic geometry, branch of GEOMETRY in which points are represented with respect to a coordinate system, such as CARTESIAN COORDINATES. Analytic geometry was introduced by René DESCARTES in 1637 and was of fundamental importance in the development of the CALCULUS by Sir Isaac NEWTON and G.W. LEIBNIZ in the late 17th cent. Its most common application—the representation of EQUATIONS involving two or three variables as curves in two or three DIMENSIONS or surfaces in three dimensions—allows problems in ALGEBRA to be treated geometrically and geometric problems to be treated algebraically. The methods of analytic geometry have been generalized to four or more dimensions and have been combined with other branches of geometry.

anarchism, political philosophy and movement that seeks the abolition of government, arguing that people, although naturally good, are corrupted by artificial institutions. Anarchism dates from the ancient Greeks, but its modern form was outlined (18th and 19th cent.) by William GODWIN, P.J. PROUDHON, and others. In Russia, given a violent and collectivist tone by Mikhail BAKUNIN, it was outlawed by the Bolsheviks after the RUSSIAN REVOLUTION. Only in the Latin countries of Europe, where it was linked to SYNDICALISM, did it gain a mass following by the end of the 19th cent. After the HAYMARKET SQUARE RIOT (1886) and the assassination of Pres. MCKINLEY, fear of anarchism caused the U.S. in 1901 to forbid anarchists from entering the country. Today anarchism remains important as a philosophical and political theory, not as an active political movement.

Anatolia, Asian part of Turkey, usually synonymous with ASIA MINOR.

Anatolian languages, subfamily of the Indo-European family of languages. See LANGUAGE (table).

anatomy, branch of biology concerned with the study of the body structure of plants and animals. Comparative anatomy considers structural similarities and differences of various organisms, forming the basis of CLASSIFICATION. Human anatomy emphasizes individual systems composed of groups of TISSUES and organs. See also PHYSIOLOGY.

Anaxagoras [ăn″əksăg′ərəs], c.500–428 B.C., Greek philosopher, thought to have been the teacher of SOCRATES. He held that an all-pervading *nous* (world-mind) ordered the physical world by combining particles from the undifferentiated mass of the universe.

Anaximander [ənăk″sĭmăn′dər], c.611–c.547 B.C., pre-Socratic Greek philosopher. His notions of the infinite or indefinite (*apeiron*) and its processes prefigured the later concept of the indestructibility of matter, while other views anticipated the theory of evolution and certain laws of astronomy.

Anchises [ănkī′sēz], in Greek mythology, Trojan shepherd; father of AENEAS by APHRODITE.

Anchorage, city (1990 pop. 226,338), Anchorage Borough, S central Alaska, at the head of Cook Inlet; inc. 1920. Founded (1915) as a railroad town, it has grown into the state's largest city as well as the administrative and commercial heart of S central and W Alaska. It is one of the nation's major defense centers and a transportation hub. Tourism is important, and there is a busy international airport. The city's rapid growth is due largely to its position as the focus of Alaska's coal, oil, and gas industries.

anchovy: see HERRING.

Andalusia, Span. *Andalucía,* autonomous region (1987 est. pop. 6,842,000), 33,675 sq mi (87,218 sq km), on the Mediterranean Sea, the Strait of Gibraltar, and the Atlantic Ocean. Spain's largest and most populous region, it occupies all of S Spain. Grapes, olives, citrus, cereals, and other crops are grown in its subtropical climate. Mineral resources include copper, iron, and zinc. It was settled (11th cent. B.C.) by the Phoenicians and later ruled by Carthage (6th cent. B.C.), Rome (3d cent. B.C.), and the Visigoths (5th cent. A.D.). In 711 the MOORS conquered Andalusia. Christian Spain ended the long reconquest of the region when GRANADA fell in 1492. In 1713 Spain ceded GIBRALTAR to Britain.

Andersen, Hans Christian, 1805–75, Danish writer of fairy tales. Poverty-ridden and a failure as an actor, Andersen won the generous patronage of King Frederick VI with his poetry. Though noted for a time as a novelist, e.g., *The Improvisatore* (1835), it was his later fairy tales that established him as Denmark's greatest author and a storyteller without peer. His sense of fantasy, power of description, and acute sensitivity contributed to his mastery of the genre. Among his many widely beloved tales are "The Little Match Girl," "The Ugly Duckling," "The Snow Queen," and "The Red Shoes."

Andersen Nexø, Martin [än′dərsĕn nĕksö], 1869–1954, Danish novelist. His famous proletarian novels *Pelle the Conqueror* (1906–10) and *Ditte, Daughter of Mankind* (1917–21) focus attention on conditions of poverty in Denmark.

Anderson, Carl David, 1905–91, American physicist; b. N.Y.C. For his discovery of the positron in 1932, he shared the 1936 Nobel Prize in physics with V.F. Hess. He is also credited as one of the discoverers of the muon (see ELEMENTARY PARTICLES) in 1936.

Anderson, Elizabeth Garrett, 1836–1917, English physician. After obtaining a private medical education under accredited physicians and in London hospitals and becoming licensed (1865) in Scotland, she opened (1866) a dispensary, later a small hospital, for women and children in London, the first in England to be staffed by women physicians. Largely through her efforts, British examining boards opened their examinations to women.

Anderson, Marian, 1897–93, African-American contralto; b. Philadelphia. She was the first African American to be named (1955) a permanent member of the METROPOLITAN OPERA COMPANY, and was also the first African American to perform in the White House. In 1958 she was an alternate delegate to the UN.

Anderson, Maxwell, 1888–1959, American dramatist; b. Atlantic, Pa. His plays, many written in verse, usually concern social and moral problems. His dramas include *What Price Glory?* (1924), *Elizabeth the Queen* (1930), *Winterset* (1935), *Anne of the Thousand Days* (1948), and *The Bad Seed* (1954).

Anderson, Sherwood, 1876–1941, American writer; b. Camden, Ohio. He was a strongly American writer, experimental and poetic, whose greatest novel, *Winesburg, Ohio* (1919), explores the loneliness and frustration of small-town lives. His other novels include *Poor White* (1920) and *Dark Laughter* (1925). Some of his finest work is in his compassionate and penetrating short stories, e.g., the collections *The Triumph of the Egg* (1921) and *Death in the Woods* (1933).

Andersonville, village (1990 pop. 277), SW Georgia, inc. 1881. It was the location of a notorious Confederate prison, now a national historic site, where dreadful conditions led to the deaths of nearly 13,000 Union soldiers. Andersonville National Cemetery, which contains the graves of the prisoners and other soldiers, is nearby.

Andes, great mountain system, extending c.4,500 mi (7,200 km) north to south in South America, generally parallel to the Pacific coast. The mountains reach a high point of 22,835 ft (6,960 m) in ACONCAGUA (highest point in the Western Hemisphere) and include many other snow-capped peaks over 22,000 ft (6,700 m). The system widens in Bolivia and Peru to form multiple ranges and a high, densely populated plateau (ALTIPLANO), where the great civilization of the INCAS had its home. Copper, silver, and tin are mined, and oil has been found in the northern foothills. The Andes are geologically young and still rising. Volcanic eruptions and earthquakes are common.

Ando Hiroshige: see HIROSHIGE.

Andorra, Fr. *Andorre,* officially Principality of Andorra, autonomous parliamentary co-principality (1992 est. pop. 55,000), 174 sq mi (450 sq km), SW Europe, between France and Spain, comprising several high valleys in the E Pyrenees. The capital is **Andorra la Vella** (1986 est. pop. 15,600). The Catalan-speaking, largely Roman Catholic native Andorrans make up about a fifth of the total population. Tourism, including the sale of consumer goods to tourists, is the principal source of income, but sheep-raising, minerals (iron, lead, marble), timber, and banking are also economically important. In 1278 Andorra was put under the joint suzerainty of a French count, whose rights passed to the president of France, and the bishop of Urgel, Spain. It is governed under the 1993 constitution, Andorra's first, by a 28-member parliament.

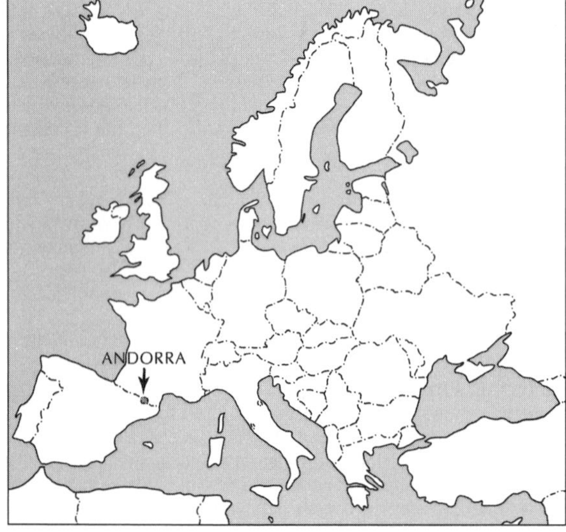

Andrássy, Julius, Count [ŏn′dräsh-shē], 1823–90, Hungarian politician. A leading figure in the unsuccessful Hungarian revolution of 1848–49, he lived in exile until 1858. He later took part (1867) in the creation of the AUSTRO-HUNGARIAN MONARCHY. As premier of Hungary (1867–71) Andrássy established Magyar supremacy over the Slavs in Hungary. He was foreign minister of the Dual Monarchy (1871–79) and signed (1879) the Dual Alliance with Germany. His son **Julius, Count Andrássy**, 1860–1929, also foreign minister, tried (1918) to obtain a separate peace for Austria-Hungary in WORLD WAR I.

Andre, Carl, 1935–, American sculptor; b. Quincy, Mass. His classic, elemental sculptures reflect the philosophy of MINIMALISM. Andre is well known for his floor pieces, e.g., *144 Pieces of Lead* (Mus. of Modern Art, N.Y.C.). In 1988 he was acquitted of the murder of his wife, Ana Mendiata.

André, John, 1751–80, British spy in the AMERICAN REVOLUTION. He was captured and hanged after negotiating with Benedict ARNOLD for the surrender of WEST POINT to the British.

Andrea del Sarto: see SARTO, ANDREA DEL.

Andreotti, Guilio [än″drāätē], 1919–, Italian political leader. A Christian Democrat, he held various ministerial posts in the 1950s and 60s. He was prime minister three times (1972c-ndash73; 1976–79; 1989–91) and also served as minister of foreign affairs (1983–89). In 1993 he was investigated for corruption and ties with the Mafia; previous investigations on similar charges had ended in his exoneration.

Andrew, Saint, one of the Twelve APOSTLES, brother of Simon PETER. He is patron saint of Russia and Scotland.

Andrew II, d. 1235, king of HUNGARY (1205–35). He was forced to issue (1222) the Golden Bull, the "Magna Carta" of Hungary, which extended privileges to the lesser nobles. He took part (1217) in the Fifth CRUSADE.

Andreyev, Leonid Nikolayevich [əndrā′yəf], 1871–1919, Russian writer. His early stories, realistic studies of everyday life, were praised by GORKY, but when the Bolsheviks took power in 1917 he broke with Gorky politically and emigrated to Finland. His popularity declined when he turned to mysticism and allegory. His fiction includes *The Red Laugh* (1905) and *The Seven That Were Hanged* (1908). His best-known play is the expressionistic *He Who Gets Slapped* (1916).

Andrić, Ivo [än′drĭch], 1892–1975, Yugoslav writer. His work includes poetry, essays, short stories, and novels, the best known being his Bosnian historical trilogy (1945) *The Bridge on the Drina, Bosnian Story,* and *Young Miss.* In 1961 he was awarded the Nobel Prize in literature.

Andromache [ăndrŏ′məkē], in Greek myth, wife of HECTOR of Troy; mother of Astyanax. After the TROJAN WAR, ACHILLES' son Neoptolemus abducted her; EURIPIDES and RACINE dramatized her captivity. Later she married Hector's brother Helenus.

Andromeda, in Greek myth, princess of Ethiopia; daughter of Cepheus and Cassiopeia. POSEIDON, angered by her mother's claim that her beauty outshone that of the nereids, sent a sea monster that could be appeased only by her sacrifice. She was rescued by PERSEUS, who slew the monster and married her. Andromeda and her parents became constellations.

Andromeda Galaxy, closest spiral GALAXY (2 million LIGHT-YEARS distant) to our MILKY WAY galaxy. They are similar in shape and composition. The Andromeda galaxy, visible to the naked eye as a faint patch in the constellation Andromeda, is about 120,000 light-years in diameter and contains at least 200 billion stars. In 1993 astronomers discovered that it apparently has a central nucleus consisting of two star clusters.

Andropov, Yuri Vladimirovich, 1914–84, Soviet public official, general secretary of the Communist party of the Soviet Union (1982–84). He was head of the K.G.B. (1967–82), became (1973) a member of the Politburo, and succeeded to the USSR's most powerful office on the death of Leonid BREZHNEV. He was an ideological conservative and potential bureaucratic reformer.

Andros, Sir Edmund, 1637–1714, British colonial governor in America. He was bitterly criticized for his high-handedness as governor (1674–81) of New York. Named (1686) governor of the Dominion of New England, Andros was deposed (1689) by Boston colonists. He was later governor (1692–97) of VIRGINIA.

anemia, condition resulting from a reduction in HEMOGLOBIN content or in number of red blood cells (erythrocytes). Although the causes of anemia vary, because of the blood's reduced capacity to carry oxygen all types exhibit similar symptoms—pallor, weakness, dizziness, fatigue, and, in severe cases, breathing difficulties and heart abnormalities. Therapy includes identifying and treating the underlying cause. See SICKLE-CELL ANEMIA.

anemone or **windflower,** wild or cultivated perennial herb (genus *Anemone*) of the BUTTERCUP family. Anemones, which contain a poisonous compound (anemonin), were once used to treat fevers, bruises, and freckles; they are often associated with evil and death. The purple- or white-blossomed wood anemone *A. quinquefolia* is also called windflower.

anesthesia, loss of sensation, especially that of pain, induced by drugs. General anesthesia, first used in surgical procedures in the 1840s, induces unconsciousness; halothane and sodium pentothal are two widely used general anesthetics. Localized or regional anesthesia is used to desensitize the area around the site of application without loss of consciousness. Regional anesthetics include spinal anesthetics, primarily for lower body surgery; epidural anesthetics for childbirth; and local anesthetics (e.g., novocaine and lidocaine) for dental procedures. Various anesthetics are often used in combination. See also ACUPUNCTURE.

angel, bodiless, immortal spirit, limited in knowledge and power, accepted in the traditional belief of Judaism, Christianity, and Islam. The three choirs of angels appear early in the Christian era; the classes are, from the highest: seraphim, cherubim, thrones; dominations, virtues, powers; principalities, archangels, angels. Angels appear in the Bible, often in critical roles, e.g., visiting Abraham and Lot (Gen. 18; 19) and announcing the Incarnation to Mary (Luke 1). The cult of guardian angels who protect individuals or nations is especially strong in the West. The angels of HELL, or devils, led by SATAN, are viewed as initiators of evil temptations.

Angel Falls, waterfall, 3,212 ft (979 m) high, on the Churún R., in the Guiana Highlands, SE Venezuela. It has the world's highest uninterrupted fall (2,648 ft/807 m).

Angelico, Fra [frä änjĕl'ĭkō], c.1400–1455, Florentine painter; b. Guido, or Guidolino, di Pietro; also known as Giovanni da Fiesole. First influenced by GENTILE DA FABRIANO and then MASACCIO, Fra Angelico developed a style remarkable for its purity of line and color. He treated none but religious subjects. His works, including the frescoes *Annunciation* and *Noli mi Tangere* (both: St. Mark's Convent, Florence), show spatial depth and sculptural clarity of form—the artistic innovations of his time. Among his paintings in the U.S. are the *Crucifixion* and *Nativity* (both: Metropolitan Mus.).

Angel Island, largest island in San Francisco Bay, Calif. It was (1863–1946) a U.S. army base and became a missile and radar site in 1952; there is also a state park. From 1910 to 1940 it was the entry point for Asian immigrants to the U.S.

Angell, Sir Norman, 1872?–1967, British internationalist and economist, b. Ralph Norman Angell Lane. He gained fame with *The Great Illusion* (1910), in which he proposed that the common economic interests of nations make war futile. After World War I he worked for a international cooperation and peace. Knighted in 1931, he was awarded the Nobel Peace Prize in 1933.

Angelou, Maya, 1928–, African-American author; b. St. Louis as Marguerite Johnson. Although a playwright, poet, and short-story writer, she is best known for her four-part autobiography (1970–81). In 1993 she read her poem "On the Pulse of Morning" at Pres. CLINTON's inauguration.

Angelus, family name and dynasty of Byzantine emperors (1185–1204) Isaac II, ALEXIUS III, and ALEXIUS IV.

angina pectoris: see under CORONARY ARTERY DISEASE.

angioplasty, any surgical repair of a blood vessel, especially **balloon angioplasty,** or **percutaneous transluminal coronary angioplasty,** a treatment of CORONARY ARTERY DISEASE. In balloon angioplasty a balloon-tipped catheter is inserted through the skin into a blood vessel and maneuvered to the clogged artery. There it is threaded into the blockage and inflated, compressing the plaque against the arterial walls. Frequent postoperative reclogging of the treated area has led to the use of such alternative techniques as **laser angioplasty,** which employs a laser to burn away or vaporize the plaque, and to clinical trials of a stainless steel coil (stent) to hold the plaque back.

angiosperm, plant in which the ovules, or young seeds, are enclosed within an ovary (that part of a FLOWER specialized for seed production), in contrast to the GYMNOSPERMS. Also known as the flowering plants, angiosperms have LEAVES, ROOTS, and STEMS, and vascular, or conducting tissue. Constituting the plant division Magnoliophyta (sometimes called Anthophyta), they are divided into dicotyledons which have two seed leaves (cotyledons) and CAMBIUM tissue in the stems, and monocotyledons which have one seed leaf and generally lack cambium tissue. The most important plant group economically, angiosperms include all agricultural crops and cereal GRAINS, all garden flowers, and almost all broad-leaved trees and shrubs.

Angkor [ăng'kôr], site of several capitals of the KHMER EMPIRE, N of Tônlé Sap, NW CAMBODIA. The ruins extend over 40 sq mi (104 sq km). The first capital was established by Yasovarman I (889–900). A new temple complex, **Angkor Wat,** was built under Suryavarman II (1113–50). This impressive temple, surrounded by a vast moat, is approached by a causeway. Its extensive sculptural ornament exhibits impeccable craftsmanship. In 1177 Angkor was sacked by the Chams and fell into ruins. Jayavarman VII (1181–c.1218) established a new capital, **Angkor Thom,** which was abandoned in 1434. The ruins, overgrown by jungle, were discovered by the French in 1861.

angle, in mathematics, figure formed by two straight lines meeting at a point; the point is known as the vertex of the angle, and the lines are its sides. Angles are commonly measured in degrees (°) or in radians. If the two sides form a single straight line but do not coincide, the angle is a *straight angle,* measuring 180° or π radians (see PI). If the sides are perpendicular, i.e., if they form half of a straight angle, the angle is a *right angle,* measuring 90° or $\pi/2$ radians. An *acute angle* is greater than 0° but less than 90°; an *obtuse angle* is greater than 90° but less than 180°; and a *reflex angle* is greater than 180°. See also TRIGONOMETRY.

Angles: see ANGLO-SAXONS.

Anglican Communion, the worldwide body of churches that are in communion with the Church of England (see ENGLAND, CHURCH OF). Composed of regional churches, provinces, and separate dioceses, the Communion is bound together by mutual loyalty as expressed in the Lambeth Conference of 1930. Member churches include the Protestant Episcopal Church in America (see EPISCOPAL CHURCH, PROTESTANT), the Scottish Episcopal Church, the Church in Wales, and the Church of England in Australia and Tasmania. Doctrinally all member churches are similar, having a ministry of three orders: deacons, priests, and bishops. Worship, though varied in form, is liturgical and sacramental, and regulated by the BOOK OF COMMON PRAYER.

Anglo-Saxon Chronicle, collective name for English monastic chronicles in Anglo-Saxon, stemming from a compilation (c.891) of earlier sources inspired by King ALFRED. The account, from the beginning of the Christian era through 1154, draws on BEDE and adds much original material. Mostly prose, it includes such poems as *The Battle of Brunanburh.*

Anglo-Saxons, name given to the Germanic-speaking peoples who settled in England at the decline of Roman rule there. The Angles probably came from Schleswig late in the 5th cent. and formed foundations for the later kingdoms of EAST ANGLIA, MERCIA, and NORTHUMBRIA. The Saxons, a Germanic tribe, settled in England at the same time; the kingdoms of SUSSEX, WESSEX, and ESSEX were outgrowths of their settlements. The Jutes, a tribe probably from the area at the mouth of the Rhine, settled in Kent and on the Isle of Wight. The term "Anglo-Saxons," denoting non-Celtic settlers of England, dates from the 16th cent. It is now used more loosely to denote any people (or their descendants) of the British Isles.

Angola, officially Republic of Angola, republic (1992 est. pop. 8,902,000), 481,351 sq mi (1,246,700 sq km), SW Africa, bordered by the Atlantic Ocean (W), Zaïre (N), Zambia (E), and Namibia (S). It includes the province of CABINDA, on the Atlantic coast, from which it is separated by a strip of land belonging to Zaïre. Major cities include LUANDA (the capital) and LOBITO. Nearly all of the land is desert or savanna, except for the densely forested valleys of the northeast and a narrow coastal strip in the west. The most prominent physical feature is the Bié Plateau (average altitude, 6,000 ft/1,830 m), which rises abruptly from the coastal lowland and slopes eastward to the CONGO and ZAMBEZI river basins. Formerly dependent on agriculture, Angola today receives over two thirds of its export earnings from oil production, chiefly from reserves offshore of Cabinda. Diamonds, natural gas, and iron ore are also important. Principal crops include coffee (the second largest export), sugarcane, corn, and wheat. Among the leading industries are food processing (notably cereals, fish, palm oil, and meat) and the manufacture of jute, cotton textiles, and paper. The Ovimbundu, Kimbundu, and Bakongo are the largest ethnic groups, and there is a sizable mixed-race population. Most of the people speak a Bantu language; the official language, however, is Portuguese. Traditional religious beliefs prevail, but there is a large minority of Roman Catholics and other Christians.

History. The first Portuguese colony in Angola was established in Luanda in 1575, and, except for a short Dutch occupation (1641–48), Angola remained under Portuguese control until its independence in 1975. (The Mbundu kingdom in central Angola was not subjugated by the Portuguese until 1902). For the Portuguese, Angola was a source of slaves for their colony in Brazil. Modern industrial development began after World War II, and Angola was upgraded from its colonial status to an overseas province in 1951. Repression of the African population continued, and in 1961 a revolt began. When this failed, guerrilla warfare was undertaken from neighboring countries, intensifying in the early 1970s, when more than 50,000 Portuguese troops were engaged against the rebels. In 1972 Angola was made an "autonomous state," and in 1973 elections were held for a legislative assembly. Independence was proclaimed in Nov. 1975, touching off a civil war among rival nationalist groups. By early 1976 the Marxist-Leninist Popular Liberation Movement of Angola (MPLA), supported by the USSR and aided by Cuban troops, controlled the government and much of the country, but the civil war with the then US-supported UNITA (see SAVIMBI, JONAS) continued. From 1979 to 1988 Angola was the object of military raids by South African troops in NAMIBIA, ostensibly striking at the bases of guerrillas seeking Namibian independence. In 1988 Cuba, South Africa, and Angola agreed to the removal of Cuban and South African troops from Angola. The South Africans left in 1988, and the Cuban withdrawal was completed in 1991. The government and UNITA signed a cease-fire agreement in 1991 that called for unified armed forces, a market economy, and free elections in 1992. When Pres. José Eduardo dos Santos and the MPLA defeated (1992) Savimbi and UNITA in an election regarded as generally fair, UNITA denounced the results as rigged. UNITA resumed fighting and won control of two thirds of Angola before a stalemate ensued.

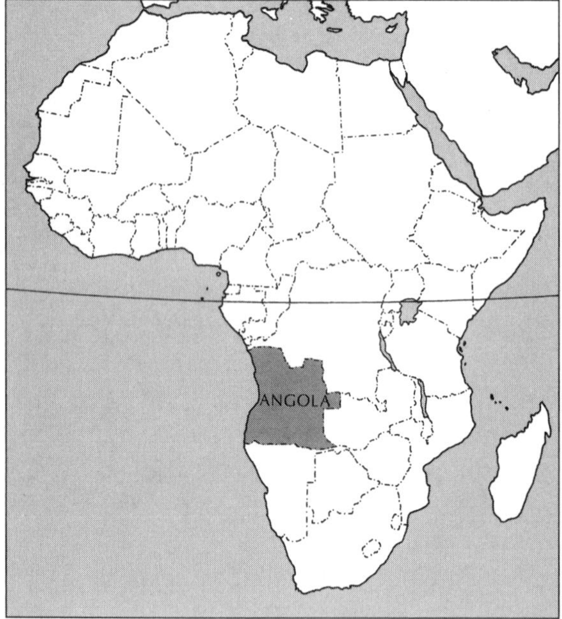

Ångström, Anders Jöns, 1814–74, Swedish physicist. Noted for his study of light, especially SPECTRUM analysis, he mapped the sun's spectrum, discovered hydrogen in the solar atmosphere, and was the first to examine the spectrum of the AURORA borealis. The length unit angstrom is named for him.

Anguilla, island and British crown colony (1992 est. pop. 7,000), 35 sq mi (91 sq km), West Indies, one of the Leeward Islands. Fishing, stock-raising, salt production, and tourism are the economic mainstays. Formerly part of the associated state of St. Kitts-Nevis-Anguilla, the island seceded in 1967 and returned to British colonial rule in 1971. A new constitution (1982) made the island largely internally self-governing.

animal, any member of the animal kingdom (Animalia). Animals are multicellular and depend on organisms that can manufacture their own food, usually by PHOTOSYNTHESIS (e.g., plants and algae). Their cells do not have cell walls. MAMMALS and other vertebrates represent only a small percentage of the animal kingdom; 95% consists of INVERTEBRATES such as sponges, INSECTS, ARACHNIDS, and worms. Most animals have nervous systems, sense organs, and specialized modes of locomotion, and are adapted for securing, ingesting, and digesting food. Although traditionally contrasted with plants, animals are now usually considered to be one of at least five kingdoms of living things (see CLASSIFICATION). The scientific study of animals is called ZOOLOGY.

animal rights movement, individuals and groups concerned with protecting animals from abuse or misuse. Its supporters have protested the use of animals for medical and cosmetics testing, the killing of animals for fur, sport hunting, and the raising of livestock in inhumane quarters. Historically rooted in the 19th-cent. antivivisection movement, the animal rights movement is closely tied to such environmental issues as the slaughter of fur seals and commercial whaling.

animism, belief that a spirit or force residing in every animate and inanimate object, every dream and idea, gives individuality to each. The related Polynesian concept of *mana* holds that the spirit in all things is responsible for the good and evil in the universe. See FETISH; SHAMAN; TOTEM.

anion: see ION.

anise, annual plant (*Pimpinella anisum*) of the CARROT family, native to the Mediterranean but widely cultivated for its aromatic and medicinal qualities. The seedlike fruits (aniseed) are used as flavoring and provide anise oil, which is used in medicinals, perfumes, beverages, and dentifrices. Biblical anise is DILL.

Anjou [äNzhōō′], region and former province, W France. Angers, the historic capital, and Saumur are the chief towns in this fertile lowland traversed by several rivers. Its vineyards produce renowned wines. Occupied by the Andecavi, a Gallic people, Anjou was conquered by the Romans and later (5th cent.) by the FRANKS. By the 10th cent. it was held by the counts of the first Angevin dynasty; it came under English rule when its ruler became (1154) king of England as HENRY II. PHILIP II of France seized (1204) Anjou from the English, and in 1246 LOUIS IX of France gave it to his brother, later CHARLES I of Naples. In 1360 Anjou became a duchy and in 1487 it was definitively annexed to France.

Ankara, city (1990 pop. 2,533,209), capital of Turkey, W central Turkey. The second largest city in Turkey, it is an administrative, commercial, and cultural center. Manufactures include processed food, farm equipment, iron and steel, textiles, and cement. Tourism and service industries are increasingly important. A Hittite trade center (18th cent. B.C.), it became (1st cent. A.D.) the capital of a Roman province; in the ruins of a temple in Ankara have been found tablets valuable as a record of AUGUSTUS's reign. The city fell to the Ottoman Turks in the 14th cent. It declined in the 19th and 20th cent., until Kemal ATATÜRK made it the capital of Turkey in 1923. Atatürk's massive limestone tomb can be seen from most of the city.

Anna, 1693–1740, czarina of Russia (1730–40); daughter of Ivan V and niece of PETER I. She succeeded her cousin Peter II. Allied with Holy Roman Emperor CHARLES VI, she intervened in the War of the POLISH SUCCESSION (1733–35) and attacked Turkey (1736). Her grandnephew, Ivan VI, succeeded her.

Annam, historic region (c.58,000 sq mi/150,200 sq km) and former state, central Vietnam. The region extended nearly 800 mi (1,290 km) along the South China Sea between Tonkin (N) and Cochin China (S). The capital was HUE. After more than 2,000 years of contact with the Chinese the peoples of the Red R. valley came under Chinese rule in 111 B.C. The Annamese drove out the Chinese in A.D. 939 and maintained their independence until the French conquest in the 19th cent. Conflict between ruling dynasties dominated this long period, ending with the establishment (1802) of the empire of VIETNAM by Nguyen-Anh, who had procured French military aid by ceding the port of DA NANG and the Con Son islands. His authority as emperor was recognized by the Chinese in 1803. Mistreatment of French nationals and Vietnamese Christians by his successor provided an excuse for French military operations, which began in 1858 and resulted in the establishment of the French colony of COCHIN CHINA and the protectorates of TONKIN and Annam. The three territories were occupied by the Japanese during WORLD WAR II. After an independence struggle against the French, most of Annam became part of South Vietnam in 1954; the rest went to North Vietnam. Annam was incorporated into united Vietnam after the VIETNAM WAR.

Annapolis, city (1990 pop. 33,187), state capital and seat of Anne Arundel co., central Md., on the Severn R. It is a port of entry and a farm-produce shipping center with seafood, boat-building, and plastics industries. Settled in 1649, it has a rich history, including a period (1783–84) as the capital of the U.S.; it has been Maryland's capital since 1694. The city has many 18th-cent. buildings and is the site of the U.S. Naval Academy and St. John's College.

Annapolis Convention, 1786, interstate convention to discuss U.S. commerce, held at Annapolis, Md. Its call for a meeting to discuss changes in the Articles of CONFEDERATION brought about the FEDERAL CONSTITUTIONAL CONVENTION.

Annapolis Royal, town (1991 pop. 633), W Nova Scotia, E Canada, on the Annapolis R. One of Canada's oldest settlements, it was founded as Port Royal by the French in 1605, destroyed (1613) by the British, and rebuilt to become the chief town of French ACADIA. Often fought over in the 1600s by the English and the French, it was finally taken (1710) by colonists from New England and renamed in honor of Queen Anne. The ruins of its fort are in Fort Anne Historic National Park.

Ann Arbor, city (1990 pop. 109,592), seat of Washtenaw co., S Mich., on the Huron R.; settled 1824, inc. 1851. It is a research and educational center, with government and industrial research firms and the huge Univ. of Michigan. Products include lasers, computers, medical and scientific equipment, and precision machinery.

Anne, 1665–1714, queen of England, Scotland, and Ireland (1702–7), later queen of Great Britain and Ireland (1707–14); daughter of JAMES II; successor to WILLIAM III. The last STUART ruler and a devout Protestant, in 1683 she married Prince George of Denmark. Her reign was one of transition to parliamentary government, but intrigue and the queen's favor could still make and unmake cabinets. The dominant event was the War of the SPANISH SUCCESSION (1702–13). Despite victories won by the duke of MARLBOROUGH (whose wife was long a favorite of the queen), the war's high cost caused political friction. None of Anne's children survived her, and by the Act of SETTLEMENT (1701) GEORGE I succeeded her. Despite her personal mediocrity, Anne's reign was marked by intellectual awakening, the popularization of Palladian architecture, and the growth of parliamentary government.

Anne, 1950–, British princess; daughter of ELIZABETH II. In 1973 she married a British army officer, Mark Phillips, and they had two children. Anne and Mark Phillips were divorced in 1992, and she married Timothy Laurence.

annealing, process in which glass, metals, and other materials are treated to render them less brittle and more workable. The material is heated and then cooled very slowly and uniformly, with the time and temperature set according to the properties desired. Annealing increases ductility and relieves internal strains that lead to failures in service.

Anne Boleyn: see BOLEYN, ANNE.

annelid worm, member of the phylum Annelida, which includes the EARTHWORMS, LEECHES, and marine worms. Also called segmented worms; they are soft-bodied, bilaterally symmetrical, and segmented. Distributed worldwide, they live in protected habitats, often in tubes manufactured with their own secretions. Reproduction is sexual or asexual; some species are HERMAPHRODITES. They range from 1/32 in. (0.5 mm) to 10 ft (3 m) in length.

Anne of Austria, 1601–66, queen consort of France. The daughter of PHILIP III of Spain, she married (1615) the French king LOUIS XIII and gained the enmity of Cardinal RICHELIEU, Louis's chief minister. As regent (1643–51) for her son LOUIS XIV, she entrusted the government to Cardinal MAZARIN.

Anne of Brittany, 1477–1514, queen of France, consort of CHARLES VIII (1491–98) and LOUIS XII (1499–1514). As duchess of Brittany from 1488, she tried to preserve independence from France by marrying by proxy (1490) Maximilian of Austria (later Holy Roman Emperor MAXIMILIAN I). Besieged (1491) by the French, she was forced to annul her marriage and to wed Charles VIII. Widowed in 1498, she then married Louis XII, and Brittany was eventually incorporated (1532) by France.

Anne of Cleves, 1515–57, fourth queen consort of HENRY VIII of England. She was the daughter of a powerful German Protestant prince, and Henry married her in 1540 for political reasons. Finding her dull and unattractive, he divorced her that same year.

Anne of Denmark, 1574–1619, queen consort of JAMES I of England.

annual rings, growth layers of WOOD produced yearly in the stems and roots of trees and shrubs. When well-marked alteration of seasons occurs (e.g., either cold and warm or wet and dry), a sharp contrast exists between the early- and late-season growth—the wood cells are larger earlier when growing conditions are better. In uniform climates, there is little visible difference between annual rings. The number of annual rings reflects the age of a tree; the thickness of each ring reflects environmental and climatic conditions.

Annunzio, Gabriele D': see D'ANNUNZIO, GABRIELE.

anode: see ELECTRODE.

anointing of the sick, SACRAMENT of the ORTHODOX EASTERN CHURCH and the ROMAN CATHOLIC CHURCH; formerly known as **extreme unction.** In it a person who is in danger of death is anointed on the eyes, ears, nostrils, lips, hands, and feet by a priest while he recites absolutions for sins. In the Eastern churches it is normally given by three priests and may be administered to the healthy to prevent sickness.

anomie, a social condition characterized by instability, the breakdown of social norms, institutional disorganization, and a divorce between socially valid goals and available means for achieving them. Introduced into sociology by Emile DURKHEIM in his study *Suicide* (1897), anomie also refers to the psychological condition—of rootlessness, futility, anxiety, and amorality—afflicting individuals who live under such conditions. The importance of anomie as a cause of deviant behavior received further elaboration by Robert K. MERTON.

anorexia nervosa: see EATING DISORDERS.

Anouilh, Jean [änwē'yə], 1910–87, French dramatist. His works contrast romantic dreams with harsh reality. Among his dramas are *Antigone* (1944), *The Waltz of the Toreadors* (1952), and *Becket* (1959).

Anselm, Saint, 1033?–1109, Italian prelate, archbishop of Canterbury, Doctor of the Church. He succeeded (1093) his friend LANFRANC as archbishop of Canterbury. In England, he quarreled with WILLIAM II and HENRY I over lay INVESTITURE and was exiled twice. An influential theologian, he was a founder of SCHOLASTICISM. His famous ontological proof deduces God's existence from man's notion of a perfect being in whom nothing is lacking. Feast: Apr. 21.

Anshan, city (1991 est. pop. 1,390,000) central Liaoning prov., NE China, on the South Manchurian RR. Its huge integrated iron and steel complex is one of the largest in China. Other manufactures include chemicals, tractors, machinery, and cement.

Ansky, Shloime, pseud. of **Solomon Seinwil Rapoport,** 1863–1920, Russian Yiddish author. He incorporated folk elements into his stories of peasants and HASIDIM, e.g., *The Dybbuk* (1916), a tale of demonic possession.

ant, INSECT (family Formicidae) belonging to the same order as the BEE and WASP. Ants have a narrow stalk joining the abdomen and thorax, and biting mouthparts (sometimes used for defense). Some ants have stings, and some can spray poison from the end of the abdomen. All ants show some degree of social organization; many nest in a system of tunnels in the soil, in constructed mounds, or in wood. Ant colonies usually include three castes: winged, fertile females; wingless, infertile females, or workers; and winged males. In some species workers may become soldiers or other specialized types. Army ants travel in columns, overrunning and devouring any animals in their path; fire ants are stinging ants that are serious pests in parts of the S U.S.

Antakya: see ANTIOCH.

Antananarivo or **Tananarive,** city (1990 est. pop. 802,000), capital of Madagascar. The country's largest city and economic and communications center, it is in a productive agricultural region whose main crop is rice. A railroad connects the city with Toamasina, the chief port. Manufactures include food products and cigarettes. Founded c.1625, it became (1797) the residence of the Merina rulers. It was taken by the French in 1895. Today it is a modern city, built on a ridge; at its top stands the old royal residence.

Antarctica, fifth largest continent, c.5,500,000 sq mi (14,245,000 sq km), asymmetrically centered on the SOUTH POLE and located almost entirely S of the ANTARCTIC CIRCLE (66°30'S). It consists of two major regions: W Antarctica, including the mountainous Antarctic Peninsula, which is structurally related to the ANDES of South America and connected to them by way of the Scotia Arc (South Georgia, South Orkney, and South Sandwich islands); and E Antarctica, a continental shield area (see PLATE TECTONICS) with a rock surface near sea level. These two regions are joined into a single continental mass by an ice cap up to 13,000 ft (4,000 m) thick that covers more than 95% of Antarctica. Vinson Massif (16,066 ft/4,897 m) is the continent's highest peak. Great ice shelves up to 4,000 ft

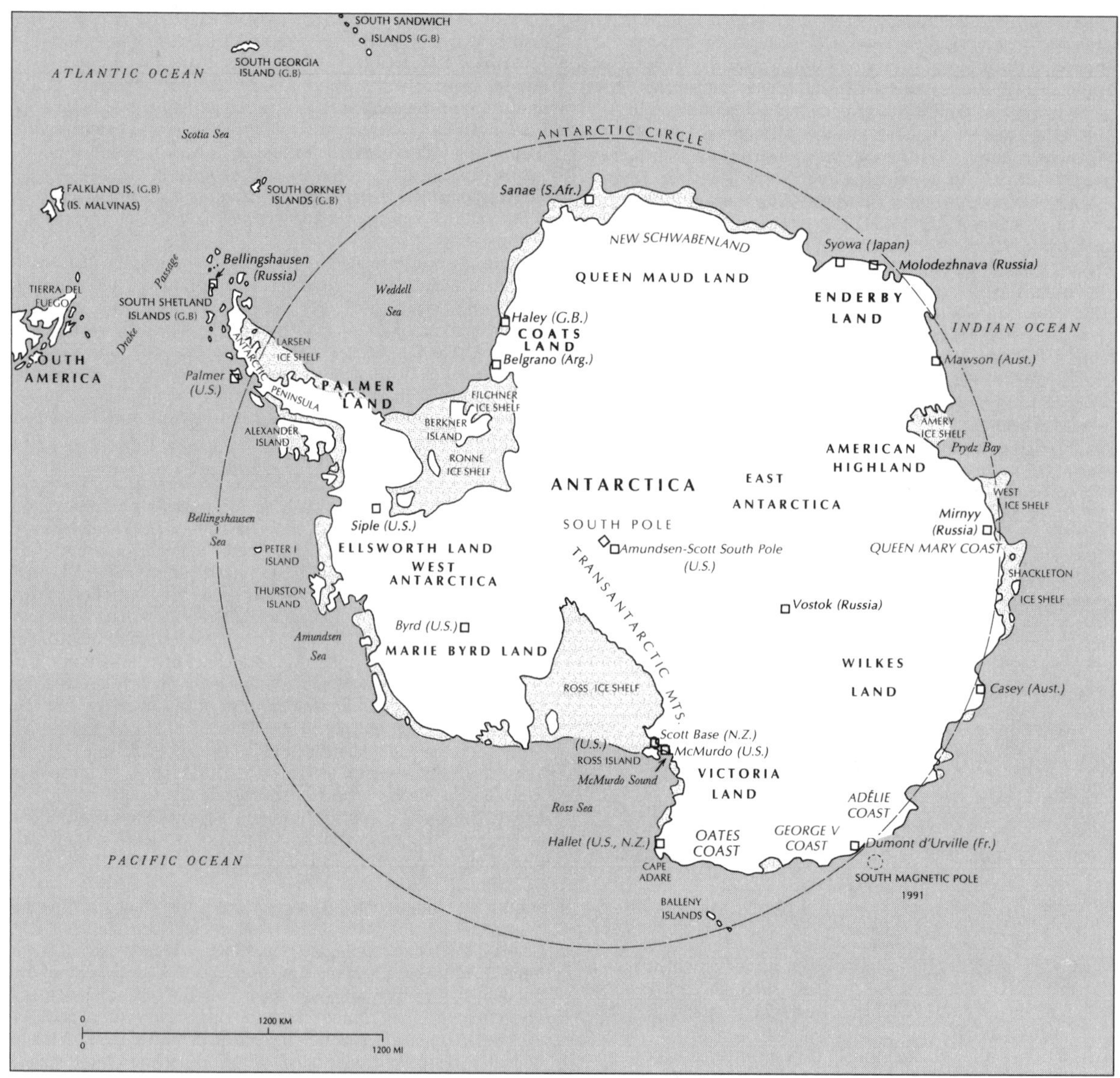

(1,220 m) thick block the ROSS and WEDDELL seas, and a belt of nearly continuous pack ice surrounds the rest of the continent. Summer temperatures (Jan.) are unlikely to be warmer than 0°F (−18°C); winter mean temperatures are −70°F (−57°C). Roald AMUNDSEN was the first explorer to reach the South Pole on Dec. 14, 1911, followed by R.F. SCOTT on Jan. 18, 1912. The first to fly over the pole was Richard E. BYRD, on Nov. 29, 1929. The success of international scientific cooperation in Antarctica during the International Geophysical Year (IGY) of 1957–58 led to the signing (1959) of the Antarctic Treaty, which prohibits military operations, nuclear explosions, and the disposal of radioactive wastes south of latitude 60°S, exclusive of the high seas. In 1985, 32 nations signed an agreement limiting human access to research zones in Antarctica, and a 1991 protocol to the 1959 treaty bans exploration for minerals and oil for 50 years.

Antarctic Circle, imaginary circle on the earth's surface at 66°30′S lat., marking the southernmost point at which the sun can be seen at the summer SOLSTICE (about June 22) and the northernmost point of the southern polar regions at which the midnight sun is visible.

Antarctic peninsula, glaciated mountain region of W ANTARCTICA, extending c.1,200 mi (1,930 km) north toward South America. It was originally named Palmer Land for Nathaniel Palmer, a U.S. captain who explored the region in 1820. The British claimed the peninsula in 1832 and it was later claimed by Argentina (1940) and by Chile (1942). In 1964, by international agreement it was named the Antarctic Peninsula.

anteater, toothless MAMMAL of three genera of the order Edentata found in tropical Central and South America. It feeds on ants, termites, and other insects. The great anteater, or ant bear (*Myrmecophaga*), has an elongated snout, a coarse-haired body about 4 ft (1.2 m) long, and a long, broad tail; the arboreal collared, or lesser, anteater (*Tamandua*) is less than half the size of the great anteater; and the arboreal two-toed anteater (*Cyclopes*) is about the size of a squirrel.

antelope, any of various hoofed ruminant MAMMALS of the CATTLE family. True antelopes are found only in Africa and Asia. Antelopes usually stand 3–4 ft (90–120 cm) at the shoulder, but range from the 12-in. (30-cm) pygmy antelope to the 6-ft (180-cm) giant eland. Antelope horns, unlike DEER horns, are unbranched and are not shed. Species of antelope include the bushbuck, with its spiral horns and oxlike body; the addax, a large desert antelope of N Africa; the horselike oryx, found in Africa and Arabia; the GNU and its close relative the hartebeest, a swift, horselike animal with U-shaped horns; and the GAZELLE.

antenna or **aerial,** system of wires or other conductors used to transmit or receive radio or other electromagnetic waves (see RADIO; TELEVISION). In a transmitting antenna, the signal from an ELEC-

TRIC CIRCUIT causes electrons in the antenna to oscillate; these moving electric charges generate ELECTROMAGNETIC RADIATION, which is then transmitted through space. The distribution pattern of the transmitted wave depends on the design of the antenna; radio broadcast-station antennas are frequently designed to emit waves in all directions, whereas those used for RADAR and for certain communication systems focus the waves in a single direction. In a receiving antenna, electromagnetic waves cause the electrons in the antenna to oscillate, inducing a signal that can be detected by an electric circuit. In general, a longer antenna is used to transmit or receive signals of longer wavelengths. Theoretically, the same antenna can be used both for sending and for receiving signals, but in practice, transmitting antennas are constructed to handle higher power loads than receiving antennas. Phased array antennas, used for long-range radar and radio astronomy, are composed of large groupings of individual antennas that are aimed electronically by changing the relative phase of the signal at each antenna.

Antheil, George [ăn'tīl], 1900–1959, American composer; b. Trenton, N.J. His early work reveals the influence of JAZZ. In 1927 a performance of his *Ballet mécanique,* scored for player piano, car horns, airplane propellers, etc., caused a furor in New York City. Other works include the opera *Transatlantic* (1930), symphonies, and film scores.

Anthony, Saint, 251?–c.350, Egyptian hermit. Living in seclusion, he resisted the many temptations of the devil. A colony of hermits grew up about him, and he ruled them as a community before going away to the desert. He was the father of Christian MONASTICISM. Feast: Jan. 17.

Anthony, Marc: see ANTONY.

Anthony, Susan B(rownell), 1820–1906, American leader of the WOMAN SUFFRAGE movement; b. Adams, Mass. She organized the first women's temperance association, the Daughters of Temperance, and with Elizabeth Cady STANTON secured the first laws in New York guaranteeing women rights over their children and control of property and wages. In 1863 she was coorganizer of the Women's Loyal League to support Lincoln's government, but after the Civil War she opposed granting suffrage to freedmen without also giving it to women. She was president (1892–1900) of the National American Woman Suffrage Association and helped compile vol. 1–3 of *The History of Woman Suffrage* (1881–86).

anthrax, infectious disease of animals that can be transmitted from animals to humans through contact or the inhalation of spores. Primarily affecting sheep, horses, hogs, cattle, and goats, anthrax is usually restricted to people who handle hides of animals (e.g., farmers, butchers, and veterinarians) or sort wool. The disease, usually fatal to animals but not humans, is caused by *Bacillus anthracis,* discovered by Robert KOCH in 1876. Louis PASTEUR developed a method of vaccinating sheep and cattle against anthrax, and the disease is now relatively rare in the U.S.

anthropological linguistics, study of the relationship between language and culture, often focusing on cultures with no written language, e.g., Native Americans. The precise relationship of language to culture is, however, a subject of controversy. See also ANTHROPOLOGY; LINGUISTICS.

anthropology, study of the origin, development, and varieties of human beings and their societies. Emerging as an independent science in the late 18th cent., it developed two divisions: physical anthropology, which focuses on human EVOLUTION and variation (see RACE), using methods of PHYSIOLOGY, anthropometry, GENETICS, and ECOLOGY; and cultural anthropology, which includes ARCHAEOLOGY, ethnology, social anthropology, and LINGUISTICS.

antianxiety drug, drug administered for the relief of ANXIETY; in larger doses, antianxiety drugs produce sleep, sedation, and anesthesia. Those frequently prescribed in the U.S. include the BENZODIAZEPINES alprazolam (Xanax) and clonazepam (Clonopin). Side effects include drowsiness and, with prolonged use, addiction.

antibiotic, any of a variety of substances, usually obtained from microorganisms, that inhibit the growth of or destroy certain other microorganisms. The foundation for the development and understanding of antibiotics was laid during the 19th cent. when Louis PASTEUR proved that one species of microorganism can kill another and Paul EHRLICH developed the idea of selective toxicity: that a specific substance can be toxic to some organisms, e.g., infectious bacteria, but harmless to others, e.g., human hosts. Further pioneering work in the 20th cent. by Alexander FLEMING, René DUBOS, and Selman WAKSMAN led to the discovery of PENICILLIN (1939) and streptomycin (1944). Mass production of antibiotic drugs began during World War II with streptomycin and penicillin. Today antibiotics are produced by various methods, including staged fermentation in huge tanks of nutrient media, synthesis in the laboratory, and chemical modification of natural substances. Antibiotics can be classified according to chemical structure, microbial origin, mode of action, or effective range. The tetracyclines are broad-spectrum drugs, effective against a wide range of bacteria (both gram-positive and gram-negative; see GRAM'S STAIN), rickettsias, and psittacosis-causing organisms. Bacitracin, penicillin, the erythromycins, and the cephalosporins work primarily against gram-positive organisms. Polymyxins and other narrow-range antibiotics are effective against only a few species. Antibiotic drugs may be injected, given orally, or applied to the skin. Some, like penicillin, are allergenic and can cause rashes or shock. Others, like the tetracylines, can alter the intestinal environment, encouraging superinfection by fungi or other microorganisms. Many antibiotics are less effective than formerly because resistant strains of microorganisms have evolved. Antibiotics have been used to enhance the growth of animals used as food, but some authorities question the practice because it encourages the development of resistant strains of bacteria infecting animals, and because continuous low exposure to antibiotics can sensitize human beings, making them unable to take such drugs later to treat infection.

antibody: see IMMUNITY; MONOCLONAL ANTIBODY.

Antichrist, in Christian belief, a person who will lead the forces of evil on earth against the forces of Jesus Christ. He will be destroyed by Jesus at the Second Coming (1 John 2.18–22; 4.3; 2 John 7; and Rev. 13).

anticline: see FOLD.

anticoagulant, substance, such as heparin or derivatives of coumarin, that inhibits blood clotting. Anticoagulants are used to treat blood clots in leg and pelvic veins, in order to reduce the risk of the clots traveling and obstructing blood flow to vital organs (e.g., the heart and lungs) and causing THROMBOSIS or STROKE.

Anti-Corn-Law League, organization formed in 1839 to work for repeal of the English CORN LAWS. Its leading figures were Richard COBDEN and John BRIGHT. The laws were repealed in 1846.

antidepressant, drug used to treat psychic depression. Antidepressants, such as fluoxetine (Prozac) and paroxetine (Paxil), act by allowing certain neurotransmitters to accumulate in the central nervous system. They are given to elevate mood, counter suicidal thoughts, and increase the effectiveness of psychotherapy. Side effects include headache, nervousness, and dry mouth.

Antietam campaign, Sept. 1862, in the U.S. CIVIL WAR. Attempting to invade Maryland and Pennsylvania, R.E. LEE sent Stonewall JACKSON to capture Harpers Ferry, which fell on Sept. 15. Lee's own advance was halted by MCCLELLAN, who attacked him at Antietam Creek, Md., on Sept. 17, the bloodiest day of the war. It was a Union victory only in that Lee's advance was stopped.

Anti-Federalists, in U.S. history, the opponents to the adoption of the Federal CONSTITUTION. Leading Anti-Federalists included George Mason, Elbridge Gerry, Patrick Henry, and George Clinton, and later, supporters of states' rights. Under Pres. Washington, many opposed the policies of the FEDERALIST PARTY and Alexander Hamilton. Under Thomas Jefferson's leadership, they formed the core of the opposition party, known as the Democratic-Republican party, subsequently the DEMOCRATIC PARTY.

antifreeze, substance added to a solvent to lower its freezing point. Antifreeze is typically added to water in the cooling system of internal combustion engines so that it may be cooled below the freezing point of pure water (32°F or 0°C) without freezing. Automotive antifreezes include ethylene glycol (the most widely used), methanol, ethanol, isopropyl alcohol, and propylene glycol.

antigen: see IMMUNITY.

Antigone [ăntĭg'ənē], in Greek legend, daughter of OEDIPUS. When her brothers Eteocles and Polynices killed each other, Creon, king of THEBES, forbade the rebel Polynices' burial. Antigone disobeyed him, performed the rites, and was condemned to death. SOPHOCLES tells her story in *Antigone*.

Antigua or **Antigua Guatemala,** town (1990 est. pop. 27,800), S central Guatemala. Now a trading center in a coffee-growing area, it was once the capital of Spanish Guatemala and, in the 16th cent., one of the richest cities in the New World. Antigua was founded in 1542, after a flood and earthquake destroyed the earlier capital, Ciudad Vieja, but was itself leveled by earthquakes in 1773. The capital was then moved to GUATEMALA City. Today Antigua is a major tourist center with fine Spanish buildings.

Antigua and Barbuda, island nation (1992 est. pop. 64,000), 171 sq mi (442 sq km), West Indies, in the Leeward Islands. It consists of Antigua (108 sq mi/280 sq km) and two smaller islands, sparsely populated Barbuda and uninhabited Redonda. The capital is St. John's. Antigua is a hilly island with farms that grow mainly sugarcane and cotton; Barbuda is a flat coral island. Tourism is the economic mainstay. The country's population is predominantly of African origin. The U.S. maintains two military bases there. Antigua was discovered by Christopher COLUMBUS in 1493. Following brief periods under the Spanish and French, it was successfully settled in 1632 by the British, who introduced sugar planting; the industry declined with the abolition of slavery in 1834. The island, with Barbuda and Redonda as dependencies, became an associated state of the Commonwealth in 1967 and achieved full independence in 1981, despite Barbudan opposition. Barbudan resentment of Antiguan dominance has resulted in unsuccessful demands for autonomy for Barbuda.

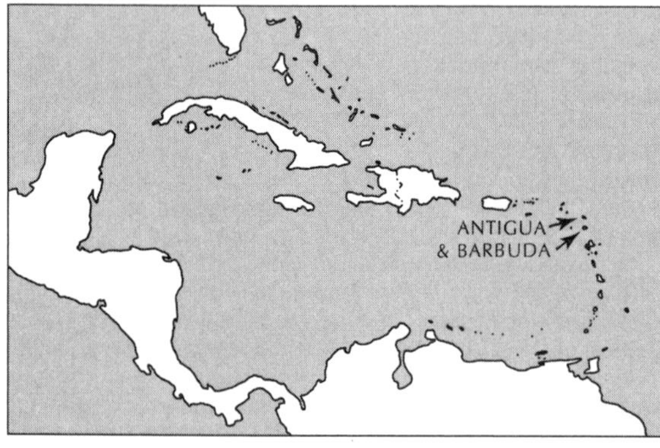

antihistamine: see ALLERGY; HISTAMINE.

Antilles: see WEST INDIES.

Anti-Masonic party, American political party founded to counter the supposed political influence of FREEMASONRY. It arose in W New York state after the disappearance (1826) of William Morgan, a former Mason who had written a book purporting to reveal Masonic secrets. Freemasons were said, without proof, to have murdered him. At Baltimore, in 1831, Anti-Masons held the first national nominating convention of any party, and issued the first written party platform. In 1834 they helped form the WHIG PARTY.

antimatter, material composed of antiparticles, which correspond to ordinary protons, electrons, and neutrons but are their "charge conjugates," i.e., they have the opposite electrical charge and magnetic moment. When matter and antimatter collide, both may be annihilated, and other ELEMENTARY PARTICLES, such as photons and pions, are produced. In 1932 Carl D. ANDERSON, while studying cosmic rays, discovered the positron, or antielectron, the first known antiparticle. Any antimatter in our part of the universe is necessarily very short-lived because of the overwhelming preponderance of ordinary matter, by which the antimatter is quickly annihilated.

antimony (Sb), semimetallic element, first described by Nicolas Lemery in 1707. Silvery blue-white, brittle, and easily powdered, it conducts heat and electricity poorly. Chief uses are as alloys and compounds in storage batteries, cable sheathing, and paint pigments. See ELEMENT (table); PERIODIC TABLE.

Antioch or **Antakya,** city (1990 pop. 124,443), S Turkey, on the Orontes R., near the Mediterranean Sea. It is a trade and processing center for a farm area where grains, cotton, grapes, and vegetables are grown. Founded (c.300 B.C.) by SELEUCUS I, king of ancient Syria, it was a military, commercial, and cultural center under Rome and an early center of Christianity. It fell (A.D. 637) to the Arabs but was retaken (1098) by the Crusaders and became a powerful principality under BOHEMOND I. It later became (1516) part of the OTTOMAN EMPIRE, was incorporated into the French mandate of Syria after World War I, and was restored to Turkey in 1939. Many important archaeological finds have been made in or near the city.

Antiochus I, 324–261 B.C., Seleucid emperor. The son of ALEXANDER THE GREAT's general SELEUCUS, he acceded to the throne in 281. He made peace with Macedonia, but lost territories in Asia Minor to Egypt in wars (274–71; 263–61). He led (273) a successful campaign against Gallic invaders in Asia Minor.

Antiochus III, c.242–187 B.C., Seleucid emperor, known as Antiochus the Great. Succeeding (223) his father, Seleucus II, he conquered Parthia, Bactria, Syria, and Palestine, entered into an alliance with PHILIP V of Macedonia, and invaded Thrace. He also gave refuge to HANNIBAL and aroused the enmity of Rome, which checked his western expansion in battles at Thermopylae and Magnesia.

Antiochus IV, c.215–163 B.C., known as Antiochus Epiphanes. Son of Antiochus II, he became king in 175. He is remembered for his infamous attempt to impose Hellenic culture on Judea, which instigated the Maccabean (see MACCABEES) Revolt (167). His preemptive war against Ptolemaic Egypt in 169–68 was lost by the intervention of Rome.

antioxidant, substance that prevents or slows OXIDATION. Antioxidants are used as FOOD ADDITIVES to retard spoilage and color changes. Studies show that antioxidants in the body, such as vitamins E and C and beta-carotene (a vitamin A precursor), can prevent cell damage and other changes caused by oxidation. Antioxidants act by scavenging the oxygen free radicals (molecules with an unpaired electron, which rapidly reacts with other molecules) that cause oxidation.

antiparticle: see ANTIMATTER.

Antipas, in the Bible: see HEROD.

Antipater [ăntĭp'ətər], d. 319 B.C., Macedonian general under ALEXANDER THE GREAT; regent of MACEDON (334–323 B.C.). After Alexander's death he defeated Perdiccas in a struggle for the regency (321). He held the kingdom together; his death was followed by the wars of the DIADOCHI.

Antipater, in the Bible: see HEROD.

antipope, person elected pope whose election was later declared uncanonical and in opposition to a canonically chosen legitimate pontiff (see PAPACY).

Anti-Saloon League, U.S. organization working for the prohibition of the sale of alcoholic beverages. Founded in 1893, it helped to secure the 18th amendment to the CONSTITUTION, establishing PROHIBITION (1919–33). In 1950 it merged with the National Temperance League.

anti-Semitism, prejudice against JEWS. Before the 19th cent. anti-Semitism was largely religious, based on the belief that Jews were responsible for Jesus' crucifixion. It was expressed in the later Middle Ages by sporadic persecutions and expulsions (e.g., the expulsion of Jews from Spain in 1492), economic restrictions (e.g., the restriction of Jews to unpopular or taboo occupations), and personal restrictions. After the Jews' emancipation during the ENLIGHTENMENT, religious and economic anti-Semitism was slowly replaced in the 19th cent. by racial prejudice, stemming from the idea of Jews as a distinct race. The cultural isolation of Orthodox Jews, rising NATIONALISM, pseudoscientific theories of Aryan racial superiority, and spurious charges of Jewish domination encouraged anti-Semitism (see POGROM). These beliefs, incorporated into Adolf Hitler's NATIONAL SOCIALISM, contributed to the extermination of 6 million Jews in the HOLOCAUST of World War II. Since the 1980s anti-Semitic nationalists have become more influential in Russia, Germany, and other European countries. In the U.S. anti-Semitism persists among some extreme right-wing groups and in the practice of excluding Jews from certain clubs, schools, and housing.

antisense, DNA or RNA manipulated in a laboratory so that its components (nucleotides) form a complementary copy (see NUCLEIC

ACID) of normal, or "sense," messenger RNA (mRNA). Antisense techniques are used to deactivate disease-causing or undesirable genes so that they cannot produce harmful or unwanted proteins. In some applications of this technique, the antisense nucleic acid segment is inserted into an inactivated or nonvirulent virus, then introduced into the cell. The antisense segment pairs with the mRNA, preventing the synthesis of protein from the mRNA. Antisense has applications in agriculture and medicine, especially in cancer and antiviral therapy.

antislavery movement: see ABOLITIONISTS; SLAVERY.

antitoxin: see TOXIN.

antitrust laws, legislation under which the U.S. government has acted to break up any large business combination alleged to be acting monopolistically to suppress competition (see TRUST, CORPORATE). The first of these laws, which were based on the constitutional power of Congress to regulate interstate commerce, was the **Sherman Antitrust Act** (1890). It declared illegal every contract, combination, or conspiracy in restraint of interstate and foreign trade. It was supplemented (1914) by the **Clayton Antitrust Act,** which prohibited exclusive sales contracts, intercorporate stock holdings, and unfair price cutting to freeze out competitors. The last provision was strengthened under the terms of the **Robinson-Patman Act** of 1936, and there have been many amendments to these laws over the years. Corporate trusts grew rapidly in the U.S. from 1880 to 1905, by which time Pres. Theodore ROOSEVELT had launched his famous "trust-busting" campaigns. An early federal success came with the Supreme Court decision of 1911 that forced the giant Standard Oil Co. to split up into independent entities. Antitrust action declined in the 1920s, but was vigorously resumed in the 1930s under Pres. F.D. ROOSEVELT. Antitrust enforcement was again deemphasized in the 1980s under presidents REAGAN and BUSH. The growth of huge CONGLOMERATES that control many companies in various, sometimes interrelated, industries has complicated enforcement of antitrust legislation. Antitrust laws have been criticized for hindering the ability of U.S. corporations to compete internationally.

antiviral drug, drug used to treat such viral infections as herpes simplex and herpes zoster, cytomegalovirus, influenza, and certain AIDS-related infections. Antiviral drugs, such as AZT and acyclovir, affect the genetic material of the virus and inhibit the ability of the virus to reproduce.

Antoine, André, 1858–1943, French theater director, manager, and critic. In 1887 he founded the Théâtre Libre to present works of NATURALISM. His work became a model for experimental theaters.

Antonello da Messina [äntōnĕl'lō dä mās-sē'nä], c.1430–1479, Italian painter. His handling of oils shows strong Flemish influence. Messina's works include *Ecce Homo* (Metropolitan Mus.) and *Pietà* (Venice). He was also an excellent portraitist.

Antonescu, Ion, 1882–1946, Romanian marshal and dictator. King CAROL II named him premier in 1940, and he promptly forced the king's abdication in favor of Carol's son, MICHAEL. In WORLD WAR II Antonescu led the nation into the AXIS camp and gave HITLER virtual control of the country. He was executed at the end of the war.

Antonioni, Michelangelo, 1912–, Italian film director. In such films as *L'Avventura* (1959), *Red Desert* (1964), *Blow-Up* (1966), and *The Passenger* (1975) he depicted modern alienation, subordinating dialogue to visual images.

Antony or **Marc Antony,** Lat. *Marcus Antonius*, c.83 B.C.–30 B.C., Roman politician and soldier. He was of a distinguished family related to Julius CAESAR, who made him a protégé. In 49 B.C. Antony became tribune. He and Quintus Cassius Longinus (see CASSIUS, family), another tribune, vetoed the bill to deprive Caesar of his army. Caesar then crossed the Rubicon, and the civil war began. After Caesar's assassination (44 B.C.), Antony, then consul, aroused the mob against the conspirators. Octavian (later AUGUSTUS) joined forces with him, but they soon fell out. However, Octavian arranged the Second Triumvirate with Antony and Marcus Aemilius Lepidus (see LEPIDUS, family). At Philippi, in 42 B.C., Antony and Octavian crushed the republicans, and the triumvirate ruled the empire for five years. Antony met CLEOPATRA in 42 B.C., and their love affair began. When Antony's wife, Fulvia, died (40 B.C.), he married Octavian's sister, OCTAVIA. In 37 B.C., Antony settled in Alexandria as the acknowledged lover of Cleopatra. In 32 B.C. the senate deprived Antony of his powers, thus making civil war inevitable. In the following year Octavian's forces defeated Antony and Cleopatra in the naval battle at Actium, and Antony returned to Egypt. When Octavian came there (30 B.C.), Antony committed suicide, and Cleopatra killed herself soon afterward. Of the many dramas on the tragedy, the best known by far is SHAKESPEARE's *Antony and Cleopatra*.

Antwerp, city (1991 est. pop. 470,050, including Berchem, Borgerhout, Deurne, Hoboken, Merksem, and Wilrijk), Flemish N Belgium, on the Scheldt R. It is one of the busiest European ports and a major center of finance, industry, and the diamond trade. Europe's chief commercial city by the mid-16th cent., it declined after its sacking (1576) by the Spanish and the closing (1648) of the Scheldt to navigation. Its modern expansion dates from 1863. In the 20th cent. it was twice occupied and heavily damaged by the Germans. Antwerp has many notable buildings, e.g., its Gothic cathedral (14th–16th cent.), and houses many important paintings, e.g., by RUBENS, MASSYS, VAN DYKE.

anxiety, anticipatory tension or vague dread persisting in the absence of a specific threat. It is characterized by increased pulse rate and blood pressure, quickened breathing, perspiration, and dryness of the mouth. Anxiety is an element of many psychic disorders including phobias, panic attacks, obsessive-compulsive disorders, and post- traumatic stress disorder. ANTIANXIETY DRUGS can effectively alleviate symptoms for many whose anxiety interferes with normal living.

Anza, Juan Bautista de [än'sä], 1735–88, Spanish explorer; b. Mexico. Accompanied by a small expedition, he blazed (1774) a route from Sonora to California. In 1776 he founded SAN FRANCISCO. He later served (1777–88) as governor of New Mexico.

Apache, indigenous people of the Southwest (see NORTH AMERICA, INDIGENOUS PEOPLES OF), six culturally related groups; most spoke dialects of the ATHABASCAN branch of the Nadene linguistic stock (see NATIVE AMERICAN LANGUAGES). Their ancestors entered the area c.1100. The NAVAHO were once joined to the Apaches. Historically the Apaches subsisted on wild game, seed and fruit gathering, livestock, and some horticulture. Men lived with and worked for their wives' families. The Apaches, known as fierce fighters, resisted the Spanish advance but increasingly fought the COMANCHES and other tribes with captured Spanish horses and arms. After the mid-19th cent. COCHISE, GERONIMO, MANGAS COLORADAS, and others led them in strong but futile efforts to stop white expansion westward. Today they live on reservations totaling over 3 million acres in Arizona and New Mexico and retain many tribal customs. Cattle, timber, tourism, and the development of mineral resources provide income. In 1982 the Apaches won a major Supreme Court test of their right to tax resources extracted from their lands. In 1990 there were 50,051 Apaches in the U.S.

apartheid [Afrik., = apartness], former system of racial segregation and white supremacy established in SOUTH AFRICA. First formalized in the 1948 Afrikaner Nationalist party platform, apartheid separated whites from nonwhites, nonwhites—"Coloureds" (persons of mixed race), "Asians" (mainly of Indian ancestry), and "Bantus" (persons of African ancestry)—from each other, and one indigenous African group from another. Under Prime Min. Hendrik VERWOERD a policy of "separate development" established nine BANTUSTANS (homelands) totaling about 14% of the country's land, most of it too poor in quality to support the designated population (roughly 75% of all South Africans). In the homelands Africans could exercise certain rights; elsewhere their activities were strictly curtailed. The policy led to international and domestic protest. In 1961 South Africa withdrew from the Commonwealth in dispute over apartheid. As a result of international economic sanctions and domestic social evolution, many lesser apartheid laws—such as those banning interracial marriage and segregating facilities—were repealed or fell into disuse by 1990. In 1991 Pres. DE KLERK obtained the repeal of the remaining laws and called for the drafting of a new constitution. In 1993 a multiracial, multiparty transitional government was approved, and fully free elections were held in 1994.

apatite, phosphate mineral $(Ca,Pb)_5(PO_4)_3(F,Cl,OH)$, transparent to opaque in shades of green, brown, yellow, white, red, and purple. Apatite, a minor constituent of many types of rock, is mined in

Florida, Tennessee, Montana, N Africa, Europe, and Russia. Large deposits are mined for use in making phosphatic fertilizers, and two varieties are used to a limited extent in jewelry.

ape, PRIMATE of the family Pongidae, or Simiidae, closely related to human beings. The small apes, the GIBBON and siamang, and the smallest of the great apes, the ORANGUTAN, are found in SE Asia; the other great apes, the GORILLA and the CHIMPANZEE, are found in Africa. They vary in size from the 3-ft (1.8-m), 15-lb (6.8-kg) gibbon to the 6-ft (1.8-m), 500-lb (227-kg) gorilla. All are forest dwellers and spend at least some time in trees; unlike MONKEYS, they can swing hand-over-hand. Their brains, similar in structure to the human brain, are capable of fairly advanced reasoning.

Apelles, fl. 330 B.C., Greek painter, the most famous in antiquity, now known only through descriptions. Perhaps his most famous work was a painting of Aphrodite rising from the sea. BOTTICELLI painted Apelles' *Calumny* (Uffizi) from ALBERTI's description.

Apennines, mountain system c.840 mi (1,350 km) long and up to c.80 mi (130 km) wide, extending the entire length of the Italian Peninsula and continuing into Sicily. The earthquake-prone mountains, long since denuded of their original forest cover, reach a high point of 9,560 ft (2,914 m) in Mt. Corno.

aphasia, language disturbance caused by a lesion of the brain, causing partial or total impairment in the individual's ability to speak, write, or comprehend the meaning of spoken or written words. Treatment consists of reeducation; the methods used include those employed in education of the deaf.

aphelion: see APSIS.

apheresis or **hemapheresis,** any procedure in which blood is drawn from a donor or patient and a component is separated out, the remaining blood components being returned to the body. See PLASMAPHERESIS.

aphid or **plant louse,** tiny, usually green, pear-shaped INSECT injurious to vegetation. Aphids feed by sucking plant juices through their beaks. Most species live in large colonies; some species live symbiotically with ants. Many inhabit swellings of plant tissues (galls) that they form with their secretions.

Aphrodite [ăfrədī'tē], in Greek mythology, goddess of love, beauty, and fertility. She was either the daughter of ZEUS and Dione, or she emerged from the sea foam. Married to HEPHAESTUS, she loved and had children by other gods and mortals, e.g., Harmonia was fathered by ARES, and AENEAS was the son of Anchises. Aphrodite was awarded the apple of discord by PARIS, leading to the TROJAN WAR. Probably of Eastern origin, she was similar in attributes to the goddesses ASTARTE and ISHTAR. The Romans identified her with VENUS.

Apia, city (1986 pop. 32,196), capital and chief port of WESTERN SAMOA.

Apicocomplexa, phylum of PROTOZOANS that are characterized by a unique body structure, the apical complex. The spore formers (class Sporozoa) are parasitic and are responsible for many human diseases. MALARIA is caused by the sporozoan *Plasmodium*. Sporozoans also infect domesticated and wild animals, as well as insects and other protozoans.

APL: see PROGRAMMING LANGUAGE.

Apocrypha, appendix to the Authorized (King James) Version of the Old Testament, containing the following books or parts of books: First and Second ESDRAS; TOBIT; JUDITH; ESTHER 10.4–16.24; WISDOM; ECCLESIASTICUS; BARUCH; DANIEL 3.24–90, 13, 14; Prayer of Manasses (see under MANASSEH); and First and Second MACCABEES. All except the Prayer of Manasses and First and Second Esdras are included in the Western canon. Protestants follow the Jewish tradition in treating these books as uncanonical. Jewish and Christian works resembling biblical books but not in the Western or Hebrew canon are called pseudepigrapha.

apogee: see APSIS.

Apollinaire, Guillaume [äpōlēnâr'], 1880–1918, French poet and critic; b. Wilhelm Apollinaris de Kostrowitzky. He was an influential innovator, whose lyric poems, e.g., *Alcools* (1913) and *Calligrammes* (1918), blend modern and traditional verse techniques. He is credited with introducing CUBISM to literature. *The Breasts of Tiresias* (1918), a play, is an early example of SURREALISM.

Apollo, in Greek mythology, one of the most important OLYMPIAN gods; son of ZEUS and Leto, twin brother of ARTEMIS. He was concerned with prophecy, medicine (he was the father of ASCLEPIUS), music and poetry (he was also the father of ORPHEUS and the patron of the MUSES), and the pastoral arts. A moral god of high civilization, he was associated with law, philosophy, and the arts. He was widely known as a god of light, Phoebus Apollo; after the 5th cent. B.C. he was often identified with the sun god HELIOS. Apollo's oracles had great authority; his chief shrine was at DELPHI, where he was primarily a god of purification. In art he was portrayed as the perfection of youth and beauty. The most celebrated statue of him is the **Apollo Belvedere**, a marble copy of the original Greek bronze, now in the Vatican in Rome.

Apollo, Project: see SPACE EXPLORATION (table).

Apollo asteroid: see ASTEROID.

Apollonius Rhodius, fl. 3d cent. B.C., epic poet of ALEXANDRIA and RHODES; librarian at Alexandria. His *Argonautica* is a four-book Homeric imitation on the Argonaut theme (see GOLDEN FLEECE; JASON).

Apollo-Soyuz Test Project: see SPACE EXPLORATION (table).

apostle [Gr., = envoy], one of the prime missionaries of Christianity. The disciples of JESUS who were chosen to be his Twelve Apostles were PETER, ANDREW, JAMES (the Greater), JOHN, THOMAS, JAMES (the Less), JUDE (or Thaddaeus), PHILIP, BARTHOLOMEW, MATTHEW, SIMON, and JUDAS ISCARIOT, who was later replaced by MATTHIAS. St. PAUL and sometimes a few others, e.g., St. BARNABAS, are also classed as apostles.

apothecaries' weight: see ENGLISH UNITS OF MEASUREMENT; WEIGHTS AND MEASURES (table).

Appalachian Mountains, major North American mountain system extending c.1,600 mi (2,570 km) SW from Canada's Quebec prov. to Alabama, with Mt. Mitchell (6,684 ft/2,037 m), in North Carolina, the highest point. Their rugged hills and valleys, the much-eroded remnants of a very old mountain mass, posed a major barrier to westward expansion in the early years of the U.S. Industries include coal mining (in the west) and tourism (see APPALACHIAN NATIONAL SCENIC TRAIL; BLUE RIDGE; Shenandoah and Great Smoky mountains under NATIONAL PARKS, table).

Appalachian National Scenic Trail, world's longest continuous hiking trail, in the Appalachian Mts., extending 2,050 mi (3,299 km) from Mt. Katahdin (Me.) to Springer Mt. (Ga.) and passing through 14 states. It was completed in 1937.

appendix, small, worm-shaped blind tube projecting from the large intestine into the lower right abdominal cavity. It has no function and is considered a remnant of a previous digestive organ. Appendicitis can occur if accumulated and hardened waste matter becomes infected; rupture of such an appendix can spread infection to the peritoneum (abdominal membrane), causing peritonitis.

Appia, Adolphe, 1862–1928, Swiss theorist of stage lighting and decor. His employment of light and shade when staging WAGNER's operas revolutionized modern scene design and stage lighting.

Appian Way, most famous of the Roman roads, built (312 B.C.) under Appius Claudius Caecus (see CLAUDIUS, Roman gens). It connected Rome with Capua and was later extended to Brundisium (Brindisi). It was the chief highway to Greece and the East.

Appius Claudius: see CLAUDIUS, Roman gens.

apple, any tree (and its fruit) of the genus *Malus* of the ROSE family. The common apple (*M. sylvestris*) is the best-known and commercially most important temperate fruit. It is native to W Asia, but has been widely cultivated from prehistoric times. Thousands of varieties exist, e.g., Golden Delicious, Winesap, Jonathan, and McIntosh. The fruit is consumed fresh or cooked, or is used for juice. Partial fermentation of apple juice (sweet cider) produces hard cider (from which applejack liquor is made); fully fermented juice yields vinegar. The hardwood is used in cabinetmaking and as fuel. The fruit of crab apple trees (which are cultivated as ornamentals) is used for preserves and jellies.

Appleseed, Johnny: see CHAPMAN, JOHN.

Appomattox, town (1990 pop. 1,707), seat of Appomattox co., central Va.; inc. 1925. Confederate Gen. Robert E. LEE surrendered to Union Gen. U.S. GRANT at nearby Appomattox Courthouse on April 9, 1865, virtually ending the CIVIL WAR. The surrender site has been made a national historical park.

apricot, tree (*Prunus armeniaca*) of the ROSE family and its fruit, native to Asia. In the U.S., it is cultivated chiefly in California. The fruit is used raw, canned, preserved, and dried, and in making a cordial and a brandy.

April: see MONTH.

apse, the termination at the sanctuary end of a church, generally semicircular, sometimes square or polygonal. In Roman temples and BASILICAS, it was a recess holding the statue of the deity. Early Christian churches placed the altar in the apse, at the eastern end. Because of its function, the apse became the architectural climax of the interior, and was often highly decorated. Chapels sometimes radiated from it.

apsis, point in the ORBIT of a smaller body where it is at its greatest or least distance from a larger body to which it is attracted. In an elliptical orbit these points are called the apocenter and pericenter; corresponding terms for elliptical orbits around the sun, the earth, and a star are, respectively, aphelion and perihelion, apogee and perigee, and apastron and periastron. The line of apsides, an imaginary straight line connecting the two apsides of an elliptical orbit, may shift because of gravitational influences of other bodies or relativistic effects (see RELATIVITY).

Apuleius, Lucius, fl. 2d cent., Latin writer. His romance *The Golden Ass* or *Metamorphoses* is the only entire Latin novel surviving. The story of a man transformed into an ass, it influenced the development of the NOVEL.

Aqaba, Gulf of, northern arm of the RED SEA, 118 mi (190 km) long and c.10 mi (16 km) wide, between ARABIA and Egypt's SINAI peninsula. The gulf, which gives Israel direct access to the INDIAN OCEAN, is entered through the Straits of Tiran. It was declared an international waterway by the UN in 1958 after Arab states opposed to Israel blockaded it (1949–56). It was blockaded again in the ARAB-ISRAELI WAR of 1967.

aquaculture, the raising and harvesting of fresh- and saltwater plants and animals. The most economically important form of aquaculture is fish farming, a billion-dollar industry that produces 10% of the food fish consumed in the U.S. Common products of aquaculture are catfish, trout, crawfish, oysters, shrimp, and salmon. Some are raised in huge freshwater tanks, others require the running water of rivers or streams, and saltwater species are raised in cages placed in coastal or deeper sea waters. The practice of aquaculture dates back to 1000 B.C. in China.

aquamarine, transparent blue to bluish-green variety of the mineral BERYL, used as a gem. Sources include Brazil, Madagascar, Russia, and parts of the U.S. Oriental aquamarine is a transparent bluish variety of CORUNDUM.

aqua regia [Lat., = royal water], corrosive, fuming yellow liquid prepared by mixing one volume of concentrated NITRIC ACID with three to four volumes of concentrated HYDROCHLORIC ACID. It was so named by the alchemists because it dissolves gold and platinum, the "royal" metals, which do not dissolve in nitric and hydrochloric acid alone.

aquatint, ETCHING technique. A metal plate is coated with resin through which acid bites an evenly pocked surface. When printed, it produces tonal effects that resemble wash drawings. Said to have been invented in the 1760s by J.B. Le Prince, aquatint is often combined with other types of etchings, as in GOYA's series of mixed aquatint etchings.

aqueduct, conduit for conveying water, built chiefly to bring fresh drinking water into cities. Aqueduct types include tunnels cut through rock, pipelines, and the conduits that top the arched, bridgelike structures that stand in many parts of Europe and are legacies of the ancient Roman water supply system. Modern aqueducts utilize gravity, pumps, and the propulsive force of very high pressures in underground tunnels to move water over great distances.

aquifer: see ARTESIAN WELL.

Aquino, (Maria) Corazon "Cory", 1933–, Philippine politician, president of the Philippines (1986–92); b. Maria Corazon Cojuangco. Her husband, **Benigno Servillano Aquino, Jr.,** 1932–83, was Pres. Ferdinand MARCOS's chief political opponent, and in 1983 he was assassinated by government agents as he returned to the Philippines from exile in the U.S. When the accused agents were acquitted, Corazon Aquino declared her candidacy for the presidency. After the election (1986), both sides claimed victory. When Marcos refused to step down, Aquino organized strikes and boycotts. With the nation on the brink of civil war, Marcos accepted asylum in the U.S. and Aquino assumed the presidency, becoming the first woman president of the country. Promised changes and improvements largely failed to materialize during Aquino's term in office, and there were six coup attempts against her.

Aquitaine [ăk'wĭtān], former duchy and kingdom in SW France. Conquered (56 B.C.) by the Romans, it fell to the VISIGOTHS in the 5th cent. In 507 Aquitaine was added to the Frankish kingdom by CLOVIS I, but later regained some independence. CHARLEMAGNE made (781) Aquitaine into a kingdom that was ruled by his son Louis (later Emperor LOUIS I). Late in the 9th cent. it became a duchy enfeoffed to the French crown. ELEANOR OF AQUITAINE's marriage (1152) to the future HENRY II of England gave Henry and his heirs control of the duchy as vassals of the French crown. France completed the recapture of Aquitaine from the English during the HUNDRED YEARS WAR.

Ar, chemical symbol of the element ARGON.

Arabia, peninsula, c.1,000,000 sq mi (2,590,000 sq km), SW Asia, containing the world's largest known reserves of oil and natural gas. It is politically divided between SAUDI ARABIA (the largest and most populous nation), YEMEN, OMAN, the UNITED ARAB EMIRATES, QATAR, BAHRAIN, KUWAIT, and several neutral zones. JORDAN and IRAQ are to the north, the RED SEA to the west, and the PERSIAN GULF to the east. Rugged mountains rising to c.12,000 ft (3,700 m) in the southwest catch what little moisture is available, making the basin-shaped interior of the peninsula one of the world's driest deserts, with less than 4 in. (10 cm) of precipitation annually.

Arabian art and architecture: see ISLAMIC ART AND ARCHITECTURE.

Arabian Gulf: see PERSIAN GULF.

Arabian Nights: see THOUSAND AND ONE NIGHTS.

Arabian Sea, ancient *Mare Erythraeum,* northwestern marginal sea of the INDIAN OCEAN, between Arabia and India. Its principal arms include the Gulf of ADEN, extended by the RED SEA, and the Gulf of Oman, extended by the PERSIAN GULF. ADEN, KARACHI, and BOMBAY are the chief ports.

Arabic languages, members of the Semitic subdivision of the Hamito-Semitic family of languages. See AFRICAN LANGUAGES (table).

Arab-Israeli Wars, conflicts in 1948–49, 1956, 1967, 1973–74, and 1982 between Israel and various Arab states. **1** The 1948–49 war reflected the opposition of the Arab states to the formation of a Jewish state in what they considered Arab territories. Newly created Israel was invaded by forces from Egypt, Syria, Transjordan (later Jordan), Lebanon, and Iraq. A UN-sponsored truce was arranged, but fighting has broken out periodically since then over the basic issue of the existence of Israel. **2** In 1956 Israel, joined by France and Great Britain, attacked Egypt after that country had nationalized the Suez Canal. Intervention by the UN, supported by the United States and the Soviet Union, forced a cease-fire. **3** In 1967, in the Six-Day War, Israel responded to Egyptian provocation with air attacks and ground victories. The result was a humiliating defeat for Egypt. **4** In the Yom Kippur War of 1973–74, Egypt, Syria, and Iraq attacked Israel on the Jewish holy Day of Atonement, catching the Israelis off guard. Israel recouped quickly and forced the Arab troops back from their initial gains, but at great cost to both sides. Again, a cease-fire stopped the fighting, but Egypt and Israel later signed the CAMP DAVID ACCORDS. **5** In 1978 Palestinian guerrillas, from their base in LEBANON, launched an air raid on Israel; in retaliation, Israel sent troops into S Lebanon to occupy a strip 4–6 mi (6–10 km) deep and thus protect Israel's border. Eventually a UN peace-keeping force was set up there, but occasional fighting continued. In 1982 Israel launched a massive attack to destroy all military bases of the PALESTINE LIBERATION ORGANIZATION in S Lebanon and, after a 10-week siege of the Muslim sector of West BEIRUT, a PLO stronghold, forced the Palestinians to accept a U.S.-sponsored plan whereby the PLO guerrillas would evacuate Beirut and go to several Arab countries that had agreed to accept them. Israel withdrew from Lebanon in 1985 but continues to maintain a Lebanese-Christian–policed buffer zone north of its border.

Arab League, association of states formed (1945) to give common expression to the political interests of Arab nations. Its 21 members include nearly all of the Arab states and the PALESTINE LIBER-

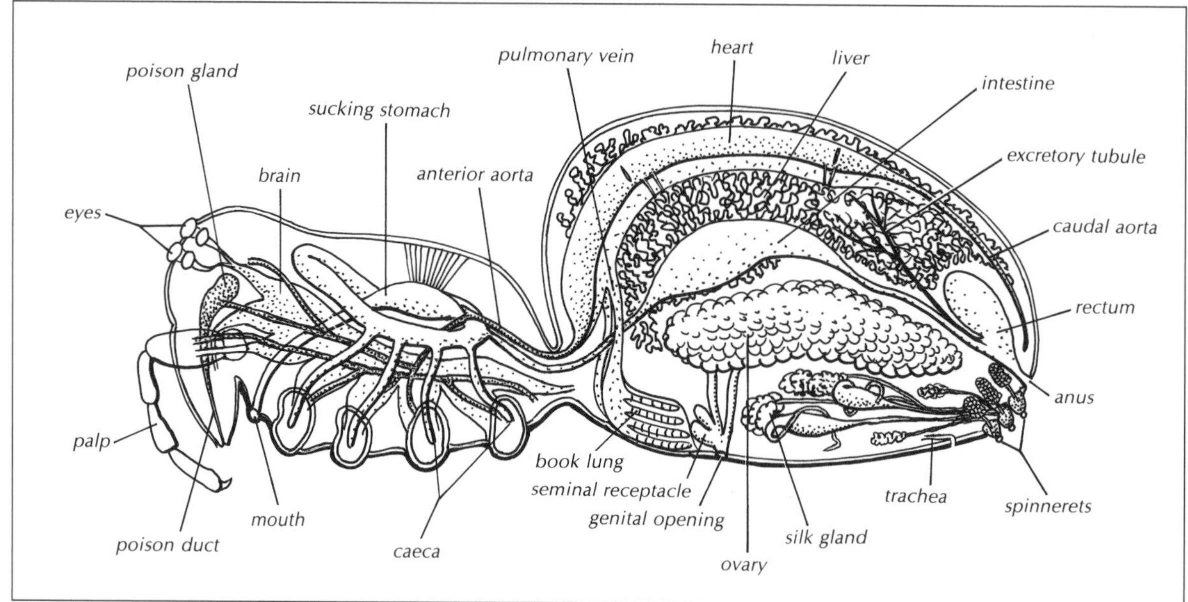

Arachnid: Internal anatomy of a spider, a representative arachnid

ATION ORGANIZATION, and its headquarters are in Cairo. Opposed to the formation of a Jewish state in Palestine, league members jointly attacked Israel in 1948 (see ARAB-ISRAELI WARS). Egypt was suspended (1979–89) because of its peace agreement with Israel, and the headquarters moved (1979–1990) to Tunis. Attempts to coordinate Arab economic life are among the league's chief activities.

Arab Maghreb Union: see under MAGHREB.

Arabs, name originally applied to the Semitic peoples of the Arabian peninsula (see SEMITE); now used also for populations of countries whose primary language is Arabic, e.g., Algeria, Egypt, Iraq, Jordan, Lebanon, Libya, Morocco, Syria, and Yemen. Socially, Arabs are divided into the settled *fellahin* (villagers) and the nomadic BEDOUIN. The invasions of Muslims from Arabia in the 6th and 7th cent. diffused the Arabic language and ISLAM, the Arabic religion. At its peak the Arab empire extended from the Atlantic Ocean across North Africa and the Middle East to central Asia. A great Arab civilization emerged in which education, literature, philosophy, medicine, mathematics, and science were highly developed. In Europe the Arab conquests were particularly important in Sicily, from the 9th to late 11th cent., and in Spain, in the civilization of the MOORS. In the 20th cent., Arab leaders have attempted to unite the Arab-speaking world into an Arab nation. Since 1945 most Arab countries have joined the ARAB LEAGUE. In 1982, member nations had a total population estimated at 43 million. Several of these countries control two thirds of the world's oil reserves and are members of OPEC (see ORGANIZATION OF PETROLEUM EXPORTING COUNTRIES). Since 1948 disputes with the state of ISRAEL have resulted in ARAB-ISRAELI WARS.

arachnid, mainly terrestrial ARTHROPOD of the class Arachnida, including the SPIDER, SCORPION, MITE, tick, and DADDY LONGLEGS. The arachnid's body is divided into a cephalothorax with six pairs of appendages and an abdomen. Most are carnivorous, and some use the first two pairs of append ages to crush and kill prey; the others are for walking. Arachnids have simple eyes and sensory bristles; they have no antennae. Respiration is through air tubes or primitive structures called book lungs.

Arafat, Yasir, 1929–, Palestinian commando leader; b. Cairo. Head of the guerrilla group Al Fatah, he became (1969) leader of the PALESTINE LIBERATION ORGANIZATION (PLO). The PLO was weakened when Arafat and his guerrillas were forced to leave their stronghold in West BEIRUT, Lebanon, after the 1982 Israeli siege (see ARAB-ISRAELI WARS). Beginning in the late 1980s, Arafat made tentative peace overtures to Israel, which ultimately culminated in a 1993 accord with Israel that called for limited Palestinian self-rule in Jericho and the GAZA STRIP.

Aragon, Louis [ärägôN′], 1897–1982, French writer. A founder of SURREALISM, he later turned to realistic social and political fiction after becoming a Communist. His works include the surrealist novel *Nightwalker* (1926), the war poems in *Heartbreak* (1941), and the series of love poems (1953, 1959, 1963) to his wife, the novelist Elsa Triolet.

Aragón, autonomous region (1988 pop. 1,208,470), 18,382 sq mi (47,609 sq km) and former kingdom, NE Spain, bordered in the north by France. Much of Aragón is sparsely populated and desertlike. Grains, sugar beets, and other crops are grown in oases and irrigated areas. Manufactures include machinery, electrical equipment, and industrial vehicles. The kingdom was founded (1035) on land won from the MOORS, and in the 12th cent. ZARAGOZA became its capital. Aragón annexed NAVARRE in 1076 and was united with CATALONIA in 1137. Its rulers (see ARAGÓN, HOUSE OF) pursued (13th–15th cent.) an expansionist policy in the Mediterranean. The marriage (1479) of Ferdinand of Aragón (later Spanish King FERDINAND V) to ISABELLA I of Castile led to the union of Aragón and Castile.

Aragón, house of, ruling family of ARAGÓN and other territories in the Middle Ages. Founded (1035) by Ramiro I, the house during the 12th cent. conquered much territory from the MOORS in Spain and also in S France. In the 13th to 15th cent. it acquired SICILY, SARDINIA, and the kingdom of NAPLES. These possessions were usually held by various branches of the house and were seldom united under one ruler as they were under ALFONSO V in 1443–58. The union of the crowns of Aragón and Castile took place in 1479, after the Spanish king FERDINAND V married ISABELLA I of Castile.

Aral Sea, inland sea, the world's sixth largest lake, c.15,000 sq mi (38,900 sq km), on the Kazakhstan-Uzbekistan border. The sea, which is fed by the AMU DARYA and SYR DARYA rivers, is generally less than 220 ft (70 m) deep and is somewhat saline. It was known to medieval Arab geographers as the Khorezm or Khwarazm Sea and to early Russian explorers, who reached it in the 17th cent., as the Sine (Blue) Sea. Since the early 1960s the sea has shrunk by two fifths due to diversion of water from its tributaries.

Aramaic [ârəma′ ĭk], Hamito-Semitic language that flourished in SYRIA and the FERTILE CRESCENT around the time of Jesus. See LANGUAGE (table).

Aramburu, Pedro Eugenio [ärämbo͞o′ro͞o], 1903–70, president of Argentina (1955–58). An army general, he participated in the overthrow of Juan PERÓN. As president, he ruled by decree, removed Peronists from important posts, and returned the country to constitutional democracy. He was kidnapped and murdered by Peronist guerrillas in 1970.

Arapaho, indigenous people of the Plains (see NORTH AMERICA, INDIGENOUS PEOPLES OF), who speak an Algonquian-Wakashan language (see NATIVE AMERICAN LANGUAGES). Sometimes called "dog eaters" by other tribes, they are divided into the Northern Arapaho (considered the parent group), the Southern Arapaho, and the GROS VENTRE. They stressed age-graded societies, the SUN DANCE, and later the GHOST DANCE. Today the Arapaho lead an agricultural life, and obtain income from leasing land for oil and gas development. In 1990 there were 6,350 Arapaho in the U.S.

Ararat, mountain, E Turkey, with two peaks, Little Ararat (12,877 ft/3,925 m) and Great Ararat (16,945 ft/5,165 m). According to tradition, it was the landing place of Noah's ark. The **kingdom of Ararat** (fl. c.9th–7th cent. B.C.), called in Assyrian Urartu, was located near Lake Van in present-day E Turkey.

Araucanians, South American agricultural peoples (see SOUTH AMERICA, INDIGENOUS PEOPLES OF) occupying most of S central Chile before the Spanish conquest (1540) and speaking languages of the Araucanian group (see NATIVE AMERICAN LANGUAGES). The INCA invaded them (c.1448–82) but were never a strong influence. The Araucanians stoutly resisted the Spanish, rebelling periodically until 1881. Some Araucanians, especially in the 18th cent., had fled to Argentina, where with captured wild horses they became plains wanderers. The Araucanians in Chile today number over 200,000; they are divided between assimilated urban dwellers and those who retain many of their traditional ways.

arbitration, industrial: see under COLLECTIVE BARGAINING.

Arblay, Madame d': see BURNEY, FANNY.

arborvitae, aromatic evergreen tree (genus *Thuja*) of the CYPRESS family, native to Asia and North America. Arborvitaes have tiny cones and flattened branchlets with scalelike leaves. The white cedar (*T. occidentalis*), popular for hedges, and the red cedar (*T. plicata*), important for lumber, both have decay-resistant wood.

Arbuthnot, John, 1667–1735, Scottish author, scientist, and physician. He is best remembered for his five "John Bull" pamphlets (1712), satires on Whig policy that introduced the character John Bull, the typical Englishman. A member of the SCRIBLERUS CLUB, he also wrote medical works.

arbutus, trailing: see TRAILING ARBUTUS.

arc, in mathematics, any part of a CURVE that does not intersect itself; in particular, a portion of the circumference of a CIRCLE.

Arcadia, region of ancient GREECE, in the central PELOPONNESUS. Its inhabitants, the Arcadians, lived a pastoral life. The largest city was Megalopolis.

Arcadius, c.377–408, Roman emperor of the East (395–408); son of THEODOSIUS I. His brother HONORIUS inherited the West, which began the division of the empire. During Arcadius's weak reign ALARIC I invaded Greece (395–97).

Arcagnolo: see ORCAGNA.

Arcaro, Eddie (George Edward Arcaro), 1916–, American jockey; b. Cincinnati. During his career (1931–62) he won 4,779 races, and his mounts won $30,039,543 in purses. He rode five Kentucky Derby, six Preakness, and six Belmont winners and twice (1941, 1948) rode Triple Crown winners.

Arc de Triomphe de l'Étoile [ärk də trēôNf' də lātwäl'], triumphal arch in Paris, in the center of the Place de l'Étoile, which is formed by the intersection of 12 avenues, one of them the Champs Élysées. It was built (1806–36) to commemorate NAPOLEON I's victories, from designs of J.F. Chalgrin. In 1920 the body of an unknown French soldier was buried there.

arch, the spanning of a wall opening by means of separate units (e.g., bricks or blocks) assembled into an upward curve that maintains stability through the mutual pressure of a load and the separate pieces. The weight of the load is converted into downward pressures (thrusts) received by the piers (abutments) flanking the opening. The blocks forming the arch are usually wedge-shaped. The arch was used by the Egyptians, Babylonians, and Greeks, chiefly for drains, and by the Assyrians in vaulted and domed chambers. The oldest known arch in Europe is a Roman drain, the Cloaca Maxima (c.578 B.C.). The Roman semicircular arch, drawn from Etruscan structures, was continued in early Christian, Byzantine, and Romanesque architecture. The pointed arch (used by the Assyrians) came into general use in the 13th cent. Possibly rediscovered independently in Europe, it became essential to the Gothic system of design. The round arch regained dominance in the RENAISSANCE. The 19th-cent. invention of steel beams for wide spans relegated the arch to a decorative function.

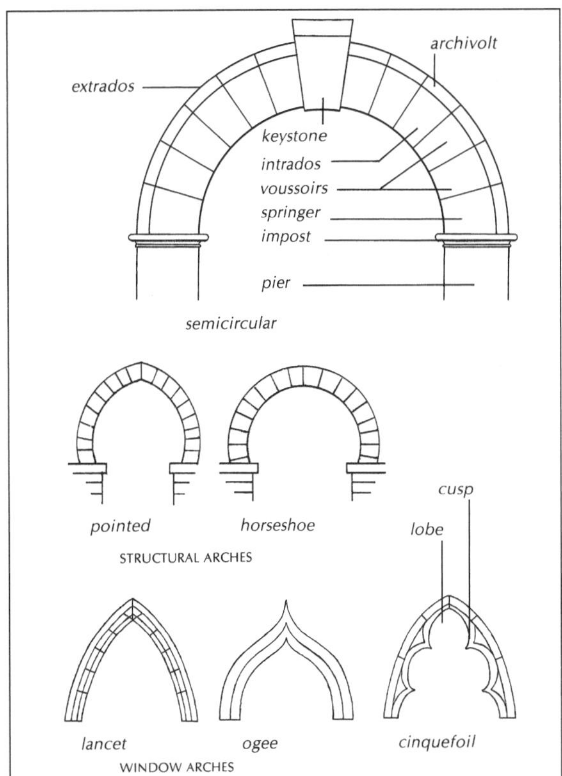

Arches

archaeology, scientific study of material remains of human cultures to derive knowledge about prehistoric times and to supplement documentary evidence of historic times. Research into the life and culture of the past began in 15th-cent. Italy with the excavation of ancient Greek sculpture. It was advanced in the 18th cent. by excavations at HERCULANEUM and POMPEII. In the 19th cent. public interest was stimulated by the acquisition of the ELGIN MARBLES and by the excavations of Heinrich SCHLIEMANN at Troy and in Greece and those of Arthur EVANS at Crete; Egyptology was born with the recovery of the ROSETTA stone. Stratigraphic excavation of such sites as BARROWS, mounds, and kitchen middens unearthed levels of material culture of the past. Scientific analysis of these material remains led Danish archaeologist Christian Thomsen to classify cultures according to the principal materials used for weapons and tools: STONE AGE, BRONZE AGE, IRON AGE. Realizing that an exact equation of technical tradition with cultural development was too rigid, later interpreters emphasized ECOLOGY and food production. Improved field techniques, new DATING methods, and the study of existing aboriginal groups have enhanced the knowledge of prehistory. See also HUMAN EVOLUTION.

archery, sport of shooting with bow and arrow. The four main types are target, field, flight, and crossbow shooting. In target shooting, the object is to score the most points with arrows aimed at the "bull's-eye"—the innermost of five to ten concentric circles. Once an important military and hunting skill, archery was revived as a sport in Europe in the 17th cent. and became popular in the U.S. in the late 1800s.

Arches National Park: see NATIONAL PARKS (table).

Archimedes [ärkĭmē'dēz], c.287 B.C.–212 B.C., Greek mathematician, physicist, and inventor. His reputation in antiquity was based on several mechanical contrivances, e.g., ARCHIMEDES' SCREW; which he is alleged to have invented. One legend states that during the Second PUNIC WAR he protected his native Syracuse from the besieging armies of Marcus Claudius MARCELLUS for three years by inventing machines of war, e.g., various ballistic instruments and mirrors that set Roman ships on fire by focusing the sun's rays on them. In modern times, however, he is best known for his work in mathematics, mechanics, and hydrostatics. In mathematics, he calculated that the value of π (see PI) is between $3^{10}/_{71}$ and $3^{1}/_{7}$; devised a mathematical exponential system to express extremely large numbers; proved that the volume of a sphere is two thirds the volume of a circumscribed cylinder; and, in calculating the areas and volumes of various geometrical figures, carried the method of exhaustion invented by EUDOXUS OF CNIDUS far enough in some cases to anticipate the invention (17th cent.) of the CALCULUS. One of the first to apply geometry to mechanics and hydrostatics, he proved the law of the lever entirely by geometry and established ARCHIMEDES' PRINCIPLE. In another legendary story, the ruler Hiero II requested him to find a method for determining whether a crown was pure gold or alloyed with silver. Archimedes realized, as he stepped into a bath, that a given weight of gold would displace less water than an equal weight of silver (which is less dense than gold); and he is said, in his excitement at his discovery, to have run home naked, shouting *"Eureka! Eureka!"* ("I have found it! I have found it!"). He was killed by a Roman soldier, supposedly while absorbed in mathematics.

Archimedes' principle, principle that states that a body immersed in a fluid is buoyed up by a force equal to the weight of the displaced fluid. The principle applies to both floating and submerged bodies, and to all fluids. It explains not only the buoyancy of ships but also the rise of a helium-filled balloon and the apparent loss of weight of objects underwater.

Archimedes' screw, a simple mechanical device used to lift water and such light materials as grain or sand, and believed to have been invented by ARCHIMEDES in the 3d cent. B.C. It consists of a large continuous screw inside a cylindrical chamber. To lift water—for example, from a river to its bank—the lower end is placed in the river, and water rises up the spiral threads of the screw as it is revolved.

Archipenko, Alexander, 1887–1964, Ukrainian-American sculptor. He recognized the aesthetic value of negative form (the void), as in the hollowed-out masses of his marble *Madonna* (Mus. Mod. Art, N.Y.C.). He taught cubist sculpture (see CUBISM) in Paris, Berlin, and New York City.

Arctic, the, northernmost area of the earth, centered on the NORTH POLE. It can be defined as embracing all lands located N of the ARCTIC CIRCLE (lat. 66°30′N) or all lands located N of the 50°F (10°C) July isotherm, which is roughly equivalent to the tree line. It therefore generally includes the ARCTIC OCEAN; the northern reaches of Canada, Alaska, Russia, and Norway; and most of Greenland, Iceland, and Svalbard. Ice sheets and permanent snow cover regions where average monthly temperatures remain below 32°F (0°C) all year; TUNDRA, which flourishes during the short summer season, covers areas where temperatures are between 32°F and 50°F (0°–10°C) for at least one month. The Arctic is of great strategic value as the shortest route between the U.S. and Russia. Since the International Geophysical Year (1957–58), rich oil and natural gas deposits have been discovered on Alaska's North Slope (see PRUDHOE BAY), Canada's Ellesmere Island (1972), and the northern areas of Siberia, in Russia. Traditionally, Robert E. PEARY was credited with being the first explorer to reach (1909) the North Pole, but this claim is disputed.

Arctic Circle, imaginary circle on the earth's surface at 66°30′N lat., marking the northernmost point at which the sun can be seen at the winter SOLSTICE (about Dec. 22) and the southernmost point of the northern polar regions at which the midnight sun is visible.

Arctic Ocean, the world's smallest ocean, c.5,400,000 sq mi (13,986,000 sq km), centering on the NORTH POLE and connecting with the Pacific through the Bering Strait and with the Atlantic through the Greenland Sea. It is covered with ice up to 14 ft (4 m) thick all year, except in fringe areas.

Ardashir I, d. 240, king of PERSIA (226?–240), founder of the Sassanid dynasty. He reunited Persia and established ZOROASTRIANISM as the state religion. His costly victory (232) over Roman Emperor Alexander Severus consolidated Persian power.

Ardennes, wooded plateau, from 1,600 to 2,300 ft (488 to 701 m) high, in SE Belgium, N Luxembourg, and N France. A traditional battleground, the Ardennes saw heavy fighting in both world wars, especially in the Battle of the Bulge (1944–45).

Arecibo Observatory, radio-astronomy facility (completed 1963) located at Arecibo, Puerto Rico; it is operated by Cornell Univ. under contract with the U.S. National Science Foundation. Its fixed antenna of spherical section, 1,000 ft (305 m) in diameter, is the largest radio-telescope antenna in the world.

Arendt, Hannah, 1906–75, German-American political theorist; b. Germany. Fleeing the Nazis in 1941, she came to the U.S. and taught at leading universities. In *The Origins of Totalitarianism* (1951), which established her as a major political thinker, Arendt traced Nazism and Communism to 19th cent. IMPERIALISM and ANTI-SEMITISM. Other works include *The Human Condition* (1958), *Eichmann in Jerusalem* (1963), and *The Life of the Mind* (1977).

Arensky, Anton Stepanovich, 1861–1906, Russian composer. A pupil of RIMSKY-KORSAKOV, he taught at the Moscow Conservatory and became (1895) conductor of the Imperial Chapel Choir. He wrote operas, symphonic music, songs, and piano works.

Arequipa, city (1993 pop. 620,471), capital of Arequipa dept., S Peru. The commercial center of S Peru and N Bolivia, it produces leather goods, alpaca wool, textiles, and foodstuffs. Founded in 1540 on an INCA site, it was largely destroyed by an earthquake in 1868 but has been restored. It is called "the white city" because of the light-colored stone, sillar, used as a building material.

Ares [âr'ēz], in Greek mythology, OLYMPIAN god of war; son of ZEUS and HERA. The Romans identified him with MARS.

Argentina [ärjəntē'nə], officially Argentine Republic, republic (1992 est. pop. 32,901,000), 1,072,157 sq mi (2,776,889 sq km), S South America, bordered by Chile (W); Bolivia (N); Paraguay, Brazil, and Uruguay (NE); and the Atlantic Ocean (SE). The second largest nation of South America, it stretches c.2,300 mi (3,700 km) from the subtropics south to TIERRA DEL FUEGO. Major cities include BUENOS AIRES (the capital), CÓRDOBA, and ROSARIO. Argentina consists of six geographical regions: (1) the Paraná Plateau in the northeast, a wet, forested area; (2) the GRAN CHACO, a flat alluvial plain; (3) the Pampa (see under PAMPAS), a vast grassland between the Atlantic and the Andean foothills; (4) the Monte, an arid region dotted with oases; (5) PATAGONIA, in the south, a bleak plateau that is the chief oil-producing region; and (6) the ANDES Mts., extending the length of the western border and including ACONCAGUA (22,835 ft/6,960 m), the highest point of South America. Most important of these is the Pampa, the chief agricultural and industrial area and site of most of the main cities. Argentina's economy is a mix of agriculture and industry. Grains and livestock are the basis of the nation's wealth; wheat corn, flax, oats, beef, mutton, hides, and wool are the major exports. Domestic oil and gas production makes the nation self-sufficient in energy. The industrial base is highly developed, providing nearly all of its consumer goods. Food processing (meat packing, flour milling, canning) is the principal industry; leather goods and textiles are also important. The population is overwhelmingly of European descent (especially Spanish and Italian), and about 90% are Roman Catholic. Spanish is the official language, but Italian is also spoken.

History. The first European explorers, notably Juan Díaz de Solís, Ferdinand MAGELLAN, and Sebastian Cabot (see under CABOT, JOHN), arrived in the early 16th cent. Buenos Aires was founded in 1536, abandoned after attacks from indigenous peoples, and refounded in 1580. The city was made the capital of a Spanish viceroyalty in 1776. The successful struggle for independence (1810–16) was led by generals Manuel BELGRANO, J.M. de Pueyrredón, and José de SAN MARTÍN. A protracted period of civil war ensued, lasting until the dictatorship of J.M. de ROSAS (1829–52). A new constitution was adopted in 1853 and, with major amendments, remained in effect until 1949, but Argentina continued to suffer political instability and military coups. It belatedly entered (1945) WORLD WAR II on the Allied side after four years of pro-Axis "neutrality." Juan PERÓN, an army colonel who, with a group of colonels, seized power in 1944, won the elections of 1946 and established a popular dictatorship with the support of the army, nationalists, and the Roman Catholic Church. His second wife, the popular Eva Duarte de Perón (see under PERÓN, JUAN) won the backing of trade unions; her popularity among the industrial working class was the major pillar of support for the Perón regime. Her death in 1952, followed by an economic downturn, led to Perón's ouster (1955) by the military. Government during the next 18 years had to contend with the continuing popularity of the Peronist movement. In 1973, Perón returned from exile and won election as president. His third wife, Isabel Martínez de Perón, was elected vice president; she succeeded him upon his death in 1974. During her presidency terrorism by the left and right grew, and inflation worsened; in 1976 she was overthrown in a military coup that established a repressive military junta. In 1982, with Gen. Leopoldo Galteri as president, Argentina occupied the FALKLAND ISLANDS, which it had long disputed with Britain. The Argentine defeat in the ensuing war with Britain led to Galtieri's resignation and to strong public criticism of the military government. In the late 1980s, the government was unable to curb an annual inflation rate of more than 1000%, and in 1989, a Peronist, Carlos Saúl Menem, was elected president. Menem reduced the government's regulation of the economy, privatized state-owned enterprises, and introduced austerity measures to control persistent inflation.

argon (Ar), gaseous element, discovered in 1894 by Sir William RAMSAY and Lord RAYLEIGH. An odorless, tasteless, and colorless INERT GAS, it makes up 0.93% of the atmosphere by volume. Argon is used in light bulbs and neon signs, in refining reactive elements, for protection in arc welding, and in the production of crystals for use in semiconductor devices. See ELEMENT (table); PERIODIC TABLE.

Argonauts: see GOLDEN FLEECE; JASON.

Argus or **Argos,** in Greek mythology. **1** Many-eyed monster who guarded IO after she was changed into a heifer. **2** Builder of the ship on which JASON and the Argonauts sailed in quest of the GOLDEN FLEECE.

Århus, city (1987 pop. 255,932), central Denmark, on Århus Bay. Founded by the 10th cent., it is a prosperous cultural center and a commercial and shipping center, manufacturing beer, metals, textiles, and machinery. Among its landmarks are its theater and the 12th-cent. Cathedral of St. Clemens.

aria, elaborate and often lengthy solo song with instrumental accompaniment, especially in an OPERA, ORATORIO, or CANTATA. The three-part *aria da capo* was developed in the 17th and 18th cent. by A. SCARLATTI, J.S. BACH, and others. The arias of W.A. MOZART often combined dramatic and lyrical elements. Later composers fused aria and RECITATIVE.

Ariadne, in Greek mythology, Cretan princess; daughter of MINOS and Pasiphaë. With her help THESEUS killed the MINOTAUR and escaped from the Labyrinth. He left with her but deserted her at Naxos. There she married DIONYSUS, who is said to have set her bridal crown among the stars.

Arianism, Christian heresy arising from the teaching of the Alexandrian priest Arius, c.256–336. To Arius, Jesus was a supernatural being, not quite human, not quite divine, who was created by God. Arianism spread and was condemned by the First Council of NICAEA (325). The conflict went on, however, and several bishops and emperors sided with Arius. The Catholic tenets of Rome and ATHANASIUS finally triumphed, and the First Council of CONSTANTINOPLE (381) upheld the decrees of Nicaea.

Arias Sánchez, Oscar, 1941–, Costa Rican politician. He was minister of national planning (1972–77), a congressman (1978–82), and president (1986–90). Intent on preserving Costa Rica's neutrality and restoring regional peace, he refused to allow Nicaraguan contras to operate from Costa Rica and negotiated an accord (1987) with other Latin American leaders that called for a cease-fire and government talks with opposition groups. In 1987 he was awarded the Nobel Peace Prize.

Ariel, in astronomy, natural satellite of URANUS.

Arion, Greek poet, fl. 7th cent.? B.C., inventor of the DITHYRAMB. His rescue from drowning by a dolphin charmed by his music is told by HERODOTUS.

Ariosto, Ludovico, 1474–1533, Italian epic and lyric poet, in the service of the Duke of Ferrara. His *Orlando Furioso* (1532), an epic treatment of the ROLAND story intended to glorify the ESTE family, greatly influenced SHAKESPEARE, MILTON, and BYRON.

Aristarchus of Samos, fl. c.310–c.230 B.C., Greek astronomer. He is said to have been the first to propose a heliocentric theory of the universe, anticipating Copernicus by 18 centuries (see COPERNICAN SYSTEM). His only surviving work, *On the Sizes and Distances of the Sun and Moon,* is celebrated for its geometric argument, even though crude observation data led to faulty estimates.

Aristide, Jean-Bertrand [ä″rēstēd′], 1953–, president of Haiti (1990–91). A radical Catholic priest who opposed the DUVALIER dictatorship, he won the 1990 presidential election by a landslide. Ousted by the military seven months after taking office, he went into exile. An agreement (1993) called for his return to power in Oct. 1993.

Aristogiton: see HARMODIUS AND ARISTOGITON.

Aristophanes [ăr″ĭstŏf′ənēz], b. c.448 B.C., d. after 388 B.C., Athenian comic poet, the greatest ancient writer of COMEDY. His plays mix political, social, and literary SATIRE. Invective, burlesque, and direct attack on persons made them suitable for the festival of DIONYSUS. Typically, his characters act naturally in preposterous circumstances; his language is economical and beautiful. Eleven surviving plays include *The Clouds, The Wasps, Lysistrata,* and *The Frogs*.

Aristotle, 384–322 B.C., Greek philosopher. He studied (367–347 B.C.) under PLATO and later (342–339 B.C.) tutored ALEXANDER THE GREAT at the Macedonian court. In 335 B.C. he opened a school in the Athenian Lyceum. During the anti-Macedonian agitation after Alexander's death Aristotle fled (323 B.C.) to Chalcis, where he died. His extant writings, largely in the form of lecture notes made by his students, include the *Organum* (treatises on logic); *Physics; Metaphysics; De Anima* [on the soul]; *Nicomachean Ethics* and *Eudemian Ethics; Politics; De Poetica; Rhetoric;* and works on biology and physics. Aristotle held philosophy to be the discerning, through the use of systematic LOGIC as expressed in SYLLOGISMS, of the self-evident, changeless first principles that form the basis of all knowledge. He taught that knowledge of a thing requires an inquiry into causality and that the "final cause"—the purpose or function of the thing—is primary. The highest good for the individual is the complete exercise of the specifically human function of rationality. In contrast to the Platonic belief that a concrete reality partakes of a form but does not embody it, the Aristotelian system holds that, with the exception of the Prime Mover (God), form has no separate existence but is immanent in matter. Aristotle's work was lost following the decline of Rome but was reintroduced to the West through the work of Arab and Jewish scholars, becoming the basis of medieval SCHOLASTICISM.

arithmetic, branch of mathematics (and the part of ALGEBRA) concerned with the fundamental operations of addition, subtraction, multiplication, and division of numbers. Conventionally, the term *arithmetic* covers simple numerical skills used for practical purposes, e.g., computation of areas or costs. The study of arithmetic also deals abstractly with the laws and properties (e.g., the ASSOCIATIVE LAW, the COMMUTATIVE LAW, and the DISTRIBUTIVE LAW) governing the various operations.

arithmetic progression: see PROGRESSION.

Arizona, state in the SW U.S.; bordered by Utah (N), New Mexico (E), Mexico (S), and, across the Colorado R., Nevada and California (W).

Area, 113,909 sq mi (295,024 sq km). *Pop.* (1990) 3,665,228, a 34.9% increase over 1980 pop. *Capital,* Phoenix. *Statehood,* Feb. 14, 1912 (48th state). *Highest pt.,* Humphreys Peak, 12,633 ft (3,853 m); *lowest pt.,* Colorado R., 70 ft (21 m). *Nickname,* Grand Canyon State. *Motto, Ditat Deus* [God Enriches]. *State bird,* cactus wren. *State flower,* blossom of the saguaro cactus. *State tree,* paloverde. *Abbr.,* Ariz.; AZ.

Land and People. Most of northern and eastern Arizona lies within the arid COLORADO PLATEAU region, and most of the south and west in the flat desert basins (many now irrigated) and jagged mountain ranges of the Basin and Range region. Major rivers are the COLORADO, Gila, and Salt. A total of 20,036,000 acres (8,108,000 hectares), or 38% of all U.S. Native American tribal lands, are in Arizona; the largest are the NAVAHO, HOPI, Fort APACHE, and Papago (TOHONO O'ODHAM) reservations. PHOENIX, TUCSON, and TEMPE are the principal cities; about 87% of the population lives in urban areas. In 1990 Arizona was 81% white, 19% Native American and others. The state has the third largest Native American population, after Oklahoma and California.

Economy. Manufacturing is the leading economic activity, with electronic and aerospace products, primary and fabricated metals, processed foods, and electrical and transportation equipment among the major manufactures. Printing and publishing are also important. Cotton is the chief irrigated crop, and some lettuce, hay, oranges, and grapefruit are also grown in the subtropical south. Large cattle and sheep ranges produce livestock and dairy products. Arizona is a leading U.S. producer of copper, and there is a small lumber industry. The state is also known for its Native American handicrafts. The hot, dry climate, spectacular scenic attractions such as the GRAND CANYON and the Petrified Forest (see NATIONAL PARKS, table), and many Native American reservations attract large numbers of tourists.

Government. The constitution provides for a governor and for a state legislature of 30 senators and 60 representatives elected for two-year terms. Arizona elects two senators and six representatives to the U.S. Congress and has eight electoral votes.

History. Early Spanish explorers included CABEZA DE VACA (1536), Marcos de Niza (1539), and Francisco Vásquez de CORONADO (1540), and several Spanish missions were founded in the late 17th cent. The region came under Mexican control after 1821, and lands north of the Gila R. passed to the U.S. territory of New Mexico at the end of the MEXICAN WAR (1846–48). Lands between the Gila R. and today's southern boundary were added through the GADSDEN PURCHASE (1853). Arizona became a separate territory in 1863, and settlement accelerated after the surrender (1866) of GERONIMO ended 25 years of Apache wars. Rapid development of irrigated agriculture, spurred by construction of the Roosevelt dam (1911), and industrial and urban expansion beginning during World War II strained limited water resources. A 1963 U.S. Supreme Court decision to increase Arizona's allocation of water from the Colorado R. led to construction (1974–91) of the huge Central Arizona project, which diverts water from the Colorado at Parker Dam and carries it across Arizona for use on farms and in the Phoenix-Tucson area.

ark, in the BIBLE. **1** Boat built by NOAH at God's command to save his family and certain animals from the Flood. **2** Ark of the Covenant, the sacred, gold-covered, wooden chest, identified by the Hebrews with God. Touching it meant death. It was carried into battle, as its presence implied victory, and was once captured by the Philistines. Restored many years later, it was placed in SOLOMON's temple.

Arkansas, state in the S central U.S.; bordered by Tennessee and Mississippi, across the Mississippi R. (E), Louisiana (S), Texas and Oklahoma (W), and Missouri (N).

Area, 53,104 sq mi (137,539 sq km). *Pop.* (1990) 2,350,725, an 2.9% increase over 1980 pop. *Capital,* Little Rock. *Statehood,* June 15, 1836 (25th state). *Highest pt.,* Magazine Mt., 2,753 ft (840 m); *lowest pt.,* Ouachita R., 55 ft (17 m). *Nickname,* Land of Opportunity. *Motto, Regnat Populus* [The People Rule]. *State bird,* mockingbird. *State flower,* apple blossom. *State tree,* pine. *Abbr.,* Ark.; AR.

Land and People. The higher terrain of the Ozark Plateau (see OZARKS) and Ouachita Mts., in the west, give way to lowlands in the east, drained mostly by the ARKANSAS and Ouachita rivers. There are many lakes, and the mineral waters of Hot Springs are preserved in the NATIONAL PARK there (see table), contributing to the state's well-developed tourist industry. Arkansas has long, hot summers and mild winters. About 53% of the population lives in urban areas. LITTLE ROCK is the leading city; other important cities are FORT SMITH and PINE BLUFF. In 1990 the population was 83% white and 16% African American.

Economy. Manufacturing, the leading contributor to the state's income, includes processed foods (especially beef and poultry), electrical equipment, chemicals, and paper and wood products. Leading agricultural commodities are soybeans, rice, cotton, poultry (Arkansas is the leading U.S. producer), and cattle. Although it boasts the country's only active diamond mine, Arkansas's most valuable mineral resources are oil, bromine, natural gas, and bauxite.

Government. According to the constitution of 1874, the government is headed by a governor elected to a two-year term. The legislature consists of 35 senators serving four-year terms and 100 representatives elected to two-year terms. Arkansas sends two senators and four representatives to the U.S. Congress and has six electoral votes.

History. The Quapaw, OSAGE, and Caddo inhabited the region when it was visited by Spanish explorers, including Hernando DE SOTO (1541–42). The French explorer Robert Cavelier, sieur de LA SALLE, founded (1682) the first permanent white settlement, Arkansas Post. In 1803 the area passed from France to the U.S. through the LOUISIANA PURCHASE, and many new settlers established cotton plantations. Arkansas soon became a separate territory (1819) and a state (1836). The state seceded from the Union in 1861 and joined the CONFEDERACY. It was readmitted to the Union in 1868 and experienced a turbulent RECONSTRUCTION era. Around the turn of the century its population grew substantially. The discovery of oil in 1921 resulted in new prosperity for Arkansas, but farmers were severely affected by the GREAT DEPRESSION of the 1930s. In 1957 Gov. Orval Faubus became the focus of world attention when he resisted the federal desegregation of Little Rock's public schools. The enrollment of African-American students was subsequently enforced by the federal government. In 1981 Arkansas passed a controversial law mandating the equal teaching of CREATIONISM and EVOLUTION in the public schools. The law was overturned in federal court the following year. In 1992 Gov. Bill CLINTON became the first Arkansas native to be elected U.S. president.

Arkansas, river, flowing SE c.1,450 mi (2,330 km) from the Rocky Mts. of Colorado to the Mississippi R. in SE Arkansas. Controlled by more than 25 dams, it is navigable to Tulsa, Okla.

Arkhangelsk [ərkhän'gĭlsk] or **Archangel,** city (1990 est. pop. 418,000), NW European Russia, on the Northern Dvina near its mouth on the White Sea. It is a leading port; though icebound much of the year, it can be made usable by icebreakers. Major exports are timber and wood products; other industries are fishing, shipbuilding, and pulp and paper. Founded as Novo-Kholmogory (1584), it was renamed (1613) for the monastery of the Archangel Michael. An Allied supply port in World Wars I and II, it was occupied (1918–20) by Allied and anti-Bolshevik forces.

Arkwright, Sir Richard, 1732–92, English inventor. His construction (1769) of a SPINNING machine, the water frame, was an early step in the INDUSTRIAL REVOLUTION. Arkwright's spinning machine led to the establishment of huge cotton mills and to the beginnings of the factory system.

Arles, kingdom of, was formed in 933, when Rudolf II united his kingdom of Transjurane BURGUNDY with Provence or Cisjurane Burgundy. Holy Roman Emperor CONRAD II annexed the kingdom to the empire in 1034, but its component parts gradually broke away. In 1378 Holy Roman Emperor CHARLES IV ceded the realm to the French dauphin (later CHARLES VI), and the kingdom for all practical purposes ceased to exist.

Arlington, county (1990 pop. 170,936), N Va., across the POTOMAC R. from WASHINGTON, D.C. A residential suburb of Washington, the county is governed as a single unit without subdivisions. Within its boundaries are Arlington National Cemetery, the PENTAGON, Marymount Univ., and Washington National Airport. Arlington was part of the DISTRICT OF COLUMBIA from 1790 to 1847.

Arlington, city (1990 pop. 261,721), Tarrant co., N Tex., midway between DALLAS and FORT WORTH; inc. 1884. Located in a rapidly growing industrial area, it produces automobiles, containers, rubber and plastic products, and other manufactures. Arlington is the home of Six Flags over Texas, a huge theme park, and the Texas Rangers baseball team. The city has a branch of the Univ. of Texas.

Armada, Spanish, 1588, fleet launched by PHILIP II of Spain for the invasion of England. Commanded by the duque de Medina Sidonia and consisting of 130 ships and a force of 30,000, the Armada was delayed by storms and finally set sail from Lisbon in May. The English fleet, under Charles Howard, sailed from Plymouth and inflicted long-range damage on the Armada but did not break its formation. Anchoring off Calais, Medina Sidonia intended to pick up Alessandro FARNESE's army in Flanders and convey it to England. But on Aug. 7 the English sent fire ships into the anchorage to scatter the Armada and then attacked the fleeing ships at close range off Gravelines. The battered Armada escaped northward, sailed around Scotland and Ireland while buffeted by storms, and returned to Spain after losing about half its ships.

armadillo, armored MAMMAL (order Edentata) found in the S U.S. and Latin America. The head and body are almost entirely covered by an armor of bony, horny plates. Armadillos are usually nocturnal and, although omnivorous, eat mostly insects. The largest species, the giant armadillo (*Priodontes giganteus*), is about 4 ft (120 cm) long; the smallest, the fairy armadillo (*Chlamyphorus truncatus*), about 6 in. (15 cm) long. The only U.S. species is the nine-banded armadillo (*Dasypus novemcinctus*), about 30 in. (76 cm) long and weighing about 15 lb (6.4 kg).

armature: see GENERATOR; MOTOR, ELECTRIC.

Armenia, officially Republic of Armenia, republic (1992 est. pop. 3,416,000), 11,500 sq mi (29,785 sq km), SW Asia, in the S Caucasus; formerly a constituent republic of the USSR. It is a mountainous country bounded by Georgia (N); Turkey (W); Azerbaijan (W and E); and Iran (S). YEREVAN is the capital; other major cities include Giumri (Leninakan), Vanadzor (Kirovakan), and St. Etchmiadzin. Major bodies of water are Lake SEVAN and the Araks and Razdan rivers. Industrial products include chemicals, metals, electrical equipment, and machinery. Grapes, cotton, and tobacco are

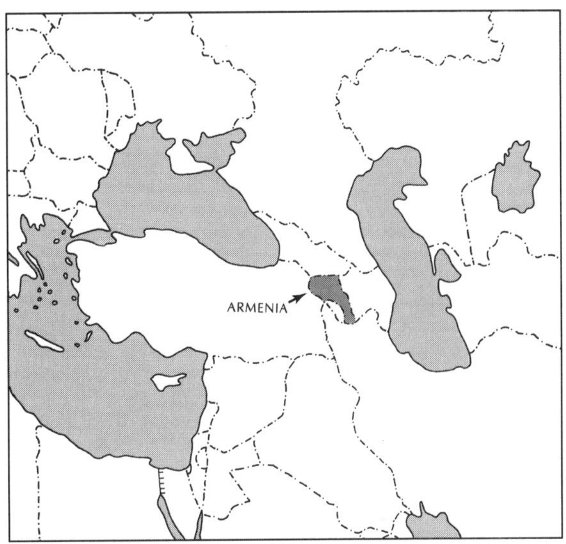

major agricultural products, and food-processing, wine-making, fishing and mining of copper, molybdenum, zinc, lead, iron, and other ores are important. In addition to the Armenian majority, there are Azeri, Russian, and Kurdish minorities. The official language is Armenian. The predominant religion is the Armenian Apostolic church, an Monophysitic Christian church (see MONOPHYSITISM.

History. Modern Armenia occupies the eastern part of ancient region and kingdom of Armenia, which also included NE TURKEY and parts of Iranian Azerbaijan. Under Persian rule (6th–4th cent. B.C.), it was conquered in 330 B.C. by ALEXANDER THE GREAT but after his death fell to Syria. Armenia was independent from 189 B.C. to 67 B.C., when it became tributary to Rome. Christianity was adopted in the 3d cent. A.D.; under Persian rule later in that century many Christians were martyred. Persia and Rome partitioned the kingdom in 387; it achieved autonomy in 886 but was invaded in the mid-11th cent. by the Byzantines and Seljuk Turks. Pushed westward, one group of Armenians founded Little Armenia, in CILICIA. In 1386–94 the Mongols, under TIMUR, seized Greater Armenia and massacred much of the population. The Ottoman Turks invaded in 1405 and by the 16th cent. held all of Armenia. Though most Armenians experienced religious persecution, Armenian merchants played an important role in the economy of the OTTOMAN EMPIRE. Eastern Armenia was long disputed by Turkey and Persia; in 1828 Persia ceded to Russia present-day Armenia. From 1894 on, a plan for Armenian extermination was pursued under Sultan ABD AL-HAMID II, culminating in the massacre of 1915. In 1918 Russian Armenia became independent under German auspices (see BREST-LITOVSK, TREATY OF), but in 1920 an autonomous Greater Armenia was created from the Turkish and Soviet Russian areas. In that year, however, Russian Armenia fell to the Communists and was made a Soviet republic; the 1921 Russo-Turkish Treaty established the present boundaries, ending Armenian independence. From 1920 to 1991 Armenia was a republic in the UNION OF SOVIET SOCIALIST REPUBLICS. In the late 1980s, under Soviet Pres. GORBACHEV's policies of *glasnost* and *perestroika,* Armenians began seeking independence. In a 1991 referendum Armenians voted overwhelmingly for independence from the USSR, and the country joined the newly established COMMONWEALTH OF INDEPENDENT STATES when the USSR collapsed (Dec. 1991). Conflicting claims to NAGORNO-KARABAKH, a largely Armenian territory within neighboring AZERBAIJAN, led to war between Armenia and Azerbaijan over the area by 1992 and an Azerbaijani economic blockade of Armenia. Levon Tar-Petrosian has been president of Armenia since 1991.

Armenian language, member of the Thraco-Phrygian sub-family of the Indo-European family of languages. See LANGUAGE (table).

Arminianism: see ARMINIUS, JACOBUS.

Arminius, Jacobus, 1560–1609, Dutch Reformed theologian; b. Jacob Harmenson. In 1603 he became a professor at the Univ. of

Leiden; there he developed his teaching, called **Arminianism.** As fully formulated after his death by Simon Episcopus, it opposed the Calvinist doctrine of predestination by asserting the compatibility of divine sovereignty and human freedom and by denying the irresistibility of God's grace. The teaching was later adopted by John WESLEY.

Armory Show, art exhibition held in 1913 at the 69th-regiment armory in New York City. Including works of the European avant-garde, e.g., DUCHAMP's *Nude Descending a Staircase,* it was a sensational introduction of modern art into the U.S. One of the most important art shows ever held in the country, it helped to change the direction of American painting.

Armstrong, (Daniel) Louis "Satchmo," 1900–1971, African-American JAZZ trumpeter, singer, and bandleader; b. New Orleans. He became known for improvisational genius and strongly influenced the melodic development of jazz. Armstrong was in large part responsible for the rise of the soloist in jazz.

Armstrong, Edwin Howard, 1890–1954, American engineer and radio inventor; b. N.Y.C. A professor at Columbia Univ. after 1930, he made numerous contributions to the development of RADIO, including the invention of the regenerative circuit (1912); the superheterodyne circuit (1918), the basic circuit of nearly all modern radio receivers; and FREQUENCY MODULATION (1925–33).

Armstrong, Neil Alden, 1930–, American astronaut; b. Wapakoneta, Ohio. He commanded the *Gemini 8* mission (Mar. 16, 1966) and the *Apollo 11* mission (July 16–24, 1969), during which he and Buzz ALDRIN became the first and second persons, respectively, to walk on the moon (see SPACE EXPLORATION, table). He was deputy associate administrator for aeronautics (1970–71) at NASA, taught aeronautical engineering (1971–79) at the Univ. of Cincinnati, and served (1985) on the National Commission on Space.

Armstrong, Samuel Chapman, 1839–93, American educator and philanthropist; b. Hawaiian Islands. Appointed an agent of the Freedmen's Bureau after the Civil War, he realized the need for vocational training of emancipated slaves and helped found (1868) the Hampton Inst., which he headed until 1893, to advance that purpose.

Arnim, Achim or **Joachim von** [är'nĭm], 1781–1831, German writer of the romantic school. He is best remembered for his work with his brother-in-law, Clemens BRENTANO, on the folk-song collection *The Boy's Magic Horn* (1806–8) and for his historical novels, notably *Isabella of Egypt* (1812). His wife, **Bettina von Arnim,** 1785–1859, b. Elisabeth Brentano, was also a writer. She corresponded with BEETHOVEN and GOETHE; her publication of *Goethe's Correspondence with a Child* (1835) reflects her own poetic imagination.

Arnold, Benedict, 1741–1801, American Revolutionary general and traitor; b. Norwich, Conn. After excellent service in the colonial assault on Quebec (1775–76) and the SARATOGA CAMPAIGN, he felt slighted regarding promotion. His plot with John ANDRÉ to betray (1780) the American post at WEST POINT was discovered, but Arnold escaped and later fought for the British.

Arnold, Matthew, 1822–88, English poet and critic; son of Thomas Arnold. He was an inspector of schools (1851–86) and professor of poetry at Oxford (1857–67). Arnold wrote superb poetry, usually dealing with the themes of loneliness and pessimism. Among his best-known verses are "Isolation: To Marguerite" (1852), "The Scholar Gypsy" (1853), and "Dover Beach" (1867). His books of literary criticism include *On Translating Homer* (1861) and *Essays in Criticism* (1865; Ser. 2, 1888). *Culture and Anarchy* (1869) is a volume of social criticism. Arnold stressed the necessity for objectivity and advocated a culture based on the best that has been thought and said in the world.

aromatic compound, any of a large class of organic compounds including BENZENE and compounds that resemble benzene in chemical properties. Aromatic compounds contain unusually stable ring structures, often made up of six carbon atoms arranged hexagonally. Some of the compounds, however, have rings with more or fewer atoms, not necessarily all carbon. Furan, for example, has a ring with four atoms of carbon and one of oxygen. Also, two or more rings can be fused, as in naphthalene. The characteristic properties of the class, notably the stability of the compounds, derive from the fact that aromatic rings permit the sharing of some electrons by all the atoms of the ring, which increases the strength of the bonds.

Aroostook War, brief conflict, 1838–39, between the U.S. and Canada concerning the Maine–New Brunswick border. An agreement (March 1839) averted full-scale war. The boundary was settled (1842) by the WEBSTER-ASHBURTON TREATY.

Arp, Jean or **Hans,** 1887–1966, French sculptor and painter. A member of avant-garde groups in Europe, Arp created abstract, organic, witty works in various media. A monumental wood relief (1950) is at Harvard Univ.

Arrhenius, Svante August [ärā'nēəs], 1859–1927, Swedish chemist. For his theory of electrolytic dissociation, or ionization (see ACIDS AND BASES), he won the 1903 Nobel Prize in chemistry. He also investigated osmosis and toxins and antitoxins. He became (1905) director of the Nobel Institute for Physical Chemistry, Stockholm.

arrhythmia, disturbance in the rate or rhythm of the heartbeat. Arrhythmias can be symptoms of serious heart disorders. Tachycardia, or fast heartbeat, can be precipitated by caffeine, shock, or emotional upset. Bradycardia, or slow heartbeat, is often present in athletes. Flutters and fibrillations, rapid uncoordinated contractions of the heart muscles, usually accompany heart disorders. Atrial fibrillation may be associated with clot formation and a risk of embolus.

arrowroot, plant (genus *Maranta*) of the family Marantaceae, found mainly in warm, swampy forests of the Americas. The term *arrowroot* also applies to the easily digested starch obtained from the true, or West Indian, arrowroot (*M. arundinacea*). Plants from other families produce similar starches, e.g., East Indian arrowroot (GINGER family); Queensland arrowroot (Canna family); Brazilian arrowroot, or tapioca (SPURGE family); and Florida arrowroot, or sago.

arrowworm, common name for Chaetognatha, a phylum of slender-bodied, transparent marine invertebrate animals widely distributed, but preferring warm, shallow seas. Most are less than 1 in. (2.5 cm) long. The head is well-developed, with eyes and other sensory organs, grasping spines, teeth, and a protective hood. Arrowworms reproduce sexually.

Arsaces [är'səsēz], fl. 250 B.C., founder of the Parthian dynasty of the **Arsacids,** which ruled Persia from c.250 B.C. to A.D. 226.

arsenic (As), semimetallic element, first described by ALBERTUS MAGNUS in the 13th cent. Arsenic has several allotropic forms (see ALLOTROPY); the most stable is a silver-gray, brittle, crystalline solid that tarnishes in air. Arsenic ores include realgar and arsenopyrite. Combined with other elements, arsenic forms strong poisons; organic compounds of arsenic were widely used medically to treat syphilis and yaws. The metal is used in the manufacture of lead shot and semiconductor devices. See ELEMENT (table); PERIODIC TABLE.

Artaxerxes [är"təzûrk'sēz], name of several ancient Persian kings. **Artaxerxes I,** d. 425 B.C. (r.464–425 B.C.), was a member of the ACHAEMENID dynasty. Artaxerxes is the Greek form of the Persian name Ardashir. He succeeded his father, Xerxes I, in whose assassination he had no part. The later weakness of the Persian empire is commonly traced to his reign. **Artaxerxes II,** d. 358 B.C. (r.404–358 B.C.), was the son and successor of DARIUS II. CYRUS THE YOUNGER attempted to assassinate him but was crushed (401 B.C.). During his reign the provinces of the empire became restless. His son, **Artaxerxes III,** d. 338 B.C. (r.358–338 B.C.), gained the throne by a general massacre of his brother's family. Throughout his reign he continued a policy of terror, and he was finally poisoned by one of his ministers.

art deco, design style popular during the 1920s and 30s, characterized by slender forms, straight lines, and a sleekness expressive of "modern" technology. The style regained popularity in the 1970s and 80s.

Artemis, in Greek mythology, goddess of the hunt. She was the daughter of ZEUS and Leto and the twin sister of APOLLO. Artemis is associated with chastity, marriage, children, wildlife, and, as a complement to the sun god Apollo, with the moon. The Romans identified her with DIANA.

arteriosclerosis, general term for a condition characterized by thickening, hardening, and loss of elasticity of the walls of the arteries. In its most common form, atherosclerosis, fatty deposits, e.g., CHOLESTEROL, build up on the inner artery walls; in some cases calcium deposits also form. The blood vessels narrow, and blood flow decreases; THROMBOSIS, HEART DISEASE, and STROKE may result. Surgical treatment is sometimes effective, but there is no specific cure. A low-cholesterol diet and control of predisposing factors, such as HYPERTENSION, smoking, DIABETES, and obesity, are usually recommended.

artesian well, deep well drilled into an inclined aquifer (layer of water-bearing porous rock or sediment), where water is trapped under pressure between impervious rock layers. When a well is drilled into the aquifer through the overlying impervious rock, pressure forces water to rise in the well. Artesian water is usually desirable for drinking. In North America, artesian systems supply water to the Great Plains and many East Coast cities. The largest artesian system is in Australia.

Artevelde, Jacob van, c.1290–1345, Flemish statesman. A conflict between the count of Flanders and EDWARD III of England cut off English wool imports, ruining the Flemish weavers and merchants. Ghent rebelled, and Artevelde, as head of its government, signed a commercial treaty with England (1338). In 1340 he had the Flemish towns recognize Edward as king of France and thus suzerain of Flanders. He was killed in a riot. His son, **Philip van Artevelde,** 1340–82, led a weavers' revolt against the count of Flanders (1381), taking Bruges and most of Flanders before being killed by the French.

arthritis, inflammation of one or more joints of the body, usually producing pain, redness, and stiffness. It disables more people than any other chronic disorder. A common form is osteoarthritis, a degenerative disease of the joints that commonly occurs with aging. Rheumatoid arthritis, an AUTOIMMUNE DISEASE of unknown cause, is a progressive, crippling joint disorder most common in women between 25 and 50. Symptomatic treatment for arthritis includes use of heat, physical therapy, and ASPIRIN or anti-inflammatory drugs such as IBUPROFEN; remission of symptoms can sometimes be achieved with gold salts, penicillamine, and short-term CORTISONE. Orthopedic surgery, including artificial joint implantation, may be done in severe cases. See also GOUT.

arthropod, invertebrate animal, having a segmented body covered by a jointed exoskeleton with paired jointed appendages; member of the phylum Arthropoda, the largest and most diverse invertebrate phylum. The exoskeleton is periodically shed (molted) to permit growth and METAMORPHOSIS. Arthropods make up more than 80% (800,000) of all known animal species; they include TRILOBITES, HORSESHOE CRABS, ARACHNIDS, SEA SPIDERS, CRUSTACEANS, INSECTS, CENTIPEDES, and MILLIPEDES.

Arthur, king of Britain: see ARTHURIAN LEGEND.

Arthur, dukes of Brittany. **Arthur I,** 1187–1203?, duke 1196–1203?, was the son of Geoffrey, fourth son of HENRY II of England. After the death of RICHARD I of England, Arthur's claim to the English crown was passed over in favor of his uncle JOHN. Arthur allied himself with PHILIP II of France, who invested Arthur with Richard's fiefs in France. Fighting ensued, and Arthur was captured (1202) by John, who is suspected of murdering him. Arthur's story is told in Shakespeare's *King John*. **Arthur III,** 1394–1458, duke 1457–58, was known as comte de Richemont before his accession. As constable of France in the HUNDRED YEARS WAR, he captured (1436) Paris from the English and helped to regain Normandy for France.

Arthur, Chester Alan, 1830?–86, 21st president of the U.S. (1881–85); b. Fairfield, Vt. A lawyer, he was appointed (1871) collector of the port of New York. His removal (1878) by Pres. HAYES angered Sen. Roscoe CONKLING and other New York Republicans, but they were placated in 1880 by Arthur's nomination as vice president on the Republican ticket with James A. GARFIELD. Succeeding to the presidency after Garfield's assassination, Arthur had an honest, efficient, and dignified administration. He supported the civil service reform act of 1883 and vetoed a Chinese exclusion bill that violated a treaty with China.

Arthurian legend, mass of stories, popular in medieval lore, concerning King Arthur of Britain and his knights. The earliest reference to Arthur is in the Welsh poem *Gododdin* (c.600), although later sources place him at the Battle of Mt. Badon, mentioned by Gildas c.540. In Nennius (c.800) he appears as a Celtic victor over Saxon invaders. The legend was greatly elaborated by GEOFFREY OF MONMOUTH in his *Historia* (c.1135), which represents Arthur as the conqueror of Western Europe. Wace's *Roman de Brut* (c.1155) infuses the story with the spirit of chivalric romance, and the *Brut* of LAYAMON (c.1200) pictures Arthur as national hero. The 12th-cent. French poet CHRÉTIEN DE TROYES introduced in *Perceval* the theme of the quest for the Holy Grail. GOTTFRIED VON STRASSBURG, a medieval German poet, wrote the first great treatment of the TRISTRAM AND ISOLDE story. The Middle English *Sir Gawain and the Green Knight* (c.1370) embodied the ideal of chivalric knighthood. Sir Thomas MALORY's *Morte d'Arthur* (1485) was the last important medieval treatment. Since Malory, the legend has appeared in the work of TENNYSON, SWINBURNE, William MORRIS, T.H. WHITE, and others. It is generally accepted that the Arthurian legend developed out of Celtic mythology, as collected in the Welsh MABINOGION. The stories may have coalesced around Irish hero tales and were probably carried to the Continent by Breton minstrels before 1000. Despite innumerable variations, the basic story has remained the same. Arthur, the illegitimate son of Uther Pendragon, king of Britain, wins recognition after his father's death by removing a sword from a stone. Merlin, the court magician, then reveals his parentage. Reigning at CAMELOT, Arthur proves a mighty and noble king. He possesses the great sword Excalibur, given him by the mysterious Lady of the Lake. His enemies include his sorceress sister, Morgan le Fay, and Sir Mordred, usually his nephew, who fatally wounds him. The dying king is borne away to Avalon, whence he will someday return. Among the knights in Arthur's court are Sir Launcelot and Sir Tristram, both involved in illicit and tragic unions, Launcelot with Arthur's wife, Guinevere, and Tristram with Isolde, the wife of his uncle, King Mark. Other figures include Sir Pelleas and Sir Gawain; Sir Galahad, Launcelot's son; Sir Percivale (or Parsifal); and other knights of the Round Table.

artichoke, name for two plants of the COMPOSITE family, both having edible parts. The French, or globe, artichoke (*Cynara scolymus*), of S Europe, is a thistlelike plant whose immature, globular flower heads are used as vegetables; only the lower parts of the fleshy bracts ("leaves") and the center ("heart") are eaten. The other artichoke plant is the JERUSALEM ARTICHOKE.

artificial insemination, technique of artificially injecting sperm-containing semen from a male into a female to cause pregnancy. The technique is widely used in the propagation of cattle, especially to produce many offspring from one prize bull. Artificial insemination is used in humans when normal fertilization cannot be achieved, as with STERILITY or IMPOTENCE in the male or anatomical disorders in the female (see IN VITRO FERTILIZATION). When combined with centrifugal separation of the sperm, it can also to used to select the sex of an offspring.

artificial intelligence (AI), the use of COMPUTERS to model the behavioral aspects of human reasoning and learning. Research in AI is concentrated in some half-dozen areas. In *problem solving,* one must proceed from a beginning (the initial state) to the end (the goal state) via a limited number of steps; AI here involves an attempt to model the reasoning process in solving a problem, such as the proof of a theorem in EUCLIDEAN GEOMETRY. In *game theory* (see GAMES, THEORY OF), the computer must choose among a number of possible "next" moves to select the one that optimizes its probability of winning; this type of choice is analogous to that of a chess player selecting the next move in response to an opponent's move. In *pattern recognition,* shapes, forms, or configurations of data must be identified and isolated from a larger group; the process here is similar to that used by a doctor in classifying medical problems on the basis of symptoms. *Natural language processing* is an analysis of current or colloquial language usage without the sometimes misleading effect of formal grammars; it is an attempt to model the learning process of a translator faced with the phrase "throw mama from the train a kiss." CYBERNETICS is the analysis of the communication and control processes of biological organisms and their relationship to mechanical and electrical systems; this study could ultimately lead to the development of "thinking" robots (see ROBOTICS). *Machine learning* occurs when a computer improves its performance of a task on the basis of its programmed application of AI principles to its past performance of that task. An outgrowth of AI research has been the EXPERT SYSTEM, a computer program that uses AI techniques to predict the outcome of events or solve problems.

artificial kidney: see DIALYSIS.

artificial life support, systems that use medical technology to aid, support, or replace a vital function of the body that has been seriously damaged. Such techniques include artificial pacemakers, dialysis machines, and respirators. The use of life-support systems to prolong the life of a patient who has suffered apparently irreversible damage to a vital organ system may raise such ethical issues as the quality of life, EUTHANASIA, and the right to die.

artificial respiration, any measure that causes air to flow in and out of a person's lungs when natural breathing is inadequate or ceases. Respiration can be taken over by mechanical devices, e.g., a respirator. In emergency situations, mouth-to-mouth (or, for a small child, mouth-to-nose) procedures are often used. The victim's mouth is cleared of foreign material, and the head is tilted back. Holding the nostrils tightly shut, the person administering artificial respiration places his (or her) mouth over that of the victim and blows air into the lungs, allowing for exhalation after each breath. Twelve vigorous breaths are administered per minute for an adult, twenty shallow breaths per minute for a child.

Artigas, José Gervasio [ärtē'gäs], 1764–1850, Uruguayan independence leader. He joined (1811) the revolution against Spanish rule and became leader in the Banda Orientale (now URUGUAY). Artigas agitated against the territory's annexation (1820) by Brazil and went into exile.

artillery, a term now applied to heavy firearms, as distinguished from SMALL ARMS. It came into use in the mid-14th cent. with the introduction in Europe of GUNPOWDER, which had been discovered many centuries earlier in China. First employed mainly against fortifications, artillery was increasingly used in the field from the early 17th cent. It was characteristically smooth-bore and muzzle-loaded, firing solid, round shot, until the late 19th cent., when breech-loaded, rifled, and shell-firing artillery became standard. Modern artillery includes a variety of long-range guns that fire their shells with rapid muzzle-velocity in a low arc; *howitzers,* which fire on a high trajectory at relatively nearby targets; *antiaircraft guns,* which fire rapidly and at high angles; armor-piercing *antitank guns;* and many field-artillery pieces and small tactical rockets used in support of infantry and other ground operations. Mobility has become a key factor in the usefulness of heavy firearms, most of which now either are self-propelled or can be towed.

art nouveau, decorative art movement begun in Western Europe that lasted from the 1880s to World War I. It was characterized by a richly ornamental, asymmetrical style of whiplash linearity, reminiscent of twining plant tendrils, and was most successful in furniture, jewelry, and book design and illustration. Its themes were symbolic and often erotic. Chief exponents included the illustrators Aubrey BEARDSLEY and Walter Crane in England; the architects Henry van de Velde and Victor HORTA in Belgium; the architect Hector Guimard and the jewelry designer René Lalique in France; the painter Gustav KLIMT in Austria; the architect Antonio GAUDÍ in Spain; the illustrator Otto Eckmann and the architect Peter BEHRENS in Germany; and the glassware designer Louis C. TIFFANY and the architect Louis SULLIVAN in the U.S.

arts and crafts, term for the field of the designing and hand fabrication of functional and decorative objects. The term was invented in late-19th-cent. England to refer to a movement, begun by William MORRIS and others, to revive the hand techniques almost obliterated by industrialization.

Aruba, island (1992 est. pop. 64,700), 69 sq mi (179 sq km), internally self-governing dependency of the Netherlands, in the Leeward Islands off the coast of Venezuela. Oranjestad is the capital. Tourism, oil refining, and offshore financial services are the mainstays of the economy. Part of the NETHERLANDS ANTILLES until 1986 and still linked with them economically, Aruba is scheduled to become independent in 1996.

arum, common name for the Araceae, a family of chiefly tropical and subtropical herbaceous herbs. The characteristic inflorescence consists of a single fleshy spike (spadix), which bears small flowers, and a typically showy flowerlike bract or modified leaf (spathe) surrounding the spadix. The largest plant inflorescence known belongs to the Sumatran krubi (*Amorphophallus titanum*) of this family; its spadix reaches a height of 15 ft (4.6 m). Among other members of the family are the decorative arum lily, or calla (genus *Zantedeschia*); the smaller, showy water arum, or wild calla (*Calla palustris*); the climbing shrub philodendron (genus *Philodendron*), a popular houseplant; and the decorative *Anthurium* and *Caladium.* Some species in this family have large, starchy edible rootstocks (corms). A major food source in the Pacific and E Asia, the corms of elephant's ear, or taro (*Colocasia esculenta*), are the main ingredient of poi. Corms of the jack-in-the-pulpit, or Indian turnip (*Arisaema triphyllum*), and tuckahoe, or Indian bread (*Petandrum* and *Orontium* species) were eaten by natives of E North America.

Aryans, speakers of Indo-European or Indo-Iranian languages. In the 2d millennium B.C., waves of warlike nomadic Aryan tribes spread from S Russia and Turkistan through Mesopotamia and Asia Minor. They invaded India c.1500 B.C., colonizing the PUNJAB. The subsequent Indo-European period was characterized by a pastoral-agricultural economy and the use of bronze objects and horse-drawn chariots. In the 20th cent., NAZI racist propaganda idealized the Aryan conquest and claimed German descent from the Aryans.

As, chemical symbol of the element ARSENIC.

asbestos, common name for any of a group of fibrous silicate minerals resistant to acid and fire. Asbestos usually occurs as veins in rocks and seems to be a product of METAMORPHISM. Chrysotile asbestos ($H_4Mg_3Si_2O_9$), a form of SERPENTINE, the most important commercial asbestos, has curly fibers. Amphibole, the other main type, has needlelike fibers. Asbestos is produced chiefly in Canada; asbestos products include brake and clutch linings, water pipe, and roofing materials. Studies have shown that amphibole asbestos particles in the air can cause lung cancer and the lung disease asbestosis, and many former and all new uses of asbestos in the U.S. have been banned.

Asbury, Francis, 1745–1816, American Methodist bishop; b. England. Arriving as a missionary in 1771, he promoted the CIRCUIT RIDER system as being particularly well suited to American frontier conditions. He became a bishop in 1784.

Ascension, volcanic, largely barren island (1991 est. pop. 1,100), 34 sq mi (88 sq km), in the S Atlantic, part of the British colony of SAINT HELENA. Georgetown is the main settlement. Ascension is the site of a U.S. missile- and satellite-tracking station and space research station.

Ascension, name given to the departure of JESUS from earth. **Ascension Thursday,** a major feast for most Christians, commemorates the event and occurs on the 40th day after Easter.

Asch, Sholem, 1880–1957, American Yiddish novelist and playwright; b. Poland. His writings often depict Jewish life in Europe and the U.S., as in *Three Cities* (1933) and *East River* (1946). Later works, e.g., *Mary* (1949), reflect the common spiritual heritage of Jews and Christians.

Ascham, Roger [ăs'kəm], 1515–68, English humanist. A leading intellectual figure of the Tudor period, he tutored Princess Elizabeth (ELIZABETH I) in the classics and later served as her secretary; he was also Latin secretary to MARY I. He wrote *Toxophilus* (1557), an essay on archery, and *The Scholemaster* (1570), a treatise on the teaching of Latin.

ASCII (American Standard Code for Information Interchange), set of codes used to represent letters, numbers, control characters, and a few symbols, originally designed for teletype systems and widely used in COMPUTERS. The seven-digit (or bit) binary number (see BINARY SYSTEM) set has 128 codes. IBM increased the number of characters to 256 (the IBM extended-ASCII set) by using eight-bit codes when it introduced its personal computer (1981); other operating systems use different eight-bit sets.

Asclepius [ăsklē'pēəs], legendary Greek physician and god of medicine; son of APOLLO and Coronis. The sick were treated in his temples; the serpent and cock were sacred to him.

ascorbic acid: see VITAMIN (table).

ASEAN: see ASSOCIATION OF SOUTHEAST ASIAN NATIONS.

Asgard, in Norse mythology, home of the gods. Also called Aesir, it consisted of luxurious palaces and halls. One of the most beautiful was Valhalla, the hall of dead heroes.

Ásgeirsson, Ásgeir [äs'kĕrsôn], 1894–1972, president of ICELAND (1952–68). He was a member of parliament (1923–52), held various cabinet posts, and served (1946–52) as governor of the International Monetary Fund.

ash, tree or shrub (genus *Fraxinus*) of the OLIVE family, mainly of north temperate regions. The ashes have small clusters of greenish flowers and long-winged, wind-dispersed fruits. The white ash (*F. americana*) is a source of durable hardwood timber used for sporting goods, furniture, and tool handles; the blue ash (*F. quadrangulata*) provides a blue dye. The mountain ash and prickly ash are not true ashes.

Ashanti or **Asante,** historic and present-day region in central GHANA, inhabited by the Ashanti, one of Ghana's major ethnic groups. In the 17th cent. the Ashanti confederation was forged, with its capital at KUMASI and with the chieftain of the Oyoko clan as king. Ashanti came into conflict with the British colonies along the coast, and the Anglo-Ashanti wars (19th cent.) resulted in the dissolution of the confederation in 1896. In 1901 Ashanti became part of the British colony of the Gold Coast. The people are noted for their goldwork and colorful kente cloth. (See also GHANA, ancient empire.)

Ashbery, John, 1927–, American poet and art critic; b. Rochester, N.Y. His poems are experimental, narrative, and strongly visual. His collections include *Some Trees* (1956), *Self-Portrait in a Convex Mirror* (1975; Pulitzer), *Shadow Train* (1981), and *April Galleons* (1987).

ashcan school: see EIGHT, THE.

Ashe, Arthur (Robert), 1943–93, American tennis player; b. Richmond. He was the first African-American man to win the U.S. Open (1968), the Australian Open (1970), and Wimbledon (1975). In the late 1960s he became active in human rights issues, particularly opposing racial discrimination. He also campaigned for AIDS-related causes after his contraction of AIDS became known in 1992. He wrote *A Hard Road to Glory* (1988), a history of blacks in sports.

Asher: see ISRAEL, TRIBES OF.

Ashgabat or **Ashkhabad,** city (1989 pop. 398,000), capital and largest city of Turkmenistan, S central Asia. Ashgabat has textile, motion picture, and machine-building industries. Founded by Russia in 1881 as a fort, the city was virtually destroyed in 1948 by an earthquake.

Ashton, Sir Frederick, 1906–1988, British choreographer and dancer; b. Ecuador. He studied in England with Léonid MASSINE and Maria Rambert. He joined (1935) the Sadler's Wells Ballet (now the Royal Ballet) as choreographer and later became director (1963–70). His precise, lyrical works include *Cinderella, Ondine,* and *A Month in the Country*.

Ashurbanipal: see ASSURBANIPAL.

Ashurnasirpal II [ä″sho͝ornä′zĭrpäl], d. 860? B.C., king of ancient ASSYRIA (884–860? B.C.). He conquered considerable territory and helped to create a centralized state.

Ash Wednesday: see LENT.

Asia, the world's largest continent, c.17,139,000 sq mi (44,390,000 sq km), joined in the west with Europe (which may be considered a peninsula of Asia) to form the great Eurasian land mass. It ranges in elevation from 29,023 ft (8,846 m) at Mt. EVEREST, the world's highest mountain, to 1,292 ft (394 m) below sea level at the DEAD SEA, the world's lowest point. It is traversed from east to west by a massive central highland region containing the Tibetan Plateau, the HIMALAYAS, the HINDU KUSH, and other great mountain systems. The continent has every type of climate, from tropical to polar and from desert to rainy. The countries of Asia are Afghanistan, Armenia, Azerbaijan, Bahrain, Bangladesh, Bhutan, Brunei, Cambodia, China, Cyprus, Georgia, India, Indonesia, Iran, Iraq, Israel, Japan, Jordan, Kazakhstan, North Korea, South Korea, Kuwait, Kyrgyzstan, Laos, Lebanon, Malaysia, the Maldives, Mongolia, Myanmar, Nepal, Oman, Pakistan, the Philippines, Qatar, Asian Russia, Saudi Arabia, Singapore, Sri Lanka, Syria, Taiwan, Tajikistan, Thailand, Asian Turkey, Turkmenistan, the United Arab Emirates, Uzbekistan, Vietnam, and Yemen; other political units are Hong Kong and Macao (see separate articles). Asia was the site of some of the world's earliest civilizations and today contains nearly 60% of the world's population. Some of the world's greatest population densities are found in S and E Asia, particularly in the great alluvial river valleys of the GANGES, in India, and the CHANG (Yangtze) and HUANG HE, in China.

Asia Minor, peninsula, W Asia, forming the Asian part of Turkey. Most of the peninsula is occupied by the Anatolian plateau, which is crossed by numerous mountains interspersed with lakes. The first civilization established there (c.1800 B.C.) was that of the HITTITES. The site of TROY and other ancient cities, Asia Minor was subjugated by many invaders, including the Persians, Macedonians, Romans, and Crusaders. Conquered by the Turks between the 13th and 15th cent. A.D., it was part of the OTTOMAN EMPIRE until the establishment of modern Turkey after WORLD WAR I.

Asian drama. Of the three major Asian dramas—Sanskrit, Chinese, Japanese—the oldest is Sanskrit (fl. 1500 B.C.–A.D. 1100).

Sanskrit drama. Sanskrit plays were written for the aristocracy, and involve music, dance, and highly stylized gesture and costume. They are full of religious and supernatural elements. Love and heroism are the most common sources of emotion, with a frequent infusion of awe produced by the supernatural. Indeed, some plays center on the supernatural, while others treat political and historical topics and ordinary people. The language of Sanskrit drama alternates between prose and lyric poetry, and Sanskrit, a literary language, is used only by important characters—inferior characters speak Prakrit, the vernacular. Few Sanskrit plays survive. The earliest known playwright was Bhasa (c.3d cent. A.D.); among the most renowned were KALIDASA, Bhavabhuti (c.8th cent.), and Harsha (7th cent.).

Chinese drama. Written for a popular audience, Chinese drama developed in the Yüan dynasty (1260–1328) from the story cycles of professional storytellers. Acting style, character types, stage properties, and other features are highly conventionalized; until the 19th cent. lines were sung or declaimed. There is, however, great narrative freedom in the plays. Although Chinese drama avoids TRAGEDY, it is frequently infused with pathos. Chinese drama is more social and less concerned with romantic love than Sanskrit, and it often propounds Confucian ethics (see CONFUCIANISM). Among the masterpieces of Chinese drama are *The Western Chamber* by Wang Shi-fu (13th cent.), *The Peony Pavilion* by T'ang Hsien-tsu (16th cent.), and *The Palace of Long Life* by Hung Sheng (17th cent.). After World War I a realistic, spoken drama developed, but under the People's Republic of China the theater (except on Taiwan) has usually devoted itself to propaganda.

Japanese drama. Japanese Nō (or Noh) drama contrasts starkly with Sanskrit and Chinese drama. Short and slow-paced, almost plotless, and tragic in mood, Nō plays are highly stylized in performance, and their language is highly symbolic. Performances integrate song, speech, music, dancing, and mime. A striking feature is the use of wood masks by principal, old, and women characters (Nō uses only male actors). Nō's invention is attributed to Kanami Kiyotsugu (1333–84), while his son Zeami Motokiyo (1363–1443) further refined Nō and wrote such classics as *The Well-Curb* and *The Lady Aoi.* In the 16th and 17th cent. two forms of drama developed that have since surpassed the difficult Nō in popularity: the puppet theater and Kabuki. Both also integrate music, movement, and language and, like Nō, Kabuki uses only male actors. The puppet theater and Kabuki, however, place greater emphasis on excitement and conflict in the plot. The most popular Kabuki play is *The Treasury of Loyal Retainers,* a tale of revenge. The puppet theater reached its peak in the 18th cent. in the work of CHIKAMATSU. In the 20th cent. many Western plays have been produced in Japan, but their influence on Japanese drama has not yet been significant. See also CHINESE LITERATURE; JAPANESE LITERATURE; SANSKRIT LITERATURE.

Asimov, Isaac, 1920–92, American biochemist and author; b. Russia. He taught biochemistry at Boston Univ., but he was best known for his many works of science fiction, e.g., *The Foundation Trilogy* (1951–53).

Asmara or **Asmera,** city (1988 est. pop. 319,000), capital of Eritrea. A commercial and industrial center, it is connected by rail with the Red Sea port of Massawa (Mesewa). Manufactures include textiles and beer. The city was occupied (1889) by the Italians, became (1900) the capital of their colony of Eritrea, and was a base for their invasion of Ethiopia (1935–36). It was taken by the British in 1941. Ethiopia annexed Eritrea in 1962; Asmara was the last part of

Eritrea wrested (1991) by Eritrean guerrillas from Ethiopian control. In 1993 the city became the capital of an independent Eritrea.

Asmoneans: see MACCABEES.

Asoka, d. c.232 B.C., Indian emperor (c.273–c.232 B.C.) of the MAURYA dynasty. One of the greatest of the ancient rulers, he brought nearly all of INDIA together. However, he sickened of war, turned (c.257 B.C.) to BUDDHISM, and thereafter professed nonviolence. He sent Buddhist missionaries as far afield as Greece and Egypt, and was largely responsible for transforming Buddhism into a world religion.

asp, popular name for several species of VIPER, one of which, the European asp (*Vipera aspis*), is native to S Europe. It is also a name for the Egyptian COBRA.

asparagus, perennial garden vegetable (*Asparagus officinalis*) of the LILY family, native to the E Mediterranean area, cultivated from antiquity and now grown in much of the world. Its green stems function as leaves, and the true leaves are reduced to scales. Its edible shoots are cut in the spring. Related species, the asparagus fern (*A. plumosus*) and smilax (*A. asparagoides*), are used for decoration.

Aspen, city (1990 pop. 5,049), alt. 7,850 ft (2,390 m), seat of Pitkin co., S central Colo., on the Roaring Fork R.; inc. 1881. Once a booming silver-mining town, it has been transformed into a modern, cosmopolitan ski resort. The Aspen Inst. for Humanistic Studies and Aspen Music School (which holds an annual music festival) are located there.

aspen: see WILLOW.

asphalt, brownish-black substance used in road making, roofing, and waterproofing. A naturally occurring mixture of HYDROCARBONS, it is commercially obtained as a residue in the DISTILLATION or refining of PETROLEUM. Asphalt varies in consistency from a solid to a semisolid, melts when heated, and has great tenacity. Used in paints and varnishes, it imparts an intense black color. Crushed asphalt rock, a natural mixture of asphalt, sand, and limestone, is used as road-building material.

asphodel, hardy, stemless herbs (genera *Asphodelus* and *Asphodeline*) of the LILY family, native to India and the Mediterranean. Both have showy flower spikes. Other asphodels include the false asphodel (genus *Tofieldia*) and the mountain asphodel, or turkey-beard (*Xerophyllum asphodeliodes*).

Aspin, Les(lie, Jr.), 1938–, U.S. politician and government official; b. Milwaukee, Wis. A Democrat, he was first elected to the U.S. House of Representatives from Wisconsin in 1970. In 1985 he became chairman of the House armed services committee. Aspin served (1993–94) as secretary of defense under Pres. CLINTON.

aspirin, acetyl derivative of salicylic acid, commonly used to lower fever; relieve headache, muscle, and joint pain; and reduce inflammation, particularly that caused by rheumatic fever and arthritis. Known side effects are nausea, vomiting, diarrhea, and gastrointestinal bleeding. ACETAMINOPHEN (Tylenol) is often substituted for aspirin. Because of aspirin's ability to inhibit the formation of blood clots, it is also used in low doses to prevent heart attack and stroke. See also ANALGESIC.

Asquith, Herbert Henry: see OXFORD AND ASQUITH, HERBERT HENRY ASQUITH, 1ST EARL OF.

ass, hoofed, herbivorous MAMMAL (genus *Equus*), related to, but smaller than, the HORSE. Unlike the horse, the ass has a large head, long ears, and small hooves. The two living species are the sandy-colored wild Asian ass (*E. hemonius*), now endangered, and the larger, gray African ass (*E. asinus*), from which domestic donkeys are descended.

Assad, Hafez al-, 1928–, president of SYRIA (1971–). He was defense minister before leading the 1970 military coup that made him premier and then president. A strong anti-Zionist, he is a major supporter of the PALESTINE LIBERATION ORGANIZATION. In 1976 he sent Syrian troops as a peacekeeping force to LEBANON, where they have become a force in Lebanese politics.

Assamese [ăs″əmez′], language belonging to the Indic group of the Indo-Iranian subfamily of the Indo-European family of languages. See LANGUAGE (table).

assault, in law, intentional attempt to use violence to do bodily harm to another. The victim must reasonably believe the perpetrator capable of such violence. See BATTERY.

assemblage: see COLLAGE.

Assemblies of God: see PENTECOSTALISM.

Assis, Joaquim Maria Machado de: see MACHADO DE ASSIS, JOAQUIM MARIA.

Association of Southeast Asian Nations (ASEAN), organization established by the Bangkok Declaration (1967), linking the nations of Indonesia, Malaysia, Philippines, Singapore, and Thailand; Brunei joined in 1984. Headquarters are in Jakarta. It seeks to promote socioeconomic progress and regional stability through cooperation in banking, trade, technology, agriculture, industry, and tourism.

associative law, in mathematics, law holding that for a given operation combining three quantities, two at a time, the initial pairing is arbitrary. Addition and multiplication are associative; thus $(a + b) + c = a + (b + c)$ and $(a \times b) \times c = a \times (b \times c)$ for any three members *a, b, c*. Subtraction and division, however, are not associative.

assonance: see RHYME.

Assurbanipal or **Ashurbanipal** [ä″so͝orbä′nēpäl, ä″sho͝or–], d. 626? B.C., king of ancient ASSYRIA (669–633 B.C.), son and successor of Esar-Haddon. He was the last of the great kings of Assyria. Under him Assyria reached the height of sumptuous living, and art and learning flourished. A few years after his reign ended, Assyria succumbed to the Medes and the Persians. His great expenditures in wars to preserve the state contributed to its collapse.

Assyria, ancient empire of W Asia, originating around the city of Ashur, on the upper Tigris R., S of its later capital, NINEVEH. At first a small Semitic city-state, Assyria flourished briefly under Tiglathpileser I (d. c.1074 B.C.). Its real importance, however, began in the 9th cent. with the conquests of ASHURNASIRPAL II, who set up an imperial administration. Later kings such as Shalmaneser III, Tiglathpileser III, and Sargon gained hegemony in the Middle East. SENNACHERIB consolidated their holdings, and Esar-Haddon (r.681–668 B.C.) defeated the Chaldaeans and conquered Egypt. Under his successor, ASSURBANIPAL (r.669–633 B.C.), Assyria reached its height of learning, art, and splendor. But Egypt broke away, and Assyria's decline was rapid. Soon after Assurbanipal's death Nineveh was sacked (612 B.C.) and Assyria was absorbed, first by Babylonia and then by the Persian empire.

Assyrian art. An Assyrian artistic style, distinct from that of BABYLONIA, began to emerge c.1500 B.C. and lasted until the fall of NINEVEH in 612 B.C. It took the form of precisely delineated, polychrome carved stone reliefs. These concerned royal affairs, chiefly hunting and war making. Predominance was given to animal forms, particularly horses and lions, which are represented in great detail. Human figures are comparatively rigid and static, but also minutely detailed. Among the best-known Assyrian reliefs are the lion-hunt alabaster carvings showing ASHURNASIRPAL II (9th cent. B.C.) and ASSURBANIPAL (7th cent. B.C.), both of which are in the British Museum. Guardian animals, usually lions and winged beasts with bearded human heads, were sculpted partially in the round for fortified royal gateways. Exquisite examples of Assyrian relief carving may be seen at the British and Metropolitan museums.

Assyrian language, Hamito-Semitic language of ancient times, in the Akkadian group. See LANGUAGE (table).

Astaire, Fred, 1899–1987, American dancer; b. Omaha, Nebr., as Frederick Austerlitz. After dancing in VAUDEVILLE with his sister, Adele, he made many films, often with Ginger Rogers, in which he displayed an elegant style of ballroom dance and tap. He also danced in movies with Eleanor Powell, Rita Hayworth, and Cyd Charisse, and on television with Barrie Chase. His influence on dancing is incalculable. Some classical dancers, notably NUREYEV and BARYSHNIKOV, have acknowledged Astaire's influence on them.

Astarte, Semitic goddess of fertility and love. Dominant in ancient Eastern religions, she was the most important goddess of the Phoenicians, corresponding to the Babylonian ISHTAR and the Greek Aphrodite. See also GREAT MOTHER OF THE GODS.

astatine (At), semimetallic radioactive element, discovered in 1931 by Fred Allison and E.J. Murphy. The heaviest known HALOGEN, it is believed to be similar to iodine in its chemical properties. Astatine-211 (half-life: 7.21 hr) is used as a radioactive tracer because it collects in the thyroid gland. See ELEMENT (table); PERIODIC TABLE.

aster, widely distributed, wild and cultivated perennial flowering plants (genus *Aster*) of the COMPOSITE family. Most species have white, pink, blue, or purple flowers that bloom in the fall. The China aster (*Callistephus chinensis*), the common aster of florists and flower gardens, and the golden asters (genus *Chrysopsis*) are in the same family.

asteroid, planetoid, or **minor planet,** small, usually irregularly shaped body orbiting the sun, most often at least partially between the orbits of Mars and Jupiter. Ceres is the largest asteroid (diameter: 470 mi/750 km) and was the first discovered (1801). Of the more than 2,000 asteroids known, most have been discovered photographically; their paths appear as short lines in a time exposure. Asteroids may be fragments of a planet shattered in the remote past; material that failed to condense into a single planet; or material from the nuclei of old comets. The Trojan asteroids revolve in the same orbit as Jupiter, kept by perturbation effects in two groups 60° ahead of and 60° behind Jupiter. A Trojan asteroid has also been found in Mars' orbit. Some asteroids, such as the Apollo asteroids, cross the earth's orbit; they may be the cause of the earth's several meteorite craters and are a possible location for future mining. The space probe Galileo, which passed near and photographed Gaspra (1991) and Ida (1993), provided the first close images of an asteroid.

asthma, chronic respiratory disorder characterized by labored breathing and wheezing resulting from obstructed and constricted air passages. Although asthma usually results from an allergic reaction (see ALLERGY), specific allergens are not always identifiable. Illness and stress may precipitate an attack. The disorder may be controlled through the use of inhaled or oral bronchodilators (albuterol, theophylline), breathing exercises, and, if possible, the identification and avoidance of allergens.

astigmatism, visual defect resulting from irregular curvature of the cornea or lens, preventing light rays from converging on the retina (see EYE). With astigmatism, some light rays focus on the retina, while others focus in front of or behind it. Congenital or caused by disease or injury, astigmatism can occur in addition to FARSIGHTEDNESS and NEARSIGHTEDNESS. It may be alleviated with corrective lenses.

Astor, John Jacob, 1763–1848, American merchant; b. Germany. At 21 he arrived in Baltimore, penniless; later he opened a small fur shop in New York City. Shrewd and ambitious, he became a leader of the China trade. His AMERICAN FUR COMPANY (1808) exercised a virtual monopoly on the fur trade in U.S. territories, and at his death Astor was the wealthiest person in the country. His great-grandson **William Waldorf Astor,** 1st **Viscount Astor,** 1848–1919, b. N.Y.C., was an American-British financier. In 1890 he moved to England, where he contributed huge sums to public causes. He was made a baron in 1916 and a viscount in 1917. His elder son, **Waldorf Astor,** 1879–1952, succeeded him as viscount and married **Nancy Witcher (Langhorne) Astor, Viscountess Astor,** 1879–1964, a British political leader who became the first woman to sit in PARLIAMENT. As a Conservative member (1919–45) she espoused temperance and reforms in women's and children's welfare, and in the 1920s she and her husband were leaders in the "Tory democracy" reform program.

astrolabe, instrument of ancient origin that measured altitudes of celestial bodies and determined their positions and motions. It typically consisted of a wooden or metal disk with the circumference marked off in degrees, suspended from an attached ring. Angular distances were determined by sighting with the alidade—a movable pointer pivoted at the disk's center—and taking readings of its position on the graduated circle. Skilled mariners used astrolabes up to the 18th cent. to determine latitude, longitude, and time of day.

astrology, form of DIVINATION based on the theory that movements of the celestial bodies (stars, planets, sun, and moon) influence human affairs and determine events. The Chaldaeans and Assyrians, believing all events to be predetermined, developed a nondeistic system of divination. The spread of astrological practice was arrested by the rise of CHRISTIANITY, with its emphasis on divine intervention and free will; but in the RENAISSANCE astrology regained popularity, in part due to rekindled interest in science and ASTRONOMY. Christian theologians attacked astrology, and in 1585 SIXTUS V condemned it. At the same time the work of KEPLER and others undermined astrology's tenets, although the practice has continued in the West. Astrology has been utilized by many Hindus for hundreds of years and continues to be relied upon in India today. One's horoscope is a map of the heavens at the time of one's birth, showing the positions of the heavenly bodies in the ZODIAC.

astronaut or **cosmonaut,** crew member on a manned spaceflight mission. The early astronauts and cosmonauts were generally trained aircraft test pilots; later astronauts and cosmonauts, however, have included scientists and physicians. As far as is possible, all conditions to be encountered in space, e.g., the physiological disorientation arising from weightlessness (see SPACE MEDICINE), are simulated in ground training. Using trainers and mock-ups of actual spacecraft, astronauts and cosmonauts rehearse every maneuver from liftoff to recovery; every conceivable malfunction and difficulty is anticipated and prepared for. Prominent Soviet and Russian cosmonauts include Yuri GAGARIN, Valentina TERESHKOVA, and Aleksei LEONOV. Prominent U.S. astronauts include Alan SHEPARD, John GLENN, Edward WHITE, Neil ARMSTRONG, Buzz ALDRIN, and John Young.

astronomical coordinate systems, four basic systems used to indicate the positions of celestial bodies on the celestial sphere. The latter is an imaginary sphere that has the observer at its center and all other celestial bodies imagined as located on its inside surface.

Equatorial. The celestial equator is the projection of the earth's EQUATOR onto the celestial sphere, and the celestial poles are the points where the earth's axis, if extended, intersects the celestial sphere. *Right ascension* (R.A.) is the angle (in hours, minutes, and seconds, with 1 h = 15°) measured eastward from the vernal EQUINOX to the point where the hour circle (the great circle passing through the celestial poles and the body) intersects the celestial equator. *Declination* is the angle (in degrees, minutes, and seconds, as are all other angles defined hereafter) measured north (+) or south (−) along the body's hour circle between the celestial equator and the body.

Horizon or Altazimuth. Altitude is the angle measured above (+) or below (−) the observer's celestial horizon (the great circle on the celestial sphere midway between the points—zenith and nadir—directly above and below the observer) to the body along the vertical circle passing through the body and the zenith. *Azimuth* is the angle measured along the celestial horizon from the observer's celestial meridian (the vertical circle passing through the nearest celestial pole and the zenith) to the point where the body's vertical circle intersects the horizon. The earth's rotation constantly changes a body's altitude and azimuth for an observer.

Ecliptic or Celestial. The ecliptic poles are the two points at which a line perpendicular to the plane of the ECLIPTIC and passing through the earth's center intersects the celestial sphere. *Celestial latitude* is the angle measured north (+) or south (−) from the ecliptic to the body along the latitude circle through the body and the ecliptic poles. *Celestial longitude* is the angle measured along the ecliptic from the vernal equinox to the latitude circle, in the same sense as R.A.

Galactic. The galactic equator is the intersection of the mean plane of our galaxy with the celestial sphere, and the galactic poles are the two points at which a line perpendicular to the mean galactic plane and passing through the earth's center intersects the celestial sphere. *Galactic latitude* is the angle measured north (+) or south (−) from the galactic equator to the body along the great circle passing through the body and the galactic poles. *Galactic longitude* is the angle measured eastward along the galactic equator from the galactic center.

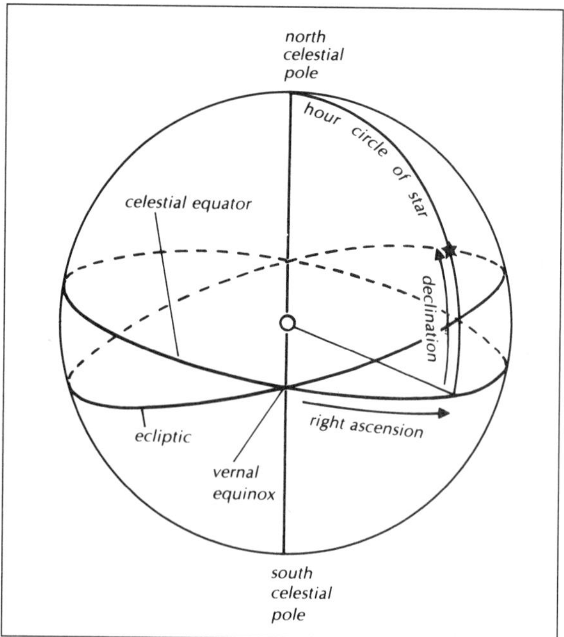

Equatorial astronomical coordinate system

astronomical unit (AU), mean distance between the earth and the sun. One AU is c.92,960,000 mi (149,604,970 km).

astronomy, branch of science that studies the motions and natures of celestial bodies, such as PLANETS, STARS, and GALAXIES; more generally, the study of matter and energy in the universe at large. Astronomy is perhaps the oldest of the pure sciences. In many primitive civilizations the regularity of celestial motions was recognized, and attempts were made to keep records and predict events. Astronomical observations provided a basis for the CALENDAR by determining the units of MONTH and YEAR. Later, astronomy served in navigation and timekeeping. The earliest astronomers were priests, and no attempt was made to separate astronomy from the pseudoscience of ASTROLOGY. Astronomy reached its highest development in the ancient world with the Greeks of the Alexandrian school in the Hellenistic period. ARISTARCHUS OF SAMOS determined the sizes and distances of the MOON and SUN and advocated a heliocentric (sun-centered) cosmology. ERATOSTHENES made the first accurate measurement of the actual size of the earth. The greatest astronomer of antiquity, HIPPARCHUS, devised a geocentric system of cycles and epicycles (a compounding of circular motions) to account for the movements of the sun and moon. Using such a system, PTOLEMY predicted the motions of the planets with considerable accuracy (see PTOLEMAIC SYSTEM). One of the landmarks of the scientific revolution of the 16th and 17th cent. was Nicholas COPERNICUS' revival (1543) of the heliocentric theory (see COPERNICAN SYSTEM). The next great astronomer, Tycho BRAHE, compiled (1576–97) the most accurate and complete astronomical observations yet produced. Johannes KEPLER's study of Brahe's observations led him to the three laws of planetary motion that bear his name (see KEPLER'S LAWS). GALILEO Galilei, the first to make astronomical use of the TELESCOPE, provided persuasive evidence (e.g., his discovery of the four largest moons of JUPITER and the phases of VENUS) for the Copernican cosmology. Sir Isaac NEWTON, possibly the greatest scientific genius of all time, succeeded in uniting the sciences of astronomy and PHYSICS. His laws of motion and theory of universal GRAVITATION, published in 1687, provided a physical, dynamic basis for the merely descriptive laws of Kepler. By the early 19th cent. the science of CELESTIAL MECHANICS had reached a highly developed state through the work of Alexis Clairaut, Jean d'ALEMBERT, Leonhard EULER, Joseph LAGRANGE, Pierre LAPLACE, and others. In 1838, Friedrich BESSEL made the first measurement of the distance to a star (see PARALLAX). Astronomy was revolutionized in the second half of the 19th cent. by techniques based on photography and the SPECTROSCOPE. Interest shifted from determining the positions and distances of stars to studying their physical composition (see STELLAR EVOLUTION). With the construction of ever more powerful telescopes (see OBSERVATORY), the boundaries of the known universe constantly increased. Harlow SHAPLEY determined the size and shape of our galaxy, the MILKY WAY. Edwin HUBBLE's study of the distant galaxies led him to conclude that the universe is expanding (see HUBBLE'S LAW). Various rival theories of the origin and overall structure of the universe, e.g., the big bang and steady state theories, were formulated (see COSMOLOGY). Since the mid-20th cent. the frontiers of astronomy have been expanded by SPACE EXPLORATION and observations in new parts of the spectrum, e.g., gamma-ray astronomy, RADIO ASTRONOMY, ultraviolet astronomy, and X-ray astronomy. The new observational techniques have led to the discovery of strange new astronomical objects, e.g., PULSARS, QUASARS, and black holes (see GRAVITATIONAL COLLAPSE).

astrophysics, application of the theories and methods of physics to the study of stellar structure, STELLAR EVOLUTION, the origin of the SOLAR SYSTEM, and related problems of COSMOLOGY. The distinction between astrophysics and modern ASTRONOMY is disappearing in scientific usage.

Asturias, Miguel Ángel [ästōō'ryäs], 1899–1974, Guatemalan writer. His major works are his novels, including *The President* (1946), a study of a dictatorship; *The Green Pope* (1954); and *The Eyes of the Interred* (1960), about banana exploitation in the Caribbean. He also wrote stories and poetry. He received the 1967 Nobel Prize in literature.

Asturias, autonomous region (1988 est. pop. 1,135,000) and former kingdom, NW Spain, S of the Bay of Biscay. The major occupations are the mining of coal, iron, and other resources; steel-making; cattle-raising; fishing; and the growing of apples for cider. When the MOORS conquered 8th-cent. Spain, Christian nobles fled to the Asturian mountains, formed a kingdom, and began the long reconquest of Spain. In the 10th cent. León became the capital of the kingdom, then known as Asturias and León. The kingdom was united (1230) with CASTILE.

Asunción, city (1990 est. pop. 608,000), S Paraguay, capital of Paraguay, on the Paraguay R. It is the nation's principal port and chief industrial and cultural center. Meat-packing is the largest industry. One of the oldest cities in South America, founded in 1537, it retains a colonial aspect. It became a center of early Jesuit missionary activity and was the most important town in the Río de la PLATA region until it was partially eclipsed by BUENOS AIRES during the 18th cent.

Aswan High Dam, one of the world's largest dams, on the Nile R., in Egypt, built (1960–70) c.4 mi (6.4 km) south of the smaller Aswan Dam (completed, 1902; enlarged, 1934). It is 375 ft (114 m) high and 11,811 ft (3,600 m) long. The dam has a hydroelectricity capacity of 10 billion kwh and stores sufficient water in impounded Lake Nasser to irrigate more than 7 million acres (2,809,400 hectares) of farmland. The USSR provided funding and engineers for the project.

asylum, refuge, most often granted by a nation to a fugitive from another nation. It is usually reserved for victims of political, religious, or other discrimination. See also EXTRADITION.

At, chemical symbol of the element ASTATINE.

Atacama, Desert of, extremely arid plateau, c.2,000 ft (610 m) high, in N Chile. It is c.600 mi (970 km) long and has great nitrate and copper wealth. Chile gained sole control of the area from Bolivia in the 1880s (see PACIFIC, WAR OF THE).

Atalanta, in Greek mythology, fleet huntress who joined the Calydonian boar hunt (see MELEAGER). She demanded that each of her suitors race her, the winner to be rewarded with marriage, the losers to die. Hippomenes finally won her by dropping three golden apples that she stopped to retrieve.

Atatürk, Kemal, 1881–1938, Turkish leader, founder of modern Turkey, first president of TURKEY (1923–38). Originally known as Mustafa Kemal, he was an army officer who took part (1908) in the Young Turk movement, distinguished himself in World War I, and, after the collapse of Ottoman power, founded the Turkish Nationalist party. With the Allies controlling the government at Constantinople (Istanbul), he set up a rival government at Ankara. He expelled the Greeks who were occupying Anatolia (1921–22), abolished the sultanate (1922), and forced the European powers to recognize the Turkish republic. He ruled for 15 years as a virtual dictator. He instituted widespread internal reforms in his efforts to Westernize his nation; those changes included abolishing the CALIPHATE (1924), which in effect disestablished Islam. In foreign affairs he pursued a moderate policy, maintaining friendly relations with Turkey's neighbors, especially Russia, with whom he established the Balkan Entente.

Atget, Eugène [ätzhĕ'], 1857–1927, French photographer. At 47 he began to produce his evocative record of Paris and its environs. He sold his work to printers and to the Paris historical monuments society. His images of the parks, vendors, bridges, and prostitutes of Paris go beyond documentation.

Athabascan, group of related indigenous North American languages forming a branch of the Nadene linguistic family, or stock. See NATIVE AMERICAN LANGUAGES (table).

Athanasius, Saint, c.297–373, patriarch of ALEXANDRIA (328–73), Doctor of the Church. At the first Council of NICAEA (325) he took part in the debate against the heresy of ARIANISM. He continued to defend the Nicene orthodoxy, especially in *Discourses Against the Arians,* and was exiled from his see five times between 335 and 365. The Athanasian CREED is no longer ascribed to him but to a 4th-cent. Western writer. Feast: May 2.

atheism, denial of the existence of God or gods and of any supernatural existence, to be distinguished from AGNOSTICISM, which holds that the existence cannot be proved. Since the 19th cent. atheism has been professed by many individuals and groups.

Athelstan or **Æthelstan** [both: ăth'əlstən], d. 939, king of WESSEX (924–39). He built his kingdom on foundations laid by his grandfather ALFRED and by 937 he was overlord of all England. Popular and able, he issued laws that attempted to impose royal authority on customary law.

Athena or **Pallas Athena,** in Greek mythology, one of the most important OLYMPIAN deities, sprung from the forehead of ZEUS. She was the goddess of war and peace, a patron of arts and crafts, a guardian of cities (notably Athens), and the goddess of wisdom.

Her most important temple was the PARTHENON and her primary festival the Panathenaea. A virgin goddess, Athena is represented in art as a stately figure, armored, and wielding her breastplate, the aegis. The Romans identified her with MINERVA.

Athens, city (1981 pop. 885,737), capital of Greece, E central Greece. Greater Athens, a transportation hub including the Aegean port of PIRAIÉVS, accounts for most of the country's industry, including textiles, machine tools, and ships. Tourism is also important. Early Athens, the center of ancient Greek civilization, was rigidly governed by aristocratic archons until the reforms of SOLON (594 B.C.) and CLEISTHENES (506 B.C.) established a democracy of its freemen. It emerged from the PERSIAN WARS (500–449 B.C.) as the strongest Greek city-state, and reached its cultural and imperial zenith in the time of PERICLES (443–429 B.C.). Its citizens included SOCRATES, AESCHYLUS, SOPHOCLES, and EURIPIDES. After defeat by its arch-rival Sparta in the PELOPONNESIAN WAR (431–404 B.C.) it began a long decline that continued under the Macedonians and Romans; yet it could still boast such citizens as ARISTOTLE, ARISTOPHANES, and PLATO. Captured (395 A.D.) by Visigoths, it became the capital of the BYZANTINE EMPIRE, then came in turn under French, Spanish, and Ottoman Turkish rule before becoming (1834) the capital of newly independent Greece. The city escaped damage in World War II. The first modern OLYMPIC GAMES were held there in 1896. Overlooking the city is its foremost landmark, the ACROPOLIS, where the ruins of the PARTHENON, the Propylaea, and the ERECHTHEUM are located.

Athens, city (1990 pop. 45,734), seat of Clarke co., NE Ga., on the Oconee R., in a piedmont area; inc. 1806. It was founded as the site of the Univ. of Georgia and has become a research center. Industries include poultry processing and the manufacture of clocks, electronic equipment, and textiles. The city has many fine CLASSIC REVIVAL houses.

athlete's foot: see RINGWORM.

Athos or **Akte,** peninsula, NE Greece, in the Aegean Sea. At its southern tip is **Mount Athos,** also called Hagion Oros, a religious community (c.30 sq mi/80 sq km) of about 20 Eastern Orthodox monasteries of the Order of St. Basil. Founded c.963, it enjoyed administrative independence under the Byzantine and Ottoman empires and was made (1927) a theocratic republic under Greek suzerainty. Women and female animals are barred.

Atlanta, capital and largest city (1990 pop. 394,017; met. area 2,833,511) of Georgia, seat of Fulton co.; settled 1837, inc. as a city 1847. Located in one of America's fastest-growing urban areas, it is the largest commercial, industrial, and financial center in the SE U.S. and the largest city in Georgia, as well as a transportation hub and a convention center. Many facilities of the federal government are located in the area, which also produces textiles, chemicals, automobiles, aircraft, clothing, and a wide variety of other goods. The city is also a center of international trade and commerce. Atlanta was captured and burned (1864) by Gen. William T. SHERMAN; rebuilt, it prospered and became the state capital in 1868. Among its educational institutions are Emory Univ., the Georgia Inst. of Technology, and Atlanta Univ. Points of interest include the Atlanta Memorial Arts Center, Grant Park, the Fernbank Museum of Natural History, and the grave of Martin Luther KING, Jr. Atlanta will be the site of the 1996 summer Olympic games.

Atlanta campaign, May–Sept. 1864, of the U.S. CIVIL WAR. W.T. SHERMAN concentrated Union forces around Chattanooga, Tenn., and on May 6 moved south with two objectives: to destroy J.E. JOHNSTON's Confederate army and to capture ATLANTA. Sherman repeatedly outflanked the Confederates, forcing them back to the Chattahoochee R. by July. J.B. HOOD, who had replaced Johnston, counterattacked but failed to halt the Union advance. Atlanta's communications were cut on Sept. 1, and Hood withdrew that night. Sherman took the city on Sept. 2.

Atlantic Charter, program of peace aims enunciated on Aug. 14, 1941, by U.S. Pres. F.D. ROOSEVELT and British Prime Min. Winston CHURCHILL. Included among the aims was the list of human rights known as the FOUR FREEDOMS.

Atlantic City, city (1990 pop. 37,986), SE N.J., an Atlantic resort and convention center; inc. 1854. On Absecon Island, a sandbar 10 mi (16 km) long, it was a fishing village until 1854, when the railroad began to transform it into a fashionable resort. It is known for its 6-mi (9.7-km) boardwalk, its convention hall, and its Steel Pier (built 1898; burned 1982). After the state legalized casino gambling there (1976), the city's economy partially revived.

Atlantic Ocean, world's second largest ocean, c.31,800,000 sq mi (82,362,000 sq km), separating North and South America from Europe and Africa. It is narrowest (c.1,600 mi/2,575 km) off NE Brazil and deepest (c.28,000 ft/8,530 m) in the Milwaukee Deep, N of Puerto Rico. The generally narrow continental shelf reaches its greatest widths off NE North America, SE South America, and NW Europe. The ocean is divided lengthwise by the Mid-Atlantic Ridge, a submarine mountain range c.300–600 mi (480–970 km) wide that extends c.10,000 mi (16,100 km) from Iceland to near the Antarctic Circle. This ridge, which has a few peaks that emerge as islands, is constantly widening, filling with molten rock, and pushing the bordering continents farther apart (see PLATE TECTONICS).

Atlantis, in Greek mythology, large island in the western sea. PLATO describes it as a UTOPIA destroyed by an earthquake. Questions as to its existence have provoked speculation over the centuries. One theory holds that it was a part of the Aegean island of THERA that sank c.1500 B.C.

Atlas, in Greek mythology, a TITAN. After the defeat of the Titans by the OLYMPIANS, he was condemned to hold the sky upon his shoulders for all eternity.

Atlas Mountains, mountain system, NW Africa, c.1,500 mi (2,410 km) long. It is widest and most rugged in Morocco, where Jebel Toubkal reaches a high point of 13,671 ft (4,167 m). The mountains are rich in phosphates, coal, iron, and oil.

atmosphere, the mixture of gases and other substances surrounding a celestial body with sufficient gravity to maintain it. Although some details about the atmospheres of the other planets and some satellites are known (see articles on individual planets), a complete description is available only for the earth's atmosphere, the study of which is called METEOROLOGY. The gaseous constituents of the earth's atmosphere are not chemically combined, and thus each retains its own physical and chemical properties. Within the first 40 to 50 mi (64 to 80 km) above the earth, the mixture is of uniform composition (except for a high concentration of OZONE at 30 mi/50 km; see OZONE LAYER). This whole region contains more than 99% of the total mass of the earth's atmosphere. Based on their relative volumes, the gaseous constituents are nitrogen (78.09%), oxygen (20.95%), argon (0.93%), carbon dioxide (0.03%), and minute traces of neon, helium, methane, krypton, hydrogen, xenon, and ozone. Additional atmospheric constituents include water vapor and particulate matter, such as various forms of dust and industrial pollutants. The earth's atmosphere is separated into certain distinct regions, each having a different temperature range. The troposphere, where air is in constant motion (see WIND), extends from the earth's surface to an altitude of 5 mi (8 km) at the poles and 10 mi (16 km) at the equator. Clouds and other WEATHER phenomena occur here. All forms of the earth's animal and plant life exist in the troposphere or in the waters beneath it. Above the troposphere, the stratosphere extends to about 30 mi (50 km), followed by the mesosphere, up to about 50 mi (80 km), the thermosphere, up to about 400 mi (640 km), and finally the exosphere. The ionosphere is in the range (50 to 400 mi/80 to 640 km) that contains a high concentration of electrically charged particles (ions), which are responsible for reflecting radio signals. Above it, out to about 40,000 mi (64,400 km) in a region called the magnetosphere, electrically charged particles are trapped by the earth's magnetic field (see AURORA; VAN ALLEN RADIATION BELTS). The atmosphere protects the earth by absorbing and scattering harmful radiation and causing extraterrestrial solid matter (see METEOR) to burn from the heat generated by air friction.

atoll: see CORAL REEFS; ISLAND.

atom, the smallest unit of a chemical ELEMENT having the properties of that element. An atom contains several kinds of particles. Its central core, the nucleus, consists of positively charged particles, called PROTONS, and uncharged particles, called NEUTRONS. Surrounding the nucleus and orbiting it are negatively charged particles, called ELECTRONS. Each atom has an equal number of protons and electrons. The nucleus occupies only a tiny fraction of an atom's volume but contains almost all of its mass. Electrons in the outermost orbits determine the atom's chemical and electrical properties. The number of protons in an atom's nucleus is called the ATOMIC NUMBER. All atoms of an element have the same atomic number and differ in atomic number from atoms of other elements. The total number of protons and neutrons combined is the atom's MASS NUMBER. Atoms containing the same number of protons but different numbers of neutrons are different forms, or ISOTOPES, of the same element. See also ATOMIC WEIGHT.

History. In the 5th cent. B.C. the Greek philosophers DEMOCRITUS and Leucippus proposed that matter was made up of tiny, indivisible particles in constant motion. Aristotle, however, did not accept the theory, and it was ignored for centuries. Modern atomic theory began with the publication in 1808 by John DALTON of his experimental conclusions that all atoms of an element have exactly the same size and weight, and that atoms of elements unite chemically in simple numerical ratios to form compounds. In 1911 Ernest RUTHERFORD explained an atom's structure in terms of a positively charged nucleus surrounded by negatively charged electrons orbiting around it. In 1913 Niels BOHR used quantum theory to explain why electrons could remain in certain allowed orbits without radiating energy. The development of QUANTUM MECHANICS during the 1920s resulted in a satisfactory explanation of all phenomena related to the role of electrons in atoms and of all aspects of their associated spectra (see SPECTRUM). The quantum theory has shown that all particles have certain wave properties. As a result, electrons in an atom cannot be pictured as localized in space but rather should be viewed as a cloud of charge spread out over the entire orbit. The electron clouds around the nucleus represent regions in which the electrons are most likely to be found. Physicists are currently studying the behavior of large groups of atoms (see SOLID-STATE PHYSICS), and the nature of and relations among the hundreds of subatomic particles (see ELEMENTARY PARTICLES) that have been discovered in addition to the proton, neutron, and electron. See also MOLECULE.

atomic bomb, weapon deriving its great explosive force from the sudden release of NUCLEAR ENERGY through the fission, or splitting, of heavy atomic nuclei. The first atomic bomb was successfully tested by the U.S. near Alamogordo, N.Mex., on July 16, 1945 (see MANHATTAN PROJECT). In the final stages of WORLD WAR II the U.S. dropped atomic bombs on Hiroshima on Aug. 6, 1945, and on Nagasaki three days later to force Japan to surrender. Atomic bombs were subsequently developed by the USSR (1949), Great Britain (1952), France (1960), China (1964), and India (1974), and a number of other nations, particularly Pakistan and Israel, are believed to have atomic bombs or the capability to produce them readily. The USSR's nuclear arsenal has been divided since 1991 among Russia, Ukraine, Kazakhstan, and Belarus. Practical fissionable nuclei for atomic bombs are the isotopes URANIUM-235 and PLUTONIUM-239, which are capable of undergoing chain reaction. If the mass of the fissionable material exceeds the critical mass, the chain reaction multiplies rapidly into an uncontrollable release of energy. An atomic bomb is detonated by bringing together very rapidly (e.g., by means of a chemical explosion) two subcritical masses of fissionable material. The ensuing explosion produces great amounts of heat, a shock wave, and intense neutron and gamma radiation. The region of the explosion becomes radioactively contaminated, and wind-borne radioactive products may be deposited elsewhere as fallout. See also DISARMAMENT, NUCLEAR; HYDROGEN BOMB.

atomic clock: see CLOCK.

atomic energy: see NUCLEAR ENERGY.

Atomic Energy Commission: see NUCLEAR REGULATORY COMMISSION.

atomic force microscope (AFM), device that uses a spring-mounted probe to image individual atoms on the surface of a material. Unlike the SCANNING TUNNELING MICROSCOPE, which is also a scanning probe microscope, the AFM can be used on materials that do not conduct electricity. In the original AFM, the probe traverses the surface, moving upward due to bumps and downward due to depressions; a LASER beam reflected from the tip of the probe measures the up and down movements, and the pattern of reflected light creates an image of the surface. Another type of AFM measures the sideways deflection of the tip caused by friction as the probe moves across the surface; differences in friction can be used distinguish different atoms and molecules on the material. A third variation employs a magnetic probe; this probe does not touch the material but moves up and down in reaction to the magnetic forces between the tip and the surface.

atomic mass: see ATOMIC WEIGHT.

atomic number, often represented by the symbol *Z,* the number of PROTONS in the nucleus of an ATOM. Atoms with the same atomic number make up a chemical ELEMENT. The elements are arranged in the PERIODIC TABLE in the order of their atomic numbers.

atomic weight, mean (weighted average) of the masses of all the naturally occurring ISOTOPES of a chemical ELEMENT; the atomic mass is the mass of any individual isotope. Atomic weight is usually expressed in atomic mass units (amu); the atomic mass unit is defined as exactly 1/12 the mass of a carbon-12 atom. Each proton or neutron weighs about 1 amu, and thus the atomic mass is always very close to the MASS NUMBER (total number of protons and neutrons in the nucleus). Because most naturally occurring elements have one principal isotope and only insignificant amounts of other isotopes, most atomic weights are also very nearly whole numbers. For the atomic weight of individual elements, see PERIODIC TABLE.

atonality, systemic avoidance of harmonies and melodies that imply a keynote (see KEY). The term designates a method of composition in which the composer deliberately rejects the principle of TONALITY in favor of another principle of order, such as the 12-tone system (see SERIAL MUSIC). The move toward atonality has its beginnings in the 19th cent., when WAGNER, Richard STRAUSS, and DEBUSSY obscured basic tonalities in their music. Atonal composers of the 20th cent. include SCHOENBERG, BERG, and IVES.

Atonement, Day of: see JEWISH HOLIDAYS.

ATP: see ADENOSINE TRIPHOSPHATE.

Atreus [āʹtrēəs], in Greek mythology, king of Mycenae; son of PELOPS, father of AGAMEMNON and MENELAUS. In retaliation for his brother Thyestes' seduction of his wife, Atreus murdered three of Thyestes' sons and served them to him at a feast. Thyestes then laid a curse on the house of Atreus. Thyestes' son AEGISTHUS killed Atreus, and Thyestes became king.

Attar: see FARID AD-DIN ATTAR.

attention deficit hyperactivity disorder (ADHD), chronic, neurologically-based syndrome characterized by any or all of three types of behavior: hyperactivity, distractibility, and impulsivity. Unlike similar behaviors caused by emotional problems or anxiety, ADHD does not fluctuate with emotional states. Often diagnosed when a child begins school, ADHD is usually accompanied by learning difficulties and social inappropriateness. Treatment may include medication such as methylphenidate hydrochloride (Ritalin), which corrects neurochemical imbalances in the brain; sugar intake is no longer considered to be a factor. Symptoms may decrease after adolescence, although adults can also have ADHD.

Attila, d. 453, king of the HUNS (434–53). From 434 he extorted tribute from the Eastern and Western Roman emperors. In 450 MARCIAN of the East and VALENTINIAN III of the West refused to pay. Valentinian's sister Honoria proposed an alliance with Attila, who took this as a marriage offer and demanded half the Western empire as dowry. Refused, he attacked Gaul but was defeated (451) by the Romans. He invaded (452) Italy but spared Rome, apparently because of a shortage of supplies and an outbreak of pestilence in his army. Although feared for his savagery, he was a just ruler.

Attlee, Clement Richard, 1st **Earl,** 1883–1967, British statesman. A lawyer and social worker, he became leader of the Labour party in 1935. During World War II he served in Winston CHURCHILL's coalition cabinet (1940–45), and in 1945 became prime minister. His government nationalized the Bank of England and much of British industry; enacted social reforms, including the National Health Service; and granted independence to Burma (now Myanmar), India, Pakistan, Ceylon (now Sri Lanka), and PALESTINE. Attlee left office in 1951. He led the opposition until 1955, when he was created Earl Attlee.

Atwood, Margaret (Eleanor), 1939–, Canadian writer. Her powerful novels are concerned with feminism and the intrusiveness of mass society. They include *The Edible Woman* (1969), *Surfacing* (1972), *Bodily Harm* (1981), *The Handmaid's Tale* (1986), and *The Robber Bride* (1993). She has also written poetry and short stories.

Au, chemical symbol of the element GOLD.

Aubrey, John, 1626–97, English antiquarian and writer. Friendly with many famous people, he left copious letters and memoranda. His most celebrated work, *Lives of Eminent Men,* was published in 1813. Only his *Miscellanies* (1696) appeared in his lifetime.

Auckland, city (1991 pop. 315,668), NW North Island, New Zealand, on an isthmus between the Pacific Ocean and the Tasman Sea. It is the country's largest city and its chief port, industrial center, and naval base. Frozen meats and dairy products are important exports. Industries include shipbuilding, food processing, oil refining, and the manufacture of automobiles and chemicals. Auckland was founded in 1840 and was the capital of New Zealand until replaced (1865) by WELLINGTON. The Univ. of Auckland is among the city's educational institutions.

Auden, W(ystan) H(ugh), 1907–73, Anglo-American poet, a major 20th-cent. literary figure. In the 1930s he was associated with SPENDER, MACNEICE, and ISHERWOOD; with the last he wrote the verse plays *The Dog Beneath the Skin* (1935), *The Ascent of F6* (1936), and *On the Frontier* (1938). Some of Auden's most original poetry appeared in the early 1930s. Later volumes, ranging in subject from politics to psychology to Christianity, include *The Double Man* (1941), *Collected Poetry* (1945), *The Age of Anxiety* (1947; Pulitzer), *Nones* (1951), and *About the House* (1965). He also wrote critical essays and opera librettos. A U.S. resident from 1939 and citizen from 1946, Auden divided his last years among England, Italy, Austria, and New York.

auditing: see under ACCOUNTING.

Audubon, John James, 1785–1851, American ornithologist; b. Les Cayes, Santo Domingo (now Haiti). After arriving in the U.S. in 1803, he began the extensive ornithological observations that would lead to the publication of his bird drawings and paintings as *The Birds of America* (1827–38). The accompanying text, called the *Ornithological Biography* (5 vol., 1831–39), was written in collaboration with the Scottish naturalist William MacGillivray. Audubon's drawings and paintings remain one of the great achievements of American intellectual history.

Aue, Hartmann von: see HARTMANN VON AUE.

August: see MONTH.

Augusta. 1 City (1990 pop. 44,639), seat of Richmond co., E Ga., on the Savannah R.; inc. 1798. The trade center for a large area of Georgia and South Carolina, it has diversified industries, including textiles, chemicals, and paper. A river trading port as early as 1717, it grew with tobacco and cotton trade. During the CIVIL WAR it housed the chief Confederate powder works. The city, a popular resort, is known for its golf tournaments and many fine old houses. **2** City (1990 pop. 21,325), state capital and seat of Kennebec co., SW Me., on the Kennebec R.; inc. as a city 1849. Shoes, fabrics, and paper products are among its manufactures. The Plymouth Company established a trading post on the site in 1628; Fort Western was built in 1754. In 1837 manufacturing began with the building of a dam. The Capitol building (1829) was designed by Charles BULFINCH and later enlarged.

Augustine, Saint [ôʹgəstēn, –tĭn; ôgŭsʹtĭn], 354–430, Doctor of the Church, bishop of Hippo (near present-day Annaba, Algeria); b. near Hippo. Brought up as a Christian by his mother, St. Monica, Augustine gave up his religion while at school in Carthage, then converted to MANICHAEISM. He taught rhetoric in Rome (after 376) and Milan (after 384). In Milan he was drawn to the teachings of St. AMBROSE and to NEOPLATONISM, and finally embraced Christianity, returning (387) to a monastic life in Tagaste. In 391 he was ordained a priest in Hippo, where he remained for the rest of his life, serving as bishop from 396. St. Augustine's influence on Christianity was immense, and theologians, both Roman Catholic and Protestant, look upon him as the founder of theology. His polemics against Manichaeism, Donatism, and Pelagianism are well known, and his autobiographical *Confessions* is a classic of Christian mysticism. *On the Trinity* systematized Christian doctrine, and *The City of God,* his monumental defense of Christianity against paganism, is famous for its Christian view of history. Feast: Aug. 28.

Augustine of Canterbury, Saint, d. c.605, Italian missionary, called the Apostle of the English, first archbishop of Canterbury (from 601). A BENEDICTINE, he was sent by Pope GREGORY I to England, where he converted King ÆTHELBERT and introduced Roman monastic practices. Feast: May 27 (May 26 in England and Wales).

Augustus, 63 B.C.–A.D. 14, first Roman emperor; a grandnephew of Julius CAESAR. Born Caius Octavius, he became on adoption by the Julian gens (44 B.C.) Caius Julius Caesar Octavianus (Octavian); Augustus was a title of honor granted (27 B.C.) by the senate. Caesar made the boy his heir without his knowledge, and after Caesar was killed (44 B.C.), Octavian became dominant at Rome. He made an alliance with ANTONY and Lepidus (d. 13 B.C.; see LEPIDUS, family) known as the Second Triumvirate and with Antony defeated the army of Marcus Junius Brutus (see BRUTUS, family) and Caius Cassius Longinus (see CASSIUS, family) at Philippi (42 B.C.). Octavian's forces next defeated POMPEY at Mylae (36 B.C.). After the naval victory at Actium (31 B.C.) over Antony and CLEOPATRA, Octavian controlled all of the Roman territories. The senate in 29 B.C. made him imperator [Lat., = commander; from it is derived *emperor*] and in 27 B.C. augustus [august, reverend]. The month Sextilis was renamed Augustus (August) in his honor. He enacted many reforms in Rome and in the provinces and tried to hold the Roman borders set by Caesar. His attempt to make a buffer state in German territory led to the revolt of Arminius, in which a Roman army was destroyed. Augustus built Roman roads, beautified Rome, and was munificent to arts and letters. He was a patron of VERGIL, OVID, LIVY, and HORACE. He also established the concept of the Pax Romana [Roman peace]. He was succeeded by his stepson TIBERIUS.

Augustus, Polish kings. **Augustus II,** 1670–1733, was king of POLAND (1697–1733) and, as Frederick Augustus I, elector of Saxony (1694–1733). He succeeded John III as king by becoming a Catholic and by giving the nobility unprecedented powers. In 1700 he involved Poland in the NORTHERN WAR. He was highly unpopular, and his death began the War of the POLISH SUCCESSION. One of its results was that his son, **Augustus III,** 1696–1763, succeeded him as king of Poland (1735–63). He was also, as Frederick Augustus II, elector of Saxony (1733–63). One of the unsuccessful claimants of the Hapsburg lands, he opposed Maria Theresa in the War of the AUSTRIAN SUCCESSION.

auk, swimming and diving BIRD of the family Alcidae, which includes the PUFFIN and guillemot. Clumsy on land, auks seldom leave the water except to nest; they return to the same nesting site every year. The largest species, the flightless great auk (*Pinguinus impennis*), was hunted for its flesh, feathers, and oil; it became extinct c.1844.

Aung San Suu Kyi, 1945–, Burmese political leader. Daughter of Burmese nationalist Aung San, who is regarded as the founder of modern Myanmar, she lived outside Myanmar after 1960. Returning in 1988 to care for her mother, she joined the opposition to U NE WIN and became leader of the National League for Democracy. She was placed (1989–) under house arrest for her outspoken criticism of the government. In 1990 her party won the parliamentary elections, but the military refused to surrender power. She was awarded the Nobel Peace Prize in 1991 for her nonviolent struggle for democracy.

Aurangzeb or **Aurangzib** [ôrʹəngzĕb", –zib"], 1618–1707, Mogul emperor of INDIA (1658–1707), son and successor of SHAH JAHAN. He ascended the throne after defeating his three brothers and imprisoning his father. The MOGUL Empire reached its greatest extent under him, but he was fanatically devoted to Islam and persecuted the Hindus (see HINDUISM) and SIKHS, thus fatally weakening Mogul control over the Indian population.

Aurelian (Lucius Domitius Aurelianus), c.212–275, Roman emperor (270–75). He succeeded Claudius II and defended the empire against the barbarians and ambitious rulers (e.g., Zenobia of Palmyra). One of Rome's greatest emperors, he regained Britain, Gaul, Spain, Egypt, Syria, and Mesopotamia and revived the glory of Rome. He was murdered, and Marcus Claudius Tacitus succeeded him.

aurochs: see CATTLE.

Aurora. 1 City (1990 pop. 222,103), N central Colo., a residential suburb of DENVER; inc. 1903. It is the fast-growing trade center for a large livestock and farming area. Electrical products, aircraft parts, and oil-field equipment are manufactured. Tourism, construction, and nearby military bases are important to the local economy. **2** City (1990 pop. 99,581), Kane co., NE Ill., on the Fox River; inc. 1837. It manufactures construction and telephone equipment, electric tools, pumps, and steel products and has rail yards and riverboat gambling. It was one of the first cities to use electricity for street lighting (1881).

aurora, luminous display of various forms and colors in the night sky. The aurora borealis (northern lights) and aurora australis (southern lights) are usually visible at latitudes within, respectively, the Arctic Circle and Antarctic Circle, but they are sometimes seen in middle latitudes. Both are seen most frequently at the time of the equinoxes and at times of great sunspot activity. Auroras occur at altitudes of 35 to 600 mi (56 to 970 km) and are thought to be caused by high-speed particles from the sun excited to luminosity after colliding with air molecules.

Auschwitz, now **Oświęcim,** Poland: see CONCENTRATION CAMP.

Ausonius (Decimus Magnus Ausonius), c.310–c.395, Latin poet; b. Bordeaux. His travel verses (*Mosella*), family sketches (*Parentalia*), and *Order of Noble Cities,* on 20 Roman cities, give portraits of people and places.

Austen, Jane, 1775–1817, English novelist. She spent her first 25 years at her father's Hampshire vicarage, writing novels published much later. *Northanger Abbey,* written early, appeared posthumously (with *Persuasion*) in 1818. Published in her lifetime were *Sense and Sensibility* (1811), *Pride and Prejudice* (1813), *Mansfield Park* (1814), and *Emma* (1816), comedies of manners, depicting the self-contained world of the English counties. Providing husbands for marriageable daughters is a central theme. Austen's work is noted for polished irony, moral firmness, and vivid characterization. She received little notice during her life, but today she is regarded as one of the masters of the English novel.

Austerlitz, Czech *Slavkov u Brna,* town, S Czech Republic, in Moravia. An agricultural center with sugar refineries and cotton mills, it was a seat of the ANABAPTISTS from 1528. At Austerlitz, NAPOLEON I won (Dec. 2, 1805) his greatest victory by defeating the Russian and Austrian armies. The town has an 18th-cent. castle and a 13th-cent. church.

Austin, Stephen Fuller, 1793–1836, Texas colonizer, known as the Father of Texas; b. Wythe co., Va. He took up the colonizing plans of his father, **Moses Austin,** 1761–1828, and began (1822) planting settlements in Texas between the Brazos and Colorado rivers. He later forwarded the Texas Revolution (1836) and was briefly secretary of state of the Republic of Texas.

Austin, city (1990 pop. 465,622), state capital and seat of Travis co., S central Tex., on the Colorado R.; inc. 1839. It is the commercial heart of a ranching, poultry, dairy, cotton, and grain area. Hydroelectric development (beginning in the 1930s) has spurred enormous industrial growth; the city now manufactures a wide variety of products, and is a center for electronic and scientific research. The Univ. of Texas' main campus is in Austin. State capital since 1870, it was capital (1839–42) of the Texas Republic.

Australasia, islands of the South Pacific, including AUSTRALIA, NEW ZEALAND, NEW GUINEA, and adjacent islands. The term sometimes includes all of OCEANIA.

Australia, smallest continent, c.2,400 mi (3,860 km) east to west and c.2,000 mi (3,220 km) north to south, only continent occupied by a single nation, the Commonwealth of Australia (1992 est. pop. 17,576,000), 2,967,877 sq mi (7,686,810 sq km). Subdivisions of the nation include the offshore island state of TASMANIA; the five mainland states of QUEENSLAND, NEW SOUTH WALES, VICTORIA, SOUTH AUSTRALIA, and WESTERN AUSTRALIA; the NORTHERN TERRITORY; and the AUSTRALIAN CAPITAL TERRITORY, containing CANBERRA, the federal capital. External territories include CHRISTMAS ISLAND, the COCOS

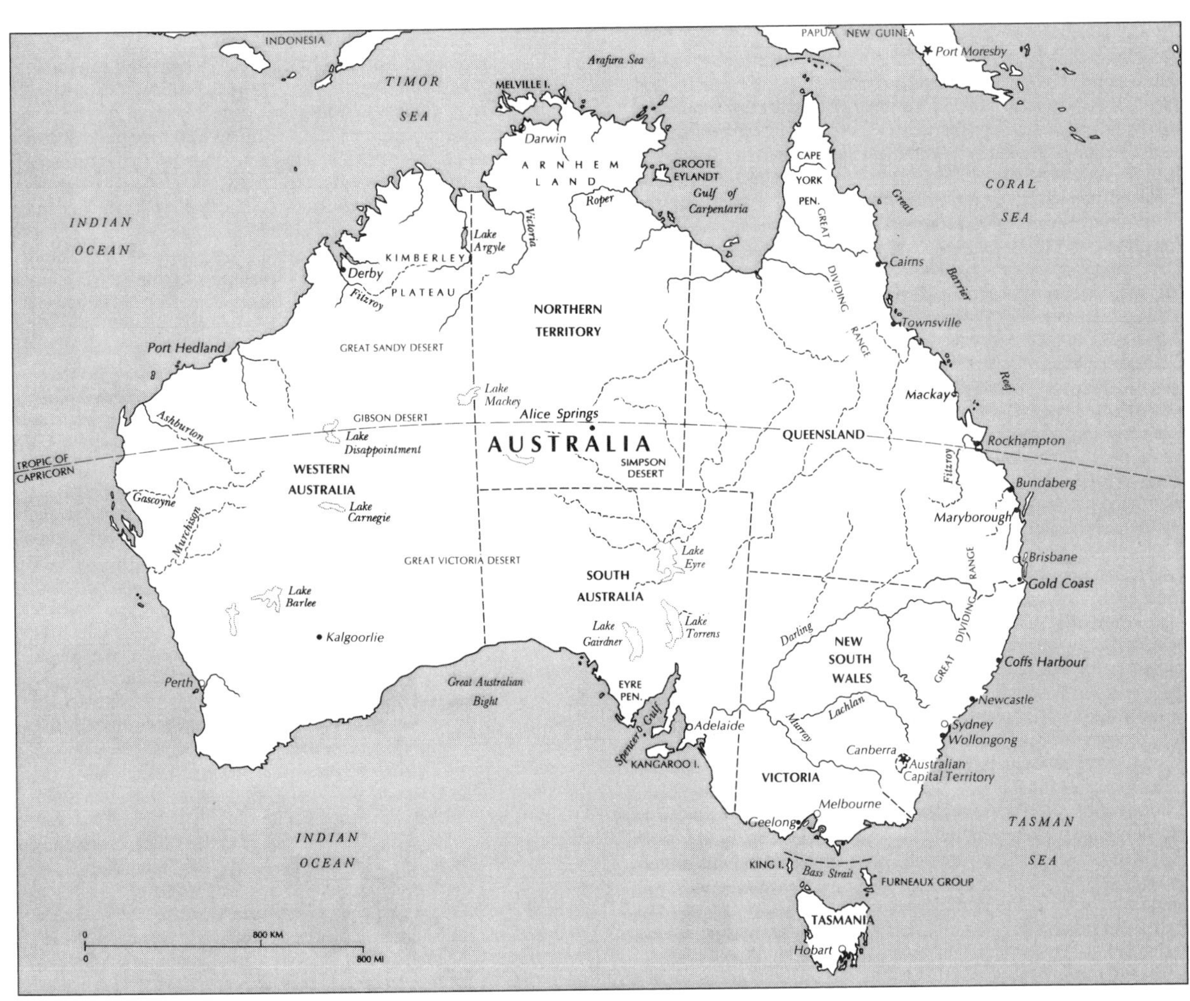

(KEELING) ISLANDS, the CORAL SEA ISLANDS, NORFOLK ISLAND, Heard and McDonald islands, and the Australian Antarctic Territory.

Geography *Australia is the flattest and driest of the continents, as well as the oldest and most isolated. Elevations range from 39 ft (12 m) below sea level at Lake* EYRE, *the lowest point, to a high point of 7,316 ft (2,230 m) at Mt.* KOSCIUSKO, *in the* AUSTRALIAN ALPS *near the New South Wales–Victoria border; much of the ancient western plateau is under 2,000 ft (610 m). Two thirds of the continent is either desert or semiarid. Humid climates are restricted to eastern coastal areas and to Tasmania. Alternating wet winters (June–August) and dry summers (November–March) occur in small areas of South Australia and Western Australia, and dry winters and wet summers alternate along the tropical northeastern coast. The* MURRAY *R. and its major tributaries, the* DARLING *and* MURRUMBIDGEE, *form the principal river system. Plant and animal life is distinctive, including many species, such as the giant* EUCALYPTUS, KOALA, KANGAROO, *and* PLATYPUS, *found only in Australia.*

Economy and People. Australia is the world's leading producer of wool and bauxite, and a significant supplier of iron ore, coal, wheat, meat, dairy products, sugar, and fruit. Manufacturing is highly developed and concentrated mainly in the coastal regions of Victoria and New South Wales. Iron, steel, automobiles, aircraft, electrical equipment and appliances, chemicals, and textiles are leading manufactures. SYDNEY, MELBOURNE, BRISBANE, ADELAIDE, and NEWCASTLE, all located along the southeastern coast, are the largest commercial and industrial centers. New South Wales and Victoria are the most populous states. Most Australians are of British and Irish ancestry. The indigenous population, the Australian aborigines and Torres Strait Islanders, totaled 257,333 in 1991. Immigration contributes significantly to population growth; in 1984 slightly more than 20% of the population had been born in Australia. Racially discriminatory immigration policies were officially ended in 1973, and there has been increased Asian immigration.

History and Government. The AUSTRALIAN ABORIGINES are thought to have come from Southeast Asia more than 40,000 years ago. The area was first visited by Europeans in the 17th cent. but attracted little interest until Capt. James COOK sailed (1770) into BOTANY BAY and claimed the entire eastern coast for Great Britain. The first settlement, a penal colony for "transported" British convicts, was established in 1788 where Sydney now stands. By the middle of the 19th cent. free colonization had replaced the old penal settlements, and the colonies of Tasmania (1825), Western Australia (1829), South Australia (1834), Victoria (1851), and Queensland (1859) had been established. Wool and wheat were early exports, and gold rushes in 1851 and 1892 attracted new settlers. In 1901 the colonies were federated as states of the Commonwealth of Australia, and in 1927 the seat of government was transferred from Melbourne to Canberra. Australia fought on the side of Britain in both world wars. In WORLD WAR II the Japanese bombed or shelled DARWIN, Port Jackson, and Newcastle, and the Allied victory in the battle of the CORAL SEA (1942) probably averted an invasion of Australia. Australia joined regional defense pacts after the war and sent troops to aid the U.S. in the VIETNAM WAR. The nation has a popularly elected bicameral parliament. Executive power rests with the governor general (representing the crown) and a cabinet and prime minister; British intervention in Australian affairs was formally abolished in 1986. In 1983 a Labor party government headed by Prime Min. Bob HAWKE came to power; it was returned to office in 1984, 1987, and 1990. After a severe recession Hawke was ousted (1991) by his party and replaced with Paul KEATING. In 1993 Keating led Labor to its fifth consecutive electoral victory.

Australian aborigines, indigenous people of Australia, thought to have come from Asia some 40,000 years ago. By the early 1990s, there were about 250,000, somewhat less than the estimated 300,000 at the time of colonization (1778). Then consisting of 500–600 groups, they were hunter-gatherers who had extensive intergroup trade and maintained intricate KINSHIP and marriage systems and an elaborate totemism (see TOTEM). Within a century, contact with British settlers led to massive depopulation and extinction for some groups. By the 1940s most aborigines had been assimilated into Australian society as laborers with limited economic and legal rights. Legislation (1976) restored some aboriginal autonomy, and improved living conditions have led to population increase. In 1992 Australia's High Court ruled that aboriginal groups could claim title to land they had once inhabited; the ruling was codified by a 1993 law that also protected existing nonaboriginal land titles.

Australian Alps, mountain chain, SE Australia, forming the southern part of the EASTERN HIGHLANDS. It reaches a high point of 7,316 ft (2,230 m) at Mt. KOSCIUSKO, the highest peak in Australia.

Australian Capital Territory (1992 est. pop. 295,000), 939 sq mi (2,432 sq km), SE Australia, an enclave within NEW SOUTH WALES containing CANBERRA, the capital of Australia. Most of it was ceded to the federal government by New South Wales in 1911 for use as the future capital; a small section on the east coast, at Jervis Bay, was ceded for use as a port in 1915. The territory is administered by the federal government and has an elected House of Assembly with advisory responsibilities.

Australian languages, aboriginal languages spoken by perhaps 130,000 persons on the continent of Australia. These languages, estimated at 100 to 600 in number, do not seem to be related to any other linguistic family and have no writing of their own. Many are already or nearly extinct.

Australopithecus: see MAN, PREHISTORIC.

Austria, Ger. *Österreich,* officially Republic of Austria, federal republic (1992 est. pop. 7,868,000), 32,374 sq mi (83,849 sq km), central Europe; bordered by Slovenia and Italy (S), Switzerland and Liechtenstein (W), Germany and the Czech Republic (N), and Slovakia and Hungary (E). VIENNA is the capital; principal cities include SALZBURG, INNSBRUCK, GRAZ, and LINZ. The ALPS traverse Austria from west to east and occupy three fourths of the country; the highest peak is the Grossglockner (12,460 ft/3,798 m). Austria is drained by the DANUBE R. and its tributaries. Forestry, cattle-raising, and dairying are the main sources of livelihood in the alpine provinces. In the rest of the country tillage agriculture predominates; the chief crops are potatoes, sugar beets, barley, wheat, rye, and oats. Manufacturing (machinery, vehicles, metals, chemicals, foodstuffs, and textiles) and mining (graphite, iron, magnesium, copper, zinc, and lignite) employ nearly half of the labor force. Tourism is very important. Divided into nine provinces, Austria has a mixed presidential-parliamentary form of government. The population is predominantly German-speaking and Roman Catholic.

History. Located at the crossroads of Europe, Austria has been from earliest times a thoroughfare and a battleground. Settled by Celts, the area was conquered (15 B.C.–A.D. 10) by Rome; overrun (from the 5th cent.) by Huns, Goths, Lombards, and Bavarians; conquered (788) by CHARLEMAGNE; taken (after 814) by the Moravians (see MORAVIA) and then the MAGYARS; and reconquered (955) by Holy Roman Emperor OTTO I, who bestowed it (976) on the house of Babenberg. Acquired in 1251 by Ottocar II of BOHEMIA, it was claimed (1282) by RUDOLF I of Hapsburg, king of the Germans, and from that time until its fall in 1918, Austrian history is that of the house of HAPSBURG. (See AUSTRIAN SECESSION, WAR OF THE; AUSTRO-HUNGARIAN MONARCHY; AUSTRO-PRUSSIAN WAR; CONGRESS OF VIENNA; FRENCH REVOLUTIONARY WARS; GERMAN CONFEDERATION; HOLY ALLIANCE; HOLY ROMAN EMPIRE; METTERNICH; SEVEN YEARS WAR; THIRTY YEARS WAR.) Following the collapse of the Austro-Hungarian monarchy at the end of WORLD WAR I, German Austria was proclaimed (1918) a republic. The Treaty of Saint-Germain (1919), which fixed its boundaries, reduced it to a small country of 7 million inhabitants, and deprived it of its raw materials, food, and markets. Unemployment, bankruptcy, and political unrest followed, and in 1934 a corporative totalitarian regime was established under Engelbert DOLLFUSS (who was assassinated) and his successor, Kurt von SCHUSCHNIGG. The nation became part of the German Third Reich in 1938, when it was occupied by German troops. After its capture (1945) by U.S. and Soviet troops, Austria was restored as a republic. Divided into zones, it was occupied by the Allies until 1955, when a peace treaty declared it a sovereign and neutral power. By the 1960s the country enjoyed unprecedented prosperity. Politically, a nearly equal balance of power between conservatives and socialists resulted in a succession of coalition governments until 1966, when the conservative People's party won a clear majority. The party was ousted in the 1970 elections by the Socialists, who, under Chancellor Bruno KREISKY, held power until 1983. Since then Austria has been ruled by Socialist-led coalition governments. In 1986 former UN Secretary General Kurt WALDHEIM was elected president despite evidence that seemed to link him with Nazi atrocities; he was succeeded (1992) by Thomas Klestil.

Austrian Succession, War of the, 1740–48, European war precipitated by the succession of MARIA THERESA to the Hapsburg lands by virtue of the PRAGMATIC SANCTION. She was challenged by the elector of Bavaria (who became Emperor CHARLES VII in 1742), PHILIP V of Spain, and AUGUSTUS III of Poland. FREDERICK II of Prussia, claiming part of Silesia, opened hostilities by invading that region. Prussia was joined by France, Spain, Bavaria, and Saxony. After being promised its Silesian claim, Prussia made a separate peace in 1742. Saxony went over to Austria in 1743, and England (at war with Spain), Holland, and Sardinia became Austrian allies. Fearing Maria Theresa's growing power, Prussia reentered the war in 1744. Maria Theresa's husband was elected emperor, as FRANCIS I, in 1745, on the death of Charles VII. France defeated the English at Fontenoy, and GEORGE II sued for peace. The war dragged on in other areas, including North America (see FRENCH AND INDIAN WARS). In 1748 the Treaty of Aix-la-Chapelle ended the war. Maria Theresa's throne was safe, but Prussia had emerged as a major European power.

Austro-Hungarian Monarchy or **Dual Monarchy,** the HAPSBURG empire from the constitutional compromise (*Ausgleich*) of 1867 until its fall in 1918. The empire was divided into two states. Cisleithania (lands W of the Leitha River) comprised Austria proper, Bohemia, Moravia, Austrian Silesia, Slovenia, and Austrian Poland. Transleithania included Hungary, Transylvania, Croatia, and part of Dalmatia. The Hapsburg monarch ruled Cisleithania as emperor of Austria and ruled Transleithania as king of Hungary. Both states elected separate parliaments for internal affairs and had independent ministries. A common cabinet dealt with foreign affairs, common defense, and common finances. The monarchy was weakened by this ethnic diversity. Czech, Italian, Slavic, and Romanian minorities desired autonomy and later sought to break free of the empire. Archduke FRANCIS FERDINAND apparently had a plan for a South Slavic partner in the monarchy, but his assassination (1914) cut short this hope and precipitated WORLD WAR I. In foreign affairs Austria-Hungary allied (1879) with Germany (see TRIPLE ALLIANCE AND TRIPLE ENTENTE) and in 1908 angered SERBIA by annexing BOSNIA AND HERCEGOVINA. The empire was dissolved at the end of World War I, and Emperor CHARLES I abdicated (1918). The Treaty of VERSAILLES and other treaties established the boundaries of the successor states.

Austronesian [ôs″trōnē′zhən, –shən], name sometimes used for the Malayo-Polynesian languages. See LANGUAGE (table).

Austro-Prussian War or **Seven Weeks War,** June 15–Aug. 23, 1866, between Austria (seconded by the various German states) and Prussia (allied with Italy). It was provoked by BISMARCK as a way of expelling Austria from the GERMAN CONFEDERATION, thereby assuring Prussian hegemony there. The pretext was a dispute between Prussia and Austria over the administration of SCHLESWIG-HOLSTEIN. Prussia quickly overran Holstein and the German states allied with Austria, and was victorious in Bohemia and Italy. The Treaty of Prague ended the war. Austria was excluded from German affairs and forced to cede Venetia to Italy. Prussia demanded no territory from Austria but annexed Hanover, Hesse, Nassau, and Frankfurt, laying the groundwork for the establishment (1871) of the German empire.

autism, developmental disorder, usually appearing before age three, characterized by impaired non-verbal and verbal communication, including abnormal speech patterns or loss of speech; lack of eye contact; a restricted range of interests; resistance to change of any kind; obsessive repetitive body movements, such as hand flapping or spinning; a lack of awareness of the existence or feelings of others; social isolation; and no comfort seeking in times of distress. Symptoms vary from child to child and can range from mild to severe. Treatment is experimental, and few autistic children show significant remission of symptoms.

autoimmune disease, general term for disorders in which the body produces antibodies (see IMMUNITY) against its own substances, resulting in tissue injury. For example, in systemic lupus erythematosus, individuals develop antibodies to their own nucleic acids and cell structures, causing dysfunction of many organs, including the heart, kidneys, and joints. Autoimmune diseases are treated by a variety of nonspecific IMMUNOSUPPRESSIVE DRUGS and STEROIDS.

automation, automatic operation and control of machinery or processes by devices that make and execute decisions without human intervention. Such devices use self-correcting control systems that employ feedback; i.e., they use part of their output to control their input. Because of their ability to store, select, record, and present data, COMPUTERS are widely used to direct automated systems. See also COMPUTER-AIDED MANUFACTURING; DATA PROCESSING; ROBOTICS.

automobile, self-propelled vehicle used for travel on land. The fundamental structure of the automobile consists of seven basic systems: the engine, usually mounted in front and driving either the two front, two rear, or all four wheels; the fuel system, using a CARBURETOR or FUEL INJECTION to produce the optimal combustible mixture of fuel and air; the electrical system, including a battery that provides a power source to the ignition; the cooling, steering and suspension, and BRAKE systems; and the TRANSMISSION, which transmits power from the engine crankshaft to the wheels by means of a series of gears. Evolving from earlier experiments with steam-powered vehicles, models using the gasoline-fueled INTERNAL-COMBUSTION ENGINE were first developed by the German engineers Karl BENZ (1885) and Gottlieb DAIMLER (1886). U.S. leadership in automobile production began with Henry FORD's founding (1903) of the Ford Motor Co., its production (1908) of the inexpensive Model T, and its development of assembly-line techniques. General Motors, Ford's principal competitor, became the world's largest automobile manufacturer in the 1920s, and U.S. dominance of the field continued until the 1970s, when it was challenged by growing sales of Japanese and German cars. Concern about pollution from gasoline combustion has led to the development of cars powered by electricity from rechargeable storage batteries and by the combustion of natural gas, but such vehicles have been limited in the distance they can travel and have only been used on a small scale, largely in metropolitan areas. See also AUTOMOBILE RACING; DIESEL ENGINE; POLLUTION; SMOG.

automobile racing, sport in which high-speed, specially constructed automobiles are raced on outdoor or indoor courses. The basic types of competition are grand prix, a series of races in several countries that leads to the designation of a world-champion driver; Indy car, with the cars used for the Indianapolis 500; stock car, using standard cars with special equipment; sprint car; sports car; and drag racing, involving acceleration tests over a ¼-mi. (.4025-km) track. The sport originated in France in 1894. The best-known U.S. race is the Indianapolis 500, first held in 1911.

autumnal equinox: see EQUINOX.

Averroës [avĕr′ōēz], Arabic *Ibn Rushd,* 1126–98, Spanish-Arabian philosopher. His greatest work, his commentaries on ARISTOTLE, remained influential in the West well into the Renaissance. Averroës held that the domains of faith and reason did not conflict, and that philosophic truth derives from reason rather than faith (see SCHOLASTICISM). In this he was opposed by St. THOMAS AQUINAS.

Avery, Milton, 1893–1965, American painter; b. Altmar, N.Y. A master colorist in the tradition of MATISSE, he is known for figurative works that display bold massing of forms and for landscapes that

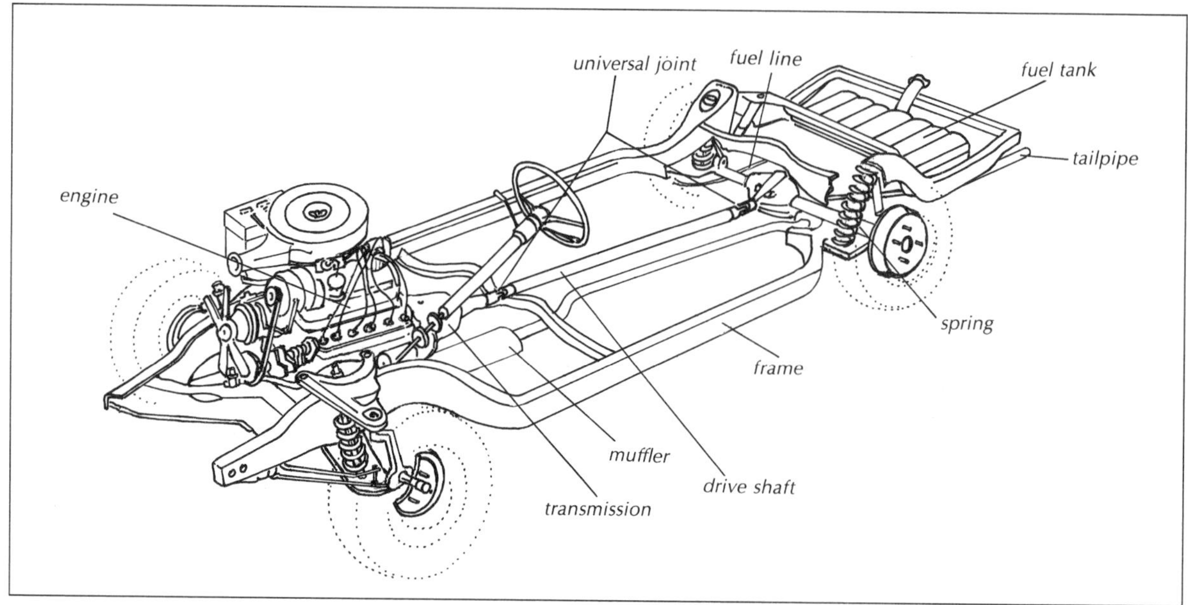

Automobile: View of a six-cylinder, gasoline-fueled engine

verge on complete abstraction, e.g., *Dunes and Sea II* (1960; Whitney Mus., N.Y.C.).

Avestan [əvĕs'tən], language belonging to the Iranian group of the Indo-Iranian subfamily of the Indo-European family of languages. See LANGUAGE (table).

aviation, operation of heavier-than-air aircraft and related activities. Aviation can be divided into military aviation (see AIRCRAFT CARRIER; AIR FORCE), air transport (commercial airline operations), and general aviation (agricultural, business, charter, instructional, and pleasure flying). The first successful flights of a motor-powered airplane carrying a human were made by Orville and Wilbur WRIGHT near Kitty Hawk, N.C. on Dec. 17, 1903. The first successful SEAPLANE was constructed in 1911–12. During the early 1900s, aviators demonstrated the feasibility of air travel to various parts of the world. World War I provided additional motivation for aviation research and development. The availability of cheap, surplus aircraft in the U.S. after the war encouraged barnstorming and stunt-flying; the result was a more airplane-conscious public. Private companies in America contracted the carrying of airmail after 1925. Technological improvements in WIND TUNNEL testing, engine and airframe design, and maintenance equipment combined in the 1930s to provide faster, larger, and more durable airplanes. The transportation of passengers became profitable, and routes were extended to include several foreign countries. Transpacific airmail service began in 1934, and was soon followed by a similar service for passengers. In 1939 the first transatlantic service for mail and passengers was inaugurated. The application of JET PROPULSION to commercial air transportation began in 1952. The first supersonic transports (SST) for passenger service were put into service during the mid-1970s, but commercial aviation was transformed by jumbo jetliners that carry hundreds of passengers on a single flight. See also AIRSHIP; BALLOON; GLIDER; HELICOPTER.

Avicenna [ăvĭsĕn'ə], Arabic *Ibn Sina*, 980–1037, Persian philosopher and physician, the most renowned philosopher of medieval Islam. His interpretation of ARISTOTLE followed that of the NEOPLATONISTS. Avicenna's *Canon of Medicine*, a classic text, was particularly influential from 1100 to 1500.

Avignon [ävēnyôN'], city (1990 pop. 86,939), capital of Vaucluse dept., SE France, on the Rhône R. It has a wine trade and many manufactures. The papal see during the Babylonian Captivity (1309–78), it was later (1378–1408) the residence of several antipopes (see PAPACY and SCHISM, GREAT). Avignon was joined to France after a plebiscite (1791). Medieval ramparts and the papal palace are highlights of the city.

avocado, tropical American broad-leaved evergreen tree (genus *Persea*) of the LAUREL family, and its pear-shaped fruit. The fruit has a tough, inedible, usually dark green skin and an oily flesh surrounding a large, hard seed. The flesh is eaten fresh, chiefly in salads.

Avogadro, Amadeo, conte di Quaregna, 1776–1856, Italian physicist. In 1811 he advanced the hypothesis (since known as Avogadro's law) that equal volumes of gases under identical conditions of pressure and temperature contain the same number of molecules. This hypothesis led to the determination by other physicists of the value of Avogadro's number, i.e., the number of molecules in one MOLE, or gram-molecular weight, of any gas.

Avogadro's number: see MOLE, in chemistry.

avoirdupois weight: see ENGLISH UNITS OF MEASUREMENT; WEIGHTS AND MEASURES, table.

Awami League, political party in PAKISTAN and BANGLADESH. Founded in 1949, it became the vehicle for the political interests of East Pakistan. When East Pakistan won independence (1971) as Bangladesh, the league became the new nation's dominant political party, but in 1981 and again in 1991 the National party defeated the league in national elections.

axiom, in MATHEMATICS and LOGIC, general statement accepted without proof as the basis for logically deducing other statements (THEOREMS). Examples of axioms used widely in mathematics are those related to equality (e.g., "If equals are added to equals, the sums are equal") and those related to operations (e.g., the ASSOCIATIVE LAW). A postulate, like an axiom, is a statement that is accepted without proof; it deals, however, with specific subject matter (e.g., properties of geometrical figures), not general statements.

Axis, 1936–45, coalition of countries in WORLD WAR II headed by Germany, Italy, and Japan. They were opposed, and defeated, by the Allies, headed by the United States, Great Britain, the Soviet Union, and China.

Ayacucho, city (1990 est. pop. 102,000), capital of Ayacucho dept., S central Peru. It is a commercial and tourist center in a region of rich gold, silver, and nickel mines. On the nearby plains of Ayacucho, Antonio José de SUCRE won (1824) a military victory that secured Peru's independence from Spain and assured the liberation of South America.

Ayala, Ramón Pérez de: see PÉREZ DE AYALA, RAMÓN.

Ayatollah Ruhollah Khomeini: see KHOMEINI, RUHOLLAH.

Ayckbourn, Alan, 1939–, English playwright. He is known for such ingenious antibourgeois FARCES as *How the Other Half Loves* (1970); *Absurd Person Singular* (1973); *The Norman Conquests* (1974), a trilogy; *Bedroom Farce* (1975), and the darker *A Small Family Business* (1987).

Aylwin Azócar, Patricio, 1918–, Chilean political leader. A founder of the Christian Democratic party (1957) and a senator (1964–73), he led a coalition that opposed PINOCHET in the late 1980s. After a national plebiscite ended military rule, Aylwin was elected president (1990). He has sought to maintain Chile's economic prosperity and strengthen civilian government.

Aymara, indigenous people of the Lake TITICACA basin in Peru and Bolivia (see SOUTH AMERICA, INDIGENOUS PEOPLES OF). Their language is classified as a separate unit (see NATIVE AMERICAN LANGUAGES). Believed to be the originators of the great culture seen in the ruins of TIAHUANACO, they were subjugated by the INCA (15th cent.) and by the Spanish (16th cent.) but retained their pastoral civilization and patrilineal society. Still dominant in the region today, the Aymara have adopted some aspects of Spanish culture and Christian belief.

Ayub Khan, Muhammad, 1907–74, president (1958–69) of PAKISTAN. After 1951 he was commander of the Pakistani armed forces, and in 1958 he led a military coup and became president. Although he inaugurated far-reaching reforms and a new constitution, unrest grew; despite his reelection in 1965, he bowed to pressure and resigned in 1969.

azalea, shrubs (genus *Rhododendron*) of the HEATH family, distinguished by typically deciduous leaves and large clusters of pink, red, orange, yellow, purple, or white flowers. Most grow in damp acid soils of hills and mountains, and are native to North America and Asia. Native American azaleas include the flame azalea (*R. calendulacea*) and the fragrant white azalea (*R. viscosa*), also called swamp honeysuckle. Most of the brilliantly flowered garden varieties are from China and Japan.

Azaña, Manuel [äthä'nyä], 1880–1940, president of Spain (1936–39). A leader of the republican revolution of 1930, he served as premier (1931–33) in the first republic. He headed the Loyalist government in the SPANISH CIVIL WAR but held little real power.

Azerbaijan or **Azerbaidzhan** [both: ä"zərbījän'], officially Republic of Azerbaijan, republic (1992 est. pop. 7,451,000), 33,428 sq mi (86,579 sq km), SW Asia, in Transcaucasia; formerly a constituent republic of the USSR. It is bounded by Russia and Georgia (N); the Caspian Sea (E); Iran (S), where the Araks R. divides it from Iranian Azerbaijan; and Armenia (W). The NAKHICHEVAN region is an exclave separated from the country by Armenia. BAKY (Baku) is the capital and largest city; other major cities include Ganje (Gyandzha) and Sumgait. The country is rich in oil and natural gas and iron, copper, lead, zinc, and other ores. Manufactures include machinery, electrical and oil drilling equipment, cement, and steel. Grains, fruit, grapes, cotton, silk, and tobacco are the major crops. In addition to the Turkic-speaking Shiite Muslim Azeri (Azerbaijani) majority, there are Russian, Armenian (largely in the Nagorno-Karabakh region), and other minorities.

History. The republic of Azerbaijan comprises the northern half of historic Azerbaijan; the southern half is in NW Iran. The area was linked to the history of ARMENIA and later PERSIA, particularly after its conquest (4th cent.) by Shapur II. Overrun later by Mongols (13th cent.) and TIMUR (14th cent.), it was divided after the fall (15th cent.) of the Timurid empire into several principalities. After 1603 the area was part of Persia until acquired by Russia between 1813 and 1828. Briefly independent after the RUSSIAN REVOLUTION, Azerbaijan was conquered (1920) by the Red Army and incorporated into the USSR. Part of the Transcaucasian Soviet Federated Republic after 1922, it became a separate constituent republic in 1936. Under Soviet Pres. GORBACHEV, Azeris began demanding greater independence from the central Soviet government. In NAGORNO-KARABAKH, a mainly Armenian territory in W Azerbaijan, Armenians demanded (1988) autonomy; fighting in the enclave led to warfare with Armenia by 1992 and spilled into Azerbaijan proper by 1993. In the aftermath of the failed coup (1991) against Gorbachev, Azerbaijan declared its independence from the USSR, and nationalist Abulfez Elchibey was elected (1992) president. Elchibey was ousted by the parliament after a military mutiny, and Heydar Aliyev, who was Azerbaijan Communist party leader from 1969 to 1982, succeeded him as president. Azerbaijan is a member of the COMMONWEALTH OF INDEPENDENT STATES.

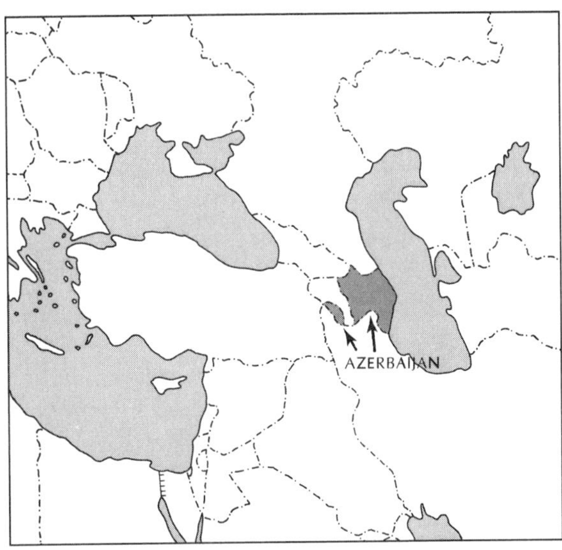

azimuth: see ASTRONOMICAL COORDINATE SYSTEMS.

Azoic time: see GEOLOGIC ERA (table).

Azores, island group belonging to Portugal (1987 est. pop. 254,000), 905 sq mi (2,344 sq km), located in the Atlantic Ocean, c.900 mi (1,448 km) W of mainland Portugal. The nine main islands are São Miguel (the largest) and Santa Maria in the southeast; Terceira, Pico, Fayal, São Jorge, and Graciosa in the center; and Flores and Corvo in the northwest. Ponta Delgado, on São Miguel, is the largest city. The islands are divided into three districts named after their capitals: Ponta Delgado, Angra do Heroísmo (on Terceira), and Horta (on Fayal). The U.S. maintains NATO air bases on the islands.

Azorín: see MARTÍNEZ RUIZ, JOSÉ.

AZT or **zidovudine,** drug used to treat patients infected with the human immunodeficiency virus (HIV), which causes AIDS; also called azidothymidine. It inhibits the virus's ability to reproduce and may decrease the frequency of infection by other diseases, enhancing the lives of HIV-infected patients, but it does not cure AIDS. Adverse effects include anemia and a reduction in the number of certain white blood cells. A drug that acts similarly to AZT, ddI (didanosine or dideoxyinosine), is used to treat patients who do not respond to or cannot tolerate AZT. A third similarly acting drug, ddC (zalcitabine or dideoxycytidine), is given in combination with AZT.

Aztec, indigenous people dominating central Mexico (see MIDDLE AMERICA, INDIGENOUS PEOPLES OF) at the time of the Spanish conquest (16th cent.), with a Nahuatlan language of the Uto-Aztecan stock (see NATIVE AMERICAN LANGUAGES). Until the founding of their capital, Tenochtitlán (c.1325), the Aztec were a poor nomadic tribe in the valley of Mexico. In the 15th cent. they became powerful, subjugating the Huastec to the north and the MIXTEC and ZAPOTEC to the south, and achieving a composite civilization based on a TOLTEC and Mixteca-Puebla heritage. Engineering, architecture, art, mathematics, astronomy, sculpture, weaving, metalwork, music, and picture writing were highly developed; agriculture and trade flourished. The nobility, priesthood, military, and merchant castes predominated. War captives were sacrificed to the many Aztec gods, including the god of war, Huitzilopochti. In 1519, when CORTÉS arrived, many subject peoples willingly joined the Spanish against the Aztecs. Cortés captured MONTEZUMA, who was subsequently murdered, and razed Tenochtitlán.

B

B, chemical symbol of the element BORON.

Ba, chemical symbol of the element BARIUM.

Baade, Walter [bä'də], 1893–1960, German-American astronomer. He presented evidence for the existence of two different stellar populations of older and newer stars. Baade knew that, at the then-accepted distance of the Andromeda galaxy, cluster-type variable stars should have appeared on photographs that he took with the 200-in. (5.08-m) telescope at Palomar Observatory. Because they did not, he correctly reasoned (1952) that the distances to this galaxy and other extragalactic systems must be doubled.

Baal [bā'əl], plural **Baalim** [Semitic, = possessor], the OLD TESTAMENT term for the deity or deities of CANAAN. First applied to local gods, it was later the name of the chief deity. His cult practiced holy PROSTITUTION and child sacrifice. In Israel it was denounced by Hebrew Prophets. The name is synonymous with evil, hence Beelzebub (see SATAN).

Baal-Shem-Tov [Heb., = master of the good name, i.e., the name of God], c.1698–1760, Jewish founder of modern HASIDISM; b. Poland as Israel ben Eliezer. He was called Baal-Shem-Tov because of his reputation as a miracle healer. Central to his teachings is the notion that one must worship God in all activities—and with joy. From his large circle of followers developed communities of modern HASIDIM.

Ba'ath movement [bä'äth], Arab movement that advocates a single, socialist pan-Arab nation. Founded in Damascus in the early 1940s and claiming to draw its philosophical tenets from Islam, Ba'athism opposed imperialism and colonialism and favored nonalignment. It spread to Iraq after the 1958 revolution. The movement spawned the Ba'ath party, a faction-riven group that has been strongest in Syria and Iraq and that governed those nations during the 1960s and 70s.

Babbage, Charles, 1792–1871, English mathematician and inventor, famous for his attempts to develop a mechanical computational aid he called the "analytical engine." Although it was never constructed and was decimal rather than binary in conception, it clearly anticipated the modern digital COMPUTER. A scientist with extremely broad interests, Babbage probed the roles of learned societies and government in advancing science, and wrote on mass production and on what is now called operational research.

Babbitt, Irving, 1865–1933, American scholar; b. Dayton, Ohio. A professor of French literature at Harvard (1912–33), he helped initiate New Humanism, a movement based on classical moderation. His works include *The New Laokoön* (1910) and *On Being Creative* (1932).

Babbitt, Milton, 1916–, American composer; b. Philadelphia. His "total serialization" attempts to apply 12-tone principles to all the elements of composition: dynamics, timbre, and rhythm, as well as melody and harmony (see SERIAL MUSIC; TWELVE-TONE MUSIC). In 1959 he became director of the Columbia-Princeton Electronic Music Center (N.Y.C.).

Babel, Isaac Emmanuelovich [bä'bəl], 1894–1941, Russian writer. A brilliant stylist, he won fame with *Odessa Tales* (1923–24), depicting Jewish ghetto life, and *Red Cavalry* (1926), which drew on his Civil War experiences. His also wrote the novel *Benia Krik* (1927) and the play *Sunset* (1928). He was arrested in 1939 and died in a labor camp.

Babel [bā'bəl], in the BIBLE, Babylonian city where NOAH's descendants (who spoke one language) tried to build a tower reaching to heaven. For this presumption they lost the ability to speak intelligibly to each other.

Bab el Mandeb, strategic strait between Arabia and NE Africa, 17 mi (27 km) wide, connecting the RED SEA with the Gulf of ADEN. It is a vital link in the MEDITERRANEAN SEA–SUEZ CANAL–INDIAN OCEAN sea lane.

Babeuf, François Noël [bäböf'], 1760–97, French revolutionary activist. In 1794 he founded a political journal that argued for economic and political equality. Imprisoned in 1795, he grew surer of his communist views. He formed a secret society called the Conspiracy of Equals and plotted to overthrow the government of the DIRECTORY. The plot was discovered, and Babeuf was executed.

Babington, Anthony, 1561–86, English conspirator. He was executed for plotting the murder of ELIZABETH I and the freeing of MARY QUEEN OF SCOTS. The proof against him convinced Elizabeth that it was necessary to behead Mary.

Babism, a 19th-cent. Persian sect, an outgrowth of SHIITE Islam that was founded by Mirza Ali Muhammad of Shiraz, who proclaimed himself the Bab [gate] in 1844. Babism, incorporating elements of SUFISM, GNOSTICISM, and Shiite Islam, centered on a belief in the coming of the Promised One. Oppressed from 1845, the movement declared its complete secession from ISLAM in 1848, and in 1863 the Babists were expelled from Persia. After 1868 a division had its center in Acre, under the leadership of BAHA ULLAH, the founder of BAHA'ISM.

baboon, large, powerful, ground-living MONKEY (genus *Papio*), also called dog-faced monkey, related to the MANDRILL. Found in the open country of Africa and Asia, baboons have close-set eyes under heavy brow ridges, long, heavy muzzles, powerful jaws, cheek pouches for storing food, and sharp, tusklike upper canine teeth. Baboons have a highly developed social structure.

Babur, 1483–1530, founder of the MOGUL empire in INDIA. A descendant of TIMUR, he invaded India from Afghanistan. He defeated (1526) the sultan of Delhi, captured Agra and Delhi, and later conquered most of N India. Babur was a poet; his autobiography is his major work.

Babylon, ancient city of Mesopotamia, on the Euphrates R. It became one of the most important cities of the ancient Middle East when HAMMURABI made it the capital of his kingdom of BABYLONIA. The city was destroyed (c.689 B.C.) by the Assyrians under SENNACHERIB, but it was rebuilt. The brilliant color and luxury of Babylon became legendary from the days of NEBUCHADNEZZAR (d. 562 B.C.). The Hanging Gardens were one of the SEVEN WONDERS OF THE WORLD. The Persians captured the city in 538 B.C.

Babylonia, ancient empire of Mesopotamia. Historically the name refers to the first dynasty of Babylon established by HAMMURABI (c.1750 B.C.) and to the Neo-Babylonian period after the fall of the Assyrian empire. Hammurabi, who had his capital at BABYLON, issued a famous code of laws for the management of the empire. Babylonian religion and cuneiform writing were derived from the older culture of SUMER and the quasi-feudal society was divided into classes. These Babylonian institutions influenced ASSYRIA and so contributed to the later history of the Middle East and of Western Europe. Babylonia degenerated into anarchy (c.1180 B.C.), but flourished once again as a subsidiary state of the Assyrian empire after the 9th cent. B.C. Later, Nabopolassar established (625 B.C.) what is generally known as the Chaldean or New Babylonian empire, which reached its height under his son NEBUCHADNEZZAR. In 538 B.C. the last of the Babylonian rulers surrendered to CYRUS THE GREAT of Persia.

Babylonian art: see SUMERIAN AND BABYLONIAN ART.

Babylonian captivity, in the history of Israel, the period from the fall of Jerusalem (586 B.C.) to the reconstruction in Palestine of a new Jewish state (after 538 B.C.). Following the capture of the city by the Babylonians, thousands of JEWS were deported to Mesopotamia. In 538 B.C. the Persian King CYRUS THE GREAT decreed the restoration of worship at Jerusalem. The century following this decree was the time of Jewish reintegration into a national and religious unit.

baby's breath, name for a plant of the PINK family, for the white bedstraw of the MADDER family, and for grape HYACINTH of the LILY family.

Bacchanalia, in Roman religion, festival honoring BACCHUS, god of wine. Originally a religious ceremony, it led to drunken, licentious excesses and was outlawed (186 B.C.).

Bacchus [băk'əs], in Greek and Roman religion, god of wine, vegetation, and fertility. His worship was celebrated in orgiastic rites such as the Bacchanalia.

Bach [bäkh], German family of distinguished musicians who flourished from the 16th through the 18th cent., its most renowned member being **Johann Sebastian Bach** (see separate article). **Johannes,** or **Hans, Bach,** 1580–1626, was a carpet weaver and musical performer at festivals. His sons and descendants were noted organists and composers. One grandson, **Johann Ambrosia Bach,** 1645–95, a musician, was the father of Johann Sebastian Bach. **Johann Christoph Bach,** 1671–1721, Johann Sebastian's eldest brother, was an organist; he took his younger brother in and taught him after their parents' death. Of the 20 children of Johann Sebastian, several were noted as musicians. The eldest son, **Wilhelm Friedemann Bach,** 1710–84, was a brilliant organist and well-known composer, but his life ended in poverty and dissolution. A younger son was **Carl Philipp Emanuel Bach,** 1714–88, also a composer and for 28 years (1740–68) the harpsichordist of Frederick the Great. He wrote an important treatise, *Essay on the True Art of Playing Keyboard Instruments* (1753). The youngest son, **Johann Christian Bach,** 1735–82, known as the "English Bach," became (1762) music master to King GEORGE III. A popular composer in the rococo style, he influenced the young MOZART.

Bach, Alexander, 1813–93, Austrian politician. As minister of the interior (1849–59) he instituted the **Bach system** for the centralization and Germanization of Hapsburg lands. It also ended internal tariffs. The system met opposition, especially in Hungary, and was replaced after 1859.

Bach, Johann Sebastian, 1685–1750, German composer and organist, one of the greatest composers of the Western world. Born into a gifted family, Bach was trained in music from childhood by his father, Johann Ambrosia, and later by his brother Johann Christoph. He held a variety of posts, serving as organist in Arnstadt (1703–7), Mühlhausen (1707–8), and Weimar (1708–17) before becoming (1717) musical director for Prince Leopold at Cöthen. After the death (1720) of his first wife, Maria Barbara Bach, he married (1721) Anna Magdalena Wülken. He had in all 20 children, several of whom became noted as musicians (see separate article). In 1723, Bach became cantor and music director of St. Thomas Church, Leipzig, a distinguished post that he held until his death. In his instrumental and choral works, Bach perfected the art of POLYPHONY and brought the era of BAROQUE music to its culmination. During his lifetime he was better known as a virtuoso organist than as a composer, but since the 19th cent. his genius has been recognized, and his reputation has grown steadily. In his early years as organist, he composed a series of works for organ that culminated in the great preludes and FUGUES written at Weimar. At Cöthen he focused on instrumental compositions, such as the Brandenburg Concertos, and keyboard works, such as Book I of the celebrated *Well-Tempered Clavier.* His superb religious compositions from the Leipzig period include the *St. John Passion* and the *Mass in B Minor,* and some 300 sacred CANTATAS, of which nearly 200 are extant. His last notable pieces are the *Musical Offering,* composed (1747) for Frederick the Great, and the *Art of the Fugue* (1749).

bachelor's button, popular name for several plants usually characterized by rounded flowers, such as the CORNFLOWER and globe AMARANTH.

Bach system: see under BACH, ALEXANDER.

backgammon, game of chance and skill played by two persons on a specially marked board divided by a space (bar) into two "tables," each of which has 12 alternately colored points (elongated triangular spaces) on which each player places 15 pieces (disks) in a prescribed formation. Two dice are thrown to determine moves. The object is to be the first to move one's pieces around and off the board. The game has very ancient roots in the Middle East.

Bacon, Francis, 1561–1626, English philosopher, essayist, and statesman. After his opposition (1584) to Queen Elizabeth I's tax program retarded his political advancement, he was favored by the earl of Essex, whom Bacon later helped to prosecute (1601). Under James I he advanced from knight (1603) to attorney general (1613) to lord chancellor (1618). In 1621 he pleaded guilty to charges of accepting bribes and was fined and banished from office; he spent the rest of his life writing in retirement. Bacon's best-known writings are his aphoristic *Essays* (1597–1625). He projected a major philosophical work, the *Instauratio Magna,* but completed only two parts: the *Advancement of Learning* (1605), later expanded in Latin as *De Augmentis Scientarum* (1623); and the *Novum Organum* (1620). His major contribution to philosophy was his application of INDUCTION, the approach used by modern science, rather than the a priori method of medieval SCHOLASTICISM.

Bacon, Francis, 1909–92, English painter; b. Ireland. Self-taught, he expressed the satirical, horrifying, and hallucinatory in such works as *Three Studies for Figures at the Base of a Crucifixion* (1944; Tate Gall., London).

Bacon, Nathaniel, 1647–76, leader of Bacon's Rebellion in colonial Virginia. Dissatisfied with the government of Sir William BERKELEY, and its neglect of frontier defense, Bacon led (1676) a popular uprising. He drove Berkeley from JAMESTOWN, but his death from malaria ended the revolt.

Bacon, Roger, c.1214–94?, English scholastic philosopher and scientist, a FRANCISCAN. A celebrated teacher at Oxford, Bacon had an interest far in advance of his times in natural science and accurate observation of phenomena, without, however, abandoning his faith. Three of his most important works, summarizing his studies, were written for Pope CLEMENT I in one year (1267–68): the *Opus majus, Opus minor,* and the *Opus tertium.* Deeply interested in alchemy, Bacon was credited by contemporaries with great learning in magic. Many discoveries have been attributed to him, including the invention of gunpowder and the first examination of cells through a microscope, but much doubt has been cast on the authenticity of such claims.

bacteria, unicellular, generally microscopic organisms having three typical forms: rod-shaped (bacillus), round (coccus), and spiral (spirillum). The cytoplasm of most bacteria—the oldest life-forms on earth—is surrounded by a cell wall; the nucleus contains DNA but lacks the nuclear membrane found in higher plants and animals. Many forms are motile, propelled by movements of a filamentlike appendage (flagellum). Reproduction is chiefly by transverse fission (MITOSIS), but conjugation (transfer of nucleic acid between two cells) and other forms of genetic recombination also occur. Some bacteria (aerobes) can grow only in the presence of free or atmospheric oxygen; others (anaerobes) cannot grow in its presence; and a third group (facultative anaerobes) can grow with or without it. In unfavorable conditions, many species form resistant spores. Different types of bacteria are capable of innumerable chemical metabolic transformations, e.g., PHOTOSYNTHESIS and the conversion of free nitrogen and sulfur into AMINO ACIDS. Bacteria are both useful and harmful to humans. Some are used for soil enrichment with leguminous plants (see NITROGEN CYCLE), in alcohol and cheese fermentation, to decompose organic wastes and clean up toxic waste sites, and in GENETIC ENGINEERING. Others, called pathogens, cause a number of plant and animal diseases, including CHOLERA, SYPHILIS, TYPHOID FEVER, and TETANUS.

bacteriological warfare: see BIOLOGICAL WARFARE.

bacteriophage or **phage,** VIRUS that infects BACTERIA, sometimes destroying them. A phage has a head composed of PROTEIN with an inner core of NUCLEIC ACID and a hollow protein tail. It infects a host by attaching its tail to the bacterial cell wall and injecting nucleic acid (DNA) into its host, whose chemical energy it uses to produce new phage particles. Eventually the bacterial cell is destroyed by lysis, or dissolution, releasing the phage particles to infect other cells. Phages are highly specific, with a particular phage infecting only certain species of bacteria; they are important tools in studies of bacterial genetics and cellular mechanisms.

Bactria [băk'trēə], ancient Greek kingdom in central Asia. Its capital was Bactra (now Balkh, in N Afghanistan). A satrapy of the Persian Empire, it fell to ALEXANDER THE GREAT in 328 B.C. It declared its independence in 256 B.C. and became a powerful state, carrying its conquests deep into N India. Later Bactria fell (c.130 B.C.) to the nomadic Sakas and did not rise again as a state.

Baden-Powell of Gilwell, Robert Stephenson Smyth Baden-Powell, 1st **Baron,** 1857–1941, British soldier, founder of the BOY SCOUTS. For his work in organizing (1908) the Boy Scout and Girl Guide movements, he received a peerage in 1929.

badger, any of several related members of the WEASEL family. Most are large, nocturnal burrowers with broad, heavy bodies, long snouts, sharp claws, and long, grizzled fur. The Old World badger (*Meles meles*), found in Europe and N Asia, weighs about 30 lb (13.6 kg) and feeds on rodents, insects, and plants. The smaller American badger (*Taxidea taxus*) has short legs and a white stripe over the forehead and around each eye; a swift burrower, it will pursue prey into their holes and may construct its own living quarters 30 ft (9.1 m) below ground level.

Badlands National Park: see NATIONAL PARKS (table).

badminton, game played by two or four persons in which a shuttlecock (small, cork hemisphere with feathers) is volleyed over a net with light, gut-strung rackets. For singles play the court measures 17 ft (5.18 m) by 44 ft (13.40 m); the doubles court is 3 ft (.91 m) wider. The game, which is generally similar to tennis, probably originated in India. It was introduced into the U.S. in the 1890s.

Badoglio, Pietro [bädô'lyō], 1871–1956, Italian soldier and premier (1943–44). In 1936 he victoriously ended the conquest of Ethiopia. After MUSSOLINI's fall he became premier and negotiated an armistice (1943) with the Allies.

Baeda: see BEDE, SAINT.

Baedeker, Karl, 1801–59, German publisher of travel guides. Issued in many editions, the "Baedekers" provided historical data. Auto touring guides were issued after 1950.

Baer, Karl Ernst von, 1792–1876, Estonian biologist. Considered a founder of modern embryology, he discovered the notochord and the mammalian egg in the ovary. His *History of the Development of Animals* (2 vol., 1828–37) presented the theory of embryonic germ layers (consisting of cells from which body tissues and organs develop) and showed that early embryonic development is similar in all animals.

Baez, Joan, 1941–, American folk singer; b. N.Y.C. Singing ballads and SPIRITUALS in a clear, soprano voice, she greatly influenced the popularity of FOLK SONG in the 1960s. She was also involved in nonviolent social action.

Baffin, William, c.1584–1622, British arctic explorer. Although he failed to find the NORTHWEST PASSAGE on two expeditions (1615–16), he discovered BAFFIN BAY. His belief that the Northwest Passage did not exist delayed arctic exploration for a time.

Baffin Bay, ice-clogged body of water with hazardous icebergs, c.700 mi (1,130 km) long, between Greenland and Baffin Island (NE Canada), linked with the N Atlantic Ocean by the Davis Strait. Visited (1585) by John Davis and explored (1616) by William BAFFIN, it was an important whaling station in the 19th cent.

Baffin Island, 183,810 sq mi (476,068 sq km), NE Canada, largest island in the Arctic Archipelago and fifth largest in the world. Largely tundra in the west and mountains in the east, it is inhabited mainly by ESKIMOS. Iqaluit, in the southeast, is the largest settlement. Early explorers were Martin FROBISHER (1576–78) and William BAFFIN (1616).

Bagehot, Walter [băj'ət], 1826–77, English social scientist. Editor (1860–77) of the highly regarded *Economist,* he studied the English banking system (*Lombard Street,* 1873) and economy (*Economic Studies,* 1880). His classic *English Constitution* (1867) distinguished effective government institutions from those in decay, while *Physics and Politics* (1872) was an early application of DARWINISM to the social sciences. He was also a noted literary critic.

Baghdad or **Bagdad,** city (1987 pop. 3,236,000), capital and largest city of Iraq, central Iraq, on both banks of the Tigris R. Most of Iraq's industries are in Baghdad; they produced refined oil, carpets, leather, textiles, and cement. The present city was founded (A.D. 762) by the ABBASIDS and became their capital. Under the caliph HARUN AR-RASHID it developed into one of the great cities of Islam. The Mongols sacked Baghdad in 1258; it became (1638) part of the Ottoman Empire, and during World War I it was captured (1917) by the British. In 1921 the city was made the capital of newly created Iraq. Baghdad is rich in archaeological remains and has several museums. Many government offices and other structures were destroyed in the PERSIAN GULF WAR.

Bagot, Sir Charles [băg'ət], 1781–1843, British diplomat. As minister to the U.S. (1815–20), he negotiated the RUSH-BAGOT CONVENTION, which limited armaments on the U.S.–Canadian border. He was later governor general of Canada (1841–43).

bagpipe, musical instrument, most widely used in Ireland and Scotland, consisting of an inflated bag, usually leather; one or two chanters (or chaunters), melody pipes with finger holes; and one or more drones, which produce one tone each. The bagpipe is an ancient instrument, probably carried E and W from Mesopotamia by Celtic migrations.

Baha'ism, religion founded by BAHA ULLAH, a doctrinal outgrowth of BABISM, with Baha Ullah as the Promised One of the earlier religion. Emphasizing simplicity and charity, Baha'is believe in the unity of all religions, in universal education, in world peace, and in the equality of men and women, and also advocate an international language and government. Baha'is have been severely persecuted in Iran under the Islamic republic, which regards the religion as an Islamic heresy. In the 20th cent. Baha'i teachings have spread across the world, particularly to Africa. The administrative center of the world faith is in Haifa, Israel; its U.S. headquarters is in Wilmette, Ill.

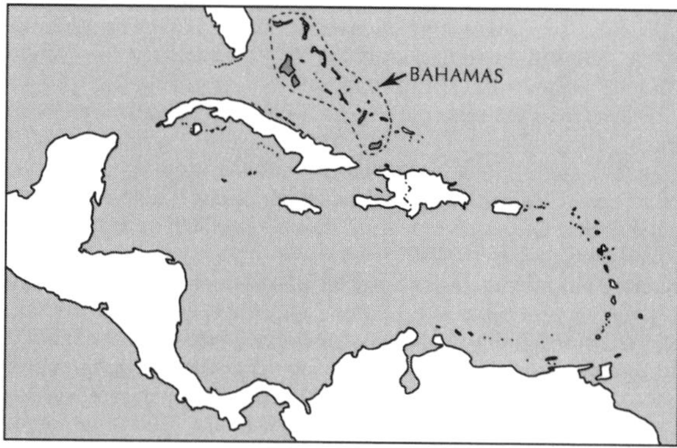

Bahamas, officially Commonwealth of the Bahamas, independent nation (1992 est. pop. 256,000), 4,403 sq mi (11,404 sq km), in the Atlantic Ocean, consisting of some 700 islands and islets and about 2,400 cays, beginning c.50 mi (80 km) off SE Florida and extending c.600 mi (970 km) SE, nearly to Haiti. Most of the islands are low, flat, and riverless, and many are uninhabited. The capital is NASSAU, on New Providence island, which, although smaller than many of the other islands, is the major population center. Other islands, called "out islands," include Grand Bahama, Great and Little Abaco, the Biminis, and Great and Little Inagua. The Bahamas' fine beaches, lush vegetation, and colorful coral reefs have made it one of the Western Hemisphere's most popular winter resort areas. Tourism is the major industry, although banking and sugar and oil refining have been developed to diversify the economy. The population is mostly black and mulatto, and the language is English.

History. Christopher COLUMBUS set foot in the New World in the Bahamas (1492), presumably on San Salvador. The British settled the Bahamas in the 1600s and imported blacks to work cotton plantations, which disappeared in the mid-19th cent., after the slaves were freed. Black Bahamians won control of the government from the white minority when Lynden PINDLING and the Progressive Liberal party came to power in 1967. Independence was granted in 1973. In the 1980s there were recurrent charges against Pindling's government of corruption and ties to drug traffickers. Elections in 1992 brought the Free National Movement, led by Hubert A. Ingraham, to power.

Bahasa Indonesia [bähä'sä], another name for Indonesian, one of the Malayo-Polynesian languages. See LANGUAGE (table).

Baha Ullah or **Baha Allah,** 1817–92, Persian religious leader, originally named Mirza Husayn Ali Nuri. One of the first disciples of

BABISM, in 1863 (shortly before being exiled to Constantinople) he declared himself to be the Promised One expected by Babists. He then founded BAHA'ISM and wrote its fundamental book, *Kitabi Ikan* (tr. *The Book of Certitude,* 1943).

Bahrain or **Bahrein** [bärān'], officially State of Bahrain, independent sheikhdom (1992 est. pop. 552,000), 231 sq mi (598 sq km), an archipelago in the PERSIAN GULF between the Qatar Peninsula and Saudi Arabia. The two main islands are Bahrain (the largest) and Al Muharraq, which are linked to each other and Saudi Arabia by causeway. The capital and chief port is AL MANAMAH. Flat and sandy, with a few low hills, Bahrain has a hot, humid climate. The economy is based on oil, and oil revenues have financed modernization projects, particularly in health and education. Oil reserves are expected to be depleted during the 1990s, and attempts are being made to establish such industries as shipyards and aluminum and turbine manufacturing. The majority of the population are Muslim Arab Bahrainis, but other Arabs and Iranians, Indians, and other Asians make up over 35% of the inhabitants. Arabic is the official language, but English, Farsi, and Urdu are also spoken.

History. Ruled successively by Portugal (16th cent.) and Persia (intermittently from 1602, and long claimed by Iran), Bahrain became a sheikhdom in 1783 and a British protected state in 1861. Independence was declared in 1971. A constitution, adopted in 1973, limited the sheikh's powers and gave women the vote, but in 1975 the sheikh dissolved the National Assembly, and elections have not been held since then. In the early 1980s Bahrain established closer ties with other Persian Gulf states, particularly Saudi Arabia.

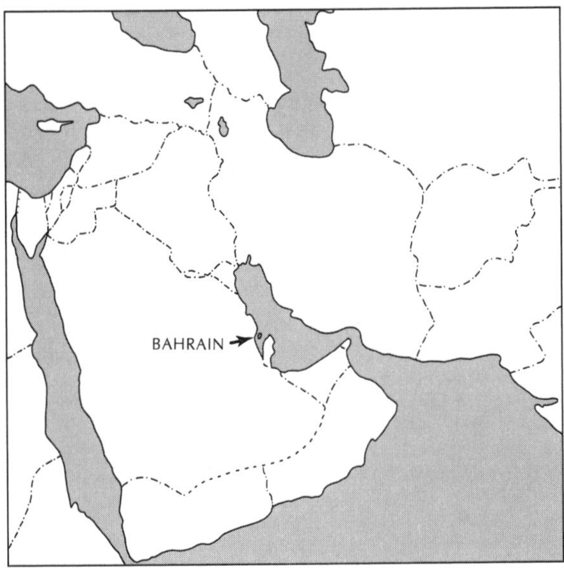

Baikal, Lake: see BAYKAL, LAKE.

Bairiki, town (1979 est. pop. 1,800) on TARAWA atoll, capital of KIRIBATI.

Baja California [bä'hä] or **Lower California,** peninsula, NW Mexico, separating the Gulf of California from the Pacific Ocean. It is c.760 mi (1,220 km) long and 30 to 150 mi (48 to 241 km) wide, and is divided between the states of Baja California (N) and Baja California Sur (S). The peninsula is generally mountainous and arid, with irrigated agriculture in the north, around Mexicali. Resort ranches and deep-sea fishing facilities along the scenic coasts support a growing tourist industry. U.S. forces occupied (1847–48) the peninsula during the MEXICAN WAR.

Bakelite for its inventor, Leo Baekeland, a synthetic thermosetting phenol-formaldehyde RESIN with an unusually wide variety of industrial applications ranging from billiard balls to electrical insulation.

Baker, Howard Henry, Jr., 1925–, U.S. public official; b. Huntsville, Tenn. As a conservative moderate Republican senator (1966–85) from Tennessee, he gained (1973) national attention as a member of the Senate committee investigating the WATERGATE AFFAIR. He became (1977) Senate minority leader and served (1981–85) as Senate majority leader after the Republican victory in the 1980 elections. He also was White House chief of staff (1987–88) under Pres. Reagan.

Baker, James A(ddison), III, 1930–, U.S. government official; b. Houston. A lawyer, Baker served (1975–76) as undersecretary in the Commerce Dept. during the Ford administration. Campaign chairman for George BUSH's unsuccessful bid for the 1980 Republican presidential nomination, he became Pres. REAGAN's chief of staff in 1981 and helped secure passage of the Kemp-Roth tax cut and other legislation. In 1985 Baker became treasury secretary, resigning in 1988 to manage Vice Pres. Bush's successful presidential campaign. Under Bush, Baker was secretary of state (1989–92), negotiating arms reduction treaties with the USSR and lending U.S. support to Germany's reunification. He was also instrumental in marshalling international opposition to Iraq's invasion of Kuwait (1990; see PERSIAN GULF WAR) and succeeded in convening (1991) a Middle East peace conference. He resigned to serve (1992–93) as White House chief of staff, with responsibility for domestic policy and for overseeing Bush's unsuccessful reelection campaign.

Baker, Dame Janet, 1933–, English mezzo-soprano. Acclaimed as an ORATORIO and LIEDER singer, she also appeared in such operas as Berlioz's *The Trojans* and Mozart's *Cosi fan tutte.* In 1991 she became chancellor of the Univ. of York, England.

Bakersfield, city (1990 pop. 174,820), seat of Kern co., S central Calif., at the S end of the SAN JOAQUIN valley; inc. 1898. Petroleum was discovered in the area in 1899. The city is an oil drilling and refining, mining, and agricultural center. Cotton, citrus fruits, potatoes, and roses are grown, and plastics and drugs are manufactured.

Baki: see BAKY.

baking soda: see SODIUM BICARBONATE.

Bakke Case: see UNIVERSITY OF CALIFORNIA REGENTS V. BAKKE.

Bakst, Léon Nicolaevich, 1866–1924, Russian painter, b. Lev Samuilovich Rosenberg. A painter of the eclectic school, he sought closer ties with the West before the Revolution through his involvement with the artists' group known as *Mir Iskusstva* or "World of Art." He is noted for his elaborate stage and costume designs for the Russian ballet, e.g., *L'Après-midi d'un Faune* (1912).

Baku: see BAKY.

Bakunin, Mikhail [bəko͞o'nyĭn], 1814–76, Russian revolutionary and leading exponent of ANARCHISM. After taking part (1848–49) in revolutions in France and Saxony, he was exiled to Siberia. He escaped (1861) to London, where he worked with Aleksandr HERZEN. In the first International Workingmen's Association he clashed with Karl MARX and was expelled (1872); their philosophical split led the International to dissolve (1876). Bakunin held that human beings are inherently good and deserve absolute freedom; he advocated the violent overthrow of existing governments. His works include *God and the State* (1882).

Baky, Baki, or **Baku,** city (1990 est. pop. 1,149,000), capital of AZERBAIJAN, SW Asia, on the Caspian Sea. Baky is a major port and a center for oil drilling, refining, and shipbuilding. Under independent Shirvan shahs the city was a medieval center of trade and crafts. It was under Persian rule from 1509 to 1806 when it was annexed by Russia. From 1920 until Azeribaijan's independence in 1991, it was part of the USSR.

Balaguer, Joaquin [bälägār'], 1907–, president of the Dominican Republic (1960–62, 1966–78, 1986–). He served in dictator TRUJILLO MOLINA's government as vice president (1957–60) and president until ousted (1962) by the military. During his second tenure, he restored financial stability, but political protest led him to resort to repression. He ran unsuccessfully for president in 1978 and 1982 but was reelected on a conservative platform in 1986 and 1990, despite his advanced age and blindness.

Balakirev, Mili Alekseyevich [bələkē'ryĕf], 1837–1910, Russian composer and conductor, leader of the group called the FIVE. His music, combining ROMANTICISM with Russian folk songs, includes the symphonic poem *Tamara.*

balalaika: see STRINGED INSTRUMENT.

balance of payments, relation between all payments in and out of a country over a given period. It is an outgrowth of the concept of BALANCE OF TRADE, which it includes; it also includes the movement of government and private capital between countries (e.g., investments and debt payments). The INTERNATIONAL MONETARY FUND was created (1945) to deal with problems relating to the balance of payments. The U.S., which has generally experienced an unfavorable balance of payments since the late 1950s, sought to improve the balance in the early 1970s through DEVALUATION of the dollar. The increase in imported oil prices (1973–74) and U.S. monetary policies in the 1980s, however, had a negative effect on the balance of payments.

balance of power, system of international relations in which nations shift alliances to maintain an equilibrium of power and prevent dominance by any single state. Its modern development began in the 17th cent. with efforts of European countries to contain the France of LOUIS XIV. The balance of power was of primary concern to European nations from 1815 to 1914, particularly to contain the rising power of GERMANY, and was attacked as a cause of WORLD WAR I. It declined with the rise of the U.S. and the USSR as superpowers after 1945, but after the 1960s, with the emergence of China and the THIRD WORLD, a revived Europe and Japan, and the later collapse of the USSR, it reemerged as a component of international relations.

balance of trade, relation between the value of a nation's exports and imports. The concept first became important in the 16th and 17th cent. with the growth of MERCANTILISM, whose theorists held that a nation should have an excess of exports over imports (i.e., a favorable balance); although challenged by Adam SMITH and other economists, the idea is still widely believed. The balance of trade is a major element in a nation's BALANCE OF PAYMENTS. In the 1980s and 90s the value of U.S. imports greatly exceeded exports, resulting in large trade deficits that complicated the U.S.'s relations with its trading partners, particularly Japan.

Balanchine, George, 1904–83, American choreographer and ballet dancer; b. Russia. A member of Sergei Pavlovich DIAGHILEV's BALLETS RUSSES (1924–28), he moved (1933) to the U.S. and helped to found (1934) the School of American Ballet. In 1948 he became artistic director and principal choreographer of the NEW YORK CITY BALLET. His many works, e.g., *Serenade, Agon,* emphasize form, often abstract. He was one of the most important figures in ballet in the 20th cent.

Balboa, Vasco Núñez de, c.1475–1519, Spanish CONQUISTADOR, discoverer of the PACIFIC OCEAN. Fleeing HISPANIOLA in 1510, he hid in a vessel that took the explorer Enciso to Panama. After reaching Darien, he seized command from Enciso and, with the aid of friendly indigenous peoples, marched across the isthmus. He reached the Pacific in Sept. 1513, claiming it and its shores for Spain. He was later accused of treason and beheaded.

Balch, Emily Green, 1867–1961, American economist and pacifist; b. Jamaica Plain, Mass. She taught at Wellesley College until her dismissal (1918) for opposing U.S. involvement in World War I. Co-founder (with Jane ADDAMS) of the Women's International League for Peace and Freedom, Balch shared the 1946 Nobel Peace Prize with J.R. Mott.

bald cypress, common name for the Taxodiaceae, a family of deciduous or evergreen CONIFERS with needlelike or scalelike leaves and woody cones. Most species are native to E Asia; some, e.g., the big trees and redwoods (see SEQUOIA) and bald cypresses, are native to North America. Almost all are cultivated for ornament. The common bald cypress (*Taxodium distichum*), valued for its softwood, forms dense forests in the SE U.S. and is common in the EVERGLADES. Bald cypresses are called "bald" because of their deciduous character, unusual in conifers. True CYPRESSES belong to a separate family.

Balder, beautiful and gracious Norse god of light; son of Odin (see WODEN) and FRIGG. Invulnerable to everything but mistletoe, he was killed by a mistletoe dart made by LOKI.

Baldwin, Latin emperors of CONSTANTINOPLE. **Baldwin I,** 1171–1205 (r.1204–5), was a leader in the Fourth CRUSADE as count of Flanders. Elected emperor of Constantinople, he was taken in battle by the Bulgarians (1205) and died in captivity. His brother, HENRY OF FLANDERS, succeeded him. **Baldwin II,** 1217–73 (r.1228–61), was the last Latin emperor of Constantinople. To obtain funds, he sold part of the True Cross to LOUIS IX of France and pawned his own son to the Venetians. When MICHAEL VIII of Nicaea stormed Constantinople, Baldwin fled to Italy.

Baldwin, Latin kings of Jerusalem. **Baldwin I,** 1058?–1118 (r.1100–18), was a brother of GODFREY OF BOUILLON, whom he accompanied in the First CRUSADE. He gained the chief ports of Palestine and aided other Latin rulers against the Muslims. His cousin and successor, **Baldwin II,** d. 1131 (r.1118–31), was also in the First Crusade. As king he warred with the Turks in N Syria. During his reign TYRE and Antioch became Jerusalem's dependents. **Baldwin III,** 1130–62 (r.1143–62), the son of Fulk of Anjou, ruled as Latin power in the East began to decay. Edessa fell (1144) to the Muslims, the Second Crusade failed, and the Turkish sultan Nur ad-Din took (1154) N Syria. His nephew **Baldwin IV** (the Leper), c.1161–85 (r.1174–85), defended his kingdom constantly against SALADIN. When his leprosy became worse, he had his child-nephew crowned (1183) **Baldwin V** (d. 1186).

Baldwin, James, 1924–87, African-American author; b. N.Y.C. His works, dealing with African Americans and relations between the races, include novels, e.g., *Go Tell It on the Mountain* (1953) and *Just Above My Head* (1979); essay collections, e.g., *Notes of a Native Son* (1955); plays; and short stories.

Baldwin, Robert, 1804–58, Canadian statesman. A reform leader in Upper CANADA, he proposed (1836) representative government for the entire country. After the reunion (1841) of Upper and Lower Canada, Baldwin and LA FONTAINE formed a coalition government (1842), and won an overwhelming victory in the 1847 election. Their second coalition (1847–51), called the "great ministry," implemented responsible government. Among its accomplishments was the Baldwin Act, which reformed local government in ONTARIO.

Baldwin, Roger Nash, 1884–1981, American civil libertarian; b. Wellesley, Mass. He helped to found (1920) the AMERICAN CIVIL LIBERTIES UNION and was its director until 1950 and its adviser on international affairs thereafter. He also taught at the New School for Social Research (1938–42) and the Univ. of Puerto Rico (1966–74).

Baldwin, Stanley, 1867–1947, British statesman. A Conservative, he was three times prime minister (1923–24; 1924–29; 1935–37). He broke the 1926 general strike and secured the abdication of EDWARD VIII. An able politician, Baldwin has been criticized for his apparent blindness to the threat to peace indicated by the rise of fascism in Europe.

Balearic Islands, archipelago and autonomous region (1991 pop. 709,138) of Spain, in the W Mediterranean Sea. The three principal islands are Majorca, Minorca, and Ibiza. All have a mild climate and are popular tourist centers. The Balearics were occupied by Moors in the 8th cent. and captured (1229–35) by James I of Aragón. They were included (1276–1343) in the independent kingdom of Majorca and reverted to the Aragonese crown under Peter IV.

Balfour, Arthur James Balfour, 1st **earl of** [băl'fŏŏr], 1848–1930, British statesman. A Conservative, he held many cabinet positions and was prime minister from 1902 to 1905. As foreign secretary under LLOYD GEORGE (1916–19), he issued the Balfour Declaration (1917), pledging British support for a Jewish national home in Palestine.

Bali, island and (with two offshore islets) province (1990 est. pop. 2,785,000), S Indonesia, c.2,200 sq mi (5,700 sq km), separated from JAVA (W) by the narrow Bali Strait. The fertile, scenic, and densely populated island is largely mountainous and volcanic, reaching a high point of 10,308 ft (3,142 m) at Mt. Agung. Rice, vegetables, fruits, and coffee are grown, and livestock is important. Industries include food processing, tourism, and handicrafts. The Balinese people retain their Hindu religion in a predominantly Muslim nation and are known for their uniquely ritualistic and beautiful music, folk drama, dancing, and architecture.

Baliol, John de [bāl'yəl], d. 1269, English nobleman; founder of Balliol College, Oxford. A regent for ALEXANDER III of Scotland, he was removed from office and later fought for HENRY III of England in the BARONS' WAR. His third son, **John de Baliol,** 1249–1315, king of Scotland (1292–96), claimed the throne at the death of MARGARET MAID OF NORWAY. EDWARD I of England supported him over ROBERT I in return for feudal overlordship, and he was crowned. In 1296 he renounced his oath of fealty, was defeated,

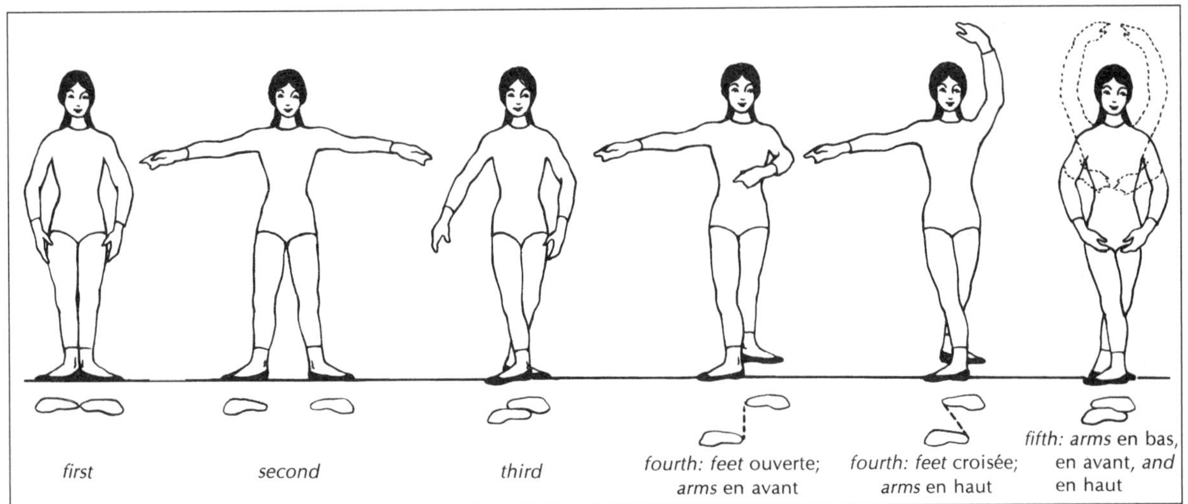

The five classical positions in ballet

and surrendered to Edward. He was imprisoned until 1299, when he retired to France. His son, **Edward de Baliol,** d. 1363, king of Scotland, invaded Scotland (1332) with the aid of EDWARD III and defeated supporters of DAVID II. After David's return from France (1341), he never held power.

Balkan Peninsula, generally mountainous land area, SE Europe, projecting south from the line of the Sava and Danube rivers between the Black, Aegean, Mediterranean, Ionian, and Adriatic seas. It comprises all or parts of nine nations—Albania, Bosnia and Hercegovina, Bulgaria, Croatia, Greece, Macedonia, Romania, Turkey, and Yugoslavia—collectively referred to as the **Balkan states.** The peninsula, which was at times part of ancient Greece and the Roman and Byzantine empires, was ruled by Turks as part of the Ottoman Empire from the late 15th cent. until the end of the BALKAN WARS in 1913.

Balkan Wars, two short wars (1912, 1913) fought for possession of the European territories of the deteriorating OTTOMAN EMPIRE (Turkey). In the first war, Serbia, Bulgaria, Greece, and Montenegro expelled Turkey from all of its European possessions except Constantinople (now İstanbul). The second war was brought on by Serbia (joined by Greece, Romania, and Turkey), which demanded that Bulgaria cede to it the larger part of Macedonia. Bulgaria lost and was forced to cede territories to all four victors. The nationalism heightened by the Balkan Wars was one of the causes of WORLD WAR I.

Ball, Lucille, 1911–89, American actress and producer; b. Jamestown, N.Y. An accomplished comedienne, she starred (1951–74) in three popular television series, beginning with *I Love Lucy.* She also headed Desilu Productions (1962–67) and Lucille Ball Productions (1967–89). Her films include *Stage Door* (1937) and *Mame* (1974).

ballad, in literature, short narrative poem usually relating a dramatic event. Folk ballads date from c.12th cent., literary ballads from the 18th. The anonymous folk ballad was originally sung, passed along orally, and changed in transmission. It was short, simple, and formulaic, often with a stock refrain. From the late 18th cent. hundreds were collected—historical, romantic, supernatural, nautical, or heroic. American ballads deal with cowboys, outlaws, folk heroes, and African Americans. Mid-20th cent. FOLK MUSIC has drawn on the tradition. The literary ballad is more elaborate, a prime example being S.T. COLERIDGE's *Rime of the Ancient Mariner.*

ballade, in literature, French 14th–15th cent. verse form, usually consisting of three eight-line stanzas and a concluding four-line envoy (a summary or address). Ballades by François VILLON and, in English, by Geoffrey CHAUCER are famous.

Balladur, Édouard, 1929–, French political leader. A Gaullist, he served under Premier POMPIDOU in the 1960s and was finance minister under Premier CHIRAC from 1986 to 1988. Appointed premier in 1993, he advocated a strict law-and-order policy, PRIVATIZATION of state-owned businesses, and promoted new taxes under an austerity budget.

ballet [Ital. *ballare,* = to dance], classic, formalized solo or ensemble dancing of a disciplined, dramatic nature, performed to music. Foreshadowed in mummeries and masquerades, it emerged as a distinct form in Italy before the 16th cent. The first ballet combining dance, decor, and special effects was presented in 1581 at the French court of CATHERINE DE' MEDICI. The 17th-cent. court ballets, danced until 1681 by males only, incorporated OPERA and drama. In 1708 the first ballet for public performance marked the appearance of a separate art form. Choreographic notation came into being and mythological themes were explored. Italian influence brought elevated and less horizontal movement, and Pierre Beauchamps established the five basic foot positions (see diagram). Marie Camargo introduced a shortened skirt, tights, and the first ballet slippers, allowing great freedom of movement. Her rival, Marie Sallé (the first female choreographer), wore a liberating, Grecian-style costume. The ballet d'action, developed c.1760 by Jean Georges Noverre, told a story through movement and facial expression. Modern ballet technique, stressing the turned-out leg and resulting variety of movement, was set down in 1820 by Carlo Blasis. With *La Sylphide* (1832) the romantic period began. Brilliant choreography emphasized the beauty and virtuosity of the prima ballerina; the male dancer functioned only as her partner until the 20th cent., when virtuoso male dancing revived. Conflicts of reality and illusion, flesh and spirit were revealed in romantic love stories and fairy tales. Under the pressure of NATURALISM in the theater, ballet declined through the mid-19th cent., but after 1875 a renaissance in romantic ballet began in Russia, where Marius Petipa and other European masters created many of the great standard ballets, e.g., *Sleeping Beauty* and *Swan Lake.* In 1909 the Russian impresario Sergei DIAGHILEV brought his Ballets Russes to Paris. In the following 20 years the Russian style, with the revolutionary music of composers like STRAVINSKY and modified by the MODERN DANCE influences of Isadora DUNCAN and others, brought a ballet renaissance to Europe and America. Paris, London, and New York City became major centers. Today Russian and English ballet continue to exemplify one major trend, toward storytelling and lavish production. In American ballet an opposing tendency toward abstraction in theme and simplicity in design, due largely to the influence of George BALANCHINE, is often displayed. In the late 20th cent. ballet enjoyed enormous popularity in the U.S.; New York City remained its center, but many companies flourished elsewhere. International touring expanded, and ballet was increasingly receptive to techniques and music from other dance forms. See articles on major dance companies and individual dancers.

Ballet Gran Folklórico de México, Mexico's national dance company. It was founded (1952) by Amalia Hernández at the National Institute of Fine Arts, Mexico City, to produce dances based on

Mexican folklore for television. Artistic excellence has led to its recognition as one of the world's finest "ethnic" ballets.

Ballets Russes: see DIAGHILEV, SERGEI PAVLOVICH.

ballistics, science of projectiles, such as bullets, bombs, rockets, and missiles. Interior ballistics deals with the propulsion and motion of a projectile within a gun or firing device. Exterior ballistics is concerned with the motion of the projectile while in flight, and includes the study of the trajectory, or curved flight path, of the projectile. Terminal ballistics is concerned with the phenomena occurring at the termination of the projectile's flight; such termination may result from impact on a solid target or explosion of the projectile. In criminology, the term *ballistics* is applied to the identification of the weapon from which a bullet was fired. Microscopic imperfections in a gun barrel make characteristic scratches and grooves on bullets fired through it.

balloon, lighter-than-air craft without a propulsion system, lifted by inflation of one or more containers with a gas lighter than air or with heated air. During flight, altitude is gained by discarding ballast, e.g., bags of sand, and lost by releasing some of the lifting gas from its container. In some late designs using air heated by a gas-fired burner, the altitude is controlled by varying the temperature of the heated air. The balloon was invented by the French brothers Joseph and Jacques Étienne MONTGOLFIER, who in 1783 caused a linen bag about 100 ft (30 m) in diameter to rise in the air. Using a Montgolfier balloon, Pilâtre de Rozier and the marquis d'Arlandes made the first manned balloon flight on Nov. 21, 1783. The Americans Ben Abruzzo, Maxie Anderson, and Larry Newman made (1978) the first successful transatlantic balloon crossing. Today WEATHER BALLOONS equipped with radio transmitters (see RADIOSONDE) and other instruments transmit meteorological readings to ground stations at regular intervals. High-altitude balloons are used in astronomy, especially in the study of cosmic rays and the photography of other planets. See also AIRSHIP; PICCARD, AUGUSTE.

balloon angioplasty: see ANGIOPLASTY.

balsa: see BOMBAX.

Balthazar: see WISE MEN OF THE EAST.

Balthus, pseud. of Balthasar Klossowski, Count de Rola, 1908–, Polish-French artist. A reclusive artist widely regarded as one of the most important modern figurative painters, Balthus is noted for his poetic, calm, yet oddly disorienting paintings. Many are extremely large with thickly built-up surfaces and feature dreamy, sensual, and enigmatically posed adolescent girls. Other typical subjects are brooding landscapes and distinctive portraits.

Baltic languages, a subfamily of the Indo-European family of languages. See LANGUAGE (table).

Baltic Sea, N Europe, arm of the Atlantic Ocean, c.163,000 sq mi (422,170 sq km), bordered by Denmark, Germany, Poland, Russia, Lithuania, Latvia, Estonia, Finland, and Sweden. Shallow and partly frozen in winter, it is connected to the Atlantic by several straits, including the Kattegat and SKAGERRAK, and by the Kiel Canal. Principal arms of the Baltic are the gulfs of Bothnia, Finland, and Riga.

Baltimore, David, 1938–, American microbiologist, b. New York City. In 1970 he and his wife, Alice Huang, discovered reverse transcriptase, an enzyme that allows RNA to synthesize DNA in RETROVIRUSES. He shared the 1975 Nobel Prize in physiology or medicine with Renato Dulbecco and Howard Temin. Appointed president of Rockefeller Univ. in 1990, he resigned the next year after a scientific fraud scandal. A paper he coauthored contained fraudulent data from another author; Baltimore was criticized for his vehement defense of the paper despite the evidence and for possibly attempting a coverup.

Baltimore, George Calvert, 1st **Baron:** see CALVERT, GEORGE.

Baltimore, city (1990 pop. 736,014; met. area 2,382,172), N Md., on the Patapsco R. estuary, a branch of CHESAPEAKE BAY; settled early 17th cent., inc. 1745. The largest city in Maryland, Baltimore is a major seaport, industrial center, and railhead. Shipbuilding, food processing, metal and oil refining, and the production of aerospace equipment and chemicals are among the leading industries. The city grew phenomenally with the opening (1818) of the NATIONAL ROAD and the founding (1827) of the Baltimore & Ohio Railroad. Largely rebuilt after a fire in 1904, it became famous for its white-stepped, red-brick row houses. Johns Hopkins Univ., Goucher College, and the Peabody Conservatory of Music are among the city's many educational institutions. Cultural features include the Baltimore Museum of Art and the Enoch Pratt Free Library. H.L. MENCKEN, Babe RUTH, and Billie HOLIDAY were among Baltimore's best-known natives. The city's sights include the first U.S. Roman Catholic cathedral (1806–21), designed by B.H. LATROBE; the Inner Harbor area, including the U.S.S. *Constellation* and the National Aquarium; and the nation's third oldest zoo.

Balts, peoples of the E coast of the Baltic Sea, namely the Latvians, Lithuanians, and now-extinct Old Prussians. The Estonians are related to the Finns rather than to the Balts. In the 13th cent. the TEUTONIC KNIGHTS and Livonian Brothers of the Sword conquered and Christianized Estonia and Latvia, which remained under German economic dominance until the 20th cent. The Lithuanians, who resisted annexation and adopted Christianity in 1387, formed a powerful state that united (1569) with Poland. Estonia passed in 1561 to Sweden and in 1721 to Russia, which by 1795 controlled all the Baltic lands. Independent after World War I, LATVIA, LITHUANIA, and ESTONIA were forcibly incorporated into the USSR in 1940. Under the more liberal policies of Soviet Pres. GORBACHEV noncommunist nationalists gained control of the Baltic states' parliaments and sought to restore the nations' independence. The Soviet government recognized their independence (1991) in the aftermath of the failed hard-line coup against Gorbachev.

Baluchi [bəlo͞o'chē], language belonging to the Iranian group of the Indo-Iranian subfamily of the Indo-European family of languages. See LANGUAGE (table).

Balzac, Honoré de [bälzäk'], 1799–1850, French writer, among the great masters of the NOVEL. Half starving in a Paris garret, he began his career by writing sensational novels to order under a pseudonym. His great work, called "The Human Comedy," written over a 20-year period, is a collection of novels and stories recreating French society of the time, picturing in precise detail individuals of every class and profession. Chief among them are *Père Goriot* (1835) and *Cousin Bette* (1847). His short stories include some of the best in the language.

Bamako, city (1987 pop. 646,163), capital of Mali, a port on the Niger R. It is a major regional trade center connected by rail to DAKAR, on the Atlantic Ocean. Manufactures include processed meat, textiles, and metal goods. Bamako was a center of Muslim learning under the MALI empire (c.11th–15th cent.). It became (1908) the capital of the Sudan, a province of French West Africa. It has a botanical and zoological park, gardens, and several educational institutions.

bamboo, plant (genus *Bambusa*) of the GRASS family, chiefly of warm or tropical regions. The genus contains the largest grasses, sometimes reaching 100 ft (30 m). Bamboo stalks are hollow, usually round, and jointed, with deciduous leaves. Bamboo is used as wood, and for construction work, furniture, utensils, fiber, paper, fuel, and innumerable other articles. Bamboo sprouts (shoots) and the grains of some species are eaten. Native American bamboo is a CANE.

banana, name for a family of tropical herbs (the Musacae), for a genus (*Musa*) of herbaceous plants, and for the fruits they produce. Bananas are probably native to tropical Asia, but are widely cultivated. They are related to the economically valuable MANILA HEMP and to the BIRD-OF-PARADISE FLOWER. Banana plants have a palmlike aspect and large leaves, the overlapping bases of which form the so-called false trunk. Only female flowers develop into the banana fruit (botanically, a berry), each plant bearing fruit only once. The seeds are sterile; propagation is through shoots from the rhizomes. Bananas are an important food staple in the tropics.

Bancroft, George, 1800–1891, American historian and public official; b. Worcester, Mass. Bancroft was secretary of the navy (1845–46) under Pres. POLK and established the U.S. Naval Academy. Later he was minister to Britain (1846–49) and Prussia (1867–74). He supported Pres. LINCOLN in the CIVIL WAR. His *History of the United States* (10 vol., 1834–74) is anti-British and intensely patriotic but remains valuable because of its extensive use of source materials.

Bancroft, Hubert Howe, 1832–1918, American historian; b. Granville, Ohio. A wealthy publisher, he produced, with a staff of researchers and writers, a prodigious history of the U.S. West, Central America, and Mexico (39 vol., 1874–90). In 1905 he presented his collection of 60,000 books, manuscripts, maps, and personal narratives to the Univ. of California, and as the Bancroft Library it remains an outstanding repository of the history of the West.

Banda, Hastings Kamuzu, 1902?–, president of MALAWI (1966–). A physician, he was a leading nationalist in Nyasaland, becoming prime minister and leading it to independence as Malawi in 1964. He became president for life under a new constitution in 1966 and suppressed opposition to his rule. The stoppage of Western aid (1992) forced him to grant a referendum (1993) on one-party rule, which he lost. The life presidency was abolished in 1993, but Banda remained in office.

Bandaranaike, Sirimavo (Ratwatte Dias) [bändränī'kē], 1916–, prime minister (1960–65, 1970–77) of SRI LANKA (formerly Ceylon). She was largely responsible for the constitution of 1972 that transformed Ceylon into the republic of Sri Lanka. In 1980 she was expelled from Parliament and stripped (1980–82) of her civil rights because of abuses as prime minister. She was an unsuccessful candidate for president in 1988.

Bandar Seri Begawan, formerly Brunei, city (1986 est pop. 50,500), capital and chief port of BRUNEI.

Bandung or **Bandoeng,** city (1990 est. pop. 1,910,000), capital of West Java prov., Indonesia, 75 miles (120 km) SE of JAKARTA. Founded by the Dutch in 1810, it became the administrative and military headquarters of the Netherlands East Indies. Third largest city in Indonesia, Bandung is an industrial hub, a famous educational and cultural center, and a tourist resort. It is a textile center and site of the country's quinine industry.

Bandung Conference, 1955, meeting of diplomats from 29 African and Asian countries held at BANDUNG, Indonesia. It promoted economic and cultural cooperation and opposed colonialism. The People's Republic of China played a prominent part.

Bangalore, city (1991 pop. 2,651,000), capital of Karnataka state, S central India. It is an industrial center producing electronic and other high-technology equipment, computer software, aircraft, textiles, and other products. Founded in 1537, it became the administrative seat of Mysore (now Karnataka) in 1831. The city has many parks and several institutes of learning.

Bangkok, city (1990 est. pop. 7,380,000), capital of Thailand, S central Thailand, on the east bank of the Chao Phraya R., near the Gulf of Thailand. Thailand's largest city, its financial and industrial hub, and a leading city of Southeast Asia, Bangkok lies in the rice-growing region. Rice, tin, teak, and rubber are shipped from the city's port. Manufactures include processed food, textiles, lumber, refined oil, motor vehicles and electrical equipment. The city is also a famous jewelry-trading center. Ethnic Chinese dominate commerce and industry. A city that contrasts ancient and modern structures, Bangkok contains the vast, walled Grand Palace and over 400 Buddhist temples and is noted for its numerous canals. It is the site of five universities, as well as the National Museum. It became the nation's capital in 1782. **Thon Buri,** part of metropolitan Bangkok, is an industrial city on the river's west bank. It was the capital of Siam (1769–82).

Bangladesh, officially People's Republic of Bangladesh, republic (1992 est. pop. 119,412,000), 55,126 sq mi (142,776 sq km), S Asia, bordered by India (W, N, and E), Myanmar (SE), and the Bay of Bengal (S). Principal cities include DHAKA (the capital) and CHITTAGONG. A low-lying alluvial region, Bangladesh is composed mainly of the combined delta of the GANGES, BRAHMAPUTRA, and Meghna rivers. The climate is tropical monsoonal, and there are frequent, devastating floods and cyclones (hurricanes). The economy is largely agricultural; jute (of which Bangladesh produces over 50% of the world supply), rice, sugarcane, and tea are the principal crops. The principal manufactures include jute products, textiles, paper, processed food, and fertilizers. Bangladesh has the highest population density in the world. The majority of the people are Bengalis. About 90% are Muslims; there are Hindu, Buddhist, and Christian minorities. The official language is Bengali, but English is also spoken.

History. Governed for centuries by Afghan, Mogul, and Muslim rulers, the area that is now Bangladesh became part of British India in the late 18th cent. When Pakistan achieved independence in 1947, Bangladesh, then called East Bengal and, after 1955, East Pakistan, became an eastern province of Pakistan, from which it is separated by more than 1,000 miles. A movement for greater autonomy was spearheaded by Sheikh Mujibar Rahman, whose AWAMI LEAGUE won a majority in the federal Pakistani assembly in 1970. The government postponed assembly sessions, and on Mar. 26, 1971, the Awami League declared the province independent as Bangladesh. Civil war ensued, and an estimated 1 million Bengalis were killed before India intervened on Bangladesh's behalf and Pakistan was defeated in Dec. 1971. Famine, disastrous weather, and political unrest have plagued Bangladesh since independence. Rahman was assassinated in a military coup in 1975. Two countercoups quickly followed, bringing to power Gen. Ziaur Rahman, who was elected president in 1978. He brought some stability to the country and reintroduced civilian rule, but was killed in an abortive coup in 1981. Another coup, led by Lt. Gen. Hossain Mohammad Ershad, and the introduction of martial law followed in 1982. Ershad declared (1983) himself president and later won (1986) a disputed election. In 1990 violent protests forced his resignation, and he was later convicted of corruption and jailed. Free elections were held in 1991. The National party, led by Khaleda Zia, Ziaur Rahman's widow, won, and she became prime minister.

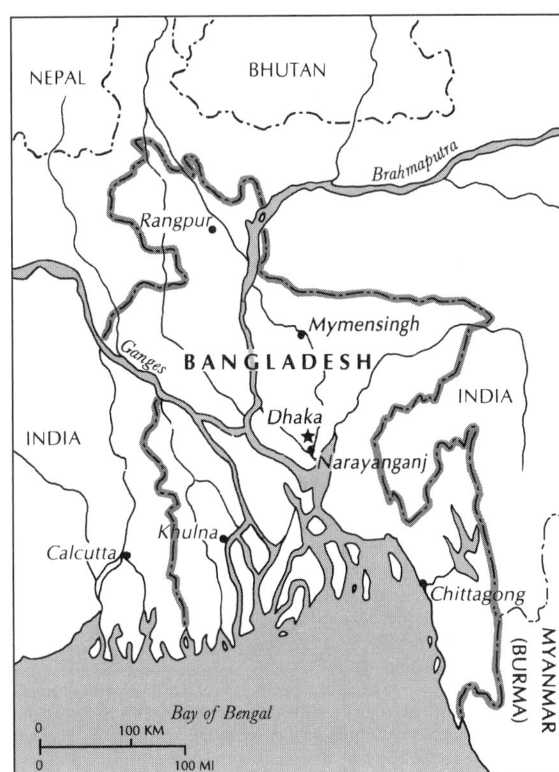

Bangor, city (1990 pop. 33,181), seat of Penobscot co., S Me., at the confluence of the Penobscot and Kenduskeag rivers; inc. as a city 1834. It is a port of entry, commercial center, and gateway to a large resort and lumber area. Shoes, paper, lumber, and electronic equipment are produced. Settled in 1769 (as Sunbury), it was an important 19th-cent. shipbuilding center with a trade in ice, lumber, and stone.

Bangui [bäng-gē'], city (1988 pop. 451,690), capital of the Central African Republic. A port and light industrial center on the Ubangi R., it handled most of the country's international trade until 1978, when an overland route was opened through Cameroon. The city is being developed as a tourist center for the country's large wildlife reserves and national parks. Bangui was founded (1889) by French explorers. It has a university (est. 1970).

banjo: see STRINGED INSTRUMENT.

Banjul, formerly Bathurst, port city (1983 pop. 44,188), capital of Gambia, on St. Mary's Island where the Gambia R. enters the Atlantic Ocean. It is Gambia's only large city and its administrative and economic center. Peanut processing, the chief industry, provides the leading export. The city was founded (1816) by the British as a trading post and a base for suppressing the slave trade.

Bank for International Settlements (BIS), financial institution established (1930) in Basel, Switzerland, by bankers and diplomats of Europe and the U.S.; there are now 27 European members plus the U.S., Canada, Japan, Australia, and South Africa. The BIS is run by a board dominated by West European central bank governors. As a meeting place for the governors of West and East European central banks, the BIS serves to promote international financial cooperation. The bank is also the representative of several important West European financial enterprises.

banking, primarily the business of dealing in money and instruments of credit. Banks were traditionally differentiated from other financial institutions by their principal functions of accepting deposits—subject to withdrawal or transfer by check—and of making loans. The deregulation of the 1980s, however, has blurred the distinctions between various U.S. financial institutions. Banking, in the form of making loans at interest, dates back to antiquity. It developed rapidly in the 18th and 19th cent. to support the expansion of industry and trade. The first bank in the U.S. was the Bank of North America, established (1781) in Philadelphia. Congress chartered the first BANK OF THE UNITED STATES in 1791 to engage in commercial banking and to act as fiscal agent of the government but failed to renew its charter in 1811. A similar fate attended the second Bank of the United States. In 1838 New York adopted the Free Banking Act, which permitted anyone to engage in banking, upon compliance with certain charter provisions. The idea spread rapidly, and from 1840 to 1863 all banking business was done by state-chartered institutions (state banks). The National Bank Act (1863) created a system of banks to be chartered by the federal government (national banks). Both types of banks continue in existence today. The FEDERAL RESERVE SYSTEM was established in 1913 to oversee the U.S. banking system. The FEDERAL DEPOSIT INSURANCE CORPORATION (FDIC; 1933) provides for insurance of bank deposits. International banking grew in importance after World War II. The International Bank for Reconstruction and Development (World Bank) makes loans to governments and private investors, and the International Monetary Fund provides members with technical assistance in international banking. Many of the world's major banks operate branches in other countries. Two major types of banks in the U.S. are commercial banks and mutual savings banks, but since the 1980s the distinctions between them have largely disappeared. The 12,000 commercial banks are the mainstay of the U.S. banking system. Known as full-service banks, they render a wide range of services, in addition to their primary functions of making loans and investments and handling demand (checking) as well as savings and other time deposits. Savings banks were exclusively state-chartered and accepted only savings deposits and made loans mainly for home mortgages. Today they have the right to offer checking accounts, either as a result of legislation or indirectly through NOW (negotiable order of withdrawal) accounts; they may be federally chartered. A similar thrift institution is the SAVINGS AND LOAN ASSOCIATION. Types of financial institutions that perform one or more banking functions include building and loan associations, CREDIT UNIONS, and the investment companies known as NONBANKS, including mortgage companies, finance companies, securities brokers, and investment bankers. By the early 1980s, sweeping changes brought about by improved communications and computers enabled the nation's nonbanks to pose a serious challenge to the traditional banks. The sharp rise of MONEY-MARKET FUNDS, the widespread use of COMMERCIAL PAPER for loans, and the creation of financial conglomerates siphoned off billions of dollars of banking business. In the late 1980s and early 1990s many U.S. banks and other financial institutions failed as a result of bad loans and a slowed economy, severely stressing the resources of the FDIC and bankrupting the Federal Savings and Loan Insurance Corporation. Computers have also enabled the development of automated teller machines and various electronic banking services, including computer programs that permit individuals to pay bills through the electronic transfer of funds.

Bank of the United States, name of two national banks created by the U.S. Congress. The first bank (1791–1811), proposed by Alexander HAMILTON and the Federalists, aroused opposition, especially from the West, for its conservative policies. Its charter was allowed to expire. Difficulties in financing the WAR OF 1812 caused the creation of a second bank (1816–36). It prospered under the management of Nicholas BIDDLE, but was viewed as a tool of Eastern commercial interests by the Jacksonians. Pres. JACKSON vetoed its rechartering and in 1833 began depositing government funds in state banks.

bankruptcy, legal proceeding to deal with the liabilities of an insolvent debtor (individual or business). Its purpose is to distribute the bankrupt's assets equitably among the creditors and, in most cases, to free the bankrupt from further liability. Bankruptcy may be instituted by the debtor (voluntary) or by the creditors (involuntary). In the U.S., bankruptcy is governed by federal laws.

Banks, Sir Joseph, 1743–1820, English naturalist and patron of the sciences. He accompanied Capt. James COOK on his voyage (1768–71) around the world, collecting biological specimens, most previously unclassified. He was chiefly responsible for making Kew Gardens an important botanical center and was president (1778–1820) of the Royal Society.

Bannister, Sir Roger (Gilbert), 1929–, British athlete. He was the first person to run the mile in under 4 min, clocking 3 min 59.4 sec at Oxford, England, in 1954. He was knighted in 1975.

Banting, Sir Frederick Grant, 1891–1941, Canadian physician. He and John MACLEOD won the 1923 Nobel Prize in physiology or medicine for isolating (1921), together with Charles BEST, the pancreatic hormone later called INSULIN. He made valuable studies of the cortex of the adrenal glands, of cancer, and of silicosis. He was knighted in 1934.

Bantu, ethnic and linguistic group of Africa. They inhabit most of Africa S of the Congo R., except the extreme southwest. The classification is primarily linguistic, and there are almost 100 Bantu languages, including Luganda, Zulu, and Swahili. Few cultural generalizations concerning the Bantu can be made. There were some highly developed Bantu states, and several Bantu confederations were formed in the 19th cent., e.g., the Zulu and the Basuto. Other Bantu peoples include the Ndebele and the Shona. In South Africa the term *Bantu* has been used to refer to the indigenous African population, which was subject to the policies of APARTHEID.

Bantu languages, group of African languages forming a subdivision of the Benue-Niger division of the Niger-Congo branch of the Niger-Kordofanian language family. See AFRICAN LANGUAGES (table).

bantustan, territory that was set aside under APARTHEID for black South Africans and slated for eventual independence. Ten bantustans (now generally referred to as homelands), covering 14% of the country's land, were created from the former "native reserves." Four were proclaimed independent—TRANSKEI (1976), BOPHUTHATSWANA (1977), VENDA (1979), and CISKEI (1981)—but no foreign government recognized them. Citizens of independent homelands lost the limited rights they had as South Africans. Under the interim South African constitution that was approved in 1993 and ended white rule. South African citizenship was restored to homeland residents and the homelands were abolished.

baobab, huge tree (*Adansonia digitata*) of the BOMBAX family, native to India and Africa. The trunk diameter of this relatively short tree is exceeded only by that of the SEQUOIA, and the trunks of living trees are hollowed out for dwellings. The bark is used for rope and cloth, the leaves yield condiments and medicines, and the gourd-like fruit (monkeybread) is eaten.

baptism [Gr., = dipping], in most Christian churches a SACRAMENT. Usually required for membership in a church, it is a rite of purification by water, invoking the grace of God to regenerate a person and cleanse him or her of sin. Formal baptism is performed by immersion (as among the BAPTISTS) or by pouring or sprinkling water on the person to be baptized. Some churches baptize infants; others withhold baptism until a relatively mature age.

Baptists, denomination of Protestant Christians holding that baptism is only for believers and solely by immersion, begun (c.1608) by English SEPARATISTS in Amsterdam. The first American congregation was founded (1639) by Roger WILLIAMS in Providence, R.I. The churches are congregational, with nongoverning general associations, e.g., the Southern Baptist Convention and the National Baptist Convention, U.S.A., Inc. Baptist churches are the largest Protestant denomination in the U.S., with over 34 million members in 1992.

Bar, Confederation of (1768–72), union formed at Bar, Podolia (now W Ukraine), by a faction of Polish nobles and the Roman Catholic clergy for the purpose of defending Polish independence and Roman Catholicism, and of opposing Russian interference in Polish affairs. It also opposed the Russian-backed king, STANISLAUS II. In 1772 the confederation fought a bitter war against Russia; it ended with the dissolution of the confederation and the First Partition of Poland.

Barabbas [bərăb'əs], bandit whose release was granted to the mob by PONTIUS PILATE instead of JESUS.

Baraka, Amiri, 1934–, African-American author and political activist; b. Newark, N.J., as LeRoi Jones. His works often express the African American's hatred for white society. Among his plays are *Dutchman, The Toilet,* and *The Slave* (all: 1964). He has also published poetry and prose, including essays and an autobiography (1984).

Barbados, island state (1992 est. pop. 255,000), 166 sq mi (430 sq km), WEST INDIES, E of St. Vincent in the Windward Islands. The capital is Bridgetown. The easternmost of the major islands in the Windward chain, Barbados is generally low-lying, rising to no more than 1,104 ft (336 m), with no rivers, but ample rainfall from June to December. The porous soil and moderate warmth are ideal for the growing of sugarcane, historically the island's major occupation. Rum and molasses are exported, there is commercial fishing, and some light industry and banking were introduced in the 1970s and early 1980s. However, the largest source of foreign exchange is tourism, the island having long been a favorite resort area. The population is mostly rural, and about 95% are of African origin.

History. Although Barbados was probably once inhabited by Arawaks, it had been depopulated when the Portuguese discovered and named it. The island was settled in the early 1600s by the British. The sugar economy that they introduced survived the abolition of slavery in 1834, and for a time Barbados served as the administrative capital of the Windward Islands. It became a separate colony of Britain in 1885 and an independent associated state of the Commonwealth in 1966. The Democratic Labor party, currently led by Prime Min. Erskine Sandiford, has been in power since 1986.

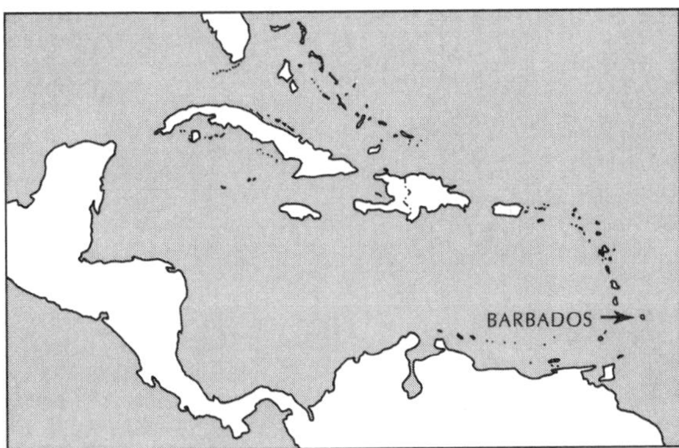

Barbarossa (Khayr ad-Din), c.1483–1546, Turkish corsair. He and his brother Aruj seized Algiers from Spain in 1518, and placed it and the other BARBARY STATES under Turkish suzerainty. As admiral of the Turkish fleet under SULAYMAN I, he twice defeated (1533, 1544) the Italian admiral Andrea DORIA and ravaged the coasts of Greece, Italy, and Spain.

Barbarossa, Frederick: see Frederick I under FREDERICK, rulers of the Holy Roman Empire.

Barbary States, term historically applied to the North African states of Tripolitania, TUNISIA, ALGERIA and MOROCCO. In the 16th cent., led by the corsair BARBAROSSA, they came under Turkish suzerainty despite efforts by Holy Roman Emperor Charles V to defeat the Turks. As Turkish hold on them weakened, they became the home base for pirates who demanded booty, ransom, and slaves from raids on Mediterranean (and occasionally Atlantic) shipping and ports. The major European naval powers in general found it more convenient to pay tribute to the Barbary States than to try to destroy them. By the 19th cent., however, opposition to them was strong, and the TRIPOLITAN WAR reflected U.S. opposition. In 1830 France captured Algiers, and c.1835 Morocco was forced to abandon plans to rebuild its fleet—in effect ending Barbary Coast piracy.

Barber, Samuel, 1910–81, American composer; b. West Chester, Pa. His music is lyrical and generally tonal. Among his major compositions are *Adagio for Strings* (1936); *Knoxville: Summer of 1915* (1947), for soprano and orchestra; and the operas *Vanessa* (1956; Pulitzer) and *Antony and Cleopatra* (1966), commissioned to open the new METROPOLITAN OPERA House, at LINCOLN CENTER (N.Y.C.).

Barbie, Klaus, 1913–91, Nazi war criminal known as the "Butcher of Lyons." Gestapo chief in Lyons, France (1942–44), he was responsible for the deaths of French Resistance members and thousands of Jews. After the war he secretly served as a U.S. army agent in Germany. In 1951, he fled Europe for Bolivia with U.S. help. Identified by Nazi-hunters in the early 1970s, he was expelled from Bolivia in 1983 after a civilian government came to power. He was tried in France, found guilty of crimes against humanity, and sentenced to life imprisonment.

Barbirolli, Sir John [bär"bərō'lē], 1899–1970, English conductor and cellist. He succeeded TOSCANINI as conductor of the New York Philharmonic (1937–42) and later conducted (1960–67) the Houston Symphony Orchestra (see ORCHESTRA, table).

barbiturate, any depressant drug derived from barbituric acid. In low doses, barbiturates have a tranquilizing effect. Increased doses are hypnotic or sleep-inducing, and still larger doses act as anticonvulsants and anesthetics. Barbiturates were widely used as SLEEPING PILLS; such use may lead to psychological dependency, physiological tolerance, and even death by overdose (see DRUG ADDICTION AND DRUG ABUSE). Barbiturates do not relieve pain.

Barbizon school, an informal association of French landscape painters that flourished c.1830–c.1870. Its name derives from the village of Barbizon, a favorite residence of members of the group. Théodore ROUSSEAU led the group, which also included Jules Dupré, Narciso Diaz de la Peña, Constant Troyon, and Charles DAUBIGNY. They rendered landscape from direct observation of nature, in a straightforward, anticlassical manner much influenced by 17th-cent. Dutch masters, including RUISDAEL and HOBBEMA. COROT and MILLET, although often linked with the group, stand outside its main line of development. The Barbizon school influenced late-19th- and early-20th-cent. American landscape painting.

Barbuda: see ANTIGUA AND BARBUDA.

Barca, surname of members of a powerful Carthaginian family. See HAMILCAR BARCA; HANNIBAL; HASDRUBAL.

Barcelona, city (1988 est. pop. 1,714,000), capital of Barcelona prov. and the chief city of CATALONIA, NE Spain, on the Mediterranean Sea. It is Spain's second largest city and largest port. Among its manufactures are textiles, machinery, motor vehicles, locomotives, and aircraft. Founded by settlers from CARTHAGE, it was held by the Romans and Visigoths; fell to the MOORS (8th cent.) and to CHARLEMAGNE (801); and was ruled from the 9th cent. by the counts of Barcelona. It reached its peak c.1400 as a center of trade, banking, and cloth-making. The center of the Catalan revolt against Spain (1640–52), it was the capital of the Catalan autonomous government (1932–39) and the seat of the Spanish Loyalist government (1938–39). Barcelona is a modern city with striking new buildings. Notable older structures include the Cathedral of Santa Eulalia (14th–15th cent.) and the Church of the Sagrada Familia (begun 1882), designed by Antonio GAUDÍ. The 1992 summer Olympic games were held in Barcelona.

bar code, computer coding system that uses a printed pattern of lines or bars to identify products, mail and packages, customer accounts, and the like. In a linear bar code system, the code itself contains no information about the item to which it is assigned but represents a string of identifying numbers or letters. When the code is read by an optical scanner linked to a computer, the computer can provide and record information about the item, such as its price or the quantity sold, from and to databases. The Universal

Product Code (UPC) uses a set of two dark (usually black) and two light (usually white) bars of specified thicknesses to represent numbers. Each item is assigned a unique numeric code, which is printed as a bar code on the item's packaging. So-called "two-dimensional" (2D) bar codes permit the encoding of information about an item in addition to an identifying code. In a 2D bar code, two axes, or directions, are used for recording and reading the codes and the bar size is reduced, increasing the space available for data in the way that a column of words improves on a column of letters. Some 2D codes do not use bars at all, such as the United Parcel Service's hexagon-based Maxicode.

Bardeen, John, 1908–91, American physicist; b. Madison, Wis. He was known for his studies of semiconductivity and other aspects of SOLID-STATE PHYSICS. The first to win a Nobel Prize twice in the same field, Bardeen shared the 1956 physics prize with Walter Brattain and William Shockley, for work in developing the TRANSISTOR, and the 1972 physics prize with Leon Cooper and John Schreiffer, for their theory of SUPERCONDUCTIVITY.

Barenboim, Daniel, 1942–, Israeli pianist and conductor; b. Argentina. He made his debut in Buenos Aires at seven. He has played chamber music and recorded widely and was music director of the Orchestre de Paris (1975–1988) and of the Bastille Opera (1987–89). In 1991 he succeeded SOLTI as music director of the Chicago Symphony, and in 1992 he became artistic director of the Berlin State Opera.

Barents Sea, arm of the Arctic Ocean, off N Norway and NW Russia, partially enclosed by Franz Josef Land (N), Novaya Zemlya (E), and Svalbard (W). Remnants of the North Atlantic Drift, a continuation of the GULF STREAM, keep its ports, including MURMANSK and Vardö, ice-free throughout the year.

Barentz or **Barents, Willem,** d. 1597, Dutch navigator. He made three expeditions to the arctic (1594, 1595, 1596–97) in search of the NORTHWEST PASSAGE. His importance lies in the extent of his explorations and the accuracy of his charts.

Bar Harbor, town (1990 pop. 4,443), SE Me., on Mount Desert Island and Frenchman Bay; settled 1763, inc. 1796. One of the most famous 19th-cent. resorts, it is near Acadia National Park (see NATIONAL PARKS, table) and has summer ferry service to Nova Scotia. A 1947 fire destroyed much of Bar Harbor. The renowned Jackson Laboratory for biological research (est. 1929) is located there.

barite, barytes, or **heavy spar,** white, yellow, blue, red, or colorless barium sulfate mineral ($BaSO_4$). Abundant worldwide in tabular crystals or in granular or massive form, barite is used as a commercial source of the element BARIUM, as a filler in the manufacture of linoleum, oilcloth, rubber, and plastics, and as a mud for sealing oil wells during drilling.

baritone: see VOICE.

barium (Ba), metallic element, isolated by electrolysis in 1808 by Sir Humphry DAVY. It is a soft, silver-white ALKALINE-EARTH METAL. Its principal ore is BARITE. Various barium compounds are used as paint pigments, rat poison, a drying agent, an X-ray imaging agent, and a water softener, and in pyrotechnics. See ELEMENT (table); PERIODIC TABLE.

bark, outer covering of the STEM of woody plants, composed of waterproof CORK cells (the outer bark) protecting a layer of food-conducting tissue (the inner bark or phloem). As the stem grows in size (see CAMBIUM), the outer bark gives way by splitting, shredding, or peeling in patterns typical of the species. Various barks are sources of textile fibers (e.g., HEMP, FLAX, and JUTE), tannin, cork, dyes, flavorings (e.g., CINNAMON), and drugs (e.g., QUININE).

Barker, Harley Granville-: see GRANVILLE-BARKER.

Bar Kokba, Simon [kōkh'bə], d. A.D. 135, leader of an unsuccessful Jewish revolt against Rome (A.D. 132–135). In excavations at MASADA, Israeli archaeologists have found letters in his handwriting.

Barlach, Ernst [bär'läkh], 1870–1938, pioneer German expressionist sculptor, graphic artist, and writer. He produced compact, angular sculptures and WOODCUTS that convey intense emotion and compassion. The NAZIS destroyed much of his work. He illustrated his own poems and plays.

barley, annual cereal plant (*Hordeum vulgare*) of the GRASS family, widely cultivated except in hot and humid climates. Barley was known to the ancients and was the chief bread grain in Europe as late as the 16th cent. Today, each of the many varieties grown has a special purpose, e.g., for stock feed, for malting, as a minor source of flour, and in soups.

Barlow, Joel, 1754–1812, American writer and diplomat; b. Redding, Conn. A CONNECTICUT WIT, he is known for his verse epic *The Vision of Columbus* (1787; rev. ed., *The Columbiad,* 1807) and his mock heroic eulogy *The Hasty-Pudding* (1793). His prose works include *Advice to the Privileged Orders* (1792) and a critique of the French Constitution of 1791. Barlow served as U.S. consul to Algiers, where he negotiated several treaties. He was killed during Napoleon I's retreat from Moscow.

bar mitzvah, Jewish ceremony in which a young male (traditionally at age 13) is initiated into the religious community and performs his first act as an adult, reading in the synagogue from the weekly portion of the TORAH. The **bat,** or **bas, mitzvah** is a comparable 20th-cent. ceremony for girls of 12 or 13.

Barnabas, Saint, Cypriot Christian apostle, relative of St. MARK; companion of St. PAUL on his first missionary journey. An epistle attributed to him is in the pseudepigrapha.

barnacle, sedentary marine animal (subclass Cirripedia), a CRUSTACEAN. Barnacles permanently attach themselves to a substrate by means of an adhesive cement. They secrete a calcareous shell around themselves and form conspicuous encrusting colonies on rocks, pilings, boats, and some marine animals (e.g., whales, turtles). The attached end of the animal is the head; jointed legs (cirri) sweep food particles through the shell opening to the mouth. Some barnacles lack shells and are PARASITES of other invertebrates.

Barnard, Christiaan Neethling, 1923–, South African surgeon. In 1958 he was appointed director of surgical research at Groote Schuur Hospital, Cape Town, where on Dec. 3, 1967, he completed the first human heart transplant. Barnard has designed artificial heart valves and developed surgical procedures for organ transplants.

Barnard, Edward Emerson, 1857–1923, American astronomer; b. Nashville. An astronomer at Lick and Yerkes observatories, he discovered 16 comets, Jupiter's satellite Amalthea (1892), and Barnard's star (1916), a star having the largest observed proper motion. He took important photographs of comets, planets, nebulae, and the Milky Way.

Barnard, Frederick Augustus Porter, 1809–89, American educator; b. Sheffield, Mass. While president (1864–89) of Columbia College (now Columbia Univ.) Barnard expanded the curriculum, added departments, and increased the enrollment from 150 to 1,500 students, turning a small undergraduate college into what would become (1896) a great university. He advocated equal education for men and women, and wrote extensively on education and other topics. He encouraged N.M. BUTLER in the founding of Teachers College, Columbia. Barnard College, for undergraduate women, is named for him.

Barnard, George Grey, 1863–1938, American sculptor; b., Bellefonte, Pa. Influenced by RODIN in his early work, e.g., *Two Natures* (Metropolitan Mus.), he is perhaps best known for his colossal statue of Abraham Lincoln (1917; now in Manchester, England). The French medieval art he purchased forms the core of the CLOISTERS collection.

Barnard, Henry, 1811–1900, American educator; b. Hartford, Conn. As a member (1837–39) of the Connecticut legislature he secured passage in 1838 of an act providing better supervision of the common schools. He and Horace MANN became leaders in the reform of the country's common schools, and Barnard did pioneer work in school inspection, recommendation of textbooks, and organization of teachers' institutes and parent-teacher associations. The first U.S. commissioner of education (1867–70), he edited and published the *American Journal of Education* (31 vol., 1855–81).

Barnard College: see COLUMBIA UNIVERSITY.

Barnes, Djuna, 1892–1982, American author; b. Cornwall, N.Y. She is best known for *Nightwood* (1936), a novel marked by horror and decay. Other works include poetry, short stories, and a verse tragedy, *Antiphon* (1958).

Barneveldt, Johan van Olden: see OLDENBARNEVELDT, JOHAN VAN.

Barnum, P(hineas) T(aylor), 1810–91, American showman; b. Bethel, Conn. In 1842 he opened his American Museum in New York

City and immediately became famous for his extravagant advertising and his exhibits of freaks, including "Gen. TOM THUMB" and the original SIAMESE TWINS. Barnum managed the hugely successful U.S. tour of the Swedish singer Jenny LIND in 1850. In 1871 (after a brief political career) he opened his famous circus, "The Greatest Show on Earth." Merged with its chief competitor in 1881, it continued as Barnum & Bailey.

Barocchio, Giacomo: see VIGNOLA, GIACOMO DA.

Baroja y Nessi, Pío [bärō'hä ē nās'sē], 1879–1956, Spanish novelist from the BASQUE PROVINCES. His popular cyclical works include *The Struggle for Existence* (3 vol., 1904), about the Madrid underworld, and *Memoirs of a Man of Action* (22 vol., 1913–34), about 19th-cent. Spain.

barometer, instrument for measuring atmospheric pressure. The mercurial barometer consists of a mercury-filled glass tube that is sealed at one end and inverted in a cup of mercury. Pressure on the surface of the mercury in the cup supports the mercury in the tube, which varies in height depending on variations in atmospheric pressure. At 32°F (0°C), standard sea-level pressure (1 standard atmosphere) is 14.7 lb/in.^{2} (1,030 g/cm^2), which is equivalent to a column of mercury 29.92 in. (76 cm) in height. The aneroid barometer contains a sealed, partially evacuated metallic box. As the air pressure on it varies, one of its surfaces expands or contracts; this motion is transmitted by a train of levers to a pointer, which shows the pressure on a graduated scale. In WEATHER forecasting, a rising barometer usually indicates fair weather; a rapidly falling barometer, stormy weather.

Baron, Salo Wittmayer, 1895–1989, American Jewish historian and educator; b. Galicia, Austria-Hungary. He taught at Columbia from 1930 to 1963, holding the first professorship of Jewish history in a U.S. university. His major work is the monumental *Social and Religious History of the Jews* (vol. I–XVII, 2d ed., 1952–80).

Barons' War, in English history, war of 1263–67 between HENRY III and his barons. In 1261 Henry reasserted his power and renounced the PROVISIONS OF OXFORD. Led by Simon de MONTFORT, the barons resorted to arms. They failed to establish control over the crown but helped prepare for the constitutional developments in the reign of EDWARD I.

baroque, in art and architecture, style developed in Europe, England, and Latin America during the 17th and 18th cent. Its essential characteristic is an emphasis on unity, a balance among diverse parts. Architecture took on the plastic aspects of sculpture and, along with sculpture, was enhanced by the chiaroscuro (high-contrast) effects of painting. Works in all media were produced on a grand scale. Illusionism increased an unequaled sense of drama, energy, and mobility of form. Baroque buildings, e.g., VERSAILLES, Christopher WREN's churches, compelled order upon overwhelming multiple forms. Throughout Europe undulating facades and complex ground plans abounded. Fountains burst forth as joyous geysers and cascades. Deep perspective was developed in painting, e.g., by RUISDAEL and de HOOCH. Chiaroscuro intensified the works of CARAVAGGIO, ZURBARÁN, Georges de LA TOUR, and REMBRANDT. Color was superbly exploited to diverse effect by VERMEER, RUBENS, CLAUDE LORRAIN, and Pietro da CORTONA. Sculptors used multiple materials for a single work, e.g., BERNINI's *Ecstasy of St. Theresa,* which also exemplifies the baroque fascination with intense emotional states. Landscape subjects were ennobled by the CARRACCI, Ruisdael, HOBBEMA, Rembrandt, Salvator ROSA and Claude Lorrain, and genre and still life by Vermeer, STEEN, de Hooch, and the LE NAINS. In the *Early Baroque* (c.1590–c.1625), the Roman artists Caravaggio, the Carracci, DOMENICHINO, and Guido Reni were preeminent; their influence spread widely to RIBERA, TERBRUGGHEN, and Rubens. The *High Baroque* (c.1625–c.1660) was dominated by Bernini, BORROMINI, Pietro da Cortona, and Claude Lorrain, and outside Italy by Rembrandt, Rubens, VELÁZQUEZ, Vermeer, HALS, VAN DYCK, Ruisdael, and Zurbarán. In the *Late Baroque* (c.1660–c.1725) Italy lost her dominant position to France. Painters such as MURILLO used lighter colors and softer forms, and the baroque style gradually gave way to the ROCOCO.

baroque, in music, the period and style of composition and performance prevailing from the last decades of the 16th cent. to the beginning of the 18th cent. The 16th-cent. revolt against the POLYPHONY of the Renaissance gave rise to an emphasis on the character of individual voices and instruments and also on the use of HARMONY in composition. Use of the older church modes was replaced by major and minor TONALITY as the basis of composition. Principal forms of vocal writing of the period included the OPERA, ORATORIO, and CANTATA; instrumental writing included the SONATA, CONCERTO, and OVERTURE. Later baroque forms were the FUGUE, choral prelude, and the toccata, a free form for keyboard instruments. Famous composers of the period include MONTEVERDI, SCHÜTZ, A. SCARLATTI, VIVALDI, A. CORELLI, J.S. BACH, PURCELL, HANDEL, and LULLY.

The baroque Trevi Fountain in Rome

Barozzi, Giacomo: see VIGNOLA, GIACOMO DA.

barracuda, slender, elongated, ferocious FISH (family Sphyraenidae) with a long snout and projecting lower jaw edged with large, sharp teeth. Found in tropical seas, barracudas will strike at anything that gleams and are excellent game fish. The great barracuda (*Sphyraena barracuda*), up to 10 ft (3 m) in length, is dangerous to swimmers.

Barranquilla, city (1985 pop. 920,695), N Colombia, on the Magdalena R., 8 mi (12.9 km) from the Caribbean Sea. Founded in 1629, it developed as a port in the mid-19th cent., with the advent of steam navigation, and is now Colombia's principal port. Manufactures include aluminum sheets, chemicals, processed foods, ships, and automobiles. The city's carnivals are renowned.

Barrie, Sir J(ames) M(atthew), 1860–1937, Scottish playwright and novelist. Best remembered for his play *Peter Pan* (1904), a fantasy about a boy who refused to grow up, Barrie was a journalist and published Scottish sketches before the success of his novel *The Little Minister* (1891). Its dramatization (1897) established him as a playwright.

Barron, James, 1769–1851, U.S. naval officer; b. Hampton, Va. He was court-martialed for failing to clear his ship, the *Chesapeake*, for action during an 1807 incident with the British ship *Leopard*. In 1820 he mortally wounded Stephen DECATUR in a duel.

Barrow, Sir John, 1764–1848, British geographer. As second secretary of the admiralty, he promoted scientific voyages and instigated arctic expeditions by John ROSS and William Parry. He helped found (1830) the Royal Geographical Society. Point Barrow, Cape Barrow, and Barrow Strait bear his name.

Barrow, city (1990 pop. 3,469), N Alaska, inc. 1958. The main trade center of N Alaska, it has government and military facilities. The population is predominantly ESKIMO, and the area has been inhabited for centuries. Hunting, fishing and whaling, and Eskimo crafts are important.

barrow, in archaeology, burial mound, built usually of earth and stone or timber, perhaps to simulate cave burial. In W Europe long barrows date from the New STONE AGE and round barrows from the BRONZE AGE. More recent Asian round barrows (STUPAS) usually house Buddhist relics. See also MOUND BUILDERS.

Barry, Philip, 1896–1949, American playwright; b. Rochester, N.Y. He is primarily known for his satirical comedies, e.g., *Holiday* (1928), *Tomorrow and Tomorrow* (1931), *The Animal Kingdom* (1932), and *The Philadelphia Story* (1939).

Barrymore, Anglo-American family of actors. The first of the name, **Maurice Barrymore,** 1847–1905, was an Englishman; b. India as Herbert Blythe. A handsome leading man, he came to the U.S. in 1875 to appear with Augustin Daly's company. His wife, **Georgiana Drew Barrymore,** 1856–93, b. Philadelphia, was a great comedienne. She began her career with the company of her parents, Louisa and John DREW, and acted with her husband in Mme Modjeska's troupe. Their elder son, **Lionel Barrymore,** 1878–1954, b. Philadelphia, was a much admired character actor remembered for his film roles in *A Free Soul* (1931; Academy Award) and *Dinner at Eight* (1933), and for his annual radio portrayal of Scrooge in *A Christmas Carol.* His sister, **Ethel Barrymore,** 1879–1959, an actress of dignity and warmth, achieved success in *Captain Jinks of the Horse Marines* (1901) and is remembered for *The Corn Is Green* (1940) and the film *None but the Lonely Heart* (1944; Academy Award). Their brother, **John Barrymore,** 1882–1942, a tempestuous matinee idol, was also a distinguished actor, famous for his electrifying *Hamlet* (1922). His films include *Grand Hotel* (1932) and *Twentieth Century* (1934).

Barth, Karl, 1886–1968, Swiss Protestant theologian, one of the leading thinkers of 20th-cent. Protestantism. A Swiss minister, he became a professor (1921–35) in Germany, and opposed the Nazi regime. Deported to Switzerland, he later taught at Basel, where he continued to expound his views, known as dialectical theology or theology of the word. Barth sought to reassert the principles of the Reformation. He saw the central concern of theology as the word of God and His revelation in Jesus, which he thought was the only means for God to reveal Himself to humans, who must listen in awe, trust, and obedience. Among his many works is his *Church Dogmatics* (vol. I–IV, 1932–62).

Barthelme, Donald, 1931–89, American writer; b. Philadelphia. He used idiosyncratic language and symbol to fit his vision of an absurd reality. His work includes the novels *Snow White* (1967) and *The Dead Father* (1975) and the short-story collections *City Life* (1971) and *Sixty Stories* (1981).

Barthes, Roland, 1915–80, French literary critic, the major theorist of semiology (see SEMIOTICS; STRUCTURALISM). In *Writing Degree Zero* (1953) he attempted to distinguish "scription," the act of writing, from conventional categories of language and style. He followed that work with controversial studies of aspects of French culture. In *Elements of Semiology* (1964), Barthes systematized the study of signs proposed earlier by Ferdinand de SAUSSURE. In his other works he applied his linguistic theories to clichés of national culture, the work of individual writers, photography, and other topics.

Bartholdi, Frédéric Auguste [bärtōldē'], 1834–1904, French sculptor; b. Alsace. He produced numerous monumental sculptures, including the *Lion of Belfort* and his most famous work, *Liberty Enlightening the World,* on Liberty Island, New York Bay (see LIBERTY, STATUE OF).

Bartholomew, Saint, one of the Twelve APOSTLES; identified with NATHANAEL. By tradition he was a missionary in India.

Bartholomew I, 1940–, Orthodox patriarch of Constantinople; b. Dimitrios Archontonis. Chief adviser and administrator for Patriarch Dimitrios I, he was elected patriarch after his predecessor's death (1991). He has worked to find common ground with Roman Catholicism and aid ORTHODOX EASTERN CHURCHES in E Europe.

Bartók, Béla [bär'tŏk], 1881–1945, Hungarian composer and collector of folk music. Utilizing folk elements, ATONALITY, and traditional techniques, he achieved an original modern style that has had great influence on 20th-cent. music. Bartók became known for his compositions for piano, e.g., *Mikrokosmos* (1926–27); for violin, e.g., *Music for Strings, Percussion, and Celesta* (1936), and for orchestra, e.g., *Concerto for Orchestra* (1943). In 1940 he emigrated to the U.S. and was commissioned by Columbia Univ. to transcribe a large collection of Yugoslav folk melodies.

Barton, Clara, 1821–1912, American humanitarian; b. Oxford, Mass. Called the Angel of the Battlefield, she set up a supply service during the CIVIL WAR, was nurse in army camps and on battlefields, and led searches for the missing. After working behind German lines for the International Red Cross in the FRANCO-PRUSSIAN WAR, she organized (1881) the American RED CROSS, which she headed until 1904.

Bartram, John, 1699–1777, pioneer American botanist; b. near Darby, Pa. He planted the first botanical garden in the U.S. His exchange of many plants with the great European botanists introduced many American plants into Europe and established some European species in the New World. In search of new plants he made many journeys around the North American continent, including trips to the Alleghenies, the Catskills, the Carolinas, and Florida.

Baruch, Bernard Mannes, 1870–1965, U.S. financier and government adviser; b. Camden, S.C. An industrial and economic adviser to the government during both world wars, Baruch was U.S. representative (1946) to the UN Atomic Energy Commission.

Baruch, book included in the OLD TESTAMENT of the Western canon and the Septuagint but not in the Hebrew Bible, and placed in the APOCRYPHA in the Authorized Version. Named for a Jewish prince, Baruch (fl. 600 B.C.), a friend of the prophet JEREMIAH and the editor of his book, it includes a message from exiled Jews to those still at home, a famous messianic allusion, a consolation, and a letter of Jeremiah.

baryon: see ELEMENTARY PARTICLES.

Baryshnikov, Mikhail [bərīy'shnikäk'v], 1948–, Russian–American dancer and choreographer; b. Riga, Latvia. He studied in Riga and performed with the KIROV BALLET (1966–74). He defected (1974) to the West, danced with the AMERICAN BALLET THEATRE (ABT; 1974–78) and the NEW YORK CITY BALLET (1978–79), and was director of the ABT (1979–89). In 1990 he founded the White Oak Dance Project, a touring dance company.

barytes: see BARITE.

Barzun, Jacques [bär'zən], 1907–, American scholar; b. France. He began teaching history at Columbia Univ. in 1928. Later he was dean of the graduate faculties (1955–58) and dean of faculties and provost (1958–67). He has written on a variety of subjects, e.g., *Darwin, Marx, Wagner* (1941).

basal metabolism: see METABOLISM.

basalt, fine-grained igneous ROCK of volcanic origin, with a high percentage of iron and magnesium, in a range of dark colors. Its texture varies depending on conditions of cooling. Most of the world's great LAVA flows (e.g., the COLUMBIA PLATEAU in the NW U.S.) are basalt. It underlies the sediment cover in the world's oceans and is believed to underlie the CONTINENTS as well. Many of the lunar rocks obtained by the Apollo astronauts are basalt.

base, in chemistry: see ACIDS AND BASES.

baseball, the "national game" of the U.S., popular also in Japan and in Cuba, Puerto Rico, Mexico, and other Latin American countries. It derives its name from the four bases, spaced 90 ft (27.43 m) apart on the inner playing field (the diamond). Cowhide-covered hard balls, wooden or aluminum bats, and padded gloves constitute the basic equipment. A game is played by two opposing teams of nine players each—a pitcher, a catcher, four infielders, and three outfielders. To win, a team must score more runs in nine innings than its opponent, a run being a complete circuit of the bases. Extra innings are played to resolve ties. A form of baseball, doubtless derived from the English games of CRICKET and rounders, was played in the early 19th cent. The belief that Abner Doubleday invented the modern game in 1839 has been largely refuted. In the U.S., two main professional associations form the major leagues. The National League (NL; organized 1876) and the American League (AL; 1900) comprise a total of 28 teams representing U.S. and two Canadian cities. Champions of each league meet annually in the World Series. Major-league baseball became truly national in scope with the westward migration of several franchises, beginning in 1953, when the Boston Braves moved to Milwaukee. During the 1960s the number of clubs expanded from 16 to 24, with two divisions in each league. In 1977 the AL added two more franchises. The NL expanded to 14 teams in 1993, and in 1994 the number of divisions in each league was increased to three. The game's greatest figures are elected to the National Baseball Hall of Fame, at Cooperstown, N.Y. (opened 1939). Baseball is also played by minor-league professional clubs and by semiprofessional, amateur, college, and school teams and since 1992 has been an Olympic sport as well.

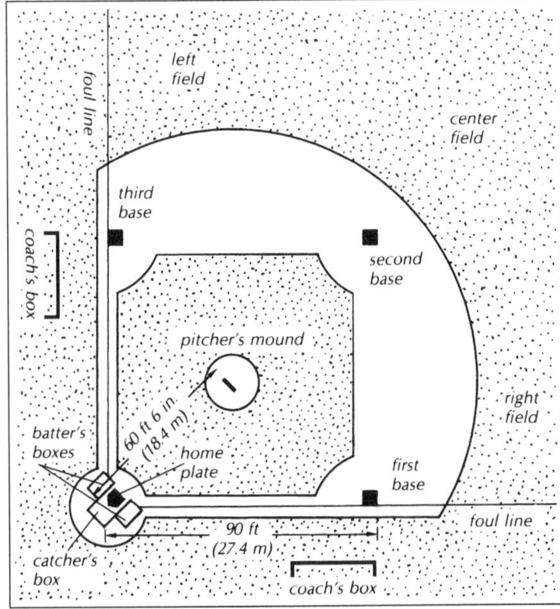

The regulation baseball field. Minimum distance to the outfield fence is 250 ft; professional baseball fields constructed since 1958 have been at least 325 ft deep along the foul lines and 400 ft deep in center field.

Basel [bä'zəl] or **Basle** [bäl], city (1990 pop. 169,587), N Switzerland, divided by the Rhine R. A river port and financial center, it is the seat of the Swiss chemical and pharmaceutical industries. Founded by the Romans, it became (7th cent.) an episcopal see and (11th cent.) a free imperial city. It was the residence of prince-bishops, expelled after Basel accepted (1523) the Reformation. Its university attracted ERASMUS (who is buried in the 11th-cent. cathedral), HOLBEIN the Younger, John CALVIN, and NIETZSCHE. The city houses a valuable collection of Holbein's work.

Basel, Council of, 1431–49, council of the Roman Catholic Church. Called primarily to discuss the HUSSITE heresy it accepted the conciliar theory that ultimate authority in the church rests in the council and not with the pope. After being denounced (1437) by Pope EUGENE IV, the council deposed him and elected (1439) AMADEUS VIII (antipope Felix V). Lacking support, Felix resigned (1449); the council then recognized Eugene's successor and dissolved.

basenji, medium-sized HOUND; shoulder height, c.17 in. (43.2 cm); weight, c.23 lb (10.4 kg). Its short, silky coat is chestnut, red, black, or black and tan, with white markings. Bred in ancient Africa and at the courts of Egypt's pharaohs, it whines rather than barks and cleans itself like a cat.

Basho (Matsuo Basho), 1644–94, usually considered the foremost Japanese HAIKU poet. He did not in fact write haiku but composed stanzas of *haikai no renga* (a sequence of linked verses, usually by a group of poets). The 17-syllable opening, and most important, stanza (*hokku*) was later separated as the verse form haiku. A master of both *hokku* and the integration of verses in a sequence, Basho imbued what was formerly a social pastime with the spirit of ZEN BUDDHISM, attending to the often lowly details of everyday life in the context of the eternal.

BASIC: see PROGRAMMING LANGUAGE.

basic oxygen process, method of producing STEEL from molten PIG IRON. A furnace similar to the one used in the BESSEMER PROCESS is employed but pure oxygen (instead of air) is used to oxidize impurities. The basic oxygen process is faster than the OPEN-HEARTH PROCESS, pollutes less than methods that use air, and also yields carbon monoxide, which can be used as a fuel or in producing various chemicals.

Basie, Count (William Basie), 1904–84, African-American JAZZ pianist and bandleader; b. Red Bank, N.J. He worked in New York City and Kansas City, where he formed (1935) a highly influential band that continues to present a powerful yet relaxed style of music featuring his own laconic piano.

Basil, Byzantine emperors. **Basil I** (the Macedonian), c.813–86 (r.867–86), was the favorite of and co-ruler (866) with MICHAEL III, whose murder (867) he ordered. Basil reformed finance and law, protected the poor, and restored the empire's military prestige. Art and architecture flourished during his rule. He tried to prevent an open break between the Eastern and Western churches. **Basil II,** c.958–1025 (r.976–1025), followed the usurpers NICEPHORUS II and JOHN I as co-ruler with his debauched brother, Constantine VIII. Basil suppressed rebellious landowners and strengthened the laws against them. He annexed (1018) Bulgaria and extended the empire east to the Caucasus. The schism between the Eastern and Western churches increased during his reign.

basil, tender herb or small shrub (genus *Ocimum*) of the MINT family, cultivated for the aromatic leaves. Common, or sweet, basil (*O. basilicum*) is used for seasoning. Holy basil and bush basil are related plants.

basilica, large Roman building used to transact business and legal matters. Often rectangular, with a roofed hall, it usually had an interior colonnade, with an APSE at one or both ends. The wide central aisle was usually higher than the flanking aisles, so that light could penetrate through the clerestory windows. Early examples are in Rome and Pompeii. In the 4th cent. Christians began to build places of worship related in form in Europe and the Middle East, e.g., the Church of the Nativity at Bethlehem (6th cent.). The massive Romanesque churches still retained the fundamental plan of the basilica.

basketball, game played generally indoors by two opposing teams of five players each. At each end of the court—usually about 92 ft (28 m) long and 50 ft (15 m) wide—is a bottomless basket made of cord net and suspended from a metal ring attached 10 ft (3.05 m) above the floor to a backboard. The ball may be passed, batted, or dribbled (bounced), but the players may not run with it. Players of one team attempt to shoot the ball through one basket while seeking to keep the opposition from scoring through the other basket. Each field goal, or basket, scores two points (sometimes three points in professional basketball); foul shots, awarded mostly for illegal body contact, count one point. Overtime periods are played to break ties. Basketball was originated (1891) in Springfield, Mass., by Dr. James Naismith of the YMCA. It quickly grew into a leading U.S. school and college sport and spread throughout the world, becoming (1936) a part of the OLYMPIC GAMES. Professional basketball gained great popularity in the U.S. after the formation (1949) of the National Basketball Association (NBA); the NBA is now made up of 27 teams in two conferences, each of which has two divisions. U.S. women's basketball has also grown enormously on the collegiate and high school levels, but attempts to form a viable women's professional league have been unsuccessful.

Baskin, Leonard, 1922–, American artist; b. New Brunswick, N.J. Known for his powerful figurative graphics and sculpture, e.g., *Man with a Dead Bird* (Mus. Mod. Art, N.Y.C.), Baskin is also an influential teacher.

Basque Country or **Basque Provinces,** Basque *Euskadi,* autonomous region (1987 est. pop. 2,143,000), Spain, comprising the provinces of Álava, Guipúzcoa, and Vizcaya, N Spain, on the Bay of Biscay, bordering France in the northeast. In Álava and Guipúzcoa the major occupations are the mining of iron, lead, copper,

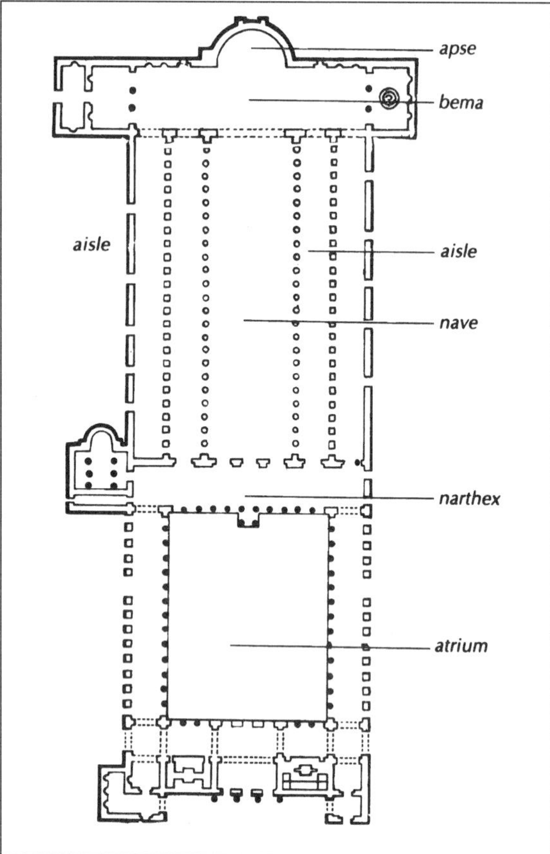

Floor plan of a basilica

and zinc; shipbuilding; metalworking; and fishing. Álava is largely agricultural. Nationalism is strong among the BASQUES, and in 1980 the provinces were granted regional autonomy. Basque terrorists and a separatist party continue to press for total independence, but they have lost support in recent years.

Basques, people of N Spain and SW France, numbering 2 million. Probably the oldest ethnic group in Europe, they preserve their ancient, unique language, and their customs and traditions. Since Paleolithic times the Basques have been genetically and culturally distinct. Long mostly peasants, shepherds, fishermen, navigators, miners, and metalworkers, they have produced such famous figures as St. IGNATIUS OF LOYOLA and St. FRANCIS XAVIER. The Basques accepted Christianity late (3d–5th cent.). In the 6th cent. they expanded northward into Gascony, to which they gave their name. The kingdom of NAVARRE, founded in 824, united almost all Basques, but after its conquest (1512) by CASTILE Basque prosperity declined. Of the Basque provinces (see BASQUE COUNTRY), only Navarre supported the Franco forces in the SPANISH CIVIL WAR (1936–39). Basque nationalism in Spain, often involving violent incidents, continued into the 1980s, but Basque terrorists and a separatist party lost support in the early 1990s.

Basra, city (1986 est. pop. 616,000), SE Iraq, on the SHATT AL ARAB. Iraq's only port, it has a commercially advantageous location near oil fields and 75 mi (121 km) from the PERSIAN GULF. Since 1948 many oil refineries have been built in the city. Basra was founded (A.D. 636) by the caliph Umar I and was a cultural center under HARUN AR-RASHID. The area around Basra was the scene of heavy fighting in the IRAN-IRAQ WAR, was bombed heavily during the PERSIAN GULF WAR, and was the site of an unsuccessful Shiite uprising after the latter conflict.

bass, any of various FISHES of the families Serranidae (sea basses) and Centrarchidae (black basses and sunfishes). Sea basses, a large, diverse family of fishes with oblong, rather compressed bodies, inhabit warm and temperate seas worldwide and are highly valued as food and game fish. The largest sea basses are GROUPERS. Sunfishes, spiny-finned, freshwater fishes with flattened bodies, are found in North America. Black basses, averaging 2 to 3 lb (.9 to 1.4 kg), are the most valuable American freshwater game fishes.

bass: see VOICE.

Bassano, Jacopo [bäs-sä'nō], c.1515–1592, Venetian mannerist painter (see MANNERISM); b. Jacopo da Ponte. Primarily a painter of biblical themes, he introduced vignettes of country life into his works, e.g., *Annunciation to the Shepherds* (National Gall., Wash., D.C.). His sons **Francesco Bassano,** 1549–92, and **Leandro Bassano,** 1558–1623, were also painters.

basset hound, short-legged, long-bodied HOUND; shoulder height, 12–15 in. (30.1–38.1 cm); weight, 25–50 lb (11.3–22.7 kg). Its short, dense coat is black, tan, or white, or a combination. The breed was developed centuries ago in France to hunt game in heavy ground cover.

bassoon: see WIND INSTRUMENT.

basswood: see LINDEN.

Bastille [băstēl'], fortress and prison in Paris, begun c.1369, now demolished. The Bastille became a hated symbol of absolutism because it was used for arbitrary and secret imprisonment by the crown. On July 14, 1789, a Parisian mob stormed the prison, hoping to seize its store of ammunition, but found only seven prisoners. This marked the start of lower-class participation in the FRENCH REVOLUTION. July 14—Bastille Day—became a national holiday in France.

bat, the only MAMMAL (order Chiroptera) capable of true flight. Numbering between 1,000 and 2,000 species, bats range in size from less than 1 in. (2.5 cm) to 15 in. (45 cm), with a wingspan of from less than 2 in. (5 cm) to 5 ft (150 cm). The body is furry and mouselike, with the forelimbs and extensions of the skin of the back and belly modified to form wings. Bats are most abundant in the tropics, and temperate species often hibernate or migrate to warmer areas in the winter. Most species frequent crevices, caves, or buildings, and are active at night or twilight; they roost during the day, often in large numbers and usually hanging by their feet. Most bats see well but depend on echolocation to navigate in the dark. Bats are fruit-eaters (fruit, nectar, pollen) or insect-eaters (fruit, insects, small animals, and fish); one species, the South American vampire bat, feeds exclusively on the blood of living animals, chiefly mammals.

Bataan, peninsula and province (1990 pop. 426,000), W Luzon, the Philippines, between Manila Bay and the South China Sea. The capital is Batanga. A mountainous jungle region with bamboo forests, Bataan has a pulp and paper mill, fertilizer plant, and oil refinery. Subsistence farming is also carried on. U.S. and Filipino troops captured on Bataan (April 1942) by the Japanese in WORLD WAR II underwent a brutal "death march" to a prison camp; thousands died.

Batavian Republic, name for the United Provinces of the Netherlands (1795–1806) after their conquest by the French in the FRENCH REVOLUTIONARY WARS. In 1806 NAPOLEON I made Batavia into the kingdom of Holland under his brother Louis Bonaparte (see BONAPARTE family).

Bates, Henry Walter, 1825–92, English naturalist and explorer. His pioneering theory of mimicry, explaining similarity among species, was used by Charles DARWIN as a proof of his theory of natural selection. During travels (1848–59) along the upper Amazon R., he collected specimens of nearly 15,000 animal species (mostly insects), more than 8,000 previously unclassified.

Bath, city (1986 est. pop. 84,400), Avon, SW England. In the 1st cent. A.D. the Romans built elaborate baths at the natural hot springs. Bath became England's most fashionable spa in the 18th cent., and the Georgian architecture and Roman baths remain tourist attractions.

batholith, enormous mass of igneous ROCK, granitic in composition, with steep walls and without visible floors. Batholiths commonly extend over thousands of square miles. Their method of formation is controversial; most appear to have moved up through the earth's crust in a molten state, shattering and incorporating the overlying rock.

Báthory [bä'tôrē], Hungarian noble family. **Stephen Báthory,** 1477–1534, a supporter of JOHN I of Hungary, was made (1529) voivode [governor] of Transylvania. His younger son, STEPHEN BÁTHORY, became (1575) king of Poland and was succeeded as prince of Transylvania by his brother, **Christopher Báthory**, 1530–81. Christopher's son and successor, **Sigismund Báthory**, 1572–1613, was mentally unbalanced. He abdicated for brief periods in 1597 and 1599 and finally in 1602. Other family members included **Elizabeth Báthory**, d. 1614, who was reputed to be a werewolf. To renew her youth, she is said to have slaughtered virgins and bathed in their blood. **Gabriel Báthory**, 1589–1613, became (1608) prince of Transylvania and was killed in a revolt by nobles against his rule.

Bath-sheba, in the BIBLE, wife of Uriah the Hittite. DAVID seduced her, effected the death of her husband, and married her. She was the mother of SOLOMON.

batik, method of decorating fabric used for centuries in Indonesia. With melted wax, a design is applied to the cloth (cotton or, sometimes, silk), which is then dipped in cool vegetable dye. Areas covered by wax do not receive the dye and display a light pattern on the colored ground. The process may be repeated several times. When the design is complete, the wax is removed in hot water. A crackling effect occurs if dye has seeped into cracks of hardened wax. The same or similar patterns have been used for c.1,000 years. Batik was brought to Europe by Dutch traders, was adopted in the 19th cent. by Western craftsmen, and is still widely used.

Batista y Zaldívar, Fulgencio, 1901–73, Cuban dictator (1933–44, 1952–59). An army sergeant, he took part in the 1933 military coup and, as army chief of staff, became de facto ruler of CUBA and its elected president (1940–44). He accepted his candidate's defeat in 1944, but in 1952 he seized power and had himself elected president (1954, 1958). His corrupt rule caused popular discontent, and he fled (1959) the country during the CASTRO revolution.

bat mitzvah: see under BAR MITZVAH.

Baton Rouge [Fr., = red stick], city (1990 pop. 219,531), state capital and seat of East Baton Rouge parish, SE La., on the Mississippi R.; inc. 1817. A deepwater port and trade hub, it is a major center of petrochemical production with large refineries and machine shops. The city was founded in 1719 and was alternately French, English, and Spanish. Acquired by the U.S. in 1815, it became state capital in 1849. The old (1882) and new (1932) capitols, many antebellum homes, and Louisiana State Univ. are among the points of interest.

Batory: see STEPHEN BÁTHORY and BÁTHORY, family.

battery, electric, device that consists of a group of CELLS that are connected to act as a source of direct current. The term is also commonly used for a single cell, such as the alkaline dry cell used in flashlights and portable tape players. A **storage battery** usually consists of several wet cells (cells with a liquid electrolyte) connected in series, and can be recharged many times. In the U.S. the lead storage battery is commonly used in automobiles. Its cells consist of alternate plates of lead (negative plates) and lead coated with lead dioxide (positive plates) immersed in a sulfuric acid solution (the electrolyte). Negative plates are connected to form a cell's negative electrode; positive plates similarly form the positive electrode.

Battle above the Clouds: see CHATTANOOGA CAMPAIGN.

Battle of Britain: see WORLD WAR II.

baud, measure of the rate at which signals are transmitted over a telecommunications link. It is equivalent to the number of elements or pulses transmitted in one second, e.g., in COMPUTER input/output, 2400 baud typically equals 2400 bits per second. Because modern data compression techniques can combine several bits in one baud, bits per second has replaced baud as a measure of MODEM speed.

Baudelaire, Charles [bōdlâr′], 1821–67, French poet whose work has been a major influence on Western poetry. His poems, classical in form, introduced symbolism (see SYMBOLISTS). Baudelaire was moody and rebellious, imbued with an intense religious mysticism, and his work reflects an unremitting inner despair. His main theme is the inseparable nature of beauty and corruption. His major work, *The Flowers of Evil* (1857), originally condemned as obscene, is recognized as a masterpiece, especially remarkable for the brilliant phrasing, rhythm, and expressiveness of its lyrics.

Baudouin I, 1930–93, king of the Belgians (1951–93). He joined his father, LEOPOLD III, in exile (1945–50) in Switzerland and became king when Leopold abdicated. He was succeeded by his brother, ALBERT II.

Bauhaus [bou′hous], school of art and architecture in Germany. It was founded at Weimar in 1919 and headed by Walter GROPIUS; its faculty included Paul KLEE, Lyonel FEININGER, Wassily KANDINSKY, Laszlo MOHOLY-NAGY, and Marcel BREUER. The teaching concentrated on functional craftsmanship applied to industrial problems of mass production. Bauhaus style was characterized by severely economic, geometric design and by respect for materials. Enormously controversial and unpopular, the school moved in 1925 to Dessau. Gropius resigned in 1928 and was succeeded by Johannes Meyer, who was replaced in 1930 by MIES VAN DER ROHE. The Bauhaus moved again to Berlin in 1932 and was closed by the NAZIS in 1933. Its influence in design of architecture, furniture, typography, and weaving found international acclaim and continued to flourish in the U.S., especially at the Chicago Institute of Design, founded by Moholy-Nagy.

Baum, L(yman) Frank, 1856–1919, American journalist, playwright, and author of juvenile stories; b. Chittenango, N.Y. His most famous work is *The Wonderful Wizard of Oz* (1900), which was made into a movie in 1938. Baum published 13 more Oz books.

bauxite, mixture of hydrated aluminum oxides usually containing oxides of iron and silicon. A noncrystalline substance formerly thought to be a mineral, bauxite is claylike, ranging from white to brown or red in color, and is the chief source of ALUMINUM and its compounds. It is widely distributed, with important deposits in Africa, South America, France, Russia, the West Indies, and the U.S.

Bavaria, Ger. *Bayern*, state (1990 est. pop. 11,222,000), 27,239 sq mi (70,549 sq km), S Germany. It is the largest state of Germany. Forestry and agriculture are important occupations, but industry, centered in MUNICH, the capital, has grown enormously since World War II. The region, whose boundaries have often varied, was conquered (15 B.C.) by the Romans and invaded (6th cent. A.D.) by the Baiuoarii, who set up a duchy. In 788 CHARLEMAGNE added Bavaria to his empire. It was ruled (788–911) by the CAROLINGIANS and in 1070 passed to the GUELPH family. In 1180 the Holy Roman Emperor bestowed the duchy on the WITTELSBACH family, who ruled it until 1918. In 1806 it became a kingdom. Bavaria joined the German Empire in 1871 and became the chief German state after Prussia. The monarchy was overthrown in 1918, and Bavaria later joined the Weimar Republic. From 1949 until German reunification in 1990, Bavaria was part of West Germany.

Bavarian Succession, War of the, between Austria and PRUSSIA, 1778–79. In 1777 Charles Theodore, the duke of Bavaria, in a secret treaty with JOSEPH II, the Holy Roman emperor, ceded Lower BAVARIA to Austria. The Bavarian heir apparent, advised by FREDERICK II of Prussia, protested the transfer. The resulting war, with no significant engagements, ended with Austria's renunciation of all but a small portion of Lower Bavaria.

Bax, Sir Arnold Edward Trevor, 1883–1953, English composer. He studied piano at the Royal Academy of Music. Known for his symphonic poems, *The Garden of Fand* (1916) and *Tintagel* (1917), he also wrote seven symphonies, each dedicated to a favorite composer. He became (1941) Master of the King's Music. Influenced by Irish folklore, he wrote poetry and prose in Ireland under the name Dermot O'Byrne.

Bayamón, city (1990 pop. 202,103), NE Puerto Rico, a residential and industrial suburb of San Juan. Bayamón was established in 1772. Fruit is a major product; manufactures include clothing, metal products, and automotive parts.

bayberry, common name for the Myricaceae, a family of chiefly temperate and subtropical aromatic trees and shrubs. The waxy gray berries of some species (mainly *Myrica cerifera*) are used to make bayberry candles, scented soap, and sealing wax. Sweet gale (*M. gale*) yields tannic acid; sweet fern (*Comptonia peregrina*) is used for medicines and tea.

Bayeux tapestry [bäyo͞o′], an embroidery chronicling the Norman conquest of England (see under WILLIAM, kings of England). It is a strip of linen, 230 ft by 20 in. (70 m by 51 cm) in the Bayeux Museum, France. Attributed to William's wife, Queen Matilda, it is a valuable document on the history and costumes of the time.

Baykal or **Baikal, Lake** [both: bīkäl′], lake, SE Siberian Russia. Nearly 400 mi (650 km) long, it is the largest (12,160 sq mi/31,494 sq km) freshwater lake in Eurasia. It is also believed to be the deepest lake in the world, its maximum known depth being 5,714 ft (1,742 m). The lake is in danger of pollution because of industrial development near its shores.

Bay of Pigs Invasion, 1961, unsuccessful invasion of Cuba by U.S.-backed Cuban exiles. On Apr. 17, 1961, about 1,500 Cuban exiles landed in the Bahía de Cochinos (Bay of Pigs) with the aim of ousting the Communist regime of Fidel CASTRO. They had been trained in Guatemala by the CIA, supplied with U.S. arms. Most were captured or killed by the Cuban army. The U.S. government was severely criticized for the attack at home and abroad. In December 1962, Cuba traded 1,113 captured rebels for $53 million in food and medicine raised by private donations in the U.S.

Bayreuth Festival: see WAGNER, RICHARD.

bazooka, military weapon consisting of a portable, lightweight tube that serves as a rocket launcher, usually operated by two soldiers. Developed by the U.S. as an infantry weapon for use against TANKS, pillboxes, and bunkers, it was widely employed during World War II and the Korean War but was later superseded by more powerful, accurate weapons, notably recoilless weapons and antitank missiles.

Be, chemical symbol of the element BERYLLIUM.

Beach, Moses Yale, 1800–1868, American journalist; b. Wallingford, Conn. As owner of the New York *Sun,* Beach vied with his chief competitor, James Gordon BENNETT of the *Herald,* in employing ingenious means of getting news fast, e.g., carrier pigeons. Rising costs led to the formation of the New York Associated Press, partly at Beach's instigation. His weekly *American Sun* was the first European edition of an American paper.

Beaconsfield, Benjamin Disraeli, 1st **earl of:** see DISRAELI, BENJAMIN.

Beadle, George Wells, 1903–89, American geneticist; b. Wahoo, Nebr. For their work on the bread mold *Neurospora crassa,* which showed that genes control cellular production of enzymes and thus the basic chemistry of cells, Beadle and Edward Tatum shared the 1958 Noble Prize in physiology or medicine with Joshua LEDERBERG.

beagle, small, compact HOUND; shoulder height, 10–15 in. (25.4–38.1 cm); weight, 20–40 lb (9.1–18.1 kg). Its short, close-lying, harsh coat is usually black, tan, and white. Developed in England to hunt hares, it was introduced into the U.S. in the 1870s.

bean, name for seeds of trees and shrubs of the PULSE family, and for various plants of the family having edible seeds or seed pods. True beans are in the genus *Phaseolus.* The COWPEA, CAROB, and CHICKPEA are sometimes considered beans. Cultivated worldwide, beans are an important food staple. They are high in protein and often used as a meat substitute.

bear, large MAMMAL of the family Ursidae, found almost exclusively in the Northern Hemisphere. Bears have large heads, bulky bodies, short, powerful, clawed limbs, and coarse, thick fur; almost all are omnivorous. In cold climates, bears do not hibernate (see HIBERNATION) but sleep most of the winter; their metabolism remains normal, and they may wake and emerge during warm spells. North American brown bears include the Kodiak bear and the grizzly. The Kodiak, the largest bear, sometimes stands 9 ft (2.7 m) high and weighs over 1,600 lb (730 kg). The grizzly, characterized by silver-tipped (grizzled) fur, is more highly carnivorous than most bears and preys on large mammals such as deer. The most widespread North American bear is the black bear, smaller than the brown bears and ranging in color from light brown to black. The large, white polar bear is an arctic species. A solitary, fearless hunter, it is a powerful swimmer and feeds mostly on marine animals.

Beard, Charles A(ustin), 1874–1948, American historian; b. near Knightstown, Ind. As a professor at Columbia Univ. he taught that history encompasses all aspects of civilization. He was particularly interested in the relationship of economics and politics and in 1913 published *An Economic Interpretation of the Constitution.* Beard helped to found the New School for Social Research. With his wife, Mary Ritter Beard (1876–1958), he wrote *The Rise of American Civilization* (2 vol., 1927) and its sequels (vol. 3 and vol. 4), *America in Midpassage* (1939) and *The American Spirit* (1943).

Beard, James, 1903–85, American cooking teacher and writer; b. Portland, Oreg. He maintained (1955–84) an influential cooking school, promoted American cuisine, and wrote some two dozen cookbooks.

Bearden, Romare, 1914–88, American painter; b. Charlotte, N.C., raised in Harlem. Rendered in vibrant, flat planes, often with collage, his works deal with the African-American experience in America. His work appears in many museum collections.

Beardsley, Aubrey Vincent, 1872–98, English illustrator and writer. His unique, largely self-taught work was influenced by Greek vase painting, Japanese woodcuts, and the French ROCOCO. He developed a superbly artificial, flat, linear, black-and-white style, illustrating macabre, often erotic themes for books, e.g., Oscar WILDE's *Salome* (1894), and periodicals, e.g., *The Yellow Book* (1894–96), for which he was art editor. He died at 26 of tuberculosis.

bearing, machine part used to reduce FRICTION between moving surfaces and to support moving loads. There are two principal types. A *plain,* or *journal, bearing* is a cylinder that supports a rotating shaft such as a motor shaft; its inner lining, the bushing, is usually made of a metal softer than that of the shaft, so that any slight misalignment of the shaft can be adjusted by an equivalent wearing of the bushing. An *antifriction bearing* is a cylinder containing a movable inner ring of small steel balls (the ball bearings used primarily in light machinery) or larger cylindrical or conical rollers. The rotating machine part fits into a center of the ring, which takes up the motion of the rotating part, distributing and reducing friction through the movement of its bearings. Magnetic bearings use magnetic repulsion to reduce friction even more.

beat frequency, half of the difference of the frequencies of two sets of waves traveling in the same direction. Sets of waves combine to form a beat, which has a varying amplitude and a fixed frequency. The number of beats occurring in one second is equal to twice the beat frequency. Beats are an example of interference, and, in sound waves, can be used for practical purposes, such as piano tuning.

beat generation, certain American artists and writers popular in the 1950s. Influenced by Eastern religions, e.g., ZEN BUDDHISM, and the rhythms of "progressive" JAZZ, they rejected traditional forms and sought expression in intense experiences and beatific illumination. Novelists in the movement included William Burroughs and Jack KEROUAC. Among the "beat" poets were Allen GINSBERG and Lawrence FERLINGHETTI.

Beatitudes, eight blessings spoken by Jesus at the beginning of the Sermon on the Mount (Mat. 5.3–12). Luke 6.20–26, a parallel passage, names four blessings and four woes.

Beatles, The, English rock music group (1959–69). Members were John Lennon (1940–80), Paul McCartney (1942–), George Harrison (1943–), and Ringo Starr (Richard Starkey) (1940–). Influenced by Americans like Elvis PRESLEY, the Beatles dominated ROCK MUSIC in the 1960s with their wit, stage presence, and music that evolved from tight rhythm and blues to allusive lyricism. The lyrics and music for their songs were written mostly by Lennon and McCartney. The group recorded numerous albums, made films, and toured widely.

Beaton, Sir Cecil, 1904–80, English stage and costume designer, photographer, writer, and painter. His credits include the designs for the Broadway shows *My Fair Lady* (1956) and *Coco* (1969), and photographic portraits of many famous people.

Beatrice Portinari, 1266–90, Florentine woman thought to be the Beatrice of DANTE's *Divine Comedy* and *Vita nuova.*

Beatrix, 1938–, queen of the Netherlands (1980–). She ascended the throne upon the abdication of her mother, JULIANA. She is married to a German, Claus von Amsberg, and has three sons.

Beaubourg, popular name for the **Centre National d'Art et de Culture Georges Pompidou,** derived from the district of Paris in which it is located. Proposed by French Pres. POMPIDOU in 1969, the center was designed by Renzo Piano and Richard Rogers and completed in 1977. Its industrial style, with architectural elements such as the steel superstructure, escalator tunnels of clear plastic, and brightly colored elevators and utility pipes exposed on the outside of the building, generated much controversy. The Beaubourg contains a modern art museum, a public library, and music and industrial design centers.

Beaufort scale, a scale of wind velocity. It was devised by Admiral

The Beaubourg, Paris

Sir Francis Beaufort of the British navy and an adaptation is used by the U.S. National Weather Service. It employs numbers from 0 to 12, representing calm, light air, light breeze, gentle breeze, moderate breeze, fresh breeze, strong breeze, moderate gale, fresh gale, strong gale, whole gale, storm, and hurricane. Zero (calm) is a wind velocity of less than 1 mi (0.6 km) per hour and 12 (hurricane) represents a velocity of over 75 mi (120 km) per hour.

Beaufort Sea, an arm of the Arctic ocean between Point Barrow, Alaska, and the Canadian Arctic Archipelago. The MACKENZIE R. flows into the sea, which is always covered with pack ice.

Beauharnais, Alexandre, vicomte de [bōärnā′], 1760–94, French general. He fought in the AMERICAN REVOLUTION and in the FRENCH REVOLUTIONARY WARS. After he was guillotined in the REIGN OF TERROR, his widow married NAPOLEON I and became the Empress JOSEPHINE. His son, **Eugène de Beauharnais,** 1781–1824, was also a French general who served with distinction under his stepfather, Napoleon. Made viceroy of Italy in 1805, he retired to Munich after Napoleon's fall. Eugène's sister, **Hortense de Beauharnais,** 1783–1837, married Louis BONAPARTE and was queen of Holland (1806–10).

Beaumarchais, Pierre Augustin Caron de [bōmärshā′], 1732–99, French dramatist. His brilliant comedies, *The Barber of Seville* (1775) and *The Marriage of Figaro* (1784), are the bases for celebrated operas by ROSSINI and MOZART, respectively. Distinguished by their clever dialogue and intricate plots, they satirize the upper class. Beaumarchais was frequently in litigation, and the pamphlets he wrote about his cases were witty and effective.

Beaumont, Francis, 1584?–1616, English dramatist, best known for collaborations with John FLETCHER. Beaumont is generally considered the superior dramatist, and to him sole authorship of *The Woman Hater* (1607) and the burlesque *Knight of the Burning Pestle* (c.1607) is usually ascribed.

Beaumont, William, 1785–1853, American physician; b. Lebanon, Conn. He was the author of *Experiments and Observations on the Gastric Juice and the Physiology of Digestion* (1833), an exhaustive account of a famous medical case involving a youth whose abdomen, opened by a gunshot, would not close. Realizing that this situation afforded a unique opportunity to study the digestive process, Beaumont conducted about 238 experiments over several years that revolutionized knowledge of this process.

Beaumont, city (1990 pop. 114,323), seat of Jefferson co., E Tex.; settled 1827, inc. 1838. A port of entry with deepwater facilities on a ship channel, Beaumont is a major oil-refining center. The world's first great oil gusher came in (1901) at nearby Spindletop, revolutionizing what is still, to a degree, a farming and lumbering economy. Lamar Univ. is located in the city.

Beauregard, Pierre Gustave Toutant, 1818–93, Confederate general in the U.S. CIVIL WAR; b. St. Bernard parish, La. In 1861, after directing the bombardment of FORT SUMTER, he was second in command at the first battle of BULL RUN. He became (1862) Confederate commander at the battle of SHILOH after the death of A.S. JOHNSTON. He later (1863) defended Charleston.

Beauvoir, Simone de [bōvwär′], 1908–86, French author. An exponent of EXISTENTIALISM, she was a close associate and companion of SARTRE. Her novels include *The Mandarins* (1955), which interprets the existential dilemma, *The Second Sex* (1949–50), a profound analysis of the status of women, and *The Coming of Age* (1970), a study of society's treatment of the aged. She also wrote a lively series of memoirs.

beaver, large, aquatic RODENT (*Castor fiber*). Once widespread in the Northern Hemisphere, beavers are from 3 to 4 ft (91 to 120 cm) long, including the distinctive broad, flattened tail; they usually weigh about 60 lb (27 kg). Known for their engineering feats, beavers create ponds by building dams of sticks, logs, and mud; they build habitations, or lodges, in the same way.

Beaverbrook, William Maxwell Aitken, 1st **Baron,** 1879–1964, British statesman and newspaper owner; b. Canada. He amassed a fortune in business before going to England in 1910. There he gained control of the *Daily Express* (1916) and the *Evening Standard* (1923), and began the *Sunday Express* (1918); these newspapers trumpeted his imperialist, isolationist views. A Conservative, he held several posts in Winston CHURCHILL's wartime cabinet (1940–45).

Beccaria, Cesare Bonesana, marchese di, 1738–94, Italian criminologist, economist, and jurist. His famous *Essay on Crimes and Punishments* (1764), arguing against CAPITAL PUNISHMENT and cruel treatment of criminals, influenced Jeremy BENTHAM and the utilitarians and stimulated penal reform throughout Europe. As an economist, Beccaria anticipated the wage and labor theories of Adam SMITH.

Becker, Boris, 1967–, German tennis player. Noted for his powerful serve-and-volley game, he gained public notice in 1985 as the teenage winner of Wimbleton. He repeated there in 1986 and 1989 and has also the U.S. (1989) and Australian (1991) opens.

Becket, Thomas: see THOMAS À BECKET, SAINT.

Beckett, Samuel, 1906–89, French novelist and playwright; b. Ireland. He won the 1969 Nobel Prize in literature. His novels, e.g., *Murphy* (1938) and *Molloy* (1951), portray an individual's entrapment by grotesque situations in an apparently normal world. In his theater of the absurd, typified by the popular but controversial *Waiting for Godot* (1952) and *Endgame* (1957), Beckett combined poignant humor with an overwhelming sense of anguish and loss.

Bécquer, Gustavo Adolfo [bā′kĕr], 1836–70, Spanish romantic poet and prose writer. His *Rhymes* (1871), published after his death, are among the finest 19th-cent. LYRIC poetry. His prose includes *Legends* (1860–64).

Becquerel, Antoine Henri [bĕkərĕl′], 1852–1908, French physicist. Professor at the École polytechnique, Paris, from 1895, he discovered RADIOACTIVITY in URANIUM in 1896. Further investigations of the phenomenon were made by Pierre and Marie CURIE, and the three shared the 1903 Nobel Prize in physics.

bedbug, small, flatbodied, blood-sucking BUG of the family Cimicidae. Distributed worldwide, bedbugs are parasites of warm-blooded animals. They are reddish-brown and about ¼ in. (6 mm) long.

Bede, Saint or **Baeda,** 673?–735, English historian, a Benedictine monk, also called the Venerable Bede. His *Ecclesiastical History of the English Nation,* in Latin, is still an important primary source for English history from 597 to 731.

Bedford, John of Lancaster, duke of, 1389–1435, English nobleman, son of HENRY IV of England and brother of HENRY V. Made protector of HENRY VI in 1422, he devoted himself to English affairs in France.

Bedlington terrier, long-legged TERRIER; shoulder height, c.16 in. (40.6 cm); weight, 22–24 lb (9.9–10.8 kg). When its thick, wiry outercoat is trimmed to the fleecy undercoat for exhibition, it resembles a lamb. It may be blue, liver, or sandy, solid or marked with tan. It was developed (19th cent.) by cross-breeding in England's Border districts.

Bedouin [Arab., = desert dwellers], primarily nomadic, Muslim Arab peoples of the Middle East. Camel- and sheep-breeding provide their main livelihood. Roving tribal groups, headed by a sheikh, traditionally traveled a defined area of land. However, the settlement policies of various governments in the 20th cent. have forced many Bedouins into a sedentary life.

bee, flying INSECT of the superfamily Apoidae, having enlarged hind feet for pollen gathering and a dense coat of feathery hairs on the head and thorax. Bees feed on POLLEN and nectar; the latter is converted to HONEY in the digestive tract. Most have stings connected to a poison gland. Bees may be social, solitary, or parasitic in the nests of other bees. Social bees include bumblebees, stingless bees, and honeybees. A typical colony of social bees has an egg-laying queen, sexually undeveloped females (workers), and fertile males (drones). Workers gather nectar, make and store honey, and protect the hive. They care for the queen and larvae and perform complex patterned dances to communicate the location of pollen sources to one another. After being fertilized by a drone, the queen spends her life (usually several years) laying eggs. Honeybees are raised commercially for honey and for the WAX they produce for their nests (combs) and as agricultural cross-pollinators. So-called "killer bees" are essentially African honeybees that are much more aggressive than common honeybees when disturbed. They were introduced into the New World in Brazil during the mid-1950s and have since spread north to the U.S.

beech, common name for the Fagaceae, a family of trees and shrubs mainly of temperate and subtropical regions in the Northern Hemisphere. The principal genera, CHESTNUT, chinquapin, beech, and OAK, are dominant forest trees valued for their hardwood timber. Some species are also grown for their fruits and as ornamentals. The beeches have smooth, silvery gray bark and pale green leaves. The American beech (*F. grandifolia*) grows over much of the NE U.S. and Canada. The European beech (*F. sylvatica*) is an important forest tree, prized for its wood and nut oil. Several of its varieties, e.g., purple and copper beeches, are cultivated in America as ornamental trees.

Beecham, Sir Thomas, 1879–1961, English conductor of international fame. He organized (1932) the London Philharmonic Orchestra and (1946) the Royal Philharmonic Orchestra, also of London, and appeared in the U.S. with the New York Philharmonic and the METROPOLITAN OPERA (see ORCHESTRA, table).

Beecher, Lyman, 1775–1863, American Presbyterian minister; b. New Haven, Conn. A preacher on temperance, he served congregations in New York, Connecticut, and Massachusetts. He was a founder of the American Bible Society (1816) and later president (1832–52) of Lane Theological Seminary, Cincinnati. Among his 13 children were Harriet Beecher STOWE and **Henry Ward Beecher,** 1813–87, American Congregational preacher, orator, and lecturer, b. Litchfield, Conn. After serving congregations in Indiana, he became pastor of the Congregational Plymouth Church in Brooklyn, N.Y., in 1847. He championed reforms, especially the abolition of slavery and woman suffrage, and advocated the theory of evolution. He was accused of adultery by Theodore Tilton. The trial (1875) ended in jury disagreement, and Beecher continued in his influential position for the rest of his life.

Beelzebub, in the Bible: see SATAN.

beer, one of the oldest known alcoholic beverages. At first brewed chiefly in the household and monastery, it has been a commercial product since late medieval times and is made today in most industrialized countries. Color, flavor, and alcoholic content (usually 3%–6%) may vary, but the process in brewing is similar: A mash of malt (usually barley), cereal adjunct (e.g., rice and corn), and water is heated and agitated. The liquid is boiled with hops and cooled. Yeast is then added, and fermentation occurs. In England ale is any light-colored beer; in the U.S. it is a pale, strongly hopped beverage. Porter is a strong, dark ale brewed with roasted malt; stout is darker, stronger, and maltier than porter. Bock beer is dark, heavy, and usually drunk in the spring. Light, or low-calorie, beer is lower in alcohol content. Ice beer is a higher-alcohol beer produced by chilling below 32°F (0°C) and filtering out the ice crystals that form.

Beerbohm, Sir Max, 1872–1956, English essayist, caricaturist, and parodist. Best known today for his witty caricatures of late Victorian writers, e.g., D.G. ROSSETTI and WILDE, he also wrote brilliant parodies, e.g., *A Christmas Garland* (1912), and a popular satire on Oxford, *Zuleika Dobson* (1911).

Beersheba, city (1989 est. pop. 128,000), S Israel, principal city of the NEGEV Desert. Beersheba is a trading center, and its manufactures include chemicals and textiles. Once one of the southernmost towns of biblical PALESTINE, Beersheba contains a well believed to have been dug by ABRAHAM. It is the seat of the Arid Zone Research Institute.

beeswax: see WAX.

beet, biennial or annual root vegetable (*Beta vulgaris*) of the goosefoot family, cultivated since pre-Christian times. Numerous varieties exist, e.g., red, or garden, beet; sugar beet; and Swiss chard. Both the roots and foliage of the red beet are edible, as is the foliage of the Swiss chard. The widely cultivated sugar beet, containing up to 20% sucrose, provides about one third of the world's sugar supply.

Beethoven, Ludwig van [bā'tōvən], 1770–1827, German composer, universally recognized as one of the greatest composers who ever lived. Young Beethoven's musical gifts were acknowledged by MOZART and HAYDN, and his piano virtuosity and extraordinary compositions won him the generous support of the Viennese aristocracy despite his notoriously boorish manners. Despite the onset (1801) of deafness, which became progressively worse and was total by 1817, his creative work was never restricted. Beethoven's work may be divided into three distinct periods. The early works, influenced by the tradition of Mozart and Haydn, include the First and Second Symphonies, the first three piano concertos, and a number of piano sonatas, including the Pathétique. From 1802, his work broke the formal conventions of classical music. This most productive middle period included the Third Symphony (Eroica); the Fourth through Eighth Symphonies; his one Violin Concerto; and his sole opera, *Fidelio.* Beethoven's final period, dating from about 1816, is characterized by works of greater depth, including the Hammerklavier Sonata; the monumental Ninth Symphony, with its choral finale based on SCHILLER's *Ode to Joy;* the *Missa Solemnis;* and the last five string quartets. A prolific composer, Beethoven produced numerous smaller works besides his major symphonies, concertos, sonatas, and quartets. His work crowned the classical period and initiated the romantic era in music.

beetle, mainly terrestrial INSECT (order Coleoptera). Beetles have chewing mouthparts; well-developed antennae; and a pair of hard, opaque, waterproof wings (elytra) which cover and protect the flight wings and the body. Some species are brilliantly colored and patterned, but most are dull. They range in size from less than 1/32 in. (1 mm) to more than 6 in. (15 cm) in length. Beetles are generally plant eaters, but some are parasitic.

beet sugar: see BEET; SUCROSE.

Menachem Begin

Begin, Menachem, 1913–92, Israeli prime minister (1977–83); b. Poland. Before Israeli independence, he commanded the Irgun, an anti-British terrorist group. He sat in the Knesset after 1949 as leader of the right-wing Herut party. In 1977 he formed a right-wing Likud coalition government. Begin signed a peace treaty with Egypt in 1979 (see CAMP DAVID ACCORDS), and he and Egyptian President Anwar al-SADAT shared the 1978 Nobel Peace Prize. In 1982 he authorized a massive Israeli invasion of LEBANON in order to destroy military bases of the PALESTINE LIBERATION ORGANIZATION located there (see ARAB-ISRAELI WARS). Israeli forces shelled BEIRUT, and Begin's government (particularly Defense Min. Ariel SHARON) was criticized for allowing the massacre of Palestinian civilians by Israel's Lebanese Christian allies. He retired in 1983.

begonia, common name for the Begoniaceae, a family of succulent, perennial herbs of the American tropics, and for members of the genus *Begonia.* Begonia species are common houseplants, some grown for their showy, variously colored leaves and others for their white, pink, or yellow flowers.

Behan, Brendan, 1923–64, Irish dramatist. An outspoken man jailed for Irish Republican Army activities, he is noted for his prison drama *The Quare Fellow* (1956); *The Hostage* (1958), a farce; and his autobiography, *Borstal Boy* (1958).

behaviorism, school of psychology that seeks to explain behavior entirely in terms of observable responses to environmental stimuli. Influenced by the conditioned-reflex experiments of PAVLOV, behaviorism was introduced in 1913 by J.B. WATSON, who, denying both the value of introspection and the concept of consciousness, emphasized laboratory techniques. B.F. SKINNER, the major modern proponent, concerned himself exclusively with the relationship of observable responses to stimuli and rewards.

behavior therapy or **behavior modification,** active psychotherapeutic approach aimed at modifying undesirable behaviors by reinforcing acceptable behavior and suppressing (by nonreinforcement) undesirable behavior. After observing the behavior and factors that trigger and maintain it, the therapist employs any of various techniques of reward and/or punishment (e.g., aversion therapy, desensitization, guided imagery). A form of PSYCHOTHERAPY developed from the work of B.F. SKINNER and others, behavior therapy is used in private and institutional therapy in group and individual settings to treat such disorders as DRUG ADDICTION, ALCOHOLISM, and PHOBIAS. It has been criticized for treating symptoms rather than causes.

Behmen, Jakob: see BOEHME, JAKOB.

Behn, Aphra, 1640–89, first professional English female author. She wrote verse under the pseudonym Astrea, adopted during a career as a spy. *The Rover* (1677), bawdy and humorous, brought her fame as a playwright. *Oroonoko* (1688) was the first English philosophical novel. Behn led a notoriously bohemian life.

Behrens, Peter [bā'rəns], 1868–1940, German architect. His utilitarian style was both clear and impressive. He is known for his factory buildings, which based a simple, effective design on the frank terms of modern construction. LE CORBUSIER, GROPIUS, and MIËS VAN DER ROHE were his students.

Behring, Emil Adolph von, 1854–1917, German physician. A pioneer in serum therapy, he received the 1901 Nobel Prize in physiology or medicine for his work on immunization against diphtheria (1890) and tetanus (1892) by injections of antitoxins (a word he introduced).

Behrman, S(amuel) N(athaniel), 1893–1973, American dramatist; b. Worcester, Mass. His sophisticated comedies include *The Second Man* (1927) and *Lord Pengo* (1962). He also wrote film scripts and biographies.

Beijing or **Peking** [Chin. = northern capital], city (1990 est. pop. 7,000,000), capital of China. It is located in central Hebei prov., but administered directly by the central government. The second largest city in China (after SHANGHAI), Beijing is the political, financial, educational, and transportation center of the country. It has become a major industrial area, with factories producing an array of heavy and light industrial goods such as iron and steel, textiles, machinery, chemicals, refined oil, and electronic equipment. A city of broad avenues, narrow lanes, and intricate residential courtyards, its landmarks include the Forbidden City, the Gate of Heavenly Peace, Tiananmen Square, and the Imperial Summer Palace; its cultural institutions include a ballet, the national library, many educational institutions, a renowned zoo, and a modern international airport. Serving (13th cent.) as KUBLAI KHAN's capital, the city became China's capital (1421–1911; 1949–). It was the site of important events such as the BOXER UPRISING (1900), the May Fourth Movement (1919), the founding of the People's Republic of China and its reestablishment as capital (1949), and the deaths of ZHOU ENLAI and MAO ZEDONG. In 1989 pro-democracy demonstrations in the city were put down by the military with substantial loss of life.

Beirut, city (1991 est. pop. 1,150,000), W Lebanon, capital of Lebanon, on the Mediterranean Sea. An important port, Beirut became a major financial center with food-processing industries. It was a Phoenician city and was called Berytus in ancient times. A prominent city under both the Seleucids and Rome, Beirut was captured by the Arabs in A.D. 635. It was part of the Latin Kingdom of Jerusalem from 1110 to 1291. After 1517 the DRUSES controlled the city under the OTTOMAN EMPIRE. It fell (1918) to France in World War I and became the capital of Lebanon in 1920 under the French mandate. Beirut suffered severe damage during the Lebanese civil war (1975–76) between Muslims and Christians and was left a divided city that was no longer an important financial center. A 1982 siege by Israeli forces led to the expulsion of PLO guerrillas from its western sector and further devastated Beirut. A multinational peacekeeping force was established after some 1,000 Palestinians were massacred by Israel's Lebanese Christian allies, but France and the U.S. withdrew (1984) after nearly 300 troops were killed (1983) in terrorist attacks. In 1990 Christian and Muslim militias withdrew, ending the division of Beirut and returning it to the control of the national government.

Béjart or **Béjard** [bāzhär'], French family of actors in a company associated (after 1643) with MOLIÈRE. The eldest was **Joseph Béjart,** c.1616–1659. His sister **Madeleine Béjart,** 1618–72, a fine actress, was Molière's mistress. Their sister, **Geneviève Béjart,** 1624–75, and brother, **Louis Béjart,** 1630–78, also acted in the company. **Armande Grésinde Béjart,** c.1640–1700, Madeleine's sister or daughter, married Molière in 1662 and played most of his heroines. After merging with two other companies, the troupe became the Comédie Française (see THEATER, table).

Béjart, Maurice, 1927–, French BALLET and opera director; b. Maurice Berger. His style incorporates JAZZ and avant-garde music, nontraditional dance forms, e.g., acrobatics, and unusual settings. He headed (1954–59) the Ballets de l'Étoile, Paris, and (1959–87) the highly influential Ballet of the 20th Century, Brussels, Belgium. In 1987 he organized the Béjart Ballet Lausanne in Lausanne, Switzerland.

Béla Kun: see KUN, BÉLA.

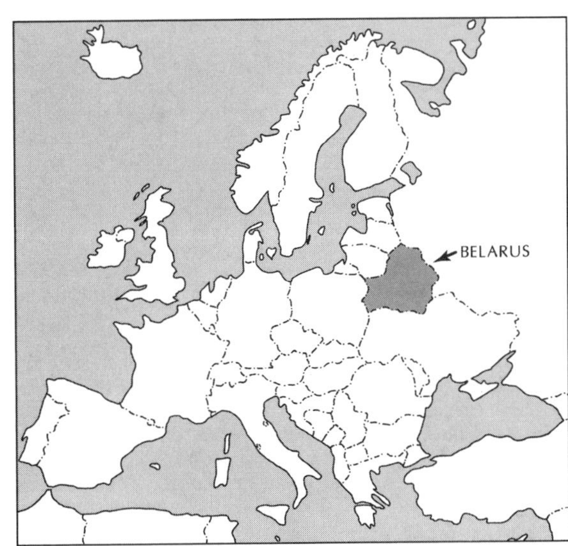

Belarus, or **Byelarus** [both: byĕ"lərōōs'], officially Republic of Belarus, republic (1992 est. pop. 10,374,000), c.80,150 sq mi (207,600 sq km), E central Europe, formerly a constituent republic of the USSR; it is sometimes called White Russia. It borders Poland

(W); Russia (E); Ukraine (S); and Lithuania and Latvia (N). MINSK is its capital and largest city; other large cities include Homyel (Gomel), Mahilyow (Mogilev), Vitsyebsk (Vitebsk), Hrodna (Grodno), and Brest. Peat, which along with other swampy soils covers one third of the land, and timber are the leading natural resources; minerals include limestone, clay, sand, chalk, and dolomite. Potatoes, flax, sugar beets, and grains are the chief agricultural products. Belarus's industries, which have grown since the 1970s as a result of the contruction of oil and gas pipelines, produce machinery, motor vehicles, chemicals, textiles, and electrical equipment. The majority of the people are Belarussians; Russians, Poles, and Ukrainians are among the minorities. The main religions are the Orthodox Eastern and Roman Catholic churches. Belarussian is the official language.

History. Settled by East Slavic tribes (5th–8th cent.), the region became part of KIEVAN RUSSIA (12th cent.), of the grand duchy of Lithuania (14th cent.), and of the Russian Empire (18th cent.) and was devastated by the Russian-Polish wars (16th–18th cent.), the Napoleonic invasion (1812), World War I (1914–18), and the Soviet-Polish war (1919–20). The last ended with the western part of the region ceded to Poland and the eastern part becoming the Belorussian Soviet Socialist Republic, or Belorussia. In 1939, the western portion was occupied by Soviet troops. During the German occupation (1941–44), Belorussia's large Jewish population (dating from the 14th cent.) was decimated. After 1945 most of W Belorussia remained part of the Belorussian SSR. Following the failure of the hard-line coup (1991) against Soviet Pres. Gorbachev, conservative Belorussian leaders were ousted. Stanislav Shushkevich became head of state, and the republic declared its independence and later joined Russia and Ukraine in initiating the establishment of the COMMONWEALTH OF INDEPENDENT STATES. The official name of the new nation in English was changed to Belarus in 1991. In 1994 former Communists in the parliament voted to replace Shushkevich with Mechislav Grib, a former national police official. Since independence Belarus has moved slowly on market reforms and maintained a neutral foreign policy.

Belau: see PALAU.

Belaúnde Terry, Fernando [bālä͞on'dā tä'rē], 1912–, president of Peru (1963–68, 1980–85). An architect, he effected social, educational, and land reforms in his first term as president. In 1968 he was deposed by an army coup and went into exile. Restored to the presidency in 1980, he attempted to combat inflation by denationalizing industries and encouraging foreign investment in the petroleum industry.

Belém or **Pará,** city (1990 est. pop. 1,203,000), N Brazil, capital of Pará state, on the Pará R. It is the chief commercial center and port of the AMAZON R. basin. Founded by the Portuguese in 1616, it prospered during the rubber boom of the late 19th cent. and again after World War II with the development of rail and highway links. The Goeldi museum holds ethnological and zoological collections of the region.

Belfast, capital city (1991 est. pop. 287,000) of Northern Ireland, on an inlet of the Irish Sea, at the mouth of the Lagan R. A port and industrial center, Belfast is known for its shipyards and linen industry. Agricultural and livestock products are the chief exports. The city was founded in 1177. French HUGUENOT settlers, who arrived in the late 17th cent., stimulated the growth of the linen industry. Since the 19th cent. the city has been scarred by violent strife between the majority Protestants and the minority Catholics, with the most recent round beginning in the late 1960s.

Bel Geddes, Norman: see GEDDES, NORMAN BEL.

Belgium, Flemish *België,* Fr. *La Belgique,* officially Kingdom of Belgium, constitutional monarchy (1992 est. pop. 10,017,000), 11,781 sq mi (30,513 sq km), NW Europe; bordered by the Netherlands and the North Sea (N), Germany and Luxembourg (E), and France (W and SW). BRUSSELS is the capital and ANTWERP the chief commercial center and port. Low-lying, except for the forested Ardennes Mts. in the south, Belgium is crossed by the MEUSE and Scheldt rivers and a network of canals. It is one of the most densely populated, heavily industrialized nations in Europe, but while the emphasis is on heavy industry, such as production of steel, chemicals, and petrochemicals, the traditional industries of lace-making and diamond-cutting continue to flourish. Iron, zinc, and other industrially important minerals are now largely imported, and coal production has declined as other fossil fuels and nuclear power have become important. Belgium is a leader in shipping, and its economy depends on its exports. Agricultural activities include cattle-raising and dairying; cereals are the chief crops, and food processing is a major source of income. Tourism is also important. Belgium is divided culturally and ethnically into Flemish-speaking Flanders in the north and French-speaking Wallonia, or Wallony, in the south. Brussels is bilingual, and German is spoken in areas bordering Germany. Virtually the entire population is Roman Catholic.

History. The Franks first appeared in the Roman province of Belgica in the 3d cent. A.D., and the area became the cradle of the CAROLINGIAN dynasty. After the death (814) of CHARLEMAGNE, most of the region was made part of LOTHARINGIA and, later, of Lower Lorraine. By the 12th cent. this had broken up into the duchies of Brabant and LUXEMBOURG, and the histories of these feudal states and of FLANDERS and Hainaut constitute the medieval history of Belgium. In the 15th cent. the area of present-day Belgium passed to the dukes of Burgundy and then to the HAPSBURGS (see NETHERLANDS, AUSTRIAN AND SPANISH). Annexed by France in 1797, the region was given to the Netherlands by the Treaty of Paris (1815). Resentment of Dutch rule led (1830) to rebellion, and an independent (1831), "perpetually neutral" (1838) state was established. Under LEOPOLD I and LEOPOLD II there was rapid industrialization and also colonization, notably in the Congo (see ZAÏRE). Belgian neutrality was violated by the Germans, who occupied the country in WORLD WAR I and WORLD WAR II. Following World War II the unpopular LEOPOLD III, who had surrendered the country unconditionally to the Germans in 1940, abdicated (1951) in favor of his son BAUDOUIN I. Postwar recovery was rapid, but crises arising from longstanding tensions between the Flemish- and French-speaking elements toppled several governments in the 1960s. Constitutional reform begun in the early 1970s created three partially autonomous regions (Flanders, Wallonia, and Brussels) and three politically recognized ethnic communities (French, Flemish, and German), but ethnic discord continued throughout the 1980s. New reforms passed in 1993 gave the regions additional autonomy and created a federal state. Since 1992 the center-left coalition government of Socialists and Christian Democrats has been led by Prime Min. Jean-Luc Dehaene. ALBERT II succeeded Baudouin I as king in 1993.

Belgrade, Serbo-Croatian *Beograd,* city (1987 est. pop. 1,131,000), capital and largest city of Yugoslavia and of its constituent republic SERBIA, at the confluence of the Danube and Sava rivers. It is the industrial, political, and cultural center of the country. Manufactures include metals, chemicals, and textiles. A harbor for Rome's Danubian fleet, it was later held by the Byzantines, Bulgars, and Serbs. After 1521 it was a major fortress of the Ottoman Turks. Belgrade became the capital of the kingdom of Serbia in 1882 and the capital of Yugoslavia after World War I. In World War II it was severely damaged by the German occupation (1941–44). Belgrade is noted for its fine parks, palaces, museums, and churches. The Kalemegdan citadel is now a military museum.

Belgrano, Manuel, 1770–1820, Argentine revolutionist. A political figure and journalist, he was a leader of the May 1810 revolution and a member of the first patriot governing junta. Later he commanded the Army of the North (1812–14, 1816–19).

Belisarius, c.505–565, Byzantine general under JUSTINIAN I. He suppressed (532) the Nika riot caused by internal political strife, and defeated (533–34) the Vandals, a Germanic tribe. In command (535) of the war against the OSTROGOTHS in Italy, he took NAPLES and ROME (536), as well as MILAN and RAVENNA (540). Justinian replaced him (548) with NARSES, but Belisarius returned (559) to drive the Bulgarians out of Constantinople. After a brief political imprisonment (562) he returned to favor.

Belize [bəlēz'], independent nation (1991 pop. 192,877), 8,867 sq mi (22,965 sq km), Central America; bordered by Mexico (N), Guatemala (S and W), and the Caribbean Sea (E). The land is generally low-lying, forested, and undercultivated, with a swampy coastline and some low mountains in the south. The capital is BELMOPAN, and the chief port and largest city is Belize (1991 pop. 44,087). The major products are mahogany and other woods, sugar, clothing, citrus fruits, and fish, but timber exports are declining due to overharvesting. The population is about equally divided between English speakers of largely African descent and Spanish speakers of Spanish-Mayan descent. English is the official language. The majority of the population are Roman Catholic, but there is a large Protestant minority.

History. Once a part of the MAYA civilization, the region was probably traversed by CORTÉS on his way to HONDURAS, but the Spanish did not colonize the area. Buccaneers founded Belize city in the early 1600s and were followed by British Jamaicans, who exploited its timber. Spain long contested British possession, but in 1859 Guatemala and Britain agreed on British Honduras's boundaries. In 1940 Guatemala declared the agreement invalid. British Honduras was granted internal self-government in 1964, but full independence was delayed by GUATEMALA's claim. Negotiations appeared to resolve that problem, though, and on Sept. 21, 1981, British Honduras, as Belize, became the last British crown colony on the American mainland to achieve independence. However, the Guatemalan-British agreement did not hold, and not until 1988 did Guatemala give de facto recognition to Belize. A British force remained in Belize to guarantee its independence but is due to be withdrawn by the end of 1994. In 1993 Manuel Esquivel, of the United Democratic party, became prime minister.

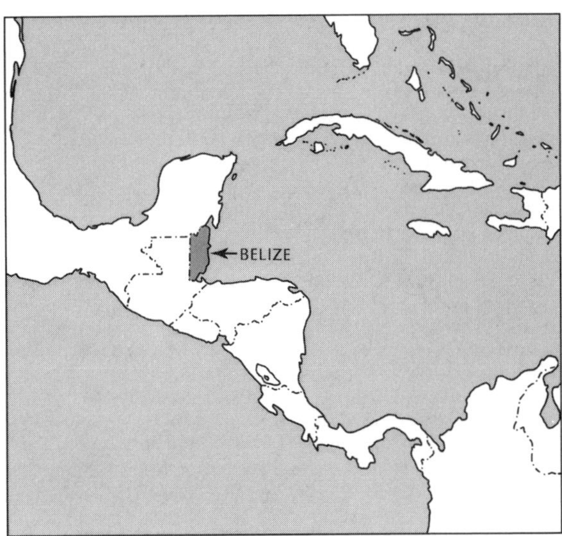

Bell, Alexander Graham, 1847–1922, Scottish-American scientist, inventor of the TELEPHONE. For many years he studied and experimented in the area of teaching the deaf to speak, conducting his own school of vocal physiology in Boston. As early as 1865 he conceived the idea of transmitting speech by electric waves, and in 1876 he perfected and demonstrated the first telephone apparatus. Under Bell's influence the magazine *Science* was founded (1880); his patronage of scientists interested in aviation resulted in the development of the HYDROFOIL.

Bell, Daniel, 1919–, U.S. sociologist. After 20 years as a journalist, he took a degree in sociology and went on to teach at Columbia and Harvard. He has written on contemporary capitalist society and the individual's place within it.

belladonna or **deadly nightshade,** poisonous perennial plant (*Atropa belladonna*) of the NIGHTSHADE family. Native to Europe and now wild in the U.S., the plant has reddish, bell-shaped flowers and shining black berries. Extracts of the leaves and roots dilate the pupils of the eye and were once so used by women—hence the name *belladonna,* meaning "beautiful lady" in Italian. Belladonna has also been employed as a poison, a sedative, and, in medieval times, a HALLUCINOGENIC DRUG. The ALKALOID drug atropine, an extract of belladonna, is frequently used to relax muscles and suppress glandular and mucous secretions.

Bellamy, Edward, 1850–98, American author; b. Chicopee Falls, Mass. He became famous with the influential *Looking Backward, 2000–1887* (1888), a utopian romance of the future under state socialism. His other works include short stories and the novels *Miss Ludington's Sister* (1884) and *Equality* (1897), a sequel to *Looking Backward.*

Bellay, Du: see DU BELLAY.

Bellerophon [bəlĕr'əfŏn, –fən], hero in Greek mythology. Given a number of seemingly impossible tasks by King Iobates, he performed them all. Most notable was the killing of the monster Chimera, accomplished with the aid of the winged horse PEGASUS. Grown proud, Bellerophon attempted to ride Pegasus to Mt. OLYMPUS, but was thrown, crippled, and blinded.

Bellini [bĕl-lē'nē], illustrious family of Venetian painters of the RENAISSANCE. **Jacopo Bellini,** c.1400–1470, was the father and teacher of Giovanni and Gentile. Few of his works survive, but two of his notebooks dealing with problems of perspective, landscapes, and antiquity are his most important legacy. **Gentile Bellini,** 1429–1507, painted contemporary Venetian life. After his visit to Constantinople in 1479, a distinct Middle Eastern flavor appeared in his paintings, including the portrait of Muhammad II (National Gall., London). **Giovanni Bellini,** c.1430–1516, became the teacher of TITIAN and GIORGIONE. His works are characterized by serenity, majesty, and luminous color. They include the altarpieces of the Frari and San Zaccaria in Venice; *St. Job* (Acad., Venice); *St. Francis in Ecstasy* (Frick Coll., N.Y.C.); and many mythological scenes.

Bellini, Vincenzo, 1801–35, Italian opera composer. His most celebrated works, *La Sonnambula* and *Norma* (both: 1831), exemplify the virtuosic bel canto tradition of 18th-cent. vocal composition (see VOICE). His last OPERA, *I Puritani* (1835), was influenced by the dramatic style of French grand opera.

Belloc, Hilaire, 1870–1953, English author; b. France. A Catholic apologist, he wrote poetry, satire, and essays, including *The Bad Child's Book of Beasts* (1896) and *The Path to Rome* (1902). With G.K. CHESTERTON he propounded distributionism, a medieval socialist philosophy.

Bellow, Saul, 1915–, American novelist; b. Canada. Moral in tone, his novels are concerned with the individual in an indifferent society. They include *Herzog* (1964), *Mr. Sammler's Planet* (1970), *Humboldt's Gift* (1975; Pulitzer), *More Die of Heartbreak* (1987), and *The Bellarosa Connection* (1989). Bellow was awarded the 1976 Nobel Prize in literature.

Bellows, George Wesley, 1882–1925, American painter; b. Columbus, Ohio. A student of Robert HENRI, Bellows is known for his direct realism. *Forty-two Kids* (Corcoran Gall., Wash., D.C.) and *Stag at Sharkey's* (Mus. Art, Cleveland) are characteristic paintings. Bellows was also noted for his lithographs (see LITHOGRAPHY), e.g., *Dempsey and Firpo.*

Belmopan, city (1991 pop. 3,558), E Belize, capital of Belize. A new city, it was constructed on the Belize R., 50 mi (80 km) inland from the former capital of then British Honduras, the port city of Belize, after that city's near destruction by a hurricane in 1961. The government was moved to Belmopan in 1970. The National Assembly Building's design is based on an ancient Mayan motif.

Belo Horizonte, city (1990 est. pop. 2,416,000), E Brazil, capital of Minas Gerais state. It is a distribution and processing center for agricultural goods and the gold, manganese, and precious stones mined in the state; a banking center; and the hub of a burgeoning industrial complex, with furniture and textile manufacturing. Brazil's first planned metropolis (built 1895–97), laid out with spacious avenues and plazas, it is a cultural center and a popular resort.

Belorussia: see BELARUS.

Belshazzar [bĕlshăz'ər], in the BIBLE, the son of NEBUCHADNEZZAR and the last king of Babylon. At his feast, handwriting appeared on the wall that was interpreted by DANIEL as a sign of doom. That night Babylon fell to Cyrus.

Belvedere, court of the VATICAN connecting it to a villa built (1485–87) for INNOCENT VIII. It was designed (1503–4) by BRAMANTE for JULIUS II, and was to include a number of buildings. It was only partially completed. Now a museum, the Belvedere contains the *Laocoön* and the *Apollo Belvedere* as well as other rare works of classical antiquity.

Bely, Andrei [byĕ'lē], pseud. of **Boris Nikolayevich Bugayev,** 1880–1934, Russian writer of the SYMBOLIST school. He attempted to fuse all the arts in the poetic *Symphonies* (4 vol., 1901–8). His best prose is contained in the novels *The Silver Dove* (1910), *Petersburg* (1912), and the experimental, Joycean *Kotik Letayev* (1917).

Bemis Heights, battle of: see SARATOGA CAMPAIGN.

Ben Ali, Zine el-Abidine, 1936–, president of Tunisia (1987–). A military officer, he was minister of national security (1984–86) and interior minister (1986–87) before becoming prime minister (Oct. 1987) under Pres. Habib BOURGUIBA. In Nov. 1987 he deposed Bourguiba and succeeded him as president.

Benares: see VARANASI.

Benavente y Martínez, Jacinto [bā"nävān'tā ē märtē'nĕth], 1866–1954, Spanish dramatist. Of his sparkling social SATIRES, the best known are *Bonds of Interest* (1907) and *The Passion Flower* (1913). His plays introduced a more natural diction. He received the 1922 Nobel Prize in literature.

Ben Bella, Ahmed, 1919–, Algerian prime minister (1962–65). A leader of the Algerian nationalist movement, he headed Algeria's first government after independence. In 1965 his government was toppled in a coup led by BOUMEDIENNE. He was imprisoned from 1965 until 1980.

Benchley, Robert Charles, 1889–1945, American humorist; b. Worcester, Mass. Drama critic for *Life* (1920–29) and the *New Yorker* (1929–40), he is best remembered as the writer and star of short, satirical films, e.g., *The Treasurer's Report* (1928). His wry commentary appears in *My Ten Years in a Quandary* (1936) and *Benchley beside Himself* (1943).

bends: see DECOMPRESSION SICKNESS.

Benedict, Saint, d. c.547, Italian monk, founder of the BENEDICTINES, called Benedict of Nursia. He became a hermit and later founded the first Benedictine monastery, at Monte Cassino. He devised the Rule of St. Benedict, the chief rule of Western MONASTICISM. Feast: July 11.

Benedict XIII, antipope: see LUNA, PEDRO DE.

Benedict XIV, 1675–1758, pope (1740–58), an Italian named Prospero Lambertini. Renowned for his learning, he protected Eastern Catholic rites from Latinization. He denounced the cruelty in the disbanding of the settlements of indigenous peoples established by the JESUITS in Paraguay.

Benedict XV, 1854–1922, pope (1914–22), an Italian named Giacomo della Chiesa. In World War I he kept the Vatican neutral and worked strenuously to restore peace. He founded the Vatican service for prisoners of war.

Benedict, Ruth Fulton, 1887–1948, American anthropologist; b. N.Y.C. A student and colleague of Franz BOAS at Columbia Univ., she did field work among Native Americans, and studied contemporary European and Asian cultures. Stressing the role of culture in personality formation, her books attacked racism and ethnocentrism. Among her writings are *Patterns of Culture* (1934), *Race* (rev. ed. 1943), and *The Chrysanthemum and the Sword* (1946).

Benedictines, monks of the Roman Catholic Church following the rule of St. BENEDICT [Lat. abbr., = O.S.B.]. Unlike earlier groups, they stress moderation rather than austerity. Their waking hours are spent in worship and work, chiefly manual labor. The first Benedictine abbey was at Monte Cassino (founded c.529), Italy. Benedictines such as St. GREGORY I, St. AUGUSTINE OF CANTERBURY, and St. BONIFACE spread the order's influence across Europe. The Cluniac and the Cistercian orders resulted from 10th- and 11th-cent. reforms among the Benedictines.

Beneš, Eduard [bĕ'nĕsh], 1884–1948, Czechoslovakian president (1935–38, 1946–48). He was a follower of T.G. MASARYK and succeeded him as president in 1935. A liberal and a nationalist, he resigned after the MUNICH PACT. After World War II he again headed the nation, but the Communist coup of 1948 brought his presidency to an end.

Benét, Stephen Vincent, 1898–43, American writer; b. Bethlehem, Pa. He is known for his vivid literary treatments of American folklore and history. Benét is famous for *John Brown's Body* (1928; Pulitzer), a long narrative ballad of the Civil War, several volumes of verse, including *Heaven and Earth* (1920) and *The Burning City* (1936), and masterful short stories, particularly "The Devil and Daniel Webster."

Ben Ezra: see IBN EZRA, ABRAHAM BEN MEIR.

Bengal, region, 77,442 sq mi (200,575 sq km), E India and Bangladesh, on the Bay of Bengal. Its inland mountains slope to the fertile GANGES-BRAHMAPUTRA alluvial plains and delta. The heavy monsoon rains and warm climate make possible two harvests a year. From the empire of ASOKA (3d cent. B.C.) Bengal passed to the Buddhist Pala kings, the Hindu Sena dynasty, and Muslims of Turkic descent. It was in MOGUL hands when Portuguese and British traders arrived (16th–17th cent.). The latter, under Robert CLIVE, defeated the Muslims in 1757 and formed the Bengal presidency. When India became independent in 1947, **West Bengal** (1991 pop. 67,982,732), 33,928 sq mi (87,874 sq km), primarily Hindu, was created as a state in India, with CALCUTTA as its capital. It has jute mills, steel plants, chemical industries, and coal reserves. **East Bengal,** overwhelmingly Muslim, became East Pakistan in 1947 and gained independence as BANGLADESH in 1971.

Bengal, Bay of, arm of the INDIAN OCEAN, off E India and W Myanmar, separated from the Andaman Sea by the Andaman and Nicobar islands. It is some 1,300 mi (2,090 km) long and 1,000 mi (1,610 km) wide, and is generally shallow. Coastal areas are subject to heavy monsoon rains and destructive cyclones. MADRAS, CALCUTTA, and CHITTAGONG are the chief ports.

Bengali, language belonging to the Indic group of the Indo-Iranian subfamily of the Indo-European family of languages. See LANGUAGE (table).

Bengasi or **Benghazi,** city (1984 pop. 485,386), a Mediterranean seaport, NE Libya. It is an administrative and commercial center. Manufactures include processed food, textiles, and cement. Bengasi was cocapital (with TRIPOLI) of Libya (1951–72). The site of Hesperides, a Greek colony (7th cent. B.C.), the city was conquered by the Romans (1st cent. B.C.), Vandals (5th cent. A.D.), Arabs (7th cent.), and Ottoman Turks (mid-16th cent.). Italy held Bengasi from 1911 until it fell (1942) to the British during WORLD WAR II.

Ben-Gurion, David [ben-go͞o'rēōn], 1886–1973, Israeli statesman and 1st prime minister (1949–53, 1955–63); b. Poland as David Grün. He settled in Palestine in 1906, devoted his life to ZIONISM, and was a founder of the Mapai (later Labor) party. During the struggle (1947–48) for independence he headed Israel's defense efforts, and once independence was achieved he became prime minister.

Benin [bĕnēn'], former kingdom, situated in present-day SW Nigeria. Ruled by the *oba* (to whose family human sacrifices were made) and by a sophisticated bureaucracy, the African state flourished (14th–17th cent.). Benin sold slaves as well as ivory, pepper, and cloth to Europeans. After a period of decline, it revived (19th cent.) with a trade in palm products. The modern Nigerian city of **Benin** (1987 est. pop. 183,000) served as the capital and was conquered and burned by the British in 1898. Iron work, carved ivory, and bronze busts made in Benin rank with the finest art of Africa.

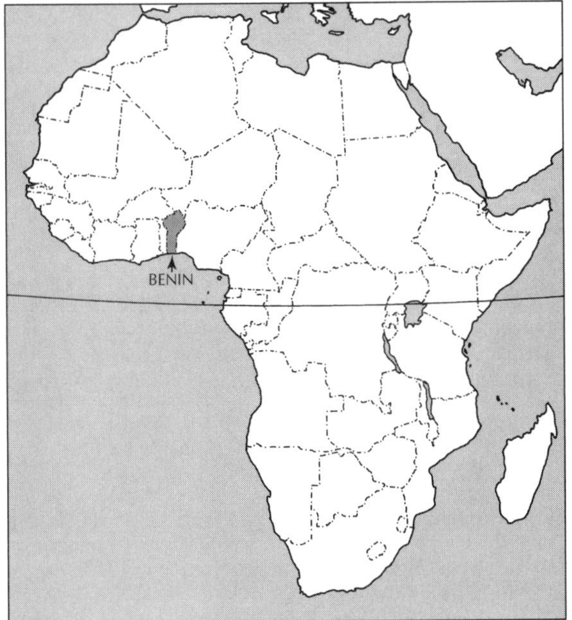

Benin, officially Republic of Benin, republic (1992 est. pop. 4,998,000), 43,483 sq mi (112,622 sq km), W Africa, formerly Dahomey; bordered by Togo (W), Burkina Faso and Niger (N), Nigeria (E), and the Bight of Benin, an arm of the Gulf of Guinea (S). PORTO-NOVO is the capital; COTONOU is the largest city and chief port. There are four major geographical zones: a narrow, lagoon-fringed coastal area in the south; a flat, fertile area crossed by the wide Lama marsh further north; forested mountains in the northwest; and savanna-covered highlands in the northeast. Benin's economy is largely agricultural, with most workers engaged in subsistence farming. Chief crops are maize, cassava, millet, sorghum, peanuts, pulses, cacao, cotton, and palm nuts; palm oil is a major export. Although there are rich mineral deposits, notably of offshore petroleum, chromite, and iron and other metal ores, only petroleum and limestone are extracted on a large scale. Most of Benin's few manufactures are processed agricultural products or consumer goods. The population is made up of four main ethnolinguistic groups—Fon, Yoruba, Voltaic, and Fulani. French is the official language, and Fon, the language of the largest ethnic group, is widely spoken. Most of the people follow traditional religions, but there are large Roman Catholic and Muslim minorities.

History. According to oral tradition, southern Benin was settled (12th or 13th cent.) by the Aja. The kingdom they founded, Great Ardra, reached its height in the 16th and early 17th cent. The Aja gradually mixed with the local people to form the Fon, or Dahomey, ethnic group. By the late 17th cent. the Dahomey were raiding their neighbors for slaves to be sold to European traders, a practice that continued until the late 19th cent. The Dahomey kingdom came under French influence in 1851 and was made part of FRENCH WEST AFRICA in 1899. Under the French, a port was constructed at Cotonou, railroads were built, and the output of palm products increased. In 1958 the area became an autonomous state (called Dahomey) within the FRENCH COMMUNITY; it gained full independence in 1960. The independent nation was plagued by governmental instability caused by economic insufficiency, ethnic rivalries, and social unrest. Beginning in 1963 a series of military coups produced several short-lived regimes. A three-member presidential council was established in 1970 but overthrown by the army, led by Maj. Mathieu Kérékou, in 1972. The country was renamed Benin in 1975. A new constitution was promulgated, providing for a national revolutionary assembly, but Benin remained essentially a one-party military dictatorship under the leadership of Kérékou, who was elected president in 1980. Unrest in 1989 and 1990 forced Kérékou to permit a multiparty democracy, and he lost the presidency to Nicéphore Soglo in a free election in 1991.

Benjamin, in the BIBLE, youngest son of JACOB and RACHEL, ancestor of one of the 12 tribes of Israel (See ISRAEL, TRIBES OF). He was the favorite of his family. The name survived in the High Gate of Benjamin of the Temple at Jerusalem. SAUL was the most noted son of the House of Benjamin.

Benjamin, Walter, 1892–1940, German essayist and critic known for his synthesis of eccentric Marxist theory and Jewish messianism. His essays on BAUDELAIRE and KAFKA and his speculation on symbolism, allegory, and the function of art in a mechanical age have profoundly affected contemporary criticism. When the Nazis invaded France, Benjamin, who had moved (1933) there, fled for Spain. Denied entry, he committed suicide.

Bennett, Arnold, 1867–1931, English novelist and dramatist, noted for realistic novels about the industrial Midlands. Influenced by ZOLA'S NATURALISM, Bennett depicted regional life in *The Old Wives' Tale* (1908) and *These Twain* (1916). His plays include *Milestones* (1912, with Edward Knoblock).

Bennett, James Gordon, 1795–1872, American newspaper proprietor; b. Scotland. His New York *Herald,* started in 1835 as a penny paper of four four-column pages, made many innovations in American journalism—editorials critical of all political parties; new fields of news, notably Wall Street finance; use of European correspondents (1838); extensive use of the TELEGRAPH; and illustrations for news articles. It gained an excellent reputation for accurate reporting, especially in the CIVIL WAR. His son, **James Gordon Bennett,** 1841–1918, b. N.Y.C., took over management of the *Herald* in 1867 and maintained its reputation. He financed (1869–71) Henry M. STANLEY'S expedition to find David LIVINGSTON in Africa and also supported (1879–81) the ill-fated expedition of the explorer George Washington De Long to the Arctic. In addition he established London and Paris daily editions of the *Herald* and helped organize (1883) the Commercial Cable Company to handle European dispatches.

Bennett, Richard Bedford, 1870–1947, Canadian prime minister (1930–35). As Conservative leader during the GREAT DEPRESSION, he signed (1932) preferential trade agreements with Britain and the dominions, and proposed (1934) reform social legislation at home. In 1941 he was created a viscount.

Benny, Jack, 1894–1974, American comedian; b. Waukegan, Ill., as Benjamin Kubelsky. His shows on radio (1932–55) and television (1950–65) made famous his miserliness, reproachful silences, and violin. His films include *To Be or Not to Be* (1942).

Benozzo Gozzoli: see GOZZOLI, BENOZZO.

Bent, Charles, 1799–1847, American fur trader; b. Charleston, Va. He helped build a prominent trading firm in the Southwest and was chosen governor of New Mexico after the U.S. occupation in the Mexican War. His brother **William Bent,** 1809–69, managed BENT'S FORT, the company's famous trading post.

Bentham, Jeremy, 1748–1832, English philosopher, jurist, political theorist; founder of UTILITARIANISM. Educated as a lawyer, Bentham devoted himself to the scientific analysis of morals and law. His *Introduction to the Principles of Morals and Legislation* (1789) held that the greatest happiness of the greatest number should govern our judgment of every institution and action. The 19th-cent. reforms of criminal law, of judicial organization, and of the parliamentary electorate owe much to Bentham's active work in English legislative reform, and his thought strongly influenced that of John Stuart MILL.

Bentley, Eric, 1916–, American critic, editor, and translator; b. England. Particularly noted for his drama criticism, he is the author of such books as *The Playwright as Thinker* (1946) and *What Is Theatre?* (1956). Bentley is also known for his translations of BRECHT and PIRANDELLO.

Bentley, Richard, 1662–1742, English critic and philologist, considered the greatest of English classical scholars. His exposure of the 4th-cent. forgery *The Epistles of Phalaris* is his most celebrated work.

Benton, Thomas Hart, 1782–1858, U.S. statesman; b. Hillsboro, N.C. As a Democratic senator (1821–51) from Missouri, he supported currency measures to benefit the common people, and drew up Pres. JACKSON's Specie Circular (1836). Benton favored Western development and opposed the extension of slavery. He served as U.S. representative (1853–55).

Benton, Thomas Hart, 1889–1975, American painter; b. Neosho, Mo.; grandnephew of Sen. Thomas Hart BENTON. The best-known American muralist of the 1930s and early 40s, he won fame for such murals as those at the New School for Social Research (N.Y.C.). Benton is noted for his dramatization of American themes, as in *July Hay* (1943; Metropolitan Mus.).

Bentsen, Lloyd (Millard, Jr.), 1921–, U.S. politician and government official; b. Mission, Tex. He was a bomber pilot in the Army Air Corps during World War II, served in the House of Representatives (1948–55), started a successful insurance business, and was elected (1970) to the U.S. Senate. In 1987 he became chairman of the Senate finance committee. He ran unsuccessfully for vice president on the Democratic ticket headed by Michael DUKAKIS in 1988. In 1993 Pres. CLINTON appointed Bentsen treasury secretary.

Bent's Fort, noted American trading post on the Arkansas R., in present-day Colorado. The trading company of Charles BENT and Ceran St. Vrain completed the fort in 1833. On a branch of the SANTA FE TRAIL, it was used by many famous MOUNTAIN MEN and by the U.S. Army during the MEXICAN WAR. By 1852 it was abandoned; its manager, William BENT, erected Bent's New Fort downstream in 1853.

Ben Yehudah, Eliezer, 1858–1922, Jewish scholar; b. Lithuania. He settled in Palestine in 1881. A leader in the revival of Hebrew as the national language, he compiled the *Dictionary of Ancient and Modern Hebrew* (16 vol.).

Benz, Karl, 1844–1929, German engineer, credited with building (1885) the first AUTOMOBILE powered by an INTERNAL-COMBUSTION ENGINE. His car had three wheels, an electric ignition, and differential gears. In 1926, Benz's company merged with that of Gottlieb DAIMLER and became the manufacturer of the Mercedes-Benz automobile.

benzene (C_6H_6), colorless, flammable toxic liquid with a strong odor. A HYDROCARBON, benzene is the parent substance of the AROMATIC COMPOUNDS. It consists of an unusually stable hexagonal ring of six carbon atoms, each of which is bonded to a hydrogen atom. Derivative compounds include phenol and aniline. Obtained from coal tar and petroleum, benzene and its derivatives are used in making dyes, drugs, and plastics. Benzene has been identified as a carcinogen.

benzodiazepine, any of a group of tranquilizers prescribed for their antianxiety, sedative, and muscle relaxing effects, including alprazolam (Xanax), diazepam (Valium), clonazepam (Klonopin), temazepam (Restoril), and triazolam (Halcion). They are considered to be highly addictive.

Ben-Zvi, Yizhak [bĕn-tsvē], 1884–1963, president of ISRAEL (1952–63); b. Russia as Issac Shimshelevitz. He settled in Palestine in 1907 and was one of the creators of the Jewish state. In 1952 he succeeded WEIZMANN as president. He was an historian and a scholar in the field of Jewish ethnology.

Beowulf [bā'əwo͝olf], oldest English epic, probably composed in the early 8th cent. by a Northumbrian bard, and drawn from Scandinavian history and folk sources. It recounts Beowulf's struggle with the water monster Grendel and Grendel's mother; the hero's victory in old age over a dragon; and his death and funeral. The poem, in alliterative verse, fuses Christian elements with a picture of old Germanic life.

Berbers, aboriginal Caucasoid peoples of N Africa who form a large part of the populations of Libya, Algeria, and Morocco. Except for the nomadic TUAREG, they are small farmers living in loosely joined tribal villages. Local industries are mining, pottery, weaving, and embroidery. They are SUNNI Muslims, speaking languages of the Hamitic group. Despite a history of conquests, their culture dates back before 2400 B.C. In classical times they formed such states as MAURETANIA and NUMIDIA. Most were Christians until the 7th-cent. Arab conquest. In the 9th cent. they supported the FATIMID dynasty; when the Fatimids left N Africa, fighting among the Berbers reduced the region to anarchy until the ALMORAVIDS and ALMOHADS imposed order. The plains Berbers were eventually absorbed by the Arabs; the mountain Berbers retained their warlike traditions, fiercely resisting French and Spanish occupation of N Africa and in the 1960s helping to drive the French from ALGERIA.

Berenson, Bernard, 1865–1959, American art critic and connoisseur; b. Lithuania. A conversationalist, wit, and arbiter of taste, Berenson selected work for many art collectors, much of it now in museums, e.g., the Isabella Stewart GARDNER Museum. Many of his judgments in art history, made in his early books, have been criticized by later scholars. His works include *Venetian Painters of the Renaissance* (1894) and *Rumor and Reflection* (1952).

Berg, Alban [bĕrk], 1885–1935, Austrian composer. A pupil and close friend of Arnold SCHOENBERG, he adopted ATONALITY and later combined the 12-tone system (see TWELVE-TONE MUSIC) with the lyric and dramatic qualities of the Viennese romantic tradition. His masterpiece, the opera *Wozzeck* (based on the play by BÜCHNER, 1925) aroused protest, but has since been acclaimed as a major 20th-cent. work. His unfinished opera *Lulu* (based on two plays by WEDEKIND) adhered more strictly to the 12-tone principle.

Bergen, city (1987 pop. 208,809), SW Norway. On North Sea inlets, it is a major shipping and shipbuilding center. Founded c.1070 by OLAF III, it was medieval Norway's largest city and a royal residence. From c.1350 to 1560 the HANSEATIC LEAGUE imposed unpopular rule on the city. Bergen was Norway's foremost city until the rise of OSLO in the 19th cent. Impressive monuments of its medieval past include Haakon's Hall (1261; largely rebuilt after World War II) and several churches.

Berger, Thomas, 1924–, American novelist; b. Cincinnati. He writes comic novels about the chasm between the American dream and middle-class reality. They include *Crazy in Berlin* (1958), *Reinhart in Love* (1962), and *Reinhart's Women* (1981); *Little Big Man* (1965); *Nowhere* (1985); *Orrie's Story* (1990); and *Meeting Evil* (1992).

Berger, Victor Louis, 1860–1929, U.S. socialist leader; b. Austria-Hungary. A Milwaukee journalist, Berger was (1911–13) the first socialist member of Congress. He was reelected (1918, 1919), but Congress excluded him for sedition, for which he was sentenced to a 20-year prison term. The U.S. Supreme Court reversed (1921) that decision, and he returned (1923–29) to Congress.

Bergman, Hjalmar [bĕr'yəmän], 1883–1931, Swedish author. His many popular works, characterized by insight into the ambivalence of human emotions, include the novel *God's Orchid* (1919) and the play *The Swedenhielm Family* (1925).

Bergman, (Ernst) Ingmar, 1918–, Swedish film director. His films, often treating man's search for God, are usually studies of human loneliness. They include *The Seventh Seal* (1956), *The Silence* (1963), *Cries and Whispers* (1972), *Autumn Sonata* (1978), and *Fanny and Alexander* (1983; Academy Award). He also wrote the screenplays for *The Best Intentions* (1992) and *Sunday's Children* (1993).

Bergman, Ingrid, 1915–82, Swedish film actress. A radiant, gifted actress, she made such films as *Casablanca* (1942), *For Whom the Bell Tolls* (1943), *Notorious* (1946), *Anastasia* (1956; Academy Award), and *Autumn Sonata* (1978).

Bergson, Henri, 1859–1941, French philosopher. He became a professor at the Collège de France in 1900. Bergson's dualistic philosophy holds that the world contains two opposing tendencies, the life force and the resistance of matter against that force. The individual knows matter through intellect but through intuition perceives the life force and the reality of time, which is not a unit of measurement but duration in terms of life experience. Bergson was awarded the 1927 Nobel Prize in literature. Among his works are *Time and Free Will* (1889) and *The Creative Mind* (1934).

Beria, Lavrenti Pavlovich, 1899–1953, Soviet leader. He became Communist party secretary in Georgia and the Transcaucasus in 1931, head of the Soviet secret police (NKVD) in 1938, and a member of the politburo in 1946. In the power struggle following the death of Joseph STALIN he was executed.

beriberi, disease caused by a deficiency of thiamine (vitamin B_1), resulting in neurological and gastrointestinal disturbances. See table under VITAMIN.

Bering, Vitus Jonassen [bār'ĭng], 1681–1741, Danish explorer in Russian employ. He explored the far northeast of SIBERIA for PETER I. In 1728 he sailed through the BERING STRAIT. In 1741 Bering

Ingrid Bergman

landed a party on the Alaskan coast. The expedition was later wrecked on Bering Island, where he died.

Bering Sea, c.878,000 sq mi (2,274,000 sq km), northern arm of the Pacific Ocean, screened from the Pacific proper by the ALEUTIAN ISLANDS. It is usually frozen from October to June. Its migratory seal herd, threatened with extinction at the time of the **Bering Sea Fur-Seal Controversy** (1886), has gradually been rebuilt following an international agreement (1911) regulating open-ocean sealing.

Bering Strait, c.55 mi (90 km) wide, connecting the Arctic Ocean and the Bering Sea and separating Siberia and Alaska. The Diomede Islands are in the strait, which is usually frozen from October to June.

Berio, Luciano, 1925–, Italian composer. He was introduced to SERIAL MUSIC by Luigi DALLAPICCOLA in 1952 and composed ELECTRONIC MUSIC from 1954. His works include a series of *Sequences* (1957–1975), each for a different instrument; *Sinfonia* (1968) and *Coro* (1976), for orchestra and voices; and *La vera storia* (1982), an opera with acrobats and a wordless soprano.

Berkeley, Busby, 1895–1975, American film director; b. Los Angeles as William Berkeley Enos. In such musicals as *42nd Street* (1933), *Footlight Parade* (1933), and *The Gang's All Here* (1942), directing either the dance sequences or the entire production, he created a striking, often surreal visual style.

Berkeley, George [bär'klē, bûr–], 1685–1753, Anglo-Irish philosopher and clergyman; b. Ireland. Going beyond the teachings of John LOCKE, Berkeley's subjective IDEALISM holds that there is no existence of matter independent of perception; the observing mind of God makes possible the continued apparent existence of material objects. Among his more important works are his *Essay towards a New Theory of Vision* (1709), *A Treatise Concerning the Principles of Human Knowledge* (1710), and *Three Dialogues between Hylas and Philonous* (1713).

Berkeley, Sir William, 1606–77, British colonial governor of Virginia (1642–52, 1660–77). Poor frontier defense and favoritism to his friends in his second term led to the rebellion (1676) of Nathaniel BACON, which he ruthlessly suppressed.

Berkeley, city (1990 pop. 102,724), W Calif., on the eastern shore of San Francisco Bay; inc. 1878. The city is the site of the main campus of the Univ. of California. Manufactures include pharmaceuticals, chemicals, and metal and other products.

berkelium (Bk), synthetic radioactive element, discovered in 1949 by Glenn SEABORG, S.G. Thompson, and Albert Ghiorso by alpha-particle bombardment of americium-241. It is in the ACTINIDE SERIES; nine isotopes exist. See ELEMENT (table); PERIODIC TABLE.

Berkman, Alexander, 1870?–1936, U.S. anarchist; b. Russia. He emigrated to the U.S. c.1887 and attempted (1892) to kill industrialist H.C. FRICK. He was imprisoned for 14 years. Deported (1919) to Russia with Emma GOLDMAN for obstructing the draft, he became disillusioned with the Bolsheviks, left Russia, and later committed suicide in France.

Berle, Milton, 1908–, American entertainer; b. N.Y.C. as Milton Berlinger. His success came with television, where his comedy routines had such broad appeal that his show is credited with contributing to the growing popularity of the medium. His extremely successful "Texaco Star Theater" (1948–54) earned him the nickname "Mr. Television."

Berlin, Irving, 1888–1989, American songwriter; b. Russia as Israel Baline. He wrote nearly 1,000 songs, many of them for Broadway musicals and reviews and films. His first big hit was "Alexander's Ragtime Band" in 1911; "God Bless America" is perhaps his best-known work.

Berlin, Sir Isaiah, 1909–, English political scientist; b. Latvia. He was a professor of social and political theory at Oxford Univ. (1957–67) and president of Wolfson College, Oxford (1966–75). His writings include *Karl Marx* (1939) and essays collected in such volumes as *Four Essays on Liberty* (1969), *Russian Thinkers* (1978), and *Against the Current* (1979).

Berlin, city and state (1991 est. pop. 3,450,000), 341 sq mi (883 sq km), in E Germany on the Spree and Havel rivers, de jure capital of the country. It is within, but administratively not a part of, BRANDENBURG. Berlin is Germany's largest city, its historic capital, and a major cultural center. The city's manufactures include electrical equipment, chemicals, and clothing. Among its many cultural institutions are the renowned Berlin Philharmonic, the gallery of the Charlottenberg Palace, with its collection of Rembrandts, and the Pergamum museum, known for classical art. Formed from two villages chartered in the 13th cent., Berlin was a leading member of the HANSEATIC LEAGUE and became prominent as a commercial, cultural, and communications center of Central Europe. It was the capital of PRUSSIA and of the German Empire after 1871 and the

The Berlin Wall

Weimar Republic (see GERMANY) after WORLD WAR I. In WORLD WAR II it was badly damaged by Allied bombing and a Soviet artillery attack. In 1945 it was divided into British, American, and French occupation zones (West Berlin) and a Soviet zone (East Berlin). The status of divided Berlin became a major COLD WAR issue, and in 1948–49 the Western powers carried out a large-scale airlift to supply West Berlin during a Soviet land and water blockade. In 1949 East Berlin was made the capital of East Germany; in 1950 West Berlin was established as a state within, and the de jure capital of, West Germany, with BONN as the de facto capital. In Aug. 1961 East German authorities erected the 29-mi (47-km) Berlin Wall along the line of partition to halt the exodus of refugees to the West. As the East German Communist regime collapsed (1989–90), the Wall was breached (Nov. 9, 1989). Upon German reunification in Oct. 1990, the new, all-German parliament held a symbolic session in Berlin in the old Reichstag building, and in 1991 it voted to move the federal government to the city. The move is to be completed by the end of the year 2000; some government offices will remain in Bonn.

Berlin, Conference of, 1884–85, international meeting aimed at settling colonial problems in Africa. Attending were all European nations, with the U.S. and Turkey. In effect, the conference legitimized the sovereignty these nations were already exercising over their African colonies.

Berlin, Congress of, 1878, international meeting called primarily to thwart Russian expansion in the OTTOMAN EMPIRE (Turkey). Included were all the European powers, RUSSIA, and Turkey, with Otto von BISMARCK as the chairman. The treaty that resulted significantly changed the existing political situation in eastern Europe. Montenegro, Serbia, and Romania were recognized as independent; Bosnia and Hercegovina were assigned to Austria-Hungary; the boundary lines between Greece and Turkey were redrawn; S Bessarabia was ceded to Russia; and Cyprus was put under British occupation. Russia was angered at Bismarck's handling of the conference, thus ending the first THREE EMPERORS' LEAGUE.

Berlioz, Louis-Hector [bĕrlyōz'], 1803–69, French romantic composer. He abandoned medical study to enter the Paris Conservatory. His *Symphonie fantastique* (1830) marked a new development in program music, and that year Berlioz won the Prix de Rome. In the next decade he wrote the symphonies *Harold in Italy* and *Romeo and Juliet.* Other works included the operas *The Damnation of Faust* (1846) and *The Trojans* (1856–59) and the successful ORATORIO *The Childhood of Christ* (1850–54). Berlioz's ideas of orchestration influenced many later composers.

Bermuda, British dependency (1992 est. pop. 60,200), 20 sq mi (52 sq km), comprising some 150 coral rocks, islets and islands, in the Atlantic Ocean, c.650 mi (1,050 km) SE of Cape Hatteras, N.C. The capital is Hamilton. Tourism is the mainstay of Bermuda's economy, but offshore banking is also important. Probably discovered by the Spanish in the early 16th cent., the islands remained uninhabited until colonists bound for Virginia were shipwrecked there in 1609. Bermuda's government became the responsibility of the British crown in 1684; internal self-government was granted in 1968. The U.S. operates a naval and air force base there. Sir John Swan, of the United Bermuda party, has been prime minister since 1982.

Bermuda Triangle, area in the Atlantic Ocean off Florida where a number of ships and aircraft have vanished. Also known as the Devil's Triangle, it is bounded at its points by Melbourne, Fla.; Bermuda; and Puerto Rico. Storms are common in the region, and investigations to date have not produced scientific evidence of any unusual phenomena involved in the disappearances.

Bern or **Berne,** city (1990 pop. 134,393), capital of Switzerland and of Bern canton, W central Switzerland, within a loop of the Aare R. A university, administrative, and industrial center, it manufactures such products as precision instruments, textiles, and machinery. It is the seat of the Universal Postal Union, the International Copyright Union, and other world agencies. Said to have been founded in 1191, it joined the Swiss Confederation in 1353 and became its leading member. Bern accepted the REFORMATION in 1528 and adopted a liberal constitution in 1831. It became the Swiss capital in 1848. Its historic buildings include a medieval clock tower and a 15th-cent. town hall.

Bernadotte, Count Folke [bĕrnädôt'], 1895–1948, Swedish internationalist. Active in the Swedish RED CROSS, which he headed after 1946, he arranged (1945) the evacuation of Danish and Norwegian prisoners from Germany. He was assassinated by Jewish extremists while serving as UN mediator in Palestine.

Bernadotte, Jean Baptiste Jules: see Charles XIV under CHARLES, kings of Sweden.

Bernanos, Georges [bĕrnänōs'], 1888–1948, French author. His novels *The Star of Satan* (1926) and *The Diary of a Country Priest* (1936) reflect his mystical, Catholic bent. A Royalist until the Spanish civil war, Bernanos condemned FRANCO's policies in *A Diary of My Times* (1938).

Bernard, Saint: see BERNARD OF CLAIRVAUX, SAINT.

Bernard, Claude [bĕrnär'], 1813–78, French physiologist. One of the great scientific investigators, he is known as the founder of experimental medicine through his work on the digestive process and on the vasomotor mechanism.

Bernard of Clairvaux, Saint, 1090?–1153, French churchman, Doctor of the Church. He founded (1115) a Cistercian monastery at Clairvaux, where he remained as abbot for the rest of his life, despite efforts to move him higher. His holiness, intellect, and eloquence made him one of the most powerful figures of his day; he brought about the condemnation of Peter ABELARD and preached the Second CRUSADE. His writings exerted a profound influence on Roman Catholic spirituality, especially that known as *devotio moderna.* He was canonized in 1174. Feast: Aug. 20.

Bernhardt, Sarah, 1844–1923, French actress; b. Rosine Bernard. Called "the divine Sarah" by Oscar WILDE, she was the queen of French romantic and classical tragedy. She became famous for her superb portrayals in *Phèdre* (1874), in Victor HUGO's *Ruy Blas* (1872), and in *Adrienne Lecouvreur* (1880). She also starred in works by SARDOU and ROSTAND, and wrote some of her own vehicles. She made tours of Europe and the U.S., including many "farewell tours" after her leg was amputated in 1915. She played Hamlet at her own Théâtre Sarah Bernhardt in 1899.

Bernini, Giovanni Lorenzo or **Gianlorenzo,** 1598–1680, Italian sculptor and architect, the dominant figure of the Italian BAROQUE. Working for the major patrons of his day, he produced brilliantly vital, dynamic sculpture in reaction against mannerist traditions (see MANNERISM) and dramatic, impressive works of architecture enriched with sculpture. For Cardinal Borghese he produced *David* (pre-1620), *Rape of Proserpine* (1622), and *Apollo and Daphne* (1625; all: Borghese Gallery, Rome). He designed churches, chapels, fountains, monuments, tombs, and statues for the popes. In 1629 he became architect of ST. PETERK'S CHURCH, designing interior details and the great, embracing, elliptical piazza in front of the church. His other Roman works include the Churches of Santa Maria della Vittoria (which houses his great sculpture the *Ecstasy of St. Theresa*) and Sant'Andrea al Quirinale, and the fountains of the Piazza Navona.

Bernoulli, Swiss family distinguished in scientific and mathematical history. **Jakob, Jacques,** or **James Bernoulli,** 1654–1705, was one of the chief developers of both the ordinary calculus and the calculus of variations. His *Ars conjectandi* (1713) was an important treatise on the theory of probability. His brother, **Johann, Jean,** or **John Bernoulli,** 1667–1748, was famous for his work on integral and exponential calculus; he was also a founder of the calculus of variations and contributed to the study of geodesics, complex numbers, and trigonometry. His son, **Daniel Bernoulli,** 1700–1782, has often been called the first mathematical physicist. His greatest work was his *Hydrodynamica* (1738), which included the principle now known as Bernoulli's principle and anticipated the law of conservation of energy and the kinetic-molecular theory of gases developed a century later. He also made important contributions to probability theory, astronomy, and the theory of differential equations. Other members of the family were noted in the fields of mathematics, physics, astronomy, and geography.

Bernoulli's principle: see AERODYNAMICS.

Bernstein, Leonard, 1918–90, American composer and conductor; b. Lawrence, Mass. He composed symphonic works (*Kaddish Symphony,* 1963); chamber music; ballets (*Fancy Free,* 1944); MUSICALS (*On the Town,* 1944; *Candide,* 1956; *West Side Story,* 1957); and choral music (*Chichester Psalms,* 1965). His *Mass* (1971), "a theater piece for singers, dancers, and players," was performed at the opening of the John F. Kennedy Cultural Center, Washington, D.C. From 1958 to 1969 he was musical director of the New York Philharmonic (see ORCHESTRA, table).

Berrettini, Pietro: see CORTONA, PIETRO DA.

Berry, Chuck (Charles Edward Anderson Berry), 1926–, American rock music guitarist, singer, and songwriter; b. San Jose, Calif. A rock music pioneer, he had a string of hits in the late 1950s, including "Maybellene" and "Johnny B. Goode." His distinctive guitar style and witty lyrics influenced England's pop renaissance.

Berryman, John, 1914–72, American poet; b. McAlester, Okla. His verse is complex, dramatic, and personal, often mirroring the anguish of a trivial age. Among his works are *Homage to Mistress Bradstreet* (1956), *77 Dream Songs* (1964; Pulitzer), *His Toy, His Dream, His Rest* (1968), and *Delusions, etc.* (1972).

Berthelot, Pierre Eugène Marcelin [bĕrtəlō'], 1827–1907, French chemist. Professor at the École Supérieure de Pharmacie and later at the Collège de France, he became a member of the French Academy in 1900. A founder of modern organic chemistry, he was the first to synthesize organic compounds (e.g., methanol, ethanol, benzene, and acetylene), thereby dispelling the old theory of a vital force inherent in organic compounds. He also worked in thermochemistry and in explosives.

Berthollet, Claude Louis, Comte [bĕrtōlā'], 1748–1822, French chemist. Noted for his ideas on chemical affinity and his discovery of the reversibility of reactions, he supported Antoine LAVOISIER's theory of combustion and collaborated with him in reforming chemical nomenclature. He analyzed ammonia and prussic acid and discovered the bleaching properties of chlorine.

beryl, extremely hard beryllium and aluminum silicate mineral ($Be_3Al_2Si_6O_{18}$), occurring in crystals that may be of enormous size and are usually white, yellow, blue, green, or colorless. It is commonly used as a gem, the most valued variety being the greenish EMERALD; the blue to bluish-green variety is AQUAMARINE. Beryl is the principal raw material for the element BERYLLIUM and its compounds.

beryllium (Be), metallic element, first isolated in 1828 independently by Friedrich WÖHLER and Antoine Bussy. The silver-gray, ALKALINE-EARTH METAL is light, strong, high-melting, and resistant to corrosion. It is used as a window material for X-ray tubes, as a shield and a moderator in nuclear reactors, and extensively in aerospace industries. See ELEMENT (table); PERIODIC TABLE.

Berzelius, Jöns Jakob, Baron, 1779–1848, Swedish chemist. He developed the modern system of symbols and formulas in chemistry, made a remarkably accurate table of atomic weights, analyzed many chemical compounds, and discovered the elements SELENIUM, THORIUM, and CERIUM. He coined the words *isomerism, allotropy,* and *protein.*

Besant, Annie (Wood), 1847–1933, English theosophist and reformer. Rejecting Christianity and advocating free thought and socialism, Besant edited the *National Reformer* with Charles Bradlaugh. Her atheism and unconventionality led the courts in 1879 to take away her children. After embracing THEOSOPHY in 1889, she went to India, where she campaigned for nationalism, founded (1898) the Central Hindu College (1898) and the Indian Home Rule League (1916), and became president (1917) of the Indian National Congress. In 1926–27, Besant proclaimed the Indian mystic Jiddu Krishnamurti to be the new Messiah. She published prolifically, particularly works on theosophy.

Bessel, Friedrich Wilhelm, 1784–1846, German astronomer and mathematician. His discovery of the parallax of the fixed star 61 Cygni, announced in 1838, was the first fully authenticated measurement of a star's distance from the earth. By 1833 Bessel had increased to 50,000 the number of stars whose positions and proper motions were accurately determined. He established a class of mathematical functions, named for him, as a result of his work on planetary perturbation.

Bessemer process, industrial process for the manufacture of STEEL from molten PIG IRON. The process is carried out in a large steel container, called the Bessemer converter. IRON is introduced through an opening in the narrow upper end. When air is forced upward through perforations in the bottom, impurities such as manganese, silicon, and carbon unite with oxygen to form oxides. The carbon monoxide burns off, and the other impurities form slag. The steel is then poured from the upper opening into molds, and the slag is left behind. The Bessemer process has been superseded by the OPEN-HEARTH PROCESS and BASIC OXYGEN PROCESS.

Best, Charles Herbert, 1899–1978, Canadian physiologist; b. West Pembroke, Me. He, Sir Frederick BANTING, and John MACLEOD were the first to isolate (1921) the hormone INSULIN from the pancreas and demonstrate its use in the treatment of diabetes mellitus. Best discovered the antiallergic enzyme histaminase, the anticoagulant heparin, and the vitamin choline.

beta blocker or **beta adrenergic blocking agent,** drug that reduces the symptoms connected with HYPERTENSION, cardiac arrhythmias, MIGRAINE headaches, and other disorders related to the sympathetic nervous system. Within the sympathetic nervous system, beta receptors are located mainly in the heart, lungs, kidneys, and blood vessels. Beta blockers compete with EPINEPHRINE for these receptor sites and interfere with the action of epinephrine, lowering blood pressure and heart rate, stopping arrhythmias, and preventing migraine headaches. Propranolol is a commonly used beta blocker.

Betancourt, Rómulo [bĕtänkōōr'], 1908–81, president of VENEZUELA (1945–48, 1959–64). He founded (1935) the left-wing party that became *Acción Democrática.* When he came to power (1945) by a military coup, he instituted universal suffrage, social reforms, and oil royalties for the government. After his exile (1948–58) by a junta, he was elected president (1959) and continued to promote his reforms.

beta particle, one of the three types of radiation resulting from natural RADIOACTIVITY; it is a high-speed ELECTRON. A NEUTRINO is emitted along with the electron. In some forms of induced, or artificial, radioactivity, the electron's antiparticle, the positron, is emitted.

betel, masticatory made from seeds of the betel palm (*Areca catechu*). Slices of the seeds (also called betel nuts), together with other aromatic flavorings and lime paste, are smeared onto a betel pepper (*Piper betle*) leaf, which is then rolled up and chewed. Betel contains a narcotic stimulant and has been chewed in S Asia since ancient times.

Bethany, village at the southeastern foot of the Mount of Olives, modern Al Ayzariyah (West Bank), 2 mi (3.2 km) E of Jerusalem. Home of LAZARUS, Martha, and MARY, it was frequently visited by JESUS and is closely associated with the final scenes of his life.

Bethe, Hans Albrecht [bā'tə], 1906–, American physicist; b. Germany; came to U.S. in 1935. He was director (1943–46) of the theoretical physics division of the Los Alamos Scientific Laboratory and scientific adviser (1958) to the U.S. at the Geneva nuclear test-ban talks. Known for his brilliant theories on atomic properties, Bethe received the 1967 Nobel Prize in physics for work on the origin of solar and stellar energy.

Bethlehem, town (1980 est. pop. 14,500), in the Israeli-occupied WEST BANK; the birthplace of JESUS. It is a place of pilgrimage and the trade center of a farming area. The biblical book of RUTH is set in Bethlehem, and it was DAVID's home. CONSTANTINE I built the Church of the Nativity (completed 333) on the traditional site of Jesus' birth. There St. JEROME produced the Vulgate text of the BIBLE. Crusaders held the town from 1099 to 1187. Annexed to the Ottoman Empire in 1571, it was part of Britain's Palestine mandate (1922–48) and then of Jordan. Israel occupied it in 1967.

Bethlehem, city (1990 pop. 71,428), E Pa., on the Lehigh R.; settled 1740–41, inc. as a city 1917. It is the site of the headquarters of the Bethlehem Steel Corp.; steel, chemicals, machines, cement, and textiles are produced. Bethlehem was settled by MORAVIAN CHURCH members and contains several early Moravian buildings. The city is noted for its Bach Choir, and Lehigh Univ. and Moravian College are located there.

Bethune, Mary McCleod, 1875–1955, African-American educator; b. Mayesville, S.C.; grad. Moody Bible Institute, Chicago, 1895. The 17th child of former slaves, she taught (1895–1903) in a series of southern mission schools until founding (1904) the Daytona Normal and Industrial Inst. for Negro Girls (later Bethune-Cookman College) and the National Council of Negro Women (1935). She was special adviser on minority affairs to Franklin D. ROOSEVELT.

Betjeman, Sir John, 1906–84, English poet, POET LAUREATE (1972–

84). His works, which combine a witty appraisal of his time with nostalgia, especially for the Victorian era, include *Mt. Zion* (1933) and *Collected Poems* (1971). He was named POET LAUREATE in 1972.

Bettelheim, Bruno, 1903–90, American psychologist; b. Austria. In the same year that he earned his Ph.D. from the Univ. of Vienna (1938) he was interned in the Dachau and Buchenwald CONCENTRATION CAMPS. Released in 1939, he emigrated to the U.S., where he published (1943) a world-famous article about the camps, "Individual and Mass Behavior in Extreme Situations." He also treated the subject in his book *The Informed Heart* (1960). He was (1944–73) director of a school for the rehabilitation of emotionally disturbed children, many of them autistic (see AUTISM), at the Univ. of Chicago. His numerous works on child psychology and child-rearing include *Love Is Not Enough* (1950), *The Empty Fortress* (1967), and *The Uses of Enchantment* (1976). He also wrote *Freud and Man's Soul* (1983), a critique of medicine's influence on psychoanalysis.

Better Business Bureau, organization established by business firms to protect and educate consumers and business people; to combat false advertising and unethical selling practices; and to support voluntary self-regulation in advertising and business. The first such local bureau was founded in Minneapolis in 1912; 200 autonomous organizations now operate in the U.S., Canada, and Israel, with the Virginia-based Council of Better Business Bureaus functioning as the U.S. national liaison office.

Betterton, Thomas, 1635?–1710, English actor and manager of the RESTORATION stage. He was a great Hamlet and Macbeth with the producer William D'Avenant's company. As a manager he presented and played in adaptations of SHAKESPEARE, notably by DRYDEN and himself. His company opened the Haymarket Theatre in 1705. His wife, **Mary Saunderson Betterton,** d. 1711, was the first woman to play Shakespeare's great female roles.

Betti, Ugo [bət'tē], 1892–1953, Italian dramatist and poet. A judge who gained literary recognition late in life, he is ranked second only to PIRANDELLO among 20th-cent. Italian dramatists. His plays, often pessimistic and moralizing, include *The Mistress* (1927), *The Flood* (1943), and *Crime on Goat Island* (1950).

Bevan, Aneurin [bĕ'vən], 1897–1960, British politician. A coal miner and trade unionist, he served as a Labour member in Parliament (1929–60). As minister of health (1945–51), he administered the National Health Service. He was leader (1951–60) of the Labour party's left wing.

Beveridge, William Henry, 1879–1963, British economist; b. India; knighted in 1919. An authority on social problems and unemployment, Beveridge was the director of the London School of Economics (1919–37). In *Social Insurance and Allied Services* (1942), he proposed a social security system "from the cradle to the grave" for all British citizens. He was made 1st Baron Beveridge of Tugwell in 1946.

Beverly Hills, city (1990 pop. 31,971), S Calif., completely surrounded by the city of LOS ANGELES; inc. 1914. Mainly residential, it is the home of many film and television personalities.

Bevin, Ernest [bĕv'ən], 1881–1951, British labor leader and statesman. He was an orphan who had earned his living from childhood. In 1921 he merged his dock workers' union with others to form the powerful Transport and General Workers' Union. A member of the Labour party, he was minister of labor in Winston CHURCHILL's wartime cabinet (1940–45). As foreign minister in the Labour government (1945–51), he worked to build up Western Europe and to establish NATO.

Bewick, Thomas [byo͞o'ĭk], 1753–1828, English wood engraver. He revived the art of original wood engraving. His chief works include illustrations for John GAY's *Fables* (1779) and for Ralph Beilby's *General History of Quadrupeds* (1790) and the print *Chillingham Bull* (1789).

Beyazid, sultans of the OTTOMAN EMPIRE (Turkey), also spelled Bayazid, Bajazet, and Bayazit. **Beyazid I,** 1347–1403 (r.1389–1402), triumphed over Byzantine Emperor Manuel II, the Turkish rulers of E Anatolia, and Sigismund of Hungary, who was on a crusade, but he was defeated (1402) by TIMUR, who routed his armies and took him prisoner. **Beyazid II,** 1447–1513 (r.1481–1512), was a peace-loving monarch who did little to advance Ottoman power but much to further Ottoman culture. With the aid of the JANISSARIES he putdown a revolt of his brother Jem, but he lost Cilicia to the Mamluks of Egypt and Cyprus to Venice.

Beyle, Marie Henri: see STENDHAL.

Bhagavad-Gita [Skt., = song of the Lord], Sanskrit poem incorporated into the MAHABHARATA, one of the classics of HINDUISM, consisting of a dialogue between Lord KRISHNA and Prince Arjuna on the eve of the battle of Kurukshetra. Arjuna is overcome with anguish when he sees his kinsmen and friends in the opposing army, but Krishna persuades him to fight by instructing him in spiritual wisdom and the means of attaining union with God (see YOGA) through selfless action, knowledge, and devotion. The *Gita* is essentially related to the UPANISHADS in content.

Bhattacharya, Bhabhani, 1906–, Indian novelist, journalist, and translator. His novels, written in English, deal with India's social problems. They include *So Many Hungers!* (1948), *A Goddess Named Gold* (1960), and *Shadow from Ladakh* (1966).

Bhave, Vinoba 1895–1982, Indian religious figure. He was a disciple of Mohandas GANDHI and after Gandhi's death (1948) was widely accepted as his successor. In 1951 he founded the Bhoodan, or land-gift, movement, seeking donations of land for redistribution to the landless.

Bhopal, city (1991 pop. 1,063,662), central India, capital of Madhya Pradesh state. Founded in 1728, Bhopal is a railway junction and industrial center, producing electrical equipment, textiles, and jewelry. Landmarks include the old fort (built 1728) and the Taj-ul-Masajid mosque, the largest in India. On Dec. 3, 1984, the worst industrial accident in history occurred there when a toxic gas leak from a Union Carbide insecticide plant killed some 4,000 people and seriously injured 30,000–40,000. The Indian government sued on behalf of over 500,000 victims and in 1989 settled for $470 million in damages and exempted company employees from criminal prosecution. The Indian judiciary rejected that exemption in 1991, and the company's Indian assets were seized (1992) after its officials failed to appear to face charges.

Bhumibol Adulyadej [po͞o'mēpôl" ädo͞ol'yädĕt"], 1927–, king of THAILAND (1946–); b. Cambridge, Mass. He became king when his brother, King Ananda, died (1946) under mysterious circumstances, and ruled with a regent until he was formally crowned King Rama IX in 1950. Although his power is largely ceremonial, he has actively promoted development projects and has intervened several times to resolve governmental crises.

Bhutan [bo͞otän'], officially Kingdom of Bhutan, kingdom (1992 est. pop. 1,660,000), 18,147 sq mi (47,000 sq km), E Asia, in the Himalayas, bordered by India (S and E), the Tibet region of China (N), and Sikkim (W). The official capital is Thimphu; Punaka is the traditional capital. Bhutan is a land of great mountain ranges, rising in the north to Kula Kangri (24,784 ft/7,554 m), and intensively cultivated valleys. The climate ranges from humid subtropical at the lower altitudes to temperate in the high mountains. Small-scale subsistence farming, with rice and other grains and potatoes the main crops, and the raising of livestock dominate the economy. Metal, wood, and leather working; papermaking; and weaving are also important. The country exports some fruit and coal, stone, and cement. Tourism, although restricted, is a significant source of income. Bhutan's people are mostly Bhutias, or Drukpas, ethnically related to Tibetans. Their religion is closely related to TIBETAN BUDDHISM; many Bhutanese live in monasteries. There is a significant Gurkha, or Nepalese, minority in S Bhutan; they are largely Hindus. The national language of Bhutan is Dzongkha.

History. In the 16th cent. the Tibetans conquered Bhutan's native tribes, and in 1720 China claimed suzerainty over the area. British interests in Bhutan date from the arrival of a trade mission in 1774. Britain annexed part of Bhutan in 1865, and in 1910 Bhutan's first hereditary king agreed to let Britain direct the country's foreign affairs; in 1949 Bhutan agreed to consult with India on foreign policy, but since the 1980s Bhutan has acted as a fully independent nation. After Communist forces occupied (1950) Tibet, Bhutan became a point of contest between China and India, and the China-Bhutan border was closed. Relations with China improved in the 1980s. Jigme Singye Wangchuk became king in 1972 (crowned 1974).

Bhutto, Benazir [bo͞ot'to], 1953–, prime minister (1988–90, 1993–)

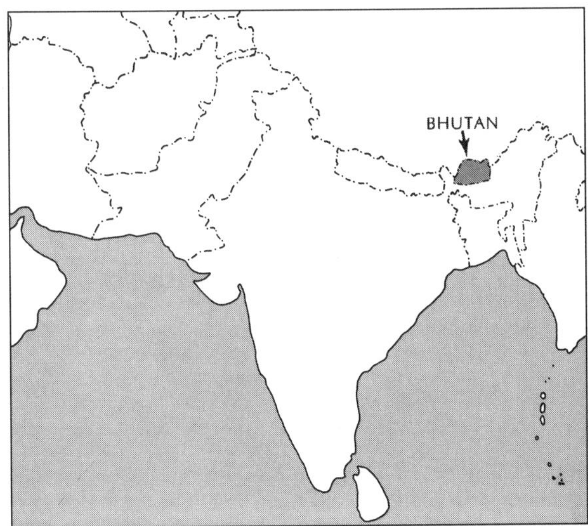

of PAKISTAN. The daughter of Zulfikar Ali BHUTTO, she lived in exile from 1984 to 1986 but returned to Pakistan to oppose Gen. Mohammad ZIA UL-HAQ, the country's military ruler. After Zia's death (1988), her party won the elections, and she became prime minister and the first female leader of a Muslim nation. She accomplished little before Pres. Ghulam Ishaq Khan dismissed (1990) her as prime minister, accusing her, her husband, Asif Ali Zadari, and her party of corruption. Zadari was held (1990–93) on various charges, and Bhutto's party lost (1990) the subsequent elections. In 1993 she again became prime minister.

Bhutto, Zulfikar Ali, 1928–79, president (1971–73) and prime minister (1973–77) of PAKISTAN. He came to power after Pakistan's defeat in the war over BANGLADESH's independence. He was overthrown (1977), tried for state crimes, and executed (1979).

Bi, chemical symbol of the element BISMUTH.

Biafra, Republic of, former African secessionist state, formed in SE Nigeria. Biafra was established in 1967 by Ibos, an ethnic group who feared they could not survive within Nigeria. The new state was led by Lt. Col. C.O. Ojukwu. Soon after secession, fighting erupted between Nigerian and Biafran forces. More than one million Biafran civilians are believed to have died of starvation during the war, which ended with Biafra's defeat in 1970.

Bialik, Hayyim Nahman [byä'lĭk], 1873–1934, Ukrainian poet and novelist who wrote mainly in Hebrew. His style—some times majestic, sometimes simple—had a great effect on modern Hebrew literature. His poems include "In the City of Slaughter" (1903). As an editor and publisher in Odessa, Berlin, and Tel Aviv, Bialik spread the ideas of the *Haskalah*, the renaissance of Jewish culture.

biathlon, a sporting event composed of two activities. The best-known type of biathlon is the winter event, combining cross-country skiing and target shooting, which has been part of Olympic competition since 1960. A combined running and swimming event, instituted in Great Britain in 1968, is also called a biathlon.

Bible, term used since the 4th cent. for the Christian Scriptures and later, by extension, for those of various religious traditions. (For the composition and canon of the Bible, see OLD TESTAMENT, NEW TESTAMENT, APOCRYPHA, and articles on individual books.) The traditional Christian view is that the Bible was written under the guidance of God and is, therefore, entirely true, literally or couched in allegory. Interpretation of the Bible is a main point of difference between Protestantism, which holds that individuals have the right to interpret the Bible for themselves, and Roman Catholicism, which teaches that individuals may read the Bible only as interpreted by the church. In the 20th cent. many Protestants have been influenced by biblical criticism that has applied scientific and historical methods to Bible study ("higher criticism"); FUNDAMENTALISM, on the other hand, emphasizes the absolute inerrancy of the Bible. Noted extant manuscripts of the Bible include Codex Vaticanus (Greek, 4th cent.), at the Vatican; Codex Alexandrinus (Greek, 5th cent.), in the British Museum; and Codex Bezae (Greek and Latin, 6th cent.), at Cambridge, England. Among the DEAD SEA SCROLLS are the oldest fragments of the Hebrew text known; the New Testament has come down to us in Greek. The first great translation of the whole Bible was the Latin Vulgate of St. JEROME. The Greek text generally accepted in the East is, for the Old Testament, the Septuagint. Great names in the history of the English Bible are John WYCLIF (d. 1384), whose name appears on two translations; William TYNDALE, whose New Testament (1525–26) was the first English translation to be printed; and Miles Coverdale, who published (1535) a translation of the entire Bible. The greatest English translation (and one of the most influential English prose works) is the Authorized Version (AV), or King James Version (KJV), of 1611, made by a group of churchmen and scholars led by Lancelot Andrewes. The Rheims-Douay Version was produced by Roman Catholic scholars at Rheims (New Testament, 1582) and Douai (Old Testament, 1610), France. In the 19th cent., the Authorized Version was revised as the English Revised Version and the American Revised Version (pub. 1880–90). American scholars published (1952) the influential Revised Standard Version (RSV). New translations are the New English Bible (1970) and such Roman Catholic translations as the Westminster Version and the New American Bible (1970); an English translation of the French Catholic Bible de Jerusalem appeared as the Jerusalem Bible (1966).

bicameral system: see LEGISLATURE.

bicarbonate of soda: see SODIUM BICARBONATE.

bicycle, light, two-wheeled vehicle driven by pedals. A model using pedals, cranks, drive rods, and handlebars was introduced c.1839 in Scotland; it was followed by the development of the hollow steel frame, ball bearings, metal wheel spokes, and rubber-rimmed wheels. The front wheel, directly powered by the pedals, was at one time much larger than the rear wheel. The first bicycle with a sprocket-chain drive powering an equal-size rear wheel was made in England in 1885; an improved pneumatic tire was invented by John B. Dunlop in 1888. Later improvements included handlebar-mounted brake cables and gearshift systems to facilitate changes in speed. The mountain bicycle, developed in the 1980s, is especially designed for travel on dirt trails and hilly countryside. The bicycle's popularity brought about major improvements in roads in 19th-cent. Europe and America, and the vehicle continues to be far more widely used than the automobile in many parts of the world today.

Bidault, Georges [bēdō'], 1899–83, French political leader. A leader of the French underground in WORLD WAR II, Bidault was a postwar premier (1949–50) and several times foreign minister. He joined the terrorist opponents of Algerian independence and fled (1962) into exile, returning to France in 1968.

Biddle, John, 1516–62, founder of English UNITARIANISM. After losing his belief in the TRINITY, he stated his conclusions in *Twelve Arguments Drawn Out of Scripture,* for which he was imprisoned (1645). He was banished for publishing his *Two-fold Catechism* (1654). Returning in 1658, he taught and preached until again imprisoned (1662).

Biedermeier, style of German furniture, 1816–48. The name derives from a humorous pseudonym used by several German poets. Comfortable and inexpensive, it featured simplified forms of the EMPIRE STYLE and the DIRECTOIRE STYLE and of some 18th-cent. English styles. Black lacquer substituted for costly ebony, and peasant-style painted decoration was applied.

Bierce, Ambrose Gwinett, 1842–1914?, American writer; b. Meigs co., Ohio. After Civil War service he turned to journalism, eventually becoming the literary arbiter of the West Coast. Bierce achieved real distinction in his short stories, collected in such volumes as *In the Midst of Life* (1891) and *Can Such Things Be?* (1893). He is equally famous for a collection of sardonic definitions, *The Devil's Dictionary* (1906). His work is marked by distilled satire, crisply precise language, and a realistically developed sense of horror. He disappeared in Mexico in 1913.

Bierstadt, Albert, 1830–1902, American painter; b. Germany. He journeyed to the West (1859) and is best known for his immense canvases emphasizing the drama of western scenery, e.g., *The Settlement of California* (Capitol, Wash., D.C.).

big bang theory: see COSMOLOGY.

Big Ben, the bell in Parliament tower (Westminster Palace), London; also the tower clock. Installed in 1856, it was named for the commissioner of works, Sir Benjamin Hall.

Big Bend National Park: see NATIONAL PARKS (table).

Bigelow, John, 1817–1911, American editor, author, and diplomat; b. Malden, N.Y. As joint owner and editor (1848–61), with William Cullen BRYANT, of the New York *Evening Post,* he wrote vigorous anti-SLAVERY editorials. Appointed consul general at Paris (1861) and later (1865–66) U.S. minister to France, he was largely instrumental in preventing French recognition of the CONFEDERACY during the CIVIL WAR.

Bigfoot or **Sasquatch,** apelike creature reportedly sighted hundreds of times in the U.S. and Canada (most often in the Pacific Northwest) since the mid-19th cent. Similar to Asia's ABOMINABLE SNOWMAN, Bigfoot is variously described as standing 7–10 ft (2–3 m) tall and weighing over 500 lb (227 kg), with footprints 17 in. (43 cm) long. Most scientists discount the existence of such a creature.

Biggs, E(dward George) Power, 1906–77, American organist; b. England. Through his many performances and recordings, he introduced the ORGAN as a serious concert instrument to the American public, most notably with music of the BAROQUE period and the 20th cent.

bighorn or **Rocky Mountain sheep,** wild SHEEP (*Ovis canadensis*) of W North America. It is a heavy, grayish brown animal with a white patch on the hindquarters; the male has curling horns. Once plentiful, bighorn have diminished in number as a result of indiscriminate hunting, disease, and habitat encroachment.

Big Island: see HAWAII, island.

bignonia, common name for the Bignoniaceae, a family of woody vines, shrubs, and trees of the American tropics. Members of the family include the tropical calabash tree, which bears large fruits used as carrying gourds (called calabashes) and whose wood is used to make pipes; and the ornamental shade trees of the genus *Catalpa,* whose wood is used for lumber.

Bigordi, Domenico: see GHIRLANDAIO, DOMENICO.

Bikini, atoll, c.2 sq mi (5.2 sq km), W central Pacific Ocean, in the MARSHALL ISLANDS. Comprising 36 islets on a reef 25 mi (40 km) long, it was used (1946–58) for U.S. nuclear-bomb tests. Bikinians were evacuated (1946), allowed to return (1969), and reevacuated (1978) when new data showed high levels of residual radioactivity. A U.S.-assisted cleanup, begun in 1988, is expected to take 10–15 years.

Biko, Steven, 1946–77, South African political leader. A leader of the radical "black consciousness" movement, he helped found the all-black South African Students Organization (1969) and the Black People's Convention (1972). Banned in 1973, he was arrested in 1977 for subversion and died brutally in police custody. See also APARTHEID.

Bilderdijk, Willem [bĭl'dərdīk], 1756–1831, Dutch poet. Ranked among the great Dutch poets, he is best known for an unfinished epic, *The Destruction of the First Creation* (1820), and other religious verse. His translations catalyzed the romantic movement in Dutch literature.

bile, bitter, alkaline fluid of a yellow, brown, or green color that aids in the digestion of fats (see DIGESTIVE SYSTEM). Composed of water, bile salts, bilirubin (a pigment), cholesterol, and lecithin, bile is secreted by the LIVER and stored in the GALL BLADDER. It is emptied into the upper intestine to breakdown fats and enable them (and fat-soluble VITAMINS) to be absorbed through the intestinal wall. Bile is also a route of excretion for cholesterol, heme, and many drugs. JAUNDICE may result if the flow of bile is impeded.

bilingual education, the sanctioned use of more than one language in U.S. education. The Bilingual Education Act (1968), confirmed by a Supreme Court decision (1974) and mandating help for students with limited English proficiency, requires instruction in the native languages of students. Critics, maintaining that some students never join the mainstream culture, have attempted to make English the "official" language of several states and cities; proponents have emphasized the preservation of ethnic heritage and culture and the need to educate non-English-speaking students in all subjects, not just English.

billiards, any of several games played with a leather-tipped stick (cue) and various numbers of balls on an oblong, cloth-covered table with raised, cushioned edges. The three main types are carom billiards, played with three balls on a pocketless table; pocket billiards (or pool), using a cue ball and 15 object balls on a table with six pockets; and snooker, similar to pool but with 21 object balls. Variants were popular in England and France in the 16th cent.

Billings, John Shaw, 1838–1913, American surgeon and librarian; b. Switzerland co., Ind. Under his direction (1864–95) the National Library of Medicine became one of the great medical library systems in the world. He initiated the *Index Catalogue* and *Index Medicus* and compiled (1889) the *National Medical Dictionary.* He also directed development of the New York Public Library (see LIBRARY, table); suggested what became punched-card technology; and supervised the 1880 and 1890 U.S. censuses.

Billings, Josh, pseud. of **Henry Wheeler Shaw,** 1818–85, American humorist; b. Lanesboro, Mass. His popular, humorous sketches in rural dialect appeared annually in the *Farmer's Allminax* (1869–80).

Billings, city (1990 pop. 81,151), seat of Yellowstone co., S Mont., on the Yellowstone R.; inc. as a city 1885. Founded in 1882 by the Northern Pacific RR, it became a shipping and fur-trading center. Oil and sugar refining, meat packing, and flour milling are now its main industries. The center of a recreational area, it is surrounded by seven mountain ranges; Yellowstone National Park (see NATIONAL PARKS, table) is nearby.

Bill of Rights, 1689, in British history, one of the fundamental instruments of constitutional law. It incorporated by statute the Declaration of Rights accepted by WILLIAM III and MARY II, and registered the results of the struggle between the STUART kings and PARLIAMENT. The Bill of Rights stated that no Roman Catholic would rule England; it gave inviolable civil and political rights to the people and political supremacy to Parliament. It was supplemented (1701) by the Act of SETTLEMENT.

Bill of Rights, in U.S. history: see under CONSTITUTION OF THE UNITED STATES.

Billy the Kid, 1859–81, American outlaw; b. N.Y.C. A large-scale cattle rustler in Lincoln co., N.M., from 1878, he was hunted and fatally shot by Sheriff Pat Garrett. Billy's real name was William H. Bonney.

Biloxi, city (1990 pop. 46,319), SE Miss., on a peninsula between Biloxi Bay and Mississippi Sound, on the Gulf of Mexico; settled 1699, inc. as a city 1896. Almost tropical in climate, it is a popular resort, with riverboat casino gambling. Fishing, especially for shrimp and shellfish, is a major industry, as is boat-building. French Old Biloxi (est. 1699) was the first white settlement in the lower Mississippi valley; New Biloxi (est. 1719) was the capital of French Louisiana until 1722. Beauvoir, the last home of Jefferson DAVIS, is nearby.

bimetallism, in economic history, a monetary system in which two commodities, usually gold and silver, were used as a standard and coined at a fixed ratio. The system was designed to create a monetary unit with more stability than one based on a single metal. In a bimetallic system, the ratio, which is determined by law, is expressed in terms of weight, e.g., 16 oz of silver equal 1 oz of gold, or a ratio of 16 to 1. The legal ratio has no relationship to the commercial value of the metals, which fluctuates constantly. This discrepancy between the commercial and face values of the two metals made bimetallism too unstable for most modern nations. The system was practiced in the U.S. and other countries (except England, where gold was used) in the 18th and 19th cent.

binary star, pair of stars that are held together by their mutual gravitational attraction and revolve about their common center of mass. True binary stars are distinct from optical doubles—pairs of stars that lie along nearly the same line of sight from the earth but are not physically associated. A visual binary is a pair of stars that can be seen by direct telescopic observation to be a distinct pair with shared motion. A spectroscopic binary cannot be distinguished telescopically as two separate stars, but spectral lines from the pair show a periodic DOPPLER EFFECT that indicates mutual revolution. An eclipsing binary has the plane of its orbit lying in the line of sight and shows a periodic fluctuation in brightness (see VARIABLE STAR) as one star passes in front of the other.

binary system: see NUMERATION.

bindweed: see MORNING-GLORY.

Binet, Alfred [bēnā'], 1857–1911, French psychologist. With Théodore Simon, Binet devised (1905–11) a series of tests of human INTELLIGENCE that, with revisions, came into wide use in schools, industry, and the army.

Bingham, George Caleb, 1811–79, American painter and politician; b. Augusta co., Va. His vigorous genre scenes accurately picture their time and locale. They include *Fur Traders Descending the Missouri* (Metropolitan Mus.) and *Raftsmen Playing Cards* (City Art Mus., St. Louis). Bingham was elected to the Missouri legislature in 1848, served as state treasurer (1862–65), and became state adjutant general in 1875.

Bingham, Hiram, 1789–1869, American Congregationalist missionary; b. Bennington, Vt. In 1819 he founded the first Protestant mission in the Hawaiian Islands. He adapted the Hawaiian language to writing and translated the Bible into Hawaiian. His son **Hiram Bingham,** 1831–1908, b. Honolulu, was also a missionary. In 1857 he founded a mission in the Gilbert Islands and later adapted the island language to writing.

Bingham, Hiram, 1875–1956, American archaeologist and statesman; b. Honolulu. At Yale Univ. (1907–23), he led expeditions that discovered the Inca cities of Vitcos and Machu Picchu. He was governor of Connecticut (1925) and U.S. senator (1925–33).

binoculars, small optical instrument, consisting of a pair of TELESCOPES mounted on a single, usually adjustable frame, that is used for magnifying distant objects. Light entering each telescope through its objective LENS is bent by a pair of PRISMS before passing through one or more additional lenses in the eyepiece. The prisms turn the image—inverted by the objective lens—right side up again and allow the distance between the objective lenses to be twice as far apart as that between the eyepieces, thus enhancing the viewer's depth perception. The usually less powerful opera and field glasses are also classed as binoculars, although both use Galilean telescopes, which do not employ prisms.

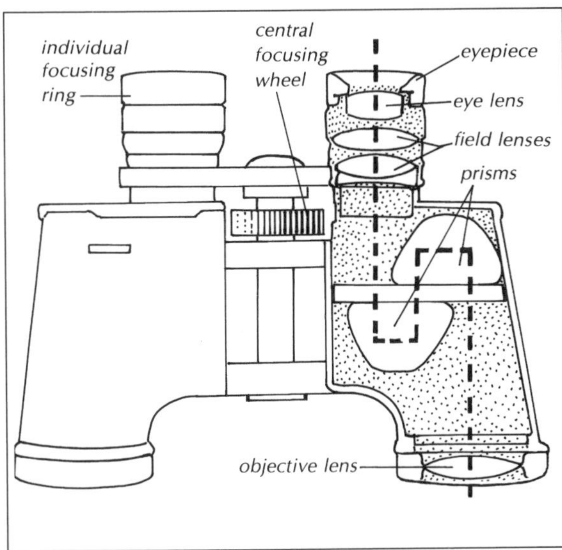

Binoculars

biochemistry, science concerned chiefly with the chemistry of biological processes. From its roots in chemistry, chiefly organic and physical chemistry, biochemistry has broadened to encompass any biological problem amenable to the investigative techniques of both chemistry and physics. Biochemists study such things as the structure and function of proteins, carbohydrates, and enzymes; the chemical regulation of metabolism; and the molecular basis of the action of genes. A milestone in the growth of the field was the elucidation of the structure of DNA.

biodiversity: see BIOLOGICAL DIVERSITY.

bioengineering, use of engineering and biological principles for the identification of the functions of living systems and for the development of (1) therapeutic devices, especially artificial body parts and systems, e.g., artificial blood vessels, PACEMAKERS, DIALYSIS equipment, and artificial limbs that function like their prototypes; and (2) equipment for monitoring the performance of healthy and diseased organisms.

bioethics, branch of ETHICS concerned with health-care and biological-sciences issues, including the morality of ABORTION, EUTHANASIA, new research in GENETIC ENGINEERING, and organ transplants. Bioethics emerged as a specialized discipline in the 1970s, and many hospitals now employ bioethicists to advise on treatment of the terminally ill and allocation of limited resources.

biofeedback, method for learning to increase one's ability to control biological responses, such as blood pressure, muscle tension, and heart rate. Sophisticated instruments are often used to measure physiological responses and make them apparent to the patient, who then tries to alter and ultimately control them without the aid of monitoring devices. Biofeedback programs have been used to teach patients to relax muscles or adjust blood flow in the case of headache, to help partially paralyzed stroke victims activate muscles, and to alleviate anxiety in dental patients.

biography, reconstruction in print of the lives of real people. With the autobiography—an individual's interpretation of his own life—it shares a venerable tradition. Ancient Egyptian and Assyrian inscriptions proclaimed the deeds of kings. Among the first biographies of ordinary individuals, the Dialogues of PLATO (4th cent. B.C.) reveal their subject, SOCRATES, by letting him speak for himself. A balanced assessment of character is achieved in PLUTARCH's *Parallel Lives* (2d cent. A.D.), where subjects are paired, e.g., DEMOSTHENES with CICERO. St. Augustine turned a searching critical judgment on himself in his *Confessions* (4th cent.). In the medieval lives of saints, human flaws were bypassed for saintly traits, but the few secular biographies of the period, e.g., Einhard's *Life of Charlemagne* (9th cent.), contain lively portraits of real people. The RENAISSANCE interest in worldly power and self-assertion is reflected in CELLINI's *Autobiography* (16th cent.). By the 17th cent. informality and intimacy had been introduced, e.g., John AUBREY's *Brief Lives.* In the 18th cent. Dr. JOHNSON's *Lives of the Poets* (1780–81) set the example for literary biographies, notably James BOSWELL's *Life of Samuel Johnson* (1791). The first definitive biography, it was drawn from personal recollection, letters, memoirs, and interviews. Later developments include the psychoanalytic biography, e.g., Sigmund FREUD's *Leonardo Da Vinci* (1910); the debunking biography, e.g., Lytton STRACHEY's *Eminent Victorians* (1918); and the thematic biography, e.g., Thomas MERTON's *Seven Storey Mountain* (1948), which follows the analogue of DANTE's *Inferno.* In the 20th cent. films and television have adapted the form to their own needs in documentaries, interviews, oral histories, and fictionalized biographies.

biological diversity or **biodiversity,** the number of species in a given habitat or ecosystem. A number of studies have suggested that a species-rich ecosystem can tolerate and recover from extreme events, such as drought, better. Scientists have variously estimated that there are from 3 to 30 million existing species, of which 1.4 million have been classified, including 750,000 insects, 41,000 vertebrates, and 250,000 plants; the remainder are other invertebrates, fungi, algae, and microorganisms. Although other species remain to be discovered, many are becoming extinct through deforestation, pollution, and human settlement. A 1992 UN treaty designed to help preserve earth's biological diversity has been signed by over 160 nations.

biological warfare, bacteriological warfare, or **germ warfare,** employment in war of microorganisms to injure or destroy human beings, animals, or crops. Although "first use" of both biological and chemical weapons (see CHEMICAL WARFARE) was prohibited by the 1925 Geneva Convention, several nations subsequently conducted research into detection and defense systems, and developed microorganisms (including strains of smallpox and the plague) suitable for military retaliation. Such organisms can be delivered by animals, especially rodents or insects, or by AEROSOL packages—built into artillery shells or the warheads of ground-to-ground or air-to-ground missiles and released into the atmosphere to infect by inhalation. Research in this area did not end after 1972, despite an agreement that year by more than 100 nations, including the U.S. and the USSR (now Russia), to prohibit the development, testing, and stockpiling of biological weapons. The treaty does allow research for defensive purposes, such as to develop antidotes to biological weapons.

biology, science dealing with living things, broadly divided into ZOOLOGY, the study of animal life, and BOTANY, the study of plant life. Subdivisions include ANATOMY and PHYSIOLOGY; GENETICS; MOLECULAR BIOLOGY, the study of cells (cytology), tissues (histology), embryonic development (see EMBRYO), and microscopic forms of life; as well as CLASSIFICATION, EVOLUTION, and paleontology (the study of FOSSILS).

bioluminescence, production of light by living organisms resulting from the conversion of chemical energy to light energy. Bioluminescent plants include certain MUSHROOMS and BACTERIA that emit light continuously. The dinoflagellates, a group of marine algae, produce light only when disturbed. Bioluminescent animals include such organisms as COMB JELLIES, annelid worms, MOLLUSKS, insects such as FIREFLIES, and FISH. Some animals seem to use luminescence in courtship and mating, to divert predators, or to attract prey.

biomass energy: see ENERGY, SOURCES OF.

biome: see ECOLOGY.

Bion, fl. 2d cent.? B.C., Greek bucolic poet, an imitator of THEOCRITUS. The *Lament for Adonis* (attributed to him) was the model for P.B. SHELLEY's *Adonais*.

bionics, study of living systems with the intention of applying their principles to the design of engineering systems. Drawing on interdisciplinary research in the mechanical and life sciences, bionics has been used to develop audiovisual equipment based on human eye and ear function, to design air and naval craft patterned after the biological structure of birds and fish, and to incorporate principles of the human neurological system in data-processing systems. Another application has been the development of artificial limbs controlled by recognition of the electrical patterns in muscle tissue.

biophysics, application of various tools, methods, and principles of physical science to the study of biological problems. In biophysics, physical mechanisms and mathematical and physical models have been used to explain life processes such as the transmission of nerve impulses, the muscle contraction mechanism, and the visual mechanism.

biopsy, examination of cells or tissues removed from a living organism to aid medical diagnosis. Samples may be removed surgically, as in excision of breast tissue, or by aspiration of cells through a special needle, as in the case of bone marrow.

biorhythm or **biological rhythm,** cyclic pattern of changes in physiology or in activity of living organisms, often synchronized with daily, monthly, or yearly environmental changes. Rhythms that vary according to the time of day (circadian rhythms), in part a response to daylight or dark, include the opening and closing of flowers and the nighttime increase in activity of nocturnal animals. Circadian rhythms also include activities that occur often during a 24-hour period, such as blood pressure changes and urine production. Annual cycles, called circannual rhythms, respond to changes in the relative length of periods of daylight and include such activities as migration and animal mating. Marine organisms are affected by tide cycles. Although the exact nature of the internal mechanism is not known, various external stimuli—including light, temperature, and gravity—influence the organism's internal clock; in the absence of external cues, the internal rhythms gradually drift out of phase with the environment.

biosphere, irregularly shaped envelope of the earth's air, water, and land, encompassing the heights and depths at which living things exist. The biosphere is a closed and self-regulating system (see ECOLOGY) sustained by grand-scale cycles of energy and materials.

Biosphere 2, privately funded ecological research project in which eight people lived sealed in a 3.15-acre (1.28-hectare) structure for two years (Sept. 26, 1991–Sept. 26, 1993). Located in Oracle, Ariz., about 35 mi (56 km) north of Tucson, and dependent on the outside only for electricity and sunlight, Biosphere 2 was designed to test the feasibility of a self-sustaining space colony. It contains over 3,500 plant and animal species and attempts to reproduce five ecosystems (see ECOLOGY)—desert, grassland, marsh, ocean, and rain forest. The human inhabitants (four men and four women) were to grow their own food and recycle their wastes but used some seed stocks as food. The project's validity was questioned by scientists who criticized the plan to use outside electricity, the presence of stores of food and animal feed, and other aspects. A decline in the oxygen level led to the pumping of oxygen into the complex in 1993. More flexible stays inside the structure, beginning in Mar. 1994, are planned.

biotechnology, the use of biological processes, as through the exploitation of living organisms or biological systems, as a component in the development or manufacture of a product, in the technological solution to a problem, and the like. For example, GENETIC ENGINEERING techniques have been used to create custom-designed bacteria capable of producing drugs and other substances. Such bacteria can be grown in quantity in "bioreactors" and then processed to extract the substance produced; specially cultured plant and animal cells can be similarly grown and processed. Often the extracted substance is not the final product and needs further chemical processing. The field of biotechnology also includes genetically enhanced livestock (see PHARMING); plants and foods with genetically engineered qualities, such as improved disease resistance or prolonged shelf life; custom-designed drugs, fertilizers, and pesticides; and therapies to repair genetic defects (see GENE THERAPY).

bipolar disorder: see MANIC- DEPRESSION.

birch, common name for some members of the Betulaceae, a family of deciduous trees or shrubs widely distributed in the Northern Hemisphere. Growing mainly in the Northeast, the genera native to the U.S. are the birches, ALDER, HAZEL, and hornbeam and hop hornbeam (both called ironwood). Some birches are valued for their fine hardwoods, e.g., the yellow birch (*Betula lutea*). White-barked birches are often used as ornamentals, notably the paper birch (*B. papyrifera*) of the N United States and Canada, whose bark was used by Native Americans for canoes and baskets. Various birches produce edible fruits, sugar, vinegar, tea from leaves, and birch beer from sap.

Bird, Larry Joe, 1956–, American basketball player; b. French Lick, Ind. Beginning in 1979, he played for the Boston Celtics of the National Basketball Association (NBA), spurring them to championships in 1981, 1984, and 1986. In 13 seasons with the Celtics, Bird scored 21,791 points and was NBA Rookie of the Year in 1980 and Most Valuable Player from 1984 to 1986. He retired in 1992.

bird, warm-blooded, egg-laying VERTEBRATE of the class Aves, having its body covered with FEATHERS and its forelimbs modified into wings. Like MAMMALS, birds have a four-chambered heart; they have a relatively large brain and acute hearing but little sense of smell. Believed to have evolved from REPTILES, birds are highly adapted for flight. Their feathers, though light, protect against cold and wet and have great strength. Intricate courtship displays are performed by many species during breeding season, when birdsong is most pronounced; singing ability is usually restricted to, or superior in, the male. Most birds build some kind of nest for their eggs, which vary in size, shape, color, and number according to species. The chief domestic birds are the CHICKEN, DUCK, GOOSE, TURKEY, and guinea fowl. Among the game birds hunted for food and sport are GROUSE, PHEASANT, QUAIL, and duck.

bird-of-paradise flower, large tropical herb (*Strelitzia reginae*) of the BANANA family, native to S Africa. Its blue and orange blossom resembles an exotic bird of that name.

Birdseye, Clarence, 1886–1956, American inventor and founder of the frozen-food industry; b. Brooklyn, N.Y. His successful experiments with food-freezing processes led to the founding (1924) of the General Foods Co. By 1949, Birdseye had perfected the anhydrous process, which reduces the time needed for food freezing from 18 to 1½ hr.

Bird Woman: see SACAJAWEA.

Birkhoff, George David, 1884–1944, American mathematician; b. Overisel, Mich. He is known for his work on linear differential equations and difference equations. His introduction of the concepts of minimal or recurrent sets of motion and establishment of their existence under general conditions began a new era in the

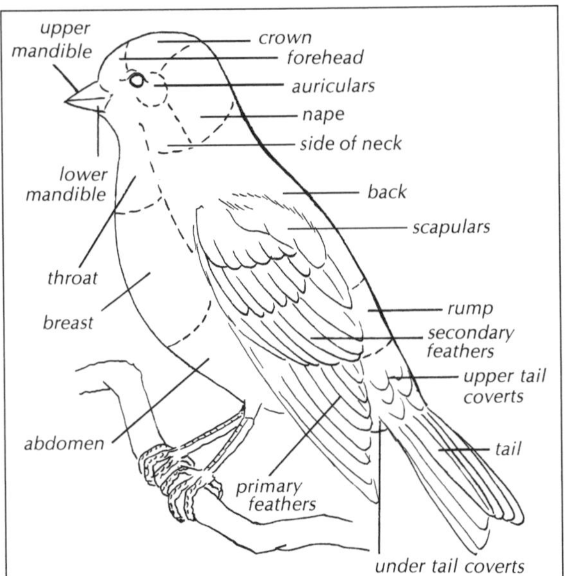

General anatomy of a bird

study of dynamical systems. He also wrote on the foundations of relativity and quantum mechanics.

Birmingham, second largest British city (1991 pop. 961,041), W Midlands, England. It is a major industrial and transportation center with such manufactures as automobiles, motorcycles, and machine tools. A market town by the 15th cent., Birmingham developed rapidly in the 17th and 18th cent. because of nearby deposits of iron and coal. In the 1870s the city underwent extensive municipal improvement, and much of the center was rebuilt after being bombed in WORLD WAR II.

Birmingham, city (1990 pop. 265,968), seat of Jefferson co., N central Ala., in the Jones Valley, near the southern end of the Appalachians; inc. 1871. The largest city in Alabama, it is the leading iron and steel center in the South. The area's coal, iron, and other resources supply its plants and factories. Its industry has diversified, and its manufactures include transportation equipment, chemicals, and textiles. Birmingham is also a governmental, research, and trade center, connected by canal with the Gulf of Mexico. It is the site of several colleges and cultural institutions.

Birney, James Gillespie, 1792–1857, American abolitionist; b. Danville, Ky. After freeing (1834) his inherited slaves, he helped organize (1835) the Kentucky Anti-Slavery Society and was active in the American Anti-Slavery Society. The acknowledged leader of ABOLITIONISTS favoring political action, he ran for president on the Liberty party line in 1840 and 1844.

birth control, practice of preventing conception for the purpose of limiting the number of births; also called contraception and family planning. The modern movement for birth control began in Britain, where the writings of MALTHUS stirred interest in the problems of overpopulation. The first birth-control clinic in the U.S. was opened in 1916 by birth-control leader Margaret SANGER. On an international level, birth control is led by the International Planned Parenthood Federation (founded 1952), and in some countries (e.g., Sweden, Japan, and China) the government provides birth-control assistance to its people in order to limit population growth. The Roman Catholic Church has provided the main opposition to the birth control movement, approving only the so-called rhythm method, or abstinence from intercourse around the time of ovulation. Other contraceptive methods include, for males, withdrawal before ejaculation; use of a condom, or sheath, over the penis; and sterilization by VASECTOMY. Contraception for women includes precoital use of spermicidal vaginal suppositories, foams, and jellies; use of a diaphragm, a cup-shaped rubber device inserted into the vagina before intercourse to prevent sperm from traveling to the egg; use of a contraceptive sponge containing spermicide in the vagina; use of an INTRAUTERINE DEVICE; "the pill" (see ORAL CONTRACEPTIVE); injection of a contraceptive every three months; and implantation under the skin of capsules that slowly release a contraceptive into the blood and are effective for up to five years. Surgical sterilization for women includes tubal ligation (sealing of the Fallopian tubes). See also ABORTION.

birth defects, abnormalities in physical and/or mental structure or function that are present at birth. They range from minor to seriously deforming and/or life-threatening, with some major defect occurring in approximately 3% of births. Defects may be genetic in origin (as in DOWN'S SYNDROME, TAY-SACHS DISEASE, SICKLE-CELL ANEMIA, and HEMOPHILIA) or may be caused by infectious agents (e.g., HERPES SIMPLEX, RUBELLA, SEXUALLY TRANSMITTED DISEASES). Other teratogenic (malformation-causing) agents include drugs or hormones taken by the mother (e.g., THALIDOMIDE; DES) and maternal illnesses (e.g., DIABETES). The mother's nutrition, alcohol and smoking habits, and exposure to toxic chemicals and radiation can also affect the developing fetus. Smoking, drugs, toxic chemicals, and the like can also damage the father's sperm, which may pass on the defect in fertilization. Certain birth defects can now be detected prenatally through AMNIOCENTESIS and CHORIONIC VILLUS SAMPLING, and surgical procedures are being explored to correct certain disorders before birth.

birthstone: see MONTH.

Biscayne National Park: see NATIONAL PARKS (table).

Bishkek, formerly **Frunze,** city (1989 pop. 616,000), capital of Kyrgyzstan (Kirghizia), central Asia, on the Chu R. Bishkek is a transportation hub and the industrial and cultural center of Kyrgyzstan. Its industries include meatpacking and other food processing, the manufacture of agricultural machinery, motor vehicles, textiles and clothing, and building materials, and metalworking. Founded (1846) as an Uzbek fortress, it was taken in 1862 by the Russians, who called it Pishpek. In 1925 it was renamed Frunze in honor of Soviet Gen. M.V. Frunze, and in 1936 it became the capital of the Kirghiz SSR. The city was renamed Bishkek in 1991.

Bishop, Elizabeth, 1911–79, American poet; b. Worcester, Mass. Her penetrating and detached poetic vision is evident in such volumes as *Poems: North and South—A Cold Spring* (1955; Pulitzer) and *Geography III* (1976).

Bishops' Wars, two brief campaigns (1639, 1640) of the Scots against CHARLES I of England. Opposing his attempt to impose episcopacy, the COVENANTERS pledged a return to Presbyterianism. They invaded England and forced Charles to sign the Treaty of Ripon (Oct. 1640). See also ENGLISH CIVIL WAR.

Bismarck, Otto von, 1815–98, German statesman, known as the Iron Chancellor; premier of Prussia (1862–90) and chancellor of Germany (1871–90). Upon becoming premier, following the wishes of WILLIAM I, he unconstitutionally dissolved parliament and illegally levied taxes for the army. In order to expel Austria from the GERMAN CONFEDERATION (as a first step toward unification of the German states), he provoked war with Denmark (1864) and Austria itself (1866) over the SCHLESWIG-HOLSTEIN question. The Austro-Prussian war resulted in a quick defeat of Austria, and Bismarck then formed the North German Confederation, from which Austria was excluded. He exploited the German states' fears of France in order to bring them into the Prussian orbit. He provoked the FRANCO-PRUSSIAN WAR (1870–71), which ended in France's humiliating defeat. Bismarck now easily brought the German states under the crown of Prussia, and William was proclaimed emperor. Bismarck became the empire's first chancellor, and ruled thereafter as virtual dictator. His system of alliance and alignments made him the acknowledged leader of Europe (see THREE EMPERORS' LEAGUE; BERLIN, CONGRESS OF; TRIPLE ALLIANCE AND TRIPLE ENTENTE). Domestically, the German economy flourished. Bismarck's struggle with the Church resulted in his cooperation with the liberals. Partly to weaken the appeal of the socialists, he initiated (1883–87) revolutionary social reforms, including child labor laws, maximum hours legislation, and extensive old age, illness, and unemployment insurance. Bismarck's economic policies resulted in the rapid growth of German industry and the acquisition of overseas colonies. The accession (1888) of WILLIAM II, a longtime enemy, brought Bismarck's career to a close; the new emperor dismissed him in 1890.

Bismarck, city (1990 pop. 49,256), state capital and seat of Burleigh co., S central N.Dak., on hills over the Missouri R.; inc. 1873, territorial capital from 1883. Bismarck developed in the 1870s when the Northern Pacific RR reached a steamboat port there. The trade center for the region, it is a major wheat, grain, and livestock producer.

bismuth (Bi), metallic element, established as a separate element by Claud J. Geoffroy in 1753. The silver-white element is the poorest heat conductor of all the metals except mercury. Its soluble compounds are poisonous; its insoluble compounds are used to treat certain gastric disorders and skin injuries. It is also used in low-melting alloys, such as Wood's metal, used in fuses and automatic sprinkler systems. See ELEMENT (table); PERIODIC TABLE.

bison, hoofed MAMMAL (genus *Bison*) of the CATTLE family, with short horns and heavy, humped shoulders. The European wisent (*B. bonasus*) is larger than the North American bison (*B. bison*), commonly called BUFFALO, which may reach a shoulder height of 5 ft (1.5 m) and a weight of 2,500 lb (1,130 kg). Bison roamed America in vast herds until slaughter by settlers for sport, hides, and meat reduced them to near extinction. They are now thriving, and some are raised for their meat.

Bison

Bissau, city (1988 est. pop. 125,000), capital of Guinea-Bissau, on the Geba estuary, off the Atlantic Ocean. It is the country's largest city, major port, and administrative center. Exports include peanuts, hardwood, palm oil, coconuts, and rubber, and there is some transit trade. Food and beverage processing is the main industry. Founded (1687) by the Portuguese as a fortified port and trading center, the city was the capital (1942–74) of Portuguese Guinea.

bit: see COMPUTER.

Bithynia, ancient country of NW Asia Minor, in present-day Turkey. At first an independent Thracian state, it became an autonomous part of the Persian empire, and after the death of ALEXANDER THE GREAT, it was an independent kingdom (3d–1st cent. B.C.). King Nicomedes IV willed it to Rome (74 B.C.). Joined with Pontus as a single colony soon afterward, Bithynia declined in the 2d cent. A.D.

bittern, migratory marsh BIRD of the HERON family. The American bittern, widely distributed in E North America, is 2 to 3 ft (61 to 91 cm) tall. When pursued, the bittern escapes detection by standing motionless with uplifted bill, its yellow and brown markings blending with the marsh grasses.

bitterroot: see PURSLANE.

bittersweet, name for two unrelated fall-fruiting, woody vines. One (*Solanum dulcamara*) belongs to the NIGHTSHADE family. Its twigs and stems yield a medicinal narcotic poison similar to belladonna. The more popular bittersweet (*Celastrus scandens*) is in the staff tree family. Both grow in North America.

bivalve, MOLLUSK of the class Bivalvia (sometimes called Pelycypoda) with a laterally compressed body and an external shell consisting of two dorsally hinged valves. Bivalves lack eyes and tentacles; most have a muscular foot, used for burrowing. Shells range in size from 1/16 in. (2 mm) to over 4 ft (120 cm). Bivalves are an important food source and include CLAMS, COCKLES, MUSSELS, OYSTERS, SCALLOPS, and SHIPWORMS.

Bizet, Georges [bēzä'], 1838–75, French operatic composer. He is celebrated for his immensely popular opera *Carmen* (1875), based on a story by MÉRIMÉE. His other works include the opera *The Pearlfishers* (1863), the Symphony in C Major (1868), and incidental music to DAUDET's *L'Arlesienne*.

Bjerknes, Vilhelm Frimann Koren [byĕrk'nĕs], 1862–1951, Norwegian physicist and pioneer in modern meteorology. He applied hydrodynamic and thermodynamic theories to atmospheric and hydrospheric conditions in order to predict future weather conditions. His work in meteorology and on electric waves was important in the early development of wireless telegraphy. He and his son **Jakob Bjerknes,** 1897–1975, evolved the polar-front theory of cyclones.

Bjørnsone, Bjørnstjerne [byörn'sōn], 1832–1910, Norwegian writer, a seminal figure in 19th-cent. Norwegian literature and a lifelong champion of liberal causes. He sought to free the Norwegian theater from Danish influence and to revive Norwegian as a literary language. As director of Bergen's Ole Bull Theater (1857–59) and of the Oslo Theater (1863–67), he recreated Norway's epic past in sagalike dramas, e.g., the trilogy *Sigurd Slembe* (1862). He was named national poet of Norway, and his poem *Yes, We Love This Land of Ours* became the national anthem. Other major works include the novel *The Fisher Girl* (1868), the epic poem *Arnljot Gelline* (1870), and the play *Pastor Sang* (1893). He received the 1903 Nobel Prize in literature.

Björnsson, Sveinn [byörn'sôn], 1881–1952, Icelandic diplomat and political leader. He served as minister to Denmark (1920–41), regent of Iceland (1941–44), and, after independence from Denmark, Iceland's first president (1944–52).

Bk, chemical symbol of the element BERKELIUM.

Black, Hugo Lafayette, 1886–1971, associate justice of the U.S. SUPREME COURT (1937–71); b. Harlan, Ala.; LL.B., Univ. of Alabama (1906). As a U.S. senator (1927–37), he was an ardent supporter of the NEW DEAL. Although his appointment to the Supreme Court was strongly opposed because he had been a member of the KU KLUX KLAN, Black led the Court in the battle for civil rights.

Black, Joseph, 1728–99, Scottish chemist and physician; b. France. Professor of chemistry at Glasgow and then at Edinburgh, he is best known for his theories of latent heat and specific heat. He discovered carbon dioxide ("fixed air") and helped establish chemistry as an exact science.

Blackbeard, d. 1718, English pirate. His name was probably Edward Teach or Thatch. Originally a privateer in the War of the SPANISH SUCCESSION, he preyed on the West Indies and along the Atlantic coast. He was killed by the British.

blackberry: see BRAMBLE.

blackbird, perching BIRD belonging to the family Icteridae, related to the BOBOLINK and ORIOLE. Except during breeding season, blackbirds travel in flocks; these may number as many as 5 million birds and often do serious crop damage. Common species are the red-winged, yellow-headed, and brewer blackbirds. The European blackbird is a THRUSH.

blackbody, in physics, an ideal substance that absorbs all and reflects none of the radiant energy falling on it. An approximate blackbody is lampblack, which reflects less than 2% of incoming radiation. A study of blackbody radiation led Max PLANCK to develop quantum theory (see QUANTUM MECHANICS) in 1900.

Black Death: see PLAGUE.

Black English, distinctive DIALECT spoken at times by as many as 80% to 90% of African Americans. Long considered merely substandard English, it is in fact a distinct form. African slaves confronting white culture, and themselves speaking many different languages, developed a PIDGIN, mixing for the most part English vocabulary and African syntax, that developed into Black English. Much in Black English that seems grammatically incorrect actually represents consistent application of African structural principles. A social, rather than regional, dialect, it is similar in all parts of the U.S., as research since the 1960s has shown. Its role in public education is a source of controversy because its effect on the process of learning to read and write is not clearly understood. In addition, its exclusive use by individuals has usually limited their opportunities for social advancement. See also GULLAH.

black-eyed bean or **black-eyed pea:** see COWPEA.

black-eyed Susan or **yellow daisy,** weedy biennial North American daisylike wildflower (*Rudbeckia hirta*) of the COMPOSITE family, with yellow rays and a dark brown center. This and other species in the genus are also called yellow coneflowers.

Blackfoot, indigenous people of the Plains (see NORTH AMERICA, INDIGENOUS PEOPLES OF), who spoke an Algonquian language of the Algonquian-Wakashan stock (see NATIVE AMERICAN LANGUAGES). The Blackfoot, so called because they wore black-dyed moccasins, were unremittingly hostile to most other Native American peoples and usually to white settlers, efficiently repelling intrusion. In the early 19th cent. they lived in a large territory around the upper Missouri and N Saskatchewan rivers, ranging W to the Rocky Mts. They developed a nomadic Plains culture, based on the horse and buffalo. Their only crop was tobacco, employed in such rituals as the SUN DANCE. The killing off of the buffalo by the whites brought the Blackfoot almost to starvation. Today they are mostly farmers and ranchers, living in Montana and Canada. In 1990 there were 32,234 Blackfoot in the U.S.

Black Forest, block mountain range, SW Germany, extending c.90 mi (145 km) along the Rhine rift valley. It is named for its cover of dark pine forests. A popular resort area, it is known for its cuckoo clock and toy industries. Baden-Baden and Freiburg are the chief cities.

Black Friday, Sept. 24, 1869, in U.S. history, day of financial panic. To corner the gold market, speculators, including Jay GOULD and James FISK, sought the support of federal officials of the GRANT administration. The attempt failed when government gold was released for sale. The drive ended on a Friday, when thousands were ruined. Other days of financial panic have also been called Black Friday.

black gum, ornamental deciduous tree (*Nyssa sylvatica*), native to E North America. The tough wood is used for wheel hubs. Black gum is also called sour gum, tupelo, and pepperidge. The genus *Nyssa* may be derived from an ancestral dogwood and is sometimes classified in the DOGWOOD family.

Black Hawk War, 1832, conflict between the U.S. and the SAC AND FOX. An 1831 treaty compelled the Sac and Fox to move W of the Mississippi, but in 1832, under Chief Black Hawk, a group returned to Illinois. Fighting ensued, and most of Black Hawk's band were killed on the Bad Axe R. (in present-day Wisconsin) by a force under Henry Atkinson.

Black Hills, forested mountains rising above the GREAT PLAINS in SW South Dakota and NE Wyoming. Harney Peak (7,242 ft/2,207 m) is the highest point. Gold mining (begun in 1874) and tourism are chief industries.

black hole: see GRAVITATIONAL COLLAPSE.

black lead: see GRAPHITE.

blackleg or **black quarter,** acute infectious bacterial disease of cattle and sometimes sheep, characterized by muscle inflammation and pain in the affected areas. TOXINS formed by the BACTERIA (genus *Clostridium*) produce severe muscle damage, and mortality is high.

black lung disease: see PNEUMOCONIOSIS.

black magic: see MAGIC.

blackmail: see EXTORTION.

Black Monday, Oct. 19, 1987, in U.S. history, day of financial panic. The DOW JONES AVERAGE fell 508.32 points, a drop of 22.6%, the largest since 1914. The point decline as well as the volume, 604.33 million shares, exceeded previous records. Among the possible causes were investors' anxiety about U.S. international trade and federal deficits, U.S. criticism of West Germany's economic policies, the cascading effect of the automatic selling of stocks, and the drop in stock-index futures triggered by computerized trading programs. Stocks throughout the world joined the slide. By mid-1988 the stock market had recovered, and the U.S. economy was largely unaffected by the crash.

Blackmore, Richard Doddridge, 1825–1900, English novelist. Though he wrote many novels, he is famous for *Lorna Doone* (1869), a romance about 17th-cent. outlaws.

Blackmun, Harry Andrew: see SUPREME COURT, UNITED STATES (table 1).

Black Muslims, popular name for members of an African-American nationalist religious movement in the U.S. Founded (1930) in Detroit, the sect, then called the Nation of Islam, was led (1934–75) by Elijah MUHAMMAD, under whom the sect greatly expanded. Its members lived austerely, and the sect advocated a separate autonomous nation within the U.S. for its adherents. In the 1960s tension between Muhammad and MALCOLM X, a Black Muslim minister, developed. Malcolm X's assassination (1965) may have been instigated by Muhammad's followers. Warith Deen Mohammed (Wallace D. Muhammad) succeeded his father as leader in 1975 and has steered the sect (renamed the World Community of Islam in the West and later the American Muslim Mission) toward SUNNI Islamic practice. A splinter group, known by the original name, the Nation of Islam, and led by Louis Farrakhan, has continued to follow the teachings of Elijah Muhammad.

Black Panther party, U.S. African-American militant political organization (founded 1966) advocating violent revolution to achieve African-American liberation. Its members became involved (late 1960s) in clashes with the police, and, after close FBI scrutiny, Huey Newton and Bobby Seale, the party's founders, were tried in a number of court cases, but were acquitted. Another leader, Eldridge Cleaver, left (1975) the party, which was torn by rival factions. By the 1980s the Black Panther party had ceased to play an important part in the African-American movement.

Black Prince: see EDWARD THE BLACK PRINCE.

black quarter: see BLACKLEG.

Black Sea, c.159,600 sq mi (413,360 sq km), SE Europe, connected with the MEDITERRANEAN SEA via the DARDANELLES and BOSPORUS. Bordered by Ukraine (N), Russia and Georgia (E), Turkey (S), and Bulgaria and Romania (W), it is c.750 mi (1,200 km) wide at its greatest extent and has a maximum depth of 7,364 ft (2,245 m). Almost tideless, it is ice-free in winter. The CRIMEA, a peninsula on its northern shore, is a major resort area. ODESSA and Constanţa are the chief ports.

Blackstone, Sir William, 1723–80, British jurist. At Oxford, after 1758, he was the first at a British university to teach English, as opposed to Roman, law. In his great work *Commentaries on the Laws of England* (1765–69) Blackstone ordered and elucidated the bulk of English law, showing it to be comparable to Roman law and to the civil law of the Continent. Although criticized, by BENTHAM among others, for a failure to analyze social and historical factors, Blackstone's work had a tremendous effect on the profession and study of law, both in Britain and in the U.S.

Black Watch or **Royal Highland Regiment,** Scottish infantry regiment. It was formed (1739–40) to guard against Scottish rebels and keep the peace. It became known as the Black Watch because of the dark colors of the regimental tartan.

Blackwell, Alice Stone: see under STONE, LUCY.

Blackwell, Elizabeth, 1821–1910, American physician; b. England. An 1849 graduate of the Geneva (N.Y.) Medical College, she was the first woman in the U.S. to receive a medical degree. She helped to found the New York Infirmary for Women and Children (1857) and its Women's Medical College (1868).

Blackwell, Henry Brown: see under STONE, LUCY.

black widow, poisonous SPIDER (genus *Latrodectus*) found in the Americas. Adults are black with a red to orange hour glass-shaped abdominal marking. The female is not quite ½ in. (1.3 cm) long; she may eat the smaller male after mating. The bite venom, a neurotoxin, is sometimes fatal to children.

bladder: see URINARY SYSTEM.

Blades, Rubén, 1948–, Panamanian singer, songwriter, and bandleader. He is internationally known for his salsa music, which often incorporates sociopolitical themes. A Harvard-trained lawyer, Blades became a candidate for the Panamanian presidency in 1993.

Blaine, James Gillespie, 1830–93, American politician; b. West Brownsville, Pa. He was a U.S. representative from Maine (1863–76), Speaker of the House (1869–75), U.S. senator (1876–81), and U.S. secretary of state (1881, 1889–92). Blaine failed to capture the 1876 Republican presidential nomination after a scandal; it was alleged that he had improperly secured a land grant for an Arkansas railroad. The leader of the "Half-Breed" Republicans who opposed the regular or "Stalwart" faction, he was the party's nominee in 1884. He was defeated by Grover CLEVELAND, in part because he failed to disavow a supporter's remark that characterized the New York Democrats as the party of "rum, Romanism, and rebellion." As secretary of state, he fostered close U.S.–Latin American relations and brought about the first Pan-American Congress.

Blair, Bonnie Kathleen, 1964–, American speed skater; b. Cornwall, N.Y. A sprint racer and an outstanding technical skater, she won five Olympic gold medals from 1988 to 1994, the most ever won by an American woman. Her total of six Olympic medals is the most ever won by any American winter-sports athlete.

Blair, Eric Arthur: see ORWELL, GEORGE.

Blair, Francis Preston, 1791–1876, American journalist and politician; b. Abington, Va. Blair was an ardent supporter of Andrew JACKSON and a member of the Kitchen Cabinet. In 1830 he founded the Washington *Globe.* He was also among the founders of the REPUBLICAN PARTY and was an adviser to Pres. LINCOLN. His son **Francis Preston Blair,** 1821–75, was a Union general in the U.S. CIVIL WAR and a U.S. senator (1871–73). Another son, **Montgomery Blair,** 1813–83, was the first U.S. solicitor in the Court of Claims (1855–57), in which capacity he served as counsel to Dred Scott in the DRED SCOTT CASE. He was also Lincoln's postmaster general (1861–64).

Blake, Eubie (James Hubert Blake), 1883–1983, African-American pianist and composer; b. Baltimore. His career has extended from ragtime (see JAZZ) to the 1980s. With the songwriter Noble Sissle he produced early African-American Broadway musicals, e.g., *Shuffle Along* (1921). His most famous songs are "Memories of You" and "I'm Just Wild about Harry."

Blake, Nicholas: see DAY LEWIS, CECIL.

William Blake engraving Elijah in the Fiery Chariot

Blake, William, 1757–1827, English poet and artist who exerted a great influence on English ROMANTICISM. His first book, *Poetical Sketches* (1783), was the only one published conventionally during his life. With the help of his wife, Catherine Boucher, he illustrated and published all his other major poetry himself. *Songs of Innocence* (1789) and *Songs of Experience* (1794), containing "The Lamb," "The Tyger," and "London," are written from a child's point of view, directly, simply, and unsentimentally. Blake was a visionary and a mystic, and in his "Prophetic Books," including *The Book of Thel* (1789), *The Marriage of Heaven and Hell* (c.1790), *Milton* (1804–8), and *Jerusalem* (1804–20), he created his own mythology in which love, energy, and imagination vie with the forces of reductive rationalism and repression. Blake's paintings and engravings, notably his illustrations of his own works, works by Milton, and the Book of Job, are realistic in their representation of human anatomy and other natural forms, but also radiantly imaginative, often depicting fanciful creatures in exacting detail. All of Blake's works were ignored or dismissed until long after his death.

Blanc, Louis [bläN], 1811–82, French socialist and journalist; b. Spain. In his *Organization of Work* (1840) he outlined an ideal social order based on the principle "From each according to his abilities, to each according to his needs." As a first stage he advocated a system of "social workshops" controlled by workers. A member of the 1848 provisional government, he was implicated in a workers' revolt and fled to England, where he wrote his *History of the French Revolution* (12 vol., 1847–64). On his return to France (1871) he became a member of the national assembly.

Blanco, Antonio Guzmán: see GUZMÁN BLANCO.

Bland-Allison Act, 1878, passed by the U.S. Congress to provide freer coinage of silver. Offered by Rep. Richard P. Bland and amended by Sen. William B. Allison, the act required the U.S. Treasury to purchase between $2 million and $4 million worth of silver bullion monthly, to be coined into silver dollars. Attempts of the Western FREE SILVER forces to replace the act with provision for unlimited coinage failed, as did attempts of the gold-standard forces to repeal it altogether. It remained law until passage (1890) of the SHERMAN SILVER PURCHASE ACT.

blank verse: see PENTAMETER.

Blantyre, city (1987 pop. 331,588), S Malawi, in the Shire Highlands. It is Malawi's main commercial and industrial center and is connected by rail to the Indian Ocean port of Beira, Mozambique. Manufactures include cement and textiles. Founded in 1876 by Scottish missionaries, it was named for the birthplace of the explorer David LIVINGSTONE.

Blasco Ibáñez, Vicente [blä'skō ēbä'nyāth], 1867–1928, Spanish novelist and politician. For his anti-monarchist activities he was imprisoned 30 times. His World War I novel *The Four Horsemen of the Apocalypse* (1916), the best known of his many in the naturalistic vein, made him world famous.

blast furnace, structure used chiefly in SMELTING, i.e., extracting METALS, mainly IRON and COPPER, from their ORES. The principle involved is that of the reduction of the ores by the action of CARBON MONOXIDE, i.e., the removal of oxygen from the metal oxide in order to obtain the metal. PIG IRON prepared in the blast furnace is converted to STEEL by the BESSEMER PROCESS. Copper ore treated in a blast furnace yields a copper sulfide mixture, which is usually further refined by electrolytic methods (see ELECTROLYSIS).

Blau, Joseph Leon, 1909–86, American Jewish scholar and educator; b. Brooklyn, N.Y. Professor of religion (1962–77) at Columbia, he examined cross-cultural influences on Judaism's development in *The Story of Jewish Philosophy* (1962), *The Jews of the United States* (ed. with S.W. BARON, 1963), and *Judaism in America* (1976).

Blaue Reiter, Der [dĕr blou'ə rī'tər] [Ger., = the blue rider], German expressionist art movement (see EXPRESSIONISM) lasting from 1911 to 1914. It was named for KANDINSKY's painting *Le cavalier bleu.* The movement was led by Kandinsky, KLEE, MARC, and MACKE, in Munich. Their works ranged from pure abstraction to romantic imagery, attempting to express spiritual truths. Common to the group was a philosophical spirit, an intellectual approach to technique, and a lyrical spontaneity. A number of their illustrations and articles were published as the *"Blaue Reiter" Album* (1911).

bleaching, the process of whitening a substance by exposure to the sun, or by chemical processes. Chemical methods include OXIDATION AND REDUCTION and ADSORPTION. In 1799 Charles Macintosh invented the first modern chemical bleach, chloride of lime, known as bleaching powder. Previous bleaching agents included chlorine, sulfuric acid, and milk. Bleaching is applied to a variety of products, including textiles, wood pulp, wood, and flour.

Blériot, Louis [blārēō'], 1872–1936, French aviator and inventor. He invented an automobile searchlight, then turned to designing and constructing monoplanes. On July 25, 1909, he was the first person to cross the English Channel in a heavier-than-air machine.

Bligh, William, 1754–1817, British admiral. He is chiefly remembered for the mutiny on his ship, the BOUNTY, in 1789. He was later governor of NEW SOUTH WALES (1805–8).

blight, any sudden, severe plant disease characterized by the withering and death of the plant; also, the causative agent of such a disease. Most blights are caused by BACTERIA (e.g., bean blights),

VIRUSES, (e.g., soybean bud blight), or a FUNGUS (e.g., chestnut blight, potato blight).

blimp: see AIRSHIP.

blindness, partial or complete loss of sight. Blindness may be congenital or caused by injury or disease. Lesions of the brain, CATARACT, GLAUCOMA, or retinal detachment can result in loss of vision, as can changes in the EYE associated with disorders such as DIABETES and HYPERTENSION. In retinitis pigmentosa, a genetically transmitted disorder, visual impairment develops in childhood and gradually progresses to complete blindness. The BRAILLE system enables the blind to read and write. See BIRTH DEFECTS; COLOR BLINDNESS.

Blixen, Karen: see DINESEN, ISAK.

Bloch, Ernest [blŏk], 1880–1959, Swiss-American composer; b. Switzerland. He taught in the U.S. and Switzerland. His music is classical, but personal and Hebraic in tone, e.g., the Hebrew rhapsody *Schelomo,* the symphonic poem *Israel* (both: 1916), and *Cinq pièces Hébraïque* (1951). He also wrote concertos, string quartets, and pieces for chorus and orchestra.

Bloch, Konrad Emil, 1912–, American biochemist; b. Germany. For his discoveries concerning the mechanism and regulation of cholesterol and fatty-acid metabolism, he shared with Feodor Lynen the 1964 Nobel Prize in physiology or medicine.

Bloch, Marc [blôk], 1886–1944, French historian. An authority on medieval feudalism, he wrote *Feudal Society* (1939, 1940), a brilliant synthesis on the subject. His other works include *French Rural History* (1931), and *The Historian's Craft* (1949). Active in the French Resistance during World War II, he was executed by the Germans.

Block, Herbert Lawrence: see HERBLOCK.

block book, book printed from engraved wooden blocks, one for each page. Although produced in Europe before and after the invention of PRINTING, block books have a richer history in China and Japan, where the large number of written characters made printing from movable type impractical.

Bloemfontein [blo͞om′fŏntān″], city (1985 pop. 104,381), capital of the Orange Free State and judicial capital of South Africa. It is a transportation and industrial center. The city was founded in 1846 by Boer settlers and was captured (1900) by the British during the SOUTH AFRICAN WAR. It was the site of negotiations that led to the founding (1910) of the Union of South Africa, and of the conference (1912) that founded the AFRICAN NATIONAL CONGRESS.

Blois [blwä], town (1982 pop. 49,422), capital of Loir-et-Cher dept., central France, known for its trade in wine and brandies. From the 10th cent. the counts of Blois were France's most powerful lords. With the accession (1498) of Louis XII (who was born in its Renaissance chateau), Blois passed to the French crown.

Blok, Aleksandr Aleksandrovich [blôk], 1880–1921, Russian poet, considered the leading Russian SYMBOLIST. Influenced by Vladimir Soloviev, he voiced mysticism and idealistic passion in *Verses about the Beautiful Lady* (1904). *The Unknown Woman* (1906) expresses his later despair. He celebrated the Bolshevik Revolution in *The Twelve* (1918) and *The Scythians* (1920).

blood, fluid that is pumped by the HEART and circulates through the body via arteries, veins, and capillaries, carrying oxygen and nutrients to the body tissues, and carbon dioxide and wastes away from them (see CIRCULATORY SYSTEM). It is also involved in tissue repair, cell METABOLISM, infection resistance, and other life-sustaining activities. Blood is made up of plasma, a colorless fluid containing red blood cells (erythrocytes), which carry on oxygen-carbon dioxide exchange; white blood cells (leukocytes), which defend the body from foreign agents; platelets that function in blood clotting; HORMONES; and essential salts and PROTEINS. There are about 6 quarts (5.6 liters) of blood in an average-sized adult male human. Blood is classified into BLOOD GROUPS. A deficiency of red blood cells is ANEMIA; abnormal proliferation of leukocytes is known as LEUKEMIA. See also BLOOD BANK; BLOOD TRANSFUSION.

blood bank, site for collecting, processing, typing, and storing whole BLOOD and blood products. Whole blood may be preserved up to 21 days without losing its usefulness in BLOOD TRANSFUSIONS. Blood plasma, the fluid portion of the blood, may be frozen and stored indefinitely. All blood donated in the U.S. is now screened for infectious agents, including the AIDS virus and several forms of HEPATITIS. Many blood banks have facilities for APHERESIS, bone marrow donations, and related procedures.

blood groups, classifications of human BLOOD based on immunological properties. The most widely used blood classification system is the ABO system, described by LANDSTEINER. It divides blood into A, B, AB, and O groups, depending on the presence of specific chemical substances on the surface of the red blood cells (A, B, or AB), or their absence (O). These substances act antigenically, i.e., to cause the formation of specific antibodies when injected into a recipient (see IMMUNITY). Because the formation of antibodies can create a potentially dangerous condition in an individual receiving a BLOOD TRANSFUSION, the blood of a donor must be compatible with that of the recipient. Another blood-group system important in blood transfusion compatibility is the RH FACTOR.

bloodhound, large HOUND; shoulder height, c.25 in. (63.5 cm); weight, 80–110 lb (36.3–49.9 km). Its short, smooth coat is black and tan, red and tan, or tawny. The skin hangs infolds on the face. The oldest hound, known in Europe over 2,000 years ago, it was brought to the U.S. in the 19th cent. It has a superb sense of smell and is used for tracking.

blood poisoning: see SEPTICEMIA.

blood pressure, force exerted by blood upon the walls of the arteries. It is initiated by the pumping action of the heart, and pressure waves can be felt at the wrist and other PULSE points. Blood pressure is strongest in the aorta, where the blood leaves the HEART, and diminishes progressively in the smaller vessels. Contraction of the heart (systole) produces the highest pressure, while heart relaxation (diastole) reduces the pressure to its lowest point. Pressure is measured at the brachial artery in the forearm (for consistency) in millimeters of mercury; pressures of about 120/80 (systolic/diastolic) are considered normal in young people. Conditions involving high blood pressure include HYPERTENSION and STROKE.

bloodstone or **heliotrope,** green CHALCEDONY spotted with red, used as a gem. It is found in India, the U.S., Brazil, and Australia.

blood substitute, substance that mimics the function of HEMOGLOBIN, the molecule that carries oxygen through the body. Blood donated by humans must be refrigerated, can be contaminated by such diseases as AIDS and hepatitis, and is often in short supply. Designers of blood substitutes hope to eliminate these problems and develop genetically engineered or chemical products that will be tolerated by people of all blood types.

blood transfusion, transfer of blood from the venous system of one person to that of another, or from one animal to another of the same species. A transfusion using a person's own blood, or autologous transfusion, can be done in some cases if the blood has been donated ahead of time or if blood lost in surgery is collected and cleansed. Transfusions are performed to replace a large loss of blood (as in hemorrhage, severe bleeding during surgery, SHOCK, and severe BURNS) and as supportive treatment in certain disorders (e.g., HEMOPHILIA). In whole blood transfusions, the BLOOD GROUPS (including the RH FACTOR) must be compatible with that of the recipient; if not, red blood cells will rupture and clump, a condition that can result in JAUNDICE, kidney damage, and death. People with blood group O are universal donors, having blood that is compatible with all other groups; those with blood group AB are universal recipients, able to accept blood from all other groups. When whole blood is not needed or is unavailable, the fluid part of the blood (plasma) may be given.

Bloody Assizes: see JEFFREYS OF WEM, GEORGE JEFFREYS, 1ST BARON.

Bloomer, Amelia Jenks, 1818–94, American reformer; b. Homer, N.Y. She edited (1848–54) the *Lily,* dedicated to women's rights and temperance. In 1851 she adopted the full trousers that became known as the Bloomer costume, or bloomers.

Bloomfield, Leonard, 1887–1949, American linguist; b. Chicago. His masterpiece, *Language* (1933), a standard text, is a clear statement of principles that have become axiomatic: that language study must always be centered in the spoken language; that the definitions used in grammar should be based on the forms of the language; and that a given language at a given time is a complete system of sounds and forms existing independently of the past, so that the history of a form does not explain its meaning.

Bloomsbury group, influential literary and intellectual group (fl.

1904–c.1939) that made Bloomsbury Square, London, its center. Its members included Lytton STRACHEY, Virginia WOOLF, Leonard Woolf, E.M. FORSTER, V. SACKVILLE-WEST, Roger FRY, Clive Bell, and John Maynard KEYNES.

Blücher, Gebhard Leberecht von [blü'khər], 1742–1819, Prussian field marshal. He helped to defeat NAPOLEON I at Leipzig (1813) and at Laon (1814). Napoleon defeated him at Ligny (June 15, 1815), but Blücher's timely arrival at WATERLOO three days later helped the duke of WELLINGTON to turn that battle into a great victory.

blueberry, widely distributed shrubs or small trees (genus *Vaccinium*) of the HEATH family, usually found in acid soils. They are related to HUCKLEBERRY and CRANBERRY. Blueberries are a popular food and are commercially important. The most cultivated are the high-bush blueberry (*V. cerymbosum*) and the low-bush blueberry (*V. augustifolium*).

bluebird, migratory BIRD of the THRUSH family. The Eastern bluebird (*Sialia sialis*), vivid blue with a red breast, usually nests in orchards or on the edge of woodlands; it eats insects and wild fruits.

bluefish, stout-bodied, delicately flavored marine FISH of the family Pomatomidae, resembling the POMPANO but more closely related to the sea BASS. Averaging 30 in. (75 cm) in length and 10 to 12 lb (4.5 to 5.5 kg) in weight, the bluefish is found in warm waters of the Atlantic and Indian oceans and Mediterranean Sea. It is an excellent game fish.

blue-green algae, common name for cyanobacteria, widespread organisms of great importance in carbon and nitrogen cycles. Blue-green algae lack cell nuclei; some are unicellular, but most are filamentous or colonial. Most are photosynthetic. They were formerly considered ALGAE and placed in the plant kingdom, but they are now usually considered MONERANS.

blue jay: see JAY.

blue laws, U.S. state laws regulating private and public conduct and morals, especially Sabbath observance. The term is derived from the blue paper on which some 17th-cent. laws were printed. Blue laws, which usually forbade work or sport on Sunday, were most common and most strict in Puritan New England. They declined after the American Revolution but many were revived in the 20th cent. during PROHIBITION. Many states retain blue laws today.

Blue Rider: see BLAUE REITER, DER.

Blue Ridge, eastern range of the APPALACHIAN MTS., extending S from S Pennsylvania to N Georgia. Heavily forested and long a barrier to early colonial expansion, the area is noted for its resorts and its scenery.

blues: see JAZZ.

Blum, Léon [blo͞om], 1872–1950, French Socialist statesman. He was premier (1936–37) in the first Popular Front government (a coalition of Radical Socialists, Socialists, and Communists) and passed important labor reforms. Arrested (1940) by the VICHY government, he was imprisoned by the Germans until 1945. Blum grew more moderate in his later years and was again premier (1946–47) in a Socialist government.

Blunt, Anthony Frederick, 1907–83, English art historian. He was director of the Courtauld Institute, professor of art at the Univ. of London, and Surveyor of the Queen's Pictures. His major writings include *Artistic Theory in Italy, 1450–1600* (1940) and *Art and Architecture in France, 1500–1700* (1953). Knighted in 1956, he was divested of the title in 1979, when it became known that he had been a Soviet agent.

Bly, Robert, 1926–, American poet; b. Madison, Minn. His personal, precisely observant poems are collected in such volumes as *The Light Around the Body* (1967) and *Loving a Woman in Two Worlds* (1985). Also a publisher, he has printed translations of lesser-known foreign poets. Since the early 1980s Bly has been active in the "men's movement," concerned with establishing a new idea of masculinity in contemporary society. His book *Iron John* (1990) deals with the passage from boyhood to manhood.

B'nai B'rith, American Jewish service organization, est. 1843. Its broad-based program includes orphanage and hospital work, disaster relief, and vocational training. The Hillel Foundation (for Jewish students), the Anti-Defamation League (est. 1913 to combat ANTI-SEMITISM), and B'nai B'rith Women are branches. It has some 500,000 members.

boa, live-bearing constrictor SNAKE of the family Boidae, which also includes the PYTHONS, found mostly in the Americas. Boas suffocate their prey by squeezing it. Best known are the boa constrictor (*Constrictor constrictor*), which lives in terrestrial habitats from S Mexico to central Argentina and averages 6 to 9 ft (1.8 to 2.7 m); and the South American anaconda, the longest (up to 25 ft/7.9 m) and thickest (3 ft/90 cm in girth) boa.

Boa constrictor

Boadicea [bō"ədĭsē'ə], d. A.D. 61, British queen of the Iceni (of Norfolk). She led the Iceni in revolt against the Romans. Her army was crushed, and she took poison.

boar: see SWINE.

Boas, Franz, 1858–1942, German-American anthropologist; b. Germany. No one has more greatly influenced American anthropology. Boas reexamined the premises of physical anthropology and pioneered in the use of statistical methods. His field work began with observations of the Central Eskimos (1883) and of indigenous British Columbian peoples (1886). Associated with the American Museum of Natural History from 1895 to 1905, he became (1899) the first professor of anthropology at Columbia Univ., a position he held for 37 years. In his studies of NATIVE AMERICAN LANGUAGES Boas stressed the importance of internal linguistic structure, and the strict methodology of his contributions gave them scientific value. Among his works are *The Mind of Primitive Man* (1911, rev. ed. 1938), *Primitive Art* (1927, repr. 1955), *Race, Language and Culture* (1940), and *Race and Democratic Society* (1945).

Boaz: see RUTH.

bobcat: see LYNX.

bobolink, American songbird (*Dolichonyx oryzivorus*) of the family Icteridae. The spring plumage of the male is black and white; after the breeding season, it is yellowish and brown-streaked like the female. In the north, bobolinks are insectivorous, but may feed on rice crops during southern migration; once hunted because of this destructive feeding habit, they are now protected.

bobsledding, sport in which a bobsled (an open, steel-bodied vehicle with runners) hurtles down an icy, steeply banked, twisting course. Sleds accommodate either two or four persons, including a driver and brakeman in each type, and can attain speeds of 90 mi (145 km) per hr. It has been an Olympic event since the first Winter Games (1924).

bobwhite, American henlike BIRD of the PHEASANT family. Bobwhites feed on insects and travel in coveys, sleeping at night in a tight circle, tails to center. In spring the coveys disperse, and each male selects a nesting territory. The characteristic call of "bob-white" functions to attract a mate and warn off other males. Hunted as game birds, bobwhites are often called QUAIL or PARTRIDGE. The eastern bobwhite quail (*Colinus virginianus*) is c.10 in. (25 cm) long; the male has mixed brown, black, and white plumage.

Boccaccio, Giovanni [bōk-kät'chō], 1313–75, Italian poet, storyteller, and humanist; b. Paris. His early works include *Filocolo* (c.1340), a vernacular prose romance; *Filostrato,* a poem infusing the Troilus and Cressida legend with a Neapolitan court atmosphere; the allegorical *Amorosa visione,* imitative of DANTE; and a psychological romance, *Amorous Fiametta.* From 1348 to 1353 he wrote his secular classic, the *Decameron,* a collection of 100 witty and sometimes licentious tales set against the somber backdrop of the Black Death. In the *Decameron,* medieval courtly themes began to give way to modern society; the masterful style of the work became a model for later Italian prose. In Florence after 1341, Boccaccio met PETRARCH, who inspired him to devote his later life to the study of Greek and other humanistic concerns, producing important critical works in anthropology, biography, and mythology.

Boccherini, Luigi [bôk-kĕrē'nē], 1743–1805, Italian composer and cellist. His masterful classical style is often compared to that of HAYDN. Boccherini wrote more than 400 works, including 4 cello concertos, some 90 string quartets, and about 125 string quintets.

Boccioni, Umberto [bŏtchō'nē], 1882–1916, Italian futurist, painter and sculptor. He was the major figure of FUTURISM (1910–14). His principal works include the painting *The City Rises* (1910) and the sculpture *Unique Forms of Continuity in Space* (1913; both: Mus. Mod. Art, N.Y.C.).

Bocskay, Stephen [bôch'kī], 1557–1606, Hungarian noble, voivode [governor] (1604–6) and prince (1605–6) of Transylvania. In 1604, with Turkish support, he led a revolt against Holy Roman Emperor RUDOLF II's attempt to impose Roman Catholicism on Hungary. In 1606 he negotiated a treaty at Vienna legalizing the partition of Hungary among the HAPSBURGS, the Turkish sultan, and the prince of Transylvania. It guaranteed constitutional and religious freedom to Hungary.

Bode's law: see TITIUS-BODE LAW.

Bodin, Jean [bôdăN'], 1530?–1596, French social and political philosopher. A lawyer, he was dismayed by the chaos resulting from conflict between Roman Catholics and Huguenots (see RELIGION, WARS OF) and argued in his most important work, *Six Bookes of the Commonweale* (1576), that the well-ordered state required religious toleration and a fully sovereign monarch. His writings made a major theoretical contribution to the rise of the modern nation-state.

Bodley, Sir Thomas, 1545–1613, English scholar and diplomat, organizer of the Bodleian Library at Oxford Univ. (see LIBRARY, table). He offered (1598) to restore Duke Humphrey's library and spent most of his life and fortune on it.

Boece (Anicius Manlius Severinus Boethius): see BOETHIUS.

Boehme [bē'mə], **Böhme,** or **Behmen, Jakob,** 1575–1624, German religious mystic. In *De signatura rerum* and *Mysterium magnum,* he describes God as the abyss, the nothing and the all, from which the creative will struggles to find manifestation and self-consciousness. Evil results when single elements of the Deity strive to become the whole. Boehme had many followers in Germany, Holland, and England.

Boeotia [bēō'shə], region of ancient GREECE, N of the Gulf of Corinth. The Boeotian League, formed (c.7th cent. B.C.) by the cities of the region, was dominated by THEBES, which fought many battles to prevent encroachment by the other great CITY-STATES. The league was disbanded when the Greeks besieged Thebes (479) and after a brief revival was defeated by ATHENS (457), which annexed the Boeotian cities. Thebes resumed leadership of the league in 446; after Thebes defeated Sparta (371) the history of Boeotia was absorbed into that of Thebes. Boeotia was the home of the poets HESIOD and PINDAR.

Boer, inhabitant of SOUTH AFRICA of Dutch or French Huguenot descent. Boers are more commonly known as Afrikaners.

Boerhaave, Hermann [bŏŏr'hävə], 1668–1738, Dutch physician and humanist. An influential clinician and teacher, he helped to revive the Hippocratic method of bedside instruction. Through post-mortem examinations he demonstrated the relation of symptoms to lesions, thereby instituting the clinico-pathological conference still in use today. His works include *Institutiones Medicinae* (1708) and *Elementa Chemiae* (1732), long used as standard texts.

Boer War: see SOUTH AFRICAN WAR.

Boethius [bōē'thēəs], **Boetius** [bōē'shəs], or **Boece** [bōēs'] (Anicius Manlius Severinus Boethius), c.475–525, Roman philosopher and statesman. A consul (510) in Rome, he became minister under Emperor Theodoric, but was falsely accused of treason, imprisoned, and sentenced to death. According to tradition, he wrote his great work, *The Consolation of Philosophy,* while awaiting execution. His treatise on ancient music was for many centuries the unquestioned authority on Western music.

bog: see SWAMP.

Bogan, Louise, 1897–1970, American poet; b. Livermore, Me. Her verse, intense, personal, and metaphysical in tone, is included in such volumes as *Collected Poems* (1954) and *The Blue Estuaries* (1968). She also wrote literary criticism.

Bogardus, James, 1800–1874, American architect; b. Catskill, N.Y. He was among the first to use cast iron in constructing facades. The Iron Building, N.Y.C., is the best known of his commercial building designs.

Bogart, Humphrey (DeForest), 1899–1957, American film actor; b. N.Y.C. He played tough, cynical heroes in such films as *The Maltese Falcon* (1941), *Casablanca* (1942), and *The African Queen* (1954; Academy Award).

Boğazköy or **Boghazkeui** [bōäz'köy], village, N central Turkey. Boğazköy was the chief center of the HITTITE empire (1400–1200 B.C.). Hugo WINCKLER found Hittite inscriptions there that greatly added to the knowledge of Hittite civilization.

Bogotá, city (1990 est. pop. 4,820,000), central Colombia, capital of Colombia. Built on a high plateau (c.8,560 ft/2,610 m), it is the financial, political, and cultural center of the republic. Manufactures include processed food and tobacco, chemical, tires, and drugs. Founded in 1538, it was long the capital of the Spanish colonial viceroyalty of New Granada and a leading Latin American religious and intellectual center. It became the capital of the independent confederation called Greater Colombia in 1819 and of what was later called Colombia in 1830. A picturesque city, it is known for its colonial architecture, its collection of pre-Colombian gold art, and its bookshops.

Bohemia, historic region (20,368 sq mi/52,753 sq km) and former kingdom, W Czech Republic, bordered by Austria (SE), Germany (W, NW), Poland (N, NE), and MORAVIA (E). The traditional capital is PRAGUE. Bohemia is the Czech Republic's most urbanized and industrialized area, with such manufactures as machinery, munitions, and textiles. Grains, sugar beets, hops, and other crops are grown, and coal, silver, and other resources are mined. Bohemia emerged (9th cent.) under the Premysl dynasty and became part (950) of the HOLY ROMAN EMPIRE. It became a kingdom within the empire in 1198 and under Emperor CHARLES IV (r.1355–78) was the empire's seat. In the 15th cent. Bohemia was the scene of the HUSSITE religious movement. The HAPSBURG dynasty of Austria dominated the kingdom after 1526; a revolt (1618) against Hapsburg rule began the THIRTY YEARS WAR. In 1627 the kingdom was demoted to an imperial crown land. After WORLD WAR I it became the core of the new nation of CZECHOSLOVAKIA. The MUNICH PACT (1938) transferred the SUDETENLAND area of Bohemia to Germany, which occupied (1939–45) all of Bohemia during WORLD WAR II. Bohemia was abolished as a province of Czechoslovakia in 1948; in 1960 it was divided into five regions and the city of Prague. With the dissolution of Czechoslovakia (1993), the region became part of the Czech Republic.

Bohemond I, c.1056–1111, prince of Antioch, Turkey (1099–1111), the son of ROBERT GUISCARD and a leader in the First CRUSADE. Breaking his oath of fealty to Byzantine Emperor ALEXIUS I, he made himself prince of Antioch. Defeated (1108) in a crusade against

Alexius, he acknowledged the emperor's suzerainty. He retired and TANCRED became regent.

Böhm, Karl, 1894–1981, Austrian conductor. He directed the Vienna State Opera (1943–45; 1954–56) and the Salzburg Festival, and appeared internationally with many orchestras, specializing in the works of Mozart and Richard Strauss.

Bohr, Niels Henrik David [bōr], 1885–1962, Danish physicist and one of the foremost scientists in modern physics. He was professor of theoretical physics at the Univ. of Copenhagen and was later director of its Institute for Theoretical Physics, which he helped to found. Bohr was awarded the 1922 Nobel Prize in physics for his work on atomic structure. Classical theory had been unable to explain the stability of the nuclear model of the ATOM, but Bohr solved the problem by postulating that electrons move in restricted orbits around the atom's nucleus and explaining how the atom emits and absorbs energy. He thus combined the quantum theory (see QUANTUM MECHANICS) with this concept of atomic structure.

Boileau-Despréaux, Nicolas [bwälō' dāprāō'], 1636–1711, French critic and poet, known for his poetic satires on the clergy, on life in Paris, and on women. His critical precepts, embodied in *L'Art poétique* (1674), established him as the champion of CLASSICISM.

boiler, device for generating steam. Two types are common: fire-tube boilers, containing long steel tubes through which the hot gases from a furnace pass and around which the water to be changed to steam circulates, and water-tube boilers, in which the conditions are reversed. A boiler must be equipped with a safety valve for venting the steam if pressure becomes too great.

boiling point, the temperature at which a substance boils, or changes from a liquid to a vapor or gas (see STATES OF MATTER), through the formation and rise to the surface of bubbles of vapor within the liquid. In a stricter sense, the boiling point of a liquid is the temperature at which its vapor pressure is equal to the local atmospheric pressure. Decreasing (or increasing) the pressure of the surrounding gases thus lowers (or raises) the boiling point of a liquid. The quantity of heat necessary to change 1 g of any substance from liquid to gas at its boiling point is known as its latent heat of vaporization.

Boise [boi'sē, –zē], city (1990 pop. 125,738), state capital and seat of Ada co., SW Idaho, on the Boise R.; inc. 1864. It is the largest city in Idaho, and a trade and transportation center. Food processing, lumber, high-technology and other light industries, construction, and government offices provide employment. In its early years a gold-mining trade center, it later became oriented toward the agriculture of the region.

Boito, Arrigo [bō'ētō], 1842–1918, Italian composer and librettist. His opera *Mefistofele* (1868, rev. 1875), influenced by Richard WAGNER's music-drama, became very popular. Boito wrote the librettos for VERDI's *Otello* and *Falstaff.*

Bok, Edward William, 1863–1930, American editor; b. the Netherlands. He founded the *Brooklyn Magazine* (later *Cosmopolitan*) in 1883. As editor (1889–1919), he made *The Ladies' Home Journal* a leading woman's magazine. His autobiographical *Americanization of Edward Bok* (1920) won a PULITZER PRIZE.

Bokassa, Jean-Bédel, 1921–, president of the CENTRAL AFRICAN REPUBLIC (1966–79). An army officer, he overthrew David DACKO in 1966, assumed the presidency, and declared (1976) the country the Central African Empire and himself Emperor Bokassa I. Erratic, opportunistic, and violent, he was ousted in 1979 and went into exile. On his return in 1987, he was arrested, convicted of murdering several political opponents, and sentenced to death (later commuted to life in prison). He was freed in 1993.

Boleslaus, Polish rulers. **Boleslaus I,** c.966–1025, king of POLAND (992–1025), was the first Polish ruler to style himself king. He succeeded his father, Mieszko I, duke of Poland. As king, he greatly expanded Polish territories. **Boleslaus II,** c.1039–1081, duke (1058–76) and king (1076–79) of Poland, sided with the pope against the Holy Roman emperor but was deposed after killing the bishop of Kraków. **Boleslaus III,** 1085–1138, duke of Poland (1102–38), reunited Poland by defeating (1109) his brother Zbigniew, who had the support of Holy Roman Emperor HENRY V. He added (1135) Pomerania and Rügen to his domains.

Boleyn, Anne, 1505–36, second queen consort of HENRY VIII of England; mother of ELIZABETH I. Henry divorced KATHARINE OF ARAGÓN to marry her. The marriage was unpopular, and when she did not produce a male heir, his ardor cooled. She was executed for alleged adultery and incest.

Bolingbroke, Henry of: see Henry IV under HENRY, kings of England.

Bolívar, Simón [bōlē'vär], 1783–1830, revolutionary leader who liberated much of South America from Spanish rule; b. Caracas, Venezuela. He joined (1810) the Venezuelan revolution against Spain and won notable victories in COLOMBIA before a royalist army crushed (1815) his forces. After fleeing to Jamaica and Haiti, he invaded (1816) VENEZUELA and met disaster, forcing his return to Haiti. Recalled (1817) to command the rebel forces, he seized the lower Orinoco basin. In 1819 he boldly defeated the Spanish at Boyacá, and he became president of Greater Colombia. Cooperating with such other rebel leaders as SUCRE and SAN MARTÍN, he won further victories, culminating (1824) in PERU at Junin and AYACUCHO, which sealed the triumph of the revolution. Now the most powerful person on the continent, Bolívar organized (1824) the government of Peru and created (1825) BOLIVIA. His vision of a united South America was not to be, however, for his dictatorial methods were widely resented and separatist movements shook the union. Venezuela and ECUADOR seceded from Greater Colombia, and he resigned (1830) as president. Although bitterly hated at the time of his death, today Bolívar is revered as Latin America's greatest hero and as its liberator.

Bolivia [bōlĭv'ēa], officially Republic of Bolivia, republic (1992 est. pop. 7,323,000), 424,162 sq mi (1,098,581 sq km), W South America. One of the two inland countries of the continent, it is bordered by Chile and Peru (W), Brazil (E, N), Paraguay (SE), and Argentina (S). SUCRE is the legal capital, but LA PAZ is the administrative capital and seat of government. Bolivia's topography is one of sharp contrasts. In the west are the ANDES, whose snow-capped peak of Illampú reaches 21,276 ft (6,485 m), and a high plateau (ALTIPLANO), 12,000 ft (3,660 m) above sea level, which is the population center of the country. The east is dominated by tropical rain forests, which, in the southeast, merge into the plains of the GRAN CHACO. In the north, on the border with Peru, is Lake TITICACA, the largest freshwater lake in South America; this region, with its ruins of TIAHUANACO, was the home of one of the great pre-Columbian civilizations. Bolivia has some of the richest mineral resources in the world. It is one of the leading producers of tin, and silver, copper, tungsten, bismuth, antimony, and zinc are also mined. Natural gas is exported, and there are major petroleum deposits. Despite these mineral riches, most Bolivians are subsistence farmers, raising sugarcane, potatoes, corn, wheat, and rice; cotton and soybeans are the major cash crops. The illegal trade in coca leaf, the source of cocaine, and processed cocaine is a major source of foreign exchange. More than half the population is pure Aymará or Quechua, but Bolivia's politics and economy are dominated by persons of European and mixed descent. Spanish is the official language; Aymará and Quechua are widely spoken. Most of the people are Roman Catholic.

History. The Aymará of Bolivia had been absorbed into the INCA empire long before the Spanish conquest of Bolivia (1538) by Gonzalo and Hernando PIZARRO. Attracted by Bolivia's mineral wealth, Spanish exploiters poured into the area, developing mines, textile mills, and great estates—all with forced native labor. Bolivia was attached to the viceroyalty of Peru until 1776 and later to that of La Plata. Revolt against Spanish rule first erupted in 1809, but Bolivia remained Spanish until the campaigns of José de SAN MARTÍN and Simon BOLÍVAR and the victory by Antonio José de SUCRE at AYACUCHO in 1824. Independence was formally proclaimed in 1825. Political instability became a hallmark of independent Bolivia, with coups and revolutions occurring, on average, more than once a year. A series of disastrous border wars, including the War of the Pacific (1879–84) against Chile and the Chaco War (1932–35) against Paraguay, cost Bolivia valuable territory, including its outlet to the sea. In 1952 the nationalistic, pro-miner Nationalist Revolutionary Movement (MNR) won control of the government, nationalizing the tin mines and launching a program of agrarian reform. They were overthrown by the military in 1964, and Bolivia resumed its history of political strife and instability, marked by recurring military coups until a civilian government assumed leadership in 1982. In 1993 Gonzalo Sánchez de Lozada, a mining entrepreneur and former planning minister, was elected president.

Böll, Heinrich [böl], 1917–85, German writer. His novels and stories present his critical, antimilitarist view of modern society. Among his works are the story collection *Traveller, If You Come to Spa* (1950) and the novels *Billiards at Half Past Nine* (1959) and *The Safety Net* (tr. 1982). Böll was awarded the Nobel Prize in literature in 1972.

Bologna, Giovanni, or **Giambologna** [bōlō'nyä, jäm"bōlō'nyä], 1524–1608, Flemish mannerist sculptor (see MANNERISM); b. Jean Bologne or Boulogne. Identified with the Italian RENAISSANCE, he is best known for *The Rape of the Sabines* (Florence), with its spiralling forms, and *Flying Mercury* (Bargello, Florence).

Bologna, city (1990 pop. 417,410), capital of Emilia-Romagna, N central Italy, at the foot of the Apennines. It is a commercial and industrial center, with such manufactures as farm and transportation equipment, metal goods, and food products. An Etruscan town, it came under Roman (189 B.C.), Byzantine (6th cent.), and papal rule. Its famous university (founded c.1088) made it an intellectual center. Political control turned on rivalries among great families (13th–15th cent.) until papal rule was restored, lasting, nearly unbroken, from 1506 until Italian unification (1860). There are many notable medieval and Renaissance buildings.

Bologne, Jean: see BOLOGNA, GIOVANNI.

Bolshevism and Menshevism, the two main branches of Russian socialism from 1903 to 1918. In 1903 the Russian Social-Democratic Workers' party split into two factions. One, led by LENIN, had a temporary majority and was thereafter known as the *Bolsheviki* [majority members]; their opponents, led by PLEKHANOV, were dubbed *Mensheviki* [minority members]. The Bolsheviks favored a small party of professional revolutionaries and the establishment of a dictatorship of the proletariat and peasantry. The Mensheviks wanted a loosely organized mass party and held that before reaching socialism Russia must develop a bourgeois-democratic stage. In the 1917 RUSSIAN REVOLUTION the Mensheviks took part in the KERENSKY provisional government, which was overthrown by the Bolsheviks in the October Revolution. The Bolsheviks became the Russian Communist party in 1918 and had suppressed all rival political groups by 1921. In 1952 the party changed its name to the Communist party of the Soviet Union. See COMMUNISM; UNION OF SOVIET SOCIALIST REPUBLICS.

Bolshoi Ballet, the principal ballet company of Russia. It began (1773) as a dancing school for the Moscow Orphanage. Opened in 1856, the Bolshoi Theatre at first competed with the Maryinsky Theatre of St. Petersburg. Alexander Gorsky revitalized it in the early 20th cent. In the 1930s, Igor Moiseyev (see MOISEYEV DANCE COMPANY) experimented with folk-dance ballets at the theater. The company is internationally acclaimed and tours with such classics as *Giselle* and *Swan Lake*.

Boltzmann, Ludwig, 1844–1906, Austrian physicist, known for his important contributions to the KINETIC-MOLECULAR THEORY OF GASES. By investigating the relationship between the temperature and the energy distribution of molecules in a gas, he laid the foundations of statistical mechanics. In 1883 he demonstrated theoretically a law (sometimes called the Stefan-Boltzmann law) describing the radiation from a BLACKBODY that had earlier been found experimentally by the Austrian physicist Josef Stefan.

Bolyai, János or **Johann** [bō'lyoi], 1802–60, Hungarian mathematician. In 1823 he independently developed hyperbolic geometry, a form of NON-EUCLIDEAN GEOMETRY. His father, **Farkas,** or **Wolfgang, Bolyai,** 1775–1856, was also a Hungarian mathematician. Farkas's *Tentamen* (1823–33), a systematic treatment of geometry, arithmetic, algebra, and analysis, contains as an appendix his son's theory of absolute space.

bombax, common name for the Bombacaceae, a family of tall, thick-trunked deciduous trees, found chiefly in the American tropics. Many members of the family are commercially important, e.g., the BAOBAB; balsa, or corkwood, which yields the lightest lumber in the world; and the ceiba tree, source of KAPOK.

Bombay, city and former province of British India, on the Arabian Sea. The region was ruled by dynasties from Central India. In the 18th cent. it came under the control of the MAHRATTAS. The islands on which the city is built were under Portuguese control from 1534, and came under the British in 1661. The surrounding areas were incorporated into Bomby Presidency (or province) after the defeat of the Mahrattas in the early 19th cent. Bombay became a state when India gained independence in 1947; it was split into the states of Gujarat and Maharashtra in 1960. The city of **Bombay** (1991 pop. 12,571,720), India's largest city and the capital of Maharashtra state, occupies two islands off the coast. It has the only natural deepwater harbor in W India. Manufactures include textiles, automobiles, chemicals, and petroleum products, and the city is the center of the Indian entertainment and financial industries. It has the largest community of PARSIS in India. Bombay was convulsed by anti-Muslim riots in 1993.

Bonaparte, Ital. *Buonaparte,* family name of NAPOLEON I of France. Besides Napoleon, this Corsican family produced many other notable figures. Napoleon's older brother, **Joseph Bonaparte,** 1768–1844, was king of Naples (1806–8), but he proved to be an inefficient administrator. As king of Spain (1808–13), he failed to cope with the PENINSULAR WAR and was forced to abdicate. He lived from 1815 to 1841 in the U.S., but died in Italy. Napoleon's brother **Lucien Bonaparte,** 1775–1840, helped Napoleon to overthrow the DIRECTORY in the coup of 18 Brumaire (1799), but later criticized him. They were reconciled while Napoleon was on Elba, and Lucien supported his brother during the Hundred Days. Another brother, **Louis Bonaparte,** 1778–1846, reluctantly married (1802) Hortense de BEAUHARNAIS; their son became NAPOLEON III. Louis was king of Holland (1806–10), but Napoleon forced him to abdicate for ignoring France's Continental System in favor of Dutch interests. Napoleon's youngest brother, **Jérôme Bonaparte,** 1784–1860, king of Westphalia (1807–13), was extravagant and irresponsible. On a visit to the U.S. he married (1803) Elizabeth Patterson, but Napoleon had the marriage annulled and married him to a German princess. Jérôme commanded a division at Waterloo and later received honors at the court of his nephew, Napoleon III.

Bonaventure or **Bonaventura, Saint,** 1221–74, Italian scholastic theologian, cardinal, Doctor of the Church, called the Seraphic Doctor. After teaching at the Univ. of Paris, he was made (1257) general of the FRANCISCANS. His writings reconcile ARISTOTLE's learning with Augustinian Christianity. His later mystical works bring the teachings of BERNARD OF CLAIRVAUX to full flower. Feast: July 15. See also AUGUSTINE, SAINT; SCHOLASTICISM.

bond, in finance, a formal certificate of indebtedness issued by governments or business corporations in return for loans. It bears a fixed rate of interest and promises to repay the funds borrowed after a certain period, usually 10 years or more. A bond is generally protected by security; debentures are bonds unsecured by a pledge against specific assets. Bonds were sold by the U.S. government to help finance both world wars and are still an important money-raising device. Bonds issued by city and state governments are exempt from federal income taxes.

bone, hard substance that forms the SKELETON in vertebrate animals. Bone consists of a gelatinous organic material called collagen, together with minerals (mainly calcium and phosphorus). In the very young, the mineral content is low and the bones are mostly cartilage, which is pliable. With age, as their mineral content increases, bones become more brittle. Bone tissue has a three-layered structure: the spongy inner layer; the compact layer surrounding the inner layer, providing support for the body; and the tough outer membrane. The inner spaces of long bones, as those in the arms and legs, are filled with marrow, important in the formation of BLOOD cells.

Bonhoeffer, Dietrich [bôn'höfər], 1906–45, German Protestant theologian. Influenced by Karl BARTH, he urged a conformation to the form of Jesus as the suffering servant in a total commitment of self to others. He was imprisoned for two years and hanged for his role in a plot to overthrow HITLER. His writings were published posthumously.

Bon Homme Richard: see JONES, JOHN PAUL.

Boniface, Saint, c.675–754?, English missionary monk and martyr, called the Apostle of Germany. From 718 he devoted himself to the conversion of pagan Germany, where he founded many bishoprics and abbeys. He was named metropolitan of Germany (731) and archbishop of Mainz (745). He was martyred by pagans in Friesland. Feast: June 5.

Boniface VIII, 1235–1303, pope (1294–1303), an Italian named Benedetto Caetani. Boniface became pope after the abdication of CELESTINE V, and, to avoid schism, he imprisoned Celestine for life. Trying to assert papal authority, Boniface interfered unsuccessfully in Sicily and further aggravated the quarrel of the GUELPHS AND GHIBELLINES. He was involved in a bitter struggle with PHILIP IV of France. The pope tried to prevent Philip from his illegal levies on the clergy with the bull *Clericis laicos* (1296), but was forced to back down. The struggle was renewed after new troubles, and Boniface issued *Ausculta fili* (1301) and *Unam sanctam* (1302), the latter being an extreme statement regarding the duty of princes to be subject to the pope. As a result, Philip sent an agent to depose Boniface at Anagni, but after the agent's companion struck the pope, the outraged townspeople drove the emissaries out. Boniface died soon afterward and was succeeded by Benedict XI. Philip later forced Pope CLEMENT V to repudiate many of the acts of Boniface. An able canon lawyer, Boniface issued (1298) a new revision of the code called the *Sext.*

Boniface, d. 432, Roman general. In AFRICA as a semi-independent governor, he was named count of Africa by VALENTINIAN III. Recalled to Rome in 427, he rebelled, causing a civil war between Africa and Rome. The struggle prepared the way for the invasion of Africa by the Vandals under GAISERIC. After a truce was arranged, Boniface attacked the Vandals and was defeated and besieged (430) at Hippo. He died of wounds received in a battle with a rival Roman general, Aetius.

Bonifácio, José [bônēfä'sēō], 1763–1838, Brazilian scientist and architect of Brazilian independence. An eminent geologist, he influenced the Portuguese prince regent, Dom Pedro, to declare (1822) Brazil an independent monarchy with himself as Emperor PEDRO I. Bonifácio served as first minister (1822–23) of the new empire, and many of his ideas were included in the 1824 constitution.

Bonin Islands, volcanic island group, c.40 sq mi (100 sq km), in the W Pacific Ocean, c.500 mi (800 km) S of Tokyo. Principal products of the sparsely populated archipelago are timber, bananas, and pineapples. The islands were claimed by Britain (1827) and Japan (1875). A Japanese stronghold in WORLD WAR II, the Bonins were captured (1945) by the U.S. They were returned to Japan in 1968.

Bonn, city (1986 est. pop. 291,000), de facto capital of Germany, North Rhine–Westphalia, W Germany, on the Rhine R. It is the administrative center of Germany, but in 1991 the German parliament voted to move the federal government to Berlin. The move is to be completed by the end of the century, but some government offices will remain in Bonn. Manufactures include ceramic and metal goods, chemicals, and pharmaceuticals. Founded (1st cent. A.D.) by the Romans, it was later (1238–1794) the residence of the electors of Cologne. From 1949 to 1990, it was the capital of West Germany (see GERMANY). BEETHOVEN was born in Bonn.

Bonnard, Pierre [bônärd'], 1867–1947, French painter, lithographer, and illustrator. He excelled at domestic interiors that emphasized light effects similar in exuberance to IMPRESSIONISM, e.g., *Bowl of Fruit* (1933; Philadelphia Mus. Art). His late works are intensely colorful.

Bonneville Salt Flats, desert area in Tooele co., NW Utah, c.14 mi (22.5 km) long and 7 mi (11.2 km) wide. It is part of Great Salt Lake Desert, the former bed of Lake Bonneville, whose area, once c.19,500 sq mi (50,500 sq km), shrank at the end of the Pleistocene epoch. The smooth salt surface of the Flats is ideal for auto racing, and several world speed records have been set there.

Bonnie Prince Charlie: see under STUART, JAMES FRANCIS EDWARD.

bonsai, the art of cultivating dwarf trees, and the plants developed by this method. Bonsai, developed over 1,000 years ago in Japan, derives from the Chinese practice of growing miniature plants. In bonsai cultivation, the plants are kept small and in true proportion to their natural models by growing them in small containers, feeding and watering only enough for healthy growth, pruning, and forming branches to the desired shape by applying wire coils. The selection of containers, the plant's position in a container, and the choice of single plants or a group are important aesthetic considerations.

Bontemps, Arna, 1902–73, African-American writer; b. Alexandria, La. He is best remembered as the author of the novel *God Sends Sunday* (1931), the basis of the play *St. Louis Woman* (1946); and of *Black Thunder* (1936), a tragic account of the slave insurrection led by Gabriel Prosser in Richmond, Va., in 1800. Bontemps was also an editor, anthologizer, and historian.

booby, large, streamlined sea BIRD of the family Sulidae, called gannets in northern waters. Boobies have heavy bodies, long, pointed wings, long, wedge-shaped tails, and short, stout legs. They fish by diving on their prey from great heights and pursuing it under water. Gullible and unwary, as its name indicates, the booby is easy prey for hunters and is diminishing in number.

Book of Changes (I Ching), ancient Chinese book of prophecy and wisdom. Its earliest parts are thought to date from the century before CONFUCIUS. It consists of eight trigrams, corresponding to the powers of nature. They are used to interpret the future with the textual help of supplementary definitions, intuitions, and Confucian commentary.

Book of Common Prayer, title given to the service book used in the Church of ENGLAND and in other churches of the ANGLICAN COMMUNION. The first Prayer Book (1549), mainly the work of Thomas CRANMER, was essentially derived from the breviary and the missal. This was revised (1552), but was suppressed under MARY I. Revised under ELIZABETH I, it was again suppressed (1645–60) by the Commonwealth and the Protectorate. A new revision was made compulsory by the Act of Uniformity (1662). The first U.S. revision was adopted by the Episcopal Church in 1789; the latest edition is that of 1979.

book of hours, form of devotional book developed in the 14th cent. containing prayers and meditations appropriate to seasons, months, days, and hours. Many are masterpieces of illumination; among the greatest is *Très Riches Heures* (c.1415; Musée Condé, Chantilly), made by the LIMBOURG BROTHERS and other artists for the renowned collector Jean, duc de Berry.

Book of the Dead, Egyptian funerary literature. The texts consist of charms, spells, and formulas for use by the deceased in the afterworld. At first inscriptions, the texts were later papyrus rolls placed inside the mummy case. Essential ideas of Egyptian religion are known through them. The earliest collection is from the XVIII dynasty (1580–1350 B.C.).

Boole, George, 1815–64, English mathematician and logician. Boolean algebra, his form of symbolic LOGIC, is central to the study of the foundations of pure mathematics and is the basis of computer technology. Boole wrote *An Investigation of the Laws of Thought* (1854), as well as works on calculus and differential equations.

Boolean algebra, an abstract mathematical system primarily used in COMPUTER science and in expressing the relationships between SETS (groups of objects or concepts). The notational system was developed by the English mathematician George BOOLE about 1850 to permit an algebraic manipulation of logical statements. Such manipulation can demonstrate whether or not a statement is true and show how a complicated statement can be rephrased in a simpler, more convenient form without changing its meaning. When used in set theory, Boolean algebra can demonstrate the relationship between groups, indicating what is in each set alone, what is jointly contained in both, and what is contained in neither. The expression of electrical networks in Boolean notation has aided the development of switching theory and the design of computers.

Boone, Daniel, 1734–1820, American frontiersman; b. near Reading, Pa. In March 1775, as advance agent for the Transylvania Company, he blazed the WILDERNESS ROAD and founded Boonesboro, Ky. In 1779 he helped defend Boonesboro against Native American tribes. Boone moved (1799) to Missouri after his land titles in Kentucky were overturned. His legendary adventures, many disproved by historical scholarship, were popularized in a so-called autobiographical account (1784) by John Filson.

Booth, family prominent in the SALVATION ARMY. **William Booth,** 1829–1912, was an evangelist in London, where he and his wife, **Catherine Mumford Booth,** 1829–90, established (1865) a movement that became (1878) the Salvation Army. Their eldest son, **Bramwell Booth,** 1856–1929, succeeded his father in 1912 as general of this organization. Another son, **Ballington Booth,** 1859–1940, was commander of the Salvation Army in Australia (1885–87) and in the U.S. (1887–96), withdrawing (1896) to found the Volunteers of America. A daughter, **Evangeline Cory Booth,** 1865–1950, commander of the Salvation Army in Canada (1895–1904) and the U.S. (1904–34), was general (1934–39) of the international Salvation Army.

Booth, Junius Brutus, 1796–1852, Anglo-American actor. He came from England to the U.S. in 1821 and became the foremost tragic actor of his day. His son **Edwin Booth,** 1833–93, b. near Bel Air, Md., toured with his father and scored great successes in Shakespearean tragedies. His 100-night run of *Hamlet* in New York City in 1864 was famous. The next year he retired briefly from the stage because of the scandal involving his brother (see below). He built Booth's Theatre in New York City (1869) and was the founder (1888) and first president of the Players' Club. Another son, **John Wilkes Booth,** 1838–65, won acclaim in Shakespearean roles but is best known as the assassin of Abraham LINCOLN. A Southern sympathizer (unlike the rest of his family) during the CIVIL WAR, he plotted with six fellow conspirators to assassinate Union leaders. On Apr. 14, 1865, he shot Pres. Lincoln during a performance of *Our American Cousin* at Ford's Theater in Washington, D.C., vaulted to the stage (breaking a leg), and escaped. A search party cornered him in a burning barn near Bowling Green, Va., on Apr. 26, and Booth was fatally shot, either by himself or by one of his pursuers.

Bophuthatswana [bäpo͞othäswä'nä], black South African homeland, or BANTUSTAN, (1990 est. pop. 2,000,000), c.17,000 sq mi (44,000 sq km), declared independent by South Africa in 1977. Mmabatho is the capital. The "state," which has seven separate areas (one on the Botswana border), is the designated homeland for the Tswana people. South Africa forcibly reinstalled Kgosi Lucas Mangope as president after a 1988 coup attempt.

borage, common name for the Boraginaceae, a family of widely distributed herbs and tropical shrubs and trees characterized by rough or hairy stems; four-part fruits; and, usually, fragrant blossoms. Species of forget-me-not (*Myosotis*) and species of heliotrope (*Heliotropium*) are cultivated in and native to North America.

Borah, William Edgar, 1865–1940, U.S. senator from Idaho (1907–40); b. near Fairfield, Ill. Sometimes called "the great opposer," he was a Republican noted for his independent stands and his interest in foreign policy. He opposed the LEAGUE OF NATIONS, but advocated disarmament. Borah also opposed economic monopolies and the growth of big government.

borax or **sodium tetraborate decahydrate,** chemical compound ($Na_2B_4O_7{\cdot}10H_2O$) occurring as a colorless, crystalline salt or a white powder. Borax is used as an antiseptic, cleansing agent, water softener, corrosion inhibitor in anti freeze, and flux for silver soldering, and in the manufacture of fertilizers, Pyrex glass, and pharmaceuticals.

Bordeaux [bôrdō'], city (1990 pop. 210,336), capital of Gironde dept., SW France, on the Garonne R. It is a busy port, accessible to the Atlantic, with important shipyards and industries. Wine is its major product, with Bordeaux the generic name of the region's wine. A prosperous Roman city, it flourished (11th cent.) as the seat of the dukes of AQUITAINE. ELEANOR OF AQUITAINE precipitated war between France and the English, who ruled the city (1154–1453). The city reached its height of prosperity in the 18th cent. It was the temporary seat of French government in 1914 and 1940.

Borden, Gail, 1801–74, American inventor; b. Norwich, N.Y. His process (patented 1856) of evaporating MILK was of great value for the army during the Civil War, and its use spread rapidly afterward. Borden also patented processes for concentrating fruit juices and other beverages.

Borden, Lizzie Andrew, 1860–1927, American woman tried for the ax murders (1892) of her father and stepmother; b. Fall River, Mass. Claiming that she was out of the house when the murders occurred, she was acquitted. The case is unsolved.

Borden, Sir Robert Laird, 1854–1937, Canadian prime minister (1911–20). He headed the Conservative government (1911–17) and a Union coalition (1917–20) during World War I. It was largely through his efforts that CANADA and other British dominions attained new self-governing status.

Bordet, Jules [bôrdā'], 1870–1961, Belgian serologist and immunologist. He received the 1919 Nobel Prize in physiology or medicine for his work in immunity. With Octave Gengou he devised (1900) the technique of the complement-fixation reaction (applied by August WASSERMANN to the diagnosis of syphilis) and discovered (1906) the bacillus of whooping cough.

Borg, Björn, 1956–, Swedish tennis player. As a teenage star he led (1975) Sweden to its first Davis Cup victory. Before losing to John McEnroe in 1981, he captured five successive Wimbledon titles, a tournament record. He also won the French Open six times (1974–75, 1978–81) and U.S. Open three times (1974–76).

Borges, Jorge Luis [bôr'hās], 1899–86, Argentine poet, critic, and short-story writer. Perhaps the foremost contemporary Spanish-American author, he wrote his early poetry, beginning with *Fervor of Buenos Aires* (1923), under the influence of *ultraísmo,* a movement for pure poetry that followed MODERNISMO. He was director of the National Library and professor of English at the Univ. of Buenos Aires. His imaginative poetry is collected in *Selected Poems: 1923–1967* (1967). His philosophical and literary essays appear in such collections as *Other Inquisitions* (1952). He is known for his original short fiction, e.g., *A Universal History of Infamy* (1935), *Ficciones* (1944), *The Book Of Imaginary Beings* (1957), and *The Book of Sand* (1975).

Borghese [bōrgā'zā], noble Roman family. It produced one pope, Paul V; several cardinals; and many prominent citizens.

Borgia [bōr'jä], Spanish-Italian family whose members included the popes CALIXTUS III and ALEXANDER VI, and Saint Francis Borgia. **Cesare Borgia,** 1476–1507, a son of Pope Alexander VI, was an outstanding figure of the Italian Renaissance. A cardinal by 1493, Cesare resigned after the death (1498) of his elder brother (in whose murder he was probably involved) and entered politics. An ally of LOUIS XII of France, he overran the cities of Romagna. He then lured his chief enemies to a castle, where he had some of them strangled. He hoped to make his position independent of the papacy, but the death of his father and the election of Pope JULIUS II were fatal to his plans. Louis XII turned against him, and Julius demanded the surrender of Cesare's lands. Cesare was imprisoned in Spain, escaped, and found refuge (1506) with the king of Navarre, for whom he died fighting at Viana. Intelligent, cruel, treacherous, and opportunistic, he has long been considered the model of the Renaissance prince, the prototype of MACHIAVELLI's *Prince*. His sister was **Lucretia Borgia,** 1480–1519. Her first marriage was annulled (1497), and her second husband, Alfonso of Aragón, was murdered (1500) by her brother, Cesare Borgia. She then married (1501) Alfonso d'Este, who became (1505) the duke of Ferrara, and set up a brilliant court. Her beauty and kindness won her much esteem. The stories of her crimes and vices are unfounded, although she is best known for her wicked legend portrayed in dramas and operas.

Borglum, (John) Gutzon (de la Mothe), 1867–1941, American sculptor; b. Idaho. His first commission was a statue of Abraham Lincoln (Capitol, Wash., D.C.). A figurative sculptor, Borglum is famous for the monumental works he designed for, and helped to carve on, mountainsides, especially the enormous busts of four U.S. presidents at MOUNT RUSHMORE NATIONAL MEMORIAL, S.D., begun in 1927.

Boris, rulers of Bulgaria. **Boris I,** d. 907, khan ruler of Bulgaria (852–89), was a Christian convert and introduced Byzantine Christianity into Bulgaria. In 889 he abdicated, entering a monastery. **Boris III,** 1894–1943, czar (1918–43), ruled constitutionally until 1935 and thereafter as a dictator. He joined the Axis in 1940 and died mysteriously soon after visiting HITLER in Berlin.

Boris Godunov: see GODUNOV, BORIS.

Borlaug, Norman Ernest, 1914–, American agronomist; b. Cresco, Iowa. Associated with the Rockefeller Foundation in Mexico from 1944, he headed a team of scientists experimenting with improvement of grains. He won the 1970 Nobel Peace Prize for his efforts to eradicate hunger and build international prosperity. His "green revolution," using improved wheat seed, new types of higher-yield rice, and more efficient use of fertilizers and water, improved food production in many less-developed countries.

Bormann, Martin, 1900–1945, German NAZI leader. In 1942 he became HITLER's private secretary. Although he was rumored to have escaped to Argentina in 1945, his skeleton was unearthed and identified in West Berlin in 1973.

Born, Max, 1882–1970, German physicist. For his statistical interpretation of QUANTUM MECHANICS, he shared the 1954 Nobel Prize in physics. Born was head (1921–33) of the physics department at the Univ. of Göttingen. After Nazi policies forced him to leave Germany, he taught at Cambridge Univ. and the Univ. of Edinburgh before returning to Germany in 1954.

Borneo, island (1985 est. pop. 7,722,000), SE Asia, world's third largest island, c.287,000 sq mi (743,330 sq km), in the Malay Archipelago. It is divided among Indonesia, which holds about 70% of the island (called Kalimantan), Brunei, and the Malaysian states of Sabah and Sarawak. Dense jungles and rain forests cover much of the mountainous island, which reaches a high point of 13,455 ft (4,101 m) at Mt. Kinabalu. The hot, humid climate has a prolonged monsoon season lasting from Nov. to May. DYAKS occupy the sparsely populated interior; Malays predominate in coastal regions. Oil, discovered in 1888, and timber are the chief resources.

Borodin, Aleksandr Porfirevich [bôrôdyēn'], 1833–87, Russian composer. He was one of the group known as The FIVE. His principal works include the SYMPHONIC POEM *In the Steppes of Central Asia* (1880) and the unfinished opera *Prince Igor*.

Boroimhe, Brian: see BRIAN BORU.

boron (B), nonmetallic element, isolated by Sir Humphry DAVY in 1807. As a dark-brown to black amorphous powder, boron is more reactive than its jet-black to silver-gray crystalline metallike form. BORAX and boric acid are common compounds. Boron is used in the shielding material and in some control rods of nuclear reactors and in a light, strong boron fiber and plastic composite material. See ELEMENT (table); PERIODIC TABLE.

Borromini, Francesco, 1599–1677, major Italian BAROQUE architect. His innovations in palace and church architecture were influential in Italy and N Europe. Among his buildings is San Carlo alle Quattro Fontane, Rome, noted for its undulating rhythm of architectural elements within a geometric plan.

Boru, Brian: see BRIAN BORU.

borzoi, tall, swift HOUND; shoulder height, 26–31 in. (66–81.2 cm); weight, c.85 lb (38.6 kg). Its long, silky coat may be flat, wavy, or curly, and any color (usually white with markings). Developed in Russia in the early 17th cent. to hunt wolves and hares, it is also called a Russian wolfhound.

Bos, Jerom: see BOSCH, HIERONYMUS.

Bosch, Hieronymus, or **Jerom Bos** [bôs], c.1450–1516, Flemish painter. His surname was van Aeken. A great influence on Pieter Brueghel, the Elder (see BRUEGEL, family), and hailed in the 20th cent. as a forerunner of SURREALISM, Bosch had a passion for the grotesque and macabre. His paintings, e.g., *Adoration of the Magi* (Metropolitan Mus.), are filled with bizarre plants, animals, and figures suggested perhaps by folk legends or moralizing religious literature. He was a favorite of PHILIP II of Spain, who collected such works as *Garden of Earthly Delights* (Prado) and the *Temptation of St. Anthony* (Lisbon).

Bose, Sir Jagadis Chunder, 1858–1937, Indian physicist and plant physiologist. Professor of physical science (1885–1915) at Presidency College, Calcutta, he is noted for his researches in plant life, especially his comparison of the responses of plant and animal tissue to various stimuli. One of his inventions is the crescograph, a device for measuring plant growth.

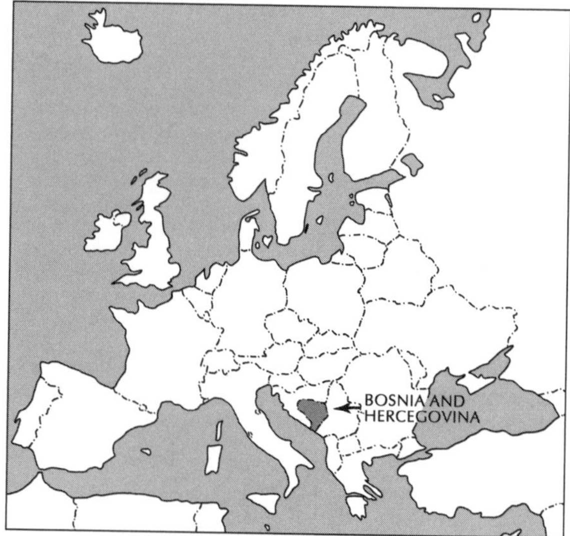

Bosnia and Hercegovina [bŏz'neə, hĕrtsəgōvē'nə], country (1991 est. pop. 4,364,000), 19,741 sq mi (51,129 sq km), S Europe, on the Balkan peninsula; formerly a constituent republic of Yugoslavia. The country is bordered by Croatia (SW, W, and N) and Yugoslavia (E and SE) and is almost entirely landlocked except for a narrow, undeveloped outlet to the Adriatic along the Neretva R. Since independence (1992), the nation has been splintered and devastated by ethnic warfare. SARAJEVO is the capital and largest city. Bosnia lies to the north of Hercegovina; both are largely within the Dinaric Alps. Despite rich deposits of lignite and iron, copper, and other ores and extensive hydroelectric resources, the republic was one of the poorer areas of Yugoslavia. About half of the land is forested; one fourth is cultivated, with grains, tobacco, and cotton among the major crops. Bosnia is ethnically diverse, but ethnic fighting since independence has displaced many, especially Bosnian Muslims. About 40% of the population are Bosnian Muslims, 30% are Serbs, and 18% are Croats; all speak Serbo-Croatian. The Serbs largely belong to the Serbian Orthodox Church, and the Croats to the Roman Catholic Church.

History. The region, part of the Roman province of Illyricum, was settled (7th cent.) by the Serbs and was independent by the 12th cent. By the late 14th cent. Bosnia reached the height of its power, but the area fell to the Turks in the late 15th cent. and many Bosnians accepted Islam. Medieval social structures and serfdom persisted into the 19th cent., when a peasant revolt (1875) led to the Russo-Turkish war of 1877–78. Bosnia and Hercegovina were placed (1878) under Austro-Hungarian administration, and Austria annexed the region in 1908. The assassination (1914) of Austrian Archduke FRANCIS FERDINAND by a Serbian nationalist in Sarajevo precipitated WORLD WAR I. Bosnia and Hercegovina were annexed to Serbia in 1918. During WORLD WAR II they were (1941–45) part of the German puppet state of CROATIA. In 1946 they were combined as one of the six constituent republics of Yugoslavia. After Slovenia and Croatia left Yugoslavia (1991), Bosnians voted (1992) for independence, and ethnic warfare erupted. Well-armed Serbs, many from the Yugoslav army, gained control of over two thirds of Bosnia, and Croats seized about half of the remainder. Both established ethnic "republics," and Serbs began exiling, imprisoning, and killing non-Serbs, especially Muslims, under a policy of "ethnic cleansing." Atrocities also occurred in Croat- and Muslim-held areas. Bosnian government forces also fought (1993) Muslim rebels for control of Bihać, a largely Muslim enclave in NW Bosnia; the rebels had signed peace accords with Serb and Croat forces. In 1993, after increased successes by government forces, regular army units from Croatia were reported fighting in Bosnia.

boson, any of a group of ELEMENTARY PARTICLES that have integral values of the quantum mechanical property called spin and are "gregarious" in that an unlimited number of them can exist in the same quantum state. Bosons, which include the PHOTON, gluon, W AND Z PARTICLES and the proposed graviton, carry the fundamental FORCES of nature. Bose-Einstein statistics describe the behavior of systems of bosons. See FERMION, STATISTICAL MECHANICS.

Bosporus, strait, c.20 mi (30 km) long and c.2,100 ft (640 m) wide at its narrowest, separating European and Asian Turkey. The fortified strait connects the Black Sea with the Sea of Marmara. As a part (with the DARDANELLES) of a passage linking the BLACK and MEDITERRANEAN seas, it is a critically important shipping lane for Russia and Ukraine. A bridge (3,524 ft/1,074 m long) spans the Bosporus at Istanbul, near the southern end of the strait.

Boston, city (1990 pop. 574,283; met. area 2,870,911), state capital and seat of Suffolk co., E Mass., on Boston Bay; inc. 1822. The largest city of New England, it is a major financial, government, and educational center, and a leading port. Industries include publishing, food processing, and the manufacture of shoes, textiles, machinery, and electronic equipment. Established by John WINTHROP as the main colony of the MASSACHUSETTS BAY COMPANY in 1630, Boston was an early center of American PURITANISM, with a vigorous intellectual life. A focus of opposition to the British, it was the scene of several actions in the AMERICAN REVOLUTION. The city prospered in the 19th cent., and shipbuilding, commercial, and industrial magnates such as the Cabots, Lowells, and Lodges patronized the arts, making Boston the "Athens of America." The arrival of many immigrants (at first mainly Irish) helped transform Boston into an industrial metropolis with expanded city limits. Today the city cherishes its landmarks, among them Paul REVERE's house, Old North Church, and Faneuil Hall. Boston's great cultural institutions include its Museum of Fine Arts, Symphony Orchestra, Public Library, and Athenaeum. Boston Univ., Northeastern Univ., New England Medical Center, and Harvard Medical School are among the institutions that make Boston world famous as an educational, medical, and research center.

Boston Massacre, 1770, incident prior to the AMERICAN REVOLUTION in which five members of a rioting crowd were killed by British soldiers sent to Boston to maintain order and enforce the TOWNSHEND ACTS.

Boston Tea Party, Boston, Mass., Dec. 16, 1773, a protest against the British tea tax retained after the repeal of the TOWNSHEND ACTS. Angry colonists disguised as Native Americans boarded three tea ships and threw the tea into Boston harbor.

Boston terrier, small, lively NONSPORTING DOG; shoulder height, 14–17 in. (35.6–43.2 cm); weight, 13–25 lb (5.9–11.3 kg). Its short, smooth coat may be brindle or black, with white markings. One of the few breeds native to the U.S., it was developed by cross-breeding in the mid-19th cent.

Boswell, James, 1740–95, Scottish author; b. Edinburgh. The son of a judge, he reluctantly studied law and practiced throughout his life. His true interest was in a literary career and in associating with the great individuals of the time. He met Samuel JOHNSON in 1763 and, having himself achieved fame with his *Account of Corsica* (1768), produced *Journal of a Tour of the Hebrides with Samuel Johnson, LL.D.* (1785). His great work, *The Life of Samuel Johnson, LL.D.* appeared in 1791. Boswell recorded Johnson's conversation so minutely that Johnson is better remembered today for his sayings than for his own literary works. The curious combination of Boswell's own character (he was vainglorious and dissolute) and his genius at biography has led later critics to call him the greatest of all biographers. Masses of Boswell manuscript, discovered in the 20th cent. near Dublin, have enhanced his reputation.

botany, science devoted to the study of plants, a major branch of BIOLOGY. In the 17th cent. the work of LINNAEUS on the CLASSIFICATION of organisms contributed greatly to the growth of the science, and the introduction of the MICROSCOPE marked the beginning of the study of plant anatomy and cells. Modern botany has expanded into all areas of biology, e.g., plant breeding and GENETICS. Practical areas of botanical study include AGRICULTURE, AGRONOMY, FORESTRY, and HORTICULTURE.

Botany Bay, inlet, New South Wales, SE Australia, just S of Sydney. It was visited in 1770 by Capt. James COOK and named for the interesting flora on its shores. Australia's first penal colony, often called Botany Bay, was at Sydney.

Botha, Louis [bō'tə], 1862–1919, South African soldier and statesman. He commanded the Boer troops in the SOUTH AFRICAN WAR (1899–1902). He was prime minister (1907–10) of the Transvaal and, as leader of the Unionist party, prime minister (1910–19) of the Union of SOUTH AFRICA.

Botha, Pieter Willem, 1916–, South African politician, prime minister (1978–84) and president (1984–89). Leader of the National party, he worked for limited reforms in his nation's policy of APARTHEID and continued the creation of BANTUSTANS as homelands for the black population. Botha also served (1965–80) as defense minister.

Bothwell, James Hepburn, 4th **earl of,** 1536?–1578, Scottish nobleman, third husband of MARY QUEEN OF SCOTS. After the murder of her secretary RIZZIO by conspirators, among them her husband, Lord DARNLEY, Mary trusted only Bothwell. Accused of murdering Darnley, Bothwell was acquitted in a rigged trial and married Mary (1567). The Scottish aristocracy attacked him and forced Mary to give him up. He fled to Denmark, where he was imprisoned and died insane.

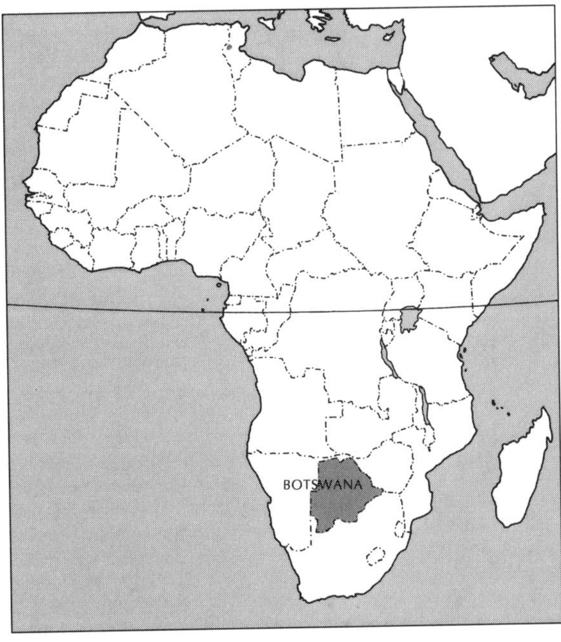

Botswana [bŏtswä'nə], officially Republic of Botswana, republic (1992 est. pop. 1,292,000), 231,804 sq mi (600,372 sq km), S central Africa, bordered by Namibia (W and N), Zambia (N), Zimbabwe (E), and South Africa (S and E). GABORONE is the capital. The terrain is mostly an arid plateau (c.3,000 ft/910 m high) of rolling land, with hills in the east, the KALAHARI Desert in the south and west, and the Okavango Swamp in the northwest. Cattle-raising is the chief agricultural activity, and beef is exported. Crop production is severely hampered by drought and lack of water resources; cotton, peanuts, and sunflowers are the main cash crops. Botswana has vast mineral resources, discovered in the 1960s, and mining has developed rapidly, making Botswana one of the wealthiest S African nations. Diamonds are the principal export, and copper, nickel, asbestos, manganese, and coal are also extracted. Because of its landlocked location, however, the country remains economically dependent on its neighbors, particularly SOUTH AFRICA. The population is mainly Tswana, who speak a Bantu language and are divided into eight major groups. English and Tswana are the official languages. The majority of Botswanans are Christian, but some adhere to traditional beliefs.

History. The region was originally inhabited by the San (Bushmen), who were supplanted by the Tswana in the 18th cent. In the early 1800s Khama, chief of the largest Tswana tribe, curbed expansion by the Zulu and Ndebele tribes into the territory and established a fairly unified state. A new threat arose in the late 19th cent. when, after gold was discovered in the region (1867), neighboring Transvaal sought to annex parts of Botswana. This move was opposed by the British, who took the area under supervision (1885) as a protectorate called Bechuanaland. A British plan to incorporate Bechuanaland into the Union of South Africa was eventually abandoned because of South Africa's apartheid policy, and in 1966, as Botswana, it gained full independence under the leadership of Sir Seretse Khama (grandson of Khama) of the Botswana Democratic party. After his death (1980), he was succeeded as president by Quett Masire, who was last reelected in 1989.

Böttger, Johann Friedrich [bôt'gər], 1682–1719, German chemist and originator of Dresden china. He developed various glazes, used gold and silver decoration, and in 1715 perfected white PORCELAIN.

Botticelli, Sandro [bôt"tĭchĕl'lē], c.1444–1510, Florentine RENAISSANCE painter; b. Alessandro di Mariano Filipepi. He was a student of Fra Filippo LIPPI, whose influence can be seen in the delicate coloration of his early work; this later gave way to the more vigorous style of Pollaiuolo (see POLLAIUOLO, family) and VERROCCHIO, e.g., *Portrait of a Young Man* (Uffizi). He became a favorite of the MEDICI and was influenced by their Neoplatonic circle. Botticelli was one of the great colorists and a master of rhythmic line. His enchanting mythological scenes, *Spring, Birth of Venus,* and *Mars and Venus* allude to the triumph of love and reason over brutal instinct. In his last years, his popularity probably declined, and he turned to religious scenes. His piety is evident in the *Nativity* (National Gall., London) and *Last Communion of St. Jerome* (Metropolitan Mus.). In the 19th cent. he was rediscovered by the PRE-RAPHAELITES.

botulism, acute, often fatal food poisoning from ingestion of food containing toxins produced by *Clostridium botulinum* bacteria. Most cases are caused by canned food that has been improperly processed. The disease causes disturbances in vision, speech, and swallowing and, ultimately, paralysis of respiratory muscles, leading to suffocation. Treatment involves the administration of antitoxin as soon as possible after exposure to contaminated food.

Bouaké, city (1983 est. pop. 275,000), central Côte d'Ivoire. It is a commercial and transportation center linked by rail to ABIDJAN. Farm products are processed in the town, and gold and manganese are found nearby. A variant spelling is Bwake.

Bouchard, Lucien, 1938–, French-Canadian separatist leader. He served under Mulroney as Canada's ambassador to France (1985–88) and environment minister (1989–90). In 1990 he broke with the Progressive Conversatives over the failed Meech Lake Accord (see CANADA) and formed the Bloc Québécois, a Quebec separatist party. In the 1993 elections the party became the second largest in the Canadian parliament.

Boucher, François [bo͞oshā'], 1703–70, French painter. Boucher's art reflected the spirit of his day: elegant, frivolous, and artificial. A prodigy, he was influenced by WATTEAU and became the most fashionable and prolific artist of his day, producing a vast number of pictures, decorations, tapestry designs, stage settings for ballet and opera, and fine ETCHINGS. His best-known works are brilliant, voluptuous decorations, e.g., those in the Frick Collection (N.Y.C.). FRAGONARD was his pupil.

Boudin, Eugène Louis [bo͞odăN'], 1824–98, French painter. His small paintings of Brittany beach scenes are noted for their pervasive clarity and directness. He painted from nature and greatly influenced MONET. Examples of his work are in the Metropolitan Museum.

Bougainville, Louis Antoine de [bo͞ogăNvēl'], 1729–1811, French navigator. He was an aide-de-camp to Gen. MONTCALM in Canada. From 1767 to 1769 he made a voyage around the world, rediscovering the SOLOMON ISLANDS, the largest of which is named for him. In the AMERICAN REVOLUTION he fought Adm. Hood at Martinique. His *Description of a Voyage around the World* (2 vol., 1771–72) popularized the theories of ROUSSEAU.

Bougainville [bo͞o'gənvĭl], volcanic island (1981 est. pop. 110,000), c.3,880 sq mi (10,050 sq km), SW Pacific, largest of the SOLOMON ISLANDS but politically part of PAPUA NEW GUINEA. Rugged and forested, it produces copra, rubber, copper, coffee, and cocoa. French navigator Louis de Bougainville explored (1768) the island, which became (1884) German, then (1914) Australian, and was held by Japan in World War II. A bloody secessionist uprising, begun in 1989, continued into the 1990s.

bougainvillea or **bougainvillaea,** chiefly tropical plant (genus *Bougainvillaea*) of the four-o'clock family. Bougainvilleas are woody vines with brilliant purple or red bracts.

Boulanger, Nadia, 1887–1979, French conductor and musician. As the teacher of such American composers as Aaron COPLAND and Virgil THOMSON, she profoundly influenced American music. She was noted for her teaching of composition and for her conducting of choral works.

Boulder, city (1990 pop. 83,312), seat of Boulder co., N central Colo.; inc. 1871. It is a major ROCKY MOUNTAIN resort, and the site of the Univ. of Colo. and the National Center for Atmospheric Research. Manufactures include aircraft and electronic equipment.

Boulez, Pierre [bo͞olĕz'], 1925–, French composer and conductor. His works apply the techniques of SERIAL MUSIC not only to melody and COUNTERPOINT but also to RHYTHM and dynamics. They include *Pli selon pli* (1957–62) and *Mémoriales* (1973–75). From 1971 to 1977 he was music director of the New York Philharmonic (see ORCHESTRA, table). He headed (1975–92) the Institute for Research and Coordination of Acoustics and Music at the BEAUBORG, Paris, where he developed equipment for the electronic manipulation of musical sound.

Boulogne, Jean: see BOLOGNA, GIOVANNI.

Boult, Sir Adrian, 1889–1983, English conductor. He led the BBC Symphony Orchestra (1930–50) and the London Philharmonic (1950–57). His handbook on the technique of conducting appeared in 1968.

Boumedienne, Houari [bo͞omĕdēĕn'], 1932?–78, Algerian president and prime minister (1965–78). He came to power in a coup that toppled Ahmed BEN BELLA. His government assumed a rigorous anti-Israeli stance.

Bounty, British naval ship, scene of a noted mutiny (1789) while on a trading voyage in the Pacific. Capt. BLIGH and 18 crew members were set adrift in a small boat; they sailed 3,618 mi (5,822 km) to TIMOR. Some of the mutineers were captured; others settled on PITCAIRN ISLAND.

Bourassa, Henri [bo͞oräsä'], 1868–1952, Canadian politician and publisher. He founded the opposition Nationalist party in QUEBEC, which caused the fall (1911) of the Liberal government of Sir Wilfrid LAURIER. He also founded (1910) and edited a Montreal daily newspaper, *Le Devoir.*

Bourassa, Robert, 1933–, Canadian political leader. Elected (1966) to the Quebec legislature, he became (1970) leader of the Quebec Liberal party and was provincial premier until 1976. Returning to politics in 1983, he again served as Quebec's premier (1986–94), advocating the province's autonomy within Canada.

Bourbaki, Nicolas, collective pseudonym of a group of French mathematicians who in 1939 began publishing a highly influential general survey of mathematics. The writers, whose identities remain secret, have attempted to develop mathematics from a few broad axioms and have divided it into general structural categories, rather than adhering to traditional mathematical classifications.

Bourbon, royal family that ruled in France, Spain, the TWO SICILIES, and Parma; a cadet branch of the CAPETIANS. It takes its name from the now ruined castle of Bourbon in France. In 1272 Robert of Clermont, sixth son of LOUIS IX of France, married the heiress of Bourbon. His son Louis was created (1327) 1st duc de Bourbon. A younger son of the first duke founded the line of Bourbon-Vendôme. His descendant Antoine de Bourbon, 1518–62, duke of Vendôme, became king of Navarre by marrying (1548) Jeanne d'Albret, later queen of NAVARRE. From his brother Louis descend the houses of CONDÉ and Conti. Antoine's son became (1589) the first Bourbon king of France as HENRY IV. His direct descendants ruled France (except from 1792 to 1814) until 1830, when CHARLES X was deposed, and died out in 1883 with Henri, comte de Chambord. The younger branch of Bourbon-Orléans gave France King LOUIS PHILIPPE. The house of **Bourbon-Spain** began in 1700 when LOUIS XIV's grandson PHILIP V ascended the Spanish throne. The succession in Spain was contested (19th cent.) by the CARLISTS against ISABELLA II. ALFONSO XIII was deposed in 1931, but the monarchy was restored in 1975 with his grandson JUAN CARLOS I. The house of **Bourbon-Sicily,** sprung from the Spanish line, was founded (1759) by Ferdinand I of the Two Sicilies and ceased to rule when Francis II was deposed (1860). The house of **Bourbon-Parma** was founded (1748) in the duchy of Parma by a younger son of Philip V of Spain. Robert, the fifth duke in the line, was deposed in 1859.

bourbon: see WHISKEY.

Bourdelle, Émile Antoine [bo͝ordĕl'], 1861–1929, French sculptor. He studied with RODIN and achieved his greatest success with Greek- and Gothic-inspired heroic monuments, e.g., *Hercules* (cast; Metropolitan Mus.), and with portrait heads.

bourgeoisie, name given in Europe to the middle class. Emerging among the merchants and craftsmen of medieval cities, it played a major role in the 16th cent. in uprooting vestiges of FEUDALISM and from the late 18th cent. in spearheading democratic reform. Following the INDUSTRIAL REVOLUTION, the high bourgeoisie (industrialists and bankers) came to be distinguished from the petty bourgeoisie (tradespeople and white-collar workers). From the time of MOLIÈRE, the bourgeoisie was ridiculed by some for its preoccupation with status and material gain. In Karl MARX's theory of class struggle, it was seen as an ultimately reactionary force trying to prevent the ascendancy of the wage-earning proletariat.

Bourguiba, Habib, 1903–, president of TUNISIA (1957–87). As leader of Tunisia's nationalist movement after 1934, he was several times imprisoned and forced to leave the country. He became premier when Tunisia achieved independence in 1956. A year later he deposed the bey and became president.

Bourke-White, Margaret, 1904–71, American photojournalist; b. N.Y.C. On the staff of *Fortune, Life,* and *Time,* she produced notable photographs of World War II, the rural South during the Great Depression, mining in South Africa, and guerrilla warfare in Korea, as well as portraits of world leaders.

Bournonville, Auguste [bo͝ornôNvēl'l], 1805–79, Danish ballet dancer, choreographer, and teacher. He studied in Copenhagen and Paris before joining (1828) the ROYAL DANISH BALLET. As a soloist, he developed a distinctive style. He choreographed over 50 works.

bourse: see STOCK EXCHANGE.

Boutros-Ghali, Boutros, 1922–, Egyptian government official and diplomat, secretary general of the UNITED NATIONS (1992–). A professor of international law at Cairo Univ. (1949–79), he became Egyptian minister of state for foreign affairs in 1977 and was part of the Egyptian delegation that negotiated (1978) the CAMP DAVID ACCORDS with Israel. He also served as Egypt's delegate to the UN and other international bodies and conferences. In May 1991, a few months before his election as UN secretary general, he was appointed Egypt's deputy prime minister for foreign affairs. The first African and Arab head of the UN, Boutros-Ghali has moved to reorganize and streamline the Secretariat (see UNITED NATIONS, table 2) and strengthen the UN's peacekeeping role.

Bovet, Daniele [bōvā'], 1907–92, Italian pharmacologist; b. Switzerland. He was awarded the 1957 Nobel Prize in physiology or medicine for work in developing antihistamines, sulfa drugs, and curare derivatives and other muscle relaxants for use in surgery. He also studied the effects of mental illness on the brain's chemistry.

Bowdler, Thomas, 1754–1825, English editor. His prudish textual expurgations, especially of Shakespeare and the Bible, gave rise to the term *bowdlerize*.

Bowen, Elizabeth, 1899–1973, Anglo-Irish author; b. Dublin. Her complex psychological novels include *The Hotel* (1927), *The House in Paris* (1936), *The Death of the Heart* (1938), and *The Heat of the Day* (1949). She also wrote short stories and reminiscences.

Bowie, James, c.1796–1836, Texas hero; b. Logan co., Ky. He was a leader of the Americans in TEXAS who opposed Mexican rule. A colonel in the Texas Revolution (1835–36), he died at the ALAMO. Legend credits him with inventing the bowie knife.

Bowles, Paul, 1910–, American author; b. N.Y.C. Originally a composer, he is best known for his fiction. A longtime resident of Morocco, Bowles often records the collision between the civilized and the primitive. Among his many works are the novel *The Sheltering Sky* (1949) and the short-story collection *The Delicate Prey* (1950). His wife, **Jane Auer Bowles,** 1917–73, b. N.Y.C., was also a writer. Her original, idiosyncratic works include *Two Serious Ladies* (1943), a novel, and *In the Summer House* (1954), a play.

bowling, indoor sport, also called **tenpins,** in which a ball is rolled at 10 maple pins down an alley of polished wood. A regulation alley is 41 to 42 in. (104.1 to 106.7 cm) wide and 60 ft (18.3 m) from the foul line to the head pin. A ball, usually weighing 16 lb (7.26 kg) and having three finger holes, is rolled at the pins, set up in a triangular array. Scoring is based on the number of pins knocked down; a perfect game is 300 points. Bowling originated in ancient Germany and was introduced in America by the Dutch. The American Bowling Congress (founded 1895) and the Women's International Bowling Congress (1916) hold yearly championships. Duck pins, candle pins, and barrel pins are similar games played with much smaller balls and pins.

Bowman, Isaiah, 1878–1950, American geographer; b. Canada. He taught at Yale (1905–15), was director of the American Geographical Society (1915–35), and was president of Johns Hopkins Univ. (1935–48). He was an adviser to Pres. Wilson at Versailles and an adviser to the Dept. of State in World War II. One of the great modern authorities on political geography, he wrote on many subjects, including the Andes, the Atacama desert, and forest physiography.

box, common name for the Buxaceae, a family of trees and shrubs with leathery green leaves, native to tropical and subtropical regions of the Old World and Central America. Boxes (genus *Buxus*) are widely cultivated as hedge plants and for their close-grained, strong hardwood. Boxwood takes a high polish and is used for wood engraving, carving, and turning, and for making musical instruments.

boxer, medium-sized, muscular WORKING DOG; shoulder height, 21–25 in. (53.3–63.5 cm); weight, 60–75 lb (27.2–34 kg). Its short, smooth coat is fawn or brindle, often with white markings. First used for fighting, the breed originated in 16th-cent. Europe and was perfected in 19th-cent. Germany.

Boxer Uprising, 1898–1900, antiforeign movement in China. By the late 19th cent. the West and Japan had wide interests in China. The dowager empress TZ'U HSI favored expelling the foreigners and encouraged an antiforeign society called I Ho Ch'uan [Chinese, = righteous, harmonious fists] or, in English, the Boxers. The movement grew menacing in 1899, and in June 1900 some 140,000 Boxers occupied Beijing and besieged Westerners and Chinese Christians there. The siege was lifted in August by an international force of British, French, Russian, U.S., German, and Japanese troops. In 1901 China was compelled to pay an indemnity of $333 million, to amend commercial treaties in favor of foreign nations, and to allow foreign troops to be posted in Beijing.

boxing, sport of fighting with fists, also called pugilism and prizefighting. Boxers compete in a roped-off area, or ring, about 20 ft (6.1 m) square, and fight for a prescribed number of 3-min rounds, separated by 1-min rest periods. Bouts may be decided by a knockout, when a floored contestant is unable to rise within 10 sec, or by the decision of the officials. Professional boxers are divided into eight weight classes, ranging from flyweight (under 112 lb/50.81 kg) to heavyweight (over 175 lb/79.38 kg). One of the oldest forms of competition known, boxing died out after the fall of Rome but was revived in England in the early 18th cent. Modern boxing began with the code of rules introduced (1865) by the marquess of QUEENSBERRY, which called for the use of gloves. In the U.S., boxing was illegal for many years before New York became the first state to legalize it (1896). Today professional boxing is regulated in each state by an athletic or boxing commission. Boxing has been an Olympic sport since 1904.

boyars, upper nobility in Russia from the 10th to the 17th cent. They occupied the highest state offices, advising the princes of Kiev through a council. Although they retained their influence after power shifted (14th–15th cent.) to Moscow, it was gradually eroded; PETER I abolished the rank.

Boyce, William, c.1710–1779, English composer. The major English-born composer of his day, he wrote symphonies, stage works, and much vocal music. His *Cathedral Music* (3 vol., 1760–68) is a compilation of English church music.

Boyd, Louise Arner, 1887–1972, American arctic explorer; b. San Rafael, Calif. She led a series of scientific explorations on the east coast of GREENLAND (1933–41). In 1955 she became the first woman to fly over the NORTH POLE.

Boyd Orr, John Boyd Orr, 1st **Baron,** 1880–1971, British nutritionist and agronomist. He made notable contributions to the science of nutrition and to the solution of world food problems, winning the 1949 Nobel Peace Prize for advocating a world food policy based on need rather than trade interests. He was director general (1946–47) of the UN Food and Agriculture Organization.

Boyle, Robert, 1627–91, Anglo-Irish physicist and chemist. Often referred to as the father of modern chemistry, he separated chemistry from alchemy and gave the first precise definitions of a chemical element, a chemical reaction, and chemical analysis. He invented a vacuum pump and used it in the discovery (1662) of what is known as **Boyle's law** (see GAS LAWS). His diverse experimental and theoretical work supplemented Sir Isaac NEWTON's achievements in establishing the dominance of mechanistic theory.

Boy Scouts, organization of boys from 7 to 18 years of age, founded (1908) in Great Britain by Sir Robert BADEN-POWELL, incorporated 1910 in the U.S. Activities of the Boy Scouts aim at mental, moral, and physical development, stressing outdoor skills and training in citizenship and lifesaving. The basic scout unit is a troop of about 15 boys, under the leadership of an adult scoutmaster. There is also a coeducational program for young adults between the ages of 14 and 21. In 1993 there were some 4.1 million Boy Scouts in the U.S. The Supreme Court affirmed the organization's right to limit membership to those who believe in God in 1993. See also GIRL SCOUTS.

boysenberry: see BRAMBLE.

Bozeman Trail, a shortcut through Native American lands from the East to the goldfields of Colorado and Montana, made by John M. Bozeman in 1862–63. The trail was used by a few parties, but after the Fetterman Massacre (1866) it was abandoned.

Br, chemical symbol of the element BROMINE.

Bradbury, Ray, 1920–, American science fiction writer; b. Waukegan, Ill. His fiction skillfully combines poetic fantasy with criticism of society and technology. His best-known works include *The Martian Chronicles* (1950), a short story collection, and the novel *Fahrenheit 451* (1953).

Braddock, Edward, 1695–1755, British general in the FRENCH AND INDIAN WARS. While on an expedition (1755) to take Fort Duquesne from the French, he was set upon by a force of some 900 French and Native Americans at the Monongahela R. Many of his troops bolted; more than half were killed, and he was mortally wounded.

Bradford, William, 1590–1657, governor of Plymouth Colony; b. England. He succeeded John CARVER as governor in 1621 and was reelected 30 times. He was largely responsible for the success of the colony. His *History of Plymouth Plantation* (first published 1856) is famous.

Bradford, William, 1663–1752, English printer in the American colonies. He emigrated (1685) and set up the first press in Philadelphia. Moving to New York City (c.1693), he became royal printer, and issued some 400 items over 50 years, including the first American BOOK OF COMMON PRAYER (1710). In 1725 he began the *Gazette,* the first New York newspaper. His son, **Andrew Bradford,** 1686–1742, b. Philadelphia, established his own press in 1712. In 1719 he began the *American Weekly Mercury,* the first Pennsylvania newspaper. Imprisoned for political publishing, he defended himself, establishing a precedent for ZENGER. **William Bradford,** 1722–91, grandson of William and nephew of Andrew, founded in Philadelphia the anti-British *Weekly Advertiser,* and became a leader of the SONS OF LIBERTY and printer to the first CONTINENTAL CONGRESS.

Bradford, city (1991 pop. 457,344), West Yorkshire, N central England. A center of the worsted industry since the Middle Ages, Bradford now also produces synthetic fabrics, machinery, automobiles, and other manufactures.

Bradley, Francis Herbert, 1846–1924, English philosopher. His metaphysics was influenced by HEGEL. In *Appearance and Reality* (1893) he held that IDEALISM, in which the world of appearance is characterized by apparent contradictions, is opposed to the absolute, in which all contradictions are transcended.

Bradley, James, 1693–1762, English astronomer. He discovered the ABERRATION OF STARLIGHT (announced in 1729) and the NUTATION, or "nodding," of the earth's axis (announced in 1748). Bradley became astronomer royal and director of the Royal Greenwich Observatory in 1742.

Bradley, Omar Nelson, 1893–1981, U.S. general; b. Clark, Mo. During WORLD WAR II, he led the U.S. 1st Army in the invasion of Normandy (1944). He was chairman (1949–53) of the Joint Chiefs of Staff and became general of the army in 1950.

Bradley, Tom (Thomas Bradley), 1917–, African-American politician; b. Calvert, Tex. A former police officer and a lawyer, he served (1963–73) on the Los Angeles city council. In 1973 he was elected mayor of Los Angeles, becoming the city's first African-American mayor. A liberal Democrat, he was reelected four times and served until 1993. He ran unsuccessfully for governor of California in 1982 and 1986.

Bradley, William (Bill), 1943–, U.S. politician; b. Crystal City, Mo. After a successful basketball career with the New York Knicks (1967–77), he was elected (1978) Democratic senator from New Jersey. He actively supported passage of the tax reform act of 1986.

Bradstreet, Anne (Dudley), c.1612–1672, American poet; b. Northampton, England; came to Massachusetts with her father and husband, both later governors of the colony. The first important woman author in America, she is known for poems that, while derivative and formal, are often realistic and genuine. Her volumes of verse include *The Tenth Muse Lately Sprung Up in America* (1650) and *Several Poems* (1678).

Brady, Diamond Jim (James Buchanan Brady), 1856–1917, American financier; b. N.Y.C. After amassing a fortune selling railroad supplies, he collected diamonds and other jewels and became famous for his lavish life-style. He funded (1912) the Brady Urological Institute at Johns Hopkins Hospital (Baltimore).

Brady, Mathew B., c.1823–1896, American photographer; b. Warren co., N.Y. Brady opened his New York City studio in 1844 and gained widespread fame as a portraitist. He photographed Pres. LINCOLN often and produced an invaluable record of the CIVIL WAR, now in the Library of Congress.

Braga, Teófilo, 1843–1924, Portuguese intellectual and political leader. His teachings and writings, e.g., his general history of Portuguese literature (10 vol., 1870–71), exerted a great influence on Portuguese intellectual life. A republican and anticlericalist, he was the first president of the new republic of Portugal (1910–11; 1915).

Braganza [brəgän'zä], royal house that ruled PORTUGAL (1640–1910) and BRAZIL (1822–89). The line was descended from Alfonso, the natural son of JOHN I, and its first king was JOHN IV. The family's Brazilian rulers were PEDRO I and his son, PEDRO II.

Bragg, Braxton, 1817–76, Confederate general in the U.S. CIVIL WAR; b. Warrenton, N.C. As commander of the Army of Tennessee, he tried unsuccessfully (1862) to invade Kentucky. In the CHATTANOOGA CAMPAIGN, he was defeated (1863) by Gen. GRANT. He then became military adviser to Jefferson DAVIS.

Bragg, Sir William Henry, 1862–1942, English physicist. He was

Matthew Brady photo of Union naval officers in the Civil War

on the faculties of the Univ. of Adelaide, Australia, the Univ. of Leeds, and the Univ. of London and director from 1923 of the Royal Institution's research laboratory. With his son, **Sir William Lawrence Bragg,** 1890–1971, he shared the 1915 Nobel Prize in physics for studies, with the X-ray spectrometer, of X-ray spectra and of crystal structure. The younger Bragg was professor of physics at Victoria Univ. (Manchester) and Cambridge and was director (1938–53) of the Cavendish Laboratory at Cambridge.

Brahe, Tycho [brä], 1546–1601, Danish astronomer. His exact observations of the planets were the basis for KEPLER'S LAWS of planetary motion. Studies of the moon's motion and of a supernova (1572) and improvements of instruments were among his contributions. Brahe never fully accepted the COPERNICAN SYSTEM, compromising between that and the PTOLEMAIC SYSTEM. In his system, the earth was the immobile body around which the sun revolved, and the five planets then known revolved around the sun.

Brahma [brä'mə], one of the supreme gods of HINDUISM; in the Hindu trinity he is the creator (see also SHIVA; VISHNU).

Brahman or **Brahma,** in VEDANTA, the ultimate reality or Self from which the world has come into being. See HINDUISM.

Brahman or **Brahmin,** member of the highest, or priestly, caste of the Hindus; see HINDUISM.

Brahmaputra, major river of S Asia, flowing c.1,800 mi (2,900 km) from the Kailas range of the Himalayas to join the GANGES R. at a vast delta on the Bay of BENGAL. It is called Yarlung Zangbo in Tibet (where it forms the principal river valley), the Brahmaputra in Assam (NE India), and the Jamuna in Bangladesh. The river's lower course is sacred to Hindus. Large craft navigate the river c.800 mi (1,290 km) upstream.

Brahms, Johannes [brämz], 1833–97, German composer, ranked among the foremost masters. He earned a living in Vienna as a moderately successful composer, incorporating the romantic impulse with classical spirit. His conservative style sparked controversy between his supporters (among them Robert and Clara SCHUMANN) and those of the dramatic romantic style of LISZT and Richard WAGNER. His four SYMPHONIES are considered among the greatest in symphonic music. Other well-known works are the *German Requiem* (1866), the Violin Concerto in D (1878), and the Piano Concerto in B Flat (1878–81). He composed in almost every genre except opera, devoting special attention to chamber music and song. His LIEDER are worldwide favorites.

Brahui, Dravidian language of Baluchistan. See LANGUAGE (table).

Braille, Louis, 1809?–1852, French inventor of the Braille system of printing and writing for the blind. Blind from an accident at age three, he attended and later taught at the Institution des Jeunes Aveugles, Paris. He evolved a system of writing with points based on Charles Barbier's method, though much simpler. The **Braille system** consists of six raised points used in 63 possible combinations; it is in use, in modified form, for printing, writing, and musical notation.

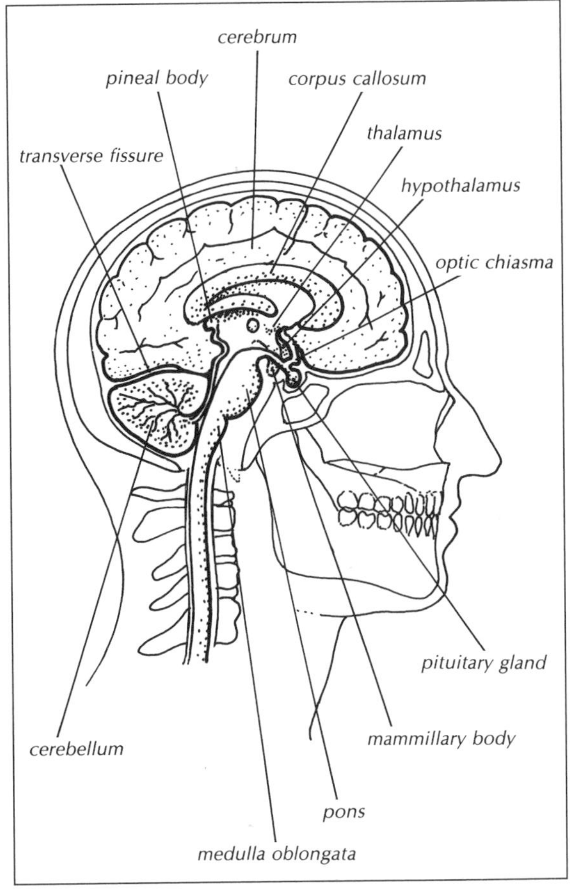

Brain

brain, supervisory center of the NERVOUS SYSTEM in all vertebrates. The brain controls both conscious behavior (e.g., walking and thinking) and most involuntary behavior (e.g., heartbeat and breathing). In higher animals, it is also the site of emotions, memory, self-awareness, and thought. It functions by receiving information via nerve cells (neurons) from every part of the body, evaluating the data, and then sending directives to muscles and glands or simply storing the information. Information, in the form of electrochemical signals, moves through complex brain circuits, which are networks of the billions of nerve cells in the nervous system. A single neuron may receive information from as many as 1,000 other neurons. Anatomically, the brain occupies the skull cavity (cranium) and is enveloped by three protective membranes (meninges). The adult brain weighs 2¼ to 3¼ lb (1–1.5 kg). It has several parts, each with a loosely associated function. The *brainstem* (hindbrain), monitoring involuntary activity (e.g., breathing), and the *cerebellum,* coordinating muscular movements and posture, are together the basic machinery for survival and reproduction. The *forebrain,* composed of the limbic system and cerebral cortex, regulates higher functions. The limbic system (including the thalamus, hypothalamus, pituitary, amygdala and hippocampus, and olfactory cortex) is associated with vivid emotions, memory, sexuality, and smell. The forebrain's cerebral cortex, in the uppermost portion of the skull, has some areas concerned with muscle control and the senses and others concerned with language and anticipation of action. The cerebral cortex is split into two hemispheres, each controlling the side of the body opposite to it. In addition, the right hemisphere is associated with perception of melody, nonverbal visual patterns, and emotion, while the left hemisphere is associated with verbal skills. Brain function is monitored by ELECTROENCEPHALOGRAPHY.

Braine, John, 1922–86, English author. His first novel, *Room at the Top* (1957), was a bitter analysis of class structure in an English factory town. His other works include *Writing a Novel* (1974).

Brain Trust, an academic group of close advisers to Franklin Delano ROOSEVELT as N.Y. governor and as U.S. president. His advisers on the NEW DEAL included Columbia professors Raymond Moley, Adolf A. Berle, Jr., and Rexford G. Tugwell.

brake, device used to slow or stop the motion of a mechanism or vehicle. Friction brakes, the most common kind, operate on the principle that friction can be used to convert the mechanical energy of a moving object into heat energy, which is absorbed by the brake. Friction brakes consist of a rotating part—such as a wheel, axle, disk, or brake drum—and a stationary part that is pressed against the rotating part to slow it or stop it. The stationary part usually has a lining, called a brake lining, that can generate a great amount of friction yet give long wear. The simplest brake form is the single-block brake, a wooden block shaped to fit against the rim of a wheel or drum. In disk brakes, two blocks press against either side of a disk that rotates with the wheel. Drum brakes have two semicircular brake shoes inside a rotating brake drum; when actuated, they press against the inner wall of the drum. Automobiles use hydraulic pressure to power disk and drum brakes (see HYDRAULIC MACHINERY). Additional braking pressure may be supplied by a "power" brake, which utilizes the vacuum created within the running engine to hold a brake shoe away from a drum. The shoe presses against the drum when the vacuum is destroyed. An antilock braking system (ABS) uses sensors to identify when a wheel is locking and then applies and releases the brake automatically several times per second to prevent lockup. ABS can prevent skids, permitting controlled stops, and decreases the amount of time and distance needed to stop a car. The air brake, invented (1868) by George WESTINGHOUSE, uses compressed air to power block brakes on trains.

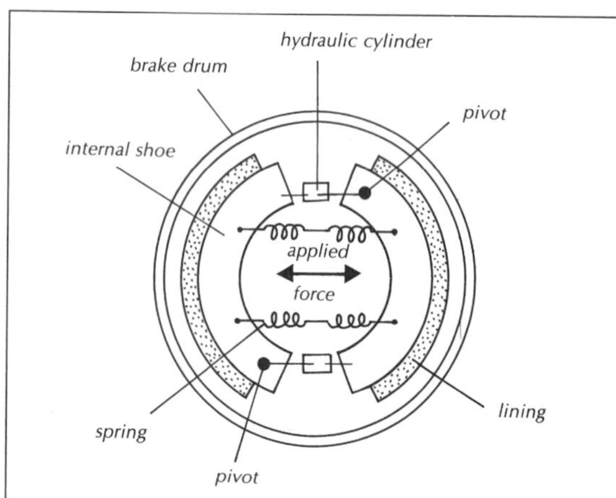

Shoe brake

Bramante, Donato, 1444–1514, Italian architect and painter. His buildings in Rome are the most characteristic examples of High Renaissance style. He favored central plans and a sense of noble severity. He designed much of Santa Maria presso San Satiro, Milan, painting its choir in perspective to give the illusion of depth. From 1499 he was in Rome, where his works include the Tempietto in the courtyard of San Pietro in Montorio; the Belvedere courtyard at the Vatican; and the original central plan for St. Peter's.

bramble, plants (genus *Rubus*) of the ROSE family, with representatives worldwide. Members include the blackberries, raspberries, loganberries, boysenberries, and dewberries. The plants are typically shrubs with prickly stems (canes) and edible fruits that botanically are not berries but aggregates of drupelets (see FRUIT). The underground parts of brambles are perennial and the canes biennial; only second-year canes bear flowers and fruits. Berries are grown commercially for sale as fresh, frozen, and canned fruit, and for use in preserves, beverages, and liqueurs. Other thorny shrubs are also called brambles.

Brampton, town (1991 pop. 234,445), S Ontario, Canada, part of the regional municipality of Peel (1991 pop. 732,798). It is one of Canada's chief automobile-producing centers.

bran, outer coat of cereal GRAINS such as wheat, rye, and corn. Various brans are used as food and livestock feed, and are important in dyeing and calico printing.

Brancusi, Constantin [bränkyōō'zē], 1876–1957, Romanian sculptor. The radical, economical style of his abstract sculptures, e.g., *The Kiss* (1908), *Sleeping Muse* (1910), and the portrait of Mlle Pogany (1923; Musée national d'art moderne, Paris), caused much controversy. *Bird in Space* (1919; Mus. Mod. Art, N.Y.C.) exemplifies his simple forms and organic, symbolic characterization.

Brandeis, Louis Dembitz, 1856–1941, associate justice of the U.S. SUPREME COURT (1916–39); b. Louisville, Ky.; LL.B., Harvard Univ. (1877). A Boston public interest attorney, he revolutionized legal practice by introducing sociological and economic facts—the "Brandeis brief"—in his arguments before the Supreme Court in *Muller* v. *Oregon* (1908). An enemy of industrial and financial monopoly, he formulated the economic doctrine of Woodrow Wilson's New Freedom. He earned a high reputation for judicial liberalism, and after 1933 he was one of the few justices who voted to uphold most of the NEW DEAL legislation.

Brandenburg, state (1990 est. pop. 2,640,000), c.10,400 sq mi (26,940 sq km), E Germany. POTSDAM is the capital. The city of BERLIN is within, but not administratively a part of, Brandenburg. A Slavic principality, it was acquired (12th cent.) by the German margrave Albert the Bear and was later ruled by electors of the HOLY ROMAN EMPIRE. In 1417 it passed to the HOHENZOLLERN family, who added (1618) the duchy of Prussia (later EAST PRUSSIA) to their holdings. The later history of Brandenburg is that of PRUSSIA. Brandenburg was (1949–90) part of East Germany and was dissolved from 1952 to 1990, when it became a state of reunified Germany.

Brandes, Georg Morris Cohen [brän'dəs], 1842–1927, Danish literary critic. He exposed Scandinavia to contemporary European thought. A disciple of TAINE and an opponent of ROMANTICISM, he helped direct Scandinavian literature toward REALISM and social consciousness. A major work is *Main Currents in Nineteenth-Century Literature* (6 vol., 1872–90).

Brando, Marlon, 1924–, American film actor; b. Omaha, Nebr. He is noted for the naturalism of his acting. His films include *A Streetcar Named Desire* (1952), *On the Waterfront* (1954; Academy Award), *The Godfather* (1972; Academy Award), *Apocalypse Now* (1979), and *A Dry White Season* (1988).

Brandt, Willy, 1913–92, German political leader; b. Herbert Ernst Karl Frahm. A Social Democrat, he opposed HITLER and fled (1933) to Norway. Returning after World War II, he was elected mayor of West Berlin (1957–66) and was (1966–69) West German foreign minister. He became chancellor of West Germany in 1969 and instituted peace talks with Eastern European countries, including East Germany. He was awarded the 1971 Nobel Peace Prize. Brandt resigned in 1974 after an East German spy was discovered within his administration.

brandy, strong alcoholic spirit distilled from wine. Manufactured in many countries, brandy is most notable in the form of cognac, made from white grapes in the Charente district of France. Most fine brandies are distilled in pot stills, blended and flavored, and stored in casks (preferably oak) to mellow. Brandies are also made from fruits other than the grape, such as plum (slivovitz) or peach.

Brandywine, battle of the, in the AMERICAN REVOLUTION, fought Sept. 11, 1777, along the Brandywine Creek in SE Pennsylvania, between Sir William Howe (see under HOWE, RICHARD HOWE, EARL) and Gen. WASHINGTON. Howe's strategy of attacking the American right flank forced Washington to retreat, and the advancing British took Philadelphia.

Branson, city (1990 pop. 3,706), Taney co., SW Mo.; inc. 1904. Primarily residential, the city has over 30 theaters that present country music and draw millions of tourists annually. Nearby is the College of the Ozarks.

Brant, Joseph, or **Thayendanegea,** 1742–1807, influential Mohawk (see IROQUOIS CONFEDERACY) chief who bound Native Americans to the British side in the AMERICAN REVOLUTION. He fought at Oriskany (1777) in the SARATOGA CAMPAIGN and joined Walter Butler in the Cherry Valley Massacre (1778). After the war he failed to settle Native American land claims in the U.S. but gained land and subsidies for Mohawks in Canada. An educated man and a Christian, Brant translated the BOOK OF COMMON PRAYER and the Gospel of MARK into Mohawk.

Braque, Georges [bräk], 1882–1963, French painter. Among the developers of FAUVISM, he later met PICASSO, and the two explored form and structure, which in turn led to CUBISM. *Nude* (1907–8; Cuttoli Coll., Paris), exemplifies the analytical stage of that movement, with its orderly decomposing of objects. After leading the way to COLLAGE, he produced works, e.g., *The Table* (Pulitzer Coll., St. Louis), that are more curvilinear in style.

Brasília, city and federal district (1990 est. pop. 1,803,000), E central Brazil, capital of Brazil. One of the world's newer cities, it was laid out (1957) in the shape of an airplane by the Brazilian architect Lúcio Costa and replaced RIO DE JANEIRO as capital in 1960. The sparsely settled region is dominated by ultramodern public buildings designed by Oscar NIEMEYER. Extensive residential developments were built in the 1960s, and highways linking Brasília with the major cities of southern and central Brazil were completed in 1982.

Braşov [bräshov′], city (1989 est. pop. 353,000), central Romania, in Transylvania, at the foot of the Transylvanian Alps. It is an industrial center known for transport vehicles, chemicals, and textiles, and a winter sports center. Founded in the 13th cent., Braşov was ceded to Romania by Hungary in 1920. It has several old churches and the remains of a 17th-cent. citadel.

brass, ALLOY having COPPER (55% to 90%) and ZINC (10% to 45%) as its essential components. Its properties vary with the proportion of copper and zinc and with the addition of small amounts of other elements. Cartridge brass is used for cartridge cases, plumbing and lighting fixtures, rivets, screws, and springs. Aluminum brass has greater resistance to corrosion than ordinary brass. Brass containing tin (naval brass) resists seawater corrosion. Brass can be forged or hammered into various shapes, rolled into thin sheets, drawn into wires, and machined and cast. See also SOLDER.

Bratislava, Ger. *Pressburg,* Hung. *Pozsony,* city (1990 est. pop. 443,000), SW Slovakia, on the Danube R. near the Austrian and Hungarian borders. The capital and largest city of SLOVAKIA, it is a major Danubian port, with textile, chemical, and armament industries. A Roman outpost by the 1st cent. A.D., it was later ruled (9th cent.) by MORAVIA. From 1541 to 1784 it was the capital of Hungary. It became part of Czechoslovakia in 1918 and capital of an independent Slovakia in 1993. Landmarks include several 13th-cent. buildings, e.g., St. Martin's Cathedral.

Braudel, Fernand, 1902–85, French historian. He studied under Lucien Febvre and was a founder of the *Annales* school of historiography. As a German prisoner-of-war during World War II, he wrote his monumental *The Mediterranean and the Mediterranean World in the Age of Philip II* (1949). After the war, he was professor at the Collège de France in Paris, (1949–72), editor of the journal *Annales*, a founder (1963) of the Maison des Sciences de l'Homme, and president of the VIth Section of the École des Hautes Études (1952–56).

Braun, Eva, 1912–45, mistress and later wife of German dictator Adolf HITLER. She entered Hitler's household in 1936, but they were married just a few days before their double suicide. She had no influence on the Nazi government.

Brauwer, Adriaen: see BROUWER, ADRIAEN.

Brazil [brəzil′], Port. *Brasil,* officially Federative Republic of Brazil, republic (1992 est. pop. 158,200,000), 3,286,470 sq mi (8,511,965 sq km), E South America, bordered by Venezuela, Guyana, Suriname, and French Guiana (N); Colombia, Peru, and Bolivia (W); Paraguay, Argentina, and Uruguay (SW); and the Atlantic Ocean (E). It is a federation of 26 states and the federal district of Brasília. The capital is BRASÍLIA, and principal cities include SÃO PAULO, RIO DE JANEIRO, RECIFE, BELO HORIZONTE, and SALVADOR. The largest

South American country and the fifth most populous country in the world, Brazil occupies nearly half the continent and has a varied topography and climate, ranging from tropical in the rain forests of the great AMAZON basin in the north to temperate in the highlands of the heavily populated east and south, which make up two thirds of the country's land and contain its chief economic centers. Brazil is the economic giant of South America and has become increasingly industrialized since the 1960s. It still depends heavily on agriculture, however, which accounts for nearly 50% of its exports. It is an important cattle producer; major commercial crops are coffee (of which it is the world's leading producer), cocoa, cotton, sugarcane, citrus fruit, corn, tobacco, bananas, and soybeans. Industrial production is led by motor vehicles, steel, cotton textiles, paper, fertilizer, cement, and machinery. The country's vast mineral wealth includes some of the finest iron resources in the world, as well as quartz, coal, manganese, chromium, industrial diamonds, uranium, and platinum. Petroleum deposits have not been fully developed; petroleum accounts for 40% of imports. The vast Amazonian rain forest was extensively cut and burned during the 1980s for wood and wood products and to clear land for farming and grazing, but the government has slowed development since the late 1980s. Inflation, which has averaged over 1000% since the late 1980s, and unchecked government spending are major economic problems. The population is diverse in origin, an amalgam of indigenous, African, and European peoples. Many native tribes live on reserves, but few are truly insulated from contemporary Brazilian society. Portuguese is the official language. Roman Catholicism is the predominant religion, but there is a large Protestant minority.

History. Although the Spaniard Vicente Yáñez Pinzón (see under PINZÓN, M.A.) and possibly others visited the coast earlier, the Portuguese, under Pedro Alvares CABRAL, claimed the land in 1500. The first permanent European settlement, at São Vicente in present-day São Paulo, was not made until 1532; development of the region now known as the Northeast began at the same time. Portuguese claims did not go unchallenged: French HUGUENOTS had to be expelled from a base in Rio de Janeiro harbor in 1567, and the Dutch held the Northeast for almost 20 years before they were driven out in 1654. When NAPOLEON invaded Portugal, Portugal's king, JOHN VI, fled (1807) to Brazil, and on his arrival (1808) in Rio de Janeiro that city became the capital of the Portuguese empire. In 1821 John returned to Portugal, leaving behind as regent his son, who in 1822 declared Brazil independent and himself Emperor PEDRO I. Forced by his restrictive policies to abdicate, he was succeeded by his son, the popular PEDRO II, whose long reign (1831–89) saw the development of Brazil as a modern nation; wars with Argentina (1851–52) and Paraguay (1865–70) brought little benefit to Brazil, however. The abolition of slavery (1888) helped bring on a bloodless revolution that established Brazil as a republic in 1889. Large-scale European immigration, an expanding coffee market, and a wild-rubber boom brought wealth to Brazil in the late 19th and early 20th cent. Later, under the presidency of Getúlio VARGAS (1930–45, 1950–54), who came to power in a revolution (1930), industrial expansion and diversification of agriculture was stressed. Brazil joined the Allies in World War II (as in World War I), enjoying a new boom (chiefly in rubber and minerals). To spur development of the interior, Juscelino Kubitschek, elected president in 1955, undertook the building of the planned city of Brasília, which replaced Rio de Janeiro as the national capital in 1960; he also inaugurated an ambitious program of highway and dam construction. Political strife and economic chaos led to a coup in 1964 and the installation of a rightist military regime. The military rulers borrowed heavily to finance industrial expansion, causing the third world's largest foreign debt and hyperinflation. In 1985 they voluntarily surrendered power to a conservative civilian government. President José SARNEY (1985–90) proved unable to cope with mounting financial problems. In 1989, in the first popular election in 29 years, Fernando Collor de Mello won the presidency. Collor's presidency was marred by corruption, and he was impeached in 1992 and resigned. Vice Pres. Itamar Augusto Franco became president. Inflation, at over 2,500% in 1993, and a recession that began in 1990 remained problems.

Brazil nut, common name for the Lecythidaceae, a family of tropical trees. Members include the West Indian anchovy pear (*Grias cauliflora*); several lumber trees of South America, e.g., the cannonball; and the Brazil nut trees (genus *Bertholletia*). Brazil nut trees are found chiefly along the Amazon and Orinoco rivers. The edible nuts are oil-rich seeds that grow clumped together in hard, grapefruit-sized, woody seed pods.

Brazzaville, city (1984 pop. 585,912), capital of the Congo. The country's largest city, and an important port on the Congo R., it receives wood, rubber, and agricultural products from the region and ships them by rail to POINTE-NOIRE on the Atlantic Ocean. The city was founded (1880) by French explorers and was the capital (1910–58) of FRENCH EQUATORIAL AFRICA. It was an important outpost of Free France in the Vichy period. A meeting there in 1944 began the process of independence for France's African colonies.

breadfruit: see MULBERRY.

Breakspear, Nicholas: see ADRIAN IV.

breast: see MAMMARY GLAND.

Breasted, James Henry, 1865–1935, American Egyptologist; b. Rockford, Ill. While Egyptology professor (1905–33) at the Univ. of Chicago and director (1895–1901) of its Haskell Oriental Museum and (after 1919) Oriental Institute, he directed research in Mesopotamia and made important discoveries in Egypt. His many books include *History of Egypt from the Earliest Times to the Persian Conquest* (rev. ed. 1928), *Dawn of Conscience* (1933), and translations of Egyptian historical records.

Brébeuf, Jean de, Saint [brābŏf'], 1593–1649, French Roman Catholic missionary, one of the JESUIT Martyrs of North America. A missionary to the HURON, Brébeuf with his colleague Gabriel Lalemant was killed by the Iroquois. Feast: Oct. 19 (in the U.S.).

Brecht, Bertolt [brĕkht], 1898–1956, German dramatist and poet; b. Berthold Brecht. In the late 1920s he turned to EXPRESSIONISM, as in *Man is Man* (1926), and began to develop his revolutionary "epic theater," designed to create—through the use of effects such as bright lights, films, and mottoes displayed on cards—a politically conscious distance between the spectator and the stage. *The Threepenny Opera* (1928), with music by Kurt WEILL, reflects Brecht's social views. During the NAZI period he went into exile in Denmark and then settled in the U.S. His later works include *Mother Courage and Her Children* (1941), *The Good Woman of Setzuan* (1943), and *The Caucasian Chalk Circle* (1955). A Marxist, Brecht lived from 1948 in East Berlin, where he directed the state-supported Berliner Ensemble.

Breckinridge, John, 1760–1806, American statesman; b. Augusta co., Va. In the Kentucky legislature, he won passage (1798) of the Kentucky Resolutions (see KENTUCKY AND VIRGINIA RESOLUTIONS). In the U.S. Senate (1801–5), he sponsored Western interests. He was attorney general (1805) under Pres. JEFFERSON. His grandson, **John Cabell Breckinridge,** 1821–75, b. Lexington, Ky., was vice president of the U.S. under Pres. BUCHANAN. He later served the CONFEDERACY as a brigadier general and as secretary of war (1865).

breeder reactor: see NUCLEAR REACTOR.

Breed's Hill: see BUNKER HILL, BATTLE OF.

Bremen, city (1989 est. pop. 535,000), N Germany, on the Weser R. It is the oldest German port city and Germany's second largest port. Shipbuilding and steel-making are among its industries; the service sector is increasingly important. Made an archbishopric in 845, it became a leading member (1358) of the HANSEATIC LEAGUE and a free imperial city (1646). It prospered as an overseas trading center during the 18th and 19th cent. During WORLD WAR II it was badly damaged, but such structures as the Gothic city hall (1405–9) and the Romanesque-Gothic cathedral (begun 1043) remain.

Brennan, William Joseph, Jr., 1906–, associate justice of the U.S. SUPREME COURT (1956–90); b. Newark, N.J.; grad. Harvard Law School (1931). He was a justice on the New Jersey supreme court from 1952 until his appointment to the U.S. Supreme Court by Pres. Dwight D. Eisenhower. In the 1970s and 80s, Brennan was the most influential liberal on an increasingly conservative Court.

Brenner Pass, Alpine Pass, 4,495 ft (1,370 m) high, connecting Innsbruck, Austria, with Bolzano, Italy. The lowest of the principal passes in the ALPS, it was an important Roman route through which many invasions of Italy were made.

Brentano, Clemens [brĕntä'nō], 1778–1842, German poet of the romantic school; brother of Bettina von Arnim. With Achim von ARNIM he collaborated on *The Boy's Magic Horn* (1806–8), a folksong collection that influenced HEINE, and the brothers GRIMM, among others. Brentano wrote plays, lyric poems, fairy tales, and novellas.

Brentano, Franz, 1838–1917, German philosopher and psychologist. He believed that mental processes are the data of psychology, to be regarded as acts rather than as passive processes. In *Psychology from an Empirical Standpoint* (1874) he tried to establish psychology as an independent science. His students included HUSSERL and FREUD.

Bresson, Robert [brĕsôN'], 1907–, French film director. His films, which tend to be austere and have spiritual themes, include *Diary of a Country Priest* (1950), *The Trial of Joan of Arc* (1961), *Lancelot of the Lake* (1976), and *Money* (1983).

Brest, city (1990 pop. 147,956), Finistère dept., NW France, on an inlet of the Atlantic Ocean. It is a commercial port and naval station. Clothing and electronic equipment are the chief manufactures; the French naval academy and a national engineering school are there. The spacious, landlocked harbor was created in 1631. During WORLD WAR II Brest was a major German submarine base and was almost completely destroyed by Allied bombing.

Brest-Litovsk, Treaty of, separate peace treaty of WORLD WAR I, signed by Soviet Russia and the Central Powers on Mar. 3, 1918, at present-day Brest, Belarus (Belorussia). It followed the removal of Russia from the war by the Bolsheviks after they seized power in Nov. 1917. By its terms, considered humiliating to the Russians, Russia ceded large areas to the Central Powers and recognized the independence of Poland, the Baltic states, Georgia, and Ukraine. Later Russia agreed to pay a large indemnity. In the general armistice of Nov. 1918, the Allies forced the Central Powers to renounce the treaty.

Brethren, German Baptist sect. Known also as Dunkers (from Ger., = to dip), they practice baptism by triple immersion. Organized in 1708, the Brethren are opposed to war and advocate a simple life. In the U.S. there are several denominations, of which the largest is the Church of the Brethren.

Breton, André [brətôN'], 1896–1966, French writer. At first a Dadaist, he later became the founder of SURREALISM, for which he wrote three manifestos (1924, 1930, 1934), and opened a studio for "surrealist research."

Breuer, Josef [broi'ər], 1842–1925, Austrian physician. His cathartic method of therapy and his theory of HYSTERIA, when developed by Sigmund FREUD, became the basis for PSYCHOANALYSIS. Together with Freud, Breuer wrote *Studies in Hysteria* (1895).

Breuer, Marcel Lajos [broi'ər], 1902–81, American architect and furniture designer; b. Hungary. In the 1920s he was associated with the BAUHAUS and won fame for his tubular chair. In the U.S. he was associated (1937–41) with Walter GROPIUS in building houses. Among his well-known buildings is the Whitney Museum, N.Y.C. (1966).

Breughel, family of painters: see BRUEGEL.

Brewster, Sir David, 1781–1868, Scottish physicist and natural philosopher. His invention of the kaleidoscope was one result of his notable light-polarization studies. He improved the spectroscope and devised the dioptic system of lighthouse illumination. Among his many writings is a major biography (1855) of Sir Isaac NEWTON.

Brezhnev, Leonid Ilyich [brĕzh'nĕf], 1906–82. Soviet leader. Rising through the Communist party, he became chairman of the presidium of the Supreme Soviet in 1960 and, when Nikita KHRUSHCHEV fell in 1964, first secretary (later general secretary) of the party. He shared power with Alexei KOSYGIN but emerged as the chief Soviet leader. In 1977, retaining his party post, he became president of the USSR. Brezhnev's hard line toward democratic or independent trends in neighboring countries, evidenced by the Soviet invasions of Czechoslovakia (1968) and Afghanistan (1979), often conflicted with his attempts at DÉTENTE with the West.

Brian Boru or **Brian Boroimhe** [both: brī'ən, brēn; bərōō, bərō], 940?–1014, king of Ireland. A clan prince, he became high king by subjugating all Ireland. He annihilated the coalition of the Norse and his Irish enemies at Clontarf in 1014, but he was murdered soon after. His victory ended Norse power in Ireland, but the nation fell into anarchy.

Briand, Aristide [brēäN'], 1862–1932, French statesman. He was premier 10 times between 1909 and 1921. After WORLD WAR I, he emerged as a leading proponent of international peace and cooperation. As foreign minister (1925–32) Briand was the chief architect of the LOCARNO PACT (1925) and the KELLOGG-BRIAND PACT (1928). He shared the 1926 Nobel Peace Prize with Gustav STRESEMANN and advocated a plan for a United States of Europe.

brick, building material made by shaping CLAY into blocks and then hardening them in a kiln. Sun-dried bricks are among the most ancient building materials. Examples from c.5,000 years ago have been discovered in the Tigris-Euphrates basin. The Romans faced brick buildings with stone or marble, but Byzantine and later European builders used the brick itself to provide a decorative surface. The many varieties of modern brick include firebrick, made of special clays that can be fired at very high temperatures.

bridge, structure spanning and giving passage over a waterway, a depression, or some other obstacle. Early bridges ranged from suspended rope walkways to arched structures of stone or brick. The mid-19th-cent. development of steel allowed for longer spans, the use of the steel truss in place of stone or masonry arches, and steel-wire suspension CABLES of great tensile strength. Movable bridges, whose center portions can be raised, are generally constructed over waterways where it is impossible to build a fixed bridge high enough for water traffic to pass under it. Military bridges—temporary structures that can be erected rapidly—include the pontoon bridge, which uses air-filled floats called pontoons to support the roadway. See also AQUEDUCT; BROOKLYN BRIDGE; GOLDEN GATE BRIDGE; VERRAZANO-NARROWS BRIDGE.

bridge, card game derived from whist, played with 52 cards by four players in two partnerships. It probably originated in the Middle East. In contract bridge, a now popular form, the cards rank from ace down to two; in bidding, suits rank spades, hearts, diamonds, and clubs. After all the cards are dealt, the auction begins. Players bid to win a stated number of tricks over six (a trick being the three cards played in rotation after the lead) with a named suit as trump or with no-trump. The highest bid becomes the contract after three consecutive passes end the bidding. The player who first named the suit (or no-trump) is the declarer; his partner's hand is the dummy and is played by the declarer face-up as he attempts to win at least enough tricks to fulfill his contract. Duplicate bridge, in which prearranged hands are played, is the main form of competitive bridge. The governing principles of bidding were delineated by Ely CULBERTSON, and the currently popular point-counting system in bidding was introduced by Charles H. GOREN.

Bridgeport, city (1990 pop. 141,686), SW Conn., on Long Island Sound; inc. 1836. A port, it is Connecticut's largest city and chief industrial center. Manufactures include electrical appliances, firearms, helicopters, engines, trucks, and aerosol sprays. Settled in 1639, it grew as a fishing community. Noteworthy is the Barnum Inst., commemorating the city's resident, P.T. BARNUM.

Bridger, James, 1804–81, American fur trapper, one of the most noted of the MOUNTAIN MEN; b. Virginia. A fur trader and guide, with Louis Vasquez he opened (1843) Fort Bridger on the OREGON TRAIL. He was a picturesque figure who won fame for his "tall tales."

Bridges, Harry, 1901–90, American labor leader; b. Australia, as Alfred Renton Bridges. Arriving in San Francisco in 1920, he became a longshoreman and militant labor organizer. In 1937 he set up the International Longshoremen's and Warehousemen's Union (ILWU), serving as its president for the next 40 years. Efforts by the U.S. government to deport him as a Communist alien failed, and he became a citizen in 1945. Bridges was convicted and sentenced (1950) to prison for perjury in denying Communist party membership, but the U.S. Supreme Court overturned the conviction in 1953. Bridges led his last major strike in 1971–72.

Bridges, Robert Seymour, 1844–1930, English lyric poet. The philosophical poem *The Testament of Beauty* (1929) is considered his greatest work. Bridges also wrote two major works on prosody and published the poems of his friend G.M. HOPKINS.

Bridgetown, city (1990 pop. 6,720), capital of BARBADOS.

Bridgman, Percy Williams, 1882–1961, American physicist; b. Cambridge, Mass. A professor at Harvard, he won the 1946 Nobel Prize in physics for his work in high pressures. He also studied electrical conduction in metals and the properties of crystals, and wrote on the philosophy of modern science.

Bright, John, 1811–89, English statesman and orator. Noted for his LAISSEZ FAIRE views, he was, with COBDEN, the greatest 19th-cent. champion of the middle class. In 1839 he helped found the ANTI-CORN-LAW LEAGUE and used his formidable oratory to urge repeal of the CORN LAWS. A member of Parliament for many years (1847–57, 1858–89), he also served in GLADSTONE's cabinets (1868–70, 1873–74, 1880–82).

brimstone: see SULFUR.

Brinkley, David McClure, 1920–, American television journalist; b. Wilmington, N.C. From 1956–70 he and Chet Huntley coanchored the *Huntley–Brinkley Report*, the popular nightly news program. Since 1981 he has hosted *ABC This Week*, a weekly news program examining national politics.

Brisbane, city (1991 est. pop. 1,327,000), capital and chief port of Queensland, E Australia, on the Brisbane R., above Moreton Bay. The third largest city in Australia, it has shipyards; oil refineries; and food-processing, textile, and automotive industries. Sugar, bananas, and bauxite are exported. Brisbane was first settled (1824) as a penal colony. The Univ. of Queensland is here.

Bristol, city (1991 pop. 376,146), Avon, SW England. A leading international port, Bristol has been a trading center since the 12th cent. Its manufactures include general and nuclear machinery, aircraft, and tobacco and food products. Although the city was heavily bombed during WORLD WAR II, many historic buildings remain.

Britain: see GREAT BRITAIN.

britannia metal, ALLOY of TIN with ANTIMONY, COPPER, and, sometimes, BISMUTH and ZINC. Similar in appearance to pewter but harder, it is used in manufacturing tableware.

British Columbia, province (1991 pop. 3,282,061), 366,252 sq mi (948,596 sq km), W Canada, bounded by Alberta (E), Montana, Idaho, and Washington (S), the Pacific Ocean and Alaska (W), and the Yukon and Northwest Territories (N). The province is almost totally mountainous, with the ROCKY MOUNTAINS in the east and the COAST MOUNTAINS along the Pacific; hydroelectric power is highly developed. The coast is deeply indented with many offshore islands, including VANCOUVER ISLAND. The chief rivers include the FRASER, the upper COLUMBIA, and the Skeena. Nearly 75% of the land is covered with forests, and lumbering and related enterprises (such as pulp and paper manufacture) are the major industries. The province is rich in copper and coal (its principal mineral resources) as well as oil, natural gas, silver, gold, iron ore, zinc, and lead. It ranks first among the provinces in fishing. Tourism is also important, with visitors attracted by the province's scenic mountain ranges. Large areas of N and central British Columbia are sparsely settled, and almost 75% of the population is crowded into the southwestern coastal strip. VANCOUVER and VICTORIA, the capital, are the chief cities.

History. The area was originally inhabited by indigenous peoples of the Pacific Northwest. In 1774 the Spaniard Juan Pérez probably sailed along the coast, and in 1778 James COOK explored the shoreline and claimed the area for Britain. Rival British and Spanish claims were resolved (1790) and George VANCOUVER mapped (1792–94) the coast for Britain. In the early 19th cent. fur traders of the NORTH WEST COMPANY and the HUDSON'S BAY COMPANY established posts in the area, and in 1846 the border with the U.S. was set at the 49th parallel. Vancouver Island became (1849) a crown colony and a new colony was formed (1858) on the mainland. The two were merged (1866) and in 1871 British Columbia voted to join the Canadian confederation. The Canadian Pacific Railway reached Vancouver in 1885, making the city a busy port. The Alaskan boundary dispute with the U.S. was settled in 1903. During the 20th cent. the province grew as its enormous wealth of natural resources was exploited. British Columbian politics were dominated since the early 1950s by the SOCIAL CREDIT party, but the New Democratic party has been in office since 1991. The province sends 6 senators (appointed) and 32 representatives (elected) to the national parliament.

British East India Company: see EAST INDIA COMPANY, BRITISH.

British Empire, overseas territories linked to Great Britain in a variety of constitutional relationships. Established over three centuries, the empire resulted primarily from commercial and political motives, and from emigration. At its height in the late 19th and early 20th cent. it included 25% of the world's population and area.

The First British Empire. The foundations of the empire were laid in the late 16th cent. by the chartered companies, commercial ventures encouraged by the crown. In the 17th cent. sugar and tobacco plantations were founded in the Caribbean and in SE North America, and religious dissenters emigrated to NE North America. An integrated imperial trade arose, involving the exchange of African slaves for West Indian molasses and sugar, English cloth and manufactures, and American fish and timber. The theories of MERCANTILISM were implanted by the NAVIGATION ACTS. The British EAST INDIA COMPANY furthered expansion into India, and during the SEVEN YEARS WAR (1756–63) Britain ousted France from Canada and India. The financial burdens of the war, however, caused difficulties in the American colonies, and the success of the AMERICAN REVOLUTION marked the end of the first British Empire.

The Second British Empire. The voyages of James COOK and further conquests in India began a new phase of British expansion. The FRENCH REVOLUTIONARY WARS and Napoleonic Wars (see NAPOLEON I) added further possessions, e.g., the Cape Colony, Ceylon, British Guiana, and Malta, and Britain's INDUSTRIAL REVOLUTION lent greater force to the ideas of free trade. Humanitarian concerns led to the abolition of the slave trade (1807) and of slavery (1833). The BRITISH NORTH AMERICA ACT of 1867, which granted CANADA internal self-rule as a dominion, inaugurated a pattern by which Britain surrendered its direct governing powers in European-settled colonies, e.g., AUSTRALIA and NEW ZEALAND. Concurrently, Britain established greater control in Africa and India.

From Empire to Commonwealth. WORLD WAR I brought the British Empire to the peak of its expansion. Imperial contributions had considerably strengthened the British war effort, and victory brought Britain mandates over new territories, e.g., Palestine, Iraq, and German territories in Africa. In 1931 the statute of Westminster officially recognized the independent and equal status under the crown of the former dominions within a British COMMONWEALTH OF NATIONS. After WORLD WAR II, self-government advanced in many parts of the empire, often as a result of violent struggle by the colonized nations. In 1947 India was partitioned and independence was granted to the new states of INDIA and PAKISTAN. Other parts of the empire, notably in AFRICA, gained independence and subsequently joined the British Commonwealth. Britain still administers many dependencies throughout the world, e.g., BERMUDA, GIBRALTAR, and HONG KONG.

British Honduras: see BELIZE.

British Imperial System of weights and measures: see ENGLISH UNITS OF MEASUREMENT; WEIGHTS AND MEASURES (table).

British Indian Ocean Territory, archipelago, c.1,180 mi (1,900 km), NE of Mauritius, in the central Indian Ocean. The islands, which form the Chagos Archipelago, were administered by MAURITIUS before they became a British dependency in 1965. Their importance is strategic; the U.S. and Britain maintain a major naval facility on the main island, DIEGO GARCIA.

British Museum, the national repository in London for treasures in science and art. It has departments of archaeology, antiquities, prints and drawings, coins and medals, and ethnography. Established (1753) with the acquisition of several collections, its exhibits now include the ROSETTA STONE, the ELGIN MARBLES, the CARYATID from the ERECHTHEUM, and the remains of a Saxon ship (c.660), with its gold and silver treasures, from the English archaeological site at Sutton Hoo. The **British Library**, est. 1973 as a separate entity, is a nonlending reference library and copyright depository. It houses one of the world's outstanding collections of rare books and manuscripts, including BEOWULF and the MAGNA CARTA. The great domed reading room at the British Museum, one of several sites now operated by the library, was finished in 1857. A new home for the library, at a separate site in London, is expected to be completed in 1996.

British North America Act, law that provided for the unification of CANADA and functioned as its constitution until 1982; passed by the British Parliament in 1867 and called the **Constitution Act, 1867** since 1982. It spelled out provincial powers and granted residual authority to the dominion government. Under it, the power of amendment was nominally vested in the British Parliament, which in practice acted only at the request of Canada's Parliament. It was superseded by the CONSTITUTION ACT, 1982.

British thermal unit (Btu), unit of energy required to raise the temperature of 1 lb of water by one degree Fahrenheit (from 59.5° to 60.5°F). 1 Btu = 251.996 calories = 778.26 foot-pounds = 1054.8 joules.

Brittany, region and former province, NW France, a peninsula between the English Channel and the Bay of Biscay. Its economy is based on farming, fishing, and tourism. Breton, a Celtic language, is spoken in some rural and traditionalist areas. Brittany got its modern name when it was settled (c.500) by Britons whom the ANGLO-SAXONS had driven from Britain. It struggled for independence from the FRANKS (5th–9th cent.), from the dukes of Normandy and the counts of Anjou (10th–12th cent.), and finally from England and France. Brittany was absorbed by France after the accession (1488) of ANNE OF BRITTANY and formally incorporated into France in 1532.

Brittany spaniel, medium-sized SPORTING DOG; shoulder height, c.19 in. (48.3 cm); weight, 30–40 lb (13.6–18.1 kg). Its dense, flat or wavy coat is dark orange and white or liver and white. It dates back hundreds of years, to France and Spain, and is the only spaniel that points its quarry.

Britten, Benjamin, Baron Britten of Aldeburgh, 1913–76, English composer. His most popular works, all written in a traditional vein, include *A Ceremony of Carols* (1942), *A Young Person's Guide to the Orchestra* (1945), and the great *War Requiem* (1962). His operas include *Peter Grimes* (1945), *The Turn of the Screw* (1954), and *Death in Venice* (1973). In 1976 Queen Elizabeth II named him a life peer.

brittle star, marine invertebrate animal (class Ophiuroidea). An ECHINODERM, it has five long, slender arms that radiate from a central disk, and the water-vascular system and tube feet common to echinoderms. Their arms break off readily, but new arms are easily regenerated. Most brittle stars are less than 1 in. (2.5 cm) across the central disk.

Brno [bûr'nô], Ger. *Brünn,* city (1990 est. pop. 392,000), central Czech Republic, at the confluence of the Svratka and Svitava rivers. The second largest Czech city and MORAVIA's chief city, it produces textiles, tractors, and other manufactures. Brno flourished (13th–14th cent.) as a free city within the kingdom of BOHEMIA. The Spielberg castle in Brno was a notorious HAPSBURG prison (1740–1855).

Broadbent, John Edward, 1936–, Canadian political leader. He was elected in 1968 to parliament and served (1975–89) as leader of the New Democratic party. In 1990 he became president of the International Centre for Human Rights and Democratic Development.

broadcasting, transmission of sound or images to a large number of RADIO or TELEVISION receivers. The first regularly scheduled radio broadcasts in the U.S. began in 1920. The sale of advertising began in 1922, establishing commercial broadcasting as an industry. A coast-to-coast hookup began early in 1924, and expansion of both audience and transmission facilities continued rapidly. By 1992, 4,963 commercial AM and 6,312 FM radio stations existed in the U.S. Experiments in broadcasting television began in the 1920s but were interrupted by World War II. By 1992 the U.S. had 1,505 television stations, and CABLE TELEVISION systems in the U.S. served over 56 million households.

Broadway, street in New York City. One of the world's longest streets, it extends c.150 mi (241 km) from lower Manhattan N to Albany. Its theater district is known as the "Great White Way" for its dazzling electric lights and signs. The world-famous intersection of Times Square is formed by Broadway, Seventh Ave., and 42d St.

broccoli, variety of CABBAGE grown for the edible immature flower panicles. It is the same variety as cauliflower (*Brassica oleracea botrytis*) and similarly cultivated.

Brock, Sir Isaac, 1769–1812, British general in Canada. As the commander (1806–12) of British forces, he defeated an American army and captured (1812) DETROIT early in the WAR OF 1812. Brock died in battle while defending the Niagara frontier.

Brodsky, Joseph (Iosif Aleksandrovich Brodsky), 1940–, Russian poet. He has lived in the U.S. since 1972 and writes in English as well as Russian. Brodsky is highly regarded for the formal technique, depth, irony, and wit displayed in his poetry, which often treats the themes of loss and exile. Among his works in English translation and in English are *A Part of Speech* (tr. 1980), *Less Than One* (tr. 1986), and *To Urania* (1988). He was awarded the 1987 Nobel Prize in literature and was named U.S. poet laureate for 1991–92.

Broglie, Louis Victor, prince de [brôglē'], 1892–1987, French physicist. From his hypothesis that particles should exhibit certain wavelike properties, wave mechanics, a form of QUANTUM MECHANICS, was developed. Experiments proved (1927) the existence of these waves; he was awarded the 1929 Nobel Prize in physics for his theory.

Broken Hill, city (1986 pop. 26,650), New South Wales, SE Australia, near the South Australia border. It is the site of one of the world's richest silver-lead and zinc deposits (first developed in 1884).

bromeliad, common name for some members of the family Bromeliaceae, chiefly epiphytic herbs and small shrubs native to the American tropics and subtropics. A typical bromeliad has strap-shaped leaves clustered in a rosette around a central cup; the flowers are found in the central cup or above it on a spike. The central cup retains water, enabling tropical bromeliads to survive dry spells. Bromeliad species such as those of the genus *Aechmea* and *Cryptanthus* are often grown as house and conservatory plants for their colorful flowers and foliage. Other members of the family include SPANISH MOSS and the PINEAPPLE.

bromine (Br), volatile liquid element, discovered in 1826 by Antoine J. Balard. A HALOGEN, it is a reddish-brown fuming liquid with an offensive odor. Bromine corrodes the skin, and its vapor irritates the eyes and the membranes of the nose and throat. The only nonmetallic element that is liquid under ordinary conditions, bromine occurs in compounds in seawater, mineral springs, and salt deposits. Its compounds are used in photographic film, in flame retardants, and in conjunction with an antiknock compound in gasoline. See ELEMENT (table); PERIODIC TABLE.

bronchitis, inflammation of the bronchial tubes caused by viral or bacterial infection or by the inhalation of irritating fumes (e.g., tobacco smoke, air pollutants). Symptoms include cough, fever, and chest pains. Acute bronchitis may subside, or, particularly with continued exposure to irritants, may persist and progress to chronic bronchitis or PNEUMONIA. Bronchitis can be treated with antihistamines, cough suppressants, bronchodilators, or ANTIBIOTICS.

Brontë, Charlotte [brŏn'tā], 1816–55, **Emily Jane Brontë,** 1818–48, and **Anne Brontë,** 1820–49, English novelists and poets. As children in a Yorkshire parsonage, the sisters created an imaginary literary world. In 1846 they published a pseudonymous collection of their poems, and in 1847 Anne's novel *Agnes Grey*, Emily's *Wuthering Heights*, and Charlotte's *Jane Eyre* all appeared. Tragedy struck, however, soon after. Emily died in Dec. 1848, and Anne (whose *Tenant of Wildfell Hall* came out in 1848) died in 1849, both from tuberculosis. Charlotte's career, however, burgeoned with *Shirley* (1849) and *Villette* (1853). She married her father's curate, Arthur Bell Nichols, in 1854 but died a year later. *The Professor* was published in 1857. Charlotte's *Jane Eyre*, the strong, violently emotional story of a governess and her passionate love for her employer, Mr. Rochester, articulates the theme of a woman's need for both love and independence; it ranks among the great English novels. Emily's *Wuthering Heights*, the intense story of the almost demonic love between Catherine Earnshaw and Heathcliff—less characters than forces—is considered a work of genius. Her lyric poems are among the best in English poetry.

bronze, ALLOY of COPPER, PHOSPHORUS, TIN, ZINC, and, sometimes, small amounts of other elements. It is harder than BRASS, and its properties depend on the proportions of its components. ALUMINUM bronze, with its high strength and corrosion resistance, is used for bearings, valve seats, and machine parts; leaded bronze is cast into heavy-duty bushings and bearings; silicon bronze is used for telegraph wires and chemical containers; and bronze with 20% to 24% tin is used for casting bells. Bronze is used for coins, medals, steam fittings, and GUNMETAL, and in artistic castings, engravings, and forgings.

Bronze Age, technological period when metals were first used to make tools and weapons. The earliest stage, when pure copper and bronze were used interchangeably, has been called the Copper Age. CASTING was well established in the Middle East by 3500 B.C.; in the New World the first bronze was cast A.D. c.1100. Development of a metallurgical industry coincided with urbanization, growth of an artisan class, and trade for raw materials, laying the foundation for the IRON AGE.

Brook, Peter, 1925–, English theatrical director. Since 1962 he has been codirector of the Royal Shakespeare Company (see THEATER, table). His innovative, controversial productions include Peter WEISS's *Marat/Sade* (1965), *A Midsummer Night's Dream* (1970), and the nine-hour *Mahabharata* (1985). He has also directed films, e.g., *Lord of the Flies* (1963), and *King Lear* (1971).

Brooke, Edward William, 1919–, U.S. senator from Massachusetts (1967–79), the first African-American U.S. senator since RECONSTRUCTION; b. Washington, D.C. A Republican, he served (1967) on the President's Commission on Civil Disorders, which investigated the causes of race riots. Although he was defeated for reelection (1978) in part because his fiscal records were investigated by the Senate Ethics Committee, he was later exonerated of any wrongdoing.

Brooke, Sir James, 1803–68, rajah of Sarawak on BORNEO. He was made (1841) rajah for helping the sultan of Brunei to suppress rebel tribes. He was succeeded by his nephew, **Sir Charles Anthony Johnson Brooke,** 1829–1917, who made the country prosperous. His son and successor, **Sir Charles Vyner Brooke,** 1874–1963, was forced out of Sarawak by the Japanese in WORLD WAR II. He ceded (1946) the country to Britain.

Brooke, Rupert, 1887–1915, English poet. His social charm, wit, and tragic death during World War I made him a legend. He wrote *Poems* (1911) and *1914 and Other Poems* (1915). The romantic patriotism of his war poems contrasts sharply with the bitterness of OWEN and SASSOON.

Brook Farm, 1841–47, experimental farm at West Roxbury, Mass.; founded by the Unitarian minister George Ripley. It was based on cooperative living and the principles of TRANSCENDENTALISM and fostered shared manual labor and a stimulating intellectual life. Nathaniel HAWTHORNE was a member, and visitors included R.W. EMERSON, Margaret FULLER, and Horace GREELEY. Brook Farm adopted the ideas of Charles FOURIER in 1844. It was disbanded shortly after its central building burned in 1846.

Brookhaven National Laboratory, scientific research center, Upton, Long Island, N.Y.; founded (1947) and operated by Associated Universities Inc. under contract to the U.S. Dept. of Energy. The laboratory's equipment includes a number of highly sophisticated nuclear reactors, particle accelerators, and computers; there is also a medical research center for work in nuclear medicine.

Brookings Institution, at Washington, D.C.; chartered in 1927 as a consolidation of the Inst. for Government Research (est. 1916), the Inst. of Economics (est. 1922), and the Robert S. Brookings Graduate School of Economics and Government (est. 1924). The institution makes social science research available to government and business by financing projects and publishing findings, sometimes working under government contract.

Brooklyn, borough of NEW YORK CITY (1990 pop. 2,300,664), 71 sq mi (184 sq km), coextensive with Kings co., SE N.Y., at the SW extremity of LONG ISLAND; settled 1636, chartered as part of New York City 1898. The largest of New York's five boroughs, it has diverse industries and a waterfront handling foreign and domestic commerce. From Dutch and Walloon settlements it became the village of Brooklyn Ferry (1816) and the city of Brooklyn (1834), absorbing settlements like Flatbush and Gravesend as it grew; it became (1855) the third largest U.S. city. Points of interest include Prospect Park, the Brooklyn Botanic Garden, and Coney Island.

Brooklyn Bridge, the first steel-wire suspension bridge in the world, built 1869–83, over the East R., linking the boroughs of Manhattan and Brooklyn in New York City. Designed by J.A. and W.A. ROEBLING, it was the world's longest suspension bridge at the time of its completion.

Brookner, Anita, 1928–, English writer and art critic. After establishing an academic career at London's Courtauld Institute of Art, she began (1980) writing fiction. Her novels are usually about middle-aged women unable to establish relationships with those around them, e.g., *Hotel du Lac* (1984) and *A Misalliance* (1986).

Brooks, Gwendolyn, 1917–, African-American poet; b. Topeka, Kans. Treating the African-American experience, her poems are in such volumes as *Annie Allen* (1949; Pulitzer) and *Riot* (1970). She is also the author of *Maud Martha* (1953), a novelette, and an autobiography (1972). Brooks was the first African-American woman to win the Pulitzer Prize for poetry.

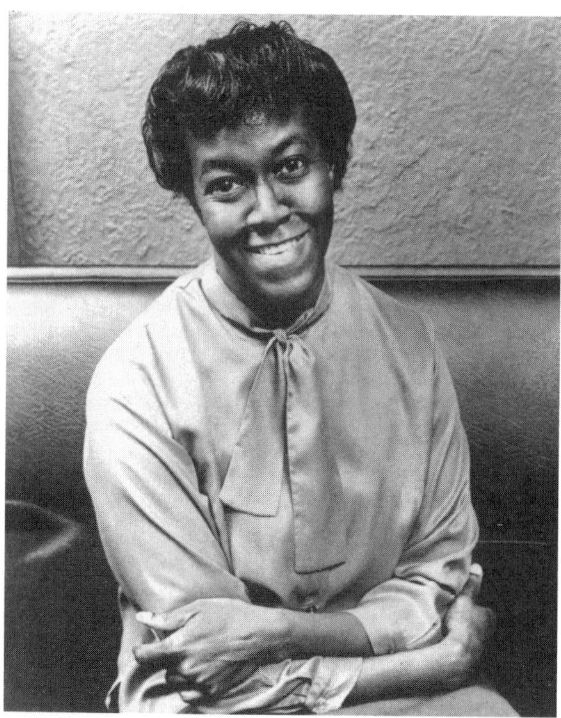

Gwendolyn Brooks

Brooks, Mel, 1927–, American film director, writer, and actor; b. N.Y.C. as Melvin Kaminsky. His comic movies, often parodies of popular film genres, include *The Producers* (1968), *Blazing Saddles* (1974), *Young Frankenstein* (1975), *High Anxiety* (1977), and *Robin Hood: Men in Tights* (1993).

Brooks, Van Wyck, 1886–1963, American critic; b. Plainfield, N.J. An extremely prolific writer, he concentrated in his early work on the influence of Puritanism on American culture, e.g., *The Wine of the Puritans* (1909), and on critical biography, e.g., *The Ordeal of Mark Twain* (1920). His masterpiece, the series *Makers and Finders: A History of the Writer in America, 1800–1915,* which began with the Pulitzer Prize-winning *The Flowering of New England* (1936), is a humanistic interpretation of American literary history.

Brouwer or **Brauwer, Adriaen** [both: brou'wər], c.1606–38, Flemish painter. His later depictions of peasant life and humorous single figures, such as *Drinkers at a Table* (Brussels) and *The Smokers* (Metropolitan Mus.), were often monochromatic.

Browder, Earl Russell, 1891–1973, American Communist leader; b. Wichita, Kan. He was the Communist party's candidate for president in 1936 and 1940. In 1946 the party expelled him for urging Soviet cooperation with the West.

Brown, Ford Madox, 1821–93, English historical painter; b. France. Closely affiliated with the PRE-RAPHAELITES, he painted *Work* (1852–63; Manchester Art Gall.) and 12 FRESCOES (in the town hall of Manchester) showing the city's history.

Brown, George, 1818–80, Canadian journalist and statesman. After emigrating from Scotland at the age of 24 he founded (1844) the Toronto *Globe* and made it a powerful political journal. A member of the Canadian assembly (1851–67), he worked for political representation by population and for the confederation of CANADA.

Brown, Jerry (Edmund Gerald Brown, Jr.), 1938–, American politician, governor of California (1975–83); b. San Francisco. A lawyer, he served (1971–75) as California's secretary of state. Although basically a liberal Democrat, as governor he gained a reputation for austerity and unpredictability. He ran unsuccessfully for the Democratic presidential nomination in 1976, 1980, and 1992 and for the U.S. Senate from California in 1982. His father, **Edmund Gerald (Pat) Brown, Sr.,** 1905–, b. San Francisco, was also governor of California (1959–67).

Brown, Jim, 1936–, American football player; b. St. Simon Island, Ga. An All-American (1956) at Syracuse Univ., he became one of the greatest fullbacks in the game's history while with the Cleveland Browns (1957–65) of the National Football League (NFL). He set NFL career records (since broken) for most yards gained rushing (12,312) and touchdowns scored rushing (106), scored a career-record 126 touchdowns, and had the second-highest career rushing average (5.22 yards per carry). After 1965 he became a movie actor.

Brown, John, 1800–1859, American ABOLITIONIST; b. Torrington, Conn. Raised in Ohio, he moved to Kansas in 1855. In 1856, in retaliation for the sack of LAWRENCE, he led the murder of five proslavery men on the banks of the Pottawatamie R., asserting that he was an instrument in the hand of God. On Oct. 16, 1859, having initiated a plan to liberate Southern slaves through armed intervention, Brown and 21 followers captured the U.S. arsenal at HARPERS FERRY, Va. (now W.Va.). It was taken the next morning by Robert E. LEE, and Brown was hanged on Dec. 2. The dignity and sincerity that he displayed during his widely reported trial led many to regard him as a martyr.

Brown, Robert, 1773–1858, Scottish botanist and botanical explorer. He went as a naturalist and collector to Australia (1801) and described its flora in his *Prodromus florae Novae Hollandiae* (1810). Librarian to the Linnaean Society and British Museum curator, he observed BROWNIAN MOVEMENT in 1827 and discovered the cell nucleus in 1831.

Browne, Charles Farrar: see WARD, ARTEMUS.

Browne, Sir Thomas, 1605–82, English author and physician. In *Religio Medici* (c.1635) he attempted to reconcile science and religion. Other works, including *Hydriotaphia: Urn Burial* (1656), express a philosophy now chiefly of historical interest. The quality of Browne's faith and his mode of expression make him an outstanding figure in English literary history.

brown hematite: see LIMONITE.

Brownian movement or **motion,** irregular, zigzag motion of minute particles of matter suspended in a fluid. First observed (1827) by the botanist Robert Brown, the effect is a result of collisions between the particles and the fluid molecules, which are in constant thermal motion.

Browning, Robert, 1812–89, English poet. His psychological portraits in verse and his experiments in diction and rhythm have made him an important influence on 20th-cent. poetry. Browning was master of the dramatic monologue, e.g., "My Last Duchess," "Fra Lippo Lippi," "Andrea del Sarto," "The Bishop Orders His Tomb." In 1846, after a secret courtship, he married the poet Elizabeth Barrett and took her to Italy, where they lived until her death in 1861. He returned to England and published *Dramatis Personae* (1864), *Dramatic Idylls* (1879–80), and *Asolando* (1889). His masterpiece is *The Ring and the Book* (4 vol., 1868–69). His wife, **Elizabeth Barrett Browning,** 1806–61, published *Poems* in 1844. This volume brought her both fame and Browning's attention. Defying her poor health and a tyrannical father, she married Browning in 1846. E.B. Browning's highly individual gift for lyric poetry is shown in *Sonnets from the Portuguese* (1850), her greatest work. Other works include *Casa Guidi Windows* (1851) and *Aurora Leigh* (1857), a novel in verse.

brown recluse spider or **violin spider,** poisonous nocturnal SPIDER, *Loxoceles reclusa,* most common in the SE and S central U.S. Adults are 3/8 in. (10 mm) long and are light brown with a dark, violin-shaped mark on the back near the head. In humans their venom kills the tissue surrounding a bite and leaves a deep sore, but only rarely does a bite result in death.

Brownsville, city (1990 pop. 98,962), seat of Cameron co., extreme S Tex., on the Rio Grande near the Gulf of Mexico, across the river from Matamoros, Mexico; inc. 1850. A deep water channel accommodates seagoing vessels, and the city has oil and gas, shrimp, and electronics industries. Fort Texas was attacked (1846) by the Mexicans, precipitating the MEXICAN WAR; it was renamed Fort Brown for its defender, Major Jacob Brown. Brownsville grew around the fort. In 1906 a group of African-American soldiers were blamed for a gun raid that killed a resident. Their controversial dishonorable discharge by Pres. Theodore ROOSEVELT was reversed in 1972.

Brown v. Board of Education of Topeka, Kansas, case decided in 1954 by the U.S. SUPREME COURT, holding that de jure segregation in public schools was a violation of the equal protection clause of the 14th amendment to the U.S. CONSTITUTION. A unanimous Court stated that racial separation, no matter how equal the facilities, branded minority children as inferior, thus hindering their development. The "separate but equal" doctrine of PLESSY V. FERGUSON was reversed. In 1955 the Court added that schools must desegregate "with all deliberate speed." The *Brown* decision gave impetus to the civil-rights movement of the 1950s and 60s, and hastened the end of segregation in all public facilities.

Bruce, Scottish royal family, descended from an 11th-cent. Norman duke, Robert de Brus, who aided WILLIAM I in his conquest of England. In the struggle following the death of MARGARET MAID OF NORWAY, the Bruces claimed succession to the Scottish throne. Robert the Bruce was a claimant in 1290, rivaled by John de BALIOL. His grandson was the famous Robert the Bruce, ROBERT I of Scotland. Edward Bruce, brother of Robert I, was crowned king of Ireland in 1316. The youngest son of Robert I succeeded him as DAVID II. He was succeeded by his nephew, ROBERT II, the first STUART king.

Bruce, earls of Elgin: see ELGIN, THOMAS BRUCE, 7TH EARL OF.

Bruce of Melbourne, Stanley Melbourne, Viscount, 1883–1967, Australian prime minister (1923–29). He advocated close relations between Australia and the empire and was later Australian delegate to the LEAGUE OF NATIONS. He was Australian high commissioner in London (1933–45).

Bruch, Max [bro͝okh], 1838–1920, German composer. His Violin Concerto in G Minor (1868) and his variations on the *Kol Nidre* (1881) for cello and orchestra are well known.

Brücke, Die [Ger., = the bridge], German Expressionist art movement lasting from 1905 to 1913 (see EXPRESSIONISM). Founded in Dresden by KIRCHNER, SCHMIDT-ROTTLUFF, and the painter Erich Heckel, the group at first lived and worked communally, developing an intense, violent style with primitive and demonic qualities. Their exhibits, influenced by *Jugendstil* (the German equivalent of ART NOUVEAU) and VAN GOGH, displayed brutally deformed, boldly colored subjects, a reaction against IMPRESSIONISM and REALISM. Unlike contemporaneous FAUVISM, Die Brücke lacked coherent definition; the group disbanded because of disagreements over a statement of its aims.

Bruckner, Anton, 1824–96, Austrian composer and organist. Influenced by Richard WAGNER'S orchestral grandeur and use of the chromatic SCALE, he employed complex, extended melody in such works as the MASSES in D Minor (1864), E Minor (1866), and F Minor (1867–71); a *Te Deum* (1881–84); and nine symphonies.

Bruegel, Brueghel, or **Breughel** [all: brö'gəl], outstanding family of Flemish genre and landscape painters. The foremost, **Pieter Bruegel,** the Elder, c.1525–69, portrayed in vibrant colors the living world of field and forest in which lively, robust peasants work and play, e.g., *The Harvesters* (Metropolitan Mus.) and *Peasant Wedding* (Vienna). BOSCH'S influence is seen in *The Fall of the Rebel Angels* (Brussels). Bruegel also painted religious histories, parables, and rhythmic landscapes based on diagonal lines unfolding into the distance. **Pieter Bruegel,** the Younger, 1564–1637, often copied his father's works and was known for his pictures of the infernal regions. His brother **Jan Bruegel,** 1568–1625, called Velvet Bruegel, specialized in still life and landscapes. He occasionally supplied floral ornament for works from RUBENS'S shop and shared his father's popularity.

Bruges or **Brugge,** city (1991 est. pop. 118,000), NW Flemish Belgium, connected by canal to the North Sea. Founded in the 9th cent., it was (13th cent.) a major port of the HANSEATIC LEAGUE. At its zenith (14th cent.) it was a great commercial center, particularly for the wool industry. It has revived as a commercial and tourist center in this century. Once (14th–15th cent.) the cradle of Flemish art, its churches and museums house many works by such masters as Jan van EYCK and Gerard David.

Bruhn, Erik [bro͞on], 1928–1986, Danish ballet dancer. He joined (1947) the ROYAL DANISH BALLET and was (1953–58) a permanent member of the American Ballet Theatre. He was known for his dramatic, precise style in such ballets as *Giselle* and *Swan Lake*.

Brummell, Beau (George Bryan Brummell), 1778–1840, English dandy and wit. A friend of the prince regent (later George IV), he popularized dark, simply cut clothes, elaborate neckwear, and trousers rather than breeches.

Brundtland, Gro Harlem, 1939–, Norwegian politician. A physician and member of the Labor party, she was environment minister (1974–79) and deputy Labor party leader (1975–81) before her election to parliament (1977). Briefly prime minister in 1981, she has since led minority governments from 1986 to 1989 and from 1990.

Brunehaut, Frankish queen: see BRUNHILDA.

Brunei [bro͞onī'] or **Brunei Darussalam,** officially State of Brunei Darussalam, sultanate (1992 est. pop. 269,000), 2,226 sq mi (5,765

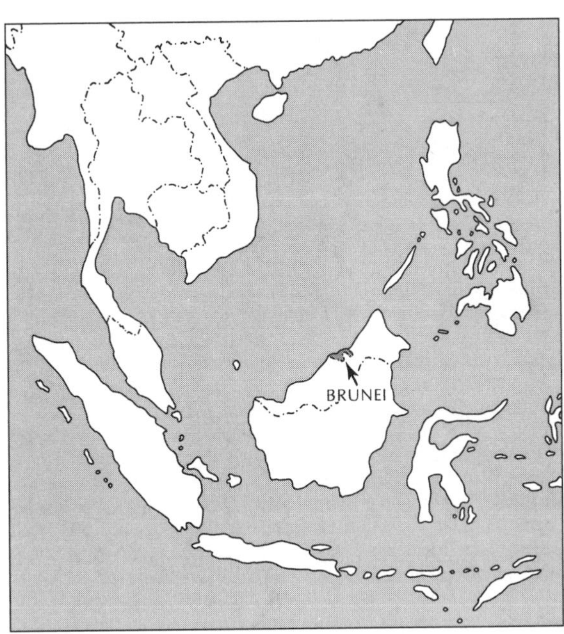

sq km), NW Borneo, in two coastal enclaves surrounded by SARAWAK, Malaysia. The capital and major port is Bandar Seri Begawan. Crude oil, natural gas, and petroleum products are the chief exports, but since independence the government has attempted to promote economic diversification. The majority of the population are Malays, but the minority Chinese dominate the economy. Malay and English are the official languages. Islam is the official religion, but there are Buddhist and Christian minorities. The native sultanate, established in the 15th cent., at one time ruled all Borneo, but its territory shrank to its present size by the late 19th cent. A British protectorate after 1888, Brunei was granted self-government in 1971 and became independent in 1984.

Brunel, Sir Marc Isambard, 1769–1849, English engineer and inventor; b. France. His most important work was the construction of the Thames Tunnel (begun 1825), in which a shield was used for the first time. His son, **Isambard Kingdom Brunel,** 1806–59, an English civil engineer, is best known for his design and construction of three oceangoing STEAMSHIPS: the *Great Western* (1838), the first transatlantic steam vessel; the *Great Britain* (1845), the first ocean screw steamship; and the *Great Eastern* (1858), the largest steam vessel of its time.

Brunelleschi's dome for the cathedral in Florence

Brunelleschi, Filippo [bro͞onĕllĕs'kē], 1377–1446, first great Italian Renaissance architect, a Florentine. After his trial panel (1401) for the bronze doors of the Florence baptistery was not accepted, he concentrated on architectural planning. His Church of San Lorenzo, Florence, with its systematic use of perspective, and his Foundling Hospital, with its series of arches supported on columns, were tremendously influential. In 1420 he began a great octagonal ribbed DOME for the cathedral in Florence, one of the great domical constructions in architectural history.

Brunhild [bro͞on'hĭld], **Brünnehilde** [brün"əhĭld'ə], or **Brynhild** [brĭn'hĭld], in Germanic mythology and literature, mighty female warrior. In the medieval NIBELUNGEN epic she is the queen of Iceland, defeated by SIEGFRIED, whose death she contrives. In the Icelandic VOLSUNGASAGA she is Brynhild, chief of the VALKYRIES. Loved and later deserted by Sigurd, she brings about his death, and destroys herself on his funeral pyre. As Brünnehilde, a Valkyrie, she figures in Richard WAGNER's operatic cycle *Ring of the Nibelungs.*

Brunhilda or **Brunehaut,** d. 613, Frankish queen, wife of Sigebert I of Austrasia. She was the real ruler, through her son and grandsons, of Austrasia and BURGUNDY. She played a leading part in the bloody war (567–613) against Neustria. Clotaire I of Neustria, her nephew, put her to death.

Brunhoff, Jean de, 1899–1937, French author and illustrator of children's books. Beginning with *The Story of Babar, the Little Elephant* (1932), he published several books about an elephant who runs away from the jungle to live in Paris. His son **Laurent de Brunhoff,** 1925–, has continued the series.

Bruno, Giordano, 1548–1600, Italian philosopher. A Dominican, Bruno was accused of heresy, left the order (c.1576), and became a wandering scholar. His works were regarded as heretical, and he was arrested (1591), tried before the INQUISITION, and burned at the stake. His major metaphysical works, *On the Infinite Universe and Worlds* and *The Infinite* (both 1584), drew heavily from Hermetic gnosticism and other works on magic and the occult. His defense of Copernicus was based not on mathematics but on animist and religious grounds. Bruno held that there are many possible modes of viewing the world, because we cannot postulate absolute truth. He was the first to state what is now called the cosmic theory: that the physical world is composed of irreducible elements (monads) in constant motion, and that the universe is infinite in scope. This view, reflected in the works of LEIBNIZ and SPINOZA, accounts for Bruno's position as a forerunner of modern science.

Brussels, Fr. *Bruxelles,* city (1991 est. pop. 140,050), capital of Belgium. An important manufacturing center, it is also a seat of the EUROPEAN UNION and of NATO. Brussels was inhabited by the Romans and later (7th cent.) by the Franks. It developed into a center of the wool trade in the 13th cent. and became (1430) the seat of the dukes of Burgundy and later (1477) of the governors of the Spanish (after 1714, Austrian) Netherlands. In 1830 it became the capital of an independent Belgium. Its historic buildings include the Maison du Roi (13th cent.), Gothic city hall (15th cent.), and parliament building (18th cent.).

Brussels sprouts, variety (*gemmifera*) of CABBAGE, producing small edible heads (sprouts) along the stem. Cultivated like cabbage, it was first developed in Belgium and France in the 18th cent.

Brut, Brute, or **Brutus,** a Trojan, the legendary first king of England, a descendant of AENEAS. His name titles long poems by Wace and LAYAMON.

Brutus, in ancient Rome, a surname of the Junian gens. **Lucius Junius Brutus**, fl. 510 B.C., was the founder of the Roman Republic. Roman historians tell how he led the Romans in expelling the TARQUINS after the rape of Lucrece and how he executed his sons for plotting a Tarquinian restoration. **Marcus Junius Brutus**, 85? B.C.–42 B.C., was the principal assassin of Julius CAESAR. He had sided with POMPEY, but after the battle of Pharsala (48 B.C.), Caesar pardoned him. Nevertheless, he joined Caius Cassius Longinus (see CASSIUS, family) in the plot against Caesar. After Caesar's murder (44 B.C.), Brutus went east and was defeated at Philippi in 42 B.C. by Octavian (later AUGUSTUS) and Antony. Brutus then committed suicide. His character has long been disputed. A lesser member of the conspiracy was **Decimus Junius Brutus**, d. 43 B.C., a partisan of Caesar against Pompey and a favorite of the dictator. After Caesar's death, Brutus was killed by ANTONY.

Brutus, Dennis, 1924–, South African poet. He was imprisoned and later (1966) exiled because of his antiapartheid activities. His poetry, collected in *Letters to Martha* (1969) and *Salutes and Censures* (1984), reflects his prison experiences, struggle for justice, and political exile.

Bryan, William Jennings, 1860–1925, American political leader; b. Salem, Ill. He was a member (1891–95) of the U.S. House of Representatives. At the 1896 Democratic national convention he made his famous "Cross of Gold" speech in defense of FREE SILVER. He was nominated for president but lost to MCKINLEY that year and in 1900; in 1908 he lost to W.H. TAFT. In 1912 he helped to elect Woodrow WILSON, who named him secretary of state (1913–15). Bryan negotiated treaties with some 30 nations providing for investigation of disputes. An advocate of religious FUNDAMENTALISM, he appeared for the prosecution in the 1925 SCOPES TRIAL. Many of the reforms he urged were later adopted, e.g., the INCOME TAX and WOMAN SUFFRAGE.

Bryant, William Cullen, 1794–1878, American poet and editor; b. Cummington, Mass. In his youth he was well known for his poems, e.g., "Thanatopsis," and "To a Waterfowl." He practiced law until 1825, when he moved to New York City. He became editor (1826), then part owner (1829–78) of the *Evening Post,* in which he advocated free trade, abolition of slavery, and other reforms. The earliest American theorist on poetry, Bryant also translated the *Iliad* (1870) and the *Odyssey* (1872).

Bryce Canyon National Park: see NATIONAL PARKS (table).

Bryn Mawr College, at Bryn Mawr, Pa.; founded 1885 by the Society of Friends. The first women's college in the U.S. to offer graduate degrees, Bryn Mawr now has a coeducational graduate school. Its library includes famous medieval and rare book collections. It shares many facilities with Haverford College, a coeducational institution nearby.

bryophyte, member of a group of primitive green land plants consisting of the MOSSES, LIVERWORTS, and hornworts. Since they lack the true stems, roots, and leaves of ferns, cone-bearing plants, and flowering plants, bryophytes must absorb moisture directly from the air or the ground. Their reproductive cycle involves alternating GAMETOPHYTE and sporophyte generations.

Brythonic [brĭthŏn'ĭk], group of languages belonging to the Celtic subfamily of the Indo-European family of languages. See LANGUAGE (table).

Brzezinski, Zbigniew [brəzhĭn'skē], 1928–, American political scientist and public official; b. Poland. While teaching (1960–77) at Columbia Univ., he became an acknowledged expert on political affairs in the Communist world. As Pres. CARTER's national security adviser (1977–81), he advocated a harder line toward the USSR. He returned to Columbia in 1981.

Btu: see BRITISH THERMAL UNIT.

bubble chamber: see PARTICLE DETECTOR.

Buber, Martin, 1878–1965, Jewish philosopher; b. Austria. He taught Jewish philosophy and religion in Germany until he was forced (1938) to leave the country; he settled in Jerusalem. The mysticism of the HASIDIM and the Christian existentialism of KIERKEGAARD influenced him. His major work, *I and Thou* (1923), which posited a personal and direct dialogue between God and the individual, has had a great impact on contemporary Christian and Jewish theology.

bubonic plague: see PLAGUE.

Bucer or **Butzer, Martin** [byōō'sər, bōōt'sər], 1491–1551, German Protestant reformer. Influenced by LUTHER's preaching, he joined (1523) the REFORMATION movement in Strasbourg. He promoted Protestant education and brought about (1536) the Wittenberg Concord on the doctrine of the Eucharist. At the invitation of Thomas CRANMER, he spent his last years in England, teaching at Cambridge.

Buchan, John, 1st **Baron Tweedsmuir,** 1875–1940, Scottish author and statesman. He wrote history, biography, and popular adventure novels, including *The Thirty-nine Steps* (1915). In 1935 he was appointed governor general of Canada.

Buchanan, Franklin, 1800–1874, U.S. naval officer; b. Baltimore. The first superintendent (1845–47) of the U.S. Naval Academy, he was the ranking officer in the Confederate navy in the CIVIL WAR. Wounded at Hampton Roads (1863), he surrendered to Adm. FARRAGUT in the battle of Mobile Bay (1864).

Buchanan, James, 1791–1868, 15th president of the U.S. (1857–61); b. near Mercersburg, Pa. A learned lawyer, he was a congressman (1821–31) and senator (1834–45) from Pennsylvania. At first a Federalist, he became a conservative Democrat and was Pres. POLK's secretary of state (1845–49) during the MEXICAN WAR. Under Pres. PIERCE, he was (1853–56) minister to Great Britain and helped draft the OSTEND MANIFESTO. In 1856 he was elected president. Believing slavery was morally wrong but not unconstitutional, he tried to keep the "sacred balance" between proslavery and antislavery factions, but his views alienated radicals in both North and South. After the 1860 election was won by Abraham LINCOLN, Buchanan was faced with the crisis of secession. Believing that states did not have the right to secede nor the federal government the right to coerce them, he promised there would be no hostile moves during negotiations. U.S. troops were, however, moved to FORT SUMTER; shortly after he left office, gunfire there set off the CIVIL WAR.

Bucharest, Rom. *București,* city (1986 est. pop. 1,989,000), capital and largest city of Romania, SE Romania, on the Dîmbovița R., a tributary of the Danube. It is Romania's chief industrial and communications center and produces farm and transport equipment, petroleum products, and textiles. Founded in the 14th cent., it became the capital of WALACHIA in 1698 and of Romania in 1861. During World War I the city was occupied (1916–18) by the Central Powers. After Romania's surrender to the Allies (Aug. 1944) in World War II, the Germans bombed it severely. Soon after, Soviet troops entered the city. Bucharest contains many old churches, e.g., Metropolitan Church (1649).

Buchman, Frank Nathan Daniel [bo͝ok'mən], 1878–1961, American evangelist; b. Pennsburg, Pa. After preaching "world-changing through life-changing" at Oxford in 1921, he became the head of a movement called the Oxford Group or Buchmanism. In 1938 he founded the controversial Moral Re-Armament movement (MRA).

Büchner, Georg [bükh'nər], 1813–37, German dramatist. A student of medicine and a political agitator, Büchner wrote a powerful drama, *Danton's Death* (1835); the fragmentary tragedy *Wozzeck* (1850), which Alban BERG adapted for his opera; and a comedy, *Leonce and Lena* (1850).

Buchwald, Art, 1925–, American newspaper columnist; b. Mount Vernon, N.Y. Specializing in political and social satire, his columns appear in about 500 newspapers. He was awarded the Pulitzer prize for commentary in 1982.

Buck, Pearl S(ydenstricker), 1892–1973, American author; b. Hillsboro, W.Va. Until 1924 she lived in China, where she, her parents, and her first husband were missionaries. She is famous for her vivid, compassionate novels about life in China, the finest of which is thought to be *The Good Earth* (1931; Pulitzer). Buck published over 85 books, including novels, children's books, plays, biographies, and non-fiction. She was awarded the Nobel Prize in literature in 1938.

buckeye: see HORSE CHESTNUT.

Buckingham, George Villiers, 1st **duke of** [vĭl'yərz], 1592–1628, English nobleman, a royal favorite. He arrived (1614) at the English court as JAMES I was tiring of Robert Carr and rose rapidly, becoming lord high admiral in 1619. By 1620 he was dispensing the king's patronage. He gained popularity with Parliament by urging war with Spain, then lost it by negotiating CHARLES I's marriage to HENRIETTA MARIA, a Catholic princess of France. He remained powerful after Charles came to the throne. After the failure of several expeditions, notably one against Cádiz (1625), he was impeached by Parliament, but the king dissolved Parliament to prevent his trial. Villiers was at Portsmouth preparing an expedition to relieve the HUGUENOTS at La Rochelle when he was killed by a discontented naval officer. His son, **George Villiers,** 2d **duke of Buckingham,** 1628–87, was a royalist in the ENGLISH CIVIL WAR. He served CHARLES II in exile, but intrigues and his marriage to the daughter of a Puritan lord caused estrangement. He regained favor after the RESTORATION and became an extremely powerful courtier. Vain and ambitious, he was noted for his temper, recklessness, and dissoluteness. He was a member of the CABAL but was dismissed for misconduct in 1674. Despite earlier opposition to JAMES II, he regained favor in 1684. A scholar with exquisite tastes, he wrote poetry and plays, including *The Rehearsal* (1671).

Buckingham Palace, residence of British sovereigns since 1837, Westminster, London. Built (1703) by the Duke of Buckingham, it was purchased (1761) by GEORGE III and remodeled (1825) by John NASH. The palace has nearly 600 rooms.

Buckle, Henry Thomas, 1821–62, English historian. Using a scientific method, he undertook the ambitious plan of writing a history of civilization rather than of battles and wars. At the time of his death, he had completed the first two volumes of his *History of Civilization in England* (1857–61), which profoundly influenced liberal thought and later historians.

Buckley, William F(rank), Jr., 1925–, American editor and writer; b. N.Y.C. A witty spokesman for the conservative viewpoint, he founded the magazine *National Review* in 1955, hosted the weekly television show "Firing Line" from 1966, and wrote a syndicated newspaper column. His books include *God and Man at Yale* (1951) and several spy novels.

buckthorn, common name for some members of the Rhamnaceae, a family of widely distributed woody shrubs, small trees, and climbing vines. The buckthorns (some species of the genus *Rhamnus*) and the jujube (*Zizyphus jujuba*) are cultivated as ornamentals. Jujube was also used as a flavoring and in confectionery. Some members of the family yield dyes; others are used for lumber, e.g., cogwood. Other American species of *Rhamnus* are the redberry, the Indian cherry, and *R. purshiana,* which yields the purgative cascara sagrada.

buckwheat, common name for some members of the Polygonaceae, a family of herbs and shrubs found chiefly in north temperate areas and having a characteristic pungent juice containing oxalic acid. Members of the family include the knotweeds and smartweeds (genus *Polygonum* or *Persicaria*), some sorrels (the common name is used also for the unrelated OXALIS), and the economically important rhubarb (genus *Rheum*) and buckwheat (genus *Fagopyrum*).

buckyball, a colloquial term for buckminsterfullerene, a roughly spherical molecule consisting of 60 carbon atoms. **Buckytube** is a generic term for cylindrical fullerenes. See FULLERENE.

bucolics: see PASTORAL.

Budapest, city (1990 pop. 2,016,100), capital and largest city of Hungary, N central Hungary, on both banks of the Danube R. About half of Hungary's industrial output comes from Budapest and its suburbs; major products include machinery, chemicals, and iron and steel. One of the capitals of the AUSTRO-HUNGARIAN MONARCHY, the city was formed in 1873 by the union of Buda and Óbuda, on the right bank of the Danube, with Pest, on the left bank. The area may have been settled in the Neolithic era. Under Roman rule from the 1st cent. A.D., the cities were destroyed by the Mongols in 1241. Buda became the capital of Hungary in 1361 and fell to the Turks in 1541. From 1686 to 1918 the cities were under HAPSBURG rule; after World War I Budapest became the capital of independent Hungary. During World War II Budapest was occupied (1944–45) by the Germans and was largely destroyed during a 14-week siege by Soviet troops. In 1956 it was the center of an unsuccessful uprising against the Communist government.

Buddha [Skt., = the enlightened one], title given to the founder of BUDDHISM, Siddhartha Gautama, c.563–c.483 B.C.; b. S Nepal. A soothsayer is said to have predicted at Siddhartha's birth that he would become a world ruler or a world teacher. His father, King Suddhodana, of the warrior caste, raised him in great luxury, but at the age of 29 Siddhartha renounced the world to become a wandering ascetic and search for a solution to the problems of death and human suffering. After six years of spiritual discipline, he achieved supreme enlightenment at the age of 35 while meditating under a pipal tree at Bodh Gaya. He spent the rest of his life teaching his doctrines and establishing a community of monks, the *sangha,* to continue his work.

Buddhism, religion and philosophy founded in India in the 6th and 5th cent. B.C. by Siddhartha Gautama, called the BUDDHA. One of the great Asian religions, it teaches the practice of MEDITATION and the observance of moral precepts. The basic doctrines include the "four noble truths" taught by the Buddha: existence is suffering; the cause of suffering is desire; there is a cessation of suffering, called NIRVANA, or total transcendence; and there is a path leading to the end of suffering, the "eightfold noble path" of right views, right resolve, right speech, right action, right livelihood, right effort, right mindfulness, and right concentration. Buddhism defines reality in terms of cause-and-effect relations, thus accepting the doctrine common to Indian religions of *samsara,* or bondage to the repeating cycle of births and deaths according to one's physical and mental actions (see KARMA). The ideal of early Buddhism was the perfected saint, *arahant* or *arhat,* purified of all desires. Of the various Buddhist schools and sects that arose, the Theravada [doctrine of the elders] school of Ceylon (now Sri Lanka) is generally accepted as representative of early Buddhist teaching. Mahayana [great vehicle] Buddhism has as a central concept the potential Buddhahood innate in all beings. Its ideal for both layman and monk is the *bodhisattva,* the perfected one who postpones entry into *nirvana* (although meriting it) until all others may be similarly enlightened. Buddhism was greatly strengthened in the 3d cent. B.C. by the support of the Indian emperor ASOKA, but it declined in India in succeeding centuries and was virtually extinct there by the 13th cent., while it spread and flourished in Ceylon (3d cent. A.D.) and Tibet (7th cent. A.D.; see TIBETAN BUDDHISM). In the 1st cent. A.D. Buddhism entered China, where it encountered resistance from CONFUCIANISM and TAOISM, and from there spread to Korea (4th cent. A.D.) and to Japan (6th cent. A.D.). Two important sects that became established in the 5th cent. A.D. and have greatly increased in popularity are ZEN BUDDHISM, featuring the practice of meditation to achieve "sudden enlightenment," and Pure Land Buddhism, or Amidism, a devotional Mahayana sect centered on the worship of the Buddha Amitabha, who vowed to save all sentient beings by bringing them to rebirth in his realm, the "Western Paradise." Buddhism still flourishes in Asia and has an influence in the modern Western world.

Budge, Don (John Donald Budge), 1915–, American tennis player; b. Oakland, Calif. He won the U.S. and Wimbledon singles titles in 1937 and 1938, and in 1938 he was the first to achieve the tennis grand slam (U.S., British, Australian, and French championships). He turned professional in 1939.

Buenos Aires, city and federal district (1991 pop. 2,780,092), E Argentina, capital of Argentina, on the Río de la Plata. It is one of the largest cities of Latin America, a major world port, and Argentina's commercial and social center. Heavily industrialized, the city is one of the world's leading exporters of processed foods. It was founded in 1536, abandoned, then resettled in 1580, and was the first Latin American city to revolt (1810) against Spanish rule. Officially independent in 1816, it became the capital of a united Argentina in 1862. It grew into an urban colossus in the late 19th cent., when railroads into the agriculturally abundant PAMPA to the west began to supplement the great inland river transportation system that linked the city with Uruguay, Paraguay, and Brazil, and immigration from Europe increased. Famous landmarks include the 19th-cent. cathedral, the opera house, and the many beautiful municipal parks.

Buffalo, city (1990 pop. 328,123; met. area 968,532), seat of Erie co., W N.Y., on Lake Erie and the Niagara and Buffalo rivers; inc. 1832. One of the major grain-distributing ports in the U.S. and a railroad hub, it has automobile, electrochemical, electrometallurgical, and steel industries. Laid out in 1803, it was almost entirely destroyed by fire in the WAR OF 1812. Transportation, particularly after the opening (1825) of the ERIE CANAL, was primary to the city's development. Its downtown area underwent major renewal in the 1970s and 80s. Buffalo is the site of a branch of the State Univ. of N.Y., the Albright-Knox Art Gallery, and other noted institutions. The Peace Bridge (1927) connects it with Fort Erie, Canada.

buffalo, name commonly applied to the North American BISON but correctly restricted to related African and Asian hoofed MAMMALS of the CATTLE family. The water, or Indian, buffalo (*Bubalus bubalis*) is a large, strong, dark gray animal with widespread curved horns, domesticated for draft. Wild forms live near rivers, where they wallow; they feed on grass and have fierce tempers.

Buffalo Bill (William Frederick Cody), 1846–1917, American scout and showman; b. near Davenport, Iowa. He worked as an army scout and hunted buffalo for railroad camps. He organized (1883) and then toured with Buffalo Bill's Wild West Show.

buffalo soldiers, name given to the African-American U.S. Army regiments commissioned by Congress to patrol the American West after the Civil War. Consisting of two infantry and two cavalry regiments, they were the first such units chartered in peacetime. The regiments continued in Army service until U.S. armed forces were integrated in 1952.

buffer, solution that can keep its *p*H, i.e., its relative acidity or alkalinity, constant despite the addition of strong acids or bases (see ACIDS AND BASES). Buffer solutions contain either a weak acid or weak base and one of their salts. See article on *p*H.

Buffon, George Louis Leclerc, comte de [büfôN′], 1707–88, French naturalist and author. From 1739 he was keeper of the Jardin du Roi (later Jardin des Plantes) in Paris, making it a center of research during the Enlightenment. His works include his monumental compendium on natural history, *Histoire naturelle* (44 vol.,

1749–1804). On his reception into the French Academy in 1753, he delivered his famous *Discours sur le style.*

bug, name correctly applied to INSECT of the order Hemiptera, although other insects are also referred to as bugs. True bugs have partially thickened, partially membranous front wings and piercing-sucking mouthparts in the form of a beak. Most bugs are terrestrial but many are aquatic (e.g., WATER BUGS). Most suck plant juices (e.g., squash bug); some suck the blood of other insects and spiders. Others feed on humans and other animals (e.g., BEDBUG).

Buganda: see UGANDA.

bugle: see WIND INSTRUMENT.

building and loan association: see SAVINGS AND LOAN ASSOCIATION.

Buisson, Ferdinand Édouard [büēsôN′], 1841–1932, French educator and 1927 Nobel Peace Prize winner. A professor of pedagogy at the Sorbonne, he produced the *Dictionnaire de pédagogie* (1882–93) and was an ardent pacifist and civil-liberties advocate.

Bujumbura, city (1986 est. pop. 273,000), capital of Burundi, W Burundi. A port on Lake TANGANYIKA, it is the country's largest city and economic center, and has a growing tourist industry. Coffee, cotton, hides, and tin ore are shipped via the lake to Tanzania and Zaïre. The city became (1899) a military post in German East Africa. After World War I it was the administrative center of Ruanda-Urundi, a Belgian MANDATE. It was called Usumbura until 1962.

Bukharin, Nikolai Ivanovich, 1888–1938, Soviet Communist leader and theoretician. After the 1917 RUSSIAN REVOLUTION he edited the newspaper *Pravda* and was a COMINTERN leader. A full member of the politburo after 1924, he lost his major party posts in 1929 for advocating slow agricultural collectivization, in opposition to the Stalinist majority. In 1938 he was tried for treason and executed.

Bulawayo, city (1983 est. pop. 429,000), SW Zimbabwe. The country's second largest city, it is an important commercial, railroad, and industrial center that produces textiles, motor vehicles, and metal products. The city was founded by the British in 1893. Nearby are the 18th-cent. ruins of Khami.

bulb, thickened, fleshy plant bud, usually formed below the soil surface, which stores food from one blooming season to the next. Bulbs have either layers (e.g., onion and hyacinth) or scales (e.g., some lilies). Structures that serve similar functions include the TUBER of the potato and the RHIZOMES of some irises. All are specialized STEMS.

Bulfinch, Charles, 1763–1844, American architect; b. Boston. He was chairman of the Boston board of selectmen (equivalent to mayor) from 1799 to 1818. He designed the first theater in New England, the Federal Street Theater (1794; now demolished). Remaining are his chief monumental works—the statehouse, Boston (1799); University Hall at Harvard (1815); and Massachusetts General Hospital (1820). Bulfinch's completion (1818–30) of the CAPITOL at Washington inspired state capitol architects throughout the U.S.

Bulfinch, Thomas, 1796–1867, American author; b. Newton, Mass. He wrote works that popularized myth and fable, e.g., *The Age of Fables* (1855) and *The Age of Chivalry* (1858).

Bulgakov, Mikhail Afanasyevich [bo͞olgä′kəf], 1891–1940, Russian author. *The White Guard* (1925), a novel, and *The Days of the Turbines* (1926), a play, are about the RUSSIAN REVOLUTION (1917). His masterpiece is *The Master and Margarita* (published in a censored edition in 1967–68; tr. 1967), a satiric, philosophical fantasy about Satan's visit to Moscow.

Bulganin, Nikolai Aleksandrovich, 1895–1975, Soviet leader. He was mayor of Moscow (1931–37), chairman of the state bank (1937–41), and defense minister under STALIN and MALENKOV, whom he succeeded as premier (1955). In 1958, forced from office by KHRUSHCHEV, he was expelled from the Communist party central committee.

Bulgaria, officially Republic of Bulgaria, republic (1992 est. pop. 8,869,000), 42,823 sq mi (110,912 sq km), SE Europe, on the E BALKAN PENINSULA. It is bordered by the Black Sea (E), Romania (N), Macedonia and Yugoslavia (W), Greece (S), and European Turkey (SE). SOFIA is the capital. Central Bulgaria is traversed from east to west by the Balkan Mts.; the Rhodope range, with the country's highest peak, Musala Mt. (9,592 ft/2,923 m), is in the southwest. The principal river is the DANUBE. Bulgaria has been considerably industrialized since World War II, but agriculture (chiefly wheat, corn, barley, sugar beets, grapes, and livestock) remains the principal occupation. The leading industries are food processing, engineering, metallurgy, and the production of machinery, chemicals, and electronics. Mineral resources include lignite, iron and lead ores, and petroleum and natural gas. The population consists chiefly of Bulgars (86%) and Turks (9%). The Bulgarian Orthodox church is the predominant religion, but most Turks and some ethnic Bulgarians are Muslims. Bulgarian is the official language.

History. In A.D. 679–80 ancient THRACE and Moesia, site of modern Bulgaria, were conquered by Eastern Bulgars, who gradually merged with earlier Slavic settlers and adopted their language. The first Bulgarian empire was established in 681, introduced to Christianity by BORIS I (r.852–89) in 865, at the height of its power under SIMEON I (r.893–927), and subjugated by the Byzantines in 1018. The second Bulgarian empire rose in 1186 and reached its apex under Ivan II (r.1218–41). In 1396 it was absorbed by the OTTOMAN EMPIRE, which ruled it for almost five centuries. Turkey's suppression of a Bulgarian revolt (1876) was one of the reasons for the RUSSO-TURKISH WAR of 1877–78. The Treaty of San Stefano, which created a large, autonomous Bulgaria, was revised by the Congress of BERLIN, which divided Bulgaria into three parts. In 1908 FERDINAND of Saxe-Coburg-Gotha proclaimed Bulgarian independence, with himself as czar. The country's borders were changed significantly by the BALKAN WARS, and Bulgarian claims in MACEDONIA prompted Bulgaria to side with Germany in WORLD WAR I. Under Boris III (r.1918–43) Bulgaria was often in political turmoil, and in 1935 Boris established a personal dictatorship. In WORLD WAR II Bulgaria again allied (1941) with Germany. The Soviet Union occupied the country in 1944, and Communists took over the government. The monarchy was abolished, and a republic proclaimed in 1946. Bulgaria's Communist dictatorship was one of the most repressive in the Soviet bloc and attempted to forcibly assimilate its Turkish minority during the 1980s. In Nov. 1989, Bulgarian president and party boss Todor I. ZHIVKOV abruptly resigned, and the National Assembly later ended the Communist party's monopoly of political power, though the ruling Socialist (formerly Communist) party was returned to power in June 1990. A new constitution (1991) established a parliamentary republic, and in the subsequent elections the Socialists lost to the Union of Democratic Forces. No party, however, was able to establish a long-term government, and major economic reforms proved difficult to enact.

Bulgarian language, member of the South Slavic group of the Slavic subfamily of the Indo-European family of languages. See LANGUAGE (table).

Bulgars, Eastern, Turkic-speaking people who appeared on the middle Volga R., E European Russia, by the 8th cent.; also called Volga or Kama Bulgars. One branch moved west into Bulgaria and there merged with the SLAVS. The Eastern Bulgars accepted ISLAM in the 10th cent. and founded a powerful state; it survived the Mongol conquests of 1237 and 1361 but disappeared after its capture by the grand duke of Moscow in 1431.

bulimia: see EATING DISORDERS.

bull, letter containing an important pronouncement of the pope. In modern times encyclicals (letters to all bishops) are usually used for doctrinal statements, whereas bulls are employed for solemn or grave pronouncements.

bulldog, thick-set NONSPORTING DOG; shoulder height, 13–15 in. (33–38.1 cm); weight, 40–50 lb (18.1–22.7 kg). Its short, flat-lying coat is brindle, white, red, or fawn. It has a low-slung body and undershot jaw and was developed in Britain for bullbaiting and pit-fighting.

bullfighting, national sport of Spain, also popular in Mexico and other Latin American countries and S France. The object is for one of the bullfighters, the matador, to kill an untamed bull with a sword in a manner largely prescribed by tradition. The matador is assisted by two mounted picadors and three capemen on foot (*banderilleros*), who sting the bull with lances and barbed sticks to spur his charge. In the final act, the matador makes daring passes at the bull with his cape, or *muleta,* before thrusting his sword between the animal's shoulder blades into the heart. Although a matador's performance is often one of grace and beauty, critics have denounced bullfighting as an inhumane spectacle. The Portuguese practice a style of bullfighting from horseback in which the bull is not killed.

Bull Moose party: see PROGRESSIVE PARTY.

Bull Run, small stream, NE Va., c.30 mi (50 km) SW of Washington, D.C.; the site of two Union defeats in the CIVIL WAR. The **first battle of Bull Run** (or Manassas) was the first major clash of the war, on July 21, 1861. On July 16, Union Gen. Irvin McDowell began to move on Confederate Gen. P.G.T. BEAUREGARD at Manassas Junction. McDowell attacked Beauregard's soldiers, who were joined by some forces of Gen. Joseph E. JOHNSTON, near the stone bridge over Bull Run and drove them to the Henry House Hill. But Confederate Gen. Stonewall JACKSON checked the Union advance and, reinforced, routed the raw Union troops. In the **second battle of Bull Run,** Aug. 29–30, 1862, Jackson was attacked by Union Gen. John Pope just as Gen. James LONGSTREET arrived with reinforcements; together they twice repulsed Pope, who withdrew to Washington. Both battlefields are in Manassas National Battlefield Park.

bull terrier, large, muscular TERRIER; shoulder height, 19–22 in. (48.3–55.9 cm); weight, 30–36 lb (13.6–16.3 kg). Its short, flat-lying, harsh coat is glossy white or brindle with white markings. It was developed for dogfighting in England c.1835.

Bülow, Hans Guido, Freiherr von, 1830–94, German pianist and conductor. He studied with LISZT, married his daughter Cosima (who left him to marry Richard WAGNER), and became a champion of BRAHMS. He was the first modern virtuoso conductor.

bulrush: see SEDGE.

Bultmann, Rudolf Karl [bo͝olt'män], 1884–1976, German existentialist theologian. Influenced by Martin HEIDEGGER, he is best known for his work on the New Testament, which he reduced—with the exception of the Passion—to basic elements of myth. His approach is termed "demythologization." His classic work is *Theology of the New Testament* (tr. 1951).

Bulwer-Lytton, Edward George Earle Lytton, 1st **Baron Lytton,** 1803–73, English novelist. Best remembered for his popular, extremely well-researched historical novels, particularly *The Last Days of Pompeii* (1834) and *Rienzi* (1835), he also wrote novels of manners and successful plays. He served in Parliament and as colonial secretary. His son, **Edward Robert Bulwer-Lytton,** 1st **earl of Lytton,** pseud. **Owen Meredith,** 1831–91, was a diplomat and poet. He was viceroy of India (1876–80) and, later, ambassador to France. His poetry includes *Lucile* (1860) and the epic fantasy *King Poppy* (1892).

Bunau-Varilla, Philippe Jean [büno'-värēyä'], 1859–1940, French engineer. He organized the company that built the PANAMA CANAL. He was a leader in the conspiracy that successfully wrested PANAMA from Colombia. As minister of the new Panamanian republic, he negotiated the treaty (1903) that gave the U.S. control of the waterway.

bunchberry: see DOGWOOD.

Bunche, Ralph Johnson, 1904–71, U.S. diplomat; b. Detroit. He was (1945) the first African American to be a division head in the U.S. Dept. of State. He entered the UN in 1946 as director of the Trusteeship Division. For his work (1947) as principal secretary of the UN Palestine Commission he was awarded (1950) the Nobel Peace Prize. He later served as undersecretary general for special political affairs (1958–71).

Bunin, Ivan Alekseyevich [bo͞o'nĭn], 1870–1953, Russian writer. He came to world attention with *The Village* (1910), a pessimistic novel of peasant life. Best known are his short stories, e.g., the title story in the collection *The Gentleman from San Francisco* (1916), an ironic study of vanity and death; and his autobiographical novel *The Well of Days* (1930). An aristocrat, he lived in exile after 1919. He received the 1933 Nobel Prize in literature.

Bunker Hill, battle of, in the AMERICAN REVOLUTION, June 17, 1775; actually fought on nearby Breed's Hill, Charlestown, Mass. Colonial militia defended the height against Gen. William Howe (see under HOWE, RICHARD HOWE, EARL) until their powder gave out. The British victory failed to break the Patriots' siege of Boston, and the gallant American defense heightened colonial morale and resistance.

Bunsen, Robert Wilhelm, 1811–99, German scientist. A professor (1852–89) at Heidelberg, he studied organic compounds of arsenic and developed a method of gas analysis from studies on blast furnaces. With Gustav KIRCHHOFF he discovered by spectroscopy the elements CESIUM and RUBIDIUM. He invented and improved various kinds of laboratory equipment, e.g., the Bunsen burner.

Bunshaft, Gordon, 1909–90, American architect; b. Buffalo. As chief designer for the firm of Skidmore, Owings, & Merrill, he was responsible for Lever House, New York City's first glass-wall SKYSCRAPER (1952), which was widely imitated. Among his other works are the Albright-Knox Art Gallery, Buffalo, and the HIRSHHORN MUSEUM, Washington, D.C.

Buntline, Ned, pseud. of **Edward Zane Carroll Judson,** 1823–86, American writer; b. Stamford, N.Y. In 1845 he founded *Ned Buntline's Own,* a sensationalist magazine. Buntline, who lived a life of violent adventure, wrote over 400 action novels that were the forerunners of America's DIME NOVELS.

Buñuel, Luis [bo͞onyo͞oĕl'], 1900–1983, Spanish film director. His critical, often witty, studies of social hypocrisy include *L'Age d'or* (1930), *Los Olvidados* (1949), *The Exterminating Angel* (1962), and *That Obscure Object of Desire* (1977).

Bunyan, John, 1628–88, English author. A tinker by trade and a Parliamentary soldier, he became a Baptist lay preacher and wrote to defend his beliefs. Arrested in 1660 for unlicensed preaching, he spent 12 years in prison. There he wrote his spiritual autobiography, *Grace Abounding to the Chief of Sinners* (1666), and other books. Imprisoned a second time, he began his masterpiece, *Pilgrim's Progress from This World to That Which Is to Come* (1678, second part 1684). An allegory of Christian's journey from the City of Destruction to the Celestial City, it is written in a prose that unites biblical eloquence with the clarity of common speech.

Bunyan, Paul, legendary American lumberjack of fantastic size and strength, hero of many "tall tales" popular in the Western timber country. His prized possession was the huge Babe the Blue Ox, whose horns were 42 ax handles apart.

Buonaparte: see BONAPARTE and NAPOLEON I.

Buonarroti, Michelangelo: see MICHELANGELO BUONARROTI.

Buoninsegna, Duccio di: see DUCCIO DI BUONINSEGNA.

buoyancy: see ARCHIMEDES' PRINCIPLE.

Burbage, Richard, 1567?–1619, first great English actor. He originated the title roles in SHAKESPEARE'S *Hamlet, King Lear, Othello,* and *Richard III.* He also acted in the premieres of many plays by Thomas KYD, BEAUMONT and FLETCHER, Ben JONSON, and John WEBSTER.

Burbank, Luther, 1849–1926, American plant breeder; b. Lancaster, Mass. He developed many new varieties of fruits, vegetables, and flowers, including the Burbank potato and the famous Shasta daisy. His methods and results are described in his books *How Plants Are Trained to Work for Man* (1921) and, with Wilbur Hall, *Harvest of the Years* (1927) and *Partners of Nature* (1939).

Burbidge, (Eleanor) Margaret, 1925–, Anglo-American astronomer. She was (1972–73) the first woman appointed director of the Royal Greenwich Observatory and was named (1982) president of the American Association for the Advancement of Science. Burbidge; her husband, Geoffrey Burbidge; William Fowler; and Sir Fred Hoyle showed (1956) how heavier elements can be built up from lighter ones in the interiors of stars.

Burckhardt, Jacob Christoph [bo͝ork'härt], 1818–97, Swiss historian, one of the founders of the cultural interpretation of history. His *Civilization of the Renaissance in Italy* (1860) remains the great classic on the Renaissance. He influenced his friend NIETZSCHE and the work of J.A. SYMONDS.

Burger, Warren Earl, 1907–, 15th chief justice of the U.S. SUPREME COURT (1969–86); b. St. Paul, Minn.; grad. St. Paul College of Law (1931). He was a judge of the U.S. Court of Appeals for the District of Columbia from 1956 until his appointment as Supreme Court chief justice by Pres. Nixon. A conservative and an advocate of judicial restraint, he led a court that was generally more conservative than the one headed by his predecessor, Earl WARREN.

Burgess, Anthony, 1917–93, English novelist; b. John Anthony Burgess Wilson. Of his surreal, darkly comic novels, the best known is the futuristic thriller *A Clockwork Orange* (1962). Others include *Inside Mr. Enderby* (1961), *MF* (1971), *Earthly Powers* (1980), and *Any Old Iron*(1989).

Burghley or **Burleigh, William Cecil,** 1st **Baron** [both: bûr'lē], 1520–98, English statesman. He was chief adviser to ELIZABETH I, whom he served faithfully for 40 years—as her chief spokesman in Parliament (1558–98) and as secretary (1558–72) and lord treasurer (1572–98). A supporter of the Anglican church, he suppressed Catholic revolts and convinced Elizabeth to execute MARY QUEEN OF SCOTS.

burglary, in COMMON LAW, the nighttime breaking into and entering of a dwelling of another to commit a FELONY. Some modern statutes have amended the common-law definition of burglary to include breaking into and entering any building during the day or night to commit any crime.

Burgoyne, John [bərgoin'], 1722–92, British general. A hero of the SEVEN YEARS WAR, he was elected to Parliament in 1761. In the AMERICAN REVOLUTION he led a poorly equipped army in the SARATOGA CAMPAIGN and surrendered (Oct. 1777).

Burgundy, historic region, E France. Dijon is the historic capital. Burgundy, centered in the fertile Saône and upper Rhone river valleys, is famous for its fine wines. The Burgundii, a tribe from Savoy, conquered (c.480) the area from Rome and established the First Kingdom of Burgundy, comprising SE France and W Switzerland. Burgundy was partitioned after it fell (534) to the Franks, but it was later united to form (933) the kingdom of ARLES. The duchy of Burgundy, roughly the area of the present region, was created in 877. In 1364 JOHN II of France bestowed it upon his son, PHILIP THE BOLD. Under Philip and his successors, JOHN THE FEARLESS, PHILIP THE GOOD, and CHARLES THE BOLD, Burgundy became a great power and acquired vast territory, including much of the Low Countries. After the accession (1477) of MARY OF BURGUNDY, most of Burgundy's possessions came under HAPSBURG rule; the duchy itself was incorporated into France.

Burke, Edmund, 1729–97, British political writer and statesman; b. Ireland. He was a member of Samuel JOHNSON's literary circle. His early writings concerned aesthetics and philosophy. In 1765 he became private secretary to the marquess of Rockingham (then prime minister) and entered Parliament. In *Thoughts on the Cause of the Present Discontents* (1770), he was the first to argue the value of political parties. As a member of Parliament he called for conciliation with the American colonists and warned against taxing them excessively. Attempting to reform the British EAST INDIA COMPANY in the 1780s, he instigated the impeachment of Warren HASTINGS, governor general of India, on corruption charges. His most famous work, *Reflections on the Revolution in France* (1790), expresses his opposition to the Revolution. Burke's writings greatly influenced 19th-cent. conservative political theory.

Burke, Kenneth (Duva), 1897–1993, American literary critic; b. Pittsburgh. A writer and music critic, he was known as a theorist of literary forms. He believed that literature is a form of "symbolic action," and his insights drew on data from the social sciences. His writings include *A Grammar of Motives* (1945) and *A Rhetoric of Motives* (1950).

Burkina Faso or **Burkina,** formerly Upper Volta, republic (1992 est. pop. 9,654,000), 105,869 sq mi (274,200 sq km), W Africa, bordered by Mali (W and N), Niger (NE), Benin (SE), and Togo, Ghana, and Côte d'Ivoire (S). The capital is OUAGADOUGOU. The country is made up of vast, semidesert plains, except in the southwest, where the low hills are covered by savanna. Rainfall is sparse, and the soil is of poor quality. Burkina Faso is an impoverished agricultural nation, with the great majority of its work force engaged in subsistence farming or livestock-raising. Cotton, oilseeds, shea (karité) nuts, live animals, meat, and hides are exported. Manganese, phosphates, and gold-bearing quartz are mined. The country is economically dependent on foreign aid, and many Burkina Faso citizens migrate for work to Côte d'Ivoire and Ghana. The Mossi, Mande, and Fulani are the largest ethnic groups. Most people adhere to traditional religious beliefs, but about 40% are Muslims and 10% Roman Catholics. French is the official language.

History. Mossi invaders from present-day Ghana conquered the region around A.D. 1100 and, although far outnumbered by their subjects, created powerful states that endured for more than 500 years. France gained control of the country in the 1890s, administering it as part of what is now MALI until 1919, when it became the separate territory of Upper Volta. From 1932 to 1947 it was divided between neighboring French territories for administrative convenience. The country gained full independence in 1960 as Upper Volta (changed to Burkina Faso in 1984). The new nation alternated between civilian and military governments. A new democratic constitution was adopted in 1978, but coups in 1980, 1982, 1983, and 1987 brought successive military factions to power. Capt. Blaise Compaoré has been head of a leftist government since 1987. In 1992 the country held its first multiparty parliamentary elections since 1978; Compaoré's party unexpectedly won over two thirds of the seats amid charges of fraud.

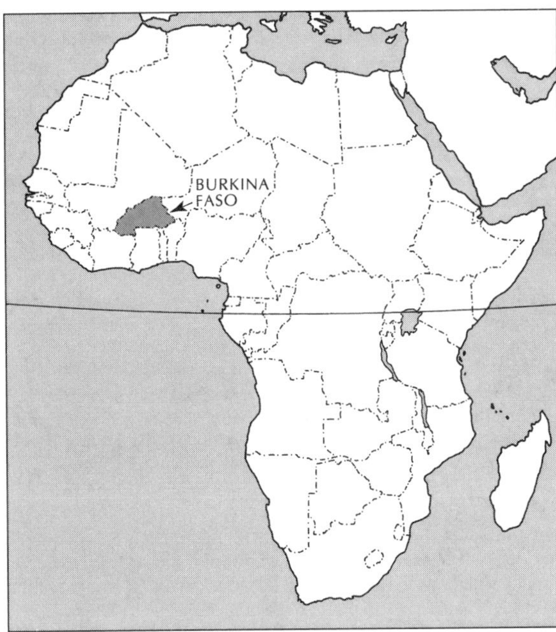

Burleigh, William Cecil, 1st **Baron:** see BURGHLEY, WILLIAM CECIL, 1ST BARON.

burlesque [Ital., = mockery; from the *burleschi* of Francesco Berni, a 16th-cent. Italian poet], an entertainment that, unlike COMEDY or FARCE, works by caricature, ridicule, and distortion, but, unlike SATIRE, has no ethical element. Early English burlesque, e.g., GAY's *Beggar's Opera* (1728), often ridiculed celebrated literary works or sentimental drama. Extravaganza and burletta were similar to burlesque; the latter was a musical production. American burlesque (from 1865) began as a variety show characterized by vulgar dialogue and broad humor; Al JOLSON, Fanny Brice, and W.C. FIELDS were famous stars. By 1920 the term had come to mean a "striptease" show. Burlesque fell victim to the popularity of nightclubs, movies, and television.

Burlington, town (1991 pop. 129,575), SE Ontario, Canada, part of the regional municipality of Halton (1991 pop. 313,136). Located on Lake ONTARIO, it is part of the rapidly growing lakefront industrial area between TORONTO and HAMILTON.

Burlington, city (1990 pop. 39,127), seat of Chittenden co., NW Vt., on Lake Champlain; settled 1773, inc. 1865. The largest city in Vermont, it has such manufactures as ordnance parts, machinery, textiles, and wood and steel products. During the WAR OF 1812, the city was the target of an abortive British naval attack. The Univ. of Vermont is in Burlington.

Burma: see MYANMAR.

Burma Road, road extending c.700 mi (1,150 km) from Kunming, Yunnan prov, S China, to Lashio, a railhead in Myanmar (Burma). A major feat of engineering, it was built (1937–38) over mountainous terrain by the Chinese. It achieved its greatest importance during WORLD WAR II, when Japan controlled the E Asian coast and it served as a vital artery for the transport of Allied military supplies to China.

Burmese, language belonging to the Tibeto-Burman subfamily of the Sino-Tibetan family of languages. See LANGUAGE (table).

Burmese cat: see under CAT.

burn, injury resulting from exposure to heat, electricity, radiation, or caustic chemicals. First-degree burns, characterized by simple reddening of the skin, can be treated locally with ice baths and ointments. Second-degree burns, characterized by formation of blisters, may require the care of a doctor to prevent infection. Third-degree burns, with destruction of upper and lower SKIN layers, are serious and often fatal; they require prompt medical attention to reduce pain and prevent SHOCK and infection. BLOOD TRANSFUSION may be necessary to replace body fluids; long-term treatment may include TRANSPLANTATION of natural or artificial skin grafts.

Burne-Jones, Sir Edward, 1833–98, English painter and decorator. A PRE-RAPHAELITE and lifelong friend of William MORRIS, he described a dreamlike, medieval world in such popular paintings as *King Cophetua and the Beggar Maid* (1884; Tate Gall., London) and *Depths of the Sea* (Birmingham Gall.).

Burnet, Sir Macfarlane, 1899–1985, Australian virologist and physician. An expert on viruses, he contributed to the understanding of influenza and the development of immunity against it. For work in immunological tolerances, specifically the reactions of the body to the transplantation of foreign living tissues, he shared with Peter MEDAWAR the 1960 Nobel Prize in physiology or medicine.

Burnett, Frances Eliza Hodgson, 1849–1924, American author; b. England. She is known for her children's books, particularly *Little Lord Fauntleroy* (1886) and *The Secret Garden* (1911).

Burney, Fanny, later **Madame D'Arblay,** 1752–1840, English novelist. *Evelina* (1778) made her famous, and she became part of Samuel JOHNSON's circle. She later wrote *Cecilia* (1782), *Camilla* (1796), and *The Wanderer* (1814). Her theme is the entry into society and the coming of age of a virtuous, inexperienced young girl. Burney's diaries and letters vividly depict English society from 1768 to 1840.

Burnham, Daniel Hudson, 1846–1912, American architect and city planner; b. Henderson, N.Y. With John W. Root, he built many major buildings in Chicago. The 20-story Masonic Temple Building (1892) was the first important skeleton SKYSCRAPER. Other projects included the "Rookery," the first suitably planned modern office building. Other works include the Flatiron Building, N.Y.C., and Union Station, Washington, D.C. Burnham and Root designed the greatly influential general plan for the 1893 Columbian Exposition at Chicago.

Burns, Arthur F., 1904–87, American economist; b. Austria. While teaching at Rutgers (1927–44) and Columbia Univ. (1944–59), he was associated (from 1933) with the National Bureau of Economic Research (president, 1957–67), where he did important work in analyzing business cycles. He served as chairman (1953–56) of the Council of Economic Advisers under Pres. Eisenhower and economic counselor (1969–70) to Pres. Nixon. As chairman (1970–78) of the board of governors of the FEDERAL RESERVE SYSTEM, he advocated fiscal and monetary restraint. He later (1981–85) served as ambassador to West Germany.

Burns, George, 1896–, b. N.Y.C. as Nathan Birnbaum, and **Gracie Allen,** 1906–64, b. San Francisco, American comedy team (1923–58). On radio (1932–50) and television (1950–58) and in films, they played an endlessly patient husband and scatterbrained wife. For his role in *The Sunshine Boys* (1975) Burns won an Academy Award.

Burns, Robert, 1759–96, Scottish poet. Raised on a farm, as a boy he read Scottish poetry, as well as POPE, LOCKE, and SHAKESPEARE. He wrote early but did not publish until, in 1786, hoping to emigrate to Jamaica, he sold *Poems, Chiefly in the Scottish Dialect*, which became an immediate success. Burns did not emigrate and spent the rest of his life in Scotland, failing as a farmer but producing hundreds of songs, among them "Flow Gently, Sweet Afton," "My Heart's in the Highlands," "Auld Lang Syne," and "Comin' thro' the Rye." Burns is noted for his humor and humanitarianism, and for the descriptive power he brings to bear on Scottish rural life. His use of dialect brought needed freshness into English poetry, but his scope far exceeds his apparent regionalism.

Burr, Aaron, 1756–1836, American political leader; b. Newark, N.J. After service in the AMERICAN REVOLUTION, he was (1791–97) U.S. senator from New York. He tied with Thomas JEFFERSON in the presidential election of 1800. Through the efforts of Alexander HAMILTON, the House of Representatives named Jefferson president and Burr vice president. Hamilton's hostility also figured in Burr's defeat (1804) for governor of N.Y. His political career ended when he mortally wounded Hamilton in a duel. Burr plotted with Gen. James WILKINSON to colonize the Southwest and was tried (1807) for treason; he was found not guilty and retired from public life.

Burroughs, Edgar Rice, 1875–1950, American novelist. He wrote *Tarzan of the Apes* (1914) and many other thrillers.

bursitis, acute or chronic inflammation of a bursa, a fluid-filled sac located close to a joint. Caused by infection, injury, or diseases like ARTHRITIS and GOUT, the inflammation produces pain, tenderness, and restricted motion. Treatment includes rest, application of heat, use of NONSTEROIDAL ANTI-INFLAMMATORY DRUGS, antibiotics, corticosteroid drugs, and occasionally surgery.

Burt, Cyril Lodowic, 1883–1971, British psychologist. Educated at Oxford and Würzburg, he made significant contributions to educational psychology and is noted for his development of factor analysis in psychological testing. After his death, some of his research on inheritance and intelligence was found to have been falsified, partially diminishing his reputation.

Burton, Richard, 1925–84, Anglo-American actor; b. Wales as Richard Jenkins. He starred in Shakespeare plays; in the musical *Camelot* (1960, 1980); and in films, e.g., *The Robe* (1953) and *Becket* (1964).

Burton, Sir Richard Francis, 1821–90, English explorer, linguist, and writer. Fluent in Arabic, he journeyed (1853) in disguise to the forbidden cities of MECCA and MEDINA. In 1858 he and J.H. SPEKE tried unsuccessfully to find the source of the NILE R. In 1865 he explored Santos, in Brazil. His works include a translation of the *Arabian Nights* (1885–88).

Burton, Robert, 1577–1640, English clergyman and scholar. His *Anatomy of Melancholy* (1621), on the causes and effects of melancholy, ranged widely into social and historical questions in an idiosyncratic, anecdotal style.

Burundi [bərŭn'dē], officially Republic of Burundi, republic, (1992 est. pop. 6,022,000), 10,747 sq mi (27,834 sq km), E central Africa, formerly part of Ruanda-Urundi, bordered by Rwanda (N), Tanzania (E), Lake Tanganyika (SW), and Zaïre (W). BUJUMBURA is the capital. The three main geographic zones are a narrow area, part of the GREAT RIFT VALLEY, in the west; a central region of mountains reaching a height of c.8,800 ft (2,680 m); and, in the east, an area of broken plateaus and somewhat lower elevations (c.4,500–6,000 ft/1,370–1,830 m), where most of the people live. Burundi is one of the smallest, most densely populated, and poorest countries in Africa. The predominant occupation is subsistence agriculture. Coffee is the most important cash crop and the major export; cotton and tea are also grown. There is a little mining, and nickel and vanadium deposits could be important in the future. Manufacturing is largely limited to basic consumer goods. The two main ethnic

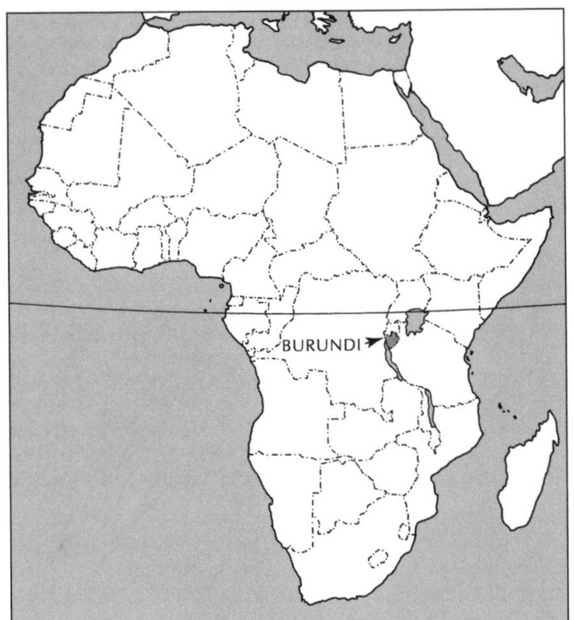

groups are the Hutu (about 85% of the population) and the Tutsi (about 14%), who, despite their relatively small numbers, historically have dominated the government and army. The remaining 1% are the Twa, who are PYGMIES. French and Kurundi (a Bantu language) are the official languages; Swahili is also spoken. A majority of the people are Christian (mostly Roman Catholic); the rest follow traditional religions.

History. The original inhabitants, the Twa (Pygmies), were followed (c.1200) and then outnumbered by the Hutu, who in turn gave way to the migrating Tutsi in the 15th cent. By the 19th cent. the Tutsi had established dominance, and a Tutsi king (mwami) ruled the country. In 1890 Burundi was incorporated into German East Africa. During WORLD WAR I it was occupied by Belgian forces, and in 1919 it became part of the Belgian League of Nations mandate of RUANDA-URUNDI (made a UN trust territory in 1946). Burundi became an independent kingdom in 1962, but the monarchy was overthrown in 1966 and a military republic established. The years following independence have been marked by bitter fighting between the Tutsi and Hutu, resulting in thousands of Hutu deaths in the 1970s. The early 1980s saw reduced military influence and efforts at Tutsi-Hutu reconciliation, but a military coup in 1987 brought Maj. Pierre Buyoya to power. In 1988 there were bloody ethnic clashes again. Subsequently, Pres. Buyoya attempted to ameliorate the Hutu's situation. In mid-1993 Melchior Ndadaye, a Hutu, won Burundi's first free presidential election, but four months later he was overthrown and killed by Tutsi soldiers. Burundi was convulsed by ethnic violence in which thousands, both Hutu and Tutsi, died, and many fled the country. The coup collapsed, but civilian authority was restored slowly. In 1994 Cyprien Ntaryamira, agriculture minister and a Hutu, was chosen as president by parliament.

Bush, George Herbert Walker, 1924–, 41st president of the U.S. (1989–93); b. Milton, Mass. A graduate of Yale Univ., he was a Navy fighter pilot in World War II and after 1953 headed an oil-drilling firm in Texas. In 1966 he was elected to the first of two terms as a Republican representative from Texas. He was ambassador to the UN (1971–73), chairman of the Republican National Committee (1973–74), chief of the U.S. liaison office in China (1974–75), and director of the CIA (1976–77). After losing the 1980 Republican presidential nomination to Ronald REAGAN, Bush served as his vice president (1981–89). In 1988, Bush and running mate Dan QUAYLE defeated Michael DUKAKIS in the presidential election. Faced with escalating budget deficits, he abandoned his electoral pledge of "no new taxes" and accepted a tax package that was designed to reduce the deficit but largely failed to do so as recession and an anemic recovery combined to produce the lowest growth rate since the GREAT DEPRESSION. In foreign affairs, he ordered an invasion of Panama (1989) to depose Manuel NORIEGA, and in 1990 he committed the U.S. to the reversal of Iraq's invasion of Kuwait, which was achieved (1991) in the PERSIAN GULF WAR. Bush signed (1991, 1992, 1993) nuclear DISARMAMENT agreements with the USSR and Russia that called for substantial cuts in nuclear arms and (1992) the NORTH AMERICAN FREE TRADE AGREEMENT with Canada and Mexico. In 1992 he was defeated in his bid for reelection by Democrat Bill CLINTON.

Bush, Vannevar, 1890–1974, American electrical engineer and physicist; b. Everett, Mass. While professor and dean of engineering at the Massachusetts Institute of Technology (1923–38), Bush designed the differential analyzer, an early computer. During World War II, he led the U.S. Office of Scientific Research and Development, directing such programs as the development of the first atomic bomb.

bushbuck: see ANTELOPE.

Bushmen: see SAN.

Bushnell, Horace, 1802–76, American Congregational minister; b. Bantam, Conn. As pastor of the North Church, Hartford, Conn. (1833–59), he repudiated the austerity of Calvinism and stressed the divine in humanity and nature. He had profound influence on liberal Protestant thought.

business cycle, a fluctuation in economic activity characterized by a period of growth, which reaches a peak and begins a downturn, followed by a period of negative growth (recession), which ends in a trough before the next upturn. French physician Clement Juglar first proposed that such cycles were an economic norm in 1862. There is no conclusive explanation of the underlying causes of business cycles, but many attempts to moderate them by altering monetary and fiscal policy have been made. Such 20th-cent. theorists as John Maurice Clark and Joseph SCHUMPETER have attempted to cure economic instability rather than merely describe it as a natural phenomenon, as 19th-cent. theorists did.

Busoni, Ferruccio Benvenuto [bo͞ozō'nē], 1866–1924, Italian pianist and composer. Influenced by LISZT, he taught widely, transcribed J.S. BACH's organ works for piano, edited Bach's *Well-tempered Clavier,* and composed piano music.

Bustamante, Sir Alexander, 1884–1977, Jamaican politician. Of Irish and African descent, he founded the country's largest trade union and (1943) the Jamaica Labour party. He served as chief minister (1953–55) and was prime minister from 1962, the year Jamaica gained independence within the British Commonwealth, until 1967. He launched an ambitious program of public works and land reform.

Buthelezi, Mangosuthu Gatsha, 1928–, black South African political leader. A Zulu chief and chief minister of the BANTUSTAN KwaZulu (1970–, initially as head of the Zululand Territorial Authority), he revived Inkatha, a Zulu cultural group, in 1975 as an antiapartheid organization, now the Inkatha Freedom party. In the 1980s he became a prominent critic of the AFRICAN NATIONAL CONGRESS (ANC) and its support for guerrilla warfare and international sanctions against APARTHEID. The early 1990s saw increasingly violent clashes between Inkatha and ANC supporters. Inkatha boycotted (1993) the multiparty talks that wrote a new South African constitution but participated in the 1994 multiracial elections.

Butler, Benjamin Franklin, 1818–93, American politician and Union CIVIL WAR general; b. Deerfield, N.H. He was made military governor of NEW ORLEANS (1862), but his harsh rule caused his removal. He commanded (1864) the Union expedition to seize Fort Fisher, N.C., but it failed, and he was removed from command. As a U.S. representative from Massachusetts he favored the radical Republican policy of RECONSTRUCTION and led the impeachment proceedings against Pres. Andrew JOHNSON.

Butler, Nicholas Murray, 1862–1947, American educator; b. Elizabeth, N.J. As president of the Industrial Education Association (1886) he helped found the institution that became Teachers College, Columbia Univ. Instrumental in the expansion of Columbia College into Columbia Univ., he was president from 1902 to 1945 and instituted the school of journalism, the medical center, and other units. An advocate of peace through education, he established the Carnegie Endowment for International Peace (president

1925–45), and shared the 1931 Nobel Peace Prize with Jane ADDAMS.

Butler, Samuel, 1612–80, English poet and satirist. His best-known work is *Hudibras* (in three parts—1663, 1664, 1678), a venomous satire against the Puritans given as the mock-heroic story of the "Presbyterian knight," Sir Hudibras.

Butler, Samuel, 1835–1902, English author, painter, and composer. After amassing a fortune in New Zealand as a sheep rancher, he returned to England, where he did work in the arts and in biology. He is best known as a writer. *Erewhon,* a novel in which he satirized English social and economic injustices, appeared in 1872, and *Erewhon Revisited* in 1901. His ironic, witty attack on Victorian life, the autobiographical *The Way of All Flesh* (1903), is ranked among the great English novels.

Butor, Michel [bütôr'], 1926–, French novelist. His experimental novels use shifting time sequences and the interior monologue. They include *Passage to Milan* (1954), *Degrees* (1960), and *Third Below* (1977).

Butte, city (1990 pop. 33,336), seat of Silver Bow co., SW Mont.; inc. 1879. Mining has dominated Butte since its founding (1862). Copper is the major resource; others are silver, zinc, manganese, molybdenum, gold, lead, and arsenic. Copper was discovered c.1880, and Marcus Daly, whose company would become Anaconda Copper Mining, and others began to exploit it. Anaconda's giant open-pit mine forced relocation of one fifth of the city. That mine was abandoned in 1982, but copper and molybdenum mining have resumed in the area.

butte, an isolated hill with steep sides and a flat top, resulting from the more rapid erosion of the surrounding areas. Many occur in the plains of the W U.S. See MESA.

butter, dairy product obtained by churning milk or cream until its fat solidifies. Cow's milk is generally the basis for butter, but milk from goats, sheep, and mares has also been used. Butter was known by 2000 B.C., and as it became a staple food various kinds of hand churns were developed. Traditional butter-making involves cooling milk in pans, allowing the cream to rise and skimming it off, letting the cream ripen by natural fermentation, then churning it. Farm-made until 1850, butter has since then increasingly become a factory product. Commercially made butter usually contains 80% to 85% milk fat, 12% to 16% water, and 2% salt. Butter without salt is known as sweet butter. The world's leading butter producers are Russia, France, Germany, the U.S., and India. Clarified butter (butterfat with milk solids removed) is widely used in Egypt and in India, where it is known as ghee. The high dietary value of butter is due to its large proportion of easily digested fat and its vitamin A and vitamin D content.

butter-and-eggs, perennial plant (*Linaria vulgaris*) of the figwort family, originally native to Europe but now common in the U.S. It has small, snapdragonlike flowers of yellow and orange and is consequently also known as wild snapdragon. Other yellow and orange flowers are sometimes called butter-and-eggs.

buttercup or **crowfoot,** common name for the Ranunculaceae, a family of chiefly annual or perennial herbs of cool regions of the Northern Hemisphere. Primitive plants, they typically have a simple flower structure. The buttercups and crowfoots comprise the largest genus (*Ranunculus*). Found mainly in the arctic, north temperate, and alpine regions, most have glossy yellow flowers and deeply cut leaves. A dozen or more species are common in every part of the U.S. The family also includes many other wildflowers and cultivated ornamentals. Some of these are the ANEMONE, CLEMATIS, COLUMBINE, LARKSPUR, and PEONY.

butterfly, flying INSECT that with the MOTH comprises the order Lepidoptera. Butterflies have coiled, sucking mouthparts; two pairs of wings that function as one; and antennae with knobs at the tips. Most feed on nectar from flowers and are active by day. The butterfly larva (caterpillar) is transformed into a pupa (chrysalis) with a hardened outer integument within which it changes into the adult (see METAMORPHOSIS). Adults of most species live only about a month.

butternut: see WALNUT.

buttonwood: see PLANE TREE.

buttress, mass of masonry built against a wall to strengthen it, particularly when a vault or arch places a heavy load or thrust on one section. The decorative possibilities were known in Mesopotamia (3500–3000 B.C.). In larger Roman buildings, internal buttresses served also as partitions; the basilica of Constantine in Rome is typical. Buttresses evolved from simple 11th-cent. piers to bold and complex Gothic structures. The flying buttress, a masonry arch, abutted the exterior wall of a building. Buttresses were often enriched with gables and sculpture; pinnacles were added to increase their weight. In cathedrals like Notre-Dame de Paris, buttresses express the elasticity and equilibrium of Gothic architecture.

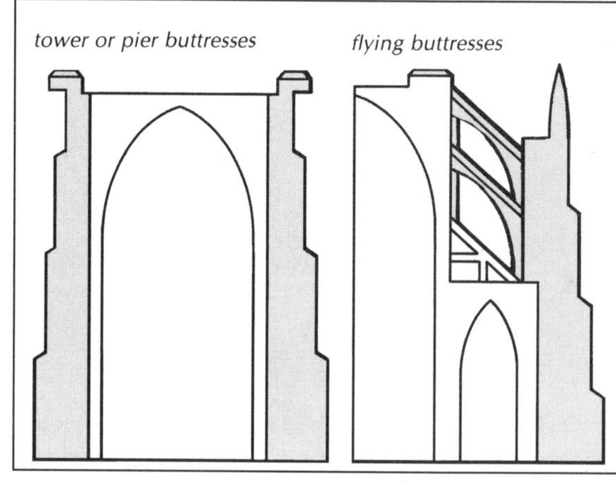

Types of buttresses

Butzer, Martin: see BUCER, MARTIN.

Buxtehude, Dietrich [bo͝oks"təho͞o'də], 1637–1707, Danish-German composer and organist. From 1668 he was organist at Lübeck, where his concerts attracted musicians from all over Germany, including J.S. BACH, whom he greatly influenced.

buzzard, HAWK of the genera *Buteo* or *Pernis.* Honey buzzards (*Pernis*) feed on insects, wasp and bumblebee larvae, and small reptiles. The term *buzzard* is often incorrectly applied to various hawks and New World VULTURES.

Byatt, A(ntonia) S(usan), 1936–, British novelist and literary critic; sister of Margaret DRABBLE. Her novels are richly complex, witty, sophisticated, and scholarly. They include *The Virgin in the Garden* (1978), *Still-Life* (1985), and *Possession* (1989), her best-known work.

Byelarus or **Byelorussia:** see BELARUS.

Byng, Julian Hedworth George, 1st **Viscount Byng of Vimy,** 1862–1935, British general. In WORLD WAR I Canadian troops under his command stormed (1917) Vimy Ridge, in N France. He was later governor general of Canada (1921–26).

Bynner, Witter, 1881–1968, American poet; b. Brooklyn, N.Y. Adept at mimicking other writers and cultures, he was coauthor of the poetic parody *Spectra* (1916) and cotranslator (from the Chinese) of *The Jade Mountain* (1929). He wrote several volumes of lyric poetry, as well as plays and essays.

Byrd, Richard Evelyn, 1888–1957, American explorer; b. Winchester, Va. He was a naval flier. In 1926 he and Floyd Bennett became the first persons to fly over the NORTH POLE. Byrd is remembered mainly for his five expeditions to ANTARCTICA: 1930, 1933, 1939–40, 1946–47, 1955–56. He was promoted to rear admiral in 1930 and set up a base in Antarctica; from there he conducted major explorations. In 1933 he spent several months close to the South Pole alone; *Discovery* (1935) and *Alone* (1938) are records of this trip. He was made commander of all U.S. Antarctic activities in 1955. His explorations form the basis of U.S. claims in Antarctica.

Byrd, Robert Carlyle, 1917–, U.S. senator from W.Va. (1959–); b. North Wilkesboro, N.C., as Cornelius Calvin Sale, Jr. Before entering the Senate, he served (1953–59) in the U.S. House of Representatives. In 1971 he defeated Sen. Edward KENNEDY for the position of Senate majority whip and was later Senate majority leader

RULERS OF THE BYZANTINE EMPIRE *(including dates of reign)*

Constantine I (the Great), 330–37	Leo IV (the Khazar), 775–80	Isaac I Comnenus, 1057–59
Constantius, 337–61	Constantine VI, 780–97	Constantine X Ducas, 1059–67
Julian (the Apostate), 361–63	Irene, 797–802	Michael VII Ducas (Parapinaces), 1067–68
Jovian, 363–64	Nicephorus I, 802–11	Romanus IV Diogenes, 1068–71
Valens, 364–78	Stauracius, 811	Michael VII Ducas (restored), 1071–78
Theodosius I (the Great), 379–95	Michael I, 811–13	Nicephorus III Botaniates, 1078–81
Arcadius, 395–408	Leo V (the Armenian), 813–20	Alexius I Comnenus, 1081–1118
Theodosius II, 408–50	Michael II (the Stammerer), 820–29	John II Comnenus, 1118–43
Marcian, 450–57	Theophilus, 829–42	Manuel I Comnenus, 1143–80
Leo I (the Great or the Thracian), 457–74	Michael III (the Drunkard), 842–67	Alexius II Comnenus, 1180–83
Leo II, 474	Basil I (the Macedonian), 867–86	Andronicus I Comnenus, 1183–85
Zeno, 474–75	Leo VI (the Wise or the Philosopher), 886–912	Isaac II Angelus, 1185–95
Basiliscus, 475–76	Alexander, 912–13	Alexius III Angelus, 1195–1203
Zeno (restored), 476–91	Constantine VII Porphyrogenitus, 913–19	Isaac II (restored) and Alexius IV Angelus, 1203–4
Anastasius I, 491–518	Romanus I Lecapenus, 919–44	Alexius V Ducas, 1204
Justin I, 518–27	Constantine VII (restored), 944–59	Theodore I Lascaris, 1204–22
Justinian I (the Great), 527–65	Romanus II, 959–63	John III Vatatzes or Ducas, 1222–54
Justin II, 565–78	Basil II Bulgaroktonos, 963	Theodore II Lascaris, 1254–58
Tiberius II Constantinus, 578–82	Nicephorus II Phocas, 963–69	John IV Lascaris, 1258–61
Maurice, 582–602	John I Tzimisces, 969–76	Michael VIII Palaeologus, 1259–82
Phocas, 602–10	Basil II (restored), 976–1025	Andronicus II Palaeologus, 1282–1328
Heraclius, 610–41	Constantine VIII, 1025–28	Andronicus III Palaeologus, 1328–41
Constantine III and Heracleonas, 641	Zoë and Romanus III Argyrus, 1028–34	John V Palaeologus, 1341–76
Heracleonas, 641	Zoë and Michael IV (the Paphlagonian), 1034–41	John VI Cantacuzenus (usurper), 1347–55
Constans II Pogonatus, 641–68	Zoë and Michael V Calaphates, 1041–42	Andronicus IV Palaeologus, 1376–79
Constantine IV, 668–85	Zoë and Theodora, 1042	John V Palaeologus (restored), 1379–91
Justinian II Rhinotmetus, 685–95	Zoë, Theodora, and Constantine IX Monomachus, 1042–50	John VII Palaeologus (usurper), 1390
Leontius, 695–98	Theodora and Constantine IX, 1050–55	Manuel II Palaeologus, 1391–1425
Tiberius III, 698–705	Theodora, 1055–56	John VII Palaeologus (restored as coemperor), 1399–1412
Justinian II (restored), 705–11	Michael VI Stratioticus, 1056–57	John VIII Palaeologus, 1425–48
Philippicus Bardanes, 711–13		Constantine XI Palaeologus, 1449–53
Anastasius II, 713–15		
Theodosius III, 716–17		
Leo III (the Isaurian or the Syrian), 717–41		
Constantine V Copronymus, 741–75		

(1977–79, 1987–88) and Senate minority leader (1980–87). Since 1989 he has chaired the appropriations committee.

Byrd, William, 1674–1744, American colonial writer and official. After inheriting extensive lands in Virginia, he served in the house of burgesses and as a Virginia council member. In 1737 he had the city that was to be Richmond laid out on one of his estates. He kept wise and witty journals and diaries, excerpts from which were published posthumously. At his death he left a library of some 4,000 volumes at his Westover estate.

Byrd, William, 1543–1623, English composer and organist. He was favored by ELIZABETH I, and, although Catholic, wrote MASSES, anthems, and other music for both English and Roman services. He performed and published music with TALLIS.

Byrne, Jane, 1934–, American politician; b. Chicago as Margaret Jane Burke. She was Chicago's consumer sales commissioner (1968–77) under Mayor Richard DALEY before being elected (1979) the first woman mayor of the city. Under Byrne, the city faced severe financial problems. In 1983 she ran for reelection but lost the Democratic primary to Harold Washington.

Byron, George Gordon Noel Byron, 6th **Baron,** 1788–1824, one of the great English romantic poets. In his life and in his poetry, Lord Byron epitomizes ROMANTICISM. Born with a clubfoot, he grew to be a dark, handsome man, beloved by, but contemptuous of, women. When an early work, *Hours of Idleness* (1807), was ridiculed by the *Edinburgh Review,* he replied with *English Bards and Scotch Reviewers* (1809), a satire that made him famous. His many love affairs before and after his ill-fated marriage (1815–16) to Anne Isabella Milbanke (notably with Lady Caroline Lamb, wife of Viscount MELBOURNE, and Claire Clairmont, SHELLEY's sister-in-law) made him notorious. Byron settled in Venice in 1817. After wandering restlessly about Europe, he died working for Greek independence. Byron's writings include long romances and stories in verse, e.g., *Childe Harold* (1812–18), *The Bride of Abydos* (1813), *The Corsair* (1814), *Manfred* (1817), *Beppo* (1818), and *Mazeppa* (1819); shorter works such as *The Prisoner of Chillon;* and lyrics. His masterpiece is *Don Juan* (1819–24), an epic-satire.

byte: see COMPUTER.

Byzantine art and architecture include not only works done in the city of Byzantium after it became the capital of the Roman Empire (A.D. 330), but also work done under Byzantine influence, as in Italy, Syria, Greece, Russia, and other Eastern countries. A blend of Hellenistic and Middle Eastern traditions, Byzantine art emphasized decorativeness and flat line harmony. Except for the interruption of ICONOCLASM (726–843), when content was restricted to ornamental forms and symbols such as the cross, the style persisted until the fall of CONSTANTINOPLE in 1453. The pillaging of Constantinople in 1204 was followed by a late flowering of Byzantine art that brought impressive achievements in MOSAIC decoration. Mosaics depicting sacred personages placed in descending order of importance were applied to all available surfaces in Byzantine churches. The stylized gestures of the figures and luminous shimmer of the gold backgrounds made the entire church a tangible evocation of celestial order. The cult of icons also played a leading role in Byzantine art. The icons were made using the ENCAUSTIC technique. Little scope was given to individuality, since the effectiveness of the image was held to depend on its fidelity to a prototype. A large group of icons has been preserved in the monastery of St. Catherine on Mt. Sinai. The development of Byzantine painting can also be seen in manuscript illumination, e.g., the 9th cent. *Homilies of Gregory Nazianzus* and the 10th-cent. *Paris Psalter.* Byzantine enamel, ivory, and metalwork objects such as reliquaries, devotional panels, and ivory caskets were highly prized throughout the Middle Ages. Byzantine architecture was based on the great legacy of Roman formal and technical achievements. The

5th cent. BASILICA of St. John of the Studion is the oldest extant church in Constantinople and an early example of Byzantine reliance on traditional Roman models. The most imposing example of Byzantine architecture is the Church of Holy Wisdom (HAGIA SOPHIA), which is the culmination of several centuries of experimentation with a unified space of monumental dimensions. These centrally planned religious structures were greatly favored and had in common a central domed space flanked by smaller domes and half-domes spanning the peripheral spaces. Two of the great achievements of Byzantine architecture are the Italian octagonal church of San Vitale in Ravenna (547) and ST. MARK'S CHURCH in Venice. In its later phases, the Byzantine prototype became more ornate, e.g., the Moscow Cathedral. Byzantine secular architecture has left few traces. Best known are the ruins of the 5th-cent. walls of Constantinople, consisting of an outer and an inner wall, each of which was originally studded with 96 towers, of which some can still be seen.

Byzantine Empire, successor state to the Roman Empire (see ROME), also called the Eastern or East Roman Empire. It was named for ancient Byzantium, which CONSTANTINE I rebuilt in A.D. 330 as his capital, Constantinople. The Roman Empire split permanently (395) into East and West, but after the Western Empire fell (476) the Eastern Empire claimed the entire Roman world. Boundaries shifted, but the core of the Byzantine Empire was ASIA MINOR and the S BALKAN PENINSULA. Throughout its 1,000 years of existence the empire was continually beset by invaders. Also, there was constant religious controversy (see ORTHODOX EASTERN CHURCH; ICONOCLASM; MONOPHYSITISM; MONOTHELETISM) and internal political strife. Nevertheless, despite a complex administration, gross violence, and moral decay, the empire carried on Graeco-Roman civilization, blended with Middle Eastern influences, while the West was in chaos. It regained vigor in the 6th-cent. reign of JUSTINIAN I, under whom Byzantine art and architecture reached their peak, but his successors lost vast lands to the LOMBARDS and ARABS. The schism between the Eastern and Western churches arose soon after CHARLEMAGNE became emperor of the West (800). The reigns of BASIL I (9th cent.) and his successors brought renewed imperial splendor and vigor until the defeat by the Seljuk TURKS (1071) and the loss of Asia Minor. The empire was further weakened by the attacks of the Norman leaders ROBERT GUISCARD and Bohemond. After a brief resurgence under ALEXIUS I, a century of decay ended with the Fourth CRUSADE, the fall of Constantinople (1204), and the breakup of the empire into NICAEA, TREBIZOND, and EPIRUS. The weak Latin empire was conquered by the Nicaean emperor MICHAEL VIII, who restored the Byzantine Empire. Gradually, however, the empire was encircled by the OTTOMAN Turks, and despite a desperate defense under CONSTANTINE XI, Constantinople fell (1453) to MUHAMMAD II. The modern era is traditionally reckoned from that date.

Byzantium, ancient city of Thrace, on the site of present-day İstanbul, Turkey. Founded by Greeks in 667 B.C., it was chosen (A.D. 330) by CONSTANTINE I as the site for Constantinople, later the capital of the BYZANTINE EMPIRE.

C

C, chemical symbol of the element CARBON.

C: see COMPUTER LANGUAGE.

Ca, chemical symbol of the element CALCIUM.

Cabal, inner circle of advisers to CHARLES II of England. Their initials form the word—Clifford of Chudleigh, Ashley (Lord Shaftesbury), BUCKINGHAM (George Villiers), Arlington (Henry Bennet), and Lauderdale (John Maitland). One or more of this group dominated court policy from 1667 to 1673.

cabala [Heb., = traditional lore], mystical Jewish system of interpretation of the Scriptures. Cabala is based on the belief that every word, letter, number, and even accent of the Scriptures contains mysteries. Cabalistic signs and writings are used as amulets and in magical practices. Cabala has two principal written sources. The first, *Sefer Yezira,* probably written in the 3d cent., is a series of monologues supposedly delivered by the patriarch Abraham. The second, *Zohar,* is a mystical commentary on the Pentateuch written by Moses de León (13th cent.) but attributed to Simon ben Yohai, a great scholar of the 2d cent. The movement appears to have arisen in 11th-cent. France and spread, most notably to Spain. After the expulsion of the Jews from Spain in 1492, cabala became messianic in emphasis, especially as developed by Isaac LURIA. This form of cabala had many adherents, including the pseudo-Messiah SABBATAI ZEVI. It was also a major influence in the development of 18th-cent. HASIDISM.

cabbage, leafy garden vegetable of many widely dissimilar varieties, all probably descended from the wild, or sea, cabbage (*Brassica oleracea*) of the MUSTARD family, found on European coasts. Cabbage is used as food for humans and animals. Varieties include BROCCOLI, BRUSSELS SPROUTS, CAULIFLOWER, collards, KALE, and kohlrabi. All grow best in cool moist climates. Chinese cabbage is a separate species.

Cabell, (James) Branch, 1879–1958, American author; b. Richmond. Popular in the 1920s, many of his anti-realistic novels, e.g., *Jurgen* (1919), are set in an imaginary medieval kingdom and can be considered moral allegories.

Cabeza de Vaca, Álvar Núñez [käbā'thä dā vä'kä], c.1490–c.1557, Spanish explorer. During an expedition to FLORIDA in 1528 he was shipwrecked on a TEXAS island and enslaved by the natives. He escaped and wandered over the Southwest, reaching Mexico in 1536. His reports of the PUEBLO towns gave rise to the myth of the Seven Cities of Cibola. He was later governor of a region of PARAGUAY but was deposed in 1544.

cabildo, Spanish autonomous municipal council, important in governing Spanish America from the 16th cent. Presided over by an alcalde, it exercised considerable legislative, executive, and judicial powers. In the 19th cent. it was an important forum for voicing nationalist ideas.

Cabinda, (1988 est. pop. 114,000), exclave of ANGOLA, from which it is separated by Zaïrian territory. Situated on the Atlantic Ocean, Cabinda has produced oil from large offshore reserves since 1968, accounting for most of Angola's output. The region, however, has not benefited from the oil wealth, fueling resentment of the government and persistent fighting by Cabindan separatists. Cabinda was the scene of heavy fighting during the war for independence from Portugal (1961–75).

cabinet, group of advisers to the head of government who are also usually the heads of administrative government departments. In Great Britain, where cabinet ministers are drawn from the majority party in the House of Commons, its modern status developed after the establishment of the sovereignty of PARLIAMENT and the emergence of party government in the 18th cent. In multiparty systems, e.g., that of France, coalition cabinets are more common. The U.S. cabinet, not specifically established by the Constitution, has evolved through custom and is now defined by statute. Its members are appointed by the president and approved by the Senate.

The first cabinet appointments (1789) were the secretaries of state, treasury, and war. The executive departments whose secretaries are in the cabinet are (in order of establishment) the departments of STATE; the TREASURY; DEFENSE (formerly departments of War and Navy); the INTERIOR; AGRICULTURE; JUSTICE; COMMERCE; LABOR; HEALTH AND HUMAN SERVICES (formerly Health, Education, and Welfare); HOUSING AND URBAN DEVELOPMENT; TRANSPORTATION; ENERGY; EDUCATION; and VETERANS AFFAIRS.

Cable, George Washington, 1844–1925, American author; b. New Orleans. He is chiefly known for his early works describing picturesque Louisiana Creole life, e.g., *Old Creole Days* (1879) and *The Grandissimes* (1880). His later essays, e.g., *The Negro Question* (1890), reflect his social concern.

cable, originally, high-strength wire cord or heavy metal chain used for hauling, towing, supporting the roadway of a suspension bridge, or securing a large ship to its anchor or mooring. Today the term often refers to an electrically conductive wire used for the transmission of electrical signals. A **coaxial cable,** virtually immune to external electromagnetic interference, consists of two concentric conductors separated by an insulator. The current in the inner conductor draws the current in the outer one toward the center, rather than letting it dissipate outwards. By means of coaxial cables a large number of telegraph and telephone messages, as well as television images (see CABLE TELEVISION), can be simultaneously transmitted. An intertwined and insulated group of wires that conducts electricity from generator to consumer is also called a cable. FIBER-OPTIC cable employs a glass fiber and carries impulses of light instead of electricity.

cable television, form of BROADCASTING that sends programs to paying subscribers by means of coaxial CABLE or a combination of FIBER-OPTIC and coaxial cable rather than through the airwaves. It originated (1949) to serve areas where reception was poor or nonexistent, and expanded rapidly in the mid-1970s with the easing of government restrictions and the use of COMMUNICATIONS SATELLITE transmission. Further programming and audience growth came in the early 1980s, when the government moved to deregulate the industry. In addition to providing the programming of the local television broadcasting stations, cable TV operators offer additional channels of movies, sports events, home-shopping services, news, and the like. The most advanced systems offer two-way, or interactive, communication; information services such as VIDEOTEX; burglar- and fire-alarm protection; and radio broadcasts that can be played on a stereophonic system.

Cabot, John, fl. 1461–98, English explorer; probably b. Genoa, Italy. Under a patent granted by HENRY VII, he sailed W from Bristol in 1497, probably seeking the riches of E Asia and the Indies, and touched the North American coast. His second expedition (1498) disappeared. English claims in NORTH AMERICA were based on his discovery. His son, **Sebastian Cabot**, b. 1483–86?, d. 1557, was an explorer in English and Spanish service. In 1509 he was part of an expedition in search of the NORTHWEST PASSAGE and may have reached HUDSON BAY. Later he explored (1526–30) the Río de la Plata region of Brazil for the Spanish. In 1548 he became governor of a joint-stock company in England (later the MUSCOVY COMPANY), which negotiated a commercial treaty with Russia.

Cabral, Pedro Alvares [kəbrăl′], c.1467–c.1520, Portuguese navigator. On an expedition to INDIA in 1500, he went far west of his course and reached BRAZIL, which he claimed for Portugal. He finally reached India, but his high-handed practices in trade and religion angered the Indians, and he returned to Portugal. His landing in Brazil, accidental or prearranged, was not the first European visit there, though the question of who actually discovered Brazil is still debated.

Cabrini, Saint Frances Xavier, 1850–1917, American nun; b. Italy. She founded in Italy the Missionary Sisters of the Sacred Heart of Jesus; in 1889 she was sent by the pope to the U.S. to aid Italian immigrants. She was the first U.S. citizen to be canonized (1946). Feast: Nov. 13 (in the U.S.).

cacao, tropical tree (*Theobroma cacao*) of the sterculia family, native to South America and now widely cultivated in the Old World. The fruit is a pod that contains a sweet pulp with rows of embedded seeds (the cocoa "beans" of commerce). Cocoa is obtained by fermenting the pods and then curing and roasting the extracted seeds. The resulting clean kernels, or cocoa nibs, are then processed. Cacao products have high food value due to their fat, carbohydrate, and protein content. CHOCOLATE is one product; other uses are in cosmetics and medicines.

cactus, common name for the Cactaceae, a family of succulent plants found almost entirely in the New World. Cactus plants have fleshy green stems that function as leaves (the leaves are typically insignificant or absent), and, usually, spines of various colors, shapes, and arrangements. The large, showy, delicate flowers are commonly yellow, white, red, or purple. Cactus fruits are berries, some of which are edible. The reduced leaf surface and fleshy stem make cacti well fitted for water storage and retention. An extensive, ramified root system makes the plants adaptable to hot, dry regions, although cacti are not restricted to the desert. Most cacti blossom briefly in the spring, sometimes for only a few hours. Blossoms are especially sensitive to light, and different species bloom at different times of the day, e.g., the night-blooming cereus, whose fragrant blossoms unfold after sunset and last one night. Many species are cultivated for food or ornamentals; the hallucinatory drug PEYOTE comes from a cactus of that name.

Cactus

CAD: see COMPUTER-AIDED DESIGN.

Cadillac, Antoine de la Mothe [kädēyäk′], c.1658–1730, French colonial governor in North America; founder (1701) of Detroit. In 1711 he became governor of Louisiana, but after quarrels in his administration, he was recalled (1716).

Cádiz [kä′dēth], city (1988 est. pop. 157,000), capital of Cádiz prov., SW Spain, in Andalusia, on the Bay of Cádiz. It is a port with such industries as shipbuilding and fishing. Founded c.1100 B.C. by the Phoenicians, it passed to Carthage (c.500 B.C.), Rome (3d cent. B.C.), the Moors (A.D. 711), and ALFONSO X of Castile (1262). It became a New World trade center but declined when Spain lost its American colonies. The clean, white city has palm-lined promenades and parks and a 13th-cent. cathedral.

cadmium (Cd), metallic element, discovered in 1817 by Friedrich Stromeyer. Cadmium is a silver-white, lustrous, malleable, ductile metal. Its major use is as an electroplated coating on iron and steel to prevent corrosion; it is also used in nickel-cadmium batteries. See ELEMENT (table); PERIODIC TABLE.

Cadmus, in Greek myth, son of Agenor; founder of THEBES. He killed the sacred dragon that guarded the spring of ARES. As instructed by ATHENA, he sowed the dragon's teeth; from them sprang the Sparti, ancestors of the Theban nobility. He married Harmonia, daughter of Ares and APHRODITE.

caecilian, legless, tailless tropical AMPHIBIAN (family Caecilidae). Most are c.1 ft (30 cm) long. Resembling earthworms superficially, but having vertebrate characteristics such as jaws and teeth, caecilians eat animals like termites and earthworms and are found in swampy places. Their eyes are nearly functionless; a groove on either side of the head contains a retractable sensory tentacle.

Caedmon, fl. 670, English poet, said by BEDE to have written early English versions of OLD TESTAMENT stories. A herdsman reputed to have received poetic powers through a vision, he later became a lay brother at the abbey of Whitby.

Caesar, (Caius) Julius, 102? B.C.–44 B.C., Roman statesman and general. Although he was born into the Julian gens, one of the oldest patrician families in Rome, Caesar was always a member of the democratic or popular party. In 82 B.C., SULLA proscribed Caesar, who fled from Rome (81 B.C.). On Sulla's death, Caesar returned (78 B.C.) to Rome and began his political career as a member of the popular party. In 69 B.C. he helped POMPEY to obtain the supreme command for the war in the East. He himself returned to Rome from Spain in 68 B.C. and continued to support the enactment of popular measures and to prosecute senatorial extortionists. In 63 B.C., as pontifex maximus, he undertook the reform of the calendar with the help of Sosigenes; the result was one of his greatest contributions to history, the Julian CALENDAR. In 60 B.C. he organized a coalition, known as the First Triumvirate, made up of Pompey, commander in chief of the army; Marcus Licinius Crassus (see CRASSUS, family), the wealthiest person in Rome; and Caesar himself. In the years 58 to 49 B.C. he firmly established his reputation in the GALLIC WARS. Caesar made explorations into Britain in 55 and 54 B.C. and defeated the Britons. By the end of the wars Caesar had reduced all Gaul to Roman control. These campaigns proved him one of the greatest military commanders of all time and also developed the personal devotion of the Roman legions to Caesar. Crassus's death (53 B.C.) ended the First Triumvirate and set Pompey and Caesar at odds. In 50 B.C. the senate ordered Caesar to disband his army, but two tribunes faithful to Caesar, Marc ANTONY and Quintus Cassius Longinus, vetoed the bill. They fled to Caesar, who assembled his army and got the support of the soldiers against the senate. On Jan. 19, 49 B.C., Caesar crossed the Rubicon, the stream bounding his province, to enter Italy, and civil war began. His march to Rome was a triumphal progress. At Pharsala in 48 B.C., Caesar defeated Pompey, who fled to Egypt, where he was killed. Caesar, having pursued Pompey to Egypt, remained there for some time, living with CLEOPATRA and establishing her firmly on the Egyptian throne. On his return to Rome, he set about reforming the living conditions of the people by passing agrarian laws and by improving housing accommodations. In 44 B.C. he became dictator for life. His dictatorial powers had aroused great resentment in his enemies, but when a conspiracy was formed against him, it was made up of his friends and protégés, among them Cimber, Casca, Cassius, and Marcus Junius Brutus (see BRUTUS, family). On March 15 (the Ides of March), 44 B.C., he was stabbed to death in the senate house. His will left everything to his 18-year-old grandnephew Octavian (later AUGUSTUS). Caesar made the Roman Empire possible by uniting the state after a century of disorder, by establishing an autocracy in place of the oligarchy, and by pacifying Italy and the provinces. He has always been one of the most controversial characters of history, either considered the defender of the rights of the people against an oligarchy or regarded as an ambitious demagogue who forced his way to power and destroyed the republic. That he was gifted and versatile there can be little doubt. His commentaries on the Gallic Wars (seven books) and on the civil war (three books) are literary masterpieces as well as classic military documents. He was married three times: to Cornelia, to Pompeia, and to CALPURNIA.

Caesarean section: see CESAREAN SECTION.

Caetano, Marcello [käətä'no͞o], 1906–80, Portuguese statesman. A law professor and close associate of António SALAZAR, he helped to plan Portugal's corporate state and served as prime minister (1968–74). His government was overthrown by a military coup, and he was exiled.

caffeine, odorless, slightly bitter ALKALOID found in coffee, tea, COLA nuts, MATÉ, and cocoa (see CACAO). In moderation, caffeine is a mild stimulant that increases urination and the heart rate and rhythm. Excessive intake can cause restlessness, insomnia, heart irregularities, and delirium.

Cage, John (John Milton Cage, Jr.), 1912–92, American composer; b. Los Angeles. He became famous for his unorthodox theories and experimental compositions. His early works featured percussion instruments, including a piano "prepared" with objects attached to the strings. His most famous work, *4'33"* (1952), in which a pianist is silent, emphasizes the "music" of the sounds of the concert hall. He also composed aleatory or "chance" music, e.g., *Music of Changes* (1951), in which elements were derived by use of the *I Ching*, and *Imaginary Landscape No. 4* (1951), scored for 12 radios tuned at random. Cage strongly influenced Philip GLASS and other minimalists and the development of PERFORMANCE ART.

Cagney, James, 1904–86, American film actor; b. N.Y.C. A tough guy in such films as *Public Enemy* (1930) and *White Heat* (1949), he also made musicals, e.g., *Yankee Doodle Dandy* (1942; Academy Award).

Caiaphas (Joseph Caiaphas) [kā'yəfəs], fl. A.D. 18–36, high priest of the Jews. In the BIBLE, he presided at the council that condemned Jesus to death. Archaeologists discovered his tomb in Jerusalem in 1990.

Cain, in the BIBLE, eldest son of ADAM and EVE, a tiller of the soil. In jealousy he killed his brother ABEL and became a fugitive.

Cain, James M., 1892–1977, American novelist; b. Annapolis, Md. His "hard-boiled" books, many made into movies, often concern middle-class lovers driven to violence. His novels include *The Postman Always Rings Twice* (1934) and *Mildred Pierce* (1941).

cairn terrier, small working TERRIER; shoulder height, c.10 in. (25 cm); weight, c.14 lb (6.4 kg). Its tough double coat has a soft, furry underlayer and a profuse, hard outercoat of any color but white. It was originally bred (19th cent.) on the Isle of Skye for hunting vermin and otters.

Cairo, city (1986 pop. 6,052,836), capital of Egypt, N Egypt, a port on the Nile R., near the head of its delta. Cairo is Egypt's administrative center and, along with ALEXANDRIA, the heart of its economy. Manufactures include textiles, food products, chemicals, and plastics. It was founded in A.D. 969 by the FATIMID dynasty as capital of Egypt. In 1517 it became part of the OTTOMAN EMPIRE. Cairo fell to NAPOLEON I in 1798 and to the British in 1801. During WORLD WAR II it was Allied headquarters in the Middle East. In the late 1970s Cairo became an important Middle Eastern financial and commercial center. Cairo has many mosques, palaces, museums, and universities, and the headquarters of the ARAB LEAGUE are there.

caisson, chamber of steel, wood, or concrete used in constructing foundations or piers in or near water. Types of caissons include open (a cylinder or box, open at the top and bottom, that is sunk and then filled with concrete) and pneumatic (a cylinder or box with an airtight bulkhead permitting people to work under it; air pressure is high enough to prevent water entry).

Calais, city (1990 pop. 75,309), N France, on the Strait of Dover. An industrial center, it has been a major seaport and communications link with England since the Middle Ages and is near the site of the Channel Tunnel. England held it from 1347 to 1558, when the Duke of GUISE recovered it. Calais was almost razed in World War II.

Calamity Jane (Martha Jane Canary), c.1852–1903, American frontier character; b. Princeton, Mo. In 1876 she appeared in Deadwood, S.D., dressed in men's clothes, and boasted of her exploits as a pony-express rider and army scout. She later toured the West in a burlesque show.

calcia: see CALCIUM OXIDE.

calcite, widely distributed calcium carbonate mineral ($CaCO_3$) that ranges from white or colorless through a great variety of colors, owing to impurities. Its crystals are noted for their perfect cleavage. Calcite also occurs in a number of massive forms, including MARBLE, LIMESTONE, and CHALK. Other forms include ICELAND SPAR, STA-

LACTITE AND STALAGMITE formations, Oriental ALABASTER, and marl. It is used as a building stone and is the raw material for quicklime (CALCIUM OXIDE) and CEMENT.

calcium (Ca), metallic element, first isolated in 1808 by Sir Humphry DAVY. It is a silver-white, soft, malleable ALKALINE-EARTH METAL. The fifth most abundant element (3.64%) of the earth's crust, it is not found uncombined but occurs in numerous compounds, e.g., APATITE, CALCITE, DOLOMITE, ICELAND SPAR, LIMESTONE, and MARBLE. Calcium acts as a reducing agent in the preparation of other metals. It occurs in most plant and animal matter, and is essential for the formation and maintenance of strong bones and teeth. Calcium helps to regulate the heartbeat and is necessary for blood clotting. See ELEMENT (table); PERIODIC TABLE.

calcium carbonate: see CALCITE; CHALK; LIMESTONE.

calcium-channel blocker, any of a class of drugs used in treating HYPERTENSION, angina pectoris (see CORONARY ARTERY DISEASE), and certain ARRHYTHMIAS. They prevent the calcium ions needed for muscle contraction from entering the cells of smooth and cardiac muscle. This causes blood vessel walls to relax and blood to flow more freely to the heart, lowering blood pressure and relieving angina pain. Some calcium-channel blockers, such as nifedipine, slow the electrical impulses that run through heart muscle, thus regulating arrhythmias.

calcium oxide or **calcia,** chemical compound (CaO), also called lime, quicklime, or caustic lime. A colorless crystalline or white amorphous substance, it has wide industrial uses, e.g., in making porcelain and glass; in purifying sugar; in preparing bleaching powder, calcium carbide, and calcium cyanamide; in water softeners; in mortars and cements; and in treating acidic soil (liming).

calculator, electronic, electronic device for performing numerical computations. Electronic calculators became available in the early 1960s, and in the early 70s miniature types, some pocket size, were marketed as consumer items. Electronic calculators have ten keys that can be used to enter numbers into the machine; additional keys are provided to enable the user to perform a range of operations, from basic arithmetic in simple devices to the generation of complex mathematical functions in more advanced types. The results are either shown on an electronic display or printed. Some of these machines are actually small COMPUTERS with limited memory and programming capabilities.

calculus, branch of MATHEMATICS that studies continuously changing quantities. It was developed in the 17th cent. independently by Sir Isaac NEWTON and G.W. LEIBNIZ. The calculus is characterized by the use of infinite processes, involving passage to a limit. The differential calculus arises from the study of the rate at which a FUNCTION, usually symbolized by y or $f(x)$, changes relative to a change in the independent variable, usually x. This relative rate can be computed from a new function—the derivative of y with respect to x, denoted by dy/dx, y', or $f'(x)$—arrived at by a process called differentiation. Formulas have been developed for the derivatives of all commonly encountered functions. For example, if $y = x^n$ for any real number n except -1, then $y' = nx^{n-1}$, and if $y = \sin x$, then $y' = \cos x$ (see TRIGONOMETRY). In physical applications, the independent variable is frequently time, e.g., if $s = f(t)$ expresses the relation between the distance s traveled and the time t elapsed, then $s' = f'(t)$ represents the rate of change of distance with time, i.e., the speed or velocity (see MOTION) at time t. Geometrically, the derivative is interpreted as the slope of the line tangent to a curve at a point. This view of the derivative yields applications, e.g., in the design of optical mirrors and lenses and the determination of projectile paths. The *integral calculus* arises from the study of the limit of a sum of elements when the number of such elements increases without bound while the size of the elements diminishes. Conventionally, the area A under the curve $y = f(x)$ between the two values $x = a$ and $x = b$ is symbolized by $A = \int_a^b f(x)dx$, called the definite integral of $f(x)$ from a to b. The area is approximated by summing the products of $f(x)$ and dx for each of the infinitely small distances (dx) that comprise the measurable distance between a and b. This method can be used to determine the lengths of curves, the areas bounded by curves, and the volumes of solids bounded by curved surfaces. The connection between the integral and the derivative is known as the Fundamental Theorem of the Calculus, which, in symbols, is $\int_a^b f(x)dx = F(b) - F(a)$, where $F(x)$ is a function whose derivative is $f(x)$. The calculus has been developed to treat functions not only of a single variable but also of several variables and is the foundation for the larger branch of mathematics known as ANALYSIS.

Calcutta, city (1991 pop. 10,916,272), capital of West Bengal state, E India, on the Hooghly R. It is India's second largest city, and the chief port and industrial center of E India. Jute is milled, and textiles, chemicals, paper, and metal products are manufactured. Nearly 60 languages are spoken in the city, which suffers from poverty, overcrowding, and high unemployment. It was founded 1696 by the British EAST INDIA COMPANY. In 1756 the nawab of Bengal captured the garrison, many of whom died when imprisoned in a small, stifling room known as the "black hole." Robert Clive retook the city in 1757. It became (1912) the capital of British India. It is one of the great cultural centers of India.

Caldecott, Randolph [kôl'dəkət], 1846–86, English artist. His colored illustrations for 16 picture books, e.g., *The House That Jack Built* and *The Grand Panjandrum Himself,* inspired the Caldecott Medal for children's-book illustration.

Calder, Alexander, 1898–1976, one of the most innovative modern American sculptors; b. Philadelphia. Famous for his MOBILES, brightly colored constellations of moving shapes, he is also known for his witty wire portraits, imaginative jewelry, colorful and complex miniature zoo (1925; Whitney Mus., N.Y.C.), and abstract immobile sculptures called stabiles.

Calderón de la Barca, Pedro [käldārōn' dā lä bär'kä], 1600–1681, Spanish dramatist, last major figure of the GOLDEN AGE. He wrote more than 100 plays, including 70 *autos sacramentales* (one-act religious plays) for the Corpus Christi festival; cloak-and-dagger thrillers; and comedies of manners like *The Mayor of Zalamea* (c.1640). His philosophical drama *Life Is a Dream* (1635) is considered a masterpiece.

Caldwell, Erskine, 1903–87, American author; b. White Oak, Ga. His realistic, earthy novels of the rural South include *Tobacco Road* (1932) and *God's Little Acre* (1933). His short stories appear in many collections, e.g., *Jackpot* (1940).

Caldwell, Sarah, 1924–, American opera director and conductor; b. Maryville, Mo. In 1957 she founded the Boston Opera Group, later renamed the Opera Company of Boston. Under her direction, the company became noted for its innovative productions of such operas as MOUSSORGSKY's *Boris Godunov* and SCHOENBERG's *Moses and Aaron.* In 1976 she became the first woman to conduct the METROPOLITAN OPERA.

calendar, system of reckoning time usually based on a recurrent natural cycle, such as the cycle of the sun through the seasons (see YEAR) or the moon through its phases (see MONTH). Because the solar year is 365 days 5 hr 48 min 46 sec and the lunar year (12 synodic months of 29.53 days) is 354 days 8 hr 48 min, people have been confronted from ancient times with the problem of the discrepancy. Because the year is not exactly divisible by months and days, the practice arose of making arbitrary divisions and inserting extra (intercalary) days or months. The Gregorian calendar, generally accepted today, evolved from the Roman calendar reformed (46 B.C.) by Julius CAESAR. In the Julian calendar April, June, September, and November had 30 days, February 28 days (29 days every fourth, or leap, year), and all other months 31 days. The date was computed by counting backward from the Kalends (the 1st day), the Nones (the 7th day in March, May, July, and October; the 5th day in other months), and the Ides (the 15th day in March, May, July, and October; the 13th day in other months); hence Jan. 10 was the 4th day of the Ides of January. Because the Julian year of 365 days 6 hr was too long, by the 16th cent. the vernal equinox was displaced from March 21 to March 11. Pope GREGORY XIII ordained that 10 days be dropped in 1582 and that years ending in hundreds be leap years only if divisible by 400. The non–Roman Catholic countries were slow to accept the Gregorian (New Style) calendar; it was adopted in England in 1752 and by the Eastern Church in the 20 cent. The Christian ecclesiastical calendar was based on the belief that JESUS' resurrection was on a Sunday, hence Easter should fall on Sunday. The First Council of NICAEA (325) decreed that Easter be the Sunday following the first full moon after the vernal EQUINOX; today the date varies from the astronomical reckoning because certain factors of the lunar period are not considered. Other calendars include the Jewish calendar (12 months, plus intercalary months 7 times in 19 years) and the Muslim lunar calendar.

Calgary, city (1991 pop. 710,677), S Alberta, Canada, at the confluence of the Bow and Elbow rivers. It is a major center for the region's expanding oil and natural-gas industry, and also an agricultural processing and wholesaling center. The Calgary Stampede, begun in 1912, is an annual rodeo usually held in July. Built at the site of a fort established (1875) by the Northwest Mounted Police, Calgary is now one of Canada's fastest growing cities. The 1988 winter Olympic games were held there.

Calhoun, John Caldwell, 1782–1850, American statesman; b. near Abbeville, S.C. He was the great defender of the agrarian South against the industrial North, and of the sovereign power of STATES' RIGHTS. After serving in the House of Representatives (1811–17) and as secretary of war (1817–25), he was vice president (1825–32) under J.Q. ADAMS and Andrew JACKSON. He and Jackson disagreed, however, over the nature of the Union, and Calhoun directed passage (1832) of South Carolina's NULLIFICATION of an increased tariff inimical to its interests. As a U.S. senator (1832–43, 1845–50), he eloquently defended slavery and SECESSION. As secretary of state (1844–45) under Pres. TYLER, he secured the admission of Texas to the Union as a slave state.

Cali, city (1985 pop. 1,492,026), W Colombia, capital of Valle del Cauca dept., on the Cali R. It is an industrial center, shipping minerals, lumber, and food products and manufacturing tires, textiles, paper, and chemicals. Founded in 1536, it has doubled its population since 1950, largely because of a regional hydroelectric power project. In the late 1980s and early 90s Cali gained notoriety for the cocaine "cartel" based there.

Caliari, Paolo: see VERONESE, PAOLO.

California, most populous state in the U.S., located in the Far West; bordered by Oregon (N), Nevada and Arizona, across the Colorado R. (E), Mexico (S), and the Pacific Ocean (W).

Area, 158,693 sq mi (411,015 sq km). *Pop.* (1990) 29,760,021, a 25.7% increase over 1980 pop. *Capital,* Sacramento. *Statehood,* Sept. 9, 1850 (31st state). *Highest pt.,* Mt. Whitney, 14,491 ft (4,417 m); *lowest pt.,* Death Valley, 282 ft (86 m) below sea level. *Nickname,* Golden State. *Motto, Eureka* [I Have Found It]. *State bird,* California valley quail. *State flower,* golden poppy. *State tree,* California redwood. *Abbr.,* Calif.; CA.

Land and People. The COAST RANGES extend along the Pacific, and in the north are the famous giant redwood forests. The SAN ANDREAS FAULT has caused severe earthquakes and tremors in the coastal region. To the west of the Coast Ranges is the fertile Central Valley, drained by the SACRAMENTO and SAN JOAQUIN rivers. Farther east is the dramatic SIERRA NEVADA range, location of Kings Canyon, Sequoia, and Yosemite national parks (see NATIONAL PARKS, table), and of Mt. WHITNEY. California is also the site of Channel Islands, Lassen Volcanic, and Redwood national parks (see table). The state's eastern section, largely desert, includes DEATH VALLEY and Joshua Tree national monuments. About 60% of the land is controlled by the federal government. The climate of California is extremely varied. In general, there are two seasons: a rainy period from October to April and a dry period from May to September. Temperatures, mainly mild, are warmer in the south than in the central and northern sections, extremely hot in the deserts, and cold in the mountains. Almost 93% of the population lives in metropolitan areas. LOS ANGELES proper is the country's second largest city, while greater Los Angeles is the second largest metropolitan area in the U.S. Other major California cities are SAN DIEGO, SAN JOSE, SAN FRANCISCO, LONG BEACH, OAKLAND, SACRAMENTO, and FRESNO. California has large, well-established Hispanic and Asian populations and the second largest Native American population (after Oklahoma). In 1990, 69% of the population was white, 9.6% was Asian, and 7.4% was African American; nearly 26% was of Hispanic descent.

Economy. California's economy is dominated by manufacturing. Leading products include transportation equipment, printed matter, primary and fabricated metals, electronic and electrical equipment, machinery, and processed foods. Leading all states in the value of its agricultural output, California produces a wide variety of fruits and vegetables, including grapes for wine and citrus fruits. More than two thirds of the farms are irrigated. The raising of cattle and the growing of cotton and flowers are also important. The most profitable minerals extracted are oil and natural gas, and asbestos, boron, gypsum, and tungsten are also important. Fishing is important along the coast. The state—and in particular, Disneyland—is a favorite destination for tourists.

Government. The constitution of 1879 provides for a governor serving a four-year term. The legislature is composed of a senate whose 40 members serve four-year terms and an assembly with 80 members elected every two years. California elects 2 senators and 52 representatives to the U.S. Congress and has 54 electoral votes.

History. The Spanish first explored the southern coast in 1542. Father Junípero SERRA, a Franciscan missionary, founded (1769) the first of many missions. American settlers began to move to California during the 1840s. After Mexico's defeat in the MEXICAN WAR California was ceded (1848) to the U.S. In the same year gold was discovered, bringing thousands of new settlers. Many Chinese laborers came to work on the Transcontinental Railroad (completed 1869), which linked the state with the East. Industry expanded rapidly during World War II. California is the nation's center of defense-related industries, many of which were hit hard in the recession of the early 1990s and by cutbacks following the end of the COLD WAR). The state is also the hub of U.S. motion-picture and television film production. Since the 1960s the area around San Jose (SILICON VALLEY) has become a center for high-technology industries. In the early 1990s California faced a continuing recession and high unemployment, revenue shortfalls, environmental problems (especially in the allocation of scarce water resources), and many urban ills.

California, Gulf of, or **Sea of Cortés,** arm of the Pacific Ocean, NW Mexico. It is c.700 mi (1,130 km) long and 50–130 mi (80–209 km) wide, and it separates BAJA CALIFORNIA from the Mexican mainland. The gulf, which is part of a structural depression that extends north to the Coachella Valley of S Calif., reaches a maximum depth of c.8,500 ft (2,590 m) in the south.

California, University of, at nine campuses, main campus at Berkeley; chartered 1868. It offers a very wide range of undergraduate and graduate training, and operates a statewide extension service. The enrollment of over 160,000 is one of the largest in the U.S. The institution began by taking over the College of California (est. 1853) at Oakland. It moved to Berkeley in 1873 and acquired or established its other branches in the 20th cent., the first being at Los Angeles (1919). The university's Scripps Institution of Oceanography, at La Jolla, became the nucleus of the campus at San Diego. Other branches are at Davis, Santa Barbara, Riverside, Irvine, and Santa Cruz, and a campus devoted entirely to medical sciences is in San Francisco. The university also operates the Los Alamos Scientific Laboratory, the Lick Observatory, and the Lawrence Berkeley and Livermore laboratories.

California holly: see CHRISTMASBERRY.

californium (Cf), synthetic, radioactive, metallic element, produced in 1950 by Glenn SEABORG and colleagues by alpha-particle bombardment of curium-242. It is in the ACTINIDE SERIES. Californium-252, produced in nuclear reactors, is a neutron source. See ELEMENT (table); PERIODIC TABLE.

Caligula, A.D. 12–41, Roman emperor (A.D. 37–41), son of Germanicus Caesar and Agrippina I. His real name was Caius Caesar Germanicus; as a small child he wore military boots, whence his nickname *caligula* = little boots. On the death of TIBERIUS the army helped make Caligula emperor. Shortly afterward he became severely ill; it is widely believed that he was thereafter insane. He earned a reputation for ruthless and cruel autocracy. He was assassinated, and CLAUDIUS I succeeded to the throne.

caliphate, the rulership of ISLAM. Since Islam is theoretically a theocracy, the caliph is ideally both temporal and spiritual leader of the Muslims. When MUHAMMAD the Prophet died, ABU BAKR was chosen as the first caliph. After the caliphate of Ali (656–61) the caliphate split between the Umayyads, who ruled from Damascus, and the ABBASIDS, who ruled from Baghdad. The Abbasids massacred the Umayyads in 750, but one member escaped to Spain, where he established the Western Caliphate, or the Caliphate of Córdoba; it lasted until 1031. A third caliphate, established by the Fatimid sect in Africa, lasted from 909 to 1171. After the rise of the

Ottoman Turks, the sultans assumed the title of caliph. The title died out with the last sultan in 1924.

calisthenics: see GYMNASTICS.

Calixtus I, Callixtus I, or **Callistus I, Saint,** c.160–c.222, pope (217–222), a Roman. As archdeacon to Pope Zephyrinus, he established the famous Calixtus Cemetery in Rome. As pope, Calixtus was opposed by the antipope Hippolytus and extended absolution to many classes of sinners thought to be unforgivable. Feast: Oct. 14.

Calixtus II, Callixtus II, or **Callistus II,** d. 1124, pope (1119–24), a Burgundian named Guy. Succeeding Gelasius II, Calixtus triumphed over the antipope Gregory VIII and ended the INVESTITURE controversy when Holy Roman Emperor HENRY V signed (1122) the Concordat of Worms. Calixtus then called (1123) the First Lateran Council.

Calixtus III, Callixtus III, or **Callistus III,** 1378–1458, pope (1455–58), a Spaniard named Alonso de Borja (Ital., Borgia). He supplied aid to John Hunyadi and SCANDERBEG to fight the Turks and quarreled with ALFONSO V of Aragón. His nepotism established the BORGIA family in Italy.

Callaghan, (Leonard) James, 1912–, British statesman. He was elected a Labour member of Parliament in 1945. Later he served as chancellor of the exchequer (1964–67), resigning when forced to accept devaluation of the pound; home secretary (1967–70); and foreign secretary (1974–76). Upon the resignation of Harold WILSON in 1976 he became prime minister. His government was plagued by inflation, unemployment, and its inability to restrain unions' wage demands. In 1979 the Labour party lost the election to the Conservatives, led by Margaret THATCHER. Callaghan resigned as party leader in 1980 and was created Baron Callaghan of Cardiff in 1987.

Callao [käyou'], city (1990 est. pop. 589,000), capital of Callao dept., W Peru, on Callao Bay of the Pacific Ocean. It is 8 mi (13 km) W of the Peruvian capital, LIMA, and, as Peru's chief seaport, handles well over half of the nation's foreign trade. Callao has survived foreign attack, tidal waves, and at least two major earthquakes, in 1746 and 1940.

Callas, Maria, 1923–77, Greek-American operatic soprano; b. N.Y.C. to Greek parents. She made her debut at Verona, Italy, in 1947 and at the METROPOLITAN OPERA in 1956. Noted for her dramatic intensity, she excelled in CHERUBINI's *Medea,* BELLINI's *Norma,* and PUCCINI's *Tosca.*

Calles, Plutarco Elias [kä'yās], 1877–1945, president of MEXICO (1924–28). His revolutionary administration initiated economic reforms, enforced anticlerical laws, and unified the government under the National Revolutionary party. After leaving office he remained political chieftain of the nation until he opposed CÁRDENAS and was exiled (1936–41).

Calley, William L.: see MY LAI INCIDENT.

Callicrates, 5th cent. B.C., Greek architect. With ICTINUS he built (447–432 B.C.) the PARTHENON at Athens. At Athens he also designed (c.427) the Temple of Nike.

Callimachus, fl. c.265 B.C., Greek poet and critic. At ALEXANDRIA he drew up a catalogue constituting a full literary history. Among his over 800 hymns, epigrams, and poems is *Aetia,* a collection of legends.

Calliope: see MUSES.

Callisto, in astronomy, natural satellite of JUPITER.

Callistus: see CALIXTUS.

Callixtus: see CALIXTUS.

Callot, Jacques [kălō'], c.1592–1635, French etcher and engraver. An influential innovator, he developed a hard varnish that allowed for more flexibility and finesse in etching. In the service of Cosimo de' Medici he created such works as the vast *Fair at Impruneta* (1620). Commissioned to engrave the sieges of Breda, Rochelle, and Ré, he was deeply affected by the scenes of carnage and in 1633 executed *Miseries of War,* his masterpiece. Callot produced nearly 1,500 plates and 2,000 drawings, influencing such masters as REMBRANDT and WATTEAU.

calorie (cal), unit of energy required to raise the temperature of one gram of water one degree Centigrade (from 14.5° to 15.5°C); 1 cal = 4.1840 joules. Nutritionists use the kilocalorie (1,000 cal) to state the heat content of food.

Calpurnia, d. after 44 B.C., Roman matron. The daughter of Lucius Calpurnicus Piso Caesoninus, she was married to Julius CAESAR in 59 B.C. She was loyal to him despite his many infidelities and his neglect.

Calvary [Lat., = a skull] or **Golgotha** [gôl'gəthə], place where JESUS was crucified, outside the walls of JERUSALEM. Its location is not certainly known. The traditional site is now occupied by the Church of the Holy Sepulcher.

Calvert, George, 1st **Baron Baltimore,** c.1580–1632, English colonizer in America. After holding high offices in England, he was granted (1623) Avalon peninsula in Newfoundland, but the colony he founded failed. In 1632 James I granted him territory that eventually became Maryland, but he died before the colony's charter was accepted.

Calvin, John, 1509–64, French Protestant theologian of the Reformation; b. Noyon, Picardy. Having studied theology and law, he experienced (1533) a "sudden conversion" and turned his attention to the cause of the REFORMATION, for which he was persecuted and hunted. His work in Geneva began in 1536, but the system he tried to impose was rejected, and he was banished (1538). After a stay at Basel and Strasbourg, he was welcomed back to Geneva in 1541. Calvin had begun the work of systematizing Protestant thought in his *Institutes of the Christian Religion* (1536). His theology diverged from Catholic doctrine in such fundamental ways as rejection of papal authority and acceptance of justification by faith alone, and the doctrine of PREDESTINATION. He also maintained that the Bible was the sole source of God's law, and that it was man's duty to interpret it and to preserve the orderly world that God had ordained. It was such a system that he sought to realize at Geneva by founding a government based solely on religious law. From his teachings grew one of the principal Christian religious systems, CALVINISM, whose extension to all spheres of human activity was extremely important in a Europe changing from an agrarian to a commercial economy.

Calvinism, term used in several different senses. It can mean the teachings of John CALVIN himself; all that developed from his doctrine and practice in Protestant countries in social, political, ethical, and theological aspects of life and thought; or the system of doctrine, distinctive in its rejection of consubstantiation in the Eucharist and in its doctrine of predestination, that was accepted by the Reformed churches (see PRESBYTERIANISM). Calvinism produced the church-dominated societies of Geneva and Puritan New England. It stressed that only those whom God elects are saved, and that a person does nothing to effect his or her salvation. The doctrine challenged LUTHERANISM in Europe, spread to Scotland, and influenced the Puritans of England and New England. It receded under rationalism (18th-19th cent.), but found new expression in the Reformed theology of Karl BARTH.

Calvino, Italo, 1923–85, Italian novelist; b. Cuba. He wrote in a variety of genres and styles. Among his works are *The Path to the Nest of Spiders* (1947), a realistic novel about World War II; *Cosmicomics* (1965), 12 science fiction tales; and *If on a Winter's Night a Traveler* (1979), a novel composed of fragments of 10 stylistically different novels.

Calvo, Carlo, 1824–1906, Argentine diplomat and historian, writer on international law. His principle known as the **Calvo Doctrine** would prohibit diplomatic intervention to enforce private claims before local remedies had been exhausted. The **Calvo Clause** found in statutes, treaties, and contracts is the concrete application of his doctrine.

Calvo Sotelo, Leopoldo, 1926–, Spanish engineer and political leader. He held (1975–77) ministerial posts before becoming (1980) deputy prime minister for economic affairs. After leading the Union of the Democratic Center to victory in 1981, he was confirmed as prime minister despite an abortive military coup in which the parliament was seized. He resigned before the 1982 elections in which the Socialist party, led by Felipe GONZÁLEZ MÁRQUEZ, was victorious.

Calypso, nymph, daughter of ATLAS, in HOMER's *Odyssey.* She entertained ODYSSEUS on the island of Ogygia for seven years before he rejected her offer of immortality and continued home.

CAM: see COMPUTER-AIDED MANUFACTURING.

Camagüey, city (1986 est. pop. 258,000), E Cuba, capital of Camagüey prov. The island's third largest city, it is a commercial and transportation center with meat-packing and other food-processing industries. Founded in the early 16th cent., it produced salted beef for Spanish fleets and was often sacked by pirates. It has retained a Spanish colonial atmosphere.

cambium, thin layer of reproductive tissue lying between the BARK and the wood of a STEM, most active in woody plants. In herbaceous plants the cambium is usually inactive; in monocotyledons (see ANGIOSPERM) it is absent. Producing thin layers of phloem on the outside and xylem on the inside (see WOOD), cambium growth increases the diameter of the stem. Its seasonal growth is responsible for ANNUAL RINGS.

Cambodia, officially Kingdom of Cambodia, constitutional monarchy (1992 est. pop. 7,296,000), 69,898 sq mi (181,035 sq km), SE Asia. It is bordered by Thailand (N and W), Laos (N), Vietnam (E), and the Gulf of Thailand (S). The capital is PHNOM PENH. The heart of the country consists of a large central alluvial plain, drained by the MEKONG R. and including the Tônlé Sap (Great Lake). Mountains flank the plain in the northwest and southwest. Cambodia has a tropical monsoonal climate ideal for growing rice, the chief crop. Corn, vegetables, peanuts, tobacco, and sugar palm are also grown. The industrial sector centers on the processing of agricultural products. Mineral resources are limited to various kinds of stone and salt. Both the industrial and agricultural sectors were devastated during the civil war and strife of the 1970s and 80s. About 90% of the population is ethnic Khmer (Cambodian). Minorities include Chinese, Vietnamese, Cham-Malays, and a number of hill tribes. Theravada Buddhism is the dominant religion; the Cham-Malays are Muslims. Khmer is the national language, but French is widely spoken.

History. The early history of Cambodia is that of the KHMER EMPIRE. After the empire's fall (15th cent.), Cambodia fell prey to Siam and later (17th cent.) to ANNAM. It was declared (1863) a French protectorate and became (1887) part of French-ruled INDOCHINA. Cambodia was occupied by the Japanese in World War II. It became self-governing (1946) and gained full independence (1953) as the Kingdom of Cambodia. NORODOM SIHANOUK led the country until he was deposed (1970) in a military coup led by Gen. LON NOL. Cambodia became (1970) the Khmer Republic and was a major battlefield of the VIETNAM WAR. The ousted Sihanouk formed a government in exile in Beijing, and the Communist KHMER ROUGE waged a successful full-scale civil war that overthrew (1975) the Lon Nol government. Sihanouk was restored as head of state, and a new socialist constitution (1976) renamed the country Democratic Kampuchea. Sihanouk was soon succeeded by Khieu Samphan, and POL POT became prime minister. The economy deteriorated following massive collectivization in which urban dwellers were evacuated to work in the countryside. Many fled to Thailand, and perhaps 1.5 million were killed or died from enforced hardships. Border conflicts (1977–78) with Vietnam led to a Vietnamese invasion and installation (1979) of a pro-Vietnamese Communist government under Heng Samrin. The country was renamed (1979–89) the People's Republic of Kampuchea. The Vietnamese withdrew in 1989, leaving the government of Prime Min. Hun Sen to face a rebel coalition (including the Khmer Rouge) supported by China and Thailand. In 1991 all factions signed an accord calling for a cease-fire, disarmament of 70% of all forces, UN peacekeepers, and UN-supervised elections. Sihanouk denounced the Khmer Rouge, aligned himself with Hun Sen, and again became head of state. The Khmer Rouge subsequently withdrew (1992) from the peace process and resumed fighting. Royalists won the largest bloc of national assembly seats (58 out of 120) in the 1993 elections, but a government that included Hun Sen's party was formed. A new constitution reestablished the monarchy, and Sihanouk became (1993) king.

Cambrai, Treaty of: see ITALIAN WARS.

Cambrian period: see GEOLOGIC ERA (table).

Cambridge, city (1991 pop. 91,933), Cambridgeshire, E central England, on the Cam R. An ancient market town that now has some light industry on its outskirts, it is famous as the site of Cambridge Univ. (est. 13th cent.). In addition to the magnificent college buildings, the city abounds in medieval churches, old inns, and narrow, winding streets.

Cambridge, city (1990 pop. 95,802), a seat of Middlesex co., E

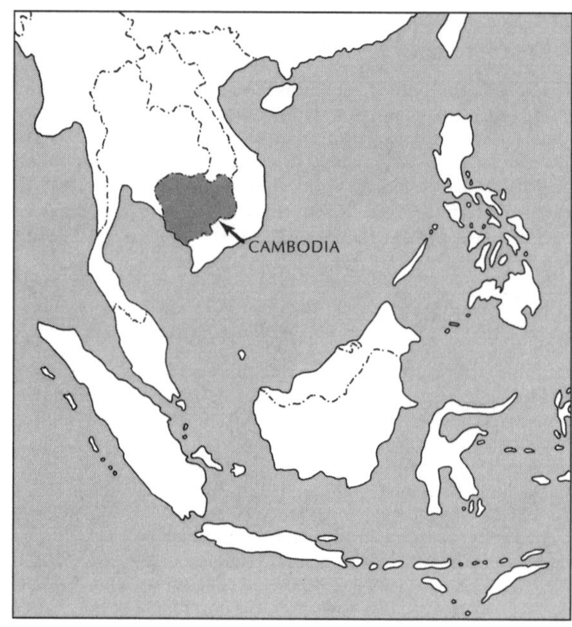

Mass., across the Charles R. from BOSTON; settled 1630 as New Towne, inc. as a city 1846. A famous educational and research center, it is the seat of Harvard Univ. (est. 1636), the Massachusetts Institute of Technology, and other colleges and seminaries. Its industries include electrical and scientific manufactures, and rubber and glass goods. Printing has been important since c.1639. The city, which was the home of such notable people as H.W. LONGFELLOW and J.R. LOWELL, has numerous historic sites.

Cambridge Platform, declaration of principles of church government and discipline, forming a constitution of the Congregational churches. Adopted (1648) by a synod in Cambridge, Mass., it is the basis of temporal church government. Connecticut Congregationalists subscribed (1708) to more centralized church government in the Saybrook Platform.

Cambridge University, at Cambridge, England. It originated in the early 12th cent., possibly earlier than OXFORD UNIV., and was organized into residential colleges by the end of the 13th cent. There are now 31 colleges (including three women's colleges). Cambridge was a center of the new learning in the Renaissance and of Reformation theology. In modern times it offers a wide range of subjects, excelling in science. The university's famous Cavendish Laboratory of experimental physics (opened 1873) has had many of the world's outstanding physicists on its faculty. The Cambridge University Press dates from the 16th cent.

Camden, city (1990 pop. 87,492), seat of Camden co., W N.J., a port of entry on the Delaware R. opposite Philadelphia; settled 1681, inc. 1828. In the 19th cent. it became a commercial, shipbuilding, and manufacturing center. Since the 1960s many important industries, e.g., steel, chemicals, and oil, have declined significantly. Of interest are Walt Whitman's home, an aquarium, and a Rutgers Univ. campus.

camel, hoofed ruminant (family Camelidae). The family consists of the true camels of Asia, the wild guanaco and domesticated ALPACA and LLAMA of South America, and the vicuña of South America. The two species of true camel are the single-humped Arabian camel, or dromedary (*Camelus dromedarius*), a domesticated animal of Arabia and N Africa; and the two-humped Bactrian camel (*C. bactrianus*) of central Asia. Their humps are storage places for fat. Ranging in color from dirty white to dark brown, camels are well adapted for desert life and can go without water for several days.

camellia, evergreen shrub or small tree (genus *Camellia*) of the TEA family, native to Asia, now widely cultivated for the white, red, or variegated showy blossoms and glossy, dark-green foliage. Teaseed oil, from the seeds of *C. sasanqua*, is used in cooking, and in soap and textile manufacturing.

Camelot, in ARTHURIAN LEGEND, the seat of King Arthur's court, frequently located in Somerset of Monmouthshire.

cameo, small relief carving, usually on striated precious or semiprecious stones or on shell. The design, often a portrait head, is cut in the light-colored vein; the dark vein becomes the background. Glass of two colors in layers may also be cameo-cut. The art originated in Asia and spread to ancient Greece and Rome; it was revived during the Renaissance and in the Victorian era.

camera, in PHOTOGRAPHY, device for recording an image on film or some other light-sensitive material. It consists of a lightproof box; a LENS through which light enters and is focused; a shutter that controls the size of the lens opening and the length of time it is open; a mechanism for moving the film between exposures; and a viewfinder, or eyepiece, that shows the user the image the lens sees. The camera developed from the **camera obscura** [Lat., = dark chamber], an artist's tool dating from the Middle Ages. It was a light-tight box with a convex lens at one end and a screen that reflected the image at the other; the artist traced the image. Joseph Nicéphore Niépce produced the first negative image in 1826. Modern cameras often employ automatic focusing and exposure controls, and some models can be computer controlled. See also PHOTOGRAPHY, STILL; POLAROID CAMERA. The **motion picture camera,** perfected in the late 1880s, comes in a variety of sizes; all operate on the same basic principle. As film goes through the camera it stops briefly to expose each frame, usually at a rate of 18 or 24 frames per second. A rotary shutter—basically a half-circle of metal that spins—usually opens and closes the aperture. A small metal device (a claw) pops into holes in the film, pulls the film down, retracts while the frame is exposed, and then repeats the process for the next frame. Modern movie cameras are powered by a tiny electric motor.

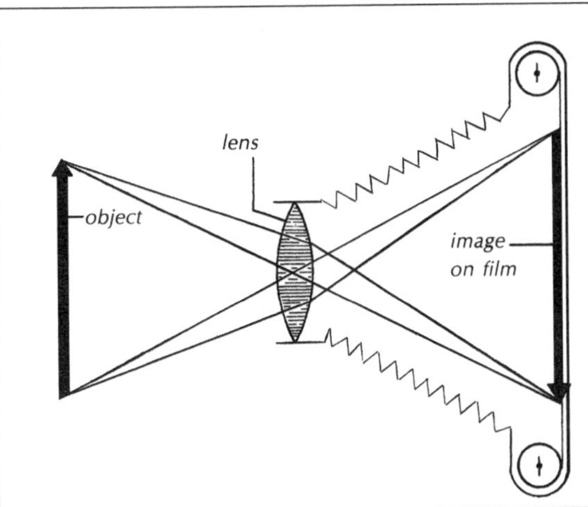

Image formed by a camera

Cameron, Julia Margaret, 1815–79, English pioneer photographer; b. India. In 1864 she began to photograph her many illustrious friends, e.g., Alfred, Lord TENNYSON and Ellen TERRY. Her superb portraits appeared as *Victorian Photographs of Famous Men and Fair Women* (rev. ed. 1973).

Cameroon, officially Republic of Cameroon, republic (1992 est. pop. 12,658,000), 183,568 sq mi (475,442 sq km), W central Africa, bordered by the Gulf of Guinea (W, SW), Nigeria (NW), Chad (NE), the Central African Republic (E), and Congo, Gabon, and Equatorial Guinea (S). Major cities are YAOUNDÉ (the capital) and DOUALA. Cameroon consists of a coastal region of swamps and dense rain forests, an interior plateau covered with forests and savanna, and an arid northern region. Volcanic peaks near the coast rise to 13,354 ft (4,070 m). The economy is based on a varied agriculture that makes the country self-sufficient in food. Cameroon is a leading producer of cocoa which, along with crude oil, coffee, bananas, palm products, cotton, rubber, timber, and aluminum, constitute the chief exports. Aluminum smelting, oil refining, and paper milling are the principal industries. Cameroon's diverse population includes more than 150 ethnic groups. French and English are the official languages. Traditional religious beliefs are dominant, but there are large minorities of Christians and Muslims, the latter in the north.

History. The first Europeans to arrive in the region were the Portuguese (1472), who developed a large-scale slave trade. By the 19th cent. palm oil and ivory had become the main items of commerce. The British established commercial hegemony over the coast in the early 1800s, but were supplanted by the Germans, who made the area a protectorate in 1884. The area was occupied by French and British troops in WORLD WAR I, after which it was divided into French and British mandates under the League of Nations. These became UN trust territories in 1946. In the 1950s guerrilla warfare, sparked by demands for independence, raged in the French Cameroons; the French granted self-government in 1957 and independence in 1960. Following a UN plebiscite in 1961, the southern zone of the much smaller British Cameroons was incorporated into the new country (the northern zone joined NIGERIA), which became a federal republic with two prime ministers and two legislatures but a single president; Ahmadou Ahidjo, who had led the French Cameroons to independence, became president of the republic. A one-party state was established in 1966, and a new constitution adopted in 1972 created a unitary state to replace the federation. Paul Biya succeeded Ahidjo as president in 1982. In 1991 a prolonged nationwide strike by the opposition led Biya to end one-party rule. Biya won a multiparty presidential election in 1992, but the result was tainted by fraud.

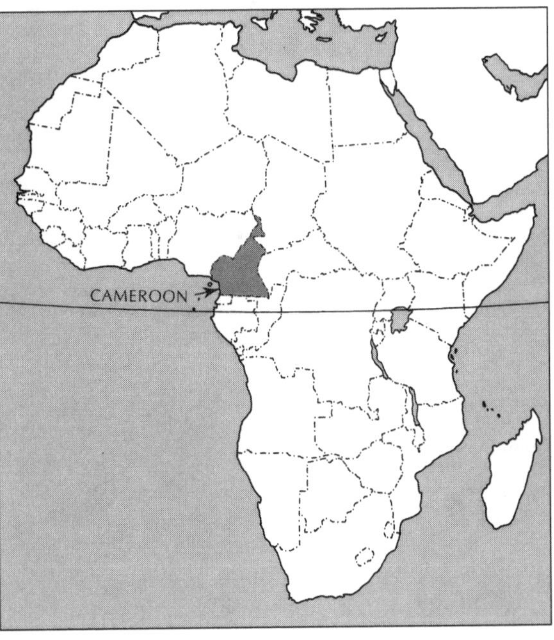

Cameroons, former German colony, W Africa, in the region that is now Cameroon and Nigeria. After World War I the colony was divided into British Cameroons and French Cameroons, both League of Nations mandates. Both colonies became UN trust territories and then achieved independence after World War II. French Cameroons and the southern part of British Cameroons became CAMEROON, and the northern section of British Cameroons joined NIGERIA.

Camões or **Camoens, Luis de** [kəmoiNsh'], 1524?–1580, Portugal's national poet and greatest literary figure. Among the events of his turbulent life were study at the Univ. of Coimbra; banishment from court (1546); loss of an eye in the Moroccan campaign; imprisonment for street-fighting; military service in India; dismissal from an official post in Macao; and shipwreck on his return (1570) to Portugal. *The Lusiads* [Port. *Os Lusíadas* = sons of Lusus, i.e., the Portuguese] (1572), a Vergilian epic encompassing the voyage of Vasco da GAMA and much of Portuguese history, is his masterpiece. Camões received a meager royal pension but died in poverty. His sonnets and lyrics appeared posthumously.

Campbell, Alexander, 1788–1866, clergyman, cofounder of the DISCIPLES OF CHRIST; b. Ireland. His father, **Thomas Campbell,** 1763–1854, came to the U.S. in 1807 and settled in Pennsylvania, where he withdrew his congregation from the Presbyterian Church. Alexander came to the U.S. in 1809 and joined his father's followers, known as Campbellites. Nominally Baptists (c.1812–c.1827), they advocated a return to scriptural simplicity and became the Disciples of Christ. Alexander founded (1840) Bethany College in West Virginia.

Campbell, Kim (Avril Phaedra Campbell), 1947–, Canadian politician, prime minister of Canada (1993). Originally a member of the SOCIAL CREDIT party, she held (1983–88) appointed and elected provincial positions in British Columbia. After joining the PROGRESSIVE CONSERVATIVE PARTY, she was elected (1988) to parliament. She served as justice minister and attorney general (1990–93) and defense minister (1993) under Prime Min. MULRONEY. In 1993 she succeeded Mulroney, becoming Canada's first woman prime minister. Shortly thereafter she and all but two of her party's candidates lost (1993) their seats in the national elections.

Campbell, Mrs. Patrick, 1865–1940, English actress; b. Beatrice Stella Tanner. She won fame in PINERO's *Second Mrs. Tanqueray* (1893). A friend of G.B. SHAW, she created the part of Eliza Doolittle in his *Pygmalion* (1913).

Campbell, Robert: see ROB ROY.

Campbell, Robert, 1808–94, Canadian explorer; b. Scotland. As a fur trader for the HUDSON'S BAY COMPANY he explored (1834–52) the Mackenzie R. region and discovered the Pelly R. At its junction with the Lewes R. to form the YUKON R. he established (1848) Fort Selkirk. Later (1850–51) he followed the Yukon as far as Fort Yukon.

Camp David, woodland camp in the Catoctin Mts., Md., used as a retreat by U.S. presidents since F.D. Roosevelt. Many important meetings have been held here, e.g., the conference that produced the CAMP DAVID ACCORDS.

Camp David accords, popular name for the 1979 peace treaty between Israel and Egypt, named for the U.S. presidential retreat (Camp David) in Maryland where the agreement was forged. It was signed Mar. 26, 1979, in Washington, D.C., by Menachem BEGIN of Israel and Anwar SADAT of Egypt, with U.S. Pres. Jimmy CARTER signing as a witness. Under the pact, which was denounced by other Arab states, Israel agreed to return the SINAI to Egypt, a transfer that was completed in 1982. In a joint letter the two sides also agreed to negotiate Palestinian autonomy measures in the occupied WEST BANK and GAZA STRIP, but virtually no progress was made on this issue until the 1990s. See also ARAB-ISRAELI WARS.

camphor ($C_{10}H_{16}O$), white, crystalline solid with a pungent odor and taste. It can be obtained from the camphor tree or synthesized from oil of TURPENTINE. Camphor is used to make CELLULOID and lacquers. In medicine it is used as a stimulant, a diaphoretic, and an inhalant; camphor ice, a mixture chiefly of camphor and WAX, is applied externally. The alcoholic solution is known as spirits of camphor.

Campi, Giulio [käm'pē], c.1500–c.1572, Italian painter and architect, founder of a school of painters at Cremona. Influenced by CORREGGIO and RAPHAEL, he did many altarpieces in Milan and Cremona. His pupils included his brothers Cavaliere **Antonio Campi,** c.1536–1591; **Vincenzo Campi,** 1532–91, a painter of portraits and still lifes; and **Bernardino Campi,** 1522–c.1590, known for frescoes in San Sigismondo, Cremona.

Campian, Thomas: see CAMPION, THOMAS.

Campin, Robert [käm'pĭn], 1378–1444, Flemish painter who with the van EYCKS was a founder of the Netherlandish school. He has been identified as the Master of Flémalle on the basis of three panels said to have come from the abbey of Flémalle, near Liège, Belgium. The *Mérode Altarpiece* (Cloisters, N.Y.C.) has also been attributed to him. His robust realism and concern for details of daily life reflected the values of the rising middle class.

Campion, Saint Edmund, c.1540–81, English JESUIT martyr. He early found favor with ELIZABETH I, but had Roman Catholic leanings and fled to the Continent, where he joined (1573) the Society of Jesus. He returned (1580) to England as a missionary and converted many, but was arrested, tortured, and executed. He was canonized in 1970. Feast: Dec. 1.

Campion or **Campian, Thomas,** 1567–1620, English poet and composer. He wrote poems and lute music, e.g., five *Books of Airs* (1601–17); a treatise on COUNTERPOINT; and a treatise on poetry.

Camus, Albert [kämü'], 1913–60, French writer and thinker; b. Algiers. His belief in the absurdity of the human condition identified him with EXISTENTIALISM, but his courageous humanism distinguished him from that group. The characters in his novels and plays, although keenly aware of the meaninglessness of the human condition, assert their humanity by rebelling against their circumstances. His best-known works are the novels *The Stranger* (1942), *The Plague* (1947), and *The Fall* (1956) and the essays *The Myth of Sisyphus* (1942) and *The Rebel* (1951). Camus was awarded the 1957 Nobel Prize in literature.

Cana, ancient town of Galilee. According to the Bible, JESUS performed his first miracle here by turning water into wine at a wedding.

Canaan, name for ancient PALESTINE. It was the Promised Land of the Israelites, which they conquered after their delivery from Egypt. Its inhabitants, who were probably related to the Amorites, were called Canaanites.

Canada, independent nation (1991 pop. 27,296,859), second largest country in the world (3,831,012 sq mi/9,922,330 sq km), occupying all of North America east of Alaska and north of a 5,335-mi-long (8,892-km) border with the U.S., and including adjacent islands of the Arctic Archipelago. It comprises 10 provinces and 2 federal territories. The provinces are ALBERTA, MANITOBA, and SASKATCHEWAN, collectively known as the Prairie Provinces; NEW BRUNSWICK, NOVA SCOTIA, PRINCE EDWARD ISLAND, and NEWFOUNDLAND, known as the Atlantic Provinces (the first three also being called the Maritime Provinces); and BRITISH COLUMBIA; ONTARIO; and QUEBEC. The territories are the YUKON TERRITORY and the NORTHWEST TERRITORIES; a new territory, NUNAVUT, will be created from the E Northwest Territories. Canada is a member of the COMMONWEALTH OF NATIONS. Its capital is OTTAWA.

Land and People. Occupying more than half of the nation's land area in the east and north is the vast CANADIAN SHIELD, a sparsely populated expanse of ancient, metamorphic rocks locally rich in iron, nickel, gold, and other minerals. Its rim extends from Labrador in the east, along the northern edge of Canada's urban-industrial heartland (the SAINT LAWRENCE R. valley and the peninsula of S Ontario), through WINNIPEG and the GREAT SLAVE and Great Bear lakes to the ice-clogged ARCTIC OCEAN in the north. Southeast of the Shield, occupying the Maritime Provinces and the island of Newfoundland, are the worn-down northern ranges of the APPALACHIAN MOUNTAINS system. To the west, in SW Manitoba and most of Alberta and Saskatchewan, are the great wheat-growing, oil-rich plains, or prairies, underlain by sedimentary rock in the Interior Lowlands region. The plains continue north through the PEACE R. and Athabasca districts to the area at the mouth of the MACKENZIE R., in the far north. West of the plains, along the western boundary of Alberta and in British Columbia and the Yukon, is the c.500-mi-wide (800-km) complex of high mountains and plateaus known as the Western Cordillera. It includes the ROCKY MOUNTAINS (E) and COAST MOUNTAINS (W), and reaches an elevation of 19,524 ft (5,951 m) at Mt. LOGAN, Canada's highest point, in the Yukon. Canada's climate ranges from temperate, with short, mild winters, in the southwest, to bitter, Arctic cold. It is temperate, with long, cold, and usually snowy winters in E Canada and the Prairie Provinces. Climatic conditions become progressively harsher to the north, where permafrost severely limits development. Most Canadians live along the southern edge of the nation, within 100 mi (160 km) of the U.S. border. More than half are concentrated in S Ontario and S Quebec. TORONTO, MONTREAL, EDMONTON, VANCOUVER, and CALGARY are the largest urban areas. The population is predominantly of British or French origin, with smaller minorities of other Europeans, some Asians, and an indigenous population of over 493,000 (many on reservations), including 28,000 Inuit (ESKIMO). Roman Catholicism and Protestantism are the largest faiths; the main Protestant sects are the United Church of Canada, Anglican Church of

Canada, and Presbyterian. French (spoken by a majority in Quebec) and English are both official languages.

Economy. Manufacturing, heavily concentrated in S Quebec and Ontario, is the chief economic activity, with major manufactures including motor vehicles, processed food, chemicals, aluminum, and iron and steel. Canada, a leading mineral exporter, produces zinc, asbestos, silver, and nickel for export, and also mines potash, sulfur, uranium, copper, and iron. Coal, oil, and natural gas are abundant in Alberta and to a lesser extent in Saskatchewan. Huge hydroelectric installations on the St. Lawrence, Churchill, Columbia, Peace, and other rivers supply additional energy in fuel-deficient regions. The extensive forest cover just north of the settled fringe supports large exports of newsprint, pulp and paper, and other forest products; and there are major exports of wheat and other grains from the Prairies, as well as fruit and meat. Tourism and financial services are also important. The U.S. is the leading trading partner and principal foreign investor. A trade agreement that took effect in 1989 will eliminate all tariffs between the U.S. and Canada by 1999. The Great Lakes–Saint Lawrence Seaway is the chief trading artery.

Government. Canada's constitution was patriated (i.e., returned to full Canadian control by the British Parliament in London) by the Canada Act (1982). It is derived from the British North America Act of 1867 (now called the Constitution Act, 1867). Under the constitution the head of state is the British monarch, acting in Canada through an appointed governor general. Legislative power is vested in a bicameral Canadian Parliament, consisting of a House of Commons (295 elected members) and a Senate (maximum 112 appointed members). The head of government is the prime minister, a member of the House. Each province has its own parliament.

History. Newfoundland and the eastern seaboard were discovered for England in 1497 by John Cabot and the mouth of the St. Lawrence R. and the Gaspé Peninsula for France in 1524 by Jacques Cartier. Port Royal (now Annapolis Royal), Canada's first known permanent mainland settlement, was founded by the French in 1605, and, traveling out from the colony of New France (made a royal colony in 1663), French fur traders, explorers, and missionaries rapidly extended French influence deep into the North American interior. British interest was sparked by the commercial efforts of the Hudson's Bay Company after 1670. Through the 18th cent. Anglo-French hostility in Europe kept spilling over into the New World (see French and Indian Wars). In 1713 Britain gained control of Nova Scotia (the heart of the French colony called Acadia), Newfoundland, and the Hudson Bay region. The rest of French Canada fell to the British in 1763, following the defeat (1759) of Gen. Montcalm by James Wolfe on the Plains of Abraham, near the city of Quebec. French residents, then in the majority, were granted rights to their own language and religion and given other concessions under the Quebec Act of 1774. Tensions mounted, however, as British settlement accelerated, especially after the American Revolution, with an influx of loyalists from the former American colonies (see United Empire Loyalists). In an effort to deal with the growing Anglo-French antagonism, Quebec was divided (1791) into English-speaking Upper Canada (now Ontario) and French-speaking Lower Canada (present-day Quebec). Following revolts in both colonies and the report by the earl of Durham in 1839, Upper and Lower Canada were again merged (1841) to form a single colony called Canada Province. The union lasted until confederation: the creation (1867), under the British North America Act, of a self-governing Dominion of Canada. Ontario and Quebec (as separate provinces), New Brunswick, and Nova Scotia were the four founding members at confederation. They were later joined by Manitoba (1870), British Columbia (1871), Prince Edward Island (1873), Alberta and Saskatchewan (1905), and Newfoundland (1949). The Northwest Territories were purchased from the Hudson's Bay Company to become (1869) a federal territory, from which the Yukon was created as a separate territory in 1898. A strong, sometimes violent French Canadian separatist movement in Quebec, seeking independence or sovereignty for the province, gathered momentum in the late 1960s. In the 1970s new regional strains arose as residents of the rapidly developing western provinces (especially oil-rich Alberta) chafed under a federal system that, in their view, deprived them of the full benefits of their resources. Such controversies pointed to the need for reform of the federal-provincial power arrangement and led to agitation for the patriation of the constitution. In 1982 Canada's constitution was returned to the Canadians, together with an amending formula and a Charter of Rights and Freedoms. In the same year first steps toward the redistribution of federal and provincial powers were taken by Prime Min. Pierre Trudeau. In 1984 Trudeau retired, and his successor, John Turner, called an election. The Progressive Conservatives won a sweeping majority, and Brian Mulroney became prime minister. Mulroney signed free trade agreements with the U.S. (1988) and with the U.S. and Mexico (1992). In 1990 the 1987 Meech Lake accord, which recognized Quebec as a "distinct society," failed to win provincial approval; a similar but broader set of constitutional revisions was rejected (1992) in a national referendum. Mulroney resigned in 1993 and was briefly succeeded by fellow party-member Kim Campbell, Canada's first woman prime minister. Elections (1993) led to a Liberal victory and a Progressive Conservative rout, and Jean Chrétien became prime minister. Two relatively new parties, the Bloc Québécois (based in Quebec) and Reform party (based in W Canada), won nearly all the remaining parliamentary seats.

CANADIAN PRIME MINISTERS SINCE CONFEDERATION
(including party and dates in office)

Sir John A. Macdonald [Conservative] 1867–73
Alexander Mackenzie [Liberal] 1873–78
Sir John A. Macdonald [Conservative] 1878–91
Sir John J. C. Abbott [Conservative] 1891–92
Sir John S. D. Thompson [Conservative] 1892–94
Sir Mackenzie Bowell [Conservative] 1894–96
Sir Charles Tupper [Conservative] 1896
Sir Wilfred Laurier [Liberal] 1896–1911
Sir Robert L. Borden [Conservative/Unionist] 1911–20
Arthur Meighen [Conservative] 1920–21
W. L. M. King [Liberal] 1921–26
Arthur Meighen [Conservative] 1926
W. L. M. King [Liberal] 1926–30
Richard B. Bennett [Conservative] 1930–35
W. L. M. King [Liberal] 1935–48
Louis St. Laurent [Liberal] 1948–57
John G. Diefenbaker [Progressive Conservative] 1957–63
Lester B. Pearson [Liberal] 1963–68
Pierre Elliott Trudeau [Liberal] 1968–79
Joseph Clark [Progressive Conservative] 1979–80
Pierre Elliott Trudeau [Liberal] 1980–84
John Turner [Liberal] 1984
Brian Mulroney [Progressive Conservative] 1984–93
Kim Campbell [Progressive Conservative] 1993
Jean Chrétien [Liberal] 1993–

Canada Act, 1982, act of the British Parliament that superseded the British North America Act of 1867 as the basic constitution of Canada. It combines the provisions of the British North America Act, subsequent amendments to that act by the British Parliament, and the Constitution Act, 1982, which established procedures by which Canadians could amend their own constitution. It was passed in response to the Canada Bill (1981), an act of Canada's Parliament that resulted from months of negotiations between the federal and provincial governments (except of Quebec). Despite protests from Canadian tribal groups and from Quebec prov., the act was signed into law by Queen Elizabeth II in Ottawa on Apr. 17, 1982.

Canada Day (July 1), national holiday of Canada; formerly Dominion Day. It is the anniversary of the union (1867) of Upper and Lower Canada, New Brunswick, and Nova Scotia as the Dominion of Canada.

Canada Company, land settlement company chartered in 1826 that acquired government land along the Lake Huron side of the Ontario peninsula, and founded Guelph and Goderick. Its first sec-

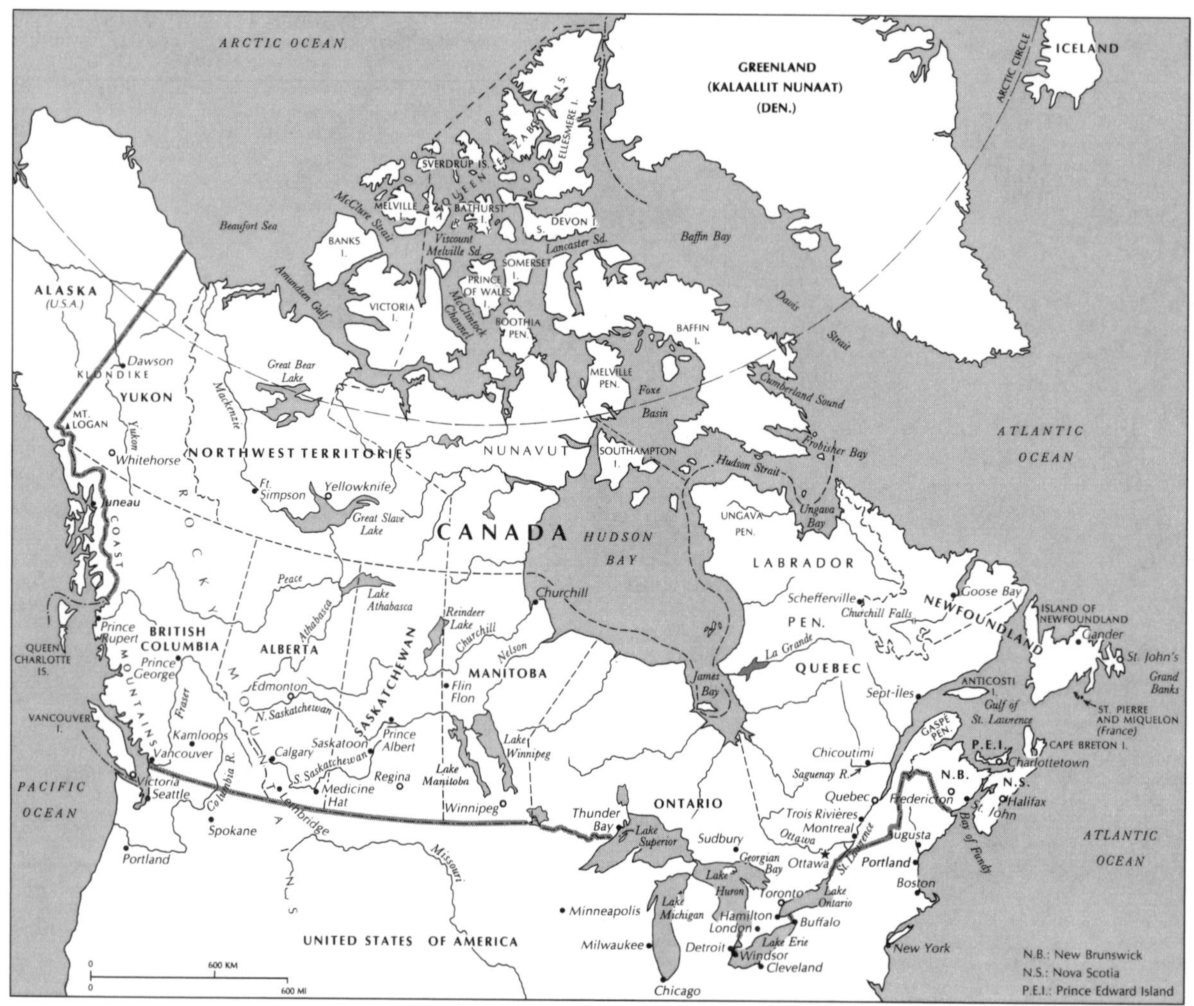

retary in Canada was the Scottish novelist John GALT. It remained in existence until the 1950s.

Canada First movement, short-lived political party founded after Canada's confederation (1867) to promote Canadian nationalism, and to encourage immigration and native industry. Its ideals were absorbed by older political parties.

Canadian football: see under FOOTBALL.

Canadian Shield or **Laurentian Plateau,** a region of ancient, mostly metamorphic rock forming the geologic nucleus of North America. Rich in minerals and water-power potential, it occupies E Canada, from the Great Lakes and the St. Lawrence N to the Arctic Ocean. It also covers much of Greenland and extends S into the U.S. as the ADIRONDACK MTS. and the Superior Highlands.

Canal, Antonio: see CANALETTO.

canal, an artificial waterway constructed for navigation or for the movement of water, e.g., irrigation, drainage of wetlands, and flood control. Irrigation canals probably date back to the beginnings of agriculture. Navigation canals developed later and for a long time were level, shallow cuts or had inclined planes up which vessels were hauled from one level to the next. The **canal lock,** a stretch of water enclosed by gates at each end, provides another means of raising or lowering vessels. When a vessel enters a lock through one gate, the gate is closed behind it. Water is let into or drained out of the lock until its level equals that of the water ahead. The vessel then passes out through the forward gate. Canal locks developed separately in China (10th cent.) and Holland (13th cent.). The GRAND CANAL of China is the world's longest canal. Europe developed a complex system of canals, and in the U.S. canal-building boomed after the opening (1825) of the ERIE CANAL. The rise of railroads, however, brought a decline in the use of canals as inland waterways. Canals have also been built to shorten sea routes, e.g., the PANAMA CANAL and the SUEZ CANAL.

Canaletto, 1697–1768, Venetian painter; b. Antonio Canal. Unsurpassed as an architectural painter, he executed such finely detailed works as *View on the Grand Canal* (National Gall., London) and *The Piazzetta, Venice* (Metropolitan Mus.). He also produced superb etchings and drawings that were not preparatory but complete in themselves. His nephew and pupil, Bernardo Bellotto, was also called Canaletto.

canary, small BIRD of the FINCH family, descended from either the wild serin finch or the wild canary (*Serinus canarius*) of the CANARY ISLANDS, MADEIRA ISLANDS, and AZORES. The wild birds are usually gray or green; breeding has yielded plain and variegated birds, mostly yellow and buff. Captive canaries are trained to sing and can live for 15 years or more.

Canary Islands, group of seven islands, 2,808 sq mi (7,273 sq km), constituting an autonomous region and two provinces of Spain, in the Atlantic Ocean off the coast of NW Africa. Tenerife, Palma, Gomera, and Hierro islands are part of Santa Cruz de Tenerife prov.; Grand Canary, Lanzarote, and Fuerteventura are part of Las Palmas prov. The islands are of volcanic origin and rise to 12,162 ft (3,707 m) in Mt. Teide, the highest point in Spain. With their warm climate and fine beaches, the Canaries are a popular tourist center.

canasta: see RUMMY.

Canberra, city (1991 pop. 278,894), capital of Australia, in the AUSTRALIAN CAPITAL TERRITORY, SE Australia. The site chosen (1908) for the capital was developed by the American architect Walter Burley

Griffin, whose plans won (1911) an international competition. Parliament first met there in 1927. The federal government is the city's largest employer.

cancer, common term for tumors (neoplasms) characterized by uncontrolled growth. Unlike normal cells, cancer cells are atypical in structure and do not have specialized functions. They compete with normal cells for nutrients, eventually killing normal tissue. Cancerous, or malignant, tissue can remain localized, invading only neighboring tissue, or can spread to other tissues or organs via the LYMPHATIC SYSTEM or blood (i.e., metastasize); virtually all tissues and organs are susceptible. Cancer symptoms, which are often nonspecific, include weakness and loss of appetite and weight. The causes are thought to include chemical agents that alter the cell's nucleic acids, e.g., nitrogen mustard; toxic substances, e.g., ASBESTOS, pollutants, substances in cigarette smoke; hormonal imbalances, possibly brought on by drugs, e.g., DES; genetic tendencies for certain types of cancer, e.g., of the breast or stomach; physical agents such as X rays and radioactivity; and VIRUSES. Methods of detection include visual observation, palpation, X-ray study, endoscopy (see ENDOSCOPE), CAT SCANS, ULTRASOUND, and BIOPSY. Tumors caught early, before metastasis, have the best cure rates. Cancer is traditionally treated by surgery, CHEMOTHERAPY, and RADIATION but more specific treatments with fewer side effects, such as hormonal products, vaccines, cryosurgery (freezing the tumor), and GENE THERAPY, have been developed or are under research. The branch of medicine concerned with diagnosis, treatment, and research into the causes of cancer is oncology.

Cancún [känkōōn], city (1990 pop. 172,425), SE Mexico, on the Yucatán peninsula. A popular coastal resort initially developed in the early 1970s, it is known for its beautiful beaches, agreeable climate, and luxurious hotels.

candytuft, low-growing Old World plant (genus *Iberis*) of the MUSTARD family, often cultivated as a rock garden and border ornamental. Candytufts have flat-topped or elongated clusters of variously colored flowers.

cane, in botany, name for a hollow or woody, usually slender, jointed plant stem (e.g., RATTAN and some bamboos) and for some tall GRASSES (e.g., SUGARCANE and SORGHUM). Giant cane (*Arundinaria macrosperma* or *gigantea*), a BAMBOO grass native to the U.S., often forms impenetrable thickets, the canebrakes of the South.

cane sugar: see SUCROSE.

Canetti, Elias, 1905–, German writer; b. Bulgaria. He has lived in England since 1938 and is best known for two works: *Auto da fé* (1935), a searing picture of humanity as degraded and evil, and *Crowds and Power* (1960), a study of mass psychology. He also wrote plays; a study of KAFKA, and autobiographical works. He was awarded the 1981 Nobel Prize in literature.

cannabis: see HEMP.

cannibalism, practice of eating human flesh, found among some peoples of Africa, South America, the South Pacific islands, and the West Indies. Victims for rites of life- or power-transfer are usually sought among alien groups, although some peoples eat part of a kinsman's corpse as a gesture of respect for the deceased. HEADHUNTING may have evolved from cannibalism. Cannibalism has also occurred among isolated groups desperate to survive, e.g. the DONNER PARTY.

Canning, George, 1770–1827, British statesman. A TORY, he served (1807–9) as foreign minister during the wars against NAPOLEON I and was influential in military affairs. After CASTLEREAGH's suicide, he was again foreign minister (1822–27). He refused to cooperate in the suppression of European revolutions, aided the MONROE DOCTRINE by recognizing the independence of Spanish colonies in America, and arranged the Anglo-French-Russian agreement that resulted in Greek independence. He was prime minister in 1827.

canning, process of hermetically sealing cooked food for future use, including meat, poultry, fruits and vegetables, seafood, milk, preserves and pickles, jams and jellies. Developed early in 19th-cent. France by Nicolas Appert, a chef, the method spread throughout Europe and the U.S., where it was patented around 1815. The process was widely used to provide foodstuffs to soldiers during the U.S. Civil War. The early glass and tin containers were later supplanted by tin-plated steel cans, mass-produced in America since 1847 and now the basis of a modern industry. In home as in factory canning, the process involves cleaning and preparing the raw product (with rapid handling necessary to prevent vitamin loss, bacterial spoilage, or enzyme changes). Once filled, the containers are thermally exhausted to release gases, then subjected to heat to destroy any microorganisms.

Cannon, Annie Jump, 1863–1941, American astronomer; b. Dover, Del. A staff assistant (from 1896) and curator of astronomical photographs (1911–38) at the Harvard College Observatory, she developed the definitive Harvard system of spectral classification (see SPECTRAL CLASS) and published spectral classifications of over 350,000 stars appearing on Harvard photographic plates. In the course of her work she discovered more than 300 variable stars, many through their spectral characteristics.

Cannon, Joseph Gurney, 1836–1926, Speaker of the U.S. House of Representatives (1903–11); b. Guilford co., N.C. A lawyer from Illinois, he ruled the House dictatorially in the interest of "Old Guard" Republicans until a bill reforming House rules (1910) broke his power.

Cannon, Walter Bradford, 1871–1945, American physiologist. He was the first to use (1897) bismuth as a contrast medium in an X-ray examination of the gastrointestinal tract. His interest in the physiological effects of emotional stimuli, especially on digestion, led to publication (1919) of his *Bodily Changes in Pain, Hunger, Fear and Rage.* Cannon also introduced (1932) the concept of homeostasis.

cannon, in warfare: see ARTILLERY.

canon, in music, a type of COUNTERPOINT in which all the instruments or voices have the same melody, beginning at different times, with successive entrances at the same or different pitches. A well-known vocal form is the round, of which the earliest known example is the medieval song *Sumer is Icumen in.* The Canon in D for string orchestra by the 17th-cent. German composer Johann Pachelbel was popular in the U.S. in the 1970s. The canon is an essential device for SERIAL MUSIC.

canonization: see SAINT.

canon law, in the ROMAN CATHOLIC CHURCH, law of the church courts, based on legislation of councils, popes, and bishops. It deals with the governance of the clergy and the church, including administration of the sacraments. The present code was promulgated in 1917, but has been undergoing revision since the 1960s. It has a long development, begun with the early letters of the popes. The greatest figure in canon law was Gratian, whose compilation was the basis of all later collections. The Council of TRENT added much to the law.

Canova, Antonio, 1757–1822, Italian sculptor. Leading examples of neoclassicism, his statues and bas-reliefs—e.g., the monuments to Clement XIV (1782–87; Church of the Apostles, Rome) and Clement XIII (1792; St. Peter's, Rome)—are executed with grace, polish and purity of contour. His portraits include two nudes of Napoleon I as a Roman emperor.

cantaloupe: see GOURD; MELON.

cantata, composite musical form similar to a short unacted opera or brief ORATORIO, developed in Italy in the BAROQUE period. In France and Italy the secular cantatas included arias and recitatives; the sacred cantatas of Germany had choral and instrumental sections. J.S. BACH utilized hymn verses in his chorale cantatas.

Canterbury, city (1991 pop. 123,947), Kent, SE England, on the Stour R. The seat of the primate of the Church of England and the spiritual center of the country, it is a major attraction. Following his arrival (597) in England, St. AUGUSTINE founded an abbey there and became the first archbishop of Canterbury. After the murder (1170) of THOMAS À BECKET, the city became the object of pilgrimage, as described in CHAUCER's *Canterbury Tales.* The magnificent cathedral (1070–1180; 1379–1503) embodies the styles of several periods. Although the city was bombed during WORLD WAR II, the cathedral and many other historic buildings survive.

Canterbury Tales: see CHAUCER, GEOFFREY.

Canticles: see SONG OF SOLOMON.

Canton: see GUANGZHOU.

Cantor, Georg, 1845–1918, German mathematician; b. Russia. His work on transfinite numbers (see INFINITY) and SET theory revolutionized mathematics and led to a critical investigation of its foundations.

Canute [kənōōt'], 995?–1035, king of England, Norway, and Denmark. The younger son of SWEYN of Denmark, he invaded England with his father in 1013 and forced ÆTHELRED to flee to Norway. On Sweyn's death (1014) he withdrew to Denmark. He reinvaded England in 1015 and, after the Danish victory at the battle of Assendun, divided the country with EDMUND IRONSIDE. On Edmund's death (1016), Canute was accepted as sole king. He gave England peace, restored the church to a high place, and codified English law. He married Emma, the widow of Æthelred. In 1018 he succeeded to the throne of Denmark. After several expeditions to Norway, he threw out OLAF II in 1028, thus becoming ruler of three kingdoms. He made his son Harthacanute king of Denmark and his son Sweyn king of Norway. Canute also established friendly relations with the HOLY ROMAN EMPIRE.

Canyon de Chelly National Monument, area near Chinle, Ariz., including a canyon known for its ruins of spectacular cliff dwellings, built in A.D. 350–1300 by the people known as the basket makers and their successors, the PUEBLO. The NAVAHO, who now live and farm there, settled in the canyon c.1700.

Canyon de Chelly

Canyonlands National Park: see NATIONAL PARKS (table).

capacitance, in electricity, the capability of a body, a system, or an ELECTRIC CIRCUIT for storing electric CHARGE. Capacitance, measured in units of farads (F) and fractions of a farad, microfarads (μF) and picofarads (pF), is expressed as the ratio of stored charge in coulombs to the applied potential difference in volts. In electric circuits, devices designed to store charge are called CAPACITORS. When alternating current flows through a capacitor, the capacitor produces a reactance, inversely proportional to the capacitance, that resists the current flow (see IMPEDANCE).

capacitor or **condenser,** device for storing electric charge. Simple capacitors usually consist of two plates made of an electrically conducting material (e.g., a metal) separated by a nonconducting material, or DIELECTRIC (e.g., air, ceramic, glass, mica, oil, paper, paraffin, or plastic). If an electric POTENTIAL (voltage) is applied to the capacitor plates, the plates will become charged, one positively and one negatively. If the externally applied voltage is then removed, the capacitor plates remain charged, and the electric charge induces an electric potential between the two plates. This phenomenon is called electrostatic INDUCTION. The capacity of the device for storing electric charge (i.e., its CAPACITANCE) can be increased by increasing the area of the plates, by decreasing their separation, or by varying the substance used as an insulator. The dielectric constant is a measure of the increase in capacitance due to a particular insulator used to separate the plates. The **Leyden jar,** a form of capacitor invented at the Univ. of Leiden in the 18th cent., consists of a narrow-necked glass jar coated on part of its inner and outer surfaces with conductive metal foil.

Cape Breton Island, island, 3,970 sq mi (10,282 sq km), in NE Nova Scotia, separated from the Canadian mainland by the Gut (or Strait) of Canso. It was discovered by the English navigator John CABOT in 1497. Under French control (1623–1763), it was renamed Île Royale and fortified (at LOUISBURG) by French loyalists (the Acadians) after the rest of NOVA SCOTIA passed to the English in 1713. It was a separate colony from 1784 to 1820, with its capital at Sydney.

Cape Canaveral, low promontory, E Florida (called Cape Kennedy, 1963–73). Since 1947 it has been the chief U.S. launching site for long-range test missiles and manned space flights.

Cape Cod, hook-shaped, sandy peninsula, SE Massachusetts, extending 65 mi (105 km) E and N into the Atlantic Ocean. It is a popular resort area. Parts of it constitute the **Cape Cod National Seashore** (44,600 acres/18,050 hectares; est. 1961). **Cape Cod Canal,** built 1910–14, cut the New York–Boston shipping distance by 75 mi (121 km).

Čapek, Karel [chä'pěk], 1890–1938, Czech writer. He wrote two brilliant satirical plays attacking technological and materialist excess: *R.U.R.* (*Rossum's Universal Robots,* 1921), which introduced the word *robot;* and *The Insect Play* (1921), written with his brother Josef. His other works include *The Makropoulos Secret* (1922), a play on which JANÁČEK based an opera; *The War with the Newts* (1936), a satirical science-fiction attack on totalitarianism; philosophical novels; travel sketches; and volumes of conversations with Thomas MASARYK. **Josef Čapek,** 1887–1945, was a writer and painter.

Cape Kennedy: see CAPE CANAVERAL.

caper, common name for members of the family Capparidaceae, chiefly Old World tropical plants closely related to the MUSTARD family. The pickled caper, used as a condiment, is the flower bud of *Capparis spinosa,* cultivated in the Mediterranean area. The family also includes the spiderflower (*Cleome spinosa*), a common garden annual.

Capetians [kəpē'shənz], royal house of France, named for HUGH CAPET, who became king in 987. His direct descendants ruled France until the death of CHARLES IV in 1328. The throne then passed to the collateral branch of VALOIS.

Cape Town or **Capetown,** city (1985 pop. 776,617), legislative capital of South Africa and capital of Cape Province, an important port on the Atlantic Ocean. It is a commercial and industrial center, linked by road, rail, and airlines to other South African cities. Situated at the foot of Table Mt. (c.3,570 ft/1, 090 m), Cape Town is a tourist resort with fine beaches and a pleasant climate. The city, founded in 1652, is the site of a fortress, church, museum, and other buildings dating to the early Dutch settlement.

Cape Verde, Port. *Cabo Verde,* officially Republic of Cape Verde, republic (1992 est. pop. 398,000), c.1,560 sq mi (4,040 sq km), W Africa, in the Atlantic Ocean, about 300 mi (480 km) W of Senegal. Cape Verde is an archipelago made up of 10 islands and 5 islets, divided into two main groups—the Barlavento, or Windward, in the north, which include Santo Antão, São Vicente, Santa Luzia, São Nicolau, Boa Vista, and Sal; and the Sotavento, or Leeward, which include São Tiago, Fogo, Maio, and Brava. Praia, the capital, is located on São Tiago, the largest island. The islands are mountainous and of volcanic origin; the only active volcano, and the archipelago's highest point, is Cano (c.9,300 ft/2,830 m), on Fogo. Farming, the main economic activity, is limited by the small annual rainfall. Occasionally, severe drought, as in the 1970s and 80s, further reduces production of the main crops (corn, bananas, sweet potatoes, beans, sugarcane, and coffee). Tuna and lobster are the major fishing catches. The main mineral resource is salt. Many of the islanders work in Portugal and the U.S., and their remittances, along with foreign assistance, help to support the weak economy. About 70% of the population is of mixed African and European descent; most of the rest are of African descent. Roman Catholicism is the main religion. Portuguese and a Portuguese-African creole are the national languages.

History. Cape Verde was discovered in 1456 by Luigi da Cadamosto, a navigator in the service of Portugal. Portuguese colonists began to settle in the islands, which were probably uninhabited, in 1462, and soon began importing West Africans as slaves. Slavery was abolished in the islands in 1876. Cape Verde became an overseas province in 1951 and gained its independence in 1975. A movement for union with Guinea-Bissau was blocked by a 1980 coup in Guinea-Bissau, which brought to power leaders opposed to the union. In 1991 the leftist party that had held power since independence lost control of parliament, and Antonio Mascarenhas Monteiro defeated Pres. Aristides Pereira, who had led the country since 1975, in a free election. The nation has been plagued with a prolonged drought that caused staggering economic problems and large-scale emigration, an 80% unemployment rate, and the need to import most of its food.

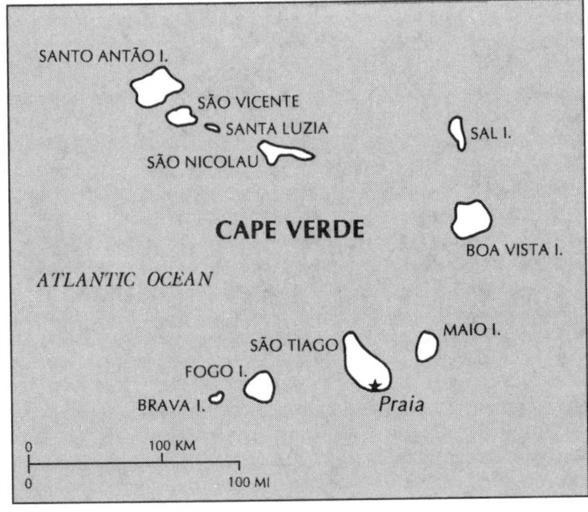

capillarity or **capillary action,** phenomenon in which the surface of a liquid is elevated or depressed when it comes in contact with a solid. The result depends on the outcome of two opposing forces, ADHESION AND COHESION. Adhesion between glass and water causes the water to rise along a glass wall until this force is balanced by the cohesive force acting to minimize the liquid's surface area (see SURFACE TENSION). When adhesion is less than cohesion, as with glass and mercury, the surface is lowered. The upward flow of water in soil and in plants is partially caused by capillarity.

capital gains tax, levy on profits earned by the sale of capital assets, such as stocks, bonds, and real estate. In the U.S., long-term gains on assets held for one year or more may be taxed at a somewhat lower rate than short-term gains if total taxable income is within a certain range.

capitalism, economic system characterized by private ownership of property and of the means of production. Generally the capitalist, or private enterprise, system embodies the concepts of individual initiative, competition, SUPPLY AND DEMAND, and the profit motive. Capitalism and SOCIALISM are the two major economic systems in the world. The modern importance of capitalism dates from the INDUSTRIAL REVOLUTION, which started in the 18th cent. when bankers, merchants, and industrialists began to displace landowners in importance, especially in Britain. By the early 20th cent. capitalism had created vast credit, manufacturing, and distributing institutions, and the social and economic effects of the system had largely transformed world culture. However, it was also held responsible for various abuses, notably the exploitation of labor. Complete freedom of economic action has been circumscribed since the late 1800s by the growth of strong labor UNIONS, the NATIONALIZATION in some countries of certain basic industries, and ANTITRUST LAWS limiting the power of MONOPOLIES, as well as by social reforms, ENVIRONMENTALISM, and legislation ensuring product safety. See also LAISSEZ-FAIRE.

capital levy: see TAXATION.

capital punishment, imposition of the death penalty by the state. Applied from ancient times in most societies, it has been used as punishment for crimes ranging in gravity from petty theft to murder. Modern opposition to capital punishment arose in France in the 18th cent. and spread through W Europe, where most nations abolished such laws in the 20th cent. In the U.S. the death penalty was applied with decreasing frequency after World War II, and in 1972 the U.S. Supreme Court voided all federal and state laws calling for the death penalty on the grounds that condemned persons were being subjected to "cruel and unusual punishment," in violation of the 8th amendment to the CONSTITUTION. The court left open, however, the possible enactment of new, constitutional laws, and since then most states have passed new measures imposing the penalty in specified kinds of murder cases.

Capitol, seat of the U.S. government, at Washington, D.C., built on an elevated site chosen by WASHINGTON and Major Pierre L'ENFANT. The building is the work of several architects. William Thornton's 1792 plan was initiated in 1793. E.S. Hallet, George Hadfield, and James Hoban succeeded Thornton. In 1814 the British burned the uncompleted building, and B.H. LATROBE and Charles BULFINCH restored and completed it (1818–30). The House and Senate wings and the dome were added (1851–65) by T.U. Walter. The dome is 288 ft (90 m) high.

Capitoline Hill or **Capitol,** highest of the seven hills of ancient Rome, historic and religious center of the city in ancient times. In the Middle Ages the Capitol remained the political center of Rome, and it is the center of municipal government in modern Rome. In the 16th cent. MICHELANGELO designed the Capitol's present plan.

Capitol Reef National Park: see NATIONAL PARKS (table).

Capone, Al(phonse), 1899–1947, American gangster; b. Brooklyn, N.Y. His crime syndicate terrorized Chicago in the 1920s, controlling gambling and prostitution there. In 1931 he was sentenced to prison for federal income-tax evasion.

Capote, Truman, 1924–84, American author; b. New Orleans. His fiction reflected a world of grotesque and strangely innocent people. He wrote novels, e.g., *The Grass Harp* (1951); short stories, e.g., *Breakfast at Tiffany's* (1958); nonfiction; and the "nonfiction novel" *In Cold Blood* (1966).

Cappadocia, ancient region of Asia Minor, in present E central Turkey. The name was applied at different times to territories of varying size. Before 1800 B.C., Cappadocia was the heart of an old HITTITE state; later, it was controlled by the Persians. During the 3d cent. B.C. it developed as an independent kingdom. In A.D. 17 Rome annexed the region.

Capra, Frank, 1897–1991, American film director; b. Sicily. *It Happened One Night* (1934), *Mr. Deeds Goes to Town* (1936), and *You Can't Take It with You* (1938), mixing "screwball" comedy and populism, won Academy Awards. Among his other films is *It's a Wonderful Life* (1946).

Caprivi Strip, panhandle area of NE Namibia, 300 mi (480 km) long and 50 mi (80 km) wide, between Botswana (S) and Angola and Zambia (N). It was obtained from Great Britain by Germany in 1890 to give German South West Africa (now NAMIBIA) access to the ZAMBEZI R.

capybara, largest living RODENT, reaching a length of 4 ft (120 cm) and a weight of 75 to 100 lb (34 to 45 kg). Found in Central and much of South America, it has coarse, scant, brownish hair flecked with yellow. An expert swimmer, the capybara is also called the water hog.

Caracalla, 188–217, Roman emperor (211–17); son of Septimius SEVERUS. Born Marcus Aurelius Antoninus; he received his nickname from the caracalla, a Gallic tunic he regularly wore. His reign was infamous for its cruelty and bloodshed. Caracalla did pacify the German frontier and extended Roman citizenship to all free inhabitants of the empire. In 217 he was murdered by his successor, Macrinus.

Caracas, city (1991 pop. 1,824,892), N Venezuela, capital and largest city of Venezuela. An extremely cosmopolitan city, it is a major industrial center, shipping through the nearby Caribbean port of La Guaira. Caracas was founded in 1567 and was the base for Spanish colonization of Venezuela. It was the birthplace of the liberators Francisco de MIRANDA and Simón BOLÍVAR. Caracas retains an old section, with many examples of colonial architecture. The oil boom of the 1950s made possible massive public building projects, transforming much of Caracas into an ultramodern metropolis famed for such futuristic complexes as University City and the Centro Bolívar government center. A cultural hub, the city is the site of a large performing arts center, three orchestras, an opera, a ballet, and three major art museums.

Caramanlis, Constantine: see KARAMANLIS, CONSTANTINE.

carambola or **star fruit,** orange fleshy fruit of *Averrhoa carambola,* a shrub of the wood sorrel family. It has prominent ridges that when cut in cross-section create a five-pointed star. It has a sour taste; its juice is used in stain remover.

Caravaggio, Michelangelo Merisi da [käräväd'jō] or **Amerigi da Caravaggio,** 1573–1610, Italian painter. After his early years in Rome doing genre paintings, e.g., *Concert of Youths* (Metropolitan Mus.) and the *Fortune Teller* (Louvre), Caravaggio devoted himself to religious works and portraits. His use of models from lower walks of life in religious works was thought irreverent, but his strong chiaroscuro technique, partially illuminating figures against a dark background, was adopted by his contemporaries. His wide influence can be seen in the works of REMBRANDT and RIBERA.

caraway, biennial plant (*Carum carvi*) of the CARROT family, cultivated in Europe and North America for its aromatic, spicy seeds. The seeds are used to flavor pastry, cabbage, sausage, cheese, and liqueurs.

carbohydrate, any member of a large class of chemical compounds that includes sugars, starches, cellulose, and related compounds. Carbohydrates are produced naturally by green plants from carbon dioxide and water (see PHOTOSYNTHESIS). Essential nutrients, they are the human body's main source of both quick and sustained energy. The three main classes of carbohydrates are monosaccharides, which are the simple SUGARS, e.g., FRUCTOSE and GLUCOSE; disaccharides, which are made up of two monosaccharide units and include LACTOSE, MALTOSE, and SUCROSE; and polysaccharides, which are polymers with many monosaccharide units and include CELLULOSE, GLYCOGEN, and STARCH.

carbon (C), nonmetallic element, known since ancient times. Pure carbon forms are amorphous carbon, found in such sources as CHARCOAL, COAL, COKE, LIGNITE, and PEAT; and the crystals GRAPHITE, a very soft, dark-gray or black, lustrous material; and DIAMOND, the hardest substance known. ORGANIC CHEMISTRY is the study of carbon compounds. All living organisms contain carbon. Carbon has seven isotopes; carbon-12 is the basis for ATOMIC WEIGHTS; carbon-14, with a half-life of 5,730 years, is used to trace chemical reactions and to date geologic and archeologic specimens (see DATING). See CARBON CYCLE; CARBON DIOXIDE; CARBON MONOXIDE; ELEMENT (table); FULLERENE; PERIODIC TABLE.

carbon cycle, in biology, the exchange of carbon between living organisms and the nonliving environment. Carbon, the central element in the compounds of which organisms are composed, is derived from free carbon dioxide found in air or dissolved water. Plants incorporate carbon into carbohydrates and other complex organic molecules by means of PHOTOSYNTHESIS; during RESPIRATION, or OXIDATION, they combine oxygen with portions of the carbohydrate molecule, releasing carbon in the form of carbon dioxide and water. Carbon is also returned to the environment when plants die and their organic material is broken down by bacteria and other microorganisms. Animals obtain carbon by feeding on plants and other animals; they release carbon through respiration and, after death, indirectly through the respiration of microorganisms that consume them.

carbon dioxide (CO_2), chemical compound, occurring as a colorless, odorless, tasteless gas that is about 1½ times as dense as air under ordinary conditions. It does not burn and will not support combustion of ordinary materials. Its weakly acidic aqueous solution is called CARBONIC ACID. The gas, easily liquefied by compression and cooling, provides the sparkle in carbonated beverages. Solid carbon dioxide, or dry ice, is a refrigerant. Dough rises because of carbon dioxide formed by the action of yeast or baking powder. Carbon dioxide is a raw material for PHOTOSYNTHESIS in green plants, and is a product of animal RESPIRATION and of the decay of organic matter. Carbon dioxide occurs both free and combined in nature, and makes up about 1% of the volume of dry air. It can cause death by suffocation if inhaled in large amounts.

carbon-14 dating: see DATING.

carbonic acid (H_2CO_3), a weak dibasic acid (see ACIDS AND BASES) formed when CARBON DIOXIDE dissolves in water; it exists only in solution. With bases it forms the CARBONATE and bicarbonate salts.

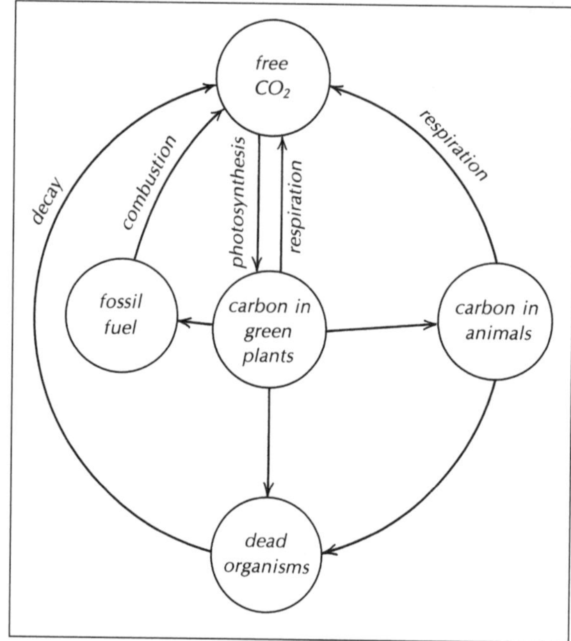

Carbon cycle

Carboniferous period: see GEOLOGIC ERA (table).

carbon monoxide, chemical compound (CO), colorless, odorless, tasteless, extremely poisonous gas that is less dense than air under ordinary conditions. It burns in air with a characteristic blue flame, producing carbon dioxide. It is a component of the artificial fuels producer gas and WATER GAS. As a reducing agent, it removes oxygen from many compounds and is used in the reduction of metals from ores. When air containing as little as 0.1% carbon monoxide by volume is inhaled, the oxygen carried by hemoglobin is replaced by the carbon monoxide, resulting in fatal oxygen starvation throughout the body.

carburetor, device in a gasoline engine that vaporizes the gas and mixes it with a regulated amount of air for efficient combustion in the engine cylinders. Land vehicles, boats, and light aircraft have a float carburetor, in which a float regulates the fuel level in a reservoir from which the fuel is continuously sucked into the intake manifold at a restriction called a venturi. In many modern vehicles, the carburetor has been replaced by a FUEL INJECTION system. See also INTERNAL-COMBUSTION ENGINE.

carcinogen, any agent that causes cancer in animal tissue. Ubiquitous indoors and out, in the workplace and at home, carcinogens can be inorganic, such as asbestos and arsenic, or organic, such as certain molds and viruses. Others include various types of radiation, such as ultraviolet and X rays. Carcinogens can be inhaled (radon and tobacco smoke), ingested (nitrites), or absorbed through the skin (DDT and other pesticides). Using a procedure called the Ames test, potential carcinogens can be tested for their propensity to damage DNA and cause mutations. It has been predicted that 30% of Americans will die of cancer caused in part by environmental carcinogens before they reach the age of 74.

carcinoma: see TUMOR.

cardamom: see GINGER.

Cárdenas, Lázaro, 1895–1970, president of MEXICO (1934–40). He fought (1913–17) as a general in the Mexican revolution and was elected president. He expropriated foreign-held properties, distributed land to peasants, and instituted reforms to benefit indigenous peoples and Mexican workers. His influence in advancing constitutional processes was great. His son, **Cuauhtémoc Cárdenas Solórzano,** 1934–, was a member of the ruling Institutional Revolutionary party and served as a senator, government minister, and governor of Michoacán. In 1988 he formed a leftist opposition group and ran unsuccessfully for president.

Cardiff, city (1991 pop. 279,055), S Glamorgan, S Wales, on the

Bristol Channel. It is capital, largest city, and chief port of Wales. The service sector is economically the most important; manufactures include machinery and processed food. Cardiff was one of the world's greatest coal-shipping ports in the 19th and early 20th cent. The ruins of Cardiff Castle, built (1090) on the site of a Roman fort, are of special interest.

cardinal, a member of the highest body within the Roman Catholic Church below the pope—the college of cardinals, having the duty of electing the pope (since 1059) and all the duties of a privy council to him. Its members are appointed by the pope and are of three classes: cardinal bishops, bishops of the seven sees around Rome and the Eastern rite patriarchs; cardinal priests, mostly archbishops outside the Roman province; and cardinal deacons, priests with functions within papal government. A cardinal's insignia resemble those of a bishop except for the red, broad-brimmed, tasseled hat, which is conferred by the pope but not subsequently worn. Pope SIXTUS V set the number of cardinals at 70. Since the pontificate of JOHN XXIII, the number has increased, but only 120 may participate in a papal election.

cardinal or **redbird,** North American songbird of the FINCH family. The eastern cardinal (*Richmondena cardinalis*) male is bright red with a black throat and face; the female is brown with red patches. Both have crests and red bills.

cardiopulmonary resuscitation (CPR), emergency procedure used to treat victims of cardiac and respiratory arrest. Special training is recommended for CPR, which combines external heart massage (to keep the blood flowing through the body) with ARTIFICIAL RESPIRATION (to keep air flowing in and out of the lungs). The victim is placed face up and prepared for artificial respiration. The person administering CPR places his or her hands (one on top of the other, with fingers interlocked) heel down on the victim's breastbone, leans forward, and presses down rhythmically about 60 times a minute. This procedure is alternated with mouth-to-mouth artificial respiration.

Cardozo, Benjamin Nathan, 1870–1938, associate justice of the U.S. SUPREME COURT (1932–38); b. N.Y.C.; A.B., Columbia Univ. (1889). A New York attorney and judge of considerable stature, on the Court he was an eloquent and influential supporter of liberal social and economic views. His published lectures are considered classics of jurisprudence.

Carducci, Giosuè, 1835–1907, Italian poet and teacher. Professor of literature at the Univ. of Bologna from 1860 to 1904, he was a scholar, editor, orator, critic, and patriot. He was awarded the 1906 Nobel Prize in literature. His verse, classic in design, with great emotional range, ranks him among leading Italian poets. His works include *Hymn to Satan* (1865) and *Lyrics and Rhythms* (1899).

Carey, George Leonard, 1935–, archbishop of Canterbury (1991–). From a working-class background, he was appointed bishop of Bath and Wells in 1987 and was enthroned as the 103d archbishop of Canterbury in 1991, succeeding Robert RUNCIE. Opposed to "extreme" liberalism in the Church of ENGLAND, he has strong ties to the church's Anglo-Catholic and evangelical wings and is a strong champion of the ordination of women. Carey became known as the "green bishop" for his environmentalism while bishop of Bath and Wells. He has written several books on religious issues.

cargo cults, nativistic religious movements in Melanesia holding that at the millennium ancestor spirits will bring cargoes of modern goods to believers. Dating from the 19th cent., these cults expanded after World War II forces left surplus goods in the islands and contact with the West increased.

Caribbean Sea, tropical sea, c.750,000 sq mi (1,942,500 sq km), an arm of the Atlantic Ocean bordered by the West Indies (N, E), South America (S), and Central America (W). Its waters are clear and warm (averaging 75°F/24°C), with almost no tidal range. Bartlett Trench (22,788 ft/6,946 m below sea level), between Cuba and Jamaica, is the deepest point. After its discovery (1493) by Christopher COLUMBUS the sea was controlled by Spain, but other European nations later established colonies on its western fringe. Since the MONROE DOCTRINE of 1823, and especially after the opening (1914) of the PANAMA CANAL, the U.S. has tried to exclude foreign powers from this strategic area (see CUBAN MISSILE CRISIS) and has often intervened in the region's domestic affairs, e.g., in the DOMINICAN REPUBLIC in 1965. See also WEST INDIES.

caribou, name in North America for the DEER (genus *Rangifer*) from which the REINDEER was domesticated. Found in arctic and subarctic regions, caribou are the only deer of which both sexes have antlers.

caricature, a satirical portrait in art or literature that, through exaggeration and distortion of features, makes its subject appear ridiculous. The comic tradition in art was established in 17th-cent. Italy by the CARRACCI. Caricature flourished in 18th-cent. England in the works of HOGARTH, ROWLANDSON, and Gillray. Expanding to include political and social satire, the genre developed into the CARTOON. Caricature was extremely popular in European and American periodicals of the 19th cent., many of which included work by such artists as DAUMIER, CRUIKSHANK, TENNIEL, and Art Young. Notable modern caricaturists include BEERBOHM, Ronald Searle, Al Hirschfeld, and David Levine. In literature, caricature has been a popular form since the ancient Greeks. Perhaps the most striking and pervasive use of literary caricature in English is in the work of Charles DICKENS.

Carleton, Guy, 1st **Baron Dorchester,** 1724–1808, British governor and commander of QUEBEC in the AMERICAN REVOLUTION. He repelled (1775) an American attack on Fort Quebec and seized (1776) Crown Point, N.Y. He was replaced (1776–77) as commander and governor, but served as commander (1782–83) of British forces in America and as governor (1786–96) of British North America.

Carl Gustaf: see Charles XVI Gustavus under CHARLES, kings of Sweden.

Carlists, partisans of Don Carlos (1788–1855) and his successors in their claims to the Spanish throne. After FERDINAND VII changed the law to enable his daughter, ISABELLA II, to succeed him (1833), his brother, Don Carlos, claimed the throne and initiated an unsuccessful civil war (1833–40). The conservative, clericalist Carlists revived the claim (1860) for Don Carlos's son, Don Carlos, conde de Montemolin (1818–61), and again (1869, 1872) on behalf of the latter's nephew, Don Carlos, duque de Madrid (1848–1909). They seized most of the Basque provinces and other territory and fought another civil war (1873–76), which failed. The Carlists supported the Nationalists in the SPANISH CIVIL WAR (1936–39), but FRANCO ended their dynastic claim in 1969 by naming the Bourbon prince, JUAN CARLOS, as his successor.

Carlos. For Spanish rulers thus named, see CHARLES.

Carlos, Don: see CARLISTS.

Carlsbad Caverns National Park: see NATIONAL PARKS (table).

Carlson, Chester Floyd, 1906–68, American inventor; b. Seattle, Wash. A patent lawyer, he invented (1938) xerography (see PHOTOCOPYING), a method of electrostatic printing, and made a fortune from the Haloid Co. (later the Xerox Corp.). The first Xerox copier was marketed in 1959.

Carlstadt, Karlstadt, or **Karolstadt,** c.1480–1541, German Protestant reformer, originally named Andreas Rudolph Bodenstein. During LUTHER's stay at Wartberg (1521–22), Carlstadt became the leader at Wittenberg and implemented his radical beliefs. Luther later accused him of betrayal. Accused of revolutionary political activity, Carlstadt fled to Switzerland, where he taught theology at Basel.

Carlyle, Thomas, 1795–1881, English author; b. Scotland. He first gained attention as an interpreter of German ROMANTICISM with his *Life of Schiller* (1825) and a translation of Goethe's *Wilhelm Meister* (1824). In 1826 he married Jane Baillie Welsh, an ambitious woman who did much to aid his career. A trenchant critic of materialism, he expressed his views in a sort of spiritual autobiography, *Sartor Resartus* (1833–34), and in his interpretative rather than historical *French Revolution* (1837). He attacked laissez-faire theory and parliamentary democracy and stressed his belief in strong government and great individuals in *On Heroes, Hero-Worship, and The Heroic in History* (1841) and *Past and Present* (1843), in an edition of the writings of Oliver CROMWELL (1845), and in a biography of Frederick the Great (1858–65). Carlyle had great influence on the literary world of his day; his style, tortuous yet effective, is unique.

Carmelites, Roman Catholic order of mendicant friars. Originating apparently as hermits on Mt. Carmel in Palestine, they were made into a Western order by St. Simon Stock (d. 1265) and became prominent in university life. An enclosed order of Carmelite nuns was established. After a decline, the Carmelites were revived by the reforms of St. THERESA of Ávila and St. JOHN OF THE CROSS in 16th-cent. Spain. The now larger reformed order is known as the Discalced Carmelites.

Carmichael, Hoagy (Hoagland Howard Carmichael), 1899–1981, American songwriter; b. Bloomington, Ind. His melodies reflect early JAZZ influence. "Stardust" (1929) is his best-known song; others include "Georgia on My Mind" and "Skylark." He also appeared in films, e.g., *To Have and Have Not* (1944).

Carnap, Rudolf, 1891–1970, German-American philosopher. One of the most influential of contemporary thinkers, he was a founder of LOGICAL POSITIVISM and made important contributions to logic, semantics, and the philosophy of science. He defined philosophy as "the logic of the sciences" and considered it a general language whose only legitimate concern could be to describe and criticize the language of the particular sciences. Through linguistic analysis he revealed the inadequacies of everyday speech. Carnap later modified this extreme view, which rejects almost all traditional philosophy. His works include *The Logical Syntax of Language* (1934) and *Introduction to Symbolic Logic* (1954).

Carnarvon, George Edward Stanhope Molyneux Herbert, 5th **earl of,** 1866–1923, English Egyptologist who, with Howard CARTER, excavated (1906–22) in the Valley of the Kings, Luxor, Egypt. The tomb of TUTANKHAMEN was their final discovery (1922).

carnation: see PINK.

Carnegie, Andrew, 1835–1919, American industrialist and philanthropist; b. Scotland, emigrated to the U.S. 1848. As a superintendent (1859–65) for the Pennsylvania RR he invested in iron manufactures. In 1873 he began to acquire firms that later became the Carnegie Steel Co., which by 1900 was producing a quarter of the steel in the U.S. and controlled iron mines, ore ships, and railroads. His partnership with Henry C. FRICK aided his success. In 1901 he sold his interests to the U.S. Steel Corp. and retired. Believing that wealth should be used for the public good, he donated c.$350 million, establishing such philanthropic organizations as the Carnegie Corp. of New York, the Carnegie Endowment for International Peace, and over 2,800 libraries.

Carnegie Corporation of New York: see FOUNDATION.

carnivorous plants: see PITCHER PLANT; VENUS'S-FLYTRAP.

Carnot, Lazare Nicolas Marguerite [kärnō'], 1753–1823, French revolutionary. He organized the republican armies and masterminded a successful strategy in the FRENCH REVOLUTIONARY WARS. A member of the DIRECTORY, he later held high posts under NAPOLEON I and wrote a classic work on fortification (1810).

Carnot, (Nicholas Léonard) Sadi, 1796–1832, French physicist, son of Lazare CARNOT. He studied the relation between heat and mechanical energy and devised an engine whose operations showed that even under ideal conditions a heat engine must reject some heat energy instead of converting it all into mechanical energy. This illustrates the second law of THERMODYNAMICS, formulated later.

Caro, Joseph ben Ephraim, 1488–1575, Jewish codifier of law; b. Spain, d. Palestine. His chief work is *Shulhan Arukh* [the table set], still an authority for Orthodox religious and legal disputes. Caro was also a cabalist (see CABALA).

carob, evergreen tree (*Ceratonia siliqua*) of the PULSE family, native to the Mediterranean but cultivated in other warm areas. Its large, red pods have been a food source since prehistoric times, and the pods and their extracts have many common names, e.g., St. John's bread and locust bean gum. Carob is used as a food stabilizer and a caffeine-free chocolate substitute; carob pods are used as livestock feed.

Carol, kings of ROMANIA. **Carol I** or **Charles I,** 1839–1914, prince (1866–81) and first king (1881–1914), was a Prussian of the Hohenzollern-Sigmaringen dynasty. He achieved full independence for Romania at the Congress of BERLIN (1878). He married ELIZABETH of Wied. **Carol II,** 1893–1953, was forced (1925) to renounce his right to succession in favor of his infant son, MICHAEL, but in 1930 he proclaimed himself king, dethroning Michael. He instituted a personal dictatorship in 1938, but was dethroned by ANTONESCU in 1940, and Michael again became king.

carol, popular, joyful hymn, celebrating an occasion such as EASTER or CHRISTMAS. English carols date from the 15th cent. Like the FOLK SONG, the carol is characterized by simplicity of thought and expression.

Carolina, city (1990 pop. 177,806), Puerto Rico. Located 7 mi (11 km) SE of San Juan, it is a residential suburb of the capital. There are tourist facilities and sugar, tobacco, and textiles are produced.

Caroline Affair. In 1837 a group of U.S. citizens sided with a Canadian rebellion headed by W.L. MACKENZIE. A small American ship, the *Caroline,* carried reinforcements and supplies to the rebels, who were on Navy Island, above NIAGARA FALLS. Loyal Canadians set fire to the ship and sent it over the falls. One American was killed. After this incident, anti-British feeling contributed to tense U.S. relations with Britain until the WEBSTER-ASHBURTON TREATY of 1842.

Caroline of Brunswick, 1768–1821, consort of GEORGE IV of England. She married George in 1795, separated from him in 1796, and lived abroad after 1814. When George became king in 1820, she returned to claim her rights as queen. The king instituted divorce proceedings on the grounds of adultery. The charges were probably true, but Caroline's persecution by a profligate husband aroused sympathy, and they were dropped.

Carolingian architecture and art. In the 8th cent. under CHARLEMAGNE changes in Western culture and art reached their apex. In architecture, the small, boxlike structures of the Merovingian period gave way to centrally planned, spacious BASILICAS. But of incalculable importance to the later Middle Ages was the new emphasis given to the western facade of the church, called the westwork. Its function is still debated, but it was flanked by symmetrical towers and was several stories high. A vaulted vestibule was below, and the room above may have been a chapel for dignitaries. The outstanding Carolingian structure still in existence is the palatine chapel at Aachen (805), in Germany, which may have been based partly on the 5th-cent. Church of San Vitale in Ravenna, Italy. The best-preserved artistic works of the period are small objects—illuminated manuscripts, ivory carving, and metalwork. They show a fusion of Anglo-Saxon and Irish ornamental motifs with figures derived from antiquity, e.g., in the Gospel book by Godescalc (783). The nervous, flickering illustrations of the Utrecht Psalter are unparalleled in early Western art. Carved ivory book covers are rare, and metalwork is rarer, but the gold altar of Sant' Ambrogio (835, Milan), the portable altar of Arnulf (Munich), several splendid book covers, and other sumptuously decorated objects provide insights into the artistic accomplishments of the period, which ended in the late 9th cent.

Carolingians, Frankish dynasty founded (7th cent.) by Pepin of Landen. They ruled as mayors of the palace under the MEROVINGIANS until 751, when PEPIN THE SHORT made himself king. His son, CHARLEMAGNE, who was crowned emperor in 800, brought the dynasty to its zenith. In 840, on the death of LOUIS I, the Treaty of Verdun split the empire among his three sons: Lotharingia went to Lothair I; Germany went to Louis the German; and France went to Charles II. In 870 Lotharingia was divided between Louis and Charles. The dynasty died out in Germany in 911 and in France in 987.

carp, freshwater, bottom-feeding FISH (*Cyprinus carpio*), largest of the MINNOW family, native to Asia but now found throughout Europe and America. Carp may be up to 3 ft (90 cm) and 25 lb (11.3 kg). They have four "whiskers" (barbels) around the mouth, and are usually dark greenish or brown with red on the fins.

Carpaccio, Vittore, c.1450–1522, Venetian painter. He was influenced by Giovanni Bellini (see BELLINI, family). The rich color and wealth of detail in his St. George series and the *Presentation in the Temple* (all: Acad., Venice) show the pageantry of 15th-cent. Venice and a fanciful view of life in Asia.

carpal tunnel syndrome: see REPETITIVE STRESS INJURY.

Carpathians or **Carpathian Mountains,** major mountain system of central and E Europe, c.930 mi (1,500 km) long. A continuation of the Alps, they curve in a great arc through the Czech Republic, Slovakia, Poland, and Ukraine, and extend into Romania as the Transylvanian Alps, or Southern Carpathians. Gerlachovka (8,737 ft/2,663 m) is the highest point.

Carpeaux, Jean-Baptiste, 1827–75, French sculptor and painter. Freedom and force distinguish his sculptures, e.g., *Ugolino* (1860–

62; Louvre) and *Neapolitan Shellfisher* (Louvre), and paintings, e.g., *Bal costumé aux Tuileries* (Louvre).

carpet or **rug,** thick fabric, originally woolen but now often synthetic, most commonly used as a floor covering. Of ancient origin, the art of carpet weaving reached its height in the handloomed Oriental carpets from 16th-cent. Persia, Turkey, and central Asia. European carpets, with many outstanding examples dating from the 17th cent. in France and the 18th cent. in England, were handmade until Erastus Bigelow introduced (1841) the power loom. Although handmade rugs are still produced, contemporary carpet manufacturing is a mechanized industry. Classifications of both antique and modern carpets include Oriental, European handwoven, velvet, chenille, rag, hooked, straw, and fiber.

carpetbaggers, Southern term for Northerners who went to the South during RECONSTRUCTION. Although regarded as transients because they carried their belongings in carpetbags, most intended to settle in the South and make money there. The African-American vote won them important posts in Republican state governments. Those who were corrupt made the term synonymous with outsiders who profit from an area's political troubles.

Carracci [kärät'chē], family of Italian painters, founders of an important school of painting. **Lodovico Carracci,** 1555–1619, a pupil of TINTORETTO, established, with his cousins and Anthony de la Tour, a school of painting in Bologna that sought to unite in one system the best characteristics of the great masters. The academy was one of the outstanding schools in Italy, and its noted pupils include DOMENICHINO. An excellent painter, Lodovico was best known for his *Sermon of John the Baptist* (Pinacoteca, Bologna) and *Vision of Hyacinth* (Louvre). His cousin **Agostino Carracci,** 1557–1602, at first a goldsmith, later joined the academy and participated in numerous joint painting commissions such as the Farnese Palace gallery. His best-known work, *Celestial, Terrestrial and Venal Love,* is in the Casino, Parma. Agostino's brother **Annibale Carracci,** 1560–1609, worked in the academy and also on the Farnese gallery, with its influential feigned architectural and sculptural forms. Among his best-known works are *The Dead Christ* (Louvre) and *The Temptation of St. Anthony* (National Gall., London).

Carranza, Venustiano, 1859–1920, Mexican political leader. He fought in the Mexican revolution and helped to overthrow (1914) Gen. HUERTA. He became president (1914) and, aided by Gen. OBREGÓN, survived a civil war (1915). When he did not enforce the reform constitution of 1917 and tried to prevent Obregón from becoming president, the latter revolted (1920). Carranza fled the capital and was murdered.

Carrel, Alexis, 1873–1944, American surgeon and experimental biologist; b. France. For his work in suturing blood vessels, in transfusion, and in transplantation of organs, he was awarded the 1912 Nobel Prize in physiology or medicine. With Charles A. LINDBERGH he invented an artificial heart, with which he kept alive a number of different kinds of tissues and organs.

Carroll, John, 1735–1815, American Roman Catholic churchman, the first Roman Catholic bishop in the U.S.; b. Maryland. A JESUIT, he supported the AMERICAN REVOLUTION and was a friend of Benjamin FRANKLIN. In 1784 he became superior of the missions in the U.S. In 1790 he was made bishop of Baltimore and in 1808 archbishop. Carroll battled anti-Catholic feeling in the U.S. and founded various educational institutions, including Georgetown Univ.

Carroll, Lewis, pseud. of **Charles Lutwidge Dodgson,** 1832–98, English writer and mathematician. He lectured on mathematics at Oxford, but his fame rests on the fantasy novels *Alice's Adventures in Wonderland* (1865) and *Through the Looking Glass* (1872). These books grew out of stories he told to children, among them Alice Liddell, the daughter of H.G. Liddell, dean of Christ Church, Oxford. An amateur photographer, Carroll photographed children.

carrot, common name for some members of the Umbelliferae (also called parsley family), a family of mainly perennial or biennial herbs of north temperate areas. Most are typified by aromatic foliage, a dry fruit that splits when mature, and an umbellate inflorescence (in which the floret stems of the flattened flower cluster arise from the same point, like an umbrella). The seeds and leaves of many of these herbs are used for seasoning or as greens, e.g., ANISE, CARAWAY, CORIANDER, CUMIN, DILL, FENNEL, and PARSLEY. The carrot, CELERY, and PARSNIP are commercially important vegetables. The common carrot (*Daucus carota sativa*) is a root crop, probably derived from the wild carrot (or QUEEN ANNE'S LACE). Carrots are rich in carotene (vitamin A), especially when cooked; in antiquity they were used medicinally. Some types, e.g., button snakeroot and sweet cicely, are used as aromatic ornamentals. A few members of the family, e.g., POISON HEMLOCK, produce lethal poisons.

Carrucci, Jacopo: see PONTORMO, JACOPO DA.

Carson, Johnny, 1925–, American television entertainer; b. Corning, Iowa. Earlier a magician, comedy writer, and quiz show host, he is best known for hosting (1962–92) *The Tonight Show.* His monologues, sketches, and interviews made it television's most popular late-night program.

Carson, Kit (Christopher Carson), 1809–68, American frontiersman; b. Madison co., Ky. In 1825 he went to Taos, N.Mex., and served as cook, guide, and hunter for exploring parties, including those of J.C. FRÉMONT. In 1853 he became an Indian agent. He was a Union general in the CIVIL WAR.

Carson, Rachel Louise, 1907–64, American writer and marine biologist; b. Springdale, Pa. Her book *Silent Spring* (1962) was an influential study on the dangers of insecticides. Some of her other popular works include *The Sea Around Us* (1951) and *The Edge of the Sea* (1954).

Carson City, city (1990 pop. 40,443), state capital, W Nev., in the Carson valley; settled 1858, inc. 1875. It is a trade center for a mining and agricultural area. The discovery (1859) of the COMSTOCK LODE brought early development. The capital of the newly created (1861) Nevada Territory, it became state capital in 1864. The U.S. Mint, closed 1893, is now the Nevada State Museum.

Cartagena, city (1985 pop. 563,949), capital of Bolívar dept., NW Colombia, a port on the Bay of Cartagena, in the Caribbean Sea. Oil-refining and the manufacture of leather, textile, and tobacco goods are major industries, and there is an expanding petrochemical complex. Founded in 1533, Cartagena became the treasure city of the SPANISH MAIN, where precious New World minerals awaited transshipment to Spain. It was often sacked despite its massive fortifications, some of which still stand. It declared its independence from Spain in 1811 and was incorporated into Colombia in 1821. Its rapid development in the 20th cent. was due largely to the discovery of oil in the Magdalena basin. One of the most picturesque of Latin American cities, with shady plazas and cobblestone streets, Cartagena attracts many tourists.

Carter, Elliott (Cook, Jr.), 1908–, American composer; b. N.Y.C. His music is organized into intellectualized contrapuntal patterns. He uses TEMPO as an element of form. His works include the ballet *Pocahontas* (1938), four string quartets (1950, 1959, 1973, 1986), and a concerto for orchestra (1969).

Carter, Howard, 1873–1939, English Egyptologist who, with Lord CARNARVON, excavated (1906–22) in the Valley of the Kings at Luxor, Egypt, and discovered (1922) the tomb of TUTANKHAMEN.

Carter, Jimmy (James Earl Carter, Jr.), 1924–, 39th president of the U.S. (1977–81); b. Plains, Ga. A graduate of the U.S. Naval Academy at Annapolis, Md. (1946), he served in the U.S. navy and in 1953 returned to his family's peanut farm, which he built into a prosperous business. As governor of Georgia (1970–75), he reorganized the state executive branch and sponsored consumer and land-use legislation. After a spectacularly successful campaign for the 1976 Democratic presidential nomination, Carter, although a Southerner and political outsider, narrowly defeated the Republican candidate, Pres. Gerald FORD; his running mate was Walter MONDALE. Carter's presidency was plagued by difficult relations with Congress, which ratified his two Panama Canal treaties (1977) giving eventual control of the canal to Panama, but would not ratify his arms limitation treaty with the Soviet Union (1979). He was successful, however, in effecting (1979) a peace treaty between Egypt and Israel (see CAMP DAVID ACCORDS). During Carter's term of office the U.S. suffered high interest rates, inflation, and then recession, all of which he had little success in controlling. In Nov. 1979 a group of Muslim militants in Teheran, Iran, took some 50 U.S. citizens hostage and held them until Jan. 1981. Carter's failure to attain their release before the 1980 presidential election contributed to his defeat by Ronald REAGAN. Since leaving office, Carter has been active in human rights issues, often serving internationally as an observer during first-time free elections. He also works with Habitat for Humanity, an organization that helps working-class people build and finance new homes.

Carter, Nick, fictional detective character in DIME NOVELS. Said to have been created by J.R. Coryell, Carter appears in over 1,000 stories by various authors.

Carteret, Sir George, c.1610–1680, British proprietor of East Jersey, part of New Jersey. He commissioned his fourth cousin, **Philip Carteret,** 1639–82, as the first governor (1665–76) of New Jersey.

Cartesian coordinates, system for representing the relative positions of points in a plane or in space. In a plane, the point *P* is specified by the pair of numbers (*x, y*) representing the distances of the point from two intersecting straight lines, referred to as the *x*-axis and the *y*-axis. The point of intersection of these axes, which are called the coordinate axes, is known as the origin. If the axes are perpendicular, as is commonly the case, the coordinate system is called rectangular; otherwise it is oblique. In either type the *x*-coordinate, or abscissa, of *P* is measured along a line parallel to the *x*-axis, and the *y*-coordinate, or ordinate, along a line parallel to the *y*-axis. A point in space may be similarly specified by the triple of numbers (*x, y, z*) representing the distances from three planes determined by three intersecting straight lines not all in the same plane. Named for the French philosopher and scientist René DESCARTES, Cartesian coordinates allow certain questions in geometry to be transformed into questions about numbers and resolved by means of ANALYTIC GEOMETRY.

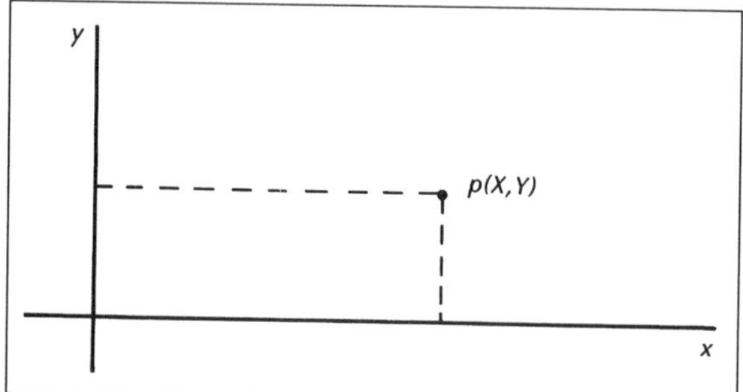

Cartesian coordinates

Carthage [kär'thĭj], ancient city of N Africa, on the Bay of Tunis and near modern Tunis. Founded (traditionally by DIDO) by Phoenicians from Tyre in the 9th cent. B.C., it eventually grew to be a mercantile CITY-STATE under an oligarchy, with explorers (e.g., Hanno) going far and wide to gather trade. Carthage's greatest weakness lay in the rivalry of two blocs of leading families who contended for control. By the 6th cent. B.C. the Carthaginians had established themselves on Sardinia, Malta, and the Balearic Islands. Their attempt to conquer Sicily in the 5th cent. B.C. was set back by the victory of Gelon of Syracuse at Himera (480 B.C.). Later Carthaginian excursions into Sicily led to the PUNIC WARS. The contest between Rome and Carthage was hotly pursued, and the greatest general involved was a Carthaginian, HANNIBAL. Nevertheless, Carthage was finally defeated at the battle of ZAMA (202 B.C.), and the Carthaginian commercial empire fell. The city itself was destroyed by Scipio Africanus Minor at the end of the Third Punic War (146 B.C.). A new city was founded in 44 B.C. and under AUGUSTUS became an important center of Roman administration. Carthage was later (A.D. 439–533) the capital of the Vandals, a Germanic tribe, and was briefly recovered (533) for the Byzantine Empire by Belisarius. Although practically destroyed by the Arabs in 698, the site was populated for many centuries afterward. LOUIS IX of France died there (1270) while on crusade.

Cartier, Sir Georges Étienne [kärtyā'], 1814–73, Canadian statesman. A leader of the French Canadians and the co-leader of the Macdonald-Cartier (see MACDONALD, Sir J.A.) ministry (1857–62), he was chiefly responsible for persuading French Canadians to accept the proposals for CANADA's confederation (1867).

Cartier, Jacques, 1491–1557, French explorer in CANADA, discoverer of the SAINT LAWRENCE R. In three voyages between 1534 and 1542 he discovered the Magdalene Islands and PRINCE EDWARD ISLAND, and ascended the St. Lawrence to the modern sites of Quebec and Montreal. French claims to the St. Lawrence valley were based on his explorations.

Cartier-Bresson, Henri [kärtēā'-brĕsôN'], 1908–, French photojournalist. His superb images convey a strong sense of the rush of time arrested. Among his many books are *The Decisive Moment* (1952) and *Henri Cartier-Bresson: Photographer* (1979).

cartoon, in the fine arts, a full-sized preliminary drawing for a work in fresco, oil, mosaic, stained glass, or tapestry. Some Italian Renaissance painters, e.g., RAPHAEL, made complete cartoons for their frescoes, and many are considered masterpieces in themselves. The use of the term *cartoon* to mean a humorous or satirical drawing began in the mid-19th cent. The first political cartoons preceded the terminology by some three centuries, appearing in 16th-cent. Germany during the Reformation. In 18th-cent. England the cartoon was an integral part of journalism. By the mid-19th cent. editorial cartoons had become regular features of American newspapers, with the work of Thomas NAST particularly influential. With the development of the color press in the late 19th cent., humorous nonpolitical cartoons became popular, soon evolving into narrative comic strips. Some noted 20th-cent. cartoonists are Bill MAULDIN, HERBLOCK, Charles ADDAMS, James THURBER, Gary Larson, and Roz Chast.

Cartwright, Edmund, 1743–1823, English inventor of a power loom (patented 1785) that made possible the weaving of wide cotton cloth and led to the development of the modern loom. Cartwright also invented a wool-combing machine (1789), a ropemaking machine (1792), and an alcohol-fueled engine (1797) and, with Robert FULTON, experimented with steam navigation.

Caruso, Enrico, 1873–1921, Italian operatic tenor. The beauty, range, and power of his voice made him one of the greatest of all singers. He sang more than 50 roles in Europe, the U.S., and Latin America, excelling in works by VERDI and PUCCINI. After his death his recordings perpetuated his fame.

Carver, George Washington, 1864?–1943, African-American agricultural chemist; b. Diamond, Mo. Born a slave, he was director (1896–1943) of agricultural research at Tuskegee Institute. Carver dedicated his life to bettering the position of African Americans and to improving the economy of the South through soil improvement and crop diversification; he discovered hundreds of uses for the peanut, sweet potato, and soybean, and devised many products from cotton waste.

Carver, John, c.1576–1621, first governor (1620) of the PLYMOUTH COLONY. A man of wealth, he was the chief figure in arranging the PILGRIMS' migration to America, hiring and provisioning the MAYFLOWER, and selecting the Plymouth site.

Carver, Raymond, 1938–88, American author; b. Clatskanie, Oreg. His short stories and poems depicted blue-collar characters and focused on everyday life. Among his volumes of short stories is *Where I'm Calling From* (1988).

Cary, (Arthur) Joyce (Lunel), 1888–1957, English author. He is best known for two trilogies exploring English social change. The first consists of *Herself Surprised* (1941), *To Be a Pilgrim* (1942), and *The Horse's Mouth* (1944). The second includes *Prisoner of Grace* (1952), *Except the Lord* (1953), and *Not Honour More* (1955).

caryatid, sculptured female figure serving as an ornamental support, in place of a column or pilaster. It was a frequent motif in architecture, furniture, and garden sculpture during the Renaissance, the 18th cent., and, notably, the CLASSIC REVIVAL of the 19th cent., when caryatids were popular as mantelpiece supports. Caryatids appeared in Egyptian and Greek architecture, the most celebrated example being the Porch of the Caryatids at the ERECHTHEUM.

Casablanca, city (1990 est. pop. 3,210,000), W Morocco, on the Atlantic Ocean. It is the country's largest city and major commercial and industrial center, producing one half of Morocco's industrial output and exporting phosphates and importing petroleum products. The Hassan II mosque (1993), one of the world's largest, is here. Almost destroyed by an earthquake (1755), rebuilt in 1757,

Casablanca was occupied by the French in 1907. In WORLD WAR II it was a site for the Allied invasion (1942) of N Africa and for a conference (Nov. 1943) between F.D. Roosevelt and Winston Churchill.

Casablanca Conference, Jan. 12–14, 1943, WORLD WAR II meeting of U.S. Pres. F.D. ROOSEVELT and British Prime Min. Winston CHURCHILL at Casablanca, French Morocco. The policy of unconditional AXIS surrender was enunciated there.

Casals, Pablo (Pau), 1876–1973, Spanish cellist and conductor, the greatest cellist of the 20th cent. He began his concert career in 1891 and conducted his own orchestra in 1919. He was especially noted for his performance of J.S. BACH's unaccompanied suites and for the music festivals he directed at Prades, France, and after 1956 in Puerto Rico.

Casanova de Seingalt, Giovanni Giacomo, 1725–98, Venetian adventurer and author. He traveled all over Europe supporting himself by gambling, spying, writing, and seducing women. In 1756 he escaped from Venice's state prison; in Paris, he became director of the lottery and amassed a fortune. In 1785 he retired to the castle of Dux, Bohemia, where he worked as a librarian. A man of wide interests, learning, and taste, Casanova left memoirs that became world-famous, although not published in full until 1960.

Casas, Bartolomé de las: see LAS CASAS.

Cascade Range, forested mountain chain in the western part of the North American cordillera, extending c.700 mi (1,130 km) from British Columbia to N California. Prominent peaks include Mts. Rainier (the highest, 14,410 ft/4,392 m), Shasta, and Hood, and volcanically active LASSEN PEAK and Mt. SAINT HELENS.

casehardening, in metallurgy, a process to harden steel by increasing the percentage of carbon at its surface. This is done by packing the STEEL in charcoal and then heating it; by heating it in a furnace with a hydrocarbon gas atmosphere; or by heating it in a molten-salt bath containing potassium and sodium cyanides.

casein, a group of proteins found especially in milk, providing many essential nutrients. When milk is treated with acid, casein separates as an insoluble white curd; it is used in cheese, adhesives, and water paints. Rennet casein curd is used to make cheese and a plastic from which imitation gemstones and other objects are made.

Cash, Johnny, 1932–, American singer; b. Kingsland, Ark. He went to Memphis in 1955 and began to record such hits as "I Walk the Line." Cash is a major figure in COUNTRY AND WESTERN MUSIC. He is noted for his performances at prisons and has appeared widely in concert, on television, and in films.

cashew, tropical American tree (*Anacardium occidentale*) of the SUMAC family, valued chiefly for its kidney-shaped nut, whose sweet, oily kernel is used for food and yields an oil used in cooking. The nut grows at the end of a red, white, or yellow pear-shaped fleshy stalk, or cashew apple, which is also eaten or pressed to extract the juice, which may be fermented to make wine. The acrid sap of the cashew tree is used to make a varnish that protects woodwork from insects.

Casimir, Polish rulers. **Casimir I,** c.1015–58, duke of POLAND (c.1040–58), reunited the Polish lands under the hegemony of the Holy Roman Empire. **Casimir II,** 1138–94, duke of Poland (1177–94), deposed his brother and secured for his descendants the hereditary right to the crown. **Casimir III,** 1310–70, king of Poland (1333–70), known as **Casimir the Great,** extended Polish territories, codified the law, improved the lot of peasants and Jews, founded (1364) Kraków Univ., and in general greatly increased royal power. **Casimir IV,** 1427–92, king of Poland and Lithuania (1447–92), successfully ended (1466) the war with the Teutonic Knights.

Caspar: see WISE MEN OF THE EAST.

Casper, city (1990 pop. 46,742), seat of Natrona co., E central Wyo., on the North Platte R.; inc. 1889. At a ford on the OREGON TRAIL, it was founded (1888) with the coming of the railroad. In 1890 an oil boom started; today Casper produces oil, gas, coal, and uranium, and is the center of a rich agricultural region. The area also attracts many tourists.

Caspian Sea, world's largest lake, c.144,000 sq mi (373,000 sq km), enclosed by Azerbaijan, Russia, Kazakhstan, Turkmenistan, and Iran, on the traditional border between Europe and Asia. The salty lake is 92 ft (28 m) below sea level and reaches a maximum depth of 3,200 ft (980 m) in the south. More than 75% of its waters are derived from the VOLGA R., whose flow is now diminished by dams and lakes. Beluga caviar is a major product of the shallow waters in the north. Baky and Astrakhan are the chief ports.

Cass, Lewis, 1782–1866, American statesman; b. Exeter, N.H. He was governor of Michigan Territory (1813–31). As secretary of war (1831–36), he favored moving Native Americans W of the Mississippi. A U.S. senator from Michigan (1845–48, 1849–57), he was the unsuccessful Democratic candidate for president in 1848. He was also (1857–60) secretary of state.

Cassander, 358–297 B.C., king of MACEDON (316–297 B.C.); one of the DIADOCHI. The son of ANTIPATER, he deposed the regent, Polyperchon. To consolidate his power, he procured the murder (316) of OLYMPIAS, mother of ALEXANDER THE GREAT, and (311) of Alexander's widow, ROXANA, and their son; he married Alexander's half sister, Thessalonica (316). One of a coalition that defeated Antigonus and DEMETRIUS I at Ipsus (301), he ruled Macedonia and Greece.

Cassandra, in Greek mythology, Trojan princess; daughter of Priam and HECUBA. She was given the power of prophecy by APOLLO, but when she spurned him he decreed that she should never be believed. A slave of AGAMEMNON after the TROJAN WAR, she was killed with him by CLYTEMNESTRA.

Cassatt, Mary, 1845–1926, American painter; b. Pittsburgh. She lived mainly in France, where she embraced IMPRESSIONISM. Her paintings are simple, vigorous, and pleasing in color. Her favorite subject was motherhood, e.g., versions of *Mother and Child* (Metropolitan Mus.; Mus. Fine Arts, Boston). She also excelled in ETCHING and pastels.

cassava or **manioc,** plant (genus *Manihot*) of the SPURGE family, native to Brazil. The roots are the source of cassava starch, cassava flour, and tapioca; they are also fermented to make an alcoholic beverage and have other uses. The raw roots of bitter cassava (*M. esculenta*), chief source of cassava flour, contain potentially lethal amounts of prussic acid, which must be dispelled in preparation. Sweet cassava roots contain less acid and can be eaten raw.

Cassini, Gian Domenico, 1625–1712, Italian-French astronomer. He determined rotational periods for the planets Jupiter, Mars, and Venus, discovered four of Saturn's satellites, and studied the division in Saturn's ring system that is named for him. He and three generations of descendants directed the Royal Observatory in Paris from its founding (1669) to the time (1793) of the French Revolution.

Cassiopeia, in Greek mythology: see ANDROMEDA.

Cassirer, Ernst, 1874–1945, German philosopher. A Neo-Kantian, he devoted himself, in *Substance and Function* (1910), to a critical-historical study of the problem of knowledge. In *Philosophy of Symbolic Forms* (3 vol., 1923–29) he characterized the human being as a "symbolic animal," holding that all cultural achievements result from the human ability to conceptualize experience in artificial signs, or symbols.

Cassius, ancient Roman family. **Quintus Cassius Longinus,** d. 45 B.C., served with ANTONY as a tribune, and in 49 B.C. vetoed the attempts of the senate to deprive Julius CAESAR of his army. Cassius died in a shipwreck. The best-known family member was **Caius Cassius Longinus,** d. 42 B.C., leader in the successful conspiracy to assassinate Julius Caesar on the Ides of March in 44 B.C. When the people were aroused by Antony against the conspirators, Cassius went to Syria and joined Marcus Junius Brutus (see BRUTUS, family). Antony and Octavian (later AUGUSTUS) met them in battle at Philippi in 42 B.C. In the first engagement, Cassius, thinking the battle lost, committed suicide.

cassowary, flightless forest BIRD of Australia and the Malay Archipelago, smaller than the OSTRICH. The plumage is dark and glossy, with a brilliantly-colored head and neck. Nocturnal and mostly herbivorous, they are fast runners. Cassowaries are notoriously vicious, and have killed people with their sharp, spikelike toenails.

Castagno, Andrea del [kästä'nyō], c.1423–57, Florentine painter. In c.1445 he began the Passion of Christ cycle for the church of Sant' Apollonia in Florence. Best known of these scenes is *The Last Supper* with its harsh perspective and metallic light. DONATELLO's influence is seen in his later heroic figures of Dante and Petrarch in the Villa Pandolfini.

castanets: see PERCUSSION INSTRUMENT.

caste, ranked hereditary social group. Rigidly restricted occupationally and socially, members may not marry outside the caste. Caste is strongest and most complex in Hindu India, where a hierarchy of thousands of distinct *jatis,* or castes, reflect religious practice, occupation, locale, culture status, or tribal affiliation. In addition, society is divided into four *varna,* or social classes—the Brahmans, priests and scholars; Kshatriyas, the military and rulers; Vaisyas, farmers and merchants; and Sudras, peasants and laborers. Below the Sudras were the untouchables, who performed the most menial tasks. Untouchability was legally abolished in 1949, and some occupational barriers have broken down, but strong social distinctions remain resistant to change, especially in rural areas.

Castelo Branco, Humberto [kəshtē'lo͝o bräng'ko͞o], 1900–1967, president of BRAZIL (1964–67). An army officer, he helped oust (1964) Pres. Goulart in a coup and became provisional president. He curtailed political freedoms but imposed economic reforms that spurred the country's growth.

Castiglione, Baldassare, Conte [kästēlyō'nā], 1478–1529, Italian author and statesman. His *Book of the Courtier* (1528), a treatise on etiquette, social problems, and intellectual accomplishments, contributed to a Renaissance ideal of aristocracy embodied in the life of Sir Philip SIDNEY.

Castile, region and former kingdom, central and N Spain, traditionally divided into Old Castile (N) and New Castile (S) and now divided between the autonomous regions of Castile and León and Castile-La Mancha. It is a vast, sparsely-populated area surrounding the highly industrialized city of MADRID. In Castile and León, which contains Old Castile, grains are grown and sheep raised. The fertile areas, especially in Castile-La Mancha, produce olive oil and grapes. Castile became a kingdom in 1035 and was united with LEÓN in 1230. Castilian kings were prominent in the fight against the MOORS, from whom they wrested New Castile. The privileges of the nobles were limited by PETER THE CRUEL (r.1350–69). In 1479 a personal union of Castile and ARAGÓN was established by ISABELLA I of Castile and her husband, Spanish King FERDINAND V. Castile was the core of the Spanish monarchy, centralized in Madrid (the capital after 1561).

casting or **founding,** the shaping of METAL by melting and pouring into a mold. Most castings are made in sand molds. Sand, mixed with a binder to hold it together, is pressed around a wooden pattern that leaves a cavity in the sand. Molten metal is poured into the cavity and allowed to solidify. *Investment casting* is used for small, complex shapes. Wax or plastic replicas of the parts are covered with sand in a box. When the whole mold is heated, the replica melts, leaving behind a cavity into which the metal is poured. *Die casting,* in which molten metal is forced under pressure into metal molds, is used to make large numbers of small, precise parts with metals of low melting points.

cast iron, form of IRON made from pig iron remelted in a small cupola furnace and poured into molds to make castings. It usually contains from 2% to 6% carbon, and scrap iron or steel is often added to vary the composition. Cast iron is used extensively to make machine parts, engine cylinder blocks, stoves, pipes, radiators, and many other products.

Castle, Vernon, 1887–1918, English dancer. He made his debut in 1907. In 1911 he married **Irene Foot,** 1893–1969, b. New Rochelle, N.Y. Together they won international acclaim for their original dances, such as the "Texas Tommy," the "Castle Walk," and the "hesitation" waltz.

castle, fortified dwelling characteristic of the Middle Ages. In the 9th cent. feudal lords began to develop private fortress-residences suitable to conditions of warfare. The castle of W Europe was a Norman creation, an outgrowth of the 10th- and 11th-cent. mound castle, which was essentially an artificial mound of earth, surrounded by a ditch, and surmounted by a blockhouse and palisade. Until the 12th cent., the only English development was the addition of a masonry keep inside the palisade, e.g., the TOWER OF LONDON. With evolving siegecraft, provisions for vigorous defense were needed. Outer masonry walls came into use, with gates, flanking towers, and earthworks. Subterranean passages and curving walls were developed. Castles were designed for security, not comfort. Defenders fought from galleries atop the walls; with successive series of defenses, the loss of one did not mean complete defeat, as those inside could retreat until they were within the keep. Gunpowder and the development of artillery rendered the castle obsolete. It was replaced by the manor house, but its effect on architecture still continues.

Castlereagh, Robert Stewart, 2d **Viscount** [kă'səlrā], 1769–1822, British statesman; b. Ireland. As acting chief secretary for Ireland, he suppressed the French-aided rebellion of 1798. He was secretary of war (1805–6, 1807–9) during the wars with NAPOLEON I, coordinating British land and sea power and, after early disasters in the PENINSULAR WAR, putting the duke of WELLINGTON in command. He resigned (1809) after what he considered to be a political betrayal by George CANNING (with whom he fought a duel). As foreign secretary (1812–22), he helped form the final coalition against Napoleon and obtained (1814) the "concert of Europe," later confirmed by the QUADRUPLE ALLIANCE. He advocated a moderate peace settlement for France, and was a dominant figure at the Congress of VIENNA. A great statesman, Castlereagh was personally cold and never popular. He became (1821) the 2d marquess of Londonderry on his father's death, but committed suicide the next year.

Castor and Pollux, in classical mythology, twin heroes called the Dioscuri; Castor was the son of LEDA and Tyndareus, Pollux the son of Leda and ZEUS. Castor was a skilled horseman, Pollux a boxer. They were famous warriors, noted for their devotion to each other. In one legend, Zeus created the constellation Gemini in their honor. Patrons of mariners, the Dioscuri were especially honored by the Romans.

castrato: see VOICE.

Castries, city (1991 pop. 51,994), capital of SAINT LUCIA.

Castriota, George: see SCANDERBEG.

Castro, Fidel, 1926–, Cuban revolutionary and political leader, premier (1959–76) and president (1976–) of CUBA. He opposed the BATISTA dictatorship and unsuccessfully attacked an army post on July 26, 1953. After being imprisoned and released (1955), he went to Mexico, where he organized the 26th of July revolutionary movement. He invaded (1956) SE Cuba and, with his brother Raúl, "Che" GUEVARA, and nine other rebels, hid out in the Sierra Maestra Mountains, from where they attracted supporters and fought a guerrilla campaign that toppled (1959) Batista. A brilliant propagandist and charismatic orator, Castro became premier and established a totalitarian government that benefited the working class at the expense of the middle class, many of whom fled. A declared Marxist-Leninist, he nationalized industry, confiscated foreign-owned property, collectivized agriculture, and increasingly depended on economic assistance from the USSR. He weathered the severance of economic and political ties by the U.S. and Latin American nations, the BAY OF PIGS INVASION (1961), a U.S. economic blockade, and the CUBAN MISSILE CRISIS (1962). He supported revolutionary movements in other Latin American countries and in Africa and became a symbol of revolution in Latin America. In 1976, under a new constitution, he became president. The end of the COLD WAR and Cuba's worsening economic difficulties and growing international isolation have greatly diminished his international stature.

Castro, Inés de, or **Inez de Castro,** d. 1355, Spanish noblewoman at the Portuguese court. Her love affair with the crown prince, Dom Pedro (later PETER I), ended in tragedy; she bore him four children but was murdered with the connivance of his father, ALFONSO IV, to preserve the legitimate succession to the throne. Her life has been a favorite theme of Portuguese and Spanish writers.

cat, carnivorous MAMMAL of the family Felidae, including the domestic cat (*Felis catus*), the great cats (e.g., LION, TIGER, LEOPARD, and CHEETAH), and the smaller wild cats (e.g., LYNX and OCELOT). Highly adapted for hunting and devouring their prey, cats have short muzzles, large eyes, sensitive whiskers, and sharp claws and teeth. Most have long tails, and all have a flexible musculo-skeletal system. Lions and cheetahs live in groups called prides, but most cats are solitary. Cats have been domesticated since prehistoric times and were often the objects of veneration or superstitious fear. Domestic cats vary in size, with males usually weighing 9–14 lb (4.1–6.4 kg) and females 6–10 lb (2.2–4.5 kg). They have coats of various lengths and many colors (black, white, and shades of red, yellow, brown, and gray) in a variety of patterns. Besides the common house cat, the species *F. catus* includes many recognized breeds maintained by selective mating. Most breeds are short-haired. **Abyssinian cats** have ruddy brown coats with ticking (marking on each hair) of darker brown or black. **Burmese cats** are small and muscular with medium- to dark-brown coats; the **Manx cat** is a variously colored, tailless breed with hind legs longer than its forelegs, elevating the rump. **Siamese cats** have almond-shaped blue eyes and white, cream, or fawn coats with brown or gray areas (points) on the feet, tail, ears, and head. The **Russian Blue cat,** with green eyes and a blue-gray coat, is distinguished by two layers of short, thick fur, and the **Rex cat,** the only curly-haired cat, has a woolly coat that may be any color. **Persian cats** are stocky and long-haired and may be a variety of colors; the other long-haired breed, the **Himalayan cat** (a Persian-Siamese cross), has Siamese coloring.

catacombs, large underground vaults and galleries serving as cemeteries for early Christians, who did not follow the Greek and Roman practice of cremation. They were built in Italy, N Africa, Asia Minor, and other Christian areas from the 1st to the 5th cent. A.D. The main ones, outside the city gates of Rome, lie from 22 to 65 ft (6.7 to 19.8 m) below ground and occupy 600 acres (240 hectares) of space in multilevel passages lined with tiers of niches for bodies. Plaster walls and ceilings were frescoed. Goths and later invaders plundered the catacombs; by the 8th cent. most bodies had been transferred to churches and the labyrinths forgotten. Rediscovery began in 1578, and preservation is now controlled by the papacy.

Catalan language, member of the Romance group of the Italic subfamily of the Indo-European family of languages. See LANGUAGE (table).

Çatal Hüyük [kətäal′ həyo͝ok′], neolithic settlement (fl. c.6500–c.5800 B.C.) on the Konya Plain in S Turkey. Excavated (1961–65) by British archaeologist James Mellaart, the 32-acre (12.8-hectare) site is divided into 12 horizons (levels of development). The settlement's rectangular dwellings were of mud brick, and its economy was apparently based on farming and some cattle raising.

Catalonia, Catalan *Catalunya,* autonomous region, NE Spain, stretching from the Pyrenees at the French border southward along the Mediterranean Sea. BARCELONA is the historic capital. Catalonia produces one third of Spain's wine; grows olives and grains; and manufactures textiles, chemicals, automobiles, airplanes, and other products. The counts of Barcelona became (9th cent.) the most powerful lords of the region, and in 1137 Catalonia was united with ARAGÓN. In the 13th and 14th cent. Catalan traders rivaled those of GENOA and VENICE. It briefly won autonomy in the 1930s and became an autonmous region in 1980.

catalpa: see BIGNONIA.

catalyst, substance that causes a change in the rate of a chemical reaction without itself being consumed by the reaction. Catalysts, which work by changing a reaction's activation energy, or minimum energy needed for the reaction to occur, are used in numerous industrial processes. Substances that increase the reaction rate are called positive catalysts, or simply catalysts, whereas substances that decrease the reaction rate are called negative catalysts, or inhibitors. The presence of a small amount of an acid or base may catalyze some reactions. Finely divided metals (e.g., platinum, copper, iron, palladium, rhodium) or metal oxides (e.g., silicon dioxide, vanadium oxide) may also serve as catalysts. Biological catalysts are called ENZYMES.

cataract, opacity of the lens of the EYE, causing impairment of vision. Most commonly caused by aging, cataracts may also be congenital or result from eye inflammations or certain diseases, such as DIABETES. Cataracts can be treated by the use of corrective lenses and, if needed, surgical removal of the lens and implantation of an artificial lens.

catastrophism, originally, the outdated geological doctrine that the physical features of the earth's surface, e.g., mountains and valleys, were formed during violent worldwide cataclysms, e.g., earthquakes and floods. This theory, easily correlated with religious beliefs, was systematized by Georges CUVIER, who argued that all living things were destroyed and replaced with wholly different forms during these cataclysmic events. In the 18th cent. the doctrine was attacked by James HUTTON, who advanced the doctrine of UNIFORMITARIANISM. Late 20th-cent. theories of meteorite or comet impacts upon the earth (see MASS EXTINCTION) have revived elements of catatrophism, and modern geological theories are somewhat of a synthesis of the two doctrines.

catbird: see MIMIC THRUSH.

catchment area or **drainage basin,** area drained by a stream or other water body. The amount of water reaching a RIVER, reservoir, or LAKE from its catchment area depends on the size of the area, amount of precipitation, and loss through evaporation and absorption.

Cateau-Cambrésis, Treaty of: see ITALIAN WARS.

catechism, originally oral instruction in religion, later written instruction. Catechisms, usually in the form of questions and answers, were used to instruct converts and children. Famous catechisms include the Lutheran Small Catechism (1529), the Anglican catechism contained in the Book of Common Prayer, and the Baltimore Catechism, which was long the standard Roman Catholic catechism in the U.S.

catecholamine, any of several structurally related compounds found in the body that help regulate the sympathetic NERVOUS SYSTEM. They include EPINEPHRINE (or adrenaline), NOREPINEPHRINE, and dopamine—substances that prepare the body to meet emergencies such as cold, fatigue, and shock. Epinephrine and isoproterenol, a synthetic catecholamine, are used as drugs to treat diseases such as EMPHYSEMA, BRONCHITIS, and ASTHMA.

categorical imperative: see KANT, IMMANUEL.

caterpillar: see BUTTERFLY.

catfish, freshwater FISH (suborder Nematognathi) with barbels, or whiskers, around a broad mouth, fleshy, rayless posterior fins, scaleless skin, and sharp defensive spines on the pectoral and dorsal fins. One species, the electric catfish, discharges electricity (see ELECTRIC FISH). Catfish range in size from a few inches to 13 ft (3.9 m) or more. Omnivorous feeders and scavengers, they are important food fish and are raised on fish farms in the S U.S.

cathedral, church in which a bishop presides, regardless of size or magnificence. Romanesque cathedrals (see ROMANESQUE ARCHITECTURE AND ART) were massive, domed, heavily vaulted structures based on the BASILICA form, reflecting the style dominant in Europe c.1050 to c.1200. The tall, wide nave was flanked by narrow side aisles, crossed by transepts, and illuminated by a clerestory pierced with small windows. The great cathedrals of the 13th and 14th cent. are the crowning achievement of GOTHIC ARCHITECTURE AND ART. These buildings are distinctive in their use of ribbed VAULTS, pointed ARCHES, ROSE WINDOWS, BUTTRESSES, geometric tracery, and STAINED GLASS, combined in a rich and complex design. In the intricacy of the glass, exterior facade, and buttresses, the building's structure is almost entirely subordinated to detail. Among the most important cathedrals are: *France*—Amiens, Beauvais, Chartres, Notre-Dame de Paris, Rheims, Rouen; *England*—Canterbury, Durham, Ely, Winchester, York; *Germany*—Cologne, Ulm; *Belgium*—Louvain; *Italy*—Florence, Milan; *Spain*—Ávila, Toledo; *Sweden*—Lund, Uppsala. A noted modern adaptation of the form is at Coventry, England (1962).

Cather, Willa Sibert, 1876–1947, American author; b. Winchester, Va. She celebrated the frontier in *O Pioneers!* (1913) and *My Ántonia* (1918), and showed the artist's need for freedom from inhibiting influences in *The Song of the Lark* (1915). Cather later turned to the North American past for *Death Comes for the Archbishop* (1927). She also wrote short stories and several essays on fiction. Her own clear, charming, and stately style is among the finest in 20th-cent. American literature.

Catherine, czarinas of Russia. **Catherine I,** 1683?–1727 (r.1725–27), was born Martha Skavronskaya, a Livonian peasant. She became the mistress of MENSHIKOV, an advisor to PETER I, and then of Peter, who married her in 1712 and had her crowned czarina in 1724. When he died without naming a successor she was raised to the throne by Menshikov, who dominated her rule. PETER II succeeded her; her daughter ELIZABETH became czarina in 1741. **Catherine II** or **Catherine the Great,** 1729–96 (r.1762–96), b. Princess Sophie of Anhalt-Zerbst, married the future PETER III in 1744. She became thoroughly Russian and was popular with pow-

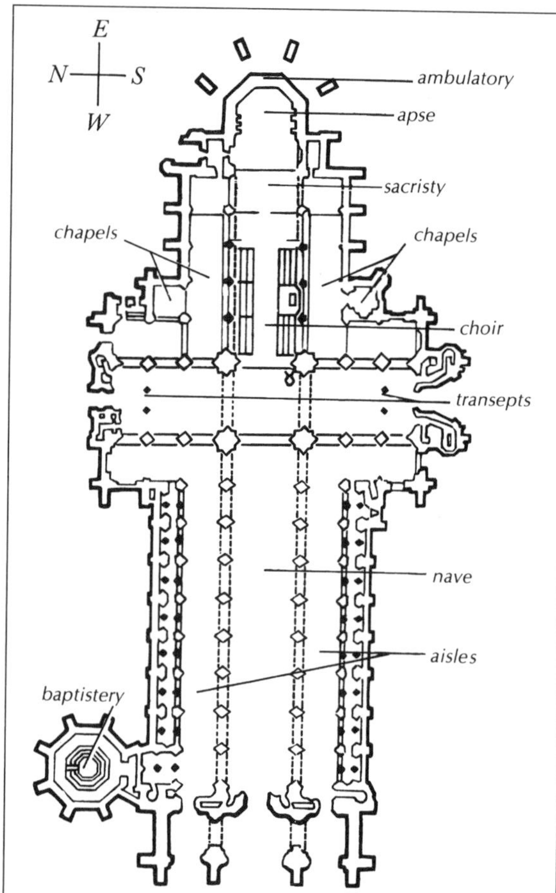

Floor plan of a cathedral

erful groups opposed to her eccentric husband. In June 1762, conspirators headed by Grigori Orlov, her lover, deposed Peter and proclaimed her ruler; shortly afterward Peter was murdered. Catherine's rule began with projects of reform, but after the peasant uprising led by PUGACHEV (1773–74) and the FRENCH REVOLUTION she strengthened serfdom and increased the privileges of the nobility within a system of provinces that survived until 1917. Her foreign policy was imperialistic: she increased Russian control of the Baltic provinces and Ukraine; began colonization of Alaska; annexed the Crimea and in two wars with Turkey made Russia dominant in SW Asia; and secured for Russia the major share in the partitions of Poland (1772, 1793, 1795). A patron of art and literature, she corresponded with VOLTAIRE and other French thinkers, and wrote memoirs, comedies, and stories. Of her many lovers, only Orlov and POTEMKIN influenced her policies. Her son, PAUL I, succeeded her.

Catherine de' Medici [mĕd'ĭchē], 1519–89, queen consort of HENRY II of France, daughter of Lorenzo de' MEDICI, duke of Urbino. Married in 1533, she was neglected in the reigns of Henry and her eldest son, FRANCIS II, but was regent (1560–63) and adviser (1563–74) for her son CHARLES IX. At first conciliatory toward the French Protestants, she later helped plan the SAINT BARTHOLOMEW'S DAY massacre. HENRY III was her son.

Catherine of Braganza, 1638–1705, queen consort of CHARLES II of England; daughter of JOHN I of Portugal. Her dowry included Bombay and Tangier. A Roman Catholic, she was never popular. Titus OATES accused her of plotting to poison the king, but Charles protected her. After his death, she returned home and in 1704 acted as regent for her brother, PETER II.

Catherine of Siena, Saint, 1347–80, Italian DOMINICAN, mystic and diplomat, Doctor of the Church. In response to a vision she entered public life and in 1376 influenced Pope GREGORY XI to end the "Babylonian captivity" of the PAPACY and return to Rome. She was later papal ambassador to Florence. Catherine caused a spiritual revival almost everywhere she went, and her mysticism contains an overwhelming love of God and humanity. She dictated *The Dialogue,* a notable mystical work. Feast: Apr. 29.

Catherine of Valois [văl'wä], 1401–37, queen consort of HENRY V of England; mother of HENRY VI; daughter of CHARLES VI of France. Some time after Henry V's death (1522), she married Owen TUDOR. The Tudor kings are descended from them.

Catherine the Great: see Catherine II under CATHERINE, czarinas of Russia.

cathode: see ELECTRODE.

cathode-ray tube, ELECTRON TUBE in which electrons are accelerated by high-voltage anodes, formed into a beam by focusing ELECTRODES, and projected toward a phosphorescent screen that forms the face of the tube. The electron beam leaves a bright spot wherever it strikes the screen. To form the screen display, or image, the electron beam is deflected in the vertical and horizontal directions either by the electrostatic effect of electrodes within the tube or by magnetic fields produced by coils located around the neck of the tube. Some cathode-ray tubes, made for COMPUTER TERMINALS and monitors, OSCILLOSCOPES, and TELEVISION receivers, can produce multiple beams of electrons and have phosphor screens that can display more than one color. See also RADAR.

Catholic Church: see ROMAN CATHOLIC CHURCH.

Catholic Emancipation, term applied to the process by which Roman Catholics in the British Isles were relieved of civil disabilities, dating back to HENRY VIII. In 1791 most of the disabilities in Great Britain were repealed. Agitation in Ireland, led by Daniel O'CONNELL, resulted in the Catholic Emancipation Act (1829), which lifted most other restrictions.

Catiline (Lucius Sergius Catilina), c.108 B.C.–62 B.C., Roman politician and conspirator. In 66 B.C. he was barred from candidacy for the consulship by accusations of misconduct in office, charges that later proved false. Feeling that he had been cheated, he concocted a wild plot to murder the consuls. He and the other conspirators were acquitted (65 B.C.). When in 63 B.C. he ran again for consul, he found CICERO, the incumbent, and the conservative party anxious to stop his election at any cost. Catiline was defeated, prompting him to try for the consulship by force. Learning of the plot, Cicero arrested the conspirators still in Rome, but Catiline had fled. On Dec. 5 they were condemned to death and executed, in spite of an appeal from Julius CAESAR to use moderation. Catiline did not surrender; he fell in battle at Pistoia a month later.

cation: see ION.

Catlin, George, 1796–1872, American traveler and artist; b. Wilkes-Barre, Pa. His trips to the American West, the first c.1832, resulted in several volumes and hundreds of portraits of Native Americans and tribal scenes. He also painted indigenous groups in South and Central America. Much of his work is housed in the Catlin Gallery of the National Gallery of Art (Wash., D.C.).

catnip or **catmint,** strong-scented perennial herb (*Nepeta cataria*) of the MINT family, native to Europe and Asia. Catnip, best known for its stimulating effect on cats, is also used to make a home-remedy tea.

Cato the Elder or **Cato the Censor** (Marcus Porcius Cato), 234–149 B.C., Roman statesman and moralist. He fought in the Second PUNIC WAR and later served as consul (195) and censor (184). He was renowned for his devotion to the old Roman ideals—simplicity of life, honesty, and courage. He told the senate to destroy Carthage and thus helped to bring on the Third Punic War, in which Carthage was vanquished. He also wrote many works, most of which are now lost. **Cato the Younger** or **Cato of Utica** (Marcus Porcius Cato), 95 B.C.–46 B.C., Roman statesman, was the great-grandson of Cato the Elder. He showed an intense devotion to the principles of the early republic. He had one of the greatest reputations for honesty and incorruptibility of anyone in ancient times, and his Stoicism put him above the graft and bribery of his day. His politics were extremely conservative. Thus he opposed Julius CAESAR and supported POMPEY. After Pompey's defeat at Pharsala in 48 B.C., Cato went to Africa to continue the struggle and took command at Utica. When Caesar clearly had gained power, Cato committed suicide, bidding his people make their peace with Caesar.

CAT scan or **computerized axial tomography,** X-RAY technique allowing relatively safe, painless, and rapid diagnosis in previously inaccessible areas of the body. An X-ray tube, rotating around a specific area of the body, delivers an appropriate amount of X radiation for the tissue being studied and takes pictures of that part of the internal anatomy from different angles. More recent scanners have a stationary X-ray tube and use deflecting coils and special reflectors to position the X-ray beam. A computer then assists in forming a composite, readable image. CAT scanning has revolutionized medicine, especially neurology, by facilitating the diagnosis of brain and spinal cord disorders, CANCER, and other conditions.

Catt, Carrie Chapman, 1859–1947, American suffragist; b. Ripon, Wis. As an organizer and president (from 1900) of the National American Woman Suffrage Association, she campaigned for a constitutional amendment on WOMAN SUFFRAGE. When the 19th amendment to the U.S. CONSTITUTION passed (1920), she organized the LEAGUE OF WOMEN VOTERS and later worked for the peace movement.

cattail or **reed mace,** perennial herb (genus *Typha*), found in open marshes. Cattails, or clubrushes, have long, narrow leaves and one tall stem with tiny male flowers above the female flowers. Pollinated female flowers form the familiar cylindrical spike of fuzzy brown fruits; the male flowers drop off. The starchy rootstocks are edible.

cattle, ruminant MAMMALS (genus *Bos*), especially a domesticated species. The term *oxen* is often used synonymously, although strictly speaking *ox* refers to a mature, castrated male used for draft purposes. Western, or European, domestic cattle (*B. taurus*) are thought to be descended from the aurochs, a large wild ox domesticated in the STONE AGE. The ZEBU is the domesticated species of Asia and Africa. A grown male is called a bull; a grown female, a cow; an infant, a calf; a female that has not given birth, a heifer; and a young castrated male, a steer. Cattle are bred for beef and DAIRYING and for use as draft animals. Beef breeds include the Angus, Charolais, and Hereford; dairy breeds include Brown Swiss, Guernsey, Holstein-Friesian, and Jersey; dual-purpose (beef-dairy) breeds include the Red Poll and Shorthorn.

Catullus (Caius Valerius Catullus), 84?–54? B.C., Roman poet, one of the greatest LYRIC poets. His poems, addressed to the faithless Lesbia, his friend Juventius, and others, include elegies (see ELEGY), EPIGRAMS, and other pieces and range from gay and tender to obscenely derisive. "On the Death of Lesbia's Sparrow" is well known.

Caucasian and **Caucasoid:** see RACE.

Caucasian languages, family of languages spoken by about five million people in the CAUCASUS region. See LANGUAGE (table).

Caucasus, great mountain system, extending c.750 mi (1,210 km) between the Black and Caspian seas, forming part of the traditional border between Europe and Asia. Mt. ELBRUS (18,481 ft/5,633 m) is the highest peak. The mountains are usually divided into North Caucasia, a region of semiarid northern slopes in SW Russia, and the southern slopes of Transcaucasia, encompassing GEORGIA, AZERBAIJAN, and ARMENIA. Oil is a major resource. The Caucasus are inhabited by a great variety of ethnic and linguistic groups, including Abkhazians, Georgians, Armenians, and Azerbaijanis in the south and Ossetians, Chechens, Ingush, Cherkess (Circassians), and Dagestani in the north. Russia gained control in the 19th cent. after a series of wars with Persia (now Iran) and Turkey. With the disintegration of the USSR, several Caucasian ethnic groups, particularly the Abkhazians, Chechens, Ingush, and Ossetians, began campaigning for independence. Fighting erupted in North Caucasia and Georgia, and Armenians and Azerbaijanis fought for control of NAGORNO-KARABAKH.

Cauchy, Augustin Louis, Baron [kōshē'], 1789–1857, French mathematician who was influential in every branch of MATHEMATICS. In calculus, he invented the notion of continuity, gave the first adequate definition of the definite integral as a limit of sums, and defined improper integrals. He provided the first comprehensive theory of complex numbers, established fundamental theorems on complex functions, published the first comprehensive treatise on determinants, and founded the mathematical theory of elasticity.

cauliflower, variety of CABBAGE (var. *botrytis*), with an edible head of condensed flowers and stems. Another cultivation of the same variety is broccoli. Both have been grown since Roman times.

Cavafy, Constantine [kävāfē'], 1863–1933, Greek poet; b. Egypt. He lived most of his life in Alexandria. The background of his poetry is a mythic, Hellenistic world peopled with historical and imaginary figures. Many of his poems treat homosexual love. Although his output was small (about 150 poems), he is one of the great modern Greek poets.

cavalry, mounted troops trained to fight from horseback. In use since the time of the ancient Hittites, horsemen remained at a disadvantage against well-disciplined infantry until the introduction (4th cent. A.D.) of the saddle. In medieval Europe the mounted KNIGHT became the typical warrior. Despite the invention of SMALL ARMS, cavalry remained important in warfare until the end of the 19th cent. The elite of the fighting forces in Europe, it was often recruited from the nobility and landed gentry. On the African, U.S., and British Indian frontiers the cavalry's mobility was essential against the lightly armed natives, but its value was drastically diminished by the development of rapid-fire rifles and machine guns. It was ultimately superseded by mobile TANK and armored units in World War II. The modern U.S. 1st Cavalry Division consists of helicoptered airborne troops.

cave, a hollow in earth or ROCK. Caves are formed by the chemical and mechanical action of water on soluble rock, by volcanic activity (the formation of large gas pockets in lava or the melting of ice under lava), and by earthquakes. LIMESTONE formations, due to their solubility, almost invariably have caves, some notable for their STALACTITES AND STALAGMITES. Among famous U.S. caves are the Carlsbad Caverns in New Mexico (see NATIONAL PARKS, table). See also SPELEOLOGY.

cave art: see PALEOLITHIC ART; ROCK CARVINGS AND PAINTINGS.

Cavendish, Henry, 1731–1810, English physicist and chemist; b. France. He determined the specific heats for numerous substances (although these heat constants were not recognized until later), did research on the composition of water and air, and studied the properties of a gas that he isolated and described as "inflammable air" (later named HYDROGEN). In a now-famous experiment (1798), he determined the value of the constant of proportionality in Newton's law of GRAVITATION.

Cavour, Camillo Benso, conte di, 1810–61, Italian statesman, premier of Sardinia (1852–59, 1860–61). Cavour introduced liberal internal reforms and involved Sardinia in the CRIMEAN WAR. He became the chief architect of Italian unification under VICTOR EMMANUEL II (see RISORGIMENTO).

Caxton, William, c.1421–1491, English printer, the first to print books in English. Apprenticed as a mercer, he was later a diplomat, and learned printing in Cologne, Germany, in 1471–72. At Bruges, Belgium (1475), he printed with Colard Mansion *The Recuyell of the Historyes of Troye,* the first book printed in English. At Westminster (1477) he printed *Dictes or Sayengis of the Philosophres,* the first dated book printed in England. He is known to have printed about 100 books, having translated about one third of them himself.

Cayenne, city (1990 est. pop. 41,500), capital of FRENCH GUIANA, on Cayenne Island. It exports timber and rum, and gives its name to cayenne pepper, found on the island. Founded (1643) by France, it was held (1808–16) by Britain and Portugal. Many residents descend from inmates of French prison colonies (1851–1946).

Cayley, Sir George, 1773–1857, English scientist, recognized as the founder of AERODYNAMICS. In his studies on the principles of flight, he experimented with wing design; distinguished between lift and drag; and formulated the concepts of vertical tail surfaces, steering rudders, rear elevators, and air screws. Although powered flight was not possible in his time, he was able to calculate the power required for various speeds and loads.

Cayman Islands, British dependency (1992 est. pop. 29,100), c.100 sq mi (259 sq km), West Indies, consisting of three main islands, of which Grand Cayman is the largest. The capital is George Town. The Caymans have prospered as a major international offshore banking center, rivaling even Switzerland. Sighted (1503) by Christopher COLUMBUS, the islands are now popular tourist attractions.

Cayuga: see IROQUOIS CONFEDERACY.

CB radio: see RADIO.

Cd, chemical symbol of the element CADMIUM.

CD: see COMPACT DISC.

Ce, chemical symbol of the element CERIUM.

Ceauşescu, Nicolae [choushĕs'kōō], 1918–89, Romanian Communist leader and president of ROMANIA (1967–89). After the Communist takeover in 1948 he rose steadily in the party and the government. At the death (1965) of GHEORGHIU-DEJ he became party leader. He maintained Romanian independence from the USSR and close ties with China and the West, but he also reduced his country to poverty while ruthlessly pursuing modernization and brutally suppressing ethnic minorities and dissidents. Ceauşescu was overthrown in 1989, and he and his wife were executed.

Cecil, Robert: see SALISBURY, ROBERT CECIL, 1ST EARL OF.

Cecil, Robert Arthur Talbot Gascoyne: see SALISBURY, ROBERT ARTHUR TALBOT GASCOYNE-CECIL, 3D MARQUESS OF.

Cecil, William: see BURGHLEY, WILLIAM CECIL, 1ST BARON.

cedar, common name for a number of mostly coniferous evergreen trees. The true cedars (genus *Cedrus*), of the PINE family, are all native to the Old World; some, e.g., the cedar of Lebanon (*C. libani*) and the fragrant deodar cedar (*C. deodara*), are cultivated elsewhere. In North America, the name cedar refers to the JUNIPER (red cedar), ARBORVITAE (white cedar), and other conifers of the CYPRESS family. Several tropical American trees (genus *Cedrela*) of the MAHOGANY family are also called cedars.

Cedar Rapids, city (1990 pop. 108,751), seat of Linn co., E central Iowa, on the Cedar R.; inc. as a city 1856. One of Iowa's chief commercial and industrial cities, it is the distribution center for an agricultural area. Its manufactures include cereals, farm machinery, communications equipment, and paper and plastic products.

Celebes or **Sulawesi,** island (1990 est. pop. 12,510,000), largest island in E Indonesia, c.73,000 sq mi (189,070 sq km), separated from BORNEO by the Makasar Strait. Irregular in shape, it comprises four large peninsulas. The terrain is almost wholly mountainous, with many active volcanoes. Valuable stands of timber cover much of the island; mineral resources include nickel, gold, diamonds, and sulfur. The inhabitants are Malayan, with some indigenous peoples in the interior. The Dutch took control of Celebes from the Portuguese in the 1600s. In 1950 it became a province of the newly created Indonesia. Makasar is the chief city and port.

celery, biennial plant (*Apium graveolens*) of the CARROT family, widely distributed and cultivated in north temperate areas. Once used as a medicine and flavoring, it is now used chiefly as a food, especially in soups and salads; the seeds are still used for seasoning.

celesta: see PERCUSSION INSTRUMENT.

celestial equator and **celestial horizon:** see ASTRONOMICAL COORDINATE SYSTEMS.

celestial mechanics, the study of the motions of astronomical bodies as they move under the influence of their mutual GRAVITATION. The calculation of such motions is complicated because many separate forces are acting at once and all bodies are moving simultaneously. Celestial mechanics is based on Isaac NEWTON's laws of motion and theory of universal gravitation. Only the problem of two isolated moving bodies mutually attracted by gravitation can be solved exactly. Because the sun is the dominant influence in the solar system, an application of the two-body problem leads to the simple elliptical ORBITS as described by KEPLER'S LAWS, which give a close approximation of planetary motion. Problems that consider the additional effects, or perturbations, of other less dominant bodies (such as the other planets in the solar system) cannot be solved exactly except in a few special cases. Methods have been devised, however, to allow successive refinements of an approximate solution to be made to almost any degree of precision.

celestial meridian, celestial pole, and **celestial sphere:** see ASTRONOMICAL COORDINATE SYSTEMS.

Celestine I, Saint, d. 432, pope (422–432), an Italian. He advanced orthodoxy by sending a delegation to the Council of Ephesus to oppose NESTORIANISM. Feast: July 27.

Celestine V, Saint, 1215–96, pope (July 5–Dec. 13, 1294), an Italian named Pietro del Murrone. Elected to end the two-year deadlock in finding a successor to Nicholas IV, Celestine was a hermit who had attracted a following of extremists (called Celestines). His papacy was chaotic and was dominated by Charles II of Naples; it lasted but five months before he resigned. His successor, BONIFACE VIII, confined Celestine for life to avert schism. Feast: May 19.

Céline, Louis Ferdinand [sālĕn'], 1894–1961, French author; b. Louis Ferdinand Destouches. He wrote sensationally misanthropic but influential novels, e.g., *Journey to the End of Night* (1932). Based on his experiences as a doctor during World War I, his works portray the vileness of humanity through frank, often obscene, language. Céline later wrote a chaotic trilogy (1957–61) recounting the last days of the Third Reich in Germany.

cell, in biology, the unit of structure and function of which all plants and animals are composed. The cell is the smallest unit in the living organism that is capable of carrying on the essential processes of life: sustaining METABOLISM for producing energy and reproducing. There are many one-celled organisms (e.g., PROTOZOANS and BACTERIA) in which the single cell performs all life functions. In higher organisms groups of cells are differentiated into specialized tissues. The cell is composed of the cytoplasm; the cell membrane, which surrounds it; and the nucleus, which is contained within it. Plant cells also have a thickened cell wall, composed chiefly of CELLULOSE. Included in the cytoplasm are mitochondria, which produce energy; lysozymes, which break down unneeded molecules; Golgi apparatuses, which synthesize, store, and secrete substances; ribosomes, the sites of protein synthesis; and CHLOROPLASTS (in green plants only), in which PHOTOSYNTHESIS occurs. The nucleus contains CHROMOSOMES, which store the genetic information for the whole cell and pass on their information to daughter cells by replicating themselves (see MITOSIS).

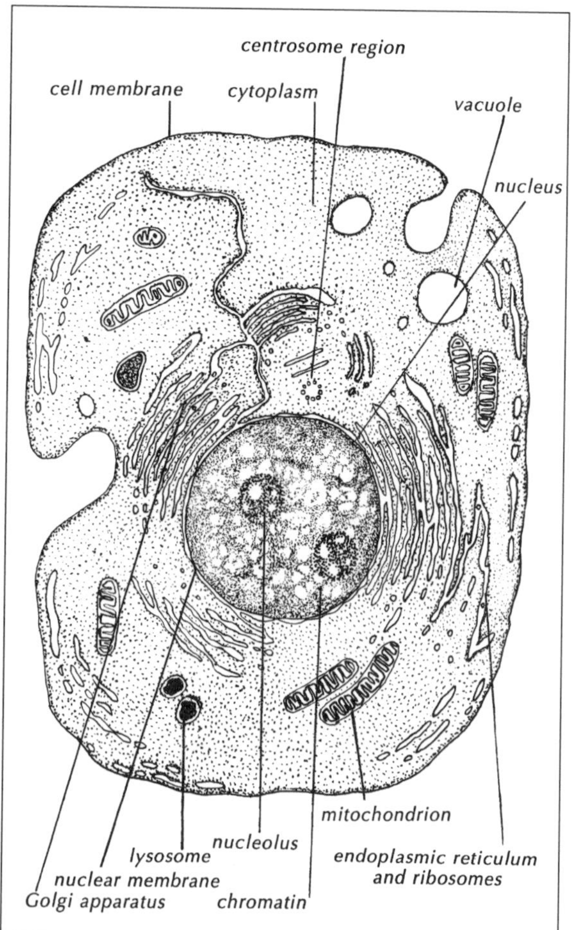

Animal cell

cell, in electricity, device that converts chemical energy into electrical energy, commonly called a battery. A cell consists of two dissimilar substances, a positive ELECTRODE and a negative electrode, and a third substance, the ELECTROLYTE, that acts chemically on the electrodes. The ELECTROMOTIVE FORCE, or voltage produced between the positive and negative electrodes, depends on the chemical properties of the substances used but not on the size of the electrodes or the amount of electrolyte. When the electrodes are connected externally by a piece of wire, electrons flow from the negative electrode, through the wire, and into the positive electrode. There are several kinds of cells, differing in electrode material and electrolyte. The Leclanché cell has a zinc negative electrode, a carbon positive electrode, and an electrolyte consisting of ammonium chloride solution. It is the basis of the common dry cell (the standard flashlight "battery"), so called because the electrolyte is in the form of a paste instead of a liquid. An alkaline dry cell, which can operate up to ten times longer than common dry cells, has a zinc negative electrode, a manganese dioxide positive electrode, and an electrolyte of potassium hydroxide. A mercury dry cell, with a zinc negative electrode, a mercuric oxide positive electrode, and a potassium hydroxide electrolyte, has a constant output voltage and may be stored for many years. Rechargeable flashlight batteries are nickel-cadmium (ni-cad) cells or alkaline cells. A wet cell contains a number of alternately positive and negative plates in a liquid electrolyte. Positive plates are connected to form the positive electrode; negative plates are similarly connected. A true BATTERY consists of a group of cells that are connected to act as a source of direct current.

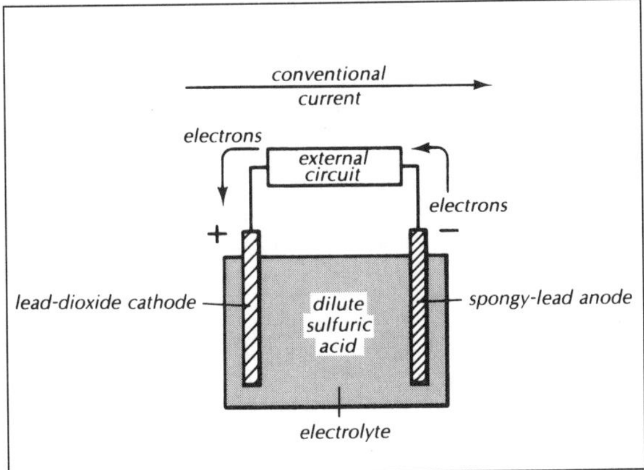

Cell, in electricity: At the lead-dioxide cathode, electrons from the circuit combine with lead dioxide and sulfuric acid to form lead sulfate and water. At the spongy-lead anode, lead reacts with sulfate ions to form lead sulfate and release electrons.

Cellini, Benvenuto [chĕlē'nē], 1500–71, Italian sculptor, metalsmith, and author. Under the patronage of Pope CLEMENT VII, he made medals, jewel settings, caskets, vases, candlesticks, metal plates, and ornaments. His work, with its decorative quality and exquisite detail, is among the best of the period. Though most of his works have perished, the famous gold and enamel saltcellar of FRANCIS I of France and the gold medallion of *Leda and the Swan* (both: Vienna Mus.) still remain. His late Florentine sculptures include the bust of Cosimo I (Bargello, Florence) and *Perseus with the Head of Medusa* (Loggia dei Lanzi, Florence). Cellini was a true RENAISSANCE man, and his autobiography (1558–62) is one of the most important documents of the 16th cent.

cello: see VIOLIN.

cellophane, thin, transparent sheet or tube of regenerated CELLULOSE. Used in packaging and for DIALYSIS, cellophane is made by mixing alkali-treated cellulose with carbon disulfide to form viscose. After aging, the viscose is forced through a slit into dilute acid. The regenerated cellulose that results has a lower molecular weight and a less orderly structure than cellulose.

celluloid, transparent, colorless synthetic PLASTIC made by treating CELLULOSE nitrate with CAMPHOR and alcohol. The first important synthetic plastic, celluloid was widely used as a substitute for more expensive substances, such as ivory, amber, and tortoiseshell. It is highly flammable and has been largely superseded by newer plastics.

cellular telephone or **cellular radio,** telecommunications system in which a portable or mobile radio transmitter and receiver, or "telephone," is linked via MICROWAVE radio frequencies to base transmitter and receiver stations that connect the user to a conventional telephone network. The geographic region served by a cellular system is subdivided into areas called cells. Each cell has a central base station and two sets of assigned transmission frequencies; one set is used by the base station, and the other by mobile telephones. To prevent radio interference, each cell uses frequencies different from those used by its surrounding cells, but cells sufficiently distant from each other can use the same frequencies. When a mobile telephone leaves one cell and enters another, the telephone call is transferred from one base station and set of transmission frequencies to the next using a computerized switching system. The first cellular telephone system began operation in Tokyo in 1979, and the first U.S. system began operation in 1983 in Chicago.

cellulose, a carbohydrate of high molecular weight that is the chief constituent of the CELL walls of plants. Raw cotton is 91% cellulose. Other important natural sources are flax, hemp, jute, straw, and wood. Cellulose has been used to make PAPER since the 2d cent. A.D. Cellulose derivatives include guncotton (fully nitrated cellulose), used for EXPLOSIVES; CELLULOID (the first PLASTIC); and cellulose acetate, used for plastics, lacquers, and fibers such as RAYON.

Celsius temperature scale: see TEMPERATURE.

Celtic Church, name given to the Christian church founded 2d or 3d cent. in the British Isles before the mission (597) of St. AUGUSTINE OF CANTERBURY from Rome. It spread in the 5th cent. through the work of St. Ninian in Scotland, St. Dyfrig in Wales, and St. PATRICK in Ireland, but was all but extinguished in England by the Saxon invasions, beginning c.450. At the Synod of Whitby (663) differences in Celtic and Roman church practices were largely resolved.

Celtic languages, subfamily of the Indo-European family of languages. See LANGUAGE (table).

Celts, Indo-European-speaking tribal groups who dominated central Europe during the IRON AGE, developing the LA TÈNE culture. Mounted raiders with iron weapons, they spread rapidly over Europe in the 6th and 5th cent. B.C. from their home in SW Germany, reaching the British Isles, France, Spain, Italy, Macedonia, and Asia Minor. Their social hierarchy included kinglike chiefs and priests known as DRUIDS. A richly ornamental art and colorful folklore were their important cultural legacies. The term *Celts* also refers to natives of areas where a Celtic language is (or, until the 20th cent., was) spoken, i.e., Ireland, the Scottish Hebrides and Highlands, the Isle of Man, Wales, Cornwall, and Brittany.

cement, hydraulic, building material typically made by heating a mixture of limestone and clay until it almost fuses and then grinding it to a fine powder. Once it is mixed with water, cement will harden even if immersed in water. The most common cement, Portland cement, is made by mixing and then heating substances containing lime, silica, alumina, and iron oxide, with gypsum added during the grinding process. Quick-setting aluminous cement is made from limestone and bauxite. See also CONCRETE.

Cenozoic era: see GEOLOGIC ERA (table).

censorship, official restriction of any expression believed to threaten the political, social, or moral order. Although most often imposed by totalitarian, autocratic, or theocratic regimes or in times of war, censorship has also long existed in the U.S. Such materials as school texts, films, and literary works have often been suppressed as morally or ideologically subversive by religious organizations, government agencies (such as the U.S. Post Office or elected local school boards) or private groups (such as the Watch and Ward Society in Boston, Anthony COMSTOCK's New York Society for the Suppression of Vice, the MORAL MAJORITY, and feminists opposed to pornography). At times, systems of self-censorship (e.g., the film industry's "Hays Code" of the 1930s) have been established to reduce the threat of outside censorship or boycott. U.S. Supreme Court rulings in 1973 and 1987 granted to state governments the right to decide what is subversive or obscene. Official secrecy, or federal censorship of information about government operations, was greatly reduced in the U.S. under the FREEDOM OF INFORMATION ACT (1966), supplemented by the Privacy Act of 1974. See also PRESS, FREEDOM OF THE; PRIVACY, RIGHT OF.

centaur, in Greek myth, a creature half-man, half-horse, descended from IXION. Most were savage followers of DIONYSUS, but some, like CHIRON, taught humans.

center of mass, the point at which all the mass of a body or group of objects is considered to be concentrated. This point is often the same as the **center of gravity** (the point at which all the weight of a body may be considered to be concentrated). The motions of several colliding elementary particles, or of the earth and moon around the sun, are sometimes analyzed from the point of view of the center of mass of the entire system of objects.

Centers for Disease Control and Prevention (CDC), agency of the U.S. Public Health Service since 1973, with headquarters in Atlanta; est. (1946) as the Communicable Disease Center. The CDC administers national programs for the prevention and control of communicable diseases, develops and implements programs for dealing with environmental health problems, directs quarantine activities, and conducts epidemiological research. It also provides consultation on an international basis for the control of preventable diseases.

centigrade temperature scale: see TEMPERATURE.

centimeter: see METRIC SYSTEM; WEIGHTS AND MEASURES, table.

centipede, invertebrate animal of the class Chilopoda, an ARTHROPOD. The flattened body is divided into a head and trunk comprised of segments (somites). The average number of legs is 35 pairs, one pair per segment except for the first one and last two. The appendages of the first segment are modified into claws equipped with poison glands, used to capture prey. The largest tropical species may reach 12 in. (30 cm) in length; temperate species are usually about 1 in. (2.5 cm) long.

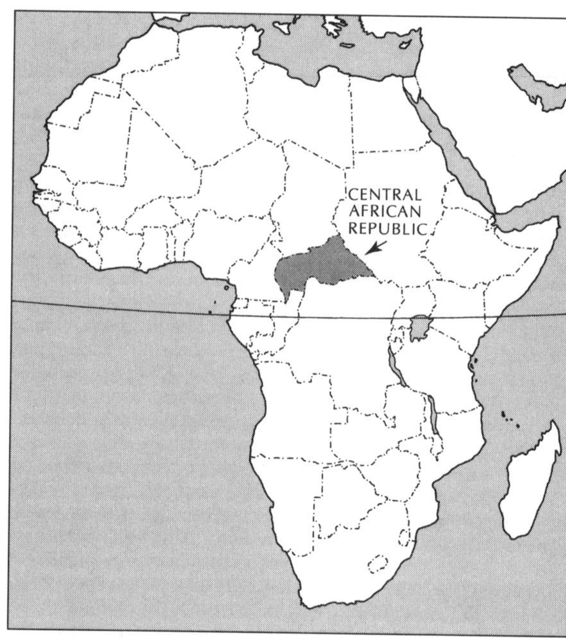

Central African Republic, republic (1992 est. pop. 3,029,000), 240,534 sq mi (622,983 sq km), central Africa, bordered by Chad (N), Sudan (E), Zaïre and Congo (S), and Cameroon (W). BANGUI is the capital. Situated on a savanna-covered plateau 2,000–3,000 ft (610–910 m) above sea level, the country has tropical forests in the south and a semidesert area in the east. Of the numerous rivers, only the Ubangi is commercially navigable. Agriculture is the chief economic activity, engaging about 90% of the people, mostly in subsistence farming. The principal cash crops and exports are cotton, tobacco, and coffee; other exports include diamonds and timber. Uranium is also mined. There are no railroads and few adequate paved roads; rivers are the chief means of transportation. The chief ethnic groups are the Mangia-Baya, Banda, Mbaka, Sara, and Azande. French is the official language, but Sango is the lingua franca. About half the population practice Christianity, with the rest roughly divided between Islam and traditional beliefs.

History. In the 19th cent. various tribes fleeing the slave trade arrived in the region. The French occupied the area in 1887 and organized it (1894) as the colony of Ubangi-Shari; it was united administratively with CHAD in 1906 and incorporated into FRENCH EQUATORIAL AFRICA in 1910. Despite periodic rebellions sparked by French concessionaires' use of forced labor, the population supported the Free French forces in WORLD WAR II. The colony was given its own territorial assembly in 1946, received autonomy and took its present name in 1958, and gained full independence in 1960 under Pres. David DACKO. In 1965 the parliamentary government was overthrown in a military coup led by Col. Jean-Bédel BOKASSA, who in 1976 changed the country's name to Central African Empire and had himself crowned Emperor Bokassa I. During his brutal regime it was alleged that he personally took part in a 1979 massacre of children protesting human rights violations. Shortly thereafter, control was regained by Dacko, who restored republican government. In 1981 Dacko was ousted in a coup led by Gen. André Kolingba, who established a dictatorial one-party state. Kolingba ended the ban on opposition parties in 1992 and Ange-Félix Patassé won the presidency in a free election in 1993.

Central America, collective term applied to the six nations of North America lying SE of Mexico—BELIZE, COSTA RICA, EL SALVADOR, GUATEMALA, HONDURAS, and NICARAGUA—and usually also including PANAMA, on the Isthmus of Panama. The region is predominantly mountainous in the interior, with an active zone of volcanoes and earthquakes marking the junction of North America's mountain systems and outliers of South America's ANDES chain. Tajumulko (13,846 ft/4,210 m), a volcano in Guatemala, is the highest point. The climate varies with altitude from tropical to cool, with heavy rainfall occurring in the east. Bananas, coffee, and cacao are the chief commercial crops. The population is mainly Spanish-speaking, Roman Catholic, and mestizo (of mixed European and indigenous descent). Though rich culturally, the area has suffered chronic political and economic problems, due largely to the persistence of a landholding system that leaves a vast gap between rich and poor.

central bank, financial institution designed to regulate and control a nation's fiscal and monetary activities. Usually state-owned, central banks issue notes to be used as legal tender, maintain adequate reserve backing for the nation's banks, and control the flow of money and precious metals. By regulating the supply of MONEY and CREDIT they influence INTEREST rates and, to some extent, the whole national economy. Most central banks are modeled after the Bank of England (1694), the first to fill a central banking role. Other notable central banks include the U.S. FEDERAL RESERVE SYSTEM, the Bank of Canada, France's Banque de France, and Germany's Deutsche Bundesbank.

Central Intelligence Agency (CIA), U.S. agency established (1947) by the National Security Act. It conducts intelligence and counterintelligence activities outside the U.S. (see INTELLIGENCE GATHERING). It also engages in domestic counterintelligence operations, but only in coordination with the FEDERAL BUREAU OF INVESTIGATION and subject to the attorney general's approval. These limitations were mandated by a 1978 executive order, issued in the wake of abuses related to the WATERGATE AFFAIR and of a presidential commission's charge (1975) that the CIA had engaged in "unlawful" domestic spying. The CIA has also been criticized for taking an active role in the internal affairs of foreign governments.

Central Powers: see WORLD WAR I.

central processing unit: see COMPUTER.

Central Valley, great trough of central Calif., c.450 mi (720 km) long and c.50 mi (80 km) wide, between the SIERRA NEVADA and COAST RANGES. The Sacramento and San Joaquin rivers drain the valley before converging in a huge delta and flowing into San Francisco Bay. California's leading agricultural area, this irrigated valley has the largest single concentration of fruit farms and vineyards in the U.S.

centrifuge, device using centrifugal force to separate substances of different density, e.g., cream from milk. Substances are placed in containers that are spun at speeds high enough to cause the heavier elements to sink. The first successful centrifuge was built in 1883 by the Swedish engineer Carl G.P. de Laval.

centripetal force and centrifugal force, action-reaction force pair associated with circular motion. Centripetal ("center-seeking") force is the constant inward force necessary to maintain circular motion. The centripetal force F acting on a body of mass m is given by the equation $F = mv^2/r$, where v is its velocity and r is the radius of its path. The centripetal force—the action—is balanced by a reaction force, the centrifugal ("center-fleeing") force, which acts not on the circling object but on the source of centripetal force, usually located at the circle's center. The two forces are equal in magnitude and opposite in direction.

cephalopod, free-swimming MOLLUSK (class Cephalopoda) with a long body and a ring of sucker-bearing arms (tentacles) encircling the mouth. The head is large, with prominent eyes. Only the NAUTILUS has an external shell; in the SQUID and CUTTLEFISH the shell is internal and reduced, and in the OCTOPUS it is completely absent. Most cephalopods are aggressive carnivores that move by means of a kind of jet propulsion.

Cepheid variables, small class of VARIABLE STARS that brighten and dim in regular periods ranging from 1 to 50 days. The periods of Cepheids, which are yellow supergiant stars that swell and contract in size, depend on their intrinsic brightness, or absolute MAGNITUDE, in a known way: the brighter the star, the greater its period. By comparing the Cepheid's absolute magnitude to its apparent magnitude, one can determine its distance. The period-luminosity relation of Cepheids make them invaluable in estimating interstellar and intergalactic distances.

ceramics, materials made of nonmetallic minerals, such as clay, that have been permanently hardened by firing at a high temperature. Most ceramics resist heat and chemicals. Ceramic materials are used in all forms of pottery, from crude earthenware to the finest PORCELAIN, and in industrial and engineering products. Ceramic products include art objects, such as figurines; ABRASIVES, such as ALUMINA; building materials, such as BRICK; cooking utensils; dinnerware; electrical equipment, such as insulators in spark plugs; and refractories, such as the heat shield on the SPACE SHUTTLE.

Cerberus [sûr'bərəs], in Greek mythology, many-headed dog with a mane and a tail of snakes; guardian of HADES. One of the 12 labors of HERCULES was to capture him.

cereal: see GRAIN; GRASS.

cerebral palsy, disorder in which muscular control and coordination are impaired, and speech and hearing problems and mental retardation may occur. It is most commonly caused by brain damage occurring before or during birth, and varies greatly in severity. Treatment involves physical, occupational, and speech therapy; braces; orthopedic surgery; and drugs to reduce muscle stiffness and spasticity.

Ceres, in astronomy: see ASTEROID.

Ceres [sēr'ēz], in Roman mythology, goddess of grain; daughter of SATURN and Ops. Her worship involved fertility rites and rites for the dead, and her chief festival was the Cerealia. She was identified with the Greek DEMETER.

cerium (Ce), metallic element, purified in 1875 by W.F. Hillebrand and T.H. Norton. Iron-gray, soft, and malleable, it is the most abundant RARE-EARTH METAL. It is used as a core for the carbon electrode of arc lamps. Cigarette- and gas-lighter flints are cerium alloys. See ELEMENT (table); PERIODIC TABLE.

CERN, officially the **European Laboratory for Particle Physics,** principal European center for research in particle physics, est. 1954 as the European Center for Nuclear Research. Seventeen European countries sponsor CERN, which straddles the Franco-Swiss border W of Geneva.

Cervantes Saavedra, Miguel de [sərvän'tēs, Span. thĕrvän' tās sä"āvāthrä], 1547–1616, Spanish novelist, dramatist, and poet, author of *Don Quixote.* Little is known of Cervantes's youth. In 1569, in the service of a cardinal, he went to Italy, where he studied literature and philosophy. At the naval battle of Lepanto (1571) his left arm was permanently crippled. Returning to Spain (1575), he was captured by Barbary pirates and sold as a slave. After many escape attempts he was ransomed at ruinous cost from the viceroy of Algiers in 1580. As a government purchasing agent (1588–97) he was jailed several times for financial irregularities. His first published work was *La Galatea* (1585), a PASTORAL romance in prose and verse. Part I of his masterpiece, *Don Quixote de la Mancha* (1605), was an immediate success. The addled idealism of Don Quixote, a country gentleman who has read too many chivalric romances, and the earthy acquisitiveness of his squire, Sancho Panza, propel them into a series of adventures involving characters from every level of society. The appearance of a spurious sequel prompted Cervantes to publish Part II in 1615. The work had an indelible effect on the development of the European NOVEL. Among his other works are poems; many plays; the *Exemplary Novels* (1613), a collection of 12 tales; and *The Travails of Persiles and Sigismunda* (1617), a prose epic.

cesarean section, delivery of an infant by surgical removal from the uterus through an abdominal incision. It is usually performed when childbirth is considered hazardous, as when the mother's pelvis is too narrow or the fetus is in an abnormal position. Subsequent deliveries were traditionally also by cesarean section, but the practice is dimishing. The name comes from the legend that Julius CAESAR was born in this manner.

cesium (Cs), metallic element, discovered by spectroscopy in 1860 by Robert BUNSEN and Gustav KIRCHHOFF. Ductile, soft as wax, and silver-white, it is the most alkaline element (see ALKALI METALS) and the most reactive metal. Cesium metal is used in photoelectric cells and various optical instruments; cesium compounds, in glass and ceramic production. The cesium-137 radioactive isotope is used to treat cancer. See ELEMENT (table); PERIODIC TABLE.

Cetewayo, Cetywayo, or **Ketchwayo,** c.1836–1884, king of the ZULUS. He succeeded his father, Mpanda, as king in 1872. Refusing to submit to British rule, he successfully resisted (1878–79) a British campaign until Zulu forces were thoroughly defeated at Ulundi (July, 1879). He spent most of the rest of his life in exile.

Ceuta [thāo͞o'tä], city (1986 pop. 71,403), c.7 sq mi (18 sq km), NW Africa, a Spanish possession, on the Strait of Gibraltar. An enclave in Morocco administered as part of Cádiz prov., Spain, Ceuta is a free port with such industries as fishing, food processing, and tourism. An ancient city, it was seized (1415) by Portugal and in 1580 passed to Spain.

Cézanne, Paul [sāzän'], 1839–1906, French painter. Strongly influenced by PISSARRO, he became a leading figure in the revolution toward abstraction. His early work is marked by heavy use of the palette knife; these fantastic, dreamlike scenes anticipate the expressionist idiom of the 20th cent. (see EXPRESSIONISM). After meeting MANET and the impressionist painters, Cézanne became interested in using color to create perspective (see IMPRESSIONISM), but he was utterly unconcerned with transitory light effects. *House of the Hanged Man* (1873–74; Louvre) is characteristic of his impressionist period. He sought to "recreate nature" by simplifying forms and utilizing color and distortion, as in *Mont Sainte-Victoire* (1885–87; Phillips Coll., Wash., D.C.), *The Kitchen Table* (1888–90; Louvre), *The Card Players* (1890–92; one version, S.C. Clark Coll., N.Y.C.), and vital portraits. He also developed a new type of spatial pattern, portraying objects from shifting viewpoints. His simple forms are always represented with almost classical structural stability, as in *Bathers* (1898–1905; Philadelphia Mus. Art), a monumental embodiment of several of his visual systems. Cézanne's influence on the course of modern art, particularly CUBISM, was enormous and profound, and his theories spawned a whole new school of aesthetic criticism.

Cf, chemical symbol of the element CALIFORNIUM.

CFC: see CHLOROFLUOROCARBON.

cgs system: see METRIC SYSTEM.

Chad, Fr. *Tchad,* officially Republic of Chad, republic (1992 est. pop. 5,239,000), 495,752 sq mi (1,284,000 sq km), N central Africa, bordered by the Central Africa Republic (S), Sudan (E), Libya (N), and Cameroon, Niger, and Nigeria (W). NDJAMENA is the capital. The terrain in the south is wooded savanna, becoming brush country near Lake Chad, on the western border. Northern Chad is a desert that merges with the S SAHARA and includes the mountainous Tibesti region. Chad is one of the poorest nations in Africa; its economy is based largely on subsistence farming, livestock-raising, and fishing. The single important cash crop is cotton, which also supports a textile industry. Deposits of petroleum, tungsten, and uranium have not been exploited. The population is made up of two distinct, often hostile, groups: settled agricultural peoples, mostly Christians but with some adherents of traditional African beliefs, in the politically dominant south; and seminomadic or nomadic Muslim peoples, including Arabs and Toubou, who engage in herding, in the north. French and Arabic are the official languages.

History. Long a focal point for trans-Saharan trade routes, the region was penetrated in the 7th cent. by Arab traders. Shortly thereafter nomads from N Africa established the state of Kanem, which reached its peak in the 13th cent. The successor state of Bornu was joined by the rival Wadai and Bagirmi empires, all of which fell to the Sudanese conqueror Rabih by the early 1890s. French expeditions moved into the region in 1890 and by 1913 had defeated the Sudanese and conquered Chad, which became a colony in FRENCH EQUATORIAL AFRICA. It gained autonomy in 1958 and full independence in 1960. Internal strife between the Muslim north and the Christian and animist south has dominated the country's affairs, flaring into guerrilla warfare (with the main Muslim group receiving active support from LIBYA, which claimed and occupied part of N Chad—the Aouzou strip—in 1973) and precipitating numerous changes of government. The country's first president, Ngarta Tombalbaye, was killed in a coup in 1975. In 1979 a coalition government, headed by Goukouni Oueddei, a former rebel from the north, assumed power, but fighting broke out again in 1980. In 1982 Goukouni's government was overthrown by the forces of former prime minister Hissène Habré. He moved to include all factions in his government and defeated the Libyans in 1987, but they retained control of the Aouzou strip. Habré was ousted (1990) by Libyan-backed rebels led by Idriss Déby, who became president. A national democracy conference established (1993) a transitional government, with Déby remaining president, and called for free elections within a year. In 1994 the International Court of Justice rejected Libya's claim to the Aouzou strip and other Chadian territory.

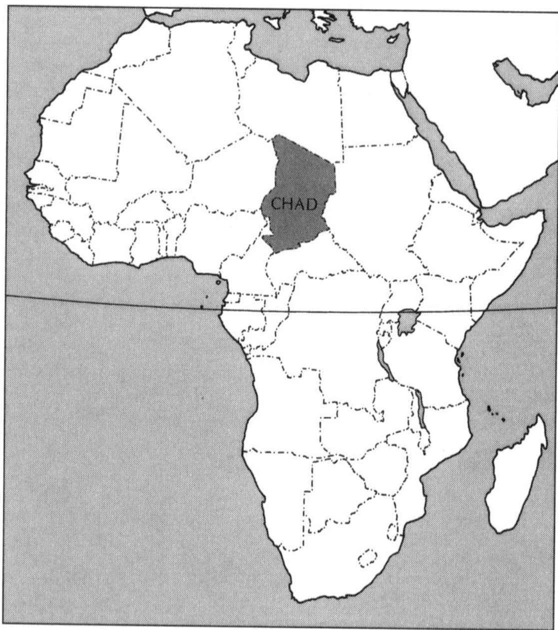

Chadwick, Sir James, 1891–1974, English physicist. He worked on radioactivity under Ernest Rutherford and was assistant director (1923–35) of radioactive research at the Cavendish Laboratory, Cambridge. For his discovery of the NEUTRON he received the 1935 Nobel Prize in physics.

Chagall, Marc, 1889–1985, Russian painter. He lived mainly in France. A forerunner of SURREALISM, he drew subject matter from Jewish life and folklore and rendered it with deceptive fairy-tale naïveté, as in *I and the Village* (1911; Mus. Mod. Art, N.Y.C.) and *The Rabbi of Vitebsk* (Art Inst., Chicago). He designed sets and costumes for STRAVINSKY's ballet *The Firebird* (1945); 12 stained-glass windows (1962) for Hadassah-Hebrew Univ. Medical Center synagogue, Jerusalem; and two vast murals for New York City's Metropolitan Opera House (1966). A museum of his work opened (1973) in Nice.

Chagas' disease, disease of South and Central America caused by the parasite *Trypanosoma cruzi.* Symptoms include fever, swelling and redness around the eyes, and, in some cases, serious or fatal inflammation of the brain and heart tissues. It usually affects children and young adults and is transmitted by infected insects, typically the assassin bug. There is no vaccine and no satisfactory treatment.

Chain, Ernst Boris, 1906–79, English biochemist; b. Germany. For their work in isolating and purifying penicillin, he and Sir Howard FLOREY shared with Sir Alexander FLEMING the 1945 Nobel Prize in physiology or medicine. Chain held various teaching and research positions in Berlin, Rome, and London and at Oxford and Cambridge.

Chalcedon, Council of, 451, 4th ecumenical council. It stated that Jesus' divine nature and human nature are distinct, but inseparably united—Jesus is both truly God and truly human. This dictum refuted EUTYCHES, and became the test of orthodoxy for the Roman Catholic Church.

chalcedony, form of QUARTZ with microscopic crystals. Some varieties of chalcedony are AGATE, BLOODSTONE, JASPER, and ONYX.

chalcopyrite or **copper pyrites,** copper and iron sulfide mineral ($CuFeS_2$), brass yellow and sometimes with an iridescent tarnish. It is found in crystal form but is most often massive. Occurring worldwide in igneous and metamorphic rocks, it is an important ore of COPPER.

Chaliapin, Feodor Ivanovich [shəyä'pyĭn], 1873–1938, Russian operatic bass. He lived outside the USSR after 1921. His powerful voice, tremendous physique, and acting ability made him one of the great performers in operatic history. He was particularly effective in MOUSSORGSKY's *Boris Godunov.*

chalk, a calcium carbonate mineral, similar in composition to limestone but softer. Chalk has been deposited throughout geologic time. The chief constituents are the shells of minute animals called foraminifera; however, the dominant component of the best-known formations, the Cretaceous chalks (e.g., the White Cliffs of Dover, England), are coccolith algae. Chalk is used to make putty, plaster, cement, quicklime, and blackboard chalk. Harder forms are used as building stones, and poor soils with high clay content are sweetened with chalk.

Challenger, U.S. space shuttle. It exploded (Jan. 28, 1986), 73 seconds into its flight, killing all seven crew members, including a civilian schoolteacher, Christa McAuliffe. The disaster was caused by a faulty gasket design. As a result of the explosion, the U.S. did not send astronauts into space for three years as NASA redesigned a number of features of the space shuttle.

Chamberlain, (Arthur) Neville, 1869–1940, British statesman. A former Conservative chancellor of the exchequer (1923–24, 1931–37), he succeeded Stanley BALDWIN as prime minister in 1937. His belief that HITLER was a rational statesman resulted in the policy of "appeasement" of the AXIS powers that culminated in the MUNICH PACT (1938). He remained in office following the outbreak of WORLD WAR II, but he resigned (1940) after the British debacle in Norway.

Chamberlain, Wilt(on Norman), 1936–, American basketball player; b. Philadelphia. Twice an All-American at the Univ. of Kansas, he starred (1959–73) in the National Basketball Association (NBA) with Philadelphia (Warriors and 76ers), San Francisco, and Los Angeles. With his height (over 7 ft 1 in./216 cm) and agility, he was the top NBA scorer in 7 consecutive seasons and the leading rebounder in 11. He set records (since broken) for most points (31,419) and highest career average (30.1).

Chamberlin, Thomas Chrowder, 1843–1928, American geologist; b. Mattoon, Ill. He taught at the Univ. of Chicago (1892–1919) and was chief geologist of the geological survey of Wisconsin (1873–82). With the American astronomer F.R. Moulton he formulated the planetesimal hypothesis of the origin of the SOLAR SYSTEM. His works include *The Origin of the Earth* (1916) and *Two Solar Families* (1928).

Chambers, Sir William, 1723–96, English architect. He designed decorative architecture for Kew Gardens. The foremost official architect of his day, he continued the neo-Palladian tradition.

chameleon, small- to medium-sized LIZARD of the family Chamaeleonidae, found in sub-Saharan Africa, with a few species in S Asia. Chameleons have laterally flattened bodies ornamented with crests, horns, or spines and bulging, independently rotating eyes. Their skin changes color in response to stimuli such as light, temperature, and emotion, not in response to background color. The so-called common chameleon (*Chamaeleo chamaeleon*) is found around the Mediterranean. The American chameleon, not a true chameleon, belongs to the IGUANA family.

Chamisso, Adelbert von [shəmī'sō], 1781–1838, German poet and naturalist; b. France as Louis Charles Adelaide de Chamisso. His poetic cycle *Frauenliebe und Leben* (1830) was set to music by SCHUMANN. His tale of Peter Schlemihl, the man who sold his shadow to the devil (1814), has become legend.

chamois, hollow-horned, hoofed MAMMAL (*Rupicapra rupicapra*) found in the mountains of Europe and the E Mediterranean. About the size of a large GOAT, it is brown with a black tail and back stripes; its horns are erect with terminal hooks. The skin was the original chamois leather, a name now also given to the skins of other animals.

chamomile or **camomile,** name for some herbs of the COMPOSITE family, especially the perennial English, or Roman, chamomile (*Anthemis nobilis*) and the annual German, or wild, chamomile (*Matricaria chamomilla*). The former is the chamomile most used for ornament and for a tea, made from the dried flower heads containing a volatile oil. The oil from wild chamomile flowers is chiefly used as a hair rinse.

Champa, kingdom of the Chams in Vietnam, fl. 2d cent. A.D.–17th cent. The Chams warred successively with China, the KHMER EMPIRE, and ANNAM. The Cham kingdom finally fell to the Annamese, and its people were scattered.

Champagne, Philippe de: see CHAMPAIGNE.

Champagne [shäNpä'nyə], region, NE France. Champagne is a generally arid, chalky plateau cut by the Aisne, Marne, Seine, Aube, and Yonne rivers. Agriculture and sheep-grazing are the traditional activities; textile and metal goods are manufactured. A small fertile area around Rheims and Epernay produces virtually all of France's celebrated champagne wine. Champagne enjoyed an early commercial prosperity, and in the Middle Ages its great fairs, particularly those at Troyes and Provins, attracted merchants from all over W Europe. Cultural life also flourished, culminating in the work of CHRÉTIEN DE TROYES and in the Gothic cathedral at RHEIMS. The county of Champagne passed to the counts of Blois in the 11th cent., and was incorporated into the French royal domain in 1314. WORLD WAR I devastated much of the region, but parts of the area have been reforested.

champagne, sparkling white wine, traditionally made from a mixture of grapes grown in the old French province of Champagne; the best is from the Marne valley. It was reputedly developed in the 17th cent. by a monk, Dom Perignon. The fermented and blended wine is bottled, then sweetened and allowed to ferment further. The carbonic acid left in the bottle after the final fermentation gives champagne its sparkle.

Champaigne or **Champagne, Philippe de** [both: shäN pä'nyə], 1602–74, French painter; b. Belgium. His best-known works, including the FRESCOES at Vincennes and the Tuileries, show the influence of RUBENS and VAN DYCK. His portraits, such as those of Richelieu and of his own daughter, a nun at Port-Royal (both: Louvre), have an air of static majesty.

Champlain, Samuel de, 1567–1635, French explorer, chief founder of New France. In 1605 he founded Port Royal, in NOVA SCOTIA, and in 1608 brought his colonists to QUEBEC. He explored as far W as Lakes Huron and Ontario, and S to Lake CHAMPLAIN, in New York, which bears his name. He extended French claims as far W as WISCONSIN.

Champlain, Lake, lake, 490 sq mi (1,269 sq km), mainly in NE U.S., extending 125 mi (201 km) south from S Quebec to form part of the New York-Vermont border. Its maximum width is 14 mi (23 km). Discovered (1609) by Samuel de CHAMPLAIN, it was the scene of battles in the FRENCH AND INDIAN WAR, the AMERICAN REVOLUTION (Crown Point; TICONDEROGA), and the WAR OF 1812.

Champollion, Jean François, 1790–1832, French Egyptologist. The founder of Egyptology, he discovered the key to Egyptian HIEROGLYPHICS while deciphering (1821) the ROSETTA stone. Sometimes called Champollion le jeune, he was trained in archaeology by his elder brother, **Jean Jacques Champollion-Figeac,** 1778–1867.

Chancellorsville, battle of, May 2–4, 1863, in the U.S. CIVIL WAR. Gen. Robert E. LEE and his Army of Northern Virginia attacked Joseph HOOKER's Union Army of the Potomac, which was entrenched near Chancellorsville, Va. Lee was brilliantly supported by Stonewall JACKSON, who in a flank attack against the Union right surprised and routed Hooker's army. Jackson was mortally wounded by his own troops. On May 3–4, Confederate generals Jubal EARLY and J.E.B. STUART drove the Union army across the Rappahannock R. Chancellorsville was Lee's last great victory; it led to his invasion of the North in the GETTYSBURG CAMPAIGN.

Chan Chan, ruins of a pre-Inca city near Trujillo, N Peru. It is believed to have been built after A.D. 800 and to have been the capital of the CHIMU civilization. Covering c.11 sq mi (28 sq km), it included at least nine self-contained, walled compounds and may once have had a population of 200,000.

Chandler, Raymond T(hornton), 1888–1959, American writer; b. Chicago. His well-plotted, brutally realistic detective novels, all featuring the tough yet honorable Philip Marlowe, include *The Big Sleep* (1939) and *The Long Goodbye* (1953).

Chandragupta (Chandragupta Maurya) [chändrəgo͝op'tə], fl. c.321–c.298 B.C., Indian emperor, founder of the MAURYA dynasty and grandfather of ASOKA. He conquered the Magadha kingdom in N India, defeated (305 B.C.) the invading army of Seleucus I, and may have expelled the last of ALEXANDER THE GREAT's army from India.

Chandrasekhar, Subrahmanyan, 1910–, American astrophysicist; b. Lahore, India (now Pakistan). He is a major figure in the research on energy transfer by radiation in stellar atmospheres. In 1983, he and William A. Fowler won the Nobel Prize in physics for work on WHITE DWARF stars.

Chang or **Yangtze,** great river of China, c.3,450 mi (5,550 km) long, and longest river in Asia; also called Chang Jiang [Mandarin, = long river]. It rises as the Jinsha in SW China, forms the Chang R. proper at Yibin, and continues generally east c.1,500 mi (2,410 km) through rich agricultural and industrial regions to enter the EAST CHINA SEA in a vast delta near Shanghai. The river is China's chief commercial artery and is navigable by ocean vessels c.600 mi (970 km), to Wuhan. The Gezhouba Dam was built near Yichang to regulate seasonally fluctuating water levels and harness the river's hydroelectric potential, and in 1993 preliminary construction began upriver on the controversial Three Gorges project, potentially the largest hydroelectric dam in the world.

Changchun [chäng'-cho͞on], city (1990 est. pop. 2,110,000), capital of Jilin prov., China, on the railroad between HARBIN and DALIAN. The former capital of the Japanese puppet state of Manchukuo (1932–45), Changchun is a major industrial city and the center of China's vehicular industry. It also produces tires, drugs, motors, and textiles. The city is a major educational and cultural center of NE China.

change ringing, a form of bell-ringing that developed during the 17th cent. in England simultaneously with the development of carillon playing in the Low Countries. A group of ringers, each ringer controlling the rope pull of one bell, use a peal (set) of 5 to 12 bells tuned to the diatonic scale; the bells are rung full circle in various predetermined orders, but without repeating any order. The result is a sound that is not melodious, but complex and compelling.

Chang Jiang: see CHANG.

Changkiakow: see ZHANGJIAKOU.

Changsha, city (1990 est. pop. 1,330,000), capital of Hunan prov., S China, on the Xiang R. Changsha is an agricultural distribution and market center producing diverse manufactures. Founded in the 3d cent. B.C., it has long been noted as a literary and educational center. It was the capital (10th cent.) of the Chu kingdom and became a treaty port in the early 1900s. MAO ZEDONG spent his early years in and around the city.

Channel Islands, archipelago (1992 est. pop. 143,000), 75 sq mi (194 sq km), 10 mi (16 km) off the coast of France in the English Channel. The principal islands are Jersey, Guernsey, Alderney, and Sark; they are dependencies of the British crown. Agriculture, dairying, and tourism are the mainstays of the economy. English is spoken, but French is the official language of Jersey. The natives speak a Norman patois and maintain Norman customs. The islands became possessions of the duke of Normandy in the 10th cent. and were joined to the English crown at the NORMAN CONQUEST. They were occupied by the Germans during WORLD WAR II.

Channel Islands National Park: see NATIONAL PARKS (table).

Channing, William Ellery, 1780–1842, American minister and author; b. Newport, R.I. A great preacher, called "the apostle of Unitarianism," he advocated tolerance in religion. His writings on slavery, war, labor problems, and education were extremely progressive and influenced many American authors, including EMERSON and other exponents of TRANSCENDENTALISM, HOLMES, and BRYANT. His works (6 vol., 1841–43) passed through many editions.

chansons de geste [Fr., = songs of deeds], a group of epic poems of medieval France written from the 11th through the 13th cent. The oldest extant chanson, and also the best and most famous, is the *Chanson de Roland* [song of Roland], composed c.1098–1100.

chant, general name for one-voiced, unaccompanied liturgical music, usually referring to melodies of the Orthodox, Roman Catholic, and Anglican branches of Christianity. The texts of Anglican chant are from the BOOK OF COMMON PRAYER, and its melodies, unlike the Roman Catholic PLAINSONG, are harmonized.

chantey or **shanty,** work song with marked rhythm, particularly one sung by sailors at work, but also by shore gangs or lumbermen. It often has solo stanzas sung by a leader, alternating with a chorus by the entire group.

Chanukah: see Hanukkah under JEWISH HOLIDAYS.

Chao Phraya [chou präyä'], **Mae Nam Chao Phraya,** or **Menam Chao Phraya,** chief river of Thailand, formed by the confluence of the Nan and Ping rivers at Nakhon Sawan. It flows generally south c.140 mi (230 km) past the capital city of Bangkok to a large delta on the Gulf of Thailand. Its valley is the country's main rice-producing region.

Chaos, in Greek mythology, the vacant, unfathomable space from which everything arose. In the OLYMPIAN myth GAEA sprang from Chaos and became the mother of all things.

chaos, in science, field of study devoted to processes that exhibit complex, apparently random behavior, such as cloud formation or fluctuations of biological populations. Attempts to predict the behavior of these systems led to the development of an interdisciplinary science, NONLINEAR DYNAMICS.

chaparral, type of plant community in which shrubs are dominant, occurring usually in areas drier than forests and wetter than deserts. The species of shrub vary in different areas. The chaparral in Colorado, E Utah, and N New Mexico is mostly deciduous, while that of S California, Nevada, and Arizona is primarily evergreen. Chaparral is well exemplified in the W and SW U.S., but similar growth is found in many other parts of the world.

Chaplin, Charlie (Sir Charles Spencer Chaplin), 1889–1977, English film actor and director. A comic genius, he became famous as the wistful Little Tramp. His films include *The Kid* (1920), *The Gold Rush* (1924), *City Lights* (1931), *The Great Dictator* (1940), and *Limelight* (1952).

Chapman, George, 1559?–1634, English dramatist, translator, and poet. A classical scholar, he translated HOMER'S *Iliad* (1612) and *Odyssey* (1614–15). His works include the tragedy *Bussy d'Ambois* (1607) and the comedy *Eastward Ho!* (1605).

Chapman, John, 1774–1845, American pioneer popularly known as Johnny Appleseed; b. Massachusetts. Raggedly dressed, he wandered for 40 years through Ohio, Indiana, and W Pennsylvania, sowing apple seeds. Chapman inspired many legends.

Chapultepec [chäpo͞ol"tāpĕk'], fortified hill, S of Mexico City. A traditional home of Spanish viceroys and Mexican rulers, it was the site of a brave defense to the death by Mexican cadets (the "boy heroes") when it was stormed and taken (1847) by U.S. forces

Charlie Chaplin

cduring the MEXICAN WAR. The castle is maintained as a historical museum.

Char, René, 1907–88, French poet. His verse and aphorisms reflect his Provençal origins and his participation in the French resistance. Marked by extreme stylistic economy, they seek to endow language with an authenticity lost in everyday use. His *Selected Poems* was published in 1982.

char: see SALMON.

charcoal, nonvolatile residue obtained when organic matter, usually wood, is heated in the absence of air. Largely pure CARBON, charcoal yields more heat per volume than wood. Charcoal obtained from bones is called bone black or animal charcoal. Finely divided charcoal, with its porous structure, efficiently filters the adsorption of gases and of solids from solution. In activated charcoal, this property is increased by heat or chemical processing. Charcoal is used in sugar refining and in water and air purification.

Charcot, Jean Martin [shärkō'], 1825–93, French neurologist. He developed at the Salpêtrière, Paris, the greatest clinic of his time for diseases of the nervous system. His insight into the nature of hysteria was credited by Sigmund Freud, his pupil, as having contributed to early psychoanalytic formulations on the subject.

Chardin, Jean-Baptiste-Siméon [shärdăN'], 1699–1779, French painter. He favored simple still lifes and unsentimental domestic interiors. His muted tones and ability to evoke textures are seen in *Benediction* and *Return from Market* (both: Louvre) and *Blowing Bubbles* and *Mme Chardin* (both: Metropolitan Mus.). His unusual abstract compositions had great influence.

charge, in ELECTRICITY, property of matter that gives rise to all electrical phenomena. The basic unit of charge, usually denoted by e, is that on the PROTON or ELECTRON; that on the proton is designated as positive ($+e$) and that on the electron is designated as negative ($-e$). All other charged ELEMENTARY PARTICLES have charges equal to $+e$, $-e$, or some whole number times one of these, with the exception of the QUARK, a particle whose charge is $\frac{1}{3}e$ or $\frac{2}{3}e$. Every charged particle is surrounded by an electric FIELD of force such that it attracts any charge of opposite sign brought near it and repels any charge of like sign. The magnitude of this force is described by COULOMB'S LAW. This force is much stronger than the gravitational force between two particles and is responsible for holding protons and electrons together in ATOMS and in chemical bonds. Any physical system containing equal numbers of positive and negative charges is neutral. Charge is a conserved quantity; the net electric charge in a closed physical system is constant. Although charge is conserved, it can be transferred from one body to another. Electric current is the flow of charge through a conductor (see CONDUCTION).

charismatics, neo-Pentecostal Christians whose worship emphasizes the gifts of the Spirit (charismata) listed by St. Paul in Corinthians, especially healing and speaking in tongues (glossolalia). Contemporary charismatics are distinguished from other Pentecostals by their origins in non-Pentecostal (especially mainline Protestant and Roman Catholic) churches during the "charismatic renewal" movements of the 1960s.

Charlemagne (Charles the Great) or **Charles I** [shär'ləmān], 742?–814, emperor of the West (800–814), Carolingian king of the Franks (768–814). The son of PEPIN THE SHORT, he consolidated his rule in his own kingdom, invaded Italy in support of the pope, and in 774 was crowned king of the Lombards. He took NE Spain from the MOORS (778) and annexed Bavaria (788). After a long struggle (772–804) he subjugated and Christianized the Saxons. In 800 he restored LEO III to the papacy and was crowned emperor by him on Christmas Day, thus laying the basis for the HOLY ROMAN EMPIRE and finalizing the split between the Byzantine and Roman empires. Charlemagne ruled through a highly efficient administrative system. He codified the law in his various dominions, and his court at AACHEN was the center for an intellectual and artistic renaissance. The end of his reign was troubled by raids by the NORSEMEN. His son, LOUIS I, was named co-emperor in 813 and succeeded on his father's death. Charlemagne's legend soon enhanced and distorted his actual achievements, and he became the central figure of a medieval romance cycle.

Charles, emperors (see HOLY ROMAN EMPIRE). **Charles II** or **Charles the Bald,** 823–77, emperor of the West (875–77) and king of the West Franks (843–77), was the son of Emperor LOUIS I by a second marriage. Louis's attempts to create a kingdom for Charles were responsible for the almost constant warfare with Charles's elder brothers, LOTHAIR I and LOUIS THE GERMAN. In 843 Charles received what is roughly modern France, and in 870 he divided LOTHARINGIA with Louis. Charles became emperor upon the death of his nephew LOUIS II. His brief reign saw the rise of the power of the nobles and serious threats by the NORSEMEN. **Charles III** or **Charles the Fat,** 839–88, emperor of the West (881–87), king of the East Franks, or Germany (882–87), and king of the West Franks, or France (884–87), was the son of Louis the German. He inherited Swabia (876) and was crowned king of Italy (881). When he became king of France, he briefly reunited the empire of Charlemagne. A weak ruler, he was deposed in 887 after he failed to stop the inroads of the Norsemen. **Charles IV,** 1316–78, Holy Roman emperor (1355–78), succeeded his father, John of Luxembourg, as king of BOHEMIA (1346) and was elected antiking to Emperor Louis IV, after whose death he made his claim. As emperor he promulgated the Golden Bull, which strengthened the German ELECTORS at the expense of the emperor. He founded Charles Univ. at PRAGUE. **Charles V,** 1500–58, Holy Roman emperor (1519–58) and, as Charles I, king of Spain (1516–56), was the son of PHILIP I and JOANNA of Castile, and grandson of Emperor MAXIMILIAN I and MARY OF BURGUNDY. Charles was the greatest of all HAPSBURG emperors. He inherited a vast empire: the Spanish kingdoms, Spanish America, Naples, Sicily, the Low Countries, and the hereditary Austrian lands. The chief problems he faced were the Protestant REFORMATION in Germany; the dynastic conflict with FRANCIS I of France, particularly for supremacy in Italy; and the Ottoman Turks, then at the height of their power. He also had difficulties with his Spanish subjects, who at first regarded him as a foreigner. Initially successful against the Protestant princes in Germany, he eventually was forced to compromise with them and to accept (1555) the Peace of Augsburg. He was more successful in promoting the Catholic REFORMATION. The imperialist struggle with France was a Pyrrhic victory for Spain. His efforts to halt the advance of the Ottomans under SULAYMAN I resulted in at best a standoff. As king of Spain, he was triumphant. The conquest of Mexico and Peru represented the high point of the Spanish empire. In 1556 Charles abdicated all his titles and retired to a monastery. His son PHILIP II received Spain, America, Naples, and the Netherlands; and his brother became emperor as FERDINAND I. **Charles VI,** 1685–1740, Holy Roman emperor (1711–40) and. as Charles III, king of Hungary (1712–40), was, before his accession, involved in both the War of the SPANISH SUCCESSION and the War of Polish Succession (1333–35). The PRAGMATIC SANCTION, whereby he settled his Hapsburg lands on his daughter MARIA THERESA, was challenged after his death. **Charles VII,** 1699–1745, Holy Roman emperor (1742–45) and, as Charles Albert, elector of BAVARIA (1726–45), refused to recognize the Pragmatic Sanction, and joined the coalition against Maria Theresa in the War of the AUSTRIAN SUCCESSION. He was elected emperor, but lost his own Bavaria to Austrian occupation.

Charles I, 1887–1922, last emperor of Austria and, as Charles IV, king of Hungary (1916–18). After his accession during WORLD WAR I, he put out peace feelers, causing friction between Germany and Austria. After Austria's defeat he was unable to save the AUSTRO-HUNGARIAN MONARCHY, and he abdicated (Nov. 1918). In 1921 he tried twice to regain the Hungarian throne, without success.

Charles, kings of England, Scotland, and Ireland, of the STUART house. **Charles I,** 1600–49 (r.1625–49), was the son and successor of JAMES I. Upon his accession, he offended his Protestant subjects by marrying HENRIETTA MARIA, a Catholic French princess. Also, the foreign ventures of his favorite, the duke of BUCKINGHAM, were unsuccessful and expensive. His reign soon became the bitter struggle between king and Parliament for supremacy that resulted in the ENGLISH CIVIL WAR. Charles supported the Anglican bishops under LAUD. Parliament, largely Puritan, controlled money grants and developed the tactic of withholding money until its grievances were redressed. Charles dismissed Parliament in 1625 and 1626, but called it again in 1628 and signed the PETITION OF RIGHT in return for a subsidy. After 1629 he ruled without Parliament. Civil and religious liberties reached a low point, and large emigrations to America took place. A crisis was reached when Charles's attempt to force episcopacy upon Scotland resulted in the BISHOPS' WARS. Eventually the Long Parliament (1640) was called. Led by John Hampton, PYM, and VANE, it secured itself against dissolution and effected the death of the earl of STRAFFORD, the abolition of STAR CHAMBER courts, and the end of arbitrary taxation. Fear of the king and of Catholics mounted, and civil war broke out. Defeated at Marston Moor (1644) and Naseby (1645), Charles surrendered to the Scottish army (1646) and finally fell into the hands of the English. He was tried by a high court controlled by his enemies, convicted of treason, and beheaded. Often stupid and obstinate, Charles brought about his own downfall as much by his weakness of character as by his religious and political beliefs. His son, **Charles II,** 1630–85 (r.1660–85), fled to France in 1646. On his father's death, he was proclaimed king of Scotland and, after accepting the terms of the COVENANTERS, was crowned there in 1651. He then marched into England but was defeated by Oliver CROMWELL and escaped to France. In 1660 he issued the conciliatory Declaration of Breda. Later that year, Gen. MONCK engineered Charles's RESTORATION to the throne. He made the earl of CLARENDON his chief minister. Episcopacy was restored and nonconformity weakened by the CLARENDON CODE, although the king favored toleration. The great London plague (1665) and fire (1666) took place during the second DUTCH WAR (1664–67). In 1667 the CABAL ministry replaced Clarendon. As a result of a secret treaty with LOUIS XIV of France, Charles entered the third Dutch War in 1672. It was unpopular, and he was forced to approve the TEST ACT (1673) and make peace (1674). His French alliance was broken by the marriage of his niece Mary to William of Orange. He intervened in the Titus OATES affair to protect the queen, CATHERINE OF BRAGANZA. In 1681 he dissolved Parliament to block passage of the Exclusion act that prevented his brother, the duke of York (later JAMES II), from succeeding him, and ruled absolutely thereafter. Although he fathered illegitimate children by several mistresses (e.g., Nell GWYN), he had no legitimate children and was succeeded by James II. His reign, the brilliant Restoration period, was marked by an increase in the power of Parliament, the rise of political parties, and advances in colonization and trade.

Charles, kings of France. **Charles I:** see CHARLEMAGNE. **Charles II** and **Charles III** (the Fat): see CHARLES II and CHARLES III, emperors of the West. **Charles III** (the Simple), 879–929 (r.893–923), was the son of LOUIS II and joint king with Eudes, count of Paris, until 898. He ceded (911) part of Normandy to the Norse leader Rollo and was defeated and imprisoned (923) by nobles who made Raoul of Burgundy king. **Charles IV** (the Fair), 1294–1328 (r.1322–28), succeeded his brother PHILIP V and was the last king of the CAPETIAN dynasty. **Charles V** (the Wise), 1338–80 (r.1364–80), the son of JOHN II, was regent during John's captivity (1356–60, 1364) in England. As regent Charles dealt with the JACQUERIE and the reformist movement of Étienne Marcel. During his reign his general Bertrand DU GUESCLIN nearly drove the English out of France. With his ministers, Charles strengthened royal power, founded a standing army, reformed taxation, and patronized the arts. His son **Charles VI** (the Mad or the Well Beloved), 1368–1422 (r.1380–

1422), was intermittently insane after 1392. France was ruled and plundered by his uncle PHILIP THE BOLD and by his brother Louis d'Orléans. Their rivalry led to a civil war that laid France open to an invasion (1415) by HENRY V of England. By the Treaty of Troyes (1420) Charles named Henry his successor. His disinherited son **Charles VII** (the Victorious or the Well Served), 1403–61 (r.1422–61), repudiated the treaty. Still called the DAUPHIN, he ruled indolently over what parts of France remained to him S of the Loire, but in 1429 JOAN OF ARC spurred him to action and had him crowned king at Rheims. In 1435 he won the alliance of Burgundy against England, and in 1453 he ended the HUNDRED YEARS WAR by expelling the English from most of France. He reorganized the army and, with the help of Jacques CŒUR, restored the finances. The PRAGMATIC SANCTION of Bourges (1438) and the suppression of the Praguerie (1440), a revolt of the nobility, strengthened royal authority. Charles's last years were troubled by the intrigues of his son, the future LOUIS XI. **Charles VIII,** 1470–98 (r.1483–98), was the son of Louis XI. His sister Anne de Beaujeu was regent during his minority and arranged his marriage (1491) to ANNE OF BRITTANY. In 1495 Charles began the ITALIAN WARS with the short-lived conquest of Naples. **Charles IX,** 1550–74 (r.1560–74), was at first under the regency of his mother, CATHERINE DE' MEDICI. Later he chose Gaspard de COLIGNY as chief adviser, but was persuaded to take part in the massacre of SAINT BARTHOLOMEW'S DAY (1572). **Charles X,** 1757–1836 (r.1824–30), known as the comte d'Artois before he succeeded his brother, LOUIS XVIII, in 1824, led the powerful ultraroyalist group before his accession and as sovereign had reactionaries as premiers. Liberal and capitalist forces joined to bring about the JULY REVOLUTION of 1830. Charles abdicated and died in exile.

Charles, kings of Hungary. **Charles I,** 1288–1342 (r.1308–42), was the grandson of CHARLES II of Naples and son-in-law of Stephen V of Hungary. In 1308 he was elected king by the Hungarian diet and thus founded the Angevin dynasty in Hungary. He reorganized the army on a feudal basis and increased the privileges of the cities. His eldest son became King Louis I of Poland. **Charles II:** see CHARLES III, king of Naples. **Charles III**: see CHARLES VI, Holy Roman emperor. **Charles IV:** see CHARLES I, emperor of Austria.

Charles, rulers of Naples. **Charles I** (Charles of Anjou), 1227–85, king of Naples and Sicily (1266–85), was a brother of LOUIS IX of France. Charles championed the papal cause against MANFRED in Naples and Sicily, and as a reward the pope crowned him (1266) king. He founded the Angevin dynasty in Naples. Heavy taxes to support his wars against the Byzantine Empire led to a rebellion (1282) in Sicily (see SICILIAN VESPERS). The ensuing war with PETER III of Aragón, who was chosen king by the rebels, continued into the reign of his son, **Charles II** (the Lame), 1248–1309, king of Naples (1285–1309). Charles II's great-grandson, **Charles III** (Charles of Durazzo), 1345–86, king of Naples (1381–86), was adopted by Joanna I of Naples, who later repudiated him in favor of Louis of Anjou (later Louis I of Naples). Charles deposed Joanna, was crowned king (1381), and repulsed Louis's attacks. In 1385 Charles was elected king of Hungary over Holy Roman emperor SIGISMUND, but he was assassinated soon afterward.

Charles II (the Bad), 1332–87, king of Navarre (1349–87). He carried on a long feud with his father-in-law, JOHN II of France, and allied himself with EDWARD III of England. Charles helped to suppress the JACQUERIE (1358) and was chosen by Étienne Marcel to defend Paris against the DAUPHIN (later King CHARLES V), but he betrayed this trust.

Charles, kings of Spain. **Charles I:** see CHARLES V, Holy Roman emperor. **Charles II,** 1661–1700, king of Spain, Naples, and Sicily (1665–1700), was a mentally retarded cripple whose mother, Mariana of Austria, ruled as regent. During his reign Spain continued to lose influence abroad and to suffer a decline in its economy and intellectual life. His choice of an heir provoked the War of the SPANISH SUCCESSION. **Charles III,** 1716–88, king of Spain (1759–88) and of Naples and Sicily (1735–59), was Spain's greatest BOURBON king. He conquered and ruled NAPLES and SICILY before becoming king of Spain. By involving Spain in the SEVEN YEARS WAR on the side of the defeated French, he lost Florida to England. But he fought on the colonists' side in the AMERICAN REVOLUTION and thereby regained (1783) Florida. His reign was noteworthy for Spain's prosperity and for his expulsion of the JESUITS. **Charles IV,** 1748–1819 (r.1788–1808), was an ineffective ruler who allowed his chief minister, GODOY, to pursue disastrous policies. Spain suffered major naval defeats by England at Cape Saint Vincent (1797) and TRAFALGAR (1805), and it suffered reverses (1808) in the PENINSULAR WAR, which forced his abdication.

Charles, kings of Sweden. **Charles IX,** 1550–1611 (r.1604–11), was the youngest son of GUSTAVUS I. As regent after the death of his brother, John III, he made Lutheranism the state religion. By his efforts the Catholic heir, SIGISMUND III of Poland, was deposed (1599). Charles became king after Sigismund's brother, John, renounced the Swedish crown. In 1600 he began the Polish-Swedish wars that ended only in 1660. His son, GUSTAVUS II, succeeded him. **Charles X,** 1622–60 (r.1654–60), was the nephew of Gustavus II. He succeeded on the abdication of his cousin, CHRISTINA. He invaded Poland (1655) but soon suffered reverses. After Denmark and Russia entered the war, Charles forced the Danes (1658) to cede territory that extended Sweden's southern boundaries to the sea. His son **Charles XI,** 1655–97 (r.1660–97), succeeded him. A council of regency ruled until he was 17. In the third of the DUTCH WARS he was defeated by FREDERICK WILLIAM of Brandenburg (1675). Under Charles, royal power was increased at the nobles' expense. **Charles XII,** 1682–1718 (r.1687–1718), was the son of Charles XI. Facing (1699) a coalition of Russia, Poland, and Denmark in the NORTHERN WAR, he forced Denmark to make peace (1700); invaded Poland and had STANISLAUS I enthroned (1704); and, with MAZEPA, invaded Russia, where his army was crushingly defeated (1708). He fled to Turkey and persuaded AHMED III to declare war on Russia (1710). After Turkey and Russia made peace (1711), Charles refused to leave Turkey and was imprisoned. At Swedish-occupied Stralsund (1714–15) he fought the Prussians and Danes. When Stralsund fell, he fled to Sweden and invaded (1716) Norway, where he was killed in battle. His sister, Ulrica Leonora, succeeded him under a new constitution that strengthened the nobles and clergy. **Charles XIII,** 1748–1818, was king of Sweden (1809–18) and Norway (1814–18). He was regent for his nephew, GUSTAVUS IV, after the assassination (1792) of his brother GUSTAVUS III. Called to the throne at the forced abdication of his nephew, Charles accepted a new constitution limiting royal power, signed treaties with Denmark and France, and ceded Finland to Russia. **Charles XIV** (Charles John; Jean Baptiste Jules Bernadotte), 1763–1844, king of Sweden and Norway (r.1818–44), was a French Revolutionary general. He served under Napoleon in Italy (1796–97), was French ambassador at Vienna (1798), and was minister of war (1799). In 1810 the aging and childless Charles XIII of Sweden adopted him, and he was elected crown prince by the Riksdag. He allied Sweden with England and Russia against NAPOLEON I and took part in his defeat at Leipzig (1813). In 1814 he forced Denmark to cede Norway, which was united with Sweden under a single king. He succeeded to the throne in 1818, having held the reins of government since 1810. His son, Oscar I, succeeded him. **Charles XV,** 1826–72 (r.1859–72), was the son of Oscar I. A liberal ruler, he agreed to such reforms as a bicameral parliament. He was succeeded by his brother, Oscar II. **Charles XVI Gustavus** (Carl Gustaf), 1946– (r.1973–), is the grandson and successor of GUSTAVUS VI and the son of Prince Gustaf Adolf of Sweden. A new Swedish constitution, passed shortly before his grandfather's death and effective in 1975, made the king a ceremonial figurehead.

Charles, 1948–, prince of Wales, eldest son of ELIZABETH II of Great Britain and heir apparent to the British throne. He was created prince of Wales in 1958. Prince Charles has become an outspoken critic of modern architecture, and in 1992 he established an architectural institute to promote more traditional approaches to building. In 1981 he married Lady Diana Spencer (see DIANA, princess of Wales); they separated in 1992. They have two sons, William and Henry.

Charles, 1771–1847, archduke of Austria, brother of Holy Roman Emperor FRANCIS II. Despite his epilepsy, he was an able Austrian commander. In 1809 he defeated NAPOLEON I at Aspern (May) but was beaten at Wagram (July).

Charles, Jacques Alexandre César [shärl], 1746–1823, French physicist. He discovered (1787) Charles's, or Gay-Lussac's, law (see GAS LAWS); invented a thermometric hydrometer; and was the first to use hydrogen gas in balloons.

Charles, Ray (Ray Charles Robinson), 1930–, African-American musician and composer; b. Albany, Ga. Blinded at age seven, he rose to fame in the 1950s singing rhythm-and-blues songs to the accompaniment of his piano and orchestra. His work, rooted in GOSPEL MUSIC, influences, and is influenced by, JAZZ.

Ray Charles

Charles Edward Stuart: see under STUART, JAMES FRANCIS EDWARD.

Charles Martel, 688?–741, Frankish ruler, illegitimate son of PEPIN of Heristal and grandfather of CHARLEMAGNE. Although never king, he ruled as mayor of the palace (714–41). He united all MEROVINGIAN kingdoms under his rule and halted the European invasion of the MOORS. His sons, PEPIN the Short and Carloman, divided the Frankish lands at his death.

Charles's law: see GAS LAWS.

Charles the Bald, French king: see Charles II under CHARLES, emperors.

Charles the Bold, 1433–77, duke of BURGUNDY (1467–77), son of PHILIP THE GOOD. He opposed the growing power of LOUIS XI of France and allied himself with England. Master of the Low Countries, Charles dreamed of reestablishing the kingdom of LOTHARINGIA, to which end he tried to acquire Alsace and Lorraine. The Swiss, roused by his actions, routed him at Grandson and Morat (1476) and in 1477 defeated and killed Charles at Nancy. Burgundy then disintegrated.

Charles the Fat, French king: see Charles III under CHARLES, emperors.

Charles the Great, Frankish king, emperor of the West: see CHARLEMAGNE.

Charleston. **1** City (1990 pop. 80,414), seat of Charleston co., SE S.C.; founded 1680, inc. 1783. On a peninsula between the Ashley and Cooper rivers, it is a major regional port. U.S. naval operations provide much employment; chemicals, steel, and other products are manufactured. The oldest city in the state, it was the scene of the first incident of the CIVIL WAR, the firing on FORT SUMTER (Apr. 12, 1861); it fell to Gen. SHERMAN's army in 1865. A major tourist center and the site of the Spoleto Festival U.S.A. Charleston is famous for its picturesque streets, houses, and other 18th-cent. monuments, reminders of its early importance as a prosperous, cosmopolitan port. **2** City (1990 pop. 57,287), state capital and seat of Kanawha co., W central W.Va., on the Kanawha R. where it meets the Elk R.; inc. 1794. The largest city in the state, it is a major chemical, glass, and metal producer. The region provides salt, coal, natural gas, clay, sand, timber, and oil for the city's manufactures. The city, which grew around Fort Lee (1788), was the home (1788–95) of Daniel BOONE. It was state capital from 1870–75 and after 1885.

Charlotte, city (1990 pop. 395,934; met. area 1,162,093), seat of Mecklenburg co., S N.C.; inc. 1768. It is the largest city in North Carolina, the commercial and industrial center of the Piedmont region, a major U.S. banking center, and a distribution hub for the Carolina textile manufacturing belt, which utilizes Catawba R. hydroelectric power. An early center of rebellion against British rule, it was the site of the signing of the MECKLENBURG DECLARATION OF INDEPENDENCE (May 1775).

Charlotte Amalie, city (1990 pop. 12,331), on St. Thomas, capital of the U.S. VIRGIN ISLANDS.

Charlottetown, city (1991 pop. 15,396), capital, chief port, and only city of Prince Edward Island, E Canada. Food processing, fishing, and tourism are major industries. Charlottetown was laid out by the British in 1768 and named for George III's queen. It was noted in the mid-1800s for the sailing ships built there. The Charlottetown Conference (1864) was the first step toward Canadian confederation. The Charlottetown Festival, held every summer in the Confederation of the Arts Centre (built 1960s), is a major cultural event.

Charon, in astronomy, natural satellite of PLUTO.

Chartism, worker's political reform movement in Great Britain, 1838–48. It derived its name from the People's Charter, drafted by the London Working Men's Association, which called for such reforms as universal male suffrage.

Chartres, city (1982 pop. 37,119), capital of Eure-et-Loir dept., NW France. The probable site of DRUIDS' assemblies, it became a royal possession (1286) and a duchy (1528). Its magnificent Gothic cathedral (12th–13th cent.) is renowned for its spires and stained-glass windows; there the Second Crusade was preached (1146) and Henry IV crowned (1594).

Charybdis: see SCYLLA AND CHARYBDIS.

Chase, Salmon Portland, 1808–73, 6th chief justice of the U.S. SUPREME COURT (1864–73); b. Cornish, N.H.; grad. Dartmouth College (1826). A zealous abolitionist, he served as U.S. senator (1849–55; 1861) and as governor of Ohio (1855–59). As chief justice he presided over the impeachment trial of Pres. Andrew JOHNSON with scrupulous fairness. His greatest achievement, however, was as secretary of the treasury (1861–64), when he created a national bank system.

Chase, William Merritt, 1849–1916, American painter; b. Williamsburg, Ind. He is known for his portraits and still lifes in oil, e.g., *Carmencita* and *Lady in Black* (Metropolitan Mus.). Chase was also an important art teacher.

château, royal or seignorial residence and stronghold of medieval France, counterpart of the English CASTLE. The fortified château culminated in the late 15th cent., e.g., Pierrefonds, near Compiègne. Sixteenth-cent. châteaux, with gardens and outbuildings, usually had a moat, but were little fortified. Notable châteaux are those of the Loire, Indre, and Cher valleys, e.g., Chambord, Amboise, Chenonceaux.

Chateaubriand, François René, vicomte de [shätōbrēäN'], 1768–1848, French writer. A founder of ROMANTICISM in French literature, he visited the U.S. in 1791 and until 1800 was an émigré in England. A Royalist, he was minister of foreign affairs (1823–24). He made his mark with *The Genius of Christianity* (1802) and two tragic love stories about Native Americans, *Atala* (1801) and *René* (1805), exemplifying the melancholy, poetic style that became typical of romantic fiction. He spent his final years with the celebrated beauty and social figure Mme Récamier, composing his *Memoirs from beyond the Tomb* (1849–50).

Chattanooga, city (1990 pop. 152,466), seat of Hamilton co., E Tenn., on both sides of the Tennessee R. near the Ga. line; inc. 1839. From a trading post (est. 1810) the port city grew into a major shipping point for salt and cotton. It was of great strategic importance in the CIVIL WAR (see CHATTANOOGA CAMPAIGN). Textile, chemical, and metal industries are important. The city is surrounded by mountains, e.g., Lookout Mt., and is a tourist center, with the world's largest freshwater aquarium.

Chattanooga campaign, Aug.–Nov. 1863, in the U.S. CIVIL WAR. Union Gen. William Rosecrans maneuvered (Aug.–Sept.) Confederate Gen. Braxton BRAGG out of strategic Chattanooga, Tenn., but Bragg routed the Union right wing at the Battle of Chickamauga (Sept. 19–20). The Union left, under Gen. George H. THOMAS, withdrew to Chattanooga, which Bragg besieged from Missionary Ridge. Rosecrans, although reinforced by Gen. Joseph HOOKER, needed help, and Gen. U.S. GRANT took command. Hooker drove the Confederates from Lookout Mt. in the Battle above the Clouds (Nov. 24). Grant attacked and carried Missionary Ridge (Nov. 25), and Bragg was forced to retreat to Georgia.

Chatterjee, Bankim Chandra, 1838–94, Indian nationalist writer. His historical novels, written in Bengali, include *Anandamath* (1882), from which India's national anthem was derived, and *Krishna Kanta's Will* (tr. 1895).

Chatterton, Thomas, 1752–70, English poet. At age 12 he was composing the "Rowley poems" and claiming they were copies of 15th-cent. manuscripts. He came to London, failed to get his work published, and killed himself at 17. An original genius as well as an adept imitator, he used 15th-cent. language but a modern approach. He was a hero to the Romantics.

Chaucer, Geoffrey, c.1340–1400, English poet. The facts of Chaucer's life are fragmentary. A London vintner's son, he served as a court page, in the army, and on frequent diplomatic missions, then held various official positions in London. His literary activity falls into three periods. In the first (to 1370), he worked largely from French models, including the *Roman de la rose,* which he partially translated. His major work from this time is the allegorical *Book of the Duchess* (1369). In the second period (to c.1387) he used Italian models, primarily DANTE and BOCCACCIO. His chief works in these years include the *House of Fame,* recounting the adventures of AENEAS after the fall of Troy; *The Parliament of Fowls,* on the mating of birds on St. Valentine's Day, thought to celebrate the betrothal of RICHARD II to Anne of Bohemia; a prose translation of BOETHIUS; the unfinished *Legend of Good Women,* on classical heroines, in which he introduced the rhymed heroic couplet; and *Troilus and Criseyde,* based on Boccaccio, one of the great love poems in English, in which he perfected the seven-line stanza later called rhyme royal. Chaucer's final period was devoted to work on his masterpiece, *The Canterbury Tales.* This unfinished work, about 17,000 lines, is one of the major poems of world literature. In it a group of pilgrims traveling to the shrine of St. Thomas à Becket decide to pass the time by telling stories. The tales include a variety of medieval genres, from the humorous fabliau to the serious homily, and vividly depict medieval attitudes toward love, marriage, and religion. Chaucer's brilliantly realized characters—the earthy Wife of Bath, the gentle Knight, the evil Summoner—are intensely alive. Chaucer's storytelling and poetic mastery were overlooked for centuries because of changes in the language after 1400, but in the 18th cent. he came to be regarded as one of the greatest English poets.

Chautauqua movement. A development in adult education similar to the LYCEUM movement, it was proposed in 1873 at the Methodist Episcopal camp meeting in Chautauqua, N.Y., by John Heyl Vincent and Lewis Miller. Eight-week summer programs offered members secular and religious instruction, and lectures by authors, explorers, musicians, and political leaders. Somewhere between revival meetings and country fairs in spirit, Chautauquas were attended by thousands each year. They were organized commercially in 1912 and persisted until c.1924.

Chavannes, Puvis de: see PUVIS DE CHAVANNES.

Chavez, Cesar Estrada, 1927–93, American agrarian labor leader; b. near Yuma, Ariz. A migrant worker, he began (1962) to organize wine-grape pickers in California. Using strikes, fasts, picketing, and marches, he won contracts from several major growers. He later launched nationwide boycotts against the table-grape and lettuce growers. In 1972 the United Farm Workers (UFW), with Chavez as president, became a member union of the AFL-CIO. A jurisdictional dispute with the TEAMSTERS was ended by a 1977 pact that defined the types of workers each union could organize.

Chavín de Huantar, archaeological site in NE Peru, probably the center of the Chavín culture (fl. c.700–c.200 B.C.), earliest civilization of the Andes. It is noted for advanced temples, painted sculptures, gold objects, and textiles.

Chavis, Benjamin Franklin, Jr. 1948–, African-American civil-rights leader; b. Oxford, N.C. A civil-rights activist from boyhood, he was wrongly jailed (1972–80) after leading a Wilmington, N.C., demonstration. Chavis was an official of the United Church of Christ before his appointment (1993) as director of the NATIONAL ASSOCIATION FOR THE ADVANCEMENT OF COLORED PEOPLE.

checkerberry: see WINTERGREEN.

checkers, game for two players, known in England as draughts. It is played on a square board composed of 64 small squares, alternately dark and light in color, with all play conducted on the dark squares. On each turn, players on opposite sides of the board may move one of their 12 pieces diagonally in a forward direction. Kings (pieces "crowned" by reaching the last rank of the board) may move either backward or forward diagonally. The object is to eliminate an opponent's pieces by "jumping" them (jumping over the squares that they occupy). The game has been played in Europe since the 16th cent., and a similar game is known to have been played in ancient times.

cheese, food known from ancient times, consisting of the curd of MILK separated from the whey. Although milk from various animals has been used for making cheese, today milk from cows, sheep, and goats is most common. In making cheese, CASEIN, the chief milk protein, is coagulated by enzyme action, by lactic acid, or by both. The many kinds of cheeses depend for their distinctive qualities on the kind and condition of the milk, the processes used in their making, and the method and extent of curing. There are two main kinds of cheeses: hard cheeses, which improve with age, and soft cheeses, made for immediate consumption. Hard cheeses include Cheddar (originally from England), Edam and Gouda (Holland), Emmental and Gruyère (Switzerland), and Parmesan and Provolone (Italy). Among the semisoft cheeses are Roquefort (France), American brick, and Muenster. Soft cheeses may be fresh (unripened), e.g., cream and cottage cheeses, or may be softened by microorganisms in a ripening process that develops flavor, e.g., Camembert, Brie, and Limburger. Cheese is a valuable source of protein, fat, insoluble minerals, and, when made from whole milk, vitamin A.

cheetah, CAT (*Acinonyx jubatus*) found in Africa, SW Asia, and India. The swiftest four-footed animal, it runs down its prey at speeds of over 60 mi (95 km) per hr, the only cat to hunt this way. Cheetahs have tawny coats with many round, black spots; the average adult weighs 100 lb (45 kg). Cheetahs are unique among cats in having nonretractile claws. Hunting has greatly reduced their numbers.

Cheever, John, 1912–82, American author; b. Quincy, Mass. A moralist whose works are often comic or surreal, he wrote about America's affluent suburbs, e.g., *The Wapshot Chronicle* (1957) and *Oh What A Paradise It Seems* (1982). Many of his stories are in *The Stories of John Cheever* (1978; Pulitzer), and selections from his journals were published posthumously in *The Journals of John Cheever* (1991).

Cheka, Russian acronym for the Extraordinary Commission for Combating Counterrevolution, Speculation, Sabotage, and Misuse of Authority, the Soviet state security service (including the secret police) established (1917) by the Bolsheviks. The Cheka was headed by Felix DZERZHINSKY. Lenin presided (1922) over its reorganization, renaming it the GPU (State Political Directorate). It became the OGPU (United State Political Directorate) in 1923 and the NKVD (People's Commissariat for Internal Affairs) in 1934. See also KGB; SECRET POLICE.

Chekhov, Anton Pavlovich [chĕ'khəv], 1860–1904, Russian writer and physician. The son of a grocer and grandson of a serf, he helped support his family, while he studied medicine, by writing humorous sketches. His reputation as a master of the short story was assured when in 1888 "The Steppe," a story in his third collection, won the Pushkin Prize. *The Island of Sakhalin* (1893–94) was a report on his visit to a penal colony in 1890. Thereafter he lived in Melikhovo, near Moscow, where he ran a free clinic for peasants, took part in famine and epidemic relief, and was a volunteer census-taker. His first play, *Ivanov* (1887), had little success, but *The Seagull* (1898), *Uncle Vanya* (1899), *The Three Sisters* (1901), and *The Cherry Orchard* (1904) were acclaimed when produced by the Moscow Art Theater. In 1901 Chekhov married the actress Olga Knipper, the interpreter of many of his characters. Three years later he died of tuberculosis. The style of his stories, novels, and plays, emphasizing internal drama, characterization, and mood rather than plot and focusing on the tragicomic aspects of banal events, had great influence.

chelicerate, member of a subphylum (Chelicerata) of ARTHROPODS comprising the HORSESHOE CRABS, ARACHNIDS, and SEA SPIDERS. Chelicerates are characterized by the absence of antennae and jaws and the presence of feeding structures (chelicera), which are modified pincerlike appendages used mainly for grasping and fragmenting food.

Chelyabinsk, city (1990 est. pop. 1,150,000), W Siberian Russia, in the southern foothills of the Urals and on the Mias R. A major industrial center, it processes ore and produces steel and farm machinery. Founded in 1736 as a Russian frontier outpost, it lies on the Trans-Siberian RR.

chemical pollutants: see POLLUTION; WASTE DISPOSAL.

chemical warfare, employment in warfare of toxic substances to damage or kill plants, animals, or human beings. POISON GAS was effectively used during WORLD WAR I, when chlorine gas and mustard gas inflicted heavy casualties on both sides. After the war the major powers continued to develop and stockpile chemical agents, but lethal types were not employed during World War II. Modern delivery systems—artillery shells, grenades, missiles, and aircraft spray systems—have increased the potential effectiveness of chemical weapons, and thousands of synthetic toxins and naturally occurring poisons have been tested for use in warfare since World War II. Besides potentially lethal chemicals that attack the skin, the blood, the nervous system, or the respiratory system, there are also nonlethal incapacitating agents that cause temporary physical disability or mental effects such as confusion, fright, or stupor. Such agents, e.g., tear gas, may be used in riot control as well as warfare. Various forms of HERBICIDES and defoliants were used during the VIETNAM WAR to destroy crops and clear away vegetation. In the early 1980s there were reports that a lethal agent, popularly called "yellow rain," was being used in Southeast Asia, but many of the reports were questioned or discredited. Iraq and Iran used chemical weapons during the IRAN-IRAQ WAR, and Iraq used them against its Kurdish minority and threatened to use them in the PERSIAN GULF WAR, but it is unclear whether their use was attempted or not. In 1993 more than 120 countries signed a treaty banning the production, stockpiling, and use of chemical weapons and establishing an independent organization to verify compliance with the treaty. See also BIOLOGICAL WARFARE.

chemistry, branch of science concerned with the properties, composition, and structure of substances and the changes they undergo when they combine or react under specified conditions. INORGANIC CHEMISTRY deals mainly with components of mineral origin. ORGANIC CHEMISTRY was first defined as the study of substances produced by living organisms; it is now defined as the study of the compounds of CARBON. PHYSICAL CHEMISTRY is concerned with the physical properties of materials; its subcategories are ELECTROCHEMISTRY; thermochemistry, the investigation of the changes in ENERGY and ENTROPY that occur during chemical reactions and phase transformations (see STATES OF MATTER); and chemical kinetics, which is concerned with the details of chemical reactions and of how equilibrium is reached between the products and reactants. Analytical chemistry is a collection of techniques that allows exact laboratory determination of the chemical composition of a given sample of material.

Chemnitz, city (1989 est. pop. 312,000), Saxony, SE Germany. Chartered in 1143, it has been a textile center since medieval times, and is now an industrial center with such manufactures as machine tools, chemicals, and vehicles. Notable buildings include a late-Gothic church. Heavily damaged in WORLD WAR II, the city has been rebuilt since 1945. It was named Karl-Marx-Stadt from 1953 to 1990.

chemosynthesis, process in which carbohydrates are manufactured from carbon dioxide and water using chemical nutrients as the energy source, rather than the sunlight used for energy in PHOTOSYNTHESIS. Most life on earth is fueled directly or indirectly by sunlight. There are, however, small ecosystems, such as those in the hot water found around hydrothermal vents on the ocean floor, that depend on bacteria whose life functions are fueled not by the sun but by simple inorganic chemicals, such as hydrogen sulfide, that seep up from the earth's crust.

chemotherapy, treatment of disease with chemicals or drugs; the term most often refers to treatment of CANCER. Traditional cancer chemotherapy poisons all body cells to some extent, but particularly targets rapidly dividing cells such as cancer cells. Its effect on other rapidly dividing cells (hair follicles, cells lining the stomach, and red blood cells) accounts for some of the common side effects. Current approaches use several drugs in combination, aimed at minimizing side effects while attacking the rapidly proliferating cells at vulnerable times. Chemotherapy is highly individualized, depending on the type of disease and its progression, the action of the agents used, and the side effects in the patient, and may be used alone or in combination with other cancer therapies, such as surgery. Knowledge from the field of molecular biology is being applied in experimental drugs that target cancer cells more specifically and inhibit their spread or "starve" them rather than poisoning them.

Cheney, Dick (Richard Bruce Cheney), 1941–, U.S. politician and government official; b. Lincoln, Nebr. A Republican, he held (1969–73, 1974–77) a series of White House posts in the Nixon and Ford administrations, eventually serving (1975–77) as Ford's de facto chief of staff. Elected to Congress from Wyoming in 1978, Cheney was a prominent conservative and became (1988) House Minority whip. He was (1989–93) secretary of defense under Pres. BUSH.

Chengchow: see ZHENGZHOU.

Chengdu or **Chengtu** [both: chŭng-do͞o], city (1990 est. pop. 2,810,000), capital of Sichuan prov., SW China, at the confluence of the Nan and Fu rivers. It is an important regional center for metallurgy, chemicals, machinery, and electronics. An ancient walled city, it was the capital of the Shu kingdom (3d cent. A.D.). The cultural hub of SW China, it is the site of Sichuan Univ. and a center of Sichuan opera.

Chénier, André [shānyā′], 1762–94, French poet; b. Constantinople. His pamphlets denouncing the excesses of the REIGN OF TERROR led to his execution. His poems, perhaps the greatest in 18th-cent. France, range from the lyrical, e.g., *La Jeune Captive* (1795) and *Élégies* (1819), to the satirical.

Chennault, Claire Lee, 1890–1958, U.S. general; b. Commerce, Tex. In 1941 he organized in China the American Volunteer Group (called the Flying Tigers). He then headed (1942–45) the U.S. air task force in China.

Cheops: see KHUFU.

Chernenko, Konstantin Ustinovich, 1911–85, Soviet political leader. A protégé of Leonid BREZHNEV, he rose through Communist party ranks in the 1950s, becoming a full member of the Central Committee (1971) and the Politburo (1974). When Yuri ANDROPOV died (1984), he was elected general secretary of the Communist party and chairman of the Presidium. His health was poor and he soon died.

Chernobyl, Ukr. *Chornobyl,* city, N Ukraine near the Belarus border, on the Pripyat R. Ten miles (16 km) to the north, in the town of Pripyat, is the Chernobyl nuclear power plant, site of the world's worst nuclear reactor accident (1986). The cooling system of the plant's No. 4 reactor failed during a test and the core overheated, resulting in an explosion and fire. Fallout contaminated wide areas of E Europe and Scandinavia, most heavily in Belarus and Ukraine. The USSR was criticized for keeping the accident secret until radioactivity was discovered in Sweden and then failing to disclose its extent. Pripyat, Chernobyl, and nearby towns were permanently evacuated as a result of the accident. Ukraine has estimated that as many as 8,000 people died as a result of the accident and its cleanup.

Chernomyrdin, Viktor Stepanovich, 1938–, Soviet and Russian government official. He held positions in the Soviet oil and gas industry and served (1985–89) as minister of the gas industry. In 1992 YELTSIN chose him as Russian prime minister in a compromise. Chernomyrdin, who opposed privatization and other economic reforms, gained increased power following the reformers' failure to win (1993) the Russian parliamentary elections.

Cherokee, once the outstanding Native American group in the SE U.S. (see NORTH AMERICA, INDIGENOUS PEOPLES OF). They spoke an Iroquoian language of the Hokan-Siouan stock (see NATIVE AMERICAN LANGUAGES). By the 16th cent. they had an advanced agricultural Eastern Woodlands culture. Soon after 1750 half the tribe died in a smallpox epidemic. In 1827 they established themselves as the Cherokee Nation, with a constitution providing for an elected, republican government. The syllabary devised by SEQUOYAH contributed to their progress. When gold was discovered on their lands, a fraudulent treaty obtained by whites bound the tribe to move West, and they were forcibly removed in 1838 to land in what is now Oklahoma. In the course of this "trail of tears," led by Chief John ROSS, thousands of Cherokees died. In Oklahoma they became the most important of the FIVE CIVILIZED TRIBES. With a 1990 population of 308,132, Cherokees constitute the largest U.S. tribe. Over 94,000 live in Oklahoma, and more than 5,000 live on a reservation in W North Carolina.

Cherokee, language belonging to the Iroquoian branch of the Hokan-Siouan linguistic family. See NATIVE AMERICAN LANGUAGES (table).

cherry, name for various trees and shrubs (genus *Prunus*) of the ROSE family, and for their fruits. Botanically, the small red-to-black fruits are drupes, or stone fruits, closely related to the PEACH, APRICOT, and PLUM. Hundreds of varieties of sweet (*P. avium*) and sour (*P. cerasus*) cherries, believed to be native to Asia Minor, are widely cultivated. Sour cherries are mostly self-fertile, and are hardier and more easily grown than sweet cherries, which must be cross-pollinated. The fruit is popular eaten raw, and in preserves, pies, ciders, and liqueurs. Species of **flowering cherry** are cultivated for their beautiful, usually double flowers; **cherry laurel** species are also cultivated as ornamentals, e.g., American cherry laurel, or mock orange (*P. caroliniana*). The wood of the wild black cherry (*P. serotina*), fine-grained and usually reddish in color, is prized for cabinetwork.

chert, cryptocrystalline variety of QUARTZ, commonly occurring in nodules. Flint—the dark variety of chert—was used by primitive peoples to make knives and spearheads, because, although it is very hard, it is easily shaped by flaking off the edges. It was long used with steel for lighting fires and later for setting off the powder in flintlock firearms.

Cherubini, Luigi [kārōōbē'nē], 1760–1842, Italian composer. He lived in Paris after 1788 and wrote operas of broad dramatic scope in the French tradition, e.g., *Médea* (1797) and *Les Deux Journées* (1800), and sacred music.

Chesapeake, city (1990 pop. 151,976), SE Va., created (1963) by merging the city of South Norfolk with all of Norfolk co. Its vast area includes residential suburbs of Norfolk, commercial farmland, and a portion of the Great Dismal Swamp. Industries include the manufacture of plywood and wood products, chemicals, fertilizers, and cement products.

Chesapeake, U.S. frigate. In June 1807, the *Chesapeake* sailed for the Mediterranean under James BARRON. H.M.S. *Leopard* stopped her and demanded the right to search for British deserters. When Barron refused, the *Leopard* opened fire; Barron had to submit, and four of his crew were impressed. The incident almost precipitated war. In the WAR OF 1812, the *Chesapeake* under James LAWRENCE fought (1813) H.M.S. *Shannon* and was taken; Lawrence's reported last command was "Don't give up the ship!"

Chesapeake Bay, major inlet on the Atlantic shoreline of the U.S. About 200 mi (320 km) long and up to 30 mi (48 km) wide, it is the drowned lower course of the Susquehannah R. and separates the DELMARVA Peninsula from mainland sections of E Maryland and E Virginia. The bay is crossed by the Chesapeake Bay Bridge-Tunnel. BALTIMORE, Md., is the chief port. Rivers feeding into the bay include the POTOMAC and the James, on which JAMESTOWN, the first permanent English settlement in the Americas, was founded in 1607. The bay was explored and charted (1608) by Capt. John SMITH.

chess, game for two players played on a square board composed of 64 small squares, alternately dark and light in color. Each player is provided with 16 pieces, or chessmen, either white or black. Various pieces are set down in a designated order in the two ranks closest to the player. Each piece is moved according to specific rules and is removed from the board when it is displaced by the move of one of the opposing pieces into its square. The objective in chess is to checkmate, or trap, the opponent's king, a piece whose mobility is limited. Chess probably originated in India. By the 13th cent. it was played throughout Europe. The first modern international chess tournament was held in London in 1851. There have been recognized world chess champions since that time, and since the 1970s championship matches, such as those in which Bobby FISCHER took the title from Boris Spassky, Anatoly KARPOV defeated Viktor Korchnoi, and Gary KASPAROV defeated Karpov and Nigel Short, have received worldwide media coverage.

Chesterfield, Philip Dormer Stanhope, 4th **earl of,** 1694–1773, English statesman and author. He was a noted wit and orator whose literary fame rests on letters to his illegitimate son Philip Stanhope (pub. 1774), aimed at educating a young man, and on letters to his godson (pub. 1890).

Chesterton, G(ilbert) K(eith), 1874–1936, English author, conservative, and Catholic apologist. A prolific writer, he produced studies of Browning (1903) and Dickens (1906); novels, including *The Napoleon of Notting Hill* (1904); detective fiction featuring Father Brown; poems; and essays, collected in *Tremendous Trifles* (1909) and elsewhere. With BELLOC he propounded the economic theory of Distributism.

chestnut, deciduous tree (genus *Castanea*) of the BEECH family, with thin-shelled, sweet, edible nuts borne in bristly burrs, widely distributed in the Northern Hemisphere. The common American chestnut (*C. dentata*), native to the E U.S., is nearly extinct from chestnut blight, a fungal disease, and edible chestnuts are now mostly imported from Italy. Several blight-resistant crosses of the American and Asian chestnuts have been developed. Some American species are called chinquapin.

Cheyenne, indigenous people of the Plains (see NORTH AMERICA, INDIGENOUS PEOPLES OF), with an Algonquian language of the Algonquian-Wakashan stock (see NATIVE AMERICAN LANGUAGES). In the 17th cent. they lived in earth-lodge villages along the Cheyenne R. After acquiring horses (c.1760) they became nomadic buffalo hunters. They were friendly to whites until prospectors swarmed into their lands when gold was found in Colorado. Cheyenne raids against intruders brought punitive actions by the U.S. army. Aroused by an unprovoked massacre at Sand Creek (1864), the Cheyenne waged bitter war that culminated in the Battle of the LITTLE BIGHORN (1876), where Cheyenne annihilated the cavalry of Gen. George CUSTER. In 1877, however, the sick and starving Cheyenne surrendered and were moved first to Oklahoma, then to Montana. In 1990 there were 11,456 Cheyenne in the U.S.

Cheyenne, city (1990 pop. 50,008), alt. 6,062 ft (1,848 m), state capital and seat of Laramie co., SE Wyo.; inc. 1868. A market and shipping center for a ranching area, it produces petroleum and plastics. It grew with the arrival (1867) of the Union Pacific RR and was made territorial capital in 1869. Its annual Frontier Days celebration (in July; first held 1897) is a famous tourist attraction.

Chiang Ch'ing: see JIANG QING.

Chiang Ching-kuo: see under CHIANG KAI-SHEK.

Chiang Kai-shek [jēäng kī-shĕk], 1887–1975, Chinese Nationalist leader. He is also called Chiang Chung-cheng. Chiang became prominent in the KUOMINTANG after the death (1925) of SUN YAT-SEN and in 1926 launched the Northern Expedition, in which the Nationalists captured Hankou, Shanghai, and Nanjing. He cooperated at first with Chinese Communists, but in 1927 reversed himself and began a long civil war with the Communists. He became head of the Nationalist government at Nanjing in 1928 and resisted the Japanese invasion of China in the Second SINO-JAPANESE WAR (1937–45). In 1949, however, the Communists drove Chiang and the Nationalists from the mainland to Taiwan. There he reorganized his military forces with U.S. aid, became (1950) president of Nationalist China (Taiwan), and instituted limited democratic political reforms. He continued to promise reconquest of the mainland, but his position was hurt when Taiwan was expelled (1972) from the UN in favor of Communist China. His son, **Chiang Ching-kuo** [jēäng jĭng-gwô], 1910–88, was also president of Taiwan

(1978–88). He was defense minister (1965–72) and premier (1972–78) before becoming president.

Chicago, Judy (Gerowitz), 1939–, American artist and founder of the Women's Art Education collective. She works in a variety of media, including such traditionally female-oriented crafts as needlework and china painting. She is best known for the multimedia installation, *The Dinner Party* (1974–78, in collaboration with various craftswomen).

Chicago, city (1990 pop. 2,783,726), seat of Cook co., NE Ill., third largest U.S. city, center of a vast metropolitan area (1990 pop. 8,065,633), on Lake Michigan; inc. 1837. A major GREAT LAKES port and the leading commercial, financial, industrial, and cultural center of the nation's interior, Chicago is a leader in steel production, printing, radio and television, and the manufacture of plastics, machinery, electronic equipment, and processed food. It has important stock, mercantile, and commodity exchanges. Downtown Chicago ("The Loop") has a dramatic skyline with some of the world's tallest skyscrapers, e.g., the Sears Tower and the John Hancock Tower. The North Side, mainly residential, stretches some 20 mi (32 km) along the lake. The West Side is a mix of European ethnic neighborhoods that developed in the 19th and early 20th cent. Most of the city's African Americans, nearly 40% of the population, live in the industrialized South Side. Leading cultural institutions include the Art Institute of Chicago, Natural History Museum, Chicago Symphony Orchestra, Univ. of Chicago, and Harold Washington Library. The city's modern development dates from the opening (1825) of the ERIE CANAL and the arrival (1852) of the railroads. A fire destroyed much of Chicago in 1871. Labor troubles, e.g., the 1886 HAYMARKET SQUARE RIOT and the 1894 Pullman strike (see DEBS, EUGENE V.; ALTGELD, JOHN P.), followed rapid industrialization. In the 1920s PROHIBITION brought a reputation for gang warfare. The SAINT LAWRENCE SEAWAY opened Chicago to ocean shipping after 1959.

Chicago, University of, at Chicago; coeducational; inc. 1890, opened 1892 primarily through the gifts of John D. ROCKEFELLER. Because of its progressive programs and distinguished faculty, it quickly achieved prominence. Significant among its facilities are the Pritzker School of Medicine; the Enrico Fermi Institute for Nuclear Studies; the McDonald Observatory, at Ford Davis, Texas; the Yerkes Observatory, at Williams Bay, Wis. The department of economics is renowned.

Chichén Itzá [chēchān' ētsä'], archaeological site in central YUCATÁN, Mexico. Probably founded c.514 by the Itzá, it was alternately abandoned and reoccupied until it was deserted for the last time in 1194. Spanning two great periods of MAYA civilization, it displays Classic and Post-Classic architectural styles and shows a strong TOLTEC influence.

chickadee, small North American BIRD of the TITMOUSE family. The lively black-capped chickadee (*Parus atricapillus*), with gray back and wings and light underparts, often swings upside down on branch tips, searching for insects.

Chickasaw, indigenous people of the Eastern Woodlands (see NORTH AMERICA, INDIGENOUS PEOPLES OF), who spoke a Muskogean language of the Hokan-Siouan stock (see NATIVE AMERICAN LANGUAGES). They lived in N Mississippi and warred with the nearby CHOCTAW, CREEK, CHEROKEE, and SHAWNEE. After 1834 they moved to Oklahoma, becoming one of the FIVE CIVILIZED TRIBES. In 1990 there were 20,631 Chickasaws in the U.S.

chicken, chief poultry BIRD, probably domesticated from a SW Asian jungle fowl. Chickens are raised commercially in highly mechanized indoor chambers and are classified by their uses. The Leghorn chicken is the main egg breed in the U.S., while a cross between the fast-growing Plymouth Rock chicken and deep-breasted Cornish hen is the most important meat breed. Some varieties are raised for their ornamental appearance, as pets, or for cockfighting.

chicken pox or **varicella,** acute infectious disease caused by the herpes zoster virus that also causes SHINGLES. Usually a disease of childhood, chicken pox is a highly contagious disorder characterized by an itchy rash of blisterlike lesions that appear two to three weeks after infection. When the lesions have crusted over, the disease is no longer communicable. Topical medication is often given to relieve the itching, and the drug acyclovir may be used to treat the disease, particularly in older patients.

chickpea, annual plant (*Cicer arietinum*) of the PULSE family, cultivated since antiquity for the edible, pealike seed. Chickpeas are used as food for humans and animals. They are boiled or roasted, and have been used as a coffee substitute. Other common names are *ceci,* garbanzo, and gram pea.

chicory or **succory,** herb (*Cichorium intybus*) of the COMPOSITE family, native to the Mediterranean and widely grown in North America and Europe. The roasted and powdered root is used as a coffee substitute and adulterant. Chicory is also used as a seasoning and in salads. French endive, or witloof, is the type that is blanched for salad. True endive, or escarole (*C. endivia*), a salad vegetable since antiquity, is cultivated in broad- and curly-leaved varieties.

chigger: see MITE.

Chihuahua, small TOY DOG; shoulder height, c.5 in. (12.7 cm); weight, 1–6 lb (0.5–2.7 kg). There are two varieties: the smooth, with a short, close-lying, glossy coat, and the long-coated, with soft-textured, flat, or slightly wavy hair. The coat is usually tan. Probably of Chinese origin, it was introduced into Mexico by Spanish settlers.

Chikamatsu Monzaemon [chē"kämä'tso͞o], 1653–1724, Japanese dramatist. Writing primarily for the puppet stage, he profoundly influenced the development of modern Japanese theater (see JAPANESE LITERATURE). His work is divided into historical romances, e.g., *Battles of Coxinga,* and domestic tragedies of love and duty, e.g., *Love Suicides at Amijima.*

Child, Julia, 1912–, American cooking teacher and writer; b. Pasadena, Calif. She has hosted a series of public television programs, most notably *The French Chef* (1962–76), her first. Her comfortable, unintimidating manner is also evident in her many cookbooks.

child abuse, physical or emotional abuse of a child by a parent, guardian, or other person. Reports of child abuse, including sexual abuse, beating, and murder, have climbed in the U.S., and some authorities believe that the number of cases is grossly underreported. **Child neglect** is sometimes included in legal definitions of child abuse to cover instances of malnutrition, desertion, and inadequate care of a child's safety. When reported, child abuse cases are complicated by inadequate foster care services and a legal system that has trouble accommodating the suggestible nature of children, who are often developmentally unable to distinguish fact from make-believe.

Childe, Vere Gordon, 1892–1957, English archaeologist; b. Australia. His synthesis of European prehistory is embodied in *The Dawn of European Civilization* (1925, 6th ed. 1957) and *The Prehistory of European Society* (1958).

Chile [chĭl'ē], officially Republic of Chile, republic (1992 pop. 13,231,803), 292,256 sq mi (756,945 sq km), S South America, bordered by Peru (N), Bolivia (NE), Argentina (E), and the Pacific Ocean (W). Long and narrow, Chile stretches 2,880 mi (4,630 km) from north to south, but is only 265 mi (430 km) at its widest point. Major cities include SANTIAGO (the capital), VALPARAISO, and CONCEPCIÓN. The ANDES Mts. extend the entire length of eastern Chile; Ojos del Salado (22,539 ft/6,870 m), the second highest point in South America, is found here. Chile has three main natural regions: the arid north, which includes the ATACAMA DESERT; the cold and humid south, with dense forests, snow-covered peaks, glaciers, and islands; and the fertile central area, Mediterranean in climate, which is the population, economic, and cultural heart of the nation. Located along an active zone in the earth's crust, Chile is subject to devastating earthquakes. With an economy based on its mineral wealth, Chile is one of the world's leading exporters of copper; other minerals include nitrates, iron ore, manganese, lead, and zinc. Manufactures include processed foods (including wine), fishmeal, textiles, and iron and steel. Chief crops are wheat, potatoes, corn, and sugar beets. Although Chile is not self-sufficient in food, fruit accounts for nearly 10% of its exports. Sheep raising, fishing, and timber production are also important. The majority of Chile's population is mestizo, but a sizable number are of European descent. More than 85% of the people are Roman Catholic. Spanish is the official language.

History. Upon arrival in the area that is now Chile, the Spaniards met stout resistance from the ARAUCANIANS who lived there, but in

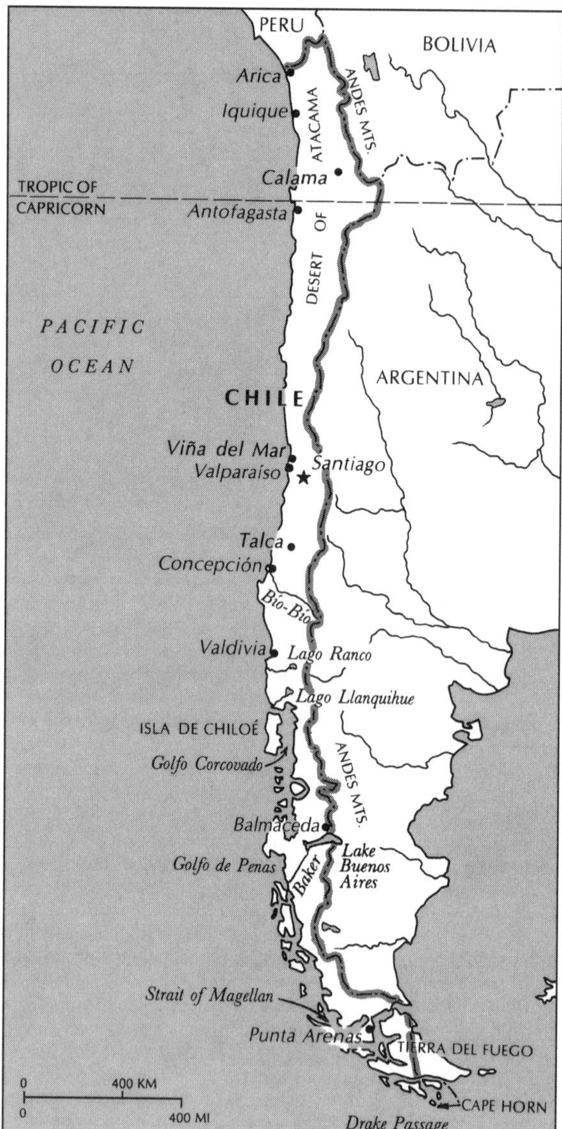

1541 Pedro de VALDIVIA succeeded in establishing the first Spanish settlement at Santiago. Despite the continued hostility of the native peoples, who were not fully conquered until the late 19th cent., the colonists established a pastoral society. In 1810 a struggle for independence from Spanish rule was initiated and finally, in 1818, following a decisive victory at Maipú by José de SAN MARTÍN, independence was proclaimed, and Bernardo O'HIGGINS, a revolutionary leader, was established as ruler. In 1879 long-standing border disputes with Bolivia and Peru led to the War of the Pacific; Chile, victorious, gained valuable mineral-rich territory. Exploitation of mineral resources, accompanied by industrialization, brought prosperity. Politically, Chile was one of the most stable and democratic nations in South America. In 1970 Salvador ALLENDE GOSSENS, a Marxist, was elected president. His attempt to transform Chile into a socialist state ended in 1973 with a U.S.-supported, bloody military coup, in which Allende lost his life. A repressive military junta, headed by Gen. Augusto PINOCHET, governed from 1973 to 1990. In a 1988 plebiscite, Chileans rejected Pinochet's bid to remain in office another eight years. Patricio Aylwin Azócar, a Christian Democrat heading a coalition of 17 center and left parties, won the presidency in 1989, but under the military-drafted constitution, Pinochet remained head of the army. In 1993 Eduardo Frei Ruiz-Tagle, the son of Allende's predecessor and a Christian Democrat, was elected president.

Chillicothe, city (1990 pop. 21,923), seat of Ross co., south-central Ohio, on the Scioto R.; founded 1796; inc. 1802. The trading center for a farm area, it also manufactures paper, shoes, and aluminum products. It became (1800) capital of the NORTHWEST TERRITORY, and (1803–10, 1812–16) capital of Ohio. Mound City National Monument (prehistoric Native American burial mounds) is nearby.

chimpanzee, black-haired APE (genus *Pan*) of the equatorial forests of central and W Africa, comprising the common chimpanzee (*P. troglodytes*) and the rarer bonobo, or pygmy chimpanzee (*P. paniscus*); considered the most intelligent of apes. The common chimpanzee is covered with long, black hair and may reach 5 ft. (1.5 m) in height and 150 lb (68 kg) in weight. Captive chimpanzees have been taught to communicate by using SIGN LANGUAGE or a computer console.

Chimu, ancient civilization on the desert coast of N Peru (see SOUTH AMERICA, INDIGENOUS PEOPLES OF) that flourished after c.1200. The Chimu were urban people with a powerful military, a complex social system, and well-planned cities such as Chan Chan, their capital. They influenced the Cuismancu empire of central Peru, but were absorbed c.1460 by the INCA.

Ch'in, dynasty: see CHINA.

China, Mandarin *Zhonghua Renmin Gongheguo,* officially People's Republic of China, republic (1992 est. pop. 1,169,620,000), 3,691,502 sq mi (9,561,000 sq km), E Asia; the most populous country in the world. It is bounded by Russia and North Korea (E), Russia and Mongolia (N), Kazakhstan, Kyrgyzstan, Tajikistan, Afghanistan, Pakistan, and India (W), and Nepal, India, Bhutan, Myanmar, Laos, and Vietnam (S). A coastline c.4,000 mi (6,440 km) long borders the Yellow and East China seas (E) and the South China Sea (S). The capital is BEIJING; other important cities include SHANGHAI, TIANJIN, and GUANGZHOU. China is the world's third largest country (after Russia and Canada). The terrain is generally rugged, with broad plains along the rivers and the southern coast. The Tibetan plateau occupies SW China and is separated from the Tarim basin of Xinjiang to the north by the massive Kunlun Mts. In N China is the vast Inner Mongolian tableland, as well as the eastern highlands and central plain of Manchuria. The two main rivers are the HUANG HE (Yellow R.), in the north, and the CHANG (Yangtze) R., in central China. The climate, harsh in the north and subtropical in the south, is mainly temperate.

Economy. The economic system was formerly centrally planned, but China is now attempting to create a "socialist market economy." The state sector has shrunk, and the economy has grown dramatically—it is now the third largest in the world. About 60% of the work force is agricultural, but their output is only about 25% of the gross domestic product. Only 15% of the land surface is suitable for farming. Principal crops are food grains, including rice, wheat, corn, millet, barley, and kaoliang (a form of sorghum); peanuts, sweet potatoes, soybeans, cotton, tobacco, and tea are also important. Hogs and poultry are widely raised, and both inland and marine fishing are important. China is one of the world's major mineral-producing countries. Reserves of coal, its most abundant mineral and principal energy source, rank among the world's largest. Once an importer of petroleum, China is now the world's fifth-ranked oil producer, and oil exports are an increasingly important source of foreign exchange. China also has extensive deposits of iron, tungsten, tin, mercury, magnesite, aluminum, salt, uranium, gold, and zinc. The country's enormous hydroelectric potential is being rapidly developed; the largest project, Gezhouba Dam, on the Chang (Yangtze) R., opened in 1981. China's manufactures include textiles, chemicals, agriculture-related products, such as farm machinery, as well as machine tools, processed foods, iron and steel, building materials, and electronic equipment. Since the 1980s light industrial and consumer items have increased greatly in importance. Rivers and canals are important arteries of transportation.

People. The population is heterogeneous. Although the Han (ethnic Chinese) constitute 92% of the total, 56 recognized minority groups exist, some occupying large and strategically important areas, including Tibet and Xinjiang. Mandarin dialects, the basis of the national language, are uniformly spoken in the north, but in the south, many dialects, including Cantonese, Wu, and Hakka, are spoken; the written language is common to all dialects. Non-

Anhui	16	Henan	15	Qinghai	12
Fujian	26	Hubei	14	Shaanxi	5
Gansu	2	Hunan	21	Shandong	18
Guangdong	25	Inner Mongolian A.R.		Shanxi	6
Guangxi		(Nei Monggol A.R.)	3	Sichuan	13
Zhuangzu A.R.	24	Jiangsu	17	Tibet	
Guizhou	20	Jiangxi	22	(Xizang A.R.)	11
Hainan	27	Jilin	9	Xinjiang Uygur A.R.	1
Hebei	7	Liaoning	8	Yunnan	19
Heilongjiang	10	Ningxia Hui A.R.	4	Zhejiang	23

Chinese minorities include the Zhuangs, Huis, Uigurs, Tibetans, and Mongols. Under Mao religious practice was discouraged, but it has revived to some degree. Traditional Chinese religion is a mix of Confucianism, Buddhism, and Taoism. There is a Muslim minority and smaller groups of Catholics and Protestants. Population growth, long a concern, has been greatly diminished by drastic, often harsh government programs to control it.

History. A protohuman toolmaker known as Peking man (*Sinanthropus pekingensis*) lived in N China about 500,000 years ago. Modern humans first appeared in the region around 20,000 years ago, establishing primitive agricultural villages by 5000 B.C. The first documented Chinese civilization was the Shang dynasty (c.1523–c.1027 B.C.), which had cities, bronze metallurgy, and a system of writing. It was succeeded by the often turbulent Chou dynasty (c.1027–256 B.C.), which nevertheless gave rise to China's golden age of philosophy, highlighted by the works of CONFUCIUS, LAO-TZE, and Mencius. The Ch'in dynasty (221–207 B.C.) united China under a centralized imperial system; construction of the GREAT WALL was begun during this period. The Han dynasty (202 B.C.–A.D. 220), considered China's imperial age, was notable for its long, peaceable rule, territorial expansion, and technological and artistic achievement. There followed four centuries of warfare among petty states and invasions by the Huns; however, despite the chaos, the arts and sciences flourished, and BUDDHISM and TAOISM developed as important Chinese religions. Political reunification, begun under the Sui (581–618), paved the way for the glorious age of the T'ang dynasty (618–906), which at its height controlled an empire stretching from Korea to Turkistan. Prosperity continued under the Sung dynasty (960–1279), a time of scholarly studies and artistic progress, marked by the invention of movable type. In the 13th cent. N China fell to the MONGOLS led by JENGHIZ KHAN. His grandson KUBLAI KHAN founded the Yüan dynasty (1260–1368) and subdued (1279) the Sung. Kublai's vast realm was visited and described by Marco POLO. After a massive peasant rebellion (14th cent.) native rule was restored with the establishment of the Ming dynasty (1368–1644). However, in 1644 foreigners from the north—the Manchus—once again conquered China, establish-

CHINESE DYNASTIES

Dynasty	Characteristics and History
Hsia c.1994–c.1523 B.C.	Semilegendary Emperor Yu built irrigation channels, reclaimed land. Bronze weapons, chariots, domestic animals used. Wheat, millet cultivated. First use of written symbols.
Shang or Yin c.1523–c.1027 B.C.	First historic dynasty. Complex agricultural society with a bureaucracy and defined social classes. Well-developed writing, first Chinese calendar. Great age of bronze casting.
Chou c.1027-256 B.C.	Classical age (CONFUCIUS, LAO-TZE, Mencius) despite political disorder. Written laws, money economy. Iron implements and ox-drawn plow in use. Followed by Warring States period, 403-221 B.C.
Ch'in 221–206 B.C.	Unification of China under harsh rule of Shih Huang-ti. FEUDALISM replaced by pyramidal bureaucratic government. Written language standardized. Roads, canals, much of GREAT WALL built.
Han 202 B.C.–A.D. 220	Unification furthered, but harshness lessened and CONFUCIANISM made basis for bureaucratic state. BUDDHISM introduced. Encyclopedic history, dictionary compiled; porcelain produced.
Three Kingdoms A.D. 220–265	Division into three states: Wei, Shu, Wu. Wei gradually dominant. Confucianism eclipsed; increased importance of TAOISM and Buddhism. Many Indian scientific advances adopted.
Tsin or Chin 265–420	Founded by a Wei general; gradual expansion to the southeast. Series of barbarian dynasties ruled N China. Continued growth of Buddhism.
Sui 581–618	Reunification; centralized government reestablished. Buddhism, Taoism favored. Great Wall refortified; canal system established.
T'ang 618–907	Territorial expansion. Buddhism temporarily suppressed. CIVIL SERVICE examinations based on Confucianism. Age of great achievements in poetry (LI PO, PO CHÜ-I, TU FU), sculpture, painting.
Five Dynasties and Ten Kingdoms 907–960	Period of warfare, official corruption, general hardship. Widespread development of printing; paper money first printed.
Sung 960–1279	Period of great social and intellectual change. Neo-Confucianism attains supremacy over Taoism and Buddhism; central bureaucracy reestablished. Widespread cultivation of tea and cotton; gunpowder first used militarily.
Yüan 1271–1368	MONGOL dynasty founded by KUBLAI KHAN. Growing contact with West. Confucian ideals discouraged. Great age of Chinese playwriting. Revolts in Mongolia, S China end dynasty.
Ming 1368–1644	Mongols expelled. Confucianism, civil service examinations, reinstated. Contact with European traders, missionaries. Porcelain, architecture (see CHINESE ARCHITECTURE), the novel and drama flourish.
Ch'ing or Manchus 1644–1912	Established by the MANCHUS. Territorial expansion but gradual weakening of Chinese power; decline of central authority. Increasing European trade; foreign powers divide China into spheres of influence. OPIUM WAR; HONG KONG ceded; BOXER UPRISING. Last Chinese monarchy.

ing the Ch'ing (MANCHU) dynasty (1644–1912), the last in China's history.

Foreign Intervention. In a relaxation of China's traditional isolationist policy, Guangzhou was opened to limited overseas trade in 1834. Dissatisfied with this restricted arrangement, Great Britain provoked the OPIUM WAR (1839–42) and easily defeated China. The Treaty of Nanking ceded HONG KONG to Britain, forced China to open several ports to unrestricted trade, and established the principle of EXTRATERRITORIALITY, by which Britons in China were granted immunity from local law enforcement. France, Germany, and Russia soon won similar concessions. The Ch'ing regime was further weakened by a series of internal rebellions, particularly the TAIPING REBELLION (1850–64), a radical military-religious movement; by defeat in the First Sino-Japanese War (1894–95); and by the subsequent further partitioning of China into foreign spheres of influence. The BOXER UPRISING (1898–1900), a final desperate effort to resist foreign influence, was crushed by an international force.

Internal Struggles. These events added impetus to growing anti-Manchu sentiment, and despite belated domestic reforms, a revolution (1911) overthrew the Ch'ing, and a republic, briefly led by SUN YAT-SEN, was established in 1912. With the death (1916) of Sun's successor, YÜAN SHIH-KAI, Chinese warlords gained control of the government; they were finally ousted in 1927, after years of civil war, by the nationalist KUOMINTANG, led by CHIANG KAI-SHEK and aided by the Communists. In 1927 Chiang inaugurated the long Chinese civil war when he purged his Communist allies, eventually forcing them on the LONG MARCH (1934–35) to Shaanxi, where they established their base. In 1931 Japan had occupied Manchuria, and in 1937 it mounted a full-scale attack against China (see SINO-JAPANESE WAR, SECOND). An uneasy coalition of Nationalists and Communists fought the Japanese, but following victory in 1945, civil war once again erupted, with the U.S. supporting the Nationalists. Beijing, followed by the other major cities, fell to the Communists in 1949, and on Oct. 1 the People's Republic of China was proclaimed with MAO ZEDONG as chairman and ZHOU ENLAI as premier. Chiang Kai-shek fled to TAIWAN, where he established a new seat for the Republic of China government.

The People's Republic. Under the Communists, high inflation was brought under control, a land reform program introduced, industry nationalized and expanded with Soviet aid, and agriculture collectivized. The Chinese People's Volunteers entered the KOREAN WAR against UN forces in 1950, participating on a large scale until the armistice of 1953. A liberal "hundred flowers" period (1957) was followed by a crackdown on intellectuals and the Great Leap Forward (1958–60), a massive industrial and agricultural development program that was intended to transform China's economy overnight but that ended in the largest famine in world history, with an estimated 20–40 million deaths. At about the same time a growing ideological rift between China and the USSR led to withdrawal of Soviet aid and technical assistance. Evidence of internal tension began to surface in the 1960s, culminating in the CULTURAL REVOLUTION of 1966–69, a massive upheaval launched by Mao to purge the revolution of liberal elements. Tension increased in the early 1970s with the revelation that Lin Biao, China's defense minister and Mao's designated heir, had died (1971) in a plane crash after an attempt to assassinate Mao. In international affairs, China's progress toward recognition as a world power was aided by its explosion of an atomic bomb (1964) and the launching of its first satellite (1970). An easing of relations with the West led to the admission of China to the UN in 1971 and to a visit to China by U.S. Pres. NIXON in 1972. Zhou Enlai and Mao Zedong died in 1976. Following the assumption of power by HUA GUOFENG, the country was shaken by the arrest, trial, and conviction (1981) of Mao's widow, JIANG QING, and three colleagues (the GANG OF FOUR). DENG XIAOPING, who came to power in 1977, adopted a program of rapid economic modernization. Liberal economic and trade policies were instituted, and the U.S. and China normalized diplomatic relations in 1979. In 1981 the Communist party publicly criticized Mao's later policies, although his thought was reaffirmed as the nation's guideline in new party and national constitutions (1982). In early 1989 China was the scene of massive demonstrations calling for democratic reforms and an end to official corruption, but in June the army brutally suppressed the Beijing demonstrators, killing perhaps 1,000. A period of repression and reaction followed, but many of the economic reforms survived and new ones have since been instituted. In 1993 a revision of the constitution called for the development of a "socialist market economy."

China, Great Wall of: see GREAT WALL OF CHINA.

China, Republic of, official name of TAIWAN.

chinchilla, small, burrowing RODENT that lives in colonies up to 15,000 ft (4,270 m) high in the Andes of Bolivia, Chile, and Peru. Its soft gray pelt is one of the costliest of all furs, and the wild chinchilla was nearly exterminated before protective laws were passed.

chinchona: see CINCHONA.

Chinese, subfamily of the Sino-Tibetan family of languages. See LANGUAGE (table).

Chinese architecture. Few buildings exist in China predating the Ming dynasty (1368–1644) because of wars, invasions, and insubstantial construction (wood and rice-paper). An exception is the Great Wall of China. Mid-20th-cent. architectural finds have clarified some of the history of Chinese architecture. As early as the neolithic period, the basic principle of supporting a roof with spaced columns rather than walls was established. Walls served merely as enclosing screens. The typical Chinese roof probably dates from c.1500 B.C., but it is known only from the Han dynasty (202 B.C.–A.D. 220), when it appeared in the familiar form—graceful, overhanging, sometimes in tiers, with upturned eaves. It rested on brackets resting in turn on columns. Roof tiles were colorfully glazed and brackets elaborately carved and painted. A characteristic ground plan has remained constant in Chinese and Japanese palaces and temples. Inside an external wall, the building complex is arranged along a central axis and is approached through a series of gates. Next come a public hall and finally the private quarters. Each residential unit was built around a central court with a garden, which became an art form in itself. The coming of BUDDHISM did not affect the style. The only distinctly Buddhist building was the PAGODA, simple and square at first, later more elaborate. A distinctive pagoda style emerged in the 11th cent. Built in three stages, it had a base, shaft, and crown, surmounted by a spire, and was often octagonal. In the Ming period the complex of courtyards, parks, and palaces became labyrinthian. BEIJING's Forbidden City remains a spectacular achievement of intricacy and decoration. After the late 19th cent. the Chinese adopted European and, later, Soviet styles, with a trend toward the massive and clearly functional in public buildings.

Chinese art, the oldest in the world, has its origins in remote antiquity (see CHINA). Excavations in Gansu and Henan have revealed a Neolithic culture with pottery painted in dynamic swirling or lozenge-shaped patterns. Bronze vessels from the Shang dynasty (2d millennium) indicate an advanced culture as well as a long period of prior experimentation. Bronzes were decorated with severe abstract as well as naturalistic representations. The advent of BUDDHISM (1st cent. A.D.) brought works of sculpture, painting, and architecture of a distinctly religious nature. Representations of the BUDDHA and the bodhisattvas became great themes in sculpture. The forms of these figures came from India, but by the 6th cent. A.D. Chinese artists had developed their own sculpture style, which reached its greatest distinction in the T'ang dynasty (618–906). Buddhist sculpture continued to flourish until the Ming dynasty (1368–1644), at which time exquisite miniature sculpture in JADE, IVORY, and GLASS was produced in China and Japan. The origins of Chinese painting are largely lost until the 5th cent. A.D. The Caves of a Thousand Buddhas, near Dunhuang, contain frescoes and scrolls dating from the 5th to 8th cent. Chinese painting achieves its effects through mastery of the line and silhouette rather than through perspective or the rendering of light and shadow. The art of figure painting reached its peak in the T'ang dynasty, which also saw the rise of Chinese landscape painting. In the Sung dynasty (960–1279) landscape painting reached its peak, reflecting contemporary Taoist and Confucian views. The human figure was diminished so as not to intrude on the orderly magnitude of nature. The monumental detail also began to emerge—a single bamboo flower or bird became the subject for a painting. The Ch'an (Zen) sect of Buddhism used rapid brush strokes and ink splashes to create intuitive works of great vigor. With the Yüan dynasty (1260–1368) and Mongol rule, the human figure assumed greater importance, and STILL-LIFE painting gained prominence. In the Ming dynasty (1368–1644) a developing connoisseurship preserved many great works of art. During the Ch'ing (1644–1912) dynasty a level of technical competence was developed that lasted until the 19th cent., but there was little innovation in painting. By the 19th cent. reliance on calligraphic techniques had produced sterile formulas in painting. Since the Communist revolution (1949), art has been used largely for propaganda purposes, and Western influence forbidden. Some artists, working in China and abroad, have nonetheless produced art of considerable individuality. The development of Chinese pottery-making followed that of painting, reaching perfection in the Sung dynasty and extreme technical elaboration in the Ming. In the minor arts, e.g., enamelware, lacquerware, jade, ivory, and textiles, the world owes an incalculable debt to the influence of Chinese art.

Chinese exclusion, policy initiated in 1882 banning U.S. entry to Chinese laborers. After the U.S. acquisition (1848) of California, there arose a need for cheap labor, and Chinese flocked there to work on the railroads. By 1867 they numbered 50,000; their number increased after the Burlingame Treaty of 1868, which permitted Chinese immigration but not naturalization. Anti-Asian prejudice and the competition with American workers led to anti-Chinese riots (1877) in San Francisco, then to the Chinese Exclusion Act of 1882, which banned Chinese immigration for 10 years. In a new treaty of 1894, China accepted another 10-year exclusion, which Congress unilaterally continued until the 1924 immigration law that excluded all Asians. In 1943 a new law extended citizenship rights, and permitted an annual immigration of 105 Chinese. The quota was abolished in 1965.

Chinese literature. The oldest written records (c.1400 B.C.) in Chinese are from the Shang dynasty, but the elaborate system of notation in use then indicates an earlier origin. Most of the oldest extant works of literature were written in the late Chou dynasty (c.1207–256 B.C.), including much of the *Five Classics* of CONFUCIANISM. Traditionally attributed to CONFUCIUS, the *Five Classics* consist of the *Spring and Autumn Annals,* a chronology of Lu, Confucius's native state; the BOOK OF CHANGES, a system of divination; the *Book of Rites,* which describes ceremonials and the ideal state; the *Book of History,* historical records; and the *Book of Songs,* a collection of poems on war, love, and peasant life written in a simple style. Other important early books include the chief literature of TAOISM, *The Way and Its Power (Tao-te ching),* traditionally ascribed to LAO-TZE, and the work of Chuang-tze. These books probably achieved their present form in the 2d cent. B.C. In time the literary and spoken languages of China diverged sharply. In poetry the freedom of the Chou dynasty was followed by the development of prescribed forms, and by the T'ang dynasty (618–906) prosodic rules and pronunciation no longer reflected the spoken language. Classical Chinese poems are usually short, unemphatic lyrics, suggesting a mood or scene by a few touches instead of a detailed picture. Historical and literary allusions abound, while intellectual themes and narratives are rather rare. The T'ang dynasty was the great age of WANG WEI, LI PO, TU FU, and PO CHÜ-I, the masters of Chinese poetry. In the succeeding Sung dynasty (960–1279), SU TUNG-P'O was perhaps the foremost poet. Much learned prose has also been written in Chinese; particularly notable are the fairly accurate and objective histories produced since the Han dynasty (202 B.C.–A.D. 220). SSU-MA CH'IEN's *Records of the Grand Historian of China* (c.100 B.C.) is the outstanding example and the model for later histories. During the T'ang and Sung dynasties popular prose and verse written in the vernacular appeared. Springing from story cycles by professional storytellers, the vernacular literature first emerged as full-fledged art in the drama of the Yüan dynasty (1260–1368; see ASIAN DRAMA). The great novels of the Ming dynasty (1368–1644) that followed took shape gradually before being given their final form, perhaps anonymously by traditional scholars. An outstanding early novel is *Romance of the Three Kingdoms,* which recounts heroic deeds and chivalrous exploits. *Journey to the West,* or *Monkey,* is an allegorical tale of the supernatural adventures of a Buddhist monk on an Indian pilgrimage. The greatest Chinese novel is *Dream of the Red Chamber,* or *Story of the Stone,* an 18th-cent. work chiefly by Ts'ao Hsüeh-ch'in, which recounts the declining fortunes of an aristocratic family. After the republican revolution (1912) writers such as HU SHIH and LU HSUN rejected classical modes of composition and advocated writing in *paihua* everyday speech. It has proved particularly effective in prose. Among the most distinguished modern Chinese writers are Lu Hsun (Lu Xun), Mao Dun (Mao Tun), Lao She, Shen Congwen (Shen Ts'ung-wen), and Ba Jin (Pa Chin). Contemporary Chinese literature has suffered from government-sponsored SOCIALIST REALISM, but since the 1980s there has been some loosening of restrictions. After the 1989 massacre in Beijing's Tiananmen Square, many writers who had supported democratic reforms fled China; most continue to publish in exile.

Ch'ing or **Manchu,** dynasty: see CHINA.

Chios: see KHIOS.

chipmunk, RODENT of the SQUIRREL family. The common Eastern chipmunk (*Tamias striatus*), about 5 to 6 in. (13 to 15 cm) long, has reddish or grayish brown upper parts with a median black stripe and two black stripes separated by a whitish band along each side. Chipmunks eat nuts, berries, and insects; food is carried in expandable cheek pouches.

Chippendale, Thomas, 1718–79, English cabinetmaker. His designs were so widely followed that much 18th-cent. English furniture is grouped under his name, but only those pieces for which the original bills survive (e.g., for Harewood House) can be assigned unquestionably to his workshop. To the sober design and fine construction of the Queen Anne and Georgian styles he added Chinese, Gothic, and ROCOCO motifs. He made chairs of many types, from geometrical to sumptuously carved; desks; mirror frames; china cabinets and bookcases; and tables with fretted galleries and cluster-column Gothic legs.

Chippewa: see OJIBWA.

Chirac, Jacques, 1932–, French political leader. He was elected to the National Assembly (1967) and held several governmental posts (1967–74) before serving as prime minister (1974–76) under GISCARD D'ESTAING. Soon breaking with Giscard, Chirac became head of the Gaullists. Mayor of Paris since 1977, he was an unsuccessful presidential candidate (1981, 1988) and again prime minister (1986–88), under MITTERRAND.

chiral molecule: see ISOMER.

Chirico, Giorgio de [kē'rēkō], 1888–1978, Italian painter; b. Greece. His powerful, disturbing paintings employ steep perspective, mannequin figures, empty space, and forms out of context to create an atmosphere of mystery and loneliness. An influence on early SURREALISM, he termed his symbolism metaphysical painting.

Chiron [kī'rŏn], in Greek mythology, a centaur; son of CRONUS. He was a wise physician and prophet whose pupils included HERCULES, ACHILLES, JASON, and ASCLEPIUS. After receiving an incurable wound, he gave his immortality to PROMETHEUS and died. ZEUS turned him into the constellation Sagittarius.

chiropractic, medical practice based on the theory that disease results from a disruption of nerve function. This interference is thought to stem primarily from displaced vertebrae, which chiropractors massage and manipulate manually in order to relieve pressure on nerves.

Chisholm, Shirley Anita St. Hill, 1924–, African-American poltician; b. Brooklyn, N.Y. A Democratic member (1964–68) of the New York state assembly, she was elected (1968) to the U.S. House of Representatives from New York, becoming the first African-American woman to serve there. She retired from Congress in 1983.

Chisholm Trail, route over which herds of cattle were driven to railheads in Kansas after the Civil War. In 1866, Jesse Chisholm, a trader, cut the trail by carting a heavy load of buffalo hides from Oklahoma to Kansas. Drovers followed the trail for 20 years with hundreds of thousands of Texas longhorns; it became celebrated in frontier stories and ballads. The trail fell into disuse as railroads and wire fencing developed, but traces of it survive.

Chippendale-style mirror in mahogany and gilt, 18th cent.

Chişinău, formerly **Kishinev,** city (1990 est. pop. 676,000), capital of Moldova, SE Europe, on the Byk R. Major industries include food and tobacco processing, the assembly of consumer goods, and the manufacture of building materials, machinery, and plastics. Founded in the early 15th cent., Chişinău came under Turkish rule in the 16th cent. Taken by Russia in 1812, it (and most of Moldova) was part of Romania between the world wars. During World War II the city's large Jewish minority was almost entirely exterminated.

chiton, marine invertebrate MOLLUSK (class Amphineura). The chiton has a low oval body covered dorsally by a slightly convex shell of eight overlapping plates. It clings tightly to hard surfaces with its broad flat ventral foot; it crawls by means of muscular undulations of the foot. The mouth, located in front of the foot, contains a toothed scraping organ, the radula. Chitons range from ½ in. to 12 in. (1.2–30 cm).

Chittagong, city (1991 pop. 2,080,195), capital of Chittagong division, SE Bangladesh, on the Karnafuli R. near the Bay of Bengal. An important rail terminus and administrative center, it is the chief port of Bangladesh, with modern facilities for oceangoing vessels. Oil (offshore installations and refineries), cotton- and jute-processing, and chemical and steel works are among its important industries. A port known since the early centuries A.D., it was controlled successively by the Hindus, Arakans, Moguls, and British. In 1991 a cyclone (hurricane) severely damaged the city and its harbor.

chivalry, system of ethical ideals that grew out of FEUDALISM and had its zenith in the 12th and 13th cent. Chivalric ethics originated chiefly in France and Spain and spread rapidly. They represented a fusion of Christian and military concepts of morality, and they still form the basis of gentlemanly conduct. The chief chivalric virtues were piety, honor, valor, courtesy, chastity, and loyalty. The knight's loyalty was due to God, to his suzerain, and to his sworn love. Love in the chivalrous sense was largely platonic. The ideal of militant knighthood was greatly enhanced by the CRUSADES, and the monastic orders of knights, the KNIGHTS TEMPLARS and KNIGHTS

HOSPITALERS, produced soldiers sworn to uphold the Christian ideal. Besides the battlefield, the tournament became an arena in which the virtues of chivalry could be proved. The code of COURTLY LOVE was developed in France and Flanders. In practice, chivalric conduct was never free from corruption, and the outward trappings of chivalry declined in the 15th cent. Medieval secular literature, such as the ARTHURIAN LEGEND and the CHANSONS DE GESTE, was concerned primarily with knighthood and chivalry. In the 19th cent. ROMANTICISM revived chivalrous ideals.

chive: see ONION.

chlamydia, genus of microorganisms that cause a variety of diseases in humans and other animals. Psittacosis, or parrot fever, caused by the species *Chlamydia psittaci,* is transmitted to people by birds, particularly parrots, parakeets, and lovebirds. In birds the disease takes the form of an intestinal infection, but in people it runs the course of a viral pneumonia. Different forms of *Chlamydia trachomatis* cause trachoma, an infection of the mucous membrane of the eyelids, and the sexually transmitted disease lymphogranuloma venereum. This same species also causes the sexually transmitted disease called chlamydia, the most common such disease in the U.S. In women, chlamydia is a common cause of pelvic inflammatory disease, which can result in infertility and an increased risk of tubal pregnancy. Men are the primary carriers, but painful urination and discharge often prompt them to get treatment before the testes can be infected and male infertility can result.

chlorine (Cl), gaseous element, discovered in 1774 by Karl SCHEELE, who thought it was an oxygen compound, and identified as an element by Sir Humphry DAVY in 1810. Chlorine is a greenish-yellow, poisonous gas with a disagreeable, suffocating odor. A HALOGEN, it occurs in nature in numerous and abundant compounds, e.g., sodium chloride (common salt). Chlorine is soluble in water; chlorine water has strong oxidizing properties. Chlorine is used in water purification, and as a disinfectant and antiseptic. Chlorinated hydrocarbons (e.g., DDT) are long-lasting pesticides and have become troublesome environmental pollutants. Many poison gases contain chlorine. Chlorine compounds used medically include chloroform and chloral hydrate. See ELEMENT (table); PERIODIC TABLE.

chlorofluorocarbon (CFC), any organic compound composed of CHLORINE, FLUORINE, and CARBON. Derived synthetically from HYDROCARBONS, many CFCs (such as some FREONS) are chemically stable, nonflammable, and relatively nontoxic. Because of such properties, these compounds have been widely used in industry and in consumer products, particularly in the production of foam for insulation and other uses, as AEROSOL propellants, as refrigerants and air conditioner coolants, and as cleansing agents in the production of electronic circuit boards. The resistance of CFCs to chemical breakdown, however, enables them to persist in the environment and migrate to the upper atmosphere. There, sunlight frees their chlorine atoms to form chlorine monoxide, which destroys the OZONE LAYER. In 1987 an international treaty called for reducing CFC use by 50% by 2000. A 1992 revision called for total elimination of CFCs in industrial countries by 1996, and by 1993 CFC emissions had dropped dramatically.

chlorophyll, green pigment in plants that gives most their color and enables them to carry on the process of PHOTOSYNTHESIS. Chlorophyll, found in the CHLOROPLASTS of the plant cell, is the only substance in nature able to trap and store the energy of sunlight. The light absorbed by chlorophyll molecules is mainly in the red and blue-violet parts of the visible spectrum; the green portion is not absorbed but reflected, and thus chlorophyll appears green.

chlorophyte, member of a division (Chlorophyta) of photosynthesizing PROTISTS that includes the green ALGAE and the stoneworts. They possess the same photosynthetic pigments (chlorophylls and carotenoids) as higher plants. Chlorophytes are typically marine or aquatic, have one to several cells and move via two whiplike flagella.

chloroplast, complex, discrete, lens-shaped structure, or organelle, contained in the cytoplasm of plant cells. Chloroplasts have submicroscopic, disklike bodies, called grana, that house CHLOROPHYLL and are the central site of the process of PHOTOSYNTHESIS.

chocolate, term for products of the seeds of the CACAO tree, used for making beverages or candy. Chocolate is prepared by a complex process of cleaning, blending, and roasting the beans, which are then ground and mixed with sugar, cocoa butter, and milk solids. A chocolate drink known to the Aztecs came to Europe through Spanish explorers c.1500, and was a fashionable beverage in 17th- and 18th-cent. England. In 1765 chocolate was first manufactured in the U.S., now the world's leading producer. The process for making milk chocolate was perfected in Switzerland c.1876.

Choctaw, indigenous people of the Eastern Woodlands (see NORTH AMERICA, INDIGENOUS PEOPLES OF), who lived mostly in central and S Mississippi and spoke a Muskogean branch of the Hokan-Siouan language stock (see NATIVE AMERICAN LANGUAGES). They had an agricultural economy and were excellent farmers. After being forced to cede their lands, they moved in 1832 to Indian Territory and became one of the FIVE CIVILIZED TRIBES. In 1990 there were 82,299 Choctaws in the U.S., with more than half living in Oklahoma.

cholera or **Asiatic cholera,** acute infectious disease caused by strains of the bacterium *Vibrio cholerae.* The bacteria, which are found in fecal-contaminated food and water and in raw or undercooked seafood, produce a TOXIN that affects the intestines, causing diarrhea, severe fluid and electrolyte loss, and, if untreated, death. Treatment consists of administration of glucose and electrolyte solutions; vaccines are of limited effectiveness. The disease remains prevalent in regions of the Third World where public sanitation is poor.

cholesterol, fat-related compound found in the tissues and blood plasma of vertebrates. A STEROID, cholesterol is found in large concentrations in the brain, spinal cord, and liver, and is a necessary component of cell membranes. It can be obtained from animal products in the diet or synthesized in the liver. Cholesterol is the major precursor of the synthesis of vitamin D and the various steroid HORMONES and can crystallize in the GALL BLADDER to form gallstones. In the blood, cholesterol travels with a protein in an organic compound called a LIPOPROTEIN. Low-density lipoproteins (LDLs) convey cholesterol from the liver to the body's tissues, and high-density lipoproteins (HDLs) convey cholesterol out of the blood stream for excretion. High levels of LDLs in the blood, or low levels of HDLs, are associated with an increased risk of heart disease; in atherosclerosis (see ARTERIOSCLEROSIS) deposits of cholesterol (mainly LDL cholesterol) accumulate inside blood vessels. Reducing consumption of foods containing cholesterol and saturated fat has been found to lower blood cholesterol levels; cholesterol levels can also be reduced with drugs (e.g., lovastatin).

Chomsky, Noam, 1928–, American linguist; b. Philadelphia. His theory of generative grammar, first proposed in *Syntactic Structures* (1957), revolutionized the study of language (see LINGUISTICS; TRANSFORMATIONAL-GENERATIVE GRAMMAR). He posits innate structures, not minimal sounds, as the basis for speech. He has written numerous linguistic works, e.g., *Reflections on Language* (1975), and books on current politics, e.g., *The Washington Connection and Third World Fascism* (1979), with Edward S. Herman.

Chongqing [chōong-chĭng] or **Chungking** [chōong-kĭng], city (1990 est. pop. 2,980,000), SE Sichuan prov., SW China, at the confluence of the Jialing and Chang (Yangtze) rivers. An industrial hub manufacturing steel and copper, refined oil, machinery, chemicals, and other products, Chongqing comprises a narrow, densely populated inner city rising on a mountain between its two rivers, and a planned industrial and residential district to the west. Long an important regional center, Chongqing became a treaty port in 1891 and was the capital of CHIANG KAI-SHEK's Nationalist government during World War II.

Chopin, Frédéric François [shôpăN′], 1810–49, Franco-Polish composer; b. Poland. He brought romantic piano music to unprecedented heights of expressiveness. In the 1830s he settled in Paris; although he remained a Polish nationalist, he never returned home. He associated with literary and artistic figures, notably George SAND, with whom he had a liaison from 1836 to 1847, when a long illness developed into tuberculosis. Chopin established the PIANO as a solo instrument free from choral or orchestral influence. In his piano CONCERTOS in E Minor (1833) and F Minor (1836), the piano dominates the orchestra. Other major works are 24 preludes (1838–39); SONATAS in B Flat Minor (1840) and B Minor (1845);

many études; and, expressing Polish nationalism, many polonaises and mazurkas.

Chopin, Kate O'Flaherty, 1851–1904, American author; b. St. Louis. Her novel *The Awakening* (1899) caused great controversy because of her treatment of female sexuality but is now highly regarded. She also wrote sketches of Creole life collected in *Bayou Folk* (1894) and *A Night in Acadie* (1897).

chordate, common name for an animal having three unique features at some stage of its development: a notochord (dorsal stiffening rod) as the chief internal support, a tubular nerve cord (spinal cord) above the notochord, and GILL slits leading into the pharynx (anterior part of the digestive tract). Grouped in the phylum Chordata, chordates are mainly vertebrates, animals of the subphylum Vertebrata (the FISHES, AMPHIBIANS, REPTILES, BIRDS, and MAMMALS), in which a backbone of bone or cartilage forms around the notochord; the rest are small aquatic invertebrates of the subphyla Urochordata (TUNICATES) and Cephalochordata (LANCELETS), in which there are no backbones.

chorea, disease causing involuntary jerky, arrhythmic movements of the face, limbs, or entire body. The childhood disease **Sydenham's chorea,** or **St. Vitus's dance,** is usually a complication of RHEUMATIC FEVER. The condition develops slowly, sometimes up to six months after the acute infection has occurred, but it resolves completely. For **Huntington's chorea,** see HUNTINGTON'S DISEASE.

chorionic villus sampling (CVS), diagnostic procedure in which a sample of chorionic villi from the developing placenta is removed from the uterus of a pregnant woman (see PREGNANCY AND BIRTH) using a fine needle inserted through the abdomen or a thin plastic catheter inserted through the cervix. Chorionic villi are fingerlike projections of a membrane surrounding the fetus and develop from the fertilized OVUM, or egg; cells in the sample are grown in the laboratory and studied to detect the presence in the fetus of such genetic BIRTH DEFECTS as TAY-SACHS DISEASE and DOWN'S SYNDROME. The sex of the child may also be ascertained. CVS is usually performed in the 10th or 11th week of pregnancy (several weeks earlier than AMNIOCENTESIS) if the parents are carriers of certain genetic diseases, if there is a family history of genetic disorders, or if the woman is over age 35.

chorus, in ancient Greek drama, the group that spoke to accent the action. It seems to have arisen from the singing of the DITHYRAMB and to have become a true dramatic chorus when THESPIS introduced the actor in the 6th cent. B.C. As TRAGEDY developed, the size and role of the chorus diminished while the importance of the actor increased. By the 2d cent. B.C. it had ceased to have anything to do with the action, and it eventually disappeared.

Chou, dynasty: see CHINA.

Chou En-lai: see ZHOU ENLAI.

Chouteau, family of American fur traders. **René Auguste Chouteau,** 1749–1829, b. New Orleans, established (1764) a trading post that became St. Louis. His half brother, **Jean Pierre Chouteau,** 1758–1849, b. New Orleans, founded (1809) the St. Louis Missouri Fur Company and settled Salina, Okla. Jean Pierre's son, **Auguste Pierre Chouteau,** 1786–1838, b. St. Louis, was a member of the company, and another son, **Pierre Chouteau,** 1789–1865, b. St. Louis, headed the reorganized company until its dissolution in 1864 and became one of the richest, most powerful people in the West.

chow chow, powerful NONSPORTING DOG; shoulder height, 18–20 in. (45.7–50.8 cm); weight, 50–60 lb (22.7–27.2 kg). Its coat has a soft, wooly underlayer and a dense, straight topcoat that stands out from the body. It may be any solid color and is the only breed with a black tongue. A hunting dog in China 2,000 years ago, it was brought to England in the 18th cent.

Chrétien, (Joseph Jacques) Jean, 1934–, Canadian politician, prime minister of Canada (1993–). A lawyer from Quebec and member of the LIBERAL PARTY, he was first elected to parliament in 1963 and served in various ministerial posts under Lester PEARSON and Pierre TRUDEAU. He lost a bid for the Liberal party leadership in 1984 but briefly served as deputy prime minister under John TURNER. Chrétien became party leader in 1990 and prime minister in 1993 after he led the Liberals to victory at the polls.

Chrétien de Troyes or **Chrestien de Troyes** [both: krātyăN' də trwä], fl. 1170, French poet, author of the first great literary treatments of the ARTHURIAN LEGEND. His narrative romances, imbued with the ideals of chivalry, include *Érec et Énide, Cligès,* and *Perceval.*

Christchurch, city (1991 pop. 292,858), E South Island, New Zealand. It is the commercial center of the productive Canterbury Plains and the third largest city in New Zealand. Lyttleton is its port. Perhaps the most English of New Zealand's cities, it has such landmarks as Hagley Park and Christchurch Cathedral. It was settled in 1850 and is the site of the Univ. of Canterbury (est. 1873).

Christian, Danish kings. **Christian I,** 1426–81, king of Denmark (1448–81), Norway (1450–81), and Sweden (1457–64), was the founder of the Oldenburg dynasty of Danish kings. In 1460 he also succeeded to Schleswig and Holstein. A weak monarch, he made concessions to the Danish nobles and lost his authority over Sweden. He was succeeded by his son John, whose son was **Christian II,** 1481–1559, king of Denmark and Norway (1513–23) and Sweden (1520–23). His massacre of Swedish nobles led to the accession of GUSTAVUS I of Sweden and the end of the Kalmar Union. Christian was deposed (1523) by the Danish nobles in favor of his uncle, Frederick I, and imprisoned (1532) until his death. **Christian III,** 1503–59, king of Denmark and Norway (1534–59), was the son of Frederick I. With Gustavus I of Sweden he defeated the German city of LÜBECK (1536), breaking the power of the HANSEATIC LEAGUE. He established (1536) Lutheranism in Denmark. Never elected king of Norway, he declared it a Danish dependency. He was succeeded by his son Frederick II. **Christian IV,** 1577–1648, king of Denmark and Norway (1588–1648), was the son of Frederick II. He made war (1611–13, 1643–45) on CHARLES IX of Sweden and had a major part in the THIRTY YEARS WAR. His son FREDERICK III succeeded him. Frederick's son was **Christian V,** 1646–99, king of Denmark and Norway (1670–99). His minister, GRIFFENFELD, dominated his reign. His son FREDERICK IV succeeded him. **Christian VI,** 1699–1746, king of Denmark and Norway (1730–46), was the son of Frederick IV. A Pietist, he carried out a peaceful foreign policy. In 1733 he established a form of serfdom. His son FREDERICK V succeeded him. **Christian VII,** 1749–1808, king of Denmark and Norway (1766–1808), was Frederick V's son. Because he was mentally ill, power was held first by his ministers and then by his son and successor, FREDERICK VI, as regent. Their reforms included the end of serfdom. **Christian VIII,** 1786–1848, king of Denmark (1839–48) and Norway (1814), was the cousin and successor of Frederick VI. He accepted a liberal Norwegian constitution. In 1836 Danish rule of SCHLESWIG-HOLSTEIN became an issue. His son FREDERICK VII succeeded him. **Christian IX,** 1818–1906, king of Denmark (1863–1906), succeeded Frederick VII, last of the Oldenburg line. In war (1864) with Prussia and Austria he lost Schleswig and Holstein. During his rule there was pressure for a more democratic constitution. His son FREDERICK VIII succeeded him. A younger son became GEORGE I of Greece. **Christian X,** 1870–1947, king of Denmark (1912–47) and Iceland (1912–44), was the son of Frederick VIII and the brother of HAAKON VII of Norway. He granted (1915) a new constitution enfranchising women. During the German occupation (1940–45) he was placed under house arrest (1943). His son FREDERICK IX succeeded him.

Christianity, all doctrines and religious groups based on the teachings of JESUS. Jesus is held by Christians to be the Son of God, the second person of the TRINITY, and the Savior of humanity. This teaching is embodied in the Bible, particularly in the New Testament. Rooted in JUDAISM, Christianity was founded in the 1st cent. in Palestine by disciples of Jesus. It was spread, despite sporadic persecution, through the Roman Empire by missionaries, notably St. PAUL, and was recognized (313) by CONSTANTINE I. The early church was plagued by heresies concerning the nature of Jesus (e.g., ARIANISM, NESTORIANISM, MONOPHYSITISM), which were condemned at councils such as the First Council of NICAEA (325). Monasticism arose in Egypt in the 3d and 4th cent. and was organized in the East by St. Basil the Great and in the West by St. BENEDICT. Christian writers, notably ORIGEN, St. ATHANASIUS, St. JEROME, and St. AUGUSTINE helped to determine and preserve the text of the Bible. In the East the church became centered in Constantinople and was largely subordinate to the emperor; in the West the PAPACY at Rome remained an independent force. From both centers Christianity grew to embrace all Europe, but in the 7th and 8th cent. lost Asia

Minor and N Africa to ISLAM. Gradually, a break developed between East and West (see ROMAN CATHOLIC CHURCH; ORTHODOX EASTERN CHURCH), and became more or less permanent after 1054. In the West the growing power and corruption of the church contributed to the Protestant REFORMATION, which splintered Christianity into numerous sects (see PROTESTANTISM). In the 20th cent. the ECUMENICAL MOVEMENT was begun to promote Christian unity.

Christian Science, religion founded upon principles of divine healing and laws expressed in the acts and sayings of JESUS, as discovered and formulated by Mary Baker EDDY and practiced by the Church of Christ, Scientist. The sect denies the reality of the material world, arguing that sin and illness are illusions to be overcome by the mind; thus, they refuse medical help in fighting sickness. Mrs. Eddy's *Science and Health with Key to the Scriptures* is the textbook of the doctrine. The church was founded in 1879 and is centered in Boston.

Christian socialism, term used in Great Britain and the U.S. for a kind of socialism growing out of the clash between Christian ideals and the effects of competitive business. In Europe it usually refers to a party or trade union directed by religious leaders in contrast to socialist unions and parties. Begun (1848) in England and led by Frederick Denison MAURICE and Charles KINGSLEY, it sought to encourage the laboring masses and the church to cooperate against capitalism. It was influenced by the Fourierists (see FOURIER, CHARLES), rather than by MARX. In the U.S. the movement was organized (1889) with the formation of the Society of Christian Socialists and was concerned more with the application of the SOCIAL GOSPEL to immediate industrial and social problems than with political socialism.

Christie, Dame Agatha, 1891–1976, English detective-story writer. Of her over 80 books, most feature one of two detectives, Hercule Poirot or Jane Marple. Her novels include *The Murder of Roger Ackroyd* (1926) and *The Pale Horse* (1962). Among her plays is the long-running *Mousetrap* (1952).

Christina, 1626–89, queen of Sweden (1632–54), daughter of GUSTAVUS II. Until 1644 she was under a regency headed by OXENSTIERNA. Because of her zeal for learning, she attracted to her court musicians, poets, and such scholars as DESCARTES. She refused to marry, naming her cousin, later CHARLES X, as her successor. In 1654 she abdicated, becoming a Catholic and settling in Rome. On the death (1660) of Charles X she returned to Sweden but failed to regain the throne. She is buried at St. Peter's in Rome.

Christmas [Christ's Mass], in the Christian calendar, the feast of the nativity of JESUS (Dec. 25). It ranks after EASTER, PENTECOST, and EPIPHANY in liturgical importance and was not widespread until the 4th cent. The customs of the yule log, caroling, mistletoe, and gifts at Christmas are English. Elsewhere, gifts are given at other times, as at Epiphany in Spain. Christmas cards appeared c.1846. The concept of a jolly Santa Claus (see NICHOLAS, SAINT) was first made popular in 19th-cent. New York City. The Christmas tree was a medieval German tradition. Midnight Mass is a familiar religious observance among Roman Catholics and some Protestants.

Christmasberry or **toyon,** evergreen tree or shrub (*Photinia arbutifolia*) of the ROSE family, found on the North American Pacific coast. White flowers precede its bright red berries. Also called California holly, it is a Christmas green.

Christmas Island, tropical island (1992 est. pop. 930), 60 sq mi (155 sq km), external territory of Australia, in the Indian Ocean. Most of the inhabitants are Chinese and Malays who had come to work the island's phosphate mine, which closed in 1987. The island was annexed by Great Britain in 1888 and transferred to Australian rule in 1958.

Christo, 1935–, Bulgarian artist; b. Christo Javacheff. His art has typically involved wrapping objects, giving them a temporary, artificial skin that both conceals and reveals, thus transforming the everyday into the ambiguous. His work includes *Running Fence* (1976), a fabric curtain that ran 24 mi (38.6 km) through the California countryside, and *The Umbrellas* (1991), 1,340 20-ft (6.1-m) tall blue umbrellas in rice fields 70 mi (113 km) north of Tokyo and 1,760 yellow ones in Tejon Pass, NW of Los Angeles.

Christ of the Andes, statue of Jesus in Uspallata Pass, the ANDES. Dedicated on March 13, 1904, it commemorates a series of peace and boundary treaties between Argentina and Chile.

Christophe, Henri [krēstôf′], 1767–1820, Haitian revolutionary leader. A freed black slave, he helped TOUSSAINT L'OUVERTURE to liberate HAITI and plotted the assassination of DESSALINES. A tyrant, he ruled (1806–20) N Haiti as King Henri I. He committed suicide.

Christopher, Saint, 3d cent.?, martyr of Asia Minor. In legend he carried a child across a river and felt the child's weight almost too heavy to bear; the child was JESUS, who was holding the world in his hands. Christopher is the patron of travelers. His feast, July 25, was dropped from the Roman Catholic liturgical calendar in 1969.

Christopher, Warren M(inor), 1925–, U.S. government official; b. Scranton, N.D. A Democrat and a lawyer in private practice, he held a number of government posts before he served (1967–69) as deputy attorney general under Pres. Lyndon JOHNSON. From 1977 to 1981 he was deputy secretary of state under Pres. CARTER and was the chief U.S. negotiator in the talks (1981) that ended the Iranian hostage crisis (see IRAN). Christopher was appointed secretary of state by Pres. CLINTON in 1993.

Christus or **Cristus, Petrus** [both: krĭs′təs], fl. 1444–c.1473, Flemish painter. A follower and probable pupil of the van EYCKS, he was noted for his introspective treatment of figures and rendering of geometric perspective. Many of his compositions are simplifications of Jan van Eyck's paintings. They include *Lamentation* (Brussels) and *Nativity* (National Gall., Wash., D.C.).

Christy, Edwin P., 1815–62, American showman; b. Philadelphia. In c.1846 he established Christy's Minstrels. The company crystallized the pattern for minstrel shows, with variety acts and white performers in blackface.

chromatography, resolution of a chemical mixture into its components by passing through a stationary system that retards each component to a varying degree. The retarding substance is usually a surface adsorbent, such as ALUMINA, CELLULOSE, or SILICA. In column chromatography the adsorbent is packed into a column, and a solution of the mixture is added at the top and washed, or eluted, down with an appropriate solvent; each component of the mixture passes through the column at a different speed. In paper chromatography the mixture to be separated is allowed to soak along the paper by capillary action, the cellulose in the paper acting as the adsorbent. In gas chromatography a liquid with a high boiling point is impregnated on an inert solid support packed into a thin metal column, and helium gas is allowed to flow through it. The solution to be analyzed is injected into the column, immediately volatized, and swept by the helium gas through the column; at this point the mixture is resolved into its components.

chromium (Cr), metallic element, discovered in 1797 by L.N. Vauquelin. A lustrous, silver-gray metal, it is comparatively rare and occurs only in compounds; the chief source is the mineral chromite. Hard and nontarnishing, chromium is used to plate other metals; in alloys (see, e.g., STEEL) with other metals it contributes hardness, strength, and heat resistance. Chromium compounds are used as paint pigments, in tanning, and in dyeing. See ELEMENT (table); PERIODIC TABLE.

chromosome, structural carrier of hereditary characteristics, found in the cell nucleus. The number of chromosomes is characteristic of each species; in sexually reproducing species, chromosomes generally occur in pairs. In MITOSIS, or ordinary cell division, each individual chromosome is duplicated and each daughter cell receives all chromosomes, a set exactly like its parent's. In MEIOSIS, the process by which germ cells (OVUM and SPERM) are formed, each daughter cell receives half the number of chromosomes, one of each pair. A fertilized egg contains two sets of chromosomes, one set from each parent. Chromosomes are made of DNA and associated proteins. They represent the linear arrangement of GENES, the units of inheritance.

chromosphere: see SUN.

chronic fatigue syndrome, syndrome that begins with flu-like symptoms followed by months or years of lethargy, weakness, and inability to concentrate. Misdiagnosed as "imaginary" for nearly a century, it has had various names, including the "yuppie flu" in the mid-1980s. Although many patients exhibit signs of brain inflammation, hormonal deficits, immune system abnormalities, and viral infections, the exact cause is unknown.

Chronicles or **Paralipomenon** [pâr″əlĭpŏm′ĭnŏn] [Gr., = things left out], two books of the OLD TESTAMENT, 13th and 14th in the Authorized Version, originally a single work in the Hebrew canon. The books contain a history of the Jewish kingdom under DAVID (1 Chron. 10–29) and SOLOMON (2 Chron. 1–9), and, after the division of the kingdom, a history of the southern kingdom of JUDAH, including the BABYLONIAN CAPTIVITY (2 Chron. 10–36).

chronometer, instrument for keeping highly accurate time. The perfection of the chronometer in 1759 by the English clockmaker John Harrison allowed navigators at sea to determine longitude accurately for the first time. A mechanical marine chronometer is a spring-driven escapement timekeeper, like a watch, but its parts are more massively built and it has devices to compensate for changes in the tension of the spring caused by changes in temperature. Modern chronometers are electronic, using quartz crystal vibrations to regulate their timekeeping.

chrysanthemum, annual or perennial herb (genus *Chrysanthemum*) of the COMPOSITE family, long grown in E Asia. The chrysanthemum is a national flower of Japan and the floral emblem of the Japanese imperial family. The red, white, or yellow flowers range from single daisylike heads to large rounded or shaggy heads. They are commercially important. Innumerable horticultural types exist, most varieties of *C. morifolium.* The pyrethrum, feverfew, marguerite, and DAISY belong in the same genus.

Chrysler, Walter Percy, 1875–1940, American industrialist, founder of the Chrysler Corp.; b. Wamego, Kans. Initially a machinist's apprentice, he became (1916) a vice president of the General Motors Corp. and in 1924 brought out the first Chrysler car. The Chrysler Corp., founded in 1925, became one of the major U.S. automobile companies.

chrysophyte, member of a division (Chrysophyta) of photosynthesizing PROTISTS that consists of the yellow-green ALGAE, golden-brown algae, and DIATOMS. Traditionally classified as plants, they differ from them in their pigmentation, in that their cell walls contain large quantities of silica, and in the way that they store food.

Chrysostom: see JOHN CHRYSOSTOM, SAINT.

chrysotile: see ASBESTOS; SERPENTINE.

Chula Vista, city (1990 pop. 135,163), San Diego co., S Calif., on San Diego Bay; inc. 1911. A port of entry located in an area of citrus and truck farms, it grew with the expanding aircraft industry in nearby San Diego. Its population, which includes many Mexican-Americans, has mushroomed since 1980.

Chun Doo Hwan, 1931–, Korean military leader, president of South Korea (1980–88). An army officer, Chun rose to power after the assassination (1979) of South Korean Pres. PARK CHUNG HEE. As president, Chun banned many of his opponents from politics and secured (1980) a new, authoritarian constitution.

Chungking: see CHONGQING.

Chunnel: see ENGLISH CHANNEL.

Church, Frederick Edwin, 1826–1900, American painter; b. Hartford, Conn. A member of the HUDSON RIVER SCHOOL, he preferred exotic foreign landscapes to native views. His large canvases are noted for their crystalline portrayal of light.

Churches of Christ, conservative body of Protestant Christians, formerly united with the DISCIPLES OF CHRIST. Highly evangelistic, they are congregational in polity and biblical in doctrine, and form one of the larger American denominations. They have about 1.7 million members in the U.S.

Churchill, John: see MARLBOROUGH, JOHN CHURCHILL, 1ST DUKE OF.

Churchill, Sarah: see under MARLBOROUGH, JOHN CHURCHILL, 1ST DUKE OF.

Churchill, Sir Winston Leonard Spencer, 1874–1965, British statesman, soldier, and author. A graduate of Sandhurst, he fought in India, the Sudan, and South Africa. In 1900 he was elected to Parliament. He was the first lord of the admiralty (1911–15) in WORLD WAR I until discredited by the failure of the Dardanelles campaign, which he had championed. He later served in several cabinet positions in the Liberal government of LLOYD GEORGE. A Conservative after 1924, he was chancellor of the exchequer from 1924 to 1929; his revaluation of the pound was a factor leading to the general strike of 1926. Out of office from 1929 to 1939, Churchill issued unheeded warnings of the threat of Nazi Germany. In 1940, seven months after the outbreak of WORLD WAR II, he replaced Neville CHAMBERLAIN as prime minister. His stirring oratory, his energy, and his refusal to make peace with HITLER were crucial to maintaining British resistance from 1940 to 1942. Before the U.S. entry into the war, he met Pres. F.D. ROOSEVELT at sea. He twice addressed the U.S. Congress, twice went to Moscow, and attended a series of international conferences (e.g., YALTA CONFERENCE). After the postwar Labour victory in 1945, he became leader of the opposition. In 1951 he was again elected prime minister; he was knighted in 1953 and retired in 1955. Churchill was the author of many histories, biographies, and memoirs, and in 1953 he was awarded the Nobel Prize in literature for his writing and his oratory.

Churchill, river, NE Canada, called the Hamilton R. until renamed (1965) for Sir Winston Churchill. It flows c.600 mi (970 km) from Ashuanipi Lake across Labrador (Newfoundland) to the Atlantic. One of the world's largest hydroelectric installations (5.2 Mw; completed 1971) is located at Churchill (formerly Grand) Falls.

Church of Christ, Scientist: see CHRISTIAN SCIENCE.

Church of England: see ENGLAND, CHURCH OF.

Church of Scotland: see SCOTLAND, CHURCH OF.

Church Slavonic, language belonging to the South Slavic group of the Slavic subfamily of the Indo-European family of languages. It is the first Slavic tongue known to be recorded in writing. From the 9th to 11th cent. A.D. the language is termed Old Church Slavonic, Old Church Slavic, or Old Bulgarian. The later Church Slavonic flourished as a literary language before the 18th cent. It is still the liturgical language of most branches of the ORTHODOX EASTERN CHURCH, but is extinct as a spoken tongue. See LANGUAGE (table).

Churriguera, José Benito [cho͞orrēgä'rä], 1665–1725, Spanish architect and sculptor. He won fame for his design (1689) for the great catafalque for Queen Maria Luisa and for his ornate retables. Associated with his brothers, he was architect for the cathedral of Salamanca and built a private palace and the urban complex Nuevo Baztán in Madrid. The term **Churrigueresque** describes late-17th- and early-18th-cent. Spanish architecture, marked by extravagance of design and capricious use of Renaissance motives. Its influence was important in the missions of Spanish colonial North America.

Chu Teh: see ZHU DE.

CIA: see CENTRAL INTELLIGENCE AGENCY.

Cibber, Colley, 1671–1757, English dramatist and actor-manager. After successes playing RESTORATION comedy, he wrote *Love's Last Shift* (1696), the first sentimental COMEDY. He wrote 30 more plays and was made poet laureate in 1730. An unpopular man, he was attacked by Alexander POPE in *The Dunciad.*

cicada, large, noise-producing INSECT (order Homoptera) with a stout body, a wide blunt head, protruding eyes, and two pairs of membranous wings. The males have platelike membranes on the thorax, which they vibrate, producing a loud, shrill sound; females are mute. The periodical cicadas (genus *Magicicada*) have the longest life cycles known of any insect, 13 years in one species and 17 in another, but winged adults only live for about one week.

Cicero or **Tully** (Marcus Tullius Cicero), 106 B.C.–43 B.C., greatest Roman orator, also a philosopher. As senatorial party leader he prosecuted CATILINE, but was later exiled himself by CLODIUS; recalled by POMPEY, he opposed Julius CAESAR. He answered Mark ANTONY in the senate with his first and second PHILIPPICS, defending the Republic. After Octavian (AUGUSTUS) took Rome, Cicero was executed. To the modern reader, his letters, to his brother and friends, are perhaps most interesting. His philosophical works are generally stoical (see STOICISM). He is best known for his *Orations against Catiline, Against Verres, On the Manilian Law,* and others. His mastery of Latin prose is unsurpassed.

Cid or **Cid Campeador** [sĭd], d. 1099, Spanish soldier whose exploits were romanticized in many literary works. He fought against the MOORS but ALFONSO VI distrusted and banished (1081) him. The Cid then served the Muslim ruler of ZARAGOZA, fighting against Moors and Christians alike. In 1094 he conquered VALENCIA and ruled there until his death.

Cilicia, ancient region of SE Asia Minor, between the Mediterranean and the Taurus range. Part of the Assyrian empire and then of the Persian empire, it was later hellenized. Roman and Byzantine rule followed. Cilicia was invaded (8th cent. A.D.) by the Arabs, and in 1080 an Armenian state (later called Little Armenia) was set up. This lasted until the area was conquered by the Turks in 1375.

ciliate or **ciliophore,** member of a subphylum (Ciliophora) comprising the most complex PROTOZOANS, including the slipper-shaped PARAMECIUM and the trumpet-shaped stentor. Ciliates are characterized by short hairlike structures (cilia) that cover the cell surface and aid in locomotion, a mouth, and a contractile vacuole for pumping waste and water from the cell.

Cimabue, Giovanni [chēmäbo͞o'ā], d. c.1302, Florentine painter; b. Cenni di Pepo or Peppi. His works constitute the transition from formal Byzantine painting to the freer expression of the 14th cent. Master of MOSAICS at the cathedral at Pisa, he kept many of the old forms while giving his figures greater naturalism. His attributed works include the *Madonna Enthroned* (Uffizi) and a *Crucifixion* (Santa Croce, Florence).

Cimarron, Territory of, now the Oklahoma panhandle. It was settled in the early 1800s by cattle ranchers, most of them squatters. After several unsuccessful attempts to create a separate territorial government for the area, Cimarron became part of Oklahoma Territory in 1890.

Cimbri: see GERMANS.

Cimmerians, ancient and little-known people who were driven (8th cent. B.C.) from the CRIMEA to the Lake Van region in present E Turkey. They swept across Asia Minor (late 7th cent.), plundering Lydia and weakening Phrygia.

cinchona or **chinchona,** evergreen tree (genus *Cinchona*) of the MADDER family, native to mountainous areas of South and Central America and widely cultivated elsewhere for its bark, the source of QUININE and other antimalarial alkaloids. The tree was named for the Countess of Chinchón, said to have been cured of a fever in 1638 by a preparation of the bark.

Cincinnati, city (1990 pop. 364,040; met. area 1,452,645), seat of Hamilton co., SW Ohio, on the Ohio R.; founded 1788, inc. as a city 1819. It is the industrial, commercial, and cultural center of a large area of Ohio and neighboring Kentucky, and a major river port and transportation center. Machine tools, processed food, electrical equipment, metal goods, and cosmetics are among its manufactures. The city was the first seat (1799) of the legislature of the NORTHWEST TERRITORY. Attractively situated in hilly terrain, it has undergone major renovation of its downtown area. Cultural institutions include its conservatory, opera, museums, and symphony orchestra. William Howard TAFT and Robert A. TAFT were born there, and it is the site of the Taft Museum.

Cincinnatus (Lucius or Titus Quinctius Cincinnatus), fl. 5th cent. B.C., Roman patriot. He was consul (460 B.C.) and dictator twice (458 and 439). According to tradition, he was called from his farm to defend Rome twice, first from foreign invaders, then from the plebeians.

cinematography: see MOTION-PICTURE PHOTOGRAPHY.

Cinna (Lucius Cornelius Cinna), d. 84 B.C., Roman politician. When SULLA left Italy, Cinna as consul (87–84 B.C.) opposed him, and slaughtered many of Sulla's followers. After Sulla set out for Rome, and before the civil war began, Cinna was murdered in a mutiny at Brundisium. His daughter Cornelia was the first wife of Julius CAESAR.

cinnabar, deep-red mercury sulfide mineral (HgS). Used as a pigment, it is principally a source of the metal MERCURY. Cinnabar is mined in Spain, Italy, and California.

cinnamon, tree or shrub (genus *Cinnamomum*) of the LAUREL family. Cinnamon spice, obtained by drying the bark of the tropical Ceylon cinnamon (*C. zeylanicum*), has been used since biblical times. *C. camphora* is the source of CAMPHOR.

CIO: see AMERICAN FEDERATION OF LABOR AND CONGRESS OF INDUSTRIAL ORGANIZATIONS.

Cione, Andrea di: see ORCAGNA.

Circe [sûr'sē], in Greek mythology, enchantress; daughter of HELIOS. In HOMER's *Odyssey* she turned ODYSSEUS' men into swine, but was forced to break the spell.

circle, closed plane CURVE consisting of all points at a given distance from a fixed point, called the center. A radius of a circle is any line segment connecting the center and the curve; the word *radius* is also used for the length r of that line segment. Both the circle itself and its length C are referred to by the term *circumference.* A line segment whose two ends lie on the circumference is a *chord;* a chord through the center is a *diameter.* The circumference of a circle is given by $C = 2\pi r$. The area A bounded by a circle is given by $A = \pi r^2$. In the religion and art of many cultures the circle frequently symbolizes heaven, eternity, or the universe. See also CONIC SECTION.

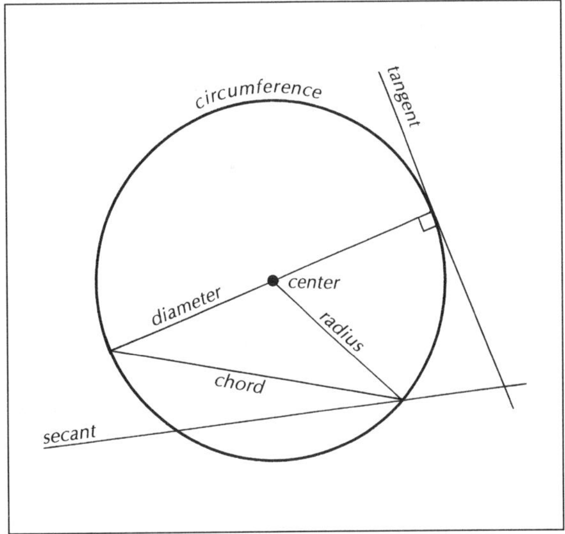

Circle

circuit breaker, electric device that, like a FUSE, interrupts a current in an ELECTRIC CIRCUIT when the current becomes too high. Unlike a fuse, which must be replaced after it has been used once, a circuit breaker can be reset after it has been tripped. When a high current passes through the circuit breaker, the heat it generates or the magnetic field it creates causes a trigger to rapidly separate the pair of contacts that normally conduct the current.

circuit rider, itinerant preacher of the Methodist denomination who served a "circuit" of 20 to 40 "appointments." The system was devised in the 18th cent. by John WESLEY for his English societies and was adapted in America by Francis ASBURY, where it aided greatly the spread of METHODISM.

circulatory system, a group of organs that transport blood and the substances it carries to and from all parts of the body. In humans the circulatory system consists of vessels (arteries and veins) that carry the blood and a muscular pump, the HEART, that drives the blood. Arteries carry the blood away from the heart; the main arterial vessel, the aorta, branches into smaller arteries, which in turn branch into still smaller vessels that reach all parts of the body. In the smallest blood vessels, the capillaries, which are located in body tissue, the gas and nutrient exchange occurs—the blood gives up nutrients and oxygen to the cells and accepts carbon dioxide, water, and wastes (see RESPIRATION). Blood leaving the tissue capillaries enters converging large vessels, the veins, to return to the heart. The human heart has four chambers and a dividing wall, or septum, that separates the heart into a right and a left heart. Oxygen-poor, carbon dioxide–rich blood from the veins returns to the right side of the heart. The heart contracts to pump the blood through pulmonary arteries to the LUNGS, where the blood receives oxygen and eliminates carbon dioxide. Pulmonary veins return the oxygen-rich blood to the left side of the heart. The left side then pumps the oxygenated blood through the branching aorta and arteries to all parts of the body. The organs most intimately related to the substances carried by the blood are the KIDNEYS, SPLEEN, and LIVER. An auxiliary system, the LYMPHATIC SYSTEM, collects lymph, or tissue fluid, from body tissues and returns it to the blood. See also ARTERIOSCLEROSIS; BLOOD PRESSURE; CORONARY ARTERY DISEASE; HEART DISEASE; SHOCK; STROKE.

circumcision, operation to remove the foreskin covering the glans of the penis. Dating from prehistoric times, it is performed by Jews as a sacramental operation eight days after the birth of a male child. It is also practiced among Muslims and other peoples and is often performed as a sanitary measure. Female circumcision, e.g.,

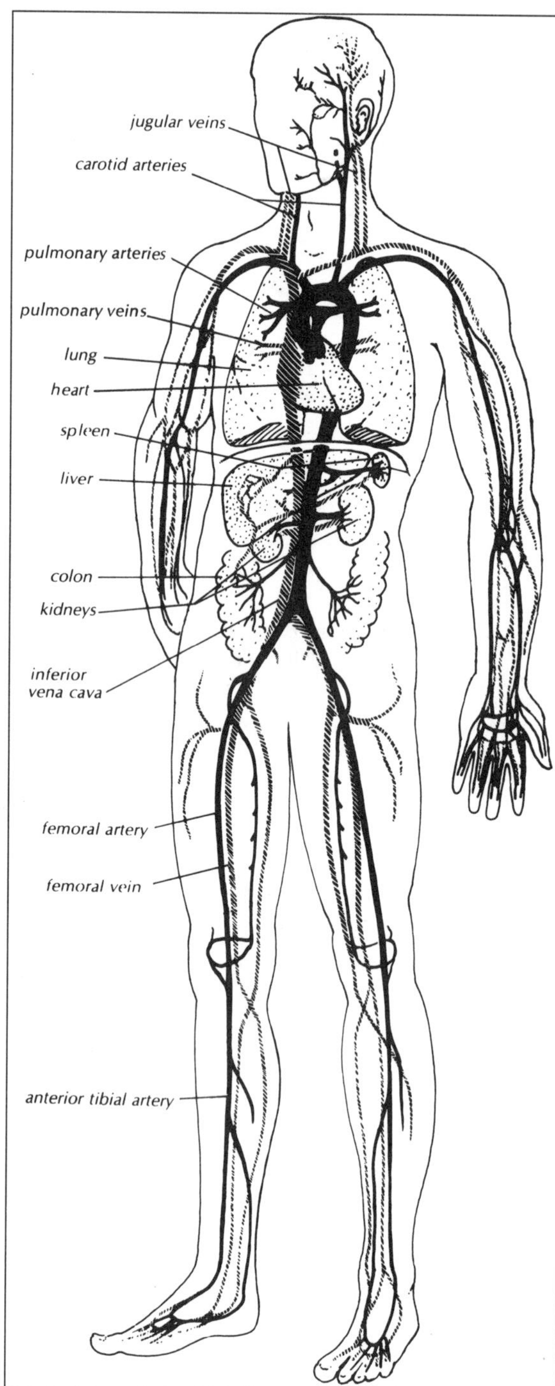

Schematic diagram of the circulatory system

excision of the labia minora and clitoris, or clitoridectomy, is found in Islam and in certain tribes of Africa, South America, and elsewhere.

circumpolar star, a star whose apparent daily path on the celestial sphere lies completely above or below an observer's horizon. A star whose declination (see ASTRONOMICAL COORDINATE SYSTEMS) is greater than 90° minus an observer's latitude will always remain above the horizon for that observer.

circus [Lat., = circle], associated historically with the horse and chariot races, gladiatorial combats, and brutal athletic contests known in ancient Rome as the Circensian games. The Roman circus was a round or oval structure, with tiers of spectators' seats enclosing the area where the action took place. The modern circus, which originated in performances of equestrian feats in a horse ring, dates from the late 18th cent. It is a tent show featuring wild and trained animals, acrobats, freaks, and clowns. The three-ring circus was originated by James A. Bailey. The most famous U.S. show was P.T. BARNUM's. Barnum and Bailey merged with Ringling Brothers in 1919. In its heyday from 1880–1920, the traveling circus declined in the 1950s and 60s. By the 1980s, however, the form had revived somewhat and more than 30 circuses were touring the U.S. and Canada.

cire perdue [Fr., = lost wax], process of hollow metal CASTING. A plaster or clay model is coated with wax and covered with a mold of perforated plaster or clay. Heat is applied, the wax melts and runs out of the holes, and molten metal (usually bronze) is poured into the space formerly occupied by the wax. When the metal is cool, the mold is broken and the core removed. Probably of Egyptian origin, the method was introduced into Greece in the 6th cent. B.C. and was used extensively from the 5th cent. The process, employed worldwide, was brought to China c.200 B.C. and was later used in casting the Benin bronzes of Africa. The great bronze masterpieces of the RENAISSANCE were produced by the cire perdue method.

cirrhosis, degeneration of LIVER tissue, resulting in fibrosis and nodule formation. Portal cirrhosis is the most prevalent form, occurring in patients with a history of ALCOHOLISM; other forms are caused by infections, such as HEPATITIS, and obstruction of BILE flow. Cirrhosis can result in gastrointestinal disturbances, emaciation, JAUNDICE, and edema. It is irreversible, but supportive treatment includes diet control, VITAMINS, diuretics (to remove accumulated fluid), and beta blockers (to control gastrointestinal bleeding). Cirrhosis is a common cause of death in the U.S.

Cisalpine Republic, 1797–1802, Italian state created by Napoleon Bonaparte, who united the two republics he had established (1796) N and S of the Po River. A French protectorate, it became the Italian Republic (1802) and, with the addition of Venetia, the Napoleonic kingdom of Italy (1805), which was broken up by the Congress of VIENNA (1815).

Ciskei [sĭskī′], black South African homeland, or BANTUSTAN (1990 est. pop. 1,000,000), 3,280 sq mi (8,500 sq km), declared independent (1981) by South Africa but not recognized as such by other nations. Bisho was the capital; the largest city was Mdantsane. Many of the Xhosa-speaking inhabitants were forcibly moved to Ciskei from Cape Province in the 1970s. South Africa took control of the homeland in 1994 after the Ciskei police mutinied, and it was reabsorbed.

Cisleithania: see AUSTRO-HUNGARIAN MONARCHY.

Citlaltépetl [sē″tlältā′petəl] or **Orizaba** [ōrēsä′bä], snow-capped, inactive volcano, highest peak (18,406 ft/5,610 m) in Mexico and third highest in North America. It last erupted in 1687.

citizens band radio: see RADIO.

citric acid cycle or **Krebs cycle,** series of chemical reactions occurring in the cells of higher plants, animals, and many microorganisms. It is essential for the oxidative metabolism of GLUCOSE and other simple sugars. The reactions take a molecule of citric acid (originating from glucose) through several intermediate products; additional organic molecules are incorporated, new molecules generated, and citric acid is regenerated. Each cycle releases hydrogen ions, which are necessary for the next stage of the metabolic process to generate chemical energy for the organism.

citron, small evergreen tree (*Citrus medica*) of the ORANGE family, and its fruit, the first of the CITRUS FRUITS introduced to Europe from E Asia. Citrons are grown in the Mediterranean, West Indies, Florida, and California. The large yellow-green, thin-rinded, and furrowed fruit contains a thick, white, and tender inner rind and a small acid pulp. The juice is used as a beverage and syrup, and the candied, preserved rind is used in confectionery and cookery.

citrus fruits, edible fruits of trees of the orange, or RUE, family; almost all native to Southeast Asia and the East Indies. The fruits are rich in vitamin C, citric acid, and sugars; the rind and blossoms yield ESSENTIAL OILS. Citrus fruits include the ORANGE, GRAPEFRUIT, LEMON, LIME, and KUMQUAT.

city-state, in ancient GREECE, autonomous political unit consisting of a city and the surrounding countryside. Greece was organized into several hundred city-states, with a variety of governments ranging from absolute monarchy to pure democracy. Only citizens participated in the government of the city-state, and citizenship was limited to those born of citizen parents. A large proportion of the population consisted of slaves. The organization of Greece into separate city-states left it open to foreign attack by large centralized states, to which it eventually became subject.

Civil Aeronautics Board: see under FEDERAL AVIATION ADMINISTRATION.

Civilian Conservation Corps (CCC), founded in 1933 by the U.S. Congress to provide work and job training for unemployed young men in conserving and developing the nation's natural resources. It was abolished in 1942.

civil law, legal system based on ROMAN LAW; also the body of law dealing with relationships between individuals, as opposed to CRIMINAL LAW, which deals with offenses against the state. After the collapse of the Roman Empire, the legal ideas and concepts of Rome were kept alive in the canon law of the medieval church and the *Corpus Juris Civilis* (6th cent.) of JUSTINIAN I. There are many later codifications of civil law principles. The most famous is the Code Napoléon (1804), the codification of the civil law of France, which has strongly influenced the law of continental Europe and Latin America, where civil law is prevalent. In contrast to COMMON LAW, prevalent in English-speaking countries (including the U.S., except Louisiana), civil law judgments are based on codified principles rather than on precedents, and civil law courts do not generally employ trial by jury or the law of evidence.

civil rights, rights protecting a person against arbitrary or discriminatory treatment. The U.S. CONSTITUTION guarantees freedom of religion, speech, and the PRESS, freedom of assembly, and rights to due process of law (e.g., HABEAS CORPUS) and equal protection under the law. After the CIVIL WAR, efforts to extend civil rights to African Americans were only in part realized by the 14th and 15th constitutional amendments. In the 20th cent. the African-American civil-rights movement, led by the NATIONAL ASSOCIATION FOR THE ADVANCEMENT OF COLORED PEOPLE, the National Urban League, Martin Luther KING, Jr., and others, was instrumental in securing legislation, notably the civil-rights acts of 1964 and 1968 and the voting rights act of 1965, prohibiting discrimination in public accommodations, schools, employment, and voting for reasons of color, race, religion, or national origin (see INTEGRATION). WOMAN SUFFRAGE was achieved in the U.S. under the 19th amendment (1920). Congress passed the Equal Rights Amendment, prohibiting discrimination on grounds of sex, in 1972, but the amendment failed to win ratification (see FEMINISM). The federal AMERICANS WITH DISABILITIES ACT, enacted in 1990, forbids discrimination against disabled persons. See also GAY RIGHTS MOVEMENT.

civil service, entire body of those employed in civil administration as distinct from the military, excluding elected officials. While competitive examinations were used to select officials in ancient China, a civil service based on merit emerged in the West with the decline of feudalism and the growth of the nation-state. Prussia (mid-17th cent.) and, later, France (especially after NAPOLEON I) developed efficient civil administrations. The term, first used to designate British administration in India, was extended to Great Britain in 1854. Civil service reform in the U.S. was spurred by the scandals of GRANT's administration. The Pendleton Act (1883) re-established the **Civil Service Commission** (first est. 1871), which sets up examinations for all positions classified as civil service; most federal jobs are so classified. As a result of reports (1949, 1955) by the Hoover Commission, the federal civil service was streamlined, and operations and activities of many agencies became part of the General Services Administration. The Hatch Act (1940), forbidding political campaigning by civil servants, was an attempt to separate civil service from politics. A 1993 revision of the act allows most civil servants to engage in political activity on their own time.

civil time: see SOLAR TIME.

Civil War, English: see ENGLISH CIVIL WAR.

Civil War, in U.S. history, conflict (1861–65) between Northern states (Union) and Southern seceded states (CONFEDERACY). It is known in the South as the War between the States, and by the official Union designation of War of the Rebellion. Many causes over a number of years contributed to what William H. SEWARD called "the irrepressible conflict": sectional rivalry, moral indignation aroused by the ABOLITIONISTS, the question of the extension of slavery into new territories, and a fundamental disagreement about the relative supremacy of federal control or STATES' RIGHTS. The MISSOURI COMPROMISE (1820) and the COMPROMISE OF 1850 were unsuccessful efforts toward a peaceful solution. The election of LINCOLN as president and the secession (Dec. 20, 1860) of SOUTH CAROLINA, soon followed by six other Southern states, precipitated war. Hostilities began when federal troops were moved to FORT SUMTER, S.C., and Confederate Gen. P.G.T. BEAUREGARD obeyed orders to fire on the fort (Apr. 12, 1861). Four more states seceded, making an 11-state Confederacy. Early battles were Confederate victories. Beauregard defeated Irvin McDowell (July 21) at the first battle of BULL RUN. In 1862, G.B. MCCLELLAN's PENINSULAR CAMPAIGN was foiled by Confederate commander Robert E. LEE. In September, however, Lee's ANTIETAM CAMPAIGN was checked by McClellan, and Lincoln drafted the EMANCIPATION PROCLAMATION. The year ended with a Union defeat (Dec. 13) at FREDERICKSBURG, and spring brought a resounding Confederate victory (May 2–4, 1863) at CHANCELLORSVILLE, where Lee, however, lost his ablest general, "Stonewall" JACKSON. Confederate fortunes turned when Lee undertook the disastrous GETTYSBURG CAMPAIGN (June–July 1863). Meanwhile, the Union navy had blockaded the Southern coast, and D.G. FARRAGUT captured New Orleans (Apr. 1862). The introduction of the ironclad warship (see MONITOR AND MERRIMAC) had ended the era of the wooden battleship, but Confederate cruisers, built or bought in England, were causing great losses to Northern commercial shipping. In the West, GRANT's great victory (Feb. 1862) at Fort Donelson was followed by a drawn battle (April 6–7) at SHILOH. Union gunboats on the Mississippi opened the way for Grant's successful VICKSBURG CAMPAIGN. Confederate Gen. Braxton BRAGG was checked at the end of the CHATTANOOGA CAMPAIGN (Aug.–Nov. 1863) and was driven back to Georgia. In the WILDERNESS CAMPAIGN (May–June 1864), Grant forced Lee toward Richmond, and besieged PETERSBURG. Union Gen. W.T. SHERMAN won the ATLANTA CAMPAIGN (May–Sept. 1864) and led a destructive march through Georgia to the sea. The Confederates evacuated Richmond after P.H. SHERIDAN's victory at Five Forks (Apr. 1, 1865). With his retreat blocked, Lee was forced to surrender to Grant at APPOMATTOX (Apr. 9, 1865). The Union victory was saddened by the assassination of Pres. Lincoln (April 14), and by the deaths of more Americans than in any other war. But the Union was saved, and slavery was abolished. The seceded states were readmitted to the Union after RECONSTRUCTION.

Cl, chemical symbol of the element CHLORINE.

cladistics, an approach to the CLASSIFICATION of living things in which organisms are defined and grouped by the possession of one or more shared characteristics that are derived from a common ancestor and that were not present in any ancestral group (as envisioned by DARWIN's idea of "descent with modification"). It is a method of reconstructing EVOLUTION that emphasizes the importance of descent and common ancestry rather than simple overall similarity.

Claflin, Tennessee: see WOODHULL, VICTORIA (CLAFLIN).

Clair, René [klâr], 1898–1981, French film director. His films, noted for wit and fantastic satire, include *Sous le Toits de Paris* (1929), *The Ghost Goes West* (1936), and *Les Belles de nuit* (1952).

clam, name for some BIVALVE mollusks, especially marine species that live buried in mud or sand and have shells (valves) of equal size. Clams burrow by means of a muscular foot, which can be extruded through the valves. Clams are highly valued as food. Some freshwater bivalves are also called clams. See also MOLLUSK.

clan, social group based on assumed unilateral descent from a common ancestor. Such groups have existed all over the world, including some that claim the parentage or special protection of an animal, plant, or other object (see TOTEM) as well as such familiar groups as the Highland clans of Scotland. Most clans are exogamous and regard marriages among their members as incest. A clan is distinguished from a lineage in that a clan merely claims common ancestry and may have several lineages; a lineage can be traced to a common progenitor. Several clans may combine into a larger social group called a phratry.

Clarendon, Edward Hyde, 1st **earl of,** 1607–74, English statesman and historian. A monarchist, he aided CHARLES I and went into exile with CHARLES II. After the RESTORATION, he was lord chancellor. Although he favored religious toleration, he was forced by Parliament to enforce the CLARENDON CODE. In 1667 Charles made him the scapegoat for various failures in the second DUTCH WAR and removed him from office. He fled England and died in exile. He wrote *History of the Rebellion.* His daughter Anne married JAMES II.

Clarendon, Constitutions of, 16 articles issued in 1164 by HENRY II of England at the Council of Clarendon. Important in the development of English law, the Constitutions extended the jurisdiction of civil over church courts. After the pope condemned them, THOMAS À BECKET, the archbishop of Canterbury, repudiated them, but for the most part they remained the law.

Clarendon Code, 1661–65, four English laws passed after the RESTORATION of CHARLES II to strengthen the position of the Church of ENGLAND. The laws resulted in a decrease in the followers of dissenting sects, especially Presbyterians. They were named for the earl of CLARENDON, who opposed but enforced them. Charles tried to court the dissenters by his unsuccessful declarations of indulgence (1662, 1672). The Code was largely superseded by the TEST ACT (1673).

Clarín: see ALAS, LEOPOLDO.

clarinet: see WIND INSTRUMENT.

Clark, George Rogers, 1752–1818, Revolutionary War general, conqueror of the Old Northwest; b. near Charlottesville, Va. He took Vincennes from the British (1779) and fought Native Americans in Ohio. His brother, **William Clark,** 1770–1838, b. Caroline co., Va., joined Meriwether Lewis (1803) as a leader of the LEWIS AND CLARK EXPEDITION. Later he was superintendent of Indian affairs, and governor of Missouri Territory.

Clark, Joe (Charles Joseph Clark), 1939–, prime minister of Canada (1979–80). He entered the Canadian House of Commons from Alberta in 1972 and became leader of the Progressive Conservative party in 1976. In the 1979 elections he led his party to victory and briefly replaced Pierre TRUDEAU as prime minister. His election represented the new political importance of W Canada, especially oil-rich Alberta. In 1983 Brian MULRONEY replaced him as party leader. Clark served as external affairs minister (1984–91) and constitutional affairs minister (1991–93) under Mulroney. In 1993 UN Secretary General Boutros-Ghali appointed him special UN representative for Cyprus.

Clark, Kenneth Bancroft, 1914–, African-American psychologist; b. Canal Zone. He is best known for his writings on the effects of school segregation on students. His 1950 report was cited in the U.S. Supreme Court decision, BROWN V. BOARD OF EDUCATION. He was the first African American to receive a permanent professorship at the City College of New York, where he taught (1942–75), and to be a member of the New York State Board of Regents (1966–86). His books include *Prejudice and Your Child* (1955), *Dark Ghetto* (1965), and *A Possible Reality* (1972).

Clark, Kenneth MacKenzie (Lord Clark of Saltwood), 1903–83, English art historian. His noted writings include *Leonardo da Vinci* (2d ed., 1952), *Landscape into Art* (1949), *Rembrandt and the Italian Renaissance* (1966), *The Romantic Rebellion* (1974), and a popular cultural survey, *Civilisation* (1970).

Clark, Mark Wayne, 1896–1984, U.S. general; b. Madison Barracks, N.Y. He was Allied commander in N Africa and Italy in WORLD WAR II, supreme commander (1952–53) of UN forces in Korea, and commander of U.S. forces in the Far East.

Clarke, Arthur C(harles), 1917–, British science fiction writer. His more than 70 popular, technologically realistic works often examine the universal search for meaning. They include *Childhood's End* (1953) and *The Songs of Distant Earth* (1983). His *2001: A Space Odyssey* (1968) was the basis of a now classic motion picture. He emigrated to Sri Lanka in 1956.

class action, lawsuit in which one or more persons represent a group (class) too large for individual suits to be practical. The decision binds all members of the group. Class action suits often involve major social issues, e.g., inmates attempting to improve prison conditions or women seeking equal pay for equal work.

classicism, term meaning clearness, elegance, symmetry, and repose produced by attention to traditional forms; absence of emotionalism, subjectivity, and excess enthusiasm; and, more precisely, admiration of Greek and Roman models. Renaissance writers, for example, looked to CICERO. In England, Francis BACON in prose and Ben JONSON in poetry strove for classical style. The movement reached its apex with Alexander POPE and the Augustans. In France neoclassicism found its highest expression in the dramas of Pierre CORNEILLE and Jean RACINE. The works of RENAISSANCE painters and of the composers F.J. HAYDN and W.A. MOZART particularly reveal the classical impulse. Classicism and ROMANTICISM are generally contrary tendencies.

classic revival, widely diffused phase of taste ("neoclassic") influencing architecture and the arts in Europe and in the U.S. in the last years of the 18th and first half of the 19th cent. Enthusiasm for antiquity and for archaeological knowledge was stimulated by the excavation of POMPEII and by expeditions in Greece. James Stuart and Nicholas Revett's *Antiquities of Athens* (1st vol., 1762) was extremely influential. In general, Roman influence predominated at first. In France, the Empire style sponsored by NAPOLEON I brought imitation of ancient Rome to a peak. In the U.S. the same spirit was seen in public buildings, e.g., Thomas JEFFERSON's Virginia capitol design (1785). American Greek revival appeared in B.H. LATROBE's Bank of Pennsylvania, Philadelphia (1799). Eventually a Greco-Roman form emerged. It was particularly dominant in the U.S., where classic colonnades were seen even on country farmhouses. Victorian romanticism after the Civil War extinguished the revival, but many major buildings, e.g., the dome and wings of the CAPITOL, remain.

classification, in biology, the systematic categorization of organisms. One aim of modern classification, or systematics, is to show the evolutionary relationships among organisms. The broadest division of organisms is into kingdoms, traditionally two—Animalia (animals) and Plantae (plants). Widely accepted today are three additional kingdoms: the Protista, comprising protozoans and some unicellular algae; the Monera, bacteria and blue-green algae; and the Fungi. From most to least inclusive, kingdoms are divided into the following categories: phylum (usually called *division* in botany), class, order, family, genus, and species. The species, the fundamental unit of classification, consists of populations of genetically similar, interbreeding or potentially interbreeding individuals that share the same gene pool (collection of inherited characteristics whose combination is unique to the species). See also LINNAEUS, CAROLUS; CLADISTICS.

Claudel, Paul [klōdĕl′], 1868–1955, French dramatist, poet, and diplomat. He was ambassador to Japan (1921–27), the U.S. (1927–33), and Belgium (1933–35). His writings reflect his profound and mystical Catholicism. His finest works include the play *Tidings Brought to Mary* (1912) and the rich lyric verse of *Five Great Odes* (1910).

Claude Lorrain [lôrăN′], whose original name was **Claude Gelée or** Gellée [zhəlá], 1600–82, French painter. The foremost landscape painter of his time, he recorded his poetic compositions in a notebook to protect them from forgeries; it was later published as *Liber Veritatis* (1777). In his later landscapes he opened up unlimited vistas, introducing lyrical variations of light to dissolve forms and draw the eye into vast panoramas. In *The Expulsion of Hagar* (1668; Munich) he defied conventional composition for strong effect. POUSSIN was indebted to him, as was J.M.W. TURNER.

Claudius I (Tiberius Claudius Drusus Nero Germanicus), 10 B.C.–A.D. 54, Roman emperor (A.D. 41–54), son of Nero Claudius Drusus Germanicus (see DRUSUS, family) and thus nephew of TIBERIUS. When CALIGULA was murdered (A.D. 41), Claudius was proclaimed emperor by the PRAETORIANS. Despite suffering from a type of paralysis, he consolidated and renewed the empire. Claudius caused MESSALINA, his third wife, to be executed. He was in turn supposedly poisoned by her successor, Agrippina II, after she had persuaded him to pass over his son Britannicus as heir in favor of NERO, her son by a former husband. Claudius was much reviled by his enemies; however, he seems to have had considerable administrative ability.

Claudius, ancient Roman gens. **Appius Claudius Sabinus Inregillenis** or **Regillensis** was a Sabine; he came (c.504 B.C.)

with his tribe to Rome. As consul (495 B.C.) he was known for his severity. **Appius Claudius Crassus** was decemvir (451–449 B.C.). Legend says that his attempt to rape VIRGINIA caused a revolt in which he was killed and which led to the fall of the decemvirs. **Appius Claudius Caecus,** censor (312–308 B.C.), constructed the first Roman aqueduct and began construction of the APPIAN WAY. **Publius Claudius Pulcher,** consul (249 B.C.), attacked the Carthaginian fleet at Drepanum and was defeated. **Appius Claudis Pulcher,** d. c.48 B.C., consul (54 B.C.), joined POMPEY in the civil war and died before the battle at Pharsala (48 B.C.).

Clausewitz, Karl von [klou'zəvĭts], 1780–1831, Prussian general and writer on military strategy. After serving in the wars against NAPOLEON I, he was appointed (1818) director of the Prussian war college. His masterpiece, *On War,* expounded the doctrines of "total war" and war as a political act (a continuation of diplomacy by other means). Published after his death, it had a major impact on military strategy and also greatly influenced political thinking.

Clausius, Rudolf Julius Emanuel [klou'zēo͞os], 1822–88, German mathematical physicist. He introduced the concept of ENTROPY and restated the second law of THERMODYNAMICS to say that heat cannot of itself pass from a colder to a hotter body. Through investigations of heat, electricity, and molecular physics, he developed the KINETIC-MOLECULAR THEORY OF GASES and formulated a theory of ELECTROLYSIS.

claustrophobia: see PHOBIA.

clavichord: see PIANO.

Clay, Cassius Marcellus, Jr.: see ALI, MUHAMMAD.

Clay, Henry, 1777–1852, American statesman; b. Hanover co., Va. He served Kentucky as U.S. senator (1806–7, 1810–11, 1831–42, 1849–52) and representative (1811–14, 1815–21, 1823–25). A leader of the "war hawks," Clay helped to bring on the WAR OF 1812. His "American system" was a national program for federal aid in internal improvements, a protective tariff, and a rechartering of the BANK OF THE UNITED STATES. Secretary of state (1825–29) under Pres. John Quincy ADAMS, he opposed the succeeding Jackson administration, especially on the bank issue. He was the presidential candidate of the National Republican party in 1832 and of the WHIG PARTY in 1844. Clay pushed the MISSOURI COMPROMISE (1820–21) through the House, and, denouncing extremists in both North and South, he was the chief shaper of the COMPROMISE OF 1850. He was called the Great Pacificator and the Great Compromiser.

clay, common name for a number of fine-grained, earthy materials that are plastic when wet. They are easily molded into a form they retain when dry, and become hard and hold their shape when subjected to heat. Chemically, clay minerals are hydrous aluminum silicates with various impurities. Clays are most commonly formed by surface weathering. In the form of BRICKS, clay has been indispensable to architecture since prehistoric times. Clays are of great industrial importance, e.g., in the manufacture of tile and pipe. Clay is one of the three principal types of soil; the others are SAND and LOAM.

Clayton Antitrust Act: see under ANTITRUST LAWS.

Clayton-Bulwer Treaty, concluded at Washington, D.C., on Apr. 19, 1850, between the U.S., represented by Secretary of State John M. Clayton, and Great Britain, represented by Sir Henry Bulwer. U.S.-British rivalries in CENTRAL AMERICA, particularly over a proposed isthmian canal, led to the treaty, which checked British expansion in Central America but prevented the U.S. from building and politically controlling a canal. The unpopular treaty remained effective until it was superseded by the HAY-PAUNCEFOTE TREATY of 1901.

Cleisthenes or **Clisthenes,** fl. 510 B.C., Athenian statesman; head of the family Alcmaeonidae. The undisputed ruler of ATHENS after 506 B.C., he instituted democratic reforms that ended civil strife there.

Cleland, John, 1709–87, English novelist. His *Memoirs of a Woman of Pleasure* (1750), commonly known as *Fanny Hill,* is traditionally considered the first great pornographic work in English and was repeatedly banned.

clematis, herb or vine (genus *Clematis*) of the BUTTERCUP family. The vines are usually profuse and varied bloomers. The Jackman clematis (*C. jackmanii*) is a large purple hybrid; the Japanese clematis (*C. paniculata*) has small white flowers. Other names for clematis are virgin's bower, traveler's joy, leatherflower, and old-man's-beard.

Clemenceau, Georges [klāmäNsō'], 1841–1929, French premier (1906–9, 1917–20), called "the Tiger." As a journalist, he passionately defended Dreyfus in the DREYFUS AFFAIR. His coalition cabinet in World War I, by reinvigorating French morale, facilitated the Allied victory. At the Paris Peace Conference, he opposed Woodrow WILSON, believing that the Treaty of VERSAILLES would not adequately protect France. Ironically, he lost the 1920 presidential election because of his perceived leniency towards Germany.

Clemens, Roger, 1962–, American baseball player; b. Dayton, Ohio. A pitcher for the Boston Red Sox since 1984, he is known for his hard fastballs, superb pitching control, and hair-trigger temper. Winner of the 1986, 1987, and 1991 Cy Young Awards, he holds the record for most batters (20) struck out in a single game (1986).

Clemens, Samuel Langhorne: see TWAIN, MARK.

Clement I, Saint, or **Clement of Rome,** d. A.D. 97?, pope (A.D. 88?–97?), martyr. Highly esteemed in his day, he may have known Saints PETER and PAUL. His letter to the Corinthians was considered canonical by some until the 4th cent. and is notable for the authority Clement assumes. He was the first Christian writer to use the phoenix as an allegory of the Resurrection. Feast: Nov. 23.

Clement V, 1264–1314, pope (1305–14), a Frenchman named Bertrand de Got. As archbishop of Bordeaux, he gained the favor of the French king PHILIP IV, who engineered his election as pope. He settled (1309) in Avignon, thus beginning the long "captivity" of the PAPACY. Dominated by Philip, he did resist attempts to condemn Pope BONIFACE VIII posthumously, but he supported Philip in suppressing the KNIGHTS TEMPLARS. He issued an important collection of canon law.

Clement VI, 1291–1352, pope (1342–52), a Frenchman named Pierre Roger. Completely pro-French, he kept an elegant court at Avignon. When the PLAGUE known as the Black Death struck (1348–50) Europe, he did much to help the sufferers and tried to stem the subsequent wave of anti-Semitism. In Roman affairs he at first favored but then opposed Cola di RIENZI.

Clement VII, c.1475–1534, pope (1523–34), a Florentine named Giulio de' Medici, a member of the MEDICI family. Weak and timorous, he seemed unaware of the threat that the REFORMATION posed to the church. Allied with FRANCIS I of France, Clement quarreled with Holy Roman Emperor CHARLES V and was captured (1527) when imperial troops sacked Rome. Peace was restored in 1529, and Clement crowned Charles emperor. Clement vacillated in the matter of granting an annulment for HENRY VIII of England and was unable to stop Henry's break with Rome.

Clement VIII, 1536–1605, pope (1592–1605), a Florentine named Ippolito Aldobrandini. Reversing a papal policy, he allied with France instead of Spain and was friendly with the French king HENRY IV. He was also known for piety.

Clement XI, 1649–1721, pope (1700–21), an Italian named Giovanni Francesco Albani. In the War of the SPANISH SUCCESSION, he supported first the claims of PHILIP V and then those of Charles of Hapsburg. Clement was known for his great learning and issued (1713) the bull *Unigenitus* to combat Jansenism (see under JANSEN, CORNELIS).

Clement XIV, 1705–74, pope (1769–74), an Italian named Lorenzo Ganganelli, a Conventual Franciscan. Bowing to the wishes of the Bourbon monarchs of France and Spain, Clement issued (1773) a brief suppressing the JESUITS.

Clemente, Roberto (Walker), 1934–72, Puerto Rican baseball player; b. Carolina, Puerto Rico. A right fielder, he played 18 years (1955–72) with the Pittsburgh Pirates. He had a lifetime batting average of .317, hit 240 home runs, and was the 11th player to reach 3,000 hits. He died in a plane crash while aiding earthquake victims in Nicaragua.

Clement of Alexandria (Titus Flavius Clemens), d. c.215, Greek theologian. A convert to Christianity, he was one of the first to attempt a synthesis of Platonic and Christian thought. He attacked GNOSTICISM, but he has himself been called a Christian gnostic for his efforts to state the faith in terms of contemporary thought. ORIGEN was his pupil.

Clement of Rome: see CLEMENT I, SAINT.

Cleon, d. 422 B.C., Athenian statesman. An antagonist of SPARTA, he won a great victory at Sphacteria (425 B.C.) but was killed in the defeat at Amphipolis. His reputation as a vulgar demagogue is due to accounts by his enemies THUCYDIDES and ARISTOPHANES.

Cleopatra, 69 B.C.–30 B.C., queen of EGYPT, one of the great romantic heroines of history. The daughter of PTOLEMY XI, she was married (as was the custom) to her younger brother, PTOLEMY XII. By revolting against him, with the aid of Julius CAESAR, she won the kingdom, although it remained a vassal of Rome. After her husband died, she married another brother, Ptolemy XIII; but she was the mistress of Caesar, and in Rome she bore a son, Caesarion (later Ptolemy XIV), said to be his. Returning to Egypt after the murder of Caesar, she was visited by Marc ANTONY, who fell in love with her. She seems to have hoped to use him to reestablish her throne's power; they were married in 36 B.C. But the Romans were hostile, and Octavian (later AUGUSTUS) defeated Antony and Cleopatra off Actium in 31 B.C. Failing to defend themselves in Egypt, Antony and Cleopatra killed themselves. PLUTARCH, SHAKESPEARE, and G.B. SHAW are among the writers who have described Cleopatra's remarkable life.

Cleopatra's needles, popular name for two red granite OBELISKS from Egypt. Originally erected at Heliopolis (c.1475 B.C.) by THUTMOSE III, they were sent separately as gifts of ISMAIL PASHA to England (1878) and the U.S. (1880).

Clergy Reserves, lands in Upper and Lower Canada (now Ontario and Quebec) set apart under the Constitutional Act of 1791 "for the support and maintenance of a Protestant clergy." "Protestant clergy" was interpreted to mean clergy of the Church of England, a view which dissatisfied other Protestant denominations and became an issue in the Rebellion of 1837. In 1854 a law provided for secularization of the reserves, but Anglican and Presbyterian churches retained their endowments.

Clerk-Maxwell, James: see MAXWELL, JAMES CLERK.

Cleveland, (Stephen) Grover, 1837–1908, 22d (1885–89) and 24th (1893–97) president of the U.S.; b. Caldwell, N.J. He was mayor of Buffalo (1882–83) and governor of New York (1883–85). An enemy of machine politics, he was named the Democratic "clean government" candidate to oppose James G. BLAINE in 1884, and was elected after a bitter campaign. As president he pursued his conscientious, independent course, offending the zealots of his party by his moderate use of the SPOILS SYSTEM. In the 1888 election, Cleveland campaigned on a lower tariff, but in spite of a popular majority he lost the election to Benjamin HARRISON. The panic of 1893 struck a hard blow at his second administration, and he angered radical Democrats by securing repeal of the SHERMAN SILVER PURCHASE ACT. The party rift widened when he refused to sign his tariff measure as altered by the protectionist Sen. A.P. Gorman. In the Pullman strike (1894), he sent in troops and broke the strike on grounds that the movement of the U.S. mail was being halted. In foreign affairs he took a strong stand on the VENEZUELA BOUNDARY DISPUTE, and refused recognition to a Hawaiian government set up by Americans. Cleveland's independence marked him as a person of integrity.

Cleveland, city (1990 pop. 505,616; met. area 1,831,122), seat of Cuyahoga co., NE Ohio, on Lake Erie, at the mouth of the Cuyahoga R.; laid out 1796, chartered 1836. Ohio's second largest city, it is a major ore port and GREAT LAKES shipping point and a major producer of metal products. It has diverse light and heavy manufacturing and is a government, corporate, and medical research center. The arrival of the canal (1827) and railroad (1851) spurred the city's growth; its location between the Pennsylvania coal and oil fields and the Minnesota iron mines led to industrialization. John D. ROCKEFELLER began his oil dynasty there. Although the city declined in the 1970s and early 80s, as indicated by its 1978 loan default, the construction of new buildings highlighted economic progress. Case Western Reserve Univ. is among its many educational institutions. The Cleveland Orchestra, Cleveland Museum of Art, and Cleveland *Plain Dealer* newspaper are well known. The city is also the future site of the Rock-and-Roll Hall of Fame.

cliff dwellers, Native Americans of the Anasazi culture who built (11th–14th cent.) large communal homes on mesas and in canyon walls along rivers in the SW U.S. Ancient ancestors of the PUEBLO, the cliff dwellers were agriculturalists who planted and irrigated fields below their highly defensible houses. Their society was communal, and their KIVA attest to religious ceremonies like those of the Pueblos. Many of the dwellings (e.g., Mesa Verde) are now part of the NATIONAL PARK system.

Clifford, Clark McAdams, 1906–, U.S. government official; b. Fort Scott, Kans. As special adviser (1946–50) to Pres. Harry S TRUMAN, he was influential in the formulation (1947) of the Truman Doctrine and the creation of the Dept. of DEFENSE. He served (1961–63) as a foreign policy adviser to Pres. John F. KENNEDY, and became (1963) chairman of the Foreign Intelligence Advisory Board, supervising U.S. espionage operations and playing a crucial role in deciding U.S. military policy in the VIETNAM WAR. Clifford served (1968–69) as secretary of state under Pres. Lyndon JOHNSON. He was (1982–91) chairman of First American Bankshares, which was secretly owned by the Bank of Credit and Commerce International (BCCI), a foreign bank that had been forbidden to purchase a U.S. bank. In 1992 he was indicted on charges stemming from BCCI's secret ownership of First American.

Clinton, Bill (William Jefferson Clinton), 1946–, 42d president of the U.S. (1993–); b. Hope, Ark., as William Jefferson Blythe, 3d. A graduate of Georgetown Univ. and Yale Law School and a Rhodes scholar, he was a lawyer and (1974–76) law professor. In 1974 he was an unsuccessful Democratic candidate for the U.S. Congress from Arkansas. In 1976 he was elected Arkansas attorney general, and in 1978 he won the Arkansas governorship, becoming the nation's youngest governor, but he failed to win reelection in 1980. He ran again in 1982 and won and was reelected twice (1986, 1990). A moderate Democrat, he headed (1990–91) the centrist Democratic Leadership Council. In 1992 he won the Democratic presidential nomination, and he and running mate Al GORE defeated Pres. George BUSH and independent candidate Ross PEROT in the presidential election. He won (1993) passage of a national service program and of tax increases and spending cuts to reduce the federal deficit. He also proposed changes in the U.S. health care system that ultimately would provide health insurance coverage to most Americans. He is married to Hillary Rodham CLINTON.

Clinton, George, 1739–1812, American statesman, vice president of the U.S. (1805–12); b. Little Britain, N.Y. As New York's first governor (1777–95) under the new state constitution, he ably managed trade and public welfare. An advocate of state sovereignty, he opposed the federal Constitution. His nephew, **De Witt Clinton,** 1769–1828, b. New Windsor, N.Y., was mayor of New York City for 10 one-year terms (between 1803 and 1815), and was governor of New York (1817–21, 1825–28). He supported public education and city planning, and sponsored the ERIE CANAL and the Champlain-Hudson Canal.

Clinton, Sir Henry, 1738?–1795, British general in the AMERICAN REVOLUTION; b. Newfoundland. Knighted in 1777, he was (1778–81) supreme commander in America. He took Charleston (1780) but did not take part in the YORKTOWN CAMPAIGN.

Clinton, Hillary Rodham, 1947–, American lawyer and political figure, wife of U.S. Pres. Bill CLINTON; b. Chicago. She was in private practice from 1977 until 1992 and is an expert on children's rights. After her husband's election as president, she co-chaired the administration task force that examined, and proposed changes in, the U.S. health system.

Clio: see MUSES.

Clisthenes: see CLEISTHENES.

Clive, Robert, Baron Clive of Plassey, 1725–74, British soldier and statesman. In the military service of the British EAST INDIA COMPANY, he won a series of brilliant victories (culminating in Plassey, 1757) that broke French power in INDIA. He brought BENGAL under British control and was its first governor. In his second term as governor (1765–67), he reduced corruption and inefficiency and reached a settlement with the states of Bihar and Orissa. On his return to England in 1767, he was accused by Parliament of having unlawfully enriched himself while in India. He was acquitted in 1773, but, in poor health, committed suicide.

clock, mechanical, electrical, or atomic instrument for measuring and indicating time. Predecessors of the clock were the sundial, the hourglass, and the clepsydra. The operation of a clock depends on a stable mechanical oscillator, such as a swinging PENDULUM or a mass connected to a spring, by means of which the energy stored in a raised weight or coiled spring advances a pointer or other indicator at a controlled rate. The heavy and bulky weight-driven clock may first have been built in the 9th cent. The introduction (c.1500) of the coiled spring made possible the construction of smaller, lighter-weight clocks. The Dutch scientist Christiaan HUYGENS invented (1656 or 1657) a pendulum clock, probably the first. Electric clocks, first made in the late 19th cent., are powered by an electric motor synchronized with the frequency of alternating current. The quartz clock, invented c.1929, uses the vibrations of a quartz crystal to drive a synchronous motor at a very precise rate. An atomic clock (invented 1948), even more precise, is indirectly controlled by atomic or molecular oscillations. Digital clocks and watches dispense with the hour-marked dial and display time as a numerical figure.

Clodius (Publius Clodius Pulcher), d. 52 B.C., Roman politician. In 62 B.C., disguised as a woman, he took part in the women's mysteries of Bona Dea in the house of Julius CAESAR, thus leading Caesar to divorce his wife Pompeia. In 58 B.C. he became tribune of the people and proved to be a demagogue. His gang of hired ruffians changed the complexion of Roman politics. He was killed by a rival gang hired by the tribune Milo.

cloisonné, method of decorating metal surfaces with enamel. Filaments of metal are attached to the surface of the object, outlining the design and forming compartments that are filled with colored paste enamels. When the piece is heated the enamels fuse with the metal, forming a glossy, colored surface. Probably invented in the Middle East, cloisonné was perfected by the Chinese, Japanese, and French.

Cloisters, the, museum of medieval art, in Fort Tryon Park, N.Y.C.; opened in 1938. A branch of the METROPOLITAN MUSEUM OF ART, it includes four French cloisters, a Romanesque chapel, and a chapter house. The core of the collection—several hundred examples of medieval French art (gathered by George Gray BARNARD)—was purchased (1925) by John D. Rockefeller, Jr. (see ROCKEFELLER, family), and presented to the museum. Later additions include the 15th-cent. *Unicorn* tapestries and CAMPIN's *Mérode Altarpiece*.

clone, group of organisms descended from a single individual through asexual REPRODUCTION. Except for changes in hereditary material due to MUTATION, all members of a clone are genetically identical. Laboratory experiments have resulted in the development of a frog from a cell of an existing animal, but it was the successful IN VITRO FERTILIZATION of human eggs that led in 1993 to the "cloning" of human embryos by dividing such fertilized eggs at a very early stage of development. This technique, which does not produce a clone but a twin, had already been used successfully with sheep and other animals. Abnormal embryos were used in the human experiment and were later discarded. The experiment provoked an outcry from ethicists, religious leaders, and others, most of whom called for banning such procedures or establishing guidelines for them.

Close, Chuck, (Charles Thomas Close), 1940–, American painter; b. Monroe, Wash. A leading figure in the PHOTOREALISM movement, he is known for huge, frontal, and photographically precise portraits.

closed-end investment company: see MUTUAL FUND.

closed shop: see UNION, LABOR.

clot-dissolving drug: THROMBOLYTIC DRUG.

Clotho: see FATES.

cloud, aggregation of minute particles of water or ice suspended in the air. Clouds form when air containing water vapor is cooled below a critical temperature called the DEW point. The resulting moisture condenses into droplets on microscopic dust particles (condensation nuclei) in the atmosphere. The air is normally cooled by expansion during its upward movement. Clouds are classified by appearance, altitude, or composition. Each cloud type is formed by specific atmospheric conditions and is, therefore, indicative of forthcoming weather. *Cirrus* clouds, generally white, and delicate and fibrous in appearance, are the highest clouds and are made of ice crystals. *Stratus* clouds, layered in appearance, are the lowest clouds and are associated with stormy weather. *Cumulus* clouds, which are vertically developed, usually with a horizontal base and a dome-shaped upper surface, are intermediate in height and are associated with fair weather. Combinations of these cloud names are common. *Cirrostratus* clouds, for example, are high-altitude layered clouds that often indicate rain or snow. Prefixes and suffixes are also used. For example, *nimbus* means rain, and *cumulonimbus* clouds, commonly called thunderheads, indicate rain showers.

cloud chamber: see PARTICLE DETECTOR.

Clouet, Jean [klo͞oā'], called **Janet** or **Jehannet,** c.1485–1540, court painter to FRANCIS I of France. He is thought to have been Flemish. None of the soft, geometrically simple drawings, portraits, and miniatures attributed to Jean Clouet can be proved to have been his. His son, **François Clouet,** c.1510–c.1572, inherited his father's position as court painter. His clear, precise draftmanship can be seen in his portraits of Francis I and Elizabeth of Austria (both: Louvre).

Clough, Arthur Hugh [klŭf], 1819–61, English poet. He is best remembered for his lyric "Say not the struggle naught availeth." Clough is the subject of "Thyrsis," an elegy written by his close friend Matthew ARNOLD.

clove, small tropical evergreen tree (*Syzygium aromaticum* or *Eugenia caryophyllata*) of the MYRTLE family and its unopened flower bud, an important spice. The buds, whose folded petals are enclosed in four toothlike lobes of the calyx, are dried and used whole or ground for cooking. Clove oil is used in flavorings, perfumes, and medicines.

clover, plant (genus *Trifolium*) of the PULSE family, mainly native to north temperate and subtropical areas. The American cultivated varieties were introduced from Europe. Clovers have been cultivated for hay and are excellent honey plants. The dried flowers and seed heads of the common white clover (*T. repens*) were used to make bread during famines in Ireland, and the leaves are used for salads in some parts of the U.S. Sweet clover is a related plant.

Clovis I, c.466–511, Frankish king (481–511), founder of the MEROVINGIAN monarchy. He rose from tribal chief to sole leader of the Salian FRANKS by dint of patience and murder. He won Gaul and SW Germany by fighting the Romans, Alemanni, Burgundians, and Visigoths. His wife, St. Clotilda, encouraged his conversion (496) to Christianity.

Clovis culture, early North American people (c.10,000–9000 B.C.) known through artifacts first unearthed in the early 1930s near Clovis, N.Mex. Their chipped flint points (Clovis points) and other stone tools were found with remains of large mammals, e.g., extinct mammoths. Clovis groups are the earliest definitively dated human populations in the Americas.

club moss, any of a family of primitive vascular plants that reached their zenith in the Carboniferous period and are now almost extinct. They resemble the more primitive nonvascular true mosses. Club mosses are usually creeping or epiphytic; many of them inhabit moist tropical or subtropical regions. Reproduction is by spores, which are clustered in small cones or borne in the axils of the scalelike leaves. Some species of *Lycopodium,* called ground pine or creeping cedar, resemble miniature hemlocks with flattened fan-shaped branches. Spores of *L. clavatum* are sold as lycopodium powder, or vegetable sulfur, a flammable yellow powder used in pharmaceuticals and fireworks. Species of *Selaginella* are grown as ornamentals, e.g., the resurrection plant.

Cluj-Napoca, Hung. *Kolozsvár,* Ger. *Klausenburg,* city (1989 est. pop. 318,000), W central Romania, in Transylvania, on the Someşul R. Romania's second largest city, it has metallurgical, consumer, and other industries. The city was founded (12th cent.) by German colonists, incorporated (1867) in the Austro-Hungarian empire, and transferred (1920) to Romania. It has noted botanical gardens and a 14th-cent. Gothic church.

Cluny Museum, Paris, 14th- and 15th-cent. Gothic and Renaissance structure built on the site of the Roman baths of Emperor Julian. Acquired and converted by the antiquarian Du Sommerard, it was left to the state at his death (1842). Its 24 galleries display medieval works of carved wood, metalwork, textiles, and stained glass, as well as superb 15th- and 16th-cent. tapestries.

cluster, star: see STAR CLUSTER.

Clytemnestra [klī'təmnĕs'trə], in Greek mythology, daughter of LEDA and Tyndareus. The wife of AGAMEMNON, she was the mother of ORESTES, ELECTRA, and IPHIGENIA. She and her lover, AEGISTHUS, murdered Agamemnon and, in revenge, were slain by Orestes. HOMER portrayed Clytemnestra as a noble woman, misled by her lover, but the Greek tragedians, particularly AESCHYLUS, depicted her as remorseless and vengeful.

Cm, chemical symbol of the element CURIUM.

Cnossus: see KNOSSOS.

Co, chemical symbol of the element COBALT.

coal, fuel substance of plant origin, composed largely of CARBON with varying amounts of mineral matter. Coal belongs to a series of carbonaceous fuels that differ in the relative amounts of moisture, volatile matter, and fixed carbon they contain; the most useful contain the largest amounts of carbon and the smallest amounts of moisture and volatile matter. The highest grade of coal is anthracite, or hard coal, which is nearly pure carbon and is used as a domestic fuel. Bituminous coal, or soft coal, with a lower carbon content, is used as an industrial fuel and in making COKE. LIGNITE and PEAT are the lowest in carbon content. Large amounts of coal were formed in the Carboniferous period of geological time (345 to 280 million years ago). It is thought that great quantities of vegetable matter collected and underwent slow decomposition in SWAMPS similar to present-day peat bogs and in lagoons. The peat that formed was converted to lignite and coal by METAMORPHISM. The pressure of accumulated layers of overlying sediment and rock forced out much of the volatile matter, leaving beds or seams of compact coal interstratified with shales, clays, or sandstones. Higher grades of coal were produced where the stress was greatest. Major U.S. coal fields are found in Appalachia, the Midwest, the Rocky Mt. region, and along the Gulf Coast. The chief coal-producing countries of Europe are Russia, Ukraine, Poland, Germany, Britain, France, and Belgium. Valuable coal deposits also exist in China, India, South Africa, and Australia.

coal tar: see TAR AND PITCH.

coast guard, special naval force assigned to seaboard duties. In peacetime the U.S. coast guard is under the jurisdiction of the Dept. of Transportation; in wartime it is under the control of the U.S. navy. In addition to suppressing contraband trade and aiding vessels in distress, the service enforces navigation rules; administers regulations governing ship construction and licensing of merchant marine personnel; and operates weather ships, an ice patrol, and navigational aids, including lighthouses, lightships, buoys, and loran stations. The UNITED STATES COAST GUARD ACADEMY, New London, Conn., provides officer training.

Coast Mountains, western range of the North American cordillera, extending c.1000 mi (1,610 km) N from W British Columbia into SE Alaska. Geologically distinct from the COAST RANGES, the range reaches a high point at Mt. Waddington (13,260 ft/4,042 m).

Coast Ranges, series of geologically related ranges forming the western edge of the North American cordillera. The highest peaks are in the St. Elias Mts. (Alaska). Other ranges are the Olympic Mts. and the Coast Ranges (Oregon), the Klamath Mts. and Coast and Los Angeles ranges (California), and the mountains of BAJA CALIFORNIA.

coaxial cable: see CABLE.

cobalt (Co), metallic element, discovered in 1735 by Georg Brandt. It is silver-white, lustrous, and hard, and can be magnetized. It is combined with other metals in the ores cobaltite and smaltite. Cobalt alloys are used in very hard cutting tools, high-strength permanent magnets, and jet engines. Radioactive cobalt-60 is used in cancer therapy and to detect flaws in metal parts. See ELEMENT (table); PERIODIC TABLE.

Cobb, Ty(rus Raymond), 1886–1961, American baseball player; b. Narrows, Ga. Cobb was the first player elected (1936) to the National Baseball Hall of Fame. An outfielder, the "Georgia Peach" is considered by many to be the greatest player in the history of the game. In a 24-year career (Detroit Tigers, 1905–26; Philadelphia Athletics, 1927–28) he set numerous major-league records that still stand, such as his lifetime batting average of .367, and 12 batting championships. A daring base runner, he stole 892 bases. He was manager of the Tigers from 1921 to 1926.

Cobbett, William, 1763?–1835, British journalist and reformer. After resigning from the army, he went (1792) to the U.S., where he championed the Federalists (see FEDERALIST PARTY) against the pro-French Republicans. On his return to England (1799) he became a radical working-class leader and champion of agrarianism. His *Political Register* was an influential reform journal. After another flight

Ty Cobb

to the U.S. to avoid the Gagging Acts, he returned to become a central figure in the agitation for Parliamentary reform. He was elected to Parliament after the Reform Bill of 1832. His most famous book is *Rural Rides* (1830).

Cobden, Richard, 1804–65, British politician, a leading spokesman for the MANCHESTER SCHOOL. After making a fortune as a calico printer, he became a major influence in the repeal of the CORN LAWS. With John BRIGHT and Robert PEEL, he managed the ANTI-CORN-LAW LEAGUE. As a member of Parliament, Cobden negotiated the "Cobden Treaty" for reciprocal tariffs with France (1859–60), and favored the Union in the U.S. Civil War.

COBOL: see PROGRAMMING LANGUAGE.

cobra, venomous SNAKE of the family Elapidae equipped with an inflatable neck hood, found in Africa and Asia. The king cobra (*Ophiophagus hannah*), or hamadryad, the largest poisonous snake, is found in S Asia; it may reach a length of 18 ft (5.5 m). Other species include the Indian cobra (*Naja naja*) and the Egyptian cobra (*Naja haja*), also called the ASP. The family also includes CORAL SNAKES.

coca, plant (genus *Erythroxylon,* particularly *E. coca*) found mainly in upland regions and on mountain slopes of South America and in Australia, India, and Africa. Certain South American peoples chew the leaves mixed with lime, which acts with saliva to release COCAINE from the leaves. In this form and concentration, the DRUG acts as a stimulant. A cocaine-free extract of the leaves is used in some soft drinks. Coca is grown commercially in Sri Lanka, Java, and Taiwan.

cocaine, ALKALOID drug derived from COCA leaves, producing euphoria, hallucinations, and temporary increases in physical energy. Prolonged use can cause nervous-system aberrations (including delusions), general physical deterioration, weight loss, and addiction (see DRUG ADDICTION AND DRUG ABUSE). Withdrawal from the drug can produce severe depression. See also CRACK.

Cochabamba, city (1985 est. pop. 317,000), W central Bolivia, c.8,400 ft (2,560 m) high in the Andes. Center of a productive agricultural region, it was founded as Villa de Oropeza in 1574 and renamed in 1786.

Cochin China, historic region (c.26,500 sq mi/68,600 sq km), S Vietnam, bounded by Cambodia (NW, N), Annam (NE), the South China Sea (E, S), and the Gulf of Thailand (W). The capital and chief city was Saigon (now HO CHI MINH CITY). Cochin China included the MEKONG delta, one of the world's great rice-growing areas, and, in the northeast, plantations where rubber, coffee, tea, oil palms, and sugarcane were grown. Originally part of the KHMER EMPIRE, Cochin China fell to ANNAM in the 18th cent. and became (1862–67) a French colony. The Japanese occupied it during WORLD WAR II. In 1954, after an independence struggle against the French, Cochin China became part of South Vietnam. At the end of the VIETNAM WAR it was incorporated into united Vietnam.

Cochise, c.1815–74, chief of the Chiricahua APACHE in Arizona, noted for courage, integrity, and military skill. From 1861, when soldiers unjustly hanged some of his relatives, he warred relentlessly against the U.S. army. Peace talks in 1872 promised him a reservation on his native territory, but after he died his people were removed.

Cockcroft, Sir John Douglas, 1897–1967, English physicist. After serving as fellow and professor of natural philosophy at Cambridge, he directed (1946–59) the British Atomic Energy Research Establishment at Harwell. He shared with Ernest Walton the 1951 Nobel Prize in physics for their pioneer work in transmuting atomic nuclei by bombarding elements with artificially accelerated atomic particles.

cocker spaniel, smallest SPORTING DOG; shoulder height, 14–15 in. (35.6–38.1 cm); weight, c.25 lb (11.3 kg). Its silky, flat, or wavy coat is moderately long and may be any solid color or combination of colors. The breed was developed from English cocker spaniels brought to the U.S. in the 1880s.

cockle, heart-shaped marine BIVALVE mollusk having ribbed, brittle shells and moving with a jumping motion produced by means of a large, muscular foot. Most species do not exceed 3 in. (7.5 cm) in length. Cockles burrow in sand or mud in shallow water. Several species are edible.

cockroach or **roach,** nocturnal, flat-bodied oval INSECT of the family Blattidae (order Orthoptera). Cockroaches have long antennae, long legs adapted for running, and a flat extension of the upper body that covers the head; some species fly. In length they range from ¼ in. to 3 in. (.6–7.6 cm). Cockroaches are not known to be disease carriers. They were extremely abundant during the Carboniferous period (about 350 million years ago) and probably were the first flying animals.

cocoa: see CACAO.

coconut, edible fruit of the coco palm tree (*Cocos nucifera*) of the PALM family, widely distributed throughout the tropics. The coco palm, which grows to a height of 60 to 100 ft (18 to 30 m) and has a crown of frondlike leaves, is one of the most useful trees in existence. It is a source of timber, and its leaves are used in baskets and for thatch. The coconut itself is a single-seeded nut with a hard, woody shell encased in a thick, fibrous husk. The hollow nut contains coconut milk, a nutritious drink, and its white kernel, a staple food in the tropics, is eaten raw and cooked. Commercially valuable coconut oil is extracted from the dried kernels, called copra, and the residue is used for fodder. Husk fibers are used in cordage and mats, and nutshells are made into containers.

Cocos (Keeling) Islands, external territory of Australia (1992 est. pop. 600), 5.5 sq mi (14.2 sq km), consisting of two separate atolls with 27 coral islets, in the Indian Ocean. The population is largely Muslim Malays. The islands were settled (1827) and developed by the Clunies-Ross family for copra production. Under British rule from late 1800s, they were a dependency of Britain's SINGAPORE colony after 1903; they were transferred to Australia in 1955. Australia purchased the Clunies-Ross interests in 1978 and leased the copra plantation to a Cocos Malay-run cooperative. The islands' residents voted to become part of Australia in 1984.

Cocteau, Jean [kôktō'], 1889–1963, French author and filmmaker. Unrivaled in the 20th cent. for versatility in the arts, he experimented in almost every artistic medium, producing poetry, fiction, drama, films, ballets, drawings, and operatic librettos. Surrealistic fantasy suffuses his work. He is best known for the novel *Les Enfants Terribles* (1929; film 1950); the plays *Orphée* (1926; film 1949) and *The Infernal Machine* (1934); and the films *The Blood of a Poet* (1932) and *Beauty and the Beast* (1945).

cod, marine, bottom-feeding FISH (family Gadidae), among the most important and abundant food fishes. The Atlantic cod (*Gadus morrhua*) averages 10 to 25 lb (4.5 to 11 kg), but specimens up to 200 lb (90 kg) have been reported. The haddock (*Melanogrammus aeglefinus*), the most important food fish in the Atlantic, is smaller, reaching a weight of 30 lb (13.6 kg). Finnan haddie is lightly smoked haddock. Commercially exploitable stocks of cod and haddock have been been depleted in recent years.

codeine, ALKALOID drug derived from OPIUM. A NARCOTIC with effects like those of MORPHINE, codeine is prescribed as an ANALGESIC and cough suppressant. It is addictive (see DRUG ADDICTION AND DRUG ABUSE).

Code Napoléon: see CIVIL LAW.

Cody, William Frederick: see BUFFALO BILL.

coelacanth: see LOBEFIN.

coelenterate, radially symmetrical, predominantly marine invertebrate animal of the phylum Cnidaria (also called Coelenterata), having a three-layered body wall, tentacles, and specialized stinging cells (nematocysts). Members of the phylum have a primitive nervous system and no specialized organs for excretion or respiration. The phylum includes the SEA ANEMONES, CORALS, JELLYFISH, and hydroids (see HYDRA). See also POLYP and MEDUSA.

coenzyme, any of a group of relatively small organic molecules that make up the non-protein portion of an ENZYME and without which the enzyme is inactive. Coenzymes participate in chemical reactions catalyzed by enzymes; although often structurally altered in the course of the reaction, coenzymes are always restored to their original form. Notable coenzymes include ADENOSINE TRIPHOSPHATE, important in the transfer of chemical energy, and VITAMINS, vital to a variety of biochemical reactions in the body, including the Krebs cycle (see CITRIC ACID CYCLE).

Coetzee, J(ohn) M(ichael), 1940–, South African writer. A white South African computer scientist, linguist, and teacher, his novels are about the human suffering that results from imperialism and APARTHEID, e.g., *In the Heart of the Country* (1976), *Waiting for the Barbarians* (1982), and *Age of Iron* (1990).

Cœur, Jacques [kör], c.1395–1456, French merchant and chief adviser to CHARLES VII of France. He amassed a fabulous fortune with which he financed the last campaigns of the HUNDRED YEARS WAR. Arrested (1451) on the concocted charge of having poisoned Agnès SOREL, the king's mistress, he escaped (1454–55) to Rome and died fighting the Turks.

coffee, name for an evergreen shrub or tree (genus *Coffea*) of the MADDER family, its seeds, and the beverage made from them. The mature, red fruit (a drupe) typically contains two seeds, or coffee beans. Varieties of Arabian coffee (*C. arabica*) supply the bulk of the world's supply; Liberian coffee (*C. liberica*) and Congo coffee (*C. robusta*) are of some commercial importance. Coffee plants require a hot, moist climate and rich soil. The harvested seeds are cleaned and roasted; heat acts on the essential oils to produce the aroma and flavor. Roasts range from light brown to the very dark Italian roast. Coffee contains CAFFEINE, a stimulant that can cause irritability, depression, and indigestion if taken in excess. The coffee plant was known before A.D. 1000 in Ethiopia, where its fruit was used for food and wine. A beverage made from ground, roasted coffee beans was used in Arabia by the 15th cent., and by the mid-17th cent. it had reached most of Europe and had been introduced into North America.

Coffin, Henry Sloane, 1877–1954, American Presbyterian clergyman; b. N.Y.C. He was pastor (1905–26) of the Madison Avenue Presbyterian Church, and president (1926–45) of Union Theological Seminary (both: N.Y.C.). His nephew **William Sloane Coffin, Jr.,** 1924–, b. N.Y.C., was chaplain (1958–75) at Yale Univ., where he was an antiwar activist, and was (1977–89) senior minister at Riverside Church (N.Y.C.).

cognac: see BRANDY.

cognitive psychology, school of psychology that examines internal mental processes, such as creativity, perception, thinking, problem solving, memory, and language. Cognitive psychologists are interested in how a person understands, diagnoses, and solves a problem, concerning themselves with the mental processes that mediate between stimulus and response. In recent years cognitive psychology has become associated with computer information processing and ARTIFICIAL INTELLIGENCE, studying parallels in the ways that both brain and computer receive, process, store, and retrieve information.

Cohan, George M(ichael), 1878–1942, American showman; b. Providence, R.I. He wrote, directed, produced, and starred in many MUSICALS, most exemplifying his favorite themes—Broadway and a flag-waving patriotism. His first successes were *Little Johnny Jones* (1904) and *Forty-five Minutes from Broadway* (1906). Best remembered for such songs as "The Yankee Doodle Boy," "Give My Regards to Broadway," and "Over There," he was also a skillful adapter of others' material, e.g., *Seven Keys to Baldpate* (1913).

coherence, a constant correlation between the phases of two or more WAVES, or parts of a single wave. Two waves are coherent and in phase if their crests and troughs are synchronized, and coherent but out of phase if the crests of one are synchronized with the troughs (or any other part of the wave except the crest) of the other. Waves are incoherent if the crests and troughs meet randomly, i.e., the correlation between the phases is not constant. Coherence underlies a variety of phenomena, such as INTERFERENCE and DIFFRACTION, and is also the basis of many of the remarkable properties of LASER radiation.

cohesion: see ADHESION AND COHESION.

Cohn, Ferdinand, 1828–98, German botanist. Considered a founder of bacteriology, he developed theories of the bacterial causes of infectious disease and recognized bacteria as plants. His writings cover such subjects as fungi, algae, insect epidemics, and plant diseases.

coin, piece of metal, usually a disk of gold, silver, nickel, bronze, copper, or a combination of such metals, issued by a government for use as MONEY. State coinage, said to have originated in Lydia in the 7th cent. B.C., enabled governments to make coins whose nominal value exceeded their value as metals. The first U.S. MINT was established in 1792. Beginning in 1965, the U.S. Treasury stopped putting silver in newly minted dimes and quarters, and reduced the amount of silver in the half-dollar. A 1970 act eliminated all silver from the half-dollar and dollar coins. U.S. law provides, however, that special mintings of both coins, containing 60% copper and 40% silver, be made for collectors.

Coke, Sir Edward [ko͝ok], 1552–1634, English jurist and political leader. After a rapid rise in Parliament he became (1593) attorney general, gained a reputation as a severe prosecutor, and was favored at the court of JAMES I. As chief justice of common pleas (from 1606) and of the king's bench (from 1613) he championed the common law against the royal prerogative. Collisions with the king and political enmities led to his dismissal in 1616. By 1620 he had returned to Parliament, where he led popular opposition to the Crown. He helped draft the PETITION OF RIGHT (1628). Coke's writings include his *Reports* (on common law) and the *Institutes*.

coke, hard, gray, porous fuel with a high CARBON content. It is the residue left when bituminous COAL is heated in the absence of air. Coke is used in extracting metals from ores in the BLAST FURNACE.

cola or **kola,** tropical tree (genus *Cola*) of the sterculia family, native to Africa but grown in other tropical areas. The fruit is a pod containing CAFFEINE-yielding seeds. Cola nuts are chewed for this stimulant. They are also exported for use in soft drinks and medicine.

Colbert, Jean Baptiste [kôlbĕr'], 1619–83, French statesman. Appointed (1665) controller general of finances by LOUIS XIV, he aimed to make France economically self-sufficient through the practice of MERCANTILISM. He encouraged industry by subsidies and tariffs, regulated prices, built roads, canals, and harbors, and expanded the navy and France's commercial potential. His power declined with the onset of Louis XIV's wars.

cold or **common cold,** viral infection of the mucous membranes of the upper respiratory tract, especially the nose and throat. There are numerous viral organisms that may cause the common cold, although there is no known cure or preventive. Treatment of symptoms includes fluids to prevent dehydration, ANALGESICS (e.g., ASPIRIN) to lessen fever, and decongestants to shrink swollen mucous membranes. Some believe that VITAMINS in large doses, especially vitamin C, may be helpful in prevention.

cold fusion or **low-temperature fusion,** nuclear fusion of deuterium, an isotope of HYDROGEN, at or relatively near room temperature. Fusion, the reaction involved in the release of the destructive energy in a HYDROGEN BOMB, requires extremely high temperatures, and investigations of fusion as a possible energy source have focused on the problems involved in designing an apparatus to contain and sustain such a reaction (see NUCLEAR ENERGY; NUCLEAR REACTOR). In 1989 B. Stanley Pons and Martin Fleischmann, chemists at the Univ. of Utah, announced that an experiment conducted at room temperature using platinum and palladium electrodes immersed in heavy water (deuterium oxide) had produced excess heat and other by-products that they ascribed to a fusion reaction. Attempts to replicate their experiment produced initially conflicting results, but several early announcements of experimental confirmation were later retracted. Pons and Fleischmann were also later criticized for having skewed data to show the emission of gamma rays at an energy level typical of fusion. Research into the possibility of cold fusion, by Fleischmann and others, nonetheless continued, because of intriguing but inconclusive experimental results and because of the desirability of producing relatively nonpolluting fusion energy in quantity at any temperature.

cold sore: see HERPES SIMPLEX.

cold war, term used to describe the political and economic struggle between the capitalist, democratic Western powers and the Soviet Union (and later other Communist nations) after the Allied victory in WORLD WAR II. The cold war period was marked by massive military buildups (including nuclear weaponry) by both sides and by intensive economic competition and strained, hostile diplomatic relations. The "hot wars" of the period included the KOREAN WAR and VIETNAM WAR. The first important post-World War II disagreement between East and West was about the reunification of GERMANY, which proved at the time to be impossible. Communications between the two sides virtually ceased, and an "iron curtain" descended between them. The U.S. rallied the other Western powers by sponsoring a series of strategic actions, including the MARSHALL PLAN, the NORTH ATLANTIC TREATY ORGANIZATION (NATO), and other regional pacts. Within the Communist bloc the Soviet Union maintained tight political, economic, and military control over its satellites, for example, by suppressing the Hungarian Revolution of 1956; by instituting (1955) the WARSAW TREATY ORGANIZATION; and by supporting Communist revolutions in CHINA, parts of Southeast Asia, and CUBA. A period of eased tensions, known as DÉTENTE, occurred in the late 1960s and the 70s, but the Soviet invasion of Afghanistan (1979), the banning of the SOLIDARITY union and other events in Poland, and Pres. REAGAN's strong anti-Communist stance worsened relations between East and West. In the late 1980s and early 90s Mikhail GORBACHEV's policies opened Soviet society to increasingly radical change and diminished the power of hard-line Communists, and the USSR permitted the collapse of Communist regimes in Eastern Europe (1989–90) and the reunification of Germany (1990). Cordial relations between the USSR and U.S., which began to act in unison internationally, led both nations' leaders to hail the end of the cold war, and the breakup of the Soviet Union in late 1991 ended Communist rule there and dramatically altered the international political landscape.

Cole, Nat "King" (Nathaniel Adams Cole), 1919–65, African-American singer and pianist; b. Montgomery, Ala. He became one of the most popular of all American singers with such hits as "The Christmas Song" and "Unforgettable." Cole appeared in films and was the first African American to have (1956) his own television series. His daughter **Natalie Maria Cole,** 1950–, b. Los Angeles, is also a popular singer.

Cole, Thomas, 1801–48, American painter; b. England. He specialized in painting the spectacular scenery of New York state, becoming a leader of the HUDSON RIVER SCHOOL. A characteristic painting is *Catskill Mountains* (Mus. Art, Cleveland). Other works are neoclassical in style.

Coleman, Ornette, 1930–, African-American musician and composer; b. Fort Worth, Tex. After playing saxophone in rhythm-and-blues bands, he became one of the most controversial figures in the JAZZ avant-garde. His impassioned, atonal music was extremely influential in the development of free jazz.

Coleridge, Samuel Taylor, 1772–1834, English poet and man of letters. After an erratic university career, he planned with Robert SOUTHEY to found a utopian community in the U.S., but the project did not materialize. In 1798 he and William WORDSWORTH published *Lyrical Ballads,* a volume whose experiments in language and subject matter (and the prefaces to later editions) make it a seminal work of English ROMANTICISM. Coleridge contributed "The Rime of the Ancient Mariner," his best-known work, as well as "Christabel" and "Kubla Khan," all poems on exotic or supernatural themes. "Dejection: An Ode" (1802) was his last great poem. A brilliant conversationalist, Coleridge lectured (notably on SHAKESPEARE), traveled, and wrote on philosophy, religion, and literature. From 1816 he lived in London at the home of Dr. James Gilman, who helped the poet control his long-standing opium addiction. *Biographia Literaria,* which includes accounts of his literary life and also critical essays, appeared in 1817; its borrowings from German idealist philosophers borders, at times, on plagiarism. This, and

Ornette Coleman

his inability to finish projects, make Coleridge a controversial figure, but he was unquestionably a major literary influence in his day and, at his best, a great poet.

Colette [kōlĕt'], 1873–1954, French novelist; b. Sidonie Gabrielle Colette. Her numerous novels, e.g., *Chéri* (1920), *The Cat* (1933), and *Gigi* (1945), are famed for their sensitive observations of women, nature, and eroticism. Colette's early *Claudine* books were published under the name of her first husband, Willy (pseud. of Henry Gauthier-Villars).

coleus, tropical plant (genus *Coleus*) of the MINT family, native to Asia and Africa. Some, with large, colorful leaves, are cultivated as houseplants.

Coligny, Gaspard de Châtillon, comte de [kōlēnyē'], 1519–72, French Protestant leader, admiral of France. With Louis I de CONDÉ, he commanded the HUGUENOTS in the Wars of Religion (see RELIGION, WARS OF) and negotiated a peace in 1570. He became a favorite adviser of CHARLES IX, thus arousing the enmity of CATHERINE DE' MEDICI. Coligny was the first victim in the massacre of SAINT BARTHOLOMEW'S DAY.

Coliseum: see COLOSSEUM.

collage [Fr., = pasting], technique in art consisting of cutting natural or manufactured materials and pasting them to a painted or unpainted surface—hence, a work of art in this medium. It was initiated in 1912 when PICASSO pasted a piece of commercially printed oilcloth to his cubist *Still Life with Chair Caning* (Mus. Mod. Art, N.Y.C.). Collage elements appear in works by GRIS and BRAQUE, and were basic to DADA and SURREALISM. Collage is related to the newer art of assemblage, in which the traditional painted canvas is abandoned in favor of the assembling of bits of material.

collateral: see CREDIT.

collective bargaining, in labor relations, procedure whereby an employer agrees to discuss working conditions by bargaining with employee representatives, usually a labor union. First developed in Britain in the 19th cent., it received an impetus in the U.S. during the 1930s through such legislation as that which created the NATIONAL LABOR RELATIONS BOARD. The process is now accepted in most Western industrialized countries as the basic method of settling disputes about wages, hours, job security, and other matters. It may be assisted by labor **mediation,** the mediator being a neutral third party who endeavors to bring the two sides together. Industrial **arbitration** is a last resort, implying the need for a third party to resolve the dispute and impose a decision on both sides. Sometimes called binding arbitration, it may be compelled by the government, as in Canada, Italy, or Britain, or it may be called for by voluntary agreement, as is often the case in the U.S.

collective farm, an agricultural producers' cooperative. In the USSR, collectivization of agriculture was initiated by STALIN in 1929, and the system initially survived the USSR's disintegration. A collective farm's land and equipment is owned by the state, which decides what will be produced. Farm workers share in state-guaranteed profits and have small private plots where they can grow goods for free-market sale. In China, the commune (first established 1958) paralleled the Soviet collective farm. Land and equipment were owned by the commune, which oversaw fulfillment of government quotas by production teams (small groups of workers). Reforms under DENG XIAOPING have led to the dismantling of most communes. China has, and the former USSR also had, state farms, whose workers are paid wages. Since the USSR's breakup the republics have slowly moved toward private ownership of land and the end of collective farming. Many barriers in Russia to private ownership of land were removed by decree in 1993. The best-known type of Israeli collective farm is the KIBBUTZ.

college of arms: see HERALDS' COLLEGE.

colleges and universities, institutions of higher education. Universities, which usually consist of several faculties or colleges, are larger than colleges, have wider curricula, are involved in research, and grant graduate and professional as well as undergraduate degrees.

Universities. Universities arose in the Middle Ages to train young men in law, theology, and medicine. Although they were usually established by royal or ecclesiastical initiative, some were founded by students. The medieval university often had thousands of students and played an important role in contemporary affairs. The most famous European universities include those at Oxford, Cambridge, and Paris (all founded in the 12th cent.), Salamanca (c.1230), Prague (1348), Vienna (1365), Uppsala (1477), Leiden (1575), and Moscow (1755). The oldest universities in the New World are the Univ. of Santo Domingo (1538), in the Dominican Republic; the Univ. of Mexico (1551), in Mexico City; and San Marcos Univ. (1551), in Lima, Peru. In the U.S., the first state university, the Univ. of North Carolina, opened in 1795. Most modern universities developed in the late 19th cent., as small private colleges expanded and tax-supported land-grant colleges and universities were founded. Institutions devoted to graduate study and research, such as Johns Hopkins Univ., were also established at that time. Women were not admitted to universities until c.1870 (see COEDUCATION); by 1900 most universities were secularized. During the 20th cent. many universities, especially in the U.S., have received large grants from government agencies for scientific and technical research.

Colleges. The earliest colleges were founded in 15th-cent. Paris as endowed residence halls for university students. It was only later, at Oxford and Cambridge, in England, that the college became the principal center of learning. Degrees, however, continued to be conferred by the university with which the college was associated. In America, however, the liberal arts college arose as a separate institution, with numerous colleges founded in the 17th and 18th cent. to train young men for the ministry, e.g., Harvard (1636), William and Mary (1693), Yale (1701), Princeton (1746), and Columbia (1754). These were joined in the next century by a number of women's colleges: Mount Holyoke (1837), Elmira (1853), Vassar (1861), Wellesley (1871), Smith (1871), Bryn Mawr (1881), and Barnard (1889). Teachers' colleges, or normal schools, also developed in the 19th cent. By the 20th cent., many American colleges had grown into universities; today, the distinction between the two has blurred, with many colleges granting graduate degrees. COMMUNITY COLLEGES have greatly expanded opportunities for higher education in the U.S. since World War II.

collie, large, agile WORKING DOG; shoulder height, 22–26 in. (55.9–66 cm); weight, 50–75 lb (22.7–34 kg). There are two types: the rough-coated (long-haired) and the smooth-coated. Both may be sable and white, blue, tricolored, or white. It was developed (17th–18th cent.) in Scotland as a sheepdog.

colligative properties, properties of a SOLUTION that depend on the number of solute particles present, but not on the chemical properties of the solute. Colligative properties of a solution include its freezing and boiling points (see STATES OF MATTER) and osmotic pressure (see OSMOSIS).

Collins, Michael, 1890–1922, Irish revolutionary leader. A member of the SINN FÉIN, he organized the guerrilla warfare that forced the British to sue for peace. With Arthur GRIFFITH he set up the Irish Free State. He was assassinated.

Collins, (William) Wilkie, 1824–89, English novelist. The author of some 30 novels, he is best known for *The Woman in White* (1860) and *The Moonstone* (1868), considered the first full-length detective novels in English.

Collodi, Carlo, pseud. of **Carlo Lorenzini,** 1826–90, Italian author. A journalist, he also wrote didactic tales for children, the most famous of which is *Pinocchio* (1883).

colloid, a mixture in which one substance is divided into minute particles (called colloidal particles) and dispersed throughout a second substance. Colloidal particles are larger than molecules but too small to be observed with a microscope; however, their shape and size (usually between 10^{-7} and 10^{-5} cm) can be determined by electron microscopy. In a true SOLUTION the particles of dissolved substance are of molecular size and thus smaller than colloidal particles. In a coarse mixture (e.g., a SUSPENSION) the particles are much larger than colloidal particles. Colloids can be classified according to the phase (solid, liquid, or gas) of the dispersed substance and of the medium of dispersion. A gas may be dispersed in a liquid to form a foam (e.g., shaving lather) or in a solid to form a solid foam (e.g., Styrofoam). A liquid may be dispersed in a gas to form an AEROSOL (e.g., FOG), in another liquid to form an emulsion (e.g., homogenized milk), or in a solid to form a gel (e.g., jellies). A solid may be dispersed in a gas to form a solid aerosol (e.g., dust or smoke in air), in a liquid to form a sol (e.g., ink), or in a solid to form a solid sol (e.g., certain ALLOYS). Colloids are distinguished from true solutions by their inability to diffuse through a semipermeable membrane (e.g., cellophane) and by their ability to scatter light (the TYNDALL effect).

Cologne, Ger. *Köln,* city (1989 est. pop. 937,000), North Rhine–Westphalia, W Germany, on the Rhine R. It is a river port and an industrial center producing electronic equipment, chemicals, and other manufactures. Founded (1st cent. B.C.) by the Romans, it flourished (4th–13th cent.) under powerful archbishops. It became a free imperial city (1475) and a member (15th cent.) of the HANSEATIC LEAGUE. The city was badly damaged in WORLD WAR II. However, such buildings as its Gothic cathedral (begun 1248) and Romanesque Church of St. Andreas still stand.

Colombia [kəlŭm'bēə], officially Republic of Colombia, republic (1992 est. pop. 34,297,000), 439,735 sq mi (1,138,914 sq km), NW South America. The only South American country with both Pacific and Caribbean coastlines, Colombia is bordered by Panama (NW), Venezuela (NE), Ecuador and Peru (S), and Brazil (SE). Major cities include BOGOTÁ (the capital), MEDELLÍN, and CALI. By far the most prominent physical features are the three great Andean (see ANDES) mountain chains (CORDILLERAS) that fan north from Ecuador, reaching their highest point in Pico Cristóbal (18,947 ft/5,775 m). The Andean interior is the heart of the country, containing the largest concentration of population as well as the major coffee-growing areas. In pre-Columbian days this was the site of the advanced civilization of the Chibcha. To the east of the Andes lies more than half of Colombia's territory—a vast, largely undeveloped lowland, including the tropical rain forests of the AMAZON basin and the savannas (LLANOS) of the ORINOCO basin. Agriculture is a major source of income: besides coffee, long Colombia's leading export, the chief cash crops are bananas, cotton, sugarcane, and tobacco. Coca and cannabis are grown for the illegal drug trade, which is a major source of foreign exchange, but trafficking has disrupted the

fabric of Colombian society. Rich in minerals, Colombia produces petroleum (since 1991 its most valuable export) and natural gas, iron, coal, gold, nickel, and emeralds. The growing manufacturing sector is led by processed foods, textiles, metal products, and chemicals. About two thirds of the population are mestizos; less than one fifth are of pure European descent. Spanish is the official language, and most of the people are Roman Catholic.

History. Conquered by the Spanish in 1530s, the region that is now Colombia became the core of the Spanish colony of NEW GRANADA, which included Panama and most of Venezuela. The struggle for independence from Spain began in 1810, lasted nine years, and ended with the victory of Simón BOLÍVAR at Boyacá in 1819. Bolívar set up the new state of Greater Colombia, which included all of New Granada and (after 1822) Ecuador. Political differences soon emerged, however, and the union fell apart. Venezuela and Ecuador became separate nations; the remaining territory eventually became the Republic of Colombia (1886), from which Panama seceded in 1903. Through the 19th and into the 20th cent., political unrest and civil strife racked Colombia. Strong parties developed along conservative (centrist) and liberal (federalist) lines, and civil war frequently erupted between the factions. As many as 100,000 people were killed before the conservatives emerged victorious in a civil war of unprecedented violence that raged from 1899 to 1902. And again, after a four-decade hiatus of political peace, in 1948 bloody strife rent the nation, costing hundreds of thousands of lives. Orderly government was finally restored as the result of a compromise between liberals and conservatives in 1958. A guerrilla insurgency arose in the 1970s and continued into the 1990s, although some groups signed peace agreements with the government. In the 1980s and early 90s the cocaine "cartels" threatened to undermine civil government through bribery, bombings, kidnappings, and the murder of government officials. In the 1990 presidential election, an outspoken enemy of the drug lords, César Gaviria Trujillo, was elected president. Although the power of the notorious Medellín drug cartel was broken in 1993, the Cali cartel remains strong. Colombia established a customs union with Venezuela in 1991 and has signed free-trade agreements with other Andean nations.

Colombo, largest city (1986 est. pop. 684,000) and capital of Sri Lanka, on the Indian Ocean near the mouth of the Kelani R. It has one of the world's largest artificial harbors, with facilities for containerized cargo. Noted for its gem-cutting and ivory-carving, Colombo also has chemical, processed food, oil refining, and other industries. A port since Greco-Roman times, it was settled by Muslims in the 8th cent. The Portuguese built (16th cent.) a fort to protect their spice trade. The city passed (17th cent.) to the Dutch and then to the British, who made it (1802) the capital of their colony of Ceylon. The city has several colleges and universities and many churches, mosques, and temples.

colonialism: see COLONIZATION; IMPERIALISM.

colonization, extension of political and economic control over an area by an occupying state that usually has organizational or technological superiority. The colonizer's nationals may migrate to the colony because of overpopulation or economic or social distress at home, but IMPERIALISM has been a major colonizing force. The colony's population must be subdued or assimilated to the colonizer's way of life, or a modus vivendi otherwise imposed. Colonization dates back at least to the Phoenicians, but it is most important historically as the vehicle of European expansion from the 15th cent. into Africa, the Americas, and Asia. The Spanish, Portuguese, English, French, and Dutch established colonies worldwide that have, for the most part, obtained independence from imperial systems only in the 20th cent. Today classic colonialism is widely considered immoral. See also MANDATES; TRUSTEESHIP, TERRITORIAL.

Colonna, a leading noble Roman family from the 12th to the 16th cent. **Sciarra Colonna,** d. 1329, was a bitter enemy of Pope BONIFACE VIII and led, with Chancellor Nogaret, the French expedition that captured (1303) Boniface. The family also produced Pope MARTIN V. **Fabrizio Colonna,** d. 1520, was a general of the HOLY LEAGUE against LOUIS XII of France in the Italian Wars. His cousin **Prospero Colonna,** 1452–1523, defeated the French at La Biocca (1522). **Marcantonio Colonna,** 1535–84, duke of Paliano, led the papal forces at LEPANTO.

colony: see COLONIZATION.

color, visual effect resulting from the eye's ability to distinguish the different wavelengths or frequencies of light. The apparent color of an object depends on the wavelength of the light that it reflects. In white, or normal, light, an opaque object that reflects all wavelengths appears white and one that absorbs all wavelengths appears black. Any three primary, or spectral, colors can be combined in various proportions to produce any other color sensation. Beams of light are combined "additively," and red, blue, and green are typically chosen as primaries. Pigments, however, combine by a "subtractive" process, i.e., by absorbing wavelengths, and artists generally choose red, blue, and yellow as their primaries. Two colors are called complementary if their light together produces white.

Colorado, one of the mountain states of the W U.S.; bordered by Wyoming (N), Nebraska (N, E), Kansas (E), Oklahoma and New Mexico (S), and Utah (W).

Area, 104,247 sq mi (270,000 sq km). *Pop.* (1990) 3,294,394, a 14% increase over 1980 pop. *Capital,* Denver. *Statehood,* Aug. 1, 1876 (38th state). *Highest pt.,* Mt. Elbert, 14,433 ft (4,402 m); *lowest pt.,* Arkansas R., 3,350 ft (1,022 m). *Nickname,* Centennial State. *Motto, Nil Sine Numine* [Nothing without Providence]. *State bird,* lark bunting. *State flower,* Rocky Mountain columbine. *State tree,* Colorado blue spruce. *Abbr.,* Colo., CO.

Land and People. Colorado has the highest mean elevation among the states (c.6,800 ft/2,100 m). The high plains of the east, an extension of the GREAT PLAINS, give way to the foothills of the ROCKY MOUNTAINS and the high Front Range. The Rockies, which run north-south across the state and are traversed by the CONTINENTAL DIVIDE, include 51 of the 80 peaks in North America over 14,000 ft (4,267 m) high. Mt. Elbert (14,433 ft/4,402 m) is the loftiest mountain in the U.S. portion of the range. The COLORADO PLATEAU in the west is an arid region with many canyons carved by the COLORADO, Gunnison, and other rivers. Most of the population (about 82%) lives in cities among the foothills, principally in and around DENVER—the leading city of the mountain states—but also in COLORADO SPRINGS, PUEBLO, and FORT COLLINS. In 1990 the state was 88% white, 12% African American and others.

Economy. Since the 1950s, manufacturing has contributed the largest share of Colorado's income. Leading industries include the manufacture of computer, transportation, and electrical equipment and aerospace products; food processing; and printing and publishing. Agriculture is dominated by the raising of cattle and sheep. Grown mostly on irrigated land, corn, wheat, hay, and sugar beets are the leading crops. Leading minerals include oil, coal, molybdenum, sand and gravel, and uranium. Gold mining has been revived recently. The state is popular year-round with tourists, especially skiers and visitors to its spectacular Rocky Mt. National Park.

Government. The constitution of 1876 provides for a governor elected to a four-year term. The legislature consists of a senate of 35 members serving four-year terms and a house with 65 members serving two-year terms. Colorado is represented in the U.S. Congress by two senators and six representatives and has eight electoral votes.

History. The cliff dwellings of Colorado's early inhabitants are preserved at Mesa Verde National Park in the southwest. Spain claimed the region comprising present-day Colorado in 1706. The U.S. acquired much of it through the LOUISIANA PURCHASE (1803) and the rest from Mexico in 1848. The discovery (1858) of gold brought many settlers, but the gold was soon extracted, and the mining settlements became ghost towns. Silver and lead were subsequently discovered, but the collapse (1893) of the U.S. silver market brought a statewide depression. Rapid urban growth occurred during and after World War II. The national energy crisis in the 1970s resulted in a dramatic expansion of Colorado's coal and oil industries, but when oil prices collapsed in the early 1980s, the economy suffered a significant downturn. In the late 1980s and early 90s Colorado grew rapidly despite the national recession. See also NATIONAL PARKS (table).

Colorado, chief river of the arid SW U.S. It flows 1,450 mi (2,334 km) from the Rocky Mts. of N Colorado to the Gulf of California, c.1000 mi (1,610 km) of its course cutting through deep canyons, including the spectacular GRAND CANYON. Use of the river, whose flow is controlled by HOOVER, Davis, Imperial, Parker, GLEN CANYON, and other dams, is allocated by treaties with Mexico and by compacts between states.

Colorado Plateau, physiographic region of the SW U.S., covering c.150,000 sq mi (388,500 sq km) in Arizona, Utah, Colorado, and New Mexico. The broad, sparsely vegetated, and semiarid plateau surfaces—one third located within Native American reservations—are cut by great canyons, including the GRAND CANYON and CANYON DE CHELLY.

Colorado Springs, city (1990 pop. 281,140), seat of El Paso co., central Colo., on Monument and Fountain creeks, at the foot of PIKES PEAK; founded 1859, inc. 1886. A year-round vacation and health resort, it manufactures electronic, mining, and aerospace equipment. Colorado College is in the city; the U.S. Air Force Academy is nearby.

color blindness, inability to distinguish colors, an inherited trait occurring almost exclusively in males. Individuals with partially defective color vision (the most common form) have difficulty distinguishing red from green. Those who are completely red-green color-blind see both colors as yellow. Totally color-blind persons see only black, white, and shades of gray.

color field painting, abstract art movement begun in the 1960s. Working toward a more intellectual aesthetic than that of ABSTRACT EXPRESSIONISM, color field painters explored their conception of the fundamental formal elements of abstract painting: pure areas of untempered color; flat, two-dimensional space; monumental scale; and the varying shape of the canvas. Painters associated with the movement include Ellsworth KELLY, Morris LOUIS, Kenneth NOLAND, and Frank STELLA.

Colosseum or **Coliseum,** common name for the Flavian Amphitheater in Rome, built A.D. c.75–80 under VESPASIAN and TITUS. Much of the four-storied oval, 617 ft (188 m) by 512 ft (156 m), still stands. Tiers of marble seats accommodated about 45,000 people. In the arena gladiatorial combats were held until A.D. 404, and according to tradition, Christians were thrown to beasts.

Colossians, EPISTLE of the NEW TESTAMENT, 12th book in the usual order, written to Christians of Colossae and Laodicea (Asia Minor) by St. PAUL (A.D. c.60), apparently in connection with a gnostic doctrine current in the churches addressed. Like EPHESIANS, it emphasizes the doctrine of the mystical body of Christ.

colossus, name given in antiquity to a statue of very great size. Examples include the Athena Parthenos on the ACROPOLIS at Athens and the **Colossus of Rhodes,** one of the SEVEN WONDERS OF THE WORLD. Among colossuses of later times, the Great Buddha at Kamakura, Japan, and the Statue of LIBERTY in New York harbor are notable. Two colossal figures of Jesus are in South America, one at Rio de Janeiro and the other, CHRIST OF THE ANDES, on the boundary of Argentina and Chile.

Colt, Samuel, 1814–62, American inventor; b. Hartford. His revolving breech pistol (patented 1835–36) was one of the standard SMALL ARMS of the world in the last half of the 19th cent. Colt also invented a submarine battery used in harbor defense and a submarine telegraph cable.

Coltrane, John, 1926–67, African-American musician; b. Hamlet, N.C. Rising to prominence with the Miles DAVIS quintet in the mid-1950s, he was until his death the dominant tenor and soprano saxophonist of the JAZZ avant-garde.

Columba, Saint, or **Saint Columcille,** 521–97, Irish missionary to Scotland, called the Apostle of Caledonia. He established a monastic center at IONA in 563 and eventually Christianized all of N Scotland. Feast: June 9.

Columbia, city (1990 pop. 98,052), state capital and seat of Richland co., central S.C., on the Congaree R.; inc. 1805. The largest city in the state, it is the trade center for a farming region, and manufactures such products as textiles, plastics, and electronic equipment. Most of the city was burned by Gen. SHERMAN's troops in 1865. The Univ. of South Carolina and several other colleges are located there.

Columbia, chief river of the NW U.S., c.1,210 mi (1,950 km) long, including 465 mi (748 km) in SW Canada. It flows generally south in British Columbia and Washington and then west, forming the Washington-Oregon boundary and entering the Pacific Ocean W of Portland, Ore. Numerous dams, including the GRAND COULEE DAM, provide hydroelectricity and irrigation. The Columbia, whose volume is greatly increased by the SNAKE and other major tributaries, was the early focus of American settlement in the Oregon country.

Columbia Plateau, physiographic region of the NW U.S., covering c.100,000 sq mi (259,000 sq km) in Washington, Oregon, and Idaho. Most of it is underlaid by thick, nearly horizontal beds of lava (mainly basalt) and partly covered with fertile loess. Arid areas south of the GRAND COULEE DAM are irrigated as part of the Columbia Basin project.

Columbia University, mainly in New York City; founded 1754 as King's College by grant of King George II. It was closed during the American Revolution but reopened as Columbia College in 1784. To reflect the addition of graduate and professional schools, the name Columbia University was adopted in 1896; Columbia College and Barnard College (for women; est. 1889 and affiliated) remained the undergraduate schools. The university also includes the College of Physicians and Surgeons, Teachers College (affiliated), and schools of journalism, law, social work, and international affairs, as well as research institutes, botanical and biological field stations, and a geological laboratory.

columbine, perennial plant (genus *Aquilegia*) of the BUTTERCUP family. Columbines have delicate foliage and red, white, yellow, blue, or purple flowers with long, nectar-secreting spurs on the petals. Wild columbine, or rockbell (*A. canadensis*), is a favorite of hummingbirds. The blue-and-white-flowered *A. coerulea* of the Rockies is Colorado's state flower.

columbium: see NIOBIUM.

Columbus, Christopher, 1451–1506, European discoverer of America; b. Genoa, Italy. In Portugal, he became a master mariner and was determined to reach India by sailing west. After eight years of supplication, he received the backing of the Spanish monarchs FERDINAND V and ISABELLA I. On Oct. 12, 1492, his ships, the *Niña, Pinta,* and *Santa María,* reached Watling Island, in the Bahama group; later they touched CUBA and HISPANIOLA. He was made an admiral and governor general of all new lands. In 1493 he set sail with 17 ships, exploring PUERTO RICO and the Leeward Islands, and founding a colony in Hispaniola. In 1498 he explored VENEZUELA, realizing that he had found a continent. Because of disreputable conditions in Hispaniola, he was replaced as governor in 1500 and returned to Spain in chains. On his last voyage (1502) he reached Central America. Although he is considered a master navigator today, he died in neglect, almost forgotten.

Columbus. 1 City (1990 pop. 178,681), seat of Muscogee co., W Ga., on the Chattahoochee R.; settled and inc. 1828. A port city situated on the FALL LINE, it has many textile mills, and manufactures iron and food products. Hydroelectric and canal development have revitalized industry in the 20th cent. Many of the city's antebellum homes have been preserved and restored. **2** City (1990 pop. 632,910; met. area 1,377,419), state capital and seat of Franklin co., central Ohio, on the Scioto R.; founded 1797, inc. as a city 1834. The largest city in Ohio, it is a major industrial and trade center in a rich farm region. Columbus took over state government from CHILLICOTHE in 1816. Transportation has been key to its development: canals, the NATIONAL ROAD (reaching Columbus in 1833), and the railroad (1850) all brought growth. The city's manufactures include appliances, machinery, and auto parts. The convention center (1993), with its vigorously disordered exterior, is notable, and Ohio State Univ. and the Columbus Gallery of Fine Arts are located in the city.

Columbus Day, holiday (traditionally Oct. 12) commemorating Christopher COLUMBUS's discovery of America. Since 1971 it has been celebrated in most of the U.S. on the Monday nearest Oct. 12.

Columcille, Saint: see COLUMBA, SAINT.

column, vertical architectural support, circular or polygonal in plan. It is generally at least four times as high as its diameter or width; stubbier masses are usually called piers or pillars. Shape, proportions, and materials of columns vary widely. Columns arranged in a row form a colonnade. The Egyptians used massive columns, closely spaced, for inner courtyards and halls. Early Greek columns had a cushionlike cap and tapering shaft. By the 7th cent. B.C., the Greek Doric had been established. In Greek, Roman, and Renaissance architecture, the various column types, with their entablatures, form the classical ORDERS OF ARCHITECTURE. The classical column has three fundamental elements: base, shaft, and capital. The capital provides a structural and decorative transition between the circular column and the rectangular entablature. In Greek buildings columns were usually indispensable, but Roman and Renaissance architects used them also as a decorative feature, mostly following fixed rules of proportions. Romanesque, Gothic, and Byzantine columns were usually structural elements, and were without canons of proportioning. Chinese and Japanese columns had, instead of capitals, ornamented brackets.

coma, deep state of unconsciousness from which a person cannot be aroused even with the most painful stimuli. It may be caused by severe brain injury, DIABETES, MORPHINE or BARBITURATE poisoning, SHOCK, or hemorrhage. Treatment is directed at the cause of the condition.

Comanche, indigenous people of a nomadic Plains culture (see NORTH AMERICA, INDIGENOUS PEOPLES OF), who ranged the Southwest from the 18th cent. They spoke a Shoshonean language of the Aztec-Tanoan stock (see NATIVE AMERICAN LANGUAGES). Excellent horsemen and warriors, they killed more whites in proportion to their numbers than any other tribe and kept their territory unsafe for whites for more than a century. They probably introduced PEYOTE to the Plains tribes (see NATIVE AMERICAN CHURCH). In 1990 there were 11,322 Comanches in the U.S.

Comaneci, Nadia [kōmänēch], 1961–, Romanian gymnast. Known for her bold routines and implacable composure, she won six medals in the 1976 Olympics, twice scoring an unprecedented perfect 10, and four medals in the 1980 Olympics. She defected to the U.S. in 1989.

combinations, in mathematics: see PERMUTATIONS AND COMBINATIONS.

comb jelly or **sea gooseberry,** solitary marine invertebrate (phylum Ctenophora) having eight radially arranged rows (combs) of ciliated plates (ctenes) on the spherical body surface and specialized adhesive cells (colloblasts) used for capturing PLANKTON. Comb jellies are carnivorous, bioluminescent, and hermaphroditic. They are weak swimmers but possess a unique sense organ controlling equilibrium (statocyst). Usually transparent, comb jellies vary from ¼ in. (0.6 cm) to more than 1 ft (30.5 cm) in length and look very much like JELLYFISH.

COMECON: see COUNCIL FOR MUTUAL ECONOMIC ASSISTANCE.

comedy, literary work, usually dramatic, aiming chiefly to amuse. Whereas TRAGEDY seeks to engage the emotions, comedy strives to entertain through ridicule of characters, customs, and institutions or through a resolution of contretemps thrown up by the plot. Dramatic comedy had its origins in Greek fertility rites. Old Comedy, culminating in ARISTOPHANES, was a series of scenes using FARCE, fantasy, parody, and SATIRE, with a final lyric celebration of unity. New Comedy (from c.4th cent. B.C.) was more realistic and romantic, less satirical and critical. MENANDER in Athens, PLAUTUS and TERENCE in Rome were its leading practitioners. In the Middle Ages comedy survived in folk plays and in the Italian COMMEDIA DELL'ARTE. In the RENAISSANCE, Elizabethan comedy drew in part on Latin comedy to produce the caustic satires of Ben JONSON and the romantic comedy of SHAKESPEARE. Classical and commedia dell'arte elements blended in France in MOLIÈRE's brilliant work. After the Puritan suppression of the theater, witty, artificial comedy reappeared during the English RESTORATION in the work of William CONGREVE and William WYCHERLEY. It descended into sentiment by the end of the 17th cent. but revived late in the 18th cent. with Oliver GOLDSMITH and R.B. SHERIDAN. Oscar WILDE typified the late-19th-cent. comedy of manners, G.B. SHAW the comedy of ideas. Trends in the 20th-cent. include the romantic comic fantasies of J.M. BARRIE and Jean GIRAUDOUX; the native Irish comedy of J.M. SYNGE and others; the absurdist works of Samuel BECKETT and Eugène IONESCO; and the so-called black comedy (the darkly humorous treatment of serious themes) of Sam SHEPARD, David MAMET, and others. The century also saw the development of such popular comedic forms as VAUDEVILLE, comic MOTION PICTURES, "stand-up comedy" (routines, often satiric, usually performed by a single individual), and of a uniquely television-related form, the situation comedy ("sit-com"), generally a kind of debased comedy of manners. Masters of nondramatic comedy include, among many, BOCCACCIO, RABELAIS, CERVANTES, VOLTAIRE, and Henry FIELDING.

Comenius, John Amos, Czech *Jan Amos Komenský,* 1592–1670, Moravian churchman and educator. Relating education to everyday life, he advocated systematizing all knowledge, teaching in the vernacular rather than Latin, and establishing a universal system of education with opportunities for women. One of his major works, *Didactica Magna* (1628–32; tr. M.W. Keatinge, 1896), expounds these principles.

comet, mostly gaseous body of small mass and enormous volume that can be seen from earth for periods ranging from a few days to several months. A comet head, on the average about 80,000 mi (130,000 km) in diameter, contains a small, bright nucleus (ice and frozen gases interspersed with particles of heavier substances) surrounded by a coma, or nebulous envelope of luminous gases. As the comet nears the sun, the particles and gases are driven off, forming a tail as long as 100 million mi (160 million km). Pushed by the SOLAR WIND, the tail streams out away from the sun. J.H. OORT hypothesized (1950) a shell of more than 100 billion comets surrounding the solar system and moving very slowly at a distance of as much as 150,000 times the sun-earth distance; a passing star, however, may gravitationally perturb a few closer to the sun. In 1951 G.P. KUIPER proposed a region of minor planets just outside Neptune's orbit as a source of comets with short orbital periods. See also HALLEY'S COMET.

comic strip, a narrative applied to a sequence of cartoons in which human and/or animal characters usually communicate by means of speech and/or thought "balloons." It is a predominantly commercial art form, which became established at the turn of the 20th cent. as a syndicated newspaper feature that boosted circulation. The first modern comic strip is acknowledged to be Richard Felton Outcault's *The Yellow Kid* (1896). While comic strips initially used humorous story lines, giving rise to their nickname, "the funnies," they later ventured into such realms as sophisticated whimsy, adventure, science fiction, and political satire, e.g., Walt Kelly's *Pogo* (1949), Charles SCHULZ's *Peanuts* (1950), and Garry TRUDEAU's *Doonesbury* (1970). The mass appeal of the comic strip was a major source of inspiration for POP ART. See also CARTOON.

Cominform: see under COMINTERN.

Comintern, acronym for Communist International, founded (1919), by V.I. LENIN to claim Communist leadership of the world socialist movement. It excluded non-Communist socialists. Its efforts to foment revolution failed, and in 1935 it began to form coalitions, or popular fronts, with bourgeois parties. The Comintern dissolved (1943) as a gesture of support for the Allied war effort. The **Cominform** (Communist Information Bureau) was organized (1947) by the USSR to coordinate the exchange of information between E European and some W European Communist parties, formerly a function of the Comintern. It was disbanded in 1956.

Commagene [kŏməjē'nē], ancient district of N Syria, on the Euphrates R. and S of the Taurus range, now in SE Asian Turkey. Once part of the Assyrian empire and later of the Persian Empire, it became independent in 162 B.C. The Roman Emperor Vespasian permanently annexed Commagene in A.D. 72.

commedia dell'arte [kōmmä'dēä dĕllär'tā], popular form of comedy in Italy (16th-18th cent.). Using improvised dialogue and masked actors in satiric song, dance, and farce, it gave rise to such traditional PANTOMIME characters as Harlequin and Columbine. Its influence on European theater, particularly French pantomine and English harlequinade, was great.

Commedia del'arte harlequin

commensalism, relationship between members of two different species of organisms in which one individual is usually only slightly benefited while the other is not affected at all. In many cases, commensalism cannot be distinguished from parasitism (see PARASITE). See also SYMBIOSIS.

Commerce, United States Department of, federal executive department charged with promoting economic and technological development. Established (1903) as the Dept. of Commerce and Labor, it became a separate department in 1913. Its divisions include the Economic Development Administration, the Bureau of the Census, the National Oceanic and Atmospheric Administration, the

National Institute of Standards and Technology, the Minority Business Development Agency, the Patent and Trademark Office, and the National Telecommunications and Information Administration.

commercial bank: see BANKING.

commercial paper, type of short-term NEGOTIABLE INSTRUMENT, usually an unsecured promissory note, that calls for the payment of money at a specified date. Because it is not backed by collateral, commercial paper is usually issued by major firms with strong credit ratings. An important source of cash for the issuing firm, it is usually payable at a lower rate of interest than the prime discount rate. The commercial paper market expanded greatly after the mid-1970s, reaching $140 billion by 1981, double the amount of four years earlier. The trend was accompanied by the rise of MONEY-MARKET FUNDS, a major buyer of commercial paper, and a resulting loss of corporate loan business by banks (see BANKING).

commodity market, organized traders' exchange in which contracts for delivery of certain products are bought and sold. Most trading is done in futures contracts, which require the holder to sell or buy goods at a future date for a specified price, and options, which are similar but give the holder the right to buy or sell. Such trading allows both hedging against serious losses in a declining market and speculation for gain in a rising market. Spot contracts, a less widely used form of trading, call for immediate delivery. In the U.S., commodity markets deal in a wide range of products, notably grains and oilseeds, livestock and meat, food and fiber, metals, petroleum, and lumber, and in financial futures, such as Treasury bonds, stocks, and currencies.

common law, system of law based on custom and precedent established by court decisions. Developed in medieval England and so called because it represented common, rather than local, custom, the common law prevails in most English-speaking nations, including the U.S. (except Louisiana, which adheres to CIVIL LAW). The formality and inflexibility of early common law often led to injustice, and in 15th-cent. England the chancellor issued the first of many decrees to restore "equity" (fairness); this was the beginning of the modern body of EQUITY law, later merged with the common law in many jurisdictions. The slowness of common-law procedure has led to adoption of numerous statutes that supersede the common law, notably in the fields of commercial, administrative, and criminal law.

Common Market: see EUROPEAN UNION.

Commons, House of: see PARLIAMENT.

Commonwealth of Independent States (CIS), association formed by most of the former republics of the UNION OF SOVIET SOCIALIST REPUBLICS to coordinate interrepublican affairs; ceremonial headquarters are in Minsk, Belarus. A council of heads of state and a council of heads of government are the chief coordinating bodies of the CIS. On Dec. 8, 1991, four months after the attempted coup against Soviet Pres. GORBACHEV, Ukraine, seeking to assure its independence and avoid renewed Russian domination, joined with the other Slavic republics (Belarus and Russia) to found the CIS. On Dec. 21, 11 of the 12 surviving Soviet republics (Georgia did not join until 1993) signed a new agreement establishing the CIS, and four days later Gorbachev resigned as president of the USSR. The agreement recognized current borders and each republic's independence, sovereignty, and equality, and established a free-market ruble zone embracing the republics' interdependent economies and a joint defense force for participating republics. Strategic nuclear weapons, in Belarus, Kazakhstan, Russia, and Ukraine, are under the joint control of those republics, with day-to-day authority in the hands of the Russian president and defense minister. Eventually all such weapons outside Russia are to be destroyed. The commonwealth proved unable to prevent conflicts between the republics, and most republics, including Russia, moved to establish independent armed forces. By the end of 1993 nearly all members had established their own currencies. Attempts to form a joint defense force were abandoned, and Ukraine proved reluctant to relinquish its nuclear arms. A pact calling for increased economic integration was signed by most CIS nations in 1993.

Commonwealth of Nations, voluntary association of Great Britain, its dependencies and associated states, and certain sovereign states that were former dependencies. The purpose of the Commonwealth (founded 1931) is consultation and cooperation. No collective decisions are binding on the 50 member states, and they may withdraw at any time. They recognize the British monarch as the symbolic head of the Commonwealth. Members are linked economically, but the system of preferential tariffs was abandoned after Britain joined (1973) the European Community. The headquarters of the Commonwealth is in London.

Commune of Paris, insurrectionary governments in Paris formed during (1792) the FRENCH REVOLUTION and at the end (1871) of the FRANCO-PRUSSIAN WAR. In the French Revolution, the commune was a major radical force in France until moderates gained control (1794–95) of the National Convention. After the Franco-Prussian War, the commune opposed the national government led by Adolphe THIERS at VERSAILLES as too conservative and ready to accept humiliating peace terms. Versailles troops laid siege to Paris, against which the *communards* (whose aims included economic reforms and whose members comprised radical republicans, socialists, anarchists, and Marxists) put up a desperate defense. Before their defeat (May 28) they shot hostages and burned the TUILERIES and the palace of justice. Severe reprisals followed, with more than 17,000 people executed, a repression that lastingly embittered French political life.

communicable diseases, illnesses caused by microorganisms (bacteria, viruses) and transmitted either directly or indirectly from one infected person or animal to another. Many diseases are spread by airborne microorganisms through contact or proximity (e.g., INFLUENZA, MEASLES, WHOOPING COUGH). Some are spread through contaminated food or water (e.g., CHOLERA, TYPHOID), while others are transmitted by an animal or insect carrier (MALARIA, RABIES). Still others are transmitted under special circumstances, such as sexual contact (e.g., SYPHILIS) or infected instruments or blood transfusion (e.g., serum HEPATITIS). Control of communicable disease includes isolation of infected persons, immunization, personal hygiene, and stringent public health and sanitation measures.

communications satellite, artificial SATELLITE that provides a worldwide linkup of RADIO and TELEVISION transmissions and TELEPHONE service; such a satellite avoids the curvature-of-the-earth limitation formerly placed on communications between ground-based facilities. The first communications satellite was NASA's *Echo 1,* an uninstrumented inflatable sphere that passively reflected radio signals back to earth. Later satellites, starting with NASA's Relay satellites and the American Telephone and Telegraph (AT&T) Company's Telstar satellites, carried with them electronic devices for receiving, amplifying, and rebroadcasting signals to earth. The U.S. launching (1963) of the first synchronous-orbit satellite (*Syncom 1*) paved the way for the formation of the International Telecommunications Satellite Organization, whose successive series of Intelsat geostationary satellites have steadily lowered the cost of transoceanic communications. Domestic communications satellites, also geostationary, have been launched by many nations, including Canada, the USSR (now Russia), and Indonesia, and by several private U.S. companies. Military satellite systems have been developed by the U.S. and NATO.

communion, a SACRAMENT in most of CHRISTIANITY, a partaking of bread and wine that repeats the actions of JESUS at the LAST SUPPER. Roman Catholics and some others believe that the substances actually and miraculously become the body and blood of Jesus (transubstantiation). Others believe that the sacrament is symbolic, but all who practice communion believe that the recipient is united mystically with Jesus. The sacrament is called the Eucharist by some (including Roman Catholics) and the Lord's Supper or Holy Communion by many Protestants.

communism, a system of social organization in which property, particularly real property and the means of production, is held in common. With an uppercase *C,* the term refers to the movement that has sought to overthrow CAPITALISM through revolution. Forms of communism existed among various tribes of Native Americans, and it was espoused by early Christian sects. During the Middle Ages the MANORIAL SYSTEM provided communal use of the village commons and cultivation of certain fields, rights the peasants fought to retain in England (14th cent.) and Germany (16th cent.). By the early 19th cent. the rise of capitalism, reinforced by the INDUSTRIAL REVOLUTION, had created a new industrial class living and working under appalling conditions. Utopian socialists such as Robert OWEN and Charles FOURIER, anarchists such as P.J. PROUDHON, and revolutionaries such as Auguste Blanqui all favored some kind of communal solution to this poverty. In Germany Karl MARX and Friedrich ENGELS published the *Communist Manifesto* (1848), the primary exposition of the doctrine that came to be known as MARXISM. It postulated the inevitability of communism arising from class war, the overthrow of capitalism, and the creation of a classless society. Marxism greatly influenced 19th-cent. SOCIALISM. The modern Communist political movement began when the Russian Social Democratic Labor party split (1903) into two factions (see BOLSHEVISM AND MENSHEVISM). The Bolsheviks, led by V.I. LENIN, called for armed revolution. After their triumph in the 1917 RUSSIAN REVOLUTION, the Bolsheviks formed the Communist party (1918), established a party dictatorship, and founded the COMINTERN (1919), which claimed leadership of the world socialist movement. In the 1930s, Joseph STALIN's policy of "socialism in one country" prevailed in the USSR, but after WORLD WAR II Stalin created "satellite" Communist states in Eastern Europe. The Chinese Communists (see CHINA), who triumphed in 1949, aided movements in Southeast Asia. U.S. opposition to these and other actions by Soviet, Chinese, and other Commmunists led to the COLD WAR, KOREAN WAR, VIETNAM WAR, and "proxy wars" elsewhere, particularly in Latin America and Africa. Economic difficulties, particularly shortages of food and other consumer goods, and the resurgence of NATIONALISM led to demands for reform and internal problems in Hungary (1956), Czechoslovakia (1968), and Poland (1956, 1981), and other Communist countries, and to the often violent suppression of protest. In the 1960s Sino-Soviet relations deteriorated, and the Communist parties of Western and THIRD WORLD countries began to assert their independence of those two powers. Popular uprisings, economic collapse, and free elections ousted Communist governments in much of Eastern Europe in 1989 and 1990, and the failed hard-line coup against Soviet Pres. GORBACHEV led to the suspension of the Communist party in the USSR and the country's subsequent disintegration in 1991. By the early 1990s traditional Communist party dictatorships held power only in China, Cuba, Laos, North Korea, and Vietnam. China, Laos, Vietnam, and, to a lesser degree, Cuba have reduced state control of the economy in order to stimulate growth. Communist parties, or their descendent parties, remain politically important in many Eastern European nations and in Russia and many other nations of the former USSR.

Communist party: see COMMUNISM.

Communism Peak or **Mount Communism,** 24,590 ft (7,495 m), highest point in Tajikistan, in the Pamir Mts. It was the highest mountain in the former USSR. Originally called Garmo Peak, it was renamed Stalin Peak (1933) and Communism Peak (1962).

community college or **junior college,** U.S. public institution of higher education characterized by a two-year curriculum leading to an associate in arts degree or to transfer to a four-year college. It prepares students for direct entry into an occupation and, because of the low tuition, local setting, and relatively easy entry requirements, has been a major force in the expansion of educational opportunities since World War II.

commutative law, in mathematics, law holding that for a given operation combining two quantities, the order of the quantities is arbitrary. Addition and multiplication are commutative, thus, $a + b = b + a$ and $a \times b = b \times a$ for any two numbers a and b. Subtraction and division, however, are not commutative.

commutator: see GENERATOR; MOTOR, ELECTRIC.

Comnenus [kŏmnē'nəs], dynasty of Byzantine emperors: ISAAC I, ALEXIUS I, JOHN II, MANUEL I, ALEXIUS II, and Andronicus I.

Comoros, the, officially Federal Islamic Republic of the Comoros, republic (1992 est. pop. 494,000), 718 sq mi (1,862 sq km), occupying most of the Comoro Islands, an archipelago in the Indian Ocean, between the African coast and Madagascar. The capital is Moroni. It consists of three volcanic main islands—Njazidja, Nzwani, and Mwali (formerly Grande-Comore, Anjouan, and Mohéli, respectively), as well as numerous coral reefs and islets. A fourth island, the largely Roman Catholic MAYOTTE, is administered by France but claimed by the Comoros. Because of poor soil, lack of natural resources, and overpopulation, the islands have severe economic problems. Most of the population is engaged in agriculture, involving subsistence crops and the production of vanilla, copra, and essential oils for export. The people are of mixed African, Arab, Malay, and Indian descent. French and Arabic are the official languages, but most people speak a local blend of Swahili and Arabic. The state religion is Islam.

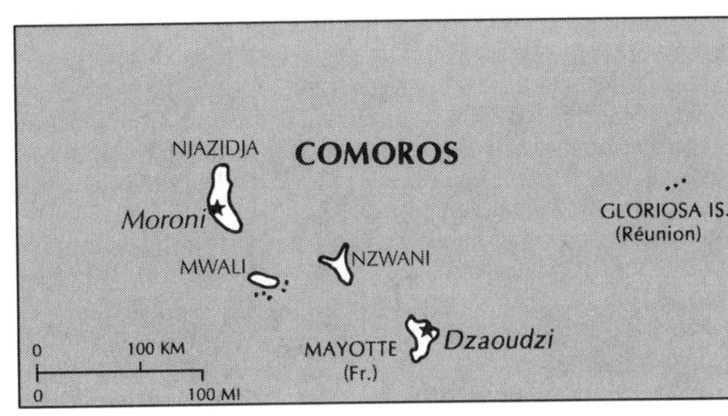

History. Originally populated by immigrants from Africa, Indonesia, and Arabia, the islands were ceded to the French between 1841 and 1909. After occupation by the British in WORLD WAR II, they were granted administrative autonomy within the French Union (1946) and internal self-government (1968). In 1975, as France was negotiating to end its rule in the islands, the Comoros unilaterally declared their independence; the island of Mayotte, however, voted to remain under French control. In 1978 the Comoros was proclaimed a federal Islamic republic; shortly thereafter, a one-party state was formed under Pres. Ahmed Abdallah Abderrahman. After his assassination in 1989, Saïd Mohamed Djohar became interim president and subsequently won election in a multiparty contest. He survived an impeachment attempt in 1991 and a coup attempt in 1992.

compact disc (CD), small plastic disk used to store information digitally; one type of OPTICAL DISK. Originally developed for audio systems as an alternative to phonograph records and audiotapes, CDs are now used for computer data storage and in video home entertainment systems. In audio CDs, the sound to be recorded is sampled thousands of times a second. Each sample is converted to a number that represents the sample's amplitude and encoded in binary form as a series of microscopic pits on the reflective surface of an aluminum disk. The disk is covered with a transparent plastic coating and is played on machine that uses an infrared LASER to read the pattern of pitted and unpitted areas on the disk's surface. Other CD formats include CD-ROM [*C*ompact *D*isk-*R*ead *O*nly *M*emory], a form of CD that is read by a computer using a CD-ROM drive and that can contain computer programs and digitized text, sound, photographs, and video; interactive CDs (CD-I, CDTV, and other formats), CD-ROM disks that require special players with built-in microcomputers; and Photo CD, a CD-ROM format for storing photographs.

comparative linguistics: see LINGUISTICS.

compass, in navigation, an instrument for determining direction. The mariner's compass, probably first used by European seamen in the 12th cent., consists of a magnetic needle freely suspended so that it turns to align itself with the magnetic north and south poles. The **gyrocompass** is a more accurate form of navigational compass, unaffected by magnetic influences, that came into wide use during World War II. It consists essentially of a rapidly spinning, electrically driven rotor suspended in such a way that its axis automatically points along the geographical meridian.

complex, in psychoanalysis, term introduced by C.G. JUNG to indicate a group of unconscious feelings and memories that result from early, highly emotional experiences and that conflict with other, conscious, ideas to influence mental activity and behavior. Two frequently cited complexes are the inferiority complex—real or imaginary handicaps, often colored by feelings of discouragement, that produce a striving to compensate; and the Oedipus complex—named by Sigmund FREUD after the myth of OEDIPUS and designating childhood hostility toward the parent of the same sex and attraction toward the parent of the opposite sex. The Oedipus complex is believed to arise as part of the psychosocial development of the personality around ages four to six.

complexity, in science, field of study devoted to the process of self-organization. The basic concept of complexity is that all things tend to organize themselves into patterns. Complexity looks for the mathematical equations that describe the middle ground between equilibrium (see STATICS) and CHAOS, such as the interplay between supply and demand in an economy or the relationship among living organisms in an ecosystem.

composite, common name for the Compositae or Asteraceae, the daisy family, which is one of the largest families of plants, consisting of some 20,000 species, mostly herbs and a few shrubs, trees, and climbing plants. The family includes many edible salad plants (e.g., LETTUCE, endive, CHICORY, salsify, and ARTICHOKES), many cultivated species (e.g., ASTERS, DAISIES, CHRYSANTHEMUMS, MARIGOLDS, and ZINNIAS), and many common weeds and wildflowers. It is often broken down into THISTLE, chicory, and RAGWEED tribes. The typical composite flower, e.g., a SUNFLOWER, is composed of a multiflowered head. The outer ring consists of the conspicuous, but sterile, often petallike ray flowers, which serve to attract insects for pollination. The central part of the head is composed of minute tubular disk flowers, usually with both stamens and pistils. A series of modified leaves (bracts) arising from the base of the flower stalk supports the head. Many composite FRUITS are highly adapted to dispersal by animals (e.g., the burr plants such as burdock and cocklebur) or by wind (e.g., the DANDELION and GOLDENROD).

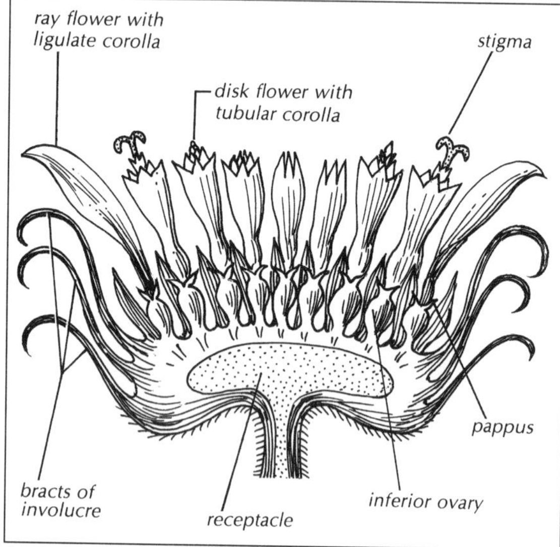

A composite flower is composed of many small flowers, often of two types (ray and disk). As in the sunflower (above), these flowers are joined by a common receptacle and surrounded by bracts (modified leaves).

composite material or **composite,** any material made from at least two discrete substances, such as concrete. Many materials are produced as composites, such as the fiberglass-reinforced plastics used for automobile bodies and boat hulls, but the term usually is used to describe any of various modern industrially manufactured composites, such as carbon fiber–reinforced plastics. Composite materials allow a blending of properties of the separate components. Carbon fiber–reinforced plastics combine the high strength and stiffness of the fiber with the low weight and resistance to fracture of the polymeric matrix. Glass, wood, and other kinds of fibers are also used, and the fibers may be layered or woven. Other modern composites include wood fiber or chunks in a concrete matrix and silicon carbide, a ceramic, in a titanium matrix.

compound, in chemistry, a substance composed of ATOMS of two or more ELEMENTS in chemical combination, occurring in fixed, definite proportion and arranged in fixed, definite structures. A compound has unique properties that are distinct from the properties of its elemental constituents and of all other compounds. A compound differs from a mixture in that the components of a mixture retain their own properties and may be present in many different proportions. The components of a mixture are not chemically combined; they can be separated by physical means. A molecular compound, e.g., WATER, is made up of electrically neutral MOLECULES, each containing a fixed number of atoms. An ionic compound, e.g., SODIUM CHLORIDE, is made up of electrically charged IONS that are present in fixed proportions and are arranged in a regular, geometric pattern called crystalline structure (see CRYSTAL) but are not grouped into molecules.

compressor, machine that decreases the volume of air or gas by the application of pressure. Compressor types range from the simple hand PUMP and the piston-equipped compressor used in gas stations to inflate tires to machines that use a rotating, bladed element to achieve compression. Compressed air exerts an expansive force that can be used as a source of power to operate pneumatic tools or to control such devices as air BRAKES. Air under compression can be stored in closed cylinders.

Compromise of 1850, an attempt at solving North-South tensions over the extension of slavery, specifically into newly annexed Texas and territory gained by the U.S. in the MEXICAN WAR. The WILMOT PROVISO of 1846, prohibiting slavery in land acquired from Mexico, caused contention. Compromise measures, largely originating with Stephen A. DOUGLAS, were sponsored in the Senate by Henry CLAY. The compromise proposed was to admit California as a free state, use popular sovereignty to decide free or slave status for New Mexico and Utah, prohibit the slave trade in the District of Columbia, pass a more stringent fugitive slave law, and settle Texas boundary claims. Chances for acceptance of these proposals were enhanced by a famous speech by Daniel WEBSTER (Mar. 17, 1850), and even more by the succession of Millard FILLMORE, a supporter of the compromise, after the death of Pres. Zachary TAYLOR. The proposals were passed as separate bills in Sept. 1850. The Compromise of 1850 was not, as had been hoped, a final solution of the question of slavery in new territories; that issue arose again in 1854 (see KANSAS-NEBRASKA ACT).

Compton, Arthur Holly, 1892–1962, American physicist; b. Wooster, Ohio. He was professor of physics at the Univ. of Chicago, where he helped to develop the atomic bomb, and was later professor and chancellor at Washington Univ., St. Louis. For his discovery of the **Compton effect** (the increase in the wavelengths of X rays and gamma rays when they collide with and are scattered from loosely bound electrons in matter), he shared the 1927 Nobel Prize in physics with Charles WILSON. Compton also made valuable studies of cosmic rays.

Compton-Burnett, Dame Ivy, 1892–1969, English novelist. Relying almost completely on highly stylized conversation, her witty novels, including *Brother and Sister* (1929) and *Mother and Son* (1955), picture a hypocritical Edwardian world.

computer, a device capable of performing a series of arithmetic or logical operations. A computer is distinguished from a calculating machine, such as an abacus or electronic CALCULATOR, by being able to store a computer program (so that it can repeat its operations and make logical decisions) and to store and retrieve data without human intervention. Computers are classed as analog or digital. An analog computer operates on continuously varying data; a digital computer performs operations on discrete data. An analog computer represents data as physical quantities and operates on the data by manipulating the quantities. In a complex analog computer, continuously varying data are converted into varying electrical quantities and the relationship of the data is determined by establishing an equivalent relationship, or analog, among the electrical quantities. Although analog computers are commonly found in such forms as speedometers and watt-hour meters, they largely have become obsolete for general-purpose mathematical computations and data storage by digital computers. Within a digital computer, data are expressed in binary notation (see NUMERATION), i.e., by a series of "on-off" conditions that represent the digits "1" and "0." A series of eight consecutive binary digits, or bits, is called a byte and allows 256 "on-off" combinations. Each byte can thus represent one of up to 256 alphanumeric characters. Arithmetic and comparative operations can be performed on data represented in this way and the result stored for later use. Digital computers are used for reservation systems, scientific investigation, data-processing applications, DESKTOP PUBLISHING, and ELECTRONIC GAMES.

Hardware. The four major physical components, or hardware, of a computer are the central processing unit (CPU), main storage, auxiliary storage, and input/output devices. Computer operations are performed in the CPU, which contains the LOGIC CIRCUITS for arithmetic and logical operations and for control of the other units that make up a computing system. The CPU also contains the registers, a relatively small number of storage locations that can be accessed faster than main storage and are used to hold the intermediate results of calculations. The main storage is contained in the storage unit, or memory, of the computer. Main storage—once made up of vacuum tubes and later of magnetic cores, each tube or core representing one bit—is now made up of tiny INTEGRATED CIRCUITS, each of which contains thousands of SEMICONDUCTORS. Each semiconductor represents one bit. Random access memory (RAM), which both can be read from and written to, is erased each time the computer is turned off. Read only memory (ROM), which cannot be written to, maintains its content at all times and is used to store the computer's control information. Programs and data that are not currently being used in main storage can be saved on auxiliary storage, or external storage. Although punched paper tape and punched cards once served this purpose, the major materials used today are magnetic tape and magnetic disks, which can be read from and written to, and the compact disc (or CD-ROM), which uses optical storage techniques and can only be read. Data are entered into the computer and the processed data made available via input/output devices. All auxiliary storage devices are used as input/output devices. For many years, the most popular input/output medium was the punched card. Although this is still used, the most popular input device is now the COMPUTER TERMINAL and the most popular output device is the high-speed PRINTER. The CPU, main storage, auxiliary storage, and input/output devices collectively make up a system. Computers are categorized by both size and the number of people who can use them concurrently. *Supercomputers* are sophisticated machines designed to perform complex calculations at the maximum speed; they are used to model very large dynamic systems, such as weather patterns. *Mainframes,* the largest and most powerful general-purpose systems, are designed to meet the computing needs of a large organization by serving hundreds of computer terminals at the same time. *Minicomputers,* though somewhat smaller, also are multiuser computers, intended to meet the needs of a small company by serving up to a hundred terminals. *Microcomputers,* computers powered by a MICROPROCESSOR, are subdivided into PERSONAL COMPUTERS and workstations, the latter typically incorporating RISC PROCESSORS. Although microcomputers were originally single user computers, the distinction between them and minicomputers has blurred as microprocessors have become more powerful. Linking multiple microcomputers together through a LOCAL AREA NETWORK or by joining multiple microprocessors together in a PARALLEL-PROCESSING system has enabled smaller systems to perform tasks once reserved for mainframes.

Software. The computer program, or software, controls the functioning of the hardware and directs its operation. See COMPUTER PROGRAM.

History. Although the development of digital computers is rooted in the ABACUS and early mechanical calculating devices, Charles BABBAGE is credited with the design of the first modern computer, the "analytical engine," during the 1830s. John Atanassoff constructed the first semielectronic digital computing device in 1939. The first fully automatic calculator was the Mark I, or Automatic Sequence Controlled Calculator, begun in 1939 at Harvard by Howard Aiken, while the first all-purpose electronic digital computer, ENIAC (Electronic Numerical Integrator And Calculator), which used thousands of vacuum tubes, was completed in 1946 at the Univ. of Pennsylvania. UNIVAC (UNIVersal Automatic Computer) became (1951) the first computer to handle both numeric and alphabetic data with equal facility; this was the first commercially available computer. First-generation computers were supplanted by the transistorized computers (see TRANSISTOR) of the late 1950s and early 1960s, second-generation machines that could perform a million operations per second. They, in turn, were replaced by the third-generation integrated-circuit machines of the mid-1960s and 1970s. The 1980s and early 90s were characterized by the development of the microprocessor and the evolution of increasingly smaller but powerful computers, such as the personal computer and PERSONAL DIGITAL ASSISTANT. See also ANALOG-TO-DIGITAL CONVERSION; ARTIFICIAL INTELLIGENCE; BAUD; BOOLEAN ALGEBRA; DIGITAL-TO-ANALOG CONVERSION; PROGRAMMING LANGUAGE; VIDEOTEX.

computer-aided design (CAD) or **computer-aided design and drafting** (CADD), the production of drawings, specifications, parts lists, and other design-related elements using special graphics- and calculations-intensive computer programs. Used in such fields as architecture, electronics, and aerospace, naval, and automotive engineering, CAD systems originally merely automated drafting but now often include three-dimensional modeling and computer-simulated operation of the model. More expensive CAD programs are often integrated with COMPUTER-AIDED MANUFACTURING systems, and less expensive ones are available for do-it-yourself home remodeling and other uses.

computer-aided manufacturing (CAM), form of AUTOMATION in which computers control the machinery on an assembly line, such as ROBOTIC milling and welding machines, and move the product from machine to machine as each step is completed. Advanced systems are integrated with COMPUTER-AIDED DESIGN systems and can manage such tasks as parts ordering, scheduling, and tool replacement.

computer graphics, the transfer of pictorial data into and out of a COMPUTER. Using ANALOG-TO-DIGITAL CONVERSION techniques, a variety of devices—such as curve tracers, digitizers, and light pens—connected to graphic COMPUTER TERMINALS can be used to store pictorial data in a digital computer. By reversing the process through DIGITAL-TO-ANALOG CONVERSION techniques, the stored data can be output on a mechanical plotting board, or plotter, or on a televisionlike graphic display terminal. Raster graphics stores and displays images as a bit map, a series of closely spaced dots (or pixels) arranged in rows and columns. Vector, or object-oriented, graphics stores the images as mathematical formulas. Images are displayed by calculating the coordinates of the end points and then drawing lines between them. Computer graphics capabilities range from the simple display of digital tabulations as line graphs and pie charts to complex animation and elaborate special effects for television and motion pictures. Computer graphics are used in architecture, art, COMPUTER-AIDED DESIGN, ELECTRONIC GAMES, FLIGHT SIMULATORS for pilot training, and MOLECULAR MODELING.

computer music: see ELECTRONIC MUSIC.

computer program, a series of instructions that a COMPUTER can interpret and execute; programs are also called software to distinguish them from hardware, the physical equipment used in DATA PROCESSING. These programming instructions cause the computer to perform arithmetic and logical operations or comparisons (and then take some additional action based on the comparison) or to input or output data in a desired sequence. In conventional computing the operations are executed sequentially; in PARALLEL PROCESSING the operations are allocated among multiple processors, which execute them concurrently and share the results. Programs are often written as a series of subroutines, which can be used in more than one program or at more than one point in the same program. Systems programs are those that control the operation of the computer. Chief among these is the operating system—also called the control program, executive, or supervisor—which schedules the execution of other programs, allocates system resources, and controls input and output operations. Processing programs are those whose execution is controlled by the operating system. Language translators decode source programs, written in a PROGRAMMING LANGUAGE, and produce object programs, which are in machine language and can be understood by the computer. These include assemblers, which translate symbolic languages that have a one-to-one relationship with machine language; compilers, which translate an algorithmic- or procedural-language program into a machine-language program to be executed at a later time; and interpreters, which translate source-language statements into object-language statements for immediate execution. Other processing programs are service or utility programs, such as those that "dump" computer memory to external storage for safekeeping and those that enable the programmer to "trace" program execution, and application programs, which perform business and scientific functions such as payroll processing, accounts payable and receivable posting, and simulation of environmental conditions.

computer terminal, a device that enables a COMPUTER to receive or deliver data. Computer terminals vary greatly depending on the format of the data they handle. For example, a simple early terminal comprises a typewriter keyboard for input and a typewriter printing element for alphanumeric output. A similar device includes the keyboard for input and a televisionlike screen to display the output. The screen can be a CATHODE-RAY TUBE or a gas plasma panel, the latter involving an ionized gas (sandwiched between glass layers) that glows to form dots which, in turn, connect to form lines. Such displays can present a variety of output, ranging from simple alphanumerics to complex graphic images used as design tools by architects and engineers. Portable terminals frequently use LIQUID CRYSTAL displays because of their low power requirements. The terminals of PEN-BASED COMPUTERS use a stylus to input handwriting on the screen. Touch-sensitive terminals accept input made by touching a pressure sensitive panel in front of a menu displayed on the screen. Other familiar terminals include store checkout systems that deliver detailed printed receipts and use laser scanners to read the BAR CODES on packages, and automatic teller machines in banks.

computer virus, rogue COMPUTER PROGRAM, typically a short program designed to disperse copies of itself to other computers and disrupt those computers' normal operations. A computer virus usually attaches or inserts itself to or in a file or the boot sector of a disk and is spread via floppy disks, networks, or on-line services. Although some viruses are harmless, others can destroy or corrupt data or cause an operating system or applications program to malfunction. Antivirus programs and hardware have been developed to combat viruses by searching for evidence of a virus program, isolating infected files, and removing viruses from a computer's software.

Comstock, Anthony, 1844–1915, American morals crusader; b. New Canaan, Conn. He secured strict New York and federal antiobscenity legislation. As an organizer and then the secretary (1873–1915) of the New York Society for the Suppression of Vice, he was responsible for the destruction of 160 tons of literature and pictures.

Comstock Lode, on Mt. Davidson, W Nev.; the richest known U.S. silver deposit, discovered in 1857 by Ethan Allen Grosh and Hosea Ballou Grosh. They died before recording claims, and in 1859 Henry Tomkins Paige Comstock laid claim to the lode. When he disposed of his holdings, the lode became a scene of furious activity, centering on VIRGINIA CITY. Wasteful mining methods and the demonetization of silver led to the lode's decline, and by 1898 it was virtually abandoned.

Comte, Auguste, 1798–1857, French philosopher and sociologist, founder of the school of philosophy known as POSITIVISM. Comte was primarily a social reformer; his goal, as set forth in *The Course of Positive Philosophy* (1830–42), was a society in which both individuals and nations could live in harmony and comfort. He regarded sociology (a term he originated) as the method by which this harmony and well-being could be achieved. Comte formulated a theory of three stages of social development: theological (belief in the supernatural), metaphysical (belief in ideas as reality), and positive (phenomena are explained by observation, hypothesis, and experimentation).

Conakry, city (1986 est. pop. 800,000), capital of Guinea, on the Atlantic Ocean. It is Guinea's largest city and its administrative, economic, and communications center. Situated on Tombo island, it is connected with the mainland by a causeway. Conakry's economy is based on its modern port; manufactures include food products and automobiles. The city was occupied by the French in 1887. Since World War II it has grown into a modern city with wide boulevards.

Conant, James Bryant, 1893–1978, American educator; b. Dorchester, Mass. President of Harvard Univ. from 1933 to 1953, he became U.S. high commissioner for Germany (1953) and ambassador to West Germany (1955–57). He published widely on American education, including *The American High School Today* (1959) and *The Education of American Teachers* (1963).

concentration, in chemistry, measure of the relative proportions of two or more quantities in a mixture (see COMPOUND). Concentrations may be expressed in a number of ways. The simplest is in terms of a component's percentage by weight or volume. Mixtures of solids or liquids are frequently specified by weight-percentage concentrations, whereas mixtures of gases are usually specified by volume percentages. Very low concentrations, such as those of various substances in the atmosphere, are expressed in parts per million (ppm). The *molarity* of a SOLUTION is the number of MOLES of solute per liter of solution. The *molality* of a solution is the number of moles of solute per 1,000 grams of solvent. The *mole fraction* of a solution is the ratio of moles of solute to the total number of moles in the solution.

concentration camp, prison or forced-labor camp outside the normal criminal system, for political prisoners, minorities, or others declared undesirable; first used by the British during the SOUTH AFRICAN WAR to confine Afrikaners. In Germany under the Nazis (see NATIONAL SOCIALISM), concentration camps were set up after 1933 to detain (without legal procedure) Jews, Communists, Gypsies, homosexuals, and others. During WORLD WAR II, extermination, or death, camps were established for the sole purpose of killing men, women, and children. In the most notorious camps—Auschwitz, Treblinka, and Majdanek in Poland, Buchenwald and Dachau in Germany—more than 6 million people, mostly Jews and Poles, were killed in gas chambers. Millions of others were also interned during the war, and a large proportion died of gross mistreatment, malnutrition, and disease. The term *concentration camp* has also been applied to similar camps operated by the Japanese during World War II, to the forced-labor camps of the USSR, and to the U.S. internment camps for Japanese-Americans during World War II.

Concentration camp survivors, Auschwitz, 1945

Concepción, city (1992 est. pop. 315,000), capital of Concepción prov., S central Chile, near the mouth of the Bío-Bío R. It is a major industrial center. Founded in 1550, it was leveled or severely damaged by at least six major earthquakes in the period from 1570 to 1960. The frequent rebuilding of the city has given it a modern aspect.

concerto, musical composition usually for orchestra and soloist (most often piano or violin) or a group of soloists. The *concerto grosso,* for a small group of soloists with full orchestra, was developed by Giuseppe Torelli, VIVALDI, and CORELLI. The BAROQUE concerto was most fully developed by J.S. BACH and G.F. HANDEL. Toward the end of the 18th cent. the solo concerto displaced the *concerto grosso,* and was fixed by W.A. MOZART in its classical form of three movements. In the 19th cent. BEETHOVEN gave greater importance to the orchestra, and LISZT unified the concerto form through the use of repeated themes.

conch, name for some tropical, marine GASTROPODS having heavy, spiral shells, the whorls of which overlap each other. The typical gastropod foot is reduced in size and the horny plate (operculum) located at the end of the foot has the appearance and function of a claw. Their shells range in color from white to red. Conchs are a valuable food source.

Concord. **1** Residential city (1990 pop. 111,348), Contra Costa co., W Calif.; settled c.1852, inc. 1906. Concord is in an oil and farm region; electronic equipment is the leading manufacture. The city is part of the growing San Francisco Bay area. **2** Town (1990 pop. 17,076), E Mass., on the Concord R.; inc. 1635. Electronic and wood products are made. The site of the 1775 battle (see LEXINGTON AND CONCORD, battles of) is marked by Daniel Chester FRENCH's bronze *Minuteman*. Concord's fine old houses were the homes of EMERSON, the ALCOTTS, HAWTHORNE, and THOREAU, among others. **3** City (1990 pop. 36,006), state capital and seat of Merrimack co., S central N.H., on the Merrimack R.; settled 1725–27, inc. 1733 as Rumford, Mass., inc. 1765 as Concord, N.H.; became state capital in 1808. Its granite quarries are famous. The city also produces electrical and leather goods and has a printing industry.

concordat, formal agreement between the pope in his spiritual capacity and the temporal authority of a state. The earliest was the Concordat of Worms (1122) which ended the INVESTITURE controversy. The most famous was the **Concordat of 1801,** reached between Napoleon and Pope PIUS VII. It reestablished the Roman Catholic Church in France and provided for the nomination of bishops by the state and the conferral of office by the pope.

concrete, structural masonry material made by mixing broken stone or gravel with sand, CEMENT, and water, and allowing the mixture to harden into a solid mass. Concrete has great strength under compression, but its tensile strength must be increased by embedding steel rods (reinforced concrete) or CABLES under tension (prestressed concrete) within the concrete structural member.

concrete music: see ELECTRONIC MUSIC.

Condé [kôNdā'], French princely family, cadet branch of the house of BOURBON. It originated with **Louis I de Bourbon, prince de Condé,** 1530–69, Protestant leader and general. He tried to topple the GUISE family from power in the conspiracy of Amboise (1560) and commanded the HUGUENOTS in the Wars of Religion (see RELIGION, WARS OF). He was slain at the battle of Jarnac. His great-grandson **Louis II de Bourbon, prince de Condé,** 1621–86, called the Great Condé, won major victories in the THIRTY YEARS WAR at Rocroi (1643), Freiburg (1644), Nördlingen (1645), and Lens (1648). In the FRONDE he turned against the government by taking command of the rebellious army of the princes in 1651 and of the Spanish army in 1653. Defeated in the battle of the Dunes (1658), he was pardoned (1659) by LOUIS XIV, for whom he fought successfully (1672–78) in the DUTCH WARS. His great-grandson **Louis Joseph de Bourbon, prince de Condé,** 1736–1818, formed the emigré "army of Condé" (dissolved 1801), which fought in alliance with France's enemies against French Revolutionary forces.

condensation: see STATES OF MATTER.

condenser: see CAPACITOR.

condominium, individually owned unit in a building or development with multiple residential or commercial occupants. Each unit (often an apartment or duplex) may be financed or sold separately by the owner, as in private housing, but the care and expense of maintaining common areas are shared, as in COOPERATIVES. Condominium sales sometimes include time-sharing, in which a number of people buy into the same condominium for use at a specified time of year (e.g., a particular month) over a period of years (e.g., 25 years). The demand for condominium housing surged in the U.S. in the 1970s and remained strong during the housing slump of the early 1980s.

condor, VULTURE found in the high peaks of the Coast Range of S California and the ANDES. Condors are the largest living birds, nearly 50 in. (125 cm) long with wingspans of from 9 to 10 ft (274 to 300 cm). Voracious eaters, they prefer carrion but will attack living animals as large as deer. California condors are extremely rare and from 1987, when the last wild bird was captured, to 1992 were only found in zoos. In 1992 zoo-raised birds were returned to the wild.

Condorcet, Marie Jean Antoine Nicolas Caritat, marquis de [kôNdôrsā'], 1743–94, French mathematician, philosopher, and political leader. He did notable work (1785) on the theory of PROBABILITY. His best-known work is *Sketch for a Historical Picture of the Progress of the Human Mind* (1795), in which he traced human development through nine epochs to the French Revolution and predicted in the tenth epoch the ultimate perfection of the human race.

conduction, transfer of HEAT or ELECTRICITY through a substance, resulting from a difference in temperature between different parts of the substance or from a difference in electric POTENTIAL. Heat may be conducted when the motions of energetic (hotter) molecules are passed on to nearby, less energetic (cooler) molecules, but a more effective method is the migration of energetic free electrons. Conduction of electricity consists of the flow of CHARGES. Metals are thus good conductors of both heat and electricity because they have a high free-electron density.

Confederacy, name commonly given to the **Confederate States of America** (1861–65), the government established by the southern states of the U.S. after their secession from the Union. When Pres. LINCOLN was elected (Nov. 1860), seven states—South Carolina, Georgia, Louisiana, Mississippi, Florida, Alabama, and Texas—seceded. A provisional government was set up at Montgomery, Ala., and a constitution was drafted; it resembled the U.S. CONSTITUTION but had provisions for STATES' RIGHTS and SLAVERY. After the firing on FORT SUMTER and Lincoln's call for troops, four more states—Arkansas, North Carolina, Virginia, and Tennessee—joined. Richmond, Va., became the capital, and Jefferson DAVIS and A.H. STEPHENS were elected president and vice president. The story of the Confederacy is the story of the loss of the CIVIL WAR. Its loyal citizens bore privations and invasion with courage. It was refused recognition by England and France. Volunteers for its army were insufficient; conscription was used but opposed. Financial troubles were heavy, and its paper money became worthless. Mounting Union victories made defeat inevitable. The Confederacy fell after R.E. LEE's surrender in Apr. 1865.

Confederation, Articles of, in U.S. history, early form of constitution ratified in 1781 and superseded (1789) by the U.S. CONSTITUTION. Its chief faults were a subordinate role for the central government and the dependence of Congress on the states both for funds and for execution of its decrees. Because of these inherent weaknesses the government commanded little respect domestically or abroad. Its most significant achievement was the ORDINANCE OF 1787.

Confessing Church, German Protestant movement. Founded (1933) by Martin NIEMOELLER in opposition to the Nazi-sponsored German Christian Church, it was later driven underground. It continues as a separate group within the German Evangelicals.

confirmation, Christian rite confirming an individual's prior initiation into the church by BAPTISM. In the Roman Catholic and Orthodox Eastern Churches, it is a SACRAMENT. In the West it is ordinarily conferred by a bishop and consists of the laying on of hands and anointing with chrism, a mixture of oil and balm. Priests confer it in the East. Lutherans and Anglicans also use confirmation.

Confucianism, moral and religious system of China. Its origins lie in the collection of sayings known as the *Analects* (see CHINESE LITERATURE), attributed to CONFUCIUS, and in ancient commentaries such as that of Mencius. Before the 3d cent. B.C., Confucianism was a system of ethical precepts for the management of society, based on the practice of *jen*—sympathy or "human-heartedness"—as shown in one's relations with others and demonstrated through adherence to *li*, a combination of etiquette and ritual. A person who wishes to be properly treated when in a subordinate role must, according to the Confucian Golden Rule, treat his own inferiors with propriety. Confucianism, with its practical social precepts, was often challenged by the supernatural religious systems of TAOISM and BUDDHISM and was eclipsed by them from the 3d to the 7th cent. A.D., but it revived under the T'ang dynasty (618–906). The Sung dynasty (960–1279) saw the development of neo-Confucianism, a metaphysical system that drew on the beliefs of Taoism and especially of ZEN BUDDHISM; during the Ming period (1368–1644) it stressed meditation and intuitive knowledge. Thereafter the system gradually weakened, and with the overthrow of the monarchy (1911–12) Confucianism declined, a process accelerated by the Communist revolution (1949). Traditional Chinese ethics and culture still stem from Confucian teachings, however.

Confucius [kənfyoo͞′shəs], Chinese *K'ung Fu-tse,* c.551–479? B.C., Chinese sage. Legend surrounds his life, but modern scholars base their accounts mainly on the *Analects,* a collection of sayings and dialogues apparently recorded by Confucius' disciples. He was born in the feudal state of Lu, in modern Shandong province. Probably because of his reformist teachings, he held only minor governmental posts. In the midst of the warfare and tyranny, he urged a system of morality and statecraft to bring about peace, stability, and just government. His supposed doctrines are embodied in CONFUCIANISM.

congestive heart failure: see HEART DISEASE.

conglomerate, a large corporation that grows mainly through acquisition of, or merger with, firms in unrelated fields. Although corporate mergers and acquisitions were common earlier, the modern conglomerate did not emerge until the 1960s, when it became popular among investors. By diversifying, the conglomerate seeks to protect itself against changing markets and economic conditions.

Congo, officially Republic of the Congo, republic (1992 est. pop. 2,377,000), 132,046 sq mi (342,000 sq km), W central Africa, bordered by Gabon (W), Cameroon and the Central African Republic (N), Zaïre (E and SE), and Cabinda (an exclave of Angola) and the Atlantic Ocean (SW). Major cities include BRAZZAVILLE (the capital) and POINTE-NOIRE. The country is largely covered by tropical rain forests and stretches of wooded savanna, and is drained by tributaries of the CONGO and Ubangi rivers. Congo serves as the commercial and transport hub of central Africa, with important road, river, and rail systems connecting inland areas with the Atlantic. Forestry and agriculture are the chief economic activities, providing sugarcane, palm oil, coffee, cocoa, and timber for export, and serving as the basis of most of the country's industry. Mining is also important, with petroleum and potash the principal exports, although reserves are being depleted. The Bakongo, the major ethnic group, are Bantu-speaking, as are the other principal groups, the Sanga, Mbochi, and Bateke. About half of the people adhere to traditional religions, and some 30% are Roman Catholic. French is the official language.

History. The region probably was first inhabited by PYGMIES, followed (15th cent.) by the Bakongo, Bateke, and Sanga. After the Portuguese navigator Diego Cão explored the coast in 1482, a slave trade developed between Europeans and the coastal African states. Portuguese traders predominated throughout the 17th cent., although French, English, and Dutch merchants competed for commercial opportunities. From 1889 the area (called French Congo and later Middle Congo) was administered by French concessionaires, who exploited its rubber and ivory, until it became a colony in FRENCH EQUATORIAL AFRICA in 1910. In 1946, after serving as a bastion for Free French forces in WORLD WAR II, Congo was granted a territorial assembly. It gained autonomy within the FRENCH COMMUNITY in 1958 and full independence in 1960. Its first president, Fulbert Youlou, was ousted in 1963, and a government with a Marxist-Leninist ideology was established. This was, in turn, overthrown in 1968, but the new military regime continued the previous government's socialist policies. Following a presidential assassination in 1977, a military council governed until 1979, when Col. Denis SASSOU-NGUESSO became president. Widespread unrest in 1990 led to a national political conference (1991) that reduced presidential power and ended the state's adherence to Marxism-Leninism. In 1992 Pascal Lissouba won the nation's first democratic presidential election, but fighting between pro-government forces and Lissouba's opponents (both largely ethnically based groups) slowed progress toward full democracy.

Congo or **Zaïre,** great river of Africa, flowing c.2,720 mi (4,380 km) generally north and west through Zaïre to the Atlantic Ocean in NW Angola. It drains much of central equatorial Africa. Its upper course, above Boyoma (Stanley) Falls, is known as the Lualaba R. Its lower course widens near Kinshasa to form lakelike Pool Malebo (Stanley Pool), from which the river descends 876 ft (267 m) through a series of rapids (Livingstone Falls) to the port of Matadi. Called the Congo for the historic KONGO kingdom near its mouth, the river was explored in the 19th cent. by David LIVINGSTONE and Henry STANLEY.

Congregationalism, a type of Protestant church organization in which each congregation, or local church, has free control of its own affairs, with Jesus alone as its head. The movement arose (16th–17th cent.) in England in a SEPARATIST revolt against formalized worship. Pilgrims brought Congregationalism to America in 1620, where it later took a leading part in the GREAT AWAKENING. There have been several mergers involving Congregational bodies, the latest (1957) forming the UNITED CHURCH OF CHRIST. There are no bishops or presbyteries.

Congress of Industrial Organizations: see AMERICAN FEDERATION OF LABOR AND CONGRESS OF INDUSTRIAL ORGANIZATIONS.

Congress of Racial Equality (CORE), civil-rights organization founded (1942) in Chicago by James Farmer. It seeks, through nonviolent direct action, to end discrimination in public accommodations, housing, and other areas. CORE first gained national recognition with the 1961 Freedom Rides, in which interracial groups traveled south by bus. It later moved toward a more separatist policy, calling for African-American economic independence within the U.S., and since the late 1970s has taken more politically conservative positions.

Congress of the United States, legislative branch of the federal government, instituted (1789) by Article 1 of the CONSTITUTION OF THE UNITED STATES. It comprises two houses, the Senate and the House of Representatives. The Senate consists of two senators from each state, who serve six-year terms. Senators were elected by state legislatures until 1913, when the 17th amendment to the Constitution required that they be chosen by popular election. Every two years one third of the Senate is elected. The House of Representatives consists of 435 members apportioned among the states according to their population in the federal census. Representatives are elected from congressional districts drawn up by the state legislatures and serve two-year terms. The House traditionally elects its presiding officer, the Speaker, by consensus of the majority party. The vice president of the U.S. is the presiding officer of the Senate, but the agenda is set by the majority leader. Most of the work in both houses is transacted by standing committees in which both majority and minority members are represented. Each chamber has an equal voice in legislation, although revenue bills must originate in the House. The Senate must ratify all treaties by a two-thirds vote; it also confirms important presidential appointees. A presidential VETO of congressional legislation can be overridden by a two-thirds vote in each house. Whenever an item of legislation is approved in varying forms by the two houses, the differences are reconciled by a joint (or conference) committee that includes members of both chambers. See also EXECUTIVE; CABINET; COURT SYSTEM IN THE UNITED STATES; SUPREME COURT, UNITED STATES.

Congress party: see INDIAN NATIONAL CONGRESS.

Congreve, William, 1670–1729, English dramatist. After publishing a novel, *Incognita* (1692), and translations, he turned to the stage. His first comedy, *The Old Bachelor* (1693), was a great success and was followed by *The Double Dealer* (1693), *Love for Love* (1695), and a tragedy, *The Mourning Bride* (1697). His masterpiece, *The Way of the World,* appeared in 1700. Congreve's plays are considered the apex of RESTORATION comedy. With brilliant language and complex plots they present amused, cynical portraits of people more concerned with manners than morals.

conic section or **conic,** curve formed by the intersection of a plane and a right circular cone, or conical surface. The ordinary conic sections are the CIRCLE, the ellipse, the parabola, and the hyperbola. When the plane passes through the vertex of the cone, the result is a point, a straight line, or a pair of intersecting straight lines; these are called degenerate conic sections. In ANALYTIC GEOMETRY every conic section is the graph of an equation of the form $ax^2 + bxy + cy^2 + dx + ey + f = 0$, where a, b, c, d, e, and f are constants and a, b, and c are not all zero.

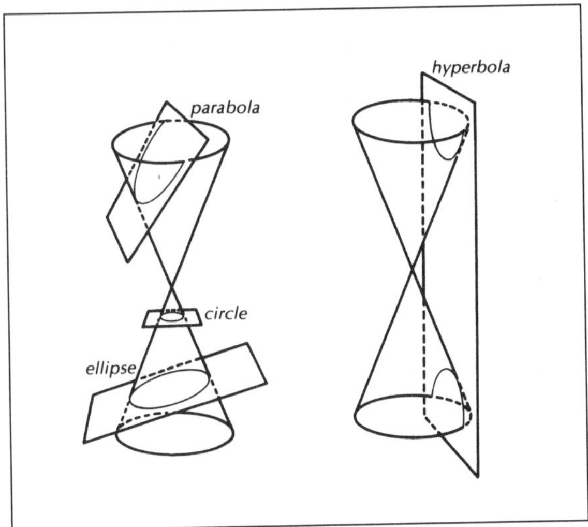

Conic sections

conifer, tree or shrub of a large division (Coniferophyta or Pinophyta) of mostly cone-bearing evergreens distributed worldwide. A few, e.g., the LARCH, are deciduous. Conifers, being GYMNOSPERMS, do not have true flowers, but some, e.g., the YEW, have globular fruits. The PINE, MONKEY-PUZZLE TREE, CYPRESS, and SEQUOIA are conifers.

conjunction, in astronomy: see SYZYGY.

conjunctivitis, disorder of the mucosal membrane that covers the eyeball and lines the eyelid, usually caused by bacteria, virus, or allergy; also called "pinkeye." Producing redness, discharge, and itching of the eyes, conjunctivitis is frequently treated with ANTIBIOTICS and sometimes CORTISONE. Before the use of silver nitrate drops in eyes of newborns, conjunctivitis was a major cause of blindness in infants.

Conkling, Roscoe, 1829–88, American politician; b. Albany, N.Y. He served New York in the U.S. House of Representatives (1859–63, 1865–67) and the U.S. Senate (1867–81). The Republican state "boss" and "Old Guard" leader, He resigned from the Senate when Pres. James A. GARFIELD ignored him in appointing a collector of the port of New York.

Connecticut, one of the New England states of the NE U.S.; bordered by Massachusetts (N), Rhode Island (E), Long Island Sound (S), and New York (W).

Area, 5,009 sq mi (12,973 sq km). *Pop.* (1990), 3,287,116, a 5.8% increase over 1980 pop. *Capital,* Hartford. *Statehood,* Jan. 9, 1788 (fifth of the original 13 states to ratify the Constitution). *Highest pt.,* Mt. Frissell, 2,380 ft (726 m); *lowest pt.,* sea level. *Nickname,* Constitution State. *Motto, Qui Transtulit Sustinet* [He Who Transplanted Still Sustains]. *State bird,* American robin. *State flower,* mountain laurel. *State tree,* white oak. *Abbr.,* Conn.; CT.

Land and People. Except for the coastal plain along Long Island Sound, Connecticut is covered with rolling hills. The western highlands, including part of the Taconic Mts., are separated from the eastern highlands by the fertile Connecticut R. valley. Almost 80% of the population lives in metropolitan areas. The principal cities are BRIDGEPORT, HARTFORD, NEW HAVEN, WATERBURY, and STAMFORD. The state's densely settled southwestern corner is part of the New York City metropolitan area. In 1990 the population was 87% white and 8.3% African American.

Economy. Although there has been significant economic decline in recent years, Connecticut continues to be a heavily industrialized state. Among its chief products are transportation equipment, including submarines manufactured at GROTON, jet engines, and helicopters; electronic and electrical equipment; munitions; medical instruments; and pharmaceuticals. Hartford has long been one of the country's leading insurance centers. The small agricultural sector is dominated by dairying and the cultivation of shade-grown tobacco.

Government. The constitution of 1965 provides for a governor elected to a four-year term. The legislature is composed of a 36-member senate and 151-seat house, with members of both serving two-year terms. Connecticut is represented in the U.S. Congress by six representatives and two senators and has eight electoral votes.

History. The Dutch discovered the Connecticut R. in 1614, but European settlement of the region was largely the work of English Puritans from Massachusetts. In the 1630s they flocked to the Connecticut valley, and in 1638–39 the towns of Hartford, Windsor, and Wethersfield adopted the FUNDAMENTAL ORDERS, which set up a government for the colony. It soon expanded to include other towns and in 1662 acquired the colony of New Haven, which had been founded in 1638. Connecticut joined the other colonies in the AMERICAN REVOLUTION and was one of the first states to ratify the Constitution. Its important shipping trade suffered from the EMBARGO ACT (1807) and the WAR OF 1812, and the state gradually turned to manufacturing. Connecticut abolished slavery in 1848 and supported the Union in the CIVIL WAR with nearly 60,000 troops. The state has prospered for most of the 20th cent., save for the Great Depression. During the early to mid-1980s, largely due to defense-related industries, Connecticut was one of the nation's wealthiest states. Prosperity gave way to economic downturn later in the decade and in the early 1990s as federal military spending declined markedly.

Connecticut Wits or **Hartford Wits,** informal association of Yale students and rectors formed in the late 18th cent. Conservative Federalists, they attacked their liberal opponents in satirical verses, e.g., *The Anarchiad* (1786–87). Members of the group included Timothy DWIGHT and John TRUMBULL.

connective tissue, supportive tissue widely distributed in the body. Consisting mainly of substances certain cells secrete, it contains relatively few cells. The connective tissue that forms TENDONS and LIGAMENTS is mainly collagen—white, inelastic protein fibers. Cartilage, vital to the skeletal system of vertebrates, is fibrous collagen in a gel; it is firm but flexible. Connective tissue found under the skin and supporting most organs contains collagen and other fibers as well. BONE connective tissue is made up largely of collagen fibers and calcium salt crystals; its structure is strong and rigid. BLOOD and lymph have a fluid connective tissue matrix.

Connelly, Marc, 1890–1980, American dramatist; b. McKeesport, Pa. His best-known play is *The Green Pastures* (1930; Pulitzer), a biblical fantasy based on African-American life in the South. He also wrote several plays in collaboration with George S. KAUFMAN.

Connolly, Maureen, 1934–69, American tennis player; b. San Diego. At 16, "Little Mo" became the youngest player to win the U.S. national singles. She twice defended (1952–53) the title successfully, won (1952–54) at Wimbledon three times, and completed (1953) the grand slam by adding the French and Australian titles.

Connors, Jimmy (James Connors, Jr.), 1952–, American tennis

Jimmy Connors

player; b. East St. Louis, Ill. In 1974, at 22, he won the Australian Open, the U.S. Open (which he also won in 1976, 1978, 1982, and 1983), and Wimbledon (which he also won in 1982). Connors has won more professional tennis tournaments than any other man.

conquistador, military leader of the Spanish conquest of the New World in the 16th cent. Francisco PIZARRO and Hernán CORTÉS were the greatest conquistadors. The word can mean any daring, ruthless adventurer.

Conrad, rulers of the HOLY ROMAN EMPIRE and its predecessor state. **Conrad I,** d. 918, German king (911–18), succeeded Louis the Child, but was plagued by feuds and rebellions in Lorraine, Swabia, and Bavaria. His failure to halt the continuing Hungarian invasions and the alienation of his nobles almost dissolved the kingdom. **Conrad II,** c.990–1039, emperor and German king (1024–39), was the first of the Frankish Salian dynasty. His election as German king was contested by Swabia, Lotharingia, and Italy; but he was crowned after three years of conflict. His reign was marked by constant revolts, but he added Burgundy to his dominions and greatly increased commerce. **Conrad III,** c.1093–1152, emperor and German king (1138–52), founder of the HOHENSTAUFEN dynasty, was set up as antiking to Emperor LOTHAIR II in 1127 but submitted to Lothair in 1135. He was elected king at Lothair's death by those opposing Henry the Proud of Bavaria and his brother Guelph, thereby setting in force the struggle between the GUELPHS AND GHIBELLINES. Conrad was never crowned. **Conrad IV,** 1228–54, emperor and German king (1237–54), king of Sicily and of Jerusalem (1250–54), was made king by his father Emperor FREDERICK II, but the struggle between Frederick and Pope INNOCENT IV kept him from being crowned. He was excommunicated in 1254 and died shortly thereafter of fever.

Conrad, d. 1192, Latin king of JERUSALEM (1192), marquis of Montferrat, a leader in the Third CRUSADE. He defended TYRE against the Saracens and became (1187) its lord. To gain the throne of Jerusalem he married the daughter of AMALRIC I, but he was immediately murdered, probably by Muslims. The title passed eventually to AMALRIC II.

Conrad, Joseph, 1857–1924, English novelist; b. Poland, as Jósef Teodor Konrad Walecz Korzeniowski. After a period at sea (during which he became a British subject), he began (1894) writing novels in English, an acquired language, and eventually became one of the greatest prose stylists in English literature. Notable early works include *The Nigger of the "Narcissus"* (1897), *Lord Jim* (1900), and the novellas *Youth* (1902), *Heart of Darkness* (1902), and *Typhoon* (1903). A master at creating character and atmosphere, Conrad acutely portrayed individuals suffering from isolation and moral disintegration, and the clash between colonized cultures and European colonizers. His best works include *Nostromo* (1904), *The Secret Agent* (1907), *Under Western Eyes* (1911), *Chance* (1913), and *Victory* (1915).

consanguinity: see KINSHIP.

conscientious objector, person who, on grounds of conscience, refuses military service. Resistance based on religious or humanitarian convictions, as among Quakers (see FRIENDS), is usually distinguished from political opposition. In World Wars I and II, the U.S. and Britain allowed objectors who were members of recognized pacifist religious denominations to substitute nonmilitary service, but imprisoned other pacifists. In the 1970s the U.S. Supreme Court allowed conscientious objection based on deeply held ethical as well as religious beliefs, but refused to accept opposition to the VIETNAM WAR as a basis for exemption.

conscription, compulsory enrollment, in war or peace, in the armed forces. The idea of compulsory military service by all of a nation's able-bodied men was introduced in the late 18th cent. during the French Revolution and enabled Napoleon to raise huge armies. Other European countries adopted such a system during the 19th cent. In the U.S. wartime conscription was used in the Civil War and both world wars, and a peacetime draft was maintained from 1945 to 1973.

conservation laws, in physics, basic laws that maintain that the total value of certain quantities remains unchanged during a physical process. Conserved quantities include MASS (or matter), ENERGY, linear MOMENTUM, angular momentum, and electric CHARGE; the theory of RELATIVITY, however, combines the laws of conservation of mass and of energy into a single law. Additional conservation laws have meaning only on the subatomic level.

conservation of natural resources, informed restraint in the human use of the earth's resources. The term *conservation,* which came into use in the late 19th cent., referred to the management, mainly for economic reasons, of such valuable natural resources as timber, fish, game, topsoil, pastureland, and minerals. It referred also to the preservation of forests, wildlife (see WILDLIFE REFUGE), park land, wilderness, and WATERSHED areas. Conservation as part of a total approach to the use of natural resources was introduced by Pres. Theodore ROOSEVELT and his chief forester, Gifford PINCHOT. They popularized the philosophy, inspired a widespread movement, and gave impetus to much legislation. A Roosevelt-appointed commission published the first inventory of the country's natural resources. POLLUTION problems and dwindling ENERGY resources gave rise in the 1960s and 70s to a related movement—ENVIRONMENTALISM—and numerous laws were passed to protect the environment and its resources. Conservation measures were originally designed to protect economic resources or the habitats of large mammal populations, such as elephants or tigers. Current thinking, however, favors the protection of entire ecological regions by the creation of "biosphere reserves" and also emphasizes the importance of reconciling human use and conservation beyond parks.

conservatism, in politics, the desire to maintain or conserve the existing order. Modern political conservatism emerged in the 19th cent., in reaction to the political and social changes of the FRENCH REVOLUTION and the INDUSTRIAL REVOLUTION. European conservatism, as formulated by Edmund BURKE and others, emphasized preserving the power of the king and landowners, limiting suffrage, and continuing the ties between church and state. Benjamin DISRAELI exemplified the conservative tendency to resort to moderate reform in order to preserve the foundations of the old order. By the 20th cent. conservatism was being redirected by erstwhile liberal manufacturing and professional groups who had achieved their political aims and had become concerned with preserving them. The new conservatism advocated economic LAISSEZ FAIRE and opposed the extension of the welfare state.

Conservative Judaism: see JUDAISM.

Conservative party, major British political party, the other being the LABOUR PARTY. The successor of the TORY party, it came into being after the REFORM BILL of 1832 and advocated the Tory policies of defense of the Church of England and protection of agricultural interests. Later, it strongly supported imperialism. The repeal of the protectionist CORN LAWS (1846) by the Conservative leader Sir Robert PEEL caused a split in the party and its exclusion from power for most of the period 1846–73. Under Benjamin DISRAELI's "Tory democracy" (1874–80), the party wooed the broadening electorate with social legislation. The dominant party during the 1920s and 30s under Stanley BALDWIN, it lost prestige with the failure of Neville CHAMBERLAIN's appeasement of Nazi Germany (1937–40), but the country rallied to his successor, Sir Winston CHURCHILL, during WORLD WAR II. In the postwar years the Conservatives led Britain into the European Community (see EUROPEAN UNION and generally continued the social programs initiated by the Labour party. In 1979 Margaret THATCHER, a Conservative, became Britain's first woman prime minister. She cut social programs and privatized many government-owned companies. Thatcher was succeeded by Conservative John MAJOR in 1990.

Considérant, Victor Prosper [kôNsēdäräN′], 1808–93, French socialist. Leader of Fourierism after the death (1837) of Charles FOURIER, he took part in the June Days uprising (1848), was forced to flee to Belgium, and later tried unsuccessfully to establish (1855–57) a Fourierist colony in Texas. His books include *Principles of Socialism* (1847).

consideration: see CONTRACT.

Constable, John, 1776–1837, leading English landscape painter. The influence of RUISDAEL and CLAUDE LORRAIN is evident in his direct observation of nature and use of broken color, both extraordinary for his day. Such works as *View on the Stour* (1819) and *The Hay Wain* (1821; National Gall., London) influenced French romantics (including DELACROIX and Bonington) and later the BARBIZON SCHOOL, as well as the general course of 19th-cent. French landscape painting. His preparatory sketches, e.g., *Weymouth Bay* (National Gall., London), are spontaneous and vigorous.

Constance, Council of: see SCHISM, GREAT.

Constant, Benjamin [kôNstäN′], 1767–1830, French-Swiss political writer and novelist; b. Switzerland. Through Germaine de STAËL he became interested in politics, and his affair with her took him to Paris (1795). He served (1799–1801) as a tribune under NAPOLEON I but lived in exile (1802–14) with de Staël after she was expelled from France. During the Bourbon restoration he served (1819–22, 1824–30) in the chamber of deputies, earning a reputation as a liberal. His most important work is the semiautobiographical novel *Adolphe* (1816).

Constanța [kônstän′tsä], city (1989 est. pop. 316,000), SE Romania, on the Black Sea. It is Romania's main seaport, with such exports as petroleum and grain; its chief naval and air base; an industrial city; and a resort. Founded (7th cent. B.C.) by the Greeks, it was ruled by the Romans, Byzantines, and Turks before passing to Romania in 1878.

Constantine, Roman emperors. **Constantine I** or **Constantine the Great,** 288?–337 (r.310–337), was born at Naissus (now Niš, Yugoslavia), the son of Constantius I and St. HELENA. When Constantius died at York in 306, his soldiers proclaimed Constantine emperor, but much rivalry for the vacated office ensued. Before the battle at the Milvian or Mulvian Bridge near Rome in 312, Constantine, who was already sympathetic toward Christianity, is said to have seen in the sky a flaming cross as the sign by which he would conquer. He adopted the cross and was victorious. The battle is regarded as a turning point for Christianity. Constantine ruled in the West and LICINIUS in the East as coemperors until they fell out in 324. Licinius lost his life in the struggle, leaving Constantine sole emperor. In a reign of peace, Constantine rebuilt the empire on a basis of absolutism. In 325 he convened the epoch-making Council of NICAEA. In 330 he moved the capital to Constantinople, a city dedicated to the Virgin. As the founder of the Christian empire, Constantine began a new era. He was baptized on his deathbed. **Constantine II,** 316–40 (r.337–40), was the son of Constantine. When the empire was divided at his father's death (337), he received Britain, Gaul, and Spain. Feeling cheated, he warred with his brother Constans I; he was killed while invading Italy.

Constantine, Byzantine emperors. **Constantine I:** see under CONSTANTINE, Roman emperors. **Constantine IV** (Pogonatus), c.652–685 (r.668–85), repelled the Muslims but had to cede land to the Bulgars. He called the Third Council of Constantinople (680), which condemned MONOTHELETISM. **Constantine V** (Copronymus), 718–75 (r.741–75), was a capable general and administrator. His support of ICONOCLASM and opposition to MONASTICISM lost him Rome. **Constantine VI,** b. c.770 (r.780–97), reigned first with his mother, IRENE, as regent and then as co-ruler (792). In 797 she had her cruel and unpopular son deposed and blinded. **Constantine VII** (Porphyrogenitus), 905–59 (r.913–59), had his reign interrupted by the usurpation of ROMANUS I (919–44). He fostered learning, law reform, and the fair distribution of land. **Constantine XI** (Palaeologus), d. 1453, was the last Byzantine emperor (r.1449–53). He proclaimed the union of the Eastern and Western churches. After a long siege Constantinople fell (1453) to Ottoman sultan MUHAMMAD II. Constantine died in the battle.

Constantine, kings of the Hellenes (Greece). **Constantine I,** 1868–1923 (r.1913–17, 1920–22), opposed the Allies in World War I and was forced to abdicate in favor of his second son, ALEXANDER. He was restored after Alexander's death, but in 1922 a military rebellion forced him to abdicate again, this time in favor of his eldest son, GEORGE II. **Constantine II,** 1940– (r.1964–73), succeeded his father, PAUL, but in 1967 was forced into exile by a military junta. He was formally deposed in 1973.

Constantine the Great: see CONSTANTINE I.

Constantinople, former capital of the BYZANTINE EMPIRE and of the OTTOMAN EMPIRE, called ISTANBUL since 1930. It was founded (A.D. 330) at BYZANTIUM as the new capital of the Roman Empire by CONSTANTINE I and became the largest, most splendid medieval European city. Built on seven hills above the BOSPORUS, it had such magnificent buildings as the church of HAGIA SOPHIA and the emperors' palace (a city in itself), and many artistic and literary treasures. It was conquered in 1204 by Crusaders (see CRUSADES), in 1261 by MICHAEL VIII, and in 1453 by MUHAMMAD II. Almost depopulated when it fell to the Turks, the city recovered quickly, and was embellished by the Ottoman sultans who built palaces and mosques. After WORLD WAR I Constantinople was occupied (1918–23) by the Allies. In 1923 Kemal ATATÜRK made ANKARA Turkey's capital.

Constantinople, Councils of, four ecumenical councils of the Roman Catholic Church. The First Council of Constantinople (381), called to confirm the victory over ARIANISM, established the orthodox teaching of the Trinity and condemned the heresy of Apollinarianism. The second council (553) was called and dominated by Byzantine Emperor JUSTINIAN I; it condemned Nestorian writings (see NESTORIANISM) and encouraged MONOPHYSITISM. The third council (680) condemned MONOTHELETISM and a former pope, HONORIUS I. The fourth council (869–70) confirmed the condemnation of PHOTIUS. The third and fourth councils are not accepted as ecumenical by the Orthodox Church.

Constantinople, Latin Empire of, 1204–61, feudal empire in the S Balkans and Greek archipelago, founded by the leaders of the Fourth CRUSADE. Its government was divided between the Crusaders and their Venetian creditors. The rulers were BALDWIN I, HENRY OF FLANDERS, ROBERT OF COURTENAY, and BALDWIN II. The empire at once began to decline from internal strife and attacks by the Bulgars, Turks, and Greek states of NICAEA and EPIRUS. It was taken (1261) by MICHAEL VIII of Nicaea, who restored the Byzantine Empire. However, Venice retained most of the Greek Isles, the Villehardouin family of France kept Achaia, and Athens came under Catalan rule.

constellation, in common usage, group of stars (e.g., URSA MAJOR) that are imagined to form a configuration in the sky; properly speaking, a constellation is a definite region of the sky in which the configuration of stars is contained. The entire celestial sphere is divided into 88 such regions, with boundaries fixed by international agreement along lines of right ascension and declination. The 12 constellations located along or near the ecliptic, or apparent path of the sun through the heavens, are known as the constellations of the ZODIAC.

constitution, fundamental principles of government of a nation, either implied in its laws, institutions, and customs, or embodied in one or more documents. The British constitution, an unwritten, flexible type, comprises the whole body of common and statutory law, practices, and customs that have evolved there; it can be

THE CONSTITUTION OF THE UNITED STATES *(Summary)*

The Preamble states the general purpose of the Constitution:

We, the people of the United States, in order to form a more perfect union, establish justice, insure domestic tranquility, provide for the common defense, promote the general welfare, and secure the blessings of liberty to ourselves and our posterity, do ordain and establish this Constitution for the United States of America.

Article I Places legislative power in a Congress composed of a Senate and House of Representatives, prescribes method of electing Congress, and empowers each house to establish its own procedural rules. Process of legislation from Congress to President is generally described. Section VIII grants Congress specific powers, e.g., to declare war. Section IX limits Congress's powers, forbidding, e.g., ex post facto laws. Section X limits powers of states and makes some state actions dependent on Congressional consent.

Article II Creates EXECUTIVE branch of government, headed by President and Vice President. Establishes ELECTORAL COLLEGE, prescribes election process, qualifications, and manner of succession when a president is incapacitated. Section II enumerates President's powers as military commander-in-chief and in foreign affairs. Section III governs President's working relations with Congress and grants President administrative power. Section IV governs impeachment of a President.

Article III Vests all judicial power in a SUPREME COURT. Congress may establish inferior courts. Section II defines the extent of federal jurisdiction and distinguishes cases in which federal jurisdiction is original, e.g., cases between states, from those in which federal courts can hear only appeals. Section III defines, and limits prosecution for, TREASON.

Article IV Governs relations between states, prescribing full faith and credit for one another's laws, equal treatment of citizens of all states, and extradition procedures. Section III governs admission of states to the Union and administration of federal territories and property. Section IV guarantees a republican (see REPUBLIC) form of government to every state.

Article V Governs the process of amending the Constitution.

Article VI Establishes the Constitution as the supreme law of the land. Federal and state officeholders shall be bound to support the Constitution; no religious test may be required for office.

Article VII States that the Constitution shall take effect when nine (of the thirteen) states have ratified it.

AMENDMENTS *(with date of ratification)*

Amendment I (1791) First of the Bill of Rights amendments (I-IX); prohibits government-established religion; guarantees freedom of worship, of speech, of the press, of assembly and to petition the government.

Amendment II (1791) For the purpose of maintaining a well-regulated militia, preserves the right to keep and bear arms.

Amendment III (1791) Prohibits peacetime quartering of troops in private dwellings without owners' consent.

Amendment IV (1791) Guarantees against unreasonable search and seizure.

Amendment V (1791) Guarantees against violations of due process in criminal proceedings. No person may be compelled to testify against himself. Grand jury process is required for criminal INDICTMENT. DOUBLE JEOPARDY is prohibited. Public taking of private PROPERTY without just compensation is prohibited.

Amendment VI (1791) Guarantees speedy, fair trial, impartial jury, right to counsel in all criminal cases. See CRIMINAL LAW.

Amendment VII (1791) Guarantees jury trial in all major civil (noncriminal) cases, and prohibits retrial of adjudicated matters.

Amendment VIII (1791) Prohibits excessive bail or fines and cruel and unusual punishment.

Amendment IX (1791) Declares that the enumeration of certain rights in the Constitution does not imply that the people do not retain all other rights.

Amendment X (1791) Reserves to the states powers that the Constitution does not give to the federal government or prohibit to the states.

Amendment XI (1798) Declares that the federal courts may not try any case brought against a state by a citizen of another state or country.

Amendment XII (1804) Revises presidential and vice presidential election rules.

Amendment XIII (1865) First of three 'Civil War' amendments; prohibits slavery.

Amendment XIV (1868) Defines U.S. citizenship. Prohibits states from violating due process (see Amendment V) or equal protection of the law.

Amendment XV (1870) Guarantees rights of citizens against U.S. or state infringement based on race, color, or previous servitude.

Amendment XVI (1913) Authorizes a federal INCOME TAX.

Amendment XVII (1913) Provides for direct popular election of Senators.

Amendment XVIII (1919) Makes PROHIBITION federal law.

Amendment XIX (1920) Guarantees women the vote in state and U.S. elections.

Amendment XX (1933) Changes Congressional terms of office and the inauguration date of the President and Vice President; clarifies succession to the presidency.

Amendment XXI (1933) Repeals Amendment XVIII, ends prohibition.

Amendment XXII (1951) Limits presidential tenure to two terms.

Amendment XXIII (1961) Permits District of Columbia residents to vote for President and Vice President.

Amendment XXIV (1964) Outlaws the POLL TAX in all federal elections and primaries.

Amendment XXV (1967) Provides for procedures to fill vacancies in the Vice Presidency; further clarifies presidential succession rules.

Amendment XXVI (1971) Lowers voting age in federal and state election to 18.

Amendment XXVII (1992) Postpones until after the next Congressional election the effect of any law that alters the compensation of members of Congress.

modified simply by an act of PARLIAMENT. The U.S. CONSTITUTION, a written, rigid type, has superior sanction to ordinary laws and can be changed only through an elaborate process of amendment. It remains abreast of the times, however, through statutes passed by

CONGRESS and interpretations and rulings of the SUPREME COURT. In modern times, countries have tended to operate under written constitutions.

Constitution Act, 1982, British law that established procedures for Canadian amendment of Canada's constitution (the previous act had required the formal approval of Britain's Parliament). It also contains a bill of rights, the Charter of Rights and Freedoms. It provisions were combined with BRITISH NORTH AMERICA ACT (1867) and previous Canadian constitutional changes in the CANADA ACT.

Constitutional Convention: see FEDERAL CONSTITUTIONAL CONVENTION.

Constitutional Union party, in U.S. history, formed when the conflict between North and South broke down older parties. Organized just before the election of 1860, it recognized "no political principle but the Constitution of the country, the union of the states, and the enforcement of laws." Party candidates John Bell and Edward EVERETT carried Kentucky, Tennessee, and Virginia in the presidential election won by Abraham Lincoln.

Constitution of the United States, document embodying the principles on which the American nation is governed. It establishes a federal REPUBLIC with sovereignty balanced between the national government and the states. Within the national government, power is separated among three branches, the EXECUTIVE, legislative (see CONGRESS), and judicial (see SUPREME COURT, UNITED STATES; COURT SYSTEM OF THE UNITED STATES). The U.S. Constitution is the supreme law of the land; no other law, state constitution or statute, federal legislation, or executive order can operate in conflict with it. Drawn up at the FEDERAL CONSTITUTIONAL CONVENTION of 1787 in Philadelphia and ratified by the required nine states by June 21, 1788, the Constitution began to function in 1789, superseding the ARTICLES OF CONFEDERATION (1781). It is relatively brief and concise, consisting of a preamble, 7 articles, and 27 amendments (see accompanying table). The **Bill of Rights,** comprising the first 10 (or in some counts, 9) amendments to the constitution, was added in 1791 to provide adequate guarantees of individual liberties. Amendments 1 through 8 prohibit certain federal actions, many of them analogous to British actions complained of in the DECLARATION OF INDEPENDENCE. The 9th amendment states that the people retain any rights not specified in the Constitution. The 10th amendment reserves to the states powers not given to the federal government and is the foundation of STATES' RIGHTS doctrine. The 27th amendment, which postpones the effect of any law that alters Congressional pay until after the next election, was originally submitted to the states with the first 10 amendments but was not ratified until 1992. After 1791, amendments to the Constitution were few. The 14th amendment—assuring that the rights of citizens cannot be abridged by the states—has been the basis for limitation of many state actions. The brevity and generality of the language of the Constitution have made it adaptable to changing times, and the mechanics of amendment are difficult. Since Chief Justice John MARSHALL's time, the U.S. Supreme Court has changed the Constitution more than the amendment process has. Arguments on the meaning of the document generally proceed from two bases: the question of the signers' intent and the need to relate the Constitution to modern conditions. Over time the Constitution has been held to mean radically different things. Thus in PLESSY V. FERGUSON (1896), the Court held racial segregation constitutional, while in BROWN V. BOARD OF EDUCATION (1954), it found the opposite. Among the concepts long subject to reexamination and reinterpretation are states' rights, due process of law, and equal protection under the law.

constructivism, Russian art movement founded c.1913 by Vladimir Tatlin (1885–1956), related to the movement known as SUPREMATISM. Naum (Pevsner) Gabo and Antoine Pevsner gave it new impetus with works derived from CUBISM and FUTURISM but related to technological society. In 1921, when all modern art movements were officially disparaged in the Soviet Union, Gabo and Pevsner went into exile. Vsevolod Meyerhold spread constructivism abroad through stage design.

Consumer Affairs, United States Office of: see CONSUMER PROTECTION.

Consumer Price Index: see INDEX NUMBER.

consumer protection, actions by government, business and private groups to safeguard the interests of the buying public. Since the 1960s consumers' rights have been extended to such broad areas as product information and safety, satisfaction of grievances, advertising claims, and a voice in governmental decisions affecting the consumer. Early legislative action by the U.S. government included the Sherman Antitrust Act (1890; see ANTITRUST LAWS); the Pure Food and Drug Act (1906); and the creation of the FEDERAL TRADE COMMISSION (1914) and the FOOD AND DRUG ADMINISTRATION (1931). The consumer movement gained significant impetus during the 1960s and 70s when consumer activists such as Ralph NADER succeeded in promoting laws that set safety standards for automobiles, children's clothing and toys, and a wide range of household products. The federal Truth in Lending Act was passed (1968) to provide consumers with full information on the cost of credit. The U.S. Office of Consumer Affairs (est. 1971) coordinates federal activities in this field, conducting investigations and surveys, acting on individual consumer complaints, and disseminating product information. The Consumer Product Safety Commission (est. 1973), another federal agency, sets national safety standards and bans hazardous products. State and local governments also have become involved in consumer protection. The Consumer Federation of America, comprising about 220 organizations, is the largest consumer advocacy group in the U.S. Consumer protection on an international scale is coordinated by the International Organization of Consumers Unions, based in The Hague, Netherlands.

contact lens, thin lens of plastic (originally glass), worn on the eyeball and used instead of eyeglasses to improve vision or, in certain cases, to correct or treat disorders. The widely used corneal lenses cover just the cornea of the eye and float on a film of tears. Those made of soft plastic can be worn for longer periods of time than the hard-plastic models. Scleral lenses, covering the entire eye, are occasionally used to treat eye injuries or infections.

contagious diseases: see COMMUNICABLE DISEASES.

continent, largest unit of land on the earth. The continents are EURASIA (EUROPE and ASIA), AFRICA, NORTH AMERICA, SOUTH AMERICA, AUSTRALIA, and ANTARCTICA. More than two thirds of the continental regions are in the Northern Hemisphere. Continental areas bounded by the sea-level contour comprise about 29% of the earth's surface. All continents contain interior plains, or PLATEAUS, underlain by the oldest rocks; where exposed to the surface, these rocks are called continental shields, or cratons. The oldest of these rocks dated by radioactivity are 3.8 billion years old, indicating that the cratons formed with the solidification of the earth's crust. The continents have grown by accretion on their edges, where huge plates of crust converge, creating MOUNTAIN belts (see CONTINENTAL DRIFT; PLATE TECTONICS).

Continental Congress, 1774–89, federal legislature of the THIRTEEN COLONIES and later of the U.S. under the Articles of CONFEDERATION. After England passed the INTOLERABLE ACTS, the First Continental Congress met (Sept. 5–Oct. 26, 1774) in Philadelphia and petitioned the king. When the Second Continental Congress met there on May 10, 1775, armed conflict had begun (see LEXINGTON AND CONCORD, BATTLES OF), but the Congress moved gradually toward independence. It finally created the Continental Army, named George WASHINGTON commander in chief, and adopted (July 4, 1776) the DECLARATION OF INDEPENDENCE.

Continental Divide, the drainage divide separating rivers flowing to different sides of a continent. In the U.S., where it is also called the Great Divide, it follows the crest of the Rocky Mts. and separates rivers draining to the Arctic, Atlantic, and Pacific oceans.

continental drift, the theory that the positions of the earth's continents have changed considerably through geologic time. The first comprehensive theory of continental drift was proposed by the German meteorologist Alfred WEGENER in 1912. On the basis of the jigsaw fit of the opposing Atlantic coasts and geologic and paleontologic correlations on both sides of the Atlantic, he advanced the theory that c.200 million years ago there was one supercontinent, Pangaea, which split into two vast land masses, Laurasia and Gondwanaland. The present continents separated in the next geologic era (the Mesozoic). A plastic layer in the interior of the earth accommodated this process, in which the earth's rotation caused horizontal alterations in the granitic continents floating on the

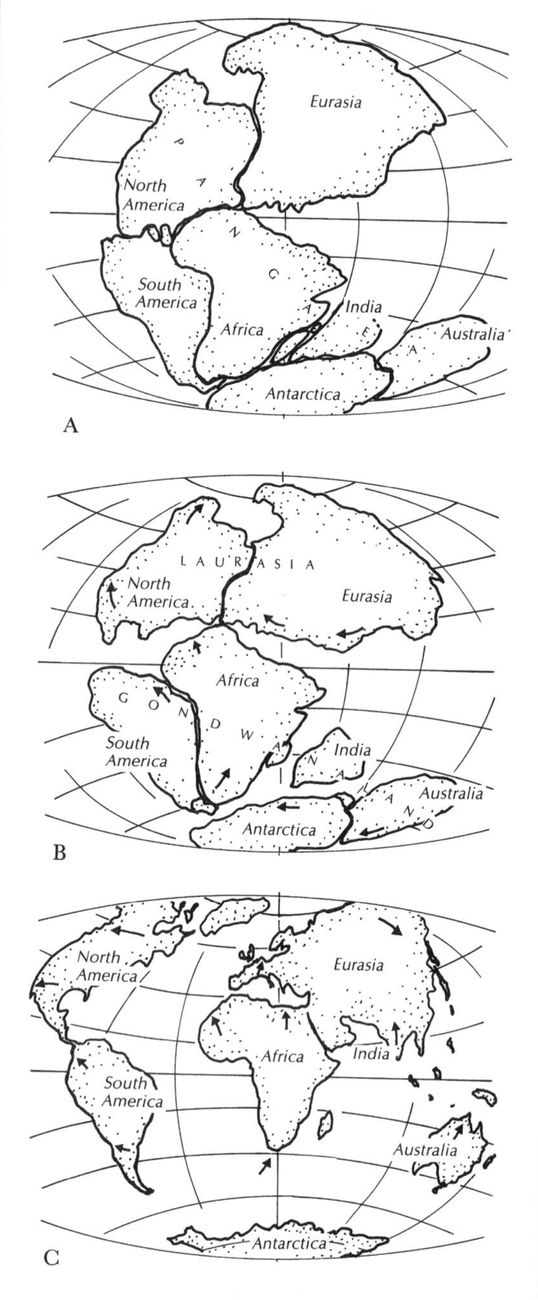

Continental drift (arrows indicate the directions of motion of the landmasses): The major present landmasses are shown in the positions they are believed to have occupied when they formed an original, single supercontinent called Pangaea (A) and, later, two separate supercontinents known as Laurasia and Gondwanaland (B). The present positions of the landmasses are shown in (C).

"sea" of the basaltic ocean floors. The frictional drag along the leading edges of the drifting continents created MOUNTAINS. Wegener's theory met controversy until 1954, when it was revived by British geophysicists seeking to explain the phenomenon of polar wandering (see MAGNETIC POLE). Since then, the modern theory of PLATE TECTONICS has evolved from and replaced Wegener's original thesis.

contrabassoon: see WIND INSTRUMENT.

contraception: see BIRTH CONTROL.

contract, in law, enforceable agreement between two or more persons to perform, or refrain from performing, a specified act. A contract is made when one party submits an offer that is accepted by the other. Generally, the parties must be mentally sound, of legal age, and acting with free will. A contract must not have an immoral or criminal purpose, or be against public policy. Certain types of contracts must be in writing. A contract must involve consideration—something of value (e.g., money or a promise) given by each party to the other. A contract is terminated when its terms have been fulfilled or when special circumstances, e.g., the death of one party, make fulfillment impossible or unlawful. The law provides several remedies for breach (failure to carry out the terms) of a contract, most often the award of money damages for losses incurred.

contralto: see VOICE.

convection, transfer of heat by the flow of a liquid or gas. A fluid expands when heated and thus undergoes a decrease in density. The warmer, less dense regions of a fluid tend to rise, in accordance with ARCHIMEDES' PRINCIPLE, through the surrounding cooler fluid. If the heat continues to be supplied, the cooler fluid that flows in to replace the rising fluid will also become heated and will rise, setting up a convection current.

Cook, George Cram: see GLASPELL, SUSAN.

Cook, James, 1728–79, English explorer. An officer in the royal navy, he set off in 1768 in the *Endeavor* to chart the transit of Venus. The trip took him around the world, and he explored the coasts of AUSTRALIA and NEW ZEALAND. In 1776 he rediscovered the Sandwich Islands and searched the West Coast of NORTH AMERICA for a passage to the Atlantic. He is credited with preventing scurvy among his crew through proper diet. Cook was killed by natives on the Hawaiian Islands.

Cook Islands, self-governing dependency of New Zealand (1992 est. pop. 18,000), 90 sq mi (234 sq km), consisting of two groups of coral islands in the South Pacific Ocean. The islanders are MAORIS and hold New Zealand citizenship. Tourism and food processing are the main economic activities; major products include citrus fruits, clothing, copra, and handicrafts. The islands were proclaimed a British protectorate in 1888, passed to New Zealand in 1901, and achieved self-government in 1965.

Coolidge, Calvin, 1872–1933, 30th president of the U.S. (1923–29); b. Plymouth, Vt. In his first year as governor of Massachusetts (1919–20) he became nationally known for using the militia to end a Boston police strike. He was U.S. vice president (1921–23) before becoming president upon the death of Warren G. HARDING. Coolidge's New England simplicity and personal honesty were appealing. His faith in laissez-faire business, economy in government, and tax cuts, and his opposition to agricultural price fixing all reflected the national mood. Through his public statements he encouraged the stock market speculation of the late 1920s and left the nation unprepared for the economic collapse that followed. He chose not to run again in 1928.

Cooper, Gary, 1901–61, American film actor; b. Helena, Mont., as Frank James Cooper. His films include *Mr. Deeds Goes to Town* (1936), *For Whom the Bell Tolls* (1943), and *High Noon* (1952; Academy Award).

Cooper, James Fenimore, 1789–1851, first major American novelist; b. Burlington, N.J., later associated with Cooperstown, N.Y. His literary career began in 1820 and covered a period of 30 years, during which he published more than 50 works. He first achieved success with the American Revolutionary novel *The Spy* (1821). Cooper's most important novels comprise *The Leatherstocking Tales,* named for their chief character, the frontiersman Natty Bumppo, nicknamed Leatherstocking. Notable for their descriptive power, mastery of native background, and idealization of the Native American, they are (in narrative order): *The Deerslayer* (1841), *The Last of the Mohicans* (1826), *The Pathfinder* (1840), *The Pioneers* (1823), and *The Prairie* (1827). Cooper is also known for his romances of American life on land and sea, e.g., *The Pilot* (1823), *The Red Rover* (1827), and *The Water-Witch* (1830). An apologist for the U.S. during his years abroad (1826–33) in works such as *Notions of the Americans* (1828), he was repelled by the abuses of democracy on his return and wrote several critical novels, e.g.,

Homeward Bound, Home as Found (both: 1838), which earned him violent criticism and many enemies. Cooper's late novels include the Littlepage trilogy (1845–46), a study of conflict between the landed and landless in New York state.

Cooper, Peter, 1791–1883, American inventor and industrialist; b. N.Y.C. He built the *Tom Thumb*, one of the earliest locomotives in the U.S., and invented practical devices and processes in the iron industry (e.g., rolling the first iron for fireproof buildings). He invested heavily in the Atlantic CABLE and headed the North American Telegraph Co., which controlled more than half the telegraph lines in the U.S. Interested in providing education for the working classes, he promoted a public school system in N.Y.C. and founded Cooper Union (1859), a free institution of higher learning and a pioneer evening engineering and art school. In 1876 he was the presidential candidate of the GREENBACK PARTY.

cooperative, nonprofit economic enterprise for the benefit of those using its services. Cooperatives are common today in such areas as insurance, food, banking and credit (see CREDIT UNION), and housing. The cooperative movement grew out of the philosophy of Robert OWEN, Charles FOURIER, and others. The first permanent consumer cooperative was founded (1844) in Britain, and workers and farmers in the U.S. formed producer cooperatives soon thereafter (see GRANGER MOVEMENT). Cooperatives of various kinds are important in Scandinavia, Israel, China, Russia, and France. See also COLLECTIVE FARM.

Coornhert, Dirck Volckerszoon [kôrn'hârt], 1522–90, Dutch humanist. His translation of the first 12 books of HOMER's *Odyssey* (1561) is the first major poetic work of the Dutch RENAISSANCE. A supporter of religious tolerance, he also wrote comedies, morality plays, and a philosophical treatise (1586).

Cope, Edward Drinker, 1840–97, American paleontologist; b. Philadelphia. He was the first to provide comprehensive descriptions of Eocene vertebrates. He and rival paleontologist Othniel Marsh, with whom he quarreled on scientific matters for 20 years, discovered the first complete dinosaur remains. Cope believed that evolution was caused by an organism's inner urge to attain a higher state of being.

Copenhagen, city (1988 pop. 468,744), capital of Denmark, E Denmark. It is a major commercial, fishing, and naval port, and Denmark's chief commercial and cultural center, with such products as ships, machinery, drugs, processed food, and the pottery known as Copenhagen Ware. Founded by the 11th cent., it survived attacks by the HANSEATIC LEAGUE and Sweden, became Denmark's capital in 1443, and expanded as a prosperous trade hub in the 16th and 17th cent. During WORLD WAR II the city was occupied (1940–45) by the Germans. Its landmarks include the 17th-cent. Charlottenborg Palace, the 19th-cent. palaces on Amalienborg Square, the round tower used by Tycho BRAHE as an observatory, and the statue of Hans Christian ANDERSEN's Little Mermaid.

Copernican system, the first modern European heliocentric theory of planetary motion; it placed the sun motionless at the center of the solar system with all the planets, including the earth, revolving around it. COPERNICUS developed his theory (which replaced the PTOLEMAIC SYSTEM) in the early 16th cent. from a study of ancient astronomical records. His system explained RETROGRADE MOTION in a natural way.

Copernicus, Nicholas, 1473–1543, Polish astronomer. After studying law and medicine at the Univ. of Cracow and at Bologna, Padua, and Ferrara, he took up (1512) his duties as canon of a cathedral in Frauenberg, East Prussia. Copernicus laid the foundation for modern astronomy with his heliocentric theory of planetary motion (see COPERNICAN SYSTEM). This theory, first presented (1512 or earlier) in a short form in his unpublished manuscript "Commentariolus," was probably completed by 1530 and was published in his classic work *De revolutionibus orbium coelestium* (1543).

Copland, Aaron, 1900–90, American composer; b. Brooklyn, N.Y. The American character of his music is apparent in his use of JAZZ and folk elements, as in the short piece for chamber orchestra, *John Henry* (1940). He wrote ballets, e.g., *Billy the Kid* (1938), *Rodeo* (1942), and *Appalachian Spring* (1944), and music for films, e.g., *Of Mice and Men* (1939). His major orchestral works are *El Salón México* (1936) and the Third Symphony (1946). Other works include *12 Poems of Emily Dickinson* (1950) and a tone poem (see SYMPHONIC POEM), *Inscape* (1967).

Copley, John Singleton, 1738–1815, American painter, considered the greatest early American portraitist; b. Boston. He painted in Boston, New York City, and Philadelphia. In 1774 he settled in London, where his style gained in subtlety and polish but lost most of the vigor and individuality of his early work. His modern reputation rests on his early American portraits, which are treasured for their pictorial qualities and as powerful records of their time and place. Among his outstanding portraits are those of Paul Revere, Samuel Adams (both: Mus. Fine Arts, Boston), and Daniel Hubbard (Art. Inst., Chicago).

copper (Cu), metallic element, known to humans since the BRONZE AGE. The reddish, malleable, ductile metal is a good conductor of heat and electricity. It has low chemical reactivity. In moist air it forms a patina, a protective, greenish surface film. The chief commercial uses are in electrical apparatus and wire, roofing, utensils, coins, metalwork, plumbing, and refrigerator and air-conditioner coils. Copper alloys include BRASS and BRONZE. Copper compounds are used as insecticides, fungicides, and paint pigments, and in electroplating. CHALCOPYRITE is the principal ore. Copper is essential for normal metabolism and hemoglobin synthesis in humans. See ELEMENT (table); PERIODIC TABLE.

Copper Age: see BRONZE AGE.

copperhead, poisonous SNAKE (*Ancistrodon contortrix*) of the E U.S. The copperhead, a PIT VIPER, detects its warm-blooded prey by means of a heat-sensitive organ behind the nostril. The head is a pale copper color; the banded, brown body may reach a length of 4 ft (120 cm).

Copperheads, in the U.S. CIVIL WAR, reproachful term for Southern sympathizers in the North. Led by C.L. VALLANDIGHAM, they were especially strong in Illinois, Indiana, and Ohio. The term was often used by Republicans to label all Democratic opponents of the Lincoln administration.

Coppola, Francis Ford, 1939–, American film director, writer, and producer; b. Detroit. Among his films are *The Godfather,* in three parts (1972, 1974, 1990), a study of an Italian-American crime family; *The Conversation* (1974); *Apocalypse Now* (1979); and *Bram Stoker's Dracula* (1992).

copra: see COCONUT.

Copt, member of the native Christian minority (5%–10%) of Egypt. Most Copts belong to the Coptic Church, an autonomous sect that adheres to MONOPHYSITISM. The Coptic language, now extinct, was the Egyptian language spoken in early Christian times.

Coptic art, Christian art in the upper Nile Valley of EGYPT. Reaching its mature phase in the late 5th and 6th cent., Coptic art was influenced by Islamic art after the Arab conquest of Egypt between 640 and 642. It shows a high degree of stylization verging on abstraction. The themes represent both Roman and Christian sources with flattened-out forms and decorative motifs. Remains of wall paintings reveal Old and New Testament scenes and images of the Mother and Child. Representative examples of Coptic art are found in sculpture, ivory, textiles, and illumination.

copyright, statutory right of the creator to exclusive control of an original literary or artistic production. The copyright holder may reproduce the work or license others to do so, and receives payments (royalties) for each performance or copy. The U.S. law (rewritten in 1978) extends protection for the creator's life plus 50 years. Books, plays, musical compositions, sound recordings, photographs, works of art, and other original creations may be copyrighted. Copyright laws first appeared in the 15th cent., when PRINTING began in Europe. The earliest American statute was passed in 1790. The U.S., with most other nations, subscribes to the 1952 Universal Copyright Convention.

coral, small, sedentary marine animal of the COELENTERATE class Anthozoa, having a horny or calcareous skeleton (also called coral). Most corals form colonies by budding, but solitary corals also exist. In both, the individual animal (polyp) secretes a cup-shaped skeleton around itself; in colonial corals, the skeleton and a thin sheet of living tissue are attached to other individuals. As a colonial coral produces more polyps, the lower members die, and new layers are built up on the old skeletons, forming CORAL REEFS. Precious red and white corals are used for jewelry.

coral reef, limestone formation produced by living animals, found in shallow, tropical marine waters. In most, the predominant animals are CORALS, which secrete skeletons of calcium carbonate (limestone) that build up over thousands of years into a massive formation that supports the living corals and a great variety of other plant and animal life. Coral reefs are formed only in the tropics where the water is warmer than 72°F (22°C). They are classified as fringing reefs (platforms continuous with the shore), barrier reefs (separated from the shore by a wide, deep lagoon), or atolls (surrounding a lagoon). Coral reefs are under many environmental pressures, including damage from coastal development, water pollution, tourism, and overharvesting of fish and crustaceans. Reefs formed by other organisms are also called coral reefs.

Coral Sea, southwest arm of the Pacific Ocean, between NE Australia, New Guinea, and Vanuatu (formerly the New Hebrides). It was the scene of a U.S. victory (1942) that checked the southward expansion of the Japanese forces in WORLD WAR II.

Coral Sea Islands, external territory of Australia, comprising scattered small islands and reefs spread over c.400,000 sq mi (1,035,995 sq km) of the South Pacific Ocean, E of the GREAT BARRIER REEF, off NE Australia. The islands, uninhabited except for a meteorological station on Willis Island, became a territory in 1969.

coral snake, New World poisonous SNAKE of the same family as the COBRAS. The venom of coral snakes, like that of cobras, is especially potent, and the mortality rate among bitten humans is high. Coral snakes are marked by alternating bands of black, red, and yellow.

Corday, Charlotte, 1768–93, French assassin of Jean Paul MARAT. A sympathizer of the GIRONDISTS, she gained access to Marat, a critic of the Girondists, under false pretenses and stabbed him (1793) in his bath. She was arrested and guillotined.

Cordeliers [kôrdəlyā′], French revolutionary club. Instrumental in the fall (1793) of the GIRONDISTS, it originally included such people as Georges DANTON. Later it drifted to the extreme left under J.R. HÉBERT. It dissolved (1794) after the extremists were executed in the REIGN OF TERROR.

Cordero, Angel Tomás, Jr., 1942–, American jockey; b. Santurce, Puerto Rico. One of the most successful jockeys, he won 7,057 races over 22 years before he retired in 1992. From 1977 to 1990 his mounts won over $5 million each year, a record. Cordero also won six Triple Crown races, including three Kentucky Derbies.

Cordilleras [Span., originally = little strings], general name for the chain of mountains in W North America, from N Alaska to Nicaragua, including the ROCKY MTS., the COAST RANGES, and the SIERRA MADRE. Some geographers use the term for any extensive group of mountain systems.

Córdoba, city (1991 pop. 1,124,700), central Argentina, on the Río Primero. It is a commercial metropolis near a major dam that has transformed the surrounding area from a ranching center to a land of grain fields, orchards, and vineyards. Settled in 1573, Córdoba was an early Argentine cultural center with a university (est. 1613). Many colonial buildings, e.g., the former city hall, remain.

Córdoba or **Cordova,** city (1988 est. pop. 302,000), capital of Córdoba prov., S Spain, in Andalusia, on the Guadalquivir R. Its industries produce beverages, textiles, and metals. Of Iberian origin, it flourished under Rome. As the seat (756–1031) of an emirate comprising most of Moorish Spain, it was a center of Muslim and Jewish culture and was renowned for its wealth, crafts, and architecture, e.g., the great mosque (begun 8th cent. and now a cathedral). Córdoba passed to Seville in 1078 and to Castile in 1236.

Corelli, Arcangelo, 1653–1713, Italian composer and violinist. He was a noted virtuoso whose technique was perpetuated by his students and in his SONATAS. He also helped to establish the typical form of the CONCERTO grosso.

Corfu: see KÉRKIRA.

coriander, annual herb (*Coriandrum sativum*) of the CARROT family, cultivated for its fruits. The dried seed is used as a spice, and contains an aromatic oil used as a flavoring, as a medicine, and in liqueurs.

Corinna, fl. c.500 B.C., Greek poet. Her verse, fragments of which remain, deals with mythological themes and is written in the dialect of BOEOTIA.

Corinth or **Kórinthos,** city (1981 pop. 22,658), S Greece, in the NE Peloponnesus, on the Gulf of Corinth. Founded after the destruction of Old Corinth by an earthquake (1858) and rebuilt after another earthquake in 1928, the modern city is a port and trading center for olives, tobacco, raisins, and wine. Ancient Corinth was one of the oldest and most powerful of the Greek CITY-STATES, dating from Homeric times. Athenian assistance to its rebellious colonies was a direct cause of the PELOPONNESIAN WAR (431–404 B.C.). Destroyed by the Romans in 146 B.C., it was restored by Julius CAESAR in 46 B.C. Later it passed to the Byzantine Crusaders, the Venetians, and the Ottoman Turks before being captured (1822) by Greek insurgents. Ruins at Old Corinth include the Temple of Apollo.

Corinthian order: see ORDERS OF ARCHITECTURE.

Corinthians, two EPISTLES of the NEW TESTAMENT, 7th and 8th books in the usual order, written to the church at CORINTH by St. PAUL. First Corinthians (A.D. 55?) is one of the longest, most important epistles. It begins with an attack on factionalism and condemns various practices, e.g., litigation among Christians. The epistle closes with five famous passages: the institution of the Eucharist (11); the doctrine of the mystical body of Christ (12); a panegyric on Christian love (13); the functions of prophecy among Christians (14); and a chapter on Jesus' resurrection (15). The shorter Second Corinthians focuses on Paul's apostleship, authority, and motives, closing with a defense of his mission. See also SACRAMENT.

Coriolanus (Gnaeus Marcius Coriolanus), Roman patrician, fl. 5th cent. B.C. According to legend he was expelled from Rome because he demanded the abolition of the people's tribunate in return for distributing state grain to the starving plebeians. He led (491? B.C.) the Volscians against Rome. Only the tears of his wife and his mother caused him to spare the city. The angry Volscians killed him.

Coriolis effect [for Gaspard Coriolis], tendency for any moving body on or above the earth's surface to drift sideways from its course because of the earth's rotational direction (west to east) and speed, which is greater for a surface point near the equator than toward the poles. In the Northern Hemisphere the drift is to the right of the motion; in the Southern Hemisphere, to the left. In most human-operated vehicles, continuous course adjustments mask the Coriolis effect. The Coriolis effect must be considered, however, when plotting ocean currents and wind patterns (see CYCLONE) as well as trajectories of free-moving projectiles through air or water.

Cork, city (1986 pop. 133,271), county town of Co. Cork, S Republic of Ireland, on the Lee R. at Cork Harbour. The second largest city in the nation, it produces tractors, rubber, leather and textile goods, and whiskey. Its exports are largely agricultural. Probably founded in the 7th cent., Cork was occupied by the Danes (9th cent.) and passed to English control in 1172. It was prominent in the nationalist disturbances of 1920. University College is located there.

cork, protective, waterproof outer covering of the stems and roots of all woody plants, produced by the cork CAMBIUM. Cork cells have regularly arranged walls impregnated with a waxy material, called suberin, that is resistant to water and gas. Cork is buoyant, resilient, light, and chemically inert; it is used for bottle stoppers and insulating materials, and in many household and industrial items. The cork OAK (*Quercus suber*), which has a thick cork layer, is the source of commercial cork.

cormorant, large aquatic BIRD related to the PELICAN, found chiefly in temperate and tropical regions. Cormorants are 2 to 3 ft (61 to 92 cm) long, with thick, dark plumage, webbed feet, and a large bill with the upper mandible hooked at the end. Expert swimmers, they pursue fish under water; in E Asia they are used to fish.

corn, in botany, name given to the leading cereal crop of any major region. In England, corn means wheat; in Scotland and Ireland, oats. In America, corn is the grain called maize, or Indian corn (*Zea mays*), a GRASS that was domesticated and cultivated long before Europeans reached the New World. Native Americans raised many varieties (e.g., sweet corn, popcorn, colored corn, and corn for cornmeal). Corn is eaten fresh or ground for meal. It is mainly used as animal fodder. The corn plant consists of the tassel (male flowers) at the top of the plant; the kernels (female flowers) on the cob, enclosed by a leafy husk, beyond which extends the silk (the threadlike stigmas and styles that catch the pollen); and the supporting pithy, noded stalk with its prop roots.

Corneille, Pierre [kôrnā'yə], 1606–84, French dramatist, a master of classical TRAGEDY. His masterpiece, *Le Cid* (1637), based on a Spanish play (see CID), took Paris by storm. Among the finest of his other tragedies are *Horace* (1640), *Cinna* (1640), and *Polyeucte* (1643). The comedy *The Liar* (1643) also had great success. A master of the grand style, Corneille exalted the will, celebrating the subordination of human passion to duty.

cornel: see DOGWOOD.

Cornell, Ezra, 1807–74, American financier, founder of Cornell Univ.; b. Westchester Landing, N.Y. He devised a method for stringing telegraph wires on poles and became founder, director, and largest stockholder of Western Union Telegraph Co. (1855). His interest in agricultural education led him to secure, with A.D. WHITE, legislation founding Cornell Univ. (1865). Its charter embraced many of his ideas, and he was responsible for the financial success of its federal land grant.

Cornell, Joseph, 1903–73, American artist; b. Nyack, N.Y. He is best known for his shadow boxes made of found objects, maps, photographs, engravings, and other materials. Influenced by SURREALISM, these constructions are personally symbolic and evocative.

cornet: see WIND INSTRUMENT.

cornflower, common herb (*Centaurea cyanus*) of the COMPOSITE family, a garden flower in the U.S. The long-stemmed, blue flower heads have radiating vase-shaped florets that yield a juice used as a dye when mixed with alum. Other names for cornflower include bluebottle, bluebonnet, ragged robin, and bachelor's button.

Cornish, dead language belonging to the Brythonic group of the Celtic subfamily of the Indo-European family of languages. See LANGUAGE (table).

corn laws, regulations dating from 1361 restricting the export and import of grain, notably in England. The corn law of 1815 was designed to maintain high prices and prevent an agricultural depression after the Napoleonic Wars. Consumer resentment led to the ANTI-CORN-LAW LEAGUE's campaign, and to their repeal by Robert PEEL in 1846.

Cornplanter, c.1740–1836, half-white chief of the Senecas who aided the British in the AMERICAN REVOLUTION. Friendly to whites, he signed (1784) the Treaty of Fort Stanwix and was given a grant of land on the Allegheny R.

Cornwallis, Charles Cornwallis, 1st **Marquess,** 1735–1805, English general. He led British forces in the AMERICAN REVOLUTION, and his defeat in the disastrous YORKTOWN CAMPAIGN ended the fighting. Later he was governor general of India (1786–94, 1805) and viceroy of Ireland (1798–1801).

Coronado, Francisco Vásquez de [kōrōnä'thō], c.1510–54, Spanish explorer. In search of the Seven Cities of Cibola, he was the first European to explore ARIZONA and NEW MEXICO. Though he found no gold, he acquainted the Spanish with the PUEBLO peoples and opened the Southwest to colonization.

coronary artery disease, condition that results when the arteries that supply the muscles of the heart (coronary arteries) are narrowed or occluded, usually by fibrous and fatty tissue deposits. When insufficient oxygen reaches the heart (especially during time of increased need, as during exercise or stress) the radiating chest pain of **angina pectoris** results. When total blockage of an artery occurs, usually due to clots or pieces of plaque blocking an already narrow artery, portions of heart muscle can die (a condition known as a myocardial infarction, or heart attack) and disrupt the electrical impulses that make the heart beat. Predisposing factors include a family history of heart disease, HYPERTENSION, high total and low-density lipoprotein (LDL) CHOLESTEROL levels, and cigarette smoking. Treatment ranges from preventive measures (lowering fat intake and giving up cigarettes) and medication to surgical procedures (coronary artery bypass and BALLOON ANGIOPLASTY).

Corot, Jean-Baptiste Camille [kôrō'], 1796–1875, French landscape painter. One of the most influential 19th-cent. painters, he celebrated the countryside without romanticizing farm labor or peasants. His Roman works have simplicity of form and clarity of lighting, as in the *Coliseum* and *Forum* (both: Louvre). Using sketches made directly from nature, he painted his later landscapes in shades of gray and green. His delicate lighting is seen in *Femme à la perle* (Louvre) and *Interrupted Reading* (Art Inst., Chicago).

Jean-Baptiste Corot landscape Paysage avec personnages et cavaliere

Corpus Christi, city (1990 pop. 257,453), seat of Nueces co., S Tex.; inc. 1852. It is a petroleum and natural-gas center, with heavy industries, e.g., refineries, smelting plants, and chemical works. Shrimp and fish processing is important, as is tourism. The first settlers arrived in the 1760s; a trading post (est. 1839) boomed in the MEXICAN WAR. The fast-growing area has a busy port and military facilities.

Corpus Juris Civilis: see ROMAN LAW.

Correggio [kərĕj'ō], c.1494–1534, Italian BAROQUE painter; b. Antonio Allegri, called Correggio after his birthplace. His early works, e.g., the *Marriage of St. Catherine* (National Gall., Wash., D.C.), were greatly influenced by the styles of MANTEGNA and LEONARDO DA VINCI. Among his many mythological scenes are the sensual *Io* (Vienna) and *Antiope* (Louvre). His most famous project, *Assumption of the Virgin* (Parma cathedral), used daring foreshortening. His illusionistic ceiling decorations, with their sense of grace and tenderness and soft play of light and color, were widely imitated in the 17th cent.

Corregidor, historic fortified island (c.2 sq mi/5 sq km) at the entrance to Manila Bay, just off BATAAN, the Philippines. It was a fortress from Spanish times; its defenses were greatly elaborated by the U.S. after the SPANISH-AMERICAN WAR (1898). During WORLD WAR II the Japanese bombarded Corregidor for five months, finally forcing the surrender (May 1942) of 10,000 U.S. and Filipino troops. The island was retaken by U.S. forces in 1945.

Corsica, island (1990 pop. 249,700), 3,367 sq mi (8,721 sq km), a department of metropolitan France, in the Mediterranean Sea SE of France. The capital is Ajaccio. Much of the island is wild, mountainous, and covered with *maquis,* whose flowers have earned Corsica the name "the scented isle." Fruit, cork, cigarettes, wine, and cheese are exported, and tourism is economically important. Native Corsican speech is a dialect of Italian. The island was granted by the Franks to the papacy in the late 8th cent., and Pope GREGORY VII ceded (1077) it to Pisa; it was taken over by Genoa in the 15th cent. Genoese rule was harsh and unpopular, and following a rebellion led (1755) by Pasquale PAOLI the island was ceded (1768) to France. With British support Paoli expelled the French and from 1794 to its recapture in 1796 it was controlled by the British. French possession was confirmed by the Congress of VIENNA in 1815. Blood feuds between clans and banditry persisted into modern times. The island has been the site of separatist movements, most recently in the 1970s and 80s.

Cortázar, Julio [kōrtä'zär], 1914–84, Argentine writer; b. Belgium. An exponent of SURREALISM who often depicted life as a maze, he is known for the novels *The Winners* (1960) and *Sixty-Two: A Model Kit* (1968), and short-story collections, e.g. *A Change of Light and Other Stories* (tr. 1980).

Cortés, Hernán, or **Hernando Cortez** [kôrtĕz'], 1485–1547, Spanish CONQUISTADOR, conqueror of MEXICO. Under a commission of the Cuban governor, Diego de VELÁZQUEZ, Cortés sailed from Cuba in 1519 to conquer the AZTEC empire of MONTEZUMA. He founded the city of Vera Cruz, burned his ships to prevent his forces from turning back, and enlisted the help of the defeated Tlaxcalans. Believing the Spanish to be descendants of the god QUETZALCOATL, Montezuma received them. Cortés took him hostage and ruled through him. Velázquez tried to recall Cortés, who defeated a force sent to retrieve him. When he returned to the capital, Tenochtitlán, he found the Aztecs in rebellion. In the famous battle known as *noche triste* [sad night], he retreated from the city with heavy losses. He returned the next year; after a three-month siege, the city fell, and with it the empire. As captain, Cortés extended his conquest to most of Mexico and N Central America. Though CHARLES V of Spain made Cortés a marqués, he refused to make him governor of Mexico. Cortés returned to Spain in 1540, where, frustrated and neglected by the court, he died.

Cortés, Sea of: see CALIFORNIA, GULF OF.

Cortes, representative assembly of SPAIN. From the 12th to the 19th cent. each region, e.g., LEÓN and CASTILE, had its own cortes. The first national Cortes met (1810) during the PENINSULAR WAR against Napoleonic rule and voted (1812) a liberal constitution revoked (1814) by the king. The Cortes was Spain's parliament (1931–39) after the fall of the monarchy but was stripped of power under Francisco FRANCO. After his death (1975) it emerged as an important element in Spanish democracy.

corticosteroid drug, any synthetic or naturally derived substance with the general chemical structure of a STEROID, used therapeutically to mimic or augment the effects of the hormones produced naturally in the cortex of the ADRENAL GLAND. Corticosteroids suppress the immune response, decrease inflammation, and stimulate the bone marrow. They are used to treat such conditions as ARTHRITIS, ASTHMA, systemic lupus erythematosus (see AUTOIMMUNE DISEASE), and HODGKIN'S DISEASE and some other forms of cancer. They are also useful in relieving the itching and inflammation of eczema, psoriasis, and insect bites. See also CORTISONE; HYDROCORTISONE.

cortisone, steroid HORMONE whose main physiological effect is on carbohydrate metabolism. It is synthesized from cholesterol in the outer layer, or cortex, of the ADRENAL GLAND and is necessary for life. Failure of the adrenal gland to synthesize cortisone (ADDISON'S DISEASE) is fatal unless cortisone is administered. The anti-inflammatory effect of the hormone makes it useful in treating asthma and other allergic reactions, arthritis, and various skin diseases.

Cortona, Pietro Berrettini da [kōrtô'nä], 1596–1669, Italian BAROQUE painter and architect. His FRESCOES and ceilings, e.g., *Allegories of the Virtues and Planets* (Pitti Palace, Florence), were influential examples of Illusionism.

corundum, aluminum oxide mineral (Al_2O_3) occurring in both gem and common varieties. The transparent gems, chief of which are RUBY and SAPPHIRE, are colorless, pink, red, blue (Oriental AQUAMARINE), green (Oriental EMERALD), yellow, and violet. Common varieties, used as ABRASIVES (e.g., emery), are blue-gray to brown. Corundum is found in North Carolina, Georgia, Montana, Myanmar, Sri Lanka, India, Thailand, South Africa, and Tanzania.

Corvinus, Matthias: see MATTHIAS CORVINUS.

Cosby, Bill, 1937–, African-American comedian and actor; b. Philadelphia. He was the first African-American actor to star in a dramatic series on television (*I Spy,* 1965–68). He has also starred in several situation comedies, including the popular *Cosby Show* (1984–92). He has won numerous Emmy awards and written several books, including *Fatherhood* (1986).

Cosgrave, William Thomas, 1880–1965, Irish statesman. A member of the SINN FÉIN, he fought in the Easter Rebellion (1916) and won election (1918) to the British Parliament. He served as president of Ireland from 1922 to 1932. **Liam Cosgrave,** 1920–, his son, was also active in Irish politics. He entered (1943) the Irish parliament as a Fine Gael member and served (1948–57) in various ministerial posts. Leader of the party from 1965 to 1977, he was prime minister from 1973 to 1977.

Cosimo de' Medici: see under MEDICI, family.

cosmetic surgery, PLASTIC SURGERY for cosmetic purposes, such as the improvement of the appearance of the face by removing wrinkles or reshaping the nose.

cosmic rays, high-energy particles bombarding the earth from outer space. The extraterrestrial origin of cosmic rays was determined (c.1911) by Victor Hess; they were so named by Robert MILLIKAN in 1925. Primary cosmic rays consist mainly of PROTONS; ALPHA PARTICLES; and lesser amounts of nuclei of carbon, nitrogen, oxygen, and heavier atoms. These nuclei cause showers of secondary cosmic rays by colliding with other nuclei in the earth's atmosphere. Some cosmic rays have energies a billion times greater than those that can be achieved in particle accelerators; cosmic rays of lower energy, however, predominate. The origin of cosmic rays is still unknown, as are the processes by which they are accelerated.

cosmology, science that aims at a comprehensive theory of the creation, evolution, and present structure of the entire universe. The PTOLEMAIC SYSTEM and the COPERNICAN SYSTEM are theories that describe the position of the earth in the universe. William HERSCHEL showed that the MILKY WAY is composed of a vast number of STARS separated by enormous distances. By studying the distribution of STAR CLUSTERS, Harlow SHAPLEY gave the first reliable estimate of the size of our galaxy (c.100,000 LIGHT-YEARS) and of the position of the sun within it (c.30,000 light-years from the center). By 1924 astronomers had recognized that some of the NEBULAE are not within our galaxy, but are separate GALAXIES at great distances from the Milky Way. After studying the RED SHIFTS in the spectral lines of the distant galaxies, Edwin HUBBLE and Milton Humason concluded that the universe is expanding (see HUBBLE'S LAW), with the galaxies flying away from one another at great speeds. The big bang theory states that all of the matter and energy in the universe was concentrated in a very small volume that exploded between 10 and 20 billion years ago, and that the resulting expansion continues today. The strongest evidence for the big bang theory is the feeble radio background radiation, discovered in the 1960s, that is received from every part of the sky. This radiation has a BLACKBODY temperature of 2.7° above absolute zero and is interpreted as the electromagnetic remnants of the primordial fireball, stretched to long wavelengths by the expansion of the universe. Data from NASA's Cosmic Microwave Background Explorer (see OBSERVATORY, ORBITING) revealed small temperature fluctuations in the radiation that are thought to be related to the "seeds" of stars and galaxies. How the homogeneous early universe implied by the uniform background radiation evolved into the present universe of clusters and superclusters of galaxies separated by enormous voids remains unanswered, as does the question of whether the universe's expansion will continue or eventually halt and reverse, with the universe collapsing in the so-called "big crunch." According to another hypothesis, the steady-state theory, the universe expands, but new matter is continuously created at all points in space left by the receding galaxies; this theory now has few adherents.

Cossa, Baldassare, c.1370–1419, Neapolitan churchman, antipope (1410–15) as John XXIII. A cardinal, he deserted Pope GREGORY XII and supported the Council of Pisa, which was intended to end the schism (see SCHISM, GREAT) between Rome and Avignon. When the antipope Alexander V died, Cossa was elected (1410). He sought the aid of SIGISMUND and helped to elect him Holy Roman emperor, then allied himself with Louis II of Anjou against Lancelot of Naples. Pressured by Sigismund, he convened the council of Constance (1414–18) and promised to abdicate if the rival popes would do so. Then, secretly, he fled, hoping to keep his position; but he was forced to return and was deposed (1415).

Cossacks, peasant-soldiers in the Russian empire who held certain privileges in return for military service. They were descended from Russians and Poles, including many runaway serfs, who settled along the Dnieper and Don rivers in the 15th and 16th cent. For taking part in 17th- and 18th-cent. peasant revolts they lost much of their early autonomy and were integrated into the Russian military. Most Cossacks fought against the Red Army in the 1918–20 civil war. Their communities were collectivized (1928–33), but many of their traditions survive.

Costa Rica, officially Republic of Costa Rica, republic (1992 est. pop. 3,187,000), 19,575 sq mi (50,700 sq km), Central America; bordered by Nicaragua (N), the Caribbean Sea (E), Panama (S), and the Pacific Ocean (W). The capital is SAN JOSÉ. The coastal

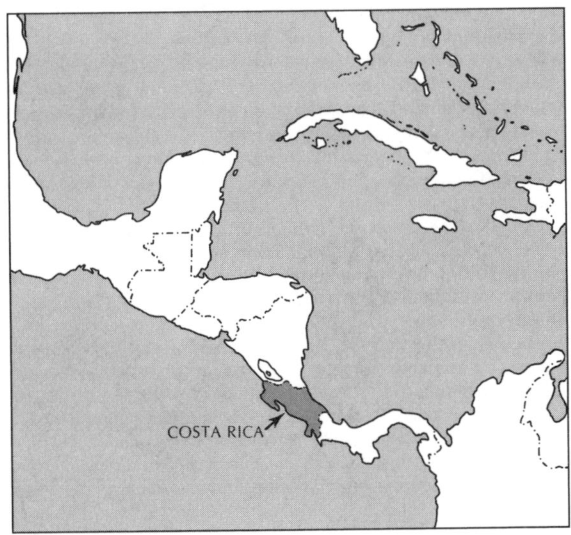

areas are hot, humid, heavily forested, and sparsely populated. A massive chain of volcanic mountains, rising to over 12,000 ft (3,658 m), traverses the country from NW to SE; nestled within it lies the *meseta central,* a broad plateau with a springlike climate, where most Costa Ricans live. Costa Rica is a largely agricultural nation, exporting coffee, bananas, sugar, and beef. Industry is being developed and manufactured goods such as textiles are increasingly exported. The people are mainly of Spanish descent and are Roman Catholic. The official language is Spanish. Costa Rica is among the most politically stable Latin American countries, with a long democratic tradition, a literacy rate over 90%, and no army as such.

History. Conquest of the area by Spain began in 1563, with the founding of Cartago. The early colonists were mainly small landowners. Gaining independence in 1821, Costa Rica was successively part of the Mexican Empire and of the Central American Federation (which also included GUATEMALA, HONDURAS, NICARAGUA, and EL SALVADOR), before becoming a sovereign republic in 1838. Coffee growing was initiated on the plateau in the early 1800s, and banana cultivation was introduced on the coast (by U.S. interests) in 1874. Costa Rica's history of orderly, democratic government began in 1889, and has been interrupted only by brief periods of junta rule, in 1917–19 and in 1948–49, after a disputed election sparked a six-week civil war. Economically, the nation has had balance-of-payments problems, e.g., in the early 1980s the cost of importing manufactured goods and oil far exceeded income received for agricultural exports. Oscar ARIAS SANCHEZ, president from 1986 to 1990, worked to preserve his nation's neutrality and to bring peace to Central America. In 1994 José María Figueres Olsen was elected president.

cost of living, amount of money needed to buy the goods and services necessary to maintain a specified STANDARD OF LIVING. The figure is based on the cost of such items as food, clothing, rent, fuel, recreation, transportation, and medical services. High inflation in the 1970s led many employers and unions to use cost-of-living increases, as measured by the Consumer Price Index (see INDEX NUMBER), as a basis for wage rates and subsequent adjustments. SOCIAL SECURITY payments and some PENSION plans are also pegged to changes in the Consumer Price Index.

Côte d'Ivoire or **Ivory Coast,** officially Republic of Côte d'Ivoire, republic (1992 est. pop. 13,497,000), 124,503 sq mi (322,463 sq km), W Africa, bordered by the Gulf of Guinea (S), Liberia and Guinea (W), Mali and Burkina Faso (N), and Ghana (E). The official capital is YAMOUSSOUKRO; the largest city, former capital, and chief port is ABIDJAN. The country consists of a coastal lowland in the south, a densely forested plateau in the interior, and high savannas in the north. Rainfall is heavy, especially along the coast. One of the most prosperous W African countries, Côte d'Ivoire enjoyed a high economic growth rate from independence until the 1980s, when falling commodities prices devalued its exports. Predominantly agricultural, the country is one of the world's largest coffee and cocoa producers. Timber from mahogany and other forests is a valuable export; rubber is also harvested. Industrialization has been steady since the 1960s; flour, palm oil, petroleum, textiles, and cigarettes are produced. The major ethnic groups are the Beti, Anyi, Malinke, Dan, and Senufo. There are also immigrants from Burkina Faso, Mali, and Guinea and people of French and Arab descent. Traditional religious beliefs predominate; about 20% of the people are Muslim and 20% Christian. French is the official language.

History. The precolonial Côte d'Ivoire was dominated by native kingdoms. Beginning in the 16th cent., the Portuguese and other Europeans engaged in a flourishing trade in slaves and ivory along the coast. The French began systematic conquest in 1870, proclaiming a protectorate in 1893. However, strong tribal resistance delayed occupation of the interior, and although Côte d'Ivoire was nominally incorporated into FRENCH WEST AFRICA in 1904, effective French control was not established until after World War I. In 1946 a mounting desire for independence led Félix HOUPHOUËT-BOIGNY to form an all-African political party. Côte d'Ivoire voted for autonomy within the FRENCH COMMUNITY in 1958 but in 1960 withdrew and declared itself independent. A one-party state until 1990, Côte d'Ivoire was headed after independence by Houphouët-Boigny. He died in office in 1993 and was succeeded as president by Henri Konan-Bédié, the national assembly speaker.

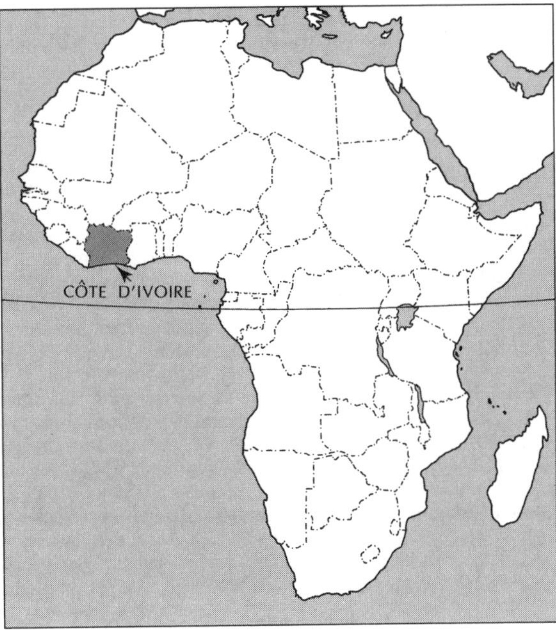

Cotonou, city (1989 est. pop. 350,000), S Benin, a seaport on the Gulf of Guinea. Although PORTONOVO is the capital, Cotonou, Benin's largest city, is the unofficial seat of government and commercial center. Its air, road, and rail connections also make it the country's communications hub. The seaport has been expanded to handle increased transit trade for Niger and Nigeria. Offshore oil-drilling is carried on nearby. Cotonou was a small state controlled by the Dahomey kingdom (see BENIN, republic) before coming under French rule (1883–1960).

Cotton, John, 1584–1652, Puritan clergyman in England and Massachusetts; b. England. When vicar of St. Botolph's Church, Boston, Lincolnshire, he was summoned (1632) to court for his Puritanism. Fleeing (1633) to Massachusetts Bay, he became a leading figure. He was chiefly responsible for expelling Anne HUTCHINSON and Roger WILLIAMS and has been viewed as an upholder of theocracy.

cotton, name for a shrubby plant (genus *Gossypium*) of the MALLOW family, for the fibers surrounding the seeds, and for the cloth woven from the spun fibers. Each of the seeds, which are contained in capsules, or bolls, is surrounded by white or cream-colored downy fibers that flatten and twist naturally as they dry. Cotton is tropical in origin but is now cultivated worldwide. It has been spun, woven, and dyed since prehistoric times. Most commercial cotton in the U.S. is from *G. hirsutum,* but some is obtained from sea-island and American-Egyptian *G. barbadense*. The chief cultivated species in Asia are *G. arboreum* and *G. herbaceum.* Cotton is planted annually by seed. Diseases and insect pests are numerous, e.g., the boll weevil, responsible for enormous losses, particularly of the highly susceptible, silky-fibered sea-island cotton, which was the leading type of cotton before the advent of this pest. Cotton is separated from its seeds by a COTTON GIN. Manufacture of cotton into cloth, textiles, and yard goods involves carding, combing, and SPINNING. Cotton is a source of CELLULOSE products, fertilizer, fuel, plastic reinforcing, automobile tire cord, pressed paper, cardboard, and cottonseed oil (used, e.g., in cooking, cosmetics, soaps, candles, detergents, paints, oilcloth, and artificial leather), which is pressed from the seeds. Used in Egypt, China, and India in ancient times, cotton has long played a significant role in world industry. Britain's need for imported cotton dictated much of its sea-domination policy as an imperial nation, and in the U.S., cotton was a principal economic cause of the CIVIL WAR.

cotton gin, machine for separating COTTON fibers from the seeds. American inventor Eli WHITNEY invented (1793) the saw gin, which was especially suited to short- and medium-staple cotton. In a modern gin, which still uses Whitney's basic design, seeds are removed as the fibers are pulled through a grid by a series of circular saws; an air blast or suction carries the clean fibers off the saws to a condenser and, finally, to the baling apparatus.

cottonmouth: see WATER MOCCASIN.

cottonwood: see WILLOW.

Coulomb, Charles Augustin de, 1736–1806, French physicist. He is known for his work on electricity, magnetism, and friction, and he invented a magnetoscope, a magnetometer, and a torsion balance that he employed in determining torsional elasticity (see STRENGTH OF MATERIALS) and in establishing COULOMB'S LAW. The unit of electric charge, the coulomb, is named for him.

coulomb (coul or C), unit of electric CHARGE. The absolute coulomb, the current U.S. legal standard, is the amount of charge transferred in 1 second by a current of 1 AMPERE; i.e., it is 1 ampere-second.

Coulomb's law, physical law stating that the electrostatic force between two point charges in free space is proportional to the product of the amount of CHARGE on the bodies divided by the square of the distance between them. If the bodies are oppositely charged, one positive and one negative, they are attracted toward each other; if the bodies are similarly charged, both positive or both negative, the force between them is repulsive.

council, ecumenical, council of church authorities accepted by the church as official. Roman Catholics recognize the following ecumenical councils (listed with their starting dates): (1) 1 Nicaea, 325, (2) 1 Constantinople, 381; (3) Ephesus, 431; (4) Chalcedon, 451; (5) 2 Constantinople, 553; (6) 3 Constantinople, 680; (7) 2 Nicaea, 787; (8) 4 Constantinople, 869; (9) 1 Lateran, 1123; (10) 2 Lateran, 1139; (11) 3 Lateran, 1179; (12) 4 Lateran, 1215; (13) 1 Lyons, 1245; (14) 2 Lyons, 1274; (15) Vienne, 1311; (16) Constance, 1414; (17) Basel and Ferrara-Florence, 1431, 1438; (18) 5 Lateran, 1512; (19) Trent, 1545; (20) 1 Vatican, 1869; (21) 2 Vatican, 1962. The Orthodox Church recognizes only the first seven councils and the continuation of 3 Constantinople (the Trullan Synod). The purpose of the first eight councils was to determine whether specific theological concepts were orthodox or heretical. The remaining councils, all held in Western Europe, have dealt chiefly with church discipline. Two of them, 2 Lyons and Ferrara-Florence, attempted to reconcile the Eastern and Western churches. In the Great SCHISM the conciliar theory developed, which held that an ecumenical council was superior to the pope; this theory was in its heyday at the Council of Constance. The 21st ecumenical council, called by Pope JOHN XXIII, advocated the reunion of all Christians with the Church of Rome (see VATICAN COUNCILS).

Council for Mutual Economic Assistance (COMECON), former international governmental organization for the coordination of economic policy among Communist nations. Founded in 1949, it adopted a formal charter in 1959 and became active in the 1960s. Its first members were Albania (which did not participate after 1961), Bulgaria, Czechoslovakia, East Germany (which ceased to be a member when Germany was reunified), Hungary, Poland, Romania, and the USSR. Joining COMECON later were Mongolia (1962), Cuba (1972), and Vietnam (1978). The fall of the Communist governments of most of the European members (1989–90) and the end of the use of the ruble as a basis for inter-member trade (1991) doomed the organization, and in 1991 it was dissolved.

counterfeiting: see FORGERY.

counterintelligence: see INTELLIGENCE GATHERING.

counterpoint, in music, the art of combining melodies each of which is independent though forming part of a homogeneous texture. The academic study of counterpoint established in the 18th cent. examined five "species" of counterpoint, or ways in which two lines of music could be interwoven: note against note; two notes against one; four notes against one; syncopation (a shifting of metrical accent in one of the lines); and florid counterpoint, which combined the other species. Early masters of contrapuntal music include PALESTRINA, LASSO, and William BYRD.

countertenor: see VOICE.

country and western music, American popular form originating in the Southeast (country) and in the West and Southwest (western), coalescing in the 1920s when recorded material became widely available. It is directly descended from the FOLK MUSIC of the English, Scottish, and Irish settlers of the SE U.S. Country music tends toward simpler forms, western toward a band style verging on swing. The music, depicting the life experience of poor rural (and now also urban) whites, has gained a national audience, largely through the "Grand Old Opry" radio broadcasts from Nashville. Although African-American GOSPEL MUSIC and blues have been influential, performers and audiences are almost all white. In the 1960s and 70s country and western influenced ROCK MUSIC's development, and since then a country and western revival has brought the form national popularity. Noted performers include Hank WILLIAMS, Patsy Cline, Merle Haggard, Johnny CASH, Willie Nelson, Loretta LYNN, Dolly Parton, Ricky Scaggs, and Garth Brooks.

Couperin, François [ko͞opərăN′], 1668–1733, French harpsichordist and composer. His graceful, delicate music represents the apex of French rococo, the reaction against BAROQUE style. He published four books of harpsichord SUITES (1713–30) and also composed much ORGAN music.

Gustave Courbet's Stonebreakers

Courbet, Gustave [ko͞orbā′], 1819–77, French painter. Always at odds with aesthetic and political authority, he audaciously chose subjects from ordinary life, as in *Wounded Man* (Louvre), which caused his work to be rejected and considered offensive. He defended his realistic works, e.g., *Funeral at Ornans* and *Stonebreakers* (both: Louvre), and went on to paint the self-congratulatory *Painter's Studio* (Louvre). Although his aesthetic theories were not destined to prevail, his influence became enormous. Today his work is admired for its frankness, vigor, and solid construction.

Courrèges, André: see FASHION (table).

courtly love, aristocratic philosophy of love that flourished in France and England during the Middle Ages, probably derived from OVID's works, various Eastern ideas, and TROUBADOUR songs. The code required a man to fall in love with a married woman of equal or higher rank, and, before consummating this love, to commit daring exploits proving his devotion; the lovers then pledged themselves to secrecy and fidelity. In reality, the code was little more than rules governing adultery. More important as a literary convention, it appears in the works of CHRÉTIEN DE TROYES and CHAUCER. See also CHIVALRY.

court system in the United States, the judicial branch of government, which applies and interprets the law. It is divided into separate federal and state systems, a division resulting from the fact that each of the 13 original colonies already had its own court system (based on the English model) when the U.S. Constitution mandated (1789) creation of a federal judiciary. The federal court system consists of three levels. At the lowest level there are district courts, which have original jurisdiction in most cases involving federal law. There are 92 districts, with at least one in each state, the District of Columbia, and Puerto Rico. The court of appeals system (est. 1891), on the second level, consists of 11 judicial circuits, which hear appeals from district courts and also deal with cases involving federal regulatory agencies. The U.S. SUPREME COURT is the ultimate arbiter of the law of the land. There are also special federal courts, such as the court of claims and court of tax appeals. While individual state court systems vary, they are also built on a hierarchical principle. At the lowest level are the inferior courts, which may include magistrate, municipal, traffic, and other courts that deal with petty civil and criminal cases. Superior courts, in which jury trials are common, handle more serious cases. The highest state court, variously called the appellate court, court of appeals, or supreme court, hears appeals from the lower courts. There are also special state courts, e.g., juvenile, divorce, probate, and small claims courts.

Cousteau, Jacques Yves, 1910–, French oceanographer and inventor. In 1943, with Emil Gagnan, he invented the self-contained underwater breathing apparatus (scuba). He founded (1945) the French navy's undersea research group, and since 1951 he has gone on annual oceanographic expeditions and produced many books and documentary films.

Cousy, Bob (Robert Joseph Cousy), 1928–, American basketball player; b. N.Y.C. In 13 seasons (1950–63) with the Boston Celtics of the National Basketball Association, he was the game's finest playmaker and a leading scorer (18.4-point average). He coached college and professional basketball from 1963 to 1973.

couvade, custom observed in some societies in which a father acts out the labor and childbirth that are actually being experienced by his wife. This may include retiring to bed, observing TABOOS, and/or appearing to feel pain. Couvade has been known since antiquity and practiced, in such places as Europe and South America, into the 20th cent. It may have begun as a way of asserting paternity or as an attempt, through magic, to draw the attention of evil spirits away from the mother and child.

covenant, in the Bible and theology, a voluntary agreement of God with humans; in law, a contract under seal or an agreement by deed; in Scottish history, a pact by opponents of episcopacy (see COVENANTERS). The Old Testament tells of several covenants between God and Israel, e.g., that culminating in the delivery of the Law of Moses. In English common law, covenants follow the same rules as other contracts; variously classified, all contain an explicit promise by the covenanter to the covenantee.

Covenanters, in Scottish history, groups of Presbyterians bound by oath to sustain one another in the defense of their religion. The first formal Covenant was signed in 1557, by Protestants trying to seize control of Scotland, and was later renewed at times of crisis, especially in the 17th cent. The Covenanters particularly opposed the imposition of the episcopate in Scotland and the use of the English Book of Common Prayer. The troubles ended with the GLORIOUS REVOLUTION (1688), which restored the Presbyterian Church in Scotland.

Covent Garden, area in London containing the city's principal produce market and the Royal Opera. The market was established (1671) on the site of a convent garden. In 1974 it was removed to Nine Elms, on the River Thames. The Royal Opera was erected on the site of the Theatre Royal built (1732) by John Rich; it was rebuilt after fires in 1808 and 1856. The Royal Ballet began performances there in 1946.

Coventry, city (1991 pop. 294,387), West Midlands, central England. It is an industrial center noted for automobile and airplane production. The city grew around a Benedictine abbey founded by Lady GODIVA and her husband in 1043. During WORLD WAR II a massive air raid (1940) destroyed the city's center and its 14th-cent. cathedral. A new cathedral was built alongside the ruins in 1962.

cow: see CATTLE; DAIRYING.

Coward, Sir Noel, 1899–1973, English playwright, actor, composer, director, and producer, known for his wit and sophistication. His works include comedies, e.g., *Private Lives* (1930) and *Blithe Spirit* (1941); musicals, e.g., *Bitter Sweet* (1929); films, e.g., *In Which We Serve* (1942) and *Brief Encounter* (1946); and many popular songs.

cowbird, New World BIRD of the BLACKBIRD and ORIOLE family. Most lay eggs in the nests of smaller birds, especially vireos, SPARROWS, and flycatchers; the host bird usually incubates the eggs and feeds the cowbird hatchlings. Cowbirds feed chiefly on insects, following cattle to capture the insects they stir up in grazing.

Cowell, Henry Dixon, 1897–1965, American composer and pianist; b. Menlo Park, Calif. Largely self-educated, he experimented with new musical resources, introducing the tone cluster on the piano, played with fist or elbow, and the technique of playing directly on the strings. His works include five *Hymns and Fuguing Tunes* (1941–45).

Cowley, Abraham, 1618–67, English METAPHYSICAL POET. In the scriptural epic *Davideis* (1656) he developed the use of the couplet as a vehicle for narrative verse. Among his principal works are the DONNE-influenced love cycle *The Mistress* (1647) and *Poems* (1656), including Pindaric odes.

cowpea, black-eyed pea, or **black-eyed bean,** annual leguminous plant (*Vigna sinensis*) of the PULSE family, native to the Old World but now cultivated in the S U.S., where it is used in cooking and, especially, as a catch crop and major forage plant. It is also grown commercially in India and China.

Cowper, William [ko͞o'pər, kou'–], 1731–1800, English poet. He led a quiet country life, interrupted by bouts of insanity. The poems contributed to John Newton's *Olney Hymns* (1779) often give way to religious despair and self-distrust. Cowper wrote on homely subjects, producing in 1785 his famous long poem *The Task,* which foreshadowed 19th-cent. ROMANTICISM in its descriptions of country life. Playfulness finds its way into many poems, including "The Diverting History of John Gilpin." His letters are considered among the most brilliant in English literature.

Cowper, William Cowper, 1st **Earl** [ko͞o'pər], 1664?–1723, English jurist. He was a leading negotiator in the union (1707) of England and Scotland. As first lord chancellor of Great Britain (1707–10, 1714–18) he contributed much to the modern system of EQUITY.

Coxey, Jacob Sechler, 1854–1951, American social reformer; b. Selinsgrove, Pa. After the panic of 1893 he gained fame by leading **Coxey's Army,** a band of jobless men who marched across the country from Ohio to Washington, D.C., to demonstrate for measures to relieve unemployment. On its arrival (May 1894), the "army" numbered only 500 instead of the threatened 100,000, and it disbanded anticlimactically when its leaders were arrested for walking on the Capitol lawn. Coxey later became an advocate of public works financed by fiat money as a remedy for unemployment and ran for president as the Farmer-Labor party candidate in 1932 and 1936.

coyote or **prairie wolf,** small, swift WOLF (*Canis latrans*) found in deserts, prairies, open woodlands, and brush country. Resembling a medium-sized dog with a pointed face, thick fur, and a black-tipped, bushy tail, the coyote is common in the central and W U.S. and ranges from Alaska to Central America and the Great Lakes; it is occasionally seen in New England. Considered dangerous to livestock, coyotes are killed each year by the thousands.

Cozens, Alexander, c.1717–1786, English draftsman; b. Russia. Probably the first English master to work entirely with landscape, he explained his system of making accidental "blot" drawings to suggest subjects in *A New Method of Assisting the Invention in*

Drawing Original Compositions of Landscape (c.1785). His son, **John Robert Cozens,** 1752–97, is known for poetic watercolor landscapes.

Cozzens, James Gould, 1903–78, American novelist; b. Chicago. His meticulously crafted novels, often concerning idealism and compromise, include *Guard of Honor* (1948; Pulitzer), and *By Love Possessed* (1957).

CPU: see COMPUTER.

Cr, chemical symbol of the element CHROMIUM.

crab, chiefly marine animal of the CRUSTACEAN order Decapoda, with an enlarged cephalothorax covered by a broad, flat shell (carapace). Extending from the cephalothorax are five pairs of legs, the first pair bearing claws (pincers). Crabs have a pair of eyes on short, movable stalks and many mouthparts. They tend to move sideways but can move in all directions. The blue crab of the Atlantic coast of the U.S. is a source of food, marketed after molting as the soft-shell crab. The giant Japanese spider crab, with a 1-ft-wide (30-cm) carapace and legs about 4 ft (122 cm) long, is the largest arthropod.

Crab Nebula, diffuse gaseous NEBULA surrounding an optical PULSAR in the constellation Taurus. It is the remnant of a SUPERNOVA explosion in 1054 and is a strong emitter of radio waves and X rays.

crack, a form of COCAINE. A less expensive, more potent, smokable form of the drug, it is the most addictive of abused substances. The drug's availability has greatly increased the number of addicts, resulting in major law enforcement problems in Western countries. See also DRUG ADDICTION AND DRUG ABUSE.

Cracow: see KRAKÓW.

crafts: see ARTS AND CRAFTS.

Craig, Sir James Henry, 1748–1812, British governor of CANADA (1807–11). His lack of sympathy with French Canadians resulted in his dissolution (1809) of Lower Canada's assembly, but his arbitrary methods served only to consolidate their position.

Craigie, Sir William A., 1867–1957, British lexicographer; b. Scotland. Generally considered the foremost lexicographer of his time, Craigie worked on the *New English Dictionary* (commonly called the *Oxford English Dictionary*) from 1897 and was joint editor from 1901 to 1933. In the U.S. he was chief editor of *A Dictionary of American English on Historical Principles* (4 vol., 1938–43).

Cram, Ralph Adams, 1863–1942, American architect; b. Hampton Falls, N.H. An ardent exponent of the Gothic, he produced collegiate and ecclesiastical works in a neo-Gothic style, e.g., part of the Cathedral of SAINT JOHN THE DIVINE, N.Y.C., and the graduate school and chapel at Princeton.

Cranach or **Kranach, Lucas** [both: krä'näkh], the Elder, 1472–1553, German painter and engraver. Called the painter of the REFORMATION, he was court painter to three electors of Saxony. Although his work is often naïve and awkward in draftmanship, it also has freshness, originality, and a warm, rich color. His paintings include *Adam and Eve* (Courtauld Inst., London) and such famous portraits as that of Elector John Frederick and *Self-Portrait* (Uffizi). His son **Lucas Cranach,** the Younger, 1515–86, inherited his shop, signature, and popularity. Their work is often indistinguishable.

cranberry, low, creeping, evergreen bog plant (genus *Oxycoccus*) of the HEATH family. The tart red berries are used for sauces, jellies, pies, and beverages. The native American, or large, cranberry (*O.* or *V. macrocarpus*) is commercially cultivated. The unrelated highbush cranberry, or cranberry tree, is in the HONEYSUCKLE family. Cranberries are often classified in the blueberry genus *Vaccinium*.

Crane, (Harold) Hart, 1899–1932, American poet; b. Garrettsville, Ohio. Although he published only two volumes, he is considered one of the most original poets of his time. His first collection, *White Buildings* (1926), was inspired by New York City. His most ambitious work, *The Bridge* (1930), is a series of long poems on the U.S., in which the Brooklyn Bridge serves as a mystical unifying symbol. An alcoholic and a homosexual, plagued by personal problems, Crane jumped overboard while returning from Mexico to the U.S. and was drowned.

Crane, Stephen, 1871–1900, often considered the first modern American writer; b. Newark, N.J. He introduced REALISM into American fiction with his grim and unpopular first novel, *Maggie: A Girl of the Streets* (1893). Crane achieved fame with his next novel, *The Red Badge of Courage* (1895), a remarkable account of a young CIVIL WAR soldier. Later a war correspondent in Cuba and Greece, he also wrote superb short stories, e.g., "The Open Boat" (1898) and "The Monster" (1899), and poetry. Vilified because of his domestic life, Crane spent his last years in Europe.

crane, large, wading marsh BIRD of the Northern Hemisphere and Africa, related to the RAILS. Cranes are known for their loud, trumpeting call and rhythmic mating dances. The North American whooping crane, a white bird almost 5 ft (152 cm) tall, was nearly extinct in 1941 and is still endangered; the gray sandhill crane, which winters W of the Mississippi, is also becoming rare.

Cranmer, Thomas, 1489–1556, English churchman. He came to the attention of HENRY VIII in 1529 by suggesting that the king might further his efforts to divorce KATHARINE OF ARAGÓN by collecting favorable opinions from the universities. He was made archbishop of Canterbury in 1533 and was completely subservient to Henry's will. While serving EDWARD VI, he shaped the doctrinal and liturgical transformation of the Church of England. He placed the English Bible in churches, and in 1552 he revised the BOOK OF COMMON PRAYER. Under the Roman Catholic MARY I, he was tried for treason, convicted of heresy, and burned at the stake.

Crashaw, Richard, 1612?–1649, English METAPHYSICAL POET. The son of an ardent Puritan minister, he converted to Catholicism and lived on the Continent. His fame rests on his intense religious verse, which combines sensuality with mysticism in a manner suggestive of baroque art. *Steps to the Temple* (1646), his major volume of poems, was enlarged to include *Delights of the Muses* (1648).

Crassus, ancient Roman family, of the plebeian Licinian gens. **Lucius Licinius Crassus,** d. 91 B.C., a noted orator and lawyer (much admired by Cicero), was consul in 95 B.C. He proposed the Licinian Law to banish from Rome all who had gained Roman citizenship by illegal means. This helped bring on the Social War (90–88 B.C.). **Marcus Licinius Crassus,** d. 53 B.C., was the best-known member of the family. Charming, avaricious, and ambitious, he became the principal landowner in Rome by organizing his private fire brigade, buying burning houses cheaply, and then putting out the fires. He gained immense prestige—along with POMPEY—for suppressing the uprising of SPARTACUS. He and Julius CAESAR drew closer together and, with Pompey, formed the First TRIUMVIRATE (60 B.C.), but Crassus and Pompey did not get along. Avid for military glory, Crassus undertook a campaign against the Parthians. His army was routed at Carrhae (modern Haran) in 53 B.C., and he was treacherously murdered.

crater: see METEORITE.

Crater Lake National Park: see NATIONAL PARKS (table).

Crawford, Joan, 1908–77, American film actress; b. San Antonio, Tex., as Lucille Le Sueur. A major Hollywood star, she made such films as *Grand Hotel* (1932), *Mildred Pierce* (1945; Academy Award), and *Humoresque* (1946).

Crawford, Thomas, 1813–57, American sculptor; b. N.Y.C. An exponent of the CLASSIC REVIVAL, he won recognition with *Armed Freedom,* a statue above the CAPITOL dome, and with the design of the WASHINGTON MONUMENT, for which he executed several figures.

Craxi, Bettino [krä'ksē], 1934–, Italian political leader. Socialist party leader from 1976, he was Italy's first socialist prime minister (1983–87). In 1993 he was charged with corruption and resigned as party leader.

crayfish or **crawfish,** edible freshwater CRUSTACEAN smaller than, but structurally similar to, the LOBSTER. Crayfish are found in ponds and streams in most parts of the world except Africa. They are scavengers and grow to 3 to 4 in. (7.6–10.2 cm) in length. Crayfish are usually brownish green; some cave-dwelling forms are colorless.

Crazy Horse, d. 1877, revered chief of the Oglala SIOUX. Resisting encroachment of whites in the mineral-rich Black Hills of South Dakota, he repeatedly defeated U.S. troops. He joined SITTING BULL and GALL to defeat George Armstrong CUSTER at LITTLE BIGHORN (1876), but finally he and 1,000 starving followers had to surrender. He was stabbed to death trying to escape from prison.

Crazy Horse Memorial, memorial to CRAZY HORSE and Native Americans, in progress at Thunderhead Mt., near Custer, S.D., in the BLACK HILLS. When finished it will consist of an equestrian statue of Crazy Horse, 563 ft (172 m) high and 641 ft (196 m) long, carved in the round out of the mountainside. Work on the memorial was begun in 1948 by American sculptor Korczak Ziolkowski (1908–82) at the invitation of Lakota Chief Henry Standing Bear.

creationism, belief in the biblical account of the creation of the world; also known as creation science. Advocates of creationism have campaigned to have it taught in U.S. public schools along with the theory of EVOLUTION, which they dispute. In 1981 a federal judge ruled unconstitutional an Arkansas law requiring the teaching of creationism, holding it to be religious in nature; a similar Louisiana law was overturned in 1982.

credit, granting of goods, services, or money in return for a promise of future payment, usually accompanied by an INTEREST charge. The two basic forms of credit are business and consumer. The chief function of business credit is the transfer of capital from those who own it to those who can use it, in the expectation that the profit from its use will exceed the interest payable on the loan. Consumer credit permits the purchase of retail goods and services with little or no down payment in cash. In installment buying and selling, the consumer agrees to make payments at specific intervals in set amounts. CREDIT CARDS are issued by local and national retailers and by banks. Cardholders usually pay an annual fee and a monthly interest charge on the unpaid balance. The major bank cards also provide short-term personal loans. See DEBT.

credit card, card or document used to obtain consumer credit when purchasing an article or service. Credit cards may be issued by a local retailer, a national retailer, or a third party, e.g., a bank or financial services company. Typically, cards issued by a retailer may be used only in its stores; third-party cards, such as those issued by a bank in association with Visa or MasterCard, are general-purpose cards and may be used at a variety of establishments. Through the revolving charge plan, cardholders can postpone payment by accepting a monthly interest charge. Consumers may also use the general-purpose cards to obtain short-term personal loans, often called cash advances. Credit-card issuers get revenue from fees paid by stores that accept their cards, from yearly fees paid by cardholders, and from interest charged on unpaid credit balances. The late 1980s and early 90s saw a dramatic increase in the number of credit cards issued by nonbanks, including the financial arms of telephone companies, automobile manufacturers, and national retailers. **Charge cards,** such as American Express, require the consumer to pay for all purchases at the end of the billing period. See also DEBIT CARD.

Crédit Mobilier of America, ephemeral construction company, involved in a major U.S. financial scandal. Oakes Ames, T.C. Durant, and other stockholders of the Union Pacific RR set up (1867) the Crédit Mobilier and awarded themselves contracts for construction on the Union Pacific that netted profits estimated at from $7 million to $23 million. To forestall investigations or interference by Congress, Ames sold or assigned shares of stock to members of Congress at par, though the shares were worth twice as much. The scandal broke during the 1872 presidential campaign and resulted in a Congressional investigation that issued censures, but there were no prosecutions.

credit union, cooperative financial institution that makes low-interest personal loans to members. It is usually composed of persons from the same occupational group or local community, such as company employees or members of labor unions and churches. Funds for lending come from members' savings deposits through the sale of shares. In the U.S. the more than 12,500 credit unions are chartered and regulated by the federal government or the states.

Cree, indigenous people of Manitoba, one branch of whom moved southwest to adopt a buffalo culture as the Plains Cree, while the other retained their deer culture as the Woodland Cree (see NORTH AMERICA, INDIGENOUS PEOPLES OF). They spoke an Algonquian language of the Algonquian-Wakashan stock (see NATIVE AMERICAN LANGUAGES). Although warlike, the Cree were friendly to fur traders, and their history closely follows that of the Hudson's Bay and North West fur companies. Today they are one of the larger Canadian tribes; another group lives in Montana. In 1990 there were 8,290 Crees in the U.S.

creed, summary of basic doctrines of faith. The following are some of the historically important Christian creeds. **1** The **Nicene Creed,** usually said to be a revision by the First Council of CONSTANTINOPLE (381) of a creed adopted by the First Council of NICAEA (325). **2** The **Athanasian Creed,** a 6th-cent. statement, no longer ascribed to St. ATHANASIUS, on the Trinity and the Incarnation. **3** The **Apostles' Creed,** similar to the Nicene Creed and dating in its present form to c.650.

Creek, confederacy of 50 Native American towns or peoples mainly in Georgia and Alabama, who spoke a Muskogean tongue of the Hokan-Siouan linguistic stock (see NATIVE AMERICAN LANGUAGES). Named for their villages on creeks or rivers, they lived a settled agricultural life, governing themselves democratically. Although they were friendly to the British in colonial times, white encroachment later aroused their hostility. In the Creek War (1813–14), they were subdued by Andrew JACKSON and lost two thirds of their territory. Eventually they were moved to Indian Territory and became one of the FIVE CIVILIZED TRIBES. Today they live largely in Oklahoma. In 1990 there were 43,550 Creeks in the U.S.

Crémazie, (Joseph) Octave [krāmäzē'], 1822–79, French Canadian poet, "the father of French Canadian poetry." His poem "Le Vieux Soldat canadien" (1855) made him famous. His poetry is patriotic and was influenced by French ROMANTICISM.

Cresson, Edith, 1934–, French politician. A Socialist, she was elected to the European parliament in 1979 and held a series of ministerial appointments (1981–86). From 1986 to 1990, she was a member of the French National Assembly and then served as French premier (1991–92), the first woman to do so.

Cretaceous period: see GEOLOGIC ERA (table).

Crete, island (1991 pop. 536,980), c.3,235 sq mi (8,380 sq km), SE Greece, in the E Mediterranean Sea and marking the southern limit of the Aegean Sea. It is now a popular tourist region composed mainly of small farms growing grains, olives, and oranges, and raising livestock; food processing is the main industry. Crete was the site of the MINOAN CIVILIZATION, which reached its peak c.1600 B.C. Invaluable archaeological finds have been made at the ruins of the palace at the ancient city of KNOSSOS. Although the island later flourished as a trading center, it played no important political role in ancient Greece. It was conquered by the Romans (68–67 B.C.) and by the Ottoman Turks (1669), but a series of revolts finally forced (1898) the Turks to evacuate. The island officially joined modern Greece in 1913, as a result of the BALKAN WARS. A British military base in WORLD WAR II, it was attacked by Germany in the first and only successful all-air invasion of the war.

cretinism: see under DWARFISM.

Crèvecoeur, J. Hector St. John [krĕvkör'], 1735–1813, American author and agriculturist; b. France. After settling in Orange co., N.Y., he wrote *Letters from an American Farmer* (1782) and other agricultural articles that described U.S. rural life of the time. He introduced the culture of the American potato into Normandy and of European crops, notably alfalfa, into the U.S. He returned to France in 1790.

Crick, Francis Harry Compton, 1916–, English scientist. He shared with Maurice Wilkins and James WATSON the 1962 Nobel Prize in physiology or medicine for establishing the function and double-helix structure of DNA, the key substance in the transmission of hereditary characteristics.

cricket, slender, chirping, hopping INSECT of the family Gryllidae. Most have long antennae, muscular hindlegs, and two pairs of fully developed wings. The males produce the characteristic song by rubbing specialized structures of their front wings together; both sexes have auditory organs on their forelegs. Common field crickets of the U.S. are brown to black and about 1 in. (2.5 cm) long.

cricket, ball and bat game played chiefly in Great Britain and the Commonwealth countries. It is played by two opposing teams of 11 contestants on a level turf, measuring about 525 ft (160 m) by about 550 ft (170 m). Two wickets are placed 66 ft (20.12 m) apart near the middle of the field, each consisting of two wooden crosspieces (bails) resting on three stumps. Batsmen of the same team defend each wicket with a paddle-shaped bat against opposing bowlers, who try to knock down the bails of the wicket. If a batsman hits the ball far enough so that he and his partner can run to exchange places, a run is scored. Batsmen are retired if the ball is caught on the fly or if the bails are knocked down. A game may require several days to complete. Cricket probably was developed in medieval England before 1400. Australia and Britain compete in a famous series.

crime, the recorded violation of major rules of social behavior codified in CRIMINAL LAW. Such law varies from one culture to the next, reflecting differences in social norms. Crime, its causes, and its prevention are the subject of criminology, a subdivision of sociology that also draws on psychology, economics, and other disciplines. One of its branches is penology, which deals with PRISON management and the rehabilitation of convicted offenders. The causes of crime may include psychological predisposition, emotional disorders, environment, or other factors. Crime tends to rise during periods of economic DEPRESSION and social upheaval and is most common in poverty areas, often as juvenile delinquency; so-called white-collar crime is committed by those of higher economic status. In the U.S. ORGANIZED CRIME developed during PROHIBITION. Crimes of violence traditionally draw the heaviest penalties, whereas "victimless crimes" (such as PROSTITUTION) are often virtually decriminalized through the failure of the authorities to prosecute.

Crimea, Ukr. and Rus. *Krym,* peninsula and autonomous republic (1991 est. pop. 2,363,000), c.10,000 sq mi (25,900 sq km), Ukraine, linked with the mainland by the Perekop Isthmus and bounded by the Black Sea (S, W) and the Sea of Azov (NE). Major cities include Simferopol (the capital), SEVASTOPOL, Kerch, and Yalta. The north is a semiarid steppe that supports wheat, corn, and cotton crops; in the south rises the Crimean, or Yaila, range. The subtropical shore along the Black Sea is famed for its resorts. Heavy industry in the Crimea includes plants producing machinery, chemicals, and building materials. The population is largely Russian.

History. In ancient times Crimea was inhabited by a CIMMERIAN people called Tauri, who were expelled (8th cent. B.C.) by the Scythians. In the 5th cent. B.C. the kingdom of the Cimmerian Bosporus emerged, later coming under Greek, then Roman, influence. The area, overrun between the 3d and 13th cent. by the Goths, Huns, Khazars, Cumans, and Mongols, became an independent TATAR khanate in the 15th cent. It was annexed by Russia in 1783. The peninsula was a battleground in the CRIMEAN WAR (1853–56), the RUSSIAN REVOLUTION, and both world wars. The Crimean Tatars were expelled from region in 1945 and were not permitted to return until the late 1980s. In 1954 the area was transferred from the Russian SFSR to Ukraine. Crimea was made (1991) an autonomous republic within Ukraine, and in 1992 there was an abortive attempt by the Russian-dominated Crimean government to declare independence.

Crimean War, 1853–56, between Russia and the allied powers of Turkey, England, France, and Sardinia. Its cause was inherent in the EASTERN QUESTION; its pretext was a quarrel between Russia and France over guardianship of Palestinian holy places. Turkey declared war on Russia after the latter occupied Moldavia and Walachia; England, France, and Sardinia joined later. The fighting centered on SEVASTOPOL, the heavily fortified base of the Russian fleet. After a long, bloody siege, the city fell and the war ended, thus checking Russian influence in the area. The war is particularly remembered for the futile battle of Balaklava and for the heroic nursing reforms of Florence NIGHTINGALE.

criminal law, body of law that defines offenses against the state and regulates their prosecution and punishment. It is distinguished from CIVIL LAW, which is concerned with relations between private parties. In the U.S., power to define crime rests with the states and with the federal government. U.S. criminal law is based on English COMMON LAW, but a number of states have enacted penal or criminal codes, and since World War II the trend is increasingly toward codification. The procedure in criminal cases is essentially the same throughout the U.S. A grand jury usually examines the evidence against a suspect and either dismisses the case or draws up an INDICTMENT. Trial is by JURY or before a judge alone. The public prosecutor (usually called the district attorney) presents the government's case, and counsel represents the accused. There is a legal presumption of innocence, and the burden of proving guilt beyond a reasonable doubt is on the prosecution. If the accused is found innocent, he or she is discharged; if guilty, the judge pronounces sentence. If convicted, the defendant may appeal; the prosecution, however, under the prohibition against DOUBLE JEOPARDY, generally cannot appeal an acquittal.

criminology: see CRIME.

crinoid, member of the class (Crinoidea) of marine invertebrate animals (ECHINODERMS) that includes the sea lilies and feather stars. Most sea lilies remain stalked and sessile for their entire lives, while feather stars break off the stalk and become mobile as adults. All crinoids live with their oral side upward. Most have a ring of 10 arms encircling the mouth, but some sea lilies have up to 40 arms and some feather stars up to 200.

Cripple Creek, town (1990 pop. 584), alt. 9,375 ft (2,858 m), seat of Teller co., central Colo.; inc. 1892. Once a great gold boom town (1901 est. pop. 50,000), it is now a summer resort and one of three Colorado towns with casino gambling. There were violent mine strikes in 1893 and 1904.

Cristus, Petrus: see CHRISTUS, PETRUS.

Crittenden Compromise, unsuccessful last-minute effort to avert the U.S. CIVIL WAR. It was proposed in Dec. 1860 by Sen. John J. Crittenden of Kentucky as a constitutional amendment mandating the use of the MISSOURI COMPROMISE line, extended to California, to divide free and slave states. It was defeated (Jan. and Mar. 1861) in Congress.

croaker, carnivorous, elongate, spiny-finned FISH of the family Sciaenidae, including the drum and weakfish (sea trout), so called because of their croaking or grunting noises. Croakers are found in the sandy shallows of temperate and warm seas. The drums are the largest and noisiest croakers—up to 150 lb (68 kg) in the common drum—and include the commercially important red drum, or channel bass. The weakfish, named for their easily torn flesh, include the common weakfish, or squeteague, of the Atlantic coast and the spotted weakfish.

Croatia [krōā'shə], Croatian *Hrvatska,* officially Republic of Croatia, republic (1991 est. pop. 4,784,000), 21,824 sq mi (56,524 sq km), S Europe, in the NW corner of the Balkan Peninsula; formerly a constituent republic of Yugoslavia. It is bordered by the Adriatic Sea (W), Slovenia (NW), Hungary (NE), Yugoslavia (E), Bosnia and Hercegovina (S and E), and Yugoslavia (S). Roughly shaped like an inverted U, Croatia is mountainous in the coastal regions of DALMATIA and Istria but flat and fertile inland in Slavonia, in the northeast. ZAGREB is the capital and largest city; other important cities include Osijek, Rijeka, and Split. Resources include petroleum, bauxite, copper, and iron, as well as timber. Tourism has been important, especially on the Adriatic coast, but was hurt by fighting in the early 1990s. The majority of population are Croats; Serbs were the largest minority but their numbers have been reduced through forced evictions. Both Croats and Serbs speak Serbo-Croatian. Most Croats are Roman Catholic; the Serbs belong largely to the Orthodox church.

History. Once part of the Roman province of Pannonia, the area

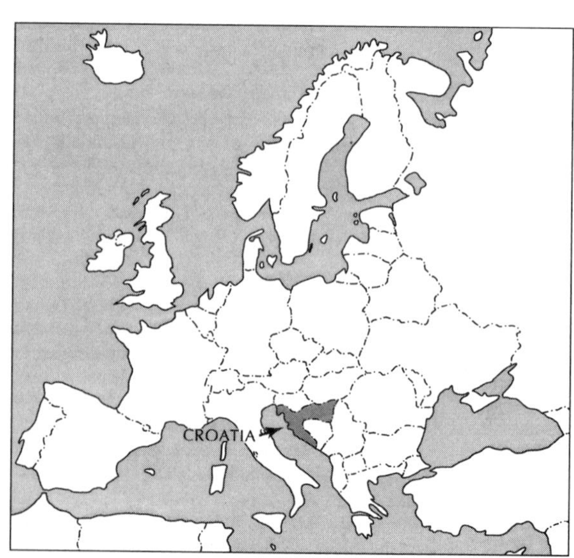

was settled by Croats in the 7th cent. Croatia was a kingdom from the 10th cent. and united with Hungary in 1102, but it retained its own diet. The Turks held most of Croatia from the 16th to 18th cent.; they were replaced by the HAPSBURGS, who ruled the area until 1918. After World War I it became part of Yugoslavia, but Serb domination led to Croatian restiveness. In World War II the Germans dismantled Yugoslavia and set up a fascist puppet state in Croatia. Thousands of Serbs were massacred under fascist rule. In 1945 the area again became part of Yugoslavia; however, Croatian nationalism persisted. In 1991, after Serbia opposed a looser Yugoslav federation, Croatia declared itself independent, with Franjo Tudjman, a former general, as president. Militias of Serbs native to the area fought for control of parts of Croatia, especially in Krajina in the west, and Yugoslav forces entered the fighting on the Serbian side. By the end of 1991 Serbs controlled about 30% of Croatia, and a truce called in early 1992 has largely held. In 1992 Croatia supported and directed Bosnian Croatians when fighting erupted in Bosnia, gaining effective control of large areas of Bosnia.

Croce, Benedetto, 1866–1952, Italian philosopher, historian, and literary critic. His *Aesthetic as Science of Expression and General Linguistic* (1902), the first part of his major work *Philosophy of the Spirit* (1902–17), was a landmark of modern IDEALISM. Croce was renowned for his works of literary criticism and AESTHETICS, cultural history, and historical methodology. A staunch anti-Fascist, he became a Liberal party leader in 1943.

crochet, construction of fabric by interlocking loops of thread or yarn using a hook. The chain stitch is used to cast on a foundation chain of the desired length, into which successive rows of stitches are worked. All stitches and patterns derive from single and double crochet. Like knitting, crochet produces a fabric that stretches. When a fine hook and thread are used, crochet can be used to produce a form of lace.

Crockett, Davy (David Crockett), 1786–1836, American frontiersman; b. near Greeneville, Tenn. He was a U.S. representative from Tennessee (1827–31, 1833–35) and died defending the ALAMO. Known for his backwoods humor, he is the supposed author of several autobiographical works, although their idiom does not match that of his own letters.

crocodile, carnivorous REPTILE (order Crocodilia) found in tropical and subtropical regions, distinguished from the ALLIGATOR by greater aggressiveness, a narrower snout, and a long, lower fourth tooth, which protrudes when the mouth is closed. Crocodiles have flattened bodies, short legs, and powerful jaws. The saltwater crocodile is often 14 ft (4.3 m) long, while the Nile, American, and Orinoco crocodiles are commonly 12 ft (3.7 m) long. Native to the Everglades and Florida Keys, the American crocodile (*Crocodylus acutus*) is an endangered species

crocus, perennial herb (genus *Crocus*) of the IRIS family, native to the Mediterranean and SW Asia. Crocuses usually bear a single yellow, purple, or white flower and have small, grasslike leaves. One species, SAFFRON, is cultivated commercially as a yellow dye. The unrelated meadow saffron, or autumn crocus, is in the LILY family, and the wild crocus, or pasqueflower, is in the BUTTERCUP family.

Croesus [krē′səs], d. c.547 B.C., last king of Lydia (560–c.546 B.C.), noted for his great wealth. He allied himself with Egypt and Babylonia against CYRUS THE GREAT of Persia, but he was defeated and captured.

Cro-Magnon man, biologically modern human being (species *Homo sapiens*), existing 40,000–35,000 years ago (see HUMAN EVOLUTION). Skeletal remains were first found (1868) in France and then in other parts of Europe. Cro-Magnon man was anatomically identical to modern humans, but differed from NEANDERTHAL MAN, who disappeared in the fossil record shortly after Cro-Magnon's appearance. Cro-Magnon's upper Paleolithic culture (see STONE AGE) produced flint and bone tools, shell and ivory jewelry, and elegant polychrome cave paintings of great vitality (see PALEOLITHIC ART).

Crompton, Samuel, 1753–1827, English inventor (1779) of a SPINNING machine that for the first time allowed the production of fine strong cotton yarns. Crompton's mule spinner, or muslin wheel, combined the best features of Richard ARKWRIGHT's water frame and James HARGREAVES's spinning jenny.

Cromwell, Oliver, 1599–1658, lord protector of England. A Puritan, he entered Parliament in 1628, standing firmly with the opposition to CHARLES I. During the first civil war (see ENGLISH CIVIL WAR), he rose rapidly to leadership because of his military ability and genius for organization. His own regiment, the Ironsides, distinguished itself at Marston Moor (1644). In 1645 he became second in command to Sir Thomas Fairfax in the New Model Army, which defeated the king at Naseby (1645). After Charles's flight to Carisbrooke (1647), Cromwell lost hope of dealing moderately with him. In the second civil war, he repelled the Scottish royalist invasion at Preston (1648). His was the leading voice demanding execution at the king's trial in 1649. After the republican Commonwealth was proclaimed, Cromwell led a cruelly punitive expedition into Ireland, where he initiated a policy of dispossessing the Irish. He defeated the Scottish royalists at Dunbar (1650) and CHARLES II at Worcester (1651). In 1653 Cromwell dissolved the Rump Parliament and replaced it with the feeble Nominated (Barebone's) Parliament, which he himself appointed. That same year the Protectorate was established and Cromwell was named lord protector. In 1657 he declined the crown. Cromwell's foreign policy was governed by the need to expand English trade and prevent the restoration of the Stuarts. He approved the Navigation Act of 1651, which led to the first (1652–54) of the DUTCH WARS; his war with Spain (1655–58) was over trade rights. Opinions of Cromwell have always varied. Although he favored religious toleration, he tolerated only Jews and non-Anglican Protestants. His military genius and force of character are recognized, but the necessities of government forced him into cruelty and intolerance. His son **Richard Cromwell,** 1626–1712, succeeded him. The army and Parliament struggled for power until the Protectorate collapsed and the Commonwealth was reestablished in 1659. He lived abroad (1660–80) and later in England under an assumed name. A man of virtue and dignity, he was forced into a situation beyond his talents.

Cronaca, Il: see POLLAIUOLO, family.

Cronkite, Walter, 1916–, American journalist; b. St. Joseph, Mo. From 1962 to 1981 he was anchorman of the Columbia Broadcasting System's evening television news program.

Cronus or **Kronos,** in Greek myth, the youngest TITAN; son of URANUS and GAEA. He led the Titans in a revolt against Uranus and ruled the world. By his sister RHEA, he fathered the great gods—ZEUS, POSEIDON, DEMETER, HERA, HADES, and HESTIA. Fated to be overthrown by one of his children, he tried unsuccessfully to destroy them. Zeus later led the OLYMPIAN gods in defeating him in a battle, described by HESIOD, called the Titanomachy. Cronus is equated with the Roman god SATURN.

Crookes, Sir William, 1832–1919, English chemist and physicist. Noted for his work on radioactivity, he invented the spinthariscope (used to make visible the flashes produced by bombarding a screen with the alpha rays of a particle of radium), the radiometer (used to measure the intensity of radiant energy), and the Crookes tube (a highly evacuated tube through which is passed an electrical discharge). He founded (1859) *Chemical News* and discovered the element THALLIUM.

croquet, lawn game in which players hit wooden balls with wooden mallets through a series of 9 or 10 wire arches (wickets). The first player to hit the posts at both ends of the field wins. Developed in France in the 17th cent., the game is popular, with varying rules, in Britain and the U.S.

Crosby, Bing, 1904–77, American singer and film actor; b. Tacoma, Wash., as Harry Lillis Crosby. His crooning voice was heard on radio and records. His many films include *Going My Way* (1944; Academy Award).

cross, widely used symbol found in such diverse cultures as those of ancient India, Egypt, and the Native Americans. Its most widespread use is among Christians, to whom it recalls the crucifixion of JESUS and humanity's redemption thereby. The oldest Christian remains contain drawings of crosses. Their use was attacked by Byzantine ICONOCLASM, but was vindicated at the Second Council of NICAEA (787). There are many types of crosses. The Latin cross, the commonest, has its upright longer than its transom. With two transoms it is called a patriarchal or archiepiscopal cross; with three, it is a papal cross. The Greek cross has equal arms. A crucifix is a cross with the figure of Jesus upon it.

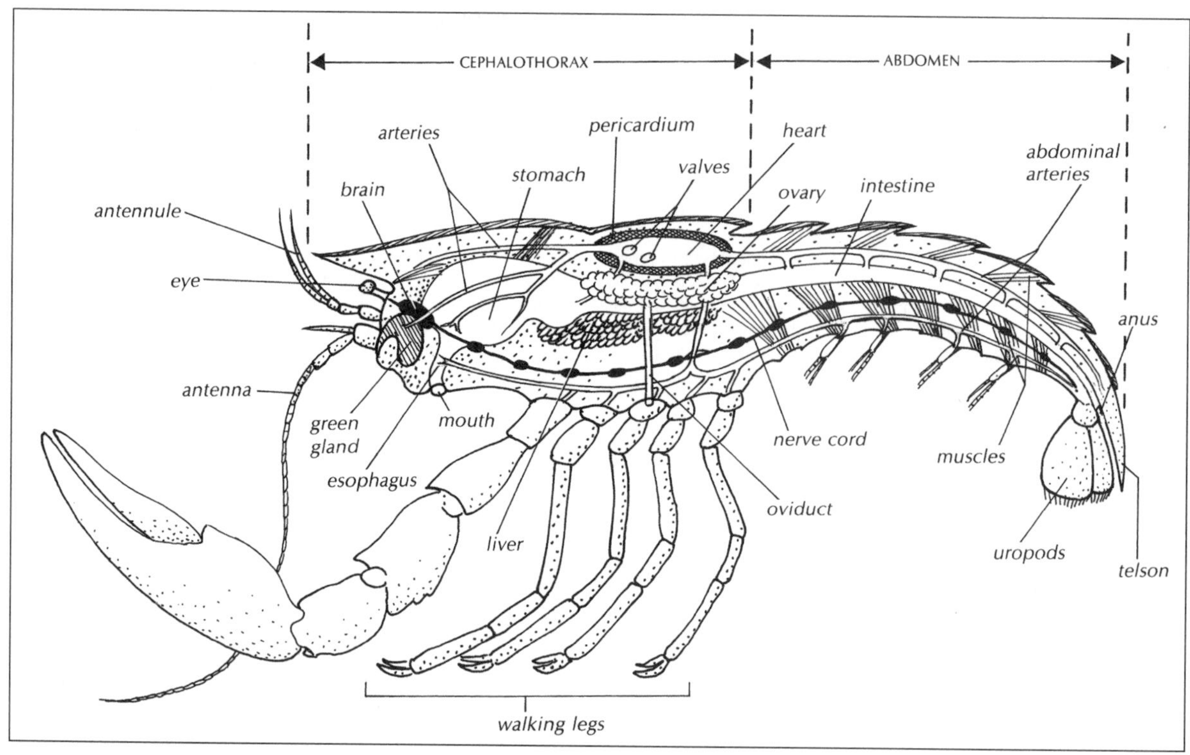

Crustacean: Internal anatomy of a female crayfish, a representative crustacean

croup, acute obstructive inflammation of the larynx in young children, usually ages three to six. Symptoms include difficulty in breathing and a high-pitched, barking cough due to swelling or spasm. The cause may be an infection, ALLERGY, or obstruction by a swallowed object. Treatment is directed at the cause.

Crow, indigenous people of the Plains (see NORTH AMERICA, INDIGENOUS PEOPLES OF), who ranged the Yellowstone R. region and spoke a Siouan language of the Hokan-Siouan stock (see NATIVE AMERICAN LANGUAGES). A hunting tribe, they cultivated only tobacco. Their highly complex social system stressed care of children. They helped the whites in the SIOUX wars. Today most Crows live in Montana, near the LITTLE BIGHORN, where tourism, ranching, and mineral leases provide tribal income. In 1990 there were 8,588 Crows in the U.S.

crow, black BIRD (family Corvidae) related to the RAVEN, MAGPIE, and JAY and among the most intelligent of birds. Known for its throaty "caw," the American, or common, crow, about 19 in. (49 cm) long with a wingspan of over 3 ft (92 cm), destroys harmful insects and rodents.

crown, circular head ornament worn by sovereigns. (The coronet is worn by nobles.) In ancient Greece and Rome crowns were merely wreaths, sometimes made of leaves, awarded in athletic or poetic contests, or in recognition of public service. The use of the crown as a symbol of royal rank is of ancient tradition in Egypt and E Asia. The medieval and modern crown, an elaboration of the DIADEM, is usually made of metal, often gold, inlaid with gems. Famous historic crowns include the Lombard iron crown (Monza, Italy), the crown of Charlemagne (Vienna, Austria), and the crown of St. Stephen of Hungary. The triple crown of the pope, known as a tiara, dates from the 14th cent.

Crozet Islands: see FRENCH SOUTHERN AND ANTARCTIC LANDS.

crucifix: see CROSS.

crucifixion, hanging on a cross, an ancient method of execution. It was used in the Middle East, but not by the Greeks. The Romans may have borrowed it from Carthage and reserved it for slaves and despised criminals. A prisoner was either nailed or tied to the cross, and, to induce more rapid death, his legs were often broken. JESUS died by crucifixion.

crude oil: see PETROLEUM.

Cruikshank, George, 1792–1878, English caricaturist, illustrator, and etcher. The most popular caricaturist of his day, he illustrated more than 850 books and contributed to the *Meteor,* the *Scourge,* and the *Satirist.* Among his best works are illustrations for *Life in London,* etchings for Grimm's *German Popular Stories,* and his drawings *The Drunkard's Children* and *The Gin Trap.*

cruise missile: see: MISSILE, GUIDED.

Crumb, George (Henry), 1929–, American composer; b. Charleston, W.Va. Crumb often incorporates mysterious voices and the sounds of such unconventional instruments as thumb pianos into his works, which include *Echoes of Time and the River* (1967; Pulitzer); *Ancient Voices of Children* (1970), one of several settings of GARCÍA LORCA's poems; and *Cosmic Dances for Amplified Piano* (1979).

Crusades, wars undertaken by European Christians between the 11th and 13th cent. to conquer the Holy Land from the Muslims. At the Council of Clermont (1095) Pope URBAN II exhorted Christendom to war, and the Crusaders took their name from the crosses distributed there. Religious motives dominated the Crusades at first, but worldly aims were never absent: The nobles hoped to capture land and loot; the Italian cities looked to expand trade with the Middle East. The **First Crusade,** 1095–99, was led by Raymond IV, count of Toulouse, GODFREY OF BOUILLON, BOHEMOND I, and TANCRED. Their victorious campaign was crowned by the conquest of Jerusalem (1099). The establishment of the Latin Kingdom of JERUSALEM and the orders of the KNIGHTS HOSPITALERS and the KNIGHTS TEMPLARS followed. The **Second Crusade,** 1147–49, preached by St. BERNARD OF CLAIRVAUX after the Christians lost EDESSA (1144) to the TURKS, ended in dismal failure. After SALADIN captured (1187) Jerusalem for Islam, the **Third Crusade,** 1189–92, led by Holy Roman Emperor FREDERICK I, PHILIP II of France, and RICHARD I of England, failed to recapture the city. A three-year truce, however, gave Christians access to Jerusalem. The **Fourth Crusade,** 1202–4, was diverted for the benefit of Venice, and the Crusaders seized Constantinople (see CONSTANTINOPLE, LATIN EMPIRE OF). In the pathetic **Children's Crusade** (1212), thousands of children set out for the Holy Land, only to be sold as slaves or to die of hunger or disease. The **Fifth Crusade,** 1217–21, was aimed at Egypt, but failed. The truce arranged with the Muslims by Holy

Roman Emperor FREDERICK II in the Sixth Crusade, 1228–29, was short-lived. Three later crusades in the 13th cent. failed to reverse the Muslim gains. In 1291 the last Christian stronghold of Akko (Acre) fell.

crustacean, invertebrate animal (class Crustacea), an ARTHROPOD. Primarily aquatic, they have bilaterally symmetrical segmented bodies covered by a chitinous exoskeleton that is periodically shed. In most, the head and thorax are fused as a cephalothorax and protected by a shield-like carapace. The head typically has two pairs of antennae, three pairs of biting mouthparts, and usually one medial and two lateral eyes. Thoracic appendages are often modified into claws and pincers with gills at their bases. Crustaceans include SHRIMP, CRAYFISH, LOBSTERS, CRABS, and BARNACLES.

Cruz, Juana Inés de la: see JUANA INÉS DE LA CRUZ.

Cruz, Ramón de la [krōōth], 1731–94, Spanish dramatist. His *sainetes,* 450 one-act comedies of middle- and lower-class life, freed Spanish drama from foreign influence.

cryogenics: see LOW-TEMPERATURE PHYSICS.

cryolite or **kryolite,** sodium and aluminum fluoride mineral (Na_3AlF_6), usually pure white or colorless but sometimes tinted pink, brown, or even black and having a waxy luster. Cryolite is used principally as a flux in the smelting of ALUMINUM, but it is also a source of soda, aluminum salts, fluorides, and hydrofluoric acid. Discovered (1794) in Greenland, it occurs almost nowhere else.

cryptography, science of translating messages into ciphers or codes. The science of breaking codes and ciphers without the key is called cryptanalysis. Cryptology is the science embracing both cryptography and cryptanalysis. The beginnings of cryptography can be traced to the HIEROGLYPHICS of early Egyptian civilization (c.1900 B.C.). Ciphering has always been considered vital for diplomatic and military secrecy. The widespread use of computers and data transmission in commerce and finance is making cryptography very important in these fields as well. Recent successes in applying certain aspects of computer science to cryptography seem to be leading to more versatile and more secure systems in which encryption is implemented with sophisticated digital electronics. Industry and the U.S. government, however, have argued over who will have ultimate control over data encryption and, as a result, over government access to encrypted private transmissions.

crystal, solid body bounded by natural plane faces that are the external expression of a regular internal arrangement of constituent atoms, molecules, or ions. The particles in a crystal occupy positions with definite geometrical relationships to each other, forming a kind of scaffolding called a crystalline lattice. On the basis of its chemistry and the arrangement of its atoms, a crystal falls into one of 32 classes; these in turn are grouped into seven systems according to the relationships of their axes. Differences in the physical properties of crystals sometimes determine the use to which they can be put in industry. See also QUASICRYSTAL.

Crystal Palace, building designed by Sir Joseph Paxton, erected at Hyde Park, London, for the Great Exhibition in 1851. It was removed to Sydenham and used as a museum until damaged by fire in 1936. The iron, glass, and wood structure greatly influenced late 19th-cent. architecture.

Cs, chemical symbol of the element CESIUM.

Cu, chemical symbol of the element COPPER.

Cuba, officially Republic of Cuba, republic (1992 est. pop. 10,847,000), 44,218 sq mi (114,524 sq km), in the Caribbean Sea, 90 mi (145 km) S of Florida. It consists of Cuba, the largest island in the WEST INDIES, and many small adjacent islands. Principal cities are HAVANA (the capital), CAMAGÜEY, SANTIAGO DE CUBA, and GUANTÁNAMO. The main island has three mountain regions, including the rugged Sierra Maestra in the east, but is predominantly level or gently rolling. The climate is subtropical. Coffee, rice, corn, citrus fruits, and an excellent tobacco are grown; nickel is mined; and there is a fishing industry. Some consumer goods, as well as chemicals and steel, are manufactured. However, despite all efforts to diversify the base, Cuba's economy remains overwhelmingly dependent on the growing of sugarcane and refining of sugar. The people are of Spanish, African, and mixed Spanish-African descent, and their language is Spanish. Roman Catholicism, the major religion, is tolerated by the regime, a one-party Marxist government dominated by its founder, Fidel CASTRO.

History. Christopher COLUMBUS discovered the island of Cuba in 1492, and Spain colonized it from 1511, using it as a base for New World exploration and as an assembly-point for its treasure fleets. Called the "Pearl of the Antilles," Cuba prospered in the 1600s and 1700s, its population swelled by immigrants from Spain and African slave laborers. When most of Spain's American possessions became independent republics in the early 1800s, Cuba remained a colony. Slavery, a major prop of the sugar-based economy, was not abolished until 1886. A TEN YEARS WAR for independence (1868–78) was inconclusive. In 1895 a new struggle, led by JOSÉ MARTÍ, culminated in the SPANISH-AMERICAN WAR and establishment of a Cuban republic in 1898. The new nation suffered recurrent periods of dictatorship during which reformist zeal gave way to corruption and repression, notably under Gerardo MACHADO (1925–33) and his successor, Fulgencio BATISTA Y ZALDÍVAR. After a long guerrilla campaign, Batista was supplanted by Fidel Castro on Jan. 1, 1959. Castro promised agrarian reform, and under his leadership the nation soon became the only Communist state in Latin America and a firm ally of the USSR. An unsuccessful U.S.-supported attempt by anti-Castro exiles to invade Cuba at the BAY OF PIGS in 1961 was followed in 1962 by a U.S.–Soviet confrontation sparked by Soviet introduction of offensive weapons onto the island (see CUBAN MISSILE CRISIS). The U.S. maintained a trade embargo against Cuba into the 1990s, provoked by Cuban support of revolutionary movements in Latin America and, later, in Africa. Domestically, Castro virtually wiped out illiteracy, but the economy required massive Soviet aid. The changes in Eastern Europe and collapse of the USSR have left Cuba isolated politically, while continued economic dependence on sugar and the U.S. embargo have hurt the economy. In 1993 the government authorized cooperatives on state farms and individual private enterprise on a limited basis.

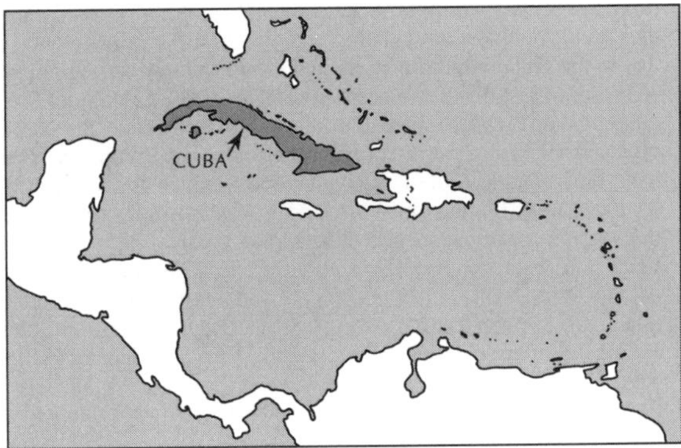

Cuban Missile Crisis, 1962, major COLD WAR confrontation between the U.S. and the Soviet Union. Following the BAY OF PIGS INVASION, the USSR secretly began building missile launching sites in Cuba. After the construction was detected by U.S. reconnaissance flights, U.S. Pres. KENNEDY demanded (Oct. 22) the withdrawal of the missiles, and imposed a naval blockade on Cuba. The Soviets agreed (Oct. 28) to dismantle the missile sites, and the crisis ended as suddenly as it had begun.

cubism, art movement, primarily in painting, that originated in Paris c.1907. In intellectual revolt against the sensual, emotional art of previous eras, the cubists used an analytical system in which three-dimensional subjects were fragmented and redefined from several different points of view simultaneously. Work from this analytic phase (1907–12), as by Pablo PICASSO and Georges BRAQUE, appealed to the intellect and has been termed conceptual realism because it shows objects as the mind, not the eye, perceives them. During the synthetic phase (1913 through the 1920s) works were composed of fewer and simpler forms, in brighter colors, and many artists introduced the *trompe l'oeil* effect of COLLAGE, as in the works of Juan GRIS. Other major exponents of cubism included Jean METZINGER, Marcel DUCHAMP, and Fernand LÉGER. Influenced also by African masks, Picasso's *Demoiselles d'Avignon* (1907; Mus. Mod. Art, N.Y.C.) contains much of the basic material of cubism.

cuckoo, BIRD of the family Cuculidae, widely distributed in temperate and tropical regions. Cuckoos are slender-bodied, long-tailed birds with down-curved bills, pointed wings, and dull plumage. Typical American cuckoos are the black-billed and yellow-billed cuckoos (*Coccyzus americanus*), known for their low, chuckling call notes. The roadrunner (*Geococcyx californianus*), a ground cuckoo of the southwest deserts, speeds over the ground at up to 15 mi (24.1 km) per hr.

cucumber, herbaceous vine (*Cucumis sativus*) of the GOURD family. Its greenish, generally cylindrical fruit is eaten fresh and pickled.

Cueva, Juan de la [kwā'vä], 1550?–1610?, Spanish dramatist. Of his 14 plays, the most famous is the comedy *The Scoundrel* (1581). By introducing national themes he laid the foundation for the drama of Spain's GOLDEN AGE.

Cui, César Antonovich [küē'], 1835–1918, Russian composer and critic. He was the nationalistic champion of The FIVE. Cui's best works were songs and short salon pieces.

Culbertson, Ely, 1893–1955, American authority on contract BRIDGE; b. Romania. A champion bridge player himself, he introduced the first successful system of bidding, wrote many books and a syndicated newspaper column on the game, and edited *Bridge World* magazine. After World War II, he wrote and lectured widely on world peace.

Cullen, Countee, 1903–46, African-American poet; b. N.Y.C. A major figure of the HARLEM RENAISSANCE of the 1920s, he applied traditional verse forms to African-American themes. His books of poetry include *Color* (1925) and *Copper Sun* (1927).

cult, ritual worship of the supernatural or its symbolic representations. It is often associated with a particular deity; for example, a cult of the ancient Middle East was that of the GREAT MOTHER OF THE GODS. The term is now often used to refer to contemporary religious groups whose beliefs and practices depart from the conventional norms of society. These groups vary widely in doctrine, leadership, and ritual, but most stress direct experience of the divine and duties to the cult community. Cults tend to proliferate during periods of social unrest; most are transient and peripheral. Many of those emerging in the U.S. since the late 1960s have been marked by renewed interest in MYSTICISM and Asian religions, but many others have had Christian roots. Such major U.S. cults as the Rev. Sun Myung MOON's Unification Church and HARE KRISHNA, a movement derived from Hinduism, have stirred wide controversy. Cults' insularity and distrust of society sometimes lead to violent conflicts with the law. In 1978, in Jonestown, Guyana, followers of Jim Jones killed a U.S. Congressman who was investigating Jones and then Jones and more than 900 others committed mass suicide. In 1993 a gunfight near Waco, Tex., between federal officers and David Koresh and his followers led to a 51-day siege that ended in a blaze that left Koresh and 82 people dead.

Cultural Revolution (1966–69), mass campaign in CHINA begun by MAO ZEDONG to revitalize the nation's revolutionary fervor and renew its basic institutions. Allied with the army, revolutionary Red Guards recruited from the youth attacked so-called bourgeois elements in cultural circles and in the bureaucracy. Lin Biao and JIANG QING were other leaders of the movement, which resulted in widespread disorder and violence. The revolution led to the fall of LIU SHAOQI and many other Communist party officials.

Cumans or **Kumans,** nomadic East Turkic people. Coming from NW Russia, they conquered S Russia and Walachia in the 11th cent. From their state along the Black Sea they traded with E Asia and Venice. After their defeat by the MONGOLS (13th cent.) many Cumans fled to Bulgaria and Hungary, and others joined the Empire of the GOLDEN HORDE.

Cumberland Gap, mountain pass through the Cumberland Mts. of the Appalachians, near Middlesboro, Ky., discovered in 1750 by Dr. Thomas Walker. Daniel BOONE's WILDERNESS ROAD to the "Old West" ran through the gap, and it was an important military objective of both sides in the CIVIL WAR. The pass was designated a national historical park in 1940.

cumin or **cummin,** low annual herb (*Cuminum cyminum*) of the CARROT family, long cultivated in the Old World for the aromatic, seedlike fruits. Cumin is an ingredient of curry powder. It yields an oil used in liqueurs and veterinary medicines. Related to the CARAWAY, cumin has similar uses in cooking.

cummings, e e (Edward Estlin Cummings), 1894–1962; b. Cambridge, Mass. His lyrical verse, eccentric in typography and language, is included in such volumes as *Tulips and Chimneys* (1923), *Is 5* (1926), and *95 Poems* (1958). *The Enormous Room* (1922) is an exceptional prose account of his World War I internment in France.

cuneiform [Lat., = wedge-shaped], system of writing developed before the last centuries of the 4th millennium B.C. in the lower Tigris and Euphrates valley, probably by the Sumerians. The characters consist of arrangements of wedge-like strokes, generally on clay tablets. The history of the script is strikingly like that of the Egyptian HIEROGLYPHIC (see also ALPHABET). Normal Babylonian and Assyrian writing used from 300 to 600 arbitrary cuneiform symbols for words and syllables, some originally pictographic. There was also an alphabetic system that made it possible to spell out a word, but because of the adaptation from Sumerian, a different language, there were many ambiguities. Cuneiform writing was used outside Mesopotamia, notably in ELAM and by the HITTITES, but was not common after the Persian conquest of Babylonia (539 B.C.). A late use was that of the ACHAEMENIDS of Persia (mid-6th–4th cent. B.C.). H.C. RAWLINSON and G.F. GROTEFEND were noted cuneiform scholars.

pictograph original	pictograph as positioned in later cuneiform	early Babylonian cuneiform	Assyrian	meaning
				heaven god
				earth
				woman
				to drink
				fish
				sun day
				donkey
				orchard
				to plow to till

Examples of the development of cuneiform

Cunningham, Merce, 1919–, American dancer and choreographer; b. Centralia, Wash. He studied and performed (1940–55) with Martha GRAHAM before forming (1953) his own company. He creates dances to the music of such avant-garde composers as John CAGE, e.g., *Sixteen Dances for Soloist and Company of Three* (1951) and *Squaregame* (1976).

Cunobelinus: see CYMBELINE.

Cuomo, Mario M(atthew), 1932–, U.S. politician; b. N.Y.C. Admitted (1956) to the New York bar, he attracted attention after he successfully mediated (1972) a local housing dispute. A Democrat, he was New York's secretary of state (1975–79), lieutenant governor (1979–83), and governor (1983–). He has supported social service program innovations and improvements in the state's infrastructure and environment and been an opponent of capital punishment. He is an often impressive orator.

Cupid: see EROS.

Curaçao [kyŏŏ'rəsō], island (1989 est. pop. 146,000), 178 sq mi (461 sq km), in the NETHERLANDS ANTILLES. Willemstad is the capital of the island group. Its refineries, among the world's largest, process oil from nearby Venezuela. Visited by Europeans in 1499, it was colonized (1527) by the Spanish and captured (1634) by the Dutch. Many Africans were imported as slaves.

curare, any of several ALKALOID plant extracts originally used as arrow poisons by indigenous South American peoples. Curare produces paralysis by interfering with the transmission of nerve impulses in skeletal muscle. Curare is also now used medically as an adjunct to general anesthesia and in diagnosing myasthenia gravis.

Curia Regis: see PARLIAMENT.

Curie, family of French scientists. **Pierre Curie,** 1859–1906, scientist, and his wife, **Marie Sklodowska Curie,** 1867–1934, chemist and physicist, b. Poland, married 1895, are known for their work on radioactivity and on radium. Pierre discovered (1883) and, with his brother Jacques, investigated piezoelectricity (a form of electric polarity) in crystals. Following Antoine BECQUEREL's discovery of RADIOACTIVITY, Marie began to study URANIUM, a radioactive element found in pitchblende. Together, the Curies discovered POLONIUM and RADIUM and determined their atomic weights and properties. For their work on radioactivity, they shared with Becquerel the 1903 Nobel Prize in physics. Marie Curie became the first person to be awarded a second Nobel Prize when she received the 1911 chemistry prize for the discovery of polonium and radium. The French scientists **Frédéric Joliot-Curie,** 1900–1958, formerly Frédéric Joliot, and **Irène Joliot-Curie,** 1897–1956, daughter of Pierre and Marie Curie, were married in 1926. They received the 1935 Nobel Prize in chemistry for artificially producing radioactive substances by bombarding elements with alpha particles. The Joliot-Curies investigated (1940) the chain reaction in nuclear fission. In 1946 they helped to organize the French atomic energy commission, of which Frédéric was the first chairman (1946–50).

Curitiba, city (1990 est. pop. 1,399,000), SE Brazil, capital of Paraná state. It handles the products of an expanding agricultural and ranching area through the Atlantic port of Paranaguá, c.70 mi (110 km) away. Founded in 1654, the city became important when immigrants developed the Paraná hinterland from the late 19th cent. The city has grown rapidly since 1950.

curium (Cm), synthetic element, first produced by alpha-particle bombardment of plutonium-239 by Glenn SEABORG and colleagues in 1944. It is a silvery metal and a very radioactive element in the ACTINIDE SERIES. Curium accumulates in bones and disrupts red blood cells. See ELEMENT (table); PERIODIC TABLE.

curlew, large shore BIRD (genus *Numenius*) of both hemispheres, usually brown and buff in color with a downcurved bill. The long-billed curlew (*N. americanus*) is found in the West.

currant, northern shrub (genus *Ribes*) of the SAXIFRAGE family. The gooseberry bush belongs to the same genus. The tart black, white, or red currant berries and the purple gooseberries are both eaten fresh or used in preserves, sauces, and pies. Dried currants were used by Native Americans in making pemmican, a travel food. Today's commercial "dried currant" is a raisin. Because gooseberries and currants are a host to blister RUST, their cultivation is discouraged.

currency: see MONEY.

Currier & Ives, American lithographers and publishers who produced highly popular hand-colored prints of 19th-cent. scenes and events in American life. **Nathaniel Currier,** 1813–88, b. Roxbury, Mass., founded the business (1835) in New York City and formed (1857) a partnership with the artist and businessman **James Merritt Ives,** 1824–95, b. N.Y.C. The business closed in 1907.

Curtis, Charles, 1860–1936, vice president of the U.S. (1929–33); b. near North Topeka, Kans. Of part Native American ancestry, Curtis was a U.S. congressman from Kansas (1892–1906). A Republican, he championed Native American rights and supported farm and veterans' benefits. He was a U.S. senator (1907–13, 1915–29) before serving as Herbert HOOVER's vice president.

Curtis, Cyrus Hermann Kotzschmar, 1850–1933, American publisher; b. Portland, Me. After starting the *Ladies' Home Journal* (1883), he founded (1890) the Curtis Publishing Company and built up a national reputation with the *Saturday Evening Post* and *Country Gentleman.* He also owned several newspapers and was a great philanthropist.

Curtiss, Glenn Hammond, 1878–1930, American inventor and aviation pioneer; b. Hammondsport, N.Y. He made (1908) the first public flights in the U.S., established (1909) the first U.S. flying school, and made (1910) a spectacular flight from Albany to New York City. He invented (1911) ailerons (see AIRFOIL) and after World War I made radical improvements in the design of planes and motors.

curve, in mathematics, the path of a point moving in space. In ANALYTIC GEOMETRY a plane curve, i.e., a curve that lies in one plane, is usually considered as the graph of an equation or function (for some examples, see CONIC SECTION). A skew, twisted, or space curve is one that does not lie all in one plane, e.g., the helix, a curve having the shape of a wire spring.

Cush, ancient kingdom of NUBIA, in what is now SUDAN. It flourished from the 11th cent. B.C. to the 4th cent. A.D. and in the 8th cent. B.C. included Egypt in its domain. Meroë, its capital, was overrun by the Ethiopians in the 4th cent., and the kingdom came to an end.

Cushing, Harvey Williams, 1869–1939, American neurosurgeon; b. Cleveland. A noted brain surgeon and a teacher at Johns Hopkins, Harvard, and Yale, he won a 1925 Pulitzer Prize for his biography of Sir William Osler. **Cushing's disease,** first described by him, is caused by hyperactivity of the cortex of the adrenal glands and affects more women than men. Symptoms include obesity, hypertension, hirsutism, and easy bruisability. Treatment is by removal of one or both adrenal glands, or, if the pituitary body is involved, by X-ray therapy or surgery.

Cushitic [kəshĭt'ĭk], group of languages belonging to the Hamitic subfamily of the HAMITO-SEMITIC family of languages. See LANGUAGE (table).

Custer, George Armstrong, 1839–76, U.S. Army officer; b. New Rumley, Ohio. He compiled an extraordinary record in the CIVIL WAR and became (1863) the youngest general in the Union army. Later he commanded the 7th Cavalry. During a campaign against the SIOUX in 1876, Custer and an entire detachment of over 200 were killed by Native Americans on the LITTLE BIGHORN R. His spectacular death made him a popular but controversial hero.

customs duty: see TARIFF.

cuttlefish, CEPHALOPOD mollusk that has 10 tentacles, 8 bearing muscular suction cups on their inner surface and 2 longer ones for grasping prey. The cuttlefish has a reduced internal shell embedded in the mantle; in some there is a degenerate internal shell of lime called cuttlebone. The body is short, broad, and flattened with lateral fins, similar to the SQUID. When disturbed, cuttlefish eject a dark ink, which hides them from predators.

Cuvier, Georges Léopold Chrétien Frédéric Dagobert, Baron [küvyā'], 1769–1832, French naturalist. A pioneer in comparative anatomy, he originated a system of zoological classification based on structural differences of the skeleton and organs. His reconstruction of the soft parts of fossils deduced from their skeletal remains greatly advanced paleontology, and he identified and named the flying reptile pterodactyl. He rejected evolutionary theory in favor of CATASTROPHISM.

Cuvilliès, François de [küvēyĕs'], 1695–1768, French architect, decorator, and engraver. He introduced French ROCOCO decoration into Germany. His Residenz-Theater (1751–53) and Amalienburg pavilion, in the park of Nymphenburg, both at Munich, represent the apex of German rococo decoration.

Cuyp or **Kuyp** [both: koip], family of Dutch painters. **Jacob Gerritszoon Cuyp,** 1594–c.1651, was a portrait and landscape painter. His stepbrother, **Benjamin Cuyp,** 1616–52, painted figures and peasant scenes in the style of REMBRANDT. Jacob's son, **Aelbert Cuyp,** 1620–91, was one of the foremost Dutch landscapists. He is famous for his simple but richly colored pastoral scenes; among the best are *Piper with Cows* and *Promenade* (both: Louvre), and *Horseman and Cows in a Meadow* (National Gall., London).

Cuza, Alexander John, or **Alexander John I,** 1820–73, first prince of ROMANIA (1859–66). He integrated Moldavia and Walachia, thereby creating Romania. He emancipated the serfs (1864) and instituted other important reforms. He was forced to abdicate in 1866.

Cuzco or **Cusco,** city (1993 pop. 257,751), S Peru, capital of Cuzco dept. It is an agricultural trading center and has woolen mills. Said to have been founded by MANCO CAPAC, it was the capital of the INCA empire, with massive, gold-decorated palaces and temples. After it was plundered by Francisco PIZARRO in 1533, the Spaniards raised a colonial city within the old walls, many of which remain visible. The city was devastated by an earthquake in 1950, but most of the historic buildings have been restored. The ruins of an Inca fortress are nearby.

cyanide, salt or ester of hydrogen cyanide (HCN) formed by replacing the hydrogen with a metal or a radical. The most common and widely used (those of sodium and potassium) are employed as insecticides, in making pigments, in metallurgy, and in gold and silver refining. Most cyanides are deadly poisons that cause respiratory failure. Symptoms include a breath odor of bitter almonds, dizziness, convulsions, collapse, and, often, froth on the mouth.

cyanobacteria: see BLUE-GREEN ALGAE.

Cyaxares [sīăk'sərēz], d. 585 B.C., king of MEDIA (c.625–585 B.C.). He made the kingdom of the Medes a major power in the Middle East. In 612 B.C. Cyaxares took NINEVEH and completely defeated the Assyrians by 605 B.C.

Cybele, in ancient Asiatic religion, GREAT MOTHER OF THE GODS. The chief centers of her early worship were Phrygia and Lydia. In the 5th cent. B.C. her cult spread to Greece and later to Rome. She was primarily a nature goddess, responsible for maintaining and reproducing the wild things of the earth. Her annual spring festival celebrated the death and resurrection of her beloved Attis, a vegetation god.

cybernetics, term coined by Norbert WIENER to refer to the general analysis of control systems and communication systems in living organisms and machines. Analogies are drawn between the functioning of the brain and nervous system and that of the COMPUTER and other electronic systems (see NEURAL NETWORK). Cybernetics overlaps the fields of AUTOMATION, computing machinery, INFORMATION THEORY, and neurophysiology.

cycad, palmlike plant of a division (Cycadophyta) of mostly tropical and subtropical cone-bearing evergreens. Cycads, known from the Permian period, are the most primitive of the living SEED-bearing plants. Some have tuberous, underground stems and crowns of leathery, glossy, fernlike leaves arising from ground level; others have high, columnar stems. Some cycads, e.g., the fern palm of the Old World tropics and the Australian nut palm, bear edible, nutlike fruits. Florida ARROWROOT, or sago, is a starch from the pith of the coontie, or sago palm (*Zamia floridens*).

Cyclades, island group (1991 pop. 95,083), c.1,000 sq mi (2,590 sq km), SE Greece, in the Aegean Sea. It includes about 220 islands, the most important of which are Tínos, Ándros, Mílos, Náxos, Kéa, and Páros. Largely mountainous, the islands are agricultural areas and tourist centers; there is some mining and quarrying. In 1829 they passed from the OTTOMAN EMPIRE to Greece.

Cycladic art [sĭklăd'ĭk], BRONZE AGE art of the central Aegean Cycladic islands. Early tomb remains include jugs, pots, and bowls decorated in geometric designs, as well as marble female fertility figures. These are frontal and geometric in style. Figures of musicians have also been found. Considerable Minoan (see MINOAN CIVILIZATION) influence is seen in the pottery of the 17th cent. B.C. found at Phylakopi in Melos.

cyclamate: see SWEETENERS, ARTIFICIAL.

cyclamen: see PRIMROSE.

cyclone, region, often called a "low," of low central atmospheric pressure relative to the surrounding pressure. The resulting pressure gradient, combined with the CORIOLIS EFFECT, causes air to circulate about the center, or core, in a counterclockwise direction north of the equator and a clockwise direction south of it. The frictional drag on near-surface air moving over land or water causes it to spiral inward toward lower pressures; this movement is compensated for near the center by rising currents, which are cooled by expansion when they reach the lower pressures of higher altitudes. The cooling, in turn, characteristically increases the relative HUMIDITY greatly and produces cloudiness. Tropical cyclones, which form over warm tropical waters, can reach a severe intensity, becoming HURRICANES. An **anticyclone** has the opposite characteristics: a "high," or region of high central pressure relative to the surrounding pressure; clockwise circulation north of the equator and counterclockwise circulation south of it; descending and diverging air that is warmed by compression as it encounters higher pressure at lower altitudes; and characteristic low humidity and little cloudiness. Both cyclones and anticyclones move across the land at speeds of 500 to 1,000 mi/day (800 to 1,600 km/day). The term *cyclone* is also sometimes used for a TORNADO.

Cyclops, plural **Cyclopes** [sīklō'pēz], in Greek mythology, immense one-eyed beings. According to HESIOD, they were smiths, sons of URANUS and GAEA, who gave ZEUS the lightning bolts that helped him defeat CRONUS. In HOMER, they were a barbarous people, one of whom (POLYPHEMUS) was encountered by ODYSSEUS in his wanderings.

cyclotron: see PARTICLE ACCELERATOR.

cymbals: see PERCUSSION INSTRUMENT.

Cymbeline or **Cunobelinus,** d. A.D. c.40, British king. His conquest of the Trinovantes (of Essex) made him the wealthiest and most powerful ruler in SE England. Cymbeline gives his name, and little else, to SHAKESPEARE's play.

Cynewulf [kĭn'əwo͝olf], fl. early 9th cent. Anglo-Saxon religious poet to whom are ascribed four didactic poems: *Juliana, The Ascension, Elene,* and *The Fates of the Apostles.*

cypress, common name for the Cupressaceae, a widely distributed family of coniferous shrubs and trees, some yielding valuable timber. Chief among them are the JUNIPER, the ARBORVITAE, and the true cypresses. The latter, found in S Europe, E Asia, and W North America, are resinous evergreens with a fragrant, durable wood and scalelike leaves and include the Monterey cypress (*Cupressus macrocarpa*), native to the region around Monterey Bay, Calif., but widely cultivated. American trees of the genus *Chamaecyparis,* also called cypresses, comprise some important timber trees, e.g., the Lawson cypress, or Port Oxford cedar (*C. lawsoniana*). The lumber called cypress in the S U.S. is mainly from BALD CYPRESS trees.

Cyprian, Saint, 200?–258, Father of the Church, bishop of CARTHAGE (c.248). He supported the papal view that Christians who had apostasized under persecution should be readmitted to the church. He was martyred in the persecution of the Roman emperor Valerian. Feast: Sept. 16.

Cyprus, Gr. *Kypros,* officially Republic of Cyprus, republic (1992 est. pop. 716,000), 3,578 sq mi (9,267 sq km), an island in the E Mediterranean Sea, c.40 mi (60 km) S of Turkey. The capital is NICOSIA. Since 1974 the nation has been divided into Turkish (in the north) and Greek (in the south) sectors. Two mountain ranges traverse the island from east to west; the highest peak is Mt. Olympus (6,406 ft/1,953 m), in the southwest. Between the ranges lies a wide plain, where grapes (used for wine), cereals, olives, tobacco, and cotton are grown. Fishing, tourism, and the raising of livestock are also important. Copper, pyrites, asbestos, and gypsum are the chief mineral resource. Manufactures include paper, chemicals, textiles, and refined petroleum. Nearly 80% of the population is Greek and Orthodox Christian, and about 18% is Turkish and Muslim. Greek, Turkish, and English are spoken.

History. Excavations have revealed the existence of a Neolithic culture on Cyprus from 4000 to 3000 B.C. Influenced by the Middle East and, after 1500 B.C., by Greece, Cyprus fell to a succession of rulers, including Assyria, Egypt, Persia, and Rome. After eight centuries (from A.D. 395) of Byzantine control, it was conquered (1191) by RICHARD I of England, who bestowed it on the French Lusignan dynasty. Annexed (1489) by VENICE and conquered (1571) by the Turks (see OTTOMAN EMPIRE), it came under British administration in 1878 and was annexed outright by Britain in 1914. The movements among Greek Cypriots for self-rule and union *(enosis)* with GREECE were a source of constant tension, erupting in 1955

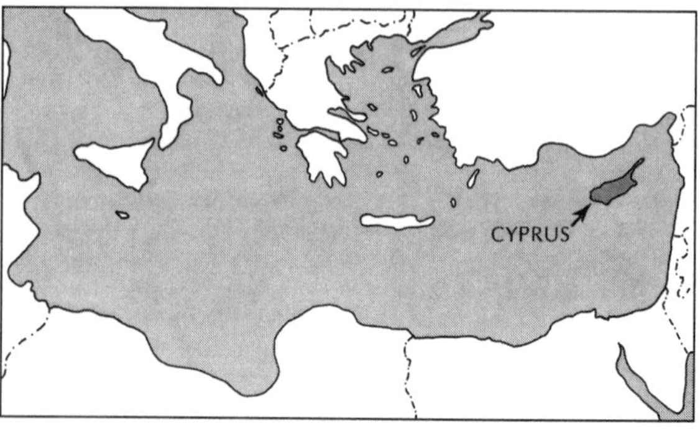

into violence that was tantamount to civil war. The conflict was aggravated by Turkish support of Turkish Cypriot demands for partition of the island. In 1959, a settlement, precluding both *enosis* and partition, provided for independence in 1960, and MAKARIOS III, leader of the Greek Cypriot nationalists, was elected president. The British retained two sovereign military enclaves, Akrotiri and Dhekelia. Large-scale fighting continued, however, and a UN peace-keeping force was sent to Cyprus in 1965. In 1974 the national guard, dominated by Greek army officers, overthrew the Makarios regime. Citing its responsibility to protect the Turkish Cypriot community, Turkey invaded Cyprus and established a Turkish state in the northern two fifths of the island. Since that time Cyprus has been a divided nation, with a self-governing Turkish community in the north and a Greek community in the south. In 1983 the Turkish state, headed by Rauf Denktash, declared itself independent as the Turkish Republic of Northern Cyprus, but it has only been recognized by Turkey. In 1993 Glafcos Clerides, a conservative, was elected president of Cyprus. Negotiations to end the division of the country have been unsuccessful.

Cyrene [sīrē'nē], ancient city near the northern coast of Africa, in Cyrenaica (now E Libya). A Greek colony (7th cent. B.C.), it was a city-state with much commerce with Greece and some development of art. Cyrene became powerful over other cities and held nominal independence until the marriage of Berenice (d. 221? B.C.) to PTOLEMY III of Egypt. It was later the center of a Roman province. The Roman emperor TRAJAN's punishment of Cyrene because of Jewish uprisings led to its decline.

Cyril and Methodius, Saints, d. 869 and 884 respectively, Greek missionaries, brothers, called Apostles to the Slavs and fathers of Slavonic literature. Sent (863) to MORAVIA, they won papal approval for the use of Slavonic in church liturgy. The **Cyrillic alphabet,** used in Russia and elsewhere, is named for St. Cyril but was probably the work of his followers. Feast: Feb. 14.

Cyrus the Great, d. 529 B.C., king of Persia, founder of ACHAEMENID power and the Persian empire. He conquered MEDIA between 559 and 549 B.C., Lydia (see CROESUS) in 546, and BABYLONIA in 538. In EGYPT he laid the basis for future Persian victories. Because he placed Jews in power in PALESTINE, creating a buffer state between Persia and Egypt, he is spoken of approvingly in the Old Testament, e.g., Dan. 6.28. He respected the religion and customs of each part of his empire.

Cyrus the Younger, d. 401 B.C., Persian prince, younger son of DARIUS II and Parysatis. His mother obtained several satrapies for him in Asia Minor when he was very young. In the PELOPONNESIAN WAR he helped LYSANDER to build a victorious fleet. When Darius died (404 B.C.) Cyrus was accused of a plot to kill his elder brother, the heir, ARTAXERXES II. Saved by his mother, he raised an army to overthrow Artaxerxes but died in battle. XENOPHON's *Anabasis* describes the revolt.

cystic fibrosis, inherited disorder of the exocrine GLANDS, affecting infants and children. It is caused by an abnormal gene that disrupts chloride transfer in and out of cells. Normally, chloride movement pulls water from the tissues. Without the water, mucus in the exocrine glands becomes thick and sticky and eventually blocks the ducts of these glands (especially the pancreas, lungs, and liver). Symptoms include a distended abdomen, diarrhea, malnutrition, and repeated incidence of respiratory infections. Treatment consists of a low-fat, high-protein diet, VITAMINS, pancreatin, and ANTIBIOTICS to ward off infection; dornase alfa (Pulmozyme) can help break up the mucus.

cytochrome, any of a class of heme-containing proteins, present in the mitochondria of plant and animal cells, that play a vital role in cellular RESPIRATION, by alternately accepting and donating electrons (as hydride ions) in oxidation reactions.

cytology, in biology, the study of the structure of all normal and abnormal components of cells and the changes, movements, and transformations of such components, using light, phase, interference, confocal, and electron microscopes.

Czech language [chěk], in the past sometimes also called Bohemian, member of the West Slavic group of the Slavic subfamily of the Indo-European family of languages. See LANGUAGE (table).

Czech Legion, in WORLD WAR I, a military force of c.40,000 to 50,000, mostly Czechs and Slovak Russians, who fought for Russia. After Russia left the war, the legion was evacuated via the Trans-Siberian RR. They did some fighting for the anti-Bolsheviks in the Russian civil war.

Czechoslovakia, former nation (1918–39, 1945–92), central Europe, divided since 1993 into the CZECH REPUBLIC and SLOVAKIA. Czechoslovakia emerged in 1918 from the ruins of the AUSTRO-HUNGARIAN MONARCHY as an independent republic comprising the Czech lands of BOHEMIA and MORAVIA, part of SILESIA, Slovakia, and, before World War II, RUTHENIA. It was largely the creation of its first and second presidents, Thomas Garrigue MASARYK and Eduard BENEŠ. Economically the most favored of the Hapsburg successor states, it also benefited from a liberal, democratic constitution (1920) and able leadership. Its weakness lay in the disaffection of the German and Magyar (Hungarian) minorities and agitation for autonomy in Slovakia. Vehemently backed by HITLER, the German nationalist minority demanded union with Germany. Faced with the threat of war, the West pursued a policy of appeasement and signed (1938) the MUNICH PACT, by which Germany obtained the Bohemian borderlands (Sudetenland). The truncated state was dissolved in 1939, when Germany made Bohemia and Moravia a "protectorate," Slovakia gained nominal independence, and Ruthenia was awarded to HUNGARY. After liberation by U.S. and Soviet forces at the end of WORLD WAR II, Czechoslovakia was restored to its pre-Munich status (except for Ruthenia, which was ceded to the USSR and became part of Ukraine) and the German population was expelled. A Communist-dominated coalition government ruled until 1949, when the Communists gained control and established a Soviet-style state. A trend toward liberalization, begun in 1963, reached its climax in 1968 with the installation of reformers Alexander DUBČEK as party leader and Ludvik Svoboda as president. In August the USSR with its Warsaw Pact allies invaded Czechoslovakia, forcing the repeal of most of the reforms and replacing Dubček with the staunchly pro-Soviet Gustav HUSÁK, who reestablished a repressive Communist dictatorship. With the Mikhail GORBACHEV's liberalization of Soviet society, and as other Eastern European Communist governments collapsed, Czechoslovakia became (1989) the scene of antigovernment demonstrations. Dissident groups formed Civic Forum which, in Dec. 1989, successfully negotiated the establishment of a multiparty government. Pres. Husák resigned, and the parliament elected the playwright Václav HAVEL, chief spokesman of Civic Forum, president. In free elections in 1990 Civic Forum won a parliamentary majority. Subsequent economic reforms were especially disruptive in Slovakia, which had a disproportionate share of subsidized state-owned heavy industry. In the 1992 parliamentary elections ethnically based parties with conflicting positions on economic and political reform triumphed in the Czech lands and Slovakia, leading to an impasse at the federal level and breakup into two separate nations, the Czech Republic and Slovakia, on Jan. 1, 1993.

Czech Republic, Czech *Česká Republika,* republic (1993 est. pop. 10,300,000), 30,443 sq mi (78,847 sq km), central Europe; bordered by Poland (N), Germany (N and W), Austria (S), and Slovakia (E). Major cities include PRAGUE (the capital), BRNO, Ostrava, Plzeň (Pilsen), and Olomouc. The republic comprises the traditional Czech lands of Bohemia and Moravia and Czech Silesia. The two main geographic regions are the Bohemian plateau (W) and the Moravian lowland (E). The Sudetes Mts. in the north separate Moravia from Czech Silesia. The country is landlocked, and the chief rivers—the ELBE, Vltava (Moldau), and Oder—are economically important. The Czech Republic is highly industrialized; major manufactures include machinery and machine tools, automobiles, metalworking, iron and steel, chemicals, electronic equipment, textiles, and footwear. Coal, lignite, and pitchblende are the main minerals. Major crops include sugar beets, potatoes, and grains. The population is largely Slavic, consisting chiefly of Czechs (81%) and Moravians (13%). Roman Catholicism is the largest religion, but there are sizable Protestant (notably HUSSITE) groups. Czech is the official language.

History. For the earlier history of the area see BOHEMIA and MORAVIA. In 1918 CZECHOSLOVAKIA emerged from the ruins of the AUSTRO-HUNGARIAN MONARCHY as an independent republic, created by uniting the Czech lands with Slovakia, inhabited by the closely related Slovaks. From the beginning, however, the minority Slovaks, who had different cultural, religious, and social traditions, sought autonomy in the highly centralized state. In 1939 the Czech lands fell under Hitler's control, and Slovakia became a German puppet state. After World War II, Czechoslovakia was reestablished, but Slovak resentment of Czech dominance persisted under Communist rule. In 1969 Czechoslovakia became, at least officially, a federal state when the Czech and Slovak socialist republics were established. With the end of Communist rule in 1990, economic reforms were begun that were especially disruptive in Slovakia, which had a disproportionate share of subsidized state-owned heavy industry. In the 1992 parliamentary elections ethnically based parties with conflicting positions on economic and political reform triumphed in the Czech lands and Slovakia, leading to an impasse at the federal level and movement toward breakup into two separate nations. Václav Klaus, prime minister of the Czech Republic, insisted on independence, rather than autonomy, for poorer Slovakia, in part to assure institution of his free-market economic program. On Jan. 1, 1993, Czechoslovakia was dissolved and the Czech Republic established. Václav HAVEL was elected (1993) its first president. The new republic quickly moved to privatize state industries.

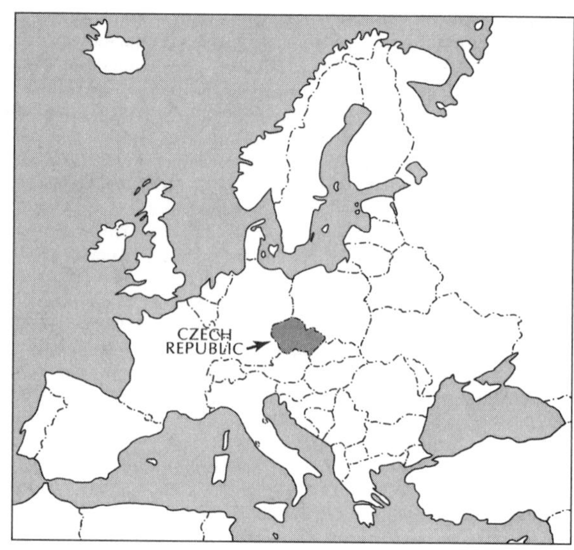

Czerny, Karl [chĕr'nē], 1791–1857, Austrian pianist. The teacher of LISZT, he is known for his technical studies for the piano.

D

Dacca: see DHAKA.

Dachau, Germany: see CONCENTRATION CAMP.

dachshund, small, short-legged HOUND; shoulder height, 5–9 in. (13–25 cm); weight, 5–20 lb (2–9 kg). It is black or chocolate with tan, or solid red. There are six varieties: smooth-haired, long-haired, wirehaired, and miniatures of each. The breed was developed in Germany over hundreds of years to hunt badgers.

Dacia, ancient region roughly corresponding to Romania, whose people were called Getae by the Greeks, Daci by the Romans. They had an advanced material culture. DOMITIAN tried to subdue them but ended by paying them tribute (A.D. 90). Under TRAJAN, Dacia became (A.D. 105) a Roman province, but AURELIAN lost it to the invading Goths (A.D. 250–70). The Roman legacy to Dacia was the Romance tongue Romanian.

Dacko, David, 1930–, president of the CENTRAL AFRICAN REPUBLIC (1960–66, 1979–81). A leader in the independence movement in French Equatorial Africa, he became the first president of the newly independent Central African Republic. He was toppled from power in 1966 by J.-B. BOKASSA but reinstated in a 1979 coup. Reelected president, he was overthrown by a military junta in 1981.

Dacron: see SYNTHETIC TEXTILE FIBERS.

Dada or **Dadaism,** international nihilistic movement among European artists and writers, 1916–22. It originated in Zürich with the French poet Tristan Tzara and stressed absurdity and the role of the unpredictable in artistic creation. Carried to New York by Jean ARP, Max ERNST, and Marcel DUCHAMP, these principles were eventually modified to become the basis of SURREALISM. Duchamp's celebrated *Mona Lisa* adorned with mustache and goatee and George GROSZ's caricatures are characteristic Dadaist works. The literary manifestations of Dada were mostly nonsense poems—meaningless and random word combinations.

daddy longlegs or **harvestman,** an ARACHNID with long slender legs, related to the SPIDERS. It has eight legs extending from a rounded or oval body. The daddy longlegs is omnivorous, feeding on plant fluids, animal tissue, and other daddy longlegs. The unrelated long-legged crane fly (an INSECT) is also called daddy longlegs.

Daedalus [dĕd'ələs], in Greek mythology, craftsman and inventor. He built the MINOTAUR's labyrinth in Crete. When King MINOS refused to let him leave, Daedalus built wax and feather wings for himself and his son Icarus. They flew away, but when Icarus came too close to the sun, his wings melted and he fell to his death. Daedalus escaped to Sicily.

daffodil: see NARCISSUS.

Daguerre, Louis Jacques Mandé [dägâr'], 1789–1851, French scene painter and physicist, inventor of the daguerreotype. Known first for his illusionistic stage sets, he was also the inventor, with C.M. Bouton, of the diorama (pictorial views seen with changing lighting). The daguerreotype, a photograph produced on a silver-coated copperplate treated with iodine vapor, was developed with J. Nicéphore NIÉPCE and ceded to the Academy of Sciences in 1839.

dahlia, tuberous-rooted, perennial plant (genus *Dahlia*) of the COMPOSITE family, native to Guatemala and Mexico, and widely cultivated. Most of the thousands of horticultural varieties are developed from one species (*D. pinnata*), the garden dahlia. Dahlias are stout, woody plants with colorful, late-blooming flowers. The tubers of the garden dahlia are a source of fructose used by diabetics.

Dahomey: see BENIN.

Daimler, Gottlieb [dām'lər], 1834–1900, German engineer, inventor, and pioneer AUTOMOBILE manufacturer. His construction (1885) of the first high-speed INTERNAL-COMBUSTION ENGINE led to the development of the automobile industry.

dairying, industry concerned with producing, processing, and distributing MILK and milk products. Ninety percent of the world's milk comes from CATTLE; the rest comes from GOATS, BUFFALO, SHEEP, REINDEER, YAKS, and other ruminants. About one third of the milk is used for BUTTER, an almost equal amount for market milk, and the rest for farm uses and the making of CHEESE, concentrated milks, ice cream, and such by-products as dried milk solids (e.g., LACTOSE and CASEIN). The rise of modern, large-scale dairying paralleled the growth of urban populations and was stimulated by the invention of the cream separator and other specialized machines, the discovery of PASTEURIZATION, and the study of cattle breeding.

daisy, name for several common wild flowers of the COMPOSITE family. The true, or English, daisy (*Bellis perennis*) is cultivated in the U.S.; its white, pink, or red flowers close at night. Other species include the purple Western daisy (*Astranthum* or *B. integrifolium*); and the common, white, or oxeye daisy of the U.S. (*Chrysanthemum leucanthemum*). Other plants called daisy include the yellow daisy, or BLACK-EYED SUSAN; the Michaelmas daisy, an ASTER; the Paris daisy, one of the plants also called marguerite; and the seaside daisy and daisy fleabane, which are fleabane species (genus *Erigeron*).

Dakar, largest city (1988 pop. 1,447,642) and capital of Senegal, on Cape Verde Peninsula, on the Atlantic Ocean. It is an economic center for a market-gardening region, and its expanding industries produce food products, fertilizers, cement, and textiles. The city is the busiest port in W Africa, also serving Mali and Mauritania, and is linked by rail and air with other Senegalese cities. Dakar became the capital of FRENCH WEST AFRICA in 1902 and was occupied by U.S. forces in World War II. The modern city is an educational and cultural center.

Dakota: see SIOUX.

Daladier, Édouard [dälädyā'], 1884–1970, French premier (1934, 1938–40). A leading radical Socialist in the 1930s, Daladier signed the MUNICH PACT with HITLER in 1938 and presided over France in the early months of WORLD WAR II, until overthrown by his failure to aid Finland. After France's fall (1940) he was arrested by the VICHY government and was tried (1942) in the war-guilt trials at Riom. In the Fourth Republic he served (1946–58) in the national assembly.

Dalai Lama, "oceanic teacher," title of the leader of TIBETAN BUDDHISM. Believed like his predecessors to be the incarnation of the Bodhisattva Avalokiteshvara, the fourteenth Dalai Lama, Tenzin Gyatso, 1935–, gave up cooperation with the Chinese and fled into exile (1959). He has traveled widely, pleading the Tibetan cause. Recipient of the 1989 Nobel Peace Prize, the Dalai Lama wrote an autobiography, *Freedom in Exile* (1990).

Dale, Sir Henry Hallett, 1875–1968, English scientist. For his study of ACETYLCHOLINE as agent in the chemical transmission of nerve impulses, he shared with Otto LOEWI the 1936 Nobel Prize in physiology or medicine. Dale also investigated the pharmacology of ergot and histamine shock. He was knighted in 1932.

d'Alembert, Jean le Rond: see ALEMBERT.

Daley, Richard Joseph, 1902–76, U.S. political leader; b. Chicago. A former (1939–46) Illinois state senator, he was elected Cook co. Democratic chairman in 1953. As mayor (1955–76) of CHICAGO, he was one of the last big city bosses; his support was often sought by state and national leaders. Daley gained national notoriety in 1968 when Chicago police brutally subdued demonstrators at the Democratic National Convention. His son, **Richard M. Daley,** 1942–, served (1980–89) as state's attorney for Cook Co., Ill., before he became mayor of Chicago in 1989.

Dali, Salvador, 1904–89, Spanish painter. Influenced by FUTURISM and CHIRICO, he became a leader of SURREALISM. His precise style enhances the dreamlike effect of his works, e.g., *Persistence of Memory* (1931; Mus. Mod. Art, N.Y.C.).

Dalian or **Dairen,** city (1990 est. pop. 2,400,000), S Liaoning prov., NE China, on the Liaodong peninsula. The city, centered on the harbor that employs 13% of its population, is China's third largest foreign-trade port. Dalian produces ships, diesel engines, machine tools, chemicals, and textiles and is a major fishing center. The municipality of **Lüda** comprises Dalian, Lüshun (the former Port Arthur, an important naval center), and surrounding areas.

Dallapiccola, Luigi, 1904–75, Italian composer. The first Italian to use ATONALITY, he is noted for his operas *The Prisoner* (1944–48) and *Odysseus* (1968); the ORATORIO *Job* (1950); and the Christmas CONCERTO (1956).

Dallas, city (1990 pop. 1,006,877), seat of Dallas co., N Tex., on the Trinity R.; inc. 1871. It is the second largest city in Texas and the eighth largest in the U.S.; with nearby FORT WORTH, it forms Texas's largest metropolitan area (1990 pop. 3,885,415). A French settlement c.1841 and a cotton market in the 1870s, it later developed into the financial center of the Southwest. Oil refineries; diverse manufactures, particularly aerospace and electronic products; meat-packing plants; corporate headquarters for oil, gas, insurance, and banking companies; and governmental offices are of major importance in its economy. The city is also a tourist and convention center. Dallas is noted as a hub of fashion and of cultural and educational institutions.

Dalmatia [dălmā'shə], historic region and province of CROATIA, extending along the ADRIATIC SEA from Rijeka to the Gulf of Kotor. Split is the capital. Dalmatia is mountainous, except for a coastal lowland whose scenic beauty attracts many tourists. Other economic activities include agriculture and fishing. A Roman province, Dalmatia was divided by the 10th cent. between the kingdoms of Croatia and Serbia. By 1420 Venice held most of the region. Various parts of Dalmatia passed (16th–20th cent.) to Hungary, the Turks, France, and Austria. After 1918 the region became part of YUGOSLAVIA. Most of Dalmatia was occupied by Italy during World War II. After Croatia declared (1991) its independence from Yugoslavia, the southern Dalmatian town of Dubrovnik was the scene of heavy fighting between Croatian and Yugoslav forces.

Dalmatian, hardy NONSPORTING DOG, known for speed and endurance; shoulder height, 19–23 in. (48.3–58.4 cm); weight, 35–50 lb (15.9–22.7 kg). It has a short, glossy coat, white with black or dark-brown spots. Probably developed in DALMATIA several hundred years ago, it was associated with horses and with horse-drawn coaches and fire engines; it remains a firemen's mascot.

Dalton, John, 1766–1844, English scientist. He taught mathematics and physical sciences at New College, Manchester. Dalton revived the atomic theory of matter (see ATOM), which he applied to a table of atomic weights and used in developing his law of partial pressures (Dalton's law). He was color-blind and studied that affliction, also known as Daltonism.

dam, barrier, commonly across a watercourse, to hold back water, often forming a reservoir or lake. Modern dams may be built for multiple purposes: to provide water for irrigation, aid flood control, furnish hydroelectric power, and improve the navigability of waterways. Rock-fill and earth dams are built with a central core—usually clay or cement, respectively—that is impervious to water. Gravity dams, usually made of concrete, use their own weight to provide resistance to the pressure of water. Single-arch concrete dams are curved upstream and are usually constructed in narrow canyons where the rocky side walls are strong enough to withstand the tremendous thrust of the dam, caused by the pressure of the water. Multiple-arch dams consist of a number of single arches supported by buttresses. Roller-compacted concrete dams, in which thin concrete layers are compacted as if they were earth, do not need full forms. See also ASWAN HIGH DAM; GRAND COULEE DAM; HOOVER DAM; TENNESSEE VALLEY AUTHORITY.

Damascene, John: see JOHN OF DAMASCUS, SAINT.

Damascus, city (1988 est. pop. 1,300,000), capital of Syria, SW Syria. The largest city in Syria, it stands in an oasis between mountains and desert and is bisected by the Barada R. Manufactures include textiles, metalware, sugar, and glass. Inhabited before 2000 B.C., it may be the oldest continuously occupied city in the world. From the 2d millennium B.C. to A.D. 395 it was ruled by the Egyptians, the Israelites, the Assyrians, the Persians, Alexander the Great, the Seleucids, and the Romans. A thriving commercial city, it early adopted Christianity. St. PAUL was converted on the road to Damascus. A provincial Byzantine capital, it fell to the Arabs in 635 and became Islamic. After 750 it was held by many conquerors, including the Saracens (12th–13th cent.) and the Ottoman Turks (1516–1918). Arab troops working with T.E. LAWRENCE helped the British take it in 1918. The French then ruled it as part of a League of Nations mandate until Syria became independent (1941). Landmarks include the Great Mosque, one of the world's largest.

d'Amboise, Jacques, 1934–, American dancer and choreographer; b. Dedham, Mass. He became (1953) a soloist with the NEW YORK CITY BALLET. He is known for American-theme works, e.g., *Filling Station, Western Symphony,* films, e.g., *Carousel* (1956), and his own ballets, e.g., *Irish Fantasy* (1964). D'Amboise founded the National Dance Institute in 1976 to bring the teaching of dance into city public schools.

Damocles [dăm'əklēz], in classical literature, courtier of DIONYSIUS

THE ELDER at SYRACUSE. To show the precariousness of power and rank, Dionysius gave a banquet at which a sword was suspended over Damocles' head by a hair.

Damon and Pythias, two youths whose loyalty to each other symbolizes true friendship. When Pythias, condemned to death by the Syracusan tyrant DIONYSIUS THE ELDER, was released to arrange his affairs, Damon stayed on as pledge. On Pythias' return, Dionysius freed them both.

Dan: see ISRAEL, TRIBES OF.

Dana, Richard Henry, 1787–1879, American author; b. Cambridge, Mass. A lawyer, poet, critic, and essayist, he was a founder of the *North American Review* and is best known for his poem *The Buccaneer* (1827). His son, **Richard Henry Dana,** 1815–82, was a writer and lawyer who wrote a classic of the days of sailing ships in *Two Years before the Mast* (1840), based on his experiences as a common sailor. *The Seaman's Friend* (1841), a manual of maritime law, grew out of his legal practice.

Da Nang, formerly Tourane, city (1990 est. pop. 371,000), central Vietnam, a port on the SOUTH CHINA SEA. It has an excellent deep-water harbor. Its manufactures include textiles and machinery. The scene (1535) of the first European landing in Vietnam, it was ceded to France by ANNAM in 1787. During the VIETNAM WAR it was the site of a huge U.S. military base.

dance, art of precise, expressive, and graceful human movement, usually performed in accord with musical accompaniment. Many primitive dances have survived in the FOLK DANCE of modern times. Native American dances, usually of a ritualistic and ceremonial nature, illustrate many of the purposes of primitive dancing. The dance of religious ecstasy, in which hypnotic and trancelike states are induced (characteristic of Africa and Asia), was represented in America by the remarkable GHOST DANCE. Native American dancing is always performed on the feet, but in islands of the Pacific and in Asia, some dances are performed in a sitting posture, with only the hands, arms, and upper parts of the body being used. In Japan, the early dances became institutionalized with a national school of dancing in the 14th cent. Soon dance became associated with the famous Nō drama (see ASIAN DRAMA). In medieval Europe, the repeated outbreaks of dance mania, associated with epidemics of bubonic plague, are reflected in the allegory of the Dance of Death. Dancing as a social activity and a form of entertainment is of relatively recent origin. In the Middle Ages, social dancing was a feature of the more enlightened courts. The BALLET first appeared at the French court in the 16th cent. Among formal social dances of the 17th cent. were the MINUET and the GAVOTTE. MODERN DANCE became part of the world of serious theatrical dance in the 20th cent. Popular national dances include the mazurka and polonaise, from Poland; the fandango and bolero, from Spain; and the WALTZ, from Germany. The U.S. initiated such dances as the cake walk, the Virginia reel, the fox trot, and the Charleston. Since the 1920s the U.S. has seen a number of dance crazes, e.g., the Lindy Hop of the 1930s, the jitterbug of the 1940s, the rock 'n' roll forms of the 1950s, the go-go dances of the 1960s, the disco dances of the 1970s, and the hip-hop styles of the 1980s and 90s. See articles on major dance companies and individual dancers.

Dance Theater of Harlem, established (1968) as an open-door school. It was founded by Arthur Mitchell of the NEW YORK CITY BALLET and is the first African-American classical dance company. Its repertoire includes mainly classics choreographed by Mitchell, Jerome ROBBINS, Antony TUDOR and others. The company tours extensively and offers community dance courses at home.

dandelion, perennial herb (genus *Taraxacum*) of the COMPOSITE family, widely distributed in temperate regions. It has a rosette of deep-toothed leaves and a bright yellow head followed in fruit by a round head of white down for wind distribution. The common dandelion (*T. officinale*) is generally considered a lawn pest in the U.S. but is also cultivated for food and medicine in the U.S. and elsewhere. The leaves are used in salads and as a seasoning; the roots are used as a coffee substitute, as a bitter tonic, and as a laxative; the flower heads are used for making dandelion wine and as forage for bees. The dandelion plant contains a white latex—a hydrocarbon—that can be converted into a combustible fuel. One species is grown commercially for latex in some nations.

Danegeld [dān'gĕld"], medieval land tax originally raised to buy off raiding Danes and later used for military expenditures. In England the tribute was first levied in 868 and then in 871 by ALFRED. Under ÆTHELRED (978–1016) it became a regular tax, and was collected by later rulers until the 12th cent.

Danelaw [dān'lô"], originally the body of law that prevailed in the part of England occupied by the Danes after the treaty of King ALFRED with Guthrum in 886. It soon came to mean also the area in which Danish law obtained. The Danelaw had four main regions: NORTHUMBRIA; the areas around and including Lincoln, Nottingham, Derby, Leicester, and Stamford; EAST ANGLIA; and the SE Midlands.

Daniel, book of the OLD TESTAMENT, 27th in the Authorized Version. It relates events and visions from the life of Daniel, a Jew of the 6th cent. B.C. Daniel and his friends, taken to BABYLON, remain faithful to the TORAH (1); Daniel interprets a dream of NEBUCHADNEZZAR (2); Nebuchadnezzar tries to punish three recalcitrant Jews (the Three Holy Children) in the fiery furnace (3); Daniel interprets a second dream of Nebuchadnezzar to foretell the latter's madness (4); Daniel interprets the handwriting on the wall at BELSHAZZAR's feast (5); he escapes from the lion's den (6); he has four apocalyptic visions (7–12). The story of Susanna and the elders, and also the stories of Daniel's revelation of the fraud connected with the Babylonian idol Bel and of his killing a dragon and subsequent miraculous escape after being thrown to lions, are in the version of Daniel in the APOCRYPHA. The book as a whole presents many critical problems.

Danilova, Alexandra [dänē'luvä], 1904–, Russian-American ballerina; b. St. Petersburg. She trained (1924–29) in St. Petersburg with DIAGHILEV, and was (1938–52) prima ballerina of the Ballet Russe de Monte Carlo. After her retirement, she taught.

Danish language, member of the North Germanic, or Scandinavian, group of the Germanic subfamily of the Indo-European family of languages. See LANGUAGE (table).

D'Annunzio, Gabriele, 1863–1938, Italian poet, novelist, dramatist, and soldier. The sensuous imagery of his early poetry, from *Canto nuovo* (1882) to *Alcione* (1904), displayed unrivaled craftsmanship. His novels, e.g., *The Child of Pleasure* (1889) and *The Triumph of Death (1894),* show the same control of language but are shallow and theatrical. Two of his plays, *La Gioconda* (1899) and *Francesca* (1902), were written for Eleonora DUSE; their affair he described in the novel *The Flame of Life* (1900). In World War I, D'Annunzio's oratory had much to do with Italy's entrance on the Allied side. In Sept. 1919 he led a march on Fiume, where he established an illegal government. He was an early exponent of fascism. See also IRREDENTISM.

Dante Alighieri [älēgyĕ'rē], 1265–1321, Italian poet, author of the *Divine Comedy.* A Florentine patrician, he fought on the side of the GUELPHS but later supported the imperial party. In 1290, after the death of his exalted Beatrice (see BEATRICE PORTINARI), he plunged into the study of philosophy and Provençal poetry. Politically active in Florence from 1295, he was banished in 1302 and became a citizen of all Italy, dying in Ravenna. The *Divine Comedy,* a vernacular poem in 100 cantos (more than 14,000 lines), was composed in exile. It is the tale of the poet's journey through Hell and Purgatory (guided by VERGIL) and through Heaven (guided by Beatrice, to whom the poem is a memorial.) Written in a complex PENTAMETER form, *terza rima,* it is a magnificent synthesis of the medieval outlook, picturing a changeless universe ordered by God. Through it Dante established Tuscan as the literary language of Italy and gave rise to a vast literature. His works also include *La vita nuova* (c.1292), a collection of prose and lyrics celebrating Beatrice and ideal love; treatises on language and politics; eclogues; and epistles.

Danton, Georges Jacques [däNtôN'], 1759–94, French Revolutionary leader. A lawyer who won immense popularity through his powerful oratory, he exercised power as a member of the Legislative Assembly (1791–92), the COMMUNE OF PARIS, and the CORDELIERS, and through his participation in the overthrow (1792) of the monarchy. In the new republic he was virtual head of the Provisional Executive Council and came to dominate the first Committee of Public Safety (1793) created by the Convention. Although initially Danton had sought foreign wars in order to spread French institutions, with France's military reverses he advocated a conciliatory foreign policy and the relaxation of the REIGN OF TERROR at home. Eclipsed by ROBESPIERRE and the extremists, he was arrested on a charge of conspiracy in 1794, subjected to a mock trial, and guillotined.

Danube, chief river of central and SE Europe, c.1,770 mi (2,850 km) long, second-longest European river after the Volga. It rises in the Brege and Brigach rivers in the BLACK FOREST of SW Germany and crosses or forms part of the borders of Austria, Slovakia, Hungary, Croatia, Yugoslavia, Romania, Bulgaria, and Ukraine before entering the BLACK SEA through a large (c.1,000 sq mi/2,590 sq km), swampy delta. The river is navigable by barges to Ulm (Germany) and connected to the Rhine and N Europe by the Rhine-Main-Danube Canal. The Sip Canal bypasses the rapids at Iron Gate gorge in the Romanian-Yugoslavian section.

Danzig: see GDAŃSK.

Daphne, in Greek mythology, a nymph loved by APOLLO. When she was pursued by him, she prayed for rescue and was transformed by GAEA into a laurel tree.

Daphnis and Chloë: see LONGUS.

Da Ponte, Lorenzo, 1749–1838, Italian poet, librettist, and teacher. He wrote the librettos to MOZART'S *Marriage of Figaro* (1786), *Don Giovanni* (1787), and *Così fan tutte* (1790). In America after 1805, he taught Italian language and culture. In 1833 he helped establish the Italian Opera House, N.Y.C.

DAR: see DAUGHTERS OF THE AMERICAN REVOLUTION.

D'Arblay, Madame: see BURNEY, FANNY.

Dardanelles, narrow strait, known as the Hellespont in ancient times, c.40 mi (60 km) long and 1–4 mi (1.6–6.4 km) wide, linking the Sea of Marmara and the Mediterranean Sea, and separating European and Asian Turkey. It forms, with the Sea of Marmara and the BOSPORUS, the only outlet of the BLACK SEA, controlling access of ships from the sea to the MEDITERRANEAN SEA–SUEZ CANAL–INDIAN OCEAN sea lane. International access by all merchant ships and by warships in peacetime is guaranteed by the Montreux Convention (1936), which also recognized Turkey's right to fortify the strait.

Dardic languages, group of languages belonging to the Indo-Iranian subfamily of the Indo-European family of languages. See LANGUAGE (table).

Dare, Virginia, b. 1587, first child born of English parents in America. She was a member of the "lost colony" of ROANOKE ISLAND that disappeared c.1591.

Dar-es-Salaam, largest city (1988 pop. 1,360,850) and capital of Tanzania, on an arm of the Indian Ocean. It is the country's chief port and economic center, connected by rail to Kigoma, in the west, and (since 1975) to LUSAKA, Zambia. The city has a variety of industries and a major oil refinery. Founded in 1866 by the sultan of ZANZIBAR, it became the capital of German East Africa in 1891 and grew rapidly after World War II. Today it has a university and several colleges.

Darío, Rubén [därē'ō], 1867–1916, Nicaraguan poet and diplomat; b. Félix Rubén García Sarmiento. His first book, *Blue* (1888), heralded the founding of MODERNISMO. Other works include *Prosas profanas* (1896) and *Autumn Poem* (1910), perhaps his masterpiece. His influence on all Spanish-language writers was enormous. He served as a diplomat in many European and Latin American countries.

Darius, several kings of ancient PERSIA. **Darius I** (the Great), d. 486 B.C. (r.521–486 B.C.), was one of the most able of the ACHAEMENIDS. He perfected a highly efficient system of administration. Around 500 B.C., when the Ionian cities rebelled against Persian rule, Darius put down the rebels and set out to punish the Greek city-states that had aided the insurrection. He met defeat in the memorable battle of MARATHON (490 B.C.); however, he consolidated Persian power in the East. He also continued Cyrus the Great's policy of restoring the Jewish state. **Darius II,** d. 404 B.C. (r.423?–404 B.C.), was not popular or successful, and he spent much time in quelling revolts. He lost Egypt (410) but secured influence in Greece. **Darius III,** d. 330 B.C. (r.336–330 B.C.), seriously underestimated ALEXANDER THE GREAT'S strength when the Macedonians invaded Persia. He was defeated by Alexander in several major battles and was forced to flee to Bactria, where the satrap had him murdered. These events ended the Persian empire and marked the beginning of the Hellenistic period in the E Mediterranean.

Dark Ages: see MIDDLE AGES.

dark matter, material that is believed to make up more than 90% of the mass of the universe but is invisible because it neither emits nor reflects ELECTROMAGNETIC RADIATION, such as light or radio signals. Its existence would explain gravitational anomalies seen in the motion and distribution of galaxies. Dark matter can only be detected indirectly, e.g., through the bending of light rays from distant stars by its gravity. It may consist of dust, planets, intergalactic gas formed of ordinary matter, or of MACHOs [*M*assive *A*strophysical *C*ompact *H*alo *O*bjects], nonluminous bodies such as burned-out stars, black holes, and brown dwarfs. Other theories hold that it is made of ELEMENTARY PARTICLES that played a key role in the formation of the universe, possibly the low-mass NEUTRINO or theoretical particles called axions and WIMPs [*W*eakly *I*nteracting *M*assive *P*articles]. See also INTERSTELLAR MATTER.

Darlan, Jean François [därläN'], 1881–1942, French admiral and politician. The leading member of Marshal PÉTAIN'S VICHY government in WORLD WAR II, he strengthened France's collaborationist ties with Germany. Later, as commander of all French forces, he was in N Africa during the Nov. 1942 Allied landings and brought French N and W Africa over to the Allied side. He was assassinated on Dec. 28.

Darling, longest river in Australia, flowing 1,702 mi (2,739 km) generally southwest across the semiarid plains of NEW SOUTH WALES to join the MURRAY R. at Wentworth. An important source of irrigation water, it rises in the rainy EASTERN HIGHLANDS and receives many tributaries; occasionally it runs dry.

Darnley, Henry Stuart or **Stewart, Lord,** 1545–67, second husband of MARY QUEEN OF SCOTS and father of JAMES I. Son of the powerful earl of Lennox, he claimed succession to the English throne through his grandmother Margaret TUDOR. His Catholic sympathies, his claim on the throne, and perhaps his handsome appearance induced Mary to marry him in 1565. He proved to be vicious and dissipated, and she did not make him royal consort. Jealous of David RIZZIO, Darnley and others murdered him. Soon Darnley was without friends. A plot was formed to murder him, probably under the earl of BOTHWELL. On Feb. 9, 1567, the house near Edinburgh where he was staying was blown up; he was found strangled in an adjoining garden the next day.

DARPA: see ADVANCED RESEARCH PROJECTS AGENCY.

Darrow, Clarence Seward, 1857–1938, American lawyer; b. Kinsman, Ohio. He had an early lucrative career in private and corporate law, but with his defense of Eugene V. DEBS and others in connection with the 1894 Pullman strike he turned to representing the underdog. He became famous as an opponent of capital punishment; none of his more than 100 clients was sentenced to death. In the SCOPES TRIAL (1925) on the teaching of evolution in public schools, he opposed fundamentalist religious tenets, arguing against William Jennings BRYAN. Darrow's writings include *Crime: Its Cause and Treatment* (1922).

Darwin, Charles Robert, 1809–82, English naturalist, grandson of Erasmus DARWIN. He firmly established the theory of organic EVOLUTION. His position as official naturalist aboard the H.M.S. *Beagle* during its world voyage (1831–36) started Darwin on a career of accumulating and assimilating data that resulted in the formulation of his concept of evolution. In 1858 he and Alfred Russel WALLACE simultaneously published summaries of their independently conceived notions of NATURAL SELECTION; a year later Darwin set forth the structure of his theory and massive support for it in his *Origin of Species.* This was supplemented by later works, notably *The Descent of Man* (1871). Darwin also formulated a theory of the origin of coral reefs.

Darwin, Erasmus, 1731–1802, English physician and poet; grandfather of Charles DARWIN. His long poem *Botanic Garden* (1789–91) expounded the Linnaean system. *Zoonomia* (1794–96) explained organic life in evolutionary terms, anticipating later theories.

Darwin, city (1990 est. pop. 73,300), capital of the Northern Territory, N Australia, on an inlet of the Timor Sea. It is the chief port and administrative center for the sparsely settled tropical north coast. Called Palmerston until 1911, it was renamed for Charles DARWIN, who discovered its site in 1839. It has been largely rebuilt since a devastating typhoon in 1974. Kakadu National Park is nearby.

Darwinism: see NATURAL SELECTION.

database: see INFORMATION STORAGE AND RETRIEVAL.

data communications, transmission of digitally encoded data from a source to a destination, particularly as applied to computers. Although telephone circuits are often used, their relatively limited frequency range makes them rather slow paths for data, a limitation offset by their availability and relatively low cost. Generally MODEMS are used to coordinate the computer and the telephone circuit. Where cost can be justified, high speed data links are constructed; these are often FIBER-OPTIC or coaxial cables designed for wide frequency range, or microwave, radio systems. Because local-area and wide-area networks link many computers together so that they can transfer and share data, a variety of techniques are used to allocate the communications resource: in time-division multiplexing, each computer is assigned a short time slot during which it can use the whole bandwidth of the network; in packet switching, multiple concurrent transmissions can take place because each data packet is tagged with the address for which it is intended; and in asynchronous transfer mode (ATM)—an advanced form of packet switching—video, data, and voice transmissions can be transmitted making it ideal for multimedia computer communications.

data processing or **information processing,** operations (e.g., handling, merging, sorting, and computing) performed upon data in accordance with strictly defined procedures, such as recording and summarizing the financial transactions of a business. In automatic or electronic data processing the operations are performed by a COMPUTER. In distributed data processing some or all of the operations are performed in different locations at computer facilities connected by telecommunications links.

date, name for a PALM (*Phoenix dactylifera*) and for its edible fruit, probably native to Arabia and North Africa and long a major food source in desert and tropical regions. The sweet, nutritious fruits grow in heavy clusters; a tree may produce up to 200 lb (90 kg) annually. Sugar and a fermented drink are made from the sap of the tree, and the seeds are sometimes used as a coffee substitute. The wood of the trunk is used in construction, and mats and baskets are woven from the leaves.

dating, in geology, archaeology, paleontology, and physics, the determination of the actual or relative age of an object, of a natural phenomenon, or of a series of events. The most common and accepted method of absolute geologic dating (establishment of actual age) is based on the natural RADIOACTIVITY of certain minerals found in rocks; because the rate of radioactive decay of any particular ISOTOPE is known, the age of a specimen can be computed from the ratio of the remaining isotope and its decay product. Relative geological dating (determination of the sequence of geological events) is accomplished by marking out the succession in which rocks were deposited, using various surface criteria. The identification of FOSSILS in a geological sample is very useful because certain assemblages of species are characteristic of specific geologic time periods. Pollen analysis, or palynology, can also establish the succession of deposits as well as the climate prevalent at the time of deposition. In archaeology and recent geology, the carbon-14 method, which measures the remaining amount of this radioactive isotope in organic matter, can date specimens as old as 35,000 years. The death of an organism ends the incorporation of this isotope (created by COSMIC-RAY bombardment) and levels of the isotope equal at a rate equal to the isotope's known decay rate. This method's accuracy has been improved by cross-checking with dendrochronology, in which the age of a piece of ancient wood can be determined by examining the ring pattern in its cross section. The pattern of individual ring widths in a sample reflects local climatic conditions occurring at the time when the piece of wood was a growing tree. By the use of overlapping patterns found in different wood samples, dating by this method has been carried back over 8,000 years.

Daubigny, Charles-François [dōbēnyē′], 1817–78, French landscape painter. Best known for his paintings of the banks of the Seine and the Oise, he was particularly successful in his atmospheric depiction of dawn, twilight, and moonlight, e.g., *Moonlight.* His son, **Karl Pierre Daubigny,** 1846–86, painted in his father's manner.

Daudet, Alphonse [dōdā′], 1840–97, French author. He is noted for his gently naturalistic portrayals of French life, as in the Provence-inspired collection of short stories, *Letters from My Mill* (1869). His semiautobiographical novel, *Le Petit Chose* (1868), touchingly describes his life at boarding school. His son, **Léon Daudet,** 1867–1942, editor of the right-wing Catholic paper *Action française,* was the author of an extensive and valuable series of memoirs.

Daughters of the American Revolution (DAR), patriotic society founded 1890 in Washington, D.C., and open to women with ancestors who aided the AMERICAN REVOLUTION. It has over 204,000 members and has done much to preserve and mark historic places. The DAR has been criticized for its conservative political policies.

Daumier, Honoré [dōmyā′], 1808–79, French caricaturist, painter, and sculptor. Daumier was the greatest social satirist of his day. His bitterly ironic approach mercilessly ridiculed bourgeois society in realistic graphic style. He produced almost 4,000 lithographs now considered masterpieces. His stylistically similar small canvases, e.g., *Third-Class Carriage* (Metropolitan Mus.), have the same dramatic intensity. His sculpture includes over 30 small, painted busts.

dauphin [dô′fĭn] [Fr., = dolphin], French title. It was borne first by the counts of Vienne and after 1350 by the eldest son of the king of France. If the dauphin died before the king, the title went to the dauphin's eldest son.

Davenport, city (1990 pop. 95,333), seat of Scott co., E central Iowa, on the Mississippi R.; inc. 1836. With the Illinois cities of Rock Island, Moline, and East Moline, it forms the Quad Cities. It prospered with the arrival (1856) of the first railroad to bridge the river. Today it produces processed food, agricultural equipment, and clothing and is a rail and commercial center. The Mississippi flooded large areas of the city in 1993.

David, Saint, d. 588?, patron saint of WALES, first abbot of Menevia (now Saint David's) in Wales. His shrine was an important place of pilgrimage in the Middle Ages, and the national Welsh festival is still celebrated on his feast, Mar. 1.

David, d. c.972 B.C., king of the ancient Hebrews (c.1012–c.972 B.C.), successor of SAUL and one of the greatest of Hebrew national heroes. To him were ascribed many of the PSALMS. Many of the interesting and beautiful narratives in the BIBLE deal with the story of David, e.g., the fight of David and GOLIATH; the friendship of David and Saul's son, Jonathan; David's love for BATH-SHEBA; and the revolt of ABSALOM.

David, kings of Scotland. **David I,** 1084–1153 (r.1124–53), fought without success for MATILDA, his niece, in the struggle for the English crown between STEPHEN and Matilda. He did realize his main aim, securing Northumberland. His rule of Scotland was felicitous. **David II** (David Bruce), 1324–71 (r.1329–71), went to France after EDWARD III and Edward de BALIOL invaded Scotland in 1332. He invaded England in 1346, was captured, and held until ransomed in 1357.

David, Jacques-Louis [dävēd′], 1748–1825, French painter. The virtual art dictator of France for a generation, he made a break with tradition that marks the beginning of "modern art." He borrowed classical forms and motifs, primarily from sculpture, to illustrate his sense of virtue. Inspired by the ideals of the FRENCH REVOLUTION, he eschewed sentiment. His *Death of Socrates* (1787; Metropolitan Mus.) and *The Oath of the Horatii* (Louvre) are major works. David's iron control was softened in his portraits, e.g., *Marat* (1793; Brussels). As First Painter to NAPOLEON I he produced paintings that are static and deadened in feeling, e.g., *The Distribution of the Eagles* (1810).

Davidson, Jo, 1883–1952, American sculptor; b. N.Y.C. He is best known for his insightful, vigorously modeled portrait busts of such leading figures as Woodrow Wilson, Mahatma Gandhi, Franklin Delano Roosevelt, and Albert Einstein.

Davies, Arthur Bowen, 1862–1928, American painter; b. Utica, N.Y. A member of the EIGHT, he favored symbolic, romantic pictures of the female nude in idyllic landscapes. Davies was the chief organizer of the 1913 ARMORY SHOW.

Davies, Robertson, 1913–, Canadian novelist. He came to international attention with the Deptford trilogy of novels (1970–75), a richly plotted study of three people's journey to self-discovery, replete with humor, mystery, magic, Jungian ideas, and grotesque characters. His other novels include *The Rebel Angels* (1982) and *The Lyre of Opheus* (1988).

Da Vinci, Leonardo: see LEONARDO DA VINCI.

Davis, Angela Yvonne, 1944–, African-American activist; b. Birmingham, Ala. She taught (1969–70) at UCLA despite state efforts to oust her for being a Communist. In 1970 she went into hiding after being accused of aiding an attempted courtroom escape that killed four persons. Apprehended, tried (1972), and acquitted, she became the vice-presidential candidate of the Communist party in 1980.

Davis, Benjamin Oliver, 1877–1970, U.S. general; b. Washington, D.C. Davis was (1940–48) the first African-American general in the U.S. Army, having risen from the rank of private. His son, **Benjamin Oliver Davis, Jr.,** 1912–, was (1954–65) the first African-American air force general and (1965–70) lieutenant general. He served (1971–75) as an assistant secretary in the Dept. of Transportation.

Davis, Bette, 1908–89, American film actress; b. Lowell, Mass., as Ruth Elizabeth Davis. An enduring Hollywood star, she made such films as *Jezebel* (1938; Academy Award), *Dark Victory* (1939), and *All About Eve* (1950).

Davis, Sir Colin (Rex), 1927–, English conductor. A clarinetist, he is self-taught as a conductor. He led the BBC Symphony (1967–71), the Royal Opera, Covent Garden (1971–86), and the Bavarian Radio Symphony Orchestra (1983–92). He was knighted in 1980.

Davis, Jefferson, 1808–89, American statesman, president of the CONFEDERACY (1861–65); b. near Elkton, Ky. A U.S. senator from Mississippi (1847–51, 1857–61) and U.S. secretary of war (1853–57), Davis left Washington after the secession (Jan. 1861) of Mississippi. As president of the Confederacy, he assumed strong centralized power, weakening the STATES' RIGHTS policy for which the South had seceded. He had many disputes with Confederate generals, and R.E. LEE surrendered without his approval. Captured (1865) by Union forces, he was imprisoned for two years but was released (1867) without prosecution.

Davis, Miles, 1926–91, African-American musician; b. Alton, Ill. He worked with Charlie PARKER in the 1940s, was a catalyst of "cool" JAZZ around 1950, led influential small bands through the 1960s, and produced jazz-rock and jazz-funk blends in the late 1960s and the 1970s. He was famous for his warm, often muted trumpet style.

Miles Davis

Davis, Richard Harding, 1864–1916, American writer; b. Philadelphia. A leading journalist and foreign correspondent, he specialized in books about his wartime experiences. His also wrote novels, e.g., *Soldiers of Fortune* (1897) and *The Bar Sinister* (1903); short stories; and plays.

Davis, Stuart, 1894–1964, American painter; b. Philadelphia. A jazz enthusiast, he often incorporated jazz tempos into the vibrant patterns of his paintings. In the 1920s Davis came under the influence of CUBISM and created, in such works as *Colonial Cubism* (Walker Art Center, Minneapolis), a brightly colored, distinctly American interpretation of the movement.

Davy, Sir Humphry, 1778–1829, English chemist and physicist. He was professor (1802–13) at the Royal Inst., London, where his electrochemical researches led to his isolation of SODIUM and POTASSIUM (1807) and BARIUM, BORON, CALCIUM, and MAGNESIUM (1808). He showed chlorine to be an element, theorized that acids characteristically contain hydrogen, and classed chemical affinity as an electric phenomenon.

Dawes, Charles Gates, 1865–1951, vice president of the U.S. (1925–29); b. Marietta, Ohio. He shared the 1925 Nobel Peace Prize for proposing the Dawes Plan that reduced defeated Germany's reparations. He was vice president under Pres. COOLIDGE.

Dawson or **Dawson City,** city (1991 pop. 972), W Yukon, N Canada, at the confluence of the Yukon and Klondike rivers. A famous gold rush town whose population reached c.20,000 in 1898, it was the territorial capital until replaced by WHITEHORSE in 1952.

Day, Clarence Shepard, 1874–1935, American essayist; b. N.Y.C. He is best known for sketches of his parents, e.g., *Life with Father* (1935) and *Life with Mother* (1937).

day: see SIDEREAL TIME; SOLAR TIME.

Dayan, Moshe [dīän'], 1915–81, Israeli military leader; b. Palestine. He directed the 1956 Sinai campaign as chief of staff and the 1967 Six-Day War as defense minister. Blamed for Israeli unpreparedness in the 1973 October War, he resigned (1974) with Golda MEIR. Later (1977–79) he was Israeli foreign minister. See also ARAB-ISRAELI WARS.

day-care center, institution for the care of children of working parents; also called day nursery, but not to be confused with NURSERY SCHOOL. Originating in Europe in the late 18th cent., day-care facilities were first established in the U.S. by private charities in the 1850s. The women's movement and other social developments during the 20th cent. have spurred the growth of day-care centers and encouraged businesses to establish them.

Day Lewis, C(ecil), 1904–72, English author. His verse was at first didactic and social, reflecting his leftist leanings, later more personal and metaphysical. His works include *Collected Poems* (1954); a translation of Vergil's *Aeneid* (1952); and detective stories written under the pseudonym Nicholas Blake. He was POET LAUREATE (1967–72).

daylight saving time (DST), time observed when clocks and other timepieces are set ahead, usually by 1 hr, so that the sun will rise and set later in the day as measured by civil time (see SOLAR TIME). DST conserves lighting power and provides more usable daylight hours for afternoon and evening activities. First adopted during World War I by the U.S. and other countries, DST in the U.S. currently extends from the first Sunday in April to the last Sunday in October.

day nursery: see DAY-CARE CENTER.

Dayton, city (1990 pop. 182,044), seat of Montgomery co., SW Ohio, on the Great Miami R.; inc. 1805. It is a port and trading hub for a fertile farm area, and an aviation center. Chief manufactures are computers, air conditioners, appliances, tools, and paper and rubber goods. The city grew with the extension of canals (1830s–40s) and railroads, and with the industrial demands of the CIVIL WAR. The WRIGHT brothers, Dayton natives, returned there after their historic first flight and established a research aircraft plant.

Dazai Osamu [dä'zī], pseudonym of **Shuji Tsushima** [shōō'jī], 1909–48, Japanese novelist. He was noted for his obsession with suicide, his ironic and gloomy wit, and his brilliant fantasy. His masterpiece, *Setting Sun* (1947), depicts the decline of Japan's nobility after World War II.

DC: see ELECTRICITY; GENERATOR; MOTOR, ELECTRIC.

D Day: see WORLD WAR II.

ddI and **ddC:** see AZT.

DDT: see INSECTICIDES.

deadly nightshade: see BELLADONNA; NIGHTSHADE.

Dead Sea, salt lake, c.390 sq mi (1,010 sq km), in the arid Jordan trough of the GREAT RIFT VALLEY, on the Israel-Jordan border. At

1,292 ft (394 m) below sea level, it is the lowest point on earth. The lake, which has no life and owes its high salinity to rapid evaporation, derives most of its inflow (now diminished because of irrigation) from the JORDAN R. Potash and bromine are commercially extracted.

Dead Sea Scrolls, documents of great historical and scholarly value, found in 1947 and later in caves above the NW Dead Sea. Archaeologists have shown that the scrolls stored in jars in the first cave at QUMRAN were written or copied between the 1st cent. B.C. and the first half of the 1st cent. A.D. Chief among the scrolls are two copies of the Book of Isaiah, almost 1,000 years older than any Hebrew biblical manuscript previously known. Another important scroll was the so-called *Manual of Discipline* for an ascetic community, which has been identified with both the ruins at nearby QUMRAN and the Essenes, a Jewish religious sect living an ascetic communal agricultural life in that region between the 2d cent. B.C. and 2d cent. A.D. Parallels between the "Qumran" scrolls and the New Testament have led some scholars to suggest a tie between the Essenes and the early Christians, including the much-disputed suggestion that Jesus and John the Baptist may have been Essenes. More recent work by other archaeologists and biblical scholars has questioned the association of the scrolls with the Qumran ruins and the Essenes.

deafness, partial or total loss of hearing. It may be present at birth (congenital) or acquired any time thereafter. Conductive deafness, one of the two major types of deafness, involves a disturbance in the transmission of sound to the nerve receptors of the inner ear. This type of deafness may be caused by infection, impacted wax, perforation of the eardrum, or otosclerosis, a chronic condition, especially in older people, that restricts the vibration of the bone leading to the inner ear. These conditions can usually be treated with ANTIBIOTICS, surgery, hearing aids, and other techniques. The other major type of deafness—perceptive, or nerve, deafness—involves damage to neural receptors in the inner ear, to nerve pathways to the brain, or to the area of the brain concerned with hearing. Usually permanent, it can be caused by infection, senility, tumors, or excessive noise, or it may be congenital. A cochlear implant, in which a tiny receiver is connected by a wire to the inner ear, can sometimes alleviate perceptive deafness. Those who cannot be helped to hear may communicate through SIGN LANGUAGE and lip reading. The first U.S. public school for the deaf was founded in 1817 by T.H. GALLAUDET. See also EAR.

Dean, James, 1931–55, American film actor, b. Fairmount, Ind. Dean was identified with restless, inarticulate youth in *East of Eden* (1953) and *Rebel without a Cause* (1954). He was killed when his racing car crashed, and his death set off a worldwide wave of cultist mourning.

Dearborn, city (1990 pop. 89,286), SE Mich., on the Rouge R., adjoining DETROIT; settled 1795, inc. as a city 1929. It is the home of the Ford Motor Co., and has automotive research and manufacturing facilties. Largely residential despite its industry, it is famous for the Edison Inst. of Technology, which includes Greenfield Village, birthplace of Henry FORD, and the Henry Ford Museum.

death, cessation of all life (metabolic) processes. Death may involve the organism as a whole (somatic death) or may be confined to cells and tissues within the organism. Somatic death has traditionally been defined as the end of cardiac activity and RESPIRATION. With advances in organ TRANSPLANTATION techniques, however, the need has arisen for a more precise definition of medical death, since the death of a donor must be established before transfer of an organ can be undertaken. The current definition is that of a 1981 U.S. presidential commission which recommended that death be defined as "irreversible cessation of all functions of the entire brain, including the brain stem," the brain stem being that part of the brain that controls breathing and other basic body functions. Some feel, however, that people in persistent vegetative states, i.e. people who have brain stem function but have lost higher brain functions (vision, abstract thought, personality) should be considered dead and allowed, through LIVING WILLS or relatives, to donate organs.

death angel: see MUSHROOM.

Death Valley National Monument, protected desert region, 2,067,628 acres (836,757 hectares), S California and S Nevada, location of the lowest point (282 ft/86 m below sea level) in the Americas. It receives less than 2 in. (5 cm) of rain a year and has recorded some of the world's highest air temperatures (134°F/57°C) and ground temperatures (165°F/74°C). The unusual plants and animals found there are of considerable scientific interest. Death Valley was a major source of borax in the late 19th cent.

debenture: see BOND.

debit card, card that allows the cost of goods or services that are purchased to be deducted directly from the purchaser's checking account. Increasingly common in the 1990s as alternatives to CREDIT CARDS, debit cards have been promoted as safer than cash and more convenient than personal checks. They are typically issued by large credit card companies through their participating banks.

de Broglie, Louis Victor, prince: see BROGLIE.

Debs, Eugene Victor, 1855–1926, American Socialist leader; b. Terre Haute, Ind. An advocate of industrial unions and a pacifist, Debs was imprisoned in 1895 for breaking an injunction during the Pullman railroad strike. Later, he was jailed (1918–21) for violating the Espionage Act. He helped to form the Socialist party and was its presidential candidate five times after 1900. Debs was widely revered as a martyr to his principles.

debt, obligation in services, money, or goods owed by one party (the debtor) to another (the creditor). A debt usually involves the payment of INTEREST. If a debtor fails to pay, a court may assign payment out of the debtor's property. In ancient times debt was associated with slavery, because the insolvent debtor and his household were often turned over to the creditor to perform compulsory services. Imprisonment for debt, which once filled prisons, was ended as such in England and the U.S. by laws enacted in the 19th cent., although imprisonment on related charges, such as concealment of assets, may still occur. The laws of BANKRUPTCY govern the distribution a debtor's assets to the creditors.

debt, public, indebtedness of a government expressed in money terms; also known as the national debt. The public debt increases whenever public spending exceeds public revenues, producing budget deficits. To finance such deficits, the government borrows from private or institutional investors or from other governments. Public loans may be in the form of short-term instruments, such as treasury certificates, long-term government bonds, or various other notes. Governments may incur debts for several reasons, most importantly for the financing of wars and the combating of the effects of recessions, but also because of an unwillingness to limit spending or increase taxes for fear of the political consequences. Heavy government borrowings exert upward pressures on INTEREST rates and may be harmful to the general economy. The rate of increase in the U.S. public debt accelerated in the 1970s, reaching $533 billion in 1975 and $908 billion in 1980. During that period, however, the debt as a percentage of the GROSS DOMESTIC PRODUCT (GDP) remained steady, at less than 30%. In the 1980s, as a result of tax cuts under Pres. REAGAN, unprecedented peacetime budget deficits led to enormous increases in the national debt, which reached $4 trillion (67% of the GDP) by the end of 1992.

Debussy, Claude Achille [dəbüsē'], 1862–1918, French composer, exponent of musical IMPRESSIONISM. He employed the whole-tone SCALE to create nuances of mood and expression, exploring unusual harmonies and dissonances. He is best known for the tone poem (see SYMPHONIC POEM) *Prelude to the Afternoon of a Faun* (1894), inspired by a poem of MALLARMÉ. Other orchestral works include *Nocturnes* (1899) and *La Mer* (1905). His piano works include *Suite Bergamasque* (1905), including *Clair de lune; Estampes* (1903); preludes; and études.

decadents, name loosely applied to the late-19th-cent. artists and writers who strove to express the morbid and macabre elements of human emotion. They claimed art should exist for its own sake. Often confused with the French SYMBOLISTS, who influenced them, they were most evident in England, where they included WILDE, DOWSON, and BEARDSLEY.

Decameron: see BOCCACCIO, GIOVANNI.

decathlon, a contest comprising 10 track-and-field events: broad jump; high jump; discus; shot put; javelin; 100-meter, 400-meter, and 1,500-meter races; 110-meter hurdles; and pole vault. An Olympic event since 1912, it has been dominated by Americans. The winner gains the traditional title "world's greatest athlete." See PENTATHLON.

Decatur, Stephen, 1779–1820, American naval officer; b. near Berlin, Md. During the TRIPOLITAN WAR, he led (1804) a daring raid into Tripoli harbor to burn the captured U.S. frigate *Philadelphia.* In the WAR OF 1812, Decatur commanded the *United States* and captured (1812) the British frigate *Macedonian.* Known for his reckless bravery and stubborn patriotism, he was mortally wounded in a duel with James BARRON.

Decatur, city (1990 pop. 83,885), seat of Macon co., central Ill., on the Sangamon R., inc. 1839. A railroad and industrial center in a rich farm area, Decatur processes soybeans and corn, repairs railway cars, and manufactures tires, tractors, machinery, and automobile equipment. Historic sites associated with Abraham LINCOLN are in and around the city.

Deccan, region of India. It is sometimes used in a wide sense for all of India S of the Narbada R. and sometimes, more specifically, for the area of rich volcanic soils and lava-covered plateaus in the northern part of the peninsula between the Narbada and Krishna rivers.

December: see MONTH.

Decembrists, Russian officers who rose against Czar NICHOLAS I in Dec. 1825. Influenced by liberal ideals while serving in W Europe during the Napoleonic Wars (see NAPOLEON I), they advocated representative democracy but disagreed on its form. Their poorly organized rebellion was crushed, but it led to increased revolutionary activity among the educated classes and an accompanying rise in police terrorism.

De Chirico: see CHIRICO, GIORGIO DE.

decibel (dB), unit of sound intensity. The faintest audible sound is arbitrarily assigned a value of 0 dB, and the loudest sounds that the human ear can tolerate are about 120 dB. The difference in decibels between any two sounds is equal to $10 \log_{10} (P_1/P_2)$, where P_1 and P_2 are the two power levels.

decimal system [Lat., = of tenths], NUMERATION system based on powers of 10 and using the digits 0, 1, 2, 3, 4, 5, 6, 7, 8, and 9. A numeral in the decimal system is written as a row of digits, with each position in the row corresponding to a specific power of 10 (see EXPONENT). A decimal point in the row divides it into increasing positive powers of 10 for positions to the left, and increasing negative powers of 10 for positions to the right. For example, 103 represents $(1 \times 10^2) + (0 \times 10^1) + (3 \times 10^0)$, or $100 + 0 + 3$; and 1.03 corresponds to $(1 \times 10^0) + (0 \times 10^{-1}) + (3 \times 10^{-2})$, or $1 + 0 + 3/100$. The decimal system was introduced into Europe c.1300. Its positional system made it an improvement over Roman numerals and simplified arithmetic computation. The METRIC SYSTEM of weights and measures is based on the decimal system, as are most systems of national currency.

Declaration of Independence, adopted July 4, 1776, by delegates of the THIRTEEN COLONIES, announcing their separation from Great Britain and the creation of the U.S. It was written almost totally by Thomas JEFFERSON. The opening paragraphs state the American ideal of government, based on the theory of natural rights. Its combination of general principles and an abstract theory of government with a detailed enumeration of specific grievances and injustices makes it one of the great political documents of history.

Declaration of London: see LONDON, DECLARATION OF.

Declaration of Rights: see BILL OF RIGHTS.

Declaration of the Rights of Man and Citizen, historic French document. It was drafted (1789) by Emmanuel SIEYÈS and embodied as the preamble in the French constitution of 1791. Influenced by the U.S. DECLARATION OF INDEPENDENCE and the ENLIGHTENMENT, it asserted the equality of all men, the sovereignty of the people, and the inalienable rights of the individual to liberty, property, and security.

declination: see ASTRONOMICAL COORDINATE SYSTEMS.

decompression sickness, physiological disorder caused by rapid decrease in atmospheric pressure that results in the release of nitrogen bubbles into body tissues. The bubbles cut off the oxygen supply, causing nausea, pain in the joints and abdomen, and, in severe cases, shock, paralysis, and even death. Also known as the bends, or altitude sickness, it affects divers, airplane pilots, and others working under compressed air. Use of a **decompression chamber** allows for a gradual reduction of pressure, preventing the accumulation of nitrogen in body tissues.

deconstruction, the exposure and undermining of the metaphysical assumptions involved in systematic attempts to ground knowledge, as in STRUCTURALISM. Deconstructionists tend to focus on close readings of texts and how the texts refer to other texts, to uncover what is left out, ignored, or silenced by the text, and reveal the illogical and paradoxical in what appears logical and stable. They also seek to disrupt hierarchical oppositions (speech and writing, truth and lie, being and nonbeing) in which one term is valued and the other denigrated and upon which texts depend. Because deconstruction is an attack on the very existence of theories and conceptual systems, deconstructionists shun logical definitions and explanations for such approaches as nonlinear presentations based on word play and puns. The term *deconstruction* was coined in the 1960s by Jacques DERRIDA, who extended the philosophical excursions of NIETZSCHE and HEIDEGGER to criticize the entire tradition of Western philosophy. In the U.S. deconstruction has been particularly influential in literary theory.

Dedekind, Julius Wilhelm Richard, 1831–1916, German mathematician, perhaps best known for the "Dedekind cut," whereby real numbers can be defined in terms of rational numbers. A student of Carl GAUSS, he led the effort to formulate rigorous definitions of basic mathematical concepts.

deduction. 1 In traditional LOGIC, the process of drawing, by reasoning, particular conclusions from more general principles assumed to be true. The Aristotelian SYLLOGISM is the classic example of deductive logic in the tradition. **2** In contemporary logic, any statement derived by a transformed rule upon an axiom; more generally, the term now refers to a process of deriving theorems from axioms, or conclusions from premises, by formal rules (transformation rules). See also INDUCTION.

Dee, John, 1527–1608, English mathematician, astrologer, and occultist. Acquitted of a charge of sorcery against Queen Mary I, he became a favorite of Queen Elizabeth I for whom he drew up valuable scientific studies about newly discovered lands. His occult studies led to his claim of having discovered the secret of ALCHEMY, which he practiced abroad.

Deep Sea Drilling Project, U.S. program (1964–83) to investigate the evolution of ocean basins by drilling and studying cores of ocean sediments and underlying oceanic crust. It used the *Glomar Challenger,* an elaborately equipped ship capable of drilling through great water depths. The OCEAN DRILLING PROGRAM, begun in 1984, succeeded it.

deer, ruminant MAMMAL of the family Cervidae, found worldwide except for Australia. Deer range in size from the MOOSE, which may be c.7 ft (2.1 m) high at the shoulder, to the pudu of South America, which is c.12 in. (30 cm) high. Antlers, bony outgrowths of the skull used as weapons during the breeding season, develop in males of most species and are shed and renewed annually. In deer lacking antlers, long, upper canine teeth are used for fighting. The white-tailed deer, a source of food and buckskin for Native Americans and white settlers, was nearly exterminated by overhunting; it is now restored in the E U.S. Other North American deer include the mule deer of the W U.S. and the closely related black-tailed deer of the Pacific Coast. Old World deer include the red deer and fallow deer.

Defense, United States Department of, federal executive department charged with coordinating and supervising all activities relating to the national security. It was organized (1949) to replace the National Military Establishment (1947), which in turn had replaced the WAR DEPARTMENT. It is the largest federal department. The secretary of defense, a civilian, oversees all policies having to do with U.S. military affairs. He is assisted by the secretaries of the army, navy, and air force, who are also civilians appointed by the president. His principal military advisers are the **Joint Chiefs of Staff,** a statutory agency within the department whose members include a chairman, the chiefs of staff of the army and air force, the chief of naval operations, and the commandant of the Marine Corps. Defense Dept. agencies include the ADVANCED PROJECTS RESEARCH AGENCY, Ballistic Missile Defense Organization, Defense Intelligence Agency, Defense Mapping Agency, and NATIONAL SECURITY AGENCY.

Defense Advanced Research Projects Agency: see ADVANCED RESEARCH PROJECTS AGENCY.

defense mechanism, any of a variety of unconscious reactions used by individuals to protect themselves from feelings of ANXIETY or enable them to modify reality to make it more tolerable. Common defense mechanisms accepted in PSYCHOANALYSIS, are denial, in which the person simply denies that the anxiety or anxiety-causing circumstance exists; repression, the prevention of unacceptable ideas from entering the conscious mind; and displacement, the release of dangerous impulses in a substitute situation or through disguised activity.

deflation: see under INFLATION.

Defoe or **De Foe, Daniel,** 1660?–1731, English writer. His poem *The True-born Englishman* (1701), a defense of William III, brought fame, but an ironic satire, *The Shortest Way with Dissenters* (1702), brought a prison term. Called the father of modern journalism, he was associated with 26 periodicals, and he wrote and published (1704–13) *The Review,* a journal, single-handedly. His three great novels—*The Life and Strange Surprising Adventures of Robinson Crusoe* (1719), based in part on the experience of Alexander SELKIRK, and often considered the first true NOVEL in English; the picaresque *Moll Flanders* (1722); and *A Journal of the Plague Year* (1722)—all appeared as memoirs, intended to be taken as true. Defoe's writing is straightforward and vivid, with a remarkable concern for detail.

defoliant: see HERBICIDE.

De Forest, Lee, 1873–1961, American inventor; b. Council Bluffs, Iowa. A pioneer in the development of wireless telegraphy, sound pictures, and television, he invented the triode (1906), which made transcontinental telephony practicable and led to the foundation of the radio industry.

Degas, Edgar (Hilaire Germain Edgar Degas) [dəgä'], 1834–1917, French painter and sculptor. Degas united the discipline of classical art with the immediacy of IMPRESSIONISM. His favorite subjects were ballet dancers, women at their toilette, café life, and the racetrack. He combined his portrayal of contemporary life with such daring compositional innovations as accidental cutoff views, off-center subjects, and unusual angles. His innovative achievement of balance is seen in *Woman with Chrysanthemums* (1865; Metropolitan Mus.) and *Foyer of the Dance* (1872; Louvre). Degas turned from oils to pastels and charcoal, perhaps because of failing eyesight. His works in sculpture include dancers and horses. He profoundly influenced such later artists as TOULOUSE-LAUTREC and PICASSO. Many of his most celebrated works, e.g., *The Bellelli Family* (1859), *The Rehearsal* (1882), and *Two Laundresses* (1882), are in the Louvre.

De Gaulle, Charles, 1890–1970, French general and statesman, first president (1959–69) of the Fifth Republic. Opposing the Franco-German armistice in WORLD WAR II, he fled (1940) to London and there organized the Free French forces and rallied several French colonies to his movement. In 1943 he became co-president (with Henri Honoré Giraud) of the French Committee of National Liberation at Algiers, and in 1945 he was elected provisional president of France. He resigned (1946) when it became apparent that the Fourth Republic's constitution would not provide for a strong executive. He become (1947) head of a new party, Rally for the French People (RFP), but dissolved it in 1953 and retired. In 1958, during the political crisis created by the civil war in ALGERIA, De Gaulle became premier with the power to rule by decree for six months. A new constitution that strengthened the presidency was drawn up, and in 1959 De Gaulle became president of the new republic. As president, he reached (1962) a settlement for Algerian independence, developed France's atomic potential, and withdrew (1966) from NATO. He supported French participation in the Common Market, but opposed British participation. Nearly toppled (1968) by worker-student demonstrations, he resigned in 1969 after a defeat on constitutional reform.

De Grasse, François Joseph Paul, comte: see GRASSE, FRANÇOIS JOSEPH PAUL, COMTE DE.

De Hooch or **De Hoogh, Pieter:** see HOOCH, PIETER DE.

dehydrated food: see FOOD PRESERVATION.

Deimos, in astronomy, natural satellite of MARS.

Deirdre [dâr'drə, dēr'–], heroine of Irish legend. Intended as the wife of Conchobar, king of Ulster, she fell in love with Naoise and fled to Scotland with him and his brothers. On their return home Conchobar killed Naoise, and Deirdre died on his grave. The story was popular with writers of the Irish literary renaissance, e.g., W.B. YEATS and J.M. SYNGE.

deists, rationalist thinkers of the 17th and 18th cent., who held that the course of nature demonstrates the existence of God, while they rejected formal religion and claims of supernatural revelation. VOLTAIRE, J.J. ROUSSEAU, Benjamin FRANKLIN, and Thomas JEFFERSON were deists. See also ENLIGHTENMENT.

Dekker, Thomas, 1572?–1632?, English dramatist and pamphleteer. His most famous play, *The Shoemaker's Holiday* (1600), is notable for its realistic depiction of London life. He collaborated with John WEBSTER, Thomas MIDDLETON (*Honest Whore,* Pt. I, 1604), Philip MASSINGER, and others. Most of his works have been lost.

de Klerk, Frederick Willem, 1936–, South African political leader. Succeeding P.W. BOTHA as National party leader and then as president in 1989, de Klerk, despite his conservative reputation, began the process of ending APARTHEID, lifting the ban on antiapartheid parties and releasing Nelson MANDELA from prison in 1990. In 1991 he obtained the repeal of all remaining apartheid laws and called for the drafting of a new constitution, a process that led to the approval of a multiracial transitional government in 1993. De Klerk and Mandela jointly were awarded the Nobel Prize for peace in 1993. Mandela succeeded de Klerk as South African president in 1994 following multiracial elections, and de Klerk became one of two vice presidents in a government of national unity.

de Kooning, Willem, 1904–, American painter and leader of ABSTRACT EXPRESSIONISM; b. Netherlands. He painted huge canvases slashed with color and charged with great energy. He is particularly known for his monumental 1950s series entitled *Woman,* e.g., the ferocious *Woman I* (Mus. Mod. Art, N.Y.C.).

Delacroix, Eugène (Ferdinand-Victor-Eugène Delacroix) [dəläkwä'], 1798–1863, French painter. He was the foremost painter of the romantic movement in France (see ROMANTICISM) and was particularly influential as a colorist. His first major work, *The Bark of Dante* (Louvre), brought him recognition as the leader of the opposition to the neoclassical school of DAVID. His dramatic interpretation of scenes from mythology, literature, political, religious, and literary history was lavish and exuberant. He was influenced by English painting and a trip to Morocco that provided him with much exotic material, e.g., *Women of Algiers* (1834; Louvre). He did many portraits of notable contemporaries, e.g., George SAND (Copenhagen), and his animals in motion, e.g., *Tiger Attacking a Horse* (Louvre), are compelling.

de la Madrid Hurtado, Miguel, 1934–, Mexican public official, president of Mexico (1982–88). As minister of planning and budget in the cabinet of José LÓPEZ PORTILLO, he was influential in planning the utilization of Mexico's oil wealth to promote economic growth. Known as a conservative technocrat, he was chosen (1981) as the candidate of the ruling Institutional Revolutionary party and served from 1982 to 1988.

de la Mare, Walter, 1873–1956, English poet and novelist. His writing often delights in the shadowy world between the real and unreal. His poetry includes *The Listeners* (1912); among his novels are *Henry Brocken* (1904) and *The Return* (1910).

De la Ramée, Louise: see OUIDA.

Delaunay, Robert [dəlōnā'], 1885–1941, French painter. He was a major figure in the movement that APOLLINAIRE termed ORPHISM. His amalgam of fauve color (see FAUVISM), futurist dynamism (see FUTURISM), and analytical CUBISM is best seen in his series of paintings of the EIFFEL TOWER.

Delaware, English name for a group of North American peoples with an Algonquian language of the Algonquian-Wakashan stock (see NATIVE AMERICAN LANGUAGES). Calling themselves the Lenni-Lenape, they claimed ancient occupation of the Delaware R. region, where most Algonquian tribes had originated. In 1682 they made a treaty of friendship with William PENN, but in 1720 the Iroquois forced them into Ohio. The Delaware sided with the British in the American Revolution; afterward they moved successively to Kansas, Texas, and the INDIAN TERRITORY. A few still live on reservations, mainly in Oklahoma. In 1990 there were 9,321 Delaware in the U.S.

Delaware, one of the mid-Atlantic states of the U.S., the country's second-smallest state (after Rhode Island). It is bordered by Maryland (W, S), and there is a short border with Pennsylvania (N); New Jersey (E) is across the Delaware Bay and Delaware R.

Area, 2,057 sq mi (5,328 sq km). *Pop.* (1990) 666,168, an 11.9% increase over 1980 pop. *Capital*, Dover. *Statehood*, Dec. 7, 1787 (first of the original 13 states to ratify the Constitution). *Highest pt.*, 442 ft (135 m), New Castle co.; *lowest pt.*, sea level. *Nickname*, First State. *Motto*, Liberty and Independence. *State bird*, blue hen chicken. *State flower*, peach blossom. *State tree*, American holly. *Abbr.*, Del.; DE.

Land and People. Delaware occupies the low-lying northeastern portion of the peninsula (DELMARVA) it shares with Maryland and Virginia. Along its entire eastern edge the state is bounded by Delaware Bay and the mouth of the DELAWARE R. The climate is equable. WILMINGTON, in the north, is the only large city and dominates the state; 73% of the population lives in urban areas. In 1990 80% of the population was white and 17% was African American.

Economy Delaware has an industrialized economy dominated by the Du Pont chemical company, in the Wilmington area. Other major industries are food processing; automobile assembly; the manufacture of nylon, clothing, metals, and rubber and plastic products; and finance. Much of the agricultural income is earned from broiler chickens, soybeans, potatoes, corn, and dairy products. Although fishing is declining, crabs, oysters, clams, and finfish are caught offshore.

Government. The constitution of 1897 provides for a governor elected to a four-year term. The general assembly consists of a senate whose 21 members serve four-year terms, and a house whose 41 members are elected to two-year terms. Delaware is represented in the U.S. Congress by two senators and one representative and has three electoral votes.

History. The area was the home of the DELAWARE when Henry HUDSON sailed up the Delaware R. in 1609. He was followed by a British explorer the following year, and control of Delaware was subsequently contested by the Dutch and the English—and later by the Swedes—until 1674, when British authority was solidified. The residents were later linked to William PENN's colony of Pennsylvania. In 1776 Delaware was one of the 13 colonies to sign the Declaration of Independence. When Eleuthère Irénée DU PONT started a gunpowder mill in 1802, the state's industrial base was established. Delaware remained loyal to the Union during the CIVIL WAR, but strong pro-Southern sentiment reflected the split between the rural south and urban north, a division that still persists. Industry expanded during both world wars and immediately after World War II. In the 1970s Delaware experienced a movement of population and industry from the cities to the suburbs. During the 1980s the state's usury laws were liberalized, and Delaware (especially the Wilmington area) became a banking center.

Delaware, a major river of the E U.S., flowing c.280 mi (450 km) from sources in the Catskill Mts., SE New York, past Trenton, N.J. (the head of navigation), Philadelphia, Pa., and Wilmington, Del., into Delaware Bay and the Atlantic Ocean. The Delaware River Basin Compact (1961) regulates water use by the heavily industrialized states through which the river flows.

De la Warr, Thomas West, 12th **Baron,** 1577–1618, 1st governor of the English colony of VIRGINIA. He arrived in the colony in 1610 and dissuaded the colonists, who were in dire need, from returning to England. Delaware is named for him.

Delhi [dĕl'ē], state (1991 pop. 9,370,475) and city (1991 pop. 7,175,000), N central India. It is located on a hot, arid plain, but irrigation supports agriculture. From ancient times the region, a crossroads, was the key to empire, and the remains of many dynasties survive. It was the chief center of the Delhi Sultanate (1192–1526). In 1638, the Mogul emperor SHAH JAHAN built a new capital there, known as Shahjahanabad (the city of Delhi, also known as "Old Delhi"). The Mahrattas held the city from 1771 to 1803, when the British took it. Points of interest include Shah Jahan's Red Fort. It was the interim capital of British India (1912–31) while the modern administrative city of New Delhi was being built.

Delian League, confederation of Greek states under the leadership of ATHENS. The first Delian League (478–404 B.C.) was formed by Athens and a number of Ionian states to oppose Persia, an object accomplished in the PERSIAN WARS. Dissent arose within the league, but by a mixture of force and persuasion Athens established supremacy, and the league in effect became an Athenian empire. The alliance was unstable, however, and with Athens' defeat (404 B.C.) in the PELOPONNESIAN WAR it came to an end. After Conan reestablished Athenian mastery of the sea, the second Delian League was formed (378 B.C.). It lasted, despite Athenian-Theban quarrels, until utterly destroyed by the victory of PHILIP II of Macedon at Chaerona (338 B.C.).

Delibes, Léo [dəlēb'], 1836–91, French composer. He wrote melodic, vividly orchestrated works, e.g., the ballets *Coppélia* (1870) and *Sylvia* (1876) and the opera *Lakmé* (1883).

Delilah: see SAMSON.

delirium tremens: see ALCOHOLISM.

Delius, Frederick, 1862–1934, English composer, of German parentage. Influenced by GRIEG, he combined ROMANTICISM and IMPRESSIONISM in music characterized by free structure and rich chromatic HARMONY. His best-known works include *Brigg Fair* (1907), *On Hearing the First Cuckoo in Spring* (1912), and *North Country Sketches* (1914). His operas include *A Village Romeo and Juliet* (1907).

Della Robbia [dĕl"ə rŏb'ēə], Florentine family of sculptors and ceramists famous for their enameled terra cotta or faïence. **Luca della Robbia,** 1400?–1482, founder of the workshop, perfected a method of making clay reliefs and sculptures permanent by coating them with a glaze made of tin, antimony, and other substances. His *Madonna and Child* (Metropolitan Mus.) is typical of his blue-and-white panels with touches of gold. The family tradition was continued by his nephew **Andrea della Robbia,** 1435–1525?, and Andrea's sons **Luca II della Robbia,** c.1480–c.1550, **Giovanni della Robbia,** 1469–c.1529, and **Girolamo della Robbia,** c.1488–1566. Andrea did the famous medallions on the Foundling Hospital, Florence, showing simple baby forms (*bambini*) on a blue background.

Delmarva, peninsula, E U.S., c.180 mi (290 km) long, between Chesapeake Bay (W) and Delaware Bay and Atlantic Ocean (E). A fertile farming area, it is divided among (and named for) three states—Delaware, Maryland, and Virginia.

Delorme or **de l'Orme, Philibert** [dəlôrm'], c.1510–70, French architect, one of the greatest Renaissance architects. Most of his work has been destroyed. After Italian travels he introduced into France a classical style that endured to the mid-18th cent. Among his works were the tomb of FRANCIS I at Saint-Denis, the TUILERIES, and the gallery at Chenonceaux.

Delors, Jacques (Lucien Jean), 1925–, French economist and politician, president (1985–) of the European Commission. Beginning in the 1940s, he held a series of posts in French banking and state planning, eventually becoming (1969) an adviser to Gaullist Prime Min. Jacques Chaban-Delmas. In 1974 he joined the Socialist party. Under Socialist Pres. François MITTERAND, Delors served as economics and finance minister (1981–83) and economics, finance, and budget minister (1983–84) and helped revive the French economy. In 1985 he was appointed president of the European Commission, the executive body of the European Community (EC), and began playing a leading role in EC affairs. Working with British commissioner Lord Cockfield, he crafted and won approval of the Single European Act (1986), which ended the need for unanimous consent by EC nations on most issues and laid the groundwork for the establishment of a single EC market by 1993. Delors has also reformed EC finances and moved the EC nations toward a single currency and greater cooperation on defense.

Delphi [del'fī], town in Phocis, GREECE, near the foot of Mt. Parnassus. It was the seat of the Delphic ORACLE, the most famous and powerful oracle of ancient Greece. The oracle, which originated in the worship of an earth-goddess, possibly GAEA, was the principal shrine of APOLLO. It was housed in a temple built in the 6th cent. B.C. The oracular messages were spoken by a priestess in a frenzied trance and interpreted by a priest, who usually spoke in verse. The oracle's influence prevailed throughout Greece until Hellenistic times. Delphi was the meeting place of the Amphictyonic League and the site of the PYTHIAN GAMES. It was later pillaged by the Romans, and the sanctuary fell into decay.

delphinium: see LARKSPUR.

delta, the alluvial plain formed at the mouth of a river where the stream loses velocity and drops part of its sediment load. No delta is formed if the coast is sinking or if ocean or tidal currents prevent sediment deposition. A deltaic plain is usually very fertile but subject to floods. The three main varieties of delta are the arcuate (e.g., that of the Nile), the bird's-foot (e.g., that of the Mississippi), and the cuspate (e.g., that of the Tiber).

Deluge: see NOAH.

De Mabuse, Jan: see MABUSE, JAN DE.

Demeter [dĭmē'tər], in Greek mythology, goddess of harvest and fertility; daughter of CRONUS and RHEA; mother of PERSEPHONE by ZEUS. She and her daughter were the chief figures in the ELEUSINIAN MYSTERIES, and her primary festival was the Athenian Thesmophoria. The Romans identified her with CERES.

Demetrius I (Demetrius Poliorcetes), c.337–283 B.C., king of MACEDON. He aided his father, Antigonus I, in the wars of the DIADOCHI until their defeat (and Antigonus's death) at Ipsus (301 B.C.). He recovered ATHENS (295) and, after murdering his competitors, seized the throne of Macedon (294). Driven out by PYRRHUS, he took refuge (285) with King Seleucis I of Syria. His son, Antigonus II, made good his claim to the throne of Macedon.

Demetrius, in Russian history: see DMITRI.

de Mille, Agnes (George), 1908?–93, American choreographer and dancer; b. N.Y.C.; niece of Cecil B. DEMILLE. She created the first major American BALLET, *Rodeo* (1942), and brought ballet techniques to MUSICALS such as *Oklahoma!* (1943). She created *Fall River Legend* (1948) for the American Ballet Theatre. De Mille wrote books on dance, including one on Martha GRAHAM (1991), and autobiographical works.

DeMille, Cecil B(lount), 1881–1959, American film director; b. Ashfield, Mass. His many "spectacle" films include *The Ten Commandments* (1923; 1956), *The Crusades* (1935), *Union Pacific* (1939), and *The Greatest Show on Earth* (1952).

Deming, W(illiam) Edwards, 1900–93, American statistician and quality-control expert; b. Sioux City, Iowa. Deming used statistics to examine industrial production processes for flaws and believed that improving product quality depended on increased management-labor cooperation as well as improved design and production processes. He greatly influenced Japanese industry as it rebuilt in the postwar years and was often critical of U.S. corporate management.

Demirel, Süleyman, 1924–, Turkish political leader. A successful engineer, he became leader of the center-right Justice party in 1964, deputy prime minister in 1965, and prime minister later the same year. Growing civil anarchy brought down his government in 1971, but he again served as prime minister during most of the late 1970s. In Sept. 1980 civil turmoil led to an army coup; Demirel was ousted, detained (1980, 1983), and banned from politics until 1987. He returned to politics as leader of the conservative True Path party and served (1991–93) as prime minister in a coalition government. In 1993 he was elected president of Turkey.

democracy, system of government in which the people—not one class, an autocrat, or a select group—share in directing the state's activities. It flourished in such Greek CITY-STATES as Athens before giving way to IMPERIALISM. The philosophy and practice of modern democracy emerged slowly in the West. Basic to it is the concept of representation of the people by elected agents. The idea that natural rights could not be taken from the people is also fundamental (see NATURAL LAW). John LOCKE, J.J. ROUSSEAU, and others developed the concept of a social contract in which sovereignty rests with the people, who undertake reciprocal obligations with a ruler; rulers violating this contract may be removed. These ideas greatly influenced British government, the AMERICAN REVOLUTION, and the FRENCH REVOLUTION. Since the 19th cent., when political democracy was established in most Western countries, emphasis has been placed on increasing the portion of the population participating in political decisions. Theorists of SOCIALISM and other doctrines have criticized this emphasis, maintaining that true democracy is not merely political but rests on economic equality and, according to some, on public ownership of wealth. Since the mid-20th cent. most political systems have described themselves as democracies, but many of them have not encouraged competing political parties and have not stressed individual rights and other elements typical of classic Western democracy. With the collapse of Communism in Eastern Europe, the fall of authoritarian dictatorships in Latin America, and the end of some one-party states in sub-Saharan Africa, however, the number of true multiparty democracies has increased.

Democratic party, American political party. Founded around Thomas JEFFERSON and opposed to Alexander HAMILTON and the Federalists, the party emphasized personal liberty and the limitation of federal government. Originally called Democratic Republicans, they were called Democrats by 1828. Backed by a coalition of Southern agrarians and Northern city dwellers. Jefferson was elected president in 1800, and the Democrats retained the presidency until 1825. A radical group of Democrats led by Andrew JACKSON won the elections of 1828 and 1832, but arguments over slavery created or deepened splits within the party, and the CIVIL WAR all but destroyed it. The party revived after the disputed election of 1876, and the end of RECONSTRUCTION brought the "solid South" into the Democratic fold. With the nomination (1896) of W.J. BRYAN on a FREE SILVER platform, the radicals again gained control, but Bryan's defeat pointed out the difficulty of reconciling the party's diverse elements. The Democrats regained (1913–21) the presidency under the liberal Woodrow WILSON, and during the Depression they swept into office with Franklin D. ROOSEVELT and initiated the NEW DEAL. When Roosevelt died in his fourth term, he was succeeded (1945) by Harry S TRUMAN, who was elected (1948) in his own right. Following the presidential victories (1952, 1956) of Republican Dwight D. Eisenhower, Democrat John F. KENNEDY narrowly won the 1960 election. After his assassination (1963) he was succeeded by Lyndon JOHNSON, whose administration was marked by civil-rights legislation and the VIETNAM WAR. The modern Democratic party had by then become an uneasy alliance of labor, minorities, middle-class reformers, and Southern Democrats. Hubert H. HUMPHREY and George MCGOVERN were the Democratic presidential nominees in 1968 and 1972 respectively, but serious Southern disaffection contributed to their defeats by Republican Richard M. Nixon. Following the WATERGATE AFFAIR, the Democrats elected (1976) the hitherto unknown Jimmy CARTER as president. Carter's inability to cope with economic problems and to free (1979–81) U.S. hostages in Iran led to his defeat (1980) by Republican Ronald REAGAN. Although the party did not win the presidency again until the election (1992) of Bill CLINTON, it remained a power in Congress and at the state level throughout the 1980s.

Democritus, c.460–c.370 B.C., Greek philosopher. His atomic theory of the nature of the physical world, known to us through ARISTOTLE's writings, was the most scientific theory proposed up to his time. He held that all living things are composed of tiny indivisible particles, called atoms, and that their constant motion explains the creation of the universe: the heavier atoms clustered together to form the earth, while the lighter ones formed the heavenly bodies.

demography, science of human population, especially of human numbers and their changes over time. By studying birth and death rates, marital and migration patterns, and population distribution, demography ascertains trends and predicts probabilities.

Demosthenes, 384–322 B.C., Greek orator. His reputation as the greatest of the Greek orators rests mainly on his orations arousing ATHENS against PHILIP II of Macedon—three *Philippics* (351–341 B.C.) and three *Olynthiacs* (349). Philip triumphed (338), and Demosthenes' cause was lost. His other orations include *On the Peace* (346), *On the False Legation* (343), and *On the Crown* (330). In 324 B.C. Demosthenes was exiled for his involvement in an obscure affair involving money taken by a lieutenant of ALEXANDER THE GREAT. Recalled after Alexander's death (323), he failed in his attempt to free Greece from Macedon, fled, and took poison to avoid capture by ANTIPATER.

demotic: see HIEROGLYPHIC.

Dempsey, Jack (William Harrison Dempsey), 1895–1983, American boxer; b. Manassa, Colo. The "Manassa Mauler" won the heavyweight title by knocking out Jess Willard in 1919 and lost it to Gene TUNNEY in 1926. In a controversial rematch (1927) Dempsey knocked Tunney down in the seventh round, but the count (now known as the "long count") was delayed by Dempsey's failure to go to his corner and Tunney won a 10-round decision.

Demuth, Charles, 1883–1935, American painter; b. Lancaster, Pa.

Known for his translucent WATERCOLORS of fruits and flowers, Demuth was one of the first painters to draw inspiration from the geometric shapes of technology.

Denali National Park: see NATIONAL PARKS (table).

dendrochronology: see DATING.

dengue fever, acute infectious disease caused by a virus and transmitted by the *Aedes* mosquito. It occurs in warm climates. Symptoms include headache, fever, and intense joint pain, followed by a generalized rash. There is no specific treatment, but the disease can be controlled by eradicating the mosquitoes and their breeding grounds.

Deng Xiaoping or **Teng Hsiao-p'ing,** [dŭng shēou-pĭng], 1904–, Chinese Communist leader. Twice purged from power (1967, 1976) and twice rehabilitated (1973, 1977), Deng was deputy premier under HUA GUOFENG. He soon became (1977) powerful as Communist party deputy chairman, and in 1979 visited the U.S. to seek closer U.S.-Chinese ties. In 1981 Deng strengthened his position in China by replacing Hua as Communist party chairman with his own protégé, HU YAOBANG. For most of the 1980s he served as head of the party and government military commissions and the newly created party Central Advisory Commission. Although not holding any of the highest ranking official posts, Deng became the most powerful Chinese leader since Mao. When Hu was forced from power, ZHAO ZIYANG, another Deng protégé, became party leader, and later when Zhao was ousted, a third Deng associate, JIANG ZEMIN, replaced Zhao. Deng has sought to loosen government control of the economy in order to promote development while insisting on tight party control of the government and politics.

De Niro, Robert, 1943–, American film actor; b. N.Y.C. After studying for the stage, he acted in films directed by Brian De Palma. In 1973, he made his first major movies, *Bang the Drum Slowly* and *Mean Streets*. Other films include *The Godfather Part II* (1974; Academy Award), *The Deer Hunter* (1979), *Raging Bull* (1981; Academy Award), *Good Fellas* (1989), and *Cape Fear* (1990).

Denis, Maurice [dənē′], 1870–1943, French painter and writer. His paintings, often on religious themes, were not as influential as his art theories. His writings include *Theories* (2 vol., 1920, 1922) and *History of Religious Art* (1939).

Denmark, Dan. *Danmark*, officially Kingdom of Denmark, kingdom (1992 est. pop. 5,164,000), 16,629 sq mi (43,069 sq km), N Europe; bordered by Germany (S), the North Sea (W), the Skagerrak (N), and the Kattegat and the Øresund (E). The southernmost of the Scandinavian countries, Denmark includes most of the Jutland peninsula as well as more than 450 islands. The FAEROE ISLANDS and GREENLAND, which are semiautonomous, lie to the northwest. COPENHAGEN is the capital and chief industrial center; other important cities are RHUS, Odense, and Ålborg. Denmark, which is almost entirely low-lying, has traditionally been an agricultural country; after 1945, however, it greatly expanded its industrial base. The main commodities raised are livestock and poultry, root crops, and cereals. The leading manufactures include food products, chemicals, machinery, metals, and electrical and electronic equipment. Fishing, shipping, and tourism are also important. Nearly all the inhabitants speak Danish, and most belong to the established Lutheran Church. Denmark is a constitutional monarchy, governed under the 1953 constitution. Legislative power is vested in the unicameral Folketing (parliament); executive authority rests with the monarch and the appointed prime minister and cabinet. The reigning monarch is Queen MARGARET II.

History. The Danes probably settled Jutland by c.10,000 B.C., but little is known of Danish history before the 9th to 11th cent. A.D., when the Danes had an important role in the VIKING raids on W Europe. Harold Bluetooth (d. c.985) was the first Christian king of Denmark, and his son, Sweyn, conquered England. Danish hegemony over N Europe was first established (12th–13th cent.) by WALDEMAR I and WALDEMAR II. Queen MARGARET I achieved (1397) the Kalmar Union of Denmark, Sweden, and Norway; the union with Sweden was largely ineffective and ended in 1523, but that with Norway lasted until 1814. The house of Oldenburg, from which the present dynasty is descended, acceded in 1448 with CHRISTIAN I, who also united Schleswig and Holstein with the Danish crown. Participation in the THIRTY YEARS WAR (1618–48) and the wars (1657–60) of FREDERICK III with Sweden caused Denmark to lose prestige. Under the Treaty of Kiel (1814) Denmark lost Norway to Sweden, and following its defeat (1864) by Prussia and Austria it was deprived of SCHLESWIG-HOLSTEIN. Of more lasting importance was the internal reform of the 19th cent. that transformed Denmark's poor peasantry into the most prosperous small farmers in Europe. Denmark was occupied (1940–45) by German forces in WORLD WAR II. In 1949 it broke a long tradition of neutrality and joined NATO, and in 1973 it joined the European Community (see EUROPEAN UNION). The Social Democratic party was dominant in the postwar era, although at times ruling in a coalition or as a minority government. From 1982 to 1993, however, a center-right coalition headed by Conservative Poul Schlüter was in power. In 1993 Poul N. Rasmussen, a Social Democrat, became prime minister of a center-left government.

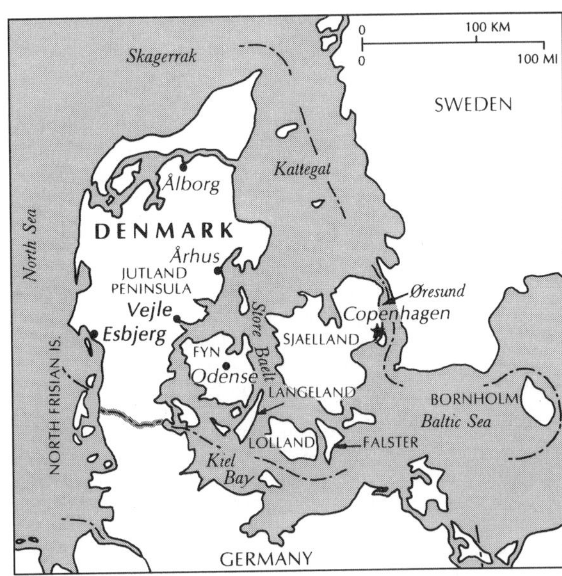

density, ratio of the MASS of a substance to its volume. Because many substances, especially gases, can be compressed into a smaller volume by increasing the pressure on them, the temperature and pressure at which the density is measured are usually specified. See SPECIFIC GRAVITY.

dentistry, treatment and care of the TEETH and associated oral structures. Dentists are concerned with tooth decay, diseases of the supporting structures (such as the gums), faulty positioning of the teeth, and tooth replacements, as well as prevention of these problems. Specialized fields of dentistry include orthodontics (corrective dentistry) and periodontics (treatment of gum diseases; see GINGIVITIS and PERIODONTITIS).

Denver, city (1990 pop. 467,610; met. area 1,622,980), state capital, coextensive with Denver co., N central Colo., on the South Platte R.; inc. 1861. Colorado's largest city, Denver is a processing, shipping, and distributing point for a large agricultural area. It is the financial and administrative center of the ROCKY MOUNTAIN region, and a hub for energy resource development. Numerous federal agencies have offices there, and it is the site of a U.S. mint. The Denver area has major stockyards and many diversified industries, including electronics and aeronautics. Tourism is also important. In the 1870s and 80s it was the center of a gold and silver boom. Its development into a major modern city began in the 1890s. Points of interest include a large park system, the state capitol, and the Denver Art Museum and other museums.

Depardieu, Gérard [dəpär″dyö′], 1948–, French actor. A versatile, highly acclaimed performer, he has made dozens of films, including *Le Dernier Métro* (1980), *The Return of Martin Guerre* (1982), and *Green Card* (1990).

De Patinir, De Patenier, or **De Patiner, Joachim:** see PATINIR, JOACHIM DE.

depreciation, in ACCOUNTING, reduction in the value of fixed assets as a result of use, damage, or obsolescence. It can be estimated in several ways. In the straight-line method, annual depreciation is simply the cost of the asset (minus its value, if any, as scrap) divided equally over its estimated lifetime. Decreasing-charge methods assign higher depreciation costs to the early years. Depreciation allows companies to cut costs of capital investment through tax savings.

depressant: see DRUG.

depression, in economics, a period of economic crisis in commerce, finance, and industry, characterized by falling prices, restriction of credit, reduced production, numerous bankruptcies, and high unemployment. A less severe crisis is usually known as a downturn, or **recession;** in the U.S. a recession is technically defined as two consecutive quarterly declines in the GROSS NATIONAL PRODUCT. A short period in which fear takes hold of the minds of businessmen is more properly called a PANIC. Depressions now tend to become worldwide in scope because of the international nature of trade and credit. Such was the case in the most severe economic reversal of the 20th cent., the GREAT DEPRESSION of the 1930s, which began in the U.S. and spread abroad. Since that time, governments have acted to stabilize economic conditions in an effort to prevent depressions, using tax and fiscal measures as well as tighter controls over BANKING and the STOCK EXCHANGES. Job-training programs and increased public welfare are other steps taken to alleviate economic slumps.

depression, a psychological disorder that can be marked by sleep and eating disturbances, lack of concentration, problems at work, intense feelings of emptiness, guilt, and worthlessness, and suicidal thoughts. A depressive illness is distinguished from a temporary "blue" mood or grief after a disappointment or loss and may have both psychological and biochemical components. The illness may have a manic phase (see MANIC-DEPRESSION). Many people improve significantly with psychological treatment and ANTIDEPRESSANT medication, often used in combination. ELECTROCONVULSIVE THERAPY may help severe cases.

depth charge, explosive device used against submarines and other underwater targets. Delivered from surface ships, it is either rolled into the water or propelled by special throwers. The charge is detonated by water pressure at a predetermined depth and, if it explodes near enough, can destroy the target by concussion.

De Quincey, Thomas, 1785–1859, English essayist. The autobiographical *Confessions of an English Opium-Eater* (1822) brought him literary eminence. A prolific contributor to various journals, he is remembered for "On the Knocking at the Gate in Macbeth" and *Autobiographic Sketches* (1853).

Derain, André [dərăN′], 1880–1954, French painter. He was an exponent of FAUVISM, as in his portrait of MATISSE (1905; Philadelphia Mus. Art). Gradually his art grew more conservative.

derivative: see CALCULUS.

Derrida, Jacques, 1930–, French philosopher. He has sought to "deconstruct" Western rationalist thought and metaphysics to reveal the incoherence of its foundations (see DECONSTRUCTION). In *Writing and Difference* (1967) and *On Grammatology* (1967) he set forth his theories, based on a broad reading of the Western tradition. In opposition to the theory of SAUSSURE (see SEMIOTICS), Derrida challenged the primacy of spoken language, emphasizing the written language's ability to alter speech and thought, creating rather than merely transmitting meaning. His writings have analyzed the work of HUSSERL, HEGEL, and other major philosophers.

dervish [Pers., = beggar], the friar or monk of ISLAM. There are numerous societies of dervishes, many quite similar to the religious orders of Western Christendom; however, dervishes do not take final vows and are never cloistered. Certain groups are characterized by the form of their mystical practice, e.g., the howling dervishes and whirling dervishes. Some form of SUFISM is the theological basis of most of the dervish sects.

Derzhavin, Gavril Romanovich [dyĭrzhä′vĭn], 1743–1816, Russian poet. An innovator in the age of classicism, he dedicated *Felitsa* (1783) to Catherine II, leading to his appointments as poet laureate and then minister of justice. His most famous lyric is the *Ode to God* (1784).

DES or **diethylstilbestrol,** synthetic nonsteroid female sex hormone having the same physiological effects as ESTROGEN. In the 1940s and 50s, DES was given in large doses to pregnant women to prevent miscarriage, but such use was banned in 1973. During the 1970s the drug was linked to vaginal cancer in some women whose mothers had taken DES during pregnancy, and it has since been implicated in various reproductive disorders and other conditions in female and male children of such mothers. The use of DES as a growth accelerator in beef cattle was banned in 1979. DES is currently used in treatment of certain breast and prostate cancers.

Desai, Morarji Ranchhodji [dēsī′], 1896–, prime minister (1977–79) of INDIA. As leader of the Janata people's party, he became prime minister after Indira GANDHI's fall from power. He was unable to maintain a working majority, however, and resigned in 1979, thereby clearing the way for Mrs. Gandhi's return to power.

desalination, process of removing soluble salts from water to render it suitable for drinking, irrigation, or industrial uses. In *distillation,* salt water is heated in one container to make the water evaporate, leaving the salt behind. The desalinated vapor is then condensed to form water in a separate container. The high fuel costs involved in vaporizing salt water can be reduced by using a vacuum to lower the boiling point or by exposing a water spray or film to high heat, a process known as flash distillation. In Hawaii the vacuum method also produces electricity in a process that vaporizes warmer, near-surface water, uses the steam to run a turbine, and condenses the steam with cold water from the ocean depths. Other desalination techniques include *electrodialysis,* the use of porous membranes to filter out negatively and positively charged salt ions; *freezing,* based on the principle that water excludes salt when it crystallizes to ice; *ion-exchange,* in which water passes through a bed of specially treated synthetic resins that are capable of extracting ions of the salt from the solution and replacing them with ions that form water; and *reverse osmosis,* in which pressure, generated by the presence of salt in the water, forces water through a membrane permeable only by pure water.

Descartes, René, 1596–1650, French philosopher, mathematician, and scientist. His philosophy is called Cartesianism (from *Cartesius,* the Latin form of his name). Often called the father of modern philosophy, he is regarded as the bridge between SCHOLASTICISM and all philosophy that followed him. Primarily interested in mathematics, he founded ANALYTIC GEOMETRY and originated the CARTESIAN COORDINATES and Cartesian curves. To algebra he contributed the treatment of negative roots and the convention of exponent notation. Descartes also contributed to optics, physiology, and psychology. His *Discourse on Method* (1637) and *Meditations* (1641) contain his important philosophical theories. Intending to extend mathematical method to all areas of human knowledge, Descartes discarded the authoritarian systems of the scholastic philosophers and began with universal doubt. Only one thing cannot be doubted: doubt itself. Therefore, the doubter must exist. This is the kernel of his famous assertion *Cogito, ergo sum* [I think, therefore I am]. From this certainty Descartes expanded knowledge, step by step, to admit the existence of God (as the first cause) and the reality of the physical world, which he held to be mechanistic and entirely divorced from the mind; the only connection between the two is the intervention of God. This is almost complete DUALISM.

descent: see KINSHIP.

desegregation: see INTEGRATION.

desert, arid region, usually partly covered by sand, supporting a limited and specially adapted plant and animal population. So-called cold deserts, caused by extreme cold and often covered perpetually by snow or ice, form about one sixth of the earth's surface. Warm deserts form about one fifth of it. The world's largest desert areas lie between 20° and 30° north and south of the equator in regions where mountains intercept the paths of the trade winds or where atmospheric conditions limit precipitation. An area with an annual rainfall of 10 in. (25 cm) or less is considered a desert, although some deserts and semideserts exist in areas of higher precipitation where moisture is lost by runoff or evaporation. The two largest deserts are the SAHARA in Africa and the great desert of central and W Australia.

De Sica, Vittorio, 1901–74, Italian film director and actor. His *Shoeshine* (1946), *The Bicycle Thief* (1948), and *Umberto D.* (1952) are classics of postwar Italian neo-realism. Among his later works is

The Garden of the Finzi-Continis (1971). He starred in ROSSELLINI's *General Della Rovere* (1959) and many other films.

desktop publishing, system for producing printed materials that consists of a PERSONAL COMPUTER or COMPUTER workstation, high-resolution printer (usually a laser PRINTER), and COMPUTER PROGRAM that allows the user to select from a variety of type fonts and sizes, column justifications, page layouts, and graphics libraries and often includes support for document creation and editing. It enables a small business or an individual to produce professional quality materials on the premises inexpensively and quickly without need of external typesetting or printing facilities.

Des Moines, city (1990 pop. 193,187), state capital and seat of Polk co., S central Iowa, on the Des Moines and Raccoon rivers; chartered 1857. Iowa's largest city, it is a major Corn Belt industrial and transportation center. Publishing and printing, food processing, insurance, and diverse manufactures are important. Drake Univ. and various state buildings are notable.

De Soto, Hernando, c.1500–42, Spanish explorer. After serving with Francisco PIZARRO in PERU, he was named governor of CUBA. In 1539 he set out to conquer Florida. In search of treasure, his group explored much of present-day GEORGIA, the Carolinas, TENNESSEE, ALABAMA, and OKLAHOMA. They were probably the first Europeans to see (1541) the MISSISSIPPI R. De Soto died on the adventurous journey and was buried in the Mississippi.

Des Prés, Josquin: see JOSQUIN DESPREZ.

Dessalines, Jean Jacques [dĕsälĕn'], c.1758–1806, emperor of HAITI (1804–6). Of African descent and born a slave, he became a shrewd general. He defeated (1803) French forces and, upon Haiti's independence (1804), ruled as a despot until he was assassinated.

detective story, type of popular fiction in which a crime, usually a murder, is solved by a detective—professional or amateur—who logically interprets the evidence. The modern detective story, complete with its conventions, is considered to have emerged in E.A. POE's "Murders in the Rue Morgue" (1841). Wilkie COLLINS's *The Moonstone* (1868) is probably the first full-length detective novel. In 1887 Arthur Conan DOYLE, in "A Study in Scarlet," introduced Sherlock Holmes, the most famous of all sleuths. Subsequent writers, too, have often used one detective in a series of works. Especially famous are G.K. CHESTERTON's Father Brown, Earl Derr Biggers's Charlie Chan, Rex Stout's Nero Wolfe, Dorothy SAYERS's Lord Peter Wimsey, Agatha CHRISTIE's Hercule Poirot and Jane Marple, and P.D. James's Adam Dalgliesh. Many writers incorporate the conventions of the detective story into the NOVEL, producing works that are witty, erudite, and filled with interesting characters. Such writers include Ngaio MARSH, C. DAY LEWIS, Josephine Tey, Arthur W. Upfield, Peter Dickinson, and Ruth Rendell. More specialized types of detective fiction include the "police procedural," by such writers as Freeman Wills Crofts, Ed McBain, and Maj Sjöwall and Per Wahlöö, which focus on the technical aspects of crime-solving; the "hard-boiled" story, such as those of Dashiell HAMMETT, Raymond CHANDLER, and Ross MACDONALD, featuring tough but honorable "private eyes"; and the psychological story, such as the novels of Georges SIMENON, in which motivation and ambience are more important than the solution to the crime. Espionage novels involving international intrigue share many conventions of detective fiction. Masters of this genre include Eric AMBLER, Graham GREENE, Ian Fleming, and John LE CARRÉ.

detector: see PARTICLE DETECTOR.

détente, relaxation of tensions between nations, applied particularly to a period of improved relations between the U.S. and USSR in the 1960s and 70s that resulted as the hostilities of the COLD WAR diminished. Détente reached its height in such agreements as the Nuclear Nonproliferation Treaty (1968), Strategic Arms Limitation Treaty (SALT I; 1972), and the Helsinki accords (1975). After the Soviet invasion of Afghanistan (1979), relations between the two superpowers worsened. The crisis in Poland, an escalation of the arms race, and Pres. REAGAN's anti-Soviet stance brought an end to détente in the early 1980s.

Detroit, city (1990 pop. 1,027,974; met. area 4,382,299), seat of Wayne co., SE Mich., on the Detroit R., between Lakes St. Clair and Erie; inc. as a city 1815. It is Michigan's largest city, the nation's seventh largest, and a major GREAT LAKES shipping and rail center. Its early carriage industry helped Henry FORD and others to make it the "automobile capital of the world." It continues to be the headquarters of major auto manufacturers, but declines in the field have caused severe unemployment in the city and its environs. Other industries include steel, pharmaceuticals, and food processing. A producer of foundry products and machine tools, tires, paint, and chemicals, it also has extensive salt mines. Detroit is the oldest city in the Midwest. A French fort and fur-trading settlement founded in 1701 by CADILLAC, it was captured (1760) by the British. U.S. control, resulting from JAY'S TREATY (1794), dates from 1796. After a devastating 1805 fire, the city was rebuilt to a plan by L'ENFANT and grew to great commercial importance in the mid-1800s. In July 1967 race riots caused several deaths and many injuries, as well as some $150 million in property damages. The city is the site of many ambitious modern building projects, e.g., the Renaissance Center. The city's educational and cultural institutions include Wayne State Univ., the Univ. of Detroit, the Detroit Inst. of the Arts, and the Detroit Symphony Orchestra. An international bridge and a vehicular tunnel link Detroit with WINDSOR, Ontario.

Deucalion [dyo͞okā'lēən], in Greek mythology, son of PROMETHEUS; father of HELLEN. Only he and his wife Pyrrha survived the flood that ZEUS caused in anger at humankind's irreverence. Later an oracle told them to cast behind them the stones of the earth. These stones became human and repopulated the world.

deuterium: see HYDROGEN.

Deuteronomy, book of the OLD TESTAMENT, fifth and last of the PENTATEUCH, ascribed by tradition to MOSES. According to the text it gives the final words of Moses to his people, and includes a review of the history of Israel since the exodus from Egypt and a number of general and particular moral principles. The book concludes with a blessing by, and the death of, Moses. Its main theme is absolute monotheism.

De Valera, Eamon [dĕ vəlâr'ə], 1882–1975, Irish statesman; b. N.Y.C. He took part in the Easter Rebellion of 1916; sentenced to life imprisonment, he was released under an amnesty in 1917 and elected president of SINN FÉIN. Again imprisoned in 1918, he escaped to the U.S., where he raised funds for Irish independence. While away, he was elected president of the revolutionary assembly, Dáil Eireann; he returned in 1920. In 1922, De Valera repudiated the treaty between Britain and Ireland that established the Irish Free State because it did not give Ireland absolute freedom, and he left the Dáil. In 1927 he reentered the Dáil with his party, FIANNA FÁIL. As prime minister (1932–48, 1951–54, 1957–58), he made Ireland a sovereign state and maintained neutrality in WORLD WAR II. He was also president of Ireland (1959–73).

devaluation, decreasing the value of one nation's currency relative to gold or the currencies of other nations. It is usually undertaken as a means of correcting a deficit in the BALANCE OF PAYMENTS. Although devaluation occurs in terms of all currencies, it is best illustrated in relation to one other currency. For example, if the U.S. is losing money in its trade with France, it may decide to devalue the dollar by 10%. If one dollar had been worth about 5.5 francs, a 10% devaluation causes it to be worth only 5 francs. Such a move causes French products to become more expensive for Americans (in theory, reducing U.S. imports) and American products to become cheaper for the French (increasing U.S. exports).

Devereux, Robert: see ESSEX, ROBERT DEVEREUX, 2D EARL OF.

Devils Island, most southerly of the Îles du Salut, in the Caribbean Sea, off FRENCH GUIANA. It was the site of a penal colony (1852–1951) used mostly for political prisoners, such as Capt. Alfred Dreyfus (see DREYFUS AFFAIR). Its name was synonymous with the system's horrors.

Devolution, War of, 1667–68, between France and Spain over the Spanish Netherlands. On the basis of a complicated legal claim, LOUIS XIV of France overran the Spanish Netherlands and Franche-Comté. The United Provinces, in alarm, formed the Triple Alliance with England and Sweden, and France was forced to make peace.

Devonian period: see GEOLOGIC ERA (table).

de Vries, Hugo, 1848–1935, Dutch botanist. He rediscovered (1900) Gregor MENDEL's laws of heredity and developed the theory of MUTATION, expounded in *The Mutation Theory* (1901–3) and in *Plant-Breeding* (1907). De Vries introduced the experimental method to the study of evolution, and maintained that new species develop via mutations and that each quality subject to change is represented by a single physical unit (which he called a pangen). His work on osmosis is also important; he coined the term *isotonic*.

dew, thin film of water that has condensed on the surface of objects near the ground. Dew forms when objects cool during the night, causing the layer of air in contact with them to cool, and then causing the condensation of the water vapor in that layer of air. Condensation occurs because the capacity of air to hold water vapor decreases as the air is cooled. FROST forms if the dew point, or temperature at which condensation begins, is below 32°F (0°C).

Dewar, Sir James, 1842–1923, British chemist and physicist; b. Scotland. Professor at the Royal Inst., London, and later director of the Davy-Faraday Research Laboratory there, he was knighted in 1904. Best known for his work on the properties of matter at very low temperatures and the liquefaction of gases, he liquefied and solidified hydrogen and invented the DEWAR FLASK.

Dewar flask [for Sir James Dewar], container for storing hot or cold substances, e.g., liquid nitrogen. It consists of two flasks, one inside the other, separated by a vacuum. The vacuum greatly reduces the transfer of heat. The common thermos bottle is an adaptation of the Dewar flask.

Dewey, George, 1837–1917, American admiral; b. Montpelier, Vt.; grad. Annapolis, 1858. During the SPANISH-AMERICAN WAR, he directed (1898) the spectacular victory over the Spanish fleet in Manila Bay in the Philippines.

John Dewey

Dewey, John, 1859–1952, American philosopher and educator; b. Burlington, Vt. He rejected authoritarian teaching methods, regarding education in a democracy as a tool to enable the citizen to integrate his or her culture and vocation usefully. To accomplish those aims, both pedagogical methods and curricula needed radical reform. Dewey's philosophy, called instrumentalism and related to PRAGMATISM, holds that truth is an instrument used by human beings to solve their problems, and that it must change as their problems change. Thus it partakes of no transcendental or eternal reality. Dewey's view of democracy as a primary ethical value permeated his educational theories. He had a profound impact on PROGRESSIVE EDUCATION and was regarded as the foremost educator of his day. He lectured all over the world and prepared educational surveys for Turkey, Mexico, and the Soviet Union. Among his works are *Democracy and Education* (1916) and *Logic* (1938).

Dewey, Melvil, 1851–1931, American library pioneer, originator of the Dewey decimal system; b. Adams Center, N.Y. As acting librarian of Amherst College (1874) he evolved his system of book classification, using the numbers 000 to 999 to cover the general fields of knowledge and narrowing the system to fit special subjects by the use of decimals. While at Columbia Univ. he established the first library school. Dewey was also librarian of the New York State Library at Albany, where he founded another important library school. He was a founder of the American Library Association.

Dewey, Thomas Edmund, 1902–71, U.S. politician, governor (1943–55) of New York; b. Owosso, Mich. Twice a Republican presidential candidate, Dewey lost in 1944 to F.D. ROOSEVELT, and in 1948, quite unexpectedly, to Harry S TRUMAN.

De Witt, Jan: see WITT, JAN DE.

dextrose: see GLUCOSE.

Dhahran, city (1980 est. pop. 15,000), NE Saudi Arabia, near the Persian Gulf. Since the discovery (1938) of oil nearby, it has grown rapidly into a modern city. In Dhahran are the headquarters of the Arabian American Oil Co. (ARAMCO), the office of the Saudi petroleum ministry, and the Univ. of Petroleum and Minerals. During the PERSIAN GULF WAR the city was the site of a coalition air base and was subjected to Iraqi missile attacks.

Dhaka or **Dacca,** city (1991 pop. 6,959,920), capital of Bangladesh, on the Burhi Ganga R. It is the nation's industrial, commercial, and administrative center, with an active trade in jute, rice, and tea. Among its manufactures are textiles, jute products, and rope, and in cottage industries, confectioneries, jewelry, and other handicrafts. It was the capital (1660–1704) of the Mogul province of Bengal. It passed under British rule in 1765, and became capital of the newly formed Bangladesh in 1971. Historic buildings include the Bara Katra palace (1644) and Lal Bagh fort (1678).

dharma. 1 In Hinduism, the religious and ethical duties of the individual; virtue, right conduct. **2** In Buddhism, religious truth, namely, Buddhist teaching. The plural, *dharmas,* refers to the constituent qualities and phenomena of the empirical world.

diabetes or **diabetes mellitus,** chronic disorder of carbohydrate metabolism involving INSULIN. Insulin-dependent diabetes (Type 1), which affects children, is usually caused by a deficient secretion of insulin and is treated by insulin injections. Noninsulin diabetes (Type 2), which affects adults, results from the inability of the cells in the body to respond to insulin and can usually be controlled with diet regulation and oral hypoglycemic (sugar-lowering) drugs. Symptoms of diabetes are elevated sugar in the urine and the blood, excessive urination, thirst, hunger, weakness, weight loss, and itching. Diabetes can lead to vascular disease, kidney disease, HYPERTENSION, and BLINDNESS. Uncontrolled diabetes leads to diabetic acidosis: ketones in the blood, confusion, unconsciousness, and possible death.

Diadochi [dīăd'əkī] [Gr., = successors], subordinates of ALEXANDER THE GREAT who, after his death (323 B.C.), struggled for control of his empire. Chief among them were Antipater, Perdiccas, Eumenes, Craterus, Antigonus, Ptolemy, Seleucus, and Lysimachus. The major events of the wars of the Diadochi were the victory of Antipater over Perdiccas for the regency (321 B.C.); the defeat of Antigonus by Lysimachus, Ptolemy, and Seleucus at Ipsus (301 B.C.); and the victory of Seleucus over Lysimachus at Corupedion (281 B.C.). At the end of the period Alexander's empire was irrevocably split, with power divided among the descendants of Ptolemy, Seleucus, and Antigonus.

Diaghilev, Sergei Pavlovich, 1872–1929, Russian Ballet impresario and art critic. With Michel FOKINE and others, he founded (1909) the Ballets Russes in Paris. His lavish productions, incorporating asymmetry and perpetual motion, revolutionized BALLET, and attracted dancers, choreographers, designers, and composers of the first rank.

dialect, variety of a LANGUAGE used by a group of speakers within a particular speech community. Every individual speaks a variety of his or her language called an idiolect. Dialects are groups of idiolects with a common core of similarities in pronunciation, grammar, and vocabulary. Adjacent dialects are mutually intelligible, yet with increasing distance differences may accumulate to the point of mutual unintelligibility. For example, in the Dutch-German speech community, there is a continuum of intelligibility from Flanders to Schleswig and from there to Styria, but Flemish and Styrian dialects are mutually unintelligible. The methods of comparative linguistics, using written texts, and of modern linguistic geography, using informants, have been used to study dialects. In recent years many linguists have focused on social dialects that reflect societal groups, occupations, or life-styles. In the U.S. much work has been done in the area of BLACK ENGLISH.

dialectical materialism, official philosophy of Communism, based on the works of Karl MARX and his followers. A reversal of HEGEL's dialectical IDEALISM, it holds that everything is material and that human beings create social life solely in response to economic needs. Thus all aspects of society are considered to reflect the economic structure, and classes in society are determined by their relationship to the means of production. Growth, change, and development take place through a naturally occurring "struggle of opposites," a process that individuals cannot influence. Application of these principles to the study of history and sociology is called historical materialism, an approach having many non-Communist advocates.

dialysis, in chemistry, transfer of dissolved solids (solute) across a semipermeable membrane, which permits or hinders diffusion of molecules according to their size. Dialysis is frequently used to separate different components of a solution. For example, in artificial kidney machines hemodialysis is used to purify the blood of persons whose KIDNEYS have ceased to function. In the machine, blood is circulated on one side of a semipermeable membrane, while dialysis fluid—containing substances necessary to the body and closely matching the chemical composition of the blood—is circulated on the other side. Metabolic waste products, such as urea, diffuse through the membrane into the dialysis fluid and are discarded, while the diffusion of substances necessary to the body is prevented. In peritoneal dialysis, the dialysis fluid is introduced into the abdominal cavity. Waste products leach from the blood vessels into the fluid, which is later drained from the patient. See also OSMOSIS.

diamond, mineral, one of two crystalline forms of the element CARBON. It is the hardest naturally occurring substance known, and inferior stones are used as ABRASIVES, in certain types of cutting tools, and as phonograph needles. Gem diamonds were first found in streambeds in India and Borneo; many now come from volcanic pipes in South Africa. Russia and Angola are also important producers. Famous diamonds include the Koh-i-noor, now among the English crown jewels; the Cullinan, from which 105 stones were cut; and the blue Hope diamond. Synthetic diamonds, produced since 1955, are now widely used industrially. A hard carbon nitride (C_3N_4) described in 1989 and synthesized in the early 1990s may be harder than diamond but has not been produced in large enough amounts for a proper test.

Diamond Head, peak, 761 ft (232 m) high, SE Oahu, Hawaii, prominent landmark of the Honolulu waterfront. It is located on the rim of an extinct volcanic crater near Waikiki Beach and is protected from commercial development.

Diana, 1961–, princess of Wales, wife of CHARLES, prince of Wales, heir to the British throne. Daughter of the 8th Earl Spencer, she worked as a kindergarten teacher in London before her marriage in 1981. She and Prince Charles separated in 1992; they have two sons, William and Henry.

Diana, in Roman mythology, goddess of the moon, forests, animals, and women in childbirth. Both a virgin goddess and an earth goddess, she was identified with the Greek ARTEMIS.

Diane de Poitiers [pwätyā'], 1499–1566, mistress of HENRY II of France. She maintained friendly relations with the queen, CATHERINE DE' MEDICI, while completely eclipsing her. She supported the king's anti-Protestant policy.

diaphragm: see RESPIRATION.

diary [Lat., = day], a daily record of events and observations. It derives its impact from its immediacy, unlike the retrospective memoir. Diaries interest historians because they depict everyday lives in a given time and place. Three of the most famous are those by Samuel PEPYS, who bore witness to the plague (1665) and great fire (1666) then sweeping London; Mary Chesnut, who chronicled in personal terms the fate of the CONFEDERACY in the American CIVIL WAR; and Anne Frank, a young German-Jewish girl who, before she died in a World War II CONCENTRATION CAMP, recorded her experiences while hiding in Holland. Important literary diaries include those of John EVELYN, André GIDE, Franz KAFKA, and Virginia WOOLF.

Diana, Princess of Wales

diatom, single-celled, microscopic plant that secretes and is enclosed by an often intricate, round-to-elongated silica shell. Golden-brown ALGAE, diatoms are found in fresh and salt water, in moist soil, and on the moist surfaces of other plants; they are the principal constituent of PLANKTON, an important food source for aquatic animals. Most exist singly, but some form colonies. When the aquatic forms die, their shells collect in the ooze on the bottom, eventually forming the material called diatomaceous earth (kieselguhr) or the more compact, chalky, light-weight rock called diatomite, used in sound and heat insulation, in making explosives, and for filters and abrasives. Most LIMESTONE and much PETROLEUM is of diatom origin.

Díaz, Porfirio, 1830–1915, Mexican dictator. In 1876 he lost the presidential election, revolted, and seized power. He ruled MEXICO ruthlessly for 35 years in the interest of the few and at the expense of the peons. He promoted prosperity by encouraging foreign investments. Growing popular discontent culminated in the 1910 revolution led by MADERO. Díaz fled and died in exile.

Dickens, Charles, 1812–70, English novelist, one of the great fiction writers in English. After a childhood of poverty, during which he had to work for a time in a blacking warehouse (a humiliation he never forgot), Dickens became a court stenographer and parliamentary reporter. His early sketches of London life were collected in *Sketches by Boz* (1836). *The Posthumous Papers of the Pickwick Club* (1836–37), a series of connected humorous sketches, promptly made Dickens famous, and the major novels that followed established him as the most popular writer of his time. They include *Oliver Twist* (1838), *Nicholas Nickleby* (1839), *The Old Curiosity Shop* (1841), *Barnaby Rudge* (1841), *Dombey and Son* (1848), *David Copperfield* (1850), *Bleak House* (1853), *Hard Times* (1854), *Little Dorrit* (1857), *A Tale of Two Cities* (1859), *Great Expectations* (1861), *Our Mutual Friend* (1865), and *The Mystery of Edwin Drood* (1870; unfinished). After an American tour in 1842, he wrote sharply about the U.S. in *American Notes* (1842) and in the novel *Martin Chuzzlewit* (1843). Working ceaselessly, Dickens gave highly successful readings from his works, edited two magazines, wrote Christmas stories, e.g., *A Christmas Carol* (1843), and managed amateur theatricals. He married Catherine Hogarth in 1836, but despite their 10 children, it was not a happy union, and they separated in 1858. Although sometimes marred by sentimentality, Dickens's novels are remarkable for their rich portraits of all aspects of society, their crusades against abuses (imprisonment for debt, legal delays, bad education), and their sharply drawn, eccentric characters, whose names—Mr. Micawber, Uriah Heep, Ebenezer Scrooge—have become household words for generations of readers.

Dickey, James, 1923–, American poet; b. Atlanta. He makes use of the ordinary in his poems, joining the natural and mechanical on such topics as war and nature. His poetry volumes include *Buckdancer's Choice* (1965) and *The Zodiac* (1976). He is probably best known for his novel *Deliverance* (1969).

Dickinson, Emily, 1830–86, one of the greatest poets in American literature; b. Amherst, Mass. The daughter of a prominent lawyer, she spent almost all of her life in her birthplace, gradually withdrawing from local activities, and spending her later years as a virtual recluse in her father's house. She composed over 1,000 unique lyrics dealing with religion, love, nature, death, and immortality, only seven of which were published during her lifetime. Her verse, noted for its aphoristic style, its wit, its delicate metrical variation, and its bold and startling imagery, has had great influence on 20th-cent. poetry. Her posthumous fame began with the first editions of her poems (1890, 1891) and her correspondence (2 vol., 1894). While her work has gone through many editions, a definitive edition of Dickinson did not appear until the 1950s, when T.H. Johnson published her poems (3 vol., 1955) and her letters (3 vol., 1958).

Dickinson, John, 1732–1808, American Revolutionary statesman; b. Talbot co., Md. He wrote *Letters from a Farmer in Pennsylvania* (1767–68) to protest the TOWNSHEND ACTS. A conservative member of the CONTINENTAL CONGRESS, he championed the rights of the small states at the FEDERAL CONSTITUTIONAL CONVENTION.

dicotyledon: see ANGIOSPERM.

Diderot, Denis [dēdərō'], 1713–84, French encyclopedist and materialist philosopher. He was enormously influential in shaping the rationalist thought of the 18th cent. His lifework, the ENCYCLOPÉDIE, for which he enlisted the leading French talents of the time, epitomized the spirit of the ENLIGHTENMENT. Also a novelist, satirist, and playwright, he produced *The Father of the Family* (1758) the first "bourgeois drama." He authored many philosophical works and in his *Salons* pioneered in modern art criticism. In his later years, he enjoyed the patronage of CATHERINE II of Russia.

Didion, Joan, 1934–, American writer; b. Sacramento, Calif. Exploring the emptiness of contemporary American life, her work includes novels, e.g., *Play It As It Lays* (1970) and *A Book of Common Prayer* (1977), and essay collections, e.g., *The White Album* (1979) and *After Henry* (1992).

Dido [dī'dō], in Roman mythology, founder and queen of CARTHAGE. Of the several versions of her story the most famous is in VERGIL's *Aeneid*, in which she loves AENEAS. When he leaves her to continue his journey to Italy, she destroys herself on a burning pyre.

Didrikson, Babe (Mildred Didrikson), 1913–56, American athlete, perhaps the greatest woman athlete of modern times; b. Port Arthur, Tex. She excelled in basketball, baseball, and track, and she won (1932) two Olympic events, the javelin and the 80-meter hurdles. As a golfer she won the U.S. (1946) and British (1947) amateur titles and the U.S. Open (1948, 1950, 1954). She married George Zaharias, a wrestler, in 1938.

Didymus: see THOMAS, SAINT.

Diefenbaker, John George, 1895–1979, prime minister of CANADA (1957–63). He was leader of the Progressive Conservatives and led them to their greatest election victory in 1958. He instituted agricultural reforms, but a recession contributed to his party's losses to the Liberals in 1962; his government fell the following year.

Diego Garcia, coral island, Indian Ocean, largest island of the Chagos Archipelago, SW of Sri Lanka. Part of the British Indian Ocean Territory, it is also claimed by Mauritius. The 11-sq-mi (28-sq-km) island, leased (1970) to the U.S., was later developed as a major U.S. naval base to guard the PERSIAN GULF oil routes and to counter increased Soviet military activities in S Asia and Africa.

dielectric, material that does not readily conduct electricity, i.e., an insulator (see INSULATION). A good dielectric resists breakdown under high voltages, does not draw appreciable power from the circuit, and has reasonable physical stability. Dielectrics are used to separate the plates of a CAPACITOR. The dielectric strength is a measure of the maximum voltage (see POTENTIAL, ELECTRIC) that a dielectric can sustain without significant CONDUCTION.

Diem, Ngo Dinh [dyĕm], 1901–63, president (1955–63) of South VIETNAM. Named (1954) premier, he ousted (1955) Bao Dai as head of state and emerged as president. His rule grew authoritarian, and he was murdered in a military coup that was apparently backed by the U.S.

Dienbienphu [dyĕn'byĕn'fōō'], former French military base, NW Vietnam, near the Laos border. It was the scene (May 1954) of the last great battle between the French and the VIET MINH, whose victory after a 56-day siege marked the end of French power in INDOCHINA.

diesel engine, type of INTERNAL-COMBUSTION ENGINE patented (1892) by the German engineer Rudolph Diesel. It is heavier and more powerful than the gasoline engine and burns fuel oil instead of gasoline. It differs from the gasoline engine in that the ignition of fuel is caused by compression of air in its cylinders instead of by a spark. The speed and power of the diesel are controlled by varying the amount of fuel injected into the cylinder. Diesels are widely used to power industrial and municipal electric generators, continuously operating pumps such as those used in oil pipelines, and ships, trucks, locomotives, and some automobiles.

dietary fiber: see FIBER, DIETARY.

diethylstilbestrol: see DES.

Dietrich, Marlene [dē'trĭkh], 1901–92, German-American film actress. She played the sultry, ageless femme fatale. Her films included *The Blue Angel* (1930), *The Scarlet Empress* (1934), *A Foreign Affair* (1948), and *Witness for the Prosecution* (1957).

diffraction, bending of radiation (such as light) around the edge of an obstacle or by a narrow aperture. Diffraction results from the INTERFERENCE of light waves that pass an opaque body, producing a fuzzy region between the shadow area and the lighted area that, upon close examination, is actually a series of light and dark lines. A **diffraction grating** contains many fine, parallel slits or scratches (about 12,000 per cm or 30,000 per in.) and disperses light into its colors. These gratings are used in diffracting SPECTROSCOPES. The atomic and molecular structure of crystals is examined by X-ray diffraction.

digestive system, in animals, a group of organs that digest food

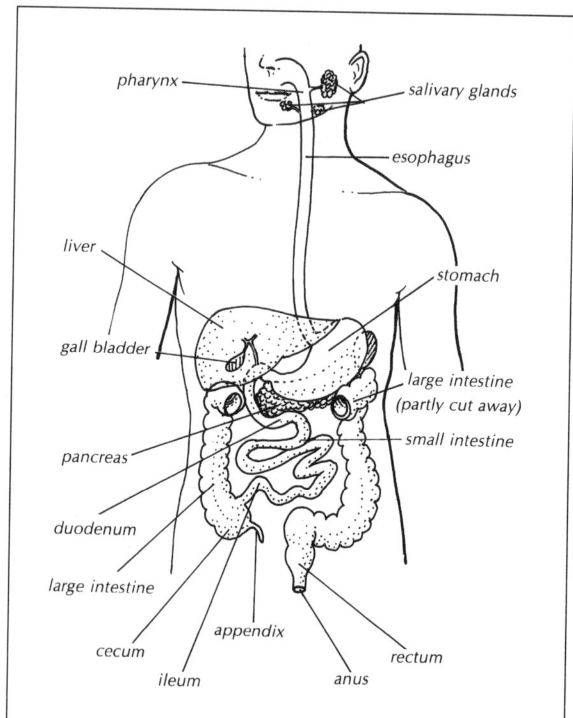

Digestive system

and eliminate wastes. Digestion converts food into a form that can be absorbed into the CIRCULATORY SYSTEM and distributed to tissues throughout the body. Digestion begins at the mouth, where chewing reduces the food to a fine texture, saliva moistens it, and an enzyme (amylase) in saliva begins the conversion of starch into simple sugars. The swallowed food passes through the PHARYNX and through a long tube, the esophagus, into the STOMACH. The food is pushed through the digestive system by peristalsis (contractions of the muscles forming the outer walls of the digestive tract). In the stomach, where digestive ENZYMES and gastric juices are secreted, sugars and alcohol are absorbed directly through the stomach wall into the bloodstream, and the remainder, in the form of a thick liquid (chyme), passes into the first section of the small INTESTINE (the duodenum). There digestive enzymes from the PANCREAS break down fats into glycerol and fatty acids, starches into sugars, and proteins into amino acids. The LIVER supplies bile, which makes fat globules smaller and more easily digested. Small glands in the intestinal wall (crypts of Lieberkühn) also secrete enzymes that continue digestion. Digested food is absorbed through small projections of the intestinal wall (villi) into the blood and lymph. Undigested material passes into the large intestine and is excreted through the anus (see EXCRETION). See also GALL BLADDER.

Digger Indians: see PAIUTE.

digital circuit, ELECTRIC CIRCUIT in which the output currents or voltages are interpreted as having one of several (often two) values, depending on which of a corresponding number of ranges they fall into. Such circuits implement logical operations or operations on representations of discrete numbers, often in binary form. See also ANALOG CIRCUIT.

digital computer: see COMPUTER.

digitalis, any of several chemically similar drugs used to treat heart failure and cardiac arrhythmias. Digitalis slows the pulse and the conduction of nerve impulses in the heart and increases the force of heart contractions and the amount of blood pumped per heartbeat. Common preparations include digitalis, digitoxin, and digoxin (from the foxglove plant *Digitalis purpurea*, the chief source of the drug), and ouabain (from the ouabaio tree).

digital-to-analog conversion, the process of changing discrete data into a continuously varying signal. The most common use is to present the output of a digital COMPUTER as a graphic display (see COMPUTER GRAPHICS) or as audio output, as in computer-generated music. See also ANALOG-TO-DIGITAL CONVERSION.

dill, annual or biennial plant (*Anethum graveolens*) of the CARROT family, native to Europe. Its pungent, aromatic leaves and seeds are used for pickling and for flavoring sauces, salads, and soups.

Dillinger, John, 1902?–34, American bank robber and murderer; b. Indianapolis (?). After his second jailbreak, he and his gang terrorized the Midwest with hit-and-run bank robberies in 1933. He was held responsible for 16 killings and was declared "public enemy number one" by the FBI, whose agents gunned him down on a Chicago street (July 1934).

Dilthey, Wilhelm, 1833–1911, German philosopher. A strict proponent of EMPIRICISM, Dilthey based what he called his "philosophy of life" on a foundation of descriptive and analytical psychology. He rejected transcendental considerations in his study of all aspects of human activity. His influence on early sociological theory is especially evident in the works of Max WEBER. Dilthey's major work is *Einleitung in die Geisteswissenschaften* [Introduction to the human sciences] (1883).

DiMaggio, Joe (Joseph Paul DiMaggio), 1914–, American baseball player; b. Martinez, Calif. A center fielder, he played his entire career (1936–51) with the New York Yankees. In 1941 "Joltin' Joe" set a major-league record by hitting safely in 56 straight games. He compiled a lifetime average of .325, hit 361 home runs, and was a superb fielder.

dime novels, swift-moving thrillers, mainly about the AMERICAN REVOLUTION, the frontier period, and the CIVIL WAR. First sold in 1860 for 10 cents, the books featured such real life adventurers as BUFFALO BILL, Ned BUNTLINE, and Deadwood Dick and such fictional characters as Nick CARTER. The quality of the novels dropped in the 1880s, and they were eclipsed by other series, pulp magazines, and comic strips in the 1890s.

dimension, in mathematics, number of parameters or coordinates required to describe points in a mathematical object (usually geometric). The space we inhabit, having height, width, and depth, is three-dimensional; a plane or surface is two-dimensional; a line or curve is one-dimensional; and a point is zero-dimensional. By means of a coordinate system, e.g., CARTESIAN COORDINATES, one can specify any point with respect to a chosen origin (and coordinate axes through the origin, in the case of two or three dimensions). By analogy, an ordered set of four, five, or more numbers is defined as representing a point in a space of four, five, or more dimensions.

Dimitrov, Georgi [dĭmē'trŏf], 1882–1949, Bulgarian Communist leader and premier (1946–49). In 1933 the NAZIS charged him with setting the REICHSTAG fire. He was acquitted and moved to the USSR, where he became a citizen. He returned to Bulgaria toward the end of World War II.

Dinesen, Isak [dē'nəsən], pseud. of **Baroness Karen Blixen,** 1885–1962, Danish author who wrote primarily in English. She is best known for her imaginative tales, which contain romantic and supernatural elements. Collections include *Winter's Tales* (1942) and *Last Tales* (1957). *Out of Africa* (1937) is an autobiographical account of her years on a coffee plantation in Kenya.

dingo, wild DOG of Australia; shoulder height, c.24 in. (61 cm). Probably introduced by aboriginal settlers thousands of years ago, it was the only large carnivorous mammal found in Australia by the first European colonists. It has large, erect ears, a wolflike head, and long legs, and is usually yellowish red, with white markings. A nocturnal hunter, it preys on small animals and often kills livestock.

Diniz, Port. *Dinis* [both: dēnēsh'], 1261–1325, king of Portugal (1279–1325). He stimulated farming and commerce and restricted the Roman Catholic Church's acquisition of land. A poet and patron of literature, he founded (1290) a university at Lisbon during his relatively peaceful reign.

Dinkins, David N., 1927–, African-American political leader; b. Trenton, N.J. After graduating (1956) from Brooklyn Law School, he went into private practice. Active in Democratic politics, he was (1986–89) Manhattan borough president and the first African-American mayor (1990–93) of New York City.

dinoflagellate: see PYRROPHYTE.

dinosaur, any of a large group of extinct REPTILES (subclass Archosauria) that dominated the earth for over 150 million years in the Mesozoic era. Dinosaurs ranged in length from the 2-ft (60-cm) *Compsognathus* to the 100 to 120-ft (30 to 37-m) *Seismosaurus*, which may have weighed as much as 100 tons (90 metric tons). They have been traditionally classified as cold-blooded reptiles, but evidence suggests that they used a range of metabolic temperature-regulating techniques. They are all thought to have been egg-layers. Saurischian (order Saurischia), or lizard-hipped, dinosaurs included meat-eating bipeds, e.g., *Allosaurus* and *Tyrannosaurus*, and plant-eating quadrupeds, e.g., *Apatosaurus* (Brontosaurus) and *Diplodocus*. Ornithischian (order Ornithischia), or bird-hipped, dinosaurs included plant-eating bipeds, e.g., *Iguanodon* and the duckbills, and armored dinosaurs, e.g., the plated *Stegosaurus* and horned *Triceratops*. Ironically, birds are related not to bird-hipped dinosaurs but to saurischian carnivores. It is not known why dinosaurs died out. Most theories postulate that drastic changes in geography, climate, and sea level, possibly resulting from catastrophic volcanic eruptions or an asteroid or comet impact, were to blame (see MASS EXTINCTION).

Diocletian (Caius Aurelius Valerius Diocletianus), 245–313, Roman emperor (284–305); b. Salona (now Split, Croatia). An army commander of humble birth, he was chosen to succeed Numerian as emperor and became sole ruler after his coemperor, Carinus, was killed (285). Diocletian appointed Maximian as his coemperor and Constantius I and Galerius as caesars (subemperors). Each of the four was given a district of the empire to rule. Under this reorganization the empire throve; Britain was restored (296), and the Persians were subjugated (298). Diocletian's unsuccessful economic policies and his persecution of Christians were the only black marks on his splendid reign. In 305 he retired to his castle at Salona.

diode, two-terminal device having a low RESISTANCE to electric current in one direction and a high resistance in the reverse direction. Diodes are thus useful as RECTIFIERS, converting alternating current (AC) into direct current (DC). Although ELECTRON-TUBE diodes were once common, almost all diodes today are SEMICONDUCTOR devices. In general, current flowing through a diode is not proportional to the voltage between its terminals. When the voltage applied in the reverse direction exceeds a certain value, a semiconductor diode breaks down and conducts heavily in the direction of normally high resistance; this effect can be exploited to regulate voltage. In another type of diode, the tunnel diode (see TUNNELING), the current through the device decreases as the voltage is increased within a certain range; this property, known as negative resistance, makes it useful as an AMPLIFIER. Some diodes are sensitive to light (see PHOTOELECTRIC CELL; PHOTOVOLTAIC CELL). A light-emitting diode (LED) produces light as current passes through it; some LEDs can act as lasers. A thermistor is a special semiconductor diode whose conductivity increases with the diode temperature.

Diogenes, c.412–323 B.C., Greek philosopher. He taught that the virtuous life is the simple life, a maxim he dramatized by living in a tub. Condemning the corruption of his contemporaries, he went about the streets looking for "an honest man." None of his writings survives.

Dione, in astronomy, natural satellite of SATURN.

Dion of Syracuse [dī'ən], 409?–354? B.C., Greek political leader in Syracuse, brother-in-law of DIONYSIUS THE ELDER. A friend of PLATO, he opposed tyranny. Leading a force from Athens, he overthrew (357 B.C.) DIONYSIUS THE YOUNGER and ruled Syracuse until he was assassinated.

Dionysius the Elder, c.430–367 B.C., tyrant of SYRACUSE. Gaining influence by supporting the poorer classes, he became (405 B.C.) TYRANT. He maintained power by exploiting Syracusan fear of the Carthaginians, leading expeditions against them in Sicily, and against Italian cities. He was succeeded by his son, **Dionysius the Younger,** fl. 368–344 B.C. Unsuited for the position by both training and temperament, he was overthrown by DION OF SYRACUSE (357). The murder of Dion permitted his return, but he was finally expelled in 344.

Dionysus [dīənī'səs], in Greek mythology, god of fertility and wine, later considered a patron of the arts. Probably of Thracian origin, Dionysus was one of the most important Greek gods and the subject of profuse and contradictory legends. He was thought to be the son of either ZEUS and PERSEPHONE or of Zeus and Semele. Dionysus was attended by a carousing band of SATYRS, MAENADS, and NYMPHS. He taught humans viticulture but was capable of dreadful revenge upon those (e.g., ORPHEUS and Pentheus) who denied his divinity. His worship was characteristically drunken and orgiastic. The chief figure in the ORPHIC MYSTERIES and other cults, Dionysus had many festivals in his honor. From the music, singing, and dancing of the Greater Dionysia in Athens developed the dithyramb and, ultimately, Greek drama. The Romans identified him with Liber and BACCHUS, who was more properly the wine god.

Diophantus, fl. c.250, Greek mathematician known as the "father of algebra." He developed the use of symbols instead of words in algebraic reasoning as well as methods for solving determinate and indeterminate equations. His chief work is the *Arithmetica.*

Dioscuri: see CASTOR AND POLLUX.

diphtheria, acute, contagious disease caused by the *Corynebacterium diphtheriae.* It is spread through respiratory droplets of infected individuals. The bacteria, lodging in the mucous membranes of the throat, secrete a potent toxin, which causes tissue destruction and the formation of a gray membrane in the upper respiratory tract that can loosen and cause asphyxiation. The toxin may also spread via the blood and damage tissues elsewhere in the body. Diphtheria can be prevented by vaccination.

Dirac, Paul Adrien Maurice, 1902–84, English physicist. He formulated (1928) a version of QUANTUM MECHANICS that took into account the theory of RELATIVITY. This theory implied the existence of an antiparticle (see ANTIMATTER) to the electron; it was discovered later and named the positron. His equation of a particle's motion is a relativistic modification of Erwin SCHRÖDINGER's basic equation of quantum mechanics. Dirac and Schrödinger shared the 1933 Nobel Prize in physics. Dirac also helped to formulate the Fermi-Dirac statistics and contributed to the quantum theory of electromagnetic radiation.

direct current: see ELECTRICITY; GENERATOR; MOTOR, ELECTRIC.

Directoire style, in French interior decoration and costume, the manner prevailing at the time of the DIRECTORY (1795–99). Influenced by Greco-Roman design, it departed from the sumptuous LOUIS PERIOD STYLES and forecast the EMPIRE STYLE. Furniture became more angular and severe; painted and waxed wood replaced marquetry. Women adopted the chemise gown, with low neckline and high waistline, and men wore tight breeches and coats with wide lapels.

Directory, five men who held (1795–99) executive power in France during the FRENCH REVOLUTION. They were chosen by the legislature and each year one director was replaced. The Directory was riddled by corruption and torn by internal squabbles. After the military reverses of 1799, the Abbé SIEYÈS, who became a director that year, helped NAPOLEON I stage the coup of 18 Brumaire (Nov. 9, 1799), which replaced the Directory with the Consulate.

dirigible: see AIRSHIP.

disarmament, nuclear. The first ATOMIC BOMBS dropped (1945) on Japan by the U.S. in WORLD WAR II demonstrated the threat to humanity posed by the possibility of nuclear war. Therefore the first resolution (1946) of the General Assembly of the UNITED NATIONS set up the UN Atomic Energy Commission to make proposals for control of atomic energy. The U.S.-sponsored Baruch Plan proposed an international agency to control all destructive uses of atomic power. Intensification of the COLD WAR made agreement impossible, and the Soviet Union became the second nuclear power (1949). After both the U.S. (1952) and the USSR (1953) exploded HYDROGEN BOMBS, UN disarmament talks were revived, and a subcommittee of the commission was established. Its Western members—the U.S., Canada, Great Britain, and France—advocated an international control system with on-site inspection. The USSR called for an immediate ban on nuclear weapons with possible later controls. The U.S., Great Britain, and the USSR began discussions on the formulation of a nuclear test-ban treaty in 1958 and agreed to suspend nuclear testing for one year. These talks, continued under U.S. Pres. John F. KENNEDY and Soviet Premier Nikita KHRUSHCHEV, led to the first test-ban treaty (1963), the Moscow Agreement, which banned testing in the atmosphere, in outer space, and under water. The two countries proposed a nonproliferation agreement that was approved (1968) by the UN General Assembly and eventually signed by over 150 nations, but North Korea threatened to withdraw (1993) from the treaty and has sought to avoid international inspections. Nonsignatory nations that have or develop nuclear weapons are not bound by the treaty. The U.S. and USSR began holding Strategic Arms Limitation Talks (SALT), which resulted in the signing (1972) of the SALT I treaty: the two powers agreed to limit antiballistic missiles and reached an interim accord on limiting offensive nuclear weapons. The SALT II talks led to an agreement tentatively approved by U.S. Pres. Jimmy CARTER and Soviet Premier Leonid BREZHNEV. Ratification by the U.S. Senate, however, was shelved (1980) after the Soviet invasion of Afghanistan. In 1982 the U.S. and USSR began a new set of talks, called START (STrategic Arms Reduction Talks). In 1987 Pres. REAGAN and Soviet leader Mikhail GORBACHEV signed the INF treaty to eliminate intermediate-range nuclear forces, and a START treaty, signed by Pres. BUSH and Gorbachev in 1991, called for additional reductions in U.S. and Soviet nuclear arsenals. In response to increasing Soviet political instability, Bush announced (1991) the elimination of most U.S. tactical nuclear arms, took strategic bombers off alert status, and called for further reductions in ballistic missiles. With the USSR's disintegration, its nuclear arms passed to Belarus, Kazakhstan, Russia, and Ukraine. The republics pledged to abide by existing treaties and remove outlying weapons to Russia. In 1993 Bush and Russian Pres. YELTSIN signed a START II treaty that called for cutting nuclear warheads by two thirds by 2003 and eliminating those weapons most likely to be used in a first strike. Ukraine, fearing Russian domination, has refused to ratify START unconditionally and relinquish all its nuclear weapons.

Disarmament Conference, 1923–37, series of international meetings for the discussion of general disarmament. Participants were the members of the LEAGUE OF NATIONS, the U.S., and the USSR. The first meeting (Feb. 1932–June 1933), at Geneva, was marked by disagreement over definitions of the categories of war materials, the reluctance of France to agree to any arms limitations, and Germany's insistence on a military parity with the other powers. The session ended in deadlock. The second session (Oct. 1933) met in Germany, but when Adolf HITLER withdrew Germany from the League of Nations, the Conference again adjourned. Thereafter, it met only sporadically until it went out of existence in 1937. By then a general military buildup preparatory to WORLD WAR II was already underway, and all hopes of disarmament had vanished.

Disciples of Christ or **The Christian Church,** a Protestant religious body founded early in the 19th cent. in the U.S. It held that the Bible alone should form the basis for faith and conduct and that individuals should interpret the Bible for themselves. The church was begun by Thomas Campbell (see under CAMPBELL, ALEXANDER), who gathered together several dissident groups. In the late 1800s the group split into the CHURCHES OF CHRIST and the more liberal Disciples of Christ, which is formally known as The Christian Church (Disciples of Christ). The latter had a U.S. membership of 1,039,692 in 1990.

Disney, Walt(er Elias), 1901–66, American film producer, a pioneer in animated cartoons; b. Chicago. He began his career as a cartoonist in 1920. In 1928 he created the character of Mickey Mouse in the cartoon short *Steamboat Willie.* His *Snow White and the Seven Dwarfs* (1938) was the first full-length animated cartoon. Others include *Fantasia* (1940) and *Alice in Wonderland* (1951). After 1950 he also produced adventure and semidocumentary nature films and began his company's development of amusement parks featuring his cartoon characters. **Disneyland,** a gargantuan amusement park in Anaheim, Calif., opened in 1955. Walt Disney World opened near Orlando, Fla., in 1971 as an amusement park and resort, and Epcot Center and Disney-MGM Studios have since been added. In 1983 a Disneyland park was opened outside Tokyo, and Euro Disneyland was opened east of Paris in 1992.

Disraeli, Benjamin, 1st **earl of Beaconsfield** [dĭzrā'lē], 1804–81, British statesman and author. Of Jewish descent, he was baptized a Christian in 1817. His political essays and novels earned him a permanent place in English literature. Elected to Parliament in 1837, he developed into an outstanding, realistic, and caustically witty politician. In 1848 he became leader of the Tory protectionists. Disraeli favored a political partnership with the working classes, and as chancellor of the exchequer (1852, 1858–59, 1866–68), he "educated his party" (now the Conservative party) to pass the fairly radical REFORM BILL of 1867, which enfranchised some 2 million men, largely of the working class, and greatly benefited his party. He became prime minister in 1868 but lost the office to GLADSTONE that same year. His second ministry (1874–80) produced many domestic reforms but is noted for its aggressive foreign policy. The annexation of the Fiji islands (1874) and the Transvaal (1877), and the wars against the Afghans (1878–79) and the ZULUS (1879), proclaimed England an imperial world power. Disraeli's purchase of controlling shares of the Suez Canal strengthened British interests in the Mediterranean. After the Russo-Turkish War, he induced Turkey to cede Cyprus to Great Britain, and through the Congress of Berlin he reduced Russian power in the Balkans. A favorite of Queen VICTORIA, he had her crowned empress of India in 1876. His policy of democracy and imperialism revitalized his party. His father, **Isaac D'Israeli,** 1766–1848, was an author, best known for *Curiosities of Literature* (6 vol., 1791–1834).

dissenters: see NONCONFORMISTS.

distaff: see SPINNING.

distillation, process used to separate the substances composing a mixture; it involves a change of state, e.g., liquid to gas, and subsequent condensation (see STATES OF MATTER). A simple distillation apparatus consists of three parts: a flask in which the mixture is heated, a condenser in which the vapor is cooled, and a vessel in which the condensed vapor, called distillate, is collected. Upon heating, the substances with a higher boiling point remain in the flask and constitute the residue. When the substance with the lowest boiling point has been removed, the temperature can be raised and the process repeated with the substance having the next lowest boiling point. The process of obtaining portions (or fractions) in this way is called fractional distillation. In destructive distillation various solid substances, such as wood, coal, and oil shale, are heated out of free contact with air, and the portions driven off are collected separately. Distillation is used in refining PETROLEUM and in preparing alcoholic beverages.

distributive law, in mathematics, a law governing the interaction of certain pairs of operations. The distributive law of multiplication over addition states that the equation $a \times (b + c) = (a \times b) + (a \times c)$ holds for all numbers a, b, c.

District of Columbia, federal district (1990 pop. 606,900), c.70 sq mi (180 sq km), on the E bank of the Potomac R., coextensive with WASHINGTON, D.C., established by congressional acts of 1790 and 1791. A 10-mi (16.1-km) square carved from Maryland and Virginia, it was reduced in 1847 when the Virginia grant was retroceded (see ALEXANDRIA; ARLINGTON). District residents were disenfranchised until the 23d amendment to the U.S. Constitution (1961) was passed, allowing them to vote in presidential elections. In 1970 the District was allowed a nonvoting delegate to Congress. A constitutional amendment giving full congressional representation passed Congress in 1978, but not enough states ratified it. Since then District officials have worked, without success, to obtain statehood. District government, under a 1974 act, is by mayor and city council, but all District legislation is reviewed by Congress.

dithyramb, in ancient Greece, hymn to the god DIONYSUS, an antiphonal choral LYRIC out of which TRAGEDY grew. It developed into the form used by poets such as Bacchylides. Later it became freer in meter and more musical.

Dittersdorf, Karl Ditters von, 1739–99, Austrian composer and violinist. An important precursor of MOZART in operatic and symphonic forms, he also wrote the comic opera *Doktor und Apotheker* (1786), his best-remembered work.

diuretic, drug that increases the rate of urine formation by the kidney, thus eliminating excess sodium and water from the body. Diuretics are given to alleviate edema (swelling from water retention) in heart, kidney, and lung disorders and to lessen the pressure in the eyeball in glaucoma.

diurnal circle, apparent path followed by a star due to the earth's rotation on its axis. The stars appear to move from east to west on the celestial sphere in concentric circular paths centered at the celestial poles (see ASTRONOMICAL COORDINATE SYSTEMS).

dividend, the part of the net earnings, or profits, of a corporation that is distributed to its stockholders. Dividends are declared by the board of directors, usually at regular intervals. In the U.S., they may be paid in bonds or stocks of a company, in notes, or in cash. Holders of preferred stock must be paid their dividends before anything is paid on common stock. Businesses being terminated may issue liquidation dividends.

divination, foreseeing future events or obtaining secret knowledge through divine sources, omens, or oracles. It is based on the belief that revelations are offered to humans in extrarational forms of knowledge: ancient Chaldeans studied birds' flight and patterns in water or entrails; the Greeks put their trust in the ORACLE. Present-day forms of divination include crystal gazing, palmistry, and astrology.

Divine, Father, c.1882–1965, African-American religious leader, founder of the Peace Mission movement; b. Georgia as George Baker. He moved (c.1915) to the North and later called himself Father Divine. Many accepted him as the personification of God. Although he was black, his movement was interracial and nonsectarian. It spread from Harlem (N.Y.C.), but faltered after his death.

Divine Comedy: see DANTE ALIGHIERI.

divine right: see under MONARCHY.

diving, deep-sea, descent into deep water for extended periods, used in a variety of commercial, scientific, and military activities. Helmeted diving suits were first devised in England in the 17th cent., and improved versions are still in use today. The scuba (acronym for Self-Contained Underwater Breathing Apparatus), invented by J.Y. COUSTEAU, which enables divers to carry their own air supply, allows much greater mobility. The bathyscaphe, developed by Auguste PICCARD, was the first self-contained diving craft; it has been replaced by the SUBMERSIBLE. Skin diving, a popular sport, is done with a face mask and snorkel (plastic tube) just below the surface, or with a scuba at greater depths.

diving, springboard and platform, sport of entering the water from a raised position, often while executing tumbles and other acrobatic maneuvers. Springboard diving is done from a flexible plank either 1 or 3 m (about 3 ft 3 in. or 9 ft 10 in.) above the water. Platform diving (or high diving) is usually done from a rigid platform projecting from a tower 10 m (32 ft 10 in.) high. Both types are scored on the basis of form, execution, and difficulty of the dive. Competitive diving, a part of most aquatic sports meets, is an Olympic event for men (since 1904) and women (since 1912).

divisionism: see POSTIMPRESSIONISM.

division of labor, in economics, the specialization of the functions and roles involved in making the separate parts of a product. It is closely tied to the standardization of production, the introduction and perfection of machinery, and the development of large-scale industry. As a result of mass-production techniques, total production is many times what it would be had each worker made the complete product. Problems created by the division of labor include job monotony, technological unemployment, and eventually chronic unemployment if the economy does not expand quickly enough to reabsorb the displaced labor.

divorce, in law, dissolution of a marriage by court judgment. Partial dissolution, leaving the parties married but allowing noncohabitation, is judicial separation. In the U.S., divorce is regulated by the states, and laws vary widely. However, generally accepted grounds are adultery, desertion, and cruelty. The trend is toward fewer and broader grounds, such as irreconcilable differences and irretrievable breakdown of the marriage. The issues of child custody, the award of alimony to one of the parties (usually the wife), and PROPERTY distribution are determined by the court. After the decree is final, both parties are free to remarry.

Dix, Dorothea Lynde, 1802–87, American social reformer; b. Hampden, Me. A pioneer in the movement for specialized treatment of the insane, she influenced the founding of state hospitals for the insane in the U.S., Canada, and Europe. Dix also did notable work in penology.

Dix, Otto, 1891–1969, German painter and draftsman. Associated with German EXPRESSIONISM, he depicted the sordid world of prostitutes and swindlers. *War* (1924) is a series of 50 etchings, fantastic visions executed with great clarity.

Djakarta: see JAKARTA.

Djibouti [jēbo͞otē′], officially Republic of Djibouti, republic (1992 est. pop. 391,000), c.8,500 sq mi (22,020 sq km), E Africa, bordered by Eritrea (N), Ethiopia (W and S), Somalia (SE), and the Gulf of Aden (E). DJIBOUTI is the capital. Largely a stony desert, the country is economically underdeveloped. Nomadic animal-herding is the chief occupation, but the government is attempting to develop agriculture and fisheries. Hides, cattle, and coffee (transshipped from Ethiopia) are the major exports, and revenue is derived from the port of Djibouti and transit fees and taxes and French military bases. Industries include the building and repairing of ships, production of compressed or liquid gas, and food processing. The population is about 40% Issa (of Somali origin) and 35% Afar (of Ethiopian origin), with the rest largely other Somali tribes, Arabs, and Ethiopian refugees. Both Issas and Afars are Muslim and speak Cushitic languages. French and Arabic are the official languages.

History. Djibouti is important for its strategic situation on the strait between the Gulf of ADEN and the RED SEA. France obtained a foothold in the area in 1862 and organized it as a colony, French Somaliland, in 1896. The colony gained territorial status in 1946 and was renamed the French Territory of the Afars and the Issas in 1967. In a 1967 referendum the Afars voted to continue ties with France, while the Issas voted for independence and eventual reunion with SOMALIA. Djibouti became independent in 1977 under Pres. Hassan Gouled Aptidon, who established a single-party state in 1981. The country has been adversely affected by warfare in and between neighboring Ethiopia and Somalia, and tensions between Afars and the Issa-dominated government led to an Afar rebellion, beginning in 1991. Limited multi-party elections were restored in 1992.

Djibouti, town, (1989 est. pop. 300,000), capital of the Republic of Djibouti. A strategically located port on the Gulf of ADEN, it is the

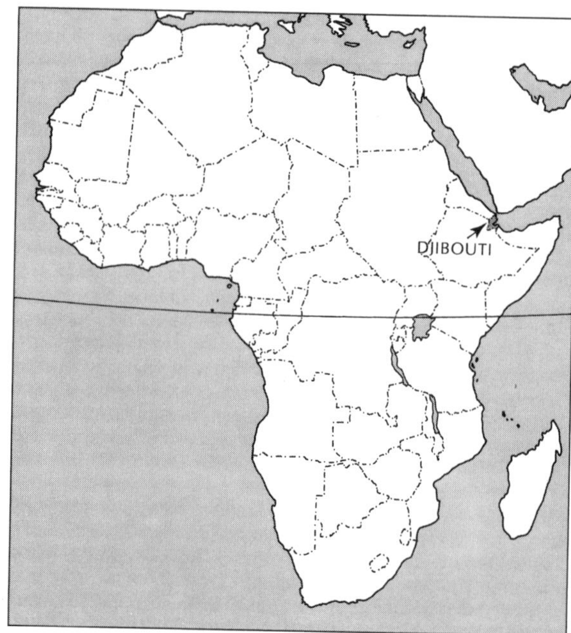

country's only large town and the mainstay of the economy. The port, linked by railroad to ADDIS ABABA, derives most of its revenue from the Ethiopian transit trade. Founded (c.1888) by the French, it was the capital of French Somaliland (1892–1945) and later of the French territory of the Afars and Issas (1945–77).

Djilas, Milovan [jē′läs], 1911–, Yugoslav political leader and writer. A leading adviser to TITO in the resistance movement during WORLD WAR II, he held high government and Communist party posts after the war but was dismissed in 1954 for criticizing the regime. He was jailed in 1956 for supporting the Hungarian revolution, and his term was extended in 1957, when *The New Class,* his critique of the Communist oligarchy, was published in the West. Released in 1961, he was arrested again in 1962 and freed in 1966. His other works include *Conversations with Stalin* (1962), *Memoir of a Revolutionary* (1973), and *Tito* (1980).

Dmitri or **Demetrius,** 1582–91, czarevich, son of IVAN IV of Russia (Ivan the Terrible). Dmitri's brother, Feodor I, succeeded Ivan, but Boris GODUNOV ruled in actuality. Dmitri was killed in 1591, possibly by Boris's order. Boris became czar when Feodor died in 1598. Four pretenders later assumed Dmitri's name. The first invaded Russia with Polish help in 1604, was crowned when Boris died suddenly, but was killed in 1606. The second invaded in 1607 and was killed in 1610. Two men claiming to be Dmitri's son were executed in 1612 and 1613. The coronation of Michael ROMANOV in 1613 ended the chaotic period, known as the Time of Troubles.

DNA or **deoxyribonucleic acid,** NUCLEIC ACID found in the nuclei of CELLS. It is the principal constituent of GENES (linear segments of DNA) and CHROMOSOMES, the structures that transmit hereditary characteristics. The amount of DNA is constant for all typical cells of any given species of plant or animal, regardless of the size or function of that cell. Each DNA molecule is a long, two-stranded chain made up of subunits, called nucleotides, containing a sugar (deoxyribose), a phosphate group, and one of four nitrogenous bases: adenine (A), guanine (G), thymine (T), and cytosine (C). In 1953 J.D. WATSON and F.H. CRICK proposed that the strands, connected by hydrogen bonds between the bases, were coiled in a double helix. Adenine bonds only with thymine (A—T or T—A) and guanine only with cytosine (G—C or C—G). The complementarity of this bonding insures that DNA can be replicated, i.e., that identical copies can be made in order to transmit genetic information to the next generation. See also HUMAN GENOME PROJECT.

DNA fingerprinting, any of several similar techniques for analyzing and comparing DNA from separate sources, used especially in law enforcement to identify suspects from hair, blood, semen, or tissue found at the scene of a violent crime. In DNA fingerprinting, DNA is extracted from a sample and cut into segments using enzymes. The segments are sorted by length by means of gel electrophoresis. Segments that contain sequences of repeated DNA bases, which have been shown to be highly variable from one individual to another, are radioactively tagged, causing them to form a visual pattern, known as a "DNA fingerprint," on X-ray film. In one version of the process, POLYMERASE CHAIN REACTION is used to produce multiple copies of segments from a limited amount of DNA, enabling a DNA fingerprint to be made from a single hair. In criminal investigations, the DNA fingerprint of a suspect's blood is compared to that of the evidence from the crime scene to see how closely they match. First developed in the mid-1980s, DNA fingerprinting has been accepted in most courts, and a number of states have established DNA fingerprint databases. It is generally regarded as a reliable forensic tool when properly done, but some scientists have called for wider sampling of human DNA to insure that the segments analyzed in the tests are indeed highly variable for all ethnic and racial groups. The techniques used in DNA fingerprinting also have applications in paleontology, archaeology, various fields of biology, and medical diagnostics.

Dnieper, Dnipro, or **Dnepr,** river in W Russia, E Belarus, and Ukraine, flowing generally S c.1,430 mi (2,300 km) into the BLACK SEA. The river, which rises W of Moscow and is the chief river of UKRAINE, was made navigable for virtually its entire length by construction (1932) of the Dniprohes dam near Zaporizhzhya (Zaporozhye). Known to the ancients as Borysthenes, the river was (9th–11th cent.) an important commercial link between the Slavs and Byzantines.

Dniester, Dnister or **Dnestr,** river, c.850 (1,370 km) long, W Ukraine and E Moldova. It rises in the CARPATHIANS and flows generally southeast through Ukraine and Moldova to an estuary on the BLACK SEA SW of Odessa. The Dniester formed the Romanian-Soviet border from 1918 to 1940, when the USSR recovered Bessarabia from Romania (see MOLDOVA).

Dnipropetrovsk, formerly **Dnepropetrovsk,** city (1990 est. pop. 1,186,000), E central UKRAINE, on the Dnieper R. A hub of rail and water transport, it is a leading producer of iron, steel, heavy machinery, chemicals, and rolling stock. Founded as Ekaterinoslav in 1787, the city was occupied (1941–43) by German forces.

Doberman pinscher, large WORKING DOG; shoulder height, 24–28 in. (61–71 cm); weight, 60–75 lb (27–34 kg). Its short, smooth coat is black, brown, or blue, with rust markings. Named for Louis Dobermann, who developed the breed in Germany c.1890, it has been used as a guard, police, and war dog.

Dobzhansky, Theodosius [dôbzhän'skē], 1900–75, American geneticist; b. Russia. After his emigration to the United States in 1927, he taught at Columbia (1940–62) and at Rockefeller Univ. (1962–71). He was known for his research in genetics and for his work with the fruit fly *Drosophila.* His most important writings were *Genetics and the Origin of Species* (1937) and *Mankind Evolving: The Evolution of the Human Species* (1962).

Doctorow, E(dgar) L(aurence), 1931–, American novelist; b. N.Y.C. Blending fiction and fact into reconstructions of eras in American history, he has been acclaimed for *The Book of Daniel* (1971), based on the ROSENBERG CASE; *Ragtime* (1975), recreating pre-World War I America; *Loon Lake* (1980), portraying American life during the Great Depression; and *Billy Bathgate* (1989).

Dodecanese, island group (1991 pop. 162,439), SE Greece, in the Aegean Sea between Asia Minor and Crete, c.1,035 sq mi (2,580 sq km). Despite its name ("twelve islands"), the Dodecanese group consists of some 20 islands, notably RHODES (site of the administrative center), Kós, Kárpathos, Kálimnos, and Pátmos. Part of ancient Greece, the islands were occupied by the Ottoman Turks (1522–1912) and by Italy before being captured by the Allies in WORLD WAR II. In 1947 they were ceded to Greece.

Dodge, Mary Mapes, 1831–1905, American writer; b. N.Y.C. She edited *St. Nicholas* magazine for children from 1873 and wrote the classic children's tale *Hans Brinker; or, The Silver Skates* (1865).

Dodge City, city (1990 pop. 21,129), seat of Ford co., SW Kans., on the Arkansas R.; inc. 1875. It is the distributing center for a wheat and livestock area. Laid out (1872) near Fort Dodge on the SANTA FE TRAIL, it was a railhead and became a rowdy cow town noted for its Boot Hill cemetery.

Dodgson, Charles Lutwidge: see CARROLL, LEWIS.

Dodoma, city (1988 pop. 203,833), central Tanzania. A centrally situated transportation hub, it was designated (1975) the administrative capital to replace DAR-ES-SALAAM, and development of the new capital is slowly proceeding. The trade center for an agricultural region, Dodoma produces processed food and furniture.

Doenitz, Karl [dön'ĭts], 1891?–1980, German admiral. He was chief naval commander during WORLD WAR II. After HITLER's death (1945) he headed the German government that negotiated the unconditional surrender to the Allies. He was imprisoned (1946–56) as a war criminal.

dog, carnivorous, domesticated MAMMAL (*Canis familiaris*) of the family Canidae. It is distinguished from other canines, e.g., WOLVES, FOXES, by its worldwide distribution in close association with humans and by the enormous genetic variability within the species. It is probable that the dog was the first animal to be domesticated over 10,000 years ago and that the earliest dogs resembled the wild Australian DINGO. For centuries dogs have been selectively bred for special purposes, notably to pursue and retrieve game, as draft animals, as guides, and as companions. There are systems for classifying and breeding dogs throughout the world, many using a variation of the British system. In the U.S. the American Kennel Club recognizes 125 of the more than 200 known breeds. The breeds are grouped into six classes: SPORTING DOG, HOUND, TERRIER, WORKING DOG, TOY DOG, and NONSPORTING DOG. A purebred dog is one that conforms to the standards of a certain breed and whose pedigree has been recorded for a certain period of time. Dogs of mixed origin are called mongrels. Dogs mate about every six months; their gestation period is about nine weeks, and litters vary from 2 to 10 puppies.

dogtooth violet, originally a name for the Old World plant *Erythronium denscansis,* now used also for several North American species of the same genus of the LILY family. The most common American species is the lilylike, yellow-flowered *E. americanum,* also called adder's tongue. Dogtooth violets are unrelated to the true VIOLETS.

dogwood or **cornel,** common name for some members of the family Cornaceae, trees or shrubs (genus *Cornus*) chiefly of north temperate and tropical mountain regions. Dogwoods have inconspicuous flowers surrounded by large, showy bracts, often mistaken for petals. The flowering dogwood (*C. florida*) and the Pacific dogwood (*C. nutallii*) are cultivated as ornamentals. Their bark, rich in tannin, is used as a QUININE substitute. The bunchberry, or dwarf cornel (*C. canadensis*), is a low, herbaceous wild flower of North America. The BLACK GUM is sometimes included in the dogwood family.

Doha, city (1986 pop. 217,294), capital of Qatar, SE Arabia, on the Persian Gulf. A fishing village before oil production began (1949) in Qatar, it has become a modern city containing almost three quarters of Qatar's population.

Dohnányi, Ernst von [dō'nänyĭ], 1877–1960, Hungarian composer, pianist, and conductor. He led the Budapest Philharmonic Orchestra (1919–44). His compositions, influenced by BRAHMS, include the suite *Ruralia Hungarica* (1924), operas, and piano music. He came to the U.S. in 1949.

doldrums or **equatorial belt of calms,** area around the earth, centered slightly north of the equator between the two belts of trade winds. The large amount of solar radiation at these latitudes results in various forms of severe weather, e.g., HURRICANES, as well as calms (periods of no wind) that can strand sailing vessels for weeks.

Dole, Robert Joseph (Bob), 1923–, U.S. politician; b. Russell, Kans. A lawyer and Republican, he was elected as U.S. representative from Kansas in 1960 and served four terms. In 1968 he was elected to the U.S. Senate. Dole was Gerald FORD's running mate in Ford's unsuccessful presidential campaign (1976) and campaigned unsuccessfully for the Republican presidential nomination in 1980 and 1988. In 1985 he became Senate majority leader; since 1987 he has been the minority leader. His wife, **Elizabeth Hanford Dole,** 1936–, b. Salisbury, N.C., is a lawyer and U.S. government official. A Republican, she was secretary of transportation (1983–89) in the Reagan administration and secretary of labor (1989–91) under

Pres. Bush. She became president of the American Red Cross in 1991.

Dole, Sanford Ballard, 1844–1921, Hawaiian statesman; b. Honolulu. He became (1894) the first president of the republic of HAWAII; after Hawaii's annexation (1898) by the U.S., he served (1900–03) as its first territorial governor.

Dolin, Anton [du'lĭn], 1904–83, English ballet dancer and choreographer. He studied (1921) with DIAGHILEV and became (1924) principal danseur. He formed (1925) his own company with Vera Nemtchimova. He joined the Vic-Wells Ballet, often dancing with Alicia MARKOVA, with whom he formed (1935, 1949) two dance companies. He danced principal roles at the Ballet Theater (N.Y.C.) and wrote several books on dance.

doll, small figure of a human being, usually a child's toy. In ancient Egypt, Greece, and Rome, dolls were used symbolically and probably also as children's playthings. In Europe, from the 15th cent., fashion dolls given as gifts by monarchs and courtiers helped spread costume styles. By the 17th cent. both boys and girls played with dolls. Sonneberg, Germany, was noted for the manufacture of wooden dolls (17th cent.) and of dolls' china heads (19th cent.). In Paris, dolls were made that could speak and close their eyes. In the 19th cent. dolls were made of papier-mâché, china, wax, hard rubber, or bisque; by the 20th cent. doll manufacturing was an important U.S. industry.

Dollfuss, Engelbert [dôl'fo͞os], 1892–1934, Austrian chancellor (1932–34). He opposed the National Socialists and the Social Democrats, and sought support from Austrian Fascists and from Italy. In Apr. 1934 Austria became a corporative state with a one-party, authoritarian system. He was assassinated (July 25) by Austrian Nazis.

Döllinger, Johann Joseph Ignaz von [döl'ĭngər], 1799–1890, German theologian, historian, leader of the OLD CATHOLICS. Ordained (1822) a Roman Catholic priest, he was long associated with the Univ. of Munich and was a leading member of the Catholic party in the Frankfurt Parliament (1848–49). He spurned the dogma of papal infallibility pronounced by the First VATICAN COUNCIL (1870) and was excommunicated (1871). While sympathetic with the Old Catholics, he never intended a separate sect to grow from the movement and never became a member of the Old Catholic Church.

dolomite. **1** White, gray, brown, or reddish calcium magnesium carbonate mineral $CaMg(CO_3)_2$, commonly crystalline. **2** Carbonate rock composed chiefly of the mineral dolomite, similar to LIMESTONE but harder and heavier. Dolomite formations are widespread and are notable in the region of the Alps called the Dolomites, where the rock was first studied. Dolomite is used chiefly as a building stone, for the manufacture of refractory furnace linings, and as magnesium carbonate for pipe coverings.

dolphin, aquatic MAMMAL, any of the small, toothed, gregarious WHALES of the family Delphinidae. They include the beaked dolphin, the killer whale, the pilot whale, and 12 freshwater species in South America and S Asia. Fishlike in form, dolphins breathe through a dorsal blowhole. They propel themselves by means of powerful flukes, steering with a dorsal fin and navigating with the aid of echolocation. Dolphins are exceptionally friendly toward humans, and their high order of intelligence and their complex language have long been the subject of study.

Domagk, Gerhard [dō'mäk], 1895–1964, German chemist and pathologist. Because of a Nazi decree, he had to decline the 1939 Nobel Prize in physiology or medicine, awarded for his discovery of the efficacy of prontosil, the forerunner of the SULFA DRUGS, in treating streptococcal infections. He received the Nobel Prize medal (but not the prize money) in 1947.

dome, a roof circular or (rarely) elliptical in plan, usually hemispherical in form, placed over a square, circular, or other space. Ancient examples are found at Mycenae and in Sicily, but the Romans were the first developers of the form. Their constructions culminated in the PANTHEON (2d cent. A.D.). The use of the pendentive, however—essential to placing a dome over a square—was discovered by the Byzantine builders of HAGIA SOPHIA at Constantinople (A.D. 532–37). Islamic architects, under Byzantine influence, built many domes. The Persian or onion dome is best seen at the TAJ MAHAL. Roman and Byzantine influences converged in the designers of the Italian RENAISSANCE. A circular drum was usually interposed between pendentive and dome, to give greater elevation; the dome was then topped with a lantern. Noted domes include BRUNELLESCHI's for the cathedral at Florence (1420–36) and MICHELANGELO's for St. Peter's, Rome (completed 1590). In the U.S. C. BULFINCH's dome for the Massachusetts state capitol, Boston, established the style. Modern domes employ a wide variety of materials and designs.

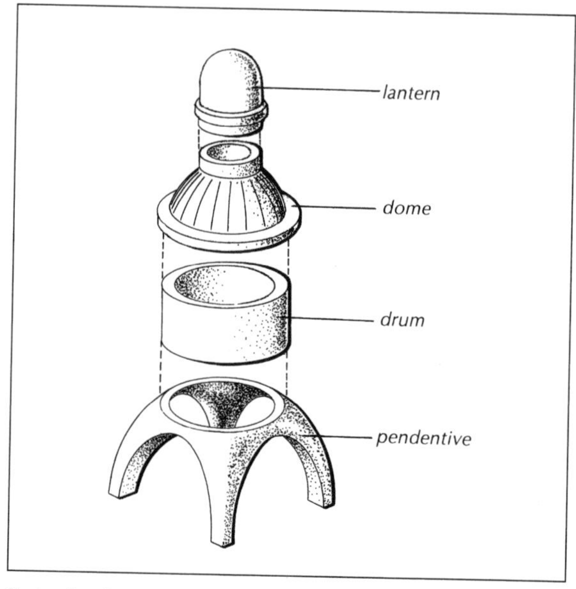

Parts of a dome

Domenichino [dōmānēkē'nō] or **Domenico Zampieri,** 1581–1641, Italian painter. An adherent of classical doctrine and a landscape painter, he produced many FRESCOES, e.g., the *Martyrdom of St. Andrew* (San Gregorio Magno, Rome).

Domenico Veneziano [vānātsyä'nō], c.1400–1461, Italian painter. His work, with rich coloring and detailed landscape settings, and his name suggest that he came from Venice. His masterpiece, the *St. Lucy Altarpiece* (central panel, Uffizi), reveals an innovative use of space; in it, he disposed of the Gothic hierarchical order and introduced figures (deity and saints) in a harmonious group.

Dome of the Rock: see MOSQUE.

Domesday Book or **Doomsday Book,** the surviving record of a census of England made (1085–86) by order of WILLIAM I. It contains extensive information on English land division and its use and inhabitants and also on economic resources in the country. It is a major source for study of the Middle Ages.

Domingo, Placido, 1941–, Spanish operatic tenor. He is best noted for his warm voice and his interpretation of lyric roles in Italian opera, although he has also sung in Wagnerian operas. Among his most famous roles are Don José in *Carmen*, Canio in *Pagliacci,* and Pinkerton in *Madama Butterfly*.

Dominic, Saint, 1170?–1221, Castilian churchman, founder of the DOMINICANS. Dominic successfully preached to the ALBIGENSES in S France. In 1216 he was given a house at Toulouse for his growing band of preachers and won the consent of Pope Honorius III to form a new order. Tradition says that the rosary was given to him by the Virgin Mary in a vision. Feast: Aug. 8.

Dominica, officially Commonwealth of Dominica, island nation (1992 est. pop. 87,000), c.290 sq mi (750 sq km), West Indies, between Guadeloupe and Martinique, largest of the Windward Islands. Dominica is mountainous and forested; of volcanic origin, it has fertile soil, a mild climate, and plentiful rainfall. The capital and chief port is Roseau. The nation exports bananas, citrus fruits, and coconut oil and is a tourist resort. Most of the people are of African descent; there is a remnant group of Caribs. Roman Catholicism is the predominant religion. English is the official language, but a French patois is widely spoken. The Caribs, who had earlier (14th cent.) wrested Dominica from the Arawaks, long fought French and British colonization. In the 18th cent. Africans were brought in as slaves to work plantations. After a long struggle for control between Britain and France, the island became a British colony in the early 1800s. It has been a fully independent member of the Commonwealth since 1978. Dominica is subject to frequent hurricanes, one of the worst of which, in 1979, left some 60,000 people homeless.

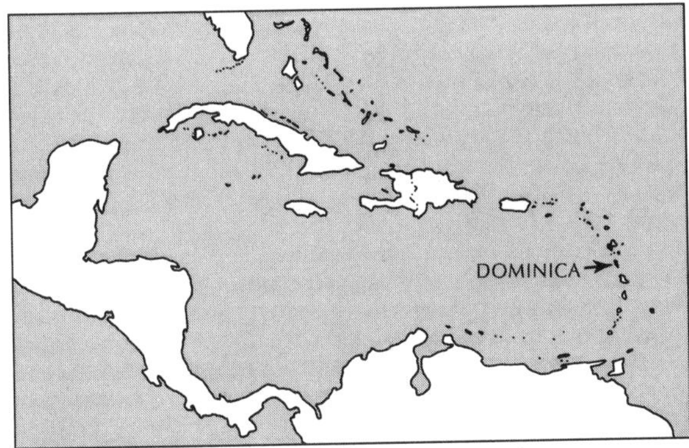

Dominican Republic, Span. *República Dominicana,* republic (1992 est. pop. 7,516,000), 18,816 sq mi (48,734 sq km), West Indies, on the eastern two thirds of the island of HISPANIOLA, which it shares with HAITI. The land ranges from mountainous to gently rolling, with fertile river valleys; the climate is subtropical. The capital and chief port is Santo Domingo. The economy has long been dominated by sugar, which still earns much of the country's foreign exchange, despite establishment of varied light industries and the development of nickel mining and tourism. Coffee, cocoa, bananas, and tobacco are also exported. About two thirds of the population is of mixed Afro-European descent, with the rest mainly of African descent. Spanish is the national language, and Roman Catholicism is the predominant religion.

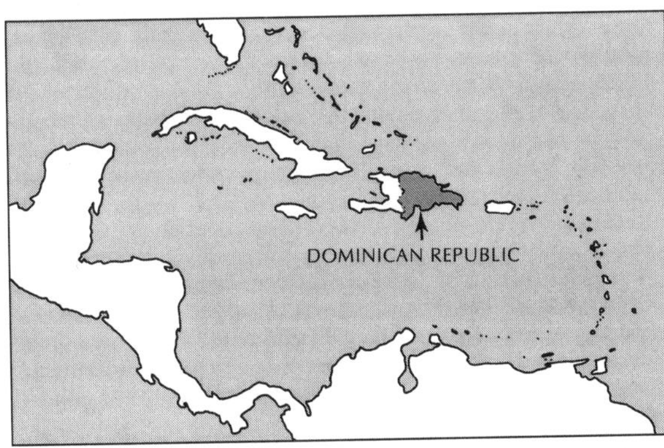

History. Part of the Spanish colony of SANTO DOMINGO during the 16th and 17th cent., and then under Haitian rule after 1821, the Dominican Republic was proclaimed in 1844. Its history has been unusually turbulent, with recurrent dictatorships and rebellions. Bankrupted by civil strife after the murder of the dictator Ulises Heureaux in 1899, the republic came under U.S. domination; U.S. marines occupied the country in 1916–24 and the U.S. exerted fiscal control until 1941. In 1930 Rafael TRUJILLO MOLINA began 30 years of corrupt dictatorship, which ended with his assassination in 1961. Democratic elections in 1962 brought to power a reform president, Juan Bosch, but right-wing opposition led to his ouster a year later. In 1965 civil war between pro- and anti-Bosch forces broke out, and U.S. troops intervened again. In 1966, elections supervised by the Organization of American States restored a degree of normality; Joaquín BALAGUER defeated Bosch, and under his regime (1966–78) considerable progress was made toward stabilizing the economy. Economic stability was also pursued by his successors, Antonio Guzmán Fernández and Jorge Blanco. Balaguer became president again in 1986. Overpopulation has been a problem for the Dominican Republic, and many people have emigrated to the U.S.

Dominicans, Roman Catholic religious order, officially named the Order of Preachers (O.P.). Founded (1216) by St. DOMINIC, the order preached against the heresy of the ALBIGENSES and produced many eminent theologians, notably St. THOMAS AQUINAS. Members are accepted not into a specific house, but into the whole order, and wear a white habit with a black mantle (worn when preaching). There is a contemplative order of nuns and a widespread third order, including many teachers.

Dominion Day: see CANADA DAY.

domino theory, notion that if one country becomes Communist, other states in the region will probably follow, like falling dominoes in a line. The analogy, first applied (1954) to Southeast Asia by Pres. EISENHOWER, was adopted in the 1960s by supporters of the U.S. role in the VIETNAM WAR. The theory was revived in the 1980s to characterize the threat perceived from leftist unrest in Central America.

Domitian (Titus Flavius Domitianus), A.D. 51–96, Roman emperor (A.D. 81–96). On the death of his brother TITUS, he succeeded to the throne. His rule became increasingly despotic and plots were formed against him. Finally his wife Domitia had him murdered.

Don, river, c.1,200 mi (1,930 km) long, SW Russia. It rises near Tula and flows southeast to within 65 mi (105 km) of the VOLGA R., to which it is connected by canal, then southwest into the Sea of Azov. It is an important artery for grain, lumber, and coal shipments and is the outlet for the industrial Donets Basin. The Don is navigable for c.850 mi (1,370 km) from Rostov-na-Donu, its chief city and port.

Donatello [dŏnətĕl'ō], c.1386–1466, Italian sculptor, a major innovator in RENAISSANCE art; b. Florence as Donato di Niccolò di Betto Bardi. He assisted GHIBERTI in Florence and worked on its cathedral. His sculptures developed from Gothic forms, e.g., the marble *David* (Bargello, Florence) to strong, humanistic expression, e.g., *St. Mark* (Orsanmichele, Florence). He developed a shallow relief technique *(schiacciato)* with which he achieved effects of spatial depth. In Rome he studied ancient monuments that influenced his sculpture. Donatello headed a vast workshop in Padua (1443–53). His late Florentine masterworks include the *Magdalen* (baptistery) and the pulpits of San Lorenzo.

Donetsk [dənyĕtsk'], city (1990 est. pop. 1,120,000), E UKRAINE, on the Kalmiius R. The hub of the Donets Basin industrial region, it has coal mines, iron and steel mills, machinery works, and chemical plants. It was founded (1870) as Yuzovka and called Stalino from 1924 to 1961.

Dong, Pham Van, 1906–, premier (1976–81) of the Socialist Republic of VIETNAM. A close associate of HO CHI MINH, he was premier of North Vietnam (1954–76) during the VIETNAM WAR and afterward helped unify the country, serving as premier (1976–81) and chairman of the council of ministers (1981–86).

Don Giovanni: see DON JUAN.

Donizetti, Gaetano, 1797–1848, Italian composer. Influenced early by ROSSINI, he later developed his own melodic, often sentimental style. His best-known operas include *Lucrezia Borgia* (1833) and *Lucia di Lammermoor* (1835). *The Daughter of the Regiment* (1840) is a comic opera.

Don Juan, legendary profligate. There are many versions of his story, but the Spanish is the most widespread. In it, Don Juan seduces the daughter of the commander of Seville and kills her father in a duel. When he jeeringly invites a statue of his victim to a feast, it comes to life and drags Don Juan to hell. The earliest-known dramatization of the story is by TIRSO DE MOLINA. Other famous treatments are by MOLIÈRE, MOZART (in his opera *Don Giovanni*), BYRON, and G.B. SHAW.

donkey: see ASS.

Donne, John, 1572–1631, English divine and greatest of the METAPHYSICAL POETS. A courtier, Donne in his first period (before 1601) wrote cynical, realistic, and sensuous lyrics, essays, and satires, including some of his *Songs and Sonnets* and the prose work *Problems and Paradoxes.* With his marriage and the end of his court career in 1601, his writing became more serious. The two *Anniversaries* (1611, 1612) reveal that his faith in the medieval order was shaken by growing scientific and philosophic doubt. In 1615 Donne took holy orders in the Anglican church. Two years later his wife died. Thereafter the tone of his poetry, e.g., *Holy Sonnets,* deepened. He wrote religious poetry, e.g., *Devotions* (1624), and became one of the great preachers of his day. From 1621 to his death he was dean of St. Paul's, London. All of Donne's poetry—love sonnets, and religious and philosophical verse—is marked by a striking blend of passion and reason. His love poetry treats the breadth, physical and spiritual, of the experience. The devotional poems are deeply concerned with death and the possibility of the soul's union with God. Original, witty, and erudite, his style is characterized by a brilliant use of paradox, hyperbole, and image. Neglected for 200 years, Donne was rediscovered in the 20th cent. and greatly influenced such poets as W.B. YEATS, T.S. ELIOT, and W.H. AUDEN.

Donner Party, group of emigrants to California who in 1846–47 met with tragedy. The party, named for its two Donner families, was trapped by snow in Oct. 1846 in the Sierra Nevada near what is today called the Donner Pass. The survivors resorted to cannibalism before their rescue, and only about half of the original party of 87 reached California.

Donoso, José, 1925–, Chilean novelist and short-story writer. His work ranges from ironically realistic studies of decadent Chilean life, e.g., the novel *Coronation* (1957), to surrealistic portrayals of bizarre subjects, written in a dense and powerful style, e.g., the novel *The Obscene Bird of Night* (1970), considered his masterpiece.

Don Quixote de la Mancha: see CERVANTES SAAVEDRA, MIGUEL DE.

Doolittle, Hilda, pseud. **H.D.,** 1886–1961, American poet; b. Bethlehem, Pa. She lived abroad after 1911 and was married to Richard ALDINGTON. One of the most original of the IMAGISTS, she wrote such volumes of verse as *Sea Garden* (1916) and *Bid Me to Live* (1960).

Doomsday Book: see DOMESDAY BOOK.

Doppler effect, change in the wavelength (and frequency) of a wave as a result of the motion of either the source or receiver of the waves. If the source and the receiver are approaching each other, the frequency of the wave will increase and the wavelength will be shortened—sounds will be higher in pitch and light will be bluer. If the source and receiver are moving apart, sounds will become lower-pitched, and light will appear redder (see RED SHIFT). Astronomers analyze Doppler shifts of light and radio waves to measure the velocities and (indirectly) distances of remote objects.

Dorchester, Guy Carleton, 1st **Baron:** see CARLETON, GUY.

Doré, Gustave, 1832–83, French illustrator, engraver, painter, and sculptor. He is best known for his fantastic, imaginative, engraved illustrations for some 120 books, including *Don Quixote* (1862) and MILTON'S *Paradise Lost.*

Doria, Andrea, b. 1466 or 1468, d. 1560, Italian admiral and statesman. He fought for France in the ITALIAN WARS until 1528, when he went over to Holy Roman Emperor CHARLES V. Doria became (1528) virtual dictator of Genoa but retained many republican institutions. He aided Charles in taking Tunis (1535), and with French aid, he recovered Corsica for Genoa (1559).

Dorians, people of ancient GREECE. They arrived in the PELOPONNESUS between 1100 and 950 B.C., drove out the ACHAEANS (see ACHAEA), and rapidly extended their influence. SPARTA and CRETE were Dorian centers. The Dorians' arrival inaugurated a period of Greek decline, but they did contribute to Greek culture, particularly in the Doric style of architecture.

Doric order: see ORDERS OF ARCHITECTURE.

dormouse, Old World nocturnal RODENT of the family Gliridae. European species hibernate for nearly six months. The common dormouse (*Muscardinus avellanarius*) of Europe and W Asia is up to 4 in. (10 cm) long with rounded ears, large eyes, and thick, reddish brown fur; it eats insects, nuts, and berries.

Dorsey, Thomas A(ndrew), 1899–1993, American gospel musician, b. Villa Rica, Georgia. He began as a blues pianist and songwriter and was later a church choir director. Widely known as the father of GOSPEL MUSIC, Dorsey combined elements of the blues with African-American religious music in his hundreds of songs, including "Take My Hand, Precious Lord."

Dortmund, city (1989 est. pop. 588,000), North Rhine–Westphalia, W Germany, a port on the Dortmund-Ems Canal. An industrial center with such manufactures as steel and machinery, it is located in the RUHR industrial district. It flourished (13th–17th cent.) as a member of the HANSEATIC LEAGUE. The city was badly damaged during WORLD WAR II, but such buildings as the Reinold church (begun in the 13th cent.) remain.

Dos Passos, John Roderigo, 1896–1970, American novelist; b. Chicago. In works such as *Manhattan Transfer* (1925) and his major opus, the trilogy *U.S.A.* (1937)—*The 42nd Parallel* (1930), *1919* (1932), and *The Big Money* (1936)—he developed a kaleidoscopic technique to portray American life, combining narration, STREAM OF CONSCIOUSNESS, biographies, and quotations from newspapers and magazines. The left-wing views that colored his early works gave way to a conservatism that is evident in his less powerful later novels, e.g., his second trilogy, *District of Columbia* (1952).

Dostoyevsky or **Dostoevsky, Feodor Mikhailovich** [dəstəyĕf-'skē], 1821–81, Russian novelist, one of the towering figures of world literature. Shortly after completing an engineering education, he published his first novel, *Poor Folk* (1846), to wide acclaim. Though less successful, his next novels, *The Double* (1846) and *White Nights* (1848), nevertheless showed the profound insight into character that marks his greatest works. Arrested in 1849 for membership in a secret political group, he was exiled to Siberia, and there served four years at hard labor and five as a soldier. His harsh experiences (recorded in *The House of the Dead,* 1862) transformed his youthful liberalism into a fervent religious orthodoxy. The existentialist *Notes from the Underground* (1864), the first major work following his return to St. Petersburg in 1859, inaugurated his most fruitful literary period. It coincided with the death of his first wife and increasing financial burdens. *Crime and Punishment* (1866), a brilliant portrait of sin, remorse, and redemption through sacrifice, was followed by *The Idiot* (1868), the story of a failed Christ figure. It was written in Germany, where Dostoyevsky had gone with his new wife, Anna Grigoryevna Snitkina, whose love and practicality enriched his later years. In *The Possessed* (1871–72) he denounced the alienated radicalism that characterized contemporary Russia. *A Raw Youth* (1875) described decay within family relationships and the inability of science to answer man's deepest needs. These themes were central to his masterpiece, *The Brothers Karamazov* (1880), in which with rare psychological and philosophical insight Dostoyevsky plumbed the depths and complexities of the human soul. His last work, it ranks as one of the finest novels ever written and is a synthesis of the author's mature vision.

Douala, city (1986 pop. 636,980), United Republic of Cameroon, on the Wuori R. estuary. Cameroon's largest city and major port, it is a commercial and transportation center handling most of the country's exports (chiefly cocoa and coffee) as well as transit trade from Chad. Douala developed as a center of the slave trade after the Portuguese arrived in 1472. It later became part of a German protectorate (1884) and of the French CAMEROONS (1919).

double bass: see VIOL; VIOLIN.

Doubleday, Abner, 1819–93, alleged originator of BASEBALL and Union general in the U.S. Civil War; b. Saratoga co., N.Y. A friend, A.G. Mills, heading a commission (1907), reported that Doubleday invented (1839) the game at Cooperstown, N.Y. The report has been generally discredited and it is now known that a children's game similar to baseball had existed long before Doubleday's time.

double jeopardy, in law, prosecution twice for the same criminal offense. Jeopardy exists when a JURY is sworn in, or when EVIDENCE is introduced. The U.S. CONSTITUTION prohibits double jeopardy; a second trial is not precluded, however, if there were procedural errors in the first trial or if the jury could not reach a verdict.

double star: see BINARY STAR.

Douglas, Sir James, 1803–77, Canadian governor of BRITISH COLUMBIA (1858–64). He commanded (1846–58) the HUDSON'S BAY COMPANY territory W of the Rockies after he founded (1843) a fort at the site of VICTORIA. Douglas served (1851–58) as governor of VANCOUVER ISLAND and was the first governor of the new crown colony of British Columbia.

Douglas, Sir James de, lord of Douglas, 1286?–1330, Scottish nobleman, called the Black Douglas and Douglas the Good. In the war of independence against England, he joined ROBERT I and made himself the terror of the border. He led a force at Bannockburn (1314) and in 1327 succeeded in ending the English campaign. After Robert died, Douglas started to Palestine to bury the king's heart but was killed fighting Moors in Spain.

Douglas, Stephen Arnold, 1813–61, American statesman; b. Brandon, Vt. A Democratic congressman (1843–47) and senator (1847–61) from Illinois, he thought disputes between North and South could be solved by SQUATTER SOVEREIGNTY and incorporated that concept into the COMPROMISE OF 1850 and the KANSAS-NEBRASKA ACT. Seeking Senate reelection in 1858, he engaged his opponent, Abraham LINCOLN, in the famous Lincoln-Douglas debates. At the Freeport (Ill.) debate, Douglas asserted that territories could exclude slavery—a doctrine that made him anathema to the South. The Democrats nominated him for president in 1860, but he ran second to Lincoln in the popular vote. A great orator, Douglas was long in the shadow of the Lincoln legend but is now held to have had a truly national vision.

Douglas, William Orville, 1898–1980, associate justice of the U.S. SUPREME COURT (1939–75), with the longest tenure in Court history; b. Maine, Minn.; LL.B., Columbia Univ. (1925). He was a member (1934–37) and chairman (1937–39) of the Securities and Exchange Commission, where he initiated a policy of reform. On the Court, he was known for his fervent support of civil rights, conservation, and free speech.

Douglas fir, tree (*Pseudotsuga menziesii*) of the PINE family, native to W North America. One of the tallest trees known (up to 385 ft/117 m), it is the leading timber-producing tree of the continent. Its usually hard, strong wood is of great commercial importance in construction.

Douglas-Home, Sir Alec (Alexander Frederick), 1903–, British politician. A Conservative, he entered Parliament in 1931 and served in government and cabinet posts, including that of foreign secretary (1960–63, 1970–74). He was prime minister from Oct. 1963 to Oct. 1964. In 1974 he was made a life peer.

Douglass, Frederick, c.1817–1895, American ABOLITIONIST; b. near Easton, Md. Escaping from slavery in 1838, he took the name Douglass from Sir Walter Scott's *Lady of the Lake.* In 1845 he published his *Narrative of the Life of Frederick Douglass,* and in 1847, after English friends had purchased his freedom, he established the *North Star* (Rochester, N.Y.), which he edited for 17 years, advocating abolition through political activism. During the CIVIL WAR he urged African Americans to join the Union ranks, and during and after RECONSTRUCTION he held several government posts.

Doukhobors: see DUKHOBORS.

Douw, Gerard or **Gerrit:** see DOU, GERARD.

Dove, Arthur Garfield, 1880–1946, American painter; b. Canandaigua, N.Y. His abstract style flowered in the 1930s in fluid, poetic canvases based on natural forms. Dove is recognized as a precursor of ABSTRACT EXPRESSIONISM.

dove: see PIGEON.

Dover, city (1990 pop. 27,630), state capital and seat of Kent co., Del., on the St. Jones R.; founded 1683, inc. 1929. In a farming and fruit-growing area, it is a shipping and canning center with light industries. Dover Air Force Base, a huge cargo facility, is a major factor in the local economy. The old statehouse (begun 1722) is notable.

Dovzhenko, Aleksandr [dōvzhĕn'kō], 1894–1956, Ukrainian film director. Ranked with EISENSTEIN and PUDOVKIN, he used MONTAGE and surreal images in such films as *Zvenigora* (1928), *Arsenal* (1929), and *Earth* (1930).

Dow Jones Average, indicators used to measure and report value changes in representative stock groupings on the New York STOCK EXCHANGE. It consists of four different averages—industrial stocks, transportation stocks, utility stocks, and a composite average of all three. Although the industrial average is the most frequently cited, it has been criticized for consisting of only blue chip stocks and for its inability to accurately adjust, in spite of a sophisticated mathematical formula, for dividends and stock splits. The average is quoted in points, not in dollars. Other averages include the Dow Jones 20 Bond Average and the Dow Jones Municipal Bond Yield Average.

Frederick Douglass

Dowland, John, 1562–1626, English composer and lutanist. His books of *Songs or Ayres* (1597–1603) made him the foremost song composer of his time.

Down's syndrome, congenital disorder characterized by moderate to severe MENTAL RETARDATION, slow physical development, and flattish skull and facial features, giving a somewhat Asian appearance (hence the alternate name for the condition, mongolism). The syndrome is caused by genetic transmittance of an extra chromosome. It can occur at any time, but the risk increases significantly with parental age, particularly if the mother is over 35. AMNIOCENTESIS or CHORIONIC VILLUS SAMPLING can be used to detect the disorder in the fetus. Few people with Down's syndrome survive beyond age 35.

Dowson, Ernest Christopher, 1867–1900, English poet. One of the best known of the DECADENTS, he wrote delicate, musical poems, the most famous of which has the refrain "I have been faithful to thee, Cynara! in my fashion."

Doyle, Sir Arthur Conan, 1859–1930, English author and creator of Sherlock Holmes, best known of all fictional detectives. The brilliantly deductive Holmes and his stolid companion, Dr. Watson, appear in *A Study in Scarlet* (1887), *The Memoirs of Sherlock Holmes* (1894), *The Hound of the Baskervilles* (1902), and others. Doyle also wrote historical romances, e.g., *The White Company* (1891), and a *History of Spiritualism* (1926).

Drabble, Margaret, 1939–, English novelist. An old-fashioned novelist, she has been compared to Henry JAMES and George ELIOT for the subtle insight she brings to the dilemmas of modern women. Her novels include *Jerusalem the Golden* (1967), *The Needle's Eye* (1972), *The Realms of Gold* (1975), *The Middle Ground* (1980), and *The Gates of Ivory* (1991). She has also published scholarly studies, e.g., *Arnold Bennett* (1974).

Draco or **Dracon,** fl. 621 B.C., Athenian politician and law codifier.

Draco's code appears to have prescribed the death penalty for even trivial offenses, and Draconian has become a synonym for harshness in legislation.

Dracula: see STOKER, BRAM.

Drago, Luis María [drä'gō], 1859–1921, Argentine statesman and jurist. His protest against coercion of Venezuela by Great Britain, Italy, and Germany (1902) became known as the **Drago Doctrine;** it stated that no public debt could be collected from a sovereign American state by armed force or through occupation of American territory by a foreign power. It was adopted in modified form at the HAGUE CONFERENCE (1907).

dragon, mythical beast, usually represented as a huge, winged, fire-breathing reptile; prominent in the folklore of many peoples. The highest achievement of a hero in medieval legend, e.g., Saint GEORGE, was slaying a dragon. The beast is usually associated with evil; the dragon of the Book of REVELATIONS gave rise to its use as a symbol of SATAN. However, it can also be benevolent, as in ancient China.

dragonfly, large predatory INSECT of the order Odonata. They have chewing mouthparts and four membranous, net-veined wings. Dragonflies are found primarily in the tropics, but occur worldwide except in polar regions. They are strong fliers with elongated bodies that may reach 5 in. (12.7 cm) in length. They prey on mosquitoes and other insects. In the Permian period one species had a wingspan of 2½ ft (76 cm).

drainage basin: see CATCHMENT AREA.

Drake, Sir Francis, 1540–96, English navigator, the first Englishman to circumnavigate the globe (1577–80). He was a leader of the marauding campaign against Spanish vessels and settlements. On one such voyage in 1577, he navigated the Strait of MAGELLAN in his ship the *Golden Hind,* and pillaged the coasts of South and North America. He sailed across the Pacific and reached England in 1580, bearing treasure of great value. He was knighted by ELIZABETH I. Drake was an admiral in the fleet that defeated the Spanish ARMADA. He was defeated by the Spanish in the WEST INDIES (1595) and died off Portobello.

Dravidian languages, family of about 20 languages that appears to be unrelated to any other known language family. They are spoken by people living in S India and N Sri Lanka. See LANGUAGE (table).

drawing, art of the draftsman, commonly used to denote works in pen, pencil, crayon, charcoal, PASTEL, or similar media in which line and form, rather than color, are emphasized. Often vigorous and spontaneous, drawings are made as preparatory studies (see CARTOON) or as finished works. Among the many artists known for their drawings are LEONARDO DA VINCI, MICHELANGELO, DÜRER, RUBENS, HOGARTH, GOYA, DAUMIER, KLEE, PICASSO, and MATISSE.

Drayton, Michael, 1563–1631, English poet. Reflecting the poetic fashions of the day, he wrote pastorals, e.g., *The Shepherd's Garland* (1593); a sonnet sequence, *Idea's Mirror* (1594–1619); poems in the form of love letters (1597); topographical poetry, e.g., *Poly-Olbion* (1612–22); and many other types.

dream, mental activity associated with the rapid-eye-movement (REM) period of sleep. It generally consists of visual images and may reflect bodily disturbances (e.g., indigestion) or external stimuli (e.g., the ringing of an alarm clock). REM sleep accounts for about half of a newborn's total sleeping time, but the proportion decreases with age to about two hours for every eight-hour period of an adult's sleep. In primitive and ancient cultures, dreams played an extensive role in myth and religion. FREUD emphasized dreams as keys to the makeup of the individual. He distinguished between the experienced content of a dream and the actual meaning of the dream, which is largely concealed from the dreamer. JUNG held that dreams are not limited to the personal UNCONSCIOUS but may also be shaped by innate mental structures, called archetypes, that originate in the collective unconscious of the human species. Research suggests that REM sleep is a way for the brain to integrate information taken in during the day, consolidating new knowledge into memory. In this scenario, impulses from the brain stem stimulate the brain, resulting in dream images that may or may not have symbolic meaning.

Drebbel, Cornelis Jacobszoon, 1572–1634, Dutch inventor, physicist, and mechanician. Among his many inventions were the first navigable SUBMARINE, a scarlet dye, and a thermostat for a self-regulating oven.

Dred Scott Case, case argued before the U.S. SUPREME COURT in 1856–57 involving the status of SLAVERY in the federal territories. Scott, a slave, had been taken to Illinois and the Wisconsin territory, where slavery was prohibited by the MISSOURI COMPROMISE. Later, in Missouri, he sued for his freedom on the basis of his residence in a free state and territory. The Supreme Court's Southern majority declared that the Compromise was unconstitutional and that Congress had no power to limit slavery in the territories. Three justices also held that an African American descended from slaves had no rights as an American citizen and therefore no standing in court. The decision further inflamed the sectional controversy leading to the CIVIL WAR.

Dreiser, Theodore [drī'sər], 1871–1945, American novelist. A pioneer of NATURALISM in American literature, Dreiser wrote novels reflecting his mechanistic view of life, which held the individual as the victim of such ungovernable forces as economics, biology, society, and even chance. Among his novels are *Sister Carrie* (1900) and *Jennie Gerhardt* (1911), both about "fallen women"; *The Financier* (1912), *The Titan* (1914), and *The Stoic* (1947), a trilogy concerning a ruthless industrialist; and *The Genius* (1915) and *The Bulwark* (1946), both about an American artist. *An American Tragedy* (1925), considered his greatest work, tells of a poor young man's futile attempts to achieve social and financial success. Dreiser also wrote short stories, autobiographical works, and nonfiction commentaries on the USSR and the U.S.

Dresden, city (1989 est. pop. 518,000), capital of SAXONY, E Germany, on the Elbe R. It is an industrial and cultural center and an inland port. Originally a Slavic settlement, it was settled (13th cent.) by Germans and later occupied by Prussia. From the 17th cent. until it was heavily bombed by the Allies in WORLD WAR II, Dresden was a showplace of art and of BAROQUE and ROCOCO architecture. It has been extensively rebuilt since 1945.

Drew, Charles Richard, 1904–50, African-American physician; b. Washington, D.C. A surgeon and a professor at Howard Univ. (1935–36; 1942–50), he developed a means of preserving blood plasma for transfusion. During World War II he headed (1940–41) the program that sent blood to Great Britain and was (1941–42) the director of the first American Red Cross Blood Bank.

Drew, John, 1827–62, American actor; b. Ireland. Having established a reputation as an Irish comedian, he maintained a stock company at the Arch Street Theatre, Philadelphia. After his death, his wife and co-star, **Louisa Lane Drew,** 1820–97, b. England, managed the theater until 1892. Her best role was as Mrs. Malaprop in *The Rivals.* Her eldest son, **John Drew,** 1853–1927, b. Philadelphia, joined Augustin Daly's company in 1875 and became one of the producer Charles Frohman's first stars. He distinguished himself in both Shakespearean and modern comedies. His sister Georgiana married Maurice Barrymore (see BARRYMORE, family).

Dreyer, Carl Theodor [drīər], 1889–1968, Danish film director. *The Passion of Joan of Arc* (1928) typifies his austere style. Among his other films are *Vampyr* (1932), *Day of Wrath* (1943), *Ordet* (1955), and *Gertrud* (1964).

Dreyfus Affair. In 1894 Capt. Alfred Dreyfus (1859–1935), a French officer, was convicted of treason by a court-martial, sentenced to life imprisonment, and sent to Devil's Island. The case had arisen with the discovery in the German embassy of a handwritten *bordereau* (schedule) that listed secret French documents and was addressed to Maj. Max von Schwartzkoppen, German military attaché in Paris. The French army was at the time permeated by anti-Semitism, and suspicion fell on Dreyfus, an Alsatian Jew. Although Dreyfus protested his innocence, interest in the case lapsed until 1896, when evidence was discovered pointing to Maj. Ferdinand Walsin Esterhazy as the real author of the *bordereau.* After the army's attempt to suppress this information failed, Esterhazy was tried (Jan. 1898) by court-martial, but was acquitted within minutes. Émile ZOLA, a leading supporter of Dreyfus, published an open letter accusing the judges of following orders from the military. Zola was sentenced to jail for libel, but fled to England. Meanwhile, the case had become a major political issue. Royalist, militarist, nationalist, and Roman Catholic elements joined the anti-Dreyfus group, while republican, socialist, and anticlerical forces allied to defend Dreyfus and to discredit the rightist government. In 1898 it was learned that much of the evidence against Dreyfus had been forged by Col. Henry of army intelligence. After Henry's suicide (Aug. 1898) and Esterhazy's flight to England, a revision of Dreyfus's sentence became imperative. A new court-martial was ordered, but the military court, unable to admit error, found Dreyfus guilty and sentenced him to 10 years in prison. However, a pardon was issued by Pres. Émile Loubet, and in 1906 the supreme court of appeals exonerated Dreyfus. In 1930 his innocence was reaffirmed by the publication of Schwartzkoppen's papers. The immediate result of the affair was to unite and bring to power the French left wing. Widespread antimilitarism and rabid anticlericalism ensued, leading in 1905 to the separation of church and state in France.

drift, deposit of clay, gravel, sand, and boulders, transported and laid down by glaciers. Some drift is stratified, or sorted by size, with coarser particles nearer the point of origin. Till, the greater part of drift, consists of unstratified heaps of rocks. Drifts can take many forms (e.g., DRUMLINS, ESKERS, MORAINES). Large sections of North America and continental Europe are covered by drift.

dromedary: see CAMEL.

drug, substance used to cure, alleviate, diagnose, or prevent disease. Before 1900 only a few drugs were used scientifically, among them alcohol, ether, MORPHINE, DIGITALIS, QUININE, IRON, IODINE, MERCURY, diphtheria antitoxin, and smallpox vaccine. Since then, and particularly since World War II, many new drugs and classes of drugs have been developed, making CHEMOTHERAPY an essential part of medical practice. Such drugs include ANTIBIOTICS; SULFA DRUGS; cardiovascular drugs, including propanolol and other BETA BLOCKERS; DIURETICS; ANTICOAGULANTS; whole blood, plasma, and blood derivatives; various smooth muscle relaxants and smooth muscle stimulants; IMMUNOSUPPRESSIVE DRUGS; HORMONES, such as thyroxine, INSULIN, and ESTROGEN; CORTISONE and other CORTICOSTEROIDS; ORAL CONTRACEPTIVES; VITAMINS; ANALGESICS; poison antidotes; and various stimulants and depressants, among them NARCOTICS, AMPHETAMINES, and BARBITURATES (see also ANESTHESIA; HALLUCINOGENIC DRUGS). Drugs are derived from many sources, organic and inorganic. Some drugs are or were originally extracted from plant or animal sources; other drugs are synthesized in the laboratory or extracted from inorganic compounds. There are two marketing classes of drugs; ethical drugs, for which prescriptions are needed, and PATENT MEDICINES, which are sold over the counter without prescription. The publication in the U.S. giving drug properties, actions, uses, dosages, and standards of strength and purity is the *United States Pharmacopoeia–National Formulary.* The *Physician's Desk Reference* compiles information supplied by drug companies about their products. The Food and Drug Administration regulates the testing and marketing of new drugs in the United States. The scientific study of drugs, their actions, and effects is PHARMACOLOGY.

drug addiction and drug abuse, chronic or habitual use of any chemical substance to alter states of body or mind for other than medically warranted purposes. Among the drugs with potential for abuse are NARCOTICS, including morphine, opium, heroin, and methadone; depressants such as ALCOHOL, BARBITURATES, and sedatives; stimulants such as COCAINE (see also CRACK) and AMPHETAMINES; HALLUCINOGENIC DRUGS; and MARIJUANA. Nicotine and CAFFEINE can also be abused, and ANABOLIC STEROIDS and HUMAN GROWTH HORMONE are often abused by athletes and bodybuilders seeking to increase muscle mass. An individual is said to be addicted if a physical dependence on a given drug develops and if withdrawal symptoms are experienced when the drug is discontinued or its dose decreased. True physical addiction is known to occur with the narcotics and depressants; psychological dependence, with or without physical symptoms, can develop with many other drugs, such as TRANQUILIZERS. The hallucinogens can also cause traumatic experiences and trigger psychotic reactions, including paranoia. Treatment for drug addiction includes METHADONE programs and participation in therapeutic communities (e.g., Synanon and Phoenix House) with other addicts who are giving up drugs (see also ALCOHOLISM). The question of what constitutes drug abuse depends on the cultural and social context. In some countries, narcotic use in the form of opium smoking is common and not considered a serious drug problem; in others, hashish or related compounds are widely used. In most industrialized nations, however, the use of many of these drugs is illegal and associated with criminal behavior.

druids, priests of ancient Celtic Britain, Ireland, and Gaul and probably of all ancient Celtic peoples. The druids constituted a priestly upper class in command of a highly ritualistic religion centering on the worship of a pantheon of nature deities. Religious ceremonies, held chiefly in oak groves and at river sources and lakes, included animal, and sometimes human, sacrifices and various forms of magic. Druids also educated the young and oversaw the community's intellectual life. They were an important cohesive force among the Celtic tribes; in Gaul they led rebellions against the Romans. Their power, although broken by the Romans, finally yielded only to Christianity.

drum, in music, PERCUSSION INSTRUMENT consisting of a frame over which one or more membranes or skins are stretched, and which acts as a resonator when the membrane is struck. The kettledrum, a metal bowl with a membrane stretched over the open side, can be tuned to a definite pitch by adjusting the tension of the head. In the snare drum, wire-covered gut strings are stretched across the head; these rattle when the drum is struck. The tom-tom is a high-pitched, tunable hand drum. The tambourine is a single-headed, small drum, usually with jingles attached to the frame, that is shaken or struck by hand.

drumlin, smooth, oval hill of glacial DRIFT, elongated in the direction of the movement of the ice that deposited it.

Drummond, William Henry, 1854–1907, Canadian poet; b. Ireland. His verse, collected in such volumes as *Poetical Works* (1912), portrays French Canadians in their own English dialect.

Drusus, Roman family of the gens Livius. An early distinguished member was **Marcus Livius Drusus,** d. 109? B.C., tribune of the people (122) with Caius Sempronius Gracchus (see GRACCHI). He successfully attacked Gracchus in the senate and became consul in 112. His son, **Marcus Livius Drusus,** d. 91 B.C., was also a leader of the senatorial party. By an increase in the franchise he won the support of the Romans and Italians, but the senate annulled Drusus' laws and brought on the Social War (90–88 B.C.) between Rome and the Italians. Drusus was assassinated. **Nero Claudius Drusus Germanicus,** 38–9 B.C., was the stepson of AUGUSTUS and father of CLAUDIUS I. He ravaged Germany E and N of the Rhine, but failed to subdue the Germans permanently. He died in Germany. His brother was the emperor TIBERIUS. Tiberius' son, **Drusus Caesar,** d. A.D. 23, earned the jealousy of Sejanus, Tiberius' minister, who tried to turn Tiberius against his son. Drusus died, perhaps of poisoning by Sejanus or by his wife under Sejanus' influence.

Druze or **Druse,** religious community primarily in Syria, Lebanon, Israel, and Jordan who believe that Hakim, the sixth Fatimite caliph (see FATIMID), is divine. Numbering about 1 million worldwide, they permit no religious conversion or intermarriage. Warring against the Ottoman Turks and the Christian Maronites, they helped prepare the way for French control of the E Mediterranean countries known as the Levant. Their defiance of the French mandate and occupation (1925–27) of Damascus led to protracted hostilities. After Syria became independent in 1944, the Druze surrendered their autonomy.

dryads: see NYMPH.

dry cell: see CELL, in electricity.

Dryden, John, 1631–1700, English poet, dramatist, and critic. He first came to notice with *Heroic Stanzas* (1659), commemorating the death of Oliver CROMWELL, but in 1660 he celebrated the restoration of CHARLES II with *Astraea Redux. Annus Mirabilis,* a long poem on the Dutch war, appeared in 1667, and in 1668 he became poet laureate. His plays include the heroic *Conquest of Granada* (1670–71); the comedy *Marriage à la Mode* (1672); and his blank-verse masterpiece, *All for Love* (1677). His great political SATIRE, *Absalom and Achitophel,* appeared in two parts (1681, 1682), and his attack on Thomas Shadwell, *MacFlecknoe,* in 1682. Five years after publishing *Religio Laici* (1682), a poetical exposition of the Protestant layman's creed, he announced his conversion to Roman Catholicism in *The Hind and the Panther.* Dryden lost his laureateship with the accession of WILLIAM III. Throughout his life, he wrote brilliant critical prefaces and discourses, notably the *Essay of Dramatic Poesy* (1668). His last years were occupied chiefly with translating Juvenal, Vergil, and others.

dry ice: see CARBON DIOXIDE.

drypoint, INTAGLIO printing process in which lines are scratched directly into a metal plate with a needle; also, the print made from such a plate. The method is often used with ETCHING. In drypoint, the burr raised by the needle produces a rich, velvety effect and allows relatively few good prints to be made. Among the greatest masters of the technique are DÜRER, REMBRANDT, WHISTLER, and PICASSO.

dry rot, FUNGUS infestation of timber, typified by the destruction of CELLULOSE, with discoloration and eventual crumbling of the wood. Dry rot requires moisture for growth and occurs in improperly seasoned wood or where ventilation is poor or humidity high.

Dual Alliance: see TRIPLE ALLIANCE AND TRIPLE ENTENTE.

dualism, in philosophy and theology, system that explains all phenomena in terms of two distinct and irreducible principles, e.g., ideas and matter (as in PLATO, ARISTOTLE, and modern METAPHYSICS) or mind and matter (as in psychology). In theology the term refers to a concept of opposing principles, e.g., good and evil. See also MONISM.

Dual Monarchy: see AUSTRO-HUNGARIAN MONARCHY.

Duarte, José Napoleón, 1925–90, president of El Salvador (1980–82, 1984–88). A Christian Democrat, he was mayor of San Salvador (1964–70). In 1972 Duarte was elected president, but was exiled by the army. He was allowed to return (1979) and in 1980 was named to the ruling military junta, which later named him president. Duarte ruled, jointly with the junta, during a period of civil war when the government was seriously opposed by leftist rebels. He was forced from office (1982) by a coalition of right-wing parties (Alvaro Alfredo Magaña succeeded him), but became president again (1984) in a controversial election that was boycotted by the left.

Dubai: see UNITED ARAB EMIRATES.

Du Barry, Jeanne Bécu, comtesse, 1743–93, mistress of LOUIS XV of France. A courtesan of illegitimate birth, she was installed (1769) at court and retained her influence until the king's death (1774). During the FRENCH REVOLUTION she was arrested for treason and guillotined.

Dubček, Alexander [do͝ob'chĕk], 1921–92, Czechoslovakian Communist leader. In 1968 he replaced NOVOTNÝ as party first secretary and instituted liberal policies that promised a gradual democratization. In Aug. 1968 Soviet forces invaded and a pro-Soviet government was installed. Dubček was removed from office in 1969. He returned (1989) to prominence during the demonstrations that ended Communist rule and served (1989–92) as parliament chairman (speaker).

Du Bellay, Joachim, 1522?–1560, French poet of the Pléiade (see under PLEIAD), author of their manifesto. Some of his finest poems, found in *Regrets* (1558) and *Antiquities of Rome* (1558) and written while he was in Rome, convey his impressions of that city and his nostalgia for France.

Dubinsky, David, 1892–1982, American labor leader; b. Russian Poland. Sent to a Siberian prison (1908) for union activity, he escaped and reached the U.S. in 1911. He worked as a cloak cutter and rose rapidly in the International Ladies' Garment Workers Union, becoming its president (1932–66). In 1936 he took the union out of the American Federation of Labor (AFL), of which he was a vice president, and into the Congress of Industrial Organizations (CIO), but he broke with the CIO in 1938 and rejoined the AFL in 1940. Dubinsky helped organize the Liberal party in 1944.

Dublin, city (1986 pop. 502,337), capital of the Republic of Ireland and county town of Co. Dublin, on Dublin Bay at the mouth of the Liffey R. It is Ireland's chief commercial, cultural, and administrative center. Its major industries include brewing, textile manufacturing, distilling, and shipbuilding. Dublin's turbulent early history was marked by the rule of the Danes, Irish, and English, who held the city from 1170 until 1800. It prospered in the late 18th cent., but declined after the Act of Union of 1800. In the 19th and early 20th cent. the city saw bloodshed in connection with nationalist efforts to free Ireland from British control. It also became the center of a Gaelic renaissance; the Gaelic League was founded (1893) there and the Abbey Theatre (see THEATER, table) began producing Irish plays. Dublin is the seat of the Irish legislature, the Dáil Éireann. Its institutions include the Univ. of Dublin (Trinity College), University College, and a national museum.

Du Bois, W(illiam) E(dward) B(urghardt), 1868–1963, African-American civil-rights leader and author; b. Great Barrington, Mass. Earning a Ph.D. from Harvard (1895), he taught economics and history at Atlanta Univ. (1897–1910; 1932–44) and was one of the first exponents of full and immediate racial equality. He cofounded (1909) the National Negro Committee, which became (1910) the NATIONAL ASSOCIATION FOR THE ADVANCEMENT OF COLORED PEOPLE, and edited the NAACP magazine, *The Crisis*, until 1932. Late in life he promoted worldwide black liberation and pan-Africanism and, in 1961, joined the Communist party and moved to Ghana. His many writings include an autobiography (1968).

Dubos, René Jules [dübō'], 1901–82, American bacteriologist and author; b. France. Associated with Rockefeller Univ. from 1927, he isolated in crystalline form the agent gramicidin, an antibiotic that destroys gram-positive bacteria (see GRAM'S STAIN). This laid the basis for a new field of chemotherapy. His works include *So Human an Animal* (1969; Pulitzer).

Dubuffet, Jean [dübüfā'], 1901–85, French painter and sculptor. His primitive, childlike, humorous paintings are often done in thick impastos of asphalt, pebbles, and glass to enrich the surface texture. *Cow with the Subtile Nose* is in the Museum of Modern Art (N.Y.C.).

Duccio de Buoninsegna [do͞ot'chō dē bwōnēnsā'nyä], fl. 1278–1319, the first great Sienese painter. He enlivened the Byzantine traditional forms by the expressive use of outline in paintings both lyrical and majestic. His only authenticated work is a large altar called *Maestà* (1311) in the Siena cathedral. His influence on Sienese painting was enormous.

Duchamp, Marcel [düshäN'], 1887–1968, French painter; brother of Raymond DUCHAMP-VILLON, half-brother of Jacques VILLON. He is particularly noted for his cubist-futurist work *Nude Descending a Staircase*, depicting continuous action with a series of overlapping figures (see CUBISM; FUTURISM). A cofounder of the DADA group, he invented ready-mades (commonplace objects), e.g., the urinal entitled *Fountain*, which he exhibited as works of art. He also invented complex, nonfunctional machines.

Duchamp-Villon, Raymond [vēyôN'], 1876–1918, French sculptor; brother of Marcel DUCHAMP and Jacques VILLON. He turned from the tradition of RODIN to CUBISM, assembling such machinelike forms as *Horse* (Paris).

duck, wild and domestic waterfowl of the family Anatidae, which also includes the GOOSE and SWAN. It is hunted and bred for its meat, eggs, and feathers. Strictly speaking, *duck* refers to the female; the male is a *drake*. Ducks range from 16 to 22 in. (36 to 56 cm) in length and have waterproof feathers, with a thick layer of down underneath, and webbed feet. They are usually divided into three groups: surface-feeding—such as the mallard, wood duck, and teal, which frequent ponds and quiet waters; diving—such as the canvasback and eider, found on bays, rivers, and lakes; and fish-eating, or mergansers, which also prefer open water.

duckbill, marsupial: see PLATYPUS.

Dudley, Robert: see LEICESTER, ROBERT DUDLEY, EARL OF.

Dufay, Guillaume [düfā'], c.1400–74, founder and leading composer of the Burgundian school of music. A singer in the papal chapel in Rome and elsewhere, he wrote chansons, MASSES, and MOTETS in the northern French tradition, with English and Italian elements.

Dufy, Raoul [düfē'], 1877–1953, French painter, illustrator, and decorator. Turning to FAUVISM c.1905, he executed glittering landscapes, seascapes, and witty views of society, painted with swift, stenographic brush strokes, e.g., *The Palm* (Mus. Mod. Art, N.Y.C.).

dugong: see SIRENIAN.

Du Guesclin, Bertrand [dü gĕklăN'], c.1320–80, French soldier, constable of France (1370–80). In the service of CHARLES V of France, he defeated CHARLES II of Navarre, and in the HUNDRED YEARS WAR reconquered much of France from the English. He was the greatest French soldier of his time.

Duisburg [düs'bo͝ork], city (1989 est. pop. 528,000), North Rhine–Westphalia, W Germany, at the confluence of the Rhine and Ruhr rivers. It is Europe's largest inland port and a steel-making center.

Founded in Roman times, it passed to the duchy of Cleves (1290) and to Brandenburg (1614). During WORLD WAR II it was an armaments center and was heavily bombed.

Dukakis, Michael S(tanley), 1933–, U.S. politician; b. Brookline, Mass. He was a member of the House of Representatives (1962–70) and governor of Massachusetts (1975–79; 1983–91). His policies included the nation's first no-fault auto insurance bill and first major state tax amnesty. In 1988 he was the Democratic candidate for president but lost the election to George BUSH.

Dukas, Paul [dükä'], 1865–1935, French composer and critic. Influenced by Richard WAGNER and DEBUSSY, he is best known for his SYMPHONIC POEM *The Sorcerer's Apprentice* (1897).

Dukhobors or **Doukhobors** [Rus., = spirit wrestlers], religious sect, prominent in Russia from the 18th to the 19th cent., originally called Christians of the Universal Brotherhood. Doctrinally somewhat like the Quakers, they rejected outward symbols of Christianity, promoted a communal, absolutely democratic attitude, and preached equality. Persecuted in Russia, many eventually moved (1898–99) to W Canada. There they prospered, but had difficulties with the Canadian government on several occasions. In 1945 they formed two groups, the Union of the Dukhobors of Canada and the Sons of Freedom.

dulcimer: see STRINGED INSTRUMENT.

Du Lhut, Daniel Greysolon, sieur: see DULUTH, DANIEL GREYSOLON, SIEUR.

Dulles, John Foster, 1888–1959, U.S. secretary of state (1953–59); b. Washington, D.C. After serving (1945–49) as U.S. delegate to the UN, he negotiated (1951) the Japanese peace treaty formally ending World War II. As secretary of state under Pres. EISENHOWER, Dulles emphasized the collective security of the U.S. and its allies through foreign economic and military aid. He encouraged the development of nuclear weapons capable of "massive retaliation." His brother, **Allen Welsh Dulles,** 1893–1969, was director (1953–61) of the CIA.

Duluth or **Du Lhut, Daniel Greysolon, sieur** [dəlo͞oth'], 1636–1710, French explorer. His explorations won the Lake SUPERIOR and upper MISSISSIPPI R. regions for France. He is remembered for his just treatment of the native peoples.

Duluth, city (1990 pop. 85,493), seat of St. Louis co., NE Minn., at the W end of Lake SUPERIOR; settled c.1852, inc. 1870. It is the commercial, industrial, and cultural center of N Minnesota. The second largest port on the GREAT LAKES, Duluth ships grain, iron ore, and bulk cargo all over the world. The discovery of iron ore (1865) in the nearby Mesabi Range transformed the former timber-shipping port.

duma, Russian representative body established (1905) after the RUSSIAN REVOLUTION. The first (1906) and second (1907) dumas were dissolved by NICHOLAS II after a few months because of their political hostility. The third (1907–12) and fourth (1912–17) were the last before the 1917 Revolution. The **State Duma** (est. 1993) is the popularly elected lower house of Russia's legislature.

Dumas, Alexandre [dümä'], known as **Dumas père** [pĕr], 1802–70, French author. After several successful historical dramas, he produced his great triumphs, *The Three Musketeers* (1844) and *The Count of Monte Cristo* (1845). Although these highly romantic novels, written with the aid of collaborators, are sometimes scorned by critics, they have delighted generations of readers and have been translated into nearly every language. His illegitimate son, **Alexandre Dumas,** known as **Dumas fils** [fēs], 1824–95, is famous for his play *La Dame aux camélias* (1852), known in English as *Camille,* which became the vehicle for many famous actresses and was the basis of VERDI's opera *La Traviata.* Dumas fils was the chief creator of the 19th-cent. comedy of manners.

Du Maurier, George Louis Palmella Busson, 1834–96, English artist and novelist. A noted *Punch* illustrator, he also penned the novels *Peter Ibbetson* (1892) and *Trilby* (1894). His granddaughter **Daphne Du Maurier,** 1907–89, wrote *Rebecca* (1938), *The Scapegoat* (1957), and other novels, as well as a family history, *The Du Mauriers* (1937).

Dumouriez, Charles François [dü-mo͞o-rēā'], 1739–1823, French general in the FRENCH REVOLUTIONARY WARS. He won victories at Valmy and Jemappes in 1792. Defeated at Neerwinden (1793), he opened negotiations with the Austrians. After turning over to them the French commissioners sent to investigate his defeat, he deserted to the Austrian lines.

Dunant, Jean Henri [dünäN'], 1828–1910, Swiss philanthropist. His published description (1862) of the suffering of wartime wounded and his plea for organizations to care for them led to the establishment (1864) of the International RED CROSS. Dunant shared the first Nobel Peace Prize (1901) with Frédérick PASSY.

Dunbar, Paul Laurence, 1872–1906, African-American author; b. Dayton, Ohio. His poetry, e.g., *Lyrics of Lowly Life* (1896), uses African-American folk materials and dialects. Dunbar also wrote of African-American life in the South in novels and stories.

Dunbar, William, c.1460–c.1520, Scottish poet. Writing in the tradition of CHAUCER and the medieval Scottish poets, he is notable for his lively verse, metrical form, and caustic satire. "Lament for the Makers" is a well-known poem.

Duncan, Isadora, 1878–1927, American dancer; b. San Francisco. Her dances based on Greek classical art had great success in Budapest (1903), Berlin (1904), and New York City (1908). She danced barefoot in a revealing modified Greek tunic with flowing scarves, to complex music. Duncan's concerts, schools, and dynamic personality greatly influenced MODERN DANCE.

Duncan, Robert, 1919–88, American poet; b. Oakland, Calif. His lyric poems are contained in such volumes as *The Opening of the Field* (1960), *Bending the Bow* (1968), and *Derivations* (1970).

Dunham, Katherine, 1910?–, American dancer, choreographer, and anthropologist; b. Chicago. She taught anthropology and directed her own dance company from the late 1930s to the 60s. Her choreography combines Caribbean and African movements and rhythms with those of MODERN DANCE, which she influenced considerably.

Dunkers: see BRETHREN.

Dunkirk, Fr. *Dunkerque,* town (1990 pop. 70,331), N France, on the North Sea. It is a major port and an important center for iron, steel, and other industries. Fought over for centuries, ruled by many, it was bought (1662) from England by Louis XIV and restored to France. In 1940, during WORLD WAR II, over 300,000 Allied troops, cut off from land retreat by the Germans, were rescued there by British ships and boats.

Dunmore, John Murray, 4th **earl of,** 1732–1809, British colonial governor of Virginia. He led (1774) an expedition against Native Americans known as Lord Dunmore's War. He opposed the colonists, and they forced (1776) his return to England.

Duns Scotus, John, c.1266–1308, Scottish scholastic philosopher, known as the Subtle Doctor. A Franciscan, he adapted Aristotelian thought to Christian theology and founded the school of SCHOLASTICISM known as Scotism, which opposed the Thomism of the followers of THOMAS AQUINAS. Duns Scotus denied that individuality comes from matter. Modifying St. ANSELM's ontological proof of the existence of God, he argued that God's possible existence must be demonstrable from sense experience. His best-known works are *On the First Principle* and two commentaries on the *Sentences* of the Italian theologian Peter Lombard.

Du Pont, French-American family. **Pierre Samuel Du Pont de Nemours,** 1739–1817, a French economist, was one of the PHYSIOCRATS. He was active in politics and diplomacy, taking part in negotiations (1783) after the AMERICAN REVOLUTION and for the LOUISIANA PURCHASE. He emigrated to the U.S. in 1799. His son, **Eleuthère Irénée Du Pont,** 1771–1834, b. Paris, set up a powder works near Wilmington, Del., in 1802. Within a few years he developed an extensive business (now E.I. du Pont de Nemours & Co.) and was appointed (1822) a director of the Bank of the United States. **Samuel Francis Du Pont,** 1803–65, b. Bergen Point, N.J., American naval officer, was a grandson of Pierre Samuel. In the Civil War he directed (1861) the naval victory at Port Royal, S.C., and against his own wishes led (1863) the unsuccessful attack on Charleston. **Pierre Samuel Du Pont,** 1870–1954, b. Wilmington, Del., was a great-grandson of E.I. Du Pont and became (1915) president of the family business. Under him the company developed scores of chemical manufactures and acquired many other industries.

duralumin, ALLOY of ALUMINUM with COPPER, MAGNESIUM, and MANGANESE. A heat treatment causes a reaction between the aluminum and magnesium, increasing hardness and tensile strength. Because of its lightness and other properties, duralumin is widely used in the aircraft industry.

Durand, Asher Brown, 1796–1886, American painter; b. near Newark, N.J. An engraver early in his career, he became a leader of the HUDSON RIVER SCHOOL. His landscapes include *Franconia Notch* (N.Y. Public Lib., N.Y.C.) and *Mountain Forest* (Corcoran Gall., Wash., D.C.).

Duras, Marguerite [dürä'], 1914–, French novelist; b. Indochina (now Vietnam). Her experimental novels include *The Sea Wall* (1950), *Destroy, She Said* (1969), and *Love* (1972). More sensual novels include *The Lover* (1985) and *Emily L.* (1989). She has also written plays and screenplays, e.g., *Hiroshima Mon Amour* (1959), and has directed films.

Durban, city (1985 pop. 634,301), Natal prov., E South Africa, on Durban Bay, an arm of the Indian Ocean. It is an industrial center, a major seaport, and a year-round resort. Industries include shipbuilding, petroleum refining, and automobile assembly. About 40% of the population is of Anglo-Indian descent. The city was settled as Port Natal by the British in 1824 and was renamed in 1835. It is the site of several educational and cultural institutions.

Dürer, Albrecht [dür'ər], 1471–1528, German painter, engraver, and theoretician, the most influential artist of the German school; b. Nuremberg. The son of a goldsmith, he was apprenticed to his father and the painter Michael Wolgemut. After travel in Switzerland and Italy he settled in Nuremberg. He became the first German artist to achieve renown outside Germany. Dürer's foremost achievement was to adapt the principles of the Italian RENAISSANCE to Northern taste. A gifted draftsman, he produced a vast number of woodcuts (see WOODCUT AND WOOD ENGRAVING) and ENGRAVINGS, achieving an unsurpassed technical mastery and expressive power in graphic media. His highly rational system of perspective and proportion served equally well his penchant for both realistic detail and visionary fantasy. His series of woodcuts of the *Apocalypse* was issued in 1498, followed by two cycles of the *Passion of Christ* and *Life of the Virgin.* After 1500 he developed as an art theoretician and produced greatly detailed engravings. From 1510 on he concentrated on the translation of lighting and tonal effects into graphic works. His humanistic inclinations were revealed in such works as *St. Jerome in His Cell* and *Melencolia I* (both: 1514). Dürer usually signed his works, and his many self-portraits reveal a self-awareness rare for his time. He produced some important altarpieces, many sensitive watercolors of wildlife and landscapes, several decorative projects, and treatises on human proportions, applied geometry, and fortifications.

Durham, John George Lambton, 1st **earl of,** 1792–1840, British statesman. A Liberal member of Parliament (1813–32), he promoted the REFORM BILL of 1832. As governor general of Canada, he prepared the masterly *Report on the Affairs of British North America* (1839), supporting Canadian self-government and reforms but opposing French Canadian nationalism.

Durham, city (1990 pop. 136,611), seat of Durham co., N central N.C., in the Piedmont area; inc. 1867. Once largely dependent on tobacco and textiles, Durham is now part (with Raleigh and Chapel Hill) of a major research and educational complex. The tobacco industry, led by James B. Duke, developed after the Civil War. Duke Univ. is in Durham.

Durkheim, Émile, 1858–1917, French sociologist, considered a founder of modern SOCIOLOGY. Influenced by the POSITIVISM of COMTE, Durkheim applied the methods of natural science (particularly empirical evidence and statistics) to the study of society. He held that the collective social mind is the source of religion and morality, that common values are the bonds of social order, and that the loss of such values leads to social and individual instability and SUICIDE. His important works include *The Rules of Sociological Method* (1895), *Suicide* (1897), and *The Elementary Forms of Religious Life* (1912).

Durrell, Lawrence, 1912–90, English author; b. India. His travels lent exotic background to many of his novels. His masterpiece is the *Alexandria Quartet* (*Justine,* 1957; *Balthazar,* 1958; *Mountolive,* 1958; and *Clea,* 1960). The quartet's excellence lies in its rich, ornamental language and in its evocation of the city of Alexandria, Egypt.

Dürrenmatt, Friedrich, 1921–, Swiss playwright and novelist. One of the most famous German-language dramatists of his generation, he wrote of a comic, grotesque world in *The Visit* (1956) and *The Physicists* (1962). Irony also informs his novels, e.g., *The Quarry* (1953) and *The Pledge* (1958).

Dušan, Stephen: see STEPHEN DUŠAN.

Duse, Eleonora [dōō'zə], 1859–1924, Italian actress. From her Juliet at age 14 to her farewell appearance (1923) in IBSEN's *Lady from the Sea,* she projected tremendous emotional power; she was BERNHARDT's only rival. For years a romantic attachment existed between her and D'ANNUNZIO.

Dushanbe, city (1989 pop. 595,000), capital of Tajikistan, W Tajikistan. A major industrial center, the city produces textiles, textile machinery, clothing, leather goods, tractor parts, and foodstuffs. It was known as Dyushambe until 1929, when it was renamed Stalinabad and became the capital of the Tadzhik SSR. The name was changed to Dushanbe in 1961.

Düsseldorf, city (1989 est pop. 569,600), capital of North Rhine–Westphalia, W Germany, at the confluence of the Rhine and Düssel rivers. It is an inland port and an industrial center producing iron and steel, machinery, and other manufactures. Chartered in 1288, it was (14th–16th cent.) a ducal residence. HEINE was born in Düsseldorf.

Dust Bowl, collectively, those areas of the U.S. prairie states subject to dust storms or the removal of unprotected topsoil by strong winds. It covered 25,000 sq mi (64,750 sq km) at its greatest extent in the 1930s, when grasslands that had been plowed for wheat in the 1920s were abandoned or returned to grazing. Irrigation, regrassing, contour farming, and other conservation measures are now widely used.

Dutch East India Company: see EAST INDIA COMPANY, DUTCH.

Dutch language, member of the West Germanic group of the Germanic subfamily of the Indo-European family of languages. See LANGUAGE (table).

Dutch Reformed Church: see REFORMED CHURCH IN AMERICA.

Dutch Wars. **1** 1652–54, war between the English and the Dutch. The long-standing rivalry between the two nations as competitors in world trade erupted into war after the British closed their possessions to Dutch traders. After a sea fight (Nov. 1652) the Dutch gained control of the English Channel, but in 1653 the English broke the control and blockaded the Dutch coast. The Dutch were defeated (July 31, 1653) and were forced to accept a humbling peace treaty. **2** 1664–67, another war between the English and the Dutch. Despite defeat, the Dutch continued to challenge English trade. The English took various Dutch colonies, including New Netherlands (later New York and New Jersey). Despite some English advances, domestic problems—the plague, the great fire, and Scottish disaffection—made them eager for peace. The resulting Treaty of Breda was a blow to English prestige. **3** 1672–78, the first of the great wars of LOUIS XIV of France. Louis was determined to crush Holland and end Dutch commercial rivalry; with secret support from CHARLES II of England, he invaded the Netherlands but was unable to take Amsterdam. After five years of fighting—with Spain, the Holy Roman emperor, and various other powers coming to Holland's aid—Louis was unable to crush Holland. France did gain some territory, including Franche-Comté, but ended up with a severely depleted treasury.

Dutch West India Company (1621–1791), trading and colonizing company chartered by the States-General of the Dutch republic in 1621 and organized in 1623. Given jurisdiction over a wide range of coast in Africa and the Western Hemisphere, it battled (1624–54) Portugal unsuccessfully for control of NE Brazil. The company founded (1626) Fort Amsterdam, which grew to be called New Amsterdam (now New York City).

Duvalier, François [düvälyā'], 1907–71, dictator of HAITI (1957–71). A physician, he served in the government and was elected president (1957) with army backing. After his reelection (1961), "Papa Doc," declared himself (1964) president for life. His long regime was a reign of terror. When he died, his son, **Jean-Claude Duvalier,** 1951–, became (1971) "president-for-life." Known as "Baby Doc," he pursued somewhat more enlightened policies but was forced (1986) to flee the country by increasing protests. France granted him asylum.

Dvořák, Antonín [dvôr'zhäk], 1841–1904, Czech composer. Much of his music is nationalistic. He is best known for his Symphony in E Minor, *From the New World* (1893), written while he was in the U.S. It conveys with great exuberance Dvořák's impressions of American scenes and folk music and at the same time evokes nostalgia for his native land. He also wrote eight other symphonies, chamber works, a violin concerto, a cello concerto, and OVERTURES.

dwarfism, condition in which an animal or plant is smaller than normal size; in humans, it usually results from a combination of genetic factors and endocrine malfunction. Pituitary dwarfism is caused by a deficiency of HUMAN GROWTH HORMONE. Typically, the pituitary dwarf, or midget, has normal body proportions, mental capacity, and sexual development. The most famous dwarf of modern times was "General" TOM THUMB. **Cretinism,** a type of dwarfism accompanied by mental retardation and body distortion, results from an insufficiency of thyroid hormone.

Dwight, Timothy, 1752–1817, American clergyman, author, and educator, grandson of Jonathan EDWARDS; b. Northampton, Mass. He became (1783) a Congregational minister in Greenfield, Conn., and was a leader of the CONNECTICUT WITS, who tried to modernize the curriculum at Yale. Dwight was a believer in theocracy and Federalism, and strongly opposed Republicanism. He was a president of Yale (1795–1817).

Dy, chemical symbol of the element DYSPROSIUM.

Dyak or **Dayak,** indigenous people of BORNEO, numbering over 1 million. Modern civilization has made little change in their customs and mode of life, including intertribal warfare and HEADHUNTING. A whole village lives in a few enormous longhouses, and crops of rice, yams, and sugarcane are grown communally. The Dyak also fish and hunt, using blowguns and poison darts. Their religious cults are animistic and shamanistic.

Dyck, Sir Anthony van: see VAN DYCK, SIR ANTHONY.

dye, natural or synthetic substance used to color various materials, especially textiles, leather, and food. Natural dyes are obtained from plants (e.g., indigo), from animals (e.g., cochineal), and from minerals (e.g., ocher). Used since ancient times, natural dyes have been largely replaced by synthetic dyes, first made in the 19th cent. Most of these are made from coal tar (see TAR AND PITCH). Although some materials, e.g., silk and wool, can be colored simply by being dipped in the dye, others, including cotton, require a mordant. The process by which dyes become "attached" to the material they color is not well understood. It is thought either that a chemical reaction takes place between the dye and the fiber or that the dye is absorbed.

Dylan, Bob, 1941–, American singer and composer; b. Duluth, Minn., as Robert Zimmerman. In the 1960s he gained recognition through his lyrics, capturing the alienation of American youth, and his harsh, insistent delivery. Influenced by Woody GUTHRIE, among others, Dylan exercised a profound influence on folk and ROCK MUSIC, his style evolving from folk to folk-rock to country. Enigmatic and reclusive, he became something of a cult figure.

dynamics, branch of mechanics that deals with the MOTION of objects; it may be further divided into kinematics, the study of motion without regard to the forces producing it, and kinetics, the study of the FORCES that produce or change motion. The principles of dynamics are used to solve problems involving work and energy, and to explain the pressure and expansion of gases, the motion of planets, and the behavior of flowing fluids (gases and liquids). Special branches of dynamics treat the particular effects of forces and motions in fluids (see FLUID MECHANICS); these include AERODYNAMICS, the study of gases in motion, and hydrodynamics, the study of liquids in motion.

dynamite, EXPLOSIVE made from NITROGLYCERIN and various amounts of an inert, absorbent filler, e.g., sawdust. Often ammonium nitrate or sodium nitrate is added. Invented in 1866 by Alfred B. NOBEL, dynamite is usually pressed in cylindrical forms and wrapped in an appropriate material, e.g., paper or plastic. The charge is set off with a detonator.

dyne: see FORCE.

dysentery, inflammation of the intestines, characterized by frequent passage of feces, usually with blood and mucus. Amoebic dysentery is caused by infestation by the ameba *Entamoeba histolytica.* Bacillary dysentery is most often caused by the *Shigella* bacillus. Spread by fecal contamination of food and water, both forms are common where sanitation is poor. Treatment of bacillary dysentery is with a broad-spectrum ANTIBIOTIC; a combination of an antibiotic and an amoebicide is necessary for successful treatment of amoebic dysentery.

dyslexia, severe and persistent difficulty in learning to read despite average or above-average intelligence, normal vision, and appropriate reading instruction. The cause is unknown, but some studies have offered evidence that dyslexia is a neurological problem. Many dyslexics have trouble matching letters to their corresponding sounds. Some common disabilities associated with dyslexia are the reversal of letters, as *b* for *d,* also called mirror writing; word reversals, as *saw* for *was*; and defects in the visual and auditory perception and memory considered necessary for reading. Dyslexia, a type of LEARNING DISABILITY, was first described (1896) by English ophthalmologist W.P. Morgan, who called the condition *word blindness.*

Dzerzhinsky, Feliks Edmundovich, 1877–1926, Soviet political leader. As a follower of LENIN, he participated in the Bolshevik revolution (Oct. 1917). He served (1917–22) as first chief of the CHEKA, the SECRET POLICE, and its successors the GPU and OGPU (1922–26), and was head of the commissariat of internal affairs (NKVD). He oversaw repressions known as the "Red Terror." Later, he was chairman of the Supreme Economic Council (1924–26), a supporter of the New Economic Policy (NEP), and a member of the Politburo.

Dzungaria, also spelled Jungaria, Sungaria, or Zungaria, steppe and desert region, NW China, in Xinjiang Uygur Autonomous Region. Since 1953 large numbers of ethnic Chinese have moved there to work the deposits of coal, iron ore, and oil. The Dzungarian Gate, used for centuries by Central Asian conquerors as an invasion route to China, is a pass at the eastern end of the Ala-Tau, a mountain chain that marks part of the Kazakhstan-China border.

E

e, irrational NUMBER occurring widely in mathematics and science, approximately equal to the value 2.71828; it is the base of natural, or Naperian, LOGARITHMS. Like π (see PI), *e* is transcendental, i.e., not a root of any algebraic equation. It is defined as the limit of the expression $(1 + 1/n)^n$ as *n* becomes infinitely large. Expressions of the form e^x, known as the exponential function, occur in applications ranging from statistics to nuclear physics.

Ead-. For Anglo-Saxon names beginning thus, see ED-; e.g., for Eadgar, see EDGAR.

eagle, large, predatory BIRD of the HAWK family, found worldwide. Similar to but larger than the BUZZARDS, eagles are solitary and believed to mate for life. Their beaks are nearly as long as their heads, and their wingspan may reach 7½ ft (228 cm). The American bald eagle (*Haliaetus leucocephalus*), an endangered species, is brown with white head, neck, and tail plumage. The golden, or mountain, eagle (genus *Aquila*), is sooty brown with tawny head and neck feathers. Unlike the bald eagle, its legs are feathered to the toes.

Eagleburger, Lawrence (Sidney), 1930–, U.S. government official; b. Milwaukee. A career diplomat, he joined the Foreign Service in 1957 and held a series of embassy, State Dept., national security, and Defense Dept. posts before serving as ambassador (1977–81) to Yugoslavia and a State Dept. assistant secretary (1981–82) and under secretary (1982–84). He was deputy secretary of state (1989–92) and secretary of state (1992–93) under Pres. Bush, becoming the first Foreign Service officer to hold those posts.

Eakins, Thomas [āʹkĭnz], 1844–1916, American painter, photographer, and sculptor; b. Philadelphia. Eakins is considered the foremost American portraitist and one of the greatest 19th-cent. artists. He sought to describe reality with absolute honesty, his study of anatomy and perspective providing a means of painting exterior reality. Eakins revived U.S. portraiture with his extraordinarily penetrating paintings and, as a teacher of artists such as HENRI, SLOAN, and GLACKENS, founded a school of native American art. Also a photographer, he used the medium as an art form, as an aid in painting, and to study motion. His paintings include *The Chess Players* (1876; Metropolitan Mus.), *The Clinic of Professor Agnew* (1889; Univ. Penn.), and portraits of Mrs. Frishmuth (1900; Philadelphia Mus.) and Miss Van Buren (1891; Phillips Coll., Wash., D.C.).

Eanes, António dos Santos Ramalho, 1935–, Portuguese army officer and president of Portugal (1976–86). In 1975 Eanes, then a colonel, headed the army group that crushed an attempted left-wing coup. A centrist, he was elected (1976) president with the support of all the major parties except the Communists. He carried out democratic and economic reforms and was reelected in 1980.

ear, organ of hearing and equilibrium. The human ear consists of outer, middle, and inner parts. The outer ear, the visible portion, includes the skin-covered flap of cartilage (auricle) and the auditory canal, which leads to the eardrum. The middle ear contains three small bones, or ossicles, known because of their shapes as the hammer, anvil, and stirrup. The Eustachian tube connects the middle ear to the throat. The inner ear contains the cochlea, which houses the sound-analyzing cells, and the vestibule, with the organs of balance. In the course of hearing, sound waves enter the auditory canal and strike the eardrum, causing it to vibrate. The waves are concentrated as they pass through the ossicles to a small opening leading to the inner ear. The vibration sets in motion fluid within the cochlea. This agitates a delicate membrane, stimulating thousands of sensory hair cells, which in turn stimulate the auditory nerve to send impulses to the brain. Three fluid-filled semicircular canals and two saclike organs, the utriculus and the sacculus, are the chief organs of balance and orientation; as with hearing, stimulation of sensory hair cells in these organs stimulates nerve impulses.

Earhart, Amelia [ârʹhärt], 1897–1937, American aviator; b. Atchison, Kans. She was the first woman to fly across the Atlantic (1928)

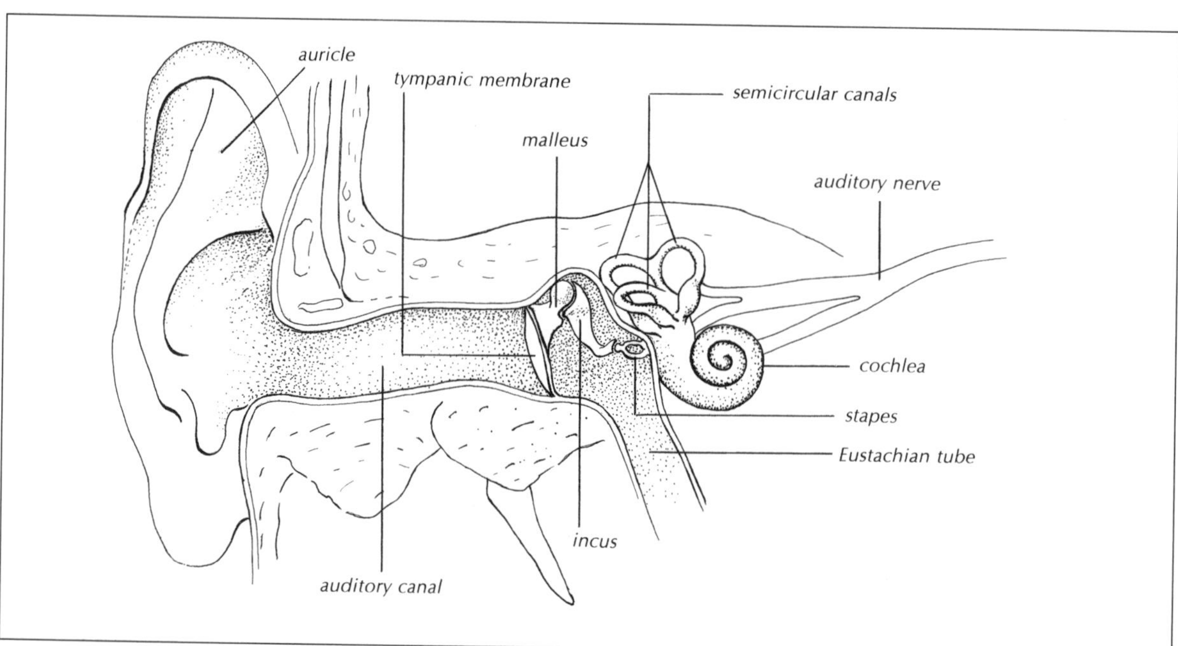

Ear

and to fly it alone (1932) and the first person to fly alone from Hawaii to California (1935). In 1937 she and Frederick J. Noonan set out to fly around the world, but they disappeared mysteriously between New Guinea and Howland Island. In 1992 a search party reported finding remnants of Earhart's plane on Nikumaroro (formerly Gardner Island), Kiribati, but their claims were disputed by people who worked on Earhart's plane.

Early, Jubal Anderson, 1816–94, Confederate general; b. Franklin co., Va.; grad. West Point, 1837. Prominent in the battle of CHANCELLORSVILLE and in the GETTYSBURG CAMPAIGN, he led (1864) a raid that reached the outskirts of Washington, D.C. Early was defeated (1864–65) by P.H. SHERIDAN in the Shenandoah Valley and was relieved of command.

Early Christian art and architecture. Among the earliest extant manifestations of Christian art are the early 3d-cent. paintings of biblical figures on CATACOMB walls in Rome. Among the main themes portrayed are the hope of resurrection and immortality, symbolized by fish and peacock motifs. After the Edict of Toleration (313) the scope of Christian art was radically enlarged. BASILICAS were covered with elaborate MOSAIC narrative cycles, e.g., Santa Maria Maggiore and Santa Pudenziana in Rome and Sant'Apollinare Nuovo in Ravenna. In Christian art the illumination of sacred texts assumed great importance. Fragments of silver and gold biblical text on purple vellum with sumptuous illuminations are still preserved, e.g., the Vienna Genesis from the first half of the 6th cent. The elaborate sculpture of the stone sarcophagus was extensively practiced, often depicting the life of Jesus. Ivory carvers decorated book covers and reliquaries and such large objects as the throne of Maximianus in Ravenna (6th cent.). After legal recognition of the faith, imposing cult edifices were erected throughout the Roman Empire. As with other art forms, Christian architecture adapted and modified existing structures from the pagan world. Church structure became centralized, emphasizing round, polygonal, or cruciform shapes. BAPTISTERIES and memorial shrines (martyria) followed the Roman style. A distinct type of Christian art and architecture was evolved in Egypt (see COPTIC ART). In the East the Byzantine emperors supported the developments of the Early Christian artistic tradition.

early man: see HUMAN EVOLUTION.

Earp, Wyatt Berry Stapp, 1848–1929, lawman and gunfighter of the American West; b. Monmouth, Ill. After serving as a policeman in Kansas, Earp was involved (1881) in the controversial gunfight at the O.K. Corral in Tombstone, Ariz.

earth, fifth largest PLANET of the SOLAR SYSTEM and the only one known to support life. Its mean distance from the SUN is c.93 million mi (150 million km). The change of seasons is caused by the tilt (23.5°) of the earth's axis to the plane of the orbit. The earth is surrounded by an envelope of gases, mostly oxygen and nitrogen, called the ATMOSPHERE. Gravitational forces have molded the earth into a spherical shape that bulges slightly at the equator (equatorial diameter: c.7,926 mi/12,760 km; polar diameter: 7,900 mi/ 12,720 km). Studies indicate that the earth consists of concentric layers that differ in size, chemistry, and density. The outer shell, or crust, consists of the CONTINENTS and the OCEAN basins. The crust is broken into vast plates that slide around on a plastic zone, or asthenosphere, within the middle shell, or mantle (see CONTINENTAL DRIFT; PLATE TECTONICS). At the center of the earth is an outer core, believed to be liquid, and an inner, solid core. The earth is estimated to be 4.5–5 billion years old, and its origin is a controversial subject. The earth has one natural satellite, the MOON.

Earth Day, April 22, a day set aside to promote ecology, encourage respect for life on earth, and highlight the problem of pollution. First observed in 1970, Earth Day is now publicly celebrated worldwide.

earthquake, trembling or shaking movement of the earth's surface. Great earthquakes usually begin with slight tremors, rapidly increase to one or more violent shocks, and diminish gradually. The immediate cause of most shallow earthquakes is the sudden release of stress along a FAULT, or fracture, in the earth's crust, resulting in the movement of opposing blocks of rock past one another. This causes vibrations to pass through and around the earth in wave form (see TSUNAMI). The subterranean origin of an earthquake is its focus; the point on the surface directly above the focus

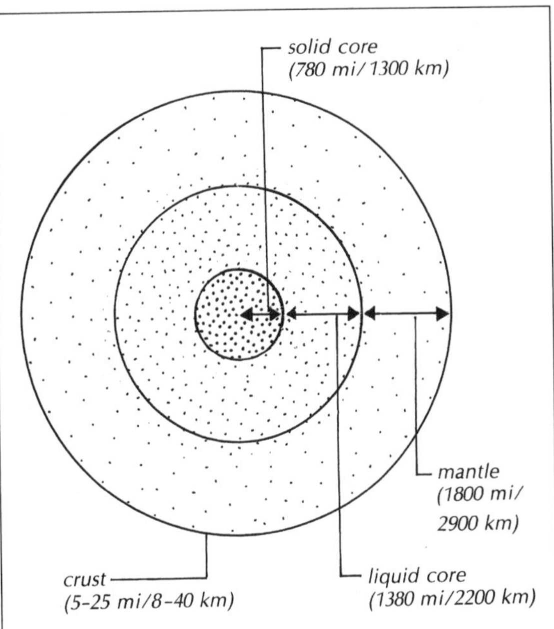

Cross-section of the earth, showing its shells

is the epicenter. Waves generated by earthquakes are of several types. Both P, or primary, waves, which are compressional and are the fastest, and S, or secondary, waves, which cause vibrations perpendicular to their motion, are body waves that pass through the earth. L, or long, waves travel along the surface and cause damage near the epicenter. Seismologists (see SEISMOLOGY) have deduced the internal structure of the earth by analyzing changes in P and S waves. The magnitude and intensity of earthquakes are determined by the use of scales, e.g., the Richter scale, which describes the amount of energy released at the focus of an earthquake.

earthworks, art form of the late 1960s and early 70s using elements of nature in situ. Often vast in scale, the works are subject to changes in temperature and light. Robert Smithson's *Spiral Jetty* (1970), a huge spiral of rock and salt crystal in the Great Salt Lake, Utah, is a classic example of the form.

earthworm, any cylindrical, segmented worm (see ANNELID WORM) of the class Oligochaeta. Ranging from 1 in. (2.5 cm) to 11 ft (330 cm) in length, earthworms burrow in the ground and swallow soil from which organic matter is extracted in the gizzard. They are important to agriculture in aerating and mixing the soil.

East Anglia, kingdom of Anglo-Saxon England, comprising the modern counties of Norfolk and Suffolk. Settled in the late 5th cent. by Angles, it became one of the most powerful English kingdoms of the late 6th cent. It became an under kingdom of MERCIA, against which it later rebelled (825), only to become a dependency of WESSEX. The Danish invading army, quartered in East Anglia (865–66), later (869) conquered the state entirely. The treaty of 886 confirmed the region as part of the DANELAW. After 917 East Anglia was an earldom of England.

East China Sea, arm of the Pacific Ocean, c.480,000 sq mi (1,243,200 sq km), bounded by China (W), Japan and the Senkaku and Ryukyu islands (E), and Taiwan (S). Vast oil deposits, first indicated in 1980, are believed to underlie much of the shallow sea floor.

Easter [from Old Eng. *Eastre,* name of a spring goddess], chief Christian feast, commemorating the resurrection of JESUS after his crucifixion. In the West it falls on a Sunday between Mar. 22 and Apr. 25 inclusive (see CALENDAR). Preceded by the penitential season of LENT, Easter is a day of rejoicing. The date of Easter is calculated differently in the Orthodox Eastern Church and usually falls several weeks after the Western date.

East Germany: see GERMANY.

Easter Island, 46 sq mi (119 sq km), in the South Pacific Ocean, W of Chile, which annexed it in 1888. The origin of the island's unusual hieroglyphs and gigantic carved heads, some weighing more than 50 tons, has been the subject of much speculation by the American psychologist Werner Wolff, the French ethnologist Alfred Métraux, and others. Thor HEYERDAHL theorized that the heads were carved by fair-skinned invaders from the East prior to the arrival (c.1680) of the island's present Polynesians; most anthropologists have rejected this idea.

Eastern Highlands, mountains and plateaus in E Australia that extend roughly parallel to the east and southeast coasts and into TASMANIA for c.2,400 mi (3,860 km). They form the continental divide and are sometimes referred to as the Great Dividing Range. Mt. KOSCIUSKO (7,316 ft/2,230 m), in the southeast is Australia's highest peak. Sections of the highlands are widely known by local names, including the Snowy Mountains, AUSTRALIAN ALPS, Blue Mts., and New England Range. Generally rugged, with few gaps and many gorges, the Eastern Highlands long hindered westward expansion across the continent.

Eastern Question, problem of the fate of the European territory, especially the Balkans, controlled by the decaying OTTOMAN EMPIRE (Turkey) in the 18th, 19th, and early 20th cent. For much of that time the Great Powers (Austria, Britain, Prussia, Russia, and France) were involved in either diplomatic intrigue or actual armed warfare to protect their national interests there. RUSSIA, in particular, was eager to expand into the area, looking for warm-water ports accessible to the Mediterranean. The other powers, especially Great Britain, were chiefly involved in thwarting Russia's ambitions. However, there were considerable shifts in alliances. The RUSSO-TURKISH WARS, in particular, resulted from the Eastern Question. In the 19th cent. the problem was exacerbated by the national aspirations of the individual Balkan peoples, who were aided or discouraged by the Great Powers, depending on what their own national interests were deemed to be. In the CRIMEAN WAR, Britain and France successfully aided Turkey in warding off Russian advances. Turkey's position, however, continued to decline. The BALKAN WARS (1912–13) set the stage for the final dissolution of the Ottoman Empire in WORLD WAR I.

Eastern Woodlands Indians: see NORTH AMERICA, INDIGENOUS PEOPLES OF.

East India Company, British, 1600–1858, company chartered by the Crown for trade with Asia. It acquired unequaled trade privileges from the Mogul emperors in India, and began to reap large profits by exporting textiles and tea. As Mogul power declined, the company intervened in Indian political affairs. Its agent, Robert CLIVE, defeated (1751–60) the rival French East India Company, and Warren HASTINGS, the first governor general of British India, assumed more control of the company. Britain took over India's administration after the INDIAN MUTINY of 1857, and the company was dissolved.

East India Company, Dutch, 1602–1798, company chartered by the States-General of the Netherlands. Granted a monopoly on Dutch trade E of the Cape of Good Hope and W of the Strait of Magellan, the company subdued local rulers; drove the British and Portuguese from Indonesia, Malaya, and Ceylon (now Sri Lanka); and dominated trade with the Spice Islands (Moluccas). When it was dissolved, its possessions became part of the Dutch empire in E Asia.

East India Company, French, 1664–1769, commercial enterprise chartered by LOUIS XIV to trade in the Eastern Hemisphere. It was merged (1719–23) into the Compagnie des Indes as part of John LAW's Mississippi Scheme. From 1741 the company was active in India, but it was dissolved after the French defeat by the British under Robert CLIVE.

East Indies, name, now seldom used, first applied to India, then to SE Asia, and finally to the islands of Indonesia.

Eastman, George, 1854–1932, American inventor and industrialist; b. Waterville, N.Y. He invented a dry-plate photographic process, roll film, and the Kodak camera (1888), as well as a process for color photography (1928). The Eastman Kodak Co. (founded 1892) was one of the first U.S. firms to mass-produce a standardized product, greatly stimulating the development of photography as a popular hobby. Eastman's philanthropies exceeded $100 million.

Eastman, Max, 1883–1969, American author; b. Canandaigua, N.Y. The editor of radical periodicals (*The Masses, Liberator*) until 1923, he later rejected Communism and wrote several books attacking it.

East Prussia, former province of Prussia, NE Germany. Königsberg (now KALININGRAD) was the capital. The area was conquered (13th cent.) by the TEUTONIC KNIGHTS from the Borussi, or Prussians. It passed (1618) to an elector of BRANDENBURG, whose son became (1701) king of PRUSSIA. From 1701 to 1945 East Prussia shared the history of Prussia. In 1945 East Prussia was divided between the USSR, becoming part of the Russian SFSR (now Russia), and Poland.

Eastwood, Clint (Clinton Eastwood, Jr.), 1930–, American actor and director; b. San Francisco. He is best known for roles in action films, where he portrays a strong, silent, often violent hero. He has starred in over thirty movies, including *Dirty Harry* (1972), *Magnum Force* (1973), and *In the Line of Fire* (1993). He directed and acted in *Play Misty for Me* (1971), *Heartbreak Ridge* (1986), and *Unforgiven* (1992; Academy Award).

eating disorders, any of several psychological disorders relating to the consumption of food, such as anorexia nervosa. Anorexia nervosa and bulimia are characterized by an abnormal fear of obesity, distorted body image, and subsequent abnormal eating patterns. Anorexia is marked by obsessive fasting; bulimia by eating binges followed by self-induced vomiting or the use of laxatives. The effects of these disorders range from mild weight loss to delayed sexual development, heart problems, depression, and even death. Both conditions have their roots in social pressures; most cases occur among middle- and upper-class adolescent girls. Some specialists distinguish a third eating disorder, binge eating disorder, which is characterized by frequent periods of uncontrolled, compulsive eating, resulting in obesity and distress; it is typically associated with anxiety or depression. Other eating disorders include rumination disorder, which generally occurs during infancy and involves repeated regurgitation; and pica, found primarily among young children and characterized by the eating of various nonnutritive substances, such as plaster, paint, or leaves.

Eaton, John Henry, 1790–1856, U.S. senator (1818–29) from Tennessee and secretary of war (1829–31); b. Halifax co., N.C. A close associate of Pres. JACKSON, he resigned as secretary after the social snubbing of his second wife, Margaret O'Neill.

Ebla, ancient city near Aleppo, Syria. The palace archive excavated (1975) there revealed that Ebla had been a major commercial center trading with much of the Middle East. The texts, written in a Canaanite language (Eblaite), date from c.2500 B.C.

ebony, common name for the Ebenaceae, a family of trees and shrubs widely distributed in warm climates. The genus *Diospyros* includes the ebony and persimmon trees. Ebony wood, valued since ancient times, is dark and hard; it is used extensively in cabinetmaking. Some species (e.g., *D. hirsuta*) have wood striped with black or shades of brown (called calamander wood or variegated ebony). The persimmons bear edible fruit that when unripe is astringent and when ripe is soft and pulpy, making it difficult to market. Persimmon wood has a limited use in the manufacture of objects (e.g., golf club heads) requiring hardwood.

eccentricity, in astronomy: see ORBIT.

Ecclesiastes [ēklē″zēăs′tēz], book of the OLD TESTAMENT, 21st in the Authorized Version, traditionally ascribed to SOLOMON but clearly written much later (3d cent. B.C. or as late as 160 B.C.). A philosophical essay, it opens with the theme that since "all is vanity," life should be enjoyed. This is followed by praise of wisdom and mercy, an emphasis on the universality of death, and a brief epilogue on the fear of God's judgment.

Ecclesiasticus, book included in the OLD TESTAMENT of the Western canon and the Septuagint but not in the Hebrew Bible, and placed in the APOCRYPHA in the Authorized Version. It is also called the Wisdom of Jesus the Son of Sirach. The original Hebrew text dates from 200–180 B.C. and was translated perhaps in 132–131 B.C. Its theme is the excellence of wisdom, and it contains several eloquent passages.

Echegaray, José [āchāgäri′], 1832–1916, Spanish dramatist, mathematician, economist, and cabinet minister. His 68 plays range from romances to melodramatic problem plays like *The Great Ga-*

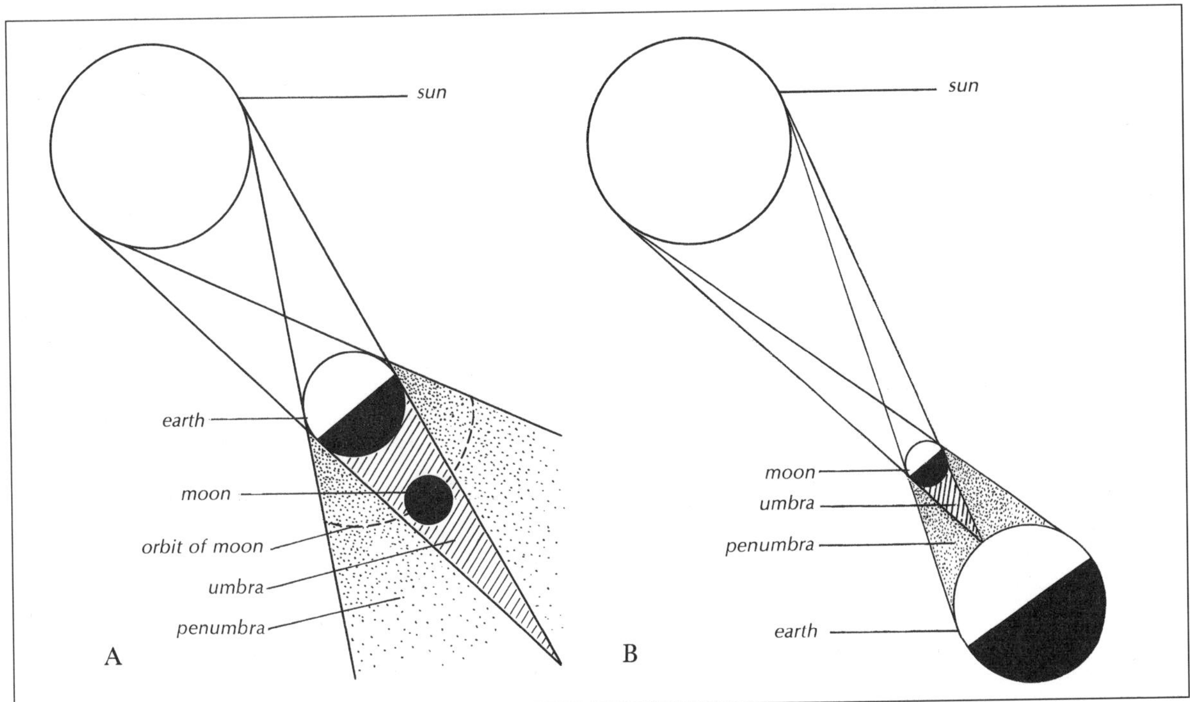

Eclipses

leoto (1881). He shared the 1904 Nobel Prize in literature with Frédéric MISTRAL.

Echeverría Álvarez, Luis [āl'värās], 1922–, president of Mexico (1970–76). A member of the Institutional Revolutionary party, he held numerous government posts, including secretary of the interior (1964–69). As president he attempted reforms but was faced with inflation, unemployment, and political violence.

echidna or **spiny anteater,** primitive, egg-laying MAMMAL, or MONOTREME, of New Guinea, E Australia, and Tasmania. Covered with sharp quills, the grayish-brown echidna protects itself by rolling into a ball. It may reach 18 in. (46 cm) in length. A rapid burrower, the echidna probes for ants and termites with its sensitive muzzle and long, sticky tongue.

echinoderm, marine invertebrate animal of the phylum Echinodermata, having external skeletons of calcareous plates just under the skin, no head, and a unique water-vascular (ambulacral) system with tube-feet. Echinoderms are radially symmetrical, lack specialized excretory organs, and reproduce sexually. Echinoderms have extensive powers of regeneration of lost or injured parts. All members of the phylum live on the sea floor. The phylum includes the STARFISH, BRITTLE STARS, SEA URCHINS and SAND DOLLARS, SEA CUCUMBERS, and CRINOIDS.

Echo, in Greek mythology, mountain NYMPH. She incurred HERA's wrath with her chatter and, as punishment, could only repeat the last words said by others. In unrequited love for NARCISSUS, she pined away until her voice alone remained.

echo, reflection of a sound wave back to its source in sufficient strength and with a sufficient time lag (at least 0.1 sec) to be separately distinguished by the human ear.

Eck, Johann Maier von, 1486–1543, German Roman Catholic theologian. Although he held humanistic ideas, he is known as the theologian who forced LUTHER, whom he disputed publicly at Leipzig (1519), into a position of open opposition to the Roman Catholic Church.

Eckhart, Meister (Johannes Eckhart), c.1260–c.1328, German mystical theologian. A DOMINICAN, he communicated his burning sense of God's nearness to human beings and began a popular mystical movement in 14th-cent. Germany. Eckhart was wrongly accused of connection with the Beghards (a group with semiheretical beliefs), and 17 of his propositions were condemned (1329) as heretical by Pope John XXII. He was perhaps the first writer of speculative prose in German, which subsequently replaced Latin as the language used for popular tracts.

eclampsia: see TOXEMIA.

eclipse, partial or total obscuring of one celestial body by the shadow of another. A **lunar eclipse** occurs when the earth blocks the sun's light from the moon; a **solar eclipse** occurs when the moon blocks the sun's light from some area on the earth. Because the earth and moon shine only by the reflected light of the sun, each casts a shadow into space in the direction away from the sun. The shadow consists of a cone-shaped area of complete darkness, called the umbra, and a larger area of partial darkness that surrounds the umbra, called the penumbra. A lunar eclipse is said to be total or partial depending on whether the moon passes completely into the umbra of the earth's shadow or remains partly in the penumbra. A solar eclipse is said to be total or partial depending on whether the observer is in the umbra or the penumbra of the moon's shadow. Total solar eclipses have particular scientific importance, providing information about the motions of the moon and about the surface phenomena of the sun and permitting tests of Albert Einstein's general theory of RELATIVITY. An annular solar eclipse occurs when the moon is so distant from the earth that the umbra of its shadow is too short to reach the earth's surface; the sun is thus seen as a bright ring completely surrounding the moon's dark disk. Solar and lunar eclipses are possible only when the moon crosses the earth's orbital plane at a time when the sun, moon, and earth are in alignment (at new and full moon; see SYZYGY).

ecliptic, the great circle on the celestial sphere (see ASTRONOMICAL COORDINATE SYSTEMS) that lies in the plane of the earth's ORBIT. Because of the earth's yearly revolution around the sun, the sun appears to move in an annual journey along the ecliptic. The obliquity of the ecliptic is the inclination (about 23.5°) of the plane of the ecliptic to the plane of the celestial equator. The constellations of the ZODIAC are those through which the ecliptic passes.

Eco, Umberto [ĕcō], 1932–, Italian author and scholar. His enormously successful novel, *The Name of the Rose* (1981), is a medieval mystery that blends detective fiction, philosophy, history, and SEMIOTICS. Among his other works are *Foucault's Pendulum*

(1989), also a novel, *A Theory of Semiotics* (1976), and *The Limits of Interpretation* (1990).

E. coli: see ESCHERICHIA COLI.

ecology, study of the interrelationships of organisms and the physical environment. Within the BIOSPHERE, the basic unit of study is the ecosystem—a community of plants and animals in an environment supplying the raw materials for life, i.e., chemical elements (or food) and water. An ecosystem is delimited by climate, altitude, latitude, water and soil characteristics, and other physical conditions. The energy for fueling life activities reaches the earth in the form of sunlight. By PHOTOSYNTHESIS green plants capture that light energy and store it in the chemical bonds of carbohydrates, fats, and proteins. Some of the energy is acquired by plant-eating animals, and a fraction of it is passed on to predatory animals. Such sequences, called food chains, overlap at many points, forming food webs. Once spent, the energy for life cannot be replenished except by further exposure of green plants to sunlight. The chemicals of life are continually recycled by such processes as photosynthesis, RESPIRATION, and nitrogen fixation (see NITROGEN CYCLE). Disruption of these cycles by natural causes such as drought or by POLLUTION can disturb the balance of an entire ecosystem. An ecosystem that has reached a stable and self-perpetuating stage is known as a *climax community.* When extensive and well-defined, the climax community is called a *biome.* Examples are TUNDRA, SAVANNA (grassland), DESERT, and forests. Stability is attained through a process known as succession, whereby a relatively simple community, such as lichen- and algae-covered rocks, gives way over time to one more complex, such as a forest or tundra.

econometrics, a technique of economic analysis that combines economic theory with statistical and mathematical methods of analysis. It is an attempt to improve economic forecasting and to make possible successful policy planning. In econometrics, economic theories are expressed as mathematical relations and then tested empirically by statistical techniques. The system is used to create models of the national economy that endeavor to predict such basic factors as GROSS NATIONAL PRODUCT, levels of unemployment, inflation rate, and federal budget deficits. The use of econometrics has grown, even though its forecasts have not always attained a high degree of accuracy.

Economic and Social Council: see UNITED NATIONS (table 2).

economics, the study of how human beings allocate scarce resources to produce various commodities and how those goods are distributed for consumption among the people in society. The essence of economics lies in the fact that resources are scarce, or at least limited, and that not all human needs and desires can be met. How to distribute these resources in the most efficient and equitable way is a principal concern of economists. The field of economics has undergone a remarkable expansion in the 20th cent. as the world economy has grown increasingly large and complex. Today, economists are employed in large numbers in private industry, government, and higher education. The development of computer sciences has further enhanced the importance of economics in modern society. Economics is usually divided into two broad categories and a number of lesser ones. **Macroeconomics** involves the study of the whole economic picture, as opposed to the parts. It analyzes aggregate data in such areas as the GROSS NATIONAL PRODUCT (GNP) and national income, general price levels, and total employment. It also examines the interplay of these forces with each other and the results of any imbalances among them. **Microeconomics,** on the other hand, looks at economic activity in the individual case, whether it be a single corporation, commodity, or consuming unit, and attempts to determine, for example, how productive resources are allocated among competing producers and how incomes are distributed among the various sectors of an economy. It is especially concerned with the price levels of particular goods and services. Some economists list a third major category, that of economic growth and development. All of these fields today make use of ECONOMETRICS, a branch dealing with statistical analysis and forecasting. The history of economics has roots in the writings of the ancient Greeks. While it is closely identified with CAPITALISM, it plays a vital role in socialist and communist countries as well. Economics was established as a major field of study in the 18th cent. by Adam SMITH, who founded the so-called classical school, which included other British economists such as David RICARDO and John Stuart MILL. While they embraced, in varying degrees, the concept of LAISSEZ-FAIRE (allowing business to follow freely the "natural laws" of economics), J.M. KEYNES in the 20th cent. developed theories that have led to governmental attempts to control BUSINESS CYCLES. In addition to Keynesian and neo-Keynesian schools, modern economic schools include the monetarists, such as Milton FRIEDMAN, who believe that the money supply exerts a dominant influence on the economy; supply-siders (see SUPPLY-SIDE ECONOMICS); and Marxist and socialist economists (see MARXISM; SOCIALISM). See also BANKING; CREDIT; DEPRESSION; INFLATION; INTEREST; MONEY; SUPPLY AND DEMAND; TAXATION.

ecosystem: see ECOLOGY.

Ecuador [ĕk'wədôr], officially Republic of Ecuador, republic (1990 est. pop. 10,933,000), 109,483 sq mi (283,561 sq km), W South America, bordered by Colombia (N), Peru (S and E), and the Pacific Ocean (W). QUITO is the capital, and GUAYAQUIL is the largest city and chief port. The ANDES Mts. dominate the landscape, extending from north to south in two parallel ranges and reaching their highest point in the peak of Chimborazo (20,577 ft/6,272 m). There are numerous active volcanoes, and earthquakes are frequent, and often disastrous, in this area. Within the mountains are high, often fertile, valleys, which support the main bulk of the population and house the major urban centers. East of the Andes is a region of almost uninhabited tropical jungle, through which run the tributaries of the Amazon R., while to the west are the hot, humid lowlands of the Pacific coast. Since completion (1972) of a trans-Andean pipeline, Ecuador has become one of Latin America's largest oil producers and exporters; oil reserves are expected to be depleted, however, early in the next century. Other exports include bananas, coffee, cocoa, fish, and forest products. Tourism is also important to the economy. Although almost one third of the work force engages in agriculture (corn, barley, rice, wheat), many foodstuffs and other goods must be imported. Manufactures are few and small-scale; in the 1980s and 90s the government attempted to stimulate economic growth by imposing austerity budgets, currency devaluation, and increased taxation. The majority of the population is indigenous or mestizo, but there are people of African or mixed African and European origin along the coast. The few Ecuadorans of entirely European-descent are mainly landholders. Spanish is the official language, although many indigenous people speak Quechua or Jarvo. Roman Catholicism is the predominant religion.

History. Entering the region that is now Ecuador in 1533, the Spanish CONQUISTADORES did not find the wealth they sought and moved on. The area became a colonial backwater, at various times subject to Peru and NEW GRANADA. It was liberated from Spanish control by Antonio José de SUCRE in the battle of Pichincha in 1822, made part of the newly formed state of Greater Colombia by Simón BOLÍVAR, and became a separate state (four times its present size) in 1830. Boundary disputes led to frequent invasions by Peru in the 19th and 20th cent., and some of them have still not been settled. Politically, Ecuador became divided between Conservatives, who supported entrenched privileges and a dominant Church, and Liberals, who sought social reforms; and its history in the 19th cent. was marked by bitter internecine struggles between the two factions. Political instability continued in the 20th cent., bringing a bewildering number of changes in government. In 1925 the army replaced the banking interests as the ultimate power. Military coups in support of various rival factions have been common. In 1979 a new constitution was promulgated, and popular presidential and legislative elections were held. Sixto Durán Ballén, a conservative, was elected president in 1992.

ecumenical council: see COUNCIL, ECUMENICAL.

ecumenical movement, a movement aimed at the unification of the Protestant churches of the world and ultimately of all Christians. In England the Evangelical Alliance (1846) was an attempt in this direction. In the U.S. the Federal Council of Churches of Christ was established in 1908. The WORLD COUNCIL OF CHURCHES (first assembly, 1948) is now the chief instrument of ecumenicity. Notable progress has been made in merging individual churches, e.g. the UNITED CHURCH OF CHRIST in the U.S. and the Church of SOUTH INDIA. Since the Second VATICAN COUNCIL (1962–65), the Roman Catholic Church has encouraged ecumenical dialogue with other churches.

Edda [ĕd'ə], title of two works in Old Icelandic. The *Poetic* (or *Elder*) *Edda,* the most valuable collection in Old Norse literature, is made up of 34 mythological and heroic lays (c.800–c.1200). The *Prose* (or *Younger*) *Edda,* probably written c.1222 by SNORRI STURLUSON, is a treatise on the art of Icelandic poetry and a compendium of Norse mythology and is the prime source on the subject.

Eddington, Sir Arthur Stanley, 1882–1944, English astronomer and physicist. He was Plumian professor of astronomy (from 1913) and director of the observatory (from 1914) at Cambridge Univ. Eddington made major contributions to the study of the evolution, motion, and internal constitution of stars and was one of the first physicists to grasp the theory of relativity, of which he became a leading exponent. A prolific writer on science, he wrote such works as *Mathematical Theory of Relativity* (1923) and *The Internal Constitution of the Stars* (1926).

Eddy, Mary Baker, 1821–1910, founder of the CHRISTIAN SCIENCE movement; b. Bow, near Concord, N.H. In frail health from childhood, she became interested in healing and faith, especially after meeting P.P. Quimby, a mental healer, in 1862. She later discarded his methods and began (1866) the Christian Science movement. *Science and Health,* the movement's textbook, appeared in 1875, and she planned the *Church Manual* and the upbuilding of the sect. As pastor emeritus of the Mother Church, Boston, and head of the whole church, she exercised great influence, even in retirement. In 1908 she founded the *Christian Science Monitor,* a daily newspaper.

Edel, (Joseph) Leon, 1907–, American literary scholar; b. Pittsburgh. For portions of his five-volume biography of Henry JAMES (1953–72) he received the Pulitzer Prize. His other works include *James Joyce: The Last Journey* (1947) and *Bloomsbury: A House of Lions* (1979).

edelweiss, perennial plant (genus *Leontopodium*) of the COMPOSITE family, found at high altitudes in the mountains of Europe, Asia, and South America. It has woolly-white floral leaves and small yellow disk flowers surrounded by silvery bracts. It is esteemed in Europe as a symbol of purity and in Switzerland is protected by law.

Eden, Sir Anthony, 1895–1977, British statesman. A Conservative, he was foreign minister from 1935 to 1938 but resigned in opposition to Neville CHAMBERLAIN's "appeasement" of the AXIS powers. Again foreign minister in Winston CHURCHILL's war cabinet (1940–45), he was instrumental in establishing the UN. After Labour's defeat in 1951, he once again became foreign minister. He succeeded Churchill as prime minister in 1955. His decision to use armed intervention in the SUEZ CANAL crisis in 1956 provoked much controversy. In poor health, he resigned in 1957. He was made a life peer in 1961.

Eden, Garden of, in the BIBLE, the first home of humans. God established the garden, with its trees of knowledge and of life, as a dwelling place for ADAM and EVE, until, having eaten of the forbidden fruit, they were banished. It has been located variously, particularly in Mesopotamia.

Edessa, ancient city of Mesopotamia (modern Urfa, Turkey). Around 137 B.C. it became the capital of the kingdom of Osroene and later came under Roman and Byzantine rule. In A.D. 639 it fell to the Arabs. Edessa was captured by the Crusaders in 1097 (see CRUSADES) but passed into Muslim hands again in 1144.

Edgar or **Eadgar,** 943–75, king of the English (957–75). His reign was one of orderly prosperity. He initiated widespread monastic reforms and granted practical autonomy to the Danes in England (see DANELAW) in return for their loyalty. His son was ÆTHELRED the Unready.

Edinburgh, Philip Mountbatten, duke of, 1921–, consort of ELIZABETH II of Great Britain; b. Greece. The son of Prince Andrew of Greece and Princess Alice, daughter of Prince Louis of Battenberg, he is a great-great-grandson of Queen VICTORIA. In 1947, the year he married Elizabeth, he took his mother's name, Mountbatten; became a British citizen; and was created duke of Edinburgh. In 1957 Elizabeth conferred upon him the title of Prince.

Edinburgh, capital city (1991 pop. 421,213) of Scotland and royal burgh. The city is divided into two sections: the Old Town, on the slope of Castle Rock, dates from the 11th cent.; the New Town spread to the north in the late 18th cent. Edinburgh is a government, finance, and tourist center. Most industry, which includes brewing and distilling, publishing, and paper milling, is situated near the city's port, Leith. Edinburgh grew up around its 11th-cent. castle and became Scotland's capital in 1437. It blossomed as a cultural center in the 18th and 19th cent., with such figures as David HUME, Robert BURNS, and Sir Walter SCOTT. It remains a cultural and educational hub and hosts an annual international arts festival.

Edison, Thomas Alva, 1847–1931, American inventor; b. Milan, Ohio. Edison was a genius in the practical application of scientific principles and one of the most productive inventors of his time—despite only three months of formal schooling and an increasing deafness throughout most of his life. Among his most important inventions were the carbon MICROPHONE (1877), the RECORD PLAYER (patented 1878), and the Kinetoscope (see MOTION PICTURES). His most significant contributions, however, were his development of the first commercially practical incandescent lamp (1879) and his design for a complete electrical distribution system for LIGHTING and power, culminating in the installation (1881–82) of the world's first central electric-light power plant in New York City. His New Jersey workshops (at Menlo Park and West Orange) were forerunners of the modern industrial research laboratory, in which teams of workers, rather than a lone inventor, systematically investigate a problem.

Edmonton, city (1991 pop. 616,741), capital of Alberta, W Canada, on the North Saskatchewan R. It is one of Canada's largest and fastest-growing cities and the chief center for Alberta's oil and petrochemical industries. Edmonton is an important agricultural processing and wholesaling center and serves as the gateway to the developing Peace R. and Athabasca frontier country. Edmonton has the world's largest mall, which has become a tourist attraction. Founded (1795) as Fort Edmonton, the city was a major western fur-trading post in the 19th cent.

Edmund, Saint (Edmund Rich), 1170?–1240, English churchman, archbishop of Canterbury. His zeal for reform antagonized HENRY

III, who secured from Rome a papal legate sympathetic to himself, with jurisdiction over Edmund. Feast: Nov. 16.

Edmund Crouchback: see under LANCASTER, HOUSE OF.

Edmund Ironside, d. 1016, king of the English (1016), son of ÆTHELRED the Unready. He was prominent in the fighting against CANUTE. On Æthelred's death, Edmund was proclaimed king although Canute received the support of over half of England. After the battle of Assandun (Oct. 18, 1016), he and Canute came to terms and partitioned England, but Edmund died the next month. His courage earned him the name Ironside.

Edom: see ESAU.

education: see AUDIOVISUAL INSTRUCTION; BILINGUAL EDUCATION; CHAUTAUQUA MOVEMENT; COLLEGES AND UNIVERSITIES; DYSLEXIA; KINDERGARTEN; LEARNING DISABILITIES; PROGRESSIVE EDUCATION; SIGN LANGUAGE; SOPHISTS; see also biographies of educators, e.g., BRAILLE, LOUIS; COMENIUS, JOHN AMOS; CONANT, JAMES BRYANT; FROEBEL, FRIEDRICH; GALLAUDET, THOMAS HOPKINS; GRAY, HANNA HOLBORN; HUTCHINS, ROBERT MAYNARD; MONTESSORI, MARIA; PESTALOZZI, JOHANN; WASHINGTON, BOOKER T.; WILLARD, EMMA.

Education, United States Department of, federal executive department established (1979) to administer and coordinate programs of federal assistance to education, previously a function of the former Dept. of Health, Education, and Welfare. It oversees and administers grants at elementary, secondary, and higher levels of education.

Edward, kings of England. **Edward I,** 1239–1307 (r.1272–1307), was the son and successor of HENRY III. He gained new claims to France through his marriage (1254) to Eleanor of Castile and was responsible for his father's victory in the BARONS' WAR. As king, his conquest of Wales (1277–82) was followed by a long, futile campaign against Scotland (1290–1307). Edward's legal reforms, notably the statutes of Westminster, earned him the title "English Justinian." He restricted private and church courts and controlled land grants to the church. His Model Parliament (1295) marked greater participation by the barons, merchants, and clergy whose resistance to war taxation had forced him to confirm previous charters (e.g., MAGNA CARTA). His son, **Edward II,** 1284–1327 (r.1307–27), was a weak king, dissipated and self-indulgent. His reign was noted for internal dissension and the loss of Scotland. His insistence on having his favorite, Piers Gaveston, at court caused rebellion among the barons, who eventually had Gaveston killed. Edward's later favorites, Hugh le Despenser and his son, virtually ruled England (1322–26). They made a truce with ROBERT I and recognized him as king of Scotland. Edward's wife, Queen ISABELLA, refused to return from France while the Despensers ruled. She entered into an adulterous alliance with Roger de MORTIMER and invaded England. The Despensers were executed and Edward forced to abdicate. He was imprisoned and almost certainly murdered by henchmen of Isabella and Mortimer. His son, **Edward III,** 1312–77 (r.1327–77), was dominated by Isabella and Mortimer until he seized power in a coup in 1330, putting Mortimer to death and forcing his mother into retirement. He supported Edward de BALIOL against the young Scottish king DAVID II, but despite his victory at Halidon Hill in 1333, the Scottish question remained unsettled. In 1337 the HUNDRED YEARS WAR began; it would dominate Edward's reign. He and his son EDWARD THE BLACK PRINCE took an active part in the war, the first phase of which ended with the treaty of London in 1359. The war was renewed after various treaties and truces, but, like the Scottish wars, was inconclusive in Edward's reign. There were many constitutional developments in Edward's long reign. The most important of these was the emergence of Commons as a distinct and powerful group in PARLIAMENT. The king's constant need for money for his wars enabled Commons to assert its power to consent to all lay taxation. The Black Death (see PLAGUE) decimated the population, producing a labor shortage that enabled the lower classes to demand higher wages and social advancement. Edward quarreled with the church, and the resulting religious unrest found a spokesman in John WYCLIF. There was rivalry between a court party headed by Edward's son JOHN OF GAUNT and the parliamentary party, headed by the Black Prince. Edward was succeeded by RICHARD II. **Edward IV,** 1442–83, son of Richard, duke of York, became king (1461–70, 1471–83) as leader of the York party (see ROSES, WARS OF THE) after his defeat of the Lancastrians and capture of HENRY VI. Edward's marriage to Elizabeth WOODVILLE (1464) and his favoritism to her family angered his cousin Richard Neville, earl of Warwick, who rebelled and fled to France, where he formed an alliance with MARGARET OF ANJOU, wife of the deposed Henry VI. They returned to England with troops and placed Henry on the throne. Their defeat by Edward (1471) led to Henry's death in the Tower (1471) and a peaceful end to Edward's reign. His son, **Edward V,** 1470–83?, was king in 1483. He was a pawn in the conflicting ambitions of his uncles, Earl Rivers and the duke of Gloucester. Gloucester had Rivers arrested, confined the king and his young brother in the Tower, had them declared illegitimate, and took the throne as RICHARD III. The boys disappeared and were presumed to have been murdered. One of the oldest and most prevalent theories—that they were smothered in their sleep by order of Richard III—is now considered anti-York propaganda of the TUDORS. **Edward VI,** 1537–53 (r.1547–53), succeeded his father HENRY VIII as king at the age of nine. He ruled under a council of regency controlled by his uncle and protector, Edward Seymour, duke of SOMERSET. During his reign Tudor absolutism was relaxed by a liberalization of the treason and heresy laws, and the government moved slowly toward Protestantism. Somerset's sympathy to the peasants led to his overthrow as regent by John Dudley, duke of Northumberland. Dudley gained ascendancy over the young king, now dying of tuberculosis, and persuaded him to settle the crown on Dudley's own daughter-in-law, Lady Jane GREY. The ensuing struggle ended with the victory of MARY I. **Edward VII,** 1841–1910, king of Great Britain and Ireland (r.1901–10), was the eldest son of Queen VICTORIA. Prince of Wales for 60 years, he was a leader of fashionable society. As king, he cooperated reluctantly in Herbert Asquith's attempt to limit the veto power of the House of Lords. He improved international understanding by traveling on the continent and by promoting an alliance with France. He and his wife, ALEXANDRA, were the parents of GEORGE V, whose eldest son, **Edward VIII** (1894–1972) was king in 1936. He was extremely popular until his announced intention of marrying Wallis Warfield Simpson (see WINDSOR, WALLIS WARFIELD, DUCHESS OF), an American suing her second husband for divorce, precipitated a crisis with the cabinet, then headed by Stanley BALDWIN. Edward insisted that he had the right to marry the woman of his choice, though her marital background made her unacceptable. The government saw in his challenge a threat to constitutional procedure and forced his abdication in 1936. As duke of Windsor, he married Wallis Warfield in 1937. He was governor of the Bahamas (1940–45).

Edwards, Jonathan, 1703–58, American theologian and metaphysician; b. Windsor, Conn. In 1729 he took sole charge of a congregation in Northampton, Mass., where he soon gained a wide following by his forceful preaching and powerful logic in support of Calvinist doctrine. A revival that he held (1734–35) effectively brought the GREAT AWAKENING to New England. His stern demands for strict orthodoxy and his inflexibility in a membership controversy resulted in his dismissal (1750) from Northampton. At Stockbridge, Mass., he completed his masterpiece, *The Freedom of the Will* (1754), which set forth metaphysical and ethical arguments for determinism. He is often regarded as the last great New England Calvinist, and his sermon *Sinners in the Hands of an Angry God* is still read today. Called (1757) to be president of the College of New Jersey (now Princeton Univ.), he died soon after.

Edward the Black Prince, 1330–76, eldest son of EDWARD III of England. He was created duke of Cornwall in 1337, the first duke ever to be created in England, and prince of Wales in 1343. Joining his father in the battles of the HUNDRED YEARS WAR, he fought at Crécy and Calais and in 1356 won the battle of Poitiers and captured JOHN II of France. It was apparently the French who first called him the Black Prince, perhaps because he wore black armor. Edward III made his French holdings a principality, and the Black Prince maintained a brilliant court at Bordeaux after 1363. He aided Peter I of Castile and León, but the taxes he was forced to levy in Aquitaine resulted in war with CHARLES V of France. Bad health forced him to resign his principalities in 1372. He opposed his brother JOHN OF GAUNT, who had become the virtual ruler of England with the aging of Edward III. The Black Prince died before his father, but his son succeeded to the throne as RICHARD II.

Edward the Confessor, d. 1066, king of the English (1042–66), son of ÆTHELRED the Unready. He grew up in France and returned to succeed Harthacanute. He was an able but not very energetic ruler, and his strife with the powerful noble Earl Godwin was heightened by his support of the Normans in England. Godwin and his family were exiled (1051) but soon returned. During their absence, Edward received William, duke of Normandy (later WILLIAM I), and apparently made him his heir. Since both William and Harold III of Norway had claims to the English throne, Edward eventually recognized Godwin's warlike son HAROLD as his heir to avoid bloodshed. Edward's piety was responsible for his name the Confessor. He was canonized in the 12th cent. Feast: Oct. 13.

Edward the Elder, d. 924, king of WESSEX (899–924). The son and successor of ALFRED, he fought with his father against the Danes and was apparently joint king with him. He gradually became ruler of all England S of the Humber.

EEG: see ELECTROENCEPHALOGRAPHY.

eel, any of a large order (Anguilliformes) of FISH with a long, snakelike body, elongate dorsal and anal fins, no pelvic fins, and scales either lacking or embedded in the skin. The male American eel reaches 2 ft (61 cm) in length; the female, 4 ft (122 cm). Most, including the morays and conger eels, are marine; one family, Anguillidae, is freshwater. All eels spawn in the sea, the eggs hatching into transparent, ribbonlike larvae that drift about feeding until they metamorphose into small eels, or elvers; freshwater species typically undertake long migrations to spawn in the sea. Freshwater eels are an important food item in some parts of the world.

eel, electric: see ELECTRIC FISH.

Égalité, Philippe: see under ORLÉANS, family.

Egbert, d. 839, king of WESSEX (802–39). He secured the submission of KENT, EAST ANGLIA, MERCIA, and NORTHUMBRIA. Historians later called him the first king of England, but there was no conception of a kingdom of England in his day.

egg: see OVUM.

eggplant, garden vegetable (*Solanum melongena*) of the NIGHTSHADE family. Native to SE Asia, it is a perennial shrub, although it is often grown in warm climates as an annual herb. It is cultivated for its ovoid fruit, which varies in size and may be purple, white, or striped.

Eglevsky, André [ĕg'lĕvskē], 1917–77, Russian-American dancer; b. Moscow. He trained in France and made his debut (1931) in London. He danced (1939–42) with the Ballet Russe de Monte Carlo and was (1951–58) premier danseur with the NEW YORK CITY BALLET. After he retired, he formed (1958) the Eglevsky Ballet in Long Island, New York.

Egmont, Lamoral, count of, 1522–68, Flemish general and statesman. Although a Catholic, he opposed the persecution of Protestants in the Low Countries. His beheading by order of the duke of ALBA caused a revolt against Spanish rule. He is the hero of GOETHE's tragedy *Egmont,* with music by BEETHOVEN.

ego: see PSYCHOANALYSIS.

egret, name for several HERON species. Egrets were nearly exterminated by hunters seeking their white, silky plumage (which develops during the mating season) for millinery. The American egret has straight plumes, c.21 in. (52.5 cm) long, on its back. The snowy egret, or snowy heron (*Leucophoyx thula*), the most beautiful and most hunted, has curved plumes on the head, breast, and back.

Egypt, Arab. *Misr,* biblical *Mizraim,* officially Arab Republic of Egypt, republic (1992 est. pop. 56,369,000), 386,659 sq mi (1,001,449 sq km), NE Africa, bordered by the Mediterranean Sea (N), Israel and the Red Sea (E), Sudan (S), and Libya (W); the Sinai peninsula, the only part of Egypt located in Asia, is separated from the rest of the country by the SUEZ CANAL. Major cities include CAIRO (the capital) and ALEXANDRIA. The principal physiographic feature is the NILE R., which flows the length of the country from south to north and separates the Libyan (Western) and Arabian (Eastern) deserts that comprise 90% of the land area. Bordering the Nile between Aswan and Cairo are narrow strips of cultivated land, home of the vast majority of Egypt's inhabitants. Although the country's industrial base has been increased considerably in the 20th cent., the economy has been severely strained by the ARAB-ISRAELI WARS and Egypt's limited farmland. Agriculture, which employs about a third of its population, depends on the Nile for its fertility. Completion of the ASWAN HIGH DAM in 1970 greatly increased arable land, which still constitutes only 5% of Egypt's total land area. Cotton is the leading cash crop. Major manufactures include refined oil, chemicals, textiles, and processed foods. The Suez Canal and tourism are sources of foreign exchange. Egypt's population is growing very rapidly, increasing by nearly a million every seven months. Its inhabitants are mainly a complex racial mixture, descended from the ancient Egyptians, Berbers, sub-Saharan Africans, Arabs, Greeks, and Turks. The majority are SUNNI Muslims, but there is a substantial minority of Coptic Christians (see COPT). Arabic is the official language.

Ancient Egypt. Egyptian civilization, one of the world's oldest, developed in the valley of the Nile over 5,000 years ago. The rival kingdoms of Upper and Lower Egypt were united as a centralized state c.3200 B.C. by a king named Menes, who established his capital at MEMPHIS. A high culture developed early, and the use of writing was introduced. During the Old Kingdom (3110–2258 B.C.) Egyptian culture and commerce flourished, and the great pyramids were built. Its fall introduced a period of anarchy, which ended c.2000 B.C. with the establishment of the Middle Kingdom, with its capital at THEBES. Civilization again flourished until in 1786 B.C. weak rulers allowed the country to pass under the rule of foreign nomads, known as the HYKSOS. The Hyksos were expelled c.1570 B.C., and the New Kingdom was established. During the XVIII dynasty (1570–c.1342 B.C.) ancient Egyptian civilization reached its zenith; a vast empire was established and THEBES and MEMPHIS became the political, commercial, and cultural centers of the world. After the XX dynasty (1200–1085 B.C.) Egypt came increasingly under foreign domination, with periods of rule by Libya, Sudan, Assyria, Nubia, and Persia. Following a brief reestablishment of native power in 405 B.C., Egypt fell without a struggle to ALEXANDER THE GREAT in 332 B.C. After Alexander's death (323 B.C.) Egypt was inherited by his general, PTOLEMY, who founded the dynasty of Ptolemies and under whom the new city of ALEXANDRIA became the intellectual and religious center of the Hellenistic world. The Ptolemies maintained a formidable empire for more than two centuries until, weakened by internal dynastic disputes, Egypt fell to Rome in 30 B.C. Christianity was readily accepted in Egypt, which became part of the Byzantine Empire about A.D. 395. With the Arab conquest (639–42) Egypt became an integral part of the Muslim world.

Modern Egypt. After 500 years as part of the CALIPHATE, Egypt was seized by the MAMLUKS in 1250 and the Ottoman Turks in 1517. The first close contact with the West occurred in 1798, when French forces under NAPOLEON occupied the country; they were expelled in 1801 by combined Ottoman and British troops. In 1805 MUHAMMAD ALI, a common soldier, was appointed pasha of Egypt; under his rule the foundations of the modern state of Egypt were established. The construction of the SUEZ CANAL (1859–69) put Egypt deeply into debt, and, although nominally still part of the OTTOMAN EMPIRE, the country was forced to appoint a French-British commission to manage its financial affairs. The British consolidated their control between 1883 and 1907, and during WORLD WAR I, when Turkey joined the Central Powers, Great Britain declared Egypt a British protectorate, which lasted until 1937.

Independent Egypt. Egypt bitterly opposed the UN partition of Palestine in 1948 and played an important role in the ARAB-ISRAELI WARS that followed. In 1952 the Egyptian army deposed King FAROUK in a coup d'état; a republic was established in 1953, and Col. Gamal Abdel NASSER became president (1954). For a brief period Egypt and Syria merged (1958) in the United Arab Republic, then were joined by Yemen in the United Arab States; the union was dissolved in 1961. Inaugurating a program of economic and social reform, modernization of the army, and construction of the Aswan High Dam, Nasser, with the aid of the USSR, strove to make Egypt the undisputed leader of the Arab world. His rallying-cry was denunciation of Israel; in 1967 Egypt lost much territory in the Six-Day War, which also shattered its economy and armed forces. Nasser died in 1970 and was succeeded by Anwar al-SADAT, who regained some of Egypt's lost territory in the Yom Kippur War (1973) and reversed a 20-year trend by ending Soviet influence and seeking closer ties with the West. In 1977 Sadat angered his Arab allies by traveling to Jerusalem as a conciliatory gesture to Israel; the two nations signed a peace treaty in 1979 (see CAMP DAVID

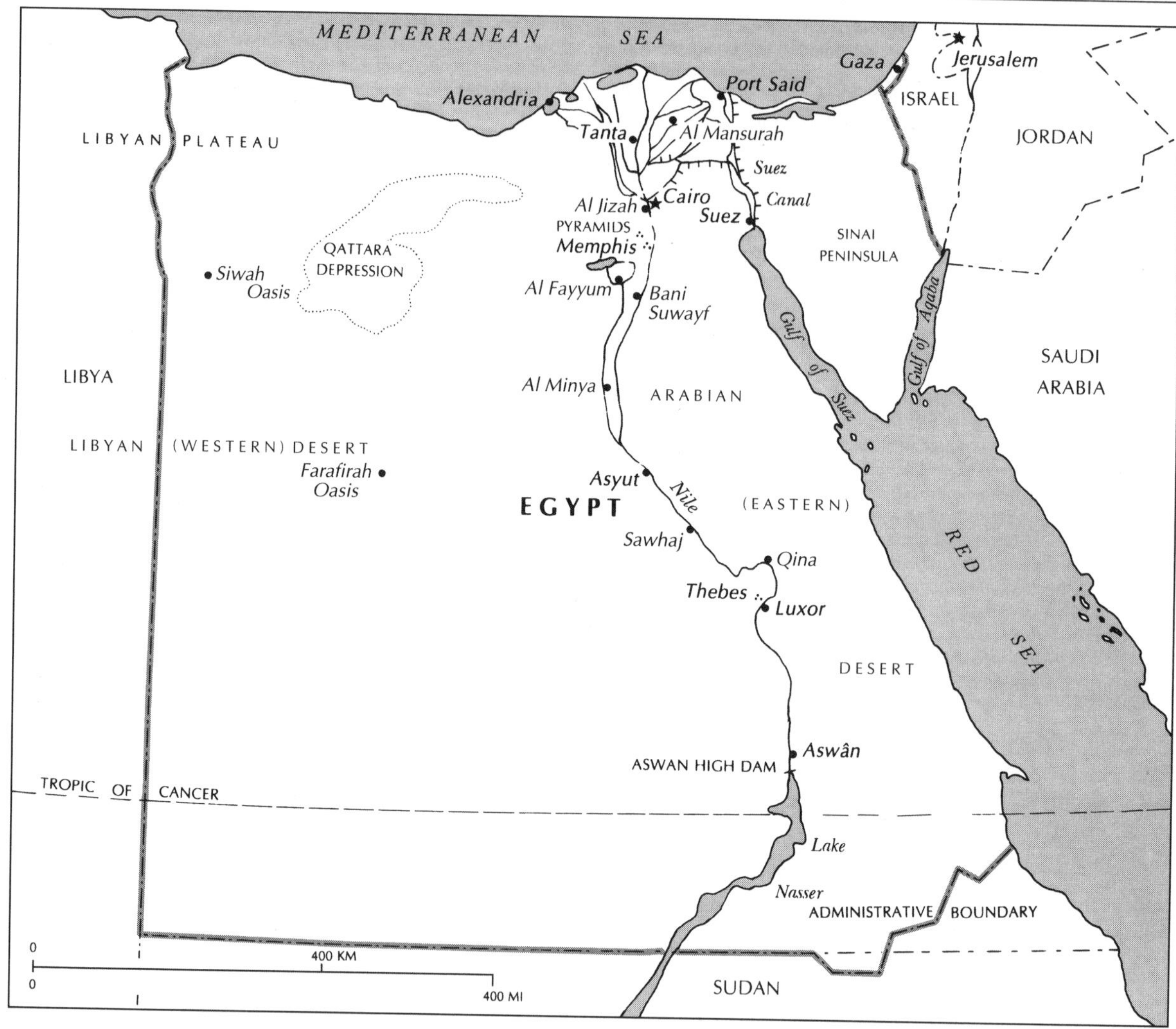

ACCORDS). In 1981 Sadat was assassinated by Muslim fundamentalists, and Hosni MUBARAK, who pledged to continue Sadat's policies, became president. The Israeli withdrawal from the Sinai and its return to Egypt, which began in 1979, was completed in 1982. In the late 1980s and early 90s Muslim fundamentalists increasingly opposed the government. Egypt's greatest problem, however, is its growing population, which is crowded into a limited area and strains the economy.

Egyptian architecture was formulated prior to 3000 B.C. Abundant clay and scarce wood led to the early development of ceramic arts and brickwork. A massive, static, serene architecture emerged. Walls were immensely thick; columns were confined to halls and inner courts. Exterior walls had few openings and were covered with HIEROGLYPHICS and pictorial carvings in brilliant colors, with symbolic motifs like the scarab beetle. The capacity of sculptors to integrate decoration into structure was highly developed. Flat stone block roofs were supported by walls or by closely spaced internal columns. No dwellings, only tombs and temples, survive. Belief in the afterlife led to massive, impressive sepulchral architecture. Of the Old Kingdom (3110–2258 B.C.) remains the MASTABA is the oldest remaining form of sepulcher. The PYRAMID of a ruler was begun as soon as he ascended the throne. Middle Kingdom (2000–1786 B.C.) tombs were tunneled out of Nile cliffs. In temples of the New Kingdom (1570–1085 B.C.), the doorway was flanked by great pylons or towers, often with statues or obelisks in front. The temple was screened from the common people by a high wall. The hall had immense columns arranged in a nave and side aisles; behind were small, restricted sanctuaries. New Kingdom temples were also carved from rock, e.g., ABU SIMBEL. Egyptian architecture consistently resisted foreign influences.

Egyptian art. The art of predynastic EGYPT (c.4000–3200 B.C.), known from funerary offerings, was largely painted pottery and figurines, ivory carvings, slate cosmetic palettes, and flint weapons. Toward the end of the predynastic period, sculptors carved monolithic figures of the gods from limestone, e.g., the Min at Coptos. In the protodynastic and early dynastic periods (3200–2780 B.C.), Mesopotamian motifs appeared. The stone bowls and vases of these periods are remarkable for fine craftsmanship. During the height of the Old Kingdom, centered at Memphis (2680–2258 B.C.), the stylistic conventions that characterize Egyptian art were developed, notably the law of frontality, in which the human figure is represented with the eye and shoulders in front view, and the head, pelvis, legs, and feet in profile. There was little attempt at linear perspective or spatial illusionism. Relief was shallow, e.g., the palette of Namer (Cairo), a masterpiece of the I dynasty showing battle scenes. In sculpture the law of frontality was also strictly followed. Working with the most durable materials they had, artists decorated tombs with domestic, military, hunting, and ceremonial scenes to enable the dead to attain a happy continuation of their previous lives. Chief examples of Old Kingdom sculpture are the *Great Chephren,* in diorite; the *Prince Ra-hetep and Princess Neferet,* in painted limestone; and the *Sheik-el-Beled,* in painted wood (all: Cairo). Painting was generally employed as an accessory to sculpture. In the Middle Kingdom, based at Thebes (2000–1786 B.C.), the forms of the Old Kingdom were retained, but the unity of style was broken to admit a new formalism and delicacy. The tomb paintings at Bani Hasan are remarkable for freedom of draftsmanship. The sculptured portraits of Sesostris III and Amenemhet III (both: Cairo) are exceptional in their revelation of inner feelings. New Kingdom art (1570–1085 B.C.) was the final development of classic Egyptian style, with monumental forms, bold design, and a controlled vitality. During the Amarna period (1372–1350 B.C.) a naturalistic style developed in sculpture, e.g., the colossal statue of IKHNATON (Cairo) and the magnificent painted limestone bust of Queen NEFERTITI (Berlin Mus.). The rich sophistication of the period is exemplified by the furnishings from the tomb of TUTANKHAMEN. The Ramesside period (1314–1085 B.C.) saw an unsuccessful attempt to return to New Kingdom styles, but the vitality of that period was lost. The following period of decline (1085–730 B.C.) is characterized by mechanical repetition of earlier forms and by satirical drawings in the papyri. In the Saite period (730–663 B.C.) a coarse, brutal style predominated. After the Assyrian conquest of Egypt (663 B.C.), all the arts but metalworking declined. Egypt proved resistant to foreign influence in art through the Ptolemaic dynasty (332–30 B.C.). Architecture remained vital, e.g., at Idfu and Philae, and the minor arts continued to flourish. Fine collections of Egyptian art in the U.S. are at the Brooklyn and Metropolitan museums in New York City.

Sphinx and pyramid at Al Jizah, Egypt

Egyptian language, extinct language of ancient Egypt that is generally classified as a member of the Hamitic subfamily of the Hamito-Semitic family of languages. See AFRICAN LANGUAGES (table).

Egyptian religion. Ancient Egyptian worship is remarkable for its reconciliation and union of conflicting beliefs. The earliest predynastic tribes venerated many deities who were at first embodied in animals (such as the sacred cat of Bubastis), but who were later gradually humanized. The most widely accepted creation myth was that of the great sun god RA (Re), who appeared out of Chaos to create a race including OSIRIS and ISIS, and their son HORUS. When a national religion arose at the end of the predynastic period (c.3200 B.C.) various priesthoods attempted to systematize the gods and myths. The reign of IKHNATON established a monotheistic cult, but POLYTHEISM was restored after his death. The most important of the many forms of Egyptian worship were the cults of Osiris, king and judge of the dead, protector of all; the sun god Ra (symbolized by the PYRAMID), said to be the direct ancestor of the kings of Egypt; and AMON, Egypt's greatest god by the XIX dynasty. With no established book of teachings such as the Bible or Koran, Egyptian conduct was guided by human wisdom and the belief in *maat*, the principle of divine justice and order, held to be reflected in civil order as administered by the state under the pharaoh. While the priesthoods and state cult grew, the populace found its expression of religious feeling in the strict rites prescribed by funerary cults (see BOOK OF THE DEAD).

Ehrenburg or **Erenburg, Ilya Grigoryevich,** [ā'rənbŏŏrk], 1891–1967, Russian writer. From 1909 to 1917 and 1921 to 1941 he lived in W Europe, where he wrote such novels as *The Love of Jeanne Ney* (1924) and *Out of Chaos* (1933). Returning to the Soviet Union in 1941, he became a war correspondent. His best-known novel, *The Fall of Paris* (1941–42), deals with the decay of French society, while *The Thaw* (1954) was the first work to discuss Stalinist repression.

Ehrlich, Paul, 1854–1915, German bacteriologist. For his work in immunology he shared with Élie Metchnikoff the 1908 Nobel Prize in physiology or medicine. He discovered salvarsan for the treatment of syphilis and made valuable contributions in hematology, cellular pathology, cancer study, and the use of dyes in microscopy and treatment of disease.

Eichmann, Adolf [īkh'män], 1906–62, German NAZI official. As head of the Gestapo's Jewish section, he oversaw the maltreatment, deportation to concentration camps, and murder (especially by the use of gas chambers) of millions of JEWS. After World War II, he escaped to Argentina, but he was located and abducted by Israeli agents in 1960. He was tried and hanged in Israel for crimes against the Jews.

Eiffel Tower, structure designed by the French engineer Alexandre Gustave Eiffel (1832–1923) for the Paris Exposition of 1889. The tower is 984 ft (300 m) high and consists of an open iron framework on four masonry piers; these piers support four columns that unite to form the shaft.

Eight, the, group of American artists in New York City, formed in 1908 to exhibit paintings. It comprised Arthur B. DAVIES, Maurice PRENDERGAST, Ernest Lawson, William GLACKENS, Everett SHINN, Robert HENRI, John SLOAN, and George LUKS. Men of widely different tendencies, they were bound by common opposition to academism and, because of their portrayal of everyday American life, were stigmatized as the "ashcan" school. They organized the ARMORY SHOW of 1913, which introduced modern European art to a reluctant but curious America.

Eijkman, Christiaan, 1858–1930, Dutch physician. For his work on the cause of BERIBERI, which led to the isolation of antineuritic vitamins, he shared with Sir Frederick Hopkins the 1929 Nobel Prize in physiology or medicine.

Eilat: see ELAT.

Eilshemius, Louis Michel [īlshē'mēəs], 1864–1941, American painter; b. near Newark, N.J. He is known for his imaginative, atmospheric American landscapes. *Approaching Storm* (Phillips Coll., Wash., D.C.) is an excellent example.

Einstein, Albert, 1879–1955, American theoretical physicist; b. Germany; recognized as one of the greatest physicists of all time. He became (1914) titular professor of physics and director of theoretical physics at the Kaiser Wilhelm Institute in Berlin. The Nazi government confiscated (1934) his property and revoked his German citizenship because he was Jewish, and in 1940 Einstein became an American citizen, holding a post at the Institute for Advanced Study in Princeton from 1933 until his death. Although an ardent pacifist, he urged Pres. F.D. ROOSEVELT to investigate the possible use of atomic energy in bombs. In one of three important 1905 papers, he explained BROWNIAN MOVEMENT on the basis of his study of the motion of atoms. His special theory of RELATIVITY (1905) dealt with systems or observers in uniform (unaccelerated) motion with respect to one another. He asserted (1911) the equality of GRAVITATION and INERTIA and formulated (c.1916) a general theory of relativity that included gravitation as a determiner of the curvature of a SPACE-TIME continuum. Einstein contributed to the development of QUANTUM MECHANICS, postulating (1905) light quanta (PHOTONS), on which he based his explanation of the PHOTOELECTRIC EFFECT, and developing the quantum theory of SPECIFIC HEAT. Working on a unified field theory, he attempted to explain gravitation and electromagnetism with one set of laws. For his work in theoretical physics, notably on the photoelectric effect, he received the 1921 Nobel Prize in physics.

einsteinium (Es), radioactive element, discovered in 1952 by A. Ghiorso and colleagues in residue from a thermonuclear explosion; a member of the ACTINIDE SERIES. Weighable amounts have since been prepared by neutron bombardment of plutonium. See ELEMENT (table); PERIODIC TABLE.

Einthoven, Willem, 1860–1927, Dutch physiologist; b. Java. He received the 1924 Nobel Prize in physiology or medicine for his invention of a string galvanometer that he used to produce the electrocardiogram (EKG), a graphic record of the action of the heart (see ELECTROCARDIOGRAPHY).

Eisenhower, Dwight David, 1890–1969, American general and 34th president of the U.S. (1953–61); b. Denison, Tex.; his nickname was "Ike." A West Point graduate, he had a meteoric rise as a military commander during WORLD WAR II. In 1942 he became chief of army operations in Washington, D.C. Later that year he was named U.S. commander of the European theater of operations, and in 1943 he became supreme commander of the Allied Expeditionary Force. Eisenhower coordinated and directed the Allied invasion of Europe in June 1944. In Dec. 1944 he was made general of the army (five-star general) and upon his return to the U.S. became army chief of staff (1945–48). He was president of Columbia Univ. from 1948 to 1950 and in 1950 was named supreme commander of the Allied forces in Europe. After organizing the defense forces of the North Atlantic Treaty Organization (NATO), Eisenhower resigned (1952) from the army to campaign for the Republican presidential nomination. Popularity as a World War II hero brought him an easy election victory over his Democratic opponent, Adlai E. STEVENSON. One of Eisenhower's first moves as president (July 1953) was to fulfill a campaign promise to end the KOREAN WAR. He and his secretary of state, John Foster DULLES, continued the TRUMAN administration's policy of containing Communism, but attempts were also made to ease cold-war tensions. In domestic affairs, Eisenhower remained aloof from the legislative process and took few initiatives. Despite a heart attack (1955) he easily won reelection in 1956. His administration then took a more active role in the growing CIVIL-RIGHTS movement. In 1957 he sent federal troops to Little Rock, Ark., to enforce a court-ordered school desegregation decision, and later Congress enacted federal civil-rights legislation. Also in 1957, the president promulgated the so-called Eisenhower doctrine, which committed the U.S. to an active role in the Middle East to protect the region from Communist aggression. Tensions with the Soviet Union increased, however, and a summit meeting (1960) with Nikita KHRUSHCHEV ended abruptly because of conflict over U.S. espionage flights over the USSR. In 1959 the coming to power of the Communist Fidel CASTRO in Cuba posed other problems, and Eisenhower broke diplomatic relations with Cuba just before leaving office in Jan. 1961.

Eisenstein, Sergei Mikhailovich, 1898–1948, Russian film director. Ranked with D.W. GRIFFITH as a cinematic genius, he pioneered the use of MONTAGE in such works as *Potemkin* (1925), *October* (1928), and *Alexander Nevsky* (1938).

eisteddfod [āstĕth′vŏd], Welsh festival involving contests in ARTS AND CRAFTS with special emphasis on music and poetry. The National Eisteddfod is held for a week in August; local festivals are held throughout the year. It dates from the 12th cent.

Ekaterinburg: see YEKATERINBURG.

Ekelöf, Gunnar, 1907–68, Swedish poet, the most important Swedish poet of the 20th cent. His verse, philosophic and mystical, reflects his interest in the French SYMBOLISTS and Asian literature. Volumes in English translation include *Selected Poems* (tr. 1971) and *A Mölna Elegy* (tr. 1979).

EKG: see ELECTROCARDIOLOGY.

Elam, ancient Asian country, N of the Persian Gulf, now in W Iran. A civilization began there in the late 4th millennium B.C., and in the early 2d millennium B.C. Elam overthrew Babylonia. Its golden age came after 1300 B.C. Around 645 B.C. Elam fell to the Assyrian king ASSURBANIPAL. Its capital was Susa.

eland: see ANTELOPE.

elastic limit: see STRENGTH OF MATERIALS.

Elat or **Eilat,** city (1989 est. pop. 26,000), S Israel, a port on the Gulf of AQABA. It is strategically located near Egypt, Jordan, and Saudi Arabia and is Israel's gateway to Africa and E Asia. The city is a center for tourism and light industry. An ancient port (perhaps identical with the 10th-cent. Ezion-geber), Elat was resettled in 1949, and its deepwater harbor was opened in 1965.

Elba, island, 86 sq mi (223 sq km), in the Tyrrhenian Sea, 6 mi (9.7 km) W of the Italian peninsula. Controlled at times by Pisa, Spain, and Naples, it was an independent principality (1814–15) under the exiled NAPOLEON I prior to his escape and return to France. Following his final defeat, Elba passed to TUSCANY.

Elbe, river, central Europe, flowing c.725 mi (1,170 km) from the N Czech Republic through E Germany before entering the North Sea through a 60-mi (97-km), two-armed estuary at Cuxhaven. Navigable for c.525 mi (845 km), the river was internationalized in 1919. Traffic declined after Germany repudiated (1938) internationalization. The division of Germany (1945–90) made the river part of the boundary between East and West Germany.

Elbrus, Mount, highest mountain of the CAUCASUS, N Georgia, considered the highest point in Europe by those who consider the area part of that continent. Its twin peaks are extinct volcanic cones 18,481 ft (5,633 m) and 18,356 ft (5,595 m) high.

El Cordobés [ĕl kōrdōvās′], 1936?–, Spanish bullfighter; b. Manuel Benítez Pérez. The highest paid matador in history, he rose to national fame in the early 1960s because of his courage and personal magnetism. He retired in 1971.

elder: see HONEYSUCKLE.

El Dorado, legendary land of the Golden Man, a place of gold and plenty sought by Spanish CONQUISTADORS in the New World from the mid-16th cent. Its location shifted as new regions were explored. Similar legends appeared in the W United States.

Eleanor of Aquitaine [ăkwĭtān′], 1122–1204, queen consort first of LOUIS VII of France and then of HENRY II of England; daughter of William X, duke of Aquitaine. Her marriage to Louis was annulled in 1152 and shortly thereafter she married Henry, then duke of Normandy, uniting her vast possessions with his. Two of her sons—RICHARD I and JOHN—became kings of England. Henry's many infidelities caused her to establish her own court (1170) at Poitiers, which became the scene of much artistic activity. She supported her sons in their unsuccessful revolt (1173) against Henry and was confined by Henry until 1185. In 1189 she helped Richard secure the throne.

electoral college, in U.S. government, the body of electors that chooses the president and vice president. During national elections, voters in each state choose between slates of electors publicly pledged to one or another of the teams of national candidates. When the electoral college meets, each state's electors (equal in number to the total of its U.S. representatives and senators) usually cast all of their ballots for the team to which they are pledged. A majority of the electoral college is required to elect. If no candidate obtains a majority, the Constitution provides that the House of Representatives will select the president from among the top three candidates. Only two presidents have been elected in the House, Thomas JEFFERSON (1800) and John Quincy ADAMS (1824). The system is often criticized for leaving open the possibility that a candidate may obtain an electoral college majority without getting a majority (or even a plurality) of the national vote. Thus, in 1888, Benjamin HARRISON was elected even though Grover CLEVELAND received a greater popular vote.

electors, in the history of the HOLY ROMAN EMPIRE, the German princes who had the right to elect the German king, who was generally crowned emperor. The number of electors varied, but in 1356 Emperor CHARLES IV issued the Golden Bull, an edict that regularized election procedures and named the electors as the archbishops of Cologne, Mainz, and Trier, the king of Bohemia, the count palatine of the Rhine, the duke of Saxony, and the margrave of Brandenburg. Later, the duke of Bavaria and the ruler of Hanover were added. After 1438 only members of the house of HAPSBURG were elected. The electoral function disappeared with the end of the Holy Roman Empire in 1806.

Electra, in Greek mythology, daughter of AGAMEMNON and CLYTEMNESTRA. She aided her brother ORESTES in avenging the murder of their father by their mother and AEGISTHUS. The tale was dramatized by AESCHYLUS, SOPHOCLES, and EURIPIDES.

electric and magnetic units, units used to express the magnitudes of various quantities in electricity and magnetism. Three systems of such units, all based on the METRIC SYSTEM, are commonly used. One of these, the mksa-practical system, is defined in terms of the units of the mks system and has the AMPERE of electric current as its basic unit. The units of this system—the VOLT, OHM, WATT, and farad—are those commonly used by scientists and engineers to make practical measurements. The two other systems, now being gradually abandoned, are both based on the cgs system. Electrostatic units (cgs-esu) are defined in a way that simplifies the description of interactions between static electric charges; there are no corresponding magnetic units in this system. Electromagnetic units (cgs-emu), on the other hand, are defined especially for the description of phenomena associated with moving electric charges, i.e., electric currents and magnetic poles.

electric arc process, method of producing STEEL from scrap metal. Electric current arcing through the scrap metal produces intense heat which quickly melts the metal and initiates the reactions that produce steel. Because little oxygen is involved, the electric arc process is ideal for producing high-grade steels that require alloying elements that would oxidize quickly in the OPEN-HEARTH PROCESS and BASIC OXYGEN PROCESS and be lost in the slag.

electric circuit, unbroken path along which an electric current may flow. A simple circuit consists of a voltage source, such as a battery (see CELL, in electricity) or a GENERATOR, whose terminals are connected to those of a circuit element, such as a RESISTOR, through which current can flow. More complex circuits include additional sources or elements and perhaps switches, so interconnected that, when appropriate switches are closed, each element is included in a closed path that also contains a source. Series, parallel, and non-series-parallel connections are illustrated in the figure. The effective RESISTANCE of two series-connected resistors is the sum of the individual resistances. The effective conductance (reciprocal of resistance) of two parallel-connected resistors is the sum of the individual conductances.

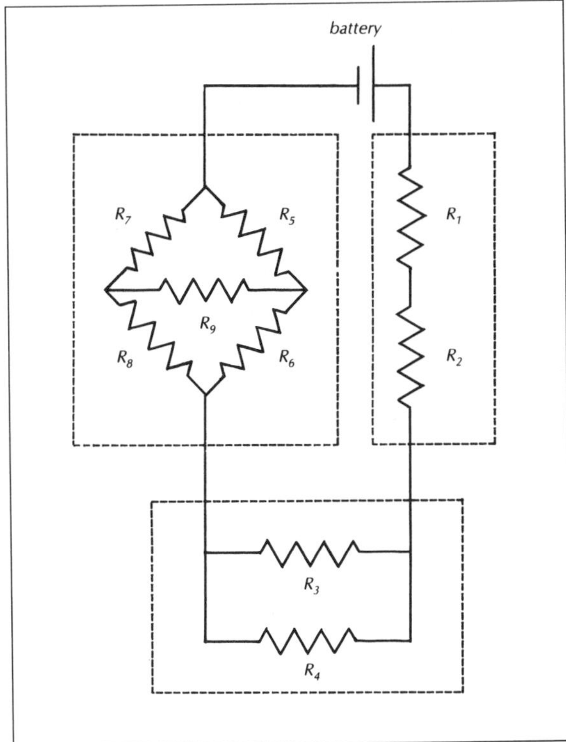

Electric Circuit: The resistances R_1 and R_2 are connected in series; the same current flows through both. The resistances R_3 and R_4 are connected in parallel; the same voltage appears across both. The resistances R_5, R_6, R_7, R_8, and R_9 are connected in a configuration that is neither series nor parallel. The three two-terminal subcircuits enclosed in broken lines are all connected in series with the battery.

electric eel: see ELECTRIC FISH.

electric fish, any of many unrelated species of FISH that have electric organs, usually made of modified muscle tissue, that are capable of producing from 450 to 600 volts of electricity. This electricity is used to detect and paralyze prey, repel enemies, navigate, and possibly communicate. Important electric fish include the electric EEL, the electric CATFISH, and the electric RAY, or torpedo.

electricity, class of phenomena arising from the existence of CHARGE. According to modern theory, most ELEMENTARY PARTICLES of matter possess charge, either positive or negative. Two particles of like charge, both positive or both negative, repel each other; two particles of unlike charge are attracted (see COULOMB'S LAW). The electric FORCE between two charged particles is much greater than the gravitational force between the particles. Many of the bulk properties of matter are ultimately due to the electric forces among the particles of which the substance is composed. Materials differ in their ability to allow charge to flow through them. Those that allow charge to pass easily are conductors (see CONDUCTION), whereas those that allow extremely little charge to pass through are called insulators (see INSULATION), or DIELECTRICS. A third class of materials, called SEMICONDUCTORS, is intermediate. Electrostatics is the study of charges, or charged bodies, at rest. When positive or negative charge builds up in fixed positions on objects, certain phenomena can be observed that are collectively referred to as static electricity. The charge can be built by rubbing certain objects together, such as silk and glass or rubber and fur; the friction between these objects causes ELECTRONS to transfer from one to another with the result that the object losing electrons acquires a positive charge and the object gaining electrons acquires a negative charge. Electrodynamics is the study of charges in motion. A flow of electric charge constitutes an electric current. In order for a current to exist in a conductor, there must be an ELECTROMOTIVE FORCE (emf), or POTENTIAL difference, between the conductor's ends. An electric CELL, a PHOTOVOLTAIC CELL, and a GENERATOR are all sources of emf. An emf source with an external conductor connected from one of the source's two terminals to the other constitutes an ELECTRIC CIRCUIT. Direct current (DC) is a flow of current in one direction at a constant rate. Alternating current (AC) is a current flow that increases in magnitude from zero to a maximum, decreases back to zero, increases to a maximum in the opposite direction, decreases to zero, and then repeats this process periodically. The number of repetitions of the cycle occurring each second is defined as the frequency, which is expressed in HERTZ (Hz). The frequency of ordinary household current in the U.S. is 60 cycles per sec (60 Hz), and electric devices must be designed to operate at this frequency. In a solid, the current consists not of a few electrons moving rapidly but of many electrons moving slowly; although this drift of electrons is slow, the impulse that causes it moves through the circuit, when the circuit is completed, at nearly the speed of light. The movement of electrons in a current is not steady; each electron moves in a series of stops and starts. In a direct current, the electrons are spread evenly through the conductor; in an alternating current, the electrons tend to congregate along the conductor surface. In liquids, gases, and semiconductors, current carriers may be positively or negatively charged.

electrocardiography, science of recording and interpreting the electrical activity of the HEART by means of a device called a cardiograph. Electrodes (leads) attached to the extremities and the left chest pick up electrical currents from heart muscle contractions. The currents are registered in wave patterns on a light-sensitive film recording known as an electrocardiogram, cardiogram, or simply EKG or ECG. Deviations in the normal height, form, or duration of the wave patterns indicate specific disorders; thus the EKG is an important aid in diagnosing many heart diseases. The first practical device for recording the activity of the heart was developed by W. EINTHOVEN in 1903, for which he won (1923) the Nobel Prize in physiology or medicine.

electrochemistry, science dealing with the relationship between electricity and chemical changes. Of principal interest are the reactions that take place between ELECTRODES and the ELECTROLYTES in electric and electrolytic cells (see ELECTROLYSIS) and that take place in an electrolyte as electricity passes through it.

electrode, terminal, usually in the form of a wire, rod, or plate, through which electric current passes between metallic and nonmetallic parts of an ELECTRIC CIRCUIT. The electrode through which current passes from the metallic to the nonmetallic conductor is called the anode; that through which current passes from the nonmetallic to the metallic conductor is called the cathode. An electrode may be made of a metal, e.g., copper, lead, platinum, silver, or zinc, or of a nonmetal, commonly carbon.

electroencephalography, science of recording and analyzing the electrical activity of the BRAIN. Electrodes placed on the scalp are connected to an electroencephalograph which amplifies the nerve impulses in the brain and prints an image in the form of characteristic wave patterns called brain waves. The recording, known as an electroencephalogram, or EEG, is an important aid in diagnosing brain disorders and malfunctions, and has contributed to understanding normal brain function, SLEEP, and the effects of DRUGS and of such activities as BIOFEEDBACK. EEGs are also used to determine brain death (see DEATH). The electrical activity of the brain was first demonstrated by the German psychiatrist Hans Berger in 1929.

electrolysis, passage of an electric current through a conducting solution or molten salt (either is a type of ELECTROLYTE) that is decomposed in the process. When a cathode, or negative electrode, and an anode, or positive electrode, are dipped into a solution, and a direct-current source is connected to the electrodes, the positive ions migrate to the negative electrode and the negative ions migrate to the positive electrode. At the negative electrode each positive ion gains an electron and becomes neutral; at the positive electrode each negative ion gives up an electron and becomes neutral. The migration of ions through the electrolyte constitutes the electric current flowing from one electrode to the other. Electrolysis is used in the commercial preparation of various substances, e.g., chlorine by the electrolysis of a solution of common salt, and hydrogen by the electrolysis of water. The electrolysis of metal salts is used for plating. See also ELECTROCHEMISTRY.

electrolyte, electrical conductor in which current is carried by IONS rather than free electrons (as in a metal). Electrolytes include water solutions of acids, bases (see ACIDS AND BASES), or SALTS; certain pure liquids; and molten salts. See also ELECTROLYSIS.

electromagnet, device in which an electric current, passing through a wire coil wrapped around a soft iron core, produces a magnetic field. The magnetic-field strength produced depends on the number of turns of the coil of wire, the size of the current, and the magnetic permeability of the core. Electromagnets made with superconducting coils (see SUPERCONDUCTIVITY) offer no resistance to an electric current and can produce a strong magnetic field. Electromagnets lose their magnetism when the current is discontinued.

electromagnetic radiation, energy radiated in the form of a WAVE caused by an electric field interacting with a magnetic field. Electromagnetic radiation is the result of the acceleration of a charged particle. It does not require a material medium and can travel through a vacuum. The theory of electromagnetic radiation was developed by James Clerk MAXWELL and published in 1865, although his ideas were not accepted until Heinrich HERTZ proved the existence of radio waves in 1887. In order of decreasing wavelength and increasing frequency, the various types of electromagnetic radiation are RADIO waves, MICROWAVES, INFRARED RADIATION, visible LIGHT, ULTRAVIOLET RADIATION, X RAYS, and GAMMA RADIATION. The possible sources of electromagnetic radiation are directly related to wavelength; long radio waves are produced by large antennas such as those used by broadcasting stations; much shorter visible light waves are produced by the motions of charges within atoms; the shortest waves, those of gamma radiation, result from changes within the nucleus of the atom. The individual quantum of electromagnetic radiation is known as the PHOTON.

electromagnetism, electromagnetic interaction, or **electromagnetic force,** a long-range force involving the electric and magnetic properties of ELEMENTARY PARTICLES. It is responsible for the repulsion of like and attraction of unlike electric charges and explains atomic structure and the properties of LIGHT and other forms of ELECTROMAGNETIC RADIATION. The electromagnetic interaction is mediated, or carried, by PHOTONS. Because its effects can be easily observed, electromagnetism is the most thoroughly studied and best understood of the four fundamental forces of nature (see also GRAVITATION; STRONG INTERACTION; WEAK INTERACTION). The same laws that govern electromagnetism on the subatomic scale also apply on a large scale in motors, generators, and electronic equipment. A moving electric charge gives rise to a magnetic field, and if its motion changes the magnetic field varies and in turn produces an electric field; this is the origin of electromagnetic radiation. **Electromagnetic fields** are generated by electric motors and household appliances and by power transmission lines. It has been suggested that such fields, particularly those around transmission lines, may cause or promote childhood cancer. A number of studies have been conducted, but the results are contradictory and a generally accepted link has not been established.

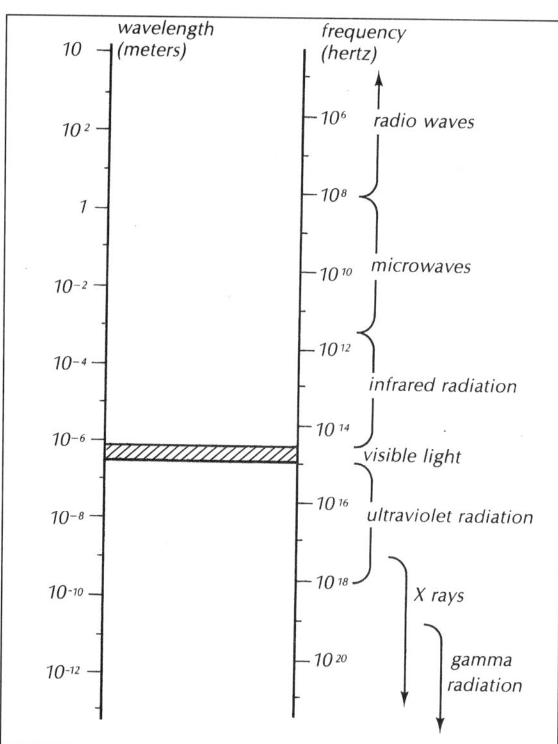

Types of electromagnetic radiation

electromotive force (emf), difference in electric POTENTIAL, or voltage, between the terminals of a source of electricity. It is usually measured in VOLTS.

electron, ELEMENTARY PARTICLE carrying a unit charge of negative electricity. An ATOM consists of a small, dense, positively charged nucleus surrounded by electrons that whirl about it in orbits, forming a cloud of charge. Ordinarily there are just enough negative electrons to balance the positive charge of the nucleus, and the atom is neutral. If electrons are added or removed, a net charge results, and the atom is said to be ionized (see ION). Atomic electrons are responsible for the chemical properties of matter (see VALENCE). The electron was discovered in 1897 by Joseph John THOMSON, who showed that cathode rays are composed of electrons. The electron is the lightest known particle having a non-zero rest mass. The positron, the electron's antiparticle (see ANTIMATTER), was discovered in 1932.

electronegativity, in chemistry, tendency for an atom to attract a pair of electrons that it shares with another atom. If the pair of electrons is not shared equally, i.e., if they spend more time with one atom than with the other atom, the favored atom is said to be more electronegative. Nonmetals have much higher electronegativities than metals; of the nonmetals, fluorine is the most electronegative, followed by oxygen, nitrogen, and chlorine.

electronic game, device or computer software that provides entertainment by challenging a person's eye-hand coordination or mental abilities. Made possible by the development of the MICROPROCESSOR, electronic games are marketed in various formats, such as hand-held one-player models, cartridges or COMPACT DISCS that are inserted in modules attached to television sets, computer software that is run on personal or network computers, and freestanding arcade versions. Most of their appeal comes from the COMPUTER

PROGRAM that synchronizes flashing lights and a variety of sounds with the action portrayed on a graphic display (see COMPUTER GRAPHICS). The games may be contested among several players, or an individual may engage in a test of skill against the computer. Game subjects include sports (e.g., baseball and football); action warfare, often space-oriented, and adventure; and such classics as contract bridge, chess, and poker.

electronic music, term applied to compositions whose sounds are either produced or modified electronically. The early examples of electronic compositions, called concrete music, were taped montages of electronically altered sound obtained by microphone from nonelectronic sources, such as voices and street noise. After the perfection of the tape recorder in the 1940s, music was composed with tones that were electronically produced as well as electronically manipulated. In 1955 the synthesizer was developed, a single unit with numerous generating and modifying capacities that enable composers to generate new sounds and to combine these sounds with great precision. Contemporary composers of electronic music include Karlheinz STOCKHAUSEN, Luciano BERIO, and Bruno Maderna. Since the 1950s, composers such as John CAGE, Milton BABBITT, and others have also experimented with COMPUTER music. Contemporary computer music may be produced using MIDI (Musical Instrument Digital Interface) or software synthesis. In MIDI a computer is used to control the output of synthesizers and signal-processing devices. In software synthesis a computer mathematically represents sounds, which are manipulated by various techniques, including filtering (which affects loudness), time delay (which affects reverberation), and frequency shifting (which affects pitch). Electronic techniques and instruments are widely employed in pop music and allow a solo artist to compose, produce, and perform music that employs a full complement of instrumental sounds.

electronics, a branch of electrical engineering; the science and technology based on and concerned with the controlled flow of electrons or other carriers of electric charge, especially in ELECTRON TUBES and SEMICONDUCTOR devices. The miniaturization (see MICROELECTRONICS) and savings in power brought about by the invention (1948) of the TRANSISTOR and the subsequent development of INTEGRATED CIRCUITS have allowed ELECTRIC CIRCUITS to be packaged more densely, making possible compact COMPUTERS, advanced RADAR and navigation systems, smaller, more reliable RADIO and TELEVISION receivers, advanced audio and video recording and reproduction systems, and CELLULAR TELEPHONES.

electron microscope, instrument that produces a highly magnified image of a small object, using an accelerated electron beam held within a vacuum to illuminate the object, and electromagnetic fields to magnify and focus the image. (By contrast, the optical MICROSCOPE uses visual light for illumination, and glass lenses for magnifying and focusing.) First developed in Gemany c.1932, the transmission electron microscope exploits the very short wavelengths of accelerated electrons, which are thousands of times shorter than those of light, to magnify an object up to one million times without losing definition. Images produced by the microscope are thrown onto a fluorescent screen or are photographed. The more recent scanning electron microscope constructs the image on a CATHODE-RAY TUBE as the surface of a specimen is gradually illuminated by a television scanning probe.

electron tube, device consisting of a sealed enclosure in which electrons flow between ELECTRODES separated either by vacuum (in a vacuum tube) or by an ionized gas at low pressure (in a gas tube). The two principal electrodes of an electron tube are called the anode and cathode. The simplest vacuum tube, the DIODE, contains only these two electrodes. When the cathode is heated, it emits a cloud of electrons, which are attracted to the positive polarity of the anode and constitute the current through the tube. Because the anode is not capable of emitting electrons, no current can flow in the reverse direction, and the diode acts as a RECTIFIER. In the vacuum triode, small signals applied to a third electrode, called a grid, placed between the cathode and anode, cause large fluctuations in the current between the cathode and anode. A triode can thus act as a signal AMPLIFIER. Although formerly the key elements of ELECTRIC CIRCUITS, electron tubes have been almost entirely displaced by SEMICONDUCTOR devices. See also CATHODE-RAY TUBE.

electron-volt (eV), unit of ENERGY used in atomic and nuclear physics; 1 eV is the energy transferred in moving a unit electric charge, positive or negative and equal in magnitude to the charge of the electron, through a potential difference of 1 volt. 1 eV = 1.60×10^{-19} joules = 1.60×10^{-12} ergs.

electroweak theory, a UNIFIED FIELD THEORY that describes two of the fundamental forces in nature, electromagnetism and the WEAK INTERACTION. The theory, for which Sheldon Glashow, Abdus Salam, and Steven Weinberg shared the 1979 Nobel Prize in physics, was confirmed in 1983 by the discovery of the W AND Z PARTICLES, two of a number of ELEMENTARY PARTICLES it predicted.

elegy, in Greek and Roman poetry, type of verse (in hexameter and pentameter couplets), written by THEOCRITUS, OVID, CATULLUS, and others; in English, a reflective poem of lamentation or regret, of no set metrical form, mourning one person, e.g., P.B. SHELLEY'S "Adonais," or all humanity, e.g., Thomas GRAY'S "Elegy in a Country Churchyard." The pastoral elegy, of which John MILTON'S "Lycidas" is the best known, has a classical pastoral setting.

element, in chemistry, substance composed of ATOMS all having the same number of PROTONS in their nuclei. This number, called the ATOMIC NUMBER, defines the element and establishes its place in the PERIODIC TABLE. Each element is assigned a symbol of one to three letters (see table). The total number of protons and NEUTRONS in the nucleus of an atom is called the MASS NUMBER. Although all atoms of an element have the same number of protons in their nuclei, they may not all have the same number of neutrons. Atoms of an element with the same mass number make up an ISOTOPE of the element. All elements have isotopes; over 1,000 isotopes of the elements are known. Although 109 elements are known, only 94 elements occur naturally on earth; the others are produced artificially (see TRANSURANIUM ELEMENTS). The chemical properties of an element are due to the distribution of electrons around the nucleus, particularly the outer, or VALENCE, electrons (the ones involved in chemical reactions). Chemical reaction does not affect the nucleus and thus does not change the atomic number. For this reason an element is often defined as a substance that cannot be decomposed into simpler substances by chemical means. See also ATOMIC WEIGHT; COMPOUND; MOLECULE.

element 105: see HAHNIUM.

element 106: see UNNILHEXIUM.

element 107: see NIELSBOHRIUM.

element 108: see HASSIUM.

element 109: see MEITNERIUM.

elementary particles, the most basic physical constituents of the universe. ATOMS are the basic units of the chemical ELEMENTS but are themselves composed of smaller particles. The first subatomic particle to be discovered was the ELECTRON, identified in 1897 by Joseph John THOMSON. The nucleus of ordinary HYDROGEN was subsequently recognized as a single particle and was named the PROTON. The third basic particle in an atom, the NEUTRON, was discovered in 1932. Although models of the atom consisting of just these three particles are sufficient to account for all forms of chemical behavior of matter, QUANTUM MECHANICS predicted the existence of additional elementary particles. A search for the positron, or antiparticle (see ANTIMATTER) of the electron, led to its detection in 1932, but a search for a particle predicted by YUKAWA HIDEKI in 1935 led to the unexpected discovery of the muon the following year. Yukawa's particle, the pion, was finally discovered in 1947. Both the muon and pion were first observed in COSMIC RAYS. As the list of particles and antiparticles grew, through further study of cosmic rays and study of the results of particle collisions produced by PARTICLE ACCELERATORS, three basic categories of elementary particles were ultimately distinguished: leptons, quarks, and bosons. Leptons and quarks are FERMIONS, the basic constituents of nuclear and atomic structure, or MATTER; BOSONS are the particles that transmit the fundamental FORCES of nature between fermions. The smallest class of elementary particles is that of the massless bosons, which comprises the PHOTON, gluon, W AND Z PARTICLES, and the hypothetical graviton. The lepton class contains twelve particles: the electron, muon, tauon, and their antiparticles, and the neutrino or antineutrino associated with each. The QUARKS, the third class,

ELEMENTS

Element	*Symbol*	*Atomic Number*	*Atomic Weight*[1]	*Melting Point (Degrees Centigrade)*	*Boiling Point (Degrees Centigrade)*
actinium	Ac	89	227.0278	1050.	3200.±300
aluminum	Al	13	26.98154	660.37	2467.
americium	Am	95	(243)	994.±4	2607.
antimony	Sb	51	121.75	630.74	1950.
argon	Ar	18	39.948	−189.2	−185.7
arsenic	As	33	74.9216	817. (28 attmospheres)	613. (sublimates)
astatine	At	85	(210)	302. (est.)	337. (est.)
barium	Ba	56	137.33	725.	1640.
berkelium	Bk	97	(247)	—	—
beryllium	Be	4	9.01218	1278.±5	2970.
bismuth	Bi	83	208.9804	271.3	1560.±5
boron	B	5	10.81	2079.	2550. (sublimates)
bromine	Br	35	79.904	−7.2	58.78
cadmium	Cd	48	112.41	320.9	765.
calcium	Ca	20	40.08	839.±2	1484.
californium	Cf	98	(251)	—	—
carbon	C	6	12.011	3550. ~	4827.
cerium	Ce	58	140.12	799.	3426.
cesium	Cs	55	132.9054	28.40	669.3
chlorine	Cl	17	35.453	−100.98	−34.6
chromium	Cr	24	51.996	1857.±20	2672.
cobalt	Co	27	58.9332	1495.	2870.
copper	Cu	29	63.546	1083.4±0.2	2567.
curium	Cm	96	(247)	1340.±40	—
dysprosium	Dy	66	162.50	1412.	2562.
einsteinium	Es	99	(252)	—	—
erbium	Er	68	167.26	1522.	2863.
europium	Eu	63	151.96	822.	1597.
fermium	Fm	100	(257)	—	—
fluorine	F	9	18.998403	−219.62	−188.14
francium	Fr	87	(223)	(27) (est.)	(677) (est.)
gadolinium	Gd	64	157.25	1313.±1	3266.
gallium	Ga	31	69.72	29.78	2403.
germanium	Ge	32	72.59	937.4	2830.
gold	Au	79	196.9665	1064.43	3080.
hafnium	Hf	72	178.49	2227.±20	4602.
hahnium[2]	Ha	105	(262)	—	−2
hassium[3]	Hs	108	(265)	—	—
helium	He	2	4.00260	<−272.2	−268.934
holmium	Ho	67	164.9304	1474.	2695.
hydrogen	H	1	1.00794	−259.14	−252.87
indium	In	49	114.82	156.61	2080.
iodine	I	53	126.9045	113.5	184.35
iridium	Ir	77	192.22	2410.	4130.
iron	Fe	26	55.847	1535.	2750.
krypton	Kr	36	83.80	−156.6	−152.30±0.10
lanthanum	La	57	138.9055	921.	3457.
lawrencium	Lw	103	(260)	—	—
lead	Pb	82	207.2	327.502	1740.
lithium	Li	3	6.941	180.54	1342.
lutetium	Lu	71	174.967	1663.	3395.
magnesium	Mg	12	24.305	648.8±0.5	1090.
manganese	Mn	25	54.9380	1244.±3	1962.
meitnerium[4]	Mt	109	(266)	—	—

[1]*Parentheses indicate most stable isotope.*
[2]*Also called unnilpentium.*
[3]*Also called unniloctium.*
[4]*Also called unnilennium.*

also number twelve: the whimsically named up, down, charm, strange, top (or truth), and bottom (or beauty) quarks and their antiparticles. Quarks are always found in pairs or triplets with other quarks or antiquarks to form particles called hadrons. More than 200 hadrons have been identified. Hadrons were earlier classified as either mesons, which include the muon and pion and consist of quark-antiquark pairs, or baryons, which consist of quark triplets. The lightest baryons are the proton and neutron; heavier baryons are known as hyperons. Elementary particles interact with one another through the four fundamental forces: GRAVITATION, electromagnetism, the WEAK INTERACTION, and the STRONG INTERACTION. Gravitation is experienced by all particles, but electromagnetism is experienced only by charged particles, such as the electron, proton, and muon. Hadrons and leptons, including the electron, muon, and the neutrinos, participate in the weak interaction associated with particle decay. The strong interaction is responsible

ELEMENTS *(Continued)*

Element	*Symbol*	*Atomic Number*	*Atomic Weight*[1]	*Melting Point (Degrees Centigrade)*	*Boiling Point (Degrees Centigrade)*
mendelevium	Md	101	(258)	—	—
mercury	Hg	80	200.59	−38.842	356.58
molybdenum	Mo	42	95.94	2617.	4612.
neodymium	Nd	60	144.24	1021.	3068.
neon	Ne	10	20.179	−248.67	−246.048
neptunium	Np	93	237.0482	640.±1	3902. (est.)
nickel	Ni	28	58.69	1453.	2732.
nielsbohrium[2]	Ns	107	(262)	—	—
niobium	Nb	41	92.9064	2468.±10	4742.
nitrogen	N	7	14.0067	−209.86	−195.8
nobelium	No	102	(259)	—	—
osmium	Os	76	190.2	3045.±30	5027.±100
oxygen	O	8	15.9994	−218.4	−182.962
palladium	Pd	46	106.42	1554.	2970.
phosphorus	P	15	30.97376	44.1 (white)	280. (white)
platinum	Pt	78	195.08	1772.	3827.±100
plutonium	Pu	94	(244)	641.	3232.
polonium	Po	84	(209)	254.	962.
potassium	K	19	39.0983	63.25	760.
praseodymium	Pr	59	140.9077	931.	3512.
promethium	Pm	61	(145)	~1168.±6	2460.
protactinium	Pa	91	231.0359	<1600.	—
radium	Ra	88	226.0254	700.	1140.
radon	Rn	86	(222)	−71.	−61.8
rhenium	Re	75	186.207	3180.	5627. (est.)
rhodium	Rh	45	102.9055	1966.±3	3727.±100
rubidium	Rb	37	85.4678	38.89	686.
ruthenium	Ru	44	101.07	2310.	3900.
rutherfordium[3]	Rf	104	(261)	—	—
samarium	Sm	62	150.36	1072.±5	1791.
scandium	Sc	21	44.9559	1541.	2831.
selenium	Se	34	78.96	217.	684.9±1.0
silicon	Si	14	28.0855	1410.	2355.
silver	Ag	47	107.8682	961.93	2212.
sodium	Na	11	22.98977	97.81±0.03	882.9
strontium	Sr	38	87.62	269.	1384.
sulfur	S	16	32.06	112.8	444.674
tantalum	Ta	73	180.9479	2996.	5425.±100
technetium	Tc	43	(98)	2172.	4877.
tellurium	Te	52	127.60	449.5±0.3	989.8±3.8
terbium	Tb	65	158.9254	1356.	3123.
thallium	Tl	81	204.383	303.5	1457.±10
thorium	Th	90	232.0381	1750.	4790.
thulium	Tm	69	168.9342	1545.±15	1947.
tin	Sn	50	118.69	231.9681	2270.
titanium	Ti	22	47.88	1660.±10	3287.
tungsten	W	74	183.85	3410.±20	5660.
unnilhexium	Unh	106	(263)	—	—
uranium	U	92	238.0289	1132.3±0.8	3818.
vanadium	V	23	50.9415	1890.±10	3380.
xenon	Xe	54	131.29	−111.9	−107.1±3
ytterbium	Yb	70	173.04	819.	1194.
yttrium	Y	39	88.9059	1522.±8	3338.
zinc	Zn	30	65.38	419.58	907.
zirconium	Zr	40	91.22	1852.±2	4377.

[1]*Parentheses indicate most stable isotope.*
[2]*Also called unnilseptium.*
[3]*Also called kurchatovium and unnilquadium.*

for the structure of the atomic nucleus, and only hadrons participate in it.

elephant, largest living land MAMMAL, of Africa and Asia. It has a massive head, thick legs, and tough, gray skin. The upper lip extends into a long, flexible trunk used for drinking, spraying, conveying food to the mouth, and touching; the large ears provide an extensive cooling surface. African bull elephants may measure 13 ft (4 m) high at the shoulder and weigh 6 to 8 tons (5400 to 7200 kg). Hunted for their great, curved ivory tusks, they have become endangered. Highly intelligent, they are used in foresting and trained as circus and zoo performers. African elephants use infrasonic frequencies (those below the range of human hearing) for communication. See also MAMMOTH; MASTODON.

elephantiasis, abnormal enlargement of any part of the body due to obstruction of the lymphatic channels in the affected area. In tropical countries, the most common cause is a disease called filariasis, the result of an infestation of small roundworms (genus *Filaria*) in the LYMPHATIC SYSTEM. The condition can also result from the sexually transmitted disease lymphogranuloma venereum.

Eleusinian Mysteries, principal religious MYSTERIES of ancient Greece, held at ELEUSIS. The secret rites, which celebrated the abduction of PERSEPHONE and her return to her mother DEMETER, symbolized the annual cycle of death and rebirth in nature, as well as the immortality of the soul. DIONYSUS was also much honored at the festival.

Eleusis [ĭlo͞o'sĭs], ancient city of Attica, GREECE, NW of ATHENS. It was the seat of the ELEUSINIAN MYSTERIES, dedicated to DEMETER. The Eleusinian games were also held there.

elevator, mechanical lift device for transporting people or goods from one level to another. The American inventor Elisha G. Otis demonstrated (1853) a safety device designed to prevent the fall of an elevator if its supporting cable should break; in 1861 he patented a steam-powered elevator. Steam was gradually replaced, first in the early 1870s by hydraulic power (see HYDRAULIC MACHINERY) and then toward the end of the 19th cent. by electricity. Safety devices were improved and automatic controls introduced as elevator speeds increased.

Elgar, Sir Edward William, 1857–1934, English composer. Among his outstanding compositions are *Variations on an Original Theme* (or *Enigma Variations,* 1899) and the Violin Concerto in B Minor. He is best known for the *Pomp and Circumstance* marches (1901–30).

Elgin, Thomas Bruce, 7th **earl of,** 1766–1841, British diplomat. While on a diplomatic mission in Constantinople (1799–1803), he arranged for the ELGIN MARBLES to be brought to England. His son **James Bruce,** 8th **earl of Elgin,** 1811–63, was governor general of Canada (1847–54). He implemented the plan for responsible government outlined by his father-in-law, the earl of DURHAM, and personally negotiated the reciprocity treaty of 1854 with the U.S. His son, **Victor Alexander Bruce,** 9th **earl of Elgin,** 1849–1917, was viceroy of India (1894–99) and colonial secretary (1905–8).

Elgin Marbles, ancient sculpture taken from the Acropolis of Athens to England in 1806 by Thomas Bruce, 7th earl of Elgin. The PARTHENON frieze by PHIDIAS and sculpture from the ERECHTHEUM are on view at the British Museum.

El Greco: see GRECO, EL.

Eliade, Mircea, 1907–86, American religious scholar and writer; b. Bucharest. A student of myths and mystical experiences, he wrote over 50 books, including a history of religious ideas, completed in 1985, and novels such as *The Forbidden Forest* (1955) and *The Old Man and the Bureaucrats* (1979). He was editor of the multivolume *Encyclopedia of Religion and Religious Belief* (1988).

Elias, Greek form of ELIJAH.

Elijah or **Elias,** fl. c.875 B.C., Hebrew PROPHET in the reign of King AHAB and an outstanding figure in the OLD TESTAMENT. Elijah's mission was to destroy the worship of foreign gods and to restore justice, and his zeal brought about a temporary banishment of idolatry. His story in the Bible has many incidents, such as his raising the widow's son from the dead, his being fed by ravens, his experience of the still, small voice on Mt. Horeb, and his departure from earth in a chariot of fire enveloped in a whirlwind. His disciple was ELISHA. In Jewish tradition, Elijah is the herald of the MESSIAH. He is also prominent in the KORAN.

Elijah ben Solomon, 1720–97, Jewish scholar, called the Gaon Eminence of Vilna; b. Lithuania. Although a student of the CABALA, he fought the spread of HASIDISM among the Jews of Lithuania and Poland, fearing that it would weaken the Jewish community. His major writings were on the HALAKAH.

Eliot, Charles William, 1834–1926, American educator and president of Harvard Univ. (1869–1909); b. Boston. His 40-year administration at Harvard Univ. developed the college into a great modern university. He extended the elective system, added new courses, required written exams, enlarged the faculty, and increased entrance requirements while raising the standards for professional degrees. He supported Elizabeth Cary Agassiz's development of Radcliffe, and was also influential in securing greater uniformity in high school curricula and college entrance requirements. Eliot published widely.

Eliot, George, pseud. of **Mary Ann or** Marian Evans, 1819–80, English novelist, a major 19th-cent. writer. She defied convention to live with her mentor, G.H. LEWES. Writing about rural life, Eliot was primarily concerned with people's moral choices and their responsibility for their own lives. Her novels include *Adam Bede* (1859) and *Silas Marner* (1861). *Middlemarch* (1871–72) is considered her masterpiece.

Eliot, John, 1604–90, English missionary in colonial Massachusetts, called the Apostle to the Indians. A Puritan, he arrived in Boston in 1631, studied the area's Native American language, began preaching, and established villages for his native converts. His translation of the Bible into an Algonquian language (1661–63) and his *Indian Primer* (1669) are prime sources of our knowledge of the peoples of the area.

Eliot, T(homas) S(tearns), 1888–1965, English poet, one of the most influential literary figures of the 20th cent.; b. St. Louis. Living in London from 1914, he became a British subject in 1927, the same year he espoused Anglo-Catholicism. He was associated with the periodicals *The Egoist* (1917–30) and his own *Criterion* (1922–39), and he had an active career in publishing. Eliot's early poems—*Prufrock and Other Observations* (1917), *Poems* (1920), and *The Wasteland* (1922)—express the anguish and barrenness of modern life. Breaking completely with the 19th-cent. poetic tradition, they drew on the 17th-cent. METAPHYSICAL POETS, along with DANTE, Jacobean drama, and the French SYMBOLISTS. Eliot's later, more hopeful, poetry includes *Ash Wednesday* (1930) and *Four Quartets* (1935–42). He was also an important critic. His plays, attempts to revitalize the verse drama, include *Murder in the Cathedral* (1935) and *The Cocktail Party* (1950). He was awarded the 1948 Nobel Prize in literature.

Elisabeth: see ELIZABETH.

Elisha [ēlī'shə] or **Eliseus** [ĕlĭsē'əs], Hebrew prophet. He continued the work of ELIJAH, but was more diplomatic and of a milder nature. Unlike Elijah, he had many disciples.

Elizabeth, 1837–98, empress of Austria and queen of Hungary, consort of FRANCIS JOSEPH. Her life was marred by tragedy, notably the death of her only son, Archduke RUDOLF. She was assassinated in Geneva by an Italian anarchist.

Elizabeth, 1709–62, czarina of Russia (1741–62); daughter of PETER I and CATHERINE I. She gained the throne by overthrowing IVAN VI. Elizabeth was hostile toward Prussia and sided against FREDERICK II of Prussia in the SEVEN YEARS WAR. She gave the nobles greater power over their serfs and in local government, while decreasing the service they owed the state.

Elizabeth, queens of England. **Elizabeth I,** 1533–1603, queen of England (1558–1603), the daughter of HENRY VIII and Anne BOLEYN, was declared illegitimate after her mother's execution; in 1544 Parliament reestablished her in the succession. Imprisoned as a rallying point for discontented Protestants, she regained some freedom by outward conformity to Catholicism. On her accession in 1558 England's low fortunes included religious strife, a huge government debt, and failure in wars with France. Her reign took England through one of its greatest eras—a period that produced such individuals as William SHAKESPEARE, Edmund SPENSER, Francis BACON, and Walter RALEIGH; a period that saw the country united to become a first-rate European power with a great navy; a period in which commerce and industry prospered and colonization began. Elizabeth's Tudor concept of strong rule and the need for popular support helped her select excellent counselors, such as Sir William Cecil (Lord BURGHLEY) and Sir Francis Walsingham. She reestablished Anglicanism, and measures against Catholics grew harsher. Important legislation enacted in her reign included stabilization of labor conditions, currency reforms, poor laws, and acts to encourage agriculture, commerce, and manufacturing. Elizabeth began a policy of peace, and her diplomatic maneuvers eventually defeated Spain and stalemated France. The Treaty of Edinburgh (1560) started a policy of supporting Protestant lords against Catholics. After the abdication of MARY QUEEN OF SCOTS from the Scottish throne, Elizabeth gave her refuge, kept her prisoner, and executed her only after numerous plots to seat Mary on the English throne. Although she had many favorites, notably the earl of LEICESTER, Elizabeth never married, but she used the possibility of marriage as a diplomatic tool. By marriage negotiations with FRANCIS, duke of Alençon and Anjou, she secured (1572) a defense alliance against

Spain and, later, French aid for the Dutch against Spain, which then emerged as England's main enemy. PHILIP II of Spain, whose marriage offer Elizabeth had refused in 1559, planned the Spanish ARMADA as a reprisal for English raids against Spanish shipping. The defeat of the Armada (1588) broke the power of Spain and strengthened England's national pride. Elizabeth's last years were darkened by the rash uprising of her favorite, Robert Devereux, 2d earl of ESSEX. She was succeeded by James VI of Scotland, son of Mary Queen of Scots, who became JAMES I of England. Vain, fickle in bestowing favors, prejudiced, vacillating, and parsimonious, she was nonetheless a great monarch, highly aware of the responsibility of rule and immensely courageous. **Elizabeth II,** 1926–, queen of Great Britain and Northern Ireland, succeeded her father, GEORGE VI, in 1952. In 1947 she married Philip Mountbatten, duke of EDINBURGH. They have four children: Prince CHARLES, Princess ANNE, Prince Andrew (b. 1960), and Prince Edward (b. 1964). In 1977 she celebrated her Silver Jubilee, the 25th anniversary of her accession to the throne. Her mother, **Elizabeth,** 1900–, queen consort to George VI, was the daughter of the 14th earl of Strathmore.

Elizabeth, 1843–1916, queen of ROMANIA, consort of CAROL I, also known as Elizabeth of Wied. Under the pseudonym Carmen Sylva she wrote extensively in several languages.

Elizabeth, city (1990 pop. 110,002), seat of Union co., NE N.J., on Newark Bay; settled 1609, inc. 1855. It is one of the largest container seaports in the world, and manufactures sewing machines, foundry products, textiles, office supplies, and chemicals. The area was purchased from the Delaware in 1664. It was the scene of several clashes during the AMERICAN REVOLUTION.

Elizabethan style, in architecture and decorative arts, transitional style of the English RENAISSANCE during which large manor houses were built. Plans tended toward symmetry, although such characteristics of TUDOR STYLE as the great hall remained. New features were added, notably broad staircases and long galleries. A famous example is Longleat, Wiltshire. Owners often designed houses themselves, and carpenters and masons amplified the plans. Renaissance, mannerist, and Flemish motifs were haphazardly adapted with no attempt at a unified classical style.

Elizabeth Woodville: see WOODVILLE, ELIZABETH.

elk, any of several members of the DEER family. It most properly designates the largest member of the family, *Alces alces,* found in N North America, where it is called MOOSE, and Eurasia. The name *elk* is used in North America to designate a different animal, the WAPITI.

Elkin, Stanley, 1930–, American novelist and short-story writer; b. N.Y.C. An offbeat comic writer with a gift for imagery and bizarre situations, Elkin demonstrates an underlying seriousness in such novels as *Boswell* (1964), *The Living End* (1979), *The Magic Kingdom* (1985), and *The MacGuffin* (1991) and the stories in *Criers and Kibitzers, Kibitzers and Criers* (1966).

Ellice Islands: see TUVALU.

Ellington, Duke (Edward Kennedy Ellington), 1899–1974, African-American jazz pianist and composer; b. Washington, D.C. He formed a band in 1918 and became nationally famous while appearing in Harlem (N.Y.C.) nightclubs. His orchestra, playing his own often complex compositions, made many innovations in the JAZZ idiom. Ellington's compositions include "Solitude" and "Mood Indigo" as well as such long concert works as *Black, Brown, and Beige* (1943).

ellipse: see CONIC SECTION.

elliptical geometry: see NON-EUCLIDEAN GEOMETRY.

Ellis Island, island, c.27 acres (10.9 hectares), N.Y.C., in Upper New York Bay, in New Jersey's waters but under New York's jurisdiction. Government property since 1808, it served (1892–1943) as the chief entry station for immigrants to the U.S. Now part of the Statue of Liberty National Monument, the island is open to tourists and has an immigration museum.

Ellison, Ralph, 1914–, African-American writer; b. Oklahoma City. His classic novel, *Invisible Man* (1952), details the struggles of a young, nameless African-American man in a hostile society. A collection of his essays, speeches, interviews, and reviews is *Going to the Territory* (1986).

Ellsworth, Lincoln, 1880–1951, American explorer; b. Chicago. He was the financial backer and colleague of Roald AMUNDSEN. With the aviator Umberto Nobile, they flew over the NORTH POLE in a dirigible in 1925. Ellsworth was the first person to fly over ANTARCTICA (1936). In 1939 he flew into interior Antarctica, viewing and claiming vast areas for the U.S.

Ellsworth, Oliver, 1745–1807, 3d chief justice of the U.S. SUPREME COURT (1796–99); b. Windsor, Conn. At the FEDERAL CONSTITUTIONAL CONVENTION (1787), he (with Roger Sherman) advanced the "Connecticut compromise," ending the struggle between large and small states over congressional representation. As U.S. senator (1789–96) he was the chief author of the bill establishing the federal court system.

elm, tree or shrub of the family Ulmaceae, found chiefly in the Northern Hemisphere. Elm trees (genus *Ulmus*) are tall and graceful, with fan-shaped crowns of finely subdividing branches and twigs. The American, or white, elm (*U. americana*) and the English, or Wych, elm (*U. campestris*) of Eurasia are widely planted as ornamental and shade trees. Both species are vulnerable to the fungus known as Dutch elm disease.

El Monte, city (1990 pop. 106,209), Los Angeles co., S Calif.; inc. 1912. Founded (1852) by pioneers on the SANTA FE TRAIL and known for its walnut groves, it is a growing residential, industrial, and commercial city in the San Gabriel Valley. Manufactures include aerospace products, electronic equipment, and plastic and metal products.

El Niño–Southern Oscillation (ENSO), large-scale climatic fluctuation of the tropical Pacific Ocean. The El Niño [Span., = the child] itself is a warm surface current that usually appears around Christmas in the Pacific off Ecuador and Peru and disappears by the end of March, but every 3–7 years it persists for as long as 18 months as part of an ENSO. Exactly what initiates an ENSO is unclear. In a typical ENSO, the strong easterly winds of the equatorial Pacific weaken, which allows warm eastward-flowing subsurface waters to rise, increasing surface temperatures 1–2°C, and sometimes as much as 4–6°C in the central and E Pacific. Along the W coast of South America, the El Niño's warm waters persist and deepen, and cold, upwelling, nutrient-rich waters fail to reach surface waters; the resulting warm, nutrient-poor waters devastate coastal fisheries. Heavy rain falls along the South American coast, and heavy rainfall also moves from the western to central Pacific, causing drier than normal conditions in Indonesia and nearby areas. An ENSO also affects the climate of the northern latitudes, particularly North America, which experiences warmer temperatures along the Pacific coast, increased rainfall in the Gulf states, and weaker Atlantic hurricanes. Severe ENSO events can be economically disruptive worldwide. In 1982–83, an ENSO caused droughts in India, Indonesia, Australia, and the Philippines, flooding in Peru and Ecuador, and devastating coastal storms in California. The ENSO that began in 1991 contributed to the record rain and flooding in the Midwest in 1993.

Elohim: see GOD.

elongation, the angular distance between two points in the sky as measured from a third point. As viewed from a third body, the elongation of two celestial bodies will be 0° when they are in conjunction and 180° when in opposition (see SYZYGY); quadrature occurs when the two bodies have an elongation of 90°. As viewed from the earth, the greatest elongations with respect to the sun of the inferior planets Mercury and Venus are 28° and 47°; the moon and the superior planets can range from 0° to 180°.

El Paso, city (1990 pop. 515,342), seat of El Paso co., extreme W Tex., on the RIO GRANDE, opposite JUÁREZ, Mex., and near the N.Mex. border; inc. 1873. Located in a region of cattle ranches and farms, the city is a port, and a commercial, industrial, and mining center. Manufactures include refined petroleum, copper, clothing, and machinery. The dry climate attracts tourists. The largest of the border cities, El Paso's history is bound up with that of MEXICO. Early settlement in the area was on the south (Juárez) bank of the river; the first house on the site of the present city was built in 1827. The arrival of railroad service in 1881 initiated the border town's growth into a modern city.

El Salvador, officially Republic of El Salvador, republic (1992 est. pop. 5,574,000), 8,260 sq mi (21,393 sq km), Central America; bordered by the Pacific Ocean (S), Guatemala (W), and Honduras (N

and E). The capital is SAN SALVADOR. Two volcanic ranges traverse the country from west to east. In between are the broad, fertile valleys that are the nation's heartland. The densely populated country is the smallest of the Latin American republics, with a weak economy overly dependent on coffee, the principal export. Cotton and sugar are also exported while oil and many manufactured goods are imported. Corn is the main subsistence crop. Light industry includes textile manufacture and food processing. The Spanish-speaking, Roman Catholic population is predominantly mestizo.

History. Spaniards conquered the area in 1524. El Salvador declared independence in 1821 and after a brief period was part of the Mexican Empire (1821–23) and then of the Central American Federation (1825–38). Becoming a separate republic in 1839 it was plagued by frequent interference from nearby states, notably GUATEMALA and NICARAGUA. The establishment of coffee cultivation in the late 19th cent. created an inequitable distribution of wealth that became the basis for future unrest and, consequently, of several repressive dictatorships. Overpopulation has been a major 20th-cent. problem. Failure of land reform in the 1970s brought increasing left-right polarization and guerrilla warfare, with U.S., Cuban, and Nicaraguan involvement. In 1982 a right-wing coalition came to power, but José Napoléon DUARTE, a Christian Democrat, was elected president in 1984. Attempts to negotiate an end to the guerrilla war were unsuccessful, and Duarte was succeeded (1989) by the right-wing ARENA party candidate, Alfredo Cristiani Burkard. Leftist parties, which had boycotted elections in the 1980s, participated in the 1991 parliamentary elections. In 1992 a peace treaty was signed with the rebels, ending the 12-year civil war, and new national elections were scheduled for 1994. Politically motivated violence remains a problem.

Elsheimer, Adam [ĕls'hīmər], 1578–1610?, German painter. Known for small paintings on copper of biblical subjects, he excelled at landscape and light effects and influenced Dutch painters. His *Good Samaritan* is in the Louvre.

Elsinore: see HELSINGØR.

Elysian fields or **Elysium,** in Greek mythology, happy otherworld in the west for heroes favored by the gods.

Elytis, Odysseus, pseud. of **Odysseus Alepoudelis,** 1911–, Greek poet; b. Crete. His poetry, joyful and sensuous, is replete with imagery of the Aegean Islands. *The Sovereign Sun* (1974) is a selection of his poems in English translation. He was awarded the 1979 Nobel Prize in literature.

Emancipation, Edict of, 1861, edict by which Czar ALEXANDER II freed all Russian SERFS (one third of the population). Serfdom was abolished, and peasants were to receive land from landlords and pay them for it. The system of payment and of land distribution, cumbersome and unjust, was reformed by STOLYPIN in 1906 in an effort to stem discontent.

Emancipation Proclamation, in U.S. history, the executive order abolishing SLAVERY in the CONFEDERACY. Pres. LINCOLN refrained at the start of the CIVIL WAR from freeing slaves lest it alienate the loyal border states. But after the successful ANTIETAM CAMPAIGN, Lincoln issued a preliminary edict and, on Jan. 1, 1863, the formal Emancipation Proclamation. It freed only those slaves residing in territory in rebellion "as a fit and necessary war measure for suppressing said rebellion." It was designed to deplete the Southern manpower reserve in slaves and to enhance the Union cause abroad, especially in Britain.

embalming, preservation of the body after death by artificial chemical means. It was highly developed in dynastic EGYPT, where immersion in a soda solution and filling of body cavities with resins and spices were common. Modern embalming grew from 17th-cent. attempts to preserve anatomical specimens. Formaldehyde, infused to replace the blood, is the most common embalming agent.

embargo, prohibition by a country of the departure of ships or certain types of goods from its ports. Instances of confining all domestic ships to port are rare, and the EMBARGO ACT OF 1807 is the sole example in U.S. history. The detention of foreign vessels, however, has often occurred as an act of reprisal or in anticipation of war. Embargoes on goods for economic and strategic purposes are also common. The U.S. has maintained an economic embargo against Cuba since 1960 in an attempt to undermine CASTRO. Both the LEAGUE OF NATIONS and the UNITED NATIONS have recognized the use of embargoes, e.g., the League's sanctions (1935) against Italy for its aggression in Ethiopia, the UN oil and arms embargoes against Rhodesia (see ZIMBABWE) and SOUTH AFRICA because of their racial policies, and the UN economic embargo against YUGOSLAVIA because of Serbian actions in CROATIA and BOSNIA.

Embargo Act of 1807, passed Dec. 22, 1807, by the U.S. Congress in answer to British and French restrictions on neutral shipping during the Napoleonic Wars (see NAPOLEON I). It forbade all international trade to and from American ports in an attempt to persuade Britain and France of the value and rights of neutral commerce. In Jan. 1808 the prohibition was extended to inland waters and land commerce to halt trade with Canada. Britain and France stood firm, however, and enforcement was difficult, especially in New England. The Nonintercourse Act (Mar. 1, 1809) and Macon's Bill No. 2 (1810) effectually dissolved the purpose of the embargo.

embezzlement: see LARCENY.

embroidery, ornamental needlework applied to all types of fabrics and worked with linen, cotton, wool, silk, gold, or silver thread. Beads, shells, feathers, or gems may be added. The art is mentioned in the Hindu Vedas and in the Old Testament; it probably antedates weaving. It was introduced into Europe from Byzantium, initiating a rich period of church embroidery (12th–14th cent.). Secular embroidery reached a height of sumptuousness in the 16th cent. By the 19th cent. embroidery had almost disappeared from male attire, and today it is used mainly on women's and children's clothing. Machine-made embroidery in no way approaches the quality of that formerly done by hand. Peasant embroidery, which has long flourished in Eastern Europe, the Balkans, Scandinavia, India, and the Americas, is still done in areas not yet penetrated by mechanization.

embryo, name for the developing young of an animal or plant. Embryology, the scientific study of embryonic development, deals with the period from fertilization until hatching or birth of an animal or, in plants, germination. In animals, early divisions produce a hollow ball of cells (a blastula), which later becomes a two-layered cuplike gastrula. In higher animals, a third (middle) layer of cells develops from one or both of the first two layers. The outer layer (ectoderm) gives rise to skin, scales, feathers, hair, nails, and the nervous system; the innermost layer (endoderm) forms the digestive glands and lining of the alimentary tract and lungs; the middle layer (mesoderm) develops into skeletal, muscular, and connective tissue and circulatory, excretory, and reproductive systems.

embryo biopsy, diagnostic procedure in which a single cell is removed from an embryo three days after it has been conceived through IN VITRO FERTILIZATION. The embryo continues to grow while the cell genes are replicated using POLYMERASE CHAIN REAC-

TION and then studied for genetic defects. The procedure allows an embryo to be tested before it is implanted into the womb when an inheritable disease is carried or exhibited one or both parents.

emerald, highly valued gem, green variety of the mineral BERYL. The finest emeralds are found in Colombia; other sources are Russia, Zimbabwe, and Australia. The Oriental emerald is the transparent green variety of CORUNDUM.

Emerson, Ralph Waldo, 1803–82, one of America's most influential authors and thinkers; b. Boston. A Unitarian minister, he left his only pastorate, Boston's Old North Church (1829–32), because of doctrinal disputes. On a trip to Europe Emerson met Thomas CARLYLE, S.T. COLERIDGE, and WORDSWORTH, whose ideas, along with those of PLATO, the Neoplatonists, Asian mystics, and SWEDENBORG, strongly influenced his philosophy. Returning home (1835), he settled in Concord, Mass., which he, Margaret FULLER, THOREAU, and others made a center of TRANSCENDENTALISM. He stated the movement's main principles in *Nature* (1836), stressing the mystical unity of nature. A noted lecturer, Emerson called for American intellectual independence from Europe in his Phi Beta Kappa address at Harvard ("The American Scholar," 1837). In an address at the Harvard divinity school (1838), he asserted that redemption could be found only in one's own soul and intuition. Emerson developed transcendentalist themes in his famous *Journal* (kept since his student days at Harvard), in the magazine *The Dial,* and in his series of *Essays* (1841, 1844). Among the best known of his essays are "The Over-Soul," "Compensation," and "Self-Reliance." He is also noted for his poems, e.g., "Threnody," "Brahma," and "The Problem." His later works include *Representative Men* (1850), *English Traits* (1856), and *The Conduct of Life* (1870).

emery: see CORUNDUM.

Emigrant Aid Company, formed (1854) to promote organized antislavery immigration to KANSAS from the Northeast. It hoped to use the concept of SQUATTER SOVEREIGNTY in the KANSAS-NEBRASKA ACT to ensure that Kansas became a free state. The name is associated exclusively with the New England Emigrant Aid Co., although Kansas aid societies in other northern states were also formed. Conceived by Eli Thayer, the company sent out 1,240 settlers. The National Kansas Committee, formed (1856) by various aid societies, became divided as to how to handle violence by proslavery forces. The movement virtually ended by 1857 and did little toward making Kansas a free state, but it captured public attention and engendered much bitterness that contributed to the CIVIL WAR.

Emmanuel Philibert, 1528–80, duke of Savoy (1553–80), called Ironhead. He succeeded his father, who had been dispossessed of his duchy by the French and the Swiss. Serving Spain, he defeated the French at Saint-Quentin (1557), and by the Treaty of Cateau-Cambrésis (1559) most of Savoy was restored to him. He made many reforms in Savoy and moved its capital to Turin, thus making it an Italian, rather than a French, state.

Empedocles, c.495–c.435 B.C., Greek philosopher. He held that everything in existence is composed of four underived and indestructible substances—fire, water, earth, and air—and that atmosphere is a corporeal substance, not a mere void. He believed that motion is the only sort of change possible and that apparent changes in quantity and quality are in fact changes of position of the basic particles underlying the observable object. Thus he first stated a principle central to modern physics.

emphysema, abnormal enlargement or distension of the air sacs of the lungs, causing difficulty in breathing. Usually chronic and progressive, the condition is associated with heredity, smoking, and long-standing respiratory ailments such as chronic bronchitis. Management is aimed at increasing lung capacity and preventing and treating infection, a common complication.

Empire State Building, in New York City, on Fifth Ave., between 33d St. and 34th St. It was designed by Shreve, Lamb, and Harmon, and built in 1930–31. With 102 stories, it was for years the tallest building in the world.

Empire style, in French interior decoration and costume, the manner prevailing in the reign of NAPOLEON I (1804–14), largely created for him by the architects FONTAINE and Percier and the artist J.-L. DAVID. Furniture was chiefly of mahogany. Walls were decorated with stucco, or with classical motifs and such imperial symbols as the emperor's monogram and representations of military trophies. The empress Josephine introduced the court dress with train, and men began to wear full-length trousers and polished top hats.

empiricism, philosophical doctrine holding that all knowledge is derived from experience, whether of the mind or of the senses. Thus it opposes the rationalist belief in the existence of innate ideas. A doctrine basic to the scientific method, empiricism is associated with the rise of experimental science after the 17th cent. It has been a dominant tradition in British philosophy, as in the works at LOCKE, HUME, and George BERKELEY. Most empiricists acknowledge certain a priori truths (e.g., principles of mathematics and logic), but John Stuart MILL and others have treated even these as generalizations deduced from experience.

empyema: see PLEURISY.

Ems dispatch, 1870 communication between King William of Prussia (later German Emperor WILLIAM I) and his premier, Otto von BISMARCK. In June 1870 the Spanish throne had been offered to Prince Hohenzollern-Sigmaringen. France having protested, the prince refused this offer, but the French ambassador, Comte Benedetti, meeting William at Ems, demanded further assurance. William rejected the request. Seeking to goad France into war, Bismarck made public the king's report of the conversation, edited in a provocative manner. France declared war on July 19, and the FRANCO-PRUSSIAN WAR began.

emu or **emeu,** large, flightless Australian BIRD (*Dromiceius novaehollandiae*) related to the CASSOWARY and OSTRICH. A swift runner, it is 5 to 6 ft (150 to 180 cm) tall. Its brownish plumage is coarse and hairlike.

emulsion: see COLLOID.

enamel, a siliceous substance that fuses with metal. Transparent or opaque, clear or colored, it adds a decorative surface. Enamel was used in making jewelry in ancient Egypt, Greece, and Rome, and was perfected in the Byzantine world, often in the CLOISONNÉ technique. Fine enamel-work was created in 12th-cent. France and Spain. The most famous enamelist was the 16th-cent. French artist Léonard LIMOUSIN. In England from the 17th cent. on, enamel was used for miniature portraits. Enamel-work declined in the 19th cent. but was revived in the 1960s.

enantiomer: see ISOMER.

encaustic, painting medium in which the binder for the pigment is wax, or wax and resin. Thought to have been widely used in ancient times, the technique is exemplified by remarkably preserved tomb paintings from Roman Egypt.

Enceladus, in astronomy, natural satellite of SATURN.

encephalitis, inflammation of the brain and spinal cord. Among the several forms of viral brain inflammation are RABIES, POLIOMYELITIS, and two types, transmitted by mosquitoes, that are known as sleeping sickness because of their characteristic prolonged COMA. Encephalitis can also follow such systemic diseases as influenza, scarlet fever, or infection with the AIDS virus. For many forms of encephalitis there is no treatment, although many types can be prevented by immunization.

Encina or **Enzina, Juan del** [ānthē'nä], 1469?–c.1530, Spanish poet and court musician. His *Églogas* (pastoral plays), which together with musical compositions and a treatise on poetry appear in *Cancionero* (1946), made him the father of Spanish RENAISSANCE drama.

enclosure of land: see INCLOSURE.

encomienda, system of tribute in Spanish America to supply adequate and cheap labor. Native peoples were required to pay tribute from their lands in return for Spanish protection. The hardships of the system soon decimated the indigenous population, however, and it died out gradually after 1542.

encyclical: see BULL.

Encyclopédie, influential 28-volume French encyclopedia, edited by Denis DIDEROT and Jean d'ALEMBERT, with the aid of QUESNAY, MONTESQUIEU, VOLTAIRE, J.J. ROUSSEAU, TURGOT, and others. It was published between 1751 and 1775. Its famous "preliminary discourse," signed by Alembert, indicated its aims and then presented definitions and histories of science and the arts. Despite attacks by the JESUITS and unofficial censorship by the printer, it was an immediate success. It championed the skepticism and rationalism of the ENLIGHTENMENT and played a major role in the intellectual preparation for the FRENCH REVOLUTION. In 1780 a five-volume supplement and two-volume index were added.

endangered species, any species of animal or plant whose ability to survive is seriously in question. Human activities can contribute to such endangerment: for example, by purposeful extermination to protect livestock; unrestricted hunting to obtain hides, feathers, or food; or the use of PESTICIDES to protect crops. Humans have contributed to the destruction of entire habitats through, e.g., STRIP MINING, oil spills, water POLLUTION, and the draining of swamps and leveling of forests for industrial and residential development. Such destruction can endanger the lives and breeding grounds of a large number of species simultaneously. Since the 1970s environmentalists have pressed for the establishment of new WILDLIFE REFUGES and for land-use planning. In the U.S. the Endangered Species Acts of 1966, 1969, and 1973 prohibit any trade in endangered species or their products and require that federal agencies assess the impact on wildlife of proposed projects.

endive: see CHICORY.

endocrine system, body control system composed of a group of glands that keeps the internal environment stable by producing chemical regulatory substances called HORMONES. In humans the major endocrine organs are the PITUITARY GLAND, THYROID GLAND, PARATHYROID GLANDS, ADRENAL GLANDS, THYMUS GLAND, PINEAL BODY, PANCREAS, ovaries, and testes (see REPRODUCTIVE SYSTEM); the KIDNEYS are also sometimes included. The endocrine, or ductless, glands secrete the hormones they produce directly into the internal environment; transmitted via the bloodstream or by diffusion, the endocrine hormones act at distant points in the body. Some, such as thyroxine from the thyroid gland, affect nearly all body cells; others, such as PROGESTERONE from the female ovary, which regulates the uterine lining, affect only a single organ. The pituitary, sometimes called the master gland, secretes hormones that regulate many of the other endocrine glands. The regulation of body function depends on the existence of specific receptor cells in target organs—cells that respond in specialized ways to minute hormonal stimuli. The hormones act by regulating cell metabolism: by accelerating, slowing, or maintaining enzyme activity in receptor cells, they control growth and development, metabolic rate, sexual rhythms, and reproduction. The quantities of hormones are maintained by feedback mechanisms that depend on interactions between the endocrine glands, blood levels of hormones, and activities of the target organs. See HYPOTHALAMUS.

endorphin, any of a group of NEUROTRANSMITTERS, affecting mood, perception of pain, memory retention, and learning. Chemically similar to opium-derived NARCOTICS, endorphins were searched for and found in the 1970s after the discovery that MORPHINE works by attaching itself to specific receptor sites in the brain. Endorphins also attach to these receptors and appear to be the brain's own natural painkillers. Besides behaving as pain regulators, endorphins are believed to contribute to euphoric feelings such as the "runner's high" experienced after prolonged exercise.

endoscope, any instrument used to look inside the body. Usually consisting of a tube attached to a viewing device, endoscopes are used to explore and biopsy such areas as the colon and the bronchi of the lungs. Endoscopes employing miniature television cameras and tiny surgical implements now allow exploration and **endoscopic surgery** through small incisions; such surgery is much less traumatic to the patient than traditional open surgery. Laparoscopic surgery, in which the endoscope is inserted through a small incision in the abdomen or chest, is used to correct abnormalities of the ovaries and as an alternative to traditional gall bladder and chest surgery. Arthroscopic surgery is endoscopic surgery performed on joints, such as the knee or shoulder.

energy, in physics, the ability or capacity to do WORK. Forms of energy include HEAT, chemical energy, and, according to the theory of RELATIVITY, MASS (see NUCLEAR ENERGY); other forms of energy are associated with the transmission of LIGHT, SOUND, and ELECTRICITY. Energy and work are measured in the same units: joules, ergs, electron-volts, calories, foot-pounds, or some other, depending on the system of measurement being used. When a force acts on a body, the work performed (and the energy expended) is the product of the force and the distance over which it is exerted. Potential energy is the capacity for doing work that a body possesses because of its position or condition. For example, a weight lifted to a certain height has potential energy because of its position in earth's gravitational field. Kinetic energy, the energy a body possesses because it is in motion, is equal to $\frac{1}{2}mv^2$, where m is its mass and v is its velocity. The average kinetic energy of the atoms or molecules of a body is measured by the TEMPERATURE of the body. Energy (or its equivalent in mass) can be neither created nor destroyed (see CONSERVATION LAWS), but it can be changed from one form into another.

energy, sources of. In contemporary usage, energy is whatever can be efficiently converted into heat or motion to provide power to run machines and vehicles and to supply heat and light. Energy sources are of two basic types, renewable and nonrenewable. Most of the industrial world is presently powered by nonrenewable fossil fuels—COAL, PETROLEUM, and NATURAL GAS—that, once used, cannot be replaced. Fission NUCLEAR REACTORS are fueled by uranium or plutonium, themselves finite energy sources. Spent uranium can be converted to fissile plutonium in a breeder reactor, however, a process that makes nuclear energy almost infinitely renewable. Nuclear technology, however, has not yet developed either failproof reactors or a safe method for disposing of nuclear wastes (see WASTE DISPOSAL). The development of nuclear fusion (whose end products are harmless) has so far been hindered by the difficulties of containing the fuels (plentiful light elements such as hydrogen) at the extremely high temperatures necessary to initiate and sustain fusion. Renewable energy sources include the energy from water and wind (see TURBINE; WATER WHEEL; WINDMILL); geothermal energy, the earth's internal heat that is released naturally in GEYSERS and VOLCANOES; tidal energy, the power released by the ebb and flow of the ocean's tides; biomass, the use of certain crops (including wood) or crop wastes either directly as fuel or as a fermentable source of fuels such as alcohol or methane; and SOLAR ENERGY, which can be stored and used directly as heat, or transformed into electricity through the use of PHOTOVOLTAIC CELLS. All these renewable energy sources are presently being tapped in some form, but none can replace fossil fuels without huge advances in the technologies needed to exploit them.

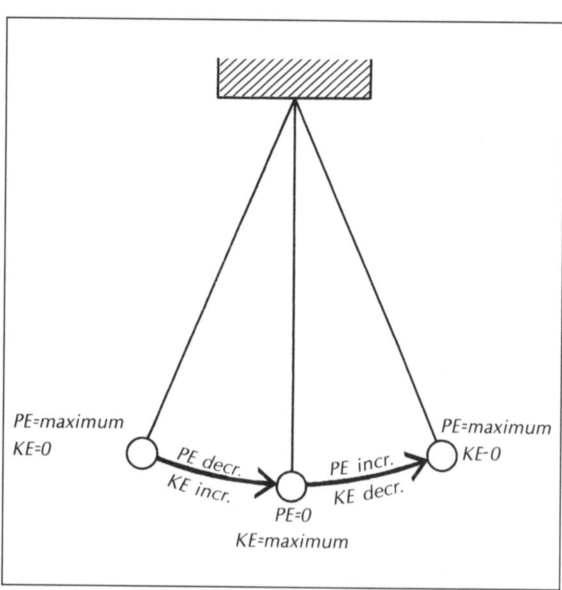

Relations between potential energy (PE) and kinetic energy (KE) for a swinging pendulum

Energy, United States Department of, federal executive department established (1977) to coordinate all national activities relating to the production, regulation, marketing, and conservation of energy. The department is also responsible for the federal nuclear weapons program and the long-term, high-risk research and development of energy technology.

Enewetak, Enewetok, or **Eniwetok,** circular atoll, central Pacific, in the MARSHALL ISLANDS. Consisting of c.40 islets surrounding a large lagoon c.50 mi (80 km) in circumference, it was used (1948–54) by the U.S. for nuclear-bomb tests. Former residents, evacuated before the tests started, began returning in the early 1970s, and the island was declared to have been rendered safe in 1980.

Engels, Friedrich, 1820–95, German social philosopher and revolutionary; with Karl MARX, a founder of modern COMMUNISM and SOCIALISM. He was the son of a textile manufacturer, and after managing a factory in Manchester, England, he wrote his first major work, *The Condition of the Working Class in England in 1844* (1845). In 1844 he met Marx in Paris, beginning a lifelong collaboration. He and Marx wrote the *Communist Manifesto* (1848) and other works that predicted the inevitable triumph of the working class. When the REVOLUTIONS OF 1848 failed, Engels settled in England. With Marx he helped found (1864) the International Workingmen's Association. Engels's financial aid enabled Marx to devote himself to writing *Das Kapital* (3 vol., 1867–94); after his death Engels edited vol. 2 and 3 from Marx's drafts and notes. Engels had enormous influence on the theories of MARXISM and DIALECTICAL MATERIALISM. His major works include *Anti-Dühring* (1878) and *The Origin of the Family, Private Property, and the State* (1884).

Friedrich Engels

engine: see AUTOMOBILE; DIESEL ENGINE; INTERNAL-COMBUSTION ENGINE; STEAM ENGINE; TURBINE.

engineering, profession devoted to designing, constructing, and operating the structures, machines, and other devices of industry and everyday life. Before the INDUSTRIAL REVOLUTION, the field was confined to the military engineer, who built fortifications and weapons, and the civil engineer, who built bridges, harbors, aqueducts, buildings, and other structures. During the early 19th cent., mechanical engineering developed to design and build manufacturing machines and the engines to power them. Major modern engineering fields include the allied pursuits of mining, metallurgical, and petroleum engineering; electrical engineering, encompassing the generation and transmission of electric power and the design of all the devices that use it; electronics engineering, dealing mainly with computers and communications equipment; chemical engineering, dealing with the design, construction, and operation of plants and machinery for making such products as acids, dyes, drugs, plastics, and synthetic rubber; and aerospace engineering, comprising the design and production of aircraft, spacecraft, and missiles. Industrial, or management, engineering is concerned with efficient production and the design of methods and processes to achieve it.

England, largest (50,334 sq mi/130,365 sq km) and most populous (1991 pop. 46,382,050) political division of the United Kingdom of Great Britain and Northern Ireland. Separated from the continent of Europe by the ENGLISH CHANNEL, the Strait of Dover, and the NORTH SEA, it is bounded by Wales and the Irish Sea (W) and Scotland (N). The Isle of WIGHT and the Scilly Islands are part of England. Inland from the white chalk cliffs of the southern coast lie gently rolling downs and wide plains. The lowlands of the east coast extend north to the reclaimed marsh of the FENS. Northern England, above the Humber R., is mountainous; the chief highlands are the Cumbrian Mts. and the Pennines, and the famous LAKE DISTRICT, in the Cumbrians, is the site of England's highest points. Central England—the Midlands—is a large plain, interrupted and bordered by hills. In the west and southwest the terrain is high and hilly. The THAMES and the Severn are the longest rivers. Among the principal cities are LONDON, the capital of the United Kingdom; BIRMINGHAM and MANCHESTER, both industrial centers; and LIVERPOOL and BRISTOL, important ports. Despite its northerly latitudes, England has a mild climate. Most of the region is subject to wet weather and some of it to severe cold, but in general life in England is conducive to a wide variety of agricultural and industrial pursuits. (For government, economy, and history of England, see GREAT BRITAIN.)

England, Church of, the established church in England and the mother church of the ANGLICAN COMMUNION. Christianity, brought by the Romans, was established in Britain by the 4th cent., but it was nearly destroyed by invasions of pagan Anglo-Saxons beginning in the 5th cent. The mission of St. AUGUSTINE OF CANTERBURY began (597) the reconversion of England and the reestablishment of its ties to the papacy. Conflicts between church and state during the Middle Ages culminated with HENRY VIII's break with Rome. The pope's refusal to annul Henry's marriage to KATHERINE OF ARAGÓN led Henry to issue the Act of Supremacy (1534), which declared the king to be the head of the Church of England. Henry suppressed the monasteries and authorized the Great Bible (1539). Under Archbishop CRANMER the First BOOK OF COMMON PRAYER was produced and adopted (1549). MARY I returned the English church to communion with Rome, but with the accession of ELIZABETH I, an independent church was restored and steered along a middle ground between Roman Catholicism and Calvinism. During the ENGLISH CIVIL WAR the Long Parliament established (1646) PRESBYTERIANISM, but with the RESTORATION (1660), the episcopacy was restored and the Prayer Book was made the only legal service book by the Act of Uniformity (1662). Since that time, despite internal controversies, e.g., the OXFORD MOVEMENT, the church has held firm. The Archbishop of Canterbury is the chief leader (primate) of the church. In polity, the High Church party holds to ritual and apostolic succession and is contravened by the Low Church party, which emphasizes the Bible and preaching. Since 1981 women have been admitted to the diaconate, and in 1992 the General Synod voted to admit women to the priesthood.

English Channel, arm of the Atlantic Ocean between France and Great Britain. Up to c.150 mi (240 km) wide in the west, it narrows to 21 mi (34 km) in the east, where it is connected to the North Sea by the Strait of Dover. Train and motor transport ferries, along with Hovercraft, provide regular channel crossings. A 32.2-mi (52-km) long tunnel connecting Folkestone, England, with Calais, France, was begun in 1987, completed in 1993, and opened in 1994. Known as the "Chunnel," it is the second longest tunnel in the world. It consists of two railway tubes and a center service tube.

English civil war, 1642–48, the conflict between CHARLES I of England and a large body of his subjects, generally called the "parliamentarians," that culminated in the defeat and execution of the king and the establishment of a republican Commonwealth. The struggle has been called the Puritan Revolution because many of the king's opponents were Puritans, and the king's defeat was accompanied by the abolition of episcopacy. The more important constitutional issue in the war was between a king who claimed to rule by divine right and a Parliament that claimed the right to govern the nation independent of the crown. Charles's father, JAMES I, temporized with Parliament due to his need for money. Sir Edward COKE upheld Parliament's rights and was dismissed by the king; Sir Francis BACON upheld the royal prerogative and was impeached by Parliament. James's last Parliament granted money with specific directions for its use. Charles I proved more intractable. Parliament tried hard to limit his power; it refused his subsidy until he signed the PETITION OF RIGHT. Charles still levied forced taxes, dissolved Parliament, and governed alone for 11 years, but his financial needs in the BISHOPS' WARS forced him to recall Parliament in 1640. Parliament recited the evils of Charles's reign in the Grand Remonstrance and tried to gather an army with a militia bill. The king organized an army himself and refused Parliament's final 19 demands. War became inevitable, and both sides bid for popular support. Charles was aided by the nobles, Anglicans, and Catholics, Parliament by the trading and artisan classes and the Scotch COVENANTERS. After initial indecisive campaigns, the victories of Oliver CROMWELL at Marston Moor and Naseby led to the king's surrender in 1645 and the end of the first civil war. His escape caused the second civil war (1647); it failed quickly. Pride's Purge (see under PRIDE, THOMAS) expelled from Parliament all those opposed to the army. The remainder, known as the Rump Parliament, sentenced and beheaded Charles for treason (1649). A quasi-democratic commonwealth was followed by Cromwell's domination in the Protectorate. The English civil war assured the emergence of the middle class, aided religious toleration, and settled the contest between king and Parliament. Its results were permanently confirmed by the GLORIOUS REVOLUTION of 1688.

English foxhound: see FOXHOUND.

English horn: see WIND INSTRUMENT.

English language, member of the West Germanic group of the Germanic subfamily of the Indo-European family of languages. See LANGUAGE (table).

English setter, large SPORTING DOG; shoulder height, c.25 in. (63.5 cm); weight, c.60 lb (27.2 kg). Its silky hair may be black, tan, and white; mixtures of lemon, liver, orange, blue, or black with white; or solid white. Developed in England as a hunting dog, it is commonly trained to point.

English sheepdog: see OLD ENGLISH SHEEPDOG.

English sparrow or **house sparrow,** small BIRD (*Passer domesticus*) of the weaver bird family, found worldwide. They are 4 to 7 in. (10 to 18 cm) long, with short, stout bills. The male is brown with black streaks above and grayish white below; the female is dull brown above and brownish white below. Chiefly seedeaters, they also eat harmful insects. Introduced (1850) in the U.S. to combat cankerworms, they have replaced many native birds in urban areas.

English springer spaniel, medium-sized SPORTING DOG; shoulder height, c.18 in. (46 cm); weight, c.45 lb (20 kg). Its medium-length, flat or wavy coat is liver and white, tan and white, or black and white. Developed in England as a field dog, it flushes game and will retrieve on land and water.

English units of measurement, principal system of a few nations, the only major industrial one being the United States. The English system actually consists of two related systems—the U.S. Customary System, used in the United States and dependencies, and the British Imperial System (see WEIGHTS AND MEASURES, table). Great Britain, the originator of the latter system, is now gradually converting to the METRIC SYSTEM. The names of the units and the relationships between them are generally the same in both systems, but the sizes of the units differ, sometimes considerably. The basic unit of length is the yard (yd); the basic unit of mass (weight) is the pound (lb). Within the English units of measurement there are three different systems of weights (avoirdupois, troy, and apothecaries'), of which the most widely used is the avoirdupois. The troy system (named for Troyes, France, where it is said to have originated) is used only for precious metals. Apothecaries' weights are based on troy weights; in addition to the pound, ounce, and grain—which are equal to the troy units of the same name—other units are the dram and the scruple. For liquid measure, or liquid capacity, the basic unit is the gallon. The U.S. gallon, or wine gallon, is 231 cubic inches (cu in.); the British imperial gallon is the volume of 10 lb of pure water at 62°F and is equal to 277.42 cu in. The British units of liquid capacity are thus about 20% larger than the corresponding American units. The U.S. bushel, or Winchester bushel, is 2,150.42 cu in. and is about 3% smaller than the British imperial bushel of 2,219.36 cu in.; a similar difference exists between U.S. and British subdivisions. The barrel is a unit for measuring the capacity of larger quantities and has various legal definitions depending on the substance being measured, the most common value being 105 dry quarts. Since the Mendenhall Order of 1893, the U.S. yard and pound and all units derived from them have been defined in terms of the metric units of length and mass, the meter (m) and the kilogram (kg); since 1959 these values are 1 yd = 0.9144 m and 1 lb = 0.45359237 kg. In the United States, the older definition of the yard as 3,600/3,937 m is still used for surveying, the corresponding foot (1,200/3,937 m) being known as the survey foot. The English units of measurement have many drawbacks: the complexity of converting from one unit to another, the differences between American and British units, the use of the same name for different units (e.g., *ounce* for both weight and liquid capacity, *quart* and *pint* for both liquid and dry capacity), and the existence of the three different systems of weights.

engraving, INTAGLIO printing process in which the lines to be printed are cut into a metal (usually copper) plate with a graver, or burin. The earliest known engravings printed on paper date from the mid-15th cent. Early master engravers include DÜRER, SCHONGAUER, and LUCAS VAN LEYDEN. During the 19th cent., steel engraving, which can produce many prints, was used to produce reproductions; it was superseded by photomechanical processes.

Eniwetok: see ENEWETAK.

enkephalin, one of several naturally occurring morphinelike substances (ENDORPHINS) in the brain.

Enlightenment, term for the rationalist, liberal, humanitarian, and scientific trend of 18th-cent. Western thought; the period is also sometimes known as the Age of Reason. The enormous scientific and intellectual advancements made in the 17th cent. by the EMPIRICISM of Francis BACON and LOCKE, as well as by DESCARTES, SPINOZA, and others, fostered the belief in NATURAL LAW and universal order, promoted a scientific approach to political and social issues, and gave rise to a sense of human progress and belief in the state as its rational instrument. Representative of the Enlightenment are such thinkers as VOLTAIRE, J.J. ROUSSEAU, MONTESQUIEU, Adam SMITH, SWIFT, HUME, KANT, G.E. LESSING, BECCARIA, and, in America, Thomas PAINE, Thomas JEFFERSON, and Benjamin FRANKLIN. The social and political ideals they presented were enforced by "enlightened despots" such as Holy Roman Emperor JOSEPH II, CATHERINE II of Russia, and FREDERICK II of Prussia. DIDEROT's *Encyclopédie* and the U.S. CONSTITUTION are representative documents of the Age of Reason.

Ennius, Quintus, 239–169? B.C., Calabrian poet, regarded by the Romans as the father of Latin poetry. He introduced quantitative hexameter and the elegiac couplet. Though he wrote in many forms, his masterpiece is the epic *Annales,* a literary history of Rome.

Enoch, in the BIBLE, father of METHUSELAH. It was said of him that he walked with God—a phrase also used of NOAH—and that, like ELIJAH, he was translated to heaven.

Ensor, James Ensor, Baron, 1860–1949, Belgian painter and etcher. Containing bizarre and powerful imagery, his early work, such as the nightmarish *Entry of Christ into Brussels* (1888), was rejected as scandalous. He produced his most inventive and original works, with weird, often gruesome compositions, until about 1900. Among his masterpieces is *The Temptation of St. Anthony* (Mus. Mod. Art, N.Y.C.). His sources included the grotesque fantasies of BOSCH and BRUEGEL. Ensor was one of the great innovators of the 19th cent.; his art opened the way for SURREALISM.

entablature, the entire unit of horizontal members above columns or pilasters in classical architecture. Its height in relation to that of the column varies with the three Greek orders: Doric, Ionic, and Corinthian. In Roman and Renaissance architecture it is about one fourth of the column height. Components are the architrave, which rests directly on the column cap, the frieze, and the cornice, or topmost member.

Entebbe, town (1991 pop. 41,638), S Uganda, on Lake VICTORIA, near KAMPALA. Founded in 1893, it was the administrative capital (1894–1962) of the British Uganda Protectorate. It is the site of a major international airport, where in 1976 Israeli airborne commandos freed the passengers held hostage on a hijacked plane.

Entente: see TRIPLE ALLIANCE AND TRIPLE ENTENTE.

enterprise zone, designated geographical district in which resident businesses are legally entitled to receive special benefits from a government, established in economically depressed areas to encourage companies to locate there. Most states enacted enterprise zone programs during the 1980s, and changes in the federal tax code in 1993 instituted tax incentives for businesses in certain locations. Typical incentives offered to attract businesses to enterprise zones include tax credits, subsidized loans, and reduced regulations. Although usually associated with urban areas, enterprise zones have also been set up in rural areas. Most enterprise zones have only been marginally successful in reviving the areas in which they are located, in part because businesses located in such zones often employ workers who live outside the area.

entomology, study of insects, an arthropod class comprising about 675,000 known species, and representing about nine tenths of all classified animal species. Insects are studied for purely biological reasons, as well as for their role as crop pollinators; carriers of viral, bacterial, fungal, and protozoal diseases; parasites of humans and livestock; destroyers of economically important plants; and predators of other destructive insects.

entrapment, instigation of a crime by a law-enforcement official in order to obtain grounds for a criminal prosecution. A person who has been induced to commit a crime in such circumstances is not regarded as criminally liable. Government undercover operations often raise questions about entrapment because the dividing line between entrapment and rightful arrest for a crime that the perpetrator was predisposed to commit may be murky.

entropy, quantity specifying the amount of disorder or randomness in a system bearing energy or information. In THERMODYNAMICS, entropy indicates the degree to which a given quantity of thermal energy is available for doing useful work—the greater the entropy, the less available the energy. According to the second law of thermodynamics, during any process the change in entropy of a system and its surroundings is either zero or positive; thus the entropy of the universe as a whole tends towards a maximum. In INFORMATION THEORY entropy represents the "noise," or random errors, occurring in the transmission of signals or messages.

environmentalism, movement to preserve the quality and continuity of life through CONSERVATION OF NATURAL RESOURCES, prevention of POLLUTION, and control of land use. U.S. conservationists began working early in the 1900s to establish state and NATIONAL PARKS, forests, and WILDLIFE REFUGES. In the decades following World War II, growing public concern about pollution problems, dwindling energy resources, and the dangers of pesticides and radiation gave rise to environmentalism—a new kind of conservationism embracing the broader concept of conserving the earth itself by protecting its capacity for self-renewal (see BIOSPHERE; ECOLOGY). The movement generated extensive legislation, notably laws regulating air quality, water quality, noise, pesticides, toxic substances, and ocean dumping; laws to protect ENDANGERED SPECIES and wilderness lands; and the National Environmental Protection Act (1970), creating the Environmental Protection Agency to develop and enforce federal standards. At the heart of the new laws was the requirement that environmental impact statements (assessments of the probable environmental consequences) be filed for all federally funded projects, and the empowering of private citizens to sue government and industry for failure to comply with governmental standards. Numerous private organizations, such as the Sierra Club, National Audubon Society, Friends of the Earth, Natural Resources Defense Council, Nature Conservancy, and Greenpeace, are actively involved in various environmental causes, from preserving the habitat of endangered species to lobbying and litigating to preserve and extend legal environmental safeguards to protesting and obstructing activities regarded as environmentally destructive. In 1992 most of the world's nations (over 150) signed two treaties on the environment: the global warming convention promotes the curbing of emissions of gases that are believed to intensify the GREENHOUSE EFFECT, and the biodiversity convention calls for protecting endangered species and sharing research, technology, and profits with nations whose plants and animals provide the genetic resources for biotechnology. The U.S. did not sign the latter treaty until 1993.

Environmental Protection Agency (EPA), independent U.S. agency in the executive branch of the government. It was established in 1970 to reduce and control air and water POLLUTION, NOISE POLLUTION, and RADIATION and to ensure safe handling and disposal of toxic substances (see WASTE DISPOSAL). The EPA engages in research, monitoring, and the setting and enforcement of national standards. It also issues statements on the impact of operations of other federal agencies that are found detrimental to environmental quality, and it supports the antipollution activities of states, municipalities, and public and private groups.

Enzina, Juan del: see ENCINA, JUAN DEL.

enzyme, protein functioning as a biological CATALYST. Enzymes accelerate (often by several orders of magnitude) chemical reactions in the cell that would proceed imperceptibly or not at all in their absence. The enzyme is not permanently modified by its participation. Most enzymes demonstrate great specificity, reacting with only one or a small group of closely related chemical compounds; several enzymes are sometimes required for efficient catalytic function. Some enzymes depend on the presence of COENZYMES for their function. For the enzyme to continue to be effective, its three-dimensional molecular structure must be maintained. Over 1,500 different enzymes have been identified, and the exact arrangement of AMINO ACIDS (subunits of a protein) has been determined for many through the technique of X-RAY CRYSTALLOGRAPHY. The molecule (substrate) that the enzyme acts upon binds to a specific site on the enzyme, so that the interactions with nearby atoms sharply reduce the energy needed to cleave and re-form the appropriate chemical bonds.

Eocene epoch: see GEOLOGIC ERA (table).

Eos, in Greek mythology, goddess of dawn. Daughter of Hyperion and Theia, she was the sister of the sun god HELIOS, and the mother of the winds. The Romans called her Aurora.

ephedrine, mild, slow-acting drug used to relieve nasal congestion from hay fever or infection of the upper respiratory tract. Nonaddictive, ephedrine may cause insomnia and restlessness.

ephemeris, table listing the positions of one or more celestial bodies for each day of the year. Early national ephemerides include the French *Connaissance des temps* (begun 1679) and the British *Nautical Almanac and Astronomical Ephemeris* (begun 1767). After 1958 the U.S. and Great Britain jointly published solar, lunar, planetary, and satellite ephemerides in identical publications, which were combined (1981) as the *Astronomical Almanac.*

Ephesians, EPISTLE of the NEW TESTAMENT, 10th book in the usual order, traditionally by St. PAUL (A.D. c.60). Some scholars believe the letter was intended as an encyclical. The most profound of the Pauline epistles, it is pervaded with the doctrine of the mystical body of Christ, Paul's analogy of the perfect union of Christians. It contains a famous metaphor of the Christian as soldier (6.10–17).

Ephesus [ĕf'əsəs], ancient Ionian Greek city of ASIA MINOR, in modern TURKEY. A wealthy seaport, it was captured in turn by Lydia, Persia, and Macedonia. It passed to Rome in 133 B.C. and was the leading city of the province of Asia. Its temple of Artemis (Diana) was one of the SEVEN WONDERS OF THE WORLD. Ephesus later became a center of Christianity and was visited by St. PAUL.

Ephraim: see ISRAEL, TRIBES OF.

epic, long, narrative poem, usually on a serious, or exalted theme, centered on a heroic figure. Early epics, e.g., the Babylonian *Gilgamesh,* HOMER's *Iliad* and *Odyssey,* and the Anglo-Saxon BEOWULF, were shaped from the legends of expanding nations. Literary epics, e.g., VERGIL's *Aeneid* and John MILTON's *Paradise Lost,* consciously imitate the earlier form. Epic conventions include a hero embodying national ideals, the performance of great deeds, the depiction of an era, divine intervention, and concern with eternal human problems. A mock epic is a satire based on an incongruous treatment of the trivial in epic terms, e.g., Alexander POPE's *Rape of the Lock.*

Epictetus, A.D. c.50–c.138, Phrygian Stoic philosopher, once a slave. His STOICISM taught that the true good is within oneself and is not dependent on external things, and he emphasized the doctrine of brotherhood. His teachings, set down by his disciple Arrian in the *Encheiridion* and *Discourses,* influenced MARCUS AURELIUS.

epic theater: see BRECHT, BERTOLT; PISCATOR, ERWIN.

Epicurus, 341–270 B.C., Greek philosopher, founder and eponym of epicureanism. He defined philosophy as the art of making life happy and subordinated METAPHYSICS to ETHICS, naming pleasure the highest and only good. For Epicurus, however, pleasure was not the heedless indulgence advocated by the followers of HEDONISM, but rather the serenity (*ataraxia*) resulting from the absence of pain. He also prescribed a code of social conduct that advocated honesty, prudence, and justice in dealing with others (because such conduct would save the individual from society's retribution, or pain). Only fragments of his writings are extant; the finest exposition of his ideas is contained in *On the Nature of Things* by the Roman poet LUCRETIUS.

Epidaurus [ĕpĭdôr'əs], ancient city of GREECE, in the NE PELOPONNESUS. It was the site of the temple of ASCLEPIUS (4th cent. B.C.), renowned for its beautiful sculpture.

epidemic: see EPIDEMIOLOGY.

epidemiology, field of medicine concerned with the study of epidemics, outbreaks of disease that affect large numbers of people. Epidemiologists, using sophisticated statistical analyses, field investigations, and complex laboratory techniques, investigate the cause of a disease, its distribution (geographic, ecological, and ethnic), method of spread, and measures for control and prevention. Epidemiological investigations once concentrated on such communicable diseases as TUBERCULOSIS, INFLUENZA, and CHOLERA, but now also encompass CANCER, HEART DISEASE, and other diseases affecting large numbers of people.

Epigoni: see SEVEN AGAINST THEBES.

epigram, short, polished saying, usually in verse, often with a satirical or paradoxical twist. Established by MARTIAL, it is particularly associated with John DONNE, Alexander POPE, Lord BYRON, and S.T. COLERIDGE. Among the most brilliant epigrammatists was Oscar WILDE, whose works are studded with epigrams, e.g., "A cynic is a man who knows the price of everything, and the value of nothing."

epilepsy, disorder resulting from rapid, uncontrolled electrical activity in one or more areas in the brain and characterized by periodic convulsive seizures. Partial, or focal, seizures involve a small area of damaged brain cells. Generalized seizures, which involve many areas of damage, include absence seizures (formerly petit mal), in which the person may appear to be daydreaming, and grand mal seizures, which last a few minutes and result in a loss of consciousness and involuntary contraction of all the muscles of the body. No organic cause can be determined for the disorder in most cases, but seizures can result from birth injury or high fever, alcohol withdrawal, tumors, and head injuries. Drug therapy includes the use of such anticonvulsants as phenytoin, phenobarbital, carbamazepine, and felbamate. Brain surgery to remove the damaged cells is most successful in infants and young children.

epinephrine or **adrenaline,** hormone secreted by the medulla of the ADRENAL GLANDS. Strong emotions, such as fear and anger, cause epinephrine to be released into the bloodstream, producing an increase in heart rate, muscle strength, blood pressure, and sugar metabolism. This reaction, often called the "fight or flight" response, prepares the body for strenuous activity. In medicine, epinephrine is used chiefly as a stimulant in cardiac arrest, as a vasoconstrictor in shock, and as a bronchodilator and antispasmodic in bronchial asthma. See also CATECHOLAMINE.

Epiphany [Gr., = showing], a prime Christian feast, celebrated Jan. 6; also called Twelfth Day or Little Christmas. It commemorates the baptism of Jesus, the visit of the Wise Men to Bethlehem, and the miracle of Cana. Its eve is Twelfth Night.

epiphyte or **air plant,** plant that grows not in the soil but on another plant, depending on it only for physical support; an epiphyte makes its own food, thus differing from a PARASITE. Epiphytes obtain moisture from the air or moisture-laden pockets of the host plant. Well-known examples are many ORCHIDS and BROMELIADS.

Epirus [ĕpī'rəs], ancient country of W GREECE, on the Ionian Sea. It reached its height in the 3d cent. B.C., under PYRRHUS. It sided with MACEDON against Rome, was sacked (167 B.C.), and passed under Roman rule. In A.D. 1204 the independent despotate of Epirus emerged, but the Turks took it over in the 15th cent. In the late 18th cent. ALI PASHA established an independent state in Epirus and Albania.

Episcopal Church, Protestant, in the United States of America, a part of the ANGLICAN COMMUNION. Anglican (Church of England) services were first held in America at Jamestown, Va., in 1607, but after the American Revolution, it was necessary for American Anglicans to organize a national church. Samuel SEABURY was consecrated (1784) as the first bishop, and the first General Convention (1789) approved the name and constitution of the church and revised the BOOK OF COMMON PRAYER for use in America. The church follows the doctrinal lines of the Anglican Communion, although the Thirty-nine Articles have been modified to fit American conditions. Since 1976 its priesthood has been open to both men and women. In 1990 church membership was 2,446,050.

epistemology, branch of philosophy dealing with the origin and nature of knowledge, a fundamental theme since the 17th cent. The rationalist view, led by DESCARTES, SPINOZA, LEIBNIZ, and others, sought to integrate a belief in the existence of certain innate ideas with an acceptance of the value of data received by experience. EMPIRICISM, expounded by HUME, LOCKE, and John Stuart MILL, denied the existence of innate ideas altogether, maintaining that all knowledge comes from human experience. KANT attempted to combine the two views. In later theories the split was reflected in IDEALISM and MATERIALISM. The empirical view has been central to PRAGMATISM, as taught by C.S. PEIRCE, William JAMES, and John DEWEY, and to the development of the modern scientific approach.

epistle, in the BIBLE, a letter of the NEW TESTAMENT. The Pauline Epistles (ascribed to St. PAUL) are ROMANS, First and Second CORINTHIANS, GALATIANS, EPHESIANS, PHILIPPIANS, COLOSSIANS, First and Second THESSALONIANS, First and Second TIMOTHY, TITUS, PHILEMON, and HEBREWS. JAMES, First and Second PETER, First, Second, and Third JOHN, and JUDE are traditionally called Catholic, or General, Epistles.

Epsom salts, a water-soluble, bitter-tasting compound ($MgSO_4{\cdot}7H_2O$) that occurs as white or colorless needle-shaped crystals. It is used as a medicinal purgative, in leather tanning, in mordant dyeing, and as a filler in cotton goods and paper. It is found in waters of mineral springs and as the mineral epsomite.

Epstein, Sir Jacob, 1880–1959, English sculptor; b. N.Y.C. After studying with RODIN in Paris, he revolted against the ornate and pretty in art, producing bold, often harsh and massive forms in stone and bronze. His best-known pieces include the Oscar Wilde Memorial (1911; Père-Lachaise, Paris), a marble *Venus* (1917; Yale Univ., New Haven, Conn.), and a *Madonna and Child* (Convent of the Holy Child Jesus, London).

Epstein-Barr virus (EBV), herpes virus that is the major cause of infectious MONONUCLEOSIS and is associated with a number of cancers, particularly lymphomas in immunosuppressed persons, including persons with AIDS. EBV affects certain salivary gland cells and white blood cells (lymphocytes) called B cells (see IMMUNITY).

Equal Employment Opportunity Commission (EEOC), U.S. agency created (1964) to end discrimination in hiring based on race, color, religion, sex, national origin, age, or disability, and to promote equal employment opportunities. If its attempts at persuasion fail to remedy unlawful practices, it is empowered to bring suit against offenders in federal court.

Equal Pay Act, U.S. law passed (1963) as an amendment to the WAGES AND HOURS ACT which prohibits discrimination based on sex that results in unequal pay for equal work.

Equal Rights Amendment: see CIVIL RIGHTS; FEMINISM.

equation, a statement, usually in symbols, that two quantities or mathematical expressions are equal, e.g., $x + 3 = 6 - y$ or $\sin^2 = 1 - \cos^2$. A numerical equation contains only numbers, e.g., $2 + 3 = 6 - 1$; a literal equation contains some letters, representing unknowns or variables. An identity is an equation that is true no matter what value is substituted for the variables, such as $x^2 - 1 = (x - 1)(x + 1)$; a conditional equation is true for only certain substitutions, e.g., only the values $+1$ and -1 make true the equation $x^2 - 1 = 0$. See also ALGEBRA.

equation of time: see SOLAR TIME.

equator, imaginary great circle around the earth, equidistant from the two geographical poles and forming the base line from which LATITUDE is reckoned. Measuring c.24,000 mi (38,600 km), the equator intersects N South America, central Africa, and Indonesia. See also ASTRONOMICAL COORDINATE SYSTEMS.

Equatorial Guinea [gĭn'ē], officially Republic of Equatorial Guinea, republic (1992 est. pop. 389,000), 10,830 sq mi (28,051 sq km), W central Africa, comprising a mainland section, Río Muni, bordered by Cameroon (N), Gabon (E and S), and the Gulf of Guinea (W); and several islands, the most important of which is Bioko (formerly Fernando Po), in the Gulf of Guinea. MALABO, on Bioko, is the capital. Río Muni, with 93% of the nation's land and 75% of the population, comprises a low-lying coastal area that rises in the interior to c.3,600 ft (1,100 m); forests of okoume, mahogany, and walnut grow along the coast. Bioko is made up of three extinct volcanoes, the loftiest of which rises to c.9,870 ft (3,010 m); the island has abundant fertile volcanic soil. The economy of Equatorial Guinea is almost exclusively agricultural. Cacao (from Bioko) and coffee and timber (from Río Muni) are the principal cash crops, but the harvest has steadily decreased since independence. Ethnically, the population is largely Fang in Río Muni, where 75% of the population lives, and Bubi on Bioko. Most of the people speak a Bantu language. Traditional religions and Roman Catholicism are both practiced.

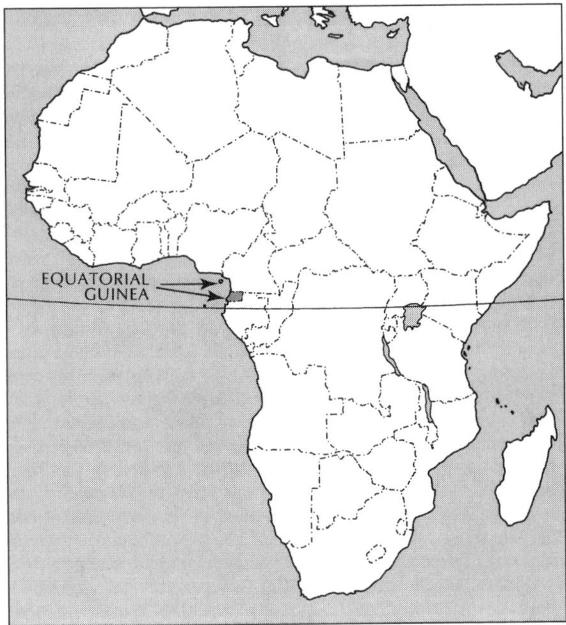

History. The island now called Bioko was discovered by Fernão do Po, a Portuguese navigator, in 1472, but Portugal ceded it to Spain in 1778. Spain formally acquired Río Muni in 1885. The boundaries of the possession were defined in a 1900 treaty, and Bioko and Río Muni, as well as several other islands, were grouped together as Spanish Guinea. In 1968 nationalist demands led to limited autonomy and then full independence (1973). The first president, Francisco Macias Nguema, imposed a brutal and despotic rule over the new nation; by the late 1970s thousands of refugees had fled the country, and the economy was virtually ruined. In 1979 a military coup led by Lt. Col. Teodoro Obiang Nguema Mbasoga overthrew Macias, who was executed, and Obiang Nguema became president. A one-party state was established in 1987, and in 1989 Obiang Nguema was elected to the presidency. Under pressure he permitted multiparty parliamentary elections in 1993, but unfair electoral laws led the major opposition parties to boycott the poll.

equestrianism, art of riding and handling a horse. Riding as a skilled sport developed in medieval times and now includes diverse styles. Horse shows, which originated (1864) in Ireland, test skills in such events as hunting, jumping, and dressage. Equestrian competition is part of the Olympics.

equilibrium: see STATICS.

equinox, either of two points on the celestial sphere where the ECLIPTIC and the celestial equator intersect (see ASTRONOMICAL COORDINATE SYSTEMS). The vernal equinox is the point at which the sun appears to cross the celestial equator from south to north; the autumnal equinox, the point where it appears to cross from north to south. These crossings occur about March 21 and September 23 and mark the beginnings of Northern Hemisphere spring and autumn. On either date night and day are of equal length (12 hr each) in all parts of the world. The equinoxes are not fixed points, but move westward along the ecliptic (see PRECESSION OF THE EQUINOXES).

equisetophyte, member of a division (Equisetophyta or Sphenophyta) of the plant kingdom consisting of the HORSETAILS and scouring rushes. The surviving genus, *Equisetum,* is descended from tree-sized fossil plants.

equity, body of legal principles and rules developed in the English Court of Chancery from the 15th cent. to correct injustices caused by the rigidity and formalism of COMMON LAW. It implies application of the standard of what seems naturally just and right rather than the strict rules of law. However, equity law gradually built its own rigid body of precedent, and today the distinction between equity and common law is much diminished.

Er, chemical symbol of the element ERBIUM.

era of good feelings, period (1817–23) in U.S. history after the decline of the FEDERALIST PARTY when there was little open party feeling. The term was coined during Pres. MONROE's goodwill tour of the North. Under the surface, however, vast sectional issues and personal rivalries were developing and broke loose in the campaign of 1824.

Erasistratus, fl. 3d cent. B.C., Greek physician. Leader of a school of medicine in Alexandria, his works were influential until the 4th cent. A.D. He suggested that air carried from the lungs to the heart is converted into a vital spirit distributed by the arteries, and he also developed a reverse theory of circulation (veins to arteries). He studied brain convolutions, named the trachea, distinguished between motor and sensory nerves, and considered plethora (hyperemia) to be the primary cause of disease.

Erasmus or **Desiderius Erasmus,** 1466?–1536, Dutch humanist. One of the great figures of the RENAISSANCE, he taught throughout Europe, influencing European letters profoundly from 1500. An ordained priest of the Roman Catholic Church, he edited the Latin and Greek classics and the writings of the Fathers of the Church, and made a Latin translation of the New Testament based on the original Greek. Among his original, satirical works, written in Latin, are *In Praise of Folly* (1509) and *The Education of a Christian Prince* (1515). He was intimate with most of the scholars of Europe; his English friends included HENRY VIII and Thomas MORE. Erasmus combined vast learning with a fine style, keen humor, moderation, and tolerance. He championed church reform but opposed the Protestant Reformation and remained a loyal Catholic. As a result, he and Martin LUTHER became bitter opponents, and in *On the Freedom of the Will* he denounced Luther's position on predestination.

Erastus, Thomas, 1524–83, Swiss Protestant theologian, originally named Lüber, Lieber, or Liebler. He opposed Calvinist doctrine and the punitive power of the church. The term **Erastianism** has come to represent approval of the dominance of civil authority in punitive matters and, by extension, complete dominance of state over church.

Erato: see MUSES.

Eratosthenes, c.275–c.195 B.C., Greek scholar. The author of works on literature, mathematics, astronomy, geography, and philosophy, he devised a world map and a system of chronology and measured the earth's circumference and tilt and the size and distance from earth of the sun and moon.

erbium (Er), metallic element, discovered by Carl G. Mosander in 1843 in the mineral gadolinite. A silvery, malleable RARE-EARTH METAL, erbium is in the LANTHANIDE SERIES. The rose-colored oxide erbia is used as a coloring agent in glazes and glass. See ELEMENT (table); PERIODIC TABLE.

Ercilla y Zúñiga, Alonso de [ärthē'lyä ē thōō'nyēgä], 1533–94, Spanish poet. His *La Araucana* (1569–89), about the conquest of the ARAUCANIANS of Chile (in which he took part), is the finest EPIC of the Spanish GOLDEN AGE.

Erechtheum, temple on the Acropolis, Athens, a masterpiece of Greek architecture. Built between c.421 B.C. and 405 B.C., it is sometimes ascribed to the architect MNESICLES. It contained sanctuaries to Athena, Poseidon, and the Athenian king Erechtheus. Of the Ionic order, the temple has three porticos; the southern one is the famous Porch of the CARYATIDS.

Erenburg, Ilya Grigoryevich: see EHRENBURG.

erg: see WORK.

ergonomics, engineering science concerned with the physical and psychological relationship between machines and people who use them. The ergonomicist assesses these interactions and attempts to improve efficiency and reduce strain and discomfort. Applications include the design of automobile interiors and the placement of machine switches and gauges.

ergot, disease of rye and other cereals caused by a fungus (*Claviceps purpurea*), which appears on heads of rye as dark purple structures called ergots. The ergots, which resemble rye seeds, contain certain active substances (ALKALOIDS) that are poisonous—ergot poisoning was epidemic in the Middle Ages, for example, because bread was often made from ergot-contaminated rye. The ergots also contain alkaloids used as drugs, e.g., ergotamine to treat migraine headaches and ergonovine to stop postpartum uterine bleeding.

Ericsson, Leif: see LEIF ERICSSON.

Eric the Red, fl. 10th cent., Norse chieftain; discoverer and colonizer of Greenland. He discovered Greenland c.982 and led (c.986) a group of 500 colonists there, founding Brattah-lid. The colony may have lasted four or five centuries.

Erie, city (1990 pop. 108,718), seat of Erie co., NW Pa., on Lake Erie; inc. as a city 1851. Pennsylvania's only GREAT LAKES port, it is a shipping point for coal, iron, and other products. Its manufactures include machinery and plastics. Laid out in 1795 on the site of a French fort, it was the launching point of the American fleet in the battle of Lake Erie (1813), during the WAR OF 1812. There are several colleges in the city.

Erie, Lake, fourth largest (9,940 sq mi/25,745 sq km) of the GREAT LAKES, separating Canada (at Ontario) and the U.S. (at New York). It is 241 mi (388 km) long, 30–57 mi (48–92 km) wide, 572 ft (174 m) above sea level, and up to 210 ft (64 m) deep. Discharge of municipal and industrial wastes from lakeside cities polluted the lake and was banned in 1972; the lake has recovered somewhat. Lake Erie was discovered by JOLLIET in 1669. British and French and, later, British and Americans fought for its control in the 18th and 19th cent.

Erie Canal, historic artificial waterway (opened 1825) between Lake Erie and the Hudson R., providing a link between the Atlantic Ocean and the Great Lakes. Its use declined after 1850 as traffic was diverted to the railroads. It was replaced (1918) by the larger New York State Barge Canal, which follows part of its course.

Erikson, Erik, 1902–, Danish-American psychoanalyst; b. Germany. He became a MONTESSORI teacher in Vienna after 1927 and trained under Sigmund and Anna FREUD, specializing in child analysis. After emigrating to the U.S. (1933), he became engaged in varied clinical work, widening the scope of psychoanalytic theory to take greater account of social, cultural, and other environmental factors. In his most influential book, *Childhood and Society* (1950), he divided the human life cycle into eight psychosexual stages of development. His famous psychohistorical studies, *Young Man Luther* (1958) and *Gandhi's Truth* (1969), explore the convergence of personal and social history.

Erinyes: see FURIES.

Eritrea [ĕrĭtrē'ə], officially State of Eritrea, republic (1993 est. pop. 3,000,000), c.48,000 sq mi (124,320 sq km), NE Africa, bordered by the Red Sea (NE), Djibouti (SE), Ethiopia (S), and Sudan (NW). It gained its independence in 1993, having been federated (1952) with and then annexed (1962) by Ethiopia. ASMARA is the capital. Eritrea is an arid coastal strip (30 mi/50 km wide) in the southeast; this narrows in the northwest, where it is bounded by the steep rise of the rugged central plateau. Most of Eritrea is sparsely populated by pastoral nomads, but there is settled agriculture in valleys of the central plateau to the north. The Red Sea ports of Assab (Aseb) and Massawa (Mesewa) are important to neighboring Ethiopia's economy. Products include citrus fruits, cereal grains, and cotton. There is little industry beyond food processing. Eritrea has deposits of gold, copper, potash, and iron ore. Eritreans are ethnically related to the inhabitants of N Ethiopia and speak Tigrinya, Arabic, and several other languages. Coptic Christianity and Islam are the main religions.

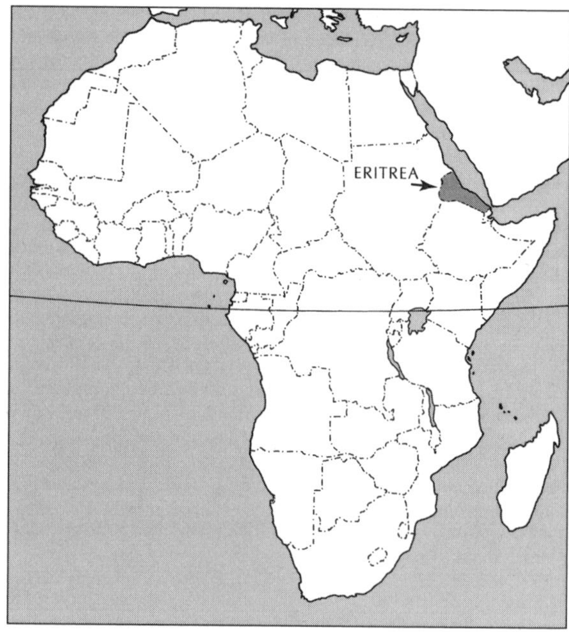

History. Eritrea was part of the ancient Ethiopian kingdom of Aksum until the 7th cent. Thereafter Ethiopian emperors maintained an intermittent presence in the area until the mid-16th cent., when the Ottoman Empire won much of the coast. In the 1880s Italy occupied the coastal areas around Assab and Massawa. Eritrea became an Italian colony in 1890 and was the main base for Italy's invasion of Ethiopia (1935–36); it was captured by the British in 1941. It was federated to Ethiopia by the UN in 1952, and in 1962 it was annexed by Ethiopia. Secessionist movements sought to end the union, and through 1970s and 80s Eritrean guerrillas fought Ethiopian forces, eventually controlling most of the countryside. In 1991 they succeeded in capturing Asmara and the ports, giving them control of Eritrea. The long war devastated many parts of the country. In 1993 Eritreans overwhelmingly voted for independence, and former guerrilla leader Isaias Aferwerki became its first president.

ermine, northern WEASEL species (*Mustela erminea*), called short-tailed weasel in North America and stoat in the Old World. Its highly-prized white winter fur is used for coats, wraps, and trimmings.

Ernst, Max, 1891–1976, German painter. A member of the DADA movement and a founder of SURREALISM, he developed several devices to express his fantastic vision. Some of his landscapes are dreamlike and whimsical, while other works reveal a satanic, allegorical imagination. *Two Children Are Threatened by a Nightingale* is in the Museum of Modern Art (N.Y.C.).

Eros, in Greek mythology, god of love in all its manifestations. According to some legends, he was one of the oldest of the gods, born from CHAOS but personifying harmony. In most stories he was the son of APHRODITE and ARES and was represented as a winged youth armed with bow and arrows. In Roman myth, under the name Cupid or Amor, he was the naked infant son and companion of VENUS.

erosion, general term for the processes by which the surface of the earth is constantly worn away, principally by the abrasive action of running water, waves, GLACIERS, and wind. Streams and ocean waves, for example, erode bedrock by their own impact or by the abrasive action of the debris they carry. Rock surfaces are eroded by glaciers moving over them or by wind driving sand and other particles against them. In the U.S. the washing away of farmland topsoil is a problem. Erosion is also caused by strip mining and the removal of vast areas of plant cover, e.g., by careless land developers. Some methods of preventing soil erosion are reforestation, terracing, and special plowing techniques.

Erskine, Thomas, 1st **Baron Erskine,** 1750–1823, British jurist. Earlier a noted commercial lawyer, Erskine is best known as a defender of radicals at the time of the French Revolution. He defended Thomas PAINE's publication of *The Rights of Man* against a charge of sedition.

Ervin, Samuel James, 1896–1985, U.S. senator from North Carolina (1954–74); b. Morgantown, N.C. A distinguished jurist, he served (1948–54) on the North Carolina supreme court. As a Senate Democrat he favored a large defense establishment and opposed civil-rights legislation. He later became a constitutional expert and a civil libertarian. He gained national attention (1973–74) as chairman of the Senate hearings that probed the WATERGATE AFFAIR.

Erving, Julius, 1950–, African-American basketball player, nicknamed "Dr. J."; b. Roosevelt, N.Y. Playing for the ABA's Virginia Squires (1971–73) and New York Nets (1973–76), and the NBA's Philadelphia 76ers (1976–87), he excelled as a shooter, rebounder, and ball-handler. He led the ABA in scoring three times (1973–74, 1976) and was named most valuable player four times (ABA, 1974–76; NBA, 1981). With 30,026 career points (in the ABA and NBA combined), he ranks third on the all-time scoring list.

Es, chemical symbol of the element EINSTEINIUM.

Esaias, variant of ISAIAH.

Esau [ē'sô], in the BIBLE, son of ISAAC. He sold his birthright for pottage to his younger twin, JACOB, who also tricked him out of their father's blessing. Also known as Edom, Esau was the ancestor of the Edomites, a tribe consistently hostile to the Jews.

escape velocity, the velocity that a body must be given in order to escape the gravitational hold of some other larger body, e.g., the earth, moon, or sun. Escape velocity depends on the mass of the larger body and the distance of the smaller body from its center. The escape velocity from the earth's surface is about 7 mi/sec (11.3 km/sec).

escarole: see CHICORY.

Eschenbach, Wolfram von: see WOLFRAM VON ESCHENBACH.

M.C. Escher lithograph Convex and Concave, 1955

Escher, Maurits Corneille [ĕsh'ər], 1898–1970, Dutch artist. Primarily a graphic artist, he composed ironic works, often visual riddles that play with the pictorially logical and the visually impossible.

Escherichia coli or **E. coli,** common bacterium that normally inhabits the intestinal tracts of humans and animals but can cause infection in other parts of the body, especially the urinary tract. One strain, sometimes transmitted in hamburger meat, can cause serious infection resulting in diarrhea, anemia, kidney failure, and death. *E. coli* is widely used in laboratory research, especially in GENETIC ENGINEERING.

Escondido [ĕskəndē'dō], city (1990 pop. 108,635), San Diego co., S Calif.; inc. 1888. One of the fastest-growing U.S. cities, it is located in an agricultural valley. Fruit packing and avocado processing are important; manufactures include cereal products, textiles, and ink. A huge wild animal park is to the south.

Escorial or **Escurial,** monastery and palace in central Spain, near Madrid. It was built (1563–84) by PHILIP II to commemorate a victory over the French. A somber, massive granite pile, it includes a monastery, church, palace, mausoleum, college, and library. Designed by Juan Bautista de Toledo and Juan de Herrera, it has a famous art collection.

Esdraelon [ĕs"drəē'lən], plain, N Israel, c.200 sq mi (520 sq km), extending SE c.25 mi (40 km) between the coastal plain near Mt. Carmel and the Jordan R. valley. Once a swampy, malarial lowland, it has been drained and turned into one of Israel's most fertile and densely populated regions. Esdraelon is also called the plain of Jezreel or of Megiddo.

Esdras, two pseudepigraphic texts included in the Western canon and the Septuagint but placed in the APOCRYPHA in the Authorized Version, where they are called First and Second Esdras. The Western canon calls EZRA and Nehemiah First and Second Esdras, respectively, and the terms Third and Fourth Esdras are then used for the pseudepigraphic books. These are a series of apocalyptic visions and revelations to Ezra. Third Esdras antedates 100 B.C.; most critics date Fourth Esdras, as a whole, after A.D. 100.

Esfahan or **Isfahan,** city (1986 pop. 986,753), central Iran, on the Zayandeh R. Esfahan has long been known for its fine carpets, hand-printed textiles, and metalwork. Industrial products include steel and refined oil. Noteworthy from SASSANID times, it reached the height of its glory under Persian Shah ABBAS I, who made it his capital in 1598 and embellished it with many fine buildings, e.g., the beautiful imperial mosque, the Lutfullah mosque, and the royal palace. The city declined after its capture (1723) by the Afghans.

Eshkol, Levi, 1895–1969, Israeli statesman; b. Ukraine as Levi Shkolnik. A leader in the General Federation of Jewish Labor and the Mapai party, he served in David BEN-GURION's cabinet as minister of finance from 1952 to 1963, when he became prime minister. He led Israel in the Six-Day War (1967) and died in office. See also ARAB-ISRAELI WARS.

esker, long (up to many miles), narrow, winding ridge of stratified sand-and-gravel DRIFT, deposited in the beds of streams flowing through or beneath GLACIERS. Eskers occur in Scandinavia, Ireland, Scotland, and New England.

Eskimo, Algonquian and European name for the native inhabitants of the coast from the Bering Sea to Greenland and of the Chukchi Peninsula, in NE Siberia. Since the 1970s the Eskimo of Canada and Greenland have adopted the name **Inuit.** The Eskimo have remained largely of pure stock and, despite their wide dispersal, are extremely uniform in language (dialects of Eskimo-Aleut), physical type (Mongolic), and culture. Probably of Asian origin, Eskimos first appeared in Greenland in the 13th cent. Before the 20th cent. they lived in small bands, and almost all property was communal. Adapted to a severe environment, they got food, clothing, oil, tools, and weapons from sea mammals. Fish and CARIBOU were also important. Summer shelters were tents of caribou or seal skins, while cold-weather shelters were built of sod, wood, or stone; the igloo, or snow hut, was seldom used. Travel was by dogsled or kayak. Most Eskimos now live in modern settlements and use guns for hunting and snowmobiles for travel. The Eskimos' traditional animist religion has a rich mythology, and their art, which includes soapstone, ivory, and bone carvings, is skillfully rendered and well developed (see ESKIMO ART).

Eskimo-Aleut, language family consisting of Aleut (spoken on the Aleutian Islands) and Eskimo (spoken in Alaska, Canada, Greenland, and Siberia). See NATIVE AMERICAN LANGUAGES (table).

Eskimo art. The art of the Eskimo peoples arose some 2,000 years ago in the Bering Sea area and in Canada. Traditional art consisted of small utilitarian objects, such as weapons and tools, as well as diminutive animals, carved and incised in walrus ivory, bone, and stone. The subjects of Eskimo art reflected their lives as hunters and fishermen, as well as their extensive mythology. Carved and painted wooden masks of the 19th cent. were used in various rituals. Modern Eskimo art dates from the late 1940s, when Canadians encouraged the development of art by native craftsmen working in traditional modes. Contemporary Eskimo art consists mainly of carved figures in smooth soapstone, ivory, and rough-surfaced whalebone, and lithographs printed with local stone that simplify and abstract the forms of the Eskimo hunters and their quarry.

ESP: see EXTRASENSORY PERCEPTION.

Esperanto: see INTERNATIONAL LANGUAGE.

Espinel, Vicente Martínez [äspēnĕl′], 1550–1624, Spanish novelist, poet, and musician of the GOLDEN AGE. He helped popularize the guitar and may have added its fifth string. His major work is the picaresque, semiautobiographical novel *History of the Life of the Squire Marcos of Obregón* (1618), the source of much of LE SAGE's *Gil Blas.*

espionage: see under INTELLIGENCE GATHERING.

essay, relatively short literary composition in prose in which the writer discusses a topic or tries to persuade the reader to accept a point of view. PLUTARCH and CICERO, among classical authors, wrote essays, but the term was first used by MONTAIGNE (1580) and Francis BACON (1597), two of the greatest essayists. The informal essay is personal, conversational, relaxed, and, frequently, humorous. Charles LAMB, William HAZLITT, and Mark TWAIN are among its masters. The formal essay, as written by Joseph ADDISON, Matthew ARNOLD, John Stuart MILL, Walter PATER, and others, is dogmatic, systematic, and expository. In the latter half of the 20th cent. the two styles of essays have tended to converge in a genre that has become more diversified in subject and conversational in tone. The magazine has been a chief vehicle for the dissemination of contemporary essays.

Essen, city (1987 pop. 620,594), North Rhine–Westphalia, W Germany, on the Ruhr R. An industrial center of the RUHR district, it was the site of the KRUPP steel works and is Germany's chief producer of electricity. The city grew up around a 9th-cent. Benedictine convent and was a small imperial state until it passed (1802) to Prussia. Badly damaged during WORLD WAR II, it was rebuilt after 1945. Landmarks include the cathedral (9th–14th cent.).

essential oils, volatile oils that occur in plants and in general give the plants their characteristic odors, flavors, or other such properties. Generally complex mixtures of organic compounds, they are used in perfumes, flavorings, and medicines. Among the plants notable for their essential oils are members of the following plant families: CARROT (e.g., ANISE, DILL, angelica), GINGER (cardamom), LAUREL (CINNAMON, CAMPHOR), MINT (peppermint, THYME), MYRTLE (CLOVE), and ORCHID (VANILLA). See also FATS AND OILS.

Essex, Robert Devereux, 2d **earl of** [dĕv′ərōō], 1567–1601, English courtier. After distinguishing himself as a cavalry officer in the Netherlands (1585–86), serving under his stepfather, the earl of LEICESTER, he became a favorite of ELIZABETH I and a rival of Sir Walter RALEIGH. In 1590 he angered the queen by his secret marriage to the young widow of Sir Philip SIDNEY. Advised by Francis BACON, he entered politics, hoping to seize power from the aging Lord BURGHLEY, but Elizabeth conferred power on Burghley's son, Robert Cecil, instead. On his own demand, Essex was sent to Ireland as lord lieutenant. There, he failed to quell the rebellion of the earl of Tyrone. On his return he was confined and later banned from court. He attempted a coup to establish his own party around the queen, but it failed and he was arrested. Elizabeth signed the warrant for his execution.

Essex, one of the kingdoms of Anglo-Saxon England. Probably settled by Saxons in the early 6th cent., Essex eventually approximated in size the modern counties of Essex, London, and Hertfordshire. King Sæbert of Essex accepted Christianity c.604, but the kingdom lapsed for a time into heathenism. Long dominated by MERCIA, Essex submitted (825) to WESSEX and became an earldom. It became part of the DANELAW in 886 but was retaken (917) by Edward the Elder of Wessex.

estate tax: see INHERITANCE TAX.

Estates-General: see STATES-GENERAL.

Este [ĕs′tā], Italian noble family, rulers of Ferrara (1240–1597) and of Modena (1288–1796), celebrated patrons of the arts. **Azzo d'Este II,** 996–1097, founded the family's greatness, and acquired Milan. His son, **Guelph d'Este IV,** d. 1101, founded the German line of GUELPHS. Among the Italian branch, **Azzo d'Este VII,** 1205–64, became (1240) chief magistrate of Ferrara. **Obizzo d'Este II,** d. 1293, was made perpetual lord of Ferrara (1264) and lord of Modena (1288). **Beatrice d'Este,** 1475–97, married Ludovico SFORZA; her sister **Isabella d'Este,** 1474–1539, was an important patron of Renaissance art. **Alfonso d'Este I,** 1476–1534, second husband of Lucrezia BORGIA (see BORGIA, family), fought for France in the Italian Wars (1494–1559). Pope JULIUS II declared (1510) his fiefs forfeited, but Alfonso aided Holy Roman Emperor CHARLES V against Pope CLEMENT VII, who was forced to recognize (1530) Alfonso's claims. His brother, **Ippolito I, Cardinal d'Este,** 1479–1520, was a patron of ARIOSTO. Alfonso's son, **Ippolito II, Cardinal d'Este,** 1509–72, built the Villa d'Este at Tivoli. In 1597 the direct male line died out and Pope CLEMENT VIII annexed (1598) Ferrara to the papal states. Another branch ruled Modena until deposed (1796) by the French.

Esterházy [ĕs′tĕrhä″zē], princely Hungarian family. **Paul, Fürst Esterházy von Galantha,** 1635–1713, took part in the defense of Vienna (1683) and the reconquest of Hungary from the Turks. His grandson, **Nikolaus Joseph, Fürst Esterházy von Galantha,** 1714–90, made (1766) F.J. HAYDN chief musical director at Eisenstadt and built the celebrated Esterházy palace there. His nephew, **Nikolaus, Fürst Esterházy von Galantha,** 1765–1833, was offered (1809) the crown of Hungary by NAPOLEON I but refused it.

Estes, Richard, 1936–, American painter; b. Evanston, Ill. One of the best-known American exponents of PHOTOREALISM, Estes is noted for his street scenes.

Esther, book of the OLD TESTAMENT, 17th in the Authorized Version. It is the story of the beautiful Jewish woman Esther (Hadassah), chosen as queen by the Persian king Ahasuerus after he has repudiated his previous wife, Vashti. Esther and her cousin Mordecai thwart the courtier Haman, who plots to massacre the Jews; Haman is hanged, and Mordecai becomes the king's chief minister. The feast of Purim (see JEWISH HOLIDAYS) celebrates this event. The historicity of the book is in question.

Estonia, Estonian *Eesti,* officially Republic of Estonia, republic (1992 est. pop. 1,607,000), 17,413 sq mi (45,100 sq km), N central Europe, from 1940 to 1991 a constituent republic of the USSR. It borders on the Baltic Sea (W); the gulfs of Riga and Finland (SW and N); Latvia (S); and Russia (E). The capital and largest city is TALLINN. Other important cities include Tartu and Narva. Industrial products include shale oil and gas, paper, and fertilizer. Fishing and farming are important. In addition to the Estonian majority, there are significant Russian and other minorities; Russians are the

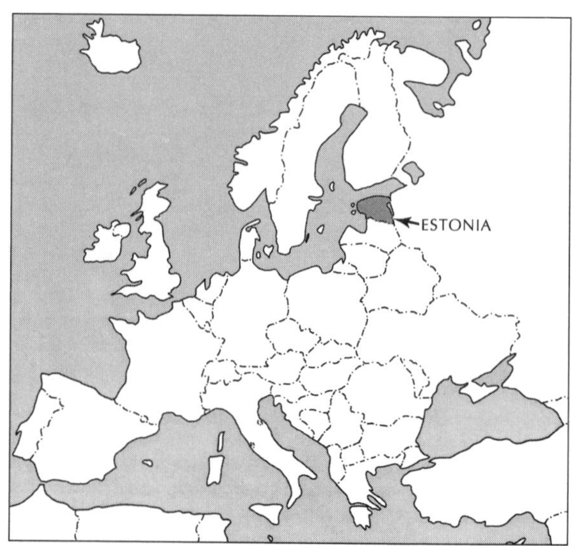

majority in NE Estonia. Estonian is the official language, and the dominant religion is evangelical Lutheranism. Since independence citizenship has generally been limited to ethnic Estonians, a practice widely criticized because it denies political and civil rights to the many Russian-speaking inhabitants.

History. The Estonians, ethnically and linguistically close to the Finns, settled the region before the 1st cent. A.D. Between the 13th and 18th cent. it was ruled in succession by Denmark, the Livonian Knights, Sweden, and Russia. Independent after 1920, it was forcibly annexed by the USSR in 1940 and was under German occupation from 1941 to 1944. Following World War II it was returned to Soviet control. In 1990 the Estonian parliament declared the Soviet annexation invalid and announced a transitional period leading to independence from the USSR. During the attempted hard-line coup against Soviet Pres. GORBACHEV, Estonia declared its immediate independence from the USSR, a status subsequently recognized by the Soviet government. In 1992 a new constitution was ratified and Lennart Meri was elected president. In 1993 Estonia signed a free-trade agreement with Latvia and Lithuania.

estrogen, any of a group of hormones produced chiefly in females by the reproductive organs and ADRENAL GLANDS. Estrogens are important in the regulation of the menstrual cycle (see MENSTRUATION) and in the development of secondary sex characteristics (pubic hair and breasts). In other animals, cyclical estrogen secretion induces estrus, or "heat." The ability of estrogens to suppress ovulation makes them major components in oral contraceptives. Estrogen replacement therapy is used to treat severe symptoms of menopause and retard OSTEOPOROSIS.

estuary, partly enclosed coastal body of water open to the ocean, so that fresh and salt water are mixed. Estuaries are extremely sensitive and ecologically important habitats, providing waterfowl sanctuaries and breeding and feeding grounds for many desirable life forms. They are often excellent harbors, and most large U.S. ports are located in them. The human impact on estuaries (e.g., landfill, sewage pollution, industrial effluents) can destroy the very properties of the estuary that facilitated development of the region.

etching, INTAGLIO process and the print produced from it. A metal plate, usually copper or zinc, is coated with a ground of acid-resistant resin or wax. The design is drawn on the ground with a needle, exposing the metal. Then the plate is submerged in acid, cutting into the exposed lines. The plate is removed frequently, and lines that are sufficiently deep are coated with varnish; others remain longer and produce darker, heavier lines when printed. In printing, the varnish is removed and the plate is warmed, coated with ink, wiped so that ink remains only in the grooves, covered with moist paper, and run through a press. Artists often alter etching plates, and several states of a work may exist. The plates have a finite life before their lines lose sharpness; many artists limit the number of prints and destroy the used plate. The art of etching evolved from ENGRAVING; both apparently originated in Germany. Among the foremost etchers are DÜRER, CALLOT, REMBRANDT, TIEPOLO, PIRANESI, GOYA, and WHISTLER.

Eteocles: see SEVEN AGAINST THEBES.

ethanol or **ethyl alcohol** (CH_3CH_2OH), a colorless liquid with characteristic odor and taste, commonly called grain alcohol or, simply, ALCOHOL. Ordinary ethanol is about 95% pure, the remaining 5% being water, which can only be removed with difficulty to give pure or absolute ethanol. Ethanol is the alcohol in beer, wine, and liquor and can be made by the FERMENTATION of sugar or starch. Denatured alcohol, for industrial use, is ethanol with toxic additives. Ethanol is used as a solvent in the manufacture of varnishes and perfumes; as a preservative; in medicines; as a disinfectant; and as a fuel and fuel additive. Ethanol is a soporific; if its presence in the blood exceeds about 5%, death usually occurs. Behavioral changes, impairment of vision, or unconsciousness occur at lower concentrations. See ALCOHOLISM.

Ethelfleda: see ÆTHELFLÆD.

ether or **aether,** in physics, a hypothetical medium for transmitting ELECTROMAGNETIC RADIATION, filling all unoccupied space. The theory of RELATIVITY eliminated the need for such a medium, and the term is used only in a historical context.

Etherege, Sir George, 1634?–1691, English dramatist. His witty *Comical Revenge; or, Love in a Tub* (1664) and *She Wou'd If She Cou'd* (1668) set the tone for the RESTORATION comedy of manners.

Ethical Culture movement, originating in the Society for Ethical Culture, founded (1876) in N.Y.C. by Felix ADLER. It stresses the ethical factor in all relations of life but insists on no definite ethical system. The society holds religious services, but members may also have other religious affiliations. The movement spread (1887) to England. In 1896 the International Union of Ethical Societies was formed.

ethics, in philosophy, the study and evaluation of human conduct in the light of moral principles, which may be viewed as the individual's standard of conduct or as a body of social obligations and duties. Theories of conscience have ascribed the moral awareness of right and wrong to divine will; to an innate sense (e.g., J.J. ROUSSEAU); or to the set of values derived from individual experience (e.g., LOCKE and MILL). Idealists such as PLATO have contended that there is an absolute good to which human activities aspire. Moral codes have frequently been based on religious absolutes, but KANT's categorical imperative attempted to set up an ethical criterion independent of theological consideration. The source of an ethical criterion has been variously equated with religion, the state (e.g., HEGEL and MARX), or the good of the individual or a group (as in the HEDONISM of EPICURUS; HOBBES; and the UTILITARIANISM of BENTHAM). Modern ethical theories include the instrumentalism of John DEWEY, for whom morality is relative to individual experience; and the intuitionism of G.E. MOORE, who postulated an immediate awareness of the morally good. More recently, Alasdair MacIntyre has cautioned against unbridled individualism and drawn on ARISTOTLE's notion of moral virtue as the mean between extremes, and Thomas Nagel has held that reason supersedes desire in moral decision making and that it is rational to choose altruism over narrow self-interest.

Ethiopia, republic (1993 est. pop. 51,000,000), 471,776 sq mi (1,221,900 sq km), NE Africa, formerly known as Abyssinia, bordered by Eritrea (N), Djibouti (NE), Somalia (E and SE), Kenya (S), and Sudan (W). ADDIS ABABA is the capital. Ethiopia may be divided into four geographic zones: from west to east they are the Ethiopian Plateau, a highland region including more than half the country and reaching a height of 15,158 ft (4,620 m) at Ras Dashan; the GREAT RIFT VALLEY, containing the Danakil Desert and several large lakes; the Somali Plateau, with heights of more than 14,000 ft (4,267 m) in the Urgoma Mts.; and the Ogaden Plateau, which is mostly desert. The Blue NILE (called the Abbai in Ethiopia) flows through the center of the Ethiopian Plateau from its source, Lake Tana, Ethiopia's largest lake. The economy is almost entirely agricultural, with most of the labor force engaged in subsistence farming. Coffee accounts for 60% of export earnings; other leading exports are oilseeds, hides and skins, and grain. Industry is limited to production of basic consumer needs. Some minerals are extracted on a small scale. Ethiopia's peoples are ethnically diverse and geographically separated. The Amhara and Tigréans (33% combined) of central and northern Ethiopia, who are Coptic Christians, are politically dominant. The largely Muslim OROMO, who live in the south and constitute about 40% of the population, are the largest ethnic group; there are also significant numbers of mainly Muslim Somalis in the east and southeast. Amharic is the official language, but English is widely spoken, and the various ethnic groups also speak their own languages.

History. According to tradition, the kingdom of Ethiopia was founded (10th cent. B.C.) by Menelik I, Solomon's first son, supposedly by the Queen of Sheba. The first recorded kingdom, however, is that of Aksum (Axum), probably founded (1st cent. A.D.) by traders from S Arabia and converted to Coptic Christianity in the 4th cent. With the rise of Islam in the 7th cent., Aksum lost control of the Red Sea routes, and a period of chaos followed. Order was restored in the 13th cent. with the founding of a new Solomonic dynasty. However, a war to expel the encroaching Somali, while successful (1543), exhausted the nation, which for the next two centuries was beset by ruinous civil wars. Finally, in 1889, MENELIK II, supported by Italy, instituted a strong rule. Claiming that Menelik had agreed to the establishment of a protectorate, Italy invaded Ethiopia in 1895 but was decisively defeated at Aduwa (1896). HAILE SELASSIE, who ascended the throne in 1930, faced a renewed

Italian threat, which culminated in a full-scale invasion in 1935. Ethiopia remained occupied until 1941, when it was liberated by the British. In 1952 the UN joined the former Italian colony of ERITREA in a federation with Ethiopia; Eritrea was annexed in 1962. In 1974 Haile Selassie was overthrown by army officers who proclaimed a socialist state and nationalized the economy. Colonel MENGISTU HAILE MARIAM brutally established (1977) himself as an authoritarian president. Under Mengistu, Ethiopia experienced serious political and economic problems, particularly a secessionist movement in Eritrea, a rebellion in Tigré prov. in the north, war with Somalia over the OGADEN, and a drought that caused widespread famine. In 1991 guerrilla successes drove Mengistu into exile. Tigréan guerrillas subsequently captured Addis Ababa, establishing an interim government with Meles Zenawi as president. The Eritreans triumphed as well, and in 1993 Eritrea became independent.

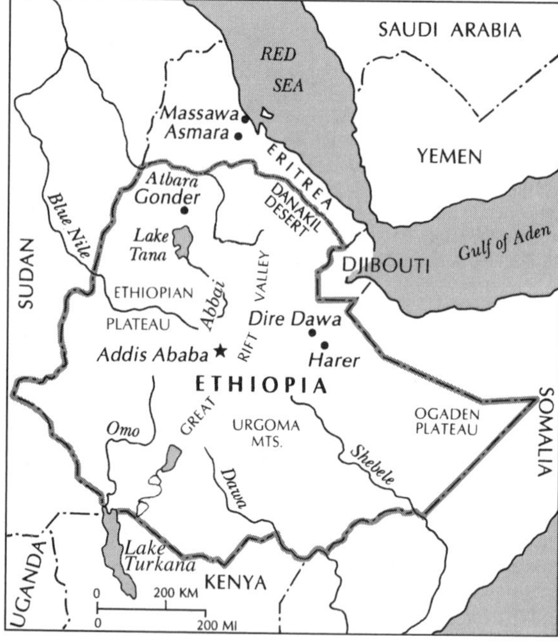

Ethiopic, extinct language of Ethiopia belonging to the Semitic subfamily of the Hamito-Semitic family of languages. See AFRICAN LANGUAGES (table).

ethnology, scientific study of the origin and functioning of humans and their cultures, usually considered a branch of cultural ANTHROPOLOGY. In the 19th cent. historical ethnology attempted to explain extant cultures by examining their early development. In the 20th cent. the comparative study of cultures has predominated.

ethology, study of animal behavior, especially its physiological, ecological, and evolutionary aspects. Originally, an organism's actions were classified as either instinctive behavior (actions not influenced by the animal's previous experiences, e.g., common reflexes) or learned behavior (actions dependent on earlier experiences, e.g., problem solving). Current emphasis is on the interaction between environmental and genetically determined responses, particularly during early development.

ethyl alcohol: see ETHANOL.

ethyne: see ACETYLENE.

Etna or **Aetna,** frequently active volcano, 10,958 ft (3,340 m), the highest in Europe, on the east coast of Sicily, S Italy. Snowcapped for much of the year, the volcano constantly threatens a densely populated agricultural area at its base. Its most recent eruption began in Dec. 1991.

Étoile, Place de l': see ARC DE TRIOMPHE DE L'ÉTOILE.

Eton, town, Berkshire, central England, on the Thames R. It is known chiefly for **Eton College** (est. 1440), the largest and most famous of the English public schools.

Etruria [ĭtrŏŏr'ēə], ancient country, W Italy, now Tuscany and W Umbria. It was the center of ETRUSCAN CIVILIZATION.

Etruscan art, the art of ETRURIA, which, by the 8th cent. B.C., spanned the area in Italy from Salerno to the Tiber R. The bronze and clay sculptures and carvings owe much to Greek sources but have a skillful, naturalistic character of their own. Sepulchral art was highly developed in centers such as Caere (Cerveteri) and Veii (Veio), as were portrait sculpture and FRESCO depictions of banquets and genre scenes. ROMAN ART absorbed the Etruscan by the 1st cent. B.C.

Etruscan civilization, highest civilization in Italy before the rise of Rome. Modern research tends to uphold the tradition of HERODOTUS that the Etruscans migrated to Italy from Lydia in Asia Minor in the 12th cent. B.C. A distinctive Etruscan culture evolved about the 8th cent. B.C., developed rapidly during the 7th cent. B.C., achieved its peak of power and wealth during the 6th cent. B.C., and declined during the 5th and 4th cent. B.C. Etruria comprised a loose confederation of city-states, including Clusium (now Chiusi), Tarquinii (Tarquinia), Veii (Veio), Volterra, and Perusia (Perugia). The Estruscans' wealth and power were in part based upon their knowledge of metalworking. They also made fine pottery. The Etruscan language cannot be classified into any known group of languages.

Eu, chemical symbol of the element EUROPIUM.

Euboea: see ÉVVOIA.

eucalyptus, evergreen shrubs or trees (genus *Eucalyptus*) of the MYRTLE family, a characteristic component of Australian flora. Also called ironbark, bloodwood, and gum tree, it is the sole food source of the KOALA and is valued for its timber and ESSENTIAL OILS. Several eucalyptus species are among the tallest trees known; *E. amygdalina regnans* reaches a height of over 300 ft (91 m).

Eucharist: see COMMUNION.

Euclid, fl. 300 B.C., Greek mathematician whose treatment of elementary plane GEOMETRY serves as the basis for most beginning courses on the subject. His great contribution was the use of a deductive system of proof in his *Elements,* a presentation of the mathematics of his day in 13 books. Studies of his work in the 19th cent. gave rise to several types of NON-EUCLIDEAN GEOMETRY.

Euclidean geometry, set of propositions in geometry that can be derived by rigorous logical steps from the five postulates stated by EUCLID in his *Elements*. The first three postulates state that it is possible (1) to draw a straight line from any point to any other point, (2) to produce a finite straight line continuously in a straight line, and (3) to describe a circle with any center and radius. The fourth postulate states that "All right angles are equal to one another," and the fifth posits that "If a straight line falling on two straight lines makes the interior angles on the same side less than two right angles, the two straight lines, if produced indefinitely, will meet on that side on which are the angles less than two right angles." A NON-EUCLIDEAN GEOMETRY replaces the fifth postulate with either of two alternative postulates.

Eudoxus of Cnidus [yōōdŏk'səs], 408?–355? B.C., Greek astronomer, mathematician, and physician. He was the first Greek astronomer to explain the movements of the planets scientifically, holding that a number of concentric spheres supported the planets in their paths. It is claimed that he calculated the length of the solar year, indicating a calendar reform similar to that made later by Julius CAESAR, and that he was the discoverer of parts of geometry included in EUCLID's work.

Eugene III, d. 1153, pope (1145–53), a Pisan named Bernard. He was driven (1146) from Rome by the agitation of Arnold of Brescia and the republicans. Eugene was a friend of BERNARD OF CLAIRVAUX and promoted the disastrous Second CRUSADE.

Eugene IV, 1383–1447, pope (1431–47), a Venetian named Gabriele Condulmer. Eugene at first opposed the Council of BASEL, but after being driven by rebellion from Rome to Florence (1434), he became conciliatory. He removed (1437) the council to Ferrara, where it proclaimed (1439) the reunion of the Eastern and Western churches (see COUNCIL, ECUMENICAL).

Eugene, city (1990 pop. 112,669), seat of Lane co., W Oreg., on the Willamette R.; inc. 1862. Located in a farming area, it has lumber, food-processing, and other industries. Tourism and convention business are important. The Univ. of Oregon is central to the city's cultural and recreational life.

Eugene of Savoy, 1663–1736, prince of the house of Savoy and general in the service of the Holy Roman Empire. He is regarded as one of the great military commanders of the modern age. He was a leading participant in the War of the SPANISH SUCCESSION, and he and the duke of MARLBOROUGH won the great battle of Blenheim (1704). He also fought the Turks and for Austria in the War of the POLISH SUCCESSION.

eugenics, study of methods to improve inherited human characteristics. It is directed chiefly at discouraging reproduction among those considered unfit (or those carrying genetic diseases) and encouraging it in the fit, although there are many difficulties in defining which traits are most desirable. The first half of the 20th cent. saw extreme coercive applications of such principles by governments ranging from miscegenation laws and enforced sterilization of the insane in the U.S. and other nations to the HOLOCAUST of Nazi Germany. In recent years, interest in eugenics has largely focused on GENETIC SCREENING.

Eugénie [yo͞ojē'nē], 1826–1920, empress of the French (1853–70), consort of NAPOLEON III. A Spanish noblewoman of great beauty, she married the emperor in 1853 and took an active part in government. After Napoleon III's deposition (1870) during the FRANCO-PRUSSIAN WAR, she fled to England.

euglenophyte, member of a small division (Euglenophyta) of photosynthetic aquatic organisms, variously classified in the protist, animal, or plant kingdoms. Most are unicellular; many have flagella and are motile. They resemble plants in that they have CHLOROPLASTS, but they also have gullets and lack cell walls, as animals do. The most characteristic genus is *Euglena,* common in ponds and pools.

Eulenspiegel, Till [oi'lən-shpē"gəl], a north German peasant clown of the 14th cent., immortalized in chapbooks describing his practical jokes. He is celebrated in Richard STRAUSS's tone poem and in stories and verse throughout Europe.

Euler, Leonhard [oi'lər], 1707–83, Swiss mathematician. The most prolific mathematician who ever lived, he worked at the St. Petersburg Academy of Sciences, Russia (1727–41, 1766–83), and at the Berlin Academy (1741–66). He contributed to areas of both pure and applied mathematics, including calculus, analysis, number theory, topology, algebra, geometry, trigonometry, analytical mechanics, hydrodynamics, and the theory of the moon's motion.

euphorbia: see SPURGE.

Euphrates, major river of arid SW Asia, formed by the confluence of the Kara and Murad rivers in E Turkey. It flows generally south, then southeast for c.1,700 mi (2,740 km) through deep canyons and narrow gorges in its upper course to a wide flood plain in Syria and Iraq. At BASRA the river joins with the TIGRIS R. to form the SHATT AL ARAB, which enters the PERSIAN GULF. An important source of irrigation for modern Syria and Iraq, the Euphrates contributed significantly to the development of many great civilizations in ancient MESOPOTAMIA. In the 1980s Turkey began constructing a series of dams on its upper course.

Eurasia, name of the great land mass that comprises the continents of EUROPE and ASIA.

Euric, d. c.484, king of the VISIGOTHS (466–c.484). He conquered the Iberian peninsula and S Gaul, made Toulouse his capital, and codified (475) Visigothic law.

Euripides, b. 480 or 485 B.C., d. 406 B.C., major Greek tragic poet. He wrote perhaps 92 plays, of which 19 are extant, including *Alcestis, Medea, Hippolytus, Andromache, The Trojan Women, Iphigenia in Tauris, The Phoenician Women, Orestes, Iphigenia in Aulis,* and *The Bacchae.* More realistic than AESCHYLUS or SOPHOCLES and rationalistic and iconoclastic toward the gods, he was interested in less-than-heroic characters. He resorted often to the device of the *deus ex machina* (god out of a machine) to resolve his plots. See also TRAGEDY.

Europa, in astronomy, natural satellite of JUPITER.

Europe, sixth largest continent, c.4,000,000 sq mi (10,360,000 sq km) including adjacent islands (1991 est. pop. 502,000,000). Actually a vast peninsula of the Eurasian landmass, it is conventionally separated from Asia by the URALS and Ural R. (E); the CASPIAN SEA and CAUCASUS (SE); and the BLACK SEA, BOSPORUS and DARDANELLES straits, and the Sea of Marmara (S). The MEDITERRANEAN SEA and Strait of GIBRALTAR separate it from Africa. The huge, young Alpine mountain chain, which includes the PYRENEES, ALPS, APENNINES, CARPATHIANS, and Caucasus, traverses the continent from west to east. MONT BLANC (15,771 ft/4,807 m) in the Alps and Mt. ELBRUS (18,481 ft/5,633 m) in the Caucasus are the highest points. The fertile European plain stretches from the Atlantic coast of France to the Urals. The climate is mild and generally humid in the west and northwest, dry in summer (Mediterranean type) in the south, and humid with cool summers in the east. Except for the north, Europe is densely populated. The countries of Europe are Albania, Andorra, Austria, Belarus, Belgium, Bosnia and Hercegovina, Bulgaria, Croatia, the Czech Republic, Denmark, Estonia, Finland, France, Germany, Greece, Hungary, Iceland, the Republic of Ireland, Italy, European Kazakhstan, Latvia, Liechtenstein, Lithuania, Luxembourg, Macedonia, Malta, Moldova, Monaco, the Netherlands, Norway, Poland, Portugal, Romania, European Russia, San Marino, Slovakia, Slovenia, Spain, Sweden, Switzerland, European Turkey, Ukraine, the United Kingdom (Great Britain and Northern Ireland), Vatican City, and Yugoslavia (see separate articles). LONDON, MOSCOW, and PARIS are the largest cities.

European Atomic Energy Community: see EUROPEAN UNION.

European Coal and Steel Community: see EUROPEAN UNION.

European Community: see EUROPEAN UNION.

European Economic Area: see EUROPEAN UNION; EUROPEAN FREE TRADE ASSOCIATION.

European Economic Community: see EUROPEAN UNION.

European Free Trade Association (EFTA), a customs union and trading bloc formed (1960) by Austria, Denmark, Britain, Norway, Portugal, Sweden, and Switzerland to promote free trade among members and seek broader economic integration of Europe. Iceland joined EFTA in 1971, and Finland in 1986. Liechtenstein, in a customs union with Switzerland, is also a member. Britain and Denmark left in 1973 to join the European Community (EC; see EUROPEAN UNION); Portugal did likewise in 1986. In 1991 the member countries of EFTA and the EC agreed to form a joint common market, the European Economic Area (EEA). Swiss voters rejected the pact in 1992, but the other EFTA nations ratified it and established the EEA in 1994; Liechtenstein must renegotiate its customs union before joining. Austria, Finland, Norway, and Sweden have applied for EC membership.

European Laboratory for Particle Physics: see CERN.

European Monetary System (EMS), arrangement by which most EUROPEAN UNION (EU) nations link their currencies to prevent large fluctuations relative to one another. It was organized in 1979 to stabilize foreign exchange and counter inflation among members. Periodic adjustments raise the values of strong currencies and lower those of weaker ones, but after 1986 changes in national interest rates were used to keep the currencies within a narrow range. The European Currency Unit (ECU) was also established. Regarded as a forerunner to a common EU currency, the ECU is a unit of accounting based on the currencies of EMS members and designed to facilitate international business within the European Community. In the early 1990s the system was strained by the differing economic policies and conditions of its members, most especially the newly reunified Germany. Britain and Italy withdrew (1992) from the exchange rate mechanism, and in 1993 the permitted range of fluctuation for the other currencies was increased (Greece has not participated in the exchange rate mechanism). In 1993 the **European Monetary Institute,** the first step in establishing an EU central bank (by 1999) and a common currency, was created.

European Organization for Nuclear Research: see CERN.

European Recovery Program: see MARSHALL PLAN.

European Space Agency (ESA), multinational agency formed in 1975 through the merger of the European Space Research Organization (ESRO) and the European Launcher Development Organization (ELDO). The financial contribution of each of the 13 member countries is determined by the projects it wishes to support. Major programs include the development of the Ariane rockets, the Spacelab scientific workshop (see SPACE EXPLORATION, table) carried into orbit by the space shuttle, and the SPACE PROBE *Giotto,* which flew by Halley's comet in 1985. **Arianespace,** a division of ESA, now conducts half of all commercial satellite launches.

European Union (EU), name given since the ratification of the

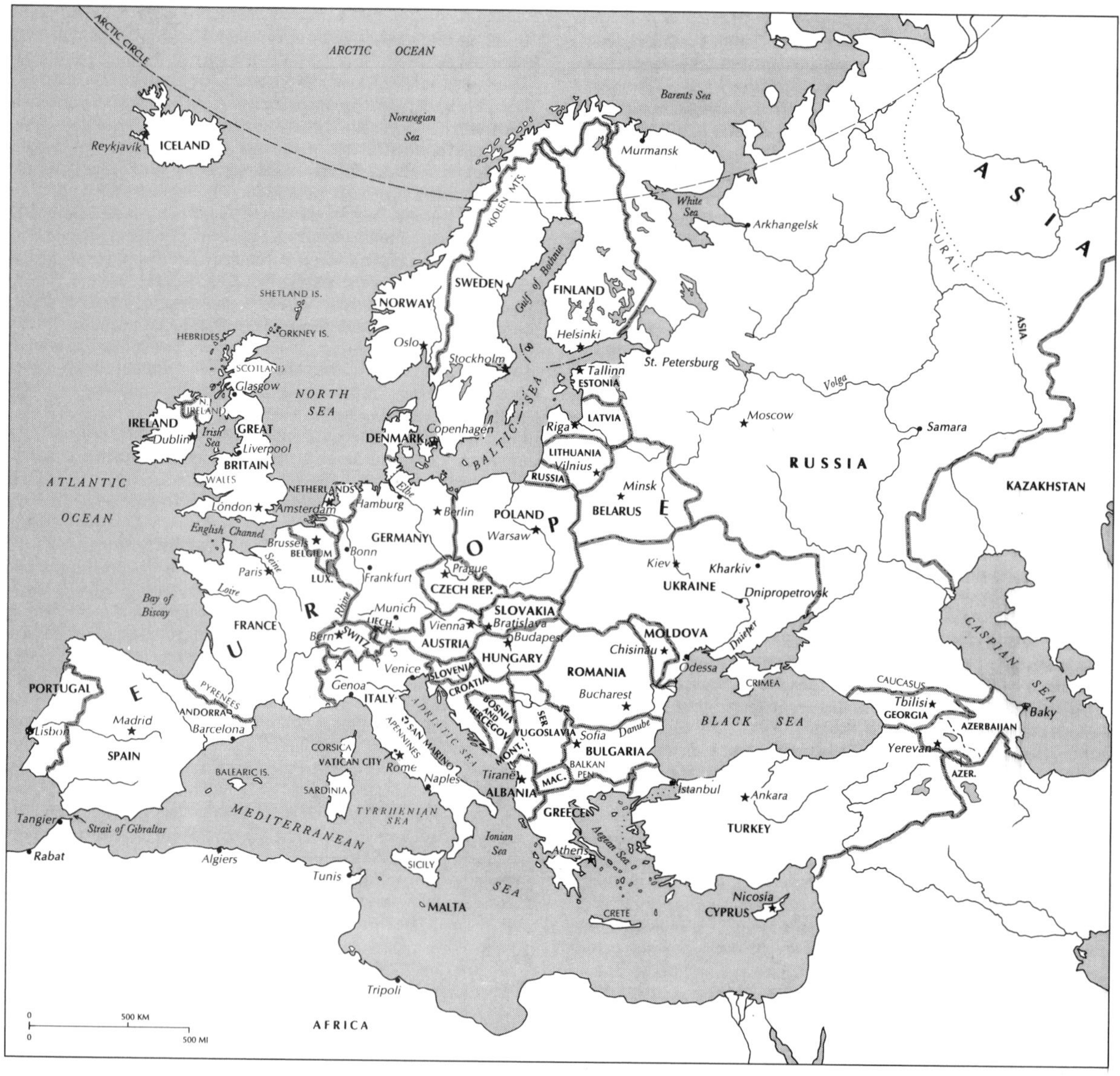

Maastricht treaty (Nov. 1993) to the **European Community** (EC) and other organizations responsible for a common EU foreign and security policy and for EU cooperation on justice and home affairs. Belgium, Britain, Denmark, France, Germany (originally West Germany), Greece, Ireland, Italy, Luxembourg, the Netherlands, Portugal, and Spain are full members. It includes the Council of the European Union (the former Council of Ministers), the European Commission, the European Parliament (directly elected by voters), and a Court of Justice. The EC, which is the core of the EU, resulted from the consolidation (1967) of three supranational groups: the European Coal and Steel Community (or Schuman Plan), established (1952) when six nations pooled their coal and steel resources to create unified products and labor markets; the Common Market, or European Economic Community (est. 1958), which sought the integration of the economies of Western Europe through the gradual elimination of internal tariff and customs barriers and the development of common price levels and a monetary union (see EUROPEAN MONETARY SYSTEM); and the European Atomic Energy Community, or Euratom (est. 1958), pledged to the common development of Europe's nuclear resources. The EC grew out of the efforts of such statesmen as Jean MONNET and Robert SCHUMAN of France and Paul Henri SPAAK of Belgium, who envisioned a unified Europe. In 1991 EC members signed the Treaty on European Union, or Maastricht treaty. It officially created the European Union, strengthened the parliament, called for the creation of an EU central bank (by 1999) and common currency, and took steps toward a common defense policy. The member countries also established a single market in 1993 and agreed to participate in a larger common market, the European Economic Area (est. 1994), with most of the EUROPEAN FREE TRADE ASSOCIATION nations.

europium (Eu), metallic element, purified by Eugène Demarcay in 1901. A silvery-white RARE-EARTH METAL, it has physical properties like those of other LANTHANIDE SERIES members, but its chemical properties resemble those of calcium. Europium is used in nuclear-reactor control rods. See ELEMENT (table); PERIODIC TABLE.

Eurydice: see ORPHEUS.

Euterpe: see MUSES.

euthanasia, either painlessly putting to death (positive, or active, euthanasia) or failing to postpone death from natural causes (negative, or passive, euthanasia), as in cases of terminal illness. The term *negative euthanasia* has come to mean the withdrawal of "extraordinary" means (e.g., intravenous feeding, respirators, and artificial kidney machines) of prolonging life. Positive euthanasia is illegal in the U.S., but physicians lawfully may refuse to prolong life when there is extreme suffering. In case of incapacitation a person's wishes concerning what life-support measures are or are not to be used to forestall death can be recorded in a LIVING WILL or preserved by a HEALTH-CARE PROXY. Whether measures used to keep the terminally ill alive are routine and justifiable or extraordinary remains a subject of debate. In the early 1990s in Michigan, Dr. Jack Kevorkian gained notoriety by assisting several people to commit suicide and became the object of a Michigan law (1992) forbidding such activity. In 1993 the Netherlands decriminalized, under a set of restricted conditions, voluntary positive euthanasia (essentially, physician-assisted suicide) for the terminally ill.

eutrophication, aging of a lake or slow-moving stream by biological enrichment of its water. In a young lake the water is cold and clear, supporting little life. With time, plant and animal life burgeon and organic remains begin to be deposited. As the lake grows shallower and warmer, marsh plants take root and begin to fill in the basin. Eventually the lake gives way to bog, finally becoming dry land. The natural aging of a lake may span thousands of years. However, wastes from human activities can accelerate the aging process, as with water POLLUTION. The prime pollutants are nitrates and phosphates, which greatly stimulate the growth of algae, producing a pungent surface scum. Decomposition of dead algae reduces the water's dissolved oxygen content, adversely affecting fish and other aquatic life forms typical of a mature lake.

Eutyches [yo͞o'tĭkēs], c.378–c.452, archimandrite in CONSTANTINOPLE, sponsor of Eutychianism (the first phase of MONOPHYSITISM) and leader of the opponents of NESTORIANISM. He taught that Jesus' humanity was absorbed in his one divine nature. Eutyches was deposed (448) but was reinstated (449) by the Robber Synod at Ephesus. The Council of CHALCEDON (1451) ended Eutychianism.

Evangelical Alliance, an association of individual Evangelical Christians of many denominations and countries, founded (1846) in London. In the U.S. the association was superseded (1950) by the NATIONAL COUNCIL OF CHURCHES OF CHRIST IN THE UNITED STATES OF AMERICA.

Evangelical United Brethren Church, Protestant denomination created (1946) by the union of the Evangelical Church and the United Brethren in Christ. Both bodies grew from evangelistic efforts, the former from the work of Jacob Albright (1807), the latter from the efforts of P.W. Otterbein and Martin Boehm (1800). The church had an episcopal government and stressed prayer, devotion to Jesus, and individual responsibility. In 1967 it became a part of the United Methodist Church.

evangelist [from Gr., = Gospel], title given to saints MATTHEW, MARK, LUKE, and JOHN. The title is now applied to Protestant preachers who preach personal conversion. Notable examples are John WESLEY, George WHITEFIELD, George FOX, Dwight Moody, and Billy GRAHAM.

Evans, Sir Arthur John, 1851–1941, English archaeologist. Keeper (1884–1908) of the Ashmolean Museum, Oxford, he excavated at KNOSSOS and uncovered remains of an ancient Cretan culture, which he called MINOAN. His writings include *The Mycenaean Tree and Pillar Cult* (1901) and *The Palace of Minos* (4 vol., 1921–35).

Evans, Mary Ann or **Marian:** see ELIOT, GEORGE.

Evans, Oliver, 1775–1819, American inventor; b. near Newport, Del. Evans developed and patented a number of grain-handling machines, including an elevator and a conveyor system, that later became standard equipment in U.S. mills. He pioneered the design of high-pressure steam engines. In 1804 he built the first land vehicle in the U.S. that moved under its own power, an engine-equipped dredge.

Evans, Walker, 1903–75, American photographer; b. St. Louis. He is noted for his studies of the rural South during the Great Depression. Many of his photographs of tenant farmers appeared in the book *Let Us Now Praise Famous Men* (1941), written by James AGEE.

Evans-Pritchard, Edward Evan, 1902–73, English social anthropologist. A specialist on Africa, he wrote *The Nuer* (1940), a classic of ethnography, and *Theories of Primitive Religion* (1965).

Evansville, city (1990 pop. 126,272), seat of Vanderburgh co., SW Ind., a port on the Ohio R.; inc. 1819. Commercial center for a coal, oil, and farm region, the city manufactures refrigeration and air-conditioning equipment, aluminum, plastics, drugs and machinery. The Univ. of Evansville and several other colleges are located there. Cultural institutions include a museum of arts and sciences and a philharmonic orchestra.

evaporation: see STATES OF MATTER.

Eve, in the BIBLE, the first woman, wife of ADAM, mother of CAIN, ABEL, and Seth. Led by the serpent to eat of the forbidden tree of knowledge, Eve tempted Adam to eat of the tree also. As punishment, they were banished from the Garden of EDEN.

Evelyn, John, 1620–1706, English diarist and author. A founder of the ROYAL SOCIETY (1660), he wrote on reforestation, natural science, art history, and numismatics. He is best known for his lifelong DIARY (pub. 1818), full of historical information on 17th-cent. England.

evening primrose, common name for a plant of the Onagraceae family, distributed worldwide. More specifically, it refers to a yellow, evening-flowering annual or biennial of the genus *Oenothera* grown in the temperate New World. The family also includes the FUCHSIA.

evening star, a common term for a bright planet, not a star, usually Venus, appearing in the western sky soon after sunset. In ancient times Venus was called Hesperus (Greek) or Vesper (Roman) when it was seen as the evening star.

Everest, Mount, 29,023 ft (8,846 m) high, highest mountain in the world, located in the central HIMALAYAS, on the Tibet-Nepal border. Named for Sir George Everest, the surveyor of the Himalayas, it was first climbed in 1953 by Sir Edmund HILLARY and Tenzing Norkay, after at least eight earlier attempts to scale it had failed.

Everett, Edward, 1794–1865, American orator and statesman; b. Dorchester, Mass. His long public career included service as congressman from Massachusetts (1825–35), governor of the state (1836–39), minister to England (1841–45), and U.S. senator (1853–54). During the CIVIL WAR he traveled throughout the North, speaking for the Union cause. He gave the principal speech at Gettysburg on the same occasion that produced Lincoln's famous GETTYSBURG ADDRESS.

Everglades, marshy, low-lying tropical area (maximum elevation 7 ft/2.1 m), S Florida, covering c.4,000 sq mi (10,000 sq km) south of Lake OKEECHOBEE and including Everglades National Park (see NATIONAL PARKS, table) and Big Cypress National Preserve. It is an area of solidly packed muck, saw grass, and marsh hummocks, and is rich in wildlife. Water from Okeechobee flows south through the Everglades to the Gulf of Mexico. The local SEMINOLE were driven out in the 1830s. From the late 19th cent., large tracts of land were drained to provide agricultural and grazing land. The Everglades have been adversely affected by agricultural development and urbanization (Miami and other cities), which have degraded and compete for the water on which its ecosystem depends. In 1988 the U.S. government sued to force Florida to restore the water quality. The state agreed to establish a cleanup program in 1992.

Evert, Chris (Christine Marie Evert), 1954–, American tennis player; b. Fort Lauderdale, Fla. Noted for her poise on the court and her strong, two-handed backhand, she captured the singles title at Wimbledon in 1974, 1976, and 1981 and won six U.S. Open singles titles between 1975 and 1982.

Everyman, late-15th-cent. English morality play. Summoned by Death, Everyman can persuade none of his friends—Beauty, Kindred, Worldly Goods—to go with him, except Good Deeds. This allegory is the basis of many later plays.

evidence, in law, material submitted to a court or other inquiring body to prove the facts in a legal dispute. The admissibility of evidence is governed by various rules. Particular evidence may be excluded on the grounds that it is irrelevant (having no bearing on the dispute), immaterial (having no impact on the substance of the dispute), or incompetent (outside the knowledge of the witness, e.g., hearsay). Rules of personal privilege excuse a witness from giving evidence relating to certain communications, e.g., between husband and wife; witnesses may also withhold self-incriminating evidence, and criminal defendants may refuse to testify. Evidence may be direct, such as that arising from personal observation, or it may be circumstantial, arising from facts that tend to prove other facts by inference. The kinds of evidence usually produced are physical objects (real evidence); written statements and documents (documentary evidence); oral testimony of the parties to the dispute (personal evidence); and technical or other specialized testimony (expert evidence). The burden of proof, i.e., the responsibility to establish a disputed fact, shifts according to the nature of the controversy: in a civil suit, each party must prove its affirmative contentions by a preponderance of the evidence; in a criminal suit, the burden of proof rests on the prosecution, which must prove each element of its case beyond a reasonable doubt.

evolution, the process in which the genetic makeup of a population changes over a long period of time by such means as mutation, the result being the emergence of distinctive characteristics and new species. This process, also known as descent with modification, constitutes organic evolution. Inorganic evolution deals with the development of the physical universe from unorganized matter (see COSMOLOGY). Organic evolution conceives of life as having begun as a simple, primordial protoplasmic mass from which arose, through time, all subsequent living forms. The first clearly stated theory of evolution, that proposed by Jean LAMARCK in 1801, included the inheritance of ACQUIRED CHARACTERISTICS as the operative force in evolution. Subsequently (1858), Alfred Russel WALLACE and Charles DARWIN independently set forth a scientifically credible theory of evolution based on NATURAL SELECTION, focusing on the survival and reproduction of those species best adapted to the environment. This theory had a profound effect on scientific thought and experimentation. Although it has undergone modification in light of later scientific developments, the theory of evolution still rests on essentially the same grounds emphasized by Darwin, supported now by research in GENETICS as well as by comparative anatomy, embryology, geography, paleontology, and biochemistry. It has been challenged by those believing in the creation theory of the universe (see CREATIONISM). See also HUMAN EVOLUTION; MUTATION.

Evtushenko, Evgeny: see YEVTUSHENKO.

Évvoia or **Euboea,** island (1991 pop. 209,132), c.1,467 sq mi (3,800 sq. km), SE Greece, separated from the mainland by the Evripos strait. Its main industries are agriculture, magnesite and lignite mining, and marble quarrying. Settled by the ancient Greeks, it was divided among seven CITY-STATES, including Eretria, and later passed to Rome, Venice, and the Ottoman Turks before its incorporation (1830) into Greece.

Ewing, (William) Maurice, 1906–74, American geophysicist; b. Lockney, Tex. Ewing's oceanographic work was critical to the acceptance of the theory of PLATE TECTONICS. In the late 1930s he conducted the first seismic studies (1935) and the first photographing (1939) of the ocean floor. At Columbia Univ. he helped to found (1949) the Lamont-Doherty Geological Observatory and was (1949–72) its first director.

excess profits tax, levy on any profit above a standard level, usually imposed during wartime to prevent businesses from making unreasonable profits. Both the U.S. and Britain levied such taxes during the world wars. A "windfall profits" tax on oil revenues and royalties, enacted by the U.S. in 1980, was actually an EXCISE TAX on production, not profits.

excise tax, governmental levy on specific goods. Introduced by Holland in the 17th cent., excise taxes spread to England (1643) and the U.S. (1791). Both the federal government and state governments impose such taxes in the U.S., chiefly on gasoline, cigarettes, and liquor, and sometimes on furs, jewelry, and other goods classed as luxury items.

excommunication, formal expulsion of a person from a religious community, especially from the Roman Catholic Church. It involves a formal decree (or anathema) and public exclusion from the church, sacraments, and society. An excommunicate may return to the church on repentance.

excretion, process of eliminating from an organism the waste products of metabolism and other materials of no use. In one-celled organisms wastes are discharged through the cell's surface. Higher plants eliminate gases through the stomata, or pores, on the leaf surface, and multicellular animals have special excretory organs. In humans the main excretory organs are the KIDNEYS and other organs of the URINARY SYSTEM, through which URINE is eliminated, and the large intestine, from which solid wastes are expelled (see DIGESTIVE SYSTEM). Excretion also takes place in the SKIN, which eliminates water and salt in the form of sweat, and the LUNGS, which expel water vapor and carbon dioxide.

executive, in government, the chief administrative officer and the branch charged with carrying out the laws, as distinguished from the legislative (see CONGRESS) and judicial branches (see COURT SYSTEM; SUPREME COURT). A further distinction is sometimes made between the executives who decide policy and civil servants who implement it. Executive areas of concern include directing relations with foreign governments, commanding the armed forces, and approving or disapproving legislative acts. In the U.S., the president, the CABINET, and functionaries of the federal administrative agencies are considered part of the executive.

executive privilege, exemption of the president from the disclosure of information to congressional or judicial inquiries. It is usually invoked to protect confidential military or diplomatic operations or private presidential discussions. Efforts by presidents since Eisenhower to gain absolute privilege have been rejected by the courts.

exercise electrocardiography: see STRESS TEST.

Exeter, city (1991 pop. 98,125), capital of Devonshire, SW England, on the Exe R. It is the market and distribution center for SW England. Strategically located, it was besieged by the Danes (9th, 11th cent.), by William the Conqueror (1068), and by Yorkists (15th cent.). Its many historic sites include Roman ruins and the massive Norman Cathedral, whose library contains the famous Old English Exeter Book. The city's center was rebuilt after heavy bombings in WORLD WAR II.

existentialism, any of several philosophical systems of the 20th cent., all centered on the individual and the individual's relationship to the universe or to God. KIERKEGAARD developed a Christian existentialism that recognized the concrete ethical and religious demands confronting the individual, who is forced each time to make a subjective commitment. The necessity and seriousness of these decisions cause him dread and despair. Following Kierkegaard, HEIDEGGER and SARTRE, both students of HUSSERL, were the major thinkers of the movement. Heidegger rejected the label of existentialism, describing his philosophy as an investigation of the nature of being in which the analysis of human existence is only a first step. For Sartre, the only self-declared existentialist among the major thinkers, existence precedes essence: there is no God and no fixed human nature; thus, each person is totally free and entirely responsible for what he or she becomes and does. This responsibility accounts for human dread and anguish. Sartre influenced the writings of CAMUS and de BEAUVOIR. A Christian existentialism was developed in France by Gabriel Marcel, a Roman Catholic. The religious thinkers Karl BARTH, Paul TILLICH, Reinhold NIEBUHR, and Martin BUBER, and the philosopher Karl JASPERS are often included in the orbit of existentialism.

exobiology, search for extraterrestrial life throughout the universe. Philosophical speculation that there might be other worlds similar to ours dates back to the ancient Chinese and Greeks. Six basic parameters determine whether an environment is suitable for life as we know it: temperature, pressure, salinity, acidity, water availability, and oxygen content. Advanced life is restricted to a narrow range of these parameters, but primitive microorganisms can exist over a much wider range. Data already collected by SPACE PROBES essentially rule out advanced life on other planets of our solar system. Some scientists, however, have estimated that as many as 50,000 planets in our galaxy have earthlike conditions and that a substantial fraction of these are likely to have cultures as technologically advanced as our own; efforts to detect radio emissions from these civilizations have so far been unsuccessful. A continuing effort is being made to detect primitive life within our solar system, e.g., the surface landings (1976) of the Viking space probes.

Exodus, second book of the OLD TESTAMENT and of the PENTATEUCH, ascribed by tradition to MOSES. It is a religious history of the JEWS during their flight from Egypt, when they began to receive the Law. The events include the bondage in Egypt and God's preparations for liberation through the agency of Moses (1–11); the exodus proper, with the institution of the Passover (see JEWISH HOLIDAYS) and the crossing of the Red Sea (12–18); and the divine legislation at Mt. Sinai (19–40), including the giving of the TEN COMMANDMENTS.

exorcism, ritual driving out of evil spirits, as distinguished from rites of propitiation or evocation. It may be applied to a person, place, or thing by use of holy water, incense, incantation, or various rites. The New Testament records Jesus' ability to drive out devils. The Roman Catholic Church regulates exorcism of demons from persons.

expert system or **knowledge-based system,** computer program that uses ARTIFICIAL INTELLIGENCE techniques to make decisions or recommendations or predict outcomes based on an analysis of data. An expert system typically has two parts: a very large database that contains specified knowledge in a given area and a set of rules (called the knowledge base) for reaching conclusions. Often the rules are an elaborate set of "if . . . then" statements. Expert systems have been applied to chemistry, geology, genetic engineering, medicine, and pharmacology.

explosive, a substance that undergoes rapid decomposition or combustion, evolving much heat and producing a large volume of gas. The heat evolved causes the gas to expand greatly, exerting the enormous pressure of explosions. Important explosives include TNT (trinitrotoluene), DYNAMITE, and NITROGLYCERIN. Chemical explosives are of two general kinds. Some, e.g., GUNPOWDER, are mixtures of readily combustible but not necessarily explosive substances, which, when set off (by ignition), undergo very rapid combustion. Others, called high explosives (e.g., TNT), are compounds whose molecules are unstable and can undergo explosive decomposition (detonation) without burning. The latter kind is used in warfare (e.g., in bombs, explosive shells, torpedoes, and missile warheads) and for blasting rock in mining and construction work. Nondetonating explosives, e.g., gunpowder and modern smokeless powders, are used as propellants for bullets and in fireworks. Nuclear explosives release energy by transformation of the atomic nucleus (see ATOMIC BOMB; HYDROGEN BOMB; NUCLEAR ENERGY).

exponent, in mathematics, a number or algebraic expression written above and to the right of another number or algebraic expression called the base. In the expressions x^2 and x^n, the number 2 and the algebraic letter *n* are the exponents, respectively, of the base *x*. A positive whole number as exponent indicates the power, or how many times the base is to be taken as a factor (e.g., $2^3 = 2 \times 2 \times 2 = 8$). Fractional and negative exponents indicate, respectively, roots and reciprocals (e.g., $8^{1/3} = 3\sqrt{8}$ and $x^{-2} = 1x^2$). A zero exponent makes any quantity equal to 1.

exponential function: see article on *e*.

expressionism, term used to describe works of art and literature in which the representation of reality is distorted to communicate an inner vision, transforming nature rather than imitating it. **1** In painting and the graphic arts, certain movements such as the BRÜCKE (1905) and BLAUE REITER (1911) are described as expressionist. In addition, certain independent artists e.g., ROUAULT, SOUTINE, VLAMINCK, KOKOSCHKA, and SCHIELE, did personal visionary paintings. GAUGUIN, ENSOR, VAN GOGH, and MUNCH were the spiritual fathers of expressionism, as were such earlier artists as El GRECO, GRÜNEWALD, and GOYA, whose works show striking parallels to modern expressionist sensibility. See also NEOEXPRESSIONISM. **2** In literature, expressionism is often considered a revolt against realism and naturalism, a seeking to achieve a psychological or spiritual reality rather than to record external events. In the novel, the term applies to KAFKA and JOYCE (see STREAM OF CONSCIOUSNESS). In drama, STRINDBERG is the forerunner of the group of early 20th-cent. dramatists to which the term is applied, e.g., Kaiser, TOLLER, and WEDEKIND. Their work was often characterized by a bizarre distortion of reality. The movement, though short-lived, gave impetus to a free form of writing and of theatrical production.

extinction, in biology, disappearance of a species of living organisms. Extinction occurs as a result of changed conditions to which the species is not suited. If no member of the affected species survives and reproduces, the entire line dies out, leaving no descendants. A species may also become extinct through its gradual evolution into a new species, as a result of natural selection for characteristics suited to new conditions. See also MASS EXTINCTION.

extortion, in law, the offense of obtaining from a person money or property not legally owed, through the use of fear, force, or authority of office. The demanding of ransom (a price for return of a captured person or property) or blackmail (money exacted by threat of exposure of criminal action or disreputable conduct) are forms of extortion.

extradition, delivery of a person, suspected or convicted of a crime, by the country of refuge to the country asserting jurisdiction. In the U.S. it also applies to the removal of a suspected criminal from one state to another. Its purpose is to prevent criminals from escaping punishment by fleeing to another jurisdiction. Extradition became common policy in the 19th cent., but since under international law it is not obligatory without a treaty, virtually all extradition occurs under the authority of specific bilateral treaties between nations. These may vary widely. Most European countries will surrender a criminal fugitive upon simple demand. The U.S. requires evidence that the accused has violated its law as well as the law of the demanding country. Like many nations, the U.S. will not surrender a fugitive wanted for a political crime (see ASYLUM).

extrasensory perception, commonly called ESP, any perception that occurs independently of the known sensory processes such as sight and smell. The main categories of ESP are telepathy, clairvoyance, and precognition. The existence of ESP is disputed, though systematic experimental research on the subject has been ongoing since 1930. See also PARAPSYCHOLOGY.

extraterritoriality, privilege of immunity from local law enforcement enjoyed by certain aliens while present in the territory of a foreign nation. It is extended to most diplomats and their families, who are considered by customary international law to be under the legal jurisdiction of their home countries and thus exempt from civil and criminal action, arrest, lawsuits, and, often, the payment of personal and property taxes. Certain transgressions, however, can result in an alien being declared persona non grata and expelled from the host country. Extraterritoriality also extends to public (i.e., state-owned) vessels in foreign territorial waterways and ports and to air space over national territory, although air space remains regulated by bilateral agreements because uniform standards of jurisdiction have not been established (see AIR, LAW OF THE).

extreme unction: see ANOINTING OF THE SICK.

extroversion and introversion, terms introduced into psychology by C.G. JUNG to identify two opposite psychological types: the extrovert, who is directed toward the external world and is most content when surrounded by people and activity, and the introvert, who is contemplative and enjoys solitude and the inner life. Jung believed that everyone has tendencies in both directions, although one direction generally predominates.

Eyck, Hubert van [văn īk], c.1370–1426, and **Jan van Eyck,** c.1390–1441, Flemish painters, brothers. Little is known of Hubert, who may have worked (1414–17) for Duke William of Bavaria and did settle in Ghent, Belgium. He is credited with an *Annunciation* and a stunningly detailed miniature diptych of the *Crucifixion and Last Judgment* (both: Metropolitan Mus.). Jan worked in the courts of Count John of Holland (1422–25) and Philip of Burgundy. His paintings are minutely descriptive, realistic depictions of portrait subjects and religious scenes with contemporary genre details. His oil technique reveals an unprecedented richness and intensity of color for the medium. The two brothers collaborated on their masterwork, the altarpiece of the Church of Saint Bavon in Ghent (completed by Jan in 1432). One or both brothers illuminated parts of the *Heures de Turin* manuscript. Jan's portrait oils include *Portrait of an Unknown Man* (1432) and *Man with the Red Turban,* perhaps a self-portrait (both: London), and the wedding picture *Giovanni Arnolfini and his Bride* (1434; National Gall., London). His splendid *Annunciation* is in Washington, D.C. (National Gall.). Jan van Eyck's influence on European painting is enormous.

eye, organ of vision. Like a camera, it has a diaphragm and variable focusing. The eyeball has three covering layers. The *sclera,* the outermost, is partially visible as the "white" of the eye. In the center of the sclera and projecting slightly is the cornea, a transparent membrane that acts as the window of the eye. The *choroid,* the layer beneath the sclera, is composed of dense pigment and blood vessels. Near the center of the visible part of the eye, the choroid forms the ciliary body, the muscles of which change the shape of the lens. The ciliary body merges with the iris, a muscular diaphragm that regulates the size of the pupil, the round opening through which light enters the eye. The iris, where it is not covered by the sclera, reveals the choroid's pigmentation, usually brown or blue (giving the eye its color). Behind the iris is the lens, a transparent, elastic, but solid ellipsoid body that bends light rays, focusing them on the *retina,* the third tissue layer. The retina is a network of nerve cells, notably the rods and cones, that send impulses along the optic nerve to the brain. The rods provide vision in dim light, while the cones respond best to bright light and provide color vision. See also ASTIGMATISM; BLINDNESS; COLOR BLINDNESS; FARSIGHTEDNESS; GLAUCOMA; NEARSIGHTEDNESS.

Eyre, Lake, largest lake in Australia, located in the continent's arid interior, in central SOUTH AUSTRALIA state. It forms the continent's lowest point, 39 ft (12 m) below sea level, and frequently runs dry. Its waters are salty.

Ezekiel or **Ezechiel** [both: ēzē'kēĕl], book of the OLD TESTAMENT, 26th in the Authorized Version, third of the Major PROPHETS, recounts the prophecies of Ezekiel, who preached (592–570 B.C.) to the Jews of the BABYLONIAN CAPTIVITY. It centers on the fall of JERUSALEM (586 B.C.): chapters 1–32 prophesy doom; 33–48, looking to restoration, end with a vision of the ideal Temple. Ezekiel stresses individual responsibility and is noted for its symbolic passages.

Ezra or **Esdras** [ĕz'drəs] and **Nehemiah** [nēəmī'ə], two books of the OLD TESTAMENT, 15th and 16th in the Authorized Version, tell the history of the JEWS from 538 B.C. to 432 B.C., from the decree of CYRUS THE GREAT permitting the return from the BABYLONIAN CAPTIVITY to the dedication of JERUSALEM's new walls. The book of Ezra concerns the return of one group, the rebuilding of the Temple, and the return of Ezra "the priest, the scribe" with orders to restore Jewish Law. Nehemiah tells of the return of Nehemiah, who was a cupbearer to ARTAXERXES I, the rebuilding of the walls, and the reading of the Law and signing of a covenant.

Ezzelino da Romano [ĕt"sālē'nō dä rōmä'nō], 1194–1259, Italian Ghibelline leader (see GUELPHS AND GHIBELLINES). He held Verona and other cities, and after 1237 he was the greatest power in N Italy. He was defeated (1258) at Milan. Placed by DANTE in the *Inferno,* he is remembered as a cruel tyrant.

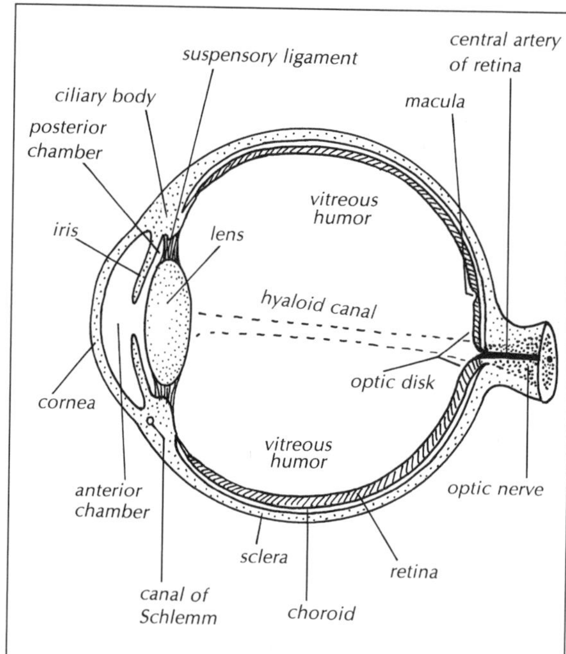

Cross-section of human eye

F

F, chemical symbol of the element FLUORINE.

Fabergé, Peter Carl, 1846–1920, Russian goldsmith. As head of the studio established by his father, he was responsible for the design of elegant jewelry and objets d'art. Fabergé was particularly well known for the richly imaginative jeweled and enameled Easter eggs he created for the Russian royal family. He died in exile in Switzerland.

Fabian Society, British organization founded (1884) to promote evolutionary socialism. Its exponents included George Bernard SHAW, Beatrice Potter WEBB, and Sidney WEBB. The Fabians rejected Marxism and denied the need for violent class struggle. After publication of the *Fabian Essays* (1889), they gained widespread recognition. The Fabian Society played a leading role in the creation of the LABOUR PARTY, of which it remains an affiliated research and publicity agency.

Fabius, ancient Roman gens. **Quintus Fabius Maximus Rullianus** or **Rullus,** d. c.291 B.C., was a renowned general, especially after his victory over the Etruscans, the Samnites, and their allies at Sentinum (295). His descendant, **Quintus Fabius Maximus Verrucosus,** d. 203 B.C., the opponent of HANNIBAL, was called Cunctator [Lat., = delayer] because of his delaying tactics, from which the term *Fabian,* referring to a waiting policy, is derived. Tired of his inaction, the Romans replaced him (216 B.C.) and were defeated at Cannae.

Fabriano, Gentile da: see GENTILE DA FABRIANO.

facsimile machine or **fax machine,** device for transmitting copies of printed images over telephone lines. A facsimile machine scans a page to make an electronic representation of its text or graphics, compresses the data to save transmission time, and transmits it to another facsimile machine. The receiving machine decrypts the signal and uses a printer (usually built in) to make a facsimile of the original page. A computer equipped with a fax MODEM, printer, and appropriate software can duplicate many functions of a facsimile machine.

Faeroe Islands or **Faröe Islands** [fâr'ō], group of volcanic islands (1992 est. pop. 48,600), 540 sq mi (1,400 sq km), Denmark, located in the N Atlantic Ocean c.850 mi (1,370 km) from mainland Denmark. There are 17 inhabited and 5 uninhabited islands; Steymoy, with Tórshavn as the capital, and Østerø are the largest islands. Inhabitants speak Faeroese, a Germanic language related to Danish. Settled by Norsemen in the 8th cent., the islands became part of Norway in the 11th cent., when they were Christianized, and passed to the Danish crown in 1380. They became a British protectorate (1940–45) in World War II and gained self-government (1948) after an aborted independence movement.

Fahd ibn Abdul Aziz, 1922–, king of Saudi Arabia (1982–). A son of IBN SAUD, the founder of Saudi Arabia, Fahd served (1962–75) as interior minister and was named (1975) crown prince by his half-brother King KHALID. He was a powerful shaper of Saudi foreign and domestic policy under Khalid, on whose death (1982) he succeeded to the throne. Fahd has encouraged limited modernization of Saudi Arabia, but the new constitution (1992) that established an appointed consultative national council left unchanged the royal family's control of the government.

Fahrenheit temperature scale: see TEMPERATURE.

Fainzilberg, Ilya Arnoldovich: see ILF, ILYA ARNOLDOVICH.

Fairbanks, Douglas, 1883–1939, American film actor; b. Denver. He starred in such swashbucklers as *The Mark of Zorro* (1920), *The Thief of Bagdad* (1924), and *The Black Pirate* (1926). His son, **Douglas Fairbanks, Jr.,** 1909–, b. N.Y.C., is an actor whose films include *The Prisoner of Zenda* (1937) and *Gunga Din* (1939).

Fairbanks, city (1990 pop. 30,843), Fairbanks North Star Borough, central Alaska, on the Chena R.; inc. 1903. Oil, gas, lumbering, and mining, as well as the Univ. of Alaska, are important to the economy. The discovery of gold (1902) and the building of the Alaska railroad caused the city to develop.

Fair Labor Standards Act: see WAGES AND HOURS ACT.

fairy, in folklore, one of a variety of supernatural beings having magical powers. Belief in fairies has existed from earliest times, but the concept and description of the creatures varies widely, from the tiny old men, or leprechauns, of Irish legend, to beautiful enchantresses like the Germanic Lorelei, to human-eating giants, or ogres. Particular kinds of fairies include the Arabic JINNI, the Scandinavian troll, the Germanic elf, and the English pixie. Although usually represented as mischievous and capricious, they could also be loving and bountiful. Among the great adapters of popular fairy tales were Charles PERRAULT, the brothers GRIMM, and Hans Christian ANDERSEN.

Faisal or **Feisal,** kings of Iraq. **Faisal I,** 1885–1933 (r.1921–33), joined (1916) with T.E. LAWRENCE in the Arab revolt against the Turks. The British, largely through the efforts of Gertrude BELL, named him king. He was generally pro-British and was succeeded by his son, Ghazi. Ghazi's son, **Faisal II,** 1935–58 (r.1939–58), was generally pro-Western in his short majority reign. He was killed in a revolution that overthrew the Iraqi monarchy.

Faisalabad, formerly **Lyallpur,** city (1981 pop. 1,104,209), NE Pakistan. The commercial center of a region that grows cotton and wheat, it produces textiles, pharmaceuticals, and other manufactures. The city was founded c.1895 by Sir James Lyall, a British civil servant and Orientalist.

Faisal ibn al Saud, 1905–75, king of Saudi Arabia (1964–75). A son of IBN SAUD, he forced his brother King Saud to abdicate in 1964 and assumed the throne. He used his country's vast oil revenues to finance far-reaching economic and social reforms. A deranged nephew assassinated him.

Falange [Span., = phalanx], Spanish political party, founded 1933. Adhering to FASCISM, the Falange, through its militia, joined the Nationalist forces of Francisco FRANCO in the SPANISH CIVIL WAR (1936–39). The party's founder, José António Primo de Rivera, son of the dictator Miguel PRIMO DE RIVERA, was executed by the Loyalists in the civil war. In 1937 Franco took control of the Falange, making it the official party of his regime. By the 1970s its power had waned.

Falashas, group of approximately 45,000 Ethiopians who practice a form of JUDAISM; they call themselves Beta Israel [house of Israel]. Their scriptures include the Old Testament and certain apocryphal books, and they adhere to certain traditions that correspond to some of those found in the MIDRASH and TALMUD. In modern times there were POGROMS against the Falashas, and some, known as the Falash Mura, converted to Christianity. In 1984 and 1991 airlifts brought thousands of Falashas to Israel, and Ethiopia subsequently agreed (1991) to permit Israel to evacuate those still remaining.

falcon, long-winged BIRD of prey (genus *Falco*) related to the HAWK. Widely distributed, falcons are typified by notched beaks. They range in size from the 6½-in. (16.5-cm) falconet to the 24-in. (60-cm) gyrfalcon. The commonest and smallest American falcon is the sparrow hawk (*F. sparverius*). Falcons lay their eggs on the ground, on cliff ledges, or in deserted hawk or CROW nests. The peregrine falcon and gyrfalcon are used in falconry.

Faliscan [fəlis'kən], extinct language belonging to the Italic subfamily of the Indo-European family of languages. See LANGUAGE (table).

Falkland Islands, Span. *Islas Malvinas,* British crown colony (1991 pop. 2,121), 4,618 sq mi (11,961 sq km), S Atlantic. Consisting of two large islands and some 200 small ones, they are economically dependent on sheep-raising. The capital is Stanley. Long claimed by Britain, they have been under British rule since 1832, when Argentine colonists were expelled, but Argentina continued to claim them. In 1982 they were seized by Argentina and retaken by British troops. From 1908 to 1985 South Georgia and the South Sandwich Islands were dependencies of the Falklands.

Falkner, William: see FAULKNER, WILLIAM.

Falla, Manuel de [fä'lyä], 1876–1946, Spanish composer. He was influenced by the IMPRESSIONISM of DEBUSSY and RAVEL but retained Spanish characteristics, e.g., the flamenco tradition. His works include *Nights in the Gardens of Spain* (1916; for piano and orchestra) and the ballets *El Amor Brujo* (1915) and *The Three-Cornered Hat* (1917).

fall line, line where waterfalls occur in rivers passing from areas of relatively hard rocks (as in the Piedmont of the E U.S.) to areas of softer rock (as in the Atlantic Coastal Plain). It is usually the head of navigation. Fall-line cities in the U.S. include TRENTON, N.J.; WASHINGTON, D.C.; RICHMOND, Va.; RALEIGH, N.C.; and AUGUSTA, Ga.

fallout: see ATOMIC BOMB; HYDROGEN BOMB.

Fall River, industrial city (1990 pop. 92,703), SE Mass., a port on Mt. Hope Bay, at the mouth of the Taunton R.; settled 1656, inc. 1854. It was once the leading cotton textile center in the U.S., and textiles and clothing are still the chief manufactures, although industry has diversified. The trial (1892) of Lizzie BORDEN took place there.

falsetto: see VOICE.

Family Compact, popular name for a small clique of wealthy, powerful men who dominated Upper Canada (see ONTARIO) from the late-18th to mid-19th cent. They controlled the government, monopolized political offices, and strongly influenced banking, land grant issues, education, the courts, and Anglican church affairs. New settlers who were thus denied political opportunity formed an opposition that became the Reform party.

family leave, social policy permitting workers to take a specified amount of time off from the job to attend to pressing family needs. The U.S. Family and Medical Leave Act (1993), which covers companies with 50 or more workers, mandates up to 12 weeks of leave per year for various family medical emergencies and for the birth or adoption of a child. Many states also have family leave laws, and in many European countries and Japan, longer periods of paid leave are common.

family planning: see BIRTH CONTROL.

family therapy, form of PSYCHOTHERAPY dealing with the improvement of family relationships and the emotional environment, based on the assumption that identified psychological problems in one member of a family are not isolated, but are the result of unhealthful interactions within the entire family unit. Unlike GROUP PSYCHOTHERAPY, which concentrates on the individual within a group, family therapy focuses on the emotional life of the family as a whole. By defining the existing family structure and clarifying patterns, conflicts, and alliances, it enables family members to develop alternative patterns of relating to each other. Treatment may include both family and individual sessions with one or a team of therapists.

Fanfani, Amintore, 1908–, Italian political leader. A Christian Democrat, he served as foreign minister (1965, 1966–68), president of the Senate (1968–73, 1976–82), and as premier (1954, 1958–59, 1960–63, 1982–83).

Fantin-Latour, Ignace Henri Jean Théodore, 1836–1904, French painter and lithographer. Master of an almost photographic technique, he is best known for portrait groups of famous contemporaries, e.g., *The Studio at Batignolles* (Louvre).

Faraday, Michael, 1791–1867, English scientist. Despite little formal education he laid the foundations of classical FIELD theory, later developed by James Clerk MAXWELL. Faraday worked (1813–62) at the laboratory of the Royal Institution in London, becoming its director in 1825. He developed the first dynamo (in the form of a copper disk rotated between the poles of a permanent magnet), the precursor of modern dynamos and GENERATORS. From Faraday's and Joseph HENRY's independent discoveries (1831) of electromagnetic INDUCTION stemmed a vast development of electrical machinery for industry. In 1825 Faraday discovered the compound BENZENE. He formulated (1834) Faraday's law, which states that the number of MOLES of substance produced at an electrode during

ELECTROLYSIS is directly proportional to the number of moles of electrons transferred at that electrode.

farce, light theater piece with characters and events exaggerated to produce broad, simple humor. An element in the plays of ARISTOPHANES, PLAUTUS, and TERENCE, it appeared as a distinct genre in 15th-cent. France. Nicholas UDALL's *Ralph Roister Doister* (1566) is an early English example. Broad, ribald humor, absurdity, and buffoonery are also found in works not considered farces, e.g., the plays of MOLIÈRE. In the 20th cent. farce found expression in films by such artists as Charlie CHAPLIN and the MARX BROTHERS and in television by such figures as Lucille BALL and the cast of *Saturday Night Live*.

Far East, term commonly used today in a restricted sense for the region comprising E Asia (i.e., CHINA, JAPAN, KOREA, MONGOLIA) and the RUSSIAN FAR EAST. It is also sometimes extended to include SOUTHEAST ASIA. As used in the 19th cent., the term denoted those portions of the Asian continent farthest removed by sea from the W European maritime powers trading there.

Fargo, city (1990 pop. 74,111), seat of Cass co., E N.D., on the Red R., opposite Moorhead, Minn.; inc. 1875. The largest city in the state, Fargo developed with the coming (1871) of the railroad. It remains a railroad hub and river port, a regional finance center, and the trade center of a great spring wheat and livestock region. North Dakota State Univ. is located in the city.

Farid ad-Din Attar [ät-tär'], d. c.1229, Persian poet, one of the greatest Muslim mystic poets. Of his many and varied works, his masterpiece is *Conference of the Birds*, an allegory surveying the philosophy and practices of SUFISM.

Farley, James Aloysius, 1888–1976, American political leader; b. Rockland co., N.Y. As Democratic National Committee chairman, he managed (1932, 1936) F.D. ROOSEVELT's presidential campaigns. He served (1933–40) as U.S. postmaster general but resigned to protest Roosevelt's third term.

Farm Credit Administration (FCA), independent U.S. agency formed (1933) to supervise and coordinate the Farm Credit System, which provides credit to American farmers and their cooperatives. The system, which is borrower-owned, includes federal land-bank and land-credit associations, intermediate credit banks, banks for cooperatives, and production credit associations.

Farmer-Labor party, U.S. political organization founded (1919) to unite agrarian and organized labor interests. It promoted nationalization of various industries and resources but garnered little support and dissolved after 1924. The Minnesota Farmer-Labor party, unaffiliated with the national party, elected a governor and several U.S. senators and congressmen in the 1920s and 30s. It merged (1944) with the Minnesota Democratic party.

Farnese [färnā'zā], Italian noble family that ruled Parma and Piacenza from 1545 to 1731. In 1534 Alessandro Farnese became pope as PAUL III. He created (1545) the duchy of Parma and Piacenza for his illegitimate son, **Pier Luigi Farnese,** 1503–47, who was assassinated by nobles. His son and successor, **Ottavio Farnese,** 1520–86, married MARGARET OF PARMA. Their son, **Alessandro Farnese,** 1545–92, duke 1586–92, was a general in the service of PHILIP II of Spain. Appointed (1578) governor in the rebellious Netherlands, he took Tournai, Maastricht, Breda, Bruges, Ghent, and Antwerp from the rebels. In 1590 he entered France to aid the Catholic League against HENRY IV of France and relieved Paris (1590) and Rouen (1592). He is considered one of the age's greatest generals. The last duke of the line, Antonio, died in 1731. His niece, **Elizabeth Farnese,** 1692–1766, married (1714) PHILIP V of Spain and for a time virtually ruled Spain. She secured (1748) Parma and Piacenza for her son Philip, who founded the line of BOURBON-Parma.

Faröe Islands: see FAEROE ISLANDS.

Farouk, 1920–65, king of Egypt (1936–52), son and successor of Fuad I. He was regarded as a corrupt playboy and was deposed by the 1952 military coup led by Gamal Abdal NASSER. His infant son, Fuad II, succeeded him briefly.

Farquhar, George, 1678–1707, English dramatist; b. Ireland. The geniality of such plays as *The Constant Couple* (1699) and his masterpiece, *The Beaux' Stratagem* (1707), mark Farquhar as a transitional figure between RESTORATION and 18th-cent. drama.

Farragut, David Glasgow, 1801–70, American admiral; b. near Knoxville, Tenn. In the U.S. CIVIL WAR, he boldly sailed (1862) up the Mississippi R. and defeated an enemy flotilla, enabling Union forces to take New Orleans. In 1864, uttering the famous cry "Damn the torpedoes [mines]," he forced the defenses of Mobile, Ala., and defeated a Confederate fleet. The outstanding naval commander of the war, Farragut was the first officer in the U.S. navy to receive the ranks of vice admiral (1864) and admiral (1866).

Farrell, James T(homas), 1904–79, American novelist; b. Chicago. In the tradition of NATURALISM, his fiction deals with life in Chicago's Irish Catholic slums. His work includes the novels of the Studs Lonigan trilogy (1932–35) and Danny O'Neill pentalogy (1936–53), short stories, and essays.

Farrell, Suzanne, 1945–, American ballet dancer; b. Cincinnati, Ohio. She was a favorite at the NEW YORK CITY BALLET (1961–69, 1974–89), where BALANCHINE created several roles for her. She also danced (1970–74) with BÉJART's Ballet of the 20th Century.

farsightedness or **hyperopia,** defect of vision in which near objects appear blurred but far objects can be seen clearly. Because the eyeball is too short or the eye's refractive power too weak, the image is focused behind the retina of the EYE, rather than upon it. Eyeglasses with convex lenses can compensate for the refractive error (see LENS).

fascism, philosophy of government that glorifies the nation-state at the expense of the individual. Major concepts of fascism include opposition to democratic and socialist movements; racist ideologies, such as ANTI-SEMITISM; aggressive military policy; and belief in an authoritarian leader who embodies the ideals of the nation. Fascism generally gains support by promising social justice to discontented elements of the working and middle classes, and social order to powerful financial interests. While retaining class divisions and usually protecting capitalist and landowning interests, the fascist state exercises control at all levels of individual and economic activity, employing special police forces to instill fear. The term was first used by the party started by MUSSOLINI, who ruled Italy from 1922 until the Italian defeat in WORLD WAR II, and has also been applied to other right-wing movements, such as NATIONAL SOCIALISM in Germany and the FRANCO regime in Spain.

fashion, the prevailing mode affecting modifications in costume. Since Asian and classical dress remained unchanged for centuries, fashion may be said to have originated in Europe around the 14th cent. Over subsequent centuries new styles, set by monarchs and prominent persons (e.g., Beau BRUMMELL), were spread by travelers, in letters, and by the exchange of the fashion DOLL. The first fashion magazine appeared c.1586 in Frankfurt, Germany; the popular American *Godey's Lady's Book* first came out in 1830. In Paris—the leading arbiter of fashion since the Renaissance—the fading influence of celebrities coincided with the rise of designer-dressmakers in the mid-19th cent. Other world fashion centers have been London, Rome, Milan, and New York. Designer fashions have traditionally been luxury goods whose possession has been largely limited to the wealthy. During the 1970s and 80s the availability of relatively inexpensive ready-to-wear collections made fashionable dressing possible for a wider range of the population. For a list of major contemporary designers, see the accompanying table.

Fassbinder, Rainer Werner, 1946–82, German film director. His more than 40 films, many of which portray post-World War II German life, include *Why Does Herr R. Run Amok?* (1969), *The Marriage of Maria Braun* (1979), *Lola* (1982), and *Veronika Voss* (1982).

Fatehpur Sikri or **Fathpur Sikri** [fətəpo͞or' sĭk'rē], historic city, Uttar Pradesh state, N India. It was founded (1569) by AKBAR as his capital and is unique in India as a largely intact masterpiece of Mogul architecture.

Fates, in Greek mythology, three goddesses who controlled human life; also called the Moerae or Moirai. They were: Clotho, who spun the web of life; Lachesis, who measured its length; and Atropos, who cut it. The Roman Fates were the Parcae; the Germanic Fates were the NORNS.

Fathers of the Church, Christian writers of antiquity whose work is generally considered orthodox. A convenient definition includes all such writers up to and including St. GREGORY I in the West and St. JOHN OF DAMASCUS in the East. The Christian church also recognized **Doctors of the Church** who exhibited great holiness and learning. The eight ancient doctors are Saints Basil the Great, GREGORY NAZIANZEN, JOHN CHRYSOSTOM, and ATHANASIUS in the East and Saints AMBROSE, JEROME, AUGUSTINE, and GREGORY I in the West.

Fatimid or **Fatimite,** dynasty founded by Said ibn Husayn of NE Syria, which claimed the CALIPHATE on the basis of descent from Fatima, daughter of MUHAMMAD the Prophet. Doctrinally, the Fatimids were related to other Shiite sects, especially the DRUZE. Around 893 a follower of Said ibn Husayn, Al-Shii, went to NW Africa and, with the support of the BERBERS, won Tunisia, Sicily, NE Algeria, and NW Libya for the Fatimids. Said ibn Husayn was then hailed as the MAHDI. In the reign (953–75) of the fourth caliph, Moizz, the Fatimids conquered Egypt, Palestine, parts of Syria, and W Arabia. In 973 Moizz moved his capital to the new city of Cairo. Reliance on mercenaries, religious intolerance, and losses to the Normans and Crusaders in the 11th cent. led to the decline of the Fatimids, who were succeeded in their last stronghold, Egypt, by the rival ABBASIDS in 1171.

fats and oils, group of organic substances that are composed of carbon, hydrogen, and oxygen and are important in the diet and in industry. They are TRIGLYCERIDES, esters of one molecule of glycerol and three fatty acids. Generally, they are called fats if they are solid at room temperature and oils if liquid. **Saturated fats,** which are usually solid, are most common in animal foods such as lard, meat, dairy products, and eggs. They are called "saturated" because they have the highest possible number of hydrogen atoms attached to their carbon atoms. In **unsaturated fats,** which generally come from plant sources and are liquid, at least one hydrogen atom is missing and a carbon-carbon double bond occurs in its stead. If there is only one double bond, the fat is **monounsaturated;** fats with two or more double bonds are **polyunsaturated.** Unsaturated fats can be "hardened" by hydrogenation, i.e., by adding hydrogen atoms to reduce the number of double bonds and produce a saturated fat that is less likely to go rancid. Fats and oils are separated from their sources by pressing, rendering, or extraction with heat or solvents. Animal fats, such as lard, can be separated from animal tissues by rendering. Vegetable oils, e.g., those from OLIVES and linseed (see LINSEED OIL), are made by pressing fruits or seeds. The finest oils, used in food, are cold pressed. Subsequent warm pressing or extraction with solvents yields industrial-grade oil, used in making SOAP and other products. Fats and oils are essential to the body as energy sources and as a component of hormones and membranes, but excessive intake may contribute to ARTERIOSCLEROSIS, colon cancer, and gallstones. It is generally recommended that people limit the amount of fat and CHOLESTEROL in their diets and substitute unsaturated fats for saturated fats. See also ESSENTIAL OILS; FAT SUBSTITUTE; PETROLEUM.

fat substitute, substance used to replace dietary fat in the manufacture of foods. Fat substitutes are made in a variety of ways, mostly by manipulating natural food products such as egg whites, whey, and oats. Fat substitutes try to mimic the texture and flavor of fat while providing fewer calories and less metabolizable fat.

Faulkner, William, 1897–1962, American novelist; b. New Albany, Miss. One of the great American writers of the 20th cent., he explored the loss of traditional values and the decay and anguish of the post-Civil War South, using the imaginary Yoknapatawpha county as a microcosm of Southern life. A brilliant literary technician, Faulkner was master of a rhetorical, highly symbolic style. He was awarded the 1949 Nobel Prize in literature. His best-known novels include *The Sound and the Fury* (1929), *The Hamlet* (1940), *A Fable* (1954; Pulitzer), and *The Reivers* (1962; Pulitzer). He also published short stories, essays, and poems.

fault, in geology, a fracture in the earth's crust in which the rocks on each side move in relation to each other. This movement can be vertical, horizontal, or oblique. Horizontal faults showing lateral displacement of points originally directly opposite each other, such as the SAN ANDREAS FAULT in California, are called strike-slip. Another type of horizontal fault, the transform fault, occurs on the ocean floor between offset portions of the mid-ocean ridge (see PLATE TECTONICS). Altered positions of rocks due to faulting can mislead the geologist, because one rock layer can appear twice in the same cross section or disappear entirely. See also EARTHQUAKE.

Faunus, in Roman myth, woodland deity, protector of herds and crops; identified with the Greek PAN. He was attended by fauns—mischievous creatures, half man, half goat.

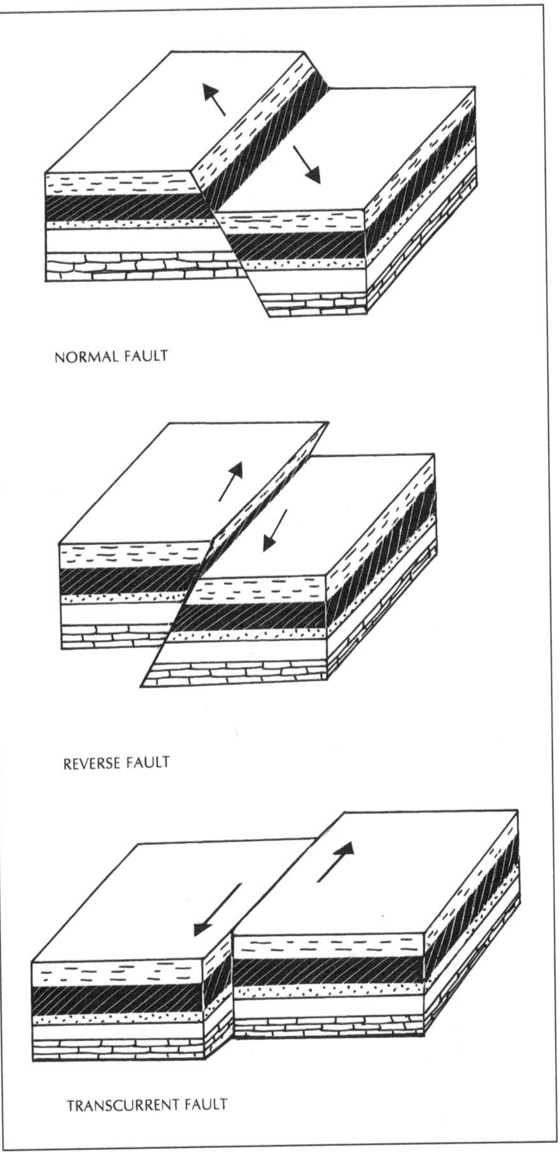

NORMAL FAULT

REVERSE FAULT

TRANSCURRENT FAULT

Types of vertical faults

Fauré, Gabriel Urbain [fōrā'], 1845–1924, French composer and teacher of RAVEL. His works include refined, intimate piano and chamber music, operas, a famous Requiem (1888), and songs, e.g., "Clair de Lune."

Faust, Faustus, or **Johann Faust** [foust], fl. 16th cent., learned German doctor who performed magic and died mysteriously. According to legend he sold his soul to the devil (Mephistopheles) in exchange for youth, knowledge, and magical power. Literary treatments of the story include the *Volksbuch* of Johannes Spies (1587), Christopher MARLOWE's *Dr. Faustus* (1593), GOETHE's masterpiece *Faust* (1808, 1833), and Thomas MANN's *Doctor Faustus* (1947). The legend inspired many composers of musical works, including BERLIOZ, GOUNOD, LISZT, SCHUMANN, and BOITO.

fauvism [fō'vĭzəm] Fr., *fauve* = wild beast, name derisively hurled at and cheerfully adopted by a group of French painters including MATISSE, ROUAULT, DERAIN, VLAMINCK, BRAQUE, and DUFY. Fauvism was essentially an expressionist style (see EXPRESSIONISM) characterized by distortion of forms and exuberant color. Although short-lived (1905–8), it was basic to the evolution of 20th-cent. art.

Fawkes, Guy: see GUNPOWDER PLOT.

fax machine: see FACSIMILE MACHINE.

FBI: see FEDERAL BUREAU OF INVESTIGATION.

Fe, chemical symbol of the element IRON.

feathers, outgrowths of the skin that constitute the protective and decorative plumage of birds and are thought to have evolved from reptilian scales in Mesozoic times. Feathers grow only along defined tracts; full grown, they lack a blood supply and have hollow shafts. Typically, barbs radiate from the distal part of the shaft (the rachis) and interlock via smaller cross-linking barbules to form a web, which gives the feather flexibility and durability. Down feathers of young birds and the protective undercoats of aquatic birds lack webs. Specializations (e.g., crests, ruffs, and topknots) and modifications (e.g., bristles) exist. Most feather colors (e.g., red, yellow, brown) are due to pigment in the feather; some (e.g., green and violet), as well as iridescent effects, are due to reflection and diffraction of light. The most important roles of feathers are in flight and heat retention.

feather star: see CRINOID.

February: see MONTH.

February Revolution, 1848, French revolution that overthrew the monarchy of LOUIS PHILIPPE and established the Second Republic. There was general dissatisfaction with the reactionary policies of the king and his minister François GUIZOT and with the poor conditions of the working class, which worsened in the economic crisis of 1846–47. After the government forbade a banquet to promote political opposition, street fighting began and government troops fired (Feb. 23, 1848) on the demonstrators, setting off the revolution. Louis Philippe abdicated on Feb. 24. A provisional government was formed and a republic was proclaimed, but the differing aims of the bourgeois revolutionaries and the radicals contributed to the revolution's eventual failure. To appease the workers and radicals, the right to work was guaranteed and national workshops were established, but deliberate mismanagement and the election of a more moderate government led to the dissolution of the workshops in May. The resulting workers' rebellion, known as the June Days, was crushed. After the completion of the republican constitution, Prince Louis Napoleon (later NAPOLEON III) was elected president. The revolution set off similar uprisings in Europe, but they failed virtually everywhere (see REVOLUTIONS OF 1848).

February Revolution, 1917, in Russian history: see RUSSIAN REVOLUTION.

Federal Art Project: see WORK PROJECTS ADMINISTRATION.

Federal Aviation Administration (FAA), U.S. government agency formed (1958) to regulate and promote air transportation. Its duties include the management of air traffic, the promulgation of safety regulations, and the setting of standards for airports and pilots. It assumed many of the functions of the **Civil Aeronautics Board,** or CAB (est. as the Civil Aeronautics Authority, 1938), and became (1967) part of the Dept. of Transportation. In 1981–82, it took over authority for the limited regulation of domestic routes and fares from the CAB, which was abolished by 1985.

Federal Bureau of Investigation (FBI), division of the U.S. Dept. of Justice charged with investigating all violations of federal law except those specifically assigned to other federal agencies. The FBI investigates espionage, sabotage, KIDNAPPING, bank robbery, CIVIL-RIGHTS violations, and fraud against the government, and conducts security clearances. Created in 1908, the bureau greatly increased its scope under the directorship (1924–72) of J. Edgar HOOVER, gaining wide popularity in the 1930s for its fight against criminal desperadoes such as John DILLINGER and against World War II saboteurs. During Hoover's controversial final years, the FBI came under attack for what many considered political bias and violation of the constitutional rights of citizens. See also INTELLIGENCE GATHERING.

Federal Communications Commission (FCC), independent U.S. agency created (1934) to regulate interstate and foreign communications, including various kinds of radio, television, wire, cable television, and satellite transmissions. The FCC is empowered to grant, revoke, renew, and modify broadcasting licenses and to assign broadcast frequencies.

Federal Constitutional Convention, in U.S. history, the meeting (May–Sept. 1787) in Philadelphia at which the CONSTITUTION OF THE UNITED STATES was drawn up. The Articles of CONFEDERATION, under which the U.S. had been governed, provided only a weak central government that had trouble conducting foreign policy, quelling internal disorders, and maintaining economic stability. Demand for a more centralized government grew steadily among the wealthy and conservative classes in many states. In 1786 a commercial conference, the ANNAPOLIS CONVENTION, disbanded with a call to convene a meeting in Philadelphia the next year for the purpose of revising the Articles. All states except Rhode Island sent delegates; George WASHINGTON presided. The major dispute at the convention was between large and small states over representation in the new Congress. A compromise proposal for a Congress with an upper house in which states were equally represented and a lower house elected by population was proposed by Oliver ELLSWORTH and Roger Sherman and finally approved. James MADISON was the chief drafter of the Constitution; Gouverneur MORRIS contributed to its style. Despite opposition, a sufficient number of states ratified the document to make it effective by the end of June 1788.

Federal Deposit Insurance Corporation (FDIC), independent U.S. agency established (1933) to promote public confidence in banks and to protect the money supply by providing a floor of insurance coverage for bank deposits in all national and state banks that are members of the FEDERAL RESERVE SYSTEM. It also examines insured state-chartered banks that are not members of the Federal Reserve. Since 1989 the FDIC has supervised the Savings Association Insurance Fund, the agency that was created to provide coverage for SAVINGS AND LOAN ASSOCIATIONS when the Federal Savings and Loan Insurance Corporation became insolvent. A sharp increase in bank failures in the late 1980s and early 1990s led to the insolvency (1991–92) of the FDIC as well, forcing it to seek government loans.

federal government or **federation,** government of a union of states in which sovereignty is divided between a central authority and component state authorities. The central government most often handles the concerns of the people as a whole, including foreign affairs, defense, coinage, and commerce; the local entities retain other jurisdictions. A successful federation usually requires a fairly uniform legal system and broad cultural affinities. The federal system is often accompanied by tensions between the central government (with its need for unity among the states) and state governments (with their desire for autonomy). Modern federations include Australia, Canada, India, Russia, Switzerland, and the U.S.

Federalist party, U.S. political faction that supported a strong federal government. During Pres. WASHINGTON's administration (1789–97), political factions appeared within his cabinet, and the group that gathered around Alexander HAMILTON was called Federalists. They were conservatives who favored strong centralized government, encouragement of industry, attention to the needs of the great merchants and landowners, and a well-ordered society. They also were pro-British in foreign affairs. The party was concentrated in New England, with a strong element in the Middle Atlantic states. After the Democratic party's victory in 1800, the Federalists remained powerful locally, but leadership passed to reactionaries rather than moderates. Federalist opposition to the EMBARGO ACT OF 1807 and to the WAR OF 1812 resulted in the HARTFORD CONVENTION, but the successful issue of the war ruined the party, and by 1824 it was virtually dead.

Federal Reserve System, central banking system of the U.S., established by the Federal Reserve Act (1913). The act created 12 regional Federal Reserve banks, supervised by a Federal Reserve Board. All national banks must belong to the system, and state banks may if they meet certain requirements. Member banks hold the bulk of the deposits of all commercial banks in the country. The Board of Governors of the Federal Reserve System is composed of seven members appointed to staggered 14-year terms by the president, who also names one of the governors as chairman but has no power to remove any member. The Federal Open Market Committee directs purchases and sales by the reserve banks of U.S. government securities in the open market. The most important duties of the Federal Reserve authorities involve the maintenance of national monetary and credit conditions through lending to member banks, open-market operations, fixing reserve requirements, and establishing discount rates. In a sense, each Federal

Reserve bank is a "banker's bank," with member banks using their reserve accounts much as bank depositors use their checking accounts. By controlling the credit market, the Federal Reserve System influences the nation's economic life. It can expand or contract the MONEY supply by buying or selling U.S. securities and by raising or lowering reserve requirements (the amount that member banks must set aside as reserves). Other important functions include the issuance of currency and coins and the setting of margin requirements (credit limits) in the stock exchanges. See also CENTRAL BANK.

Federal Trade Commission (FTC), independent U.S. agency established in 1914 and charged with keeping business competition free and fair. Its duties include enforcing ANTITRUST LAWS, preventing the dissemination of false and deceptive advertising, regulating the labeling and packaging of commodities, and gathering data concerning business conditions and making it available to Congress, the president, and the public. It may require corporations to submit information about their business practices if there is substantial evidence of wrongdoing. It is also empowered to issue cease-and-desist orders and to take violators to court.

Federal Writers' Project: see WORK PROJECTS ADMINISTRATION.

federation: see FEDERAL GOVERNMENT.

Feininger, Lyonel, 1871–1956, American painter; b. N.Y.C. Living in Europe, he was an illustrator and caricaturist before turning to easel painting in 1907. Feininger exhibited with the BLAUE REITER group and taught at the BAUHAUS in Germany (1919–32). He returned to the U.S. in 1937. Feininger developed a geometric style with interlocking translucent planes, often portraying sailboats or skyscrapers.

Feisal: see FAISAL.

feldspar or **felspar,** a group of potassium-, sodium-, and calcium-aluminum silicate minerals ($KAlSi_3O_8$, $NaAlSi_3O_8$, and $CaAl_2Si_2O_8$) and their isomorphic mixtures. The three pure members are called, respectively, orthoclase, albite, and anorthite. As constituents of crystalline rocks, the feldspars form much of the earth's crust. Pure feldspar is colorless and transparent, but impurities commonly make it opaque and colorful. Potassium feldspars are used in making porcelain and as a source of aluminum in making glass. The plagioclase feldspars (those ranging in composition from albite to anorthite) are commonly gray and occasionally red. MOONSTONE is a gem variety.

Felix V, antipope: see AMADEUS VIII.

Feller, Bob (Robert William Andrew Feller), 1918–, American baseball player; b. Van Meter, Iowa. A pitcher famous for his fastball, he won 266 games (1936–56) with the Cleveland Indians. He threw 3 no-hit and 12 one-hit games.

Fellini, Federico [făl-lē'nē], 1920–93, Italian film director. His films, noted for their extravagant visual fantasy, include *La Dolce Vita* (1960), *8½* (1963), *Juliet of the Spirits* (1965), *Fellini Satyricon* (1969), *Amarcord* (1973), *City of Women* (1980), and *Voices of the Moon* (1990).

felony, in CRIMINAL LAW, an offense more serious than a MISDEMEANOR, from which it is distinguished by the severity of the prescribed punishment. State laws vary, but in most U.S. jurisdictions (and in federal statutes), felonies are those crimes punishable by death or by imprisonment for more than one year. Felonies are usually tried by a JURY.

felspar: see FELDSPAR.

Femgericht: see VEHMGERICHT.

feminism, movement for women's political, social, and educational equality with men. Early leaders, including Mary WOLLSTONECRAFT in England and Elizabeth Cady STANTON and Susan B. ANTHONY in the U.S., demanded full legal and economic equality for women. Gradually, women in the U.S. won the right to own property and to enter the professions, and in 1920, after a prolonged struggle for WOMAN SUFFRAGE led by Carrie Chapman CATT and others, they obtained the right to vote through the passage of the 19th amendment to the U.S. CONSTITUTION. Women were fully enfranchised in Britain by 1928 and throughout most of the world by 1950. Betty FRIEDAN and the NATIONAL ORGANIZATION FOR WOMEN played prominent roles in the resurgence of feminism in the U.S. from the 1960s, stressing equal pay and employment opportunities, DAY-CARE CENTERS, the right to ABORTION, and the need to end SEXUAL HARASSMENT and sex

Federico Fellini

stereotyping. The movement failed in one of its key goals, that of securing ratification of the federal Equal Rights Amendment, and legalized abortion also energized an anti-abortion, anti-feminist backlash in the U.S. that succeeded in restoring some restrictions on abortion. Nonetheless, much of what feminists sought in the 1960s was gained.

fencing, sport of dueling with foil, épée, and saber. The weapons and rules of modern fencing evolved from combat weapons and their usage. The foil, a light, flexible weapon with a blunted point, was originally used for practice. The épée, or dueling sword, is a straight, narrow, stiff weapon without cutting edges. The saber, a light version of the old cavalry broadsword, has a flexible, triangular blade with theoretical cutting edges. Fencing matches may be conducted among individuals or between teams, generally of nine players (three for each weapon). Points are made by touching the opponent. Protective clothing includes heavy canvas jackets, wire-mesh masks, and gloves. In women's fencing, only the foil is used. Fencing was first developed as a sport by the Germans in the 14th cent. It was included in the first modern Olympic games in 1896.

Fenian movement [fē'nēən], a secret revolutionary society organized c.1858 in Ireland and the U.S. to achieve Irish independence from England by force. The famine of the 1840s, which forced vast numbers of Irishmen to emigrate, brought to a crisis Irish discontent with English rule. In Ireland the Fenian movement was led by James Stephens. It appealed to the nonagrarian population and was opposed by the Roman Catholic Church. The various Fenian risings and acts of terrorism led at first to suppression by the British but eventually drew Parliament's attention to Irish problems. The movement in the U.S. was led by the émigré Irish revolutionary John O'Mahony. In 1865 a group of embittered Irish-American Fenians unsuccessfully attempted to invade Canada. The movement continued until 1914, but its influence was largely drawn into new organizations, notably the SINN FÉIN.

Fenians, a professional military corps that roamed over ancient Ireland (c.3d cent.) in the service of the high kings. They figure in the legends that developed around FINN MAC CUMHAIL and OSSIAN.

fennel, common name for several herbs, particularly those of the genus *Foeniculum* of the CARROT family. Their licorice-scented foliage and seeds are used for flavoring. Sweet fennel has a thickened leaf base and is eaten like CELERY.

Fens, the, also **Fenland,** fertile agricultural district, E England, reclaimed from The Wash, an arm of the North Sea. First Romans, then Saxons, attempted to drain the low-lying original swampland. Effective drainage began in the 17th cent. under Cornelius Vermuyden, a Dutch engineer, and continued into the 19th cent. A drainage-improvement program was completed in the 1960s to deal with continued land sinkage.

Ferber, Edna, 1887–1968, American author; b. Kalamazoo, Mich. Her colorful novels of American life include *So Big* (1924; Pulitzer),

Show Boat (1926), and *Giant* (1952). She also wrote plays with G.S. KAUFMAN, e.g., *Stage Door* (1936).

Ferdinand, rulers of the HOLY ROMAN EMPIRE. **Ferdinand I,** 1503–64, emperor (1558–64), king of BOHEMIA (1526–64) and of HUNGARY (1526–64), was the younger brother of Emperor CHARLES V; he increasingly acted as Charles's agent in the Hapsburg lands. In Hungary he fought against rival claimants who had the support of Ottoman Sultan SULAYMAN I, to whom he eventually was forced to pay tribute. In Bohemia, Ferdinand vigorously pushed Catholic reform and established HAPSBURG absolutism. In Germany he dealt with the Peasants' War and other rebellions and negotiated the Peace of Augsburg (1555). Charles abdicated in his favor in 1558. **Ferdinand II,** 1578–1637, emperor (1619–37), king of Bohemia (1617–37) and of Hungary (1618–37), was the grandson of Ferdinand I. In 1619 the Bohemian nobles rebelled and elected FREDERICK THE WINTER KING, thus beginning the THIRTY YEARS WAR. Ferdinand defeated Frederick in 1620, but the war continued. Ferdinand was almost certainly responsible for the murder (1634) of his leading general, WALLENSTEIN. **Ferdinand III,** 1608–57, emperor (1637–57), king of Hungary (1626–57) and of Bohemia (1627–57), was nominal head after 1634 of the imperialist forces in the Thirty Years War. After he succeeded his father, Ferdinand II, as emperor, the war took a disastrous turn. The Peace of WESTPHALIA, which he was forced to accept (1648), virtually ended the central power of the Holy Roman Empire. Ferdinand spent the last years of his reign healing the wounds of war and reforming the imperial bureaucracy.

Ferdinand, 1861–1948, czar of Bulgaria (1908–18), after being ruling prince (1887–1908). He declared Bulgarian independence from Turkey in 1908 and was a victor in the first of the BALKAN WARS (1912–13). His fortunes later declined, and in 1918 he was forced to abdicate in favor of his son, BORIS III.

Ferdinand, kings of Bohemia and Hungary: see FERDINAND, rulers of the Holy Roman Empire.

Ferdinand, kings of Portugal. **Ferdinand I,** 1345–83 (r.1367–83), the son of PETER I, had ambitions for the throne of CASTILE that led to three disastrous wars between 1369 and 1382. In 1372 he allied himself with JOHN OF GAUNT of England, but their two wars against Castile resulted in defeat. The final war ended with the marriage of Ferdinand's daughter, Beatrice, and John I of Castile. After Ferdinand's death and a national revolution, the throne of Portugal went to his half brother, JOHN I. **Ferdinand II,** 1816–85 (r.1837–53), was the king consort of Maria II of Portugal and was regent for their son, Peter V. He was more interested in his art collection than in governing the country.

Ferdinand, 1865–1927, king of ROMANIA (1914–27); nephew and successor of CAROL I. He took Romania (1916) into WORLD WAR I on the Allied side. In 1918 he acquired Bessarabia, and in 1919 he successfully intervened in Hungary against the Communist government of Bela KUN. During his reign agrarian reforms and universal male suffrage were instituted.

Ferdinand, Spanish kings. **Ferdinand I** (the Great), d. 1065, king of CASTILE (1035–65) and of LEÓN (1037–65), inherited the former kingdom and conquered the latter. He reduced the Moorish kings of Zaragoza, Badajoz, SEVILLE, and TOLEDO to vassalage and introduced church reforms. Prior to his death he divided his kingdom among three sons. **Ferdinand III,** 1199–1252, king of Castile (1217–52) and León (1230–52), permanently united the two kingdoms in 1230. He crusaded against the MOORS and completed the reconquest of Spain, except for the kingdom of GRANADA, by 1248. **Ferdinand IV,** 1285–1312, king of Castile and León (1295–1312), conquered GIBRALTAR (1309) from the Moors with the help of ARAGÓN, but he failed in his attempt to take Algeciras. **Ferdinand V** (the Catholic), king of Castile and León (1474–1504, jointly with his wife, ISABELLA I), king of Aragón (as Ferdinand II, 1479–1516), king of Sicily (1468–1516), and king of Naples (1504–16), with his wife completed the unification of Spain by conquering Granada in 1492. In that fateful year they also expelled the JEWS and sponsored COLUMBUS's discovery of the New World. Ferdinand fought France in the ITALIAN WARS and captured NAPLES. After Isabella's death (1504), he kept control of Castile by acting as regent for their daughter, JOANNA. He increased the powers of the throne by curbing the nobles and the CORTES. During his reign Spain became an Atlantic power and revolutionized European commerce. He left a vast empire to his grandson, Holy Roman Emperor CHARLES V. **Ferdinand VI,** c.1712–59, king of Spain (1746–59), kept the nation out of the SEVEN YEARS WAR during his lifetime. After the death (1758) of his beloved queen, Maria Barbara de Braganza, Ferdinand did not recover from his grief and soon followed her in death. **Ferdinand VII,** 1784–1833, king of Spain (1808–32), was forced by NAPOLEON I to renounce his throne and was imprisoned in France during the PENINSULAR WAR (1808–14). His name became the rallying cry of Spanish nationalists who resisted the French invaders and proclaimed (1812) a liberal constitution. But when he was restored to the throne (1814), Ferdinand proved to be a thorough reactionary; he abolished the new constitution but was forced to reinstate it by a revolution (1820). Backed by France's military intervention, he revoked the constitution again (1823) and ruthlessly repressed Spanish liberals. Ferdinand's death caused no less trouble than his reign: he had excluded his brother, Don Carlos, from the throne and thus brought on the CARLIST wars.

Ferdinand, kings of the TWO SICILIES. **Ferdinand I,** 1751–1825 (r.1816–1825), had previously been king of Naples as Ferdinand IV and king of Sicily as Ferdinand III. He had succeeded (1759) to the kingdoms when his father became king of Spain as CHARLES III. He opposed the French, who drove him from Naples to Sicily in 1799 and 1806. Restored (1815) in Naples, he abolished Sicilian autonomy and proclaimed himself king of the Two Sicilies. His rule was despotic. His grandson, **Ferdinand II,** 1810–59 (r.1830–59), initially tried to improve the kingdom's wretched state but soon drifted into absolutism. He bombarded Messina (1848) and Palermo (1849) to quell disorders, thus earning the nickname "King Bomba."

Ferdinand the Catholic: see Ferdinand V under FERDINAND, Spanish kings.

Fergana Valley or **Ferghana Valley** [fyĕrgənä'], region, c.8,500 sq mi (22,000 sq km), in Uzbekistan, Tajikistan, and Kyrgyzstan, central Asia. It is one of the most densely populated agricultural and industrial areas in central Asia, with important oil, coal, natural gas, and iron deposits. The valley belonged to a succession of central Asian empires and prospered until the 16th cent. from caravan trade along the traditional silk route between China and the Mediterranean. It was acquired by Russia in 1876 and became part of the USSR after the Russian Revolution. The region was divided when the Uzbek, Tadzhik, and Kirghiz SSRs were established in the 1920s.

Ferlinghetti, Lawrence, 1919–, American poet and publisher; b. Yonkers, N.Y. His City Lights Bookshop in San Francisco was a center for BEAT GENERATION writers. Among his volumes of verse is *A Coney Island of the Mind* (1958).

Fermat, Pierre de [fĕrmä'], 1601–65, French mathematician and magistrate. Although his work in mathematics was done for recreation, he was a founder of modern NUMBER THEORY and PROBABILITY theory. Many developments in number theory resulted from unsuccessful attempts to prove **Fermat's Last Theorem,** a conjecture that states that the equation $x^n + y^n = z^n$, where x, y, and z are nonzero integers, has no solutions for n when n is an integer greater than 2. In 1993 British mathematician Andrew Wiles described an apparent (but as yet unverified) proof of the conjecture.

fermentation, process by which a living cell can obtain energy through the anaerobic breakdown of glucose and other simple sugar molecules. Of the many different kinds of glucose fermentation, two kinds predominate: one, in microorganisms and animal cells, produces lactic acid as the sole end product; the other, in brewer's yeast and some bacteria, yields ethyl alcohol and carbon dioxide. Alcoholic fermentation to produce intoxicating beverages was practiced in antiquity. By 1500 B.C. production of beer from germinating cereals (malt) and of wine from crushed grapes was an established technical art in most of the Middle East. The modern science of BIOCHEMISTRY emerged directly from 19th-cent. studies of fermentation.

fermented milk, whole or skim milk curdled and thickened by lactic-acid-producing microorganisms. It was used in many forms by early nomadic herdsmen, especially in Asia, S and E Europe, Scandinavia, Africa, and South America. Yogurt, acidophilus milk, cultured buttermilk, and kumiss (koumiss) are forms of fermented milk.

Fermi, Enrico, 1901–54, American physicist; b. Italy; came to U.S., 1938. He contributed to the early theory of beta decay and the NEUTRINO and to quantum statistics and discovered the element NEPTUNIUM. For his experiments with RADIOACTIVITY, he was awarded the 1938 Nobel Prize in physics. Fermi created (1942) the first self-sustaining chain reaction in uranium and worked on the atomic bomb at Los Alamos (see MANHATTAN PROJECT). He later helped develop the hydrogen bomb and served on the General Advisory Committee of the U.S. Atomic Energy Commission.

Fermi National Accelerator Laboratory (Fermilab), physical science research center (est. 1968) located near Batavia, Ill. Universities Research Association operates it under contract to the U.S. Dept. of Energy. Work at Fermilab is devoted to the study of elementary particles, principally through the use of a synchrotron particle accelerator capable of accelerating protons up to energies of 500 billion electron-volts.

fermion, any of a group of subatomic particles that have half-integral values of the quantum mechanical property called spin and are "antisocial," in that two of them cannot exist in the same quantum state. Fermions include the leptons and QUARKS, which are the basic components of matter. The proton, neutron, electron, and neutrinos are fermions. Fermi-Dirac statistics describe the behavior of systems of fermions. See BOSON; ELEMENTARY PARTICLES; STATISTICAL MECHANICS.

fermium (Fm), radioactive element, discovered in 1952 by Albert Ghiorso and colleagues in residue from a thermonuclear explosion. Its physical properties are largely unknown; its chemical properties are similar to those of other ACTINIDE SERIES members. See ELEMENT (table); PERIODIC TABLE.

fern, any plant of the division Polypodiophyta (sometimes called Filicophyta or Pterophyta), consisting of several thousand species found worldwide, usually in tropical rain forests. Most common living ferns belong to the polypody family (Polypodiaceae) and are characterized by triangular fronds subdivided into many leaflets (pinnae) and smaller pinnules. Except for ornamentals, the only commercially important ferns are tree ferns (families Dicksoniaceae and Cyatheaceae), whose trunks are used in construction; the starchy pith is used as stock feed. Ancestors of modern ferns were the dominant vegetation during the Carboniferous era. They, and such relatives as CLUB MOSSES and HORSETAILS, are the most primitive plants to have developed a true vascular system. Ferns reproduce by alternation of generations (see REPRODUCTION), and although no present-day ferns reproduce by seed, there is some fossil evidence that fernlike plants are the ancestors of seed plants (GYMNOSPERMS and ANGIOSPERMS).

Fernández de Lizardi, José Joaquín [fārnän'dās dā lēsar'dē], 1776–1827, Mexican writer. A dramatist and poet, he is best known for his picaresque satire *The Itching Parrot* (1816–30), considered the first Spanish-American novel.

Ferrara, city (1990 pop. 141,404), in Emilia-Romagna, N Italy, an industrial and agricultural center on a marshy plain. It was the site of an ESTE family principality (13th cent.). Its commerce and art flourished during the Renaissance. The 12th-cent. cathedral, 14th-cent. castle, and several palaces are notable.

Ferrara-Florence, Council of: see COUNCIL, ECUMENICAL.

Ferraro, Geraldine A(nne), 1935–, U.S. politician; b. N.Y.C. A Democrat, she served three terms in the House of Representatives (1979–84). In 1984, as Walter MONDALE's running mate, she became the first woman nominated for the vice presidency by a major party in the U.S. In 1993 she was appointed U.S. representative on the UN Human Rights Commission.

ferret, domesticated polecat (*Mustela putorius*), a WEASEL common in the Old World. Used for centuries to hunt rats, mice, and rabbits, the ferret is related to the wild North American black-footed ferret (*M. nigripes*), which was nearly extinct by 1986, when the last wild black-footed ferrets were trapped. Since then they have been bred in captivity; the process of reestablishing them in the wild was begun in 1991.

Fertile Crescent, historic region of the Middle East, flanked by the Nile R. (W) and the Tigris and Euphrates rivers (E). A well-watered area, it includes parts of Israel, Lebanon, Jordan, and Iraq. It was the cradle of many ancient civilizations, e.g., EGYPT and MESOPOTAMIA.

fertility drug, any of a variety of substances used to increase the potential for conception and successful pregnancy by correcting various functional disorders. In the male, inadequate sperm production can often be remedied by administering thyroid hormones and, sometimes, pituitary hormones. In the female, failure to ovulate, a common cause of female sterility, can sometimes be treated with the administration of gonadotropic hormone and, in some cases, clomiphene citrate. Clomiphene often induces more than one ovum per month and can result in multiple births. In cases of repeated miscarriage or bleeding during pregnancy, PROGESTERONE has been found effective.

fertilization, in biology, sexual reproductive process involving the union of two unlike sex cells (gametes)—the ovum, or egg (female), and sperm (male)—followed by fusion of their nuclei. The principle of fertilization is the same in all organisms. The ovum absorbs the first sperm to make successful contact, and the two nuclei fuse, combining the hereditary material of both parents; the subsequent EMBRYO develops into a new individual. In lower plants and animals, the sperm swims to the egg through an external medium or through fluid in the female reproductive tract. In some higher plants, POLLINATION enables the sperm to contact the egg. In higher animals, sperm contact initiates cell division in the fertilized egg (zygote).

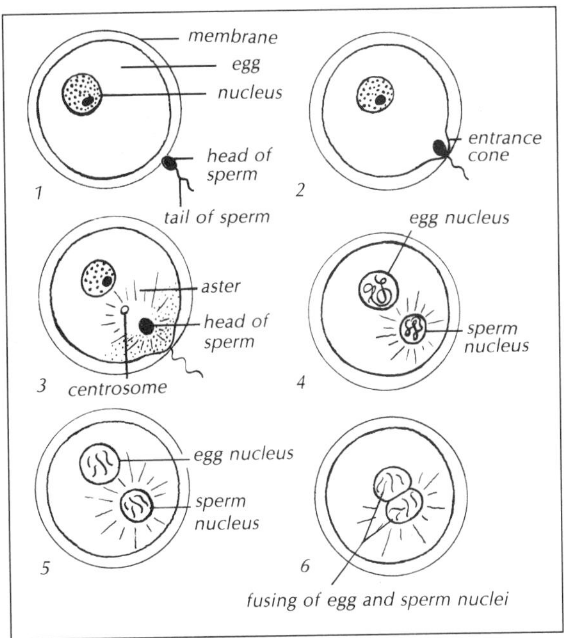

Fertilization of an egg cell

fertilizer, organic or inorganic material added to the soil to replace or increase plant nutrients. Organic fertilizers—including animal and green manure, fish and bone meal, guano (seabird excrement), and compost—are decomposed by soil microorganisms, and their elements are freed for plant use (see HUMUS). Most inorganic or chemical fertilizers contain the major nutrients (nitrogen, phosphorus, and potassium) in proportions required by the crop. Properly used, fertilizers increase crop yields and have helped make up for the world decrease in farmland. There are concerns, however, that inorganic nitrogenous fertilizers, in suppressing nitrogen-fixing bacteria, create a cycle in which more and more fertilizer is needed. In addition, nitrogen fertilizers that wash from farms into lakes and streams promote overgrowth of aquatic vegetation and cause EUTROPHICATION. See also NITROGEN CYCLE.

Festus (Sextus Pompeius Festus), fl. at some time between A.D. 100 and 400, Roman lexicographer. His surviving work, *On the Meaning of Words,* an abridgment of the lost glossary of Marcus Verrius Flaccus, is important as a primary source for Roman scholarship and antiquities.

fetal alcohol syndrome (FAS), pattern of physical, developmental, and psychological abnormalities seen in babies born to mothers who consumed alcohol during pregnancy. Abnormalities include low birth weight, facial deformities, and mental retardation, and there appears to be an association with impulsive behavior, anxiousness, and an inability on the part of the affected children to understand the consequences of their actions. FAS affects 1 to 2 babies per 1,000 born worldwide.

fetal tissue implant, implantation of tissue from a FETUS into a patient. In experimental procedures, fetal brain tissue has been implanted in the brains of patients with PARKINSON'S DISEASE so that the fetal tissue will supply chemicals lacking in the diseased brain. Because fetal cell therapy uses tissue from freshly aborted fetuses, the procedure is controversial. The successful transplantation of fetal ovaries in experiments with mice led to the suggestion in 1994 that human fetal ovaries could be implanted in infertile women, a possibility that troubled many ethicists and others.

fetish, inanimate natural or cultural object believed to have magical power, either from a will of its own or from a god that has transformed the object into an instrument of its desires. A fetish with great power is often declared TABOO.

fetus, term used to describe the unborn offspring in the uterus of vertebrate animals after the embryonic stage. In humans, the fetal stage begins seven to eight weeks after fertilization of the egg, when the EMBRYO assumes the basic shape of the newborn and all the organs are present, and continues until birth. Births before 36 weeks after conception are considered premature. See also PREGNANCY AND BIRTH.

Feuchtwanger, Lion [foikht'väng-ər], 1884–1958, German historical novelist. He achieved fame with *The Ugly Duchess* (1923), *Jud Süss* (1925), and the *Josephus* trilogy (1923–42). Feuchtwanger left Germany in 1933 and lived in the U.S. after 1940. His novels are noted for imaginative historical reconstruction and character portrayal.

feudalism, a political and social system in Western Europe from the end of CHARLEMAGNE's empire (late 9th cent. A.D.) to the rise of absolute monarchies. It had a local agricultural economy with the manor as its unit. In the MANORIAL SYSTEM, the VILLEIN and SERF held land from the lord of the manor, the seigneur or suzerain, in return for services, dues, and an oath of fealty. The king owned all land. Under him came a hierarchy of nobles, the highest holding land from the king, and those of lesser rank from the nobles above them. Landholding was by fief and was ceremonially acquired by INVESTITURE. The unsettled conditions of the time necessitated warriors for the lord and protection for the vassal. Gradations of vassalage were based on landholding and military service, from the single serf to private armies of hundreds. The KNIGHT was the typical warrior, with the squire below him and counts, dukes, and other nobles above him. The system, rooted in the decay of Roman institutions, spread from France to Spain, to Italy, and later to Germany and E Europe. WILLIAM I (the Conqueror) brought (1066) the Frankish form of feudalism to England. Feudalism waned as powerful monarchies broke down local systems, but it lingered in France until the French Revolution, in Germany and Japan until the 19th cent., and in Russia until 1917 (although serfdom was abolished officially in 1861).

Feuerbach, Ludwig Andreas, 1804–72, German philosopher. At first a follower of HEGEL, he abandoned IDEALISM for materialism, a progression that influenced Karl MARX in the development of DIALECTICAL MATERIALISM. Feuerbach rejected the "illusionistic" nature of religion and established a naturalistic-humanistic ethic that held humanity and nature to be the proper study of philosophy. His best-known work, *The Essence of Christianity* (1841), was translated into English by George ELIOT.

Feuerbach, Paul Johann Anselm von, 1775–1833, German jurist. A criminal-law theorist, he argued in *Critique of Natural Law* (1796) that law was the positive mandate of the state, and not to be confused with natural morality. Feuerbach saw a dual role for criminal law as protector both of society (through its deterrent function) and of the individual (through its exact definition of crimes). In 1813 he drafted an influential liberal criminal code in Bavaria.

Feuillants, political club of the FRENCH REVOLUTION. Emerging in July 1791, the group advocated a constitutional monarchy. After the fall (Sept. 1792) of the monarchy, it was suppressed by the JACOBINS.

Feynman, Richard Phillips, 1918–88, American physicist; b. N.Y.C. He shared (1965) the Nobel Prize in physics for his work on quantum electrodynamics. Feynman also explained, with Murray GELL-MANN, the WEAK INTERACTION. He worked on the early development of the atomic bomb and developed the Feynman diagram, a system of notation used to describe and calculate subatomic reactions.

Fez, city (1990 est. pop. 1,012,000), N central Morocco. It is located in a rich agricultural region. The city is noted for its Muslim art and its handicraft industries. It has given its name to the brimless felt caps that were formerly characteristic items of Muslim dress in the Middle East. Fez reached its zenith under the Marinid sultans in the mid-14th cent. It consists of the old city (founded A.D. 808) and the new city (founded 1276), connected by walls; there is also a European suburb. The city has more than 100 mosques.

Fianna Fáil, Irish political party, organized in 1926 by opponents of the Anglo-Irish treaty (1921) that established the Irish Free State. Led by Eamon DE VALERA, the party gained control of the government in 1932 and advocated separation from Great Britain. Except for 1948–51 and 1954–57, it held power until 1973. It returned to power under John LYNCH (1977–79), Charles HAUGHEY (1979–81, Mar.–Dec. 1982, 1987–92), and Albert REYNOLDS (1992–). Since 1989 the party has shared power in coalition governments with the Progressive Democrats (1989–92) and with Labor (1993–).

fiber, threadlike strand, usually pliable and capable of being spun into a yarn. Fibers are classified as either natural (including animal, vegetable, and inorganic) or artificial (see SYNTHETIC TEXTILE FIBERS). Animal fibers, e.g., SILK, WOOL, and goat hair (mohair), consist mainly of proteins. Vegetable fibers, e.g., COTTON, consist mainly of cellulose. ASBESTOS is the chief natural inorganic fiber; FIBERGLASS also is of inorganic origin. Artificial fibers are made either by synthesizing POLYMERS, as in nylon, or by altering natural fibers, as in RAYON. Fibers are used for textiles, e.g., cotton, silk, wool; cordage, e.g., hemp; brushes, e.g., animal hairs; filling, e.g., horsehair; and plaiting, e.g., sisal. The invention of SPINNING and weaving machinery during the INDUSTRIAL REVOLUTION greatly increased the demand for fibers.

fiber, dietary, or **roughage,** bulky part of food that cannot be broken down by enzymes in the small intestine, consisting of cellulose, pectin, and other materials. Although it has little nutritional value, fiber's bulk prevents constipation and minimizes intestinal disorders. People with a high-fiber diet statistically have lower colon cancer rates and lower levels of CHOLESTEROL and triglycerides in the blood. Almost all dietary fiber comes from plants, particularly legumes, green leafy vegetables, whole fruits, and bran and whole grains.

fiberglass, thread made from glass. Molten glass is forced through a kind of sieve, thus spinning it into threads. Strong, durable, and impervious to many caustics and to extreme temperatures, fiberglass fabrics are widely used in industry. Some, resembling silk and cotton, are used for drapery. Boat hulls and auto bodies molded of fiberglass combined with plastic are rustproof.

fiber optics, transmission of messages or information by light pulses along hair-thin glass fibers. Cables of optical fibers can be made smaller and lighter than conventional cables of copper wires or coaxial tubes, yet they can carry much more information, making them useful for transmitting large amounts of data between computers and for carrying data-intensive television pictures or many simultaneous telephone conversations. Optical fibers are immune to electromagnetic interference (from lightning, nearby electric motors, and similar sources) and to crosstalk from adjoining wires, and tapping into them is more easily detected. They also require fewer repeaters over a given distance than copper wire does to keep a signal from deteriorating. In addition to communications, optical fibers are used to transmit light in automobiles and aircraft, in medical equipment, and in other products.

Fibonacci, Leonardo [fēbōnät'chē]; b. c.1170, d. after 1240; Italian mathematician, known also as Leonardo da Pisa. The Fibonacci SEQUENCE 0, 1, 1, 2, 3, 5, 8, 13, 21, . . . , in which each term is the sum of the two preceding terms, occurs in higher mathematics in various connections.

Fichte, Johann Gottlieb, 1762–1814, German philosopher. He received early recognition for *A Critique of All Revelation* (1788), erroneously attributed to KANT. His later works, including *The Vocation of Man* (1800), developed a transcendental IDEALISM that considered the individual ego as the source of experience and postulated an absolute ego or moral will of the universe, from which everything derives. An important influence on Friedrich SCHELLING and G.W. HEGEL, Fichte is best remembered for his political theories. His *Addresses to the German People* (1808) established him as a leader of liberal nationalism, and he became a hero to the revolutionaries of 1848.

fiction: see NOVEL; SHORT STORY.

Fiedler, Arthur, 1894–1979, American conductor; b. Boston. A versatile German-trained instrumentalist, he formed (1924) the Boston Sinfonietta, a group dedicated to performing little-heard compositions. In 1929 he inaugurated annual concerts at Boston's Esplanade bandshell. Fiedler became director of the Boston Pops Orchestra in 1930; for almost 50 years he led it to enormous international popularity with an astute blend of classical and popular music concerts featuring a wide variety of guest artists.

Fiedler, Leslie, 1917–, American critic; b. Newark, N.J. He is probably best known for *Love and Death in the American Novel* (1960), a Freudian literary analysis. His other works include *An End to Innocence* (1955), essays; *Nude Croquet* (1969), stories; and *Freaks* (1978), a historical study.

fief: see FEUDALISM.

Field, Cyrus West, 1819–92, American merchant, promoter of the first Atlantic CABLE; b. Stockbridge, Mass. In 1853 he retired with a modest fortune from the paper business. The next year he conceived the idea of the cable and organized English and American companies to lay it. The first message was transmitted on Aug. 16, 1858; the cable failed three weeks later, but he raised new funds and succeeded in laying a new cable in 1866. He later promoted other oceanic cables, notably one via Hawaii to Asia and Australia.

Field, Eugene, 1850–95, American writer; b. St. Louis. He was known for his wittily urbane newspaper column "Sharps and Flats." Among his books are *A Little Book of Western Verse* (1889) and *With Trumpets and Drums* (1892). Field's children's poems include "Little Boy Blue" and "Wynken, Blynken, and Nod."

Field, Marshall, 1834–1906, American merchant; b. Conway, Mass. As a partner in the firm of Field, Leiter, and Co. (founded 1881), he amassed one of the largest private fortunes in the U.S. and pioneered in many modern retailing practices. His large philanthropies included the Art Institute of Chicago, Univ. of Chicago, and the Chicago Museum of Natural History. His grandson, **Marshall Field III,** 1893–1956, was owner (1940–48) of the New York city liberal newspaper *PM* and later of the Chicago *Sun* and *Times*.

field, in physics, region throughout which a force may be exerted; examples are the gravitational, electric, and magnetic fields that surround, respectively, masses, electric charges, and magnets (see GRAVITATION; ELECTRICITY; MAGNETISM). Fields are used to describe all cases in which two bodies separated in space exert a force on each other.

field hockey: see HOCKEY, FIELD.

Fielding, Henry, 1707–54, English novelist and dramatist. *Tom Thumb* (1730) was the most notable of his early comedies, farces, and burlesques. Two satires, *Pasquin* (1736) and *The Historical Register for 1736* (1737), in which he attacked the government of Robert WALPOLE, ended his dramatic career by provoking the Licensing Act of 1737, which censored the stage. Turning to the NOVEL, he achieved success with *Joseph Andrews* (1742), a parody of Samuel RICHARDSON's *Pamela;* and *Jonathan Wild* (1743), the ironic history of a highwayman. His masterpiece, *Tom Jones* (1749), presents in the foundling Tom and his guardian, Squire Allworthy, Fielding's ideal person, in whom goodness and charity are combined with common sense. Memorable characters, brilliant plotting, and moral vision make it one of the greatest English novels. Fielding's last works were *Amelia* (1751) and the *Journal of a Voyage to Lisbon* (1755).

field mouse: see VOLE.

Field Museum of Natural History, at Chicago, est. 1893 with gifts of Marshall Field and others. It is noted for its exhibits of animals in their natural settings, displays of plant life, and anthropological and geological collections. The museum sponsors expeditions and conducts research.

Field of the Cloth of Gold, meeting place of HENRY VIII of England and FRANCIS I of France, near Calais, France (1520). Both kings brought large retinues, and the name given the site indicates the splendor of the pageantry. The political results were negligible, because Henry had decided to ally himself with Holy Roman Emperor CHARLES V rather than with Francis.

Fields, W.C., 1880–1946, American film actor; b. Philadelphia as William Claude Dukenfield. He played a series of drunken, misanthropic, yet wistful rascals in such comedies as *It's a Gift* (1934), *My Little Chickadee* (1940), and *The Bank Dick* (1940).

fifth force, postulated fifth basic FORCE of nature (the four known forces of nature are gravity, electromagnetism, and the strong and weak interactions). Proposed in 1986 to account for gravitational discrepancies observed during some experiments, it was said to result in a repulsive effect about 1,000 times less powerful than gravity, and its strength was said to fall off quickly with distance, having a range of about 700 ft (200 m). The results of some initial experiments supported the possibility that the fifth force might exist, but later investigations, including a large-scale, highly accurate oceanic experiment, provided no evidence of such a force.

Fifty-four forty or fight, in U.S. history, phrase commonly used by American extremists in the controversy with Great Britain over the OREGON region. They held that U.S. rights extended to lat. 54°40′N, the recognized southern boundary of Russian America. The phrase was used by Democrat James POLK in his successful 1844 presidential campaign. In 1846 the boundary was set at 49°N.

fig, plant (genus *Ficus*) of the MULBERRY family, comprising over 600 species of vines, shrubs, and trees. Fig plants bear hundreds of tiny female flowers inside a fleshy receptacle, which ripens into a soft, pear-shaped fruit containing masses of tiny seeds. The common fig (*F. carica*), native to the Mediterranean region and cultivated from early times for its commercially valuable fruit, has been naturalized elsewhere in mild, semiarid climates. Some edible varieties can be pollinated only by the fig wasp.

Figueiredo, João Baptista de Oliveira [fēgārā'dō], 1918–, Brazilian general and politician, president of Brazil (1979–85). He was named (1974) to head the national intelligence service and in 1979 was chosen to succeed Ernesto Geisel as president. Figueiredo liberalized Brazil's military regime and moved the nation cautiously toward democracy.

Figueres Ferrer, José [fēgā'rās fār-rār'], 1906–90, president of COSTA RICA (1948–49, 1953–58, 1970–74). In 1948 he led a revolt to ensure the presidency of newly elected Otilio Ulate and served as provisional president. His administrations enacted social legislation and economic reforms.

figured bass, in music, a system of shorthand notation in which figures are written below the notes of the bass part to indicate the chords to be played; also called thorough bass and basso continuo. It arose in the 17th cent. and was widespread until after the time of J.S. BACH as a means of notating an accompaniment on the harpsichord or ORGAN.

Fiji or **Viti,** officially Republic of Fiji, republic (1990 pop. 759,567), c.7,000 sq mi (18,130 sq km), comprising c.320 islands (c.105 inhabited) in the SW Pacific Ocean (see PACIFIC OCEAN map). The two largest islands are Viti Levu, the site of Suva, the capital; and Vanua Levu. The climate is tropical. Sugarcane, copra, ginger, tropical fruits, taro, and cotton are the chief crops. Gold and fish are also significant exports. Tourism is important. The original Fijians, of Melanesian origin in the west and Polynesian origin in the east, are now almost equaled in number by Indians, who first came (1870–1916) to the islands as indentured workers for the British. The native Fijians are largely Christian; those of Indian origin are about three quarters Hindu and one quarter Muslim. The official language is English; Fijian and Hindi are also spoken.

History. The islands were visited by the Dutch navigator Abel TASMAN (1643) and by Capt. James COOK (1774). The first European settlement was established in 1804, and the islands were annexed by Britain in 1874. Fiji gained independence as a Commonwealth member in 1970. Following two coups (1987) by native army officers opposed to a government dominated by Indians, Fiji declared itself a republic and left the Commonwealth. In 1990 a new constitution granted non-urban Melanesians a disproportionate say in the government. In 1992 Sitiveni Rabuka, who had led the 1987 coups, became prime minister.

filbert: see HAZEL.

Filipepi, Alessandro di Mariano: see BOTTICELLI, SANDRO.

Fillmore, Millard, 1800–1874, 13th president of the U.S. (1850–53); b. Summerhill, N.Y. A U.S. representative from New York (1833–35, 1837–43), Fillmore was elected (1848) vice president on the WHIG PARTY ticket with Zachary TAYLOR. Succeeding to the presidency on Taylor's death, Fillmore signed the COMPROMISE OF 1850 and tried to enforce the FUGITIVE SLAVE ACT. He emphasized nonintervention in foreign disputes and signed a treaty opening Japan to Western commerce. Fillmore unsuccessfully strove to make the Whigs a national party, in order to conciliate the sectional struggle. In 1856 he was the presidential candidate of the KNOW-NOTHING MOVEMENT, which tried vainly to unite the North and South.

finch, BIRD of the family Fringillidae, found worldwide except Australia, considered the most highly developed of birds. Finches are typified by stout, conical bills, used to open the seeds that comprise their main diet; many also eat insects. Highly diversified, finches are classified in three groups: those with triangular bills, e.g., CANARY, SPARROW, and the birds called finch, e.g., bullfinch and goldfinch; those with thick, rounded bills, e.g., CARDINAL; and those whose mandibles cross at the tips, e.g., crossbill. Because their seed diet does not depend on weather, many finches are year-round residents in colder areas.

Fingal: see FINN MAC CUMHAIL.

fingerprint, an impression or image of the underside of the end of a finger or thumb, which has ridges that form a pattern unique to each person. Traditionally, impressions have been taken using ink and paper, but in live-scan fingerprinting electronic images produced by a video scanner are converted by computer into binary codes, which can be more readily compared. Fingerprinting as an identification device dates from antiquity, but sophisticated modern methods are based on work by the English scientist Sir Francis GALTON and others during the late 19th cent. Fingerprint identification is used extensively in criminal investigation, the armed services, government employment, and banking. In the U.S. a national fingerprint file and database is maintained by the FEDERAL BUREAU OF INVESTIGATION.

fingerprinting, DNA: see DNA FINGERPRINTING.

Finland, Finnish *Suomi,* officially Republic of Finland, republic (1992 est. pop. 5,004,000), 130,119 sq mi (337,009 sq km), N Europe; bordered by the Gulf of Bothnia and Sweden (W), Norway (N), Russia (E), and the Gulf of Finland and the Baltic Sea (S). HELSINKI is the capital. There are three main geographical zones: a low-lying coastal strip in the south and west that includes most of the major cities; a vast forested interior plateau, dotted with some 60,000 lakes; and a thinly wooded or barren region north of the ARCTIC CIRCLE, part of LAPLAND. Since World War II, manufacturing has replaced agriculture as the principal sector of the economy. Chief manufactures are forest products (about 70% of Finland is forested), iron, steel, petroleum products, machinery, chemicals, and processed food. Finland is also known for its design of glass, ceramics, and stainless-steel cutlery. Financial and other services are also important. Finnish and Swedish are both official languages, and most of the population belongs to the established Evangelical Lutheran Church. Finland is governed by an elected president and a 200-member unicameral parliament (*Eduskunta*).

History. Beginning in the 1st cent. A.D., Finland was settled by nomadic hunters and fishers, who forced the small number of Lapps living in the central and southern regions to move to the far north, where they live today. Sweden conquered the area in the 13th cent. but allowed the Finns considerable independence, raising Finland to the rank of grand duchy in 1581. During the Napoleonic Wars, Finland was invaded by Russia, which annexed it in 1809. As a Russian grand duchy, Finland was again allowed wide-ranging autonomy. Finnish nationalism became a strong force early in the 19th cent.; an elected parliament was established in 1906, and Finnish independence was proclaimed in 1917. In the civil war that followed (1918), the nationalist White Guard, led by C.G.E. MANNERHEIM and aided by German troops, defeated the leftist Red Guard, supported by the Soviets. A republic was established in

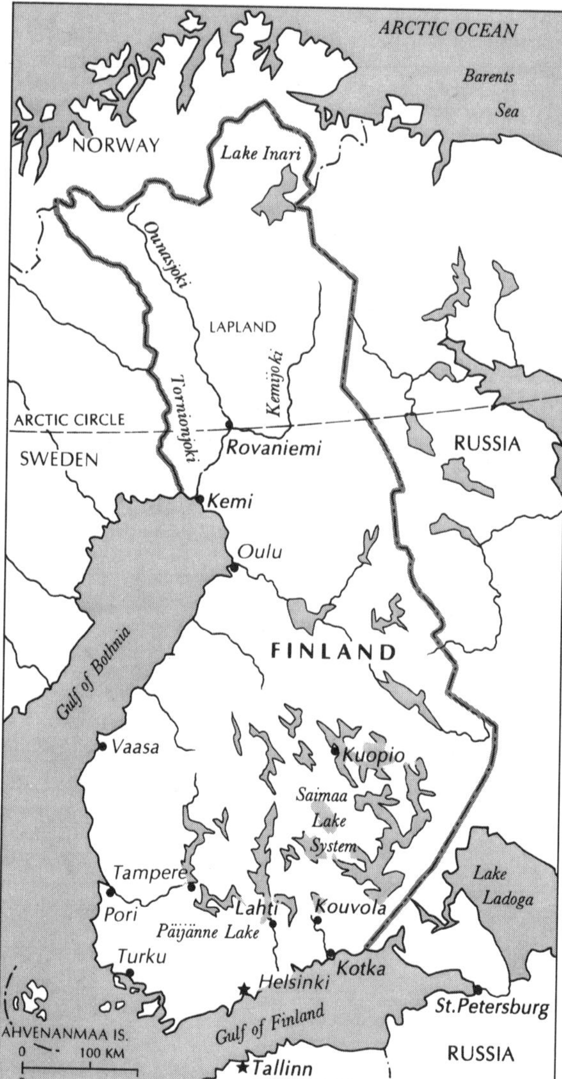

1919. After the start of WORLD WAR II, Soviet troops invaded Finland (1939), which, despite heroic resistance, was defeated (1940). Hoping to recover territories lost in the conflict, Finland joined the German attack (1941) on the USSR but was forced to capitulate (1944). The armistice required Finland to expel the Germans, and in the ensuing Finnish-German warfare, N Finland was devastated. The peace treaty signed in 1947 ceded additional Finnish territory to the USSR, and a treaty signed in 1948 pledged Finland to defend the USSR from attack along their common border. In the postwar years Finland, led by Pres. U.K. KEKKONEN from 1956, sought to remain neutral and maintain good relations with the USSR while preserving its independence. In 1981 Mauno K. Koivisto succeeded Kekkonen as president. The country began developing closer relations with Western Europe in the late 1980s. The economic collapse of the USSR caused economic difficulties in Finland, which had traded extensively with the Soviets, but Soviet political disintegration led to the scrapping of the 1948 defense treaty and to a pledge by Russia to treat Finland as an equal. Since 1991 Esko Aho, a centrist, has been prime minister, heading the first nonsocialist government since the 1960s. Martti Ahtisaari, a diplomat, became Finland's first popularly elected president in 1994.

Finlay, Carlos Juan, 1833–1915, Cuban physician. He suggested (1881) the mosquito as the carrier of YELLOW FEVER and specified (1882) the correct species, now known as *Aëdes aegypti.* A commission headed by Walter REED inaugurated (1900) experiments that proved his theory.

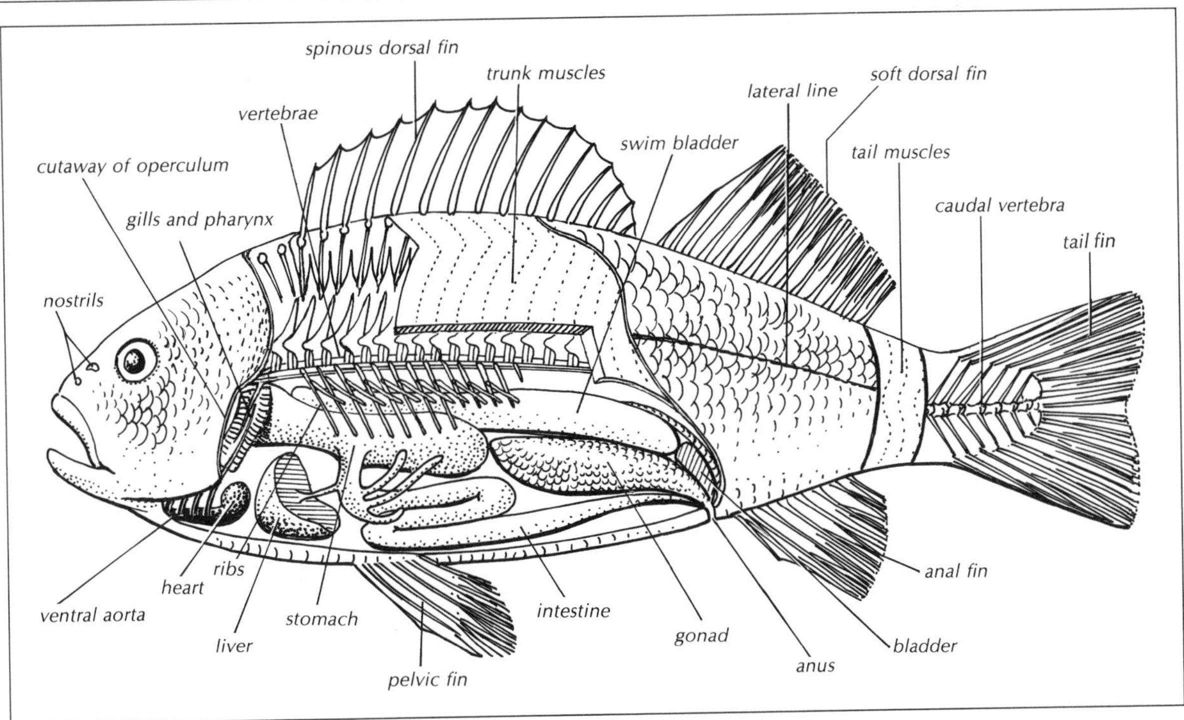

Anatomy of a ray-finned fish

Finney, Albert, 1936–, English film actor. He has starred in such varied films as *Tom Jones* (1963), *Murder on the Orient Express* (1974), and *Shoot the Moon* (1982).

Finnish language, also called Suomi, member of the Finnic group of the Finno-Ugric languages. These languages form a subdivision of the Uralic subfamily of the URALIC AND ALTAIC family of languages. See LANGUAGE (table).

Finn mac Cumhail, Fionn mac Cumhail, or **Finn MacCool** [all: fĭn məkōōl'], semimythical Irish hero, celebrated in OSSIAN's narrative poems and in the Fenian ballads, so called after the professional fighters Finn is said to have led in the 3d cent.

Finno-Ugric languages [fĭn'ō-ōōgrĭk], group of languages forming a subdivision of the Uralic subfamily of the URALIC AND ALTAIC family of languages. See LANGUAGE (table).

fiord: see FJORD.

fir, tree (genus *Abies*) of the PINE family, found chiefly in the alpine regions of the Northern Hemisphere. Tall, pyramidal evergreens, firs have short, flat, stemless needles and erect, cylindrical cones. They are valued for their fragrance and beauty. The balsam fir is a popular Christmas tree.

Firbank, (Arthur Annesley) Ronald, 1886–1926, English author. An eccentric aesthete, he wrote unconventional satiric novels, e.g., *Vainglory* (1915), *Valmouth* (1919), and *Prancing Nigger* (1924), that influenced WAUGH, COMPTON-BURNETT, and Aldous HUXLEY.

Firdausi [fərdou'sē], c.940–1020, Persian poet, author of the *Book of Kings*, the first great work of Persian literature; b. Abdul Kasim Mansur. The *Book of Kings* is an epic poem recounting the history of Persia from the arrival of the Persians to that of the Arabs. It is noted for its even rhyme, stately cadences, and continuous flow.

firearm: see ARTILLERY; GUN; SMALL ARMS.

firefly or **lightning bug,** small, luminescent, nocturnal, carnivorous BEETLE of the family Lampyridae. They emit heatless flashes of green-yellow to red-orange light (see BIOLUMINESCENCE); these are sexual signals produced by special organs on the abdomen. Firefly larvae prey on snails and earthworms, and some are beneficial to agriculture. Larvae and wingless females are called glowworms.

Firestone, Harvey Samuel, 1868–1938, American industrialist; b. Columbiana co., Ohio. He began to manufacture rubber tires in 1896. The Firestone Fire & Rubber Co., which he organized in 1900, became a leader of the rubber industry and one of the largest tire manufacturers in the U.S.

Firth, Raymond William, 1901–, English social anthropologist; b. New Zealand. A professor at the Univ. of London (1944–68), he conducted research in the Pacific and in West Africa, focusing on social organization and economic systems. His works include *We the Tikopia* (1936, rev. ed. 1957) and *Symbols: Public and Private* (1973).

Fischer, Bobby (Robert James Fischer), 1943–, American chess player; b. Chicago. In 1972 at Reykjavik, Iceland, he won the world chess championship from Boris Spassky of the USSR. Fischer subsequently disputed match rules with the International Federation of Chess, and in 1975 Anatoly KARPOV of the USSR was declared champion by default. In 1992 Fischer again beat Spassky in an exhibition match in YUGOSLAVIA and was charged with violating U.S. economic sanctions against that nation.

Fischer-Dieskau, Dietrich, 1925–, German baritone. He is one of the foremost singers of German LIEDER, noted for his interpretations of Brahms, Schubert, Schumann, and Wolf.

Fischer-Tropsch process, method, discovered (1923) by the German coal researchers Franz Fischer and Hans Tropsch, for the synthesis of hydrocarbons and other aliphatic compounds. A mixture of hydrogen and carbon monoxide is reacted in the presence of an iron or cobalt catalyst. Much heat is evolved, and such products as methane, synthetic gasoline and waxes, and alcohols are made, with water or carbon dioxide as by-products.

Fish, Hamilton, 1808–93, American statesman; b. N.Y.C. A Whig congressman (1843–45) and senator (1851–57) from New York, Fish served as Pres. GRANT's secretary of state (1869–77) and was one of the ablest persons ever to hold that office. He arranged the Treaty of WASHINGTON (1871), which settled long-standing disputes with Britain, and he kept U.S.-based filibustering expeditions against Cuba from escalating into war with Spain.

fish, limbless, aquatic, VERTEBRATE animal with fins, internal gills, and skin with a glandular secretion that decreases friction. Most fish have scales and are cold-blooded. A typical fish is torpedo-shaped, with a head containing a brain and sensory organs, a muscular-walled trunk with a cavity containing internal organs, and a muscular tail. Most fish propel themselves through water with weaving movements and control direction with fins. Although some fish, such as sharks, bear live young, most fish eggs are fertilized and hatch in water. There are over 20,000 species in three classes: Agnatha, the most primitive fishes, jawless and without paired pelvic and pectoral fins (e.g., LAMPREY); Chondrichthyes, cartilaginous fishes, with skeletons of cartilage but no swim bladder or lungs (e.g., SHARK, RAY); and Osteichthyes, bony fishes, the most highly developed. Bony fishes have a bony skeleton and a swim bladder or lungs, and are divided into fleshy-finned (e.g., LOBEFIN, LUNGFISH) and ray-finned fishes (e.g., BASS, TUNA). The largest fish is the whale shark (*Rhincodon typus*), reaching 50 ft (15 m) in length and found worldwide in tropical seas; the smallest is the ½-in. (1.3-cm) goby (family Gobiidae) of the Philippines.

Fisher, Irving, 1867–1947, American economist; b. Saugerties, N.Y. A professor at Yale Univ. (1890–1935), he is known for his pioneering work in monetary economic theory; his theory of the "compensated dollar" to stabilize purchasing power; and his development of the INDEX NUMBER, a measurement of price levels.

Fisher, Saint John, c.1469–1535, English prelate, cardinal, bishop of Rochester (1504–34). For opposing the divorce of HENRY VIII and KATHARINE OF ARAGÓN and other acts of the English REFORMATION, Fisher was imprisoned in 1534. To show his support Pope PAUL III created (1535) Fisher a cardinal, but an enraged Henry quickly had Fisher beheaded. He was canonized in 1935. Feast: June 22.

Fisher, M(ary) F(rances) K(ennedy), 1908–92, American culinary writer. In her youth, she lived in France, where she was inspired by the literary gastronome Brillat-Savarin. Her writings, including *Serve It Forth* (1937) and *With Bold Knife and Fork* (1979), are culinary essays offering recipes, philosophical reflections, reminiscences, and anecdotes.

fish farming: see AQUACULTURE.

Fisk, James, 1834–72, American financial speculator; b. Pownal, Vt. He became wealthy during the Civil War by dealing in cotton and established (1866) a brokerage house in New York City. After taking part in the struggle against Cornelius VANDERBILT for control of the Erie RR, he and Jay GOULD made millions by manipulating Erie stock. They also engineered an attempt to corner the gold market in 1869, causing the BLACK FRIDAY scandal. At the age of 37, Fisk was killed by a rival for the attentions of an actress.

fission: see ATOMIC BOMB; NUCLEAR ENERGY.

Fitch, John, 1743–98, American inventor; b. Windsor, Conn. An early experimenter with steam engines and steamboats (see STEAMSHIP), he is believed to have designed (1786) the first practical steamboat. Nevertheless, he failed to receive either the opportunity to commercialize his invention or the recognition he justly deserved.

FitzGerald, Edward, 1809–83, English author. His masterpiece is his translation of *The Rubaiyat of Omar Khayyam* (1859; rev. 1868, 1872, 1879). Other works are *Euphranor* (1851), a Platonic dialogue; and *Polonius* (1852), aphorisms.

Fitzgerald, Ella, 1918–, African-American singer; b. Newport News, Va. She was a popular big band and solo artist. Principally a JAZZ singer with a sweet and effortless style, she is a noted interpreter of the songs of George GERSHWIN and Cole PORTER, among others.

Fitzgerald, F(rancis) Scott (Key), 1896–1940, American author, one of the great American writers of the 20th cent.; b. St. Paul, Minn. The literary spokesman of the "jazz age," he wrote about people whose lives resembled his own. He and his wife, Zelda, lived a celebrated life, glittering and dissipated, in New York City and the French Riviera, but his later years were plagued by financial worries and his wife's insanity. Fitzgerald's novels are *This Side of Paradise* (1920); *The Beautiful and Damned* (1922); *The Great Gatsby* (1922), his masterpiece about the corruption of the American dream; *Tender Is the Night* (1934); and *The Last Tycoon* (1941), an unfinished work reflecting his last years in Hollywood. He also published four short-story collections.

Fitzgerald, Garrett, 1926–, Irish politician. An economist, he was elected (1969) to parliament as a Fine Gael member. He was foreign affairs minister (1973–77), then party leader (1977–87), and later prime minister (1981–82; 1983–87). A moderate nationalist, he was a driving force behind the 1985 Anglo-Irish agreement on Northern Ireland.

Five, The, group of five 19th-cent. Russian composers: BALAKIREV, CUI, MOUSSORGSKY, BORODIN, and RIMSKY-KORSAKOV. They drew on Russian history, literature, and folklore to write music of a distinctly national character.

Five Civilized Tribes, name used since the mid-19th cent. for the CHEROKEE, CHICKASAW, CHOCTAW, CREEK, and SEMINOLE settled in INDIAN TERRITORY under the Removal Act of 1830. Living on communally held land, each tribe had a written constitution, a tripartite government, and a public school system. A later federal policy of detribalization resulted in the loss of their governmental functions, except advisory, and the division of tribal land into individual holdings.

Five Nations: see IROQUOIS CONFEDERACY.

Five-Power Treaty: see NAVAL CONFERENCES.

fjord or **fiord,** coastal inlet characterized by sheer parallel walls, often extending far below the water surface, and by many branches. They are probably glaciated valleys subsequently drowned by the sea. Norway's fjords are noted for their grandeur; Sognafjord is 4,000 ft (1,220 m) deep and over 100 mi (160 km) long.

flag, piece of cloth, usually bunting or similar light material, plain, colored, or bearing a device, varying in size and shape but often oblong or square, used as an ensign, standard, or signal or for display or decorative purposes, and generally attached at one end (the hoist) to a staff or a halyard by which it may be hoisted. The portion from the hoist to the free end is the fly; the top quarter of the flag next to the staff is the canton. Flags have been used since ancient times. Early flags had a religious significance that persisted historically. For example, the ensign of Great Britain, the Union Jack, is formed by the crosses of St. GEORGE, St. ANDREW, and St. PATRICK, the national saints, respectively, of England, Scotland, and Ireland. Armies and navies use flags for signaling: the white flag is used universally for truce; the black, in early times, was a symbol for piracy; the red symbolizes mutiny or revolution; the yellow is a sign of infectious diseases. Shipping lines have their own flags. Striking a flag signifies surrender, and the flag of the victor is hoisted above that of the vanquished. A flag flown at half-mast is a symbol of mourning. The inverted national ensign is a signal of distress. The first flag of the U.S. was raised at Cambridge, Mass., by George WASHINGTON on Jan. 2, 1776. Today, the U.S. flag has 13 stripes, denoting the 13 original colonies, and 50 stars, for the 50 states. The U.S. states and territories also have their own flags.

Flag Day (June 14), anniversary of the adoption of the American flag in 1777. It is not a legal holiday.

Flagstad, Kirsten, 1895–1962, Norwegian soprano. In 1935 she appeared at the METROPOLITAN OPERA in Richard WAGNER's *Die Walküre* and thereafter was regarded as the greatest living Wagnerian soprano.

Flaherty, Robert Joseph, 1884–1951, American film director; b. Iron Mountain, Mich. His pioneering documentaries include *Nanook of the North* (1922) and *Man of Aran* (1934).

flamingo, large pink or red tropical wading BIRD (order Ciconiiformes), similar to the related HERON and STORK but with webbed feet and a unique, down-bent bill. Ranging in height from 3 to 5 ft (90 to 150 cm), the flamingo has a long neck and legs and a broad wingspan.

Flanders, former county in the Low Countries extending along the North Sea and W of the Scheldt R.; the name is also used for all Flemish (Dutch) areas of Belgium. Flanders became a French fief in the 9th cent. Virtually independent, it was the hub of medieval Europe's cloth industry but was weakened by civil strife and by rebellion against France. By the 15th cent., although Flemish art and commerce flourished under the Burgundians, it was little more than a French province. It passed in turn to the Spanish Hapsburgs and Austria before being partitioned among France (1797), the Netherlands (1815), and Belgium (1830); parts of W Flanders had earlier been annexed (1668–78) to France. Its strategic location has made Flanders a key battleground; occupation by the Germans in WORLD WAR II led to the dramatic British evacuation at DUNKIRK (1940).

flatfish, member of the order Pleuronectiformes, bottom-living FISH of the Atlantic and Pacific. Adult flatfish have an unusual, flattened body with both eyes on one side of the head. They lie with the blind, generally whitish, side on the ocean bottom; the eyed, colored side faces up. Soles are generally small, warm-water flatfishes with small eyes and mouths and few or no teeth. Flounders, generally larger, are known for the ability to change their color to match the background. The European sole (*Solea solea*) and many flounders, including the flukes (genus *Paralichthys*) and the large, voracious, cool-water halibuts (genus *Hippoglossus*), are important food fish.

Flathead: see SALISH.

flatworm, soft-bodied, bilaterally symmetrical invertebrate of the phylum Platyhelminthes. Among the most primitive organisms, flatworms are divided into the free-living, primarily aquatic class of turbellarians (including PLANARIANS) and the exclusively parasitic classes of FLUKES and TAPEWORMS.

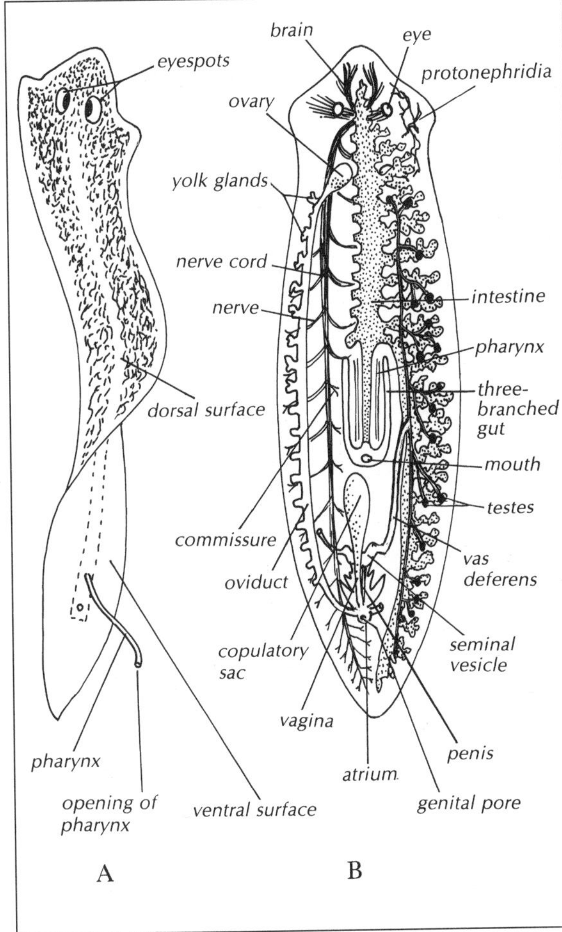

Flatworm: External (left) and internal (right) anatomy of a planaria, a representative flatworm

Flaubert, Gustave [flōbĕr′], 1821–80, French novelist, a master of the realistic novel. A scrupulous writer, intent on finding the exact word (*le mot juste*) and achieving complete objectivity, he published his masterpiece, *Madame Bovary,* in 1857, after five years of work. Portraying the frustrations of a romantic young woman married to a dull provincial doctor, it resulted in his prosecution on moral grounds. His other works include the novels *Salammbô* (1862), *A Sentimental Education* (1869), and the satirical *Bouvard and Pécuchet* (1881) and *Three Tales* (1877), one of which is the great novella "A Simple Heart."

flax, common name for an annual herb of the Linaceae family, especially members of the genus *Linum,* and for the fiber obtained from such plants. Native to Eurasia, flax was the major source of cloth fiber until the growth of the COTTON industry (c.1800). The flax of commerce is obtained from several varieties of *L. usitatissimum.* Exposure to water or dew and sun loosens the fiber from the woody tissue in a process known as retting. After washing, drying, beating, and combing, fibers are obtained for use in making fabric (see LINEN), threads, and cordage. Flax seeds are crushed to make LINSEED OIL, and the remaining linseed cake is used for fodder. Dried seed is also used in medicines.

Flaxman, John, 1755–1826, English sculptor and draftsman. After designing Wedgwood pottery, he produced figure drawings from Greek vases to illustrate works by Homer and Dante; these were engraved by William BLAKE. He is known for his memorial sculptures, e.g., Sir Joshua REYNOLDS.

flea, small, blood-sucking wingless INSECT of the order Siphonaptera. Adult fleas eat only blood and are external PARASITES of mammals and birds. They have hard bodies flattened from side to side, piercing and sucking mouthparts, and strong legs for jumping. Certain rat fleas carry TYPHUS and bubonic PLAGUE; other fleas transmit TAPEWORMS to humans.

Flémalle, Master of: see CAMPIN, ROBERT.

Fleming, Sir Alexander, 1881–1955, Scottish bacteriologist. He discovered PENICILLIN (1928) and lysozyme (1922), an antibacterial substance found in body secretions. Professor of bacteriology at the Univ. of London, he shared the 1945 Nobel Prize in physiology or medicine with Ernst CHAIN and Sir Howard FLOREY for work on penicillin. Fleming was knighted in 1944.

Flemish language, member of the West Germanic group of the Germanic subfamily of the INDO-EUROPEAN family of languages. It is one of the official languages of Belgium. See LANGUAGE (table).

Fletcher, John, 1579–1625, English dramatist, thought to have worked with SHAKESPEARE on *Two Noble Kinsmen* and *Henry VIII.* His most important collaboration was with Francis BEAUMONT. Their chief works—*Philaster, A Maid's Tragedy, A King and No King,* and *The Scornful Lady* (1607–13)—developed the romantic tragicomedy, which was popular through the 18th cent.

Fleury, André Hercule de [flörē′], 1653–1743, French Roman Catholic cardinal, chief minister of LOUIS XV. As virtual ruler of France (1726–43), he restored financial order. He strove for peace abroad but was drawn into the wars of the POLISH SUCCESSION and the AUSTRIAN SUCCESSION.

flight simulator, device providing a controlled environment in which a flight trainee can experience conditions approximating those of actual flight. The simulator, complete with a replica of an aircraft's cockpit, simulates an aircraft's rolling, pitching, and yawing motions. A computer coordinates the instrument readings, the student's control inputs, the position of the simulator, information about the aircraft's characteristics, and information about the terrain over which it is supposed to be flying. Video displays simulate conditions outside the cockpit. Simulators are also now used to increase the competence of experienced pilots with new aircraft and to expose them to potential adverse weather and equipment failure conditions.

Flinders Petrie, Sir William Matthew: see PETRIE.

Flinders Ranges, mountain chain, SOUTH AUSTRALIA state, Australia. They extend 260 mi (418 km) between Lake Torrens and Lake Frome and reach a high point of 3,900 ft (1,189 m) at St. Mary's Peak. Uranium and copper are mined there.

Flint, city (1990 pop. 140,761), seat of Genesee co., SE Mich.; inc. 1855. Established (1819) as a fur-trading post, it later became a site of cart and carriage making. Since 1902 it has been an international automobile manufacturing center; many major auto makers, e.g., General Motors, began there.

flint: see CHERT.

Flood, in the Bible: see NOAH.

Florence, Ital. *Firenze,* city (1990 pop. 413,069), capital of TUSCANY, central Italy, on the Arno R. It is a commercial, industrial, and tourist center known for fine handicrafts. Of Roman origin, it became prominent after gaining autonomy in the 12th cent. It was a center of GUELPH AND GHIBELLINE strife (13th cent.) but nonetheless grew in size and power through war with other cities. Meanwhile, trade in silks, tapestries, and jewelry brought great wealth. The MEDICI family dominated Florence from the 15th to 18th cent., their rule interrupted by two revolutions (1494–1512, led by SAVONAROLA; and 1527–30). The artistic and intellectual life of the city flowered from the 14th to 16th cent., with DANTE, BOCCACCIO, DONATELLO, LEONARDO DA VINCI, RAPHAEL, and MICHELANGELO among the many born or active there. Florence passed (1737) to the house of Hapsburg-Lorraine, was annexed (1860) to Sardinia, and was the capital of Italy (1865–71). Among its many glorious works of architecture are the cathedral of Santa Maria del Fiore; the nearby baptistry; the churches of Santa Croce, Santa Maria Novella, and San Lorenzo; and the Pitti Palace, the Palazzo Vecchio, and the UFFIZI, all of which house masterpieces of RENAISSANCE art.

Florey, Howard Walter (Baron Florey of Adelaide), 1898–1968, British pathologist; b. Australia. For their work in purifying PENICILLIN and demonstrating its effectiveness against harmful bacteria, he and Ernst CHAIN shared with Alexander FLEMING the 1945 Nobel Prize in physiology or medicine. He was professor of pathology at Oxford Univ. from 1935 to 1962 and was knighted in 1944.

Florida, state in the extreme SE U.S. A long peninsula between the Atlantic Ocean (E) and the Gulf of Mexico (W), Florida is bordered by Georgia and Alabama (N).

Area, 58,560 sq mi (151,670 sq km). *Pop.* (1990) 12,937,926, a 32.8% increase over 1980 pop. *Capital,* Tallahassee. *Statehood,* Mar. 3, 1845 (27th state). *Highest pt.,* 345 ft (105 m), Walton co.; *lowest pt.,* sea level. *Nickname,* Sunshine State. *Motto,* In God We Trust. *State bird,* mockingbird. *State flower,* orange blossom. *State tree,* Sabal palmetto palm. *Abbr.,* Fla.; FL.

Land and People. The highest elevations are found in the northwest, the Florida Panhandle. Central Florida has rolling hills and abounds in lakes, of which Lake OKEECHOBEE is the largest. The EVERGLADES, which includes Big Cypress Swamp, is a unique wilderness area extending over much of S Florida. The small islands of the FLORIDA KEYS extend southwest from the end of the mainland. The state is noted for its mild climate and abundant sunshine. The extreme south of Florida and the state of Hawaii are the only places in the U.S. with tropical climates. Florida has one of the highest rates of population increase in the country, partly because many retired persons have settled in the state. It also has one of the larger Hispanic populations in the country (more than 12% of the total population). In 1990, 83% of the population was white and 14% African American. Almost 85% of the population lives in urban areas. MIAMI is a leading international trade and financial center and the state's second largest city; JACKSONVILLE is the largest city. Other important cities are TAMPA, SAINT PETERSBURG, ORLANDO, and FORT LAUDERDALE.

Economy. Because of Florida's warm climate, extremely long coastline, and many beaches, as well as such attractions as Walt Disney World and other resorts near Orlando, tourism is the main source of income. Florida is one of the country's leading agricultural states, producing citrus fruits, winter vegetables, and cattle. Industry is dominated by agricultural processing and the manufacturing of electrical, electronic, and transportation equipment and chemicals. By the early 1990s, foreign trade had also become an important factor in Florida's economy. The state leads the U.S. in phosphate production; petroleum, natural gas, and sand and gravel are also extracted. The large fishing industry catches mostly shellfish.

Government. The constitution (adopted 1968) provides for a governor elected to a four-year term. The legislature is composed of a house of 120 members elected for two years and a senate of 40 members elected for four years. Florida sends 23 representatives and 2 senators to the U.S. Congress and has 25 electoral votes.

History. Seeking the fabled Fountain of Youth, the Spanish explorer PONCE DE LEÓN became the first European to land (1513) in Florida. The first permanent settlement, SAINT AUGUSTINE, was founded by the Spanish in 1565 and is the oldest city in the U.S. Subsequently, Spain and England fought for control of the strategic peninsula. In 1819 Spain reluctantly ceded Florida to the U.S. As settlers arrived, the increasingly displaced SEMINOLE rebelled, but they were defeated in the Second Seminole War (1835–42), and most were forcibly removed to Oklahoma. However, small bands fled to the Everglades and Lake Okeechobee area, where they still live on reservations. With the arrival (1880s) of railroads, Florida experienced its first real-estate boom, followed by a second during the 1920s. After the Cuban Revolution (1958–59), a huge influx of Cubans fled to Miami; another wave followed in 1980. The establishment (1947) of a rocket-launching site at CAPE CANAVERAL brought the aerospace industry to Florida, making it one of the fastest-growing states in the SUN BELT. In 1992 parts of S Florida were devastated by Hurricane Andrew.

Florida Keys, chain of small islands and reefs extending into Florida Bay c.150 mi (240 km) southwest from the southern shore of Florida. A motor causeway traverses the keys, linking the mainland and the city of KEY WEST on the outermost island (Key West), which is c.90 mi (150 km) N of Cuba, separated by the Straits of Florida. The largest of the Florida Keys is Key Largo. Commercial fishing and tourism are the principal industries.

flotation process, process for concentrating the metal-bearing mineral in an ORE. Crude ore is ground to a fine powder and mixed with water and reagents. When air is blown through the mixture, mineral particles cling to the bubbles, which rise to form a froth on the surface. The froth is skimmed off and the water and chemicals removed, leaving a clean concentrate. Among the minerals effectively concentrated by this method are sulfide and phosphate ores.

flounder: see FLATFISH.

flower, specialized part of seed plants that contains reproductive organs. The basic floral parts (sepal, petal, stamen, and pistil) are modified leaves, typically arranged concentrically and attached at their bases to the tip of the stem. The outermost, green sepals (the calyx) encircle a whorl of usually showy, colored petals (the corolla), within which POLLEN-bearing stamens surround a central ovary-bearing pistil. After fertilization, each ovule (the part that contains the egg) in the ovary becomes a SEED, and the ovary becomes the FRUIT. The number and arrangement of floral parts varies greatly among groups of plants and are important bases for classification. In general, the higher a plant is on the evolutionary scale, the greater the flower's complexity and efficiency for reproduction.

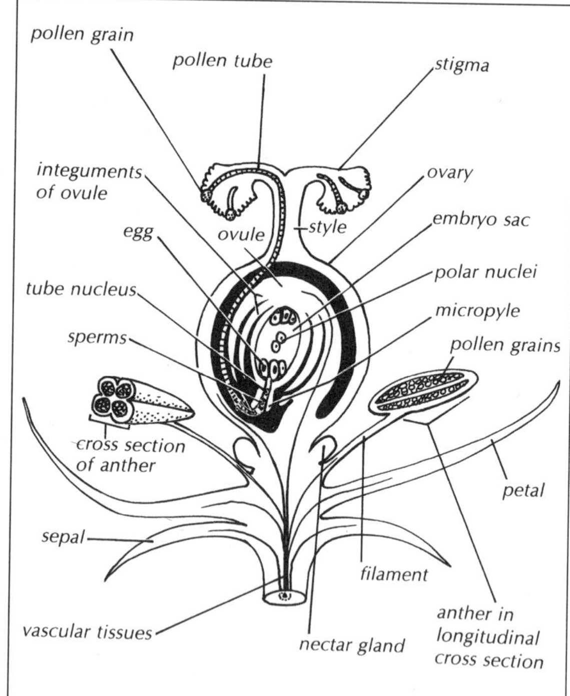

Flower: Longitudinal cross-section of a flower at the time of fertilization, showing a pollen grain and pollen tube

Floyd, Carlisle, 1926–, American composer; b. Latta, S.C. He is known for his folk opera *Susannah.* Other operas, written in a conservative style, include *Wuthering Heights* (1958), *Of Mice and Men* (1970), and *Bilby's Doll* (1976). *The Passion of Jonathan Wade* (1962; revised version, 1991) is less conservative and more musically eclectic in its revised version.

fluid mechanics, branch of MECHANICS dealing with the properties and behavior of fluids, or substances that flow, i.e., liquids and gases. The larger part of the field is fluid dynamics (study of fluids in motion), which itself is divided into hydrodynamics (study of liquids in motion) and AERODYNAMICS (study of gases in motion).

fluke, FLATWORM of the class Trematoda. Flukes, which are related to the TAPEWORM, are internal and external parasites that cause many diseases. Adults cling to their hosts with sucking disks and bear an external cuticle resistant to digestion by the host. Some species of FLATFISH are also called flukes.

fluorescence, LUMINESCENCE in which light of a visible color is emitted from certain substances, called phosphors, when irradiated by electromagnetic radiation, especially ultraviolet light. Unlike PHOSPHORESCENCE, the light is emitted only while the stimulation continues.

fluoridation, process of adding a fluoride to a community water supply to preserve the TEETH of the inhabitants. Tooth enamel ordinarily contains small amounts of fluorides, which, when augmented with fluoridated water, can greatly reduce tooth decay in children. While studies have proved fluoridation safe at levels of one part per million, opponents assert that such action constitutes compulsory medication and that those wanting fluoride can use it individually.

fluorine (F), gaseous element, first prepared in 1886 by Henri Moissan. Fluorine is a yellowish, poisonous, highly corrosive HALOGEN gas. It is the most chemically active nonmetallic element and the most electronegative of all the elements. FLUORITE is its chief commercial source. The addition of one part per million of soluble fluorides (salts of hydrofluoric acid) to public water supplies reduces tooth decay. Fluorine compounds are used in ceramic and glass manufacturing, in refrigeration and air-conditioning systems, and as lubricants. TEFLON is an inert, heat-resistant FLUOROCARBON. See ELEMENT (table); PERIODIC TABLE.

fluorite or **fluorspar,** calcium fluoride mineral (CaF_2), occurring in various colors in crystal, granular, and massive forms. Its crystals sometimes exhibit fluorescence. Found mainly in England, Germany, Mexico, Kentucky, and Illinois, fluorite is used as a flux in metallurgy, in preparing hydrofluoric acid, and in making opal glass and enamel. Some colorless crystals are used to make lenses and prisms.

fluorocarbon, any organic compound composed of FLUORINE and CARBON. Derived synthetically from HYDROCARBONS, many fluorocarbons, such as TEFLON, and the chemically related CHLOROFLUOROCARBONS, such as FREON-12, are chemically stable, nonflammable, and relatively nontoxic. Fluorocarbons have been widely used as lubricants, in materials used in bearings, and in low-adhesion surfaces.

flute: see WIND INSTRUMENT.

fluxional molecule, molecule that exhibits rapid intramolecular rearrangements of its component atoms. As with structural ISOMERS, fluxional compounds maintain the same number of component atoms. At equilibrium, fluxional molecules may manifest many different isomers and fluctuate rapidly among them.

fly, name for a variety of winged INSECTS, but properly restricted to members of the order Diptera. True flies have sucking and piercing mouthparts and, in most species, one pair of wings. All flies undergo complete METAMORPHOSIS. Most are harmful as disease carriers or crop destroyers. The order includes the FRUIT FLY, GNAT, MOSQUITO, and TSETSE FLY.

flying buttress: see BUTTRESS.

flying fish, torpedo-shaped FISH (family Exocoetidae) of warm seas that has well-developed pectoral fins that can be held rigid and used to glide short distances over the water. Specially adapted tail fins, vibrated in taxiing along the water surface to gain momentum, and (in some species) enlarged pelvic fins also help in "flight." The largest species is the 18-in. (45-cm) California flying fish.

flying saucer: see UNIDENTIFIED FLYING OBJECT.

flying squirrel, nocturnal SQUIRREL adapted for gliding. Flying squirrels do not actually fly. Most are found in Asia, but there are two North American species (genus *Glaucomys*), which together are found in forests over much of the continent. The gliding mechanism is a fold of skin extending along each side of the body. When the animal extends its limbs in leaping, the flaps stretch out taut like a parachute.

Fm, chemical symbol of the element FERMIUM.

FM: see MODULATION.

Fo, Dario, 1926–, Italian playwright, actor, director, and songwriter. Fo developed a form of satirical farce influenced by Berthold BRECHT and Antonio GRAMSCI that is less formal than traditional COMMEDIA DELL'ARTE. In 1968 Fo and his wife, actress Franca Rame, began presenting plays on contemporary issues; the most famous is *Accidental Death of an Anarchist* (1970).

foam: see COLLOID.

Foch, Ferdinand [fôsh], 1851–1929, marshal of France. In WORLD WAR I he halted the German advance at the Marne (1914) and fought at Ypres (1915) and the Somme (1916). In 1917 he became chief of the French general staff, and in Apr. 1918 he assumed the unified command of the British, French, and U.S. armies.

fog, aggregation of water droplets just above the earth's surface, i.e., a cloud near the ground. A light or thin fog is usually called a mist. Fog may occur either when the moisture content of the air is increased beyond the saturation point or when the air is cooled below the DEW point. In either case, excess moisture condenses on microscopic dust particles (condensation nuclei) in the atmosphere.

Fokine, Michel [fôkēn', Rus. fô'kyĭn], 1880–1942, Russian–American choreographer and ballet dancer; b. St. Petersburg. He choreographed for NIJINSKY and PAVLOVA in Russia and for DIAGHILEV in Paris. He is considered the founder of modern ballet. His works include *Les Sylphides* (1909), *The Firebird* (1910), and *Petrouchka* (1911).

Fokker, Anton Herman Gerard [fôk'ər], 1890–1939, German-American aircraft manufacturer; b. Java. His factories in Germany produced triplanes and biplanes used in World War I; he also invented an apparatus allowing machine-gun bullets to be fired through a rotating propeller without intercepting the blades. He later turned to developing commercial aircraft and came to the U.S. in 1922.

fold, in geology, bent or deformed arrangement of stratified rocks. Arches, or upfolds, are known as anticlines; depressions, or downfolds, are called synclines. An imaginary line drawn along the crest of an anticline or the trough of a syncline is its axis; the two sides curving away from the axis are the limbs. The complex causes of folding include large-scale crustal movements (see PLATE TECTONICS).

Foley, Thomas S(tephen), 1929–, U.S. politician, Speaker of the U.S. House of Representatives (1989–); b. Spokane, Wash. Elected to the House as a Democrat from Washington state in 1964, he served as chairman of the House Democratic caucus (1976–80) and of the agriculture committee (1975–80). Foley held the House leadership positions of majority whip (1981–86) and majority leader (1987–89) before he became Speaker of the House in 1989.

Folger, Henry Clay, 1857–1930, American industrialist and collector of Shakespeareana. With the help of his wife, **Emily Jordan Folger,** 1858–1936, he acquired one of the largest and most valuable collections of its sort in the world. They endowed the Folger Shakespeare Library.

folk art, artwork of a culturally homogeneous people made by artists without formal training. Often nationalistic in character, it generally involves craft processes, e.g., in America, QUILTING and sculpture of figureheads, weather vanes, and cigar-store figures. Paintings in the tradition of PRIMITIVISM are also in the folk idiom. Much folk art has a rough-hewn, idiosyncratic, or awkward quality often admired and imitated by sophisticated artists.

folk dance, primitive, tribal, or ethnic form of the dance, sometimes the survival of an ancient ceremony or festival. The term includes characteristic national dances, country dances, and figure dances in costume. Examples include children's games such as "The Farmer in the Dell," as well as the Spanish fandango, the Bohemian polka, the Irish jig, and the American Virginia reel. The English musician Cecil James Sharp made a notable collection of English folk songs and dances, and the American Folk Dance Society has preserved American country dances.

folklore, body of customs, legends, beliefs, and superstitions passed on by oral tradition, including folk tales, dances, songs, and medicine. The study of folklore became significant in the 19th cent. as a result of the rise of European ROMANTICISM and nationalism. Today most anthropologists see the many manifestations of folklore as imaginative expressions by a people of its desires, attitudes, and cultural values and regard folk heroes (e.g., Paul BU-

NYAN in the U.S. and ROBIN HOOD in England) as reflections of the civilizations from which they sprang.

folk song, music of anonymous composition, transmitted orally. The germ of a folk song is assumed to be produced by an individual and altered in transmission as a group expression. National and ethnic individuality is seen in folk music, but little is wholly indigenous. That of the U.S. reveals transplanted European and African sources. Interest in folk music grew in the 19th cent., although earlier scholars had worked in the field. Béla BARTÓK made great contributions in notating the folk music of central Europe. The phonograph and tape recorder facilitated transcription and collection of folk song. The music often shows the influence of formal composition, and songs of traceable authorship, e.g., "Dixie," are often considered folk songs. Since the 1950s folk music has been a significant influence and source for much popular vocal and instrumental music. Singers like Woody GUTHRIE and Joan BAEZ have performed folk songs and their own compositions in the idiom. Types of folk song include the work songs found in all cultures, e.g., sea CHANTEYS and SPIRITUALS.

Fonda, Henry, 1905–82, American actor; b. Grand Island, Nebr. Among his films are *Young Mr. Lincoln* (1939), *The Grapes of Wrath* (1940), *Mr. Roberts* (1955), and *On Golden Pond* (1981; Academy Award).

Fonda, Jane, 1937–, American actress; b. N.Y.C. The daughter of Henry FONDA, she has starred in such films as *Klute* (1971; Academy Award), *Julia* (1977), *The China Syndrome* (1979), and *On Golden Pond* (1981). She is also known for her liberal politics and for her exercise and weight-loss books and videos. Previously married to Roger Vadim and Tom Hayden, she married Ted TURNER in 1991.

Fongafale, town (1973 est. pop. 870), capital of TUVALU.

Fontaine, Pierre François Léonard [fôNtĕn'], 1762–1853, French architect. Working from 1794 with Charles Percier, he was a developer of the Empire style in France.

Fontainebleau, school of, group of 16th-cent. artists who decorated the royal palace at Fontainebleau, in France. Chief in importance were Il ROSSO, Francesco PRIMATICCIO, and Sabastiano Serlio. An Italian development of MANNERISM, the style of the Fountainebleau school was refined to the point of artificiality. Its subjects were allegorical and symbolic, in keeping with the tastes of FRANCIS I's court.

Fontana, Domenico, 1543–1607, Italian architect. In Rome he designed (1588) the LATERAN palace and the Vatican library. His other work included the fountain Acqua Felice (1587), the erection of an Egyptian obelisk before St. Peter's (1586), and the royal palace, Naples (1600).

Fontanne, Lynn: see LUNT, ALFRED, AND LYNN FONTANNE.

Fonteyn, Dame Margot [fŏntān'], 1919–91, English ballerina, b. Margaret Hookham. She studied in London and was *prima ballerina assoluta* of the ROYAL BALLET. Her performances in *Sleeping Beauty* and *The Firebird* were renowned, and her partnership (after 1962) with Russian dancer Rudolf NUREYEV brought her new recognition.

Foochow: see FUZHOU.

food additives, substances added to foods during processing to prevent spoilage or to enhance appearance, taste, texture, or nutritive value. By quantity the most common food additives are flavorings (e.g., spices and synthetic flavors) and sweeteners (e.g., sucrose, corn syrup, fructose, and dextrose). Other additives include colorings, preservatives, emulsifiers (which keep processed foods from separating), and stabilizers (which prevent the formation of ice crystals). In the U.S. the FOOD AND DRUG ADMINISTRATION is responsible for testing and regulating food additives.

Food and Agricultural Organization: see UNITED NATIONS (table 3).

Food and Drug Administration (FDA), agency in the Public Health Service division of the U.S. Dept. of HEALTH AND HUMAN SERVICES. Established in 1928, it is charged with protecting public health by ensuring that foods are safe and pure, cosmetics and other chemical substances harmless, and products safe, effective, and honestly labeled. All new medicinal drugs must be licensed for use by the FDA.

food chain: see ECOLOGY.

food preservation. Because most foods remain edible for only a limited time, food preservation has been practiced since the remotest times. Early products of conservation were cheese, butter, wine, bacon, pemmican, raisins, and parched grains. Advances in the methods used came with scientific investigations of the microorganisms that cause food spoilage, especially in the work of Louis PASTEUR. Basic methods of modern food preservation include dehydration, freeze-drying, heating (e.g., CANNING and PASTEURIZATION), refrigeration (both freezing and chilling), hermetic sealing to remove air, and GAMMA RADIATION to destroy microorganisms and retard spoilage. Such preserving agents as salt, vinegar, sugar, smoke, and alcohol are also used, often in combination. Other common preservatives are chemical agents.

food pyramid or **Food Guide Pyramid,** diagram used in nutrition education that fits food groups into a triangle and notes that, for a healthful diet, those at the base should be eaten more frequently than those at the top. At the base of the pyramid are breads, cereals, rice, and pasta. Above these are the vegetable and fruit groups. Next are the dairy group and a group including meats, eggs, nuts, and dry beans. Oils and sweets are at the apex, with a recommendation that they be used sparingly.

fool's gold: see PYRITE.

Foot, Michael, 1913–, British politician. He entered Parliament in 1945 and became a spokesman for the Labour party's radical left wing. Editor of the party organ, the *Tribune,* he served as secretary of state for employment (1974–75) and Speaker of the House of Commons (1976–79). He succeeded James CALLAGHAN as Labour party leader (1980–83) and tried to maintain the party's traditional policies in the face of the opposition of more conservative members, who broke away and formed the SOCIAL DEMOCRATIC PARTY.

foot-and-mouth disease: see HOOF-AND-MOUTH DISEASE.

football, any of several games in which two opposing teams attempt to score points by moving an inflated ball past a goal line or into a goal area. The games, differing greatly in their rules, include SOCCER (association football) and RUGBY, English games from which **American football** developed. The American game is played by two teams of 11 players each on a field that measures 100 by 53⅓ yd (91.4 by 48.8 m). At each end of the field is an end zone 10 yd (9.14 m) deep, in which stand H-shaped goal posts. Play is directed toward gaining possession of the football and moving it (by running or passing) across the opponent's goal line, thereby scoring a touchdown, worth six points. Points are also scored by kicking the ball over the crossbar between the goal posts (a field goal, worth three points); downing a player with the ball behind the player's own goal line (a safety, worth two points); and a conversion following a touchdown. In professional ball the conversion is made by kicking the ball over the goal posts (one point); in college and high school ball, the conversion is by a kick (one point) or by a pass or run (two points). The offensive team, led by the quarterback, must gain 10 yd in four tries (downs) or yield possession of the ball. The defending team tries to stop the ball carrier from advancing by tackling. Blocking and tackling make football one of the most rugged of sports, and players must wear heavy protective gear. The first intercollegiate football match in America (more like a 50-person soccer game) was played (1869) between Princeton and Rutgers at New Brunswick, N.J. Harvard began to play a rugby-type game in the 1870s, and within the next decade the distinctive American version evolved. A professional football association was formed in 1920 and renamed the National Football League (NFL) in 1922. Buoyed by the tremendous popularity of professional football after World War II, the NFL absorbed two rival leagues (1949 and 1966) and grew to 28 teams in two conferences by the early 1980s. The league will expand to 30 teams in 1995. The annual Super Bowl game for the league championship has been a major sports spectacle since its introduction in 1967. The World League of American Football was a short-lived NFL affiliate that played (1991–92) during the NFL's off-season. It had ten teams, including three in Europe and one in Canada. It is scheduled to be replaced with a six-team all-European league in 1995. **Canadian football** is similar to the U.S. game except that the field and the end zone are larger, measuring 110 by 65 yd (100 by 59 m) and 25 yd (23 m) deep, respectively; a team consists of 12 players; and only three downs are allowed. The Canadian Football League

(CFL), formed in 1959, is the major professional circuit. **Gaelic football,** played primarily in Ireland, is perhaps the roughest of the football-type games. The object is to punch, dribble (bounce), or kick the ball into (3 points) or directly over (1 point) the rectangular goal-net. A team is made up of 15 players. **Australian football** is played on a large oval field. Each team of 18 players attempts to kick the egg-shaped ball past a set of goal posts. The ball may be advanced by punches, kicks, or dribbles.

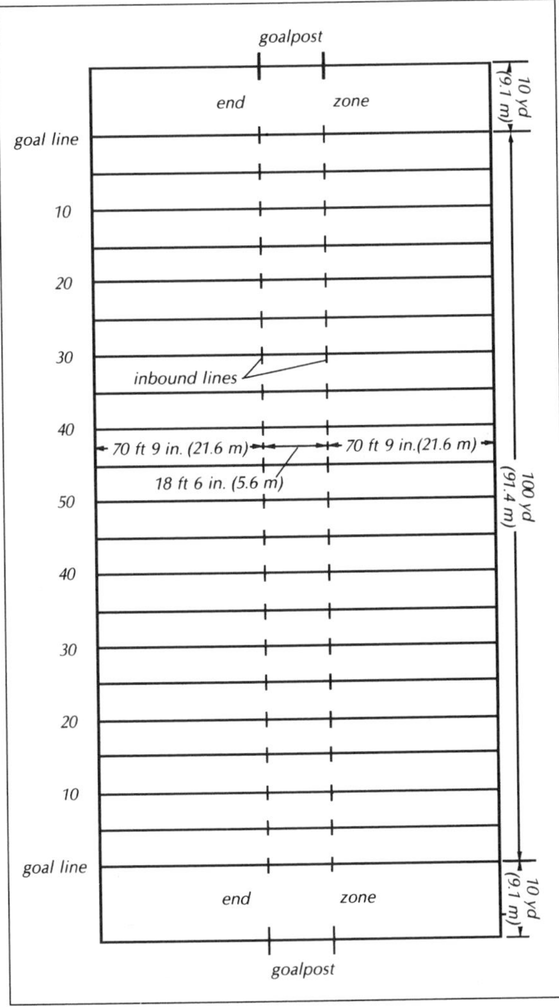

A professional football field. College teams use a similar field except that the inbound lines are 53 ft 4 in. (16.3 m) from the sidelines

foot-pound: see TORQUE; WORK.

Forbidden City: see CHINESE ARCHITECTURE; BEIJING.

force, in physics, a quantity that produces a change in the size or shape (see STRENGTH OF MATERIALS) or the MOTION of a body. Commonly experienced as a "push" or "pull," force is a vector quantity, having both magnitude and direction. The study of forces in equilibrium is STATICS; that of forces and motion is DYNAMICS. Four basic types of force are known in nature. The gravitational force (see GRAVITATION) and the electromagnetic force (see ELECTROMAGNETISM) both have an infinite range. The STRONG INTERACTION is a short-range force holding the atomic nucleus together, and the WEAK INTERACTION is a short-range force associated with radioactivity and particle decay. In the METRIC SYSTEM forces are measured in such units as the dyne (cgs system) and the newton (mks system), which cause accelerations of, respectively, 1 cm/sec^2 on a 1-gram mass and 1 m/sec^2 on a 1-kg mass. In ENGLISH UNITS OF MEASUREMENT, the pound (lb) is used. A 1-lb force equals 444,823 dynes; 1 dyne equals 10^{-5} newtons.

force bill, name of several laws in U.S. history, notably the federal act of Mar. 2, 1833, and the Reconstruction acts of 1870–71. The first force bill was passed in response to South Carolina's ordinance of NULLIFICATION. It empowered Pres. JACKSON to use the military, if necessary, to enforce the laws of Congress, specifically the tariff measures at issue. The second set of force bills strengthened the RECONSTRUCTION program of the radical Republicans by imposing strict penalties on those who tried to obstruct it. The act of May 31, 1870, penalized anyone who tried to prevent qualified citizens (in this case African Americans) from voting and placed congressional elections under exclusive federal control. The act of Apr. 20, 1871, in response to KU KLUX KLAN activities, declared acts by armed combinations tantamount to rebellion and empowered the president to suspend habeas corpus in lawless areas.

Ford, Edsel Bryant: see under FORD, HENRY.

Ford, Ford Madox, 1873–1939, English author; b. Ford Madox Hueffer. He wrote over 60 works, including novels, poems, criticism, travel essays, and reminiscences, and edited the *English Review* (1908–11) and *Transatlantic Review* (1924). His most important novels are *The Good Soldier* (1915) and a tetralogy published together as *Parade's End* (1950).

Ford, Gerald Rudolph, 1913–, 38th president of the U.S. (1974–77); b. Omaha, Nebr., as Leslie Lynch King, Jr. (he later took the name of his stepfather). A Republican congressman from Michigan (1949–73), he served (1965–73) as Republican minority leader in the House and was (1968, 1972) permanent chairman of the Republican National Convention. In 1973 Ford became the first appointed vice president of the U.S. (see CONSTITUTION) when he succeeded Spiro T. AGNEW. When Nixon resigned (Aug. 9, 1974) amidst the WATERGATE AFFAIR, Ford became president; one month later he issued a pardon to Nixon. As president, Ford continued Nixon's foreign policy and advocated anti-inflationary measures and limited social spending at home. A presidential candidate in 1976, he lost the election to Democrat Jimmy CARTER. His defeat was attributed to an economic recession and high inflation and to his pardon of Nixon.

Ford, Henry, 1863–1947, American industrialist, pioneer automobile manufacturer; b. Dearborn, Mich. While working as a machinist and engineer with the Edison Co., in his spare time he built (1892) his first automobile. In 1903 he organized the Ford Motor Co. By cutting production costs, controlling raw materials and distribution, adapting the assembly line to automobiles, and featuring an inexpensive, standardized car, Ford became the largest automobile producer in the world. In 1908 he designed the Model T; over 15 million cars were sold before the model was discontinued (1928), and a new design, the Model A, was created to meet growing competition. In 1914 Ford created a sensation by paying his workers five dollars for an eight-hour day, considerably above the average, and by beginning a profit-sharing plan that would distribute up to $30 million annually among his employees. He stubbornly resisted union organization until 1941. He retired in 1945. His numerous philanthropies included the FORD FOUNDATION. His son, **Edsel Bryant Ford,** 1893–1943, was president of the company from 1919 until his death. Henry's grandson, **Henry Ford II,** 1917–1987, who became president in 1945 and chairman in 1960, modernized the firm, and, for the first time in company history, recruited outsiders for high positions. He retired in 1980.

Ford, John, 1586–c.1640, English dramatist. The most important playwright during the reign of Charles I, he wrote (1627–33) three major tragedies: *'Tis Pity She's a Whore, The Broken Heart,* and *Love's Sacrifice.*

Ford, John, 1895–1973, American film director; b. Cape Elizabeth, Me. He won Academy Awards for *The Informer* (1935), *The Grapes of Wrath* (1940), *How Green Was My Valley* (1941), and *The Quiet Man* (1952). His many Westerns include *Rio Grande* (1950) and *The Searchers* (1956).

Ford Foundation: see FOUNDATION.

foreign exchange, methods and instruments used to adjust the payment of debts between two nations that employ different currency systems. A nation's BALANCE OF PAYMENTS has an important effect on the exchange rate of its currency. The rate of exchange is the price in local currency of one unit of foreign currency and is determined by the relative supply and demand of the currencies in the foreign exchange market. The chief demand for foreign exchange comes from importers and exporters, purchasers of foreign securities, government agencies, and international corporations. Exchange rates were traditionally fixed under the gold standard and later by international agreements, but in 1973 the major industrial nations of the West adopted a system of "floating" rates that allows for fluctuation within a limited range. See also EUROPEAN MONETARY SYSTEM; INTERNATIONAL MONETARY SYSTEM.

Foreign Legion, French volunteer armed force composed chiefly, in its enlisted ranks, of foreigners. Its international composition and practice of not inquiring into enlistees' backgrounds surrounded it with an aura of romance. Created by King LOUIS PHILIPPE (1831) to pacify Algeria, it was used throughout the French colonial empire and during both world wars. Today its headquarters are in S France.

Forester, C(ecil) S(cott), 1899–1966, English novelist. He is best known for stories of the royal navy in the days of sail, especially for those centering on Capt. Horatio Hornblower. Forester also wrote *The African Queen* (1935).

forestry, the management of forests for WOOD, water, wildlife, forage, and recreation. Due to wood's economic importance, forestry has been chiefly concerned with timber management, especially reforestation, maintenance of extant forests, and fire control. The U.S. Forest Service manages the National Forest System (federally owned forest reserves), emphasizing sustained yield (achieved by balancing reforestation and logging) and multiple use.

forgery, in law, fabrication or alteration of a written document with intent to deceive or defraud. Most instances of forgery occur in connection with instruments for payment of money, such as checks, but the crime may also involve documents of title (e.g., deeds) or public documents (e.g., birth and marriage certificates). Counterfeiting (the manufacture of false money with intent to deceive) may be regarded as a special variety of forgery.

forging: see WELDING.

formaldehyde or **methanal** (HCHO), a colorless, flammable, poisonous gas with a suffocating odor. Pure gaseous formaldehyde is uncommon, because it readily polymerizes into solid paraformaldehyde. Formalin, a 40%-by-volume solution of formaldehyde in water, is used as an antiseptic, disinfectant, and preservative for biological specimens. Formaldehyde is also used to make DYES, PLASTICS (e.g., BAKELITE), and synthetic RESINS.

Forrest, Edwin, 1806–72, American actor, the nation's first theatrical idol; b. Philadelphia. His New York City debut as Othello (1826) established him as a great tragedian, noted for bold and forceful acting. His rivalry with the English actor W.C. MACREADY resulted in a riot (1849) in New York by Forrest partisans in which many were killed.

Forrestal, James Vincent, 1892–1949, U.S. secretary of the navy (1944–47) and secretary of defense (1947–49); b. Beacon, N.Y. After the reorganization (1947) of the war and navy departments, Forrestal became the first secretary of defense. Illness forced his resignation, and he later committed suicide.

Forster, E(dward) M(organ), 1879–1970, English novelist. With sensitivity, subtlety, and an impeccable style, he brought new depths to the English novel of manners. *Where Angels Fear to Tread* (1905) was followed by *The Longest Journey* (1907), *A Room with a View* (1908), *Howards End* (1910), and *Maurice* (1913–14, published 1971). His last novel, *A Passage to India* (1924), is his best-known work. He also published short stories and nonfiction, including *Aspects of the Novel* (1927).

forsythia, shrub (genus *Forsythia*) of the OLIVE family, native to Europe and Asia. Producing abundant bell-shaped yellow or white flowers, which appear before the leaves, forsythia bushes are often cultivated as ornamentals in hedges and along borders.

Fortaleza, city (1990 pop. 1,824,991), NE Brazil, capital of Ceará state. An Atlantic port at the mouth of the Paejú R., which bisects the city, it ships coffee and other products of Brazil's interior and has processing and textile industries. It is also known for traditional handicrafts, e.g., lacemaking. The city first achieved importance in the 17th cent. as a center of the great colonial sugar plantations.

Fort Collins, city (1990 pop. 87,758), seat of Larimer co., N Colo., on the Cache la Poudre R., at the foot of the ROCKY MOUNTAINS.; inc. as a city 1883. The area was settled (1864) around a fortification built to protect a trading post. The city, trade center for a rich farming area, has diversified industries and is the seat of Colorado State Univ.

fortification, system of defense structures for protection from enemy attacks. The art developed in earliest times with the building of simple earthworks, which soon evolved into walls, palisades, and elaborate stockades. City walls appeared very early in the Middle East, notably in Mesopotamia and Phoenicia. Major advances in permanent fortification were made by the Romans, who built walls along the Danube and Rhine rivers and in England, e.g., HADRIAN'S WALL. The GREAT WALL OF CHINA was an even more ambitious undertaking. The advent of siegecraft, using such devices as battering rams and catapults, reduced the effectiveness of large-scale fortification, but in the Middle Ages CASTLES and citadels remained defensible against all but a lengthy siege. In the 15th cent. the development of ARTILLERY further diminished the value of fixed fortifications, and military engineers had to devise new methods of defense based on detached forts that created an entrenched camp over a wide area. This ring system of fortification failed in Belgium in World War I, however, as did the French MAGINOT LINE in World War II. The development of air power, heavy artillery, and mechanized warfare eventually brought an end to such defense systems. In both the Korean and Vietnam wars, the theory of fortification largely returned to the idea of temporary, even improvised, shelter, intended mainly to delay the enemy's advance.

Fort Knox [for Henry KNOX], U.S. military reservation, 110,000 acres (44,515 hectares), Hardin and Meade cos., N Ky.; est. 1917 as a training camp and became a permanent post in 1932. The U.S. Depository (built 1936) holds the bulk of the nation's gold bullion in steel and concrete vaults.

Fort Lauderdale, city (1990 pop. 148,377), seat of Broward co., SE Fla., on the Atlantic coast; settled around a fort built (c.1837) in the Seminole War, inc. 1911. The city has more than 270 mi (435 km) of natural and artificial waterways and one of the largest marinas in the world. A major beach resort, it has a performing arts center and art and science museums. Products include electronic devices, boats and yachts, and various light manufactures.

Fort McHenry, U.S. military post, Baltimore harbor, Md. Its defense against British bombardment in the WAR OF 1812 inspired Francis Scott KEY to write "The STAR-SPANGLED BANNER." It is now a national monument and historic site.

FORTRAN: see PROGRAMMING LANGUAGE.

Fort Sill, U.S. military reservation, Comanche co., SW Okla., 4 mi N of Lawton; est. 1869 by Gen. Philip SHERIDAN. Now a 95,000-acre (38,445-hectare) field artillery and missile base, it was once (1870s) a base of operations for campaigns against Native American peoples and for maintaining law and order in the region. Various tribes were resettled on the reservation, and GERONIMO is buried there.

Fort Smith, city (1990 pop. 72,798), seat of Sebastian co., NW Ark., at the Okla. line, where the Arkansas and Poteau rivers join; inc. 1842. A military post (est. 1817) and gold rush supply point (1848), it was a lawless area cleansed by "Hanging Judge" Isaac Parker. The modern city is a rail and trade center and has diverse manufactures, including refrigerators and heating and electrical equipment. The city has a 22-block historic district. Fort Smith National Historic Site is there.

Fort Sumter, fortification in Charleston harbor, S.C., site of the first clash (Apr. 12, 1861) of the CIVIL WAR. The Confederates were victorious, but the fort was retaken by Union forces in 1865. It is now a national monument.

Fort Wayne, city (1990 pop. 173,072), seat of Allen co., NE Ind., where the St. Joseph and St. Marys rivers join to form the Maumee R.; inc. 1840. It is a railroad, wholesale, and distribution hub with electronics and automotive industries. The MIAMI had their chief town on the strategic site. A French fort (built before 1680) was replaced by one built (1794) by Anthony WAYNE.

Fort Worth, city (1990 pop. 447,619), seat of Tarrant co., N Tex., 30 mi (48 km) W of DALLAS, with which it forms Texas's largest metropolitan area (1990 pop. 3,885,415); settled 1843, inc. 1873. Established as an army post in 1847, it became a cattle town after the Civil War. Completion (1876) of the railroad made it a meat-packing and shipping point. Wheat (late 19th cent.) and oil (discovered 1919 W of the city) furthered its development. Today it is a major N Texas industrial city, with large oil and gas facilities and aerospace and electronics industries. The Dallas–Fort Worth airport (opened 1974 between the cities) is one of the world's largest. Texas Christian Univ., the Kimball Art Museum, and the Amon Carter Museum of Western Art are among the city's well-known institutions.

Foscolo, Ugo, 1778–1827, Italian writer. A novel recounting his political disillusionment with Napoleon Bonaparte (see NAPOLEON I), *The Last Letters of Jacopo Ortis* (1798–1802), together with his criticism and lyrics (e.g., *Sepulchres,* 1807), strongly influenced Italian letters.

Foss, Lukas, 1922–, American composer, pianist, and conductor; b. Germany as Lukas Fuchs. As conductor of the Buffalo Philharmonic Orchestra (1963–71), he was noted for performing avant-garde compositions. His own early works were traditional; his later interest in modern techniques is seen in *Elytres* (1964) and *Fanfare* (1973). He was music director of the Brooklyn Philharmonic from 1971 to 1991 and of the Milwaukee Symphony Orchestra from 1981 to 1986.

fossil, remains or imprint of a plant or animal preserved from prehistoric times by natural methods and found mainly in sedimentary rock, asphalt, coal, and amber. Fossilization of skeletal structures or other hard parts is most common. Conditions for fossilization include quick burial in an originally moist sediment or other material that prevents both weathering and decay. Shells and bones embedded in hardened sediment can be dissolved by water, leaving a natural mold. Sometimes these molds are filled with mineral deposits, forming natural casts. Fossil footprints and trails and coprolites, or fossil excrement, can reveal much about the lives and feeding habits of ancient animals. Many insects and other ARTHROPODS have been preserved whole in amber; in 1993 DNA was extracted from an amber-encased weevil from the Cretaceous period. Entire large animals of the late Pleistocene have been found frozen, notably in Siberia. In California the LA BREA tar pits have yielded many skeletons. The study of fossils is called paleontology.

fossil fuel: see ENERGY, SOURCES OF.

Foster, Stephen Collins, 1826–64, American songwriter and composer; b. Lawrenceville, Pa. He had little training. Writing songs for the E.P. CHRISTY minstrel troupe, he acquired a knowledge of African American life, but sensing prejudice against "Ethiopian songs" he was reluctant even to put his name to them. Because of their utter simplicity, his African-American dialect songs are often thought of as folk music. His songs include "Oh! Susannah," "Camptown Races," "My Old Kentucky Home," and "Old Black Joe."

foster care, generally, care of children on a full-time, temporary basis by persons other than their own parents. Also known as boarding-home care, foster care is intended to offer a supportive family environment to children whose natural parents cannot raise them because of the parents' physical or mental illness, the child's behavioral difficulties, or problems within the family environment, e.g., abuse, alcoholism, or crime. Children may be placed by an agency in group homes or with families, who receive some payment toward care. The child's parents may retain their parental rights, and the child may ultimately return home. Under permanent foster care the agency has guardianship; the child may then be available for adoption by the foster parents or others. Foster care has been extended in recent years to include care for elderly persons, on a fee basis, in the homes of people who are not family members.

Foucault, Jean Bernard Leon [fo͞okō′], 1819–68, French physicist. Investigating the speed of light, he determined its velocity in air and found that its speed in water and other media decreased in proportion to the index of refraction. He originated the Foucault PENDULUM, with which he demonstrated the earth's rotation, invented (1852) the GYROSCOPE, and with the physicist Armand Fizeau took the first clear photograph of the sun.

Foucault, Michel, 1926–84, French philosopher and historian. Highly influential, he is known for historical studies, e.g., *Madness and Civilization* (1961), that reveal the sometimes disturbing power relations in social practices. Works such as *The Order of Things* (1966) and *Archaeology of Knowledge* (1969) analyze systems of knowledge, uncovering their unconscious rules and relations to one another. His last writings, e.g., *History of Sexuality*, vol. 2 (1984), examine the self's relationship to itself.

Fouché, Joseph [fo͞oshā′], b. 1759 or 1763, d. 1820, French police minister (1799–1802, 1804–10). An opportunist, he sided with every party in power from the FRENCH REVOLUTION through the BOURBON restoration. He was indispensable to NAPOLEON I, who created him duke of Otranto in 1809. Sometimes considered the father of the modern police state, he created a ruthlessly efficient system of criminal and political police. After the second Bourbon restoration, he was exiled and died in obscurity.

Foucquet: see FOUQUET.

foundation, institution through which private wealth is contributed and distributed for public purposes. Foundations have existed since Greek and Roman times, when they honored deities. The medieval European church had many foundations, and the Arab *waqf* (pious endowment) developed with the growth of Islam. Modern European foundations are generally smaller than those in the U.S. and are closely regulated by the state. There were a few early American foundations, e.g., those endowed by Benjamin FRANKLIN (1791) and by James Smithson (1846; to form the SMITHSONIAN INSTITUTION), but foundations in the U.S. developed rapidly after the Civil War. From 1896 to 1918 many wealthy Americans created private foundations for the public benefit, e.g., Andrew CARNEGIE and John D. ROCKEFELLER, Sr. The larger of the modern U.S. foundations have devoted themselves to broad areas, e.g., the Carnegie Corporation of New York (est. 1911) concentrates on American education and underprivileged groups; the Rockefeller Foundation (est. 1913) works in the areas of hunger, overpopulation, education, equal opportunity, cultural improvement, and ecology; and the Ford Foundation (est. 1936) concentrates on world peace, democratic government, economic well-being, education, and the scientific study of humanity. More recent foundations include the John D. and Catherine T. MacArthur Foundation (est. 1979), best known for its annual awards to creative individuals (often called "genius" prizes).

founding: see CASTING.

Fouquet or **Foucquet, Jean** or **Jehan** [fo͞okā′], c.1420–c.1480, French painter and illuminator. Court painter to CHARLES VII and LOUIS XI, he produced delicate religious paintings, court portraits, and an illuminated BOOK OF HOURS for Étienne Chevalier (Chantilly) that is regarded as his masterpiece.

Four Freedoms. On Jan. 6, 1941, Pres. F.D. ROOSEVELT, in a message to Congress proposing LEND-LEASE legislation, stated that Four Freedoms should prevail throughout the world—freedom of speech and expression, freedom of worship, freedom from want, and freedom from fear. These were substantially incorporated (Aug. 1941) in the ATLANTIC CHARTER.

Four Horsemen of the Apocalypse, allegorical figures in REVELATION in the BIBLE. One interpretation of the rider on the white horse is that he represents Jesus. The rider on the red horse is war; on the black horse, famine; and on the pale horse, death.

Fourier, Charles [fo͞oryā′], 1772–1837, French social philosopher. He held that social harmony could be achieved in a society based on the "phalanx," an economic unit of 1,620 people sharing a communal dwelling and dividing work according to their natural inclinations. The many Fourierist communities included BROOK FARM. After Fourier's death Fourierism was led by V.P. CONSIDÉRANT.

Fourier, Jean Baptiste Joseph, Baron, 1768–1830, French mathematician and physicist, noted for his researches on heat diffusion and numerical equations. He originated the Fourier series, which allowed discontinuous functions to be represented by a trigonometric series.

Four-Power Treaty: see NAVAL CONFERENCES.

Fourteen Points, formulation of a peace program, presented (Jan. 1918) by Pres. WILSON near the end of WORLD WAR I. The program called for a just, unselfish peace that would offer self-government to the European national groups and pave the way for general disarmament and open agreements between nations. The program had two purposes: to reach the people and liberal leaders of the

Central Powers, in the hope that their influence would help shorten the war, and to provide an actual framework for the peace discussions. The first aim was successful, but despite the enormous moral authority the Fourteen Points conferred on Wilson, the program's important points were lost in the compromises that came out of the peace treaty (see VERSAILLES, TREATY OF).

Fourth of July, Independence Day, or **July Fourth,** U.S. patriotic holiday commemorating the adoption of the DECLARATION OF INDEPENDENCE. Celebration of it began during the AMERICAN REVOLUTION.

Fowler, Henry Watson, 1858–1933, English lexicographer. He and his brother, Francis G. Fowler (1870–1918), collaborated on *The King's English* (1906), *The Concise Oxford Dictionary of Current English* (1911), and *The Pocket Oxford Dictionary* (1924). After the death of his brother, H.W. Fowler completed alone the invaluable reference work *A Dictionary of Modern Usage* (1926).

Fowles, John, 1926–, English novelist. A cerebral writer, he is interested in manipulating the novel form. His books include *The Collector* (1963), *The French Lieutenant's Woman* (1969), *Mantissa* (1982), and *A Maggot* (1985).

Fox: see SAC AND FOX.

Fox, Charles James, 1749–1806, British statesman and orator, for many years the outstanding parliamentary proponent of liberal reform. A WHIG, he entered Parliament in 1768. He was a close friend of the prince of Wales (later GEORGE IV) and an enemy of GEORGE III and William PITT. Three times foreign secretary (1782, 1783, 1806), Fox opposed British intervention in the FRENCH REVOLUTION. He advocated legislative independence for Ireland, enlargement of the franchise, and parliamentary reform. Abolition of the slave trade, which he proposed and urged, was passed in 1807.

Fox, George, 1624–91, English religious leader, founder of the Society of FRIENDS. In 1646 he underwent a mystical experience that convinced him that Christianity was an inner light by which Jesus directly illumines the believing soul. Beginning to preach in 1647, he was often persecuted and imprisoned but won many followers. He organized his sect in 1668; the first London Yearly Meeting was held in 1671. His journal (1694, with a preface by William Penn) has appeared in various editions.

Fox, Margaret: see SPIRITISM.

fox, carnivorous MAMMAL of the DOG family, found in much of the Northern Hemisphere. It has a pointed face, thick fur, and bushy tail. Most fox species belong to the red fox group (genus *Vulpes*). The common red fox (*V. vulpes*) of North America inhabits areas of forest mixed with open country from the Arctic to the S U.S.

fox terrier, long-legged TERRIER; shoulder height, c.15 in. (38.1 cm); weight, 15–19 lb (6.8–8.6 kg). There are two types: the smooth, with a dense, short, flat coat, and the wirehaired, with a longer, harsh, wiry coat. Both are white, with black or black-and-tan markings. The breed was perfected in 19th-cent. England to hunt foxes.

Foxe, John, 1516–87, English clergyman, author of the noted *Book of Martyrs.* A Protestant, he fled to the Continent in the reign of MARY I. There, a Latin edition of his history was published in 1559. An expanded English edition (1563) appeared in the reign of ELIZABETH I. The book praised the Protestant martyrs of Mary's reign.

foxhound, sturdy, medium-sized HOUND. The **English foxhound,** shoulder height, 21–25 in. (53.3–63.5 cm), weight, 60–70 lb (27.2–31.8 kg), with a short, glossy coat that is usually black, tan, and white. Probably developed from 14th-cent. French hounds, it was first used in packs to hunt foxes in the 17th cent. The slightly smaller **American foxhound** was developed over 300 years ago.

Foyt, A.J. (Anthony Joseph Foyt, Jr.), 1935–, American auto racing driver; b. Houston. Foyt was the first person to win the Indianapolis 500 race four times (1961, 1964, 1967, 1977). He has also won the Daytona 500 and, with Dan Gurney, the 24 Hours of Le Mans. He has been U.S. Auto Club driving champion seven times.

Fr, chemical symbol of the element FRANCIUM.

Fra: see ANGELICO, FRA; LIPPI, FRA FILIPPO.

fractal geometry, branch of MATHEMATICS concerned with irregular patterns made of parts that are in some way similar to the whole, e.g., twigs and tree branches, a property called self-similarity or self-symmetry. Unlike conventional GEOMETRY, which is concerned with regular shapes and whole-number dimensions, such as lines (one-dimensional) and cones (three-dimensional), fractal geometry deals with shapes found in nature that have non-integer, or fractal, dimensions—linelike rivers with a fractal dimension of about 1.2 and conelike mountains with a fractal dimension between 2 and 3. The theory of fractals developed from Benoit MANDELBROT's study of COMPLEXITY and CHAOS. Fractal geometry has been applied to such diverse fields as the stock market, chemical industry, meteorology, and COMPUTER GRAPHICS.

fraction, in arithmetic, an expression representing a part, or several equal parts, of a unit. In writing a fraction, e.g., 2/5 or $\frac{2}{5}$, the number after or below the bar, called the denominator, indicates the total number of equal parts into which the unit has been divided; the number before or above the bar, called the numerator, indicates how many of these parts are being considered. The present notation for fractions is of Hindu origin, but Egyptians used some types of fractions before 1600 B.C. The DECIMAL SYSTEM uses another way to represent fractions, e.g., 0.75 for $\frac{3}{4}$, often simplifying arithmetical computation.

Fragonard, Jean-Honoré [frägônär'], 1732–1806, French painter. Influenced by BOUCHER, he was admitted to the Académie royale in 1765 for *Coresus and Callirrhoë* (Louvre). Thereafter he painted polished, delicately erotic scenes of love for the court of LOUIS XV. Representative works are *Love's Vow* and *The Swing* (both: Wallace Coll., London) and the *Music Lesson* (Louvre). He is esteemed for the freedom of his brushstroke, the vitality of his portraiture and landscapes, and his virtuosity in depicting the gaiety and charm of the age of Louis XV.

Frame, Janet, 1924–, New Zealand author of such complex, disturbing novels as *Owls Do Cry* (1957), *Faces in the Water* (1961), *Living in the Maniototo* (1979), and *The Envoy from Mirror City* (1985), of poems, e.g., *The Pocket Mirror* (1967), and of short stories.

France, Anatole [fräNs'], pseud. of **Jacques Anatole Thibault,** 1844–1924, French author, the most prominent French man of letters of his day. His early fiction displayed allusive charm and subtle irony, as in *The Crime of Sylvestre Bonnard* (1881), *Thaïs* (1890), and *At the Sign of the Reine Pédauque* (1893). After the DREYFUS AFFAIR (in which he supported ZOLA), he concentrated more on political satire, notably in the novel *Penguin Island* (1908), an allegory of French history. He was elected to the French Academy in 1896 and received the Nobel Prize in literature in 1921.

France, officially French Republic, republic (1992 est. pop. 57,287,000), 211,207 sq mi (547,026 sq km), W Europe; bordered by the English Channel (N), the Atlantic Ocean and Bay of Biscay (W), Spain (SW), the Mediterranean Sea (S), Switzerland and Italy

RULERS OF FRANCE SINCE 987 *(including dates of reign)*

The Capetians

Hugh Capet, 987–96
Robert II (the Pious), son of Hugh Capet, 996–1031
Henry I, son of Robert II, 1031–60
Philip I, son of Henry I, 1060–1108
Louis VI (the Fat), son of Philip I, 1108–37
Louis VII (the Young), son of Louis VI, 1137–80
Philip II (Augustus), son of Louis VII, 1180–1223
Louis VIII, son of Philip II, 1223–26
Louis IX (Saint Louis), son of Louis VIII, 1226–70
Philip III (the Bold), son of Louis IX, 1270–85
Philip IV (the Fair), son of Philip III, 1285–1314
Louis X (the Quarrelsome), son of Philip IV, 1314–16
John I (the Posthumous), son of Louis X, 1316
Philip V (the Tall), son of Philip IV, 1317–22
Charles IV (the Fair), son of Philip IV, 1322–28

House of Valois

Philip VI, grandson of Philip III, 1328–50
John II (the Good), son of Philip VI, 1350–64
Charles V (the Wise), son of John II, 1364–80
Charles VI (the Mad or the Well Beloved), son of Charles V, 1380–1422
Charles VII (the Victorious or the Well Served), son of Charles VI, 1422–61
Louis XI, son of Charles VII, 1461–83
Charles VIII, son of Louis XI, 1483–98
Louis XII, descendant of Charles V, 1498–1515
Francis I, cousin and son-in-law of Louis XII, 1515–47
Henry II, son of Francis I, 1547–59
Francis II, son of Henry II, 1559–60
Charles IX, son of Henry II, 1560–74
Henry III, son of Henry II, 1574–89

House of Bourbon

Henry IV (of Navarre), descendant of Louis IX, 1589–1610
Louis XIII, son of Henry IV, 1610–43
Louis XIV, son of Louis XIII, 1643–1715
Louis XV, great-grandson of Louis XIV, 1715–74
Louis XVI, grandson of Louis XV, 1774–92

The First Republic

The National Convention, 1792–95
The Directory, 1795–99
The Consulate (Napoleon Bonaparte, First Consul, 1802–4), 1799–1804

The First Empire

Napoleon I (Napoleon Bonaparte), 1804–15

Bourbon Restoration

Louis XVIII, grandson of Louis XV, 1814–24
Charles X, grandson of Louis XV, 1824–30

House of Bourbon-Orléans

Louis Philippe, descendant of Louis XIII, 1830–48

The Second Republic

Louis Napoleon Bonaparte, nephew of Napoleon I, president, 1848–52

The Second Empire

Napoleon III (Louis Napoleon Bonaparte), 1852–70

The Third Republic *(presidents)*

Louis Jules Trochu (provisional), 1870–71
Adolphe Thiers, 1871–73
Marie Edmé Patrice de MacMahon, 1873–79
Jules Grévy, 1879–87
Sadi Carnot, 1887–94
Jean Paul Pierre Casimir-Périer, 1894–95
Félix Faure, 1895–99
Émile François Loubet, 1899–1906
Armand Fallières, 1906–13
Raymond Poincaré, 1913–20
Paul Eugène Louis Deschanel, 1920
Alexandre Millerand, 1920–24
Gaston Doumergue, 1924–31
Paul Doumer, 1931–32
Albert Lebrun, 1932–40

The Vichy Government

Henri Philippe Pétain, chief of state, 1940–44

The Provisional Government

Charles De Gaulle, president, 1944–46

The Fourth Republic *(presidents)*

Georges Bidault (provisional), 1946
Vincent Auriol, 1947–54
René Coty, 1954–58

The Fifth Republic *(presidents)*

Charles De Gaulle, 1958–69
Georges Pompidou, 1969–74
Valery Giscard d'Estaing, 1974–81
François Mitterrand, 1981–

(E, SE), and Germany, Luxembourg, and Belgium (NE). PARIS is the capital; other major cities include MARSEILLES, LYONS, TOULOUSE and NICE. One of the country's major natural features is the Massif Central, a rugged mountain area occupying south-central France. North of this and of the LOIRE R. is the Paris basin, a fertile depression drained by the SEINE and Marne rivers. To the southeast is the RHÔNE valley, which widens into a plain near its delta on the MEDITERRANEAN. To the southwest is the great Aquitanian plain, drained by the Garonne and Dordogne rivers. The main mountain ranges are the French ALPS, with France's highest peak, MONT BLANC (15,771 ft/4,807 m), the Vosges and the Jura mountains in the east, and the PYRENEES in the southwest.

Economy. France is one of the world's major economic powers. Agriculture is important, and about 60% of the land is used for farming. Over half of the value of agricultural output derives from livestock; leading crops are sugar beets, wheat, corn, barley, and potatoes. Only Italy produces more wine. Iron ore and bauxite are the leading minerals. Major industrial products include chemicals, textiles, steel, foods (particularly cheese), motor vehicles, aircraft. Tourism is important, as is the production of luxury goods such as perfume. The railroads, utilities, many banks, and some key industries are nationally owned, but there has been some recent movement toward PRIVATIZATION. France has the world's second largest number of operating nuclear power plants, which produce over 75% of its electricity.

People. France has great ethnic diversity. French is the universal language, but Alsatian (a German dialect), Flemish, Breton, Basque, and Catalan are still spoken in various sections. Roman Catholicism is the dominant religion.

Government. Metropolitan (European) France is composed of 96 departments (including the island-department of CORSICA), grouped into 22 regions and subdivided into districts, municipalities, and cantons. Together with the overseas departments and territories, they constitute the French Republic. The Fifth French Republic is governed under a constitution adopted in 1958 and amended in

1962. It provides for a strong president, directly elected to a seven-year term, and a bicameral parliament.

Early History. The area known as GAUL was conquered (58–51 B.C.) by the Romans under Julius CAESAR. Beginning in the 3d cent. A.D., the Gallo-Roman civilization that had developed was overrun by Germanic invaders, including the FRANKS under CLOVIS I, who defeated (486) the last Roman governor. Under the MEROVINGIAN and CAROLINGIAN dynasties, the Franks ruled Gaul until 987, when powerful feudal lords established HUGH CAPET as king. Under the Capetian kings, who reigned until 1328, France experienced a rebirth that reached its height in the 13th cent. Its leading role in the CRUSADES established its cultural supremacy in most of Europe, and the HUNDRED YEARS WAR (1337–1453) evicted the English from French soil. The 16th cent. brought religious conflict and civil wars, but in the 17th cent. two great statesmen, Cardinal RICHELIEU and Cardinal MAZARIN, reestablished French power, and under LOUIS XIV (r.1643–1715) France became the greatest power in Europe.

The Ancien Régime and the New France. Burdened by remnants of FEUDALISM and a system of outworn privileges, France under LOUIS XV (r.1715–74) hovered on the verge of bankruptcy. The SEVEN YEARS WAR (1756–63) drained the treasury and cost France its empire in India and North America. French support of the AMERICAN REVOLUTION proved a financial disaster. The result was the upheaval that shook Europe from 1789 to 1815 (see FRENCH REVOLUTION; FRENCH REVOLUTIONARY WARS; NAPOLEON I). During this time a constitutional monarchy was created (1791); war with much of Europe began, accompanied by the growth of radical factions in France (1792); ROBESPIERRE presided over the REIGN OF TERROR (1793–95); and a reaction ushered in the DIRECTORY (1795–99), which was terminated by Napoleon's coup d'etat. Making himself emperor (1804), Napoleon led his armies as far as Moscow before his final defeat in the WATERLOO CAMPAIGN (1815).

Modern France. France emerged as a uniform, bureaucratic state dominated by the bourgeoisie. The Bourbon Restoration (1814–30) was short-lived. The JULY REVOLUTION of 1830 enthroned LOUIS PHILIPPE, who was overthrown in turn by the FEBRUARY REVOLUTION of 1848. Louis Napoleon headed the Second Republic and later (1852) made himself emperor as NAPOLEON III. Defeat in the FRANCO-PRUSSIAN WAR (1870–71) led to his downfall and the establishment of the Third Republic. In WORLD WAR I France, led by CLEMENCEAU, bore the brunt of the fighting in the West. In WORLD WAR II defeat by Germany (1940) was followed by occupation; Marshal PÉTAIN headed the collaborationist VICHY government in unoccupied France, while Gen. Charles DE GAULLE led the "Free French" resistance. In 1944 the Allies expelled the Germans from France. The Fourth Republic, proclaimed in 1946, was weakened by the defeat (1954) of French troops in INDOCHINA and a war for independence in ALGERIA. De Gaulle was returned to power as first president (1958–69) of the Fifth Republic. Seeking to restore French prestige in world affairs, De Gaulle stressed independence from the U.S. and NATO in military affairs. His conservative policies were continued by his successors, Georges POMPIDOU and Valéry GISCARD D'ESTAING. In 1981, after 23 years of Gaullist dominance, Socialist François MITTERRAND was elected president and embarked on a program that included administrative decentralization and nationalization of banks and industry. In 1986 the Socialists lost their parliamentary majority, and Mitterrand was forced to appoint Jacques CHIRAC, a Gaullist, as premier. Chirac reversed the Socialist program with a policy of reprivatization and opposed Mitterrand in the 1988 presidential election. Mitterrand won, and the Socialists regained control of the national assembly. Mitterrand turned increasingly to foreign affairs and pursued a more moderate economic program. Rising unemployment and other economic difficulties, as well as several corruption scandals, led to a resounding Socialist defeat in 1993. Conservatives captured nearly 85% of the seats in the national assembly, and Édouard BALLADUR, a Gaullist, became premier.

Franceschi, Piero de': see PIERO DELLA FRANCESCA.

Francis, Saint, or **Saint Francis of Assisi,** 1182?–1226, founder of the FRANCISCANS; b. Assisi, Italy. The son of a wealthy merchant, he underwent a conversion at age 22 and became markedly devout and ascetic. In 1209 he began to preach and was given permission by Pope INNOCENT III to form an order of friars. The friars traveled about Italy and soon began preaching in foreign countries, including (1219–20) the Holy Land. In 1221 Francis gave up command of the order, and in 1224 he became the first known person to receive the stigmata (wounds corresponding to those of the crucified Jesus). Francis exemplified humility, love of poverty, and joyous religious fervor; he is also associated with a simple love of nature and humanity and is often depicted preaching to birds. Stories about him were collected in *The Little Flowers of St. Francis.* Feast: Oct. 4.

Francis, rulers of the HOLY ROMAN EMPIRE. **Francis I,** 1708–65, emperor (1745–65), duke of Lorraine (1729–37), and duke of Tuscany (1737–65), exchanged Lorraine for Tuscany in 1735 as part of the settlement of the War of the POLISH SUCCESSION. In 1736 he married MARIA THERESA, heiress to the HAPSBURG lands. He became emperor at the end of the War of the AUSTRIAN SUCCESSION, but the real rulers were Maria Theresa and Chancellor Kaunitz. **Francis II,** 1768–1835, was the last Holy Roman emperor (1792–1806) and, as Francis I, the first emperor of Austria (1804–35) and king of Bohemia and Hungary (1792–1835). When NAPOLEON I forced the dissolution of the Holy Roman Empire, Francis took the title emperor of Austria. Later he helped defeat Napoleon and, guided by METTERNICH, presided over the Congress of VIENNA. His reign was exceedingly reactionary and repressive.

Francis I, emperor of Austria: see FRANCIS II, Holy Roman emperor.

Francis, kings of France. **Francis I,** 1494–1547 (r.1515–47), was the cousin, son-in-law, and successor of LOUIS XII. He resumed the ITALIAN WARS and recovered Milan by a brilliant victory at Marignano (1515). A candidate for Holy Roman emperor (1519), Francis lost to CHARLES V, who became his lifelong rival. A planned alliance with HENRY VIII of England failed to occur at the FIELD OF THE CLOTH OF GOLD (1520), and Francis was captured in his first war (1521–25) against Charles V. To gain his freedom Francis renounced many territorial claims. He then created the League of Cognac, consisting of Francis, Henry VIII, Venice, Florence, and the papacy; they were all allied against Charles V, but a second war (1527–29) gained little, and a third war (1536–38) proved inconclusive. In 1542 Francis, allied with the Turkish sultan SULAYMAN I, again attacked Charles, who was supported by Henry VIII. The resulting peace treaties only confirmed earlier French losses. Francis was a typical Renaissance monarch, unscrupulous, spendthrift, and dissolute, but is also known for his support of the arts. He was a patron of François RABELAIS, and LEONARDO DA VINCI worked at his court. Francis was succeeded by his son HENRY II. His grandson, **Francis II,** 1544–60 (r.1559–60), married (1558) MARY QUEEN OF SCOTS, and during his reign the government was run by her relatives, the GUISE family. Their ruthless persecution of the Protestants caused the HUGUENOTS to launch the ill-fated Amboise Conspiracy (1560) in an effort to displace them.

Francis, 1554–84, French prince, duke of Alençon and Anjou, youngest son of HENRY II of France. Although ill-shapen and pockmarked, he was considered as a husband for ELIZABETH I of England. Offered (1580) the rule of the Low Countries by WILLIAM THE SILENT, leader of the Netherlands' revolt against Spain, he invaded the Netherlands but withdrew in 1583.

Francis, Dick, 1920–, English novelist. Formerly a professional champion steeplechase jockey, he parlayed his knowledge of horse racing into successful mysteries, including *Twice Shy* (1982), *Break In* (1986), and *The Edge* (1988).

Franciscans, members of several Roman Catholic religious orders following the rule (approved 1223) of St. FRANCIS. There are now three orders of Franciscan friars. The Friars Minor (O.F.M.), formerly called Observants, and the Friars Minor Conventual (O.M.C.) split (1517) as a result of a reform. Further reform (1525) created the Capuchins (O.M.Cap.). The Franciscans include an order of nuns, the Poor Clares, and a third order including both laity and religious members. Franciscans are educators and missionaries.

Francis de Sales, Saint, 1567–1622, French Roman Catholic preacher, Doctor of the Church, key figure in the Catholic Reformation in France (see REFORMATION, CATHOLIC). He became (1602) bishop of Geneva and is credited with many conversions of Protestants by his eloquent preaching. With St. Jane Frances de Chantal, he founded the Order of the Visitation for women. His *Intro-*

duction to the Devout Life is a religious classic, and he is the patron saint of Roman Catholic writers. Feast: Jan. 24.

Francis Ferdinand or **Franz Ferdinand,** 1863–1914, Austrian archduke, heir apparent to his great-uncle, Emperor FRANCIS JOSEPH. He and his wife, Sophie, were assassinated (1914) in SARAJEVO by Gavrilo Princip, a Serbian nationalist. The consequent Austrian ultimatum to Serbia led directly to WORLD WAR I.

Francis Joseph or **Franz Josef,** 1830–1916, emperor of Austria (1848–1916) and king of Hungary (1867–1916). He subdued Hungary (1849) but lost (1859) Lombardy to Sardinia, and later he lost Venetia to Italy in the AUSTRO-PRUSSIAN WAR of 1866. After reorganization (1867), his empire became the AUSTRO-HUNGARIAN MONARCHY. Francis Joseph joined (1879) in an alliance with Germany (see TRIPLE ALLIANCE AND TRIPLE ENTENTE). His reign was disturbed by the tragic deaths of his son, RUDOLF; his brother, MAXIMILIAN, emperor of Mexico; and his wife, ELIZABETH. He died during World War I and was succeeded by CHARLES I.

Francis Xavier, Saint, 1506–52, Basque JESUIT missionary, called the Apostle to the Indies. A friend of St. IGNATIUS OF LOYOLA, with whom he and five others formed the Society of Jesus, he spent the last 11 years of his life as a missionary in India, Southeast Asia, and Japan. He is considered one of the greatest Christian missionaries, possessing both profound mysticism and common sense. Feast: Dec. 3.

francium (Fr), radioactive element, discovered in 1939 by Marguerite Perey as a disintegration product of actinium. Some of the 21 known isotopes of this rare ALKALI METAL are prepared by bombarding thorium with protons, deuterons, or alpha particles. See ELEMENT (table); PERIODIC TABLE.

Franck, César Auguste [fräNk], 1822–90, Belgian-French composer and organist. As a teacher in Paris, he influenced an entire generation of composers. His distinctive music, drawing on the techniques of BACH, includes his famous Symphony in D minor (1886–88).

Franco, Francisco [fräng'kō], 1892–1975, Spanish general, *caudillo* [leader] of Spain (1939–75). An army chief of staff (1934–36) and a political conservative, he joined (1936) the Nationalist rebellion against the republic and invaded Spain from Morocco. He became head of the rebel government (1936) and of the fascist FALANGE party (1937). With German and Italian help, he won the SPANISH CIVIL WAR in 1939, dealt ruthlessly with Loyalist opponents, and established a corporate state. He kept Spain a nonbelligerent in World War II, and in 1947 he declared Spain a kingdom and himself regent. He named (1969) Prince JUAN CARLOS as his successor and, despite social unrest, retained power until his death.

Franco-German War: see FRANCO-PRUSSIAN WAR.

Franconia, one of the five basic or stem duchies of medieval Germany, S Germany. It became (9th cent.) a duchy that included the cities of Mainz, Würzburg, Frankfurt, and Worms. Partitioned in 939, it remained politically fragmented. Most of Eastern Franconia passed (1803–15) to Bavaria.

Franco-Prussian War or **Franco-German War,** 1870–71, war provoked by BISMARCK as part of his plan to create a unified German empire. Bismarck surmised that his publication of the EMS DISPATCH would goad the French government into declaring war (on July 19, 1870) on Prussia and that the other German states would fall into line behind Prussia. A brilliant campaign led by von MOLTKE brought a string of German victories, culminating in the French rout at Sedan, where the emperor, NAPOLEON III, was captured (Sept. 1). In Paris, Napoleon was deposed and a provisional government was formed, but French resistance was made useless after the surrender of the French commander, Marshal Bazaine, at Metz (Oct. 27). Paris, however, held out until Jan. 1871, when the Prussian siege finally succeeded. France was forced to pay a huge indemnity and to give up most of Alsace and Lorraine. Again Paris resisted, until the COMMUNE OF PARIS was crushed militarily by the new French government. The war had far-reaching consequences. The German Empire was proclaimed (at Versailles on Jan. 18, 1871), and Prussian militarism and imperialism had triumphed.

Frank, Anne, 1929–45, Jewish diarist; b. Germany. Her family fled Nazi rule for Amsterdam in 1933. After Germany occupied the Netherlands, they hid (1942–44) in a secret room in a warehouse until betrayed to the Nazis. The moving diary she kept while in hiding was discovered (1947) and became an international bestseller. She died at the Bergen-Belsen CONCENTRATION CAMP.

Frank, Jacob, c.1726–1791, Polish Jewish sectarian and adventurer; b. Ukraine as Jacob ben Judah Leib. He founded the Frankists, a heretical Jewish sect that was an anti-Talmudic outgrowth of the mysticism of SABBATAI ZEVI.

Frankenthaler, Helen, 1928–, American painter; b. N.Y.C. A one-time student of Jackson POLLOCK, she is known for her lyrical and sensuous stained canvases.

Frankfort, city (1990 pop. 25,968), state capital and seat of Franklin co., N central Ky., cut by the Kentucky R.; est. 1786, became capital 1792. In the bluegrass country, it is the trade center for a tobacco and livestock area and produces whiskey, electronic and automotive parts, and other manufactures. Many fine old homes and the graves of Daniel BOONE and his wife are in the city.

Frankfurt or **Frankfurt am Main,** city (1989 est pop. 625,300), Hesse, central Germany, on the Main R. A port and an industrial center producing chemicals, pharmaceuticals, and other manufactures, it is also a world financial center—the German central bank and European Monetary Institute are here—and the site of major international trade fairs. Founded (1st cent. A.D.) by the Romans, it became a royal residence (8th cent.) under CHARLEMAGNE and the coronation place (1562–1792) of the Holy Roman emperors. In the 19th cent. it was the seat of the diet of the GERMAN CONFEDERATION. The city was the original home of the ROTHSCHILD family and the birthplace of GOETHE.

Frankfurt an der Oder, city (1989 est. pop. 87,900), Brandenburg, E Germany, a port on the Oder R. It is an industrial center, agricultural market, and rail hub. Manufactures include textiles, machinery, and foodstuffs. Chartered in 1253, the city was sacked (1631) by the Swedes in the THIRTY YEARS WAR and was severely damaged in WORLD WAR II.

Frankfurter, Felix, 1882–1965, associate justice of the U.S. SUPREME COURT (1939–62); b. Austria; LL.B., Harvard Univ. (1906). A professor (1914–39) at Harvard Law School, he espoused liberal causes, helping to found the AMERICAN CIVIL LIBERTIES UNION and supporting the NEW DEAL. Appointed to the Court by Pres. F.D. ROOSEVELT, Frankfurter tempered liberalism with judicial restraint, holding that government could limit civil liberties to protect itself and that the Court should not interfere in political issues.

Frankfurt Parliament, 1848–49, national assembly convened as a result of the liberal revolution that swept Germany. Its members were popularly elected, and its aim was the unification of Germany. It offered the imperial crown to FREDERICK WILLIAM IV of Prussia, but he refused the offer because it came from a popularly elected parliament. Thereafter, the movement foundered and most members withdrew.

Frankfurt School, the researchers associated with the Institute of Social Research at the Univ. of Frankfurt, Germany, founded (1923) as a Marxist-oriented center for research in philosophy and the social sciences. Influenced by PSYCHOANALYSIS and EXISTENTIALISM, such members as Theodor ADORNO, Walter BENJAMIN, and Herbert MARCUSE developed a version of Marxism known as "critical theory," formulated aesthetics, and critiqued capitalist culture.

frankincense: see INCENSE-TREE.

Franklin, Aretha, 1942–, American singer; b. Memphis, Tenn. She began singing in the choir of her father's church. Known as "Queen of Soul," she recorded such hits as "Respect," "Chain of Fools," and "Who's Zoomin' Who."

Franklin, Benjamin, 1706–90, American statesman, printer, scientist, and writer; b. Boston. He went (1723) to Philadelphia as a printer and won attention for his wit and commonsense philosophy, especially as expressed in *Poor Richard's Almanack* (pub. 1732–57). He helped establish (1751) an academy that became the present Univ. of Pennsylvania, and he served as deputy postmaster general of the colonies (1753–74). His famous experiment with a kite in a thunderstorm proved the presence of electricity in lightning. Franklin proposed a plan of union for the colonies at the ALBANY CONGRESS (1754) and was agent for several colonies in England. Returning (1775) to America, he helped draft the DECLARATION OF INDEPENDENCE, which he signed. During the AMERICAN REVOLUTION he was a successful American agent in France and was appointed (1781) a commissioner to negotiate the peace with Brit-

Aretha Franklin

ain. Franklin's last great public service was his attendance at the FEDERAL CONSTITUTIONAL CONVENTION (1787). His autobiography is well known. Benjamin's illegitimate son, **William Franklin,** c.1730–1813, was the last royal governor of New Jersey and a Loyalist in the American Revolution.

Franklin, Sir John, 1786–1847, British explorer in N Canada. He explored the arctic coast of CANADA on expeditions in 1819–22 and 1825–27, during which he founded Fort Franklin. After serving as governor of Van Diemen's Land (now TASMANIA) (1836–43), he set out to look for the NORTHWEST PASSAGE in 1845. His entire expedition of 129 men was lost, their ships apparently frozen in the ice. The tragedy inspired over 40 searches, from which much geographical information was gained.

Franklin, John Hope, 1915–, African-American historian; b. Rentiesville, Okla. Educated at Fiske University and Harvard, he was president of Phi Beta Kappa (1973–76) and the American Historical Association (1978–79). His works include *From Slavery to Freedom* (1947) and *Racial Equality in America* (1976).

Franklin, State of, government (1784–88) formed by the inhabitants of what is now E TENNESSEE after NORTH CAROLINA ceded (1784) its western lands to the U.S. Unable to secure congressional recognition, the government under John SEVIER passed out of existence when the terms of its officers expired. The area reverted temporarily to North Carolina.

Franklin Institute, in Philadelphia, chartered in 1824 "for the promotion of the mechanic arts" and noted for its lecture series, trade exhibitions, and work on governmental, industrial, and scientific problems. Its renowned science museum opened in 1934.

Franks, group of Germanic tribes that settled by the 3d cent. along the Rhine. The Salian Franks, under CLOVIS I, moved into GAUL and overthrew (486) the Romans. Clovis united them with the Ripuarian Franks, and they accepted Christianity and founded the MEROVINGIAN dynasty. Their conquests eventually encompassed most of western and central Europe, including the kingdoms of Neustria, Austrasia, and Burgundy. In the 8th cent. the rule of the CAROLINGIAN dynasty was culminated by the reign of CHARLEMAGNE. In 870 the kingdom of the West Franks became France and that of the East Franks became Germany.

Franz Josef or **Franz Joseph:** see FRANCIS JOSEPH.

Fraser, Douglas Andrew, 1916–, American labor leader; b. Scotland. He began working in a Detroit auto plant at 18. After becoming active in the United Auto Workers, he rose through the ranks as a union executive and earned wide respect as chief negotiator with the Chrysler Corp. While president of the UAW (1977–83), Fraser led the union in granting wage concessions in exchange for greater job security during the severe auto-industry slump of 1981–82. He became (1980) the first union leader to be elected to the board of directors of an American company (Chrysler).

Fraser, John Malcolm, 1930–, Australian political leader and prime minister (1975–83). In 1955 he was elected to Parliament. In 1975 he became the leader of the opposition Liberal-Country party and prime minister after the Labor government of Gough WHITLAM was dismissed. Fraser's conservative policies included cuts in government spending. He resigned from Parliament in 1983.

Fraser, major river of British Columbia, Canada, flowing in a zigzag course c.850 mi (1,370 km) from a source in the Rocky Mts. near Yellowhead Pass, Alta., to a fertile delta on the Strait of Georgia at Vancouver, B.C. The Fraser contains the chief spawning grounds in North America for the Pacific salmon. Early explorers were Sir Alexander MACKENZIE (1793) and the fur trader Simon Fraser (1808).

fraternity and sorority, in American colleges, student societies formed for social, literary, or religious purposes, with initiation by invitation and occasionally by a period of trial called hazing. Sororities are for women. Usually named with two or three Greek letters, fraternities and sororities are also known as Greek-letter societies. **Phi Beta Kappa,** the oldest of these societies, was founded (1776) at the College of William and Mary (Williamsburg, Va.) and became a scholarship honor society. Because of their entrance policies, which can be discriminatory, fraternities and sororities are forbidden on some campuses.

fraud, in law, willful misrepresentation intended to deprive another of some right. Fraud may be actual (involving actual deceit) or constructive (involving abuse of a relationship of trust). The remedy granted the plaintiff in most cases of fraud is either damages for the loss incurred or cancellation of the fraudulent CONTRACT (or sometimes both).

Frazer, Sir James George, 1854–1941, Scottish anthropologist. He is best known for *The Golden Bough* (1890), a comparative study in folklore, magic, and religion that showed parallel beliefs in primitive and Christian cultures. The monumental work had a great impact on early 20th-cent. thought.

Frederick, rulers of the HOLY ROMAN EMPIRE. **Frederick I** or **Frederick Barbarossa,** c.1125–90, emperor (1155–90) and German king (1152–90), was of the HOHENSTAUFEN dynasty, but his mother was a GUELPH, and Frederick was chosen emperor in the hope that he could end the discord between the GUELPHS AND GHIBELLINES. His coronation was delayed by unrest in Germany and by the revolutionary commune of Rome (1143–55). He restored peace, placated his Guelph cousin, HENRY THE LION, by restoring Bavaria to him, and was crowned in 1155. He failed in his efforts to restore imperial power in Italy; he was forced to recognize the LOMBARD LEAGUE, and Pope Alexander III, whom he had opposed, excommunicated him. In Germany, however, he succeeded in breaking the power of Henry the Lion in 1180–81. In 1189 he joined the Third CRUSADE and was drowned in Cilicia, in Turkey. **Frederick II,** 1194–1250, emperor (1220–50) and German king (1212–20), king of Sicily (1197–1250), and king of Jerusalem (1229–50), was one of the most arresting figures of the Middle Ages. He was a patron of art and science and greatly expanded commerce. His intense struggle with the papacy led to the ruin of the house of Hohenstaufen. With his rule the great days of the German empire ended and the rise of states in Italy began. He was the son of Emperor Henry VI and Constance, heiress of Sicily. Both died while he was an infant, and the imperial crown passed him by, but he was made king of Sicily. After OTTO IV became emperor in 1209, he alienated Pope INNOCENT III by asserting imperial authority in Italy, and Innocent retaliated by crowning Frederick as German king (1212). Otto was deposed (1215) and, after long negotiations, Frederick was crowned emperor in 1220. His long-delayed crusade, when it finally took place (1228–29), turned out to be a state visit that culminated in Frederick's being crowned king of Jerusalem. The sporadic fighting between emperor and pope turned into a serious breach in 1239, and INNOCENT IV excommunicated (1245) Frederick and declared him deposed. Just as the war had turned in his favor, Frederick died of dysentery. **Frederick III,** 1415–93, emperor (1452–93) and German king (1440–93), was generally a weak ruler but made considerable progress toward reuniting the HAPSBURG family lands within his own branch. His greatest success was the acquisition of Burgundy through the marriage of his son, later Emperor MAXIMILIAN I, to MARY OF BURGUNDY, daughter of Charles the Bold. After 1490 Frederick relinquished most of his duties to Maximilian. He was the last emperor crowned at Rome.

Frederick, Danish kings. **Frederick III,** 1609–70, king of Denmark and Norway (1648–70), was the son of CHRISTIAN IV. After disastrous wars (1657–60) with CHARLES X of Sweden, the monarchy was made hereditary and the burghers strengthened at the expense of the nobles. Frederick's son, CHRISTIAN V, succeeded him. **Frederick IV,** 1671–1730, king of Denmark and Norway (1699–1730), was the son of Christian V. In the NORTHERN WAR he failed to recover S Sweden but obtained Schleswig and Lauenburg. His son, CHRISTIAN VI, succeeded him. **Frederick V,** 1723–66, king of Denmark and Norway (1746–66), was Christian VI's son. He encouraged commerce and industry, but the peasants' condition remained poor. His son, CHRISTIAN VII, succeeded him and was the father of **Frederick VI,** 1768–1839, king of Denmark (1808–39) and Norway (1808–14). In the FRENCH REVOLUTIONARY WARS England's attack on Denmark led him to ally himself with NAPOLEON I. At the Congress of Vienna (1814–15) he lost Norway to Sweden. His cousin CHRISTIAN VIII succeeded him. The son of Christian VIII, **Frederick VII,** 1808–63, was king of Denmark and duke of Schleswig, Holstein, and Lauenberg (1848–63). He accepted a constitution ending absolute monarchy. The SCHLESWIG-HOLSTEIN issue continued, leading to war with Prussia under his successor, CHRISTIAN IX. **Frederick VIII,** 1843–1912, king of Denmark (1906–12), was the son of Christian IX. He fought in the 1864 war with Prussia. His son CHRISTIAN X succeeded him. Another son became HAAKON VII of Norway. **Frederick IX,** 1899–1972, king of Denmark (1947–72), was the son of Christian X. Because he had no son, the Danish constitution was amended in 1953 to permit the succession of his daughter, who became Queen Margaret II.

Frederick, German kings: see FREDERICK, rulers of the Holy Roman Empire.

Frederick II or **Frederick the Great,** 1712–86, king of Prussia (1740–86), son and successor of FREDERICK WILLIAM I. He spent a miserable youth, ill-treated and despised by his father, and at one time was imprisoned for desertion. Once king, however, he displayed unexpected qualities of leadership and decision, becoming one of the great military generals of all time. His exploits in the War of the AUSTRIAN SUCCESSION (1740–48) and the SEVEN YEARS WAR (1756–63) made Prussia the greatest military power in Europe. He was the prime mover in the first Partition of POLAND (1772), which vastly increased his kingdom. He was less successful in the War of the BAVARIAN SUCCESSION (1778–79), in which he was thwarted by Emperor Joseph II. A "benevolent despot," Frederick promoted important legal and social reforms. He was a great patron of the arts and surrounded himself with intellectuals. His taste for French culture and his stormy friendship with VOLTAIRE are well known. He was a champion of religious liberty, and his philosophy was materialistic and skeptical. He wrote mediocre poetry and excellent prose (in French), and he composed passable music, especially for the flute, which he played well. He was childless and was succeeded by his nephew, FREDERICK WILLIAM II.

Frederick Augustus, electors of Saxony: see Augustus II (for Frederick Augustus I) and Augustus III (for Frederick Augustus II) under AUGUSTUS, kings of Poland.

Frederick Barbarossa: see Frederick I under FREDERICK, rulers of the Holy Roman Empire.

Frederick Henry, 1584–1647, prince of Orange, son of WILLIAM THE SILENT. He succeeded (1625) his brother MAURICE OF NASSAU as stadtholder of the United Provinces. In 1635 he signed a pact with France and Sweden against the Hapsburgs in the THIRTY YEARS WAR. During his rule commerce, science, and art (see HALS; REMBRANDT) flourished, and his title was made hereditary in his family. He was succeeded by his son, William II.

Fredericksburg, battle of, in the U.S. CIVIL WAR, fought Dec. 13, 1862, at Fredericksburg, Va., Union troops under Gen. Ambrose Burnside were repulsed in their efforts to reach Richmond by the forces of R.E. LEE, Stonewall JACKSON, and James LONGSTREET. It was a major Union defeat, with more than 12,000 Union casualities.

Frederick the Great: see FREDERICK II, king of Prussia.

Frederick the Winter King, 1596–1632, king of Bohemia (1619–20, or during one winter; hence his sobriquet) and elector palatine (1610–20) as Frederick V. The Protestant diet of Bohemia deposed the Catholic King Ferdinand (Holy Roman Emperor FERDINAND II) and named Frederick king, thus precipitating the THIRTY YEARS WAR. When he did not receive the expected Protestant support, he was defeated (1620) at White Mountain and forced to give up all his lands. He was the father of Prince RUPERT and of the Electress SOPHIA, the forebear of the British ruling family the Hanovers.

Frederick William, kings of Prussia. **Frederick William I,** 1688–1740 (r.1713–40), created a strong, absolutist state, instituting administrative reforms and rigid economy. He also built up the Prussian army, but except for a brief intervention in the Northern War (1700–21), he observed peace. He was a coarse man who had contempt for his gifted son, who succeeded him as FREDERICK II (Frederick the Great). **Frederick William II,** 1744–97 (r.1786–97), was the nephew and successor of Frederick II. He was defeated in the FRENCH REVOLUTIONARY WARS and signed a separate peace (1795) with the French. He participated in the second and third partition of POLAND (1793, 1795) and was a patron of MOZART. His son, **Frederick William III,** 1770–1840 (r.1797–1840), suffered crushing defeat by the French, and the Treaty of Tilsit (1807) made Prussia virtually a French vassal. Though he was weak and vacillating, he surrounded himself with able administrators who made valuable reforms. He grew increasingly reactionary in his old age. **Frederick William IV,** 1795–1861 (r.1840–61), was the son and successor of Frederick William III. A romanticist, mystic, and half-hearted liberal, he nonetheless crushed the REVOLUTION OF 1848 and refused the imperial crown because it was offered by a popularly elected body, the FRANKFURT PARLIAMENT. In 1857 his mental imbalance necessitated the regency of his brother and successor, William I.

Frederick William, 1620–88, elector of Brandenburg (1640–88), known as the Great Elector. He rebuilt his devastated state after the THIRTY YEARS WAR and added greatly to his domains. He secured East Pomerania and other territories in 1648 and secured full sovereignty over Prussia in 1660. He was succeeded by his son Frederick, who in 1701 crowned himself "king in Prussia" and styled himself Frederick I.

Fredericton, city (1991 pop. 46,466), capital of New Brunswick, E Canada, on the St. John R. Wood products are a major manufacture. It was founded (1783) by UNITED EMPIRE LOYALISTS at the site of Ste. Anne, an abandoned village of French ACADIA. It became provincial capital in 1785.

Freedom of Information Act (1966), law requiring that U.S. government agencies release their records to the public on request, unless the information sought falls into a category specifically exempted, such as national security, an individual's right to PRIVACY, or internal agency management. The act provides for court review of agency refusals to furnish identifiable records. The states also have similar laws. The U.S. and some states have also adopted so-called sunshine laws that require governmental bodies, as a matter of general policy, to hold open meetings, announced in advance.

freedom of the press: see PRESS, FREEDOM OF THE.

free fall, in physics, the state of a body moving solely under the influence of gravitational forces (see GRAVITATION). A body falling freely toward the surface of the earth undergoes an acceleration (see MOTION) equal to 32 ft/sec^2 (9.8 m/sec^2).

Freeman, Douglas Southall, 1886–1953, American historian; b. Lynchburg, Va. A retired newspaper editor, he wrote superb works on the CIVIL WAR, including *R.E. Lee* (4 vol., 1934–35; Pulitzer) and *Lee's Lieutenants* (3 vol., 1942–44). He also wrote a biography of George Washington (7 vol., 1949–57; Pulitzer).

Freeman's Farm, battle of: see SARATOGA CAMPAIGN.

Freemasonry, teachings and practices of the secret fraternal order known as the Free and Accepted Masons. There are 4.75 million members worldwide, mostly in the U.S. and other English-speaking countries, and no central authority. Its ideals include fellowship, religious toleration, and political compromise. Drawing on guild practices of medieval stonemasons, the order's first Grand Lodge was organized in London (1717). In America, Masons were active in the Revolution and continued as a force in later politics. In Europe, they included VOLTAIRE, GOETHE, HAYDN, MAZZINI, and GARIBALDI. Freemasonry's identification with 19th-cent. bourgeois liberalism led to reaction, e.g., in the U.S., the ANTI-MASONIC PARTY; its anticlericalism brought the hostility of the Roman Catholic Church. Totalitarian states have always suppressed Freemasonry. Masons have a complex systems of rites and degrees, subsidiary organizations for women and children, and lodges noted for their parades and fraternal gatherings.

freesia: see IRIS.

free silver, in U.S. history, a political movement for the unlimited coinage of silver. Supported by silver-mining interests, by indebted agrarian classes of the South and West, and later by Populists (see POPULIST PARTY) and Democrats, free silver was a hotly contested issue in the late 19th cent. Debtors believed that more money in circulation would permit them to pay their debts with inflated dollars. The BLAND-ALLISON ACT (1878) and the SHERMAN SILVER PURCHASE ACT (1890) were compromises that failed to satisfy the silverites. The defeat of free-silver champion W.J. BRYAN in the presidential elections of 1896 and 1900, coupled with increasing gold supplies and returning prosperity, minimized the issue thereafter.

Free-Soil party, U.S. political party born in 1847–48 to oppose the extension of SLAVERY into territories newly gained from Mexico. In 1848 the Free-Soil party ran Martin VAN BUREN and C.F. Adams (see ADAMS, family) for president and vice president; by polling 300,000 votes it gave New York state to the Whigs and thus made Zachary TAYLOR president. After the COMPROMISE OF 1850 seemed to settle the slavery-extension issue, the group known as the Barnburners left the Free-Soilers to return to the Democratic party, but radicals kept the Free-Soil party alive until 1854, when the new REPUBLICAN PARTY absorbed it.

Freetown, city (1985 pop. 469,776), capital of Sierra Leone, W Sierra Leone, on the Atlantic Ocean. It is the nation's largest city and chief port. Industries include food processing and oil refining. A highway link to MONROVIA, Liberia, was under construction in the early 1980s. Freetown was founded in 1792 by former slaves from Nova Scotia; descendants of liberated slaves (called Creoles), though a minority, play a leading role in the modern city.

free verse, loose term for verse free of conventional limitations and metrical restrictions. Cadence, particularly of common speech, is often substituted. The term comes from the *vers libre* of Jules Laforgue, Arthur RIMBAUD, and others who rejected the classical alexandrine. The term has been applied to the King James translation of the Bible and is associated with Walt WHITMAN, Ezra POUND, T.S. ELIOT, and other modern poets.

free will, in philosophy, the doctrine that the will of an individual can and does determine some of his acts. PLATO held that actions are determined by the extent of a person's understanding. Christian ethics have long disputed the extent of human dependence on the power of God: St. AUGUSTINE, LUTHER, and John CALVIN followed the doctrine of predestination or divine grace, while St. THOMAS AQUINAS held that God's omnipotence does not include the predetermination of human will. Later advocates of free will have referred to common practice: Individuals believe they determine their actions and hold one another accountable for doing so. Modern psychology has introduced the concept of the UNCONSCIOUS as a motivating force.

freezing: see STATES OF MATTER.

Frege, Gottlob [frā'gə], 1848–1925, German philosopher and mathematician. Frege was one of the founders of symbolic logic (see LOGIC) and a major influence on Bertrand RUSSELL and Russell's student Ludwig WITTGENSTEIN. He demonstrated that mathematics is derived solely from deductive logic and is not synthetic, as Kant had posited. He also believed that verbal conceptualizations can be translated into logical form. After Russell and others had pointed out some serious contradictions in vol. 2 of his major work, *The Basic Laws of Arithmetic* (1893–1903), Frege virtually ceased to produce original work. Nevertheless, his contributions to the development of modern mathematical theory and the theory of meaning are of prime importance.

Frémont, John Charles, 1813–90, American explorer, soldier, and political leader; b. Savannah, Ga. His enthusiastic reports of his Western explorations (1841–44) created wide interest in that region. He was a leader (1846) in the revolt of California against Mexico until he quarreled with S.W. KEARNY in Kearny's contest for command with Robert Stockton. Frémont was U.S. senator from California (1850–51) and Republican candidate for president in 1856. He commanded the Western Dept. in the CIVIL WAR but was removed because of his radical policy toward slaveholders. He lost his fortune (1870) in a railroad venture. Later, he was governor (1878–83) of Arizona Territory. He was called the Pathfinder.

Fremont, city (1990 pop. 173,339), W Calif., on San Francisco Bay; inc. 1956. Long an agricultural center with vineyards, it still has breweries and canneries, but the 1963 opening of an automobile-assembly plant transformed it into a fast-growing industrial city.

French, Daniel Chester, 1850–1931, American sculptor; b. Exeter, N.H. After executing his first large work, *The Minute Man* (1875; Concord, Mass.), he received many commissions for public statues. His most famous is the heroic figure of Abraham Lincoln in the LINCOLN MEMORIAL (Wash., D.C.).

French and Indian Wars, 1689–1763, a series of colonial campaigns in North America between England and France, corresponding to wars between European alliances in the worldwide struggle for empire. In America, seaboard strongholds and western forts were seized, and the settlers engaged in guerrilla warfare with Native Americans. *King William's War* (1688–97), linked to the War of the GRAND ALLIANCE, consisted chiefly of frontier attacks on the British colonies. *Queen Anne's War* (1702–13) corresponded to the War of the SPANISH SUCCESSION, and *King George's War* (1744–48) to the War of the AUSTRIAN SUCCESSION. The last and most important conflict, called simply the *French and Indian War* (1754–63), was linked to the SEVEN YEARS WAR. Jeffrey AMHERST took Louisbourg (1758), and Quebec and Montreal also fell (1759–60) to the British. The war ended French control in Canada and the West (see PARIS, TREATY OF). After the wars the American colonies felt less dependent militarily on the British; they began to concentrate on their own problems and institutions and to think of themselves as American rather than British.

French Community, established in 1958 to replace the FRENCH UNION. Its purpose was to create a political federation for France and all its overseas departments and territories. However, since all of France's African colonies chose total independence, the French Community never achieved its aims. After 1962 it operated primarily as a vehicle for fostering military, economic, technical, and cultural cooperation among its members and is now largely inactive.

French East India Company: see EAST INDIA COMPANY, FRENCH.

French Equatorial Africa, former French federation of territories in W central Africa (1910–58), comprising what are now GABON, CHAD, the CENTRAL AFRICAN REPUBLIC, and CONGO. It was dissolved (1958) when the members became republics within the FRENCH COMMUNITY.

French Guiana [gēăn'ə, –än'–], Fr. *La Guyane française,* French overseas department (1992 est. pop. 128,000), 35,135 sq mi (91,000 sq km), NE South America, bordered by the Atlantic Ocean (N), Suriname (E), and Brazil (S and E). CAYENNE is the capital. The population, largely Creole, is concentrated along the coast. French is the official language, but Creole, Taki-Taki, and other languages and dialects are also spoken. The economy rests on the export of shrimp, timber, and rum; there are deposits of gold and bauxite. A rocket-launching base for communications satellites is located at Kourou, on the coast. French settlement dates from 1604; following periods of Dutch and British rule, French authority was restored in 1815. Guiana was made an overseas department in 1947. French Guiana was used as a penal colony during the French Revolution, and permanent penal camps were established under Napoleon III; DEVILS ISLAND, off the coast, was especially notorious. Since the early 1970s there have been increasing local demands for autonomy, fueled in part by high unemployment and divisions between the white European elite and Creole majority.

French horn: see WIND INSTRUMENT.

French language, member of the Romance group of the Italic subfamily of the Indo-European family of languages. See LANGUAGE (table).

French Polynesia, overseas territory of France (1992 est. pop. 206,000), 105 islands in the South Pacific. The capital is Papeete, on TAHITI. It comprises the Society Islands, Marquesas Islands, Austral Islands, Tuamotu Islands, and Gambier Islands. Tropical fruits are grown, vanilla and copra exported. Tourism is important. The inhabitants are mainly indigenous Polynesians, known as Demis. French is the official language, but native languages are commonly spoken. The population is about 60% Protestant and 30% Roman Catholic. There is a governor, council, and elected assembly.

French Revolution, political upheaval that began in France in 1789 and eventually affected the whole world. Historians differ widely as to its causes. Some see it as an intellectual movement born from the liberal ENLIGHTENMENT of the 18th cent.; some, as a rebellion of the underprivileged classes against feudal oppression; others, as the assertion of the new capitalist bourgeoisie against an outdated and restricted social and economic system—in the fixed order of the ancien régime, France was still ruled by two privileged classes, the nobility and the clergy, who refused to give up any of their privileges and supplemented their dwindling funds by exacting dues from the more productive bourgeoisie. The immediate cause of the revolution was without doubt the bankrupt state of the public treasury. The wars of the 17th and 18th cent., an iniquitous and inefficient system of taxation, intervention in the AMERICAN REVOLUTION, and waste had resulted in a gigantic public debt, which neither NECKER, nor Calonne, nor Loménie de Brienne was able to reduce. As a last resort LOUIS XVI called the STATES-GENERAL, which, it was hoped, would pass the necessary fiscal reforms. It convened at VERSAILLES on May 5, 1789, for the first time since 1614. From the start the deputies of the third estate—the commons—joined by many members of the lower clergy and by a few nobles, pressed for sweeping political and social reforms that far exceeded the assembly's powers. Defying the king, they proclaimed themselves the National Assembly (June 17), and, on an indoor tennis court, took an oath not to separate until a constitution had been drawn up. The king yielded and legalized the Assembly, but his dismissal of Necker led to the storming of the BASTILLE by an excited Paris mob (July 14). Louis XVI, ever anxious to avoid bloodshed, gave in once more; Necker was recalled; the Commune was established as the city government of Paris; and the National Guard was organized. On Aug. 4, 1789, the Assembly abolished all feudal privileges. Meanwhile, rumors of counterrevolutionary court intrigues were exploited by extremist demagogues, and on Oct. 5 a mob marched to Versailles and forcibly moved the royal family and the Assembly to Paris. There the Assembly drafted a constitution (1791) that created a limited monarchy with a unicameral legislature (the Legislative Assembly) elected by voters who had the requisite property qualifications; the preamble was the famous DECLARATION OF THE RIGHTS OF MAN AND CITIZEN. Earlier, anticlerical legislation had been capped when the clergy was required to take oaths to civil authority (1790), a measure that alienated many pious rural districts from the Revolution. The king decided to join those nobles who had already fled abroad (émigrés), but his flight (June 20–21, 1791) was arrested at Varennes. Brought back in humiliation to Paris, Louis accepted the new constitution. In the Legislative Assembly, the republican GIRONDISTS and the extreme JACOBINS and CORDELIERS gained the upper hand. "Liberty, Equality, Fraternity" became a catch phrase. Elsewhere, the émigrés were inciting other European courts to intervene. The Declaration of Pillnitz played into the hands of the Girondists, who hoped that a foreign war would rally the nation to the republican cause. With the declaration of war on Austria (April 20, 1792), the FRENCH REVOLUTIONARY WARS began. Early reverses and rumors of treason by the king and Queen MARIE ANTOINETTE brought the lower classes, especially those in Paris, into action. In Aug. 1792 a mob stormed the TUILERIES palace and an insurrectionary commune replaced the legally elected one (see COMMUNE OF PARIS); all police power was seized by the Paris commune (dominated by DANTON and MARAT); the Assembly suspended the king and ordered elections for a National Convention to draw up yet another constitution; and hundreds of royal prisoners were killed by "spontaneous" mobs in the September massacres (Sept. 2–7, 1792). On Sept. 21 the Convention abolished the monarchy, set up the First Republic, and proceeded to try the king for treason. Louis's conviction and execution (Jan. 1793) led to royalist uprisings, notably in the Vendée, and was followed by the REIGN OF TERROR, in which ROBESPIERRE and his associates triumphed in turn over the more moderate Girondists and over his rivals Danton and J.R. HÉBERT. The republican constitution never became active; the Committee of Public Safety and the Revolutionary Tribunal reigned supreme. Robespierre's final excesses frightened the Convention into the coup d'etat of 9 Thermidor (July 27, 1794), which resulted in his execution and a period of relative reaction. Under the new constitution of 1795, the DIRECTORY came into existence. Its rule was marked by corruption, intrigues, runaway inflation, bankruptcy, and a fatal dependence on the army; it was ended by Napoleon Bonaparte's coup d'etat of 18 Brumaire (see NAPOLEON I). With the establishment of the Consulate (followed in 1804 by Napoleon's empire), the victory of the bourgeoisie became final. With the French Revolutionary Wars and the Napoleonic Wars, the French Revolution tore down the medieval structures of Europe, opened the paths of 19th-cent. liberalism, and hastened the advent of nationalism.

French Revolutionary Wars, 1792–1802, general European war precipitated by the FRENCH REVOLUTION, which had aroused in foreign lands the hostility of monarchs, nobles, and clergy, all of whom feared the spread of republican ideas to the lower classes. They looked upon war as the only way to restore LOUIS XVI (still nominally king of France) to his full powers. For their part, the revolutionaries in France looked upon war as a way of ensuring permanence to their revolution by spreading it abroad. Thus, with both sides wanting it, war seemed inevitable. In August 1791 Austria and Prussia called for the restoration of Louis, an act that angered French public opinion. The radical GIRONDISTS assumed power in March 1792, and on Apr. 20, 1792, France declared war on Austria. Meeting little resistance at first, allied Austrian and Prussian armies invaded France, but the cannonade at Valmy (Sept. 20) revealed the superiority of French artillery and proved a turning point. The French overran the Austrian Netherlands, invaded Germany, and seized Savoy and Nice from Sardinia. Louis XVI was executed (Jan. 21, 1793), an act that led to the formation of the First Coalition (Austria, Prussia, Great Britain, Holland, Spain). The French, led by Lazare CARNOT, raised new armies and by the end of 1793 had driven the allies from France. Holland,

Prussia, and Spain all made peace in 1795. Napoleon Bonaparte contributed stunning French victories in Italy, and by 1797 only Britain remained in the war. Bonaparte's strike against Britain in Egypt was disastrous, and the English destroyed (1798) the French fleet at Aboukir. In 1798 a Second Coalition was formed, consisting of Britain, Russia, Austria, Turkey, Portugal, and Naples. The French victory over the Russians at Zürich took Russia out of the war. Napoleon Bonaparte, back in France, declared himself First Consul (November 1799). In 1800 Bonaparte inflicted a heavy defeat on the Austrians at Marengo, and the Second Coalition collapsed (1801) when Austria consented to the Peace of Luneville. Once more, only the British persevered. They expelled the French from Egypt and destroyed the Danish fleet. (The Danes had refused to abide by British rules of neutrality.) But the British public was weary of fighting, and in 1802 the Treaty of Amiens concluded the war. The French Revolutionary Wars had transformed the political landscape of Europe. With their victories the French had created a whole series of new political entities: the Batavian Republic (Holland), the Helvetic Republic (Switzerland), the Parthenopian Republic (Naples), the Cisalpine Republic (various Italian states), and the Roman Republic (the Papal States). Peace was short-lived, however; in 1803 the Napoleonic Wars began (see NAPOLEON I).

French Southern and Antarctic Lands, overseas territory of France, including Adélie Land, which covers c.200,000 sq mi (520,000 sq km) in ANTARCTICA, and a number of islands in the S Indian Ocean. The largest of these is Kerguelen (1,318 sq mi/3,414 sq km). One of 300 islands in the Kerguelen Archipelago, it is a base for research, seal hunting, and whaling. The Crozet Islands, to the west, and Saint Paul and Amsterdam islands, to the northeast, are also part of the territory.

French Union, former political entity (1946–58) that comprised metropolitan France (France proper and Corsica) and its overseas territories. It replaced the colonial system and was superseded by the FRENCH COMMUNITY.

French West Africa, former federation of French territories in W Africa (1895–1959) that consisted of present-day BENIN, BURKINA FASO, GUINEA, CÔTE D'IVOIRE, MALI, MAURITANIA, NIGER, and SENEGAL. It was dissolved in 1959 as the territories moved toward independence.

Freneau, Philip, 1752–1832, American writer; b. N.Y.C. America's first professional journalist, he was a propagandist for the AMERICAN REVOLUTION and Jeffersonian democracy. His fame rests on such lyrical poems as "The Wild Honeysuckle," "The Indian Burial Ground," and "Eutaw Springs." His poem *The British Prison Ship* (1781) recorded his captivity on a British brig.

Freon, trade name for any of a special class of chemical compounds used as refrigerants, air conditioner coolants, and solvents. Freons are HYDROCARBON derivatives that contain fluorine, and often chlorine and bromine as well. They are generally colorless, odorless, nontoxic, noncorrosive, and nonflammable. Though usually unreactive, freons can undergo reactions in the upper atmosphere that damage the earth's OZONE LAYER. The most commonly used is Freon-12, or dichlorodifluoromethane (CCl_2F_2).

frequency: see HARMONIC MOTION; WAVE.

frequency modulation: see MODULATION.

fresco, the art of painting on plaster. Pure fresco is painted on damp, fresh lime plaster. The binder is in the lime, which, in drying, forms a calcium carbonate that incorporates the pigment with the material of the wall. Fresco does not permit a large palette or delicate transitional tones, as does oil, but its clear, luminous color and permanence make it ideal for monumental murals. An ancient technique, fresco was employed in the Minoan palace at KNOSSOS and used by the Romans for decoration, notably at POMPEII. It was perfected by the masters of the Italian RENAISSANCE, who customarily prepared a CARTOON and transferred the design to wet plaster. For large frescoes the plaster was applied to small sections daily, each painted in a day. Fresco was revived in 20th-cent. Mexico with the work of José Clemente OROZCO, Diego RIVERA, and other artists.

Frescobaldi, Girolamo, 1583–1643, Italian composer. He became organist at St. Peter's Church, Rome, in 1608, and at the Medici court, Florence (1628–34). His style traveled to Germany and influenced organists through J.S. BACH. He wrote many ORGAN works and some instrumental and vocal music.

Fresnel, Augustin Jean [frānĕl'], 1788–1827, French physicist and engineer. His investigations of light, especially interference phenomena in POLARIZED LIGHT and double refraction, supported the wave theory of light and the concept of transverse vibrations in light waves. He also devised a way of producing circularly polarized light.

Fresno, city (1990 pop. 354,202), seat of Fresno co., S central Calif.; founded 1872, inc. 1885. It is the financial hub of the SAN JOAQUIN Valley. Grapes, figs, cotton, and vegetables are grown in the area, and Fresno co. leads all U.S. counties in the value of agricultural products sold. The city is also a railroad, marketing, and processing center with light industries.

Freud, Sigmund, 1856–1939, Austrian psychiatrist, founder of PSYCHOANALYSIS; b. Vienna. M.D., 1881, Univ. of Vienna. Early in his career Freud collaborated with Josef BREUER on the use of HYPNOSIS in the treatment of HYSTERIA. The therapy was based on the hypothesis that the symptoms of hysterical patients—directly traceable to apparently forgotten psychic traumas in early life—represented undischarged emotional energy. The two men separated over Freud's growing conviction that this energy was sexual in nature. Rejecting hypnosis, Freud devised the technique of free association, which allowed material repressed in the UNCONSCIOUS to emerge to conscious recognition. Although his early work was poorly received, after 1906 he was joined by other psychiatrists, including C.G. JUNG and Alfred ADLER. Both, however, resigned from the International Psychoanalytic Association (founded 1910) between 1911 and 1913 in protest against Freud's emphasis on infantile sexuality and the Oedipus complex (see COMPLEX). Although they and others who broke away later objected to aspects of Freudian theory, the basic structure of their analysis remained Freudian. With the Nazi occupation of Austria, Freud fled (1938) to England, where he died. His theory has had enormous impact, influencing anthropology, education, art, and literature. His writings include *The Interpretation of Dreams* (1900), *Beyond the Pleasure Principle* (1920), and *Moses and Monotheism* (1939).

Freud, Anna, 1895–1982, Austrian-British psychoanalyst. She continued the work of her father, Sigmund FREUD, and was a pioneer in the psychoanalysis of children. She received her training in Vienna before emigrating (1938) with her father to England, where she founded and directed a clinic for child therapy. Her writings include *The Psychoanalytical Treatment of Children* (1946), *Normality and Pathology in Childhood* (1965), and *The Writings of Anna Freud* (7 vol., 1973).

Freyja [frā'yä] or **Freya** [frā'ä], Norse goddess of love, marriage, and fertility. She was also a deity of the dead and was the sister of the god Frey.

Frick, Henry Clay, 1849–1919, American industrialist; b. Westmoreland co., Pa. In 1871 he organized Frick & Co. to operate coke ovens and soon held a key place in the coal industry. Andrew CARNEGIE acquired heavy interests in Frick's company, and Frick in turn played a key role in organizing (1892) the Carnegie Steel Co.; he expanded that company and acquired railroads and iron-ore lands. His strong anti-union policies resulted in the Homestead strike. After a struggle with Carnegie for control, Frick resigned and became a director of U.S. Steel Corp. He willed his mansion in New York City, housing his art collection, to the public as a museum.

friction, resistance offered to the movement of one body past another body with which it is in contact. The amount of friction depends on the nature of the contact surfaces and on the magnitude of the force pressing the two bodies together, but not on the surface area of the contact surfaces. The coefficient of friction is the ratio of the force necessary to move one body horizontally over another at a constant speed to the weight of the body. Fluid friction, observed in the flow of liquids and gases, is minimized in airplanes by a modern, streamlined design (see AERODYNAMICS).

Friday: see WEEK.

Friedan, Betty Naomi, 1921–, American feminist; b. Peoria, Ill. In 1963 she galvanized the women's movement by publishing *The Feminine Mystique,* an attack on the notion that women find fulfillment only through childbearing and homemaking. Founder of the NATIONAL ORGANIZATION FOR WOMEN (1966), she also helped organize the National Women's Political Caucus (1970). In *The Second Stage* (1981) she evaluated the progress of FEMINISM, remaining a moderate and criticizing its radical elements. *The Fountain of Age* (1993) is an affirmation of the vitality of old age.

Betty Friedan

Friedman, Milton, 1912–, American economist and a leading spokesman for the monetarist school of economics; b. Brooklyn, N.Y. A staunch conservative and opponent of the beliefs of J.M. KEYNES, Friedman developed the theory that changes in monetary supply precede, rather than follow, changes in overall economic activity. A professor at the Univ. of Chicago (1946–77), he received the 1976 Nobel Prize in economics. His writings include *Capitalism and Freedom* (1962). See ECONOMICS.

Friedrich, Caspar David, 1774–1840, German romantic landscape painter. His mystical, pantheistic attitude toward nature is best seen in *Capuchin Friar by the Sea* and *Man and Woman Gazing at the Moon* (both: Berlin).

Friends, Religious Society of, religious body originating in England in the 17th cent. under George FOX. He believed that a person needed no spiritual intermediary but could find understanding and guidance through "inward light" supplied by the Holy Spirit. Commonly called Quakers, members refused to participate in Church of ENGLAND services, take oaths, or bear arms, and were often subject to persecution. They spread to Asia, Africa, and America, where they found refuge in Rhode Island and a colony established (1682) in Pennsylvania by William PENN. In the 19th cent. American Friends split into Orthodox, Hicksite, and Conservative groups, but the old lines of division have since grown considerably less. Their meetings are periods of silent meditation in which those urged by the spirit can offer prayer or exhortation. Friends are active in education and social welfare and believe in complete equality.

Frigg or **Frigga,** Norse mother goddess and the wife of WODEN. Of great importance in GERMANIC RELIGION, she was queen of the heavens, a deity of love and the household.

Friml, (Charles) Rudolf, 1879–1972, American composer; b. Prague. He lived in the U.S. after 1906. Best known of his 33 light operas are *The Firefly* (1912), *Rose Marie* (1924), and *The Vagabond King* (1925).

Frisch, Karl von, 1886–1982, Austrian zoologist. For his pioneering work in comparative behavioral psychology, particularly his studies of the complex communication between insects, he shared the 1973 Nobel Prize in physiology or medicine with Konrad LORENZ and Nikolaas TINBERGEN. An important implication of his work is that behavioral continuity exists between animal communication and human language.

Frisch, Max, 1911–91, Swiss writer. His novels *I'm Not Stiller* (1954), *Homo faber* (1957), *A Wilderness of Mirrors* (1964), and *Man in the Holocene* (tr. 1980) deal with the individual's search for personal identity. *The Firebugs* (1953) and *Andorra* (1961) are his best-known plays. His *Journal 1966–1971* was published in English in 1974.

Frisch, Ragnar, 1895–1973, Norwegian economist who, with Jan TINBERGEN, won the first Nobel Prize in economics (1969) for pioneering work in the development of ECONOMETRICS.

Frisian language, member of the West Germanic group of the Germanic subfamily of the Indo-European family of languages. See LANGUAGE (table).

Frobisher, Sir Martin, 1535?–1594, English mariner. He was licensed by ELIZABETH I for three expeditions to search for the NORTHWEST PASSAGE (1576, 1577, 1578). He reached Frobisher Bay and S BAFFIN ISLAND but erroneously believed that he had found Cathay. He commanded a ship in Sir Francis DRAKE'S WEST INDIES expedition (1585) and was knighted for his services in the defeat of the Spanish ARMADA (1588).

Froebel, Friedrich Wilhelm August [frā'bəl, frō–], 1782–1852, German educator and founder of the KINDERGARTEN system. Having little formal schooling himself, he stressed pleasant surroundings, self-directed activity, and physical training for children. Influenced by SCHELLING, he also insisted upon spiritual training as a fundamental principle. He founded (1816) the Universal German Educational Institute to train teachers and opened the first kindergarten in 1837. The most important of his several books on education is *The Education of Man* (1826).

frog, tailless, freshwater AMPHIBIAN (order Anura) found worldwide. Some frogs require moisture and are highly aquatic; others, such as TOADS, are more terrestrial. Frogs have bulging eyes, short, neckless bodies, long, muscular hind legs for jumping, webbed feet for swimming, and smooth skin, usually green or brown. They capture insects and other food with a sticky, forked tongue. Most frogs lay eggs in early spring, and by the end of summer METAMORPHOSIS to a four-legged adult is complete. True frogs belong to the Ranidae family, which includes the bullfrog (*Rana catesbeiana*) and other North American frogs.

Froissart, Jean [frəwäsär'], c.1337–1410?, French chronicler, poet, and courtier. He traveled widely and knew many important people. His famous chronicle covers the history of Western Europe from the early 1300s to 1400, roughly the first half of the HUNDRED YEARS WAR. In it he describes events with brilliance and gusto. His disregard for accuracy and highly partisan spirit limit the chronicle as pure history, but it brings an era to life.

Fromm, Erich, 1900–1980, American psychoanalyst and author; b. Germany. He emigrated (1934) to the U.S., where he practiced psychoanalysis and lectured at various institutions, including Bennington College and New York University. Fromm held that the individual is a product of society and that in industrial society human beings have become estranged from themselves. His many works include *Escape from Freedom* (1941), *The Sane Society* (1955), and *Beyond the Chains of Illusion* (1962).

Fronde [frôNd], 1648–53, series of outbreaks in France during the minority of LOUIS XIV. They were caused by the efforts of the PARLEMENT of Paris (the chief judicial body) to limit royal authority (as championed by Cardinal MAZARIN), by the ambitions of discontented nobles, and by the excessive fiscal burden on the people. The **Fronde of the Parlement,** 1648–49, began with Parlement's refusal to register a fiscal edict that would have required the magistrates of high courts to give up four years' salary. Parlement then drew up a reform document limiting royal authority. The royal court secretly fled Paris, and government forces under Louis II, prince de CONDÉ, blockaded the city until a compromise peace between Parlement and the monarchy was arranged. The arrest of the overbearing Condé by the order of Mazarin, his former ally, precipitated the much more serious **Fronde of the Princes,** 1650–53. Although Condé was released and Mazarin fled into exile (1651), Condé, with the support of several powerful nobles and the provincial parlements of S France, waged open warfare on the government and even concluded an alliance with Spain, then at war with France. Defeated at Faubourg Saint-Antoine (1652), Condé was given shelter in Paris. His arrogance soon alienated the Parisians, and the Fronde disintegrated. In 1652 the king returned to Paris, followed by Mazarin in 1653. The last attempt of the nobility to resist the king by arms, the Fronde resulted in the strengthening of the monarchy and the further disruption of the French economy.

Frondizi, Arturo, 1908–, president of Argentina (1958–62). A liberal and anti-Peronist, he supported a policy of economic austerity. Because he allowed Peronists to participate in the elections of 1962, outraged anti-Peronist elements in the army arrested him and annulled the elections.

front, in meteorology, the boundary between adjacent air masses. If a cold air mass pushes a warm air mass ahead of it, a cold front exists; a warm front is the reverse situation. A stationary front is one in which neither air mass pushes against the other. An occluded front exists when a cold front catches up to a warm front; the warm air mass lying between the two cold air masses is thus forced to rise.

Frontenac, Louis de Buade, comte de Palluau et de [frŏn-'tănăk], 1620–98, French governor of New France (1672–82, 1696–98). Although his independent policy displeased King LOUIS XIV and his powers as governor were reduced, he advanced French exploration in Canada, established new forts and posts, subdued (1696) the IROQUOIS CONFEDERACY, and held QUEBEC against the British in the first FRENCH AND INDIAN WAR.

Frost, Robert, 1874–1963, one of the most popular American poets of the 20th cent.; b. San Francisco; moved to Lawrence, Mass., 1885. He went to England in 1912 and won his first acclaim there. After publishing *A Boy's Will* (1913) and *North of Boston* (1914), he returned to the U.S. and settled in New Hampshire. While Frost wrote movingly of the people and landscape of New England, his lyrical, dramatic, and often deeply symbolic verse goes far beyond regional poetry. His volumes of poetry include *New Hampshire* (1923), *A Witness Tree* (1942), *Steeple Bush* (1947), and *In the Clearing* (1962). Frost was awarded the Pulitzer Prize for poetry in 1924, 1931, 1937, and 1943, and in 1961 he read his poem "The Gift Outright" at Pres. Kennedy's inauguration. His complete poems were published in 1967.

frost or **hoarfrost,** ice formed by the condensation of atmospheric water vapor on a surface whose temperature is below 32°F (0°C). In the formation of frost, water vapor is changed directly to a solid (see DEW). Frost appears as a light, feathery deposit of ice, often in a delicate pattern.

frostbite or **chilblains,** tissue injury caused by exposure to cold, usually affecting the hands, feet, ears, or nose. Extreme cold causes the small blood vessels in the extremities to constrict, resulting in slowed blood circulation and stagnation, which deprive tissues of nutrients. The condition is aggravated by inactivity and dampness. Severe, untreated frostbite may result in GANGRENE.

frozen foods: see FOOD PRESERVATION.

fructose, levulose, or **fruit sugar,** simple SUGAR found in honey and fruit. Sweeter than SUCROSE, fructose is a carbohydrate with the same formula as GLUCOSE, but with a different structure (see ISOMER). An equimolar mixture of fructose and glucose, called invert sugar, is obtained by the breakdown of sucrose and is the major component of honey.

fruit, matured ovary of a FLOWER, containing the seed. After FERTILIZATION takes place and the embryo plantlet has begun to develop, the surrounding ovule becomes a seed and the ovary wall around the ovule (pericarp) becomes the fruit. Fruits are classified into four types: simple, aggregate, multiple, and accessory. Simple fruits are either fleshy or dry. Fleshy fruits are either berries (the entire pericarp is fleshy, e.g., the blueberry, tomato, and banana) or drupes (the inner layer of the pericarp becomes a pit or stone around the seed, e.g., the peach and walnut). Dry fruits are divided into those whose hard, papery shells either split to release the mature seeds (dehiscent), e.g., the PEA, or do not split (indehiscent), e.g., the NUT or GRAIN. Aggregate fruits (e.g., the raspberry) are masses of small drupes (drupelets), each developed from separate ovaries of a single flower. Multiple fruits (e.g., the pineapple) develop from ovaries of many flowers in a cluster. Accessory fruits contain tissue derived from parts other than the ovary, e.g., the apple, the edible portion of which is actually a swollen stem.

fruit fly, very small, winged INSECT (families Tephritidae and Drosophilidae) in the order Diptera (see FLY). Fruit flies lay their eggs in plant tissue. In some species the larvae feed directly on the fruit pulp; in others they feed on yeasts growing in the fruit. Some spe-

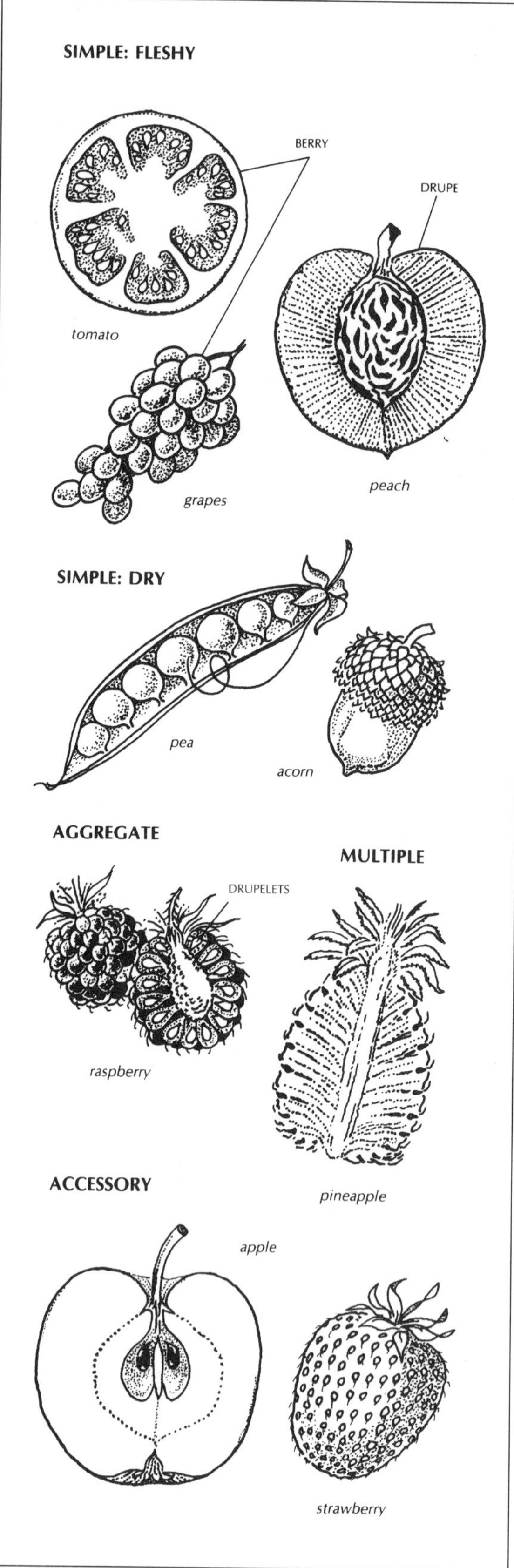

Types of fruit

cies cause damage to important crops, e.g., the Mediterranean fruit fly (*Ceratitis capitata*), a serious pest of citrus fruits. The vinegar fly (*Drosophila melanogaster*) is often used in the laboratory study of GENETICS because of its ten-day life cycle and large chromosomes.

Frunze: see BISHKEK.

Fry, Christopher, 1907–, English dramatist and film writer, one of the few 20th-cent. playwrights to employ verse successfully. His plays include *The Lady's Not for Burning* (1949) and *A Sleep of Prisoners* (1951). His screenplays include *Ben Hur* (1959; Academy Award) and *The Bible* (1966).

Fry, Elizabeth (Gurney), 1780–1845, English prison reformer and philanthropist. A Quaker, she worked from 1813 to improve the conditions of women in Newgate prison. Such innovations as segregation of the sexes and education and employment programs in British prisons were largely due to her efforts. She also founded soup kitchens in London.

Fry, Roger Eliot, 1866–1934, English art critic and painter. A champion of the modern French schools of art (see POSTIMPRESSIONISM), he emphasized analysis of the formal qualities in a work of art. His writings include *Vision and Design* (1920) and *Cézanne* (1927).

Fuchs, Klaus Emil, 1911–88, British physicist and Communist spy; b. Germany. An acknowledged Communist, he passed information to the USSR while working on the atomic bomb in the U.S. (1944–45) and in the atomic research center at Harwell, England, as head of the physics division. He was arrested in 1950 and imprisoned until 1959, when he went to East Germany. He was director of the Institute for Nuclear Physics from 1959 to 1979.

fuchsia, shrub or herb (genus *Fuchsia*) of the EVENING PRIMROSE family, a tropical American plant cultivated for its pendulous, brilliant, red-to-purple and white flowers. Most garden fuchsias are hybrids.

fuel cell, electric CELL in which the chemical energy from the oxidation of a gas fuel is converted directly to electrical energy in a continuous process. The fuel cell differs from a battery in that its reactants are supplied from an external source. In the hydrogen and oxygen fuel cell, hydrogen and oxygen gas are bubbled into separate compartments connected by a porous disk through which an ELECTROLYTE, such as aqueous potassium hydroxide (KOH), can pass. Inert graphite electrodes, mixed with a catalyst such as platinum, are dipped into each compartment. When the two electrodes are electrically connected, an OXIDATION AND REDUCTION reaction takes place in the cell: hydrogen gas is oxidized to form water at the anode; electrons are liberated in this process and flow through the external circuit to the cathode, where the electrons combine with the oxygen gas and reduce it. Fuel cells are characterized by high efficiency, cleanliness, and lack of noise. They have been used to generate electricity in spacecraft, prototype electric power plants, and experimental motor vehicles.

fuel injection, system in an INTERNAL-COMBUSTION ENGINE that delivers fuel or a fuel-air mixture to the cylinders by means of pressure from a pump. It was originally used in DIESEL ENGINES because of diesel fuel's greater viscosity and the need to overcome the high pressure of the compressed air in the cylinders. A diesel fuel injector sprays an intermittent, timed, metered quantity of fuel into a cylinder, distributing the fuel throughout the air within. Fuel injection is also now used in gasoline engines in place of a CARBURETOR. In gasoline engines the fuel is first mixed with air, and the resulting mixture is delivered to the cylinder. Modern fuel injection systems use computers to regulate the process. Fuel injection results in more efficient fuel combustion, improving fuel economy and engine performance and reducing polluting exhaust emissions.

Fuentes, Carlos [fwän'tās], 1928–, Mexican novelist and short-story writer. He synthesizes reality and fantasy in such experimental novels as *Where the Air is Clear* (1958), *A Change of Skin* (1967), *Terra Nostra* (1975), *The Old Gringo* (1984), and *The Campaign* (1991).

Fuessli, Johann Heinrich: see FUSELI, HENRY.

Fugard, Athol (Harold Lanigan), 1932–, South African playwright, actor, and director. An Afrikaner opposed to APARTHEID, Fugard has written of the suffering and common humanity of blacks, Coloureds, and poor whites in his country in such powerful plays as *The Blood Knot* (1961), *Boesman and Lena* (1969), *A Lesson from Aloes* (1978), *Master Harold . . . and the Boys* (1982), and *Playland* (1993).

fugitive slave laws, in U.S. history, the federal acts of 1793 and 1850 providing for the return between states of escaped slaves. Northern states relaxed enforcement of the 1793 law as they abolished SLAVERY, greatly angering the South, and the law was circumvented by the UNDERGROUND RAILROAD. Many Northern states also passed personal-liberty laws allowing fugitives jury trial; others forbade state officials to aid in capturing or jailing fugitives. As a concession to the South, the COMPROMISE OF 1850 strengthened the fugitive slave law. "All good citizens" were required to obey it on pain of heavy penalty; jury trial and the right to testify were prohibited to fugitives. The ABOLITIONISTS and new personal-liberty laws defied these provisions. Notable fugitive slave trials stirred up public opinion in both the North and South. Northern NULLIFICATION of the fugitive slave laws was cited in 1860 by South Carolina as a cause of secession. Congress repealed both laws in 1864, during the CIVIL WAR.

fugue [from Ital., = flight], in music, a form of composition, originally choral, in which the basic principle is imitative COUNTERPOINT of several voices. Its main elements are: a theme or subject, stated first in one and then in all voices; continuation of a voice after the subject, accompanying the subject statements in other voices; and passages built on a *motif,* a short phrase derived from the subject or countersubject. First established by Flemish composers in the 15th cent., the fugue was highly developed by J.S. BACH. The CANON is a short form of fugue.

Fuji, Mount, or **Fujiyama,** volcano 12,389 ft (3,776 m) high, highest point on HONSHU, Japan. The mountain, which last erupted in 1707, is sacred to many Japanese and is a traditional goal of pilgrimage. In 1982 a wall was erected to halt erosion of the perfectly formed, snow-capped cone, long a source of inspiration to Japanese artists.

Fujimori, Alberto, 1938–, president of Peru (1990–). An economist and the son of Japanese immigrants, he won the presidency in a upset victory. As president he slashed inflation by cutting subsidies and raising prices. In 1992 he suspended congress and declared emergency rule to combat corruption and SHINING PATH guerrillas.

Fukuoka [fo͝okō͞o'ôkä], city (1990 pop. 1,237,107), capital of Fukuoka prefecture, N Kyushu, Japan. Having grown from Hakata, one of Japan's most important medieval ports, the modern city is also a vital commercial and steel and textile producing center as well as the seat of several universities. The city has three noted shrines, including a 16th-cent. Shinto shrine.

Fulani, people of W Africa, numbering approximately 14 million. They are of mixed African and Berber origin. First recorded as living in the Senegambia region, they are now scattered throughout the area of the Sudan from Senegal to Cameroon. The Fulani became zealous Muslims (11th cent.) and from 1750 to 1900 engaged in many holy wars in the name of Islam. In the first part of the 19th cent., the Fulani carved out two important empires. One, based on Massina, for a time controlled TIMBUKTU; the other, centered at Sokoto, included the HAUSA States and parts of Bornu and W Cameroon. The Fulani emir of Sokoto continued to rule over part of N Nigeria until the British conquest in 1903.

Fulbright, J(ames) William, 1905–, U.S. senator from Arkansas (1945–75); b. Sumner, Mo. A Democrat, he was elected to the House of Representatives (1942) and then to the Senate (1944). He became known internationally for the Fulbright Act (1946), which provided for the exchange of students and teachers between the U.S. and other countries. As chairman (1959–74) of the Senate Foreign Relations Committee, he opposed the VIETNAM WAR.

Fuller, Margaret, 1810–50, American writer and lecturer; b. Cambridge, Mass. One of the most influential literary figures of her day, she was a leading exponent of TRANSCENDENTALISM and edited (1840–42) its journal, *The Dial. Woman in the Nineteenth Century* (1845) expresses her feminist views. Her essays as first literary critic of the New York *Tribune* are collected in *Papers on Literature and Art* (1846). In 1847 she went to Rome, where she married the Marchese Ossoli, a follower of MAZZINI, and with him took part in the REVOLUTION OF 1848–49, writing about it for the *Tribune.* Returning to the U.S. (1850), she, her husband, and their baby were drowned in a shipwreck.

Fuller, Melville Weston, 1833–1910, 8th chief justice of the U.S. SUPREME COURT (1888–1910); b. Augusta, Me. He was the first chief justice with academic legal training, having attended (1854–55), but received no degree from, Harvard Law School. On the Court he tended toward a strict construction of the Constitution.

Fuller, R(ichard) Buckminster, 1895–83, American architect and engineer; b. Milton, Mass. He is noted for his revolutionary technological designs aimed at deriving maximum output from minimum material and energy—the *Dymaxion* principle. Examples are his self-contained "4-D" house (1928), Dymaxion automobile (1933), and designs for geodesic domes.

fullerene, any of a class of carbon molecules in which the carbon atoms are arranged in the form of a closed, hollow sphere, cylinder, or the like. A fullerene molecule may have as few as 32 atoms of carbon, but the most common and most stable is **buckminsterfullerene** (C_{60}), a soccerball-shaped molecule consisting of 60 carbon atoms and named after R. Buckminster FULLER because of the resemblance of its molecular structure to his geodesic domes. Fullerenes were first identified in 1985 as products of experiments in which graphite was vaporized using a laser, and they have since been discovered in nature, where they resulted from lightning strikes. Fullerenes have been used experimentally as superconductors and to produce tiny diamonds and thin diamond films.

Fullerton, city (1990 pop. 114,144), S Calif., SE of Los Angeles; inc. 1904. Oil was discovered nearby in 1892, but the city's main growth followed the building of the Santa Ana Freeway in the 1950s. Its diversified manufactures include aerospace, electrical, and electronic components.

Fulton, Robert, 1765–1815, American inventor, engineer, and painter; b. near Lancaster, Pa. A person of many talents and a mechanical genius, he was successively an expert gunsmith, a landscape and portrait painter, and a maker of torpedoes and submarines. In 1807 his *Clermont,* launched on the Hudson R. was the first commercially successful steamboat (see STEAMSHIP) in America; although Fulton had predecessors, e.g., John FITCH, he is popularly considered the steamboat's inventor.

function, in mathematics, a relation that assigns to each member x of some set X (the domain) a unique member y of some set Y (the range); y is said to be a function of x, usually denoted $f(x)$ (read "f of x"). In the equation $y = f(x)$, x is called the independent variable and y the dependent variable. Although a function f assigns a unique y to each x, several x's may yield the same y; e.g., if $y = f(x) = x^2$ (where x is a number), then $f(2) = f(-2) = 4$. If this never occurs, then f is called a one-to-one, or injective, function.

functional group, in organic chemistry, group of atoms within a molecule that is responsible for certain properties of the molecule and reactions in which it takes part.

functionalism, in anthropology and sociology, theory stressing the interdependence of all of a society's behavior patterns and institutions. Implicit in the work of late 19th-cent. French sociologist Émile DURKHEIM, it was developed in England by anthropologists B. MALINOWSKI and A.R. RADCLIFFE-BROWN and applied more broadly by U.S. sociologist Talcott PARSONS. Although functionalism has the virtue of stressing the interrelatedness of a society with its institutions, beliefs, and customs, it has been criticized for celebrating the status quo and not paying enough attention to conflict and change as features of social life.

fundamentalism. 1 In Protestantism, conservative religious movement that arose among members of various denominations early in the 20th cent. Its aim is to maintain traditional interpretations of the Bible and what its adherents believe to be the fundamental doctrines of the Christian faith. The movement developed (1909) in reaction to the emergence of liberal theology, which attempted to recast Christian teachings in light of the scientific and historic thought of the time. **2** In Islam, term encompassing various modern Muslim leaders, groups, and movements opposed to secularization in Islam and Islamic countries and seeking to reassert traditional beliefs and practices. There are both SHIITE and SUNNI fundamentalist leaders and groups, such as the Ayatollah KHOMEINI and the MUSLIM BROTHERHOOD.

Fundamental Orders, in U.S. history, the basic law of the Connecticut colony, 1639–62. A preamble and 11 orders presented a binding and compact frame of government that put the welfare of the community above that of individuals.

Fundy, Bay of, large inlet of the Atlantic Ocean, c.170 mi (270 km) long and 30–50 mi (50–80 km) wide, NE Canada, between New Brunswick and Nova Scotia. It is famous for its tidal bore and for high tides that reach 40–50 ft (12–15 m), creating the reversing falls of the St. John R.

fungal infection, infection caused by a fungus. Some, such as SMUT and MILDEW, affect plants. Others, such as lumpy jaw, affect animals. In humans, fungi cause the skin infections RINGWORM and athlete's foot and the vaginal yeast infection candidiasis. Other fungi take advantage of the body when it has been weakened by diseases such as AIDS or DIABETES and cause infections such as candidiasis of the throat (thrush) or aspergillosis. Some fungal infections are regional. The lung disease histoplasmosis occurs in the central and SE U.S., and VALLEY FEVER occurs in the SW U.S.

fungicide, substance used to prevent or destroy a FUNGUS. Made from sulfur or copper compounds, organic salts of iron, zinc, and mercury, or other chemicals, fungicides are used on seeds, soil, wood (to prevent dry rot), and fabrics (to prevent mildew). Human FUNGAL INFECTIONS are treated with fungicides, called antifungals or antimycotics in medicine, such as nystatin and clotrimazole.

fungus, member of a kingdom (Fungi) of non-photosynthesizing organisms that live as PARASITES, symbionts, or SAPROPHYTES. Fungi are multicellular (with the exception of YEASTS); the body of most consists of slender cottony filaments, or hyphae. All fungi are capable of asexual REPRODUCTION by cell division, budding, fragmentation, or SPORES. Those that reproduce sexually alternate a sexual generation (GAMETOPHYTE) with a spore-producing one. The three divisions of fungi are the zygomycetes (e.g., black bread MOLD), the ascomycetes (e.g., yeasts, powdery mildews, TRUFFLES, and blue-green molds such as *Penicillium*) and deuteromycetes (the imperfect fungi, e.g., species that cause RINGWORM), and the basidiomycetes (e.g., MUSHROOMS, smuts, and puffballs). Fungi help decompose organic matter (important in soil renewal) and are valuable as a source of ANTIBIOTICS, vitamins, and various industrial chemicals and for their role in FERMENTATION.

fungus infection: see FUNGAL INFECTION.

Funk, Casimir [fo͝ongk], 1884–1967, American biochemist; b. Warsaw, Poland; came to U.S., 1915. Credited with discovering VITAMINS, he stirred public interest with his 1912 paper on vitamin-deficiency diseases. He coined the term *vitamine* and later posited the existence of four such materials (B_1, B_2, C, and D). He contributed to knowledge of the hormones of the pituitary and sex glands and stressed the importance of balance between hormones and vitamins.

fur, hairy covering of an animal, especially that with thick, soft, close-growing underfur next to the skin and a coarser protective layer of guard hair above it. The term includes sheepskins with their hair, and curled pelts, e.g., Persian lamb. Used for clothing since prehistoric times, furs were traditionally luxury goods in the more populous, temperate regions of the world, where wild animals are scarce. The most prized furs include sable, mink, and chinchilla, but many others, e.g., beaver, fox, rabbit, and ocelot, are also valued, and breeding and hunting industries are important in North America and Asia. Following the exploitation (17th–19th cent.) of N American and Asian wilderness areas, depleting the sea otter and threatening the fur seal, conservationists and humane groups have protested trapping for fur. In 1969 the U.S. government passed the ENDANGERED SPECIES Act, banning importation or sale of pelts of such animals as the polar bear, jaguar, and tiger. Since World War II synthetic furs have become increasingly popular because of their realistic appearance, their relatively low cost, and public awareness of endangered species.

Furies or **Erinyes** [ērĭn'ē-ēz], in Greek mythology, goddesses of vengeance. Born from the blood of URANUS, they punished wrongs committed against blood relatives regardless of the motivation, as in the case of ORESTES. Named Megaera, Tisiphone, and Alecto, they were usually represented as crones with bats' wings, dogs' heads, and snakes for hair.

Furtwängler, Wilhelm, 1886–1954, German conductor, in Lübeck, Mannheim, Berlin, and with the New York Philharmonic (see ORCHESTRA, table). He was renowned for his interpretations of BRAHMS and Richard WAGNER.

fuse, electric, safety device used to protect an ELECTRIC CIRCUIT against an excessive current. A fuse consists of a low-melting-point alloy strip enclosed in a suitable housing and connected in series with the circuit that it protects. Because of its electrical RESISTANCE, the alloy strip is heated by electric current; if the current exceeds the safe value for which the fuse was designed, the strip melts, opening the circuit and stopping the current. See also CIRCUIT BREAKER.

Fuseli, Henry [fyōō'zĭlē], 1741–1825, Anglo-Swiss painter and draftsman, also known as Johann Heinrich Fuessli or Füssli. His paintings were grotesque and visionary, e.g., *Nightmare* (1782). His drawings reveal his romantic fascination with the terrifying and the weird.

fusel oil, oily, colorless liquid with a disagreeable odor and taste. A mixture of ALCOHOLS and fatty acids formed during the alcoholic FERMENTATION of STARCH, fusel oil may occur as an unwholesome impurity in imperfectly distilled liquor. It is used as a solvent in making lacquers and enamels.

Fushun [fōō-shōōn], city (1990 est. pop. 1,350,000), NE Liaoning prov., NE China, in a highly industrialized area 36 mi (60 km) from SHENYANG. It is the coal-mining center of China and has one of the largest opencut coal mines in the world. Oil production and refining are also major industries. The city was developed by Russia until 1905 and by Japan until 1945.

fusion: see COLD FUSION; HYDROGEN BOMB; NUCLEAR ENERGY.

Füssli, Johann Heinrich: see FUSELI, HENRY.

futures market, a commodity exchange (see COMMODITY MARKET) where contracts for the future delivery of grain, livestock, and precious metals are bought and sold. Speculation in futures serves to protect both the developers and the users of the commodities from unfavorable and unpredictable price fluctuations. The U.S. futures market now includes Treasury bills and government guaranteed mortgages, or Ginnie Maes, thereby allowing speculation on changes in future interest rates.

futurism, Italian school of painting, sculpture, and literature that flourished from 1909, when Filippo Marinetti's first manifesto of futurism appeared, until the end of World War I. It portrayed the dynamic character of 20th-cent. life, glorified war and the machine age, and favored the growth of FASCISM. The futurists' representation of forms in motion influenced many painters, including Marcel DUCHAMP and Robert DELAUNEY, and such movements as CUBISM and Russian CONSTRUCTIVISM.

Fuzhou or **Foochow** [both: fōō-jō], city (1990 est. pop. 1,290,000), capital of Fujian prov., E China, a port on the Min R. delta c.25 mi (40 km) from the coast. It consists of an old walled city dating from the T'ang dynasty and a modern riverside town. Its industries include food processing (tea, sugar, and fruit), chemicals, and textiles. The city's lacquerware and handicrafts are famous throughout China. Long a center for China's foreign commerce and a treaty port following the OPIUM WAR (1839–42), it was designated a "special economic zone" in 1979 to spur foreign investment.

fuzzy logic, a multivalued (as opposed to binary) LOGIC. Classical logic holds that everything can be expressed in binary terms: 0 or 1, black or white, yes or no; in terms of BOOLEAN ALGEBRA, everything is in one set or another but not in both. Fuzzy logic allows for values between 0 and 1, shades of gray, and maybe; it allows partial membership in a set. When the approximate reasoning of fuzzy logic is used with an EXPERT SYSTEM, logical inferences can be drawn from imprecise relationships. It is used, for example, to optimize automatically the wash cycle of a washing machine by sensing the load size, fabric mix, and quantity of detergent. Fuzzy logic is used to control passenger elevators, household appliances, cameras, automobile subsystems, and SMART WEAPONS.

G

Ga, chemical symbol of the element GALLIUM.

Gable, Clark, 1901–60, American film actor; b. Cadiz, Ohio. For years a box-office attraction, he made such films as *It Happened One Night* (1934), *Gone with the Wind* (1939), and *The Misfits* (1960).

Gabo, Naum [gä'bō], 1890–1977, Russian sculptor, architect, and theorist; brother of Antoine PEVSNER. He wrote the *Realist Manifesto* (1920), proposing that new concepts of time and space be incorporated into art. His sculptural experiments with CONSTRUCTIVISM were often transparent, geometric abstracts.

Gabon [gäbôN'], officially Gabonese Republic, republic (1991 pop. 1,079,980), 103,346 sq mi (267,667 sq km), W central Africa, bordered by the Atlantic Ocean (W), Equatorial Guinea and Cameroon (N), and Congo (E and S). LIBREVILLE (the capital) and Port-Gentil are the only large cities. Lambaréné, on the Ogooué, is the site of the famous hospital established by Albert SCHWEITZER in 1913. Gabon is situated astride the equator. The coastline is a narrow, low-lying strip; the interior is made up of mountain ranges and high plateaus. Much of the country is drained by the Ogooué R., which flows into the Atlantic. The economy is based on oil production, which provides the highest per capita income in sub-Saharan Africa and accounts for two thirds of export earnings. Other minerals extracted include manganese, uranium, and gold. Forest products are also important. Agricultural output is low, and much food needs to be imported. The peoples of Gabon include the Fang (the most numerous group), Omiéné, Batoka, and Eshira. French is the official language and a number of Bantu dialects are also spoken. Most of the people follow traditional beliefs, but there are many Christians in the cities.

History. The region that is now Gabon was inhabited in Paleo-

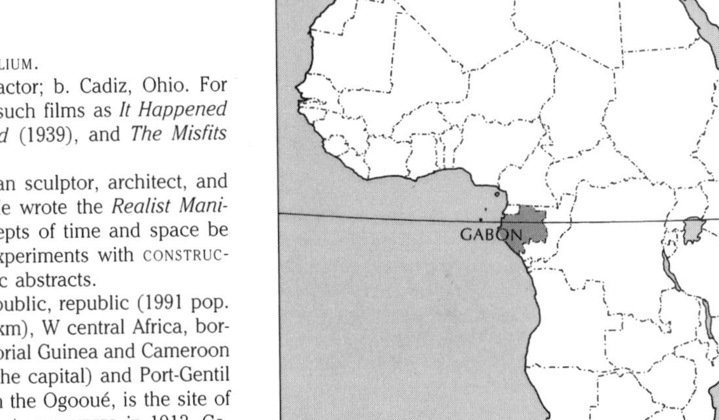

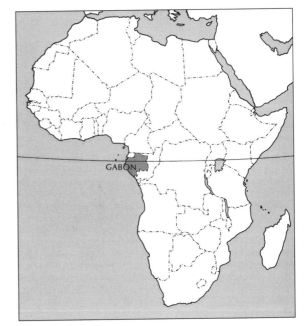

lithic times. The Omiéné were living there by the 16th cent., the Fang by the 18th, and from the 16th to 18th cent. Gabon was part of the Loango empire, which stretched from the Ogooué to the Congo (Zaïre) rivers. Portuguese navigators arrived in the Ogooué estuary in the 1470s, and Gabon soon became an important center of a slave trade that flourished until the 1880s. By the late 18th cent., the French had gained a dominant position in the area, and, despite resistance from the Fang, Gabon became part of the French Congo in 1889 and of FRENCH EQUATORIAL AFRICA in 1910. Held by the Free French in WORLD WAR II, Gabon became an overseas territory in 1946 and self-governing in 1958. It achieved full independence in 1960 but retained close ties with France. In 1967 the country adopted a one-party political system with Omar Bongo as president. Independent legislative candidates were permitted in 1980, but not until 1990, when unrest forced Bongo to agree, did multiparty legislative elections occur. Amid charges of fraud, Bongo's party won a majority of the seats. Bongo won (1993) reelection in disorganized polling that also prompted fraud charges.

Gaborone, city (1992 est. pop. 140,000), capital of Botswana. Primarily an administrative center with mining-related industries, it is located on the country's main rail line and has a small international airport. The city was founded c.1890 by Gaborone Matlapin, an African chief. It became the capital of newly independent BOTSWANA in 1966.

Gabriel, archangel, the divine herald. In the BIBLE he appears to DANIEL; to Zacharias, father of JOHN THE BAPTIST; and to the Virgin MARY in the Annunciation. Christian tradition makes him the trumpeter of the Last Judgment. In Islam, Gabriel reveals the KORAN to MUHAMMAD, becoming the angel of truth.

Gabriel, Jacques Ange [gäbrēĕl′], 1689–1782, French architect of the ROCOCO. His work is characterized by classical repose, purity of form, and restraint. He worked for 30 years for LOUIS XV at VERSAILLES, Compiègne, and other royal residences. He also designed Place Louis XV (now Place de la Concorde), Paris (1753), and worked on the LOUVRE.

Gabrieli, Andrea, c.1510–86, Italian organist and composer. He wrote MADRIGALS, MOTETS, MASSES, *ricercari,* and canzones for organ and was important in developing multiple-choir technique, which was further refined by his nephew **Giovanni Gabrieli,** c.1555–1612. Giovanni was most important in the development of the CONCERTO style, and he published (1597) the first printed music with dynamic indications.

Gadda, Carlo Emilio, 1893–1973, Italian novelist. His complex style combined literary language, slang, dialects, deliberate misspellings, foreign words, and imitations of various prose styles. *That Awful Mess on Via Merulana* (1957) is considered his masterpiece.

Gaddi, celebrated family of Florentine artists. **Gaddo Gaddi,** c.1260–c.1333, a painter and mosaicist, is thought to have produced the MOSAICS in the portico of Santa Maria Maggiore, Rome. His son, **Taddeo Gaddi,** c.1300–c.1366, was a pupil and assistant to GIOTTO and chief Florentine painter after Giotto's death. His works include painting in Santa Croce and Santa Felicità, Florence. Taddeo's son, **Agnolo Gaddi,** c.1350–1396, possessed a somewhat rigid, Giottesque style. His frescoes include *Life of the Virgin* (cathedral, Prato).

Gadhafi, Moammar: see QADDAFI, MUAMMAR AL-.

gadolinium (Gd), metallic element, extracted in oxide form by J.C.G. de Marignac in 1880. This silver-white, malleable, ductile, lustrous RARE-EARTH METAL is found in gadolinite, MONAZITE, and bastnasite. It is paramagnetic at room temperature but becomes strongly ferromagnetic when cooled. See ELEMENT (table); PERIODIC TABLE.

Gadsden, James, 1788–1858, American railroad promoter and diplomat; b. Charleston, S.C. He advocated a southern rail system and a railroad to the Pacific. Appointed minister to Mexico (1853), he negotiated the GADSDEN PURCHASE, but he was recalled (1856) for exceeding his instructions.

Gadsden Purchase, strip of land bought (1853) by the U.S. from Mexico. Pres. Franklin PIERCE wished to ensure U.S. possession of the Mesilla Valley near the Rio Grande—the most practicable southern route for a railroad to the Pacific. James GADSDEN negotiated the purchase for $10 million of the area of about 30,000 sq mi (77,700 sq km) that now forms extreme S New Mexico and Arizona S of the Gila R.

Gaea, in Greek mythology, the earth; daughter of CHAOS, mother and wife of both URANUS (the sky) and Pontus (the sea). She was mother, by Uranus, of the CYCLOPES, the TITANS, and others, and, by Pontus, of five sea deities. She helped cause the overthrow of Uranus by the Titans and was worshiped as the primal goddess, the mother of all things.

Gaelic [gā′lĭk], or Goidelic, group of languages belonging to the Celtic subfamily of the Indo-European family of languages. Gaelic is spoken in highland Scotland, in Ireland, and on the Isle of Man. See LANGUAGE (table).

Gaelic football: see under FOOTBALL.

Gagarin, Yuri Alekseyevich, 1934–68, Soviet cosmonaut. He became the first person to achieve orbital spaceflight when, on Apr. 12, 1961, he circled the earth once in *Vostok 1.* He died (Mar. 27, 1968) in the crash of a jet trainer.

Gage, Thomas, 1721–87, British general, commander of the British forces in North America (1763–75). As governor of Massachusetts (1774–75) he tried to enforce the INTOLERABLE ACTS. His measures brought on the battles of LEXINGTON AND CONCORD, which began the AMERICAN REVOLUTION.

Gaines's Mill: see SEVEN DAYS BATTLES.

Gainsborough, Thomas, 1727–88, English portrait and landscape painter. Greatly influenced by VAN DYCK, he was celebrated for the elegance, vivacity, and refinement of his portraits. His favorite subject was landscape, and he produced some of the first great landscape paintings in England. Gainsborough had few English rivals as a colorist. In his last years he excelled in fancy pictures, a pastoral genre with idealized subjects, e.g., *The Mall* (1783; Frick Coll., N.Y.C.). Among his well-known works are *Perdita* (Wallace Coll., London), *The Blue Boy* (Huntington Art Gall., San Marino, Calif.), and *Lady Innes* (Frick Coll., N.Y.C.).

Gaiseric or **Genseric,** c.390–477, king of the Vandals and Alani (428–77). He left Spain for Africa (429), subdued a large territory, and took CARTHAGE (439). Recognized as independent of Rome, he persecuted Roman landowners and clergy. In 455 he sacked Rome, and he frustrated Roman expeditions against him. By the time he made peace with ZENO (476), he held N Africa, Sicily, Sardinia, Corsica, and the Balearic Islands.

Gaitskell, Hugh Todd Naylor, 1906–63, British statesman. During WORLD WAR II he served in the ministry of economic warfare (1940–42) and on the Board of Trade (1942–45). He entered Parliament as a Labour member in 1945 and later was chancellor of the exchequer (1950–51). In 1955 he succeeded ATTLEE as party leader. He favored moderation of party policies.

Gaius [gā′əs, gī′–], fl. 2d cent., Roman jurist. His textbook *Institutes* is a major source of our knowledge of early ROMAN LAW.

galactic cluster: see STAR CLUSTER.

Galápagos Islands or **Archipiélago de Colón,** archipelago of 13 large and several smaller islands belonging to Ecuador, c.650 mi (1,045 km) W of the country in the Pacific Ocean. The islands were claimed by Ecuador in 1832. They are largely desolate lava piles with little vegetation, except on the upper slopes, but are of special interest to naturalists for their large tortoises, land and marine iguanas, flightless cormorants, and other unusual wildlife. Charles DARWIN, who visited the islands in 1835, gathered evidence there that supported his theory of natural selection.

Galatians, epistle of the NEW TESTAMENT, possibly the earliest written (A.D. c.48), 9th book in the usual order, by St. PAUL to Christians of central Asia Minor. Some scholars date it after A.D. 52. In answer to the belief that circumcision and the Law of MOSES are essential, Paul argues, in a passage central to Christianity, that salvation can be achieved through faith alone.

galaxy, large aggregation of gas, dust, and typically billions of stars. It is held together by the gravitational attraction between its parts, and its rotational motion prevents it from collapsing on itself. A typical spiral galaxy is shaped like a flat disk, about 100,000 light-years in diameter, with a central bulge, or nucleus, containing old stars; winding through the disk are the characteristic spiral arms of dust, gas, and young stars. An elliptical galaxy, lacking spiral arms entirely and containing little or no gas and dust, resembles the nucleus of a spiral galaxy. A small minority of galaxies are classified as irregular, i.e., showing no definite symmetry or nucleus. One theory suggests that irregulars evolve into spirals or ellipticals, depending on the initial amount of rotational motion. Some galaxies radiate a large fraction of their energy in forms other than visible light, such as radio waves, X rays, and infrared and ultraviolet radiation; their optical counterparts may be faint or undetectable. Gravitation also holds clusters of galaxies together; the Local Group cluster includes the MILKY WAY (containing the sun and solar system) and the ANDROMEDA GALAXY, both spirals, and the irregular MAGELLANIC CLOUDS. See also HUBBLE'S LAW.

Galbraith, John Kenneth, 1908–, American economist and public official; b. Ontario, Canada. He taught economics at Harvard (1934–39, 1949–75, except for time in government service). An adviser to Pres. J.F. KENNEDY, he was (1961–63) U.S. ambassador to India. A Keynesian economist (see KEYNES), he advocated government spending to fight unemployment and using more of the nation's wealth for public services and less for private consumption. His widely read books include *The Affluent Society* (1958; rev. ed., 1985), *The New Industrial State* (1967; 3d rev. ed., 1978), and *The Anatomy of Power* (1983).

Galdós, Benito Pérez: see PÉREZ GALDÓS, BENITO.

Galen, c.130–c.200, physician and writer; b. Pergamum, of Greek parents. He resided chiefly in Rome and was personal physician to several emperors. Credited with some 500 treatises (at least 83 extant), Galen correlated earlier medical knowledge with his own discoveries (based on experiments and animal dissections). He showed that arteries carry blood, not air, and added greatly to knowledge of the brain, nerves, spinal cord, and pulse. His virtually undisputed authority discouraged original investigation and hampered medical progress until the 16th cent.

galena or **lead glance,** lustrous, blue-gray lead sulfide mineral (PbS). It is the chief ore and principal source of LEAD. Distributed worldwide, it frequently contains silver and other accessory metals.

Galicia [gəlĭsh'ēə], historic region (32,332 sq mi/83,740 sq km), SE Poland and W Ukraine. The Polish section covers Rzeszów and the greater part of Krakow provinces; the Ukranian section includes Lviv (Lvov), Ivano-Frankovsk, and Tarnopol oblasts. Mainly agricultural, Galicia also has minerals, notably oil. Originally the duchy of Galich and Vladimir, the region was annexed to Poland in the 14th cent., passed to Austria in 1772, and won limited autonomy in 1861. A battleground in WORLD WAR I, after the war Galicia was contested (1918–20) by newly independent Poland and the new Ukrainian republic with Polish title to the region confirmed by the Polish-Soviet Treaty of Riga (1921). In 1939 most of E Galicia was annexed to Ukraine.

Galicia, Galician *Galiza,* autonomous region (1987 est. pop. 2,858,000), NW Spain, on the Atlantic Ocean, S of the Bay of Biscay and N of Portugal. It includes the provinces of La Coruña, Lugo, Orense, and Pontevedra. In this largely mountainous area, fishing, stock-raising, and food processing are the major occupations. Galicia passed from Rome to the German Suevi (5th–6th cent.), the MOORS, and ASTURIAS (8th–9th cent.).

Galilee, region, N Israel, roughly the portion north of the plain of Esdraelon. Galilee was the chief scene of the ministry of Jesus. After the destruction of Jerusalem (A.D. 70), it became the main center of Judaism in PALESTINE. Zionist colonization of the area began at the end of the 19th cent. and accelerated after World War II. The chief city is NAZARETH. The **Sea of Galilee,** also called **Lake Tiberias** or **Lake Kinneret,** is a lake (64 sq mi/166 sq km) in NE Israel. About 700 ft (210 m) below sea level, it has a saline character and is fed and drained by the JORDAN R. Some fishing is carried on, and some of its water is pumped to S Israel for irrigation. In the Old Testament the lake was called the Sea of Chinnereth or Chinneroth; in the New Testament, Galilee, Gennesaret, or Tiberias.

Galileo (Galileo Galilei), 1564–1642, Italian astronomer, mathematician, and physicist. At the age of 19 he discovered the principle of isochronism—that each oscillation of a pendulum takes the same time despite changes in amplitude. Soon thereafter he became known for his invention of a hydrostatic balance and his treatise on the center of gravity of falling bodies. He found experimentally that bodies do not fall with velocities proportional to their weights, a conclusion received with hostility because it contradicted the accepted teaching of ARISTOTLE. Galileo discovered that the path of a projectile is a parabola, and he is credited with anticipating Isaac NEWTON's laws of motion. In 1609 he constructed the first astronomical telescope, which he used to discover the four largest satellites of Jupiter and the stellar composition of the Milky Way, and in 1632 he published his *Dialogue Concerning the Two Chief World Systems,* a work that upheld the COPERNICAN SYSTEM rather than the PTOLEMAIC SYSTEM and marked a turning point in scientific and philosophical thought. Brought (1633) before the INQUISITION in Rome, he was made to renounce all his beliefs and writings supporting the Copernican theory. His last book, *Dialogues Concerning Two New Sciences* (1638), contains most of his contributions to physics.

Galileo, in space exploration: see SPACE PROBE, table.

Gall, c.1840–94, SIOUX war chief; b. South Dakota. Chief lieutenant of SITTING BULL in the defeat of George CUSTER at LITTLE BIGHORN (1876), Gall later surrendered and worked for better relations between Native Americans and whites.

Galla: see OROMO.

Gallant, Mavis, 1922–, Canadian writer. An expatriate writer living in France, she has contributed to *The New Yorker* since the 1950s. Her publications include short stories, two novels, *Green Water, Green Sky* (1959) and *A Fairly Good Time* (1970), and one play, *What Is to Be Done?* (1983).

Gallatin, Albert, 1761–1849, U.S. public official and financier; b. Switzerland. An innovative secretary of the treasury (1801–14), he reshaped U.S. financial policy to Jeffersonian principles. Under Pres. MADISON he urged the use of federal money to expand the internal economy. A key figure in negotiating the Treaty of GHENT, he was also minister to France (1816–23) and to Great Britain (1826–27). In 1842 he founded the American Ethnological Society.

Gallaudet [gă"lôdĕt'], American family of educators of the deaf. **Thomas Hopkins Gallaudet,** 1787–1851, b. Philadelphia, founded (1817) the first free school for the deaf in the U.S. His oldest son, **Thomas Gallaudet,** 1822–1902, an Episcopal priest, founded St. Ann's Church for Deaf-Mutes, N.Y.C., and the Gallaudet Home for aged deaf-mutes, Poughkeepsie, N.Y. The youngest son, **Edward Miner Gallaudet,** 1837–1917, opened a school for deaf-mutes (now Gallaudet College) in Washington, D.C.

gall bladder, small, pear-shaped sac attached to the LIVER by the cystic duct. The gall bladder stores and concentrates BILE, which is produced by the liver and functions in fat digestion. Fatty foods stimulate intestinal cells to produce a hormone that causes the gall bladder to contract, forcing the bile into the common bile duct and the intestine, where fats are absorbed. Components of bile sometimes crystallize in the gall bladder, forming gallstones.

Gallic Wars, campaigns in Gaul led by Julius CAESAR as proconsul of Gaul (58–51 B.C.). Caesar's first campaign was to prevent the Helvetii from entering SW GAUL. Next, the Aedui asked Caesar's help against the German Ariovistus, whom Caesar routed. In 57 B.C. Caesar pacified Belgica (roughly Belgium). In 56 B.C. he attacked the Veneti, and in the following year he went to the Low Countries and repelled a German invasion. He invaded (54 B.C.) Britain and the next winter put down a revolt of Belgian tribes led by Ambiorix. In 53 B.C. all central Gaul raised a revolt, organized by VERCINGETORIX. With incredible speed and brilliant tactics, Caesar crossed the Alps and suppressed the Gauls. The prime source of the Gallic Wars is Caesar's own commentaries, *De bello Gallico.*

Gallipoli campaign, April 1915–January 1916, Allied expedition in Turkey in WORLD WAR I. Planned by Winston CHURCHILL, British first lord of the admiralty, its purpose was to gain the Dardanelles, capture Constantinople, and make contact with Russia. Poor Allied cooperation and strong Turkish resistance forced the Allies into an evacuation that was the only successful operation in a disastrous campaign.

Gallitzin [gəlĭt'sĭn], Russian princely family. **Vasily Vasilyevich Gallitzin,** d. 1619, sent to offer the Russian throne to Prince Ladislaus of Poland, was imprisoned by King SIGISMUND III for refusing to help him gain the throne; he died in prison. **Vasily Vasilyevich Gallitzin,** 1643–1714, was the lover and chief adviser of Sophia Alekseyevna, regent for PETER I. He was exiled to Siberia after her downfall (1689). **Boris Alekseyevich Gallitzin,** 1654–1714, tutor to PETER I, headed the government during Peter's first foreign tour. **Dmitri Mikhailovich Gallitzin,** 1665–1737, helped ANNA, daughter of IVAN IV, gain the throne providing she agreed to limit her power; she began to rule absolutely and sentenced him to death, then exiled him instead. **Dmitri Alekseyevich Gallitzin,** 1735–1803, Russian ambassador at Paris (1765–73), was a friend of DIDEROT and VOLTAIRE. **Aleksandr Nikolayevich Gallitzin,** 1773?–1844, a statesman of liberal tendencies, was a counselor to ALEXANDER I. **Nikolai Dmitryevich Gallitzin,** 1856–1925, headed the council of ministers of NICHOLAS II from 1916 until the RUSSIAN REVOLUTION of 1917.

gallium (Ga), metallic element, discovered spectroscopically by P.E. Lecoq de Boisbaudran in 1875. Solid gallium is blue-gray; the liquid form is silver. It is chemically similar to ALUMINUM. Gallium compounds are used in transistors, lasers, and diodes. See ELEMENT (table); PERIODIC TABLE.

gallotanic acid: see TANNIN.

Gallup, George Horace, 1901–84, American public-opinion statistician; b. Jefferson, Iowa. He founded the American Institute of Public Opinion (1935) at Princeton, N.J., and originated the Gallup POLL to measure voter sentiment and gauge the national mood on various issues.

Galsworthy, John, 1867–1933, English novelist and dramatist. He is best remembered for his novels of the Forsyte family, grouped in three trilogies, *The Forsyte Saga* (1922), *A Modern Comedy* (1928), and *End of the Chapter* (1934). Dealing with three generations of a complacent upper-middle-class family from the 1880s to the 1920s, the novels focus on Soames Forsyte, the "man of property." Galsworthy also wrote highly successful dramas on social problems, including *The Silver Box* (1906), *Strife* (1909), and *Justice* (1910). He was awarded the 1932 Nobel Prize in literature.

Galt, John, 1779–1839, Scottish novelist. Known chiefly for his novels of Scottish country life, e.g., *The Ayrshire Legatees* (1821) and *The Entail* (1823), he also wrote a biography of BYRON (1830) and founded (1827) the town of Guelph in Canada.

Galton, Sir Francis, 1822–1911, English scientist and cousin of Charles DARWIN. In his *Hereditary Genius* (1869) he presented evidence that talent is an inherited characteristic; this led him to found the EUGENICS movement. His system of classifying fingerprints is basically that still in use.

Galvani, Luigi, 1737–98, Italian physician. A noted surgeon and researcher in comparative anatomy, he concluded, from his observation that a frog's leg contracted when touched by two different metals in a moist environment, that animal tissues generate ELECTRICITY. Although he was eventually proved wrong by Alessandro VOLTA, the controversy stimulated research in electrotherapy and on electric currents. Many electrical terms derive from his name.

galvanizing, process of coating a metal, usually iron or steel, with a protective coating of ZINC. Galvanized iron is usually prepared by dipping or electroplating. Pure iron, copper iron, and various steels are often galvanized, because the zinc coating resists oxidation and moisture.

galvanometer, instrument used to determine the presence, direction, and strength of electric current in a conductor. Galvanometers are based on the discovery (1819) by Hans OERSTED that a magnetic needle is deflected by the presence of an electric current in a nearby conductor. When an electric current is passing through the conductor, the magnetic needle tends to turn at right angles to the conductor, so that its direction is parallel to the lines of induction around the conductor and its north pole points in the direction in which these lines of induction flow. In general, the extent to which the needle turns is dependent upon the current strength. In the modern d'Arsonval galvanometer, the magnet is fixed and the coil is movable. If a pointer is attached to the moving coil so that it passes over a suitably calibrated scale, the galvanometer can be used to quantitatively measure the current passing through it. A direct current (DC) AMMETER measures direct current by allowing a known percentage of the current to pass through a galvanometer. A DC VOLTMETER measures direct voltage (see POTENTIAL, ELECTRIC) between two points by allowing current to flow through a galvanometer connected in series with a high resistance. The current through the galvanometer is then proportional to the voltage (see OHM'S LAW).

Galveston, city (1990 pop. 59,070), seat of Galveston co., on Galveston Island, SE Tex.; inc. 1839. It has a fine natural harbor at the entrance to Galveston Bay; causeways connect it with the mainland and Texas City. Oil refining and shipbuilding lead its industries. From its deepwater port goods are exported all over the world. Settled from the 1830s but known to Europeans centuries earlier, it also is a noted resort center with fine beaches and many tourist attractions, including Moody Gardens. The city was devastated by a 1900 hurricane. A massive seawall has helped to protect it, but hurricanes since have still caused much damage.

Gama, Vasco da, c.1469–1524, Portuguese navigator, the first European to travel by sea to INDIA (1497–99). At the order of MANUEL I, he commanded four vessels, reached Calicut, and opened up a lucrative spice trade, thus beginning the Portuguese empire. He returned with 20 ships in 1502 and established Portuguese power in India and Africa. His methods were harsh, and he was not a good administrator. He was sent back to India as viceroy in 1524 but soon died.

Gambetta, Léon [gäNbĕtä'], 1838–82, French republican leader. He opposed the Second Empire of NAPOLEON III and was prominent in the provisional government following the empire's fall (1870) in the FRANCO-PRUSSIAN WAR. He bitterly fought French capitulation and after 1871 helped to create the Third Republic. He pursued a moderate policy between the radicals and the monarchists and was premier (1881–82).

Gambia, The [găm'bēə], officially Republic of The Gambia, republic (1993 pop. 1,025,867), 4,361 sq mi (11,295 sq km), W Africa, the continent's smallest independent state. It is a narrow strip of land on both banks of the Gambia R., bordered by the Atlantic Ocean on the west and surrounded on the remaining three sides by Senegal. The capital is BANJUL, on St. Mary's Island, near the mouth of the Gambia R. A low-lying country, it ranges from sandy beaches along the coast to a swampy river valley in the interior. The economy is overwhelmingly dependent on the export of peanuts, which provide 90% of its earnings. Rice and other grains are produced for local consumption. Tourism also is important. The population is primarily Muslim, including the Malinke (Mandingo; the most numerous group), Fulani (Fula), and Wolof. English is the official language, but the Malinke language is common and Wolof also is spoken.

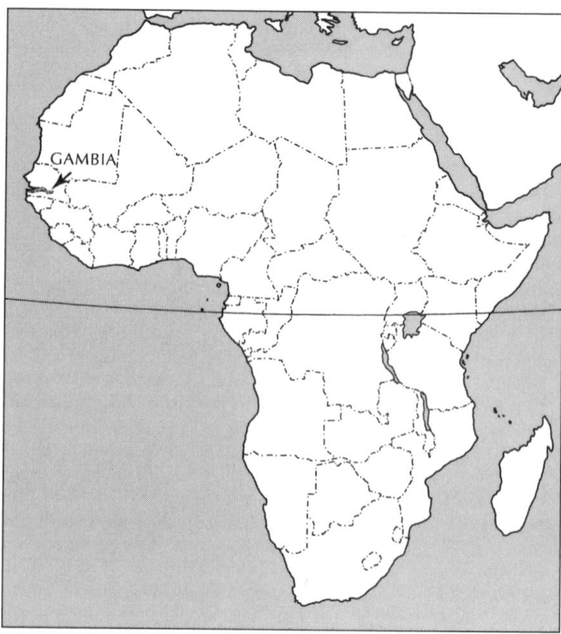

History. Prior to the arrival of Portuguese explorers in the mid-15th cent., the area that is now Gambia was part of the MALI empire. English merchants won trading rights from the Portuguese in

1588, and in the early 17th cent. British companies founded settlements along the Gambia R. In 1816 the British purchased St. Mary's Island, where they established Bathurst (now Banjul), and in 1843 the territory became a crown colony. The French, who controlled the neighboring interior (now Senegal), failed in negotiations to acquire the Gambia R. settlements, which, in 1894, became a British protectorate. Gambia achieved self-government in 1963 and independence in 1965, under Dawda Kairaba Jawara; it became a republic in the Commonwealth of Nations in 1970. Independent Gambia has largely been a successful parliamentary democracy, but in 1981 there was an attempted coup against Jawara that was suppressed only with the help of Senegalese troops. The country joined (1981) with SENEGAL in a confederation known as Senegambia, which, while maintaining individual sovereignty, aimed at cooperation in foreign policy, security, communications, and monetary and economic affairs, but Gambia's reluctance to move toward union led Senegal to dissolve (1989) the confederation.

games, theory of, group of mathematical theories applying statistical logic to the choice of strategies in a game. A game consists of a set of rules governing a competitive situation in which two or more individuals or groups attempt to maximize their own winnings or minimize those of their opponents. Game theory, first developed by John VON NEUMANN, is applied to many fields, e.g., military problems and economics.

gametophyte, phase of a plant life cycle in which the egg (see OVUM) and SPERM (gametes) are produced. In many lower plants the gametophyte phase is the dominant life form; for example, the familiar MOSSES are the gametophyte form of the plant. The union of egg and sperm gives rise to the sporophyte phase, in which spores are formed; spores, in turn, give rise to the gametophyte. In mosses the sporophyte is a capsule atop a slender stalk that grows out of the top of the gametophyte. The alternation between the gametophyte and sporophyte phase is known as alternation of generations.

gamma globulin: see GLOBULIN.

gamma radiation, radiation emitted in one of the three types of natural RADIOACTIVITY. It is the most energetic form of ELECTROMAGNETIC RADIATION, with a very short wavelength of less than 10^{-10} m. Gamma rays are essentially very energetic X RAYS emitted by excited nuclei. They often accompany alpha or beta particles, because a nucleus emitting those particles may be left in an excited (higher-energy) state. Gamma-ray sources are used in medicine to treat cancer, for diagnostic purposes, and to sterilize equipment and supplies, in industry in the inspection of castings and welds, and in food processing to kill microorganisms and retard spoilage.

gamma-ray astronomy, study of celestial objects by analysis of the most energetic ELECTROMAGNETIC RADIATION they emit. Gamma rays are difficult to observe from ground-based telescopes due to atmospheric interference, and high-altitude balloons, sounding ROCKETS, and orbiting OBSERVATORIES are therefore used. Gamma-ray astronomy is particularly useful in the study of black holes (see GRAVITATIONAL COLLAPSE), COSMIC RAYS, PULSARS, QUASARS, NEUTRON STARS, and SUPERNOVAS. Gamma-ray astronomy can be considered an extension of X-RAY ASTRONOMY to the extreme shortwave end of the spectrum.

Gamow, George [găm'ôf], 1904–68, Russian-American theoretical physicist and author; b. Odessa; came to U.S., 1933. He is best known as an author who popularized abstract physical theories. Gamow devised (1928) a theory of radioactive decay and applied nuclear physics to problems of stellar evolution. He also proposed an important theory on the organization of genetic information in the living cell.

Gandhi, Indira, 1917–1984, prime minister of India (1966–77, 1980–84); daughter of Jawaharlal NEHRU. After serving as her father's aide and rising through the ranks of the Congress party, she became prime minister on the death of SHASTRI. India's defeat of Pakistan in 1971 assured Indian dominance of the subcontinent. Gandhi's administration, increasingly authoritarian, was marked by stress on social programs and government planning. Faced with opposition, she declared an "emergency" in 1975, jailing opponents and suspending civil liberties. Forced from office in 1977, she made a triumphant return in 1980, stressing agricultural development and stronger international relations. She was assassinated (1984) by SIKH members of her bodyguard unit following an attack on the Golden Temple in Amritsar, the Sikhs' holiest shrine. Her son, Rajiv GANDHI, succeeded her as prime minister.

Gandhi, Mohandas Karamchand, 1869–1948, Indian political and spiritual leader, called the Mahatma [great-souled] and regarded as the father of independent INDIA. After practicing law in South Africa, where he fought for the rights of the Indian population there, he returned (1915) to India. Already regarded as a leader in the nationalist movement, he began working for Indian independence from Great Britain. He gave up Western ways to lead a life of abstinence and spirituality. He asserted the unity of all people under one God and preached Christian and Muslim ethics along with the Hindu. He became a proponent of satyagraha [passive resistance] as a way to end British rule. His efforts led the British to jail him several times, but so great was his following that his threats to fast until death usually forced his release. In the INDIAN NATIONAL CONGRESS, India's chief political party, he led the fight to rid the country of the CASTE system; he especially defended the rights of the untouchables. In 1942 the British jailed him after he refused to cooperate during World War II. In 1944 he was released and became a major figure in the postwar negotiations that resulted in Indian independence in 1947. He was deeply distressed by the religious partition of the country into India and Pakistan. When violence broke out between Hindus and Muslims, he resorted to fasts and visits to the troubled areas in efforts to end the violence. He was on one such prayer vigil in New Delhi when he was fatally shot by a Hindu extremist who objected to Gandhi's tolerance for the Muslims.

Gandhi, Rajiv, 1944–91, Indian political leader. He succeeded his mother, Indira GANDHI, as prime minister after her assassination (1984) and led the Congress party (see INDIAN NATIONAL CONGRESS) to a sweeping election victory. A proponent of free enterprise, he presided over the government during a period of robust economic growth. He also unsuccessfully attempted to mediate an end to Tamil-Sinhalese violence in SRI LANKA, sending Indian peacekeeping forces there in 1987. Allegations of corruption and arrogance diminished his popularity, however; in 1989 the Congress party lost its parliamentary majority and he resigned as prime minister. Gandhi was assassinated by Tamil separatists in 1991.

Ganges [găn'jēz] or **Ganga,** chief river in India, c.1,560 mi (2,510 km) long, considered sacred by Hindus. It rises in the Himalayas and flows generally east-southeast through a wide and densely populated plain to join the BRAHMAPUTRA R. in Bangladesh. The combined river then continues through a vast and fertile delta on the Bay of BENGAL, which it enters as the Padma and other distributaries. Hardwar, Allahabad, and Varanasi (Benares) are especially holy bathing sites along its banks. The Ganges is a major source of water for irrigation in both India and Bangladesh.

Gang of Four, term of opprobrium given by the Chinese Communist authorities to four persons held responsible for the excesses of the CULTURAL REVOLUTION (1966–69). They were also accused of trying to seize power after the deaths (1976) of MAO ZEDONG and ZHOU ENLAI. The most notable of the Gang of Four was JIANG QING, Mao's widow. The others were Wang Hongwen, Yao Wenyuan, and Zhang Chunqiao. They were imprisoned in 1976, tried in 1980, and sentenced in 1981. Sentences ranged from death (later commuted to life in prison) to 20 years in prison.

gangrene, local death of body tissue. Dry gangrene, the most common form, follows a disturbance of blood supply to the tissues, e.g., in DIABETES or destruction of tissue from injury. Moist gangrene results from an invasion of toxin-producing bacteria that destroy tissue. Treatment includes rest and ANTIBIOTICS; excision of the diseased area or, in advanced cases, amputation of the affected part may be necessary.

gannet: see BOOBY.

Ganymede, in astronomy, natural satellite of JUPITER.

Ganymede [găn'ēmēd], in Greek mythology, a beautiful youth carried off by ZEUS to be cupbearer to the gods.

Gaon of Vilna: see ELIJAH BEN SOLOMON.

gar, cylindrical, mostly freshwater FISH (family Lepisosteidae) with hard, diamond-shaped scales, a long jaw, and long, sharp teeth, found in the U.S. and Central America. The largest species is the

9-ft (2.7-m) alligator gar (*Lepisosteus spatula*) of the Mississippi valley.

garbanzo: see CHICKPEA.

Garbo, Greta, 1905–90, Swedish-American film actress; b. Sweden as Greta Gustafson. She was noted for her beauty and her dramatic intensity. Her films include *Queen Christina* (1933), *Anna Karenina* (1935), and *Camille* (1936).

García Lorca, Federico [gärthē'ä lôr'kä], 1898–1936, Spanish lyric poet and dramatist. His work reflects the spirit of his native Andalusia and his own passionate response to life. *Gypsy Ballads* (1928) made him the most popular Spanish poet of his generation, while *Lament for the Death of a Bullfighter* (1935) and *The Poet in New York* (1940) evidenced his growing maturity of thought. His plays, notably the tragedies *Blood Wedding* (1933) and *The House of Bernarda Alba* (1936), ensure his continuing international reputation. García Lorca was shot by FRANCO's soldiers at the outbreak of the SPANISH CIVIL WAR.

García Márquez, Gabriel [gärsē'ä mär'kās], 1928–, Colombian writer. His works, generally chronicling the physical and moral collapse of Macondo, an imaginary town, include *Leaf Storm and Other Stories* (1955) and the novels *One Hundred Years of Solitude* (1967), *The Autumn of the Patriarch* (1975), and *Chronicle of a Death Foretold* (tr. 1982). *The General in His Labyrinth* (1989) is a novelized treatment of the last years of Simón Bolívar. García Márquez was awarded the 1982 Nobel Prize in literature.

García Moreno, Gabriel [gärsē'ä mōrā'nō], 1821–75, president of ECUADOR (1861–65, 1869–75). A fervent Roman Catholic, he guaranteed (1862) the Church's independence and granted it control over education. His despotism in crushing liberal opposition led to his assassination.

Garcilaso de la Vega [gärthēlä'sō dā lä vā'gä], 1503?–1536, Spanish lyric poet. He typified the courtly poet-soldier of Spain's GOLDEN AGE. His sonnets, elegies, odes, and eclogues, published after his death in battle, introduced Italian RENAISSANCE poetic forms into Spain.

Garden Grove, city (1990 pop. 143,050), S Calif., a residential suburb of LONG BEACH and LOS ANGELES, on the Santa Ana R.; founded 1877, inc. 1956. The city is in a citrus fruit area. Nearby defense installations provide much employment. The "Crystal Cathedral," an enormous glass church, is there.

gardenia, evergreen shrub or tree (genus *Gardenia*) of the MADDER family, native to the Old World tropics. Gardenias' heavily fragrant and showy blossoms make them popular corsage and greenhouse plants. Most of the cultivated types are varieties of *G. jasminoides*, also called Cape jasmine but unrelated to true JASMINE.

Gardner, Erle Stanley, 1889–1970, American writer; b. Malden, Mass. His many detective novels are noted for their fast action and clever legal devices. His most famous character, Perry Mason, is, like Gardner himself, a lawyer.

Gardner, Isabella Stewart, 1840–1924, American art collector, b. N.Y.C. The wealthy leader of a cultural salon, she sponsored artists and the connoisseur Bernard BERENSON, who advised her in collection. She willed her collection and the building that houses it to Boston as a museum.

Gardner, John Champlin, Jr., 1933–82, American novelist; b. Batavia, N.Y. A scholar of medieval literature, he drew on his academic knowledge and religious concerns to create fiction that is both popular and philosophically interesting. His works include *Grendel* (1971), *The Sunlight Dialogues* (1972), *October Light* (1976), and *Mickelsson's Ghosts* (1982), novels, and *On Moral Fiction* (1978), criticism.

Garfield, James Abram, 1831–81, 20th president of the U.S. (March–Sept., 1881); b. Cuyahoga co., Ohio. He served in the Union army until 1863, when he became a Republican member of the U.S. House of Representatives, and followed his party's radical RECONSTRUCTION program. Elected president in 1880, he declared war on the leading faction of his party by appointing James G. BLAINE secretary of state (passing over the "Stalwarts" of the influential Roscoe CONKLING); won a victory with his appointment for port collector of New York; and began prosecution of frauds in the U.S. postal service. But on July 2, 1881, he was shot by a disappointed office seeker, Charles J. Guiteau. Garfield died Sept. 19 and was succeeded by Vice President Chester A. ARTHUR.

Garibaldi, Giuseppe, 1807–82, Italian patriot and soldier, a leading figure in the RISORGIMENTO; b. France. He fled to South America (1835) after a republican plot failed and fought (1842–46) in the Uruguayan civil war. Returning to Italy, he fought for Sardinia against Austria (1848) and for MAZZINI's Roman republic (1849), then found asylum in the U.S. Returning (1851) to Italy, he renounced his republican views and supported a united Italy under VICTOR EMMANUEL II of Sardinia. In 1860, with Victor Emmanuel's connivance, Garibaldi led 1,000 volunteer "red shirts" in a spectacular conquest of Sicily and Naples. He then relinquished his conquests to Sardinia, and Victor Emmanuel was proclaimed (1861) king of Italy. In 1862 and 1867 he tried unsuccessfully to take Rome, which had remained outside the new kingdom. He was elected (1874) to the Italian parliament.

Garland, Hamlin, 1860–1940, American author; b. near West Salem, Wis. Raised in the Midwest, he wrote of the difficulties of prairie life in tales, e.g., *Main-Travelled Roads* (1891); novels, e.g., *A Little Norsk* (1892); and autobiographical works, e.g., *A Daughter of the Middle Border* (1921; Pulitzer).

Garland, Judy, 1922–69, American singer and film actress; b. Grand Rapids, Mich., as Frances Gumm. Her films include *The Wizard of Oz* (1939), *Meet Me in St. Louis* (1944), and *A Star Is Born* (1954).

Garland, city (1990 pop. 180,650), N Tex., a suburb of DALLAS; inc. 1891. Since World War II it has grown from an agricultural community into a center for electronics research and the production of aerospace equipment.

garlic: see ONION.

Garmo Peak: see COMMUNISM PEAK.

Garneau, François Xavier, 1809–66, French-Canadian historian. His *History of Canada* (3 vol., 1845–48) is a well-written, scholarly work covering the period from the exploration and settling of Canada by the French to the union of the two Canadas in 1841. Garneau may have written the history to disprove Lord Durham's claim that French Canadians were "without history and without a literature."

Garner, Erroll Louis, 1921–77, American jazz pianist and composer; b. Pittsburgh. He wrote about 200 songs, including "Misty," "Dreamy," and "Solitaire." He developed a unique style of piano playing and toured throughout the world from the 1940s through the 1960s.

Garner, John Nance, 1868–1967, vice president of the U.S. (1933–41); b. Red River co., Tex. In Congress from 1902, he became Speaker of the House (1931) and was vice president for Franklin D. ROOSEVELT's first two terms.

garnet, name applied to a group of silicate minerals $(Fe,Mg,Ca,Mn)_3(Al,Fe,Cr)_2(SiO_4)_3$ used chiefly as gems and abrasives. The most common gem varieties are red, but garnets are also yellow, brown, and green. They are found in many types of rock throughout the world.

Garnett, Richard, 1835–1906, English author and distinguished librarian at the British Museum (1851–99). He wrote essays, novels, and poems, and biographies of MILTON, CARLYLE, EMERSON, and COLERIDGE, and discovered previously unknown poems by P.B. SHELLEY. His son, **Edward Garnett,** 1868–1937, was a critic who corresponded with and encouraged many writers. Edward's wife, **Constance (Black) Garnett,** 1862–1946, made important translations from Russian of TOLSTOY, DOSTOYEVSKY, and others. Their son, **David Garnett,** 1892–1981, wrote the imaginative *Lady into Fox* (1923) and other novels.

Garrick, David, 1717–79, English actor, manager, and dramatist, the greatest actor of 18th-cent. England. A pupil of Samuel JOHNSON, he accompanied Johnson to London in 1737. His formal debut (1741) as Richard III made him the idol of London, where his straightforward manner and diction revolutionized acting styles. Noted for his versatility, he played contemporary drama as well as Shakespearean roles; his King Lear was especially praised. As manager (1747–76) of the Drury Lane Theatre, he initiated many reforms in stagecraft.

Garrison, William Lloyd, 1805–79, American abolitionist; b. Newburyport, Mass. He founded the *Liberator* in 1831 and for 35 years campaigned for immediate and complete abolition of slavery. Favoring moral persuasion over violence or political involvement, he helped organize (1833) the American Anti-Slavery Society and was its president (1843–65). He advocated Northern secession from the Union because the Constitution permitted slavery, and he opposed the Civil War until Lincoln issued the EMANCIPATION PROCLAMATION in 1862. Although he was considered the foremost antislavery leader during the 19th cent., evidence indicates that less famous ABOLITIONISTS were more effective.

Garvey, Marcus, 1887–1940, African-American proponent of black nationalism; b. Jamaica. In 1914 he founded the Universal Negro Improvement Association to foster worldwide unity among blacks and establish the greatness of their African heritage. Rejecting any notion of integration in countries where blacks were a minority, he urged a "back to Africa" movement. Garvey's brilliant oratory and his newspaper, *Negro World,* made him the most influential African-American leader of the early 1920s, but his influence declined after his misuse of funds intended to establish an African-American steamship company resulted in a mail fraud conviction. He was jailed (1925) and deported to Jamaica (1927), dying in relative obscurity.

Gary, city (1990 pop. 116,646), NW Ind., on Lake Michigan, near Chicago. Once one of the world's great steel centers, Gary was founded by the U.S. Steel Corp., which bought the land in 1905. Its location midway between western iron ore sources and eastern and southeastern coal areas made it ideal for industry. During the nationwide steel strike of 1919, federal troops occupied the city for several months. In recent years the city has looked for new industries to revitalize its economy.

gas, in physics: see KINETIC-MOLECULAR THEORY OF GASES; STATES OF MATTER.

Gasca, Pedro de la [gäs'kä], c.1485–1567?, Spanish colonial administrator in PERU (1547–50). Sent by Holy Roman Emperor CHARLES V to restore order, he repealed the New Laws of LAS CASAS, which were meant to protect indigenous peoples, and pardoned their violators. He put down (1548) a revolt by Gonzalo PIZARRO and restored the semblance of order in Peru.

Gascony, region, SW France. The sandy, swampy Landes along the ocean, the Pyrenees, and the hilly Armagnac region are the main geographic areas. Fishing, stock raising, wine making, and tourism are the chief industries. Auch is the historic capital. The Vascones, or BASQUES, invaded the area and set up a duchy in 601. In 1154 Gascony, along with AQUITAINE, came under English rule; and France did not recover it completely until the end (1453) of the HUNDRED YEARS WAR. It later passed to Henry of Navarre (later HENRY IV of France) and was united with the royal domain in 1607.

Gaskell, Elizabeth Cleghorn (Stevenson), 1810–65, English author. In addition to her excellent but controversial *Life of Charlotte Brontë* (1857), she is known for her novels about social conditions, e.g., *Mary Barton* (1848), and village life, e.g., *Cranford* (1853) and *Wives and Daughters* (1866).

gas laws, physical laws describing the behavior of a gas (see STATES OF MATTER) under various conditions of volume (V), pressure (P), and absolute, or Kelvin, TEMPERATURE (T). Boyle's, or Mariotte's, gas law states that under constant temperature $PV = k_1$. Charles's, or Gay-Lussac's, law states that under constant pressure $V = k_2T$. A third law states that under constant volume $P = k_3T$. The constants k_1, k_2, and k_3 are dependent on the amount of gas present and, respectively, on the temperature, pressure, and volume of the gas. These three laws can be combined into a single law, or equation of state: $PV = kT$ or $Pv = RT$, in which v is the specific volume equal to V/n, n is the number of moles of the gas, k is a proportionality constant, and R is the universal gas constant, equal to 8.3149×10^3 joules/kg-mole-degree in mks units. These laws are formulated for so-called ideal or perfect gases. Real gases are described more accurately by the van der Waals equation: $(P + a/v^2)(v - b) = RT$, in which a and b are specific constants for each gas.

gasoline, light, volatile fuel oil; called petrol in Britain. A mixture of HYDROCARBONS obtained in the fractional DISTILLATION and "cracking" of PETROLEUM, it is used as a fuel for INTERNAL-COMBUSTION ENGINES, for cooking, and as a solvent. The quality of gasoline used in engines is rated by OCTANE NUMBER. To increase octane rating, additives containing lead were once widely used. Because of the health hazard of lead as an environmental pollutant and the harmful effect it has on pollution-control devices, however, AUTOMOBILE design and gasoline composition were changed. Lead additives are now banned in the U.S. Compounds such as methyl tertiary butyl ether (MTBE), which raises octane ratings and promotes more thorough combustion, and ethanol, used in gasohol, are now added to reduce pollution. Detergents are added to clean fuel injectors and improve engine performance. Alternatives to gasoline as a vehicular fuel, such as NATURAL GAS and electricity from storage batteries, have also been used on a small scale, particularly in urban areas, where distances are shorter and air pollution greater.

gasoline engine: see INTERNAL-COMBUSTION ENGINE.

Gaspar: see WISE MEN OF THE EAST.

Gaspee, British revenue cutter, burned June 10, 1772, at Gaspee Point, Narragansett Bay, R.I. Colonists burned the *Gaspee* in defiance of the enforcement of revenue laws.

Gaspé Peninsula or **Gaspésie,** tongue of land, E Quebec, Canada, 60–90 mi (97–145 km) wide, projecting c.150 mi (240 km) E into the Gulf of St. Lawrence. The coast is famous for its bold headlands and picturesque coastal settlements. The interior is a mountainous wilderness, completely forested, that reaches a high point of 4,160 ft (1,268 m) in the Shickshock Mts.

gastropod, MOLLUSK of the class Gastropoda. It usually has a coiled or spiraled one-piece shell (univalve), although it may be reduced or absent. The head has sensory tentacles and a mouth with a rasplike tongue (radula). The ventral surface of the animal is modified into a large, flattened foot, which, along with other soft body parts, can be withdrawn into the shell; in most cases, the opening is covered by a plate (operculum). Most gastropods are marine, but there are forms that live in fresh water and on land. The class includes the ABALONE, CONCH, SNAIL, SLUG, WHELK, LIMPET, PERIWINKLE, and SEA SLUG.

Gates, Bill (William Henry Gates, 3d), 1955–, American businessman; b. Seattle. At 19 Gates founded (1974) the Microsoft Corp. with Paul Allen. Since 1980, when Microsoft purchased the rights to an existing computer operating system and adapted it for the International Business Machines Corp.'s new PERSONAL COMPUTER, Gates has built the company into one of the world's largest producers of microcomputer software.

William Gates

Gates, Horatio, 1727–1806, American Revolutionary general; b. England. A colonial hero after his successful SARATOGA CAMPAIGN (1777), he commanded Patriot forces in the Carolinas until the disgraceful defeat (1780) at Camden, S.C.

Gates of the Arctic National Park: see NATIONAL PARKS (table).

Gatling, Richard Jordan, 1818–1903, American inventor; b. Winton, N.C. He invented and manufactured agricultural implements but is remembered as the creator of a rapid-firing gun, the precursor of the modern machine gun (see SMALL ARMS). He offered it to the Union army, but it was not accepted for use until 1866, after the Civil War had ended.

GATT, General Agreement on Tariffs and Trade: see UNITED NATIONS (table 3).

Gaudier-Brzeska, Henri [gōdyā'-bərzĕskä'], 1891–1915, French sculptor. The chief exponent of VORTICISM in sculpture, he is known for his draftsmanship, animal figures, and abstracts.

Gaudí i Cornet, Antonio [gaudē' ē kōr'nĕt], 1852–1926, Spanish architect, working mainly in Barcelona. He created startling architectural forms paralleling the development of ART NOUVEAU or MODERNISMO. Many of his buildings resemble sculptural configurations. His use of color and mixed materials is seen in his masterpiece, the Expiatory Church of the Holy Family (1882–1930). He also made many technological innovations.

Gauguin, Paul [gōgăN'], 1848–1903, French painter and woodcut artist; an influential founder of modern art. At 35 he left his career as a stockbroker and devoted himself to painting. Allied with the impressionists (see IMPRESSIONISM), in 1888 he and Émile Bernard proposed a synthetist theory emphasizing flat planes and bright, non-naturalistic color with symbolic or primitive subjects. *The Yellow Christ* (Albright-Knox Gall., Buffalo) is characteristic of this period. In 1891 he went to Tahiti, where he painted some of his finest works and wrote *Noa Noa* (tr. 1947), an autobiographical novel. He returned to France briefly but died in poverty and despair in the South Seas. Gauguin rejected the tradition of Western naturalism, using nature as a starting point from which to abstract figures and symbols. His color harmonies and profound sense of mystery can be seen in such paintings as *The Day of the God* (Art Inst., Chicago), *La Orana Maria* (1891; Metropolitan Mus.), and *By the Sea* (1892; Nat. Gall., Wash., D.C.). He also revived the art of woodcutting and did some fine lithographs and pottery pieces.

Gaul, Lat. *Gallia,* ancient name for the land S and W of the Rhine, W of the Alps, and N of the Pyrenees. The name was extended by the Romans to include N Italy and is derived from its settlers of the 4th and 3d cent. B.C.—invading CELTS, called Gauls by the Romans. Julius CAESAR conquered Gaul in the GALLIC WARS (58–51 B.C.). He is the best ancient source on Gaul, and he has immortalized its three ethnic divisions: Aquitania in the S, Gaul proper (central France), and Belgica in the N. Gaul was rapidly Romanized.

Gaunt, John of: see JOHN OF GAUNT.

Gauss, Carl Friedrich [gous], 1777–1855, German mathematician, physicist, and astronomer; b. Johann Friederich Carl Gauss. Considered the greatest mathematician of his time and the equal of ARCHIMEDES and Isaac NEWTON, Gauss made many discoveries before age twenty. His greatest work was in NUMBER THEORY; his *Disquisitiones Arithmeticae* (completed 1798; pub. 1801) is a masterpiece. Extremely rigorous in his work, Gauss refused to publish any result without a complete proof. Thus, many discoveries were not credited to him and were remade by others later, e.g., the work of János Bolyai and Nikolai LOBACHEVSKY in NON-EUCLIDEAN GEOMETRY, Augustin CAUCHY in complex variable analysis, Carl Jacobi in elliptic functions, and Sir William Rowan HAMILTON in quaternions. Gauss early discovered, independently of Adrien LEGENDRE, the method of least squares. In 1801, when the asteroid Ceres was discovered by the Italian astronomer Giuseppe Piazzi, Gauss calculated its orbit on the basis of only a few accurate observations, and it was found the next year precisely where he had predicted. His *Theoria motus corporum celestium* (1809) treats the calculation of the orbits of planets and comets from observational data. From 1807 until his death, Gauss was director of the astronomical observatory at Göttingen. Geodetic survey work done for the governments of Hanover and Denmark from 1821 led him to an interest in space curves and surfaces, as well as to the invention of the heliotrope, a device to measure distances by means of reflected sunlight. Gauss's collaboration with the German physicist Wilhelm Weber in research on electric and magnetic phenomena led to his invention, in 1833, of the electric telegraph.

Gautier, Théophile, 1811–72, French poet, novelist, and critic and exponent of art for art's sake. His finely crafted poems, notably *Enamels and Cameos* (1852), foreshadowed the revolt against ROMANTICISM by the PARNASSIANS and SYMBOLISTS.

gavotte, originally a peasant DANCE of the Gavots, in upper Dauphiné, France. A circle dance with lively, skipping steps, it was used by LULLY in court ballets and by COUPERIN and J.S. BACH in their keyboard suites.

Gay, John, 1685–1732, English playwright and poet, best known for *The Beggar's Opera* (1728), about thieves and prostitutes, and satirizing society and then-fashionable Italian opera. Its sequel, *Polly* (1729), was suppressed by the government. Gay's verse appeared in *Fables* (1727, 1738).

Gay-Lussac, Joseph Louis, 1778–1850, French chemist and physicist. He and the French chemist Louis Jacques Thénard were the first to isolate BORON. Gay-Lussac discovered (1802) independently that at constant pressure the volume of an enclosed gas is directly proportional to its temperature, a law known as Charles's law or as Gay-Lussac's law (see GAS LAWS). He was the first to formulate (c.1808) the law of combining volumes, which states that gases combine by volume in simple multiple proportion.

Gay-Lussac's law: see GAS LAWS.

gay rights movement, organized efforts to end the criminalization of homosexuality and protect the CIVIL RIGHTS of homosexuals. The modern gay rights movement in the U.S. grew out of the Stonewall riot (June 1969) in New York City, which resulted from a police raid on a gay bar. A number of groups formed to work for the repeal of laws prohibiting consensual homosexual conduct; for legislation barring discrimination against gays in housing and employment; and for greater acceptance of homosexuals among the rest of the population. By the early 1990s 26 states had repealed their antisodomy laws. Laws protecting homosexuals from discrimination also had been enacted, but largely at the local level; by 1993 only eight states had such laws. Opposition to such laws, particularly from conservative religious groups, has often been strong, and opponents have often gained repeal of gay rights measures. In 1993 the Defense Dept., at Pres. Clinton's order, changed the ban on homosexuals in the military to a ban on homosexual activity. See also HOMOSEXUALITY.

Gaza Strip, coastal region of the Middle East (1992 est. pop. 681,000), c.140 sq mi (370 sq km), on the Mediterranean Sea, adjoining Egypt and Israel. Densely populated and impoverished, it is mainly inhabited by Palestinian refugees; there is also a small minority of Israeli settlers. The strip was part of the British mandate for PALESTINE from 1917 to 1948, passed to Egyptian control in 1949, and has been occupied by Israel since the 1967 ARAB-ISRAELI WAR. Autonomy for the region, promised by the CAMP DAVID ACCORDS (1978), has yet to be granted. The Palestinian uprising (*intifada*) began in Gaza in 1987. A 1993 accord between Israel and the PALESTINE LIBERATION ORGANIZATION called for limited self-rule in the area by mid-1994.

gazelle, delicate, graceful ANTELOPE (genus *Gazella*) inhabiting arid, open country, usually in Africa. Standing 2 to 3 ft (60 to 90 cm) high at the shoulder, the fawn-colored gazelle often has heavily ringed horns that curve back and inward. Gazelles are powerful jumpers and very swift. Closely related is the reddish-brown **impala** (*Aepyceros melampus*), the most powerful jumper of all antelopes, able to leap 10 ft (3 m) into the air and travel 30 ft (9 m) in a single bound.

Gd, chemical symbol of the element GADOLINIUM.

Gdańsk or **Danzig,** city (1989 est. pop. 461,000), N Poland, on a branch of the Vistula R. and on the Gulf of Gdańsk. It is a major port on the BALTIC SEA, with some of the world's largest shipyards. Its other industries include mechanical engineering, machine building, chemicals and metallurgy. An old Slavic settlement, it was the capital of Pomerelia (see POMERANIA) from the 10th cent. and a member of the HANSEATIC LEAGUE from the 13th cent. The city was later ruled by Poland and Prussia and in 1919 was made a free city. HITLER's demand (1939) for Danzig's return to Germany and his subsequent invasion of Poland began WORLD WAR II. The city was restored to Poland in 1945. In both 1970 and 1980 workers' strikes in Gdańsk spread to other cities, causing major political changes in Poland.

GDP, gross domestic product. See under GROSS NATIONAL PRODUCT.

Ge, chemical symbol of the element GERMANIUM.

gear, toothed wheel, cylinder, or cone, usually mounted on a shaft, that transmits motion from one part of a machine to another. When the teeth of two gears are meshed, the turning of one shaft will cause the other shaft to rotate. By meshing two gears of different diameters, a variation in both speed and torque is obtained.

Geddes, Norman Bel, 1893–1958, American designer; b. Adrian, Mich., as Norman Melancton Geddes. He was known for imaginative designs for the New York City stage, notably *The Miracle* (1924), and for numerous industrial products. His daughter, **Barbara Bel Geddes,** 1922–, b. N.Y.C., is an actress. She appeared in the play *Cat on a Hot Tin Roof* (1955), the film *Vertigo* (1959), and was a regular (1978–84, 1985–90) on the television series *Dallas.*

Geelong, city (1991 pop. 152,800), Victoria, SE Australia, on an inlet of Port Phillip Bay, near Melbourne. One of Australia's chief ports and industrial centers, its manufactures include refined oil, automobiles, fertilizer, and processed meat.

Gehrig, Lou(is), 1903–41, American baseball player; b. N.Y.C. As first baseman (1925–39) for the New York Yankees, he had a lifetime batting average of .340, hit 493 home runs, and batted .361 in seven World Series. Known as the "Iron Horse," he set a record by playing in 2,130 consecutive league games. His career was ended by a rare disease, AMYOTROPHIC LATERAL SCLEROSIS, which took his life at 37.

Geiger counter: see PARTICLE DETECTOR.

Geisel, Theodor Seuss: see SEUSS, DR.

gelatin or **animal jelly,** foodstuff obtained from connective tissue (found in hoofs, bones, tendons, ligaments, and cartilage) of vertebrate animals by the action of boiling water or dilute acid. It is largely composed of the protein collagen. Pure gelatin is brittle, transparent, colorless, tasteless, and odorless. It dissolves in hot water and congeals when cooled. Gelatin is widely used to give food a proper consistency, in photographic emulsions, and as a coating for pills. Vegetable gelatin, or AGAR, is made from seaweed.

Gelée, Claude: see CLAUDE LORRAIN.

Gell-Mann, Murray, 1929–, American theoretical physicist; b. N.Y.C. In 1953 he and, independently, the Japanese team of T. Nakano and Kazuhiko Nishijima proposed the concept of "strangeness" to account for certain particle-decay patterns. In 1961 Gell-Mann and Yuval Ne'eman independently introduced the "eightfold way," or SU(3) symmetry, a tablelike ordering of all subatomic particles. The 1964 discovery of the omega-minus particle, which filled a gap in this ordering, brought the theory wide acceptance and led to Gell-Mann's being awarded the 1969 Nobel Prize for physics. In 1963 Gell-Mann and George Zweig independently postulated the existence of the QUARK, an even more fundamental particle with a fractional electric charge.

Gemara: see TALMUD.

Gemayel, Amin, 1942–, president of LEBANON (1982–88). A lawyer and a member of the Christian Phalange party, he served in the Lebanese parliament from 1970. In 1982, after the assassination of his brother, President-elect Bashir Gemayel, he was elected president. He had no real authority and accomplished little. With parliament deadlocked (1988) over his successor, Gemayel appointed Gen. Michel Aoun interim president, an act that led to two years of warfare and political instability.

Gemini, Project: see SPACE EXPLORATION, table.

gene, the unit by which inheritable characteristics are transmitted to succeeding generations in all living organisms. Genes are contained by, and arranged along the length of, the CHROMOSOME. The gene is composed of deoxyribonucleic acid (see DNA) arranged in a definite sequence and interspersed with sequences of "nonsense" DNA, called introns, that have no known function. Each chromosome of each species has a definite number and arrangement of genes, which govern both the structure and metabolic functions of the cells, and thus of the entire organism. A genome is the sum total of the genes contained in an organism's full set of chromosomes. They provide a blueprint for the synthesis of enzymes and other proteins and specify when these substances are to be made. Alteration of the number or arrangement of the genes can result in MUTATION, a change in the inheritable traits. See also GENETIC ENGINEERING; GENETICS; HUMAN GENOME PROJECT.

General Agreement on Tariffs and Trade (GATT): see UNITED NATIONS (table 3).

General Assembly: see UNITED NATIONS (table 2).

generator, electrical device used to convert mechanical energy to electrical energy. It operates on the principle of electromagnetic INDUCTION. The generator moves a conductor through a magnetic field and directs the current produced by the induced voltage to an external circuit. In the simplest generator the conductor is an open coil of wire rotating between the poles of a permanent magnet. During a single rotation, one side of the coil passes through the magnetic field, first in one direction and then in the other, so that the induced current is alternating current (AC), moving first in one direction, then in the other. Each end of the coil is attached to a separate metal slip ring that rotates with the coil. Brushes resting on the slip ring pass the current to the external circuit. To obtain direct current (DC), i.e., current that flows in only one direction, a commutator is used in place of slip rings. The commutator is a single slip ring split into left and right halves that are insulated from each other and attracted to opposite ends of the coil. Current leaves the generator through the brushes in only one direction and pulsates from no flow to maximum flow and back again. In practice, generators have many coils and several magnets. The whole assembly carrying the coils is called the armature, or rotor; the stationary parts constitute the stator. Except for magnetos, which use permanent magnets, AC and DC generators use electromagnets. AC generators are often called alternators.

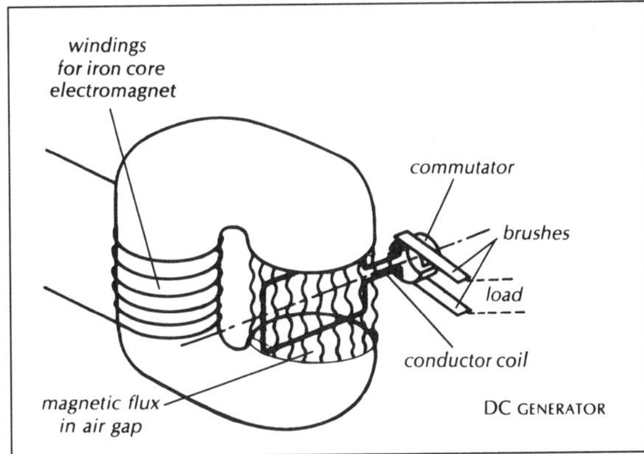

Generator: The rotation of the conducting coil of wire in a magnetic field causes a current to be induced in the coil. In the DC generator, a split-ring commutator changes the direction of the current with each half rotation, resulting in a pulsing direct current.

Genesis, first book of the OLD TESTAMENT and of the PENTATEUCH, ascribed by tradition to MOSES. It tells of the origin of the world and of humans (1–11), including the stories of humanity's disobedience and fall, CAIN and ABEL, and NOAH; the career of God's special servant ABRAHAM (12–24), including the story of Hagar and ISHMAEL, the sacrifice of ISAAC, and Abraham's journey to CANAAN and God's promises to him; the career of Isaac (25–26); and the life of JACOB, called Israel (27–50), with the story of his son JOSEPH and the migration of the family to Egypt. Sources of Genesis include Babylonian and Egyptian folklore. Controversy over its interpretation and literary history has been extensive.

gene splicing: see GENETIC ENGINEERING.

Genet, Edmond Charles Édouard [zhənā'], 1763–1834, French Revolutionary minister to the U.S. (1793–94), known as Citizen Genet. His plans to raise troops against Spanish FLORIDA and to commission privateers against Britain were not approved by Pres. WASHINGTON, and the U.S. demanded (1793) his recall. Genet remained in the U.S. rather than face a changed political situation in France.

Genet, Jean, 1910–86, French dramatist. While in prison, he attracted attention with his autobiographical narratives about homosexuality and crime, e.g., *Our Lady of the Flowers* (1943). He was pardoned (1948) from a sentence of life imprisonment through the intervention of French literary figures. His plays *The Balcony* (1956), *The Blacks* (1958), and *The Screens* (1961) are classic examples of the theater of the absurd.

gene therapy, the use of GENES and the techniques of GENETIC ENGINEERING in the treatment of a genetic disorder or chronic disease. There are many techniques of gene therapy, most of them still in experimental stages. One technique for treating hereditary problems involves removing cells from a patient, fortifying them with healthy copies of the defective gene, and reinjecting the fortified cells into the patient. Another involves inserting a gene into an inactivated or nonvirulent virus and using the virus's infective capabilities to carry the desired gene into the patient's cells. A LIPOSOME, a tiny fat-encased pouch that can traverse cell membranes, is also sometimes used to transport a gene into a cell. Once inserted into body cells, the gene may produce an essential chemical that the patient's body cannot, remove or render harmless a substance or gene that is causing or contributing to disease (see ANTISENSE), or expose certain cells, especially cancerous cells, to attack by conventional drugs. Like drugs, gene therapy techniques must be approved by the federal government in the U.S.

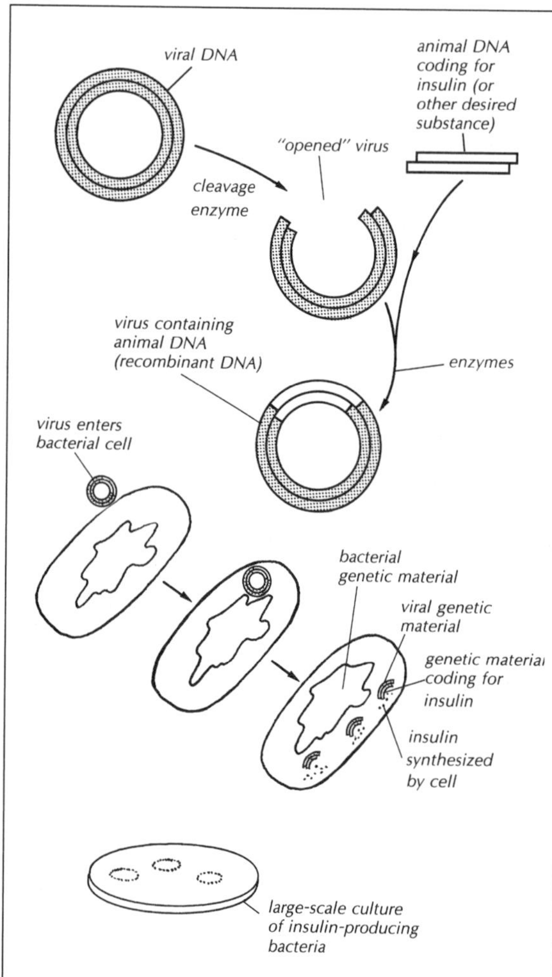

Genetic engineering: Gene-splicing techniques

genetic engineering, group of research techniques that manipulate the DNA (genetic material) of cells in order to change hereditary traits or produce biological products. The techniques include the use of hybridomas (hybrids of rapidly multiplying cancer cells and cells that make small amounts of a desired antibody) to make MONOCLONAL ANTIBODIES, gene splicing or recombinant DNA technique (in which the DNA of a desired gene is inserted into the DNA of a bacterium, which then reproduces itself, yielding more of the desired gene), and POLYMERASE CHAIN REACTION (which makes perfect copies of DNA fragments). Genetically engineered products include bacteria designed to efficiently break down oil slicks and industrial waste products, drugs (growth hormone, human insulin, interferon), plants that are resistant to diseases and insects, and, in forensics, DNA FINGERPRINTING techniques. Because genetic engineering involves techniques used to obtain patents on human genes and to create patentable living organisms, it has raised many legal and ethical issues. Questions have also been raised about the safety of releasing into the environment genetically altered organisms that might disrupt ecosystems.

genetics, scientific study of heredity. The science arose in 1900, with rediscovery of MENDEL's work on traits that are inherited as if each were a separate, independent unit. Geneticists probing the physical basis of the transmission of inherited characteristics study the unit of inheritance, the GENE; the various forms of a gene that governs a trait (alleles); the array of genes along a CHROMOSOME; and the set of genes characteristic of each species (the genome). Since the discovery (1953) of the structure of DNA, work on NUCLEIC ACIDS has begun to explain how genes determine life processes by directing the synthesis of proteins. It has also explained MUTATION as alterations in gene or chromosome structure. See also GENETIC ENGINEERING; HUMAN GENOME PROJECT.

genetic screening, testing for genetic disorders. Most commonly, prospective parents or a fetus are tested when a specific genetic disorder is suspected (e.g., TAY-SACHS DISEASE or SICKLE-CELL ANEMIA). Genetic screening begins with a complete medical history of both parents. If the parents decide to conceive or have already conceived, diagnostic tests, such as CHORIONIC VILLUS SAMPLING and AMNIOCENTESIS, can be performed on the fetus to detect various genetic disorders. In the case of a positive finding, the parents can elect to abort the fetus. As researchers identify more genetic markers for diseases and develop blood tests for them, concern has arisen over the use of such tests to deny people health and life insurance, employment, and the like. A 1993 National Academy of Sciences report called for the establishment of ethical guidelines on the use of genetic screening.

Geneva, city (1990 pop. 165,404), capital of Geneva canton, SW Switzerland, on the Lake of Geneva, divided by the Rhône R. A cultural, financial, and administrative center, it manufactures watches, jewelry, and precision instruments. The city was settled by the Celts and later held by the Romans. In the 16th cent. it was the focal point of the Reformation under John CALVIN; by the 18th cent. it had become an intellectual center, the residence of J.J. ROUSSEAU and others. Geneva joined (1815) the Swiss Confederation. The LEAGUE OF NATIONS and the GENEVA CONFERENCES met there. It is the seat of such bodies as the World Health Organization and the International Red Cross.

Geneva Conference. **1** International conference held Apr.–July 1954 to bring peace to KOREA and INDOCHINA. The chief participants were the U.S., the USSR, Great Britain, France, China, the two Koreas, and various factions from Indochina. No permanent agreement on Korea resulted, but three agreements were reached on Indochina (see VIETNAM; VIETNAM WAR). **2** So-called summit conference, held in July 1955, attended by the leaders of the U.S., the USSR, Britain, and France. A wide agenda of issues was discussed (e.g., disarmament, unification of Germany, increased cultural and economic ties). Although no substantive agreements resulted, the conference ended on a note of optimism and is regarded as a major step in the ending of the COLD WAR. **3** Conference, beginning Oct. 1958, attended by the U.S., the USSR, and Britain; its purpose was to reach an accord on the banning of nuclear testing. Since then, most international meetings at Geneva have been concerned with the general problem of nuclear arms. See DISARMAMENT, NUCLEAR.

Geneva Conventions, series of treaties signed (1864–1949) in Geneva, Switzerland, providing for humane treatment of combatants and civilians in wartime. The first convention, signed by 16 nations, covered the protection of sick and wounded soldiers and medical personnel and facilities. Later conventions extended

(1906) the first to naval warfare and covered (1929) the treatment of prisoners of war. As a result of World War II, particularly of the conduct of Germany and Japan, four conventions were adopted in 1949 to strengthen and codify earlier treaties and safeguard civilians.

Genghis Khan: see JENGHIZ KHAN.

genie: see JINNI.

Gennesaret: see Galilee, Sea of, under GALILEE.

Genoa, city (1990 pop. 706,754), capital of Liguria, NW Italy, on the Italian RIVIERA. Italy's chief port, it handles heavy passenger and freight traffic. Iron and steel, chemicals, oil refineries, and shipyards long led the economy, but the service sector is increasingly important. It became (10th cent.) a free commune and its maritime power grew; rivalry with Pisa ended (1284) in naval victory. In decline, it fell to many, including Napoleon (1805–14). The medieval Cathedral of San Lorenzo and the doges' palace are notable.

Gentile da Fabriano [dä fäbrēä'nō], c.1370–1427, Italian painter, a foremost exponent of the international Gothic style. His elegant, lavishly gilt Strozzi altarpiece (Uffizi) exhibits his jewellike colors and courtly style. He worked throughout Italy. His later paintings reflect Florentine realism, e.g., *John the Baptist* (Lateran Basilica, Rome).

Gentileschi, Orazio [jäntēlĕ'skē], c.1562–1647, Tuscan painter. Influenced by CARAVAGGIO, he developed a cooler, more lyrical style. In 1626 he settled in England, at the invitation of CHARLES I. His principal works include *The Annunciation* (San Siro, Genoa) and *Flight into Egypt* (Louvre). His daughter, **Artemisia Gentileschi,** c.1597–c.1651, was known for her spirited execution, e.g., *Judith and Holofernes* (Uffizi) and *Mary Magdalen* (Pitti Gall., Florence).

gentlemen's agreement, in U.S. history, an agreement between the U.S. and Japan in 1907 that Japan should stop the emigration of its laborers to the U.S. and that the U.S. should stop discrimination against the Japanese. This agreement was ended in 1924 by the act of Congress excluding immigration from Japan, just as immigration from China had been previously excluded.

geocentric system: see PTOLEMAIC SYSTEM.

geochemistry, study of the chemistry of the earth, especially the study of the absolute and relative abundances of the elements and their distribution and movement. Such studies have provided insights into the evolution of the oceans and atmosphere, the ages of rocks, the chemical evolution of life, and, more recently, the effects of the massive introduction of pollutants into the environment.

geodesy or **geodetic surveying,** subdivision of GEOPHYSICS that determines the earth's size and shape, the position of points on the earth's surface, and the dimensions of areas so large that the curvature of the earth must be taken into account. In a process called triangulation, a base line between two points, many miles apart, is measured, and a third point is determined by the angle it makes with each end of the base line. Triangulation is now increasingly done using signals from geodetic satellites in space.

Geoffrey IV, known as **Geoffrey Plantagenet,** 1113–51, count of Anjou (1129–51). He married (1128) MATILDA, daughter of HENRY I of England. On Henry's death (1135) he claimed and conquered (1144) Normandy in his wife's name. After 1139 Matilda tried to conquer England from her cousin King STEPHEN. Her son by Geoffrey became HENRY II of England. In 1147 Geoffrey went on a crusade with LOUIS VII of France.

Geoffrey of Monmouth, c.1100–1154, English author. His *Historia Regum Britanniae* (c.1135), a supposed chronicle of the kings of Britain, is a major source of ARTHURIAN LEGEND, giving the first coherent account of Arthur.

Geoffroy Saint-Hilaire, Étienne [zhôfrwä' săNtēler'], 1772–1844, French zoologist. He was professor (1793–1840) at the Museum of Natural History in Paris and a member of Napoleon's scientific staff in Egypt. His theory that all animals conform to a single plan of structure was strongly opposed by the naturalist Georges CUVIER, and they held a widely publicized debate in 1830.

geologic era, major unit of geologic time. For the purpose of dating rock formations and the fossils contained within them, the earth's history has been divided into eras, which are further subdivided into periods and, in some cases, epochs (see table).

geology, science of the EARTH's history, composition, and structure. Branches include mineralogy (see MINERAL), PETROLOGY, geomorphology (the origin of landforms and their modification by dynamic processes), GEOCHEMISTRY, GEOPHYSICS, sedimentation, structural geology, economic geology, and engineering geology. Historical geology includes stratigraphy (the interrelationships of layered ROCKS) and paleontology (the study of FOSSILS). Geological observations have been made since ancient times, but modern geology began in the 18th cent., notably with James HUTTON's doctrine of UNIFORMITARIANISM, which, in its opposition to CATASTROPHISM, laid the groundwork for much of modern geological science. The systematic survey in the mid-20th cent. of the OCEAN floors brought radical changes in concepts of crustal evolution (see PLATE TECTONICS).

geometric progression: see PROGRESSION.

geometry, branch of MATHEMATICS concerned with the properties of and relationships between points, lines, planes, figures, solids, and surfaces. Elementary EUCLIDEAN GEOMETRY of two and three dimensions (plane and solid geometry) is based largely on EUCLID's *Elements* (c.300 B.C.), a systematic presentation of the geometry of its time. Although Euclid's basic assumptions have been judged insufficiently rigorous by David HILBERT and others, his axiomatic method of proof has been adopted throughout mathematics and in other fields as well. In the 17th cent., René DESCARTES invented CARTESIAN COORDINATES to express geometric relations in algebraic form; he thus founded ANALYTIC GEOMETRY, from which developed algebraic geometry, concerned with geometrical objects defined by algebraic relations between their coordinates. Other branches of geometry include descriptive geometry, which is concerned with the two-dimensional representation of three-dimensional objects; differential geometry, in which the concepts of the CALCULUS are applied to curves, surfaces, and other geometrical entities; projective geometry, which is concerned with those properties of geometrical figures that remain unchanged under projection, e.g., from one plane to another; and NON-EUCLIDEAN GEOMETRY. TOPOLOGY, perhaps the most general type of geometry, is often considered a separate branch of mathematics.

geomorphology: see GEOLOGY.

geophysics, study of the structure, composition, and dynamic changes of the EARTH and its ATMOSPHERE, based on the principles of physics. Applied geophysics uses seismic, electrical, gravimetric, magnetic, and radiometric techniques for geological exploration and prospecting.

geopolitics, method of political analysis stressing the importance of geographical factors (e.g., natural boundaries and access to waterways) in determining national interests and international relations. The term received wide attention through the works of the German geographer Karl Haushofer, who popularized H.J. Mackinder's theory of a Eurasian "heartland" central to world dominance. The NAZIS used Haushofer's ideas to justify their expansion in central Europe. Geopolitical considerations have been used to justify other expansionist policies, such as MANIFEST DESTINY.

George, Saint, 4th cent.?, patron of England. Possibly a soldier in the Roman army who died a martyr in Asia Minor, he was adopted by England in the Middle Ages. In legend he is the slayer of a dragon. Feast: Apr. 23.

George, kings of Great Britain and Ireland. **George I** (George Louis), 1660–1727 (r.1714–27), was the great-grandson of JAMES I. He was the first British sovereign of the house of HANOVER under the Act of SETTLEMENT. His dual role as elector of Hanover and king of England, his German manners, and his inability to speak English made him unpopular. His indifference to government led to the first real cabinet and the rise of the WHIGS to power. In 1718 the QUADRUPLE ALLIANCE guaranteed the Hanoverian succession. His son, **George II** (George Augustus), 1683–1760 (r.1727–60), was more active in government than his father. In the War of the AUSTRIAN SUCCESSION, he personally led his troops in battle, the last British monarch to do so. His wife, Caroline of Ansbach, furthered the dominancy of Robert WALPOLE. During his reign the Whigs united behind the policy of William PITT (the Elder) in the SEVEN YEARS WAR. His grandson, **George III,** 1738–1820 (r.1760–1820), ended the long Whig control of government by securing Pitt's resignation in 1761. George wanted to rule personally, and he found an amenable minister (1770–82) in Lord NORTH, whose policy of

GEOLOGIC ERAS		
Time	*Geologic Developments*	*Life Forms*
Azoic Time. From the formation of the earth.		
4,550-3,800 million years ago	Crust and oceans forming. Lack of ATMOSPHERE allows bombardment.	No life forms.
Precambrian Time. Traditionally divided into two eras, Archeozoic and Proterozoic.		
3,800-700 million years ago	Permanent crust formed, with vast deposits of metallic minerals. Metamorphic rocks in massive formations, e.g., CANADIAN SHIELD. Erosion, sedimentation begin.	Earliest life marine (blue-green ALGAE). PHOTOSYNTHESIS begins to develop oxygen-rich atmosphere. Wormlike forms possible. First recognizable fossils.
Paleozoic Era. Age of INVERTEBRATES and marine forms. Six periods.		
Cambrian: 700-500 million years ago	Sedimentary rock (sandstone, shale, limestone, conglomerate) forms in shallow seas over continents. Climate generally mild, but North America tropical.	First FOSSILS of animals with hard parts, e.g., shells, skeletons, All fauna marine; every invertebrate phylum represented. Animal ability to secrete CALCIUM leads to shell, skeleton formation. TRILOBITE dominant.
Ordovician: 500-435 million years ago	North America, Europe, Africa moving together (see PLATE TECTONICS; CONTINENTAL DRIFT). Seas at greatest extent over North America. Rocks chiefly sedimentary.	Marine ecosystems develop; fossil evidence of deepwater life forms. MOLLUSKS, some CORALS. Fishlike VERTEBRATES appear.
Silurian: 435-395 million years ago	Shallow flooding deposits sediments. Later withdrawal of water leaves oxidized "red beds," salt deposits.	Earliest land plants. In seas, coral reefs, ARTHROPODS, CRINOIDS. Fish develop first vertebrate jaw. SHARKS appear.
Devonian: 395-345 million years ago	Continents drier at beginning. Europe, North America collide, causing mountain building (orogeny). South pole in central Africa.	Fish dominant: armored fish, lungfish. Toward end of period first land animals, AMPHIBIANS. Plant life, including lowland forests of giant PSILOPHYTA plants, highly developed, uniform over planet.
Carboniferous: 345-280 million years ago	Climate warm, moist; COAL-forming sediments laid down in vast swamps. Severe continental collisions cause orogeny, e.g., in URALS.	FERNS, fernlike trees, primitive CONIFERS among flora in swamps, INSECTS, e.g., cockroaches, flourish. First REPTILES appear toward end.
Permian: 280-230 million years ago	Land, e.g., E North America, rising. Atmosphere, oceans cooler. Glaciation in southern hemisphere. General aridity. Appalachians thrust up at end.	Insects evolve toward modern types. Reptiles flourish. Ferns, conifers persist in cool air.
Mesozoic Era. Age of reptiles. Three periods.		
Triassic: 230-195 million years ago	Climate warming; semiarid to arid. Continental plates, joined c.200 million years ago in supercontinent Pangaea, begin to break into continents; FAULTS, tilting widespread.	Fewer species, higher populations. Ammonites, clams, snails present. First DINOSAURS. First MAMMALS may have evolved.
Jurassic: 195-140 million years ago	North America, Africa separate; ocean basins open. Erosion reduces Appalachians. Plate subduction (Pacific under North American) causes folding, orogeny in W North America.	Climate warmer than present. CYCADS appear. GINKGOES, HORSETAILS among flora. Reptiles dominant on land, in sea and air. Archaeopteryx, first BIRD, appears. First mammal fossils.
Cretaceous: 140-65 million years ago	Extensive submergence of continents leaves overlapping marine rocks. Chalk deposits. South America, Africa separate; North Atlantic widening. Cycles of orogeny.	Dinosaurs, large reptiles climax, then disappear. Snakes, lizards appear. Revolution in plants: flowering plants (ANGIOSPERMS); modern trees. Flora uniformity that lasts into Eocene.

coercion led to the AMERICAN REVOLUTION. The notable TORY ministry of the younger William PITT (1783–1801) saw the end of royal attempts to control the ministry. George III's reign witnessed a great expansion of empire and trade, the beginning of the INDUSTRIAL REVOLUTION, and a flowering of arts and letters. The king's insanity led to the regency (1811) of his son **George IV,** 1762–1830 (r.1820–30). Ruling through Tory ministers, he was hated for his extravagance and dissolute habits. He aroused particular hostility when he attempted (1820) to divorce his long-estranged wife, CAROLINE OF BRUNSWICK. He was succeeded by his brother, WILLIAM IV. **George V** (George Frederick Ernest Albert), 1865–1936 (r.1910–36), was the second son of EDWARD VII. He was always interested in the affairs of the British empire and in 1911 traveled to India. During WORLD WAR I (1917) he gave up all his German titles and changed the name of the royal house from Saxe-Coburg-Gotha to WINDSOR. His second son, **George VI** (Albert Frederick Arthur George), 1895–1952, king of Great Britain and Northern Ireland (r.1936–52), became king on the abdication of his brother, EDWARD VIII. During WORLD WAR II he worked to keep up British morale by visiting bombed areas, war plants, and theaters of war. He and his wife, ELIZABETH, had two daughters: ELIZABETH II and Princess MARGARET. Like his father, he was held in deep affection by his people.

George, kings of the Hellenes (Greece). **George I,** 1845–1913 (r.1863–1913), was the second son of Christian IX of Denmark and was elected king of Greece after the deposition (1862) of OTTO I. He introduced (1864) a democratic constitution and expanded the Greek domain. He was assassinated. **George II,** 1890–1947 (r.1922–23, 1935–47), did not succeed his father, CONSTANTINE I, but was passed over (1917) because of his pro-German sympathies. The crown fell to his younger brother ALEXANDER. In 1922

GEOLOGIC ERAS *(Continued)*

Time	*Geologic Developments*	*Life Forms*
Cenozoic Era. Age of mammals, modern seed plants. Traditionally divided into two periods, Tertiary (Paleocene/Eocene, Oligocene, Miocene, and Pliocene epochs) and Quaternary (Pleistocene and Holocene epochs).		
Paleocene/Eocene: 65-37 million years ago	Seas withdraw; Europe emergent. Volcanism forms Rockies, other ranges. Erosion fills basins, laying BAUXITE deposits in W North America. Greenland, North America split.	Most common modern plants present. Modern birds. Early horses, pigs, rodents, whales. Number of PRIMATE types greatly increases. Hardwoods, redwoods in W North America. Climate warm, humid.
Oligocene: 37-23 million years ago	North America largely dry; red bed sedimentation; erosion in Rockies. African, European plates collide, causing Alpine orogeny. Arabia, Africa split at Red Sea rift. California collides with mid-Pacific ridge.	Archaic mammals disappearing. Modern horses, pigs, true CARNIVORES, rhinoceroses, elephants begin to appear. Cats, dogs evolving. Modern grasses.
Miocene: 23-5 million years ago	Coastal submergence; volcanism raises CASCADES, western North American plateaus. Himalayas, Alps, Andes, built up. South America, Antarctica separate; cold transantarctic current isolates southern continent.	Climate cooler; forests reduced, grassy plains increase. Mammals include hyena, bear, seal, raccoon. Giant ape widespread. Giant hog develops, then disappears.
Pliocene: 5-1.8 million years ago	Volcanism creates isthmus between North and South America. Outlines of North America roughly modern. Polar, Alpine ice caps sizable. Uplifting, tilting in W North America continues.	Cooler, drier climate. Life forms begin to take on modern appearance. Climax, maybe initial decline, of mammals. Manlike apes. Earliest human artifacts, OLDUVAI GORGE skeletal finds from this epoch.
Pleistocene: 1.8 million-10,000 years ago	Great age of GLACIERS. Polar, Alpine ice advances in 4 or 5 separate glacial periods. Glacial DRIFT widespread. Land forms altered; lakes created by ice retreats.	Extinction of mammals, including mastodon, mammoth, sabertooth carnivores. Rise of man (*Homo sapiens*) c.100,000 years ago; Cromagnon c.35,000 years ago. Horse, camel disappear from Americas. See also STONE AGE.
Holocene or Recent: 10,000 years ago to present	Glaciers retreat. Climate warmer; DESERTS form in some areas. Many scientists argue that Holocene is only another interglacial episode of the Pleistocene epoch.	Human civilization; mankind begins to affect climate, geology. Extinction of other species continues.

George did become king, but hostility towards the dynasty forced him into exile in 1923 and Greece was declared a republic. He was restored in 1935 and instituted a dictatorship under John Metaxas. George was in exile during World War II, and his return to Greece in 1946 failed to halt the civil war then raging. He was succeeded by his brother PAUL.

George, David Lloyd: see LLOYD GEORGE, DAVID.

George, Henry, 1839–97, American economist, founder of the single-tax movement; b. Philadelphia. His own poverty and his observation of avarice as a newspaperman bolstered his reformist ideas. Believing that the great contrast between poverty and wealth lay in the fact that the rental of land and the unearned increase in land values profited only a few individuals, not the community, George proposed a single tax on land to meet all costs of government. His theories, published in *Progress and Poverty* (1879), have influenced tax legislation in many countries.

George, Stefan [gāôrg'ə], 1868–1933, German poet. He was influenced poetically by Greek classical forms and the French SYMBOLISTS and intellectually by NIETZSCHE. His esoteric, pure verse appeared in such volumes as *Algabal* (1892), *Book of the Shepherds* (1895), *The Soul's Year* (1897), and *The Seventh Ring* (1907). George's aesthetic ideal called for a controlled humanism. He devoted himself to the purifying of German language and culture and had great influence on younger poets through his verse and through *Blätter für die Kunst* (founded 1892), the literary organ of his circle.

Georgetown, city (1985 est. pop. 75,000), N Guyana, capital of Guyana, on the Atlantic Ocean at the mouth of the Demerara R. Guyana's largest city, it exports bauxite and other products of the interior. Settled in the 1600s by the Dutch, who called it Stabroek, it was taken and renamed by the British in 1812. It still has canals and other Dutch features.

Georgia, Georgian *Sakartvelo,* officially Republic of Georgia, republic (1992 est. pop. 5,571,000), c.26,900 sq mi (69,700 sq km), SW Asia, in W Transcaucasia; formerly a constituent republic of the USSR. It borders the Black Sea (W); Azerbaijan (E); Turkey and Armenia (S); and Russia (N). The capital is TBILISI. A mountainous country rich in minerals and coal, Georgia produces many manufactures, particularly iron and steel, machinery, and chemicals. Agricultural products include tea, citrus fruits, and tobacco. The BLACK SEA coast is a popular resort area. In addition to the Georgian majority, which comprises about 70% of the population, there are

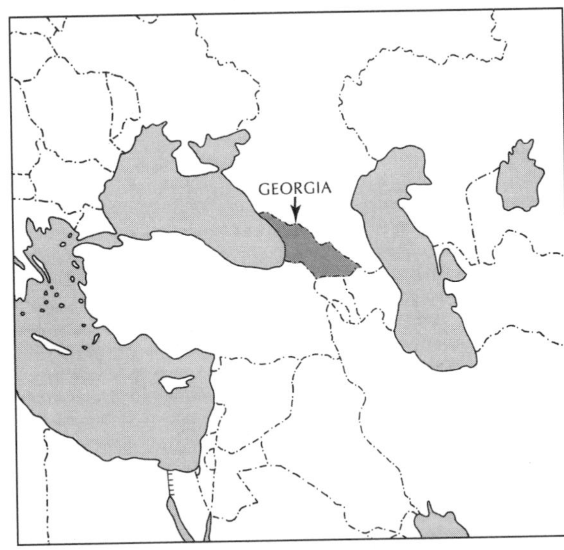

Armenian, Russian, Ossetian, and other minorities. Georgian, a Caucasian language, and Russian are spoken. Most Georgians are members of the Eastern Orthodox church.

History. The kingdom of Georgia, dating from the 4th cent. B.C., reached its height in the 12th and 13th cent. A.D. In 1555 W Georgia fell to Turkey and E Georgia to Persia. Under Russian sway after 1783, Georgia was briefly independent (1918–21). In 1991 a nationalist-dominated parliament declared Georgia independent from the USSR. Pres. Zviad Gamsakhurdia was subsequently accused of dictatorial rule, and fighting between the opposition and his supporters led to his ouster (1992). Eduard SHEVARDNADZE agreed to head an interim government and was later elected head of state, but unrest and fighting continued into 1993 in Gamsakhurdia's home region of Mingrelia, in W Georgia. There have also been conflicts with separatists in South Ossetia, in central Georgia, and in Abkhazia, in NW Georgia. In 1993 Abkhazian separatists ousted Georgian forces from Abkhazia. Georgia did not join the COMMONWEALTH OF INDEPENDENT STATES until 1993.

Georgia, state in the SE U.S.; bordered by Florida (S), Alabama (W), Tennessee and North Carolina (N), and South Carolina and the Atlantic Ocean (E).

Area, 58,876 sq mi (152,489 sq km). *Pop.* (1990) 6,478,216, an 18.6% increase over 1980 pop. *Capital,* Atlanta. *Statehood,* Jan. 2, 1788 (fourth of original 13 states to ratify the Constitution). *Highest pt.,* Brasstown Bald, 4,784 ft (1,459 m); *lowest pt.,* sea level. *Nickname,* Empire State of the South. *Motto,* Wisdom, Justice, and Moderation. *State bird,* brown thrasher. *State flower,* Cherokee rose. *State tree,* live oak. *Abbr.,* Ga.; GA.

Land and People. The mountains of the north, part of the APPALACHIAN MOUNTAINS system, give way to the transitional Piedmont Plateau and its fertile, gently rolling hills. The southern half of the state is covered by the low-lying coastal plain; just offshore are the popular resorts of the Georgia SEA ISLANDS. Along the border with Florida is the OKEFENOKEE SWAMP, a huge wilderness area with unique flora and fauna. The climate is temperate but variable throughout the state. About 63% of the population lives in urban areas; ATLANTA, the largest city, is the major commercial and financial center of the southeast. Other major cities are COLUMBUS, SAVANNAH, and MACON. In 1990, 71% of the population was white and the rest predominately African American (27%).

Economy. Service industries and manufacturing are of prime economic importance. Major manufactures include cotton textiles, apparel, carpets, transportation equipment, processed foods, and paper. The heavily wooded state is a leading producer of lumber, pulpwood, and resins and turpentine. Georgia also provides 60% of the world's kaolin and is known for its fine marble. Principal crops are peanuts (Georgia is the largest U.S. producer), tobacco, corn, and cotton.

Government. The constitution (adopted 1945) provides for a governor serving a four-year term. The general assembly consists of a 56-seat senate and a 180-seat house, both of whose members serve two-year terms. Georgia sends 11 representatives and 2 senators to the U.S. Congress and has 13 electoral votes.

History. The region was inhabited by the CREEK and CHEROKEE when it was visited (c.1540) by Hernando DE SOTO. Subsequently, both England and Spain claimed control of the area, and British settlers led by James E. OGLETHORPE arrived in 1733. The British captured much of Georgia during the AMERICAN REVOLUTION. Following the war, cotton cultivation, based on the plantation system and slavery, began to dominate the economy. In 1861 Georgia seceded from the Union and joined the CONFEDERACY. The state suffered considerable damage during the CIVIL WAR, with the burning of Atlanta (1864) and Gen. W.T. SHERMAN's destructive march to the sea. By the 1880s the textile industry was transforming the state's economy from agriculture to manufacturing. In the early 1960s Georgia was the first state of the deep South to proceed with integration without a major curtailment of its public-school system. In 1976 Jimmy CARTER became the first native Georgian to be elected U.S. president. From the 1970s to early 90s, Georgia's cities, especially Atlanta, experienced significant growth, further heightening the disparity between the urban centers and rural areas of the state.

Georgian style, several trends in English architecture during the reigns (1714–1820) of George I, George II, and George III. The first half of the period (c.1710–c.1760) was dominated by Neo-Palladianism (see PALLADIO). Colin Campbell's *Vitruvius Brittanicus* (1715) inspired a return to CLASSICISM, based on the works of Inigo JONES and Palladio. His Mereworth Castle, Kent, epitomizes the style. A second generation of architects carried the Palladian tradition through the Georgian period. In the first half of the 18th cent., a BAROQUE countercurrent, stemming from Christopher WREN's designs, was carried on by Sir John VANBRUGH, Nicholas HAWKSMOOR, and James GIBBS. In the second half, the CLASSIC REVIVAL was led by Sir William CHAMBERS, Robert ADAM, and Sir John Soane. A standard type of house construction, red brick with white stone courses and cornices and white painted trim, came to be known as Georgian. Notable buildings of the period include Soane's Bank of England and Gibbs's St. Martin's-in-the-Fields. American builders of the period followed British models closely.

geothermal energy: see ENERGY, SOURCES OF.

Gephardt, Richard A(ndrew), 1941–, U.S. congressman; b. St. Louis. A lawyer, he was elected to the U.S. House of Representatives as a Democrat from Missouri in 1976. Influential on foreign trade issues, he has championed restrictions on imports as a means of protecting American jobs. Gephardt ran unsuccessfully for the 1988 Democratic presidential nomination. He became House majority leader in 1989.

geranium, herb or shrub of the family Geraniaceae. More specifically, the name refers to the popular garden and greenhouse geranium (genus *Pelargonium*), grown for its colorful flowers and ornamental, sometimes scented foliage. Its long, beak-shaped fruits give it the name stork's-bill. The family also includes the true geraniums (genus *Geranium*) and the heron's-bills (genus *Erodium*). Geraniums also are cultivated for the aromatic oils extracted from their foliage and flowers.

gerbil, desert RODENT (subfamily Gerbillinae) found in the hot, arid regions of Africa and Asia. Gerbils have large eyes and powerful, elongated limbs upon which they can spring. Sandy, gray, or red-brown, gerbils are 3 to 5 in. (7.6 to 12.7 cm) long, excluding the long tail, and are popular pets.

geriatrics, study of the medical problems of the aged. Aging cells are more susceptible to the accumulation of CALCIUM, CHOLESTEROL, and other substances that may cause tissue deterioration, and thus the elderly are more prone to disease and decreased physiological functioning. Many disabilities of aging are related to CIRCULATORY SYSTEM deterioration, but studies have shown that proper nutrition and exercise contribute to prolonging good health and circulation. The study of old age is known as GERONTOLOGY.

Géricault, Jean Louis André Théodore [zhārĕkō'], 1791–1824, French painter. After studying in Rome he exhibited in Paris his famous *Raft of the Medusa* (Louvre), a turbulent painting of shipwrecked men at sea that ushered in French ROMANTICISM. He later went to England, where he did such fine horse paintings as *The Village Forge* (Louvre). He also modeled small figures and made excellent lithographs.

German Confederation, 1815–66, union of 39 German states created by the Congress of VIENNA to replace the old HOLY ROMAN EMPIRE. It comprised 35 monarchies and 4 free cities. It was little more than a loose union for the purpose of mutual defense, with its main organ a central diet under the presidency of Austria. The confederation was dominated by the strong influence of Austria and Prussia. The Austro-Prussian War (1866) destroyed the confederation, and the North German Confederation that replaced it was under the sole leadership of Prussia.

Germanic languages, subfamily of the Indo-European family of languages, of which English, Dutch, and German, are members. See LANGUAGE (table).

Germanic law, customary laws of the ancient Germans, codified (5th–9th cent.) after the Germanic tribes invaded the Roman Empire. Enacted cooperatively by ruler and people, they deal chiefly with penal law and legal procedure, although there are many laws pertaining to landholding. The Germans regarded law as personal, not territorial, and therefore continued to govern the Romans under their rule by ROMAN LAW.

Germanic religion, pre-Christian religious practices among the tribes of W Europe, Germany, and Scandinavia. There was no one religion common to all the Scandinavian and Teutonic peoples, but descriptions from TACITUS and the EDDAS point to certain basic polytheistic features. In early times two groups of gods were worshiped, the Aesir and the Vanir; later they coalesced to form a single pantheon of 12 principal deities, headed by WODEN (Odin) and including Tiw (Tyr), Thor (Donar), Balder, Frey, FREYJA, and FRIGG. Their home was Asgard. There, in the palace Valhalla, Woden and his warrior maidens (the Valkyries) gave banquets to dead heroes. Unlike the gods of most religions, the ancient Nordic deities were subject to Fate (the Norns), and tradition held that they were doomed to eventual destruction by the forces of evil in the form of giants and demons, led by Loki. After a ferocious battle at Ragnarok, the universe would end in a blaze of fire; but a new cosmos was to rise from the ashes of the old, and a new generation of gods and humans would dwell in harmony. The Germanic temples were attended by priests, who oversaw magic rites (e.g., divination) and prayer. Conversion of the Germans to Christianity began as early as the 4th cent. A.D., but it took many centuries for the new religion to spread throughout N Europe.

germanium (Ge), semimetallic element, isolated from argyrodite by Clemens Winkler in 1886. Gray-white, lustrous, and brittle, it is chemically and physically similar to SILICON. It is used as a SEMICONDUCTOR in TRANSISTORS and integrated circuits. The oxide, transparent to infrared radiation, is used in optical instruments. See ELEMENT (table); PERIODIC TABLE.

German language, member of the West Germanic group of the Germanic subfamily of the Indo-European family of languages. See LANGUAGE (table).

German measles: see RUBELLA.

Germans, a large ethnic complex of ancient Europe, a basic stock in the composition of the modern peoples of Scandinavia, Germany, Austria, Switzerland, the Low Countries, and England. They lived in N Germany and along the Baltic Sea, expanding south, southeast, and west in the early Christian era. CAESAR and TACITUS wrote of their warlike attributes, culture, and distribution. The Teutons and Cimbri, whom the Roman general Marius defeated (102–101 B.C.), may have been Germans. German tribes increasingly troubled the Roman Empire, with Vandal attacks in the west and OSTROGOTH attacks in the east. Among the tribes were the Alemanni, the FRANKS, the Angles, the Burgundii, the LOMBARDS, the SAXONS, and the VISIGOTHS. The Scandinavians included the Icelanders, who produced the first Germanic literature.

German shepherd, large, muscular WORKING DOG; shoulder height, c.25 in. (64 cm); weight, 60–85 lb (27.2–38.5 kg). It has a dense undercoat and a harsh outercoat that is usually black, gray, or black and tan. Developed as a sheepherder and perfected in Germany c.1900, it has been used in war, in police work, and as a guide dog for the blind.

German wirehaired pointer, large SPORTING DOG; shoulder height, c.24 in. (61 cm); weight, c.60 lb (27 kg). It has a woolly undercoat and a harsh, wiry, flat-lying outercoat of liver and white. An all-purpose retrieving pointer, it was developed in Germany in the mid-19th cent.

Germany, officially Federal Republic of Germany (1992 est. pop. 80,387,000), 137,900 sq. mi. (357,161 sq km), central Europe; bordered by the Netherlands, Belgium, and France (W), Switzerland and Austria (S), the Czech Republic and Poland (E), and Denmark and the North and Baltic seas (N). BERLIN is the de jure capital and largest city. The de facto capital is BONN, but in 1991 the German parliament voted to move the federal government to Berlin. N Germany is a plain drained by the Ems, Weser, ELBE, and ODER rivers. Its chief cities are BREMEN, HAMBURG, and Berlin. South of the N German plain, the country rises to highlands, including the mineral-rich Harz mountains and Thuringian uplands. The chief rivers are the Weser and the Main; major cities are FRANKFURT, LEIPZIG, and CHEMNITZ. Germany is mountainous, with the BLACK FOREST on the west and the Bavarian Alps on the south. The Main, Neckar, and DANUBE are the principal rivers; major cities are MUNICH, STUTTGART, and NUREMBERG. A fourth geographical region is the heavily industrialized valley of the RHINE R., which rises in the Swiss Alps and flows north through W Germany. Its chief cities are MAINZ, Bonn, and COLOGNE. Manufacturing, which includes transportation equipment, electrical machinery, metal and chemical products, and automobiles, and service industries dominate the economy. The main religions are Protestant (45%, predominant in the N and E) and Roman Catholicism (37%, chiefly in the W and S).

Government. Germany is a federal republic comprising 16 states, each with its own parliament. The federal government includes a president, a cabinet headed by a chancellor (who is the head of government), and a bicameral legislature with 662 members. Germany is a member of the EUROPEAN UNION and the NORTH ATLANTIC TREATY ORGANIZATION.

Economy. After World War II, West Germany became one of the world's primary industrial powers, with an export-oriented economy. Principal manufactures were machinery, chemicals, motor vehicles, and electric and electronic equipment. East Germany, which rapidly industrialized in the postwar years, was considered a prosperous Eastern European nation, but by 1990 its infrastructure was obselete and its industries uncompetitive by Western standards. At reunification it was estimated that Germany would have to invest $500 billion in the East German economy, and the costs of restructuring the East strained German resources in the early 1990s.

History to 1949. In antiquity, Rome conquered (1st cent. B.C.–1st cent. A.D.) SW Germany but was stopped from further conquest by Germanic tribes who lived to the northeast. Germanic tribes later (4th–5th cent.) overran most of the Roman Empire, and by the 6th cent. one of these tribes, the FRANKS, had created a vast empire in Germany and Gaul (see MEROVINGIANS; CAROLINGIANS; CHARLEMAGNE). In the 8th cent. Christianity was spread among the Germans by St. BONIFACE. A successor state, the HOLY ROMAN EMPIRE, was founded in the 10th cent., but Germany remained a loose federation of small principalities and cities. The Holy Roman Empire, weakened by the Protestant REFORMATION (16th cent.) and the THIRTY YEARS WAR (1618–48), was finally swept aside (1806) by NAPOLEON I. The Congress of VIENNA (1814–15) created the GERMAN CONFEDERATION, another loose federation of German states, in which PRUSSIA and Austria emerged as rivals. Prussia, under Otto von BISMARCK, finally achieved the unification of Germany after victories in the AUSTRO-PRUSSIAN WAR (1866) and the FRANCO-PRUSSIAN WAR (1870–71). In 1871 King WILLIAM I of Prussia was proclaimed emperor of Germany, and the new German empire rapidly became the chief economic and military power on the Continent. Its industrial, colonial, and naval expansion threatened British and French interests and helped bring about WORLD WAR I. Badly defeated, Germany accepted (1919) the harsh Treaty of VERSAILLES and established the Weimar Republic. This was beset from the beginning by extremist agitation, mass unemployment, and severe inflation. In 1933 Adolf HITLER was appointed chancellor, and within a year he had established an absolute dictatorship. WORLD WAR II began with Germany's invasion of Poland (1939) and ended, in Europe, with the German surrender in 1945. The defeated country was divided into four Allied occupation zones, but dissension between the USSR and the West led to the formation (1949) of the Federal Republic of Germany (West Germany) in the U.S., French, and British zones and of the German Democratic Republic (East Germany) in the Soviet zone.

West Germany. The Federal Republic of Germany was established in 1949, with Konrad ADENAUER as its first chancellor. The country gained most of the attributes of national sovereignty in 1952 and full independence in 1955. Aided by the MARSHALL PLAN, West Germany recovered quickly from World War II. Politics in the early years were dominated by insistence on reunification, to be achieved through democratic elections, and nonrecognition of East Germany. The government (1969–74) of Willy BRANDT, while upholding the goal of a united Germany, made significant steps toward improving relations with Eastern Europe, including the signing of a nonaggression pact with the USSR (1970) and a treaty with East Germany (1973). Brandt was succeeded (1974) by Helmut SCHMIDT (reelected 1976 and 1980). Over a decade of political dominance by the Social Democrats ended when the Christian Democrat Helmut KOHL became chancellor in 1982.

East Germany. The German Democratic Republic was established in 1949, with Otto Grotewohl as its first prime minister.

Economic hardships led (1953) to a workers' uprising that was suppressed by Soviet forces. Under Walter ULBRICHT, who emerged as leader in the 1950s, the Berlin Wall was erected (1961) to halt the flow of millions of East Germans to the West. Ulbricht's successor, Erich HONECKER, ruled one of the most politically repressive police states in the Soviet bloc. In 1989, East Germans fled west by way of Hungary and Czechoslovakia, and antigovernment demonstrations spread throughout the country. Honecker was ousted, and his successors opened (1989) the West German border, dissolved the secret police, and promised multiparty elections.

Reunification. A strong drive for reunification developed in East and West Germany in 1990. In East Germany, conservative parties supporting reunification won the elections, and the new government and the force of events proceeded to dismantle the state. Economic union with the West occurred in July, and on Oct. 3, 1990, political reunification took place under what had been the West German constitution. In new national elections (Dec. 1990), the conservative coalition headed by Kohl retained power. The economy of the East largely collapsed, and the costs of reunification pushed Germany into recession and led to increased social tensions.

germination, process by which the plant embryo within the SEED resumes growth after a period of dormancy and the seedling emerges. Food stored in the endosperm or in the cotyledons (see ANGIOSPERM) provides energy in the early stages of growth until the seedling can make its own.

germ warfare: see BIOLOGICAL WARFARE.

Geronimo, c.1829–1909, leader of the Chiricahua APACHE; b. Arizona. After the Chiricahua Reservation was abolished (1876), he repeatedly led raids, was captured, and escaped. Finally surrendering in 1886, he and his followers were deported as prisoners of war to Florida. Geronimo was removed to Fort Sill, Okla., became a Christian and a prosperous farmer, and appeared in Pres. Theodore Roosevelt's inaugural procession.

gerontology, study of old age and the aging process, concerned with the physical aspects of aging as well as with the special economic and social problems of the elderly. Gerontology emerged as a major field of study in the 20th cent. as the steady increase in average life expectancy swelled the numbers of older people in the population, especially in developed countries. The medical specialty that focuses on the health and diseases of the elderly is called GERIATRICS.

Gerry, Elbridge [gĕr'ē], 1744–1814, vice president of the U.S. (1813–14); b. Marblehead, Mass. He supported patriotic activities before and during the AMERICAN REVOLUTION, and sat in the CONTINENTAL CONGRESS (1766–85) and the FEDERAL CONSTITUTIONAL CONVENTION (1787), where he opposed a strong central government. Elected governor of Massachusetts in 1810, he won again in 1811. His second term was marked by the grotesque rearrangement of election districts, called a GERRYMANDER after him. He was elected vice president on the ticket with James MADISON. His grandson **Elbridge Thomas Gerry,** 1837–1927, b. N.Y.C., was a reformer. A position as legal advisor to the American Society for the Prevention of Cruelty to Animals led to his founding (1875), with the help of Henry Bergh, the New York Society for the Prevention of Cruelty to Children (sometimes called the Gerry Society). He devoted most of his life to this cause, which became national in scope.

gerrymander, in U.S. politics, rearrangement of lines and boundaries of voting districts to favor the party in power. The term, which described this political art as practiced by Massachusetts Jeffersonians, originated while Elbridge GERRY was governor. Gerrymandering was limited somewhat by the Supreme Court in 1964. The term has also been used to describe the similar creation of voting districts to favor the election of a candidate from a specific racial or ethnic group.

Gershwin, George, 1898–1937, American composer; b. Brooklyn, N.Y. His scores to MUSICALS, including *Lady, Be Good!* (1924) and *Of Thee I Sing* (1931; Pulitzer), made him famous. In his extended compositions, e.g., *Rhapsody in Blue* (1923) and *An American in Paris* (1928), he blended traditional with folk and JAZZ elements. Gershwin wrote the music for the folk opera *Porgy and Bess* (1935). His brother, **Ira Gershwin,** 1896–1983, wrote lyrics to many of his compositions. After George's death, he collaborated with Harold Arlen on the film *A Star is Born* (1954).

Gesner, Konrad von, 1516–65, Swiss scientist and bibliographer. He was an important reviver of the classical school of zoological description that culminated in the work of Carolus LINNAEUS. His illustrated *Historia animalium* (5 vol., 1551–58, 1587), influenced biology and the arts and is considered the foundation of zoology as a science.

gesneria, herb or shrub, chiefly tropical and subtropical, of the family Gesneriaceae, cultivated for its showy, often tubular blossoms. The family includes the AFRICAN VIOLETS, the African Cape primrose (genus *Streptocarpus*), and the gloxinia (*Sinningia speciosa*) of Brazil, not to be confused with the genus *Gloxinia,* which is not cultivated.

Gestalt, school of psychology that interprets phenomena as organized wholes, rather than as aggregates of distinct parts. It maintains that the significance of a structured whole (e.g., in visual perception) does not depend on its specific constituent elements; thus a drawn figure still has meaning when there are gaps in the drawing. Gestalt, which has made substantial contributions to the study of learning, memory, thinking, and human personality and motivation, was brought to the U.S. in the 1930s by refugee psychologists from Germany. There the movement had received impetus from psychologists Max Wertheimer, Wolfgang Köhler, and Kurt Koffka, in protest against the prevailing scientific approach to analysis, with its detachment from human values. *Gestalt therapy*, developed after World War II by Frederick Perls, believes that a person's inability to successfully integrate the parts of his or her personality into a healthy whole may lie at the root of psychological disturbance. In therapy the analyst encourages clients to release their emotions and to recognize these emotions for what they are.

Gesta Romanorum, medieval collection of Latin stories, each with a moral, probably older than the extant 14th-cent. manuscript. CHAUCER and others used it as a source.

Gethsemane [gĕthsĕm'ənē], olive grove or garden, E of Jerusalem, near the foot of the Mount of OLIVES. It was the scene of the agony and betrayal of JESUS.

Getty, J(ean) Paul, 1892–1976, American business executive, one of the richest people in the world; b. Minneapolis, Minn. After inheriting his father's oil business, he became (1956) director and principal owner. His personal worth was estimated at $3 billion. An ardent art collector, he founded (1954) the J. Paul Getty Museum in Malibu, Calif., and bequeathed it an endowment of $750 million, making it the world's richest museum (see GETTY CENTER). Getty lived in Britain from the early 1950s until his death.

Getty Center, art complex in Brentwood, Calif. Consisting of six buildings on 124 acres (50 hectares) outside Los Angeles, it was designed by Richard MEIER and is scheduled for completion in 1996. It will combine a new J. Paul Getty Museum with a library and archives, conservation and art historical institutes, and educational and computer centers.

Gettysburg Address, Nov. 19, 1863, famous speech by Abraham LINCOLN at the dedication of the CIVIL WAR cemetery at Gettysburg, Pa. Lincoln eloquently stated his grief for the fallen soldiers and the principles for which they had given their lives. The brief address is perhaps the most quoted speech of all time, including among many memorable phrases: "and that government of the people, by the people, for the people, shall not perish from the earth."

Gettysburg campaign, June–July 1863, a series of battles that marked the turning point of the U.S. CIVIL WAR. After his victory at CHANCELLORSVILLE, Confederate Gen. Robert E. LEE undertook a second invasion of the North, crossing the Potomac into Pennsylvania and fighting at Harrisburg and Chambersburg. Union forces under George G. MEADE were massing N of the Potomac. The two forces met just W of Gettysburg in the greatest battle of the war (July 1–3, 1863). On July 1 the Union was driven to Cemetery Hill, south of the town. On July 2 the Confederates took the Peach Orchard but were repulsed in assaults on Cemetery Ridge and Cemetery Hill; they briefly held Culp's Hill. On July 3 Lee ordered George E. PICKETT's division forward in its famous but disastrous charge against the Union center. Tremendous losses resulted, and on July 4 Lee withdrew. Union losses totaled 23,000 killed or wounded; Confederate, 25,000.

geyser, HOT SPRING from which water and steam are ejected periodically to heights ranging from a few to several hundred feet. The generally accepted explanation is that rainwater, collected under pressure in hot rocks below ground, turns partly to steam and causes the water above it to overflow, thereby reducing the pressure and forcing an eruption. Notable geysers are found in Iceland; North Island, New Zealand; and Yellowstone National Park, U.S. (see NATIONAL PARKS, table). Geothermal generating plants use geysers to produce electricity. Geyserlike features have been observed on Neptune's moon Triton, some of them ejecting material to a height of 5 mi (8 km).

Ghana, ancient empire, W Africa, in the savanna region now occupied by E Senegal, SW Mali, and S Mauritania. The empire was founded c.6th cent. by Soninke peoples and lay astride the trans-Saharan caravan routes. Its capital was Kumbi Salih. It prospered from trade, mostly in salt and gold, and from tribute. Invaded by the Almoravids in 1076, it disintegrated by the 13th cent. Modern GHANA takes its name from the ancient empire.

Ghana, officially Republic of Ghana, republic (1992 est. pop. 16,185,000), 92,099 sq mi (238,536 sq km), W Africa, bordered by the Gulf of Guinea (S), Côte d'Ivoire (W), Burkina Faso (N), and Togo (E). Major cities include ACCRA (the capital) and KUMASI. The coastal region and the far north are savanna areas; in between is a forest zone. Lake Volta, in central Ghana, is one of the world's largest dammed lakes. Cacao is the principal crop in Ghana's predominantly agricultural economy; other exports include minerals (gold, diamonds, and bauxite) and timber. Aluminum smelting, food processing, and lumber production are the principal industries, and coffee and tobacco are widely grown. The population includes various linguistic groups, chiefly the Akan (Ashanti and Fanti), Mole-Dagbani, Ewe, and Ga-Adangme. Numerous indigenous tongues are spoken, but English is the official language. About 40% of the people are Christians, 10% are Muslims (mainly in the north), and the rest follow traditional religions.

History. In precolonial times the region comprised a number of independent kingdoms, including the ASHANTI confederation in the interior and the Fanti states along the coast. The first European fort

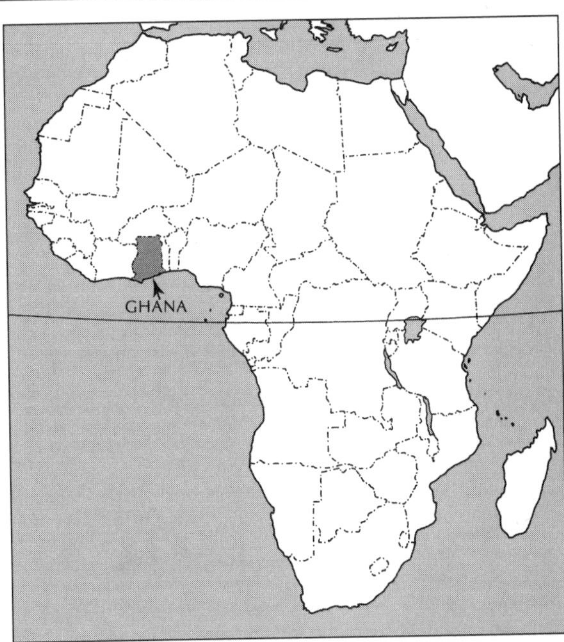

was established by the Portuguese at Elmina in 1482, and for more than three centuries European nations engaged in a brisk but highly competitive trade in gold and slaves. The expanding Ashanti kingdom forced the withdrawal of the Danes (1850) and the Dutch (1872), but the British allied themselves with the Fanti, defeated the Ashanti in 1874, and organized the coastal region as the Gold Coast colony. After renewed fighting between the British and the Ashanti, Britain made the kingdom a colony in 1901, at the same time declaring a protectorate over the Northern Territories, a region north of Ashanti. After World War I part of the German colony of TOGOLAND, mandated to Britain, was administered with the Gold Coast. In 1951, in the face of rising nationalist activity, Britain granted a new constitution and held general elections, from which Kwame NKRUMAH, the colony's leading nationalist figure, emerged as premier. The state of Ghana, named after a medieval African empire (see separate article) and including British Togoland, which had voted to join it, became an independent country within the Commonwealth of Nations in 1956. In 1969 Nkrumah transformed Ghana into a republic and named himself president for life. Increasingly repressive and beset by a deteriorating economy, Nkrumah was overthrown by a coup in 1966. The ensuing years saw a succession of coups. By the late 1970s the economy had slid into chaos, and corruption was rife. In 1979 Jerry RAWLINGS led a military coup, and after conducting a harsh anti-corruption campaign, he stepped aside and permitted a return to elected civilian government. Continuing corruption and economic decline led Rawlings to seize power again in 1981. Economic reforms (1983) helped revive the economy, and in 1992 Rawlings became president after a free election under a new constitution.

Ghats, two mountain ranges, S India, forming the eastern and western edges of the DECCAN plateau. Anai Mudi (8,841 ft/2,695 m) is the highest point. The **Western Ghats,** c.1,000 mi (1,600 km) long, extend southeast from near Bombay to the southern tip of India. Their densely forested western slopes receive abundant rainfall from onshore monsoon winds and are the source of many easterly-flowing rivers, including the Godavari, Kistna, and Caudery. The **Eastern Ghats,** facing the Bay of Bengal, form a series of hills extending c.900 mi (1,450 km) southwest from the Mahanadi valley.

Ghazali, al-, 1058–1111, Islamic philosopher, considered the greatest theologian in ISLAM, well known in medieval Europe as Algazel. Of Persian origin, he abandoned teaching to wander for 10 years as a Sufi mystic (see SUFISM), attempting to reconcile MYSTICISM with orthodox Islam. His great compendium of Muslim thought, *Restoration of the Sciences of Religion,* outlines an orthodox system for the attainment of unity with God.

Ghelderode, Michel de [gĕldərōd'], 1898–1962, Belgian dramatist. A satirist and exquisite poet, he is considered one the most original French-language playwrights of modern times. A wide variety of influences—MAETERLINCK, medieval morality plays, Flemish painting, puppet theater, COMMEDIA DELL'ARTE, the Elizabethans, and Edgar Allan POE—reveal themselves in such masterpieces as *Chronicles of Hell* (1929), *Pantagleize* (1929), and *Hop Signore!* (1935).

Ghent, city (1991 est. pop. 231,000), W Belgium, at the confluence of the Scheldt and Leie rivers. It is a major port and a banking and textile-manufacturing center. One of Belgium's oldest cities, founded in the 7th cent., it was the capital of FLANDERS. It was a medieval wool-producing city and was virtually independent until 1584. Thereafter it was ruled by the HAPSBURGS, until the French Revolution. It is noted for its many medieval and Renaissance buildings.

Ghent, Treaty of, 1814, agreement ending the WAR OF 1812 between the U.S. and Great Britain. Stipulating the restoration of territory taken by either party during hostilities, it was a diplomatic victory for the U.S.

Gheorghiu-Dej, Gheorghe [gāô'gyo͞odāzh], 1901–65, Romanian Communist leader. He was secretary general of the Communist party (1945–54, 1955–65), premier (1952–55), and chief of state (1961–65). He maintained a measure of independence within the Soviet sphere.

Ghibellines: see GUELPHS AND GHIBELLINES.

Ghiberti, Lorenzo [gēbĕr'tē], c.1378–1455, Florentine sculptor. In 1401 he won the competition to produce a bronze portal for the baptistery in Florence, defeating BRUNELLESCHI. He designed the north portal to match Andrea PISANO's earlier Gothic portal and was constrained by its rigid quatrefoil framework. The reliefs, executed between 1403 and 1424, depict the life of Jesus, the Evangelists, and the Church Fathers. Ghiberti also produced sculptural figures for the Church of Or San Michele before he began work on the baptistery's east portal, a task that took him 23 years. These later reliefs were more modern in form and structure. His *Comentarii* is the earliest known autobiography of an artist.

Ghirlandaio or **Ghirlandajo, Domenico** [both: gĕrländä'yō], 1449–94, Florentine painter whose family name was Bigordi. His religious narrative paintings, e.g., *Madonna with the Vespucci Family* (Church of the Ognissanti, Florence), reveal superlative technique and a keen eye for contemporary detail. With BOTTICELLI in Rome he decorated parts of the SISTINE CHAPEL. Among his pupils was MICHELANGELO, who probably assisted with Ghirlandaio's great FRESCO cycle of the life of Mary and St. John the Baptist in Santa Maria Novella, Florence. His famous realistic portrait *Grandfather and Grandson* is in the Louvre.

Ghose, Aurobindo [gōsh], 1872–1950, Indian mystic philosopher, known as Sri Aurobind. He spent his early years as an agitator for Indian independence. He experienced mystic visions, retired from political activism, and formulated what became Purna, or Integral, Yoga. In 1926 he retired into seclusion in his ashram at Pondicherry.

ghost dance, ritual central to the messianic religion instituted c.1870 among the PAIUTE by their prophet WOVOKA. The religion, which prophesied the end of white expansion westward and the return of land to Native Americans, spread to most of the western tribes. The ritual was danced for five successive days and was accompanied by hypnotic trances. The SIOUX performed the ritual prior to their massacre at WOUNDED KNEE in 1890—wearing "ghost shirts" that they thought would protect them from bullets.

Giacometti, Alberto [jäkōmĕt'tē], 1901–66, Swiss sculptor and painter. Associated with SURREALISM, he is known for his bronze sculptures of elongated human figures, e.g., *Man Walking* (Albright-Knox Gall., Buffalo).

Giambologna: see BOLOGNA, GIOVANNI.

giant, in mythology, manlike being of great size and strength; a brutish power of nature, lacking the stature of gods and the civilization of humanity. In many cultures, e.g., Greek, Scandinavian, and Native American, giants were believed to be the first race of people that inhabited the earth.

giant schnauzer: see SCHNAUZER.

giant sequoia: see SEQUOIA.

Gibbon, Edward, 1734–94, English historian. He is the author of *The History of the Decline and Fall of the Roman Empire* (6 vol., 1776–88), one of the most influential historical works of modern times. Gibbon also wrote a subtle and interesting autobiography, *Memoirs of His Life and Writings* (1796). He served in Parliament from 1774 to 1783.

gibbon, small APE (genus *Hyloblates*) found in the forests of SE Asia. Gibbons are highly adapted to arboreal life. Their arms are extremely long, and they swing through the trees with great speed and agility. Gibbons live in permanent families consisting of a male, a female, and their young; they are very territorial.

Gibbs, James, 1682–1754, English architect. An exponent of the GEORGIAN STYLE, he is noted for London churches, e.g., St. Mary-le-Strand (1714–17) and St. Martin's-in-the-Fields (1721–26); the latter inspired steepled churches in the American colonies. He also designed the circular Radcliffe Camera, Oxford.

Gibbs, Josiah Willard, 1839–1903, American mathematical physicist; b. New Haven, Conn. A professor of mathematical physics at Yale, his studies in physical chemistry and thermodynamics have profoundly affected industry, notably in the production of ammonia. He formulated the concept of chemical potential, was influential in developing vector analysis, and did work in statistical mechanics.

Gibraltar, British dependency (1992 est. pop. 29,700), 2.25 sq mi (5.8 sq km), on a narrow, rocky peninsula extending into the Mediterranean Sea from SW Spain. The town of Gibraltar lies at the northwest end of the Rock of Gibraltar. Although Gibraltar is a free port with some transit trade, its major importance is strategic, and its status has long been a subject of dispute between Great Britain (which has maintained possession since 1704) and Spain.

Gibran, Kahlil [jəbrän'], 1883–1931, Lebanese poet and novelist. He wrote in both English and Arabic. Fusing elements of Eastern and Western mysticism, he achieved lasting fame with such aphoristic, poetic works as *The Prophet* (1923) and *The Garden of the Prophet* (1934).

Gibson, Althea, 1927–, American tennis player; b. Silver, S.C. In 1948 she won the first of 10 straight national Negro women's singles titles. The first African American to play in the U.S. nationals (1950) and at Wimbledon (1951), she captured both of those championships in 1957 and 1958.

Gibson, Charles Dana, 1867–1944, American illustrator; b. Roxbury, Mass. As an illustrator of various contemporary magazines, he delineated aristocratic social ideals and created an ideal woman, the famous "Gibson Girl."

Gide, André [zhēd], 1869–1951, French author. A leader of French liberal thought, he was one of the founders (1909) of the influential *Nouvelle revue française.* He was controversial for his frank defense of homosexuality and for his espousal (and later disavowal) of communism. In his major novels—*The Immoralist* (1902), *Lafcadio's Adventures* (1914), and *The Counterfeiters* (1926)—he shows individuals seeking out their own natures, which may be at odds with prevailing ethical concepts. He was also known for his journals (1889–1949). Gide received the Nobel Prize in literature in 1947.

Gideon, Gedeon, Jerubbaal, or **Jerubbesheth,** in the BIBLE, one of the greater judges of Israel, a strong opponent of the BAAL cult. He refused the kingship because of his belief that God was the king of Israel. He also defeated the Midianite (see MIDIAN) oppressors and appeased the rival Emphramites (see ISRAEL, TRIBES OF).

Gideon v. Wainwright, case decided in 1963 by the U.S. SUPREME COURT. Florida had denied Clarence Gideon free counsel in a criminal trial, and he had defended himself. The Court held that the right to counsel, guaranteed in federal trials by the 6th amendment to the U.S. CONSTITUTION, is fundamental to a fair trial, and that the state's failure to provide counsel for a FELONY defendant violated due process under the 14th amendment.

Gielgud, Sir John, 1904–, English actor. He excelled in plays by SHAKESPEARE (notably *Hamlet*), WILDE, and PINTER, and won praise for film and television roles, e.g., *Arthur* (1981; Academy Award), *Brideshead Revisited* (1981), and *Prospero's Books* (1991).

Gierek, Edward, 1913–, Polish Communist leader. He replaced Władysław GOMULKA as first secretary of the party in 1970 after food riots had broken out. A failing economy and labor unrest led to his ouster in 1980 (see SOLIDARITY). In 1981 he was expelled from the Communist party and interned after martial law was declared.

gift tax: see under INHERITANCE TAX.

gila monster, venomous LIZARD (*Heloderma suspectum*) found in the deserts of the SW U.S. and NW Mexico. It averages 18 in. (45 cm) in length, with a large head, stout body, and thick tail that acts as a food reservoir; its skin is covered with beadlike scales. It and the beaded lizard (*H. horridum*) are the only known venomous lizards.

Gilbert, Cass, 1859–1934, American architect; b. Zanesville, Ohio. His 60-story Woolworth Building (1913) in New York City exerted great influence on the growth of the SKYSCRAPER. Among his other conspicuous works are the Federal Courts Building (N.Y.C.) and the Supreme Court Building (Wash., D.C.).

Gilbert, Sir Humphrey, 1537?–1583, English soldier, navigator, and explorer; half brother of Sir Walter RALEIGH. He was knighted (1570) for services in Ireland. His *Discourse* (1576), arguing the existence of the NORTHWEST PASSAGE, long motivated English exploration. In 1583 he reached NEWFOUNDLAND and claimed it for England. He disappeared at sea near the AZORES.

Gilbert, William, 1544–1603, English scientist and physician. Noted for his studies of ELECTRICITY and MAGNETISM, he coined the word *electricity* and was the first to distinguish between electric and magnetic phenomena. In his *De Magnete* (1600) he described methods for strengthening natural magnets (lodestones) and for using them to magnetize steel rods by stroking, and he concluded that the earth acts like a giant magnet with its poles near the geographic poles. From 1600 he was president of the College of Physicians and court physician to Elizabeth I and James I.

Gilbert, Sir William Schwenck, 1836–1911, English playwright and poet. With the composer Sir Arthur SULLIVAN he wrote a series of popular, satiric operettas, including *Trial by Jury* (1875), *H.M.S. Pinafore* (1878), *The Pirates of Penzance* (1879), *Patience* (1881), *Iolanthe* (1882), *Princess Ida* (1884), *The Mikado* (1885), *Ruddigore* (1887), *The Yeomen of the Guard* (1888), and *The Gondoliers* (1889). Gilbert was a metrical craftsman, and his lyrics are often scintillatingly funny.

gilds: see GUILDS.

gill, external respiratory organ of most aquatic animals, the basic function of which is oxygen–carbon-dioxide exchange. Gill structure and location vary among animals of different groups. In fishes, gills are located at the rear of the mouth and contain capillaries; in higher aquatic invertebrates, they protrude from the body surface and contain extensions of the vascular system; in mollusks, they are inside the mantle cavity; in aquatic insects, they occur as projections from the walls of the air tubes. In amphibians, gills are usually present only in the larval stage; in higher vertebrates, they occur merely as rudimentary, nonfunctional gill slits, which disappear during embryonic development.

Gillespie, Dizzy (John Birks Gillespie), 1917–93, African-American jazz musician; b. Cheraw, S.C. With Charlie PARKER he led the bop movement in JAZZ in the 1940s. His trumpet style blended spectacular facility with taste and intelligence.

Gilson, Étienne, 1894–1978, French philosopher and historian. After teaching in Paris, Gilson founded (1929) the Institute of Medieval Studies at the Univ. of Toronto and was long a member of its faculty. He was also one of the leaders of the neo-Thomist movement in Catholic philosophy. His works include *The Philosophy of St. Thomas Aquinas* (1919) and *The Spirit of Medieval Philosophy* (2 vol., 1932).

ginger, common name for perennial herbs of the tropical and subtropical family Zingiberaceae. Many are important for their aromatic oils. Ginger (*Zingiber officinale*) is cultivated for its root, which is candied or dried for medicines and spice. Turmeric (*Curcuma longa*) and the seeds of cardamom (*Elettaria cardamomum*) are similarly used, and often combined with ginger to make a curry.

gingivitis, inflammation of the gums, characterized by red, swollen, spongy gums that bleed easily. It may be acute, chronic, or recurrent. Chronic gingivitis usually results from bacteria, although other factors, such as poor dentition, prolonged use of the drug phenytoin, vitamin C deficiency, or DIABETES, may also contribute to it. If left untreated, gingivitis can lead to PERIODONTITIS.

Dizzy Gillespie

Gingrich, Newt(on Leroy), 1943–, U.S. politician; b. Harrisburg, Pa. A history professor, he was elected as a U.S. representative from Georgia in 1978. He became a leader of conservative House Republicans who supported the use of confrontational tactics against House Democrats and helped force Speaker Jim WRIGHT's resignation (1989) by questioning his financial dealings. Gingrich became House minority whip in 1989.

ginkgo or **maidenhair tree,** deciduous tree (*Ginkgo biloba*) with fan-shaped leaves. A sacred plant in its native China and Japan, ginkgo is a "living fossil," the only remaining species of a large group of GYMNOSPERMS (division Ginkophyta) that existed in the Triassic period. Today the ginkgo is valued in the U.S. and Europe as an urban tree because of its exceptional tolerance for smoke, low temperatures, and minimal water supply (although the female plant, with its malodorous fruit, is not as desirable an ornamental as the male). Ginkgo seeds are esteemed as a food in E Asia.

Ginsberg, Allen, 1926–, American poet of the beat generation; b. Paterson, N.J. He is best known for *Howl* (1956), a long poem attacking American values. Other volumes include *Kaddish and Other Poems* (1961), *Collected Poems, 1947–1980* (1984), and *White Shroud: Poems 1980–1985* (1986).

Ginsburg, Ruth (Joan) Bader: see SUPREME COURT, UNITED STATES (table 1).

ginseng, plant (genus *Panax*) of the family Araliaceae. True ginseng (*P. schinseng*) is prized by the Chinese for its curative properties. It and a North American ginseng (*P. quinquefolius*), used as a substitute for true ginseng, have been nearly exterminated by commercial exploitation.

Giono, Jean [jônō], 1895–1970, French novelist. His works—particularly the pastoral trilogy *Hill of Destiny* (1920), *Lovers Are Never Losers* (1929), and *Harvest* (1930)—describe Provençal life, emphasizing closeness to nature.

Giorgione [jōrjô'nā], c.1478–1510, Venetian painter. With TITIAN he was a student of Giovanni Bellini (see BELLINI, family). Few details remain of his life. He undertook important commissions in oil and FRESCO and died of the plague in his 30s. He was a major innovator, greatly influencing the principal painters of his time. His frescoes are virtually destroyed, and only a few oils are ascribed to him with certainty. Luminous colors, a liberated, self-expressive style, and the poetic rendition of a bucolic fantasy world are the chief hallmarks of his works, which include *The Three Philosophers* (Vienna), *Tempesta* (Acad., Venice), and *Concert Champêtre* (Louvre).

Giotto (Giotto di Bondone) [jôt'tō], c.1266–c.1337, Florentine painter and architect. More than any other artist, he may be said to have determined the course of painting in Europe. Giotto turned from the formulas of Byzantine painting to the study of nature, achieving lifelike, expressive faces and the illusion of movement. He designed a great number of works, many of which have disappeared. In Rome in 1300 he executed the MOSAIC of the *Navicella* (now in St. Peter's, Rome), and in 1304 began the 38 FRESCOES in the Scrovegni (Arena) Chapel (Padua). Among the greatest works in Italian art, these scenes from the *Life of the Virgin,* the *Life of Christ,* the *Last Judgment,* and *Virtues and Vices* illustrate Giotto's dramatic sense and power of narration. Returning to Florence, he did the frescoes of *St. John the Baptist* and *St. John the Evangelist* (Peruzzi Chapel, Church of Santa Croce) and the *Life of St. Francis* (Bardi Chapel). He achieved a remarkable representation of space, allying figures and background harmoniously without using a system of perspective, e.g., in *Madonna in Glory* (Uffizi) and *Death of the Virgin* and *Crucifixion* (both: Berlin). Chief architect of the cathedral in Florence, in his last years he designed the campanile called "Giotto's Tower." His reforms in painting were carried throughout Italy by his many pupils and followers, and his popularity is attested to in literature by DANTE, PETRARCH, BOCCACCIO, and others. His well-known *Wedding of St. Catherine* (Uffizi) was badly damaged in the flood of 1966.

Giotto, in space exploration: see SPACE PROBE, table.

Giovanni Bologna: see BOLOGNA, GIOVANNI.

Giovanni da Fiesole: see ANGELICO, FRA.

Giovanni di Paolo [dē pä'ōlō], c.1403–1483, major Italian painter of the Sienese school. Like other Sienese painters of his era, he paid scant attention to the artistic innovations made in Florence. He had an inclination toward fantasy and a disregard for perspective. *Paradise* and *Creation of the World* (both: Metropolitan Mus.) and six expressive scenes from the life of St. John the Baptist (Art Inst., Chicago) are typical of his work.

Giovanni Gondola: see GUNDULIĆ, IVAN.

giraffe, African ruminant MAMMAL (*Giraffa camelopardalis*) living in open SAVANNA S of the SAHARA. The tallest animal (up to 18 ft/5.5 m), the giraffe browses in the tops of ACACIA and MIMOSA trees. The legs and neck are elongated; the skin is patterned in large, sandy-to-chestnut spots on a lighter background. Giraffes travel in small herds.

Giraudoux, Jean [zhērōdo͞o'], 1882–1944, French dramatist and novelist. Mostly imaginative interpretations of Greek myths, his plays include *Tiger at the Gates* (1935) and *Electra* (1937). *The Madwoman of Chaillot* (1945) is a bitter satire on 20th-cent. materialism. Among his novels are *Les Provinciales* (1909) and *My Friend from Limousin* (1922).

Girl Scouts, recreational and service organization est. 1912 in Savannah, Ga., by Juliette Gordon Low, originally modeled on the BOY SCOUTS and Girl Guides of Sir Robert BADEN-POWELL. The membership is divided into four age groups between 6 and 17. Activities stress good citizenship, service to others, health, international friendship, and the arts. There are some 3.3 million members.

Girondists [jĭrŏn'dĭsts] or **Girondins,** group of moderate republicans in the FRENCH REVOLUTION, so called because their early leaders were mostly from the Gironde dept. Notable members were Jacques Brissot de Warville, Charles DUMOURIEZ, and Jean Marie Roland de la Platière. Representing the educated, provincial middle class, they favored a constitutional government and a continental war, splitting with the JACOBINS on the second issue. They were unable to prevent the execution of the king, and their position was weakened after the treason of Dumouriez. In June 1793 many Girondists were arrested and executed; the leftist MOUNTAIN was thus assured of complete control.

Giscard d'Estaing, Valéry [zhēskär' dĕstăN'], 1926–, president of France (1974–81). A member of the national assembly from 1955, he was finance minister (1962–66, 1969–74) under DE GAULLE and POMPIDOU. As president he was unsuccessful in dealing with inflation and rising unemployment. He lost the 1981 election to MITTERRAND but later held a seat (1984–89) in the national assembly.

Gish, Lillian, 1896–93, American actress; b. Springfield, Ohio. She is best known for such silent films as *The Birth of a Nation* (1915), *Broken Blossoms* (1919), and, with her sister, Dorothy Gish (1898–1968), *Orphans of the Storm* (1921).

Gissing, George, 1857–1903, English novelist. Influenced by Charles DICKENS, he wrote grim treatments of social issues that reflect his own unhappy life, as in *The Private Papers of Henry Ryecroft* (1903). His best-known work is *New Grub Street* (1891), depicting the plight of the poor, alienated artist.

Giuliani, Rudolph William, 1944–, American politician; b. Brooklyn, N.Y. A crime-busting Republican prosecutor in the Justice Dept. in the 1970s, he was U.S. attorney for New York's Southern District from 1983 to 1989. Giuliani narrowly won the New York City mayoral election in 1993, defeating the incumbent, David DINKINS, who had bested him by a slim margin in 1989.

Giulini, Carlo Maria, 1914–, Italian conductor. A disciple of TOSCANINI, he was first known as a conductor of opera, chiefly in Milan and Rome. In 1968 he made his orchestral debut, with the New York Philharmonic. After holding posts with the Chicago Symphony and Vienna Symphony, he was (1978–84) musical director of the Los Angeles Philharmonic (see ORCHESTRA, table).

Giulio Romano, c.1492–1546, Italian painter, architect, and decorator, a founder of MANNERISM; b. Giulio Pippi. A favorite pupil of RAPHAEL, Giulio painted many FRESCOES from Raphael's designs. In the service of the duke of Mantua, he designed the Church of San Benedetto and rebuilt the Palazzo del Te, decorating it with illusionistic and somewhat melodramatic frescoes. His well-known oils include *The Stoning of St. Stephen* (Church of Santo Stefano, Genoa).

Giza [gē'zə] or **Al Jizah** [äl jē'zö], city (1990 est. pop. 2,680,000), N Egypt, a suburb of CAIRO. It is a manufacturing and agricultural trade center, the seat of Egypt's motion-picture industry, and a resort. Nearby are the Great SPHINX and the PYRAMID of KHUFU (Cheops).

Gjellerup, Karl Adolf [yĕl'əro͝op], 1857–1919, Danish novelist. His novels range from the naturalistic, idealistic *Minna* (1889) to the Buddhist-influenced *Pilgrim Kamanita* (1906). He shared the 1917 Nobel Prize in literature with Henrik PONTOPPIDAN.

glacier, mass of ice formed in high mountains and polar regions by the compacting of snow and kept in constant movement by the pressure of the accumulated mass. The four main types are *valley,* or *mountain, glaciers,* tongues of ice moving from mountain snowfields into stream valleys; *piedmont glaciers,* formed by the spread of one or the convergence of several valley glaciers; *ice caps,* flattened, somewhat dome-shaped glaciers covering mountains and valleys alike; and *continental glaciers,* huge ice sheets that give rise to ICEBERGS. Glaciers alter topography greatly by their erosive action, by their transport of various debris, and by the various forms of DRIFT they leave behind.

Glacier Bay National Park: see NATIONAL PARKS (table).

Glacier National Park: see NATIONAL PARKS (table).

Glackens, William James, 1870–1938, American painter; b. Philadelphia. An illustrator for various periodicals, Glackens first showed his paintings with the EIGHT and is known for his portrayals of the contemporary scene. His dark early style yielded to a brighter palette influenced by French IMPRESSIONISM, e.g., *Parade, Washington Square* (Whitney Mus., N.Y.C.).

gladiators [Lat., = swordsmen], in ancient Rome, class of professional fighters who performed for exhibition. There were various types of gladiators, armed and armored differently. Gladiators fought each other and also wild beasts. They were slaves or prisoners, including Christians, or impoverished freedmen. Forbidden by CONSTANTINE I, gladiatorial games continued nonetheless until A.D. 405.

gladiolus: see IRIS.

Gladstone, William Ewart, 1809–98, British statesman, the dominant personality of the LIBERAL PARTY from 1868 to 1894. As chancellor of the exchequer (1852–55, 1859–66), he secured measures for economic retrenchment and free trade. He was prime minister four times (1868–74, 1880–85, 1886, 1892–94) and achieved notable reforms: passage of the Irish land act; establishment of competitive examinations for the civil service, and of vote by secret ballot; abolition of the sale of army commissions; parliamentary reform; and educational expansion. His advocacy of HOME RULE for Ireland wrecked his third ministry. A great orator and master of finance, he was deeply religious and brought a high moral tone to politics; nonetheless, he was passionately disliked by Queen VICTORIA.

gland, organ that manufactures chemical substances. A gland may vary from a single cell to a complex system. The glands of the ENDOCRINE SYSTEM, e.g., the thyroid, adrenals, and pituitary, secrete hormones directly into the bloodstream. Sweat, salivary, and other so-called exocrine glands secrete substances onto external or internal body surfaces, usually through ducts. Mixed glands such as the LIVER and PANCREAS have both endocrine and exocrine functions.

glanders, highly contagious, fatal bacterial disease of horses, mules, and donkeys that can be transmitted to humans. The bacterium, *Actinobacillus mallei,* primarily infects the skin, lungs, and nasal membranes, causing lumps, or nodules, to form in the infected area. These nodules enlarge, form ulcers, and release bacteria-laden pus to other parts of the body. Infected animals must be destroyed to prevent the spread of the disease.

Glaser, Milton, 1929–, American graphic designer; b. N.Y.C. His constantly changing style, which draws widely on art history, has had enormous international influence. Glaser's work includes the design of posters, e.g., Bob Dylan (1966); book and record covers; periodicals; type; and interiors.

Glasgow, city (1991 pop. 654,542), Strathclyde, S central Scotland, on the River Clyde. It is Scotland's leading seaport and largest city and the center of the Clydeside industrial belt. Manufactures include electronic equipment, chemicals, textiles, carpets, and machine tools. Economically depressed in the early 1980s, by the late 1980s it had become a lively cultural center. Founded in the late 6th cent. by St. Mungo (St. Kentigern), Glasgow began its modern commercial growth with the tobacco trade in the 18th cent. Nearby coal fields and its location on the Clyde contributed to its industrial growth in the early 19th cent.

glasnost: see GORBACHEV, MIKHAIL SERGEYEVICH; UNION OF SOVIET SOCIALIST REPUBLICS.

Glaspell, Susan, 1882–1948, American author; b. Davenport, Iowa. She and her husband, George Cram Cook, organized (1915) the Provincetown Players. Glaspell wrote novels, short stories, and plays, e.g., *Alison's House* (1930; Pulitzer).

Glass, Philip, 1937–, American composer; b. Baltimore. He was influenced by Eastern music, and in 1968 he formed the Philip Glass Ensemble. His music, blending standard notation and tonality with electronics, is repetitive and of great duration. His best-known works are his operas, including *Einstein on the Beach* (1976; with Robert Wilson), *Satyagraha* (1980), and *The Voyage* (1992).

glass, hard substance, usually brittle and transparent, composed chiefly of silicates and an alkali fused at high temperatures. Metallic oxides impart color. In prehistoric times objects were fashioned from natural glass such as obsidian (a volcanic substance) and rock crystal (a transparent quartz). The oldest extant manufactured glass is from Egypt, c.2000 B.C. Many types were made in Roman times, but little is known of European glassmaking from the fall of Rome until the 10th cent., when STAINED GLASS appeared. Methods have changed little since ancient times. The materials are fused at high temperatures in seasoned fireclay containers, boiled down, skimmed, and cooled several degrees; then the molten glass is ladled or poured into molds and pressed, or it is blown or drawn. The shaped glass is annealed to relieve stresses caused by manipulation, then slowly cooled. Until the 17th cent. the finest glass was made in Venice; later France and England became centers of glassmaking. In the 20th cent. many new types have been developed, including fiberglass and safety glass, but in some uses glass has been superseded by PLASTIC. Despite mass production, glassmaking by hand remains a valued art.

glaucoma, disease of the EYE characterized by an excess of fluid within the eyeball, causing increased pressure on the retina and impairment of vision ranging from slight abnormalities to BLINDNESS. It most commonly develops gradually after the age of 40 but can sometimes occur abruptly. It is treated with drugs (such as pilocarpine) that decrease intraocular pressure.

Glazunov, Aleksandr Konstantinovich, 1865–1936, Russian composer. With RIMSKY-KORSAKOV he completed BORODIN's *Prince Igor.* His own early works reflected nationalism, but Western influences became more prominent later.

Gleizes, Albert Léon [glĕz], 1881–1953, French cubist painter, illustrator, and writer. A leading cubist, he used a rich palette and wrote the first tract on the principles of CUBISM, *Du Cubisme* (1912), with Jean METZINGER.

Glen Canyon Dam, 710 ft (216 m) high, 1,560 ft (475 m) long, N Arizona, on the COLORADO R. Completed in 1964, it is one of the world's largest concrete dams and impounds Lake Powell.

Glendale. 1 City (1990 pop. 148,134), Maricopa co., S central Ariz., adjacent to Phoenix; inc. 1910. One of the fastest-growing U.S. cities, it is located in a rich agricultural region and is a fruit and vegetable shipping and processing center. Luke Air Force Base is in Glendale. **2** City (1990 pop. 180,038), Los Angeles co., S Calif., a suburb of Los Angeles; inc. 1906. It has an aerospace industry and other defense-oriented manufactures, as well as a film industry. Forest Lawn Memorial Park, a large cemetery containing numerous art reproductions, is located in Glendale.

Glendower: see OWEN GLENDOWER.

Glenn, John Herschel, Jr., 1921–, U.S. astronaut and politician; b. Cambridge, Ohio. He was the first American and the third person to be put into orbital spaceflight when, on Feb. 20, 1962, he circled the earth three times in *Friendship 7* (*Mercury-Atlas 6*). After retiring (1964) from NASA and the U.S. marine corps, he was elected (1974, 1980, 1986, 1992) to the U.S. Senate as a Democrat from Ohio. He made unsuccessful bids for the Democratic presidential nomination in 1984 and 1988.

glider, type of aircraft resembling an airplane but having at most a small auxiliary propulsion plant and often no means of propulsion at all. Modern gliders typically have very slender wings and streamlined bodies. An unpowered glider is usually launched by an elastic shock cord, a rope, or a cable attached to its front and pulled by a launching crew, a tow car, or a tow plane; its relative low weight and large wing area permit it to keep flying for long periods and updrafts of air are used to gain altitude. The type of craft built especially for soaring and sustained flight is called a sailplane. See also HANG GLIDING; LILIENTHAL, OTTO.

Glière, Reinhold Moritzovich [glēĕr'], 1875–1956, Russian composer and teacher of PROKOFIEV and KHACHATURIAN. His romantic, impressionistic compositions show folk influences. The ballet *The Red Poppy* (1927) is well known.

Glinka, Mikhail Ivanovich [glēn'kä], 1804–57, first of the nationalistic school of Russian composers. His operas *A Life for the Czar* (1836) and *Russlan and Ludmilla* (1842) introduced a characteristically Russian style.

global warming, gradual increase of the temperature of earth's lower atmosphere as a result of human activity. A layer of atmospheric gases (carbon dioxide, methane, nitrous oxide, and ozone; called greenhouse gases) allows radiation from the sun to reach the earth unimpeded and traps INFRARED RADIATION from the earth's surface. This process, called the GREENHOUSE EFFECT, keeps the earth's temperature at a level suitable for life. Growth in industry, agriculture, and transportation since the Industrial Revolution, however, has produced gases that have augmented the earth's thermal blanket. Some researchers believe that continued production of greenhouse gases will lead to global temperature increases, which could melt the polar ice sheets, resulting in a rise in sea level and damage to coastal development and estuaries; dry soils, producing profound changes in agriculture; endanger many species; and spawn more frequent tropical storms. Despite controversy over this scenario, many nations have acted to decrease greenhouse-gas production and control deforestation, which also contributes to higher levels of carbon dioxide.

Globe Theatre, London playhouse, built 1598, where most of SHAKESPEARE's plays were presented. It burned down in 1613, was rebuilt, and was destroyed by the Puritans in 1644.

globular cluster: see STAR CLUSTER.

globulin, any of a very large family of PROTEINS widely distributed in animals and plants. The gamma globulins, isolated from mammalian blood serum, are the antibodies of the immune system (see IMMUNITY). Gamma globulin injections are given to people exposed to a disease (e.g., infectious hepatitis) to create a temporary immunity to the disease or reduce its severity and to people whose bodies cannot produce antibodies.

glockenspiel: see PERCUSSION INSTRUMENT.

Glorious Revolution, in English history, the events of 1688–89 leading to the deposition of JAMES II and the accession of WILLIAM III and MARY II. James's overt Catholicism and the birth of a Catholic heir united Whigs and Tories against him. Seven Whig and Tory leaders sent an invitation to the Dutch prince, William of Orange, and his consort, Mary, the Protestant daughter of James, to come to England. When William and Mary landed, James's army deserted him and he fled to France (Dec. 1688). William and Mary accepted the BILL OF RIGHTS (1689), which assured the ascendancy of parliamentary power over royal power.

Gloucester, city (1990 pop. 28,716), NE Mass., on Cape Ann; settled 1623, inc. as a city 1873. Its fine harbor has been used by fishing ships for over three centuries, and it is still a great fishing port with many related industries. The picturesque city is a resort center and artists' colony. Points of interest include the bronze *Fisherman,* a memorial to Gloucester sailors lost at sea, and Hammond Castle Museum.

gloxinia: see GESNERIA.

glucagon, polypeptide HORMONE secreted by the islets of Langerhans in the PANCREAS. It tends to counteract the action of INSULIN, i.e., it raises the concentration of glucose in the blood, by promoting GLYCOLYSIS. The actions of glucagon are mediated by cyclic adenosine monophosphate, which is synthesized from adenosine triphosphate.

Gluck, Christoph Willibald von [glo͝ok], 1714–87, German-born operatic composer. With *Orfeo ed Euridice* (1762) he revolutionized OPERA, establishing lyrical tragedy as a vital form that unified dramatic, emotional, and musical elements. *Alceste* (1767) followed. In Paris he produced (1774) *Iphigénie en Aulide,* his first serious opera with a French libretto. His last important work, *Iphigénie en Tauride* (1779), is often considered his masterpiece. Gluck's emphasis on dramatic impact and musical simplicity became incorporated into French operatic tradition.

glucose, dextrose, or **grape sugar** (empirical formula: $C_6H_{12}O_6$), white crystalline SUGAR; somewhat less sweet-tasting than SUCROSE (table sugar), it is found in fruits and honey. Glucose is the major source of energy in animal metabolism. It requires no digestion prior to absorption into the bloodstream. A monosaccharide (see CARBOHYDRATE), glucose can be obtained by HYDROLYSIS of a variety of more complex carbohydrates, e.g., MALTOSE, CELLULOSE, or GLYCOGEN. It is commercially made from cornstarch (see STARCH) and is used in sweetening candy, chewing gum, jellies, and various foods. Glucose present in urine may be a symptom of DIABETES.

glutton: see WOLVERINE.

glycogen, highly branched POLYMER of GLUCOSE that is made and stored in the LIVER and MUSCLE cells of humans and the higher animals and in the cells of lower animals. During short periods of strenuous activity, energy is released in the muscles by direct conversion of glycogen to lactic acid. See also CARBOHYDRATE.

glycolysis, process in all higher animals and most microorganisms in which glucose is broken down. Beginning with a single molecule of glucose, glycolysis is a series of chemical reactions requiring eleven different ENZYMES and eventually yielding two molecules of lactic acid, which then enter the CITRIC ACID CYCLE. The reactions of glycolysis also generate the high-energy substance ADENOSINE TRIPHOSPHATE. Glycolysis is the primary means by which many anaerobic organisms obtain energy.

gnat, small, two-winged INSECT of the order Diptera (see FLY). Gnats include black flies, crane flies, midges, MOSQUITOES, and others. Gnats often assemble in large mating swarms. Some gnats are suspected carriers of pinkeye and yaws.

gnathustomulid, member of a phylum (Gnathustomulida) of microscopic worms that have elongated bodies and cilia and are hermaphroditic. They live largely in sandy marine sediments. They resemble flatworms, but their feeding mechanism differs, and their epithelial cells each have only one cilium.

gneiss, coarse-grained, imperfectly layered metamorphic ROCK characterized by alternating dark and light bands that differ in mineral content. Gneisses result from the metamorphism of many igneous or sedimentary rocks and are the most common types of rocks found in Precambrian regions.

Gnosticism, dualistic religious and philosophical movement of the late Hellenistic and early Christian eras. The term designates a variety of sects, all promising salvation through an occult knowledge [Gr. *gnōsis*] that they claimed was revealed to them alone. Christian ideas were quickly incorporated into these syncretistic systems, and by the 2d cent. A.D. several posed a serious threat to Christianity; much of early Christian doctrine was formulated in reaction to this danger. Gnosticism taught that the spirit was held captive by evil archons but that through the use of secret formulas it could be freed at death and restored to the heavenly abode. Gnosticism eventually merged with MANICHAEISM, which adopted many of its ideas. The Mandaeans, in modern Iran and Iraq, are the only Gnostic sect extant.

GNP: see GROSS NATIONAL PRODUCT.

gnu or **wildebeest,** large ANTELOPE (genus *Connochaetes*) living in herds on African grasslands. A swift runner, it has hindquarters like those of a horse and a head and humped shoulders like those of a buffalo. A beard, mane, long tail, and large curving horns are characteristic of both sexes. The brindled gnu, or blue wildebeest (*C. taurinus*), weighs c.500 lb (225 kg) and stands 4½ ft (135 cm) at the shoulder.

goat, ruminant MAMMAL (genus *Capra*) of the CATTLE family, with hollow horns, coarse hair, and a characteristic "beard," closely related to the SHEEP. Found in mountainous terrain and arid climates worldwide, goats live in herds and feed on grass and shrubs. They have been bred for centuries for their highly nutritious milk and valuable hair and wool, the source of mohair and cashmere. Wild goats include the IBEX.

goatsucker, medium-sized, primarily nocturnal BIRD (order Caprimulgiformes) found in temperate and tropical regions. Goatsuckers have long, pointed wings, weak feet, and small, gaping bills fringed with bristles. Most are brown, gray, or black and have monotonous songs. They feed mainly on insects. All fly at night except the nighthawk, which is active at dawn and dusk. One species, the whippoorwill, common in the E U.S., hibernates during the winter instead of migrating.

Gobi, one of the world's great deserts, c.500,000 sq mi (1,295,000 sq km), extending c.1,000 mi (1,610 km) east to west across Central Asia, in SE Mongolia and N China. It is from 3,000 to 5,000 ft (910 to 1,520 m) high, with cold winters, short hot summers, and fierce sand and wind storms. Grassy fringe areas support a small population of nomadic Mongol herders, and there are important deposits of oil at Yumen (China) and Saynshand (Mongolia) and coal at Tawan-Tolgoi (Mongolia). The Kerulen R. is the largest permanent stream.

God, divinity of the three great monotheistic religions, JUDAISM, CHRISTIANITY, and ISLAM, as well as many other world religions. In the Old Testament various names for God are used, *Elohim* most commonly. The four-letter form YHWH is the most celebrated; the Hebrews considered it ineffable and in reading substituted the name *Adonai* [my Lord]. The reconstruction *Jehovah* was based on a mistake, and the form *Yahweh* is not now regarded as reliable. The general conception of God is that of an infinite being (often a personality but not necessarily anthropomorphic) who is supremely good, who created the world, who knows all and can do all, who is transcendent over and immanent in the world, and who loves all human beings. (The Old Testament concept of God is less unified and consistent.) The majority of Christians believe God lived on earth in the flesh as Jesus Christ (see JESUS; TRINITY). Muslims call God *Allah,* the name of God in Arabic, the language of the Koran, but it is also used by Arabic-speaking Christians. The several famous arguments for the existence of God are based on causality, design and purpose in the universe, and the nature of divine being; many have held, however, that God's existence must be accepted on faith. Some philosophers have extended the name God to such concepts as world soul, cosmic energy, and mind.

Godard, Jean-Luc [gôdär'], 1930–, French film director. His highly personal films are marked by a free-wheeling approach to content and style. *Breathless* (1959), noted for its elliptical editing, was followed by films like *My Life to Live* (1962), *Weekend* (1967), and *Every Man for Himself* (1980).

Goddard, Robert Hutchings, 1882–1945, American physicist and rocket expert; b. Worcester, Mass. In 1926 he completed and successfully fired the world's first liquid-fuel rocket. Goddard designed and built early high-altitude rockets, the first practical automatic steering device for rockets, and many other rocket devices. He was one of the first persons to develop a general theory of rocket action and to prove experimentally the efficiency of rocket propulsion in a vacuum.

Godden, Rumer, 1907–, English novelist. Subtle characterization marks her novels, which include *Black Narcissus* (1939), *The River* (1946), *In This House of Brede* (1969), and *The Dark Horse* (1982).

Her sister **Jon Godden,** 1908–, is a novelist whose works include *In the Sun* (1965).

Gödel, Kurt [gö'dəl], 1906–78, Czech-American mathematician and logician. He came to the U.S. in 1940. Gödel is best known for his work in mathematical logic, particularly his proof (1931) of a theorem stating that the various branches of mathematics are based in part on propositions that are not provable within mathematics itself, although they may be proved by means of logical systems external to mathematics.

Godfrey of Bouillon [bo͞oyôN'], c.1058–1100, crusader, duke of Lower Lorraine. He was prominent in the First CRUSADE at the siege of Jerusalem (1099) and was elected ruler of the city after its capture. Known for piety and simplicity, he was the subject of many legends and CHANSONS DE GESTE. He was succeeded by his brother BALDWIN I.

Godfrey of Strasbourg: see GOTTFRIED VON STRASSBURG.

Godiva, Lady [gōdī'və], fl. c.1040–c.1080, wife of Leofric, earl of Mercia. According to legend, she rode naked through the town of Coventry to persuade her husband to lower the heavy taxes. The only person who looked at her as she rode became known as Peeping Tom.

Godolphin, Sidney Godolphin, 1st **earl of,** 1645–1712, English statesman. Possessed of considerable financial knowledge, he early established a friendship with the duke of MARLBOROUGH, and their political fortunes were closely linked. He was first lord of the treasury under CHARLES II, JAMES II, WILLIAM III (1689–96, 1700–1701), and Queen ANNE (1702–10).

Godoy, Manuel de [gōthoi'], 1767–1851, Spanish statesman. As chief minister (1792–97, 1801–8) of CHARLES IV, he made peace with France (1795) and led the Spanish army to victory over Portugal (1801). His alliance with NAPOLEON I against England resulted in the Franco-Spanish naval defeat at TRAFALGAR (1805). An unscrupulous, corrupt politician, he was overthrown (1808) when France invaded Spain in the PENINSULAR WAR, and he went into exile in France.

Godunov, Boris [gədo͞onôf'], c.1551–1605, czar of Russia (1598–1605). A favorite of IVAN IV, Boris was regent for Feodor I, Ivan's son, and probably had Ivan's younger son, DMITRI, murdered. On Feodor's death an assembly of the ruling class made Boris czar. He ruled capably, but popular distrust and famine (1602–4) undermined his reign. In 1604 a pretender claiming to be Dmitri invaded Russia; Boris died, and his son, Feodor II, could not defend the throne.

Godwin, William, 1756–1836, English author and political philosopher. Rationalism, materialism, and anarchism mark his *Enquiry Concerning Political Justice* (1793) and his novels, including *The Adventures of Caleb Williams* (1794) and *Fleetwood* (1805). In 1797 he married the feminist Mary WOLLSTONECRAFT. Their daughter, Mary SHELLEY, married the poet P.B. SHELLEY, who was influenced by Godwin's works.

Godwin-Austen, Mount: see K2.

Goebbels, Paul Joseph [göb'əls], 1897–1945, German NAZI propagandist. One of HITLER's original followers, he became propaganda minister in 1933, which gave him complete control over the German radio, press, cinema, and theater; later he also regimented all German culture. A master of the "big lie," he directed his most virulent propaganda against the JEWS. He killed himself and his family after Germany's defeat in World War II.

Goering or **Göring, Hermann Wilhelm** [gö'rĭng], 1893–1946, German NAZI leader. One of HITLER's earliest followers, Goering founded and headed (1933–36) the Gestapo (secret police) after Hitler came to power. He was air minister after 1937, and he directed the German economy as a virtual dictator. Hitler designated him as his successor in 1939. In WORLD WAR II he was responsible for the total air war. He was severely criticized for not being able to counter the Allies' bombing raids, and in 1943 Hitler relieved him of all duties and offices. He was sentenced to death for his WAR CRIMES at the Nuremberg trials, but he killed himself two hours before he was to be hanged.

Goes, Hugo van der [go͞os], d. 1482, Flemish painter. His *Monforte Altarpiece* (c.1472; Berlin) reveals a classic sonority in color and serenity. Later works, e.g., the great *Portinari Altarpiece* (c.1476; Uffizi), show tension and dissonance in color and spatial arrangement. His *Death of the Virgin* (c.1480; Bruges) is remarkable for its staring, melancholy apostles.

Goethals, George Washington [gō'thəlz], 1858–1928, American army engineer; b. Brooklyn, N.Y. After serving on inland water projects, he became (1907) chief engineer of the PANAMA CANAL. After overcoming geological, climatic, and labor problems, he completed (1919) the canal ahead of schedule. For the next two years he was governor of the Canal Zone.

Goethe, Johann Wolfgang von [gö'tə], 1749–1832, German poet, dramatist, novelist, and scientist whose genius embraced most fields of human endeavor. His autobiography, *Poetry and Truth* (1811–13), describes his happy childhood. He studied law at Leipzig (1765) and at Strasbourg (1770–71), where he met HERDER and began his lifelong study of plants and animals. Lasting influences from this period were J.J. ROUSSEAU and SPINOZA, who appealed to his mystic feeling for nature. Goethe first won attention with the drama *Götz von Berlichingen,* a product of STURM UND DRANG, and *The Sorrows of Young Werther* (1774), an epistolary novel of morbid sensibility written after his unrequited love for Charlotte Buff. In 1775 Goethe was invited to visit Charles Augustus, duke of Saxe-Weimar, at whose court he was to spend the rest of his life. For 10 years Goethe was chief minister of state at Weimar. A trip to Italy (1786–88) fired his enthusiasm for the classical ideal. Written under this impact were *Egmont* (1788), *Roman Elegies* (1788), *Torquato Tasso* (1789), *Hermann and Dorothea* (1797), and the final version of the drama *Iphigenia in Tauris* (1787). A major work, *The Apprenticeship of Wilhelm Meister* (1796), became the prototype of the German novel of character development; also acclaimed is Goethe's psychological novel *Elective Affinities* (1809). The first part of his dramatic poem *Faust,* one of the great works of world literature, was published in 1808; the second, after his death. The friendship of SCHILLER made a deep impression on Goethe. His many relationships with women inspired some of his finest lyrics. The collection *West-Eastern Divan* (1819) also reflects his readings of the Persian poet HAFIZ. Increasingly aloof in his later years from national or literary partisanship, Goethe became more and more the Olympian divinity to whose shrine at Weimar all Europe flocked. His approach to science combined sensuous experience with poetic intuition; well known is his stubborn attack on Newton's theory of light (1810). Most of his works have been translated into English, notably by Thomas CARLYLE.

Goffman, Erving, 1922–88, American sociologist; b. Manville, Alta. He developed a performance-oriented theory of behavior in *The Presentation of Self in Everyday Life* (1959). *Asylums* (1961), which dealt with personality changes among inmates of a mental asylum, led to his study of other institutions. He taught at the universities of California and Pennsylvania.

Gogh, Vincent Van: see VAN GOGH, VINCENT.

Gogol, Nikolai Vasilyevich [gô'gəl], 1809–52, Russian writer. His first success was *Evenings on a Farm Near Dikanka* (1831–32), a collection of fanciful tales set in his native Ukraine. *Mirgorod* (1835) included "Taras Bulba," a novella of 17th cent. COSSACK life. He next wrote several tales of St. Petersburg; the most famous is "The Overcoat." His fame as a dramatist rests on *The Inspector-General* (1836), a satire on provincial folly. The culmination of his inventive gift was *Dead Souls* (1842), a picaresque novel about a rogue who buys the names of dead serfs in order to mortgage them.

Goidelic: see GAELIC.

Golan Heights, strategic upland region in SW Syria, c.500 sq mi (1,250 sq km), bordering S Lebanon, NE Israel, and NW Jordan, formally annexed by Israel in 1981. Elevations range from c.6,500 ft (2,000 m) in the north to below sea level along the Sea of Galilee (Lake Tiberias) and the Yarmuk R. in the south. The Golan Heights were fortified and used for artillery attacks on Israel after 1948. The region was captured by Israel during the Six-Day War in 1967 (see ARAB-ISRAELI WARS).

gold (Au), metallic element, known since prehistoric times. Chemically inactive, this very ductile and most malleable METAL can be beaten into thin sheets of gold leaf. Only silver and copper conduct electricity better. Gold is usually hardened by alloying with other metals; it also often occurs in nature as an alloy. The gold content of an alloy is stated in carats; by definition, pure gold is 24 carats, and thus a 75% gold alloy is 18 carats. Gold is found widely distributed, mostly in metallic form as dust, grains, flakes, or nuggets. It occurs in quartz veins or lodes, usually in association with silver or other metals, and in alluvial placer deposits. Chief producers are South Africa, Russia, Canada, and the U.S. Possibly the first metal used by humans, gold was valued for ornaments, and magical powers were attributed to it. Alchemists of the Middle Ages tried to transmute baser metals into gold (see ALCHEMY). The search for gold stimulated European exploration of the Western Hemisphere. For discussion of its monetary function, see BIMETALLISM; COIN; MONEY. See also ELEMENT (table); PERIODIC TABLE.

Goldberg, Rube (Reuben Lucius Goldberg), 1883–1970, American cartoonist; b. San Francisco. A humorous and political cartoonist, he is known for drawings of wildly intricate machines that perform simple tasks. He was also a sculptor.

Golden Age, [Span. *Siglo de Oro*], in Spanish literature, the period between c.1500 and c.1680, when many of the masterpieces of Spanish literature were produced. During the 16th cent. Spain became a dominant European power, and the spirit of the RENAISSANCE invaded its life and letters. Spanish writers assimilated the foreign influences to produce a distinctive literature characterized by patriotism, realism, and, occasionally, mysticism. The greatest single work of the period was *Don Quixote de la Mancha* (1605, 1615), by CERVANTES. Other important writers of the Golden Age were ALARCÓN Y MENDOZA, CALDERÓN, ERCILLA, ESPINEL, GARCILASO DE LA VEGA, GÓNGORA, GRACIÁN, St. JOHN OF THE CROSS, LOPE DE VEGA, MORETO, QUEVEDO, ROJAS ZORILLA, ST. THERESA of Ávila, and TIRSO DE MOLINA.

Golden Ass, The: see APULEIUS, LUCIUS.

golden calf, in the BIBLE, an idol erected by the Israelites on several occasions. AARON made one while MOSES was on Mt. Sinai. JEROBOAM I made two, and HOSEA denounced a calf in Samaria. A bull cult was widespread in CANAAN at the time of the Israelite invasion.

Golden Fleece, in Greek mythology, magic fleece of the ram that carried Phrixus and Helle from Boeotia. Helle fell into the sea (which became the Hellespont), but Phrixus arrived safely in Colchis. He then sacrificed the ram, which became the constellation Aries. Its fleece, hung in a wood guarded by a dragon, was later sought by JASON and the Argonauts.

Golden Gate Bridge, one of the world's longest suspension bridges, built (1933–37) across the entrance (Golden Gate) of San Francisco Bay, Calif. It has a main span of 4,200 ft (1,280 m) and a total length of 9,266 ft (2,824 m).

Golden Horde, Empire of the, Mongol state comprising most of Russia, founded in the mid-13th cent. by the Mongol leader Batu Khan (see TATARS). The name derives from the magnificence of the Mongol camp on the Volga, where the empire had its capital. The Russian principalities were tributaries of the khan, who confirmed princely succession and exacted taxes. In the early 14th cent., Islam became the official religion of the empire. Warfare among its leaders and attempts by the Russian princes to end tributary payments weakened the empire. TIMUR conquered it in the late 14th cent.

golden retriever, large SPORTING DOG; shoulder height, c.23 in. (58 cm); weight, 60–75 lb (27.2–34.1 kg). Its water-repellent double coat is golden-brown. Developed in Scotland in the 19th cent. mainly to hunt waterfowl, this hardy breed is also used as a guide dog.

goldenrod, any species of the genus *Solidago* of the COMPOSITE family, chiefly North American weedy herbs with small, mostly yellow flowers growing along a slender stem. Once incorrectly thought to cause hay fever, it grows wild in many parts of the U.S. and is the state flower of Kentucky and Nebraska. Goldenrod has been used in dyes and teas.

Golden Rule, saying of JESUS, "As ye would that men should do to you, do ye also to them likewise."

goldfish, freshwater FISH (genus *Carassius*) popular in home aquariums. Native to China, it was domesticated centuries ago from its wild form, an olive-colored carplike fish up to 16 in. (40 cm) long. Marketed goldfish are 1 to 4 in. (2.5 to 10 cm) long and most commonly orange in color; breeders have developed bizarre varieties with unusual tails, double or triple fins, bulging eyes, and a range of colors.

Golding, Sir William (Gerald), 1911–93, English novelist. His novels, concerned especially with the dark side of human nature, include the nightmarish *Lord of the Flies* (1954), *The Spire* (1964), and *Rites of Passage* (1980). He was awarded the 1983 Nobel Prize for literature and was knighted in 1988.

Goldman, Emma, 1869–1940, American anarchist; b. Russia; emigrated to the U.S. in 1886. With the anarchist Alexander BERKMAN, she published the paper *Mother Earth.* Between 1893 and 1917 she was imprisoned several times on such charges as inciting to riot, publicly advocating birth control, and obstructing the draft. She and Berkman were deported (1919) to Russia; disagreeing with the Soviet government, she left in 1921.

Goldmark, Peter Carl, 1906–77, Hungarian-American engineer. Emigrating to the U.S. (1933), he joined (1936) the Columbia Broadcasting System, where he perfected the first commercial color television system. He also developed the 33⅓ (LP) phonograph and the scanning system used (1966) by the Lunar Orbiter space probe to radio photographs back to the earth.

Goldoni, Carlo, 1707–93, Italian dramatist, author of over 260 works, including opera. He created a new Italian COMEDY of character, an advance on the COMMEDIA DELL'ARTE. Among his most notable plays are *The Mistress of the Inn* (1753), *The Accomplished Maid* (1756), and *The Fan* (1763).

Goldsmith, Oliver, 1730?–74, Anglo-Irish author. One of Samuel JOHNSON's circle, he made his name with *Citizen of the World* (1762), a series of whimsical essays; the philosophical poem *The Traveler* (1764); and the nostalgic pastorale *The Deserted Village* (1770). His reputation, however, rests on two comedies, *The Good-natur'd Man* (1768) and *She Stoops to Conquer* (1773), and on his novel *The Vicar of Wakefield* (1766). The comedies injected realism into the dull, sentimental theater of the day and, like the novel, are imbued with humor and warm humanity.

Goldwater, Barry Morris, 1909–, U.S. senator (1953–65, 1969–87); b. Phoenix, Ariz. He was the leader of the extreme conservative wing of the Republican party during the 1950s and 1960s. He ran for president in 1964 but was decisively defeated by Lyndon B. JOHNSON. His son **Barry Morris Goldwater, Jr.,** 1938–, b. Los Angeles, was a U.S. congressman from California (1968–83).

Goldwyn, Samuel, 1882–1974, American film producer; b. Poland as Samuel Goldfish. In 1916 he formed Goldwyn Pictures, which merged with L.B. MAYER's company to become Metro-Goldwyn-Mayer in 1924. Goldwyn also produced films independently, e.g., *The Best Years of Our Lives* (1946).

golem [Heb., = something shapeless], in medieval Jewish legend, a robotlike servant made of clay and given life by means of a charm, particularly the name of God.

golf, game in which players hit a small, hard ball with specially designed clubs over an outdoor course (links). The object is to deposit the ball in a cup, or hole, using as few strokes as possible. The standard course, usually more than 6,000 yd (about 5,500 m) in length, is divided into 18 holes, each consisting of a tee, from which the ball is initially driven; the fairway, bounded by tall grass (the rough) and containing natural or artificial obstacles (hazards) such as water and sand traps; and the green, a smooth surface on which the cup (4.5 in/11.43 cm in diameter) is located. A set of 14 golf clubs typically includes 3 or 4 woods, 8 to 10 irons, 1 or 2 wedges, and a putter for use on the green. Although its origin is unknown, golf is identified with Scotland, where it was played as early as 1457. The British Open Tournament was established in 1860. The game may have been played in America in the 17th cent., but the first permanent club, at Yonkers, N.Y., was not organized until 1888. In the 20th cent. golf experienced a tremendous increase in popularity. The professional tour, led by such stars as Arnold PALMER and Jack NICKLAUS, emerged as a major attraction after World War II, and the women's professional tour grew in popularity in the 1980s and early 90s.

Golgi, Camillo [gôl'jē], 1844–1926, Italian physician. For his work on the structure of the nervous system, he shared with Santiago Ramón y Cajal the 1906 Nobel Prize in physiology or medicine. Golgi stained nerve tissue with silver nitrate to delineate (1883) certain nerve cells (Golgi cells) in the central nervous system; observed (1909) the Golgi apparatus, a part of the cytoplasm distinguishable by staining; and recognized that the three types of malaria are caused by different protozoan organisms.

Golgotha: see CALVARY.

Goliad, city (1990 pop. 1,946), seat of Goliad co., S Tex., on the San Antonio R., a market town in a farm area. During the Texas Revolution (1836) it was the scene of the infamous "Goliad massacre" of Texan prisoners by Mexican troops. A Spanish mission (est. 1749) and presidio are tourist attractions.

Goliath, in the BIBLE, gigantic Philistine who challenged the Israelites. The young DAVID accepted the challenge and killed him with a stone from a sling.

Gomorrah: see SODOM AND GOMORRAH.

Gompers, Samuel, 1850–1924, American labor leader; b. England. After emigrating to the U.S. in 1863, he worked as a cigar maker and joined the local union. In 1881 he helped found the labor organization that became the American Federation of Labor in 1886. From 1886 until his death (except during 1895), he was president of the AFL. He directed the successful battle with the KNIGHTS OF LABOR and kept the AFL free of radical and socialistic elements; he also won higher wages, shorter hours, and more freedom for workers. A man of great personal integrity and the leading spokesman of the labor movement, he did much to make organized labor respected. See AMERICAN FEDERATION OF LABOR AND CONGRESS OF INDUSTRIAL ORGANIZATIONS.

Gomułka, Władysław, 1905–82, Polish Communist leader. As first secretary of the Communist party (1956–70), he liberalized Poland while retaining close ties to the USSR. He resigned as the result of food riots.

Goncharov, Ivan Aleksandrovich [gənchərôf′], 1812–91, Russian novelist. A government official, he wrote the satirical novel *Oblomov* (1859), a classic study of indolence. Other novels are *A Common Story* (1847) and *The Precipice* (1869).

Goncourt, Edmond Louis Antoine Huot de [gôNkŏŏr′], 1822–96, and **Jules Alfred Huot de Goncourt,** 1830–70, French authors, brothers. Together they wrote social history, art criticism, and influential naturalistic novels, e.g., *Renée Mauperin* (1864) and *Mme Gervaisais* (1869). From 1851 they published the highly successful *Journal des Goncourt,* for 40 years providing an intimate account of Parisian society. Their work paved the way for both NATURALISM and IMPRESSIONISM. In his will, Edmond provided for the founding of the Goncourt Academy and its annual prize for fiction.

Gondwanaland: see CONTINENTAL DRIFT.

gong: see PERCUSSION INSTRUMENT.

Góngora y Argote, Luis de [gōn′gōrä ē ärgō′tā], 1561–1627, Spanish poet. A major figure of Spain's GOLDEN AGE, he wrote sonnets, ballads, and the long pastoral *Solitudes* (1613), his masterpiece. His complex, artificial style, characterized by innovative use of metaphor, latinate vocabulary, and classical and mythological allusions, exemplifies the baroque tendencies that came to be known as *Gongorism.*

gonorrhea, infectious disease involving chiefly the mucous membranes of the genitourinary tract, caused by the bacterium *Neisseria gonorrheae.* A SEXUALLY TRANSMITTED DISEASE, gonorrhea causes inflammation of the genital organs and urethra and, if untreated, sterility. The disease is treated with ANTIBIOTICS, but the bacterium has developed strains that are resistant to antibiotic treatment.

Gonzaga [gōntsä′gä], Italian princely house that ruled Mantua (1328–1708), Montferrat (1536–1708), and Guastalla (1539–1746). **Francesco Gonzaga,** 1466–1519, marquis of Mantua, married Isabella d'ESTE and made numerous alliances in the ITALIAN WARS. His son, **Federico Gonzaga,** 1500–40, was made (1530) duke of Mantua and acquired Montferrat. In 1627 this senior branch became extinct, and the succession was disputed by a cadet line that had acquired the French duchies of Nivernais and Rethel, and by another junior branch that ruled Guastalla. War broke out between France and Spain over the issue, and the Nivernais branch won (1631). It in turn became extinct in 1708.

Gonzales, Pancho (Richard Alonzo Gonzales), 1928–, American tennis player; b. Los Angeles. Known for his powerful service, he won (1948–49) two U.S. national singles titles. His early professional career was unsuccessful, but he rose to prominence in 1954, remaining the professional champion (except for 1960) until 1961.

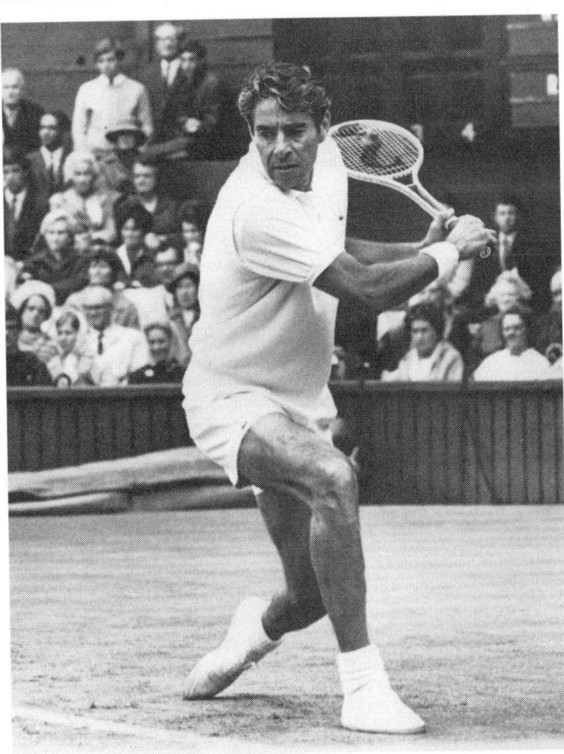

Pancho Gonzalez

González Márquez, Felipe, 1942–, prime minister of Spain (1982–). A lawyer and first secretary (1974–79, 1979–) of the Spanish Socialist party, González led the Socialists to a landslide victory in the 1982 parliamentary elections to become head of Spain's first leftist government since the SPANISH CIVIL WAR. The Socialists were returned to power in 1986, 1989, and, as a minority government, 1993. In 1986 he led Spain into the European Community.

Goodall, Jane, 1934–, British ethologist. An authority on chimpanzees, she has studied their behavior and social patterns since establishing (1960) a research camp in Tanzania. Her books include *My Friends the Wild Chimpanzees* (1967) and *The Chimpanzees of Gombe* (1986).

Good Friday, anniversary of JESUS' death on the cross, the Friday before Easter. Among Christians it is a day of mourning and penitence. In the Orthodox, Roman Catholic, and Anglican churches, the saying of Mass is suspended.

Goodman, Benny (Benjamin David Goodman), 1909–86, American clarinetist and bandleader; b. Chicago. He formed (1934) a big band and went on to become the "King of Swing," performing for radio, motion pictures, and records. He also led small ensembles, e.g., with Teddy Wilson (piano), Gene Krupa (drums), and Lionel Hampton (vibraphone), and was successful as a classical clarinetist. See also JAZZ.

Goodyear, Charles, 1800–60, American inventor and originator of vulcanized RUBBER; b. New Haven, Conn. He experimented for years to find a way to keep rubber from sticking and melting in hot weather; in 1839 he discovered vulcanization, patenting it in 1844. Goodyear worked and died in poverty.

goose, large, wild or domesticated swimming BIRD related to the DUCK and SWAN. Strictly speaking, the term *goose* applies to the female and *gander* to the male. In North America the wild, or Canada, goose (*Branta canadensis*) is known by its honking call and V-shaped, migrating flocks in spring and fall. Geese have been domesticated since ancient times; the popular Toulouse, or gray, goose is descended from the European graylag (*Anser anser*).

gooseberry: see CURRANT.

gopher or **pocket gopher,** burrowing RODENT (family Geomyidae) found in North and Central America. The gopher is gray, buff, or dark brown; its combined head and body length is 5 to 12 in. (13 to 30 cm). It has extremely long teeth and large claws. The name *pocket gopher* refers to the fur-lined pouches that open on the outsides of its cheeks, used to carry food and nesting material.

Gorbachev, Mikhail Sergeyevich, 1931–, Soviet political leader, last president of the USSR (1988–91). A specialist in agriculture, he was elected to the Communist party's central committee in 1971 and became a full member of the POLITBURO in 1980. Succeeding CHERNENKO as general secretary of the Communist party in 1985, he was elected president of the USSR in 1988 and to a new, more powerful presidency in 1989. Confronted with deteriorating economic conditions, Gorbachev introduced policies whose guiding principles *glasnost* [openness] and *perestroika* [restructuring] were intended to liberalize and revitalize Soviet socialism and society. The changes succeeded in democratizing Soviet politics but produced few economic benefits and unleashed long-suppressed ethnic conflicts and separatist movements. In foreign affairs he vastly improved relations with the U.S. and ended Soviet interference in Eastern European nations, most of which subsequently elected non-Communist governments. In 1990 he was awarded the Nobel Peace Prize. The imminent signing of a treaty transferring many powers to the republics led hard-liners in Gorbachev's government to attempt (Aug. 1991) to overthrow him. In the aftermath Gorbachev aligned himself with Boris YELTSIN and other reformers and resigned from the Communist party. He agreed to even greater power-sharing with the republics and tried to prevent the USSR's disintegration but met with little success. The agreement (Dec. 8, 1991) by Belarus, Russia, and Ukraine to form the COMMONWEALTH OF INDEPENDENT STATES, the decision of all but one of the remaining republics to join, and Russia's expropriation of union ministries and property left Gorbachev without function or authority, and he resigned Dec. 25, 1991. In 1993 he became head of the International Green Cross, a newly established environmental organization.

Gorboduc, legendary early British king mentioned by GEOFFREY OF MONMOUTH. He divided his kingdom between his sons Ferrex and Porrex, causing great strife. *Gorboduc, or Ferrex and Porrex* (1561), was the first English blank-verse tragedy.

Gordian, name of three Roman emperors. **Gordian I** (Marcus Antonius Gordianus Africanus), d. 238, was made coemperor (238) with his son. After a reign of only 22 days, he committed suicide after learning that his son and colleague, **Gordian II,** 192–238, had been killed in battle. The latter's son, **Gordian III,** c.223–244, then became emperor. Philip the Arabian had him murdered in 244.

Gordian knot: see GORDIUS.

Gordimer, Nadine, 1923–, South African writer. Her novels, often bleak studies of South African life, include *The Voice of the Serpent* (1953), *A Guest of Honour* (1970), *Burger's Daughter* (1979), *July's People* (1981), and *My Son's Story* (1990). She has also written short stories. In 1991 Gordimer was awarded the Nobel Prize for literature.

Gordius, in Greek mythology, king of Phrygia. The pole of his wagon was fastened to the yoke with a knot that defied efforts to untie it. An oracle stated that he who untied this Gordian knot would rule Asia. According to legend, ALEXANDER THE GREAT simply cut the knot with his sword.

Gordon, Charles George, 1833–85, British soldier and administrator. After serving in the CRIMEAN WAR, he commanded the Chinese army that suppressed the TAIPING REBELLION; afterwards he was popularly known as "Chinese Gordon." He was governor of the Egyptian Sudan (1877–80). Later (1885), while trying to crush the power of the MAHDI, he was killed in the siege of KHARTOUM.

Gordon setter, large SPORTING DOG; shoulder height, 23–27 in. (58.4–68.6 cm); weight, 45–75 lb (20.4–34.1 kg). Its long, shiny coat is black, with tan markings. Developed in Scotland and popularized there by the fourth duke of Gordon in the early 1800s, it was brought to the U.S. in 1842.

Gore, Al(bert, Jr.), 1948–, vice president of the U.S. (1993–); b. Washington, D.C. A moderate Democrat, he served (1977–85) as a U.S. representative from Tennessee before he was elected (1984) U.S. senator from Tennessee. He ran unsuccessfully for the Democratic presidential nomination in 1988. Gore was reelected to the Senate in 1990. In 1992 Bill CLINTON chose Gore as his vice-presidential running mate. He has sought to draw attention to environmental concerns and to promote the development of nationwide information systems and the streamlining of the federal government.

Goren, Charles Henry, 1901–91, American expert on contract BRIDGE; b. Philadelphia. His first book on the game, *Winning Bridge Made Easy* (1936), outlined his point-count system for determining the strength of a hand; it became the standard. He later gave up his law practice to concentrate on bridge and wrote a daily newspaper column, as well as many books and magazine articles. A master player, he won, on average, a major tournament a year from 1937 to 1965, placing second many times when he didn't win.

Gorgon, in Greek myth, one of three hideous sisters, Stheno, Euryale, and Medusa (the only mortal one, killed by PERSEUS). Winged and snake-haired, they turned all who looked at them to stone. They were much represented in Greek art.

gorilla, largest APE (*Gorilla gorilla*), native to the forests of equatorial W Africa. Males range from 5 to 6 ft (150 to 190 cm) in height and weigh c.450 lb (200 kg) in the wild; they have prominent sagittal crests and brow ridges and enormous canine teeth. Females are about half the size of males, and their features are less developed. Their shaggy coats are brown or black. Though extremely muscular and powerful, gorillas are quiet and retiring; they are chiefly vegetarian.

Göring, Hermann Wilhelm: see GOERING, HERMANN WILHELM.

Gorky, Arshile [gôr'kē], 1904–48, American painter; b. Armenia. His early work is figurative and refined. Later he was influenced by SURREALISM and began (c.1940) to create abstractions of mysterious organic forms. His work was influential in the development of ABSTRACT EXPRESSIONISM.

Gorky, Maxim or **Maksim** [gôr'kē] [Rus., = bitter], pseud. of **Aleksey Maximovich Pyeshkov,** 1868–1936, Russian writer. Born in poverty, he wandered the Volga region, educating and supporting himself, from the age of eight. *My Childhood* (1913), *In the World* (1916), and *My Universities* (1923) describe his early years. His first story appeared in 1892. In *Sketches and Stories* (1898) he wrote of the vigor and nobility of peasants, workers, and vagabonds. In 1902 *The Lower Depths,* the first and greatest of his 15 plays, was performed by the Moscow Art Theater. Gorky's friendships with the writers ANDREYEV, CHEKHOV, and TOLSTOY date from this time; he later published memoirs of all three. When the 1905 Revolution failed he was forced into exile. *Mother* (1906), which became the prototype of the revolutionary novel, was written in the U.S. After living in Capri (1907–13) Gorky returned to Russia in 1914. In the period of turmoil after the RUSSIAN REVOLUTION (1917), he used his friendship with LENIN and his post as head of the state publishing house to aid writers and artists. In 1921 he went abroad again, returning in 1928. *The Life of Klim Samgin* (1927–36), a four-part novel often considered his masterpiece, was unfinished at his death. Gorky's work, vital and optimistic, combines realism with a strong poetic strain. He is considered the father of Soviet literature and the founder of the doctrine of SOCIALIST REALISM.

Gorky: see NIZHNY NOVGOROD.

Gospel [M.E., = good news; cf. *evangel* from Gr., = good news], one of the four biographies of JESUS in the NEW TESTAMENT: MATTHEW, MARK, LUKE, and JOHN. The first three are called Synoptic Gospels because they present a comprehensive view, agreeing in subject matter and order. Many church liturgies include a solemn reading of the Gospel for the day. The honor paid to the Gospels resulted in some of the glories of book illumination, e.g., the Book of Kells.

gospel music, American musical form that developed in Protestant churches of the South. It is performed today by Americans of all backgrounds, but African-American gospel music is more important. Rooted in field and work songs, and owing less to the Protestant hymns than do African-American SPIRITUALS, gospel is an intense, joyful music. Its form derives from the call-and-response singing of preacher and congregation in African-American churches; the message is conveyed with tight control, at other times with abandon. Gospel and JAZZ were considered antithetical in African-American society until both forms gained general acceptance by the mid-20th cent.; together they influence "soul" and ROCK MUSIC. Major gospel performers include Mahalia JACKSON, Sister Rosetta Tharpe, the Clouds of Joy, and the Dixie Hummingbirds. Popular artists influenced by gospel music include Ray CHARLES and Aretha FRANKLIN.

Gossaert or **Gossart, Jan:** see MABUSE, JAN DE.

Göteborg [yötəbôr'yə], city (1988 pop. 432,021), capital of Göteborg och Bohus co., SW Sweden, on the Kattegat. Sweden's most important seaport, it has shipyards and fisheries as well as such manufactures as wood and paper products, iron and steel, and ball bearings. Founded in 1604 by CHARLES IX, it was a major commercial center from the 17th cent. Early in the 20th cent., it became the terminus of an important transatlantic shipping service.

Gothic architecture and art. The character of the Gothic visual aesthetic was one of immense vitality; it was spikily linear and restlessly active. Informed by the scholasticism and mysticism of the Middle Ages, it reflected the exalted religious hysteria, the pathos, and the self-intoxication with logical formalism that were the essence of the medieval. The Gothic style was the dominant structural and aesthetic mode in Europe for 400 years. Making its appearance (c.1140) in the Île-de-France, the style owes much to prior experimentation in Normandy (see NORMAN ARCHITECTURE). Ribbed vaulting (see VAULT) and pointed ARCHES had been used in Romanesque construction but without such purposeful and constant application. The important Gothic rib delineated the vaults and clarified the entire structure. Unlike the Romanesque, Gothic construction emphasized light and soaring spaces. The introduction (c.1180) of flying BUTTRESSES reduced wall surfaces by relieving them of part of their structural function, making possible the huge stained-glass windows that gave High Gothic church walls the appearance of curtains. The High Gothic cathedral was based on the traditional basilican plan, but single units were integrated into a unified spatial scheme. The exterior view was dominated by twin towers crowning a facade decorated with sculptures. Additional towers, a profusion of flying buttresses, and pinnacles rose around the upper part of the edifice. The first landmark Gothic structure is the ambulatory of the abbey of Saint-Denis (1140–44). The influence of its large areas of glass and use of space was imitated in such cathedrals as those of Sens, Noyon, Laon, and Paris. The High Gothic phase is marked by the Cathedral of Chartres (begun after 1194). In the mid-13th cent., the Rayonnant style further reduced opaque wall surfaces for windows and stone tracery, e.g., Sainte-Chapelle, Paris. Interesting variations on Gothic style appeared in Western Europe. The early English style (late 12th–early 13th cent.) retained much of the ponderous mural style of Norman architecture, e.g., Salisbury Cathedral. Romanesque proportions were dominant in Italy, but the French style inspired German churches, e.g., in Cologne, as well as Spanish Gothic architecture. The latter was also influenced by Moorish tradition, e.g., in Toledo. In the 14th and 15th cent. these trends culminated in the flamboyant style, e.g., The Church of Saint-Maclou, Rouen; the decorated style in England, e.g., Ely Cathedral; and the even more flamboyant perpendicular style, e.g., the choir of the cathedral at Gloucester. After the 14th-cent. economic crises and the Black Death, building slowed, but the Gothic tradition never completely died. It was revived in the 19th cent. (see GOTHIC REVIVAL). All the other arts of the Gothic period were dominated by architecture. Sculpture and stained glass were integrated into the churches. By the 13th cent., sculpture became more important, more humanized, and less united with architecture. The tendency toward mannerisms in gesture and greater realism reached monumental form in the *Well of Moses* (1395–1403; Dijon), by Claus Sluter. Monumental fresco painting was rare in the Gothic period, though STAINED GLASS and tapestry assumed great importance and showed a stylistic development parallel to that of sculpture. The Paris school was the center of Gothic painting and manuscript illumination. The *Pietà* of the Avignon school (Louvre; c.1460) is noted for its originality of expression. The elegant International Style was developed at this time, and panel painting dominated all other forms of painting. The culmination of Gothic art in the 15th cent. was marked by SCHONGAUER, Lochner, FOUQUET, and the van EYCKS.

Gothic language, dead language belonging to the Germanic subfamily of the Indo-European family of languages. One of the earliest literary remains in any Germanic tongue is the Gothic Bible of Ulfilas. See LANGUAGE (table).

Gothic revival, term designating a return to building styles of the Middle Ages, most important in the U.S. and England. Early works were in the late ROCOCO manner of Horace WALPOLE's "gothick" house, Strawberry Hill (1770). By 1830, architects were copying the originals more literally. A.W.N. Pugin's *Contrasts* (1836) and *True Principles of Pointed or Christian Architecture* (1841) were basic texts. Pugin advocated adherence to the methods of medieval builders to achieve structural clarity. John RUSKIN elaborated on these ideas. The movement came into conflict with the CLASSIC REVIVAL. The Church of England, supporting the Gothic style, provided for the restoration of many medieval religious buildings. In 1840 Pugin and Sir Charles Barry won a competition with Gothic designs for the houses of parliament. VIOLLET-LE-DUC led the exponents of Gothic design in France. In the U.S. the picturesque aspect of the style dominated. Gothic works include James Renwick's ST. PATRICK'S CATHEDRAL (N.Y.C.). The revival foundered because of the impossibility of reproducing Gothic buildings without a medieval economy or technology.

Goths: see OSTROGOTHS; VISIGOTHS.

Gottfried von Strassburg (Godfrey of Strasbourg) [gôt'frēt fən shtrăs'bŏŏrkh], fl. 13th cent., German poet. His unfinished Middle High German epic *Tristan* (c.1210) ranks him among the great medieval poets. See TRISTRAM AND ISOLDE.

Gottschalk, Louis Moreau, 1829–69, American pianist and composer; b. New Orleans. He achieved extraordinary international success as a performer. His compositions often use African-American and Creole rhythms and Spanish subjects. They include the piano pieces *The Last Hope* and *The Dying Poet*.

gouache: see WATERCOLOR PAINTING.

Gould, George Jay: see under GOULD, JAY.

Gould, Glenn, 1932–82, Canadian pianist and composer. A prodigy, he was noted for his interpretations of J.S. BACH and the romantic composers. After 1964 he concentrated on recording rather than performing.

Gould, Jay, 1836–92, American speculator; b. Delaware co., N.Y. From country-store clerk he rose to control half the railroad mileage in the Southwest, New York City's elevated lines, and the Western Union Telegraph Co. Aided by James FISK, he defeated Cornelius VANDERBILT for control of the Erie RR, but public protest over Gould's stock manipulations resulted in his expulsion in 1872. He then bought into the Union Pacific and other western railroads, and by sharp practice gained control of four lines, creating the Gould system. His scheming with Fisk to corner the gold market in 1869 caused the BLACK FRIDAY panic, and Gould's name became synonymous with autocratic business practice. His son, **George Jay Gould,** 1864–1923, b. N.Y.C., inherited his holdings. To compete with E.H. HARRIMAN, he bought or built railroads from coast to coast, but his unsound financing collapsed in the panic of 1907.

Gould, Stephen Jay, 1941–, American paleontologist and science writer; b. N.Y.C. With Niles Eldredge, Gould proposed (1972) the evolutionary theory of "punctuated equilibrium," which states that in geologic time and strata, the appearance of a new species occurs suddenly and without the continuous slow accretion of tiny variations, due to the nature of the evolutionary process and the relationship between the evolutionary and geologic time scales (see EVOLUTION; NATURAL SELECTION); and that the new species then persists virtually unchanged in the fossil record for perhaps millions of years. The "missing links" in evolutionary development sought since the time of Charles DARWIN are thus unlikely to be found. Elaboration of these concepts has led to extensive scientific debate. Gould has taught at Harvard Univ. since 1967 and has written many books and essays, including *The Mismeasure of Man* (1981) and *Wonderful Life* (1989).

Gounod, Charles François [gōō'nō], 1818–93, French composer of the romantic operas *Faust* (1859) and *Romeo and Juliet* (1867). He also wrote ORATORIOS and CANTATAS.

gourd, common name for some members of the Cucurbitaceae family, of tropical, subtropical, and temperate regions. The family is known for its many edible and otherwise useful plants, almost all annual herbs that grow as vines. Among these are *Cucurbita* species, including the PUMPKIN and summer squashes (varieties of *C. pepo*) and the winter squashes (*C. maxima*); and *Cucumis* species, including the CUCUMBERS, gherkins (*C. anguria*), and all MELONS except the WATERMELON. The edible fruit of the loofah, or California okra (*Luffa cylindrica*), is dried for the inner fibrous network, which is used as a scrubbing sponge. The term *gourd* is applied to those members of the family whose fruits have hard, durable shells used for ornament and as utensils, e.g., cups, dippers, and bowls. The Old World genus *Lagenaria* includes the calabash, dipper, and bottle gourds.

Gourlay, Robert Fleming [gŏŏr'lē], 1778–1863, Scottish writer and agitator in Canada. After emigrating to ONTARIO in 1817, he opposed the control of land grants by the FAMILY COMPACT clique and was imprisoned and banished (1819) by it. His conviction was nullified (1842), and he returned briefly (1856–60) to Canada.

gout, condition that manifests itself as recurrent attacks of acute ARTHRITIS, distinguished from other forms of arthritis by the presence of increased uric acid in the body. It may become chronic and deforming. Gout usually begins with an acute attack of pain, inflammation, extreme tenderness, and redness in the affected joint. Treatment includes anti-inflammatory drugs, high liquid intake, and medication that increases uric acid excretion by the kidneys.

Gower, John, 1330?–1408, English poet, a friend of CHAUCER. His three major works are *Speculum meditantis* or *Miroir de l'omme,* an allegorical manual in French; *Vox clamantis,* in Latin; and *Confessio amantis* (c.1390), in English, a collection of stories illustrating the Seven Deadly Sins.

Gowon, Yakubu, 1934–, Nigerian head of state (1966–75). In 1966 he was appointed commander in chief of the armed forces and head of the military government. He led (1967–70) the fight against secessionist BIAFRA, and after the Nigerian victory he attempted a policy of reconciliation. He was deposed while abroad in 1975 and went in exile into England.

Goya y Lucientes, Francisco José de, 1746–1828, Spanish painter and graphic artist, the greatest painter of his age. After studying in Zaragoza, Madrid, and Rome, Goya designed a series of ROCOCO tapestries full of gaiety and charm, enhanced by earthy realism. The candor of observation revealed in these early works was later to make him the most graphic and savage of satirists. He became court painter to CHARLES III and CHARLES IV, and his royal portraits, painted with extraordinary realism, show his contempt for his subjects. In 1793 a severe illness left him deaf, and thereafter his works were cheerless. Two of his most celebrated paintings, *Maja Nude* and *Maja Clothed* (both: Prado) are from this period, as was his chief religious work, FRESCOES for the Church of San Antonio de la Florida, Madrid. It is in his ETCHINGS and AQUATINTS that his disillusionment is clearly seen. His *Caprichos* are a grotesque social satire; his *Disasters of War,* a series of etchings suggested by the Napoleonic invasions of Spain, are an indictment of human evil and corruption. Also inspired by the Napoleonic invasions is his compelling painting, *The Third of May 1808* (1814–15; Prado). At 70 Goya retired to his villa, decorating it with "Black Paintings" of macabre subjects, e.g., *Satan Devouring His Children, Witches' Sabbath,* and *The Three Fates* (all: Prado).

Goyen, Jan Josephszoon van, 1596–1656, Dutch landscape painter. His grayish-green landscapes of harbors, canals, riverbanks, and winter scenes sacrifice minute detail for atmospheric effects, e.g., *Banks of a Canal* (Louvre).

Goytisolo, Juan [goitēsō'lō], 1931–, Spanish writer. His novels, often realistic portrayals of post–civil war Spanish society, include *The Young Assassins* (1954), *The Party's Over* (1962), and *Makbara* (1980).

Gozzoli, Benozzo [gôt'tsōlē], 1420–97, Florentine painter; b. Benozzo di Lese. He was apprenticed to Fra ANGELICO. His famous *Journey of the Magi* (Medici Palace) depicts a magnificent cavalcade, with Lorenzo de' Medici as one of the Magi.

Gracchi [grăk'ī], two Roman statesmen and social reformers, brothers. **Tiberius Sempronius Gracchus,** d. 133 B.C., the elder brother, became alarmed at the growth of wealth of the few. He stood for the tribunate of the people in 133 B.C. as an avowed reformer and was the author of the Sempronian Law to redistribute the public lands. At the next election Tiberius renominated himself, but the senate had the election postponed. In a great riot on the following day Tiberius was killed. His brother, **Caius Sempronius Gracchus,** d. 121 B.C., became the organizer of the reform movement begun by Tiberius. Elected (123) tribune of the people, he initiated a series of remarkable social reforms. Caius was reelected (122) tribune, but the following year was defeated for reelection. Repeal of his measures was proposed, and in the ensuing riots Caius was killed.

Grace, 1929–82, princess consort of Monaco; b. Philadelphia as Grace Patricia Kelly. She was a major film star until 1956, when she married RAINIER III, the ruling prince of Monaco. She won the 1954 Academy Award for her performance in *The Country Girl.*

grace, in Christian theology, the free favor of God toward people, necessary for their salvation. Differing conceptions of grace led to challenges by the 5th-cent. heresy Pelagianism and by 16th-cent. CALVINISM. There is also cleavage in Christianity about the role of sacraments. Roman Catholics and Orthodox Christians hold that sacraments confer grace; Protestants, that they are merely signs, not sources, of grace.

Graces, in Greek mythology, personifications of beauty and charm; daughters of ZEUS and the oceanid NYMPH Eurynome. Also known as the Charites, they were named Aglaia, Thalia, and Euphrosyne. The Romans called them the Gratiae.

Gracián, Baltasar [gräthyän'], 1601–56, Spanish JESUIT writer of the GOLDEN AGE. His masterpiece is the allegorical, pessimistic novel *El criticón* (3 parts, 1651–57), which contrasts an idyllic primitive life with the evils of civilization. It brought him exile and disgrace.

grackle, New World BIRD of the family Icteridae, which includes the BLACKBIRD and BOBOLINK. The common grackle of the Atlantic coast is black with metallic hues. It eats grains and insects but is also a cannibalistic nest robber.

Graf, Steffi, 1969–, German tennis player. Graf won her first major title, the French Open, in 1987. In 1988 she captured the Grand Slam (Australian, French, and U.S. opens and Wimbledon) and the women's singles gold medal in the Olympics. Graf has subsequently won the Australian Open three times (1989–90, 1994), U.S. Open twice (1989, 1993), French Open once (1993), Wimbledon four times (1989, 1991–93) and a silver medal in the 1992 Olympics.

graffito, or **sgraffito,** decorative medium in which a plaster surface is scratched to uncover a darker, contrasting color. The technique was known to the ancient Egyptians and Greeks. During the Renaissance, Italian architects used graffito to decorate the surfaces of buildings. A graffito (pl. graffiti) also refers to an irreverent inscription on a wall in a public space. Archaeologists used the term to designate informal writings on ancient monuments. In the second half of the 20th cent., the term has been applied to many acts of property defacement involving paint and other graphic media.

grafting, horticultural practice of uniting the cambial layers, or CAMBIUM, of two closely related plants so that they grow as one. The scion (the piece grafted onto the stock or rooted part) may be a single bud or a cutting with several buds; the stock may be a whole plant or a root. The primary reason for grafting is to propagate HYBRIDS that do not bear seed or do not grow true from seed. It is also used to increase fruit tree productivity by adding to the numbers of buds, to grow a plant in an unfamiliar environment by using a stock adapted to that environment, and to combat diseases and pests by using resistant stock.

Graham, Billy (William Franklin Graham), 1918–, American evangelist; b. Charlotte, N.C. Ordained (1939) a minister in the Southern Baptist Church, he began his career as an evangelist in 1944. A fiery and persuasive preacher, he has had highly successful evangelistic campaigns that have brought him international attention. The Billy Graham Evangelical Association publishes *Decision* magazine and produces material for radio, television, and films.

Graham, Martha, 1894–1991, American dancer, teacher, and choreographer; b. Pittsburgh, Pa. She studied and made her debut (1920) with the Denishawn companies, and then formed (1929) her own troupe. She was a leading figure in MODERN DANCE; her works include *Appalachian Spring* (1944) and *The Archaic Hours* (1969).

Graham, Thomas, 1805–69, Scottish chemist. His research in diffusion in both gases and liquids led to his formulation of Graham's law. The first to work in colloidal chemistry, he observed that some

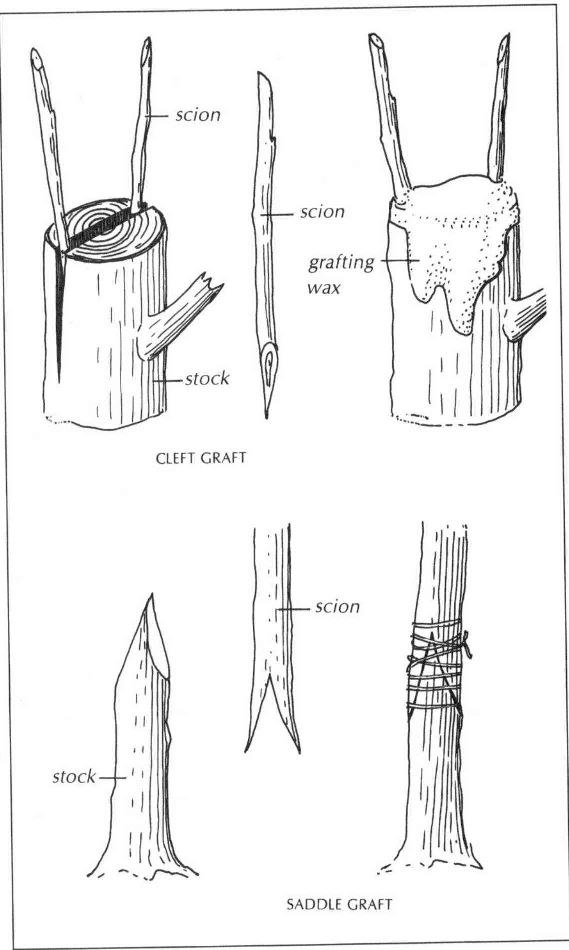

Two methods of grafting

Martha Graham, "Lamentation," 1935

substances pass through a membrane more slowly than others, thus discovering DIALYSIS. His studies of phosphoric acid led to the present chemical concept of polybasic acids.

Grahame, Kenneth, 1859–1931, English author. His humorous works include *The Golden Age* (1895) and, his children's classic *The Wind in the Willows* (1908).

grain, in agriculture, the caryopsis, or dry FRUIT, of a cereal GRASS, the seedlike fruits of BUCKWHEAT and other plants, and the plants bearing such fruits. Grains, whole or ground into meal or flour, are the main food of humans and domestic animals. The food content is mostly carbohydrate, but some protein, oil, and vitamins are present. Low in water content, grains can be stored for long periods. The primary grain crops—including WHEAT, RICE, and CORN—together occupy about half of total world cropland.

Grainger, Percy Aldridge, 1882–1961, Australian-American pianist and composer. He settled in the U.S. in 1914. A friend of GRIEG, he is noted for settings of folk melodies.

gram: see METRIC SYSTEM; WEIGHTS AND MEASURES, table.

Gramme, Zénobe-Théophile, 1826–1901, Belgian electrical engineer. Model-maker for a Parisian manufacturer of electrical devices, he developed (1869), with little knowledge of electrical theory, an improved, practical direct-current dynamo. By reversing its principle, he invented the electric engine. In 1872, working with others, he transmitted direct-current electricity over a long distance.

Gramm-Rudman-Hollings Act, U.S. budget deficit reduction measure of 1985. The law provided for automatic spending cuts to take effect if Congress failed to reach established targets. Because the automatic cuts were declared unconstitutional, a revised version of the act was passed in 1987; it failed to result in reduced deficits. A 1990 revision of the act changed its focus from deficit reduction to spending control.

Gramsci, Antonio, 1891–1937, Italian political theorist. After rejecting Socialism, Gramsci helped found (1921) the Italian Communist party. As party chief (1924) he was elected to the chamber of deputies (1924–26). When MUSSOLINI outlawed the party, Gramsci was arrested (1926) and spent his remaining years in prison (1926–37), where his writings, *Letters from Prison* (1947), *The Modern Prince* (1949), and *Prison Notebooks* (1971) proved him to be one of the leading Marxist thinkers of the century.

Gram's stain, laboratory staining technique that distinguishes between two groups of bacteria, gram-negative and gram-positive, by identifying differences in their cell-wall structure. Pinpointing the type of bacterial pathogens involved in disease (see BACTERIA) can be valuable in determining treatment.

Granada, city (1988 est. pop. 263,000), capital of Granada prov., S Spain, in Andalusia, at the confluence of the Darro and Genil rivers and at the foot of the Sierra Nevada. Now the center of a mineral-rich agricultural region, Granada flourished as the seat (1238–1492) of the kingdom of Granada, the last refuge of the MOORS, driven south by the Christian reconquest of Spain. The city is dominated by the Alhambra, a Moorish citadel and palace, and also contains a cathedral and the palace of Holy Roman Emperor CHARLES V.

Granados, Enrique [gränä'thōs], 1867–1916, Spanish composer and pianist; b. Cuba. He created the Spanish piano manner later used by FALLA. *Goyescas* (1912–14), a set of piano pieces, is his outstanding work.

Gran Chaco, lowland plain, c.250,000 sq mi (647,500 sq km), in Paraguay and adjacent parts of Bolivia and Argentina. It is sparsely populated and one of the hottest places in South America, with alternating flood and drought seasons. Resources include oil (in the east) and quebracho, a source of tannin.

Grand Alliance, War of the, 1688–97, war between France and members of the League of Augsburg (known as the Grand Alliance after 1689). League members included the Holy Roman emperor, the German states, Spain, Sweden, the Dutch Netherlands, Savoy, and England (after WILLIAM III ascended the throne). They attempted to thwart the territorial incursions of LOUIS XIV. Despite some English victories, France was generally successful. But as the war dragged on, both sides wearied of it. The Treaty of Ryswick, which ended the war, forced France to give up most of its conquests. See FRENCH AND INDIAN WARS.

Grand Army of the Republic (GAR), organization established by Union veterans of the U.S. CIVIL WAR in 1866. At its peak in 1890, it had more than 400,000 members. Its principal goals were to aid fellow veterans and their families, obtain pension increases, and preserve the memory of fallen comrades (they secured the adoption of MEMORIAL DAY in 1868). They exerted a strong influence on the REPUBLICAN PARTY until 1900. The last member died in 1956.

Grand Banks, submarine plateau off SE Newfoundland, Canada. Shallow and frequently fog-bound, the waters in the area are rich in cod, halibut, haddock, and other marine life, making it one of the most important fishing grounds in the world. There are also oil deposits.

Grand Canal, world's longest and oldest constructed waterway, extending c.1,000 mi (1,600 km) from Tianjin (the port for Beijing) in N China to Hangzhou and the CHANG (Yangtze) R. valley in the south. The canal, which was started in the 6th cent. B.C., was lengthened A.D. c.610 and again extended in the 13th cent. Long in decline, it was dredged, widened, and renovated after 1958.

Grand Canary: see CANARY ISLANDS.

Grand Canyon, world-famous gorge cut by the COLORADO R., NW Arizona. It is up to 1 mi (1.6 km) deep, 4–18 mi (6–29 km) wide, and more than 200 mi (320 km) long. Multicolored layers of rock in the canyon wall record more than 2 million years of geologic time. Trails wind from the rim of the gorge to its floor. The most spectacular section of the canyon is part of Grand Canyon National Park (see NATIONAL PARKS, table) and is one of the principal tourist attractions in the U.S., visited each year by nearly 4 million people.

Grand Canyon National Park: see NATIONAL PARKS (table).

Grand Coulee Dam, concrete dam, 550 ft (168 m) high and 4,173 ft (1,272 m) long, on the COLUMBIA R., Washington. Built 1933–42, it impounds **Franklin D. Roosevelt Lake** (130 sq mi/337 sq km), one of the largest reservoirs in the U.S., and supports a hydroelectric installation that was expanded during the early 1980s into one of the largest in the world (more than 9.7 Mw capacity).

grandfather clause, provision in constitutions of seven Southern states (adopted 1895–1910) exempting from rigid economic and literacy requirements those persons eligible to vote on Jan. 1, 1867, and their descendants. Since African Americans had not yet been enfranchised on that date, the provision effectively barred them from the polls while granting voting rights to poor and illiterate whites. The clause was ruled unconstitutional by the Supreme Court in 1915. The term *grandfather clause* is now applied to any kind of legal exemption based on prior status.

grand jury: see under JURY.

Grand Prairie, city (1990 pop. 99,616), Dallas and Tarrant cos., N Texas; inc. 1909. A rapidly growing city between Dallas and Fort Worth, it is a distribution hub with a large aerospace industry. Other manufactures include mobile homes, metal goods, plastics, and automobiles. A wildlife park and the Six Flags over Texas amusement park are there.

Grand Rapids, city (1990 pop. 189,126), seat of Kent co., W central Mich., on the Grand R.; inc. 1850. The commercial center for a farm and orchard area, the city is famous for furniture manufacturing (begun 1859), which is still one of its leading industries. Gravel, gypsum, and appliances are among its other products. Grand Rapids is the gateway to a large recreational area of Michigan.

Grand Teton National Park: see NATIONAL PARKS (table).

Grange, Red (Harold Edward Grange), 1903–91, American football player; b. Forksville, Pa. As an All-American halfback (1923–25) at the Univ. of Illinois, he scored 31 touchdowns and gained 3,367 yards. In his professional career with the Chicago Bears (1925–35), he scored 1,058 points. Later he became a radio and television sportscaster.

Granger movement, American agrarian movement named for the National Grange of the Patrons of Husbandry, founded in 1867. Its local units were called granges and its members grangers. Originally established for social and educational purposes, the granges became political forums seeking to correct economic abuses through cooperative enterprise. The "Granger laws," regulating railroads and grain storage facilities, established the constitutional principle of public regulation of private utilities. After 1876 other groups adopted the agrarian protest and the granges reverted to their social role.

granite, coarse-grained ROCK composed chiefly of QUARTZ and FELDSPARS, of varying color. It is commonly believed to be igneous (having solidified from a molten state), but some granites show evidence of being metamorphic in origin (see METAMORPHISM). Formed at depth, granite masses are exposed at the earth's surface by crustal movements or erosion of overlying rocks. Very coarse-grained granite, called pegmatite, may contain minerals and gems of economic value.

Grant, Cary, 1904–86, American film actor; b. England as Archibald Leach. Debonair and charming, he appeared in such films as *Bringing Up Baby* (1938), *The Philadelphia Story* (1940), and *North by Northwest* (1959). In 1970 he received the Academy Award for general excellence.

Grant, Ulysses Simpson, 1822–85, commander in chief of the Union army in the U.S. Civil War, 18th president of the U.S. (1869–77); b. Point Pleasant, Ohio, as Hiram Ulysses Grant. He graduated from West Point in 1843. Upon the outbreak of the CIVIL WAR, he was commissioned colonel, then brigadier general, of a regiment of volunteers and fought his first battle at Belmont, Mo., on Nov. 9, 1861. In Feb. 1862 he captured Fort Henry and Fort Donelson in Tennessee, providing the first major Union victory, and he was at once promoted to major general. In Apr. 1862 he barely escaped defeat at the Battle of SHILOH. The VICKSBURG CAMPAIGN (1862–63), which ended Confederate control of the Mississippi, was one of his greatest successes. Called to the supreme command in the West (Oct. 1863), he thoroughly defeated the Confederate forces under Braxton BRAGG at CHATTANOOGA. Pres. LINCOLN made him commander in chief, with the rank of lieutenant general, in Mar. 1864. He directed the Union army in the WILDERNESS CAMPAIGN (May–June 1864), wearing out the Confederates by sheer attrition; he received Robert E. LEE's surrender at APPOMATTOX on Apr. 9, 1865. He was made full general in 1866, the first U.S. citizen after Washington to hold that rank. Grant was elected president in 1868, defeating Horatio Seymour, and reelected in 1872, defeating Horace GREELEY. His administration was characterized by corruption, special-interest legislation, and vigorous pursuit of a punitive RECONSTRUCTION program; in foreign affairs, however, much was accomplished by his able secretary of state, Hamilton FISH. Grant's *Personal Memoirs* (2 vol., 1885–86) rank among the great military narratives of history.

Granville-Barker, Harley Granville, 1877–1946, English dramatist and critic. A major avant-garde producer of plays in the early 1900s, he also wrote realistic plays, e.g., *Waste* (1907) and *The Madras House* (1910), and the monumental *Prefaces to Shakespeare* (6 vol., 1927–74).

grape, common name for the family Vitaceae, mostly climbing shrubs of tropical, subtropical, and temperate zones. The WINE grape (*Vitis vinifera*), known since ancient times, probably originated around the Mediterranean and in W Asia; it is now grown also in temperate regions of the Americas. Grapes grown east of the Rockies are usually hybrids of this species and disease-resistant American grapes, or are varieties of native species. Raisins are dried grapes. The genus *Parthenocissus,* native to the U.S., includes the VIRGINIA CREEPER (*P. quinquefolia*) and Boston IVY (*P. tricuspidata*).

grapefruit, evergreen tree (*Citrus paradisi*) of the RUE family and its globular CITRUS FRUIT, which grows in grapelike bunches and weighs from one to five pounds (0.45 to 2.27 kg). It is believed that the pomelo (*C. maxima*), long a popular fruit in parts of Asia, was introduced into the West Indies, where a mutation produced the grapefruit.

graphics: see COMPUTER GRAPHICS; ENGRAVING; ETCHING; PRINTING; WOODCUT AND WOOD ENGRAVING.

graphite, plumbago, or **black lead,** mineral, one of two crystalline forms of the element CARBON, occurring in various parts of the world. Dark gray or black, greasy, and soft, with a metallic luster, it is a good conductor of electricity. It is used to make crucibles and electrodes; mixed with clay, it is the so-called lead of pencils.

Grass, Günter [gräs], 1927–, German writer and artist; b. Danzig (Gdańsk, Poland). Antimilitarism and social criticism are expressed in his novels *The Tin Drum* (1959) and *Dog Years* (1963). His early works are symbolic; later writings, such as *From the Diary of a Snail* (1973), reflect his political activism. *The Flounder* (1977) is a highly acclaimed novel treating politics, feminism, and the art of cooking.

grass, any plant of the family Gramineae, a widely distributed group of mostly annual and perennial herbs. The grass family is of far greater economic importance than any other. It includes the cereal grasses, e.g., WHEAT, RICE, CORN, OATS, BARLEY, and RYE, which provide the GRAIN that is the staple food in most countries and the major type of feed; most hay and pasture plants, e.g., SORGHUM and bluegrass; SUGARCANE; and species of REED and BAMBOO used for thatching and construction. In addition, plants of the grass family provide raw material for the production of many liquors and PAPER items, form climax vegetation (see ECOLOGY) in areas of low rainfall (see PAMPAS; PRAIRIE; SAVANNA; STEPPE; VELDT), and help to prevent EROSION.

Grasse, François Joseph Paul, comte de [gräs], 1722–88, French admiral. His blockade of the York and James rivers during the AMERICAN REVOLUTION effectively bottled up Gen. CORNWALLIS at Yorktown and led to the great American victory of the YORKTOWN CAMPAIGN.

grasshopper, slender, winged, singing INSECT of two families in the order Orthoptera, having powerful hind legs adapted for jumping and initiating flight and chewing mouthparts. Usually only males produce a song, but both sexes possess auditory organs. They range from ½ to 4 in. (1–10 cm) in length. The long-horned grasshopper family includes the KATYDID; the smaller, short-horned family includes the LOCUST.

Grasso, Ella Tambussi, 1919–81, American politician, governor of Connecticut (1975–81); b. Windsor Locks, Conn. She served Connecticut in the legislature (1952–56) and as secretary of state (1958–70). She was elected to the U.S. House of Representatives in 1970. Elected governor in 1974, she was the first American woman to achieve the office of governor in her own right.

Gratiae: see GRACES.

Grattan, Henry, 1746–1820, Irish statesman. Entering the Irish Parliament in 1775, he became known as a brilliant orator. He helped achieve nominal legislative independence for the Irish Parliament, and he helped gain Catholics the right to vote in Ireland. When hopes that Catholics could sit in Parliament were dashed, he retired (1797). He sat in the British Parliament from 1805 but took little part.

Graves, Michael, 1934–, American architect; b. Indianapolis. A member of the New York "Five" group in the 1960s, he emerged in the 1970s as a leading proponent of architectural POSTMODERNISM. His projects include the Portland Building, Portland, Oreg.; the Walt Disney Co. Corporate Headquarters, Burbank, Calif.; and the Newark Museum, Newark, N.J. He is also known for his furniture and furnishings designs.

Graves, Robert, 1895–1985, English poet, novelist, and critic. He was first successful with his war memoir *Good-bye to All That* (1929). Best known for his poetry and for novels on Roman history, *I, Claudius* (1934) and *Claudius the God* (1934), he also wrote studies of myth, e.g., *Greek Myths* (2 vol., 1955), criticism, and translations of APULEIUS and HOMER.

gravitation, the attractive FORCE existing between any two particles of matter. Because this force acts throughout the universe, it is often called universal gravitation. Isaac NEWTON was the first to recognize that the force holding any object to the earth is the same as the force holding the moon and planets in their orbits. According to Newton's law of universal gravitation, the force between any two bodies is directly proportional to the product of their MASSES and inversely proportional to the square of the distance between them. The constant of proportionality is known as the gravitational constant (symbol *G*) and equals 6.670×10^{-11} newton-M^2/kg^2 in the mks system of units. The measure of the force of gravitation on a given body on earth is the WEIGHT of that body. In the general theory of RELATIVITY, gravitation is explained geometrically: matter in its immediate neighborhood causes the curvature of the four-dimensional SPACE-TIME continuum. See also CELESTIAL MECHANICS.

gravitational collapse, in astronomy, theoretically predicted final stage in the life history of a star (see STELLAR EVOLUTION). Gravitational collapse may begin when a star has depleted its steady sources of nuclear energy and can no longer produce the expansive force, which is a result of normal gas pressure, that supports the star against the compressive force of its own GRAVITATION. As the star shrinks in size (and increases in density), it may assume one of several forms, depending upon its mass. A low-mass star may become a WHITE DWARF; a more massive star may explode as a SUPERNOVA and become a NEUTRON STAR. If the core remaining after a supernova is more than three times the sun's mass, however, the star can collapse without limit to an indefinitely small size. According to the general theory of RELATIVITY, space becomes curved in the vicinity of matter; the greater the concentration of matter, the greater the curvature. When the radius of a star decreases below a certain limit (the Schwarzschild radius, or event horizon) determined by its mass, the extreme curvature of space seals off contact with the outside world. The former star is now a **black hole.** Because light and other forms of energy and matter are permanently trapped inside a black hole by the enormous pull of gravitation, a black hole can be observed only indirectly. For example, in some BINARY-STAR systems, such as the X-ray source Cygnus X-1, the smaller and invisible companions are strong emitters of X-rays and are suspected of being black holes. Gas flows from the larger component of the binary and forms an accretion disk around the black hole. As the gas from this disk spirals into the black hole, it is accelerated by the collapsed star's enormous gravitational pull; as this happens, the matter becomes compressed and heated to the extreme temperatures at which X rays are emitted.

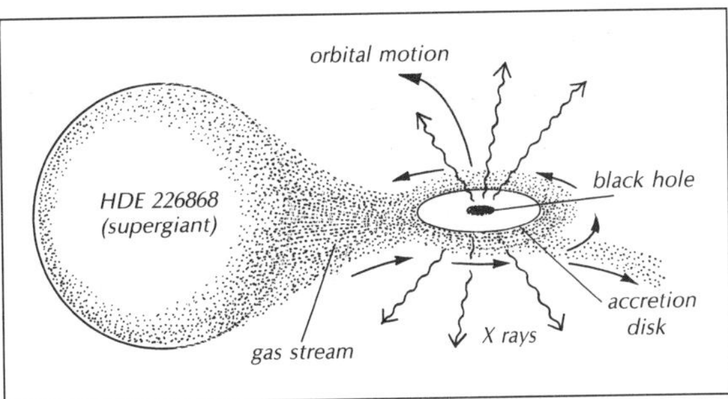

Gravitational collapse: The X-ray source Cygnus X-1 is believed to be a black hole (a massive star that has undergone gravitational collapse and cannot now be seen directly) orbiting around an optically observed supergiant star (HDE 226868).

Gray, Asa, 1810–88, leading American botanist and taxonomist; b. Oneida, N.Y. Professor of natural history at Harvard and a prolific author, he (with the botanist John Torrey) helped to revise LINNAEUS's taxonomy, basing his version mainly on fruit anatomy rather than gross morphology. His writings include the *Manual of Botany* (8th centennial ed. 1950), the standard reference for E U.S. flora; *Structural Botany* (6th ed. 1879); and *The Elements of Botany* (1887).

Gray, Elisha, 1835–1901, American inventor; b. Barnesville, Ohio. He patented many electrical devices, most having to do with the telegraph. In 1875, experimenting with transmitting musical notes, he hit on the idea of transmitting the human voice. In early 1876 he filed for a patent caveat, just hours after the registration of Alexander Graham BELL's final telephone patent.

Gray, Hanna Holborn, 1930–, American historian, president of the Univ. of Chicago (1978–93); b. Germany. Her father, the eminent historian Hajo Holborn, fled the Nazis in 1934 and settled in the U.S. A Renaissance and Reformation scholar, Gray became provost of Yale in 1974 and acting president in 1977. Her appointment to Chicago made her the first woman to head a major American university.

Gray, Thomas, 1716–71, English poet. A scholar of Greek and history, he spent a secluded life at Cambridge. His first important poems, written in 1742, include "Ode on a Distant Prospect of Eton College." The meditative "Elegy Written in a Country Churchyard" (1751) is probably the most quoted poem in English. Horace WALPOLE published Gray's Pindaric odes in 1757. Gray's verse illustrates the evolution of 18th-cent. English poetry from CLASSICISM to early ROMANTICISM.

Graz [gräts], city (1991 pop. 232,155), capital of Styria prov., SE Austria, on the Mur R. Probably founded in the 12th cent., it was built around the Schlossberg, a mountain peak, on which stand the famous Uhrturm clock tower and the ruins of a 15th-cent. fortress. The second largest city in Austria, Graz produces iron and steel, precision and optical instruments, and machinery. Noteworthy are its Gothic structures and the Johanneum museum. The astronomer Johannes KEPLER taught at the university.

Great Awakening, series of religious revivals that swept over the American colonies about the middle of the 18th cent. Beginning in the 1720s, Theodorus Frelinghuysen and Gilbert Tennent made local stirrings in New Jersey. In New England the movement was started (1734) by Jonathan EDWARDS. It was spread by a tour (1739–41) of George WHITEFIELD and reached the South with the preaching (1748–59) of Samuel Davies. The Great Awakening led to bitter doctrinal disputes, but it also resulted in missionary work among Native Americans and in the founding of new educational institutions. It encouraged a democratic spirit in religion.

Great Barrier Reef, largest coral reef in the world, in the CORAL SEA, off the coast of Queensland, NE Australia. It is c.1,250 mi (2,000 km) long and is separated from the mainland by a shallow lagoon up to 100 mi (161 km) wide. The reef is composed of hundreds of individual reefs and has many islets, coral gardens, and unusual marine life. In some places it is more than 400 ft (122 m) thick.

Great Basin, desert region, in Nevada, Utah, and parts of adjoining states, forming the northern half of the **Basin and Range** physiographic province. It was explored (1843–45) and named by J.C. FRÉMONT, who recognized it as a basin of interior drainage (i.e., without outlet to the sea). GREAT SALT LAKE, Sevier, and Utah are the chief lakes. The basin is sparsely populated. Industries include defense-related manufacturing, tourism, mining, and ranching.

Great Basin National Park: see NATIONAL PARKS (table).

Great Bear Lake, largest lake of Canada and fourth largest of North America, c.12,275 sq mi (31,800 sq km), on the Arctic Circle in the Mackenzie district of the Northwest Territories. The lake, which is ice-bound for eight months of the year, is 190 mi (310 km) long, 25–110 mi (40–177 km) wide, and drains west through the Great Bear R. to the MACKENZIE R. Port Radium, in the east, was a radium-mining boom town in the 1930s.

Great Britain, officially United Kingdom of Great Britain and Northern Ireland, constitutional monarchy (1991 pop. 54,156,067), 94,226 sq mi (244,044 sq km), on the British Isles, off W Europe. It comprises England, Wales, and Scotland on the island of Great Britain, and Northern Ireland on the island of Ireland. The capital is LONDON. Great Britain is one of the world's leading industrial nations. It lacks most of the raw materials needed for industry, however, and must also import about 40% of its food supplies. Thus, its prosperity is heavily dependent on the export of manufactured goods in exchange for raw materials and foodstuffs, and it has long been an extremely active trading nation. Manufacturing and service industries employ more than one third of the total work force. Major industries include mechanical and electrical engineering, food processing, iron and steel, paper and printing, motor vehicles, chemicals, textiles, and aircraft. Production of oil from NORTH SEA wells began in 1975, and by 1979 the country was self-sufficient in petroleum. Coal is also mined in large quantities. Almost 30% of the land is arable, and almost half is suitable for meadows and pastures. Chief commodities are dairy products and beef cattle and other livestock, including many sheep, which are raised for meat and wool. The coal, gas, electricity, railroad, shipbuilding, nuclear energy, and aerospace industries, which were mainly publicly owned until the late 1970s, have undergone increasing PRIVATIZATION. Great Britain is the fourth most populous nation in Europe; the greatest population concentration is in England. English is the universal language, but Welsh is widely spoken in Wales and some Gaelic in Scotland. The Church of England is the established church in England; the Presbyterian Church is legally established in Scotland. There are also large numbers of Roman Catholics and Methodists and smaller minorities of Muslims, Jews, Hindus, Sikhs, and Buddhists. Immigration has made Great Britain a multiracial society; Indian, Pakistani, West Indian, African, Chinese, and other minorities total 2.7 million. The hereditary monarch plays a largely ceremonial role in the government. Sovereignty rests in PARLIAMENT, which consists of an elected House of Commons and a nonelected House of Lords. Effective power resides in the Commons, where the leading party usually provides the executive—the cabinet, headed by the prime minister. For physical geography, see ENGLAND; IRELAND, NORTHERN; SCOTLAND; WALES; for the early history of Scotland (to 1707) and Wales (to 1536), prior to incorporation in Great Britain, see separate articles.

Early English History. Little is known of the earliest inhabitants of Britain, but the great structure at STONEHENGE is evidence of their advanced BRONZE AGE culture. The first Celtic invaders arrived in Britain in the early 5th cent. B.C. In A.D. 43 the emperor CLAUDIUS I began the Roman conquest of Britain, which prospered and grew under four centuries of Roman rule. With the disintegration of the empire by the early 5th cent., Germanic peoples—the ANGLO-SAXONS and the Jutes—initiated waves of invasion and settlement that gradually coalesced into a group of small kingdoms. Raids by VIKINGS (Danes), begun in the late 8th cent., turned into full-scale invasion in 865, and by 1016 the Dane CANUTE ruled all of England. The conquest of England in 1066 by the Norman WILLIAM I (see NORMAN CONQUEST) ushered in a new era in English history with the introduction of FEUDALISM. Conflict between the kings and the nobles over abuse of royal power came to a head under King JOHN, whose unprecedented financial demands and unpopular church and foreign policies resulted in the MAGNA CARTA (1215), a landmark in English constitutional history. The HUNDRED YEARS WAR with France, which began in 1337, and the Black Death (see PLAGUE), which first arrived in Britain in 1348, hastened the breakdown of the feudal system. Dynastic wars (see ROSES, WARS OF THE) weakened both the nobility and the monarchy and ended with the accession (1485) of the TUDOR family. Under the Tudors, England flourished and was introduced to RENAISSANCE learning. HENRY VIII (r.1509–47) began the English Reformation by breaking with the papacy and establishing the Church of England. He also brought about the union (1536) of England and Wales. The English Renaissance reached its peak during the reign of ELIZABETH I, a time of great artistic achievement and overseas expansion. At her death (1603) the crowns of England and Scotland were united by the accession to the English throne of the Stuart JAMES I (James VI of Scotland). Under the STUARTS a bitter power struggle between the monarchy and Parliament culminated in the ENGLISH CIVIL WAR (1642–48). The victory of the parliamentarians led to the execution (1649) of CHARLES I, abolition of the monarchy, and establishment of the Commonwealth and the Protectorate under Oliver CROMWELL. Following Cromwell's death, CHARLES II was invited (1660) to become king (see RESTORATION). The old issues of religion, money, and royal prerogative were not laid to rest, however, until the GLORIOUS REVOLUTION (1688) ousted JAMES II and placed (1689) WILLIAM III and MARY II on the throne. The BILL OF RIGHTS confirmed that sovereignty resided in Parliament. In 1707 the Act of Union legally united the kingdoms of Scotland and England.

The Empire. In the 18th cent. Britain began to play a more active role in world affairs, emerging from the SEVEN YEARS WAR (1756–63) as possessor of the world's greatest empire (see BRITISH EMPIRE). It suffered a serious loss in the AMERICAN REVOLUTION (1775–83), but it was preeminent in INDIA, settled AUSTRALIA, and acquired still more territories in the wars against NAPOLEON I. A vain attempt to solve the longstanding Irish problem (see IRELAND) brought about the union (1801) of Great Britain and Ireland. The INDUSTRIAL REVOLUTION, in the late 18th and early 19th cent., transformed social and economic life. Under Queen VICTORIA (r.1837–1901) Britain reached the height of its commercial, political, and economic leadership. The country's aggressive diplomacy in Europe culminated in the CRIMEAN WAR, and social and political reforms were also begun. The dominant figures on the political scene were the prime ministers Benjamin DISRAELI and William GLADSTONE.

The 20th Century. In the early 20th cent., growing military and

economic rivalry with Germany led Britain to ally itself with France and Russia (see TRIPLE ALLIANCE AND TRIPLE ENTENTE), and in 1914 Britain entered WORLD WAR I. Despite British victory, the war drained the nation of wealth and manpower, and in the postwar years Britain faced severe economic problems. In an effort to settle the thorny Irish problem, Northern Ireland was created in 1920 and the Irish Free State in 1921–22. Prime Min. Neville CHAMBERLAIN pursued a policy of appeasement toward the rising tide of German and Italian aggression, but this failed. In 1939 the Germans invaded Poland, and Britain entered WORLD WAR II by declaring war on Germany. The nation sustained intensive bombardment in the Battle of Britain, but the British people, inspired by Prime Min. Winston CHURCHILL, rose to a supreme war effort. Following the defeat (1945) of Germany, the Labour party, led by Clement ATTLEE, gained power and launched a program, including nationalization of industry, to revive the war-damaged economy. The postwar years brought independence to many former colonies, and Britain's status as a world military and economic power gradually declined. In the early 1970s the country underwent its worst economic crisis since World War II, and although the situation eased somewhat with the discovery of oil in the North Sea, the early 1980s saw a continuation of the problems of inflation and unemployment accompanied by a weakening currency. Conservative Margaret THATCHER became (1979) Britain's first woman prime minister. Opposed to the Labour welfare state, she cut social programs, privatized many state-owned businesses, and sought to break the power of organized labor. In 1982 she led the nation in a successful undeclared war with Argentina over the disputed FALKLAND ISLANDS. In the mid and late 1980s, the economy grew and unemployment decreased, but economic conditions again worsened in the 1990s, with unemployment rising to 9.4% by early 1992. Thatcher was succeeded as prime minister by Conservative John MAJOR in 1990.

Great Dane, very large, powerful WORKING DOG; shoulder height, up to 36 in. (91.4 cm); weight, up to 150 lb (68.1 kg). Its short coat may be brindle, fawn, black, or white with black patches. Developed in Germany over 400 years ago, it was used as a boarhound.

Great Depression, the severe U.S. economic crisis of the 1930s, supposedly precipitated by the 1929 stock market crash. Certain

RULERS OF ENGLAND AND GREAT BRITAIN *(including dates of reign)*

Saxons and Danes Egbert, 802–39 Æthelwulf, son of Egbert, 839–58 Æthelbald, son of Æthelwulf, 858–60 Æthelbert, 2d son of Æthelwulf, 860–65 Æthelred, 3d son of Æthelwulf, 865–71 Alfred, 4th son of Æthelwulf, 871–99 Edward (the Elder), son of Alfred, 899–924 Athelstan, son of Edward, 924–39 Edmund, 3d son of Edward, 939–46 Edred, 4th son of Edward, 946–55 Edwy, son of Edmund, 955–59 Edgar, younger son of Edmund, 959–75 Edward (the Martyr), son of Edgar, 975–78 Æthelred (the Unready), younger son of Edgar, 978–1016 Edmund (Ironside), son of Æthelred, 1016 Canute, by conquest, 1016–35 Harold I (Harefoot), illegitimate son of Canute, 1037–40 Harthacanute, son of Canute, 1040–42 Edward (the Confessor), younger son of Æthelred, 1042–66 Harold II, brother-in-law of Edward the Confessor, 1066	**House of Tudor** Henry VII, descendant of Edward III, 1485–1509 Henry VIII, son of Henry VII, 1509–47 Edward VI, son of Henry VIII, 1547–53 Mary I, daughter of Henry VIII, 1553–58 Elizabeth I, younger daughter of Henry VIII, 1558–1603 **House of Stuart** James I (James VI of Scotland), descendant of Henry VII, 1603–25 Charles I, son of James I, 1625–49 **Commonwealth and Protectorate** Council of State, 1649–53 Cromwell, Oliver, lord protector, 1653–58 Cromwell, Richard, lord protector, 1658–59
House of Normandy William I (the Conqueror), by conquest, 1066–87 William II (Rufus), 3d son of William I, 1087–1100 Henry I, youngest son of William I, 1100–1135 **House of Blois** Stephen, grandson of William I, 1135–54	**House of Stuart (restored)** Charles II, son of Charles I, 1660–85 James II, younger son of Charles I, 1685–88 William III, grandson of Charles I; ruled jointly with Mary II, 1689–94; ruled alone, 1694–1702 Mary II, daughter of James II; ruled jointly with William III, 1689–94 Anne, younger daughter of James II, 1702–14
House of Plantagenet Henry II, grandson of Henry I, 1154–89 Richard I (Coeur de Lion), 3d son of Henry II, 1189–99 John, youngest son of Henry II, 1199–1216 Henry III, son of John, 1216–72 Edward I, son of Henry III, 1272–1307 Edward II, son of Edward I, 1307–27 Edward III, son of Edward II, 1327–77 Richard II, grandson of Edward III, 1377–99	**House of Hanover** George I, great-grandson of James I, 1714–27 George II, son of George I, 1727–60 George III, grandson of George II, 1760–1820 George IV, son of George III, 1820–30 William IV, 3d son of George III, 1830–37 Victoria, granddaughter of George III, 1837–1901
House of Lancaster Henry IV, grandson of Edward III, 1399–1413 Henry V, son of Henry IV, 1413–22 Henry VI, son of Henry V, 1422–61, 1470–71 **House of York** Edward IV, great grandson of Edward III, 1461–70, 1471–83 Edward V, son of Edward IV, 1483 Richard III, brother of Edward IV, 1483–85	**House of Saxe Coburg** Edward VII, son of Victoria, 1901–10 **House of Windsor** *(family name changed during World War I)* George V, son of Edward VII, 1910–36 Edward VIII, son of George V, 1936 George VI, 2d son of George V, 1936–52 Elizabeth II, daughter of George VI, 1952–

causative factors are generally accepted: overproduction of goods; a tariff and war-debt policy that curtailed foreign markets for American goods; and easy money policies that led to overexpansion of credit and fantastic speculation on the stock market. At the depth (1933) of the Depression, 16 million people—one third of the labor force—were unemployed. The effects were felt in Europe and contributed to Adolph HITLER's rise in Germany. The policies of the NEW DEAL relieved the situation, but complete recovery came only with the heavy defense spending of the 1940s. See also DEPRESSION.

Great Dividing Range, crest line of the Eastern Highlands of Australia, forming most of that continent's drainage or continental divide. It is also widely used as an alternate name for the EASTERN HIGHLANDS.

Great Elector, the: see FREDERICK WILLIAM.

Greater Antilles: see WEST INDIES.

Great Falls, city (1990 pop. 55,097), seat of Cascade co., N central Mont., at the confluence of the Missouri and Sun rivers, near the falls that gave the city its name; inc. 1888. A hydroelectric power center and farm market, it refines oil, copper, and zinc and mills flour. Malmstrom Air Force Base is nearby.

Great Lakes, group of five connected freshwater lakes, E central North America, together covering c.95,000 sq mi (246,000 sq km). The lakes—SUPERIOR, MICHIGAN, HURON, ERIE, and ONTARIO—and their connecting waterways extend 1,160 mi (1,876 km) along the U.S.-Canadian border. With the SAINT LAWRENCE SEAWAY they form the **St. Lawrence & Great Lakes Waterway,** a major shipping artery that is navigable (except from December to April, when blocked by ice) for 2,342 mi (3,770 km) by ocean-going vessels of 27-ft (8.2-m) draft. The lakes range in elevation from 602 ft (183 m) in the west to 246 ft (75 m) in the east, the greatest drop (167 ft/51 m) occurring between lakes Erie and Ontario at NIAGARA FALLS.

Great Mother of the Gods, in ancient Middle Eastern religion (and later in Greece, Rome, and W Asia), mother goddess, the great symbol of the earth's fertility. As the creative force in nature, she was worshiped under many names, including ASTARTE (Syria), CERES (Rome), CYBELE (Phrygia), DEMETER (Greece), ISHTAR (Babylon), and ISIS (Egypt). The later forms of her cult involved the worship of a male deity (her son or lover, e.g., ADONIS, OSIRIS), whose death and resurrection symbolized the regenerative power of the earth.

Great Plains, semiarid region of level and rolling terrain, located E of the Rocky Mts. and extending more than 1,500 mi (2,415 km) from Texas N into Canada. Elevations range from c.6,000 ft (1,829 m) in the west to c.1,500 ft (457 m) at the eastern boundary, which coincides roughly with the 100th meridian of longitude (running from E Oklahoma through the central Dakotas). Ranching and wheat farming, begun in the late 1800s, ended centuries of habitation by Native Americans and huge bison herds. Coal, oil, and natural gas deposits underlie the Plains.

Great Rift Valley, huge depression, currently thought to be the product of PLATE TECTONICS, extending c.3,000 mi (4,830 km) across most of E Africa and into SW Asia. In Africa it consists of an eastern arm, occupied in part by Lakes Turkana (Rudolf) and MALAWI (Nyasa), and a western arm, occupied in part by Lakes TANGANYIKA, Kivu, Edward, and Albert. In SW Asia it forms the RED SEA, the Gulf of AQABA, the DEAD SEA, and the JORDAN and Al Biqa valleys. Flanked in places by high cliffs and volcanoes (Mts. KENYA and KILIMANJARO), the floor of the rift ranges in elevation from c.1,300 ft (395 m) below sea level, in the Dead Sea, to c.6,000 ft (1,830 m) above sea level, in S Kenya.

Great Salt Lake, largest salt lake in North America, in NW Utah. The shallow lake (c.13–24 ft/4–7.3 m deep) has ranged in size from 1,000 sq mi (2,600 sq km), during 1955–75, to 2,500 sq mi (6,500 sq km) in the mid-1980s. The Weber, Jordan, and Bear rivers, which feed it, are diverted for use farther east. The lake's waters have a salt content (10%) that is greater than sea water and support no life except brine shrimp and colonial algae.

Great Slave Lake, second largest lake of Canada, c.10,980 sq mi (28,400 sq km), in the Mackenzie district of the Northwest Territories. The deepest lake (2,015 ft/614 m) in North America, it is c.300 mi (480 km) long, 12–68 mi (19–109 km) wide, and drains W through the MACKENZIE R. Gold is mined at YELLOWKNIFE, in the north, and some lead and zinc on the southern shore.

Great Smoky Mountains or **Great Smokies,** range of the APPALACHIAN MTS., on the North Carolina–Tennessee border, named for a smokelike haze that frequently envelops them. They rise to a high point of 6,642 ft (2,024 m) at Clingmans Dome and are partly within Great Smoky Mountains National Park (see NATIONAL PARKS, table).

Great Smoky Mountains National Park: see NATIONAL PARKS (table).

Great Society: see JOHNSON, LYNDON BAINES.

Great Wall of China, fortifications winding c.1,500 mi (2,400 km) across N China from Gansu prov. to the Yellow Sea. It is an amalgamation of many walls, first united (3d cent. B.C.) by the Ch'in dynasty. The present form dates substantially from the Ming dynasty (1368–1644) and averages 25 ft (7.6 m) in height. Successive invasions of China by northern nomads proved the wall to be of little military utility.

grebe, swimming BIRD found on or near quiet waters in much of the world. Resembling both the related LOON and unrelated DUCK, it has short wings, a vestigial tail, and long, individually webbed toes on feet that are set far back on a short, stubby body. Grebes are poor fliers and clumsy on land. They have complex courtship rituals, including dancing in pairs on the water.

Greco, El [ĕl grĕk'ō], c.1541–1614, Greek painter in Spain; b. Candia, Crete, as Domenicos Theotocopoulos. By 1577 he was established in Toledo after having painted in Rome and studied in Venice under TITIAN. He left portraits of Toledo's proud nobility; their ascetic faces are seen in the foreground of the *Burial of the Count Orgaz* (Church of San Tomé, Toledo). El Greco's flamelike lines, accentuated by vivid highlights, elongated and distorted figures, and full, vibrant color produced dynamic representations of religious ecstasy. Among his great works are *Baptism, Crucifixion,* and *Resurrection* (all: Prado) and a long series of paintings of St. FRANCIS. To his last period belong such works as the *Adoration* and *View of Toledo* (both: Metropolitan Mus.). El Greco undoubtedly influenced VELÁZQUEZ and is ranked among the great inspired, visionary artists.

Greece, Gr. *Hellas* or *Ellas,* officially Hellenic Republic, republic (1992 est. pop. 10,064,000), 50,944 sq. mi (131,945 sq km), SE Europe. Occupying the S Balkan Peninsula, it is bordered by the Ionian Sea (W), the Mediterranean Sea (S), the Aegean Sea (E), Turkey and Bulgaria (NE), Macedonia (N), and Albania (NW). ATHENS is the capital and largest city; other major cities include THESSALONÍKI and PIRAIÉVS. About 75% of the country is mountainous, the major range being the Pindus Mts., in the north. Central Greece includes the low-lying plains of Thessaly, Attica, and Boeotia, as well as Greece's highest point, Mt. OLYMPUS (9,570 ft/2,917 m). The southern portion of the country is the PELOPONNESUS. Of the total land area, almost 20% is in islands, notably CRETE, the DODECANESE (including RHODES), and the CYCLADES. Industry has replaced agriculture as the leading source of income. Principal manufactures include building materials, textiles, food products, chemicals, paper and printed material, refined petroleum, and ships. The chief farm products are corn, wheat, citrus fruits, olives and olive oil, grapes, tobacco, sugar beets, and tomatoes; large numbers of sheep and goats are raised. Tourism is also important. Modern Greek is the official language, and the established religion is the Greek Orthodox Church. Ethnic Greeks constitute over 98% of the population. Government is by a unicameral parliament of 300 members, who elect a president for a 5-year term. Greece became a full member of the European Community (see EUROPEAN UNION) in 1981. The country left the military wing of NATO in 1974 but rejoined it in 1980.

Ancient Greece. The region had seen the rise and fall of splendid cultures, e.g., the MINOAN CIVILIZATION and the MYCENEAN CIVILIZATION, before the arrival of Greek-speaking peoples. By 1000 B.C. Achaeans, Aeolians, Ionians, and Dorians had settled in the region that is modern Greece, where they developed many independent, often warring, CITY-STATES. Taking to the sea, by the 8th cent. B.C. they had created a network of colonies from Asia Minor to Spain (see MAGNA GRAECIA). The 5th cent. B.C. began with attempted invasions of Greece by the Persians. Greek success in the PERSIAN WARS (500–449 B.C.) ushered in the golden age of Greek history. Athens, in particular, grew dramatically and, in the age of PERICLES (c.495–429 B.C.), experienced a surge of cultural development rarely equaled in world history. Although Athens succumbed to SPARTA in the PELOPONNESIAN WAR (431–404 B.C.), Athenian thought prevailed, and the culture that was to be the fountainhead of Western civilization lived on. When PHILIP II of Macedon conquered Greece (338 B.C.) at Chaeronea, he paved the way for his son, ALEXANDER THE GREAT, who spread Greek civilization across the known world. By 146 B.C. the remnants of the Greek states had fallen to Rome, but when the Roman Empire was split (A.D. 395), the BYZANTINE EMPIRE, formed from the eastern portion, was thoroughly Greek in tradition. HELLENISTIC CIVILIZATION, centered at ALEXANDRIA, Egypt, and other cities, also preserved the Greek heritage.

Modern Greece. Turkish incursions and Norman attacks began in the 11th cent., and Greece was absorbed into the OTTOMAN EMPIRE in 1456. Under Ottoman rule Greece languished in obscurity and poverty until the successful Greek War of Independence (1821–32) and the establishment of a constitutional monarchy. Greece acquired the Ionian Islands (1864), Thessaly and part of Epirus (1881), and Crete (1913); in the BALKAN WARS (1912–13) it obtained SE MACEDONIA and W THRACE. Pressured by the Allies, Greece entered WORLD WAR I in 1917 and after the war was awarded most of European Turkey and the Bulgarian coast. The period between the world wars was marked by political turmoil: monarchs were enthroned and dethroned; a republic proclaimed in 1924 collapsed in 1935; and in 1936 a right-wing dictatorship was established under George METAXAS. During WORLD WAR II Greece was occupied (1941–44) by the German army. Civil war erupted in 1946, but massive U.S. military and economic aid ensured the victory of royalist forces over Communist rebels. A coup d'etat by rightist army officers in 1967 resulted in the rise to power of George PAPADOPOULOS, who abolished (1973) the monarchy and was, in turn, overthrown by another military coup. Civilian government was restored in 1974, and a new constitution adopted in 1975. In 1981 the electoral victory of Andreas Papandreou (see under PAPANDREOU, GEORGE) and the Pan-Hellenic Socialist Movement (Pasok) ended 35 years of pro-Western, conservative rule and gave Greece its first

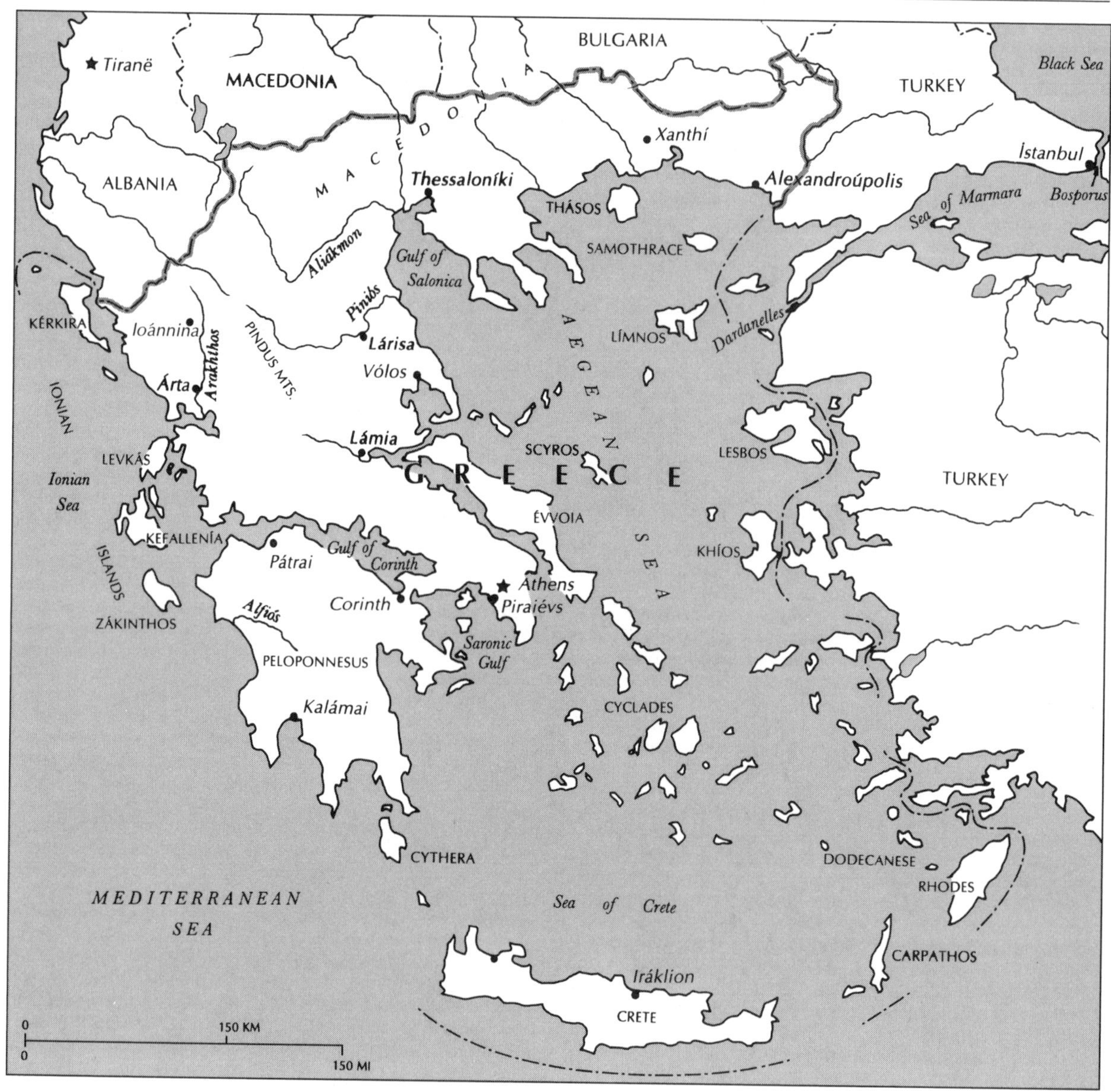

socialist government. In 1989 Pasok lost its parliamentary majority amid charges of corruption, but three elections were needed before the conservative New Democratic party secured a parliamentary majority of one vote in 1990. Constantine Mitsotakis became premier, and Constantine KARAMANLIS was elected president. Facing a record deficit and high inflation, Mitsotakis instituted an austerity program and moved to sell or liquidate state-owned companies. The economic hardships that resulted led Greek voters to return Papandreou and Pasok to power in 1993.

Greek Anthology, collection of epigrammatic poems representing Greek literature from the 7th cent. B.C. to the 10th cent. A.D. It began with Meleager's *Garland* (c.90–80 B.C.) and was added to by others. A 10th-cent. version, the *Palatine Anthology,* is the chief modern source.

Greek architecture arose on the shores of the Aegean Sea. When the Dorians migrated into Greece (c.1000 B.C.), true Hellenic culture began; by the 6th cent. B.C., a definite Dorian system of construction existed. All the great works were produced between 700 B.C. and the Roman occupation (146 B.C.). The major masterpieces were erected between 480 B.C. and 323 B.C., including the reign of PERICLES, when CALLICRATES, MNESICLES, and ICTINUS flourished. Of the three great styles or ORDERS OF ARCHITECTURE, the Doric was earliest and the one in which most of the monuments were erected. Early examples (6th cent. B.C.) are found in Sicily and Paestum in Italy; after 500 B.C. the Doric was perfected at Athens in the Hephaesteum (465 B.C.), the PARTHENON (c.447–432 B.C.), and the Propylaea (437–432 B.C.). The Greek colonies of Asia Minor evolved the second great order, the Ionic order, stamped with Middle Eastern influences. After 500 B.C. it appeared in Greece proper, challenging with its slender columns and carved enrichments the sturdy, simple Doric. The most important Ionic buildings were at Miletus. In Greece, the ERECHTHEUM was the one major Ionic structure. The third, or Corinthian, order, appeared in this period. Even more ornate, it was little used. Examples are the Choragic monument (c.335 B.C.) and the Tower of the Winds (100 B.C.–35 B.C.), both at Athens. The Greeks used finely cut stone joints rather than mortar. Marble was used after the 5th cent. B.C. Earlier, rough stone was covered with a marble dust and lime coating. Although Greek buildings were long thought to have been left white, traces of decorative coloring have been found. Cities often had an acropolis, a citadel and temple site built on a steep hill. The standard Greek temple had a simple rectangular chamber with an entrance porch flanked by columns. The sides and ends would then be surrounded with a colonnade, sometimes doubled. A body of traditional mathematical formulas was developed to ensure harmony of proportions. The Greeks built temples, monumental tombs, agoras [public meeting places], stoas [colonnaded shelters], stadiums, palaestrae [gymnasiums], propylaeas [city gates], and amphitheaters. After Athens and Sparta declined, the more opulent and florid Hellenistic architecture arose (4th–3d cent. B.C.); from this style the Romans doubtless acquired their concepts of monumental architecture.

Greek art. The Aegean basin was a center of artistic activity from early times (see AEGEAN CIVILIZATION). Two great cultures—the MINOAN CIVILIZATION and the MYCENEAN CIVILIZATION—developed complex and delicate art forms. After the invasion of the Dorians and other barbarians (before 1000 B.C.), the curvilinear designs and naturalistic representations of the Mycenean age were replaced by geometric schemes with linear patterns. The transformation is seen in late geometric (c.900–700 B.C.) pottery. Between 700 and 600 B.C., Asian influence led to the use of floral and arabesque patterns and monster and animal themes. Then, during the archaic period (c.660–480 B.C.), sculpture became the principal form of artistic expression. The statues of nude walking youths, *kouroi,* suggesting Egyptian prototypes but distinct in stylization and tension of movement, e.g., *Kouros* (Metropolitan Mus.), date from this period. Draped female figures show Asian influence, e.g., *Hera of Samos* (Louvre). The outstanding Athenian school of black-figure vase painting led by Execias depicted mythological and contemporary scenes. A greater concern with three-dimensional space and naturalistic detail emerged with red-figure vase painting (c.525). Euthymides and Euphronius were early masters. The early classical period revealed new insight into the structure of the human form (c.480–450 B.C.). e.g., the sculptures from the temple of Zeus at Olympia, the bronze *Charioteer* (museum; Delphi), and the *Zeus* or *Poseidon* (Athens, National Mus.). During the Golden Age, the height of the classical period (450–400 B.C.), Polykleitos arrived at a rational norm for the ideal figure. The magnificent sculptures from the ACROPOLIS and its PARTHENON, thought to have been designed by PHIDIAS, exemplify this ideal. In the late classical period (400–300 B.C.), there was more emphasis on emotion in art. The works attributed to PRAXITELES are elegant and graceful; to SCOPAS, strongly emotional; and to LYSIPPOS, individualized, though their sculptures largely survive as fragments or Roman copies. The works of the painters of the period, e.g., Apollodorus and APELLES, are known only through description. The Hellenistic period began with the conquests of Alexander the Great. Masterpieces of the period include the *Nike (Victory) of Samothrace* and *Aphrodite of Melos* (both: Louvre); the *Pergamum Frieze* (Berlin Mus.); the Roman copies of the *Odyssey Landscape* (Vatican), a painting with great spatial illusionism; and the *Laocoön and his Sons* (Vatican). Despite its decline, Greek culture and art inspired Western art throughout history.

Greek language, member of the Indo-European family of languages. Modern Greek is derived from the standard Greek or koinē of the Hellenistic world. See LANGUAGE (table).

Greek religion. Although its exact origins are lost in time, Greek religion is thought to date from about the 2d millennium B.C., when the culture of Aryan invaders fused with those of the Aegean and Minoan peoples who had inhabited the region of Greece from Neolithic times. As portrayed in Homer's *Iliad,* the classical Greek pantheon, also called Homeric or Olympian (for Mt. Olympus, home of the gods), was a blend of Minoan, Egyptian, Asian, and other elements. The Greek deities had supernatural powers, particularly over human life, but were severely limited by the relentless force of fate (Moira). The gods were most important in their role as guardians of the city-states and as those who could provide information, through divination rites, about one's future on earth. Often the favorable response or reward expected did not materialize, and the civil strife that followed the classical period (from c.500 B.C.) placed the old gods on trial. The popular religion of the Greek countryside rose, emphasizing the promise of afterlife and elaborate rites offered by such cults as the Eleusinian and ORPHIC MYSTERIES. The Dionysian excesses of these mystery rites were offset by the virtues of moderation ascribed to Apollo. Later Greek philosophical inquiry sought a more logical connection between nature and humanity, leading to the rationalization of the early myths and the final destruction of the Homeric pantheon. The vacuum was eventually filled by Christianity.

Greeley, Horace, 1811–72, American newspaper editor; b. Amherst, N.H. He founded the New York *Tribune* in 1841. As editor for over 30 years, he advocated a protective tariff, the organization of labor, temperance, a homestead law, and women's rights, and opposed monopoly, land grants to railroads, and SLAVERY. His editorials were widely quoted, and thousands acted on his advice, "Go West, young man, go West." He was one of the first members of the new REPUBLICAN PARTY, although he denounced Pres. LINCOLN's border-state policy and embarrassed the administration by his antiwar sentiments. Following the Civil War he favored African-American suffrage and amnesty for all Southerners; he defied public opinion by signing the bail bond to release Jefferson DAVIS from prison. He ran for president in 1872 as the candidate of the LIBERAL REPUBLICAN PARTY but was soundly defeated by the incumbent, U.S. GRANT.

Greely, Adolphus Washington, 1844–1935, American army officer and explorer; b. Newburyport, Mass. Between 1881 and 1884 he commanded the Lady Franklin Bay Expedition to establish one of a chain of arctic meteorological stations. He and his party mapped a stretch of Greenland's coast, crossed Ellesmere Island, and achieved a northern record of 83°24′. After two relief efforts failed, a ship found only Greely and six others alive. Later, as the army's chief signal officer, he built telegraph communications in U.S. possessions. He directed relief operations after the San Francisco earthquake in 1906.

Green, Henry, 1905–74, English novelist; b. Henry Vincent Yorke. His enigmatic, comic novels include *Living* (1929), *Caught* (1943), *Loving* (1945), and *Concluding* (1948).

Green, Julian, 1900–, French novelist, of American parentage. Such novels as *The Closed Garden* (1927) and *The Dark Journey* (1929) concern vice and madness. Others are *Moïra* (1950) and *Each in His Darkness* (1960). In 1971, he was elected to the Académie Française.

Green, William, 1872–1952, American labor leader; b. Coshocton, Ohio. He rose through the ranks of the United Mine Workers of America (UMW), serving (1912–24) as secretary-treasurer. In 1924 he was elected president of the AFL (see AMERICAN FEDERATION OF LABOR AND CONGRESS OF INDUSTRIAL ORGANIZATIONS), a post he held until his death. He organized skilled labor into craft unions and led the AFL in the struggle with the CIO after the groups split in 1935. Green wrote *Labor and Democracy* (1939).

Greenaway, Kate, 1846–1901, English illustrator. Her fanciful colored drawings of child life influenced children's clothing and illustrated books. She provided text and pictures for many books, e.g., *Under the Window* (1879).

Greenback party, a U.S. political organization founded (1874–76) to promote currency expansion. Its principal members were Southern and Western farmers stricken by the Panic of 1873. They nominated Peter COOPER for president in 1876, but he received only 81,737 votes. Uniting with labor in the Greenback-Labor party (1878), they polled over 1 million votes and elected 14 representatives to Congress. Thus encouraged, and with a broadened program that included woman suffrage, federal regulation of interstate commerce, and a graduated income tax, they nominated James B. WEAVER for president (1880). But the return of prosperity had allayed discontent, and their vote declined to a little over 300,000. Following the 1884 election the party dissolved. Many members later joined the Populists.

Green Bay, city (1990 pop. 96,466), seat of Brown co., NE Wis., at the mouth of the Fox R., on Green Bay; inc. 1854. A major GREAT LAKES port and rail center, it is on the site of a French trading post and mission (1634); permanent settlement, the state's oldest, dates from 1701. It was a fur-trading center and gateway to the upper Midwest occupied by the French (1717), British (1761), and Americans (1816). Today it produces paper, food products, and automobile parts. It is home to the Packers professional football team.

Greene, Charles Sumner, 1868–1957, and **Henry Mather Greene,** 1870–1954, American architects; b. Brighton, Ohio. The Greene brothers modified aspects of the ARTS AND CRAFTS movement, the shingle style, and Asian architecture to fit the relaxed climate and lifestyle of California. They were pioneers in the development of the bungalow-style residence in southern California, e.g., the Gamble House (1908) in Pasadena.

Greene, (Henry) Graham, 1904–91, English novelist. A Catholic convert with intense moral concerns, he wrote novels that are essentially parables of the damned. Those that are thrillers, e.g., *Orient Express* (1932), he called "entertainments." His major works are *Brighton Rock* (1938) and *The Heart of the Matter* (1948). A superb journalist, he set novels in sites of topical interest, e.g., *The Quiet American* (1955) in Indochina. He is also known for his short stories, plays, film criticism, and film scripts, including *The Third Man* (1950).

greenhouse effect, process whereby heat is trapped at the surface of the earth by the atmosphere. Energy from the sun passes through the atmosphere, warming the earth and providing the wavelengths used in PHOTOSYNTHESIS. Much of the incoming energy is reradiated in the form of heat, some directly and some as a result of either the METABOLISM of living things or human industrial activities. This heat (infrared radiation) is prevented from leaving the earth by atmospheric carbon dioxide, water vapor, and ozone (acting like the glass in a greenhouse), and much of it goes back into the ground. An increase in atmospheric carbon dioxide of 10% over the past century has led some authorities to predict a long-term warming of the earth's climate. Over 150 nations have signed a 1992 treaty designed to reduce the emission of gases that are believed to intensify the greenhouse effect and result in global warming.

Greenland, officially Kalaallit Nunaat (1992 est. pop. 57,400), largest island in the world, c.840,000 sq mi (2,175,600 sq km), self-governing overseas division of Denmark, lying largely within the Arctic Circle off NE Canada. The capital is Nuuk (formerly Godthb). An ice sheet c.14,000 ft (4,300 m) deep in places covers more than four fifths of the land area. Fishing, shrimping, and sealing are the principal economic activities. Extensive oil deposits have been detected beneath its southwestern offshore waters, but the fragile arctic environment, great depths, and icebergs make drilling difficult. Most people live along the coast in the SW, where the climate is warmed by the North Atlantic Drift. Almost 20% of the people were born outside Greenland; the others are of mixed Inuit and Danish ancestry. A majority of the population are Lutherans. Greenland is internally self-governing; Denmark is responsible for foreign affairs, defense, and the judicial system. Greenlandic (Inuit) and Danish are the official languages.

History. Greenland was named and settled (c.982) as a self-governing colony by ERIC THE RED, a Norseman. The colony was neglected by Norway in the 14th and 15th cent., and the colonists had either died out or had been assimilated with the Eskimos when Greenland was rediscovered, with no trace of the Norsemen, in the 16th cent. by the British explorers Martin FROBISHER and John Davis. It was recolonized, beginning in 1721, by Norway and became a Danish colony in 1815. Greenland became an integral part of Denmark in 1953 with representatives in the *Folketing* (Parliament), and was granted home rule in 1979. Since then the local parliament has been controlled by left-wing parties favoring greater autonomy and internal economic development. In 1985 the island withdrew from the European Community.

Green Mountain Boys, popular name of armed bands led by Ethan ALLEN that used threats, intimidation, and violence to prevent the New Hampshire Grants (land that is now Vermont) from becoming part of New York state. In the AMERICAN REVOLUTION, under Allen, they captured Fort TICONDEROGA (1775) and won an important victory at Bennington (1777).

Greenough, Horatio [grē′nō], 1805–52, American sculptor and writer; b. Boston. As a writer, he heralded modern concepts of functionalism in architecture. As a sculptor, he is famous for a colossal statue of George Washington (Smithsonian Inst.).

Green party, any of the political parties established in various countries to oppose the destructive environmental effects of many modern technologies and the economic systems and institutions that drive them. Many Green parties also advocate PACIFISM and support HUMAN RIGHTS. The German Green party, founded in West Germany in 1979, had some political successes in the 1980s and merged with a group from the former East Germany in 1993. There are 26 Green parties in Europe; a U.S. group has existed since 1973.

Greenpeace, international environmental organization, founded 1971. It seeks to promote environmental awareness and end environmental abuse through nonviolent confrontations with governments and companies. It often uses media exposure to draw attention to its causes.

Green Revolution, popular term referring mainly to the large increases achieved in GRAIN production in certain developing countries—especially Mexico, India, Pakistan, and the Philippines—from the late 1960s into the 1980s. The increases were achieved by using high-yielding and high-protein HYBRIDS, chemical FERTILIZERS, and new crop strategies and harvesting methods. The dependence on costly fertilizers, pesticides, and irrigation, which poor farmers cannot afford and that may be ecologically harmful, has been criticized.

Greensboro, city (1990 pop. 183,521), seat of Guilford co., N central N.C.; settled 1749, inc. 1808. The state's third largest city, it has an important textile industry, produces tobacco and machinery, and is a regional financial, insurance, and distribution center. The Revolutionary War battle of Guilford Courthouse was fought nearby. The city has several colleges. It is the birthplace of Dolley MADISON and O. HENRY.

Greenspan, Alan, 1926–, U.S. economist, chairman of the Federal Reserve Board (1987–); b. N.Y.C. A private economic consultant (1954–74, 1977–87), Greenspan served (1974–77) as chairman of the president's Council of Economic Advisers during the Ford administration. From 1981 to 1983 he chaired the bipartisan National Commission on Social Security Reform, which reformed the financing of the U.S. social security system to assure its solvency. In 1987 Pres. Reagan appointed him chairman of the Federal Reserve Board; he was reappointed by Pres. Bush in 1991. Influenced by the philosophy of Ayn RAND, Greenspan is a strong free-market supporter and opponent of government intervention in the economy. As Federal Reserve chairman, he has emphasized fighting inflation.

Greenville, city (1990 pop. 58,282), seat of Greenville co., NW S.C., on the Reedy R., in the Piedmont; laid out 1797, inc. as a city 1907. A major industrial and commercial center of the SE U.S., in the heart of a region of mill towns, it has huge textile mills and diverse manufactures, and processes farm products. Textile Hall is the scene of the biennial Southern Textile Exposition. Furman Univ. and Bob Jones Univ. are in the city.

Greenwich, borough (1991 est. pop. 212,000) of Greater London, SE England, on the Thames R. The system of geographic longitude and time-keeping worked out at its old Royal Observatory (1675–1958) have become standard in most of the world; the prime meridian (0° longitude) passes through the observatory. Other points of interest are the Royal Naval College (begun 17th cent.) and the National Maritime Museum.

Greenwich Mean Time (GMT): see SOLAR TIME.

Greenwich meridian: see PRIME MERIDIAN.

Greenwich Village, district of lower Manhattan, N.Y.C. An influx of artists and freethinkers in the early 1900s established the area's reputation for bohemianism.

Greer, Germaine, 1939–, Australian feminist and writer. She moved to England (1964), earned a Ph.D. from Cambridge, and taught at the Univ. of Warwick (1967–73). Her book *The Female Eunuch* (1970), an analysis of attitudes toward women and a call for an end to sexual repression, made her a leading spokeswoman for FEMINISM. She has also written *The Change: Women, Aging, and the Menopause* (1992).

Gregorian chant: see PLAINSONG.

Gregory I, Saint (Saint Gregory the Great), c.540–604, pope (590–604), Doctor of the Church. A Roman prefect, he became a monk and, although he resisted promotion, eventually pope. His rule was notable for the enforcement of papal supremacy and the establishment of the temporal position of the pope. He attacked Donatism in Africa, refused to recognize the title *ecumenical* of the patriarch of Constantinople (an act that helped split East and West), and treated (592) with the invading LOMBARDS after the Byzantine exarch failed to defend Rome. Gregory encouraged monasticism, made laws for the lives of the clergy, and sent missionaries to England. His writings include letters, commentaries on the Book of Job, saints' lives, and *Pastoral Care.* He also contributed to the development of Gregorian chant or PLAINSONG. Feast: Sept. 3.

Gregory VII, Saint, d. 1085, pope (1073–85), an Italian named Hildebrand. A Benedictine, he became notable under Pope Gregory VI and under LEO IX launched his reform program, aimed at correcting corruption and laxity in the church. As chief figure in the curia under Leo's successors, he transferred the papal election from the Romans to the college of cardinals and formed an alliance with the Normans of S Italy. As pope he pressed his reforms by condemning clerical marriage, simony, and lay INVESTITURE, and he sent papal legates throughout Europe to enforce his actions. Opposition was widespread, and a powerful antireform party grew among laymen who feared church domination. In Germany, HENRY IV joined the antireform party and was excommunicated (1076) by Gregory. Losing support, Henry humbled himself before Gregory at Canossa, but in 1080 the two again fell out. Henry, again excommunicated, set up Guibert of Ravenna (Clement III) as antipope, and Gregory's appeal to the Christian world failed. When the German civil war ended, Henry marched into Italy and took Rome (1083). Gregory retired into the Castel Sant' Angelo until the Normans under ROBERT GUISCARD rescued him, then followed the Norman withdrawal and died in Salerno after a year of exile. His reform was a turning point in church history. It elevated the moral level of the church and began the successful struggle against lay investiture. Feast: May 25.

Gregory IX, 1143?–1241, pope (1227–41), an Italian named Ugolino di Segni. Elected at age 84, he excommunicated (1227) Holy Roman Emperor FREDERICK II for not undertaking a crusade. Imperialists in Rome revolted and forced Gregory into exile until 1230. In a dispute over Italian liberties, he again excommunicated (1239) Frederick and ordered him dethroned. Frederick blocked Gregory's call for a general council and was preparing to attack Rome when Gregory died at age 98.

Gregory XI, 1330–78, pope (1370–78), a Frenchman named Pierre Roger de Beaufort. After receiving prophetic admonitions from St. Bridget of Sweden and St. CATHERINE OF SIENA, he determined to move the papacy from Avignon back to Rome. But the Avignon court was opposed, and the papal states were in chaos. After sanctioning a foray into Italy by Robert of Geneva, Gregory returned to Rome (Jan. 1377), thus ending the Babylonian Captivity of the popes. The elections after his death began the Great SCHISM.

Gregory XII, c.1327–1417, pope (1406–15), a Venetian named Angelo Correr. Gregory negotiated with the Avignon antipope, Benedict XIII (see LUNA, PEDRO DE), to end the Great SCHISM, but failed, whereupon the Council of Pisa elected a second antipope. The Council of Constance accepted Gregory's resignation (1415), deposed the two antipopes, and elected MARTIN V pope (1417).

Gregory XIII, 1502–85, pope (1572–85), an Italian named Ugo Buoncompagni, best known for the reformed, or Gregorian, CALENDAR. He was prominent at the Council of TRENT (1545, 1559–63). As pope he proposed the deposition of Queen Elizabeth I of England and took an interest in the education of the clergy and the conversion of Protestants. He issued a new edition of the canon law and patronized the Jesuits.

Gregory, Lady Augusta (Persse), 1859–1932, Irish dramatist, a founder and director of the Abbey Theatre, Dublin. Her plays include *Spreading the News* (1904), *The Gaol Gate* (1906), *The Rising of the Moon* (1907), and *The Workhouse Ward* (1908). Her *Our Irish Theater* (1913) is a key document of the Irish Literary Renaissance.

Gregory Nazianzen, Saint [nāzēăn'zĭn], c.330–390, Cappadocian theologian, Doctor of the Church, one of the Four Fathers of the Greek Church. Active in the struggle against ARIANISM, he was chosen bishop of Constantinople (379), but he retired after the First Council of CONSTANTINOPLE. Feast: Jan. 2.

Gregory of Nyssa, Saint, c.330–95, Christian theologian. Influenced by his brother Saint Basel and friend Saint Gregory Nazianzen, he entered monastic life and became Bishop of Cappadocia in E central Turkey. Against Arian opponents (see ARIANISM), he championed the Nicene doctrine of the single substance (ousia) of the members of the Trinity at the First Council of CONSTANTINOPLE (381). His writings include many anti-Arian tracts and apologias for rigorous Christian asceticism.

Gregory of Tours, Saint, 538–94, French historian, bishop of Tours (from 573). His masterpiece, *History of the Franks,* is a universal history with an important account of contemporary events. Feast: Nov. 17.

Grenada [grĭnā'də], island nation (1992 est. pop. 83,600), in the West Indies, consisting of the main island of Grenada (120 sq mi/311 sq km), the southernmost of the Windward Islands; and the southern group of the sparsely settled archipelago known as the Grenadines. The capital and main port, Saint George's, is on Grenada, a volcanic, mountainous island. The economy is primarily agricultural; cocoa, bananas, nutmeg, mace, sugar, coconuts, cotton, and limes are exported. The people, mainly of African or mixed descent, speak English (the official language) or a French patois. Almost 65% of the inhabitants are Roman Catholics, with Anglicans making up more than 20% of the population. Settlement of Grenada, delayed by hostile Caribs, was begun by the French in 1650, but the island was taken over in 1783 by the British, who established sugar plantations and imported African slaves. Grenada became self-governing in 1967 and an independent state within the Commonwealth in 1974. A coup in 1979 installed a Marxist government headed by Maurice Bishop, who allied the nation with Cuba. In 1983 the overthrow and execution of Bishop led to an invasion by the U.S., with token forces from other Caribbean nations, that restored democratic rule. Nicholas Brathwaite, of the National Democratic Congress, has been prime minister since 1990.

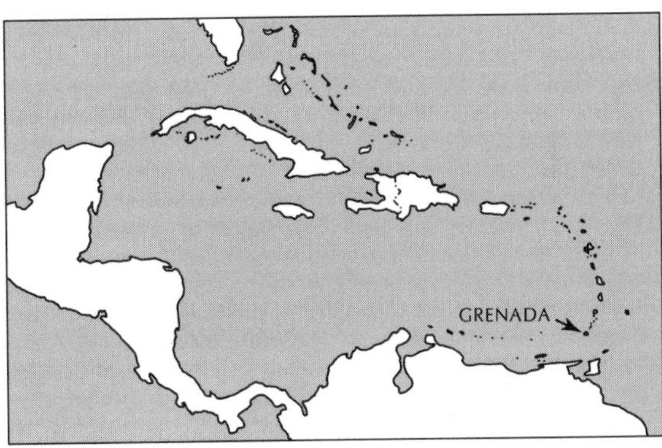

grenade, small bomb designed to be thrown by hand or shot from a modified rifle or a grenade launcher. It may be filled with gas or chemicals but more often holds an explosive charge that fractures the casing into lethal fragments. First used in the 15th cent. (by "grenadiers"), the grenade later fell into disuse until the 20th cent., when it became a standard infantry weapon.

Grenoble, city (1990 pop. 150,758), capital of Isère dept., SE France. A leading resort at the foot of the Alps and site of the 1968 winter Olympics, it is important for its nuclear-research center, hydroelectric power, and science-based industries and research institutes, linked to the noted University of Grenoble (est. 1339). It passed from the dauphins of Viennois to the crown in 1349.

Grenville, George, 1712–70, British statesman. While prime minister (1763–65), he provoked reformers by persecuting John WILKES and aroused opposition by attempting to tax the American colonies through the STAMP ACT. His son **George Nugent Temple Grenville,** 1st **marquess of Buckingham,** 1753–1813, was lord lieutenant of Ireland (1782–83, 1787–89). His brother **William Wyndham Grenville, Baron Grenville,** 1759–1834, was foreign secretary to William PITT (1791–1801). In 1806 he formed the "ministry of all talents," which abolished the slave trade (1807).

Grenville, Sir Richard, 1542?–1591, English naval hero. In 1585 he commanded the fleet carrying the first colonists to ROANOKE ISLAND. On an expedition to capture Spanish treasure ships off the Azores in 1591, his ship, the *Revenge,* became separated from the rest of the fleet. He tried to break through the Spanish line, but he was mortally wounded and died in Spanish captivity.

Gresham, Sir Thomas, 1519?–1579, English merchant and financier. Founder of the Royal Exchange, he accumulated a private fortune while serving as an adviser to ELIZABETH I. His name was given to **Gresham's law,** the economic principle (formulated long before his time) that "bad money drives out good." When depreciated, mutilated, or debased coinage (or currency) circulates concurrently with money of high value in terms of precious metals, the good money automatically disappears because of hoarding.

Gretzky, Wayne, 1961–, Canadian ice hockey player. He has played on the Edmonton (Alta.) Oilers (1978–88) and Los Angeles Kings (1988–). In 1981–82 he set single-season National Hockey League (NHL) marks for goals scored (92), assists (120), and points (212), becoming the first player to achieve more than 200 points, and in 1984–85 he set a new single-season assists record (135). He also holds the lifetime goals, assists, and points records and has been NHL scoring champion and most valuable player nine times.

Greuze, Jean-Baptiste [gröz], 1725–1805, French genre and portrait painter. He is best known for his moralizing pictures, e.g., *The Broken Pitcher* (Louvre). His portraits, e.g., that of his wife (*The Milkmaid*) and of Napoleon I (both: Versailles), are more interesting.

Grey, Charles Grey, 2d **Earl,** 1764–1835, British statesman. In 1796 he became foreign secretary in the "ministry of all talents" and WHIG leader of the House of Commons, putting through the measure to abolish the slave trade (1807). As prime minister (1830–34), he secured passage of the REFORM BILL of 1832 by threatening to force WILLIAM IV to create enough Whig peers to carry it in the House of Lords. His grandson, **Albert Henry George Grey,** 4th **Earl Grey,** 1851–1917, was a Liberal member of the House of Commons (1880–86). Later he was a successful governor general of Canada (1904–11).

Grey, Lady Jane, 1537–54, queen of England for nine days; grandniece of HENRY VIII. She was married to the son of the duke of Northumberland, who persuaded EDWARD VII to make her his successor. She was proclaimed queen in 1553, but the English people rallied behind MARY I, and Jane was imprisoned. Her life might have been spared, but her father, the duke of Suffolk, joined Thomas Wyatt's rebellion, and she was beheaded.

Grey, Zane, 1875–1939, American writer; b. Zanesville, Ohio. He is known for his enormously popular melodramatic tales of the West, especially *Riders of the Purple Sage* (1912).

greyhound, tall, swift sight HOUND; shoulder height, c.26 in. (66 cm); weight, c.65 lb (29.5 kg). Its short, smooth coat may be any of various colors. Developed in Egypt c.5,000 years ago, the breed was known before the 9th cent. in England, where it was bred by aristocrats to hunt such small game as hares. Today it is widely used in racing.

Grieg, Edvard Hagerup [grēg], 1843–1907, Norwegian composer who developed a strongly nationalistic style. He founded (1867) the Norwegian Academy of Music. His best-known works are the Concerto in A Minor for piano and orchestra (1869); the CANTATA *Olav Trygvason* (1873); the SUITE of incidental dramatic music, *Peer Gynt* (1876); and settings of Norwegian FOLK SONGS.

Griffes, Charles Tomlinson, 1884–1920, American composer; b. Elmira, N.Y. His impressionistic compositions include *The Pleasure-Dome of Kubla Khan* (1920) and *Roman Sketches* (1915–16), including *The White Peacock*.

griffin, in ancient and medieval legend, creature with an eagle's head and wings and a lion's body. Originating in Middle Eastern legend, it is often found in Persian art. It is thought to have symbolized strength and vigilance.

Griffith, Arthur, 1872–1922, Irish statesman, founder of SINN FÉIN. Through his newspaper, the *United Irishmen,* he advocated the creation of an Irish assembly. He was the first president (1922) of the Irish Free State.

Griffith, D(avid) W(ark), 1875–1948, American film director. A cinematic genius, he innovated cross-cutting, close-ups, long shots, moving-camera shots, and flashbacks in such films as *The Birth of a Nation* (1915) and *Intolerance* (1916).

Grimké, Angelina Emily, 1805–79, and **Sarah Moore Grimké,** 1792–1873, American abolitionists and feminists; b. Charleston, S.C. Sisters from an aristocratic slaveholding family, they were converted to the Quaker faith, moved north, and became the first women to speak publicly on the issues of slavery and women's rights. Angelina became a persuasive orator, and Sarah published influential works on abolition (1836) and the equality of the sexes (1838).

Grimm, Jakob, 1785–1863, German philologist and folklorist, a founder of comparative philology. Aside from his study of Germanic languages (see GRIMM'S LAW) and his writings on German grammar and mythology, he is best known for the collection of folk tales known as *Grimm's Fairy Tales* (1812–15), compiled with his brother, **Wilhelm Grimm,** 1786–1859.

Grimmelshausen, Hans Jakob Christoffel von [grĭm'əlshou"zən], 1625–76, German novelist. His satirical *Adventuresome Simplicius Simplicissimus* (1669) is a picaresque romance, noted for its vigor, humor, and realism.

Grimm's law, principle of relationships in Indo-European languages, first formulated by Jakob GRIMM in 1822. It demonstrates that the regular shifting of consonants in groups took place once in the development of English and the other Low German languages and twice in German and the other High German languages. Thus, the unaspirated voiceless stops *(k, t, p)* of the ancient, or classical, Indo-European languages (Sanskrit, Greek, Latin) became voiceless aspirates *(h, th, f)* in English and mediae *(h, d, f)* in German; unaspirated voiced stops *(g, d, b)* became voiceless stops *(k, t, p)* in English and voiceless aspirates *(kh, ts, f)* in German; and aspirated voiced stops *(gh, dh, bh)* became unaspirated voiced stops *(g, d, b)* in English and voiceless stops *(k, t, p)* in German.

Gris, Juan [grēs], 1887–1927, Spanish cubist painter; b. José Victoriáno Gonzalez. A developer of synthetic CUBISM, he painted simple forms that reflect an architectonic design. His later works were more sumptuous and decorative. Most of his works are still life oils and COLLAGES.

Griswold v. Connecticut, case decided in 1965 by the U.S. SUPREME COURT, establishing a right to privacy in striking down a Connecticut ban on the sale of contraceptives. The Court, through Justice DOUGLAS, found a "zone of privacy" created by several amendments to the U.S. CONSTITUTION guaranteeing against governmental intrusion into the homes and lives of citizens. The *Griswold* decision was important in later cases, such as ROE V. WADE.

Gromyko, Andrei Andreyevich [grōmē'kō], 1909–89, Soviet diplomat and government official. After holding such posts as ambassador to the U.S. (1943–46) he became foreign minister (1957–85). In the 1970s he helped arrange U.S.–Soviet summit talks. He became (1973) a member of the ruling politburo, taking the position of first deputy premier (1983–85) and president (1985–88).

Gronchi, Giovanni [grôn' kē], 1887–1978, Italian politician. He broke (1922) with MUSSOLINI. A founder of the Christian Democratic party, he was minister for commerce, industry, and labor (1944–46), speaker of the chamber of deputies (1948–55), and president of Italy (1955–62).

Grooms, Red, 1937–, American artist; b. Nashville. A painter and filmmaker, he pioneered in the theatrical art form known as the "happening." He is best known for his witty environmental constructions, e.g., *Ruckus Manhattan* (1975).

Gropius, Walter [grō'pēo͝os], 1883–1969, German-American architect, a leader of modern functional architecture. In Germany his glass-wall Fagus factory buildings (1910–11) at Alfeld were among the most advanced works in Europe. In 1918 he became director of the Weimar School of Art and reorganized it as the BAUHAUS. He designed (1926) a complete new set of buildings for it in Dessau, as well as the Staattheater in Jena (1923), residences, and industrial buildings. In the U.S. after 1937, he taught at Harvard until 1952.

gross domestic product: see under GROSS NATIONAL PRODUCT.

Grosseteste, Robert [grōs'tĕst], c.1175–1253, English prelate. A founder of the Oxford Franciscan school, he made Oxford a center of learning. As bishop (1235) of Lincoln, he resisted the efforts of HENRY III to control church appointments and supported the reforms of Simon de MONTFORT. He also censured Pope INNOCENT IV for excessive exactions and for appointing foreigners to English sees. His writings include treatises on the sciences, pastoral works, and poems. His studies of ARISTOTLE were the basis for the SCHOLASTICISM of THOMAS AQUINAS and ALBERTUS MAGNUS.

gross national product (GNP), a nation's total output of goods and services in a given period, usually one year. In estimating the GNP, only the final value of a product is counted (e.g., automobiles, but not the steel that they contain). The three major components of GNP are consumer purchases, private investment (including over-

Fagus factory buildings, designed by Gropius

seas investment but excluding foreign investment in a nation's economy), and government spending. The GNP is reported quarterly in the U.S. and was used as a barometer of the nation's economic health, but in 1991 the government switched to emphasizing the **gross domestic product** (GDP), which is similar but covers only goods and services produced inside a nation's borders. The GDP, which also is reported quarterly, is regarded as a better indicator of the performance of a country's economy and is used as such by most industrialized nations. The government continues to report the GNP, but about a month after the GDP.

Gros Ventre, name used by the French for two distinct bands of Native Americans of the Plains (see NORTH AMERICA, INDIGENOUS PEOPLES OF). The nomadic Atsina band of ARAPAHO spoke an Algonquian language of the Algonquian-Wakashan stock; the settled Hidatsa, speaking a Siouan branch of Hokan-Siouan, were closely allied with the MANDAN, an agricultural people with whom they live on a reservation in North Dakota.

Grosz, George [grōs], 1893–1959, German-American painter; b. Germany. Early associated with DADA, he was famous for savage post–World War I caricatures of bourgeois society. He became a U.S. citizen in 1938 and painted traditional landscapes and figures. Deeply affected by the horrors of World War II, he created a symbolic series of ravaged figures, e.g., *Street Scene* (Philadelphia Mus. Art).

Grotefend, Georg Friedrich [grō'təfĕnt], 1775–1853, German archaeologist and philologist. His greatest achievement was deciphering inscriptions of Persian CUNEIFORM.

Grotius, Hugo [grō'shəs], 1583–1645, Dutch jurist and humanist. His *Concerning the Law of War and Peace* (1625) is considered the first definitive text on INTERNATIONAL LAW. Drawing on the Bible and classical history, he argued that natural law prescribes rules of conduct for nations, as for individuals. While not condemning all war, he maintained that only certain causes justified it, and he devoted much attention to the concept of more humane warfare.

Groton, city (1990 pop. 45,144), SE Conn., on the Thames R., opposite New London; settled c.1650, inc. 1705. Shipbuilding and pharmaceuticals are its major industries; it is famous for the construction of submarines. The *Nautilus,* the first nuclear submarine, was launched there in 1954.

ground-effect machine: see AIR-CUSHION VEHICLE.

groundhog: see WOODCHUCK.

ground laurel: see TRAILING ARBUTUS.

Group of Seven (G7), international organization (est. 1985) of the world's major industrial powers: the U.S., Canada, France, Germany, Great Britain, Italy, and Japan. It discusses and coordinates economic and commercial matters and works to aid the economies of other nations. The leaders of the G7 nations meet annually in member countries.

grouper, large, carnivorous FISH of the sea BASS family, abundant in tropical and subtropical seas and highly valued as food. Most have bright markings that change in color and pattern to match the background. The largest is the spotted jewfish (up to 600 lb/270 kg). The red grouper and black grouper form the bulk of the commercial catch.

group psychotherapy, a means of altering behavior and emotions that is based on the use of group interactions. The technique was developed in the 1930s and received further impetus during World War II, when there was a great need for a prompt method of treating many patients simultaneously. The therapy can take many forms, depending upon the predisposition and training of the therapist, but is generally carried out in formal groups of 5 to 12 people; the members may be heterogeneous or homogeneous. The group becomes a "sample" social setting, reproducing conditions of interpersonal relationships in general; its members jointly participate in observing personal motivation and styles of interaction. Members can also try new behaviors and learn to deal with the consequences of these within the group. Group therapy may be combined with individual treatment.

grouse, henlike terrestrial BIRD of the family Tetraonidae, found in the colder parts of the Northern Hemisphere. It is protectively plumaged in reds, browns, and grays. The American ruffed grouse (*Bonasa umbellus*), often miscalled PARTRIDGE or PHEASANT, is a forest bird noted for the drumming sound made by the courting male. The ptarmigan (*Lagopus lagopus*) is an arctic species that migrates to the NW U.S. in winter, when its rusty brown plumage changes to white.

Grove, Lefty (Robert Moses Grove), 1900–1975, American baseball player; b. Lonaconing, Md. He won 300 games and struck out over 2,200 batters as a left-handed pitcher for the Philadelphia Athletics (1925–33) and Boston Red Sox (1934–41). In 1931 he won 31 games and lost 4, for a winning percentage of .866, a record that stood for many years.

Grundtvig, Nikolai Frederik Severin [grŏŏnt'vĭg], 1783–1872, Danish writer, churchman, and educator. He founded the folk high school, a form of adult education designed to foster patriotism and religious conviction in young adults. His many literary works include the epoch-making *Northern Mythology* (1808), a loose retelling of the Old Norse myths. In his poems, songs, and hymns, he treated historical, mythological, and religious subjects.

Grünewald, Mathias [grün'əvält], c.1475–1528, German religious painter; b. Mathis Gothart Neithart. Possessed of unique expressive power, he used stylistic components such as silhouette and unusual color, the striking contrast of light and shadow, and the exaggeration of the human form to convey anguish and terror. His most frequent subject was the crucifixion of Jesus, and his masterpiece is the *Isenheim Altarpiece* (1515; Colmar, France).

grunion: see SILVERSIDES.

Guadalajara, city (1990 pop. 1,628,617), SW Mexico, capital of Jalisco state. A spacious, beautiful city (called the "Pearl of the West"), it is Mexico's second largest city. Although it is a modern metropolis with varied manufactures, it retains many old colonial structures, notably a cathedral and a governor's palace. Its location on a plain more than 5,000 ft (1,524 m) high and its mild, dry climate have made it a popular health resort. Founded c.1530, Guadalajara was a center of the movement for independence from Spain. It has suffered several earthquakes.

Guadalcanal, island c.2,510 sq mi (6,500 sq km), in the SW Pacific

Ocean, largest of the SOLOMON ISLANDS and site of the national capital, Honiara. The largely mountainous and forested island is of volcanic origin. Coconuts are grown, and some gold has been mined. In bitter fighting during WORLD WAR II, U.S. forces seized (1942–43) the island and its airstrip, Henderson Field, from Japanese troops.

Guadalupe Hidalgo, Treaty of, 1848, peace treaty between the U.S. and Mexico that ended the MEXICAN WAR. It confirmed U.S. claims to TEXAS. Mexico ceded most of the present SW U.S. for $15 million and the assumption by the U.S. government of claims against Mexico by U.S. citizens.

Guadalupe Mountains National Park: see NATIONAL PARKS (table).

Guadalupe Victoria, 1786?–1843, first president of MEXICO (1824–29); b. Manuel Félix Fernández. A general, he fought against Spanish rule, and after Mexican independence (1821) he and SANTA ANNA overthrew the ITURBIDE regime. His administration was marred by factional strife.

Guadeloupe, overseas department of France (1992 est. pop. 409,000), 687 sq mi (1,779 sq km), in the Leeward Islands; comprising Basse-Terre, Grande-Terre, and smaller islands. Visited (1493) by Columbus, it was settled (17th cent.) by the French, who eliminated the native Caribs, imported African slaves, and made it a major sugar producer. Sugar remains important, as are tourism, bananas, livestock raising, and fishing. The population is mainly of African or mixed descent. French is the official language, but a French patois is widely spoken.

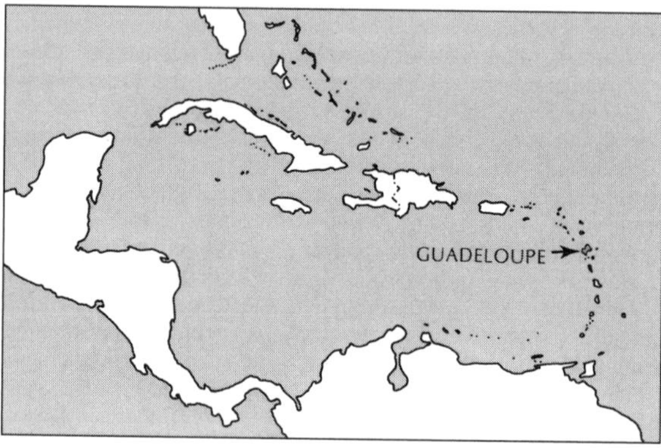

Guam [gwäm], island (1990 pop. 141,039), 209 sq mi (541 sq km), W Pacific, southernmost of the Marianas island group; an unincorporated U.S. territory. AGANA is the seat of government. Guam is tropical and partly mountainous. The island is a major military base, and providing goods and services to the installations is a major industry. There is tourism (largely from Japan) and some light industry. Subsistence agriculture also is practiced. Guamanians, who are chiefly of Chamorros (mixed Spanish, Filipino, and Micronesian) stock, are U.S. citizens but cannot vote in U.S. elections. About one fourth of the population are military personnel and their dependents. Administered by the U.S. Dept. of the Interior, Guam has an elected governor and legislature. Discovered (1521) by MAGELLAN, it belonged to Spain until it was surrendered to the U.S. in 1898. Guam was occupied by the Japanese from 1941 to 1944. Typhoons devastated Guam in 1976 and 1992, and the island suffered a severe earthquake in 1993. In 1987 Guamanians voted to seek commonwealth status with the U.S.

Guangzhou or **Canton,** city (1990 est. pop. 3,580,000), capital of Guangdong prov., S China, a major deepwater port on the Pearl R. delta. Among the largest cities in the country, Guangzhou is the transportation, industrial, and trade center of S China. It has shipyards, a steel complex, and factories producing many heavy and light industrial products. Its exports include textiles, paper, cement, sugar, and traditional handicrafts. Guangzhou has a large international airport and is linked with HONG KONG by rail and hovercraft. It became a part of China in the 3d cent. B.C. and was later the first Chinese port regularly visited by European traders. The seat (1913) of SUN YAT-SEN's revolutionary movement, Guangzhou was a Nationalist center in the 1920s, and its fall (1950) to Communist armies signalled the Communist victory in all of China. Foreign trade expositions have been held there since 1957. Guangzhou remains a major marketplace for China's foreign trade and for foreign investment in S China.

Guantánamo, city (1986 est. pop. 175,000), SE Cuba, in Oriente prov. Founded in the 19th cent. by French refugees from Haiti, it is now a sugar- and coffee-processing center. It is c.20 mi (32 km) inland from its port, Caimanera, on well-protected **Guantánamo Bay,** which is also the site of a large U.S. naval station established in 1903. Since the revolution of 1959, Cuba has refused to accept the token annual U.S. rent for the naval base and has pressed for its surrender.

Guaraní, people in N and E South America (see SOUTH AMERICA, INDIGENOUS PEOPLES OF) of the Tupi-Guaraní linguistic stock (see NATIVE AMERICAN LANGUAGES). Those who live in S Brazil and Paraguay are called Guaraní; those in the Amazon region are called Tupí or Tupinambá. At the time of the Spanish conquest (16th cent.), communities of both groups had a chief and a powerful SHAMAN. The Guaraní grew corn and manioc. In ancient times they practiced ritual CANNIBALISM. Although their material culture was not advanced, they had a rich body of folklore. Early Jesuit missionaries founded among them the agricultural settlements called reductions, using native labor under the absolute, but usually benevolent, rule of priests. Guaraní is widely spoken in Paraguay; most Tupí have been assimilated into European culture.

Guardi, Francesco [gwär'dē], 1712–93, Venetian painter of landscapes and architectural scenes. A follower of CANALETTO, he developed a freer style. His work ranges from architectural scenes to delightful, spontaneous *capricci*.

Guatemala, officially Republic of Guatemala, republic (1992 est. pop. 9,784,000), 42,042 sq mi (108,889 sq km), Central America; bordered by Mexico (N and W), Belize and the Caribbean Sea (E), Honduras and El Salvador (SE), and the Pacific Ocean (SW). The capital is GUATEMALA CITY. A highland region occupies the southern half of the country and is the most densely populated area. Much of northern Guatemala is covered by a vast tropical forest, the Petén. Coffee exports accounts for more than half of the nation's revenue. Sugar, cotton, tobacco, vegetables, fruit, and beef also are exported. Industry, particularly the assembly of clothing for the U.S. market, is being expanded. The mainly Roman Catholic population is about evenly divided between Maya and mestizos. The official language is Spanish, although many indigenous people speak only their own dialects. The literacy rate and per capita income are extremely low.

History. After defeat of the Quiché (MAYA) in 1523–24, Spain established a prosperous colony in the area, with its capital (from 1542) at ANTIGUA. After independence (1821) Guatemala became the nucleus of the Central American Federation and, after dissolution of the federation in 1839, a separate republic. Ruled through the 19th cent. by a series of usually repressive dictators, Guatemala has alternated in the 20th cent. between economic reform and reaction. A conservative coup in 1954 owed its success to U.S. military intervention. From 1970 into the early 1980s, the country was dominated by conservative military elements. A leftist insurgency, begun in the 1960s, persisted into the 1990s, despite army efforts to crush it, but the rebels have had limited success at best. Peace talks, begun in 1991, have proved unsuccessful. In 1985 a civilian, Vinicio Cerezo Arévalo, was elected president, but the military retained considerable influence. He was succeeded (1991) by Jorge Serrano Elías, a right-wing businessman with military ties. Serrano adopted economic reforms, but they resulted in a decline in living standards and led to antigovernment protests. In 1993 he attempted to institute rule by decree, but the army withdrew its support and forced him to resign. Ramiro de León Carpio, the attorney general for human rights, was elected by the congress to succeed Serrano and won passage of constitutional reforms.

Guatemala, city (1990 est. pop. 2,250,000), S central Guatemala, capital of Guatemala. The largest city in Central America, it is the nation's commercial and industrial center, with a cosmopolitan atmosphere and many modern public buildings, as well as Spanish colonial structures and large native markets. It was constructed in a highland valley in 1779, after the former capital, ANTIGUA, was

destroyed by earthquakes. Guatemala City itself suffered that fate in 1917–18 and has since been completely rebuilt.

guava, small evergreen tree or shrub (genus *Psidium*) of the MYRTLE family, native to tropical America and grown for its ornamental flowers and edible fruit. Species include the common tropical guava (*P. guajava*) and the strawberry guava (*P. cattleyanum*). The guava is grown commercially in Florida and California and is made into jellies and beverages.

Guayaquil, city (1990 pop. 1,531,229), capital of Guayas prov., W Ecuador, on the Guayas R. near its mouth on the Gulf of Guayaquil, an inlet of the Pacific Ocean. It is Ecuador's largest city and its chief port and manufacturing center. Founded by Sebastián de Benalcázar in 1535, it was liberated from Spain by Antonio José de SUCRE in 1821, and in 1822 was the site of a meeting between Simón BOLÍVAR and José de SAN MARTÍN that determined the course of South American independence. The climate is hot and humid, and yellow fever was a problem until the early 20th cent.

Guðmundsson, Kristmann [gvü'thmünsôn], 1902–83, Icelandic novelist who wrote in both Norwegian and Icelandic. His psychologically insightful works include *The Bridal Gown* (1927) and *The Square* (1965).

Gudrun [goo'droon] or **Kudrun** [koo–], in Germanic literature. **1** Heroine of the VOLSUNGASAGA. **2** Heroine of a Middle High German epic influenced by the *Nibelungenlied* (see NIBELUNGEN). **3** Principle character of the Icelandic *Laxdaelasaga.*

Guelphs [gwĕlfs], German dynasty of the Middle Ages. It traced its descent from the Swabian count Guelph, or Welf, in the 9th cent. Eventually the Guelphs became the dukes of Bavaria and Saxony, and were the rivals of the house of HOHENSTAUFEN. In Italy the dynasty was represented by the ESTE family. The Guelphs came to represent the papal faction in the longtime struggle between the GUELPHS AND GHIBELLINES.

Guelphs and Ghibellines [gĭb'əlēnz], opposing political factions in Germany and Italy in the later Middle Ages. The names designated the papal (Guelph) party and the imperial (Ghibelline) party during the long struggle between the papacy and the Holy Roman emperors; they also designated two rival German families, the Welfs or GUELPHS, and the HOHENSTAUFEN. In Germany the rivalry began under Emperor HENRY IV and last flared at the election of Emperor OTTO IV. In Italy the terms were used from the 13th to the 15th cent., and the rival factions plunged the country into internal warfare. Among the Ghibellines were EZZELINO DA ROMANO and the VISCONTI family of Milan. Milan itself was Guelph, as were, generally, Florence and Genoa. Cremona, Pisa, and Arezzo were usually Ghibelline. Venice remained neutral.

Guernica [gärnē'kä], town (1981 pop. 17,836), in the Basque prov. of Vizcaya, N Spain. The Guernica oak, under which the diet of Vizcaya met, symbolizes the Basques' lost liberty. One of PICASSO's greatest paintings commemorates the 1937 destruction of Guernica by German bombers aiding FRANCO during the SPANISH CIVIL WAR.

Guernsey: see CHANNEL ISLANDS.

Guerrero, Vicente [gār-rā'rō], 1782–1831, Mexican revolutionary leader. He won guerrilla victories over Spanish forces but accepted ITURBIDE's conservative leadership of the Mexican independence movement. He and SANTA ANNA led (1828) a successful revolt against Iturbide, and Guerrero served briefly (1829) as president, but he was forced to retreat and was finally captured and shot.

Gueux [gö] [Fr., = beggars], 16th-cent. Dutch revolutionary party. In 1566 over 2,000 nobles and burghers vowed to resist Spanish repression in the NETHERLANDS. Called "these beggars" at the court of the Spanish regent, MARGARET OF PARMA, they adopted the sobriquet. The "Beggars of the Sea," crews of Dutch privateers chartered in 1569 by WILLIAM THE SILENT to harass Spanish shipping, raised the siege of LEIDEN in 1574.

Guevara, Ernesto, 1928–67, Cuban revolutionary leader; b. Argentina. A physician and political activist, "Che" Guevara became (1956) Fidel CASTRO's chief lieutenant and a guerrilla leader in the Cuban revolution (1959). He served as minister of industry (1961–65), then left Cuba to foster revolutions in other countries. Captured in Bolivia (1967), he was executed.

Guggenheim, family of American industrialists and philanthropists. **Meyer Guggenheim,** 1828–1905; b. Aargau canton, Switzerland, emigrated (1847) to the U.S. and prospered as a merchant in Philadelphia. His real fortune came from metal smelting and refining, beginning when he was nearly 60. Seven sons—Isaac, Daniel, Murry, Solomon, Benjamin, Simon, and William—contributed to the expansion of the family enterprises. **Daniel Guggenheim,** 1856–1930, b. Philadelphia, combined (1901) the Guggenheim interests with the American Smelting and Refining Co. The Daniel and Florence Guggenheim Foundation for aeronautical research represented his main philanthropy. **Simon Guggenheim,** 1867–1941, established (1925), with his wife, the John Simon Guggenheim Memorial Foundation to assist scholars, writers, and artists. **Solomon Robert Guggenheim,** 1861–1949, created a foundation that established (1937) the SOLOMON R. GUGGENHEIM MUSEUM.

Guggenheim Museum: see SOLOMON R. GUGGENHEIM MUSEUM.

Guicciardini, Francesco [gwētchärdē'nē], 1483–1540, Italian historian and statesman. He served in the Florentine government and under Pope LEO X before taking up writing. Breaking with medieval tradition, he removed history from the realm of literature and related it to the development of states. His history of Italy (1492–1534) is the masterwork of Italian historical literature of the RENAISSANCE.

Guidi, Tommaso: see MASACCIO.

guilds or **gilds,** economic and social associations of persons engaged in the same business or craft, typical of Western Europe in the Middle Ages. Membership was never by class, but by profession or trade. The primary function of guilds was to establish local control over a profession or craft by setting standards of workmanship and price, by protecting the business from competition, and by gaining status in society for guild members. Merchant guilds in some cases developed into intercity leagues for the promotion of trade, such as the medieval HANSEATIC LEAGUE. By the 17th cent. the power of the guilds had withered in England. They were abolished in France in 1791 and elsewhere in Western Europe during the 19th cent.

guild socialism, form of socialism in Great Britain that advocated industrial self-government through national worker-controlled guilds. The theory began (1906) with Arthur J. Penty, who sought to revive the spirit of medieval craft guilds and argued that workers should strive for control of industry rather than for political reform. Several guilds were started, but the movement ended after the collapse (1922) of the National Building Guild, its most powerful component.

Guillén, Jorge [gēlyän'], 1893–1984, Spanish poet. He settled in the U.S. in 1939. His difficult, classic verse appears in *Cántico* (1928), *Clamor* (1957), and *Affirmation: A Bilingual Anthology* (1968). He also wrote the essays in *Language and Poetry* (1961).

Guinea [gĭn'ē], Fr. *Guinée,* officially Republic of Guinea, republic (1992 est. pop. 7,784,000), 94,925 sq mi (245,856 sq km), W Africa, bordered by Guinea-Bissau, Senegal, and Mali (N), Côte d'Ivoire (E), Sierra Leone and Liberia (S), and the Atlantic Ocean (W). CONAKRY is the capital. A humid and tropical country, Guinea comprises an alluvial coastal plain; the mountainous Fouta Jallon region; a savanna interior; and the forested Guinea Highlands, which rise to c.5,800 ft (1,770 m) in the Nimba Mts. Guinea is predominantly agricultural. Coffee, bananas, palm kernels, and pineapples are the leading cash crops; the main subsistence crop is rice. Some of the world's largest bauxite deposits lie in Guinea, the world's third largest producer; iron ore, gold, and diamonds also are mined. Poor administration and transportation have hampered industrialization, and Guinea, despite its mineral wealth, remains one of the world's poorest nations. Most sectors of the economy were placed under state control after independence (1958), but large-scale PRIVATIZATION was initiated in 1991. The main ethnic groups are the pastoral Fulani and the agrarian Malinké and Susu. Islam is the chief religion, but there are animist and Roman Catholic minorities. French is the principal language, but indigenous tongues also are spoken.

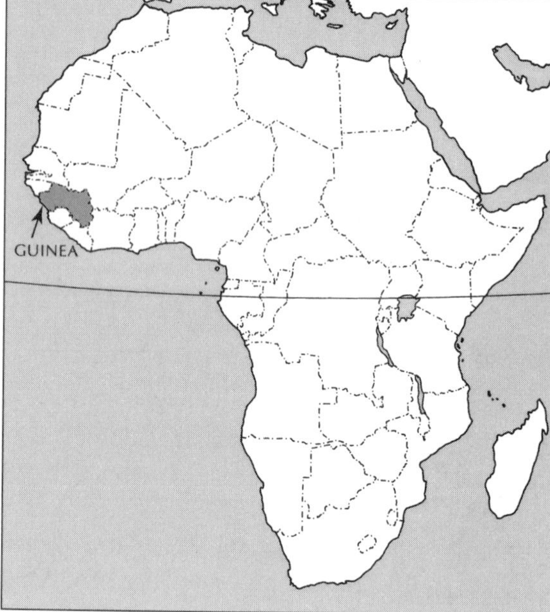

History. Part of present-day Guinea belonged to medieval GHANA, and later to the MALI empire. As in other W African states, Portuguese exploration of the Guinea coast in the mid-15th cent. led to the development of a slave trade involving also the French and British. France proclaimed a protectorate over the Boké area of Guinea in 1849 and, after extending its control over much of the rest of Guinea, annexed it under the name Rivières du Sud (rivers of the south). In 1895, as French Guinea, it became part of French West Africa. Exploitation of Guinea's rich bauxite deposits began just before World War II, accompanied by the growth of a radical labor movement led by Ahmed Sékou TOURÉ. Under his leadership Guinea was the only French colony to reject (1958) self-government within the FRENCH COMMUNITY and to vote instead for full independence. Touré created a one-party socialist state in which he, as head of the government and the ruling party, had ultimate authority. Over time his rule became increasingly repressive. When Touré died (1984) a military clique seized power, and Col. (now Major Gen.) Lansana Conté became president. Conté has reduced state control of the economy and, under foreign and domestic pressure, liberalized the political system. Conté won (1993) a multiparty presidential election that was boycotted by some opposition groups and was marred by fraud.

Guinea-Bissau [–bĭs″sou′], officially Republic of Guinea-Bissau, republic (1992 est. pop. 1,047,000), 13,948 sq mi (36,125 sq km), W Africa, bordered by the Atlantic Ocean (W), Senegal (N), and Guinea (E and S), and including the Bijagós Archipelago and several islands in the Atlantic. The capital is BISSAU. Guinea-Bissau is largely a low-lying coastal plain, with many rivers and swampy estuaries. Farming is the leading occupation, producing rice, palm oil, cassava, sugarcane, coconuts, and peanuts. Cashew nuts and fishing are leading exports. The population is largely comprised of four ethnic groups: the Balante, Fulani, Malinke, and Mandyako. A majority of the people hold traditional beliefs, but about one third are Muslim, and about 5% are Christian. Portuguese is the official language, but Criould and indigenous tongues are spoken.

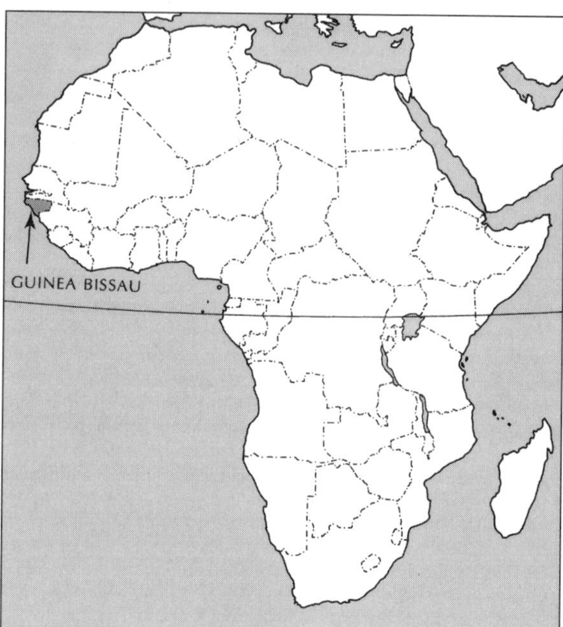

History. First visited by the Portuguese in 1446–47, the area that is now Guinea-Bissau developed in the 16th cent. as a slave-trading center. It was administered as part of the CAPE VERDE islands until 1879, when it became the separate colony of Portuguese Guinea. In 1951 it was constituted an overseas province. A nationalist movement was organized in 1956, and a war for independence began in the early 1960s. After more than 10 years of fighting, independence was proclaimed in 1973 and recognized by Portugal in 1974. The following year some 100,000 refugees of the war returned. Ties with Cape Verde had been close, with eventual union a goal. However, a coup in 1980, which brought João Bernardo Vieira to power, led to a breakdown of those relations. Since then the country's economy has slowly moved away from socialism. Popular pressure led the ruling party to agree (1991) to the introduction of multiparty democracy; free elections are expected to be held in 1994.

guinea pig, domesticated form of the cavy (*Cavia porcellus*), a South American RODENT unrelated to the pig. Guinea pigs have rounded bodies and large heads, are 6 to 10 in. (15 to 25 cm) long, and weigh 1 to 2 lb (450 to 900 grams). There are short- and long-haired varieties and many color combinations.

Guinevere: see ARTHURIAN LEGEND.

Guinness, Sir Alec, 1914–, English actor. Noted for his versatility, he has appeared in such films as *Kind Hearts and Coronets* (1949; he performed eight parts); *The Bridge on the River Kwai* (1957; Academy Award); and, for television, *Tinker, Tailor, Soldier, Spy* (1980) and *Smiley's People* (1982), dramatizations of novels by John LECARRÉ.

Guise, French ducal family, founded as a cadet branch of the house of Lorraine by **Claude de Lorraine,** 1st **duc de Guise,** 1496–1550. His daughter, MARY OF GUISE, married JAMES V of Scotland and was the mother of MARY QUEEN OF SCOTS. His sons **François de Lorraine,** 2d **duc de Guise,** 1519–63, and **Charles de Guise, Cardinal de Lorraine,** c.1525–74, controlled French politics in the reign of FRANCIS II, the first husband of Mary Queen of Scots.

They championed the Roman Catholic cause against the Protestant HUGUENOTS and harshly suppressed the Huguenot conspiracy of Amboise (1560). After Francis's death they opposed the tolerant policies of the regent, CATHERINE DE' MEDICI, and provoked the Wars of Religion (see RELIGION, WARS OF). François's son **Henri de Lorraine,** 3d **duc de Guise,** 1550–88, helped Catherine de' Medici plan the massacre of Huguenots on SAINT BARTHOLOMEW'S DAY (1572). He formed the Catholic League to oppose Protestantism and revived the League in 1585 to block the accession of the Protestant Henry of Navarre (later HENRY IV). Because of Guise's designs on the throne, King HENRY III brought about the assassinations of Guise and his brother **Louis de Lorraine, Cardinal de Guise,** 1555–88. Henri was succeeded by his son, **Charles de Lorraine,** 4th **duc de Guise,** 1571–1640. Charles's son **Henri de Lorraine,** 5th **duc de Guise,** 1614–64, was the archbishop of Rheims. He conspired against Cardinal RICHELIEU (1641) and fought in Naples against Spain (1647–48; 1654). He was grand chamberlain at the court of LOUIS XIV.

guitar: see STRINGED INSTRUMENT.

Guitry, Lucien Germain [gētrē'], 1860–1925, the most versatile French actor of his day. His son, **Sacha Guitry,** 1885–1957, was an actor; popular playwright, e.g., *Nono* (1905); and film director.

Guiyang or **Kweiyang** [both: gwā-yäng], city (1990 est. pop. 1,530,000), capital of Guizhou prov., SW China. A major transport and industrial center, it produces textiles, fertilizers, machine tools, and petroleum products. The city's population includes numerous minority nationalities.

Guizot, François [gēzō'], 1787–1874, French statesman and historian. A university professor, he served LOUIS PHILIPPE as minister of public instruction (1832–37). Becoming the chief power in the ministry (1840), he was named premier in 1847, but his acceptance of the established order led to his overthrow in the FEBRUARY REVOLUTION of 1848. He devoted the rest of his life to writing. His *History of the Revolution in England* (6 vol., 1826–56) illustrates his critical approach and his admiration for the British experience.

GULAG, system of forced-labor prison camps in the USSR, from the Russian acronym for Chief Administration of Corrective Labor Camps, a department of the KGB (Soviet SECRET POLICE). Established in 1918, the vast penal network reached its peak under STALIN, when deaths of political prisoners from starvation and other forms of maltreatment were estimated in the millions. The system was publicized in the writings of SOLZHENITSYN.

Gulf Stream, warm ocean current of the N Atlantic Ocean off E North America, originating in the Gulf of Mexico, passing through the Straits of Florida, and moving northeastward until it merges with the NORTH ATLANTIC DRIFT at lat. 40°N and long. 60°W. The Gulf Stream has an average speed of 4 mi (6.4 km) per hour. At its beginning the water temperature is 80°F (27°C), but it decreases as it moves north.

Gulf War: see PERSIAN GULF WAR; IRAN-IRAQ WAR.

gull, aquatic BIRD of the family Laridae (which also includes the TERN), found near all oceans and many inland waters. White with gray or black plumage, gulls are larger and bulkier than terns, and their tails are squared rather than forked. They have long, narrow wings adapted for soaring, webbed feet for swimming, and hooked bills.

Gullah, a creole language spoken by the Gullahs, African Americans of the Carolina Sea Islands and the Middle Atlantic coast of the U.S. It is a mixture of 17th- and 18th-cent. English and a number of West African languages.

gum tree, name for the EUCALYPTUS and for other trees, e.g., sweet gum (WITCH-HAZEL family) and BLACK GUM.

gun, a device that discharges shot, shells, or bullets from a straight tube. A gun using the explosion of GUNPOWDER or some other explosive substance to propel the projectile is called a firearm; types include ARTILLERY (large firearms), MORTAR, and SMALL ARMS. Certain other guns use compressed air produced by a spring-operated plunger (e.g., BB gun) or a lever-and-pump system (e.g., air rifle) to propel the projectile.

gun control, government limitation of the purchase and ownership of firearms. The availability of guns is controlled by nations and localities throughout the world. In the U.S. the "right of the people to keep and bear arms" is guaranteed by the Constitution, but has been variously interpreted. Some states and localities have enacted strict licensing and other control measures, and federal legislation (1968) prohibited the sale of rifles by mail. Gun control has continued to be widely debated, however, and often opposed, notably by the NATIONAL RIFLE ASSOCIATION. The growing number of gun-related crimes propelled congressional passage (1993) of the "Brady bill" (named for James Brady, the press secretary wounded in the 1981 assassination attempt on Pres. Reagan) after years of controversy. It requires a five-day waiting period and background check before a handgun purchase.

Gundulić, Ivan [go͝ondo͞o'lĭch], or **Giovanni Gondola** [gōndə'lä], 1588–1638, Croatian poet. His finest work, *Osman* (1626), an epic of the Polish wars against the Turks, shows early Slavic nationalism and the influence of ancient song.

gunmetal, a BRONZE, an ALLOY of COPPER, TIN, and a small amount of ZINC. Originally used to make guns, it is now employed in casting machine parts. The percentages of the three elements are varied, depending on the intended use.

gunpowder, explosive mixture of saltpeter (75%), sulfur (10%), and charcoal (15%). It is believed to have originated as early as the 9th cent. in China, where it was used for making fireworks, and to have been introduced into Europe in the 14th cent. Its use revolutionized warfare. Gunpowder was the only explosive in wide use until the mid-19th cent., when it was superseded by NITROGLYCERIN-based EXPLOSIVES.

Gunpowder Plot, conspiracy to blow up the English Parliament and JAMES I on Nov. 5, 1605, the opening day of Parliament. An uprising of English Catholics was to follow. In preparation, gunpowder was stored in the cellar of the House of Lords. The plot was exposed when a conspirator warned a relative not to attend Parliament that day. One of the plotters, Guy Fawkes, was arrested as he entered the cellar. The others were either seized and killed outright or imprisoned and executed. The plot only worsened the plight of English Catholics. Guy Fawkes Day is celebrated today in England on Nov. 5.

Gupta [go͝op'tə], Indian dynasty (c.320–c.550) founded by CHANDRAGUPTA I (r.c.320–c.330). At its height, the dynasty ruled much of what is modern India.

Gurkha, ethnic group of NEPAL. Predominantly Tibeto-Mongolians, they speak Khas, a Rajasthani dialect of Sanskritic origin; practice Hinduism; and claim descent from the RAJPUTS of N India. By the 18th cent. they had expanded east from their small state of Gurkha throughout Nepal. Many Gurkha soldiers have served in Indian and British armies.

Gustavus, kings of Sweden. **Gustavus I,** 1496–1560 (r.1523–60), was the founder of the modern Swedish state and the VASA dynasty. After his father, a Swedish senator, was killed (1520) in a massacre ordered by the Danish king, CHRISTIAN II, Gustavus escaped from prison and defeated the Danes. His election as king by the Riksdag (1523) ended the Kalmar Union of Denmark, Sweden, and Norway. In 1527 he founded a national Protestant church. With a newly strengthened navy, he defeated LÜBECK (1537), freeing Swedish commerce from the power of the HANSEATIC LEAGUE. In 1544 he made the throne hereditary in the Vasa family, ending the election of Swedish kings. His son Eric XIV succeeded him. **Gustavus II** (Gustavus Adolphus), 1594–1632 (r.1611–32), was the son of CHARLES IX. Aided by his chancellor, OXENSTIERNA, he ended the Kalmar War with Denmark (1613) and forced Russia to cede Ingermanland (1617). In the THIRTY YEARS WAR he obtained much of Polish Livonia and several Baltic ports (1629), then invaded German Pomerania, defeating TILLY near Leipzig (1631). At Lützen (1632) the Swedes defeated WALLENSTEIN, but Gustavus was killed. His daughter, CHRISTINA, succeeded him. **Gustavus III,** 1746–92 (r.1771–92), was the son of Adolphus Frederick. To quell civil strife he imposed (1772) a new constitution restoring the royal prerogatives lost by his successors. In a war with Russia and Denmark (1788–90), he was victorious. He planned a coalition to aid the French royalists but was assassinated by an agent of the nobles. His son, **Gustavus IV,** 1778–1837 (r.1792–1809), succeeded him under the regency of his uncle, later CHARLES XIII. After he joined (1805) the Third Coalition against NAPOLEON I he lost Swedish Pomerania to France and Finland to Russia (1808). His despotism, mental imbalance, and disastrous policies led to his forced abdication when the Russians threatened Stockholm (1809). Charles XIII became king and made peace with Russia. Gustavus was exiled, and his descendants barred from succession. **Gustavus V,** 1858–1950 (r.1907–50), was the son of Oscar II. During his reign Sweden prospered and avoided involvement in two world wars. He was succeeded by his son, **Gustavus VI** (Gustaf Adolf), 1882–1973 (r.1950–73). He participated in archaeological expeditions in Sweden, Greece, and China, and his work as a botanist earned him admission (1958) to the British Royal Academy. His grandson, Carl Gustaf, succeeded him as CHARLES XVI GUSTAVUS.

Gustavus Adolphus: see Gustavus II under GUSTAVUS, kings of Sweden.

Gutenberg, Johann, c.1397–1468, German printer, believed to have been the first European to print with movable type. Laurens Janszoon Koster of Holland and Pamfilo Castaldi of Italy are thought by some to have preceded him. Gutenberg's name did not appear on any of his work, and details of his life are scant. He is thought to have trained as a goldsmith. He may have invented PRINTING in Strasbourg in 1436 or 1437, but the work attributed to him, including the MAZARIN BIBLE (1455), was done in Mainz. He had to give up his press and types to Johann Fust for debt.

Guthrie, Sir Tyrone, 1900–1971, English director and producer. Noted for his experimental Shakespearean productions, he headed the Old Vic and Canada's Shakespeare Festival before founding (1963) the Guthrie Theater in Minneapolis.

Guthrie, Woody (Woodrow Wilson Guthrie), 1912–67, American folk singer, guitarist, and composer; b. Okemah, Okla. He wrote over 1,000 songs, chiefly on social and political themes, and strongly influenced younger performers like Bob DYLAN. His son, **Arlo Guthrie,** 1947–, b. N.Y.C., also is a folk singer and composer.

Guyana [gīăn'ə, –än–], officially Cooperative Republic of Guyana, republic (1992 est. pop. 739,000), 83,000 sq mi (214,969 sq km), NE South America, bordered by the Atlantic Ocean (N), Suriname (E), Brazil (S and W), and Venezuela (W). GEORGETOWN is the capital. The climate is hot and humid, and rainfall is heavy. There is a cultivated coastal plain and a forested, hilly interior. Agriculture and mining are the principal economic activities, with the processing of bauxite (nationalized in the 1970s) and sugarcane the largest industries. The population, primarily of Indian (51%) and African and mixed (43%) descent, with about 4% native peoples, is concentrated along the coast. English is the official language, and indigenous American languages also are spoken. Christianity, Hinduism, and Islam are the main religions.

History. Originally settled by the Dutch in the 17th cent., the region was awarded to the British in 1815 and united as British Guiana in 1831. Full independence was gained in 1966 under the leadership of Prime Min. (later Pres.) Forbes Burnham. Guyana became a republic in 1970 and embarked on a socialist path that ultimately led to economic ruin. In 1978 the Guyana jungle was the site of a mass suicide involving over 900 American exiles who were members of Rev. Jim Jones's People's Temple. Burnham was succeeded at his death (1985) by Desmond Hoyte, who gradually reversed the government's socialist policies. Both Burnham and Hoyte were accused of using electoral fraud to stay in power. In 1992 Hoyte lost the presidency to Cheddi Jagan, a former prime minister (1957–64) and ex-Marxist.

Three-frame gyroscope

Guzmán Blanco, Antonio [gōōsmän' blän'kō], 1829–99, Venezuelan dictator (1870–88). Instrumental in deposing (1863) PAEZ as dictator, he served (1863–68) as Liberal vice president and led a counterrevolution (1870) that made him president. A benevolent despot, he reformed government administration and brought about material progress. His regime was overthrown in 1888.

Gwyn or **Gwynn, Nell** (Eleanor Gwyn), 1650–87, English actress, notable for her charm in comic roles. From 1669 she was the mistress of CHARLES II and bore him two sons.

gymnastics, exercises for the balanced development of the body, usually practiced in a gymnasium, so named for the training place for the OLYMPIC GAMES of ancient Greece. Modern gymnastics dates from the early 19th cent., when several *Turnplätze* were established in Berlin, then spread throughout the Continent, to England, and to the U.S. Now a popular modern Olympic sport, gymnastics includes floor exercises, the horse, the vault, parallel and uneven bars, horizontal bar, balance beam, and rings.

gymnosperm, plant in which the SEEDS are exposed to the air during all stages of development, in contrast to ANGIOSPERMS. Gymnosperms, which include the PINES, are woody plants with STEMS, ROOTS, LEAVES, and vascular, or conducting, tissue (xylem and phloem). Gymnosperms are always pollinated by wind, and many have their seed-bearing structures organized into cones. Traditionally constituting the plant division Pinophyta, the group includes the CYCADS, CONIFERS, and GINKGOS.

gynecology, branch of medicine specializing in disorders of the female REPRODUCTIVE SYSTEM. Modern gynecology deals with disorders of MENSTRUATION, menopause, disease and maldevelopment of reproductive organs, hormonal and fertility problems, and BIRTH CONTROL devices. A related branch of medicine is **obstetrics,**

which specializes in the care of women during PREGNANCY and childbirth.

gypsies or **gipsies,** nomadic people found on every continent but most prominent in Spain and the Balkans. Despite much wandering they still cling to their identity and customs. Some still travel in small caravans, although many now live in settled communities. They often earn a living as metalworkers, musicians, horse or car dealers, auto mechanics, and fortune-tellers. Most are Roman Catholic or Eastern Orthodox Christian. Their Indo-Iranian language, Romany, and their blood groupings are related to those found in NW India and adjoining areas, where they probably originated. They went to Persia in the 1st millennium A.D. and have since divided into the Gitanos, Kalderash, Manush, Rom, and other groups. They had spread throughout Europe by the 16th cent. and appeared in North America in the late 1800s. Estimates of the number of gypsies range widely, but there are perhaps 10 million worldwide; half a million died in Nazi CONCENTRATION CAMPS during World War II. Since the end of Communist rule in E Europe, they have faced increased discrimination and persecution there, particularly in Romania.

gypsum ($CaSO_4 \cdot 2H_2O$), the most common sulfate mineral, occurring in many places and forms. It is very soft; the massive variety ALABASTER and the lustrous variety satin spar are easily worked into decorative objects. Plaster of Paris, used to make casts, molds, and wallboard, is made from gypsum.

Gypsy language: see ROMANY.

gyroscope, symmetrical mass, usually a wheel, mounted so that it can spin about an axis in any direction. A spinning gyroscope will resist changes in the orientation of its spin axis. Gyroscopes are used in ship stabilizers to counteract rolling, and a gyroscope is the nucleus of most automatic steering systems, such as those used in airplanes, missiles, and torpedoes. See also COMPASS.

H

H, chemical symbol of the element HYDROGEN.

Ha, chemical symbol of the element HAHNIUM.

Haakon [hä'kən, Nor. hô'ko͞on], kings of Norway. **Haakon I** (the Good), c.915–61 (r. c.935–61), was the son of HAROLD I. Raised as a Christian in England, he tried unsuccessfully to introduce Christianity into Norway after seizing power from his brother Eric Bloodyaxe. Eric's sons succeeded him. **Haakon IV** (Haakon Haakonsson), 1204–63 (r.1217–63), was the illegitimate son of Haakon III. Under him medieval Norway reached its zenith. Iceland and Greenland were acquired, legal reforms were carried out, and Old Norse literature flowered (see SNORRI STURLUSON). His son, MAGNUS VI, succeeded him. **Haakon VII,** 1872–1957 (r.1905–57), was born Prince Charles, second son of FREDERICK VIII of Denmark. He was chosen king when Norway separated from Sweden. During the German occupation of Norway (1940–45), he headed a government in exile in London. He was succeeded by his son OLAF V.

Haarlem, city (1991 est. pop. 150,000), capital of N Holland prov., W Netherlands. It has heavy industry but is best known as a flower-growing center and exporter of bulbs, chiefly tulips. Leading masters, e.g., HALS, van OSTADE, and van RUISDAEL, painted there. Among its many historic buildings are the 15th-cent. Groote Kerk (church) and the city hall (begun 1250).

Habakkuk, Habacuc, or **Habbacuc** [all: həbäk'ək], book of the OLD TESTAMENT, 35th in the Authorized Version, 8th of the Minor PROPHETS. It is a set of poems on the punishment of the wicked by God, using the Chaldaeans (Babylonians) as His instrument, and on the triumph of divine justice and mercy.

habeas corpus [Lat., = you should have the body], in law, a writ issued by a court commanding that a person held in custody be brought before a court so that it may determine whether the detention is lawful. Meant to ensure that a prisoner is accorded due process of law, it does not determine guilt or innocence. Habeas corpus originated in medieval England and was regarded highly by the British colonists in America as a safeguard against illegal imprisonment. It is guaranteed by the U.S. CONSTITUTION and may be suspended only in time of rebellion or invasion.

Haber, Fritz, 1868–1934, German chemist. During World War I he directed Germany's chemical warfare activities, which included the introduction of poison gas. After the Nazi rise to power (1933), he went into exile in England. He won the 1918 Nobel Prize in chemistry for his discovery of the Haber process for synthesizing ammonia from its elements.

Habsburg, family: see HAPSBURG.

haddock: see COD.

Hades [hā'dēz], in Greek mythology. **1** The ruler of the underworld, commonly called PLUTO. **2** The world of the dead, ruled by Pluto and PERSEPHONE. Guarded by CERBERUS, it was either underground or in the far west and was separated from the land of the living by five rivers. One of these was the STYX, across which the dead were ferried. Three judges decided the fate of souls; heroes went to the ELYSIAN FIELDS, evildoers to TARTARUS.

Hadewijch [hä'dəvīkh], fl. early 13th cent., Dutch mystical poet, a nun. Her works are a monument both to early Dutch literature and to Roman Catholic mysticism.

Hadrian. For popes of this name, see ADRIAN.

Hadrian or **Adrian,** A.D. 76–138, Roman emperor (117–138); b. Spain. His name in full was Publius Aelius Hadrianus. A ward of TRAJAN, Hadrian distinguished himself as a commander and as an administrator. He was chosen as Trajan's successor. Hadrian's reign was vigorous and judicious. Abandoning the aggressive policy of Trajan in Asia, he withdrew to the boundary of the Euphrates in Palestine. In 132 he put down the insurrection of the Hebrew leader BAR KOKBA with great severity. Hadrian traveled extensively in the empire, stabilizing government and adorning the cities. In Germany he built great protective walls, and in Britain he had HADRIAN'S WALL built. He also patronized the arts; his regard for the youth Antinoüs was recorded by sculptors and architects. As his successor he chose Antoninus Pius.

Hadrian's Wall, ancient Roman wall, 73.5 mi (118.3 km) long, across Great Britain from Wallsend to Bowness. Built (A.D. c.122–26) by Emperor HADRIAN and extended by Emperor SEVERUS a century later, the wall demarcated the northern boundary and defense line of Roman Britain. Fragments of it remain.

Haeckel, Ernst von [hĕ'kəl], 1834–1919, German biologist and philosopher. He was an early exponent in Germany of Charles DARWIN's theory of EVOLUTION. Based on his interpretations of Darwin's theory, he evolved a mechanistic form of MONISM. His theory of recapitulation postulated a hypothetical ancestral form represented by the gastrula stage of embryonic development. Although many were later proved incorrect, his theories attracted a following and stimulated research.

haemo-. For words beginning thus, see HEMO-.

Hafiz [häfēz'], d. 1389?, Persian poet; b. Shams ad-Din Muhammad. Traditionally interpreted allegorically by Muslims, his poems are passionate lyrics, usually *ghazals* (groups of rhyming couplets), on such themes as love and drink.

hafnium (Hf), metallic element, discovered by X-ray spectroscopy in 1923 by Dirk Coster and Georg von Hevesy. Lustrous, silvery, and ductile, it is chemically similar to ZIRCONIUM; the two elements are among the most difficult to separate. Hafnium is used for nuclear-reactor control rods. See ELEMENT (table); PERIODIC TABLE.

Hagar: see ISHMAEL.

Hagen, Walter, 1892–1969, American golfer; b. Rochester, N.Y. He won 11 major championships: the U.S. Open twice (1914, 1919) and, during the 1920s, the British Open four times and the Professional Golfers' Association five times. He played on five Ryder Cup teams.

Haggai [hăg'āī] or **Aggeus** [ăgē'əs], book of the OLD TESTAMENT, 37th in the Authorized Version, 10th of the Minor Prophets. Dated 520–519 B.C., it calls on the JEWS, newly returned from the Babylonian exile, to renew work on restoring the Temple.

Haggard, Sir Henry Rider, 1856–1925, English novelist. He is known for his highly popular romantic adventure stories, particularly *King Solomon's Mines* (1885) and *She* (1887).

Hagia Sophia [Gr., = Holy Wisdom] or **Santa Sophia,** Turkish *Aya Sofia,* originally a Christian church at Constantinople (now Istanbul), later a MOSQUE, now a museum of Byzantine art. The supreme masterpiece of Byzantine architecture, the present structure was built (A.D. 532–37) by Anthemius of Tralles and Isidorus of Miletus for the emperor JUSTINIAN I. After the Turkish conquest of Constantinople (1453), it became a mosque. The interior mosaics were obscured under layers of plaster and painted ornament, and Christian symbols were obliterated. Four MINARETS were added at the outer corners. The nave is covered by a lofty DOME carried on pendentives; its weight thus rests on four huge arches and their piers. The east and west arches are extended by half-domes and domed exedrae. A vast oblong interior is thus created. The dome is 102 ft (31 m) in diameter and 184 ft (56 m) high, with a corona of 40 arched windows flooding the interior with light. The original decorations and gold mosaics have been largely restored.

Hague, The, city (1991 est. pop. 445,000), capital of S Holland; seat of the Dutch government, the Dutch supreme court, and the International Court of Justice (see UNITED NATIONS, table 2). It grew around a palace begun c.1250 by William, count of Holland. Seat (from 1586) of the States General of the United Provinces of the Netherlands and residence (17th–18th cent.) of their stadtholders, it became a major diplomatic and intellectual center. It was the Dutch royal residence from 1815 to 1948. Site of the HAGUE CONFERENCES, the city is known as a center for the promotion of peace. Landmarks include the 14th-cent. Gevangenenpoort prison, the 17th-cent. Mauritshuis, and the Peace Palace (1913).

Hague Conferences, two international conferences (1899, 1907) held at The Hague, the Netherlands, on the problems of armaments and the rules of modern warfare. They adopted various conventions that were later ratified by many nations. Although they failed to prevent WORLD WAR I, they were an example for both the LEAGUE OF NATIONS and the UNITED NATIONS. The first conference created the HAGUE TRIBUNAL.

Hague Tribunal, popular name for the Permanent Court of Arbitration, established by the first HAGUE CONFERENCE (1899). Headquartered in The HAGUE, it consists of a permanent group of jurists from which a panel is selected whenever contending nations agree to submit a dispute to arbitration. It has ruled in more than 20 international disputes, including the Venezuela Claims (1904). After World War I it was largely eclipsed in importance by the WORLD COURT.

Hahn, Otto, 1879–1968, German chemist and physicist. Noted for important work on radioactivity, he received the 1944 Nobel Prize in chemistry for splitting (1939) the uranium atom and discovering the possibility of chain reactions. The development of the atomic bomb was based on this work.

hahnium (Ha), artificial radioactive TRANSURANIUM ELEMENT. Claims for its production have been made by a Soviet group at Dubna who in 1967 bombarded americium with neon to obtain, apparently, the Ha^{260} and Ha^{261} isotopes, and by an American group at the Univ. of California, Berkeley, who in 1970 bombarded californium with nitrogen nuclei to obtain the Ha^{260} isotope. It is also called unnilpentium (Unp). See ELEMENT (table); PERIODIC TABLE.

Haida, indigenous people of the Northwest Coast (see NORTH AMERICA, INDIGENOUS PEOPLES OF) who live on islands off British Columbia and speak a language of the Nadene stock (see NATIVE AMERICAN LANGUAGES). Before the arrival (early 19th cent.) of white fur traders, their clan society practiced the POTLATCH. The Haida are noted for their artwork and dugout canoes. By 1880 disease had reduced 8,000 Haida to 2,000. Today many have left their islands for mainland life. In 1990 there were 1,805 Haidas in the U.S.

Haidar Ali or **Hyder Ali,** 1722–82, Indian Muslim ruler. A peasant by birth, he rose through army ranks and by 1761 was the virtual ruler of the state of Mysore. His efforts to expand his domain met with British opposition. He defeated the British in 1769, but in 1781 he was defeated near Madras.

Haifa [hī'fä], city (1988 est. pop. 225,000), NW Israel, on the Mediterranean Sea. It is a major industrial center, a railroad hub, and one of the main ports of Israel. Haifa is known to have existed by the 3d cent. A.D. and was destroyed (1191) by SALADIN. The city's revival began in the late 18th cent.; development of its port in the 20th cent. led to its main growth. It is the world center of BAHA'ISM.

Haig, Alexander Meigs, Jr., 1924–, U.S. general and public official, U.S. secretary of state (1981–82); b. Philadelphia. A career military officer, he served as Pres. NIXON's civilian chief of staff during the WATERGATE AFFAIR. Later he was (1974–79) NATO commander, and in 1981, became Pres. REAGAN's secretary of state. His sudden resignation (1982) was attributed to disagreements over foreign policy. In 1988, he ran unsuccessfully for the Republican party's nomination for president of the U.S.

Haig, Douglas Haig, 1st **earl,** 1861–1928, British field marshal. In WORLD WAR I he became (1915) commander in chief of the British expeditionary force in France, but he received little support from LLOYD GEORGE. He was much criticized for the staggering losses suffered in the battle of the Somme and the Passchendaele campaign (see YPRES, BATTLES OF).

haiku, unrhymed Japanese poem recording the essence of a keenly perceived moment linking nature and human nature. Usually consisting of 17 symbol-sounds, it was adapted by the IMAGISTS and other Western writers as a three-line poem of five, seven, and five syllables.

hail, solid form of precipitation that can occur at any time of year, usually in a cumulonimbus cloud and often during a THUNDERSTORM. Large hailstones are spherical or irregularly spherical in shape and are composed of alternate hard and soft layers of ice. Hail usually forms when raindrops are blown up to high (cold) areas in a cloud and freeze. As they fall, they become coated with more water drops; they are then blown back up and refrozen, adding an additional layer. This process is repeated until the wind currents can no longer support the weight of the hailstone. Hailstones are generally less than 0.5 in. (1.3 cm) in diameter, although larger ones are occasionally observed.

Haile Selassie [hī'lē səlăs'ē], 1891–1975, emperor of ETHIOPIA (1930–74). The grandnephew of Emperor MENELIK II, and a Coptic Christian, he forced (1916) the abdication of Lij Yasu, a Muslim convert, and placed Menelik's daughter, Zauditu, on the throne. In 1928 he was crowned king, and after Zauditu's mysterious death in 1930, he became emperor. During the Italian invasion (1935–36) he personally led his troops against the enemy. He lived in exile in England until 1941, when he returned and claimed the throne. After World War II he instituted social and political reforms, such as establishing a national assembly in 1955. In 1974, however, he was deposed by an army coup, and he later died under mysterious circumstances.

Hainan [hī'nän'], island and province (1990 pop. 6,557,000), c.13,100 sq mi (33,940 sq km), S China, 30 mi (50 km) offshore in the SOUTH CHINA SEA. Haikou is its capital and largest city. Hainan is the second largest island (after TAIWAN) off China's coast and is the home of the Li and Miao people. Rubber production and fishing are major industries, and rice, sugar, tobacco, coffee, and fruit are cultivated during a year-round tropical growing season. Incorporated into China in the 13th cent., Hainan was occupied by Japan during World War II. The island was created a province and a special economic area in 1988 to spur development of its natural resources and of tourism.

Haiphong [hīfŏng'], city (1990 est. pop. 456,000) NE Vietnam, on a large branch of the Red R. delta c.10 mi (16 km) from the Gulf of Tonkin. One of the largest ports in Southeast Asia, it was developed (1874) by the French and became their chief naval base in INDOCHINA. During the VIETNAM WAR Haiphong was severely bombed (1965–68, 1972) and its harbor mined. Its shipyards, textile mills, cement factories, and other industrial installations have since been rebuilt.

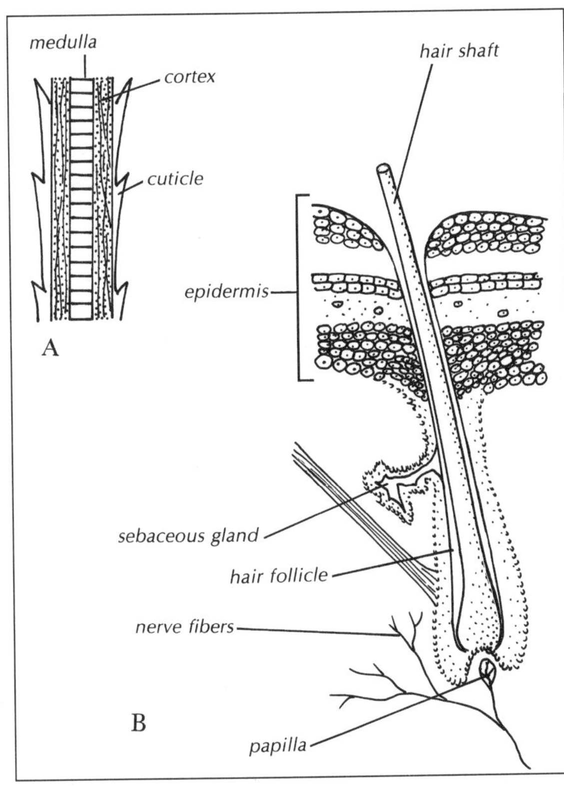

A. cross-section of a hair shaft B. General structure of a hair

hair, slender, threadlike outgrowth from the skin of mammals. Some animals grow a dense profusion of hair known as FUR or WOOL. Insulation from cold, protection against dust and sand, and camouflage are among the functions of hair. Each hair originates in a deep, pouchlike hair follicle, which contains the bulb-shaped root of the hair. The papilla, a net of nerves and capillaries that supplies the hair, extends into an indentation at the base of the root. Here newly dividing cells force older cells upward, where they die and harden into the hair shaft. The shaft has two layers, the colorless cuticle and the cortex, which contains pigment and the protein keratin. Hair is lubricated by oil from sebaceous glands in the follicle.

Haiti, Fr. *Haïti,* officially Republic of Haiti, republic (1992 est. pop. 6,431,000), 10,700 sq mi (27,713 sq km), West Indies, occupying the western third of the island of HISPANIOLA, which it shares with the DOMINICAN REPUBLIC. The capital and main seaport is PORT-AU-PRINCE. The densely populated, mostly mountainous country has the lowest per-capita income in the Americas, with about 50% of the population unemployed and 75% living in poverty. It has few manufacturing industries and a high rate of emigration. Subsistence farming (cassava, rice, yams) is the principal occupation; coffee is the main export. About 95% of the population is of African descent, and French and Creole (a French dialect that is predominant) are spoken. Haiti is a largely Roman Catholic nation in which some *vodun* (voodoo) rites are still practiced.

History. Nominally part of the Spanish colony of SANTO DOMINGO from the early 1500s, eastern Hispaniola remained virtually unsettled until the mid-17th cent., when French colonists, importing African slaves, developed sugar plantations in the north. Under French rule from 1697, Haiti (then called Saint-Domingue) became one of the world's richest sugar and coffee producers. However, after the 1780s, rebellion; class war among African, mulatto, and white Haitians; and invasions by French and British forces shredded the nation's social and economic fabric. In 1801 a former slave, TOUSSAINT L'OUVERTURE, conquered the whole island and abolished slavery; in 1804 Haiti became the second independent nation in the Americas. Ruled until 1859 by self-styled emperors, it lost control of eastern Hispaniola in 1844. Haiti's subsequent history is one of economic poverty, dictatorship, and occasional anarchy, with a period of U.S. military occupation (1915–34). In 1957 François "Papa Doc" DUVALIER was elected president. Supported by a personal police force, the Tontons Macoutes, he imposed an especially repressive rule, relaxed to some degree only after his death (1971), when he was succeeded by his son, Jean-Claude Duvalier. He fled the country in 1986, and a period of social and political unrest followed. In 1991 Jean-Bertrand ARISTIDE, a popular priest, became president after free elections, but the army ousted him later that year. The Organization of American States called for his restoration and imposed an economic embargo, but the army appointed a series of civilian leaders while retaining real power. In 1993 a UN-sponsored oil embargo led to an agreement that called for Aristide's return, but the army blocked implementation of the accord.

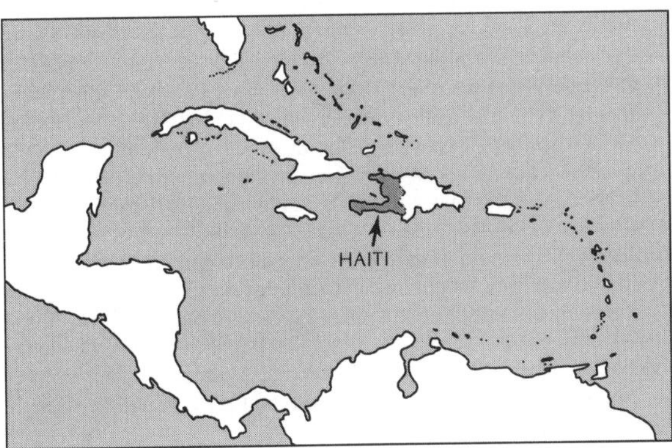

Hakluyt, Richard [hăk'lo͞ot], 1552?–1616, English geographer. He promoted English discovery and colonization, especially in North America, and published many accounts of exploration and travel. His chief work is *The Principal Navigations, Voyages, Traffics, and Discoveries of the English Nation* (3 vol., 1598–1600). The Hakluyt Society (founded 1846) continues to publish narratives of early exploration.

halakah or **halacha,** legal portion of the TALMUD and of post-Talmudic literature concerned with personal, communal, and international activities, as well as with religious observance. The term usually refers to the Oral Law, as codified in the MISHNA.

Hale, Edward Everett, 1822–1909, American author; b. Boston. A Unitarian minister, he was a social reformer and chaplain of the U.S. Senate (1903–9). His best-known work is the short novel *The Man without a Country* (1863).

Hale, George Ellery, 1868–1938, American astronomer; b. Chicago. He was the founder of the Yerkes, Mt. Wilson, and PALOMAR OBSERVATORIES (and director of the first two), each in its time housing the largest telescope in the world. His observatories also employed the latest in photographic and spectrographic techniques. He invented (1890) the spectroheliograph, which led to the discovery of magnetic fields and vortices in sunspots, and founded (1895) the *Astrophysical Journal,* still the leading publication in its field.

Hale, Nathan, 1755–76, American Revolutionary soldier; b. Coventry, Conn. Sent to Long Island to get information on the British, he was captured and hanged without trial. On the gallows he is said to have declared, "I only regret that I have but one life to lose for my country."

Hale, Sarah Josepha (Buell), 1788–1879, American author, editor, and feminist; b. near Newport, N.H. Editor of *Godey's Lady's Book* for over 40 years, she is best known as the author of the poem "Mary Had a Little Lamb" (1830).

Haleakala National Park: see NATIONAL PARKS (table).

half-life: see RADIOACTIVITY.

Haliburton, Thomas Chandler, pseud. **Sam Slick,** 1796–1865, Canadian author. A judge and historian, he is known for his series about Sam Slick, Yankee peddler, collected in *The Clockmaker* (1836) and later volumes.

halibut: see FLATFISH.

Halicarnassus [hăl"ĭkärnă'səs], ancient city of Caria, SW Asia Minor (modern Bodrum, Turkey). In the 4th cent. B.C., the widow of King Mausolus built him a tomb there that was one of the SEVEN WONDERS OF THE WORLD. The historians HERODOTUS and Dionysius of Halicarnassus were born there.

Halifax, city (1991 pop. 114,455), capital of Nova Scotia, E Canada, overlooking one of the world's great natural harbors. It is the largest city in the Atlantic provinces and Canada's principal ice-free port and naval base on the eastern seaboard. Much of E Canada's trade passes through the port when the Great Lakes–St. Lawrence Seaway is closed by ice in winter. Founded in 1749 by the British as a rival to France's naval stronghold at LOUISBURG, Halifax played a major role in the AMERICAN REVOLUTION and the WAR OF 1812. It continued to be used by the British fleet until 1906 and was a naval base during both world wars. In 1917 a munitions ship was rammed in the harbor and exploded, killing 1,800 and destroying the northern part of the city. Major landmarks in Halifax include the Citadel, a massive fortress (built 1794–97), and St. Paul's Church (1750), the oldest Anglican church in Canada.

Hall, G(ranville) Stanley, 1844–1924, American psychologist and educator; b. Ashfield, Mass. He organized (1882) at Johns Hopkins Univ. a leading psychological laboratory and founded the *American Journal of Psychology* (1887). As first president (1889–1920) of Clark Univ., he developed its education courses. His most important work is *Adolescence* (2 vol., 1904).

Hall effect, phenomenon in which an electric current applied perpendicularly to a magnetic field generates an electric field that is perpendicular to both the current and the magnetic field, discovered by Edwin H. Hall in 1879. It was believed that the voltage across the generated electric field was in direct proportion to the current, to the magnetic field, and to the conducting material. Klaus von Klitzing demonstrated (1980) that, under the special conditions of low temperature, high magnetic field, and two-dimensional electronic systems (in which the electrons are confined to moving in planes), the voltage difference increases in a series of steps as magnetic field is increased. This is known as the quantized Hall effect. Von Klitzing was awarded the 1985 Nobel Prize in physics for his work. Hall effect devices are used as sensors in robotics, electric propulsion, automobiles, telecommunications equipment, and DC motors.

Haller, Albrecht von, 1708–77, Swiss scientist and poet. Haller's research at the Univ. of Göttingen in experimental physiology, on which he based his theory of irritability, or contractility, of muscle tissue, is set forth in *A Dissertation on the Sensible and Irritable Parts of Animals* (1732). Back in his native Bern, he wrote extensively, notably *Elementa physiologiae corporis humani* (8 vol., 1757–66).

Halley, Edmund, 1656–1742, English astronomer. He was the first to predict the return of a comet, using Isaac NEWTON's gravitational theory to calculate the orbit of the great comet of 1682 (now known as HALLEY'S COMET). He was also the first to point out the use of a transit of Venus in determining the sun's parallax. Halley financed the publication (1687) of Newton's *Principia.* In 1720 he became astronomer royal.

Halley's comet or **Comet Halley,** periodic COMET named for Edmund HALLEY, who observed it in 1682 and identified it with those seen in 1531 and 1607. It returned in 1759, close to the time Halley predicted, as well as in 1835 and 1910. It was sighted again in late 1982 and returned to its closest approach to the sun early in 1986.

Halloween: see ALL SAINTS' DAY.

hallucinogenic drug, ALKALOID substance that alters consciousness; also called psychotomimetic, or, popularly, psychedelic or mind-expanding drug. Hallucinogens include mescaline, or PEYOTE; psilocin and psilocybin, from the mushrooms *Psilocybe mexicana* and *Stropharia cubensis;* LSD (lysergic acid diethylamide); BELLADONNA; and MANDRAKE. MARIJUANA has hallucinogenic properties but is pharmacologically distinct. Hallucinogens have been used by primitive societies in both the Old and New Worlds to facilitate meditation, cure illness, placate evil spirits, and enhance mystical and magical powers. They produce a wide range of effects, from pleasant to very disturbing, depending on dosage, potency, and the personality and environment of the drug taker. Effects include altered perception of time and space and of the color, detail, and size of objects; also the experience of imaginary conversations, music, odors, tastes, and other sensations. Hallucinogens are not physically habit-forming, but tolerance, i.e., the need to take increased quantities to induce the original effect, may develop.

halo, in meteorology, circle of light surrounding the moon or sun. A halo occurs when sunlight or moonlight is refracted or reflected by ice crystals in the atmosphere, usually in a thin layer of high cirrostratus clouds. In general, a white halo results when the light is reflected, and colored rings (showing the colors of the spectrum, with red on the inside) result when the light is refracted.

halogen, any of the five chemical elements in group VIIa of the PERIODIC TABLE. FLUORINE, CHLORINE, BROMINE, IODINE, and the radioactive ASTATINE are nonmetallic, monovalent negative ions and exist in pure form as diatomic molecules. The first four elements exhibit an almost perfect gradation of physical properties. Fluorine is the least dense and chemically the most active, displacing other halogens from their compounds and oxygen from water. Iodine is the least active. The halogens form numerous compounds with each other and with other elements, such as hydrogen halides, metal halides (SALTS), and halocarbons.

halon, any of a group of organic compounds formerly widely used as fire suppressants. Halons, which are bromofluorocarbons, dissipate quickly, leave no residue, and are nontoxic. They were used on fires involving flammable gases and electrical amd electronic equipment. Because halons destroy atmospheric ozone (see OZONE LAYER), however, their production was phased out.

Hals, Frans, c.1580–1666, Dutch painter of portraits and genre scenes; b. Belgium. Although his reputation was established early, Hals spent most of his life in poverty. His scenes from everyday life were painted in the first half of his career. In the 1620s and 30s he painted group portraits, e.g., *Banquet of the Officers of the St. George Militia* (1616; Haarlem) with vivacity and informality, and some important single portraits, e.g., *Lucas de Clercq* (Rijks Mus., Amsterdam). He worked rapidly, employing Caravaggesque lighting to capture momentary effects (see CARAVAGGIO). At 84 he painted two masterpieces, *The Governors of the Almshouse* and *Lady Regents of the Almshouse* (both: Haarlem), which have the same brilliant lighting and cool clarity as his gayer canvases. His notable paintings include *The Merry Drinker* (Rijks Mus.) and *The Smoker* (Metropolitan Mus.). Five of his sons were painters, the foremost being **Frans Hals,** c.1618–c.1669, a painter of still lifes and rustic scenes. **Dirk Hals,** c.1591–1656, brother of the elder Frans Hals, specialized in festivals and drinking scenes, e.g., his *Merry Party* (National Gall., London).

Ham: see NOAH.

hamadryads: see NYMPH.

Haman: see ESTHER.

Hamburg, city (1989 est. pop. 1,603,000), coextensive with, and capital of, Hamburg state, N Germany, on the Elbe and Alster rivers. It is Germany's largest and busiest port. Manufactures include copper, ships, and machinery. Founded in the 9th cent., it formed (13th cent.) an alliance with LÜBECK that became the basis of the HANSEATIC LEAGUE. The city was largely destroyed by fire in 1842. Severely damaged during WORLD WAR II, it has been rebuilt and is now a modern cultural center. Felix MENDELSSOHN and Johannes BRAHMS were born in Hamburg.

Hamilcar Barca, d. 229 or 228 B.C., Carthaginian general, father of HANNIBAL. In the First PUNIC WAR, he gave a good account of himself in Sicily. He ruthlessly put down (238) a revolt of mercenaries and became virtual dictator of CARTHAGE. In 237 he set out to conquer Spain but fell in battle.

Hamilton, Alexander, 1755–1804, U.S. statesman; b. West Indies. In the AMERICAN REVOLUTION he was Gen. WASHINGTON's secretary and aide-de-camp and served brilliantly in the YORKTOWN CAMPAIGN.

As a delegate (1782–83) to the CONTINENTAL CONGRESS, he pressed for a strong national government. After serving as a New York delegate to the FEDERAL CONSTITUTIONAL CONVENTION (1787), he did much to get the Constitution ratified, particularly by his contributions to *The Federalist.* As secretary of the treasury (1789–95) under Pres. Washington, Hamilton sponsored legislation to pay off the debt of the Continental Congress and to charter the BANK OF THE UNITED STATES. To raise revenue he advocated a tariff on imported manufactures and excise taxes. By these measures he hoped to strengthen the federal government and tie it to persons of wealth. In foreign affairs Hamilton sought close ties with Britain and opposed the FRENCH REVOLUTION. Opposition to Hamilton and his supporters, who were known as Federalists, gathered around Thomas JEFFERSON, and the FEDERALIST PARTY was swept under in the election of 1800. Hamilton was killed in a duel by Aaron BURR, whose bids for the presidency (1800) and for New York governor (1804) Hamilton had thwarted.

Hamilton, Emma, Lady, c.1765–1815, English beauty. She was the mistress and, later, wife of Sir William Hamilton, the English ambassador to Naples. After 1798 she was the mistress of Horatio NELSON, whose daughter she bore in 1801. George ROMNEY painted many portraits of her.

Hamilton, Sir William Rowan, 1805–65, Irish mathematician. A child prodigy, he had mastered 13 languages by the age of 13. Hamilton was one of the most creative mathematicians of his time. In *Theory of Systems of Rays* (1828), he unified the field of optics under the principle of varying action, which he later extended to dynamics and which is of fundamental importance in modern physics, particularly quantum theory. His later years were devoted to the development of his theory of quaternions.

Hamilton, city (1991 pop. 318,499), S Ontario, Canada, on Lake Ontario, part of Hamilton-Wentworth municipality (1991 pop. 451,665). A major GREAT LAKES shipping port, it is Canada's chief iron and steel center and manufactures automobiles and heavy machinery. The city, hemmed into the narrow coastal plain by the Niagara escarpment, was founded in 1778 by UNITED EMPIRE LOYALISTS.

Hamites, African people of Caucasoid descent, inhabiting the Horn of Africa (chiefly Somalia and Ethiopia), the W Sahara, and parts of Algeria and Tunisia. They are believed to have been the original settlers of N Africa, having come from S Arabia and farther east. Eastern Hamites include the ancient and modern Egyptians, the OROMO and most other Ethiopians, and the Somali. Northern Hamites include the BERBERS, the TUAREG of the Sahara, and other groups.

Hamitic languages, subfamily of the Hamito-Semitic family of languages. See AFRICAN LANGUAGES (table).

Hamito-Semitic languages, family of languages spoken by people in N Africa, much of the Sahara, parts of E central and W Africa, and W Asia (especially the Arabian peninsula). See AFRICAN LANGUAGES (table); LANGUAGE (table).

Hammarskjöld, Dag [häm'ərshōld"], 1905–61, Swedish statesman, secretary general (1953–61) of the UNITED NATIONS. He was chairman of the board of the Bank of Sweden (1941–48) and deputy foreign minister (1951) before joining Sweden's UN delegation. As secretary general he greatly extended the influence of the UN with his peacekeeping efforts, particularly in the Middle East and Africa. He was on a mission to the Congo (now ZAÏRE) when his plane crashed in northern Rhodesia (now Zambia) in 1961.

Hammer, Armand, 1898–1990, American business executive; b. N.Y.C. He worked for his father's pharmaceutical business in the U.S. and in the USSR, where he also manufactured pencils. On his return (1930) to the U.S., Hammer invested in whiskey, cattle, and broadcasting, and later expanded the Occidental Petroleum Corporation into a multibillion-dollar business. He was noted for being on friendly personal terms with most Soviet leaders (except Stalin). His art collection is housed in the Armand Hammer Museum of Art and Cultural Center in Westwood, Calif.

Hammerstein, Oscar, 2d, 1895–1960, American lyricist and librettist; b. N.Y.C. He collaborated on many MUSICALS with Vincent Youmans, Rudolf FRIML, Sigmund Romberg, Jerome KERN, and Richard RODGERS. His grandfather **Oscar Hammerstein,** 1846–1919, was a well-known German-American operatic impresario. He built the Harlem Opera House (1888) and the Manhattan Opera House (1906) in New York City and introduced many singers to the U.S.

Hammett, Dashiell, 1894–1961, American writer; b. St. Mary's co., Md. He originated the "hard-boiled" detective novel—realistic, fast-paced, sophisticated. His novels include *The Maltese Falcon* (1930) and *The Thin Man* (1932).

Hammurabi [hämo͞orä'bē], fl. 1792–1750 B.C., king of BABYLONIA. He founded an empire that was eventually destroyed by raids from Asia Minor. His code of laws, found on a column at Susa, is one of the greatest of the ancient codes.

Hampton, part of the Greater London borough of Richmond upon Thames, SE England, on the Thames R. It is the site of **Hampton Court Palace,** begun by Cardinal WOLSEY in 1514. After his fall it was taken by HENRY VIII, and it remained a royal residence until the time of GEORGE II. Much of it is open to the public. The King's Apartments were damaged by fire in 1986 but have been restored. The **Hampton Court Conference,** held in 1604 in the reign of JAMES I, considered reforms of the Established Church for which its Puritan clergy had petitioned, but few concessions were made. The conference authorized the King James version of the BIBLE.

Hampton Court Palace, London

Hampton, city (1990 pop. 133,793), SE Va., a port of HAMPTON ROADS at the mouth of the James R.; settled 1610 by colonists from JAMESTOWN, inc. 1849. Seafood packing and shipping, light industry, and nearby military installations contribute to the economy. On the site of a Native American village, Hampton is one of the oldest English settlements in the U.S.

Hampton Roads, channel, 4 mi (6.4 km) long, SE Va., through which the James, Nansemond, and Elizabeth rivers pass into CHESAPEAKE BAY. A superb natural harbor, it houses the largest naval complex in the world. NEWPORT NEWS and HAMPTON are on its north shore, NORFOLK and PORTSMOUTH on the south.

hamster, nocturnal RODENT with external cheek pouches for holding food. The common, or European, hamster (*Cricetus cricetus*), about 12 in. (30 cm) long, is reddish brown with white patches on the nose, cheeks, throat, and flanks. The Syrian, or golden, hamster (*Mesocricetus auratus*) of E Europe and W Asia is familiar as a laboratory animal and pet. Hamsters are serious agricultural pests in much of their range.

Hamsun, Knut [häm'so͝on], 1859–1952, Norwegian novelist. His youthful wanderings, including two visits to the U.S., provided the theme for many of his novels, especially *Hunger* (1890), which established him. He is best known for the lyrically beautiful *Pan* (1894), expressing his interest in irrational forces, and for his masterpiece, *The Growth of the Soil* (1917), reflecting his love of nature and concern for the effect of material conditions on the individual spirit. He was awarded the 1920 Nobel Prize in literature but lost popularity during World War II because of his NAZI sympathies.

Han, dynasty: see CHINA.

Hancock, John, 1737–93, political leader of the AMERICAN REVOLU-

TION; b. Braintree, Mass. He opposed the STAMP ACT (1765) and advocated resistance to the British. Hancock was a member (1775–80) and president (1775–77) of the CONTINENTAL CONGRESS, and he was the first to sign the DECLARATION OF INDEPENDENCE. He was later governor of Massachusetts (1780–85, 1787–93).

Hand, Learned, 1872–1961, American jurist; b. Albany, N.Y. A federal judge from 1909 to 1951, Hand, a noted defender of free speech, was often known as the "tenth justice of the Supreme Court." He published *The Spirit of Liberty* (1952) and *Bill of Rights* (1958).

Handel, George Frideric, 1685–1759, English composer; master of the BAROQUE celebrated for his ORATORIO *The Messiah;* b. Germany as Georg Friedrich Handel. By 1705 he had produced two OPERAS in Hamburg; he spent the next four years in Italy, where he absorbed Italian style. Moving to England in 1712, he wrote music, including the celebrated *Water Music* (1717), for GEORGE I. He presented operas in London until 1741. Among his 46 operas are *Julius Caesar* (1724), *Atalanta* (1736), and *Serse* (1738), with its tenor ARIA now known as *Largo. The Messiah* was presented in Dublin in 1742. Its contemplative character sets it apart from the rest of his 32 oratorios, which include *Acis and Galatea* (1720), *Esther* (1732), *Saul* (1739), and *Judas Maccabeus* (1747). He also composed about 100 Italian solo CANTATAS; numerous orchestral works, among them the Twelve Grand Concertos (1739); harpsichord SUITES; organ CONCERTOS; and the anthem "Zadok, the Priest" (1727), used at all British coronations since that of George II.

Handke, Peter, 1942–, Austrian novelist and playwright. His controversial, avant-garde works often reflect his ironical sense of the constricting limitations of language and of reason. They include the plays *Kaspar* (1968) and *They Are Dying Out* (1973) and the novels *The Goalie's Anxiety at the Penalty Kick* (1972), *A Sorrow Beyond Dreams* (1974; play, 1977), and *The Left-Handed Woman* (1976).

Handy, W(illiam) C(hristopher), 1873–1958, African-American songwriter and bandleader; b. Florence, Ala. He was among the first to set down the blues (see JAZZ) and became famous with "Memphis Blues" and "St. Louis Blues."

Hangchow: see HANGZHOU.

hang gliding, form of gliding done using a kitelike wing. The hang glider consists of a Rogallo wing about 18 ft (5.5 m) across and weighing about 35 lb (15.9 kg). The pilot is suspended below the glider and typically jumps from an elevated point to begin the flight. Also called sky surfing, the sport began in California in the late 1960s.

Hangzhou or **Hangchow** [both: häng-jō], city (1990 est. pop. 1,340,000), capital of Zhejiang prov., E China. Long a famous silk- and tea-producing center, Hangzhou has become an important regional industrial complex. Manufactures include textiles, iron and steel products, and motor vehicles. The city is also one of China's most popular tourist centers. The scenic West Lake, wooded hills, and shrines and monasteries dating from the 10th cent. A.D. are all located in the city. As the capital (1132–1276) of the Southern Sung dynasty, it was a famous cosmopolitan center of commerce and culture. Almost destroyed (1861) in the TAIPING REBELLION, it was rebuilt as a modern city.

Hanna, Marcus Alonzo (Mark Hanna), 1837–1904, American capitalist and politician; b. Lisbon, Ohio. He managed the 1896 presidential campaign of William MCKINLEY and was a Republican senator from Ohio (1897–1904).

Hannibal, b. 247 B.C., d. 183 or 182 B.C., Carthaginian general, one of the great military geniuses of all time; son of HAMILCAR BARCA, of the great Barca family. In 221 B.C. he succeeded his brother-in-law, HASDRUBAL, as commander in Spain. During the second PUNIC WAR, he set out to invade Italy with a small force of picked troops, crossed the Alps with a full baggage train and elephants, and with his cavalry overran the Po valley. He wiped out a Roman force and in 217 set out toward Rome. After defeating the Romans again at Lake Trasimeno, he went to S Italy and gained many allies. At Cannae (216 B.C.) he won one of the most brilliant victories in history, but he failed to get proper support from CARTHAGE and could not take Rome. In 207 B.C. his brother Hasdrubal was defeated on the Metaurus R., and Hannibal had to draw back. Recalled (203) to defend Carthage against Scipio Africanus Major (see SCIPIO, family), he was decisively beaten at the battle of ZAMA (202). After peace was concluded (201 B.C.), he became chief ruler in Carthage and governed well; but Rome demanded him as a prisoner, and he went into exile, finally poisoning himself to avoid being given to the Romans.

Hanoi, city (1990 est. pop. 1,089,000), capital of Vietnam, N Vietnam, on the Red R. A major transportation and industrial center, it produces such manufactures as machine tools, plywood, textiles, and chemicals. It became the seat of the Chinese rulers of Vietnam in the 7th cent. and the capital of French INDOCHINA in 1887. When the French withdrew in 1954, Hanoi became the capital of North Vietnam. It was heavily bombed during the VIETNAM WAR. After the North Vietnamese victory, it became the capital of united Vietnam. A cultural center with several universities and institutes, it is noted for its European-style buildings and tree-lined avenues.

Hanover, former kingdom and former province of Germany. Its chief cities included Hanover, Osnabrück, and Stade. In 1692 Duke Ernest Augustus of Calenburg became elector of Hanover. His son succeeded (1714) to the British throne as GEORGE I (see also HANOVER, HOUSE OF), uniting Britain and Hanover in a personal union. NAPOLEON I broke up the electorate, but in 1813 Britain regained possession. In 1815 it was made a kingdom. On the accession (1837) of Queen VICTORIA, Hanover was separated from Britain because of the SALIC LAW of succession. As a result of the AUSTRO-PRUSSIAN WAR (1866), Hanover was made a Prussian (from 1871 a German) province. After World War II it was incorporated into Lower Saxony.

Hanover, city (1989 est. pop. 499,000), capital of Lower Saxony, central Germany, on the Leine R. and the Midland Canal. A transshipment and industrial center with such manufactures as iron and steel and tires, it is noted for its annual industrial fair. It was chartered in 1241 and became a member (1386) of the HANSEATIC LEAGUE and the capital (1692) of the electorate of Hanover (see HANOVER, former kingdom). Badly damaged during WORLD WAR II, the city has been rebuilt since 1945. Historic buildings include the 14th-cent. Marktkirche and the 17th-cent. Leineschloss, which now houses the parliament of LOWER SAXONY.

Hanover, house of, ruling dynasty of Hanover (see HANOVER, former kingdom), which descended from the GUELPHS and in 1714 acceded to the British throne in the person of GEORGE I, elector of Hanover, through a claim based on descent from JAMES I. George I's succession was based on the Act of SETTLEMENT. There were six Hanoverian British monarchs. With VICTORIA, the last Hanoverian ruler of Britain, the crowns of Hanover and Britain were separated.

Hansa towns: see HANSEATIC LEAGUE.

Hansberry, Lorraine, 1930–65, African-American playwright; b. Chicago. Her famous play *A Raisin in the Sun* (1959) deals with the problems of an African-American family in modern America. Many of her writings were collected in *To Be Young, Gifted, and Black* (1969).

Hanseatic League, mercantile league of medieval N German towns. It came into existence gradually as the Hansas—companies of merchants dealing with foreign lands—and the cities from which they operated drew closer together as a way of protecting themselves from foreign competition and piracy. In the 13th cent. more than 70 German cities joined in treaties of mutual protection. The Hanseatic League was formally organized in 1358, and in 1370 it won a trade monopoly in all of Scandinavia. The league prospered in the following centuries but went out of existence in the 17th cent. BREMEN, HAMBURG, and LÜBECK are still known as Hanseatic cities.

Hansen's disease: see LEPROSY.

Hanson, Howard, 1896–1981, American composer, teacher, and conductor; b. Wahoo, Nebr. He directed the Eastman School of Music, Rochester, N.Y. (1924–64). His romantic works include symphonies and the opera *Merry Mount* (1934).

hantavirus, any of a genus (*Hantavirus*) of viruses that are transmitted by rodents and can cause flulike symptoms and—in more severe cases—shock, kidney failure, internal bleeding, fluid accumulation in the lungs, and death. Infection typically results from exposure to the excrement of a rodent host, and sometimes responds to treatment with the drug ribavirin. Hantavirus-caused illness occurs largely in Asia and Europe, particularly in China and

Korea. In 1993, after an outbreak of a sometimes fatal flulike illness in the SW U.S., a previously unknown hantavirus was identified as the cause.

Hanukkah: see under JEWISH HOLIDAYS.

Hapsburg or **Habsburg** [hăps'bûrg], ruling house of AUSTRIA (1282–1918). The family originally held lands in Alsace and NW Switzerland, and Otto (d. 1111) took the name Hapsburg when he was made count. In 1273 Count Rudolf IV became king of the Germans as RUDOLF I; his war with Ottocar II of Bohemia resulted in Ottocar's defeat (1278) and confirmation of Hapsburg possession of Austria, Carniola, and Styria. These lands and the Austrian ducal title were declared hereditary in 1282, and in 1335 Carinthia, too, was claimed. The possessions were divided (1365) between the Albertine and the Leopoldine lines but were reunited under Holy Roman Emperor MAXIMILIAN I in the late 15th cent. Tyrol (1363), NE Istria (1374), and Trieste (1382) were added to the Hapsburg domain. From the election (1438) of Albert II as German king, the head of the Hapsburgs, with one exception, was chosen German king and Holy Roman emperor. Through marriage the Hapsburgs gained most of the Low Countries, and Hapsburg power reached its zenith under Emperor CHARLES V, who had inherited (1516) the crown of Spain. Charles was succeeded in Spain by his son, PHILIP II, and in Austria by his brother, Emperor FERDINAND I. The Spanish Hapsburgs died out in 1700. In Austria the PRAGMATIC SANCTION (1713) guaranteed the indivisibility of the Hapsburg domains and the succession of MARIA THERESA. Her son, Emperor JOSEPH II, began the line of **Hapsburg-Lorraine.** In 1806 Holy Roman Emperor FRANCIS II abdicated and assumed the title emperor of Austria. In 1867 the Hapsburg empire was reorganized into the AUSTRO-HUNGARIAN MONARCHY, which was dissolved at the end of WORLD WAR I.

Harald, kings of Norway: see HAROLD.

Harare, formerly **Salisbury,** largest city (1983 est. pop. 681,000) and capital of Zimbabwe. One of Africa's most modern cities, it is the country's commercial and communications center and the market for an agricultural region. Industries include textiles and clothing, processed food, steel, and chemicals. The city is connected by rail with BULAWAYO and the Mozambique port of Beira. Founded by the British in 1890, it was the capital of the Federation of Rhodesia and Nyasaland (1953–63). In 1982 it was renamed Harare (after a 19th-cent. African chief).

Harbin, city (1990 est. pop. 2,830,000), capital of Heilongjiang prov, NE China, on the Sungari R. It is the main trade, industrial, and transportation center of NE China and the main port on the Sungari. Harbin is part of the great Manchurian complex of metallurgical, machinery, chemical, oil, and coal industries. It is also an important producer of tractors, turbines, and precision instruments. Harbin's strong resemblance to Russian cities is due to settlers who came to the city after Russia was granted (1896) a concession there and after the RUSSIAN REVOLUTION (1917). Most of its European population, once one of the largest in the East Asia, left the city following the rise to power of the Chinese Communists.

Hardenberg, Friedrich von: see NOVALIS.

Harding, Warren Gamaliel, 1865–1923, 29th president of the U.S. (1921–23); b. Blooming Grove (now Corsica), Ohio. An Ohio Republican, Harding was elected (1914) to the U.S. Senate and was a compromise choice as Republican presidential candidate in 1920. His administration had one achievement—the calling (1921) of the Washington NAVAL CONFERENCE. He had promised to appoint a cabinet of the "best minds," but in 1923 came rumors of government scandals. Harding died suddenly (Aug. 1923) in San Francisco on his way back from Alaska. He thus was spared the public exposure of the TEAPOT DOME scandal and the humiliation of seeing his cabinet appointees Albert B. Fall and Harry M. Daugherty brought to the bar of justice. Harding's administration has been called one of the most corrupt in U.S. history. He was succeeded by Calvin COOLIDGE.

Hardouin, Jules: see under MANSART, FRANÇOIS HARDOUIN.

hardware: see COMPUTER.

Hardwick, Elizabeth, 1916–, American writer; b. Lexington, Ky. A founder and editor of the *New York Review of Books,* she has published two autobiographical novels; *A View of My Own: Essays in Literature and Society* (1962); and *Seduction and Betrayal: Women and Literature* (1974).

Hardy, Thomas, 1840–1928, English novelist and poet, one of the great English writers of the 19th cent. He won success with *Far from the Madding Crowd* (1874). His other major novels are *The Return of the Native* (1878), *The Mayor of Casterbridge* (1886), *Tess of the d'Urbervilles* (1891), and *Jude the Obscure* (1896), the last two his masterpieces. Set in the harsh landscape of Hardy's native Dorsetshire ("Wessex" in the books), they are generally gloomy, naturalistic studies of character and environment. Adverse criticism led Hardy to turn to poetry after 1896, and he expressed his pessimism in books such as *Wessex Poems* (1898), *Moments of Vision* (1917), and *The Dynasts* (written 1903–8), an epic historical drama in verse.

hare, herbivorous MAMMAL of the family Leporidae, which also includes the RABBIT, native to Eurasia, Africa, and North and Central America. The term *hare* is especially applied to the genus *Lepus,* sometimes called true hares. Hares generally have longer ears and hind legs than rabbits and move by jumping rather than running. They are usually brown or grayish in color, but northern species acquire a white coat in winter. Most North American hares are very large and are called jackrabbits.

Hare Krishna, communalistic religious movement, officially the International Society for Krishna Consciousness, founded (1966) by A.C. Bhaktivedanta Swami Prabhupada (1896–1977). Claiming thousands of followers, the movement teaches devotion to the Hindu god Krishna (see HINDUISM) as a means of attaining spiritual enlightenment, particularly through the practice of chanting the MANTRA *Hare Krishna* [O Lord Krishna].

Hargreaves, James, 1720?–78, English engineer. His 1764 invention of the spinning jenny doubled production in carding, a process preparatory to SPINNING.

Hari, Mata: see MATA HARI.

Hariri, Abu Muhammad al-Kasim al- [härē'rē], 1054–1122, Arab writer. *Assemblies of al-Hariri,* his principal work and one of the most popular Arabic books, is an episodic tale of an old rogue, Abu Zaid, who earns his living by his wits.

Harlem, section of New York City. Established (1658) as Nieuw Haarlem by the Dutch, Harlem remained rural until the 19th cent., when it became a fashionable residential district. A rapid influx of African Americans beginning c.1910 made it one of the largest African-American communities in the U.S., and in the 1920s it became a center of art and literature (see HARLEM RENAISSANCE). Harlem deteriorated after World War II into an economically depressed area with a high rate of unemployment.

Harlem Renaissance, term used to describe a flowering of African-American literature in the 1920s. During the great migration of African Americans from the rural South to the industrial North (1914–18), some settled in the HARLEM district of New York City, as did the musicians who brought JAZZ from the South, and Harlem became a sophisticated artistic and literary center. In his magazine *Crisis,* W.E.B. DUBOIS urged racial pride among African Americans, and writers, many living in Harlem, began producing fine original works about African-American life. Their work constituted a fresh, new subject that attracted white readers and publishers. Writers associated with the Harlem Renaissance include Arna BONTEMPS, Langston HUGHES, Claude MCKAY, Countee CULLEN, James Weldon JOHNSON, Zora Neale HURSTON, and Jean TOOMER. The Renaissance faded with the onset of the Great Depression of the 1930s.

Harmodius and Aristogiton [härmō'dēəs, ăr"ĭstōjī'tən], d. c.514 B.C., Athenian tyrannicides. Their attempt to assassinate the tyrant Hippias and his brother Hipparchus ended with Hipparchus dead but Hippias unhurt. Harmodius was killed instantly; Aristogiton was captured and executed later. Although they had been motivated by a personal quarrel, they became heroes of ATHENS and were given public recognition after the expulsion (510 B.C.) of Hippias.

harmonic motion, regular vibration, or back-and-forth motion, in which the acceleration of the vibrating object is directly proportional to the displacement of the object from its equilibrium position but oppositely directed. A single object vibrating in this manner is said to exhibit simple harmonic motion; examples are a PENDULUM swinging in a small arc, a mass bouncing at the end of a spring, and the motion of air molecules when a sound wave passes. Simple harmonic motion is periodic, i.e., it repeats itself at regular intervals. The time required for one complete vibration of the object is the period of the motion. The inverse of the period is the frequency, or the number of vibrations per unit of time. The maximum displacement of the object from its central position of equilibrium is the amplitude of the motion. See WAVE.

harmony, in music, simultaneous sounding of two or more tones and, especially, the study of chords and their relations. POLYPHONY, or the interweaving of several independent melodic lines, prevailed in composition until the 16th cent., when interest centered on harmonic chord construction, or the relationship between one tone and the tone or tones being played at the same time. In 1722 Jean Philippe RAMEAU presented the idea that different groupings of the same notes were inversions of the same chord. In the 18th cent. the concept of TONALITY became firmly established. Using the principle of MODULATION, later composers developed freer concepts of tonality, until some in the 20th cent. discarded traditional tonality altogether. See also ATONALITY; SERIAL MUSIC.

Harmsworth, Alfred Charles William: see NORTHCLIFFE, ALFRED CHARLES WILLIAM HARMSWORTH, VISCOUNT.

Harmsworth, Harold Sidney: see ROTHERMERE, HAROLD SIDNEY HARMSWORTH, 1ST VISCOUNT.

Harnett, William Michael, 1848–1892, American painter; b. Ireland. He is known for the spectacular *trompe l'oeil* (eye-deceiving) realistic effects he achieved in his still lifes, e.g., *After the Hunt* (Calif. Palace of the Legion of Honor, San Francisco).

Harold, 1022?–1066, king of England (1066). The son of Godwin, earl of Wessex, he belonged to the most powerful noble family in the reign of EDWARD THE CONFESSOR. After Harold's succession in 1053 to the earldom of Wessex, he aspired to the throne. In c.1064 he was shipwrecked on the French coast and was forced to take an oath (which he later renounced) supporting WILLIAM I's claim to the English throne. In 1065 he sided with the Northumbrians against his brother Tostig. The family was thus divided at the death of the king, who named Harold his heir. William at once invaded England from the south, and Tostig, with HAROLD III of Norway, invaded from the north. Harold defeated them in a battle in which both Harold III and Tostig were killed. The king then met William in the battle of HASTINGS, fought valiantly, and was killed.

Harold or **Harald,** kings of Norway. **Harold I** or **Harold Fairhair,** c.850–c.933 (r.872–c.933), was the son of Halfdan the Black, king of Vestfold (SE Norway). He became Norway's first king by defeating other petty kings. During his reign, raids on Europe and migration to Iceland reached their peak. His son HAAKON I succeeded him by defeating another son. **Harold III** or **Harold Hardrada** [stern council], d. 1066 (r.1046–66), half brother of OLAF II. He joined (1042) the revolt against MAGNUS I and was made joint king (1046), becoming sole king at Magnus's death (1047). After invading N England, he died in battle with HAROLD of England. **Harold V,** 1937– (r.1991–), became king upon the death of his father, OLAF V.

harp, STRINGED INSTRUMENT of ancient origin, the strings of which are plucked with the fingers. During the 15th cent. the harp came to be made in three parts, as it is today: sound box, neck, and pillar. The strings are stretched between the sound box and the neck, into which are fastened the tuning pegs. The diatonic harp was perfected c.1810 with the invention of double-action pedals, which can raise pitch by a semitone or a tone.

Harpers Ferry, town (1990 pop. 308), Jefferson co., easternmost W. Va., at the confluence of the Shenandoah and Potomac rivers; inc. 1763. The U.S. Arsenal (est. 1796) was seized in the famous raid by John BROWN on Oct. 16, 1859. Because of its strategic SHENANDOAH VALLEY location and its arms production, its industry was repeatedly destroyed by both sides during the CIVIL WAR; the town never recovered. The Harpers Ferry National Historical Park preserves Civil War historical sites.

harpsichord: see PIANO.

Harpy, in Greek mythology, a predatory monster with the head of a woman and the body, wings, and claws of a bird.

Harriman, Edward Henry, 1848–1909, American railroad executive; b. Hempstead, N.Y. A stockbroker, he gained positions of power in the Illinois Central RR (1883) and Union Pacific (1898). After securing control of the Southern Pacific and the Central Pacific, he tried to seize the Chicago, Burlington & Quincy but was blocked by J.J. Hill in a famous financial struggle. He later joined with Hill and J.P. Morgan (see MORGAN, family) to organize the Northern Securities Co., a holding company formed to prevent railroad competition; in 1904 the trust was ordered dissolved by the U.S. Supreme Court. His son was W. Averell Harriman.

Harriman, W(illiam) Averell, 1891–1986, U.S. businessman and public official; b. N.Y.C. A Democrat, he was ambassador to the USSR (1943–46), secretary of commerce (1946–48), governor of New York state (1955–59), undersecretary of state (1963–65), and ambassador-at-large (1965–68). He was also (1968) chief U.S. negotiator at the Paris peace talks on Vietnam.

Harris, Frank, 1856–1931, British-American author; b. Galway, Ireland. He is best known for his scandalously frank, highly unreliable autobiography, *My Life and Loves* (3 vol., 1923–27). He also wrote novels, a series of biographical sketches of literary figures (1915–27), and a biography of Oscar WILDE (1916).

Harris, Joel Chandler, 1848–1908, American regionalist writer; b. Eatonton, Ga. His popular tales, narrated by the former slave Uncle Remus, drew upon African-American folklore, dialect, and humor to capture the authentic life of Southern African Americans. Volumes include *Uncle Remus: His Songs and His Sayings* (1881), *The Tar Baby* (1904), and *Uncle Remus and Br'er Rabbit* (1906).

Harris, Patricia Roberts, 1924–85, African-American U.S. public official; b. Mattoon, Ill. Named secretary of housing and urban development (1977) by Pres. CARTER, she was the first African-American woman to serve in a cabinet post. From 1979 to 1981 she was secretary of health, education, and welfare (health and human services after 1980).

Harris, Roy, 1898–1979, American composer; b. Lincoln co., Okla. Vital, melodic, and personal expression is characteristic of his works, including his First Symphony (1934); *When Johnny Comes Marching Home* (1934), a choral work; Cumberland Concerto (1951); and his Piano Quintet (1936).

Harrisburg, city (1990 pop. 52,376), state capital and seat of Dauphin co., SE Pa., on the Susquehanna R.; settled c.1710 as a trading post; inc. 1791. A commercial and transportation center, it produces steel and processed foods. Iron and coal mines are nearby. Harrisburg became the state capital in 1812; its capitol building (1906) is noteworthy. A 1979 nuclear accident at nearby THREE MILE ISLAND focused national attention on the area.

Harrison, Benjamin, 1833–1901, 23d president of the U.S. (1889–93); b. North Bend, Ohio. A grandson of William Henry HARRISON, he commanded an Indiana volunteer regiment in the CIVIL WAR, became a corporate lawyer, and served (1881–87) as U.S. senator from Indiana. The Republicans chose him (1888) as presidential candidate against Grover CLEVELAND. After what has been called the most corrupt campaign in U.S. history, he was elected by the electoral college, though Cleveland had won the popular vote. He approved all regular Republican measures, including the highly protective McKinley Tariff Act. The first Pan-American Conference was held (1889) during his administration. Defeated (1892) for reelection by Cleveland, he later represented Venezuela in the VENEZUELA BOUNDARY DISPUTE.

Harrison, William Henry, 1773–1841, 9th president of the U.S. (Mar. 4–Apr. 4, 1841); b. Charles co., Va. Following service against Native Americans in the Old Northwest, Harrison was governor (1800–1812) of the Indiana Territory and engaged the forces under TECUMSEH in the battle of Tippecanoe (1811). In the WAR OF 1812, he recaptured Detroit from the British and defeated a combined force of British and Native Americans in the battle of the Thames (1813). He was a U.S. congressman (1816–19) and senator (1825–28) from Ohio. Gaining the WHIG PARTY presidential nomination in 1840, he and his running mate, John TYLER, ran a "rip-roaring" campaign with the slogan "Tippecanoe and Tyler too." On becoming president he selected a brilliant Whig cabinet, but he died after only a month in office. He was the grandfather of Benjamin HARRISON.

Hart, Lorenz Milton, 1895–1943, American lyricist; b. N.Y.C. His lyrics were witty, literate, and expressive. He collaborated with Richard RODGERS on such MUSICALS as *Connecticut Yankee* (1927) and *Pal Joey* (1940).

Hart, Moss, 1904–61, American dramatist; b. N.Y.C. He collaborated with George S. KAUFMAN on such comedies as *You Can't Take It with You* (1936; Pulitzer) and *The Man Who Came to Dinner* (1939), and with Kurt WEILL and Ira GERSHWIN on the musical *Lady in the Dark* (1941).

Harte, (Francis) Bret(t), 1836–1902, American author; b. Albany, N.Y. At 19 he went to California, where he helped establish the *Overland Monthly,* in which his short stories and poems first appeared. Harte is best known for his picturesque stories of Western local color, e.g., "The Luck of Roaring Camp" and "The Outcasts of Poker Flat." He was U.S. consul in Germany and Scotland (1878–85) and spent his last years in England.

hartebeest: see ANTELOPE.

Hartford, city (1990 pop. 139,739), state capital, central Conn., on the Connecticut R.; settled as Newtown 1635–36 on the site of a Dutch trading post (1633); inc. 1784. It is a world-famous insurance center and a commercial, industrial, and cultural hub. Manufactures include typewriters, precision instruments, and computers. Part of the Connecticut colony (1639), Hartford was an important depot in the AMERICAN REVOLUTION and was the scene of the 1814–15 HARTFORD CONVENTION. The old statehouse (1796), the capitol (1878), and the Wadsworth Atheneum are noteworthy. Harriet Beecher STOWE, Mark TWAIN, and Wallace STEVENS were among its notable residents.

Hartford Convention, Dec. 15, 1814–Jan. 4, 1815, meeting held in Hartford, Conn., to consider the problems of New England in the WAR OF 1812. It was an outgrowth of the disaffection of New England Federalists with government policy and with the expenses of the war. The sessions were held in secret, and the moderates prevailed. The proposal to secede from the Union was discussed and rejected, and New England's grievances were aired, but the war's successful conclusion made any recommendation a dead letter. The convention confirmed STATES' RIGHTS as the refuge of sectional groups and sealed the destruction of the FEDERALIST PARTY, which never regained its lost prestige.

Hartford Wits: see CONNECTICUT WITS.

Hartmann von Aue [härt'män fən ou'ə], c.1170–c.1220, German poet whose name is also spelled von Ouwe. Among his works are the chivalric romances *Erec* and *Iwain,* the religious legend *Gregorius,* and the idyl *Poor Henry,* used by LONGFELLOW for his *Golden Legend.*

Harun ar-Rashid, c.764–809, 5th and most famous ABBASID caliph (786–809). His empire included all of SW Asia and the northern part of Africa. He was a patron of the arts, and during his reign Baghdad was at its apogee. He figures prominently in the *Thousand and One Nights.*

Harunobu (Suzuki Harunobu), 1725–70, Japanese color-print artist of the *ukiyo-e* school (see JAPANESE ART). He was the first to use a wide range of colors effectively in printing, and in 1765 he developed multicolored calendar prints from wood blocks. His subjects include actors, courtesans, and domestic life.

Harvard University, mainly at Cambridge, Mass. The oldest American college, Harvard College was founded (1636) with a grant from the Massachusetts Bay Colony and named (1638) for its first benefactor, John Harvard. Intended as a training ground for Puritan ministers, it evolved a more generalized program of education. Supported largely by private gifts, Harvard's expansion into one of the world's great universities occurred mainly during the administration (1869–1910) of Charles W. ELIOT, when the elective system was introduced and graduate education was developed. Besides Harvard College the university has many graduate schools. The Harvard University Library is among the nation's largest and finest (see LIBRARY, table). Affiliated with the university is Radcliffe College for women (est. 1879), whose students are instructed by the Harvard faculty.

harvestman: see DADDY LONGLEGS.

Harvey, William, 1578–1657, English physician, considered by many to have laid the foundation for modern medicine. A physician at St. Bartholomew's Hospital in London and at the court, he was the first to demonstrate the function of the heart and the complete circulation of the blood. His renowned *On the Movement of the Heart and Blood in Animals* (1628) describes his theories, which were not fully substantiated until 1827. Harvey also contributed greatly to comparative anatomy and embryology.

Hasdrubal [hăz'drōōbəl], d. 221 B.C., Carthaginian general. He succeeded his father-in-law, HAMILCAR BARCA, as commander in Spain, increased the Carthaginian empire, and founded Cartagena. He was succeeded by his brother-in-law HANNIBAL.

Hasidim [Heb., = the pious], term used by the rabbis to describe those Jews who maintained the highest standard of religious observance and moral action. The term has been applied to three distinct movements. **1** The first Hasidim, also called the Assideans or Hasideans, were members of a sect that developed between 300 B.C. and 175 B.C. Rigid adherents of Judaism, they led the resistance to the Hellenizing campaign of Antiochus IV of Syria and were important in the revolt of the MACCABEES. **2** In 12th- and 13th-cent. Germany there arose the Hasidei Ashkenaz, a group with messianic and mystical elements, influenced by SAADIA BEN JOSEPH. **3** The third movement of Hasidim was that founded in the 18th cent. by BAAL-SHEM-TOV and known as HASIDISM.

Hasidism, Jewish movement founded in Poland in the 18th cent. by BAAL-SHEM-TOV. Its name derives from HASIDIM. The movement arose in reaction to persecutions and to the academic formalism of rabbinical Judaism. It encouraged joyous religious expression through music and dance and taught that purity of heart was more pleasing to God than learning. Although the Talmudists pronounced Hasidism heretical in 1772, it continues to be a strong force in Jewish life. Since the HOLOCAUST the U.S. and Israel have been the main centers of Hasidism. The various Hasidic communities are staunch defenders of tradition against the increased secularism in modern Jewish life.

Hasmoneans: see MACCABEES.

Hassam, Childe, 1859–1935, American painter and etcher; b. Boston. Hassam, who studied in Paris, produced sprightly landscapes and interiors that show the strong influence of IMPRESSIONISM, e.g., *Isles of Shoals* (Metropolitan Mus.).

Hassan II, 1929–, king of Morocco (1961–). He succeeded his father, MUHAMMAD V. An abortive coup (1971) led him to yield some of his powers to parliament. After 1976 his country fought for control of WESTERN SAHARA; in 1982, bolstered by U.S. military support, Morocco began the economic development of Western Sahara.

hassium (Hs), artificial radioactive TRANSURANIUM ELEMENT. Report of its production has been made by a West German group at Darmstadt, who in 1984 bombarded lead with iron ions to obtain the Hs^{265} isotope. It is also called unniloctium (Uno). See ELEMENT (table); PERIODIC TABLE.

Hastings, Warren, 1732–1818, first governor general of British India (1774–1784). His aggressive policy of judicial and economic reform rebuilt British prestige in India but created powerful enemies at home, including Edmund BURKE and Charles James FOX. He was impeached (1787) on charges of extortion and other crimes. After a long and costly trial, he was acquitted (1795).

Hastings, borough (1986 est. pop. 81,100), E Sussex, SE England. Today a seaside resort and residential city, it was occupied in Roman times and probably earlier. The battle of Hastings (1066) between the Norman invaders of England and the Anglo-Saxon defenders, the first and most decisive victory of the NORMAN CONQUEST, took place nearby.

Hatta, Mohammad, 1902–80, Indonesian statesman. With SUKARNO, he fought for Indonesian independence from the Netherlands. He served (1945–48, 1950–56) as vice president of Indonesia but broke with Sukarno and resigned in 1956.

Hatteras, Cape, promontory on Hatteras Island, N.C. The site of frequent storms and shipwrecks, it is known as the "Graveyard of the Atlantic." The cape is part of **Cape Hatteras National Seashore,** one of the longest stretches of undeveloped shoreline on the U.S. Atlantic coast.

Haughey, Charles James, 1925–, Irish political leader and prime minister (1979–81, Mar.–Dec. 1982, 1987–92). In 1970 Haughey, a member of the FIANNA FÁIL party and finance minister, was charged with smuggling arms to Northern Ireland, but he was later acquitted. After the resignation (1979) of Prime Min. John LYNCH, Haughey was named as his successor. He resigned after Fianna Fáil's 1981 electoral loss but briefly returned to office in 1982. In 1987 Haughey and Fianna Fáil again returned to power; after 1989 he led a Fianna Fáil–Progressive Democrat coalition. In 1992 accusations of Haughey's involvement in a ten-year-old wiretapping scandal led to his resignation.

Hauptmann, Gerhart [houpt'män], 1862–1946, German dramatist, novelist, and poet. He inaugurated the naturalist movement in German theater with his plays *Before Dawn* (1889) and *The Weavers* (1892), then turned to the romantic with *Hannele* (1893) and *The Sunken Bell* (1897). His prose works include the novels *The Fool in Christ, Emanuel Quint* (1910), and *The Heretic of Soana* (1918). A leading figure in German literature for three generations, he was awarded the 1912 Nobel Prize in literature.

Hausa, African ethnic group numbering about 23 million, chiefly in N Nigeria and S Niger. The Hausa, who are almost exclusively Muslim, practice agriculture and carry on a widespread trade. Their language is a lingua franca of W Africa. Formerly organized as the **Hausa States,** they were long vassals of the Muslim state of Bornu and were conquered by SONGHAI (1513) and by the FULANI (early 19th cent.). The Hausa are a major force in Nigerian politics.

Hausa language, member of the Chad group of languages, frequently assigned to the Hamitic subfamily of the Hamito-Semitic family of languages. See AFRICAN LANGUAGES (table).

Haussmann, Georges Eugène, Baron [ōsmän'], 1809–91, French civic official and city planner. Noted for his bold plan for PARIS under NAPOLEON III, he is largely responsible for the city's appearance, its wide streets, broad vistas, parks, and avenues radiating from focal points.

Havana, Span. *La Habana,* city (1987 est. pop. 2,125,000), W Cuba, capital of Cuba and La Habana prov. The largest city and chief port of the WEST INDIES, it is Cuba's political and industrial center, with shipyards, assembly plants, oil and sugar refineries, rum distilleries, and cigar factories. It is a popular winter resort, although tourism from the U.S. ended after the Cuban revolution of 1959. One of the oldest cities in the Americas, Havana was founded by the Spanish before 1520. It has often been invaded and held by foreign forces. The sinking of the U.S. battleship *Maine* in its harbor sparked (1898) the SPANISH-AMERICAN WAR. The modern part of Havana has wide avenues and impressive public buildings. Much of the old colonial city has been preserved. A major landmark is Morro Castle.

Havel, Václav, Czech playwright, president of CZECHOSLOVAKIA (1989–92) and the CZECH REPUBLIC (1993–). His experimental, absurdist plays attacking totalitarianism became popular in Prague and abroad but were suppressed after the Soviet invasion in 1968. Havel became a prominent dissident and was arrested several times and imprisoned twice. He was the principal spokesman for the Civic Forum, an opposition group, when it succeeded in forcing (1989) the Communist party to share power, and he became interim president of Czechoslovakia. In 1990 Havel was elected to a two-year term as president. He resigned in 1992 when the breakup of Czechoslovakia, which he opposed, became inevitable. He was elected president of the new Czech Republic in 1993.

Hawaii, 50th state of the U.S., a group of eight major islands and numerous islets in the central Pacific Ocean, c.2,100 mi (3,380 km) SW of San Francisco.

Area, 6,450 sq mi (16,706 sq km). *Pop.* (1990) 1,108,229, a 14.8% increase over 1980 pop. *Capital,* Honolulu. *Statehood,* Aug. 21, 1959 (50th state). *Highest pt.,* Mauna Kea, 13,796 ft (4,208 m); *lowest pt.,* sea level. *Nickname,* Aloha State. *Motto, Ua Mau Ke Ea O Ka Aina I Ka Pono* [The Life of the Land Is Perpetuated in Righteousness]. *State bird,* Hawaiian goose. *State flower,* hibiscus. *State tree,* candlenut. *Abbr.,* HI.

Land and People. The islands, of volcanic origin, are ringed with coral reefs. Oahu, site of HONOLULU, the capital and only large city, is the most populous and economically important island. On HAWAII Island are located MAUNA KEA, a huge extinct volcano, and MAUNA LOA, a large active volcano in Hawaii Volcanoes National Park. Haleakala, one of the world's largest volcanic craters, on MAUI Island, is part of Haleakala National Park. (See NATIONAL PARKS, table.) Other principal islands are Kahoolawe, KAUAI, LANAI, MOLOKAI, and Nihau. The islands are generally fertile, largely covered in luxuriant vegetation, and enjoy a mild climate. In 1990 over 60% of Hawaii's ethnically diverse population was of Asian descent, including people of Japanese, Chinese, and Filipino origin. There is a small minority of indigenous Hawaiians; about 33% of the population is white.

Economy. Service industries, especially tourism and military installations, dominate the economy of Hawaii. The leading agricultural products are sugarcane and pineapples—both cultivated on large corporate plantations—and cattle and dairy products. Sugar refining and pineapple canning are the basis of the leading industry, food processing, which is supplemented by petroleum refining and printing and publishing.

Government. The constitution (adopted 1950) provides for a governor serving a four-year term. The legislature consists of a senate with 25 members elected to four-year terms and a house with 51 members serving two-year terms. Hawaii sends two representatives and two senators to the U.S. Congress and has four electoral votes.

History. It is believed that the Polynesians who first settled the islands had arrived by c.750 A.D. The first European to discover (1778) the islands was Capt. James COOK. In 1810 King KAMEHAMEHA I united the islands under his sovereignty, ushering in a prosperous period of agriculture and trade. However, American and European traders introduced devastating infectious diseases that greatly reduced the native population. Missionaries and American planters who arrived in 1820 established sugar plantations and increasingly dominated the islands' economy and government. The monarchy was overthrown in 1893, and Hawaii became a U.S. territory in 1900. On Dec. 7, 1941, Japanese aircraft made a surprise attack on the naval base at PEARL HARBOR, plunging the U.S. into WORLD WAR II. Since the war's end and statehood (1959), Hawaii has enjoyed sustained economic and population growth. In 1992 Kauai was devastated by a hurricane.

Hawaii, island (1990 pop. 120,217), 4,037 sq mi (10,456 sq km), largest and southernmost island of the state of HAWAII, coextensive with Hawaii co. Geologically the youngest Hawaiian island, it consists of three volcanic mountains—MAUNA KEA (13,796 ft/4,205 m, the state's highest point), MAUNA LOA, and Hualalai. The northern coasts have rugged cliffs; the western and southern coasts are generally low, with many beaches. Hawaii includes tropical rain forests, grasslands, and barren lava flows. Sugarcane and pineapples are its principal products. Hilo is the largest city. The Kona district (noted for its coffee) and Hawaii Volcanoes National Park are on the island.

Hawaii Volcanoes National Park: see NATIONAL PARKS (table).

hawk, name for smaller members of the Accipitridae family, diurnal BIRDS of prey, distinguished from the related FALCONS by their broader, rounded wings. Hawks have keen sight, sharply hooked bills, and powerful feet with curved talons. The hunting hawks, or accipiters, include the goshawk, which feeds on small MAMMALS and birds, and the destructive chicken hawk. Buteos, or BUZZARDS, are a diverse group of larger hawks; they feed on RODENTS and REPTILES. The term *hawk* is also applied to many falcons and a number of unrelated birds, e.g., the nighthawk (a GOATSUCKER) and certain GULLS and jaegers.

Hawke, Bob (Robert James Lee Hawke), 1929–, Australian prime minister (1983–91). A former president of the Australian Council of Trade Unions (1970–80) and a member of Parliament, he became leader of the Australian Labor party (ALP) in 1983 and led the ALP to victory in 1983, 1984, 1987, and 1990. He was replaced as prime minister by fellow ALP member Paul KEATING in 1991 when a recession caused his government to lose popular support.

Hawkes, John (Clendennin Burne, Jr.), 1925–, American writer; b. Stamford, Conn. His novels often mix everyday reality with menacing hallucinations. They include *The Lime Twig* (1951), *Blood Oranges* (1971), *The Passion Artist* (1979), *Adventures in the Alaskan Skin Trade* (1985), and *Sweet William* (1993).

Hawking, Stephen William, 1942–, British theoretical physicist. His key area is astronomical bodies known as black holes (see GRAVITATIONAL COLLAPSE). Hawking has worked on the formation, size, and radiation of black holes as well as research supporting the big bang theory (see COSMOLOGY). He wrote *A Brief History of Time* (1988).

Hawkins, Coleman, 1904–69, African-American musician; b. St. Joseph, Mo. He established the tenor saxophone as a major JAZZ instrument. His huge tone, vigorous attack, and evolving improvisatory style made his influence pervasive, even among avant-garde musicians.

Hawkins or **Hawkyns, Sir John,** 1532–95, English admiral. As a slave trader, he sold Africans at a profit in Spanish ports. As treasurer and comptroller of the navy, he improved ship construction. In the great defeat of the Spanish ARMADA, he commanded the *Victory* and was knighted for his services. His son, **Sir Richard Hawkins,** 1562–1622, served under his father and Sir Francis DRAKE. While on a raiding expedition in South America, he was captured and sent to a Spanish prison (1597–1602). He later served in Parliament.

Hawks, Howard Winchester, 1896–1977, American film director; b. Goshen, Ind. He directed his first film in 1926 and is noted for crisp dialogue and visual clarity. His credits include *Scarface* (1932), *Bringing Up Baby* (1938), *To Have and Have Not* (1944), *The Big Sleep* (1946), *Red River* (1948), and *Gentlemen Prefer Blondes* (1953).

Hawksmoor or **Hawksmore, Nicholas,** 1661–1736, English architect involved in the development of most of the great English BAROQUE buildings. He assisted Christopher WREN at Chelsea Hospital and St. Paul's, and Sir John VANBRUGH at Castle Howard and Blenheim Palace. His London churches (1714–30) include St. George's, Bloomsbury, and Christ Church, Spitalfields.

Hawley-Smoot Tariff Act, enacted 1930 by the U.S. Congress. It brought the U.S. tariff to its highest point in history. The retaliatory tariffs of foreign nations caused a sharp decline in U.S. foreign trade. The act was sponsored by Rep. Willis C. Hawley (Oreg.) and Sen. Reed Smoot (Utah).

Hawthorne, Nathaniel, 1804–64, a master of American fiction; b. Salem, Mass. Hawthorne created highly symbolic fiction that penetratingly explored complex moral and spiritual conflicts. In early life he wrote the unsuccessful novel *Fanshawe* (1829) and the acclaimed short-story collection *Twice-Told Tales* (1837; 2d series, 1842). He lived briefly (1841) at BROOK FARM, basing his later novel *The Blithedale Romance* (1852) on the experience. After his marriage (1842) to Sophia Peabody, he settled in Concord, Mass., where he wrote the tales collected in *Mosses from an Old Manse* (1846). In the novels *The Scarlet Letter* (1850), his masterpiece, and *The House of the Seven Gables* (1851), he examined the gloomy, brooding spirit of Puritanism. His last novel, *The Marble Faun* (1860), is set in Italy. His works include two juvenile books, *A Wonder Book* (1852) and *Tanglewood Tales* (1853). He also helped establish the American short story as an art form.

Hay, John (Milton), 1838–1905, American author and statesman; b. Salem, Ind. After serving as assistant private secretary to Pres. LINCOLN, Hay wrote *Pike County Ballads* (1871) and, with John G. Nicolay, *Abraham Lincoln: A History* (10 vol., 1890). As secretary of state (1898–1905) under presidents MCKINLEY and Theodore ROOSEVELT, he was responsible for the OPEN DOOR policy in China and for the HAY-PAUNCEFOTE TREATIES.

Haydn, Franz Joseph [hī'dən], 1732–1809, Austrian composer, one of the great masters of classical music. Haydn's early years in poverty ended when his compositions brought him to the attention of some of Vienna's aristocrats. He became musical director to the princes Esterházy, serving for 29 years, received commissions, traveled, and formed a close friendship with MOZART, a bond that influenced the music of both. His string quartets and symphonies expanded C.P.E. BACH's three-part SONATA form, affecting the development of classical music. Haydn wrote over 100 symphonies, many of which are called by names, e.g., The "Clock" Symphony (1794), over 80 string quartets, over 50 sonatas, and many other pieces; two great ORATORIOS, *The Creation* (1798) and *The Seasons* (1801), were written in his old age.

Hayek, Friedrich August von [hī'ĕk], 1899–1992, British economist; b. Austria. An opponent of governmental control of the economy, he taught at the universities of London (1931–50), Chicago (1950–62), and Freiburg (1962–70). He shared the 1974 Nobel Prize in economics with Gunnar MYRDAL for his work in the theory of money and economic fluctuations. Hayek became a British subject in 1938.

Hayes, Helen, 1900–93, American actress; b. Washington, D.C., as Helen Hayes Brown. Called the First Lady of the American Theater, she starred in such plays as *Dear Brutus* (1918), *Victoria Regina* (1936), and *A Touch of the Poet* (1958) and such films as *The Sin of Madelon Claudet* (1932; Academy Award) and *Airport* (1969; Academy Award).

Hayes, Rutherford Birchard, 1822–93, 19th president of the U.S. (1877–81); b. Delaware, Ohio. A lawyer, he became (1858) city solicitor of Cincinnati. In the CIVIL WAR he took part in some 50 engagements and rose in rank to a major general of volunteers (1865). Hayes served (1865–67) as a Republican in Congress and was three times elected (1867, 1869, 1875) governor of Ohio. In 1876, chosen as the Republican candidate for president, he ran against Democrat Samuel J. TILDEN. In the election the returns of South Carolina, Louisiana, Florida, and Oregon were disputed, and Congress created an electoral commission to decide the result. The commission awarded all the disputed returns to Hayes, thus giving him a majority of one in the electoral college. Indignation over this partisan decision affected Hayes's administration, which was generally conservative and efficient and no more. He withdrew federal troops from Louisiana and South Carolina, ending the RECONSTRUCTION era. An advocate of hard money, he vetoed the BLAND-ALLISON ACT, which was passed nonetheless.

Haymarket Square riot, outbreak of violence in Chicago on May 4, 1886. Amid American labor's drive for an eight-hour working day, a demonstration was staged by anarchists in Haymarket Square. A crowd of some 1,500 people gathered; when police attempted to disperse them, a bomb exploded and rioting ensued. Eleven people were killed, and more than 100 others wounded. Eight anarchists were tried, but no evidence was found to link them to the bomb. They were, however, convicted of inciting violence. Four were hanged, one committed suicide, and three—after having served seven years in prison—were pardoned (1893) by Gov. John P. ALTGELD.

Hay-Pauncefote Treaties, negotiated in 1899 and 1901 by U.S. Secy. of State John HAY and Lord Pauncefote of Preston, British ambassador to the U.S. The first treaty was amended (1900) by the U.S. Senate and was rejected by the British. The second treaty, superseding the CLAYTON-BULWER TREATY, gave the U.S. the right to construct and fully control an Isthmian canal in CENTRAL AMERICA. It retained nominally the principle of neutrality under the sole guarantee of the U.S. and provided that the canal would be open to ships of all nations on equal terms, but it omitted a clause contained in the first draft forbidding fortifications.

Hayward, city (1990 pop. 111,498), Alameda co., W Calif.; settled 1851, inc. 1876. A rapidly growing San Francisco Bay area city, it is an important distribution and processing center for an agricultural area. Its manufactures include steel and chemicals. A California State Univ. campus is located there.

Haywood, William Dudley, 1869–1928, American labor leader, known as Big Bill Haywood; b. Salt Lake City, Utah. At age 15 he began work as a miner, and in 1900 he became secretary-treasurer of the Western Federation of Miners. In 1905 he helped organize the INDUSTRIAL WORKERS OF THE WORLD. Forced out of the Socialist party because of his militancy, he preached the doctrines of class struggle and mass action. Haywood was convicted of sedition during World War I but escaped to the Soviet Union. He wrote an autobiography, *Bill Haywood's Book* (1929).

hazel, shrub or small tree (genus *Corylus*) of the BIRCH family, grown as an ornamental and for its edible nuts. Species include the American hazel (*C. americana*) and European hazels (*C. maxima* and *C. avellena*); hazelnuts, usually known as filberts, are chiefly from the European trees. WITCH HAZEL is not related to hazel.

Hazlitt, William, 1778–1830, English essayist and critic. His penetrating literary criticism is collected in *Characters of Shakespeare's Plays* (1817), *Lectures on the English Poets* (1818), *Lectures on the English Comic Writers* (1819), *Table Talk* (1821–22), and *The Spirit of the Age* (1825). His *Dramatic Literature of the Age of Elizabeth* (1820) renewed interest in SHAKESPEARE and Elizabethan drama. Among his masterful essays are "On Going a Journey" and "On the Feeling of Immortality in Youth."

Hazzard, Shirley, 1931–, Australian novelist. She has lived in the U.S. since 1951. Noted for her insight, sensitivity, and poetic style, she has published two collections of short stories and three novels, *The Evening of the Holiday* (1966), *The Bay of Noon* (1970), and *The Transit of Venus* (1980).

H.D.: see DOOLITTLE, HILDA.

He, chemical symbol of the element HELIUM.

head-hunting, widespread practice of taking and preserving the head of a slain enemy, occurring from ancient times into the 20th cent. It may have evolved from CANNIBALISM. Taking a head was believed to strengthen one's own tribe and weaken the enemy's. Heads were also secured as tokens of courage and manhood. North American tribes took only the scalp; the JIVARO of South America preserve the skin to make so-called shrunken heads.

Head Start, U.S. educational program for disadvantaged preschool children, established under the Economic Opportunity Act of 1964. The program was initially aimed at preparing poor children for elementary school, but it was later extended to children above the poverty level, whose parents paid according to their income.

Health and Human Services, United States Department of, federal executive department that administers government health and SOCIAL SECURITY programs. It is the reorganized successor (1980) to the Dept. of Health, Education, and Welfare. It includes the Public Health Service, CENTERS FOR DISEASE CONTROL AND PREVENTION, FOOD AND DRUG ADMINISTRATION, NATIONAL INSTITUTES OF HEALTH, Social Security Administration, and the Health Care Financing Administration, which administers Medicare and Medicaid.

health-care proxy, legal document in which a person assigns to another the responsibility to make medical decisions in case of incapacitation. In many states the person who is designated in a health-care proxy also has the authority to withhold life-sustaining medical treatment. See also LIVING WILL.

Health, Education, and Welfare, United States Department of: see EDUCATION, UNITED STATES DEPARTMENT OF; HEALTH AND HUMAN SERVICES, UNITED STATES DEPARTMENT OF.

health insurance, prepayment plan providing medical services or cash indemnities for medical care; it may be voluntary or compulsory. Compulsory accident and sickness insurance was initiated (1883–84) in Germany by Bismarck and adopted by Britain, France, Chile, the USSR (now Russia), and other nations after World War I. In 1948 Britain instituted the most comprehensive compulsory health plan to date, including free medical care from any doctor participating in the system; a small charge for some services has been instituted since then. Canada has provided nearly free hospital service since 1958 and more comprehensive coverage since 1967. National health insurance has been widely adopted in Europe and parts of Asia. In the U.S., where the medical profession opposed government health insurance, voluntary cooperative or commercial programs developed, offering limited benefits to group or individual subscribers. Blue Cross and Blue Shield, the largest such insurers, covering hospital care and doctors' fees, respectively, are nonprofit agencies. In 1965 the federal government established two plans: Medicare, for persons age 65 and over, providing basic hospital insurance and supplementary insurance for doctors' and other health-care bills; and Medicaid, for low-income persons, operated by the states and covering hospital, physician, and other services. The U.S. is the only Western industrial nation without some form of comprehensive national health insurance. In 1993 Pres. Clinton proposed a health insurance program that would ultimately provide coverage for most citizens. See also MANAGED HEALTH CARE.

health maintenance organization (HMO), type of prepaid medical service in which members pay a monthly or yearly fee for all health care, including hospitalization. Most HMOs involve physicians engaged in group practice. Because costs to patients are fixed in advance, preventive medicine is stressed, to avoid costly hospitalization. "Open-ended" HMOs offer members the option of seeing a doctor who is not part of the HMO, but the patient must pay additional costs. In 1993 there were 45.3 million Americans enrolled in HMOs. See also MANAGED HEALTH CARE.

Heaney, Seamus [hē'nē], 1939–, Northern Irish poet. Rooted in his own life and in that of Ireland, balanced between the personal and the topical, Heaney's carefully crafted poems are extremely evocative yet clear and direct. His volumes of verse include *North* (1975), *Field Work* (1979), *Station Island* (1985), and *Seeing Things* (1991). Many of his critical and autobiographical pieces in prose were collected in *Preoccupations* (1980).

hearing: see EAR.

Hearn, Lafcadio, 1850–1904, American author; b. Ionian Islands; came to U.S., 1869. Partially blind and discontented, he wrote about the macabre and exotic, e.g., *Stray Leaves from Strange Literature* (1884). In 1890 he went to Japan, where he became a citizen and wrote 12 books.

Hearne, Samuel, 1745–92, British fur trader and explorer of N Canada. Working for the HUDSON'S BAY COMPANY, he explored the Coppermine River area in 1770. He opened up unknown territory and proved that there was no short NORTHWEST PASSAGE.

Hearst, William Randolph, 1863–1951, American journalist and publisher; b. San Francisco. During his lifetime Hearst established a vast publishing empire that included 18 newspapers in 12 cities and 9 successful magazines (including *Good Housekeeping* and *Harper's Bazaar*). His use of flamboyant pictures, shrieking typography, and mass-appeal news coverage, together with a policy of buying distinctive talent from other papers and selling papers at a penny, made him the leader in "penny journalism" by 1900. His papers' wild reports of Cuba's struggle for independence from Spain helped bring about the SPANISH-AMERICAN WAR. A flamboyant figure, later in life he became stridently conservative. His huge castle at San Simeon, Calif., is now a state museum.

heart, muscular organ that pumps blood to all parts of the body. The pear-shaped human heart is about the size of a fist and lies just left of center within the chest cavity. The contractions of heart muscle, or myocardium, are entirely self-stimulated. The heart is divided into two cavities by a wall of muscle; each cavity is divided in turn into two chambers, the upper ones called atria, the lower ones ventricles. Blood from the veins, high in carbon dioxide but low in oxygen, returns to the right atrium. It enters the right ventricle, which contracts, pumping the blood through the pulmonary

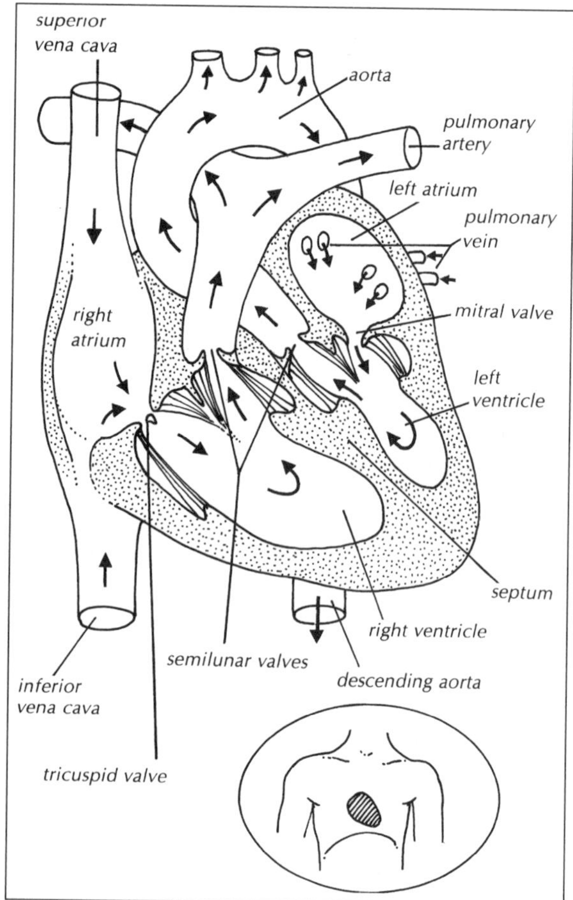

Cross-section of the heart, with arrows indicating direction of blood flow

artery to the LUNGS. Blood rich in oxygen and poor in carbon dioxide returns from the lungs to the left atrium and enters the left ventricle, which contracts, forcing the blood into the aorta, from which it is distributed throughout the body. The blood is prevented from backing up by a series of valves. See CIRCULATORY SYSTEM. See also CORONARY ARTERY DISEASE; TRANSPLANTATION, MEDICAL.

heart, artificial, external or surgically implanted mechanical device designed to replace a patient's diseased heart. The first one used on a human being, the Jarvik-7, was implanted (1982) in Dr. Barney Clark, who lived for 112 days; another patient, William Schroeder, lived 620 days. Two major drawbacks of the Jarvik-7 were the danger of stroke from clots formed in the artificial heart and the need for the patient to be hooked to the external air compressor that powered the pump. By 1989 such devices had largely become a bridge to human heart transplants. A related device, the **ventricular assist device** (VAD), or "artificial ventricle," is an internally implanted pump designed to aid a person with a failing left ventricle; unlike an artificial heart, it does not require removal of the patient's heart. In 1991 doctors implanted the first portable VAD; it was powered by a battery pack. Its pump used a special interior lining to promote the growth of a surface like that lining blood vessels, reducing the risk of the formation of blood clots, which can cause stroke. See also TRANSPLANTATION, MEDICAL.

heart disease, any of several abnormalities of the HEART and its function in maintaining blood circulation. Among the most common causes of heart disease are BIRTH DEFECTS of the heart; infectious diseases, such as RHEUMATIC FEVER; degenerative changes due to CORONARY ARTERY DISEASE; and HYPERTENSION. These and other forms of cardiovascular disease, alone or in combination, can lead to congestive heart failure, a condition in which the heart cannot pump sufficient blood to meet the demands of the body. The various forms of heart disease may also cause disturbances in normal heartbeat, called arrhythmias.

heart-lung machine, device that maintains the circulation and oxygen content of the BLOOD when connected with the arteriovenous system. Used in open-heart surgery to bypass the CIRCULATORY SYSTEM of the HEART and LUNGS, the oxygenator repeatedly draws off blood from the veins, reoxygenates it, and pumps it into the arterial system.

heat, internal ENERGY of a substance, associated with the positions and motions of its component molecules, atoms, and ions. The average kinetic energy of the molecules or atoms, which is due to their motions, is measured by the TEMPERATURE of the substance; the potential energy is associated with the state, or phase, of the substance (see STATES OF MATTER). Heat energy is commonly expressed in CALORIES, BRITISH THERMAL UNITS (Btu), or joules (see WORK). Heat may be transferred from one substance to another by three means: CONDUCTION, CONVECTION, and RADIATION. See also HEAT CAPACITY; SPECIFIC HEAT; THERMODYNAMICS.

heat capacity or **thermal capacity,** ratio of the change in HEAT energy of a unit mass of a substance to the change in TEMPERATURE of the substance. The heat capacity is a characteristic of a substance; it is often expressed in CALORIES per gram per degree Celsius or BRITISH THERMAL UNITS per pound per degree Fahrenheit. See also SPECIFIC HEAT.

Heath, Sir Edward Richard George, 1916–, British statesman. A Conservative, he was prime minister from 1970 to 1974. His attempts to reduce soaring inflation by enforcing wage controls led to bad relations with the trade unions and a confrontation with the miners' union (Nov. 1973–Feb. 1974) that forced the nation into a three-day workweek. In 1975 Heath lost the party leadership to Margaret THATCHER. In the 1980s he was a vocal and bitter critic of Thatcher's government.

heath, common name for some plants of the family Ericaceae, composed chiefly of evergreen shrubs native to the Old World. Heaths form the characteristic vegetation of many regions with acid soils, particularly moors, swamps, and mountain slopes. They are valued for their edible fruit, e.g., BLUEBERRY, CRANBERRY, and HUCKLEBERRY; as a source of flavoring, e.g., WINTERGREEN; and for their showy blossoms, e.g., RHODODENDRON, AZALEA, and TRAILING ARBUTUS. The names *heath* and *heather* are often used interchangeably, although true heaths (genus *Erica*) have needlelike foliage and white, rose, or yellow flowers, and heathers, such as the common heather of Scotland (*Calluna vulgaris*), have scalelike foliage and rose-colored flowers.

heather: see HEATH.

heat pump, device for controlling the air temperature in buildings. A heat pump operates like a reversible air conditioner. In summer, air flowing across the colder, heat-absorbing side of a REFRIGERATION apparatus is chilled and ducted through the building, and the heat is vented through an apparatus outdoors. In winter, the flow of the refrigerant is reversed. It absorbs heat through the outdoor apparatus, and the heat is released using the indoor apparatus and ducted through the building. Heat pumps are inefficient when the outside temperature is below freezing.

heaven, in Judaeo-Christian belief, the state of bliss in which the just see God face to face. Many Christians believe that after the RESURRECTION the glorified human body will be reunited forever with the soul in heaven, a realm popularly thought to contain material delights. Islam is accused of teaching of a heaven filled with delights of the flesh, but the passages in the Koran describing it may be allegorical.

heavy spar: see BARITE.

heavy water: see HYDROGEN.

Hebe [hē'bē], in Greek religion, goddess of youth; daughter of ZEUS and HERA and wife of HERCULES.

Hébert, Jacques René [āběr'], 1757–94, French revolutionary. The editor of a virulent paper, *Le Père Duchesne,* he led the CORDELIERS after MARAT's death. He was largely responsible for the price ceilings during the REIGN OF TERROR. His power over the Paris commune threatened ROBESPIERRE, who had him and his followers guillotined on a concocted charge of conspiracy. His fall marked the triumph of the propertied middle class.

Hebrew language, member of the Canaanite group of the Semitic subdivision of the Hamito-Semitic family of languages. In 1948 it became the official language of Israel. See LANGUAGE (table).

Hebrews. For history, see JEWS; for religion, see JUDAISM.

Hebrews, epistle of the NEW TESTAMENT, 19th book in the usual order, traditionally ascribed to St. PAUL; few modern scholars accept his authorship. It was written before A.D. 96. Most modern scholars feel it is addressed to Christians lapsing into indifference. The first part (1.1–4.13) argues Jesus' superiority to the angels and to MOSES; the second (4.14–10.18) treats Jesus' ministry and sacrifice, which supersedes all other sacrifices and serves to expiate sin.

Hebrides, the, group of more than 500 islands, W and NW Scotland. Less than a fifth of the islands are inhabited. They form two groups: the Outer Hebrides (known administratively as the Western Isles) and the Inner Hebrides, including SKYE and IONA. The main economic activities are fishing, farming, sheep grazing, and the manufacture of tweeds and other woolens. The islands were ruled by the Norwegians (8th–13th cent.) and by Scottish chiefs (13th–16th cent.) until they were acquired by the Scottish crown.

Hebron, city (1990 est. pop. 80,000), in the Israeli-occupied WEST BANK, near Jerusalem. Grapes, grains, and vegetables are grown in the area, and the main industries include tanning, food processing, and glass blowing. According to the Bible, the cave of Machpelah in Hebron is the burial place of ABRAHAM and his family, and the city was King DAVID's capital for seven years. Hebron has been occupied by Israel since the 1967 ARAB-ISRAELI WAR.

Hecate, in Greek mythology, goddess of ghosts and witchcraft. An attendant of PERSEPHONE, she was a spirit of black magic, able to conjure up dreams and the spirits of the dead. She haunted graveyards and crossroads.

Hecht, Ben, 1894–1964, American writer; b. N.Y.C. A controversial figure, he worked on Chicago newspapers and in the film industry in Hollywood. He wrote novels, stories, and plays. His best-known work, written with Charles MacArthur, is *The Front Page* (1928), an irreverent drama of newspaper life.

Hector, in Greek mythology, greatest Trojan hero of the TROJAN WAR, eldest son of Priam and HECUBA and husband of Andromache. In HOMER's *Iliad* he was killed by ACHILLES in revenge for the death of Patroclus.

Hecuba, in Greek mythology, queen of TROY; wife of Priam, to whom she bore 19 children, including HECTOR, PARIS, Troilus, and CASSANDRA. After the TROJAN WAR she was taken as a slave by ODYSSEUS.

She is an important character in EURIPIDES' plays *Hecuba* and *The Trojan Women*.

hedgehog, usually brown or yellow Old World MAMMAL of the family Erinaceidae, related to MOLES and SHREWS. Spiny hedgehogs, of Africa and Eurasia, are covered with stiff spines; they can roll into a ball when attacked, becoming invulnerable to predators. The European hedgehog (*Erinaceus eropaeus*) is nocturnal, living in a burrow (often in hedgerows) and hibernating in winter. It is about 9 in. (23 cm) in length. Like a hog, it roots in the ground for food; it eats worms, insects, mice, frogs, and poisonous snakes.

hedonism, in philosophy, the doctrine that pleasure is the highest good. Ancient hedonism equated pleasure variously with the gratification of sensual desire (as in the teaching of Aristippus and the Cyreniacs, c.435–360 B.C.) and with the intellectual serenity brought on by the rational control of desire (as in the teaching of EPICURUS). Modern British hedonism, expressed first in UTILITARIANISM, represents a social universalism, stressing that the aim of life is the greatest happiness for the greatest number.

Hegel, Georg Wilhelm Friedrich, 1770–1831, German philosopher. His all-embracing philosophical system, set forth in such works as *Phenomenology of Mind* (1807), *Science of Logic* (1812–16), and *Encyclopedia of the Philosophical Sciences* (1817), includes theories of ethics, aesthetics, history, politics, and religion. Hegel posited an enveloping absolute spirit at the center of the universe that guides all reality, including human reason. His absolute IDEALISM envisages a world-soul, evident throughout history, that develops from, and is known through, a process of change and progress now known universally as the Hegelian dialectic. According to its laws, one concept (thesis) inevitably generates its opposite (antithesis); their interaction leads to a new concept (synthesis), which in turn becomes the thesis of a new triad. Thus, philosophy enables human beings to comprehend the historical unfolding of the absolute. Hegel's application of the dialectic to the concept of conflict of cultures stimulated historical analysis and, in the political arena, made him a hero to those working for a unified Germany. He was a major influence on subsequent idealist thinkers and on such philosophers as KIERKEGAARD and SARTRE; perhaps his most far-reaching effect was his influence on Karl MARX, who substituted materialism for idealism in his formulation of DIALECTICAL MATERIALISM.

hegira or **hejira** [Arab. *hijra*, = breaking off of relations], flight of the Prophet MUHAMMAD in Sept. 622 from his native city, MECCA (because of its hostility toward him), to Yathrib (later renamed MEDINA). The Muslim era is dated from the first day of the lunar year in which the hegira took place. The abbreviation A.H. is used before years of the hegira, as A.D. is in Christendom.

Heidegger, Martin, 1889–1976, German philosopher. A student of HUSSERL, whom Heidegger succeeded as professor of philosophy at Freiburg, he was also influenced by KIERKEGAARD, DILTHEY, and NIETZSCHE. Heidegger's analysis in his major work, *Being and Time* (1927), of the concepts of "care," "mood," and the individual's relationship to death, relates the authenticity of being, as well as the anguish of modern society, to the individual's confrontation with his own temporality. Although he rejected the title, Heidegger is regarded as one of the founders of 20th-cent. EXISTENTIALISM; he influenced the work of SARTRE, DERRIDA, and others. His later work included studies of poetry and of dehumanization in modern society.

Heidelberg, city (1989 est. pop. 131,000), Baden-Württemberg, SW Germany, on the Neckar R. Its manufactures include machinery and precision instruments. First mentioned in the 12th cent., it was the residence of the electors and capital of the PALATINATE until the 18th cent. Its famous university (est. 1386) is the oldest in Germany. Since 1952 the city has been the headquarters of the U.S. army in Europe.

Heifetz, Jascha, 1901–87, Russian-American violinist. A child prodigy in Europe, he emigrated (1917) to the U.S., becoming a greater artist in maturity. He combined reasoned interpretation with virtuoso technique.

Heilbroner, Robert L., 1929–, American economist; b. N.Y.C. He has successfully popularized economics and explained economic theory to the lay reader. His works include *The Worldly Philosophers* (1953), *The Limits of American Capitalism* (1966), and *The Nature and Logic of Capitalism* (1985).

Heimlich maneuver, emergency procedure used to treat choking victims whose airway is obstructed by food or another substance. It forces air from the lungs through the windpipe, pushing the obstruction out. If the victim is standing, the rescuer wraps his (or her) arms around the victim's waist; making a fist with one hand and placing the thumb side of the fist against the abdomen just above the navel, the rescuer grasps his fist with the other hand and presses in with firm, quick, upward thrusts.

Heine, Heinrich [hī'nə], 1797–1856, German poet. His early poems, e.g., *Book of Songs* (1827), established him as a romantic, and his travel sketches, beginning with *Harz Journey* (1826), reveal a mixture of poignant emotion and barbed wit. A supporter of the social ideals of the FRENCH REVOLUTION, he left Germany for Paris in 1831. From there he continued to disseminate French revolutionary ideas in Germany and was the leading figure in the literary movement Young Germany. Heine worked in Paris as a correspondent for German newspapers and died there after years of severe illness. His lyrics have been used in some 3,000 compositions by SCHUMANN, SCHUBERT, and many others; his best-known song is "Die Lorelei." His later verse satires *Atta Troll* (1843) and *Deutschland* (1844) reflect his reaction, as a German of Jewish descent, to German anti-Semitism. Virtually all his work has been translated into English.

Heinlein, Robert (Anson MacDonald), 1907–88, American science fiction writer; b. Butler, Mo. His best-known novel, *Stranger in a Strange Land* (1961), about a young man who is raised by Martians and returns to Earth, became a 1960s cult classic. Other books include *Green Hills of Earth* (1951) and *I Will Fear No Evil* (1971).

Heisenberg, Werner, 1901–76, German physicist. A founder of QUANTUM MECHANICS, he is famous for his uncertainty principle, which states that it is impossible to determine both the position and momentum of a subatomic particle (such as the electron) with arbitrarily high accuracy. The effect of this principle is to convert the laws of physics into statements about relative, instead of absolute, certainties. Heisenberg's matrix mechanics, a form of quantum mechanics, was shown to be equivalent to Erwin SCHRÖDINGER's wave mechanics. Heisenberg received the 1932 Nobel Prize in physics for his work in nuclear physics and quantum theory.

Hekla [hěk'lä], active volcano, c.4,900 ft (1,490 m) high, SW Iceland, on the Mid-Atlantic Ridge. Hekla regularly emits steam and has several craters. The most destructive known eruption occurred in 1766; the most recent in 1947.

Helen, in Greek mythology, the most beautiful of women; daughter of ZEUS and LEDA, sister of CLYTEMNESTRA and of CASTOR AND POLLUX. Courted by many suitors, she married MENELAUS. When PARIS awarded the apple of discord to APHRODITE, the goddess gave him Helen; he carried her off to Troy, precipitating the TROJAN WAR. After the war she returned to Sparta with Menelaus, by whom she bore Hermione.

Helena, Saint, c.248–328?, mother of CONSTANTINE I. Converted to Christianity in 313, she is said to have discovered the True Cross and the Holy Sepulcher in Jerusalem. Feast: Aug. 18.

Helena, city (1990 pop. 24,569), state capital and seat of Lewis and Clark co., W central Mont., on the eastern slope of the CONTINENTAL DIVIDE; inc. 1870. A commercial center in a ranching and mining area, its manufactures include machine parts and paints. Helena's main street is the site of Last Chance Gulch, where gold was discovered in 1864.

helicopter, type of aircraft in which the lift is obtained by means of one or more power-driven horizontal propellers called rotors. In a single-rotor helicopter the reaction torque from the spinning rotor is compensated by a small vertical rotor near the tail. On twin-rotor craft the rotors spin in opposite directions, so that their reaction torques cancel each other. The helicopter is steered in any direction by inclining the axis of the main rotor in that direction. Because of its maneuverability and ability to land and take off in small areas, the helicopter is used in warfare and in a wide range of services, e.g., air-sea rescue, fire fighting, crop sowing, and traffic control. See SIKORSKY, IGOR.

heliocentric system: see COPERNICAN SYSTEM.

Heliopolis [Gr., = city of the sun], ancient city, N EGYPT, in the Nile delta, 6 mi (10 km) below Cairo. It was the center of sun worship, and its god RA or Re was the state deity until THEBES became the capital (c.2100 B.C.), when the gods AMON and Ra were combined as Amon-Ra. Its famous schools declined after the founding of Alexandria (332 B.C.)

Helios [hē'lēŏs], in Greek mythology, the sun god; son of the TITANS Hyperion and Theia; father of PHAËTHON. Each morning he left a palace in the east and crossed the sky in a golden chariot, then returned along the river Oceanus. He was a national god in Rhodes, where a COLOSSUS represented him. In Rome he was known as Sol and was an important god.

Helios, in space exploration: see SPACE PROBE, table.

heliotrope, in mineralogy: see BLOODSTONE.

helium (He), gaseous element, first observed spectroscopically in the SUN during a solar eclipse in 1868. Its noncombustibility and buoyancy make this extremely unreactive, INERT GAS the most suitable of gases for BALLOONS and AIRSHIPS. Deep-sea divers often breathe a helium-and-oxygen mixture; because helium is less soluble in human blood than nitrogen, its use reduces the risk of the bends (see DECOMPRESSION SICKNESS; DIVING, DEEP-SEA). Liquid helium is essential for low-temperature work (see LOW-TEMPERATURE PHYSICS; SUPERFLUIDITY). Helium is also used in arc welding and gas-discharge lasers. Abundant in outer space, helium is the product of hydrogen fusion in STARS. See ELEMENT (table); PERIODICTABLE.

hell, in Christian theology, eternal abode of those damned by God. Souls in hell are led by SATAN and deprived forever of the sight of God. In legend it is a place of fire and brimstone, where the damned undergo physical torment. Islam has a similar hell. In the ancient Jewish Sheol or Tophet, souls wander about unhappily, but Sheol later became much like the Christian hell. The ancient Greeks believed souls went to an underworld called Hades.

Helladic culture: see MYCENAEAN CIVILIZATION.

Hellen, in Greek mythology, ancestor of the Hellenes, or Greeks; son of DEUCALION and Pyrrha. His sons Dorus, Xuthus, and Aeolus were the progenitors of the principal Greek nations—the DORIANS, Ionians, Achaeans (see under ACHAEA), and Aeolians.

Hellenism, the culture, ideals and pattern of life of classical Greece, especially of Athens during the age of PERICLES; also, later thought and writing drawing on these ideals. It is often contrasted with austere, monotheistic Hebraism. The Hellenic period ended in the 4th cent. B.C. and was followed by HELLENISTIC CIVILIZATION.

Hellenistic civilization, spread of HELLENISM through the Mediterranean and Middle East and into Asia after ALEXANDER THE GREAT'S conquests. While the Greek city-states stagnated, their culture flourished elsewhere, notably at ALEXANDRIA. The city's influence on art, letters, and commerce was so great that the era is sometimes called the Alexandrian age. PERGAMUM and other cities also were important. Navigators extended the known world, and commercial wealth was reflected in ornate, grandiose architecture. Social divisions were extreme, but education was more widespread than ever before, with Greek the language of culture. A division between popular and learned writing appeared. The libraries of Alexandria and Pergamum were great learning centers, and writers like CALLIMACHUS, LUCIAN, and THEOCRITUS flourished. Philosophical disputation abounded, with STOICISM and Epicureanism (see EPICURUS) especially important. The highest achievement of the age may have been the preservation of Greek culture for the Romans. As Rome overshadowed the Mediterranean world, Hellenistic civilization was absorbed rather than extinguished.

Heller, Joseph, 1923–, American writer; b. Brooklyn, N.Y. He is best known for the novel *Catch-22* (1961), a wildly comic tale of military absurdities. He has also written a play and the novels *Something Happened* (1974), *Good as Gold* (1979), *God Knows* (1984), and *Picture This* (1988).

Heller, Walter, 1915–87, American economist; b. Buffalo, N.Y. Professor at the Univ. of Minnesota since 1946, he was chairman (1961–64) of the Council of Economic Advisers under Pres. J.F. KENNEDY and consultant to Pres. L.B. JOHNSON until 1969. He advocated deficit spending to spur economic growth, and federal revenue sharing with the states. His writings include *Monetary vs. Fiscal Policy* (1969; with Milton FRIEDMAN) and *The Economy* (1976).

Hellman, Lillian, 1905–84, American dramatist; b. New Orleans. Her finely crafted plays include *The Children's Hour* (1934), *The Little Foxes* (1939), and *Watch on the Rhine* (1941). She is also noted for her autobiographical works, e.g., *An Unfinished Woman* (1969), *Pentimento* (1973), *Scoundrel Time* (1976).

Helmholtz, Hermann Ludwig Ferdinand von, 1821–94, German scientist. An investigator of thermodynamics, electrodynamics, and vortex motion in fluids, he extended the application of the law of conservation of energy and in 1847 formulated it mathematically. A pioneer in physiological optics, Helmholtz invented (1851) the ophthalmoscope. He was professor of physics at the Univ. of Berlin.

Helms, Jesse, 1921–, U.S. politician; b. Monroe, N.C. A radio broadcasting executive, Helms gained prominence in the 1960s as a staunchly conservative Raleigh (N.C.) radio commentator. Elected (1972) to the U.S. Senate as a Republican from North Carolina, he gained notoriety for his outspoken, often unyielding support of right-wing causes in the Senate. Helms was chairman of the Senate agriculture committee from 1981 to 1986.

helots: see SPARTA.

Helsingør or **Elsinore,** city (1988 pop. 56,643), E Denmark, on the Oresund. It is an industrial center, fishing port, and summer resort. Known since the 13th cent., it served as a toll port from the 15th to the 18th cent. Kronborg castle (now a maritime museum), the setting of Shakespeare's *Hamlet,* is used to stage performances of the play.

Helsinki, city (1988 pop. 490,101), capital of Finland, S Finland, on the Gulf of Finland. Though blocked by ice from January to May, it is a natural seaport and the nation's administrative, cultural, and commercial center, with machine shops, shipyards, food-processing plants, and textile mills. Founded in 1550 by GUSTAVUS I of Sweden, it was devastated by fire in 1808 but was rebuilt and became the capital in 1812. Its university became (19th cent.) a center for Finnish nationalist activity against Russian rule. Landmarks include the railway station (designed by Eliel SAARINEN) and the sports stadium, site of the 1952 OLYMPIC GAMES.

Hemingway, Ernest, 1899–1961, one of the great American writers of the 20th cent.; b. Oak Park, Ill. With the publication of his novel

Ernest Hemingway

The Sun Also Rises (1926), he was recognized as a leading spokesman of the "lost generation" of American expatriates in post–World War I Paris. Writing in a direct, terse style, Hemingway focused on courageous people living essential, dangerous lives. His other major novels include *A Farewell to Arms* (1929), a tragic wartime love story, and *For Whom the Bell Tolls* (1940), based on an incident in the SPANISH CIVIL WAR, in which he was a correspondent. He is also famous for his vigorous short stories, e.g., "The Killers" and "The Snows of Kilimanjaro." In 1945 he settled in Cuba, where he wrote the novella *The Old Man and the Sea* (1952; Pulitzer). His other writings include the nonfiction works *Death in the Afternoon* (1932) and *Green Hills of Africa* (1935). In 1954 he was awarded the Nobel Prize in literature. He later moved to Idaho, where, plagued by illness, he committed suicide.

hemlock, coniferous evergreen tree (genus *Tsuga*) of the PINE family, native to North America and Asia. The common hemlock of E North America (*T. canadensis*) has small cones and short, dark-green leaves that give the branchlets a flat appearance. It is grown as an ornamental and has been valued as a source of tanbark. The wood of a Western hemlock (*T. heterophylla*) is used for construction. POISON HEMLOCK is an herb of the CARROT family.

hemoglobin, respiratory pigment found in the red blood cells of all vertebrates and some invertebrates (see BLOOD). It is produced in the bone marrow and carries oxygen to the body from the LUNGS. An inadequate amount of circulating hemoglobin results in a condition called ANEMIA.

hemophilia, hereditary disorder in which the clotting ability of the BLOOD is impaired and excessive bleeding results. Unable to form or maintain a sufficient blood clot, a hemophiliac may bleed uncontrollably after a small cut or bruise, after rigorous exertion, or even spontaneously. Hemophilia is genetically transmitted through females but usually affects only males. It is treated by transfusing the missing clotting factor; manufactured clotting factor also is now available. In the 1980s, before donated blood was routinely screened for the AIDS virus, some hemophiliacs contracted AIDS through transfusions of contaminated blood.

hemorrhoids or **piles,** dilation of the veins in or about the anus, often producing itching, bleeding, and pain. A common disorder associated with conditions such as constipation, pregnancy, and diarrhea, hemorrhoids can be treated with warm baths, ointments, and suppositories; in severe cases, injections, freezing, laser surgery, or traditional surgery may be necessary.

hemp, annual herb (*Cannabis sativa*) native to Asia and widely cultivated in Europe. It is often grown for the fiber made from its stems and for the narcotic drugs hashish and MARIJUANA, made primarily from the female flowers. Of major importance in many kinds of cord, hemp fiber is used in making paper, cloth, and other products. Hemp seed is used as bird food, and oil from the seeds is used in the manufacture of paints, varnishes, and soap.

Henderson, Rickey, 1957–, American baseball player, b. Chicago. A power-hitting outfielder with blazing speed, he holds the career base-stealing record. He played with the Oakland Athletics (1979–84) and achieved fame with the New York Yankees (1985–90). Plagued by injuries, he was traded (1990) to the Athletics and then (1993) the Toronto Blue Jays. He rejoined the Athletics in 1994.

Henie, Sonja [hĕn′ē], 1912–69, Norwegian-American figure skater; b. Norway. Ten times the world's figure-skating champion, she won Olympic championships in 1928, 1932, and 1936. She later became a popular professional skater and movie actress.

Henley, William Ernest, 1849–1903, English poet, critic, and editor, best known as the author of the poems "Invictus" and "England, My England." He also wrote plays with R.L. STEVENSON and edited literary reviews.

Henri, Robert, 1865–1929, American painter; b. Cincinnati. A member of the EIGHT, he rebelled against academic art and excelled in dramatic portraits, e.g., *Spanish Gypsy* (Metropolitan Mus.) and *Young Woman in Black* (Art Inst., Chicago). One of the foremost American art teachers, he imbued such students as George BELLOWS, Rockwell KENT, and Edward HOPPER with his dynamic concepts.

Henrietta Maria, 1609–69, queen consort of CHARLES I of England, daughter of HENRY IV of France. Her dealings with the pope, foreign powers, and army officers increased Parliament's suspicion of Charles and fear of a Catholic uprising, and helped to precipitate (1642) the ENGLISH CIVIL WAR.

Henry, rulers of the HOLY ROMAN EMPIRE. **Henry I** or **Henry the Fowler,** 876?–936, German king (919–36), was the first of the Saxon line, precursors to the Holy Roman emperors. After succeeding CONRAD I as German king, he won LOTHARINGIA from its allegiance to France (925), defeated the MAGYARS (933), and fortified his frontiers. St. Matilda, his queen, founded many monasteries. **Henry II,** 973–1024, emperor (1014–24) and German king (1002–24), was the last of the Saxon line. He was duke of Bavaria and succeeded his third cousin, OTTO III. In 1004 he entered Italy and was crowned king of Lombardy. He carried on a long warfare with BOLESLAUS I of Poland. After being crowned (1014) emperor, Henry was forced to assert his control over Italy. Both he and his empress, Kunigonde, are saints of the Roman Catholic Church. **Henry III,** 1017–56, emperor (1046–56) and German king (1039–56), served jointly as king with his father, CONRAD II, and acceded after his father's death. Under Henry the medieval Holy Roman Empire probably attained its greatest power and solidity. He defeated (1041) the Bohemians and maintained control over SAXONY and Lotharingia. The four Germans he named to the papal throne greatly increased the power of the papacy. His son, **Henry IV,** 1050–1106, emperor (1084–1105) and German king (1056–1105), was the central figure in the long struggle between the Holy Roman Empire and the papacy, which had been greatly strengthened by his father. His appointment of bishops in 1075 was condemned by Pope GREGORY VII. Henry declared Gregory deposed, and Gregory in turn excommunicated Henry. Even though Henry recanted, an antiking, Rudolf of Swabia, was named by a faction of German nobles, and civil war broke out. Henry was again excommunicated, but he invaded Italy, defeated the pope's forces, and was crowned emperor (1084) by the antipope, Guibert of Ravenna. His continuing battles with the pope, however, endangered the monarchy. With the blessing of Pope PASCHAL II, **Henry V,** 1081–1125, emperor (1111–25) and German king (1105–25), forced his father, Henry IV, to abdicate (1105), but he soon fell out with the pope. In 1111 he took Paschal and his cardinals prisoner. To secure his release the pope crowned Henry emperor and made other concessions. The conflict continued but was finally resolved by the Concordat of Worms (1122). **Henry VI,** 1165–97, emperor (1191–97) and German king (1190–97), was the son and successor of FREDERICK I. As the husband of Constance, heiress of Sicily, he gained control (1194) of that kingdom. He also took RICHARD I of England prisoner and forced him to swear fealty. He died while preparing to lead a Crusade. **Henry VII,** c.1275–1313, emperor (1312–13) and German king (1308–13), was a minor count of the house of Luxembourg when he was named king. As emperor he tried vainly to end the strife between the GUELPHS AND GHIBELLINES. He died while on a futile campaign to secure imperial authority in S Italy.

Henry, kings of England. **Henry I,** 1068–1135 (r.1100–1135), was the youngest son of WILLIAM I. On the death of his brother WILLIAM II, he had himself elected and crowned king while his older brother, ROBERT II, duke of Normandy, was on crusade. In 1101 Robert invaded England, but Henry bought him off. Henry invaded Normandy in 1105, defeated his brother, and became duke of Normandy. In the meantime he had been involved in a struggle with ANSELM over lay investiture. His later years were marked by his attempts to obtain the succession for his daughter MATILDA. Under Henry's reign of order and progress, royal justice was strengthened. **Henry II,** 1133–89 (r.1154–89), was the son of Matilda and GEOFFREY IV, count of Anjou. Founder of the Angevin, or Plantagenet, line, he became duke of Normandy in 1150 and in 1152 married ELEANOR OF AQUITAINE, thus gaining vast territories in France. In 1153 he invaded England and forced STEPHEN to acknowledge him as his heir. As king he restored order to war-ravaged England, subdued the barons, centralized the power of government in royalty, and strengthened royal courts. Henry's desire to increase royal authority brought him into conflict with THOMAS À BECKET, whom he had made (1162) archbishop of Canterbury. The quarrel, which focused largely on the jurisdiction of the church courts, came to a head when Henry issued (1163) the Constitutions of CLARENDON, defining the relationship between church and state, and ended (1170) with Becket's murder, for which Henry was forced by public indignation to do penance. During his reign he gained northern counties from Scotland and increased his French holdings. He was also involved in family struggles. Encouraged by their mother and LOUIS VI of France, his three oldest sons, Henry, RICHARD I, and Geoffrey, rebelled (1173–74) against him. The rebellion collapsed, but at the time of Henry's death, Richard and the youngest son, JOHN, were in the course of another rebellion. **Henry III,** 1207–72 (r.1216–72), was the son of John. He became king under a regency and was granted full powers of kingship in 1227. In 1230, against the advice of the chief justiciar, Hubert de Burgh, he led an unsuccessful expedition to Gascony and Brittany. He dismissed Hubert in 1232 and began a reign of extravagance and general incapacity, spending vast sums on futile wars in France. Henry's absolutism, his reliance on French favorites, and his subservience to the papacy aroused the hostility of the barons. His attempt to put his son, Edmund, earl of Lancaster, on the throne of Sicily (given to Henry by the pope) eventually led to the BARONS' WAR. Simon de MONTFORT, the barons' leader, won at Lewes and summoned (1265) a famous PARLIAMENT, but Henry's son EDWARD I led royal troops to victory at Evesham (1265), where de Montfort was killed. By 1267 the barons had capitulated, Prince Edward ruled the realm, and Henry was king in name only. **Henry IV,** 1367–1413, (r.1399–1413), was the son of JOHN OF GAUNT. In 1387 he joined the opposition to RICHARD II and was one of the five "lords appellant" who ruled England from 1388 to 1389. In 1398 Richard banished Henry and, after John's death in 1399, seized the family's vast Lancastrian holdings. Counting on the king's unpopularity and his absence in Ireland, Henry invaded England and successfully claimed the throne, thus establishing the Lancastrian dynasty. His reign was spent suppressing rebellions, notably by Richard's followers; by the Scots; by the Welsh under OWEN GLENDOWER; and by Sir Henry PERCY. He left the kingdom militarily secure but in debt. His son, **Henry V,** 1387–1422 (r.1413–22), presided over the privy council during his father's illness. As prince of Wales (Shakespeare's "Prince Hal"), he led armies against Owen Glendower and figured largely in the victory over the Percys. The early years of his reign were troubled by the rebellion of the Lollards (see LOLLARDRY). Determined to regain lands he believed to be his, he invaded France in 1415, thus reopening the HUNDRED YEARS WAR. After announcing his claim to the French throne, he met and defeated a superior French force at the famous battle of AGINCOURT. By 1420 he had conquered Normandy, married CATHERINE OF VALOIS, and persuaded her father, CHARLES VI of France, to name him his successor. He fell ill and died in 1422. As king he ruled with justice and industry, restoring civil order and the national spirit. Though his wars left the crown in debt, his charm, military genius, and care for his less fortunate subjects made him a popular hero. His son, **Henry VI,** 1421–71 (r.1422–61, 1470–71), became king when he was not yet nine months old. During his early years England was under the protectorate of two of his uncles. After their defeat at Orléans by JOAN OF ARC, the English attempted to protect their French interests by crowning Henry king of France at Paris in 1431, but their cause was hopeless. Henry's rule was dominated by factions, and there were many riots and uprisings indicating public dissatisfaction with the government. The struggle between the faction headed by Henry's wife, MARGARET OF ANJOU, and Edmund Beaufort, duke of Somerset, and that headed by Richard, duke of York, developed into the dynastic battle between the LANCASTERS and YORKS known as the Wars of the ROSES. Henry went insane in 1453. In 1455 Somerset was killed in the battle of St. Albans, and the Yorkists gained control of the government. Margaret had control from 1456 until 1460, when the Yorkists won a victory at Northampton and Henry was taken prisoner. York, who had been named Henry's successor, was killed at Wakefield in 1460, but his son EDWARD IV defeated the Lancastrians and was proclaimed king. Later he fled to Holland, and Henry was briefly (1470–71) restored. In 1471 Edward retook the throne, and Henry was murdered in the Tower of London. Henry was a mild, honest, pious man, a patron of literature and the arts, and the founder (1440) of Eton College. He was also unstable, weak-willed, and politically naïve. **Henry VII,** 1457–1509 (r.1485–1509), became head of the house of Lancaster at Henry VI's death. In 1485 he invaded England from France and defeated the forces of RICHARD III at the battle of Bosworth Field. The next year he married Edward IV's daughter, Elizabeth, thus uniting the houses of York and Lancaster and founding the TUDOR dynasty. Although his accession marked the end of the Wars of the Roses, the early years of his reign were disturbed by Yorkist attempts to regain the throne, e.g., the impersonations of Lambert SIMNEL and Perkin WARBECK. He consolidated English rule in Ireland (1494) and effected a peace treaty with Scotland (1499), which was followed by the marriage of his daughter Margaret to JAMES IV of Scotland. He established the Tudor tradition of autocratic rule tempered by justice and increased the powers of the STAR CHAMBER court. His son **Henry VIII,** 1491–1547 (r.1509–47), married his brother Arthur's widow, KATHARINE OF ARAGÓN, who bore him a daughter, MARY I. His chief minister, Thomas WOLSEY, concluded an alliance with FRANCIS I of France. but Henry (despite the FIELD OF THE CLOTH OF GOLD) joined (1522) Emperor CHARLES V in a war against France. England prospered internally under Wolsey, who had almost complete control. The court became a center of learning, and the pope gave Henry the title "Defender of the Faith" for a treatise he wrote against Martin LUTHER. By 1527 Henry, desiring a male heir, wished to marry Anne BOLEYN, but Pope CLEMENT VII, under the control of Katharine's nephew, Charles V, resisted his demands for a divorce. Wolsey's failure in this affair caused his downfall, and Thomas Cromwell became chief minister. An anti-ecclesiastical policy was adopted, and the subservient Thomas CRANMER became archbishop of Canterbury. He immediately pronounced Henry's marriage to Katharine invalid. Papal powers were transferred to the king, who became the supreme head of the English church. The break with Rome was now complete, and the Church of ENGLAND was established. Anne, whom Henry immediately married, had one daughter, ELIZABETH I. The marriage ended in 1536, when Anne was convicted of adultery and beheaded. Ten days later Henry married Jane SEYMOUR, who died in 1537 giving birth to EDWARD VI. The king dealt harshly with rebellions against the abolition of papal supremacy and the dissolution of the monasteries. In 1537 he licensed the publication of the Bible in English. His marriage (1540) to ANNE OF CLEVES (whom he disliked and soon divorced) led to the execution of Cromwell. He then married Catherine HOWARD, who suffered (1542) Anne Boleyn's fate. In 1543 Catherine PARR became his sixth queen. In 1542 war with Scotland began again, and Henry made unsuccessful attempts to unite the two kingdoms. Wales was officially incorporated into England (1536), but the conquest of Ireland proved too expensive. The end of Henry's reign saw a gradual move toward Protestantism. Henry remained immensely popular, despite his advancement of personal desires under the guise of public policy or moral right. His political insight, however, grew steadily better, and the power of Parliament increased. He gave England a comparatively peaceful reign.

Henry, kings of France. **Henry I,** c.1008–1060 (r.1031–60), was the son and successor of ROBERT II. He unwisely invested his brother Robert with the duchy of Burgundy, setting up a powerful rival to the French kingdom. Henry also fought with William, duke of Normandy (later WILLIAM I of England). **Henry II,** 1519–59 (r.1547–59), succeeded his father, FRANCIS I. Weak and pliant, he was dominated by Anne de Montmorency, by his mistress DIANE DE POITIERS, and by François and Charles de GUISE. Henry resumed his father's wars against Holy Roman Emperor CHARLES V and continued them against Charles's son PHILIP II of Spain. He was killed accidentally in a tournament and was succeeded by FRANCIS II. **Henry III,** 1551–89 (r.1574–89), was the son of Henry II and CATHERINE DE' MEDICI. He helped his mother plan the SAINT BARTHOLOMEW'S DAY massacre (1572) and was elected (1573) king of Poland. Assuming the French crown on the death of his brother CHARLES IX, Henry was faced with an ongoing civil war between Roman Catholics and Protestants, who were called HUGUENOTS (see RELIGION, WARS OF). In 1576 he made concessions to the Protestants that caused Henri, 3d duc de GUISE, to form the Catholic League. When the Protestant Henry of Navarre (later HENRY IV of France) became (1584) legal heir to the throne, Guise forced Henry III to suppress Protestantism and to exclude Navarre from the succession. In the ensuing War of the Three Henrys, Navarre defeated a royal army at Coutras (1587). Guise then revolted against the weakened Henry III, who was expelled (1588) from Paris by the mob. The king arranged the assassination of Guise, joined forces with Navarre, and attempted to retake Paris. During the siege he was assassinated by a fanatical monk, Jacques Clément. Henry III was the last male member of the house of VALOIS. **Henry IV,** 1553–1610, king of France (1589–1610) and, as Henry III, king of Navarre (1572–1610), was the first BOURBON monarch of France. Raised as a Protestant, he became (1569) the nominal head of the Huguenots. To save himself from the Saint Bartholomew's Day massacre (1572), Henry renounced his faith. He returned to Protestantism in 1576, however, and led a combined force of Protestants and moderate Catholics against Henry III and the Catholic League (for the resulting conflict see under **Henry III,** above). Henry became heir to the throne in 1584 and became king after Henry III was assassinated (1589). He defeated the Catholic League at Arques (1589) and Ivry (1590) but abandoned the siege of Paris when the league received aid from Spain. In 1593 Henry again abjured Protestantism, allegedly with the remark "Paris is well worth a Mass." He entered the city in 1594, and his conciliatory policy soon won him general support. He waged a successful war (1595–98) against Spain, and by the Edict of NANTES (1598) established political rights and a measure of religious freedom for the Huguenots. The rest of his reign was spent restoring order, industry, and trade. He was assassinated by a fanatic, François Ravaillac. In 1600 Henry had married MARIE DE' MEDICI, and he was succeeded by their son LOUIS XIII. Henry IV's gallantry, wit, and concern for the common people have become legendary.

Henry, German kings: see HENRY, rulers of the Holy Roman Empire.

Henry, Joseph, 1797–1878, American physicist; b. Albany, N.Y. A professor of philosophy at Princeton (then the College of New Jersey), he was later (from 1846) the first secretary and director of the Smithsonian Institution. Henry improved the electromagnet, invented and operated the first electromagnetic telegraph, and discovered self-inductance. The unit of inductance is often called the *henry* in his honor. Independently of Michael FARADAY, he discovered the principle of the induced current.

Henry, O.: see O. HENRY.

Henry, Patrick, 1736–99, political leader in the AMERICAN REVOLUTION; b. Hanover co., Va. A brilliant orator, he served in the Virginia house of burgesses (1765–74) and the CONTINENTAL CONGRESS (1774–76) and was governor of Virginia (1776–79). The phrases "If this be treason, make the most of it" and "Give me liberty or give me death" are attributed to him. He later worked to add the Bill of Rights to the Constitution.

Henry E. Huntington Library and Art Gallery: see under HUNTINGTON, COLLIS POTTER.

Henry of Flanders, c.1174–1216, Latin emperor of CONSTANTINOPLE (1206–16) after his brother, BALDWIN I. Ablest of the Latin emperors, he fought off the Bulgarians.

Henry of Navarre: see Henry IV under HENRY, kings of France.

Henryson, Robert, c.1425–c.1506, Scottish poet. His *Testament of Cresseid* is a harshly moral epilogue to CHAUCER's *Troilus and Criseyde.* His *Moral Fables of Aesop,* on the other hand, are macabre and drily humorous.

Henry the Fowler: see Henry I under HENRY, rulers of the Holy Roman Empire.

Henry the Lion, 1129–95, Guelphic duke of SAXONY (1142–80) and of BAVARIA (1156–80). Bavaria and Saxony were restored to him by Holy Roman Emperor FREDERICK I in an effort to end the strife between the GUELPHS AND GHIBELLINES. He supported Frederick in Italy and Christianized the Wendish lands. By 1180 the growth of his power had alarmed the emperor, who seized his two duchies and subdivided them into small principalities. Henry later regained Brunswick and Lüneburg in Saxony. His son became emperor as OTTO IV.

Henry the Navigator, 1394–1460, prince of Portugal, patron of exploration. The son of Portuguese King JOHN I, he established (1416) at Sagres a base for sea exploration, an observatory, and a school for geographers and navigators. Henry's sea captains explored the W African coast, rounding Cape Verde (1444) and reaching as far as present-day Sierra Leone. Their return with gold and slaves made for a lucrative and popular business, although he forbade (1455) the kidnapping of Africans. His promotion of navigation and exploration provided the groundwork for the development of Portugal's sea power and colonial empire.

Henze, Hans Werner [hĕn'tsə], 1926–, German composer. He was influenced early by STRAVINSKY, HINDEMITH, and BARTÓK and experimented with TWELVE-TONE MUSIC. His leftist politics are manifested in such works as *Essay on Pigs* (1969). He has written SYMPHONIES and OPERAS, e.g., *The Young Lord* (1964) and *The English Cat* (1983).

hepatitis, any of several viral inflammations of the liver that cause nausea, fever, weakness, loss of appetite, and, usually, JAUNDICE. Two forms are most common: hepatitis A (infectious), spread through contaminated food or water; and hepatitis B (serum), usually transmitted by sexual activity, transfusion of infected blood or transplantation of infected tissue, or use of shared syringes by drug addicts or of poorly sterilized medical and dental instruments. A third type, hepatitis C, is also transmitted by contaminated blood transfusions and tissue transplants. Although rarer, hepatitis C is more likely to become chronic and to result in CIRRHOSIS. Hepatitis can also occur as a complication of other diseases or as a toxic reaction to alcohol, drugs, or other chemicals. VACCINATION for hepatitis B is recommended for all infants and others at risk for the virus; a hepatitis A vaccine has also been developed. Chronic hepatitis B and C may be treated with INTERFERON.

Hepburn, Katharine, 1909–, American actress; b. Hartford, Conn. She has enhanced the screen with her individual and commanding presence since 1932. Her films include *Morning Glory* (1933; Academy Award), *The Philadelphia Story* (1940), *The African Queen* (1951), *The Lion in Winter* (1968; Academy Award), and *On Golden Pond* (1981; Academy Award).

Katharine Hepburn

Hephaestus, in Greek mythology, OLYMPIAN god; son of HERA and ZEUS; husband of APHRODITE. Originally a Middle Eastern fire god, in Greece he was the divine smith and god of craftsmen, worshiped in centers such as Athens. Usually a comic figure, he was represented as bearded, with mighty shoulders but lame. He worked at huge furnaces, aided by CYCLOPES. The Romans identified him with VULCAN.

Hepplewhite, George, d. 1786, English cabinetmaker. His work is noted for light, curvilinear forms; painted or inlaid decoration with ribbon and rosette motifs; slender, tapering legs; chair backs in shield and oval forms; and the use of satinwood, painted beechwood, and mahogany. His small pieces, e.g., inlaid work tables, are especially prized.

Hepworth, Dame Barbara, 1903–75, English sculptor. Working primarily in stone or bronze, she sought perfection of form and surface technique. Her smooth, usually nonfigurative sculptures are reminiscent of those of Jean ARP.

Hera, in Greek mythology, queen of OLYMPIAN gods; daughter of CRONUS and RHEA; wife and sister of ZEUS; mother of ARES and HEPHAESTUS. A jealous wife, she plagued Zeus, his mistresses, and his progeny, e.g., HERCULES. Hera was powerful and widely worshiped as the protectress of women, marriage, and childbirth. The Romans identified her with JUNO.

Heracles: see HERCULES.

Heraclitus, c.535–c.475 B.C., Greek philosopher. He taught that there is no permanent reality except the reality of change, a position illustrated by his famous maxim "You cannot step twice in the same river." Thus the only possible real state is the transitional one of becoming. He believed fire to be the underlying substance of the universe and all other elements to be transformations of it.

Heraclius, c.575–641, Byzantine emperor (610–41). He recovered provinces from Persia (622–28) but lost them (629–42) to the Arabs. MONOTHELETISM resulted from his efforts to reconcile MONOPHYSITISM with the Orthodox Church. He began the reorganization of the empire into military provinces.

Herakles: see HERCULES.

heraldry, system in which inherited symbols, or devices, called charges are displayed on a shield, or escutcheon, for the purpose of identifying individuals or families. In the Middle Ages the herald, often a tournament official, had to recognize knights by their shields. As earlier functions of the herald grew obsolete, his chief duties became the devising, inscribing, and granting of armorial bearings. Heraldry proper, developed by noblemen using personal insignia on seals and shields, was a feudal institution. It is thought to have originated in Germany in the late 12th cent. and to have been imported into England by the Normans (see NORMAN CONQUEST). The CRUSADES and the tournaments that drew together knights from many countries caused heraldry to flourish in Europe. The embroidering of family emblems on the surcoat worn over chain mail in the 13th cent. accounts for the term "coat of arms." The use of armorial bearings spread rapidly thereafter. In England the regulation of heraldry was assigned to the HERALDS' COLLEGE (chartered 1483). Arms were borne by families, corporations, guilds, colleges, cities, and kingdoms, and the tradition still persists.

Herat, city (1984 est. pop. 161,000), capital of Herat prov., NW Afghanistan, on the Hari Rud. Located in a fertile valley, the city is renowned for its fruits, textiles, and carpets. It is the site of the 12th-cent. Great Mosque. Herat's strategic location on ancient trade routes made it an object of conquest. Long part of the Persian empire, Herat fell to Jenghiz Khan (1221), Timur (1383), and the Uzbeks (early 16th cent.). In 1881 it was confirmed as part of a united Afghanistan. Soviet troops occupied (1979–89) the city and demolished many of its buildings.

herbal medicine, use of natural plant substances to treat illness. The practice has existed since prehistoric times and is used today by up to 80% of the world's population as a primary form of medicine. Herbs may be used directly as teas or extracts, or they may be used in the production of drugs. Modern medicines that come from plants include aspirin from willow bark (*Salix* species) and digitalis from foxglove (*Digitalis purpurea*).

Herbert, George, 1593–1633, English METAPHYSICAL POET and Anglican priest. His devotional poems, combining reverence with a homely familiarity with religious experience, were published after his death (1633) as *The Temple.*

Herbert, Victor, 1859–1924, Irish-American cellist, composer, and conductor. After coming to the U.S. (1886), he conducted the Pittsburgh Symphony Orchestra (1898–1904). His major successes were melodious OPERETTAS, including *Babes in Toyland* (1903), *The Red Mill* (1906), and *Eileen* (1917).

herbicide, substance that kills plants or inhibits their growth. Nonselective herbicides, generally toxic, are used to clear all plants from a broad area; selective herbicides attack weeds without permanently harming crops. Scientists are using GENETIC ENGINEERING to develop crop varieties with increased tolerance for herbicides. Inorganic compounds such as common salts have long been used as herbicides; c.1900 certain sulfates, ammonium and potassium salts, and other compounds began to be used as selective herbicides. The 1940s saw the development of 2,4-D (2,4-trichlorophenoxyacetic acid), an organic compound that is a highly selective systemic herbicide. Such herbicides are now widely used. Several such compounds, including 2,4,5-T (2,4,5-trichlorophenoxyacetic acid), have been banned by the Environmental Protection Agency as potentially dangerous. 2,4,5-T was used in Agent Orange (a defoliant employed by U.S. forces in Vietnam), which has been linked to some diseases suffered by veterans. Since Agent Orange, heightened awareness of possible ecological and health dangers attributable to herbicides has resulted in reevaluation of many compounds and has called indiscriminate use into question.

Herblock (Herbert Lawrence Block), 1909–, American cartoonist; b. Chicago. Widely syndicated, his work has appeared in the Washington *Post* since 1946 and has been collected in numerous volumes. Known for his witty political drawings, he won the Pulitzer Prize in 1942 and 1954.

Herculaneum, ancient city at the foot of Mt. Vesuvius, S Italy, buried along with POMPEII when Vesuvius erupted in A.D. 79. Since the first ruins of the popular Roman resort were found in 1709, the most important excavations have been the Villa of the Papyri, a basilica, and a theater.

Hercules, Heracles, or **Herakles,** most popular Greek hero, famous for strength and courage. The son of Alcmene and ZEUS, he was hated by HERA, who sent serpents to his cradle; he strangled them. Later Hera drove Hercules, mad and he slew his wife and children. He sought purification at the court of King Eurystheus, who set him 12 mighty labors: killing the Nemean lion and HYDRA; driving off the Stymphalian birds; cleaning the Augean stables; capturing the Cerynean hind, Cretan bull, mares of Diomed, Erymanthian boar, cattle of Geryon, and CERBERUS; and procuring the girdle of Hippolyte and the golden apples of the Hesperides. He was later involved in the Calydonian hunt (see MELEAGER) and the Argonaut expedition (see JASON). At his death he rose to OLYMPUS, where he was reconciled with Hera and married HEBE. Represented as a powerful man cloaked with a lion's skin and carrying a club, he was widely worshiped. He is the hero of plays by SOPHOCLES, EURIPIDES, and SENECA.

Herder, Johann Gottfried von, 1744–1803, German philosopher, critic, and clergyman. He was an influential critic and a leader of the STURM UND DRANG movement. While studying at Königsberg, he was influenced by Immanuel KANT, and later he gained notice with *Fragments Concerning Current German Literature* (1767). He became court preacher at Weimar through the influence of GOETHE, whose work was greatly influenced by Herder's *On the Origin of Language* (1772). At Weimar, Herder became the chief theorist of German ROMANTICISM and produced his anthology of foreign folk songs, *Voices of the People* (1778–79). His vast work *Outlines of the Philosophy of Man* (1784–91) developed a major evolutionary approach to history, propounding the uniqueness of each historical age.

Heredia, José María [ārā'thēä], 1803–39, Cuban lyric poet and prose writer. Such poems as "Niagara" (1825) typify his romantic melancholy and joy in nature. Exiled (1823) as a revolutionary, he spent two years in New York City before settling in Mexico. He also wrote stories, essays, and plays.

hermaphrodite, animal or plant with both female and male reproductive systems, producing both eggs and sperm. Some hermaphrodites undergo self-FERTILIZATION, in which egg and sperm of the same individual fuse, as in self-pollinating plants; others may undergo cross-fertilization, in which egg and sperm of different individuals fuse, as in the earthworm. Protandric hermaphrodites (e.g., oyster and sage plant) produce both eggs and sperm but at different times.

hermeneutics, branch of philosophy dealing with the theory of understanding and interpretation. "Understanding" is viewed as a circular process whereby one can understand the whole only in terms of the parts, but the parts only from the whole. First used to interpret biblical texts in the early 19th cent., the theory was extended by SCHLEIERMACHER beyond scriptural interpretation, and by the end of the century DILTHEY construed it as the general methodology for all the social sciences and humanities. Both held that a universal human capacity for empathy—the personal experience of that which has been expressed by someone else—was the bridge between past and present. In the 20th cent. HEIDEGGER and his student Hans-Georg Gadamer rejected this psychological foundation, instead basing their hermeneutics on the study of linguistic phenomena such as translation and etymology.

Hermes, in Greek mythology, son of ZEUS and Maia; messenger of the gods and conductor of souls to HADES. He was also the god of travelers, of luck, music, eloquence, commerce, young men, cheats, and thieves. He was said to have invented the lyre and flute. The riotous Hermaea festival was celebrated in his honor. Hermes was represented with winged hat and sandals, carrying the caduceus. He is equated with the Roman MERCURY.

Hermitage, museum in Saint Petersburg (Leningrad), one of the world's foremost houses of art. It was reconstructed in the neoclassical style in the 19th cent. from the original palace built by CATHERINE II. Although opened to the public in 1852, it contained only the imperial collections until 1917. It now has over 40,000 drawings; 500,000 engravings; and 8,000 paintings of the Flemish, French, Dutch, Spanish, and Italian schools. It also contains many superb modern works, notably by PICASSO and MATISSE, and the art of many civilizations. Russian art is exhibited separately in Mikhailovsky Palace.

hermit crab, primarily marine animal (a CRUSTACEAN) distinguished from the true CRAB by its long, soft, spirally coiled abdomen terminating in an asymmetrically hooked tail. Most occupy the empty shells of GASTROPODS and are marine scavengers. The largest species reaches 1 ft (30 cm) in length.

hernia, protrusion of an internal organ or part of an organ through the wall of a body cavity. It may be present at birth or acquired after heavy strain on the musculature in such areas as the lower abdomen (inguinal hernia), diaphragm (hiatus hernia), or region around the navel. Surgery is sometimes recommended to alleviate symptoms and prevent the hernia from becoming caught and strangulated (cut off from the blood supply).

hero, in Greek mythology, famous person worshiped after death as quasi-divine. Heroes might be actual great people, real or imaginary ancestors, or "faded" deities (ancient gods demoted to human status). Most hero worship, performed at night with blood sacrifices, was celebrated at the supposed place of the hero's tomb.

Herod, dynasty reigning in Palestine at the time of Jesus. **Antipater,** fl. c.65 B.C., founded the family fortune. He was an Idumaean, who gained a stronghold in Palestine. His son **Antipater,** d. 43 B.C., was favored by Julius CAESAR, who made him (c.55 B.C.) virtual ruler of all of Palestine. The son of the second Antipater was **Herod the Great,** d. 4 B.C., who gave the family its name. He was friendly with Marc ANTONY, and secured (37 B.C.–4 B.C.) the title king of Judaea; after the battle of Actium he made peace with Octavian (later AUGUSTUS), who thereafter showed him great favor. Herod made great efforts to mollify the Jews by publicly observing Hebrew laws and by building a temple, but also promoted hellenization. In his last years Herod became bloodthirsty, and around the time of Jesus' birth, he ordered the massacre of the innocents. His son **Herod Antipas,** d. after A.D. 39, tetrarch of Galilee and Peraea, was the Herod who executed JOHN THE BAPTIST and who was ruling at Jesus' death. He repudiated his wife to marry his niece Herodias, wife of his half-brother Herod Philip. He was eventually banished by CALIGULA in A.D. 39. **Herod Agrippa I,** d. A.D. 44, was the nephew of Herod Antipas and a man of some ability. His son, **Herod Agrippa II,** d. c.A.D. 100, was a poor ruler who alienated his subjects. The Herods are usually blamed for the state of virtual anarchy in Palestine at the beginning of the Christian era. The prime source is the history by JOSEPHUS.

Herodotus [hērŏd'ətəs], 484?–425? B.C., Greek historian, called the Father of History; b. Halicarnassus, Asia Minor. His history of the PERSIAN WARS, the first comprehensive attempt at secular narrative history, marks the start of Western historical writing. The work is written in an anecdotal style of great charm and offers a rich diversity of information about the ancient world.

heroic couplet: see PENTAMETER.

heroin, NARCOTIC drug synthesized from MORPHINE. In many parts of the world, it is used as an analgesic (for relief of pain), particularly for the terminally ill. In the U.S. its manufacture and importation are restricted, and its use in medicine remains under investigation. Heroin predominates in illicit narcotics traffic. See DRUG ADDICTION AND DRUG ABUSE.

Heron, mathematician: see HERO OF ALEXANDRIA.

heron, BIRD of the family Ardeidae, large wading birds, including the BITTERN and EGRET, found in many temperate regions but most numerous in tropical and subtropical areas. Herons have sharp, serrated bills, broad wings, and long legs. Their plumage is soft and drooping, and (especially at breeding time) they may have long, showy plumes on their heads, breasts, and backs.

Hero of Alexandria or **Heron** [hēr'ŏn], fl. A.D. 62, mathematician and inventor. His origin is uncertain, although he wrote in Greek on the measurement of geometric figures and invented many contrivances operated by water, steam, or compressed air, including a fountain and a fire engine.

herpes simplex, virus causing infection of the skin characterized by one or more blisters filled with clear fluid that usually appear around the lips (cold sores). The initial infection, probably occurring during infancy or childhood, subsequently becomes dormant. The reappearance of blisters may be triggered by such factors as fever, exposure to sunlight, menstruation, or pregnancy. Genital herpes, a type of SEXUALLY TRANSMITTED DISEASE, can be treated with the drug acyclovir.

Herrick, Robert, 1591–1674, considered the greatest of the English Cavalier poets. A country clergyman, he never married, and the many women in his poems are probably fictitious. Most of his work appeared in *Hesperides* (1648), which included the sacred songs called *Noble Numbers*. A disciple of JONSON, Herrick shows classical influence, but his greatness rests on simplicity and sensuousness. Among his best-known lyrics are "Upon Julia's Clothes" and "Corinna's Going a-Maying."

herring, important marine or freshwater food FISH of the family Clupidae, including the sardine, menhaden, and SHAD. Herrings are relatively small but very abundant; they swim in large schools. The adult common herring (*Clupea harengus*) of the N Atlantic is about 1 ft (30 cm) long, with silvery sides and blue back. The menhaden, of the Atlantic coast of North America, is a commercially important source of oil and fish meal. Of the smaller herrings and related species, the anchovies and sardines are the most important. Herring species have been depleted by overfishing. They also fluctuate in response to natural conditions, e.g., the anchovies off Peru are adversely affected by EL NIÑO.

Herschel, family of distinguished English astronomers. **Sir William Herschel,** 1738–1822, originally Friedrich Wilhelm Herschel, b. Germany, discovered (1781) the planet Uranus, which led (1782) to his position as private astronomer to the king. The large reflecting telescopes that he constructed, including one with a 40-ft (12.2-m) focal length, far surpassed in size those of his contemporaries. He concluded from the motion of double stars that they are held together by gravitation and that they revolve around a common center, thus confirming the universal nature of Isaac NEWTON's theory of gravitation. He discovered the Saturnian satellites Mimas and Enceladus (1789) and the Uranian satellites Titania and Oberon (1787). His research on nebulae suggested a possible origin of new worlds from gaseous matter, and his catalog of nebulae (including some objects that are now known to be galaxies or star clusters) increased those known from about 100 to 2,500. His sister, **Caroline Lucretia Herschel,** 1750–1848, discovered eight comets and three nebulae. For her arrangement of her brother's catalog of star clusters and nebulae, she received (1828) the Royal Astronomical Society's gold medal. Sir William's son, **Sir John Frederick William Herschel,** 1792–1871, spent four years (1834–38) at the Cape of Good Hope cataloging 1,707 nebulae and clusters and 2,102 pairs of double stars. He published (1864) a consolidated catalog of 5,079 nebulae and clusters; revised by Johann Dreyer as *A New General Catalogue of Nebulae and Star Clusters* (NGC; 1888), it is still a standard reference. In photography, he was the first to use sodium thiosulfate as a fixing agent, and he introduced the terms *positive image* and *negative image*.

Hersey, John (Richard), 1914–93, American writer; b. China. A former war correspondent, he examined WORLD WAR II events in *Hiroshima* (1946) and the novels *A Bell for Adano* (1944; Pulitzer) and *The Wall* (1950). His later novels include *The Walnut Door* (1977) and *Antonietta* (1991).

Herskovits, Melville Jean, 1895–1963, American anthropologist; b. Bellefontaine, Ohio. A professor at Northwestern Univ. (from 1927), he did his fieldwork in Africa and pioneered in applying principles of modern cultural anthropology to African-American ethnology. His works include *The Myth of the Negro Past* (1941) and *The Human Factor in a Changing Africa* (1962).

Hertz, Heinrich Rudolf, 1857–94, German physicist. He confirmed James Clerk MAXWELL's electromagnetic theory and produced and studied electromagnetic waves (radio waves), which he showed are long transverse waves that travel at the speed of light and can be reflected, refracted, and polarized like light. The unit of frequency, the hertz, is named for him.

Hertzog, James Barry Munnik, 1866–1942, South African political leader. A Boer, he served (1910–12) in BOTHA's cabinet in the newly created Union of SOUTH AFRICA, but opposition to Botha's cooperation with the British led him to form the Nationalist party. As prime minister (1924–39) he instituted various methods of racial segregation, or APARTHEID.

Hertzsprung-Russell diagram [for astronomers Ejnar Hertzsprung and Henry Norris RUSSELL], graph showing the LUMINOSITIES, or absolute MAGNITUDES, of the STARS of a cluster or galaxy plotted against their surface temperatures (or some temperature-dependent characteristic such as SPECTRAL CLASS or color). The majority of stars lie on a diagonal band—the main sequence—that extends from hot stars of high luminosity, in the upper-left corner, to cool stars of low luminosity, in the lower-right corner. The concentration of stars in certain distinct regions of the H-R diagram indicates that definite laws govern stellar structure and STELLAR EVOLUTION.

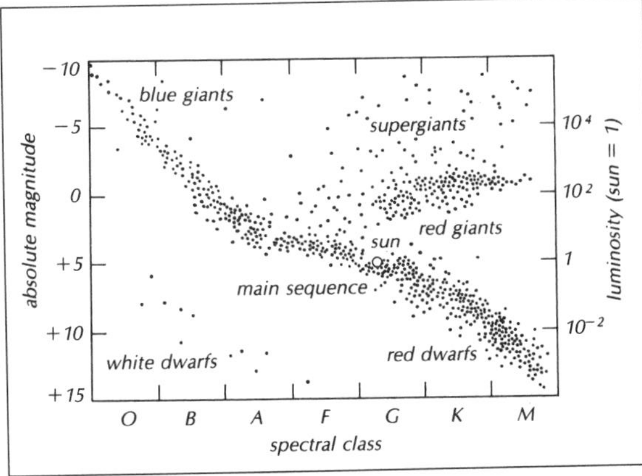

The Hertzsprung-Russell (H-R) diagram shows the absolute magnitudes of stars as a function of their spectral class, which is related to their temperature. Most stars fall along a diagonal, the main sequence, that extends from cool, dim red dwarfs to hot, bright blue giants.

Herzen, Aleksandr Ivanovich, 1812–70, Russian revolutionary leader and writer. A civil servant, he was sent to the provinces (1834) for participating in a socialist group. He left Russia permanently in 1847. In England he set up the first free Russian press abroad; his weekly journal *Kolokol* (1857–62) was banned in Russia but widely read. His books include *My Past and Thoughts* (1855).

Herzl, Theodor [hĕr'tsəl], 1860–1904, Hungarian Jew, founder of modern ZIONISM. As a newspaper correspondent covering the DREYFUS AFFAIR, he became convinced that the only solution to European ANTI-SEMITISM was the establishment of a Jewish national state. He organized the first Zionist World Congress (1897) and was its president until his death.

Herzog, Werner, 1942–, German film director. His visionary, ironic films, often treating bizarre historical incidents, include *Aguirre the Wrath of God* (1973), *Stroszek* (1977), *Heart of Glass* (1977), *Nosferatu* (1979), and *Fitzcarraldo* (1982).

Hesiod, fl. 8th cent.? B.C., Greek poet, self-described as a Boeotian farmer. His *Works and Days* is filled with maxims for farmers, to inculcate righteousness and efficiency. Also ascribed to him is the *Theogony*, a genealogy of the gods. Hesiod and HOMER codified much of Greek myth.

Hesse, Hermann [hĕs'ə], 1877–1962, German novelist and poet. An ardent pacifist, he became a Swiss citizen after the outbreak of World War I. The spiritual loneliness of the artist is a major theme in Hesse's symbolic novels, which include *Peter Camenzind* (1904), *Demian* (1919), *Steppenwolf* (1927), and *Narziss und Goldmund* (1930). *The Glass Bead Game* (1943) and *Siddhartha* (1922) reflect his interest in Asian mysticism. In 1946 he was awarded the Nobel Prize in literature.

Hesse, Philip of: see PHILIP OF HESSE.

Hesse, state (1990 est. pop. 5,661,000), 8,150 sq mi (24,064 sq km), central Germany. Weisbaden is the capital. Hesse is largely agricultural, with heavily forested areas. Fine wines are produced along the Rhine valley. Industries include textiles, chemicals, metallurgy, and mining. Hesse emerged (1247) as a landgraviate under the Holy Roman emperor and was divided (1567) among several lines; Hesse-Kassel and Hesse-Darmstadt were the most important. In the 18th cent. the rulers of Hesse raised revenue by letting mercenaries, called Hessians, for hire. Hesse-Kassel was made (1803) an electorate and was annexed (1866) to PRUSSIA. Hesse-Darmstadt joined (1871) the German Empire and was ruled by its own dynasty until 1918.

Hestia, in Greek mythology, goddess of the hearth; daughter of CRONUS and RHEA. Widely worshiped, she was a kind deity who represented personal and communal security and happiness. The Romans identified her with VESTA.

Heyerdahl, Thor, 1914–, Norwegian explorer and anthropologist. Seeking evidence that ancient cultures could have been diffused by transoceanic travelers, he sailed across the Pacific (1947), the Atlantic (1970), and the Persian Gulf (1977) in replicas of primitive crafts. He described these voyages in *Kon Tiki* (tr. 1950), *The Ra Expeditions* (tr. 1971), *The Tigris Expedition* (tr. 1981) and *Easter Island: The Mystery Solved* (1989). His work is controversial.

Heyward, DuBose, 1885–1940, American author; b. Charleston, S.C. His story of African-American life on the Charleston waterfront, *Porgy* (1925), was dramatized (1927) by Heyward and his wife, Dorothy, and made into the folk opera *Porgy and Bess* (1935), with music by George GERSHWIN.

Heywood, Thomas, 1574?–1641, English dramatist, best known for *A Woman Killed with Kindness* (1603), one of the finest domestic tragedies. A prolific playwright, he also wrote *Apology for Actors* (1612), a response to Puritan attacks.

Hezekiah, d. c.686 B.C., king of Judah (c.715–c.686 B.C.). The successor to AHAZ, he resisted two invasions by SENNACHERIB of Assyria. He was one of the best of Judah's kings, abolishing idolatry and listening to ISAIAH and MICAH.

Hf, chemical symbol of the element HAFNIUM.

Hg, chemical symbol of the element MERCURY.

Hialeah, city (1990 pop. 188,004), SE Fla., NW of Miami; inc. 1925. It has printing and diversified manufacturing industries. Nearby Miami International Airport is a major employer. Hialeah Park race track is in the city.

hiatus hernia: see HERNIA.

Hiawatha, fl. c.1550, legendary chief of the Onandaga, credited with founding the IROQUOIS CONFEDERACY. He is the hero of a well-known poem by Henry Wadsworth LONGFELLOW.

hibernation, protective practice, among certain animals, of spending part of the cold season (when normal body temperatures cannot be maintained and food is scarce) in a state of relative dormancy. Hibernating animals can store enough food in their bodies to survive this period, during which no growth occurs and body activities are at a minimum. Cold-blooded animals (poikilotherms) assume the temperature of the environment and must hibernate when temperatures fall below freezing; frogs and fishes, for example, bury themselves in ponds below the frost line. Most warm-blooded animals (homoiotherms) can survive freezing environments by metabolic control of their body temperatures, although many seek insulation in sheltered places, e.g., bears and bats in caves. Studies have shown that, in addition to living off stored fat, hibernating bears maintain muscle mass and healthy bones by recycling body waste products that normally would be excreted.

hibiscus: see MALLOW.

Hickok, Wild Bill (James Butler Hickok), 1837–76, American frontier marshal; b. near Ottawa, Ill. After becoming marshal of Hays (1869) and Abilene (1871), in Kansas, he gained repute as a marksman from his encounters with outlaws. After his murder in Deadwood (now in South Dakota) by Jack McCall, he became a legend.

hickory, deciduous, nut-bearing tree (genus Carya) of the WALNUT family, native to E North America and Southeast Asia. The shagbark hickory (*C. ovata*) is valued for its edible hickory nuts and strong, resilient wood, often used for golf clubs, tool handles, and furniture. The pecan tree (*C. illinoensis*) and the paper-shelled pecans, the cultivated varieties with unusually thin-shelled nuts, yield pecans, which are among the most popular and commercially important nuts in the U.S.

Hicks, Edward, 1780–1849, American painter and preacher; b. Bucks co., Pa. Untrained in art, he painted primitive works of great charm and appeal. Hicks's fame rests on the nearly 100 versions of his painting *The Peaceable Kingdom.*

Hidalgo y Costilla, Miguel [ēthäl'gō ē kōstē'yä], 1753–1811, Mexican priest and revolutionary hero. In 1810 he rebelled against Spanish rule and, with a huge, almost entirely native army, won the initial battles. But he was defeated (1817) by a royalist army at Calderón Bridge and was captured, defrocked, and executed.

Hidatsa: see MANDAN; GROS VENTRE.

Hideyoshi (Hideyoshi Toyotomi) [hēdäō'shē], 1536–98, Japanese warrior and dictator. He was a general in the dictator Nobunga's service, and after Nobunga's death (1582) he set out to unify Japan. In 1580 he came to terms with IEYASU, and by 1590, with the defeat of the Hojo clan, he was the ruler of a unified Japan. Hideyoshi fostered foreign trade and beautified his capital, Osaka. In 1592 his campaign against China subdued only Korea.

hieratic: see HIEROGLYPHIC.

hieroglyphic [Gr., = priestly carving], type of writing used in ancient EGYPT. Similar pictographic styles of Crete, Asia Minor, and Central America and Mexico are also called hieroglyphics. Interpretation of Egyptian hieroglyphics, begun by J.F. CHAMPOLLION, is virtually complete; the other hieroglyphics are still imperfectly understood. Hieroglyphics are conventionalized pictures used chiefly to represent meanings that seem arbitrary and are seldom obvious. Egyptian hieroglyphics were already perfected in the first dynasty (3110–2884 B.C.), but they began to go out of use in the Middle Kingdom and after 500 B.C. were virtually unused. There were basically 604 symbols that might be put to three uses (although few were used for all three purposes): as an ideogram, as when a sign resembling a tree meant "tree"; as a phonogram, as when an owl represented the sign *m,* because the word for owl had *m* as its principal consonant; or as a determinative, an unpronounced symbol placed after an ambiguous sign to indicate its classification (e.g., an eye to indicate that the preceding word has to do with looking or seeing). The phonograms provided a basis for the development of the ALPHABET.

Examples of hieroglyphics

Higginson, Thomas Wentworth, 1823–1911, American author; b. Cambridge, Mass. A minister and abolitionist, he was also a versatile writer whose books include an account of his CIVIL WAR experiences, a novel, and literary biographies. With M.L. Todd he was the editor of Emily DICKINSON's *Poems* (1890–91).

Highlands, mountainous region, N Scotland. Famous for its rugged beauty, it consists roughly of that part of Scotland north of the imaginary line from Dumbarton to Stonehaven, excluding the Orkneys, the Shetlands, and lower coastal areas. Farming, fishing, and distilling are the main occupations; tourism is also important. Early history is not well known, but by the 11th cent. the Scottish monarchy was centered in the Lowlands, and the Highland lairds were left to run their own affairs. In the early 18th cent. Highlanders strongly supported the JACOBITE uprisings. Until the 19th cent. the Scottish Gaelic language was the core of a Highland culture marked by the clan system and distinctive dress (kilt, tartan, etc.). In 1975 the former counties of the region were reorganized into Highland, one of Scotland's nine administrative units.

Hilbert, David, 1862–1943, German mathematician. After work on the theory of invariants, he developed a new approach that foreshadowed 20th-cent. abstract algebra. Hilbert also made important contributions to algebraic number theory and to functional analysis, particularly in the area of integral equations. His presentation in a 1900 speech of a list of 23 unsolved problems of mathematics stimulated much investigation by 20th-cent. mathematicians. Hilbert taught (1895–1930) at Göttingen Univ., where his breadth of mind and personality attracted to him many students who became important mathematicians.

Hildebrand: see GREGORY VII, SAINT.

Hildegard of Bingen, 1098–1179, German nun, mystic, and cultural figure, known as the Sibyl of the Rhine. An aristocrat and child visionary, she entered religious life (c.1116) and became abbess in 1136. Her theological magnum opus, *Scivias* (c.1151), contains 26 visions. She also wrote a medical encyclopedia, works of natural history, and musical compositions. Widely proclaimed a saint, she has not been canonized.

Hill, Joe, 1879–1915, Swedish-American union organizer; b. Sweden, as Joseph Hillstrom. He came to the U.S. in 1902 and, as a maritime worker, joined the INDUSTRIAL WORKERS OF THE WORLD in 1910. He wrote many labor songs, including "Casey Jones" and "The Union Scab." Found guilty in 1915 of murdering a prominent Salt Lake City man, Hill was executed. He has become a legendary hero of radical labor.

Hillary, Sir Edmund Percival, 1919–, New Zealand mountain climber and explorer. In 1953 he and Tenzing Norkay of Nepal became the first people to reach the summit of Mt. EVEREST. He led (1958) a party in the first successful overland trek to the South Pole since 1912.

Hillel, fl. 30 B.C.–A.D. 10, Jewish scholar; b. Babylonia. President of the SANHEDRIN, he fostered a systematic, liberal interpretation of Hebrew Scripture and was the spiritual and ethical leader of his generation. SHAMMAI opposed his teachings.

Hillel, organization: see B'NAI B'RITH.

Hilliard, Nicholas, 1537–1619, English miniature painter. The first true miniaturist in England, he was court painter to ELIZABETH I and JAMES I. His meticulous portraits on card, vellum, and the backs of playing cards are elegant and subtle.

Himalayan cat: see under CAT.

Himalayas [hŭmäl'əyəz, hĭmələ'əz], great mountain system of Asia, extending c.1,500 mi (2,410 km) through Pakistan, India, Tibet, Nepal, Sikkim, and Bhutan. For most of its length it comprises two nearly parallel ranges separated by a wide valley in which the INDUS R. flows west and the BRAHMAPUTRA (Yarlung Zangbo) flows east. The northern range is called the Trans-Himalayas. The southern range has three parallel zones: the perpetually snow-covered Great Himalayas, where Mt. EVEREST, the highest mountain in the world, rises to 29,023 ft (8,846 m); the Lesser Himalayas, with elevations of 7,000 to 15,000 ft (2,130 to 4,570 m); and the southernmost Outer Himalayas, 2,000 to 5,000 ft (610 to 1,520 m) high. The Himalayas are associated with many legends in Indian mythology. Simla, Naini Tal, Mussoorie, and Darjeeling are popular summer retreats from the heat of the Indian plains to the south.

Himmler, Heinrich, 1900–1945, German NAZI leader. He was a Nazi from the founding (1920) of the party, and after HITLER came to power, he headed (1936–45) the secret police, or Gestapo. The most ruthless of the Nazi leaders, Himmler was responsible for the death of millions in forced-labor and CONCENTRATION CAMPS. He was also held in fear by members of the Nazi party. In the last years of WORLD WAR II, he was the virtual dictator of German domestic affairs. He was captured by the British in 1945 but committed suicide by taking poison.

Hims or **Homs,** city (1991 est. pop. 435,000), W central Syria. It is a commercial center located in a fertile plain where wheat, grapes, and other crops are grown. The city's manufactures include refined oil and flour and fertilizer. In ancient times called Emesa, it was the site of a temple to BAAL and gained prominence when a temple priest, Heliogabalus, became (A.D. 218) Roman emperor. The Arabs took the town in 636 and renamed it. From the 16th cent. to 1918 the Ottoman Turks ruled it. The French then held it as part of a League of Nations mandate until Syria gained independence (1941).

Hindemith, Paul, 1895–1963, German-American composer and violist; b. Germany. He combined traditional and experimental techniques in a distinctive style. The NAZIS banned his compositions (1937) because of their dissonance and modernity, and he emigrated to the U.S. Hindemith's early compositions are contrapuntal and often atonal (see COUNTERPOINT; ATONALITY). Later he returned to a tonality some have called neoclassical. His best-known work is a symphony (1934) drawn from his opera *Mathis the Painter* (1938). In addition to other operas, sonatas, and chamber works, he wrote *Ludus Tonalis* (1943) for piano and the song cycle *The Life of Mary* (1923, 1948).

Hindenburg, Paul von, 1847–1934, German field marshal and president (1925–34). In WORLD WAR I he won victories on the eastern front, especially the battle of Tannenberg (1914), making him the greatest German hero of the war. Although a monarchist, he supported the new republican government in 1918 and was elected president in 1925. In the election of 1932 he defeated HITLER and was reelected, but he was persuaded to appoint (1933) Hitler chancellor. He was figurehead president until his death.

Hindenburg: see AIRSHIP.

Hindi [hĭn'dē], language belonging to the Indic group of the Indo-European family of languages. It is the official language of India. See LANGUAGE (table).

Hinduism, Western term for the religious beliefs and practices of innumerable sects to which the vast majority of the people of India belong. Arising initially as a synthesis of indigenous religion and the religion brought to India c.1500 B.C. by the ARYANS, Hinduism developed in syncretism with the religious and cultural movements of the Indian subcontinent. Hindu belief is generally characterized by the CASTE system and the acceptance of the VEDA as sacred scripture. The Veda, which comprises the liturgy and interpretation of sacrificial ritual, culminates in the UPANISHADS, mystical and speculative works that state the doctrine of BRAHMAN, the absolute reality or Self, and its identity with the individual soul, or *atman.* The goal of Hinduism, like that of other Eastern religions, is liberation from the cycle of rebirth and the suffering brought about by one's own actions (see KARMA); this can be effected by following spiritual YOGA, practices leading to knowledge of reality and union with God. Early Brahmanism, the religion of the priests, or Brahmans (who through Vedic ritual sacrifice established a proper relation to the gods), was challenged in the first millennium B.C. by non-Vedic systems such as BUDDHISM and JAINISM. To meet the challenge, the Brahmans recognized popular devotional movements and showed greater concern for the people. Writings like the laws of MANU regulated DHARMA (duty) according to one's class (priest, warrior, farmer or merchant, laborer) and stage in life (celibate student, householder, forest recluse, one who completely renounces societal ties). The post-Vedic Puranas deal with this structure of individual and social life and also describe the repeating cycle of birth and dissolution of the universe, represented by the divine trinity of Brahma, the creator; Vishnu, the preserver; and Shiva, the destroyer. In medieval times, TANTRA and devotional sects flourished, producing poet-saints who wrote religious songs and epics. This literature still plays an essential part in Hinduism, as does the practice of *puja,* or worship of enshrined deities such as Vishnu and his incarnations Rama and Krishna, Shiva, Ganesha, and Devi (also called Kali, Sarasvati, or Lakshmi). Many modern Hindu leaders, e.g., Swami Vivekananda, Mohandas GANDHI, and Aurobindo GHOSE, have stressed the necessity of uniting spiritual life with social concerns. A Hindu revival in the late 20th cent. has led to a political movement to replace the secular Indian state with a Hindu one and to renewed tensions between Indian Hindus and Muslims.

Hindu Kush, one of the highest mountain systems in the world, extending c.500 mi (800 km) west from Pamir Knot, N Pakistan, into NE Afghanistan. Tirich Mir (25,236 ft/7,692 m) is the highest point. Meltwater from the permanently snow-covered peaks feeds the headstreams of the AMU DARYA and INDUS rivers. Several high-altitude passes, followed by trade routes, cross the mountains, once called the Caucasus Indicus.

Hindustani, subdivision of the Indic group of the Indo-Iranian subfamily of the Indo-European family of languages. See LANGUAGE (table).

Hines, Earl "Fatha," 1905–83, African-American jazz pianist and composer; b. Duquesne, Pa. In the 1920s, while working for Louis ARMSTRONG, Hines transformed the role of the piano in JAZZ by making it a solo instrument. His nickname came from a radio announcer's acknowledgment of his role as "the father of modern jazz piano."

hip-hop: see RAP MUSIC.

Hipparchus, fl. 2d cent. B.C., Greek astronomer; b. Bithynia (present-day Turkey). Ptolemy's geocentric theory of the universe (see PTOLEMAIC SYSTEM) was based largely on the conclusions of Hipparchus. In Ptolemy's *Almagest,* Hipparchus is credited with discovering the PRECESSION OF THE EQUINOXES, the eccentricity of the sun's apparent orbit, and certain inequalities of the moon's motions. He also made the first known comprehensive chart of the heavens.

Hippocrates, c.460–c.370 B.C., Greek physician, recognized as the father of medicine. He is believed to have been born on the island of Cos, where he later practiced and taught. Hippocrates based medicine on objective observation and deductive reasoning. Although he accepted the belief that disease results from an imbalance of the four bodily humors, he maintained that the humors were glandular secretions and that outside forces influenced the disturbance. He taught that medicine should build the patient's strength through diet and hygiene, resorting to more drastic treatment only when necessary. The **Hippocratic Oath,** an ethical code formulated in ancient Greece and still administered to medical graduates in many modern universities, cannot be directly credited to him, but it does represent his ideals and principles.

Hippolytus: see PHAEDRA.

hippopotamus, river-dwelling MAMMAL (*Hippopotamus amphibius*) of tropical Africa, related to the pig (see SWINE). The male stands about 5 ft (160 cm) at the shoulder and weighs about 5 tons (4,500 kg). The broad, short-legged body has a thick brown or gray hide, and the eyes are near the top of the head, so the animal can see when submerged. Hippopotamuses live in small herds, feeding on aquatic plants. Hunted for meat and hides, they are endangered.

Hirohito, 1901–89, emperor of Japan. Made regent in 1921, he succeeded his father, Taisho, as emperor in 1926. Hirohito helped persuade the Japanese government to accept unconditional surrender at the end of WORLD WAR II. In 1946 he renounced the idea of imperial divinity and was stripped of all but ceremonial powers by a new constitution. His son, AKIHITO, succeeded him.

Hiroshige (Ando Hiroshige) [hērō'shēgā"], 1797–1858, Japanese painter and color-print artist of the *ukiyo-e* school (see JAPANESE ART). Among his works is a landscape series, *Fifty-three Stages of the Tokaido Highway* (1833), and rain, mist, and moonlight scenes that influenced WHISTLER.

Hiroshima, city (1990 pop. 1,085,677), capital of Hiroshima prefecture, SW Honshu, Japan. Founded c.1594, the city is divided by the Ota R. into six islands. A commercial and industrial center, it manufactures ships, motor vehicles, steel, rubber, and furniture. Hiroshima was the target (Aug. 6, 1945) of the first ATOMIC BOMB ever dropped on a city: casualties numbered nearly 130,000 and 90% of the city was leveled. Most of Hiroshima has been rebuilt, but a gutted area, the "Peace City," has been set aside as a memorial.

Hirsch, Samson Raphael, 1808–88, German rabbi and chief exponent of Neo-Orthodoxy. He sought to combine traditional Jewish studies with secular learning (*Nineteen Letters,* 1836) and condemned the Reform movement (see JUDAISM) for breaking with tradition.

Hirshhorn Museum and Sculpture Garden, Washington, D.C., opened 1974. Part of the SMITHSONIAN INSTITUTION, it was designed by Gordon BUNSHAFT to house 6,000 pieces of the huge art collection of industrialist Joseph H. Hirshhorn, who gave them to the nation in 1966; the remainder of his collection was bequeathed to the museum upon his death in 1981. It was Washington's first museum devoted exclusively to modern art and is very rich in sculpture, POP ART, OP ART, COLOR FIELD PAINTING, and PHOTOREALISM.

Hishikawa Moronobu: see MORONOBU.

Hispaniola, 29,530 sq mi (76,483 sq km), subtropical island with abundant rainfall, in the WEST INDIES. It is divided between HAITI (W) and the DOMINICAN REPUBLIC. The island was discovered in 1492 by Columbus and has at times been known as Española and Saint-Domingue.

Hiss, Alger, 1904–, U.S. public official; b. Baltimore. He served (1936–47) in the Dept. of State, becoming a foreign policy coordinator. In 1948 Whittaker Chambers, an editor who was a confessed Communist courier, accused Hiss of helping to transmit confidential government documents to the Soviets. Hiss denied the charges and was indicted for perjury by a grand jury. His first trial ended in a hung jury, but in a second trial (1950) he was found guilty and served four years in prison. In 1992 a high-ranking Russian official said he had found no evidence in the archives of the former USSR that Hiss had been a spy.

Hissarlik: see TROY.

histamine, organic compound derived from the amino acid histidine. Histamine is released from certain cells upon tissue injury or by the action of certain antibodies (see IMMUNITY). It then tends to dilate capillaries and to make them more permeable, which may lead to edema (tissue swelling) and hives, accompanied by severe itching. This reaction, common to many allergies, can often be controlled with ANTIHISTAMINES.

histology, study of the groups of specialized cells called TISSUES, found in most multicellular plants and animals. Histologists study tissue organization at all levels, from the whole organ to the molecular components of cells. Histological techniques include tissue culture, fixing and staining, light and electron microscopy, and X-ray diffraction. In medicine, histological techniques are used to identify diseased tissue.

historical linguistics: see LINGUISTICS.

Hitchcock, Alfred, 1899–1980, Anglo-American film director; b. London. A master of suspense, he made such films as *The Lady Vanishes* (1938), *Notorious* (1946), *Strangers on a Train* (1951), *Psycho* (1960), and *Frenzy* (1972).

Alfred Hitchcock

Hitler, Adolf, 1889–1945, German dictator, founder and leader of NATIONAL SOCIALISM, or Nazism; b. Austria. In World War I he served in the Bavarian army, was gassed and wounded, and received the Iron Cross (first class) for bravery. The war embittered him, and he blamed Germany's defeat on the Jews and Marxists. Settling in Munich, he joined with other nationalists to found (1920) the Nazi party. In the famous "beer-hall putsch" (1923), Hitler attempted to overthrow BAVARIA's republican government, but the army put down the revolt, and Hitler was imprisoned. He thus became known throughout Germany and used his nine months in prison to write *Mein Kampf* [my struggle], filled with anti-Semitism, power worship, disdain for morality, and his strategy for world domination. It became the bible of the Nazi party. The Nazi movement grew slowly until 1929, when the economic depression brought it mass support. Hitler made prime use of his frenzied but magnetic oratory of hate and power, his insight into mass psychology, and his mastery of deceitful strategy, or the "big lie." He used his virulent ANTI-SEMITISM and anti-Communism to win the support both of the workers and of the bankers and industrialists. Although he was defeated when he ran for president in 1932, Pres. Paul von HINDENBURG was persuaded to name him chancellor (1933), and the REICHSTAG gave him dictatorial powers. With other Nazi leaders, among them GOERING, HIMMLER, and GOEBBELS, he crushed the opposition and took control of all facets of German life. Anti-Semitism was enacted into law, and CONCENTRATION CAMPS were established. In 1934, voters approved the union of the presidency and chancellorship in Hitler's person. His aggressive foreign policy, abetted by English and French appeasement, culminated in the triumph of the MUNICH PACT (1938). As he prepared Germany for war, he bullied smaller nations into making territorial concessions. He became allied with MUSSOLINI in Italy, and he helped FRANCO come to power in Spain. Austria was absorbed into the "Third Reich," and Czechoslovakia was dismembered. In 1939 he signed a nonaggression pact with the Soviet Union that gave him a free hand to invade Poland. With that act WORLD WAR II began, and Hitler took complete control of Germany's war efforts. At first Germany was triumphant, but the tide turned, and by July 1944 the German military situation was desperate. Despite a well-planned assassination attempt against him, in which he was injured, Hitler remained in charge and insisted that Germany fight to the death. As the Third Reich collapsed, Hitler remained in an underground bunker in Berlin while the Russians approached the city. On April 29, 1945, he married his longtime mistress, Eva BRAUN, and on April 30 they committed suicide. He left Germany a devastated nation. Hitler's legacy is the memory of the most dreadful tyranny of modern centuries.

Hittite, language belonging to the Anatolian subfamily of the Indo-European family of languages. See LANGUAGE (table).

Hittites, ancient people of Asia Minor and Syria who flourished from 1600 to 1200 B.C. The Hittites, a people of Indo-European connection, were supposed to have entered Cappadocia around 1800 B.C. The Hittite empire, with its capital at BOĞAZKÖY (also called Hattusas), was the chief power and cultural force in W Asia from 1400 to 1200 B.C. It was a loose confederation that broke up under the invasions (c.1200 B.C.) of the Thracians, Phrygians, and Assyrians. The neo-Hittite kingdom (c.1050–c.700 B.C.) that followed was conquered by the Assyrians. The Hittites were one of the first peoples to smelt iron successfully. They spoke an Indo-European language.

HIV or **human immunodeficiency virus:** see AIDS.

Ho, chemical symbol of the element HOLMIUM.

Hoban, James, c.1762–1831, American architect; b. Ireland. He designed and built (1792–99) the WHITE HOUSE, which he rebuilt after the British burned it in 1814. He was also a supervising architect in the building of the CAPITOL.

Hobbema, Meindert [hôb'əma], 1638–1709, Dutch painter, considered the last of the great 17th-cent. Dutch landscape painters (see landscape painting). His paintings of woodland scenes, country villages, water mills, and other rustic subjects are full of life and luminosity, with bold execution and color. His best-known works include *The Mill* (Louvre) and *Entrance to a Village* (Metropolitan Mus.).

Hobbes, Thomas, 1588–1679, English philosopher. Hobbes developed a materialist and highly pessimistic philosophy that was denounced in his own day and later but has had a continuing influence on Western political thought. His *Leviathan* (1651) presents a bleak picture of human beings in the state of nature, where life is "nasty, brutish, and short." Fear of violent death is the principal motive that causes people to create a state, contracting to surrender their natural rights and to submit to the absolute authority of a sovereign. Although the power of the sovereign derived originally from the people, Hobbes said—challenging the doctrine of the divine right of kings—the sovereign's power is absolute and not subject to review by either subjects or ecclesiastical powers. Hobbes's concept of the SOCIAL CONTRACT led to investigations by other political theorists, notably LOCKE, SPINOZA, and J.J. ROUSSEAU, who formulated their own radically different theories of the social contract.

Hobby, Oveta Culp, 1905–, U.S. public official and publisher; b. Killeen, Tex. She was (1943–45) the first director of the Women's Army Corps and served (1953–55) as the first secretary of the Dept. of Health, Education, and Welfare. She was editor (1952–53, 1955–83), president (1955–65) and (1965–83) chairman of the board of the Houston *Post.*

Ho Chi Minh [hô chē mĭn], 1890–1969, Vietnamese nationalist leader, president of North VIETNAM (1954–69). In 1911 he left Vietnam and lived in London, the U.S., and France, where he became (1920) a founding member of the French Communist party. He later lived in Moscow, but he returned to Vietnam in World War II and organized a Vietnamese independence movement, the Viet Minh. He raised an army to fight the Japanese, and in the French Indochina war (1946–54), he defeated the French colonial regime. After the Geneva Conference (1954), which divided Vietnam, Ho became the first president of North Vietnam. In his last years he led the North's struggle to defeat the U.S.-supported government of South Vietnam (see VIETNAM WAR).

Ho Chi Minh City, formerly **Saigon,** city (1989 pop. 3,169,135), S Vietnam, on the Saigon R. It is a large river port and industrial center producing textiles, ships, processed foods, motor vehicles, and other goods. An ancient settlement in the KHMER EMPIRE, Saigon grew into a city under French rule in the 19th cent. It became the capital of South Vietnam in 1954. Military headquarters for U.S. and South Vietnamese forces during the VIETNAM WAR, it was heavily damaged and faced the overcrowding created by the influx of over 1 million refugees. It was renamed at the end of the war. Built in the European style, it is the seat of several universities.

hockey, field, outdoor stick-and-ball game similar to SOCCER. It is played on a field measuring 50 to 60 yd by 90 to 100 yd (46 to 55 m by 82 to 91 m) by two teams of 11 players each. Teams attempt to advance the ball down the field with their wooden sticks. A point is scored by delivering the ball past the goalkeeper through the goal posts, which are joined by a net. Of ancient origin, field hockey was played in England for centuries before it spread to other countries. In the U.S., field hockey for women has been popular since 1901, especially in colleges and high schools.

hockey, ice, winter skating sport in which players use sticks to propel a rubber disk into a net-enclosed goal. A rough sport, it is played chiefly by men, who wear heavy protective gear. The rink, which is divided into three zones (attacking, neutral, and defending), measures up to 200 ft (61 m) in length and 98 ft (30 m) in width. A team consists of six players, including a goalie, all of whom wear ice skates. Play is directed toward advancing the disk (called a puck) with flat-bladed sticks and striking it into the goals at each end of the rink. A goal counts one point. A player who violates the rules is removed to the penalty box for two minutes or more while his team plays shorthanded. Ice hockey originated in Canada in the 1870s and later spread to the U.S. and other northern countries. It has been an Olympic event since 1920. The professional National Hockey League (founded 1917) is made up of 26 teams representing U.S. and Canadian cities. The annual Stanley Cup playoffs determine the league championship.

Hockney, David, 1937–, English artist. He has lived in the U.S. since the 1960s. His realistic, witty, clearly illuminated compositions often contain elements of POP ART. A superb draftsman, he has executed several print series, designed stage sets, and produced mosaic-like photo montages.

Hodgkin, Sir Alan Lloyd, 1914–, English biophysicist. For their work in analyzing the electrical and chemical events in nerve-cell discharge, he and Andrew HUXLEY shared with Sir John Eccles the 1963 Nobel Prize in physiology or medicine. He was a research professor of the Royal Society (1952–69) and professor of biophysics at Cambridge Univ. (1970–81).

Hodgkin, Dorothy Mary Crowfoot, 1910–, English chemist and X-ray crystallographer; b. Egypt. She received the 1964 Nobel Prize in chemistry for determining the structure of biochemical compounds (particularly of vitamin B_{12}) used to control pernicious anemia. In 1933 she and J.D. Bernal made the first X-ray photograph of a protein (pepsin). She was president (1977–78) of the British Association for the Advancement of Science.

Hodgkin's disease, chronic malignant disorder of the lymph nodes; the commonest form of lymphoma. Symptoms vary but often include enlargement of one or more lymph nodes, particularly in the neck region, followed by fatigue, loss of weight, and fever. As the disease progresses, other lymph nodes and organs may become involved. It is often treated effectively with radiation and CHEMOTHERAPY.

Hoffa, James Riddle, 1913–1975?, American labor leader; b. Brazil, Ind. In 1957 he became president of the TEAMSTERS UNION, which was expelled from the AFL-CIO that year because of evidence of union corruption. Hoffa's power continued to grow, however, and by 1964 he was able to effect the trucking industry's first national contract. In the same year he was convicted in two separate trials for jury tampering and fraud. Imprisoned in 1967, he retained the Teamster presidency until 1971, when Pres. Nixon commuted his sentence, with the proviso that he not engage in union activity until 1980. Hoffa disappeared in 1975 and is widely assumed to have been murdered.

Hoffman, Dustin, 1937–, American actor; b. Los Angeles. He began his career on Broadway but became popular with his first major film, *The Graduate* (1967). Known for his acute characterizations, he has appeared in such films as *Midnight Cowboy* (1969), *Kramer vs. Kramer* (1980; Academy Award), *Tootsie* (1982), and *Rain Man* (1989; Academy Award).

Hoffman, Malvina, 1887–1966, American sculptor; b. N.Y.C. She was a pupil of RODIN. Her most notable achievement is a series of 100 bronze statues of racial types (Field Mus., Chicago). She is also known for her spirited figures and her portrait busts.

Hoffmann, Ernest Theodor Amadeus [hŏf'män], 1776–1822, German romantic novelist and composer. His gothic tales of madness, grotesquerie, and the supernatural include *The Serapion Brethren* (1819–21) and *Kater Murr, the Educated Cat* (1821–22). OFFENBACH's opera *Tales of Hoffmann* is based on three of his stories.

Hofmann, Hans, 1880–1966, American painter; b. Germany. After emigrating to the U.S. in 1930, he opened two art schools (N.Y.C. and Provincetown, Mass.) that were central to the development of ABSTRACT EXPRESSIONISM. His own exuberant canvases combine violent, clashing colors.

Hofmannsthal, Hugo von [hōf'mänstäl], 1874–1929, Austrian dramatist and poet. *Electra* (1903), *Der Rosenkavalier* (1911), and *Ariadne auf Naxos* (1912) are librettos written for Richard STRAUSS. Also notable are his *Poems* (1903), the tragedy *The Tower* (1925), and his adaptation of *Everyman* (1911).

hog: see SWINE.

Hogan, Ben, 1912–, American golfer; b. Dublin, Tex. One of the game's leading money winners, he won nine major championships, beginning with the Professional Golfers' Association title in 1946. His greatest victories, notably a sweep of the U.S. Open, British Open, and Masters crowns in 1953, came after recovery from a near-fatal automobile accident in 1949. Hogan was the first since Bobby JONES to capture four U.S. Open titles.

Hogarth, William, 1697–1764, English painter, satirist, engraver, and art theorist. His first real success came in 1732 with a series of six morality pictures, *The Harlot's Progress,* first painted and then engraved. *The Rake's Progress* (1735) followed. In the series *Marriage à la Mode,* considered his masterpiece, he depicts the inane, profligate existence of a fashionable couple with great detail and brilliant characterization. His *Analysis of Beauty* (1753) is a treatise on the ROCOCO aesthetic. In such prints as *Gin Lane,* he satirizes cruelty and stupidity. His portraits *The Shrimp Girl* (National Gall., London) and *Captain Coram* (1740) are masterpieces of British painting.

hog cholera, infectious viral disease of swine; also called swine fever. Perhaps the most serious disease of hogs in North America, it is characterized by listlessness, temperature increase, muscle tremors, and convulsions. Mortality is high; recovered hogs are permanently stunted.

Hohenstaufen [hō"ənshtou'fən], German princely family of the 11th to 13th cent. They were dukes of Swabia from 1079; German kings and Holy Roman emperors, 1138–1254; and kings of Sicily, 1194–1266. Their chief rivals were the Guelphs (see GUELPHS AND GHIBELLINES), who sided with the papacy in the long struggle between emperor and pope.

Hohenzollern, German princely family that ruled from the 11th cent. until 1918. They ruled BRANDENBURG (1415–1918), PRUSSIA (1525–1918), and Germany (1871–1918). They comprised two main branches (the Swabian and the Franconian) and held various titles, including that of burgrave, margrave, duke, and elector. In 1701 Frederick I styled himself "king in Prussia," and thereafter the members of the Franconian branch held that title. After Germany was unified in 1871, three Hohenzollern emperors (or kaisers), WILLIAM I, FREDERICK III, and WILLIAM II, reigned.

Hohokam, ancient agricultural culture of S Arizona (c.300–1200 A.D.). The Hohokam are noted for their extensive irrigation systems but also built sunken ball-courts, pyramidal mounds, and other structures similar to those of central Mexico. Most archaeologists believe that Hohokam culture evolved from local antecedents, although they did trade with more southerly groups. Their fate and possible ancestry of the PIMA and TOHONO O'ODHAM (Papago) is widely disputed.

Hokan-Siouan, linguistic stock, or family, whose member languages are spoken by indigenous peoples in North America. See NATIVE AMERICAN LANGUAGES (table).

Hokkaido, island (1990 pop. 5,643,515), Japan, second largest (c.30,130 sq mi/78,040 sq km), northernmost, and most sparsely populated of Japan's major islands. It is separated from HONSHU island by the Tsuguru Strait and from SAKHALIN (held by Russia but also claimed by Japan) by the Soya Strait. The rugged, partly volcanic interior reaches a high point of 7,511 ft (2,289 m) at Asahi-dake. Forests, providing lumber, pulp, and paper, cover much of the island, and there are important coal, iron ore, and manganese deposits. The AINU, the original inhabitants, became a minority after Japan began a policy of settling the island after 1868. SAPPORO is the chief city.

Hokusai (Katsushika Hokusai), 1760–1849, Japanese painter, draftsman, and wood engraver, one of the foremost *ukiyo-e* print designers (see JAPANESE ART). He used over 50 different names. His prodigious output included book illustrations, printed cards, and landscapes in a variety of styles. His technical excellence and observant delineation of contemporary life can be seen in *Mangwa, or Ten Thousand Sketches* (15 vol., 1814–78) and *Views of Mt. Fuji.*

Katsushika Hokusai woodblock print Fuji in Clear Weather

Holbein, Hans [hôl'bīn], the Elder, c.1465–1524, German painter and draftsman. His early work is heavily influenced by the Flemish style, e.g., the *Life of the Virgin* (Augsburg Cathedral). Later altarpieces, done after 1500, e.g., those of the *Basilica of St. Paul* and of *St. Catherine* (both: Augsburg), show Italian influence. He also designed STAINED GLASS windows and remarkable silverpoint drawings. His younger son, **Hans Holbein,** the Younger, c.1497–1543, an outstanding portrait and religious painter of the northern RENAISSANCE, started his career early. In Basel, Switzerland, he illustrated ERASMUS's *Praise of Folly* and in 1519 was admitted to that city's painters' guild. During this period he decorated many buildings and painted the *Passion Scenes* and the celebrated *Dead Christ* (both: Basel); the altarpiece of the *Madonna with St. Ursus and a Bishop Saint* (Solothurn, Switzerland); and his famous *Madonna of the Burgomaster Meyer* (Darmstadt, Germany). In these works and in the portraits of Erasmus and Boniface Amerbach (Basel), he shows his full genius. The larger conception, monumental composition, and idealization of characters show Italian influence. In England from 1526 to 1528, he painted a fine group of portraits, including one of Sir Thomas More (Frick Coll., N.Y.C.), all of which reveal his exquisite gift for characterization. He returned to England in his last years and did his famous portrait of Christine of Denmark and *The French Ambassadors* (both: National Gall., London). He was also court painter to HENRY VIII and painted numerous portraits of the king and his wives. His preliminary drawings and woodcuts are also famous.

Hölderlin, Friedrich [höl'dərlĭn], 1770–1843, German lyric poet. He is considered a link between the classic and romantic schools. Before his mind failed at 36, he wrote lofty yet subjective poetry modeled on classic Greek verse. *Hyperion* (1797–99) is an elegaic novel in prose; he also wrote a dramatic fragment, *The Death of Empedocles* (1799).

holding company: see TRUST.

Holiday, Billie, 1915–59, African-American singer; b. Baltimore as Eleanora Fagan. She began singing in 1930 and earned a supreme position among modern JAZZ singers with her emotional impact and highly personal approach to a song. Her life was complicated by the drug addiction that eventually destroyed her career and hastened her death.

Holinshed, Raphael or **Ralph** [hŏl'ĭnz-hĕd"], d. c.1580, English chronicler. With the assistance of William Harrison and Richard Stanihurst, he wrote the famous *Chronicles of England, Scotland,*

and Ireland (1577), from which SHAKESPEARE and other Elizabethan dramatists drew material for plays.

holistic medicine, system of health care based on a concept of the "whole" person as one whose body, mind, spirit, and emotions are in balance with the environment. Stressing personal responsibility for health, a holistic approach may include conventional medicine and various nontraditional methods of diagnosis and therapy, e.g., ACUPUNCTURE, BIOFEEDBACK, faith healing, folk medicine, megavitamin therapy, MEDITATION, and YOGA. Surgery and prescription drugs are generally avoided; instead, patients are encouraged to establish self-regulated regimes to control such illness-related factors as poor diet, smoking, alcohol intake, and stress. See also ALTERNATIVE MEDICINE.

Holland, former county of the HOLY ROMAN EMPIRE and, from 1579 to 1795, the chief member of the United Provinces of the Netherlands. Its name has been popularly applied to the entire Netherlands. Since 1840 the area has been divided into two provinces, North and South Holland. The original county was created in the 10th cent. and was controlled (14th–15th cent.) in turn by the WITTELSBACH family, BURGUNDY, and the HAPSBURGS. Holland led (16th–17th cent.) the struggle for Dutch independence, and its history became virtually identical with that of the Netherlands.

Hollerith, Herman, 1860–1929, American inventor; b. Buffalo, N.Y. He developed a system that used cards with punched holes to encode data, as well as machines to punch and tabulate the cards. In 1896 he founded the Tabulating Machine Company, predecessor of the International Business Machines Company (IBM).

holly, common name for trees and shrubs of the Aquifoliaceae family, widely distributed but most numerous in Central and South America. Many are cultivated as ornamentals. The English holly (*Ilex aquifolium*) and the American holly (*I. opaca*) are popular for their hard white wood and decorative spiny leaves and red berries. Some hollies are sources of tea, such as MATÉ, and medicinal preparations.

hollyhock: see MALLOW.

Hollywood. **1** Community (1985 est. pop. 250,000), part of the city of LOS ANGELES, S Calif., on the slopes of the Santa Monica Mts.; inc. 1903, consolidated with Los Angeles 1910. Long the center of the U.S. movie industry (its first film was made c.1911), it draws many tourists, but most film and television companies have moved to nearby areas or the suburbs. Its crowded and lively Hollywood Blvd. and Sunset Strip are famous. **2** City (1990 pop. 121,697), Broward co., SE Fla., on the Atlantic coast, N of Miami; inc. 1925. A resort and retirement center, it has electronics and building-materials industries. Most of Port Everglades, the area's largest port, is located there.

Holmes, Oliver Wendell, 1809–94, American author and physician; b. Cambridge, Mass.; father of Oliver Wendell HOLMES, Jr. A professor at Harvard medical school (1847–82), he wrote a number of important medical papers. Holmes's most familiar poems include "Old Ironsides," "The Chambered Nautilus," and the ironic "Deacon's Masterpiece." His witty series of sketches, originally published in the *Atlantic Monthly*, were collected in *The Autocrat of the Breakfast-Table* (1858) and other volumes. Holmes also wrote pioneering psychological novels, e.g., *Elsie Venner* (1861), and biographies.

Holmes, Oliver Wendell, Jr., 1841–1935, associate justice of the U.S. SUPREME COURT (1902–32); b. Boston; LL.B., Harvard Univ. (1886). A profound scholar, Holmes achieved international recognition in 1881 with publication of *The Common Law*, in which he attacked prevailing views of jurisprudence. He was associate justice (1882–99) and chief justice (1899–1902) of the Massachusetts supreme judicial court. On the U.S. Supreme Court, he advocated "judicial restraint." From his eloquent and frequent disagreements with his more conservative colleagues over the nullification of social legislation, Holmes came to be known as the Great Dissenter.

Holmes, Sherlock: see DOYLE, SIR ARTHUR CONAN.

holmium (Ho), metallic element, discovered independently by J.L. Soret and M. Delafontaine in 1878 and by Per Teodor Cleve in 1879. The soft, malleable, lustrous, silvery metal is in the LANTHANIDE SERIES. Holmium and its oxides and salts have no commercial uses. See ELEMENT (table); PERIODIC TABLE.

Holocaust, name given to the period (1933–1945) of persecution and extermination of European Jews by Nazi GERMANY. After Adolf HITLER's rise to power in 1933, most Jews who did not flee Germany were sent to CONCENTRATION CAMPS. With the outbreak of WORLD WAR II, Hitler began to implement his "final solution of the Jewish question": the extermination of Jews in all countries conquered by his armies. By the end of the war, 6 million Jews had been systematically murdered and a creative religious and secular community destroyed. A U.S. HOLOCAUST MEMORIAL MUSEUM was dedicated and opened in 1993 in Washington, D.C. See also ANTI-SEMITISM; NATIONAL SOCIALISM; WAR CRIMES.

Holocaust Memorial Museum, in Washington, D.C., designed by James Ingo Freed; opened 1993. Using a harsh architectural vocabulary, the museum immerses visitors in the era of the HOLOCAUST, memorializing its victims by tracing the history of the Holocaust in artifacts, recorded oral histories, documentary films, and photographs.

Holocene epoch: see GEOLOGIC ERA (table).

Holofernes: see JUDITH.

holography, method of reproducing a three-dimensional image of an object by means of light-wave patterns recorded on a photographic plate or film. The object is illuminated with a coherent beam of light produced by a LASER. Before reaching the object, the beam is split into two parts: the reference beam is recorded directly on the photographic plate, and the other is reflected from the object and then is recorded. On the photographic plate the two beams create an INTERFERENCE pattern, exposing the plate at points where they arrive in phase. When this photographic recording, called a hologram, is later illuminated with coherent light of the same frequency as that used to form it, a three-dimensional image of the object becomes visible and the object can be photographed from various angles. Color holograms are formed using three separate exposures with laser beams of each of the primary colors (see COLOR). In **acoustical holography,** a coherent beam of ultrasonic waves (see SOUND), instead of light, is used. The resulting interference pattern is recorded with microphones to form a hologram, which, when viewed with laser light, produces a visible three-dimensional image. Holography has been combined with microscopy to study very small objects; it also is used in industry for stress and vibrational analysis.

Holst, Gustav, 1874–1934, English composer. GRIEG, Richard STRAUSS, and VAUGHAN WILLIAMS were early influences. His outstanding works are *The Planets* (1914–16), an orchestral SUITE; *The Hymn of Jesus* (1917), for chorus and orchestra; and the orchestral piece *Egdon Heath* (1927).

Holt, Helen Maud: see under TREE, SIR HERBERT BEERBOHM.

Holy Alliance, 1815, agreement among the emperors of Russia and Austria and the king of Prussia. It was part of the complex redesign of the political fabric of Europe after the fall of the Napoleonic empire and was an attempt by conservative monarchs to preserve the social order. It was engineered by METTERNICH, and eventually almost all the princes of Europe signed the agreement. Although it accomplished nothing specific, it became a symbol of reaction. Opposition to it was a major aim of British foreign policy.

Holy Ghost or **Holy Spirit,** in Christian doctrine, the third person of the TRINITY, sometimes described as the aspect of God immanent in this world, in people, and in the church. Its descent upon the APOSTLES, giving them the gift of tongues (Acts 2), is commemorated on Pentecost (Whitsunday). The dove is the symbol of the Holy Ghost.

Holy League, alliance formed (1510–11) by Pope JULIUS II during the ITALIAN WARS to expel LOUIS XII of France from Italy. It included Venice, the Swiss cantons, the Spanish king FERDINAND V, HENRY VIII of England, and Holy Roman emperor MAXIMILIAN I. It fell apart after Julius's death (1513).

holy orders, in Christianity, the traditional degrees of the clergy, conferred by the Sacrament of Holy Order. The Roman Catholic Church, like the Church of England, has three orders: bishop, priest, and deacon, and like the Orthodox Eastern churches it has permanent deacons, who serve in local parishes. The bishop heads a diocese consisting of many parishes; a priest may be the head of a parish or a member of a religious order. Monsignor and cardinal are honorary titles, unidentified with any particular office.

Holy Roman Empire, designation for the political entity that originated at the coronation as emperor of German king OTTO I in 962 and endured until the renunciation of the title by FRANCIS II in 1806. It was the successor state to the empire founded in 800 by CHARLEMAGNE, who claimed legitimate succession to the Roman Empire. In theory, just as the pope was the vicar of God on earth in spiritual matters, so the emperor was God's temporal vicar; hence he claimed to be the supreme temporal ruler in Christendom. Actually, the power of the emperors never equaled their pretensions. Their suzerainty never included the East, and it ceased early over France, Denmark, Poland, and Hungary. Their control over England, Sweden, and Spain was never more than nominal, and their control over Italy was always in contention. The core of the empire was the various German principalities, plus Austria, Bohemia, and Moravia. Switzerland, the Netherlands, and parts of northern Italy were at times included. Its rulers were chosen by the princes of Germany until 1356, after which they were elected by a fixed number of ELECTORS. They elected the German king (later known as king of the Romans). He became emperor only when crowned by the pope in Rome. After 1562, however, emperors-elect dispensed with coronation by the pope and were crowned at Frankfurt. Emperors held immediate jurisdiction only over their hereditary family domains (e.g., the Saxon dynasty over Saxony) and over the imperial free cities. The rest of the empire they controlled only to the extent to which they influenced the imperial Diet. Important also was the relative power of the papacy at any given period. The conflict between pope and emperor was a never-ending one. A longtime dispute was over the right of INVESTITURE, an issue finally settled in the church's favor by the Concordat of Worms (1122). Political control of Italy was another source of conflict. In addition to being a spiritual leader, the pope was also a great temporal power there; and popes were generally jealous of efforts by the emperors to extend their political control over the various Italian states. The feud between the GUELPHS AND GHIBELLINES dramatized the conflict. Although the emperorship was technically an elective office, after 1438 the HAPSBURG dynasty became permanently entrenched. Thereafter, the hereditary domains of the Hapsburgs were the primary concerns of the emperors. The domain of CHARLES V, for example, stretched around the globe, far beyond the boundaries of the Holy Roman Empire. The empire was seriously weakened by the REFORMATION, which generally aligned the German Protestant princes against the emperors, who championed Roman Catholicism. The THIRTY YEARS WAR ended with the virtual dissolution of the empire in the Peace of WESTPHALIA (1648), which recognized the sovereignty of all the states of the empire. Thereafter, the title was largely honorific; the Hapsburg emperors remained powerful monarchs, but because of their hereditary domains and not because of the empire. In the 18th cent. the prestige of the empire was further weakened by the military triumphs of LOUIS XIV of France, whom the emperors opposed. Also, the male Hapsburg line died out, creating a crisis that culminated in the War of the AUSTRIAN SUCCESSION and the SEVEN YEARS WAR. In the end, the husband of MARIA THERESA, heiress to the Hapsburg lands, became emperor as FRANCIS I. Whatever power remained in the office, however, was exerted by Maria Theresa herself and her advisers. The empire ended in 1806 as the result of the triumphs of NAPOLEON I in the French Revolutionary Wars. Francis II, grandson of Maria Theresa and Francis I, renounced his title and styled himself Francis I, emperor of Austria. After the fall of Napoleon (1815), no attempt was made to resurrect the Holy Roman Empire.

HOLY ROMAN EMPERORS *(including dates of reign)*	
Saxon dynasty	
Otto I, 936–73	Otto III, 983–1002
Otto II, 973–83	Henry II, 1002–24
Salian or Franconian Dynasty	
Conrad II, 1024–39	Henry IV, 1056–1105
Henry III, 1039–56	Henry V, 1105–25
Lothair II, duke of Saxony, 1125–37	
Hohenstaufen Dynasty and Rivals	
Conrad III, 1138–52	
Frederick I, 1152–90	
Henry VI, 1190–97	
Philip of Swabia, 1198–1208	
antiking: Otto IV (Guelph), 1198–1208	
Otto IV (king, 1208–12; emperor, 1209–15), 1208–15	
Frederick II (king, 1212–20; emperor, 1220–50), 1212–50	
Conrad IV, 1237–54	
antiking: Henry Raspe, 1246–47	
antiking: William, count of Holland, 1247–56	
Interregnum, 1254–73	
Richard, earl of Cornwall, and Alfonso X of Castile, rivals	
Hapsburg, Luxemburg, and Other Dynasties	
Rudolf I (Hapsburg), 1273–91	
Adolf of Nassau, 1292–98	
Albert I (Hapsburg), 1298–1308	
Henry VII [Luxemburg], 1308–13	
Louis IV (Wittelsbach), 1314–46	
Charles IV (Luxemburg), 1346–78	
Wenceslaus (Luxemburg), 1378–1400	
Rupert (Wittelsbach), 1400–10	
Sigismund (Luxemburg), 1410–37	
Hapsburg Dynasty	
Albert II, 1438–39	Matthias, 1612–19
Frederick III, 1440–93	Ferdinand II, 1619–37
Maximilian I, 1493–1519	Ferdinand III, 1637–57
Charles V, 1519–58	Leopold I, 1658–1705
Ferdinand I, 1558–64	Joseph I, 1705–11
Maximilian II, 1564–76	Charles VI, 1711–40
Rudolf II, 1576–1612	
Interregnum, 1740–42	
Wittelsbach-Hapsburg and Lorraine Dynasties	
Charles VII (Wittelsbach-Hapsburg), 1742–45	
Francis I (Lorraine), 1745–65	
Hapsburg-Lorraine Dynasty	
Joseph II, 1765–90	Francis II, 1792–1806
Leopold II, 1790–92	

Holy Week: see LENT.

homeopathy, system of medicine based on the law of similars—that like is cured by like. In homeopathy a drug that produces the same symptoms as a disease (e.g., quinine given to a healthy person mimics malaria) is used in small doses to treat that disease. Developed by German physician Samuel Hahnemann (1755–1843), it was popular through the early 20th cent. Although U.S. medical schools no longer recognize this approach, it is used by some European and Asian physicians, and many Americans use homeopathic treatments.

Homer, principal figure of ancient Greek literature, the first European poet. Two epic poems are ascribed to him, the *Iliad* and the *Odyssey.* Among the greatest works of Western literature, they are the prototype for all later EPIC poetry. Modern scholars generally agree that they were written for an aristocratic audience by a single poet in Asia Minor before 700 B.C. The *Iliad* tells of an episode in the TROJAN WAR: the wrath of ACHILLES and its tragic consequences, including the deaths of Patroclus and Hector. The *Odyssey,* beginning ten years after the fall of Troy, tells of ODYSSEUS's wanderings on his way home to Ithaca, of his wife and son's plight, and of their reunion. The atmosphere of adventure and fate contrasts with the heavier tone and tragic grandeur of the *Iliad.* Also attributed to Homer, wrongly, were the HOMERIC HYMNS. According to legend, Homer was blind.

Homer, Winslow, 1836–1910, American painter; b. Boston. Homer first won acclaim as a magazine illustrator, especially for his CIVIL WAR portrayals. In 1876 he gave up illustration to devote himself to painting. He found inspiration in the American scene and, above all, in the sea. Homer's paintings are direct and realistic and have a splendid sense of color. His powerfully dramatic seascapes in watercolor are unsurpassed and hold a unique place in American art, e.g., *Breaking Storm* (Art Inst., Chicago) and *The Hurricane* (Metropolitan Mus.).

Homeric Hymns, hexameter poems, c.800–400 B.C., wrongly attributed to HOMER by the ancients. They are important sources of knowledge about Greek religion.

Home Rule, in Irish and English history, political slogan adopted by Irish nationalists in the 19th cent. to describe their basic objective of self-government for Ireland. The modern movement began in 1870 and was strengthened by the rise of C.S. PARNELL, who unified the Irish party in PARLIAMENT. The First Home Rule Bill, introduced (1886) by GLADSTONE, failed to pass; the Second was passed (1893) by Commons but defeated by Lords. At this point advocates of constitutional means to Home Rule began to lose ground to republicans and revolutionaries. The Third Home Rule Bill passed (1912) by Commons led to threats of civil war from Protestant Ulster, and Lords excluded Ulster from its provisions. The bill never took effect because continuing agitation led to recognition of the Irish Free State with dominion status in 1921, and other ties with Britain were gradually broken (see IRELAND, REPUBLIC OF). The six counties of Northern Ireland remained part of Great Britain, governed under the Fourth Home Rule Bill (1920).

home rule, in the U.S., system adopted in many states by which a city or county is given the right to draft and amend its own charter. It may be either provided for in the state constitution or adopted through an act of the legislature. Home rule was a response to the rapid expansion of cities in the 19th cent. and the need for autonomous city government. The first municipal home-rule clause was adopted by Missouri in 1875.

home schooling, practice of teaching children in the home rather than in public or private schools; the children's parents usually are the teachers. In the U.S. the practice grew rapidly in the 1980s; by the early 1990s some 350,000 children were being educated at home. The laws regulating home schooling differ from state to state. Advocates of home schooling are often disenchanted with public education, and many wish to teach religious precepts forbidden in public settings. Critics have questioned the quality of such education and argue that it deprives children of necessary social interactions.

Homestead. **1** City (1990 pop. 26,866), Dade co., SE Fla.; inc. 1913. A Miami suburb, it is a trade center for surrounding citrus and vegetable farms and a gateway to Everglades National Park (see NATIONAL PARKS, table) and the FLORIDA KEYS. In 1992 a hurricane leveled much of Homestead and nearby areas. **2** Borough (1990 pop. 4,179), Allegheny co., SW Pa., on the Monongahela River just S of Pittsburgh; inc. 1880. Once a major steel producer, it declined rapidly in the 1980s. The Homestead strike (1892), one of the bitterest labor disputes in U.S. history, occurred here.

Homestead Act, 1862, passed by the U.S. Congress. It gave title to 160 acres (65 hectares) of unoccupied public land to each homesteader on payment of a nominal fee and required five years of residence; land could also be acquired after six months' residence at $1.25 an acre. The government had previously sold land in the West to settlers for revenue purposes.

homicide, killing of one human being by another human being. In law, there are four categories of homicide. Two of them, murder and manslaughter, are criminal; both are homicide committed without justification or excuse, but manslaughter is distinguished from murder by the absence of malice aforethought. Noncriminal homicides are justifiable homicide, or killing in circumstances authorized under law (e.g., executing a condemned prisoner), and accidental, negligent, or excusable homicide, which is killing unintentionally by misadventure or without gross negligence (e.g., in the course of unsuccessful surgery).

Homo erectus, early human species dating from 1.6 million to 250,000 years ago (see HUMAN EVOLUTION). The species was indistinguishable from contemporary humans from the neck down, except for its slight stature. The size of its braincase, however, was intermediate between *Homo habilis* and *Homo sapiens*. Its culture included stone tools and the first use of fire. The first fossils, found (1891) in Java, were called *Pithecanthropus*, or Java man.

homosexuality, sexual interest in members of one's own sex. Female homosexuality is known as lesbianism. Many male and female homosexuals prefer to be called "gay," a term that has been associated with homosexuality since the early 1900s. Although many people consider homosexuality a moral offense and homosexual sex is illegal in some states and nations, it is no longer considered a psychiatric disorder, and genetic and neural evidence that sexual orientation has a physiological basis is growing. Societal attitudes toward homosexuality have varied greatly, historically and culturally. It was celebrated in ancient Greece and respected historically in Japan. In European cultures, religious and secular laws against homosexuality began in the Middle Ages as prohibitions against any kind of sexual activity not aimed a procreation. Since the "Stonewall Rebellion" in 1969, many groups have formed to fight for the civil rights of homosexuals (see GAY RIGHTS MOVEMENT). Condemnatory attitudes toward homosexuality have complicated efforts to combat AIDS in places like the U.S., where the disease initially appeared among homosexuals.

Homs: see HIMS, Syria.

Honda Soichiro, 1906–91, Japanese automobile executive. A mechanic and race car driver, he was a self-taught engineer. Honda founded a motorcycle company in the 1940s and began producing cars in the 1950s. His company's clean-burning CVCC engine created an automotive revolution, and its cars won a large share of the U.S. market.

Honduras, officially Republic of Honduras, republic (1992 est. pop. 5,093,000), 43,277 sq mi (112,088 sq km), Central America; bordered by the Caribbean Sea (N), Nicaragua (E and S), El Salvador and the Pacific Ocean (SW), and Guatemala (W). The capital is TEGUCIGALPA. Over 80% of the land is mountainous; in the east are the swamps and forests of the Mosquito Coast. Bananas, grown on plantations established by U.S. companies in the 1800s, now account for more than 50% of annual export earnings. Coffee, timber, meat, and shrimp are also exported, and some manufacturing is being attempted, but the general economy remains seriously underdeveloped, and the country is dependent on U.S. aid. The people, of whom about 90% are mestizo, are Spanish-speaking and Roman Catholic.

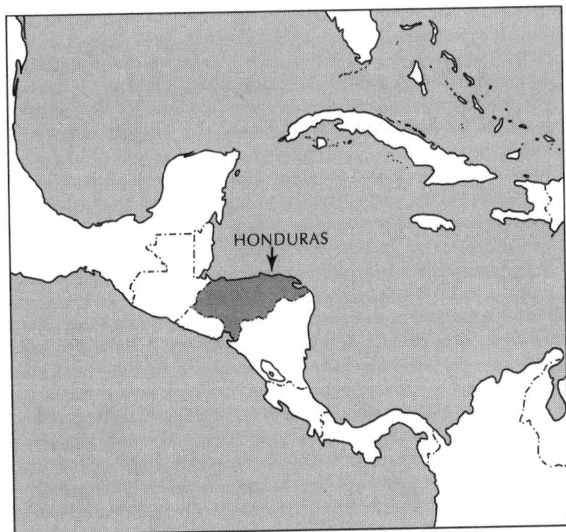

History. At one time an important center of Mayan culture (see MAYA), the region was colonized after 1524 by the Spanish, who established mines in the highlands. Honduras gained independence in 1821 and, after brief periods as part of the Mexican Empire and the CENTRAL AMERICAN CONFEDERATION, became a separate republic in 1838. Its history has been turbulent, marked by frequent coups (nearly one a year) and trouble with neighbors, most recently a four-day war with EL SALVADOR (1969) and border clashes with NICARAGUA (1981). Foreign influence and conservative government were the rule from the 1890s to the 1950s, when a labor code and other reforms were adopted. From 1963 to the early 1980s, rightist-to-moderate army elements dominated the nation's politics. A new constitution (1982) brought free elections, but the army remains the most important power in the country. Carlos Roberto Reina became president in 1994.

Honecker, Erich [hŏn'ĕkər], 1912–, East German communist leader. Imprisoned under the Nazis, he joined the East German Communist party after World War II. He rose in the party bureaucracy and supervised the construction of the Berlin Wall (1961). Honecker succeeded Walter ULBRICHT as party leader in 1971 and became head of state in 1976. Demonstrations in 1989 led to his ouster, and he was charged (1990) with corruption and treason but not tried. Following German reunification he was charged with corruption and with manslaughter in the killing of East Germans fleeing west, and he fled (1991) to the USSR. He returned to Germany to face trial in 1992 but was released because of ill health and went to Chile.

Honegger, Arthur [hŭn'ĕgər], 1892–1955, Swiss-French composer. One of the Parisian group "les SIX," he is known for *Pacific 231* (1923) and the operas *Judith* (1926) and *Antigone* (1927; libretto by COCTEAU).

honey, sweet, viscous fluid made by honeybees from the nectar of flowers and containing 70% to 80% sugar. It has been a major sweetening agent since earliest times. The worker bee transforms the sucrose of nectar into the simple sugars fructose and glucose by the enzyme action of its honey sac, and stores the honey to thicken in the wax cells of the hive. The excess of the colony's requirement may be extracted by humans for use as food. The flavor and color of honey depend on the kind of flower that produced the nectar, e.g., alfalfa, clover, orange, or tupelo.

honeydew melon: see MELON.

honey locust, deciduous tree (*Gleditsia triacanthos*) of the PULSE family, native to the eastern half of the U.S. Often grown as a shade tree or as an ornamental, the honey locust has fragrant flowers, compound leaves, branching thorns, and brown pods with edible pulp. Its durable wood is used chiefly for fence posts and crossties.

honeysuckle, common name for vines and shrubs of the family Caprifoliaceae. Found in the Northern Hemisphere, the family includes the honeysuckles, elders, snowberries, viburnums, and weigelas. The true honeysuckles (genus *Lonicera*) include the well-known trumpet honeysuckle (*L. sempervirens*), with fragrant scarlet blossoms, and the Japanese honeysuckle (*L. japonica*), with white to yellow blossoms, now a noxious weed. Elders and viburnums usually have showy clusters of white flowers, and some produce edible berries, e.g., the North American elder (*Sambucus canadensis*), whose berries are used in preserves and wine.

Hong Kong, Mandarin *Xianggang,* British crown colony (1993 est. pop. 6,020,000), land area 399 sq mi (1,034 sq km), adjacent to Guangdong prov., SE China, on the estuary of the Pearl R., 40 mi (64 km) E of MACAO and 90 mi (145 km) SE of GUANGZHOU. The colony comprises Hong Kong island, ceded by China in 1842 and the site of the capital, Victoria; Kowloon peninsula, ceded in 1860; and the New Territories, a mainland area adjoining Kowloon that was leased in 1898 for 99 years along with Deep Bay, Mirs Bay, and some 235 offshore islands. Hong Kong is a free port, a bustling trade center, a shopping and banking hub, and one of the greatest trading and transshipment centers in E Asia. It has also become a leading light industrial manufacturing center, utilizing the abundant cheap labor available. The textile and clothing industry is the colony's largest; plastics and electrical and electronic goods are also produced. Only about one seventh of the land is arable, and food and water must be imported, much of it from China. Some 98% of the population is ethnic Chinese; there are important British and American communities. Traditional Chinese religions are practiced by about 90% of the people; about 10% are Christians. Both Cantonese and English are widely spoken.

History. Hong Kong was a sparsely populated area when it was occupied by the British during the OPIUM WAR (1839–42). As a colony it prospered as an East-West trading center and as the commercial gateway to and distribution center for S China. Conquered (1941) by the Japanese during WORLD WAR II, it was reoccupied by the British in 1945. Hong Kong is one of the most severely crowded urban areas in the world. Hundreds of thousands of refugees streamed into the city after 1949, and thousands more from Vietnam and S China flooded Hong Kong in the late 1970s, sparking stringent new controls on the Chinese border (1980). In 1991 Hong Kong's first direct legislative elections (but for only 30% of the seats) were won almost entirely by liberal, pro-democracy candidates; no pro-China candidate was elected. British efforts to introduce further democratic reforms have met with strong objections from China. In 1997 Britain will return the entire colony to China, and Hong Kong will become a Special Administrative Region.

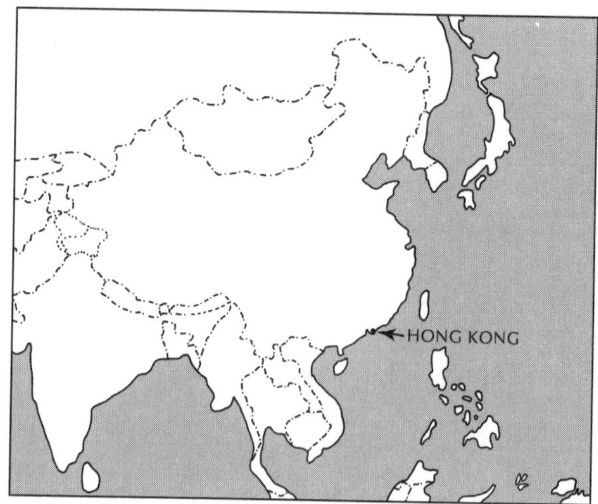

Honiara, city (1986 pop. 30,413), capital of the SOLOMON ISLANDS, on GUADALCANAL.

Honolulu, city (1990 pop. 365,272; Honolulu co. 1990 pop. 836,231), capital of HAWAII, on the SE coast of the island of Oahu. The city and county are legally coextensive. Famous for its beauty and ethnic diversity, it is the economic center of the Hawaiian Islands and the crossroads of the Pacific. The first European to see it was an Englishman, Captain William Brown. Honolulu grew into a Hawaiian royal residence and became the capital of the kingdom of Hawaii in 1845. In the 19th cent. it was a busy whaling and trading port occupied successively by Russian, British, and French forces. It remained the capital upon U.S. annexation (1898) of the islands and the coming (1959) of statehood. During WORLD WAR II its naval base, PEARL HARBOR, was the staging area for U.S. forces in the Pacific and the site of the 1941 Japanese bombing. After the war, tourism, industrial diversification, and luxury building accelerated. Defense activities are still important. Sugar processing and pineapple canning are important industries. Waikiki Beach and nearby Diamond Head crater are famous. Notable institutions include the Univ. of Hawaii, Bishop Museum, Kawaiahao Church (1841), and Iolani Palace (the only royal palace in the U.S.).

Honorius I, pope (625–38), an Italian. He wrote a letter apparently supporting the heresy of MONOTHELETISM. The pope and letter were declared heretical at the Third Council of CONSTANTINOPLE. The letter is held not to affect papal infallibility because Honorius was not speaking ex cathedra.

Honorius, 384–423, Roman emperor of the West (395–423), which he inherited from his father, THEODOSIUS I, as his brother ARCADIUS inherited the East. Honorius had his guardian, STILICHO, murdered (408). After the Visigoths under ALARIC I invaded Italy and sacked Rome (410), Honorius made peace (412) with them. In 421 he was forced to accept as co-ruler his general Constantius, who had married his sister, Galla Placidia. The West declined markedly during his weak reign.

Honshu, island (1990 pop. 98,352,000), largest (c.89,000 sq mi/230,510 sq km) and most populous island in Japan. It is c.800 mi (1,290 km) long and from 30 to 150 mi (50 to 240 km) wide, with a climate ranging from subtropical in the south to cold-temperate in the north. Rugged mountains, reaching 12,389 ft (3,776 m) at Mt. FUJI, cover most of the island. The population is concentrated in a series of small coastal plains along the south, including the Kanto, or Kwanto, Plain (c.5,000 sq mi/12,950 sq km), site of the great

TOKYO-YOKOHAMA industrial complex, the Kinki district (OSAKA-KOBE), and the Nobi Plain (NAGOYA).

Hooch or **Hoogh, Pieter de** [both: hōkh], b. c.1629, d. after 1677, Dutch genre painter. His paintings of intimate interiors, with rooms opening into other rooms or outdoors, display his ability to handle complicated lighting. One of his finest works is *Courtyard of a Dutch House* (National Gall., London).

Hood, John Bell, 1831–79, Confederate general in the American CIVIL WAR; b. Owingsville, Ky. Hood was named (1864) Confederate commander in the ATLANTA CAMPAIGN. He later marched into Tennessee but was defeated (Dec. 1864) at Nashville.

Hood, Raymond Mathewson, 1881–1934, American architect; b. Pawtucket, R.I. His traditional design vocabulary changed to meet the challenges of European modernists in the 1920s. He was co-winner (1922) of the Chicago Tribune Tower international competition with a neo-Gothic design (completed 1925). His McGraw-Hill skyscraper (1931) in New York City is an fine example of the INTERNATIONAL STYLE.

Hood, Thomas, 1799–1845, English poet, noted for his compassion for the poor and unfortunate in such poems as "The Song of the Shirt" and "The Bridge of Sighs." He also wrote much humorous verse and prose and edited several prominent magazines.

hoof-and-mouth disease or **foot-and-mouth disease,** highly contagious viral disease of cattle, sheep, goats, and other cloven-hoofed animals. Symptoms include fever, loss of appetite and weight, and blistering on mucous membranes. The disease is spread both through direct contact and indirectly by way of contaminated food, water, soil, and other materials. Humans seldom contract the disease but may be carriers, as may rats, dogs, birds, and wild animals. Although there are vaccines for the disease, epidemics still cause enormous losses.

Hoogh, Pieter de: see HOOCH, PIETER DE.

Hooke, Robert, 1635–1703, English physicist, mathematician, and inventor; considered the greatest mechanic of his age. He improved astronomical instruments, watches, and clocks, and first formulated the theory of planetary movements as a mechanical problem. He devised (1684) a practicable telegraph system; invented the spiral spring in watches and the first screw-divided quadrant; and constructed the first arithmetical machine and Gregorian telescope. He stated Hooke's law on elasticity (see STRENGTH OF MATERIALS) and anticipated the law of universal GRAVITATION.

Hooker, Joseph, 1814–79, Union general in the U.S. CIVIL WAR; b. Hadley, Mass. Given command (Jan. 1863) of the Army of the Potomac, he was decisively defeated by Gen. R.E. LEE at CHANCELLORSVILLE. He later served in the CHATTANOOGA CAMPAIGN.

Hooker, Richard, 1554?–1600, English theologian and Anglican clergyman. His *Of the Laws of Ecclesiastical Polity* helped to formulate the intellectual concepts of Anglicanism and influenced civil ecclesiastical government.

Hooker, Thomas, 1586–1647, Puritan clergyman in colonial America; b. England. Emigrating (1633) to Massachusetts, he became unhappy with the strict theological rule there. In 1635–36 he and his followers founded HARTFORD, Conn.

Hooke's law: see STRENGTH OF MATERIALS.

Hooks, Benjamin Lawson, 1925–, African-American civil-rights leader; b. Memphis, Tenn. In 1972 Pres. NIXON named Hooks, a lawyer and Baptist minister, to the FEDERAL COMMUNICATIONS COMMISSION, making him its first African-American member. From 1977 to 1993 he was executive director of the NATIONAL ASSOCIATION FOR THE ADVANCEMENT OF COLORED PEOPLE.

hookworm, any of a number of parasitic nematode worms found in tropical and subtropical climates. The hookworm larva usually penetrates the exposed skin of humans and other mammals and migrates to the small intestine, where it attaches itself by means of hooks and feeds on the host's blood. Hookworm infestation causes ANEMIA, diarrhea, and abdominal pain and is treated with drugs.

Hoover, Herbert Clark, 1874–1964, 31st president of the U.S. (1929–33); b. West Branch, Iowa. Before 1914 he was a mining engineer and consultant. During World War I he headed food and relief bureaus in Europe. As secretary of commerce (1921–29) under HARDING and COOLIDGE, he fostered trade associations and supported such engineering projects as the St. Lawrence Waterway and the Boulder (now Hoover) Dam. He easily won the 1928 Republican presidential nomination and defeated Democrat Alfred E. SMITH. His administration was dominated by the GREAT DEPRESSION, ushered in by the stock market crash of Oct. 1929. Believing that the economy would regenerate spontaneously, Hoover was reluctant to extend federal activities. But he did begin a large public works program, and the RECONSTRUCTION FINANCE CORPORATION was created (1932). Congress, controlled by Democrats after 1930, passed the Emergency Relief Act and created the federal home loan banks. In 1932 some 15,000 ex-servicemen, known as Bonus Marchers, marched on Washington to demand immediate payment of their World War I bonus certificates. Hoover ordered federal troops to oust them from government property. The U.S. took part in the London NAVAL CONFERENCE of 1930 and the abortive DISARMAMENT CONFERENCE. In 1931 Hoover proposed a one-year moratorium on reparations and war debts to ease the financial situation in Europe. He ran for reelection in 1932 but was overwhelmingly defeated by Franklin D. ROOSEVELT. Later Hoover coordinated (1946) food supplies to war-ravaged countries and headed (1947–49) the Hoover Commission, which recommended administrative reforms of the executive branch. He headed a second commission (1953–55), which studied policy and organization.

Hoover, J(ohn) Edgar, 1895–1972, U.S. director of the FEDERAL BUREAU OF INVESTIGATION (1924–72); b. Washington, D.C. As director, he built an efficient crime-detection system and attacked organized crime. After World War II he targeted Communist activities and became a controversial figure because of FBI harassment of left-wing dissenters.

Hoover Dam, formerly **Boulder Dam** (1933–47), one of the world's major dams, c.726 ft (221 m) high and 1,244 ft (379 m) long, on the COLORADO R. between Nevada and Arizona. Built from 1931 to 1936, the multipurpose dam impounds **Lake Mead**. It has a hydroelectric capacity of 1.3 Mw.

Hoover Institution on War, Revolution, and Peace, at Stanford Univ., Palo Alto, Calif. Established (1919) as the Hoover War Library by Herbert HOOVER, it houses collections that include source material from World Wars I and II. It conducts research, publication, and advanced study.

hop, herbaceous perennial vine of the MULBERRY family, widely cultivated since early times for brewing purposes. The commercial hop (*Humulus lupulus*), native to Eurasia, is grown for the cone-like female flowers, called hops, used to impart a bitter flavor to beer. Oil of hops is used in perfumes, and the stem is used for fiber.

Hope, Bob, 1903–, American comedian, b. England as Leslie Townes Hope. Hope debuted as a comedian on radio (1935). He later teamed with Bing CROSBY and Dorothy Lamour for six successful "Road" films (1940–53) and has appeared in other movies and on television. He made frequent entertainment tours of U.S. military bases.

Hopi, PUEBLO people of the Southwest (see NORTH AMERICA, INDIGENOUS PEOPLES OF) who occupy several MESA pueblos in NE Arizona, numbering 11,173 in 1990. Most speak Hopi, a Uto-Aztecan language (see NATIVE AMERICAN LANGUAGES). Geographically isolated, they resisted European influence more than other Pueblo tribes and participated in Popé's revolt (1680) against the Spanish. In the 1820s the NAVAHO began to encroach on their lands. Sedentary farmers and sheep herders, they retain clan structure and rituals, including the KACHINA ceremony and snake dance; at the same time, the Hopi have a high level of education. In 1975 the federal government began procedures to separate Navaho and Hopi lands, requiring several thousand Navahos to relocate but also assigning some formerly Hopi territory to the Navaho. A court decision in 1992 assigned most of the land still in dispute to the Navaho.

Hopkins, Gerard Manley, 1844–89, English poet. His intense poems and experiments in prosody have profoundly influenced 20th-cent. poetry. Hopkins was a convert to Catholicism and a Jesuit priest, and his poems and letters often show his inner conflict and deep dissatisfaction with himself as a poet and a servant of God. His mature work began with "The Wreck of the *Deutschland*" and includes "God's Grandeur" and "The Windhover." Edited by Robert BRIDGES, his *Poems* was published posthumously in 1918.

Hopkins, Harry Lloyd, 1890–1946, American public official; b. Sioux City, Iowa. An intimate friend and close adviser of Pres.

Franklin D. ROOSEVELT, he headed the Federal Emergency Relief Administration (1933) and the WORKS PROGRESS ADMINISTRATION (1935). He was secretary of commerce (1938–40).

Hopper, Edward, 1882–1967, American painter; b. Nyack, N.Y. A student of HENRI, he gained an early reputation with his etchings. His realistic paintings of streets and houses, often without figures, have an atmosphere of loneliness and an almost menacing starkness. A characteristic oil is *Early Sunday Morning* (1930; Whitney Mus., N.Y.C.).

Horace (Quintus Horatius Flaccus), 65 B.C.–8 B.C., Latin poet, one of the greatest LYRIC poets. His benefactor, MAECENAS, gave him the famous Sabine farm where he spent most of his later life, writing poetry reflecting the civilized spirit of the Augustan age and his own genial disposition and love of nature. His poetry consists of two books of *Satires,* four books of *Odes,* the *Epodes,* two books of *Epistles,* the *Carmen Saeculare* (a hymn), and the *Ars Poetica* (on literary matters). Horace's SATIRE was gentler than that of JUVENAL. He was a master of poetic form, and his later verse shows a completely individual adaptation of Greek meters to Latin. Horace has remained a major influence on English poetry.

Horatius (Horatius Cocles), legendary Roman hero. With two companions he held Lars Porsena's Etruscan army at bay while the Romans cut the Sublician bridge behind him. He then swam the Tiber to safety. The story is related in MACAULAY's *Lays of Ancient Rome.*

horehound, aromatic Old World perennial herb (*Marrubium vulgare*) of the MINT family. It has woolly white foliage and tiny, clustered white flowers. The dried leaves and flowers are used in making candy and cough and cold remedies.

hormone, chemical messenger released in minute amounts by the endocrine, or ductless, glands and carried by the bloodstream to target tissues, where it produces either rapid or long-term effects (see ENDOCRINE SYSTEM). Most hormones fall into two major categories: PEPTIDES (chains of amino acids) and LIPIDS (including STEROIDS). Since the lack of any hormone may cause serious disorders, many hormones are now synthesized for use in treating such deficiencies.

Hormuz, Strait of, strategic waterway, 30 to 50 mi (48 to 80 km) wide, between the PERSIAN GULF and the Gulf of Oman, controlling ocean traffic to and from the oil-rich Persian Gulf area. Located in the strait are Qishm Island (Iran) and three other islands—Greater Tunb, Lesser Tunb, and Abu Musa—seized by Iran (1971) but also claimed by the United Arab Emirates.

Horn, Cape, southernmost point of South America, S Chile, known for its strong currents and stormy climate. "Rounding the Horn" was a great hazard in the era of sailing ships.

Horne, Marilyn, 1934–, American mezzo-soprano; b. Bradford, Pa. She is noted for the power and smoothness of her voice. Her memorable operatic roles include Adalgisa in BELLINI's *Norma* and the title role in BIZET's *Carmen.*

horned lizard or **horned toad,** broad, flat-bodied LIZARD (genus *Phrynosoma*) found in arid regions from SW Canada to Guatemala. The body is 3 to 5 in. (7.6 to 12.7 cm) long, with spines on the head, sides, and back. Horned lizards are protectively colored, usually in dull grays or browns.

hornet: see WASP.

Horney, Karen, 1885–1952, American psychiatrist; b. Germany. Deviating from orthodox Freudian analysis, she emphasized environmental and cultural, rather than biological, factors in the genesis of NEUROSIS. She founded the American Institute of Psychoanalysis in 1941. Her works include *The Neurotic Personality of Our Time* (1937) and *Neurosis and Human Growth* (1950).

Hornsby, Rogers, 1896–1963, American baseball player and manager; b. Winters, Tex. One of the game's greatest hitters, he played shortstop, second base, and other positions for the St. Louis Cardinals (1915–26), managing the team to a World Series victory in 1926. He subsequently played or was player-manager for the New York Giants, Boston Braves, Chicago Cubs, and St. Louis Browns before retiring as a player in 1937. "Rajah" Hornsby won seven National League batting titles, and his .424 average in 1924 remains the modern record. His lifetime batting average of .358 is second only to Ty COBB's .367.

horoscope: see ASTROLOGY; ZODIAC.

Horowitz, Vladimir, 1904–89, Russian-American virtuoso pianist. He made his Russian debut at 17 and first appeared in the U.S. in 1928. He was noted for his interpretations of CHOPIN, RACHMANINOFF, and LISZT.

horse, hoofed, herbivorous MAMMAL of the family Equidae, the single living genus of which is *Equus,* which includes the domestic horse, the wild Przewalski's horse, the ASS, and the ZEBRA. All are swift, plains-dwelling herd animals with teeth adapted for grinding coarse grass. The species can interbreed (see MULE), but offspring are usually sterile. The modern horse evolved in North America (where it later became extinct) and spread over the world. It was hunted by early humans and domesticated by Asian nomads in the 3d millennium B.C. The fast, light southern breeds may have originated independently of the heavier northern draft breeds, and the small breeds called ponies may have evolved from a wild European race. Until the mid-20th cent. horses were widely used for warfare, agriculture, and transportation. Today light breeds are used for show and sport.

horse chestnut, common name for some trees and shrubs of the family Hippocastanaceae, found in north temperate zones and South America. The horse chestnut tree (*Aesculus hippocastanum*) is often cultivated for shade and ornament. The family includes the buckeyes; the prevalence of the Ohio buckeye (*A. glabra*) has given Ohio its nickname, the Buckeye State. The soft wood of horse chestnuts and buckeyes is used for paper pulp and woodenware and in carpentry.

horsemanship: see EQUESTRIANISM.

horsepower: see POWER.

horseradish, perennial herb (*Armoracia rusticana*) of the MUSTARD family, native to central and S Europe. Once used medicinally against scurvy, today it is grown mainly for its pungent roots, which are used in a popular condiment.

horseshoe crab, large marine invertebrate animal (class Merostomata), an ARTHROPOD. It has a heavy, dark brown, domed exoskeleton divided into a broad horseshoe-shaped front part (prosoma), a tapered middle region (opisthosoma), and a spiky, taillike part (telson). Also known as king crabs, horseshoe crabs swim or burrow using five pairs of walking legs. The largest reach 2 ft (61 cm) in length.

horsetail, plant of the genus *Equisetum,* the single surviving genus of a large group of primitive vascular plants that flourished during the Carboniferous period. Found in temperate and tropical regions, horsetails seldom grow to over 3 ft (91 cm), although FOSSIL evidence indicates that many extinct species were treelike in size. They have whorls of small, scalelike leaves around a green, hollow, jointed stem. Some species bear shoots with spore-bearing cones at the top for reproduction. The scouring rush (*E. hyemale*), common in North America and Eurasia, is so called because it has a coarse texture suitable for scouring.

Horta, Victor, Baron, 1861–1947, Belgian architect. His Tassel House, Brussels (1892–93), was the earliest monument of ART NOUVEAU. He also designed the Maison du Peuple (1896–99), the market and communal complex in Brussels.

Horthy de Nagybánya, Nicholas [hôr'tĭ də nŏ'dyəbä"nyŏ], 1868–1957, Hungarian admiral and regent. He led (1919) the counterrevolutionary forces in Hungary against Béla KUN and was regent (1920–44). After he tried to make peace with the USSR in WORLD WAR II, the Germans forced him to resign and took him to Germany. He died in Portugal.

horticulture, science of cultivating fruits, vegetables, flowers, and ornamental plants; a branch of AGRICULTURE. Horticulture usually refers to small-scale gardening and AGRONOMY to the large-scale growing of field crops. Although many horticultural practices are ancient, relatively recent knowledge of GENETICS, plant PHYSIOLOGY and PATHOLOGY, BIOCHEMISTRY, ECOLOGY, ENTOMOLOGY, and SOILS, and the practical application (e.g., in plant breeding) of this knowledge, have made horticulture an extremely complex science. See also BOTANY.

Horus, in ancient EGYPTIAN RELIGION, sky god, god of light and goodness. The son of OSIRIS and ISIS, he avenged his father's murder by defeating Set, the god of evil and darkness.

Hosea [hōzē'ə, –zā'ə] or **Osee** [ōsē'], book of the OLD TESTAMENT, 28th in the Authorized Version, first of the Minor PROPHETS. It consists of the career and sermons of Hosea, who preached against the sins of the northern kingdom of Israel in the 8th cent. B.C., focusing on apostasy, decadence, punishment, and redemption.

Hosokawa Morihiro, 1938–, Japanese politician, grandson of KONOYE FUMIMARO. A member of the Liberal Democratic party (LDP), he was elected (1971) to the upper house of the Japanese parliament and won (1983) the governorship of Kumamoto prefecture, Kyushu. He broke with the LDP in 1992 to found the reformist Japan New party. When former opposition parties won the 1993 elections, he became prime minister. Hosokawa won passage (1994) of electoral reforms designed to reduce political corruption.

Hostos, Eugenio María de [ō'stōs], 1839–1903, Latin American philosopher, sociologist, writer, and political and educational reformer. In Santo Domingo, Puerto Rico, he founded (1879–88) the first normal school and introduced advanced teaching methods; while in Chile he was instrumental in having women admitted to the university. He wrote some 50 volumes of prose.

hot spring, natural discharge of groundwater with an elevated temperature. Most hot springs (including GEYSERS) result from water passing through or near recently formed, hot, igneous rocks. Hot springs are used as a source of geothermal energy in California, Iceland, and Italy. See also HYDROTHERMAL VENT.

Hot Springs National Park: see NATIONAL PARKS (table).

Hotspur: see PERCY, SIR HENRY.

Hottentots: see KHOIKHOI.

Houdin, Jean Eugène Robert [o͞odăN'], 1805–71, French magician. Famed for his optical illusions, he liked to explain the natural causes of these and other "magic" tricks.

Houdini, Harry, 1874–1926, American magician; b. Hungary as Erich Weiss. He took his stage name from the French magician HOUDIN. He was world-famous for his escapes from every sort of bond and sealed container and for his exposure of fraudulent spiritualistic mediums.

Houdon, Jean-Antoine [o͞odôN'], 1741–1828, French neoclassical sculptor. In creating sculptural documents of his time, he developed a kind of portrait remarkable for elegance, measured realism, and depiction of individuality. He did portrait busts of such statesmen as Thomas Jefferson, Benjamin Franklin, and Prince Henry of Prussia and a full-length sculpture of Voltaire. His later works reveal his study of antique form, e.g., *The Bather* (Metropolitan Mus.). He exerted a strong influence for generations.

hound, class of dogs bred to hunt animals. Most hunt by scent, their quarry ranging from such large game as bear or elk to small game and vermin. Some long-legged breeds that hunt mainly by sight are also classed as hounds. A third variety, treeing hounds, track by scent and pursue tree-climbing animals. Many scent hounds have coats patterned in "hound colors": black, white, and tan. See individual breeds, e.g., AFGHAN HOUND, BASENJI, BASSET HOUND, DACHSHUND, FOXHOUND, WHIPPET.

Houphouët-Boigny, Félix [o͞ofwā'-bwä'nyē], 1905–93, president of CÔTE D'IVOIRE (1960–93). When Côte d'Ivoire (Ivory Coast) became a constituent member of the French Community in 1958, he was its president. Two years later he led the country to full independence and became president of the new republic. In 1990, in the first election involving opposition parties, he won a seventh five-year term; he died in office.

hour circle: see ASTRONOMICAL COORDINATE SYSTEMS.

House of Commons: see PARLIAMENT.

House of Lords: see PARLIAMENT.

House of Representatives, United States: see CONGRESS OF THE UNITED STATES.

Houses of Parliament: see WESTMINSTER PALACE.

house sparrow: see ENGLISH SPARROW.

Housing and Urban Development, United States Department of (HUD), federal executive department established (1965) to administer programs that provide aid for housing and community development. It grants loan assistance for low-income housing programs, insures mortgages, and encourages the participation of private home-building and mortgage-lending industries in urban development projects.

Housman, A(lfred) E(dward), 1859–1936, English poet and scholar. A failure at Oxford and a recluse, he nevertheless became a leading classicist, editing Manilius, Juvenal, and Lucan. He is best known for the poetry that appeared in two volumes, *A Shropshire Lad* (1896) and *Last Poems* (1922). In such lyrics as "To an Athlete Dying Young" and "When I was One-and-twenty," he handled with vivid economy the themes of mortality and the passing of youth. His brother, **Laurence Housman,** 1865–1959, was also a writer, particularly noted for his play *Victoria Regina* (1934).

Houston, Samuel, 1793–1863, Texas statesman; b. near Lexington, Va. He was sent (1823, 1825) by Tennessee to the U.S. Congress as a Democrat and in 1827 became the state's governor. When his wife left him, however, he resigned (1829) and later moved to Texas. After Texas declared its independence from Mexico, Houston commanded the revolutionary troops and defeated the Mexicans at the battle of San Jacinto (Apr. 21, 1836). He was the first president of the Republic of TEXAS (1836–38), serving again from 1841 to 1844. After Texas joined the U.S., he was U.S. senator (1846–59). Elected (1859) governor of Texas, he opposed secession and was removed from office in 1861.

Houston, city (1990 pop. 1,630,553; met. area 3,301,937), seat of Harris co., SE Tex., a deepwater port on the Houston Ship Channel; inc. 1837. The fourth largest city in the U.S., it is the largest city in the South and Southwest; a commercial, industrial, and financial hub; and one of the world's great oil centers. It has numerous space and science research firms, petrochemical works, shipyards, grain elevators, breweries, mills, and factories. The city is also a major corporate and medical research center. Settled in 1836, it was capital (1837–39) of the Texas Republic. It was a 19th-cent. railhead and grew rapidly after the opening (1914) of the ship channel linking it to the Gulf of MEXICO. Coastal oil fields and other natural resources poured money into Houston. World War II shipbuilding and the opening (1961) nearby of NASA's Manned Spacecraft Center (renamed the Lyndon B. Johnson Space Center, 1973) furthered its growth. Houston is noted for its art museums, numerous universities and cultural institutions, and the Astrodome stadium (opened 1965).

Hovercraft: see AIR-CUSHION VEHICLE.

Hovhaness, Alan [hōvhä'nəs], 1911–, American composer; b. Somerville, Mass. Many of his compositions are based on Armenian culture. He is also interested in unusual sonorities. His works include *Ukiyo-Floating World* (1965), a symphonic poem, *Dawn at Mt. Tahoma* (1973), for string orchestra, and *Mt. Katahdin* (1987), a piano sonata.

Howard, Catherine, 1521?–1542, fifth queen consort of HENRY VIII of England. Niece of the powerful Thomas Howard, 3d duke of Norfolk, she married the king in 1540. She was accused of adultery in 1541 and later beheaded.

Howard, Henry: see SURREY, HENRY HOWARD, EARL OF.

Howard University, at Washington, D.C.; founded 1867 to provide education for newly emancipated slaves. Although predominantly an African-American university, it has always been open to all qualified students. The Founders Library has noted collections of materials on African-American literature and history.

Howe, Elias, 1819–67, American inventor; b. Spencer, Mass. He was apprenticed (1838) to a Boston instrument- and watchmaker, at whose suggestion he turned his attention to devising a SEWING MACHINE. He exhibited his first in 1845, patented another in 1846, and sold a third (1846) in England. After several patent infringement suits, he obtained (1854) a judgment for royalty.

Howe, Gordie (Gordon Howe), 1928–, Canadian hockey player. Possibly the greatest and most durable forward in the history of hockey, he played (1946–71) for the Detroit Red Wings of the National Hockey League (NHL). With his two sons he joined (1973) the Houston Aeros and then (1977) the New England Whalers of the World Hockey Association, ending his career in 1980 with the Hartford Whalers of the NHL. Howe's NHL career records include most seasons (26) and most games (1,767).

Howe, Irving, 1920–93, American critic; b. N.Y.C. An "Old Left" social critic, he also wrote literary criticism. His books include *Politics and the Novel* (1957), *World of Our Fathers* (1976), a study of Jewish immigrants to the U.S., and *Socialism in America* (1985).

Howe, Julia Ward: see under HOWE, SAMUEL GRIDLEY.

Howe, Richard Howe, Earl, 1726–99, British admiral. He defended the English Channel in the SEVEN YEARS WAR. In the AMERICAN REVOLUTION he commanded (1776–78) the North American fleet. He is best remembered for his victory over the French fleet in the battle called the First of June in 1794. His brother, **William Howe,** 5th **Viscount Howe,** 1729–1814, was a British general. In the American Revolution he was commander in chief in the colonies (1775–78). He commanded the successful battle of Long Island (1776), defeated WASHINGTON at the battle of the BRANDYWINE (1777), and resigned in 1778.

Howe, Samuel Gridley, 1801–76, American reformer and philanthropist; b. Boston. He founded and ran for 44 years the New England Asylum for the Blind (later the Perkins Institute), where he was the first to educate a blind deaf-mute successfully, and advocated reforms in the treatment of the insane and mentally retarded. His wife, **Julia Ward Howe,** 1819–1910, b. N.Y.C., was a social reformer and a widely published author who wrote the words of "The Battle Hymn of the Republic" (1861). With her husband, she edited the abolitionist paper *Commonwealth.*

Howells, William Dean, 1837–1920, American novelist and critic; b. Martins Ferry, Ohio. A printer, journalist, and biographer of Lincoln, he won recognition with the first of many travel books, *Venetian Life* (1866), written after five years as consul to Venice. On his return to the U.S., he was associated with such periodicals as the *Atlantic Monthly* and *Harper's Magazine.* In his novels and in his criticism, Howells was a champion of REALISM in American literature. Among his works the realistic novels *A Modern Instance* (1882) and *The Rise of Silas Lapham* (1885) are regarded as his major achievements. The friend and editor of Mark TWAIN, Howells sponsored such younger American realists as Stephen CRANE and Frank NORRIS, and his essays on realist European writers helped to mold American taste. An amazingly prolific writer, he wrote novels, plays, criticism, reminiscences, and short stories.

howitzer: see ARTILLERY.

Hoxha, Enver [hô'jä], 1908–85, Albanian Communist leader and general. One of the founders (1941) of the Albanian Communist party, he became its first secretary in 1954. After World War II he held important government posts, including premier (1946–54), foreign minister (1946–53), and commander of the armed forces (1944–54).

Hrdlicka, Ales [hûrd'lĭchkä], 1869–1943, American anthropologist; b. Bohemia. A curator (1910–42) at the SMITHSONIAN INSTITUTION, he founded and edited (1918–43) the *American Journal of Physical Anthropology.* His investigations of the evolution and migrations of early human beings produced *Physical Anthropology* (1919), *Anthropometry* (1920), *Old Americans* (1925), and *Alaska Diary, 1926–1931* (1943), among other works.

Hs, chemical symbol of the element HASSIUM.

Hs-. For some Chinese names beginning thus, see S-; e.g., for Hsi, see SI.

Hsia, dynasty: see CHINA.

Hua Guofeng or **Hua Kuo-feng** [both: hwä gwô-fŭng], 1920–, Chinese Communist leader. He succeeded (1976) ZHOU ENLAI as premier and MAO ZEDONG as chairman of the Chinese Communist party. Hua was ousted as premier (1980) and party chairman (1981) when the followers of Vice Premier DENG XIAOPING consolidated their power. In 1982 Hua was removed from the party's politburo.

Huang He, Hwang Ho, or **Yellow River,** great river of N China, c.3,000 mi (4,830 km) long, sometimes called "China's Sorrow" for the devastating floods once common along its lower course. From the Kunlun Mts. in W China, it flows generally east, with a "great northern bend" (around the Ordos Desert), to a mouth on the Bo Hai, an arm of the YELLOW SEA north of the Shandong Peninsula. The river is named for the great quantities of yellow silt that it carries from China's fertile loessland region and has deposited seaward over the millennia to form a great, now densely populated delta called the North China Plain. A 50-year construction program, designed to control future flooding and harness the river for increased irrigation and hydroelectric production, was initiated in 1955.

Hubbard, L. Ron: see SCIENTOLOGY.

Hubble, Edwin Powell, 1889–1953, American astronomer; b. Marshfield, Mo. As a staff member (from 1919) at Mt. Wilson Observatory, Hubble used the 100-in. (254-cm) telescope there to discover that there are large-scale galaxies beyond the Milky Way and that they are distributed almost uniformly in all directions. In what is now known as HUBBLE'S LAW, he was the first to offer observational evidence supporting the theory of the expanding universe.

Hubble's law, statement that the greater the distance between any two GALAXIES, the greater is their relative speed of separation. In other words, the universe is expanding roughly uniformly. This empirical finding is more consonant with the big bang theory of the universe's origin than with the steady state theory (see COSMOLOGY). The law was first proposed in 1929 by Edwin HUBBLE, who observed that the more distant a galaxy, the greater is its RED SHIFT, and hence its velocity relative to our galaxy.

Hubble Space Telescope, U.S. astronomical observatory put into orbit in 1990 from the SPACE SHUTTLE *Discovery.* Built 1978–90 at a cost of $1.5 billion, the telescope (named for astronomer E.P. HUBBLE) was expected to provide the clearest view yet obtained of the universe. A flaw in the telescope's 94.5-in (2.4-m) light-gathering mirror, discovered after the telescope was in orbit, initially limited its effectiveness. In 1993, however, astronauts repaired the telescope, replacing critical instruments and adding corrective optics while in orbit.

Hubble Space Telescope

huckleberry, shrub (genus *Gaylussacia*) of the HEATH family, native to the Americas. Huckleberry, often confused with BLUEBERRY, is grown as an ornamental or for its fruit. The common huckleberry (*G. baccata*) is particularly valued for its blue or black fruit.

Hudson, Henry, fl. 1607–11, English explorer. Sailing for the Dutch EAST INDIA COMPANY in search of the NORTHWEST PASSAGE, he explored (1609) the HUDSON R., giving the Dutch their claims to the area. Sailing for the English, he reached (1610) HUDSON BAY. He was abandoned at sea by a mutinous crew.

Hudson, William Henry, 1841–1922, English author and naturalist; b. Argentina of American parents. The romance *Green Mansions* (1904), set in a South American jungle, is a classic. *Far Away and Long Ago* (1918) is autobiographical. He described nature with great sensitivity, force, and beauty.

Hudson, river in New York state, flowing generally south c.315 mi (510 km) from Lake Tear of the Clouds on Mt. Marcy in the Adirondack Mts. to the Atlantic Ocean at New York City. It is tidal, and navigable by ocean vessels, to Albany, 150 mi (240 km) upstream. First sighted (1524) by VERRAZANO, it was explored (1609) by Henry HUDSON and became part of the first all-water trans-Appalachian route when linked (1825) to the GREAT LAKES by the ERIE CANAL. Many industries are located along its banks, which are also associated with the well-known HUDSON RIVER SCHOOL of painting and Washington IRVING's legend of Rip Van Winkle.

Hudson Bay, shallow sea, N Canada, covered by ice from October to mid-July. Explored and named (1610) by Henry HUDSON, the bay (which extends south as James Bay) is c.850 mi (1,370 km) long and c.650 mi (1,050 km) wide. It connects with the Atlantic Ocean through Hudson Strait and with the Arctic Ocean through Foxe Channel. The Hudson Bay region has been a rich source of furs since the late 1600s (see HUDSON'S BAY COMPANY).

Hudson River school, group of American landscape painters, working from 1825 to 1875. Influenced by European ROMANTICISM's attitude toward nature, they were attracted to the grandeur of the Hudson River valley's scenery and painted its awesome beauty along with other spectacular vistas from the American landscape. Thomas COLE was the leader of the group during its most active years. Other members of the school were BIERSTADT, DURAND, KENSETT, S.F.B. MORSE, Henry Inman, F.E. CHURCH, and, in his early work, George INNESS.

Hudson's Bay Company, corporation chartered (1670) by the English crown to operate a fur trade monopoly and settlements in the HUDSON BAY region of North America and to discover a NORTHWEST PASSAGE to E Asia. The company's traders failed to find a passage, but they did establish a monopoly of the Canadian fur trade after the company's amalgamation (1821) with the NORTH WEST COMPANY ended their violent rivalry (see RED RIVER SETTLEMENT). The united company ruled a vast territory extending from the Atlantic to the Pacific, and its fortunes peaked under Sir George SIMPSON's governorship (1821–56). An internal reorganization (1863) passed its stock from a few to many holders. The company's fur monopoly was curtailed by the transfer (1869) of its territory to the new dominion government in return for £300,000. In the late 19th and early 20th cent. it was transformed from a fur-trading agency to a gigantic corporation with many varied business interests. The company was split up into separate organizations in 1930.

Hue [hwā], city (1990 est. pop. 211,000), S Vietnam, on the Hue R. near the South China Sea. The third largest city in Vietnam, it is the market center for a rich farming region and has a cement plant nearby. Hue was probably founded in the 3d cent. A.D. In the 16th cent. it became the seat of the dynasty that ruled ANNAM. The French took Hue in 1883. In 1954 it became part of South Vietnam. During the VIETNAM WAR it was the scene of fighting in which c.4,000 civilians were killed and most of the city destroyed. After the war it was incorporated into united Vietnam; it has since been rebuilt.

Huerta, Victoriano [wār'tä], 1854–1916, Mexican president (1913–14). As commander of federal forces, he overthrew Pres. MADERO and set up a dictatorship marked by corruption and violence. Numerous revolts forced him to resign (1914) as president and to flee into exile.

Hufstedler, Shirley Mount, 1925–, American jurist and U.S. secretary of education (1979–81); b. Denver. She was a county and state judge in California (1961–68) and a federal judge (1968–79). In 1979 Pres. CARTER named her the first secretary of education.

Huggins, Sir William, 1824–1910, English astronomer. A pioneer in spectroscopic photography, he helped develop the combined use of the telescope, spectroscope, and photographic negative. He adapted the gelatin dry-plate negative for use in astronomical photography, making possible exposures of any length. Huggins proved that while some nebulae are clusters of stars, others are uniformly gaseous. He made (1866) the first spectroscopic observations of a nova.

Hugh Capet, c.938–996, king of France (987–96), first of the CAPETIANS. He inherited (956) a vast domain in France from his father, Hugh the Great, and in 987 was elected king. He spent much of his reign fighting with Charles I of Lower Lorraine, the ignored Carolingian claimant.

Hughes, Charles Evans, 1862–1948, American jurist and statesman; b. Glens Falls, N.Y.; LL.B., Columbia Univ. (1884). After presiding over the enactment of much progressive legislation as governor of New York (1907–10), he was appointed (1910) associate justice of the U.S. SUPREME COURT. He resigned in 1916 to run for president, but he was narrowly defeated by Woodrow Wilson. As U.S. secretary of state (1921–25), he greatly increased U.S. diplomatic prestige. In 1930 he was appointed 11th chief justice of the U.S. Supreme Court, serving until 1941; he was moderately conservative, although he frequently voted to uphold controversial NEW DEAL legislation.

Hughes, Howard Robard, 1905–76, U.S. business executive; b. Houston. At 20 he inherited patent rights to an oil tool drill that, manufactured by the Hughes Tool Co., formed the basis of his financial empire. A pilot, he set several aviation records and in the 1930s formed the Hughes Aircraft Corp. His interests extended to the motion picture industry, and he produced such films as *Hell's Angels* (1930) and *The Front Page* (1931). He later gained control of RKO Studios and of Trans World Airways (TWA). A billionaire, he became a recluse in his later years.

Hughes, (James) Langston, 1902–67, African-American poet; b. Joplin, Mo. A major figure in the HARLEM RENAISSANCE, he depicted urban African-American life. His collections of verse include *The Weary Blues* (1926) and *One-Way Ticket* (1949). Among his other works are plays, children's books, and novels.

Hughes, Ted, 1930–, English poet, Poet Laureate of England (1984–). He attempts in tightly controlled verse to bring order out of violence and passion. His works include *The Hawk in the Rain* (1957), *Crow: From the Life and Songs of the Crow* (1971), *Moortown* (1980), and *Wolfwatching* (1989). He was married to Sylvia PLATH.

Hughes, Thomas, 1822–96, English author. His novel of school life, *Tom Brown's School Days* (1857), is a classic, idealizing Dr. Thomas Arnold, headmaster of Rugby school.

Hughes, William Morris, 1864–1952, Australian statesman; b. England. He was minister for external affairs (1904) in the first Labour government and was later attorney general (1908–9, 1910–13, 1914–21). As prime minister (1915–23) of Australia, he strongly supported Britain in WORLD WAR I.

Hugo, Victor Marie, Vicomte [hyōō'gō], 1802–85, French poet, dramatist, and novelist and 19th-cent. France's leading literary figure. The preface to his drama *Cromwell* (1827) placed him at the head of the romantic school, and the production of his unconventional poetic drama *Hernani* (1830) produced a riot between champions of ROMANTICISM and CLASSICISM. Other plays are *Le Roi s'amuse* (1832) and *Ruy Blas* (1838). His principal poetic works, e.g., *Autumn Leaves* (1831), *Rays and Shadows* (1840), and *Contemplations* (1856), demonstrate his musical powers and highly personal voice. His two great epic novels, *The Hunchback of Notre Dame* (1831) and *Les Misérables* (1862), for which he is best known in English, portray the sufferings of humanity with great compassion and power. Originally a monarchist, Hugo later became an ardent republican, and his opposition to NAPOLEON III led to his exile in 1851. In 1870 he returned in triumph to Paris, where his final years were marked by public veneration; he is buried in the Panthéon.

Huguenots [hyōō'gənŏts], French Protestants, followers of John CALVIN. Protestants founded (1559) a Presbyterian church in France and soon became one of the nation's most industrious and economically advanced elements. They emerged victorious over Roman Catholic forces in the Wars of RELIGION (1562–98) and by the Edict of NANTES (1598) received some religious and political freedom. Cardinal RICHELIEU captured their strongholds, however, and the Peace of Alais (1629) stripped them of their political power. In 1685 LOUIS XIV revoked the Edict of Nantes, and countless Huguenots fled to Protestant Europe and to America.

Huizinga, Johan [hoi'zĭnga], 1872–1945, Dutch historian. Noted for his work on the cultural history of the late Middle Ages, he wrote the classic *Waning of the Middle Ages* (1919). He considered the Renaissance the death of the MIDDLE AGES rather than the birth of the modern world.

Hull, Bobby (Robert Marvin Hull, Jr.), 1939–, Canadian hockey player. Considered the best left wing in the sport's history, he played 15 seasons (1957–72) with the Chicago Black Hawks. His total of 610 goals was third best among National Hockey League players. He later played (1972–80) for the Winnipeg Jets, then of the World Hockey Association, and scored 303 goals.

Hull, Cordell, 1871–1955, American statesman; b. Overton co. (now Pickett co.), Tenn. A U.S. congressman (1907–21, 1923–31) and senator (1931–33) from Tennessee, he served (1933–44) as secretary of state under Pres. F.D. ROOSEVELT. Hull sought sound international economic relations and in WORLD WAR II backed the creation of a world organization to maintain peace. He was awarded the 1945 Nobel Peace Prize.

Hull House: see ADDAMS, JANE.

human evolution, theory of the origins of the human species, *Homo sapiens.* Humans and their immediate ancestors, known as hominids, are notable for their bipedal locomotion, slow rate of maturation, large brain size, and—at least among the more recent hominids—the development of a relatively sophisticated capacity for language, tool use, and social activity. About 5 million years ago, humans and apes began to develop along separate lines. The earliest known hominid fossils are of the genus *Australopithecus* (at least 4 million years ago). They were short and small-brained and were the first primates to walk on two feet. The first member of the genus *Homo* was *Homo habilis* (at least 2 million years ago), a small, gracile species exhibiting marked expansion of the brain. By about 1.6 million years ago, *H. habilis* had evolved into the larger, more robust, and larger-brained HOMO ERECTUS, the first hominid known to have migrated off the African continent. Between 400,000 and 250,000 years ago, NEANDERTHAL MAN and the archaic forms of *Homo sapiens* that replaced it evolved. By 35,000 years ago in Europe (see CRO-MAGNON MAN), the transition to fully modern humans was complete. Among hominids there is evidence of increasing intelligence, behavioral flexibility, and cultural complexity in the fossil record. Tool use, once thought to be the hallmark of the genus *Homo*, is now known to be common in chimpanzees. Nevertheless, tools of increasing complexity accompany the evolution of the human species. With the emergence of modern humans, there is an explosion of technological innovations and artistic activities.

Human Genome Project, international scientific effort to map all of the approximately 100,000 GENES on the 23 human chromosomes and, eventually, to sequence the 3 billion DNA base pairs that make up these genes. Begun in 1990 and centered in the U.S. and France, the study's goal is to understand the basis of genetic diseases like muscular dystrophy and Alzheimer's disease and to gain insight into human evolution. The 15-year, $3 billion project will also compare human genomes (the full set of genes and traits) with those from the bacterium ESCHERICHIA COLI, a FRUIT FLY, and a NEMATODE worm, in order to study the many genetic similarities shared by all species.

human growth hormone (HGH) or **somatotropin,** glycoprotein hormone released by the anterior PITUITARY GLAND that is necessary for normal skeletal growth in humans (see PROTEIN). Evidence suggests that the secretion of HGH is regulated by the release of certain peptides by the HYPOTHALAMUS of the brain. HGH is known to act on many aspects of cellular metabolism, but its most obvious effect is the stimulation of the growth of cartilage and bone in children. An HGH deficiency before puberty results in pituitary dwarfism; an excess results in gigantism. Excess HGH after puberty has little effect on skeletal growth but results in a disease known as acromegaly. Pituitary dwarfism can be treated by injections of synthetic growth hormone produced by GENETIC ENGINEERING in bacteria. HGH is also used illegally by bodybuilders and athletes to increase muscle mass.

human immunodeficiency virus: see AIDS.

humanism, philosophical and literary movement in which human values and capabilities are the central focus. The term originally referred to a point of view particularly associated with the RENAISSANCE, with its emphasis on secular studies (the humanities), a conscious return to classical ideals and forms, and a rejection of medieval religious authority. BOCCACCIO, ERASMUS, and PETRARCH were outstanding humanists. In modern usage, humanism often indicates a general emphasis on lasting human values, respect for scientific knowledge, and cultivation of the classics.

human papillomavirus (HPV), any of a family of more than 60 viruses that cause various growths, including plantar warts and genital warts, a sexually transmitted disease. Detectable warts can be removed but often recur. Genital warts caused by certain types of HPV are associated with cancer of the cervix, vulva, vagina, and penis.

human rights, universal rights held to belong to individuals by virtue of their being human, encompassing civil, political, economic, social, and cultural rights and freedoms, and based on the notion of personal human dignity and worth. Conceptually derived from the theory of NATURAL LAW and originating in Greco-Roman doctrines, the idea of human rights appears in some early Christian writers' works and is reflected in the MAGNA CARTA (1215). The concept winds as a philosophical thread through 17th- and 18th-cent. European and American thought, including the DECLARATION OF INDEPENDENCE (1776) and the French DECLARATION OF THE RIGHTS OF MAN AND CITIZEN (1789). The UN's Universal Declaration of Human Rights (1948) reasserted the concept after the horrors of WORLD WAR II, and human rights have since become a universally espoused yet widely disregarded concept. Organizations such as Amnesty International and Human Rights Watch promote human rights and denounce human rights abuses.

Humboldt, Alexander, Freiherr von, 1769–1859, German naturalist and traveler. From 1799 to 1804 he made his renowned expedition with A.J.A. Bonpland to Central and SOUTH AMERICA and CUBA, a journey that did much to lay the broad foundations for the sciences of physical geography and meteorology. Humboldt explored the ORINOCO R. and the sources of the AMAZON R., and conducted experiments. He wrote *Voyage of Humboldt and Bonpland* (1805–34) and *Kosmos* (1845–62).

Hume, David, 1711–76, Scottish philosopher and historian. Hume carried the EMPIRICISM of LOCKE and George BERKELEY to the logical extreme of radical SKEPTICISM. He repudiated the possibility of certain knowledge, finding in the mind nothing but a series of sensations, and held that cause-and-effect in the natural world derives solely from the conjunction of two impressions. Hume's skepticism is also evident in his writings on religion, in which he rejected any rational or natural theology. Besides his chief work, *A Treatise of Human Nature* (1739–40), he wrote *Political Discourses* (1752), *The Natural History of Religion* (1755), and a *History of England* (1754–62) that was, despite errors of fact, the standard work for many years.

humidity, moisture content of the atmosphere, a major element of climate. Humidity measurements include *absolute humidity,* the mass of water vapor per unit volume of natural air; *relative humidity* (usually meant when the term *humidity* alone is used), the ratio of the actual water-vapor content of the air to its total capacity at a given temperature; and *specific humidity,* the mass of water vapor per unit mass of natural air. Relative humidity is usually measured by means of a HYGROMETER. The National Weather Service's **temperature-humidity index** gives a single numerical value that serves as a measure of comfort (or discomfort) during warm weather. When the index is at 70, most people feel comfortable; at 75 about one half are comfortable; at 80 most are uncomfortable.

hummingbird, small, colorful BIRD with a long, slender bill, of the New World family Trochilidae, found chiefly in the mountains of South America. Hummingbirds vary in size from the 2¼-in. (6-cm) fairy hummingbird of Cuba, the smallest of all birds, to the 8½-in. (21.6-cm) giant hummer of the Andes. They are usually seen hovering or darting (at speeds of up to 60 mi/97 km per hr) in the air, beating their wings at 50 to 75 beats per sec. Constant feeding supplies their enormous energy needs. At night they lapse into a state of torpor similar to HIBERNATION.

Humperdinck, Engelbert, 1854–1921, German composer and teacher, friend and associate of Richard WAGNER. He is known chiefly for his first opera, *Hänsel und Gretel* (1893), loved for its fairy-tale subject and folk-based music.

Humphrey, Doris, 1895–1958, American modern dancer and choreographer; b. Oak Park, Ill. She was a soloist with the Denishawn companies until 1927, when she formed a company with Charles WEIDMAN. A foremost figure in MODERN DANCE, she choreographed *Water Study* (1928) and *Theater Piece No. 2* (1956).

Humphrey, Hubert Horatio, 1911–78, U.S. vice president (1965–69); b. Wallace, S.D. He served as mayor of Minneapolis (1945–48) and U.S. senator from Minnesota (1949–64, 1971–78). A strong advocate of civil rights, he was vice president under L.B. JOHNSON. In 1968 he was the Democratic presidential candidate but lost a close election to Richard M. NIXON.

humus, organic matter decayed to a relatively stable, amorphous state. An important component of fertile SOIL, it affects physical properties such as soil structure, water retention, and EROSION resistance. Humus is formed when soil microorganisms decompose animal and plant material into elements usable by plants (see FERTILIZER).

Hundred Days, in French history, the period (Mar. 20 to June 28, 1815) that began when NAPOLEON I reentered Paris after his exile on Elba. It ended when LOUIS XVIII was restored after Napoleon's defeat in the WATERLOO CAMPAIGN.

Hundred Years War, 1337–1453, conflict between England and France. Its basic cause was a dynastic quarrel between the kings of England, who held the duchy of Guienne, in France, and resented paying homage to the kings of France. There were several immediate causes: a quarrel between EDWARD III of England and PHILIP IV of France over a part of Guienne held by France; English attempts to control the commercially important FLANDERS, a French possession; fishing disputes in the English Channel; and Philip's support of Scotland in its dispute with England. The war began in 1337, when Edward, assuming the title King of France, invaded France. The English won a sea battle at Sluis (1340) and land battles at Crécy (1346), Calais (1347), and Poitiers (1360), where King John II of France was captured. The Treaty of Brétigny (1360) awarded England Calais, Aquitaine, and a large ransom for the captured king. In return, England gave up its claim to the French crown. The war resumed in 1369, when nobles in Aquitaine rebelled over the oppressive tax policies of EDWARD THE BLACK PRINCE. By 1373 DU GUESCLIN had won back most of the English claims. The conflict then languished until 1415, when HENRY V of England defeated France's best knights at AGINCOURT. He then allied himself with Burgundy and went on to subdue Normandy. In the Treaty of Troyes (1420), CHARLES VI of France was forced to recognize Henry as regent and heir to the throne of France, disinheriting his own son, the dauphin. By 1429 the English and their Burgundian allies controlled practically all of France N of the Loire and had Orléans under siege. French fortunes were reversed that year, however. JOAN OF ARC lifted the siege of Orléans and saw the dauphin crowned as CHARLES VII at Rheims. Her capture and execution did not end the string of French victories. In 1435 Charles obtained an alliance with Burgundy, and by 1450 France had reconquered Normandy. By 1451 all of Guienne except Bordeaux was in French hands. Bordeaux fell in 1453, leaving the English only Calais (which they retained until 1558). Domestic difficulties, specifically the Wars of The ROSES, kept England from making any further attempts to conquer France. The Hundred Years War inflicted untold misery on the French people. Famine, the Black Death, and roving bands of marauders decimated the population. An entirely new France emerged. The virtual destruction of the feudal nobility allowed the monarchs to unite the country more solidly under the royal authority and to ally themselves with the newly rising middle class. England ceased thinking of itself as a continental power and began to develop as a sea power.

Hungarian language, member of the Ugrian group of the Finno-Ugric languages, which form a subdivision of the URALIC AND ALTAIC family of languages. See LANGUAGE (table).

Hungary, Hung. *Magyarország,* officially Republic of Hungary, republic (1992 est. pop. 10,333,000), 35,919 sq mi (93,030 sq km), central Europe; bordered by Slovakia (N), Ukraine (NE), Romania (E), Yugoslavia, Croatia, and Slovenia (S), and Austria (W). The capital is BUDAPEST. The DANUBE R. forms part of the border with Slovakia, then turns south and bisects the country. East of the Danube lies the Great Hungarian Plain (Hung. *Alföld*); W of the river are the Little Alföld and the Transdanubian region. Lake Balaton, the largest lake in Europe, is a leading resort area. Traditionally agricultural, Hungary has become heavily industrialized since World War II, producing machinery, textiles, metal goods, chemicals, and motor vehicles. Major farm products are corn, wheat, sugar beets, barley, potatoes, grapes and other fruit, livestock, and poultry. Bauxite and coal are the most important mineral resources. The people are largely ethnic Hungarians; GYPSIES are the largest minority (5.8%). About two thirds of the population is Roman Catholic, but there is a large Protestant minority and nearly 100,000 Jews (the largest Jewish population in central Europe). Hungarian is the official language.

History. Most of the area that is now Hungary and TRANSYLVANIA was conquered in the late 9th cent. A.D. by the MAGYARS, a Finno-Ugric people from beyond the Urals; Christianization was completed by St. STEPHEN (r.1001–38), first king of Hungary. A feudal society developed, controlled by a few powerful nobles, the magnates. Hungary was ruled after 1308 by the Angevin dynasty and after 1386 by other foreign houses. In 1526 the Ottoman Turks defeated the Hungarians at the battle of Mohács. In the long wars that followed, the Turks dominated most of Hungary, while Transylvania was ruled by noble families (see BÁTHORY and RÁKÓCZY). By 1711, however, all Hungary had fallen under HAPSBURG control. A short-lived independent Hungarian republic (1849) under Louis KOSSUTH was overthrown by Austrian and Russian troops, and in 1867 the AUSTRO-HUNGARIAN MONARCHY was established, in which Austria and Hungary were nearly equal partners. After the collapse of the Dual Monarchy in WORLD WAR I, Hungary was proclaimed (1918) an independent republic and was drastically reduced in area and population by the Treaty of Trianon (1920). The Communist dictatorship (1919) of Béla KUN was put down by Romanian intervention, and in 1920 Adm. Nicholas HORTHY DE NAGYBÁNYA became regent of a kingless Hungarian kingdom. In WORLD WAR II Hungary joined (1941) the AXIS and was invaded (1944) by the USSR. A republican constitution was adopted in 1946, but a Communist coup d'etat in 1948 set up a totalitarian people's republic in 1949. In 1956 a popular anti-Communist revolution, led by former premier Imre NAGY, was suppressed by Soviet forces. However, the Soviet-supported counter-government of János KÁDÁR, one of Nagy's ministers, slowly liberalized the country's economic, political, and cultural life. "Goulash communism" made Hungary the most prosperous Soviet-bloc nation, but economic stagnation and decline set in during the 1970s and 80s. In 1988 Kádár was replaced as party leader by a moderate reformer. In 1990 the conservative Hungarian Democratic Forum (HDF) and its allies won a parliamentary majority. József Antall became prime minister, and Árpád Göncz, a writer and former dissident, was elected president. The new government embarked on the privatization of Hungary's state enterprises, selling interests in more than half of such businesses by 1993. Antall died in 1993 and was succeeded as prime minister by Péter Boross.

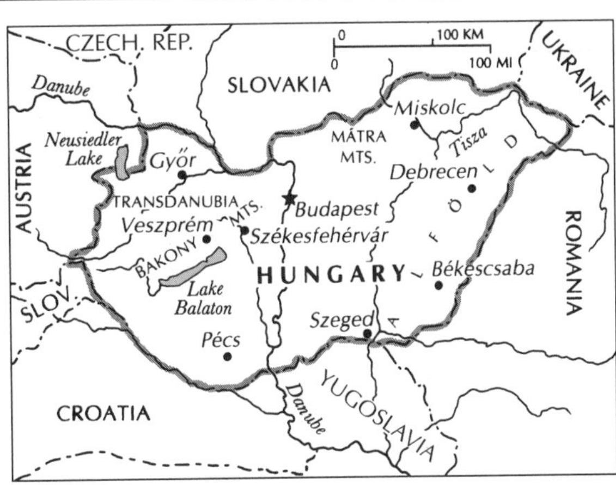

Huns, nomadic people who originated in north-central Asia. Although in customs they resemble the MONGOLS and MAGYARS, they appear not to have been related ethnically to other groups. Short and somewhat Mongolic in appearance, the Huns were organized into ravaging military hordes riding small, rapid horses. In the 3d cent. B.C. they invaded China, where part of the GREAT WALL was built to exclude them. They appeared in the Volga valley c.372; the Goths were pushed west, where they destroyed the Roman Empire. Most of European Russia, Poland, and Germany paid tribute to ATTILA, the greatest Hun king. Defeated (451) in Gaul, the Huns ravaged Italy until Attila's death (453), after which little is known of them.

Hunt, Holman: see HUNT, WILLIAM HOLMAN.

Hunt, (James Henry) Leigh, 1784–1859, English writer. Hunt edited liberal weeklies, notably the *Examiner* (1808–21), and wrote many critical articles. He befriended the important writers of his time, among them KEATS and SHELLEY. His own fame rests on his essays, his lyrics "Abou Ben Adhem" and "Jenny Kissed Me," and his autobiography (1850).

Hunt, Richard Morris, 1828–95, American architect, an exponent of 19th-cent. eclecticism; b. Brattleboro, Vt.; brother of W.M. HUNT. In New York City he founded the first studio to train architects. Most of his work imitated historical styles, e.g., the Lenox Library, N.Y.C., and mansions in New York and Newport, R.I.

Hunt, William Holman, 1827–1910, English painter. He was a founder of the PRE-RAPHAELITE brotherhood, and his sincere devotion to its principles can be seen in such paintings as *The Light of the World* (Oxford Univ.).

Hunt, William Morris, 1824–79, American painter; b. Brattleboro, Vt. A disciple of the BARBIZON SCHOOL, which he introduced into Boston, he exerted great influence on American art. His paintings include portraits, landscapes, and figure pieces, e.g., *Girl at a Fountain* (Metropolitan Mus.).

Huntington, Collis Potter, 1821–1900, American railroad builder; b. near Torrington, Conn. He helped organize the Central Pacific RR and eventually gained for himself and his partners practical control of transportation in the West, consolidated (1884) in the Southern Pacific RR. Most of his vast fortune was left to his nephew **Henry Edwards Huntington,** 1850–1927, b. Oneonta, N.Y., who endowed his estate at San Marino, Calif., for public use. It is the site of the **Henry E. Huntington Library and Art Gallery,** which has one of the largest collections of incunabula in America. It also excels in rare American and British documents, manuscripts, and books, and in 18th-cent. paintings.

Huntington, Henry Edwards: see under HUNTINGTON, COLLIS POTTER.

Huntington, city (1990 pop. 54,844), seat of Cabell co., W W.Va., on the Ohio R.; founded 1871 as the western terminus of the Chesapeake & Ohio RR. It is a river port and commercial center with a large bituminous coal trade. Glass and chemical industries and railroad yards are important.

Huntington Beach, city (1990 pop. 181,519), Orange co., S Calif., on the Pacific coast, across from Santa Catalina Island (see SANTA BARBARA ISLANDS), in a vegetable- and citrus-growing area; inc. 1909. It has oil refineries and aerospace, communications, and other industries. Its fine beaches are well known.

Huntington Library and Art Gallery: see under HUNTINGTON, COLLIS POTTER.

Huntington's disease, formerly **Huntington's chorea,** hereditary disease of the central nervous system, beginning usually in middle age and characterized by involuntary jerky movements, personality changes, and progressive mental deterioration. It is caused by a mutated gene on chromosome 4. The child of a person with Huntington's has a 50% chance of inheriting the gene, which inevitably leads to the disease.

Huntsville, city (1990 pop. 159,789), seat of Madison co., N Ala.; inc. 1811. A major space research center, Huntsville is the site of the Redstone Arsenal, the U.S. Army's missile and rocket center; NASA's Marshall Space Flight Center; and the Alabama Space and Rocket Center, the world's largest space museum. Local industry also includes tires, glass, and electrical equipment. Alabama's first constitution was written (1819) in Huntsville. Numerous antebellum buildings remain.

Huron, confederation of four Native American groups of the Eastern Woodlands (see NORTH AMERICA, INDIGENOUS PEOPLES OF) who spoke Wyandot, an Iroquoian language of the Hokan-Siouan stock (see NATIVE AMERICAN LANGUAGES). Numbering about 20,000 in the 17th cent., they lived in palisaded villages near Georgian Bay in Ontario and grew tobacco. In the mid-17th cent. the Iroquois (see IROQUOIS CONFEDERACY) hunted them down relentlessly. In 1750 they settled in Ohio; there they were known as the Wyandot to the British, with whom they sided in the AMERICAN REVOLUTION. In 1867 they were removed to NE Oklahoma, where some hundreds now live as citizens, the tribe having been terminated in 1959. In 1990 there were 1,947 Wyandots in the U.S.

Huron, Lake, second largest (23,010 sq mi/59,596 sq km) of the GREAT LAKES and fourth largest lake in the world, on the U.S.-Canada border. It is 206 mi (332 km) long and up to 183 (295 km) wide, with a surface elevation of 580 ft (177 m). It receives the waters of Lake Superior through the St. Marys R. and of Lake Michigan through the Straits of Mackinac, and it drains S into Lake Erie through the St. Clair R.–Lake St. Clair–Detroit R. system.

hurricane, tropical CYCLONE formed over the North Atlantic, E North Pacific, W South Pacific, and Indian oceans in which the winds attain speeds greater than 75 mph (121 km/hr). A tropical cyclone passes through two stages, tropical depression and tropical storm, before reaching hurricane force. An average of 3.5 tropical storms per year become hurricanes; one to three of these approach the U.S. coast. Hurricanes usually develop between July and October. A hurricane is nearly circular in shape, and its winds cover an area about 500 mi (800 km) in diameter. As a result of the extremely low central air pressure (around 28.35 in/72 cm of mercury), air spirals inward toward the hurricane's eye, an almost calm area about 20 mi (30 km) in diameter. Hurricanes, which may last from 1 to 30 days, usually move westward in their early stages and then curve northward toward the pole. Deriving their energy from warm tropical ocean water, hurricanes weaken after prolonged contact with colder northern ocean waters, becoming extratropical cyclones; they decay rapidly after moving over land areas. The high winds, coastal flooding, and torrential rains associated with a hurricane may cause enormous damage. Tropical cyclones that form over the E North Pacific Ocean and its seas are called typhoons; those over the Indian Ocean and its seas, cyclones.

Hurston, Zora Neale, 1901–60, African-American writer; b. Eatonville, Fla. An anthropologist who sympathetically interpreted African-American folktales in such collections as *Mules and Men* (1935) and *Tell My Horse* (1938), Hurston also wrote two novels, *Jonah's Gourd Vine* (1934) and *Their Eyes Were Watching God* (1937).

Husák, Gustav [ho͝o'säk], 1913–91, Czechoslovakian Communist leader. After the Soviet invasion of 1968, he succeeded (1969) DUBČEK as Communist party leader and later served as president (1975–89). He reestablished close ties with the USSR and reinstituted tight party control over the government. Widespread opposition to Communist rule forced Husák to resign as president in 1989. He was succeeded by Václav HAVEL, a former dissident.

Husayn ibn Ali, 1856–1931, Arabian political and religious leader. He led the revolt against the Turks and made himself (1916) king of the Hejaz, but he was overthrown (1924) by IBN SAUD. His effort to claim the title of caliph was also unsuccessful. He was the father of ABDULLAH of Jordan and FAISAL I of Iraq.

Hu Shih [ho͞o shŭr], 1891–1962, Chinese philosopher in Republican China. He promoted vernacular literature to replace writing in the classical style. He was ambassador to the U.S. (1938–42) and chancellor of Peking Univ. (1946–48).

husky: see SIBERIAN HUSKY.

Huss, John [hŭs], Czech *Jan Hus,* 1369?–1415, Czech religious reformer. A priest, he was influenced early by the writings of John WYCLIF. Huss attacked the abuses of the clergy and was supported by Holy Roman Emperor WENCESLAUS, who made him rector of the Univ. of Prague (1409). Huss, however, incurred the hostility of the archbishop of Prague, who had him excommunicated in 1410. He then wrote his chief works, including *De ecclesia,* in exile near Tabor. Because Huss denied the infallibility of an immoral pope and asserted the ultimate authority of Scripture over the church, he is generally considered a forerunner of the Protestant REFORMATION. The Emperor SIGISMUND invited him to defend his views at the Council of Constance (1414–18) and granted him a safe-conduct. In 1414 Huss presented himself at the council, which refused to recognize his safe-conduct, tried him as a heretic, and burned him at the stake.

Hussein I, 1935–, king of JORDAN (1953–). He has maintained a moderate course in his relations with the West and other Arab leaders. The loss of W Jordan to Israel in the 1967 ARAB-ISRAELI WAR led to hostility between Hussein and the Palestinian guerrilla movement and to a civil war (1970) in Jordan that Hussein won, achieving stronger control of the country. In 1974 he agreed to relinquish all Jordanian claims to the WEST BANK to the PALESTINE LIBERATION ORGANIZATION.

Hussein, Saddam, 1937–, Iraqi political leader. A member of the Ba'ath party, Hussein played a prominent part in the 1968 coup that brought the party to power. He became party leader and president in 1979 and has ruled Iraq ruthlessly since. He used the nation's oil revenues to make Iraq a major Arab military power and led the country into the IRAN-IRAQ WAR and PERSIAN GULF WAR.

Husserl, Edmund, 1859–1938, German philosopher, founder of PHENOMENOLOGY. A student of Franz BRENTANO, Husserl offered a descriptive study of consciousness for the purpose of discovering the laws by which experiences are had, whether of the objective world or of pure imagination. He concluded that consciousness has no life apart from the objects it considers. In his later work he moved toward IDEALISM, denying that objects exist outside of consciousness. His chief works were *Logical Investigations* (1900–1901) and *Ideas for a Pure Phenomenology* (1907). His most prominent pupil was Martin HEIDEGGER.

Hussites, 15th-cent. religious reformers in Bohemia and Moravia, followers of John HUSS. In the Four Articles of Prague (1420), they called for freedom of preaching, communion in both bread and wine, limits to church property holding, and civil punishment of mortal sin. Papal and imperial forces opposed the reformers in the Hussite Wars, during which the Hussites split into two factions, the moderate Ultraquists and the radical Taborites. The Ultraquists were reconciled to the church in 1436, but the Taborites remained obstinate and were finally defeated at Lipany (1534). During the REFORMATION some Ultraquists became Lutherans. The MORAVIAN CHURCH probably descended from the Taborites.

Huston, John, 1906–87, American film director; b. Nevada, Mo. His films include *The Maltese Falcon* (1941); *The Treasure of the Sierra Madre* (1947), with his father, the actor Walter Huston (1884–1950); *The African Queen* (1951); *Moby Dick* (1956); and *The Dead* (1987).

Hutchins, Robert Maynard, 1899–1977, American educator; b. Brooklyn, N.Y. He was president (1929–45) and chancellor (1945–53) of the Univ. of Chicago. Chairman of the board of editors for the *Encyclopaedia Britannica* after 1943, he was an enthusiast for adult education and in 1946 promoted the "Great Books" program. He later directed various research foundations, including the Center for the Study of Democratic Institutions (Santa Barbara, Calif.). His books include *The Higher Learning in America* (1936) and *The Learning Society* (1968).

Hutchinson, Anne (Marbury), c.1591–1643, religious leader in New England; b. England. She emigrated (1634) to Massachusetts Bay, where her brilliant mind won her a following. Believing that a person justified by grace could discover God's will not only through the Bible but directly through the spirit as well, she broke with Puritan orthodoxy. Banished as a heretic (1637), she helped found present-day Portsmouth, R.I. She later moved to what is now Pelham Bay Park, N.Y.C., where she was killed by Native Americans.

Hutton, James, 1726–97, Scottish geologist who formulated controversial theories of the origin of the earth (see UNIFORMITARIANISM) that paved the way to modern geology. His great work was *The Theory of the Earth* (2 vol., 1795). John Playfair, in his *Illustrations of the Huttonian Theory of the Earth* (1802), simplified Hutton's theories.

Huxley, Aldous Leonard, 1894–1963, English author; grandson of T.H. HUXLEY. After writing critical essays and symbolist poetry, he turned to the novel. *Crome Yellow* (1921), *Antic Hay* (1923), and *Point Counter Point* (1928) all depict social decadence. *Brave New World* (1932) describes a nightmarish 25th-cent. Utopia. Other works include *Eyeless in Gaza* (1936) and *Ape and Essence* (1948). In later years he was strongly interested in mysticism and Eastern philosophy. Huxley also published many short stories and essays.

Huxley, Andrew Fielding, 1917–, British physiologist; half-brother of Aldous HUXLEY; grandson of Thomas HUXLEY. He and Alan HODGKIN shared with Sir John Eccles the 1963 Nobel Prize in physiology or medicine for their analysis of the electrical and chemical events in nerve-cell discharge. He served as president of the Royal Society (1980–85).

Huxley, Thomas Henry, 1825–95, English biologist and educator. He gave up his own biological research to become an influential science publicist and was the principal exponent in England of Charles DARWIN's theory of EVOLUTION. An agnostic (see AGNOSTICISM), he doubted all things not immediately open to logical analysis and scientific verification. However, he placed human ethics outside the scope of materialistic evolutionary processes and believed that progress was achieved by the human control of evolution.

Hu Yaobang, 1915–89, Chinese Communist leader. An associate of DENG XIAOPING, he served as general secretary of the Chinese Communist party (1980–87) until protest demonstrations forced him to resign. ZHAO ZIYANG replaced him.

Huygens, Christiaan [hoi'gəns], 1629–95, Dutch mathematician and physicist; son of Constantijn HUYGENS. He improved telescopic lenses, was the first to interpret correctly the ring structure surrounding SATURN, and discovered its satellite Titan. He was the first to use a pendulum in clocks. Huygens developed a wave theory of LIGHT opposed to Isaac NEWTON's corpuscular theory and formulated Huygens's principle of light waves, which holds that every point on a wave front is a source of new waves. He discovered the polarization of light (see POLARIZED LIGHT) in calcite.

hyacinth, bulbous herb (genus *Hyacinthus*) of the LILY family, native to the Mediterranean region and South Africa. The common hyacinth, cultivated primarily in Holland, has a single spike of fragrant flowers in shades of red, blue, white, or yellow. The smaller, related grape hyacinth (*Muscari*), mostly blue-flowered, is also commonly cultivated.

Hyatt, John Wesley, 1837–1920, American inventor; b. Starkey, N.Y. He is known especially for his development of CELLULOID, which he manufactured with his brothers, beginning in 1872. Among his other inventions were the Hyatt filter, a means of chemically purifying water while it is in motion, and a widely used type of roller bearing.

hybrid, term used by plant and animal breeders for the offspring of a cross between two different subspecies or species. In genetics it is the term for the offspring of parents differing in any genetic characteristic.

Hyde, Edward: see CLARENDON, EDWARD HYDE, 1ST EARL OF.

Hyde Park, town (1990 pop. 21,230), Dutchess co., SE N.Y., on the Hudson R.; settled c.1740, inc. 1821. Franklin D. ROOSEVELT was born there and is buried on the Roosevelt estate. The Roosevelt Library (1941) contains a wealth of historical material. The town also contains the mansion of Frederick W. Vanderbilt (grandson of Cornelius VANDERBILT), two state parks, and a culinary institute.

Hyderabad, former state, S central India. It is now divided among the states of Karnataka, Maharashtra, and Andhra Pradesh. Located almost entirely on the Deccan plateau, it has cotton, grain, and rice crops and deposits of iron and coal. The seat of an ancient Hindu civilization, it fell to the MOGULS in the 17th cent. In 1948 a plebiscite endorsed union with India rather than independence under its Muslim prince. In 1950 it was divided among neighboring states. **Hyderabad,** city (1991 pop. 4,280,261), capital of Andhra Pradesh state, is an administrative and commercial center. Its historic structures include the 16th-cent. Char Minar ("four minarets") and Old Bridge.

Hyderabad, city (1981 pop. 702,539), S Pakistan. The third largest city in Pakistan, it has food-processing, textile, metalworking, and other industries. It was founded in 1768 and was the capital of the emirs of Sind. The British EAST INDIA COMPANY occupied it when the Sind became (1839) a British protectorate. The birthplace of the MOGUL emperor AKBAR is nearby.

hydra, freshwater organism (class Hydrazoa) widely distributed in lakes, ponds, and sluggish streams; a COELENTERATE. Hydras are small, cylindrical, solitary animals, about 1 in. (2.5 cm) long, that attach themselves temporarily to submerged objects by means of a disk at the anal end. Tentacles equipped with stinging cells (nematocysts) surround the mouth; hydras use them to stun their prey.

Hydra, in Greek mythology, many-headed water serpent. When one of its heads was cut off, two new ones appeared. It was killed by HERCULES, who burned the neck after decapitation.

hydrangea: see SAXIFRAGE.

hydraulic machinery, machines that derive their power from the motion or pressure of water or some other liquid. Water or oil under pressure is commonly used as a source of power for many types of machines. The hydraulic press, used, e.g., to form three-dimensional objects from sheet metal or plastics and to compress large objects, consists of two cylinders of different size, each filled with liquid and fitted with a piston, and each connected to a pipe filled with the same liquid. According to Pascal's law, pressure exerted upon the smaller piston is transmitted undiminished through the liquid to the surface of the larger piston, which is forced upward. A small pressure exerted on the smaller piston creates a stronger force on the larger piston, because the area of the latter is larger and the distance it moves is less. The same principle is used to power the hydraulic jack, which is used to lift heavy loads. The hydraulic ELEVATOR is also an application of Pascal's law.

hydraulics, branch of engineering that studies the mechanical properties of fluids. There are two subdivisions. *Hydrostatics,* the study of liquids at rest, involves the problems of buoyancy and flotation, pressures on dams and submerged devices, and hydraulic presses. *Hydrokinetics,* the study of liquids in motion, is concerned with such matters as friction and turbulence generated in pipes by flowing liquids and the use of hydraulic pressure in machinery.

hydrocarbon, any organic compound composed solely of CARBON and HYDROGEN. Hydrocarbons include aliphatic compounds, in which the carbon atoms form a chain, and AROMATIC COMPOUNDS, in which the carbon atoms form stable rings. The aliphatic group is divided into alkanes (e.g., METHANE and PROPANE), alkenes, and alkynes (e.g., ACETYLENE), depending on whether the molecules of the compounds contain, respectively, only single bonds, one or more carbon-carbon double bonds, or one or more carbon-carbon triple bonds. PETROLEUM distillation yields useful fractions that are hydrocarbon mixtures, e.g., NATURAL GAS, GASOLINE, KEROSENE, home heating oil, lubricating oils, PARAFFIN, and ASPHALT. Coal TAR is also a source of hydrocarbons. Hydrocarbon derivatives contain additional elements, e.g., oxygen, and include ALCOHOLS, aldehydes, ketones, carboxylic acids, and halocarbons.

hydrochloric acid, chemical compound formed by dissolving hydrogen chloride (HCl) in water. Most hydrochloric acid produced has a concentration of 30% to 35% hydrogen chloride by weight. Hydrochloric acid is a strong acid (see ACIDS AND BASES) and reacts with most common metals, releasing hydrogen and forming a metal chloride. The major use of hydrochloric acid is in the manufacture of other chemicals. It is also used in pickling (cleaning) metal surfaces, e.g., iron, before galvanizing.

hydrocortisone or **cortisol,** steroid HORMONE produced by the ADRENAL GLAND and involved in carbohydrate and protein metabolism and in response to stress. Like CORTISONE it is used to treat ADDISON'S DISEASE, inflammatory and rheumatoid diseases, allergies, and some cancers. Low- potency hydrocortisone, available over the counter, is used to treat skin irritations.

hydrodynamics: see FLUID MECHANICS.

hydroelectric power: see POWER, ELECTRIC.

hydrofoil, finlike device, attached by struts to the hull of a watercraft, that lifts the moving craft above the water's surface. The term also designates the vessel itself. Like an aircraft wing, the foil develops lift as it passes through the water; the hull is raised above the surface, and the reduced water drag permits greater speed. Some hydrofoil vessels are capable of traveling faster than 70 mph (113 km/hr). Hydrofoil vessels are used as ferries and naval craft. A type of hydrofoil called a stabilizer is used on oceangoing passenger ships to minimize the effect of wave action on the vessel.

hydrogen (H), gaseous element, discovered by Henry CAVENDISH in 1766. The first element on the PERIODIC TABLE, hydrogen is colorless, odorless, tasteless, slightly soluble in water, and highly explosive. The hot flame produced by a mixture of oxygen and hydrogen is used in welding and in melting quartz and glass. Normal hydrogen is diatomic (see ALLOTROPY). The most abundant element in the universe, hydrogen is the major fuel in fusion reactions of the SUN and other STARS. Atmospheric hydrogen has three isotopes: *protium* (nucleus: one proton), the most common; *deuterium,* or heavy hydrogen (nucleus: one proton and one neutron), used in particle accelerators and as a tracer for studying chemical-reaction mechanisms; and *tritium* (nucleus: one proton and two neutrons), a radioactive gas used in the hydrogen bomb, in luminous paints, and as a tracer. Hydrogen's principal use is in the synthesis of AMMONIA; liquid hydrogen has been greatly used as a rocket fuel, in conjunction with oxygen or fluorine. Deuterium oxide, or heavy water, is used as a moderator in nuclear reactors. See ELEMENT (table).

hydrogen bomb, weapon deriving a large portion of its energy from the nuclear fusion of hydrogen isotopes. In fusion lighter elements are joined together to form heavier elements, and the end product weighs less than the components forming it. The difference in mass is converted into energy. Because extremely high temperatures are required to initiate fusion reactions, a hydrogen bomb is also known as a thermonuclear bomb. The structure of a hydrogen bomb is as follows: an ATOMIC BOMB is surrounded by a layer of lithium deuteride (a compound of lithium and deuterium) and then by a tamper, or thick outer layer, frequently of fissionable material, that holds the contents together in order to obtain a larger explosion. The atomic explosion produces neutrons that fission the lithium into helium, tritium, and energy, and creates the extremely high temperature needed for the subsequent fusion of deuterium with tritium, and of tritium with tritium. Explosion of the neutron bomb, which has a minimal atomic trigger and a nonfissionable tamper, produces blast effects and a hail of lethal neutrons but almost no radioactive fallout. The first thermonuclear bomb was exploded in 1952 at ENEWETAK by the U.S., the second in 1953 by the USSR. See also DISARMAMENT, NUCLEAR.

hydrogen chloride: see HYDROCHLORIC ACID.

hydrogen cyanide: see CYANIDE.

hydrogen peroxide: see PEROXIDE.

hydrology, study of water and its properties, including its distribution and movement in and through the land areas of the earth. The hydrologic cycle consists of the passage of water from the oceans into the atmosphere; onto, through, and under the lands; and back to the ocean. Hydrology is mainly concerned with the part of the cycle that follows the precipitation of water onto the land and precedes its return to the oceans. See also METEOROLOGY; OCEANOGRAPHY.

hydrolysis, chemical reaction of a compound with WATER, usually resulting in the formation of one or more new compounds. The most common hydrolysis occurs when a salt of a weak acid or weak base (or both) is dissolved in water. Water ionizes into negative hydroxyl ions (OH^-) and positive hydrogen ions (H^+), which become hydrated to form positive hydronium ions (H_3O^+). The salt also breaks up into positive and negative ions, and the formed ions recombine.

hydrometer, calibrated glass float used to determine the SPECIFIC GRAVITY of a liquid. It usually consists of a thin glass tube that is weighted at one end so that it will float upright in a liquid. The scale reading on the tube that is level with the surface of the liquid in which the hydrometer floats indicates the number of times heavier or lighter the liquid is than water, i.e., the specific gravity of the liquid. The hydrometer is based on ARCHIMEDES' PRINCIPLE.

hydrophobia: see RABIES.

hydrophone, device, used in SONAR apparatus and in certain underwater weapons, that receives underwater sound waves and converts them to electrical energy. The voltage generated can then be read on a meter or played through a loudspeaker. It is the marine equivalent of the MICROPHONE.

hydroponics, growing of plants without soil, in water (and sometimes a sterile medium, e.g., sand) containing balanced concentrations of essential nutrients. Hydroponics can increase yields of commercial crops because plants are grown closer together than in the field; it also almost eliminates weeds and pests. The technique is limited by the support required to hold a given plant upright.

hydrothermal vent, crack along a rift or ridge in the deep ocean floor that spews out water heated by the magma under the earth's crust. Giant tube worms, yellow mussels, and pink sea urchins are found in the unique ecological systems that surround the vents. All of these animals live on bacteria that use CHEMOSYNTHESIS to produce energy from dissolved hydrogen sulfide. The vents' hot springs leach out valuable subsurface minerals and deposit them on the ocean floor. Some scientists believe such vents may have been the source of life on earth.

hydroxide, chemical compound that contains the hydroxyl (—OH) radical. The term refers especially to inorganic compounds. Organic compounds that have the hydroxyl radical as a functional group are referred to as ALCOHOLS. Most metal hydroxides are bases. ALKALI METAL hydroxides, such as sodium hydroxide (NaOH), are strong bases and are very soluble in water. The ALKALINE-EARTH METAL hydroxides are less basic, and magnesium hydroxide (MILK OF MAGNESIA) is only slightly basic. Some hydroxides, such as aluminum hydroxide [$Al(OH)_3$], exhibit AMPHOTERISM.

hyena, chiefly nocturnal MAMMAL of the family Hyaenidae of Africa and SW Asia. Known for its cry, which sounds like maniacal laughter, it feeds mostly on carrion and can crush bones with its strong teeth and jaws. Three species are generally recognized: the spotted hyena (*Crocuta crocuta*) of sub-Saharan Africa; the smaller striped hyena (*Hyaena hyaena*) of Asia and N Africa; and the brown hyena (*H. brunnea*) of S Africa.

hygrometer, instrument used to measure the moisture content of a gas, as in determining the relative HUMIDITY of the air. The most common type of hygrometer is the dry- and wet-bulb psychrometer. It consists of two identical mercury THERMOMETERS, one of which has a wet wick around its bulb. The sling type of psychrometer is swung around in the air. Water evaporating from the wick absorbs heat from the bulb, causing the thermometer reading to drop. The observer, after reading the dry-bulb temperature and the drop in the wet-bulb temperature, can determine the relative humidity from appropriate tables. Among other kinds of hygrometers are ones that use human hair or electrical resistance, rather than thermometers, to determine moisture content.

Hyksos [Egyptian, = rulers of foreign lands], invaders of ancient EGYPT, now substantiated as the XV–XVII dynasties. A northwestern Semitic people, they entered Egypt c.1720–1710 B.C. and subdued the Middle Kingdom pharaohs. The Hyksos established a peaceful, prosperous reign. Their introduction of Canaanite deities and Asian artifacts broke down the isolationism of Egypt.

hyperactivity, excessive physical activity of emotional or physiological origin, usually seen in young children; one of the components of ATTENTION DEFICIT HYPERACTIVITY DISORDER.

hyperbola: see CONIC SECTION.

hyperbolic geometry: see NON-EUCLIDEAN GEOMETRY.

Hyperion, in astronomy, natural satellite of SATURN.

hypertension, elevated blood pressure resulting from an increase in the amount of blood pumped by the heart or from increased resistance to the flow of blood through the small arterial blood vessels (arterioles). When the cause is unknown, the condition is called primary, or essential, hypertension. When a cause can be identified (e.g., a disorder of the adrenal glands, kidneys, or arteries), the condition is known as secondary hypertension. Factors such as heredity, obesity, and emotional stress are thought to play a role. Known as the "silent killer," hypertension often produces few overt symptoms; it may, however, result in damage to the heart, eyes, kidneys, or brain and ultimately lead to heart failure or STROKE. Treatment of hypertension includes diets to reduce weight and alcohol intake, increased exercise, and various drugs, such as DIURETICS, BETA BLOCKERS, ACE INHIBITORS, and CALCIUM-CHANNEL BLOCKERS (see also BIOFEEDBACK). Recent research has questioned the importance of dietary salt as a major contributor to hypertension, and other studies point to low calcium intake as a cause.

hypertext, technique for organizing computer databases or documents to facilitate the nonsequential retrieval of information. Related pieces of information are connected by predefined or user-created links that allow a user to follow associative trails across the database. The linked data may be in a text, graphic, or audio format, allowing MULTIMEDIA presentations. Hypertext applications offer a variety of tools for very rapid searches for specific information. See also INFORMATION STORAGE AND RETRIEVAL.

hypnosis, altered state of consciousness characterized by focused concentration similar to that experienced when daydreaming or concentrating and oblivious to distraction. It allows access to the highly suggestible subconscious mind by quieting the conscious mind. Research has shown electrical changes in the brain during hypnosis; the brain waves of a hypnotized person are usually different from those of a person in the normal waking state. Most people can be hypnotized, although the ability varies from person to person. Techniques vary but usually involve deep relaxation accompanied by the focusing of the mind (as on an object or the voice of the hypnotist). Hypnosis is occasionally used as an aid in medical practice, especially for anesthesia and pain relief; in psychotherapy, e.g., to help patients recall traumatic events and overcome denial; and in BEHAVIOR THERAPY, to assist people in breaking unwanted habits (e.g., smoking, overeating).

hypoglycemia, abnormally low level of blood glucose (sugar), the body's chief energy source (hence the term *low blood sugar*). It is most often caused by an oversecretion of insulin from the pancreas triggered by stress, exercise, fasting, or disorders of the adrenal or pituitary glands, liver, or pancreas; in persons with diabetes it may result from an overdose of insulin. Symptoms range from weakness, fatigue, shakiness, and anxiety to mental disturbances, convulsions, and coma. Acute episodes are relieved by ingestion of glucose or sucrose. Long-term treatment involves control of causative factors and diet regulation.

hypothalamus, important supervisory center in the BRAIN. The hypothalamus regulates body temperature, BLOOD PRESSURE, heartbeat, METABOLISM of fats and carbohydrates, and blood-sugar level. It participates, with other brain centers, in the control and monitoring of several other functions, such as water balance and certain motor responses. The hypothalamus is also thought to be involved in the expression of emotions and in sexual behaviors.

Hypsilanti: see YPSILANTI.

hysterectomy, surgical removal of the uterus, sometimes including the removal of the cervix, Fallopian tubes, and ovaries (see REPRODUCTIVE SYSTEM). It is performed in cases of malignant tumors or of benign growths causing bleeding and pain. Hysterectomy does not interfere with sexual activity, but since it eliminates the possibility of childbearing, it is avoided in younger women when more conservative treatment is feasible.

hysteria, any of several psychological conditions. In conversion hysteria, or conversion disorder, a psychological conflict is converted into a bodily disturbance. Symptoms, which have no underlying physical cause, may include limb paralysis, blindness, or convulsive seizures. Dissociative hysterical neuroses, or dissociative disorders, include multiple personality disorder and AMNESIA. Hysterical personality, or histrionic personality disorder, is characterized by excessive emotionality and attention-seeking. Because of the broad and confusing use of the term (and the popular use of *hysterics*), the term *hysteria* is gradually being replaced in psychiatry.

I

I, chemical symbol of the element IODINE.

Iacocca, Lee (Lido Anthony Iaccoca), 1924–, American business executive; b. Allentown, Pa. In 1946 he joined the Ford Motor Co., where he rose to president (1970–78). He left Ford after a dispute with Henry FORD II and became president (1978–79) and chairman (1979–92) of the Chrysler Corp., reviving it through shrewd financial policies and with a loan guarantee and tax concessions granted by Congress.

iambic pentameter: see PENTAMETER.

Iapetus, in astronomy, natural satellite of SATURN.

Iaşi [yäsh] or **Jassy** [yä'sē], city (1989 est. pop. 330,000), E Romania, in Moldavia, near the Moldova border. The center of a farming region, it produces chemicals, drugs, plastics, and textiles. It was (1565–1859) MOLDAVIA's capital. In World War II its large Jewish population was massacred by the Nazis.

Ibadan, city (1987 est. pop. 1,144,000), SW Nigeria. The second largest city of Nigeria, it is a major commercial and industrial center, producing metal products, furniture, soap, and handicrafts. The center of a rich agricultural area, it is a market for cocoa, which, with cotton, is grown in the region. Founded in the 1830s, it developed into the most powerful Yoruba city-state before coming under British protection in 1893.

Iberian Peninsula, SW Europe, c.230,400 sq mi (596,740 sq km). Occupied by Spain and Portugal, it is separated from the rest of Europe (NE) by the PYRENEES and from Africa (S) by the Strait of GIBRALTAR.

ibex, wild goat (genus *Capra*) found in rugged, mountainous country from central Asia to the Himalayas, S Europe, and NE Africa. Surefooted and agile, ibexes live in small herds and feed on vegetation. They are sturdily built, with brown to gray coats and heavy horns of varying size; the chin is bearded and the tail short. The adult ibex stands from 2½ to 3½ ft (76 to 106 cm) at the shoulder.

ibis, wading BIRD with long, slender, downcurved bill, found in warmer regions of the world. Its body is usually about 2 ft (61 cm) long; most feed on fish and other aquatic animals. The sacred ibis of ancient Egypt (*Threskiornis aethiopica*), a white and black bird, no longer frequents the NILE basin, although it inhabits other parts of Africa.

Ibiza: see BALEARIC ISLANDS.

Ibn al-Haytham [ĭb'ən äl-hĭthäm'] or **Alhazen** [ălhəzen'], 965–c.1040, Egyptian mathematician, physicist, and astronomer; b. Persia. His *Optics,* which influenced the work of Johannes KEPLER and René DESCARTES, introduced the important idea that light rays emanate in straight lines in all directions from every point on a luminous surface. In mathematics, al-Haytham elucidated and extended EUCLID's *Elements*.

Ibn Ezra, Abraham ben Meir, 1098–1164, Jewish grammarian, commentator, poet, philosopher, and astronomer; b. Spain. Best known as a biblical critic, he was the inspiration for Robert BROWNING's poem "Rabbi Ben Ezra."

Ibn Gabirol, Solomon ben Judah, c.1021–1058, Jewish poet and philosopher, also known as Avicebron; b. Spain. He wrote hundreds of poems, both sacred and secular; much of his religious poetry has been incorporated into the Judaic liturgy. His great philosophical work *The Fountain of Life* greatly influenced Christian thought.

Ibn Khaldun [ĭb'ən khäldōōn'], 1332–1406, Arab historian; b. Tunisia. Considered the greatest of Arab historians, he wrote *Kitab al-Ibar* [universal history], in which he treated history as a science and outlined a philosophy of history.

Ibn Saud [ĭ'bən säōōd'], c.1888–1953, founder of SAUDI ARABIA and its first king. As leader of the WAHHABI sect he claimed ancient rights in the area. By 1912 he had conquered the Nejd, and he triumphed over HUSAYN IBN ALI and became king of the Hejaz in 1924. In 1932 he combined his conquests into the kingdom of Saudi Arabia.

Ibo, ethnic group in Nigeria, chiefly from SE Nigeria and numbering about 15 million. Receptive to Christianity and education under British colonialism, they became heavily represented in professional, managerial, and technical occupations. They played a major role in securing (1963) Nigerian independence. Political conflict in the 1960s caused the Ibos to secede from Nigeria and form the Republic of BIAFRA. Civil war followed, and by 1970 Biafra had been defeated.

Ibrahim Pasha, 1789–1848, Egyptian general, son of MUHAMMAD ALI. He led Turkish forces against the WAHHABIS in Arabia (1816–19) and rebel Greeks (1825–28). After his father turned against the Turks, he conquered Syria (1832–33), but Britain and Austria forced its return to Turkey (1838).

Ibsen, Henrik [ĭb'sən], 1828–1906, Norwegian dramatist, probably the most influential figure in modern theater. He was stage manager and playwright of the National Stage in Bergen (1851–57) and director of the Norwegian Theater in Oslo (1857–62). Because his early plays went unrecognized or were greeted with hostility, he went to Italy in 1864, and it was there and in Germany that he wrote the bulk of his dramas. Ibsen's work can be divided into three periods. The first phase, that of poetic drama, deals primarily with historical themes, folklore, and romantic pageantry, and includes the tragedy *Brand* (1866) and the existentialist *Peer Gynt* (1867). Then came the realistic social plays for which he is best known, e.g., *A Doll's House* (1879), *Ghosts* (1881), *An Enemy of the People* (1882), *The Wild Duck* (1884), and *Hedda Gabler* (1890), in which Ibsen rebelled against sterile and restrictive social conventions. The final period is characterized by a strong emphasis on symbolism, e.g., *The Master Builder* (1892) and *John Gabriel Borkman* (1896), which blend an introspective realism with folk poetry.

ibuprofen, nonsteroidal anti-inflammatory drug that reduces pain, fever, and inflammation. Available over the counter, it is commonly used to treat rheumatoid arthritis, gout, and painful menstruation. Side effects include intestinal upset, which can lead to gastritis and ulcers.

Icarus: see DAEDALUS.

ICBM: see MISSILE, GUIDED.

iceberg, mass of ice that has become detached from an ice sheet or GLACIER and is floating in the ocean. Only about one ninth of its total mass projects above the water. Rocks dropped to the ocean floor by melting icebergs have been studied to determine the range of icebergs during glacial periods. Because of the 1912 collision of the ocean liner TITANIC with an iceberg, a constant census of icebergs is maintained and their locations reported to nearby ships.

ice hockey: see HOCKEY, ICE.

Iceland, Icel. *Island,* officially Republic of Iceland, republic (1992 est. pop. 259,000), 39,698 sq mi (102,819 sq km), the westernmost state of Europe, occupying an island in the Atlantic Ocean just S of the Arctic Circle. REYKJAVÍK is the capital. Iceland, whose coasts are indented by deep fjords, is a plateau averaging 2,000 ft (610 m) in height and culminating in vast icefields. There are about 200 volcanoes, many still active. Hot springs abound and are used for inexpensive heating. Only about one fourth of the island is habitable, and most settlements are on the coast. The climate is relatively mild and humid in the west and south, and polar and tundralike in the north and east. Fishing is the most important industry, with codfish and herring the chief exports. Agriculture is limited (hay, potatoes, turnips), but sheep, horses, and cattle are grazed extensively. Aside from aluminum smelting there is little heavy industry, and imports provide most of the country's needs. The Lutheran Church is established, and 95% of the people are members. Icelandic (Old Norse) is the official language; Old Norse literature reached its greatest flowering in Iceland.

History. Iceland was settled (c.850–75) by the Norse (see VIKINGS). A general assembly, the ALTHING, was established in 930, making it the world's oldest functioning parliamentary body, and Christianity was introduced c.1000. Norwegian rule was imposed after 1261, and in 1380 Iceland, with Norway, passed to the Danish crown, inaugurating a national decline that lasted to 1550. The 17th and 18th cent. were disastrous: pirate raids destroyed trade; epidemics and volcanic eruptions killed a large part of the population; and a private trade monopoly, created in Copenhagen in 1602, caused economic ruin. The 19th cent. brought a rebirth of national culture and a strong independence movement led by Jón Sigurðsson. A constitution and limited home rule were granted in 1874, and Iceland became a sovereign state in personal union with DENMARK in 1918. In WORLD WAR II British and U.S. forces defended the island. Icelanders voted in 1944 to end the union with Denmark, and an independent republic was proclaimed on June 17, 1944. Disputes with Britain over fishing rights in Iceland's waters resulted in three "cod wars" and a four-month break in diplomatic relations before a settlement was reached in 1976. In 1980 Vigdís Finnbogadóttir was elected to the presidency (a largely ceremonial post), becoming the world's first popularly elected female head of state, and she has held the office since then. David Oddsson, of the conservative Independence party, has been prime minister since 1991.

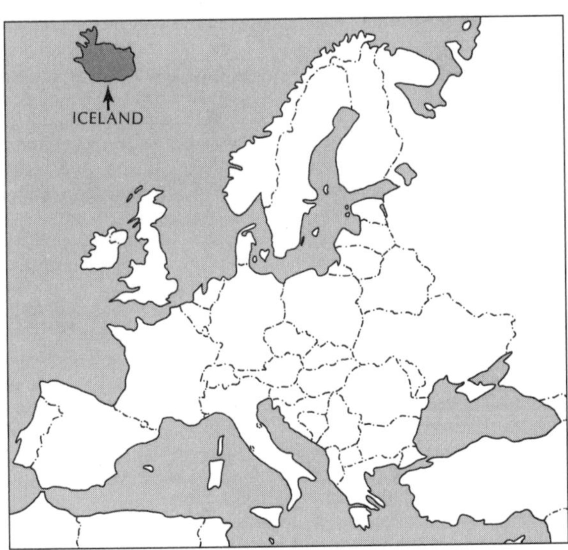

Icelandic language, member of the North Germanic, or Scandinavian, group of the Germanic subfamily of the Indo-European family of languages. See LANGUAGE (table).

Iceland spar, colorless variety of crystallized CALCITE known for its properties of transparency and double refraction, found primarily in Iceland. It is used chiefly in the manufacture of Nicol prisms.

ice skating: see SKATING.

Ickes, Harold LeClaire, 1874–1952, American statesman; b. Blair co., Pa. A Republican, he was secretary of the interior (1933–46) under F.D. ROOSEVELT and Harry TRUMAN. He was also head (1933–39) of the PUBLIC WORKS ADMINISTRATION.

iconoclasm [Gr., = image breaking], opposition to the religious use of images. Religious pictures and statues were an early feature of Christian worship. Opponents of their use claimed that they led to idolatry. Iconoclasm flourished in Asia Minor in the 8th and 9th cent. and was favored by several Byzantine emperors. Opponents of iconoclasm were Popes Gregory II and ADRIAN I and Empress IRENE, who restored the images. Iconoclasm was rejected at the Second Council of NICAEA (787). The controversy led Byzantine artists toward spiritual expression rather than naturalism.

Ictinus, fl. 2d half of 5th cent. B.C., Greek architect. With CALLICRATES as his associate, he built the PARTHENON on the Acropolis at Athens (447–432 B.C.).

id: see PSYCHOANALYSIS.

Idaho, mountain state in the NW U.S.; bordered by Montana and Wyoming (E), Utah and Nevada (S), Oregon and Washington (W), and the Canadian province of British Columbia (N).

Area, 83,557 sq mi (216,413 sq km). *Pop.* (1990) 1,006,749, a 6.6% increase over 1980 pop. *Capital,* Boise. *Statehood,* July 3, 1890 (43d state). *Highest pt.,* Borah Peak, 12,662 ft (3,862 m); *lowest pt.,* Snake R., 710 ft (217 m). *Nickname,* Gem State. *Motto, Esto Perpetua* [It Is Perpetual]. *State bird,* mountain bluebird. *State flower,* syringa. *State tree,* white pine. *Abbr.,* ID.

Land and People. Over 60% of the mountainous and heavily forested land of Idaho is controlled by the federal government, much of it in national forests, Yellowstone National Park (see NATIONAL PARKS, table), and recreation areas such as Craters of the Moon National Monument. The ROCKY MOUNTAINS' lofty peaks, including the Bitterroot, Salmon R., and Sawtooth ranges, dominate the terrain. The SNAKE R. flows through S Idaho in a great arc, creating the state's most extensive valley. Among the river's spectacular gorges is Hell's Canyon, North America's deepest (7,900 ft/2,408 m). The climate ranges from hot summers in the arid south to cold, snowy winters in the mountainous north. About 57% of the state's population lives in urban areas. The largest city is BOISE, followed by POCATELLO and IDAHO FALLS. The population is (1990) nearly 95% white.

Economy. Agriculture is the most important sector of the economy. Cattle are the leading product, and dairy goods are also important. The chief crops are potatoes (Idaho is the leading U.S. producer), peas, sugar beets, wheat, hay, and barley. Lumber and wood products, processed foods, and chemicals are the major manufactures. Tourism has also become important, and the state attracts many campers and outdoor sports enthusiasts. Idaho is the country's leading silver producer, and it also extracts significant quantities of zinc, phosphate, lead, and gold.

Government. The constitution (adopted 1889) provides for a governor serving a four-year term. The legislature consists of a 42-seat senate and 84-seat house, with members of both bodies elected to two-year terms. Idaho sends two representatives and two senators to the U.S. Congress and has four electoral votes.

History. Probably the first whites to enter the area were members of the LEWIS AND CLARK EXPEDITION (1805), but they were not far ahead of fur trappers, who established trading posts and by the 1840s had depleted the fur supply. Present-day Idaho was part of Oregon country, over which the U.S. gained control in 1846. With the discovery of gold and silver during the early 1860s, settlers poured in. In the late 19th cent. the growth of ranching, violent labor conflicts in the mines, and the arrival of railroads were concurrent with the development of cities. In recent years, the Snake R. projects have provided a huge hydroelectrical capacity and a greatly expanded water supply for irrigated agriculture. In the late 1980s the state rebounded from recession earlier in the decade, largely by attracting many new businesses, notably high-technology firms.

Idaho Falls, city (1990 pop. 43,929), seat of Bonneville co., SE Idaho, on the Snake R.; inc. 1900. The chief city of the upper Snake Valley, it is the commercial center of a farm and ranch region. The Idaho National Engineering Laboratory, a government facility, is a major employer. The city's industries produce steel and building materials, and tourism is important. Idaho Falls was settled (1860) by MORMONS.

idealism, in philosophy, the attempt to account for all objects in nature and experience as representations of the mind, and sometimes to assign to such representations a higher order of existence. It is opposed to MATERIALISM and NATURALISM. Early idealism (e.g., that of PLATO) conceived a world in which eternal ideas constituted reality; in modern times idealism (e.g., that of George BERKELEY in the 18th cent.) has come to refer the source of ideas to the individual's consciousness. In KANT's transcendental idealism, the phenomenal world of human understanding opposes a world of things-in-themselves, while the later German idealists (e.g., FICHTE, SCHELLING, and HEGEL) treated all reality as the creation of mind or spirit. More recent idealists include F.H. BRADLEY and CROCE.

Ides: see CALENDAR.

Idrisi [ĭdrē'sē] or **Edrisi** [ĕ–], b. 1099?, d. after 1154, Arabian geographer. After many travels, he came to the court of Roger II of Sicily. His monumental work, *Kitab Rujjar* (the Book of Roger; 1154), contains his description of the earth, supplemented by reports of travelers sent out by Roger.

Ieyasu (Ieyasu Tokugawa) [ēā'yäsōō], 1542–1616, Japanese dictator, founder of the TOKUGAWA shogunate. He helped the dictators Nobunga and HIDEYOSHI to unify Japan and received (1590) a fief near Edo (Tokyo). He became the most powerful daimyo, or baron, by defeating his rivals in the battle of Sekigahara (1600) and became shogun in 1603. Ieyasu encouraged foreign trade; one of his advisers was an Englishman, Will Adams.

Ignatius of Antioch, Saint, d. c.107, bishop of Antioch (Turkey) and Christian martyr. He wrote epistles to Christian communities in Rome and Asia Minor to combat heresy. He stressed the virgin birth, the TRINITY, and the role of the bishop, and was the first Christian writer to use the word *Catholic.* Feast: Oct. 17.

Ignatius of Constantinople, Saint, c.800–877, Greek churchman, patriarch of CONSTANTINOPLE. A son of Byzantine Emperor MICHAEL I, he was castrated and imprisoned by Emperor LEO V to prevent his accession. In 846 or 847 he was made patriarch and opposed ICONOCLASM. In 858 Ignatius was replaced with PHOTIUS, but on the accession (867) of BASIL I, Ignatius again became patriarch and was confirmed by the Fourth Council of CONSTANTINOPLE. Feast: Oct. 23.

Ignatius of Loyola, Saint, 1491–1556, Spanish churchman, founder of the JESUITS. A soldier, he was converted in 1521 and began to study religion. In 1534, in Paris, he and six others took vows of poverty and chastity and were later (1537) ordained. They were received (1538) by the pope, and in 1540 Ignatius won papal approval for his *Formula* for a new religious order. In 1541 he was elected general of the order, a post he held until his death. Ignatius was a leader in the Catholic Reformation (see REFORMATION, CATHOLIC), but he was more interested in education and missionary work than in converting Protestants. His *Spiritual Exercises* are a major devotional work. Feast: July 31.

igneous rock: see ROCK.

Iguaçu Falls or **Iguassú Falls,** on the Argentina-Brazil border, one of the world's greatest waterfalls, with a drop of c.210 ft (64 m), located on the Iguaçu R. near its confluence with the PARANÁ R. Nearby is the great ITAÍPU Dam and one of the world's largest hydroelectric power complexes.

iguana, large LIZARD (family Iguanidae) found in tropical America and the GALAPAGOS ISLANDS. The common iguana (*Iguana iguana*), a tree-living species found along streams from Mexico to N South America, is bright green with a crest of spines from the neck to the striped tail. Its tail accounts for two thirds of its length (3–6 ft/90–180 cm).

IJsselmeer [ī'səlmār"], shallow freshwater lake, NW Netherlands, created when much of the old Zuider Zee, an inlet of the North Sea, was enclosed in 1932 by two dams totaling 19 mi (31 km) in length. During the next half century, more than 850 sq mi (2,200 sq km) of fertile farmland, in five polders (tracts), was reclaimed from the IJsselmeer.

Ikhnaton [ĭknä'tən] or **Akhenaton** [ä"kənä'tən], d. c.1354 B.C., Egyptian king (c.1372–54) of the XVIII dynasty; son of Amenhotep III. A religious innovator, he abandoned polytheism to embrace an absolute solar monotheism, holding that the sun alone was God and he the sun's physical son. Under him a new school of artists abandoned convention and returned to nature (to glorify the sun). His fanaticism was his undoing; he defaced earlier monuments, arousing the anger of the priests and the people. Neglecting the provinces, he left to his successors only EGYPT and the upper NILE valley, not the empire he had inherited. Of the art works of his reign, the bust of his wife, NEFERTITI, is the most famous.

Ilf, Ilya Arnoldovich [ēlf], pseud. of **Ilya Arnoldovich Fainzilberg,** 1897–37, Russian writer. Ilf and Yevgeny Petrovich PETROV wrote the satirical novels *The Twelve Chairs* (1928) and *The Little Golden Calf* (1931). *Little Golden America* (1936) is a humorous account of their trip to the U.S.

Iliad: see HOMER.

Ilion or **Ilium:** see TROY.

Illia, Arturo [ēl'yä], 1900–83, president of Argentina (1963–66). A physician, he was elected president with only 25% of the vote. He was unable to deal with the country's deteriorating economy or with the Peronists. In addition, he canceled Argentina's petroleum contracts with foreign countries. He was deposed by military leaders in 1966.

Illinois, confederation of Native American tribes of the Eastern Woodlands (see NORTH AMERICA, INDIGENOUS PEOPLES OF), who spoke an Algonquian language of the Algonquian-Wakashan stock (see NATIVE AMERICAN LANGUAGES). In the mid-17th cent. 6,500 Illinois lived in the N Illinois area, but by 1750 warfare had reduced them to 2,000. They were all but exterminated in retaliation for the supposed assassination of PONTIAC by a member of the Illinois. In 1833 the survivors, largely Peorias, moved West, and their descendants live on a reservation in NE Oklahoma. In 1990 there were 1,365 Peorias in the U.S.

Illinois, midwestern state in the N central U.S.; bordered by Lake Michigan, Indiana, and—across the Ohio R.—Kentucky (E), Missouri and Iowa, across the Mississippi R. (W), and Wisconsin (N).

Area, 56,400 sq mi (146,076 sq km). *Pop.* (1990) 11,430,602, a 0.1% increase over 1980 pop. *Capital,* Springfield. *Statehood,* Dec. 3, 1818 (21st state). *Highest pt.,* Charles Mound, 1,235 ft (377 m); *lowest pt.,* Mississippi R., 279 ft (85 m). *Nicknames,* Inland Empire; Prairie State. *Motto,* State Sovereignty—National Union. *State bird,* cardinal. *State flower,* native violet. *State tree,* white oak. *Abbr.,* Ill.; IL.

Land and People. Most of Illinois consists of broad, fertile, level plains drained by more than 275 rivers. The state's temperate climate is marked by cold winters and hot summers. Almost 85% of the population lives in urban areas. CHICAGO, the third largest city in the U.S. and the center of the third largest metropolitan area, is by far the leading city of Illinois and the entire Midwest and is a major center of heavy industry, transportation, commerce, and finance. Other important cities are ROCKFORD, PEORIA, and SPRINGFIELD. In 1990 the state was 78% white and 15% African American.

Economy. Illinois has long had one of the U.S.'s most productive economies. Prosperous industrial and agricultural sectors are supported by a superb transportation complex, including GREAT LAKES shipping, and since 1959 the port of Chicago has been linked to the Atlantic via the SAINT LAWRENCE SEAWAY. Manufacturing is the leading source of income, with machinery (including machine tools and transportation equipment), electrical and electronic equipment, steel and other metals, and chemicals the principal products. Illinois is the leading U.S. producer of soybeans; is second to Iowa in output of hogs and corn; and earns considerable income from cattle, hay, and wheat. Much heavy industry is supported by Illinois's extensive bituminous coal deposits, the fifth largest in the country, and by petroleum deposits in the south. The state is the U.S.'s leading producer of fluorspar.

Government. The constitution (adopted 1970) provides for a governor elected to a four-year term. The legislature consists of a senate whose 59 members serve terms of both four and two years, and a house with 118 members elected for two years. Illinois elects 20 representatives and 2 senators to the U.S. Congress and has 22 electoral votes.

History. The ILLINOIS, SAC AND FOX, and other Native American peoples lived in the area when French explorers, including Father Jacques MARQUETTE and Louis JOLLIET, explored the region during the late 17th cent. It passed from France to Britain in 1763, but it was ceded to the U.S. at the end of the AMERICAN REVOLUTION and was part of the NORTHWEST TERRITORY before becoming (1809) a separate territory. The BLACK HAWK WAR (1832) virtually ended the tenure of Native Americans in Illinois. During the mid-19th cent. Abraham LINCOLN launched his political career in Illinois, which was just becoming a major industrial state. Chicago, with its huge steel mills and stockyards, attracted thousands of European immigrants. The late 19th cent. saw the growth of the GRANGER MOVEMENT among farmers and violent labor strife in industry. In 1937 new oilfields were discovered, further enhancing industrial growth. In the 1980s much of Illinois's heavy industry suffered a serious decline, although the state continued to benefit from industrialization of its downstate area. In 1980 the first U.S. president born in Illinois, Ronald Reagan, was elected. Flooding along the Mississippi inundated large areas of W Illinois in 1993.

Ilium: see TROY.

Illyria and **Illyricum,** ancient regions of the Balkan peninsula occupied by Indo-European–speaking tribes, including the Dalmatians and Pannonians. Warlike and piratical, they withstood (6th cent. B.C.) Greeks attracted by their mines and later attacks by Macedonians. The Romans conquered them and set up (168–167 B.C.) the province of Illyricum. Today Illyria means the Adriatic coast N of central Albania.

imaginary number: see NUMBER.

imagists, group of English and American poets (c.1909–c.1917) who rebelled against the exuberance and sentimentality of 19th-cent. verse. Influenced by CLASSICISM, Chinese and Japanese poetry, and the French SYMBOLISTS, they advocated a hard, clear, concentrated poetry, free of artificialities and replete with specific physical analogies. The group included Ezra POUND, Richard ALDINGTON, Amy LOWELL, and Hilda DOOLITTLE.

imam [Arab., = leader], in ISLAM, a recognized leader or a religious teacher. Any pious Muslim may function as imam. The term is also used as a synonym for *caliph,* God's vice-regent. Among SHIITES the belief arose that a hidden or unrecognized imam, or true caliph (the MAHDI), would return at the end of the world to restore the true CALIPHATE.

immunity, ability of an organism to resist foreign substances called *antigens*—viruses, bacteria, bacterial toxins, or certain nonliving substances—in the body. Immunity is present in all vertebrates and some invertebrates. Invasion by an antigen triggers the production of proteins called antibodies by special white blood cells (lymphocytes) located chiefly in the spleen and lymph nodes (see LYMPHATIC SYSTEM). The process is highly specific, with different lymphocytes recognizing only certain antigens and producing antibodies against only that particular antigen. Lymphocytes called B cells produce the antibodies, which circulate in the blood (humoral immunity). The antibodies neutralize antigens by removing them from the body's circulation, causing them to clump, or making them more susceptible to other immune cells. Other lymphocytes, which mature in the THYMUS GLAND and are called T cells, are active in cell-mediated immunity, i.e. they activate other cells that cause direct destruction of antigens or assisting B cells. Immunity has been found to be important not only in resisting infectious disease, but also in defense against CANCER, in successful organ TRANSPLANTATION, in ALLERGIES, and in AUTOIMMUNE DISEASES. See also IMMUNOLOGY; IMMUNOSUPPRESSIVE DRUG.

immunity, diplomatic: see EXTRATERRITORIALITY.

immunology, study of the resistance of organisms to disease or INFECTION caused by viruses, bacteria, and their by-products, such as endotoxins and exotoxins (see TOXIN). Immunologists study behavior of pathogenic (disease-causing) substances, resistance to infection, and defensive measures used by organisms to fight invading pathogens (see IMMUNITY). Current research includes study of the use of immune globulins (proteins that function as antibodies) and the study of the lymphocytes, called T cells, that are attacked by the AIDS virus (HIV).

immunosuppressive drug, substance that suppresses the activity of the body's immune system. Such drugs can be administered to prevent the body's rejection of a transplanted organ (see TRANSPLANTATION, MEDICAL). They are also used to treat AUTOIMMUNE DISEASES such as rheumatoid arthritis and to suppress temporarily the proliferation of white blood cells in LEUKEMIA. Their benefits must be weighed against the fact that they suppress the immune system in general, leaving the body open to other disease.

impala: see under GAZELLE.

impatiens: see JEWELWEED.

impeachment, formal accusation by a legislature against a public official, to remove him from office. The term loosely includes both the bringing of charges, or articles, and the trial that may follow. Impeachment developed in England in the 14th cent. In the U.S. the House of Representatives (see CONGRESS) can bring articles of impeachment against federal officials, including the president. Trial is by the Senate, which must convict by a two-thirds margin of the members present. There have been 15 federal impeachments and 7 convictions. Andrew JOHNSON was the only president to be impeached (1868), but he was acquitted by the Senate. Richard NIXON resigned (1974) the presidency before the House could bring charges against him.

Imperial Conference, assembly of representatives of the self-governing members of the BRITISH EMPIRE, held about every four years until WORLD WAR II. The assemblies were first called Colonial Conferences (1887–1902) and were concerned with defense problems. More formalized meetings were held later (1907–37) to discuss defense and economic problems. Since the war, Commonwealth policy has been coordinated through regular meetings of the prime ministers of Commonwealth nations.

imperialism, broadly, the extension of rule or influence by one government, nation, or society over another. Evidence of the existence of empires dates back to the dawn of written history, when local rulers extended their realms by conquering other states. Ancient imperialism reached its climax under the Roman Empire, but it was an important force elsewhere, e.g., the Middle East, N Africa, and central Asia. In the West, imperialism was reborn with the emergence of the modern nation-state and the age of exploration and discovery. European COLONIZATION of the Western Hemisphere and Africa from the 15th to 17th cent. was followed in the 18th cent. by attempts to regulate the trade of colonies in the interests of the mother country. Later, the growth of manufacturing after the INDUSTRIAL REVOLUTION introduced a new form of imperialism, as industrial nations scrambled for raw materials and new markets for manufactured products. The inequities of the system produced a growing opposition by the end of the 19th cent., when Marxists argued that imperialism was the ultimate state of capitalism. After WORLD WAR I, anti-imperialist feeling grew rapidly, and since WORLD WAR II nearly all of the countries once subject to Western control have achieved independence. Contemporary debate centers on neo-imperialism, with many less-developed countries contending that their economic development is largely determined by the developed countries through unfair trading practices, control over capital, and the power of multinational corporations.

Imperial Valley, low-lying depression in a desert area S of the Salton Sea, S California, extending S into NW Mexico. Irrigated by water diverted from the Colorado R. by the All-American Canal, it is an important U.S. source of cotton, citrus, dates, and winter vegetables. Completion of HOOVER DAM (1936) ended periodic inundation there.

impetigo, highly contagious skin infection affecting mainly infants and children, caused either by hemolytic streptococcus or staphylococcus. The rash consists of red spots or blisters that rupture, discharge, and become encrusted. ANTIBIOTIC ointment is usually effective.

impotence, inhibited sexual excitement in a man during sexual activity that, despite an unaffected desire for sex, results in inability to attain or maintain a penile erection. Impotence can result from psychological factors (performance anxiety or fear of abandonment or unwanted pregnancy), sociocultural factors (negative sexual attitudes or religious beliefs) or, less frequently, physical causes such as hormonal abnormalities, DIABETES, DRUGS, and ALCOHOLISM. Treatment of impotence depends on the underlying cause. Impotence should be distinguished from STERILITY (inability to produce sperm adequate for reproduction). See also SEX THERAPY.

impressionism, in music, a French movement of the late 19th and early 20th cent. It was begun by Claude DEBUSSY as a reaction to the emotionalism of romantic music. Using new chord combinations and exotic rhythms and scales, Debussy developed a style in which atmosphere and mood take the place of strong emotion or a story. The influence of impressionism is evident in the music of RAVEL, DELIUS, FALLA, and SATIE.

impressionism, in painting, late-19th-cent. French school. It was generally characterized by the attempt to depict transitory visual impressions, often painted directly from nature, and by the use of broken color to achieve brilliance and luminosity. The movement began with MONET, Pierre Auguste RENOIR, and SISLEY, who met regularly with CÉZANNE, PISSARRO, MORISOT, and, later, DEGAS and MANET. They repudiated academic standards, the romantics' emphasis on emotion, and literary and anecdotal subject matter; they also rejected the role of the imagination. Dubbed "impressionists" by hostile journalists after Monet's painting *Impression: Sunrise, 1872,* they observed nature closely, with scientific interest. Impressionist objectivity proved to be limiting, but the movement produced an aesthetic revolution, influencing many later painters.

In, chemical symbol of the element INDIUM.

Inca, pre-Columbian empire in W South America (see SOUTH AMERICA, INDIGENOUS PEOPLES OF) whose language was QUECHUA (see NATIVE AMERICAN LANGUAGES). From its center at CUZCO (Peru), the empire at its height dominated the entire Andean region, extending 2,000 mi (3,200 km). It was a closely knit state ruled by an emperor who required total obedience but looked after his subjects' welfare. The state owned almost everything and could draft people to work in mines or on public projects. Priests, government servants, the aged, sick, and widowed were supplied from imperial storehouses. The large royal family formed the nobility; a privileged, Quechua-speaking "Inca class" governed colonies. Lesser officials formed a minor nobility. The empire was administratively divided and subdivided, down to local communities. Surveys and census reports were recorded on knotted strings called *quipas*. The Incas' pantheistic, ritualistic religion sometimes incorporated human sacrifice. By terracing and irrigation, Inca engineers made a difficult terrain fertile; the llama and alpaca were domesticated. Remarkable feats of construction were accomplished in such cities as MACHU PICCHU, using clay models, tools such as plumb bobs, and wooden rollers to transport huge stone blocks. A network of roads included bridges, ferries, and relay stations. The Inca also made elaborate tapestries, fine polished pottery, and complex metalwork. Inca history begins when the legendary MANCO CAPAC brought his people from mountain caves into the Cuzco valley. In their early period (c.1200–c.1440) the Inca subjugated neighboring peoples. Their great conquests (1440–93) came under Pachacuti and his son Topa Inca. The present Ecuador was won by Huayna Capac, the last of the great Inca emperors. At his death (1525) his sons fought over the empire; just as Atahualpa triumphed, Francisco PIZARRO arrived (1532) to begin the Spanish conquest. Pizarro executed Atahualpa and entered Cuzco. Despite resistance and the rebellion (1536–37) of the second Manco Capac, the Inca were subdued, and their culture was eventually Hispanicized. Only in recent years have efforts been made to integrate their descendants (about 50% of the population) into the national life of Peru.

incense-tree, common name for deciduous shrubs and trees of the family Burseraceae, found chiefly in tropical America and NE Africa. The incenses frankincense and myrrh are prepared from the resin exuded by some species. Frankincense, or olibanum, derived mainly from *Boswellia carterii,* is used medicinally and for fumigation. Myrrh, prepared especially from *Commiphora erythraea* and common myrrh, *C. myrrha,* is used medicinally and in perfumes and was used by the ancients in embalming. Frankincense and myrrh, together with GOLD, were the gifts of the WISE MEN OF THE EAST.

Inchon, city (1985 pop. 1,386,911), NW South Korea, on the Yellow Sea. The country's second largest port, Inchon is a major industrial center, producing steel, coke, textiles, chemicals, and fertilizers. Fishing is an important industry. Population growth and transportation links have merged Inchon and SEOUL into one urban area. During the KOREAN WAR, U.S. troops landed (Sept. 15, 1950) there to launch a UN counteroffensive against the North Koreans.

inclination, in astronomy: see ORBIT.

inclined plane: see MACHINE.

inclosure or **enclosure,** in British history, the process of inclosing (with fences, ditches, hedges, or other barriers) land formerly subject to common rights. In England the practice dated from the 12th cent. and accompanied the breakdown of the MANORIAL SYSTEM. Its great development came in the 14th cent. with the rapid expansion of the Flemish wool trade and the resulting monetary advantages of fenced sheep pastures. Inclosure reached its peak in the 17th cent. Though hard on the small farmer, it produced more efficient farming.

income tax, assessment levied on individual or corporate income. The first modern income tax was levied (1799–1816) in Britain to fund the Napoleonic Wars, but it did not become permanent until 1874. Similarly, the U.S. imposed a temporary income tax during the CIVIL WAR; the system became permanent with the adoption of the 16th amendment (1913) to the CONSTITUTION. Since 1919 most U.S. states have adopted the tax, as have several cities, beginning with Philadelphia (1939). See also TAXATION.

Independence, city (1990 pop. 112,301), seat of Jackson co., W Mo., a suburb of Kansas City; inc. 1849. Its manufactures include electrical equipment, cement, machinery, and oil products. The city was a MORMON settlement (1831) and a starting point for Western expeditions in the 1830s and 40s. Harry S TRUMAN lived there and is buried on the grounds of the Truman Library.

Independence, American War of: see AMERICAN REVOLUTION.

Independence, Declaration of: see DECLARATION OF INDEPENDENCE.

Independence Day: see FOURTH OF JULY.

Independence Hall, building in Philadelphia, in Independence National Historical Park. The DECLARATION OF INDEPENDENCE was proclaimed here, and it was the site of the CONTINENTAL CONGRESS and the FEDERAL CONSTITUTIONAL CONVENTION.

independent counsel, in U.S. law, a judicially appointed investigator of charges of misdeeds by high government officials. Originally termed special prosecutor, the position was created by the 1978 Ethics in Government Act. Prompted by the WATERGATE AFFAIR, the purpose of the law was to avoid the conflict of interest that might develop if the executive branch investigated its own officials. The request for the appointment of an independent counsel, however, had to be made by the attorney general. The act expired in 1992.

Independent Treasury System. When Pres. Andrew JACKSON transferred (1833) government funds from the BANK OF THE UNITED STATES to state banks, rampant speculation followed and led to the Panic of 1837. In 1840, under Pres. VAN BUREN, an independent treasury isolated from all banks was set up, but in 1841 the Whigs repealed the law, and it was not until 1846 that the Democrats restored the Independent Treasury System. The Act of 1846 ordered that public revenues be retained in the Treasury building or in subtreasuries in various cities. The Treasury was to pay out its own funds and be completely independent of the banking and financial system of the nation; all payments in and out were to be in specie. In practice the system created problems in prosperous times by amassing surplus revenue, and thus restraining legitimate expansion of trade; in depressed times, the treasury's insistence on being paid in specie reduced the amount of specie available for private credit. The large expenditures of the CIVIL WAR also revealed problems, and Congress created (1863–64) national banks. The Independent Treasury was later used to stabilize the money market, but the Panic of 1907 proved the attempt futile. The Federal Reserve Act of 1913 marked the end of the system.

index number, in ECONOMETRICS, a figure reflecting a change in value or quantity, as compared with a standard or base. The base usually equals 100, and the index number is usually expressed as a percentage. For example, if a commodity cost twice as much in 1980 as it did in 1970, its index number would be 200, relative to 1970. An example of index numbers in the U.S. is the Consumer Price Index (CPI), which measures a "market basket" of goods and services bought by a typical urban family. The CPI, as a barometer of INFLATION and the COST OF LIVING, triggers increases in Social Security benefits and the wages of many union workers.

India, officially Republic of India, federal republic (1991 pop. 843,930,861), 1,269,413 sq mi (3,287,782 sq km), S Asia, occupying most of the Indian subcontinent, bordered by Pakistan (W); Afghanistan, China, Nepal, and Bhutan (N); and Myanmar (E); Bangladesh forms an enclave in the NE. Jutting into the INDIAN OCEAN, southern India has a shoreline of about 3,500 mi (5,630 km) along the Bay of BENGAL in the east and the ARABIAN SEA in the west. The capital is NEW DELHI; other important cities include CALCUTTA, BOMBAY, DELHI, MADRAS, and BANGALORE.

Land and People. The land may be divided into three topographical zones: the towering HIMALAYAS in the north; the fertile, densely populated Indo-Gangetic alluvial plain in the north-central section; and the southern peninsula, dominated by the uplands of the DECCAN plateau. The GANGES R., sacred to the Hindus, flows through the heart of the nation. Economically, India often seems like two separate countries: village India, supported by primitive agriculture, where tens of millions live below the poverty level; and urban India, one of the most heavily industrialized areas in the world.

Although the traditional textile industry is still important, the emphasis is on heavy industry, which produces iron and steel, machine tools, transportation equipment, and chemicals. Computer software is an increasingly important export. About 70% of the work force is engaged in agriculture, growing rice, wheat, peanuts, corn, and millet for subsistence; cash crops are sugarcane, tea, oilseeds, cotton, tobacco, and jute. The opium poppy is also grown, both for the legal pharmaceutical market and illegal drug trade; cannabis is produced as well. Improved irrigation, the introduction of chemical fertilizers, and the use of high-yield strains of rice and wheat have led to record harvests, and by the late 1970s India was self-sufficient in grain, becoming an exporter in the early 1980s. India has perhaps more cattle per capita than any other country, but their economic value is severely limited by the Hindu prohibition against their slaughter. Among the country's rich mineral resources are coal, zinc, iron, manganese, mica, bauxite, and lead. India is the world's second most populous country (after China). The ethnic composition is complex, but two major strains predominate: the Aryan, in the north, and the Dravidian, in the south. More than 1,500 languages and dialects are spoken; Hindi (spoken throughout the north) and English (used in politics and commerce) are the official languages, and 14 other languages are recognized by the constitution. The population is overwhelmingly Hindu, but there are significant numbers of Muslims (more than 10% of the population), Christians, Buddhists, Sikhs, Jains, and Parsis. About 80% of the population is rural. The caste system, under which people are socially classified at birth, is an important facet of Hinduism, and thus a dominant feature of Indian life; the 1950 constitution abolished the lowest caste, known as untouchables, but caste conflicts remain a serious problem.

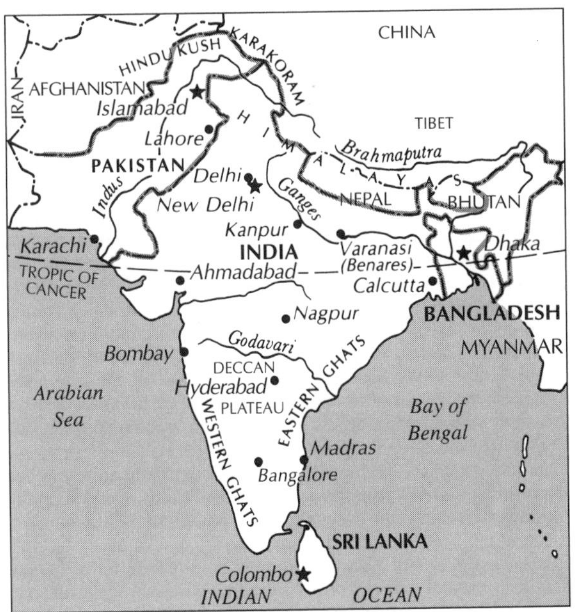

History. The INDUS VALLEY CIVILIZATION (c.2500–c.1500 B.C.) was the first to flourish on the Indian subcontinent (in present-day Pakistan). It fell c.1500 B.C. to Aryan invaders from the northwest, who dominated the area for 2,000 years and developed HINDUISM, the socioreligious system that is the basis of India's institutions and culture. Under the MAURYA dynasty (c.325–c.183 B.C.)—especially ASOKA (d. 323 B.C.), who established Buddhism as the state religion—Indian culture had its first great flowering. A golden age of Hindu culture was achieved under the GUPTA dynasty, in the 4th–5th cent. A.D., considered India's classical period. By the 10th cent. Muslim armies from the north were raiding India, and in 1192 the Delhi Sultanate, the first Muslim kingdom in India, was established. The small Muslim kingdoms that succeeded it were swept away by BABUR, a great Muslim invader from Afghanistan, who established the MOGUL empire in 1526. Portugal, which captured Goa in 1510, was the first European nation to gain a foothold in India, but the British, French, and Dutch were soon vying with the Portuguese for Indian trade. With the weakening of the Mogul empire in the 18th cent., the struggle was renewed—this time between France and Britain, with the British EAST INDIA COMPANY emerging dominant. In 1857, after the bloody INDIAN MUTINY against the British, the East India Company was abolished and control of India was transferred directly to the British crown. Discontent with British rule became intense during the early 20th cent., and the INDIAN NATIONAL CONGRESS (founded 1885), led by Mohandas GANDHI and Jawaharlal NEHRU, mounted a movement for independence. The British instituted a program of gradual power-sharing, but Congress leaders, frustrated by the slow pace, organized the Quit India movement during World War II. The desire of the Congress to maintain a united front against Britain was frustrated, however, by the MUSLIM LEAGUE, which demanded the partition of India into separate Hindu and Muslim states. Finally, in 1947, British India was divided into two independent nations: India, with Nehru as prime minister, and PAKISTAN, under Muhammad Ali JINNAH. More than 1 million people died in the ensuing disorder. Hostile relations between the nations led to the INDIA-PAKISTAN WARS (1947–48, 1965, 1971). A specific dispute was jurisdiction over KASHMIR, which both countries claimed. India was also involved in a border conflict (1962) with China. A sovereign republic from 1950, India became a leader of the nonaligned nations. Indira GANDHI (Nehru's daughter), who became prime minister in 1966, precipitated a crisis in 1975 when, after being convicted of campaign fraud, she declared a state of emergency and suspended civil liberties. Her Congress party was defeated in national elections in 1977, but the new ruling coalition, the Janata party, was beset by factionalism and economic difficulties. Gandhi was reelected in 1980 but faced continued runaway population growth, labor strife, and intercaste violence. In 1984 over 1,000 people were killed when she ordered an attack on armed Sikh separatists in Amritsar. Four months later she was assassinated by Sikhs in her bodyguard. Her son Rajiv GANDHI succeeded her. Although India grew economically, Rajiv Gandhi became increasingly unpopular. In 1989 he lost his majority in parliament and resigned. Two subsequent, short-lived coalition governments led to new elections (1991), during which Rajiv Gandhi was assassinated and no party won a majority. The Congress party formed a government under P.V. Narasimha RAO, who took steps to diminish the state's role in the economy. Religious conflict sparked by militant Hindus and exploited by Hindu political parties was a persistent problem in the 1980s and led to bloody riots in 1992.

Indiana, midwestern state in the N central U.S.; bordered by Lake Michigan and the state of Michigan (N), Ohio (E), Kentucky, across the Ohio R. (S), and Illinois (W).

Area, 36,291 sq mi (93,994 sq km). *Pop.* (1990) 5,544,159, a 1% increase over 1980 pop. *Capital,* Indianapolis. *Statehood,* Dec. 11, 1816 (19th state). *Highest pt.,* 1,257 ft (383 m), Wayne co.; *lowest pt.,* Ohio R., 320 ft (98 m). *Nickname,* Hoosier State. *Motto,* Crossroads of America. *State bird,* cardinal. *State flower,* peony. *State tree,* tulip poplar. *Abbr.,* Ind.; IN.

Land and People. Along the shores of Lake MICHIGAN are the sand formations of Indiana Dunes National Lakeshore, which give way to the glaciated lake area, separated by the Wabash R. from the fertile plains that cover most of the state. Nearly 65% of the population lives in urban areas. The largest city is INDIANAPOLIS, followed by FORT WAYNE, EVANSVILLE, GARY, and SOUTH BEND. In 1990 about 91% of the population was white and about 8% was African American.

Economy. Manufacturing, the leading source of income, is concentrated in the Calumet region along Lake Michigan, adjacent to Chicago, where cities such as Gary produce steel and other manufactures, including electrical and transportation equipment, machinery, chemicals, and primary metals. Most of these industries have recently suffered significant recessionary reversals. About three quarters of the land is devoted to agriculture, with corn, sorghum, grains, soybeans, hogs, and cattle the major products. Indiana is the nation's leading producer of building limestone and has rich coal deposits and some petroleum.

Government. The constitution of 1851 provides for a governor elected to a four-year term. The general assembly consists of a senate whose 50 members serve four-year terms and a house whose 100 members are elected to two-year terms. Indiana sends 10 representatives and 2 senators to the U.S. Congress and has 12 electoral votes.

History. The remains of the MOUND BUILDERS, Indiana's earliest known inhabitants, have been found along the state's rivers and bottomlands. Subsequently, the area was occupied mainly by the MIAMI, DELAWARE, and Potawatomi. The first Europeans to explore the area were the French, notably Robert Cavalier, sieur de LA SALLE, in 1679. Vincennes, the first French settlement, was established in 1725. The region was ceded (1763) to Britain, which in turn ceded it to the U.S. at the end of the AMERICAN REVOLUTION. Part of the NORTHWEST TERRITORY, Indiana was the site of major battles with Native Americans, including Fallen Timbers (1794) and Tippecanoe (1811). During the 1840s canals and railroads strengthened Indiana's link with the East, providing the impetus for industrial development that began during the 1860s and continued into the 20th cent. The opening (1959) of the SAINT LAWRENCE SEAWAY, linking the Great Lakes with the Atlantic Ocean, and of a new harbor on Lake Michigan (1970) have increased the importance of shipping in Indiana's economy. The recession of the late 1980s and early 90s was particularly severe in Indiana's industrial north; in and around Indianapolis diversification of industry spurred economic growth.

Indian Affairs, Bureau of (BIA), created in 1824 in the War Dept. with jurisdiction over trade with and defense against Native Americans and over resettlement of Native Americans on reservations. In 1849 the bureau was transferred to the Dept. of the INTERIOR, where the primary function of the agency became the administration of reservation lands. On some reservations and Alaskan Native areas the BIA still is responsible for health and social services, education and job training, reclamation and development projects, or law enforcement.

Indianapolis, city (1990 pop. 731,327; met. area 1,249,822), state capital and seat of Marion co., central Ind., on the White R. By far the state's largest city, it is the chief processing point in a large agricultural region and an important grain and livestock market. Its manufactures include chemicals, drugs, telephone and electronic equipment, and automotive and aircraft parts. An insurance center, it has numerous educational and medical facilities. Indianapolis is a transportation hub and a center of the trucking industry. The Indianapolis Motor Speedway is the scene of the world-famous annual 500-mile automobile race. Urban renewal projects in the 1970s and 80s have produced many modern, multistory buildings.

Indian art and architecture is essentially traditional and religious. Each work of art is both a symbol and a manifestation of a god or his powers. In both Buddhist and Hindu art, symbolism in every gesture, posture, and attribute contains many levels of meaning (see BUDDHISM; HINDUISM). The earliest Indian art emerged in the Indus R. valley during the 2d half of the 3d millennium B.C. The Indus valley civilization (c.2500–c.1500 B.C.) produced early examples of city planning and drainage systems, as well as many statuettes and square seals with naturalistically rendered bulls as decorations. From the MAURYA dynasty the most famous architectural remains are the edict pillars, over 50 ft (15 m) high, surmounted by lotus flowers and animal figures. Also dating from this period are the stone ogival chaitya windows found at a sanctuary near Bodh Gaya. The early classic period of the Sunga dynasty (2d–1st cent. B.C.) and early Andhra dynasty (1st cent. B.C.) has left the earliest extant STUPAS, mounds surrounded by railings and gateways covered with ornament. Between the 2d and 5th cent. A.D., art from the Gandhara and Mathura regions developed. Gandhara art presents the first human images of the BUDDHA and was profoundly influenced by 2d-cent. Hellenistic art (see HELLENISTIC CIVILIZATION). Ornate stupas and monasteries held colossal gilt figures and imported glassware. Mathura created a wholly Indian sculptural art, usually employing reddish limestone. Symmetrical heavier Buddhas smile benignly at worshipers. The GUPTA period (A.D. 320–600) was the golden age of Buddhist art. Smooth, elegant reliefs cover the facades and interiors of remaining chaitya halls. The murals in the caves at Ajanta depict the joys of secular life and the beauty of the spiritual. From the 6th cent. on, with the Hindu dynasties, temples were built that were so exuberantly embellished with sculpture that their style is called "sculptural architecture." The Dravidian-style temple is constructed in five pyramidal *raths* (temples). Skilled CIRE-PERDUE sculptures were produced until the late 19th cent. Most Indian wall paintings, except for fragments from the caves of Ajanta, were destroyed, but examples of manuscript illumination remain. Jain manuscript illuminations are brightly colored and have the characteristic protruding farther eye. Rajput painting is characterized by an interest in nature and sinuous grace in the human form. Little of the glorious tradition of Indian artistic achievement survived British rule. A revival of Indian themes in the 20th cent. has produced such artists as Rabindranath Tagore, Nandalal Bose, and Ram Kinker.

Indian literature. Oral literature in the vernacular languages of India is of great antiquity, but it was not until about the 16th cent. that an extensive written literature appeared. Its development was spurred by the emergence of Hindu pietistic movements that encouraged the popularizing of SANSKRIT LITERATURE, e.g., the RAMAYANA was put into popular verse form. Among Muslims, classical Persian poetry was the basis for Urdu verse written for the Mogul court. In the early 19th cent., with the establishment of vernacular schools and the importation of printing presses, a great impetus was given to popular prose. Today literature is written in all the important languages of India, Pakistan, and Bangladesh, and there is a large literature in English. Among the best-known writers of the 19th and 20th cent. are Rammohun Roy, Bankim Chandra CHATTERJEE, Rabindranath TAGORE, Mohandas GANDHI, Jawaharlal NEHRU, R.K. NARAYAN, Raja RAO, and Bhabhani BHATTACHARYA.

Indian Mutiny, 1857–58, also known as the Sepoy Rebellion, revolt of the Indian soldiers (sepoys) in the British army in BENGAL that became a widespread uprising against British rule in India. The Bengali soldiers resented British annexation (1856) of Oudh, their homeland. They were also angered by the issuing of cartridges coated in beef fat (which violated Hindu law) and pork fat (which violated Muslim law). Fighting quickly spread all over N India; the rebels besieged Lucknow and conquered Kanpur and Delhi. British reconquest was completed by March 1858. Various reforms resulted, the most important being the transfer of rule from the East India Company to the British crown.

Indian National Congress, Indian political party, founded in 1885 to promote economic reforms. It became the spearhead of the Indian movement for independence from Great Britain. Its membership became overwhelmingly Hindu, as most Muslim members left it for the MUSLIM LEAGUE. In 1919, led by Mohandas GANDHI, it adopted a policy of satyagraha (nonviolent resistance) toward the British. The party was outlawed during WORLD WAR II for refusing to support the British war effort, and most of its leaders were jailed. After India achieved independence (1947), Jawaharlal NEHRU headed both the government and the party. Its dominance continued after Nehru's death (1964) under Shri Lal Bahadur SHASTRI and Nehru's daughter, Indira GANDHI. In 1969 the party split: the conservative wing became the Old Congress party; Indira Gandhi's followers became the New Congress party, winning a landslide victory in 1971. But this party was also to split. After its electoral defeat in 1977, Mrs. Gandhi withdrew and in 1978 formed a new faction, the Congress-I (for Indira) party, which brought her back into power in Jan. 1980. She was assassinated in 1984 by her Sikh bodyguards. Her son Rajiv GANDHI succeeded her as prime minister (1984–90) and leader of the party until his assassination in 1991. P.V. Narasimha RAO succeeded him as party leader.

Indian Ocean, world's third largest ocean, c.28,350,000 sq mi (73,427,000 sq km), between S Asia, Antarctica, E Africa, and SW Australia. It is c.4,000 mi (6,400 km) wide at the equator and reaches a maximum depth of 25,344 ft (7,725 m) in the Java Trench S of Indonesia. Its major arms include the Arabian Sea, Red Sea, Gulf of Aden, Persian Gulf, Bay of Bengal, and Andaman Sea. A complex series of mid-oceanic submarine ridges intersect to enclose deep-sea basins, their summits rising to the surface in places to form the Andaman, Nicobar, Seychelles, and other island groups.

Indian philosophy. Systematized Indian philosophy begins in the period of the UPANISHADS (900–500 B.C.). The rise of BUDDHISM (from the 5th cent. B.C.) led to the development of philosophical tenets presented in the form of sutras, concise aphorisms intended to serve as a memory aid and as a basis for oral elaboration. There are six classical schools that accept the authority of the VEDA. The first, *Nyaya* (6th cent. B.C.), is a school of logic and epistemology. *Vaisheshika* (3d cent. B.C.) posits a sixfold classification of reality (substance, quality, activity, generality, particularity, inherence). The *Samkhya* system (6th cent. B.C.) expounds two basic metaphysical principles: *purusha* (soul) and *prakriti* (matter or nature). *Purusha* appears bound to *prakriti* but may become free through the realization that it is distinct from *prakriti.* The YOGA system of Patanjali (2d cent. B.C.), which accepts Samkhya metaphysics and the concept of a supreme soul, presents an eight-stage discipline of self-control and MEDITATION. The *Purva Mimamsa* school (2d cent. B.C.) sets forth principles of interpretation of the Vedic texts. The different schools of *Uttara Mimamsa,* or VEDANTA, all based on the *Brahma-Sutras* of Baradayana (early cent. A.D.), epitomize the teachings of the Upanishads. The three main heterodox schools not based on the Veda and Upanishads are BUDDHISM, JAINISM, and the materialist school called *Charvaka* or *Lokyata.* The latter, the only Indian school to reject the ideas of KARMA and spiritual liberation, held that only this world exists and that religious ideas are delusion.

Indian pipe, common name for the genus *Monotropa* and the Monotropaceae, a family of low, flowering plants with a funguslike appearance found in north temperate zones. These chlorophylless SAPROPHYTES are yellowish- or waxy-white in color and, with their scalelike leaves and nodding flowers, resemble pipes. The related, bright-red snow plant (*Sarcodes sanguinea*) of the Sierra Nevadas shoots up and blooms as soon as the snow melts.

Indians, American: see MIDDLE AMERICA, INDIGENOUS PEOPLES OF; NORTH AMERICA, INDIGENOUS PEOPLES OF; SOUTH AMERICA, INDIGENOUS PEOPLES OF; and individual peoples. See also AMERICAS, PREHISTORY OF THE; NATIVE AMERICAN LANGUAGES.

Indian Territory, in U.S. history, name of land set aside for Native Americans by the Indian Intercourse Act (1834). In the 1820s the U.S. government began moving the CHEROKEE, Creek, Seminole, Choctaw, and Chickasaw W of the Mississippi R. The act of 1834 designated the area of present-day Oklahoma, N and E of the Red River, as well as Kansas and Nebraska, for them. Other tribes moved there also. In 1854 the territory was delimited by the creation of the Kansas and Nebraska territories, and it was abolished in 1907 with the entrance of Oklahoma into the Union.

Indian wars, in American history, term referring to the series of conflicts, beginning in colonial times, between European settlers and their descendants and indigenous North American peoples. After 1815 the U.S. government began removing Native Americans to reservations W of the Mississippi R., a policy that often triggered war. The Indian wars W of the Mississippi reached their height between 1869 and 1878. WOUNDED KNEE (1890) is often called the last battle of the Indian wars.

India-Pakistan Wars, the series of conflicts between INDIA and PAKISTAN since 1947, when the Indian subcontinent was partitioned as British rule there ended. The roots of the conflict lie in the long-standing hostility between the Hindus and Muslims. More than one million people are believed to have died in the religious rioting that took place immediately after partition, and many millions more were forced to relocate. The status of KASHMIR was particularly troublesome. An uneasy peace was worked out and lasted until 1965, when fighting broke out in the Rann of Kutch, a border region between India and West Pakistan. Fighting spread to Kashmir and the Punjab, but a UN-sponsored cease-fire went into effect in 1966. In 1971 East Pakistan, with the support of India, revolted against the rule of West Pakistan. Again, brutal fighting and massive relocations took place. East Pakistan declared itself independent as BANGLADESH, and 1974 Pakistan recognized that status.

Indic languages, group of languages belonging to the Indo-Iranian subfamily of the Indo-European family of languages. See LANGUAGE (table).

indictment, in law, formal written accusation of crime, affirmed by a grand JURY and presented by it to a court for trial of the accused. The 5th amendment to the U.S. CONSTITUTION guarantees the use of an indictment (thus safeguarding the right to a preliminary hearing by a grand jury) in all trials for capital or other infamous crimes. In practice, however, the tendency has been to allow prosecution of many crimes on "information" (an accusation presented directly by the prosecutor without consideration by a grand jury).

indium (In), metallic element, discovered spectroscopically in 1863 by Ferdinand Reich and H.T. Richter. Soft, malleable, ductile, lustrous, and silver-white, it remains liquid over a wide temperature range. Indium wets glass and can be used to form a mirror surface more corrosion-resistant than one of silver. See ELEMENT (table); PERIODIC TABLE.

Individual Retirement Account (IRA), tax-sheltered retirement plan, originally created (1974) to assist individuals not covered by company pensions. Under the U.S. tax law of 1981, individuals were permitted to contribute up to $2,000 per year (increased from $1,500) to such accounts and coverage was extended to employees already in corporate pension programs. Since 1987 there have been limitations on who can make tax-deductible contributions to an IRA. IRA monies may be placed in high-yield investments, with tax deferred until money is withdrawn.

Indo-Aryan, variant name for Indic languages. Broader uses referring to racial stocks are now obsolete. See LANGUAGE (table).

Indochina, term used in a wide sense for the entire SE Asian peninsula occupied by MYANMAR, MALAYSIA, THAILAND, LAOS, CAMBODIA, and VIETNAM, whose cultures reflect the long-term influence of neighboring India (W) and China (N). The term is also used in a more restricted sense for the colonial empire developed by France in the eastern part of the peninsula after 1862. During World War II France offered greater self-government to the various states it ruled there, within a French federation of Indochina. Vietnamese nationalists rejected the offer (which Laos and Cambodia accepted), demanding (1945) the complete independence of the colony of COCHIN CHINA and of the TONKIN and ANNAM protectorates, or what is now Vietnam. After a long and bitter war, the French were defeated at DIENBIENPHU (1954) and subsequently lost control of all Indochina at the GENEVA CONFERENCE (1954). See also VIETNAM WAR.

Indochina War: see VIETNAM WAR.

Indo-European, family of languages to which English belongs. It includes more speakers than any other language family. See LANGUAGE (table).

Indo-Iranian, subfamily of the Indo-European family of languages. See LANGUAGE (table).

Indonesia, officially Republic of Indonesia, republic (1992 est. pop. 195,684,000), c.740,000 sq mi (1,916,600 sq km), SE Asia, comprising more than 3,000 islands stretching along the equator from the Malaysian mainland to New Guinea; the main islands are JAVA, SUMATRA, Kalimantan (Indonesian BORNEO), CELEBES (Sulawesi), BALI, TIMOR, the MOLUCCAS (Maluku), and Irian Jaya (West New Guinea). Indonesia is the fourth largest country in the world by population. The capital is JAKARTA, on Java. The islands are mountainous and dotted with volcanoes, both active and dormant; the climate is tropical, with abundant rainfall. About 55% of the work force is engaged in agriculture, and fertile soil sustains a rich yield; principal crops are rice, fruit, cassava, peanuts, rubber, and coffee. Indonesia's natural resources are among the richest in the world; the nation is a leading producer of petroleum, its most valuable export; liquefied natural gas, tin, bauxite, nickel, and gold also are important. Products of the vast rain forests include hardwoods (rapid deforestation has caused international concern), rubber, palm oil, and cinchona. Primarily a supplier of raw materials, the country has little industry beyond oil, mining, and textiles. An aircraft industry was established in 1986, however, and development of other high-technology manufactures is planned. The population is mainly Malayan and Papuan, with an important Chinese minority, and is unevenly distributed among the islands. Over 50% of the people live on Java, which has about 7% of the nation's land area, and the government has undertaken (since 1969) to resettle Javans on Sumatra and other islands. Islam is the predominant religion; there is a Christian minority (about 10%). The official language is Bahasa Indonesia (a Malay lingua franca), but Javanese, English, Dutch, and more than 250 other tongues are spoken.

History. Early in the Christian era, Indonesia came under the influence of Indian civilization, and after the 7th cent. important Bud-

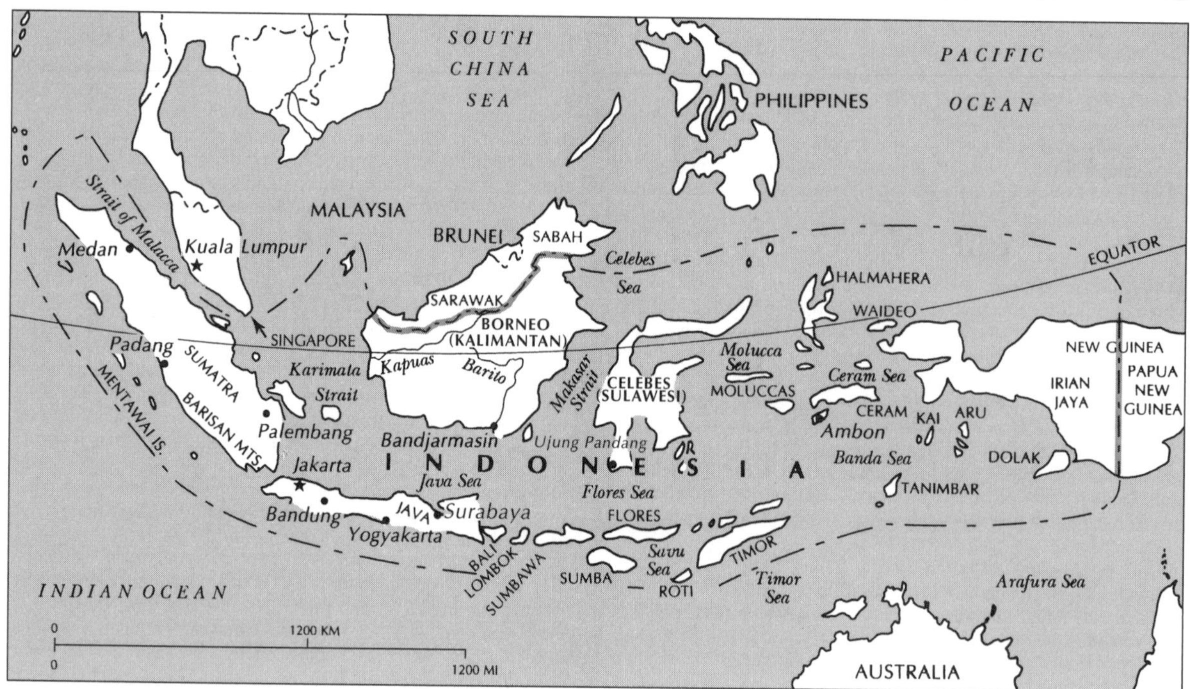

dhist and Hindu kingdoms arose, notably the 13th-cent. Majapahit empire of Java. Arab traders first arrived in the 14th cent., and by the end of the 16th cent., Islam had become the dominant religion. Reduced by internal dissension to a number of small, weak states, the area was easy prey for Europeans (Portuguese, 1511; Dutch, 1596; British, 1600) lured by the rich spice trade. By the 17th cent. the Dutch EAST INDIA COMPANY emerged as the dominant power, and in 1799 the Netherlands assumed direct control of the area, thereafter known as the Netherlands (or Dutch) East Indies. Agitation for independence began early in the 20th cent. Following Japanese occupation of the islands in World War II, nationalist leader SUKARNO proclaimed (1945) an independent Indonesian republic; after four years of intermittent, sometimes heavy fighting, the Dutch finally transferred sovereignty in 1949. Netherlands New Guinea became part of Indonesia in 1963 and was renamed Irian Jaya in 1973. Indonesia forcibly annexed Portuguese East Timor in 1976, a move not recognized by the UN and opposed by the inhabitants. An abortive Communist coup in 1965 led to an anti-Communist takeover by the military, under Gen. SUHARTO, who was elected president in 1968 and reelected in 1973, 1978, 1983, and 1988. Under Suharto, who moved Indonesia closer to the West, the priority has been economic rehabilitation and growth. In recent years government corruption has increased, and Suharto has relied on repression to control dissent.

inductance, quantity that measures the electromagnetic INDUCTION of an ELECTRIC-CIRCUIT component. The self-inductance L of a circuit component determines the magnitude of the ELECTROMOTIVE FORCE (emf) induced in it as a result of a given rate of change of current through the component. The mutual inductance M of two components, one in each of two separate but closely located circuits, determines the emf that each may induce in the other for a given current change. Inductance is expressed in units of henrys. A device designed to produce an inductance, e.g., a wire coil, is called an inductor.

induction, in ELECTRICITY and MAGNETISM, common name for three distinct phenomena. **Electromagnetic induction** is the production of an ELECTROMOTIVE FORCE (emf) in a conductor as a result of a changing magnetic FIELD about the conductor. Such a variation may be produced by relative motion between the conductor and the source of the magnetic field, as in an electric GENERATOR, or by varying the strength of the entire field. Changing the current in a given circuit can also induce emf in a nearby circuit unconnected with the original circuit; this is called mutual induction and is the basis of the TRANSFORMER. **Electrostatic induction** is the production of an unbalanced electric CHARGE on an uncharged metallic body as a result of a charged body being brought near it without touching it. If the charged body is, e.g., positively charged, electrons in the uncharged body will be attracted toward it; if the opposite end of the body is then grounded, electrons will flow into it to replace those drawn to the other end. The body thus acquires a negative charge after the ground connection is broken. **Magnetic induction** is the production of a magnetic field in a piece of unmagnetized iron or other ferromagnetic substance when a magnet is brought near it. The magnet causes the individual particles of the iron, which act like tiny magnets, to line up so that the sample as a whole becomes magnetized.

induction, in LOGIC, the process of reasoning from the particular to the general. Francis BACON proposed induction as the logic of scientific discovery and DEDUCTION as the logic of argumentation. In fact, both processes are used together regularly in the empirical sciences: by the observation of particular events (induction) and from already known principles (deduction), new hypothetical principles are formulated and laws induced.

inductor: see INDUCTANCE.

indulgence, in the Roman Catholic Church, the pardon of temporal punishment due for SIN. Indulgences are granted out of the Treasury of Merit won for the church by Jesus and the saints. Until their sale was made unlawful by the Council of TRENT (1562), the abuse of indulgences was common, and it was this abuse that Martin LUTHER first denounced.

Indurain, Miguel, 1964–, Spanish bicycle racer. The best competitive bicyclist of the early 1990s, he scored consecutive victories in the Tour de France (1991–93) and Giro d'Italia (1992–93). Known for his extremely strong legs, he excels at time trials.

Indus, chief river of Pakistan, c.1,900 mi (3,060 km) long, site of the prehistoric INDUS VALLEY CIVILIZATION. It rises in the TIBET region of China, flows west across Jammu and KASHMIR, India, then southwest through Pakistan, where it receives the "five waters" of the PUNJAB (the Chenab, Jhelum, Ravi, Beas, and Sutlej rivers), to an infertile clay delta on the Arabian Sea SE of Karachi. The unnavigable Indus is harnessed for irrigation and hydroelectricity by the Jinnah, Sukker, and Kotri dams. A treaty (1960) between India and Pakistan regulates withdrawals of water from the river and its tributaries.

industrial policy, government-sponsored economic program in which public and private sectors coordinate their efforts to develop new technologies and industries. The government may provide support through subsidies, preferential tariffs, tax credits, or development banks. This approach to industrial development has been used in many E Asian countries and some W European ones. Although government involvement is often viewed with suspicion in the U.S., subsidies or other support are provided in the areas of defense, energy, transportation, agriculture, and home construction. The federally sponsored semiconductor industry consortium, Sematech (est. 1987), is credited with aiding the revival of U.S. semiconductor manufacturers.

industrial pollutants: see POLLUTION; WASTE DISPOSAL.

Industrial Revolution, term usually applied to the social and economic changes that mark the transition from a stable agricultural and commercial society to a modern industrial society. Historically, it is used to refer primarily to the period in British history from c.1750 to c.1850. Dramatic changes in the social and economic structure took place as inventions and new technology created the factory system of large-scale machine production and greater economic specialization. The laboring population, formerly employed mainly in agriculture, increasingly gathered in great urban factory centers. The same process occurred at later times and in different degrees in other countries. The crucial development of the Industrial Revolution in Britain was the use of steam for power, made possible by the STEAM ENGINE (1769) of James WATT. Cotton textiles was the key industry early in this period. The presence of large quantities of coal and iron proved a decisive factor in Britain's rapid industrial growth. Canals and roads were built, and the advent of the railroad and steamship widened the market for manufactured goods. New periods of development came with electricity and the gasoline engine, but by 1850 the revolution was accomplished, with industry having become a dominant factor in British life. The effects of the Industrial Revolution were worldwide. France (after 1830), Germany (after 1850), and the U.S. (after the Civil War) were transformed by industrialization. Europeans introduced the revolution to Asia at about the turn of the century, but only Japan eventually grew into an industrial giant. The RUSSIAN REVOLUTION had as a basic aim the introduction of industrialism. The Industrial Revolution has changed the face of nations, providing the economic base for population expansion and improvement in living standards, and it remains a primary goal of less developed countries. But with it have also come a host of problems, including labor-management conflicts, worker boredom, and environmental pollution.

Industrial Workers of the World (IWW), revolutionary industrial union organized in Chicago in 1905 by 43 labor organizations. It became the chief organization in the U.S. representing the doctrines of SYNDICALISM. Leaders included E.V. DEBS, W.D. HAYWOOD, and Daniel De Leon. The aim of the IWW, whose members were known as Wobblies, was to unite all skilled and unskilled workers for the purpose of overthrowing CAPITALISM and rebuilding society on a socialistic basis. It opposed arbitration and COLLECTIVE BARGAINING, favoring direct action. After 1908 the IWW became an organization largely of the unskilled, reaching its peak strength (60,000 to 100,000 members) on the eve of World War I. Wartime strikes led to suppression by the federal government, including arrest of its entire leadership, and it declined rapidly thereafter.

Indus valley civilization, c.2500–c.1500 B.C., ancient civilization that flourished along the Indus R. in present-day Pakistan. Its chief cities were Mohenjo-Daro and Harappa, where archaeologists have unearthed impressive public and private buildings that are evidence of a complex society based on a highly organized agriculture supplemented by active commerce. The arts flourished, and examples in copper, bronze, and pottery have been uncovered. Also found were examples of a pictograph script that long baffled archaeologists but was finally deciphered in 1969. The fate of the Indus valley civilization remains a mystery, but it is believed that it fell victim to invading Aryans.

inequality, in mathematics, statement that one expression is less than or greater than another. The symbols $<$ (less than), $>$ (greater than), $\leq$ (less than or equal to), and $\geq$ (greater than or equal to) are used to indicate inequalities, as in $3 < 5$ and $2x + 1 \geq 7$. Like EQUATIONS, inequalities containing variables can be solved; the solutions are also inequalities. For instance, $2x + 1 \geq 7$ has the solution $x \geq 3$, because any number greater than or equal to 3 can be substituted for x to make the left side greater than or equal to 7.

Indus Valley pictograph script

inert gas or **noble gas,** any of the elements in group 0 of the PERIODIC TABLE. In order of increasing atomic number, they are HELIUM, NEON, ARGON, KRYPTON, XENON, and RADON. Sometimes called the rare gases (although argon makes up 1% of the atmosphere), they are colorless, odorless, and tasteless. Inert gases have very low chemical activity because their outermost, or valence, electron shell is complete, containing two electrons in the case of helium and eight in the remaining cases.

inertia, in physics, the resistance of a body to any alteration in its state of MOTION, i.e., the resistance of a body at rest to being set in motion or of a body in motion to any change of speed or of direction. See MASS.

Inez de Castro: see CASTRO, INÉS DE.

infallibility, in Christian thought, the inability of the church to err, believed since early Christian times to be guaranteed by Scripture. As proclaimed at the first VATICAN COUNCIL (1870), Roman Catholics believe in the infallibility of the pope when he speaks *ex cathedra* on faith and morals. The Orthodox hold that ecumenical councils are infallible. Protestants largely reject the infallibility of the church.

infantile paralysis: see POLIOMYELITIS.

infection, invasion of plant or animal tissues by pathogenic (disease-producing) microorganisms, such as BACTERIA, fungi (see FUNGAL INFECTION), VIRUSES, VIROIDS, and PROTOZOANS. Bacteria can destroy certain immune system cells or produce toxins that damage host tissues and interfere with normal metabolism. Viruses can cause either cellular degeneration, as in RABIES, or cellular proliferation, as in WARTS. Many invading organisms produce substances that cause allergic sensitivity in the host (see ALLERGY). IMMUNITY is the capacity of the host to resist infection.

inferiority complex: see COMPLEX.

infertility: see STERILITY.

infinity, in mathematics, that which is not finite; it is often indicated by the symbol ∞. A SEQUENCE of numbers is said to approach infinity if the numbers eventually become arbitrarily large, i.e., larger than any specified number. The word *infinite* is also used to describe a SET with more than any finite number of elements, e.g., the set of points on a line or the set of all prime numbers (see NUMBER THEORY). Georg CANTOR showed that there are different orders of infinity, the infinity of points on a line being of a greater order than that of prime numbers, and developed the theory of transfinite numbers as a means of distinguishing them.

inflation, in economics, a persistent and relatively large increase in the general price level of goods and services. It results from an increase in the amount of circulating currency beyond the needs of trade. The oversupply of currency thus created, in accordance with the law of SUPPLY AND DEMAND, decreases the value of money, or, more accurately, increases the prices of goods and services. Inflation may occur in times of economic or political upheaval, and it commonly occurs during war, when governments borrow and when there is a limited supply of consumer goods. Under less extreme circumstances, inflation stimulates business and helps wages to rise, but usually not as fast as prices; hence, real wages diminish. As a rule, annual price increases of less than 2% or 3% have not been considered inflationary. The 1970s brought the onset of worldwide inflation (often occurring as stagflation), commonly attributed to the soaring cost of petroleum. Double-digit inflation (i.e., 10% or more) became common in many countries and caused severe economic dislocations. In the early 1980s, however, recession lowered the inflation rate in the U.S., and it has remained relatively moderate since then. The opposite of inflation is **deflation,** a time of falling prices, curtailed business activity, and high unemployment (see DEPRESSION).

influenza, acute, highly contagious disease caused by a number of different viruses. The disease usually begins abruptly with fever, muscular aches, and inflammation of the respiratory mucous membranes; its more severe forms are bacterial PNEUMONIA and BRONCHITIS. Influenza epidemics have decimated large populations; an outbreak in 1918 killed over 20 million people. An injection with influenza virus vaccine can confer temporary immunity.

information storage and retrieval, the systematic process of collecting and cataloging data so that they can be located and displayed upon request. COMPUTERS and DATA PROCESSING have made possible the high-speed, selective retrieval of large amounts of information in such diverse fields as banking, law enforcement, jurisprudence, and medicine. There are several basic types of information-storage-and-retrieval systems. *Document-retrieval systems* store entire documents; these are usually retrieved by title or through a series of key words that denote the category to which they belong. Full-text searching, the capability of retrieving on the basis of any word in the document, is increasingly common and in used in many electronic encyclopedias. *Database systems* store the information as a series of discrete records that are, in turn, divided into discrete fields (e.g., name, height, and weight); records can be searched and retrieved on the basis of the content of the fields (e.g., all people who weigh more than 150 lb/68 kg). The data are stored within the computer, either in main storage or auxiliary storage, for ready access. *Reference-retrieval systems* store references to documents; references relevant to a particular request are retrieved and printed in a list. Such a system can therefore provide an index to literature from a wide variety of sources (e.g., books, periodicals, technical journals) on a particular subject (e.g., hypertension). *Image-retrieval systems* store drawings and photographs that either have been sketched directly on a graphics COMPUTER TERMINAL or have been input through a scanning device. The digitized images can be retrieved for viewing on a graphics terminal or drawn with a plotter or a printer. Such systems are proving increasingly important in COMPUTER-AIDED DESIGN and DESKTOP PUBLISHING. See also HYPERTEXT.

information theory, mathematical theory that explains aspects and problems of communication. A communication system in information theory consists of a message source, an encoder, a channel over which the message is transmitted, a decoder, and a message recipient. *Information* is a measure of the probability of a message being selected from the set of all possible messages. Information thus is distinct from meaning—a string of nonsense words and a meaningful sentence may be equivalent with respect to information content. Numerically, information is measured in bits (short for *binary digits*). One bit is equivalent to the choice between two equally likely choices. When several choices are equally likely, the number of bits is equal to the LOGARITHM of the number of choices taken to the base two. When the various choices are not equally probable, the situation is more complex. The mathematical expression for information content closely resembles the expression for ENTROPY in thermodynamics. The greater the information in a message, the lower its randomness, or "noisiness," and hence the smaller its entropy. For any given channel information theory defines a limiting capacity or rate at which it can carry information, expressed in bits per second. Once the information content and channel capacity are calculated, coding techniques can be defined to control errors in the channel. The theory succeeds remarkably in outlining the engineering requirements and limitations of communications systems.

informed consent, in medicine, a patient's written consent to a surgical or medical procedure or other course of treatment, given after the physician has told the patient all of the potential benefits, risks, and alternatives involved. The concept of informed consent is based on the principle that a physician has a duty to disclose to a patient information that allows the patient to make a reasonable decision regarding his or her own treatment.

infrared astronomy, study of celestial objects by means of INFRARED RADIATION. Although it was shown as early as the late 18th cent. that IR radiation could be detected, modern IR astronomy did not begin until the late 1950s because of the lack of appropriate equipment. Most progress has resulted from data obtained from orbiting OBSERVATORIES. Among the findings are the existence of dust trails in comet orbits, a new class of galaxies that are dim in the visible region of the SPECTRUM but 50 to 100 times brighter in the infrared, clouds of millimeter-sized particles around distant stars, and a bulge near the center of the MILKY WAY.

infrared radiation, ELECTROMAGNETIC RADIATION having a wavelength in the range of 750 to 1,000,000 nanometers, thus occupying that part of the electromagnetic spectrum with a frequency less than that of red visible LIGHT and greater than that of MICROWAVES. Infrared radiation is thermal, or heat, radiation and is generally produced by any body having a temperature above 10K. It has many of the same properties as visible light, such as being reflected or refracted. Infrared radiometers serve as the basis for heat-seeking devices in missiles and night vision devices. Medical uses of infrared radiation include thermal imaging, or thermography, which is also used in industry.

Inge, William [ĭnj], 1913–73, American playwright; b. Independence, Kans. His realistic dramas, often dealing with midwestern small-town life, include *Come Back, Little Sheba* (1950), *Picnic* (1953; Pulitzer), and *Bus Stop* (1955).

Ingemann, Bernhard Severin [ĭng'əmän], 1789–1862, Danish poet and novelist. His historical novels helped revive national literary consciousness, and the religious *Morning and Evening Songs* (1839) contains some of the finest lyrics in Danish.

Inglewood, city (1990 pop. 109,602), Los Angeles co., S Calif.; founded 1873, inc. 1908. A residential and industrial suburb of Los Angeles, it is located in an oil-producing area. Manufactures include machinery, aircraft parts, and electronic equipment. The Northrop Inst. of Technology and Los Angeles Forum, home of the Lakers basketball team, are there.

Ingres, Jean Auguste Dominique [ăN'grə], 1780–1867, French painter. A student of J.L. DAVID and an unparalleled draftsman, he won the Prix de Rome in 1801. The extraordinary sensuality of his work, e.g., the portrait of Mme Rivière (Louvre) and *Jupiter and Thetis* (1811; Musée Granet, Aix-en-Provence), put him at odds with the strict neoclassicists of his day. Ingres was also a portraitist, and his pencil portraits, e.g., *Paganini* (1819), are among his finest works. He was hailed as the bulwark of Davidian classicism for his *Vow of Louis XIII* (cathedral, Montauban), but his true inspiration had always been RAPHAEL. His followers, the *Ingristes,* lacked his genius, but many later artists (DEGAS, RENOIR, and PICASSO) have acknowledged their debt to him. His works include rigidly academic paintings, e.g., *The Apotheosis of Homer* (1827; Louvre), and intimate, sensual nudes, e.g., *The Turkish Bath* (1852–63; Louvre).

inheritance tax, assessment made by a state on the portion of an estate received by an individual; it differs from an estate tax, which is a federal tax levied on an entire estate before it is distributed to individuals. A related federal levy is the **gift tax,** designed to prevent people from avoiding inheritance and estate taxes by giving away property before death. The U.S. tax law of 1981 greatly reduced estate and gift taxes by raising exemptions (from $175,000 to $600,000) and lowering rates.

initiation, ritual transition from one status to another, as from childhood to adulthood, with attendant ceremonies and ordeals. A dominant theme is the symbolism of death and rebirth. Testing the initiate's worthiness to enter the new status, it often involves special instructions, restrictions, seclusion, and/or mutilation. Among the most important social institutions of traditional, preliterate societies, it continues in such modern contexts as fraternal orders and SECRET SOCIETIES.

initiative, referendum, and recall, processes by which voters can directly influence the making of laws and the removal of public officials. An **initiative** is the originating of a law or constitutional amendment by obtaining a prescribed number of signatures on a petition. It is then either voted on in a special election or the next general election, or taken up by the legislature. **Referendum** is a vote of final approval on a specific law or policy. **Recall** is a petition method for removing an elected official, before his or her term has expired, by requiring a special election.

injunction, in law, formal court order directing a party to perform or refrain from performing a specified act. It is often used where money damages cannot satisfy a plaintiff's claim. Developed in EQUITY courts, injunctions were at first only prohibitory; but the practice of issuing positive orders in negative guise (e.g., "Do not allow the wall to stand," meaning "Tear down the wall") led to acceptance of the mandatory (affirmative) injunction. Injunctions are granted in many circumstances, usually by a judge sitting without a jury, and are enforced by contempt of court proceedings.

Inkatha Freedom party: see BUTHELEZI, MANGOSUTHU GATSHA.

inlaying, process of ornamenting a surface by setting into it a material of a different color or substance. Of ancient origin, inlaying of materials such as wood, stone, ivory, glass, metal, and mother-of-pearl has been used on a wide variety of architectural and decorative objects.

Inner Mongolian Autonomous Region, region (1990 pop. 21,457,000), c.460,000 sq mi (1,200,000 sq km), N China. The capital is Hohhot. Bounded on the N by the Republic of Mongolia and Russia, the region is home to the Mongolian nationality, which comprises about 16% of the population. Its extensive grasslands are a major center of stock raising. Mineral extraction is an important industry; steel, machinery, and light industrial products are also manufactured.

Inness, George, 1825–94, American landscape painter; b. Newburgh, N.Y. His early work is in the manner of the HUDSON RIVER SCHOOL, e.g., *Delaware Water Gap* (Montclair Mus., N.J.). He soon discovered a personal style that was freer, more intimate, and richer in color. A Swedenborgian, Inness sought the mystical in nature, portraying it through a wide range of light effects. Among his principal works are *Rainbow After a Storm* (Art Inst., Chicago) and *June* (1882; Brooklyn Mus., N.Y.C.).

Innis, Roy (Emile Alfredo), 1934–, African-American CIVIL-RIGHTS leader; b. St. Croix, Virgin Islands. A member of the CONGRESS OF RACIAL EQUALITY (CORE) since 1963, he has served as its national director (1968–82) and chairman (1970–). In the late 1960s he abandoned an integrationist approach to civil rights for the ideology of black power and a revived black nationalism, but he later supported Pres. REAGAN's policies and criticized Jesse JACKSON.

Innocent I, Saint, d. 417, pope (401–17), an Italian. He was champion of papal supremacy. In 410, he tried but failed to halt ALARIC's sack of Rome. Feast: July 28.

Innocent II, d. 1143, pope (1130–43), a Roman named Gregorio Papareschi. Opposed by the antipope Anacletus II, Innocent won the support of BERNARD OF CLAIRVAUX and Holy Roman Emperor LOTHAIR II and prevailed over Anacletus's successor, Victor IV. He convened the Second Lateran Council (1139) and condemned the teachings of Peter ABELARD and Arnold of Brescia.

Innocent III, 1160?–1216, pope (1198–1216), an Italian named Lotario di Segni, one of the most prominent figures of medieval history. A learned theologian, he held the theory that supremacy of the spirit over the flesh meant that the pope, as church ruler, should be superior to lay rulers of states—a theory not held in present Roman Catholic doctrine. To establish papal supremacy, Innocent was active in political affairs. In the Holy Roman Empire, he arbitrated the dispute of PHILIP OF SWABIA and OTTO IV in Otto's favor (1201); later favored Philip (1207–8); crowned Otto (1209) after Philip's murder, only to excommunicate him (1210) and bring about the election of FREDERICK II, who was his ward. In England, Innocent, by naming Stephen Langton archbishop of Canterbury, infuriated King JOHN; in the quarrel, Innocent put England under interdict and excommunicated (1209) the king. John submitted and received England and Ireland as a fief from the pope. Later, Innocent declared that MAGNA CARTA was not binding on John because it was extorted by force and without the knowledge of his overlord (Innocent). In France the pope could not establish political power over PHILIP II but did force him to bow to canon law in the matter of a divorce. In Italy he reclaimed papal territories and was recognized as overlord of Tuscany. Thus, in all Europe he went far to put his theory of papal monarchy into effect, though history was to make his victories hollow. He promoted the Fourth CRUSADE and protested when the Crusaders attacked the Byzantine Empire; nevertheless, he recognized the Latin Kingdom of Constantinople, which they set up, and tried to spread the Latin rite there, embittering relations between the Eastern and Western churches. Similarly, he protested when the crusade he had started against the ALBIGENSES was turned to political and economic ends; he later urged St. DOMINIC's mission. Innocent was vigorous in administering internal church affairs and dominated the Fourth Lateran Council (1215). He wrote extensively, and his *De contemptu mundi* on the contempt of this world was popular in the Middle Ages.

Innocent IV, d. 1254, pope (1243–54), a Genoese named Sinibaldo Fieschi. His papacy was preoccupied by a contest with the HOHENSTAUFEN rulers. He opposed Holy Roman Emperor FREDERICK II and had to flee to Lyons, where he convened (1245) the First Council of Lyons, which declared Frederick deposed. Innocent supported pretenders to Frederick's throne and, after Frederick's death, continued the struggle against the emperors Conrad IV and MANFRED.

Innocent VIII, 1432–92, pope (1484–92), a Genoese named Giovanni Battista Cibò. His close friend Giuliano della Rovere (later Pope JULIUS II) largely directed papal affairs. Innocent failed to organize a crusade against the Turkish sultan BEYAZID II, but in 1490 wrung a peace agreement from Beyazid by threatening to recognize Beyazid's brother, Djem, as sultan.

Innocent XI, 1611–89, pope (1676–89), an Italian named Benedetto Odescalchi. Noted for his saintliness, he argued with LOUIS XIV of France over papal authority and denounced Louis's Gallican statement (1682) that kings are not subject to the pope. He condemned the king's revocation of the Edict of NANTES (1685). He was beatified in 1956.

Innsbruck, city (1991 pop. 114,996), capital of TYROL prov., SW Austria, on the Inn R. Established in the 12th cent., it became an important trans-Alpine trading post. Today it is an industrial center and a summer and winter resort. The winter Olympic games were held in Innsbruck in 1964 and 1976. The city's historic buildings include the Hofkirche, a 16th-cent. Franciscan church, and the 15th-cent. Fürstenburg castle.

inoculation: see VACCINATION.

Inonu, Ismet, 1884–1973, Turkish statesman. The chief of staff of the Turkish nationalist army in 1920, he repelled Greek forces at Inonu. He was premier (1923–37) and then president (1938) of the Turkish Republic. He kept Turkey neutral during World War II, westernized Turkish society, and encouraged democracy. Out of power during the 1950s, he returned in the 1960s, when his Republican People's party led several coalition governments.

inorganic chemistry, branch of CHEMISTRY dealing with all the elements and their compounds, except for most carbon compounds, which are studied in ORGANIC CHEMISTRY. Branches of inorganic chemistry include bioinorganic chemistry, coordination chemistry, geochemistry, inorganic technology, nuclear science and energy, reaction kinetics and mechanisms, solid-state chemistry, and synthetic inorganic chemistry.

Inouye, Daniel K., 1924–, U.S. politician; b. Honolulu. A senator from Hawaii since 1962, he was a member of the WATERGATE committee (1972–74) and served as chairman of the committee investigating the IRAN-CONTRA AFFAIR (1987).

input-output analysis, a tabular technique, devised by Wassily LEONTIEF, that statistically analyzes how a nation's industries interact. It determines the impact on supplier industries of production changes in any single industry. These techniques can be used to measure the impact of changing demand in any industry throughout the economy.

Inquisition, tribunal of the Roman Catholic Church formed to suppress heresy. In 1233 Pope GREGORY IX established the papal Inquisition to combat the heresy of the ALBIGENSES. The Inquisition used judicial torture but rarely condemned prisoners to burn; imprisonment was the norm. To deal with Protestantism, PAUL III assigned (1542) the Inquisition to the Holy Office. This was replaced (1965) by the Congregation for the Doctrine of the Faith, which governs vigilance in matters of faith. The **Spanish Inquisition,** independent of the papal Inquisition, was established (1478) by the Spanish monarchs to punish converted Jews and Muslims who were insincere. Headed by people such as Tomás de TORQUEMADA, it was notoriously harsher than the medieval Inquisition and much freer with the death penalty. Soon every Spaniard came to fear its power. It was finally abolished in 1834.

insanity, in law, a mental disorder so severe as to render its victim incapable of managing his or her affairs, e.g., incapable of entering into a CONTRACT. In CRIMINAL LAW, insanity may relieve a person from the legal consequences of his or her acts. Determining factors in establishing insanity are the ability to distinguish right from wrong and the capacity to control one's conduct. Some courts accept "irresistible impulse" as a defense. Present insanity is that which renders a defendant incapable of understanding legal proceedings; past insanity refers to the defendant's mental state at the time of the alleged crime. In criminal cases, state laws provide for various means of determining insanity. A defendant found not guilty by reason of insanity is committed to a mental institution. Long-standing controversy over the insanity defense came into focus in the 1982 trial of John Hinckley, Jr., who, after attempting to assassinate Pres. Reagan, was found not guilty by reason of insanity. The plea is rarely employed in the U.S.

insect, invertebrate animal of the class Insecta, an ARTHROPOD. There are more than 700,000 known species. Insects have a chitinous exoskeleton; a segmented body composed of a head (with three pairs of mouthparts, compound and simple eyes, and sensory antennae); a trisegmented thorax (with three pairs of jointed legs and two pairs of wings); and an abdomen (with reproductive appendages). They breathe through a complex network of air tubes (tracheae) opening on the sides of the body. Reproduction is usually sexual, although PARTHENOGENESIS is also common. Some 80% of insect species undergo complete METAMORPHOSIS. Insects are both harmful to humans (as disease carriers and agricultural pests) and beneficial as pollinating agents, as predators on harmful species, and as food in some parts of the world. Fossil records show that insects have undergone relatively little change for 200 million years. The class includes the BEETLES; the MOTHS and BUTTERFLIES; the WASPS, ANTS, and BEES; the FLIES and MOSQUITOES; the true BUGS; APHIDS; and the COCKROACHES and GRASSHOPPERS.

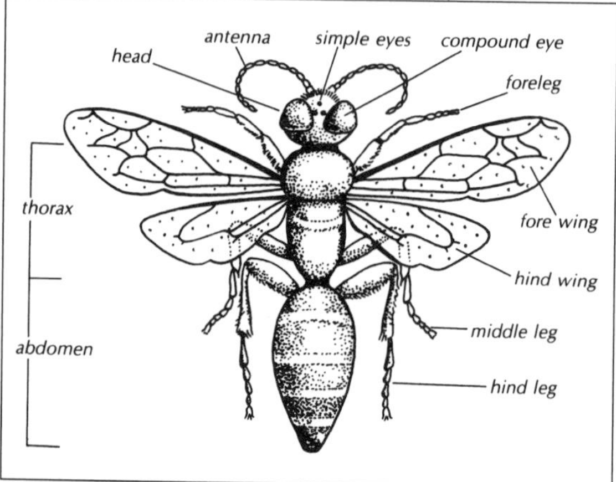

Insect: General anatomy of a wasp, an insect of the order Hymenoptera

insecticide, agent used to kill insect pests. Insecticides have helped increase the yield and improve the quality of crops, but there has been concern about the dangers of chemical insecticide residues in the ecosystem (see ECOLOGY) and in foodstuffs. Such concerns have led to governmental regulation and the replacement of some toxic insecticides that persist in the environment (e.g., DDT and other chlorinated hydrocarbons) with compounds that break down more quickly into less toxic forms. The liabilities of chemical insecticides have encouraged interest in biological controls, which turn natural processes and mechanisms against pest insects and have few if any harmful side effects. Biological controls include using predators, parasites, and pathogens to kill target insects or using synthetic hormones to disrupt pests' normal life processes. Increasingly, biological and chemical methods are coordinated in INTEGRATED PEST MANAGEMENT programs.

insider trading, stock market transactions made with the knowledge of nonpublic information about corporate activity. In the U.S., it has been illegal since 1934. The SECURITIES AND EXCHANGE COMMISSION regards it as unfair to investors who are not privy to such information. Several insider trading scandals shook Wall Street in the mid-1980s.

installment buying and selling: see CREDIT.

instinct, in psychology, term used to indicate an unlearned behavior that is elicited by a specific stimulus and that generally fulfills a vital need of the organism. Instinctive behaviors may include aspects of fighting, escape, courtship, and food-gathering activities; these behaviors are often modified—especially in higher animals—by past experience, as well as by innate regulatory mechanisms. The role of instinct in human behavior is poorly understood, but it is apparently highly modified by the socialization process and individual INTELLIGENCE.

Institut de France [ăNstētü' də fräNs], cultural institution of the French state. Founded in 1795 by the DIRECTORY, it replaced five learned societies that had been suppressed in 1793 by the Convention. Today it is made up of five academies—the French Academy (Académie Française; language and literature), the Académie des Inscriptions et Belles-Lettres (history and archaeology), the Académie des Sciences (physical and mathematical sciences), the Académie des Beaux-Arts (fine arts), and the Académie des Sciences morales et politiques (moral and political sciences). The awards and prizes given by these academies have encouraged endeavor in various fields.

Institutional Revolutionary party (PRI), Span. *Partido Revolucionario Institucional,* Mexican political party. Established (1929) as the National Revolutionary party by former president CALLES, it brought together the country's governmental, military, and agricultural leaders in a program of socioeconomic reform. Since its inception all Mexican presidents and most officials have belonged to the PRI, which has sometimes been accused of corruption and electoral fraud. Its victory margins decreased in the 1980s and 90s, and it has been forced to concede some state elections to its opponents, but the party remains Mexico's dominant political group.

instructional television: see AUDIOVISUAL INSTRUCTION.

insulation, use of materials to inhibit or prevent the CONDUCTION of heat or of electricity. Common heat insulators are ASBESTOS, CELLULOSE fibers, FEATHERS, FIBERGLASS, FUR, stone, WOOD, and WOOL; all are poor conductors of heat. In the conduction of electricity from point to point, the conductor acts as a guide for the electric current and must be insulated at every point of contact with its support to prevent escape, or leakage, of the current. Good electrical insulators, or DIELECTRICS, include dry air, dry COTTON, GLASS, PARAFFIN, PLASTICS, PORCELAIN, RESIN, RUBBER, and VARNISHES.

insulin, HORMONE secreted by the islets of Langerhans in the PANCREAS. A protein of 21 amino acids in two cross-linked chains, insulin was the first protein to be sequenced (1951), and its synthesis was reported by several groups in the mid-1960s. Insulin was also one of the first products to be manufactured using GENETIC ENGINEERING. In general, insulin acts to metabolize glucose (sugar). It also increases protein synthesis in muscle. Insufficient insulin in the body results in DIABETES, a condition treated by the administration of insulin or drugs that stimulate insulin secretion.

insurance or **assurance,** system for indemnifying or guaranteeing an individual against loss. Reimbursement is made from a fund to which many individuals exposed to the same risk have contributed specified amounts, known as premiums, so that payment for the loss is divided among many, not falling heavily upon the actual loser. The essence of the contract of insurance, called a policy, is mutuality. The amount of the premium is determined by the operation of the law of averages, as calculated by actuaries. Reinsurance, whereby losses are distributed among many companies, was devised to meet the enormous claims resulting from disasters. Insurance may now be obtained against almost any conceivable risk. Fire insurance usually covers damage from lightning; other insurance against the elements includes hail, tornado, flood, and drought. Life insurance, originally conceived to protect a wage-earner's family when he or she died, has developed policies that provide a lump sum at the end of a term of years or payment of benefits to a terminally ill person. Annuity policies, which pay the insured a yearly income after a certain age, are also available. Automobile insurance compensates not only for fire and theft, but also for damage to the car and for injury to the victim of an accident (liability insurance, now required in many states). Under no-fault insurance plans, automobile-accident victims are compensated by their own company, eliminating the need for a lawsuit, except in serious cases. Bonding, or fidelity insurance, protects an employer against dishonesty or default by an employee. In group insurance, employees pay a lower premium than they would as individuals. By investing premium payments in a wide range of revenue-producing projects, insurance companies have become a major supplier of capital. Many forms of insurance, such as SOCIAL SECURITY, workers' compensation, and unemployment benefits, are government-sponsored. Devices resembling modern insurance seem to have originated in ancient times. By the mid-14th cent. marine insurance was common in the maritime nations of Europe. The first life-insurance policy is believed to have been issued in England in 1583, and Lloyds, perhaps the world's best-known insurer, began issuing marine insurance in London in the 1600s. The first insurance company in the American colonies was founded at Charlestown, S.C., in 1735. See also HEALTH INSURANCE.

intaglio, design cut into stone or other material, or etched or engraved in a metal plate, producing a concave effect that is the reverse of relief or CAMEO. Intaglio PRINTING techniques include ENGRAVING and ETCHING.

integer: see NUMBER; NUMBER THEORY.

integral calculus: see CALCULUS.

integrated circuit, miniature ELECTRIC CIRCUIT containing large numbers of electronic devices—including TRANSISTORS, RESISTORS, CAPACITORS, and DIODES—and packaged as a single unit with leads extending from it for input, output, and power-supply connections. All the electronic devices are formed by selective treatment (doping) of a single chip of SEMICONDUCTOR material. Integrated circuits are used as computer memory circuits and MICROPROCESSORS. They are categorized according to the number of transistors or other active circuit devices they contain; an active circuit device is one that receives power from a source other than its input signal. An ordinary, or small-scale, integrated circuit (SSI) may contain up to several tens of such devices; a medium-scale integrated circuit (MSI), many tens to several hundred; a large-scale integrated circuit (LSI), several hundred to a few thousand; an extra-large-scale integrated circuit (ELSI), a few thousand or more; and a very-large-scale integrated circuit (VLSI), several hundred thousand or more. The first VSLI device was introduced in 1981.

integrated pest management (IPM), planned program that coordinates economically and environmentally acceptable methods of pest control with judicious and minimal use of toxic pesticides. IPM programs assess local conditions, including climate, crop characteristics, the biology of the pest species, and soil quality, to determine the best method of pest control. Tactics employed include better tillage to prevent soil erosion and introduction of beneficial insects that eat harmful species.

integration, in U.S. history, the goal of eliminating discrimination and segregation of African Americans from the rest of American society. After RECONSTRUCTION, white dominance, codified in segregation (Jim Crow) laws, was reestablished in the South: African Americans were denied the vote and an equal share in community life. In 1896 the Supreme Court upheld the principle of separate but equal treatment (PLESSY V. FERGUSON), and by 1920 segregation affected education, transportation, hospitals, churches, housing, and public facilities. The rising CIVIL-RIGHTS movement opposed segregation, and in the late 1940s the federal government gradually moved toward integration. Following the Supreme Court's momentous decision in BROWN V. BOARD OF EDUCATION (1954) that public school segregation is inherently unequal and denies African Americans equal protection under the law, the 17 segregationist states and the District of Columbia were ordered to desegregate their schools. In some places the order met with resistance, lawsuits, and even violence: in Arkansas, federal troops enforced integration (1957) over Gov. Orval Faubus's objections, while Gov. George C. WALLACE tried in vain (1963) to block African-American enrollment at the Univ. of Alabama. Another milestone was the successful bus boycott (1955–56) in Montgomery, Ala., led by civil-rights activist Martin Luther KING, Jr., to end segregation in transportation. Freedom riders then tackled segregation in interstate transportation. Segregated lunch counters, restaurants, beaches, and other public places were also challenged with increasing effect in both the North and South during the 1960s. The Civil Rights Act of 1964, prohibiting discrimination in voting, education, employment, and public facilities, together with the 1965 Voting Rights Act, for the first time gave the federal government the power to enforce desegregation—by denying federal funds to segregated programs and schools or by overseeing elections, for example. The Civil Rights Act of 1968 barred discrimination in the sale or rental of housing. Desegregation of schooling proceeded slowly, but despite setbacks such as widespread opposition to school busing as a means of effecting integration, by the 1980s relatively few African-American students in the U.S. still remained in schools that were completely segregated. Despite real achievements in integration, racial tensions remain one of the U.S.'s most intractable problems, in large part because personal biases and racial stereotyping (by and of all races) cannot be altered by legislation or lawsuits. See also AFFIRMATIVE ACTION.

intelligence, in psychology, the general mental ability involved in processes such as calculating, reasoning, classifying, learning, the use of language, and adjusting to new situations. It is widely accepted that although potential intelligence is related to heredity, the environment is a critical factor in determining the extent of its expression. Since the concept of intelligence is elusive, it has generally been defined by psychologists as that which is measured by intelligence tests. Alfred BINET and Théodore Simon developed the first modern intelligence test in 1905 for the French school system. Currently, the most widely used intelligence tests are the Wechsler Intelligence Scale for Children (WISC) and the Wechsler Adult Intelligence Scale (WAIS). Others commonly used in the past include the Army Alpha Test, first administered to recruits in World War I, and the Revised Stanford-Binet Intelligence Tests, developed by Lewis Terman in the 1930s. One criticism of intelligence tests is that test items may be meaningless or more difficult for members of different sociocultural groups. Test findings in the U.S., however, closely correlate with career and academic achievement. In response to the criticism that intelligence is an attribute of the entire personality and cannot be measured in isolation, "pure" intelligence tests have given way to tests that also measure special aptitudes and personality factors. Recent theories have sought to broaden the definition of intelligence by identifying different types of intelligence, e.g., linguistic and interpersonal intelligence.

intelligence gathering, securing of military, political, or other information, usually about one nation for the benefit of another. It includes the analysis of diplomatic reports, publications, statistics, and broadcasts, as well as **espionage,** or spying, a clandestine activity. French revolutionary Joseph FOUCHÉ developed (1799–1802) the first modern political espionage system, and FREDERICK II of Prussia is considered the father of modern military espionage, which was to play an important role in WORLD WAR I. The efficient British system was the keystone of Allied intelligence in WORLD WAR II. The Office of Strategic Services, the first U.S. espionage agency (1942), was succeeded (1947) by the CENTRAL INTELLIGENCE AGENCY, the NATIONAL SECURITY AGENCY, and other intelligence-gathering bodies. Modern techniques include RECONNAISSANCE SATELLITES, long-distance photography, sophisticated sensing and listening ("bugging") devices, and computer analysis. Defense against espionage is principally a function of counterintelligence specialists. In the business world the massive task of information-gathering that is a normal part of marketing may occasionally include so-called industrial espionage, an attempt by one company to discover another's secrets.

interest, charge for the use of money, usually figured as a percentage of the principal and computed annually. Such charges have been made since ancient times, and they fell early into disrepute. The Jews and the Christian church forbade interest charges, or usury, as it was called, within their own groups. Gradually the distinction was made between low interest rates and high ones, which came to be known, and condemned, as usury. In the U.S. state usury laws set ceilings on interest, but in 1981, when rates soared to record highs, many legislatures increased or abolished such ceilings in order to attract lenders. High interest rates can dampen the economy by making it more difficult for consumers, businesses, and home buyers to secure loans, as happened in 1981 when the prime rate—the rate that banks charge their best customers—climbed past 20%, with most other rates a few points lower. Economists differed over the causes of such extraordinary rates, but inflationary expectations, federal budget deficits, and the restrictive monetary policies of the FEDERAL RESERVE SYSTEM were important factors.

interference, in physics, the effect obtained when two systems of WAVES reinforce, neutralize, or in other ways interfere with each other. Interference is observed in waves both in a material medium (such as SOUND) and in ELECTROMAGNETIC RADIATION. *Constructive interference* occurs when two waves in the same phase combine. The waves reinforce each other, and the amplitude of the resulting wave is equal to the sum of the amplitudes of the interfering waves. When the phases of the two waves are shifted by 180°, i.e., the maximum positive amplitude of one wave coincides with the maximum negative amplitude of the other wave, *destructive interference* occurs, which results in the canceling of the waves when they have the same amplitude. See DIFFRACTION.

interferon, any of a group of proteins produced by cells in the body in response to viruses. Interferon impairs the growth and replication of the attacking virus and has been shown to have some antitumor properties. Interferons used as drugs include alpha interferon, for HEPATITIS B and C and Kaposi's sarcoma (a cancer associated with AIDS), and beta interferon, for MULTIPLE SCLEROSIS.

Interior, United States Department of the, federal executive department (est. 1849) principally charged as the custodian of the nation's natural resources. Among the many divisions whose chiefs report to the secretary of the interior are the Bureau of Land Management, which must reconcile the often conflicting demands (e.g., for conservation or economic use) made upon U.S. public land; the Bureau of Mines, which sets safety regulations in mining; the Bureau of Reclamation, which oversees water and power projects; the National Park Service, which maintains NATIONAL PARKS and monuments; the Fish and Wildlife Service; the Bureau of INDIAN AFFAIRS (est. 1824); and the Geological Survey.

Interlingua: see INTERNATIONAL LANGUAGE.

internal-combustion engine, engine in which combustion of fuel takes place in a confined space, producing expanding gases that are used to provide mechanical power. The most common internal-combustion engine is the four-stroke reciprocating engine used in AUTOMOBILES. Here, mechanical power is supplied by a piston fitting inside a cylinder. On a downstroke of the piston, the first stroke, fuel that has been mixed with air (by FUEL INJECTION or using a CARBURETOR) enters the cylinder through an intake valve; the piston moves up to compress the mixture at the second stroke; at ignition, the third stroke, a spark from a spark plug ignites the mixture, forcing the piston down; in the exhaust stroke, an exhaust valve opens to vent the burned gas as the piston moves up. A rod connects the piston to a crankshaft. The reciprocating (up and down) movements of the piston rotate the crankshaft, which is connected by gearing to the drive wheels of the automobile. The ignition spark is provided by an electrical system whose power comes from a battery, which also supplies power to the starting system, a small electric motor that turns the crankshaft until the engine takes over. The engine is cooled by water circulating around the cylinders and is lubricated by motor oil driven around the moving engine parts by an oil pump. The two-stroke engine, which combines intake and compression in the first stroke and power and exhaust in the second, is used in lawn mowers and for small vehicles such as motorcycles. Other variations of the internal-combustion engine include the Wankel engine, which replaces the piston and cylinder with a triangular rotor moving inside an oval chamber, and the DIESEL engine. (For a description of an external-combustion engine, see STEAM ENGINE.)

Internal Revenue Service (IRS), division of the U.S. Dept. of the TREASURY, established in 1862. It is responsible for the assessment and collection of federal taxes other than those levied on alcohol, tobacco, firearms, and explosives, and collects most of its revenues through the individual and corporate INCOME TAX.

International Atomic Energy Agency: see UNITED NATIONS (table 3).

International Bank for Reconstruction and Development or **World Bank:** see UNITED NATIONS, table 3.

International Civil Aviation Organization: see UNITED NATIONS (table 3).

International Court of Justice: see UNITED NATIONS (table 2).

International Criminal Police Organization: see INTERPOL.

international date line, imaginary line on the earth's surface, generally following the 180° meridian of LONGITUDE, where, by international agreement, travelers change dates. Traveling eastward across the line, one subtracts one day; traveling westward, one adds a day. The date line is necessary to avoid a confusion that would otherwise result. For example, if an airplane were to travel westward with the sun, 24 hours would elapse as it circled the globe, but it would still be the same day for those in the airplane, while it would be one day later for those on the ground below.

International Development Association: see UNITED NATIONS (table 3).

International Finance Corporation: see UNITED NATIONS (table 3).

International Fund for Agricultural Development: see UNITED NATIONS (table 3).

International Labor Organization: see UNITED NATIONS (table 3).

international language, sometimes called universal language, a language intended to be used by people of different linguistic backgrounds to facilitate communication. Latin was an international language during the Middle Ages and Renaissance. During the 18th cent., French was known as the language of diplomacy, and English is often said to fill such a role today in world commerce. Many artificial languages, i.e., languages constructed by human agents, have also been promoted as international languages. It has been estimated that since the 17th cent. several hundred efforts have been made to create such artificial tongues. Among the best known of these is Esperanto, invented by Dr. Ludwig L. Zamenhoff of Poland and first presented to the public in 1887. It has enjoyed some recognition as an international language, being used, for example, at international meetings and conferences. The vocabulary of Esperanto is formed by adding various affixes to individual roots and is derived from Latin, Greek, the Romance languages, and the Germanic languages. The grammar is based on that of European languages but is regular and greatly simplified. The spelling is phonetic. A simplified form of Esperanto is Ido, short for Esperandido. Another well-known artificial language is Interlingua. Created in the early 20th cent., it is derived from English and the Romance languages in both grammar and vocabulary. Later (1932), the British scholar C.K. Ogden developed Basic English, a simplified form of English with a vastly reduced vocabulary.

international law, body of laws considered legally binding among national states; also known as the law of nations. It is based both on customary usages and on provisions of multilateral or bilateral agreements. It is influenced, but not made, by the writings of jurists, unratified conventions, and decisions of the WORLD COURT, the INTERNATIONAL COURT OF JUSTICE, and other tribunals. Since it is not enforced by any supernational sovereign body, some theorists, including HOBBES, have denied it true legal status. But it is recognized in practice, and enforcement is by virtue of world opinion, third-state intervention, sanctions of international organizations like the UN, and, in the last resort, war. In some areas, such as WAR CRIMES, international law governs individuals as well as states. The development of international law coincides with the rise of national states after the Middle Ages, and the first comprehensive formulation of international law, *Concerning the Law of War and*

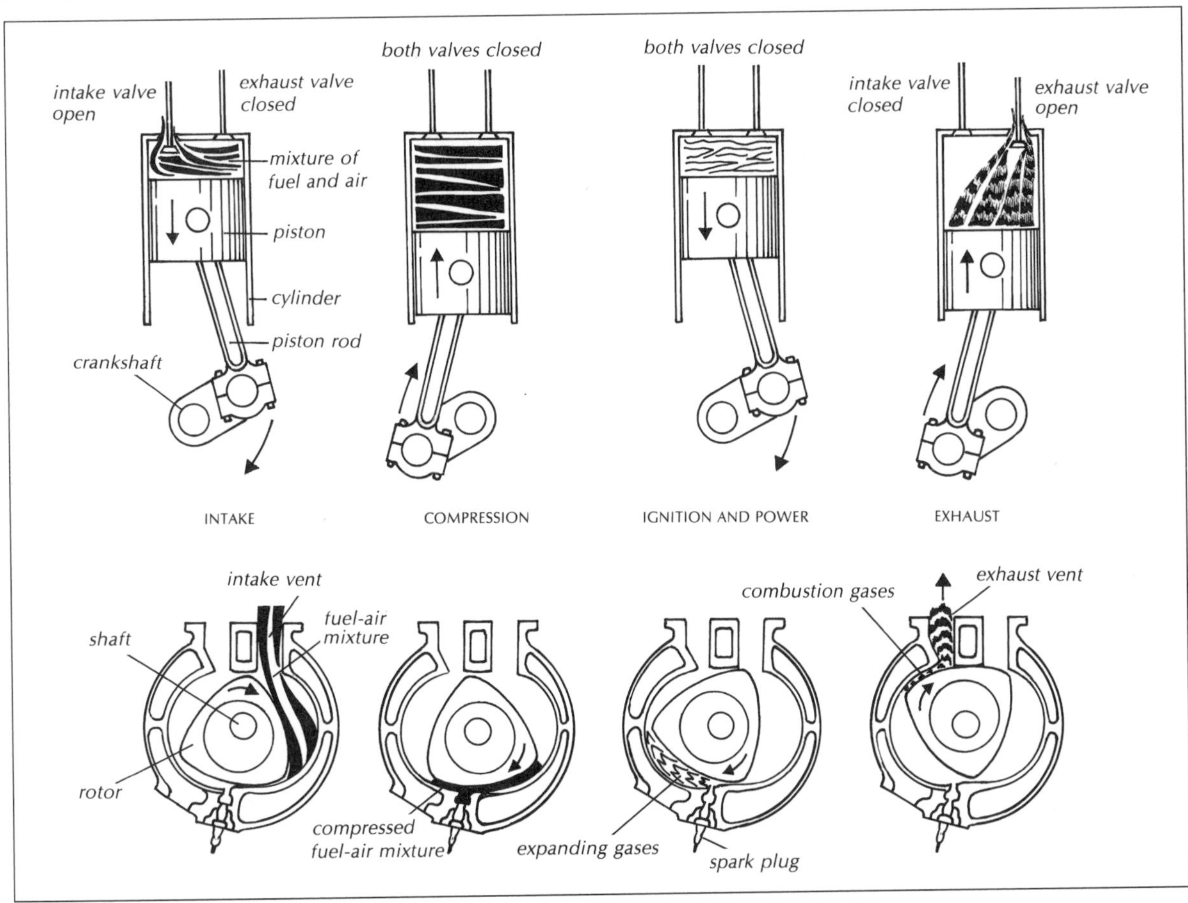

Internal-combustion engine

Peace, by Hugo GROTIUS, appeared in 1625; among the principles that he enunciated as the basis of international law are the sovereignty and legal equality of all states. International law thereafter grew largely through treaties among states. Following the Napoleonic period, the 1815 Congress of VIENNA reestablished and expanded international law. The GENEVA CONVENTION (1864) and the HAGUE CONFERENCES (1899, 1907), dealing with the rules of war, are other landmarks in development of an international legal code. The 20th cent. presented new problems: Two world wars led to the formation of the LEAGUE OF NATIONS, and then of the UNITED NATIONS, as a body capable of compelling obedience to international law; nuclear proliferation exacerbated the need for international arms treaties (see DISARMAMENT, NUCLEAR); and burgeoning space exploration has led to creation of the field of SPACE LAW. See also AIR, LAW OF THE; SEA, LAW OF THE.

International Maritime Organization: see UNITED NATIONS (table 3).

International Monetary Fund: see UNITED NATIONS (table 3).

international monetary system, rules and procedures by which different national currencies are exchanged for each other in world trade. The first formal international monetary system of modern times was the gold standard, in effect during the late 19th and early 20th cent. Gold served as an instrument of exchange and the only standard of value. The international gold standard broke down in 1914, however, partly because of its inherent lack of liquidity. It was replaced by a gold-bullion standard, but that, too, was abandoned in the 1930s. In the decades following World War II, international trade was conducted under a gold-exchange standard. Under this system, nations fixed the value of their currencies not to gold but to some foreign currency, which was in turn fixed to and redeemable in gold. Most nations fixed their currencies to the U.S. dollar. During the 1960s, however, a severe drain on U.S. gold reserves led to the introduction (1968) of the so-called two-tier system. In the official tier, the value of gold was set at $35 an ounce; in the free-market tier, the price was free to fluctuate according to supply and demand. At the same time, the International Monetary Fund (IMF) created SPECIAL DRAWING RIGHTS as a new reserve currency. In the early 1970s new troubles plagued the international monetary system, resulting in the temporary adoption of "floating" exchange rates based largely on SUPPLY AND DEMAND. Finally, under a 1976 agreement IMF members accepted a system of controlled floating rates and took steps to diminish the importance of gold in international transactions, including elimination of the official price. Since the 1970s the U.S. dollar, Japanese yen, German Deutchmark, and the EUROPEAN MONETARY SYSTEM's European Currency Unit have played the most important roles in international trade. See FOREIGN EXCHANGE.

International style, in architecture, form that originated in the 1920s and became the dominant mode of public architecture in the 1950s and 60s. Structure was regularized, mass lightened, and ornament suppressed, often resulting in an austere framework of steel or concrete, great expanses of glass, and white-walled interiors. Outstanding examples of the International style are the BAUHAUS (1926) at Dessau, by GROPIUS, and the Barcelona pavilion (1929), by MIËS VAN DER ROHE. In the U.S., exponents of the style included Richard NEUTRA and Philip JOHNSON.

International System of Units: see METRIC SYSTEM.

International Telecommunication Union: see UNITED NATIONS (table 3).

International Union for the Conservation of Nature and Natural Resources or **World Conservation Union,** international organization founded (1948) to encourage the preservation of wildlife and wild environments. It lists ENDANGERED SPECIES worldwide and promotes ecological and environmental research.

Internet, the: see NETWORK.

Interpol, acronym for the International Criminal Police Organization, a worldwide clearinghouse for police information. Established in Vienna in 1923, it was reconstituted in Paris in 1946. Focusing on counterfeiting, forgery, smuggling, and the narcotics trade, it serves more than 150 member nations, providing information about international criminals and helping to apprehend them.

Interstate Commerce Commission (ICC), independent U.S. government agency (est. 1887) responsible for regulating the economics and services of specified carriers engaged in transportation between states. The first U.S. regulatory agency, it was formed in response to malpractices in the railroad industry. Its jurisdiction has gradually expanded to include trucking, bus lines, water carriers, freight forwarders, pipelines not regulated by other agencies, and express agencies, and it controls rates and enforces laws against discrimination in these areas. Its safety functions were transferred to the Dept. of TRANSPORTATION in 1967, and since the 1980s the ICC has had a reduced role in regulating trucking, bus lines, and railroads.

interstellar matter, matter in a galaxy between the stars. About 1% is tiny interstellar grains, believed to be frozen water vapor and carbon dioxide. The grains may appear optically as bright reflection or dark NEBULAE. The rest of the matter is gas, mostly hydrogen and helium, but many molecules have been detected by RADIO ASTRONOMY techniques.

intestine, muscular, hoselike portion of the DIGESTIVE SYSTEM extending from the lower end of the STOMACH to the anal opening. In humans the fairly narrow small intestine is a tubelike structure that winds compactly back and forth within the abdominal cavity. The contraction of its muscular walls (peristalsis) propels food onward while digestion is completed. Innumerable minute projections (villi) in the intestinal lining absorb the altered food for distribution by the BLOOD and LYMPHATIC SYSTEMS to the rest of the body. In the lower right abdominal cavity, the small intestine joins the large intestine (colon), where most of the water content of the remaining mass is absorbed.

Intolerable Acts, name given by American patriots to five laws (including the QUEBEC ACT) adopted by the British Parliament in 1774, limiting the geographical and political freedom of the colonists. Four of the laws were passed to punish Massachusetts for the BOSTON TEA PARTY.

Intracoastal Waterway, toll-free, sheltered water route, extending 2,455 mi (3,951 km) along the U.S. Atlantic Coast (Trenton, N.J.–Key West, Fla.) and the Gulf Coast (NW Florida–Brownsville, Tex.), with open-water extensions of 645 mi (1,038 km) N to Boston and along the W Florida coast. Authorized by Congress in 1919 and maintained by the Army Corps of Engineers, the waterway has a minimum depth of 12 ft (4 m) for most of its length and is used by commercial and pleasure boats.

intrauterine device (IUD), variously shaped BIRTH CONTROL device, usually of plastic, which is inserted into the uterus by a physician. The IUD may contain copper or progesterone. Apparently the IUD creates a hostile environment for the fertilized egg.

Inuit: see ESKIMO.

invertebrate, any multicellular animal lacking a backbone. Invertebrates include all animals except the fishes, amphibians, reptiles, birds, and mammals, which are in the phylum Chordata (see CHORDATE). The major invertebrate groups are the segmented or ANNELID WORMS, ARTHROPODS, COELENTERATES, ECHINODERMS, FLATWORMS, MOLLUSKS, NEMATODES, and SPONGES.

investiture, in FEUDALISM, the ceremony by which a lord "invested" a vassal with a fief, usually by giving him a symbolic stone or clod. In clerical investiture, the symbols were the pastoral ring and staff. Since bishops and abbots were both spiritual and temporal lords, kings and popes disputed the right of investiture in the Middle Ages. Lay investiture—the investiture of a cleric by a temporal lord—became a bitter quarrel between Pope GREGORY VII and Holy Roman Emperor HENRY IV when Gregory forbade (1075) it. After a long conflict, HENRY V and Pope CALIXTUS II resolved the issue in the Concordat of Worms. In England, WILLIAM II began a long struggle over investiture that was settled (1107) by a compromise between HENRY I and St. ANSELM which gave investiture to the church and homages from church revenues to the king.

in vitro fertilization, technique for conception of a human embryo outside the mother's body. Several ova, or eggs, are removed from the mother's body and placed in special laboratory culture dishes (Petri dishes); sperm from the father are then added. If fertilization occurs, a fertilized ovum, after undergoing several cell divisions, is either transferred to the mother's or a surrogate mother's body for normal development in the uterus, or frozen for later implantation. First developed by Drs. Patrick C. Steptoe and Robert G. Edwards of Great Britain (where the first "test-tube baby" was born under their care in 1978), the technique was devised for use in cases of infertility when the woman's fallopian tubes are damaged and cannot be surgically repaired or the man's sperm count is low. It is also now used to enable parents with other reproductive problems (e.g., inability to produce eggs, poor sperm quality, or endometriosis) to bear a child. The technique has raised legal, ethical, and religious issues, including concerns regarding custody of frozen embryos in cases of divorce and questions regarding the appropriateness of the procedure by the Roman Catholic Church. See also ARTIFICIAL INSEMINATION; FERTILIZATION; REPRODUCTIVE SYSTEM; SURROGATE MOTHER.

Io, in astronomy, natural satellite of JUPITER.

Io, in Greek mythology, princess of Argos. She was turned into a heifer by ZEUS to protect her from HERA's jealousy. Hera claimed the heifer and had the many-eyed monster ARGUS guard it. When HERMES killed Argus, Hera's gadfly drove Io until she came to rest in Egypt. There Zeus returned her to human form. Io has been identified with the Egyptian ISIS.

iodine (I), nonmetallic element, discovered in 1811 by Bernard Courtois. The least active of the HALOGENS, it is a dark-gray to purple-black solid that, when heated, sublimes directly to the vapor state. The violet-colored vapor has a characteristic irritating odor. Tincture of iodine and iodoform have important medical uses. Silver iodide is used in photography. Starch turns deep-blue in the presence of iodine; this is a test for either substance. Thyroid-gland hormones contain iodine; inadequate dietary iodine results in goiter, a swelling of the thyroid. Thyroid defects are treated with iodine-131. See ELEMENT (table); PERIODIC TABLE.

ion, atom, or group of atoms, having a net electric charge, acquired by gaining or losing one or more electrons or protons. A simple ion consists of only one charged atom; a complex ion consists of an aggregate of atoms with a net charge. Because the electron and proton have equal but opposite unit charges, the charge of an ion is always expressed as a whole number of positive or negative unit charges. If an atom or group loses electrons or gains protons, it will have a net positive charge and is called a cation. If an atom or group gains electrons or loses protons, it will have a net negative charge and is called an anion. See also ACIDS AND BASES; ELECTROLYTE.

Iona, island, 3.5 mi (5.6 km) long and 1.5 mi (2.4 km) wide, NW Scotland, one of the Inner HEBRIDES. Tourism is the main industry. The island is famous as the early center of Celtic Christianity. In 563 St. COLUMBA founded a monastery there and spread Christianity to Scotland.

Ionesco, Eugène [yŏnĕs'kō], 1912–, French playwright; b. Romania. His works express the absurdity of bourgeois values and the futility of human endeavor in a universe ruled by chance. *The Bald Soprano* (1950), a classic of the theater of the absurd, was followed by *The Lesson* (1951), *The Chairs* (1952), and *Rhinoceros* (1959).

Ionia [īō'nēə], ancient Greek region of ASIA MINOR, on the E Mediterranean (in present-day TURKEY), and including the Aegean Islands. It was here that the Ionians, Greek colonists driven from the mainland by the Dorians, established colonies before 1000 B.C. There came to be 12 important cities—among them MILETUS, SÁMOS, and EPHESUS. After invasions by Cimmeria and Lydia, the cities came under Persian rule (546 B.C.). In 500 B.C. they revolted against DARIUS I; Athens and Eritrea came to their aid, and the PERSIAN WARS resulted. Ionia was conquered by ALEXANDER THE GREAT in 335 B.C. The cities remained rich and important during the Roman and Byzantine empires, but after the Turkish conquest (15th cent. A.D.) their culture was destroyed.

Ionic order: see ORDERS OF ARCHITECTURE.

ionization chamber: see PARTICLE DETECTOR.

ionosphere: see ATMOSPHERE.

Iowa, midwestern state in the N central U.S.; bounded by the Mississippi R., across which lie Wisconsin and Illinois (E); Missouri (S); Nebraska and South Dakota, from which it is separated by the Missouri R. (W); and Minnesota (N).

Area, 56,290 sq mi (145,791 sq km). *Pop.* (1990) 2,776,755, a 4.7% decrease from 1980 pop. *Capital,* Des Moines. *Statehood,* Dec. 28, 1846 (29th state). *Highest pt.,* 1,670 ft (509 m), Osceola co.; *lowest pt.,* Mississippi R., 480 ft (146 m). *Nickname,* Hawkeye State. *Motto,* Our Liberties We Prize and Our Rights We Will Maintain. *State bird,* Eastern goldfinch. *State flower,* wild rose. *State tree,* oak. *Abbr.,* IA.

Land and People. Most of Iowa is composed of gently rolling prairies, covered with some of the world's most fertile soil and lying between the high bluffs of the MISSISSIPPI and MISSOURI rivers. Because of its location in the center of the North American landmass, Iowa has a typical continental climate characterized by seasonal extremes in temperatures. Over 60% of the population of this traditionally agricultural state lives in urban areas. DES MOINES is the largest city, followed by CEDAR RAPIDS and DAVENPORT. In 1990, nearly 97% of the population was white.

Economy. The state has one of the country's most important and prosperous agricultural sectors. Iowa's deep black soil yields huge quantities of corn, soybeans, oats, hay, wheat, and barley, which help support its cattle and hogs and supply its large food-processing industry. Manufacturing is a large source of income; tires, nonelectrical and farm machinery, electronic equipment, and chemicals are among the principal products.

Government. The constitution of 1857 provides for a governor serving a four-year term. The general assembly consists of a senate whose 50 members serve four-year terms and a house with 100 members elected for two-year terms. Iowa elects two senators and five representatives to the U.S. Congress and has seven electoral votes.

History. The earliest known inhabitants of present-day Iowa were the MOUND BUILDERS, whose remains are preserved at Effigy Mounds National Monument. The SAC AND FOX, Iowa, and SIOUX tribes lived there when French explorers arrived during the late 17th cent., including Robert Cavelier, sieur de LA SALLE, in 1681–82. The U.S. obtained the area by the LOUISIANA PURCHASE (1803), and after the BLACK HAWK WAR (1832) Native Americans were forced to cede all their lands to whites, who rushed to settle the prairies. Among the many settlers who came both from New England and N Europe were a group of German Pietists who established (1855) at Amana a communal society that still exists. With its large rural population, Iowa proved to be fertile ground for such reform movements as the GRANGER MOVEMENT, GREENBACK PARTY, and POPULIST PARTY during the late 19th cent. Since World War II, Iowa has registered a gradual decline in farm population that has been more than balanced by a steady increase in its urban population; however, it remains basically a rural state. In 1993 record rains caused widespread flooding in Iowa.

Iphigenia [ĭf″əjənī′ə], in Greek myth, daughter of CLYTEMNESTRA and AGAMEMNON. When his ships were becalmed en route to the TROJAN WAR, Agamemnon sacrificed Iphigenia to ARTEMIS. In another version, Artemis saved her and made her a priestess at Taurus. Later, Iphigenia saved her brother, ORESTES, and the two fled to Greece. EURIPIDES dramatized both legends.

Ipsambul: see ABU SIMBEL.

Iqbal, Muhammad [ĭkhbäl′], 1873–1938, Indian poet, philosopher, and political leader. Because he advocated an independent homeland for India's Muslims, he is regarded as the spiritual founder of PAKISTAN. In his poetry and essays he urged regeneration of Islam through love of God and active development of the self.

Ir, chemical symbol of the element IRIDIUM.

IRA: 1 in economics, see INDIVIDUAL RETIREMENT ACCOUNT. **2** in Irish history, see IRISH REPUBLICAN ARMY.

Iran, officially Islamic Republic of Iran, known as Persia until 1935, republic (1992 est. pop. 61,183,000), 636,290 sq mi (1,648,000 sq km), SW Asia, bordered by Armenia, Azerbaijan, the Caspian Sea, and Turkmenistan (N), Afghanistan and Pakistan (E), the Persian Gulf and Gulf of Oman (S), and Turkey and Iraq (W). TEHERAN is the capital. Iran lies on a high plateau (alt. c.4,000 ft/1,200 m) surrounded by the Elburz and ZAGROS mountain ranges; there are great salt deserts in the interior. The climate is continental, with hot summers and cold winters. Iran is subject to numerous and often severe earthquakes. The country is one of the world's leading oil producers, and revenues from petroleum contribute 90% of the nation's wealth. Although only about 10% of the land is arable, agriculture supports about a third of the population. Wheat is the most important crop, and fruit, nuts, and hides are among the major exports. Textiles are Iran's second most important industrial product, and traditional handicrafts (such as carpet weaving) still play a role in the economy. Iran's culturally diverse population, with Persian, Turkic (including Azerbaijani), Kurdish, Tatar, and Arab strains, is mainly urban. Islam is the official religion; about 98% of Iranians are Shiite Muslims, although most of the Kurds and Arabs are Sunnites. Farsi (Persian) is the official language; a number of other tongues, including Azeri, Kurdish, Arabic, English, and French are also spoken.

History. Village life began on the Iranian plateau as early as c.4000 B.C. The Persian empire, founded (c.550 B.C.) by CYRUS THE GREAT, was succeeded, after Greek and Parthian occupation, by the SASSANID dynasty in A.D. 226 (see PERSIA). Iran's history may be said to have begun in 641, when the Arabs overthrew the Sassanids, introduced Islam, and incorporated Persia into the CALIPHATE. Persia was later invaded by the Turks (10th cent.), JENGHIZ KHAN (13th cent.), and TIMUR (14th cent.). The Safavid dynasty (1502–1736), which reached its height under ABBAS I, restored internal order and established the Shiite form of Islam as the state religion. Persia then entered into a long period of decline during which it steadily lost territory and fell under the domination of the European powers. The discovery of oil in the early 1900s intensified European interest, and the Anglo-Russian Entente of 1907 divided Persia into British and Russian spheres of influence until after World War I. In 1921 Reza Khan, an army officer, overthrew the decadent Kajar dynasty, and, as REZA SHAH PAHLEVI, established the Pahlevi dynasty in 1925; in 1941 he abdicated in favor of his son MUHAMMAD REZA SHAH PAHLEVI. In the 1950s the power of the shah was challenged by Premier Muhammad MUSSADEGH, a militant nationalist who nationalized the oil industry and forced the shah to flee the country. However, with strong Western backing, monarchist elements ousted Mussadegh in 1953. In the 1960s the shah initiated a modernization program that was designed to improve economic and social conditions, but which brought social and political unrest. The regime, supported by the U.S., became increasingly repressive, and in 1979 popular opposition forced the shah to leave. Ayatollah Ruhollah KHOMEINI, an Shiite leader exiled since 1964, returned and established an Islamic republic. Hundreds of the shah's supporters were tried and executed, others fled the country, and the westernization of Iran was reversed. On Nov. 4, 1979, Iranian militants seized the U.S. embassy in Teheran, held the occupants hostage, and demanded the return of the shah from the U.S. After the shah's death (1980) in Egypt, an agreement was negotiated that freed the hostages on Jan. 20, 1981. Meanwhile, a full-scale border war with Iraq erupted in Sept. 1980 (see IRAN-IRAQ WAR), severely reducing Iran's oil production and disrupting its economy. The government was also beset by internal violence and unrest among ethnic minorities. The war ended with a cease-fire in 1988. In 1989, Khomeini died and was replaced as supreme religious leader by Iran's Pres. Ali Khamenei; Akbar Hashemi RAFSANJANI became president. Rafsanjani has diminished the influence of fundamentalist and revolutionary factions and placed greater emphasis on economic development but has also embarked a military buildup.

Iran-contra affair, in U.S. history, secret government arrangement to provide funds to the Nicaraguan contra rebels from profits gained by selling arms to Iran. Aid to the contras had been prohibited by Congress, and discovery of the arrangement in 1986 shook the administration of Ronald REAGAN. Most directly involved were Adm. John Poindexter and Marine Lt. Col. Oliver North, both of the NATIONAL SECURITY COUNCIL (NSC). It was unclear to what degree higher officials, particularly Reagan and Vice Pres. BUSH, were involved. North said he believed Reagan was largely aware of the secret arrangement, and the independent prosecutor's report (1994) said that Reagan and Bush had some knowledge of the affair or its coverup but no evidence could be found to link them to any crime. A presidential commission was critical of the NSC,

while congressional hearings uncovered a web of official deception, mismanagement, and illegality. A number of criminal convictions resulted, including those of North and Poindexter, but North's and Poindexter's were vacated on appeal for technical reasons. Former State Dept. and CIA officials pleaded guilty in 1991 to withholding information about the contra aid from Congress, and Caspar Weinberger, the former defense secretary, was charged (1992) with the same offense. In 1992 Pres. Bush pardoned Weinberger and other government officials who had been indicted or convicted for withholding information on or obstructing investigation of the affair.

Iran-Iraq War, Persian Gulf War, or **Gulf War,** 1980–88. In 1975, a militarily weaker Iraq signed over to Iran partial control of the SHATT AL-ARAB waterway. With the fall (1979) of MUHAMMAD REZA SHAH PAHLEVI (1979), Iran's military crumbled. Iraq seized (Sept. 1980) 90 sq mi (230 sq km) of Iranian territory in the Shatt al-Arab but failed to win the swift victory predicted by many; a bloody war of attrition set in. Iraq's use (1984) of chemical weapons (see CHEMICAL WARFARE) drew worldwide outrage. The scope of the conflict increased, and the ships of neutral nations in the Persian Gulf were attacked by both sides. By 1987 U.S. forces in the gulf began flying limited sorties against Iranian oil rigs and naval vessels. Iran and Iraq finally accepted a UN peace plan, and fighting between the two nations ceased in Aug. 1988. Estimates of the number of dead range up to 1.5 million. In 1990 Iraq, concerned with securing its forcible annexation of Kuwait (see PERSIAN GULF WAR), agreed to accept the 1975 treaty, withdraw its troops from Iranian territory, and exchange all prisoners of war. A treaty was not signed, however, and both sides still hold thousands of POWs, despite several prisoner exchanges since 1988.

Iranian languages, group of languages belonging to the Indo-Iranian subfamily of the INDO-EUROPEAN family of languages. See LANGUAGE (table).

Iraq, officially Republic of Iraq, republic (1992 est. pop. 18,446,000), 167,924 sq mi (434,924 sq km), SW Asia, bordered by the Persian Gulf, Kuwait, and Saudi Arabia (S), Jordan and Syria (W), Turkey (N), and Iran (E). Principal cities include BAGHDAD (the capital), BASRA, and MOSUL. Iraq is an almost landlocked country, its only outlet to the sea a short stretch of coast on the PERSIAN GULF. It is composed of a mountainous region in the northeast and the vast Syrian Desert, inhabited by a few nomadic shepherds, in the southwest; in-between is the heart of the country, a fertile lowland region watered by the TIGRIS and EUPHRATES rivers. Although about one third of the labor force is engaged in agriculture, oil production, notably in the great fields of Mosul and Kirkuk, dominates the economy, producing nearly 95% of its income. Iraq is among the largest oil producers of the Mideast. Its petroleum resources were nationalized in 1972, and oil revenues have been used to promote industrialization and to transform Iraq into a military power. The country has a small, diversified industrial sector, with textiles, shoes, processed food, and building materials among its products. Iraq is the world's leading exporter of dates; other crops include cotton, cereals, and vegetables. Agriculture depends largely on irrigation. Most of the population are Muslim Arabs, divided religiously into the Sunnis of central Iraq and Shiites of the south. The Kurds, who inhabit the north (see KURDISTAN), are the principal minority. Arabic is the official language in most of the country; Kurdish is official in northern sections; Assyrian and Armenian are spoken by some.

History. Modern Iraq is approximately coextensive with ancient

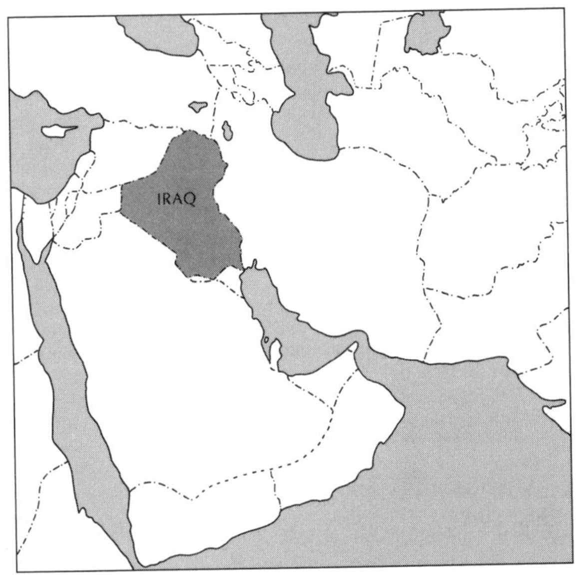

MESOPOTAMIA, and prior to the Arab conquest in the 7th cent. A.D. was the site of a number of flourishing civilizations, including SUMER, AKKAD, ASSYRIA, and BABYLONIA. In the 8th cent., as capital of the ABBASID caliphate, Baghdad became an important center of learning and the arts. Mesopotamia fell to the Ottoman Turks in the 16th cent. The British invaded Iraq in World War I, and in 1920 the country became a LEAGUE OF NATIONS mandate under British administration. Iraq was made a kingdom under FAISAL I in 1921, and the British mandate was terminated in 1932, although British military bases remained. Meanwhile, the first oil concession had been granted in 1925, and in 1934 the export of oil began. Domestic politics were marked by turbulence, and the country experienced seven military coups between 1936 and 1941. Following an army coup in 1958, Iraq became a republic under Gen. Abdul Karim Kassem. The chronic Kurdish problem flared up in 1962, when tribes demanding an autonomous KURDISTAN gained control of much of N Iraq. The rebellion collapsed (1975), but intermittent warfare has continued. In 1968 a coup brought the Ba'ath party to power, and in 1979 Saddam HUSSEIN became party leader and Iraq's president. Iraq launched (1980) a costly war against Iran that ended (1988) in a stalemate (see IRAN-IRAQ WAR). In 1990 Iraq invaded Kuwait, which it had previously claimed, provoking the PERSIAN GULF WAR; the war ended (1991) with Iraq ousted from Kuwait. Following the war, Iraqi Shiites and Kurds revolted. The uprisings were crushed, but both groups were provided (1992) with limited UN protection, which proved ineffective in the case of the Shiites.

Ireland, Irish *Eire,* second largest island (32,598 sq mi/84,429 sq km) of the British Isles. It lies W of the island of GREAT BRITAIN, from which it is separated by the North Channel, the Irish Sea, and St. George's Channel. It is divided politically into Northern Ireland and the Republic of Ireland; physically, it is composed of a large, fertile central plain roughly enclosed by a highland rim. Heavy rains (over 80 in./203 cm annually in some areas) account for the brilliantly green grass that makes Ireland the "emerald isle." The interior is dotted with lakes and wide stretches of river called loughs. The longest river is the Shannon.

History. Celtic tribes in ancient Ireland established a distinctive culture (see CELT) that, in its full flower after the introduction (5th cent. A.D.) of Christianity by St. PATRICK, produced superb works of art and literature. Beginning in the 8th cent., Norsemen (see VIKINGS) invaded the area, remaining until the Irish king BRIAN BORU broke their strength in 1014; Ireland then remained free from foreign interference for 150 years. But in the 12th cent. Pope Adrian granted overlordship of Ireland to HENRY II of England, initiating an Anglo-Irish struggle that lasted for nearly 800 years. The bitter religious contention between Irish Catholics and Protestants began in the 16th cent. after England tried to impose Protestantism on a largely Catholic Ireland. Irish rebellions flared up repeatedly—under HENRY VIII, ELIZABETH I, and Oliver CROMWELL. The Act of Union (1800) united England and Ireland; the Irish parliament was abolished, and Ireland was represented in the British parliament. Agitation by the Irish leader Daniel O'CONNELL resulted in passage of the CATHOLIC EMANCIPATION Act in 1829. But political developments were dwarfed by the Great Potato Famine (1845–49), in which nearly a million Irish died of starvation and disease; another 1,600,000 emigrated (1847–54) to the U.S. Irish desire for domestic control persisted. The failure of the British government to implement HOME RULE, complicated by the fear in largely Protestant Ulster of Catholic domination, led to the Easter Rebellion of 1916. The militant SINN FÉIN, founded (1905) among Irish Catholics, emerged as the dominant nationalist group, declaring themselves the Dáil Éireann (Irish Assembly) and proclaiming an Irish republic (1918). Outlawed by the British, the Sinn Féin went underground and waged guerrilla warfare. In 1920 a new Home Rule bill provided for partition of Ireland, with six counties of Ulster remaining part of the United Kingdom as Northern Ireland (see IRELAND, NORTHERN). In 1922 a treaty gave the remainder of Ireland dominion status within the British Empire as the Irish Free State (see IRELAND, REPUBLIC OF).

Ireland, Northern, political division of the United Kingdom of Great Britain and Northern Ireland (1991 pop. 1,577,836), 5,642 sq mi (14,147 sq km), comprising six counties of Ulster in NE Ireland. The capital is BELFAST, one of Britain's chief ports. Farming is the principal occupation. Shipbuilding, food processing, and the manufacture of textiles are the leading industries; Northern Ireland's fine linens are famous. The majority of the population is Protestant, but about 40% is Catholic. English is the official language.

History. Northern Ireland's relatively distinct history began in the 17th cent. when the British crown, after suppressing an Irish rebellion, populated much of Ulster with Scottish and English settlers, giving the area a Protestant character in contrast to the rest of Ireland. The question of political separation did not arise, however, until proposals for HOME RULE for Ireland, first broached in 1886 by British prime minister William GLADSTONE, aroused fears in largely Protestant Ulster of domination by the Catholic majority in the south. The situation continued to deteriorate, and by World War I civil war was imminent. The Government of Ireland Act (1920) attempted to solve the problem by enacting Home Rule separately for the two parts of Ireland. Ulster thus became the province of Northern Ireland, but the Irish Free State (now the Republic of Ireland), established in the remainder of Ireland in 1922, refused to recognize the finality of the partition. The situation remained relatively stable until the late 1960s, when protest by the Catholic minority against economic and political discrimination led to widespread violence by the "provisional" wing of the IRISH REPUBLICAN ARMY (IRA) on one side and the Ulster Defense Asso-

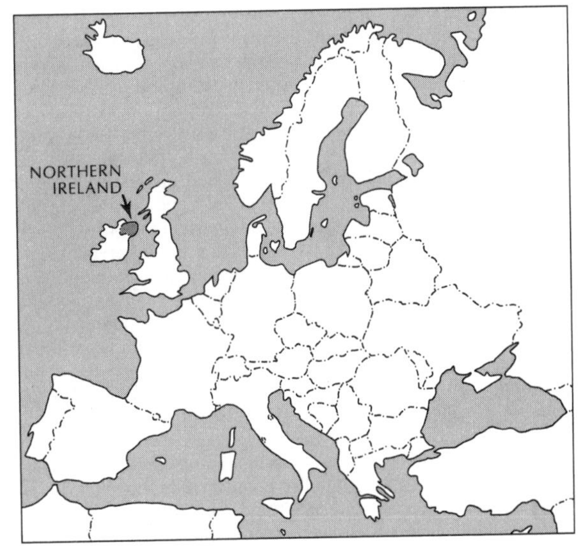

ciation, a Protestant terrorist group, on the other. In reply, the British government sent in British troops in 1969 and suspended the Ulster parliament in 1972 and assumed direct rule of the province (except for a period in 1973–74). Protestant and Catholic extremists rejected several efforts at power-sharing, and sectarian conflict marked by bloodshed continued. In 1982 an elective assembly was established with the aim of eventually ending direct rule, but a boycott sparked by the Anglo-Irish Agreement (1985), which granted the Irish republic a consultative role in certain Northern Irish affairs, led to its dissolution (1986). A 1993 Anglo-Irish declaration offered to open negotiations to all parties that renounce violence. See IRELAND; IRELAND, REPUBLIC OF.

Ireland, Republic of, independent republic (1992 est. pop. 3,521,000), 27,136 sq mi (70,282 sq km), occupying all but the northeastern corner of the island of Ireland in the British Isles; formerly the Irish Free State (1922–37) and Eire (1937–49). DUBLIN is the capital. Agriculture, primarily stock and poultry raising, engages 70% of the land and less than 15% of the people; crops include flax, oats, wheat, turnips, potatoes, sugar beets, and barley. Tourism is the second largest source of income. Industry produces linen and laces (for which Ireland is famous), food products, beer and ale, and textiles, particularly woolens. Gaelic and English are the official languages, but English is more widely spoken. About 95% of the population is Roman Catholic, but there is no established church.

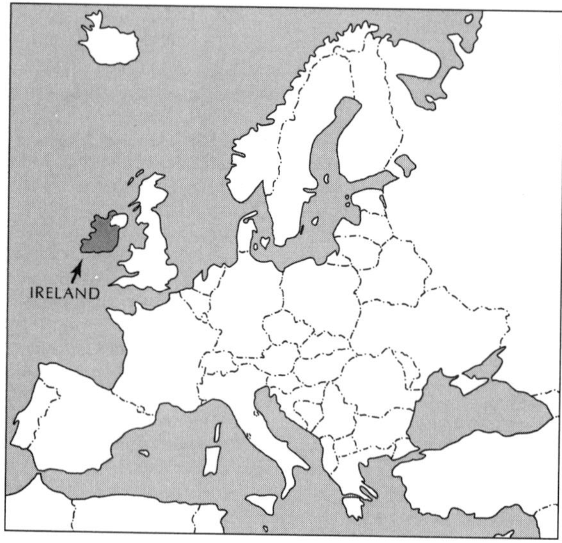

History. The establishment by treaty with GREAT BRITAIN of the Irish Free State in 1922 completed the partition of Ireland into two states (Northern Ireland was created in 1920) and resulted in civil war between supporters of the treaty and opponents. The anti-treaty forces, embodied in the IRISH REPUBLICAN ARMY (IRA) and led by Eamon DE VALERA, were defeated, but the IRA continued as a secret terrorist organization. De Valera and his Fianna Fáil party finally entered the Dáil (parliament) in 1927, and de Valera became prime minister in 1932. Under his administration a new constitution was promulgated (1937), establishing the sovereign state of Ireland, or Eire, within the British Commonwealth. In World War II Eire, remaining neutral, denied the use of Irish ports to the British, although many Irish served voluntarily in the British armed forces. In 1948 Ireland demanded total independence from Great Britain; the Republic of Ireland was proclaimed in 1949 and the country withdrew from the Commonwealth. In the late 1960s problems flared up with Northern Ireland, aggravated by the terrorist activities in Northern Ireland of the IRA, which was headquartered in the republic. In 1973 the country joined the European Community (see EUROPEAN UNION). The Fianna Fáil dominated the country's politics until a Fine Gael coalition came to power in 1973; the two parties have tended since to alternate in power. Since 1993 a Fianna Fáil–Labor coalition government led by Prime Min. Albert REYNOLDS has been in office. In 1985 the republic began participating in Northern Irish affairs relating to legal, political, and security matters through an intergovernmental committee set up under a British-Irish agreement. See also IRELAND; IRELAND, NORTHERN.

Irene, c.750–803, Byzantine empress (797–802). As regent for her son, CONSTANTINE VI, she neglected wars in her zeal to suppress ICONOCLASM. Her son's misconduct enabled her to depose him (797), have him blinded, and ascend the throne. Her accession gave CHARLEMAGNE a pretext for having himself crowned emperor (800). Irene was deposed (802) and died in exile.

iridium (Ir), metallic element, discovered by Smithson Tennant in 1804. Chemically very unreactive, iridium is a very hard, usually brittle, extremely corrosion-resistant, silver-white metal used in chemical crucibles, surgical tools, and pivot bearings. The international kilogram standard is an iridium-platinum alloy. See ELEMENT (table); PERIODIC TABLE.

iris, common name for members of the genus *Iris* of the Iridaceae, a family of perennial herbs that includes the CROCUS, freesia (genus *Freesia*), and gladiolus (genus *Gladiolus*). The family is typified by modified stems (BULBS, corms, and RHIZOMES) and by linear or sword-shaped leaves. Distributed worldwide except in the coldest regions, the family is closely related to the LILY and AMARYLLIS families. The cultivated irises, freesias, and gladioli show a wide variety of colors in their usually perfumed blossoms. The many species of wild iris are often called flags. Orrisroot, a violet-scented flavoring used in dentrifices, perfumes, and other products, is made from the powdered rhizomes of several European species.

Irish Land Question, name given in the 19th cent. to the problem of Irish land ownership, which went back many centuries. In the 12th cent. a feudal landholding system was imposed on Ireland. The TUDORS, CROMWELL, and WILLIAM III continued land confiscations; the result was the creation of an absentee landlord class and an impoverished Irish peasantry. The 18th-cent. penal laws increased the difficulty of landowning by Catholics; Catholic Emancipation did not help much, although it did bring Irish Catholics into the British Parliament. Irish hatred for England grew through the great famine of the 1840s and the influx of speculators after the Encumbered Estates Act of 1849. The violent FENIAN MOVEMENT, the Reform Act of 1867, and support by GLADSTONE led to the First Land Act (1870). The National Land League, led by Michael Davitt and C.S. PARNELL, fought for passage of the Land Act of 1881, which gave the three "F's"—fair rent, fixity of tenure, and freedom from sale. Land purchase by the tenant became the main issue. Agitation by the Irish Union League led to passage of the Wyndham Act (1903), which provided loans at reduced rates for tenants who wanted to buy land, and bonuses for landlords willing to sell. By 1921 Irish tenants owned two thirds of the land, the rest was confiscated by law and given to them.

Irish language, also called Irish Gaelic, member of the Goidelic group of the Celtic subfamily of the Indo-European family of languages. See LANGUAGE (table).

Irish Republican Army (IRA), nationalist organization dedicated to the unification of Ireland. It was organized by Michael COLLINS after the Easter Rebellion of 1916 (see IRELAND) and became the military wing of the SINN FÉIN party. Despite the establishment of the Irish Free State (1922), the IRA refused to accept a separate Northern Ireland under British rule. With popular support lessened by its violent actions and pro-German agitation during WORLD WAR II, it was outlawed by both Irish governments and became a secret organization. In 1969 it split into an "official" majority, which disclaimed violence, and a terrorist "provisional" wing, whose attacks on British troops in Northern Ireland, random bombings, and other acts of terror in England and elsewhere have become, along with attacks by Protestant extremists, an unabated cycle of Northern Irish violence.

Irish setter, large SPORTING DOG; shoulder height, c.26 in. (66 cm); weight, 50–70 lb (22.7–31.8 kg). The long, silky coat of the American variety is solid red; that of its Irish counterpart is often red and white. It was developed in 18th-cent. Ireland as a field hunter.

Iron, Ralph: see SCHREINER, OLIVE.

iron (Fe), metallic element. Iron is a lustrous, ductile, malleable, silver-gray metal. A good conductor of heat and electricity, it is attracted by a magnet and is itself easily magnetized (see MAGNETISM). Iron is abundant in the universe; it is found in many stars, including the sun. It is the fourth most common element in the earth's crust, of which it constitutes about 5% by weight, and is believed to be the main component of the earth's core. Iron is rarely found uncombined in nature except in METEORITES, and it rusts readily in moist air. LIMONITE and hematite are the chief iron ores; other ores include MAGNETITE, taconite, and siderite. Iron ores are refined in a BLAST FURNACE to produce pig iron, which can be remelted and poured into molds to make CAST IRON, commercially purified to make WROUGHT IRON, or alloyed with carbon and other elements to make STEEL. Iron compounds are used as paint pigments, in dyeing, and in ink manufacture. A component of HEMOGLOBIN, the oxygen-carrying pigment of red BLOOD cells in vertebrates, iron is important in nutrition; one cause of ANEMIA is iron deficiency. See ELEMENT (table); IRON AGE; PERIODIC TABLE.

Iron Age, technological period from the first general use of iron to modern times. In Asia, Egypt, and Europe it followed the BRONZE AGE; Europeans brought it to the Americas. Hammered iron was known in Egypt before 1350 B.C., and after the fall of the HITTITE empire (1200 B.C.), migrants carried iron technology to S Europe and the Middle East. Smelting was known in the ETRUSCAN CIVILIZATION. After the Early Iron Age (c.800–500) in central Europe, migrating CELTS spread the use of iron into W Europe and the British Isles, where Late Iron Age peoples used it for tools, vehicles, coinage, and art objects (see LA TÈNE). Metal technology increasingly influenced culture up to the INDUSTRIAL REVOLUTION and beyond.

Iron Guard, Romanian nationalistic, anti-Semitic terrorist organization founded in 1924. Although officially banned in 1933, it continued under different names. It helped Ion ANTONESCU to take power in 1940, preparing the way for the Nazi takeover of the country in WORLD WAR II.

Iroquoian, branch of Native American languages, belonging to the Hokan-Siouan linguistic family of North America. See NATIVE AMERICAN LANGUAGES (table).

Iroquois Confederacy or **Iroquois League,** confederation of five indigenous North American peoples, or nations, Mohawk, Oneida, Onondaga, Cayuga, and Seneca; founded c.1570. After the Tuscarora joined, c.1722, it became known collectively as the Six Nations. The Iroquois speak Iroquoian languages of the Hokan-Siouan stock (see NATIVE AMERICAN LANGUAGES. In the early 17th cent. the Iroquois inhabited New York N and W of the Hudson R., numbering c.5,500. Materially, politically, and militarily their culture was the most advanced in the Eastern Woodlands. The Iroquois conceived of themselves as living in a metaphorical long house in which each nation had a role, e.g., the Mohawks guarded the eastern door. By absorbing neighboring tribes in territorial wars, the League came to number 16,000 by the late 17th cent. Led by CORNPLANTER, Red Jacket, and Joseph BRANT, all but the Oneida and Tuscarora sided with the British in the AMERICAN REVOLUTION. Today the Iroquois live mostly in Ontario and in New York, where in the 1970s and early 80s they occupied disputed lands. Some, however, have become urban—many Mohawks, for instance, have worked as structural steelworkers. The Oneida opened a gambling casino near Syracuse, N.Y., in 1993. There were 49,038 Iroquois in the U.S. in 1990.

irrational number: see NUMBER.

Irrawaddy, one of the great rivers of Asia and the chief river of Myanmar, c.1,000 mi (1,600 km) long, formed by the confluence in N Myanmar of the Mali and Nmai rivers. It flows south, receiving the Chindwin R. just below Mandalay, to form a vast delta (c.200 mi/320 km wide) beginning at Henzada, c.180 mi (290 km) from the Andaman Sea. The river is navigable up to Myitkyina and serves as Myanmar's economic lifeline.

irredentism, originally, the nationalist movement for annexation to Italy of predominantly Italian areas—*Italia irredenta* [unredeemed Italy]—retained by Austria after 1866. It was a strong motive for Italy's entry into WORLD WAR I. The term is also applied to similar movements in other nations.

irrigation, in AGRICULTURE, artificial watering of the land, using water diverted from rivers and lakes or pumped from underground (see DAM). Modern large-scale irrigation is often part of a multipurpose project that may also produce hydroelectric power and provide systems for water supply and flood control. Surface irrigation delivers water to a field directly from a canal, well, or ditch. In surface-pipe irrigation, the water is piped to the field and distributed via sprinklers or smaller pipes. Drip irrigation delivers a small, measured amount of water to each plant through narrow plastic tubes and helps prevent the two major problems caused by irrigation: waterlogging, saturation of the soil as a result of inadequate drainage; and soil salinization, the accumulation of salts deposited by irrigation water. In addition, extensive irrigation (137 billion gallons a day in the U.S.) has contributed to concerns about water supply, water rights of those downstream, and aquatic habitats of endangered species.

Irtysh, river, c.2,650 mi (4,260 km) long, NE Kazakhstan and central Russia, chief tributary of the OB R. It rises as the Kara-Irtysh in NW China and flows through Kazakhstan and past Semey (Semipalatinsk) into W Siberia, past Omsk and Tobolsk to join the Ob near Khanty-Mansiysk.

Irvine, city (1990 pop. 110,330), Orange co., SW Calif.; inc. 1971. One of the fastest-growing U.S. cities, it has important electronics research and development facilities and service and retailing industries. Irvine is also the site of a Univ. of California campus.

Irving, Sir Henry, 1838–1905, English actor and manager; b. John Henry Brodribb. As the innovative manager (1878–1903) of the Lyceum Theatre, London, he reigned supreme on the English stage, appearing with his leading lady, Ellen TERRY, in Shakespearean and contemporary productions. He was the first English actor to be knighted (1895).

Irving, John, 1942–, American novelist; b. Exeter, N.H. The combination of sex, violence, social satire, and grotesque comedy in his novels gives him an affinity with the black humorists. *The World According to Garp* (1978) made him an overnight success. Other novels include *The Hotel New Hampshire* (1981), *The Cider House Rules* (1985), and *A Prayer for Owen Meany* (1989).

Irving, Washington, 1783–1859, American author; b. N.Y.C. His earliest works, *Letters of Jonathan Oldstyle, Gent.* (1802–3) and *Salmagundi* (1807–8; written with William Irving and J.K. Pauling), were collections of amusing essays. Under the pseudonym Diedrich Knickerbocker he wrote *A History of New York* (1809), perhaps America's first great book of comic literature. Irving's reputation at home and abroad was established with the essays in *The Sketch Book of Geoffrey Crayon, Gent.* (1820), including such tales as "Rip Van Winkle" and "The Legend of Sleepy Hollow." While a diplomat in Madrid (1826–29), he wrote several works on Spanish subjects, among them the charming sketches in *The Alhambra* (1832). After returning to the U.S. he wrote a number of books on the American West, e.g., *A Tour of the Prairies* (1835). Except for a term as U.S. minister to Spain (1842–46), Irving spent most of his later years at his estate, Sunnyside, near Tarrytown, N.Y. There he completed several works, including his biography of George Washington (5 vol., 1855–59). A gentle satirist who was master of a graceful, sophisticated style, Irving created some of the most popular essays and tales in American literature.

Irving, city (1990 pop. 155,037), N Tex., a suburb of DALLAS; inc. as a city 1952. Building supplies, chemicals, electronic equipment, and aircraft parts are manufactured there. Its Texas Stadium is home to the Dallas Cowboys professional football team. The Dallas–Fort Worth Airport (opened 1974) borders Irving on the west. The Univ. of Dallas is in the city.

Isaac, Byzantine emperors. **Isaac I,** c.1005–1061 (r.1057–59), first of the COMNENUS dynasty, was proclaimed emperor by the army. He abdicated after losing popularity and failing in war. **Isaac II** (Angelus), d. 1204 (r.1185–95, 1203–4), was made emperor by the people. He repulsed the Normans but failed to suppress a Bulgar rebellion. He was deposed and blinded by his brother, ALEXIUS III, but the army of the Fourth CRUSADE restored him as co-ruler with his son, ALEXIUS IV. After their overthrow by ALEXIUS V, the Crusaders sacked Constantinople.

Isaac, in the BIBLE, a patriarch, only son of ABRAHAM and SARA. He married REBECCA, and their sons were ESAU and JACOB. ISHMAEL was his half-brother. As a supreme act of faith, Abraham offered Isaac at an early age as a sacrifice to God—a deed prevented by divine intervention. Some scholars have questioned Isaac's historicity.

Isabella, Spanish queens. **Isabella I** (the Catholic), 1451–1504, queen of Castile and León (1474–1504) and queen of Aragón (1479–1504), with her husband, FERDINAND V, established the unified Spanish kingdom. She suppressed the lawless Castilian nobles by reviving the medieval HERMANDAD, administered the holdings of powerful religious military orders, and placed the INQUISITION under royal control. Isabella was a prime mover (1492) in the expulsion of the JEWS, the conquest of GRANADA from the MOORS, and discovery of the New World by COLUMBUS. Together she and Ferdinand advanced learning and the arts, especially architecture. The accession of **Isabella II,** 1830–1904, queen of Spain (1833–68), caused the CARLIST wars. Her marriage (1846) to Francisco de Asis, which contravened Anglo-French agreements regarding the choice of husbands for certain Spanish princesses, contributed to a rift between England and France. Frequent conflicts between moderates and liberals led to her deposition (1868). In 1870 she abdicated her rights in favor of her son, ALFONSO XII.

Isabella, 1296–1358, queen consort of EDWARD II of England; daughter of PHILIP IV of France. Neglected and mistreated by her husband, she hated the royal favorites, the Despensers, who had seized her lands. While in France (1325), she formed a liaison with Roger de MORTIMER. They invaded England in 1326, forced Edward to abdicate, and caused his murder. They ruled corruptly until EDWARD III seized power in 1330.

Isabella Stewart Gardner Museum: see GARDNER, ISABELLA STEWART.

Isaiah [īzā'yə, īsā'] or **Isaias** [īsā'yəs], book of the OLD TESTAMENT, 23d in the Authorized Version, first and longest of the Major Prophets, a collection of prophecies attributed to Isaiah, apparently a nobleman in the kingdom of Judah (c.740 B.C.). The book falls into two sections of metrical prophecies (1–35; 40–66) divided by a prose section. The first set of poems deals with prophecies against the Assyrians and other nations; those affecting ISRAEL and JUDAH announce destruction and subsequent redemption. The second poetic section is a prophecy of redemption of the kingdom of Israel, delivered from captivity and from sin. The book contains many of the most beautiful passages in the Bible (among them prophecies thought by Christians to refer to Jesus) and may be the result of diverse authorship.

Iscariot: see JUDAS ISCARIOT.

Ise [ē'sä], city (1990 pop. 104,162), Mie prefecture, S Honshu, Japan. One of the foremost religious centers of SHINTO, it is the site of the shrines of Ise. Said to have been built in 4 B.C., the three shrines, set deep in a forest, exhibit an archaic style of architecture without Chinese or Buddhist influence. One houses the Sacred Mirror of the imperial regalia.

Iseult: see TRISTRAM AND ISOLDE.

Isfahan: see ESFAHAN.

Isherwood, Christopher, 1904–86, English author. His experiences in Germany gave him material for *The Last of Mr. Norris* (1935) and *Goodbye to Berlin* (1939; reissued as *The Berlin Stories,* 1946). These form the basis of John Van Druten's play *I Am a Camera* (1951) and the musical *Cabaret* (1966). He collaborated with AUDEN on three plays and on *Journey to a War* (1939). He moved to the U.S. in 1939. His later writings include *Essentials of Vedanta* (1969) and *My Guru and His Disciple* (1980).

Ishmael [ĭsh'māĕl], in the BIBLE, son of ABRAHAM and Hagar, half brother to ISAAC, and ancestor of 12 tribes in N Arabia. Through SARA's jealousy, he and his mother, who was Sara's handmaid, were sent into the desert. Hence the name Ishmael came to mean "outcast." According to tradition, the Arabs are the descendants of Ishmael.

Ishtar, ancient fertility deity, the most widely worshiped goddess in Babylonian and Assyrian religion. Ishtar was important as a mother goddess, goddess of love, and goddess of war. Her cult spread throughout W Asia, and she became identified with various other earth goddesses (see GREAT MOTHER OF THE GODS).

Isis, nature goddess whose worship, originating in ancient Egypt, gradually extended throughout the lands of the Mediterranean world and became one of the chief religions of the Roman Empire. The worship of Isis, together with that of her brother and husband, OSIRIS, and their son, HORUS, resisted the rise of Christianity and lasted until the 6th cent. A.D.

Islam [Arab., = submission to, or having peace with, God], the religion of which MUHAMMAD was the prophet. An adherent of Islam is a Muslim [Arab., = one who submits]. The youngest of the three great monotheistic world religions (the others being JUDAISM and CHRISTIANITY), Islam is the dominant religion throughout large portions of Asia and Africa, especially North Africa, the Middle East, Central Asia, Pakistan, Bangladesh, Malaysia, and Indonesia (the world's largest Muslim country). In 1990 there were some 935 million Muslims worldwide, less than one fifth of whom were Arab; there are an estimated 6 million Muslims in the U.S. Its salient feature is its devotion to the Koran, or Qur'an, a book believed to be the revelation of God to Muhammad. Since the Koran is in Arabic, this language is used in Islam all over the world; hence the custom of referring to God as Allah, His name in Arabic. The ethos of Islam is its attitude toward God: to Him Muslims submit; Him they praise and glorify; and in Him alone they hope. He is awesome, transcendent, almighty, just, loving, merciful, and good. No creature may be compared to Him, and to Him alone do Muslims pray. Muhammad is the last and greatest of God's prophets, who also include ADAM, NOAH, ABRAHAM, MOSES, and JESUS. According to the Muslim eschatology, there will be a judgment at the end of the world; heaven awaits the believers and hell the nonbelievers. The ordinary pious Muslim does not distinguish faith from works; both are indispensable and mutually supplementary. There are five essential duties in Islam. (1) A Muslim must affirm that "There is no god but God, and Muhammad is the Messenger of God." (2) Five times daily he must pray facing MECCA: at dawn, at noon, in midafternoon, at dusk, and after dark. (3) A Muslim must give alms generously. (4) A Muslim must keep the fast of RAMADAN, which is the ninth month of the Muslim year. (5) Once in his life a Muslim must, if he can, make the pilgrimage (hajj) to Mecca. There are also a prohibition of alcohol and pork and injunctions against gambling, usury, fraud, slander, and the making of images. The Sunna, the way or example of the Prophet, supplements the Koran. It consists of the collected sayings and anecdotes of Muhammad. The Ijma, or the agreement of Islam, is expressed in Muhammad's saying "My community will never agree in an error" and is the principle that has enabled Islam to resolve apparent contradictions and maintain both a flexibility and its unity with the past. The Koran, the Sunna, and the Ijma are the three foundations of Islam. Islam does not recognize a priestly class, but religious and legal officers have acquired an authority similar to that of the clergy in Christian and Jewish communities. The fundamental division of Islam into SUNNI and SHIITES dates from disputes over the succession to the CALIPHATE in the first centuries of the Muslim era. The WAHHABIS are the only important modern separatist Sunni sect. The Shiites, by contrast, have fathered countless sects, including the Assassins, DRUZE, FATIMIDS, Ismailis, and Karmathians. However, there is a remarkable community of feeling in Islam even today, when Muslims are divided politically into many groups. Historically, Muslim thought shows three major tendencies: legalism, rationalism, and mysticism; philosophy has never been distinct from theology. The greatest period of Muslim thought and culture was the 9th to 11th cent. In recent years Islam has seen a resurgence of FUNDAMENTALISM among both Sunni and Shiites, most notably in Iran, Sudan, Algeria, Tunisia, and Eygpt.

Islamabad, city (1988 est. pop. 200,000), capital of Pakistan. Construction of Islamabad [city of Islam], which replaced KARACHI as the capital, began in 1960. Points of interest include the Grand National Mosque and the botanical gardens.

Islamic art and architecture. In the century after the death (A.D. 632) of the prophet MUHAMMAD, his Arab followers spread his teachings through Egypt and North Africa, as far west as Spain and as far east as Sassanid Persia. Because of their rapid expansion and the paucity of their artistic heritage, the Muslims derived their unique style from a synthesis of the arts of the Byzantines, the Copts, the Romans, and the Sassanids. The great interior surface of the Mosque of Damascus (715) was covered with stone MOSAICS in the Byzantine technique. No human figures were depicted, but there were crowns, fantastic plants, realistic trees, and empty towns. In A.D. 750 the ABBASID dynasty moved the capital to Baghdad, and immediately Persian influence became stronger. In the ruins of Samarra lusterware fragments have been found. The Great Mosque of Al Qayrawan (c.862) is decorated with square luster tile. The 9th cent. saw the development of metalwork in Egypt, and skilled craftsmanship can be seen in rock-crystal carving, a Sassanid art. From the 10th to 13th cent. great strides were made in the minor arts in Egypt. calligraphy, bookbinding, papermaking, and illumination were developed. The Kufic script was animated with floriated, interlaced, and anthropomorphic designs. Early in the 13th cent. a school of secular manuscript painting arose near Baghdad with pictures of two types: those that illustrate scientific works, descending from late Hellenistic models, and those that illustrate anecdotal tales and whose miniatures represent the true spirit of CARICATURE. After the Mongol invasions there was a revitalization of art through Chinese taste and artifacts. Textiles and CARPETS were again manufactured throughout Islam, and Turkish ceramics reached their peak in the "Iznik" ware of the 16th and 17th cent. Early Islamic architecture used the Syrian cut-stone technique of building, as in the Mosque of Damascus, and popularized the DOME (see MOSQUE). Sassanid building techniques such as the squinch were combined with the mosque form. In the 10th cent. the FATIMIDS introduced into Egypt the decorative stalactite ceiling and placed emphasis on decorative flat moldings. The cruciform Mosque of Hasan, in Cairo (1536), reflects Persian influence, while the square Char Minar of Hyderabad (1591), with its large ARCHES, arcades, and MINARETS, is characteristic of the Indian style of the Delhi Sultanate. The art of Islamic Spain used faïence and lacy, pierced-stone screen windows. Turkish architects were influenced by the Byzantine church of HAGIA SOPHIA. In general, all Islamic art and architecture is the result of synthesis rather than origination, with decoration of the surface the most important factor in every work. Interlaced lines and brilliant color characterize the style. See also MOGUL ART AND ARCHITECTURE.

island, relatively small (compared to a CONTINENT) body of land completely surrounded by water. The largest, in descending order, are GREENLAND, NEW GUINEA, BORNEO, MADAGASCAR, BAFFIN ISLAND, SUMATRA, HONSHU, and GREAT BRITAIN. Islands are either *continental,* caused by partial submergence of coastal highlands or by the sea breaking through an isthmus or peninsula, or *oceanic,* originating from the ascension of the ocean floor above water through volcanic activity or other earth movements. Tropical oceanic islands sustained above sea level by coral growth are called atolls (see CORAL REEFS).

Isle Royale National Park: see NATIONAL PARKS (table).

Ismail, 1486–1534, shah of PERSIA (1502–24), founder of the Safavid dynasty. He restored Persia to the position of a sovereign state and established SHIITE Islam as the state religion, thus incurring the wrath of the Sunnite Ottoman Turks and the Uzbeks.

Ismail Pasha, 1830–95, ruler of Egypt (1863–79), the first to bear the title khedive (viceroy); son of IBRAHIM PASHA. His grandiose schemes, including building the SUEZ CANAL, forced him to submit (1876) to joint Anglo-French management. He was deposed (1879) in favor of his son, Tewfik Pasha.

Isocrates [īsŏk'rətēz], 436–338 B.C., Greek orator, pupil of SOCRATES. A great teacher, he taught every young orator of his time. His most celebrated oration is *Panegyricus,* in which he urges Hellenic unity against Persia.

Isolde: see TRISTRAM AND ISOLDE.

isomer, in chemistry, one of two or more compounds having the same molecular formula (i.e., the same number of atoms of each element in a molecule) but different structures (arrangements of atoms in the molecule). Isomers have the same number of atoms of each element in them and the same atomic weight but differ in other properties. **Structural isomers,** e.g., ETHANOL (CH_3CH_2OH) and dimethyl ether (CH_3OCH_3), differ in the way the atoms are joined together in their molecules. **Stereoisomers** have the same basic arrangement of atoms in their molecules but differ in the way the atoms are arranged. Geometric isomers, which are stereoisomers that differ in the positioning of groups about a double bond or some other feature that gives the molecule a certain amount of structural rigidity, differ in physical properties such as melting and boiling points. Optical isomers, also called enantiomers or chiral molecules, are stereoisomers in which the two molecules are mirror images of each other and, each being asymmetrical, cannot be superposed on each other; optical isomers differ in the direction in which they rotate light passed through the molecules and can have different properties. Spearmint leaves and caraway seeds get their distinctive odors from different optical isomers of the compound carvone, and it has been theorized that one optical isomer of THALIDOMIDE produced sedation and the other caused birth defects.

```
     H   H               H           H
     |   |               |           |
 H — C — C — OH      H — C — O — C — H
     |   |               |           |
     H   H               H           H

      ethanol           dimethyl ether
```

Isomers

isotope, one of two or more atoms having the same ATOMIC NUMBER but differing in ATOMIC WEIGHT and MASS NUMBER. The nuclei of isotopes of the same element have the same number of PROTONS (equal to the element's atomic number) but have different numbers of NEUTRONS. The isotopes of a given element have identical chemical properties but slightly different physical properties. A radioactive isotope, or radioisotope, is a natural or artificially created isotope having an unstable nucleus that decays, emitting alpha, beta, or gamma rays (see RADIOACTIVITY) until stability is reached. For most elements, stable and radioactive isotopes are known.

Israel [as understood by Hebrews, = striven with God], in the Bible, name given JACOB. The Hebrews adopted the name as a national designation. Under REHOBOAM, in 931 B.C., the Israelite kingdom broke into a northern kingdom called Israel and a southern one called JUDAH.

Israel, officially State of Israel, republic (1992 est. pop. 4,748,000, including Israelis in occupied Arab territories), 7,992 sq mi/20,700 sq km (excluding occupied Arab territories), SW Asia, bounded by Lebanon (N), Syria and Jordan (E), the Mediterranean Sea and Egypt (W), and the Gulf of Aqaba (S). The capital is JERUSALEM; other major cities are TEL AVIV–JAFFA and HAIFA. There are four land regions: the Mediterranean coastal plain; a mountain area in the northeast; the semiarid NEGEV in the south; and, in the extreme east, a portion of the GREAT RIFT VALLEY, including the DEAD SEA, which at 1,292 ft (394 m) below sea level is the lowest point on earth. Despite adverse conditions, extensive irrigation has enabled agriculture to flourish. Fresh fruits and vegetables are the major export crops. A wide variety of industrial goods is produced, including textiles, chemicals, military and electronic equipment, and machinery; Israel is second only to Belgium in processing diamonds. The manufacture of high technology items (computers, software, and telecommunications equipment) and biotechnology have also become significant. Tourism is also important. The standard of living is high for a Middle Eastern nation, but a high trade deficit, heavy defense expenditures, and inflation rates of 50% to 100% in the 1980s have put the economy under a great strain. About 85% of the population are Jews, about half of whom are immigrants from Europe, North America, Asia, and North Africa. The non-Jewish population consists mainly of Muslim, and a smaller group of Christian, Arabs. The official languages are Hebrew and Arabic, but English and many European languages are widely spoken. Israel is highly urbanized. About 7% of the people live on COLLECTIVE FARMS known as *kibbutzim, moshav ovdim,* and *moshav shitufim.*

History. For the earlier history of the region, see PALESTINE. In November 1947 the United Nations divided Palestine, then under British mandate, into Jewish and Arab states. Six months later the British withdrew, and on May 14, 1948, the state of Israel was proclaimed. The neighboring Arab states of Lebanon, Syria, Jordan, Egypt, and Iraq rejected both the partition of Palestine and the existence of the new nation. In the war that followed (1948–49), Israel emerged victorious and with its territory increased by one half. Arab opposition continued, however, and full-scale fighting broke out again in 1956 (the Sinai campaign), 1967 (the Six-Day War), and 1973 (the Yom Kippur War). Israel emerged from these conflicts (see ARAB-ISRAELI WARS) with large tracts of its neighbors'

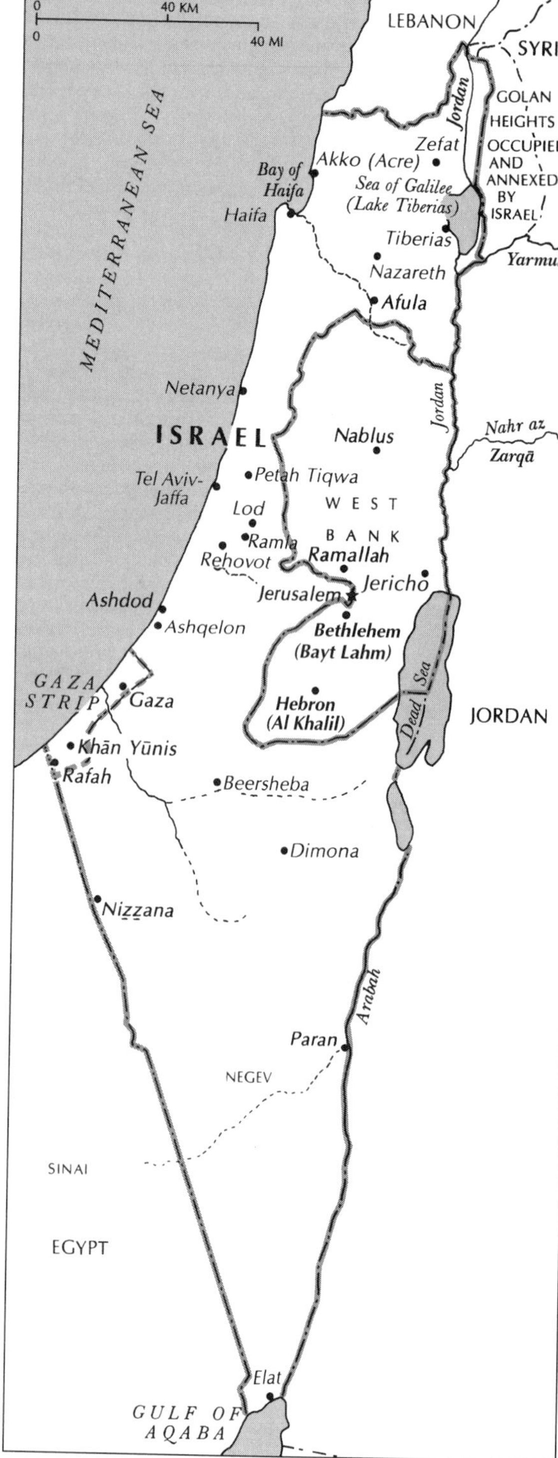

territories. In 1978 Israeli Prime Min. Menachem BEGIN and Egyptian Pres. Anwar al-SADAT signed the CAMP DAVID ACCORDS; a peace treaty between Egypt and Israel was signed (1979) in Washington, D.C., and Israel withdrew from the SINAI by 1982. Little progress was made, however, with respect to the GAZA STRIP and WEST BANK, and in 1981 Israel annexed the GOLAN HEIGHTS (captured from Syria in 1967). Israel's fierce, intermittent fighting with the PALESTINE LIBERATION ORGANIZATION (PLO) in LEBANON led to a devastating Israeli invasion in 1982. Israel withdrew in 1985 but maintained a 6–12 mi (10–20 km) security zone there just north of the border. Begin retired in 1983 and was succeeded by Yitzhak SHAMIR. Indecisive elections in 1984 and 1988 resulted in an awkward coalition government, led by Labor party leader Shimon PERES (1984–86) and Shamir (1986–90). In June 1990, after the coalition collapsed, Shamir formed a right-wing government. In the late 1980s and early 1990s there were increasingly violent clashes between Palestinians and Israeli troops in the occupied territories. Soviet Jews began emigrating to Israel in large numbers in 1990, strapping Israel's resources, and Iraq launched missiles at Israel during the PERSIAN GULF WAR. In 1992 the Labor party and its allies won the largest bloc of seats in parliament, and Yitzhak RABIN became prime minister. Israel began peace talks with Syria, Jordan, and the Palestinians in 1991 and signed (1993) an accord with the PLO that called for Palestinian self-rule in the Gaza Strip and Jericho.

Israel, Tribes of, in the BIBLE, the 12 tribes of Hebrews named for 10 sons of JACOB (Reuben, Simeon, Judah, Zebulun, Issachar, Dan, Gad, Asher, Naphtali, and Benjamin) and the two sons of Jacob's son JOSEPH (Ephraim and Manasseh). The 13th tribe, Levi (the third of Jacob's sons), was set apart and had no one portion of its own. After the break in the Hebrew kingdom under REHOBOAM, the tribes of Judah, Benjamin, and some Levites formed a southern kingdom called Judah; the other 10 tribes formed a northern kingdom called Israel. These 10 were later (721 B.C.) conquered and transported to Assyria. They became known as the 10 lost tribes; numerous conjectures have been advanced as to their fate, and they have been identified with various peoples.

Israëls, Jozef [ēs'räëls], 1824–1911, Dutch genre painter. He used dramatic, silver-gray light to express the melancholy character of his themes, e.g., *Toilers of the Sea* (Amsterdam) and *Expectation* (Metropolitan Mus.).

Issachar: see ISRAEL, TRIBES OF.

Isserles, Moses ben Israel, c.1525–1572, Polish rabbi, annotator, and philosopher, known as Remah. He is best known for his works on Jewish law (see HALAKAH), notably his additions to the code of Joseph CARO, which made the code acceptable to Ashkenazic Jews.

İstanbul, city (1990 pop. 6,748,435), capital of İstanbul prov., NW Turkey, on both sides of the Bosporus where it enters the Sea of Marmara. The city was known both as İstanbul (since 1453) and as Constantinople until 1930, when the one official name İstanbul was declared; before A.D. 330 its site was occupied by BYZANTIUM. Turkey's largest city and chief seaport, it produces textiles, glass, shoes, motor vehicles, and other manufactures. The part of İstanbul corresponding to historic Constantinople is built on seven hills rising on the south side of the Golden Horn, an inlet of the BOSPORUS. Points of interest include the HAGIA SOPHIA, once a church and mosque; the Seraglio, the palace of the Ottoman sultans; and many museums. In 1973 the Bosporus Bridge was the first to unite the city's European and Asian sections.

Itaípu, city (1981 est. pop. 80,000), S Brazil, on the Paraná R., which forms the E boundary of Paraguay. The rapidly growing city was created after 1973 to house workers building the Itaípu Dam and power complex, one of the world's largest hydroelectric projects. A joint Brazilian-Paraguayan venture, the complex was engineered to generate 12,600 megawatts, as much power as the ASWAN and GRAND COULEE dams combined.

Italian East Africa, former federation of Italian territories in E Africa that comprised the colonies of ERITREA and Italian Somaliland (see SOMALIA) and the kingdom of ETHIOPIA. Formed in 1936, when Italian forces conquered Ethiopia, it lasted until the territories were freed of Italian rule by the British in 1941.

Italian language, member of the Romance group of the Italic subfamily of the Indo-European family of languages. See LANGUAGE (table).

Italian Wars, 1494–1559, efforts by the great European powers, chiefly France and Spain, to control the small, independent states of Renaissance Italy. In 1494 CHARLES VIII of France invaded Italy and seized Naples, only to be forced to retreat by a coalition of Spain, Holy Roman Emperor MAXIMILIAN I, the pope, Venice, and Milan. In the second phase (1494–1504), LOUIS XII of France occupied Milan, Genoa, and (jointly with Spain) Naples. In 1508 Pope JULIUS II formed an alliance with France, Spain, and Maximilian I against Venice. The pope and Louis soon fell out, and in 1510 the pope formed the HOLY LEAGUE, this time including the Swiss, for the purpose of expelling France from Italy. Julius died in 1513, and the league dissolved. In 1515 the great victory of FRANCIS I at the battle of Marignano reestablished French power in Italy. The wars between Francis and Emperor CHARLES V began in 1521. In 1526, after being defeated and captured, Francis was forced to renounce all claims in Italy. Once freed, however, he formed the League of Cognac with the pope, HENRY VIII of England, Venice, and Florence. In retaliation, Charles V sacked Rome (May 1527). The pope capitulated, and the war ended (1529) with the Treaty of Cambrai. France again was forced to renounce its Italian claims. The death of Francis (1547) and the Treaty of Cateau-Cambrésis (1559) effectively ended France's exploits in Italy and left Spain supreme there.

Italic languages, subfamily of the Indo-European family of languages. See LANGUAGE (table).

Italy, Ital. *Italia,* officially Italian Republic, republic (1990 pop. 57,576,429), 116,303 sq mi (301,225 sq km), S Europe; bordered by France (NW), the Ligurian and Tyrrhenian seas (W), the Ionian Sea (S), the Adriatic Sea (E), Slovenia (NE), and Austria and Switzerland (N). It includes the large Mediterranean islands of SICILY and SARDINIA. VATICAN CITY and SAN MARINO are independent enclaves on the Italian mainland. ROME is the capital. About 75% of the country is mountainous or hilly, and 20% is forested. N Italy, made up of a vast plain contained by the ALPS in the north, is the richest region, with the best farmland, largest industrial centers, and a flourishing tourist trade; Gran Paradiso (13,323 ft/4,061 m), the highest peak wholly within Italy, is located here. Central Italy has great historic and cultural centers, such as Rome and FLORENCE. S Italy is generally the poorest and least developed area. The Italian peninsula, bootlike in shape, is traversed for its entire length by the APENNINES. Italian is the major language, though there are small German-, French-, and Slavic-speaking minorities. Almost all Italians are Roman Catholic.

Economy. Largely agricultural until World War II, Italy industrialized rapidly after 1950. By the early 1970s industry contributed about 40% of the national product, compared with only 11% for agriculture. Chief manufactures include iron and steel, refined petroleum, chemicals, textiles, motor vehicles, and machinery. Principal farm products include wheat, corn, sugar beets, rice, tomatoes, citrus fruits, olives and olive oil, and livestock. Wine production is important. Tourism is a major source of foreign exchange. Mineral resources are limited, and 75% of energy needs must be imported. An increasing problem for the country's economic health, and one that may hinder its further integration into the EUROPEAN UNION, is the large state sector, which is inefficient and rife with patronage and corruption.

Government. Under the 1948 constitution, legislative power is vested in a bicameral parliament, consisting of a 630-member chamber of deputies and a senate of 315 elected and 5 life members. All legislators were formerly elected by a system of proportional representation that fostered political corruption, but reforms enacted in 1993 assigned 75% of the seats to winner-take-all districts. The council of ministers, headed by the premier, is the country's executive.

History. After the expulsion of the Etruscans from what is now central Italy, ancient Italian history (5th cent. B.C.–5th cent. A.D.) is largely that of the Roman Empire, of which Italy was the core. Like the rest of the empire, Italy was overrun by barbarian tribes in the early 5th cent. A.D. The Eastern emperors struggled over its remains, but Byzantine rule was soon displaced (569) by that of the LOMBARDS, except in Rome, where Pope GREGORY I (r.590–604) laid the foundation for the PAPAL STATES. The persisting Lombard threat against Rome brought the intervention of PEPIN THE SHORT (754, 756) and CHARLEMAGNE (800), who established Frankish hegemony over Italy. The German king OTTO I invaded (961) Italy and was crowned (962) emperor by the pope; this union of Italy and Germany marked the beginning of the HOLY ROMAN EMPIRE. Southern Italy, conquered (11th cent.) by the Normans, eventually passed to the Angevins of NAPLES and the Aragonese kings of Sicily. North and central Italy saw the rise of separate city-states; these, despite constant internecine warfare, built huge commercial empires, dominated European finance, and produced the great cultural flowering known as the RENAISSANCE. Beginning in the late 15th cent., Italy became the battleground of French, Spanish, and Austrian imperialism. By the 18th cent. Italian subjection to foreign rule, notably by the Spanish BOURBONS and the Austrian HAPSBURGS, was complete and remained so until the FRENCH REVOLUTIONARY WARS and NAPOLEON I redrew the map of Italy. After the Congress of VIENNA (1814–15), Austria, whose influence in Italy was now paramount, could not long suppress the burgeoning nationalistic movement for unification (see RISORGIMENTO). Unification was ultimately achieved under the house of SAVOY, largely through the efforts of CAVOUR, GARIBALDI, and VICTOR EMMANUEL II, who became king of Italy in 1861. Italy later acquired Venetia (1866) and Rome and its environs (1870). Though a member of the TRIPLE ALLIANCE, Italy entered (1915) WORLD WAR I on the Allied side and in the peace treaty obtained additional territory, including S TYROL, TRIESTE, and Istria. After the war, political and social unrest encouraged the growth of fascism, and in 1922 MUSSOLINI seized power. He created a totalitarian corporative state, conquered Ethiopia (1936), seized Albania (1939), and entered (1940) WORLD WAR II as an ally of Germany. In 1943 Italy surrendered to the Allies. Italy became a republic in 1946, and the king was exiled. The 1947 peace treaty deprived Italy of its colonies and considerable territory. Trieste was regained in 1954. The postwar era has seen a succession of short-lived, pro-Western coalition governments; the Communists (now the Democratic Party of the Left), although strong electorally, have been excluded from ministerial positions. The MAFIA and organized crime have had a persistent corrupting influence on postwar Italian society, and in the late 1970s leftist guerrilla terrorism plagued the country, most notably in the kidnapping and murder (1978) of former premier Aldo MORO. The 1992 parliamentary elections resulted in centrist, four-party minority government led by Giuliano Amato, a Socialist. Corruption probes, begun in 1992, led to the arrest of hundreds of business and political figures and the investigation of many others, including several party leaders and former prime ministers. A large vote, in a 1993 referendum, in favor of ending proportional representation in Italy's senate was regarded as a call for political change, and Prime Min. Amato resigned. Carlo Azeglio Ciampi, head of Italy's central bank, succeeded him, and legislation was passed that largely ended proportional representation in parliament. In new elections in 1994, a coalition of conservatives and neo-fascists, led by Silvio Berlusconi, won a majority of the seats in parliament.

Itháki or **Ithaca,** island (1981 pop. 3,646), c.37 sq mi (96 sq km), W Greece, one of the Ionian Islands. Olive oil, currants, and wine are produced there. It is traditionally celebrated as the home of ODYSSEUS.

Ito Hirobumi, prince, 1841–1909, Japanese statesman and architect of Japan's modernization. After visiting the West, he created the new government and constitution (1889). He was prime minister (1892–96; 1898, 1900–01) and formed the Seiyukai party (1900). While serving as resident-general of Korea, he was assassinated.

Iturbide, Agustín de [ētōorbē'thā], 1783–1824, Mexican revolutionary leader. In 1821, while commanding royalist troops, he agreed to the Plan of Iguala and the Treaty of Córdoba, assuring MEXICO's independence from Spain. He favored a conservative state and had himself proclaimed emperor (1822), but radical rebels forced him to abdicate and go into exile (1823). When he returned illegally to Mexico, he was executed.

IUD: see INTRAUTERINE DEVICE.

Ivan [ēvän'], rulers of Russia. **Ivan III** (the Great), 1440–1505, grand duke of Moscow (1462–1505), was the creator of the consolidated Muscovite (Russian) state. He subjugated Novgorod and other territories and in 1480 freed Muscovy from allegiance to the GOLDEN HORDE. He married Sophia, niece of the last Byzantine emperor, and claimed Moscow as the successor to the Roman and Byzantine empires. **Ivan IV** (the Terrible), 1530–84, grand duke of Moscow (1533–84), had himself crowned czar in 1547. He began trade with England, engaged in an unsuccessful war with Poland and Sweden to improve his access to the Baltic Sea, and began Russia's eastward expansion; Siberia was conquered during his reign. In later years he grew tyrannical and paranoid. He formed a special corps, the *oprichniki,* with which he conducted a reign of terror against the BOYARS. In one of his rages he killed his son and heir, Ivan (1581). He married seven times, disposing of his wives by forcing them to take the veil or ordering their murder. His sons Feodor I and DMITRI survived him, but his favorite, Boris GODUNOV, took power. **Ivan V,** 1666–96, czar (1682–90), succeeded his brother, Feodor III, ruling with PETER I under the regency of his sister, Sophia Alekseyevna. Feebleminded, he was excluded from affairs of state. He was father of Czarina ANNA, who was succeeded by her infant grand-nephew, **Ivan VI,** 1740–64, a German by birth. Deposed (1741) by Czarina ELIZABETH, Ivan VI was murdered in 1764 by order of CATHERINE II.

Ivanov, Lev [ēvä'nôf], 1834–1901, Russian dancer, teacher, choreographer, and ballet-master. He worked with Marius PETIPA and was a major force in the development of the classic romantic ballet in Russia. He choreographed *The Nutcracker* (1892) and, with Petipa, revised *Swan Lake* (1877). He influenced Michel FOKINE.

Ives, Charles, 1874–1954, American composer; b. Danbury, Conn. An organist who entered the insurance business, Ives composed music advanced in style, anticipating some of the innovations of SCHOENBERG and STRAVINSKY, but generally unpublished. In 1939 performance of his second piano SONATA, *Concord* (1909–15), won him recognition. His works, which include chamber, orchestral, and choral pieces and about 150 songs, draw on American folk music.

Ives, James Merritt: see CURRIER & IVES.

ivory, type of dentin present only in ELEPHANT tusks. Major sources are Africa and Asia. Ivory was long used for carvings and inlay work and as a surface for miniature painting. The ancient civilizations of Egypt, Assyria, Babylon, Greece, Rome, India, China, Japan, Byzantium, and early Christian Europe produced works in ivory. In modern times it has also been used to make keys for pianos and other instruments, billiard balls, and handles. The diminishing elephant population (largely the result of their slaughter for ivory) and efforts to protect existing herds led to an international treaty (1990) banning the ivory trade and the increasing use of alternative materials, such as PLASTIC and certain specially designed substitutes, as ivory stocks are depleted. In the past, teeth or tusks of such animals as the hippopotamus, walrus, narwhal, sperm whale, and wild boar were also called ivory.

Ivory Coast: see CÔTE D'IVOIRE.

ivy, name applied loosely to any trailing or climbing plant, particularly cultivated forms; more properly, the English ivy (*Hedera helix*) and some other members of the family Araliaceae. The evergreen English ivy, grown in many varieties, is a popular ornamental vine; its berries are poisonous. The GRAPE family also includes some ivies, most notably the VIRGINIA CREEPER and Boston ivy. Kenilworth ivy (*Cymbalaria muralis*), of the figwort family, is often used as ground cover.

Iwo Jima, volcanic island, c.8 sq mi (21 sq km), W Pacific, largest and most important of the Volcano Islands. Annexed by Japan in 1891, the island, site of a Japanese air base, was captured (Feb.–Mar. 1945) by U.S. marines at great cost. American administration ended in 1968. Iwo Jima is uninhabited, except for a small military force. The island's Mt. Suribachi is an extinct volcano.

IWW: see INDUSTRIAL WORKERS OF THE WORLD.

Ixion, in Greek mythology, king of the Lapithes. He murdered his bride's father to avoid paying him the bride price. When no one on earth would purify him, Zeus took Ixion to Olympus and purified him. Ixion attempted to seduce Hera, but Zeus created a phantom of her and by it Ixion fathered the CENTAURS. In punishment he was chained for eternity to a fiery wheel in Tartarus.

İzmir, formerly **Smyrna,** city (1990 pop. 1,762,849), capital of İzmir prov, W Turkey, on the Gulf of İzmir, an arm of the Aegean Sea. It is Turkey's second largest seaport and an industrial center with varied manufactures. Settled during the Bronze Age (c.3000 B.C.), it was colonized (c.1000 B.C.) by Ionians and destroyed (627 B.C.) by the Lydians. Under Macedon and Rome it prospered. It changed hands many times from the 7th to 15th cent. A.D., when the Ottoman Turks conquered it. Greece contested the city after the collapse (1918) of the OTTOMAN EMPIRE; when the Treaty of Lausanne confirmed it as Turkey's, the large Greek population was evacuated, making İzmir mostly Turkish. Earthquakes in 1928 and 1939 caused severe damage to the city.

J

Jabbar, Kareem Abdul-: see ABDUL-JABBAR, KAREEM.

jackal, carnivorous MAMMAL (genus *Canis*) related to the DOG and WOLF and similar in size and behavior to the COYOTE. Some authorities classify jackals in a separate genus (*Thos*). Jackals are found in Africa and S Asia, where they inhabit deserts, grasslands, and brush country. They forage by night and spend the day in holes or hidden in grass or brush.

jack-in-the-pulpit: see ARUM.

jackrabbit, popular name for several North American HARES.

Jackson, Andrew, 1767–1845, 7th president of the U.S. (1829–37); b. Waxhaw Settlement, on the border of North and South Carolina. Jackson helped to draft the Tennessee constitution and was elected (1796) to the U.S. Congress. In the WAR OF 1812 he defeated the CREEK at Horseshoe Bend (Mar. 1814), was made a major general, and decisively defeated seasoned British troops at New Orleans (Jan. 8, 1815). In 1818 he led a reprisal against the Seminoles in Florida and captured Pensacola, involving the U.S. in serious trouble with Spain and Britain. The conduct of Old Hickory, as he was called, pleased the people of the West. He was the greatest hero of his time and became associated with increased popular participation in government. This so-called Jacksonian democracy almost won him the presidency in 1824, but the election ended in the House of Representatives, with a victory for J.Q. ADAMS. Jackson was elected president in 1828 and brought a strong element of personalism to Washington. His Kitchen Cabinet was powerful, and the SPOILS SYSTEM developed. Jackson and Vice Pres. J.C. CALHOUN differed on NULLIFICATION, and Calhoun resigned (1832). Jackson's fight against the BANK OF THE UNITED STATES was an important issue in the election of 1832, in which he defeated Henry CLAY. He then transferred federal assets from the bank to chosen state, or "pet," banks. In 1836 he issued the Specie Circular, which said that all public lands must be paid for in specie and which hastened the Panic of 1837.

Jackson, Jesse Louis, 1941–, African-American political leader, clergyman, and CIVIL-RIGHTS activist; b. Greenville, S.C. He was executive director (1966–71) of Operation Breadbasket, founder and national president (1971–83) of People United to Save Humanity (Operation PUSH), and the first serious African-American candidate in the presidential primaries (1984; 1988). An advocate of statehood for the District of Columbia, he was elected (1990) as one of the District's nonvoting "shadow" senators.

Jackson, Mahalia, 1911–72, African-American singer; b. New Orleans. Living in Chicago from 1927, she sang in churches and revival meetings and began to make recordings. By the 1950s her powerful, joyous GOSPEL MUSIC style had gained her an international reputation.

Jackson, Michael, 1958–, American singer and composer; b. Gary, Ind. At eight, he was the lead singer of his family's group, The Jackson Five. He has achieved great popularity as an adult performer. His album "Thriller" broke all records by selling over 30 million copies. In 1993 he was charged in a civil suit with sexual abuse, which he denied. The suit was settled out of court in 1994.

Jackson, Stonewall (Thomas Jonathan Jackson), 1824–63, Confederate general in the U.S. CIVIL WAR; b. Clarksburg, Va. At the first battle of BULL RUN he earned his sobriquet when he and his brigade stood "like a stone wall." He conducted the brilliant Shenandoah Valley campaign (May–June 1862) and joined Gen. R.E. LEE for the SEVEN DAYS BATTLES. Serving under Lee, Jackson flanked the Union army to set up the Confederate victory at the second battle of Bull Run (Aug. 1862) and fought in the ANTIETAM CAMPAIGN and at Fredericksburg. At CHANCELLORSVILLE (May 1863) Jackson again flanked the Union army en route to a smashing Confederate victory, but he was mortally wounded by fire from his own troops. He was Lee's ablest and most trusted lieutenant.

Jackson, William Henry, 1843–1942, American artist and pioneer photographer of the West; b. Keeseville, N.Y. From 1858 Jackson recorded the scenic grandeur and historic sites of the American West. His Yellowstone photographs influenced the decision to make the area the first NATIONAL PARK.

Jackson, city (1990 pop. 196,637), state capital and seat of Hinds co., W central Miss., on the Pearl R.; inc. 1833. The state's largest city, it has processed-food, wood-products, metal, glass, and other industries, and is the center of the state's oil industry. Jackson is also a major southern rail and distribution center. It became capital in 1821 and was named for Andrew JACKSON. A center for the VICKSBURG CAMPAIGN in the CIVIL WAR, it was largely destroyed by SHERMAN's forces. The old capitol (1839) is now a museum. During the 1960s it was the site of many demonstrations for CIVIL RIGHTS.

Jackson Hole, fertile Rocky Mt. valley, NW Wyoming, partly in Grand Teton National Park (see NATIONAL PARKS, table). Named for the trapper David Jackson, who wintered (1828–29) there, the valley is a resort area that supports a diverse wildlife and is the wintering ground for large elk herds.

Jacksonville, city (1990 pop. 635,230), coextensive (since 1968) with Duval co., NE Fla., on the St. Johns R. near its mouth on the Atlantic; settled 1816, inc. 1832. The largest city in Florida, it is a major port and rail, air, and highway hub, with shipyards and extensive freight-handling facilities. Lumber, paper, processed food, computer components, and chemicals are leading products. Naval operations are important, as is insurance, banking, and tourism. The city's growth was interrupted by the SEMINOLE War and the CIVIL WAR, and the city was destroyed by fire in 1901 and rebuilt. Points of interest include the Gator Bowl, a Confederate monument, and several museums, and a large outdoor jazz festival is held annually.

Jack the Ripper, name given to a 19th-cent. London murderer. In 1888 he was responsible for the death and mutilation of seven East End prostitutes. Although a manhunt was undertaken and the police received letters purportedly from the Ripper, he was never found. Many theories regarding his identity have been advanced.

Jacob, in the BIBLE, ancestor of the Hebrews, the younger of the twin sons of ISAAC and REBECCA. By bargain and trickery, Jacob got the birthright and the blessing that was intended for his twin, ESAU. Jacob had two wives, Leah and her younger sister, RACHEL. On the banks of the Jabbok, he wrestled with an angel and received the name of Israel. He was the ancestor of the 12 tribes of Israel (see ISRAEL, TRIBES OF).

Jacob, François, 1920–, French biologist. By studying the genetic basis of lysogeny (see BACTERIOPHAGE), he and Elie Wollman discovered (1961) a new class of genetic elements, the episomes. Studies of the regulation of bacterial enzyme synthesis led Jacob and Jacques MONOD to propose (1961) the concepts of messenger RNA (see NUCLEIC ACID) and the operon. For this work Jacob and Monod shared with André LWOFF the 1965 Nobel Prize in physiology or medicine.

Jacobean style, an early phase of English Renaissance architecture and decoration, a transition between the ELIZABETHAN STYLE and the pure Renaissance style introduced by Inigo JONES. Under James I (r.1603–25) Renaissance motifs, communicated through German and Flemish carvers, were freely adopted, but some Gothic influence lingered. Columns and pilasters, round-arch arcades, and other classical elements mixed with characteristic English ornamental detail. The style influenced furniture design and other arts. Holland House, London, and Knole House, Kent, are noted Jacobean buildings.

Jacobins, political club of the FRENCH REVOLUTION. Formed in 1789, the club was named after the monastery of the Jacobins (Parisian name of the Dominicans), where it met. The members were mainly bourgeois and at first included moderates such as Honoré de MIRABEAU. With the FEUILLANTS, the Jacobins were (1791–92) the chief parties in the Legislative Assembly. They sought to limit the power of the king, and many had republican tendencies. The group split on the issue of war in Europe, which the majority, the GIRONDISTS, sought. The minority, supported by the lower classes of Paris, opposed the war and grew more radical and republican. In the National Convention, which proclaimed the French republic, these Jacobins and other extremist opponents of the Girondists were called the MOUNTAIN. After contributing heavily to the fall (1793) of the Girondists, the Jacobins, under Maximilien ROBESPIERRE, instituted the REIGN OF TERROR, which they used not only against counterrevolutionaries, but also against their former allies, the CORDELIERS and Georges DANTON. The Jacobins lost power on the fall (1794) of Robespierre, but their spirit lived on in revolutionary doctrine.

Jacobites, adherents of the exiled branch of the house of STUART after the GLORIOUS REVOLUTION of 1688. They took their name from the Latin form (*Jacobus*) of the name James. The Jacobites sought the restoration of JAMES II, then advanced the claims of his descendants until 1807, when the direct Stuart line ended. They included many Catholics, high churchmen, and extreme Tories. After the death of Queen ANNE (1714), Henry St. John and the 6th earl of Mar attempted a rising known as "the '15" (1715) to crown the Old Pretender, James Edward STUART; they were defeated in the disastrous battles of Preston and Sheriffmuir. The second major Jacobite rising, called "the '45," occurred when the Young Pretender, Charles Edward Stuart, invaded (1745) England and was crushed at the battle of Culloden Moor.

Jacquerie [Fr., = collection of *Jacques,* a nickname for the French peasant], 1358, a revolt of the French peasantry. The uprising stemmed from poor economic conditions, high taxation, and pillaging during the HUNDRED YEARS WAR. It was brutally crushed by CHARLES II of Navarre and other nobles.

jade, common name for either of two minerals, both white to green in color, used as gems. Jadeite $NaAl(SiO_3)_2$, rarer and costlier, is found in Myanmar, China, Japan, and Guatemala. Nephrite $Ca_2(Mg,Fe)_5Si_8O_{22}(OH,F)_2$ occurs in New Zealand, Central Asia, Siberia, and parts of North America. Jade was much used by primitive peoples to make implements and has been prized by the Chinese and Japanese as the most precious of gems.

jaguar, large CAT (*Panthera onca*) found from the SW U.S. to S central Argentina. It has a yellow or tawny coat with black rings and spots; some rings surround spots, a feature which distinguishes it from a LEOPARD. An adult male may be 4½ ft (1.4 m) long (excluding the long tail), stand 2½ ft (76 cm) high at the shoulder, and weigh 200 lb (90 kg). Mainly forest dwellers, jaguars are also found in rocky, semidesert areas and on the PAMPAS.

jai alai, also called pelota, handball-like game of Spanish Basque origin. It is played as either singles or doubles on a three-walled court (*fronton*) with a hard rubber ball (*pelota*) that is hurled with a wicker basket (*cesta*) attached to the player's arm. The sport is popular in Latin America and is played in some states (e.g., Florida and Connecticut) where jai alai betting is legal.

Jainism, the religion of Jina, a religious system of India practiced by about 2 million followers. It arose in the 6th cent. B.C. in protest against the ritualism of HINDUISM and the authority of the VEDA and was established by a succession of 24 saints, the last of whom was Vardhamana (called Mahavira or Jina), apparently a historical figure. He preached asceticism and concern for all life as a means of escaping from the transmigration of souls that results from one's past actions (see KARMA) and of achieving NIRVANA. Early Jainism spread from NE India, converting the emperor CHANDRAGUPTA and other rulers, according to tradition. In time, elements of Hinduism were adopted, including the CASTE system and a number of Hindu deities. Contemporary Jains are known for charitable works and their eschewal of any occupation that even remotely endangers animal life.

Jakarta or **Djakarta,** city (1988 est. pop. 8,800,000), capital and largest city of Indonesia, NW JAVA. It is the administrative, commercial, industrial, and transportation center of the country; industries include food processing, ironworks, automobile assembly, textiles, and chemicals. Resembling a Dutch town, with its many canals and drawbridges, Jakarta has an old quarter and a new suburb. Its port, the largest in Indonesia, handles most of the country's export-import trade. Founded (c.1619) as the Dutch EAST INDIA COMPANY fort of Batavia, it became capital of the newly established nation in 1949 and was renamed Jakarta. It is the site of the Univ. of Indonesia. Notable museums include the National Museum, with its superb collection of Asian porcelain, and Jakarta Museum (the former Batavia City Hall).

Jakobson, Roman, 1896–1982, Russian-American linguist and literary critic. His early work, grounded in structural linguistics, contributed to the development of the "Prague school" of linguistics, which argued for a historical emphasis in the study of speech sounds. He came to the U.S. in 1943. He later worked on distinctive-feature theory, which defines speech sounds by the presence or absence of specific phonetic qualities. Among his works is *Framework of Language* (1980).

Jamaica, island republic (1992 est. pop. 2,507,000), 4,232 sq mi (10,962 sq km), West Indies, S of Cuba and W of Haiti. The capital is KINGSTON. Most of Jamaica is an elevated plateau with a mountainous spine reaching 7,402 ft (2,256 m) in the Blue Mts., but there are low-lying plains along the north and south coasts. Jamaica is the second-ranking world supplier of bauxite and alumina, which account for half of its foreign exchange. Tourism, stimulated by the island's subtropical climate and excellent beaches, is the second largest source of exchange. The most important agricultural product is sugar, from which molasses and rum are produced. Other export crops are coffee, bananas, citrus fruits, and tobacco. A large majority of the people are of African descent. The chief religion is Protestantism, with Roman Catholic and spiritualist minorities. The official language is English, although most Jamaicans speak an English creole.

History. Discovered by COLUMBUS in 1494 and first settled (1509) by Spaniards, Jamaica was captured by England in 1655; formal cession was in 1670. A large African slave population worked sugar plantations in the 18th cent., when Jamaica was a leading sugar producer. The decline of sugar after the abolition (1838) of slavery created economic hardship, civil unrest, and British suppression (1865–84) of local autonomy. Black rioting, sparked by poverty and British racial policies, recurred periodically, reaching a peak in 1938. In 1944 universal adult suffrage was introduced. After a brief period (1958–62) as part of the WEST INDIES Federation, in 1962 Jamaica became an independent member of the Commonwealth. After 1972 a move toward socialism under Prime Minister Michael Manley led to violence between extremist factions and produced an economic crisis. Edward Seaga, a moderate, took office in 1980 and restored some measure of economic stability. In 1989 Manley's party returned to power with a more conservative program. Manley resigned in 1992, due to ill health, and was succeeded by P.J. Patterson, who subsequently won his own electoral mandate in 1993.

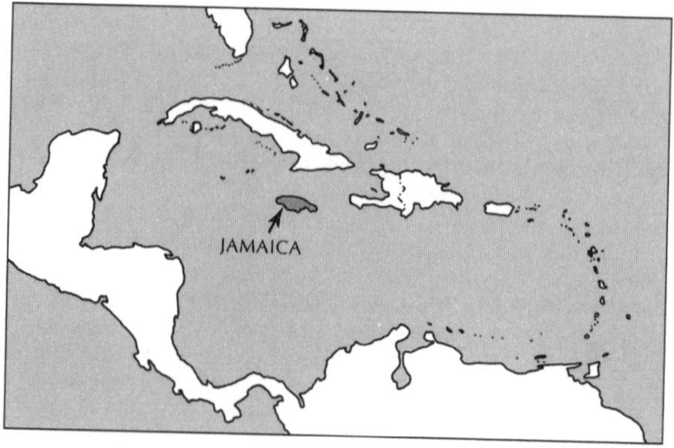

James, Saint, d. A.D. c.43, one of the Twelve APOSTLES; called St. James the Greater. The son of Zebedee and brother of St. JOHN, he is venerated widely, especially (as Santiago) in Spain.

James, Saint (the Less or Little), one of the Twelve APOSTLES. He was the son of Alphaeus and Mary.

James, Saint, the "brother" of Jesus, according to St. Paul. Since belief in the perpetual virginity of Mary precludes a blood relationship, he is assumed to have been a stepbrother. The Roman Catholic Church identifies him with St. James the Less. He apparently opposed the imposition of Jewish Law on Gentile Christians and is probably the author of the Epistle of James.

James, kings of England, Scotland, and Ireland. **James I,** 1566–1625 (r.1603–25), the son of Lord DARNLEY and MARY QUEEN OF SCOTS. He succeeded (1567) to the Scottish throne on the forced abdication of his mother. During his minority, Scotland was ruled by regents, and he was the creature of successive combinations of his mother's pro-French Catholic party and the Protestant faction, which favored an alliance with England. He began his personal rule in 1583. Allying himself with ELIZABETH I, he accepted calmly his mother's execution in 1587. He succeeded Elizabeth in 1603. At the Hampton Court Conference of 1604 (which commissioned the translation that resulted in the Authorized or King James Version of the BIBLE), he displayed an uncompromising anti-Puritan attitude. His inconsistent policy toward English Catholics (which resulted in the GUNPOWDER PLOT) angered them as well as Protestants. After the death (1612) of his able minister Robert Cecil, earl of SALISBURY, he asserted his divine right, battling with Sir Edward COKE and relying on incompetent favorites, e.g., George Villiers, 1st duke of BUCKINGHAM. These actions, his extravagance, and his refusal to recognize the importance of Parliament furthered discontent and led to the ENGLISH CIVIL WAR. In 1611 he dissolved Parliament, ruling without it (except for the Addled Parliament, 1614) until 1621. In 1624 he acceded to its wish for war with SPAIN. His reign saw the beginnings of colonization in North America. He was succeeded by CHARLES I. **James II,** 1633–1701 (r.1685–88), was the second son of Charles I and the brother and successor of CHARLES II. He escaped to France (1648) in the English Civil War. At the RESTORATION (1660) he returned to England and was made lord high admiral, serving (1655; 1672) in the DUTCH WARS. In about 1668 he became a Roman Catholic. After his resignation as admiral because of the TEST ACT (1673) and his marriage to the staunchly Catholic Mary of Modena (1673), he became increasingly unpopular. His daughter MARY married the Protestant William of Orange (later WILLIAM III), and they became, after James, heirs presumptive to the English throne. Exiled after the false accusations of a Popish Plot (1678) by Titus OATES, he was recalled in 1680. After the failure of Parliament to exclude him from succession and the abortive RYE HOUSE PLOT, Charles II's death brought him to the throne in 1685. His unpopularity was increased by the Bloody Assizes of Baron JEFFREYS OF WEM, his attempts to fill important positions with Roman Catholics, and his autocratic methods with a hostile Parliament. The birth of his son, James Edward STUART, as a possible Catholic heir, led to the GLORIOUS REVOLUTION of 1688, in which William of Orange became king. James fled to France. In 1689 he attempted to restore himself in Ireland but was defeated (1690) at the battle of the Boyne. He died in exile.

James, kings of Scotland. **James I,** 1394–1437 (r.1406–37), was the son of ROBERT III. Fearful for his safety because of the ambitions of the king's brother, Robert Stuart, duke of Albany, Robert III sent James to France in 1406. The prince was captured by the English and held captive until 1424. Treated as a royal guest, he was well educated. Ransomed by several Scottish nobles, he returned to Scotland and governed energetically. He brought peace by ruthless methods, exterminating members of the Albany family. James's popularity was lessened by his vindictiveness, cupidity, and quick temper; he was assassinated by a group of nobles. He is thought to be the author of a number of fine poems. His son, **James II,** 1430–60 (r.1437–60), had successive earls of Douglas as regents during his minority. Allying himself with William Douglas, the 6th earl, he was ruling in his own right by 1450. When he discovered (1452) William in a conspiracy, he killed him. After the ensuing revolt, he seized the Douglas lands. He invaded England in the Wars of the ROSES and was accidentally killed. His son, **James III,** 1452–88 (r.1460–88), was seized at his mother's death by the Boyd family, who ruled until 1469. A cultivated king, James lacked the force necessary in a turbulent period. He fought with his brother, Alexander STUART, who, aided by other nobles, rebelled in 1482. The nobles rebelled again in 1488 and murdered James at Sauchieburn. His son, **James IV,** 1473–1513 (r.1488–1513), was a popular and able monarch who brought progress and stability to Scotland. In 1503 he married Margaret Tudor, daughter of HENRY VII of England. Scottish relations with England deteriorated with the accession of HENRY VIII. James invaded England in 1513 and was killed in the battle of Flodden, in which the Scottish aristocracy was almost annihilated. His son, **James V,** 1512–42 (r.1513–42), was the object of a struggle between his regents. Held captive, he escaped (1528) and allied himself with France against Henry VIII. He married MARY OF GUISE in 1538. War with England broke out in 1542. James's nobles gave him little support, and his army was routed at Solway Moss. He died shortly thereafter and was succeeded by his infant daughter, MARY QUEEN OF SCOTS. For **James VI,** king of Scotland (r.1567–1625), see James I, under JAMES, kings of England, Scotland, and Ireland.

James, Alice, 1848–92, American diarist and the sister of Henry and William JAMES; b. N.Y.C. Although she did not receive a formal education and suffered several breakdowns, her diaries, written from 1886 to 1892, contain astute observations on her times and family.

James, Henry, 1843–1916, American novelist; b. N.Y.C.; brother of William JAMES. He settled in London in 1876 and became a British citizen in 1915. In his early novels, such as *Daisy Miller* (1879) and *The Portrait of a Lady* (1881), he compared the sophisticated culture of Europeans with the naïve quality of Americans. In his next period, James dealt with revolutionaries, as in *The Bostonians* (1886) and *The Princess Casamassima* (1886). He also wrote several powerful short novels, such as *The Aspern Papers* (1888) and *The Turn of the Screw* (1898). He returned to the international theme in his last novels, *The Wings of the Dove* (1902), *The Ambassadors* (1903), and *The Golden Bowl* (1904), widely considered his masterpieces. He was also a fine short-story writer and a noted critic. Considered one of the great masters of the novel, James is particularly noted for his portrayals of the subtleties of character and for his complex style.

James, Jesse, 1847–82, American outlaw; b. Clay co., Mo. From 1866 Jesse and his brother Frank headed a band of outlaws whose trail of robberies and murders led through many central states. He was killed by a gang member seeking a reward.

James, William, 1842–1910, American philosopher and psychologist; b. N.Y.C.; son of the theologian Henry James and brother of the novelist Henry JAMES. He taught first psychology and then philosophy at Harvard Univ. His *Principles of Psychology* (1890) was a brilliant and epoch-making work. Although he is often considered the founder of PRAGMATISM, James gave that title to C.S. PEIRCE. According to James, the truth of a proposition is judged by its practical outcome. His "radical empiricism" rejected all transcendental principles and directly influenced the instrumentalism of John DEWEY. James maintained a lifelong interest in religion and psychical research. His works, noted for their literary quality, include *The Will to Believe* (1897), *The Varieties of Religious Experience* (1902), and *Pragmatism* (1907).

James, EPISTLE of the NEW TESTAMENT, 20th book in the usual order, traditionally placed among the Catholic or General Epistles and ascribed to St. James the Less. A practical work, it gives diverse admonitions in no special order, among them two general ethical principles: "Be doers of the word, not hearers only" (1.19–27) and "Faith without works is dead" (2.14–26).

Jameson, Sir Leander Starr, 1853–1917, British colonial administrator in South Africa. In 1895 he led the unauthorized Jameson Raid into the Boer colony of the Transvaal, an act that helped to precipitate the SOUTH AFRICAN WAR. He was captured and turned over to the British, who imprisoned him briefly. He later returned to South Africa, where he was prime minister of the Cape Colony (1904–8).

Jamestown, former village, SE Va., first permanent English settlement in America; est. May 14, 1607, by the London Company on a peninsula (now an island) in the James R.; named for the reigning English king, JAMES I. Disease, starvation, and attacks by Native Americans decimated the settlement, and the remaining colonists prepared to return; but new settlers and supplies were sent, and

Lord DE LA WARR arrived in 1610. John SMITH was an early colonial leader. John ROLFE began the cultivation of tobacco there in 1612; in 1614 he married POCAHONTAS, assuring peace with the indigenous people. The first representative government in the colonies met there (1619); Jamestown was capital of VIRGINIA through most of the 17th cent. The village was almost entirely destroyed during Bacon's Rebellion (1676; see BACON, NATHANIEL). The site, which contains the old church tower (c.1639), some original gravestones, and many replicas of the early settlement, is mainly administered by the U.S. government.

Jami, Nur ad-Din Abd ar-Rahman [jä'mē], 1414–92, Persian poet and DERVISH. Among his works are *Seven Thrones,* a collection of poems including "Salaman and Absal," and *Abode of Spring,* a collection of short stories.

Janáček, Leoš [yä'nächěk], 1854–1928, Czech composer, theorist, and collector of Slavic folk music. His works include the operas *Jenufa* (1904), *Katia Kabanova* (1921), and *The Makropulos Affair* (1926); a song cycle; and a MASS.

Janet: see CLOUET, JEAN.

Janissaries, elite corps of war captives and Christian youths in the service of the OTTOMAN EMPIRE (Turkey). Converted to Islam and trained under the strictest discipline, they eventually became powerful enough to make and unmake sultans. By the 17th cent. membership was largely hereditary. Their power came to an abrupt end in 1826 when Sultan MAHMUD II had them massacred in their barracks.

Jansen, Cornelis [yän'sən], 1585–1638, Dutch Roman Catholic theologian, bishop of Ypres. He sought to reform Christian life by a return to St. AUGUSTINE. From his posthumous *Augustinus* (1640) arose the movement called **Jansenism,** which stressed greater personal holiness. The movement, centered in France, caused great controversy within the Roman Catholic Church because of its advocacy of an extreme form of PREDESTINATION and its discouragement of frequent communion. It was attacked in papal bulls (1705, 1713), and the Jansenist convent of Port-Royal, near Paris, was closed. Jansenists are still found in the Netherlands.

Jansky, Karl Guthe, 1905–50, American radio engineer; b. Norman, Okla. While trying to determine the causes of radio communications static for Bell Telephone Laboratories, Jansky discovered (1931) radio waves from extraterrestrial sources—a discovery that led to the development of the science of RADIO ASTRONOMY; By 1932 he had concluded that the source of the interference was located in the direction of the center of the Milky Way galaxy.

January: see MONTH.

Janus, in Roman mythology, custodian of the universe, god of beginnings. The guardian of gates and doors, he held sacred the first hour of the day, first day of the month, and first month of the year (which bears his name). He is represented with two bearded heads set back to back.

Japan, Jap. *Nihon* or *Nippon,* country (1991 pop. 124,017,137), 142,811 sq mi (369,881 sq km), occupying an archipelago off the coast of E Asia. The capital is TOKYO. Japan proper has four main islands; these are, from north to south, HOKKAIDO, HONSHU (the largest island, where the capital and major cities are located), SHIKOKU, and KYUSHU. Many smaller islands lie in an arc between the Sea of Japan and the East China Sea, and the Pacific Ocean. Honshu, Shikoku, and Kyushu enclose the Inland Sea. Mountains, including a number of volcanoes, cover two thirds of Japan's surface; the most famous peak is Mt. FUJI. The land is also marked by short, rushing rivers, forested slopes, irregular lakes, and small, rich plains. Rainfall is abundant, and typhoons and earthquakes are frequent.

Economy. Mineral resources are meager. Many rapid streams provide hydroelectric power, and nuclear energy is produced. High-speed train service now extends to many parts of the country. Japan's farming population has been declining steadily and now comprises about 8% of the total labor force. Arable land (less than 16% of the country's area) is intensively cultivated; rice and other cereals are the main crops. Fishing is highly developed, and the annual catch is one of the largest in the world. Since its defeat in World War II, Japan has developed into one of the world's great economic powers. The world's leading producer of ships and automobiles, it also ranks high in the production of steel, electronic equipment, and textiles. Japan's industry depends heavily on imported raw materials, especially petroleum and iron and aluminum ore. Japan's successful exports have produced huge foreign trade surpluses that have created strains with the U.S. and W European nations.

People. The Japanese are primarily descended from various peoples who migrated from Asia in prehistoric times; the dominant strain is N Asian or Mongolic. The principal religions are SHINTO and BUDDHISM, and Japanese thought has also been deeply affected by CONFUCIANISM. The present educational system, established after World War II, has created a highly educated and skilled population.

Government. The constitution, which went into effect in 1947, established a democratic form of government. It declares the emperor to be the symbolic head of state and renounces Japan's right to declare war. The national diet, which has sole legislative power, is composed of the 512-member house of representatives and the 252-member house of councilors. Reforms passed in 1994 will reduce lower-house membership to 500. Executive power rests with the prime minister, who is elected by the diet, and his appointed cabinet. Japan is divided into 47 prefectures, each governed by a popularly elected governor and a legislature.

History. In legend, Japan was founded in 660 B.C., but reliable records date only to about A.D. 400. By the 5th cent. Japan was unified by the Yamato clan, and the foundations of a centralized imperial state were laid by the 8th cent. Court culture was influenced first by Chinese learning and institutions and then by a rebirth of native Japanese culture. By the 9th cent. the powerful Fujiwara family ruled as regents, and imperial authority was undermined. The 12th cent. ushered in Japan's medieval period, with the development of feudalism, the rise of a warrior class called the SAMURAI, and the establishment of military rule under Minamoto Yoritomo, the first SHOGUN. After civil war between rival warrior clans, the country was unified in 1600 under a new shogun, Tokugawa IEYASU. For more than 250 years the TOKUGAWA family ruled over a Japan internally at peace and largely cut off from the outside world. In 1853 the U.S. naval officer Matthew C. PERRY arrived in Japan to force the opening of trade with the West, and in 1868 the shogunate collapsed, when the Meiji Restoration returned formal power to the Emperor MEIJI. A new government was established under the able leadership of former samurai. Adopting the techniques of Western civilization, Japan modernized rapidly into an industrial state and military power. A constitutional monarchy and a parliament (diet) were established by the constitution of 1889. The success of Japan in the First Sino-Japanese War (1894–95) and the RUSSO-JAPANESE WAR (1904–5) brought the nation to international prominence. An Anglo-Japanese alliance was formed in 1902. Japan annexed Korea in 1910, established a puppet-state in MANCHURIA in 1932, and began the Second SINO-JAPANESE WAR (1937–45) by invading N China. Japan formed a military alliance with Germany and Italy in WORLD WAR II and opened hostilities against the U.S. with an attack on PEARL HARBOR in 1941. After rapid initial success, the Japanese were defeated by the Allies. Following the dropping of atomic bombs by the U.S. on HIROSHIMA and NAGASAKI, Japan surrendered in Aug. 1945 and was occupied by U.S. forces. The signing of a peace treaty in 1951 led to full Japanese sovereignty over the main islands in 1952. The U.S. returned the BONIN and nearby islands to Japan in 1968 and the RYUKYU ISLANDS (Okinawa) in 1972. The LIBERAL DEMOCRATIC PARTY (LDP) dominated postwar politics, but beginning in the 1970s various scandals increasingly tarnished its image. TAKESHITA NOBURU served as prime minister (1987–1989) until, amid reports of scandal, he resigned, and Uno Sosuke replaced him. Uno resigned after a sex scandal and an election defeat, and Kaifu Toshiki became (1989) prime minister. In 1991 MIYAZAWA KIICHI succeeded Kaifu as prime minister. Miyazawa's government fell in 1993 after the LDP split over political reforms. No party won a majority in the subsequent elections, but an opposition coalition formed a government, and HOSOKAWA MORIHIRO became prime minister.

Japan, Sea of, arm of the Pacific Ocean, c.405,000 sq mi (1,048,950 sq km), located between Japan, Korea, and the Russian Far East. A branch of the warm Japan Current flows northeast through the sea, modifying climatic conditions and keeping coastal ports ice-

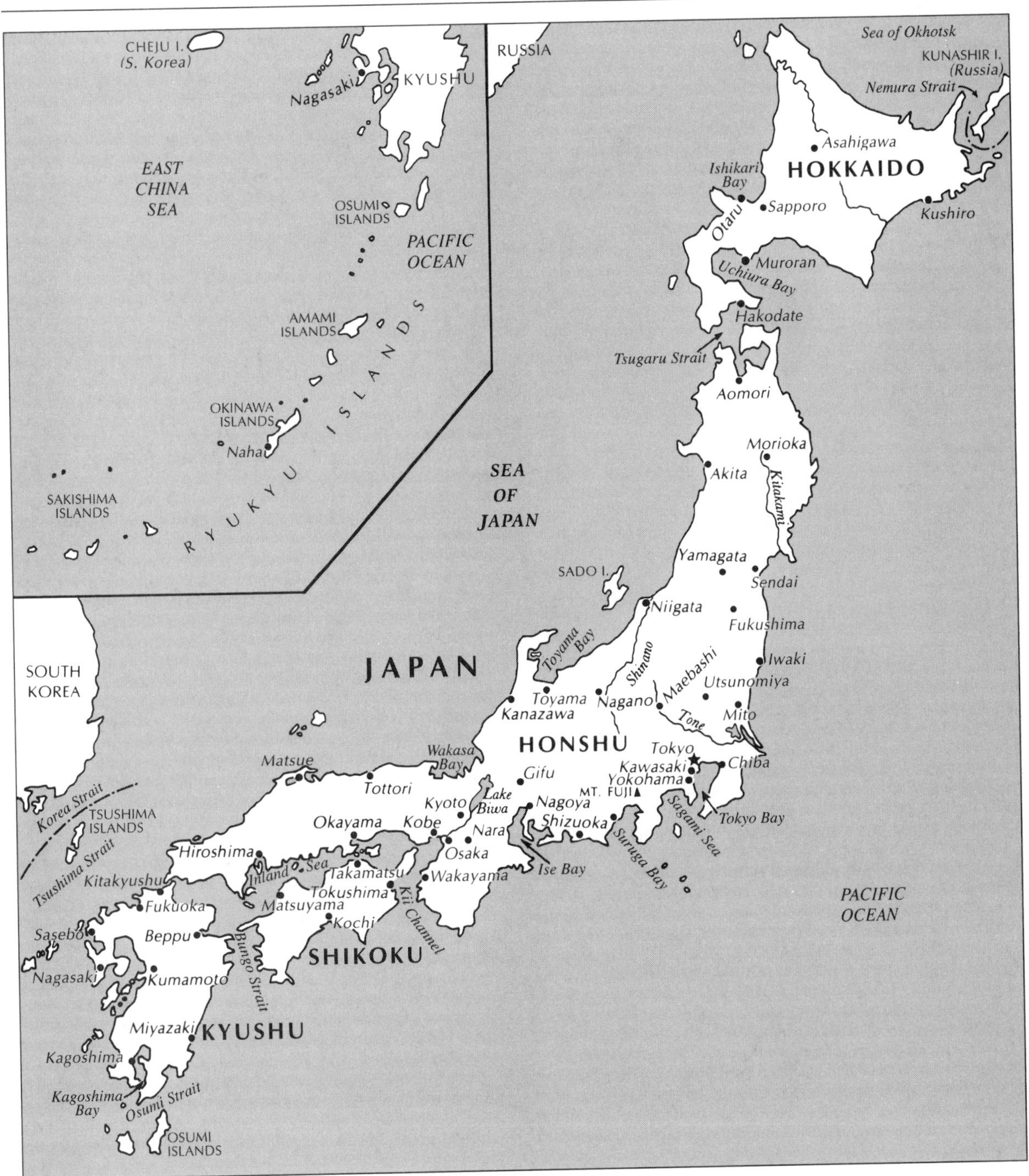

free as far north as VLADIVOSTOK, Russia's only major all-year outlet to the Pacific Ocean sea lanes.

Japanese, language of uncertain origin that is spoken by more than 100 million people, most of whom live in Japan. Japanese appears to be unrelated to any other language; however, some scholars see a kinship to Korean, and others link Japanese and Korean to the ALTAIC languages (see URALIC AND ALTAIC LANGUAGES).

Japanese architecture. Evidence of neolithic building in Japan remains. Chinese religious architecture came to Japan with BUDDHISM in the 6th cent. Parts of the monastery of Horyu-ji, near Nara, illustrate the first epoch of Japanese architecture (6th–8th cent.), characterized by gravity and simple, vital construction, sparsely ornamented. Wood has always been the favored material. Interior columns and thin woodwork and plaster walls were characteristic. Vitality and grace are communicated by the refined curvatures in columns and overhanging roofs. Emulation of the Chinese style is seen in the monastery of Todai-ji (begun 745), with its great hall housing the daibutsu (colossal Buddha), fronted by twin pagodas. Distinctively Japanese architecture dates from the late Heian period (898–1185). The Phoenix Hall at Uji, near Kyoto, represents the apogee of Japanese design, with its airiness and beautiful situation near a lotus lake. In the 13th cent. a renewed interest in CHINESE ARCHITECTURE came with the emergence of ZEN BUDDHISM. Japanese temple design adhered to the Chinese symmetrical pattern. In front of the main building stood an impressive gateway. Accessory structures included the PAGODA. The Shinto temple was small and simple; greatest importance was attached to the landscape setting. Regard for the environment was seen also in secular building, as in the housing schemes called *shinden-zukuri,* in which buildings connected by corridors surrounded a garden and pond. The Japanese upper-class dwelling was unexcelled for refinement and simplicity. Exterior walls were usually movable panels; interiors were subdivided by screens. Important rooms contained a *tokonoma,* an alcove for display of flower arrangements. European architectural influence entered Japan after 1868. In the 20th cent. the Japanese began to influence the development of the INTERNATIONAL STYLE in MODERN ARCHITECTURE. Important Japanese architects include Tange Kenzo and Kurokawa Kisho.

Japanese Netsukes, ivory, 18th–19th cent.

Japanese art. The earliest Japanese art, probably dating from the 3d and 2d millennia B.C., consisted of monochrome pottery in a cord pattern (*jomon*). This was replaced by bronze bells with simple designs, clay tomb figures (*haniwa*), and some painted burial chambers. With the introduction of BUDDHISM in the 6th cent., and throughout its history, Japanese art relied on Chinese forms and techniques. In the Nara period (710–784) traditional technical methods of Japanese painting were established. The work was executed on thin silk or soft paper with Chinese ink or watercolors. Mounted on silk brocade or paper, the paintings were of two types: hanging scrolls (*kakemono*) and horizontal scrolls (*emakimono*). The Jogan period (794–897) witnessed the beginning of an indigenous style of art. The Fujiwara period (898–1185) was marked by the crystallization of the *Yamato-e* tradition of painting, based on national rather than Chinese taste. The famous scroll *Tale of Genji* reflects the extreme sensitivity and overrefinement of the court of that period. The Kamakura period (late 12th–14th cent.) restored vigor and realism, as seen in scrolls like *Tales of the Heiji Insurrection* (13th cent.; Mus. of Fine Arts, Boston). Here, unlike in Chinese painting, humanity occupies the most important role. In the Momoyama period (1568–1615) architectural sculpture achieved unprecedented grandeur. The KANO family of artists succeeded in fusing Chinese ink-painting technique with Japanese decorative quality. During the Edo period (1615–1867) miniature sculptures called *netsuke* became popular. In the 18th cent., influenced by Dutch engravers, a new type of art arose in the form of woodblock prints known as *ukiyo-e* pictures of the fleeting or floating world. *Ukiyo-e* color-print designers won worldwide renown, the best known being HARUNOBU and HIROSHIGE. Mid-19th-cent. contacts with European culture enervated Japanese art, and in the 20th cent. a great number of painters and sculptors have been strongly influenced by Western styles.

Japanese literature. Although Japanese and Chinese are different languages, the Japanese borrowed and adapted Chinese ideographs early in the 8th cent. so that their spoken language could be written. This system was used in the writing of *Records of Ancient Matters* (712), the sacred book of SHINTO, but other works of the period were written in pure Chinese. The addition of two phonetic syllabaries (*kata-kana* and *hiragana*) during the Heian era (794–1185) opened a golden age in which Japanese literature, written in Japanese, reached its first peak of development. Much of the Heian literature was written by women, notably MURASAKI SHIKIBU, a noblewoman whose *Tale of Genji* (early 11th cent.) is ranked with the world's greatest novels. The four basic forms of Japanese drama were evolved (see ASIAN DRAMA) from the 12th to the 17th cent. Under the TOKUGAWA shogunate (17th–19th cent.) the written language was standardized, and freer verse forms, e.g., the HAIKU, began to replace the *tanka,* the classical form. While Heian literature dealt mostly with the aristocracy, the Tokugawa era was concerned with the bourgeoisie. CHIKAMATSU's plays are the first tragedies about common people in world literature. Other important writers were the poet Matsuo Basho (1648–94) and the novelist Ihara Saikaku (1642–93). Modern Japanese literature reflects the influence of the West, and many 20th-cent. writers have faced the problem of reconciling Japanese tradition with that influence. They include TANIZAKI JUNICHIRO, KAWABATA YASUNARI (who won the 1968 Nobel Prize in literature), MISHIMA YUKIO, ABE KOBO, and Ooka Shohei.

japanning: see LACQUER.

Japheth: see NOAH.

Jarrell, Randall, 1914–65, American poet; b. Nashville, Tenn. His poetry, e.g., *Losses* (1948), *The Woman at the Washington Zoo* (1960), reflects a sensitive, tragic world view. Among his other works are children's books; a novel; and critical essays, which were collected in *Poetry and the Age* (1953).

Jaruzelski, Wojciech [yärōōzĕl'skē], 1923–, Polish military and political leader. He fought in World War II, became a general in 1956, and began his rise in the Communist party in 1960. During the 1981 crisis involving the trade union SOLIDARITY, Jaruzelski became premier and party leader. Known as a moderate, he sought a compromise but finally ordered a military crackdown, placed Poland under martial law, and ordered the arrest of Solidarity leader Lech WALESA. Backed by Soviet leadership, his government outlawed Solidarity and put down attendant protest demonstrations and strikes (1982). Martial law was lifted in 1983, and in 1985 he was elected president by the parliament after stepping down as premier. Narrowly reelected (1989) by a parliament that included members of Solidarity, Jaruzelski resigned his Communist party posts. He resigned as president the following year and was succeeded by Walesa.

jasmine or **jessamine,** plant (genus *Jasminum*) of the OLIVE family, chiefly of Old World tropical and subtropical regions but cultivated in other mild areas and greenhouses. The blossoms, mostly yellow or white and usually fragrant, are used in scenting tea; the oil is used in perfumery.

Jason, one of the greatest heroes of Greek mythology. Raised by the centaur CHIRON, Jason claimed the kingdom of Iolcus, which his uncle, Pelias, had stolen from his father, Aeson. Pelias agreed to return it if Jason gathered the GOLDEN FLEECE, owned by King Aeëtes of Colchis. In quest of it, Jason assembled the Argonauts, sailed in the *Argo,* and had many adventures. In Colchis, they captured the fleece with the help of Aeëtes' daughter, MEDEA, who loved Jason. Medea returned with Jason, married him, and helped him to secure the throne. When he later tried to divorce her, she brutally destroyed his betrothed, Creusa; Creusa's father; and, in some versions, her own children. The gods then caused Jason to wander for many years. The story of Jason and Medea appears frequently in literature, notably in EURIPIDES.

jasper, opaque, impure CHALCEDONY, usually red but also yellow, green, and grayish blue, used as a gem. Ribbon jasper has colors in stripes.

Jaspers, Karl, 1883–1969, German philosopher. Generally placed within the orbit of EXISTENTIALISM, Jaspers believed that genuine philosophy must spring from the study of a person's individual existence, which he viewed as enclosed by an all-embracing, transcendental reality he called "the encompassing." Among his works are *Man in the Modern Age* (1931) and *Philosophy* (3 vol., 1932).

jaundice, abnormal condition in which body fluids and tissues, particularly the skin and eyes, take on a yellowish color as a result of excess bilirubin, a substance normally removed from the bloodstream by the LIVER and eliminated from the body in BILE. Causes include excessive disintegration of red blood cells (as in some types of ANEMIA); damage to liver cells by disease (e.g., CIRRHOSIS, HEPATITIS); and bile duct blockage (e.g., by gallstones or tumors). Jaundice in the newborn may indicate an RH FACTOR reaction.

Java, island (1990 pop. 107,573,749), Indonesia, c.51,000 sq mi (132,090 sq km), one of the world's most densely populated regions. It constitutes only one seventh of Indonesia's area but contains nearly two thirds of the population. A chain of volcanic, forested mountains traverses the island east to west, rising to 12,060 ft (3,676 m) at Mt. Semeru. The climate is warm and humid, and the volcanic soil is exceptionally productive, yielding two or three crops a year when irrigated. Most of Indonesia's industry is on Java, and lumbering and mining also are important. From the 10th to 15th cent. the island was the center of Hindu-Javanese culture, from which it derives today's highly developed art forms. It was under Dutch rule from 1619 to 1946.

Java man: see HOMO ERECTUS.

Jay, John, 1745–1829, American statesman, 1st chief justice of the U.S. SUPREME COURT (1789–95); b. N.Y.C. A lawyer, he guided the drafting of the New York State constitution. He was president (1778–79) of the CONTINENTAL CONGRESS and one of the commissioners who negotiated (1781–83) peace with Great Britain (see PARIS, TREATY OF). As secretary of foreign affairs (1784–89), he advocated strong central government. During his tenure as chief justice, he was sent (1794) on a mission to England, where he negotiated what became known as JAY'S TREATY. Jay was also governor of New York for two terms (1795–1801).

jay, BIRD (family Corvidae) related to the CROW and found in Europe, Asia, and the Americas. The blue jay (*Cyanocitta cristata*) of central and E North America has a grayish blue crest and upper parts, and bright blue wings with white and black markings. The Canada jay (*Perisoreus canadensis*), gray with a white throat and forehead and no crest, is found in northern coniferous forests and swamps.

Jay's Treaty, concluded in 1794 between the U.S. and Britain to settle difficulties arising mainly out of violations of the Treaty of PARIS of 1783 and to regulate commerce and navigation. The treaty, signed in England by John JAY and Lord GRENVILLE, provided for British evacuation of posts in the Old Northwest, unrestricted navigation of the Mississippi, and equal privileges for American and British vessels in Great Britain and the East Indies. It placed severe restrictions on U.S. trade in the West Indies and did not allow indemnity for Americans whose slaves were carried off by Britain's evacuating armies. Because the treaty failed to protect American seamen against impressment, or to secure recognition of the principles of international maritime law, it aroused indignation in the U.S., and appropriations to put it into effect were delayed until 1796.

jazz, American musical form, developed c.1890 from African-American work songs, SPIRITUALS, and other forms whose harmonic, melodic, and rhythmic elements were mainly African. It came to general notice in the 1920s, when whites adapted or imitated it. Jazz began in the South and spread north and west. The *blues* has remained a vital part in all periods. Blues generally employs a 12-bar construction and a "blue" SCALE thought to be African in origin. Vocal blues have earthy, direct lyrics. The tempo may vary, and the mood ranges from despair to cynicism to satire. Major early blues artists were Blind Lemon Jefferson, Ma Rainey, and Bessie SMITH. W.C. HANDY popularized blues. *Ragtime,* a syncopated, polyphonic genre (fl. 1890s–1910s), spread through sheet music and piano rolls (see POLYPHONY). Scott JOPLIN was its most famous exponent. *New Orleans* or *Dixieland* jazz developed from military music, blues, and the French tradition in New Orleans. Pioneer musicians like Buddy Bolden and Jelly Roll Morton performed at functions from funerals to dances. In World War I musicians went north up the Mississippi, seeking work. In Chicago, King Oliver, Louis ARMSTRONG, and others introduced jazz to a wider audience, and young whites like the cornetist Bix Beiderbecke were drawn to it. At the end of the 1920s a new phenomenon, *swing,* emerged. The small New Orleans band had played polyphony, but swing involved larger groups (14–18) featuring soloists with arranged backgrounds. The bands of Count Basie, Duke ELLINGTON, and Benny GOODMAN were especially notable. *Bop* (bebop), a 1940s revolt against the formulas of swing, was rhythmically complex and harmonic, rather than melodic, at base. Charlie PARKER and Dizzy GILLESPIE were the leaders. In the 1950s *progressive jazz,* with bop's harmonics but simpler melody and rhythm, flourished, chiefly on the West Coast, inspired largely by the swing giant Lester YOUNG. Stan Getz and Dave Brubeck were key figures. *Hard bop,* a second wave, was led by such musicians as Sonny Rollins and John COLTRANE. An exploratory avant-garde of the 1960s coexisted with the efforts of Miles DAVIS and others to bring ROCK MUSIC into jazz, and in the 1970s reached into the past to create a music with elements of all jazz styles, epitomized in the work of the Art Ensemble of Chicago. Wynton MARSALIS was the most prominent of several younger artists who sparked a jazz resurgence in the 1980s that was less avant-garde and more traditional. Almost all jazz styles remain current today.

Jeanneret, Charles Édouard: see LE CORBUSIER.

Jeffers, Robinson, 1887–1962, American poet; b. Pittsburgh. After 1914 he lived on the California coast. His virile, intense poetry includes *Roan Stallion* (1925) and *The Double Axe* (1948). He is also known for his adaptations of Greek tragedy, e.g., *Medea* (1947), *The Cretan Woman* (1954).

Jefferson, Thomas, 1743–1826, 3d president of the U.S. (1801–9); b. Goochland (now in Albemarle) co., Va. A member (1769–75) of the Virginia house of burgesses, he was a leader of the patriot faction. At the Second CONTINENTAL CONGRESS he drafted the DECLARATION OF INDEPENDENCE, a historic document that reflects his debt to John LOCKE and other philosophers. In 1779 he became governor of Virginia, guiding that state through the troubled last years of the AMERICAN REVOLUTION. A member (1783–84) of the Continental Congress, Jefferson drafted a plan for decimal coinage and drew up an ordinance for the Northwest Territory that formed the basis for the ORDINANCE OF 1787. In 1785 he became minister to France. Appointed secretary of state (1790–93) in Pres. WASHINGTON's cabinet, Jefferson defended agrarian interests against the Federalist policies of Alexander HAMILTON and led a group called the Republicans—antecedents of the present DEMOCRATIC PARTY. He served as vice president (1797–1801) and protested the passage of the ALIEN AND SEDITION ACTS by writing the Kentucky Resolutions (see KENTUCKY AND VIRGINIA RESOLUTIONS). The Republicans triumphed at the polls in 1800, but Aaron BURR, who had been slated to become vice president, tied Jefferson in the presidential vote. Jefferson was finally chosen president by the House of Representatives, largely on the advice of Hamilton, who considered Jefferson less dangerous than Burr. Jefferson was the first president inaugurated in Washington, a city he had helped to plan. He instituted a republican simplicity in the city and cut federal expenditures. He believed that the federal government should be concerned mainly with foreign affairs, leaving local matters to the states and local authorities. Usually strict in interpreting the Constitution, he pushed through the LOUISIANA PURCHASE of 1803, an action that it did not expressly authorize. He also planned the LEWIS AND CLARK EXPEDITION. During his second administration, difficulties arose from attacks on neutral U.S. shipping by the warring powers of Britain and France. With such measures as the EMBARGO ACT of 1807 he tried to use economic pressure to gain a solution, but this aroused strong opposition in the U.S. In retirement after 1809 at his beloved home, Monticello, Jefferson brought about the founding of the Univ. of Virginia and continued his lifelong interests in science, architecture, philosophy, and the arts.

Jefferson City, city (1990 pop. 35,481), state capital and seat of Cole co., central Mo., on the Missouri R., near the mouth of the Osage R.; inc. 1825. State government is the major employer; the city is also the processing center for an agricultural area. Printing and various manufactures are important. The state capital since 1826, its Renaissance-style capitol (1917) contains murals by Thomas Hart BENTON.

Jefferson Memorial, monument in Washington, D.C., honoring Thomas JEFFERSON. Dedicated in 1943, the domed white marble structure was designed by the American neoclassical architect John Russell Pope; it houses a 19-ft (5.8-m) statue of Jefferson by Rudulph Evans.

Jeffreys of Wem, George Jeffreys, 1st **Baron,** 1645?–1689, English judge under CHARLES II and JAMES II; noted for his cruelty. In the Bloody Assizes following the rebellion (1685) of the duke of

MONMOUTH, he caused nearly 200 persons to be hanged, some 800 transported, and many more imprisoned or whipped.

Jehannet: see CLOUET, JEAN.

Jehoshaphat [jēhŏsh'əfăt], **Josaphat,** or **Joshaphat,** king of Judah (c.873–849 B.C.), son and successor of King Asa. He was an ally of King AHAB of Israel and his successors and was the first king of Judah to make a treaty with the kingdom of Israel. The **Valley of Jehoshaphat,** mentioned in Joel as a place of judgment, has been identified by tradition with the northern extension of the vale of Kidron to the east of JERUSALEM.

Jehovah: see GOD.

Jehovah's Witnesses, international sect founded in the U.S. in the late 19th cent. by Charles Russell. They were called Russellites before 1931. Their doctrine centers on the imminent second coming of Jesus. Witnesses refuse to salute the flag, bear arms, or participate in government. All members are considered ministers, and believers engage in active proselytizing. In 1991 they reported a U.S. membership of 858,367.

Jekyll, Gertrude, 1843–1932, British artist, landscape gardener, and crafts artist. She was associated with William Robinson and Edwin LUTYENS in developing an informal style of garden. Her works include *Wood and Garden* (1899) and *Garden Ornament* (1918).

Jellicoe, John Rushworth Jellicoe, 1st **Earl,** 1859–1935, British admiral. As commander in chief of the Grand Fleet (1914–16) in WORLD WAR I, he was engaged in the inconclusive battle of Jutland (1916). He was later first sea lord (1916–17) and governor general of New Zealand (1920–24).

jellyfish, free-swimming stage (see POLYP AND MEDUSA) of invertebrate animals (COELENTERATES) of the classes Hydrozoa and Scyphozoa of the phylum Cnidaria. Many jellyfish are colored and are considered to be among the most beautiful of animals. They have bell- or umbrella-shaped bodies with a clear, jellylike material filling most of the space between the upper and lower surfaces. A mouth is located on the underside and tentacles dangle from the bell margin. Most catch their prey with stinging cells located in the tentacles and most are marine, living in ocean depths and along the coasts.

Jena [yā'nä], city (1989 est. pop. 108,000), Thuringia, SE Germany, on the Saale R. Its industries include pharmaceuticals and precision and optical instruments. Known since the 9th cent., the city gained international repute in the 18th and 19th cent., when SCHILLER, HEGEL, FICHTE, and SCHELLING taught at its university (est. 1557). GOETHE also lived there.

Jenghiz Khan or **Genghis Khan** [jĕng'gĭz kän], 1167?–1227, Mongol conqueror. After uniting the Mongol tribes, he conquered (1213–15) most of the Chin empire of N China. From 1218 to 1224 he subdued Turkistan, Transoxania, and Afghanistan and raided Persia and E Europe. A brilliant military leader, he ruled one of the greatest land empires of history from his capital at KARAKORUM. After his death his empire was divided among his sons and grandsons.

Jenkins, Roy (Harris), 1920–, British politician. A member of the House of Commons (1948–87), he was first elected as a Labour member and was minister of aviation (1964–65), home secretary (1965–67, 1974–76), and chancellor of the exchequer (1967–70) in Labour governments. He served (1977–81) as president of the Commission of the European Community. In 1982 he was elected to Parliament as a member of Britain's new SOCIAL DEMOCRATIC PARTY, which he had helped to found. In 1987 he became chancellor of Oxford Univ. and was created Baron Jenkins of Hillhead.

Jeremiah or **Jeremias,** book of the OLD TESTAMENT, 24th in the Authorized Version, 2d of the Major PROPHETS. It tells of the career of Jeremiah, a prophet who preached (c.628–586 B.C.) in Jerusalem. His message was a summons to moral reform, personal and social, backed by threats of doom. Jeremiah was allowed to stay in Jerusalem after its fall to Babylon (586 B.C.), and continued prophesying in Egypt. The prophecies in the book were arranged by his secretary Baruch, and are not in strict chronological order. They include prophecies against Gentile nations and well-known Messianic passages (in 14, 23, 30, 32).

Jericho, ancient city of Palestine, in the Jordan valley N of the Dead Sea, near modern Ariha, or Jericho, in the Israeli-occupied WEST BANK. According to the Bible, JOSHUA took Jericho from the Canaanites and destroyed it. It later fell to HEROD, the Muslims, and others. Excavations of the original site, begun early in the 20th cent., reveal the world's oldest known settlement, dating perhaps from c.8000 B.C. Nearby, a Hellenistic fortress and Herod's palace have been excavated.

Jeroboam I [jĕrəbō'əm], first king of the northern kingdom of Israel (c.922–901 B.C.). When SOLOMON's son, REHOBOAM, became king, Jeroboam led the secession of the ten tribes who formed the northern kingdom of Israel. He was notorious for fostering idolatry.

Jerome, Saint, c.347–420?, Christian scholar, Father of the Church, Doctor of the Church. Following a vision (375) in Antioch (Turkey), he renounced his pagan learning and fled to the desert, where he undertook scriptural studies. He was ordained (378) and, after serving as secretary to Pope Damasus I, began a new version of the BIBLE at the pope's request. From 386 he lived in Bethlehem, revising his Latin translations of the Bible and translating some portions from the Hebrew. All this became the basis for the Vulgate. He also wrote exegetical works, tracts, and biographies of Christian writers. Feast: Sept. 30.

Jersey: see CHANNEL ISLANDS.

Jersey City, city (1990 pop. 228,537), seat of Hudson co., NE N.J., a port on a peninsula formed by the Hudson and Hackensack rivers and Upper New York Bay, opposite lower Manhattan; settled before 1650; inc. 1836. It is a great center of shipping, commerce, and manufacturing. There are docks, oil refineries, railroad shops, warehouses, and many factories. Located on the site of a 17th-cent. Dutch trading post, it grew with the arrival (1840s) of the railroad. Liberty State Park, on the city's waterfront, is the site of a science museum and provides an excellent view of New York harbor.

Jerubbaal or **Jerubbesheth:** see GIDEON.

Jerusalem, city (1991 est. pop. 535,000, including East Jerusalem), capital and largest city of Israel, on a high ridge W of the Dead Sea and the Jordan R. A holy city for Jews, Christians, and Muslims, Jerusalem is an administrative, cultural, and tourist center. Manufactures include cut and polished diamonds, plastics, and clothing. The eastern part of Jerusalem is the Old City; the New City, to the south and southwest, has been largely developed since the 19th cent. and is the site of the Knesset, Israel's parliament. Archaeology indicates that Jerusalem was already settled in the 4th millennium B.C. DAVID captured it (c.1000 B.C.) from the Jebusites (Canaanites), and after SOLOMON built the Temple there (10th cent. B.C.), Jerusalem became the spiritual and political capital of the Hebrews. The city fell to many conquerors, e.g., Babylonia (586 B.C.) and Rome (63 B.C.), and it was the scene of JESUS' last ministry. The Roman emperor TITUS destroyed the rebuilt (Second) Temple (A.D. 70) to punish rebellious Jews. The Muslims, who believe that MUHAMMAD ascended to heaven from the city, treated it well after they captured it in 637. It was conquered by the Crusaders in 1099 and was recaptured (1187) by the Muslims under SALADIN. Jerusalem was the capital (1922–48) of the British mandate of PALESTINE. During the ARAB-ISRAELI WARS, the city was divided (1949–67); the Old City became part of Jordan and the New City became the capital of Israel. In 1967 Israel captured the Old City and formally annexed it. Israel reaffirmed its annexation of the Old City in 1980, an action not accepted by many nations. The Old City contains many holy places of Christianity, e.g., the Church of the Holy Sepulcher; of Islam, e.g., the Dome of the Rock (688–91); and of Judaism, e.g., the Western (or Wailing) Wall (part of the Second Temple compound).

Jerusalem, Latin kingdom of, feudal state founded by GODFREY OF BOUILLON after the conquest of Jerusalem in the First CRUSADE (1099). Antioch, Edessa, and Tripoli were the kingdom's great fiefs. Jerusalem comprised the counties of Jaffa and Ashqelon, the lordships of Krak, Montreal, and Sidon, and the principality of Galilee. The nominally elective kingship and the law, as in the Assizes of Jerusalem, were ideally feudal. In practice, the great feudal lords rarely supported the king in his wars. The rise of the great military orders, e.g., KNIGHTS TEMPLARS, further weakened royal power. Edessa fell (1144), then Jerusalem (1187), and lastly Akko (1291). Godfrey's brother BALDWIN I was Jerusalem's first king, followed by BALDWIN II, the Angevin kings Fulk, BALDWIN III, AMALRIC I, and BALDWIN IV, and, finally, BALDWIN V (d. 1186). Later kingship was nominal only.

Jerusalem artichoke, perennial (*Helianthus tuberosus*) of the COMPOSITE family. A species of SUNFLOWER, it is the only root plant of economic importance to have originated in North America. Its potato-like tubers, most favored as a food in Europe and China, contain inulin, a valuable source of FRUCTOSE for diabetics. The tubers are also used to produce ALCOHOL.

Jerusalem cherry: see NIGHTSHADE.

jessamine: see JASMINE.

Jesuit, a member of the Society of Jesus (see JESUS, SOCIETY OF), a Roman Catholic religious order of priests and brothers. Jesuits are noted as educators, theologians, and missionaries.

Jesus or **Jesus Christ,** 1st-cent. Jewish teacher and prophet; in Christian belief, the Son of God, the second person of the TRINITY. The name *Jesus* is Greek for the Hebrew *Joshua,* a name meaning "Savior"; Christ is the Greek word for the Hebrew *Messiah,* meaning "Anointed." Traditional CHRISTIANITY says Jesus was God made man, wholly divine, wholly human; he was born to MARY, a virgin, and died to atone for humanity's sins; his resurrection from the dead provides man's hope for salvation. The principal sources for his life are the four Gospels of MATTHEW, MARK, LUKE, and JOHN. There are also several brief references to Jesus in non-Christian sources, e.g., TACITUS. According to the Gospels, Jesus was born a Jew in Bethlehem to Mary, wife of Joseph, a carpenter of Nazareth. His date of birth is now reckoned have been between 8 B.C. and 4 B.C. When he was about 30, Jesus began a public ministry as a preacher, teacher, and healer. His activity was centered around Galilee, and he gathered a small band of disciples. Jesus preached the coming of the Kingdom of God, often in PARABLES, and called on his hearers to repent. The Gospels also describe miracles he performed. His uncompromising moral demands on his hearers, his repeated attacks on the Pharisees (see JEWS) and scribes, and his sympathy for social outcasts and the oppressed kindled popular enthusiasm. In the third year of his mission, while in Jerusalem for Passover, he was betrayed to the authorities by one of his companions, JUDAS ISCARIOT. After sharing the LAST SUPPER (a Passover seder) with his disciples, he was arrested. The Gospels indicate that he was interrogated by Jewish authorities and handed over to the Romans, who crucified him, perhaps as an agitator. On the third day, his tomb was found empty, and an angel (or a man) announced that he had risen from the dead. According to the Gospels, Jesus later appeared to several of his disciples, and after 40 days he ascended into heaven. In Islam, Jesus is highly regarded as a prophet who restated divine religion, and Hindus acknowledge him as an avatar.

Jesus, Society of, religious order of the Roman Catholic Church founded (1534–39) by St. IGNATIUS OF LOYOLA. Its members, called Jesuits, have a highly disciplined structure and are especially devoted to the pope. They were a major force in the Counter Reformation (see REFORMATION, CATHOLIC) and were leaders in European education. Their missionary work in China, Paraguay, and Canada was remarkable. In 1773, under pressure from the Bourbon monarchies, Pope CLEMENT XIV suppressed the order, but it was restored in 1814. Jesuits have a tradition of learning and science, e.g., St. Robert Bellarmine and TEILHARD DE CHARDIN.

jet propulsion, propulsion of a body, such as an airplane, by a force developed in reaction to the ejection of a high-speed jet of gas. The jet-driven turbine, or turbojet, consists of four basic parts: compressor, combustion chambers, TURBINE, and propelling nozzles. In the combustion chambers the combustion of a fuel, mixed with air coming from the compressor, generates expanding gases, which spin the rotor of the turbine. The axis of the turbine is connected by a shaft directly to the axis of the compressor; thus the turbine drives the compressor. The gas, after passing through the turbine, is exhausted into the atmosphere through a nozzle at high speed. In the fanjet, or turbofan, the turbine powers a set of vanes that force air rearward for both combustion and extra thrust. In the propeller-driven turbine, or turboprop, the turbine not only drives the compressor, but also turns an outside propeller. The ramjet engine relies on its own forward motion to compress the air that enters it. The similar scramjet, designed for hypersonic speeds, uses hydrogen for fuel and could, in theory, propel a craft into orbit. Jet propulsion is also produced by a ROCKET engine.

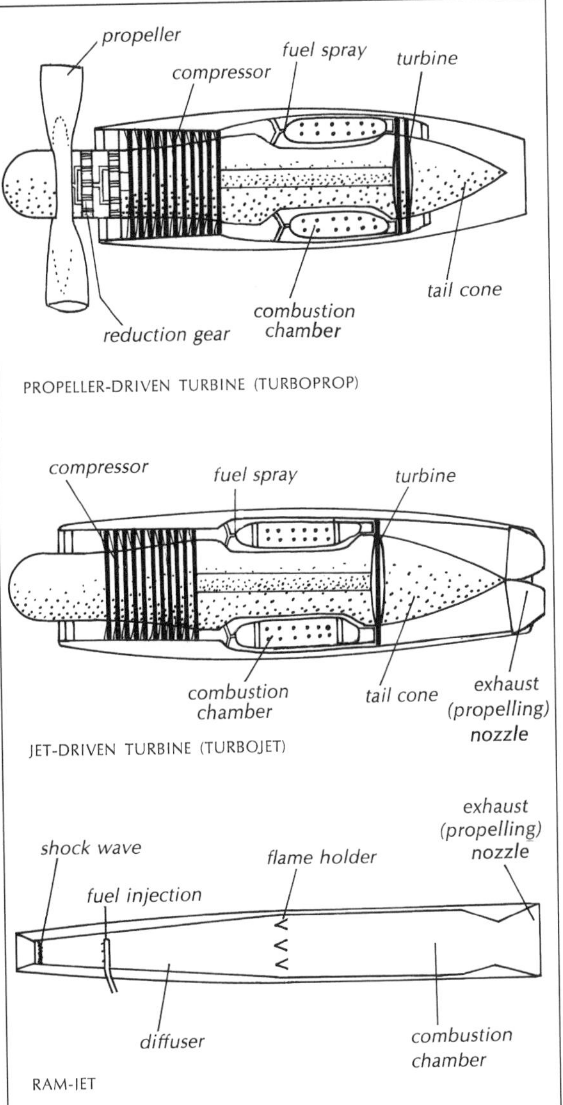

Jet propulsion engines

jet stream, narrow, swift air currents at altitudes of 7 to 8 mi (11.3 to 12.9 km). The two major jet streams, one in each hemisphere, circle the globe (although discontinuous at some points), varying between 30° and 40° in latitude. They flow in easterly directions in wavelike patterns, with speeds averaging 35 mph (56 km/hr) in summer and 75 mph (120 km/hr) in winter, although speeds as high as 200 mph (320 km/hr) have been recorded. Eastbound aircraft fly with the jet stream (a tail wind) to gain speed and save fuel; westbound aircraft avoid the jet stream (a head wind).

jewelweed, common name for the Balsaminaceae, a family of widely cultivated annual and perennial herbs. The principal genus is *Impatiens,* found in tropical and north temperate regions and so named because its seed capsules burst when touched; certain species are also commonly called touch-me-not. Some species are grown as ornamentals, e.g., the common impatiens (*I. wallerana,* of African origin), various New Guinea species hybrids, and the garden balsam (*I. balsamina*).

Jewett, Sarah Orne, 1849–1909, American author; b. S. Berwick, Me. She is noted for her perceptive, gently humorous studies of small-town New England life. The most memorable of her short-story collections is *The Country of the Pointed Firs* (1896); her best-known novel is *A Country Doctor* (1884).

Jewish holidays. There are seven major holidays in the Jewish calendar. **Rosh Hashanah,** the New Year, falls on the 1st and 2d days of the Hebrew month Tishri (Sept.–Oct.). It is spent in solemn prayer, and a *shofar,* or ram's horn, is blown in the synagogue. Rosh Hashanah begins the Ten Days of Penitence, which end with **Yom Kippur,** on the 10th of Tishri. This is the Day of Atonement, a day of fasting and praying for forgiveness for the past year's sins. **Sukkoth,** or the Feast of Tabernacles, is the fall harvest festival; it begins on the 15th of Tishri and lasts eight days (seven in Israel). Meals are eaten in a *sukkah,* a booth with a roof of thatch, to recall the shelters of the Jews when they wandered in the wilderness. The day after Sukkoth is Simhath Torah [Heb., = rejoicing of the law], celebrating the annual completion of the reading of the TORAH. **Hanukkah,** or **Chanukah,** recalls the victory of Judas Maccabeus (see MACCABEES) and the rededication of the Temple in Jerusalem. It lasts for eight days, beginning on the 25th of Kislev (Dec.). The Festival of Lights, it is marked by the lighting of candles in a *menorah,* an eight-branched candlestick, to commemorate the miracle of a small vial of oil that burned for eight days. **Purim,** the Feast of Lots, on the 14th of Adar (Feb.–Mar.), celebrates the deliverance of the Persian Jews from a general massacre (according to the Book of ESTHER, which is read in the synagogue on this holiday). The day is one of merrymaking, feasting, and wearing costumes. **Passover,** or **Pesach,** from the 14th to the 22d of Nisan (14th to 21st of Nisan in Israel; Mar.–Apr.), possibly a spring festival originally, recalls the exodus of the Jews, led by MOSES, from Egypt. Throughout the holiday, *matzah* (unleavened bread) is eaten. At the *seder,* a special Passover meal, the *Haggadah,* telling the story of the deliverance from Egypt, is read. **Shavuot,** on the 6th and 7th of Sivan (the 6th of Sivan in Israel; May–June), the Feast of Weeks, is an agricultural festival. The Book of RUTH, which tells of a grain harvest, is read in the synagogue. Traditionally, Shavuot also commemorates the receiving of the TEN COMMANDMENTS.

Jews, accepted designation of believers in JUDAISM; originally represented in the Bible as the descendants of Judah and the dominant group in Judea. In the Bible, Jewish history begins with the patriarchs ABRAHAM, ISAAC, and JACOB in CANAAN. Jewish agricultural tribes lived in Egypt until MOSES led them away from the persecutions of Ramses II and eventually back to Canaan. DAVID, an early Jewish king from the tribe of Judah, defeated the enemies of the Jews, expanded his territory, and brought peace and prosperity to his people. His son SOLOMON built the first Temple and was famous for his wealth and wisdom. After Solomon's death the Jewish kingdom split into two smaller kingdoms, ISRAEL and JUDAH. In 722 B.C. the Assyrians conquered Israel, sending most Israelites into exile (see ISRAEL, TRIBES OF). Judah also was conquered. Under Babylonian rule the Temple was destroyed (586 B.C.), but it was rebuilt by 516 B.C. The MACCABEES (2d and 1st cent. B.C.) restored Jewish independence for a time, but Roman domination followed (see ROME), and Jerusalem was destroyed (A.D. 70). After the fall of the Roman Empire, Jews migrated to Western Europe. From the 9th to 12th cent. their conditions improved, particularly in Spain, but the period from the Crusades to the 18th cent. was one of intermittent persecution in Europe, where the Jews served as a convenient scapegoat in troubled times (see ANTI-SEMITISM; INQUISITION). The rise of capitalism improved their economic condition, and Jews gained political emancipation in the 17th cent. in Holland and later in other countries. With the coming to power of the NAZIS in Germany, in 1933, persecution of the Jews became increasingly widespread and violent (see HOLOCAUST). The establishment of Israel in PALESTINE in 1948 created the Jewish state envisioned by ZIONISM but also led to war with Palestinian Arabs and neighboring Arab countries opposed to the creation of Israel (see ARAB-ISRAELI WARS). The population of Jews worldwide before WORLD WAR II was 16 million; 6 million died in the Holocaust. In 1990 the world Jewish population was estimated at 17.8 million: U.S., 6 million; Israel, 3.5 million; Europe and the former USSR, 3.5 million; and the remainder in Africa and other parts of the Americas and Asia. See also FALASHAS; HASIDIM; SEPHARDIM.

Jezebel: see AHAB.

Jiang Qing or **Chiang Ch'ing** [both: jēäng chĭng], 1913–91, Chinese Communist leader, wife of MAO ZEDONG. She became prominent as a radical during the CULTURAL REVOLUTION (1966–69) and was appointed (1969) to the politburo. After Mao's death, she was one of the GANG OF FOUR arrested (1976) for planning a coup. In 1981 she was convicted and received a death sentence, which was suspended for two years and then commuted to life imprisonment in 1983. After her death the government reported that she had been released from prison for medical reasons in 1984.

Jiang Zemin, 1926–, Chinese government official, general secretary of the Chinese Communist party (1989–) and president of China (1993–). Trained as an engineer, Jiang held positions in industry, becoming electronics industry minister in 1983. In 1985 he became mayor of Shanghai and deputy secretary of the Shanghai Municipal party (secretary after 1988). A member of the Chinese politburo since 1987, he was named to succeed ZHAO ZIYANG as Communist party general secretary after the army crushed (1989) pro-democracy demonstrations in Beijing and other cities. A protégé of DENG XIAOPING (he replaced Deng as head of the powerful government and party military commissions in 1989–90), Jiang is regarded as a pragmatist. He was named president of China in 1993.

Jidda or **Jedda,** city (1988 est. pop. 1,500,000), W Saudi Arabia, on the Red Sea. It is the port of MECCA and annually receives a huge influx of pilgrims; the oil industry is economically important. Present-day Jidda is not more than three centuries old, but Old Jidda, c.12 mi (19 km) south of the modern city, was founded c.646 by the caliph Uthman. Jidda was ruled by the Turks until 1916 and was conquered by IBN SAUD in 1925.

Jiménez, Juan Ramón [hēmā'nāth], 1881–1958, Spanish poet. Early identified with MODERNISMO, as in his *Elejías* (1908) and the distinctive prose poems of *Platero and I* (1914–17), he later adopted a simpler, sparer style suffused with mysticism, as in *Eternidades* (1918) and *Total Season* (1946). Jiménez left Spain during the civil war to live first in the U.S., then in Puerto Rico. He was awarded the 1956 Nobel Prize in literature.

Jiménez de Quesada, Gonzalo [hēmā'nĕth dā kāsä'thä] c.1499–1579, Spanish CONQUISTADOR in Colombia. Commissioned to explore the Magdalena R. in search of EL DORADO, he set out in 1536. He defeated the Chibcha and founded (1538) BOGOTÁ as the capital of New Granada (now COLOMBIA). In 1550 he was made marshal of New Granada and councillor of Bogotá for life. His 1569 expedition in search of El Dorado was disastrous.

Jinan or **Tsinan** [both: jē-nän], city (1990 est. pop. 2,320,000), capital of Shandong prov., E China, 3 mi (4.8 km) S of the HUANG HE. Over 100 natural springs are located in Jinan, which is also a regional manufacturing center producing metals, trucks, machinery, chemicals, textiles, and paper.

Jinnah, Muhammad Ali, 1876–1948, founder of PAKISTAN. He at first supported the INDIAN NATIONAL CONGRESS and its advocacy of Hindu-Muslim unity, but after 1934 he led the MUSLIM LEAGUE in its agitation for a separate Muslim nation. He gained power during World War II by supporting British war efforts. In the postwar independence negotiations he was successful in his insistence on the creation of Pakistan (1947) as the homeland for India's Muslims.

jinni [jĭnē'], plural **jinn,** in Arabic and Islamic folklore, spirit or demon with supernatural powers, especially of changing size and shape. Both good and evil, jinn are popular figures in Middle Eastern literature, particularly in the *Thousand and One Nights. Genie* is the English form.

Jívaro, indigenous people of Ecuador (see SOUTH AMERICA, INDIGENOUS PEOPLES OF). They engage in farming, hunting, fishing, and weaving. Each patrilineal family group lives in a large, isolated communal house. The Jívaro, who were once famous for the practice of ritual head shrinking, long resisted conquest.

Joanna (the Mad), 1479–1555, Spanish queen of CASTILE and LEÓN (1504–55). Because of her insanity the kingdoms were ruled by two regents, her husband, PHILIP I (1504–6), and her father, FERDINAND V (1506–16). Her son Charles (later Holy Roman Emperor CHARLES V) was proclaimed joint ruler of Castile in 1516, and Joanna was confined to a castle for life.

Joan of Arc, 1412?–31, French saint and national heroine, called the Maid of Orléans. A farm girl, she began at a young age to hear the "voices" of St. Michael, St. Catherine, and St. Margaret. When she was about 16, the voices exhorted her to bear aid to the DAUPHIN, later CHARLES VII of France, then kept from the throne by the English in the HUNDRED YEARS WAR. Joan journeyed in male attire to meet the dauphin and conquered his skepticism as to her divine mission. She was furnished with troops, but her leadership provided spirit and morale more than military prowess. In May 1429 she raised the siege of Orléans, and in June she defeated the English at Patay. After considerable persuasion the dauphin agreed to be crowned at Rheims, and Joan was at the pinnacle of her fortunes. In Sept. 1429 she unsuccessfully besieged Paris. The following spring she went to relieve Compiègne but was captured by the Burgundians and sold to the English, who were eager for her death. To escape responsibility, the English turned her over to the ecclesiastical court at Rouen, where she was tried for heresy and witchcraft by French clerics who supported the English. Probably her most serious crime was the claim of direct inspiration from God; in the eyes of the court this refusal to accept the church hierarchy constituted heresy. Only at the end of the lengthy trial did she recant. She was condemned to life imprisonment, but shortly afterward she retracted her abjuration. She was then turned over to the secular court as a relapsed heretic and was burned at the stake (May 30, 1431) in Rouen. The proceedings of the original trial were annulled in 1456. Joan was canonized in 1920. Her career lent itself to numerous legends, and she has been represented in much art and literature. Feast: May 30.

Job [jōb], book of the OLD TESTAMENT, 18th in the Authorized Version. Based on a folktale, it may have been written between 600 and 400 B.C. It discusses, in dialogue or dramatic form, the problem of good and evil in the world. In the prologue (1–2), Satan obtains God's permission to test the "upright man" Job; accordingly, all Job has is destroyed, and he is physically afflicted. The main part of the book (3–31) consists of speeches by Job and three friends who come to "comfort" him. A fourth speaker, Elihu (32–37), who accuses Job of arrogant pride, is followed by God himself (38–42), who rebukes Job and his friends. Job is restored to happiness. The ethical problem of the book is not explicitly resolved; rather, the author intended to criticize a philosophy that associated sin with the sufferer.

Jobs, Steven Paul, 1955–, American businessman; b. San Francisco. Working with Stephen Wozniak, he created the company that produced the Apple computer in 1976. He resigned (1985) and founded the NeXT Computer Company.

Jocasta: see OEDIPUS.

Joel, book of the OLD TESTAMENT, 29th in the Authorized Version, 2d of the Minor PROPHETS. Dated variously from the 9th to the 3d cent. B.C., it predicts a plague of locusts, followed by blessings, this being a Messianic prophecy.

Joffre, Joseph Jacques Césaire [zhô'frə], 1852–1931, marshal of France. French commander in chief from 1911, he deserves partial credit for the victory of the Marne (1914) in WORLD WAR I. After the Germans nearly captured Verdun (1916), Joffre was replaced by Robert Georges Nivelle.

Joffrey, Robert: see ROBERT JOFFREY BALLET.

Johannesburg, largest city (1985 est. pop. 1,609,000) of South Africa, TRANSVAAL prov., on the southern slopes of the WITWATERSRAND. The sprawling city, situated in the nation's major gold-mining region, is a manufacturing and commercial center and a transportation hub. Founded (1886) as a gold-mining settlement, it grew rapidly and had c.100,000 people by 1900.

John, Saint, one of the Twelve APOSTLES, traditional author of the fourth GOSPEL, three EPISTLES, and the REVELATION. He and St. James the Greater were sons of Zebedee; Jesus called them Boanerges, or Sons of Thunder. With PETER, they were closest to Jesus, witnessed the Transfiguration, and were at Gethsemane. Jesus, dying, committed the Virgin Mary to John's care. He may be the same as St. John of Ephesus (d. A.D. c.100). He is variously known as St. John the Evangelist, St. John the Divine, and the Beloved Disciple.

John VIII, d. 882, pope (872–82), a Roman. He strenuously opposed St. Ignatius, patriarch of Constantinople, and when Ignatius died, he recognized PHOTIUS as patriarch, momentarily solving the differences between East and West. John crowned the emperors CHARLES II (the Bald; 875) and CHARLES III (the Fat; 881). He was murdered by relatives.

John XII, c.937–964, pope (955–64), a Roman named Octavian. Elected pope before age 20, John led a notoriously immoral life. He was allied with OTTO I and crowned him (962) the first German emperor, but later sided with Berengar II of Italy. Otto conquered Rome, deposed John, and elected Leo VIII as pope. John retook Rome (964) but was soon murdered.

John XXIII, antipope (1410–15): see COSSA, BALDASSARRE.

John XXIII, 1881–1963, pope (1958–63), an Italian named Angelo Giuseppe Roncalli. He was a papal diplomat in the Balkans and Middle East (1925–44), papal nuncio to France (1944–53), and in 1953 was named cardinal and patriarch of Venice. As pope he showed great concern for church reform, the promotion of peace, world social welfare (expressed in his encyclical *Mater et Magistra*), and for dialogue with other faiths. The convening (1962) of the Second VATICAN COUNCIL was the high point of his reign. His heartiness, his overflowing love of humanity, and his freshness of approach to ecclesiastical affairs made John one of the best-loved popes of modern times.

John, Byzantine emperors. **John I** (Tzimisces), c.925–76 (r.969–76), began his reign by murdering NICEPHORUS II. He extended Byzantine power against the Russians and Arabs. **John II** (Comnenus), 1088–1143 (r.1118–43), succeeded his father, ALEXIUS I. He failed to cancel Venetian trade privileges but won military victories. **John III** (Ducas Vatatzes), d. 1254 (r.1222–54), succeeded his father-in-law, Theodore I. During his reign the empire thrived, and he almost reunited the Byzantine territories. **John IV** (Lascaris), b. c.1250, d. after 1273, succeeded his father, Theodore II, under a regent (1258–61). Michael Palaeologus became co-ruler (1259), had the boy emperor blinded and imprisoned (1261), and succeeded as MICHAEL VIII. **John V** (Palaeologus), 1332–91 (r.1341–76, 1379–91), had his throne usurped during his minority by **John VI** and later by his son Andronicus IV. He lost territory to the Ottoman Turks and recognized their suzerainty (1371). **John VI** (Cantacuzene), c.1292–1383 (r.1341–54), usurped the throne of John V, calling to the Ottoman Turks for aid. He later abdicated. **John VII** (Palaeologus), c.1370–1408, grandson of John V, briefly usurped (1390) the throne of John V with Turkish help and later became co-ruler (1394–1403) with his uncle MANUEL II. **John VIII** (Palaeologus), 1390–1448 (r.1425–48), son of Manuel II, ruled an empire reduced to the city of Constantinople. He sought in vain to secure Western aid against the Turks by agreeing at the Council of Florence (1439) to a union of the Eastern and Western churches. His brother and successor, CONSTANTINE XI, was the last Byzantine emperor.

John, 1167–1216, king of England (1199–1216); youngest son of HENRY II. After his brother RICHARD I left on the Third CRUSADE, John conspired unsuccessfully with PHILIP II of France to supplant Richard as king. On Richard's death, John ascended the throne to the exclusion of his nephew ARTHUR I of Brittany, who, with the aid of Philip II, began a revolt in France. Although Arthur was captured (1202), John lost many of his French possessions to Philip. John's refusal to accept a new archbishop of Canterbury led to his excommunication (1209). To regain papal favor, he surrendered (1213) his kingdom to Pope INNOCENT III, and received it back as a papal fief. In England his abuse of feudal custom in raising money aroused intense opposition from the barons. They rebelled in 1215 and compelled John to set his seal to the MAGNA CARTA. He was succeeded by his son HENRY III.

John, kings of France. **John I** (the Posthumous), 1316, was the posthumous son of LOUIS X and lived only five days. He was succeeded by his uncle PHILIP V. **John II** (the Good), 1319–64 (r.1350–64), was the son of PHILIP VI. His reign was troubled by the HUNDRED YEARS WAR with England and by his quarrels with CHARLES II of Navarre. Captured (1356) by the English at Poitiers, John was released (1360) by the Treaty of Brétigny for a ransom and hostages. In 1364 one of the hostages escaped, and John, to save his honor, returned to England, where he died. His son CHARLES V succeeded him.

John, kings of Hungary. **John I** (John Zápolya), 1487–1540 (r.1526–40), voivode [governor] of Transylvania (1511–26), was the son of Stephen ZÁPOLYA. He succeeded King Louis II, who was killed at the battle of Mohács (1526). The succession was challenged by Ferdinand of Austria (later Holy Roman Emperor FERDINAND I), but John prevailed and was confirmed as king by the Turkish sultan, who exercised real power. His son and successor, **John II** (John Sigismund Zápolya), 1540–71 (r.1540–71), was crowned as an infant. Sultan SULAYMAN I invaded (1541) Hungary and made John prince of TRANSYLVANIA under Turkish suzerainty. Deposed (1551) by Austrian interests, John was restored (1556) by Turkish pressure. During his reign Transylvania adopted (1564) Calvinism as the state religion.

John, kings of POLAND. **John II** (John Casimir), 1609–72 (r.1648–68), succeeded his brother, LADISLAUS IV. During John's reign, known as the Deluge, Poland lost the E Ukraine to Russia, Livonia to Sweden, and East Prussia to Brandenburg. Wars against Cossacks, Turks, Tatars, Russia, Transylvania, and Sweden occupied much of his time. He abdicated in 1668 and retired to a monastery. **John III** (John Sobieski), 1624–96 (r.1674–96), was the champion of Christian Europe against the Turks. In 1683 he relieved the Turkish siege of Vienna, and in 1684 he formed a Holy League with the pope, the Holy Roman emperor, and Venice. He failed to wrest Moldavia and Walachia from Turkey. He was succeeded as king by the elector of Saxony, whose accession as AUGUSTUS II marked the virtual end of Poland's independence.

John, kings of PORTUGAL. **John I** (the Great), 1357?–1433 (r.1385–1433), illegitimate son of PETER I and half-brother of FERDINAND I, led a popular revolt in 1384 against the regency established in the name of Ferdinand's daughter Beatrice and withstood a Castilian siege of Lisbon. Elected king the next year, he defeated the Castilians and assured Portugal's independence. His reign was one of the most glorious in Portuguese history. **John II** (the Perfect), 1455–95 (r.1481–95), was an astute politician and a patron of Renaissance culture. He supported Portuguese exploration and in 1494 agreed to set bounds for Portuguese and Spanish colonization. **John III** (the Fortunate), 1502–57 (r.1521–57), ruled at the height of the Portuguese empire, when its colonization of BRAZIL began and its Asian territories were extended. But the decline of agriculture and population portended Portugal's stagnation following his reign. **John IV,** 1604–56 (r.1640–56), became king of independent Portugal upon the revolt from Spain (1640). He consolidated his position against Spain by concluding alliances with France and other nations. **John V** (the Magnanimous), 1689–1750 (r.1706–50), maintained Portugal's alliance with England and kept the peace. Gold from Brazil permitted him to become a great patron of arts and letters and he beautified Lisbon. Wealth also made him independent of the CORTES, and he ruled with increasing absolutism. **John VI,** 1769–1826 (r.1816–26), was regent for his mother, Maria I, who was insane. He lost a war to France (1801) and eventually fled (1807) to Brazil. He returned (1821) after a revolution and the proclamation of a liberal constitution, but he did everything he could to modify it. In 1825 he recognized Brazil's independence.

John, Elton (Hercules), 1947–, English popular singer, pianist, and composer; b. Reginald Kenneth Dwight. By the mid-1970s he had become famous by presenting his own and other composers' songs in spectacularly staged productions. His songs include "Benny and the Jets" and "Rocket Man."

John, three epistles of the NEW TESTAMENT, 23d, 24th, and 25th books in the usual order, ascribed to St. JOHN, the disciple. First John was clearly written by the author of the GOSPEL. Second and Third John are generally agreed to be by the same person. First John is a homily on the blending of mystical and practical religion. Second John, the Bible's shortest (13 verses) book, warns against false teachers who deny JESUS' historicity. Third John protests the failure of a church leader to receive teaching missionaries.

John, Gospel according to Saint, fourth book of the NEW TESTAMENT, clearly set off from the other three Synoptic GOSPELS, although John may have used both MARK and LUKE as sources. The evangelist seems to have two aims—to show that JESUS is the vital force in the world, now and forever, and that he lived on earth to reveal himself in the flesh. In a philosophical prologue, Jesus is identified with the Word (Logos). The book recounts selected incidents from Jesus' ministry and (13–21) the Passion and RESURRECTION. The influence on CHRISTIANITY of the Gospel of John, particularly with reference to its enunciation of Jesus' position in the TRINITY, has been enormous.

John Birch Society, right-wing, anti-Communist organization in the U.S. It was founded (1958) by Robert Welch. Among its objectives are the repeal of social security legislation and of the graduated income tax, and the impeachment of certain government officials.

John Bull: see ARBUTHNOT, JOHN.

John Chrysostom, Saint [krĭs'əstəm], c.347–407, Doctor of the Church, greatest of the Greek Fathers. Made (398) patriarch of CONSTANTINOPLE, he came to be admired for his eloquence, ascetic life, and charity. After attempting church reform and denouncing the ways of the imperial court, John was illegally deposed (403) by the Empress Eudoxia and Bishop Theophilus. Recalled briefly, he was again sent into exile, where he died. His writings, notable for their purity of Greek style, greatly influenced Christian thought. Feasts: Nov. 13 in the East; Sept. 13 in the West.

John Damascene, Saint: see JOHN OF DAMASCUS, SAINT.

John Henry, legendary African-American famous for his strength, celebrated in ballads and tales. In one version of the story he outworks a steam drill but dies from the strain. The legend may have some historical basis.

John Maurice of Nassau, 1604–79, Dutch general and colonial administrator; grandnephew of WILLIAM THE SILENT. As governor-general of BRAZIL (1636–43) for the DUTCH WEST INDIA COMPANY he took NE Brazil from Portugal; rebuilt RECIFE; and, to ensure the supply of slave labor, seized Portuguese strongholds on the Guinea coast. He later held commands in the THIRTY YEARS WAR and the DUTCH WARS.

Johnny Appleseed: see CHAPMAN, JOHN.

John of Austria, 1545–78, Spanish admiral and general, illegitimate son of Holy Roman Emperor CHARLES V. In 1571 he won the famous naval victory of LEPANTO over the Turks. Appointed governor-general of the NETHERLANDS (1576–78), he tried to stamp out rebellion.

John of Austria, 1629–79, Spanish general, illegitimate son of Philip IV. He was viceroy of Sicily (1648–51) and fought rebels (1656–58) in the Spanish NETHERLANDS, where he lost the battle of the Dunes (1658). His campaign (1661–64) to reconquer Portugal also failed. In 1677 he overthrew the Spanish regency of the queen-mother Mariana but ruled only briefly.

John of Damascus, Saint, or **Saint John Damascene,** c.675–c.749, Syrian theologian, Father of the Church, Doctor of the Church. He wrote against ICONOCLASM and defended orthodoxy. *The Fountain of Wisdom* is his theological masterpiece. Feast: Dec. 4.

John of Gaunt, 1340–99, duke of Lancaster, fourth son of EDWARD III of England. He acquired the Lancaster holdings (see LANCASTER, HOUSE OF) through marriage and became one of the most influential nobles in England. He served under his brother EDWARD THE BLACK PRINCE in the HUNDRED YEARS WAR and by his second marriage (1371) gained a claim on the throne of Castile. For a short time John, in effect, ruled England for his aging father; he remained powerful under his nephew RICHARD II. From 1386 to 1388 he fought in vain to make good his Castilian claims. Returning (1389) to England, John helped to restore peace between Richard II and the barons. In 1396 he married Catherine Swynford; they were ancestors of the TUDORS. John was the patron of CHAUCER. His eldest son was HENRY IV.

John of Lancaster, duke of Bedford: see BEDFORD, JOHN OF LANCASTER, DUKE OF.

John of Leiden, c.1509–1536, Dutch Anabaptist leader. In 1534, following a revolt in Münster by ANABAPTISTS, he set up a theocracy and led, as "king," a communistic and polygamous state until expelled (1535) by the prince bishop. He and the other leaders were tortured and executed.

John of Luxemburg, 1296–1346, king of Bohemia (1310–46), son of Holy Roman Emperor HENRY VII. He was elected king after the death of his father-in-law, Wenceslaus II. Although blind, he fought on the French side at Crécy in the HUNDRED YEARS WAR, where he was killed.

John of the Cross, Saint, 1542–91, Spanish mystic and poet, Doctor of the Church. He was a founder of the Discalced CARMELITES and a friend of St. THERESA of Ávila. His reforming zeal antagonized the hierarchy, and he was imprisoned in 1577. In his cell he wrote *Spiritual Canticle* and began *Songs of the Soul,* which are among the finest creations of Spanish literature. After escaping (1578), he went to Andalusia, where he wrote masterly prose treatises on mystical theology, notably *The Dark Night of the Soul* and *The Ascent of Mount Carmel.* Feast: Dec. 14.

John Paul II, 1920–, pope (1978–), a Pole named Karol Wojtyła. Archbishop of Kraków, he was elected pope in Oct. 1978. He was the first non-Italian pope in 450 years and the first Polish pope. Conservative on doctrine, John Paul traveled widely early in his reign, e.g., to Poland and the U.S. in 1979. Following a trip to E Asia (1981), he was shot at the Vatican on May 13, 1981, by a Turkish terrorist. John Paul has continued to travel and has worked for ecumenism, e.g., his 1982 trip to Britain, where he held an ecumenical service in Canterbury Cathedral. He has also been an outspoken commentator on world events, opposing the imposition (1981) of martial law in Poland and criticizing the inadequacies and injustices of both capitalism and communism in two encyclicals (1981, 1991). His predecessor, **John Paul I,** 1912–78, pope (1978), an Italian named Albino Luciani who had been patriarch of Venice, was elected pope in Aug. 1978 and reigned for only 34 days before his death.

Johns, Jasper, 1930–, American artist; b. Augusta, Ga. Influenced by Marcel DUCHAMP, Johns sought to transform common objects into art by placing them in an art context. His paintings of flags and targets (1954–59) heralded POP ART. His later works, such as *Seasons* (1987), have become increasingly self-referential, using recurrent motifs as symbols to engage the viewer.

Jasper Johns

Johns Hopkins University, The, mainly at Baltimore, Md.; incorporated (with Johns Hopkins Hospital) 1867; opened 1876. Patterned after a European university, it emphasized graduate research over collegiate instruction, becoming a model for programs at other institutions. The hospital became the nucleus of Johns Hopkins's famous medical school (est. 1893). It has a noted school of advanced international studies (Washington, D.C.).

Johnson, Andrew, 1808–75, 17th president of the U.S. (1865–69); b. Raleigh, N.C. A self-educated tailor, he rose in Tennessee politics to become congressman (1843–53), governor (1853–57), and U.S. senator (1857–62). In Washington, Johnson voted with other Southern legislators on questions of slavery, but after Tennessee seceded (June 1861) he remained in the Senate and vigorously supported Pres. LINCOLN, who appointed him (1862) military governor of Tennessee. As a Southerner and a war Democrat, he was an ideal choice as a running mate to Lincoln on the successful Union ticket in 1864, and he succeeded to the presidency after Lincoln's assassination. As president he was denounced by the radical Republicans for his RECONSTRUCTION program, and in 1866 his political power began to decline sharply. When Johnson tried to force Secy. of War Edwin M. Stanton—whom he rightly suspected of conspiring with congressional leaders—out of office, the radical Republicans sought to remove the president. On Feb. 24, 1868, the House passed a resolution of IMPEACHMENT against him. The most important of the charges, which were purely political, was that he had violated the Tenure of Office Act in the Stanton affair. On Mar. 5 the Senate was organized as a court to hear the charges. The president himself did not appear. In spite of tremendous pressure brought to bear on several senators, the Senate failed to convict by one vote. Johnson's administration had some accomplishments, notably the purchase (1867) of Alaska. After his presidency he was returned (1875) to the Senate from Tennessee, but died shortly afterward.

Johnson, Earvin "Magic," 1959–, African-American basketball player; b. Lansing, Mich. He joined the Los Angeles Lakers of the National Basketball Association (NBA) in 1979 and became one of the best and best-liked players in the NBA. In his 12 years with the Lakers, he won three most-valuable-player awards (1987, 1989–90), and the team won five NBA championships (1980, 1982, 1985, 1987–88) in eight appearances in the finals. He retired (1991) when he learned he was infected with the AIDS virus, but he played briefly during the 1992 pre-season.

Johnson, Eyvind, 1900–1976, Swedish novelist and short-story writer. He is probably best known for his cycle of four autobiographical novels, *The Novel about Olof* (1934–37), which is noted for its psychological penetration. Other novels include *Return to Ithaca* (1946) and *Steps into Silence* (1973). He shared the 1974 Nobel Prize in literature with his countryman Harry MARTINSON.

Johnson, James Weldon, 1871–1938, African-American author; b. Jacksonville, Fla. A lawyer, he was a founder and secretary (1916–30) of the NAACP. He was American consul (1906–12), first in Venezuela and then in Nicaragua. His books include the novel *Autobiography of an Ex-Coloured Man* (1912), such poetry as *God's Trombones* (1927), and an autobiography (1933).

Johnson, Lyndon Baines, 1908–73, 36th president of the U.S. (1963–69); b. near Stonewall, Tex. As a Democratic congressman from Texas (1937–49) he supported Pres. F.D. ROOSEVELT's New Deal. He was elected senator in 1948 and became majority leader following the 1954 elections. After losing the 1960 presidential nomination to J.F. KENNEDY, Johnson agreed to become Kennedy's running mate. After Kennedy's assassination (Nov. 22, 1963) Johnson was immediately sworn in as president. Announcing that he would carry out the late president's programs, he skillfully prodded Congress into enacting (1964) an $11 billion tax cut and a sweeping Civil Rights Act. Elected (1964) to a full term, he launched a program of social and economic welfare programs to create what he termed the Great Society. It included Medicare and Medicaid (see HEALTH INSURANCE), federal aid to education, increased antipoverty programs (including HEAD START), and the 1965 Voting Rights Act. The Dept. of TRANSPORTATION and the Dept. of HOUSING AND URBAN DEVELOPMENT were created. Johnson's domestic achievements, however, were soon obscured by foreign affairs. When North Vietnam allegedly attacked (Aug. 1964) U.S. destroyers, Congress passed the TONKIN GULF RESOLUTION, which gave the president authority to take any action necessary to protect U.S. troops. Johnson began (Feb. 1965) the bombing of North Vietnam and increased U.S. forces in South Vietnam to nearly 550,000 (1969). The VIETNAM WAR aroused widespread opposition in Congress and among the public, and rioting (1968) in the African-American ghettos of U.S. cities further marred his presidency. In 1965 Johnson sent U.S. troops into the DOMINICAN REPUBLIC. He announced (Mar. 1968) that he would not run for reelection and retired to his Texas ranch. In 1934 he had married Claudia Alta Taylor (nicknamed Lady Bird), b. 1912; they had two children, Lynda Bird (now Mrs. Charles S. Robb) and Luci Baines.

Johnson, Philip Courtelyou, 1906–, American architect and historian; b. Cleveland. He wrote *The International Style* (1932) with Henry-Russell Hitchcock and became a major advocate of the new architecture. His glass house in New Canaan, Conn. (1949), reveals the influence of MIËS VAN DER ROHE, with whom he collaborated on the Seagram Building (1958), N.Y.C. He designed the New York State Theater at Lincoln Center (1964) and the American Telephone and Telegraph Headquarters Building (1978; now the Sony Building), both in New York City.

Johnson, Samuel, 1709–84, English author. The leading literary scholar and critic of his day, he helped to define the great period of English literature known as the Augustan Age. He is as celebrated for his brilliant conversation as for his writing. He began writing for London magazines around 1737, on literary and political subjects. The anonymously published poem *London* (1738) won the praise of POPE, and his reputation was further enhanced by his poetic satire *The Vanity of Human Wishes* (1749) and his moral essays in *The Rambler* (1750–52). Johnson's place was permanently assured by his great *Dictionary of the English Language* (1755), the first comprehensive English lexicon. *Rasselas,* a moral romance, appeared in 1759, and the *Idler* essays between 1758 and 1760. In 1763 Johnson met James BOSWELL, and his life thereafter is documented in Boswell's great biography (1791). With Joshua REYNOLDS he founded (1764) "The Club"; this elite gathering, with such members as GOLDSMITH, BURKE, and GARRICK, was dominated by Johnson, whose wit and aphorisms are still remembered. In 1765 he published his edition of SHAKESPEARE, the model for later editions. His last works include an account (1775) of a trip with Boswell to the Hebrides and the perceptive 10-volume *Lives of the Poets* (1779–81). He was England's first complete man of letters, and his influence was incalculable.

Johnson, Uwe [yŏn'zŏn], 1934–84, German novelist. He grew up in East Germany but emigrated (1959) to West Berlin. Using an experimental prose style that presents several viewpoints of the same event, his works examine the problems of humanity in a divided Germany. Among his best-known novels are *Speculations About Jacob* (1959), *Two Views* (1965), and the novel series *Anniversaries* (1970–74).

Johnson, Virginia E.: see MASTERS AND JOHNSON.

Johnson, Walter (Perry), 1887–1946, American baseball player; b. Humboldt, Kans. A right-handed pitcher, he spent his entire playing career (1907–27) with the Washington Senators. The "Big Train" won 416 games (second highest total on record) and established several pitching marks, including most shutouts (113), most strike-outs (3,508), and most consecutive scoreless innings (56). He won 20 or more games in 12 seasons (32 in 1912 and 36 in 1913). Johnson later managed the Senators (1929–32) and the Cleveland Indians (1933–35).

Johnston, Albert Sidney, 1803–62, Confederate general in the U.S. CIVIL WAR; b. Washington, Ky. Confederate commander in the West, he attacked (Apr. 6, 1862) Gen. GRANT at SHILOH. Johnston was killed in the battle, and the South lost one of its ablest generals.

Johnston, Joseph Eggleston, 1807–91, Confederate general in the U.S. CIVIL WAR; b. Prince Edward co., Va. He took part in the first battle of BULL RUN and was commander in the PENINSULAR CAMPAIGN until May 1862. Given command in the West, he was unable to stem the Union success in the VICKSBURG CAMPAIGN and the ATLANTA CAMPAIGN, and he was relieved of command (July 1864). Later reinstated, he surrendered (Apr. 26, 1865) to Gen. SHERMAN.

Johnstown, city (1990 pop. 28,134), SW Pa., on the Conemaugh R.; settled 1770, inc. as a city 1936. Located in a beautiful mountain region, its industries produce coal, metal products, and chemicals. Major U.S. steel producers dominated the city until the 1980s; the city grew with the industry after the Civil War. Johnstown is remembered for the disastrous flood of May 31, 1889, when about 2,200 died after a dam break.

John the Baptist, Saint, d. A.D. c.28–30, Jewish prophet, the forerunner of JESUS; son of Zacharias and Elizabeth, a kinswoman of the Virgin MARY. He preached in the Jordan valley, baptizing many, including Jesus, whom he recognized as the Son of God. Herodias, wife of HEROD, and her daughter (traditionally called SALOME) had him beheaded.

John the Fearless, 1371–1419, duke of Burgundy (1404–19), son of PHILIP THE BOLD. Continuing his father's feud, he had Louis, duc d'Orléans, assassinated (1407) and won control of the French government. In 1411 civil war broke out between the Orléanists, or Armagnacs, and the Burgundians. Forced to flee Paris (1413), John did not aid the now Armagnac-controlled government against HENRY V of England and in 1418 took advantage of French defeats to retake Paris and seize the king, CHARLES VI. John was assassinated at a meeting with the DAUPHIN (later CHARLES VII) and was succeeded by his son PHILIP THE GOOD.

joint, in anatomy, juncture between two bones. Some joints are immovable, e.g., those connecting bones of the skull. Hinge joints provide a forward and backward motion, as at the elbow and knee. Pivot joints permit rotary movement, as in the turning of the head from side to side. Ball-and-socket joints, like those at the hip and shoulder, allow the greatest range of movement. Ease of movement is aided by elastic cartilage, lubricating synovial fluid, and, in some joints, a cushioning, fluid-filled sac (bursa) that reduces friction. Joints are subject to injury and to diseases such as ARTHRITIS. The use of artificial joints is now common, particularly in hip-joint and knee-joint replacement.

Joint Chiefs of Staff: see under DEFENSE, UNITED STATES DEPARTMENT OF.

Joinville, Jean, sire de [zhwăNvēl'], 1224?–1317?, French chronicler. His memoir of LOUIS IX (whom he served as a close adviser) is an invaluable record of the king, feudal France, and the Seventh CRUSADE, written in a simple, delightful style, with a sharp eye for graphic detail.

Joliet, Louis: see JOLLIET, LOUIS.

Joliot-Curie, Frédéric and **Irène:** see CURIE, family.

Jolley, Elizabeth, 1923–, Australian writer; b. England. A nurse during World War II, she later emigrated to Western Australia. Although writing since childhood, her first book, *Five Acre Virgin and Other Stories*, did not appear until 1976. Her novels, such as *Miss Peabody's Inheritance* (1983), *Foxybaby* (1986), and *The Sugar Mother* (1988), are studies of comic eccentricity written in a traditional style but animated by feminist concerns.

Jolliet or **Joliet, Louis** [both: jō'lēĕt"], 1645–1700, French explorer; b. Quebec prov., Canada. He discovered, with Jacques MARQUETTE, the upper MISSISSIPPI R. in 1673.

Jolson, Al, c.1886–1950, American entertainer; b. Russia as Asa Yoelson. He made famous such songs as "Swanee," "Sonny-Boy," and "Mammy," the last sung in *The Jazz Singer* (1927), the first major film with sound.

Jonah, Jonas, or **Jona,** book of the OLD TESTAMENT, 32d in the Authorized Version, 5th of the Minor Prophets. It tells of a Hebrew PROPHET in the reign of Jeroboam II (c.793–753 B.C.) sent to reform NINEVEH. To avoid the command, he sails for Tarshish, but his disobedience brings a storm; the crew throw him overboard. Swallowed by a "great fish," he is cast up after three days and fulfills his mission. Jonah's escape is seen as foreshadowing Jesus' RESURRECTION.

Jones, Bobby (Robert Tyre Jones, Jr.), 1902–71, American golfer; b. Atlanta. A lawyer, he played golf as an amateur and won the U.S. Open (1923, 1926, 1929–30), the U.S. Amateur (1924–25, 1927–28, 1930), and the British Open (1926–27, 1930). The first golfer to win the U.S. Open and British Open in the same year (1926), he was the only player ever to score what was then the grand slam of golf, taking the open and amateur titles in both the U.S. and Britain in 1930. Still an amateur, he retired that year with 13 major championships.

Jones, Casey (John Luther Jones), 1864–1900, American locomotive engineer celebrated in song; b. Fulton co., Ky. He received his nickname from Cayce, Ky., where he went to work. Driving the *Cannon Ball* express from Memphis, Tenn., to Canton, Miss., he applied the brakes in time to save the lives of the passengers in a wreck at Vaughan, Miss., but he was killed.

Jones, Sir Edward Burne: see BURNE-JONES.

Jones, Ernest, 1879–1958, English psychoanalyst; b. Wales. Founding the London Clinic for Psycho-Analysis in 1925, he was instrumental in introducing the study of PSYCHOANALYSIS into England and the U.S. He is considered an authoritative biographer of Sigmund FREUD.

Jones, Inigo, 1573–1652, one of England's first great architects. He studied Renaissance and Palladian buildings in Europe. After designing settings for court masques, he became in 1615 the king's surveyor of works and began (1616) the Queen's House, Greenwich, the first English design to embody Palladian principles (see PALLADIO, ANDREA). He then built (1619–22) the royal banquet hall, Whitehall. In many houses in London and in the country he broke from the prevailing JACOBEAN STYLE, marking a starting point for the Renaissance and Georgian periods in England.

Jones, James, 1921–77, American novelist; b. Robinson, Ill. Written in the tradition of NATURALISM, his powerful novels include *From Here to Eternity* (1951), his best-known work; *Some Came Running* (1957); and *The Thin Red Line* (1962).

Jones, James Earl, 1931–, African-American actor; b. Tate co., Miss. He gained Broadway stardom with his powerful portrayal of a prizefighter in *The Great White Hope* (1968) and excelled in *Othello* (1963, 1982), Athol FUGARD's *A Lesson from Aloes* (1980), and August WILSON's *Fences* (1987). He has also appeared in films and on television.

Jones, John Paul, 1747–92, American naval hero; b. Scotland. In the AMERICAN REVOLUTION he raided British shipping in the waters off Great Britain. He captured the British warship *Drake* (1778) and, while commanding the *Bon Homme Richard,* the *Serapis* (1779). When he was asked to surrender his badly damaged ship in the latter battle, Jones defiantly replied, "Sir, I have not yet begun to fight."

Jones, LeRoi: see BARAKA, AMIRI.

jonquil: see NARCISSUS.

Jonson, Ben, 1572–1637, English dramatist and poet, known for his linguistic brilliance. An actor, he produced his first important play, *Every Man in His Humour,* in 1598 and *Every Man out of His Humour* in 1599. *The Poetaster* (1601) satirized fellow playwrights. After collaborating with CHAPMAN and MARSTON on *Eastward Ho!* (1604), he entered his great period, marked by the comic masterpieces *Volpone* (1606), *Epicoene* (1609), *The Alchemist* (1610), and *Bartholomew Fair* (1614)—all characterized by biting satire and intriguing plots. A moralist, he sought to teach improvement through exaggerating the foibles and passions (humors) of his characters. Jonson became a favorite of JAMES I and wrote court MASQUES, as well as two Roman tragedies, *Sejanus* (1603) and *Catiline* (1611). After *The Devil Is an Ass* (1616), his dramatic career declined. Jonson's nondramatic poetry includes the collections *Epigrams* (1616); *The Forrest* (1616), notable for the songs "Drink to me only with thine eyes" and "Come, my Celia, let us prove"; and *Underwoods* (1640). His many followers are known as the "sons of Ben."

Joos of Ghent: see JUSTUS OF GHENT.

Jooss, Kurt [yus], 1901–79, German dancer, producer, and choreographer. His most famous ballet was the expressionistic, antiwar *Green Table* (1932). He was in England during the Hitler era and returned to Germany after World War II. He has influenced the development of psychological themes in ballet.

Joplin, Scott, 1868–1917, African-American ragtime pianist and composer; b. Texarkana, Tex. The best-known ragtime composer (see JAZZ), he wrote such works as "Maple Leaf Rag" (1899) and the ragtime opera *Treemonisha* (1911).

Jordaens, Jacob [yôr'däns], 1593–1678, Flemish baroque painter; b. Belgium. His works include portraits and religious and allegorical paintings. The influence of CARAVAGGIO is evident in his early work, e.g., *The Artist's Family* (Hermitage, Saint Petersburg). His later works show increased grandeur and richness, e.g., *Triumph of Bacchus* (Kassel, Germany). In his last years he stressed the classical element in BAROQUE art, as seen in the rigidly composed *Christ and the Doctors* (Mainz, Germany).

Jordan, Barbara Charline, 1936–, African-American lawyer, public official, and educator; b. Houston. As a Democratic member of the U.S. House of Representatives (1973–79), she achieved national renown as a member of the House Judiciary Committee when it investigated (1974) the WATERGATE AFFAIR. In 1979 she became professor of public affairs at the Univ. of Texas.

Jordan, David Starr, 1851–1917, American biologist and educator; b. near Gainesville, N.Y. He was president of Indiana Univ. (1885–91) and the first president of Stanford Univ. (1891–1913). A peace advocate, he opposed U.S. entry into World War I. He was director of the World Peace Foundation (1910–14) and president of the World Peace Congress (1915). His writings include *Imperial Democracy*.

Jordan, Michael (Jeffrey), 1963–, African-American basketball player; b. Brooklyn, N.Y. Joining the Chicago Bulls of the National Basketball Association (NBA) in 1984, he became the premier guard of the late 1980s and early 1990s. Jordan was the NBA's leading scorer for seven straight years (1987–93) and holds the career record for scoring average (32.3 points per game). He was NBA's most valuable player for three years (1988, 1991–92) and led the Bulls to three NBA championships (1991–93). He retired in 1993.

Jordan, Vernon Eulion, Jr., 1935–, African-American civil-rights leader; b. Atlanta. A graduate of Howard Univ. Law School, he was executive director (1970–71) of the United Negro College Fund and president (1970–81) of the National Urban League. Jordan was seriously wounded (1980) by a sniper in Fort Wayne, Ind. In 1981 he joined a Washington law firm.

Jordan, officially Hashemite Kingdom of Jordan, kingdom (1992 est. pop. 3,557,000), 37,737 sq mi (97,740 sq km), SW Asia, bordered by Israel (W), Syria (N), Iraq (NE), and Saudi Arabia (E, S). AMMAN is the capital and largest city. Pre-1967 Jordan fell into three main geographical regions: East Jordan, which encompasses about 92% of the country's land area; the Jordanian Highlands (highest point, 5,755 ft/1,754 m); and West Jordan (the WEST BANK), part of historic Palestine. In the Arab-Israeli War of 1967, Israel captured and occupied the West Bank, and Jordan has since renounced its claim to the area (see below). Jordan's economy is largely agricultural, although less than 5% of the land is arable. The principal crops are vegetables, wheat, and citrus fruits; olives are grown for oil. Manufactures are limited to such items as foodstuffs, clothing, and cement, and there is some oil refining. Phosphate rock and potash are the only minerals produced in quantity. The annual cost of Jordan's imports far exceeds its earnings from exports. Aqaba, on the Gulf of AQABA, is the only seaport. The inhabitants of Jordan are mostly of Arab descent (about two thirds are of Palestinian descent), and Arabic is the official language (English is also spoken among the upper and middle classes). About 95% of the people are Sunni Muslims. Under the 1952 constitution, the king is the most powerful figure in the country; he appoints a cabinet (headed by a prime minister). The bicameral parliament was dissolved in 1974 and not reconvened until 1984; the 1989 elections were first in 22 years. Political parties were again permitted to field candidates in 1993.

History. This section deals primarily with the region east of the

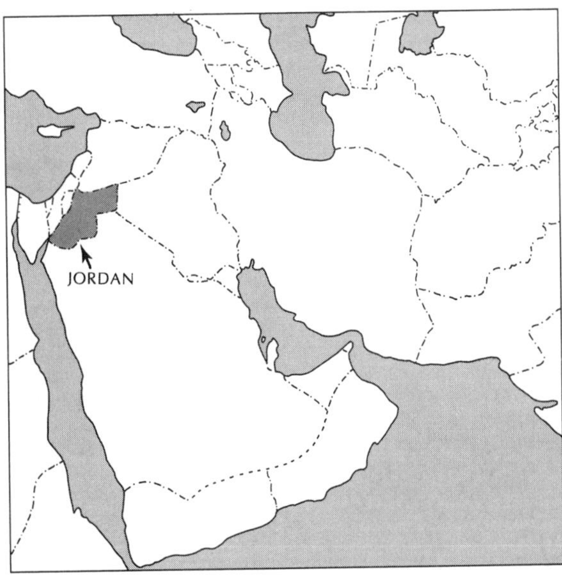

Jordan River; for the history of the area to the west, see PALESTINE. The region of present-day Jordan was conquered successively by the Seleucids (4th cent. B.C.), Romans (mid-1st cent. A.D.), and Muslim Arabs (7th. cent.). After the Crusaders captured (1099) Jerusalem, it became part of the Latin Kingdom of Jerusalem. The Ottoman Turks gained control in 1516, and what is now Jordan remained in the OTTOMAN EMPIRE until World War I. In 1920 Transjordan (as it was then known) was made part of the British mandate of Palestine. The country gained independence in 1946, and the name was changed (1949) to Jordan, reflecting its acquisition of land W of the Jordan R. during the Arab-Israeli War of 1948. ABDULLAH ibn Husain, a member of the Hashemite dynasty that headed Jordan since 1921, was assassinated in 1951. His grandson, HUSSEIN I, became king the following year. Jordanian forces were routed by Israel in the 1967 war (see ARAB-ISRAELI WARS), and Jordan lost the West Bank. Growing hostility between Hussein and the Palestinian guerrilla organizations operating in Jordan reached a climax during a brief civil war in 1970, and the guerrilla bases were destroyed the following year. Under pressure from Arab states, Hussein renounced (1974; reaffirmed 1988) Jordanian claims to the West Bank in order to allow the PALESTINE LIBERATION ORGANIZATION eventually to organize a state in this territory. Jordan also joined the most other Arab countries in opposing the 1979 peace treaty between Egypt and Israel. Jordan was officially neutral in the PERSIAN GULF WAR, but many Jordanians supported Iraq. Since 1991 Jordan has been involved in peace talks with Israel.

Jordan, river, Palestine, c.200 mi (320 km) long. It is formed by headwaters converging in N Israel, flows south between Israel and the GOLAN HEIGHTS and through the Sea of GALILEE (Lake Tiberias) into a below-sea-level valley called the Ghor (a continuation in Asia of Africa's GREAT RIFT VALLEY), where it forms the boundary between Israel and the WEST BANK (W) and the country of Jordan (E), and empties into the DEAD SEA. The river becomes increasingly saline to the south and is not navigable. Much of its water and that of the Yarmuk, its chief tributary, is diverted for irrigation. It is often mentioned in the Bible as the scene of Jesus' baptism.

Josaphat, in the Bible: see JEHOSHAPHAT.

Joseph, Saint, husband of the Virgin, a carpenter, a descendant of the house of DAVID. He is highly honored by Orthodox and Roman Catholics as the chaste spouse of the Virgin MARY and the foster father of JESUS. Feast: Mar. 19.

Joseph, rulers of the HOLY ROMAN EMPIRE. **Joseph I,** 1678–1711, emperor (1705–11), king of Hungary (1687–1711) and of Bohemia (1687–1711), became emperor during the War of the SPANISH SUCCESSION and died before it ended. He vigorously supported the Spanish claims of his brother, who succeeded him as Emperor CHARLES VI. **Joseph II,** 1741–90, emperor (1765–90), king of Bohemia and Hungary (1780–90), was the son of MARIA THERESA and Emperor Francis I, whom he succeeded. Until his mother's death in 1780, he exerted little authority, but once in power he instituted far-reaching social, economic, and religious reforms, including the law (1781) abolishing serfdom. His aim was to abolish hereditary and ecclesiastical privileges by creating a centralized and unified state administered by a civil service based on merit. He liberalized the legal codes, reformed tax policies, and founded hospitals, orphanages, and insane asylums. He was idolized by the common people but opposed by the nobles and the clergy, and most of his reforms did not outlive him. Nevertheless, he left a freer state than the one he had found on his accession. His foreign policy, focused on attempts to annex Bavaria and his military adventures in Turkey, was generally not successful.

Joseph, kings of Bohemia and Hungary: see JOSEPH, rulers of the Holy Roman Empire.

Joseph, in the BIBLE, the favored son of JACOB and RACHEL. He was sold into slavery by his brothers, who were jealous of their father's favoritism toward him. Taken to Egypt, Joseph rose to authority in the house of Potiphar, only to be imprisoned on the false accusations of Potiphar's wife. Released after interpreting Pharaoh's dream, Joseph rose in Pharaoh's favor. He was reunited with his family when, as governor of Egypt, he helped them during a famine.

Joseph (Chief Joseph), c.1840–1904, chief of a band of NEZ PERCÉ. Joseph was among those chiefs who peacefully resisted a land cession treaty fraudulently obtained (1863) by the U.S. When fighting broke out (1877), he and several hundred Nez Percé undertook a heroic 1,000-mi (1,600-km) retreat to Canada but were forced to surrender just 30 mi (48 km) from their goal. He spent the rest of his life on the Colville reservation, Wash.

Josephine, 1763–1814, empress of the French (1804–9) as the consort of NAPOLEON I. Born Marie Josèphe Rose Tascher de La Pagerie, in Martinique, she married (1779) Alexandre de BEAUHARNAIS, who was executed (1794) in the FRENCH REVOLUTION. In 1796 she married Napoleon, but he had their childless marriage annulled (1809) so that he might marry the Austrian princess MARIE LOUISE. Josephine thereafter lived in retirement.

Josephus, Flavius [jōsē'fəs], A.D. 37–A.D. 95?, Jewish historian. A soldier, he took part in the war between the Romans and Jews and won the favor of the Roman general VESPASIAN. His works include *The Jewish War, Antiquities of the Jews,* and *Against Apion* (a defense of the Jews).

Joshua or **Josue,** book of the OLD TESTAMENT, sixth in the Authorized Version, a historical sequel to DEUTERONOMY, telling of the occupation of Palestine by the Hebrews. The chief figure is Joshua, MOSES' successor as leader of Israel. The book may be divided into three sections: the conquest of the Promised Land (1–12), the allotment of the land by tribes (13–22), and the farewell sermon and death of Joshua (23–24). The fall of Jericho (6) is a famous passage.

Josquin Desprez or **Des Prés** [both: dāprā'], c.1440–1521, Flemish composer, regarded as the greatest of his age. His earlier works were contrapuntal (see COUNTERPOINT); his later, more chordal. He was noted for his chansons and MOTETS.

Joule, James Prescott, 1818–89, English physicist. He established the mechanical theory of HEAT and was the first to determine the relationship between heat energy and mechanical energy (the mechanical equivalent of heat). Joule discovered the first law of THERMODYNAMICS, which is a form of the law of conservation of ENERGY. The mechanical unit of WORK, the joule, is named for him.

joule: see WORK.

Jove: see JUPITER.

Jovian, c.331–64, Roman emperor (363–64). He made a humiliating peace with Persia and restored Christianity to the privileged position it had held before JULIAN THE APOSTATE's reign.

Joyce, James, 1882–1941, Irish novelist. Perhaps the major 20th-cent. writer in English, Joyce was a master of language, exploiting its total resources. Educated in Dublin Jesuit schools, he lived after 1902 on the Continent, returning to Ireland only briefly. *Dubliners,* his short stories, was suppressed in Ireland because of topical references and published in London (1914). He spent World War I in Zürich, working on *A Portrait of the Artist as a Young Man* (1916), his first novel. Publication of *Ulysses,* written 1914–21, was delayed by obscenity charges; it did not appear in the U.S. until 1933. After 1922, Joyce worked on *Finnegans Wake* (1939). He died in Zürich in 1941. With each major work, Joyce's profundity and complexity grew. *Dubliners* centers on moments of spiritual insight he called epiphanies. *A Portrait* is a fairly realistic autobiographical account of young Stephen Dedalus's growing realization that he must free himself from the narrowness of Irish society. *Ulysses* recounts the events of June 16, 1904, in the actions and thoughts of the salesman Leopold Bloom, his wife, Molly, and Stephen Dedalus, now a teacher. The book follows the design of HOMER's *Odyssey* in theme and image. With its shifts in consciousness, its rich allusion, and its play with language, it is a difficult but rewarding celebration of life. *Finnegans Wake* seems at times to present the dreams of a Dublin publican, at times to represent a universal consciousness. Less read, it is not well understood. The Joyce canon includes three volumes of poems, *Chamber Music* (1907), *Pomes Penyeach* (1927), and *Collected Poems* (1937); the Ibsenesque play *Exiles* (1918); and *Stephen Hero* (1944), a fragmentary draft of *A Portrait.*

Joyner-Kersee, Jackie, 1962–; American track-and-field athlete; b. East St. Louis, Ill. She won the silver medal in the heptathlon in the 1984 Olympics, won the gold medal and set the world record in the event in 1988, and won the gold again in 1992. She also won a gold medal (1988) and bronze medal (1992) in the long jump.

József, Attila [yō'zhĕf], 1905–37, Hungarian poet. Born in poverty, he published his first book at 17 and in 1930 joined the illegal Communist party. After periods of schizophrenia he committed suicide. His compassionate poetry deals with political and existential themes.

Juana Inés de la Cruz [dā lä kro͞os], 1651–95, Mexican poet. Considered the greatest lyric poet of the colonial period, she was an intellectually precocious girl who entered a convent at 16. Her classical and scientific studies were criticized by her superiors, including the bishop of Puebla, whose objections to women's education she answered in a spirited autobiographical letter (1691). The long poem *First Dream* (1680) was her major achievement. She also wrote plays, both religious and worldly. Her last years were devoted to the spiritual life; she died aiding victims of an epidemic.

Juan Carlos I [hwän kär'lōs], 1938–, king of Spain (1975–). The grandson of ALFONSO XIII, he married (1962) Princess Sophia of Greece. Francisco FRANCO named him (1969) his successor as ruler. Upon Franco's death (1975), he became the first Spanish king since his grandfather was deposed in 1931. Personally popular, he has proven to be a strong force for Spanish political stability and democracy. In Feb. 1981 he successfully foiled a right-wing military coup.

Juárez, Benito [hwä'rās], 1806–72, Mexican statesman. A lawyer of Native American descent, he helped to overthrow (1855) SANTA ANNA's dictatorship and to limit the privileges of the church and army. He led the liberals to victory in the War of the Reform (1858–61) and, as president (1857–65, 1867–72), oversaw the transfer of political power in MEXICO from the creoles to the mestizos. Juárez defeated France's attempt (1864–67) to establish a Mexican empire and tried to implement reforms.

Juárez or **Ciudad Juárez,** city (1990 pop. 797,679), N Mexico, on the Río Grande, opposite El Paso, Texas. A cotton-processing center and resort at the desert's edge, it has grown rapidly since the 1970s as assembly plants exporting to the U.S. have favored the area. First called El Paso del Norte, it was a base for Spanish colonial expansion northward and later served as the headquarters of Benito JUÁREZ, for whom it was renamed in 1888.

Juda: see JUDAH.

Judaea or **Judea** [both: jo͞odē'ə], Greco-Roman name for S Palestine. At the time of Jesus, it was both part of the province of Syria and a kingdom ruled by the HERODS.

Judah or **Juda,** in the BIBLE, fourth son of JACOB and LEAH and the eponymous ancestor of one of the 12 Tribes of Israel (see ISRAEL, TRIBES OF). Judah is a distinctive figure, a leader in the family counsels. His tribe gave its name to the kingdom of Judah.

Judah, more southerly of two kingdoms created by the division of the kingdom of the JEWS under REHOBOAM. Judah, which lasted from 931 B.C. to 586 B.C., had its capital in JERUSALEM and was ruled by the house of DAVID.

Judah ha-Levi or **Halevy,** c.1075–1141, Spanish rabbi, poet, philosopher, and physician. His poems—secular, religious, and nationalist—are filled with a serene and lofty spirit. In his great philosophic work, *Sefer ha-Kuzari* (tr. *Kuzari,* 1964), he attempts to establish the superiority of the Jewish religion.

Judah ha-Nasi [prince] or **Judah I,** A.D. 135?–220?, religious and political leader of the Palestinian Jews and head of the SANHEDRIN. He collected and edited the Oral Law, which he compiled as the MISHNA.

Judaism, the religious beliefs and practices and the way of life of the JEWS. Central to these is the notion of monotheism, adopted by the biblical Hebrews. In this early period there also developed a belief in the ultimate coming of God's kingdom on earth, a time of peace and justice. With the destruction (586 B.C.) of the First Temple and the consequent Babylonian captivity came the expectation of national restoration under the leadership of a MESSIAH. In Babylonia the Israelites were exposed to, and adopted, new ideas, e.g., the personification of evil (Satan) and the resurrection of the dead. In the post-exilic period (not later than the 5th cent. B.C.) the practice of publicly studying the TORAH, or Pentateuch, and of writing expositions on it, began; these were later collected in the MISHNA and TALMUD. The conquests of Alexander the Great brought other new ideas, most significantly that of the immortality of the soul. Conflict over the acceptable level of Hellenization led to the revolt of the MACCABEES. As conditions of life deteriorated, apocalyptic beliefs grew: national catastrophe and the Messianic kingdom were seen as imminent events. Out of these beliefs grew both Christianity and classical, or rabbinic, Judaism. Rabbinic Judaism, which evolved over five centuries (until A.D. c.500), replaced the Temple with the SYNAGOGUE (the Second Temple was destroyed in A.D. 70), the priesthood with the RABBI, and sacrificial ceremony with the prayer service. Emphasis was placed on study of the Torah, on the growing need for national restoration in the Promised Land, and on the function of this world as preparatory for the world to come. In the medieval period two new developments arose: the CABALA, influenced predominantly by NEOPLATONISM, and, opposed to it, rationalism, whose principal exponent was MAIMONIDES. Although the Jewish Middle Ages extended into the 18th cent., the general European Renaissance had its Jewish counterpart, e.g., in the work of the poet Judah ABRAVANEL. At the same time, the influence of the SEPHARDIM, particularly the Marranos, came to be felt, generally as a liberalizing force. The 18th cent. produced both the great traditional rabbinic figure ELIJAH BEN SOLOMON (the Gaon of Vilna) and the untraditional figures BAAL-SHEM-TOV, the founder of HASIDISM, and Moses MENDELSSOHN, spiritual progenitor of the later Reform movement. With the 19th cent. came the question of how Jews were to maintain tradition when the non-Jewish world demanded its abandonment. In Eastern Europe this problem was dealt with by the Haskalah, or Jewish enlightenment, movement, whose members, e.g., Nachman KROCHMAL, sought to revitalize Jewish life by recreating it along the lines of the best in European culture. Finally, in reaction to the needs of a persecuted people and to growing nationalistic desires, ZIONISM arose, promising a return to the Holy Land. Ultimately, it was HALAKAH (the law) over which Jews divided; Orthodoxy regards halakah as derived from God and therefore authoritative, whereas Reform sees it as binding only in its ethical content. The Conservative movement assumes a middle position, maintaining most of the traditional rituals but recognizing a need for change in accordance with overriding contemporary considerations. Reconstructionist Judaism, a 20th-cent. movement, accepts all forms of Jewish practice, regarding Judaism as a culture rather than a theological system. See also JEWISH HOLIDAYS.

Judas, in the Bible. **1** See JUDE, SAINT. **2** Judas Maccabeus: see MACCABEES. **3** See JUDAS ISCARIOT.

Judas Iscariot [ĭskâr'ēət], JESUS' betrayer, one of the Twelve APOSTLES. The chief priests paid him 30 pieces of silver, for which he led soldiers to Gethsemane and identified Jesus to them by kissing him. Later he repented and killed himself. The blood money bought a potter's field. The name *Iscariot* suggests he may have belonged to an anti-Roman sect, the Sicarii, and may have betrayed Jesus out of disappointment that Jesus was not the political Messiah he had looked for.

Judas Maccabeus: see MACCABEES.

Judd, Donald (Clarence), 1928–94, American sculptor; b. Excelsior Springs, Mo. Associated with MINIMALISM, he was known for his geometric works in wood or steel painted with industrial pigments.

Jude, Saint, or **Saint Judas,** one of the Twelve APOSTLES. Jude is an English form used to distinguish him from JUDAS ISCARIOT; he is also called Lebbaeus and Thaddaeus.

Jude, epistle of the NEW TESTAMENT, next to last book of the Bible. A Catholic, or general, EPISTLE, it warns against some heresy that led to immorality and has a close literary relationship with Second PETER.

Judea: see JUDAEA.

Judges, book of the OLD TESTAMENT, seventh in the Authorized Version, the sequel to JOSHUA. It tells of the Hebrews from Joshua's death until the time of SAMUEL. The religious interpretation, stated in an introduction, is that the book recounts Israel's successive apostasies and their consequences. The judges, primarily military leaders of the tribes, include Deborah, GIDEON, Jephthah, and SAMSON.

Judith, book included in the OLD TESTAMENT of the Western canon and the Septuagint but not in the Hebrew Bible, and placed in the APOCRYPHA in the Authorized Version. It tells of an armed attack on the Jewish city of Bethulia and of how Judith, a beautiful widow, saved the city by killing Holofernes, the enemy leader. The book probably antedates 100 B.C.

judo: see MARTIAL ARTS.

Judson, Edward Zane Carroll: see BUNTLINE, NED.

jujitsu: see MARTIAL ARTS.

jujube: see BUCKTHORN.

Julia, feminine name in the Julian gens. **1** Died 54 B.C., daughter of Julius CAESAR and wife of POMPEY. She maintained the bond between them, but after her death they became open enemies. **2** 39 B.C.–A.D. 14, daughter of AUGUSTUS and wife, in turn, of Marcus Claudius Marcellus (d. 23 B.C.), Marcus Vipsanius Agrippa, and TIBERIUS. Her infidelities caused her banishment by Augustus. Soon after Tiberius became emperor, she died of starvation.

Juliana, 1909–, queen of the Netherlands (1948–80). She succeeded her mother, WILHELMINA, and abdicated in favor of her eldest daughter, BEATRIX.

Julian the Apostate, 331?–363, Roman emperor (361–63); nephew of CONSTANTINE I. A scholar, writer, and general, he sponsored far-reaching legislation. He decreed religious toleration but tried unsuccessfully to restore paganism. Killed in battle, he was succeeded by JOVIAN.

Julius I, Saint, pope (337–52), a Roman. When asked for his opinion on ARIANISM, he summoned a council at Rome (340). The Arians did not come, and Julius wrote them a letter, chiding them for lack of sincerity; the letter was remarkable as an early claim to papal jurisdiction over the whole church. Feast: April 12.

Julius II, 1443–1513, pope (1503–13), an Italian named Giuliano della Rovere. A warrior, he completed the work of his enemy, Cesare BORGIA, of restoring the Papal States to the church and took a vigorous part in the ITALIAN WARS. Julius assembled (1512) the Fifth Lateran Council, which abolished simony in the college of cardinals. An art patron, he favored RAPHAEL (who painted his portrait), MICHELANGELO, and BRAMANTE. He laid the cornerstone of St. Peter's Cathedral. Worldly as Julius was, he was one of the first to try to break the hold of Renaissance corruption on Rome.

Julius Caesar: see CAESAR, JULIUS.

July: see MONTH.

July Revolution, revolt in France in July 1830 against CHARLES X. The attempt of the ultraroyalists under Charles to return to the ancien régime provoked opposition from the more liberal middle class. When Charles's minister, Jules Armand de Polignac, issued the July Ordinances, which controlled the press, dissolved the newly elected chamber of deputies, and reduced the electorate, insurrection followed. Charles fled and abdicated, and LOUIS PHILIPPE was proclaimed king.

June: see MONTH.

Juneau, city (1990 pop. 26,751), state capital, SE Alaska, in the Alaska Panhandle; settled by gold miners 1880, inc. 1900. Lying at the foot of two lofty peaks, it has an ice-free harbor. Government, fishing, lumber, and tourism are important to the economy. Alaska's capital since 1906, the city is one of the largest in area in the U.S. (3,108 sq mi/8,050 sq km) and the only mainland U.S. state capital not accessible by land.

Jung, Carl Gustav [yo͝ong], 1875–1961, Swiss psychiatrist, founder of analytical psychology. Jung met Sigmund FREUD in 1907, and became the first president of the International Psychoanalytic Association when it was formed. He broke with Freud in 1912, when Jung published his revolutionary *Psychology of the Unconscious,* which postulated two dimensions of the UNCONSCIOUS—the personal (repressed or forgotten content of an individual's mental and material life), and what he termed the collective unconscious (those acts and mental patterns shared either by members of a culture or universally by all human beings). Under certain conditions these manifest themselves as archetypes—images, patterns, and symbols that are often seen in dreams or fantasies and that appear as themes in mythology, religion, and fairy tales. In *Psychological Types* (1921) Jung elucidated EXTROVERSION AND INTROVERSION. He held the most significant task for any person to be the achievement of harmony between the conscious and the unconscious. The definitive edition of his collected works in English translation was published between 1951 and 1979.

Jünger, Ernst [yŭng'ər], 1895–, German writer. His early works, e.g., *Storm of Steel* (1920), glorify war. Later he opposed HITLER and militarism. His war diaries express a mystical plea for peace, as in *On the Marble Cliffs* (1939) and *Heliopolis* (1949). *The Glass Bees* (1957) and *Aladdin's Problem* (1983) are late novels.

junior college: see COMMUNITY COLLEGE.

juniper, aromatic evergreen tree or shrub (genus *Juniperus*) of the CYPRESS family, widely distributed over the north temperate zone. Many are important sources of lumber and oil. The insect-repellent wood of the red cedar (*J. virginiana*) is especially valuable for closets, furniture, and posts; the oil is used in medicine and perfumery. The common juniper (*J. communis*) and its varieties (e.g., dwarf and pyramidal) are grown ornamentally; its fruits are used to flavor gin.

Junius, pseud. of an English political writer. His letters, sent to the London *Public Advertiser* (Jan. 1769–Jan. 1772), attacked GEORGE III and his ministers and centered on the John WILKES controversy. His identity remains a mystery.

junk bond, a BOND that involves greater than usual risk as an investment and pays a relatively high rate of interest, typically issued by a company lacking an established earnings history or having a questionable credit history. Junk bonds became a common means for raising business capital in the 1980s, when they were used to help finance the purchase of companies, especially by LEVERAGED BUYOUTS. See also MILKEN, MICHAEL R.

Juno, in Roman mythology, wife and sister of JUPITER; great goddess of the state. Like the Greek HERA, she was the protectress of women.

Jupiter, in astronomy, 5th PLANET from the sun, at a mean distance of 483.6 million mi (778.3 million km), and largest planet in the solar system, with an equatorial diameter of 88,700 mi (142,800 km). It is a gaseous planet with an atmosphere composed mostly of hydrogen and helium, with traces of methane, ammonia, and other gases, and about five or six zones each of counterflowing eastward- and westward-flowing winds. The most prominent atmospheric features (all in the southern hemisphere) are the Great Red Spot, a storm at least 300 years old and measuring c.30,000 by 10,000 mi (48,000 by 16,000 km), and three large white ovals that formed in 1939. Jupiter has 16 known natural satellites, 12 of which are of small diameter. The four larger Galilean satellites were discovered by GALILEO in 1610. **Callisto** (diameter: 2,995 mi/4,820 km), the most distant and the least active geologically of the four, has a heavily cratered surface. **Ganymede** (diameter: 3,279 mi/5,276 km), second most distant of the four and the largest satellite in the solar system, has heavily cratered regions, tens of miles across, that are surrounded by younger, grooved terrain. **Europa** (diameter: 1,942 mi/3,126 km) is a white, highly reflecting body whose smooth surface is entirely covered with dark streaks up to 70 km in width and from several hundred to several thousand kilometers in length. **Io** (diameter: 2,257 mi/3,632 km), the closest to Jupiter of the four, is the most active geologically, with eight active volcanoes that are probably energized by the tidal effects of Jupiter's enormous mass. The red color of **Amalthea** (diameter: 150 mi/240 km), a small, elongated satellite interior to Io's orbit that was discovered (1892) by Edward BARNARD, probably results from a coating of sulfur particles ejected from Io. Four SPACE PROBES have encountered the Jovian system: *Pioneers 10* and *11* (1973 and 1974) and *Voyagers 1* and *2* (both 1979). The latter two discovered Io's volcanoes, a thin ring system surrounding Jupiter, and three of the smaller satellites. The U.S. launched (1989) the space probe *Galileo* to orbit and study Jupiter and send a probe into its atmosphere.

Jupiter, in Roman mythology, supreme god; also called Jove; son of SATURN and Ops; brother and husband of JUNO. Originally an agricultural god, he developed into the prime protector of the state and was identified with the Greek ZEUS.

Jurassic period: see GEOLOGIC ERA (table).

jury, in COMMON LAW, a group of laymen summoned to study the EVIDENCE and determine the facts in a dispute tried in a court of law. The jury was probably brought to England by the NORMAN CONQUEST (11th cent.). Early juries consisted of people with personal knowledge of a dispute. Eventually, formally produced evidence became the basis for decision by an objective jury. The use of the jury system, which by the 18th cent. had become an important protection against judicial and administrative tyranny, spread to territories colonized by England. The sixth and seventh amendments to the U.S. CONSTITUTION provide for a jury trial in most criminal and civil cases. A grand jury of 12 to 23 members usually considers the evidence and determines whether a trial is justified (see INDICTMENT). A petit (petty) jury, usually of 12 members, sits at the trial proper and, after hearing the evidence, reaches a verdict. Traditionally, the verdict was required to be unanimous, but today some states allow majority verdicts.

Justice, United States Department of, federal executive department established (1870) to help the U.S. attorney general enforce federal laws, to furnish legal counsel in federal cases, and to construe laws under which other federal executive departments act. Its solicitor general represents the federal government in SUPREME COURT cases. The department's divisions include Antitrust, Civil, Civil Rights, Criminal, Environment and Natural Resources, and Tax; its agencies include the FEDERAL BUREAU OF INVESTIGATION, the Drug Enforcement Administration, the Bureau of Prisons, and the Immigration and Naturalization Service.

Justin I, c.450–527, Byzantine emperor (518–27). He strongly opposed MONOPHYSITISM and had close relations with the Western Church. Lacking education, he entrusted government to his nephew, who succeeded him as JUSTINIAN I.

Justinian I, 483–565, Byzantine emperor (527–65), nephew of JUSTIN I. His heavy taxes and the discontent of the Monophysites (see MONOPHYSITISM) involved internal political factions in the Nika riot, which was crushed (532) by Empress THEODORA. She was helped by two generals, BELISARIUS and NARSES, who had recovered Africa and Italy for the empire. Justinian advocated caesaro-papism, i.e., the supremacy of emperor even over church, and called the Second Council of Constantinople (553) in a fruitless effort to reconcile the Monophysites to the church. His chief accomplishment was the codification of ROMAN LAW. His many public works included the church of HAGIA SOPHIA.

Justin Martyr, Saint, A.D. c.100–c.165, Christian apologist. He opened a school of Christian philosophy at Rome, where he was martyred. Two undisputed works remain, both philosophic defenses of Christian doctrine—the *Apology* and the *Dialogue*. Feast: June 1.

Justus of Ghent, fl. c.1460–c.1480, Flemish religious and portrait painter, known as Jodocus or Joos of Ghent. His simple, quiet style provides a clear link between Flemish and Italian art, e.g., the *Adoration of the Magi* (Metropolitan Mus.).

jute, tropical annual (genus *Corchorus*) of the LINDEN family, and its fiber. Although the fiber, of comparatively low CELLULOSE content, is weak and deteriorates quickly, it is the principal coarse fiber in commercial production; chief sources are *C. capsularis* and *C. olitorius*. India, with its hot climate and abundant cheap labor, is the unrivaled world producer and processor. Easily dyed and spun, jute is used for coarse fabrics, especially burlap and sacking, and for twine, rope, and insulation.

Jutland, Battle of, May 31, 1916, only major naval engagement between the British and German fleets in WORLD WAR I off the coast of Jutland, in Denmark. The outnumbered German fleet performed brilliantly and escaped in the fog. The tactics of the British commander, Admiral Jellicoe, and the heavy British losses caused much controversy.

Juvenal (Decimus Junius Juvenalis) [jo͞o'vənəl], fl. 1st–2d cent. A.D., Roman satiric poet. His verse established a model for the SATIRE of indignation. Written from the stern viewpoint of older standards, his 16 satires denounce a lax and luxurious society, tyranny, affectations, and immorality; the form is terse, polished, and epigrammatic.

K

K, chemical symbol of the element POTASSIUM.

K2 or **Mount Godwin-Austen,** the world's second highest peak, 28,250 ft (8,611 m) high, in the Karakorum range, N Kashmir, at the China-India border. It was discovered in 1856 and first climbed in 1954 by an Italian team led by Ardito Desio.

Kaaba or **Caaba,** in ISLAM, the most sacred sanctuary, the center of the Muslim world and the chief goal of pilgrimage. It is a small building in the Great Mosque of MECCA, nearly cubic in shape, built to enclose the Black Stone, the most venerated Muslim object. The Kaaba was a pagan holy place before MUHAMMAD, and many legends surround its origin. Nonbelievers are forbidden to approach it. Muslims face the Kaaba when praying.

Kabalevsky, Dmitri, 1904–87, Soviet composer. His many works, melodic and harmonically conservative, include the opera *Colas Breugnon* (1938); the SUITE *The Comedians* (1940); the OPERETTA *The Sisters* (1967), and piano and chamber works.

kabbalah: see CABALA.

Kabuki: see *Japanese drama* under ASIAN DRAMA.

Kabul, city (1989 est. pop. 1,400,000), capital of Afghanistan and its largest city and economic and cultural center, E Afghanistan, on the Kabul R. Manufactures include textiles, beet sugar, ordnance, and machinery, but warfare has limited economic activity since 1979. Strategically located, the city, whose history dates back more than 3,000 years, became Afghanistan's capital in 1773. It has been destroyed and rebuilt many times. It has an old quarter, with narrow, crooked streets, and a modern section. Kabul has a university (est. 1931), numerous colleges, and a fine museum. Soviet troops occupied the city from 1979 to 1989, and Kabul has been torn by factional fighting since the ouster (1992) of Najibullah.

kachina, among PUEBLO peoples, the spirit of the life forces. Elaborately costumed tribesmen, impersonating kachinas, visit Pueblo villages early in the year. They dance, sing, and give gifts to children. Dolls that the HOPI and ZUÑI carve and dress like the dancers are also called kachinas.

Kádár, János [kä'där], 1912–89, Hungarian Communist leader. He was imprisoned (1951–54) for alleged pro-Titoism. In the 1956 uprising (see HUNGARY) he first joined the cabinet of Imre NAGY but then formed a counter-government with support from the USSR, which crushed the revolt. He was premier (1956–58, 1961–65) and first secretary of the Communist party (1956–88).

Kafirs: see XHOSA.

Kafka, Franz [käf'kä], 1883–1924, German novelist and short-story writer, of a Jewish family; b. Prague. In remarkably clear and precise prose, Kafka presents a world at once real and dreamlike in which modern people, burdened with guilt, isolation, and anxiety, make a futile search for personal salvation. Among his symbolic novels are *The Trial* (1925), *The Castle* (1926), and *Amerika* (1927). Important stories include "The Metamorphosis" (1915), "A Country Doctor" (1919), and "In the Penal Colony" (1920), all translated into English, as are his diaries (1948–49) and several volumes of correspondence.

Kahlo, Frida, 1907–54, Mexican painter. Drawing on personal experiences, she portrayed the harshness and pain of women's lives in stark, often shocking works, including many self-portraits. Kahlo was also influenced by Mexican culture, aspects of which she painted in bright colors, with a mixture of realism, surrealism, and symbolism. She was married to Diego RIVERA.

Kahn, Louis Isadore, 1901–74, American architect; b. Estonia. From the 1920s he worked on many housing projects, e.g., Carver Court (1944), Coatesville, Pa. He also designed the Yale Univ. Art Gallery, the Salk Institute, La Jolla, Calif., and the Kimbell Art Museum, Fort Worth, Tex., and exerted wide influence as a professor.

Kakinomoto no Hitomaro [kä'kē'nō'mō'tō nō hē'tō'mä'rō], d. 710?, early Japanese lyric poet. The greatest poet in the *Manyoshu,* the oldest extant Japanese poetry anthology, he is known for the unusualy wide range of his verse forms, his sense of humanity, and his empathy with nature.

Kalahari, arid desert area, c.100,000 sq mi (259,000 sq km), in Botswana, E Namibia, and N South Africa, with a yearly rainfall ranging from 5 in. (12.7 cm) in the southwest to 20 in. (50.8 cm) in the northeast. The nomadic San (Bushmen) and Khoikhoi are the principal inhabitants.

Kalamazoo, city (1990 pop. 80,277), seat of Kalamazoo co., SW Mich., on the Kalamazoo R. where it meets Portage Creek; inc. as a city 1883. It has paper, metal, and pharmaceutical industries, and the area produces celery and other crops, grains, and dairy goods. Western Mich. Univ. and two colleges are located there.

kale, borecole, and **collards,** common names for nonheading types of CABBAGE (mostly of the variety *acephala*), cool-weather crops of the MUSTARD family. They are grown for their edible greens and, in Europe, for fodder.

Kalends: see CALENDAR.

Kalevala, Finnish national epic. It recounts the exploits of three semidivine brothers in mythical Kaleva, land of the heroes. Known to scholars as early as 1733, the folk verses that make up the epic were collected in the 19th cent. by Zakarias Topelius and E. Lönnrot. The effect of the *Kalevala* on Finnish art has been great.

Kali [Hindi, = the Black One], important goddess in popular HINDUISM and TANTRA, associated with destructive forces.

Kalidasa [kä"lĭdä'sə], fl. 5th cent.?, Indian dramatist and poet, the greatest figure in classical SANSKRIT LITERATURE. His three surviving plays—*Shakuntala, Vikramorvasi,* and *Malavikagnimitra*—are court dramas in verse and relate fanciful or mythological tales of romantic love ripened by adversity. He also wrote fine epic and lyric poetry.

Kalimantan: see BORNEO.

Kaliningrad, formerly Königsberg, city (1990 pop. 404,000), W European Russia, on the Pregolya R., in a Russian exclave surrounded by Poland and Lithuania. An ice-free Baltic seaport and naval base, it produces ships, machinery, and other manufactures. Königsberg, in E Prussia, was founded (1255) as a fortress of the TEUTONIC KNIGHTS and joined (1340) the HANSEATIC LEAGUE. The Univ. of Königsberg (founded 1544) reached its greatest fame when KANT taught there. The city became part of the USSR in 1945 and was renamed for the Soviet leader Mikhail Kalinin. Most of the population is now Russian.

Kamakura, city (1990 pop. 174,299), central Honshu, Japan, on Sagami Bay. A religious center and resort, Kamakura is famous for its 42-ft (12.8-m) high bronze Buddha, cast in 1252. The city was the seat of Yoritomo, the first SHOGUN, and his descendants (1192–1333); under the Ashikaga Shogunate (1333–1573), it was the government headquarters of E Japan.

Kamchatka, peninsula, c.750 mi (1,210 km) long, NE Russia, projecting southwest from the Asian mainland between the Sea of Okhotsk (W) and the Bering Sea and Pacific Ocean (E). It is traversed by two parallel ranges containing the only active volcanoes in Russia and has a cold and humid climate. Fishing (notably for crabs), sealing, fur trapping, mining, and lumbering are the main occupations. The population is predominantly Russian, with large Koryak minorities.

Kamehameha I [kämä'hämä'hä], c.1738–1819, Hawaiian king. He was king of the island of Hawaii after 1790 and through conquest became (1810) ruler of all the Hawaiian islands.

Kamenev, Lev Borisovich [kä'mĭnyĭf], 1883–1936, Soviet Communist leader; b. L.B. Rosenfeld. After the RUSSIAN REVOLUTION (1917) he was a member of the first politburo of the Communist party. When LENIN died (1924), Kamenev, STALIN, and ZINOVIEV excluded TROTSKY from power, but in 1925 the Stalinist majority defeated Kamenev and Zinoviev, who joined Trotsky's opposition. In 1936 Kamenev, with Zinoviev and others, was tried for treason and executed.

Kampala, largest city (1991 pop. 773,463) and capital of Uganda, on Lake VICTORIA. It is linked by railroad to SW Uganda and Mombasa, Kenya, and by ships crossing the lake to ports in Kenya and Tanzania. The city is built on and around six hills. An international airport is nearby, at ENTEBBE. Kampala, which grew up around a British fort constructed in 1890, replaced Entebbe as the capital in 1962.

Kampuchea: see CAMBODIA.

Kanarese [känərēz'], Dravidian language of India. See LANGUAGE (table).

Kandahar or **Qandahar,** city (1989 est. pop. 203,000), capital of Kandahar prov., S Afghanistan. The country's second largest city, it is a market for sheep, cotton, grain, and dried fruit. Manufactures include textiles and processed food. Possibly founded by Alexander the Great, the city was the capital (1748–73) of the kingdom of Afghanistan and was occupied (1839–42, 1879–81) by the British in the Afghan wars. After the 1979 Soviet invasion of Afghanistan, the Soviets and Afghan rebels engaged (1981) in heavy fighting in Kandahar.

Kandinsky, Wassily, 1866–1944, Russian abstract painter and theorist. Regarded as the originator of abstract art (see ABSTRACT EXPRESSIONISM), he developed his ideas concerning the power of pure color and nonrepresentational painting in Paris, where he came in contact with neo-impressionism (see POSTIMPRESSIONISM) and FAUVISM. In his study *Concerning the Spiritual in Art* (1912), he examined the psychological effects of color. He was a founder of the BLAUE REITER. In the 1920s his style evolved from pure bursts of color to more precise geometric compositions. In 1922 he joined the BAUHAUS faculty; later he wrote *Point and Line to Plane* (1926), which includes an analysis of geometric forms in art.

Kandy, city (1985 est. pop. 125,000), capital of Central prov., Sri Lanka, on the Kandy Plateau. It is a mountain resort and the trade center for an area producing tea, rubber, rice, and cacao. The capital of the Sinhalese kings after 1592, Kandy was held temporarily by the Portuguese (16th cent.) and the Dutch (18th cent.). The British captured it in 1815. Nearby Kandy are the Univ. of Sri Lanka (est. 1942) and noted botanical gardens.

kangaroo, hopping MARSUPIAL of the family Macropodidae, found in Australia, Tasmania, and New Guinea. Kangaroos have powerful hind legs, long feet, short forelimbs, and long, muscular tails for maintaining balance. The female has a pouch in which she suckles the newborn kangaroo (joey). The chief grazers of Australian plains, kangaroos are diurnal and live in herds. Great red kangaroo males may attain a height of 7 ft (210 cm) and weigh over 200 lb (90 kg). Smaller members of the kangaroo family include the rabbit-sized wallabies and pademelons. Kangaroos have been extensively hunted as pests and for their valuable hides.

Kano [kä'nō], family or school of Japanese painters. **Kano Masanobu,** c.1434–c.1530, the forerunner of the school, painted landscapes, birds, and figure pieces. Done chiefly in inks, his work is Japanese in spirit, with Chinese technical influence. His son, **Kano Motonobu,** c.1476–1559, was the actual founder of the school. He introduced heavily stressed outlines and bold decorative patterns into Chinese-style ink paintings that appealed to the warrior class. **Kano Eitoku,** 1543–90, grandson of Motonobu, painted screens with energy, ease, and inventiveness, using brilliant colors against gold-leaf backgrounds. **Kano Tanyu,** 1602–74, first known as Morinobu, was the grandson of Eitoku and was called the reviver of the Kano school. He was the official painter of the Tokugawa government (1621) and established a school of his own. His *Confucius and Disciples* is in the Museum of Fine Arts, Boston. See also JAPANESE ART.

Kano, city (1987 est. pop. 538,000), N Nigeria. It is the commercial center for an agricultural region that produces cotton, cattle, and peanuts. A rapidly growing city, it is the chief industrial center of N Nigeria, manufacturing a variety of consumer goods, and is known for its leatherwork. Kano is connected by rail with LAGOS and has an international airport. One of the seven Hausa city-states, Kano reached the height of its power in the 17th and 18th cent. The British captured the city in 1903. In 1981 it was the site of an uprising by Moslem separatists, in which nearly 1,000 were killed.

Kanpur, city (1991 pop. 2,111,284), Uttar Pradesh state, N central India, on the Ganges R. An industrial center, it produces chemicals, textiles, and other manufactures. It was a village until the Nawab of Oudh ceded it to the British in 1801. During the INDIAN MUTINY (1857) the entire British garrison, including women and children, was killed.

Kansas, midwestern state occupying the center of the coterminous U.S.; bordered by Missouri (E), Oklahoma (S), Colorado (W), and Nebraska (N).

Area, 82,264 sq mi (213,064 sq km). *Pop.* (1990) 2,477,574, a 4.8% increase over 1980 pop. *Capital,* Topeka. *Statehood,* Jan. 29, 1861 (34th state). *Highest pt.,* Mt. Sunflower, 4,039 ft (1,232 m); *lowest pt.,* Verdigris R., 680 ft (207 m). *Nickname,* Sunflower State. *Motto, Ad Astra per Aspera* [To the Stars Through Difficulties]. *State bird,* Western meadowlark. *State flower,* native sunflower. *State tree,* cottonwood. *Abbr.,* Kans.; KS.

Land and People. Kansas is part of the GREAT PLAINS and is famous for its seemingly endless fields of wheat. The land rises more than 3,000 ft (914 m) from the eastern alluvial prairies to the semiarid high plains of the west, which stretch toward the foothills of the ROCKY MOUNTAINS. Kansas has a typical continental climate characterized by seasonal extremes in temperatures, blizzards, tornadoes, and severe thunderstorms. Nearly 70% of the population lives in urban areas. WICHITA, one of the country's leading aircraft-manufacturing centers, is the largest city, followed by KANSAS CITY (adjacent to Kansas City, Mo.) and TOPEKA. In 1990, 90% of the population was white and 6% was African American.

Economy. Kansas is the country's leading producer of wheat and the second leading producer of sorghum. Corn and hay are also important crops. Cattle, raised on the abundant grazing lands, constitute the most profitable agricultural commodity. Meatpacking and the dairy industry are major economic activities, although food processing is surpassed in value by the production of transportation and computer equipment and nonelectrical machinery. Kansas is the country's leading producer of helium and also extracts petroleum, natural gas, and salt.

Government. The constitution (adopted 1859) provides for a governor elected for a four-year term. The legislature consists of a senate with 40 members serving four-year terms and a house with 125 members serving two-year terms. Kansas is represented in the U.S. Congress by two senators and four representatives and has six electoral votes.

History. When the Spanish explorer Francisco Vásquez de CORONADO visited the area in 1541, it was inhabited by Native Americans, including the Kansa, WICHITA, and PAWNEE, whose nomadic life, based on buffalo-hunting, was transformed after the Spanish introduced the horse. The U.S. acquired the land through the LOUISIANA PURCHASE (1803). As settlement proceeded during the 19th cent., Kansas became the center of national controversy on the question of slavery, and by the 1850s sentiment reached the level of armed warfare among settlers, including the abolitionist John BROWN, earning it the name "bleeding Kansas." Kansas fought with the Union in the CIVIL WAR and suffered the highest rate of fatal casualties of any northern state. After the war, thousands of new settlers arrived to farm the prairies. As part of the DUST BOWL, Kansas sustained serious land erosion during the drought of the 1930s. During World War II, airplane manufacturing became very important, and industry continued to grow into the 1980s. As the state has become increasingly urban and suburban, however, more emphasis has also been placed on the financial and service sectors concentrated in and around its major cities.

Kansas City, two adjacent cities: one (1990 pop. 149,767), seat of Wyandotte co., NE Kans. (inc. 1859); the other (1990 pop. 435,146), in NW Mo. (inc. 1850), the largest city in Missouri. Ports at the junction of the Missouri and Kansas rivers, they form a commercial, industrial, cultural, and transportation center. The cities are a huge market for crops and livestock with stockyards, grain elevators, refineries, and mills. Transportation equipment, chemicals, and petroleum and paper products are among the manufactures. The area was the starting place for many Western expeditions, and several early 19th-cent. settlements were the predecessors to today's cities. Points of interest in Kansas include an agricultural museum, a Shawnee mission (1839), and a unique mall in the city's center; among those in Missouri are the Nelson-Atkins Museum of Art, Thomas Hart Benton's home, and several theaters.

Kansas-Nebraska Act, bill passed (1854) by the U.S. Congress to establish the Kansas and Nebraska territories. Controversy over SLAVERY and conflict over the route of the proposed transcontinental railroad had delayed territorial organization of the region. Four attempts to organize a single territory had been defeated by Southern opposition to the MISSOURI COMPROMISE, which would have barred slavery from the territory. Finally, Sen. Stephen A. DOUGLAS presented a bill that made concessions to the South. It created two territories, Kansas and Nebraska, and called for "popular sovereignty" (see SQUATTER SOVEREIGNTY). An amendment repealed the antislavery clause of the Missouri Compromise. The squatter sovereignty provision caused both pro-slavery and antislavery forces to try to swing the popular decision in Kansas in their favor (see EMIGRANT AID COMPANY). The tragedy of "bleeding Kansas" resulted, and sectional division reached a point that precluded reconciliation and culminated in the CIVIL WAR.

Kant, Immanuel, 1724–1804, German philosopher, one of the greatest figures in the history of METAPHYSICS. After 1755 he taught at the Univ. of Königsberg and achieved wide renown through his teachings and writings. According to Kant, his reading of HUME woke him from his dogmatic slumber and led him to become the "critical philosopher," synthesizing the rationalism of LEIBNIZ and the SKEPTICISM of Hume. Kant proposed that objective reality is known only insofar as it conforms to the essential structure of the knowing mind. Only objects of experience, phenomena, may be known, whereas things lying beyond experience, noumena, are unknowable, even though in some cases we assume a priori knowledge of them. The existence of such unknowable "things-in-themselves" can be neither confirmed nor denied, nor can they be scientifically demonstrated. Therefore, as Kant showed in the *Critique of Pure Reason* (1781), the great problems of metaphysics—the existence of God, freedom, and immortality—are insoluble by scientific thought. Yet he went on to state in the *Critique of Practical Reason* (1788) that morality requires belief in their existence. Kant's ETHICS centers in his categorical imperative, or absolute moral law, "Act as if the maxim from which you act were to become through your will a universal law." His *Critique of Judgment* (1790) considered the concepts of beauty and purposiveness as a bridge between the sensible and the intelligible worlds. Kant's influence on modern philosophy has continued to the present day. His work fostered the development of German IDEALISM by FICHTE, SCHELLING, and HEGEL. The Neo-Kantianism of the late 19th cent. applied his insights to the study of the physical sciences (Hermann Cohen, Ernst CASSIRER) and to the historical and cultural sciences (Heinrich Rickert); his influence is also seen in the thought of DILTHEY; in the pragmatism of DEWEY and William JAMES; in the theology of SCHLEIERMACHER; and in GESTALT psychology.

Kantorovich, Leonid Vitalievich, 1912–86, Soviet economist and mathematician. He applied linear programming to economics and proposed the adoption of widely used Western economic techniques. He shared the 1975 Nobel Prize in economics with Tjalling C. Koopmans for work on optimum allocation of resources. His books include *Management Science* (1939) and *Functional Analysis* (1977).

Kaohsiung [gou-shyōōng], city (1988 est. pop. 1,343,000), S Taiwan. It is the second largest city of Taiwan, the leading port in S Taiwan, and a heavy industrial center. Its manufactures include petroleum products, metals, ships, and fertilizer. The city was developed by the Japanese, who occupied Taiwan in 1895.

Kapitza, Pyotr Leonidovich, 1894–1984, Soviet physicist. He trained in England under Ernest RUTHERFORD and contributed to LOW-TEMPERATURE PHYSICS. Forbidden to leave the USSR again, he was placed under house arrest when he refused (1946) to work on atomic weapons. He was finally released (1955) and worked on research supporting Soviet space projects. He shared the 1978 Nobel Prize in physics for his work on the superconductivity of liquid helium.

Kaplan, Mordecai Menahem, 1881–1983, American rabbi, educator, and philosopher; b. Lithuania. He is the originator of Reconstructionist JUDAISM and the founder of its Society for the Advancement of Judaism.

kapok, tropical tree of the BOMBAX family, and the resilient fiber obtained from its seeds. The water- and decay-resist ant fiber, obtained chiefly from *Ceiba pentandra,* is used as a stuffing, especially for life preservers, and for insulation against sound and heat.

Karachi, largest city (1981 pop. 4,901,627), and former capital of Pakistan, capital of Sind prov., on the Arabian Sea near the Indus R. delta. It is Pakistan's chief seaport and industrial center, with such manufactures as automobiles, refined petroleum, and steel. Developed (18th cent.) as a port and trade center by Hindu merchants, it passed (1843) to the British, who made it the seat of the Sind government, a military outpost, and a major seaport. It was Pakistan's capital from independence (1947) until 1959, when RAWALPINDI became the interim capital pending completion of ISLAMABAD. Points of interest include the tomb of Muhammad Ali JINNAH, Pakistan's founder.

Karadjordjević or **Karageorgevich,** Serbian dynasty descended from KARAGEORGE that ruled from 1842 to 1945. It alternated with its longtime rival, the OBRENOVIĆ dynasty.

Karageorge, 1768?–1817, Serbian patriot, founder of the KARADJORDJEVIĆ dynasty; b. George Petrović. After defeating the Turks, he was proclaimed (1808) hereditary chief of the Serbs. He was murdered, probably at the instigation of Miloš Obrenović.

Karageorgevich: see KARADJORDJEVIĆ.

Karajan, Herbert von [käräyän′], 1908–89, Austrian conductor. He was musical director of the Berlin Philharmonic from 1955 to 1989. He was noted for his recording activity.

Karakorum, ruined city, central Mongolia, MONGOL capital (c.1220–67) under JENGHIZ KHAN. The ruins were discovered in 1889 by N.M. Yadrinstev, a Russian explorer. A nearby site, also called Karakorum, was the UIGUR capital.

Karamanlis or **Caramanlis, Constantine,** 1907–, Greek political leader. A conservative, he was premier from 1955 to 1963. He took Greece into NATO and worked to settle the CYPRUS problem. In exile during the rule (1967–74) of the military junta, he formed the New Democratic party. Returning to Greece in 1974, he again served as premier (1974–80) and then as president (1980–85, 1990–).

Karamzin, Nikolai Mikhailovich [kərəmzēn′], 1766–1826, Russian writer. Karamzin made the Russian literary language more polished and rhythmic. His sentimental story, "Poor Liza" (1792), forecast the novel of social protest. His greatest work was his *History of the Russian State* (11 vol., 1818–24).

karate: see MARTIAL ARTS.

Kariba Dam, one of the world's largest dams, S central Africa, impounding the ZAMBEZI R. to form **Kariba Lake** (c.175 mi/280 km long and 20 mi/32 km wide), on the Zambia-Zimbabwe border. The dam, 420 ft (128 m) high and 1,900 ft (579 m) long, was built (1955–59) to provide hydroelectricity and serves as a bridge between Zimbabwe and Zambia.

Karl-Marx-Stadt: see CHEMNITZ.

Karloff, Boris, 1887–1969, Anglo-American actor; b. England as William Henry Pratt. A fine actor with a superb speaking voice, he won fame as the monster in such horror films as *Frankenstein* (1931) and *The Bride of Frankenstein* (1935).

Karlstadt: see CARLSTADT.

karma [Skt., = action, work, or ritual], basic concept common to HINDUISM, BUDDHISM, and JAINISM. The doctrine holds that one's state in this life is the result of physical and mental actions in past incarnations and that present action can determine one's destiny in future incarnations. Karma is a natural, impersonal law of moral cause and effect; only those who have attained NIRVANA, or liberation from rebirth, can transcend karma.

Karnak, village, central Egypt, on the Nile R., 1 mi (1.6 km) E of LUXOR. Remains of the pharaohs abound at Karnak. Most notable is the Great Temple of AMON; its huge hypostyle hall (388 ft by 170 ft/118 m by 52 m) has 134 columns arranged in 16 rows. The temple was largely conceived and built, on an older foundation, in the XVIII dynasty.

Karpov, Anatoly, 1951–, Russian chess master. Karpov won (1975) the world championship by default when Bobby FISCHER, the title-

Boris Karloff

holder, refused to agree to terms for a match. He successfully defended (1978, 1981) his title against Viktor Korchnoi but lost (1985) to Gary KASPAROV. Karpov again won (1993) the World Chess Federation championship when Kasparov formed a rival chess association.

Karsavina, Tamara [kərsä′vyĭnə], 1885–1978, Russian dancer. She made her debut (1902) in St. Petersburg, joined (1909) DIAGHILEV in Paris, and created principal roles in *Firebird* and *Petrouchka*. She often danced with NIJINSKY and was a leading exponent of Michel FOKINE's theories.

Karst, barren limestone plateau, W Slovenia, extending c.50 mi (80 km) southeast from the lower Soča (Isonzo) Valley. Characterized by underground drainage, caves, sinkholes, deep gullies, and other features associated with dissolution and collapse of carbonate rocks, the name has become a generic term used to describe any area where similar landforms occur.

Kasavubu, Joseph, 1917?–1969, 1st president (1960–65) of the Republic of the Congo (now ZAÏRE). Under his leadership the Congo gained independence from Belgium. Kasavubu won a struggle for power with Premier LUMUMBA but was ousted by Gen. MOBUTU in 1965.

Kashmir [kăshmēr′], disputed territory, S Asia, administered since 1972 as the Indian state of Jammu and Kashmir (1991 pop. 7,718,000; c.54,000 sq mi/139,900 sq km; capital Srinagar), the only predominantly Muslim Indian state, and the Pakistani Azad Kashmir (1981 est. pop. 1,980,000; c.32,000 sq mi/82,900 sq km; capital, Muzaffarabad). Known for its beauty, Kashmir is covered with lofty, rugged mountains, including sections of the HIMALAYAN and Karakorum ranges. The heart of the region is the Vale of Kashmir, where wheat and rice are grown. After years of Buddhist and Hindu rule, Kashmir was converted to Islam in the late 14th cent., and became part of the MOGUL empire in 1586. The British installed a Hindu prince as ruler in 1846. Since the partition of India in 1947, control of the territory has been contested by India and Pakistan (see INDIA-PAKISTAN WARS), with occasional interference by China. The present division of the territory was drawn up in 1972. In the late 1980s unrest grew in Indian Kashmir as Muslim militants, some supporting independence and others union with Pakistan, resorted to guerrilla attacks. In 1990 the region was placed under army rule in an attempt to suppress the insurgency; the army has used often brutal measures to maintain Indian rule.

Kashmiri [kăshmē′rē], language belonging to the Dardic group of the Indo-Iranian subfamily of the Indo-European family of languages. See LANGUAGE (table).

Kasimir. For Polish rulers thus named, see CASIMIR.

Kasparov, Gary, 1963–, Armenian chess player; b. Azerbaijan as

Garri Kimovich Wainshtein. In Sept. 1984 he challenged Anatoly KARPOV for the world championship and appeared likely to win when the match was halted amid controversy in Feb. 1985. He won a rematch (Sept.–Nov. 1985), becoming the youngest world champion ever. He later broke with the World Chess Federation and formed a rival association; in 1993 he defended against Nigel Short. Kasparov is noted for his aggressive style of play.

Kassebaum, Nancy Landon: see under LANDON, ALFRED MOSSMAN.

Katanga: see SHABA.

Katayev, Valentin Petrovich [kətī'əf], 1897–1987, Russian novelist, playwright, poet, and short-story writer; brother of Yevgeny Petrov (see under ILF, ILYA). In *The Embezzlers* (1926), a novel, and *Squaring the Circle* (1928), a play, he satirized Soviet economic conditions. His four-part novel, *Black Sea Waves* (1936–61), portrays Russian life from 1905 through World War II. *The Holy Well* (1966) and *Broken Life* (1972) are memoirs.

Katayev, Yevgeny Petrovich: see PETROV, YEVGENY PETROVICH.

Katharine of Aragón, 1485–1536, first queen consort of HENRY VIII of England; daughter of Ferdinand V of Castile and León and ISABELLA I of Castile. In 1501 she married Arthur, eldest son of HENRY VII. He died in 1502; a papal dispensation allowed Henry VIII, his brother, to marry Katharine in 1509. Only one of her six children (MARY I) survived infancy, and Henry became impatient for a male heir. Also, with the collapse of the English-Spanish alliance in 1525, Katharine's political influence waned. In 1527 Henry tried to have the marriage annulled, a move that led to the English REFORMATION. After his secret marriage (1533) to Anne BOLEYN, Henry had a court declare his first marriage invalid. Katharine was confined at various estates; she refused to recognize the divorce or the break with Rome.

Katmai National Park: see NATIONAL PARKS (table).

Katmandu, city (1981 pop. 235,160), capital of Nepal, central Nepal, c.4,500 ft (1,370 m) above sea level, in a fertile Himalayan valley. Nepal's administrative and commercial center, it lies on an ancient route from India to China. Ruled by the Newars, it fell (1768) to the GURKHAS. Landmarks include the royal palace, temples, and Sanskrit libraries.

Katsushika Hokusai: see HOKUSAI.

katydid, name for some large, singing, winged INSECTS of the long-horned GRASSHOPPER (family Tettigoniidae). Katydids are green or pink and range from 1¼ to 5 in. (3 to 12.5 cm) in length. They are nocturnal and arboreal. The song of the male, which supposedly sounds like "Katy did, Katy didn't," is produced by rubbing together specialized structures on the front wings.

Katyn [kətĭn'], village, W European Russia, W of Smolensk near the Belarus border. It was occupied by the Germans in World War II. In 1943 the German government announced that the mass graves of 4,250 Polish officers had been found in a nearby forest and blamed Soviet forces for the massacre. The Soviet government asserted that the Poles had been killed by the Germans. In 1990 the USSR admitted that Soviet secret police had killed the Poles, and in 1992 Russian officials released documents that showed STALIN had ordered the killings.

Kauffmann, Angelica, 1741–1807, Swiss neoclassical painter and graphic artist. A protégée of Sir Joshua REYNOLDS and one of the original members of the Royal Academy, she was a fashionable portraitist and decorator. After her marriage in 1781 she lived in Italy. Her works include *Religion* (National Gall., London) and the etching *La Pensierosa*.

Kaufman, George S., 1889–1961, American playwright; b. Pittsburgh. He collaborated on over 40 plays, including *Beggar on Horseback* (1924; with Marc CONNELLY), *Dinner at Eight* (1932; with Edna FERBER), and *Of Thee I Sing* (1932; with Morrie Ryskind and George GERSHWIN; Pulitzer). Many of his most famous plays were written with Moss HART, e.g., *You Can't Take It with You* (1936; Pulitzer), *The Man Who Came to Dinner* (1939).

Kauai [kou″wī'], island (1990 pop. 51,177), 549 sq mi (1,422 sq km), N Hawaii. Formed by extinct volcanoes, it is the oldest Hawaiian island, with Kawaikini (5,170 ft/1,576 m high) its tallest peak. Most people live along the coast; Lihue (1990 pop. 5,536) is the largest town. Sugarcane, rice, and pineapples are the chief crops, and tourism is important. An independent kingdom when visited (1778) by Capt. James COOK, it became (1810) part of the kingdom of HAWAII. The island was devastated by a hurricane in 1992.

Kaunda, Kenneth [koun'də], 1924–, African political leader, president of ZAMBIA (1964–91). He led the nationalist movement in Northern Rhodesia. When it became independent (1964) as Zambia he became its first president and gained prominence as an opponent of white minority rule in neighboring Rhodesia (see ZIMBABWE) and in South Africa. In 1972 he proclaimed a one-party state. Discontent with one-party rule and deteriorating economic conditions led to several coup attempts against him, and in 1990 opposition parties were again legalized. He was overwhelmingly defeated for reelection in 1991.

Kawabata Yasunari [käwä'bätä], 1899–1972, Japanese novelist. Written in a lyrical, impressionistic style, his novels are distinguished by a masterful use of imagery. Often they treat, in a delicate, oblique fashion, the relationship of men to women, of humanity to nature. His novels include *Snow Country* (tr. 1956) and *The Sound of the Mountain* (tr. 1970). In 1968 Kawabata became the first Japanese author to receive the Nobel Prize in literature.

Kawasaki, city (1990 pop. 1,173,606), Kanagawa prefecture, central Honshu, Japan, on Tokyo Bay. Located in the Tokyo-Yokohama industrial area, it has steel mills, shipyards, oil refineries, and factories producing electrical machinery, motors, petrochemicals, and cement. Heigenji Temple, dedicated to the Buddhist priest Kukai, is in Kawasaki.

Kazakhstan, officially Republic of Kazakhstan, republic (1992 est. pop. 17,104,000), c.1,050,000 sq mi (2,719,500 sq km), central Asia, formerly a constituent republic of the USSR. It borders on Russia (N); China (E); Kyrgyzstan, Uzbekistan, and Turkmenistan (S); and the Caspian Sea and European Russia (W). The capital is Almaty (Alma-Ata); other large cities are Qaraghandy (Karaganda), Shymkent (Chimkent), Semey (Semipalatinsk), and Öskemen (Ust-Kamenogorsk). Kazakhstan produces much wool, cattle, and wheat and is rich in coal, oil, gas, and such minerals as chromium, silver, tungsten, lead, zinc, and copper. The Turkic-speaking Muslim Kazakhs (Qazaqs) comprise only 40% of the population; ethnic Russians make up 38% of the population, and other groups include Germans, Ukrainians, Tatars, and Uzbeks. The official language is Kazakh, but Russian remains the primary language of commerce and government.

History. The region was ruled by the MONGOLS from the 13th to 18th cent. and then by Russia. In 1916 the Kazakhs rebelled against Russian rule, and were in the process of establishing a Western-style state when the Bolshevik Revolution occurred in 1917. The region became part of the USSR in 1920 and a constituent republic in 1936. As the USSR broke up following the hard-line coup against Soviet Pres. GORBACHEV (1991), Kazakhstan declared its independence—it was one of the last republics to do so—and joined the COMMONWEALTH OF INDEPENDENT STATES. Nursultan A. Nazarbayev, president of Kazakhstan since 1990, has moved to privatize the economy since independence.

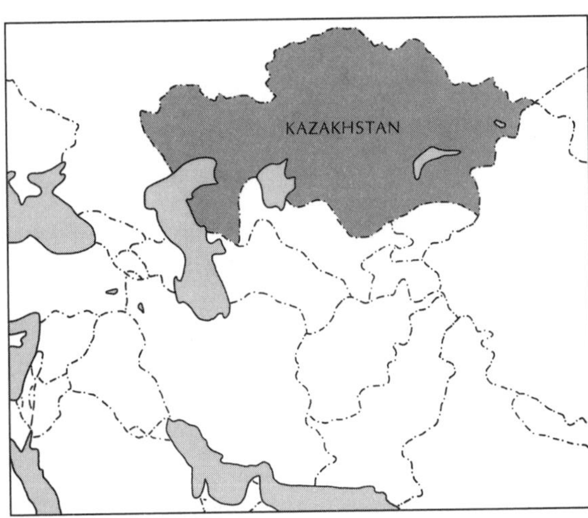

Kazan, Elia, 1909–, American stage and film director, producer, and writer; b. Turkey as Elia Kazanjoglous. A founding member of the Actors' Studio (see STRASBERG, LEE), he directed *A Streetcar Named Desire* (1947; film, 1951), *Death of a Salesman* (1949), and the film *On the Waterfront* (1954). He has also written several novels, e.g., *The Anatolian* (1982), and an autobiography (1988).

Kazan, city (1990 est. pop. 1,001,000), capital of Tatarstan, E European Russia. A major port on the Volga R., it has shipyards, chemical and explosives factories, and other industries. Founded in 1401, it became (1445) the capital of a powerful TATAR khanate that was conquered (1552) by IVAN IV of Russia. TOLSTOY and LENIN studied at the Univ. of Kazan (founded 1804).

Kazantzakis, Nikos [kä"zändzä'kēs], 1883–1957, Greek writer; b. Crete. Of an intensely poetic and religious nature, he produced his most ambitious work in *The Odyssey, a Modern Sequel* (1938), a verse tale that explores the world views of BUDDHA, JESUS, NIETZSCHE, LENIN, and others. He is, however, better known for two earthy, realistic novels, *The Greek Passion* (1938) and *Zorba the Greek* (1946), both of which were filmed.

Kean, Edmund, 1787?–1833, English actor. His violent acting style expressed the romantic ideal. Popular in the U.S. and England, he was famous for Shakespearean roles. His Shylock in *The Merchant of Venice* was a landmark in theater history. His son, **Charles John Kean,** 1811?–1868, was best known for his spectacular and historically accurate productions. Charles's wife, **Ellen Tree Kean,** 1806–80, was a noted comedienne.

Kearny, Stephen Watts, 1794–1848, American general in the MEXICAN WAR; b. Newark, N.J. Made (1846) commander in the West, Kearny captured Santa Fe and Los Angeles and was military governor of California until 1847. His nephew, **Philip Kearny,** 1814–62, commanded the 1st New Jersey Brigade in the U.S. CIVIL WAR. He fought in the PENINSULAR CAMPAIGN and at the second battle of BULL RUN. In Sept. 1862 he was killed when he unwittingly crossed Confederate lines at Chantilly.

Keating, Paul, 1944–, Australian politician. A trade-union official and Labor party member, he was elected to parliament in 1969. He was (1983–91) federal treasurer (treasury minister) and deputy prime minister (1990–91) under Prime Min. HAWKE and pushed free-market economic policies designed to spur growth. In mid-1991 he challenged Hawke for the party leadership but lost and resigned his posts. Continuing recession, however, eroded support for Hawke, and Keating replaced him (Dec. 1991) and later (1993) won re-election. As prime minister, Keating has emphasized Australia's ties with Asia and sought to end the British monarch's role as head of state.

Keaton, Buster (Joseph Francis Keaton), 1895–1966, American film actor and director; b. Piqua, Kans. A comic genius, he made such silent films as *Sherlock Junior* (1924), *The Navigator* (1924), and *The General* (1927).

Keats, John, 1795–1821, English poet, considered one of the greatest English poets. Apprenticed to a surgeon in 1811, he soon came to know Leigh HUNT and in 1816 gave up surgery for poetry. His first volume of poems appeared in 1817; it included "On First Looking into Chapman's Homer." The long poem *Endymion,* published in 1818, was vigorously attacked by the critics. Keats's passionate love for Fanny Brawne began in 1818, but he had contracted tuberculosis and they did not marry. Shortly after the publication of *Lamia, Isabella, The Eve of St. Agnes, and Other Poems* (1820), Keats went to Italy for his health and died there at the age of 25. Keats's poems are unequaled for dignity, melody, and richness of imagery. They include "Ode to a Nightingale," "Ode on a Grecian Urn," "To Autumn," "Ode on Melancholy," and the unfinished epic "Hyperion." "The Eve of St. Agnes" and "La Belle Dame sans Merci" are examples of romantic medievalism at its best. His sonnets include "When I have fears that I may cease to be" and "Bright star, would I were stedfast as thou art."

Keble, John, 1792–1866, English clergyman and poet. His poetical work *The Christian Year* (1827), based on the BOOK OF COMMON PRAYER, won him a professorship of poetry at Oxford (1831–41). J.H. NEWMAN called his sermon "National Apostasy" (1833) the start of the OXFORD MOVEMENT.

Keeling Islands: see COCOS (KEELING) ISLANDS.

Kefauver, (Cary) Estes, 1903–63, U.S. political leader; b. Madisonville, Tenn. A Democratic congressman (1939–49) and senator (1949–63) from Tennessee, he led (1950–51) a Senate committee investigating crime and supported civil-rights legislation. He was the unsuccessful Democratic candidate for vice president in 1956.

Kekkonen, Urho Kaleva [kĕ'kōnĕn], 1900–86, president of Finland (1956–81). Leader of the Agrarian party (from 1965 the Center party), he held various cabinet posts from 1936 and was prime minister (1950–56). He resigned the presidency for reasons of health and was succeeded (1982) by Mauno Koivisto.

Kekulé von Stradonitz, Friedrich August [kā'ko͝olā], 1829–96, German organic chemist. A professor at Bonn, he is most noted for his representation of the molecular structure of BENZENE as a ring. Such rings are the basic structural feature of AROMATIC COMPOUNDS.

Keller, Helen Adams, 1880–1968, American author and lecturer; b. Tuscumbia, Ala. Blind and deaf from the age of two, she was put (1887) in the care of Anne Sullivan (see MACY, ANNE SULLIVAN), who became her teacher and lifelong companion. Keller made rapid progress and in 1904 was graduated from Radcliffe College with honors. She published and lectured widely to raise funds for the training of the blind and for other social causes.

Kellogg-Briand Pact, or Pact of Paris, agreement reached in 1928 by 15 nations (and eventually ratified by 62 nations) who agreed to settle all conflicts by peaceful means and who renounced war as an instrument of national policy. U.S. Secy. of State Frank Billings Kellogg and French Foreign Minister Aristide BRIAND were its sponsors. Its effectiveness was vitiated by its failure to provide measures of enforcement. Ultimately, the pact proved to be meaningless, especially as nations adopted the practice of waging undeclared wars.

Kelly, Ellsworth, 1923–, American painter; b. Newburgh, N.Y. He paints flat color areas, usually with sharp, geometric contours, e.g., *Atlantic* (1956; Whitney Mus., N.Y.C.).

Kelly, George, 1887–1974, American playwright; b. Philadelphia. His best-known plays, satires on American middle-class life, include *The Torch-Bearers* (1922) and *Craig's Wife* (1925; Pulitzer).

Kelly, Grace (Patricia): see GRACE, princess consort of Monaco.

Kelvin, William Thomson, 1st **Baron,** 1824–1907, British mathematician and physicist; b. Ireland. He was professor (1846–99) of natural philosophy at the Univ. of Glasgow. His work in THERMODYNAMICS coordinating the various existing theories of heat established the law of the conservation of ENERGY as proposed by James JOULE. He discovered the Thomson effect in thermoelectricity and introduced the Kelvin scale, or absolute scale, of TEMPERATURE. His work on the transmission of messages by undersea cables made him a leading authority in this field.

kelvin: see METRIC SYSTEM; TEMPERATURE.

Kelvin temperature scale: see TEMPERATURE.

Kemp, Jack (French), 1935–, U.S. politician and government official; b. Los Angeles. A professional football quarterback for 13 seasons (1957–69), primarily with the San Diego Chargers and Buffalo Bills, he was elected as a U.S. representative from New York in 1970. A conservative Republican, he championed supply-side economics and urban ENTERPRISE ZONES, coauthored the 1981 Kemp-Roth tax cut bill, and ran unsuccessfully for the 1988 Republican presidential nomination. He was (1989–93) secretary of housing and urban development under Pres. BUSH.

Kempis, Thomas à: see THOMAS À KEMPIS.

Kenai Fjords National Park: see NATIONAL PARKS (table).

Kendall, George Wilkins, 1809–67, American journalist; b. near Amherst, N.H. A partner in founding (1837) the New Orleans *Picayune,* he was an active exponent of the MEXICAN WAR, in which he served. His reports, sent back to his paper by private express, earned him a reputation as the first modern war correspondent.

kendo: see MARTIAL ARTS.

Keneally, Thomas, 1935–, Australian novelist. His strong, often violent novels are usually set in a specific historical period, e.g., *The Chant of Jimmie Blacksmith* (1972), about an aborigine run amok in the Australia of 1900. His other novels include *The Confederates* (1979) and *Flying Hero Class* (1991). *Schindler's List* (1982) novelizes the story of Oskar Schindler, a businessman who saved the lives of many Jews during the HOLOCAUST.

Kennan, George Frost, 1904–, U.S. diplomat and historian; b. Milwaukee, Wis. A formulator of the policy of "containment" toward the USSR, he was ambassador to Moscow (1952) until the Russians demanded his removal. He later served (1961–63) as ambassador to Yugoslavia. His works include *American Diplomacy, 1900–1950* (1951), his memoirs (2 vol., 1967–72), and the autobiographical *Sketches from a Life* (1989).

Kennedy, American family, active in U.S. government and politics. **Joseph Patrick Kennedy,** 1888–1969, b. Boston, engaged in banking, shipbuilding, and motion-picture distribution before serving as chairman of the Securities and Exchange Commission (1934–35) and head of the U.S. Maritime Commission (1936–37). He was U.S. ambassador to Great Britain (1937–40). His son **John Fitzgerald Kennedy** was president of the U.S. (see separate article). His son **Robert Francis Kennedy,** 1925–68, b. Brookline, Mass., served (1961–64) as U.S. attorney general. He resigned after Pres. Kennedy's death and was elected (1964) U.S. senator from New York. In 1968 he sought the Democratic presidential nomination, but after winning the California primary he was mortally wounded by a gunman, Sirhan B. Sirhan. Joseph Kennedy's youngest son, **Edward Moore Kennedy,** 1932–, b. Boston, has served as U.S. senator from Massachusetts since 1962. A spokesman for liberal causes, he has advocated such reforms as national health insurance and tax reform. His political future was marred somewhat by the Chappaquiddick incident (July 1969) in which Mary Jo Kopechne, a passenger in a car he was driving on an island near Martha's Vineyard, Mass., was drowned when the car ran off a bridge. Kennedy unsuccessfully challenged Pres. Jimmy CARTER for the 1980 Democratic presidential nomination.

Kennedy, Anthony M.: see SUPREME COURT, UNITED STATES (table 1).

Kennedy, John Fitzgerald, 1917–63, 35th president of the U.S. (1961–63); son of Joseph P. Kennedy; brother of Robert Francis Kennedy and Edward Moore Kennedy (see KENNEDY, family); b. Brookline, Mass. After enlisting in the U.S. navy in World War II, he served with distinction as commander of a PT boat in the Pacific. He was a Democratic congressman from Massachusetts (1947–53) and in 1952 won a seat in the U.S. Senate. The next year he married Jacqueline Lee Bouvier (see ONASSIS, JACQUELINE BOUVIER). Kennedy narrowly lost the Democratic vice presidential nomination in 1956 and in 1960 won the party's presidential nomination. He defeated Republican Richard NIXON, becoming at 43 the youngest man to be elected president. His domestic program, the New Frontier, called for tax reform, federal aid to education, medical care for the aged under Social Security, and the extension of civil rights. Many of his reforms, however, stalled in Congress, and foreign-affairs crises occupied much of his time. He was much criticized for his approval for the abortive BAY OF PIGS INVASION (1961) of Cuba. In Oct. 1962 U.S. reconnaissance planes discovered Soviet missile bases there. In the ensuing CUBAN MISSILE CRISIS, Kennedy ordered a blockade of Cuba and demanded the removal of the missiles. After a brief and tense interval, the USSR complied with his demands. The next year the U.S. and the Soviet Union signed a limited treaty banning nuclear tests. Kennedy also increased the number of U.S. military advisers in South Vietnam to about 16,000 (see VIETNAM WAR). He established the Alliance for Progress to give economic aid to Latin America and created the PEACE CORPS. He also pressed hard to achieve racial INTEGRATION in the South. On Nov. 22, 1963, Kennedy was shot and killed in Dallas, Tex. Vice Pres. Lyndon JOHNSON succeeded him as president. The WARREN COMMISSION, appointed to investigate the assassination, concluded that it was the work of a single gunman, Lee Harvey Oswald. In 1979, however, the House Select Committee on Assassinations, relying in part on acoustical evidence, concluded that a conspiracy was "likely" and that it may have involved organized crime.

Kenneth I, d. 858, traditional founder of the kingdom of Scotland. He united (c.843) the thrones of Dalriada and the Picts.

Kensett, John Frederick, 1818–72, American painter; b. Cheshire, Conn. Famous for delicately colored landscapes, he was a member of the HUDSON RIVER SCHOOL.

Kent, Rockwell, 1882–1971, American artist and writer; b. Tarrytown, N.Y. Kent is known for his stark, powerful graphic art and paintings. His major works include *Toilers of the Sea* (Art Inst., Chicago) and *Winter* (Metropolitan Mus.). Among his books are *Wilderness* (1921) and *Salamina* (1935).

Kent, kingdom of, one of the kingdoms of Anglo-Saxon England. Kent was settled (mid-5th cent.) by the Jutes, who overcame the British inhabitants. Their kingdom comprised essentially the area of the present county of Kent. King ÆTHELBERT of Kent established hegemony over England south of the Humber R. and became a Christian. Kent was later subject to King OFFA of MERCIA and in 825 became part of WESSEX. The kingdom remained an advanced area of pre-Norman England because of the archbishopric of CANTERBURY and because of steady intercourse with the Continent.

Kentucky, one of the so-called border states of the S central U.S.; bordered by West Virginia (E), Tennessee (S), the Mississippi R., across which lies Missouri (SW), and Illinois, Indiana, and Ohio, all across the Ohio R. (W, N).

Area, 40,395 sq mi (104,623 sq km). *Pop.* (1990) 3,685,296, a 0.7% increase over 1980 pop. *Capital,* Frankfort. *Statehood,* June 1, 1792 (15th state). *Highest pt.,* Black Mt., 4,145 ft (1,264 m); *lowest pt.,* Mississippi R., 257 ft (78 m). *Nickname,* Bluegrass State. *Motto,* United We Stand, Divided We Fall. *State bird,* cardinal. *State flower,* goldenrod. *State tree,* Kentucky coffee tree. *Abbr.,* Ky.; KY.

Land and People. Coal-rich E Kentucky is part of the APPALACHIAN MOUNTAINS system. The mountains give way in the west to the rolling agricultural plains and rocky hillsides of the Pennyroyal, the famous Bluegrass region, where thoroughbreds are raised, and low flatlands along the MISSISSIPPI R. The climate is generally mild. About 52% of the population lives in urban areas. LOUISVILLE is the largest city, followed in size by LEXINGTON. In 1990 the population was 92% white and 7% African American.

Economy. Manufacturing accounts for most of Kentucky's income, with nonelectrical machinery, apparel, electrical equipment, and chemicals among the principal products. Finance, insurance, and real estate also now play significant roles in the state's economy. Tobacco has long been the state's chief crop. Other major agricultural products are cattle, soybeans, dairy products, corn, and hay. Kentucky leads the nation in the production of bituminous and lignite coal, and stone, petroleum, and natural gas are also extracted. The Kentucky Dam, on the TENNESSEE R., is a major part of the TENNESSEE VALLEY AUTHORITY. Tourism is of growing importance, partly because of such attractions as Mammoth Cave National Park (see NATIONAL PARKS, table) and the annual Kentucky Derby thoroughbred race, held in Louisville.

Government. The constitution of 1891 provides for a governor elected to a four-year term. The general assembly consists of a senate whose 38 members serve four-year terms and a house with 100 members elected to two-year terms. Kentucky is represented in the U.S. Congress by six representatives and two senators and has eight electoral votes.

History. Early settlers began crossing the mountains to settle in Kentucky during the 1760s, and in 1775 Daniel BOONE helped to blaze the WILDERNESS ROAD. After Kentucky became (1792) the first state west of the Appalachians to join the Union, it prospered from river traffic on the Mississippi and Ohio. Residents of this border state were torn over the question of slavery, and although Kentucky remained in the Union, its residents fought on both sides in the CIVIL WAR. Coal mining, which began on a large scale during the 1870s, was well established by the early 20th cent. Mining areas, especially Harlan co., became the scene of violent labor strife when the United Mine Workers of America attempted to unionize the mines during the 1930s. Mining subsequently entered a decline, but because of the national energy crisis of the 1970s, Kentucky enjoyed new prosperity from the revival of its coal-mining industry during the 1970s and 80s.

Kentucky and Virginia Resolutions, in U.S. history, resolutions passed in 1798 and 1799 by the Kentucky and Virginia legislatures in opposition to the ALIEN AND SEDITION ACTS. The Kentucky Resolutions, written by Thomas JEFFERSON, stated that the federal government had no right to exercise powers not delegated to it by the Constitution. A further resolution declared that the states could nullify objectionable federal laws. The Virginia Resolutions, written by James MADISON, were milder. Both were later considered the first notable statements of the STATES' RIGHTS doctrine.

Kenya [kĕn'yə, kēn'–], officially Republic of Kenya, republic (1992 est. pop. 26,164,000), 224,960 sq mi (582,646 sq km), E Africa, bordered by Somalia (E), the Indian Ocean (SE), Tanzania (S),

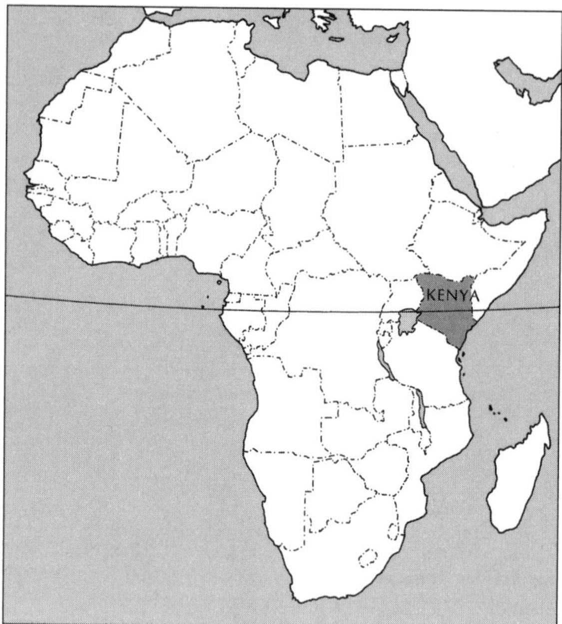

Lake Victoria (SW), Uganda (W), the Sudan (NW), and Ethiopia (N). Principal cities are NAIROBI, the capital, and MOMBASA, the chief port. Kenya, which lies astride the equator, has five main regions: a narrow, dry coastal strip; bush-covered plains in the interior; high-lying scrublands in the northwest; fertile grasslands and highland forests in the southwest; and the GREAT RIFT VALLEY in the west, location of some of the country's highest mountains, including MT. KENYA (17,058 ft/5,199 m), and of Lake Turkana (Rudolf). Except for the temperate highlands, the climate is hot and dry. The great majority of Kenyans engage in subsistence farming. Coffee, tea, petroleum products, cereals, and fresh vegetables, fruits, and flowers are the chief exports. Large numbers of cattle are pastured in the grasslands. Industry, which is expanding, includes oil refining, food processing, and the manufacture of consumer goods, cement, and textiles. Tourists, attracted by Kenya's protected wildlife in Tsavo National Park, are an important source of income. The Kikuyu, Luhya, Luo, Kalenjin, Kamba, and 35 other indigenous ethnic groups make up 97% of the population. Many of the people follow traditional beliefs, but about 65% are Christian and about 6% Muslim. Swahili is the official language, but English is used in commerce.

History. Anthropological discoveries indicate that humans, perhaps the first on earth, probably inhabited southern Kenya some 2 million years ago. In the Kenya highlands farming and domestic herds can be dated to 1000 B.C. Arab traders settled on the coast by the 8th cent. A.D., establishing several autonomous city-states. The Portuguese, who first visited the Kenya coast in 1498, gained control of much of it but were expelled by Arabs in 1729. In 1886, under a British-German agreement on spheres of influence in E Africa, most of present-day Kenya passed to Britain, and in 1903, after a railroad opened up the interior, the first European settlers moved in. Under Britain, Europeans controlled the government, and Indians, who had arrived earlier, were active in commerce, while Africans were largely confined to subsistence farming or to work as laborers. Protests by Africans over their inferior status reached a peak in the so-called MAU-MAU emergency (1952–56), an armed revolt against British rule. After the rebellion Britain increased African representation in the legislative council, and in 1963 Kenya gained independence. The country became a republic in 1964, with Jomo KENYATTA as president. The first decade of independence was marked by disputes among ethnic groups (especially the Kikuyu and the Luo), by the exodus of many Europeans and Asians, and by sporadic fighting with Somalia over boundary issues. Daniel arap MOI of the Kenya African National Union succeeded to the presidency after Kenyatta's death in 1978. A stable democracy in 1978, Kenya under Moi became a one-party state and, increasingly, a dictatorship. Undermined by growing internal opposition and international resistance to supplying aid to his government, Moi agreed to end one-party rule in 1991, but social and political unrest, especially tribal conflicts that Moi's government has been accused of promoting, continued. Moi was reelected president (1992) in a multiparty election that his opponents denounced as fraudulent.

Kenya, Mount, or **Mount Kirinyaga,** extinct volcano, 17,058 ft (5,199 m) high, in Kenya. The snow-capped peak, located near the equator, is the second-highest mountain in Africa, after KILIMANJARO.

Kenyatta, Jomo, 1893?–1978, 1st president of KENYA (1964–78). One of the best-known African leaders, he founded various pan-African nationalist movements. He was imprisoned by the British in 1953 following the MAU MAU uprising and was exiled in 1959. He was released in 1961 to negotiate Kenya's independence (1963).

Kepler, Johannes, 1571–1630, German astronomer. He was professor of mathematics at Graz (1593–98) and court mathematician to Holy Roman Emperor Rudolf II. In 1596 he wrote *Mysterium cosmographicum,* which led to exchanges with GALILEO and Tycho BRAHE. His *Astronomia nova* (1609) contained the first two of what became KEPLER'S LAWS; the third law appeared in 1619 in his *Harmonice mundi.* These laws were the result of calculations based on Brahe's accurate observations, which Kepler published in the *Tabulae Rudolphinae* (1627).

Kepler's laws, three mathematical statements by Johannes KEPLER that accurately describe the revolutions of the planets around the sun. The first law states that the shape of each planet's orbit is an ellipse (see CONIC SECTION), with the sun at one focus. The second law states that if an imaginary line is drawn from the sun to the planet, the line will sweep out equal areas in space in equal periods of time for all points in the orbit. The third law states that the ratio of the cube of the semimajor axis of the ellipse (i.e., the average distance of the planet from the sun) to the square of the planet's period (the time it needs to complete one revolution around the sun) is the same for all the planets. Newton gave a physical explanation of Kepler's laws with his laws of MOTION and law of GRAVITATION. See also CELESTIAL MECHANICS.

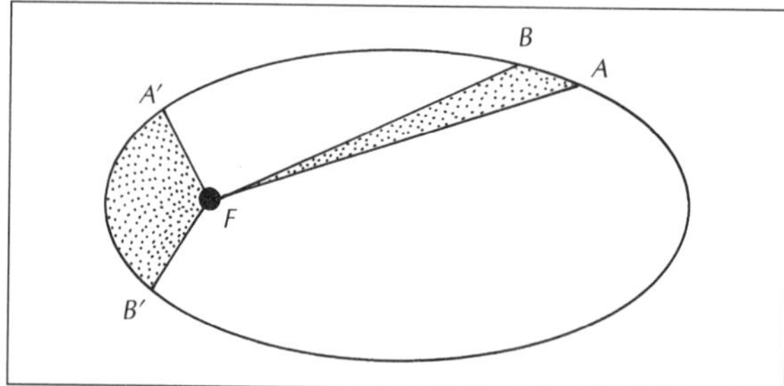

Kepler's law: Schematic representation of Kepler's second law. The areas ABF and A′B′F are equal and are swept out in equal intervals of time by a planet orbiting around the sun (at F).

Kerensky, Aleksandr Feodorovich, 1881–1970, Russian revolutionary. He was prime minister in the provisional government that followed the Feb. 1917 RUSSIAN REVOLUTION, but his failure to withdraw Russia from WORLD WAR I or to deal with economic problems enabled the Bolsheviks (see BOLSHEVISM) to overthrow him in Nov. 1917. He fled to Paris and then (1940) to the U.S.

Kerguelen Island: see FRENCH SOUTHERN AND ANTARCTIC LANDS.

Kérkira or **Corfu,** island (1991 pop. 105,043), 229 sq mi (593 sq km), NW Greece, in the Ionian Sea. Its industries include agriculture, fishing, and tourism. Settled c.730 B.C. by Corinthians, it later concluded a rebellious alliance with Athens that helped to precipitate (431 B.C.) the PELOPONNESIAN WAR.

Kern, Jerome, 1885–1945, American composer; b. N.Y.C. Among his successful MUSICALS were *Show Boat* (1927; with Oscar HAMMERSTEIN 2d) and *Roberta* (1933). He wrote many famous songs, including "Smoke Gets in Your Eyes."

kerosene or **kerosine,** a colorless, thin oil that is less dense than water. It is a mixture of HYDROCARBONS commonly obtained in the fractional DISTILLATION of PETROLEUM, but also from coal, oil shale, and wood. Once the most important refinery product because of its use in lamps, kerosene is now used chiefly as a carrier in insecticide sprays and as a fuel in jet engines.

Kerouac, Jack, 1922–69, American writer; b. Lowell, Mass. A leader of the BEAT GENERATION, he wrote of the frenetic pursuit of new experience. His best-known work is the novel *On the Road* (1957). He also wrote other novels and poetry.

Ketchwayo: see CETEWAYO.

kettledrum: see DRUM.

Kew Gardens, Surrey, S England, on the Thames just W of London; officially, Royal Botanic Gardens. Founded in 1761 by a member of the royal family and presented to the nation in 1841, the gardens cover 288 acres (117 hectares) and contain thousands of plant species, four museums, and laboratories and greenhouses.

Key, Francis Scott, 1779–1843, American poet, author of the STAR-SPANGLED BANNER; b. Carroll co., Md. A lawyer, he was U.S. attorney for the District of Columbia (1833–41).

key, in music, is used to indicate the scale from which the tonal material of a composition is derived. To say that a composition is in the key of C major means that it uses as its basic tonal material the tones of the C-major scale and that its harmony employs the chords built on the tones of that scale. MODULATION to another key may be utilized within the composition. A term usually used synonymously with *key* is TONALITY; absence of a feeling of key is ATONALITY.

Key Largo, island: see FLORIDA KEYS.

Keynes, John Maynard, Baron Keynes of Tilton [kānz], 1883–1946, English economist and monetary expert. His theories, known as Keynesian economics, are the most influential economic formulation of the 20th cent. In 1919 he represented the British treasury at the peace conference ending WORLD WAR I, but he resigned in protest over the VERSAILLES Treaty's economic provisions. He gained world fame with *Economic Consequences of the Peace* (1919). His departure from the classical concepts of a free economy dates from 1929, when he endorsed a government public-works program to promote employment. In the 1930s his theories prompted several nations to adopt spending programs, such as those of the NEW DEAL, to maintain high national income. His chief work, *The General Theory of Employment, Interest, and Money* (1936), advocates active government intervention in the market and, during recessionary times, deficit spending and easier monetary policies to stimulate business activity. At the Bretton Woods Conference (1944) he helped to win support for the creation of a world bank. He was raised to the peerage in 1942.

Key West, city (1990 pop. 24,832), seat of Monroe co., S Fla., on an island at the SW end of the FLORIDA KEYS, c.150 mi (240 km) from Miami, 90 mi (145 km) from Cuba. It is the southernmost city of the continental U.S., a resort and artists' colony and fishing center. Winslow HOMER painted there; Ernest HEMINGWAY, whose home is a museum, wrote there.

KGB, abbreviation of the Russian name of the USSR's Committee for State Security, the Soviet SECRET POLICE from 1953–54 to 1991. It and the MVD, the Ministry of the Interior, were the two organizations sharing responsibility for order and security. The KGB was responsible for security troops, the loyalty of government employees and the elite, and espionage and subversive activities abroad. The origins of the KGB were in the CHEKA, founded under LENIN and headed by Felix DZERZHINSKY. Reorganized in the 1920s as the OGPU (United State Political Directorate), its functions were transferred (1934) to the NKVD (People's Commissariat for Internal Affairs). The NKVD became notorious as the instrument of STALIN's state terror. In 1943 the NKVD was split into the predecessor organizations of the KGB and MVD, which were briefly reunited after Stalin's death under Lavrenti BERIA. Under KHRUSHCHEV, the KGB's arbitrary powers were reduced, and it was subjected to party control. In the aftermath of the attempted coup (1991) against Soviet Pres. GORBACHEV, in which KGB leaders played a major role, reformers were named to head the KGB and Interior Ministry. The KGB was renamed and restricted to counterintelligence, economic crimes, and air and rail security. Foreign intelligence gathering was assigned to the new Central Intelligence Service. With the USSR's collapse, Russia absorbed the KGB's remnants, combining most of them under the Security and Internal Affairs Ministry. YELTSIN ordered the ministry replaced with a new Federal Counterintelligence Service in 1993.

Khachaturian, Aram Ilich, 1903–78, Russian composer of Armenian parentage. His colorful music uses Armenian and Asian folk elements. He is best known for the ballet *Gayané* (1942), including the popular *Sabre Dance.*

Khalid ibn Abd al-Aziz al-Saud, 1913–82, king of Saudi Arabia (1975–82). He became king after the assassination of his half-brother FAISAL. The son of IBN SAUD, the founder of Saudi Arabia, he was the third of Ibn Saud's sons to become king. He continued the widespread economic and social reforms begun by Faisal. His half-brother FAHD succeeded him.

Kharkiv or **Kharkov,** city (1990 est. pop. 1,620,000), NE Ukraine, at the confluence of the Kharkiv, Lopan, and Udy rivers in the upper Donets valley. It is the second largest Ukrainian city and a main rail junction. Manufactures include metals, machinery, and chemicals. Founded in 1656 as a military outpost, it became a center of commerce and culture. From 1919 to 1934 it was the capital of UKRAINE, until superseded by KIEV.

Khartoum, city (1983 pop. 473,597), capital of Sudan, a port at the confluence of the Blue Nile and White Nile rivers. Food, cotton, gum, and oil seeds are processed; textiles, clothing, and glass are produced. Khartoum is a railroad hub, with road connections to the adjacent cotton-growing region and an international airport. Founded in 1821 as an Egyptian army camp, it developed as a trade center and slave market. British forces resisted a long siege here in which Gen. Charles GORDON was killed (1885). The headquarters for the Bank for African Development, Khartoum is the economic link between the N and S African nations.

Khasbulatov, Ruslan Imranovich, 1942–, Russian politician. A Chechen from the Caucasus region, he was an academic economist in Moscow before his election (1990) to the Russian Congress of People's Deputies and parliament. A supporter of Boris YELTSIN, he served as his deputy (1990–91) and was elected chairman (speaker) of the congress and parliament in 1991. Increasingly critical of Yeltsin's economic program after 1991, he led the legislators in their power struggle with Yeltsin in 1993. He was imprisoned when parliament's attempt to oust Yeltsin by force was crushed by the army.

Khayyam, Omar: see OMAR KHAYYAM.

Khazars, ancient Turkic people who appeared in Transcaucasia in the 2d cent. A.D. and subsequently settled in the lower Volga region. They rose to great power; the Khazar empire at its height (8th–10th cent. A.D.) extended from the northern shores of the Black Sea and the Caspian Sea as far west as Kiev. The Khazars maintained friendly relations with the Byzantine Empire. Their empire came to an end in 965, when they were defeated by the duke of Kiev. In the 8th cent. the Khazar nobility embraced Judaism and thus are believed by some to be the ancestors of many East European Jews.

Khíos or **Chios,** island (1991 pop. 52,691), c.350 sq mi (910 sq km), E Greece, in the Aegean Sea. Its main industries are agriculture and marble quarrying. Colonized by Ionians, the island was independent by 479 B.C. It claims to be the birthplace of HOMER and is famed for its scenic beauty.

Khmer Empire, ancient kingdom of SE Asia, roughly corresponding to modern CAMBODIA and LAOS; fl. 6th–15th cent. It reached its greatest extent in the ANGKOR period (A.D. 889–1434), which produced exquisite architecture and sculpture. Khmer civilization was formed largely by Indian influences. The Khmers fought repeated wars against CHAMPA and the Annamese. The empire declined after invasions from Thailand.

Khmer Rouge, Cambodian Communist guerrilla force. Aided by Vietnamese Communists, it waged a war (1970–75) that toppled LON NOL. Under POL POT, it undertook a ruthless collectivization drive in which perhaps 1.5 million people died. Border fighting with Vietnam led to a Vietnamese invasion (1978–79), the ouster of the Khmer Rouge, and installation of the Heng Samrin regime. The Khmer Rouge, however, continued to field an army of c.30,000 near the Thai border and retained UN recognition as the official

Cambodian government. In 1982 it formed a coalition with former premier NORODOM SIHANOUK and non-Communist leader Son Sann. Khieu Samphan officially succeeded Pol Pot as head of the Khmer Rouge in 1985, but Pol Pot is believed to remain the real leader. All Cambodian factions signed (1991) a treaty calling for UN-supervised elections and disarming 70% of all forces, but the Khmer Rouge withdrew (1992) from the peace process and resumed fighting.

Khoikhoi, people of Namibia and Cape Province, South Africa. Formerly called Hottentots by whites, they speak a Khoisan language close to that of the San (Bushmen). A pastoral, nomadic people, they were decimated as Dutch colonialists took over their lands beginning in the 17th cent.; most of the c.40,000 survivors live in villages in Namibia.

Khomeini, Ruhollah [kōmānē'], 1900–89, Iranian ayatollah (religious leader); b. Ruhollah Hendi. A SHIITE Muslim, he adopted the name Khomeini in 1930. After teaching at a theological school in Qom, he was arrested (1963) and exiled to Turkey and Iraq before moving to Paris in 1978. Following the revolution that deposed MUHAMMAD REZA SHAH PAHLEVI, Khomeini returned in triumph to Iran in 1979, declared an Islamic republic, and began to exercise ultimate authority in the nation. His rule was marked by the holding of U.S. hostages (1979–81) and by war with Iraq (1980–88).

Khorezm [khərĕz'əm] or **Khwarazm,** ancient central Asian state; now in NW Uzbekistan. Part of the empire of CYRUS THE GREAT (6th cent. B.C.), Khorezm was conquered by the Arabs and converted to Islam in the 7th cent. A.D. Briefly independent (late 12th cent.), it ruled from the Caspian Sea to Bukhara and Samarkand, but fell to JENGHIZ KHAN (1221), to TIMUR (late 14th cent.), and then to the Uzbeks (early 16th cent.), who called it the khanate of Khiva.

Khosru, kings of PERSIA. **Khosru I,** d. 579 (r.531–79), was the greatest of the Sassanid monarchs and extended Persian rule E to the Indus River and W across Arabia, and N and NW by taking part of Armenia and Caucasia from the Byzantines. **Khosru II,** d. 628 (r.590–628), of the Sassanid dynasty, conquered much Byzantine territory before being assassinated by his son and successor, Kauadh II Shiruya.

Khrushchev, Nikita Sergeyevich [khrŏŏshchôf'], 1894–1971, Soviet leader. Of Ukrainian peasant origin, he joined the Communist party in 1918, becoming a member of its central committee in 1934. As first secretary of the Ukrainian party (from 1938) he carried out STALIN's purge of its ranks. As a full member of the politburo (after 1939) he was a close associate of Stalin. In the power struggle after Stalin's death (1953) he emerged as first secretary of the party. At the 1956 party congress he delivered a "secret" report denouncing Stalin's policies and personality. The new atmosphere of freedom, however, led to uprisings in Poland and Hungary that year. In 1957 he replaced BULGANIN as premier, becoming head of both state and party. As part of his policy of "peaceful coexistence" in the COLD WAR, he toured the U.S. in 1959 and met with Pres. EISENHOWER; but in 1960 he cancelled the Paris summit conference after a U.S. reconnaissance plane was shot down over the USSR. Repeated crop failures, his retreat in the CUBAN MISSILE CRISIS (1962), and the ideological rift with China led to his removal from power in Oct. 1964.

Khufu [khōō'fōō] or **Cheops** [kē'ŏps], fl. c.2680 B.C., Egyptian king, founder of the IV dynasty. He ruled for 23 years and built the greatest PYRAMID at Gizeh.

Khyber Pass, narrow, steep-sided mountain pass, c.3,500 ft (1,070 m) high and 28 mi (45 km) long, on the Pakistan-Afghanistan border. For centuries the main western land approach to India, it was used by ALEXANDER THE GREAT, TIMUR, and other conquerors. A modern highway and a railroad (built 1920–25) with 34 tunnels link Peshawar, Pakistan, with the Afghan capital, Kabul.

kibbutz, economically most important type of Israeli COLLECTIVE FARM. The land is held by the Jewish National Fund and rented at a nominal fee; all other property (except certain personal possessions) is collectively owned. Planning and work is collective, and collective living is the rule. Elected officials administer social and economic affairs. About 5% of Israel's population live on kibbutzim.

Kickapoo, indigenous people of North America (see NORTH AMERICA, INDIGENOUS PEOPLES OF) speaking an Algonquian language of the Algonquian-Wakashan stock (see NATIVE AMERICAN LANGUAGES). Living in SW Wisconsin, they added buffalo hunting to their Eastern Woodlands culture. In the 18th cent., numbering 3,000, they moved to Illinois. For siding with the British in the WAR OF 1812, they lost their lands to the U.S. From Missouri and Kansas some went to Mexico c.1852. After the Civil War the Mexican Kickapoo harassed U.S. border settlements. Today small groups of Kickapoo live in Oklahoma, in Kansas, and along the Texas-Mexico border. In 1990 there were 3,577 Kickapoo in the U.S.

Kid, Thomas: see KYD, THOMAS.

Kidd, William (Captain Kidd), 1645?–1701, British pirate. Commissioned (1695) as a privateer to guard English ships in the Red Sea and Indian Ocean, he turned pirate. He was tried for piracy and murder and hanged in England. Legends of his barbaric cruelty and buried treasure are unsubstantiated.

Kidder, Alfred Vincent, 1885–1963, American archaeologist; b. Marquette, Mich. His excavations (1915–29) at Pecos, N.Mex., laid the foundation for modern archaeological field methods. He conducted (1927–50) a broad-scale research program in the Guatemalan highlands that established the framework of Mayan stratigraphy. His writings include *Introduction to the Study of Southwestern Archaeology* (1924), regarded as the first comprehensive archaeological study of a New World area.

kiddush [Heb., = sanctification], Jewish ceremonial blessing indicating the beginning of the Sabbath or a Hebrew festival, usually said at mealtime.

kidnapping, in law, unlawful taking away of someone by force, threat, or deceit, to detain the person against his or her will. Public outcry at the kidnapping and murder of the son of Charles A. LINDBERGH in 1932 led to adoption of severe penalties for the offense, now punishable by the U.S. government and most states by death or life imprisonment. Traditionally done for ransom, in recent years kidnapping has also been used by political extremists as a means of extorting concessions from governments, e.g., the release of political prisoners.

kidney, one of a pair of small, bean-shaped organs of the URINARY SYSTEM, located near the spine at the small of the back. The kidneys extract water and urea, mineral salts, toxins, and other waste products from the blood with filtering units called nephrons. From the nephrons the collected waste (URINE) is sent to the bladder for excretion. One kidney must function properly for life to be maintained. Kidney diseases include nephritis, inflammation of the kidneys caused by infection or degenerative changes in the renal capillaries, and nephrosis, a condition resulting from lesions in the renal tubules characterized by general edema and by protein in the urine. See also DIALYSIS; TRANSPLANTATION, MEDICAL.

kidney machine: see DIALYSIS.

Kiel [kēl], city (1989 est. pop. 241,000), N Germany, on Kiel Bay, capital of SCHLESWIG-HOLSTEIN. Germany's chief naval base from 1871 to 1945, it is now a shipping and industrial center producing ships, textiles, metal products, and printed materials. Kiel was chartered in 1242 and joined the HANSEATIC LEAGUE in 1284. It passed to Denmark in 1773 and to Prussia in 1866. A naval mutiny at Kiel touched off a socialist revolution in Germany in 1918.

Kierkegaard, Søren, 1813–55, Danish philosopher and religious writer, a precursor of 20th-cent. EXISTENTIALISM and a major influence on modern Protestant theology. Kierkegaard described the various stages of existence as the aesthetic, the ethical, and the religious; advancing through this "existential dialectic," the individual becomes increasingly aware of his relationship to God. This awareness leads to despair as he realizes the antithesis between temporal existence and eternal truth. Reason is no help in achieving the final religious stage; a "leap of faith" is required. Kierkegaard's works, largely ignored in his own lifetime, include *Either/Or* (1843), *Fear and Trembling* (1843), *Philosophical Fragments* (1844), and *Concluding Unscientific Postscript* (1846).

Kiev [kē'ĕf], Ukr. *Kyyiv,* city (1990 est. pop. 2,620,000), capital of UKRAINE, on the Dnieper R. It Ukraine's largest city and a major port. Industries include food processing, metallurgy, machinery, and chemicals. One of the oldest European cities, it was a commercial center as early as the 5th cent. and became the capital of KIEVAN RUSSIA in the 9th cent. Invaded (1240) by the Mongols, it paid tribute to the GOLDEN HORDE until it passed (14th cent.) under the control of LITHUANIA. It became (17th cent.) part of the Russian Empire and later (1920) of the USSR. During the German occupation (1941–44) thousands of Kiev's residents, including 50,000 Jews, were massacred. Reconstruction of the city ended c.1960. Its architectural treasures include the 11th-cent. Cathedral of St. Sophia.

Kievan Russia, medieval state of the Eastern Slavs. Earliest forerunner of Russia and the USSR, it included most of present-day UKRAINE and BELARUS and part of NW European Russia. In about 862 Rurik, a Varangian (Scandinavian) warrior, founded a dynasty at NOVGOROD. His successor, Oleg (d. 912), seized Kiev, establishing the Kievan state, and freed the Eastern Slavs from the sway of the KHAZARS. Under Sviatoslav (d. 972) Kievan power reached the lower Volga and N Caucasus. VLADIMIR I (r.980–1015) introduced Christianity. Under his son, YAROSLAV (r.1019–54), the state reached its cultural and political apex, but after Yaroslav's death it was weakened by internal strife and ultimately fell to the Mongols (1237–40).

Kigali, town (1990 est. pop. 913,481), capital of Rwanda. Founded by Germany in 1907, it is the country's main administrative and economic center and has an international airport. A tin-smelting plant processes cassiterite (tin ore), which is mined in the vicinity.

Kikuyu, Bantu-speaking agricultural people of northern Kenya, inhabiting highlands NE of Nairobi; they number over 5 million. The most influential of Kenya's peoples, they fought the British during the 1950s MAU MAU rebellion. Dwelling traditionally in family homesteads, more recently in villages, they have a patrilineal social organization with much emphasis on age groups. Kikuyu tribal customs are described in Jomo KENYATTA's *Facing Mount Kenya* (1938).

Kilauea [kē'läwā'ə], volcanic crater, Hawaii island, on the southeastern slope of MAUNA LOA in Hawaii Volcanoes National Park (see NATIONAL PARKS, table). It is c.8 mi (13 km) in circumference and 3,646 ft (1,111 m) deep, with a lake of molten lava c.740 ft (230 m) below its rim. Its most recent eruption began in 1983.

Kilimanjaro, highest mountain of Africa, NE Tanzania. An extinct volcano, it rises in two snow-capped peaks, Kibo (19,340 ft/5,895 m) and Mawenzi (17,564 ft/5,354 m).

killer whale: see DOLPHIN.

Kilmer, Joyce, 1886–1918, American poet; b. New Brunswick, N.J. He is known chiefly for his poem "Trees," in *Trees and Other Poems* (1914).

kilogram: see METRIC SYSTEM; WEIGHTS AND MEASURES, table.

Kimhi or **Kimchi** [kĭm'khē], family of Jewish scholars and grammarians in Spain and France. **Joseph ben Isaac Kimhi,** 1105?–1170?, wrote a biblical commentary, translations from Arabic, and poetry, and made grammatical reforms. His *Sefer ha-Berit* is an anti-Christian polemic. His son **Moses Kimhi,** d. 1190?, wrote *Paths of Knowledge,* a grammatical text used by 16th-cent. Christian Hebraists for its philological information. Another son, **David Kimhi,** known as Redak, 1160?–1235?, was the author of a noted Hebrew grammar, a biblical dictionary, and learned commentaries that were included in standard editions of the Hebrew Bible.

Kim Il Sung, 1912–, North Korean political leader. Trained in Moscow, he was North KOREA's first premier (1948–72) and led his nation in the KOREAN WAR. In 1972 he became president under a revised constitution. His son, **Kim Jong Il,** 1942–, has been groomed as his successor. Active in the Korean Worker's party leadership since 1964, Kim Jong Il became secretary of its central committee in 1973. In 1991 he was appointed supreme commander of the armed forces.

Kim Young Sam, 1927–, South Korean political leader. An opponent of military rule and National Assembly member (1954–79), he was (1980–85) banned from politics and twice put under house arrest. Kim was an unsuccessful presidential candidate in 1987 but shrewdly merged his party with the ruling Democratic Liberals (1990) and won the presidency in 1992. He initiated a series of political and economic reforms.

kindergarten, system of preschool education designed (1837) by Friedrich FROEBEL. In an educational situation less formal than elementary school, children's play instincts are organized constructively through songs, stories, games, simple materials, and group activities, to develop habits of cooperation and application. In the U.S. kindergartens are generally part of the public school system. The first American kindergarten was established in 1856, the first public kindergarten in 1873.

kinematics: see DYNAMICS.

kinetic energy: see ENERGY.

kinetic-molecular theory of gases, physical theory that explains the behavior of gases by assuming that any gas is composed of a very large number of very tiny particles, called molecules, that are very far apart compared to their sizes. The molecules are assumed to exert no forces on one another, except during rare, perfectly elastic collisions. A gas corresponding to these assumptions is called an ideal gas. The analysis of the behavior of an ideal gas according to the laws of mechanics leads to the GAS LAWS. The theory also shows that the absolute TEMPERATURE is directly proportional to the average kinetic energy of the molecules. Pressure is seen to be the result of large numbers of collisions between molecules and the walls of the container in which the gas is held. See THERMODYNAMICS.

kinetics: see DYNAMICS.

King, Billie Jean, 1943–, American tennis player; b. Long Beach, Calif., as Billie Jean Moffitt. Outstanding in both singles and doubles play, she won 6 singles and 10 doubles championships at Wimbledon by 1979, and took the U.S. Open singles crown 4 times between 1967 and 1974. King has been instrumental in improving the status of women's professional tennis.

King, Martin Luther, Jr., 1929–68, African-American clergyman and civil-rights leader; b. Atlanta, Ga. An active Baptist minister and a moving orator, he first gained national prominence by advocating passive resistance to segregation and leading a year-long boycott (1955–56) against the segregated bus lines in Montgomery, Ala. He subsequently set up the Southern Christian Leadership Conference as a base for nonviolent marches, protests, and demonstrations for African-American rights, such as the 1963 March on Washington and the 1965 voter-registration drive in Selma, Ala. King was awarded the 1964 Nobel Peace Prize, but his leadership was challenged as civil-rights activists became more militant. In the late 1960s he intensified his opposition to the war in Vietnam and to economic discrimination. While planning a multiracial Poor People's March for antipoverty legislation, he was shot and killed in Memphis, Tenn. James Earl Ray was convicted of the murder. King's wife, **Coretta Scott King,** 1927–, b. Heiberger, Ala., carried on his civil-rights work after his assassination. She wrote *My Life with Martin Luther King* (1989).

King, Rufus, 1755–1827, American political leader; b. Scarboro, Me. As a delegate (1784–87) to the CONTINENTAL CONGRESS, he helped draft the ORDINANCE OF 1787; and he attended the FEDERAL CONSTITUTIONAL CONVENTION. A Federalist, he served (1789–96, 1813–25) as U.S. senator from New York. He also was minister to Great Britain (1796–1803, 1825–26).

King, William Lyon Mackenzie, 1874–1950, prime minister of CANADA (1921–30, 1935–48). He was editor (1900–1908) of the *Labour Gazette* and minister of labor (1909–11) in the Liberal government before he succeeded (1919) Wilfred LAURIER as party leader. As prime minister during World War II, King directed the Canadian war effort and signed agreements with the U.S. providing for joint defense.

King Arthur: see ARTHURIAN LEGEND.

King George's War: see FRENCH AND INDIAN WARS.

King Philip's War, 1675–76, the most devastating INDIAN WAR in NEW ENGLAND. Named for King Philip, chief of the Wampanoag Indians, the war began when the English executed three Native Americans for murder. It involved several Native American peoples and all the New England colonies before the tribes were defeated.

Kings, books of the OLD TESTAMENT, called First and Second Kings in the Authorized Version, where they occupy 11th and 12th place. They continue the history of 1 and 2 SAMUEL from the death of DAVID to the destruction of the southern kingdom of JUDAH (i.e., from 1000 to 560 B.C.). They include the reign of SOLOMON (1 Kings 1–11); a parallel account of the two Hebrew kingdoms (1 Kings 12–2 Kings 17), including the stories of the house of AHAB and the prophets ELIJAH and ELISHA; and the end of the southern kingdom (2 Kings 18–25).

Kings Canyon National Park: see NATIONAL PARKS (table).

Kingsley, Charles, 1819–75, English author and clergyman. His views on CHRISTIAN SOCIALISM were expressed in the novel *Alton Locke* (1850). A remark by Kingsley denigrating the Roman Catholic clergy produced a controversy with J.H. NEWMAN and led to Newman's *Apologia.* Kingsley's novels include *Westward Ho!* (1855) and, for children, *The Water Babies* (1863).

Kingston, city (1989 est. pop. 661,000), SE Jamaica, capital of Jamaica. It is the island's commercial hub, chief port, and largest city. Founded in 1693 on one of the Caribbean's best-protected harbors, near the early capital of Port Royal, Kingston replaced Spanish Town as Jamaica's capital in 1872. Tourism, oil refining, and food processing are major industries. The city's botanical gardens are famous.

Kingstown, city (1990 est. pop. 29,500), capital of SAINT VINCENT AND THE GRENADINES.

King William's War: see FRENCH AND INDIAN WARS.

Kinnock, Neil (Gordon), 1942–, British politician, leader of the LABOUR PARTY (1983–92). First elected to Parliament in 1970, he became a left-wing critic of Labour Prime Mins. Harold WILSON and James CALLAGHAN. A protégé of Michael FOOT, he rose in the party hierarchy, becoming (1979) spokesman for education in the Labour shadow cabinet. In 1983 he was chosen party leader. Kinnock moved Labour to more centrist positions, neutralizing the party's extreme left and reducing the challenge posed by the Liberal and Social Democratic parties, but he could not lead Labour to victory at the polls.

Kino, Eusebio Francisco [kē'nō], c.1644–1711, Jesuit missionary explorer in the U.S. Southwest; b. Segno, in the Tyrol. He was cosmographer on a 1681 mission to colonize lower CALIFORNIA. It failed, and he settled at Pinero Alta (now N Sonora and S Arizona), exploring and mapping the region.

Kinsey, Alfred Charles, 1894–1956, American biologist; b. Hoboken, N.J. He is known for his studies, based on over 10,000 personal interviews with assorted Americans, of human sexuality; this work was summarized in *Sexual Behavior in the Human Male* (1948) and *Sexual Behavior in the Human Female* (1953), which he wrote with colleagues. He taught at the Univ. of Indiana from 1920, and founded and directed (1942–56) the university's Institute for Sex Research.

Kinshasa, largest city (1984 pop. 2,653,558) and capital of Zaïre, W Zaïre, a port on the Congo (Zaïre) R. It is the country's communications and commercial center, with rail links upriver to Matadi, motorboat service to Brazzaville, Congo Republic, and an international airport. Founded in 1881 by Henry M. STANLEY, who named it Leopoldville (after Leopold II of Belgium), the city became the capital of the Belgian Congo in 1926. A rebellion there in 1959 launched the country's drive for independence. Modern Kinshasa (so named in 1966) is an educational and cultural center.

kinship, relationship between persons by blood or MARRIAGE; also, a system of rules based on such relationships and governing marriage, descent, inheritance, and, sometimes, residence. All societies recognize consanguinity (relationship by blood or by descent from a common ancestor) and affinity (relationship to a spouse's cosanguineous relatives). Marriage between persons in lineal consanguinity (in direct line of descent, e.g., father and daughter) or between brother and sister is considered incest and is almost universally void under church, civil, and common law, while marriage between persons of collateral consanguinity (sharing a common ancestor but not in direct line of descent, e.g., first cousins) may be allowed. Every individual is classified by kinship lines, or descent. Social organization is often dominated by descent groups based on links through females (matrilineal), males (patrilineal), or both (bilateral). In some societies the concept of kinship extends beyond the family to groups or clans in which consanguinity is hypothetical or even mythological, but which are governed by all the laws of descent.

Kiowa, indigenous people of the Plains (see NORTH AMERICA, INDIGENOUS PEOPLES OF), speaking a probable Aztec-Tanoan language (see NATIVE AMERICAN LANGUAGES). They had a pictographic calendar and worshiped a stone image, the *taimay.* Nomads, they acquired horses c.1710. Forced from the Black Hills by the CHEYENNE and SIOUX, they joined the COMANCHE in raids as far south as Mexico. In the 19th cent. they opposed white settlers and migrating eastern tribes until subdued (1874) by the U.S. Army. In 1990 there were 9,421 Kiowas in the U.S. The **Kiowa Apache,** a small group long associated with the Kiowa, live with them on an Oklahoma reservation.

Kipling, Rudyard, 1865–1936, English author; b. India. Kipling's popular works interpret India in all its heat, strife, and ennui. His romantic view of English imperialism is reflected in such well-known poems as "Mandalay," "Gunga Din," and *Recessional* (1897). His works include poems, in *Departmental Ditties* (1886) and *Barrack-Room Ballads* (1892); stories, in *Plain Tales from the Hills* and *Soldiers Three* (both 1888); a novel, *The Light That Failed* (1890); and children's stories, such as *The Jungle Book* (1894), *Captains Courageous* (1897), and *Kim* (1901). He received the 1907 Nobel Prize in literature.

Kipnis, Alexander, 1891–1978, Russian-American operatic bass; b. Russia. He performed in Berlin, Chicago, and New York City and was noted in the role of Boris Godunov.

Kirchhoff, Gustav Robert [kĭrkh'hôf], 1824–87, German physicist. He was professor of physics at the universities of Breslau, Heidelberg, and Berlin. He and Robert BUNSEN, working with the spectroscope, discovered the elements CESIUM and RUBIDIUM. Kirchhoff explained the Fraunhofer lines in the solar spectrum (see SUN) and formulated KIRCHHOFF'S LAWS describing current and voltage in an electric circuit.

Kirchhoff's laws, pair of laws stating general restrictions on the current and voltage (see POTENTIAL, ELECTRIC) in an ELECTRIC CIRCUIT or network. The first states that at any given instant the sum of the voltages around any closed path, or loop, in the network is zero. The second states that at any junction of paths in a network the sum of the currents arriving at any instant is equal to the sum of the currents flowing away.

Kirchner, Ernst Ludwig [kĭrkh'nər], 1880–1938, German expressionist painter and graphic artist. Inspired by primitive sculpture; late Gothic WOODCUTS; and the art of MUNCH, VAN GOGH, and the Fauves (see FAUVISM), he co-founded the BRÜCKE. His works, e.g., *The Street* (1913; Mus. of Mod. Art, N.Y.C.), show startling contrasts of pure color and aggressive forms. His woodcuts are powerful creations of the expressionist vision.

Kirghizia or **Kirghizstan:** see KYRGYZSTAN.

Kirghizstan: see KYRGYZSTAN.

Kiribati, officially Republic of Kiribati, independent nation (1991 pop. 71,137), 342 sq mi (886 sq km), consisting of 33 islands scattered across 2,400 mi (3,860 km) of the Pacific Ocean near the equator. It includes islands in the Gilbert, Phoenix, and Line groups and Banaba (formerly Ocean) Island, whose residents were moved to Rabi Island, FIJI, and are Fiji citizens. The population is nearly all Micronesian, with about 30% concentrated on TARAWA, site of the capital, Bairiki. Fishing and the growing of taro and bananas form the basis of the mainly subsistence economy. Copra became the chief export after mining of Banaba's once thick phosphate deposits ended in 1979. Languages spoken are English (official) and Gilbertese. Most of the people are Christian, about evenly divided between Roman Catholics and Protestants. A Commonwealth member, the country is a republic with a president, a cabinet, and a unicameral legislature. The islands were administered (1892–1916) with the Gilbert Islands as a British protectorate that became (1916) the British Gilbert and Ellice Islands colony. They gained self-rule in 1971, and, after the Ellice Islands gained (1978) independence as TUVALU, the remaining islands were granted independence (1979) as Kiribati. U.S. claims to several islands, including Kanton (formerly Canton) and Enderbury, were abandoned in 1979. A rapidly growing population has led to plans for resettling people from the central islands to the comparatively underpopulated Line Islands. See PACIFIC OCEAN map.

Kirinyaga, Mount: see KENYA, MOUNT.

Kirkland, (Joseph) Lane, 1922–, American labor leader, president (1979–) of the AMERICAN FEDERATION OF LABOR AND CONGRESS OF INDUSTRIAL ORGANIZATIONS (AFL-CIO); b. Camden, S.C. He was an executive assistant (1961–69) to AFL-CIO Pres. George MEANY and, from 1969, secretary treasurer of the AFL-CIO. Succeeding Meany as president, he made consolidation of the labor movement a major goal, overseeing the reentry of the United Automobile Workers (1981) and TEAMSTERS UNION (1987) into the AFL–CIO.

Kirkpatrick, Jeane (Duane Jordan), 1926–, U.S. public official; b.

Duncan, Okla. A Democrat, she was professor of political science at Georgetown Univ. when Pres. REAGAN chose her (1981) to be the U.S. representative to the UNITED NATIONS. She gained a reputation for independent thought, often criticizing the UN itself. She returned to Georgetown Univ. in 1985.

Kirov, Sergei Mironovich, 1886–1934, Soviet political leader. Kirov engaged in revolutionary activities after joining (1904) the Russian Social Democratic party. He headed (from 1926) the Leningrad Communist party organization and became a member of the Politburo (1930). His assassination triggered STALIN's Great Terror (1934–38).

Kirov Ballet, officially (since 1991) the St. Petersburg Ballet, one of the two major ballet companies of Russia (the other is the BOLSHOI). Originally the Imperial Russian Ballet, it was instrumental in developing much of classic ballet's technique and repertoire under the direction of Marius PETIPA. It declined after the Russian Revolution (1917). Agrippina Vaganova helped restore it to prominence, and it was renamed (1935) the Kirov Ballet. Famous for its classical elegance, the company declined again by the 1970s when limitations on artistic freedom prompted Rudolf NUREYEV, Natalia MAKAROVA, and Mikhail BARYSHNIKOV to defect. The political changes of the late 1980s and early 90s, which allowed the company to perform many previously forbidden Western ballets, reinvigorated it.

Kishinev: see CHIŞINĂU.

Kissinger, Henry Alfred, 1923–, U.S. secretary of state (1973–77); b. Germany. An expert in international affairs and nuclear defense, he was national-security adviser (1969–75) to Presidents NIXON and FORD, and played a major role in the formulation of U.S. foreign policy. He arranged Nixon's visit (1972) to China, shared (1973) the Nobel Peace Prize for negotiating a cease-fire with North Vietnam, and helped arrange a cease-fire in the 1973 ARAB-ISRAELI WAR.

Kitagawa Utamaro: see UTAMARO.

Kitakyushu [kētä'kyo͞osho͞o], a port city (1990 pop. 1,026,467), Fukuoka prefecture, N Kyushu, Japan, on the Shimonoseki Strait between the Inland Sea and the Korea Strait. Kitakyushu is one of Japan's major manufacturing and railroad centers and has a great variety of industries producing iron and steel, textiles, chemicals, machinery, ships, and porcelain. It is also the base for a deep-sea fishing fleet. The city is connected by tunnel and bridge with Shimonoseki on Honshu.

Kitasato Shibasaburo, 1852–1931, Japanese physician. With Emil BEHRING he studied the tetanus bacillus and developed (1890) an antitoxin for diphtheria. He discovered (1894) the infectious agent of bubonic plague, which he described simultaneously with Alexandre Yersin.

Kitchener, Horatio Herbert Kitchener, 1st **Earl,** 1850–1916, British field marshal and statesman. In 1896 he began the Anglo-Egyptian reconquest of the Sudan that culminated in a victory at Omdurman (1898). He served under F.S. Roberts in the SOUTH AFRICAN WAR and, when Roberts returned (1900) to England, was left to face continued guerrilla warfare. By extending blockhouses, interning civilians, and denuding the land—methods that received much criticism—he secured Boer submission (1902). In WORLD WAR I he was secretary for war and, despite strained relations with the cabinet, carried out the vast expansion of the British army. He was drowned on a mission to Russia when his ship was sunk by a German mine.

Kitchener, city (1991 pop. 168,282), S Ontario, Canada, in the Grand R. valley, adjoining the smaller city of Waterloo. Major manufactures include processed food, and metal, leather, and rubber goods. Called Berlin until 1916, Kitchener was settled in 1806 by MENNONITES from Pennsylvania. It is renowned in Canada for its annual Oktoberfest.

Kitt Peak National Observatory, astronomical observatory (founded 1958) located at an altitude of 7,000 ft (2,130 km) on the Papago (Tohono O'Odham) reservation, SW of Tucson, Ariz.; it is administered by the Association of Universities for Research in Astronomy under contract with the U.S. National Science Foundation. Principal instruments include the Mayall 158-in. (4.01-m) reflector and the 60-in. (1.52-m) Robert McMath Solar Telescope, the largest of this type. The observatory's ten telescopes are supplemented at Kitt Peak by four other telescopes operated by other institutions.

Horatio Herbert Kitchener

Kitwe, city (1987 est. pop. 449,000), N central Zambia, near Zaïre; founded 1936. It is the main commercial and industrial center of a rich mining region known as the Copper belt. Manufactures include food products, clothing, and plastics.

kiva, large, underground chamber used by PUEBLO men for secret ceremonies. A modern kiva is a rectangular or circular structure with a fire pit in the center and a timbered roof; it is accessible by ladder. An opening in the floor represents the entrance to the lower world and the place through which life emerged into this world.

kiwi or **apteryx,** flightless BIRD (genus *Apteryx*) of New Zealand related to the OSTRICH and EMU. The size of a large chicken, the kiwi has short legs and coarse, dark plumage that hides rudimentary wings. There are three living species, all protected.

Klee, Paul [klā], 1879–1940, Swiss painter, graphic artist, and art theorist. His sophisticated theories of abstraction, combined with his inventiveness, give his works the appearance of great innocence. Associated with the BLAUE REITER, he became aware of new theories of color use, and thereafter his whimsical and fantastic images show a luminous, subtle color sense. Characteristic works are the witty *Twittering Machine* (1922; Mus. Mod. Art, N.Y.C.) and the disturbing *Revolutions of the Viaducts* (1937; Hamburg). His *Pedagogical Sketchbooks* (tr. 1944) define his approach to art.

Klein, (Christian) Felix, 1849–1925, German mathematician, noted for his work in geometry and on the theory of functions. His "Erlangen Programm" (1872) for unifying the diverse forms of geometry through the study of equivalence in transformation groups was influential for over 50 years. Klein was a prolific writer and lecturer on the theory, history, and teaching of mathematics.

Klein, Melanie, 1882–1960, British psychoanalyst; b. Vienna. As the first major child psychoanalyst, Klein developed the technique of play therapy in the analysis of children. Her writings include *The Psychoanalysis of Children* (1932) and *Narrative of a Child Analysis* (1961).

Kleist, Heinrich von [klīst], 1777–1811, German dramatic poet. Among his comedies are *The Broken Pitcher* (1806) and *Amphitryon* (1807). Other works include *Penthesilea* (1808), *Kätchen von Heilbronn* (1810), and the masterful tragedy *The Prince of Homburg* (1821). Kleist's terse, dynamic style and sense of conflict are also evident in stories and in novellas, e.g., *Michael Kohlhass* (1808). His unhappy life ended in suicide.

Klemperer, Otto, 1885–1973, German conductor. Working in Prague, in Berlin, and later in Los Angeles and Pittsburgh, he was celebrated for his interpretations of Beethoven, Mahler, and Richard Strauss.

Klimt, Gustav [klĭmt], 1862–1918, Austrian painter, the foremost exponent of ART NOUVEAU in Vienna. His greatest works were portraits and landscapes of exotic and erotic sensibility, with symbolic themes and extravagant rhythms.

Kline, Franz, 1910–62, American painter; b. Wilkes-Barre, Pa. His large canvases of dynamically painted black-and-white grids, sometimes with notes of bright color, are among the important achievements of ABSTRACT EXPRESSIONISM.

Klondike, region in the YUKON TERRITORY, NW Canada, near the Alaska border, the scene of a great gold rush in the late 1890s. The area is crossed by the Klondike R., which enters the YUKON R. at DAWSON, the principal town. Rich placer-gold deposits were discovered in Rabbit (now Bonanza) Creek, a tributary of the Klondike, in 1896. When news of the find reached the U.S. in July 1897, thousands rushed to the virtually uninhabited region by a variety of difficult overland and river routes, swelling its population to c.25,000 in 1898 and causing near-famine conditions during winter months. Some $100 million in gold was mined there in about 10 years. The area still produces small amounts of gold, together with some silver, lead, and other minerals.

Klopstock, Friedrich Gottlieb [klŏp'shtŏck], 1724–1803, German poet, important for his influence on GOETHE and the STURM UND DRANG. A major work is *The Messiah* (1748–73). His lyrical *Odes* (1747–80) influenced German song composition.

knight, in medieval history, an armed and mounted warrior of the nobility or, under FEUDALISM, of the landholding class. Knighthood was conferred by the overlord by a blow on the neck or shoulder with the flat of a sword. A class of landless knights, created by primogeniture, formed in the CRUSADES such great military religious orders as the KNIGHTS TEMPLARS and KNIGHTS HOSPITALERS. Secular orders of knights also appeared, e.g., the Order of the Garter in Britain and the Golden Fleece in Burgundy. As feudalism waned, knightly service was often commuted into the cash payment known as SCUTAGE. Feudal knighthood ended in Germany in the early 16th cent., and earlier in Britain and France. In modern Britain, knighthood is conferred by the sovereign on commoners or nobles for civil or military achievements. A knight is addressed as Sir; a woman, knighted in her own right, as Dame.

Knights Hospitalers, members of the military religious order of the Hospital of St. John of Jerusalem, called also the Knights of St. John, of Jerusalem, of Rhodes, or of Malta. The order grew out of an 11th-cent. pilgrims' hospital in the Holy Land (see PALESTINE). As a military order it grew rich and powerful. After the Saracen conquest (1291) of Akko, the Knights took RHODES (1310), which they defended (1480) against the Ottoman sultan MUHAMMAD II but yielded (1522) to SULAYMAN I. Emperor CHARLES V gave them Malta (1530), which they defended against the Turks. After the Turkish defeat (1571) at LEPANTO, the Hospitalers engaged peacefully in hospital work until Napoleon seized Malta (1798). The order as constituted in the 19th cent. bears little relation to the old order.

Knights of Jerusalem: see KNIGHTS HOSPITALERS.

Knights of Labor, American labor organization started in Philadelphia in 1869. Becoming a national body in 1878, it was organized on an industrial basis, welcoming women and African Americans, and even employers. Among its aims were an eight-hour day, abolition of child and convict labor, and equal pay for equal work. The Knights of Labor attained its peak membership of 702,000 in 1886, but unjust blame for the HAYMARKET SQUARE RIOT of that year, together with factional disputes and weak management, resulted in its virtual extinction by 1900.

Knights of Malta and Knights of Rhodes: see KNIGHTS HOSPITALERS.

Knights of St. John of Jerusalem: see KNIGHTS HOSPITALERS.

Knights Templars, members of the military religious order of the Poor Knights of Christ, also called Knights of the Temple of Solomon. Like the KNIGHTS HOSPITALERS and the TEUTONIC KNIGHTS, they rose during the CRUSADES. From a band of nine knights united (c.1118) to protect pilgrims, the order grew large and rich. They were famous for dashing military exploits. After the city of Akko fell (1291), they went to Cyprus. Their wealth made them the bankers of Europe and led to persecution (1308–14) by PHILIP IV of France. The last grand master and their other leaders were burned as heretics (1314), and the order came to an end.

Knossos or **Cnossus** [nŏs'əs], ancient city on the N coast of CRETE. Occupied long before 3000 B.C., it was the center of MINOAN CIVILIZATION, known mainly from study of the great palace of Knossos. In Greek legend, it was the capital of King MINOS and the site of the labyrinth. Knossos was destroyed, probably by invaders, c.1400 B.C., but it later flourished as a Greek city until the 4th cent. A.D.

Know-Nothing movement, U.S. political movement in the mid-19th cent. The increased immigration of the 1840s had resulted in concentrations of Roman Catholic immigrants in the Eastern cities. The Democrats welcomed them, but local nativist societies were formed to combat "foreign" influences and uphold the "American" view. The American Republican party, formed (1843) in New York, spread to neighboring states as the Native American party and became a national party in 1845. Many secret orders sprang up, and when outsiders made inquiries of supposed members, they were met with a statement that the person knew nothing; hence members were called Know-Nothings. The Know-Nothings sought to elect only native Americans to office and to require 25 years of residence for citizenship. Allied with a faction of the WHIG PARTY, they almost captured New York in the 1854 election and swept the polls in Massachusetts and Delaware. In 1855 they adopted the name American party and dropped much of their secrecy. The issue of slavery, however, split the party, and many antislavery members joined the new REPUBLICAN PARTY. Millard FILLMORE, the American party's presidential candidate in 1856, won only Maryland, and the party's national strength was broken.

Knox, John, 1514?–1572, Scottish religious reformer, founder of Scottish PRESBYTERIANISM. A Catholic priest, he had attached himself by 1545 to the reformer George Wishart and soon became a Protestant. In England (1549–53) Knox preached, was a royal chaplain briefly, and helped prepare the second Book of Common Prayer. After the accession (1553) of MARY I, he went into exile, chiefly in Geneva, where he consulted with John CALVIN. In 1557 the Scottish Protestant nobles made their first covenant (see SCOTLAND, CHURCH OF) and invited (1559) Knox to return to lead their fight against the regent, MARY OF GUISE. After a civil war, the reformers forced the withdrawal of Mary's French forces and won their freedom as well as dominance for the new religion. They tried (1560) to abolish the pope's authority and condemn the practices of the old church. Knox verbally attacked the Roman Catholic MARY QUEEN OF SCOTS, and, after her abdication (1567), the acts of 1560 were confirmed and Presbyterianism was established in Scotland. Knox's single-minded zeal made him the outstanding leader of the Scottish Reformation and an important influence in Protestant movements elsewhere.

Knoxville, city (1990 pop. 165,121), seat of Knox co., E Tenn., on the Tennessee R.; settled c.1785, inc. 1876. Trade center for a farm, coal, and marble area, it produces processed meats, seat belts, chemicals, and other goods. It was territorial capital (1792–96) and twice (1796–1812, 1817–18) state capital. The city was occupied by federal troops during the CIVIL WAR. The city is a tourist center; Great Smoky Mts. National Park (see NATIONAL PARKS, table) is nearby, and the 1982 World's Fair was held there. It is the site of the Univ. of Tennessee.

koala, arboreal, nocturnal MARSUPIAL (*Phascolarctos cinereus*) native to Australia. Bearlike in appearance, it has thick, gray fur, a tailless body 2 to 2½ ft (60 to 75 cm) long, a black nose, and large, furry ears. Its diet consists of only one species of eucalyptus (see MYRTLE) at a particular stage of maturation. The koala has been hunted for food and fur and is now endangered.

Kobe [kō'bā], city (1990 pop. 1,477,423), capital of Hyogo prefecture, S Honshu, Japan. A leading Japanese port, industrial center, and railway hub, it has shipyards, steel mills, vehicle-assembly and food-processing plants, and many factories. Kobe was heavily bombed during WORLD WAR II but has been rebuilt and enlarged. It is a cultural center, with colleges, universities, temples, and shrines.

Kobuk Valley National Park: see NATIONAL PARKS (table).

Koch, Edward Irving, 1924–, mayor of NEW YORK CITY (1977–89); b. N.Y.C. A Democrat, he served (1969–77) as a U.S. congressman from New York and was elected mayor of New York City in 1977.

He is credited with avoiding the city's bankruptcy during the financial crisis of the late 1970s. Reelected mayor in 1981 and 1985, he was defeated in the 1989 primary election by David N. DINKINS, who was then elected mayor.

Koch, Kenneth [kōk], 1925–, American poet, novelist, and playwright; b. Cincinnati, Ohio. He is noted for his "anti-symbolic" poems and books on teaching poetry-writing to children and the elderly, e.g., *Rose, Where Did You Get That Red?* (1973) and *I Never Told Anybody* (1977).

Koch, Robert, 1843–1910, German bacteriologist. He devised a method of staining bacteria with aniline dyes and developed bacteriological culture techniques still used. He established the bacterial cause of many infectious diseases, including anthrax (1876), tuberculosis (1882), conjunctivitis (1883), and cholera (1884), and studied sleeping sickness, malaria, bubonic plague, rinderpest, and other diseases. For developing tuberculin as a test of tuberculosis he received the 1905 Nobel Prize in physiology or medicine.

Kodály, Zoltán [kô'dī], 1882–1967, Hungarian composer and collector of folk music. With BARTÓK he collected thousands of Hungarian FOLK SONGS and dances. His best-known works are the opera *Háry János* (1926; orchestral suite, 1927); the *Psalmus Hungaricus* (1923); and *Missa Brevis* (1945). His method for teaching music to children is widely employed.

Koestler, Arthur, 1905–83, English writer; b. Hungary. A Communist in the 1930s, he left the party over the STALIN purge trials and became a spokesman of the non-Communist left, combining a brilliant journalistic style with a sense of commitment. His best-known novel, *Darkness at Noon* (1941), describes the purge of a Bolshevik "deviationist." He is also known for his essay "The Yogi and the Commissar" and for philosophical studies, e.g., *The Ghost in the Machine* (1968).

Koffka, Kurt: see GESTALT.

Kohl, Helmut, 1930–, German political leader, chancellor of West Germany (1982–90) and of Germany (1990–). A member of the Christian Democratic party, Kohl led (1976–82) the opposition in the Bundestag (lower house of parliament). Conservative and pro-American, he replaced Social Democrat Helmut SCHMIDT as chancellor in 1982. During his administration, West Germany prospered economically and became increasingly influential in world affairs. With the accession of East Germany to the Federal Republic of Germany in 1990, Kohl became chancellor of a reunited Germany. The economic collapse in the east and the cost of unification, however, created social and economic problems that proved difficult to handle.

Köhler, Wolfgang: see GESTALT.

Koivisto, Mauno Henrik, 1923–, Finnish politician, president of Finland (1981–94). A Social Democrat, he served as finance minister (1966–67, 1972) and prime minister (1968–70, 1979–80). Appointed interim president in 1981, he later won (1982, 1988) election to the office. He sought close ties with the West while maintaining a policy of neutrality and good relations with the USSR and, subsequently, Russia.

Kokoschka, Oskar [kōkôsh'kä], 1886–1980, Austrian expressionist painter and writer. Influenced by KLIMT's elegant work, he developed an expressionist style that emphasizes psychological tension, e.g., the portrait of Hans Tietze and his wife (1909; Mus. Mod. Art, N.Y.C.). His striking landscapes include *Jerusalem* (Detroit Inst. Arts).

kola: see COLA.

Kolonia, town (1980 pop. 5,549), capital of the Federated States of MICRONESIA, on the island of Pohnpei (formerly Ponape).

Komodo dragon: see MONITOR.

Kongo, kingdom in W Central Africa that flourished from the 14th to 17th cent. in the region that is now ANGOLA and ZAÏRE. It was ruled by a *manikongo,* or king, and its capital was Mbanza (later São Salvador). After 1491 Kongo was increasingly under the influence of the Portuguese, who attempted to Christianize the kingdom. Their rapaciousness, particularly that of the slave traders, played a major part in weakening the kingdom. After 1665 the *manikongo* was little more than a Portuguese vassal.

Königsberg: see KALININGRAD.

Konoye Fumimaro [kōnoyä], 1891–1945, Japanese premier (1937–39, 1940–41). He pressed China for concessions in the Second SINO-JAPANESE WAR and proclaimed (1938) Japan's goal of a "new order in East Asia." Konoye concluded (1940) an alliance with the Axis powers but resigned after he failed to reach an agreement with the U.S. His suicide prevented his trial as a war criminal after WORLD WAR II.

Konrad, Gyorgy, 1933–, Hungarian novelist. In his semi-autobiographical first novel, *The Case Worker* (1969), and other writings, he has examined the social and spiritual problems of life under Communism. Among his works are *The City Builder* (1975) and *A Feast in the Garden* (1989), a novel of the HOLOCAUST.

Kook, Abraham Isaac, 1864–1935, Jewish scholar and philosopher; b. Latvia. In his view, PALESTINE and ZIONISM were necessary to Judaism. As chief rabbi of the Ashkenazic community of Palestine from 1921, he was one of the first Orthodox rabbis to apply Talmudic learning to current problems and was sympathetic toward Jewish mysticism.

Kooweskoowe: see ROSS, JOHN.

Köprülü, family of humble Albanian origin, several members of which served as grand viziers in the OTTOMAN EMPIRE (Turkey) in the 17th and 18th cent. The name is also spelled Kiuprilu, Koprili, and Kuprili. The most eminent member of the family was **Mehmed Köprülü,** 1583–1661, who became grand vizier to Sultan MUHAMMAD IV in 1656 and gained complete authority. He regained some of the former Ottoman prestige by restoring internal order, reforming finances, and rebuilding the Ottoman military forces.

Koran or **Quran** [Arab., = reading], the sacred book of ISLAM and one of the world's most influential books. According to Islamic belief, the Koran was revealed by God to the Prophet MUHAMMAD in separate revelations during the Prophet's life at Mecca and Medina. The canonical text was established A.H. 30 (A.D. 651–52) under the caliph Uthman. The revelations are divided into 114 *suras* [chapters]. The Arabic of the Koran is the classic language.

Korea, Korean *Choson,* historic country (85,049 sq mi/220,277 sq km), E Asia. A peninsula 600 mi (966 km) long, Korea separates the Yellow Sea (W) from the Sea of Japan (E). It is bounded by the Korea Strait (S), and its land boundaries with China and Russia (N) are marked by the great YALU and Tumen rivers. The land is largely mountainous, rising in the northeast to its highest point at Mt. Paektu (9,003 ft/2,744 m). Some 3,420 islands, mostly uninhabited, lie off the coast. Korea has great mineral wealth, with 80% to 90% of it concentrated in the north. Of the peninsula's five major minerals—gold, iron ore, coal, tungsten, and graphite—only the last two are found principally in the south. North Korea, which has some 300 different kinds of minerals, is especially rich in iron and coal. It ranks among the world leaders in production of graphite, gold, tungsten, magnesite, zinc, molybdenum, and other minerals. Only about 20% of Korean land is arable; rice (the chief crop), barley, wheat, corn, soybeans, and grain sorghums are extensively cultivated. The fishing waters off Korea are among the best in the world, and fish remains the chief source of protein in the Korean diet. The economy was shattered by the war of 1950 to 1953, but huge amounts of foreign aid and intensive government programs in both north and south sped postwar reconstruction. Important industrial advances were made in the 1960s and 70s, and South Korea now has one of the most rapidly growing economies in Asia, with its gross national product exceeding that of the north by more than five times by the early 1990s. South Korean manufactures include textiles, clothing, processed foods, electrical and electronic equipment, automobiles, chemicals, ceramics, and a variety of consumer products. Major North Korean products include iron, steel, machinery, textiles, and chemicals. Most Koreans are Confucianists or Buddhists; there are many Christians in the south. Korean is spoken in both parts of the country; English is widely taught in the south.

History. Korea was founded in 2333 B.C. The kingdom of Koguryo, one of the three native states, arose in Manchuria near the Yalu R. in the 1st cent. A.D. The kingdom of Silla emerged A.D. c.350 and unified the peninsula in the 7th cent. The Koryo dynasty ruled a united Korea from 935 until Mongol invasions from China in the 13th cent. forced an alliance under Mongol control. The Yi dynasty (1392–1910) built a new capital at Hanyang (now SEOUL) and established CONFUCIANISM as the official state doctrine. Japa-

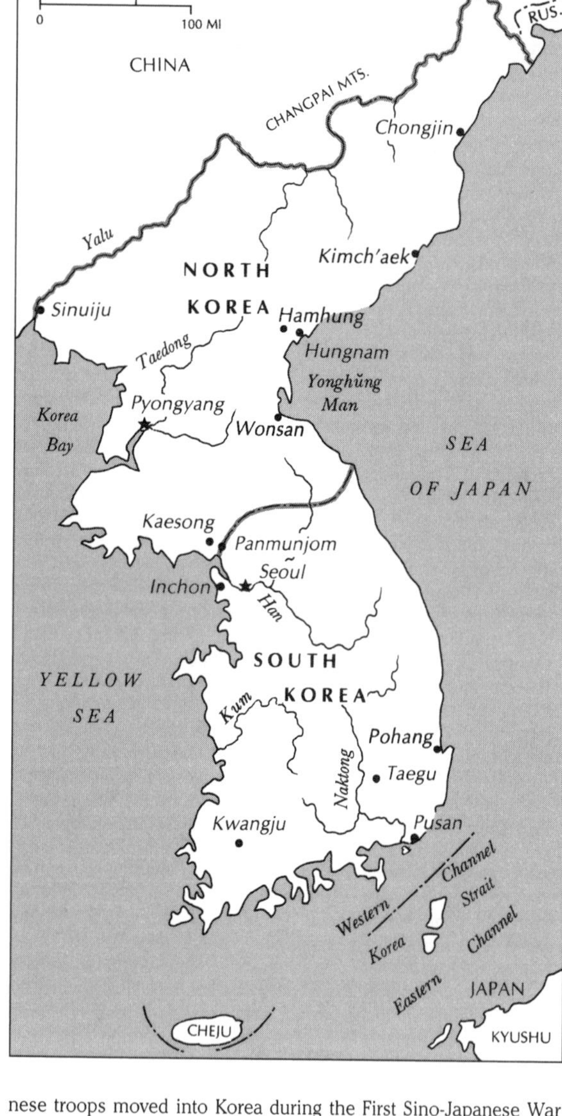

nese troops moved into Korea during the First Sino-Japanese War (1894–95) and the RUSSO-JAPANESE WAR (1904–5), and Japan formally annexed (1910) the country, which remained under Japanese colonial rule until 1945. During World War II the Allies promised Korea independence, and after the war the country was divided into two zones of occupation, with Soviet troops north and Americans south of the line of lat. 38°N. In 1948 two separate regimes were established—the Republic of Korea in the south, and the Democratic People's Republic under Communist rule in the north. Since the KOREAN WAR (1950–53) the peninsula has remained two independent nations divided roughly at the 38th parallel. Since 1990 there have been increasing contacts between the governments of the two Koreas. In 1991 both nations joined the UN after the North dropped its opposition to such a move. **North Korea,** officially Democratic People's Republic of Korea (1992 est. pop. 22,227,000), 46,540 sq mi (120,538 sq km), has its capital at PYONGYANG, the largest city. After the Korean War the Communist government launched an ambitious program of industrialization. North Korea maintained close relations with the USSR and the People's Republic of China, both of which provided aid for reconstruction. Postwar politics have been dominated by KIM IL SUNG, who kept the country isolated, heavily armed, and thoroughly collectivized. A personality cult has glorified Kim, and his son, Kim Jong Il, has been groomed to succeed him. By the early 1990s the rapid economic growth of North Korea's early years had given way first to stagnation, then to hardship, and there was widespread dissatisfaction with the repressive regime. The North was also increasingly isolated as the USSR, once a key ally, was dissolved and China, now its most important ally, improved ties with the economically more successful South. In 1991 the U.S., Japan, and South Korea accused the North of developing nuclear weapons. North Korea initially refused to permit international inspections and threatened (1993) to withdraw from the nuclear nonproliferation treaty, but it agreed to inspections in 1994. **South Korea,** officially Republic of Korea (1992 est. pop. 44,149,000), 38,022 sq mi (98,477 sq km), has its capital at Seoul, the largest city; PUSAN is the chief port. Syngman RHEE, elected the first president in 1948, was forced to resign in 1960 by a popular uprising against his authoritarian rule. A military junta under Gen. PARK CHUNG HEE seized power in 1961 and had by 1975 assumed near-dictatorial powers. In the 1960s foreign trade, especially with Japan, replaced American aid. Ties with the U.S. were temporarily strained by alleged Korean influence peddling in the U.S. Congress and by Pres. CARTER's decision (later suspended) to withdraw U.S. troops from South Korea. In 1979 Pres. Park was assassinated in an apparent coup attempt; soon after, Lt. Gen. CHUN DOO HWAN led a military coup and took control. Despite widespread opposition to his government's repressive measures, Chun was elected president and reelected under a new constitution in 1981. Roh Tae Woo, Chun's chosen successor, became (1988) president after an election in which the opposition was divided. He attempted to improve relations with opposition politicians and with the North and established diplomatic relations with the USSR (1990) and China (1992). In 1992 Kim Young Sam, a former opposition leader who had merged his party with Roh's, was elected president, becoming the first civilian to hold the office since the Korean War.

Korean, language of uncertain relationship that is spoken by about 36 million people, most of whom live in Korea. It is thought by some scholars to be akin to JAPANESE, by others to be a member of the Altaic subfamily of the URALIC AND ALTAIC family of languages (see LANGUAGE, table), and by still others to be unrelated to any known language.

Korean War, conflict between Communist and non-Communist forces in Korea from June 25, 1950, to July 27, 1953. At the end of WORLD WAR II, Korea was divided at the 38th parallel into Soviet (North Korean) and U.S. (South Korean) zones of occupation. In 1948 rival governments were established. When North Korean forces invaded South Korea, the UN authorized member nations to aid South Korea. Gen. Douglas MACARTHUR commanded the UN forces until 1951, when he was replaced by Gen. Matthew B. RIDGWAY. In Oct. 1950 Chinese Communist forces joined the North Korean army. Fighting centered around the 38th parallel. In 1951 negotiations for a cease-fire were begun at Panmunjom; it was achieved on July 27, 1953.

Kornberg, Arthur, 1918–, American biochemist. For his discovery of the mechanisms in the biological synthesis of DNA, he shared with Severo OCHOA the 1959 Nobel Prize in physiology or medicine. He has done research at the National Institutes of Health (1942–52), Washington Univ. (1953–59), and Stanford Univ. (1959–).

Korolev, Sergei Pavlovich, 1907–66, Soviet rocket designer. His role as chief designer of the Soviet space program was revealed only after his death. After he successfully launched two intercontinental ballistic missiles in Aug. 1957, Soviet premier Nikita Khrushchev allowed him to attempt the orbiting of a test satellite; as a result, *Sputnik 1,* the first artificial earth satellite, was orbited successfully on Oct. 4, 1957. Korolev also directed the launching of the USSR's first unmanned space probes and manned space missions.

Koror, island (1990 est. pop. 10,500), capital of PALAU.

Kosciusko, Thaddeus, 1746–1817, Polish general and patriot. He fought for the colonists in the AMERICAN REVOLUTION and then returned to Poland, where he became a champion of independence. In 1794 he led an unsuccessful rebellion against Russian and Prussian control of Poland.

Kosciusko, Mount, 7,316 ft (2,230 m) high, in SE New South Wales, Australia. It is the highest point in Australia.

kosher [Heb., = proper], term applied to food that is in accordance with Jewish dietary laws. Animals that chew their cud and have cloven hooves (e.g., cows and sheep) are kosher; rules governing their slaughter and preparation also apply to fowl. Proper preparation of kosher meats includes complete drainage of blood. Kosher fish are those with scales and fins. Milk products may not be cooked or eaten with, or immediately after, meat or poultry. The origins of and motivations for Jewish dietary laws and customs have been variously explained as hygienic, aesthetic, folkloric, ethical, and psychological.

Kosinski, Jerzy, 1933–91, Polish-American writer; b. Łodz, Poland. His best-known work is *The Painted Bird* (1965), a novel depicting a boy's nightmarish wanderings among brutal peasants during World War II. His other novels, e.g., *Steps* (1968) and *The Devil Tree* (1973), echo the theme of character disintegration through cruelty and revenge.

Kosovo [kô'sôvô] or **Kosova** [kô'sôvä], former autonomous province, 4,126 sq mi (10,686 sq km), S Yugoslavia, in Serbia. Priština is the chief city. A largely mountainous region, its major occupations are agriculture, stock raising, forestry, and lead and silver mining. Its population is about 90% Albanian, with Serbian and Montenegrin minorities. Most of the region was incorporated into Italian-held Albania from 1941 to 1944. Serbia abolished Kosovo's autonomy in 1989–90 in reaction to a campaign for constituent republic status for the region and began repressing Albanians and encouraging Serbian migration into the region. In response Albanians pressed for Kosovo's complete independence, elected a "parliament" in 1992, and boycotted (1992) Serbian elections. At **Kosovo Field,** the fertile central valley of Kosovo, the Ottoman Turks defeated Serbia and its allies in 1389; Serbia and Bulgaria then passed under Ottoman rule. On the same site in 1448 the Turks defeated an army led by John Hunyadi.

Kossuth, Louis, Hung. *Kossuth Lajos,* 1802–94, Hungarian revolutionary hero. A fiery orator, Kossuth was one of the leaders of the Hungarian revolution of 1848 (see HUNGARY). His principles were liberal and nationalistic. When Austria prepared to move against the Hungarians, he became head of the government of national defense. He served as president of the newly formed Hungarian republic from Apr. to Aug. 1849 but was forced to resign after Russian troops intervened in favor of Austria. Thereafter he lived in exile.

Kosygin, Aleksei Nikolayevich [kəsē'gĭn], 1904–81, Soviet leader. Appointed to the central committee of the Communist party in 1939, he became first deputy chairman of the USSR council of ministers in 1960 and succeeded Nikita KHRUSHCHEV as premier in 1964, sharing power with Leonid BREZHNEV until the mid-1970s.

Koufax, Sandy (Sanford Koufax), 1935–, American baseball player; b. N.Y.C. A left-hander with overwhelming speed and a brilliant curve, he played (1955–66) with the Dodgers, first in Brooklyn and then in Los Angeles. He struck out 2,396 batters, pitched four no-hitters (including a perfect game), and won the Cy Young Award three times as the game's top pitcher. At the peak of his career (he won 26 and 27 games his last two seasons), he was forced into premature retirement because of a chronic arm ailment.

koumiss: see FERMENTED MILK.

Koussevitzky, Serge, 1874–1951, Russian-American conductor. He came to the U.S. in 1924 and conducted (1924–49) the Boston Symphony Orchestra. He directed (from 1936) the Berkshire Symphonic Festivals (the Berkshire Festival). A champion of modern music, he commissioned and performed new works by COPLAND, BARBER, William SCHUMAN, and others.

Kr, chemical symbol of the element KRYPTON.

Krakatoa or **Krakatau,** active volcano, W Indonesia, forming an island (c.5 sq mi/13 sq km) in Sunda Strait, between Java and Sumatra. The volcano, which rises to 2,667 ft (813 m), is famous for its 1883 eruption, one of the most violent of modern times, which scattered debris as far as Madagascar. The associated TSUNAMI swept over nearby coastal areas, causing great loss of life.

Kraków or **Cracow,** city (1989 est. pop. 743,000), S Poland, on the Vistula R. It is a river port and industrial center producing metals, machinery, textiles, and chemicals. Founded c.700, the city was (1320–1596) the residence of Poland's kings. Its university was founded in 1364. Ruled at various times by Austria, Prussia, and Russia, Kraków reverted to Poland in 1919. On a hill, the Wawel, are the royal castle (rebuilt 16th cent.) and a Gothic cathedral (rebuilt 14th cent.).

Sandy Koufax

Kranach, Lucas: see CRANACH, LUCAS.

Kravchuk, Leonid Makarovich, 1934–, president of UKRAINE (1991–). An ideologist in the Ukrainian Communist party, he was elected (1990) chairman of Ukraine's Supreme Soviet. A cautious pragmatist and an opponent of Ukrainian nationalists, he did not initially oppose the coup against GORBACHEV, but afterward he quit the Communist party and advocated Ukraine's independence. In Dec. 1991 he became Ukraine's first popularly elected president, as Ukrainians simultaneously voted for independence. Kravchuk was a leading force in the establishment of the COMMONWEALTH OF INDEPENDENT STATES. He has clashed with the parliament over the slow pace of economic reform.

Krebs, Sir Hans Adolf, 1900–1981, English biochemist; b. Germany; emigrated to England, 1933. For his studies of intermediary metabolism he shared with Fritz Lipmann the 1953 Nobel Prize in physiology or medicine. These studies included the elucidation of the cycle of chemical reactions called the CITRIC ACID CYCLE, or Krebs cycle, the major source of energy in living organisms.

Krebs cycle: see CITRIC ACID CYCLE.

Kreisky, Bruno [krī'skē], 1911–90, Austrian political leader. A lifelong socialist who fled Nazi-ruled Austria, he was foreign minister (1959–66), Socialist party chairman (1967–83), and chancellor of Austria (1970–83). As chancellor, he increased Austria's role in world affairs and presided over a growing economy.

Kreisler, Fritz [krīs'lər], 1875–1962, Austrian-American violinist. From about 1901 he was perhaps the most popular violinist in the U.S. He composed OPERETTAS and numerous famous violin pieces, e.g., *Tambourin Chinois*.

kremlin, Rus. *kreml,* citadel or walled center of a city. A medieval kremlin protected against attack and was a city in itself. Those of MOSCOW and several other cities still stand. Moscow's, called simply the **Kremlin,** occupies 90 acres (36.4 hectares). Along its crenellated walls, built in the 15th cent., are palaces; one houses the tsars' crown jewels, another the parliament building. Inside the Kremlin are three cathedrals and a bell tower. The tsars' residence until St. Petersburg became the capital (1712), the Kremlin was the Soviet political and administrative center from 1918 to 1991, when the USSR disintegrated. It now houses Russian government offices.

Křenek, Ernst, 1900–91, Austrian-American composer. In the 1920s he composed in a neoclassical style. His jazz opera *Johnny Strikes*

Up (1926) was a great success. After a neo-Romantic period, he adopted the TWELVE-TONE system, as in his opera *Karl V* (1933). In 1937 he moved to the U.S. The operas *Dark Waters* (1950) and *Sardakai* (1969), and *Eleven Transparencies* (1956) for orchestra and ELECTRONIC MUSIC, are among later pieces.

Krishna [Skt., = black], popular deity in HINDUISM; the eighth avatar, or incarnation, of Vishnu.

Krleža, Miroslav, 1893–1981, Croatian novelist, playwright, and poet. He captured the concerns of a revolutionary era in Yugoslavia in his trilogy of social dramas about the Glembay family (1928–32) and in novels like *The Return of Philip Latinovicz* (1932) and *Banners* (1963–65), a multivolume saga of the Croatian bourgeoisie beginning in the early 20th cent.

Krochmal, Nachman Kohen [krôkh'mal], 1785–1840, Jewish secular historian and writer; b. Galicia. He was a leader of the Haskalah, or Jewish enlightenment, and a founder of Conservative JUDAISM.

Kroeber, Alfred Louis, 1876–1960, American anthropologist; b. Hoboken, N.J. A major figure in the founding of modern anthropology, he clearly set forth the relationship between cultural patterns and the individual. His major works include *The Nature of Culture* (1952) and *Style and Civilization* (1957).

Kronecker, Leopold, 1823–91, German mathematician. After making a fortune in business, he became a noted algebraist. He was a pioneer in the field of algebraic NUMBERS and formulated the relation between number theory, the theory of equations, and elliptic functions.

Kronos: see CRONUS.

Kropotkin, Prince Piotr Alekseyevich, 1842–1921, Russian anarchist. A noted geographer, he was imprisoned (1874–76) for political activities and fled Russia. Kropotkin settled in England, but after the February 1917 RUSSIAN REVOLUTION returned to Russia. When the Bolsheviks took power, he retired from political life. His writings include *Mutual Aid* (1902), which holds that cooperation rather than competition is the norm in both animal and human life, and *Memoirs of a Revolutionist* (1899).

Kruger, Paul, 1825–1904, South African Transvaal statesman, known as Oom Paul. He was a founder (1852) of the Transvaal, and after its annexation by Britain (1877) he was a leader of the Boer settlers there. He led the Boer Rebellion (1880) that forced Britain to restore independence and was president (1883–1900) of the Transvaal. In the SOUTH AFRICAN WAR (1899–1902) he went to Europe, where he made vain attempts to enlist aid for his country.

Krupp [kro͝op], family of German armament manufacturers who flourished in the 19th and 20th cent. **Friedrich Krupp,** 1787–1826, built a small steel plant at Essen c.1810. His son, **Alfred Krupp,** 1812–87, the "cannon king," specialized in armaments and acquired mines all over Germany. Under Alfred's son, **Friedrich Alfred Krupp,** 1854–1902, the family extended its operations. The husband of his daughter, Bertha Krupp (after whom the Big Bertha guns were named), took the name **Gustav Krupp von Bohlen und Halbach,** 1870–1950. He took over what was then a public company and made it the center of Nazi rearmament in the 1930s. In 1943, HITLER converted the company back into a family holding, and **Alfred Krupp von Bohlen und Halbach,** 1907–67, son of Gustav and Bertha, ran the company until the end of World War II. He was convicted (1948) as a war criminal but was released from prison (1951) and allowed to resume control of the firm. After his death, Krupp became a public corporation and the family ceased (1968) to control it.

kryolite: see CRYOLITE.

krypton (Kr), gaseous element, discovered by William RAMSAY and M.W. Travers in 1898. It is a rare INERT GAS used to fill electric lamp bulbs and various electronic devices, and to detect heart defects. From 1960 to 1983 the definition of a meter was based on the emission spectrum of the krypton-86 isotope. See ELEMENT (table); PERIODIC TABLE.

Kuala Lumpur, largest city (1990 est. pop. 1,750,000) and capital of Malaysia, S Malay Peninsula, at the confluence of the Klang and Gombak rivers. It is a transport hub and trade and industrial center in a tin-mining and rubber-growing district. Founded (1857) by Chinese miners, it became the capital of the Federated Malay States (see MALAYSIA) in 1896.

Kublai Khan [ko͞o'blī kän], 1215?–1294, Mongol emperor, founder of the Yüan dynasty of China. He succeeded (1260) his brother Mangu as khan of the empire founded by their grandfather JENGHIZ KHAN. Kublai Khan defeated (1279) the Sung dynasty of China, but his campaigns against Japan, Southeast Asia, and Indonesia failed. His rule was nominal except in Mongolia and China. He improved public works and established a magnificent capital at Cambuluc (now Beijing), where Marco POLO visited him.

Kübler-Ross, Elisabeth, 1926–, Swiss-American physician; M.D., Univ. of Zürich, 1957. After settling in the U.S. in 1958, she taught psychiatry and specialized in treating the terminally ill. Her best-selling book *On Death and Dying* (1969), describing five psychological stages experienced by the dying (denial, anger, "bargaining for time," grieving, and acceptance), has greatly influenced the humane treatment and counseling of terminally ill patients and the rise of HOSPICE care for dying persons.

Kudrun: see GUDRUN.

Kuhn, Richard, 1900–1967, Austrian chemist. Awarded the 1938 Nobel Prize in chemistry for his work on the carotinoids and on vitamins, he was unable, because of the Nazis, to accept the award until after World War II. He isolated vitamins B_2 (riboflavin) and B_6.

Kuhn, Thomas Samuel, 1922–, American philosopher and historian of science; b. Cincinnati, Ohio. In his influential *The Structure of Scientific Revolutions* (1962), he distinguished between normal science, which solves puzzles while operating within a particular "paradigm," and revolutionary science, which occurs rarely and requires that one paradigm be abandoned for another. This insight was derived, in part, from his analysis of the Copernican revolution.

Kuhn, Walt, 1880–1949, American painter; b. N.Y.C. He is known for his boldly interpretive studies of backstage and circus life, e.g., *Blue Clown* (Whitney Mus., N.Y.C.). Kuhn was one of the organizers of the famed ARMORY SHOW.

Kuiper, Gerard Peter or **Gerrit Pieter,** 1905–73, American astronomer; b. Netherlands. Kuiper discovered a carbon dioxide atmosphere on Mars (1948), URANUS's satellite Miranda (1948), and NEPTUNE's satellite Nereid (1949). He proposed (1951) the existence of a disk-shaped region of minor planets outside the orbit of Neptune (now called the Kuiper belt) as a source for short-period COMETS. See also OORT, JAN HENDRICK.

Ku Klux Klan, designation mainly given to two distinct American secret societies. The first, founded in the South in 1866, opposed RECONSTRUCTION. Organized by ex-Confederates and led by Nathan B. Forrest, it used elaborate disguises and rituals, augmented by whippings and lynchings, to terrorize African Americans and their supporters. Forrest disbanded the Klan in 1869, but its members continued to keep African Americans from the polls. The second Klan, organized in 1915, had a wider scope: embracing anti-Catholic, anti-Semitic, nativist, and fundamentalist impulses, it spread to the North, fueled by the militant patriotism of World War I. In the mid-1920s it had 4 to 5 million members; it declined rapidly thereafter but contributed to the 1928 defeat of Alfred E. SMITH, a Catholic. The Klan revived in reaction to civil-rights activism in the 1960s, using violence against civil-rights workers in the South. Despite its split into competing factions, the Klan became involved in racial confrontations late in the 1970s. The various factions continue to recruit new members, largely in response to AFFIRMATIVE ACTION programs, unstable economic conditions, and other factors, but intimidation, rather than violence, is the Klan's main tactic and its success is often limited.

Kulkulcán: see QUETZALCOATL.

Kumasi, city (1984 pop. 348,880), capital of the Ashanti Region, central Ghana. The nation's second largest city, it is a commercial and transportation center in a cocoa-producing region. It was founded c.1700 as the capital of the ASHANTI confederation and is the seat of the Ashanti kings. Points of interest include a British fort (1897).

kumiss: see FERMENTED MILK.

kumquat, evergreen shrub (genus *Fortunella*) of the RUE family, cultivated for its small, orange-yellow CITRUS FRUITS, eaten fresh or in preserves. Kumquats, with their sweet-scented white flowers, are also grown as ornamentals in warm areas of the U.S.

Kun, Béla [ko͞on], 1886–1939?, Hungarian Communist leader. In

1919, when Count Karolyi's government resigned, the Communists and Social Democrats formed a coalition government under Kun. He raised a Red Army that overran SLOVAKIA. The Allies forced him to evacuate Slovakia, and a counterrevolution broke out. Kun was defeated by a Romanian army of intervention. He went (1920) to the USSR and probably died in prison or Siberia.

Kundera, Milan, 1929–, Czech writer. His first novel, *The Joke* (1967), is about a student whose joking reference to Trotsky earns him a sentence at hard labor. It brought Kundera into official disfavor in Prague and resulted in the loss of his citizenship. He moved to France and became a French citizen in 1980. He has also written poems, plays, short stories, and other novels, e.g., *The Book of Laughter and Forgetting* (1979), *The Unbearable Lightness of Being* (1984), and *Immortality* (1990).

Küng, Hans, 1928–, Swiss Roman Catholic theologian. A professor at Tübingen Univ. and an adviser (1962–65) to the Second VATICAN COUNCIL, he has consistently criticized papal authority. His *Infallible? An Inquiry* (1971) rejects papal infallibility. In 1979 Küng was stripped of his right to teach as an official Roman Catholic theologian. He has written many other books, including *Why I Am Still a Christian* (1987).

Kunitz, Stanley (Jasspon) [kyo͞onĭts], 1905–, American poet and editor; b. Worcester, Mass. His complex poems are in such volumes as *Intellectual Things* (1930), *Selected Poems, 1928–1958* (1958; Pulitzer), and *Next-to-Last Things* (1985). He has edited reference books (with Howard Haycraft), e.g., *Twentieth Century Authors* (1942).

Kuniyoshi, Yasuo [ko͞on″ēyō′shē], 1892?–1953, American painter; b. Japan. Considered Asian in spirit but Western in technique, his paintings, drawings, and prints are rich in symbolism and fantasy, but often somber in color.

Kunming, city (1990 est. pop. 1,520,000), capital of Yunnan prov., SW China. It comprises an old walled city, a modern commercial suburb, and a residential and university section. Kunming is an industrial, administrative, commercial, cultural, and transportation hub of SW China. On its outskirts is a famed Ming dynasty temple.

Kuomintang, Chinese political party. It was organized (1912) by Sung Chiao-jen to succeed the Revolutionary Alliance and was outlawed (1913) after gaining a majority in the first national assembly elected in China. Under SUN YAT-SEN it established revolutionary secret governments in Guangzhou in 1918 and 1921. In 1924 it formed an alliance with the Communists under Sun's Three People's Principles (nationalism, democracy, and livelihood). After Sun's death (1925), it was led by CHIANG KAI-SHEK, who purged the Communists (1927) and captured the capital, Beijing, in 1928. The Kuomintang ruled China until 1949, fighting the Japanese invaders and the Communists. Defeated by the latter, its members fled to the island of TAIWAN, which they continued to rule under Chiang, under Chiang Ching-kuo, his son, and under LEE TENG-HUI. In 1991 Lee ended emergency rule on Taiwan, which had permitted Kuomintang delegates elected to the National Assembly in 1947 to retain their seats.

Kuprin, Aleksandr Ivanovich [ko͞o′prĭn], 1870–1938, Russian novelist and short-story writer. His best-known novels are *The Duel* (1905), an attack on Russian military life, and *The Pit* (1924), a sensational exposé of prostitution.

kurchatovium (Ku): see RUTHERFORDIUM.

Kurdistan, extensive plateau and mountain region in SW Asia (c.74,000 sq mi/191,660 sq km), inhabited mainly by Kurds and including parts of E Turkey, N Syria, NE Iraq, S Armenia, and NW Iran. Ethnically and linguistically close to the Iranians, the **Kurds,** who number about 20 million, were traditionally nomadic herders but are now mostly seminomadic or sedentary. The majority are devout SUNNI Muslims and speak Kurdish. The Kurds have traditionally resisted subjugation by other nations. Kurdistan was conquered by the Arabs and converted to Islam in the 7th cent. The region was held by the Seljuk Turks in the 11th cent., by the Mongols from the 13th to 15th cent., and then by the Ottoman Empire. Since World War I the Kurds have struggled unsuccessfully in the various countries in which they live for self-determination and independence. In 1946 a short-lived, Soviet-backed Kurdish republic was formed in Iran. There were Kurdish uprisings in Iraq in the 1960s, 70s, and 80s, and since the mid-1980s Kurdish guerrillas have fought the Turkish government. After the PERSIAN GULF WAR, Kurdish groups again rose against Iraq but were crushed, and perhaps 1.5 million fled to Turkey and Iran. Returning under UN protection, they established (1992) an "autonomous region" in N Iraq. There was also fighting in the early 1990s between Turkish and Iraqi Kurds.

Kuril Islands or **Kuriles,** island chain, NE Asia, part of Russia; the southernmost islands are claimed by Japan as the Northern Territories. The islands extend c.775 mi (1,250 km) S from the KAMCHATKA Peninsula to near HOKKAIDO, Japan, and are cold, damp, and sparsely populated. They were divided between Japan and Russia in 1855. In 1875 Japan gave up nearby SAKHALIN for Russian concession of the northern Kuriles; the entire chain was occupied by the USSR in 1945.

Kurosawa Akira [ko͞orō′säwä], 1910–, Japanese film director. With *Rashomon* (1950), he gained international recognition, becoming the best known Japanese filmmaker in the West. He blends Eastern and Western styles, has often adapted the works of foreign authors (including Dostoyevsky, Gorky, and Shakespeare), and is known for his impressive use of wide screen cinematography. His other films include *Ikiru* (1952), *Seven Samurai* (1954), *Yojimbo* (1961), *Dersu Uzala* (1976), *Kagemusha* (1980), *Ran* (1985), and *Rhapsody in August* (1991).

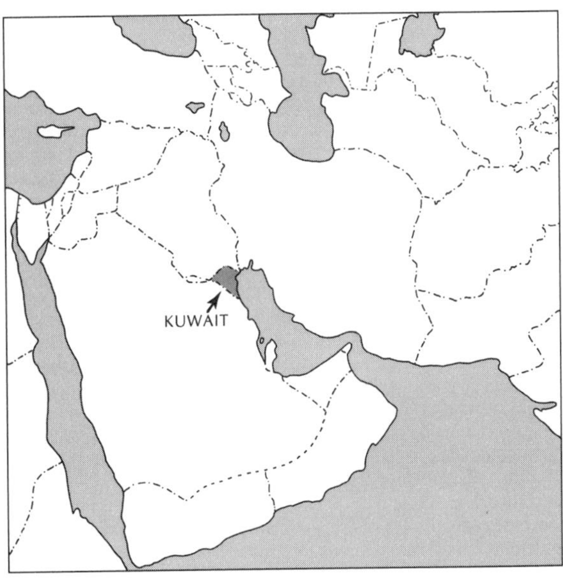

Kuwait, officially State of Kuwait, independent sheikhdom (1992 est. pop. 1,378,000), 6,177 sq mi (16,000 sq km), NE Arabian peninsula, at the head of the Persian Gulf, bounded by Saudi Arabia (S) and Iraq (N and W). The capital is KUWAIT. It is a sandy and barren country. With more than 10% of the world's estimated oil reserves, Kuwait is a leading exporter of petroleum and has used some of the enormous profits for social improvements. In the 1960s the government launched a program of industrial diversification, successfully introducing oil refining and production of natural gas and fertilizers. The population is predominantly Arab and Sunni Muslim, although only half the inhabitants are native-born.

History. Kuwait, settled by Arab tribes in the early 18th cent., has been ruled since its inception by the al-Sabah dynasty. Nominally an Ottoman province, the sheikhdom became a British protectorate in 1897, remaining so until independence in 1961. Oil production began in the 1940s and was controlled by a joint British-American firm until 1974, when Kuwait nationalized most of the operations. Kuwait took part in the Arab oil embargo against nations that supported Israel in the 1973 Arab-Israeli War, and is a member of the ORGANIZATION OF PETROLEUM EXPORTING COUNTRIES (OPEC). In Aug. 1990 Kuwait was invaded and forcibly annexed by Iraq, an act that led to and was reversed by the PERSIAN GULF WAR. Widespread looting and intentional destruction by Iraqi troops and the fighting during the war devastated Kuwait, particularly its oilfields, but by the end of 1992 the country had repaired nearly all the damage and its oil output was at about the prewar level. In 1992 opposition candidates won a majority of the seats in parliament.

Kuwait or **Al-Kuwait,** city (1990 est. pop. 151,000), capital of Kuwait, situated on a Persian Gulf inlet. The city was modernized after oil was discovered in 1938 and was heavily damaged in the PERSIAN GULF WAR. Its port, Mina al-Ahmad, has refineries and shipyards. The country's first university (est. 1966) is there.

Kuybyshev: see SAMARA.

Kuyp, family of Dutch painters: see CUYP.

Kuznets, Simon, 1901–85, American economist; b. Russia. After emigrating (1922) to the U.S., he worked for the National Bureau of Standards (1927–63) and taught at the Univ. of Pennsylvania (1930–54), Johns Hopkins (1954–60), and Harvard (1960–71). Generally credited with having developed the GROSS NATIONAL PRODUCT as a measure of economic output, he was awarded the 1971 Nobel Prize in economics. *National Income and Its Composition, 1919 to 1938* (1941) is considered his major work.

Kwajalein: see MARSHALL ISLANDS.

Kwakiutl, indigenous people of the Northwest Coast (see NORTH AMERICA, INDIGENOUS PEOPLES OF) who live in Vancouver Island and adjacent British Columbia, Canada. They speak a Wakashan language of the Algonquian-Wakashan stock (see NATIVE AMERICAN LANGUAGES). In the 19th cent. they conducted elaborate POTLATCH ceremonies. Numbering c.15,000 before European contact, they are now reduced to a few thousand, mostly fishermen and farmers.

Kwangju, city (1985 pop. 905,896), capital of South Cholla prov., SW South Korea. A regional agricultural and commercial center, Kwangju has rice mills and produces automobiles, textiles, and beer. There are several ancient tombs and temples in the area. In 1980 Kwangju was seized for several days by rebels protesting martial law in South Korea; government troops eventually suppressed the uprising.

Kwanzaa or **Kwanza,** secular seven-day festival in celebration of the African heritage of African Americans, beginning on Dec. 26. Developed by Maulana Karenga and first observed in 1966, Kwanzaa is based in part on traditional African harvest festivals but particularly emphasizes the role of the family and community in African-American culture. Each day is dedicated to a particular principle (unity, self-determination, collective work and responsibility, cooperative economics, purpose, creativity, and faith), and on each day one of the candles on a seven-branched candelabrum is lighted. The celebration also includes the giving of gifts and a karamu, or African feast.

kwashiorkor, protein deficiency disorder of children, prevalent in overpopulated parts of the world where the diet consists mainly of starchy vegetables, particularly Africa, Central and South America, and S Asia. Such a diet is deficient in certain amino acids, which make up PROTEINS vital for growth. Depending on the extent, onset, and duration of the deficiency, manifestations include skin changes, edema, severely bloated abdomen, diarrhea, and generally retarded development.

Kweiyang: see GUIYANG.

Kyd or **Kid, Thomas,** 1558–94, English dramatist. His fame rests on *The Spanish Tragedy* (c.1586), which initiated the Elizabethan revenge TRAGEDY. Popular through the 17th cent., *The Spanish Tragedy* is noted for its action, rhetoric, and character delineation.

Kyoto [kyō'tō], city (1990 pop. 1,461,140), capital of Kyoto prefecture, S Honshu, Japan. Founded in the 8th cent., it was Japan's capital from 794 to 1868. The cultural heart of Japan, the city has magnificent art treasures and is the seat of Kyoto Univ. and other institutions of higher learning. Along with Osaka, it has undergone an economic and cultural revival. Kyoto is a religious center, noted especially for its ancient Buddhist temples. Rich in historic interest, its buildings include the old imperial palace and Nijo Castle, the former palace of the Ashikaga SHOGUNS. Industries include electronics, chemicals, and the manufacture of tools and cameras. The city is famous for its silk, cloisonné, bronzes, damascene work, and porcelain.

Kyrgyzstan, Kirghizstan, or **Kirghizia,** officially Republic of Kyrgyzstan, republic (1992 est. pop. 4,568,000), c.79,000 sq mi (204,600 sq km), central Asia, formerly a constituent republic of the USSR. It borders China (SE), Kazakhstan (N), Uzbekistan (W), and Tajikistan (SW). The capital is BISHKEK (formerly Frunze). A mountainous country, it has rich pasturage for livestock. Cotton, sugar beets, and other crops are grown. Among its mineral resources are coal, oil, natural gas, antimony, mercury, uranium, and gold. Industries include the extraction and processing of its many resources, food processing, steel manufacture, and metallurgy. The Kyrgyz (or Kirghiz), a nomadic, Turkic-speaking, Sunni Muslim people with Mongol strains, comprise a little over half the population; Russians, Uzbeks, and others make up the rest. The official language is Kyrgyz, but Russian is also spoken.

History. The Kyrgyz emigrated in the 17th cent. from the region of the upper Yenisei R., where they had lived since the 7th cent. The region was annexed (1855–76) by Russia and became part of the USSR in 1921 when Bolshevik forces subdued the nomadic Kyrgyz. The area became an autonomous republic of the USSR in 1926 and a constituent republic in 1936. In 1991, following the attempted hard-line coup against Soviet Pres. Gorbachev, the republic declared its independence as Kyrgyzstan; as the central Soviet government collapsed, it joined the COMMONWEALTH OF INDEPENDENT STATES. In 1993 a new constitution, establishing a unicameral parliament and separate heads of state and government, was adopted. Askar Akayev, who has been president of Kyrgyzstan since 1990, has sought more radical economic and political reforms than the other Central Asian republics.

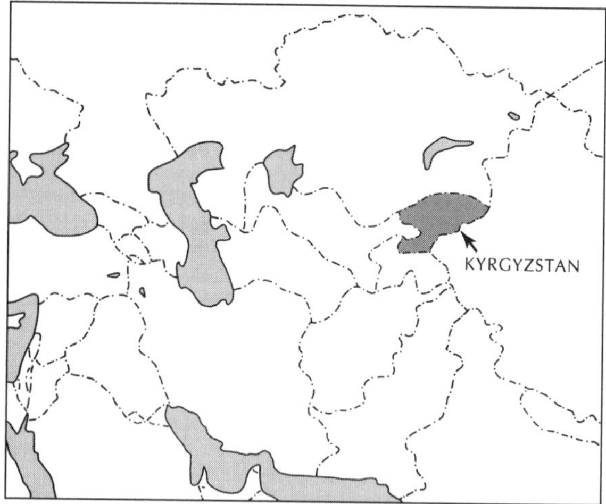

Kyushu, island (1990 pop. 13,064,955), c.16,205 sq mi (42,133 sq km), southernmost and third largest of the main islands of Japan. It is mainly of volcanic origin, with a scenic, mountainous interior rising to 5,886 ft (1,794 m) at Kuju-san. There are many hot springs. Coal, mined in the north, contributed to the early development of the principal industrial cities (KITAKYUSHU, FUKUOKA, and Omuta). NAGASAKI is the chief port.

Kyzyl Kum or **Kizil Kum,** desert, central Asia, in Kazakhstan and Uzbekistan, SE of the ARAL SEA. Seminomadic tribes inhabit most of the region, which has gold and natural gas deposits and supports agricultural settlements in the river valleys and irrigated oases.

L

La, chemical symbol of the element LANTHANUM.

Labor, United States Department of, federal executive department established (1913) to administer and enforce statutes that promote the welfare, improve the working conditions, and advance the employment opportunities of the American workforce. Its major divisions include the Bureau of International Labor Affairs, the Employment and Training Administration, the Employment Standards Administration, the Bureau of Labor Statistics, the Pension and Welfare Benefits Administration, and the OCCUPATIONAL SAFETY AND HEALTH ADMINISTRATION.

Labor Day, holiday celebrated in the U.S. and Canada on the first Monday in September to honor the laborer.

labor law, legislation affecting workers and the conditions of employment. The earliest English factory law (1802) dealt with the health, safety, and morals of child textile workers. Labor unions were legalized in Britain in 1825, but agreements among their members to seek better hours and wages were punishable as conspiracy until 1871. In the U.S. early legislation was aimed at improving working conditions, but labor organizing was discouraged by the federal doctrine of conspiracy until this was superseded by state laws, beginning in 1842. A wide range of labor legislation has been enacted over the years—including laws prohibiting night work and work in hazardous occupations for women and children; laws establishing MINIMUM WAGES in certain occupations; and laws regulating interstate commerce to discourage sweatshop labor and child labor. Congress exempted (1916) UNIONS from the antitrust laws, and the use of injunctions in labor disputes was outlawed in 1932, although later reinstated. A landmark in legislation favorable to trade unions was achieved in the Wagner Act of 1935, which established the right of workers to organize and required employers to accept COLLECTIVE BARGAINING. In 1938 the Fair Labor Standards Act provided for minimum wages and overtime payments for workers in interstate commerce. The outbreak of strikes after World War II, however, brought demands for more restrictive labor legislation, culminating in passage of the Taft-Hartley Labor Act (1947), which declared illegal such union practices as the secondary boycott, the closed shop, and jurisdictional strikes (see STRIKE). Further restrictions were imposed in 1959 by the Landrum-Griffin Act. The Civil Rights Act (1964) prohibited race-, sex-, and religion-based discrimination in employment, and age discrimination was barred in 1967. Concern over workplace safety led to the act (1970) that established the OCCUPATIONAL SAFETY AND HEALTH ADMINISTRATION, and a 1974 law created a federal agency to insure many pension plans. The AMERICANS WITH DISABILITIES ACT (1990) barred job discrimination against otherwise qualified disabled individuals.

labor union: see UNION, LABOR.

Labour party, major British political party, the other being the CONSERVATIVE PARTY. Spurred by the increased enfranchisement of the working class (1867, 1884) and with the help of the FABIAN SOCIETY and the Trades Union Congress, the Labour Representation Committee was founded in 1900; it was renamed the Labour party in 1906. Its espousal of mildly socialist policies led to its quick rise to official opposition status in Parliament in 1922. In 1924 it formed its first ministry, under Ramsey MACDONALD. During the early 1930s a new group of Labour leaders, including Clement (later Earl) ATTLEE and Ernest BEVIN, called for increased nationalization of industry. Labour won the 1945 election, and the Attlee government enacted many social reforms, including a national health service. Harold WILSON, prime minister in 1964–70 and 1974–78, held the party together despite a widening split over economic and foreign policy issues. His successor, James CALLAGHAN, was unable to prevent a decisive Labour defeat at the polls in 1979, and, in 1981, a number of centrist members withdrew and formed the SOCIAL DEMOCRATIC PARTY. In 1983 Neil KINNOCK became leader of the Labour party. Kinnock moved the party toward the political center, but Labour lost the 1987 and 1992 elections. John SMITH succeeded Kinnock as party leader in 1992.

Labrador: see NEWFOUNDLAND.

Labrador retriever, large SPORTING DOG; shoulder height, c.23 in. (58.4 cm); weight, 60–75 lb (27.2–34.1 kg). Its short, oily coat, either black, brown, or yellow, resists cold weather and icy water. Widely used to hunt waterfowl, it was developed in Newfoundland and brought to England in the early 1800s.

La Brea, formerly Rancho La Brea, area, S California, known for its asphalt (tar) pits. Now within the boundaries of Hancock Park, Los Angeles, the pits are an extensive source of Pleistocene plant and animal fossils.

Lacan, Jacques, 1901–81, French psychoanalyst. Although known for his unorthodox treatment methods, he was a critic of modern, particularly U.S. psychoanalytic revisionism. He adhered to orthodox Freudian ideas, holding that there is a constant, unresolveable conflict between the ego and the UNCONSCIOUS, and that the true intent of PSYCHOANALYSIS is analysis, not cure. His collection *Écrits* (1966) was highly influential, especially in linguistics and literary criticism.

lacquer, solution of film-forming materials, natural or synthetic, usually applied as an ornamental or protective coating. Quick-drying synthetic lacquers are used to coat such products as automobiles, furniture, and textiles. Lacquer-work was one of the earliest industrial arts of Asia. It was highly developed in India; the Chinese inlaid lacquer-ware with ivory, jade, coral, or abalone. The art spread to Korea, then to Japan, where it took new forms. The ware, which is often given more than 40 coats of lacquer, may be decorated in color, gold, or silver and enhanced by relief, engraving, or carving. In the 17th cent. the technique known as japanning was used to make Western European imitations of lacquer-ware. Commercial production of lacquer-ware in the 19th cent. resulted in a decline in quality.

lacrosse, soccerlike ball and goal game, played by two teams of 10 players each on a field 60 to 70 yd (54.86 to 64.01 m) wide and 110 yd (100.58 m) long. The hard rubber ball is received, carried, and passed in the pocketlike head of the stick (crosse). Teams attempt to advance the ball until it can be hurled with the crosse or kicked into the opponent's goal (counting one point). Only the goalkeeper may touch the ball with the hands, and no field player may enter the crease, an area surrounding the goal. Lacrosse is a game of rough physical contact; fouls are penalized by disqualification or temporary suspension (as in ice HOCKEY) that leave the penalized team with a player handicap. Of Native American origin, the game was developed in Canada and introduced (1870s) into the U.S., where it is a popular college sport in the East.

lactose or **milk sugar** (empirical formula: $C_{12}H_{22}O_{11}$), white crystalline SUGAR formed in the mammary glands of all lactating animals and present in their milk. A disaccharide (see CARBOHYDRATE), lactose can be broken down by HYDROLYSIS into GLUCOSE and galactose. When milk sours, the lactose in it is converted by bacteria to lactic acid. Lactose is less sweet-tasting than SUCROSE and, unlike sucrose, is not found in plants and is not fermented by ordinary yeast.

Ladin: see RHAETO-ROMANIC.

Ladino: see SEPHARDIM.

Ladislaus I, king of Bohemia: see LADISLAUS V, king of Hungary.

Ladislaus II, king of Bohemia: see ULADISLAUS II, king of Hungary.

Ladislaus V or **Ladislaus Posthumous,** 1440–57, king of HUNGARY (1444–57) and, as Ladislaus I, king of Bohemia (1453–57). The posthumous son of the German king Albert II, he was duke of Austria by birth. His guardian, Holy Roman Emperor FREDERICK III, refused to let him leave his custody until 1452. Ladislaus was crowned (1453) king of Bohemia but governed none of his realms. George of Podebrad was regent in Bohemia; John Hunyadi and later Ulrich, count of Cilli, were regents in Hungary.

Ladislaus, Polish rulers. **Ladislaus I,** 1260–1333, duke (1306–20) and king (1320–33) of POLAND, unified the kingdom after 82 years of division. **Ladislaus II** or **Ladislaus Jagiello,** 1350?–1434, king of Poland (1386–1434) and grand duke of Lithuania (1378–1401), acceded to the Polish crown by marrying Queen Jadwiga, at which time he was baptized and agreed to convert Lithuania to Christianity. He defeated (1410) the TEUTONIC KNIGHTS. **Ladislaus III,** 1424–44, king of Poland (1434–44) and, as Uladislaus I, king of Hungary (1442–44), led two crusades against the Turks (1443, 1447); the first was successful, the second ended with his defeat and death at the battle of VARNA. **Ladislaus IV,** 1595–1648, king of Poland (1632–48), struggled with his subjects and nobles, and fought wars with the Swedes, Russians, and Turks.

ladybird beetle or **ladybug,** small, brightly colored BEETLE. Generally under ¼ in. (6 mm) long, ladybugs are hemispheric in shape, have short legs, and are red or yellow with black spots or black with red or yellow spots. Ladybugs and their larvae feed on destructive, plant-eating insects; adults are frequently used in pest control.

lady's-slipper: see ORCHID.

laetrile, name given the chemical amygdalin, found in the kernels of many fruits, notably APRICOTS, bitter ALMONDS, and PEACHES. The subject of controversy for many years, laetrile has been purported by some to be a cure for CANCER. In 1981 the U.S. National Cancer Institute reported laetrile to be ineffective against cancer.

La Farge, John, 1835–1910, American artist and writer; b. N.Y.C. He was primarily engaged in mural painting and the design and manufacture of STAINED GLASS, e.g., his works in Trinity Church, Boston. La Farge also created notable oils, watercolors, and drawings. A man of the widest culture, he did much to establish a tradition of American fine arts and is known for his many urbane pieces of art criticism.

Lafayette or **La Fayette, Marie Joseph Paul Yves Roch Gilbert du Motier, marquis de,** 1757–1834, French general and statesman. Enthusiastic about the AMERICAN REVOLUTION, he sailed (1777) to America and was made a major general by the CONTINENTAL CONGRESS. A close friend of Gen. WASHINGTON, he served at Brandywine, VALLEY FORGE, and in the YORKTOWN CAMPAIGN. In the FRENCH REVOLUTION, Lafayette became (1789) commander of the militia (later the National Guard) and tried unsuccessfully to moderate between the contending factions. Given command (1792) of the army of the center, he was relieved of command after he had spoken in favor of the monarchy. He fled France and was imprisoned in Austria. Freed in 1797, he later made a triumphal tour (1824–25) of the U.S. He led the moderates in France during the JULY REVOLUTION of 1830. The modern French flag was created by Lafayette in 1789.

La Fayette, Marie Madeleine Pioche de La Vergne, comtesse de, 1634–92, French novelist of the classical period. Her chief and only surviving work, *La Princesse de Clèves* (1678), analyzing a woman's renunciation of an illicit love, is the first great French novel.

Laffite or **Lafitte, Jean,** c.1780–1826?, leader of a band of privateers and smugglers. He preyed on Spanish commerce from bases in Louisiana and Texas. He and his followers aided U.S. troops against the British at the battle of NEW ORLEANS (1815).

La Follette, Robert Marion, 1855–1925, U.S. senator from Wisconsin (1906–25); b. Primrose, Wis. A Republican, he was a U.S. congressman (1885–91) from Wisconsin; later, as governor (1901–6), he introduced reforms that became known as the Wisconsin Idea. As senator he was at odds with the Republican leadership and generally supported Pres. WILSON's reforms, but he voted against the U.S. entry into World War I and opposed the League of Nations. In 1924 he ran for president on the PROGRESSIVE PARTY ticket and polled 5 million votes. His son **Robert Marion La Follette, Jr.,** 1895–1953, was a U.S. senator from Wisconsin (1925–47). Another son, **Philip Fox La Follette,** 1897–1965, was governor of Wisconsin (1931–33, 1935–39).

La Fontaine, Jean de, 1621–95, French poet. His *Selected Fables* (1668–94), 12 books of some 230 fables drawn largely from AESOP, place him among the masters of world literature. Told with wit and acumen, in brilliant verse and narrative, the fables have achieved worldwide success. Although their charm and simple facade have made them popular with children, most are sophisticated satires and serious commentaries on French society. Other works include *Tales and Novels in Verse* (1664–74), humorous tales drawn largely from BOCCACCIO and ARIOSTO; comedies and librettos for opera; and poems on classical themes.

LaFontaine, Sir Louis Hippolyte, 1807–64, Canadian statesman. The leader of the Reform party in Lower Canada (Quebec), he and Robert BALDWIN headed two ministries (1842–43, 1847–51) that enacted reforms and achieved responsible government. He was chief justice (1853–64) of Lower Canada.

Lagerkvist, Pär Fabian [lä'gərkvĭst], 1891–1974, Swedish writer, winner of the 1951 Nobel Prize in literature. His concern with good and evil and with man's search for God is expressed in such novels as *The Hangman* (1933) and *Barabbas* (1950), and the play *Man Without a Soul* (1936). His verse collections include *Evening Land* (1953).

Lagerlöf, Selma [lä'gərlöv], 1858–1940, Swedish novelist. Her novels, often set in her native Värmland and based on legends and sagas, include *The Story of Gösta Berling* (1891) and *The Ring of the Lowenskolds* (1925–28). She also wrote the children's classic *The Wonderful Adventures of Nils* (1906). She received the 1909 Nobel Prize in literature, the first woman to be thus honored.

Lagos, largest city (1989 est. pop. 1,274,000) and former capital of Nigeria, on the Gulf of Guinea. It comprises four islands and four mainland sections, connected by bridges and causeways. Lagos is Nigeria's chief port and industrial center, a road and rail terminus, and site of an international airport. An old Yoruba town, Lagos grew as a trade center and seaport from the 15th cent. It was a center of the slave trade until Britain annexed the city in 1861. Because of severe congestion in the modern city and its peripheral location, Nigeria announced (1976) plans to create a new federal capital at ABUJA, and the government was moved there in 1991.

Lagrange, Joseph Louis, Comte [lägräNzh'], 1736–1813, French mathematician and astronomer; b. Italy. He was director of mathematics (1766–87) at the Berlin Academy of Sciences. After moving to Paris, he became (1793) chairman of the French commission on weights and measures and was influential in the adoption of the decimal system as the basis for the metric system. Under Napoleon, Lagrange was made senator and count. His contributions to mathematics included work on the calculus, the calculus of variations, number theory, the solutions of equations, and the application of calculus to probability theory. In astronomy, he made theoretical calculations on the libration of the moon and on the motions of the planets and satellites of Jupiter. He also did research on the nature and propagation of sound and on the vibration of strings. His chief work was the *Mécanique analytique* (1788).

LaGuardia, Fiorello Henry, 1882–1947, mayor of NEW YORK CITY

Fiorello LaGuardia

(1934–45); b. N.Y.C. A Republican, he was a U.S. congressman (1917–19, 1923–33) and was elected mayor (1933) on the Fusion ticket. Known as "the Little Flower" (from his first name), he achieved numerous municipal reforms. His courage and energy gave him a national reputation.

Lahore, city (1981 pop. 2,707,215), capital of Punjab prov., E central Pakistan, on the Ravi R. Pakistan's second largest city, it is the commercial center of an agricultural region and has such industries as filmmaking, food processing, and steel making and produces many handicrafts. In 1206 India's first Muslim emperor was crowned in Lahore. The city flourished (16th cent.) as a capital of the MOGUL empire, was annexed by the Sikhs in 1767, and passed to the British in 1849. The palace and mausoleum of Emperor Jehangir and the Shalimar gardens are among the splendid remains of the Mogul period.

Lahr, Bert, 1895–1967, American comic actor; b. N.Y.C. as Irving Lahrheim. He is remembered as the Cowardly Lion in the film *The Wizard of Oz* (1939) and as Estragon in Samuel BECKETT's *Waiting for Godot* (1956).

Laing, R(onald) D(avid), 1927–89, British psychiatrist. He studied schizophrenia for over thirty years and came to view it as a culturally-conditioned, family-induced internal conflict, a controversial idea. He directed (1962–65) London's Langham Clinic, a therapeutic community where hierachical distinctions between doctors and patients were essentially eliminated.

laissez faire [Fr., = leave alone], in economics and politics, a doctrine holding that an economic system functions best when there is no interference by government. It is based on the belief that the natural economic order tends, when undisturbed by artificial stimulus or regulation, to secure the maximum well-being for the individual and therefore for the community. The principles of laissez faire were formulated by the French PHYSIOCRATS in the 18th cent. in opposition to MERCANTILISM. In Britain, Adam SMITH, Jeremy BENTHAM, and J.S. MILL developed laissez faire into a tenet of classical economics and a philosophy of individualism. During the 19th cent. the so-called MANCHESTER SCHOOL of economics popularized the doctrine of free trade and brought laissez faire into politics (e.g., by securing repeal of the CORN LAWS). In time, laissez faire came to be perceived as promoting monopoly rather than competition and as contributing to "boom-and-bust" economic cycles, and by the mid-20th cent. the principle of state noninterference in economic affairs had generally been discarded. Nevertheless, laissez faire, with its emphasis shifted from the value of competition to that of profit and individual initiative, remains a bulwark of conservative political thought, influential in the 1980s in such government administrations as that of Ronald REAGAN in the U.S. and Margaret THATCHER in Britain.

Laius: see OEDIPUS.

lake, body of standing water occupying a depression in the earth. Most lakes are freshwater bodies; a few (e.g., the GREAT SALT LAKE, the DEAD SEA), however, are more salty than the oceans. The GREAT LAKES of the U.S. and Canada are the world's largest system of freshwater lakes. The CASPIAN SEA is the world's largest lake. Most lake basins were formed by the erosive action of GLACIERS on bedrock. Other sources include volcanic calderas and natural and human-made dams in streams and RIVERS. Lakes are transient geologic features, eventually disappearing because of climatic changes, erosion of an outlet, and EUTROPHICATION.

Lake Clark National Park: see NATIONAL PARKS (table).

Lake District, scenic mountain region, c.30 mi (50 km) wide, NW England. It includes 15 lakes, among them Ullswater, Derwentwater, and Windermere, and reaches a high point of 3,210 ft (978 m) in Scafell Pike. Many writers and artists have lived there, including William WORDSWORTH, Samuel Taylor COLERIDGE, and Robert SOUTHEY, who are known as the Lake Poets.

Lake of the Woods, island-studded resort lake on the U.S.–Canadian border, 1,485 sq mi (3,846 sq km), extending c.70 mi (110 km) N from N Minnesota into SW Ontario and SE Manitoba. The one third that belongs to the U.S. separates the northernmost point in the coterminous 48 states from Minnesota.

Lakewood, city (1990 pop. 126,481), N central Colo., a suburb of DENVER; inc. 1969. It is primarily residential, with light industries producing electronic and medical equipment. Corporate and federal government offices are important.

Lamarck, Jean Baptiste Pierre Antoine de Monet, chevalier de, 1744–1829, French naturalist. Regarded as the founder of invertebrate paleontology, he is noted for his study and classification of invertebrates and for his evolutionary theories; the latter were first made public in his *Système des animaux sans vertèbres* (1801). **Lamarck's theory of evolution,** or **Lamarckism,** asserted that all life forms have arisen by a continual process of gradual modification throughout geological history. It was based on the theory of ACQUIRED CHARACTERISTICS, which held that new traits in an organism develop because of a need created by the environment and that they are transmitted to its offspring. Although the latter hypothesis was rejected as the principles of heredity were established, Lamarck's theory was an important forerunner of Charles DARWIN's theory of EVOLUTION.

Lamartine, Alphonse Marie Louis de [lämärtēn′], 1790–1869, French romantic poet, novelist, and statesman. Drawing on traditional and contemporary sources, his best-known work, *Poetic Meditations* (1820), including the well-known poem "Lake," is noted for its musical lyricism and affinity for nature. Other poetic volumes include *Harmonies* (1830) and the narrative *Jocelyn* (1836). Lamartine wrote *The History of the Girondists* (1847), in praise of the GIRONDISTS, and after the FEBRUARY REVOLUTION of 1848 he briefly headed the provisional government. Among his later works is the novel *Graziella* (1849).

Lamb, Charles, 1775–1834, English essayist. A boyhood friend of COLERIDGE, he was a clerk in India House (1792–1825). He lived with his sister, Mary Ann Lamb, who was subject to violent fits of insanity. With her he wrote *Tales from Shakespeare* (1807). Lamb established his reputation as a critic with *Specimens of English Dramatic Poets* (1808) and as an essayist with *Essays of Elia* (collected 1823, 1833). The essays cover a variety of topics and maintain throughout Lamb's singular tone—intimate, familiar, and humorous.

lamb: see SHEEP.

Lamentations, book of the OLD TESTAMENT, 25th in the Authorized Version, directly after JEREMIAH, to whose author it has been ascribed since ancient times. It is a series of poems mourning the destruction of JERUSALEM by Babylon.

Lampedusa, Giuseppe di, 1896–1957, Italian novelist. A Sicilian prince, he drew on family history for his acclaimed novel *The Leopard* (1958), about the demise of an aristocratic society after the unification of Italy.

lamprey, primitive marine and freshwater FISH (family Petromyzontidae) lacking a sympathetic nervous system, spleen, and scales. Although unrelated, the lamprey externally resembles the EEL. Most lampreys are parasitic bloodsuckers, attaching themselves to other fish by means of horny teeth set in a circular, jawless mouth; an anticoagulant in the saliva keeps the blood fluid. Some freshwater lampreys eat flesh as well. They are abundant in the Great Lakes, where they are considered pests by the fishing industry.

lamp shell, common name for animals in the phylum Brachiopoda, marine invertebrates resembling but not related to CLAMS. Found in shallow seas, lamp shells attach themselves to objects by means of a short stalk (pedicel) and feed by means of a characteristic tentacled organ (lophophore) surrounding the mouth. The lophophore creates currents that draw water, with food and oxygen, into the shell. Lamp shells are usually from 1 to 2 in. (2.5–5 cm) across.

LAN: see LOCAL AREA NETWORK.

Lanai [lənī′], island, 141 sq mi (365 sq km), central Hawaii. Mt. Lanaihale (3,370 ft/1,027 m) is its highest point; Lanai City (1990 pop. 2,400) its chief town. Purchased (1922) by a fruit company, it was long a major pineapple-growing center. The company's corporate successor, which owns most of Lanai, has promoted tourism and developed its lands on a limited basis.

Lancaster, Burt(on Stephen), 1913–, American film actor; b. N.Y.C. His films include *All My Sons* (1948), *From Here to Eternity* (1953), *Elmer Gantry* (1960; Academy Award), *The Birdman of Alcatraz* (1962), *The Swimmer* (1968), *Atlantic City* (1980), and *Tough Guys* (1986).

Lancaster, city (1990 pop. 55,551), seat of Lancaster co., SE Pa., on the Conestoga R.; settled c.1709 by German MENNONITES; inc. as a city 1818. A farming market town, it has stockyards and various light industries. Tourism and outlet retailing are important. Lancaster's rich history includes involvement in the AMERICAN REVOLUTION, service as state capital (1802–12), and development of the Conestoga wagon, later modified into the prairie schooner. James BUCHANAN lived there; his home (1828) is a national shrine.

Lancaster, house of, royal family of England. The line was founded by the second son of HENRY III, **Edmund Crouchback,** 1245–96, who became earl of Lancaster in 1267. His nickname "Crouchback," or crossed back, refers to the fact that he went on crusade and was entitled to wear the cross. His son **Thomas, earl of Lancaster,** 1277?–1322, led the barons against his cousin EDWARD II and was (1314–18) the virtual ruler of England. Defeated at the battle of Borough bridge, he was beheaded for treason. Thomas's brother, **Henry, earl of Lancaster,** 1281?–1345, was chief adviser to the young EDWARD III. His son, **Henry, duke of Lancaster,** 1299?–1361, was made duke in 1351 for excellent service in the HUNDRED YEARS WAR. When he died without male heirs, JOHN OF GAUNT inherited the Lancastrian lands by marrying Henry's daughter Blanche. John's son Henry deposed (1399) RICHARD II and became king as HENRY IV. Other Lancastrian kings were HENRY V and HENRY VI. Claims by the rival house of YORK led to the Wars of the ROSES; the Lancastrian claims passed to the house of TUDOR.

lancelet, small, fishlike lower CHORDATE, related to the VERTEBRATES. Usually about 1 in. (2.5 cm) long, with a transparent body tapering at both ends, the lancelet has no distinct head and no paired fins. A filter feeder that lives in shallow marine waters, it is usually found buried in the sand with only the mouth end projecting. The lancelet has a nerve cord but no heart, no brain, and no eyes. LAMPREY larvae resemble the lancelet.

Lanchow: see LANZHOU.

Land, Edwin Herbert, 1909–91, American inventor and industrialist; b. Bridgeport, Conn. He became interested in POLARIZED LIGHT and invented (1932) a material to eliminate glare, now known by the trademark Polaroid. In 1937, Land established the Polaroid Corp. to manufacture such products as sunglasses, camera filters, and headlights. He also developed a process for three-dimensional pictures (1941); invented the polaroid camera (1947), which takes and prints photos in one step; and introduced "instant" color photographs (1963).

Landau, Lev Davidovich, 1908–68, Soviet physicist. He was head of the theoretical department of the USSR Academy of Sciences. A leader in Soviet space technology, he helped make the first Soviet atomic bomb. For his contributions to LOW-TEMPERATURE PHYSICS, especially his development of a theory of SUPERFLUIDITY, and his pioneering studies on gases, he received the 1962 Nobel Prize in physics.

Landis, Kenesaw Mountain, 1866–1944, American jurist and commissioner of baseball (1921–44). A U.S. district judge in N Illinois (1905–22), he assumed the new post of baseball commissioner in the wake of the "Black Sox Scandal," a revelation that players in the 1919 World Series had been bribed. Landis strictly ruled organized baseball until his death, restoring public confidence in the game.

Landon, Alf(red) Mossman, 1887–1987, American politician; b. West Middlesex, Pa. He was governor of Kansas (1933–37) and the 1936 Republican candidate for president. His daughter, **Nancy Landon Kassebaum**, 1932–, b. Topeka, Kans., was elected (1978) U.S. senator from Kansas.

Landowska, Wanda [ländôf'skä], 1877–1959, Polish-French harpsichordist and pianist. She founded the École de Musique Ancienne, near Paris, giving many concerts between 1919 and 1940. She came to the U.S. in 1940 and is largely responsible for the revival of interest in the harpsichord.

Landrum-Griffin Act: see LABOR LAW.

Landseer, Sir Edwin Henry, 1802–73, English painter of animals. He is best known for his sentimental, humanized paintings of dogs, e.g., *Dignity and Impudence* (Tate Gall., London).

landslide, rapid slipping of a mass of earth or rock from a higher elevation to a lower level due to gravity and water lubrication. In humid climates, slow-moving earthflows can block roads and cause property damage. The more spectacular mudflows that pour down canyons in areas subject to erosion cause severe damage as well as loss of life.

landsmaal: see NORWEGIAN LANGUAGE.

Landsteiner, Karl, 1868–1943, American medical researcher; b. Austria; came to U.S., 1922. For discovering human BLOOD GROUPS he was awarded the 1930 Nobel Prize in physiology or medicine. His research in immunology and the chemistry of antigens and serological reactions led to contributions in hemolysis and in methods of studying poliomyelitis. With Alexander Wiener and Philip Levine he identified the RH FACTOR (1940).

Lanfranc, d. 1089, Italian churchman and theologian, archbishop of Canterbury (1070–89). He founded an illustrious school at Bec (c.1040) and wrote *Concerning the Body and Blood of the Lord,* a treatise on the Eucharist (see COMMUNION) that became a medieval classic. An associate of WILLIAM I of England, he reluctantly became archbishop of Canterbury. In England his reforms included establishing ecclesiastical courts, strengthening the monasteries, and shifting bishoprics from small towns to important cities.

Lang, Fritz, 1890–1976, German-American film director; b. Austria. Among his German films are *Metropolis* (1926), a science-fiction classic, and *M* (1930), a study of a child-murderer. His Hollywood work includes *Fury* (1936), *Ministry of Fear* (1944) and *The Big Heat* (1953).

Lange, Dorothea, 1895–1965, American photographer; b. Hoboken, N.J. Lange's *Migrant Mother* (1936) is typical of her powerful documentary portraits of rural America in the Depression years. She also recorded the Japanese-American internment (1941).

Dorthea Lange's Migrant Mother, *1936*

Langland, William, c.1332–c.1400, putative author of *The Vision of William concerning Piers the Plowman (Piers Plowman)*, a tremendously popular Middle English allegorical poem in unrhymed alliterative verse. Consisting of three dream visions, it is both a social satire and a vision of the simple Christian life.

Langley, Samuel Pierpont, 1834–1906, American scientist; b. Roxbury, Mass. He invented the bolometer, an instrument for recording variations in heat radiation, and with it he measured the distribution of heat in the solar and lunar spectra. From these studies he concluded that the solar constant of radiation was in fact a variable. Director (from 1867) of the Allegheny Observatory and secretary (from 1887) of the Smithsonian Inst., Langley founded (1890) the Smithsonian Astrophysical Observatory.

Langmuir, Irving, 1881–1957, American chemist. He introduced atomic-hydrogen welding, invented a gas-filled tungsten lamp, and contributed to the development of the radio vacuum tube. For his work in surface chemistry, in which he developed an important technique for studying layers of molecules one molecule thick, he

MAJOR LANGUAGES OF EUROPE, ASIA, AND SOME ISLANDS OF THE PACIFIC AND INDIAN OCEANS (**Asterisk indicates a dead language*)

Caucasian Languages (*spoken in the Caucasus region, Turkey, and Iran*)	
NORTHERN	Abkhaz, Adyghe (including Circassian and Kabardin), Chechen
SOUTHERN	Georgian
Dravidian Languages (*spoken in S India and N Sri Lanka*)	
	Brahui, Kanarese, Malayalam, Tamil, Telugu
Hamito-Semitic or **Afroasiatic Languages** (*spoken in W Asia; for languages of this family spoken in Africa, see the Hamito-Semitic classification in the table of* AFRICAN LANGUAGES)	
SEMITIC	
North Semitic	
Akkadian	Old Akkadian,* Assyrian,* Babylonian*
Canaanite	Hebrew,* Israeli Hebrew, Moabite,* Phoenician,* Punic*
Ugaritic	Ugaritic*
Aramaic	Biblical Aramaic,* Nabataean,* Palestinian,* Palmyrene,* Samaritan,* Syriac
South Semitic	Classical Arabic,* Modern Arabic, South Arabic (or Himyaritic, including Sabaean* and Minaean*)
Indo-European Languages (*spoken originally in an area between and including India and Europe, but now spoken on every continent and on a number of islands*)	
ANATOLIAN	Hieroglyphic Hittite,* Hittite (Kanesian),* Luwian,* Lycian,* Lydian*, Palaic*
BALTIC	Lettish (or Latvian), Lithuanian, Old Prussian*
CELTIC	
Brythonic	Breton, Cornish,* Welsh
Continental	Gaulish*
Goidelic (or Gaelic)	Irish (or Irish Gaelic), Manx, Scottish Gaelic
GERMANIC	
East Germanic	Burgundian,* Gothic,* Vandalic*
North Germanic (or Norse or Scandinavian)	Old Norse*, Danish, Faeroese, Icelandic, Norwegian, Swedish
West Germanic	
High German	German, Yiddish
Low German	Afrikaans, Dutch, English, Flemish, Frisian, Plattdeutsch
GREEK	Aeolic,* Arcadian,* Attic,* Byzantine Greek,* Cyprian,* Doric,* Ionic,* Koinē,* Modern Greek
INDO-IRANIAN	
Dardic	Kafiri, Kashmiri, Khowar, Kohistani, Romany (or Gypsy), Shina
Indic (or Indo-Aryan)	Pali,* Prakrit,* Sanskrit,* Vedic*
Central Indic	Hindi, Hindustani, Urdu
East Indic	Assamese, Bengali, Bihari, Oriya
NW Indic	Punjabi, Sindhi
Pahari	Central Pahari, Eastern Pahari (or Nepali), Western Pahari
South Indic	Marathi (including the major dialect Konkani), Singhalese (or Sinhalese)
West Indic	Bhili, Gujarati, Rajasthani (has many dialects)
Iranian	Avestan,* Old Persian*
East Iranian	Baluchi, Khwarazmian,* Ossectic, Pamir dialects, Pushtu (or Afghan), Saka (or Khotanese),* Sogdian,* Yaghnobi
West Iranian	Kurdish, Pahlavi (Middle Persian),* Parthian,* Persian (or Farsi), Tajiki
ITALIC	
Non-Romance	Faliscan*, Latin*, Oscan*, Umbrian*
Romance (or Romanic)	
Eastern Romance	Italian, Rhaeto-Romanic (including Romansh, Ladin, and Friulian), Rumanian, Sardinian
Western Romance	Catalan, French, Ladino, Portuguese, Provençal, Spanish

won the 1932 Nobel Prize in chemistry. He discovered that particles of dry ice and iodide added to certain clouds could produce rain or snow.

Langtry, Lillie, 1853–1929, English actress; b. Jersey, Channel Islands. Called the Jersey Lily, she was noted for her great beauty and her liaison with EDWARD VII. *Lady Windermere's Fan* was written for her by Oscar WILDE.

language, systematic communication by vocal symbols. It is a universal characteristic of the human species. The earliest forms of language known are no more "primitive" than modern forms. Because language is a cultural system, individual languages classify objects and ideas differently. There are some 6,500 spoken languages, but about 2,000 have fewer than 1,000 speakers. The smallest have only a few members; the largest, in approximate descending order based on the number of native speakers, are North Chinese vernacular (Mandarin), English, Spanish, Hindustani, Bengali, Arabic, Russian, and Portuguese. Differences within languages are DIALECTS. Languages change continuously, but various factors, especially literacy, lead to the development of a community's standard language, usually one dialect, e.g., London English. Literary and colloquial standards may differ, and a group jargon may be unintelligible to outsiders; the differences are primarily in vocabulary. Groups of related languages are called families and stocks. For a survey of the important languages by family, see the table accompanying this article and the AFRICAN LANGUAGES and NATIVE AMERICAN LANGUAGES articles. See also LANGUAGE ACQUISITION.

language acquisition, the process of learning a native or a second language. Although how children learn to speak is not perfectly understood, most explanations involve both the observation that children copy what they hear and the inference that human beings have a natural aptitude for understanding grammar. Children usually learn the sounds and vocabulary of their native language through imitation, and grammar is seldom taught to them; that they rapidly acquire the ability to speak grammatically supports the theory of Noam CHOMSKY and others that children are able to learn the grammar of a particular language because all intelligible languages are founded on a "deep structure" of universal grammatical rules that corresponds to an innate capacity of the human brain. People learning a second language pass through some of the same stages as do children learning their native language.

langue d'oc [läNg dôk'] and **langue d'oïl** [dôē], names of the two principal groups of medieval French dialects, *oc* and *oïl* being their respective words for *yes. Langue d'oc* was spoken south of a line running, roughly, from Bordeaux to Grenoble. Also called PROVENÇAL, it was the language of the great medieval TROUBADOURS. The *langue d'oïl* of the Paris region developed into modern French.

MAJOR LANGUAGES OF EUROPE, ASIA, AND SOME ISLANDS OF THE PACIFIC AND INDIAN OCEANS *(Continued)*
*(*Asterisk indicates a dead language)*

SLAVIC (or SLAVONIC)	
East Slavic	Belarussian (or White Russian), Russian, Ukrainian
South Slavic	Bulgarian, Church Slavonic,* Macedonian, Serbo-Croatian, Slovenian
West Slavic	Czech, Kashubian, Lusatian (or Sorbian or Wendish), Polabian,* Polish, Slovak
THRACO-ILLYRIAN	Albanian, Illyrian,* Thracian*
THRACO-PHRYGIAN	Armenian, Grabar (Classical Armenian),* Phrygian*
TOKHARIAN (was spoken in W China)	Tokharian A (or Agnean),* Tokharian B (or Kuchean)*

Luorawetlan Languages *(spoken in E Siberia)*

	Chukchi, Kamchadal, Koryak

Malayo-Polynesian or **Austronesian Languages** *(spoken in the Malay Peninsula; Madagascar; Taiwan; Indonesia; New Guinea; Melanesia, Micronesia, and Polynesia; the Philippines; and New Zealand)*

WESTERN	Balinese, Batak, Bikol, Bugi, Dayak, Ilocano, Indonesia (or Bahasa Indonesia), Javanese, Madurese, Malagasy, Malay, Sundanese, Tagalog, Visayan
EASTERN	
Melanesian	Fijian, Malo, Marovo, Mono
Micronesian	Chomorro, Caroline, Gilbertese, Marianas, Marshallese
POLYNESIAN	Hawaiian, Maori, Samoan, Tahitian, Tongan

Sino-Tibetan Languages *(spoken in central and SE Asia)*

CHINESE	Amoy-Swatow, Cantonese, Hakka, Fukienese, Mandarin Chinese, Wu
THAI (or TAI)	Lao, Shan, Thai (or Siamese)
TIBETO-BURMAN	Burmese, Bodo, Garo, Kachin, Karen, Lolo, Lushai, Tibetan

Southeast Asian or **Austroasiatic Languages** *(spoken in SE Asia)*

ANNAMESE-MUONG	Muong, Vietnamese (or Annamese)
MON-KHMER	Cambodian (or Khmer), Cham, Khasi, Mon (or Talaing), Nicobarese, Sakai, Samang
MUNDA	Santali

Uralic and Altaic Languages *(spoken discontinuously in Eurasia from E Europe to the Pacific Ocean)*

ALTAIC	
Turkic	
Eastern	Uigur, Uzbek
Southern	Azeri (or Azerbaijani), Chuvash, Turkish, Turkmen
Western	Kazakh, Kazar, Kireghiz, Noghay, Tatar
Mongolian	Buryat, Kalmuck, Khalkha (or Mongol proper)
Tungusic	Manchu, Tungus
URALIC	
Finno-Ugric	
Finnic	Cheremiss, Estonian, Finnish (or Suomi), Karelian, Lapp, Mordvinian, Permian tongues
Ugrian (or *Ugric*)	Hungarian (or Magyar), Ostyak, Vogul
Samoyedic	Samoyed

Note: The numerous aboriginal languages of Australia and the numerous Papuan languages have not as yet been studied sufficiently to be classified with any certainty as far as relationships with each other are concerned. They are, however, unrelated to the other languages of the world.

The non-related languages of the world include Ainu, Basque, Japanese, and Korean, as well as the dead languages Elamite, Etruscan, Hurrian, Meroitic, and Sumerian.

Both *langue d'oïl* and *langue d'oc* dialects persisted, however, in some rural areas as *patois,* or popular, provincial speech.

Lanier, Sidney, 1842–81, American poet and musician; b. Macon, Ga. An accomplished flutist, he wrote a study of the interrelation of music and poetry, *The Science of English Verse* (1880). His own melodic verses, e.g., "Corn," "Song of the Chattahoochee," were published in *Poems* (1887).

Lansing, city (1990 pop. 127,321), state capital, S Mich., at the confluence of the Grand and Red Cedar rivers; inc. 1859. It was made state capital in 1847. The arrival of the railroad in the 1870s and the automobile industry in 1897 spurred its growth. Automobiles and automobile parts are the main manufactures. Michigan State Univ. is in East Lansing, a suburb.

lanthanide series, RARE-EARTH METALS with atomic numbers 58 through 71 in group IIIb of the PERIODIC TABLE. They are, in order of increasing atomic number, CERIUM, PRASEODYMIUM, NEODYMIUM, PROMETHIUM, SAMARIUM, EUROPIUM, GADOLINIUM, TERBIUM, DYSPROSIUM, HOLMIUM, ERBIUM, THULIUM, YTTERBIUM, and LUTETIUM. Although they closely resemble LANTHANUM and each other in their chemical and physical properties, lanthanum (at. no. 57) is not always considered a member of the series.

lanthanum (La), metallic element, discovered in 1839 by C.G. Mosander. It is a silver-white, soft, malleable, ductile, and chemically active RARE-EARTH METAL. Lanthanum is used in making ductile cast IRON and as an alloy in cigarette-lighter flints. It occurs in MONAZITE. See ELEMENT (table); PERIODIC TABLE.

Lanzhou or **Lanchow** [both: län-jō], city (1990 est. pop. 1,510,000), capital of Gansu prov., W China, on the HUANG HE. The transport and industrial center of NW China, it has a large oil refinery and a plutonium gas-diffusion plant. Its products include petrochemicals, textiles, and machinery. The city is a center for China's Muslims. Since 1960, it has been the center of China's atomic energy industry.

Laocoön [lāŏk'ōŏn], in Greek mythology, priest of APOLLO who warned the Trojans not to touch the wooden horse made by the Greeks during the TROJAN WAR. He and his two sons were crushed by sea serpents as they sacrificed to POSEIDON, and the Trojans brought the horse into the city. The death struggle of the family is portrayed in a famous Greek sculpture by Agesander, Athenodorus, and Polydorus, now in the Vatican.

Laos [lä'ōs], officially Lao People's Democratic Republic, republic (1992 est. pop. 4,440,000), 91,428 sq mi (236,800 sq km), SE Asia, bordered by China (N), Vietnam (E), Cambodia (S), and Thailand and Myanmar (W). The capital is VIENTIANE. Except for lowlands along the MEKONG R., where most of the people live, and three sparsely populated plateaus, the terrain is mountainous and thickly forested. The climate is monsoonal. Economically, the country is one of the least developed in Asia. There are no railroads, few roads, and practically no mining or industry, although textiles have become a major export. The predominantly rural population is engaged primarily in fishing and subsistence agriculture. Rice (by far the chief crop), corn, vegetables, coffee, tobacco, sugarcane, and cotton are important. Illegal opium poppies and cannabis are produced in the northwest (the "golden triangle"). Ethnic Lao, related to the Thai, make up about half the population; minorities include ethnic Thai, Vietnamese, and Chinese as well as a number of tribal mountain groups. Lao is the official language; French and English are also widely spoken. Buddhism is the most widely practiced religion.

History. Part of the KHMER EMPIRE, Laos was infiltrated in the 13th cent. by Lao people from Yunnan, China, and by the 17th cent. a powerful Lao kingdom called Lan Xang held sway over much of SE Asia. After 1707 internal dissension split the kingdom, which passed to Siam (early 18th cent.) and then became (1893) a protectorate in the French-ruled union of INDOCHINA. After occupation by Japanese forces in World War II Laos became (1949) a semiautonomous state within the FRENCH UNION. It received independence in 1953. By that time the Pathet Lao, a Communist nationalist movement aided by the Vietminh (Vietnamese Communists), had gained control of N Laos, establishing a rival government headed by Prince Souphanouvong. A protracted civil war followed, and after 1965 the VIETNAM WAR increasingly spilled over into Laos. A cease-fire was finally signed in 1973, and a coalition government was formed under Premier Souvanna Phouma. It soon collapsed, however, and the Pathet Lao took over the government in 1975 and abolished the monarchy. Souphanouvong became president, and Kaysone Phomvihane, head of the Communist party, became premier. A flood of refugees, including most of the professional and commercial classes, fled the country. Laos became increasingly dependent on Vietnam for military and economic assistance, and the two countries signed a 25-year treaty of friendship in 1977. In the early 1990s Laos abandoned economic communism for capitalism, but the party retained tight political control. Kaysone became president in 1991, but he died the following year and Nouhak Phoumsavan became president and Khamtay Siphandon party leader.

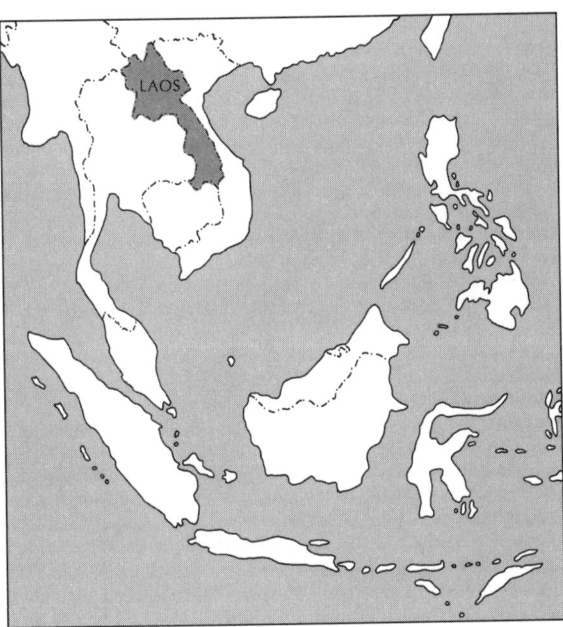

Lao-tze or **Lao-tzu** [lou-dzŭ], b. c.604 B.C., legendary Chinese philosopher. It is uncertain that Lao-tze [Chin., = old person or old philosopher] is an historical figure. According to legend and to sources from the 1st cent. B.C., he was a royal librarian named Li Erh. He is traditionally cited as the author of the *Tao-te-ching,* the central text of TAOISM, but modern scholars date that work as a whole from the 4th cent. B.C.

La Paz, city (1992 pop. 1,883,122), W Bolivia, administrative capital of Bolivia since 1898. (The constitutional capital is SUCRE.) It is the nation's largest city and its commercial center. Manufactures include clothing and processed food. Situated in a narrow Andean river valley at an elevation of c.12,000 ft (3,660 m), it is the highest capital city in the world. It was founded in 1548 and was a key point on colonial trade routes. Tourist attractions in the area include Lake TITICACA.

laparoscopic surgery: see ENDOSCOPE.

lapis lazuli, gem composed of lazurite and other minerals in shades of blue, usually flecked with PYRITE. Most often found in massive form in metamorphosed limestones, it has been used since ancient times for beads and small ornaments. Lapis lazuli was the original pigment for ultramarine and was the "sapphire" of the ancients.

Laplace, Pierre Simon, marquis de, 1749–1827, French astronomer and mathematician. On the basis of Isaac NEWTON's gravitational theory, he made mathematical studies of the motions of comets, the moon, Saturn, Jupiter, and Jupiter's satellites, as well as of the theory of tides. His research results, which together with those of Joseph LAGRANGE and earlier mathematicians established Newton's theory beyond a doubt, were published in his famous *Mécanique céleste* (5 vol., 1799–1825). His more popular *Exposition du système du monde* (1796) gave scientific form to the nebular hypothesis of the origin of the solar system.

Lapland, vast region of N Europe, largely within the Arctic Circle, occupying N Norway, N Sweden, N Finland, and the Kola Peninsula of Russia. The climate is severe, and the vegetation cover a sparse tundra except in the forested southern zone. Reindeer, an essential foodstuff, were seriously contaminated by the 1986 Chernobyl nuclear disaster, dealing the region a severe economic blow. There are important high-grade iron ore deposits at Gällivare and Kiruna (Sweden), copper deposits at Sulitjelma (Norway), and nickel and apatite deposits in Russia. The **Lapps** or **Laplanders,** the indigenous population, number about 60,000 and are concentrated mainly in Norway; they call themselves the Sami. They speak a Finno-Ugric language, and are believed to have originated in central Asia and to have been pushed into the northern extremities of Europe by the later migrations of Finns, Goths, and Slavs.

larceny, in law, unlawful taking and carrying away of another's property with intent to deprive the owner of its use or to appropriate it to one's own or someone else's use. Grand larceny, usually classed as a FELONY, is distinguished from petty larceny, usually a misdemeanor, by the value of the property involved. Robbery (the taking and carrying away of property by force or threat of force) and embezzlement (wrongful use of legally entrusted property) are both classed as larceny in most modern statutes.

larch, non-evergreen CONIFER (genus *Larix*) of the PINE family, found in the Northern Hemisphere. The needles of the larch are borne in characteristic radiating clusters. The Western larch (*L. occidentalis*), of North America, achieves great height; its wood is used for interior construction and cabinetmaking. The American larch, or tamarack (*L. laricina*), also a source of timber, is often cultivated for its beauty.

Lardner, Ring(gold) Wilmer, 1885–1933, American writer; b. Niles, Mich. A sports reporter (1907–19), he became known for short stories in a racy sports idiom, e.g., *You Know Me, Al* (1916). His later stories, cynical and pessimistic, yet humorous, include *What of It?* (1925) and *First and Last* (1934).

Laredo, city (1990 pop. 122,899), seat of Webb co., S Tex., on the Rio Grande; founded 1755, inc. 1852. It is the major port of entry on the U.S.-Mexico border; import-export trade thrives, and tourism is important. Ranching, oil, and smelting operations are also important. Laredo has many ties with its Mexican sister city, NUEVO LAREDO. It was a post on the Mexican road to SAN ANTONIO, and during the MEXICAN WAR it was the capital of a "Republic of the Rio Grande."

lark, perching BIRD of the mainly Old World Alaudidae family. Skylarks, the best known of the larks, are c.7 ¼ in. (18.2 cm) long and similar in coloration (grays and browns above and light underneath) and nesting habits (meadows, plains, and other open areas). The horned lark belongs to the only species native to North America, *Eremophila alpestris;* the prairie lark is a subspecies. On the ground, these larks run rather than hop; in flight, they have a melodious song. The MEADOWLARK belongs to another family.

Larkin, Philip, 1922–85, English poet. His poems display a subtle wit and his fine eye for the ordinary in English life. His volumes include *The Less Deceived* (1955), *The Whitsun Weddings* (1964), and *High Windows* (1974). He also wrote novels and jazz criticism.

larkspur, any north temperate, Old-World annual (genus *Consolida*) of the BUTTERCUP family. *Consolida* species were formerly classified in the genus *Delphinium,* which includes the similar annual, biennial, and perennial herbaceous plants commonly called larkspurs or delphiniums. Plants of both genera are popular garden plants. In many cultivated larkspurs and delphiniums the spurred flowers, usually blue, pink, or white, rise in a spire above the leaves.

La Rochefoucauld, François, duc de [rôshfōōkō'], 1613–80, French author. As head of an ancient family, he opposed RICHELIEU and was later active in both FRONDES, which gives his *Mémoires* (1662) historical interest. However, his place in French literature rests on the *Maxims* (1665), a collection of several hundred lucid and polished moral maxims expressing his pessimistic view that selfishness is the source of all human behavior.

larynx, organ of voice in mammals. An extension of the trachea, the human larynx is a small, boxlike chamber with walls of cartilage bound by muscles and membranes. The vocal cords, a pair of elastic folds in the mucous-membrane lining, lie within the larynx. During speech the cords are stretched across the larynx; outgoing breath, forced between them, vibrates and produces voice. The sound varies with the tension of the cords and the space between them.

La Salle, Robert Cavelier, sieur de [läsäl'], 1643–87, French explorer in NORTH AMERICA. He commanded Fort Frontenac, developed trade, and built many forts. In 1682 he and his lieutenant, Henri de Tonti, descended the MISSISSIPPI to its mouth. La Salle took possession of the whole valley, naming it LOUISIANA. After three futile attempts to find the mouth of the Mississippi by sea, he was murdered in a mutiny.

Las Casas, Bartolomé de [läs kä'säs], 1474–1566, Spanish missionary in Latin America. Ordained a priest (1510), he worked to improve the condition of the indigenous peoples and to end their enslavement and forced labor. He converted uncivilized tribes, tried but failed to establish (1520–21) a model native colony, and visited Spain to urge government action. Chiefly through his efforts, a humanitarian code known as the New Laws was adopted (1542) to protect the native peoples in Spanish colonies. The New Laws were later so altered, however, as to be ineffective.

Lascaux: see PALEOLITHIC ART.

laser [acronym for *l*ight *a*mplification by *s*timulated *e*mission of *r*adiation], device for the creation and amplification of a narrow, intense beam of coherent LIGHT. In a laser, the atoms or molecules of a crystal, such as ruby or garnet—or of a gas, liquid, or other substance—are excited so that more of them are at higher energy levels than are at lower energy levels. If a PHOTON whose frequency corresponds to the energy difference between the excited and ground states strikes an excited atom, the atom is stimulated, as it falls back to a lower energy state, to emit a second photon of the same (or a proportional) frequency, in phase with (see WAVE; COHERENCE) and in the same direction as the bombarding photon. This process is called stimulated emission. The bombarding photon and the emitted photon may then each strike other excited atoms, stimulating further emission of photons, all of the same frequency and phase. This process produces a sudden burst of coherent radiation as all the atoms discharge in a rapid chain reaction. First built in 1960, lasers now range in size from semiconductor lasers as small as a grain of salt to solid-state and gas lasers as large as a building. The light beam produced by most lasers is pencil-thin and maintains its size and direction over very large distances. Lasers are widely used in industry (for cutting and boring metals and other materials), in medicine (for self-cauterizing surgery), and in communications, scientific research, and HOLOGRAPHY. They are an integral part of such familiar devices as BAR-CODE scanners, laser PRINTERS, and COMPACT DISC players. See also MASER.

laser disc: see VIDEODISC.

laser printer, a COMPUTER printer that produces output by a process similar to PHOTOCOPYING. Rather than using reflected light from an image (as in xerography), it uses the data sent from the computer to turn a laser beam on and off as it scans a charged drum. The drum then attracts toner powder to the areas not exposed to the light. Finally, the toner is fused to paper over the belt by heated rollers. Faster, quieter, and with more attractive results than standard printers, they have made an impact on business since they have become more generally available (1984) for PERSONAL COMPUTERS. See also DESKTOP PUBLISHING.

Laski, Harold Joseph, 1893–1950, British political scientist and economist. He taught (1920–50) at the London School of Economics and served on the executive committee of the FABIAN SOCIETY (1922–36) and of the LABOUR PARTY (from 1936). He was chairman of the party (1945–46) and held various government posts. His many works include *Karl Marx* (1921), *Democracy in Crisis* (1933), and *Faith, Reason, and Civilisation* (1944).

Lassalle, Ferdinand, 1825–64, German socialist. Although partially influenced by MARXISM, Lassalle's theory of state socialism differed from it in contending that once universal suffrage was achieved, the state could be forced to establish workers' cooperatives. He played a key role in founding (1863) the first workers' political party in Germany, the forerunner of the Social Democratic party.

Lassen Peak, intermittently active (1914–21) volcano in the CASCADE RANGE in N California, a part of Lassen Volcanic National Park (see NATIONAL PARKS, table). It was the only active volcano in the coterminous U.S. until the eruption (1980) of Mt. SAINT HELENS.

Lassen Volcanic National Park: see NATIONAL PARKS (table).

Lasso, Orlando di, 1532–94, Dutch composer, also Orlandus Lassus or Roland de Lassus. He represents the culmination of Renaissance music. A famous singer and choirmaster, he published his first books of MADRIGALS in Antwerp in 1555 and subsequently held positions in other cities. Lasso brought Flemish POLYPHONY to its highest development. His more than 2,000 works are in every form known in his day—MASSES, MOTETS, chansons, madrigals, and others.

Last Supper, repast taken by JESUS and his disciples on the eve of the passion (Mat. 26.17–30; Mark 14.12–26; Luke 22.7–39; John 13–17; 1 Cor. 11.23–29). At that time Jesus instituted the SACRAMENT called COMMUNION.

Las Vegas, city (1990 pop. 258,295), seat of Clark co., S Nev.; inc. 1911. The largest city in Nevada, it is one of the fastest-growing urban areas in the U.S. Revenue from gambling, entertainment, theme parks, and other tourist industries forms the backbone of its economy, although in the 1970s diversified industry began to play a more important role.

László V, king of Hungary: see LADISLAUS V.

La Tène, ancient Celtic site on Lake Neuchâtel, Switzerland, that gives its name to cultures of the late IRON AGE. The earliest Tenian culture (6th cent.–late 5th cent. B.C.), drawn from Greek and Etruscan civilizations, spread as far as the British Isles in the first great CELT migrations. An important late Tenian site includes lake dwellings at Glastonbury, S England.

latent heat: see BOILING POINT; MELTING POINT.

Lateran, group of buildings, SE Rome, on land presented to the church by CONSTANTINE I. The Lateran basilica is the cathedral of Rome, the pope's church, the first-ranking church of the Roman Catholic Church. Officially it is the Basilica of the Savior, familiarly St. John Lateran. Built perhaps before 311, it has been often rebuilt or restored. Much of the decoration, including the mosaics of the apse, is medieval. The Lateran baptistery (c.4th cent.) has been much restored. The Lateran palace, the papal residence until the 14th cent., was demolished in the 16th cent. to make way for the smaller present palace. The palace now houses a historical museum.

Lateran Treaty, 1929, concordat between the Holy See and Italy. In 1871 the unity of Italy was perfected by limiting papal sovereignty to a few buildings. The papacy objected to the loss of Rome and the Papal States, creating the dilemma called the Roman Question. The Lateran Treaty resolved the matter by creating the new sovereign state of VATICAN CITY. It also recognized Roman Catholicism as the only state religion of Italy. The treaty was signed for the pope by Cardinal Pietro Gasparri, and for Italy by Benito MUSSOLINI.

Lateur, Frank: see STREUVELS, STIJN.

latex: see RUBBER.

Latimer, Hugh, 1485?–1555, English Protestant martyr. Bishop of Worcester under HENRY VIII, he refused to recant his Protestantism when the Roman Catholic MARY I became queen. With Nicholas RIDLEY, he was burned at the stake.

Latin America, collective term for the 20 republics of South and Middle America where Romance languages are generally spoken. It includes Portuguese-speaking BRAZIL, French-speaking HAITI, and Spanish-speaking ARGENTINA, BOLIVIA, CHILE, COLOMBIA, COSTA RICA, CUBA, DOMINICAN REPUBLIC, ECUADOR, EL SALVADOR, GUATEMALA, HONDURAS, MEXICO, NICARAGUA, PANAMA, PARAGUAY, PERU, URUGUAY, and VENEZUELA. It is also sometimes extended to include PUERTO RICO and the French WEST INDIES and, less frequently, BELIZE, GUYANA, FRENCH GUIANA, and SURINAME.

Latin Empire of Constantinople: see CONSTANTINOPLE, LATIN EMPIRE OF.

Latin Empire of Jerusalem: see JERUSALEM, LATIN EMPIRE OF.

Latin language, the language of ancient Rome, a member of the Italic subfamily of the Indo-European family of languages. As the standard language of most of the Roman Empire, it spread widely and developed into the Romance languages. To this day Latin survives as the official tongue of Vatican City and as the official language of communication of the Roman Catholic Church. See LANGUAGE (table).

Latins, in ancient times, inhabitants of Latium. Rome early became a dominant city in Latium, and Roman hegemony was definitely established by 338 B.C. The Latins were admitted to Roman citizenship in 90 B.C.

latitude, angular distance from the EQUATOR of any point on the earth's surface. The equator is latitude 0°, and the poles are 90°N and S, respectively. One degree of latitude is about 69 mi (110 km), increasing slightly poleward as a result of the earth's polar flattening. See also LONGITUDE.

La Tour, Georges de, 1593–1652, French painter. Named painter to the king in 1639, he executed religious and GENRE pictures that showed Dutch modifications of CARAVAGGIO's style. His minutely descriptive early works include *St. Jerome* (Stockholm). An example of his nocturnal scenes, dramatically illuminated by a candle or hidden light source, is *Education of the Virgin* (Frick Coll., N.Y.C.). He discarded detail for simple sculptural forms in his later work, e.g., *Repentant St. Peter* (Cleveland Mus.).

Latrobe, Benjamin Henry, 1764–1820, considered the first professional architect in the U.S.; b. England. He arrived in the U.S. in 1796. In 1803 Pres. JEFFERSON appointed him surveyor of public buildings. Beside houses in Philadelphia, Washington, and other cities, he did monumental work, introducing Greek forms, an important element of the CLASSIC REVIVAL. His design (1799) for the Bank of Pennsylvania, Philadelphia, was based on an Ionic temple. This and his Roman Catholic cathedral in Baltimore (1805–18), the first U.S. cathedral, are among the leading monumental works of his time.

Latter-Day Saints, Church of Jesus Church of: see MORMONS.

Latvia, Lettish *Latvija,* officially Republic of Latvia, republic (1992 est. pop. 2,729,000), 24,590 sq mi (63,688 sq km), north central Europe, formerly a constituent republic of the USSR. It borders on Estonia (N); Lithuania (S); the Baltic Sea and Gulf of Riga (W); and Russia (E) and Belarus (SE). The capital and largest city is RIGA; other large cities include Daugavpils and Liepaja. Dairying, stock raising, and timbering are major occupations. Industries include shipbuilding, metallurgy, and the manufacture of machines, chemicals, and electrical equipment. The majority of the people are Letts and Latgalians (both widely known as Latvians), but there is a significant Russian and smaller Belarussian, Ukrainian, and Polish minorities. Citizenship is restricted to those who or whose parents were citizens in 1940; others can apply if they have been residents for 16 years and speak Lettish (Latvian). Lettish is the official language, but Russian is widely spoken.

History. The region was conquered and Christianized by the Livonian Knights (13th cent.) and later fell to Poland (1561), Sweden (1629), and Russia (1721–95). German merchants and landowners had reduced the population to servitude, but in 1819 serfdom was abolished. Russian replaced German as the official language in 1885. Latvia became independent in 1920 but was forcibly annexed by the USSR in 1940. It was occupied (1941–44) by the Germans in World War II. After the war Latvia was returned to Soviet rule, and the economy was nationalized. In 1990 the Latvian parliament voted in favor of independence from the Soviet Union, and following the attempted coup (1991) against Soviet Pres. GORBACHEV the Soviet government recognized Latvia's independence. In 1993 Latvia signed a free-trade agreement with Estonia and Lithuania. Guntis Ulmanis became president in 1993.

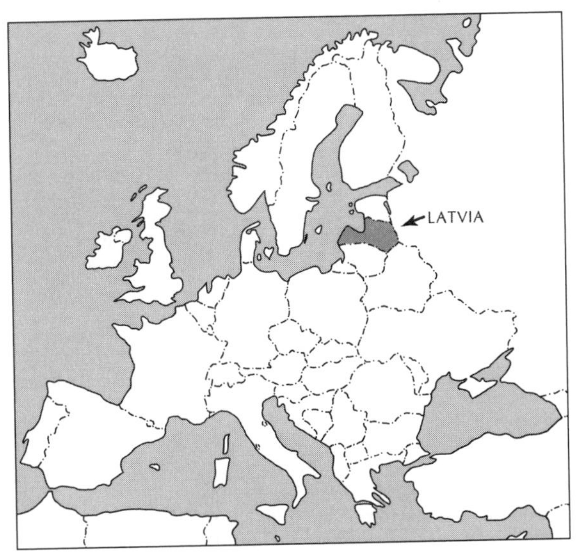

Latvian language: see LETTISH.

Laud, William, 1573–1645, English prelate. Laud was hostile to the Puritans and worked with CHARLES I to eliminate them from important positions in the church. Named (1633) archbishop of Canterbury, he tried to standardize Anglican ritual along High Church lines. He persecuted and imprisoned many nonconformists and supported Charles to the end. He was impeached (1640) by the Long Parliament and condemned (1644) to death by the Commons.

Laue, Max Theodor Felix von, 1879–1960, German physicist. Laue was awarded the Nobel Prize in physics in 1914 for his discovery of X-ray diffraction in crystals.

laughing gas: see NITROUS OXIDE.

Laughton, Charles, 1899–1962, Anglo-American actor; b. England. A versatile character actor, he appeared in such films as *The Private Life of Henry VIII* (1933), *Mutiny on the Bounty* (1935), and *Advise and Consent* (1962).

Laurasia: see CONTINENTAL DRIFT.

laurel, common name for the family Lauraceae, trees and shrubs found chiefly in tropical Southeast Asia and America; most are evergreen. The true laurel (*Laurus nobilis*), also called bay or sweet bay, is native to the Mediterranean, and is the source of bay leaf, a seasoning. Laurel symbolized victory and merit to the ancients. Other members of the family include the sassafras (*Sassafras albidum*), the aromatic bark of which is used for tea, and the spicebush (*Lindera benzoin*), both of the U.S.; and the AVOCADO of Central America, now widely grown in the U.S. Members of the Asian genus *Cinnamomum* are cultivated largely for their aromatic bark (see CAMPHOR; CINNAMON).

Laurel and Hardy, American film comedy team. Its members were Stan Laurel, 1890–1965, b. England as Arthur Stanley Jefferson, and Oliver Hardy, 1892–1957, b. Atlanta, Ga. Their zany comic routines often involved pantomime. Among their films are *Sons of the Desert* (1933), *Babes in Toyland* (1934), and *A Chump at Oxford* (1940).

Laurence, (Jean) Margaret, 1926–87, Canadian author. Her novels of character include *This Side Jordan* (1960), *A Jest of God* (1966), and *The Diviners* (1974). She also wrote stories, essays, and works on African literature.

Laurencin, Marie [lōräNsăN′], 1885–1956, French painter and printmaker. Her elegant, highly personal style consists of simplification of form, flat and decorative surface, and delicate pastel colors, e.g., *The Assembly* (1910).

Laurentian Plateau: see CANADIAN SHIELD.

Laurier, Sir Wilfrid [lô′rēā, Fr. lōrya′], 1841–1919, prime minister of CANADA (1896–1911), the first French Canadian to hold the office. He worked for French-English political cooperation and became (1887) the Liberal opposition leader. As prime minister he advanced Western development, the railroads, preferential tariffs, and Canada's defenses.

Lautrec, Henri de Toulouse: see TOULOUSE-LAUTREC, HENRI DE.

lava, molten ROCK erupted on the earth's surface by a VOLCANO or through a fissure in the earth. It solidifies into igneous rock that is also called lava. Before reaching the surface, lava is known as magma. See also PUMICE.

Laval, Pierre, 1883–1945, French politician. Entering politics as a Socialist, Laval later became an Independent and was premier (1931–32, 1935–36). In 1935 he proposed a plan to halt Italy's conquest of Ethiopia by appeasing MUSSOLINI. After the fall of France in WORLD WAR II, Laval was vice premier (1940) in the VICHY government, but he was dismissed on suspicion of trying to overthrow Marshal PÉTAIN. Outspoken in favor of collaboration with Nazi Germany, Laval was reinstated (1942) with dictatorial powers. He agreed to draft labor for Germany and began a reign of terror. In 1945 he surrendered to the Allies and was executed for treason. His poorly conducted trial was denounced by many.

Laval, city (1991 pop. 314,398), coextensive with Île-Jésus, a 94-sq-mi (243-sq-km) island, S Quebec, E Canada. A mainly residential suburb of MONTREAL, the city was created in 1966 through amalgamation of 14 small communities on the island.

Lavalleja, Juan Antonio [läväyā′hä], c.1786–1853, Uruguayan revolutionary leader. He led the small group—the Thirty-three Immortals—that declared (1825) Uruguay's independence from Brazil. Denied the presidency of the new nation, he revolted twice (1832, 1834) against Pres. Fructuoso Rivera and joined in the civil war (1843–51). From the war two dominant political parties emerged: the Blancos (whites), which he led; and the Colorados (reds), under Rivera.

Laver, Rod(ney George), 1938–, Australian tennis player. He won the grand slam of tennis (Australian, U.S., British, and French titles) in 1962 and 1969, the only person to do so twice. In 1971 he became the first professional tennis player to earn over $1 million. His many national championships included four at Wimbledon.

Laveran, Charles Louis Alphonse, 1845–1922, French physician. While an army surgeon in Algiers, he discovered (1880) the parasite that causes MALARIA. For his work on protozoa in the causation of disease he received the 1907 Nobel Prize in physiology or medicine.

Lavoisier, Antoine Laurent [lävwäzyā′], 1743–94, French chemist and physicist. A founder of modern chemistry, he was one of the first to use effective quantitative methods to study reactions. His classification of substances is the basis of the distinction between chemical elements and compounds and of the system of chemical nomenclature. He proposed the oxygen theory of combustion, thereby discrediting the PHLOGISTON THEORY, and described oxygen's role in respiration. Concerned with improving social and economic conditions in France, he held various government posts; he was guillotined during the Reign of Terror.

Law, John, 1671–1729, Scottish financier in France. Law gained (1717) a commercial monopoly in LOUISIANA and formed the Compagnie d'Occident, or Mississippi Company, which was enlarged (1719) as the Compagnie des Indes. In 1720 Law's bank (the royal bank since 1718) was merged with the trading company, and a rash of speculation followed. This so-called Mississippi Scheme collapsed (Oct. 1720), and ruined many investors. Law died in disgrace in Venice. The "Mississippi Bubble" discredited the idea of a national bank, but encouraged colonization in Louisiana.

law, rules of conduct of organized society, enforced by threat of punishment. Early examples from Babylonia (the code of HAMMURABI), India (Laws of MANU), and Palestine (Mosaic code) suggest a universal tendency of religious and ethical systems to produce a legal order. ROMAN LAW developed the distinction between public law, in which the state is directly involved, and private law, concerned with disputes between persons. Roman influence survived in the canon law of the Catholic Church and in the laws of FEUDALISM, and it is the basis of modern CIVIL LAW. In England, law made by royal judges became COMMON LAW, later modified by the laws of EQUITY. The work of Sir William BLACKSTONE in the 18th cent., which stressed the natural rights of human beings, greatly influenced U.S. law, which is distinguished by the coexistence of federal and state systems.

Lawrence, D(avid) H(erbert), 1885–1930, English author. Holding that industrial culture dehumanizes, he glorified union with nature and its corollary, sexual fulfillment. His great novels are *Sons and Lovers* (1913; restored ed. 1992), *The Rainbow* (1915), and *Women in Love* (1921). After World War I, Lawrence wrote about the idea of a superhuman leader for humanity. The novels of this period, e.g., *The Plumed Serpent* (1926), are considered failures. His controversial and sexually explicit *Lady Chatterley's Lover* (1928) was long banned. Lawrence wrote in a sensuous, lyrical style, brilliantly conveying the specific, and greatly influenced 20th-cent. fiction. His works include poetry, short stories, essays, plays, travel books, and criticism.

Lawrence, Ernest Orlando, 1901–58, American physicist; b. Canton, S.D. He was a professor at the Univ. of California and director of its radiation laboratory. For his invention and development of the cyclotron (see PARTICLE ACCELERATOR) and his studies of atomic structure and transmutation, he received the 1939 Nobel Prize in physics.

Lawrence, Gertrude, 1898–1952, English actress; b. Alexandre Dagmar Lawrence-Klasen. On the musical stage from childhood, she charmed audiences in shows such as *Private Lives* (1931) and *The King and I* (1951).

Lawrence, James, 1781–1813, U.S. naval hero; b. Burlington, N.J. Commanding the *Chesapeake* in the WAR OF 1812, he was defeated by the British frigate *Shannon* outside Boston harbor. His dying words, "Don't give up the ship!" became famous.

Lawrence, Sir Thomas, 1769–1830, English portrait painter. He succeeded Sir Joshua REYNOLDS as painter in ordinary to the king, became an Academician, and was knighted in 1815. After doing portraits of state and church officials in Austria and Italy, he became president of the Royal Academy. Among his best portraits are the *Calmady Children* (Metropolitan Mus.), *Pinkie* (Huntington Gall., San Marino, Calif.), and the portraits of Mrs. Siddons and Benjamin West (National Gall., London) and George IV and Princess Caroline (National Portrait Gall., London).

Lawrence, T(homas) E(dward), 1888–1935, British adventurer, soldier, and scholar, known as Lawrence of Arabia. After the outbreak of World War I, he was attached to the intelligence section of the British army in Egypt. In 1916 he joined the Arab forces under Faisal al Husein (FAISAL I) and became a leader in their revolt against Turkish domination. After the war he was a delegate to the Paris Peace Conference, where he sought in vain to achieve independence for the Arabs. By this time Lawrence had become something of a legendary figure. In 1922 he joined the Royal Air Force under an assumed name. Lawrence wrote about his Arabian adventures in *The Seven Pillars of Wisdom* (1935; abr. ed., *Revolt in the Desert,* 1927). He also published a translation of the *Odyssey* (1932).

Lawrence. 1 City (1990 pop. 65,608), seat of Douglas co., NE Kans., on the Kansas R.; founded 1854, inc. 1858. A focus of historical controversy, it was the center of Free State activity, suffered (1856) a proslavery raid, and was sacked and burned (1863) by William QUANTRILL. The Univ. of Kansas dominates the city's economic and cultural life, but agriculture and light industry are also important. **2** City (1990 pop. 70,207), a seat of Essex co., NE Mass., on the Merrimack R.; settled 1655, inc. as a city 1853. Textiles, clothing, and electrical equipment are among its manufactures. Laid out by a group of Boston capitalists in 1845, with mills, a dam, and workers' dwellings, it became a great textile center of the 19th cent. It was the scene (1912) of a famous mill strike.

Lawrence Berkeley Laboratory (LBL; est. early 1930s) and **Lawrence Livermore Laboratory** (LLL; est. 1952), nuclear-science research centers, founded by Ernest LAWRENCE and located, respectively, in Berkeley and Livermore, Calif. The Univ. of California operates them with funds provided by the U.S. Dept of Energy. LBL's work centers on the study of atomic nuclei and makes use of four major particle accelerators, but it also does research on environmental problems and energy technology. LLL carries out research on nuclear weaponry, the effects of radiation, controlled thermonuclear reactions, lasers, materials, and climate.

lawrencium (Lr), radioactive element, first prepared in 1961 by A. Ghiorso and co-workers by boron nuclei bombardment of californium. It is an ACTINIDE-SERIES element. In 1965 a Soviet group prepared a different isotope by the reaction of oxygen-18 with americium-243. See ELEMENT (table); PERIODIC TABLE.

Layamon, fl. c.1200, first major Middle English poet. His *Brut* gives a history of Britain from the fall of Troy to Brutus' arrival in Britain through the death of Cadwaladr (a semilegendary Welsh king, d. 664?). Important in the development of the ARTHURIAN LEGEND, it contains the first mention of LEAR and CYMBELINE.

Lazarsfeld, Paul F., 1901–76, Austrian-American sociologist; b. Vienna. After beginning as a mathematician, he established a research center for social psychology. Emigrating (1933) to the U.S., he studied the social effects of mass media. A founder of the Bureau of Applied Social Research, he authored a groundbreaking study of American voting patterns and, with his collaborator, Robert K. MERTON, introduced innovations in sociological method and the use of statistics in social research.

Lazarus. 1 Brother of MARY and Martha of Bethany; he was brought back to life by JESUS. **2** Beggar in a parable who was spurned in life by a rich man. After death, the rich man, parching in hell, pleads in vain that Lazarus, now in heaven, be permitted to give him a drink.

Lazarus, Emma, 1849–87, American poet; b. N.Y.C. A spokeswoman for Judaism, she wrote a book of poems, *Songs of a Semite* (1882). Her sonnet about the Statue of LIBERTY, "The New Colossus," is engraved on the statue's pedestal.

L-dopa or **levadopa,** drug used to alleviate symptoms of PARKINSON'S DISEASE and related syndromes, particularly rigidity, slow movements, and trembling, resulting from a deficiency of dopamine in the brain. Introduced into the bloodstream, L-dopa is probably converted to dopamine by neurons in the brain.

lead (Pb), metallic element, one of the earliest known metals, used by the ancient Egyptians and Babylonians. A poor conductor of heat and electricity, lead is silver-blue, dense, relatively soft, and malleable, with low tensile strength. It is used in lead-acid storage batteries (see CELL, in electricity), SOLDER, and plumbing, and as protective shielding against X rays and radiation from nuclear reactors. The principal lead ores are GALENA, cerussite, and anglesite. Lead compounds (all poisonous) include tetraethyl lead (formerly used as a gasoline antiknock additive) and oxides used in mordants and pigments. Continued exposure to lead—through inhalation of fumes or sprays and ingestion of food containing lead—can result in a cumulative chronic disease called **lead poisoning.** It was once a serious occupational hazard, but protective equipment and other precautionary measures have reduced its incidence. Lead poisoning remains a serious problem in children, who are more susceptible to it. Causes may include ingestion of paint chips from peeling walls or pipes or inhalation of contaminated dust during home renovation. Lower doses may be treated by altering the diet to counteract lead's effects and and cleaning the person's environment to reduce intake. Higher doses are treated with chelating agents, drugs that remove lead from the body. See ELEMENT (table); PERIODIC TABLE.

lead glance: see GALENA.

lead poisoning: see under LEAD.

Leadville, city (1990 pop. 2,629), alt. c.10,200 ft (3,110 m), seat of Lake co., central Colo.; inc. 1878. The quintessential western boom town, it began as the site of a gold rush (c.1860–62). A silver boom followed, from 1877 to 1893, when the population reached 40,000, and a second gold boom came in the late 1890s. Some mining and smelting continue, but tourism and agriculture are also important.

leaf, the chief food-manufacturing organ of higher plants, a lateral

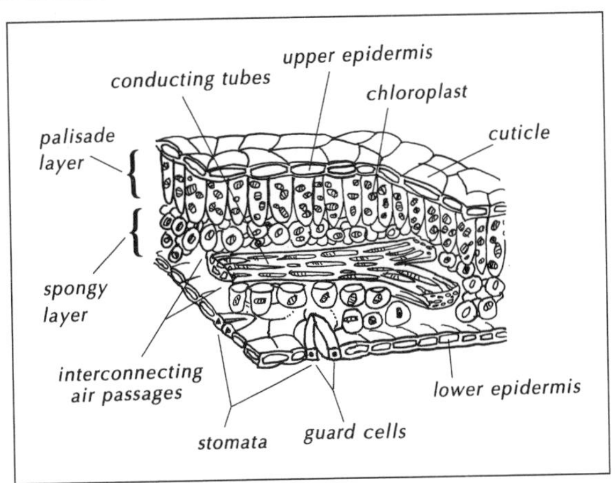

A. General structure of a leaf B. Microscopic cross-section of the leaf blade

outgrowth of the STEM. The typical leaf consists of a stalk, or petiole, and a thin, flat, expanded portion (needlelike in most CONIFERS), or blade. The blade, veined with sap-conducting tubes (xylem and phloem), consists of upper and lower layers of epidermal cells, including cells that control the size of tiny pores (stomata) that are used in gas exchange and TRANSPIRATION. Between the two layers are cells, rich in CHLOROPHYLL, that conduct PHOTOSYNTHESIS.

leaf insect, tropical herbivorous INSECT, about 4 in. (10 cm) long, whose flattened, green, irregularly shaped body gives it a leaflike appearance. The related WALKING STICK resembles a twig.

League or **Holy League,** during the Wars of Religion (see RELIGION, WARS OF), organization of French Catholics aimed at the suppression of Protestantism. Founded (1576) by Henri, 3d duc de Guise, it was dissolved (1577) by King HENRY III. Although revived (1585), it failed to survive HENRY IV's military successes.

League of Nations, a former international organization, formed after WORLD WAR I to promote international peace and security. The basis of the League, the Covenant, was written into the Treaty of VERSAILLES and other peace treaties and provided for an assembly, a council, and a secretariat. A system of colonial mandates was also set up. The U.S., which failed to ratify the Treaty of Versailles, never became a member. Based in Geneva, the League proved useful in settling minor international disputes, but was unable to stop aggression by major powers—e.g., Japan's occupation of Manchuria (1931), Italy's conquest of Ethiopia (1935–36), and Germany's seizure of Austria (1938). It collapsed early in World War II and dissolved itself in 1946. The League established the first pattern of permanent international organization and served as a model for its successor, the UNITED NATIONS.

League of Women Voters, public service organization, an outgrowth (1920) of the National American Women Suffrage Association. Founded to educate women in the intelligent use of their newly acquired suffrage, it later broadened its scope to include the improvement of the political process in general. Its activities include educational and research campaigns on local, state, and national levels. Men were admitted after 1974; the league has 110,000 members.

Leah, in the Bible, Laban's elder, uglier daughter, RACHEL's sister and JACOB's first wife.

Leakey, family of anthropologists and archaeologists whose work in East Africa indicated that human EVOLUTION centered there rather than in Asia. **Louis Seymour Bazett Leakey,** 1903–72, b. Kenya, began excavating at OLDUVAI GORGE, Tanzania, in 1931. There he and his wife, **Mary Douglas Leakey,** 1913–, b. England, discovered stone tool and hominid fossil evidence that pushed back the dates for early humans. Notable finds were *Zinjanthropus* (1959), dated at 1.75 million years of age (now generally regarded as Australopithecine), and *Homo habilis* (1961). Mary Leakey has more recently discovered *Homo* fossils over 3.75 million years old. Louis Leakey's evolutionary interpretations of these discoveries were frequently controversial. He popularized archaeology in his lectures and books, including *Adam's Ancestors* (4th ed. 1953) and *Unveiling Man's Origins* (1969). In 1972 their son, **Richard (Erskine Frere) Leakey,** 1944–, b. Kenya, discovered near Lake Turkana (Lake Rudolf), Kenya, yet another type of hominid skull, which may represent a transition between *Australopithecus* and *Homo* genera. He was (1974–89) director of the National Museums of Kenya and headed (1989–94) Kenya's wildlife service. With Roger Lewin he published *Origins Reconsidered* (1992).

leap year: see CALENDAR.

Lear, legendary English king. GEOFFREY OF MONMOUTH claimed to have translated Lear's story from Old English records, but it probably had its origins in Celtic mythology. It is the subject of SHAKESPEARE's tragedy *King Lear.*

Lear, Edward, 1812–88, English humorist and artist. He is best known for his illustrated limericks and nonsense verse, collected in such volumes as *A Book of Nonsense* (1846).

learning disabilities, in education, any of various disorders involved in understanding or using spoken or written language, including difficulties in listening, thinking, talking, reading, writing, spelling, or ARITHMETIC. They may affect people of average or above-average intelligence. Learning disabilities include conditions referred to as perceptual handicaps, minimal brain dysfunction (MBD), DYSLEXIA, developmental aphasia, and attention deficit hyperactivity disorder; they do not include learning problems due to physical handicaps (e.g., impaired sight or hearing, or orthopedic disabilities), MENTAL RETARDATION, emotional disturbance, or cultural or environmental disadvantage. Techniques for remediation are highly individualized, including the simultaneous use of several senses (sight, hearing, touch), slow-paced instruction, and repetitive exercises to help make perceptual distinctions. Students are also assisted in compensating for their disabilities; for example, one with a writing disability may use a tape recorder for taking notes or answering essay questions. Behavior often associated with learning disabilities includes short attention span and impulsiveness. School programs for learning-disabled students range from a modified or supplemental program in regular classes to placement in a special school, depending upon the severity of the disability.

leather, skin or hide of animals, cured by TANNING to prevent decay and to impart flexibility and toughness. Early peoples used pelts preserved with grease or smoke for garments, tents, and containers. Since the 18th cent. machines have been used to split the tanned leather into the desired thicknesses of flesh layers and grain (hair-side) layers. Pelts are prepared by dehairing, cleaning, tanning, and treating with fats to ensure pliability. Finishes include glazing, staining or dye coloring, enameling or lacquering (as for patent leather), and sueding (buffing to raise a nap). Artificial leather, made since c.1850, is now mainly manufactured from vinyl PLASTIC.

Leavis, F(rank) R(aymond), 1895–1978, English teacher and author. He wrote critical works, including *The Great Tradition* (1948), and essays on society like *Mass Civilization and Minority Culture* (1930). His wife, **Q(ueenie) D(orothy) Leavis,** 1900–1982, was also a critic of note.

Lebanon, officially Republic of Lebanon, republic (1992 est. pop. 3,439,000), 4,015 sq mi (10,400 sq km), SW Asia, bounded by the Mediterranean Sea (W), Syria (N, E), and Israel (S). The capital is BEIRUT. Much of the terrain is mountainous, with two main ranges—the Lebanon in the west and the Anti-Lebanon in the east—paralleling the coast; the fertile Al Biqa valley lies between them. Until the disruption caused by the civil war of 1975–76, Lebanon had a service-oriented economy, and Beirut, a free port, was the financial and commercial center of the Middle East. Through the 1980s the commercial and industrial life of Lebanon was in severe disarray, but by the early 1990s the economy had at least partially revived. Banking, food processing, and the manufacture of textiles and chemicals are now economically important. Principal crops are grains, olives, and citrus fruits. Remittances from Lebanese working abroad are an important source of foreign exchange. Most Lebanese are Arabs; there is a small Armenian minority. Arabic is the official language, but French and English are also widely spoken. The population is divided between Muslims, mainly Sunni and Shiite, and Christians (mainly Maronites), who make up about one quarter of the total.

History. The site of the ancient maritime city-state of PHOENICIA, the area later fell to successive Middle Eastern powers. Christianity was introduced under the Roman Empire and persisted even after the coming of Islam with the Arab conquest (7th cent.). In the late 11th cent. Lebanese Christians aided the Crusaders (see CRUSADES) in the region. The area came under the Ottoman Turks in the 16th cent., and after the Turkish defeat in WORLD WAR I it became part of a French mandate known as Greater Lebanon. Since independence in 1945, Lebanon has been plagued by civil strife and problems with its neighbors. A member of the ARAB LEAGUE, it took little part in the ARAB-ISRAELI WARS that followed Israel's independence in 1948, but the stage was set for future problems when many Palestinians fled Israel and settled in S Lebanon. Meanwhile, Lebanon's internal equilibrium was shaken (1958) by a rebellion against pro-Western policies, and U.S. forces were called in briefly. In 1975 civil war erupted between leftist Muslims, aided by the PALESTINE LIBERATION ORGANIZATION (PLO), and conservative Christians. In 1976 Syrian troops intervened, and a cease-fire was declared, but Israel and the PLO engaged in a sporadic border war in S Lebanon. In 1978, following a limited Israeli invasion, a UN peacekeeping force was placed in S Lebanon. Fighting continued, however, and in 1982 Israel invaded Lebanon, forcing out many members of the PLO and causing widespread devastation. A massacre of Palestinians by Lebanese Christians during the Israeli occupation of Beirut led to worldwide criticism of Israel and the establishment of a multinational peacekeeping force in Beirut. In Oct. 1983 terrorist bombings killed over 230 U.S. Marines and French troops in their respective compounds, and both nations subsequently withdrew their remaining forces. When the Lebanese parliament in 1988 proved unable to elect a successor to the Christian president, Amin Gemayel. Gemayel, on the expiration of his term, appointed a Christian general, Michel Aoun, as interim president, but Muslims challenged his legitimacy. In 1989 Arab governments brokered a peace agreement that produced a new constitution that increased the political power of the Muslim majority. Elias Hrawi, a Christian, was elected president, but Aoun refused to step down and fighting between Christian factions for and against Aoun broke out. In 1990, at Hrawi's request, Syrian troops attacked Aoun's position. Aoun took refuge in the French embassy and later fled to France, ending the civil war. Hrawi signed (1991) a treaty of friendship and cooperation with Syria that essentially guaranteed Syrian domination of Lebanon's foreign relations. In 1993 fighting again erupted between Shiite Hezbollah guerrillas and Israel in S Lebanon.

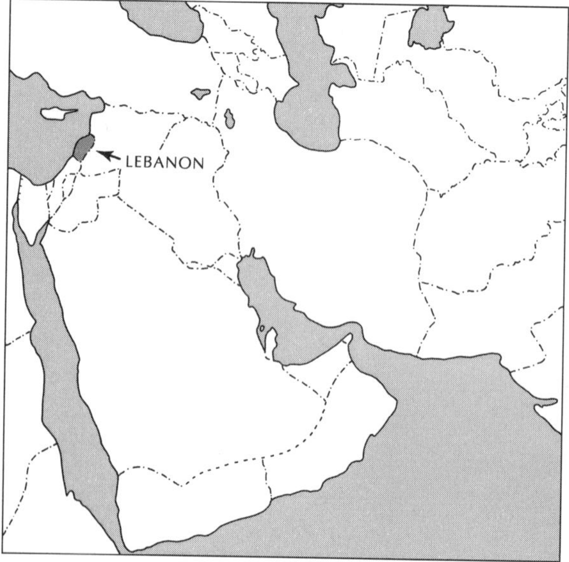

Le Brun, Charles, 1619–90, French painter, decorator, and architect. Influenced by POUSSIN, he developed a more decorative form of CLASSICISM. His first royal commission, *The Family of Darius*

before Alexander (1661), gained him the favor of LOUIS XIV. He became painter to the king (1662), controlling artistic theory and production in France for two decades. Head of the Gobelins works, he designed royal furnishings and was director of the Académie royale. The atmosphere of richness and splendor he created can be seen at VERSAILLES.

Lebrun, Élisabeth Vigée: see VIGÉE-LEBRUN.

le Carré, John, pseud. of **David John Moore Cornwall,** 1931–, English novelist. He is noted for his bleak, complex studies of international espionage. His novels include *The Spy Who Came In from the Cold* (1963), *Tinker, Tailor, Soldier, Spy* (1974), *The Little Drummer Girl* (1983), and *The Night Manager* (1993).

Leconte de Lisle, Charles Marie [ləkôNt' də lēl], 1818–94, French poet, the leading PARNASSIAN. Anti-Christian and a pessimist, he saw death as the only reality and drew his inspiration from antiquity, as in *Poèmes antiques* (1852), *Poèmes barbares* (1872), and *Poèmes tragiques* (1884).

Le Corbusier [lə kôrbüzyā'], pseud. of **Charles Édouard Jeanneret** [zhänərā'], 1887–1965, French architect; b. Switzerland. His buildings and writings had a revolutionary effect on the international development of MODERN ARCHITECTURE. After 1915 he began to produce radical schemes for houses and apartments, drawing inspiration from industrial forms. In 1923, at Vaucresson, near Paris, the first building (a villa) was constructed according to his principles. His book *Towards a New Architecture* (1923) gained wide circulation. His plan for a "vertical city" was partially realized in the Unité d'Habitation, Marseilles (1946–52). His most ambitious work was the main buildings for the capital of the Punjab, Chandigarh (begun 1951). Other buildings include a chapel at Ronchamp (1950–55) and the Visual Arts Center, Harvard Univ. (1961–62).

LED (light-emitting diode): see DIODE.

Leda, in Greek mythology, wife of Tyndareus, king of SPARTA, mother by him of CLYTEMNESTRA. In most legends Leda was seduced by ZEUS, who appeared as a swan. She bore two eggs: from one issued CASTOR AND POLLUX, from the other HELEN.

Lederberg, Joshua, 1925–, American geneticist; b. Montclair, N.J. For their studies establishing that sexual recombination occurs in bacteria, he and Edward Tatum shared the 1958 Nobel Prize in physiology or medicine with George BEADLE. Lederberg and his student Norman Zinder discovered the process called transduction, by which certain viruses transfer a chromosome from one bacterial cell to another. From 1978 to 1990 he was president of Rockefeller Univ.

Le Duan [lā dwän], 1908–86, Vietnamese Communist leader. Imprisoned by the French colonial regime, he later rose in North Vietnam's Communist party to become (1959) first secretary. After HO CHI MINH's death (1969), Le Duan emerged as the leader of North Vietnam's ruling collective. In 1976, after Vietnam's reunification, he was renamed party leader and served until his death.

Lee, Ann, 1736–84, English religious visionary, founder of the SHAKERS in America. In 1758 she joined the "Shaking Quakers," and, claiming revelation in a vision (c.1770) that the second coming of Christ was fulfilled in her, she became their leader. Lee led (1774) a band to America, where in 1776 the first Shaker settlement was founded at Watervliet, N.Y.

Lee, Charles, 1731–82, American Revolutionary general; b. England. When he was captured (1776) by the British in Basking Ridge, N.J., he gave them a plan to defeat the Americans. His treason was not discovered, and he was exchanged and rejoined (1778) Gen. WASHINGTON's army. At the battle of MONMOUTH (1778), he ordered a retreat that prevented an American victory and was suspended and later (1780) dismissed.

Lee, Francis Lightfoot, 1734–97, American Revolutionary leader, signer of the DECLARATION OF INDEPENDENCE; b. Westmoreland co., Va. As a member (1758–76) of the Virginia house of burgesses, he urged resistance to Britain. He served (1775–79) in the CONTINENTAL CONGRESS.

Lee, Henry, 1756–1818, American Revolutionary soldier, known as "Light-Horse Harry Lee"; b. Prince William co., Va. A daring cavalry officer, he fought in the Carolina campaign after 1780. He was the father of Robert E. LEE and the cousin of Richard H. LEE.

Lee, Richard Henry, 1732–94, American revolutionary leader; b. Westmoreland co., Va. A member (1774–79, 1784–87) of the CONTINENTAL CONGRESS, he signed the DECLARATION OF INDEPENDENCE and later opposed the federal Constitution on the STATES' RIGHTS issue. He was U.S. senator from Virginia (1789–92).

Lee, Robert E(dward), 1807–70, Confederate general in the U.S. CIVIL WAR, son of Henry LEE; b. Westmoreland co., Va. He served with distinction in the MEXICAN WAR, was superintendent at West Point (1852–55), and led (1859) the U.S. marines who captured John BROWN at Harpers Ferry. After the secession of the lower South, he declined the field command of U.S. forces. After Virginia's secession, however, he was given (June 1862) command of the Army of Northern Virginia and immediately took the offensive in the SEVEN DAYS BATTLES. He crushed the Union army at the second battle of BULL RUN, but Gen. G.B. MCCLELLAN halted Lee's first invasion of the North in the ANTIETAM CAMPAIGN. Lee repulsed Union advances at the battles of FREDERICKSBURG and CHANCELLORSVILLE, where he lost his ablest lieutenant, Stonewall JACKSON. His second invasion of the North ended in defeat in the GETTYSBURG CAMPAIGN (1863). He repulsed Gen. U.S. GRANT's direct assaults in the WILDERNESS CAMPAIGN (May–June 1864), but in July Grant laid siege to Petersburg. Lee became (Feb. 1865) general in chief of all Confederate armies, but the South was near collapse. He surrendered (Apr. 9, 1865) to Grant at APPOMATTOX Courthouse. After the war he was president of Washington College (now Washington and Lee Univ.). Lee was idolized by his soldiers, and many historians consider him to be the greatest general of the Civil War.

Lee, Spike (Shelton Jackson Lee), 1957–, American filmmaker: b. Atlanta, Ga. He celebrates the richness of African-American culture while examining racism and other social problems. Lee's films include *She's Gotta Have It* (1986), *Do the Right Thing* (1989), *Jungle Fever* (1991), and *Malcolm X* (1992).

leech, segmented or ANNELID WORM with a cylindrical or slightly flattened body having suckers at both ends; it usually feeds on blood, which it stores in pouches large enough to hold several months' supply. Most are aquatic. Leeches were once used to bleed patients suffering from almost any ailment; they are still used in some regions to treat bruises.

Leeds, city (1991 pop. 680,722), W Yorkshire, N central England, on the Aire R. Lying between manufacturing and agricultural regions, Leeds is a center of communications, transportation, and regional government. Manufactures include woolens, locomotives, and farm implements. Triennial music festivals are held in the classical town hall (1858).

leek: see ONION.

Lee Teng-hui, 1923–, Taiwanese political leader and agricultural expert. He was a member of the Joint Commission on Rural Reconstruction (1957–61), a minister without portfolio (1972–78), mayor of Taipei (1978–81), governor of Taiwan province (1981–84), and vice president (1984–88). In Jan. 1988 he succeeded to the presidency at the death of Chiang Ching-kuo (see under CHIANG KAI-SHEK). He has permitted increasing political democratization in Taiwan and has used Taiwan's economic success to diminish its international isolation.

Leeuwenhoek, Antony van [lā'vənho͝ok"], 1632–1723, Dutch student of natural history. He made over 247 MICROSCOPES, some of which magnified objects 270 times. He examined microorganisms and tissue samples and gave the first complete descriptions of bacteria, protozoa, spermatozoa, and striped muscle. He also studied capillary circulation and observed red blood cells.

Leeward Islands: see WEST INDIES.

Le Gallienne, Eva [ləgăl'yən], 1899–1991, American actress and producer; b. England. She founded the Civic Repertory Theatre (1926) and, with Margaret WEBSTER, the American Repertory Theatre (1946). She produced classical revivals and was an outstanding interpreter of IBSEN.

Legendre, Adrien Marie [ləzhäN'drə], 1752–1833, French mathematician, noted especially for his work on number theory and elliptic integrals. He invented the method of least squares independently of Carl GAUSS and was the first to state it in print (1806).

Léger, Alexis Saint-Léger: see PERSE, SAINT-JOHN.

Léger, Fernand [lāzhā], 1881–1955, French painter. A modified CUBISM is apparent in much of his work. In paintings such as *The City* (1919; Philadelphia Mus. of Art) he celebrated the machine in a naïve, energetic style, using flat tones of pure color, black, white, and gray.

Legionnaire's disease, infectious, sometimes fatal, disease characterized by high fever, dry cough, lung congestion, and subsequent PNEUMONIA, and kidney and liver damage. The disease struck over 180 people attending an American Legion convention in Philadelphia in July 1976—hence the name. It is caused by several species of *Legionella* bacteria, which are inhaled via contaminated water droplets produced by air-conditioning cooling systems. The disease is treated with the ANTIBIOTIC erythromycin.

legislature, representative assembly empowered to enact statute law and to levy taxes. In a DEMOCRACY its members are elected by the general populace. One of the oldest is the English PARLIAMENT, a bicameral legislature whose lower (House of Commons) and upper (House of Lords) chambers derive from class divisions. In the U.S. CONGRESS, which is also bicameral, the House of Representatives and the Senate were established on federal principles. The Israeli Knesset is an example of a unicameral legislature.

legume, name for any plant of the PULSE family; more generally, any vegetable harvested from such a plant. Botanically, a legume—a pod that splits along two sides, with the seeds attached to one of the sutures—is the characteristic FRUIT of the pulse family.

Lehár, Franz [lĕ'här], 1870–1948, Hungarian composer of OPERETTAS. He is best known for *The Merry Widow* (1905), *The Count of Luxembourg* (1909), and *Gypsy Love* (1910), works filled with gaiety and engaging melodies.

Lehmann, Lilli [lā'män], 1848–1929, German operatic soprano. She began as a coloratura, but became a great Wagnerian singer (see WAGNER, RICHARD) with a repertory of 170 roles. She also interpreted LIEDER and was a teacher.

Lehmann, Lotte, 1888–1976, German-American soprano. After singing in Berlin and Vienna, she made her American debut in Chicago (1930) and sang with the METROPOLITAN OPERA, New York City (1934–45). She was noted for her performances in operas by Richard STRAUSS.

Leibniz or **Leibnitz, Gottfried Wilhelm, Baron von,** 1646–1716, German philosopher and mathematician. His career as a scholar embraced the physical sciences, law, history, diplomacy, and logic, and he held diplomatic posts (from 1666) under various German princes. Leibniz also invented the CALCULUS, concurrently with but independently of NEWTON. His philosophical writings, including *Theodicy* (1710) and *Monadology* (1714), popularized by the philosopher Christian von Wolff, were orthodox and optimistic, claiming that a divine plan made this the best of all possible worlds (a view satirized by VOLTAIRE in *Candide*). According to Leibniz, the basic constituents of the universe are simple substances he called monads, infinite in number, nonmaterial, and hierarchically arranged. His major work, *New Essays on Human Understanding,* a treatise on John LOCKE's *Essay concerning Human Understanding,* was written in 1704 but because of Locke's death published only in 1765. A critique of Locke's theory that the mind is a blank at birth, it exerted great influence on KANT and the German ENLIGHTENMENT. Modern studies have tended to focus on Leibniz's contributions to mathematics and logic; manuscripts published in the 20th cent. show him to be the founder of symbolic logic (see LOGIC).

Leicester, Robert Dudley, earl of [lĕs'tər], 1532?–1588, English courtier and favorite of Queen ELIZABETH I. He aided (1553) the plot to place Lady Jane GREY on the throne, but was pardoned. After the accession (1558) of Elizabeth, he became a privy councillor, and was rumored to be Elizabeth's most likely choice for a husband. Though his wife's suspicious death (1560) darkened his reputation and his remarriage (1578) temporarily estranged the queen, he retained Elizabeth's confidence. Later he led (1585–87) an unsuccessful expedition against the Spanish in the Netherlands.

Leicester [lĕs'tər], city (1991 pop. 270,493), county town of Leicestershire, central England. Of industrial importance as early as the 14th cent., it now manufactures shoes, hosiery, machinery, and other products. It was, in turn, a town of the Romans, the early Britons, and the Danes. Extensive Roman and medieval remains are found there.

Leiden or **Leyden,** city (1991 est. pop. 112,000), W Netherlands. Among its various manufactures, the textile industry has flourished since the 16th cent. It is famous for its university (est. 1575), the nation's oldest, a center (17th–18th cent.) of science, medicine, and Protestant theology. Leiden took part in the Dutch revolt against the Spanish and was saved (1574) by WILLIAM THE SILENT. It is the birthplace of REMBRANDT.

Leif Ericsson, fl. 999–1000, Norse discoverer of America; b. probably in Iceland; son of ERIC THE RED. Information about his travels is taken from Norse SAGAS. One states that he was blown off course on a trip to GREENLAND c.1000 and landed in an area that he named Vinland (probably in either NOVA SCOTIA or NEW ENGLAND).

Leinsdorf, Erich, 1912–93, American conductor; b. Austria. Associated with the METROPOLITAN OPERA (1938–43) and New York City Opera (1956–62), he also led the Boston Symphony Orchestra (1962–69) and appeared widely as a guest conductor.

Leipzig, city (1989 est. pop. 545,000), Saxony, SE Germany. It manufactures textiles, electrical equipment, machine tools, chemicals, and other goods. It has been a commerical center since medieval times and became a cultural center in the 17th and 18th cent. LEIBNIZ and Richard WAGNER were born there; J.S. BACH (now buried in the 15th-cent. Church of St. Thomas), Robert SCHUMANN, Felix MENDELSSOHN, and the young GOETHE worked there. A monument commemorates the victory over NAPOLEON I in the Battle of Leipzig (1813). In 1989 demonstrations in the city sparked the downfall of the Communist East German government and the subsequent German reunification.

leishmaniasis, any of a group of tropical diseases caused by parasites of the genus *Leishmania.* The parasites infect the very white blood cells that normally would defend the body from such invaders. Leishmaniasis is spread by blood-sucking sand flies that bite, leaving deep, disfiguring sores. If the parasites spread to internal organs, death can result.

Lem, Stanislaw, 1921–, Polish writer. Lem's writings, including many translated works of SCIENCE FICTION, reflect his philosophical concern over the moral implications of modern science and technology, and also reflect his acute sense of comedy and irony. Among his works are the novels *Memoirs of a Space Traveler* (1957), *Solaris* (1961), and *The Futurological Congress* (1983).

Lemaître, Georges, Abbé, 1894–1966, Belgian astrophysicist and cosmologist. He posited that the universe began as a condensed primeval atom that exploded, creating the force by which the universe is still expanding.

Lemercier, Jacques [ləmĕrsyā'], c.1585–1654, French architect, a major contributor to classical French style. He was a designer of Jesuit churches, and his chief surviving work is the church of the Sorbonne, Paris (1635). He also designed Cardinal RICHELIEU's Paris residence, later transformed into the Palais-Royal, and the town of Richelieu.

lemming, mouselike RODENT of arctic or northern regions, inhabiting tundra or open meadows. All are about 5 in. (13 cm) long, with stout bodies, thick fur, and short tails. Two or three times per decade, Norway lemmings (*Lemmus lemmus*) undergo a population explosion that forces them to set out in search of food. Crossing bodies of water by swimming, some reach the ocean and drown—giving rise to folklore about lemmings committing mass suicide.

lemon, yellow-skinned CITRUS FRUIT of a small tree (*Citrus limon*) of the RUE family. High in VITAMIN C, lemons prevent scurvy. Products include citric acid, juice, oil, polish, pectin, and flavorings. Lemons grow best in a mild climate, e.g., the Mediterranean, California, and Florida.

LeMond, Greg(ory James), 1961–, American bicycle racer; b. Los Angeles. In 1986 LeMond became first American to win the Tour de France, a three-week, 2,500-mi (4,000-km) race and cycling's premier event. Seriously injured in a 1987 hunting accident, he returned to racing and won the Tour de France in 1989 and 1990. He was also world champion twice (1983, 1989) and won the Tour Du Pont in 1992.

lemur, prosimian, or lower PRIMATE, of the related families Lemuridae and Indriidae, found only on Madagascar and adjacent islands. Lemurs have monkeylike bodies, long, bushy tails, pointed muzzles, large eyes, and flat nails, except the second toe, which has a stout claw. Most are arboreal. Best known is the ring-tailed lemur (*Lemur catta*), which is atypically terrestrial.

Lena, river, easternmost of the great rivers of Siberia, Russia, c.2,670 mi (4,300 km) long. It flows generally north, then northeast, from a source near Lake BAYKAL to empty into the ARCTIC OCEAN through a delta c.250 mi (400 km) wide. The river, which is navigable for 2,135 mi (3,436 km) in summer, is frozen at its mouth from Oct. to June.

Le Nain [lə năN'], family of French painters consisting of three brothers. **Antoine Le Nain,** 1588?–1648, painted colorful miniatures of family scenes. **Mathieu Le Nain,** 1607–77, was painter to the city of Paris, specializing in portraiture and depicting the city militia. **Louis Le Nain,** 1593?–1648, conceived the famous genre scenes in which peasant life is treated sympathetically and realistically. The brothers collaborated on much of their work, e.g., *The Forge* and *Peasant's Repast* (both: Louvre).

Lendl, Ivan, 1960–, Czech-American tennis player. Known for his powerful forehand, punishing serve, and poker-faced style, he was a dominant singles player in the 1980s. Lendl won all the grand slam tournaments except Wimbledon: the Australian (1989–90), French (1984, 1986–87), and U.S. opens (1985–87).

lend-lease, WORLD WAR II arrangement whereby the U.S. furnished necessary supplies, including food, machinery, and services, to its allies. The Lend-Lease Act (1941) empowered the president to sell, lend, lease, and transfer such material under whatever terms he deemed proper. It was originally intended to aid Britain and the Commonwealth countries, and China. By the war's end virtually all the Allies (including the USSR) were part of it. Total lend-lease aid exceeded $50 billion. By 1972 the U.S. had reached settlements with all the nations that had received lend-lease aid.

L'Enfant, Pierre Charles [läNfäN'], 1754–1825, American architect; b. France. On Pres. WASHINGTON's request he submitted (1791) plans for the new capital city at Washington. He was dismissed due to various personal antagonisms, but in 1889 the plans were exhumed from the archives, and in 1901 the capital was developed along their lines.

Vladimir Lenin

Lenin, Vladimir Ilyich, 1870–1924, Russian revolutionary, founder of Bolshevism, and major force behind the founding of the USSR. Born in the Volga region, the son of a school inspector named Ulyanov, he was deeply influenced by his brother Aleksandr, who was executed in 1887 for plotting to kill the czar. Lenin abandoned the law to devote himself to Marxist study and agitation among workers, and was arrested and exiled to Siberia in 1895. There he married Nadezhda K. Krupskaya. In 1900 they left Russia for W Europe; about this time he took the name Lenin. Lenin's insistence that only a disciplined party of professional revolutionaries could bring socialism to Russia (expressed in his 1902 pamphlet *What Is to Be Done?*) led the Russian Social-Democratic Workers' party, meeting in London in 1903, to split into two factions: the Bolsheviks, led by Lenin, and the Mensheviks (see BOLSHEVISM AND MENSHEVISM). Lenin returned to Russia on the outbreak of the 1905 Revolution but left in 1907. He continued to write and to engage in Social-Democratic party politics in W Europe. When WORLD WAR I began he saw it as an opportunity for worldwide socialist revolution. In March 1917 the RUSSIAN REVOLUTION broke out and he returned to Petrograd, where in November (October according to the Old Style) he led the Bolsheviks in overthrowing KERENSKY's provisional government. As chairman of the Council of People's Commissars he became virtual dictator; his associates included STALIN and TROTSKY. Among the Soviet government's first acts were the signing of the Treaty of BREST-LITOVSK with Germany and the distribution of land to the peasants. The Bolsheviks (who became the Communist party) asserted that the October Revolution had created a proletarian dictatorship; in fact, it was the party that ruled. Political opposition was suppressed, but civil war, complicated by foreign invasion and war with Poland, continued until late 1920. In 1919 Lenin established the Third International, or COMINTERN, to further world revolution. His policy of "war Communism," prevailing until 1921, brought extensive nationalization, food rationing, and control over industry. In an attempt to boost the economy, he launched the NEW ECONOMIC POLICY (NEP), which allowed some private enterprise. Lenin's death in 1924 precipitated a power struggle in which Stalin was victorious. Lenin's main contributions to Marxism were his analysis of IMPERIALISM and his concept of a revolutionary party as a highly disciplined unit. He was one of the greatest and most practical revolutionists of all time.

Leningrad: see SAINT PETERSBURG.

Lenôtre or **Le Nôtre, André** [lənō'ə], 1613–1700, French landscape architect. Working for LOUIS XIV, he brought to full development the spacious formal French garden, at the palace of VERSAILLES, the TUILERIES, and other sites.

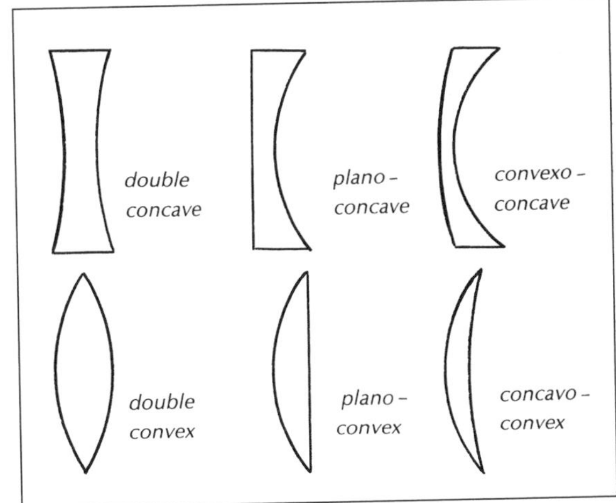

Lenses

lens, a device for forming an image of an object by the REFRACTION, or bending, of light. In its simplest form it is a disk of transparent substance, commonly glass or plastic, with its two surfaces curved or with one surface plane and the other curved. Generally each curved surface—called *convex* if curved outward and *concave* if curved inward—of a lens is made as a portion of a spherical surface; the center of the sphere is called the center of curvature (C) of the surface. All rays of light passing through a lens are refracted except those that pass directly through a point called the optical center. A divergent lens (thicker at the edges than at the center) bends parallel light rays passing through it away from each other. The image formed by a diverging lens is always erect (upright), smaller than the object, and virtual (located on the same side of the lens as the object). A convergent lens (thicker at the center than at the edges) bends parallel light rays toward one another; if they are parallel to the principal axis of the lens, they converge to a common point, or focus (F), behind the lens. The image formed by a converging lens depends on the position of the object relative to the lens's focal length (distance between the focus and the optical center) and its center of curvature. See ABERRATION, in optics; CAMERA; MICROSCOPE; TELESCOPE.

Lent [from Old Eng. *lencten*, = spring], Christian period of fasting and penitence preparatory to EASTER. Lent begins on Ash Wednesday, the 40th weekday before Easter Sunday. Of the Sundays of Lent, the fifth is Passion Sunday, and the last is Palm Sunday. The week preceding Easter is Holy Week and includes GOOD FRIDAY. Lent ends at midnight on Holy Saturday.

lentil, Old World annual (*Lens culinaris*) of the PULSE family. Its pods contain two dark seeds—lentils—unusually high in PROTEIN content; the seeds are ground into meal or used in soups. One of the first food plants cultivated in Europe, lentils are increasingly grown for food in the U.S.

Lenya, Lotte, 1900–1981, Austrian actress; b. Caroline Blamauer. She was married to the composer Kurt WEILL and was the foremost interpreter of his songs, appearing in *The Threepenny Opera* and *Mahagonny*.

Leo I, Saint (Saint Leo the Great), c.400–461, pope (440–61), an Italian. One of the greatest pontiffs and a doctor of the Church, Leo waged a campaign against schism and heresy. He attacked MANICHAEISM in Italy and, in a conflict with St. Hilary of Arles, asserted his authority over all bishops. He defended church teaching against NESTORIANISM and MONOPHYSITISM. In 452 he persuaded ATTILA not to attack Rome. Feast: Nov. 10.

Leo III, Saint, d. 816, pope (795–816), a Roman. After being physically attacked by the family of his predecessor, ADRIAN I, Leo escaped to CHARLEMAGNE and won his support. Leo crowned (800) Charlemagne emperor at Rome, thus initiating the Holy Roman Empire. Seeking East-West unity, he declared the *Filioque* phrase of the Nicene CREED liturgically dispensable. Feast: June 12.

Leo IX, Saint, 1002–54, pope (1049–54), a German named Bruno. A relative of Holy Roman Emperor CONRAD II, Leo, aided by Hildebrand (later Pope GREGORY VII), launched a program of clerical reform. Leo was also concerned with the heresy of Berengar of Tours and was defeated (1053) by the Normans in S. Italy. Michael Cerularius, patriarch of Constantinople, attacked (1053) the pope, and Leo excommunicated him in 1054, beginning the formal schism between East and West. Feast: Apr. 19.

Leo X, 1475–1521, pope (1513–21), a Florentine named Giovanni de' Medici. Son of Lorenzo de' MEDICI, he was famous for his patronage of RAPHAEL, the continuation of St. Peter's by BRAMANTE, and his literary circle. The Fifth Lateran Council, which he called, failed to effect the desired reforms, and the Protestant REFORMATION began when Martin LUTHER posted (1517) his 95 theses. Leo excommunicated the reformers, notably with the bull *Exsurge Domine* (1520), but failed to deal effectively with the crisis.

Leo XIII, 1810–1903, pope (1878–1903), an Italian named Gioacchino Pecci. He devoted himself to forming Catholic attitudes appropriate to the modern world and issued encyclicals to that end. *Immortale Dei* (1885) charted the course for Catholics as responsible citizens in modern democratic states. *Rerum novarum* (1891), a most important encyclical, outlined Catholic social ideals, pointing to the abuses of capitalism and the deficiencies of Marxism. To meet intellectual attacks on the Church, he wrote *Aeterni Patris* (1879), which declared the philosophy of St. THOMAS AQUINAS official, and he founded the Inst. of Thomistic Philosophy at Louvain. In his reign, the conflict in Germany between the government and the church (the Kulturkampf) was ended (1887) with a victory for the church.

Leo, Byzantine emperors. **Leo I** (the Great or the Thracian), d. 474 (r.457–74), enlisted Isaurians to break the power of Germans in his army. His naval attack on the Vandals failed (468). **Leo III** (the Isaurian or the Syrian), c.680–741 (r.717–41), deposed Theodosius III. He checked the Arab threat, ended anarchy in the empire, and issued a civil code, the *Ecloga*. His ICONOCLASM alienated Popes Gregory II and Gregory III, who ended Byzantine suzerainty over Rome. **Leo IV** (the Khazar), d. 780 (r.775–80), succeeded his father, CONSTANTINE V. Leo's widow, IRENE, became regent for their son, CONSTANTINE VI. **Leo V** (the Armenian), d. 820 (r.813–20), made a 30-year truce with the BULGARS. Reviving iconoclasm, he deposed the patriarch Nicephorus (815) and persecuted St. Theodore of Studium. **Leo VI** (the Wise or the Philosopher), 862?–912 (r.886–912), modernized the code of JUSTINIAN I in his *Basilica* (887–93). By renewing (906) the schism with the patriarch PHOTIUS he forced Photius's resignation.

León, Juan Ponce de: see PONCE DE LEÓN, JUAN.

León, region and former kingdom, NW Spain, E of Portugal and Galicia. It includes the provinces of León, Salamanca, and Zamora. The climate is harsh; the sparse population engages in coal mining, stock raising, agriculture, and linen manufacturing. The kings of ASTURIAS took the region (8th–9th cent.) from the MOORS, and the city of León became (10th cent.) their capital. The kingdom of León was permanently joined (1230) with CASTILE.

León, city (1990 pop. 872,453), central Mexico. Founded in the 1570s, it is in a fertile river valley c.5,600 ft (1,700 m) high. It is a commercial, agricultural, and mining center and is noted for its shoe manufactures.

León, city (1988 est. pop. 136,000), W Nicaragua, on Lake Managua. The nation's second largest city, it is a major commercial hub. Founded in 1524, it was colonial Nicaragua's political center and, after independence (1821), a stronghold of liberal forces. Its bitter rivalry with conservative Granada led to the founding (1855) of a "neutral" capital, MANAGUA. It is the seat of the Univ. of Nicaragua and is noted for its 18th-cent. cathedral, which houses the tomb of Rubén DARIO.

Leonardo da Vinci [də vĭn'chē], 1452–1519, Italian painter, sculptor, architect, musician, engineer, and scientist, probably the supreme example of RENAISSANCE genius. Born in Vinci, Tuscany, he was the illegitimate son of a Florentine notary and a peasant girl. His precocious artistic talent brought him to VERROCCHIO's workshop in 1466, where he met BOTTICELLI and GHIRLANDAIO. The culmination of his art in this first period in Florence is seen in the magnificent, unfinished *Adoration of the Magi* (Uffizi), with its characteristic dramatic movement and chiaroscuro. In c.1482 Leonardo went to the court of Ludovico SFORZA in Milan and there composed most of his *Trattato della pittura* and the notebooks that demonstrate his versatile genius. The severe plagues in 1484 and 1485 drew his attention to town planning, and his drawings and plans for domed churches reflect his concern with architectural problems. In 1483, Leonardo and his pupil Ambrogio de Predis were commissioned to execute the famous *Madonna of the Rocks* (two versions: 1483–c.1486, Louvre; 1483–1508, National Gall., London). The now badly damaged *Last Supper* (c.1495–1498; Milan) was executed during the period when he was experimenting with the FRESCO medium, and this partly accounts for its damage. Despite this, a sublime spiritual content and power of invention mark it as one of the world's masterpieces. Leonardo's model for an equestrian monument to Francesco Sforza was never cast, and in 1500 he returned to Florence, where he did much theoretical work in mathematics and pursued his anatomical studies in the hospital of Santa Maria Nuova. As a military engineer for Cesare BORGIA he studied swamp reclamation and met Niccolò MACHIAVELLI. In c.1503 he executed the celebrated *Mona Lisa* (Louvre). Then, as architect and engineer in Milan to the French king LOUIS XII, he continued his scientific investigations into geology, botany, hydraulics, and mechanics. In 1510–11 he painted *St. Anne, Mary, and the Child* (Louvre), a work that exemplifies his handling of *sfumato*—misty, subtle transitions in tone. His enigmatic *St. John the Baptist* (c.1513; Louvre) was executed for Pope LEO X and his brother Giuliano de' Medici in Rome. Shortly after 1515, Leonardo accepted an invitation from FRANCIS I of France to settle in the castle of Cloux. Here he pursued his own researches until his death. His versatility and creative power, as well as the richness and originality expressed in his notebooks, drawings, and paintings, mark him as one of the great minds of all time.

Leoncavallo, Ruggiero, 1858–1919, Italian composer. His one great success was the opera *I Pagliacci* (1892), a classic example of Italian *verismo*, opera based on a realistic plot.

Leonov, Aleksei Arkhipovich, 1934–, Soviet cosmonaut and Russian general. While serving as copilot of *Voskhod 2* (Mar. 18–19, 1965), he became the first person to perform extravehicular activity. Leonov was also command pilot for *Soyuz 19* in the *Apollo-Soyuz Test Project* (July 15–21, 1975). He became an air force major general in 1975.

Leontief, Wassily [lē'ŏntēf], 1906–, American economist; b. Russia. He was at Harvard from 1931 to 1975. He is best known for developing the input-output method of economic analysis, used by most industrialized nations, for which he won (1973) the Nobel Prize in economics.

leopard, large carnivore (*Panthera pardus*) of the CAT family, found in Africa and Asia. Its yellowish fur is patterned with black spots and rings. Black leopards, a color variant, are called PANTHERS. The largest male leopards are about 7 ft (2.3 m) long, including the tail. They live mainly in forests and are solitary and nocturnal, preying on small animals and livestock.

Leopardi, Giacomo, conte, 1798–1837, Italian poet and scholar. His fame rests mainly on his *Canti* (songs), written between 1816 and 1836. Lyrical, lofty, and pessimistic, they are patriotic and contemptuous of Italian rulers of the day. He is regarded as the outstanding 19th-cent. Italian poet.

Leopold, rulers of the HOLY ROMAN EMPIRE. **Leopold I,** 1640–1705, emperor (1658–1705), king of Bohemia (1656–1705) and of Hungary (1655–1705), fared badly against Louis XIV of France in the third (1672–78) of the Dutch Wars and in the War of the Grand Alliance (1688–97). He was more successful against the Ottomans, and the Treaty of Karlowitz (1699) greatly increased his domains. He made VIENNA a cultural center. **Leopold II,** 1747–92, emperor (1790–92) and king of Hungary and Bohemia (1765–90), was the younger son of MARIA THERESA and Emperor Francis I, and the brother of Emperor JOSEPH II, whom he succeeded. His defense (1791) of his brother-in-law, Louis XVI of France, helped to precipitate the FRENCH REVOLUTIONARY WARS, which spelled the end of the Holy Roman Empire.

Leopold, kings of the Belgians. **Leopold I,** 1790–1865 (r.1831–65), was the youngest son of Francis Frederick, duke of Saxe-Coburg-Saalfeld. After the death (1817) of his wife, Princess Charlotte, daughter of the English prince regent, Leopold lived in England until elected king of newly formed Belgium. In 1832 he married a daughter of LOUIS PHILIPPE of France; their daughter became the wife of MAXIMILIAN, emperor of Mexico. Leopold introduced ministerial responsibility, electoral reform, and a national bank. **Leopold II,** 1835–1909 (r.1865–1909), was the son of Leopold I. With the aid of H.M. STANLEY he founded (1884–85) the Congo Free State (see ZAÏRE) under his personal rule. Using slave labor he amassed a huge fortune, until scandal forced him to turn the Congo over to the Belgian government. In Belgium, labor unrest forced the granting (1893) of universal male suffrage. His nephew, ALBERT I, succeeded him. **Leopold III,** 1901–83 (r.1934–51), was the son of Albert I. He led the Belgian army in resisting the German invasion in May 1940, but surrendered on May 28 over cabinet opposition. Held by the Germans until 1945, he was accused of collaboration on his return to Belgium and forced into exile in Switzerland while his brother, Prince Charles, acted as regent. He was allowed to return in 1950 but soon abdicated in favor of his son, BAUDOUIN I.

Leopold, kings of Bohemia and Hungary: see LEOPOLD, rulers of the Holy Roman Empire.

Lepanto, battle of, Oct. 7, 1571, naval battle between the Christians and Turks fought in the Gulf of Patras, off Lepanto, Greece. The fleet of the Holy League, commanded by JOHN OF AUSTRIA, virtually destroyed the fleet of the OTTOMAN EMPIRE (Turkey), ending the threat of Turkish naval supremacy in the Mediterranean.

Lepidus, family of the ancient Roman patrician gens Aemilia. **Marcus Aemilius Lepidus,** d. 77 B.C., was given a proconsulship in Gaul, but raised an army in N Italy. He was defeated, and fled from Italy. His son, **Marcus Aemilius Lepidus,** d. 13 B.C., supported ANTONY and, with Antony and Octavian (AUGUSTUS), formed the Second Triumvirate. Octavian became suspicious of Lepidus and curbed his powers.

Leppard, Raymond (John), 1927–, English conductor, composer, and harpsichordist. Best known for "realizing" 17th-cent. Venetian opera, he has led the English Chamber Orchestra (1959–77), BBC Philharmonic (1973–80), and Indianapolis Symphony (1987–). He has also composed film scores, e.g., for *Lord of the Flies* (1963).

leprosy or **Hansen's disease,** chronic infectious disease, caused by *Mycobacterium leprae,* affecting the skin and superficial nerves. It is found mainly, but not exclusively, in tropical regions. The disease produces numerous skin and nerve lesions, which, if left untreated, enlarge and may result in severe disfigurement. Leprosy is treated—successfully in most cases—with dapsone and other drugs. In 1993 the World Health Organization began a campaign to eliminate leprosy by 2000.

lepton: see ELEMENTARY PARTICLES.

Lerdo de Tejada, Miguel [lĕr'thō dā tāhä'thä], d. 1861, Mexican public official. He initiated (1856) the Ley Lerdo, providing for the forced sale of church property, and helped to draft the liberal constitution of 1857. His brother, **Sebastián Lerdo de Tejada,** 1820?–1889, succeeded JUÁREZ as president (1872–76) and incorporated the new reform laws in the constitution of 1874. He was overthrown by Gen. DÍAZ.

Lermontov, Mikhail Yurevich [lyĕr'məntŭf], 1814–41, Russian romantic poet and novelist. His poem "Death of a Poet" (1837), protesting the death of PUSHKIN in a duel, led to his banishment to the Caucasus, whose stirring landscape became a vital element in his work. The Byronic poem "The Angel" (1832), the narrative *The Demon* (1841), and *Mtsyri* (1840) are among the works on which his poetic reputation, second only to Pushkin's, rests. His novel *A Hero of Our Time* (1840), about a disenchanted nobleman, is a classic of psychological realism. Lermontov was killed in a duel.

Le Sage, Alain René [lə säzh'], 1668–1747, French novelist and dramatist. His masterpiece, *Gil Blas* (1715–35), a rambling picaresque romance, was unusual for its realism and attention to detail. It was a major influence on the development of the realistic NOVEL. The satirical comedy *Turcaret* (1709) is his best dramatic work.

lesbianism: see HOMOSEXUALITY.

Lesbos or **Lésvos,** island (1991 pop. 103,700), c.630 sq mi (1,630 sq km), E Greece, in the Aegean Sea, near Turkey. It has vast olive groves and also produces wine, wheat, and citrus fruits; fishing and tanning are important. A center of BRONZE AGE civilization, it was settled c.1000 B.C. by the Aeolians and became a brilliant cultural center of ancient Greece. It was the home of SAPPHO, ARISTOTLE, and EPICURUS.

Lesotho [ləsō'tō], officially Kingdom of Lesotho, formerly Basutoland, kingdom (1992 est. pop. 1,848,000), 11,720 sq mi (30,355 sq km), S Africa, enclave within South Africa. MASERU is the capital. The eastern two thirds of Lesotho is dominated by the Drakensberg mountain range, with elevations of more than 11,000 ft (3,353 m); the rest of the country is a narrow, rocky tableland. Only a small percentage of the land is arable, but corn, sorghum, and wheat are extensively cultivated. Sheep, cattle, and Angora goats are raised. Mineral resources include some diamonds. Industry is limited to light manufacturing. Lesotho is heavily dependent on SOUTH AFRICA for economic support, and more than 100,000 Sotho work in South African mines. The population is homogeneous, with nearly 100% belonging to the Sotho group. Some 80% are Christian. Non-Sothos are barred from owning land. English and Sesotho, a Bantu tongue, are official languages; Zulu and Xhosa are also spoken.

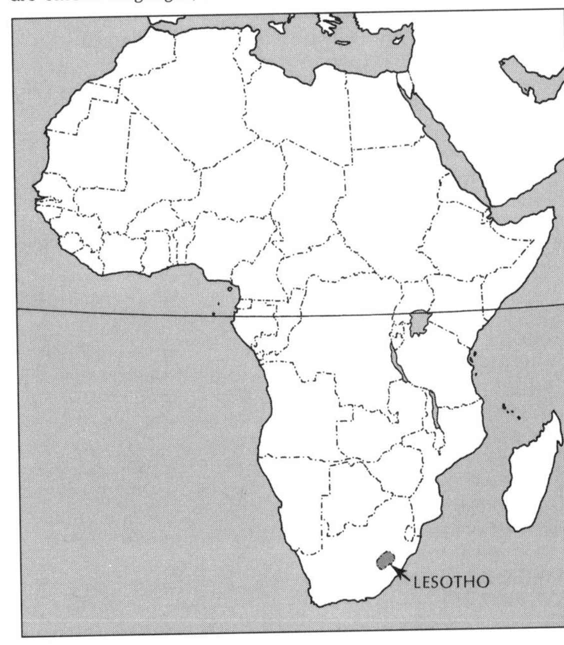

History. The region that is now Lesotho was originally inhabited by the San (Bushmen). In the 17th and 18th cent. refugees from various tribal wars entered the area, and in the early 19th cent. they were welded together into the Basuto nation by the paramount chief, Moshesh, who founded Lesotho's royal line. Threatened by Boer incursions, in 1868 Moshesh placed his people under British protection. Basutoland, as the territory was known, resisted plans for its incorporation into the newly created Union of South Africa (1910) and ultimately gained independence as the kingdom of Lesotho (1966). Chief Leabua Jonathan, prime minister since independence, suspended the constitution in 1970 when the opposition Congress party appeared to win the elections, and effectively reduced the king to a figurehead. A coup led by Major Gen. Justin Lekhanya toppled Jonathan in 1986. In 1991 Lekhanya was forced to resign, and Col. Elias Tutsoane Ramaena came to power as chairman of a military council. A free election resulted in a Basotho Congress party landslide, and Ntsu Mokhehle became (1993) prime minister.

Lesseps, Ferdinand Marie, vicomte de, 1805–94, French diplomat and engineer. After retiring from consular service, he organized a company and supervised (1859–69) the building of the SUEZ CANAL. In 1878 he headed another company formed to build the PANAMA CANAL. Its bankruptcy (1888) led to his conviction for misappropriation of funds. Later observers have felt he was guilty only of negligence.

Lesser Antilles: see WEST INDIES.

Lessing, Doris, 1919–, British novelist; b. Iran. Her themes include Africa, Communism, women, and global catastrophe. The series collectively titled *The Children of Violence* includes *The Four-Gated City* (1969). Other novels are *The Golden Notebook* (1962) and a series of science-fiction novels entitled *Canopus in Argos: Archives,* of which *The Making of the Representative for Planet 8* (1982) is best known.

Lessing, Gotthold Ephraim, 1729–81, German philosopher and dramatist, a leader of the ENLIGHTENMENT. His critical essays, *Hamburgische Dramaturgie* (1767–69), attacked French classical theater and held SHAKESPEARE up as a model for German playwrights. His own plays include *Miss Sara Sampson* (1755), *Minna von Barnhelm* (1763), *Emilia Galotti* (1772), and *Nathan the Wise* (1779), a plea for the peaceful coexistence of religious faiths. In *Education of the Human Race* (1780), he applied Enlightenment ideas of progress and evolution to religion. His *Laokoon* (1766) is a classic of modern aesthetics.

letterpress: see PRINTING.

Lettish or **Latvian,** language belonging to the Baltic subfamily of the Indo-European family of languages. See LANGUAGE (table).

lettuce, garden annual (*Lactuca sativa* and varieties) of the COMPOSITE family. Long cultivated as a salad plant and unknown in the wild state, lettuce is possibly derived from the weed called wild lettuce (*L. scariola*). Three types of lettuce are grown: head, leaf, and Cos, or romaine (the most heat-tolerant).

leukemia, any of a variety of cancerous disorders of blood-forming tissues (bone marrow, lymphatics, spleen), characterized by the abnormal proliferation of white blood cells and consequently a crowding out of other blood elements. There are many types, each named after the type of cell affected, whether the disease is chronic or acute, and whether it affects children or adults. No one cause of leukemia is known, but genetic abnormalities, certain viruses, and exposure to toxic chemicals are implicated in certain subtypes. Symptoms include weakness, fever, bleeding, and susceptibility to infection. CHEMOTHERAPY is effective against some forms of leukemia, especially those occurring in children. Transfusions and bone marrow transplants are also often effective. New therapies made possible by genetic engineering techniques are being studied. See also CANCER.

levadopa: see L-DOPA.

Le Vau, Louis [lə vō], 1612–70, French architect, involved in most of the important building projects for LOUIS XIV. He worked (after 1655) on the LOUVRE, and designed the palace of VERSAILLES and the chateau of Vaux-le-Vicomte.

lever: see MACHINE.

leveraged buyout, the takeover of a company, financed by borrowed funds. Often, the target company's assets are used as security for the loans acquired to finance the purchase. The acquiring company or group then repays the loans from the target company's profits or by selling its assets. Many leveraged buyouts have been financed through JUNK BONDS.

Leverrier, Urbain Jean Joseph [ləvĕryā'], 1811–77, French astronomer. On the basis of calculations derived from the perturbations of the motions of the planet Uranus, he and John Couch ADAMS independently and accurately predicted the presence of a transuranian planet; Leverrier's prediction, published first, led directly to the discovery (1846) of the planet NEPTUNE.

Levertov, Denise, 1923–, American poet; b. England. Her clear, spare poems are included in such collections as *The Double Image* (1946), *Here and Now* (1957), *Relearning the Alphabet* (1970), and *A Door in the Hive* (1989).

Lévesque, René [lāvĕk'], 1922–87, French-Canadian separatist leader, premier of Quebec (1976–85). Originally a member of the Liberal party, he helped form (1968) Le Parti Québécois, which advocated Quebec's secession from Canada. In 1980 Quebec voters rejected a sovereignty-association scheme in a provincial referendum, but Lévesque's popularity in Quebec remained high. He resigned as party leader and premier (1985) when the party voted to temporarily abandon the goal of separation.

Levi: see LEVITES.

Levi, Primo, 1919–87, Italian writer. He was a chemist of Jewish descent. His writings focus on the 20th-cent. Jewish experience. His works include his 1947 memoir, *Survival in Auschwitz; The Reawakening* (1963); and *The Periodic Table* (1984). He committed suicide.

Lévi-Strauss, Claude, 1908–, French anthropologist. The founder of structural anthropology, he believes that all cultures order the elements of the universe into systems. Structuralism compares the formal relationships among the elements in each system, revealing structural similarities underlying all cultures. Structuralism has influenced linguistics and other social sciences, as well as criticism in literature and the arts. His major works include *Structural Anthropology* (1958), *The Savage Mind* (1962), *Totemism* (1962), *Mythologiques* (4 vol., 1964–71), and *The View from Afar* (1985).

Levites, among the ancient Hebrews, a religious caste of priests, descended from Levi, son of JACOB. They alone of the tribes received no allotment of land in CANAAN. With the unification of worship at JERUSALEM, the Levites became temple servants with hereditary assignments. LEVITICUS is named for them.

Leviticus [lĭvĭt'əkəs], book of the OLD TESTAMENT, third of the five books of the PENTATEUCH ascribed by tradition to MOSES, essentially a collection of liturgical legislation, including laws on the installation of priests (8–10) and on purity and impurity, e.g., dietary laws (11–16).

levulose: see FRUCTOSE.

Lévy-Bruhl, Lucien, 1857–1939, French philosopher, psychologist, and ethnologist. Known for his work on the mentality of preliterate peoples, he wrote such works as *How Natives Think* (1910) and *Primitive Mentality* (1922).

Lewes, George Henry [lo͞o'ĭs], 1817–78, English author. As the editor of the *Fortnightly Review,* he gained fame as a critic. His most noted work is his *Life of Goethe* (1855). In 1854 he began living with Mary Ann Evans (George ELIOT), whose work he encouraged.

Lewis. For rulers thus named, see LOUIS.

Lewis, Carl, 1961–, American sprinter and jumper; b. Birmingham, Ala. In the 1984 Olympics he won four gold medals, in the 100 meters, the 200 meters, the long jump, and the 4×100 meter relay. This duplicated Jesse OWENS's celebrated feat in the 1936 Berlin Olympics. In 1988 Lewis won three more Olympic medals (two gold and a silver), and in 1992 he won two gold medals. He set a new world record (9.86 sec) in the 100 meters in 1991.

Lewis, Cecil Day: see DAY LEWIS, CECIL.

Lewis, C(live) S(taples), 1898–1963, English author, noted for his exposition of Christian tenets. His works include *The Allegory of Love* (1936), on medieval romantic love, and the ironic *Screwtape Letters* (1942). He also wrote outer-planet fantasies with moral overtones, e.g., *Out of the Silent Planet* (1938), and criticism.

Lewis, Jerry Lee, 1935–, American singer and composer; b. Ferriday, La. Combining country music elements with an energetic performance style, he was an early star of ROCK MUSIC. His songs include "Whole Lotta Shakin' Goin' On" and "Great Balls of Fire."

Lewis, John L(lewellyn), 1880–1969, American labor leader; b. Lucas co., Iowa. He worked as a coal miner and rose through the union ranks to become president (1920) of the United Mine Workers of America (UMW). Forceful and eloquent, Lewis built up the union and won the loyalty of the miners. He was an important figure in the AFL until he founded (1935) the CIO, which he headed until 1940 (see AMERICAN FEDERATION OF LABOR AND CONGRESS OF INDUSTRIAL ORGANIZATIONS). At first a supporter of Pres. F.D. Roosevelt, Lewis became his principal labor critic, backing Wendell Willkie in the 1940 election. In 1942 Lewis pulled the UMW out of the CIO. During World War II he led the coal miners in several strikes, arousing public anger, and drew a heavy fine in 1948 for failing to obey a court order ending a protracted strike. In the 1950s Lewis, becoming less aggressive, sought accommodation with the depressed coal industry. He resigned the UMW presidency in 1960.

Lewis, Meriwether, 1774–1809, American explorer; b. near Charlottesville, Va. Friend and secretary to Pres. JEFFERSON, Lewis headed (1803–6) the LEWIS AND CLARK EXPEDITION. In 1807 he was made governor of the Louisiana Territory.

Lewis, (Percy) Wyndham, 1886–1957, English author and painter; b. Maine. He was associated with VORTICISM, but his own paintings, which are in several important museums, were often more conventional. He also wrote iconoclastic essays and novels like *The Revenge for Love* (1937).

Lewis, Sinclair, 1885–1951, American novelist; b. Sauk Centre, Minn. A brilliant satirist, he offered a devastating picture of middle-class American life. He achieved notice with *Main Street* (1920), a satire on small-town midwestern life. *Babbitt* (1922), a portrait of an average American destroyed by conformity, is considered his greatest book. Lewis satirized the medical profession in *Arrowsmith* (1925; Pulitzer) and attacked hypocritical religiosity in *Elmer Gantry* (1927). Among his 22 novels are *Dodsworth* (1929), *It Can't Happen Here* (1935), and *Cass Timberlane* (1945). In 1930 he became the first American to win the Nobel Prize in literature.

Lewis, Sir (William) Arthur, 1915–91, British economist; b. St. Lucia, West Indies. After teaching at the London School of Economics and the Univ. of Manchester, he was (1959–63) an administrator at the Univ. of the West Indies in Jamaica and (1963–83) a professor at Princeton Univ. A specialist in the economy of developing nations, he was a co-winner of the 1979 Nobel Prize in economics, becoming the first black Nobel laureate in a category other than peace.

Lewis and Clark Expedition, 1803–6, U.S. expedition that explored the LOUSIANA PURCHASE and the land beyond to the Pacific Ocean. Led by Meriwether LEWIS and William Clark (see under CLARK, GEORGE ROGERS), it was dispatched to find a land route to the Pacific, strengthen U.S. claims to the OREGON territory, and gather information on Native Americans and the country. The group started up the Missouri R. from ST. LOUIS in May 1804, and in 1805 their Shoshone woman guide, SACAJAWEA, led them across the Rockies. They descended the Clearwater, Snake, and Columbia rivers and built Fort Clatsop, where they wintered, on the Pacific coast. On their return they separated for a time, Lewis descending the Marias R. and Clark the Yellowstone. Reunited, they arrived in St. Louis in Sept. 1806. Their well-documented expedition opened vast new territories to the U.S.

Lexington, city (1990 pop. 225,366), seat of Fayette co., N central Ky., in the bluegrass region; inc. 1832. It is the major U.S. center for the raising of thoroughbred horses, and a tobacco and bluegrass seed market. Shipping of Kentucky's coal and other products is important, and there are diversified manufactures. The Univ. of Kentucky is in Lexington; "Ashland," the home of Henry CLAY (1806, rebuilt 1850s), is notable.

Lexington and Concord, battles of, Apr. 19, 1775, opening battles of the AMERICAN REVOLUTION. To seize colonial military stores at CONCORD, the British marched from Boston and were met at Lexington by colonial militia. After a brief engagement, the colonials withdrew. The British marched to Concord, where they fought another battle and began a harried retreat to Boston that cost them over 200 casualties.

Leyden, Lucas van: see LUCAS VAN LEYDEN.

Leyden jar: see CAPACITOR.

Lhasa [lä-sŭ], city (1986 est. pop. 84,500), capital and chief trade center of Tibet Autonomous Region, SW China. The center of TIBETAN BUDDHISM before the Chinese occupied Tibet in 1951, Lhasa was known as the Forbidden City because of its remoteness and the hostility of the Lamaist clergy to foreigners. Located here are the magnificent Potala, former palace of the Dalai Lama; the Drepung monastery, one of the largest in the world; and the outwardly unimpressive, but extremely holy, Jokang temple.

Lhasa apso, small NONSPORTING DOG; shoulder height, c.11 in. (27.9 cm); weight, 13–15 lb (5.9–6.8 kg). Its heavy, straight, long coat may be any of various colors, with shades of gold preferred. Developed centuries ago in Tibet, it was given as a gift to dignitaries by the Dalai Lamas.

Li, chemical symbol of the element LITHIUM.

Liaquat Ali Khan [lēä'kət älē' kän], 1895–1951, first prime minister of PAKISTAN (1947–51). He was the chief lieutenant of Muhammad Ali JINNAH and a leader of the Muslim League. After Pakistan was created in 1947, he served as prime minister until he was assassinated in 1951.

libel and slander, in TORT law, two forms of defamation (unjustified disparagement of the good name and reputation of an individual). Defamation is classed as libel when it is in some permanent form, such as writing or a picture; when it is oral, it is classed as slander. In both cases, it must be revealed to a third party. A statement is generally not defamatory if it is true, but under some statutes a defendant must prove good motives in the utterance. Certain privileged situations (e.g., testimony in a court of law) shield a defamer from liability. The usual remedy for defamation is monetary damages.

Liberal Democratic party (LDP), Japanese political party. It began as the conservative Liberal party, which, under YOSHIDA SHIGERU, became the dominant political force in Japan (1949) and retained power after the 1952 elections. The Liberals merged (1955) with the newly created Japan Democratic party. Retaining control of the Japanese government for 38 years, the LDP supported Japan's alliance with the U.S. and fostered close links between Japanese business and government. It lost its parliamentary majority in the 1993 elections, which put a coalition government in power, but remained Japan's largest political party.

Liberal party, British political party. An outgrowth of the WHIG party, it was supported by the bulk of the industrial and business classes enfranchised by the REFORM BILL of 1832. Lord John Russell, a leading Liberal, became prime minister in 1846. The party advocated LAISSEZ FAIRE and initially opposed social legislation. Under William GLADSTONE, however, it accepted electoral and social reforms and, in 1884, took up the cause of Irish HOME RULE. Herbert Asquith (see OXFORD AND ASQUITH, 1ST EARL OF), a Liberal imperialist, became prime minister in 1908. He was followed by David LLOYD GEORGE, who led a coalition government during WORLD WAR I. By the 1930s the Liberals had become a small third party. In 1981 it entered into an alliance with the newly formed SOCIAL DEMOCRATIC PARTY, later (1988) merging with it to form the Social and Liberal Democratic party.

Liberal party, Canadian political party. Reform parties dominated politics in several provinces after confederation (1867), but a strong national party was hampered by Liberal weakness in Quebec. The party's only prime minister in the next 30 years was Alexander MACKENZIE. Louis RIEL's execution, however, angered Quebec, and Wilfrid LAURIER moderated the anticlericalism of Quebec Liberals. He became prime minister in 1896 and forged an English-French coalition that appealed to the middle class. Liberal W.L.M. KING led Canada for much of the 1920s, 30s, and 40s. His successor, Louis ST. LAURENT, lost much of the party's western base, but Lester PEARSON slowly rebuilt the party. Constitutional questions and Quebec dominated Pierre TRUDEAU's tenure. John TURNER briefly succeeded Trudeau as prime minister and led the party until 1990, when Herb Grey and then Jean CHRÉTIEN became party leader. In 1993 dissatisfaction with the economy returned the Liberals to power.

Liberal Republican party, U.S. political party formed in 1872 by Republicans unhappy with the corruption and policies of Pres.

Grant's administration. Among its leaders were Carl SCHURZ, Horace GREELEY, and Charles SUMNER. The party nominated Greeley for president, a choice acceptable to the Democrats, but Greeley proved unpopular with many party leaders and Grant easily won reelection.

liberation theology, doctrine that belief in the Christian Gospel requires that one support the struggles of the poor for freedom and economic justice. Many leftist Catholics, especially in South America, have advocated this mixture of religion and politics, but conservatives, including Pope JOHN PAUL II, have criticized the concept, especially when it is used to support violent revolution and Marxism.

Liberia, officially Republic of Liberia, republic (1992 est. pop. 2,462,000). 43,000 sq mi (113,370 sq km), W Africa, bordered by the Atlantic Ocean (SW), Sierra Leone (NW), Guinea (N), and Côte d'Ivoire (E). MONROVIA is the capital. Liberia has three geographic regions: a flat coastal plain, a dominant interior area of densely forested foothills, and a northern mountain area with elevations of over 4,500 ft (1,370 m). Liberia's economy, formerly dependent on subsistence farming and rubber production, is now based primarily on exports of iron ore. Other exports are rubber, timber, coffee, cocoa, and diamonds. The government derives a sizable income from registration of foreign ships while exercising no control over them, a practice that has made the Liberian merchant marine appear to be one of the world's largest. The descendants of American settlers, though not numerous, long wielded considerable political influence. The indigenous African population is made up of diverse ethnic groups and mainly practices traditional religions. Islam and Christianity are significant minority faiths. English is the official language, but tribal tongues are widely spoken.

History. Liberia was founded in 1821 as a haven for freed American slaves by the AMERICAN COLONIZATION SOCIETY. The first American settlers arrived in 1822, and some 15,000 were eventually settled. The colony became independent in 1847. Constitutional issues, mounting foreign debts (the government was bankrupt by 1909), and the loss of disputed territory threatened the stability of the new nation, but with U.S. help, independence was preserved. In 1930 revelations of government connivance in a slave trade from Liberia resulted in the downfall of the regime and proposals for international control. Such action was averted, however, by the leadership of presidents Edwin Barclay (1930–44) and William V.S. Tubman (1944–71); the latter opened Liberia to international investment, gave tribal peoples a greater voice in the country's affairs, and improved living standards. In 1979, after years of political stability, a government proposal to increase the price of rice (the main staple) produced widespread violence. A year later a coup led by soldiers of African origin ended 100 years of rule by Americo-Liberians; Pres. William R. TOLBERT (who had succeeded Tubman in 1971) was assassinated, and the country was placed under military rule, with 28-year-old Samuel K. Doe assuming the presidency. Doe's tyrannical rule and his favoritism toward his own ethnic group precipitated a civil war in 1990. In late 1990 Doe was captured by rebels and executed; fighting subsequently broke out between the rebel factions. Peacekeeping forces led by Nigeria largely ended the fighting, but progress toward peace stalled, with the peacekeepers controlling Monrovia and environs and rebel forces under Charles Taylor controlling most of the rest of Liberia. A 1993 accord established a cease-fire and interim government and called for multiparty elections in 1994. Implementation of the accord, however, was slow, and the emergence of new armed groups threatened to disrupt the pact.

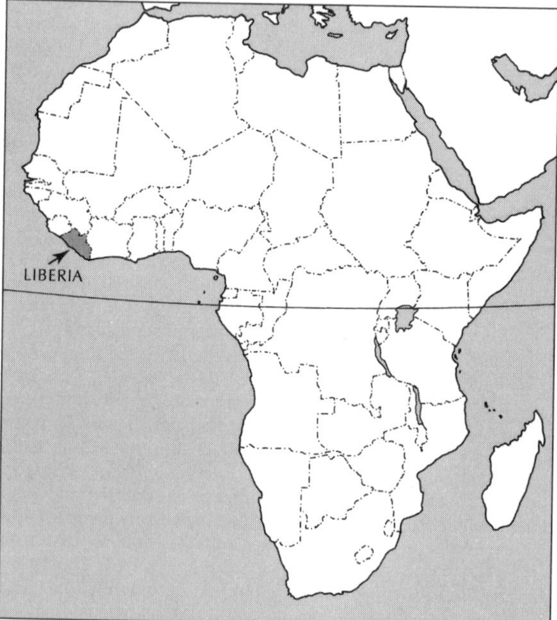

Liberty, Statue of, colossal (152-ft/46-m) statue on Liberty Island, N.Y.C., in Upper New York Bay, in New Jersey waters but under New York jurisdiction. Designed by F.A. BARTHOLDI, it was presented to the U.S. by the Franco-American Union to commemorate the AMERICAN REVOLUTION. Dedicated in 1886, it became a national monument in 1924 and was extensively restored in 1986.

Liberty Bell, historic relic housed near Independence Hall, Philadelphia. Hung in 1753, it was rung in July 1776 to proclaim the DECLARATION OF INDEPENDENCE. It was hidden (1777–78) from the British in Allentown, Pa., and later returned. The bell was cracked in 1835 and again in 1846.

library, place containing an organized collection of written, artistic, or other kinds of materials. The earliest known library was a collection of clay tablets in Babylonia in the 21st cent. B.C. Other early libraries were the Babylonian library at Nineveh of King ASSURBANIPAL (d. 626? B.C.) and the sacred library in the Temple at JERUSALEM. In 330 B.C. the first public library in Greece was established in order to preserve accurate examples of the works of the great dramatists. The most famous libraries of antiquity were those at ALEXANDRIA, in Egypt, and PERGAMUM. Roman libraries were brought from Greece, Asia Minor, and Syria as the result of conquests (1st and 2d cent. B.C.). The great Roman public libraries were the Octavian (destroyed A.D. 80) and the Ulpian, founded in the reign of TRAJAN. Early Christian libraries were located in monasteries; those founded in Britain by Anglo-Saxon monks produced fine manuscript illumination. The Arabs (9th–15th cent.) collected many fine libraries. In the RENAISSANCE, nobles like Lorenzo de' Medici (see MEDICI, family) had great libraries, and many of the major university libraries, e.g., Bologna and Oxford, were created. The Vatican Library, the oldest public library in Europe, was founded in the 15th cent. In the U.S., the Boston Public Library opened in 1653 and was followed by the Library Company of Philadelphia in 1731, a circulating library. In 1833 the first U.S. tax-supported library opened in Peterborough, N.H. The American Library Association, formed in 1876, spurred improvements in library methods and the training of librarians. Libraries in the U.S. and Britain benefited greatly from the philanthropy of Andrew CARNEGIE, who strengthened local interest in libraries by making his grants contingent upon public support. Among the innovations of the late 19th cent. were free public access to books and branch libraries. In the early 20th cent. traveling libraries, or "bookmobiles," began to take books to readers in rural areas. Modern innovations include reader's advisory services, interlibrary loans, lecture series, public book reviews, and the maintenance of special recording and juvenile collections. Two widely used systems of classification are the Dewey decimal system of Melvil DEWEY and the Library of Congress system. Since the 1930s a number of technological tools have been developed that have revolutionized library science. These include microphotographic techniques for text preservation (microfilm; microfiche); photocopiers; and COMPUTER data banks that enable libraries to store vast amounts of information (see INFORMATION STORAGE AND RETRIEVAL) and produce comprehensive indexes and catalogs.

Libreville, city (1985 est. pop. 236,000), capital of Gabon, a port on the Gabon R. estuary, near the Gulf of Guinea. It is an administrative center and has petroleum and plywood industries. Founded in 1843 as a French trading station to which freed slaves were sent, it was named Libreville [Fr., = freetown] in 1848. It was the chief port of FRENCH EQUATORIAL AFRICA until the development of Pointe-Noire in the 1930s.

Libya, officially Socialist People's Libyan Arab Jamahirya, republic (1992 est. pop. 4,485,000), 679,358 sq mi (1,759,540 sq km), N Africa, bordered by Algeria and Tunisia (W), the Mediterranean Sea (N), Egypt and Sudan (E), and Chad and Niger (S). The principal cities are TRIPOLI (the capital) and TOBRUK. Most of Libya is part of the SAHARA desert; the population is restricted to a coastal strip along the Mediterranean and a few widely scattered oases in the Libyan desert, in the east, and the Fazzan region, in the south. The discovery of oil in 1958 transformed Libya from a poor agricultural country into one of the world's leading petroleum producers, with vast sums to spend on social, agricultural, and military development. The discovery of oil in 1958 transformed Libya from a poor agricultural country into one of the world's leading petroleum producers, with vast sums to spend on social, agricultural, and military development. Petroleum accounts for 95% of export earnings and more than 50% of national income; Libya is also an important producer of natural gas. Major crops include cereals, olives, fruits, dates, and vegetables. The majority of the inhabitants are Arabs, but there are scattered communities of Berbers and, in the southwest, many of mixed Berber and African descent. Of the work force of about one million, over 25% are resident foreigners. Islam is the official religion (most Libyans are SUNNI Muslims), and Arabic is the official language.

History. At various times in its history the territory that is now Libya was occupied by Carthage, Rome, Arabia, Morocco, Egypt, and Spain. It was part of the Ottoman Empire from 1551 to 1911, serving in the 18th cent. as a base for pirates who, in return for immunity, provided large revenues to the local ruler. Libya was seized by Italy in 1911, but Libyan resistance continued until the 1930s. During WORLD WAR II, as an Italian colony, it was one of the main battlegrounds of N Africa (see NORTH AFRICA, CAMPAIGNS IN), passing under an Anglo-French military government when the Axis was defeated in the area in 1943. In accordance with a UN decision, in 1951 the country became independent as the United Kingdom of Libya, with King Idris I as ruler. Idris was ousted in 1969 in a coup d'etat led by Col. Muammar al-QADAFFI, who established an anti-Western dictatorship. British and American bases were closed in 1970, and unification was sought, unsuccessfully, with several other Arab countries. An implacable foe of Israel, Qadaffi used Libya's vast oil wealth to help support the Palestinian guerrilla movement, particularly radical elements. In 1979 Libya intervened in Uganda to help keep Idi AMIN in power, and in 1981 it dispatched troops into neighboring CHAD (Libya had occupied the disputed Aozou Strip, in N Chad, in 1973), withdrawing most of them later that year. Qaddafi's forces continued to take sides in Chadian fighting, eventually occupying much of N Chad, but they were pushed back somewhat in 1987. In 1990 the dispute over the Aozou Strip was submitted to the International Court of Justice. As a member of OPEC (see ORGANIZATION OF PETROLEUM EXPORTING COUNTRIES) Libya has been a leading exponent of limiting production and increasing prices of petroleum. In the late 1980s the U.S. took action against Libya for its backing of terrorist activities against U.S. citizens, including an air strike (1986) on Qaddafi's residence and other sites in Libya. Since 1986 Libya has attempted to form a union with the Arabic countries of the MAGHREB, especially Algeria and Tunisia. In 1992 the UN Security Council accused Libya of supporting state terrorism and called for a ban on air flights and arms sales to it unless suspects in the LOCKERBIE and another airplane bombing were turned over to the U.S., Britain, and France.

lichee: see LITCHI.

lichen, complex organism consisting of blue-green or green ALGAE living symbiotically with a FUNGUS, usually sac fungi. Lichens commonly grow on rocks or trees. The body, or thallus, is composed of fungal filament, or hyphae. The fungi obtains food from the algae and, in turn, absorbs and retains the water that is used by the algae for PHOTOSYNTHESIS. Reproduction of the algae and fungi is usually simultaneous. Lichens can withstand great extremes in temperature and can be found in deserts and the polar regions.

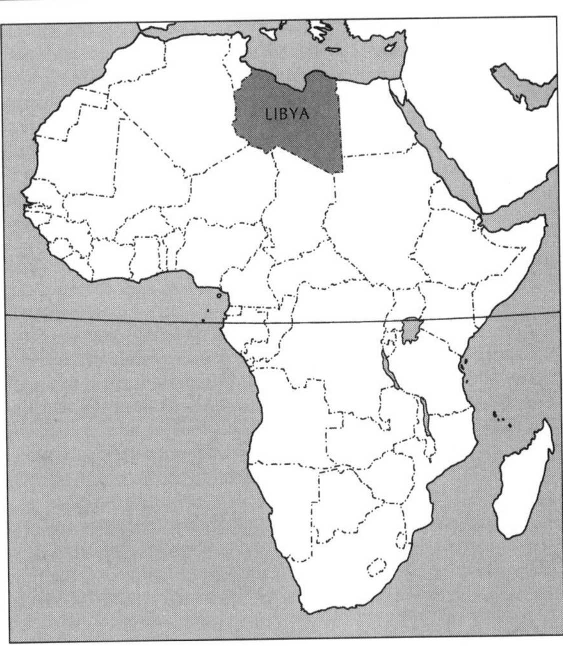

Lichtenstein, Roy, 1923–, American painter; b. N.Y.C. Linked to the POP ART movement, he derives his subject matter from sources such as comic strips. One of his ironic, sophisticated works is *Preparedness* (Guggenheim Mus., N.Y.C.).

Licinius, 250–325, Roman emperor. Coemperor (308) with Galerius, he allied himself with CONSTANTINE I and defeated Maximin in 313, thus becoming sole ruler in the East. He was later defeated and put to death by Constantine.

Licinius (Caius Licinius Calvus Stolo), fl. 375 B.C., tribune to whom the Licinian Rogations are attributed. They strictly limited the amount of public land that one person might hold, limited grazing rights, regulated debts, and ordained that one consul must be a plebeian.

licorice, European, blue-flowered perennial (*Glycyrrhiza glabra*) of the PULSE family; also, the sweet substance obtained from its roots, used medicinally and as a flavoring. It is cultivated chiefly in the Middle East.

Lidice [lĭ'dyĭtsĕ], village, NW Czech Republic. In 1942, in reprisal for the assassination of Nazi official Reinhard Heydrich, the Germans razed Lidice, killed the men, and deported the women and children. After the war a new village was built near the old one, now a memorial.

Lie, Trygve Halvdan [lē], 1896–1968, Norwegian statesman, first secretary general (1946–53) of the UNITED NATIONS. He served in ministerial posts and was foreign minister of his government in exile during World War II before being elected to the UN. His support of UN action during the KOREAN WAR earned him the enmity of the USSR. On leaving the UN he resumed an active role in Norwegian politics.

Liebermann, Max, 1847–1935, German GENRE painter and etcher. Influenced by the BARBIZON painters, Frans HALS, and Jozef ISRAËLS, he developed a style close to IMPRESSIONISM. He depicted the working classes, landscapes, and outdoor groups. Among his works is *Ropewalk* (Metropolitan Mus.).

Liebig, Justus, Baron von [lē'bĭkh], 1803–73, German chemist. As professor (1824–52) at Giessen, he was among the first to establish a chemical teaching laboratory, where some of the leading 19th-cent. chemists were trained. A professor (1852–73) at Munich, he improved methods of organic analysis and discovered chloral; he was also one of the discoverers of chloroform. His work in agricultural chemistry aided in the development of artificial fertilizers.

Liechtenstein, officially Principality of Liechtenstein, principality

(1992 est. pop. 28,600), 61 sq mi (157 sq km), W central Europe, in the Alps between Austria and Switzerland; the Rhine R. forms its western boundary. Vaduz is the capital. Liechtenstein produces machinery and other metal goods, pharmaceuticals, precision instruments, ceramics, and textiles. Most of the firms are owned and operated by Swiss. Tourism and revenues from some 25,000 foreign corporations nominally headquartered in Vaduz because of low taxes and bank secrecy, are important sources of income. Roman Catholicism is the state religion; German is the national language. The 1921 constitution established a parliament elected by male suffrage; not until 1986 did women receive the vote at both the national and local levels.

History. The principality was created in 1719 as a fief of the HOLY ROMAN EMPIRE. A member of the GERMAN CONFEDERATION from 1815, it became independent in 1866. It is closely linked with SWITZERLAND and is represented abroad by the Swiss government. In 1989 Prince Hans-Adam II succeeded his father, Franz Josef II, as sovereign.

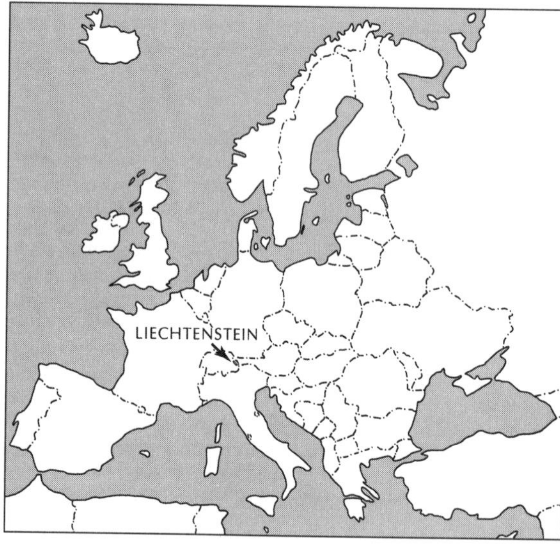

lieder [Ger., = songs], songs written in the German vernacular. Although the term encompasses centuries of musical history, it is popularly used to denote German art songs of the 19th cent. These songs, usually for a single voice, have as lyrics poems by such authors as GOETHE. The most noted composers of lieder are SCHUBERT, SCHUMANN, and BRAHMS.

lie detector, instrument designed to determine whether a subject is lying or telling the truth, generally by detecting evidence of the slight increase in body tension believed to occur when a person knowingly lies. Various devices developed in the 20th cent. and used mainly in police work measure blood pressure, respiration, pulse, electrical changes on the skin, and voice frequencies. Lie detectors are not considered infallible, and test results are not usually accepted as evidence in U.S. courts. The use of lie detectors to screen employees and job applicants is highly controversial.

Liège, city (1991 est. pop. 199,000), E Belgium, at the confluence of the Meuse and Ourthe rivers. The cultural center of French-speaking Belgium, it is a transportation hub and an industrial city whose manufactures include metal goods, armaments, and motor vehicles. It was largely rebuilt after considerable damage in World War II.

Lifar, Serge, 1905–86, Russian dancer, teacher, choreographer, director, and dance historian. He was primarily self-taught and danced (1923–29) with DIAGHILEV. He created (1929) the title role in BALANCHINE's *The Prodigal Son.* He was the principal dancer and ballet-master of the Paris Opéra (1929–44, 1947–58). His own works include *Phèdre* (1950) and *Le Grand Cirque* (1969).

ligament, strong band of CONNECTIVE TISSUE that joins BONES to other bones or to cartilage in the JOINT areas. Ligaments tend to be pliable but not elastic, permitting limited movement while holding attached bones in place. Fibrous sheets supporting internal organs are also ligaments.

light, that part of ELECTROMAGNETIC RADIATION to which the human eye is sensitive. The wavelengths of visible light range from c.400 to c.750 nanometers. If white light, which contains all wavelengths, is separated into a SPECTRUM, each wavelength is seen to correspond to a different COLOR. The scientific study of the behavior of light is called OPTICS; it covers REFLECTION of light by a MIRROR or other object, REFRACTION of light by a LENS or PRISM, and DIFFRACTION of light as it passes by an opaque object. Christiaan HUYGENS proposed (1690) a theory that explained light as a WAVE phenomenon. Isaac NEWTON, however, held (1704) that light is composed of tiny particles, or corpuscules, emitted by luminous bodies. By combining his corpuscular theory with his laws of mechanics, he was able to explain many optical phenomena. Newton's corpuscular theory of light was favored over the wave theory until important experiments, which could be interpreted only in terms of the wave theory, were done on the diffraction and INTERFERENCE of light by Thomas YOUNG (1801) and A.J. FRESNEL (1814–15). In the 19th cent. the wave theory became the dominant theory of the nature of light. The electromagnetic theory of James Clerk MAXWELL (1864) supported the view that visible light is a form of ELECTROMAGNETIC RADIATION. With the acceptance of the electromagnetic theory of light, only two general problems remained. It was assumed that a massless medium, the ETHER, was the carrier of light waves, just as air or water carries sound waves. The famous experiments (1881–87) by A.A. MICHELSON and E.W. Morley, in which they tried unsuccessfully to measure the velocity of the earth with respect to this medium, failed to support the ether hypothesis. With his special theory of RELATIVITY, Albert EINSTEIN showed (1905) that the ether was unnecessary to the electromagnetic theory. Also in 1905, Einstein, in order to explain the PHOTOELECTRIC EFFECT, suggested that light, as well as other forms of electromagnetic radiation, travel as tiny bundles of energy, called light quanta, or PHOTONS, that behave as particles (see QUANTUM MECHANICS). Light thus behaves as a wave, as in diffraction and interference phenomena, or as a stream of particles, as in the photoelectric effect. The theory of relativity predicts that the speed of light in a vacuum (186,282 mi/sec = 299,792.458 km/sec) is the limiting velocity for material particles.

light-emitting diode: see DIODE.

lightning, electrical discharge accompanied by THUNDER, commonly occurring during a THUNDERSTORM. The discharge may take place between two parts of the same cloud, between two clouds, or between a cloud and the earth. Lightning may appear as a jagged streak (forked lightning), as a vast flash in the sky (sheet lightning), or, rarely, as a brilliant ball (ball lightning). The electrical nature of lightning was proved by Benjamin FRANKLIN in his famous kite experiment of 1752. Space probes have photographed lightning on Jupiter and recorded indications of it on Venus, Saturn, Uranus, and Neptune.

lightning bug: see FIREFLY.

light-year, in astronomy, the distance (5.87×10^{12} mi/9.46×10^{12} km) that LIGHT travels in one sidereal YEAR.

lignite or **brown coal,** carbon-containing fuel intermediate between COAL and PEAT, brown or yellowish in color and woody in texture. Lignite contains more moisture than coal and tends to dry and crumble when exposed to air. It burns with a long, smoky flame but little heat.

lignum vitae, tropical American evergreen tree (genus *Guaiacum*). Its dense, durable wood, chiefly from *G. sanctum* and *G. officinale,* is used where strength and hardness are required, e.g., in ship construction and for butcher blocks.

lilac, Old World shrub or small tree (genus *Syringa*) of the OLIVE family, noted for its fragrant, cone-shaped masses of lavender or white flowers. Many variations in form, e.g., double flowers, and color, e.g., rosy pink, have been hybridized from the familiar common lilac (*S. vulgaris*).

Lilienthal, Otto [lēlyəntäl], 1848–96, German aeronautical engineer. A pioneer in experiments with gliders, making more than 2,000 flights, he based his developments largely on observations of birds. He died as a result of a crash landing.

Lilith, Jewish female demon, probably originally the Assyrian storm demon Lilitu. In Jewish folklore she is a vampirelike child-killer and the symbol of lust.

Liliuokalani [lēlēo͞o"ōkälä'nē], 1838–1917, last reigning queen of the Hawaiian islands (1891–93). Her rule caused a revolt of sugar planters (mostly Americans), who deposed her. She wrote many songs, including the popular "Aloha Oe" or "Farewell to Thee."

Lille, city (1990 pop. 172,142), capital of Nord dept., N France. Long known for its textiles, it is the heart of a large, industrially developed metropolitan area. Once chief city of the county of Flanders and home of the 16th-cent. dukes of Burgundy, Lille was captured by the duke of Marlborough (1708) and restored to France by the Treaty of Utrecht (1713).

Lillehammer [lĭ'ləhämər], town (1985 pop. 21,935), S Norway. A lakeside resort and commercial center in an agricultural valley, it was the site of the 1994 winter Olympic games.

Lillie, Beatrice, 1898–1989, English comedienne; b. Canada. She won an international reputation for sophisticated wit in revues, radio and television shows, and films.

Lilly, John: see LYLY, JOHN.

Lilongwe [lēlông'gwā], city (1987 pop. 233,973), capital of Malawi. Located in a fertile agricultural area, it became Malawi's capital in 1966, and government buildings, an international airport, and a railroad link were built.

lily, common name for the family Liliaceae, perennial plants having showy flowers and erect clusters of narrow, grasslike leaves. The lily family is distributed worldwide but is particularly abundant in warm temperate and tropical regions. Most species grow from BULBS or other forms of enlarged underground STEMS. Common wildflowers in the family are ASPHODEL, DOGTOOTH VIOLET, LILY OF THE VALLEY, and TRILLIUM. Ornamentals of commercial importance include lilies, HYACINTHS, MEADOW SAFFRON, SQUILL, and TULIPS; food plants of commercial importance are ASPARAGUS and plants of the ONION genus. YUCCA and ALOE species are popular SUCCULENTS. True lilies include the Madonna lily (*Lilium candidum*) of Europe; the white trumpet lily (*L. longiflorum*) of Japan, which includes the Easter, or Bermuda, lily (var. *eximium*); the tiger lily (*L. tigrinum*) of China; and the Turk's-cap lily (*L. superbum*) and leopard lily (*L. pardalinum*), both of North America.

lily of the valley, fragrant, spring-blooming perennial (genus *Convallaria*) of the LILY family. It has dainty, bell-shaped, white or pink flowers on a stalk between two shiny leaves and grows in the shade. There are two species: the widely cultivated *C. majalis,* native to Europe, and *C. montana,* which grows in the Appalachian Mts.

Lima, city (1993 pop. 6,397,431), W Peru, capital of Peru. Its port is CALLAO. Lima is Peru's largest city, and its urban area is the nation's economic center, with oil-refining and diversified manufacturing industries. Founded by Francisco PIZARRO in 1535, Lima was the magnificent capital of Spain's New World empire until the 19th cent. Rebuilt several times, it retains the architectural styles of several periods but is dominated by modern buildings erected since World War II. Its focal point is the central Plaza de las Armas, with its huge palace and cathedral. The Univ. of San Marcos (est. 1551) is one of the finest in South America.

Limbourg brothers [lăNbo͝or'], fl. 1380–1416, Pol, Jan, and Herman, Franco-Flemish manuscript illuminators. In 1411 they became court painters to Jean, duc de Berry for whom they did their Gothic masterpiece, the *Très Riches Heures* (c.1415; Musée Condé, Chantilly). This exquisite BOOK OF HOURS shows scenes of daily life, and profoundly influenced Flemish painting.

lime: see CALCIUM OXIDE.

lime, small, shrublike tree (*Citrus aurantifolia*) of the RUE family. Its bright-green fruit, smaller and more acid than the LEMON, has long been used to prevent scurvy. The plant grows well in rocky or sandy soils. It is the most frost-sensitive of the CITRUS FRUITS, and chief production areas are in tropical regions.

Limerick, city (1986 pop. 56,279), Co. Limerick, SW Republic of Ireland, on the Shannon estuary. Industries include fishing, food processing, and lacemaking. Taken by the English in the late 12th cent., it was JAMES II's last Irish stronghold after the GLORIOUS REVOLUTION. Preserved there is the Treaty Stone on which the document granting Irish Catholics political and religious liberty was signed in 1691.

limestone, sedimentary rock composed of calcium carbonate. It is ordinarily white but may be colored brown, yellow, or red by iron oxide and blue, black, or gray by carbon impurities. Most limestones are formed from the skeletons of marine invertebrates; a few are chemically precipitated from solution. Organic acids acting on underground deposits lead to formations such as those in Carlsbad Caverns and Mammoth Cave national parks (see NATIONAL PARKS, table). Limestone is used in iron extraction, in cements and building stones, and as a source of lime (see CALCIUM OXIDE). Limestone varieties include CHALK, DOLOMITE, MARBLE, OOLITE, and travertine.

limner, the work of untrained, generally anonymous artists in the American colonies. Their work often showed flat, awkward figures in richly detailed costumes and landscape settings. The limner tradition extended into the 19th cent.

limonite or **brown hematite,** yellowish to dark brown mineral [$FeO(OH) \cdot nH_2O$] occurring worldwide in deposits formed by the alteration of other minerals containing iron. It is used as a pigment (in ocher) and as an ore of IRON. Both iron rust and bog iron ore are limonite.

Limousin or **Limosin, Léonard** [lēmo͞ozăN', lēmôzăN'], c.1505–c.1577, French painter, celebrated member of a Limoges, Belgium, family of enamel artists. He did plates, vases, goblets, medals, and portraits for Francis I and Henry II of France. Remarkable for their elegance, precise techniques, and intense color, his works include plaques of the French kings, Diane de Poitiers, Martin Luther, and John Calvin. His art is best studied at the Louvre.

limpet, GASTROPOD mollusk with a flattened conical shell and a muscular foot with which it clings tightly to rocks. Although occasional specimens reach 4 in. (10 cm) in length, most are smaller. Limpets are found mainly in cooler waters of the Atlantic and Pacific oceans.

Lincoln, Abraham, 1809–65, 16th president of the U.S. (1861–65); b. Hardin co. (now Larue co.), Ky. Born in a log cabin in the backwoods, Lincoln was almost entirely self-educated. In 1831 he settled in New Salem, Ill., and worked as a storekeeper, surveyor, and postmaster while studying law. The story of his brief love affair there with Anne RUTLEDGE is now discredited. In 1834 he was elected to the state legislature, and in 1836 he became a lawyer. He served one term (1847–49) in Congress as a Whig; in 1855 he sought to become a senator but failed. In 1856 he joined the new REPUBLICAN PARTY. He ran again (1858) for the Senate against Stephen A. DOUGLAS, and in a spirited campaign he and Douglas engaged in seven debates. Lincoln was not an ABOLITIONIST, but he regarded slavery as an evil and opposed its extension. Although he lost the election, he had by now made a name for himself, and in 1860 he was nominated by the Republicans for president. He ran against a divided Democratic party and was elected with a minority of the popular vote. To the South, Lincoln's election was a signal for secession. By Inauguration Day seven states had seceded, and four more seceded after he issued a summons to the militia. It is generally agreed that Lincoln handled the vast problems of the CIVIL WAR with skill and vigor. Besides conducting the war, he faced opposition in the North from radical abolitionists, who considered him too mild, and from conservatives, who were gloomy over the prospects of success in the war. His cabinet was rent by internal hatred, and the progress of the war went against the North at first. In 1863 he moved to free the slaves by issuing the EMANCIPATION PROCLAMATION, but preserving the Union remained his main war aim. His thoughts on the war were beautifully expressed in the GETTYSBURG ADDRESS (1863). In 1864 Lincoln ran for reelection against George B. MCCLELLAN and won, partly because of the favorable turn of military affairs after his appointment of Gen. U.S. GRANT as commander-in-chief. Lincoln saw the end of the war but did not live to implement his plan for RECONSTRUCTION. On Apr. 14, 1865, while attending a play at Ford's Theater, in Washington, D.C., he was shot by the actor John Wilkes Booth (see under BOOTH, JUNIUS BRUTUS). He died the next morning. As time passed a full-blown "Lincoln legend" grew, and he became the object of adulation and a symbol of democracy. His wife, **Mary Todd Lincoln,** 1818–82, b. Lexington, Ky., met and married Lincoln in 1842. The harsh portrayal of her by Lincoln's biographer William H. Herndon is certainly exaggerated. Only one of their four sons, **Robert Todd Lincoln,** 1843–1926, b. Springfield, Ill., reached manhood. He served as secretary of war (1881–85) and minister to Great Britain (1889–93). A corporation lawyer for railroad interests, he was president of the Pullman Co. (1897–1911).

Lincoln, city (1990 pop. 191,972), state capital and seat of Lancaster co., SE Nebr.; inc. 1869. It is the railroad, trade, and industrial center for a large grain and livestock area. Many insurance companies have home offices there. The Univ. of Nebraska is in the city; points of interest include the capitol (completed 1934) and the home of W.J. BRYAN.

Lincoln Center for the Performing Arts, New York City, was constructed between 1959 and 1972. The complex includes the Metropolitan Opera, Avery Fisher (formerly Philharmonic) Hall, New York State Theater, Juilliard School (including Alice Tully Hall for recitals), Vivian Beaumont Theater, Library-Museum for the Performing Arts, a band shell, and several Fordham Univ. buildings. Among the architects were W.K. Harrison, Eero SAARINEN, Philip JOHNSON, and Max Abramowitz, and the stage designer Jo MIELZINER. In 1991 a 28-story tower with dormitory rooms, rehearsal studios, movie theater, and other facilities was added to the complex.

Lincoln Memorial, monument in Washington, D.C., built 1914–17. Designed by the American architect Henry Bacon and styled after a Greek temple, it houses a heroic statue of Abraham LINCOLN by Daniel Chester FRENCH and two murals by the American painter Jules Guerin.

Lind, Jenny, 1820–87, Swedish soprano. She became a noted operatic singer in Europe before 1849, when she abandoned opera for concert and oratorio until 1870. Under the management of P.T. BARNUM, she toured (1850–52) the U.S. Known as the "Swedish nightingale," she was one of the great coloraturas of her period.

Lindbergh, Charles Augustus, 1902–74, American aviator who made the first solo nonstop transatlantic flight; b. Detroit. An air reserve officer, he astounded the world on May 21, 1927, by landing in Paris after a flight from New York in his *Spirit of St. Louis.* In the U.S. he received unprecedented acclaim. After the kidnapping and murder of their son in 1932, he and his wife moved to England. In 1936, Lindbergh collaborated with Alexis CARREL in inventing a perfusion pump (artificial heart). In 1938–39 he advocated U.S. neutrality in a European war; when his speeches were branded as pro-Nazi, he resigned his commission, but later flew combat missions in the Pacific. His wife, **Anne Spencer Morrow Lindbergh,** 1906–, b. Englewood, N.J., is a writer. Her works include *North to the Orient* (1935) and *Listen! the Wind* (1938), accounts of flights made with her husband; *Gift from the Sea* (1955), a poetic study of women's problems; and volumes of diaries and letters.

linden, a woody shrub or tree of the family Tiliaceae, including the tropical genus *Corchorus,* from which JUTE is obtained. The name most often refers to deciduous trees (genus *Tilia*) known as linden, lime tree, or basswood, valued for ornament and shade. Their light, strong wood is useful for woodenware and excelsior and in BEE culture; their flowers yield an excellent honey. Fiber made from the tough inner BARK, or bast (hence the name basswood), is used in caning and wickerwork.

Lindner, Richard, 1901–78, American painter; b. Germany. He emigrated to the U.S. in 1941. He is noted for his strangely erotic, almost sadistic images. Mainly of women and strongly influenced by CUBISM, they are painted in harsh, sharply defined colors, e.g., *Ice* (1966; Whitney Mus., N.Y.C.).

Lindsay, (Nicholas) Vachel, 1879–1931, American poet; b. Springfield, Ill. He lived as a modern-day troubadour, selling his drawings and poems as he traveled. His best poetry is virile and strong, with a fine spoken music. Volumes include *The Congo* (1914) and *Collected Poems* (1938).

linen, fabric or yarn made from FLAX, probably the first vegetable FIBER known. Linen fabric dating from 5000 B.C. has been found in Egyptian tombs. Egyptian, Greek, and Jewish priests wore linen to symbolize purity. Brought to N Europe by the Romans, it became the chief European textile of the Middle Ages. French HUGUENOTS carried the art of working flax to Ireland, still the major producer of fine linen. Power looms were first used to weave linen in 1812, but many textile inventions were not applicable to linen thread because its inelasticity made it break readily. Thus the expense of linen weaving relative to that of cotton limits its use. It is woven into fabrics ranging from heavy canvas to sheer handkerchief linen.

linguistics, scientific study of LANGUAGE, covering structure (grammar, PHONETICS, morphology) as well as the history of the relations of languages to one another and language's cultural place in human behavior. Before the 19th cent. language study was mainly a field of philosophy. The German philologist Wilhelm von Humboldt felt that language arose spontaneously from the human spirit: thus languages are different as humans are different. In 1786 Sir William Jones suggested the affinity of Sanskrit and Persian with Greek, opening the study of genetic relationships between languages. With his revelation the school of comparative historical linguistics began. In the 19th cent. Jakob GRIMM, Rasmus Rask, and others did much study establishing the existence of the Indo-European language family. In the 20th cent. the structural or descriptive school of linguistics emerged. The father of structural linguistics, Ferdinand de SAUSSURE, believed in language as a systematic structure linking thought and sound; he thought of language sounds as a series of purely arbitrary linguistic signs. A more recent school, TRANSFORMATIONAL-GENERATIVE GRAMMAR, has received wide notice through the works of Noam CHOMSKY.

Linnaeus, Carolus, 1707–78, Swedish botanist and taxonomist, considered the founder of the binomial system of nomenclature and the originator of modern scientific CLASSIFICATION of plants and animals. In *Systema naturae* (1735) and *Genera plantarum* (1737) he presented his classification system, which remains the basis for modern taxonomy. His more than 180 works also include *Species plantarum* (1753), books on the flora of Lapland and Sweden, and the *Genera morborum* (1763), a classification of diseases.

Linotype: see PRINTING.

linseed oil, amber-colored oil extracted from linseed, the seed of the FLAX plant. The oil obtained from hydraulically pressed seeds is pale in color and practically odorless and tasteless. Oil that has been boiled or extracted by application of heat and pressure is darker, with a bitter taste and unpleasant odor. Linseed oil is used as a drying oil in paints and VARNISHES and in making linoleum, oilcloth, and certain inks. See also FATS AND OILS.

Linz, city (1991 pop. 202,855), capital of Upper Austria, NW Austria, a major port on the Danube R. Manufactures include steel, machinery, and electrical equipment. A Roman settlement, it became (15th cent.) a provincial capital of the Holy Roman Empire. Anton BRUCKNER was organist at the 17th-cent. baroque cathedral. Other historic buildings include the Romanesque Church of St. Martin (8th cent.).

lion, large carnivore (*Panthera leo*) of the CAT family, found in open country in Africa, with a few surviving in India. The tawny-coated male lion usually has a long, thick mane and may reach 9 ft (2.7 m) in length and 400 lb (180 kg) in weight. Lions live in prides of up to 30 individuals. Females do most of the hunting, preying on zebra, antelope, and domestic livestock.

Lipchitz, Jacques [lēpshēts′], 1891–1973, French sculptor; b. Lithuania. Associated with the cubists (see CUBISM), he originated vibrant skeletal constructions and transparent sculptures. During the late 1930s allegories of struggle preoccupied him, e.g., *The Rape of Europa.* His later sculpture includes *The Spirit of Enterprise* (Fairmont Park, Philadelphia) and his celebrated semi-automatics—masses of clay or plasticine molded underwater.

Li Peng, 1928–, Chinese political leader. He has been minister of the Electric Power Industry (1981–82), a member of the Communist party central committee (1982–) and politburo (1985–), acting prime minister (1987–88), and prime minister (1988–). More politically orthodox than some of his contemporaries, he favors greater central economic planning and slower economic growth. He took an active role in the suppression of the 1989 pro-democracy demonstrations.

lipids, natural products in living systems that are insoluble in water but soluble in organic solvents. Major classes of lipids include fatty acids, glycerol-derived lipids (including fats and oils), sphingosine-derived lipids associated with the nervous system, steroids, terpenes, certain aromatic compounds, and long-chain alcohols and waxes. The fat-soluble VITAMINS can be classified as lipids.

Li Po or **Li Tai Po,** c.700–762, Chinese poet. He is known for his unconcern for worldly preferment and love of retirement and wandering. Extremely fecund and facile, he wrote of the grief of lovers parted by duty, the beauty of the countryside, and the solace and wisdom found in wine.

lipoprotein, any organic compound that is composed of both protein and the various fatty substances, e.g. fatty acids and steroids such as cholesterol, classed as LIPIDS. There are several types of lipoproteins present in human blood, including low-density (low protein to fat ratio) lipoproteins (LDL) and high-density (high protein to fat ratio) lipoproteins (HDL). LDLs transport CHOLESTEROL to cells that need it and deposit excess cholesterol in the cells lining the blood vessels, forming the plaque that increases the risk of ARTERIOSCLEROSIS. HDLs transport cholesterol from the tissues to the liver for excretion, retarding the formation of plaque and lowering the risk of arteriosclerosis.

liposome, microscopic, fluid-filled pouch formed by mixing LIPIDS with water or water solutions. Liposomes are used to deliver certain drugs (e.g., insulin and some cancer drugs) to the body. Liposomes have also been used experimentally to carry normal genes into a cell in order to replace defective, disease-causing genes.

Lippi [lēp'pē], two 15th-cent. Italian painters. **Fra Filippo Lippi,** c.1406–1469, called Lippo Lippi, was one of the foremost Florentine painters of the early RENAISSANCE. He may have studied under MASACCIO, and his graceful narrative style influenced northern Italian painters. He is best known for his many easel paintings, e.g., *Virgin Adoring the Christ Child* (Uffizi) and *Madonna with Saints* (Louvre). His most important works are the FRESCOES of the lives of St. Stephen and St. John the Baptist (Prato cathedral). His son, **Filippino Lippi,** c.1457–1504, studied under BOTTICELLI. He completed Masaccio's frescoes in the Brancacci Chapel, Florence, and his early works, e.g., *Madonna Enthroned* (Uffizi), echo Masaccio's style. His later works, e.g., the frescoes in Santa Trinita (Florence), the *Adoration of the Magi* (Uffizi), and the dramatic frescoes of St. John and St. Philip (Santa Maria Novella, Florence), were greatly influenced by Botticelli and echo his graceful expression and refinement of line.

Lippmann, Walter, 1889–1974, American journalist; b. N.Y.C. After serving on the editorial staff of the New York *World* (1921–31), he began writing a highly influential syndicated column, first for the New York *Herald Tribune* (1931–62), later for the Washington *Post* (1962–67). This and his many books made him famous as an analyst of moderate detachment and incisiveness.

Lippold, Richard, 1915–, American sculptor; b. Milwaukee. His abstract constructions of wire and sheet metal are precisely engineered, intricate works in which light plays an integral part. An outstanding example is *Orpheus and Apollo* (Avery Fisher Hall, Lincoln Center, N.Y.C.).

liqueur, strong alcoholic beverage made of nearly neutral spirits flavored with herbs, fruits, or other materials, and usually sweetened. The alcoholic content ranges from c.27% to 80%. Cordials are prepared by steeping fruit pulps or juices in sweetened alcohol. Liqueurs include anisette, benedictine, chartreuse, crème de menthe, and kirsch.

liquid: see STATES OF MATTER.

liquid crystal, liquid whose component particles, atoms or molecules, tend to arrange themselves with a degree of order far exceeding that of ordinary liquids and approaching that of solid crystals. As a result, liquid crystals have many of the optical properties of solid crystals. Moreover, because its atomic or molecular order is not as firmly fixed as that of a solid crystal, a liquid can be easily modified by electromagnetic radiation, mechanical stress, or temperature, with corresponding changes in its optical properties. This characteristic has made possible liquid crystal displays (LCDs) such as those used on digital clocks, electronic calculators, portable televisions, and notebook computers.

Lisbon, Port. *Lisboa,* city (1987 est. pop. 831,000), W Portugal, capital of Portugal on the Tagus R. near the Atlantic Ocean. Lisbon is Portugal's largest city and its cultural, administrative, commercial, and industrial hub. It is set on seven terraced hills and has one of the best harbors in Europe. Its manufactures include textiles, chemicals, and steel. Held by Rome from 205 B.C., it fell (714) to the MOORS, who were expelled in 1147. It became the capital c.1260 and reached its height in the 16th cent. with the establishment of Portugal's empire. Earthquakes, notably in 1755, have destroyed many of the city's old buildings, but some remain, e.g., the Castelo de São Jorge, the Church of St. Roque, and the monastery at Belém. The old quarter, the picturesque Alfama, surrounds the 12th-cent. cathedral (rebuilt later).

LISP: see PROGRAMMING LANGUAGE.

Lister, Joseph Lister, 1st **Baron,** 1827–1912, English surgeon. He introduced to surgery the principle of antisepsis, an outgrowth of Louis PASTEUR's theory that bacteria cause infection, and he founded (1865) modern antiseptic surgery. Using carbolic acid as an antiseptic agent in conjunction with heat sterilization of instruments, he dramatically decreased post operative fatalities. He developed absorbable ligatures and the drainage tube, both now in general use for wounds and incisions.

Liszt, Franz [lĭst], 1811–86, Hungarian composer. A revolutionary figure of romantic music, acknowledged as the greatest pianist of his time, he studied with CZERNY and enthralled audiences with his expressive, dramatic playing. Liszt taught most of the major pianists of the next generation. In his compositions he favored program music, originating the SYMPHONIC POEM, e.g., *Les Préludes* and *Mazeppa* (both: 1856). In his Sonata in B Minor (1853) he developed the technique of transformation of themes and thereby changed the concept of the SONATA form. He influenced Richard WAGNER and Richard STRAUSS. His piano works include six Paganini Études (1851); concertos; and 20 Hungarian Rhapsodies.

Li Tai Po: see LI PO.

litchi or **lichee,** Chinese tree (*Litchi chinensis*) of the soapberry family, also cultivated in other warm countries. It has a small, aromatic pulpy fruit in a thin, rough shell. The best-known Chinese fruit, it is eaten fresh, dried, preserved, or canned.

liter: see WEIGHTS AND MEASURES, table.

lithium (Li), metallic element, discovered in 1817 by J.A. Arfvedson. A soft, silver-white corrosive ALKALI METAL, lithium is the least dense metal. Lithium compounds are used in lubricating greases, special glasses, and ceramic glazes; as brazing and welding fluxes; and in the preparation of plastics and synthetic rubber. Lithium salts are used in medicine to treat MANIC-DEPRESSION. See ELEMENT (table); PERIODIC TABLE.

lithography, type of planographic or surface printing used as an art process and in commercial PRINTING, where the term is synonymous with offset printing; it is also used in the manufacture of INTEGRATED CIRCUITS. Lithography was invented c.1796 by Aloys SENEFELDER, and the Bavarian limestone he used is still considered the best material for art printing. Lithography is based on the antipathy of oil and water. A drawing is made in reverse on the ground (flat) surface of the stone with a crayon or ink that contains soap or grease. The image produced on the stone will accept printing ink and reject water. Once the grease in the ink has penetrated the stone, the drawing is washed off and the stone kept moist. It is then inked with a roller and printed on a lithographic press. As a process, lithography is probably the most unrestricted, allowing a wide range of tones and effects. Several hundred fine prints can be taken from a stone. The medium was employed by many 19th-cent. artists, including GOYA, DELACROIX, DAUMIER, DEGAS, WHISTLER, and TOULOUSE-LAUTREC. Among American artists noted for their lithographs are A.B. DAVIES, George BELLOWS, and CURRIER AND IVES. The medium remains popular with contemporary artists. **Photolithography** is frequently used in the commercial reproduction of art works. With the process, a photographic negative is exposed to light over a gelatin-covered paper, and those portions of the gelatin that are exposed become insoluble. The soluble portions are washed away, and the pattern to be printed is transferred to a stone or metal plate. In color lithography or color photolithography, a stone or plate is required for each color used. The term photolithography is also applied to a process used in INTEGRATED-CIRCUIT manufacture. Light is shined through the non-opaque portions of a pattern, or photomask, onto a piece of specially coated silicon or other SEMICONDUCTOR material. The portions of the coating that were exposed to light harden, and the unhardened coating is removed, as by an acid bath. The uncovered silicon is altered to produce one layer of the integrated circuit. Advances in this technique have replaced visible and ultraviolet light frequencies with electron and X-ray beams, which permit smaller feature sizes in the patterns.

Lithuania, Lithuanian *Lietuva,* officially Republic of Lithuania, republic (1992 est. pop. 3,789,000), 25,174 sq mi (65,201 sq km), N central Europe, from 1940 to 1991 a constituent republic of the USSR. It borders on the Baltic Sea (W), Latvia (N), Belarus and Poland (E), and the Kaliningrad oblast (SW, a Russian exlcave). The capital and largest city is VILNIUS; other large cities include Kaunus and Klaipeda (Memel). Lithuania is a flatland drained by the Nemen R. Dairying, stock raising, and the growing of such crops as grains and flax are agriculturally important. Among its industries are shipbuilding, metallurgy, food processing, and the manufacture of machinery, textiles, and chemicals. The majority of the population is Lithuanian; minorities include Russians and Poles. Lithuanian is the official language, and Russian and Polish are spoken. Roman Catholicism and Lutheranism are the main faiths.

History. The Lithuanians may have settled along the Neman (Nemanus) as early as 1500 B.C. In the 13th cent., to protect themselves against the Livonian and Teutonic knights, they formed a strong, unified state which, by absorbing neighboring Russian principalities, became one of the largest in medieval Europe. Between 1386 and 1569, Lithuania gradually merged with Poland. In 1795 it came under Russian control. Independence was declared in 1918, but Poland held Vilnius from 1920 to 1939. In 1940, the USSR forcibly annexed Lithuania. During the German occupation (1941–44) in WORLD WAR II, Lithuania's large Jewish minority was virtually exterminated. The country was returned to Soviet rule after the war. In 1990 Sajudis, a noncommunist coalition, won control of the Lithuanian parliament, and Vytautus Landsbergis became president. The parliament declared Lithuania independent, but the USSR imposed an economic embargo that compelled Lithuania to suspend enforcement of the declaration. In Jan. 1991 the Soviet army unsuccessfully attempted to oust Lithuania's government. After the failed hard-line coup against Soviet Pres. GORBACHEV, the USSR recognized Lithuania's independence. In 1992 the Democratic Labor (former Communist) party defeated Sajudis, and Algirdas Brazauskas, a former Communist, was elected president (1993). Lithuania signed a free-trade agreement with Estonia and Latvia in 1993.

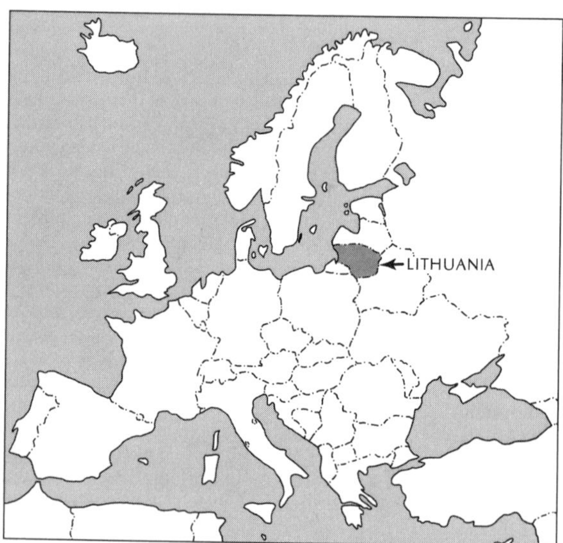

Lithuanian, a language belonging to the Baltic subfamily of the Indo-European family of languages. See LANGUAGE (table).

litmus, organic dye usually used as an indicator of acidity or alkalinity (see ACIDS AND BASES). Naturally pink in color, it turns blue in alkaline solutions and red in acids. Litmus paper is paper treated with the dye.

Little Bighorn, river, flowing c.90 mi (145 km) from N Wyo. to join the Bighorn R. in S Mont. **Little Bighorn National Battlefield,** in SE Montana, commemorates the famous Battle of the Little Bighorn on June 25–26, 1876, in which Col. George CUSTER and most of his force were killed by Sioux and Cheyennes.

Little Entente, loose alliance formed in 1920–21 by Czechoslovakia, Romania, and Yugoslavia and supported by France. Its aims were to contain Hungary and to prevent the restoration of the HAPSBURGS. Romania and Yugoslavia were also members of the Balkan Entente (1934). The general purposes of both ententes were to preserve the territorial status quo and to encourage closer economic ties. The Little Entente was successful until the rise of HITLER in Germany and was ended by the MUNICH PACT (1938).

Little Richard, 1935–, American musician and singer; b. Macon, Ga. as Richard Wayne Penniman. One of the first rock musicians in the 1950s, he recorded "Tutti Frutti," "Long Tall Sally," and "Good Golly Miss Molly." His music influenced, among others, the BEATLES. See also ROCK MUSIC.

Little Rock, city (1990 pop. 175,795), state capital and seat of Pulaski co., central Ark., a port on the Arkansas R.; inc. 1831. It is the administrative, commercial, industrial, and cultural center of the state. Agricultural-products, bauxite, and lumber industries are important. A river crossing before 1819, Little Rock became territorial capital in 1821. It was a center of world attention in 1957, when federal troops enforced a school-desegregation order.

Little Turtle, c.1752–1812, chief of the MIAMI; b. Indiana. Noted for his military skill, he defeated the U.S. army in several engagements but counseled against the disastrous battle with Gen. Anthony WAYNE at Fallen Timbers (1794). He reluctantly signed the Treaty of Greenville (1795), ceding much of Ohio to the U.S. Later he refused to join TECUMSEH's confederacy against the whites.

Liu Shaoqi or **Liu Shao-Ch'i** [both: lyōō shou-chē], 1893?–1969, Chinese Communist leader. An expert on organization and party structure, he was chairman and head of state of the Chinese People's Republic (1959–68). Liu was criticized during the Cultural Revolution (1966–69) and was removed from power in 1968. He was posthumously rehabilitated (1980) by DENG XIAOPING and a collection of his writings was published in 1982.

liver, largest glandular organ of the body. It lies on the right side of the abdominal cavity, beneath the diaphragm, and is made up of four unequal lobes. Liver tissue consists of thousands of tiny lobules, in turn made up of hepatic cells, the basic metabolic cells. The liver is thought to perform over 500 functions involving the DIGESTIVE SYSTEM, EXCRETION, blood chemistry and detoxification, and the storage of vitamins and minerals. Of the liver's many digestive system functions, the production of BILE (for fat digestion) and storage of glucose (see GLYCOGEN) are particularly important.

Liverpool, city (1991 pop. 452,450), Merseyside, NW England, on the Mersey R. It is one of Britain's greatest ports and largest cities and a major outlet for industrial exports. Food processing and the manufacture of electrical equipment and chemicals are major industries. Chartered in 1207, the city was once famous for its pottery and its textile industry.

liverwort, member of a group of small, flowerless, primitive green land plants that are alternately considered a class (Marchantiopsida) or division (Hepatophyta) of BRYOPHYTES. They are characterized by horizontal growth and are related to the MOSSES. Usually growing in moist places, liverworts are considered intermediate between the aquatic ALGAE and the terrestrial mosses and FERNS. The ancients believed that liverworts could cure diseases of the liver, hence their name.

Livingston, family of American statesmen, diplomats, and jurists. **Robert R. Livingston,** 1654–1728, b. Scotland, emigrated to America in 1673 and made his home in Albany, N.Y. He acquired extensive landholdings and influence in the colony. His grandson, **Robert R. Livingston,** 1718–75, was a judge of New York's supreme court (1763–75) and a delegate to the Stamp Act Congress. His son, **Robert R. Livingston,** 1746–1813, b. N.Y.C., conducted the negotiations that led to the LOUISIANA PURCHASE and financed the steamboat experiments of Robert FULTON. A brother, **Edward Livingston,** 1764–1836, b. Livingston Manor, N.Y., was a U.S. congressman (1795–1801) and mayor of New York City before moving to Louisiana. He served again as a congressman (1823–29) and then as a senator (1829–31) before becoming secretary of state under Pres. JACKSON. Another grandson of Robert R. Livingston (1654–1728) was **Philip Livingston,** 1716–78, b. Albany, who signed the DECLARATION OF INDEPENDENCE and was active in the CONTINENTAL CONGRESS. He was one of the original promoters of King's College (now Columbia Univ.). His brother, **William Livingston,** 1723–90, attended the First and Second Continental Congresses and was New Jersey's first governor (1776–90). His influence played a large part in New Jersey's prompt ratification of the U.S. Constitution.

Livingstone, David, 1813–73, Scottish explorer in Africa. While a medical missionary in what is now BOTSWANA (1841–52), he crossed the KALAHARI desert and discovered the ZAMBEZI R. In 1855 he discovered VICTORIA FALLS. He set out to seek the source of the NILE in 1866. H.M. STANLEY went in search of him, finding him in 1871. Stanley then joined him on a journey (1871–72) to the north end of Lake TANGANYIKA. Livingstone died in an African village; his body is buried in Westminster Abbey.

living will, document in which a person, in case of incapacitation, expresses in advance his or her wishes concerning the use of medical measures to prolong life. Typically living wills are used to reject "extraordinary" measures, such as intravenous feeding and mechanical respirators, when death appears imminent. The use of living wills was affirmed by a 1990 U.S. Supreme Court decision. Family members and medical personnel sometimes challenge a living will because of unclear or legally invalid instructions, concern over possible legal consequences, or the emotional difficulty involved in withholding treatment. See also HEALTH-CARE PROXY.

Livonia, city (1990 pop. 100,850), SE Mich., a suburb of DETROIT; founded 1835, inc. 1950. Its manufactures include automobile bodies, tools and dies, and paints.

Livy (Titus Livius), 59 B.C.–A.D. 17, Roman historian; b. Patavium (Padua). His life work was a history of Rome (entitled *Books from the Founding of Rome*) from its founding in 753 B.C. to DRUSUS (9 B.C.). Of the original 142 books, 35 are extant. While Livy's accuracy is often questionable, he has achieved a long popularity because of his vivid depictions, freedom of expression, and masterly style.

lizard, REPTILE of the order Squamata, which also includes the SNAKE, distributed worldwide (except for the Arctic) but most common in warm climates. Lizards typically have four legs with five toes on each foot, although a few are limbless, retaining internal vestiges of legs. They also differ from snakes in having ear openings, movable eyelids, and less flexible jaws. Several, most notably CHAMELEONS, undergo color changes under the influence of environmental and emotional stimuli. Lizards range in size from species under 3 in. (7.6 cm) long to the 10-ft (3-m) Komodo dragon (see MONITOR).

Ljubljana, Ger. *Laibach,* city (1987 est. pop. 233,000), capital of SLOVENIA, on a tributary of the Sava R. Located in W central Slovenia, it is the country's largest city and an industrial and transportation center. Manufactures include textiles, chemicals, and electronic equipment. The city has a medieval fortress and several fine palaces and churches. Known as Emona in Roman times, Ljubljana passed (1277) to the Hapsburgs. In 1919 it became part of the Kingdom of the Serbs, Croats, and Slovenes (later Yugoslavia). In 1946 Ljubljana became the capital of the Yugoslav constituent republic of Slovenia, which declared its independence in 1991.

llama, South American domesticated hoofed MAMMAL (*Lama glama*) of the CAMEL family. It resembles a large, long-eared, long-necked sheep and provides the indigenous people of the Andes with wool, milk, and meat. Its usefulness as a pack animal is enhanced by its ability to work at exceptionally high altitudes. In the U.S. llamas have also been used as guard animals for sheep flocks.

llanos, Spanish American term for prairies, applied specifically to the plains of the ORINOCO R. basin, in Venezuela and Colombia. They are low-lying and hot, with wet and dry seasons. Cattle ranching, farming, and oil and gas drilling are important.

Lleras Camargo, Alberto [lyä'räs kämär'gō], 1906–90, president of COLOMBIA (1945–46, 1958–62). After his first brief term as Liberal president, he became (1948) the first secretary general of the Organization of American States. In 1957 he helped to depose dictator Rojas Pinilla and to institute bipartisan Liberal-Conservative rule, ending 10 years of bloody political strife in the nation.

Lleras Restrepo, Carlos [lyä'räs rästrä'pō], 1908–, president of COLOMBIA (1966–70). He was Liberal party leader during Colombia's bloody civil war (1948) and became so again in 1961. His government reduced inflation, diversified the economy, and instituted land reform.

Llewelyn ap Gruffydd [lo͞oĕl'ĭn äp gro͞o'f ĭth], d. 1282, Welsh prince; last independent ruler of Wales. By 1263 he had recovered much of Wales from the English. He sided with Simon de MONTFORT in the BARONS' WAR and was recognized (1267) by HENRY III as prince of Wales. In 1277 he submitted to EDWARD I, but was killed in a subsequent revolt.

Lloyd, Chris Evert: see EVERT, CHRIS.

Lloyd, Harold, 1893–1971, American film actor; b. Burchard, Kans. A bespectacled innocent, he blundered into hair-raising situations in such silent comedies as *Safety Last* (1923) and *The Freshman* (1925).

Lloyd George, David, 1st **Earl Lloyd-George of Dwyfor,** 1863–1945, British statesman. Elected as a Liberal to Parliament in 1890, he served until 1945. He gained a reputation as an anti-imperialist and as the author of far-reaching social reforms, proposed in 1905 and while chancellor of the exchequer (1908–15) under Herbert Asquith. Replacing (1916) Asquith as prime minister during WORLD WAR I, he formed a strong war cabinet, waged war aggressively, and played a moderating role in shaping the Treaty of VERSAILLES. His coalition fell (1922) when the Conservatives withdrew. He later (1926–31) led the remnants of the LIBERAL PARTY and played a quixotic part in politics in the 1930s and the early months of WORLD WAR II.

Lloyd Webber, Sir Andrew, 1948–, British composer. A member of a successful musical family, he began composing musicals as a teenager. His first success was *Jesus Christ Superstar* (1970). Among his other musicals are *Evita* (1976), a fictional biography of Eva PERON, *Cats* (1981), based on poems by T.S. ELIOT, *The Phantom of the Opera* (1986; Tony Award), and *Sunset Boulevard* (1993).

loam, soil composed of sand, silt, clay, and organic matter in evenly mixed variously sized particles. Loams are more fertile than sandy soils and are not stiff and tenacious like clay soils. Their porous texture permits high moisture retention and air circulation, and most agriculturally important soils are loams. Loam soils are classified as sand, silt, or clay loams, depending on the largest component. Loam is often popularly confused with HUMUS.

Lobachevsky, Nikolai Ivanovich, 1793–1856, Russian mathematician. Independently of János Bolyai he developed (1826) hyperbolic geometry, one type of NON-EUCLIDIAN GEOMETRY.

lobefin, name for several lunged, fleshy-finned, bony FISHES, predecessors of the AMPHIBIANS. Lobefins were considered extinct until 1938, when a live coelocanth (*Latimeria chalumne*), a marine lobefin, was caught off S Africa. Coelocanths are brown to blue and 5 ft (150 cm) long, with circular, overlapping scales, a laterally flattened three-lobed tail, a spiny dorsal fin, and a vestigial lung.

Lobito, city (1983 est. pop. 150,000), W central Angola, on the Atlantic Ocean. It is Angola's chief port, with such exports as ores, grains, and coffee. Industries include shipbuilding and food processing. Founded (1843) by the Portuguese and built mainly on reclaimed land, the city became a commercial center after the completion (1929) of the Benguela RR, but declined in the 1970s due to damage of port facilities during the war of independence from Portugal.

lobster, large marine CRUSTACEAN with five pairs of jointed legs, the first pair bearing large pincerlike claws of unequal size adapted to crushing the shells of its prey. The dark-green common American lobster (*Homarus americanus*) is found from Labrador to North Carolina, but especially along the New England coast. When lobster is cooked, the shell turns bright red; the meat is considered a delicacy.

local area network (LAN), a network dedicated to sharing data among several single-user computer workstations or PERSONAL COMPUTERS. A LAN can have from two to several hundred such nodes, each separated by distances of from several feet to as much as a mile, and should be distinguished from connections among computers over public carriers, such as telephone circuits, that are used for other purposes. See also MODEM.

Local Group of galaxies: see GALAXY.

Locarno Pact, 1925, agreement reached at Locarno, Switzerland, by Great Britain, France, Germany, Italy, Belgium, Czechoslovakia, and Poland. It guaranteed the demilitarized status of the RHINELAND and the common borders of Belgium, France, and Germany, all as specified by the Treaty of VERSAILLES of 1919. Germany, Poland, and Czechoslovakia also signed border agreements. The "spirit of Locarno" was widely hailed as ushering in an era of international peace and good will. In 1936, however, HITLER denounced the pact, and Germany remilitarized the Rhineland, a step toward WORLD WAR II.

lock, canal: see CANAL.

Locke, John, 1632–1704, English philosopher, founder of British EMPIRICISM. Locke's two most important works, *Essay concerning Human Understanding* and *Two Treatises on Civil Government,* both published in 1690, quickly established him as the leading philosopher of freedom. In the *Essay* he opposed the rationalist belief in innate ideas, holding that the mind is born a blank upon which all knowledge is inscribed in the form of human experience. He distinguished the primary qualities of things (e.g., extension, solidity, number) from the secondary qualities (e.g., color, smell, sound), which he held to be produced by the direct impact of the world on the sense organs. The primary qualities affect the sense organs mechanically, providing ideas that faithfully reflect reality; thus science is possible. Later empiricists such as HUME and George BERKELEY based their systems largely on Locke's theory of knowledge. In political theory he was equally influential. Contradicting HOBBES, Locke maintained that the original state of nature was happy and characterized by reason and tolerance; all human beings were equal and free to pursue "life, health, liberty, and possessions." The state formed by the SOCIAL CONTRACT was guided by the natural law, which guaranteed those inalienable rights. He set down the policy of checks and balances later followed in the U.S. CONSTITUTION; formulated the doctrine that revolution in some circumstances is not only a right but an obligation; and argued for broad religious freedom. Much of the liberal social, economic, and ethical theory of the 18th cent. was rooted in Locke's social-contract theories. One of the major influences on modern philosophical and political thought, he epitomized the ENLIGHTENMENT's faith in the middle class, in the new science, and in human goodness.

Lockerbie, rural village (1988 est. pop. 3,000), SW Scotland, near the English border. On Dec. 21, 1988, a terrorist bomb exploded in flight on a Frankfurt–New York Pan Am Boeing 747. The plane crashed around Lockerbie, killing all 259 aboard and 11 village inhabitants. The refusal of Libya to let the U.S. and Britain try the Libyan intelligence agents accused of involvement in the bombing led (1992) to UN sanctions against LIBYA.

lockjaw: see TETANUS.

Lockyer, Sir Joseph Norman, 1836–1920, English astronomer. One of the first to make a spectroscopic study of the sun and stars, he devised (1868) a way of observing solar prominences in daylight; he also identified helium in the sun and applied the name *chromosphere* to the layer of gas around the sun. He was director (1890–1913) of the Solar Physics Observatory and was the founder and first editor (1896–1919) of *Nature,* considered the world's leading general scientific periodical.

locomotive, vehicle used to a pull a train of unpowered RAILROAD cars. From their invention in the early 19th cent. until the early years of the 20th, all locomotives were powered by STEAM ENGINES fueled by wood or coal, with a rod-and-piston arrangement to move the drive wheels. The front wheel assembly (the swivel truck) and the wheels mounted under the cab were unpowered. **Electric locomotives,** introduced c.1895, obtained their power from an electric trolley, or pantograph, running on an overhead wire, or from a third rail. Electric locomotives are used chiefly on steep grades and on runs of high traffic density. Although very efficient, they are not more widely used because of the cost of electrifying larger railroad systems. In parts of Europe and in Japan, however, high-speed electric locomotives are widely used. American railroads today are largely powered by **diesel-electric locomotives** (introduced c.1924). These use a DIESEL ENGINE to drive an electric generator, which feeds electric motors that turn the driving wheels. **Gas turbine–electric locomotives** are similar to the diesel-electric but use a gas TURBINE to drive the generator.

locust, in botany, deciduous tree or shrub (genus *Robinia*) of the PULSE family, native to the U.S. and Mexico. The black locust (*R. pseudoacacia*), a popular ornamental, has fragrant flowers; its durable wood is used for treenails in shipbuilding and for fenceposts, turning, and fuel. The CAROB, thought to be the biblical locust tree, and the HONEY LOCUST belong to other genera in the same family.

locust, in zoology, migratory INSECT of the short-horned GRASSHOPPER family. Locust migration is an occasional event. Under certain environmental conditions, which also lead to population increases, young locusts develop into a short-winged migratory form, gather in huge swarms, and, at maturity, take to the air. The swarms can include more than 100 billion insects. When they finally settle, the resulting agricultural devastation is enormous.

lodestone: see MAGNETITE.

Lodge, Henry Cabot, 1850–1924, U.S. senator from Massachusetts (1893–1924); b. Boston. He wrote several historical works and was a U.S. congressman (1887–93). A conservative Republican senator, he welcomed war with Spain in 1898, bitterly criticized Pres. WILSON's peace policy, and opposed U.S. entry into the LEAGUE OF NATIONS. His grandson, **Henry Cabot Lodge, Jr.,** 1902–85, was also a Republican senator from Massachusetts (1937–44, 1947–53). In 1952 he lost a bid for reelection to John F. KENNEDY. Later he served as U.S. representative to the UN (1953–60). He was ambassador to South Vietnam (1963–64, 1965–67) and West Germany (1968–69), and chief U.S. representative (1969) at the Paris peace talks on Vietnam.

Łódź [lo͞oj], city (1989 est. pop. 851,000), central Poland. Łódź is Poland's second largest city and the center of its textile industry. Other manufactures include chemicals and radios. The city was chartered in 1423, passed to Prussia (1793) and Russia (1815), and reverted to Poland in 1919.

Loewi, Otto, 1873–1961, American physiologist and pharmacologist; b. Germany. For his discovery of the chemical transmission of nerve impulses he shared with Sir Henry DALE the 1936 Nobel Prize in physiology or medicine. Loewi investigated the physiology and pharmacology of metabolism, the kidneys, the heart, and the nervous system. He was professor of pharmacology at the Univ. of Graz, Austria (1909–38), and New York Univ. (1940–61).

Logan, James, c.1725–80, Mingo chief; b. Pennsylvania. A friend of whites until they killed (1774) his family, he led Native Americans of the Ohio and Scioto rivers on retaliatory raids, resulting in Lord DUNMORE's War. An eloquent speech in which he refused to participate in a peace treaty is famous.

Logan, Mount, 19,524 ft (5,951 m), highest mountain in Canada and second highest in North America, in SW Yukon Territory, at the center of a vast glacial expanse. Named for Sir William Logan, a Canadian geologist, it was first climbed in 1925.

logarithm, the power to which a number, called the base, must be raised in order to obtain a given positive number. For example, the logarithm of 100 to the base 10 is 2, because $10^2 = 100$. Common logarithms use 10 as the base; natural, or Napierian, logarithms (for John NAPIER) use the number *e* (see separate article) as the base.

logic, systematic study of valid inference. Classical, or Aristotelian, logic is concerned with the formal properties of an argument, not its factual accuracy. Aristotle, in his *Organon,* held that any logical argument could be reduced to a sequence of 3 propositions (2 premises and a conclusion), known as a SYLLOGISM, and posited 3 laws as basic to all logical thought: the law of identity (*A is A*); the law of contradiction (*A cannot be both A and not A*); and the law of the excluded middle (*A must be either A or not A*). Aristotle assumed a correspondence linking the structures of reality, the mind, and language, a position known in the Middle Ages as REALISM. The opposing school of thought, NOMINALISM, represented by WILLIAM OF OCCAM, maintains that language and logic correspond to the structure of the mind only, not to that of reality. John Stuart MILL in the 19th cent. helped to formulate the scientific method of IN-

DUCTION, i.e., movement from specific perceptions to generalizations. Aristotelian logic basically held sway in the Western world for 2,000 years, but since the 19th cent. it has been largely supplanted as a field of study by symbolic logic, which replaces ordinary language with mathematical symbols. Symbolic logic draws on the concepts and techniques of mathematics, notably SET theory, and in turn has contributed to the development of the foundations of mathematics. In the early 20th cent. Bertrand RUSSELL and Alfred North WHITEHEAD attempted to develop logical theory as the basis for mathematics. See also DEDUCTION.

logical positivism, also known as scientific EMPIRICISM, modern school of philosophy that in the 1920s attempted to introduce the methodology and precision of mathematics to the study of philosophy, much as had been done in symbolic logic (see LOGIC). Led by the Vienna Circle, a group including the philosophers Rudolf CARNAP and Moritz Schlick and the mathematician Kurt GÖDEL, the logical positivists held that metaphysical speculation is nonsensical; that logical and mathematical propositions are tautological; and that moral and value statements are merely emotive. The function of philosophy, they maintained, is to clarify concepts in both everyday and scientific language. The movement received its inspiration from the work of FREGE, Bertrand RUSSELL, WITTGENSTEIN, and G.E. MOORE. The Vienna Circle disintegrated in the late 1930s after the Nazis took Austria, but its influence spread throughout Europe and America, and its concept, particularly its emphasis on the analysis of language as the function of philosophy, has been carried on throughout the West.

logic circuit, ELECTRIC CIRCUIT whose output depends upon the input in a way that can be expressed as a function in symbolic LOGIC; it has one or more binary inputs (capable of assuming either of two states, e.g., "on" or "off") and a single binary output. Logic circuits that perform particular functions are called gates. Basic logic circuits include the AND gate, the OR gate, and the NOT gate, which perform the logical functions *AND, OR,* and *NOT.* Logic circuits, which are mainly used in digital COMPUTERS, can be built from any binary electric or electronic devices, including switches, RELAYS, ELECTRON TUBES, solid-state DIODES, and TRANSISTORS.

Lohengrin [lō'ən-grĭn], in medieval German story, knight of the Holy Grail, son of Parzival. He rescues and marries Princess Elsa but is doomed to leave her. An epic poem (c.1285–90), ascribed to WOLFRAM VON ESCHENBACH, tells the story. Richard WAGNER based his libretto for the opera *Lohengrin* (1850) on this source.

Loire [lwär], longest river of France, flowing c.630 mi (1,015 km) in a wide arc N and W to the Atlantic from the Cévennes Mts. of SE France. It crosses the MASSIF CENTRAL through deep gorges and, at Orléans, enters a broad valley in the nation's agricultural heartland. It widens at Nantes into an estuary c.35 mi (55 km) long. Important in French history, the Loire valley is noted for its elegant châteaux.

Loki [lō'kē], in Norse mythology, the personification of evil. He constantly sought to overthrow the gods of ASGARD. His worst exploit was the murder of BALDER.

Lollardry or **Lollardy,** medieval English movement for church reform, led by John WYCLIF, whose "poor priests" spread his ideas in the late 14th cent. Opposed to the great wealth of the church, Lollards taught that the clergy should be poor, that believers could interpret the Bible for themselves, that the doctrine of transubstantiation was false, and that clerical and monastic celibacy was unnatural. In the early 15th cent. the movement gained momentum and was put down by statute (1401) and by force (1414). The Lollards then went underground and survived until the 16th cent. Many Lollard ideas were reflected by the HUSSITES.

Lombardi, Vince(nt Thomas), 1913–70, American football coach; b. N.Y.C. He played football at Fordham Univ., coached in high school and college, then entered professional football. In 1959 he became head coach of the Green Bay Packers, developing them into the dominant professional team of the 1960s and winning five national championships. In 1969 he coached the Washington Redskins to a second-place finish.

Lombard League, alliance formed in 1167 by the communes of Lombardy against Holy Roman Emperor FREDERICK I when he tried to assert his authority in Lombardy. Previously, some communes had favored the emperor, others had favored Pope ALEXANDER III. The league, which was supported by the pope, defeated (1176)

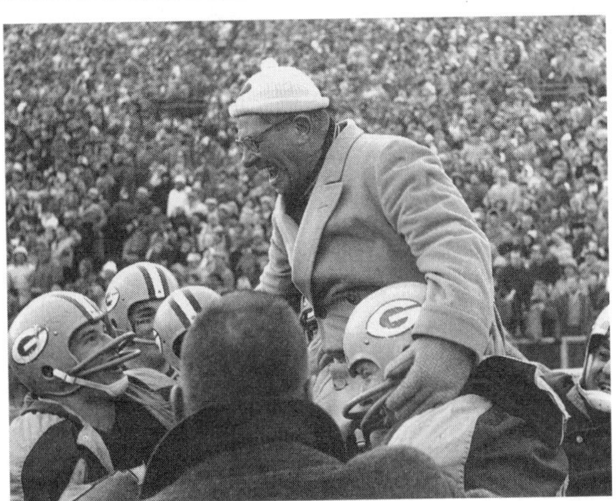

Vince Lombardi

Frederick at Legnano, but after the peace (1183) it tended to split into rival factions. The league was revived in 1226 against the Emperor FREDERICK II, who in 1237 defeated it at Cortenuova. The Lombard communes then took opposing sides, favoring either the popes or the HOHENSTAUFEN.

Lombards, ancient Germanic people. The Byzantines allowed the Lombards to settle (547) in the area of modern Hungary and E Austria. In 568 they invaded N Italy and established a kingdom, with Pavia as its capital. Soon they spread into central and S Italy, where the duchies of Spoleto and Benevento were set up independently. However, the Byzantines still held much of the Adriatic coast, and the PAPACY kept Rome and the PAPAL STATES. The Lombard kingdom reached its height in the 7th and 8th cent., and paganism and ARIANISM gave way to Catholicism. King Liutprand consolidated the kingdom and reduced Spoleto and Benevento to vassalage. His successors took RAVENNA (751) and threatened Rome (772). CHARLEMAGNE then defeated the Lombards; he was crowned (774) with the Lombard crown at Pavia. Of the Lombard kingdom only Benevento remained; it was conquered by the Normans in the 11th cent.

Lombardy, region (1990 pop. 8,911,995), c.9,200 sq mi (23,830 sq km), N Italy. MILAN is the capital. Lombardy has Alpine peaks and glaciers, and upland pastures that slope to the rich Po valley. Agriculture is important, but Lombardy is also Italy's industrial heart, with such manufactures as steel, textiles and clothing, and machinery. In 569 the area became the center of the kingdom of the LOMBARDS, for whom the region is named. In the 11th cent. autonomous communes arose, and Lombard merchants did business throughout Europe. Spanish rule (1535–1713) was followed by Austrian (1713–96) and French (1796–1814). In 1815 the Lombardo-Venetian kingdom was established under Austrian rule. Lombardy passed to Sardinia in 1859 and in 1861 became part of the new kingdom of Italy.

Lomé, city (1985 est. pop. 400,000), capital of Togo, on the Gulf of Guinea. It is the country's administrative, communications, and economic center, and the chief port. Lomé is linked by road, rail, and air to other towns in Togo, and it has an international airport. It was a small village until it became (1897) the capital of the German colony of Togo.

London, Jack (John Griffith London), 1876–1916, American author; b. San Francisco. A sailor, gold-seeker in the Klondike, and war correspondent, he created romantic yet realistic and often brutal fiction. Among his many popular novels are *The Call of the Wild* (1903), *The Sea-Wolf* (1904), *White Fang* (1905), and the partially autobiographical *Martin Eden* (1909). A socialist, London expressed his views in many tracts and in several novels, e.g., *The Iron Heel* (1907). In later years he was beset by alcoholism and financial problems, and he committed suicide at 40.

London, capital city (1991 pop. 6,378,600) of Great Britain and chief city of the COMMONWEALTH OF NATIONS, SE England, on both sides of the Thames R. The city is made up of 32 boroughs and the

Corporation of London (The City). The City, 1 sq mi (2.6 sq km), the historical and commercial core of London, has its own constitution and elects its own lord mayor. London is one of the world's foremost financial, commercial, industrial, and cultural centers, and one of its greatest ports. Little is known of the city prior to Queen BOADICEA's revolt against the Romans in A.D. 61. The Roman legions withdrew in the 5th cent. Celts, Saxons, and Danes contested the area, but it was not until 886 that London emerged as an important town under King ALFRED. Under the Normans and Plantagenets the city became self-governing and grew commercially and politically. By the 14th cent. it had become the political capital of England. The reign of ELIZABETH I brought London great wealth, power, and influence as the center of England's RENAISSANCE in the age of SHAKESPEARE. A plague (1665) was followed by a fire (1666) that virtually destroyed the city. Sir Christopher WREN played a large role in rebuilding London, designing over 50 churches, notably SAINT PAUL'S CATHEDRAL. London grew enormously in the 19th cent., acquiring great prestige in the Victorian era as the capital of the BRITISH EMPIRE. The city was heavily bombed during WORLD WAR II in raids that killed thousands of civilians. Many of the bombed areas were subsequently rebuilt with tall, modern buildings. London's cultural institutions include the BRITISH MUSEUM, NATIONAL GALLERY, TATE GALLERY, and VICTORIA AND ALBERT MUSEUM. Among its landmarks are the remains of the city's Roman walls, BUCKINGHAM PALACE, the Houses of PARLIAMENT, the TOWER OF LONDON, Trafalgar Square, and WESTMINSTER ABBEY.

London, city (1991 pop. 303,165), SE Ontario, Canada, on the Thames R. An important industrial and commercial center, with manufactures including electrical goods and automotive parts, the city has streets and bridges named for those of London, England. London was settled in 1826. Earlier (1792), Governor John Simcoe had tried unsuccessfully to have the capital of Upper Canada (now Ontario) located at the site.

London, Declaration of, international code of MARITIME LAW, especially as related to war, proposed in 1909. At Britain's invitation, the leading European powers, the U.S., and Japan met at London in 1908. The declaration they issued comprised 71 articles dealing with such controversial points as blockade and contraband. It was primarily a restatement of existing law, but in its high regard for neutrals it represented an advance. The code never went into effect officially.

London Bridge, granite bridge formerly over the Thames in London. It replaced (1831) earlier wood (10th cent.) and stone (12th cent.) bridges. In 1968 it was dismantled and moved to Lake Havasu City, Ariz. A new concrete bridge replaced it.

London Conference, any of numerous international meetings held at London, England, only some of which are discussed here. **1** 1830–31, at which the chief powers of Europe discussed the status of GREECE and later the Belgian revolt against the Dutch king. Greece was recognized as a fully independent nation, and the conference ordered the separation of BELGIUM and the NETHERLANDS. **2** 1838–39, followed up on the 1830–31 conference by preparing the final Dutch-Belgian separation treaty. Luxembourg and Limburg were divided between the Dutch and Belgian crowns. **3** 1908, see LONDON, DECLARATION OF. **4** 1933, also known as the World Monetary and Economic Conference. Its purpose was to check the world depression by stabilizing the world's currencies. It was a total failure. **5** 1954, see PARIS PACTS.

Londonderry, Robert Stewart, 2d **marquess of:** see CASTLEREAGH, ROBERT STEWART, 2D VISCOUNT.

Londonderry, city (1989 est. pop. 100,000), NW Northern Ireland, on the Foyle R. Northern Ireland's second largest city, it is a naval base and seaport and is known for its linen manufactures. It grew up around an abbey founded (546) by St. COLUMBA. When it was turned over (1613) to the corporations of the City of LONDON, its name was changed from Derry. The city underwent a 105-day siege by JAMES II in 1689 and in recent years has been the scene of Protestant-Catholic conflict.

Long, Huey Pierce, 1893–1935, American politician; b. Winnfield, La. As LOUISIANA governor (1928–31), the "Kingfish" used ruthless and demagogic methods to establish dictatorial power and achieve his program of social and economic reform. Elected to the U.S. Senate in 1930, he continued to control the Louisiana government from Washington through his hand-picked successor as governor. A presidential aspirant, he gained national support for his "Share the Wealth" program. He was assassinated in Baton Rouge, La., by Dr. Carl A. Weiss in Sept. 1935. His son, **Russell Billiu Long,** 1918–, b. Shreveport, La., served (1948–87) as U.S. senator from Louisiana.

Long Beach, city (1990 pop. 429,433), S Calif., on San Pedro Bay, S of Los Angeles; inc. 1888. With an excellent harbor, it is one of the largest U.S. ports and a tourist center. Oil (discovered 1921) is found both underground and offshore. Diverse manufactures include aircraft, missiles, and electronics equipment, and there is a large shipyard and drydock. Points of interest include the ocean liner *Queen Mary,* which has been converted into a museum, hotel, and tourist center.

Longfellow, Henry Wadsworth, 1807–82, American poet; b. Portland, Me. A professor of modern languages, he taught at Bowdoin College (1829–35) and Harvard Univ. (1836–54). One of the most popular poets of his time, Longfellow created a body of romantic American legends in such long narrative poems as *Evangeline* (1847), *The Song of Hiawatha* (1855), *The Courtship of Miles Standish* (1858), and *Paul Revere's Ride* (1861). Among his best-known shorter poems are "The Village Blacksmith," "Excelsior," and "A Psalm of Life." His often sentimental and moralizing verse has a unique metrical quality produced by his use of unorthodox, "antique" rhythms.

Longinus, fl. 1st cent.? A.D., Greek writer of *On the Sublime,* a monument of literary criticism defining the qualities that would now be called "loftiness of style." It is the source for SAPPHO's second ode.

Long Island, in SE New York, largest island of the coterminous U.S. (1,723 sq mi/4,463 sq km). It is 118 mi (190 km) long and 12–20 mi (19–32 km) wide. Its western end, site of the American defeat in the Battle of Long Island (Aug. 27, 1776), is part of New York City. The southern shore, fringed by sandy barrier beaches, is a popular recreation area.

Long Island, battle of, Aug. 27, 1776, in the AMERICAN REVOLUTION. To protect New York City and the lower Hudson valley from the British on Staten Island, Gen. WASHINGTON sent troops to defend Brooklyn Heights, on Long Island. The British under Sir William Howe (see under HOWE, RICHARD HOWE, EARL) laid siege, and Washington, seeing the position was hopeless, evacuated his army to Manhattan.

longitude, angular distance on the earth's surface measured along the EQUATOR east or west of the PRIME MERIDIAN, which is at 0°. All other points have longitudes from 0° to 180° east or west. Meridians of longitude (imaginary lines drawn from pole to pole) and parallels of LATITUDE form a grid by which any position on the earth's surface can be specified.

Long March, the journey of c.6,000 mi (9,660 km) undertaken by the Red Army of China in 1934–35. Escaping from Nationalist forces in Jiangxi prov., some 90,000 men and women marched W to Guizhou prov. Led by MAO ZEDONG, they then pushed on to Shaanxi prov. in the north, despite natural obstacles and harassment by Nationalist troops. More than half the marchers were lost in this almost incredible one-year trek.

Long Parliament: see ENGLISH CIVIL WAR.

Longstreet, James, 1821–1904, Confederate general in the U.S. CIVIL WAR; b. Edgefield dist., S.C. He fought at FREDERICKSBURG and ANTIETAM, and in the WILDERNESS CAMPAIGN. His delay in taking the offensive at GETTYSBURG is said to have cost Gen. R.E. LEE the battle. He participated in the defense of Richmond and surrendered at APPOMATTOX.

Longueuil, [lôNgö'yə], city (1991 pop. 129,874), S Quebec, E Canada, on the St. Lawrence R. The city, now a residential suburb of MONTREAL, is at the eastern end of the Jacques Cartier Bridge. It was originally settled as a seigniory in 1657.

Longus, fl. 3d cent. A.D., Greek writer. The popular PASTORAL romance *Daphnis and Chloë,* about the love of a goatherd and shepherdess, is attributed to him.

Lon Nol, 1913–85, Cambodian general and political leader. As premier, he led (1970) a coup that deposed NORODOM SIHANOUK and assumed control of the government. His government was overthrown (1975) by Communist guerrillas in a bloody civil war. Lon Nol fled and settled in Hawaii.

loofah: see GOURD.

loon, migratory aquatic BIRD, found in fresh and salt water in the colder parts of the Northern Hemisphere. Its strange, laughing call carries for great distances. Expert swimmers and divers, loons walk on the land with difficulty. Their long, sharp beaks are well adapted for catching fish.

Lope de Vega Carpio, Félix [lō'pā dā vā'gä kär'pyō], 1562–1635, Spanish dramatist, poet, and novelist, founder of modern drama, one of the great figures of Spain's GOLDEN AGE. As a peasant boy of 12 he wrote the first of some 1,800 plays, of which almost 500 are extant. His turbulent life included countless love affairs, scandals, and service in the Spanish ARMADA. His masterworks are such *comedias* as *Peribáñez* (c.1607) and *Fuenteovejuna* (c.1613), which combine the serious and the comic in treating themes of honor, justice, and the conflict between peasant and nobleman. He expounded his dramatic precepts in *The New Art of Writing Plays* (1609): he kept his plays fairly short to hold the audience's attention, invented startling turns of plot, and wrote so as to be understood by ordinary people. In 1614 Lope took religious orders. He completed *La Dorotea* (1632), a novel partly based on his life and amorous adventures, in his last years.

López de Mendoza, Iñigo, marqués de Santillana: see SANTILLANA.

López Portillo y Pacheco, José [lō'pĕz pôrtē'yō ē pächä'kō], 1920–, Mexican political leader and president (1976–82). A lawyer and university professor, he wrote novels and works on political theory. He served (1973–75) as finance minister under Pres. ECHEVERRÍA, whom he succeeded. As president, López Portillo developed Mexico's oil reserves, but faced a national financial crisis at the end of his term. He also served as a mediator in Pan-American disputes.

loran [*lo*ng-*ra*nge *n*avigation], long-range, accurate radio navigational system used by a ship or aircraft to determine its geographical position. The measured time-of-arrival difference between signals transmitted from two geographically separated ground stations determines the hyperbolic curve on which the receiver is situated. By taking a similar time-difference reading from a second pair of stations whose curve intersects that of the first pair, a definite geographical fix may be obtained. Loran will eventually be replaced by the Global Positioning System (see NAVIGATION SATELLITE.

Lorca, Federico García: see GARCÍA LORCA.

Lord's Prayer or **Our Father,** principal Christian prayer taught by Jesus to his disciples (Mat. 6.9–13; Luke 11.2–4). English translations vary. After the Second VATICAN COUNCIL, Roman Catholics added a version of the doxology ("For thine is the kingdom," etc.) adopted earlier by most Protestants.

Lord's Supper: see COMMUNION.

Loren, Sophia, 1934–, Italian film actress; b. Sophia Scicoloni. A beautiful leading lady, she has appeared in such films as *Two Women* (1961; Academy Award), *Yesterday, Today, and Tomorrow* (1963), and *A Very Special Day* (1977).

Lorentz, Hendrik Antoon, 1853–1928, Dutch physicist. For his explanation of the Zeeman effect (a change in spectral lines in a magnetic field), which was based on his postulating the existence of ELECTRONS, he shared with Pieter Zeeman the 1902 Nobel Prize in physics. He extended the hypothesis of George Fitzgerald, an Irish physicist, that a body's length contracts as its speed increases (the Fitzgerald-Lorentz contraction) and formulated the Lorentz transformation, by which space and time coordinates of one moving system can be correlated with the known space and time coordinates of any other system. This work influenced, and was confirmed by, Albert EINSTEIN's special theory of RELATIVITY.

Lorenz, Konrad, 1903–89, Austrian zoologist and ethologist. For his work in ETHOLOGY, particularly his studies of the organization of individual and group behavior patterns, he shared the 1973 Nobel Prize in physiology or medicine with Karl von FRISCH and Nikolaas TINBERGEN. With Oscar Heinroth, Lorenz discovered imprinting, a rapid and nearly irreversible learning process occurring early in life. His controversial book *On Aggression* (1966) maintains that aggressive impulses are to a degree innate, and draws analogies between human and animal behavior.

Lorenzetti, two brothers who were major Sienese painters. **Pietro Lorenzetti,** c.1280–c.1348, was influenced by Giovanni Pisano (see under PISANO, NICOLA) and by GIOTTO's profound emotion and simple grandeur of form. His works include the magnificent *Birth of the Virgin* (c.1342; Opera del Duomo, Siena). **Ambrogio Lorenzetti,** d. 1348?, was the more inventive brother. Also influenced by Pisano and Giotto, he had a remarkable ability to depict spatial depth. His greatest work is the cycle of FRESCOES (1337–39) in the Palazzo Pubblico, Siena, which consists of allegories of good and bad government and is a revealing portrait of 14th-cent. Italian life.

Ambrogio Lorenzetti's fresco Good Government in the City, *14th cent.*

Lorenzo de' Medici: see under MEDICI, family.

Lorenzo Monaco [mō'näkō], c.1370–1425?, a leading early 15th-cent. Italian painter; b. Siena as Piero di Giovanni. His *Adoration of the Magi* (Uffizi), with its elongated figures and rich pageantry, reflects the international Gothic style.

Loria, Isaac ben Solomon: see LURIA, ISAAC BEN SOLOMON.

loricifer, member of a phylum (Loricifera) of microscopic animals that live in marine gravel and sand. The sexes are separate and they have a large brain and a spiny head, which can be retracted into the body.

Lorrain, Claude: see CLAUDE LORRAIN.

Los Alamos, uninc. town (1990 pop. 11,455), north-central N.Mex., on a long mesa extending from the Jemez Mts. It was chosen (1942) for atomic research, and the first atomic bombs were produced there. Government control ended in 1962. The Los Alamos National Laboratory is now operated by the Univ. of California and is a national historic landmark.

Los Angeles, city (1990 pop. 3,495,398; met. area 8,863,164; 1992 greater met. area est. 15,000,000), seat of Los Angeles co., S Calif., on the Pacific Ocean, with a harbor at San Pedro Bay. The second largest city in the U.S., it is the shipping, communications, and financial hub of a rich agricultural area. The Spanish visited the site in 1769 and founded a town in 1781. At times the capital of Alta California, it was captured by the U.S. from Mexico in 1846 and incorporated in 1850. Late-19th-cent. railroad development and the discovery of oil in the 1890s spurred growth. In the 20th cent., the motion-picture industry and, later, the radio and television industry have been important. Today Los Angeles is a major industrial, technological, and research center, as well as the largest U.S. port. The city is especially important in the area of electronic and aerospace products; other manufactures include drugs, military ordnance, processed food, and chemicals. Its greater metropolitan area, which ranks second only to that of New York in size, covers five counties and 34,000 sq mi (88,000 sq km). Automobile density is high, and SMOG has been a major problem. Los Angeles grew by absorbing neighboring communities; it now surrounds the independent municipalities of Santa Monica, Beverly Hills, and San Fernando. The city, which attracts thousands of tourists yearly, is noted for its parks; for many and varied museums; for its enormous

Music Center and Convention Center; for the fossil-rich La Brea Tar Pits; for its ethnic communities; for its climate and beaches; and for its educational institutions, including the Univ. of Southern California and the Univ. of California at Los Angeles. The 1932 and 1984 summer Olympics were held in the city. In 1992 the city was torn by rioting following not-guilty verdicts in a local police brutality trial. An earthquake centered in Northridge in N Los Angeles damaged many structures in the city and surrounding areas in 1994.

Los Angeles County Museum, Los Angeles, Calif.; opened 1913. Its holdings, which include the collection of William Randolph HEARST, contain French and English furnishings, and paintings by FRAGONARD, MATISSE, and other masters.

lost tribes: see ISRAEL, TRIBES OF.

lost-wax casting: see CIRE PERDUE.

Lot, nephew of ABRAHAM. Warned of Sodom's coming destruction (see SODOM AND GOMORRAH), Lot fled with his family. His wife, disobeying God's orders, looked back at the city and was turned into a pillar of salt.

Lothair, Frankish and German emperors. **Lothair I,** 795–855, emperor of the West (840–55), was the son and successor of LOUIS I, with whom he was coemperor after 817. A grandson of CHARLEMAGNE, he was in almost constant territorial wars with his father and his three brothers, Pepin, CHARLES II (Charles the Bald), and LOUIS THE GERMAN. Eventually, the Treaty of Verdun (843) subdivided Charlemagne's empire among the brothers. **Lothair II,** also called **Lothair III,** 1075–1137, Holy Roman emperor (1133–37) and German king (1125–37), was the first elected monarch. With the help of his son-in-law, Henry the Proud, he defeated the antiking Frederick of HOHENSTAUFEN and Frederick's brother Conrad (who succeeded him as CONRAD III), thereby clearing the way to being crowned emperor. He Christianized NE Germany.

Lotharingia [lŏthərĭn'jə], name given to the northern portion of the lands assigned (843) to Emperor of the West LOTHAIR I in the first division of the CAROLINGIAN empire. it comprised roughly the present Netherlands, Belgium, Luxembourg, Lorraine, Alsace, and NW Germany, including Aachen and Cologne. Lothair I, in turn, gave the land to his son King Lothair (d. 869), for whom the kingdom was named. After King Lothair died, Lotharingia was divided between the East Frankish and West Frankish kingdoms (i.e., Germany and France). Throughout history the territories composing Lotharingia have been contested between Germany and France. Only one part of it, the duchy of Lorraine (the modern form of Lotharingia), has remained a consistent political entity.

Loti, Pierre [lôtē'], pseud. of **Julien Viaud,** 1850–1923, French novelist. His most enduring novels are *An Iceland Fisherman* (1886), a tale of Breton fishermen, and *Ramuntcho* (1897), a story of French Basque peasant life.

lotus: see WATER LILY.

loudspeaker or **speaker,** device used to convert electrical energy into sound. It consists essentially of a thin flexible sheet called a diaphragm that is made to vibrate by an electric signal from an AMPLIFIER. The vibrations create sound waves in the air around the speaker. In the common dynamic speaker, the diaphragm has a cone shape and is attached to a wire coil suspended in a magnetic field. A signal current in the suspended coil creates another magnetic field that interacts with the already existing field, causing the coil and the diaphragm attached to it to vibrate. Quality sound systems employ three different sized speakers. The largest one, the woofer, reproduces low frequencies; the medium-sized one, called a mid-range speaker, reproduces middle frequencies; the smallest one, called a tweeter, reproduces high frequencies. They are typically contained in a single cabinet (used in pairs for STEREOPHONIC SOUND), but a pair of small cabinets with a mid-range speaker and tweeter and a third cabinet with a single woofer is also now common, and some home entertainment systems use five such small cabinets for more realistic sound reproduction.

Louganis, Greg E., 1960–, American diver; b. San Diego, Calif. He won gold medals in springboard diving and platform diving in the 1984 Olympics and repeated in both categories in 1988 despite a head injury during the competition.

Louis, Frankish and German emperors. **Louis I** or **Louis the Pious,** 778–840, emperor of the West (814–40), son and successor of CHARLEMAGNE, tried to create a kingdom for Charles (later Emperor CHARLES II), his son by a second marriage, and thereby caused several revolts by his elder sons, Pepin I, LOTHAIR I, and LOUIS THE GERMAN. Eventually he partitioned his empire between Lothair and Charles. **Louis II,** d. 875, emperor of the West (855–75) and king of Italy (844–75), was the son of Emperor Lothair I. His title as emperor had little meaning since he ruled only in Italy, and even there his reign was constantly challenged by independent Lombard dukes and by Arab invaders of S Italy. He supported his brother Lothair, king of LOTHARINGIA, in a dispute with the pope and briefly (864) occupied Rome; but he subsequently submitted to the pope. He unsuccessfully tried to claim Lotharingia after Lothair's death. **Louis IV** or **Louis the Bavarian,** 1287?–1347, Holy Roman emperor (1328–47) and German king (1314–47), was in constant struggle with the papacy. When he was elected German king, a minority faction elected Frederick the Fair of Hapsburg. Louis defeated Frederick in 1322, but the pope refused to recognize or crown him, so Louis had himself crowned emperor by "representatives of the Roman people." In 1346 Pope Clement VI declared him deposed and secured the election of CHARLES IV. Louis was successfully resisting his rival when he died in a hunting accident.

Louis, Frankish kings and kings of France of the Carolingian, Capetian, Valois, and Bourbon dynasties.

Carolingian dynasty. **Louis I:** see Louis I under LOUIS, Frankish and German emperors. **Louis II** (the Stammerer), 846–79, son of CHARLES II, emperor of the West, was the king of France (r.877–79). His succession was shared by his sons Carloman and **Louis III,** c.863–882, (r.879–882), who defeated the Normans at Saucourt (881). **Louis IV** or **Louis d'Outremer** [Fr., = Louis from overseas], 921–54, (r.936–54), was the son of King CHARLES III. He spent his youth in exile in England and was recalled by the nobles under the duke Hugh the Great at the death of King Raoul. His energy and independence displeased Hugh, who waged war on the king but was forced to submit in 950. Louis was succeeded by his son Lothair, whose own son **Louis V** (the Sluggard), c.967–987 (r.986–87), was the last French king of the CAROLINGIAN dynasty. He died childless and was succeeded by HUGH CAPET.

Capetian dynasty. **Louis VI** (the Fat), 1081–1137 (r.1108–37), succeeded his father, PHILIP I. He was almost continuously at war with HENRY I of England in Normandy, and in 1124 resisted an invasion by Holy Roman Emperor HENRY V. Louis strengthened royal authority by suppressing robber barons, favoring the church, and issuing royal charters to towns to gain their support. His son and successor, **Louis VII** (the Young), c.1120–1180 (r.1137–80), married ELEANOR OF AQUITAINE before his accession. He quarreled with the papacy over an appointee to the archbishopric of Bourges but capitulated in 1144. Louis left (1147) on the Second CRUSADE but returned (1149) when the enterprise failed. In 1152 he had his marriage annulled, and Eleanor's subsequent marriage to Henry Plantagenet (later HENRY II of England) resulted in Henry's claim to Aquitaine and recurrent warfare between Louis and Henry. Louis's son PHILIP II succeeded him. Philip II's son **Louis VIII,** 1187–1226 (r.1223–26), was invited by English lords in rebellion against their king, JOHN, to become king of England. He invaded (1216) England, but was defeated in 1217 and withdrew. He seized (1224) Poitou from the English and resumed (1226) the crusade against the ALBIGENSES. His son and successor, **Louis IX** or **Saint Louis,** 1214–70 (r.1226–70), began his reign under the regency of his mother, Blanche of Castile. In 1240–43 he secured the submission of Poitou and Toulouse, and repulsed a weak invasion by HENRY III of England. Louis left on the Seventh Crusade against Egypt in 1248, but was captured in 1250. Ransomed, he remained in the Holy Land until 1254 to strengthen Christian defenses. Returning to France, he reached peaceful agreements with England's HENRY III and with James I of Aragón. In 1270 he undertook the Eighth Crusade, but he died after landing in Tunis. He was succeeded by his son, PHILIP III. Under Louis IX, France enjoyed unprecedented prosperity and peace. He curbed private warfare, simplified administration, improved tax distribution, and encouraged the use of ROMAN LAW. Louis was an ideal Christian monarch, pious and ascetic, yet a good administrator and diplomat. He was canonized in 1297. Feast: Aug. 25. **Louis X,** Fr. **Louis le Hutin** [the quarrelsome], 1289–1316 (r.1314–16), was the son and successor of PHILIP IV.

Dominated by his uncle, Charles of Valois, Louis made concessions to the barons in the form of charters. His posthumous son, John I, died soon after birth, opening the succession to PHILIP V.

Valois dynasty. **Louis XI,** 1423–83 (r.1461–83), was the son and successor of CHARLES VII. As DAUPHIN, he was involved in a revolt against his father called the Praguerie (1440), and his constant intrigues led to his exile from court. His measures as king to curb the power of the great nobles aroused (1465) the League of the Public Weal, headed by CHARLES THE BOLD, Francis II of Brittany, and others, against the crown. Louis successfully defended Paris but in Oct. 1465 granted the demands of the rebels. Soon he ignored the settlement, and in 1467 a new coalition against the king was formed by Charles the Bold, now duke of Burgundy, and Francis II, with the support of EDWARD IV of England. Louis forced Francis to sign (1468) a peace, but fell prisoner to Charles, who exacted important concessions from him. After his release, Louis involved himself in English affairs against Edward IV. He aided the restoration of HENRY VI and, after Edward regained the throne, halted Edward's invasion (1475) of France by buying him off. Louis also united the enemies of Charles the Bold and, after Charles's death (1477), took Burgundy, Picardy, Boulogne, Artois, and Franche-Comté from Charles's daughter, Mary of Burgundy. Despite his revocation (1461) of his father's PRAGMATIC SANCTION of Bourges, he intervened freely in church affairs. A born diplomat, Louis checked his foreign and domestic enemies and set up an efficient central administration. He also encouraged industry and expanded trade. Fearing assassination, he spent his last years in virtual self-imprisonment near Tours. He was succeeded by his son, CHARLES VIII. **Louis XII,** 1462–1515 (r.1498–1515), succeeded his cousin Charles VIII and ensured the continuation of the personal union of France and Brittany by having his first marriage annulled and marrying ANNE OF BRITTANY, Charles VIII's widow. Thereafter Louis tried to assert his claims in Italy (see ITALIAN WARS). He conquered Milan and Genoa, but failed to secure Naples, which he had conquered with the Spanish king FERDINAND V. His Italian territories were attacked (1511) by the HOLY LEAGUE of Pope JULIUS II. Louis abandoned Milan, and in 1513 his armies were defeated at Novara and Guinegate. In 1514 he made a truce with all his enemies save Holy Roman Emperor MAXIMILIAN I. Louis tried to rule France with justice and moderation, and was known as the Father of the People. He was succeeded by his cousin and son-in-law, FRANCIS I.

Bourbon dynasty. **Louis XIII,** 1601–43 (r.1610–43), succeeded his father, HENRY IV, under the regency of his mother, MARIE DE' MEDICI, and married (1615) ANNE OF AUSTRIA. Even after being declared of age in 1614, he was excluded from state affairs by his mother. In 1617 he caused the assassination of her minister, Concino Concini, with the help of his own favorite, the duc de Luynes. Marie was forced into retirement, but was temporarily reconciled with Louis when he entrusted the government to her protégé, Cardinal RICHELIEU. Melancholy and retiring by nature, Louis gave full support to Richelieu and to his successor, Cardinal MAZARIN. His son and successor, **Louis XIV,** 1638–1715 (r.1643–1715), began his reign under the regency of his mother, Anne of Austria, but real power was in the hands of Cardinal Mazarin. Although Louis's majority was declared (1651), he did not take control of the government until the cardinal's death (1661). The centralizing policies of Richelieu and Mazarin had prepared the ground for Louis, under whom absolute monarchy, based on the theory of divine right, reached its height. Gathering power into his own hands, he forced the nobility into financial dependence on the crown, curtailed local authorities, and used the bourgeoisie to build a centralized administration. Under his minister, Jean Baptiste COLBERT, industry and commerce were expanded according to MERCANTILISM. Under the war minister, the marquis de LOUVOIS, the foundations of French military greatness were laid. In foreign policy Louis strove for supremacy. His marriage (1660) to the Spanish princess Marie Thérèse served as a pretext for the War of DEVOLUTION (1667–68), which netted him part of Flanders. In the Third Dutch War (1672–78), Louis gained Franche-Comté, but depleted his treasury. Over the next 10 years he seized, on various pretexts, a number of cities, notably Strasbourg (1681). Fear of Louis's rapacity resulted in two great European wars, the War of the GRAND ALLIANCE and the War of the SPANISH SUCCESSION. These left France in debt and weakened it militarily. In religion, Louis resorted in the 1680s to the persecution of French Protestants, or HUGUENOTS, which culminated (1685) in the revocation of the Edict of NANTES, after which many Huguenots fled France. Despite his orthodoxy, Louis resisted papal interference in France, and his quarrels with the papacy neared schism (1673–93). He had many mistresses, among them Mlle de La Vallière and Mme de MONTESPAN. In 1684 he married Mme de MAINTENON, who was a great influence on him in later years. Louis was a supporter of the arts and was a patron of writers and artists such as MOLIÈRE and LE BRUN. The architect Jules MANSART supervised the building of Louis's lavish palace at VERSAILLES. Because of the brilliance of his court, Louis is often called the Sun King. His great-grandson **Louis XV,** 1710–74 (r.1715–74), succeeded him under the regency of Philippe II d'ORLÉANS. André Hercule de FLEURY was the young king's chief adviser from 1726. After Fleury's death (1743), Louis was influenced by a succession of favorites, such as Mme de POMPADOUR. As a result of the king's marriage (1725) to the Polish princess Marie Leszcynska, France took part in the War of the POLISH SUCCESSION (1733–35), and eventually obtained the duchy of Lorraine. Louis was also involved in the War of the AUSTRIAN SUCCESSION (1740–48) and in the SEVEN YEARS WAR (1756–63). In the latter, France lost most of its colonial empire and reached a low point in its prestige on the continent. The expense of the wars and Louis's extravagant court left the government nearly bankrupt. The failure by the monarchy to solve its fiscal problems and to effect needed reforms led directly to the French Revolution. The saying "Après moi le déluge" [after me, the flood], though wrongly attributed to Louis, aptly sums up his reign. His grandson and successor, **Louis XVI,** 1754–93 (r.1774–92), was unsuited to provide the leadership needed to control the situation he inherited. Shy, dull, and corpulent, he preferred hunting and working in his locksmith's workshop to council chambers. Reforms begun by his minister A.R.J. TURGOT were opposed by the court faction and by the PARLEMENT, which had been revived by Louis to pacify the privileged classes. Louis was forced to dismiss (1776) Turgot and replaced him with Jacques NECKER, but the costly French involvement in the AMERICAN REVOLUTION increased the debt greatly and led to Necker's resignation (1781). His successors were unable to ward off bankruptcy, and Louis recalled Necker in 1788. In 1789 the king called the STATES-GENERAL, an act which led to the FRENCH REVOLUTION. Louis's mismanagement of this assembly caused the third, or lowest, estate to declare itself the National Assembly, and when the king sent troops to Paris, rumors began that he intended to suppress it. After the dismissal of Necker, violence erupted as Parisians stormed (July 1789) the BASTILLE. Although outwardly accepting the revolution, Louis refused to approve the abolition of feudal rights and allowed the reactionary plotting of his queen, MARIE ANTOINETTE. In Oct. 1789 a mob marched on Versailles and forced the royal family to move to the TUILERIES palace in Paris. Louis's position was definitely ruined when the royal family attempted to escape (June 1791) and was caught at Varennes. Its flight was considered proof of treasonable action. Louis was forced to accept the constitution of 1791, which reduced him to a figurehead. Early French losses in the war with Austria and Prussia increased suspicion of the king. The royal family was imprisoned in the Temple (Aug. 1792), and the monarchy was abolished (Sept.). Incriminating evidence against Louis was discovered, and he was tried by the Convention, which had replaced the National Assembly. Condemned to death by a majority of one, he was guillotined on Jan. 21, 1793, facing death with steadfast courage. His son **Louis XVII,** 1785–1795?, was titular king of France (1793–95) and is known in popular legend as the "lost dauphin." In 1792 revolutionaries imprisoned him with the royal family in the Temple. After the execution of Louis XVI, the comte de Provence (later Louis XVIII) proclaimed Louis king, but he remained imprisoned until his death. Various stories of his escape and fate opened the way to a series of impostors who claimed to be the lost DAUPHIN. Most historians disregard their claims because evidence indicates that the boy died in prison. **Louis XVIII,** 1755–1824 (r.1814–24), was the brother of Louis XVI. Known as the comte de Provence, he fled (1791) from the French Revolution and intrigued against the revolutionaries from abroad. After the death of

Louis XVII (1795), he was proclaimed king by French émigrés. With the assistance of Charles de TALLEYRAND, he was restored (1814) to the French throne by the allies after their entry into Paris, and he granted a constitutional charter. Forced to flee on the return of NAPOLEON I from Elba, Louis returned with the allies after Napoleon's defeat at Waterloo. His chief ministers were at first moderates, but he later relied on ultraroyalists. This reactionary trend was continued by his successor, CHARLES X.

Louis I or **Louis the Great,** 1326–82, king of HUNGARY (1342–82) and of POLAND (1370–82). He succeeded his father, CHARLES I, in Hungary and his uncle, CASIMIR III, in Poland. Two successful wars (1357–58, 1378–81) against Venice gained him Dalmatia and Ragusa, and the rulers of Serbia, Walachia, Moldavia, and Bulgaria became his vassals. Louis brought Hungarian power to its peak, and fostered art and learning. In Poland, however, he was unable to prevent revolts. His daughter Mary succeeded him in Hungary, his daughter Jadwiga in Poland.

Louis I, 1838–89, king of Portugal (1861–89). His reign was marked by political turmoil over a growing republican movement, but Portugal progressed considerably in its commercial and industrial development.

Louis, Joe, 1914–81, American boxer; world heavyweight champ (1937–49); b. Lafayette, Ala., as Joseph Louis Barrow. He turned professional in 1934 and in 1937 won the world heavyweight championship over James J. Braddock. He avenged (1938) his only early defeat with a first-round knockout of Max Schmeling. The "Brown Bomber" defended his title a record 25 times, scoring 21 knockouts. After a brief retirement he returned to the ring in 1950 but lost to Ezzard Charles and Rocky MARCIANO. He lost only 3 of 71 professional bouts.

Louis, Morris, 1912–62, American painter; b. Baltimore. Associated with COLOR FIELD PAINTING, Louis is noted for soaking poured paint through unsized canvas, often in transparently colored columns or muted organic patterns.

Louisburg, town (1991 pop. 1,261), Nova Scotia, E Canada, on CAPE BRETON ISLAND. Its ice-free port, guarded by the great fortress of Louisbourg (built 1720–40), served as headquarters for the French fleet in ACADIA. The stronghold played a major role in the struggle for control of North America between France and England until it was captured and destroyed by the British in 1758. The restored fort is a popular tourist attraction.

Louisiana, state in the S central U.S.; bounded by Mississippi, with the Mississippi R. forming about half of the border (E), the Gulf of Mexico (S), Texas (W), and Arkansas (N).

Area, 48,523 sq mi (125,675 sq km). *Pop.* (1990) 4,219,973, a 0.4% increase over 1980. *Capital,* Baton Rouge. *Statehood,* Apr. 30, 1812 (18th state). *Highest pt.,* Driskill Mt., 535 ft (163 m); *lowest pt.,* New Orleans, 5 ft (2 m) below sea level. *Nickname,* Pelican State. *Motto,* Union, Justice and Confidence. *State bird,* Eastern brown pelican. *State flower,* magnolia. *State tree,* cypress. *Abbr.,* La.; LA.

Land and People. Most of Louisiana consists of lowlands: the Gulf coastal zone, threaded by bayous and marshy rivers, and the MISSISSIPPI delta plains, in the southwest. Inland are rolling prairies and pine-covered hills. The state has long, hot summers and brief, cool winters. Over 68% of the population lives in urban areas. NEW ORLEANS, the largest city, is the leading U.S. port and a major regional industrial and commercial center. Other important cities are BATON ROUGE and SHREVEPORT. Louisiana has an unusually diverse population: the Cajuns of the delta region are descendants of French-speaking Acadians (see ACADIA) expelled (1755) from NOVA SCOTIA; the Creoles are descended from the original Spanish and French settlers; and the state has the second-highest percentage of African Americans (30.8% in 1990), after Mississippi.

Economy. A mild climate and rich alluvial soil make Louisiana one of the country's leading producers of soybeans, sugarcane, rice, corn, and cotton; sweet potatoes and cattle are also important. Louisiana is the third largest U.S. oil producer and a leading producer of natural gas; most wells are offshore. Rich in minerals, Louisiana leads the nation in the production of salt and sulfur. The state is also a leader in the fur and pelt industry. Industry is dominated by oil refining and chemical manufacturing; food processing and the manufacture of transportation and electronic equipment are also important. Fishing and lumbering are also important. Louisiana is popular with tourists, especially during the annual MARDI GRAS festival in New Orleans.

Government. The constitution (adopted 1974) provides for a governor serving a four-year term. The legislature consists of a 39-seat senate and 105-seat house, with members of both bodies elected to four-year terms. Louisiana is represented in the U.S. Congress by two senators and seven representatives and has nine electoral votes.

History. Present-day Louisiana was part of the region claimed (1682) by Robert Cavelier, sieur de LA SALLE, for France. The first permanent European settlement was founded (1714) at NATCHITOCHES, and subsequently New Orleans thrived as an important port city. The area was ceded (1763) to Spain before the U.S. acquired it by the LOUISIANA PURCHASE (1803). Huge sugar and cotton plantations based on slavery were developed, and in 1861 Louisiana seceded from the Union and joined the CONFEDERACY. The state's economy was dramatically changed by the discovery of oil and natural gas early in the 20th cent. A vast federal flood-control system was constructed on the Mississippi R. after the devastating flood of 1927. For much of the 20th cent. the controversial Long family (see LONG, HUEY PIERCE) dominated Louisiana politics. An increase in the state's industrial development, begun at the end of World War II, slowed in the 1980s. The collapse of the oil market in 1986 led to attempts to diversify Louisiana's economy, and the state has recently confronted environmental problems largely caused by degradation of its freshwater marshlands.

Louisiana Purchase, 1803, U.S. acquisition from France of the region of LOUISIANA. Uneasy at news that Spain had secretly retroceded Louisiana to aggressive Napoleonic France, Pres. JEFFERSON in 1802 dispatched Robert R. LIVINGSTON and James MONROE to purchase NEW ORLEANS and West FLORIDA for $2 million. The French, to whom Louisiana was of diminishing importance, offered to sell the entire territory to the surprised envoys for $15 million. The treaty of cession was dated Apr. 30, 1803, and the U.S. flag was raised over New Orleans on Dec. 20. The Louisiana Purchase, extending from the Mississippi R. to the Rocky Mts. and from the Gulf of Mexico to British North America, doubled the area of the U.S.

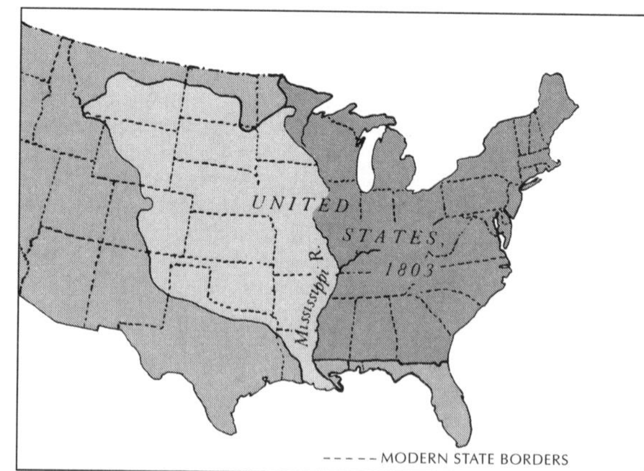

Louisiana Purchase (1803)

Louis Napoleon: see NAPOLEON III.

Louis period styles, 1610–1793, series of modes of interior decoration and architecture in France. The Louis XIII (1610–43) style was a transition from the Italian-influenced BAROQUE to the classical dignity of the Louis XIV [*Louis Quatorze*] (1643–1715) style. Colbert, Louis's chief minister, set up manufactories of textiles, furniture, and ornaments, and chose Charles LE BRUN to direct the Gobelins tapestry works and to decorate the palace of Versailles. Le Brun and J.H. Mansart (see under MANSART, FRANÇOIS) created splendid interiors filled with massive furniture. The Régence style, named for the regency of Philippe II, duc d'Orléans (1715–23), used delicate, curved lines and bronze reliefs. The Louis XV [*Louis Quinze*] period (1723–74) was noted for ROCOCO ornament and chinoiserie. In the Louis XVI [*Louis Seize*] period (1774–93) the CLASSIC REVIVAL style replaced excess with simplicity.

Louis Philippe, 1773–1850, king of the French (1830–48), the son of Philippe Égalité (see Louis Philippe Joseph, duc d'Orléans, under ORLÉANS, family). Known as the duc d'Orléans before his accession, he joined the army of the FRENCH REVOLUTION, but deserted (1793) and remained in exile until the Bourbon restoration (1814). He figured in the liberal opposition to LOUIS XVIII and CHARLES X, and after the JULY REVOLUTION of 1830 he was chosen king. Although a constitutional monarch, Louis Philippe gained considerable personal power by splitting the liberals, and eventually a conservative ministry to his liking came to power. It was dominated (1840–48) by François GUIZOT. The king promoted friendship with Britain by supporting (1831) Belgian independence, but the Spanish marriages (1846) of ISABELLA II and her sister violated an earlier Franco-British agreement. In France, Louis Philippe became increasingly unpopular with both the right and the left. His opponents began a banquet campaign against the government that led to the FEBRUARY REVOLUTION of 1848. The king abdicated in favor of his grandson, but a republic was declared. Louis Philippe fled to England, where he died. He was known as the "citizen king" because of his bourgeois manner and dress.

Louis the Bavarian: see Louis IV under LOUIS, Frankish and German emperors.

Louis the German, c.804–876, king of the East Franks (817–76), son of Emperor LOUIS I, who gave him BAVARIA in 817. In the shifting conflict among his father and his brothers, LOTHAIR I, Pepin I, and CHARLES II, he sided first with one, then with the other. Eventually the Treaty of Verdun (843) gave him the kingdom of the East Franks (roughly modern Germany). Later, part of Lothair's territory of LOTHARINGIA came to him. He survived several revolts by his sons, Louis the Younger, Carloman, and Charles the Fat (later Emperor CHARLES III).

Louis the Great: see LOUIS I, king of Hungary.

Louis the Pious: see Louis I under LOUIS, emperors.

Louisville, city (1990 pop. 269,063), seat of Jefferson co., NW Ky., at the falls of the Ohio; settled 1778, inc. 1828. Named for LOUIS XVI of France, Louisville developed as a fort, portage place, river port, and commercial center. During the CIVIL WAR it was a base for federal forces. It is the largest city in Kentucky, and an important industrial, financial, marketing, and shipping center, with large distilleries and cigarette factories as well as many other plants. Churchill Downs, scene of the Kentucky Derby, is there.

Lourdes, town (1982 pop. 17,425), SW France. Each year, millions visit the Roman Catholic shrine where the Virgin Mary is said to have appeared (1858) to St. Bernadette.

Louvois, François Michel Le Tellier, marquis de [lo͞o vwä'], 1641–91, French statesman under LOUIS XIV. With his father, **Michel Le Tellier,** 1603–85, whom he replaced (1677) as war minister, Louvois shared in the reforms that made France the most powerful military force in Europe. They closely coordinated the infantry, artillery, and corps of engineers, and introduced the bayonet and the flintlock rifle. After the death (1683) of J.B. COLBERT, Louvois became Louis's chief adviser and helped to shape France's aggressive policies.

Louvre [lo͞o'vrə], Paris, foremost French museum of art. The building was a royal fortress built by PHILIP II in the late 12th cent. In 1546 a new building was erected on the site by FRANCIS I, designed by Pierre Lescot. LEONARDO's *Mona Lisa* and other works by Italian artists came into the royal collections. In 1606, under HENRY IV, the Grande Galerie was completed. Art was collected with state funds, and more buildings were constructed, including the colonnade, completed in 1670 by Louis Le Vau and Claude Perrault. In 1793 the Grande Galerie was officially opened, with the area beneath serving as artists' studios and workshops. A new entrance complex beneath the main courtyard, designed by I.M. PEI and crowned by a glass pyramid, opened in 1989, and the exhibition space and underground facilities were greatly expanded in 1993. The museum is famous for its collection of Greek, Roman, and Egyptian antiquities, and old masters such as REMBRANDT, RUBENS, TITIAN, and LEONARDO. Its famous sculptures include the NIKE, or *Victory of Samothrace,* and the *Venus of Milo.* The Jeu de Paume, which formerly housed impressionist art, is an exhibition hall for contemporary art.

Lovelace, Richard, 1618–1657?, English Cavalier poet. An ardent royalist, he was imprisoned under Oliver CROMWELL and died in extreme poverty. He is remembered chiefly for two much-quoted lyrics, "To Althea, from Prison" and "To Lucasta, Going to the Wars." His poems were published in 1649 and 1660.

Lovell, Sir (Alfred Charles) Bernard, 1913–, English radio astronomer. He was the leader of the team that built at Jodrell Bank, near Manchester, England, what was then the largest steerable radio telescope (completed 1957). The telescope (since been surpassed in size) is now a part of the NUFFIELD RADIO ASTRONOMY LABORATORIES, which Lovell directed (1945–81).

Lowell, Abbott Lawrence, 1856–1943, American educator; b. Boston; brother of Percival LOWELL and Amy LOWELL. As president (1909–33) of HARVARD UNIV. he developed the undergraduate college, modifying (1914) the elective system, establishing (1917) a general examination in the major subject, and instituting (1917) the tutorial system for upperclassmen. He also established (1931) a "house plan" like that in English universities. A defender of academic freedom, he wrote *Essays on Government* (1889, new ed. 1969) and *Conflicts of Principle* (1932).

Lowell, Amy, 1874–1925, American poet; b. Brookline, Mass.; sister of Percival LOWELL and Abbott Lawrence LOWELL. After writing the conventional verse in *A Dome of Many-Colored Glass* (1912), she went to England (1913), where she became a leader of the IMAGISTS. Notable for its rendering of sensuous images, her poetry is included in such volumes as *Sword Blades and Poppy Seeds* (1914) and *What's o'Clock* (1925; Pulitzer). Lowell also wrote perceptive literary criticism and a two-volume biography of KEATS (1925).

Lowell, Francis Cabot, 1775–1817, pioneer American cotton manufacturer; b. Newburyport, Mass. A Boston merchant, he studied (1810) textile machinery in England, then designed the first power loom in America and built the first U.S. factory, at Waltham, Mass., to perform all operations involved in converting raw cotton into cloth. LOWELL, Mass., was named for him.

Lowell, James Russell, 1819–91, American man of letters; b. Cambridge, Mass. His poetry ranges from the didactic—*The Vision of Sir Launfal* (1848)—to the satiric—*The Bigelow Papers* (1848; 2d series, 1867)—to the critical—*A Fable for Critics* (1848). A professor of modern languages at Harvard (1855–76), he was also the editor of the *Atlantic Monthly* (1857–61) and the *North American Review* (1864–72). He later turned to scholarship and criticism, and his essays were collected in *Fireside Travels* (1864), *Among My Books* (1870; 2d series, 1876), and *My Study Windows* (1871). As U.S. minister to London (1877–85), Lowell did much to increase European respect for American letters and institutions, and his speeches in England, published as *Democracy and Other Addresses* (1887), are among his best work.

Lowell, Percival, 1855–1916, American astronomer; b. Boston; brother of Abbott Lawrence LOWELL and Amy LOWELL. His contention that there was a planet beyond Neptune was confirmed (1930) by the discovery of Pluto. The observations that he and his assistants made at the Lowell Observatory (Flagstaff, Ariz.), which he founded in 1894, led him to interpret certain linear features seen on the planet Mars as artificial waterways, or canals, and thus to believe that Mars was inhabited.

Lowell, Robert, 1917–77, American poet; b. Boston. His poetry is intense, richly symbolic, and often autobiographical. Volumes include *Lord Weary's Castle* (1946; Pulitzer), *Life Studies* (1959), *The Dolphin* (1973; Pulitzer), and *Day by Day* (1977). His other works include translations, e.g., Racine's *Phèdre* (1969), and plays.

Lowell, city (1990 pop. 103,439), a seat of Middlesex co., NE Mass, at the confluence of the Merrimack and Concord rivers; settled 1653, inc. as a city 1836. The city developed around its great textile mills. Its modern manufactures include electronic equipment, chemicals, machine parts, and rubber and plastic products. It is the site of Lowell National Historic Park, which contains industrial and historical museums. James WHISTLER, whose birthplace is preserved, was born there.

Lower Saxony, state (1990 est. pop. 7,239,000), 18,295 sq mi (47,384 sq km), N Germany. HANOVER is the capital. Lower Saxony was formed (1946) by the merger of the former Prussian province of Hanover with the former states of Brunswick, Oldenburg, and Schaumburg-Lippe. The state is drained by the Weser, Ems, Aller, Leine, and Elbe rivers and has several North Sea ports. Farming and cattle-raising are important occupations. Manufactures include iron and steel, textiles, and machinery. The region, although considered a geographic entity, had no historic unity after the dissolution of the duchy of HENRY THE LION of Saxony in 1180.

Lowie, Robert Harry or **Robert Heinrich,** 1883–1957, American anthropologist; b. Vienna. Lowie was known for his ethnological studies of indigenous North American peoples, especially the Plains tribes. His other works include the theoretical classics *Primitive Society* (1920, 2d ed. 1947) and *Social Organization* (1948).

Lowry, (Clarence) Malcolm, 1909–57, English novelist. He is famous for *Under the Volcano* (1947), a subtle, complex, highly autobiographical study of dissolution, set in Mexico. After his death, a reworking of his first novel, *Ultramarine* (1933), poetry, and short stories appeared.

low-temperature fusion: see COLD FUSION.

low-temperature physics or **cryogenics,** branch of physics concerned with the production and maintenance of extremely low temperatures, and with the effects that occur under such conditions. Low temperatures are achieved by removing energy from a substance. By using a succession of liquefied gases, a substance may be cooled to as low as 4.2K, the boiling point of liquid helium. Still lower temperatures may be reached by successive magnetization and demagnetization. Temperatures as low as about one millionth of a degree above absolute zero on the Kelvin scale were attained in 1991 by using infrared lasers first to reduce the energy level of cesium atoms in a vacuum and then to induce further energy loss in the atoms. Some unusual conditions, notably SUPERCONDUCTIVITY, SUPERFLUIDITY, and large-scale quantum mechanical effects, prevail at cryogenic temperatures.

Loyang: see LUOYANG.

Loyola, Ignatius of: see IGNATIUS OF LOYOLA, SAINT.

Lr, chemical symbol of the element LAWRENCIUM.

LSD or **lysergic acid diethylamide,** HALLUCINOGENIC DRUG, an extremely potent drug causing physiological and behavioral changes. Reactions to LSD, such as heightened sense perceptions, anxiety, and hallucinations, are influenced by the amount of the drug taken and the user's personality and expectations. Prolonged psychic disturbances have been reported with LSD use, and there is some evidence linking it with chromosome damage.

Lu, chemical symbol of the element LUTETIUM.

Luanda, city (1989 est. pop. 1,460,000), capital of Angola, a port on the Atlantic Ocean. Angola's largest city, Luanda is an administrative and manufacturing center that produces a variety of consumer goods. A refinery processes petroleum from nearby wells. Founded (1575) by the Portuguese, it was the center (16th–19th cent.) of a slave trade to Brazil. A modern city, it is the seat of the Univ. of Angola. The 17th-cent. fort of São Miguel is among its points of interest.

Lubbock, city (1990 pop. 186,206), seat of Lubbock co., NW Tex.; settled 1879, inc. 1909. On a branch of the Brazos R., it is a trade center for a grain and cotton region of W Texas and E New Mexico. Lubbock's growing industry includes the manufacture of electronic and oil-field equipment.

Lübeck, city (1989 est. pop. 211,000), Schleswig-Holstein, N Germany, on the Trave R. near its mouth on the Baltic Sea. It is a major port and has such industries as shipbuilding and food processing. Chartered c.1158, it headed (13th–17th cent.) the HANSEATIC LEAGUE. Its medieval Gothic architecture, damaged during WORLD WAR II, has been restored. The writers Thomas and Heinrich MANN were born in Lübeck.

Lubumbashi, city (1984 pop. 543,268), capital of Shaba region, SE Zaïre, near the Zambian border. It is a commercial and industrial center, situated on a transcontinental railroad. Founded in 1910 as Elisabethville, it prospered from the region's copper-mining industry. As capital of the secessionist state of Katanga (now SHABA), it was the scene of heavy fighting in the early 1960s.

Lucan (Marcus Annaeus Lucanus), A.D. 39–65, Latin poet, nephew of SENECA. Ten books of his epic *Bellum civile* (on the civil war between POMPEY and CAESAR), wrongly called *Pharsalia,* survive; they were esteemed by later writers.

Lucas, George W., Jr., 1944–, American film director and producer. His early successes included *American Graffiti* (1973). He wrote and directed *Star Wars* (1977), produced its two sequels (and co-wrote one of them), and produced *Raiders of the Lost Ark* (1981) and the two subsequent Indiana Jones films. His films are noted for the innovative use of special effects. He owns film production, special effects, and other entertainment companies.

Lucas van Leyden [vän lī'dən], 1494–1533, Dutch historical and Genre painter and engraver. Dutch paintings of daily life begin with Lucas. His art is noted for its realism, dramatic power, and careful execution. Lucas produced more than 200 ETCHINGS, ENGRAVINGS, and designs for woodcuts, e.g. *Adam and Eve* (1519). His paintings include *Virgin Enthroned* (Berlin).

Luce, Henry Robinson, 1898–1967, American publisher; b. China. In 1923, with Briton Hadden, he founded *Time,* a weekly news magazine featuring capsulated news accounts written in a brisk, adjective-laden style. His other periodicals included *Fortune* (1930), *Life* (1936), and *Sports Illustrated* (1954). His wife, **Clare Booth Luce,** 1903–87, b. N.Y.C., was a playwright and diplomat. She was best known for her witty, satirical play *The Women* (1936). She was a U.S. representative from Connecticut (1943–47) and later served (1953–56) as ambassador to Italy.

Lucian (Lucianus), b. c.125, d. after 180, Greek prose writer. Most characteristic of his vigorous and witty satire are his dialogues (*Dialogues of the Gods, Dialogues of the Dead, The Sale of Lives*) dealing with ancient mythology and contemporary philosophy. His fantastic *True History* influenced SWIFT and RABELAIS.

Luciani, Sebastiano: see SEBASTIANO DEL PIOMBO.

Lucifer: see SATAN.

Lucilius, Gaius, c.180–102? B.C., the father of Latin SATIRE. He influenced HORACE, PERSIUS, and JUVENAL.

Lucretius (Titus Lucretius Carus), c.99–c.55 B.C., Roman poet and philosopher. His poetry constitutes one great didactic work in six books, *De rerum natura* [on the nature of things]. In dignified hexameter verse he set forth arguments based on the philosophy of DEMOCRITUS and EPICURUS. Using the so-called atomic theory of the ancients, he argued that a person need not fear gods or death because everything, even the soul, is made up of atoms controlled by natural laws; thus there is no immortality, consciousness ending with death. Though not the same as modern atomic theory, Lucretius' teachings have been upheld in many respects by later investigation.

Lucullus (Lucius Licinius Lucullus Ponticus), c.110 B.C.–56 B.C., Roman general. He served in the Social War (90–88 B.C.) under Sulla, who made him his favorite. Lucullus defeated MITHRIDATES VI of Pontus. He then provoked great unpopularity in Rome by reforming the provincial finances. In 66 B.C. POMPEY replaced Lucullus, who retired to Rome and became known for showy elegance; hence the term *Lucullan.*

Lüda: see DALIAN.

Luddites, bands of laborers who rioted (1811–16) in the industrial areas of England; named for the mythical Ned Ludd or King Ludd. Starting in Nottinghamshire, rioters destroyed textile machines, to which they attributed high unemployment and low wages. The riots were harshly suppressed.

Ludendorff, Erich, 1865–1937, German general. As chief of staff to Field Marshal HINDENBURG in WORLD WAR I, he was largely responsible for German military strategy. After 1916 he also intervened in civilian matters. He supported the Nazis in the 1920s and wrote pamphlets idealizing the "Aryan" race and attacking the pope, Jews, Jesuits, and Freemasons.

Ludwig: for German rulers thus named, see LOUIS.

Ludwig, Christa, 1928–, German mezzo-soprano. She starred at the Vienna State Opera (from 1955) and the METROPOLITAN OPERA (1959–93). Possessing an expressive voice of considerable range, she is a noted interpreter of MAHLER.

luffa: see GOURD.

luge, type of small sled in which one or two persons race down snowy hillsides or steeply banked, curving chutes. Steering is accomplished by shifting weight, pulling straps attached to the runners, and use of the feet. Lugeing is an Olympic event for both men and women.

Lugones, Leopoldo [lōōgō'nās], 1874–1938, Argentine poet. He expressed his adherence to MODERNISMO in *The Golden Mountains* (1897) and *Twilight in the Garden* (1905). His prose includes history and short stories.

Lu Hsun, 1881–1936, Chinese author; b. Chou Shu-jen. Lu sought to awaken the Chinese to the values of Western science and philosophy. His gift for satire and his use of the vernacular made him popular. At first attacked as bourgeois by the Communists, he was later called the GORKY of China.

Luke, Saint, early Christian, traditional author of the third GOSPEL and of the ACTS OF THE APOSTLES. A Gentile called by St. PAUL "the beloved physician," he accompanied Paul to Rome.

Luke, Gospel according to Saint, third book of the NEW TESTAMENT, composed late in the 1st cent. A.D., ascribed since the 2d cent. to St. LUKE. A literary composition, it shows the thoughtful use of several sources, including MARK. Luke contains a unique account of the birth and boyhood of JESUS. The GOSPEL shows Pauline influences, e.g., with regard to the equality of human beings and the universality of salvation.

Luks, George Benjamin [lōōks], 1867–1933, American painter; b. Williamsport, Pa. One of the EIGHT, he is known for his portraits, painted with dash and verve, and his genre scenes, e.g., *The Spielers* (Addison Gall., Andover, Mass.).

Lully, Jean Baptiste [lülē'], 1632–87, French operatic composer; b. Italy. After 1652 he was a chamber composer and conductor for LOUIS XIV. He wrote BALLETS and in 1672 obtained a patent for the production of OPERA. Among his operas are *Cadmus et Hermione* (1673), *Alceste* (1674), and *Amadis* (1684). He established the form of the French OVERTURE and set French operatic style until GLUCK.

Lumière, Louis Jean [lümyĕr'], 1864–1948, and **Auguste Lumière,** 1862–1954, French inventors, brothers. In 1895 they patented and demonstrated the Cinématographe, the first documented device for photographing, printing, and projecting films.

luminescence, the emission of light by sources other than a hot, incandescent body. It is caused by the movement of electrons within a substance from more energetic states to less energetic states. Among several types are chemiluminescence, electroluminescence, and triboluminescence, which are produced, respectively, by chemical reactions, electric discharges, and the rubbing or crushing of crystals. See also BIOLUMINESCENCE; FLUORESCENCE; PHOSPHORESCENCE.

luminism, American art movement of the 19th cent., related to IMPRESSIONISM, that sought to render the mystical effect of diffused light on the landscape. Luminists included KENSETT, FitzHugh Lane, and Frederick E. CHURCH.

luminosity, the rate at which energy of all types is radiated by a STAR in all directions. A star's luminosity varies approximately as the square of its radius and the fourth power of its absolute surface temperature. See MAGNITUDE; SPECTRAL CLASS.

Lumumba, Patrice Emergy, 1925–61, 1st prime minister of the Republic of the Congo (now ZAÏRE). Shortly after becoming (1960) prime minister, he clashed with KASAVUBU and MOBUTU. He was arrested and died under mysterious circumstances.

Luna, Pedro de, 1328?–1423?, Spanish cardinal, antipope (1394–1417) as Benedict XIII. He supported the election of URBAN VI, but deserted him for Robert of Geneva, who as Antipope Clement VII, launched the Great SCHISM. On Robert's death, Luna was elected to succeed him. He refused to abdicate at the Council of Pisa (1409), but was deposed by the Council of Constance (1417). To his death he continued to claim he was the rightful pope.

Luna, in space exploration: see SPACE PROBE, table.

Lunar Orbiter: see SPACE PROBE, table.

Lunar Rover: see SPACE EXPLORATION, table.

lungfish, lung-bearing FISH, often resembling an EEL, found in rivers in South America, Africa, and Australia. Like the LOBEFIN, it is ancestrally related to the four-footed land animals. The most primitive living lungfish is a stout-bodied Australian species, 5 ft (150 cm) long with paired fins set on short stumps. African species, which hibernate in hard clay during the dry season, breathe through gills in water. Other species will drown if held under water.

lungs, pair of elastic organs used for breathing in vertebrate animals. In humans, they are located on either side of the heart, filling much of the chest cavity. Air enters each lung through a large tube, or bronchus, which divides and subdivides into a network of bronchioles. These tiny tubules lead to cup-shaped air sacs known as alveoli, each of which is surrounded by a net of capillaries. As blood flows through the capillary net, carbon dioxide passes into the alveoli and oxygen diffuses into the bloodstream. Covered by a thin membrane, the pleura, which allows them to move freely during breathing, the lungs are expanded (inhalation) and contracted (exhalation) by the combined movement of the diaphragm and the rib cage. Diseases of the lungs include bronchitis, pleurisy, and pneumonia. See RESPIRATION.

Lunt, Alfred, 1893–1977, b. Milwaukee, **and Lynn Fontanne** [fŏntăn'], 1887–1983, b. England, American acting team. Married in 1922, they appeared together from 1924, excelling in sophisticated comedy, e.g., *Design for Living* (1933).

Luoyang or **Loyang,** city (1990 est. pop. 1,190,000), NW Henan prov., China, on the Luo R. Since 1949 it has become an important industrial city producing mining machinery, tractors, ball bearings, and other products. A major cultural center, it was the capital of several ancient dynasties, e.g., the Eastern Chou kingdom (770–256 B.C.) and the T'ang dynasty (A.D. 618–906). The famous Buddhist caves of Longmen (6th cent. A.D.), with their stone carvings, are nearby.

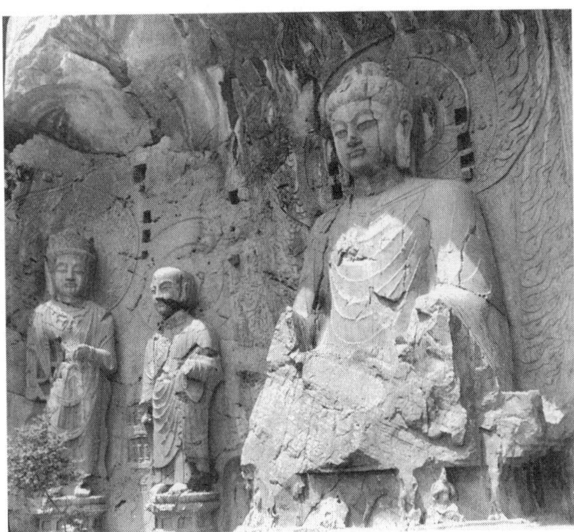

Buddhist caves of Luoyang

lupus erythematosus: see AUTOIMMUNE DISEASE.

Luria or **Loria, Isaac ben Solomon,** 1534–72, Jewish cabalist, surnamed Ashkenazi, called Ari [lion]; b. Jerusalem. He settled (c.1570) at Safed, Palestine, where he led an important school of mysticism that combined Messianism with older cabalistic doctrines (see CABALA). Luria was concerned with the nature of, and the connection between, earthly redemption and cosmic restoration.

Lusaka, largest city (1987 est. pop. 819,000) and capital of Zambia, S central Zambia. Located in a productive farm area, it is a commercial center and a transportation hub, at the junction of highways to Tanzania, Malawi, and Zimbabwe. Founded in 1905, the city developed after 1935, when it became the capital of what was then the British protectorate of Northern Rhodesia.

Lusitania, British liner sunk off the Irish coast by a German submarine on May 7, 1915. Of the 1,195 lives lost, 128 were U.S. citizens. Even though the Germans had warned Americans not to take passage on British ships, the incident contributed to the rise of American sentiment in favor of entering WORLD WAR I on the side of the Allies.

lute: see STRINGED INSTRUMENT.

lutetium (Lu), metallic element, discovered independently by Georges Urbain in 1907 and by Carl Auer von Welsbach in 1908. A silver-white RARE-EARTH METAL and LANTHANIDE-SERIES element with few commercial uses, it is found in MONAZITE. See ELEMENT (table); PERIODIC TABLE.

Luther, Martin, 1483–1546, German leader of the Protestant REFORMATION. In 1505, Luther completed his master's examination and began the study of law. Several months later, after what seems to have been a sudden religious experience, he entered an Augustinian monastery at Erfurt, was ordained (1507) a priest, and was assigned (1508) to the Univ. of Wittenberg. In 1510, on a mission to Rome, he was shocked by the spiritual laxity in high ecclesiastical places. Returning to Wittenberg, he developed a great spiritual anxiety about his salvation, but in his study (1513) of the Scriptures, especially St. Paul, he found a loving God who bestowed upon sinful humans the free gift of salvation, received by faith alone, and not by works. This resolved his turmoil. From 1516 he protested the dispensation of INDULGENCES, then being preached by John Tetzel, whose arrival in Saxony in 1517 prompted Luther to post his historic 95 theses on the door of the castle church. While these were appreciated by many within Germany, they were a threat to the church. Several attempts at reconciliation failed, and Luther broadened his position to include widespread reforms. He supported the new nationalism by advocating German control of the German church. When a bull of condemnation (*Exsurge Domine*) was issued, he burned it publicly and was excommunicated in 1521. Summoned before the Diet of Worms (1521), Luther was forced to take refuge in the Wartburg after the diet ordered his seizure. There, under the protection of Elector Frederick III of Saxony, Luther translated the New Testament into German and began a translation of the entire Bible. He then returned to Wittenberg, where he stayed for most of the remainder of his life. His opposition to the Peasants' War (1524–25) cost him some popular support. Nevertheless, through his forceful writings and preaching, his doctrines spread. He married (1525) a former nun, Katharina von Bora, and raised six children. Luther worked to build a competent educational system and wrote extensively on church matters, including a liturgy, hymns, and two catechisms, but his uncompromising attitude in doctrinal matters helped break the unity of the Reformation. Controversies with Huldreich ZWINGLI and John CALVIN eventually divided the Protestants into the Lutheran and the Reformed churches. Under his sanction, Philip MELANCHTHON wrote a Lutheran confession of faith, the Augsburg Confession, at the Diet of Augsburg in 1530. About this time control of the Lutheran Church passed further into the hands of the Protestant princes, and Luther's last years were troubled with ill health and the plagues of political and religious disunion. He left behind an evangelical doctrine that spread throughout the Western world. In Germany his socio-religious concepts laid a new basis for German society, and his writings helped to fix the standards of the modern German language.

Lutheranism, branch of Protestantism that arose as a result of the REFORMATION, whose religious faith is based on the principles of Martin LUTHER, although he opposed such a designation. Luther's conservative attitudes, as distinguished from those of Calvinists, held that the Scriptures contained all that was necessary for salvation, which came by faith alone. His two catechisms contain the principal statements of faith. Baptism is necessary for spiritual regeneration, and the sacrament of the Lord's Supper (see COMMUNION) was also retained, although transubstantiation was replaced by consubstantiation. Some churches are episcopal, e.g., in Sweden, and others have a synodal form of organization, but unity is based on doctrine rather than structure. In Germany, Lutheranism has had close associations with political life, and it is the established church of the Scandinavian countries. Lutherans in America first formed (1638) a congregation at Fort Christina (Wilmington, Del.). In the 18th cent. exiles from the Palatinate established German Lutheran churches throughout the mid-Atlantic colonies, and Heinrich Melchior MÜHLENBERG formed (1748) the first American synod in Pennsylvania. The American Lutheran Church, the Lutheran Church-Missouri Synod, and the Lutheran Church in America comprise most of the nearly 8.4 million American Lutherans. World membership in the Lutheran church is more than 70 million.

Luthuli, Albert John, 1898?–1967, South African political leader. A ZULU chief and a Christian, he opposed racial discrimination in South Africa and advocated nonviolence and passive resistance against APARTHEID. He was banished by the white government, but he retained the loyalty of black South Africans. He won the 1960 Nobel Peace Prize.

Lutyens, Sir Edwin Landseer, 1869–1944, English architect. His sprawling Edwardian country house designs, such as Deanery Garden, Sonning (1899–1902), combined the best features of open planning with traditional forms and exquisite craftsmanship. In collaboration with landscape designer Gertrude JEKYLL, Lutyens laid out many romantic English gardens, which serve as ideal settings for his houses. Along with Herbert Baker, Lutyens began the planning and design of the imperial capital of New Delhi, India, in 1912. His monumental Viceroy's House (1912–31) is considered his masterpiece, with Asian motifs superimposed on an overall Beaux-Arts classicism. Lutyens has been particularly admired by postmodern architects for his ability to manipulate traditional forms in an inventive manner.

Luxembourg or **Luxemburg,** officially Grand Duchy of Luxembourg, constitutional monarchy (1992 est. pop. 392,000), 998 sq mi (2,586 sq km), W Europe; bordered by Belgium (W and N), Germany (E), and France (S). The city of LUXEMBOURG is the capital. The grand duchy is drained by tributaries of the Moselle R. The ARDENNES Mts. extend into N Luxembourg. Part of the Luxembourg-Lorraine iron-mining basin is in the southwest, and Luxembourg is a major iron and steel producer. Other manufactures include food products, leather goods, textiles, and chemicals. Grains and potatoes are grown, and livestock, especially cattle, are raised. Luxembourg is an important financial center. The people, chiefly Roman Catholic, speak French (the official language), Letzeburgesch (a Low German dialect), and German. The ruling house of NASSAU came to the throne in 1890; the present grand duke, Jean, succeeded his mother in 1964.

History. The medieval county of Luxembourg (originally Lützelburg), which lay between the Meuse and Moselle rivers and included parts of present-day BELGIUM, was one of the largest fiefs of the HOLY ROMAN EMPIRE. It rose to prominence when its ruler was elected emperor as Henry VII in 1308, and it was raised to the status of duchy in 1354. Conquered by PHILIP THE GOOD of Burgundy in 1443, the duchy passed in 1482 to the Hapsburgs and in 1797 to the French. The Congress of Vienna (1814–15) made Luxembourg a grand duchy under the king of the Netherlands. Luxembourg joined Belgium in revolt (1830) against the Netherlands, and after Belgian independence the greater part of the grand duchy became (1839) part of Belgium (the present Belgian Luxembourg prov.). The remainder became autonomous in 1848. Although neutral, Luxembourg was occupied by the Germans in both world wars. Since World War II Luxembourg has played an active role in fostering Western European integration, joining the Benelux Economic Union and the Common Market (see EUROPEAN UNION). It is a member of NATO.

Luxembourg or **Luxemburg,** capital (1987 est. pop. 77,000) of the Grand Duchy of Luxembourg. A commercial, industrial, administrative, and cultural center, the picturesque city developed around a 10th-cent. castle. Of note are the Cathedral of Notre Dame and the city hall (both 16th cent.). Several EUROPEAN COMMUNITY institutions are there.

Luxemburg, Rosa, 1871–1919, German revolutionary; b. Russian Poland. While a student, she helped to found (1892) the Polish Socialist party. After 1898 she was a leader in the German Social Democratic party, and became a brilliant writer and orator. She and Karl Liebknecht founded (c.1916) the Marxist SPARTACUS PARTY, forerunner to the German Communist party. Arrested in the Spartacist uprising of 1919, she and Liebknecht were murdered by soldiers.

Luxor, city (1986 pop. 125,404), central Egypt, on the Nile R., 1 mi (1.6 km) E of KARNAK. The temple of Luxor (623 ft/190 m long), the city's greatest monument of antiquity, was built under Amenhotep III and altered by later pharaohs. Many temples and burial grounds, including the Valley of the Tombs of the Kings, are nearby.

Luzon, island (1980 est. pop. 23,900,000), Philippines, largest (40,420 sq mi/104,688 sq km) and most populous of the Philippine Islands. Much of it is mountainous, rising to a high point of 9,606 ft (2,928 m) at Mt. Pulog. Most of the population is concentrated in

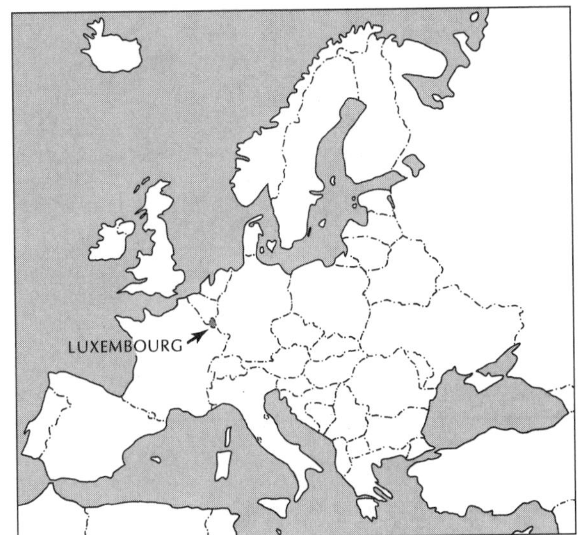

the MANILA metropolitan area and between the mountains in the low-lying central Luzon Plain, c.100 mi (160 km) long and 40 mi (65 km) wide, along the Pampanga and Agno rivers. Rice, sugarcane, coconuts, tobacco, and corn are important crops. Manufacturing is centered around Manila, where the major industries produce textiles, chemicals, and metal products. During WORLD WAR II Japan invaded Luzon in 1941, and in early 1942 the Allied forces made their last stand there on BATAAN peninsula and the offshore island of CORREGIDOR.

Lviv, Rus. *Lvov,* city (1991 est. pop. 600,000), W Ukraine, at the watershed of the Western Bug and Dniester rivers and in the northern foothills of the Carpathian Mts. Chief city of the W UKRAINE, it has such industries as oil refining and automobile manufacturing. Founded c.1256, it became a commercial center on the trade route from VIENNA to KIEV. Its famous university was established in 1661. Lviv was held by the Poles, Turks, and Swedes (14th–18th cent.). In 1772 it passed to Austria and, as Lemberg, became the capital of the region of GALICIA. Held by Poland (and known as Lwów) after 1919 and by the USSR after 1939, it was occupied for much of WORLD WAR II by the Germans, who exterminated most of the Jewish population. In 1945, Poland formally ceded the city to the USSR.

Lvov, Georgi Yevgenyevich, Prince [lyəvôf′], 1861–1925, Russian public official. He headed the provisional government formed after the Feb. 1917 RUSSIAN REVOLUTION but resigned in favor of KERENSKY in July. Lvov later emigrated to Paris.

Lvov: see LVIV.

Lwoff, André, 1902–, French microbiologist. In the 1920s his study of the morphogenesis of protozoa led to the discovery of extranuclear inheritance in these organisms. After World War II he conducted experiments that enabled him to explain the phenomena of lysogenic bacteria (see BACTERIOPHAGE). For his contributions to molecular biology, Lwoff shared with François JACOB and Jacques MONOD the 1965 Nobel Prize in physiology or medicine.

Lyallpur: see FAISALABAD.

lycanthropy, in folklore, assumption by a human, through witchcraft or magic, of the form and nature of an animal. Belief in lycanthropy has been widespread since ancient times. One of the best-known superstitions is a belief in werewolves, persons who consume human flesh or blood and change to and from wolves. The term *lycanthropy* also applies to a psychosis in which victims believe themselves to be animals.

lyceum, 19th-cent. American association for popular instruction of adults by lectures, concerts, and other methods. The National American Lyceum (1831) developed from lectures given by Josiah Holbrook, and soon leaders of the time lectured to lyceum audiences on the arts, sciences, history, and public affairs, stimulating interest in general education. The movement became a powerful force in social and educational reform. After the Civil War, the CHAUTAUQUA MOVEMENT took its place.

lycopodiophyte, member of a division (Lycopodiophyta or Lycophyta) that comprises the primitive vascular plants known as CLUB MOSSES, spike-moss, and quillworts. Some species are known only as fossils.

Lydgate, John, c.1370–c.1450, English poet, one of the most versatile and prolific medieval writers. He wrote Chaucerian poems, e.g., *Complaint of the Black Knight;* long translations; and fables and other short poems.

lye: see SOAP.

Lyell, Sir Charles, 1797–1875, English geologist. He helped win acceptance of James HUTTON's theory of UNIFORMITARIANISM and of Charles DARWIN's theory of EVOLUTION. Lyell's *Principles of Geology* (3 vol., 1830–33) went into 12 editions in his lifetime. His research led him to divide the Tertiary period into the Eocene, Miocene, and Pliocene epochs.

Lyly or **Lilly, John,** 1554?–1606, English dramatist and prose writer, best known for his novel *Euphues,* published in two parts (*The Anatomy of Wit,* 1578; *Euphues and His England,* 1580), in which he tried to establish an ideal prose style, actually artificial and convoluted. Lyly's plays introduced prose as a vehicle for comic dialogue.

Lyme disease, bacterial infection that causes symptoms ranging from a rash, fever, and headache to a painful swelling of the joints that resembles arthritis. First identified in 1975 in Lyme, Conn., the disease is caused by the spirochete *Borrelia burgdorferi* and is transmitted by the deer tick, *Ixodes dammini.* The disease is usually successfully treated with antibiotics, especially in its early stages. If untreated it can cause permanent damage to the heart and nervous system.

lymphatic system, network of vessels carrying lymph, or tissue fluid, from the TISSUES into the veins of the CIRCULATORY SYSTEM. Lymph, a colorless fluid similar to blood but containing no red blood cells or platelets and considerably less protein, is continuously passing through the walls of the capillaries. It transports nutrients and oxygen to the cells and collects waste products. It also transports large molecules, such as proteins, and bacteria, which cannot enter the small pores of the circulatory system. Most of the lymph passes back into the venous capillaries; however, a small amount is returned to the blood via the lymphatic system. The lymphatic system is composed of fine capillaries that lie adjacent to the blood capillaries. These merge first into larger tributaries called trunks, and then into two still larger vessels called ducts. Ducts feed into the circulatory system in the region of the collarbone, returning the lymph to the bloodstream there. Along the lymphatic network, in the neck, armpit, groin, abdomen, and chest, are small reservoirs, the lymph nodes, which collect bacteria and other deleterious agents and act as a barrier against the entrance of these substances into the blood. The lymphatic system, like the circulatory system, absorbs nutrients from the small intestine. Enlarged lymph nodes may be a sign of infection or various kinds of cancer, including breast cancer and Hodgkin's disease.

Lynch, John, 1917–, prime minister of the Republic of Ireland (1966–73, 1977–79). He entered the Dáil (parliament) in 1948 as a member of the FIANNA FÁIL party and later served as minister for education (1957–59) and minister for industry and commerce (1959–65). Lynch led Fianna Fáil from 1966 until 1979, when he resigned the party leadership and was replaced as prime minister by Charles HAUGHEY.

Lynd, Robert Staughton, 1892–1970, American sociologist; b. New Albany, Ind. A teacher at Columbia Univ. (1931–61), he was noted for his studies of Muncie, Ind. (*Middletown,* 1929; *Middletown in Transition,* 1937).

Lynn, Loretta, 1935–, American singer and songwriter; b. Butcher Hollow, Ky. One of the most successful modern country-music singers, she had 22 top-ten hits from 1962 to 1971. *Coalminer's Daughter* (1978) is her autobiography.

lynx, any of several small, ferocious CATS found in N North America and N Eurasia. Lynxes have small heads with tufted ears and heavy bodies with long legs and short tails; they have yellow-brown to grayish fur. Nocturnal hunters, they prey mainly on small animals. The Canadian lynx may be over 3 ft (90 cm) in length and weigh up to 40 lb (18 kg). The smaller North American spotted lynx (*Felis rufa*) is also known as a bobcat.

Lyons, Fr. *Lyon* [both: lyôN′], city (1990 pop. 415,487), capital of Rhône dept., E central France. A leading city in European silk and rayon production, it has many industries, e.g., metal and machine, and is a leader in banking and education. There, during Roman rule, Christianity was introduced into Gaul. Lyons was ruled by its archbishops until c.1307, when it passed to the French crown. In the 12th cent. the WALDENSES were organized there. During World War II the French resistance movement was based (1940–44) in Lyons.

Lyons, Councils of: see COUNCIL, ECUMENICAL.

lyre: see STRINGED INSTRUMENT.

lyric, in ancient Greece, a poem accompanied by music, usually a lyre. The term now refers to any short poem expressing personal emotion: SONNET, ODE, song, or ELEGY. The Greek monody or individual song was developed by SAPPHO and ALCAEUS, the choral lyric by PINDAR, the Latin lyric by CATULLUS and HORACE. The lyric became common in Christian hymns, in FOLK SONGS, and in TROUBADOUR songs. Renaissance lyric reached a peak in the sonnets of PETRARCH and SHAKESPEARE, and the short poems of RONSARD and DONNE. The lyric was a popular form for the expression of personal emotion among 19th-cent. poets in Europe (e.g., KEATS, LAMARTINE) and the U.S. (e.g., WHITMAN, DICKINSON). Among the lyric poets of the 20th cent. are W.B. YEATS, Edna St. Vincent MILLAY, Dylan THOMAS, and Robert LOWELL.

Lysander [līsăn′dər], d. 395 B.C., Spartan naval commander. He was responsible for the capture of the Athenian fleet (405 B.C.) and the final submission (404) of ATHENS to SPARTA that ended the PELOPONNESIAN WAR.

Lysenko, Trofim Denisovich, 1898–1976, Soviet agronomist. As president (1938–56, 1961–62) of the Lenin Academy of Agricultural Science, he was the scientific and administrative head of Soviet agriculture; he also directed (1940–65) the Institute of Genetics of the Soviet Academy of Sciences. He rejected Mendelian genetics in favor of the doctrine of ACQUIRED CHARACTERISTICS. His ideas were presented and accepted as Marxist orthodoxy until after the death of Joseph STALIN, when they were severely criticized.

lysergic acid diethylamide: see LSD.

Lysippos [līsĭp′əs], fl. late 4th cent. B.C., Greek sculptor, head of the Sicyon school. He modified the proportions for the human figure set by POLYKLEITOS, and Hellenistic sculpture was based on this more slender form with its new sense of movement. Many copies were made of the 1,500 works he was said to have produced, but no originals remain.

Lytton, Edward George Earle Lytton Bulwer-Lytton, 1st **Baron:** see under BULWER-LYTTON.

Lytton, Edward Robert Bulwer-Lytton, earl of, pseud. **Owen Meredith:** see under BULWER-LYTTON.

M

Ma, Yo-Yo, 1955–, American cellist; b. Paris. A prodigy who gave a public recital in Paris at age six, he studied in New York with the cellist Leonard Rose and appeared at Carnegie Hall in 1964. He is noted for his interpretive power and stage presence.

Maas, river, Europe: see MEUSE.

Maastricht Treaty: see EUROPEAN UNION.

Mabinogion, collective title given medieval Welsh stories found in two manuscripts, the *White Book of Rhydderch* (c.1300–1325) and the *Red Book of Hergest* (c.1375–1425). *The Four Branches of the Mabinogi* includes three Arthurian romances—*Geraint, The Lady of the Fountain,* and *Peredur*—and other material making it an invaluable source of ARTHURIAN LEGEND.

Mabuse, Jan de [mäbüz′], c.1478–c.1533, Flemish painter; b. Jan Gossaert or Gossart. He was among the first Flemish painters to represent the nude and classical mythology in the Italian manner. *A Donor and His Wife* (Brussels) and *Neptune and Amphitrite* (Berlin) are characteristic paintings.

Mac, Mc, or **M'** [Irish, = son], element in names derived from Irish and Scottish Gaelic patronymics. In most of these names the second element was a forename (e.g., *Macdonald,* in various spellings). Notions that some forms of the prefix are more typically Scottish or Irish are fallacious.

macadamia, edible fruit of an evergreen tree (*Macadamia ternifolia*) native to Australia but also grown in other tropical regions. The small, edible kernel of the nut is white and crisp.

Macao [məkou′], Port. *Macau,* Chinese *Aomen,* Portuguese administered territory (1992 est. pop. 473,000), 6 sq mi (15.5 sq km), adjoining Guangdong prov., SE China, on the estuary of the Pearl R., 40 mi (64 km) W of HONG KONG and 65 mi (105 km) S of GUANGZHOU. It consists of a rocky, hilly peninsula (c.2 sq mi/5 sq km), connected by a 700-ft wide isthmus to China; and two small islands. Macao is a free port and a leading trade, tourist, and gambling center. Fishing and textiles are also important. The population is overwhelmingly Chinese and adheres mainly to traditional Chinese beliefs. Portuguese is the official language, but Cantonese is the native and commercial language. The oldest permanent European settlement in Asia, it became a Portuguese trading post in 1557. In 1849 Portugal proclaimed it a free port. Macao has many Chinese refugees. Historic structures, including fine examples of Italian and Portuguese architecture, dot the city. Macao will revert to China in 1999, becoming a special administrative region with an independent capitalist economy for a period of 50 years.

macaroni: see PASTA.

MacArthur, Douglas, 1880–1964, American five-star general; b. Little Rock, Ark. He fought in France in WORLD WAR I and was army chief of staff (1930–35). During WORLD WAR II he commanded the Allied forces in the Southwest Pacific and directed the postwar occupation of Japan. In the KOREAN WAR, as commander of the UN military forces, he became involved in a policy dispute with Pres. TRUMAN, who removed him from command in April 1951. He was an unsuccessful contender for the Republican presidential nomination in 1948 and 1952.

Macaulay, Thomas Babington, 1800–1859, English historian. He sat in Parliament (1830–34, 1839–47, 1852–56), served in India with the EAST INDIA CO. (1834–38), and was secretary of war (1839–41). His greatest work is his *History of England from the Accession of James the Second* (5 vol., 1849–61), a vivid recreation of the social world of the 17th cent. An unprecedented success, it was also criticized for its Whig and Protestant bias. Macaulay was elevated to the peerage in 1857.

Macbeth, d. 1057, king of Scotland (1040–57). Macbeth seized the Scottish throne by killing Duncan I in battle, but was himself defeated and killed by Duncan's son, who reigned as MALCOLM III. He is the subject of Shakespeare's *Macbeth.*

Maccabees, also called **Hasmoneans** and **Asmoneans,** Jewish family (in Palestine) of the 2d and 1st cent. B.C. who restored Jewish political and religious life. When the Syrian ruler Antiochus IV stripped and desecrated the Temple of Jerusalem and began a religious persecution, **Mattathias of Modin** and his five sons, together with many HASIDIM, began a guerrilla war. On Mattathias' death (166 B.C.), leadership passed to his son **Judas Maccabeus** (from whose surname the family name derives), who occupied Jerusalem and rededicated the Temple; the feast of Hanukkah (see JEWISH HOLIDAYS) celebrates this event (165 B.C.). Judas was defeated by DEMETRIUS I of Syria and killed (161? B.C.). The Maccabees remained in power—mostly peacefully—until 63 B.C., when Pompey conquered Palestine for Rome.

Maccabees, two books included in the OLD TESTAMENT of the Western canon, but not in the Hebrew Bible, and placed in the APOCRYPHA in the Authorized Version. First Maccabees is an account of the struggles of the house of Maccabees against Antiochus IV of Syria. Second Maccabees is a devout history of the persecutions of Antiochus and the career of Judas Maccabeus.

McCarthy, Joseph Raymond, 1908–57, U.S. senator from Wisconsin (1947–57); b. near Appleton, Wis. He achieved national prominence and power with his sensational and unsubstantiated accusations against those U.S. officials (frequently in high positions) he termed "Communists." After the Senate "condemned" him (1954), his influence steadily declined.

McCarthy, Mary Therese, 1912–89, American writer; b. Seattle, Wash. Her novels, known for their wit, intellect, and acerbity, include *The Groves of Academe* (1952) and *The Group* (1963). Among her nonfiction works are *Venice Observed* (1956), *Vietnam* (1967), and *How I Grew* (1987). She was married to Edmund WILSON.

McClellan, George Brinton, 1826–85, Union general in the U.S. CIVIL WAR; b. Philadelphia. Appointed general in chief (1861), he was criticized for overcaution in the unsuccessful PENINSULAR CAMPAIGN and removed from command. Called on again (1862), he checked Lee in the ANTIETAM CAMPAIGN, but he allowed the Confederates to withdraw across the Potomac and was again removed. He ran against LINCOLN for president in 1864 but was soundly defeated.

McClintock, Barbara, 1902–92, American geneticist. She discovered that certain genetic material, called "transposable elements," could shift position on a chromosome from generation to generation, altering the expression of a gene, and thus provided a key for understanding cell differentiation. At first ignored, her research was later recognized as a major contribution to DNA research. In 1983 she was awarded the Nobel Prize for physiology or medicine.

McClure, Sir Robert John Le Mesurier, 1807–73, British arctic explorer. As commander (1850–53) of one of two ships searching the Arctic Archipelago for the lost party of Sir John FRANKLIN, he discovered McClure Strait and proved the existence of the NORTHWEST PASSAGE.

McClure, Samuel Sidney, 1857–1949, American editor and publisher; b. Ireland. He established (1884) the McClure Syndicate, the first newspaper syndicate in the U.S. As editor, he made *McClure's Magazine* (which he founded in 1893) a great success, publishing articles by the MUCKRAKERS.

McCormack, John, 1884–1945, Irish-American tenor; b. Ireland. Coming to the U.S. in 1909, he sang with the Boston and Chicago operas, appeared in concerts, and made many famous recordings, often of simple, sentimental songs.

McCormick, Cyrus Hall 1809–84, American inventor; b. Rockbridge co., Va. The reaper that he invented in 1831 contained the straight reciprocating knife, guards, reel, platform, divider, main-drive wheel, and other innovations that are essential features of every harvesting machine.

McCullers, Carson, 1917–67, American author; b. Columbus, Ga. She often explored spiritual isolation in her fiction, using outcasts and misfits as main characters. Her works include the novels *The Heart Is a Lonely Hunter* (1940) and *The Member of the Wedding* (1946; dramatized, 1950), and the short-story collection *The Ballad of the Sad Cafe* (1951; dramatized by Edward ALBEE, 1963).

McCulloch v. Maryland, case decided in 1819 by the U.S. SUPREME COURT. A Maryland tax on all banks not chartered by the state had been levied on operations of the Second BANK OF THE UNITED STATES. Chief Justice MARSHALL found that the power to charter a bank was implied from Congress's power over federal fiscal operations; the state could not impede it. This exposition of the doctrine of implied powers, based on a "loose constructionist" interpretation of the U.S. CONSTITUTION, expanded the scope of federal power.

MacDiarmid, Hugh, pseud. of **Christopher Murray Grieve,** 1892–1978, Scottish poet and critic. A Communist and Scottish nationalist, he rejuvenated indigenous literature. His works include the long poem *A Drunk Man Looks at the Thistle* (1962). His *Complete Poems, 1920–76* (2 vol., 1978) was published posthumously.

Macdonald, Sir John Alexander, 1815–91, 1st prime minister of the Dominion of CANADA. A Conservative leader of Upper Canada, he was prime minister of the Liberal-Conservative coalition that brought about confederation (1867) of the Canadian provinces. As dominion prime minister (1867–73, 1878–91) he established strong links with Britain. Although he resigned (1873) over the PACIFIC SCANDAL, he was returned (1878) to office.

Macdonald, Ramsay, 1866–1937, British statesman. An organizer of the LABOUR PARTY, he was elected (1906) to the House of Commons, where he was party leader (1911–14). Discredited for his pacifism during World War I, he was defeated (1918), but returned to Parliament in 1922. In Jan. 1924 he became prime minister in the country's first Labour government, but in December Labour was defeated amid charges it was pro-Communist. In 1929 Macdonald again became prime minister in a Labour government, but in 1931 formed the coalition National government, which leaned on Conservative support. He resigned the premiership to Stanley BALDWIN in 1935.

Macdonald, Ross, pseud. of **Kenneth Millar,** 1915–83, American author; b. Los Gatos, Calif. Featuring the tough but compassionate private detective Lew Archer, his novels include *The Galton Case* (1959), *The Chill* (1964), *The Good-bye Look* (1969), *The Underground Man* (1971), and *Sleeping Beauty* (1973).

Macdonald-Wright, Stanton, 1890–1973, American painter; b. Charlottesville, Va. With the artist Morgan Russell, he founded synchromism (1912), an American abstract movement related to ORPHISM that employed harmonizing colors and geometric forms.

MacDowell, Edward Alexander, 1861–1908, American composer; b. N.Y.C. His outstanding works are four piano sonatas and his *Indian Suite* (1897) for orchestra. *Woodland Sketches* (1896) and *Sea Pieces* (1898) for piano are popular. The MacDowell Colony for artists, writers, and composers (Peterborough, N.H.) was founded by his widow.

mace: see NUTMEG.

Macedon [măs'ədŏn], ancient country of N GREECE, the modern region of MACEDONIA. The first known population included Anatolian and Hellenic peoples. By the 7th cent. B.C. a Greek-speaking family had set themselves up as rulers of a state in W Macedon. Hellenic influences grew, and the state became stronger until, with the great victory of PHILIP II at Chaeronea (338 B.C.), Macedon became master of Greece. Expanding upon Philip's conquests, his son, ALEXANDER THE GREAT, forged his fabulous empire, at the same time spreading Hellenistic civilization. When Alexander died (323 B.C.) his successors, the DIADOCHI, engaged in incessant warfare that split the empire and drained Macedon. Finally Antigonus II (r.277–239 B.C.) restored Macedon economically, and Antigonus III (r.229–221 B.C.) reestablished Macedonian hegemony. But PHILIP V and PERSEUS were defeated in the Macedonian Wars (215–168 B.C.) by Rome, which divided Macedon into four republics. After a pretender, Andriscus, tried to revive a Macedonian kingdom, Macedon was made the first Roman province (146 B.C.). It never again had political importance in ancient times.

Macedonia, region, SE Europe, on the BALKAN PENINSULA, divided among Greece, Bulgaria, and the republic of Macedonia (formerly part of Yugoslavia). It extends north from the Aegean Sea between Epirus (W) and Thrace (E) and includes parts of the Pindus and Rhodope mountains. Tobacco and other crops are grown, livestock is raised, and iron and other metals are mined. Site of the ancient kingdom of MACEDON, the region fell under Roman control in 146 B.C. With Rome's division (A.D. 395) Macedonia came under Byzantine rule. The Slavs settled there in the 6th cent. The region was contested (9th–14th cent.) by Constantinople, Bulgaria, Serbia, and others, before falling to the Ottoman Turks. In the 19th cent. Macedonia was claimed by Greece, Serbia, and Bulgaria; the latter supported terrorist bands opposing Ottoman rule. The BALKAN WARS (1912–13) established roughly the present boundaries, although disputes over the region continued. Bulgaria, an Axis power in World War II, occupied (1941–44) all of Macedonia. The prewar boundaries were later restored. In 1992 Yugoslav Macedonia declared its independence, but international recognition came slowly when Greece opposed the new nation's use of the name *Macedonia.* See also MACEDONIA, republic.

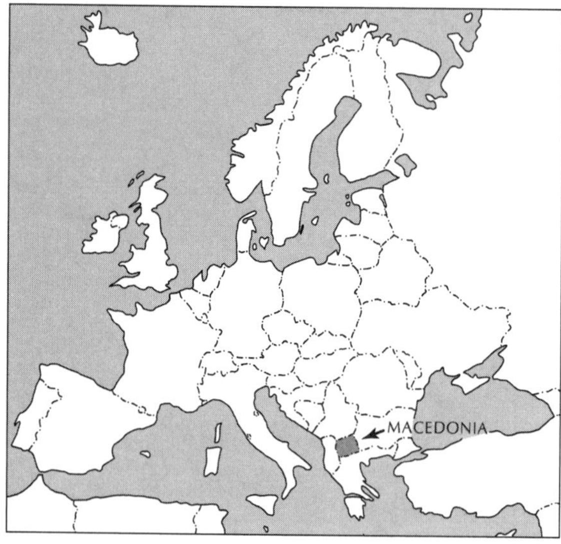

Macedonia, Macedonian *Makedoniya,* officially Republic of Macedonia, independent republic (1992 est. pop. 2,174,000), 9,925 sq mi (25,713 sq km) in the S central Balkan peninsula; formerly a constituent republic of Yugoslavia. Macedonia is bordered by Yugoslavia (N), Albania (W), Greece (S), and Bulgaria (E). The largest cities are SKOPJE (the capital), Bitola (Bitolj), and Prilep. The country is largely mountainous and is bisected by the Vardar R. valley. After Albania, Macedonia is the poorest and most economically underdeveloped nation in the Balkans. The chief crops are grains, tobacco, and cotton. Sheep and goats are raised, and chromium is mined. Industries include metallurgy, timbering, and the manufacture of chemicals, cement, and textiles. The population is about two-thirds Macedonian, and many belong to the Orthodox Church. There is a sizable Albanian Muslim minority, concentrated mainly in W Macedonia. Macedonian (related to Bulgarian) is the official language.

History. For Macedonian history prior to independence, see MACEDONIA, region, and YUGOSLAVIA. Macedonian leaders did not initially favor independence for their constituent republic, but after SLOVENIA and CROATIA left the federation Macedonians grew wary of Serbian domination in a smaller Yugoslavia. In 1991 Macedonians voted for independence from Yugoslavia, and the government sought (1992) international recognition of its independence when the European Community (EC) recognized Croatia and Slovenia. Greece, fearing possible Macedonian claims on Greek Macedonia, sought a change in the new nation's name and was able to slow, but not prevent, international recognition of Macedonia. In 1992 a small group of UN peacekeepers were sent to the country to discourage possible fighting in KOSOVO from spilling into Macedonia.

McEnroe, John (Patrick, Jr.), 1959–, American tennis player; b. West Germany. With three straight U.S. Open victories by 1981 and a Wimbledon title that year, he gained top world ranking. He also won the 1984 U.S. Open and the 1983–84 Wimbledon titles and has been a leading doubles player. The young McEnroe was known for his on-court temper displays.

McGillivray, Alexander, 1759–93, CREEK chief; b. Ala., son of a Scots trader and French-Creek mother. Educated in Charleston, S.C., he returned to Creek country as a British agent during the AMERICAN REVOLUTION. He signed (1784) a treaty with Spain to gain an annuity and arms, which he used against American settlers until Pres. Washington made him a brigadier general by the Treaty of New York (1790). A skilled diplomat, he acknowledged U.S. sovereignty and promised peace, but in 1792 he resumed Spanish-subsidized attacks.

McGovern, George Stanley, 1922–, U.S. senator from South Dakota (1963–81); b. Avon, S.D. He was among the first senators to oppose the VIETNAM WAR. He ran for president on the Democratic ticket in 1972, on a platform promising to end the war, cut defense spending, and provide a guaranteed annual income for all Americans, but he was defeated by Richard M. NIXON.

McGraw, John J(oseph), 1873–1934, American baseball manager; b. Cortland co., N.Y. He starred (1891–1900) at third base for the Baltimore Orioles. As manager (1902–32) of the New York Giants, the fiery McGraw became one of the outstanding figures of baseball, leading the Giants to 10 pennants and 3 World Series victories (1905, 1921–22).

MacGregor, Robert: see ROB ROY.

McGuffey, William Holmes, 1800–1873, American educator; b. near Claysville, Pa. He helped organize the Ohio public schools but is now chiefly remembered as the compiler of the first four of the six McGuffey Eclectic Readers. Estimated sales of six editions from 1836 to 1920 totaled 122 million copies. Concerned with traditional morality, they greatly influenced the shaping of the mid-19th-cent. American mind.

Mach, Ernst [mäkh], 1838–1916, Austrian physicist and philosopher. He did his major work in the philosophy of science, striving to rid science of metaphysical assumptions, and influenced the development of LOGICAL POSITIVISM. He also did work in ballistics; the MACH NUMBER is named for him.

Mácha, Karel Hynek [mä'khä], 1810–36, Czech poet. The romantic EPIC *May* (1836), considered the finest lyric work in Czech, reveals his fatalism, love of nature, and national pride. His only novel is *Gypsies* (1835–36).

Machado, Antonio [mächä'thō], 1875–1939, Spanish poet, essayist, and dramatist. His poetry, including *Solitudes* (1902), *Castilian Fields (1912),* and *Poesías completas* (1917, 1928), was influenced by Castilian life and the death of his young wife. He also wrote philosophical and literary essays, and, with his brother, the poet and dramatist **Manuel Machado,** 1874–1947, several plays. In the SPANISH CIVIL WAR, however, they were on opposing sides; in 1939 Antonio, a Loyalist, fled to France, where he died.

Machado, Gerardo, 1871–1939, Cuban president (1925–33). He tried to free CUBA from political and economic dependence on the U.S. by taxing U.S. investments and developing Cuba's economy. When he resorted to terrorism to crush opposition, the U.S. intervened (1933), and he fled.

Machado de Assis, Joaquim Maria [məshä'dōō dĭ əsēz'], 1839–1908, Brazilian novelist, considered Brazil's greatest writer. In this subtly ironic novels he displayed his keen psychological insight and his pessimistic vision. His novels include *Epitaph of a Small Winner* (1881), *Philosopher or Dog* (1891), and *Dom Casmurro* (1900).

Machaut, Guillaume de [mäshō'], c.1300–1377, French poet and composer. His chivalric experience is seen in *Le livre du voir dit* (1361–65), a long poem of courtly love with musical interpolations. He wrote lais, ballads, rondeaux, and virelais, and used COURTLY LOVE texts for his secularized MOTETS. His innovative, polyphonic MASS led to the great masses of JOSQUIN DESPREZ and PALESTRINA.

Machel, Samora Moïsés, 1933–86, president of Mozambique (1975–86). He was army commander (1966–74) and president (1970–86) of Frelimo, a revolutionary group that fought to free Mozambique from Portuguese rule. The first president of independent Mozambique (1975), he worked to convert the nation into a Marxist society and attempted to gradually end fighting with South Africa through a non-aggression treaty (1984).

Machiavelli, Niccolò, 1469–1527, Italian political philosopher and statesman. As defense secretary of the Florentine republic he substituted a citizens' militia for the mercenary system. Through diplomatic missions he became acquainted with power politics, meeting such leaders as Cesare BORGIA. When the MEDICI family returned to power (1512) he was dismissed, and briefly imprisoned and tortured. He then retired to his country estate, where he wrote on politics. His most famous work, *The Prince* (1532), describes the means by which a leader may gain and maintain power. His "ideal" prince is an amoral and calculating tyrant capable of unifying Italy. Despite the ruthless connotation of the term *Machiavellian,* such works as the *Discourses* (1531) and the *History of Florence* (1532) express republican principles. Machiavelli also wrote poems and plays, notably the comedy *Mandragola* (1524).

machine, any arrangement of stationary and moving mechanical parts used to perform some useful WORK or a specialized task. By means of a machine, a small force can be applied to move a much greater resistance or load; the force, however, must be applied through a much greater distance than it would if it could move the load directly. The mechanical advantage of a machine is the factor by which it multiplies any applied force. The simplest machines are (1) the *lever,* consisting of a bar supported at some stationary point (the fulcrum) along its length, and used to overcome resistance at a second point by application of force at a third point; (2) the *pulley,* consisting of a wheel over which a rope, belt, chain, or cable runs; (3) the *inclined plane,* consisting of a sloping surface, whose purpose is to reduce the force that must be applied to raise a load; (4) the *screw,* consisting essentially of a solid cylinder around which an inclined plane winds spirally, whose purpose is to fasten one object to another, to lift a heavy object, or to move an object by a precise amount; and (5) the *wheel and axle,* consisting of a wheel mounted rigidly upon an axle or drum of smaller diameter, the wheel and axle having the same axis. The more complicated machines are merely combinations of these simple machines. Machines used to transform other forms of energy (as heat) into mechanical energy are known as engines, e.g., the STEAM ENGINE or the INTERNAL COMBUSTION ENGINE. The electric MOTOR transforms electrical energy into mechanical energy; its operation is the reverse of that of the electric GENERATOR. In the past, the first machines, e.g., the catapult, were built to improve war-making capacity. The first manufacturing machines, powered by steam engines, appeared during the 18th cent., causing the onset of the INDUSTRIAL REVOLUTION.

machine gun: see SMALL ARMS.

machine tool, power-operated tool used for shaping or finishing metal parts by removing chips, shavings, large pieces, or extremely small particles. Machine tools vary in size from hand-held devices used for drilling and grinding to large stationary machines that perform a number of different operations. The lathe, for example, can turn, face, thread, and drill. The working surfaces of a machine tool are made of such substances as high-speed steels, sintered carbides, and diamonds—substances that can withstand the great heat generated by the action of the working surface against the workpiece. Modern machine tools are often numerically or computer controlled.

Mach number, ratio between the speed of an object, usually an airplane, and the speed of SOUND in the medium in which the object is traveling. A plane traveling at Mach 3.0 is traveling at three times the speed of sound.

Machu Picchu, fortress city of the ancient INCAS, in a high saddle between two peaks c.50 mi (80 km) NW of Cuzco, Peru. The extraordinary pre-Columbian ruin, 5 sq mi (13 sq km) of terraced stonework linked by 3,000 steps, was probably the last Inca stronghold after the Spanish Conquest; it was virtually intact when discovered by Hiram BINGHAM in 1911.

Machu Picchu, Peru

McIntire, Samuel, 1757–1811, American architect and woodcarver; b. Salem, Mass. He designed houses for the ship-owning aristocracy of Salem. The interiors featured beautifully carved cornices and mantelpieces, inspired by the style of Robert ADAM. His public buildings include Assembly Hall, Salem. He also produced many works of sculpture.

McKay, Claude, 1890–1948, African-American writer; b. Jamaica. A major figure in the HARLEM RENAISSANCE, he is best known for poems on racial themes, e.g., *Harlem Shadows* (1922). He also wrote the novels *Banjo* (1929) and *Banana Bottom* (1933).

Macke, August [mä'kə], 1887–1914, German painter. A brilliant colorist, he exhibited with the BLAUE REITER group. In 1914 he went to Tunisia with Paul KLEE, doing watercolors of prismatic patterns. His works include *Farewell* (Cologne).

Mackenzie, Sir Alexander, 1764?–1820, Scottish explorer in Canada. A fur trader, he followed (1789) an unknown river (later named after him) to the Arctic Ocean. He discovered (1793) the Fraser River while pioneering the first overland route through the Canadian Rockies to the Pacific.

Mackenzie, Alexander, 1822–92, prime minister of CANADA (1873–78). A Scottish immigrant (1842), he was elected (1861) to the Canadian assembly and headed (from 1867) the Liberal opposition to the J.A. MACDONALD dominion government; when it fell (1873) because of the PACIFIC SCANDAL he became the first Liberal prime minister. He strengthened the provincial governments, expanded trade, and encouraged immigration.

Mackenzie, Sir William, 1849–1923, Canadian railroad builder. A railroad construction contractor, he and Sir Donald Mann began (c.1888) to organize the Canadian Northern Railway, which became (1918) part of Canadian National Railways.

Mackenzie, William Lyon, 1795–1861, Canadian insurgent leader. A Scottish immigrant (1820), he published (1824–34) the *Colonial Advocate,* which attacked the FAMILY COMPACT clique. As leader of the Reform party he became (1834) the first mayor of TORONTO. After the Reform party's defeat he led (1837) an armed rebellion in Toronto that was quickly put down. He fled to the United States but was imprisoned for violating the neutrality laws. After a general amnesty (1849) he returned to Canada and served in the assembly.

Mackenzie, one of the world's great rivers, NW Canada, flowing c.1,120 mi (1,800 km) generally NW from Great Slave Lake to enter the Arctic Ocean through a vast delta. Navigable only in summer (June-October), it drains the northern portion of the GREAT PLAINS and is the main channel of the c.2,600 mi (4,180 km) Finlay-Peace-Mackenzie river system. Oil, discovered at Norman Wells in the 1930s, and natural gas, found in the delta region in the 1970s, are major resources of the area.

Mackenzie King, William Lyon: see KING, WILLIAM LYON MACKENZIE.

mackerel, open-sea FISH of the family Scombridae, including the albacore, bonito, and TUNA. Mackerel have deeply forked tails, narrowed where they join the body, finlets behind the dorsal and anal fins, and streamlined bodies. They are superb, swift swimmers of generally large size and are important commercially as food. They travel in schools feeding on fish, especially HERRING, and SQUID, and migrate between deep and shallow waters. The largest mackerel is the tuna (up to ¾ ton/680 kg); among the smallest (1½ lb/0.675 kg) is the common mackerel of the Atlantic. Stocks of many mackerel species have been depleted through overfishing.

McKim, Charles Follen, 1847–1909, American architect; b. Chester co., Pa., a founder of the firm that became (1879) McKim, Mead, and White. The firm adhered to classical architecture and its Renaissance derivatives, and McKim's spirit and taste guided it. Among the firm's best-known buildings are the Boston Public Library (1888–95) and the Pierpont Morgan Library in New York City.

McKinley, William, 1843–1901, 25th president of the U.S. (1897–1901); b. Niles, Ohio. As congressman from Ohio (1877–91), he strongly advocated a protective tariff, and the McKinley Tariff Act of 1890 cost him his congressional seat. With the support of Ohio political boss Marcus A. HANNA, McKinley was elected governor in 1891 and 1893. Again with Hanna's help, he won the Republican nomination for president in 1896. Running against William Jennings BRYAN on a platform advocating a protective tariff and endorsing the gold standard, McKinley was elected. His administration was marked by adoption of the highest tariff rate in U.S. history, annexation of Hawaii, the OPEN DOOR policy in China, and the Currency Act of 1900, which consolidated the gold standard. Foreign affairs were dominated by the brief SPANISH-AMERICAN WAR, from which the U.S. emerged a world power. McKinley was reelected in 1900. He was shot in Buffalo, N.Y., by Leon Czolgosz, an anarchist, on Sept. 6, 1901, and died on Sept. 14.

McKinley, Mount, 20,320 ft (6,194 m), S central Alaska, the highest point in North America. The snow-capped peak was part of Mount McKinley National Park (est. 1917) before becoming part of Denali National Park and Preserve (see NATIONAL PARKS, table) in 1980. It was first scaled in 1913 by American explorer Hudson Stuck.

Mackintosh, Charles Rennie, 1868–1928, Scottish architect, artist, and furniture designer. His decorative and graphic works epitomize the sumptuous ART NOUVEAU. His few buildings, however, display Scottish simplicity and subtlety.

MacLeish, Archibald, 1892–1982, American poet; b. Glencoe, Ill. His early poems range from expressions of postwar disillusionment, e.g., *The Pot of Earth* (1925), to a long narrative on Mexico's conquest, *Conquistador* (1932; Pulitzer). His 1930s work reflects his concern with the rise of fascism, e.g., *Frescoes for Mr. Rockefeller's City* (1933) and the verse play *Panic* (1935). His later works include the verse drama *J.B.* (1958; Pulitzer), a retelling of the story of Job; and volumes of poetry, including *Collected Poems 1917–1952* (1952; Pulitzer). During the administration of Franklin D. ROOSEVELT, MacLeish was librarian of Congress (1939–44) and undersecretary of state (1944–45).

MacLennan, Hugh, 1907–90, Canadian writer. His novels, including *Two Solitudes* (1945), *The Watch That Ends the Night* (1959), and *Return of the Sphinx* (1967), use Canadian life as a paradigm of the human condition.

Macleod, John James Rickard, 1876–1935, Scottish physiologist. For their discovery of INSULIN (together with Charles BEST) and studies of its use in treating diabetes, he and Sir Frederick BANTING shared the 1923 Nobel Prize in physiology or medicine.

McLuhan, (Herbert) Marshall, 1911–80, Canadian communications theorist and educator. He taught in Canada and the U.S., gaining fame in the 1960s with his proposal that electronic media, especially television, were creating a "global village" in which "the medium is the message," i.e., the means of communications has a greater influence on people than the information itself. His books include *The Gutenberg Galaxy* (1962) and *Understanding Media* (1964).

Macmillan, (Maurice) Harold, 1894–1986, British statesman. A Conservative, he entered Parliament in 1924 and later served as minister of housing and local government (1951–54), minister of defense (1954–55), foreign secretary (1955), and chancellor of the exchequer (1955–57). As prime minister (1957–63) he strove to improve East-West relations and to gain Britain's entry into the Common Market. In 1963 a scandal linked his minister of war, John Profumo, to a call girl and a Soviet official. He served as chairman (1963–74) of the Macmillan publishing house. In 1984 he was made an earl.

McNamara, Robert Strange, 1916–, U.S. secretary of defense (1961–68); b. San Francisco. He was president (1960–61) of the Ford Motor Co. At the Defense Dept. he modernized management techniques and deemphasized nuclear weapons. His doubts about the VIETNAM WAR led him to resign (1968) from the cabinet. He later served (1968–81) as president of the World Bank.

McNaughton, Andrew George Latta 1887–1966, Canadian general. He was Canadian chief of staff (1929–35) and commander of Canadian forces in Britain during WORLD WAR II. He served as defense minister (1944–46) and in other posts.

MacNeice, Louis, 1907–63, Irish poet and classicist. A poet of social protest in the 1930s, he later wrote with irony of the futility of modern life. His books of poetry include *Springboard* (1945), *Ten Burnt Offerings* (1952), and *Solstices* (1961). He also translated AESCHYLUS and GOETHE.

Macon, city (1990 pop. 106,612), seat of Bibb co., central Ga., on the Ocmulgee R.; inc. 1823, named for Nathaniel Macon. It is the processing and shipping center for an agricultural area. It produces textiles, insulation, explosives, and other manufactures. Sidney LANIER was born there.

McPherson, Aimee Semple, 1890–1944, U.S. evangelist; b. Ontario. She opened (1923) the Angelus Temple in Los Angeles and was a founder (1927) of the International Church of Foursquare Gospel. In 1926 her disappearance and reappearance, with a bizarre tale of kidnapping, led to a trial for fraud. Although she was acquitted, her business dealings resulted in numerous other legal actions. She died from an accidental overdose of sleeping pills.

Macpherson, James, 1736–96, Scottish author. He wrote *Fragments of Ancient Poetry Collected in the Highlands of Scotland* (1760), supposedly translations from Gaelic, and two epic poems, *Fingal* (1761) and *Temora* (1763), represented as the work of OSSIAN, a 3d-cent. bard. The works were mainly Macpherson's own, and they strongly influenced romanticism.

macramé, decorative knotting technique. Named for an Arabic word for knotted fringe, it arose in the 13th cent. and reached Europe during the next hundred years. A traditional sailors' pastime, after decades of obscurity it was revived in the 1960s for wall hangings, jewelry, and other objects.

Macready, William Charles, 1793–1873, English actor and manager. His portrayal of Richard III (1819) established him as a major tragedian. His 1849 U.S. tour was marred by a riot by supporters of his rival Edwin FORREST.

macroeconomics: see under ECONOMICS.

Macy, Anne Sullivan, 1866–1936, American educator; b. Feeding Hills, Mass. Partially blinded by a childhood infection, she attended Perkins Institution for the Blind, learned the manual alphabet, and was chosen (1887) to teach Helen KELLER. Macy based her instruction on a system of touch teaching, pioneering in techniques of education for the handicapped, and helped promote the newly founded (1921) American Foundation for the Blind.

Madagascar, officially Democratic Republic of Madagascar, formerly Malagasy Republic, republic (1992 est. pop. 12,596,000), 226,658 sq mi (587,045 sq km), in the Indian Ocean, separated from E Africa by the Mozambique Channel. The nation comprises Madagascar, the world's fourth largest island, and several small islands. ANTANANARIVO (Tananarive) is the capital. The island of Madagascar is a largely deforested highland plateau fringed by a lowland coastal strip; mountains in the north rise to more than 9,000 ft (2,745 m). The economy is predominantly agricultural, producing rice (the staple crop), coffee, vanilla, cloves, cassava, and sugarcane. Large numbers of livestock and poultry are raised. Manufacturing, mostly confined to food-processing and textiles, is becoming more diversified. Chromite, graphite, and phosphates are extracted. The two main population groups are of Indonesian and African descent. French and Malagasy, an Indonesian tongue spoken by all the people, are the official languages. About 40% of the population is Christian, 5% is Muslim, and the rest follow traditional beliefs.

History. Africans and Indonesians first reached Madagascar about 2,000 years ago; they were joined in the 9th cent. A.D. by Muslim traders from E Africa and the COMORO Islands. The first Europeans to visit the island were the Portuguese (1500), but it was the French who established footholds, beginning in 1642. In the 19th cent. the rulers of the Merina kingdom, one of several that had developed on the island, opened the island to European traders and Christian missionaries who, in return, helped spread Merina control and culture; by the end of the century the Merina kingdom included almost the entire island. In 1885 France established a protectorate over Madagascar, but the Merina resisted fiercely, and it was not until 1904 that the French fully controlled the island. In WORLD WAR II Madagascar was aligned with Vichy France until taken (1942) by the British and turned over to a Free French regime (1943). A major uprising against the French in 1947–48 was crushed, but the independence movement gained momentum in the 1950s, and in 1958 the country, renamed the Malagasy Republic, gained autonomy. Full independence came in 1960, with Philibert Tsiranana as president. In 1972 widespread protests over economic failures prompted the autocratic president to step aside. Political strife continued, however. In 1975 power was seized by a military directorate, headed by Pres. Didier Ratsiraka, a Marxist one-party state was established, and the country was renamed the Democratic Republic of Madagascar. Economic failure led the government to permit the return of a free-market economy in 1987, and growing opposition to Ratsiraka's rule in the 1980s led to the legalization (1990) of opposition political parties. After demonstrations and a lengthy general strike (1991), Ratsiraka agreed to share power with opposition leader Albert Zafy in a transitional government. In a free election (1993) Zafy defeated Ratsiraka for the presidency.

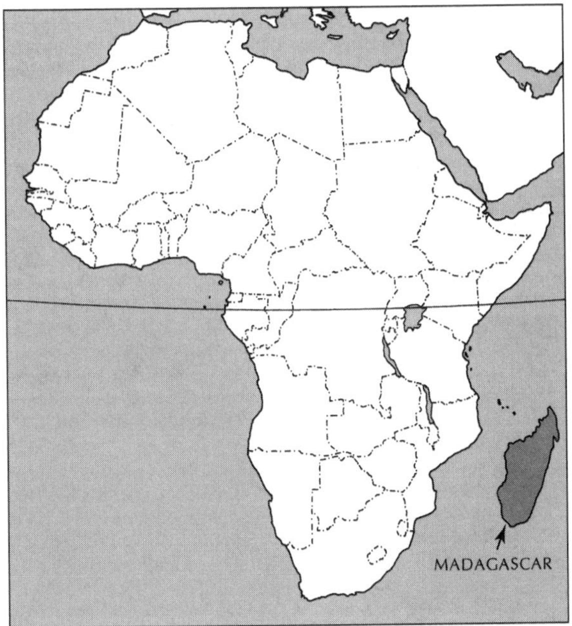

Madariaga, Salvador de [mäthäryä'gä], 1886–1978, Spanish writer and diplomat. He headed the disarmament section of the League of Nations (1922–27); later he was the Spanish Republic's ambassador to the U.S. (1931) and France (1932–34) and chief delegate to the League of Nations (1931–36). After the SPANISH CIVIL WAR he exiled himself to England. His many books include *The Genius of Spain* (1923), *Don Quixote* (1934), *Bolívar* (1951), *Anatomy of the Cold War* (1955), novels, poetry, plays, historical and psychological studies, and memoirs (1974).

madder, common name for the family Rubiaceae, chiefly tropical and subtropical trees, shrubs, and herbs, especially abundant in N South America. The family is important economically for several tropical crops, e.g., COFFEE and QUININE (from CINCHONA), and for many ornamentals, e.g., the madder, GARDENIA and bedstraw. True madder (*Rubia tinctorum*), also called turkey red, is a dye plant native to S Europe. The herb's long, fleshy root was the principal source of various brilliant red dye pigments until artificial production of alizarin, the pigment chemical in madder. The bedstraws (genus *Galium*), formerly used for mattress filling because of their pleasing odor, have clusters of tiny white or yellow flowers.

Madeira Islands, archipelago (1990 est. pop. 290,000), 308 sq mi (798 sq km), coextensive with Funchal dist., Portugal, in the Atlantic Ocean c.350 mi (560 km) off Morocco. Madeira, the largest island, and Porto Santo are inhabited; the Desertas and Selvagens are not. Madeira is a scenic, year-round resort. The islands produce sugarcane and Madeira wine. Known to the Romans, they were rediscovered (15th cent.) under HENRY THE NAVIGATOR.

Madero, Francisco Indalecio, 1873–1913, president of MEXICO (1911–13). A champion of democracy and social reform, he led (1910) the revolution that swept through Mexico and overthrew (1911) the DIAZ regime, but he failed to implement notable reforms. Revolts broke out, and Gen. HUERTA treacherously assassinated Madero's brother, seized power, and arrested and imprisoned Madero. He was killed while allegedly attempting to escape.

Madison, James, 1751–1836, 4th president of the U.S. (1809–17); b. Port Conway, Va. An early opponent of British colonial measures, he helped draft the Constitution for the new state of VIRGINIA (1776), served in the Continental Congress (1780–83, 1787), and was a member of the Virginia legislature (1784–86). He was active in the call for the ANNAPOLIS CONVENTION (1786), and his contributions at the FEDERAL CONSTITUTIONAL CONVENTION (1787) earned him the title "master builder of the Constitution." A principal contributor to the *Federalist Papers,* he was largely responsible for securing ratification of the Constitution in Virginia. As a congressman from Virginia (1789–97), he was a strong advocate of the Bill of Rights. A steadfast enemy of the financial measures of Alexander HAMILTON, he was a leading Jeffersonian and drew up the Virginia resolutions protesting the Alien and Sedition Acts (see KENTUCKY AND VIRGINIA RESOLUTIONS). After Jefferson triumphed in the presidential election of 1800, Madison became (1801) his secretary of state. He succeeded Jefferson as president in 1809. The unpopular and unsuccessful WAR OF 1812, known disparagingly as "Mr. Madison's War," was the chief event of his administration. His term in office witnessed the beginning of postwar national expansion and the rise of Jacksonian democracy. Retiring in 1817, he lived quietly at Montpelier with his wife, **Dolley Madison,** 1768–1849, b. Guilford, co., N.C., as Dolley Payne. She married Madison in 1794 (her first husband had died in 1793). As official White House hostess for Thomas Jefferson (who was a widower) and for her husband, she was noted for the magnificence of her entertainments, as well as for her charm, tact, and grace.

Madison, city (1990 pop. 191,262), state capital and seat of Dane co., S central Wis., on an isthmus between Lakes Monona and Mendota; inc. 1856. It is a trading center in a rich agricultural area, and produces meat products, machinery, medical equipment, and other goods. The city, noted for its parks along the attractively wooded lakeshore and for the elaborate capitol building, is the seat of the Univ. of Wisconsin.

Madonna (Madonna Louise Ciccione), 1958–, American singer and actress: b. Rochester, Mich. Her albums, and the music videos from them, e.g., *Madonna* (1983) and *Like a Virgin* (1984), secured her position as a sexual and pop icon.

Madras, city (1991 pop. 5,361,468), capital of Tamil state, SE India, on the Bay of Bengal. An industrial center, it has chemical and automobile plants, tanneries, and textile mills. It was largely built around a 17th-cent. British outpost and became a trade center. The city's cultural institutions include the Univ. of Madras (est. 1857).

Madrid, city (1988 est. 3,103,000), capital of Spain and of Madrid autonomous region and prov., central Spain, on the Manzanares R. A modern city of broad, tree-lined avenues, Madrid also has old quarters with picturesque winding streets. The city is Spain's chief transportation and administrative center and the focus of modern industrial development. It became the capital of Spain in 1561 under PHILIP II but remained small until expanded in the 16th cent. under the Bourbons (especially CHARLES III). Two of the city's most famous landmarks—the royal palace and the PRADO—date from that period. Madrid's resistance against the French in the PENINSULAR WAR in 1808 was immortalized in two of GOYA'S best-known paintings (now in the Prado), and the city again played an heroic role in the SPANISH CIVIL WAR (1936–39) by holding out against an Insurgent siege for 29 months.

madrigal, name for two different forms of Italian music. The poetic madrigal of the 14th cent. consisted of one to four strophes of three lines each, followed by a two-line strophe (ritornello). These early examples were restrained and featured three or four voices in homophony, i.e., with one voice carrying the melody. The 16th-cent. madrigal was a musically unrelated, free poetic imitation of the earlier form. The classic madrigals of Giovanni Gabrieli, Orlando di LASSO, and others were polyphonic and usually written for five voices, with their musical expression closely allied to the text. A final phase, exemplified by Carlo Gesualdo and Claudio MONTEVERDI, featured use of the chromatic scale of twelve tones and special effects (such as multiple choirs) devised to intensify the expression of the text. The polyphonic madrigal also flourished in Elizabethan England.

Maecenas (Caius Maecenas), d. 8 B.C., Roman statesman and patron of letters under AUGUSTUS. His famous literary circle included HORACE, VERGIL, and PROPERTIUS. His name is the symbol of the wealthy benefactor of the arts.

maenads, in Greek and Roman mythology, female devotees of DIONYSUS or BACCHUS. Waving the thyrsus, they roamed the mountains and forests, and performed frenzied, ecstatic dances. They are also known as Bacchae.

Maerlant, Jacob van [mär'länt], c.1235–c.1300, Flemish poet, the earliest important figure of Dutch literature. He wrote lyric poems and chivalric verse romances as well as long didactic poems, chief of which is *The Mirror of History*.

Maeterlinck, Maurice [mätĕrlăNk'], 1862–1949, Belgian author who wrote in French. His 60-odd volumes, with their suggestion of universal mystery and sense of impending doom, can be read as a SYMBOLIST manifesto. Major works include the plays *Pelléas et Mélisande* (1892) and *Monna Vanna* (1902); the allegorical fantasy *The Blue Bird* (1909); and the essay *The Life of the Bee* (1901). He was awarded the Nobel Prize in literature in 1911.

Mafia, name given, probably in the 1800s, to organized, independent groups of brigands in Sicily. Following a feudal tradition, the Mafia disdained all legal authorities, sought justice through direct action (as in the vendetta), and observed a rigid code of secrecy, practices that enabled Mafiosi to rise in ORGANIZED CRIME after coming to the U.S. as Italian immigrants in the late 19th and early 20th cent. The Mafia survived MUSSOLINI's attempt to stamp it out in Italy before World War II, and it and other Italian organized crime organizations remained influential in Sicily and S Italy, often assassinating justice officials who prosecuted them in the 1980s and 1990s. In the U.S., the Mafia was reputedly active in both illegal and legal (or "front") operations in the 1980s.

Mafikeng, formerly Mafeking, town (1970 pop. 6,900), N central South Africa. It is the market for a cattle-raising and dairy-farming area and is an important railroad depot. In the SOUTH AFRICAN WAR (1899–1902), a British garrison here withstood a 217-day Boer siege. Formerly in Cape Province, Mafikeng was incorporated into BOPHUTHATSWANA in 1980.

Magdalen: see MARY, in the Bible, 2.

Magdeburg, city (1989 est. pop. 291,000), capital of Saxony-Anhalt, central Germany, on the Elbe R. It is a large inland port and an industrial center producing metal products, textiles, processed food, and other goods. Founded by the 9th cent., it accepted the REFORMATION in 1524. During the THIRTY YEARS WAR it was sacked and burned by imperial forces; 85% of the population perished. Rebuilt under the electorate of BRANDENBURG, it became a Prussian fortress in the 17th cent. During WORLD WAR II it was badly damaged. Landmarks include an 11th-cent. Romanesque church.

Magellan, Ferdinand, c.1480–1521, Portuguese navigator, leader of the first expedition to circumnavigate the globe. Of noble birth, he was backed by CHARLES I of Spain to reach the MOLUCCAS by sailing west. He began in 1519 with five ships and explored the Río de la Plata, wintering in PATAGONIA. He then sailed through the straits which bear his name and headed NW across the Pacific, reaching the Marianas and the PHILIPPINES, where he was killed by natives. His voyage proved the roundness of the earth and revealed the Americas as a new world.

Magellan, Strait of, c.330 mi (530 km) long and 2½–15 mi (4–24 km) wide, N of Cape HORN. Separating TIERRA DEL FUEGO from mainland South America, it was important in the days of sailing ships. The strait was discovered (1520) by Ferdinand MAGELLAN.

Magellan, in space exploration: see SPACE PROBE (table).

Magellanic Clouds, two irregular GALAXIES that are the nearest extragalactic objects (nearly 200,000 LIGHT-YEARS distant). They are visible to the naked eye in the southern skies. The Large Magellanic Cloud, about 7° in angular diameter, is located mostly in the constellation Dorado; in 1987 it became the site of the first supernova visible to the naked eye since 1604. The Small Magellanic Cloud, about 4° in diameter, is almost completely in the constellation Tucana.

Maghreb or **Magrib,** Arabic term for NW Africa. It is generally applied to all of MOROCCO, ALGERIA, and TUNISIA, but more specifically it pertains only to the area of the three countries that lies between the Atlas Mts. and the Mediterranean Sea. The **Arab Maghreb Union** was established in 1989 and includes Algeria, Libya, Mauritania, Morocco, and Tunisia. Envisioned initially by Muammar al-QADDAFI as an Arab superstate, it is eventually expected to function as a N African common market.

Magi [mā'jī], priestly caste of ancient Persia. Magian priests headed ZOROASTRIANISM. The Magi were revered by classic authors as wise men, and their reputed power over demons gave rise to the word *magic*. For the Magi of Mat. 2, see WISE MEN OF THE EAST.

magic, practice of manipulating the course of nature by controlling supernatural forces through ritual and spell. The spell, or incantation, unlocks the full power of the ritual. Black magic is intended to harm or destroy; white magic is to benefit the community (as in fertility rites) or an individual, especially one suffering the effects of black magic. Sympathetic magic treats an image (sticking pins in a doll representing one's enemy), while contiguous magic deals with things that have touched a person (clothing, hair, or even a footprint); the two can be used together.

magic realism, primarily Latin American literary movement that arose in the 1960s. Magic realist writers mingle realistic portrayals of events and characters with elements of fantasy and myth, creating a world that is at once familiar and dreamlike. Its best-known proponent is the Colombian novelist Gabriel GARCÍA MÁRQUEZ, notably in his *One Hundred Years of Solitude* (1967). Other magic realist writers include Guatemala's Miguel Ángel ASTURIAS, Argentina's Julio CORTÁZAR, and Mexico's Carlos FUENTES; non–Latin American writers include Italo CALVINO and Salman RUSHDIE.

Maginot Line [măzh'ĭnō], fortifications on the eastern border of France, running from the Swiss border to the Belgian. Named for André Maginot, minister of war (1929–32), who directed its construction, it was considered impregnable. The Germans, however, flanked it in 1940 during WORLD WAR II.

maglev: see MAGNETIC LEVITATION.

magma: see LAVA.

Magna Carta or **Magna Charta** [Lat., = great charter], the most famous document of British constitutional history, issued (1215) by King JOHN at Runnymede under compulsion by the barons. The purpose was to insure feudal rights and to guarantee that the king could not encroach on baronial privileges. The document also guaranteed the freedom of the church and the customs of the towns; implied laws protecting the rights of subjects and communities, which the king could be compelled to observe; and vaguely suggested—at least to later generations—guarantees of trial by jury and HABEAS CORPUS. After John's death (1216) the charter was reissued with significant omissions. In later centuries parliamentarians portrayed it as a democratic document, but in the 19th cent. some scholars maintained that it was reactionary in that it merely guaranteed feudal rights. It is now generally recognized that the charter showed the viability of opposition to the excessive use of royal power. There are four extant copies of the original.

Magna Graecia [măg'nə grē'shə] [Lat., = great Greece], Greek colonies in S Italy, founded in the 8th cent. B.C., on both coasts, S of the Bay of Naples and the Gulf of Taranto. They included Tarentum, Cumae, and Heraclea, and brought the Etruscans and Romans into early contact with Greek civilization. Unlike the related cities of Greek Sicily, Magna Graecia did not thrive and by 500 B.C. had begun a rapid decline.

Magnasco, Allessandro [mägnäs'kō], 1667–1749, Italian painter. His gloomy, storm-torn landscapes and ruins with small figures and flickering light are primarily religious, e.g., *The Baptism of Christ* (National Gall., Wash., D.C.).

magnesia, common name for the chemical compound magnesium oxide (MgO). The fine powder is used in soaps, cosmetics, pharmaceuticals, and as a filler for rubber goods. Because of its refractory properties (it melts at c.2800°C), it is used in crucibles and ceramics. Crude magnesia is prepared by roasting DOLOMITE or MAGNESITE. Magnesia is also extracted from seawater.

magnesite, white, yellow, or gray magnesium carbonate mineral ($MgCO_3$). It is formed through the alteration of olivine or SERPENTINE by waters carrying carbon dioxide; through the replacement of calcium by magnesium in DOLOMITE or LIMESTONE; and through precipitation from magnesium-rich water that has reacted with sodium chloride. It is used for floorings, as a stucco, and to make firebrick, Epsom salts, face powder, boiler wrappings, and disinfectants.

magnesium (Mg), metallic element, discovered as an oxide by Sir Humphry DAVY in 1808. A ductile, silver-white, chemically active ALKALINE-EARTH METAL, it is the eighth most abundant element in the earth's crust. Its commercial uses include lightweight alloys in aircraft fuselages, jet-engine parts, rockets and missiles, cameras, and optical instruments. The metal is used in pyrotechnics. Magnesium is found in plant chlorophyll and is necessary in the diet of animals and humans. See ELEMENT (table); PERIODIC TABLE.

magnesium hydroxide: see MILK OF MAGNESIA.

magnesium oxide: see MAGNESIA.

magnet: see MAGNETISM.

magnetic levitation or **maglev,** support and often propulsion of objects or vehicles by magnetic fields. Magnetic levitation suspends an object free of contact with any surface, making it particularly appropriate for high-speed (275–300 mph/435–475 kph) transportation, where it greatly reduces friction and allows for fast, quiet operation. In a typical maglev train, the vehicle, which resembles a railroad or monorail car, travels along a guideway. Lifting force is produced by arrays of electromagnets in both the train and guideway. In one version, magnets of like polarity repel each other to lift the train above the guideway; in another, magnets of opposite polarity attract the part of the car suspended below the guideway up toward the guideway, raising the rest of the car above it. Continuously changing the polarity of alternate magnets along the guideway generates a series of attractions and repulsions that moves the train. The enormous amount of electrical power needed by a maglev train is an obstacle to its wide use, but the use of superconducting magnets (see SUPERCONDUCTIVITY) reduces energy needs. First proposed in 1909 by Robert GODDARD, maglev trains have been the subject of research since the 1960s in the U.S., Britain, Japan, Germany, and South Korea, and Japan has begun construction on the first leg of a Tokyo-Osaka maglev line.

magnetic pole, either of two points on the earth, one in the Northern Hemisphere and one in the Southern; each point attracts one end of a compass needle and repels the opposite end. Studies of magnetism in rocks indicate that in the geological past the earth's magnetic field has reversed its polarity often and that rock movement (due to CONTINENTAL DRIFT and PLATE TECTONICS) relative to the magnetic poles has occurred.

magnetic resonance, in physics and chemistry, absorption or emission of ELECTROMAGNETIC RADIATION in the electrons or atomic nuclei of a sample of atoms in response to simultaneous adjustments in a magnetic field and electromagnetic radiation (usually radio waves) applied to the sample. The resonance refers to the enhancement of the absorption that occurs when the correct combination of field and frequency is reached. Most magnetic resonance phenomena depend on the fact that both the proton and the electron behave like microscopic magnets—a property that can be ascribed to an intrinsic rotation, or spin. Types of magnetic resonance include electron paramagnetic resonance (EPR), also known as electron spin resonance (ESR), involving the magnetic effect of electrons, and nuclear magnetic resonance (NMR), involving the magnetic effects of protons and neutrons in the nuclei of atoms. The NMR resonant frequency provides information about the molecular material in which the nuclei reside, and NMR is used in chemistry and physics to analyze samples of solids and liquids, as well as in medicine to analyze tissues removed from the body.

Magnetic resonance imaging (MRI) is a noninvasive diagnostic technique that uses NMR to image the structure of the body. The patient is placed in the field of an electromagnet, which causes the nuclei of certain atoms in the body (especially those of hydrogen) to align magnetically. The patient is then subjected to radio waves, which cause the aligned nuclei to "flip"; when the radio waves are withdrawn the nuclei return to their original positions, emitting radio waves that are then detected by a receiver and analyzed by computer. Unhampered by bone and capable of producing images in a variety of planes, MRI is used in the diagnosis of brain tumors and disorders, spinal disorders, multiple sclerosis, and cardiovascular disease. The procedure is considered to be without risk to the patient.

magnetic resonance imaging (MRI): see under MAGNETIC RESONANCE.

magnetism, FORCE of attraction or repulsion between various substances, especially those containing iron and certain other metals, such as nickel and cobalt; ultimately it is due to the motion of electric charges. Any object that exhibits magnetic properties is called a magnet. An ordinary magnet has two poles where the magnetic forces are the strongest; these poles are designated as a north (north-seeking) pole and a south (south-seeking) pole, because a magnet freely rotating in the earth's magnetic field tends to orient itself along a north-south line. The like poles of different magnets repel each other, and the unlike poles attract each other. Whenever a magnet is broken, a north pole appears at one of the broken faces and a south pole at the other, such that each piece has its own north and south poles. It is impossible to isolate a single magnetic pole, regardless of how small the fragments become. (The possibility of the existence of a single magnetic pole, or monopole, is still unresolved, but experiment has failed so far to detect one.) In the 18th cent. Charles COULOMB found that the magnetic forces of attraction and repulsion are directly proportional to the product of the strengths of the poles and inversely proportional to the square of the distances between them. As with electric charges, the effect of this magnetic force acting at a distance is expressed in terms of a field of force. A picture of the magnetic field lines can be obtained by placing a piece of paper over a magnet and sprinkling iron filings on it. The individual pieces of iron become magnetized by entering a magnetic field, i.e., they act like tiny magnets, lining themselves up along the magnetic field lines. The connection between magnetism and ELECTRICITY was discovered in the early 19th cent. Hans OERSTED found (1820) that a wire carrying an electrical current deflects the needle of a magnetic compass because a magnetic field is created by the moving electric charges constituting the current. André AMPÈRE showed (1825) that magnets exert forces on current-carrying conductors. In 1831 Michael FARADAY and Joseph HENRY independently discovered electromagnetic INDUCTION—the production of a current in a conductor by a change in the magnetic field around it. The magnetic properties of matter are also explained by the motion of charges. Because the electron has both an electric charge and a spin, it can be considered a charge in motion, giving rise to a tiny magnetic field. In many atoms, all the electrons are paired within energy levels, so that the electrons in each pair have opposite (antiparallel) spins, and their magnetic fields cancel. In some atoms there are more electrons with spins in one direction than the other, resulting in a net magnetic field for the atom as a whole. Placed in an external field, the individual atoms will tend to align their fields with the external one. Because of thermal vibrations the alignment is not complete, and materials, called paramagnetic substances, that contain such atoms react only weakly to a magnetic field. Materials such as iron, nickel, or cobalt that respond strongly to a magnetic field are called ferromagnetic. In a ferromagnetic substance there are also more electrons with spins in one direction than in the other. The individual magnetic fields of the atoms in a given region, called a domain, tend to line up in one direction, so that they reinforce each other. Materials such as bismuth and antimony that are repelled by a magnetic field are called diamagnetic. In a diamagnetic substance, an external magnetic field accelerates the electrons moving in one direction and retards those moving in the opposite direction; this situation produces an induced magnetization opposite indirection to the external field. See also ELECTROMAGNET; ELECTROMAGNETIC RADIATION.

magnetite, lustrous, black, magnetic iron mineral (Fe_3O_4), occurring as crystals, masses, and sand in Sweden, South Africa, Italy, and parts of the U.S. It is an important ore of IRON. Lodestone is a naturally magnetic variety that exhibits polarity.

magnetohydrodynamics (MHD), study of the motions of electrically conducting fluids and their interactions with magnetic fields. The principles of magnetohydrodynamics are of particular importance in PLASMA physics.

magneto-optical disk: see OPTICAL DISK.

magnetosphere: see ATMOSPHERE; VAN ALLEN RADIATION BELTS.

magnitude, measure of the brightness of a celestial object. Apparent magnitude is that determined on the basis of an object's relative brightness as seen from the earth. Objects differing by one magnitude differ in brightness by a factor of 2.512 (the 5th root of 100). The brightest stars have a magnitude of about +1; the sun's magnitude is −26.8. Absolute magnitude, a measure of the intrinsic luminosity, or true brightness, of an object, is the apparent magnitude an object would have if located at a standard distance of 10 PARSECS.

magnolia, common name for the genus *Magnolia,* and for the Magnoliaceae, a family of deciduous or evergreen trees and shrubs, often with showy flowers, chiefly found in temperate regions. Native American species of the chiefly Asian genus *Magnolia* include the umbrella tree (*M. tripetala*), the cucumber tree (*M. acuminata*), the sweet, or swamp, bay (*M. virginiana*), and the bull bay (*M. grandiflora*), also called southern magnolia. Many other, imported magnolias are also cultivated in the U.S. The tulip tree, or yellow poplar (*Liriodendron tulipfera*), the only other member of the family native to the U.S., is prized for cabinetwork and furniture because of its yellowish soft wood.

Magnus, Norwegian kings. **Magnus I** (the Good), 1024–47, king of Norway (1035–47) and Denmark (1042–47), was the son of OLAF II. He succeeded CANUTE'S sons Sweyn of Norway and Harthacanute of Denmark. In 1046 he was forced to share the Norwegian crown with his uncle, HAROLD III, who became sole king on his death. **Magnus VI** (the Law Mender), 1238–80, king of Norway (1263–80), was the son of HAAKON IV. He made peace with ALEXANDER III of Scotland by ceding (1266) the Hebrides and the Isle of Man for a large sum. His legal reforms introduced the concept of crime as an offense against the state rather than the individual, thus discouraging personal vengeance and making the king the source of justice; defined the limits of church and state power; and created a new royal council and nobility. His sons, Eric II (r.1280–99) and Haakon V (r.1299–1319), succeeded him. **Magnus VII** (Magnus Ericsson), 1316–73?, king of Norway (1319–43) and Sweden (1319–63), succeeded his grandfather, Haakon V of Norway, and was elected by the Swedish nobles to succeed his exiled uncle, King Birger of Sweden. He was declared of age in 1332. Educated in Sweden, he neglected Norway and was forced to recognize (1343) his son, later Haakon VI, as his successor as king of Norway. He lost part of Sweden (1356) to his son Eric but regained it on Eric's death (1359). After Haakon married MARGARET I, daughter of WALDEMAR IV of Denmark, the Swedish nobles deposed Haakon and Magnus, choosing Albert of Mecklenburg as king (1363). Magnus was imprisoned until 1371.

magpie, name for certain BIRDS of the CROW and JAY family. The black-billed magpie (*Pica pica*), of W North America, has iridescent black plumage and white wing patches and abdomen. Other species are found in Europe, Asia, and Africa. Magpies are scavengers and often collect small, bright objects. In captivity they can learn to imitate some words.

Magrib: see MAGHREB.

Magritte, René [mägrēt'], 1898–1967, Belgian surrealist painter. Influenced by CHIRICO, he developed a style in which a misleading realism is combined with mocking irony. Works such as *The Red Model* (1935; Modern Mus., Stockholm) are elaborate fantasies constructed around common situations.

Magyars, the dominant people of Hungary, who speak a Finno-Ugric language. The nomadic Magyars migrated c.460 from the Ural Mts. to the N Caucasus, where they remained until forced into present-day Romania late in the 9th cent. by the Pechenegs, a Turkic group. Under their leader Arpad, the Magyars defeated the Bulgars but were pushed northward (c.895) into Hungary. They conquered Moravia and penetrated Germany until checked (955) by Holy Roman Emperor OTTO I. In the 11th cent. they adopted Christianity.

Mahabharata [məhä'bär'ətə], classical Sanskrit epic, probably composed between 200 B.C. and A.D. 200. Traditionally ascribed to the sage Vyasa, the 18-book work is the longest poem in world literature and the foremost source on classical Indian civilization. Although there are many subplots and irrelevant tales, the *Mahabharata* is primarily the fabulous account of a dynastic struggle and great civil war in the kingdom of Kurukshetra. The BHAGAVAD-GITA, a religious classic of Hinduism, is contained within the epic.

Mahan, Alfred Thayer, 1840–1914, American naval officer and historian; b. West Point, N.Y. In works like *The Influence of Sea Power upon History, 1660–1873* (1890), he argued that naval power was the key to success in international politics. His works had a major influence on the growth of world naval power.

Mahdi [Arab., = he who is divinely guided], in Sunni ISLAM, the restorer of faith. It is believed that he will appear at the end of time to restore justice on earth and establish universal Islam. Among SHIITES the concept of the Mahdi centers on the IMAM. Throughout Islamic history, many reformers claiming to be the Mahdi have arisen. One such was **Muhammad Ahmad,** 1844–85, a Muslim religious leader in the Anglo-Egyptian Sudan. In 1881 he declared himself to be the Mahdi, but he died soon after capturing KHARTOUM. Lord KITCHENER defeated his followers at Omdurman in 1898.

Mahfuz, Nagib, or **Naguib Mahfouz,** [both: mäkhfōōs'], 1911–, Egyptian novelist and short-story writer. One of Egypt's major contemporary writers, he was awarded the 1988 Nobel Prize for literature. He depicts urban life in such novels as *Midaq Alley* (1947), *Palace of Desire* (1957), *The Search* (1964), *Miramar* (1967), and *Children of Gebelawi* (1969). Among his volumes of short stories is *God's World* (tr. 1973).

Mahicans, a confederacy of Native Americans of the Eastern Woodlands (see NORTH AMERICA, INDIGENOUS PEOPLES OF) with an Algonquian language of the Algonquian-Wakashan stock (see NATIVE AMERICAN LANGUAGES). They occupied both banks of the Hudson R., almost to Lake Champlain. The MOHEGANS were a tribe of the Mahican group; both have been called Mohicans. By 1664 the Mohawk had driven the Mahicans E to Massachusetts. Their complete dispersal was hastened when their enemies were armed by the Dutch.

Mahler, Gustav [mä'lər], 1860–1911, Austrian composer and conductor; b. Austrian Bohemia. In Budapest, Hamburg, Vienna, and in New York (1908–11) he set conducting standards that have become legendary. He wrote nine symphonies; songs; and song cycles, mostly with orchestral accompaniment. Of the cycles, *Songs of a Wayfarer* (1883–85), *Kindertotenlieder* [songs of dead children] (1901–4), and *Das Lied von der Erde* [song of the earth] (1907–10) are most notable. Following BRUCKNER in the Viennese symphonic tradition, he added folk elements and expanded the form in length, emotional contrast, and orchestral size.

Mahmud II, 1784–1839, Ottoman sultan (1808–39). An able ruler, he was unable to halt the disintegration of the OTTOMAN EMPIRE (Turkey). During his reign the EASTERN QUESTION assumed increasing importance. He was a vigorous reformer who began the Westernization of Turkey and ruthlessly destroyed (1826) the JANISSARIES. He was unable to defeat the Greek rebels in their War of Independence or to prevent Egypt from attaining virtual independence.

mahogany, common name for the Meliaceae, a family of chiefly tropical shrubs and trees, from which the valuable hardwood called mahogany is obtained. Principal sources of the hardwood, often used for furniture, are trees of the American genus *Swietenia* and the W African genus *Khaya.* Varying in color from golden to deep red-brown, the woods are usually scented, close-grained, and resistant to termites.

Mahrattas or **Marathas,** Marathi-speaking people of W central India. From their homeland in Maharashtra (see INDIA) these Hindu warriors rose to power in the 17th cent. Led by SIVAJI they resisted the MOGULS under AURANGZEB. Expanding into the DECCAN and S India, they became the strongest rival to British supremacy but then split into several warring groups. The British conquered them in 1818.

maidenhair tree: see GINKGO.

Mailer, Norman, 1923–, American writer; b. Long Branch, N.J. He won early renown with his World War II novel *The Naked and the Dead* (1948). His sharp views of American society are reflected not only in such semiautobiographical novels as *An American Dream* (1966) but also in *The Armies of the Night* (1968; Pulitzer), a journalistic account of the 1967 peace march on Washington, and *The Executioner's Song* (1979; Pulitzer), a novelistic treatment of the convicted killer Gary Gilmore. *Harlot's Ghost,* a long novel about the CIA, was published in 1991.

Maillol, Aristide [mäyôl'], 1861–1944, French sculptor, WOODCUT artist, and painter. Allied with the NABIS, he later turned to sculpture. His idealized, massive female nudes, e.g., *The River* (Mus. Mod. Art, N.Y.C.), show classical influence.

Maimonides [mīmŏn'ĭdēz] or **Moses ben Maimon,** 1135–1204, Jewish rabbi, physician, and philosopher, one of the greatest Hebrew scholars; b. Spain. He is sometimes called Rambam (from *R*abbi *M*oses *B*en *M*aimon). His great work *Mishneh Torah,* known in English as the *Strong Hand,* represents his effort to organize for the layman as well as for rabbis and judges the vast mass of Jewish oral law, or MISHNA. His contribution to Western philosophy, however, rests on his influential *Guide to the Perplexed,* in which he attempted to reconcile Aristotle's theories with those of Jewish theology and thereby helped to introduce Aristotle to the Christian philosophers of the Middle Ages (see SCHOLASTICISM).

Maine, largest of the New England states of the NE U.S.; bordered by New Hampshire (W), the Canadian provinces of Quebec (NW) and New Brunswick (NE), and the Atlantic Ocean (S, SE).

Area, 33,215 sq mi (86,027 sq km). *Pop.* (1990) 1,227,928, a 9.2% increase over 1980 pop. *Capital,* Augusta. *Statehood,* Mar. 15, 1820 (23d state). *Highest pt.,* Mt. Katahdin, 5,268 ft (1,607 m); *lowest pt.,* sea level. *Nickname,* Pine Tree State. *Motto, Dirigo* [I Direct]. *State bird,* chickadee. *State flower,* white pine cone and tassel. *State tree,* Eastern white pine. *Abbr.,* Me.; ME.

Land and People. Located within the forested New England upland, Maine occupies a glacially smoothed plateau that slopes gradually south and east toward the Atlantic Ocean from higher lands in the north and west. Occasional peaks such as Mt. Katahdin and the mountains of Mt. Desert Island rise above the surrounding plateau. Waterfalls and lakes, relics of the Pleistocene Ice Age, interrupt many of the more than 5,000 rivers and streams. Winters are cold, with heavy snow over the northern interior; summers are cool. Most of the largely rural (over 55%) population lives in the south and the southwest. PORTLAND is the largest city. In 1990 the population was over 98% white.

Economy. Maine is a predominantly industrial state; the leading manufactures are wood and paper products, textiles, leather goods (especially shoes), sardines and other canned goods, and transportation and electrical equipment. During the 1980s, service and financial industries, many centered in the Portland area, became more important. Potatoes, dairy products, eggs, broiler chickens, blueberries, and apples are the major farm products. Picturesque coastal resorts and Mt. Desert Island, in Acadia National Park (see NATIONAL PARKS, table), attract a large summer tourist population. There are lobster, sardine, and other fisheries along the coast.

Government. The 1820 constitution provides for a governor elected every four years and a legislature of 35 senators and 151 representatives elected every two years. Maine sends two senators and two representatives to the U.S. Congress and has four electoral votes.

History. Short-lived settlements were established by the French (1604) on the St. Croix R. and by the English (1607–8) under George Popham at Fort St. George (site of Phippsburg). Further French settlement was prevented after Sir Samuel Argall destroyed a colony (1613) on Mt. Desert Island. Ferdinando Gorges attempted settlement after receiving a grant (1620) and royal charter (1639). The Massachusetts Bay Colony claimed jurisdiction (1647) and purchased (1677) proprietary rights from Gorges's heirs. As part of Massachusetts, Maine developed early fishing, lumbering, and shipbuilding industries, and was designated (1775) one of three admiralty districts of that state in the AMERICAN REVOLUTION. Commerce expanded rapidly after the war, followed by industry after commercial activity was interrupted by the EMBARGO ACT of 1807 and the WAR OF 1812. Statehood was achieved in 1820 through the MISSOURI COMPROMISE. The WEBSTER-ASHBURTON TREATY of 1842 ended the chronic Northeast Boundary Dispute. Economic and population growth, slowed after the Civil War as the nation expanded to the west, accelerated in the 1970s as new highways attracted commuters and industries to the southwest from the nearby Boston area. The economy received a boost when long-standing land claims against the state by Native Americans were settled (1980) for $81.5 million, and the tribes began to buy land and make investments. Maine's population grew by 13.2% in the 1970s and 9.2% in the 1980s, the largest increases since the 1840s.

Maine, U.S. battleship sunk (Feb. 15, 1898) in Havana harbor, killing 260, in an incident that helped precipitate the SPANISH-AMERICAN WAR. The cause of the explosion was never satisfactorily explained, and separate American and Spanish inquiries produced different results. But the American jingoistic press blamed the Spanish government, and "Remember the Maine" became the rallying cry of the war.

Maintenon, Françoise d'Aubigné, marquise de [măNtə nôN'], 1635–1719, second wife of LOUIS XIV of France. Educated as a Protestant, she later became a devout Roman Catholic and at 16 married the poet Paul Scarron. After his death (1660) she was the governess of the children of Louis XIV and Mme de MONTESPAN. She gained considerable influence over Louis, and in 1684 she was morganatically married to the king.

Mainz [mīnts], (1989 est. pop. 175,000), capital of Rhineland-Palatinate, W Germany, on the Rhine R., opposite the mouth of the Main R. It is an industrial center with such manufactures as chemicals, drugs, and machinery, and a trade center for Rhine wines. The site (1st cent. B.C.) of a Roman camp, it became (746) the seat of the first German archbishop, St. BONIFACE. Johann GUTENBERG made it (15th cent.) the first printing center of Europe. It was (1873–1918) a fortress of the German Empire. Badly damaged during WORLD WAR II, it has been rebuilt since 1945. Historic buildings include the 10th-cent. Romanesque cathedral.

Maisonneuve, Paul de Chomedey, sieur de [māzônnöv'], 1612–76, founder and first French governor of MONTREAL (1642–63). Commanding a detachment of French soldiers, he landed (1642) on Montreal Island and founded the city of Ville Marie, later Montreal.

maize: see CORN.

majolica, type of glazed pottery often associated with Spain, Italy, and Mexico. A tin enamel is applied to a fired piece of earthenware, forming a white, opaque, porous surface on which a design is then painted. After a transparent glaze is applied, the piece is fired again. Used since Babylonian days, majolica was made by 14th-cent. Hispano-Moresque potters and popularized in mid-15th-cent. Italy by the DELLA ROBBIA family. It is still used in folk art.

Major, John, 1943–, British political leader. From a working-class background and lacking a university education, he made a successful career in banking and was elected to Parliament as a Conservative in 1979. A protégé of Margaret THATCHER, he served as her foreign secretary (1989) and chancellor of the exchequer (1989–90). In Nov. 1990 he was elected to succeed Thatcher as prime minister and leader of the CONSERVATIVE PARTY. He has been more cautious and pragmatic than his predecessor. In 1992 he led the Conservatives to victory in parliamentary elections.

Majorca [məjôr'kə], Span. *Mallorca,* island (1987 est. pop. 606,000), 1,405 sq mi (3,639 sq km), Spain, largest of the BALEARIC ISLANDS, in the W Mediterranean. Palma is the chief city. A separate kingdom (1276–1343), the island is now a popular resort noted for its fine scenery and architecture.

Majorian, d. 461, West Roman emperor (457–61). He tried to protect the people from unfair taxation. His expedition (461) against GAISERIC failed. His general RICIMER, who had enthroned him as puppet emperor, became jealous of his power and murdered him. This began the decline of the empire.

Majuro, atoll (1986 est. pop. 12,800), c.3.5 sq mi (9 km), capital (comprising over 60 islets) of the MARSHALL ISLANDS.

Makarios III, 1913–77, Orthodox Eastern archbishop and first president of CYPRUS (1960–77). As archbishop of Cyprus he led the movement that culminated in the island's independence in 1960. As president he maintained a policy aimed at reducing conflict between the Greek and Turkish populations on the island. He survived four assassination attempts and was turned out of office briefly in 1974.

Makarova, Natalia, 1940–, Russian ballet dancer. She studied in Leningrad (Saint Petersburg) and danced (1959–70) with the KIROV BALLET in such classic ballets as *Giselle* and *Swan Lake*. She also danced (1970–72) with the AMERICAN BALLET THEATRE. After 1972, she made guest appearances in London and the U.S., retiring in 1989.

Makemie, Francis [məkĕ'mē], c.1658–1708, American clergyman, considered the founder of Presbyterianism in America; b. Ireland. Ordained (c.1682) as a missionary to America, he preached from the Carolinas to New York and organized two Presbyterian churches in Maryland. In 1706 he formed the first presbytery in the country in Philadelphia.

Malabo, formerly Santa Isabel, city (1983 pop. 31,630), capital of Equatorial Guinea, on Bioko Island (formerly Fernando Po), in the Gulf of Guinea. The island's chief port and commercial center, Malabo exports cacao, coffee, and other agricultural products. The city was founded in 1827 by the British as a base for the suppression of the slave trade and was called Port Clarence, or Clarencetown.

Malacca, Strait of, c.500 mi (800 km) long and c.30 to 200 mi (50 to 320 km) wide, between Sumatra and the Malay Peninsula. SINGAPORE is the chief port. The strait, one of the world's most important sea passages, links the INDIAN OCEAN and the SOUTH CHINA SEA.

Malachi [mălәkī, –kē], **Malachias** [măl″әkī'әs], or **Malachy** [măl'әkē], book of the OLD TESTAMENT, 39th and last in the Authorized Version and 12th of the Minor PROPHETS. The anonymous author (probably c.460 B.C.) rebukes the people and the priests and prophesies the Day of Judgment.

malachite, green copper carbonate mineral $Cu_2CO_3(OH)_2$, found in crystal and, more commonly, massive form. It is used as a gem, a COPPER source, and, when ground, a pigment. It occurs associated with other copper ores in the U.S., Chile, Russia, Zimbabwe, Zaïre, and Australia.

Malamud, Bernard, 1914–86, American author; b. Brooklyn, N.Y. Often reflecting a concern with Jewish tradition, his works include the novels *The Natural* (1952; made into a movie in 1984), *The Fixer* (1966; Pulitzer), *Dubin's Lives* (1979), and *God's Grace* (1982) and such short-story collections as *The Magic Barrel* (1958).

malamute: see ALASKAN MALAMUTE.

malaria, infectious parasitic disease characterized by high fever, severe chills, enlargement of the spleen, and sometimes ANEMIA and JAUNDICE. It can be acute or chronic and is frequently recurrent. Widespread throughout tropical and subtropical areas of the world, malaria is transmitted by the *Anopheles* mosquito, which picks up the causative *Plasmodium* parasite from the blood of an infected person and transfers it to that of a healthy person. Quinine, the traditional treatment, has largely been replaced by modern antimalarials, including chloroquine, primaquine, and mefloquine. In strains that have developed resistance to the new antimalarials, quinine is again the drug of choice.

Malatesta, Italian family that ruled Rimini and neighboring cities from the 13th to 16th cent. Among its members was the hunchback Gianciotto Malatesta, who killed his wife, Francesca da Rimini, when he learned of her love affair with his brother, Paolo. Their story was immortalized in DANTE's *Divine Comedy.* **Sigismondo Pandolfo Malatesta,** (1417–68), was a patron of the arts and a bitter enemy of the papacy.

Malawi [mәlä'wē], officially Republic of Malawi, republic (1992 est. pop. 9,605,000), 45,200 sq mi (117,068 sq km), E central Africa, bordered by Zambia (W), Tanzania (N), and Mozambique (E, S, and SW). Principal cities are LILONGWE (the capital) and BLANTYRE. About one fifth of the country is occupied by Lake Malawi (Lake Nyasa), in the Great Rift Valley; the remainder is largely a high plateau. The economy is overwhelmingly agricultural, and per capita income is very low. Most of the farmland is given to subsistence crops, but large estates produce tobacco, tea, sugar, peanuts, cotton, and corn for export. Large numbers of poultry, goats, cattle, and pigs are raised. Malawi's extensive mineral resources, including uranium, coal, and bauxite, are largely unexploited. Most of the population are members of various Bantu-speaking ethnic groups. Many follow traditional beliefs, although 75% are nominally Christian. Chichewa and English are the official languages.

History. The Malawi kingdom, established in the Shire R. valley in the 15th cent., conquered much of modern Rhodesia and Mozambique in the 18th cent. It declined shortly thereafter, and a flourishing slave trade developed. Missionary activity and the threat of Portuguese annexation led Britain in 1889 to proclaim a protectorate in the area (known from 1907 to 1964 as Nyasaland). The British ended the slave trade and established large coffee-growing estates. In 1915 a small-scale revolt against British rule was easily suppressed, but it was an inspiration to other Africans intent on ending foreign domination. In 1953 the Federation of Rhodesia and Nyasaland (linking Nyasaland, Northern Rhodesia, and Southern Rhodesia) was formed despite the protests of Nyasaland's natives, who feared the white-dominated policies of Southern Rhodesia (now ZIMBABWE). The Federation was dissolved in 1963, and Nyasaland became independent as Malawi in 1964. It became a republic in 1966 under Hastings Kamuzu BANDA, president for life and the autocratic ruler of a one-party state. Malawi alienated its black neighbors by maintaining friendly relations with white-run governments in S Africa, but its relations with black African nations have improved since. In 1992 there were violent protests against Banda's rule, and Western nations suspended aid to the country. In a 1993 referendum Malawians voted for an end to one-party rule, and parliament passed legislation establishing a multiparty democracy and abolishing the life presidency.

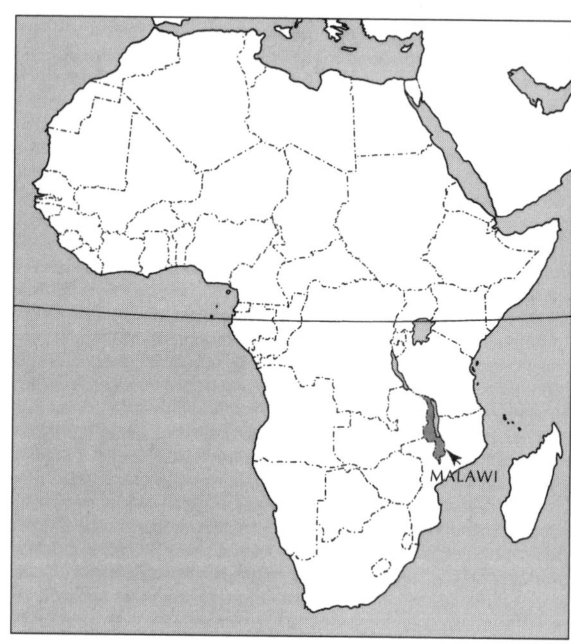

Malawi, Lake,or **Lake Nyasa,** freshwater lake, c.360 mi (580 km) long, bounded by steep mountains, in the GREAT RIFT VALLEY of E Africa. It is drained in the south by the Shire R., a tributary of the Zambezi.

Malayalam [mä″lәyä'lәm], Dravidian language of India. See LANGUAGE (table).

Malay language: see MALAYO-POLYNESIAN LANGUAGES.

Malayo-Polynesian languages, family of languages spoken in the Malay Peninsula; Madagascar; Taiwan; Indonesia; New Guinea; the Melanesian, Micronesian, and Polynesian Islands; the Philippine Islands; and New Zealand. See LANGUAGE (table).

Malay Peninsula, southern extremity (c.70,000 sq mi/181,300 sq km) of the continent of Asia, between the Andaman Sea of the Indian Ocean and the Strait of Malacca (W), and the Gulf of Thailand and the South China Sea (E). It forms part of Thailand (N) and part of Malaysia (S); at its southern tip is the island of Singapore. A mountain range (7,186 ft/2,190 km at its highest point), from which many swift rivers flow east and west, forms the backbone of the peninsula. More than half its area is covered by tropical rain forest. It is a major rubber and tin producer; other products include timber, rice, and coconut products. Malays, who probably came from S China c.2,000 B.C., form a majority of the population. Chinese are almost as numerous. Indians and Thais are important minorities, and aborigines are found in the hills and jungles. Thais, Indians, and Indonesians invaded the peninsula periodically from the 8th cent. until the primacy of a Malay state was established c.1400. Later in the 15th cent. the Malays were converted to Islam. European contacts began in the 16th cent. In 1511 the Portuguese seized the prime Malay state of Malacca, which fell to the Dutch in 1641. The British dominated the southern part of the peninsula from 1826 and acquired suzerainty over much of the central portion from Siam in 1909. In 1948 the British part of the peninsula became the Federation of Malaya (see MALAYSIA).

Malaysia, independent federation (1992 est. pop. 18,411,000), 128,430 sq mi (332,633 sq km), SE Asia, consisting of **Peninsular Malaysia** (also called West Malaysia or Malaya), on the Malay Peninsula; and, about 400 mi across the SOUTH CHINA SEA, **East Malaysia** (made up of the states of SABAH and SARAWAK), on the

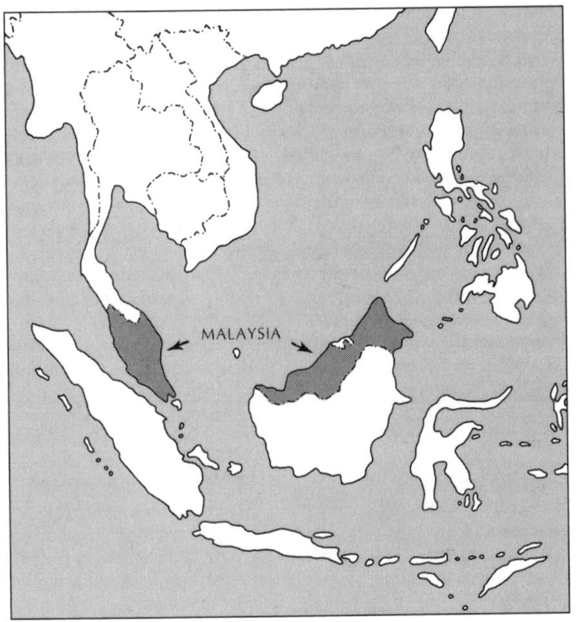

island of BORNEO. Peninsular Malaysia is bordered by Thailand (N), the South China Sea (E), Singapore (S), and the Strait of Malacca and the Andaman Sea (W); East Malaysia is bordered by the South China and Sulu seas (N), Brunei (NE), the Celebes Sea (E), and Indonesia (S and W). The capital of Malaysia is KUALA LUMPUR. Both Peninsular and East Malaysia have densely forested, mountainous interiors flanked by coastal plains; the climate is tropical. Politically the country is a federal parliamentary democracy with a constitutional monarch elected by the hereditary rulers of the sultanates from which the country was formed. Malaysia has a high standard of living by SE Asian standards, largely due to a steadily expanding industrial sector. The country is a major world producer of tin and rubber; steel, electronics equipment, palm oil, lumber, and petroleum are other important products. PRIVATIZATION of many state-owned businesses began in 1992 as part of a plan to cut government expenditures and expand free enterprise. Although it has only 31% of the country's area, Peninsular Malaysia has more than 80% of its people. The majority of the polyglot population are ethnic Malays and Chinese; there is a sizable Indian (mainly Tamil) minority. The official language is Malay, but Chinese, English, Tamil, Hindi, and tribal dialects are widely spoken. Islam, practiced by the Malays, is the established religion. Many Chinese follow traditional beliefs, and the Indian minority is mainly Hindu.

History. The region may have been part of the Buddhist Sri Vijaya kingdom (8th–13th cent.), converted (15th cent.) to Islam as part of a Muslim Malay state. The Malayan Peninsula was first visited by Europeans in the 16th cent. Malacca, on the west coast, was occupied by Portugal (1511) and the Dutch (1641). The British acquired Pinang island in 1786, uniting it in 1826 with Malacca and Singapore as the STRAITS SETTLEMENT. By the beginning of the 20th cent. Britain had established many protectorates on the Malayan Peninsula, as well as in North Borneo (Sabah) and Sarawak. After the Japanese occupation during World War II, Britain united all its territories on the peninsula in the Union of Malaya (1946); Sabah and Sarawak became crown colonies. In 1948, in response to pressure from the ethnic Malays, who feared the reorganization would increase Chinese and Indian influence, Britain created the Federation of Malaya. A largely Chinese-led Communist insurrection was not fully suppressed until 1960. Meanwhile, the Federation of Malaya became an independent state within the Commonwealth in 1957. In 1963 it formed the Federation of Malaysia with SINGAPORE, Sarawak, and Sabah; Singapore was forced to withdraw in 1965. The struggle between the Muslim Malays and the ethnic Chinese continued, and bloody riots in 1969 led to a 22-month suspension of parliament. Since then, political balance has been maintained by a multiracial National Front coalition, led since 1981 by Prime Min. Mahathir Mohamad, but there have been restraints on personal and political freedoms and the independence of the judiciary has been compromised.

Malcolm III (Malcolm Canmore), d. 1093, king of Scotland (1057–93); son of Duncan I; successor to MACBETH. In aid of Edgar Atheling, pretender to the English throne, Malcolm waged wars against England that helped ensure Scottish independence and made possible church reorganization by his wife, Margaret of Scotland.

Malcolm X, 1925–65, African-American religous and political leader, also known as El-Hajj Malik El-Shabazz; b. Malcolm Little in Omaha, Neb. Convicted of burglary (1946), he adopted the BLACK MUSLIM faith in prison, and on his release (1952) became a Muslim minister and charismatic advocate of black separatism. Following a split (1963) with Black Muslim leader Elijah MUHAMMAD and a pilgrimage to Mecca, he converted to orthodox Islam and founded (1964) the Organization of Afro-American Unity, which promoted black nationalism but admitted the possibility of interracial brotherhood. In 1965 he was assassinated in Harlem, N.Y.C., purportedly by Black Muslims. The *Autobiography of Malcolm X* (1964) is a classic of the 1960s black power movement.

Maldives [mălʹdīvz], officially Republic of Maldives, formerly Maldive Islands, republic (1992 est. pop. 234,000), 115 sq mi (298 sq km), 19 atolls in the N Indian Ocean, about 420 mi (675 km) SW of Sri Lanka. They comprise nearly 2,000 coral islands, of which about 200 are inhabited. Malé is the capital and largest island. The islands are covered with tropical vegetation, particularly coconut palms. Although some fruit, corn, and other grains are cultivated, most food staples must be imported. The chief sources of revenue are fishing, tourism, coconut products (especially copra), and shipping. There is some fish processing and limited industrial development. The inhabitants are of mixed Indian, Sinhalese, and Arab descent. ISLAM is the official religion. Divehi (a Sinhalese dialect) is spoken; English is also widely used.

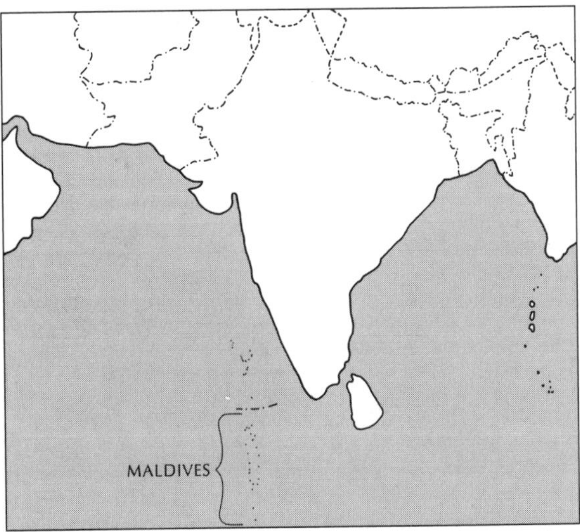

History. The Maldives were originally settled by peoples from S Asia; Islam was introduced in the 12th cent. From the arrival of the Portuguese in the 16th cent., the islands were intermittently under European influence. In 1887 they became a British protectorate and military base but retained internal self-government. The Maldives achieved full independence as a sultanate in 1965, but in 1968 the ad-Din dynasty, which had ruled since the 14th cent., was ended, and a republic was declared. In 1976 Britain closed its air force base on the island of Gan, but a Soviet offer to lease the facility was rejected. In 1978 Maumoon Abdul Gayoom was elected president. A coup attempt (1988) by Tamil mercenaries was quashed with the help of Indian forces.

Malé, city (1990 est. pop. 55,100), capital of MALDIVES.

Malenkov, Georgi Maksimilianovich, 1902–1988, Soviet leader. An aide of STALIN, he became a full member of the politburo and a deputy premier in 1946. As premier (1953–55) he pursued a conciliatory foreign policy and curtailed the power of the secret police. He was forced to resign as premier (1955) in favor of BULGANIN; removed from other posts in 1957; and expelled from the party in 1961.

Malevich, Casimir or **Kasimir** [mälyā'vĭch], 1878–1935, Russian painter, the founder (1913) of SUPREMATISM. His nonobjective paintings are geometric forms on a flatly painted surface, e.g., *White on White* (Mus. Mod. Art, N.Y.C.).

Mali, officially Republic of Mali, republic (1992 est. pop. 8,641,000), 478,764 sq mi (1,240,000 sq km), the largest country in W Africa, bordered by Algeria (N), Niger (E and SE), Burkina Faso and Côte d'Ivoire (S), and Guinea, Senegal, and Mauritania (W). BAMAKO is the capital. With the SAHARA desert in the north, much of the country is arid and barely supports grazing (mainly cattle, sheep, and goats). The south, watered by the NIGER and Senegal rivers (both important transportation arteries), contains fertile areas where peanuts and cotton, the chief cash crops, are grown. Subsistence crops include rice, corn, sorghum, and millet. Fish from the Niger and livestock are exported. Industry is limited mainly to food processing, cotton ginning, and textile production. Salt, gold, and phosphates are mined on a small scale, but extensive mineral resources remain unexploited. Six ethnic groups make up most of the population. There are also TUAREG and Moor minorities who, with Tuaregs in NIGER, fought for autonomy in the early 1990s. About 90% of the people are Muslims; most of the remainder are animists. French is the official language, but Bambara is spoken by most of the population.

History. Several extensive empires and kingdoms dominated the early history of the region. Among them, the medieval empire of Mali, a powerful state and one of the world's chief gold suppliers, reached its peak in the early 14th cent. Such cities as TIMBUKTU and Djenné became important centers of trade and culture. The SONGHAI empire of Gao rose to prominence in the late 15th cent. but was shattered by a Moroccan army in 1590, after which the vast region broke up into petty states. Despite a resurgence of Islam and the opposition of Muslim emperors, French conquest of the Mali area was virtually complete by 1898, and Mali, then called French Sudan, became part of FRENCH WEST AFRICA. Between the two World Wars a nationalist movement developed, and the militant Sudanese Union, led by Modibo Keita, emerged as the leading political force. A 1958 referendum created the autonomous Sudanese Republic, which joined (1959) with Senegal in the Mali Federation. The union ended in 1960, when the new Republic of Mali obtained full independence and broke with the FRENCH COMMUNITY. With Keita as president, Mali became a one-party, socialist state. It withdrew from the franc zone in 1962 but was forced by financial problems to return to the French bloc in 1967. Keita was overthrown by junior army officers in 1968, and Lt. Moussa Traoré assumed power as head of a military regime. In the early 1970s Mali's agrarian economy was devastated by a severe drought that struck the SAHEL region of Africa. The resulting famine contributed to the deaths of nearly 100,000 people. In 1979 a new constitution established a one-party state, and Traoré was reelected president. Mali fought a brief border war with Burkina Faso in 1985. Traoré was overthrown in 1991, and in 1992 Alpha Oumar Konaré became Mali's first democratically elected president.

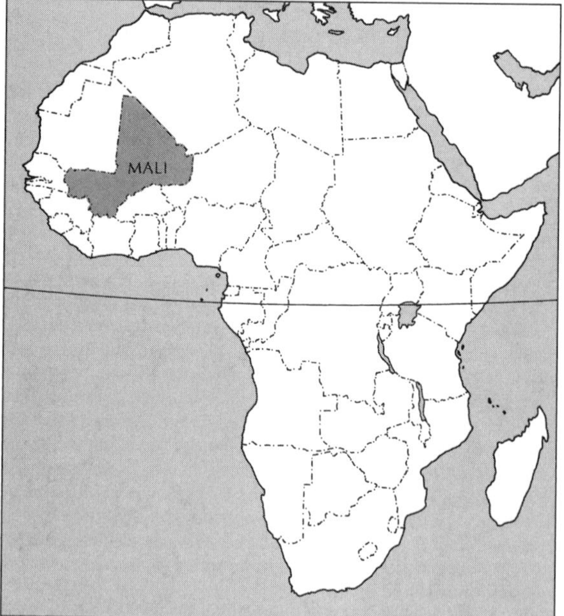

Malinowski, Bronislaw [mălĭnŏf'skē], 1884–1942, English anthropologist; b. Poland. He was the founder of "functionalism," the theory that cultures should be studied in terms of their particular internal dynamics. After studying (1914–18) Trobriand Islanders he did research in Africa and the Americas. His writings include *Argonauts of the Western Pacific* (1922), *Crime and Custom in Savage Society* (1926), and *Magic, Science and Religion* (1948).

Mallarmé, Stéphane [mällärmā'], 1842–98, French poet. The chief forebear of the SYMBOLISTS, he held that poetry should be transcendental, approaching the abstraction of music. His language defies traditional syntax and is exceedingly obscure. Major works include *Herodias* (1869) and *The Afternoon of a Faun* (1876). Mallarmé was the center of a literary group that gathered every Tuesday, and his theories had a major influence on modern French writing.

Malle, Louis, 1932–, French film director. His varied work includes *The Lovers* (1958), *Murmur of the Heart* (1971), *Atlantic City* (1980), *My Dinner with André* (1980), *Au Revoir les Enfants* (1988), and *Damage* (1992).

Mallea, Eduardo [mäyā'ä], 1903–82, Argentine writer. His novels, many dealing with alienation, include *The Bay of Silence* (1940), *Posesión* (1958), and *Gabriel Andaral* (1971). Also of note are the *History of an Argentine Passion* (1935) and the stories collected in *City on the Motionless River* (1936).

mallow, common name for the Malvaceae, a family of widely distributed shrubs and herbs, abundant in the American tropics and typified by mucilaginous sap and showy flowers with a prominent column of fused stamens. The family includes the true mallows (genus *Malva*) of the Old World, and the false mallows (genus *Malvastrum*), and rose, or swamp, mallows (genus *Hibiscus*) of North America. Introduced *Hibiscus* species include the rose of Sharon (*H. syriacus*), a popular ornamental, and okra, or gumbo (*H. esculentus*), whose mucilaginous pods are used as a vegetable. The most popular ornamental of the family, the hollyhock (*Althea rosea*), originally a Chinese perennial, is widely cultivated in many varieties and colors. The European marsh mallow (*A. officinalis*) is used medicinally and was formerly used in the confection marshmallow, now usually made from syrup, gelatin, and other ingredients. Economically the most important plant of the family is COTTON.

Malmö, city (1988 pop. 230,785), capital of Malmöhus co., S Sweden, on the Øresund. It is a major naval and commercial port. Founded in the 12th cent., it was an important trade center in Danish hands until it passed to Sweden in the mid-17th cent. Its castle is now a museum.

malnutrition, insufficiency of one or more nutrients necessary for health. Primary malnutrition is caused by a lack of essential foodstuffs (usually VITAMINS, MINERALS, or PROTEINS) in the diet. Such a lack can be caused by regional conditions such as drought and overpopulation or by poor eating habits. Secondary malnutrition is caused by failure to absorb or utilize nutrients, as in disease of the gastrointestinal tract, KIDNEY, or LIVER; by failure to satisfy increased nutritional requirements, as during PREGNANCY; or by excessive excretion, as in diarrhea. Malnutrition can cause such conditions as ANEMIA and KWASHIORKOR.

Malory, Sir Thomas, d. 1471, English author of *Morte d'Arthur,* originally called *The Book of King Arthur and His Knights of the Round Table* and consisting of eight romances. The printer William CAXTON gave it the misleading title in 1485. It became the standard source for later versions of the ARTHURIAN LEGEND.

Malpighi, Marcello [mälpē'gē], 1628–94, Italian anatomist. A pioneer in the use of the MICROSCOPE, he made many valuable observations on the structure of plants and animals. He completed William HARVEY's theory of circulation by his observation of the movement of blood through capillaries; this and his study of lung structure appeared in *De pulmonibus* (1661). He is noted also for studies of gland structure, of the brain and other organs, of the embryology of the chick, and of the anatomy of the silkworm.

malpractice, a failure to provide professional services with the skill exhibited by careful, responsible providers, resulting in injury, loss, or damage to the contracting party. Claims of malpractice are most common against medical professionals, and most suits are for negligence in providing the expected level of care. In recent decades such suits have increased, leading to vastly higher malpractice insurance rates. Proposed solutions to the increased cost burden of such rates include compensation review boards, no-fault statutes, and limits on awards for damages.

Malraux, André [mälrō'], 1901–76, French man of letters and statesman. He participated with the Communists in the Chinese civil war (1925–27) and with the Loyalists in the Spanish civil war (1936–39); these experiences are the source for his outstanding social novels, *Man's Fate* (1933) and *Man's Hope* (1937). An intellectual with a broad knowledge of archaeology, art history, and anthropology, he wrote extensively on art and civilization in such works as *The Voices of Silence* (1951) and *The Metamorphosis of the Gods* (1957). Malraux was a resistance leader during World War II, and he served under Charles DE GAULLE as minister of information (1945) and minister of cultural affairs (1958–68).

malt, a grain (usually BARLEY) steeped in water, partially germinated, then dried and cured. It is used in brewing to convert cereal starches to sugars by means of the ENZYMES (chiefly diastase) produced during germination.

Malta, officially Republic of Malta, republic (1992 est. pop. 359,000), 122 sq mi (316 sq km), in the Mediterranean Sea S of Sicily, comprising the islands of Malta, Gozo (Ghawdex), and Comino (Kemmuna). Valletta is the capital. The economy is supported by tourism, light industry, agriculture, and shipbuilding. The polyglot population is a mixture of Arab, Sicilian, Norman, Spanish, Italian, and English. Maltese (a Semitic language) and English are the official languages, but Italian is widely spoken. Roman Catholicism is the state religion. Malta is governed by a unicameral parliament, a prime minister, and a cabinet.

History. In ancient times Malta belonged successively to the Phoenicians, Greeks, Carthaginians, Romans, and Saracens. The Normans of SICILY occupied it c.1090, and in 1530 Holy Roman Emperor CHARLES V granted Malta to the KNIGHTS HOSPITALERS, who held it until it was surrendered (1798) to NAPOLEON I. Taken (1800) by the British, the island became of great strategic importance as a military and naval base after the opening (1869) of the SUEZ CANAL. In WORLD WAR II Malta sustained heavy Axis bombing but was never subdued. Limited self-government began in 1921, and Malta became fully independent in 1964. The last British forces withdrew in 1979. In elections in 1987, the Nationalist party came into power, with Edward Fenech Adami as prime minister; the 1992 elections returned the Nationalists to office. In foreign affairs Malta has policy of neutrality and has sought to maintain good relations with both Libya and Italy.

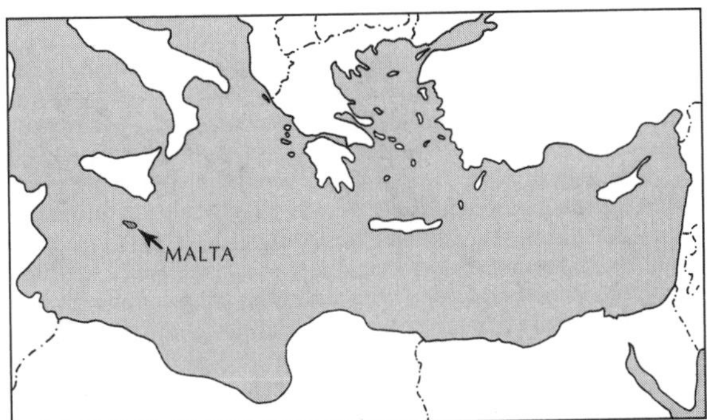

Maltese, very small TOY DOG; shoulder height, c.5 in. (12.7 cm); weight, 2–7 lb (.9–1.4 kg). Its silky white coat hangs down almost to the ground. Probably an ancient breed, closely resembling lap dogs of ancient Greece and Rome, it was very popular in Europe by the 19th cent.

Malthus, Thomas Robert [măl'thəs], 1766–1834, English economist, sociologist, and pioneer in modern population study. In *An Essay on the Principle of Population* (1798; rev. ed. 1803) he contended that poverty and distress are unavoidable because population increases faster than the means of subsistence. As checks on population growth, he accepted only war, famine, and disease but later added "moral restraint" as well. His controversial theory was adapted by neo-Malthusians and influenced such classical economists as David RICARDO.

maltose or **malt sugar** (empirical formula: $C_{12}H_{22}O_{11}$), crystalline SUGAR involved in brewing beer. Maltose can be produced from STARCH by HYDROLYSIS in the presence of diastase, an enzyme found in MALT. A disaccharide (see CARBOHYDRATE), maltose is hydrolyzed to GLUCOSE by maltase, an enzyme present in YEAST. The glucose thus formed can be fermented by another enzyme in yeast to produce ETHANOL.

Malvinas, Islas: see FALKLAND ISLANDS.

Mamelukes: see MAMLUKS.

Mamet, David, 1947–, American playwright; b. Chicago. He taught drama and produced some of his early plays at Goddard College. His work, which deals with the success and failure of the American dream, has sharp and insightful dialogue. He wrote *American Buffalo* (1975), *Glengarry Glen Ross* (1984, Pulitzer; screenplay, 1992), and *Oleanna* (1992), as well as screenplays for *The Postman Always Rings Twice* (1981) and *Homicide* (1991).

Mamluks or **Mamelukes,** Egyptian warrior caste dominant for over 700 years. They were originally slaves brought to Egypt by Fatimid caliphs in the 10th cent. Many were freed and rose to high rank. Aybak was the first Mamluk to actually become ruler (1250). For 250 years after that, Egypt was ruled by Mamluk sultans chosen from the caste of warriors. In 1517 the Ottoman Turks captured Cairo and put an end to the Mamluk sultanate. The Mamluks maintained their vast landholdings and their private armies, however, and remained provincial governors. As Turkish rule weakened, they reasserted their power, and by the 18th cent. they were virtual rulers again. NAPOLEON I defeated them in 1798, but their final defeat came in 1811 when they were massacred by MUHAMMAD ALI.

mammal, warm-blooded animal of the class Mammalia, the highest class of VERTEBRATES, found in terrestrial and aquatic habitats. The female has mammary glands, which secrete milk for the nourishment of the young after birth. In most mammals the body is partially or wholly covered with hair, the heart has four chambers, and a muscular diaphragm separates the chest from the abdominal cavity. Except for the egg-laying MONOTREMES (e.g., the PLATYPUS), mammals give birth to live young. In some MARSUPIALS and higher mammals the young receive prenatal nourishment through a placenta. Terrestrial mammals include carnivores (e.g., CAT, DOG, BEAR); rodents (e.g., BEAVER, SQUIRREL); hoofed animals (e.g., HORSE, RHINOCEROS, DEER, SWINE, CATTLE); primates (e.g., human being, MONKEY, LEMUR); and others, such as the BAT and ELEPHANT. Aquatic mammals include the carnivorous SEAL and WALRUS and the omnivorous WHALE and DOLPHIN.

mammary gland or **breast,** organ of the female mammal that produces milk for nourishment of the young. Mammary glands develop during puberty and distend during pregnancy in preparation for nursing. They are sometimes considered part of the REPRODUCTIVE SYSTEM.

mammoth, name for several prehistoric ELEPHANTS of the extinct genus *Mammuthus,* found in Eurasia and North America in the Pleistocene epoch. The imperial mammoth of North America was about 13½ ft (4.1 m) high at the shoulder. As depicted in Cro-Magnon cave paintings in S France, the mammoth had a shaggy coat, complex molar teeth, slender tusks, and a long trunk.

Mammoth Cave National Park: see NATIONAL PARKS (table).

Man, Isle of, island (1991 pop. 69,788), 227 sq mi (588 sq km), off Great Britain, in the Irish Sea. The capital is Douglas. The coast is rocky, with precipitous cliffs, the scenery varied and beautiful, and the climate very mild, making the island a popular resort. It was variously ruled until 1765, when it became a dependency of the British crown. It is, however, not subject to acts of the British Parliament and has its own legislature, the Tynwald.

man, prehistoric: see HUMAN EVOLUTION.

managed health care, system of health care delivery that aims to control costs by assigning set fees for services, monitoring the need for such procedures as tests and surgical operations, and stressing preventive care. Managed health care systems include HEALTH MAINTENENCE ORGANIZATIONS; preferred provider organizations (PPOs), networks of doctors and hospitals that adhere to given guidelines and fees in return for recieving a certain number of patients; and point of service (POS) plans, which are similar to PPOs but allow patients to go outside the network for treatment, usually at a higher cost. The term is also used to describe more traditional health insurance plans that require that more expensive procedures be reviewed and approved by a plan official before they are performed.

Managua, city (1985 est. pop. 650,000), W Nicaragua, capital of Nicaragua, on the southern shore of Lake Managua. The nation's largest city and commercial and industrial center, it became the capital in 1855 to end a feud between the cities of LEÓN and Granada. There has been much rebuilding since 1972, when earthquakes almost leveled the city and took some 10,000 lives, but the old city center has been largely unrestored.

Manassas, battle of: see BULL RUN.

Manasseh or **Manasses.** **1** First son of Joseph and eponymous ancestor of one of the 12 tribes of ISRAEL. **2** King of Judah (c.696–c.642 B.C.). He fostered foreign cults. The **Prayer of Manasses,** one of the pseudepigrapha, placed in the APOCRYPHA in the Authorized Version, is given as his penitential prayer.

Manasseh ben Israel, 1604–57, Jewish scholar and communal leader; b. Portugal. A Marrano (see SEPHARDIM), he returned to Judaism in Holland, where he served as a rabbi and started (1627) the first Hebrew press. He obtained Oliver CROMWELL's unofficial assent for Jews to settle in London, where they had been forbidden to live since 1290.

manatee: see SIRENIAN.

Manaus, city (1990 est. pop. 1,114,000), NW Brazil, capital of Amazonas state, on the Rio Negro. Surrounded by jungle, it is the westernmost of Brazil's major cities, the commercial center of the upper AMAZON region, and a major river port accommodating oceangoing vessels. Founded in 1669, it grew rapidly during the rubber boom of the late 19th cent. Since the 1970s, increased interest in development of the Amazon basin has brought Manaus new importance. Its opera house is renowned.

Manchester, city (1991 pop. 404,861), Greater Manchester, NW England, on the Irwell, Medlock, Irk, and Tib rivers. The Manchester Ship Canal provides access to oceangoing vessels. The center of England's most densely populated area, Manchester was long the nation's leading textile city, but other industries, including chemicals and pharmaceuticals, are now more important. A Celtic and Roman town, it was chartered in 1301. Parliamentary representation was achieved in 1832. Important in liberal thought, the city was the center of the MANCHESTER SCHOOL of economics in the 19th cent. and the site of the founding (1821) of the influential daily the *Manchester Guardian.*

Manchester, city (1990 pop. 99,567), S N.H., on the Merrimack R.; settled 1722, inc. as a city 1846. Now the state's largest city, it was a major 19th-cent. textile producer. Since the Depression and the shift of much industry to the South, the city has diversified its manufactures, which include electronic and electrical equipment and shoes.

Manchester school, group of 19th-cent. English economists, led by Richard COBDEN and John BRIGHT, who advocated free trade and held that the state should interfere as little as possible in economic matters (see LAISSEZ FAIRE).

Manchu, inhabitants of Manchuria descended from the Jurchen, a tribe known in Asia since the 7th cent. Originally pastoral nomads, they swept into N China in the 12th cent., but were driven out in the 13th cent. by the MONGOLS. They settled in the Sungari valley, developing an agrarian civilization and increasing their territory. In 1644 they conquered China and founded the Ch'ing dynasty . When the dynasty ended (1912), they merged with the Chinese.

Manchuria [mănchŏŏr'ēə], Mandarin *Dongbei* [northeast], region (1988 est. pop. 94,781,000), c.600,000 sq mi (1,554,000 sq km), NE China. Comprising (since 1956) the provinces of Heilongjiang, Jilin, and Liaoning—it had previously included part of Inner Mongolia—Manchuria is bordered by Russia, North Korea, and Mongolia. It has timber resources and mineral deposits, including oil, coal, gold, magnesium, and uranium. A major manufacturing and agricultural center, Manchuria produces steel, heavy machinery, motor vehicles, chemicals, and aircraft in the highly industrialized cities and grains, beans, soybeans, and sweet potatoes in the fertile Manchurian plain. It is the traditional home of peoples that have invaded and sometimes ruled N China, notably the MANCHU. Controlled successively by Russia, Chinese warlords, Japan, and the Soviet Union in the 20th cent., Manchuria was occupied by the Communists in 1948. Important strategically, it was developed as a major industrial region, but its huge state enterprises stagnated during the economic reforms of the 1980s.

Manco Capac, legendary founder of the INCA dynasty of Peru; one of four brothers who, with their four sisters, conquered the peoples of the Cuzco valley. Manco Capac's son may be the Sinchi Roca who authorities accept as the first historical Inca chief (c.1105–c.1140). **Manco Capac** was also the name of the last Inca ruler. A puppet emperor crowned in 1534 by the Spanish conqueror Francisco PIZARRO, he raised a huge army and in 1536 besieged Spanish-occupied CUZCO. Abandoning the siege after ten months, he fought a bloody guerrilla war against the Spanish until he was murdered in 1544.

Mandalay, city (1983 pop. 532,985), central Myanmar, on the Irawaddy R. Myanmar's second largest city, it is a major transportation hub. It dates from c.1850 and was the capital of the Burman kingdom from 1860 until Britain annexed the kingdom in 1885. Mandalay is a center of Burmese Buddhism. Much of the city was destroyed by British bombing in World War II, but numerous Buddhist monuments, notably the Arakan pagoda, remain.

Mandan, indigenous people of the Plains (see NORTH AMERICA, INDIGENOUS PEOPLES OF), who spoke a Siouan language of the Hokan-Siouan stock (see NATIVE AMERICAN LANGUAGES). Said to have come from the east, by mid-18th cent. they lived in North Dakota. The Mandan were agricultural people with distinctive cultural traits, including a myth of origin in which their ancestors climbed from beneath the earth on the roots of a grapevine. Their numbers were severely depleted in the 19th cent. by war and epidemics; in 1990 there were 1,207 Mandans in the U.S. Today, Mandans, Arikaras, and Hidatsas (a band of GROS VENTRE) live together on reservations in North Dakota.

Mandarin, a high official of imperial China. Mandarin Chinese, the language spoken by the official class, was based on the Beijing dialect. It is now the official language of China.

mandates, system of national trusteeships established (1920) under the LEAGUE OF NATIONS to administer former territorial possessions of Germany and Turkey after WORLD WAR I. Its long-term goal was self-government in the administered territories, which included Iraq, Syria, Lebanon, Palestine, several African countries, and various Pacific islands. The mandates system was superseded by the TRUSTEESHIP system of the UNITED NATIONS.

Mandela, Nelson Rolihlahla, 1918–, South African political leader. A lawyer, he joined (1944) the AFRICAN NATIONAL CONGRESS (ANC), co-founded the Congress Youth League, and was prominent in the nonviolent "defiance campaign" against South Africa's APARTHEID laws. After the shooting of demonstrators at Sharpeville (1960), he organized a paramilitary group to engage in guerrilla warfare against the government. Although acquitted (1961) of treason, he was subsequently convicted (1964) of sabotage and sentenced to life imprisonment. Released in 1990, he led the ANC in its negotiations with Pres. F.W. DE KLERK for an end to apartheid and the establishment of a multiracial government. Mandela and de Klerk were jointly awarded the Nobel Prize for peace in 1993. After South Africa's first multiracial elections (1994), Mandela was elected as the nation's new president. Mandela married his second wife, **Winnie Mandela,** 1936?–, b. Nomzamo Winifred Madikizela, in 1958. A social worker, she became active in the ANC and was her husband's principal champion while he was in prison. She herself was (1962–85) imprisoned and declared a "banned" person several

Nelson Mandela

times. She was convicted (1991) in the 1988 kidnapping and beating of four young men, one of whom died. In 1992 the Mandelas separated.

Mandelbrot, Benoit B., 1924–, French mathematician; b. Poland. Largely self-taught and considered something of a maverick, he did pioneering work in the area of CHAOS theory and conceived, developed, and applied FRACTAL geometry.

Mandelstam, Osip Emilyevich [män'dĭlshtəm], 1891–1938?, Russian poet. A leader of the ACMEISTS, he wrote fatalistic, meticulously constructed lyrics, collected in *Stone* (1913) and *Tristia* (1922). He died a political prisoner.

Mandeville, Bernard, 1670–1733, English author; b. Holland. A physician, he wrote on medical and ethical subjects. His argument in *The Fable of the Bees* (1714), an expansion of his poem *The Grumbling Hive* (1705), that the efforts of self-seeking individuals are the mainspring of commercial-industrial society, influenced 19th-cent. UTILITARIANISM.

mandolin: see STRINGED INSTRUMENT.

mandrake, herbaceous perennial plant (genus *Mandragora*) of the NIGHTSHADE family, native to the Mediterranean and Himalayan regions. True mandrakes contain several ALKALOIDS of medicinal value, and they have been used as pain-killers. Magical powers have often been attributed to the root, which crudely resembles the human form.

mandrill, large MONKEY (*Mandrillus sphinx*) found in the forests of central W Africa, related to the BABOON. The fur of the mandrill is mostly dark brown, but the bare face and buttocks are patterned in colors particularly spectacular in the adult male—bright red, blue, black, purple, and pale yellow.

man-eater: see SHARK.

Manet, Édouard [mänā'], 1832–83, French painter. He was influenced by VELÁZQUEZ and GOYA, and later by Japanese printmakers. In 1861 the Salon accepted his *Guitarist.* Two years later, with the exhibition of *Luncheon on the Grass* (Louvre), he was violently attacked; the painting depicts a nude woman enjoying a picnic in the woods with two fully clothed men. Manet's masterpiece, *Olympia* (1863; Louvre), an arresting portrait of a courtesan, elicited outrage and abuse from critics and public. This hostility from the art establishment attended his work throughout his life. His subject matter and technical innovations were considered heresy, but he profoundly influenced IMPRESSIONISM. Although often called an impressionist, he did not employ broken color, or sketchy brush strokes. All his work was a successful attempt to describe the natural immediacy of the eye's perception, and he worked in broad, flat areas of color. His major works include *The Balcony* (1869) and *The Fife Player* (1866; both Louvre).

Manfred, c.1232–1266, last HOHENSTAUFEN king of Sicily (1258–66); illegitimate son of Holy Roman Emperor FREDERICK II. He was regent in Sicily for his brother, CONRAD IV, and for his nephew, Conradin. In 1254 he was forced to restore the kingdom of the papacy, but he soon rebelled. Assuming the leadership of antipapal forces, Manfred reconquered Sicily and S Italy, and had himself crowned (1258) at Palermo. Pope Urban IV reacted by investing Charles of Anjou with Sicily as CHARLES I. Manfred was defeated by Charles and killed at Benevento (1266), and Conradin was later captured and executed (1268).

manganese (Mn), metallic element, first isolated by J.G. Gahn in 1774. It is pinkish-gray and chemically active, and resembles iron. It is a unique deoxidizing and desulfurizing agent in the manufacture of steel, is widely used in making other alloys, and is used as an octane-enhancing gasoline additive. Manganese nodules found on the deep ocean floor are a potentially rich and extensive resource. They form when manganese oxides and other metallic salts precipitate around a rock or shell nucleus. See ELEMENT (table); PERIODIC TABLE.

Mangas Coloradas, c.1797–1863, chief of the Mimbrenos APACHE of SW New Mexico. Noted for his intelligence and great stature, he united the tribes (1837) against white scalp-hunters paid by Mexico. When the U.S. acquired the area in 1846, he pledged peace, but after a flogging by gold miners he led his people in continuous warfare until he was killed by Union soldiers.

mange, contagious skin disease of animals, caused by parasitic MITES that burrow into the skin, HAIR follicles, or sweat glands. This leads to itching, inflammation, hair loss, and secondary bacterial infection. The disease is also called scabies, scab, and barn itch.

mango, evergreen tree of the SUMAC family, native to tropical E Asia but now grown in both hemispheres. The trees grow rapidly and can attain heights of up to 90 ft (27 m); they are densely covered with glossy leaves and bear small, fragrant yellow or red flowers. The aromatic, slightly acid fruit, a fleshy drupe with a thick, greenish to yellow-red skin, is an important food in the tropics.

mangrove, large, tropical evergreen tree (genus *Rhizophora*) found on muddy tidal flats and along shorelines, most abundant in tropical Asia, Africa, and the SW Pacific. Aerial roots, produced from the trunk, become embedded in the mud and form a tangled network that serves as a prop for the tree and a means of aerating the roots. The fruit is a conical, reddish-brown berry with a single seed; it germinates inside the fruit while it is still on the tree, forming a primary root that quickly anchors the seedling in the mud.

Manhattan: see NEW YORK CITY.

Manhattan Project, the wartime effort to design and build the first nuclear weapons (see ATOMIC BOMB). A $2-billion effort, centered at Oak Ridge, Tenn., and Hanford, Wash., was required to obtain sufficient amounts of the two necessary isotopes, uranium-235 and plutonium-239. The design and building of the bombs took place at Los Alamos, N.Mex., where J. Robert OPPENHEIMER directed a large group of American and European-refugee scientists. Following the test explosion of a plutonium device on July 16, 1945, near Alamogordo, N.Mex., a uranium bomb and a plutonium bomb were dropped on, respectively, HIROSHIMA (Aug. 6) and NAGASAKI (Aug. 9).

manic-depression or **bipolar disorder,** severe mental disorder involving manic episodes (characterized by an abnormally elevated or irritable mood, grandiosity, sleeplessness, extravagance, and a tendency toward irrational judgment) that are usually accompanied by episodes of DEPRESSION (possibly including lethargy, a sense of worthlessness, lack of concentration, and guilt). It occurs in males and females equally and is found more frequently in close relatives of people with the disorder. Therapy includes LITHIUM (to control mania and stabilize mood swings) and ANTIDEPRESSANTS. ELECTROCONVULSIVE THERAPY has been useful in cases where other treatments have had little success.

Manichaeism or **Manichaeanism,** religion founded by Mani (A.D. c.216–c.276), a visionary prophet, probably of Persian origin. After his martyrdom, his religion spread rapidly throughout the Roman Empire and Asia. Manichaeism synthesized elements from earlier religions such as GNOSTICISM, ZOROASTRIANISM, and Christianity; it taught dualism between good and evil, the transmigration of souls, and the possibility of salvation. St. Augustine was a Manichee until his conversion. The religion survived in the West until the 6th cent. and in the East until about the 13th cent.

Manifest Destiny, 19th-cent. doctrine that the U.S. had the duty and right to expand its territory and influence throughout North America. It reflected a growing spirit of confidence during a period of population increase and westward movement. The concept was invoked as justification for the SPANISH-AMERICAN WAR (1898).

Manila, city (1990 pop. 1,587,000), capital of the Philippines, SW Luzon, on Manila Bay. The Philippine capital before 1948 and after 1976, it is the country's second largest city, its chief port and transport center, and the focus of its commercial, industrial, and cultural activities. Manufactures include automobiles, textiles, and chemicals. Founded in 1571 and developed by Spanish missionaries, Manila was taken (1898) by the U.S. in the SPANISH-AMERICAN WAR. During WORLD WAR II it was occupied (1942) by the Japanese; many 17th-cent. buildings were destroyed in the Allied assault (1945); only the Church of San Agustin (1606) survived. Among the city's outstanding modern buildings is the Philippine Cultural Center complex.

Manila hemp, plant (*Musa textilis*) of the BANANA family, native to the Philippines, and the cordage fiber obtained chiefly from it. Manila hemp, or abacá, yields exceptionally strong, durable, saltwater-resistant fibers, useful for cordage and fabrics. It is unrelated to true HEMP.

manioc: see CASSAVA.

Manitoba, province (1991 pop. 1,091,942), 251,699 sq mi (651,900 sq km), west-central Canada, bordered by the Northwest Territories (N), Hudson Bay and Ontario (E), Minnesota and North Dakota (S), and Saskatchewan (W). Manitoba is the easternmost of the Prairie Provinces. The northern section, around HUDSON BAY, is a treeless tundra, and central and S Manitoba contain numerous lakes (Winnipeg, Manitoba, Winnipegosis) and rivers (Nelson, Churchill, Hayes), which flow northeast into the bay. In the south, where most of the population is centered, are extensive fields of wheat, barley, oats, and flax. Grain is shipped in quantity from the port of Churchill, on Hudson Bay. Vegetables, sugar beets, and sunflowers are also grown, and dairying has become significant. Although agriculture remains important, manufacturing has replaced it as the leading provincial industry. Foods, clothing, refined oil, transportation and electrical equipment, fabricated metals, chemicals, and pulp and paper are major products. WINNIPEG is the capital and largest city.

History. In 1670 the area of present-day Manitoba was given to the HUDSON'S BAY COMPANY, which built fur-trading posts on Hudson Bay. The French also established posts, but British claims to the area were confirmed in 1763. Rivalry between the NORTH WEST COMPANY and the Hudson's Bay Company led to violence after Lord SELKIRK established the RED RIVER SETTLEMENT. Immigration to the area increased after the two companies merged (1821) and after the area was sold (1870) to the confederation of Canada. This purchase was unsuccessfully resisted by a revolt led by Louis RIEL, and Manitoba became a province in 1870; it was enlarged in 1881 and 1912. In the 20th cent. many immigrants, notably Ukrainians, settled in the province. Control of the provincial government has alternated between the New Democrats and the Progressive Conservatives since the late 1960s. In 1988 the New Democrats again lost power to the Conservatives. Manitoba sends 6 senators (appointed) and 14 representatives (elected) to the national parliament.

Manley, Norman, 1893–1969, prime minister of Jamaica (1959–62). An internationally known lawyer of Irish and African descent, he, with his cousin Alexander BUSTAMANTE, dominated Jamaican politics for many years. Manley was chief minister (1955–59) before being designated prime minister. His son, **Michael Norman Manley,** 1923–, was prime minister from 1972 to 1980, and partially nationalized foreign-owned industry and established close ties with Cuba and the USSR. In 1989 he again became prime minister when his party won control of the government with a moderate program. Manley resigned in 1992 due to poor health.

Mann, family of German writers. **Heinrich Mann,** 1871–1950, wrote novels of sharp social criticism such as *Professor Unrat* (1905; tr. *The Blue Angel*) and the trilogy *The Poor* (1917), *The Patrioteer* (1921), and *The Chief* (1925). His brother, **Thomas Mann,** 1875–1955, is an outstanding German literary figure of the 20th cent. whose novels developed themes relating inner problems to changing European cultural values. His first novel, *Buddenbrooks* (1901), brought him fame. Translations of his shorter fiction, collected in *Stories of Three Decades* (1936), including *Tonio Kröger* (1903) and the classic *Death in Venice* (1912), reflect Mann's preoccupation with the proximity of creative art to neurosis, with the affinity of genius and disease, and with the problem of artistic values in bourgeois society. These themes are featured in his major work, *The Magic Mountain* (1924). His tetralogy *Joseph and His Brothers* (1933–43) is a brilliant study of psychological and mythological elements in the biblical story. Later works include *Doctor Faustus* (1947), *The Holy Sinner* (1951), and *Confessions of Felix Krull* (1954). Translations of Mann's major political writings denouncing fascism are published in *Order of the Day* (1942); his major literary essays are collected in *Essays of Three Decades* (1947). He left HITLER's Germany in 1933 and lived in the U.S. after 1938, moving to Switzerland in 1953. He received the Nobel Prize in literature in 1929. Thomas Mann's daughter, **Erika Mann** (1905–69), was an actress and author and was married to the poet W.H. AUDEN. His son, **Klaus Mann** (1906–49), was a novelist, essayist, and playwright. His works include *Alexander* (1929), *Pathetic Symphony* (1936), and the autobiographical *Turning Point* (1942).

Mann, Horace, 1796–1859, American educator; b. Franklin, Mass. While serving as secretary of the Massachusetts state board of education, he started a movement for better teaching and better-paid teachers, established state normal schools, and improved schoolhouses and equipment. After serving (1848–53) in the U.S. House of Representatives, he became (1853) the first president of Antioch College, where he demonstrated the practicality of coeducation and set high academic standards.

Mannerheim, Baron Carl Gustav Emil, 1867–1951, Finnish field marshal and president (1944–46). He fought the Bolsheviks in 1918 and was briefly regent (1919). In 1939–40 and 1941–44 he headed the Finnish forces against the USSR. The **Mannerheim Line** of defense, across the Karelian Isthmus, was planned by him; Soviet forces broke through it in 1940.

mannerism, a style in art and architecture (c.1520–1600), originating in Italy as a reaction against the equilibrium of form and proportion characteristic of the High RENAISSANCE. Artists such as PONTORMO, Il ROSSO, and PARMIGIANO created elongated, elegant figures, contorted into uncomfortable poses. Mannerists confused scale and spatial relationships and created strange tunnel-like spaces, e.g., in the works of TINTORETTO and El GRECO. Lighting was harsh, and color, acrimonious. Sculptors such as Giovanni BOLOGNA, CELLINI, and Jean Goujon of France created sinuous, bizarre forms. In architecture, the style used unbalanced proportions and arbitrary arrangements of decorations, e.g., in the Laurentian Library (Florence), designed (c.1525) by MICHELANGELO, and the UFFIZI, planned by VASARI. The ZUCCARO brothers gave mannerism an academic formalism, but by the end of the 16th cent. it gave way to the BAROQUE.

Manning, Henry Edward, 1808–92, English Roman Catholic churchman. An Anglican pastor, he became an adherent of the OXFORD MOVEMENT and in 1851 followed John Henry NEWMAN into the Roman Catholic Church; he was later ordained. Made archbishop of Westminster (1865) and a cardinal (1875), he disagreed violently with Newman over the enunciation of papal infallibility, which Manning favored. A strong advocate of social reform, he was influential in the labor movement, and in 1889 he supported the London dock strike and then single-handedly settled it.

manorial system or **seignorial system,** a socio-economic system of medieval Europe (fl. 11th–15th cent.), which regulated the landholding and production of peasants. It was based on the holding of lands from a lord *(seigneur)* in return for fixed dues in kind, money, and services. Unlike FEUDALISM, the manorial system lacked the military or political concept of the fief, and it declined with the emergence of towns, a money economy, and centralized monarchies. In its simplest form the system consisted of the division of land into self-sufficient estates, each held by a lay or ecclesiastical lord, who lent it to peasants for cultivation. The peasant might be personally free although his land was not (see VILLEIN), or servile (see SERF). The estate was divided into arable land held by peasants, meadow held in common, and woodland held by the lord. The manor was an administrative and political unit, with a court presided over by the lord and systems of taxation and public works.

Mansard: see MANSART.

mansard roof, type of roof so named because it was frequently used by François MANSART, but used earlier, e.g., at the LOUVRE (early 16th cent.). It was characteristic of French Renaissance and, later, of European and American Victorian architecture. The roof's two-section slope, with the lower slope almost vertical, allows a higher, more useful, interior.

Mansart or **Mansard, François** [mäNsär'], 1598–1666, French classical architect. His Hôtel de la Vrillière (1635) was long a model for the elegant Paris house. Surviving works include the château of Maisons and, in Paris, the alterations to the Hôtel Carnavalet. His pupil and grand-nephew **Jules Hardouin Mansart,** 1646–1708, was also an architect. In 1699 he was named chief architect for the royal buildings for LOUIS XIV. At VERSAILLES he built the Galérie des Glaces, the Grand Trianon, the palace chapel, and the vast orangery. As a town planner he designed in Paris the Place des Victoires (1684–86) and the Place Vendôme (1699). The Dôme des Invalides (1706) in Paris is perhaps his greatest achievement.

Mansfeld, Peter Ernst von, 1580?–1626, commander in the THIRTY YEARS WAR. In the service of FREDERICK THE WINTER KING he defeated TILLY (1622). He became a Dutch mercenary in 1623. With an English subsidy (1625) he recruited a force to fight on the Protestant side but was defeated by WALLENSTEIN.

Mansfield, Katherine, 1888–1923, English author; b. New Zealand as Kathleen Beauchamp. Considered a master of the short story, she shows the influence of CHEKHOV in her stories, which are simple in form and evocative in substance. Collections include *Bliss* (1920), *The Garden Party* (1922) and *Something Childish* (1924).

Mansfield, Michael Joseph, 1903–, U.S. senator from Montana (1953–77); b. N.Y.C. He served as a Democrat from Montana in the U.S. House of Representatives (1943–53). As Senate majority leader (1961–77), a position he held longer than any other senator, he helped win passage of major civil-rights legislation and liberal reform programs. He also served as ambassador to Japan from 1977 to 1989.

Manship, Paul, 1885–1966, American sculptor; b. St. Paul, Minn. His works, often taking subjects from classical mythology, are noted for their emphatic musculature and polished contours, e.g., *Prometheus* (Rockefeller Center, N.Y.C.).

manslaughter: see HOMICIDE.

Mansur, al- (Muhammad ibn Abi-Amir al-Mansur billah), 914–1002, Moorish regent of CÓRDOBA. Known in Spanish as Almanzor, he became royal chamberlain (978) and controlled the caliphate. He campaigned against the Christian states of N Spain, sacking BARCELONA (985) and razing the city of LEÓN (988).

manta: see RAY.

Mantegna, Andrea [mäntĕ'nyä], 1431–1506, Italian painter of the Paduan school. Married to the daughter of Jacopo Bellini (see BELLINI, family), he was the greatest artist in N Italy outside of Venice. His passion for the antique is evidenced in all his work, and he was one of the first artists to collect Greek and Roman works. A rigorous draftsman and anatomist and a perfectionist in perspective, he nevertheless gave his statuesque forms intense life. Among his celebrated early works is the St. Luke altarpiece (Milan). His illusion of sky on the ceiling of the bridal chamber of the Gonzaga palace (Mantua) was widely imitated in the BAROQUE period. About 1497 he did *Parnassus* and *Triumph of Virtue* (Louvre) for Isabella d'Este. His *Adoration of the Shepherds* is in the Metropolitan Museum. Mantegna is also noted for his drawings and copper-plate engravings. He recaptured the art of Roman inscriptions in his initial letters for STRABO's *Geography,* and his lettering influenced the development of printing.

mantis: see PRAYING MANTIS.

Mantle, Mickey (Charles), 1931–, American baseball player; b. Spavinaw, Okla. A switch-hitter and one of the great sluggers in baseball history, he played center field during most of his career (1951–68) with the New York Yankees. His 536 home runs place him among the leaders in that category, and he was named the American League's most valuable player in 1956 (when he led the American League in batting average, home runs, and runs batted in), 1957 (when he batted .365, his highest average), and 1962. Mantle hit a record 18 home runs in World Series play.

mantra, in HINDUISM and BUDDHISM, mystic word used in ritual and MEDITATION. It is believed to have power to bring into being the reality it represents. The *bija-mantra* seed-sounds used in TANTRA are syllables having occult affinity for particular deities; use of such mantras usually requires initiation by a guru, or spiritual teacher.

Mantua, city (1990 pop. 54,808), in LOMBARDY, N Italy. It is an agricultural, industrial, and tourist center. A Roman town, it was a free commune (12th–13th cent.) and flourished (1328–1708) under the GONZAGA family. Italy regained it (1866) after Austrian and French rule. Its splendid Gonzaga palace (13th–18th cent.) has many outstanding works of art.

Manu, in Hindu legend, a divinely inspired lawgiver. Traditionally ascribed to him are the *Laws of Manu,* compiled (probably between 200 B.C. and A.D. 200) from diverse ancient sources and providing detailed rules, presumably for Brahmans (priests), governing ritual and daily life. See also HINDUISM.

Manuel, Byzantine emperors. **Manuel I** (Comnenus), c.1120–80 (r.1143–80) was the son of John II. In the Second CRUSADE (1147–49) he made a truce with the Turks to protect his western provinces. Later he made peace (1158) with William I of Sicily. Manuel supported Pope ALEXANDER III against Holy Roman Emperor FREDERICK I, and tried to reunite the empires and churches of the East and West. His neglect of Asia Minor brought a crushing defeat (1176) by the Turks. Manuel encouraged Western merchants in Constantinople. His son, ALEXIUS II, succeeded him. **Manuel II** (Palaeologus), 1348?–1425, (r.1391–1425), reigned over an empire reduced by the Turks to CONSTANTINOPLE and its environs. TIMUR's victory over the Ottoman sultan BEYAZID I (1402) temporarily saved Constantinople. Manuel's son, JOHN VIII, ruled during his father's last years.

Manuel, kings of Portugal. **Manuel I,** 1469–1521 (r.1495–1521), had a reign notable for Portugal's advances in overseas exploration, especially Vasco da GAMA's epochal voyage (1497–99) to India. Wealth from the Indies made Portugal the West's leading commercial nation. In order to marry the Spanish princess Isabel, Manuel agreed (1496) to expel the JEWS, but he first attempted their forcible conversion. He was unable to prevent the departure of some Jews and their massacre in Lisbon (1506). **Manuel II,** 1889–1932, (r.1908–10), became king after the assassination of his father and brother. In 1910 a republican revolution deposed him. He was the last king of Portugal.

Manx, virtually extinct language belonging to the Goidelic or Gaelic group of the Celtic subfamily of the Indo-European family of languages. See LANGUAGE (table).

Manx cat: see under CAT.

Manzoni, Alessandro, 1785–1873, Italian novelist and poet. His most famous work, *The Betrothed* (1825–26), a romantic novel of 17th-cent. Milan, had gone through 118 editions by 1875, and greatly influenced the development of Italian prose. He also wrote tragedies and poetry, including the celebrated *Fifth of May* (1821), on the death of Napoleon. VERDI's *Requiem* commemorates the poet's death.

Maori, Polynesian people of New Zealand, making up about 8% of the nation's population. They speak a language related to Tahitian and Hawaiian. Believed to have migrated from POLYNESIA in canoes in early times, the Maori established an agricultural society. In the 19th cent., after wars against European encroachment, they were reduced to 100,000 and later even fewer. Their population has since increased to 250,000; today, they are economically self-sufficient while maintaining their cultural identity.

Maori language, spoken by the MAORI people of New Zealand, belonging to the Polynesian subfamily of the Malayo-Polynesian family of languages. See LANGUAGE (table).

Mao Zedong or **Mao Tse-tung** [both: mou dzŭ-do͝ong], 1893–1976, founder of the People's Republic of China. Born in Hunan prov., he was one of the original members of the Chinese Communist party. Mao organized unions for the KUOMINTANG, but after the Communist-Kuomintang split (1927) he worked to establish rural soviets and to build the Red Army. He led (1934–35) the LONG MARCH from Jiangxi N to Yan'an in Shaanxi prov. and became head of the Chinese Communist party. In 1949, when the Communists had seized most of the mainland, Mao became the first chairman of the People's Republic of China. In 1958 he launched the Great Leap Forward, a program for industrial growth; after it failed he was replaced (1959) as chairman by LIU SHAOQI, but still retained his party leadership. Mao successfully attacked Liu by directing the CULTURAL REVOLUTION (1966–69), a period of widespread agitation. In the 1970s he consolidated his position as China's most powerful figure. Mao's policies often strained relations with the USSR, but his ideas on revolutionary struggle became very influential in the Third World. In 1972 he developed closer ties with the West by meeting U.S. Pres. NIXON in Beijing.

maple, common name for the genus *Acer* of the Aceraceae, a family of deciduous trees and shrubs of the Northern Hemisphere, characterized by winged seeds. Maples are popular as shade trees and noted for their brilliant fall colors. Several species provide close-grained, hardwood timber, e.g., the sugar maple (*A. saccharum*) and the black maple (*A. nigrum*); these trees are also the main source of maple syrup. In the spring, their sap is drawn off, strained, and concentrated by boiling to produce syrup and sugar. Other well-known species include the box elder (*A. negundo*), a shade tree, and the swamp, or red, maple (*A. rubrum*).

maple sugar: see SUCROSE.

map projection, transfer of the features of the earth's surface or those of another spherical body onto a flat sheet of paper. Only a globe can represent surface features correctly with reference to area, shape, scale, and direction. Projection from a globe to a flat map always causes some distortion. A grid or net of two intersecting systems of lines corresponding to parallels and meridians must be drawn on a plane surface. Some projections (equidistant) aim to keep correct distances in all directions from the center of the map. Others show areas (equal-area) or shapes (conformal) equal to those on the globe of the same scale. Projections are cylindrical, conical, or azimuthal in geometric origin. See also MERCATOR MAP PROJECTION.

Mapp v. Ohio, case decided in 1961 by the U.S. SUPREME COURT, overturning a conviction based on evidence gained by entering a house without a search warrant. The Court held that the exclusionary rule (based on the 4th amendment to the U.S. CONSTITUTION), which bars the use in federal courts of EVIDENCE obtained through illegal searches and seizures, extended also to the state courts.

Maputo, formerly **Lourenço Marques,** city (1991 est. pop. 1,215,000), capital of Mozambique, a port on the Indian Ocean. The country's largest city and economic center, it is linked by rail with South Africa and Zimbabwe. Manufactures include food products, cement, and furniture; the chief exports are coal, cotton, sugar, and chrome. The city's excellent beaches are a tourist attraction. Founded in the late 18th cent., it became the capital in 1907 and was renamed (1976) after independence.

maquiladoras, assembly plants along the U.S.-Mexico border, generally owned by non-Mexican corporations, that produce finished goods for the U.S. market. Originating in the 1960s but significant only since the 1980s, they depend on low-cost labor, advantageous tariffs, and their proximity to the U.S. A multibillion dollar industry, maquiladoras constitute one of Mexico's primary sources of export income and have stimulated migration to the border cities.

Maracaibo, city (1991 pop. 1,207,513), NW Venezuela, capital of Zulia state, at Lake MARACAIBO's outlet to the Caribbean Sea. It is the nation's oil capital and a major commercial and industrial center, exporting textiles, soap, and lumber and other inland products. Founded in 1571, Maracaibo developed slowly until 1918, when foreign interests began to exploit the vast petroleum resources of the area. Lake Maracaibo bridge, one of the world's longest bridges, is south of the city.

Maracaibo, Lake, large, brackish lake, c.5,100 sq mi (13,210 sq km), NW Venezuela, extending c.110 mi (180 km) inland from the Caribbean. It is one of the world's richest oil-producing regions. The city of Maracaibo is at the lake's outlet to the sea.

Marat, Jean Paul [märä'], 1743–93, French revolutionary. A doctor, he turned to politics when the FRENCH REVOLUTION began (1789) and founded the journal *L'Ami du peuple,* in which he bitterly attacked all who were in power. Outlawed, he fled to England (1790, 1791) and also hid in the Paris sewers, thereby worsening a skin disease; it required treatments in warm baths. He continued to publish in secret and helped to inflame the public. Elected (1792) to the Convention, he supported the JACOBINS against the GIRONDISTS. Marat was murdered in his bath by an admirer of the Girondists, Charlotte CORDAY.

Marathi [mərä'tē], language belonging to the Indic group of the Indo-Iranian subfamily of the Indo-European family of languages. See LANGUAGE (table).

Marathon, village and plain of ancient Greece, NE of ATHENS, site of an Athenian victory (490 B.C.) in the PERSIAN WARS. In legend, the plain was the scene of the victory of THESEUS over a great bull. See also MARATHON RACE.

marathon race, long-distance endurance race, named for MARATHON, Greece, from which, in 490 B.C., the runner Pheidippides carried news to Athens of a Greek victory over the Persians. Included in the first modern Olympic games (1896), the marathon was standardized at 26 mi, 385 yd (42.2 km) in 1908. Annual marathons in Boston, New York City, and elsewhere attract thousands of distance runners.

Boston Marathon, 1937

marble, a ROCK formed by the METAMORPHISM of LIMESTONE. The term is loosely applied to any limestone or DOLOMITE that takes a good polish and is otherwise suitable as a building or ornamental stone. Its color varies depending on the types of impurities present. It has been used since ancient times for statuary, monuments, and facing stones. Like all limestones, it is corroded by water and acid fumes and is therefore ultimately uneconomical for use in exposed places.

Marbury v. Madison, case decided in 1803 by the U.S. SUPREME COURT. In a dispute over federal appointments, Chief Justice MARSHALL held that the statute that was the basis for the remedy sought gave the Court authority denied it by Article III of the U.S. CONSTITUTION. This decision, the first to invalidate an act of Congress, established the doctrine of judicial review, vastly expanding the judiciary's power.

Marc, Franz, 1880–1916, German painter. A leader of the BLAUE REITER group, he developed a rich chromatic symbolism to depict a mystical world of animals. *Blue Horses* (Walker Art Center, Minneapolis) is representative.

Marc Antony: see ANTONY.

marcasite or **white iron pyrites,** mineral closely resembling and having the same chemical composition (FeS_2) as PYRITE; paler in color, it becomes darker upon oxidation. Marcasite occurs worldwide in marls, clays, and limestones.

Marceau, Marcel [märsō'], 1923–, French mime. Famed for his sad-faced clown character, Bip, he has performed frequently with his company in the U.S. since 1955.

Marcellus, Marcus Claudius, c.268–208 B.C., Roman consul. He besieged Syracuse in the Second PUNIC WAR and took the city in 212. He also captured (211) the town of Capua. Earlier (222), he had killed the king of the Insubrian Gauls in single combat.

March, earl of: see MORTIMER, ROGER DE, EARL OF MARCH.

March: see MONTH.

Marcian, 396–457, the last Theodosian to be East Roman emperor (450–57). He called the Council of CHALCEDON (451). By refusing tribute to ATTILA he brought on the HUN invasion.

Marciano, Rocky, 1924–69, American boxer; b. Brockton, Mass., as Rocco Francis Marchegiano. He turned professional (1947) and won the world heavyweight championship (1952) by knocking out Jersey Joe Walcott. A powerful puncher, he won 43 of his 49 professional bouts by knockouts. He retired in 1956 as the only heavyweight champion who never lost a professional bout. He died in a plane crash.

Marcion, fl. A.D. 144, early Christian bishop, founder of the Marcionites, the first great Christian heresy to rival Catholic Christianity. He taught that there were two gods, the stern creator God of the OLD TESTAMENT and the superior merciful God of the NEW TESTAMENT, and he rejected the Old Testament entirely. Marcionism, which stressed ascetic practices, influenced and was later absorbed by MANICHAEISM.

Marcomanni: see GERMANS.

Marconi, Guglielmo, Marchese, 1874–1937, Italian physicist. For his development of wireless telegraphy (see RADIO), he shared with Karl Braun the 1909 Nobel Prize in physics. Marconi sent (1895) long-wave signals over a distance of more than a mile and received (1901) the first transatlantic wireless signals.

Marco Polo: see POLO, MARCO.

Marcos, Ferdinand Edralin, 1917–89, president and prime minister of the PHILIPPINES (1965–1986). He maintained close ties with the U.S. and attempted to suppress Muslim rebels and Communist and liberal opposition to his rule. Marcos proclaimed (1972) martial law, and assumed (1973) virtual dictatorial rule under a new constitution. Opposition strength continued to grow, despite the lifting of martial law in 1981. After defeating Corazon AQUINO in the controversial 1986 election, he was accused of election fraud and forced by a popular uprising to leave the Philippines.

Marcus Aurelius (Marcus Aelius Aurelius Antoninus), 121–180, Roman emperor and philosopher. He was adopted by the emperor Antoninus Pius and succeeded him in 161, ruling jointly with his adoptive brother, Lucius Verus. Sole emperor after 169, he spent most of his reign repressing rebellions and attacks by the Parthians, Germans, and Britons. He was a humanitarian ruler who nevertheless accepted the then-prevalent view of the Christians as the empire's chief enemies. His spiritual reflections, the *Meditations,* are considered a classic work of STOICISM. They were strongly influenced by the thought of EPICTETUS.

Marcuse, Herbert, 1898–1979, American political philosopher; b. Germany. A founder of the Frankfurt Institute of Social Research, he fled from Nazis (1934) to the U.S. He taught at Harvard and other universities before becoming (1965) professor of philosophy at the Univ. of California at San Diego. He is known for his synthesis of Marxist and Freudian theory, expounded in *Eros and Civilization* (1954), *One Dimensional Man* (1964), and other books. He was a hero to American radicals of the 1960s.

Mardi Gras, last day before the fasting season of Lent. It is the French name for Shrove Tuesday. Carnivals are held in some countries, usually lasting a week or more before Mardi Gras itself. Among the most celebrated carnivals are those of New Orleans, Rio de Janeiro, Nice, and Cologne.

Margaret, Danish queens. **Margaret I,** 1353–1412, queen of Denmark, Norway, and Sweden, was the daughter of WALDEMAR IV of Denmark. Married (1363) to Haakon VI of Norway (d. 1380), the son of MAGNUS VII, she was regent for her son OLAF V in Denmark (1375–87) and Norway (1380–87). After he died (1387), she defeated and captured (1389) the Swedish king, Albert, and persuaded the Danish, Norwegian, and Swedish diets to accept her grandnephew, Eric of Pomerania, as king. He was crowned (1397), and the Kalmar Union was established. Margaret remained the actual ruler of all three kingdoms until her death. **Margaret II** (Margrethe), 1940–, queen of Denmark (r.1972–), is the daughter of King FREDERICK IX and Queen Ingrid (daughter of GUSTAVUS VI of Sweden). She became queen under a new constitution (1953) allowing female succession. She and her husband, Comte Henri de Laborde de Monpezat, have two sons.

Margaret, 1930–, British princess; sister of ELIZABETH II. Her 1960 marriage to Antony Armstrong-Jones (later earl of Snowdon) produced two children: Viscount Linley (b. 1961) and Sarah (b. 1964). It ended in divorce in 1978.

Margaret Maid of Norway, 1283–90, infant queen of Scotland (1286–90); daughter of Eric II of Norway; granddaughter of ALEXANDER III of Scotland, whom she succeeded. Her early death led to an English attempt to subjugate Scotland.

Margaret Maultasch [moul'täsh] [Ger., = pocket mouth], 1318–69, countess of Tyrol, called the Ugly Duchess. She expelled her first husband from Tyrol, received a secular annulment, and married (1342) his son. The act offended the nobles, who rebelled. Margaret eventually abdicated (1363), and Tyrol passed to the HAPSBURGS. Lion FEUCHTWANGER used her story in his novel *The Ugly Duchess*.

Margaret of Angoulême: see MARGARET OF NAVARRE.

Margaret of Anjou, 1430?–1482, queen consort of HENRY VI of England. In the first 16 years of the Wars of the ROSES, she defended the cause of her husband and her son Edward against the house of YORK. Captured (1471) by the Yorkist EDWARD IV, she returned (1476) to France where she died in poverty.

Margaret of Austria, 1480–1530, Hapsburg princess, regent of the NETHERLANDS; daughter of MAXIMILIAN I. First betrothed to the future CHARLES VIII of France, she was married (1497) to John of Spain (d. 1497) and (1501) to Philibert of Savoy (d. 1504). In 1507 she became guardian of her nephew, the future Holy Roman Emperor CHARLES V, and regent of the Netherlands, mediating between her father and his Dutch subjects.

Margaret of Navarre or **Margaret of Angoulême** [äNgōōlām'], 1492–1549, sister of FRANCIS I of France. Married (1527) to Henri d'Albret, king of Navarre, she was a patron of writers such as François RABELAIS. She wrote the *Heptaméron,* an original collection of 72 stories in the manner of Boccaccio.

Margaret of Parma, 1522–86, Spanish regent of the NETHERLANDS; illegitimate daughter of Holy Roman Emperor CHARLES V. She was married (1536) to Alessandro de' Medici (d. 1537) and (1538) to Ottavio Farnese (see FARNESE, family), duke of Parma. In 1559 she became regent of the Netherlands under her half brother, PHILIP II. She resigned in 1567, opposing the duke of ALBA's harsh suppression of the nationalist revolt led by WILLIAM THE SILENT.

Margaret of Valois [välwä'], 1553–1615, queen of France and Navarre; daughter of HENRY II. Her marriage (1572) to the Protestant Henry of Navarre (later HENRY IV of France) was a prelude to the massacre of Protestants on SAINT BARTHOLOMEW'S DAY. She became estranged from her husband and her brother, HENRY III, and took up arms against them. Captured (1586) by royal troops, she was confined (1587–1605) at Usson, where she assembled a literary circle. In 1599 Margaret agreed to have her marriage annulled, and she spent her last years in Paris. Her writings show much literary ability.

Margaret Tudor, 1489–1541, queen consort of JAMES IV of Scotland; sister of HENRY VIII of England. She married James in 1503, and after his death (1513) their infant son, JAMES V, became king. Margaret remarried twice and played a large part in Scottish politics, her affiliation varying with her personal interest. JAMES I of England was her descendant.

Mari, ancient city of Mesopotamia, on the middle Euphrates R. Discovered in the 1930s, the site has since been excavated. Evidence of habitation dates to the 3d millennium B.C. Mari was the commercial and political focus (c.1800 B.C.) of W Asia, and the inhabitants were referred to as Amorites in the Old Testament. HAMMURABI conquered (c.1700 B.C.) Mari, which never regained its former status.

Maria, queens of PORTUGAL. **Maria I,** 1734–1816 (r.1777–1816), was married (1760) for political reasons to her uncle, PETER III, who ruled jointly with her. Together they brought down the powerful minister POMBAL and freed his enemies from jail or exile. The deaths of Peter (1786) and her eldest son, Joseph (1788), contributed to unhinging her mind, and her second son, later JOHN VI, assumed power (1792) and became regent (1799). **Maria II,** 1819–53 (r.1834–53), was designated queen by her father, PEDRO I of Brazil, on condition that she marry her uncle, Dom Miguel, but he usurped the throne (1828) before she could return to Portugal. Her father led an invading army into Portugal and deposed Miguel in the Miguelist Wars (1832–34), restoring Maria as queen. Her reign was torn by dissent and revolutions.

Marianas trench, Marianas trough, or **Marianas deep,** depression in the Pacific Ocean, 210 mi (338 km) SW of Guam. The deepest (36,198 ft/11,033 m) part of any ocean, it was reached (1960) by two men in a U.S. navy bathyscape.

Maria Theresa, 1717–80, Austrian archduchess, queen of Bohemia and Hungary (1740–80); consort of Holy Roman Emperor FRANCIS I. The daughter of Emperor CHARLES VI, she succeeded (1740) to the HAPSBURG lands by the PRAGMATIC SANCTION of 1713. Her succession was contested in the War of the AUSTRIAN SUCCESSION, in which she lost Silesia to Prussia but secured (1745) the election of her husband as emperor. Aided by her chancellor, Wenzel Anton Kaunitz, she allied Austria with France in the SEVEN YEARS WAR (1756–63) and joined in the partition (1772) of Poland. With her son, JOSEPH II (with whom she jointly ruled after 1765), Maria Theresa carried out agrarian reforms and centralized the administration. During her reign Vienna developed as a center for music and the arts. Among her 16 children were Emperors JOSEPH II and LEOPOLD II, and MARIE ANTOINETTE of France.

Marie Antoinette, 1755–93, queen of France, wife of LOUIS XVI; daughter of Holy Roman Emperor FRANCIS I. In 1770 she married the DAUPHIN, who became king in 1774. The marriage, made to strengthen France's ties with Austria, was not popular and was unconsummated for seven years. Unhappy, the queen surrounded herself with a dissolute clique and threw herself into a life of pleasure and extravagance. Her notorious reputation led to several scandals. The famous solution to the bread famine, "Let them eat cake," is unjustly attributed to the queen. Although she contributed to the downfall of A.R.J. TURGOT in 1776, her influence on Louis in the first two years of the FRENCH REVOLUTION has been exaggerated. She was brought (Oct. 1789) to Paris with the king from VERSAILLES and was seized at Varennes when the royal family tried to escape (1791). The king's apathy led her to negotiate first with the comte de MIRABEAU and later with Antoine Barnave, and she secretly urged Austrian intervention in France. After the TUILERIES palace was stormed (Aug. 1792), the king and queen were imprisoned and charged with treason. The king was executed in Jan. 1793; Marie Antoinette's son (see LOUIS XVII) was taken from her. In October she was tried by a revolutionary tribunal and guillotined (Oct. 16).

Marie de' Medici, 1573–1642, queen of France; daughter of Francesco de' MEDICI, grand duke of Tuscany. She became the second wife of HENRY IV in 1600 and after his assassination (1610) became regent for her son LOUIS XIII. She chose as minister her favorite, Concino Concini, who dissipated the treasury by extravagance. Exiled after Concini's murder (1617), Marie was reconciled with her son in 1622. She tried (1630) to gain the dismissal of her former protégé and the king's minister, Cardinal RICHELIEU, but Louis exiled her again. Her daughter, HENRIETTA MARIA, married CHARLES I of England.

Marie Louise, 1791–1847, empress of the French (1810–15), as consort of NAPOLEON I; daughter of Holy Roman Emperor FRANCIS II. She married Napoleon in 1810 and was the mother of NAPOLEON II. After her husband's defeat the Congress of VIENNA awarded her the duchies of Parma, Piacenza, and Guastalla, which she ruled (1816–47) ineptly. She remarried twice.

marigold, plant (genus *Tagetes*) of the COMPOSITE family, mostly Central and South American herbs cultivated as garden flowers. Two common annuals are the large-flowered, strong-scented, yellow or orange African marigold (*T. erecta*) and the smaller, yellow or orange and red French marigold (*T. patula*). Both are native to Mexico and Guatemala.

marijuana or **marihuana,** relatively mild, nonaddictive drug with hallucinogenic properties, obtained from the flowering tops, stems, and leaves of the HEMP plant. Resins found on the surface of the female plant are used to prepare the most potent form of marijuana, hashish. The primary active substance is tetrahydrocannabinol (THC). Marijuana produces a dreamy, euphoric state of altered consciousness, with feelings of detachment and gaiety. The appetite is usually enhanced, while the sex drive may increase or decrease. Adverse reactions are relatively rare, and most can be attributed to adulterants frequently found in marijuana preparations. Marijuana has been used experimentally to reduce nausea from cancer CHEMOTHERAPY and in the treatment of GLAUCOMA, but in 1992 the Drug Enforcement Administration declined to reclassify marijuana so that it could be prescribed by doctors. Marinol, a synthetic form of THC, is approved for use in reducing the nausea caused by chemotherapy. In the U.S. there were a number of successful efforts, especially in the 1970s, to reduce criminal penalties for possession and use of marijuana, but many of the resulting laws have since been modified or repealed.

Marin, John, 1870–1953, American painter; b. Rutherford, N.J. A leading watercolorist, he frequently painted scenes of New York and Taos and Maine seascapes. He rendered these with powerful zigzag strokes, often enclosed by angular abstract forms, and used a wide variety of color effects.

marine biology, study of ocean plants and animals and their ecological relationships. Marine organisms are classified according to their mode of life as nektonic (free-swimming), planktonic (floating), or benthic (bottom-dwelling). Their distribution depends on the chemical and physical properties of seawater (e.g., temperature, salinity, and dissolved nutrients), ocean current, and penetration of light. See also OCEANOGRAPHY.

Mariner, in space exploration: see SPACE PROBE, table.

marines, troops that serve on board ships of war or in conjunction with naval operations. A British marine corps was established in 1664, reflecting the need for skilled riflemen aboard military vessels. The present U.S. marine corps was created by Congress in 1798 and now functions as a complete operating unit within the U.S. navy. It has been prominent in all U.S. wars, beginning with the TRIPOLITAN WAR (1800–1815) in North Africa. Highly trained in amphibious landing operations, it has also been used between wars to quell disturbances abroad and to serve as a temporary occupying force, notably in the Caribbean and Central America. The corps won special distinction during the Pacific island invasions of WORLD WAR II and in the KOREAN WAR and VIETNAM WAR.

Maris, Roger (Eugene), 1934–85, American baseball player; b. Hibbing, Minn. With the New York Yankees in 1961 he hit 61 home runs, surpassing Babe RUTH's major-league record by one. At the time, baseball commissioner Ford C. Frick ruled that Ruth's record would stand because it was achieved in a 154-game schedule, compared with a 162-game schedule for Maris, but in 1991 major-league baseball recognized Maris as the official home-run record holder. In 12 seasons (1957–68) Maris had 275 home runs.

maritime law, body of law governing navigation and overseas commerce. It is based on customs and usages that developed between trading nations and were compiled beginning in the late Middle Ages. It is part of the international law only insofar as it determines relations between nations. In the U.S., maritime cases (except for collision at sea) are under exclusive federal jurisdiction. See also SEA, LAW OF THE.

Maritime Provinces, Canada, term applied to NOVA SCOTIA, NEW BRUNSWICK, and PRINCE EDWARD ISLAND, which, before the formation of the Canadian confederation (1867), were politically distinct from Canada proper.

Marius, Caius, 155 B.C.–86 B.C., Roman general. He was seven times consul and won a reputation in wars against the Germans. The rival of SULLA, he fled Rome when Sulla got the command against MITHRIDATES VI. With the help of CINNA, Marius returned to Rome and fought Sulla in a bloody civil war that Sulla won.

marjoram or **sweet marjoram,** Old World perennial aromatic herb (*Marjorana hortensis*) of the MINT family, cultivated for flavoring and for origanum oil, used in perfumed soaps. The closely related European wild marjoram (*Origanum vulgare*) is the spice usually sold as OREGANO.

Mark, Saint, Christian apostle, traditional author of the 2d GOSPEL. Christians in Jerusalem met at his mother's house. He accompanied St. PAUL and St. BARNABAS to Cyprus. Traditionally, he was an associate of St. PETER, who is thought to have provided him with many of his facts. The Alexandrian church claims Mark as its founder; he is patron saint of Venice.

Mark, Gospel according to Saint, second book of the NEW TESTAMENT, simplest and earliest of the GOSPELS (probably A.D. c.70), used as a source by MATTHEW and LUKE. It may be divided into the beginning of the ministry of JESUS (1.1–1.13), his first two years of preaching (1.14–6.56), his third year (7–13), and the Passion and RESURRECTION (14–16).

Markham, Edwin, 1852–1940, American poet; b. Oregon City, Oreg. He is best known for his poem "The Man with the Hoe" (1899), inspired by MILLET's painting. His other work includes the verse in *Lincoln and Other Poems* (1901).

Markova, Dame Alicia [märkō'vä], 1910–, English ballerina. She joined (1925) DIAGHILEV and became (1932) prima ballerina with the Vic-Wells Ballet in London. She formed (1935) her own dance company with Anton DOLIN and appeared with other companies in such classic roles as *Giselle*.

Alicia Markova

Marlborough, John Churchill, 1st **duke of,** 1650–1722, English general and statesman, one of the greatest military commanders in history. Under JAMES II he crushed the rebellion (1685) of the duke of MONMOUTH. During the GLORIOUS REVOLUTION he supported WILLIAM III against JAMES II but later (1692–98) fell into William's disfavor. Marlborough's power peaked in the reign of Queen ANNE. Created duke (1702), he was involved in many victories in the War of the SPANISH SUCCESSION, including Blenheim (1704), Ramillies (1706), Oudenarde (1708), and Malplaquet (1709). Politically he favored the WHIGS during the war; when they fell he was dismissed (1711). On the accession of GEORGE I in 1714, Marlborough resumed chief command of the army. His wife, **Sarah Churchill, duchess of Marlborough,** 1660–1744, was a favorite of Queen Anne. Born Sarah Jennings, she married John Churchill in 1677. She wielded great influence at Anne's court until they quarreled in 1705. After her husband's death she supervised the building of Blenheim Palace.

Marley, Bob, 1945–81, Jamaican reggae musician. As a member of the Wailers, and later on his own, he propelled REGGAE to worldwide popularity. His songs often express his commitment to nonviolence and to RASTAFARIANISM.

marlin, open-sea FISH related to the SAILFISH and SWORDFISH (family Istiophoridae), prized by sportsmen. The blue marlin (genus *Makaira*) of the Gulf Stream may reach 1,000 lb (454 kg) in weight. The marlin's upper jaw extends into a long spike, which it uses to club the fish on which it feeds.

Marlowe, Christopher, 1564–93, English dramatist and poet. A major Elizabethan figure, he broke with TRAGEDY modeled on SENECA. His dramas have heroic themes, usually that of a great character destroyed by his own passions and ambition. Marlowe introduced blank verse as the medium for drama, paving the way for SHAKESPEARE. His most important plays are *Tamburlaine the Great* (c.1587), *Dr. Faustus* (c.1588), *The Jew of Malta* (1589), and *Edward II* (c.1592). His best-known nondramatic works are the long poem *Hero and Leander* (1598, finished by George CHAPMAN) and the lyric "Come live with me and be my love."

Marne, battle of the, two WORLD WAR I battles that took place at the Marne River, in France. In the first (Sept. 6–9, 1914), the German advance on Paris was halted by the Allies. In the second (July 1918), the last great German advance of the war was decisively repulsed by the Allies.

Marprelate controversy, a 16th-cent. English religious argument. Under the pseudonym Martin Marprelate, several Puritan pamphlets appeared (1588–89), satirizing the Church of England's authoritarianism and starting a flood of literature from both Martinist and anti-Martinist factions.

Marquand, J(ohn) P(hilips), 1893–1960, American author; b. Wilmington, Del. His gently satirical novels, often dealing with the rich in NEW ENGLAND, include *The Late George Apley* (1937; Pulitzer) and *Point of No Return* (1949).

Marquette, Jacques, 1637–75, French missionary and explorer in NORTH AMERICA, a Jesuit priest. He accompanied (1673) Louis JOLLIET on a journey down the MISSISSIPPI R., proving the existence of a water highway from the ST. LAWRENCE to the GULF OF MEXICO.

Marrakesh, city (1990 est. pop. 1,517,000), W central Morocco. The city is renowned for leather goods and is a principal commercial center of Morocco. It was founded (1062) by the ALMORAVIDS. The French captured the city in 1912. Beautifully situated near the ATLAS Mts., Marrakesh has extensive gardens, a 14th-cent. palace, and a former palace of the sultan, now a museum of Moroccan art. The minaret of the famous Koutoubya mosque dominates the city.

marriage, socially sanctioned union of one or more men with one or more women, called monogamy when only one partner of each sex is involved and polygamy when the marriage includes more than one wife or (more rarely) more than one husband. In many societies, marriage has been the focus of creating and consolidating ties between families, with marriages often arranged by parents and the partners sometimes pledged in childhood. In the West; marriage has traditionally been supervised by the churches; in the Roman Catholic Church it has been declared a SACRAMENT. Civil unions are now permitted in most societies. In Anglo-American LAW, marriage differs from other CONTRACTS in that it may be terminated by a court (through DIVORCE), but not by the partners agreeing between themselves. Most marriages are solemnized by some ritual that conforms to law, but in the U.S. a few states still recognize "common-law" marriages entered into by partners without any ceremony. All states establish age and other requirements for marriage, as well as conditions for legal dissolution of a marriage that detail certain rights and obligations of the partners, particularly with regard to PROPERTY. Anglo-American law was formerly characterized by the view that husband and wife were one legal personality, in effect, that of the husband. Since the mid-19th cent. the rights of married women to own property, enter into contracts, bring legal suits, and otherwise act independently of their husbands have gradually expanded. See also KINSHIP. In part because of economic advantages of marriage (coverage by a spouse's health insurance, tax advantages) and the rights and recognition afforded one considered next-of-kin, many GAY RIGHTS advocates are pressing for laws that would allow gay couples to marry.

Marryat, Frederick [măr'ēăt], 1792–1848, English novelist. His 24 years of service in the British navy provided background for his thrilling tales of sea adventure, e.g., *Frank Mildmay* (1829) and *Mr. Midshipman Easy* (1836).

Mars, in astronomy, 4th PLANET from the sun, at a mean distance of 141.6 million mi (227.9 million km). It has a diameter of 4,223 mi (6,796 km) and a thin atmosphere composed largely of carbon dioxide. The surface of Mars is highly diverse: the younger, lower terrain of the northern hemisphere is sparsely cratered, whereas the older, higher terrain of the southern hemisphere is often densely cratered and contains numerous channels tens of miles wide and hundreds of miles long. It also has numerous volcanoes—including Olympus Mons (c.370 mi/600 km in diameter and 16 mi/26 km tall), the largest in the solar system—and lava plains. Dust storms, often local but sometimes global in extent, have been observed moving across the Martian surface. Mars has two known satellites, **Phobos** and **Deimos,** both discovered by the American astronomer Asaph Hall in 1877; both are very small, irregular ellipsoids. SPACE PROBES that have encountered Mars include *Mariners 4, 6, 7,* and *9* (1965, 1969, 1971); *Vikings 1* and *2* (1976); and several Soviet Mars spacecraft. Experiments on the Viking landing craft detected no definite evidence of life.

Mars, in Roman mythology, god of war and of the state; originally an agricultural god; father of ROMULUS and husband of Bellona. The martial Romans considered him second in importance only to JUPITER. His festivals were held in March (named for him) and October. Mars was identified with the Greek ARES.

Mars, Soviet space probe: see SPACE PROBE, table.

Marsalis, Wynton, 1961–, African-American jazz trumpeter and bandleader; b. New Orleans. He early acquired a reputation for astounding technique and emerged as a leading jazz and classical player. His older brother, **Branford Marsalis**, 1960–, b. New Orleans, is a brilliant jazz, rock, pop, and classical saxophonist and bandleader, known for his improvisations and technique.

Marseilles [märsā'], city (1990 pop. 800,550), capital of Bouches-du-Rhône dept., SE France. France's second city and a major seaport, it is an important industrial center and produces many food products. It is the oldest French town, settled (c.600 B.C.) by Phocaean Greeks and annexed by Rome in 49 B.C. During the CRUSADES (11th–14th cent.), Marseilles was a commercial center and transit port for the Holy Land. Taken by Charles I of Anjou (13th cent.), it was absorbed by PROVENCE and bequeathed to the French crown in 1481. It grew as a port in the 19th cent., with the opening of the SUEZ CANAL and the conquest of Algeria. It is known for its great avenue, the Canebière, and for the Chateau d'If (1524), a castle in its harbor.

Marsh, Dame Ngaio, 1899–1982, New Zealand detective novelist. Her many books, acute in characterization and literary in style, include *A Man Lay Dead* (1934), *Artists in Crime* (1938), *False Scent* (1959), and *Photo Finish* (1980).

Marsh, Reginald, 1898–1954, American painter; b. Paris. An illustrator, scene designer, and easel and mural painter, he is known for his lively paintings of Manhattan street life, e.g., *"Why Not Use the 'L'?"* (1930; Whitney Mus., N.Y.C.).

marsh: see SWAMP.

Marshall, Alfred, 1842–1924, English economist. While a professor (1885–1908) at Cambridge Univ., he systematized the classical economic theories and made new analyses of his own, thus laying the foundation of the neoclassical school of economics. He was concerned with theories of cost, value, and distribution, and developed a concept of marginal utility. His *Principles of Economics* (1890) became a standard work.

Marshall, George Catlett, 1880–1959, American army officer and statesman; b. Uniontown, Pa. He was a staff officer in WORLD WAR I, an aide to Gen. PERSHING (1919–24), and army chief of staff (1939–45). He helped direct Allied strategy in WORLD WAR II and was named general of the army (five-star general) in 1944. As secretary of state (1947–49), he organized and directed the European Recovery Program (the MARSHALL PLAN) to promote postwar recovery in Europe, for which he received the 1953 Nobel Peace Prize. He also served briefly as secretary of defense (1950–51).

Marshall, John, 1755–1835, 4th chief justice of the U.S. SUPREME COURT (1801–35); b. Virginia. A noted lawyer and a delegate to the Virginia assembly, Marshall defended the new U.S. Constitution. As a special envoy to France (1797–98), he was involved in the XYZ AFFAIR. Returning home, he served in Congress (1799–1800) and as secretary of state in Pres. John ADAMS's beleaguered Federalist administration. Appointed chief justice, Marshall established the prestige and independence of the Supreme Court and formulated basic principles of constitutional law. In MARBURY V. MADISON he established the Court's power to determine the constitutionality of legislation; in the Dartmouth College Case he dealt with the inviolability of contract; and, as an opponent of STATES' RIGHTS, in MCCULLOCH V. MARYLAND and Gibbons v. Ogden he established the superiority of federal authority under the Constitution. In these and many other cases, the breadth and wisdom of his interpretations earned him the appellation the Great Chief Justice.

Marshall, Thurgood, 1908–93, associate justice of the U.S. SUPREME COURT (1967–91); b. Baltimore, Md.; grad. Howard Law School (1933). As chief counsel for the NAACP Legal Defense and Educational Fund, he became an influential civil-rights lawyer, arguing 32 cases before the Supreme Court and winning 29 of them, including BROWN V. BOARD OF EDUCATION OF TOPEKA, KANSAS, which led to the end of de jure segregation in public schools. He was appointed to the U.S. Court of Appeals for the Second Circuit by Pres. Kennedy in 1961 and served (1965–67) as solicitor general of the U.S. under Pres. Johnson. In 1967 he became the first African-American Supreme Court justice when Johnson appointed him to the Court. During his tenure as associate justice he was particularly concerned with civil rights and economic justice and was a strong opponent of CAPITAL PUNISHMENT.

Marshall Islands, officially Republic of the Marshall Islands, independent island group (1991 pop. 48,091), c.70 sq mi (181 sq km), consisting of c.1,225 atolls and reefs, in the central Pacific; formerly part of the U.S. Trust Territory of the PACIFIC ISLANDS. The U.S. is responsible for their defense. The main atolls are MAJURO, the capital; Arno; Ailinglaplap; Jaluit; and Kwajalein, site of a U.S. military missile range. The predominantly Micronesian, mainly Protestant population depends for the most part on U.S. aid, tourism, fishing, and subsistence farming. English is the official and Marshallese, a Malayo-Polynesian tongue, the native language; Japanese is also spoken.

History. The islands were named after a British captain who visited them in 1788. They were annexed (1885) by Germany and were seized (1914) by Japan, which received (1920) a League of Nations mandate over them. In WORLD WAR II, U.S. forces occupied (1943–44) the islands and they were included (1947) in the U.S.-administered trust territory. After the war both ENEWETAK and BIKINI atolls were used as U.S. nuclear-weapons test sites, and Kwajalein is presently used for testing U.S. intercontinental ballistic missiles. In 1983 the U.S. gave $183.7 million to the Marshall Islands for damages caused by the tests. The Marshalls became self-governing in 1979 and achieved free-association status in 1986. See PACIFIC OCEAN map.

Marshall Plan or **European Recovery Program,** a coordinated effort by the U.S. and many nations of Europe to foster European economic recovery after WORLD WAR II. First urged (June 5, 1947) by U.S. Secy. of State George C. MARSHALL, the program was administered by the Economic Cooperation Administration (ECA) and from 1948 to 1951 dispensed more than $12 billion in American aid.

marsh mallow: see MALLOW.

Marsilius of Padua, d. c.1342, Italian political philosopher. His tract *Defender of the Peace* (1324), written for Holy Roman Emperor LOUIS IV in his struggle with Pope John XXII, argued that the power of kings and of the church comes from the people and is subject to their control, and that the church should be under the civil ruler. The work was repeatedly condemned by the Holy See.

Marston, John, 1576–1634, English satirist and dramatist. After his early verse satires were suppressed (1599), he turned to drama, writing *Antonio and Mellida* (1599); *Antonio's Revenge* (1599); *The Malcontent* (1604), his masterpiece; and *The Dutch Courtezan* (1605). He collaborated (1605) with JONSON and CHAPMAN on *Eastward Ho!*

marsupial, member of the order Marsupialia, the pouched MAMMALS (sometimes considered a subclass, Metatheria). All but the New World OPOSSUMS and an obscure South American family are found only in Australia, Tasmania, and New Guinea and on nearby islands. Unlike that of higher mammals, the marsupial embryo is generally not connected to its mother by a placenta. The young are born in an undeveloped state and crawl to the mother's nipples, which are in a pouch (marsupium) formed by a fold of abdominal skin. The order includes the KANGAROO, KOALA, TASMANIAN DEVIL, and WOMBAT.

Martha: see MARY, in the Bible, 3.

Martha's Vineyard, island (1990 pop. 11,541), c.100 sq mi (260 sq km), SE Massachusetts, off the southern coast of CAPE COD. Settled in 1642, it was an important whaling and fishing center in the 18th and early 19th cent. before developing as a summer resort in the late 1800s.

Martí, José [märtē], 1853–95, Cuban poet and patriot. He achieved fame with his modernist poetry, e.g., *Ismaelillo* (1882) and *Plain Verses* (1891). A lifelong advocate of Cuban independence, he lived in other Latin American countries and in the U.S. (1881–95), where he founded the Cuban Revolutionary party. He was killed at the start (1895) of the final Cuban insurrection against Spain.

Martial (Marcus Valerius Martialis), A.D. c.40–c.104, Roman poet; b. Spain. His verses, characterized by a twist of wit at the end of each and by original meter and form, became models for the modern EPIGRAM.

martial arts, any of various forms of self-defense, usually weaponless, based on techniques originally developed in ancient China, India, and Tibet. In modern times they have come into wide use for self-protection and as competitive sports. The basic system, jujitsu, teaches skills that enable one to overcome a physically superior opponent. Judo, a Japanese sport created in 1882, makes use of jujitsu principles. Other popular forms include kung fu, karate, and tae kwon do, all of which emphasize blows with the feet and the side of the hand, and kendo, in which bamboo "swords" covered with leather are used.

Martin, Saint, c.316–397, bishop of Tours. Born a heathen, he was converted (c.360) and was a hermit until acclaimed (371) bishop against his will. St. Martin's summer, occurring in mid-November, is the English counterpart of American Indian summer. Feast: Nov. 11.

Martin I, Saint, d. 655?, pope (649–55?), an Italian. Defying Byzantine Emperor Constans II, he called a council that condemned MONOTHELETISM. The emperor banished him to the Crimea, where he died. He was acclaimed a martyr. Feast: Apr. 13.

Martin V, 1368–1431, pope (1417–31), a Roman named Oddone Colonna. His election at the Council of Constance ended the Great SCHISM. Martin rehabilitated Rome and papal power and restored church unity. He rejected the view that councils are supreme in the church, but at the request of the Council of Constance he did call a council at Pavia (1423–24). Later, he summoned another council that began (1431) at Basel. Martin was ineffectually opposed by the Spanish antipope Benedict XIII (Pedro de LUNA) and his successor.

Martin, Homer Dodge, 1836–97, American painter; b. Albany, N.Y. Influenced first by the HUDSON RIVER SCHOOL, then by the BARBIZON SCHOOL, Martin painted melancholy, poetic landscapes, subtle in color and treatment of light. A typical example is *Sea at Villerville* (Kansas City Art Inst.).

Martin, William McChesney, Jr., 1906–, American banker; b. St. Louis. In 1938 he became the first salaried president of the New York Stock Exchange. Appointed chairman of the board of governors of the FEDERAL RESERVE SYSTEM by Pres. Truman, Martin served (1951–70) under six successive administrations. He opposed an excessive expansion of the monetary supply and fought to keep the CENTRAL BANK free of political control.

Martin du Gard, Roger [märtăN′ də gär], 1881–1958, French novelist. His fame rests on *The World of the Thibaults* (1922–40), an eight-part novel cycle that explores the conflicts of French society in the early 20th cent. He was awarded the Nobel Prize in literature in 1937.

Martineau, Harriet [mär′tĭnō], 1802–76, English writer. She is best known for her *Illustrations of Political Economy* (9 vol., 1832–34) and *Illustrations of Taxation* (1834), collections of stories that interpret economics to the layman.

Martínez de la Rosa, Francisco [märtē′nĕth dā lä rō′sä], 1787–1862, Spanish dramatist, poet, statesman, and historian. His play *The Conspiracy of Venice* (1834) is a landmark of romantic drama in Spain.

Martínez Ruiz, José [rōōēth′], pseud. **Azorín,** 1873?–1967, Spanish writer. Collections of his descriptive essays include *España* (1909) and *Castilla* (1912). Among his other works are the autobiographical novels *Antonio Azorín* (1903) and *The Writer* (1942), plays, and short stories.

Martínez Sierra, Gregorio [syā′rä], 1881–1947, Spanish dramatist, novelist, and poet. His best-known play is *The Cradle Song* (1911); his most popular novel is *Ana María* (1907). He often wrote with his wife, the poet María Lejárraga.

Martini, Simone, or **Simone di Martino,** c.1283–1344, major Sienese painter. His work is admired for its Gothic spirituality combined with a vibrancy and a great elegance of line. His earliest known work (1315) is the *Maestà (Madonna and Child Enthroned with Saints and Angels),* in the Palazzo Pubblico, Siena. He painted (1328) one of the first commemorative portraits, the impressive image of the soldier Guidoriccio da Fogliano (Palazzo Pubblico, Siena). Simone's *Annunciation* (1333; Uffizi) is famous for its refined use of outline. His FRESCOES at Assisi include lively scenes from the life of St. Martin.

Martinique, overseas department of France (1992 est. pop. 372,000), 425 sq mi (1,101 sq km), in the Windward Islands. Sugar and rum are exported. This rugged volcanic island, discovered (c.1502) by Columbus, was settled (from 1635) by the French, who eliminated the native Caribs and introduced African slaves. It became a French department in 1946.

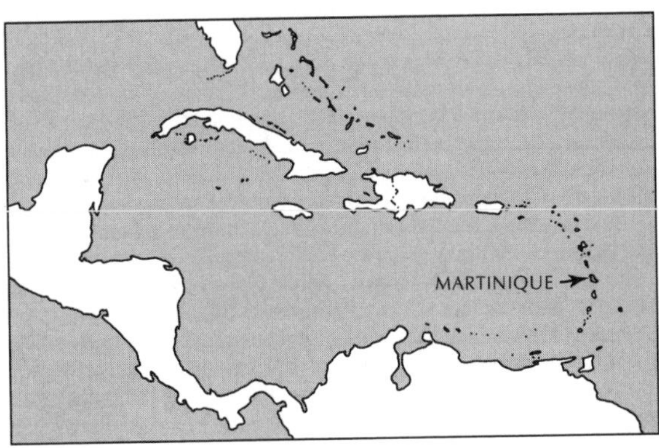

Martins, Peter, 1946–, Danish ballet dancer and choreographer. He performed with the ROYAL DANISH BALLET (1965–69), then joined the NEW YORK CITY BALLET. In 1983 Martins retired from dancing and became joint (now sole) artistic director of the City Ballet.

Martinson, Harry, 1904–78, Swedish writer. He is best known for his long narrative poem *Aniara* (1956), about a journey in space, and his novel *The Road* (1948). He shared the 1974 Nobel Prize in literature with Eyvind JOHNSON.

Marvell, Andrew, 1621–78, English METAPHYSICAL POET. Marvell, who served as MILTON's assistant in the Latin secretaryship and was a member of Parliament, was a leading wit and satirist of his time. Today he is known for his brilliant lyric poetry, including "The Garden," "Bermudas," and "To His Coy Mistress," and for his "Horatian Ode" to CROMWELL.

Marx, Karl, 1818–83, German social philosopher and revolutionary; with Friedrich ENGELS, a founder of modern SOCIALISM and COMMUNISM. The son of a lawyer, he studied law and philosophy; he rejected the idealism of G.W.F. HEGEL but was influenced by Ludwig FEUERBACH and Moses Hess. His editorship (1842–43) of the *Rheinische Zeitung* ended when the paper was suppressed. In 1844 he met Engels in Paris, beginning a lifelong collaboration. With Engels he wrote the *Communist Manifesto* (1848) and other works that broke with the tradition of appealing to natural rights to justify social reform, invoking instead the laws of history leading inevitably to the triumph of the working class. Exiled from Europe after the REVOLUTIONS OF 1848, Marx lived in London, earning some money as a correspondent for the New York *Tribune* but dependent on Engels's financial help while working on his monumental work *Das Kapital* (3 vol., 1867–94), in which he used DIALECTICAL MATERIALISM to analyze economic and social history; Engels edited vol. 2 and 3 after Marx's death. With Engels, Marx helped found (1864) the International Workingmen's Association, but his disputes with the anarchist Mikhail BAKUNIN eventually led to its breakup. MARXISM has greatly influenced the development of socialist thought; further, many scholars have considered Marx a great economic theoretician and the founder of economic history and sociology.

Marx Brothers, American comedy team. The major members were **Groucho** (Julius), 1895–1977; **Harpo** (Arthur), 1893–1964; and **Chico** (Leonard), 1891–1961; all b. N.Y.C. Their anarchic brand of humor depended on slapstick, sight gags, and outrageous puns and wisecracks. They starred in such films as *Horse Feathers* (1932), *Duck Soup* (1933), and *A Night at the Opera* (1935). **Zeppo**

(Herbert), 1901–79, left the team in 1935; **Gummo** (Milton), 1893–1977, left after their vaudeville days.

Marxism, economic and political philosophy originated by Karl MARX and Friedrich ENGELS. The *Communist Manifesto* (1848), by Marx and Engels, suggests many of the premises rigorously developed in Marx's *Das Kapital* (3 vol., 1867–94). The Marxist philosophical method, DIALECTICAL MATERIALISM, reverses the dialectical idealism of G.W.F. HEGEL. Marxism holds that the primary determinant of history is economics. It views the history of society as "the history of class struggle" in which the bourgeoisie, or capitalist class, which replaced the feudal nobility, will inevitably by supplanted by the proletariat, or working class. The capitalist class flourishes by extracting surplus value, or profit, from the commodities produced by the working class. Marxist theory predicts that the contradictions and weaknesses within capitalism will cause increasingly severe economic crises and deepening impoverishment of the working class, which will ultimately revolt and seize control of the means of production. In the resulting classless society, the coercive state will be replaced by rational economic cooperation. Marxism greatly influenced the development of SOCIALISM. After the 1917 RUSSIAN REVOLUTION, however, many socialists dissociated themselves from Soviet COMMUNISM. Communist regimes, while claiming Marxist orthodoxy, have often veered sharply from it. The evolution of laissez faire CAPITALISM in its various forms and the improved conditions for workers in industrialized societies are believed by some to discredit Marxist economic predictions, and Marxism's close association with Communism has already popularly discredited it. Aspects of Marxist theory have, nonetheless, powerfully influenced Western philosophy, history, art, literary criticism, and sociology.

Mary, queens of England. **Mary I** (Mary Tudor), 1516–58 (r.1553–58), was the daughter of HENRY VIII and KATHARINE OF ARAGÓN. Following her parents' divorce, Mary was forced to acknowledge herself illegitimate and to renounce the Roman Catholic Church. The pope later absolved her from these statements, and she remained loyal to Rome. Mary succeeded her half brother, EDWARD VI, after the unsuccessful attempt to put Lady Jane GREY on the throne. Her marriage (1554) to Philip of Spain (later PHILIP II), a consequent Spanish alliance, and the reestablishment of papal authority followed. All this, together with the religious persecution of Protestants, which earned her the name "Bloody Mary," and the loss (1558) of Calais to France, gained her the hostility of the English people. **Mary II,** 1662–94, queen of England, Scotland, and Ireland (1689–94), was the daughter of JAMES II and Anne Hyde. Reared as a Protestant, she married (1667) William of Orange and became joint sovereign with him (see WILLIAM III) after the GLORIOUS REVOLUTION. She actually ruled only during William's absences.

Mary, 1867–1953, queen consort of GEORGE V of England. Married in 1893, she was the mother of EDWARD VIII and GEORGE VI.

Mary, in the Bible. **1 The Virgin,** mother of JESUS, the principal saint, called Our Lady. Her name is the Hebrew *Miriam.* The events of her life mentioned in the NEW TESTAMENT include the archangel GABRIEL's annunciation to her of Jesus' birth; her visitation to Elizabeth, mother of JOHN THE BAPTIST; Jesus' nativity; and her station at the Cross upon which Jesus was crucified. According to Scripture she was first betrothed, then married, to St. JOSEPH and was the cousin of Elizabeth. Tradition has it that Mary was the daughter of Saints Joachim and Anne. From ancient times she has been highly honored by Christians. The Orthodox, Roman Catholic, and Anglican churches all teach the perpetual virginity of Mary, placing a nonliteral interpretation on New Testament references to Jesus' "brothers." The Roman Catholic Church has also proclaimed (1854) the dogma of the Immaculate Conception, which states that Mary was conceived and born without original sin. From earliest times her intercession was believed to be efficacious, and she is called upon to meet every kind of need. Her principal feasts are the Assumption (Aug. 15), the Birthday of Our Lady (Sept. 8), the Immaculate Conception (Dec. 8), the Purification (Feb. 2), and the Annunciation or Lady Day (Mar. 25). Apparitions of the Virgin have been reported at Guadalupe Hidalgo, Mexico (1531), Paris (1830), LOURDES, France (1858), and Fatima, Portugal (1917). **2 Mary Magdalene** [măg'dələn; formerly, môd'lən, hence *maudlin,* i.e., tearful], Christian saint. She appears in the NEW TESTAMENT as a woman whose evil spirits are cast out by JESUS, as a watcher at the CROSS, as an attendant at Jesus' burial, and as one of those who found the tomb empty. A universal tradition identifies her with the repentant prostitute who annointed Jesus' feet. Some also identify her with Mary of Bethany. Feast: July 22. **3 Mary of Bethany,** sister of LAZARUS and Martha. She sat at Jesus' feet while Martha served. She has come to symbolize the life of contemplative love of God.

Maryland, one of the mid-Atlantic states of the U.S.; bounded by Delaware and the Atlantic Ocean (E), the District of Columbia (S), Virginia and West Virginia (S, W), and Pennsylvania (N).

Area, 10,577 sq mi (27,394 sq km). *Pop.* (1990) 4,781,468, a 13.4% increase over 1980 pop. *Capital,* Annapolis. *Statehood,* Apr. 28, 1788 (7th of the original 13 states to ratify the Constitution). *Highest pt.,* Backbone Mt., 3,360 ft (1,025 m); *lowest pt.,* sea level. *Nickname,* Old Line State. *Motto, Fatti Maschii, Parole Femine* [Manly Deeds, Womanly Words]. *State bird,* Baltimore oriole. *State flower,* black-eyed Susan. *State tree,* white oak. *Abbr.,* Md.; MD.

Land and People. Maryland is divided by Chesapeake Bay, into which the Susquehanna and POTOMAC rivers empty, and which separates the more rural Eastern Shore from the rest of the state. Much of Maryland is covered by low coastal plains, which give way to the rolling Piedmont plateau and then to the higher hills of the BLUE RIDGE, in the west. The coastal area has mild winters and hot summers, while the uplands are cooler. Almost 50% of the population lives in the greater BALTIMORE area, which forms a continuous urbanized zone with nearby WASHINGTON, D.C.; over 80% of the population lives in urban areas. Other important cities are Frederick and Salisbury. In 1990 the state's population was 71% white and 25% African American.

Economy. Service industries are the largest state employer, ahead of finance, insurance, real estate, and government. Industry, however, is the principal source of income, with processed foods, electronic equipment, chemicals, and primary metals the leading manufactures. Maryland is an important producer of broiler chickens, greenhouse and nursery products, dairy goods, corn, and soybeans. Although fishing in the Chesapeake Bay has declined, primarily due to water pollution, it is still an important resource. Baltimore is one of the country's leading ports. Coal is mined in the west.

Government. The constitution of 1867 provides for a governor elected to a four-year term. The general assembly consists of a 47-seat senate and 141-seat house, with members of both bodies serving four-year terms. Maryland is represented in the U.S. Congress by two senators and eight representatives and has 10 electoral votes.

History. Giovanni da VERRAZANO probably visited (1524) the Chesapeake region. In 1632 Charles I of England granted a royal charter to George CALVERT, 1st Baron Baltimore, whose sons led (1634) settlers to the colony, conceived as a haven for persecuted Catholics. The Algonquian-speaking natives withdrew gradually, and in 1767 the demarcation of the MASON-DIXON LINE ended a long-standing boundary dispute with Pennsylvania. Maryland was one of the 13 colonies to sign the Declaration of Independence, and after the American Revolution, Maryland and Virginia contributed (1791) land for the new national capital in the DISTRICT OF COLUMBIA. Because it was a border state, Maryland's residents were strongly divided over the slavery question, and military rule was imposed to guarantee that the state remain in the Union. After the Civil War, industry revived, and it continues to be the dominant economic force in the state. The opening (1952) of the Chesapeake Bay Bridge spurred development of the Eastern Shore. The expansion of government-related businesses helped to boost the economy in the 1970s and early 80s. Maryland experienced tremendous suburban growth in the 1980s, especially outside Washington, D.C.

Mary Magdalene: see under MARY, in the Bible.

Mary of Burgundy, 1457–82, daughter and heiress of CHARLES THE BOLD of Burgundy. Her marriage (1477) to Maximilian of Austria (later Holy Roman Emperor MAXIMILIAN I) established the HAPSBURGS in the Low Countries. On her father's death (Jan. 1477) LOUIS XI of France seized Burgundy and Picardy, and prepared to annex the Low Countries and the rest of Mary's inheritance. In May she married Maximilian, who came to her aid with an army. Mary's premature death left her young son, Philip (later PHILIP I of Castile), her heir. In 1493 Maximilian regained control of the Low Countries, but Burgundy and Picardy remained French.

Mary of Guise, 1515–60, queen consort of JAMES V of Scotland; mother of MARY QUEEN OF SCOTS. She was regent for her daughter from 1554. Earlier she had aligned herself with France by arranging Mary's marriage to the DAUPHIN. As regent, she began suppressing Protestantism in Scotland, backed by the French. Civil war ensued (1559), and the Protestants, with English support, prevailed.

Mary Queen of Scots (Mary Stuart), 1542–87, daughter of JAMES V of Scotland and MARY OF GUISE. She became queen of Scotland on the death (1542) of her father, just six days after her birth. Mary was sent by her mother to France, where she grew up and married (1558) the French DAUPHIN (later FRANCIS II). After his death in 1560, she returned to Scotland as queen in 1561. Despite harsh attacks by John KNOX, she refused to abandon her Roman Catholicism, and her charm and intelligence won many over. To reinforce her claim to succeed ELIZABETH I on the English throne, she married (1565) her English cousin Lord DARNLEY. Soon despised by Mary, he joined a conspiracy of Protestant nobles who murdered her trusted counselor, David RIZZIO. Mary, however, talked Darnley over to her side and escaped to loyal nobles. Their son, James, was born soon after. At this period she fell in love with the earl of BOTHWELL. Darnley, widely disliked, was murdered in 1567; Bothwell, widely suspected of the murder, was acquitted and married Mary. Outraged Scots flew to arms, and Mary surrendered and abdicated (1567) in favor of her son, James VI (later JAMES I of England), naming the earl of Murray as regent. She escaped (1568) and gathered a large force, but was defeated by Murray and fled to England. Although welcomed by Elizabeth, she became a prisoner and was involved in several ill-fated plots against Elizabeth with English Catholics, the Spanish, and others. In 1586 a plot to murder Elizabeth was reported. Charged with being an accomplice, Mary was brought to trial; she defended herself with eloquence, although there was little doubt of her complicity. Elizabeth reluctantly signed the death warrant, and Mary was beheaded at Fotheringhay Castle on Feb. 8, 1587. Mary's reported beauty and her undoubted courage have made her a particularly romantic figure in history. She is the subject of much literature.

Mary Tudor, queen of England: see Mary I under MARY, queens of England.

Masaccio [mäzät'chō], 1401–1428?, Italian painter, one of the foremost figures of the Florentine RENAISSANCE; b. Tommaso Guidi. Most of his works have perished, but four remain that are his without question: a polyptych (1426) for the Church of the Carmine, Pisa; the great *Trinity* fresco in Santa Maria Novella, Florence, which revolutionized the understanding of perspective in painting; the *Virgin with St. Anne* (Uffizi), an early work in collaboration with MASOLINO DA PANICALE; and his masterpiece, the FRESCOES in the Brancacci Chapel of Santa Maria del Carmine (Florence), a major monument in the history of art. These frescoes were a training school and inspiration to generations of painters such as MICHELANGELO and RAPHAEL. Masaccio imparted a new sense of grandeur and austerity to the human figure. He used light to give dimension and achieved a classic sense of proportion. He also created a diversity of character within a unified group.

Masada, ancient mountaintop fortress in the Judaean Desert, Israel. Ornately renovated (37–31 B.C.) by Herod the Great, it was seized (A.D. 66) by Jewish Zealots in their revolt against Rome. When 1,000 Zealots were overcome (A.D. 73) by 15,000 Roman soldiers, all but two women and five children killed themselves to escape capture. Masada was excavated (1963–65) by Israeli-led international archaeologists.

Masai, largely nomadic pastoral people of E Africa, chiefly in Kenya and Tanzania. Cattle and sheep form the basis of the economy they have maintained in resistance to cultural change. Masai society is patrilineal; polygyny is practiced. Boys are initiated into a warrior age-group responsible for herding and other tribal labors; only after serving as a warrior may a man marry. The Masai, who are characteristically tall and slender, live traditionally in the kraal, a compound within which are mud houses.

Masaryk, Thomas Garrigue, 1850–1937, principal founder and first president of Czechoslovakia (1918–35). A philosophy professor at the Univ. of Prague, he led the Czech independence movement from 1907 and became the first president of the new republic after WORLD WAR I. An ardent liberal and democrat, he was revered by the Czech people, although he was always faced with strong opposition from extremist groups. Edward BENEŠ succeeded him as president. Among Masaryk's writings is *The Making of a State* (1927). His son, **Jan Masaryk,** 1886–1948, became foreign minister of the Czech government-in-exile in London during WORLD WAR II. He kept that post after his government's return to Prague in 1945. His death, shortly after the Communist coup in 1948, was officially described as suicide by leaping from a window, although the exact circumstances have been subject to speculation ever since.

Mascagni, Pietro [mäskä'nyē], 1863–1945, Italian operatic composer. He is known for *Cavalleria rusticana* (1890), a classic example of Italian *verismo*, or realism of plot.

Masefield, John, 1878–1967, English poet. A seaman and journalist, he gained fame with the poetry collections *Salt-Water Ballads* (1902), containing "Sea Fever" and "Cargoes," and *Ballads* (1903). His major works are long narrative poems, including *The Everlasting Mercy* (1911), *Dauber* (1913), and *Reynard the Fox* (1919). Masefield also wrote plays, in both verse and prose; novels; literary studies; war sketches; and adventure stories for boys. He was POET LAUREATE from 1930 to 1967.

maser acronym for *m*icrowave *a*mplification by *s*timulated *e*mission of *r*adiation, device, first operated in 1954, for the creation and amplification of high-frequency radio waves. The waves produced by the maser are coherent, i.e., all of the same frequency, direction, and phase relationship. Used as an oscillator, the maser provides a very sharp, constant signal and thus serves as a time standard for atomic clocks. The maser can also serve as a relatively noise-free amplifier. The optical maser is now called a LASER.

Maseru, city (1986 pop. 109,382), capital of Lesotho, on the Caledon R. It is a trade and transportation hub linked with South Africa's rail network. Manufactures include candles and carpets. Maseru was a small trading town when Moshesh I, paramount chief of the Basuto, chose it for his capital in 1868 and placed the kingdom under British protection.

Mashhad, city (1986 pop. 1,463,508), NE Iran. It is an industrial and trade center and a transportation hub. Formerly known as Tus, the city was attacked by the Oghuz Turks (12th cent.) and by the Mongols (13th cent.). It recovered by the 14th cent. and prospered under the Safavids. Shah ABBAS I embellished Mashhad with many fine buildings, and NADIR SHAH made it the capital of Persia in the 18th cent.

Masinissa or **Massinissa** [both: măsĭnĭs'ə], c.238–148 B.C., king of NUMIDIA. He fought with the Romans in the Second PUNIC WAR and led his cavalry to victory at the battle of ZAMA. His goading of CARTHAGE brought on the Third Punic War.

Masolino da Panicale [pänēkä'lā], 1383–c.1447, Florentine painter of the early RENAISSANCE; b. Tommaso di Cristoforo Fini. His paintings incorporated his feeling for decorative color with strong modeling and spatial organization. He began the FRESCOES in the Brancacci Chapel that were continued by his pupil MASACCIO. Among the works attributed to him are a *Madonna and Christ in Glory* (Naples) and *Saints* (Philadelphia Mus.).

Mason, George, 1725–92, American Revolutionary statesman; b. Fairfax, Va. He wrote the Virginia declaration of rights (1776), the model for the first part of Jefferson's DECLARATION OF INDEPENDENCE. He was active in drafting the U.S. Constitution (1787), but, unhappy with several provisions, he campaigned against its ratification. The bill of rights he advocated was the basis for some of the first 10 amendments to the Constitution. His grandson, **James Murray Mason,** 1798–1871, was a U.S. senator from Virginia (1847–61). As Confederate commissioner to England, he was one of the principals in the TRENT AFFAIR (1861).

Mason-Dixon Line, boundary between Pennsylvania and Maryland, surveyed (1763–67) by the English astronomers Charles Mason and Jeremiah Dixon and extended (1779) to present-day West Virginia. Before the Civil War it was popularly designated as the boundary between the "slave states" and the "free states," and it is still used on occasion to distinguish the South from the North.

Masons, Free and Accepted: see FREEMASONRY.

Maspero, Gaston Camille Charles, 1846–1916, French Egyptologist, founder of the French School of Oriental Archaeology at Cairo. He was noted for excavations at LUXOR and KARNAK, and for his works *The Dawn of Civilization* (1884), *The Struggle of Nations* (1897), and *The Passing of the Empires* (1900).

masque, courtly form of dramatic spectacle popular in 17th-cent. England. Characterized by the use of masks and the mingling of actors and spectators, it employed pastoral and mythological themes, with an emphasis on music and dance. The foremost writer of masques was Ben JONSON.

Mass, religious service of the Roman Catholic Church, a performance of the SACRAMENT of the Eucharist (see COMMUNION). The Mass was traditionally based on the Latin rite of Rome, which became the official rite of most Roman Catholic churches. Since the Second VATICAN COUNCIL (1962–65) the Roman Mass liturgy has undergone extensive revision, including the use of vernacular languages in place of Latin. Mass is usually said in a church at an altar containing relics, and two lighted candles are essential. Among the types of Masses are High Mass, celebrated in its full form by a priest, assisted by a deacon and choir; Low Mass, much commoner, said by one priest; and a REQUIEM, a proper Mass said for the dead. Some of the sung portions of the Mass are chanted solo at the altar with choral response. There are also nine hymns for the choir; four of these change with the occasion and are related in theme, with texts usually from the PSALMS; there are also five invariable choral pieces: Kyrie eleison, Gloria in excelsis, Credo, Sanctis, and Agnus Dei. PLAINSONG is permitted for all texts, but latitude is granted the choir. A musical setting for the five ordinary hymns, called a Mass, has been an important musical form. Among the composers who have produced masses are PALESTRINA, J.S. BACH, HAYDN, MOZART, VERDI, and STRAVINSKY.

mass, in physics, the quantity of matter in a body regardless of its volume or of any forces acting on it. There are two ways of referring to mass, depending on the laws of physics defining it. The *gravitational mass* of a body may be determined by comparing the body on a beam balance with a set of standard masses; in this way the gravitational factor is eliminated (see GRAVITATION; WEIGHT). The *inertial mass* of a body is a measure of the body's resistance to acceleration by some external force. All evidence seems to indicate that the gravitational and inertial masses are equal. According to the special theory of RELATIVITY, mass increases with speed according to the formula $m = m_0/\sqrt{1-v^2/c^2}$, where m_0 is the rest mass (mass at zero velocity) of the body, v its speed, and c the speed of light in vacuum. The theory also leads to the Einstein mass-energy relation $E = mc^2$, where E is the energy and m the relativistic mass.

Massachusetts, most populous of the New England states of the NE U.S.; bordered by New York (W), Vermont and New Hampshire (N), the Atlantic Ocean (E), and Rhode Island and Connecticut (S).

Area, 8,257 sq mi (21,386 sq km). *Pop.* (1990) 6,016,425, a 4.9% increase over 1980. *Capital,* Boston. *Statehood,* Feb. 6, 1788 (6th of original 13 states to ratify the Constitution). *Highest pt.,* Mt. Greylock, 3,491 ft (1,065 m); *lowest pt.,* sea level. *Nickname,* Bay State. *Motto, Ense Petit Placidam Sub Libertate Quietem* [By the Sword We Seek Peace, But Peace Only under Liberty]. *State bird,* chickadee. *State flower,* mayflower. *State tree,* American elm. *Abbr.,* Mass.; MA.

Land and People. The state's heavily indented coastline has many natural harbors. Offshore are the resort islands of MARTHA'S VINEYARD and NANTUCKET. The low coastal plain gives way inland to gently rolling uplands bisected by the fertile Connecticut R. valley. In the west are the Berkshire Hills. The temperate climate is variable. Massachusetts is the country's third most densely populated state; over 84% of the population lives in urban areas. BOSTON, the largest city, is one of the country's leading commercial and educational centers. WORCESTER and SPRINGFIELD are also important cities. In 1990 the state was 90% white and 5% African American.

Economy. By the early 1990s services and trade had become the most important sectors of the economy, although industry remains economically important. Chief among the state's manufactures are electrical, electronic, and industrial equipment; machinery; plastic products; fabricated metals; leather goods; and textiles. Shipping, printing, and publishing are also important. Leading agricultural products include cranberries, greenhouse and nursery items, vegetables, dairy products, and eggs. Fishing fleets bring in a varied catch. The Atlantic coast, including CAPE COD National Seashore, and the Berkshires attract many visitors.

Government. According to the constitution of 1780, the governor is elected to a four-year term. The legislature is composed of a 40-member senate and 160-member house, both with two-year terms. The state sends ten representatives and two senators to the U.S. Congress and has 12 electoral votes.

History. The PILGRIMS landed in 1620. Despite early difficulties, the PLYMOUTH COLONY took firm hold and was followed by the MASSACHUSETTS BAY COMPANY colony. The early Puritan settlers (see PURITANISM) were primarily agricultural, although a merchant class soon formed. By the mid-18th cent. the colony had become the center of a lively and prosperous seagoing traffic in molasses, rum, and African slaves—the so-called triangular trade. The colonists sorely felt British restrictions imposed by the STAMP ACT (1765) and TOWNSHEND ACTS (1767). Following the BOSTON MASSACRE (1770) and the BOSTON TEA PARTY (1773), the AMERICAN REVOLUTION started with fighting at LEXINGTON AND CONCORD in April 1775. After independence, the industrial revolution took hold in Massachusetts, with the development of a thriving textile industry. During the 19th cent. the state was the center of many of the country's religious, philosophical, and social movements, including TRANSCENDENTALISM, UNITARIANISM, and abolitionism (see ABOLITIONISTS). Following the Civil War, there began a huge influx of immigrants, of whom the Irish were a dominant group. The early 20th cent. was marked by intense labor strife, including the unsuccessful Boston police strike (1919). The decline of the state's textile and shoe industries since World War II was largely offset by the growth of computer- and defense-related industries into the 1980s. In 1989, however, Massachusetts was hit by the nationwide recession and the burden of a huge state budget, and the state struggled to regain economic prosperity in the 1990s.

Massachusetts Bay Company, English chartered company (1628) that established the Massachusetts Bay colony on a grant of land between the Charles and Merrimack rivers and extending westward to "the South Sea." Puritan colonists sailed for New England in 1630 and founded their chief settlement at Boston as a religious and political refuge. The company and colony were synonymous until 1684, when the company was dissolved.

Massasoit, c.1580–1661, powerful chief of the Wampanoags of New England. Faithful to his treaty (1621) with the PILGRIMS, he befriended Roger WILLIAMS. Massasoit's son, Metacomet, was the leader of KING PHILIP'S WAR.

Masséna, André [mäsänä'], 1758–1817, marshal of France. He won the battle of Rivoli (1797) in NAPOLEON I's Italian campaign and defeated (1799) the Russians at Zürich. He was later defeated in the PENINSULAR WAR (1808–14). Napoleon made him duke of Rivoli and prince of Essling. After Napoleon's fall, Massena supported LOUIS XVIII. He was neutral during the HUNDRED DAYS.

Massenet, Jules [mäsənā'], 1842–1912, French composer. Among his 20 OPERAS, *Manon* (1884) exemplifies his sensuous style and contains accompanied spoken dialogue instead of traditional recitative. Others are *Werther* (1892) and *Thaïs* (1894).

mass extinction, the EXTINCTION of a large percentage of the earth's species, opening ecological niches for other species to fill. There have been at least ten such events. The worst occurred approximately 250 million years ago, at the end of the Permian period, when more than 60% of all the earth's plant and animal species were lost. The most famous mass extinction was that of the Cretaceous period, 65 million years ago, when the dinosaurs and many other plants and animals disappeared. Scientists theorize that mass extinctions result from drastic environmental changes (e.g. fire, acid rain, global cooling) that follow events such as meteorite or comet impacts or massive volcanic eruptions.

Massif Central, diverse mountainous plateau, c.33,000 sq mi (85,470 sq km), occupying almost one sixth of France. It rises to a high point of 6,187 ft (1,866 m) in the Puy de Sancy of the once-volcanic Auvergne Mts. and also includes the rugged Cévennes Mts. (SE) and the plateaus of the Causses (SW). Clermont-Ferrand and St. Étienne are major cities.

Massine, Léonide [mäsēn′], 1895–1979, Russian-American choreographer and ballet dancer; b. Moscow. He was the principal dancer and choreographer for DIAGHILEV (1914–21, 1925–28) and the Ballet Russe de Monte Carlo (1932–42). His works include *Parade* (1917) and *Jeux d'Enfants* (1943).

Massinger, Philip, 1583–1640, English dramatist. Many of his plays, largely collaborations, are lost. He is best known for two realistic domestic comedies, *A New Way to Pay Old Debts* (1625) and *The City Madam* (1632). A harsh moralist, he attacked the evils of a frivolous society.

mass number, represented by the symbol *A*, the total number of nucleons (NEUTRONS and PROTONS) in the nucleus of an ATOM. All atoms of a chemical ELEMENT have the same ATOMIC NUMBER but may have different mass numbers (from having different numbers of neutrons in the nucleus). Atoms of an element with the same mass number make up an ISOTOPE of the element. Isotopes of different elements may have the same mass number but different numbers of protons.

Masson, André [mäsôN′], 1896–1987, French painter and graphic artist. An exponent of SURREALISM until 1928, he developed "automatic writing"—spontaneous linear expressions of his personal mythology.

Massys, Matsys, Messys, or **Metsys, Quentin** [mäsīs′, mätsīs′, mĕ–, mĕt–], c.1466–1530, Flemish painter. Influenced by Italian art and Jan van EYCK, he developed a calm, measured style with solid figures and soft textures. The influence of LEONARDO DA VINCI's grotesque head studies is seen in the *Ugly Duchess* (National Gall., London). His son **Jan Massys,** c.1509–1575, did satirical and elegant works, e.g., *Judith* (Mus. Fine Arts, Boston). Another son, **Cornelis Massys,** d. after 1560, a landscape painter and engraver, did *Arrival in Bethlehem* (Metropolitan Mus.).

mastaba, in EGYPTIAN ARCHITECTURE, a sepulchral structure built above ground. Mastabas of the early dynastic period (3200–2680 B.C.), evidently modeled on contemporary houses, were elaborate and had many compartments. Better known are those of the Old Kingdom (2680–2181 B.C.), which elaborated on the predynastic burial-pit and mound form. The typical mastaba was rectangular and flat-roofed, with inward sloping walls. The superstructure was solid except for the offering chamber—a decorated chapel—and the serdab—a smaller chamber containing a portrait statue of the deceased.

mastectomy, surgical removal of breast tissue, usually done as treatment for breast cancer. There are many types of mastectomy. In general, the farther the cancer has spread, the more tissue is taken. The radical mastectomies of the past (which removed not only the breast, but underlying chest muscle and lymph nodes) have largely been replaced by less drastic, but equally effective procedures. For small tumors, lumpectomy, removing just the tumor and a margin of tissue, may be performed. A partial, or segmental, mastectomy removes the cancer, some breast tissue, the lining over the chest, and usually some lymph nodes from under the arm; total or simple mastectomy removes the whole breast; modified radical mastectomy takes the breast, lining over the chest muscles, and lymph nodes. Breast reconstruction can be done using the patient's own tissue or breast implants. Saline implants are currently used; controversial SILICONE-gel implants are undergoing further testing.

Masters, Edgar Lee, 1869–1950, American poet; b. Garnett, Kans. He is best known for *The Spoon River Anthology* (1915), a group of free-verse epitaphs revealing the secret lives of small-town Americans. He also wrote such biographies as *Lincoln the Man* (1931) and *Whitman* (1937).

Masters and Johnson, pioneering research team in the field of human sexuality, consisting of the gynecologist **William H(owell) Masters,** 1915–, b. Cleveland, and the psychologist **Virginia E(shelman) Johnson,** 1925–, b. Springfield, Mo. Authors of *Human Sexual Response* (1966), *Human Sexual Inadequacy* (1970), and *Homosexuality in Perspective* (1979), they established a sex-therapy program in St. Louis (1970), which became a model for clinics elsewhere, and trained other therapists in clinical counseling. They were married from 1971 to 1993.

mastiff, very large, powerful WORKING DOG; shoulder height, 27–33 in. (68.6–83.8 cm); weight, 165–185 lb (74.9–83.9 kg). Its short coat may be silver-fawn, apricot, or dark fawn brindle with black markings. It was developed as a fighting dog and guardian in England over 2,000 years ago.

mastodon, name for several prehistoric MAMMALS of the extinct genus *Mammut,* from which ELEPHANTS are believed to have evolved. Long-jawed mastodons about 4½ ft (137 cm) high, with four tusks, lived in Africa during the Oligocene epoch. Later forms were larger, with long flexible trunks and two tusks. Forest dwellers, mastodons fed by browsing.

Masudi [mäsōō′dē], d. 956, Arab historian, geographer, and philosopher; b. Baghdad. He traveled in many lands and wrote the comprehensive *Muruj adh-Dhahab* [meadows of gold], a history of the world from the creation to A.D. 947.

Masur, Kurt, 1927–, German conductor. He is noted for his performances of the German composers whose works form the core of the symphonic repertoire and of modern E European and Russian composers. Beginning in 1948 he held a series of positions as conductor and musical director in East Germany; in 1970 he became conductor of the Leipzig Gewandhaus Orchestra. He succeeded Zubin MEHTA as musical director of the New York Philharmonic Orchestra (see ORCHESTRA, table) in 1991. Masur played a prominent part in the events in Leipzig (1989) that contributed to the collapse of Communist East Germany.

Matabele: see NDEBELE.

Mata Hari, 1876–1917, Dutch dancer and spy for Germany in WORLD WAR I; b. Margaretha Geertruida Zelle. A member of the German secret service in Paris, she obtained military secrets from high Allied officers. The French tried and executed her.

maté, yerba maté, or **Paraguay tea,** name for a South American evergreen tree (*Ilex paraguensis* and related species) of the HOLLY family and for a tea brewed from the young leaves and tender shoots. Less astringent than genuine TEA, maté is a stimulant containing considerable caffeine. It is the most popular beverage in much of South America.

materialism, in philosophy, a widely held system of thought that explains the nature of the world as entirely dependent on matter, the final reality. Early Greek teaching, e.g., that of DEMOCRITUS, EPICURUS, and the proponents of STOICISM, conceived of reality as material in nature. The theory was renewed and developed beginning in the 17th cent., especially by HOBBES, and in the 18th cent. LOCKE's investigations were adapted to the materialist position. The system was developed further from the middle of the 19th cent., particularly in the form of DIALECTICAL MATERIALISM and in the formulations of LOGICAL POSITIVISM.

mathematics, deductive study of numbers, geometry, and various abstract constructs.

Branches. Mathematics is very broadly divided into foundations, algebra, analysis, geometry, and applied mathematics. The term *foundations* is used to refer to the formulation and analysis of the language, AXIOMS, and logical methods on which all of mathematics rest (see LOGIC); SET theory, originated by Georg CANTOR, now constitutes a universal mathematical language. ALGEBRA, historically, is the study of solutions of one or several algebraic equations, involving POLYNOMIAL functions of one or several variables; ARITHMETIC and NUMBER THEORY are areas of algebra concerned with special properties of the integers. ANALYSIS applies the concepts and methods of the CALCULUS to various mathematical entities. GEOMETRY is concerned with the spatial side of mathematics, i.e., the properties of and relationships between points, lines, planes, figures, solids, and surfaces. TOPOLOGY studies the structures of geometric objects in a very general way. The term *applied mathematics* loosely designates a wide range of studies with significant current use in the empirical sciences. It includes COMPUTER science, mathematical physics, PROBABILITY theory, and mathematical STATISTICS.

History. The earliest records indicate that mathematics arose in response to the practical needs of agriculture, business, and industry in the 3d and 2d millennia B.C. in Egypt and Mesopotamia and, possibly, India and China. Between the 6th and 3d cent. B.C., the Greeks THALES, PYTHAGORAS, PLATO, ARISTOTLE, EUCLID, ARCHIMEDES, and Zeno of Elea profoundly changed the nature of mathematics, introducing abstract notions such as INFINITY and irrational NUMBERS and a deductive system of proof. Their work was carried on in the 2d and 3d cent. A.D. by HERO OF ALEXANDRIA, PTOLEMY, and Diophantus. With the decline of learning in the West, the development of mathematics was continued in the East by the Chinese, the Indians (who invented the numerals now used throughout the civilized world), and the Arabs. Their writings began to reach the West in the 12th cent., and by the end of the 16th cent. Europeans had made advances in algebra, TRIGONOMETRY, and such areas of applied mathematics as mapmaking. In the 17th cent. decimal fractions (see DECIMAL SYSTEM) and LOGARITHMS were invented, and the studies of projective geometry and probability were begun. Blaise PASCAL, Pierre de FERMAT, GALILEO, and Johannes KEPLER made fundamental contributions. The greatest advances of the century, however, were the invention of ANALYTIC GEOMETRY by René DESCARTES and of the calculus by Sir Isaac NEWTON and, independently, G.W. LEIBNIZ. The history of mathematics in the 18th cent. is dominated by the development of the methods of the calculus and their application to physical problems, both terrestrial and celestial, with leading roles being played by the BERNOULLI family, Leonhard EULER, Joseph LAGRANGE, and Pierre de LAPLACE. The modern period of mathematics dates from the beginning of the 19th cent., and its dominant figure is Carl GAUSS, who made fundamental contributions to algebra, arithmetic, geometry, number theory, and analysis. In that century NON-EUCLIDEAN GEOMETRY was invented independently by Nikolai LOBACHEVSKY, János Bolyai, and, in another form, G.F.B. RIEMANN, whose work was of great importance in the development of the general theory of relativity. Number theory and abstract algebra received significant contributions from Sir William Rowan HAMILTON, M.S. Lie, Georg Cantor, Julius DEDEKIND, and Karl WEIERSTRASS. Weierstrass and Augustin CAUCHY brought new rigor to the foundations of the calculus and of analysis. In the 20th cent. there have been two main trends. One is toward increasing generalization and abstraction, exemplified by investigations into the foundations of mathematics by David HILBERT, Bertrand RUSSELL and Alfred North WHITEHEAD, and Kurt GÖDEL. The other trend is toward concrete applications to such areas as linguistics and the social sciences, as well as computer science, made possible by the work of John VON NEUMANN, Norbert WIENER, and others.

Mather, Richard, 1596–1669, English Puritan clergyman. He fled (1635) to Massachusetts because of his Puritan beliefs and was pastor of Dorchester until his death. His son, **Increase Mather,** 1639–1723, b. Dorchester, Mass., became (1664) pastor of North Church, Boston, where he was an outstanding upholder of the old Puritan theocracy. During the Restoration period he was a bitter opponent of Edward Randolph and Sir Edmund ANDROS over the withdrawal of the Massachusetts charter. He was president of Harvard College (1685–1701). His son, **Cotton Mather,** 1663–1728, b. Boston, assisted his father and succeeded him as pastor of North Church, Boston. By his writings he became one of the most celebrated New England Puritan ministers. Although his works helped stir up hysteria during the Salem witch trials of 1692, he was also a promoter of learning and a power in the state.

Mathewson, Christy (Christopher Mathewson), 1880–1925, American baseball player; b. Factoryville, Pa. One of the game's great right-handed pitchers, he played (1900–1916) for the New York Giants and later managed the Cincinnati Reds. During his career he won 373 games and struck out 2,499 batters. He was a victim of poison gas in France in World War I, but survived until his death from tuberculosis.

Matilda or **Maud,** 1102–67, queen of England, daughter of HENRY I. In 1114 she married Holy Roman Emperor HENRY V. After his death she married (1128) Geoffrey IV of Anjou. At her father's death (1135) her cousin STEPHEN seized the English throne. In 1139 Matilda and her half brother Robert, earl of Gloucester, challenged Stephen, and she was elected "Lady of the English" in 1141. Unable to establish her rule, she withdrew her claim in 1148 in favor of her son Henry (later HENRY II).

Matisse, Henri, 1869–1954, French painter, sculptor, and lithographer, considered, with PICASSO, one of the two foremost artists of the modern era. His contribution to 20th-cent. art is inestimable. He explored IMPRESSIONISM, e.g., *The Dinner Table* (1897; Niarchos Coll., Athens); neo-impressionism, e.g., *Luxe, calme et volupté* (1905, private coll.) (see POSTIMPRESSIONISM); and made variations on the old masters in the Louvre. In 1905 he began using pure primary color as a significant structural element, e.g., *The Green Line* (1905; State Mus., Copenhagen). A leader of FAUVISM, he always used color in bold patterns and different sorts of expressive abstraction, e.g., *The Blue Nude* (1907; Baltimore Mus. of Art). In his last years he made brilliant paper cutouts, e.g., *Jazz* (Philadelphia Mus. of Art), and decorated the Dominican chapel at Vence, France, with fresh, joyous windows and murals.

matriarchy, familial and political rule by women. Many anthropologists now reject the claims of Lewis MORGAN and others that early society was matriarchal, although some contemporary feminists have theorized that a primitive matriarchy once existed. Claims for such a matriarchy are based largely on research on societies in which women are the major contributors to subsistence, on societies with matrilineal descent, and on myths of ancient female rule. Such societies and myths have many aspects, however, that cast doubt on the validity of the claims. Most anthropologists have also concluded that patriarchy, or male dominance, is not natural or biological but culturally constructed because of the diverse forms it takes across cultures.

Matsu and Quemoy, islands off the coast of China, c.100 to 150 mi (160 to 240 km) W of Taiwan, which controls them. Matsu is a single island, while Quemoy is a group consisting of Quemoy, Little Quemoy, and 12 islets in Xiamen Bay. The islands remained Chinese Nationalist outposts after the Communist victory in mainland China in 1949 and were bombarded several times from the mainland.

Matsuo Basho: see BASHO.

Matsys, Quentin: see MASSYS, QUENTIN.

Mattathias: see MACCABEES.

matter, anything that has mass. Because of its mass, all matter has WEIGHT, if it is in a gravitational field, and INERTIA. The three common STATES OF MATTER are solid, liquid, and gas; scientists also recognize a fourth, PLASMA. Ordinary matter consists of ATOMS and MOLECULES. See also ELEMENT; ELEMENTARY PARTICLES.

Matterhorn, distinctive pyramidal peak, 14,690 ft (4,478 m) high, in the Alps, on the Swiss-Italian border, near Zermatt. It was first climbed in 1865 by Edward Whymper.

Matthew, Saint, one of the Twelve APOSTLES, also called Levi, a publican (tax collector) from Capernaum. The attribution to him of the first GOSPEL is most likely incorrect.

Matthew, Gospel according to Saint, 1st book of the NEW TESTAMENT, now generally accepted as postdating MARK. Containing more allusions to the OLD TESTAMENT than the other GOSPELS, it was clearly written for Jewish Christians, to prove that JESUS was the promised Messiah.

Matthew of Paris or **Matthew Paris,** d. 1259, English historian, a monk of St. Albans. He wrote *Chronica majora* great chronicle, a history of the world (containing a hostile portrait of King JOHN), and *Historia Anglorum,* a history of England.

Matthias, Saint, APOSTLE chosen by lot to replace JUDAS ISCARIOT by the remaining disciples.

Matthias, 1557–1619, Holy Roman emperor (1612–19), king of Bohemia (1611–17) and of Hungary (1608–18); son of Emperor MAXIMILIAN II. The ill health of his brother Emperor Rudolf II gave Matthias the opportunity to increase his political authority, and he was recognized as head of the house of HAPSBURG in 1606 and as emperor in 1617. His conciliatory policy toward the Protestants gave rise to an opposing Catholic faction led by his brother the Archduke Maximilian and by the Archduke Ferdinand (later Emperor FERDINAND II). Old and ailing, Matthias was unable to prevent their takeover, and he was succeeded by Ferdinand.

Matthias Corvinus, 1443?–1490, king of Hungary (1458–90) and Bohemia (1478–90), son of John Hunyadi. After succeeding LADISLAUS V in Hungary, he took up arms against George of Podebrad, king of Bohemia, and the latter's successor, Ladislaus II. Matthias had himself crowned (1469) king of Bohemia, but the Bohemian diet did not recognize him. In 1478 a compromise allowed both Matthias and Ladislaus to keep the title of king. Matthias made war (1477, 1479, 1482) on Holy Roman Emperor FREDERICK III, but most of his conquests were lost after his death.

Matthiessen, F(rancis) O(tto), 1902–50, American critic; b. Pasadena, Calif. An American literature scholar, he taught at Harvard

Univ. (1929–50). His books include *American Renaissance* (1941), *Henry James* (1944), and *Theodore Dreiser* (1951).

Maugham, W(illiam) Somerset, 1874–1965, English author. An expert storyteller, he wrote with irony and, frequently, cynicism. His first success was the humorous play *Lady Frederick* (1907), followed by *The Circle* (1921) and others. His masterpiece, the partly autobiographical novel *Of Human Bondage,* appeared in 1915. Other novels include *The Moon and Sixpence* (1919), based on the life of GAUGUIN, and the satirical *Cakes and Ale* (1930). He also wrote many well-known short stories (e.g., "Miss Thompson") and literary essays.

Maui [mou'ē], second largest island (1990 est. pop. 82,500), 728 sq mi (1,886 sq km), of HAWAII, consisting of two mountainous peninsulas joined by an isthmus. The highest point is Haleakala volcano (10,023 ft/3,055 m) in Haleakala National Park. Wailuku (1990 pop. 10,688) is the largest town. Tourism and sugarcane and pineapple farming are economically important.

Mauldin, Bill (William Henry Mauldin), 1921–, American cartoonist; b. Mountain Park, N.Mex. Famous during World War II for his sardonic cartoons depicting the enlisted man's life, he won two Pulitzer Prizes (1945, 1959). Since 1962 he has worked at the Chicago *Sun-Times.* His books of cartoons include *Up Front* (1945) and *Brass Ring* (1971).

Mau Mau, secret terrorist organization in KENYA, comprising chiefly members of the Kikuyu tribe. In 1952 the Mau Mau began bloody reprisals against the Europeans. By 1956 British troops had driven the Mau Mau into the hills, and later the entire Kikuyu tribe was relocated.

Mauna Kea, dormant volcano, Hawaii island, 13,796 ft (4,205 m) high, highest point in the Hawaiian Islands. It has many cinder cones on its flanks and a great crater at the summit. At the peak of Mauna Kea, where the dry air is ideal for optical and infrared astronomical observations, are several major telescopes, including the 150-in (3.8-m) United Kingdom Infrared Telescope, the largest such designed expressly for infrared observations, and the 142-in (3.6-m) Canada-France-Hawaii reflector.

Mauna Loa, intermittently active volcano, Hawaii island, 13,680 ft (4,170 m) high, in Hawaii Volcanoes National Park (see NATIONAL PARKS, table). One of its many craters is KILAUEA.

Maupassant, Guy de [mōpäsäN'], 1850–93, French author. He poured out a prodigious number of short stories, novels, plays, and travel sketches until 1891, when he went mad; he died in a sanitarium. Writing in a simple, objective style reminiscent of FLAUBERT, Maupassant is an exemplar of French psychological realism. His influence on all European literature was enormous. His best works are some 300 short stories, many unsurpassed in their genre. Among his masterpieces are "Tallow Ball," "The Necklace," and "The Piece of String." His novels include *A Life* (1883), *Bel-Ami* (1885), and *Pierre et Jean* (1888).

Maurer, Alfred Henry, 1868–1932, American painter; b. N.Y.C. Influenced by FAUVISM and CUBISM, he generally painted female heads and balanced, restrained still lifes, e.g., *Still Life with Pears* (Addison Gall., Andover, Mass.).

Mauretania, ancient district of Africa in Roman times, usually including most of present-day N Morocco and W Algeria. In the 2d cent. B.C. Bocchus, father-in-law of Jugurtha of Numidia, established the kingdom of Mauretania. The Roman Emperor AUGUSTUS put Juba II on the throne in 25 B.C., and the Emperor CLAUDIUS I made the region into two Roman provinces, but the native chiefs were never wholly subdued. By the end of the 5th cent. A.D., Roman control over Mauretania had ended.

Mauriac, François [mōryäk'], 1885–1970, French author. Imbued with a profound but nonconformist Catholicism, his novels include *The Desert of Love* (1925), *Thérèse* (1927), and *Vipers' Tangle* (1932). Other works include lives of Racine (1928) and of Jesus (1936); the play *Asmodée* (1938); several collections of essays; and memoirs. Mauriac received the 1952 Nobel Prize in literature.

Maurice of Nassau, 1567–1625, prince of Orange (1618–25); son of WILLIAM THE SILENT. In the independence struggle of the NETHERLANDS he took the offensive against the Spanish under Alessandro Farnese (see FARNESE, family). His victories led (1609) to a 12-year truce, making the United Provinces virtually independent. He broke with his chief adviser, OLDENBARNEVELDT, over the split between the Calvinists and the more liberal Remonstrants; Oldenbarneveldt, a leader of the Remonstrants, was executed in 1619. Maurice's campaigns against Spain after hostilities resumed (1621) had little success. His brother FREDERICK HENRY succeeded him.

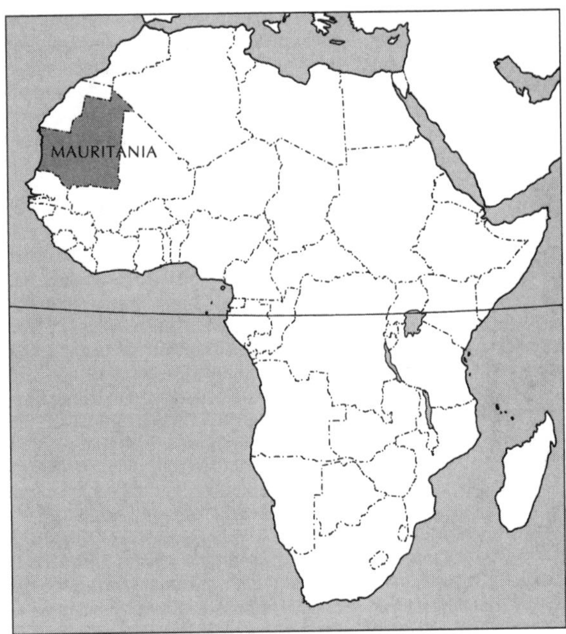

Mauritania, officially Islamic Republic of Mauritania, republic (1992 est. pop. 2,059,000), 397,953 sq mi (1,030,700 sq km), NW Africa. It is bordered by the Atlantic Ocean (W), Morocco (N), Algeria (NE), Mali (E and SE), and Senegal (SW). NOUAKCHOTT is the capital. Most of the country is low-lying desert, forming part of the SAHARA, but some fertile soil is found in the semiarid SAHEL of the southwest, along the Senegal R. The economy is divided between a traditional agriculture sector and a modern mining industry developed in the 1960s. Irrigated crops include millet, dates, rice, and sorghum. Stock raising (cattle, sheep, goats, and camels) was sharply reduced by the great drought of the 1970s and 80s. The fishing industry, based in the Atlantic, is growing, and fish processing is now important. Shipments of iron ore account for a large portion of export earnings. Nearly a third of the population are nomadic Moors, of Berber and Arab background; another third are mostly Africans, many of whom live as agriculturalists near the Senegal R.; and the rest are of mixed Moor and African descent. Islam is the state religion; Arabic and Wolof are official languages.

History. Settled by Berbers in the 1st millennium A.D., the region was the center of the ancient empire of GHANA (700–1200) and later became part of the empire of MALI (14th–15th cent.). By this time the Sahara had encroached on much of Mauritania, limiting agriculture and reducing the population. In the 1440s Portuguese navigators established a fishing base, and from the 17th cent. European traders dealt in gum arabic along the southern coast. France gained control of S Mauritania in the mid-19th cent., declared a protectorate over the region in 1903, and made it a separate colony in FRENCH WEST AFRICA in 1920, but did little to develop the economy. Nationalist political activity began after World War II, and Mauritania gained full independence in 1960. A Muslim state was created in 1961 under Makhtar Ould Daddah as president. His rule was troubled by ethnic tensions between the Fulani and the Arab-Berber group, by economic problems aggravated by the severe drought in the Sahel, and by worker-student protests. The military deposed Ould Daddah in 1978, and military governments subsequently ruled the country. A 1975 agreement with Spain and Morocco giving Mauritania control over the southern third of the Spanish (Western) Sahara ignited a conflict in the former colony. The Polisario Front, a pro-independence guerrilla group backed by Algeria, waged war against Mauritanian troops until 1979, when Mauritania renounced its claims to the area and signed a peace treaty with the front. Slavery was only officially abolished in 1980, and racial unrest erupted in the late 1970s and persisted into the 1980s, aggravated by government repression of black Mauritanians. In 1984 Col. Maouiya Ould Sidi Ahmed Taya became president after a coup. A new constitution approved in 1991 called for an elected president and national assembly, and the government legalized political parties. In 1992 Taya won election as president in balloting marred by widespread cheating.

Mauritius [môrĭsh'ēəs, –rĭsh'əs], island country (1992 est. pop. 1,092,000), 790 sq mi (2,046 sq km), in the SW Indian Ocean, c.500 mi (800 km) E of Madagascar. The capital is PORT LOUIS. The island of Rodrigues and two groups of small islands are dependencies of Mauritius. Surrounded by coral reefs, the principal island consists of a central plateau and volcanic mountains that rise to c.2,700 ft (820 m). The one-crop economy is based on sugarcane, which represents about 40% of export earnings. Tea production, light industry, and tourism are being developed in a government program to diversify the economy. The fishing industry is also being expanded. About 70% of the population are of Indian descent; the rest are of Creole (mixed French and African), French, or Chinese descent. Over half the people are Hindu, about 30% are Christian, and 17% are Muslim. English is the official language, but Creole, French, and other languages are commonly used.

History. Originally uninhabited, Mauritius was occupied by the Dutch (1598–1710), who named it after Prince Maurice of Nassau. It was settled (1715) by the French, who established a colony called Île de France. The French imported large numbers of African slaves to work the sugarcane plantations. In 1810 the British captured the island and restored the Dutch name. After slavery was abolished in 1833 the British imported indentured laborers from India, whose descendants constitute a majority of the population today. Extension of the franchise in 1947 gave political rights to the Indians, who favored independence. They were opposed by the French and Creoles, who feared domination by the Indian majority. Sir Seewoosagur Ramgoolam's pro-independence Labour party won control of the assembly in 1967, and independence was granted in 1968. In 1982 the left-wing Mauritius Militant Movement (MMM) came to power, and Aneerood Jugnauth became prime minister. The following year a split in the MMM led Jugnauth to form a new party, and he has remained in office at the head of a series of coalition governments.

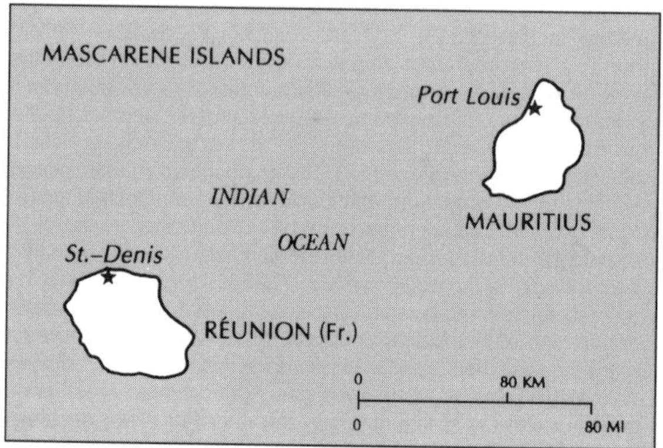

Maurois, André [mōrwä'], 1885–1967, French author; b. Émile Herzog. He is noted for his biographies of Shelley, Byron, Disraeli, Chateaubriand, Washington, and others. His novel, *The Silence of Colonel Bramble* (1918), about British military life, was also highly successful. His *Memoirs* appeared in 1970.

Maury, Matthew Fontaine, 1806–73, American hydrographer and naval officer; b. near Fredericksburg, Va. His wind and current charts of the Atlantic cut sailing time on many routes, and his *Physical Geography of the Sea* (1855) was the first classic work of modern oceanography. Maury was director of the U.S. Naval Observatory from 1844 to 1861.

Maurya, ancient Indian dynasty, c.325–c.183 B.C., founded by CHANDRAGUPTA. His grandson, ASOKA, brought nearly all of India, along with Afghanistan, under one rule. Under the Maurya dynasty Indian arts and sciences flowered.

Mauss, Marcel, 1872–1950, French sociologist and anthropologist. His contributions to the theory of sacrifice and classification rest on his works with Henri Hubert and his uncle, Émile DURKHEIM. He also contributed to the theory of gift exchange, and played a role in founding the journal *Année Sociologique* and the Institut d'Ethnologie in Paris.

Mavrokordatos or **Mavrocordatos, Alexander,** 1791–1865, Greek statesman and premier (1833–34, 1841, 1843–44, 1854–55). He was a leading patriot in the Greek War of Independence (1821–29) against Turkey and wrote the Greek declaration of independence.

Maxim, family of inventors and munitions makers. **Sir Hiram Stevens Maxim,** 1840–1916, b. near Sangerville, Me., invented the Maxim machine gun (1884; see SMALL ARMS), a smokeless powder, and a delayed-action fuse. He became a British citizen in 1900. His brother **Hudson Maxim,** 1853–1927, b. Orneville, Me., developed a high explosive, smokeless powder, and a propellant for torpedoes. Sir Hiram's son **Hiram Percy Maxim,** 1869–1936, b. Brooklyn, N.Y., created (1908) the Maxim silencer for explosive weapons.

Maximian (Marcus Aurelius Valerius Maximianus), d. 310, Roman emperor, with DIOCLETIAN (286–305). Both emperors abdicated in 305 in favor of Constantius I and Galerius, but the death (306) of Constantius caused a complicated struggle for power. Maximian at first aided his son Maxentius in this struggle. He later revolted against CONSTANTINE I and in 310 was forced to commit suicide.

Maximilian, rulers of the HOLY ROMAN EMPIRE. **Maximilian I,** 1459–1519, emperor and German king (1493–1519), son and successor of Emperor FREDERICK III, attempted to aggrandize his Hapsburg lands, chiefly through marriage diplomacy, thus involving himself in wars through most of his reign. His marriage (1477) to MARY OF BURGUNDY led to war with Louis XI of France over her vast holdings (Burgundy, the Netherland provinces, and Luxembourg) and with Louis's successor, Charles VIII. A later marriage involved him in the ITALIAN WARS. He arranged the marriage of his son Philip, later PHILIP I of Castile, into the Spanish royal family. That marriage later gave his grandson, Emperor CHARLES V, one of the largest territorial inheritances in history. He also arranged the marriages that assured HAPSBURG succession to the Bulgarian and Hungarian thrones. **Maximilian II,** 1527–76, emperor (1564–76), king of Bohemia (1562–76) and of Hungary (1563–76), was the son and successor of FERDINAND I. He was sympathetic to Lutheranism and allowed considerable religious freedom, while at the same time encouraging Catholic reform. In 1568 he made a truce with Turkey whereby he agreed to pay tribute to the sultan for his share of Hungary. He died while preparing to invade Poland, where he had been elected rival king to STEPHEN BÁTHORY.

Maximilian, 1832–67, emperor of Mexico (1864–67). An Austrian archduke, he was escorted (1864) to MEXICO by French soldiers to establish an empire for NAPOLEON III, but the Mexicans were hostile to him and loyal to Pres. JUÁREZ. Although the French drove Juárez's army from the capital, the empire disintegrated when French troops withdrew (1866–67). Maximilian's wife, Carlotta (1840–1927), went to Europe seeking help from Napoleon III. Her pleas were in vain, and Maximilian was captured and executed.

Maxwell, James Clerk, 1831–79, Scottish physicist. In 1871 he became the first professor of experimental physics at Cambridge, where he organized the Cavendish Laboratory. Maxwell's notable work in ELECTRICITY and MAGNETISM was summarized in his *A Treatise on Electricity and Magnetism* (1873). He developed the theory of the electromagnetic field on a mathematical basis and concluded that electric and magnetic energy travel in transverse waves that propagate at a speed equal to that of light; light is thus only one type of ELECTROMAGNETIC RADIATION. Maxwell's theoretical study (1859) of Saturn's rings foreshadowed his later investigations of heat and the kinetic theory of gases.

Maxwell, Robert, 1923–91, British businessman; b. Czechoslovakia as Jan Ludwik Hoch. Fleeing the Nazis (1939), he settled in England, purchased (1951) Pergamon Press, and served (1964–70) in Parliament. In the 1980s he created a diversified media empire, anchored by the Mirror Newspaper Group. After his mysterious drowning, he was found to have bankrupted his companies and looted their pension plans in an attempt to prop up his debt-ridden businesses.

Maxwell, William (Keepers, Jr.), 1908–, American novelist; b. Lincoln, Ill. Handling traditional themes, e.g., growing up, the impact of death, he writes of Midwesterners in the early 20th cent. His novels include *They Came Like Swallows* (1937), *Time Will Darken It* (1948), *So Long, See You Tomorrow* (1980), and *The Outermost Dream* (1989).

May: see MONTH.

Maya, related tribes of CENTRAL AMERICA (see MIDDLE AMERICA, INDIGENOUS PEOPLES OF) occupying the YUCATÁN and E Chiapas in Mexico, much of Guatemala and Belize, and W Honduras, and speaking Mayan languages (see NATIVE AMERICAN LANGUAGES). They may derive from the OLMEC, or they may have originated c.1000 B.C. among nomadic tribes in N central Petén, Guatemala, where there are evidences of a once-flourishing agricultural people. Among indigenous American cultures the Maya emerge as undisputed masters of abstract knowledge, with a system of hieroglyphic writing that they used to record political and dynastic history. Their system of mathematics was an achievement not equaled for centuries in Europe. The 365-day Mayan year was so divided as to be more accurate than that of the Gregorian CALENDAR. Sculpture, used in architecture, reached a beauty and dignity unequaled in aboriginal America. Most of the population, estimated at 14 million in the 8th cent., lived in suburban agricultural communities. Mayan history is divided into three periods. From early in the Pre-Classic period (1500 B.C.?–A.D. 300), corn was cultivated. Late in that period the calendar, chronology, and hieroglyphic writing developed. In the Early Classic (300–600), Mayan culture spread throughout the area. The greatest Mayan accomplishments in art and science occurred in the Late Classic (600–900) at such centers as Copán, Honduras; Palenque, in Chiapas; and UXMAL, in the Yucatán, all abandoned in the following century. At the beginning of the Post-Classic period (900–1697) an invasion by Kulkulcán (see QUETZALCOATL), who conquered CHICHÉN ITZÁ, brought TOLTEC elements into Mayan culture. The Toltec took Chichén Itzá, but were absorbed c.1200 by the Maya. In 1283 Mayapán became the civil capital. The century preceding the Spanish conquest (1546) was dominated by civil wars and a series of calamities. Today some 4 million Maya retain many elements of their culture combined with that of the CONQUISTADORS. Numerous Mayan-derived dialects are spoken, and agriculture and religious practices owe much to Mayan tradition. A 1994 uprising in Chiapas, Mexico, drew most of its strength from the support of Mayan peasants.

Mayakovsky, Vladimir Vladimirovich [mī"əkôf'skē], 1893–1930, Russian poet and dramatist. *A Cloud in Trousers* (1915), a poem written almost entirely in metaphors, typifies his early style. With the drama *Mystery-Bouffe* (1918) he welcomed the RUSSIAN REVOLUTION (1917), but his satirical plays *The Bedbug* (1928) and *The Bathhouse* (1929) express the disillusionment with Soviet life that contributed to his suicide.

May Day, first day of May. Its celebration probably originated in the spring fertility festivals of India and Egypt. The festival of Flora, Roman goddess of spring, ran from Apr. 28 to May 3. In medieval England, May Day's chief feature was the Maypole, which dancers circled. The Second Socialist International designated (1889) May Day as the holiday for radical labor; it was an important holiday in the USSR.

Mayer, Julius Robert von, 1814–78, German physician and physicist. From a consideration of the generation of animal heat, he was led to determine the relationship between HEAT and WORK. As a result he announced (1842), independently of James JOULE, the mechanical equivalence of heat, a result of the law of conservation of ENERGY.

Mayer, Louis B(urt), 1885–1957, American movie producer; b. Russia. Mayer began his career as a theater operator in Haverhill, Mass. In 1924 he merged his Louis B. Mayer Corp. with Metro Pictures Corp., which he had organized, and eventually with Goldwyn Pictures Corp. to form Metro-Goldwyn-Mayer. One of the most powerful film tycoons in early Hollywood, he was known for his strict paternalistic management of his studio and stars.

Mayflower, ship that in 1620 brought the PILGRIMS from England to New England. Under Capt. Christopher Jones, she sailed from Southampton on Sept. 16, sighted land (Cape Cod) on Nov. 19, and landed at Plymouth on Dec. 26. Before disembarking, the colonists drew up the **Mayflower Compact,** an agreement providing for the temporary government of the colony by the will of the majority.

mayflower, in botany: see TRAILING ARBUTUS.

Mayo, Charles Horace, 1865–1939, b. Rochester, Minn., and his brother, **William James Mayo,** 1861–1939, b. Le Sueur, Minn., American surgeons, specializing, respectively, in goiter and cataract operations and in abdominal surgery. From a small clinic in Rochester opened by their father, William Worrall Mayo, the brothers developed the internationally known **Mayo Clinic.** In 1915 they established the Mayo Foundation for Medical Education and Research as a branch of the graduate school of the Univ. of Minnesota.

Mayotte, island (1991 pop. 94,410), 144 sq mi (374 sq km), French territorial collectivity, Indian Ocean, in the Comoro chain. Dzaoudzi is the capital. It exports seafood, perfume oils, vanilla, coffee, and copra. When the largely Muslim COMOROS republic became independent (1975), Mayotte, mostly Roman Catholic, decided to remain French.

Mayr, Ernst, 1904–, American zoologist, b. Germany. He emigrated to the U.S. in 1932. In 1940 he proposed that *species* be defined as "groups of actually or potentially interbreeding natural populations which are reproductively isolated from other such groups." With T. DOBZHANSKY and G.G. SIMPSON, he helped formulate the *synthetic theory* of EVOLUTION, combining DARWIN's theory with the genetic principles of Gregor MENDEL.

Mays, Willie (Howard, Jr.), 1931–, American baseball player; b. Fairfield, Ala. An outfielder (1951–72) with the New York (later, San Francisco) Giants, he hit 660 home runs (third-highest total on record) and led the National League in home runs four times. He was twice voted (1954, 1965) most valuable player. In his last season (1973) Mays sparked the New York Mets to the pennant.

Mazarin, Jules [mäzäräN'], 1602–61, French statesman. An Italian, born Giulio Mazarini, he was a papal nuncio to France (1634–36) and entered French service under Cardinal RICHELIEU. Although never ordained a priest, Mazarin was made a Roman Catholic cardinal. After the death (1643) of LOUIS XIII, he was the chief minister of the regent, ANNE OF AUSTRIA, to whom he may have been secretly married. He gained favorable terms at the Peace of WESTPHALIA (1648), but his centralizing policy in France provoked the uprisings of the FRONDE. In 1659 he ended the war with Spain by negotiating the Peace of the Pyrenees.

Mazarin Bible, considered the first important work printed by Johann GUTENBERG and the earliest European book printed from movable type. It was completed at Mainz, Germany, not later than 1455. The text was in Latin, in a Gothic type related to Old English, illuminated by hand, on vellum and paper. The first copy to recapture attention was in the library of Cardinal MAZARIN. The book is popularly known as the Gutenberg Bible.

Mazepa, Ivan, c.1640–1709, hetman [leader] of the COSSACKS in the Russian UKRAINE. He tried to maintain Ukrainian autonomy, but the demands of PETER I threatened it. When war began between Russia and Sweden (1700) he secretly contacted pro-Swedish elements in Poland. In 1708 he openly joined CHARLES XII when the Swedes entered Ukraine, but few Cossacks followed him. After the Swedish defeat (1709) Mazepa fled Ukraine.

Mazzini, Giuseppe [mät-sē'nē], 1805–72, Italian patriot and revolutionist, a leading figure in the RISORGIMENTO. A proponent of Italian unity under a republican government, he wrote revolutionary propaganda from exile, chiefly in London after 1837. He believed that unity should be achieved by revolution and war based on direct popular action. His influence on Italian liberals was enormous, and his literary style is remarkably fine. He returned to Italy during the REVOLUTIONS OF 1848 and took part in the Roman republic of 1849. He organized unsuccessful uprisings in Milan (1853) and in S Italy (1857). He supported GARIBALDI's expedition to Sicily (1860) but, unlike Garibaldi, he remained a republican.

Mazzola, Francesco: see PARMIGIANO.

Mbabane [əmbäbä'nā], town (1986 pop. 38,290), administrative capital of Swaziland, in the Mdimba Mts. The city serves as the commercial hub for an agricultural region.

Mboya, Thomas Joseph [mboi'ə], 1930–69, Kenyan political leader. After KENYA gained (1963) its independence, he held a number of high posts. He was widely regarded as a likely successor to Jomo KENYATTA, but he was assassinated in 1969.

Thomas Mboya

Mc-. Names beginning thus are entered as if spelled Mac-. See MAC.

Md, chemical symbol of the element MENDELEVIUM.

Mead, George Herbert, 1863–1931, American philosopher and psychologist; b. South Hadley, Mass. Mead's philosophy, social behaviorism, was related to that of John DEWEY. It placed great importance on the role of language and conduct. Mead's works include *The Philosophy of the Present* (1932) and *Mind, Self, and Society* (1934).

Mead, Margaret, 1901–78, American anthropologist; b. Philadelphia. A student of Franz BOAS and Ruth BENEDICT, she won world fame through studies of child-rearing, personality, and culture. Her primary field work was among peoples of OCEANIA. Affiliated with the American Museum of Natural History from 1926 until her death, after 1954 she was also adjunct professor of anthropology at Columbia Univ. Some of her widely read books are *Coming of Age in Samoa* (1928), *Growing Up in New Guinea* (1930), *Male and Female* (1949), *Culture and Commitment* (1970), and the autobiographical *Blackberry Winter* (1972).

Mead, Lake, reservoir, 247 sq mi (640 sq km), on the Colorado R. in Arizona and Nevada, the largest in the U.S., chief feature of **Lake Mead National Recreation Area.** Impounded by HOOVER DAM, it is 115 mi (185 km) long, 1–8 mi (1.6–12.9 km) wide, and up to 589 ft (180 m) deep, and has a shoreline of 550 mi (885 km).

Meade, George Gordon, 1815–72, Union general in the U.S. CIVIL WAR; b. Spain. He distinguished himself in 1862 at the SEVEN DAYS BATTLES, BULL RUN, and ANTIETAM, and later at FREDERICKSBURG and CHANCELLORSVILLE. In command of the Army of the Potomac from 1863, he won the important battle of GETTYSBURG, although he was criticized for not following up his victory.

Meade, James Edward, 1907–, British economist. An expert on theories of international trade, he taught (1947–57) at the London School of Economics and later at Cambridge Univ. For his work in the early 1950s on foreign-trade and balance-of-payments problems, he was a co-recipient, with Bertil OHLIN, of the 1977 Nobel Prize in economics.

meadowlark, North American meadow BIRD of the family Icteridae, which includes the BLACKBIRD, ORIOLE, and COWBIRD. Unlike other members of the family, the meadowlark (also called meadow starling) does not travel in flocks, and eats harmful insects rather than grain. The eastern species, *Sturnella magna,* is known for its clear, whistling song. It is c.10 in. (25 cm) long and has black-streaked brown coloring above and yellow below.

meadow saffron or **autumn crocus,** perennial garden ornamental (*Colchicum autumnale*) of the LILY family, native to Europe and N Africa and now naturalized in the U.S. Its poisonous corms and seeds yield the drug colchicine. The purplish fall flowers resemble those of the unrelated true CROCUS and true SAFFRON (of the IRIS family).

Meany, George, 1894–1980, American labor leader, president (1955–79) of the AMERICAN FEDERATION OF LABOR AND CONGRESS OF INDUSTRIAL ORGANIZATIONS; b. N.Y.C. A plumber, he rose in 1934 to the presidency of the New York State Federation of Labor. Elected secretary-treasurer of the AFL in 1939, he held that post until becoming president in 1952. When the AFL and CIO merged in 1955, he was elected head of the new federation. Angered by Democratic party reforms in 1972, he support neither of the major presidential candidates, a decision that contributed to Pres. Richard Nixon's landslide victory. Meany broke with Nixon, however, and was an early advocate of his removal from office. A supporter of Jimmy Carter in the 1976 election, Meany later denounced Pres. Carter's economic policies.

measles or **rubeola,** highly contagious viral disease spread by droplet spray from the mouth, nose, and throat during the infectious stage (beginning two to four days before the rash appears and lasting two to five days thereafter). Early symptoms (fever, redness of eyes) are followed by characteristic white spots in the mouth and a facial rash that spreads to the rest of the body. Although one attack confers lifelong immunity, immunization is advisable because of the possibility of serious secondary infection. See also RUBELLA.

Mecca, city (1990 est. pop. 689,000), W Saudi Arabia. The birthplace A.D. c.570 of MUHAMMAD, it is the holiest city of ISLAM, and non-Muslims may not enter Mecca. It developed as a caravan city about two centuries before Muhammad's birth. It was an ancient center of commerce. Muhammad's flight (the hegira) from Mecca in 622 is the beginning of the Muslim era. Mecca was taken by the Ottoman Turks in 1517 and fell to IBN SAUD in 1924. At the city's center is the Great Mosque, the Haram, which encloses the KAABA, the most sacred Islamic sanctuary and the goal of Muslim pilgrimage. The commerce of the city depends almost wholly on the nearly 2 million pilgrims each year. In 1979 Muslim fundamentalists seized the Great Mosque; the government retook it by force after a two-week siege.

mechanics, branch of PHYSICS concerned with MOTION and the FORCES causing it. The field includes the study of the mechanical properties of matter, such as DENSITY, elasticity (see STRENGTH OF MATERIALS), and VISCOSITY. Mechanics is divided into STATICS, which deals with bodies at rest or in equilibrium, and DYNAMICS, which deals with bodies in motion. Isaac NEWTON, who derived three laws of motion and the law of universal GRAVITATION, was the founder of modern mechanics. For bodies moving at speeds close to that of light, Newtonian mechanics is superseded by the theory of RELATIVITY, and for the study of very small objects, such as ELEMENTARY PARTICLES, QUANTUM MECHANICS is used.

Mecklenburg Declaration of Independence, document, widely regarded as spurious, alleged to have been adopted at Charlotte, N.C., by the citizens of Mecklenburg co. on May 20, 1775. The anti-British resolutions actually adopted (May 31, 1775) imply, but do not declare, independence.

Medan [mādän'], city (1990 pop. 1,730,752), capital of North Sumatra prov., Indonesia, 15 miles (25 km) from the mouth of the Deli R., site of its port. The largest city in SUMATRA, it is the marketing, commercial, and transportation center of a rich agricultural area with great tobacco, rubber, and palm oil estates. Manufactures include machinery and tile.

Medawar, Peter Brian, 1915–87, British zoologist; b. Brazil. During World War II he developed a method for joining the ends of severed nerves; later he did experimental work in transplanting living tissue from one body to another. Working on a theory of Sir Macfarlane BURNET, he proved that under certain circumstances an organism can overcome its normal tendency to reject foreign tissue or organs. For this work he and Burnet shared the 1960 Nobel Prize in physiology or medicine.

Medea, in Greek mythology, princess of Colchis; famed for her skill in sorcery. She fell in love with JASON and helped him obtain the GOLDEN FLEECE. After marrying Jason she returned with him to Iolcus and bore him two children. Years later, when Jason wished to marry Creusa, the vengeful Medea sent her an enchanted gown, which burned her to death. Then she killed her own children. Her story was dramatized by EURIPIDES.

Medellín, city (1985 pop. 1,480,382), capital of Antioquia dept., W central Colombia. Virtually isolated in its remote mountain valley until the mid-19th cent., it is now one of Colombia's chief cities and manufacturing centers. Its leading products include textiles, steel, food products, and automobiles. Coal, gold, and silver are mined in the surrounding region. Medellín has three universities and a world-famous orchid garden. In the 1980s and early 90s the city was notorious as the headquarters of a "cartel" of cocaine traffickers.

Media, ancient country of W Asia, in a region now in W Iran and S Azerbaijan. Its inhabitants were the Medes, an Indo-European people, who extended their rule over PERSIA in the reign of Sargon (d. 705 B.C.) and captured NINEVEH in 612 B.C. Their capital was Ecbatana. Media was forcibly annexed (c.550 B.C.) to Persia by CYRUS THE GREAT.

mediation, labor: see under COLLECTIVE BARGAINING.

Medicaid: see HEALTH INSURANCE.

Medicare: see HEALTH INSURANCE.

Medici [mĕ'dĭchē], Italian family that directed the destinies of Florence from the 15th cent. until 1737. Of obscure origin, they gained immense wealth as merchants and bankers, became affiliated through marriage to the major houses of Europe, and produced three popes (LEO X, CLEMENT VII, and Leo XI) and two queens of France (CATHERINE DE' MEDICI and MARIE DE' MEDICI). Until 1532 the democratic constitution of Florence was outwardly upheld, but the Medici exerted actual control over the government without holding any permanent official position. They were exiled from Florence in 1433–34, 1494–1512, and 1527–30. Through their patronage of the arts they helped to make the city a great repository of European culture. The first important member of the family was **Giovanni di Bicci de' Medici,** 1360–1429, whose sons founded the two branches of the family.

Senior Line. His elder son, **Cosimo de' Medici** (Cosimo the Elder), 1389–1464, was the first Medici to rule Florence. Exiled from Florence in 1433, he returned in 1434 and doubled his wealth through banking. He ended Florence's traditional alliance with Venice and supported the SFORZA family in Milan. His chief fame is as a patron to such artists as BRUNELLESCHI, DONATELLO, and GHIBERTI, and as the founder of the Medici Library. He was succeeded as head of the family by his son, **Piero de' Medici,** 1416–69, nicknamed Il Gottoso [the gouty] because of ill health. In 1466 Piero put down a conspiracy against him by the Pitti family. His son and successor, **Lorenzo de' Medici** (Lorenzo the Magnificent), 1449–92, was one of the towering figures of the Italian RENAISSANCE. He had little success in business, however, and his lavish entertainments depleted his funds. In 1478 Pope SIXTUS IV helped to foment the Pazzi conspiracy against him. Lorenzo's brother Giuliano was murdered, but Lorenzo escaped with only a wound, and the plot collapsed. In spite of the attacks of Girolamo SAVONAROLA, Lorenzo allowed him to continue preaching. Lorenzo was a patron of BOTTICELLI and MICHELANGELO. His second son later became pope as Leo X. His successor was his eldest son, **Piero de' Medici,** 1471–1503. Piero was driven (1494) from Florence by the democratic party led by Savonarola during the invasion of Italy by CHARLES VIII of France. Piero's brother, **Giuliano de' Medici,** 1479–1516, duke of Nemours (1515–16), entered Florence in 1512 when the HOLY LEAGUE restored the Medici as rulers. After his death, control over Florence was exercised by Pope Leo X through Piero's son **Lorenzo de' Medici,** 1492–1519, duke of Urbino (1516). Lorenzo was the father of Catherine de' Medici. Giuliano's and Lorenzo's statues by Michelangelo adorn their tombs in the Church of San Lorenzo in Florence. After 1523 Pope Clement VII headed the Medici family and controlled Florence through **Ippolito de' Medici,** 1511–35, Giuliano's illegitimate son, and **Alessandro de' Medici,** 1510?–37, probably the illegitimate son of Lorenzo de' Medici (d. 1519). The Medici were banished (1527) from Florence as a result of the invasion of Italy by Holy Roman Emperor CHARLES V, but Pope Clement restored them to power in 1530. Clement soon favored Alessandro, who became head of the republic (1531) and hereditary duke (1532). In 1535 Ippolito was sent by the Florentines to present their grievances to the emperor, but he died on the way, possibly poisoned at Alessandro's command. Alessandro, who had married Margaret of Austria (see MARGARET OF PARMA), was assassinated by a relative, **Lorenzino de' Medici,** 1515–47, and the leadership of the family passed to Cosimo I de' Medici, of the younger branch.

Younger Line and Grand Dukes of Tuscany. This line descended from **Lorenzo de' Medici,** d. 1440, younger son of Giovanni di Bicci de' Medici. Lorenzo's great-grandson **Giovanni de' Medici,** 1498–1526, called Giovanni delle Bande Nere [of the black bands], was a famous condottiere. He fought for Pope Leo X in the ITALIAN WARS, but later changed sides and fought for FRANCIS I of France. His nickname probably derives from the black bands of mourning he put on his banners after Leo's death. His older son, **Cosimo I de' Medici,** 1519–74, succeeded Alessandro de' Medici as duke of Florence in 1537. He acquired (1555) SIENA and was made (1569) grand duke of Tuscany. His son, **Francesco de' Medici,** 1541–87, grand duke 1574–87, devoted himself to alchemy and allowed the HAPSBURGS of Spain and Austria to establish a virtual protectorate over his kingdom. He was the father of Marie de' Medici. His brother, **Ferdinand I de' Medici,** 1549–1609, grand duke 1587–1609, built the famous Villa Medici at Rome and created a free port at Leghorn. His son, **Cosimo II de' Medici,** 1590–1621, grand duke 1609–21, was a patron of GALILEO. Cosimo's grandson, **Cosimo III de' Medici,** 1642–1723, grand duke 1670–1723, headed a corrupt and bigoted regime. His son, **Gian Gastone de' Medici,** 1671–1737, grand duke 1723–37, was the last male member of the family. He ruled a Tuscany that had fallen from glory into decadence and impoverishment. In 1735 his succession was settled on Francis of Lorraine (later Holy Roman Emperor FRANCIS I).

Medici, Giovanni de', 1475–1521: see LEO X.

Medici, Giulio de': see CLEMENT VII.

medicine, science and art of diagnosing, treating, and preventing disease. For centuries its treatment was coupled with magic and superstition. The more scientific practice of medicine, however, began in ancient Asian civilizations. In Sumer, the Laws of HAMMURABI established the first known code of medical ethics. In China, the ancient practice of ACUPUNCTURE and ideas about the circulation of blood presuppose familiarity with anatomy, vascular systems, and the nervous system. The Greeks advanced medical knowledge in anatomy and physiology, diet, exercise, and other areas, and provided the Hippocratic oath, still used today (see HIPPOCRATES). The Romans improved public health through their sophisticated sanitation facilities, and GALEN provided a final synthesis of the medicine of the ancient world. After a period of decline during the Middle Ages, when medical knowledge was kept alive mainly by Arab and Jewish physicians, VESALIUS proved that there were errors in Galen's work and again opened medicine to discovery. In the 17th cent., William HARVEY demonstrated the circulation of blood and the role of the heart as a pump. With the introduction of the compound microscope, minute forms of life were discovered and a major step was made toward diagnosing disease. In the 18th cent., Edward JENNER introduced the concept of VACCINATION, and surgery was transformed into an experimental science. The beginnings of modern medicine date from the 19th cent., with the development of the germ theory of disease; the use of antiseptics and ANESTHESIA in surgery; and a revival of public-health measures and better sanitation. Medicine in the 20th cent. has been characterized by an increased understanding of IMMUNITY, the ENDOCRINE SYSTEM, and the importance of VITAMINS and nutrition; advances in SURGERY, organ TRANSPLANTATION, and diagnostic techniques (see X RAY; CAT SCAN; ULTRASOUND; MAGNETIC RESONANCE); the use of DRUGS, especially ANTIBIOTICS; and the development of GENE THERAPY. Advances have also been notable in the treatment of mental illness through both PSYCHOTHERAPY and the administration of drugs (see ANTIDEPRESSANTS; PSYCHIATRY). With growing specialization and complex diagnostic and therapeutic technology, modern medicine faces problems in the allocation of both personnel and capital. The cost of medical care in the U.S. has been financed by various forms of private coverage (see HEALTH INSURANCE; HEALTH MAINTENANCE ORGANIZATION; MANAGED HEALTH CARE) and government programs (e.g., Medicare for those over age 65, Medicaid for the poor, and public vaccination programs). The great rise in health care costs in recent years has led to reevaluation of the current system and consideration of a nationwide health insurance plan.

Medina, city (1990 est. pop. 500,000), W Saudi Arabia. It is situated in an oasis c.110 mi (180 km) inland from the Red Sea. Before the flight (the hegira) of MUHAMMAD from MECCA to Medina, the city was called Yathrib. Muhammad used it as a base for converting and conquering Arabia. It came under the sway of the Ottoman Turks in 1517. In 1924 it fell to IBN SAUD. Medina's large mosque contains the tombs of Muhammad and his daughter Fatima.

meditation, religious discipline in which the mind is focused on a single point of reference. It may be a means of invoking divine GRACE, as in the contemplation by Christian mystics of a spiritual theme, question, or problem; or it may be a means of attaining conscious union with the divine, e.g., through visualization of a deity or inward repetition of a prayer or MANTRA (sacred sound). Employed since ancient times in various forms by all religions, the practice gained greater notice in the postwar U.S. as interest in ZEN BUDDHISM rose. In the 1960s and 70s the Indian Maharishi Mahesh Yogi popularized a mantra system called Transcendental Meditation (TM). Meditation is now used by many nonreligious adherents as a method of stress reduction; it is known to lessen levels of cortisol, a hormone released in response to stress. The practice has been shown to enhance recuperation and improve the body's resistance to disease.

Mediterranean fruit fly: see FRUIT FLY.

Mediterranean Sea, strategically important sea between Europe, Africa, and Asia, c.965,000 sq mi (2,499,350 sq km), opening to the Atlantic Ocean through the Strait of GIBRALTAR; to the BLACK SEA through the DARDANELLES, the Sea of Marmara, and the BOSPORUS; and to the RED SEA through the SUEZ CANAL. It is c.2,400 mi (3,900 km) long, up to 1,000 mi (1,600 km) wide, and reaches a maximum depth of c.14,450 ft (4,400 m) off Greece. The sea has little variation in tides. It was the focus of Western civilization from earliest times (see AEGEAN CIVILIZATION) until the 15th cent. when open-ocean shipping around Africa became common. It was revitalized as a trade route in 1869 by the opening of the Suez Canal and since then by its proximity to Middle East and North African oil fields.

Medusa: see GORGON.

medusa, in zoology: see POLYP AND MEDUSA.

meerschaum or **sepiolite,** hydrous magnesium silicate mineral ideally, $Mg_8(H_2O)_4(OH)_4Si_{12}O_{30}$ resembling white clay. It is found in many parts of the world and is used primarily to make pipes and cigar and cigarette holders. Meerschaum pipes, often carved into ornate forms, become dark brown with use.

megalithic monuments, ancient structures of one or more huge stone slabs, mostly in W Europe and the British Isles, dating 2000–1500 B.C. Slabs may be 65 ft (20 m) long and weigh 100 tons. Erected singly, in rows, or in a circle (see STONEHENGE), they probably served religious or funerary purposes. A dolmen, or chamber tomb, was usually covered to form a BARROW.

Megiddo [məgĭd'ō], ancient city, Palestine, on the S edge of the plain of Esdraelon. Inhabited since the 4th millennium B.C., it has been the scene of many battles throughout history, from the victory of THUTMOSE III (c.1468 B.C.) to that of Gen. Edmund ALLENBY in World War I. The plain is called the valley of **Megiddon** in the Bible.

Mehemet. For persons thus named, see MUHAMMAD.

Mehta, Zubin [mā'tə], 1936–, Indian-American conductor; b. Bombay. A flamboyant stylist, he specializes in late romantic and early modern music. After conducting in Montreal and Los Angeles, he was music director of the New York Philharmonic (see ORCHESTRA, table) from 1978 to 1991. He has also been music director of the Israel Philharmonic since 1968.

Meier, Richard (Alan), 1934–, American architect. He was one of the New York "Five" or "white" architects, whose design vocabulary recalls LE CORBUSIER and the modernism of the 1920s. Meier is noted for his country houses, which are often built in dramatic natural settings. At the High Museum (1983) in Atlanta, he has successfully adapted his characteristic design idiom to a public building.

Meiji [mā'jē], 1852–1912, reign name of the emperor of Japan (1867–1912). His given name was Mutsuhito. Just after his accession a revolution called the **Meiji restoration** occurred (1868). The TOKUGAWA shogunate, a military dictatorship that controlled Japan, had declined, and opposition to it had grown. Some daimyo, or barons, disgruntled by foreign intrusions, demanded the creation of a new government and favored using Western armaments to expel the foreigners. In 1867 the shogun finally surrendered to the emperor, and subsequent rebellions were put down. The restoration caused the downfall of feudalism, and a centralized administration was set up. The court was moved from Kyoto to Tokyo, and the emperor entrusted (1868) government to Westernizers such as Shigenobu OKUMA. Soon after a new constitution was adopted (1889), Japan emerged as a modern industrial state.

Meinecke, Friedrich [mī'nĕkə], 1862–1954, German historian. A nationalist and a liberal, he believed that the state must serve cultural needs and promote individualism. His works include *Machiavellism* (1924) and *The German Catastrophe* (1946).

meiosis, process of nuclear division in a cell by which the CHROMOSOMES (genetic material) are reduced to half their original number. Meiosis occurs only during formation of germ cells (OVUM and SPERM). An ordinary body cell contains two of each type of chromosome (diploid). Meiosis produces cells with one chromosome of each pair (haploid). In FERTILIZATION, two haploid cells are united; the resulting zygote then contains a diploid number of chromosomes.

Meir, Golda [māēr'], 1898–1978, Israeli prime minister (1969–74); b. Russia as Golda Mabovitch. After a teaching career in the U.S., she settled in Palestine (1921), where she became active in the labor movement and later served as Israel's minister of labor (1949–56) and of foreign affairs (1956–66). As prime minister she sought peace for Israel and resigned in 1974 after she and Moshe DAYAN were criticized for the country's lack of preparation for the 1973 ARAB-ISRAELI WAR.

meistersinger [Ger., = mastersinger], member of a 15th–16th-cent. German musical and poetical guild. Candidates for the rank of *Meister* were judged in public contests. Richard WAGNER's opera *Die Meistersinger von Nürnberg* faithfully represents guild practices.

Meitner, Lise [mīt'nər], 1878–1968, Austrian-Swedish physicist and mathematician. She discovered the PROTACTINIUM-231 isotope and investigated the disintegration products of radium, thorium, and actinium and the behavior of beta rays (see RADIOACTIVITY). Her conclusion, from experimental research in bombarding the uranium nucleus with slow-speed neutrons, that fission of the nucleus had occurred, contributed to the development of the ATOMIC BOMB.

meitnerium (Mt), artificial radioactive TRANSURANIUM ELEMENT. Report of its production was made by a West German group at Darmstadt, who in 1982 bombarded bismuth with iron ions to obtain the Mt^{267} isotope. It is also called unnilennium (Une). See ELEMENT (table); PERIODIC TABLE.

Meknès [mĕknĕs'], city (1990 est. pop. 750,000), N central Morocco. It has a noted carpet-weaving industry as well as woolen mills, cement and metal works, oil distilleries, and food-processing plants. Meknès was founded c.1672 by Sultan Ismail, who built many palatial buildings, of which little survives. A European town is laid out beside the old one.

Mekong, one of the great rivers of Southeast Asia, c.2,600 mi (4,180 km) long. It rises as the Za Qu in Tibet and flows generally south through SW China, then circuitously across or along the borders of Myanmar, Laos, Thailand, and Cambodia. It enters the SOUTH CHINA SEA through several mouths across a vast, fertile delta (c.75,000 sq mi/194,250 sq km) near HO CHI MINH CITY (Saigon), in S Vietnam. Its densely populated lower valley, in Cambodia and Vietnam, is one of the world's great rice-growing regions. PHNOM PENH is a major port.

Melanchthon, Philip [məlăngk'thən], 1497–1560, German scholar, humanist, and religious reformer. His name is the Greek rendering of the German Schwarzerd [black earth]. A man of great intellect and wide learning, he was professor of Greek at the Univ. of Wittenberg when he met Martin LUTHER, and they soon became associates. His *Loci communes* (1521) was the first systematic presentation of the principles of the REFORMATION and clarified the new gospel to those outside the movement. A mediator between Luther and the humanists, he also represented him at many conferences and wrote the Augsburg Confession (1530). Melanchthon was more conciliatory than Luther, as evidenced by his friendship with John CALVIN and his willingness to compromise on doctrinal issues. For his role in creating the German schools, he is known as preceptor of Germany.

Melanesia, one of the three main divisions of OCEANIA, in the SW Pacific Ocean, NE of Australia and S of the equator. It includes the SOLOMON ISLANDS, VANUATU, TUVALU, NEW CALEDONIA, the Bismarck Archipelago, FIJI, and the Admiralty Islands. The Melanesians are largely of Australoid stock and speak languages of Malayo-Polynesian origin.

Melbourne, William Lamb, 2d **Viscount,** 1779–1848, British statesman, prime minister (1834, 1835–39, 1839–41). A Whig with aristocratic views, he conceded reforms such as the Poor Law (1834) and the Municipal Corporations Act (1835), but resisted more radical demands. A favorite of the young Queen VICTORIA, he taught her important lessons in statecraft. His wife, **Lady Caroline Lamb,** 1785–1828, wrote several minor novels, but is best known for her love affair with Lord BYRON.

Melbourne, city (1991 est. pop. 3,153,500), capital of Victoria, SE Australia, on Port Phillip Bay, at the mouth of the Yarra R. Australia's second largest city, it is a commercial and industrial center with such manufactures as ships, automobiles, farm machinery, textiles, and electrical equipment. The city was settled in 1835 and named (1837) for the British prime minister, Lord MELBOURNE. It was the seat of the Australian federal government (1901–27). The population, once primarily British, has changed since World War II with immigration from E and S Europe. Melbourne was the site of the 1956 Olympic games. The Melbourne Cup Race is run annually.

Melchior: see WISE MEN OF THE EAST.

Melchior, Lauritz [mĕl'kēôr], 1890–1973, Danish heroic tenor. A great singer and actor, he was (1926–50) the leading Wagnerian tenor (see WAGNER, RICHARD) at the METROPOLITAN OPERA.

Meleager [mĕlēā'jər], hero of Greek mythology. At his birth a prophecy said that he would die when a certain log in the fire burned. His mother hid the log, and Meleager grew to be a famous warrior. When ARTEMIS sent a huge boar to ravage his land, Meleager led a band of heroes, including CASTOR AND POLLUX, THESEUS, and JASON, in the Calydonian hunt, and killed the boar. Meleager gave its pelt to the huntress ATALANTA, and when his uncles tried to take it he killed them. In revenge his mother burned the hidden log, and Meleager died.

Melilla [mālē'lyä], city (1991 pop. 56,600), Spanish possession, on the Mediterranean coast of Morocco, NW Africa. It is a fishing port and an export point for iron ore. Held by Spain since 1496, it was the site of the revolt that began (1936) the SPANISH CIVIL WAR.

Mellon, Andrew William, 1855–1937, American financier, industrialist, and public official; b. Pittsburgh. With his brother, Richard, he took over (1886) his father's banking firm and later established other banks. He expanded his holdings in key American industries, such as oil, locomotives, coal, hydroelectricity, bridge-building, public utilities, steel, and insurance, and played a key role in founding the huge Aluminum Co. of America. In 1921 he resigned as president of the Mellon National Bank to become U.S. secretary of the Treasury, serving until 1931, under three presidents. He was also (1931–32) ambassador to Great Britain. In 1937 he donated his art collection to the public, with funds for constructing the NATIONAL GALLERY OF ART (Wash., D.C.).

melodrama [Gr., = song-drama], originally a spoken text with musical background, as in Greek drama. Popular in the 18th cent., it was varied to include drama interspersed with music, e.g., *The Beggar's Opera* by John GAY. ROUSSEAU's *Pygmalion* (1762) helped create a vogue for romantic nonmusical plays often ending in the triumph of virtue. The term now applies to all plays with overdrawn characterizations, smashing climaxes, and sentimental appeal, including such "tearjerkers" as Mrs. Henry Wood's *East Lynne.* True musical melodrama has been written in the 20th cent. by such composers as SCHOENBERG and Richard STRAUSS.

melon, fruit of *Cucumis melo,* a plant of the GOURD family, native to Asia but now widely cultivated in warm regions. Many varieties exist, differing in taste, color, and skin texture—e.g., Persian, honeydew, casaba, muskmelon, and cantaloupe. The true cantaloupe (var. *cantalupensis*) is a hard-shelled melon grown in Mediterranean countries; cantaloupes of the U.S. are varieties of the muskmelon.

melting point, temperature at which a substance changes its state from solid to liquid (see STATES OF MATTER). Under standard atmospheric pressure, different pure crystalline solids will each melt at a different specific temperature; thus melting point is a characteristic of a substance and can be used to identify it. The quantity of heat necessary to change 1 gram of any substance from solid to liquid at its melting point is known as its latent heat of fusion.

Melville, Andrew, 1545–1622, Scottish religious reformer and scholar. An academic, he became (1590) rector of St. Andrews and reorganized the Scottish universities. More importantly, as successor to John KNOX, he was largely responsible for the introduction of a presbyterian system into the Scottish church. A foe of prelacy and royal supremacy, he struggled to assert church independence.

Melville, Herman, 1819–91, one of the greatest American writers; b. N.Y.C. His experiences on a whaler (1841–42) and ashore in the Marquesas (where he was captured by cannibals) and other South Sea islands led to the writing of *Typee* (1846), *Omoo* (1847), and other widely popular romances. Melville's masterpiece, *Moby-Dick; or, The Whale* (1851), the tale of a whaling captain's obsessive search for the white whale that had ripped off his leg, is at once an exciting sea story, a heavily symbolic inquiry into good and evil, and one of the greatest novels ever written. Both *Moby-Dick* and the psychological novel *Pierre; or, The Ambiguities* (1852) were misunderstood at the time of their publication and badly received. Although disheartened by his failure to win an audience, by ill health, and by debts, Melville continued to produce such important works as *The Piazza Tales* (1856), a collection including the stories "Benito Cereno" and "Bartleby the Scrivener," *The Confidence Man* (1857), and the novella *Billy Budd, Foretopman* (1924). After holding the position of customs inspector in New York City for 19 years, Melville died in poverty and obscurity. Neglected for many years, his work was rediscovered c.1920.

Memling or **Memlinc, Hans,** c.1430–1494, Flemish religious and portrait painter; b. Germany. His religious works are rather bland, reflecting Roger van der WEYDEN's figure types without their intensity. They include the *Adoration of the Magi Triptych* and the *St. Ursula Shrine* panels (both: Bruges). Memling's portraits are more original, combining accuracy of representation with varied backgrounds of flowers and animals.

Memorial Day, U.S. holiday observed late in May. Formerly known as Decoration Day, it was instituted (1868) to honor the CIVIL WAR dead, but it now commemorates all war dead.

Memphis, ancient city of EGYPT, capital of the Old Kingdom (c.3100–c.2258 B.C.), at the apex of the NILE delta, 12 mi (18 km) from Cairo. The PYRAMIDS and other monuments are nearby. Memphis declined and fell into ruin under the Arabs.

Memphis, city (1990 pop. 610,337), seat of Shelby co., SW Tenn., on a bluff above the Mississippi R., at the mouth of the Wolf R.; est. (by Andrew JACKSON and others) 1819, inc. 1826. The largest city in the state, it is a major river port, rail center, and market for lumber, cotton, and livestock. Textiles, pianos, heating equipment, and motor vehicle parts are among its manufactures. Strategically important in the CIVIL WAR, it fell to Union forces in 1862. The city has numerous medical, educational, and cultural institutions, including the National Civil Rights Museum, located in the motel where Martin Luther KING, Jr., was assassinated. The site of the famous Beale St., Memphis is associated with such musicians as W.C. HANDY and Elvis PRESLEY. The Great American Pyramid, a 32-story glass-encased sports arena and museum complex built in 1991, dominates the city's riverfront.

Menam Chao Phraya: see CHAO PHRAYA.

Menander, 342?–291? B.C., Greek poet, most famous writer of New COMEDY. His ingenious plays, based on love plots, have highly developed characters. Through imitations by PLAUTUS and TERENCE he influenced 17th-cent. COMEDY.

Mencken, H(enry) L(ouis), 1880–1956, American author; b. Baltimore. He was a journalist, notably on Baltimore's *Sun* papers (1906–56). He and George Jean NATHAN edited the *Smart Set* (1914–23) and started (1924) the *American Mercury,* which Mencken alone edited (1925–33). His ascerbic critical essays, aimed mainly at the complacent bourgeoisie, were collected in *Prejudices* (6 vol., 1919–27). He also wrote many other critical and autobiographical works. In philology, he compiled the monumental *The American Language* (1919; 4th ed., 1936; supplements).

H.L. Mencken

Mendel, Gregor Johann, 1822–84, Austrian monk noted for his experimental work on heredity. At the Augustinian monastery in Brno (1843–68) he conducted experiments, chiefly on garden peas and involving a controlled pollination technique and a careful statistical analysis of his results, that produced the first accurate and scientific explanation for hybridization. His findings, published in 1866, were ignored during his lifetime, but were rediscovered by three separate investigators in 1900. Mendel's conclusions have become the basic tenets of GENETICS and a notable influence in plant and animal breeding. **Mendelism** is a system of heredity based on his conclusions. Briefly summarized, the Mendelian system states that an inherited characteristic is determined by the combination of two hereditary units (now called genes), one from each of the parental reproductive cells, or gametes.

Mendeleev, Dmitri Ivanovich [mĕndəlā'əf], 1834–1907, Russian chemist. He formulated (1869) the periodic law and invented the PERIODIC TABLE, a system of classifying the elements that allowed him to predict properties of then-unknown elements. He was a professor (1868–90) at the Univ. of St. Petersburg, a government adviser on the development of the petroleum industry, and the director of the bureau of weights and measures.

Mendele mocher sforim [mĕn'dələ mōkh'ər sfô'rĭm], pseud. of **Sholem Yakob Abramovich,** 1836–1917, Russian Yiddish novelist who also wrote in Hebrew. He is considered the father of modern Hebrew literature, and his Yiddish style was influential. His novels include *The Travels of Benjamin the Third* (1878).

mendelevium (Md), artificial radioactive element, detected in 1955 by A. Ghiorso and colleagues, who produced it one atom at a time by alpha-particle bombardment of einsteinium-253. Little is known about its properties. See ELEMENT (table); PERIODIC TABLE.

Mendelssohn, Felix, 1809–47, German composer, a major figure in 19th-cent. music; grandson of Moses MENDELSSOHN. A prodigy, he composed his first mature work, the Overture to *A Midsummer Night's Dream,* at 17. In 1829 he conducted a performance of the *St. Matthew Passion* that revived interest in J.S. BACH. Mendelssohn's music is characterized by emotional restraint, refinement, and sensitivity, and by adherence to classical forms. Of his five symphonies, the *Scottish* (1830–42), *Italian* (1833), and *Reformation* (1830–32) are best known. His Violin Concerto in E Minor (1844) is popular, as are his ORATORIOS and piano pieces.

Mendelssohn, Moses, 1729–86, German-Jewish philosopher, leader in the movement for cultural assimilation; grandfather of Felix MENDELSSOHN. He was a close friend of the playwright G.E. LESSING. His works on esthetics were highly regarded in his time.

Menelaus [mĕnəlā'əs], in Greek myth, king of SPARTA; husband of HELEN; brother of AGAMEMNON. When PARIS abducted Helen to Troy, Menelaus asked the Greek kings to join him in the TROJAN WAR. At its end he returned to Sparta with Helen.

Menelik II, 1844–1913, emperor of ETHIOPIA (1889–1913). In 1896 he crushed the Italian invasion at Aduwa, thereby establishing Ethiopian independence. His conquests greatly expanded the size of Ethiopia.

Menem, Carlos Saúl, 1930–, president of Argentina (1989–). A follower of PERÓN), he was a provincial governor (1973–76, 1983–89) before and after his imprisonment after the 1976 coup. As president, he addressed Argentina's economic crisis by reducing subsidies for the poor and stimulating the free market.

Mengistu Haile Mariam, 1937–, Ethiopian army officer and dictator (1977–91). He took a leading part in the 1974 coup that deposed Emperor HAILE SELASSIE and by 1977 had ruthlessly consolidated his power as dictator. He established close ties with the USSR and Cuba, which gave him military aid, and his regime undertook a Marxist program, including the nationalization of industry and collectivization of agriculture. His authoritarian, often brutal rule was plagued by uprisings in the northern provinces of ERITREA and Tigre, famine, and war with SOMALIA. Mengistu went into exile in 1991 as the army was overwhelmed by Eritrean and Tigrean rebels.

meningitis or **cerebrospinal meningitis,** acute inflammation of the membranes covering the BRAIN or spinal cord, or both. It can be caused by BACTERIA, a VIRUS, PROTOZOAN, YEAST, or FUNGUS, usually introduced from elsewhere in the body. Symptoms include fever, headache, vomiting, neck and back rigidity, delirium, and convulsions. Examination of the cerebrospinal fluid by means of a spinal tap permits a specific diagnosis. ANTIBIOTICS have reduced mortality and decreased the incidence of such complications as brain damage and paralysis. Infant VACCINATION for haemophilus influenzae type B (HIB), a bacterium that is the major cause of meningitis in children, is recommended.

Menninger, Karl Augustus [mĕn'ĭnjər], 1893–90, and **William Claire Menninger,** 1899–1966, American psychiatrists, brothers; b. Topeka, Kans. In 1920, Karl and his father, Charles Frederick (1862–1955), founded in Topeka the Menninger Clinic, conceived with the idea of collecting many specialists in one center. They were joined in 1926 by William. The Menninger Foundation, established (1941) for research, training, and public education in psychiatry, became a psychiatric center of the U.S. Karl was instrumental in founding (1946) the Winter Veterans' Administration Hospital, which includes the largest psychiatric training program in the world.

Mennonites, Protestant sect arising among Swiss ANABAPTISTS and for a time called Swiss Brethren. They derive their name from MENNO SIMONS, a Dutch reformer. The group seceded (1523–25) from the state church in Zürich after rejecting its authority and infant baptism. They believed in nonresistance, refused to take oaths, and held the Bible as their sole rule of faith. Their distinctive beliefs were embodied in the Dordrecht Confession of Faith (1632). Mennonites have two sacraments, baptism (for adults only) and the Lord's Supper. The sect spread to Russia, France, and Holland. In America Mennonites first settled (1683) at Germantown, Pa. One of the most conservative divisions of the Mennonite Church is the **Amish** Church, which, under Jacob Ammann broke away (late 17th cent.) from the main body in Europe. The principal U.S. Amish groups are the Old Order Amish, who hold services in German and adhere to traditional customs (e.g., wearing plain clothing and shunning modern education and technology), and the Conservative Amish, who hold services in English as well as German and have adopted some innovations.

Menno Simons, 1496?–1561, Dutch religious reformer. In 1536 he left the Roman Catholic priesthood because of his disbelief in infant baptism and other Catholic teachings. He organized and led the less aggressive division of ANABAPTISTS in Germany and Holland. The name MENNONITES is derived from his name, although he did not actually found the sect.

menopause, period in a woman's life when the amount of ESTROGEN produced by the ovaries decreases, resulting in changes in, and ultimately cessation of, MENSTRUATION. It usually occurs between ages 45 and 55 and signals the end of the childbearing years. It may be accompanied by "hot flashes" and vaginal changes (especially decrease in moisture).

Menotti, Gian-Carlo [mānôt'tē], 1911–, Italian operatic composer. His major works include *The Old Maid and the Thief* (1939) and *Amahl and the Night Visitors* (1951), both written for radio broadcast; *The Saint of Bleecker Street* (1950); *Tamu-Tamu* (1973); and other operas with dramatic impact and superb polytonality. In 1958 he instituted the Festival of Two Worlds at Spoleto, Italy. He became artistic director of the Rome Opera in 1993.

Menshevism: see BOLSHEVISM AND MENSHEVISM.

Menshikov, Aleksandr Danilovich, Prince [mĕn'shĭkəf], 1672?–1729, Russian field marshal and statesman. Friend and chief advisor to PETER I, he held various governorships, becoming notorious for his financial misdeeds. On Peter's death (1725) he helped CATHERINE I (who had been his mistress before marrying Peter) to accede to the throne; he, however, became the real ruler. After the accession of PETER II (1727) he was removed from power and exiled to Siberia.

menstruation, periodic flow of bloody fluid which is part of the human female's reproductive cycle. In this cycle (menstrual cycle), the hormone ESTROGEN, secreted by the ovaries (egg-producing organs), first acts to thicken the lining (endometrium) of the uterus (the muscular organ that carries developing young). After 8 to 10 days the ovary releases an egg and begins to secrete the hormone PROGESTERONE. If the egg is fertilized, it will embed itself in the thick uterine lining. If the egg is not fertilized, the secretion of progesterone declines, and the lowered level of progesterone causes the uterine lining to be sloughed off. The menstrual cycle, which is repeated approximately every 28 days, is the result of complex interactions between ovarian and pituitary hormones and the nervous system. Menstruation commences at puberty (about age 12) and ceases at MENOPAUSE (about age 45 to 55).

mental retardation, subnormal mental development, manifested from birth or early childhood. Although mental retardation has traditionally been diagnosed in the U.S. by significantly lower than normal scores on INTELLIGENCE tests, other characteristics such as social maturity and ability to sustain personal and social independence are now used to evaluate mental competence. Many of the mentally retarded can achieve some language development and can be taught to perform manual tasks of moderate complexity. See also DOWN'S SYNDROME.

Menuhin, Yehudi, 1916–, British violinist; b. N.Y.C. He has been a British subject since 1985. He made his debut in San Francisco at age 7 and has appeared around the world. In 1957 he initiated his own music festival at Gstaad, Switzerland, and in 1963 founded the Yehudi Menuhin School of Music in Suffolk, England. He has toured internationally with the Menuhin Festival Orchestra. Menuhin is an active promoter of Eastern music and little-known works. In 1993 he was created Baron Menuhin of Stoke D'Abernon.

Menzies, Sir Robert Gordon, 1894–1978, Australian statesman. As head of the United Australian party and founder (1944) of the Liberal party, he was prime minister (1939–41, 1949–66). He pursued a firmly anti-Communist policy.

Mephistopheles: see FAUST.

mercantilism, an economic policy of the major trading nations from the 16th to the 18th cent., based on the premise that national wealth and power were best served by increasing exports and collecting precious metals in return. State action, an essential feature of the mercantile system, was used to accomplish its purposes—to sell more than it bought to accumulate bullion and raw materials. Under a mercantilist policy, a government exercised much control over economic life by regulating production, encouraging foreign trade, levying duties on imports to gain revenue, making treaties to obtain exclusive trading privileges, and exploiting the commerce of the colonies. In England, HENRY VIII, ELIZABETH I, and Oliver CROMWELL pursued mercantilist policies; in France, J.B. COLBERT was the chief exponent. Superseding the medieval feudal organization in Western Europe, mercantilism did not decline until the coming of the INDUSTRIAL REVOLUTION and the doctrine of LAISSEZ FAIRE.

Mercator, Gerardus, Latin form of his real name, **Gerhard Kremer,** 1512–94, Flemish geographer, mathematician, and cartographer. He surveyed Flanders and made terrestrial and celestial globes. He was named (1552) to the chair of cosmography of Duisburg, Germany, where he subsequently lived. In 1568 his first map using the projection that bears his name appeared (see MAP PROJECTION). He began (1585) a great atlas, published (1594) by his son.

Mercator map projection, a cylindrical MAP PROJECTION of the features of the earth's surface that can be constructed only mathematically. The parallels of LATITUDE, which on the globe are equal distances apart, are drawn with increasing separation as their distance from the EQUATOR increases in order to preserve shapes. However, areas are exaggerated with increasing distance from the equator. For instance, Greenland is shown with enormously exaggerated size, although its shape is preserved. The poles themselves cannot be shown on a Mercator projection. This type of projection gives an incorrect impression of the relative sizes of the world's countries.

Mercia, kingdom of Anglo-Saxon England, consisting generally of the area of the Midlands. Settled (c.500) by the Angles, it extended its leadership over S England in the reign of Penda (d. 654). This hegemony was strengthened under OFFA (r.757–96), but declined after his death. The eastern part became (886) part of the DANELAW; the western part fell under the control of ALFRED of Wessex.

mercury (Hg) or **quicksilver,** metallic element, known to the ancient Chinese, Hindus, and Egyptians. Silver-white and mirrorlike, it is the only common metal existing as a liquid at ordinary temperatures. Mercury is used in barometers, thermometers, electric switches, mercury-vapor lamps, and certain batteries; a mercury alloy, called an amalgam, is employed in dentistry. Mercury compounds have been used as insecticides, in rat poisons, and as disinfectants. Not easily discharged from the body, the metal is a cumulative poison; its ingestion in more than trace amounts in contaminated food or its absorption by the skin or mucous membranes results in **mercury poisoning,** which can cause skin disorders, hemorrhage, liver and kidney damage, and gastrointestinal disturbances. Workers in many industries have been affected, and mercury POLLUTION of rivers, lakes, and oceans, usually through the discharge of industrial wastes, has become a serious environmental problem. Most mercury pesticides have been withdrawn from the U.S. market, and in 1972 more than 90 nations approved an international ban on the dumping of mercury in the ocean, where the metal has tended to work its way into the food cycle of aquatic life and to reach dangerous levels in certain food fish. See ELEMENT (table); PERIODIC TABLE.

Mercury, in astronomy, nearest PLANET to the sun, at a mean distance of 36.0 million mi (57.9 million km). It has a diameter of 3,031 mi (4,878 km), a cratered, lunarlike surface, and almost no atmosphere. Because its greatest ELONGATION is 28°, it can never be seen more than 2 hours after sunset or 2 hours before sunrise. The observed motion (43′ each century) of Mercury's perihelion (closest point to the sun) is more than can be explained by planetary perturbations (see CELESTIAL MECHANICS) using Newton's theory of gravitation but is in nearly exact agreement with the prediction of the general theory of RELATIVITY. Mercury has no known satellites. The only SPACE PROBE to study Mercury was *Mariner 10,* which made three encounters in 1974–75. In 1991 radar photographs of Mercury from earth strongly suggested that the planet has polar ice.

Mercury, in Roman mythology, god of commerce and messenger of the gods; identified with the Greek HERMES.

Mercury, Project: see SPACE EXPLORATION, table.

mercury poisoning: see under MERCURY.

Meredith, George, 1828–1909, English novelist and poet. His first distinguished novel, *The Ordeal of Richard Feverel* (1859), was followed by *Evan Harrington* (1860), *The Egoist* (1879), *Diana of the Crossways* (1885), and others. *Modern Love* (1862), a series of 50 poems, traces the dissolution of a marriage. His 1877 lecture *On the Idea of Comedy and the Uses of the Comic Spirit* (pub. 1897) is highly regarded. Written in a witty, oblique style, his works contain penetrating analyses of individual character and social institutions.

Meredith, Owen: see under BULWER-LYTTON.

Merezhkovsky, Dmitri Sergeyevich [mârĭshkôf'skē], 1865–1941, Russian writer. Enormously influential in pre-Revolutionary Russia, he is best known for his study of TOLSTOY and DOSTOYEVSKY (1901–2) and for the philosophical novel trilogy *Christ and Antichrist* (1896–1905). With his wife, the poet Zinaida Gippius, he emigrated to Paris in 1918.

Meridian, city (1990 pop. 41,036), seat of Lauderdale co., E Miss.; settled 1831; inc. 1860. It is the trade and transportation center for a farm, livestock, and timber area. Electronic equipment and textiles are produced. Temporary state capital (1863), it was destroyed (1864) by Gen. SHERMAN. The nearby Meridian Naval Air Station is economically important.

meridian circle: see TRANSIT INSTRUMENT.

Mérimée, Prosper [mārēmā'], 1803–70, French romantic author. His concise, understated style was most fully realized in such short novels as *Carmen* (1846, the basis for BIZET's opera) and *Colomba* (1852). His short story "Mateo Falcone" (1829) is a masterpiece of the genre.

Merleau-Ponty, Maurice, 1908–61, French philosopher. Influenced by Edmund HUSSERL, he advocated a form of PHENOMENOLOGY but, unlike most phenomenologists, affirmed the material reality of a world that transcends one's consciousness of it. In the 1940s and 50s he was sympathetic to the historical materialism of Karl MARX, but later he turned his attention to the study of language and meaning. His major works are *The Structure of Behavior* (1942) and *Phenomenology of Perception* (1945).

Merman, Ethel, 1909–84, American musical comedy star, noted for her booming voice; b. Astoria, N.Y., as Ethel Zimmerman. Her greatest successes were *Annie Get Your Gun* (1946), *Call Me Madam* (1950), and *Gypsy* (1958).

Merovingian art and architecture [mĕr″əvĭn'jēən]. Named for Merovech, founder of the first Germanic-Frankish dynasty (5th cent.–751), the Merovingian period was marked by a decline of classical tradition, and the absorption of a radically new element into the artistic mainstream—the abstract and brilliantly ornamental style of the nomadic barbarian tribes. Their art was confined to small, portable objects. The Central European and Eastern settlers introduced CLOISONNÉ and excelled at enamelwork and metalwork. Merovingian architecture, monumental sculpture, and painting were based on classical and Early Christian traditions. Little remains of the structures, but larger churches were said to be based on the basilican plan, with characteristic Merovingian timber roofs. Their most original device was the use of a bell tower. Merovingian stone sculpture simplified antique forms. Animal motifs were common, and manuscript illumination elaborated initial letters based on animal forms. The human figure became an abstract sign.

Merovingians, dynasty of Frankish kings that flourished from the 5th cent. to 751. They traced their descent from the semilegendary Merovech, or Meroveus, chief of the Salian Franks. His grandson, CLOVIS I, founded the Frankish monarchy in 481. His descendants divided his domains into Austrasia, Neustria, AQUITAINE, BURGUNDY, Paris, and Orléans. These territories were often combined and sometimes reunited under a single Merovingian ruler. Dagobert I (c.612–c.639) was the last Merovingian to exercise personal power. His successors, the "idle kings," left governing to the mayors of the palace, the CAROLINGIANS. In 751 PEPIN THE SHORT deposed Childeric III, the last Merovingian king.

Merrimack: see MONITOR AND MERRIMACK.

Merton, Robert K(ing), 1910–, American sociologist; b. Philadelphia. His early work includes studies of deviant behavior as social adaptation. After joining (1944) the Columbia Univ. faculty, he teamed with Paul F. LAZARSFELD, as associate director of the Bureau of Applied Social Research. He worked on sociological theory and developed improved methods of conducting social scientific research. His wide-ranging writings include works on mass media and the sociology of science.

Merton, Thomas, 1915–68, American religious writer and poet; b. France. A Roman Catholic convert, he became a Trappist monk in 1941 and was later ordained a priest. He died in an accident in Thailand. Merton is best known for his autobiography, *The Seven Storey Mountain* (1948), and two volumes on Trappist life, *The Waters of Siloe* (1949) and *The Sign of Jonas* (1953).

Merwin, W(illiam) S(tanley), 1927–, American poet; b. N.Y.C. His

Merovingian belt buckle

volumes of poetry include *A Mask for Janus* (1952), *The Carrier of Ladders* (1970; Pulitzer), *Opening the Hand* (1983), and *Selected Poems* (1988). Merwin is also known for his translations, e.g., *The Cid* (1959).

Mesa, city (1990 pop. 288,091), S central Ariz., 15 mi (24 km) from PHOENIX, in the Salt R. valley; founded by MORMONS 1878, inc. 1883. The city's population multiplied fivefold from 1960 to 1980 and 89% from 1980 to 1990. It has electronics, aircraft, metal, and machine-tool industries. Citrus and farm products are packed and processed. Tourism is also important.

mesa, name given in the SW U.S. to a small, isolated, flat-topped hill with two or more steep, usually perpendicular sides. Mesas are thought to have formed when a relatively hard surface rock layer protected those beneath it from the regional erosion that wore away the surrounding rock. The rock layers composing mesas are more or less horizontal. See also BUTTE.

Mesa Verde National Park: see NATIONAL PARKS (table).

Mesolithic period: see under STONE AGE.

meson: see ELEMENTARY PARTICLES.

Mesopotamia [Gr., = between rivers], ancient region of W Asia around the Tigris and Euphrates rivers, now in Iraq. Called the "cradle of civilization," the heart of the area was a plain rendered fertile in ancient times by canals. Settlements have been found in N Mesopotamia, which probably date from 5000 B.C., and urban civilization later arose in S Mesopotamia in city states such as Erech and Ur (see SUMER). AKKAD emerged (c.2340 B.C.) as the region's first empire and was followed by BABYLONIA and ASSYRIA. Mesopotamia was still important in the Byzantine Empire and in the Abbasid caliphate, but the Mongols devastated the area in A.D. 1258. Today it is largely arid and barren, but its rich oil fields have international importance.

Mesopotamian art: see ASSYRIAN ART; PHOENICIAN ART; SUMERIAN AND BABYLONIAN ART.

mesosphere: see ATMOSPHERE.

Mesozoic era: see GEOLOGIC ERA (table).

Mesquite, city (1990 pop. 101,484), Dallas co., N Texas, a Dallas suburb; inc. 1887. One of the fastest-growing U.S. cities, it had a population increase of over 50% in the 1980s. Mesquite is home to several major corporate headquarters; telephone equipment is a leading manufacture.

mesquite, spiny tree or shrub (genus *Prosopis*) of the PULSE family, native to tropical and subtropical regions. The seedpods of *P. juliflora* contain an edible, sweet pulp that is used as forage and to make bread and a fermented drink; the durable wood is used for fence posts and to lend a smoky flavor to grilled foods. Mesquite roots may penetrate 50 ft (15 m) into the ground for water, enabling the plant to grow in sites unsuited to most crops.

Messalina (Valeria Messalina), d. A.D. 48, corrupt Roman empress, wife of CLAUDIUS I, who had her killed after a scandal in which she publicly married her lover.

Messenia [mĕsē'nēə], ancient region of SW GREECE, in the PELOPONNESUS, corresponding to modern Messinias. From the 8th cent. B.C. Messenia was engaged in a series of revolts against Spartan domination, and it was finally freed when THEBES defeated Sparta at the battle of Leuctra (371 B.C.). Excavation has revealed an important center of MYCENAEAN CIVILIZATION at the Messenian city of PYLOS.

Messiaen, Olivier [mĕsyäN'], 1908–92, French composer and organist. He was a noted teacher and theorist. His works, which reflected his religious mysticism, include *L'Ascension* (1935) and *Des canyons aux étoiles* (1974) for orchestra; *Le Banquet céleste* (1936), for organ; *Oiseaux exotiques* (1956); *Turangalila* (1949), a symphony in 10 movements, and *St. Francis of Assisi,* (1983), an opera.

Messiah or **Messias** [Heb., = anointed], in Judaism, a man who is to be sent by God to restore Israel and reign righteously over all humanity. The idea developed among the Jews especially in adversity; self-proclaimed messiahs, e.g., SABBATAI ZEVI and Jacob FRANK, always attracted some followers. Jewish Messianic expectations generally focused on a kingly figure of the house of DAVID who would be born in Bethlehem. JESUS may have considered himself, and is generally considered by Christians, to be the Messiah promised by the Bible; the name *Christ* is Greek for "Messiah." Expectation of a redeemer is also found in some ancient Middle Eastern texts and among Buddhists, Zoroastrians, Confucians, and Muslims (see MAHDI).

Messier catalog, systematic list of 103 nebulous celestial objects published (1771, 1780, 1781) by the French astronomer Charles Messier. Of these, 33 were identified by later observers as galaxies, 55 as star clusters, and 11 as true nebulae; the 4 others are a double star; an asterism, or small group of stars; a patch of the Milky Way; and a duplicate observation. Objects on the list include the CRAB NEBULA (M1) and the ANDROMEDA GALAXY (M31).

Messys, Quentin: see MASSYS, QUENTIN.

metabolism, sum of all living processes in living systems. Two subcategories of metabolism are anabolism, the building up of organic molecules from simpler ones, and catabolism, the breaking down of complex substances, often accompanied by the release of energy. Thus the energy required for anabolism is obtained from catabolic reactions. Basal metabolism, the heat produced by an organism at rest, represents the minimum amount of energy required to maintain life at normal body temperature.

metal, chemical ELEMENT displaying certain properties, notably metallic luster, the capacity to lose electrons and form a positive ION, and the ability to conduct heat and electricity (see CONDUCTION), by which it is normally distinguished from a nonmetal. The metals comprise about two thirds of the known elements. Some elements, e.g., arsenic and antimony, exhibit both metallic and nonmetallic properties, and are called metalloids. Metals fall into groups in the PERIODIC TABLE determined by similar arrangements of the orbital electrons and a consequent similarity in chemical properties. Such groups include the ALKALI METALS (Group Ia in the periodic table), the ALKALINE-EARTH METALS (Group IIa), and the RARE-EARTH METALS (LANTHANIDE and ACTINIDE series). Most metals other than the alkali metals and the alkaline-earth metals are called transition metals (see TRANSITION ELEMENTS). The oxidation states, or VALENCE, of the metal ions vary from +1 for the alkali metals to +7 for some transition metals. Chemically, the metals differ from the nonmetals in that they form positive ions and basic oxides and hydroxides. Upon exposure to moist air, a great many metals undergo corrosion, i.e., enter into a chemical reaction, the oxygen of the atmosphere uniting with the metal to form the oxide of the metal, e.g., rust on exposed iron. See also ALLOY; METALLURGY.

metalloid: see METAL; PERIODIC TABLE.

metallurgy, science extracting metals from their ores. The processes employed depend upon the chemical nature of the ORE to be treated and upon the properties of the METAL to be extracted. When an ore has a low percentage of the desired metal, a method of physical concentration, e.g., the FLOTATION PROCESS, must be used before the extraction process begins. Because almost all metals are found combined with other elements in nature, chemical reactions are required to set them free. These chemical processes are classified as *pyrometallurgy,* the use of heat for the treatment of an ore, e.g., in SMELTING and roasting; *electrometallurgy,* the preparation of certain active metals by ELECTROLYSIS; and *hydrometallurgy,* or leaching, the selective dissolution of metals from their ores. Modern metallurgical research is concerned with preparing radioactive metals, with obtaining metals economically from low-grade ores, with obtaining and refining rare metals hitherto not used, and with formulating ALLOYS.

metamorphic rock: see METAMORPHISM; ROCK.

metamorphism, in geology, process of change in the structure, texture, or composition of ROCKS caused by heat, deforming pressure, and/or hot, chemically active fluids. In general, metamorphic rock is coarser, denser, and less porous than the rock from which it was formed. The change in texture commonly results in a rearrangement of MINERAL particles into a parallel alignment called foliation, probably the most characteristic property of metamorphic rocks; it is seen in SLATE, SCHIST, and GNEISS. Local metamorphism is usually caused by the intrusion of a mass of igneous rock into older rock. Regional metamorphism accompanies mountain-building activity associated with large-scale crustal movements.

metamorphosis, in zoology, a term used for a series of distinct stages in the development from egg to adult. For example, an insect such as the butterfly is active and wormlike (a caterpillar) in its larval stage. In its next stage (pupal) the insect is surrounded by an outer covering (a cocoon); it is outwardly inactive but undergoes many changes in internal organization. Eventually the insect emerges transformed into its adult stage (a butterfly). Metamorphosis is called complete when there is no suggestion of the adult in the larval stage. In incomplete metamorphosis, the successive larval stages resemble the adult, as in the GRASSHOPPER. Many species change their habitat after undergoing complete metamorphosis (e.g., the toad lives in water in its tadpole stage and on land in its adult stage).

metaphysical poets, name first used by Samuel JOHNSON (1744) for a group of 17th-cent. English lyric poets. Their hallmark is the metaphysical conceit, wit, learned imagery, and subtle argument. Most important were John DONNE, George HERBERT, Henry VAUGHAN, Abraham COWLEY, Richard CRASHAW, and Andrew MARVELL. They considerably influenced 20th-cent. poetry.

metaphysics, branch of philosophy concerned with the ultimate nature of existence. Ontology (the study of the nature of being), cosmology, and philosophical theology are its main branches. The term comes from the metaphysical treatises of ARISTOTLE, who presented the First Philosophy (as he called it) after the *Physics* [Gk. *meta-physic,* = after physics]. Metaphysical systems in the history of philosophy have included Aristotelian SCHOLASTICISM and the rationalistic systems of the 17th cent. (e.g., those of DESCARTES, SPINOZA, and LEIBNIZ). KANT, in the 18th cent., held scientific metaphysical speculation to be an impossibility but considered metaphysical questions a moral necessity. His work influenced that of FICHTE, SCHELLING, and HEGEL. Since the mid-19th cent. philosophy has generally denied validity to metaphysical thought. Modern interest in metaphysics has centered on analyzing the metaphysical systems that inform prevailing modes of thought. See also LOGICAL POSITIVISM.

Metastasio, Pietro, 1698–1782, Italian poet and librettist. He became court poet at Vienna in 1729. With his predecessor, Apostolo Zeno, he created the rigid *opera seria* (see OPERA). His works include the melodrama *Attilio Regolo* (1750) and many librettos, including *La clemenza di Tito* (1734, music by Mozart) and *The Shepherd King* (1751).

Metcalfe, Charles Theophilus Metcalfe, 1st **Baron,** 1785–1846,

British governor-general of CANADA (1843–45). In his administration the ministry of Robert BALDWIN and L.H. LAFONTAINE resigned (1843), and he formed a Conservative government that won an election. He was forced to retire (1845) because of ill health.

Metellus, ancient Roman family of the plebeian gens Caecilia. It was one of the families that controlled the senate. **Quintus Caecilius Metellus Macedonicus,** d. 115 B.C., conquered (148 B.C.) Macedonia and pacified (146 B.C.) Greece. **Quintus Caecilius Metellus Numidicus,** d. 91? B.C., a leader of the senatorial party and consul (109 B.C.), conducted the Numidian War against Jugurtha. He antagonized Marius and was exiled (100 B.C.). His son, **Quintus Caecilius Metellus Pius,** d. c.63 B.C., continued his father's opposition to Marius. In 89 B.C. he fought in the Social War and in the civil war that followed defended Rome against Marius and Lucius Cornelius CINNA. In 83 B.C. Metellus joined SULLA and defeated the Marians in Umbria and Cisalpine Gaul. He warred unsuccessfully (79–72 B.C.) against Sertorius in Spain.

meteor, small piece of extraterrestrial matter that becomes visible as a "shooting star" or "falling star" when it enters the earth's atmosphere. While still outside the atmosphere, it is called a meteoroid. As a meteor it is heated to incandescence through friction (due to collisions with air molecules) and usually disintegrates completely before reaching the earth; those meteors large enough to reach the ground are called METEORITES. A meteor of considerable duration and brightness is known as a fireball; a fireball that explodes in the air is called a bolide. The frequency of meteors increases when the earth, in its orbit, annually passes through a swarm of particles generated from the breakup of a comet. The meteors of such a **meteor shower** all appear to originate at a single point, or radiant, in the sky. Some of the better-known showers (named for the constellations in which their radiants are located) and their approximate dates are: Lyrids, Apr. 21; Perseids, Aug. 12; Orinoids, Oct. 20; Taurids, Nov. 4; Leonids, Nov. 16; Geminids, Dec. 13.

meteorite, large METEOR that survives the intense heat of atmospheric friction and reaches the earth's surface. Meteorites may have originated as fragments of asteroids. They are classified in three general categories. The siderites, or irons, are composed entirely of metal (chiefly nickel and iron). The aerolites, or stony meteorites, show a diversity of mineral elements including large percentages of silicon and magnesium oxides; the most abundant type of aerolite is the chondrite, so called because the metal embedded in it is in the form of grainlike lumps, or chondrules. The siderolites, or stony irons, which are rarer than the other types, are of both metal and stone in varying proportions. When a meteorite reaches the earth, the tremendous force of impact with the earth's surface causes great compression, heating, and partial vaporization of the outer part of the meteorite and of the materials in the ground; expansion of the gases thus formed and of steam produced from groundwater causes an explosion that shatters the meteorite and carves out a **meteorite crater** in the ground. One of the best-preserved craters is Meteor, or Barringer, Crater, near Winslow, Arizona, c.¾ mi (1½ km) in diameter and 600 ft (180 m) deep. The largest meteorite ever discovered, the 60-ton Hoba West, rests where it was found (in 1920), near Grootfontein, Namibia.

meteorology, branch of science that deals with the ATMOSPHERE of a planet, particularly that of the earth. Meteorology is based on the scientific measurement of various atmospheric conditions with a wide assortment of instruments. Air temperature is measured with the THERMOMETER; air pressure with the BAROMETER; wind direction with the weather vane; wind speed with the anemometer; high-altitude air-pressure and wind information with the WEATHER BALLOON; relative humidity with the HYGROMETER; precipitation with the rain gauge; and cloud formations and weather fronts with both radar and high-altitude WEATHER SATELLITES. The meteorologist uses the data collected from many geographical locations to create a weather map. On a typical map the various weather elements are shown by figures and symbols. Isobars are drawn to show areas of equal pressure, and FRONTS and areas of precipitation are also indicated. Meteorologists also analyze the data collected with computer models in order to predict, or forecast, the WEATHER for the next few hours and the next few days. Long-range weather forecasts, which are more general and less accurate, are also made for future periods of several months.

meter: see METRIC SYSTEM; WEIGHTS AND MEASURES, table.

methadone, synthetic NARCOTIC, similar in effect to MORPHINE, used primarily in the treatment of narcotic drug addiction. Given to addicts, it blocks the euphoric action of HEROIN without itself causing euphoria and causes less severe and hazardous withdrawal symptoms than other narcotic drugs (although critics of methadone therapy point out that methadone patients are still addicts). Methadone is also used as an ANALGESIC, especially in patients who are terminally ill.

methanal: see FORMALDEHYDE.

methane (CH_4), colorless, odorless, gaseous HYDROCARBON formed by the decay of plant and animal matter. It occurs naturally as the chief component of NATURAL GAS, as the firedamp of coal mines, and as the marsh gas released in swamps and marshes. Methane can also be made synthetically by various means. It is combustible and can form explosive mixtures with air. Used for fuel in the form of natural gas, methane is also an important starting material for making solvents and certain FREONS.

Methodism, the doctrines, polity, and worship of those Protestant denominations that have developed from the movement started in England by the teaching of John WESLEY. He, with his brother Charles, George WHITEFIELD, and others, formed (1729) a group at Oxford that met for religious exercises. From their resolution to conduct their lives and study by "rule and method," they were given the name Methodists. Influenced by the Moravians, the Wesleys began (1738) evangelistic preaching, often in barns, houses, and open fields. The moving of preachers from one appointment to another was the beginning of the system of itinerancy. John Wesley was essentially a follower of Jacobus ARMINIUS, but Whitefield was unable to accept Arminian doctrine and broke away (1741) to form the Calvinistic Methodists. The first annual conference (1744) drew up the Articles of Religion, which stressed repentance, faith, sanctification, and full, free salvation for all. The group adopted a constitution in 1784 and withdrew from the Church of England in 1791 to become the Wesleyan Methodist Church. In America Methodism began after 1766 in New York with the preaching of Philip Embury and spread rapidly under Francis ASBURY. The first conference was held in 1773, and the Methodist Episcopal Church in America was formed in 1784. In both England and the U.S., Methodists splintered into many groups, but significant progress toward unity has been made in the 20th cent. Among U.S. Methodist bodies the United Methodist Church is the largest, with nearly 9 million members.

Methodius, Saint: see CYRIL AND METHODIUS, SAINTS.

Methuselah [mēthyo͞o'zələ], descendant of Seth; son of ENOCH. GENESIS says he lived 969 years.

metric system, system of weights and measures planned in France and adopted there in 1799. Now used by most of the countries of the world, it is based on a unit of length called the meter (m) and a unit of mass called the kilogram (kg). The meter is now defined as the distance light travels through a vacuum in 1/299,792,458 of a second. The kilogram is defined as the mass of the International Prototype Kilogram, a platinum-iridium cylinder kept at Sèvres, France, near Paris. Other metric units can be defined in terms of the meter and the kilogram (see WEIGHTS AND MEASURES, table). Fractions and multiples of the metric units are related to each other by powers of 10, allowing conversion from one unit to a multiple of it simply by shifting a decimal point. This avoids the lengthy arithmetical operations required by the ENGLISH UNITS OF MEASUREMENT. The prefixes in the accompanying table have been accepted for designating multiples and fractions of the meter, the gram (= 1⁄1000 kilogram), and other units. Several other systems of units based on the metric system have been in wide use. The cgs system uses the centimeter (= 1⁄100 meter) of length, the gram of mass, and the SECOND of time as its fundamental units; other cgs units are the dyne of FORCE and the erg of WORK or energy. The mks system uses the meter of length, the kilogram of mass, and the second of time as its fundamental units; other mks units include the newton of force, the joule of work or energy, and the watt of POWER. The units of the mks system are generally much larger and of a more practical size than the comparable units of the cgs system. ELECTRIC

AND MAGNETIC UNITS have been defined for both these systems. The International System of Units (officially called the Système International d'Unités, or SI) is a system of units adopted by the 11th General Conference on Weights and Measures (1960). Its basic units of length, mass, and time are those of the mks system; other basic units are the AMPERE of electric current, the kelvin of temperature (a degree of temperature measured on the Kelvin TEMPERATURE scale), the candela (see PHOTOMETRY) of luminous intensity, and the MOLE, used to measure the amount of a substance present. All other units are derived from these basic units.

PREFIXES FOR BASIC METRIC UNITS

Prefix	Abbreviation	Power of 10	Equivalent
MULTIPLES			
yotta	Y	10^{24}	septillion
zetta	Z	10^{21}	sextillion
exa-	E	10^{18}	quintillion
peta-	P	10^{15}	quadrillion
tera-	T	10^{12}	trillion
giga-	G	10^{9}	billion
mega-	M	10^{6}	million
kilo-	k	10^{3}	thousand
hecto-	h	10^{2}	hundred
deka-	da	10^{1}	ten
FRACTIONS			
deci-	d	10^{-1}	tenth part
centi-	c	10^{-2}	hundredth part
milli-	m	10^{-3}	thousandth part
micro-	μ	10^{-6}	millionth part
nano-	n	10^{-9}	billionth part
pico-	p	10^{-12}	trillionth part
femto-	f	10^{-15}	quadrillionth part
atto-	a	10^{-18}	quintillionth part
zepto-	z	10^{-21}	sextillionth part
yocto-	y	10^{-24}	septillionth part

Metropolitan Museum of Art, New York City, the foremost art museum in the U.S.; founded 1870, opened 1880. Owned by the city, it is largely supported by private endowment. The museum's most outstanding collections include European paintings and sculpture of the Renaissance, baroque, and modern periods. It has extensive Egyptian holdings, e.g., the Temple of Dendur, and a vast collection of Asian works. Much of its collection of medieval art is housed at the CLOISTERS. Its American Wing contains a comprehensive array of U.S. arts and crafts of all periods, its Costume Institute includes thousands of authentic costumes and accessories, and its Michael C. Rockefeller Wing houses a large collection of primitive art. The museum is also known for its collections of Greek pottery, Greek and Roman sculpture, and graphic arts.

Metropolitan Opera Company, term used in referring collectively to the organizations that have produced OPERA at the Metropolitan Opera House, New York City. The original opera house was on West 39th Street. The company's first presentation, on Oct. 22, 1883, was a performance of Charles GOUNOD's *Faust.* In 1966 the Met moved to LINCOLN CENTER FOR THE PERFORMING ARTS, opening with a performance of Samuel BARBER's *Antony and Cleopatra.* A galaxy of great stars have sung at the Met, e.g., Enrico CARUSO, Kirsten FLAGSTAD, Feodor CHALIAPIN, Maria CALLAS, Joan SUTHERLAND, and Luciano PAVAROTTI. Conductors of the opera orchestra have included Gustav MAHLER and Arturo TOSCANINI. Managers have included Giulio Gatti-Casazza (1898–1908) and Rudolf Bing (1940–72).

Metsu or **Metzu, Gabriel** [mĕt'sü], 1630?–1667, Dutch genre painter. He is best known for his quiet, charming interiors. His fine draftsmanship and exquisite handling of light and texture can be seen in *Music Lesson* (The Hague) and *Duet* (National Gall., London).

Metsys, Quentin: see MASSYS, QUENTIN.

Metternich, Clemens Wenzel Nepomuk Lothar, Fürst von [mĕt'ərnĭkh], 1773–1859, Austrian statesman. He became foreign minister in 1809 and secured (1812) a temporary alliance with France. Later he developed a policy of substituting Austrian for French supremacy, and Austria joined the QUADRUPLE ALLIANCE (1814). Metternich, a conservative, was the guiding spirit at the Congress of VIENNA (1814–15) and succeeding European congresses. The period 1815–48 has been called the Age of Metternich. He sought to maintain a balance of power in Europe, and to make Austria supreme in Italy and in the newly formed GERMAN CONFEDERATION. His system depended on censorship, espionage, and the suppression of revolutionary and nationalist movements.

Metzinger, Jean, 1883–1956, French painter and writer. With GLEIZES he wrote *Du cubisme* (1912) (see CUBISM). His paintings employ cubist faceting that is never wholly abstract, e.g., *The Dancer* (Albright-Knox Art Gall., Buffalo).

Metzu, Gabriel: see METSU, GABRIEL.

Meunier, Constantin [mönyā'], 1831–1905, Belgian sculptor and painter. His paintings express the dignity of labor. He is best known for his bronze reliefs and monuments, e.g., the unfinished *Monument to Labor* (Brussels), which includes reliefs, statues, and a group, *Maternity.*

Meuse or **Maas,** river, one of the chief waterways of N Europe, c.560 mi (900 km) long. It rises in NE France, flows through an important mining and industrial region of Belgium, and into the S Netherlands, where it branches out to form a common delta with the RHINE R.

Mexicali, city (1990 pop. 602,390), NW Mexico, capital of Baja California state. Located across the U.S. border from Calexico, Calif., in agricultural area, its economy is dominated by assembly plants producing goods for export to the U.S.

Mexican art and architecture were highly developed before the Spanish conquest (see PRE-COLUMBIAN ART AND ARCHITECTURE). With the arrival of the Spanish, native peoples were introduced to European art and building techniques. During the 17th cent., native artists became adept at religious oil paintings, wax figures, and polychrome wood sculpture, and, mingling European and indigenous traditions, Mexican paintings achieved the unique mellowness and richness of color of the Mexican baroque. The first great native Mexican artist was Baltasar de Echave, the Elder (c.1548–1620), who founded the first indigenous school (1609). During the mid-17th cent., sculpture and architecture gained ascendancy and the Churrigueresque (named for José CHURRIGUERA) became the dominant style. The 18th cent. produced such important painters as José Ibarra and Miguel Cabrera. In the 19th cent., the landscapes of José María VELASCO and the satirical prints of José Guadalupe POSADA reaffirmed a national style. During the regime of Emperor MAXIMILIAN (1864–67), the heavy splendor of French Second Empire architecture was introduced. French influence continued under the administration of Porfirio DÍAZ (1876–1911), when ART NOUVEAU was also introduced. Since the 1910 revolution, Mexican art has manifested a strongly revolutionary tone, as in the murals of the modern Mexican masters Diego RIVERA, José Clemente OROZCO, and David Alfaro SIQUEIROS. In abstract painting, Rufino TAMAYO is outstanding. Contemporary Mexican artists continue to produce a variety of works in many styles and techniques. Modern architecture in Mexico combines contemporary schools with native elements in such notable achievements as the Ciudad Universitaria, outside Mexico City. Folk arts, including textiles, pottery, and silverwork, have flourished throughout Mexican history. See also NATIONAL MUSEUM OF ANTHROPOLOGY; SPANISH COLONIAL ART AND ARCHITECTURE.

Mexican War, 1846–48, armed conflict between the U.S. and Mexico. The immediate cause of the war was the U.S. annexation of TEXAS (Dec. 1845); other factors included the existence of long-standing claims by U.S. citizens against MEXICO and the American ambition to acquire CALIFORNIA. In 1845 Pres. Polk sent John SLIDELL to Mexico to purchase California and New Mexico. When the mission failed, Polk prepared for war, and in Mar. 1846 Gen. Zachary TAYLOR occupied Point Isabel, on the Rio Grande. This was viewed as an act of aggression by the Mexicans, who claimed the Nueces R. as the boundary, and Mexican troops crossed the Rio Grande

and shelled (May 3) Fort Brown. Polk pronounced these actions an invasion of American soil, and the U.S. declared war on May 13, 1846. Meanwhile, Taylor had won victories at Palo Alto and Resaca de la Palma (May 8 and 9); he took Matamoros (May 18), Monterrey (Sept. 20–24), and Buena Vista (Feb. 1847). Gen. S.W. KEARNEY occupied Santa Fe (Aug. 1846) and advanced to find that California was already under American rule. In the final campaign of the war, Gen. Winfield SCOTT captured Veracruz (Mar. 1847), defeated Gen. SANTA ANNA at Cerro Gordo (April), and stormed CHAPULTEPEC. On Sept. 14, 1847, American troops entered Mexico City, where they remained until peace was restored. The Treaty of GUADALUPE HIDALGO (Feb. 2, 1848) ended the war. Mexico ceded two fifths of its territory to the U.S. and received an indemnity of $15 million.

Mexico, officially United Mexican States, republic (1990 pop. 81,140,922), 761,600 sq mi (1,972,544 sq km), S North America; bordered by the U.S. (N), the Gulf of Mexico and the Caribbean Sea (E), Belize and Guatemala (SE), and the Pacific Ocean (W). Principal cities include MEXICO CITY (the capital), GUADALAJARA, and MONTERREY. The country is predominantly mountainous, and no more than 15% of the land is considered arable. There is lowland in the southeast and along the coasts, but the heart of the country is the extensive Mexican plateau, with elevations generally above 4,000 ft (1,220 m). Fringed by the ranges of the SIERRA MADRE, the plateau (except for the arid north) is a region of broad, shallow lakes where more than half of the country's population is concentrated. To the south is a chain of extinct volcanoes, including POPOCATÉPETL, Ixtacihuatl, and ORIZABA, which at 18,406 ft (5,610 m) is Mexico's highest point. Since World War II Mexico has had considerable economic growth, but in the mid-1980s it suffered a severe depression due in part to a drop in world oil prices. By the early 1990s, however, debt relief, diversification, foreign investment, and PRIVATIZATION of many industries long owned by the Mexican government had begun to produce an economic upturn. Agriculture engages about a quarter of Mexico's active work force and is slowly being modernized. Major irrigation projects have increased yields. Cotton, coffee, sugar, and tomatoes are the major export crops, and much corn, wheat, sugarcane, beans, and citrus fruits are grown. Livestock raising and fishing are also significant. Mexico has considerable mineral resources, including vast petroleum reserves and zinc, sulfur, silver, antimony, copper, and manganese. Industries, usually in or near the larger cities, produce iron and steel, motor vehicles, engines, processed foods, refined petroleum and petrochemicals, chemical fertilizers, and other products. Assembly factories (MAQUILADORAS) along the U.S. border are a major source of foreign income. Tourism is also economically important. The population has grown rapidly in the 20th cent., more than quadrupling from 1940 to 1990. The great majority of the people are of mixed Spanish and indigenous descent, but a sizable minority are of purely indigenous descent. The official language is Spanish, but many Mexicans still speak only indigenous tongues. Over 95% of the people are Roman Catholic.

History. Before the arrival of the Spanish in the early 16th cent., great indigenous civilizations (the AZTEC, MAYA, TOLTEC, MIXTEC, ZAPOTEC, and OLMEC) flourished in Mexico. Arriving in 1519, Hernán CORTÉS overthrew the Aztec empire (1521) and captured its ruler, MONTEZUMA. The territory became the viceroyalty of New Spain in 1535. Spanish conquerors exploited the mineral wealth of the land, using as laborers the native population and a growing mestizo class; at the same time they extended Spanish rule to the remainder of Mexico and to what is now the southwestern U.S. A rebellion led (1810–15) by Miguel HIDALGO Y COSTILLA failed, but in 1821 Spain accepted Mexican independence, and an "empire," headed by Augustín de ITURBIDE, was established in 1822. In 1823 army officers overthrew the empire and established a federal republic. The early years were marked by turmoil and corruption. Texas broke free of Mexican rule in 1836, and in the ensuing MEXICAN WAR (1846–48) with the U.S., Mexico lost much territory. Internally, the republic was torn by strife among contending political leaders, and in 1855 a democratic reform movement, led by Benito JUÁREZ, overthrew the dictatorship of Antonio López de SANTA ANNA and drafted a liberal constitution. Civil war followed, and in 1864 NAPOLEON III of France, who had colonial ambitions, established another ill-starred Mexican empire, under the Hapsburg prince MAXIMILIAN; it collapsed in 1867, and Maximilian was killed. Then followed the long reformist dictatorship of Porfirio DÍAZ, who ruled Mexico with a firm hand for most of the 35 years after 1876. Díaz promoted economic growth and provided a degree of stability, but his encouragement of the concentration of wealth in the hands of a few spawned a new generation of revolutionaries. Among these were Emiliano ZAPATA, Francisco "Pancho" VILLA (whose raid into the U.S. in 1916 resulted in a brief retaliatory U.S. invasion of Mexico), and Francisco I. MADERO, who toppled Díaz in 1911 but was himself overthrown and murdered in 1913. A foundation for reform was laid by Venustiano CARRANZA's constitution of 1917. In 1929 Plutarco Elías CALLES founded the National Revolutionary party (renamed the Institutional Revolutionary party, or PRI, in 1946), which has governed Mexico ever since (although it suffered heavy setbacks in the 1988 elections). During the presidency of Lázaro CÁRDENAS (1934–40), land was redistributed, illiteracy reduced, power projects initiated, and some industries nationalized. Cárdenas's successors have tended to stress industrial development, which has benefited the middle and upper classes. In 1982 the faltering economy caused the government to devalue the peso and nationalize the banks; the country's enormous foreign debt hampered economic growth. In 1988 Carlos SALINAS GORTARI was elected president amid charges of widespread fraud. Salinas opened Mexico to foreign investment, signed the NORTH AMERICAN FREE TRADE AGREEMENT with the U.S. and Canada, and oversaw a general improvement in the economy. A Mayan-based uprising (1994) in the southern state of Chiapas, however, provided a reminder of the poverty in which many Mexicans still live.

PRESIDENTS OF MEXICO SINCE THE CONSTITUTION OF 1917

PRESIDENT	DATES IN OFFICE
Venustiano Carranza	1917-20
Adolfo de la Huerta	1920
Álvaro Obregón	1920-24
Plutarco Elías Calles	1924-28
Emilio Portes Gil	1928-30
Pascual Ortiz Rubio	1930-32
Abelardo L. Rodríguez	1932-34
Lázaro Cárdenas	1934-40
Manuel Ávila Camacho	1940-46
Miguel Alemán	1946-52
Adolfo Ruiz Cortines	1952-58
Adolfo López Mateos	1958-64
Gustavo Díaz Ordaz	1964-70
Luis Echevarría Álvarez	1970-76
José López Portillo	1976-82
Miguel de la Madrid Hurtado	1982-88
Carlos Salinas de Gortari	1988-

Mexico, Gulf of, arm of the Atlantic Ocean, c.700,000 sq mi (1,813,000 sq km), off SE North America. Oil and natural gas occur along the coast and offshore on the continental shelf. TAMPA, PENSACOLA, MOBILE, NEW ORLEANS, GALVESTON, and CORPUS CHRISTI are major U.S. ports; TAMPICO and VERACRUZ are important Mexican ports.

Mexico, National Autonomous University of, at Mexico City. Founded 1551 by Charles I of Spain (Holy Roman Emperor CHARLES V), it is one of the two oldest universities in the New World. In the 19th cent. the government suppressed it several times for being a center of reactionary politics; the last time it was closed from 1865 to 1910. After its reopening, it was reorganized as a legally autonomous institution. The university offers a variety of programs in the arts and sciences and professional fields. The ultramodern, colorfully decorated structures of the main campus are renowned architecturally.

Mexico City, city (1990 pop. 8,236,960; 1991 met. area est. 20,899,000), central Mexico, capital and largest city of Mexico; it has the largest population of the world's cities. Mexico City is on the Mexican plateau, in the Valley of Mexico, at an elevation of c.7,800 ft (2,380 m), and is ringed by mountains. It is the nation's political, cultural, and commercial hub and its main center of both light and heavy industry. Entrapment of industrial, automobile, and other emissions by the surrounding mountains has made the air among the world's most polluted; in 1991 the government banned vehicles from part of the city and closed a refinery as part of a program to improve air quality. The oldest part of the city surrounds a large central plaza from which wide avenues radiate to the environs. Structures such as a 16th-cent. cathedral and the colonial-baroque National Palace (both on the plaza), 19th cent. public buildings, skyscrapers, and the boldly modern University City reflect a rich, 400-year architectural heritage. Mexico City was founded soon after the conquest of Mexico (1521) at the site of the AZTEC capital, Tenochtitlán, and was the capital of New Spain before Mexico's independence (1821). The city was captured (1847) by U.S. troops during the MEXICAN WAR, was conquered (1863) by the French army, and was occupied (1914–15) by rebel forces during the Mexican Revolution. In 1957 and 1985 earthquakes caused extensive damage to the capital. Mexico City was host to the 1968 OLYMPIC GAMES.

Meyerbeer, Giacomo, 1791–1864, German operatic composer, noted for his spectacular French grand operas *Robert le Diable* (1831) and *Les Huguenots* (1836). Two opéras comiques, *North Star* (1854) and *Dinorah* (1859), are noteworthy.

Mezzogiorno, region, S Italy, comprising six modern regions and the islands of SICILY and SARDINIA. The APPENINES render much of the land untillable, but agriculture is the mainstay of the generally underdeveloped economy. The chief crops are grains, fruits, olives, grapes, and vegetables. The port cities of Bari and NAPLES are important industrial centers. The region's income, educational level, and standard of living is considerably lower than that of N Italy.

mezzo-soprano: see VOICE.

mezzotint, method of copper or steel ENGRAVING in tone. The mezzotint plate is given an overall, even grain by burring the surface with a curved, saw-toothed tool. The picture is then developed in light and shade with a scraper and a burnisher. The resulting print is softly tonal, with no sharp lines. Said to have been invented by Ludwig von Siegen c.1640, the process became prominent in 18th-cent. England, where it was often used to reproduce paintings.

Mg, chemical symbol of the element MAGNESIUM.

Miami, Native American group with an Algonquian language of the Algonquian-Wakashan stock (see NATIVE AMERICAN LANGUAGES). Although of Eastern Woodlands culture (see NORTH AMERICA, INDIGENOUS PEOPLES OF), they shared the Plains trait of buffalo hunting. In the 18th cent. enemies drove them to NW Ohio, from which they retired to Indiana, numbering c.1,700. Chief LITTLE TURTLE led them in the INDIAN WARS of the Old Northwest. Most Miami moved (1867) to a reservation in Oklahoma; the land has since been divided among them. In 1990 there were 4,477 Miamis in the U.S.

Miami, city (1990 pop. 358,548; met. area 1,937,094), seat of Dade co., SE Fla., on Biscayne Bay; inc. 1896. Tourism is its main industry, and there are extensive recreational and convention facilities. A famous resort and cruise-ship port, it is also the processing and shipping center for an agricultural region. Aircraft rebuilding and repair and aluminum products are among its industries. First settled in the 1870s, it was developed into a recreational center after 1896. Miami's first boom occurred during the Florida land speculation in the 1920s. In the 1960s the city became a focus for Caribbean immigration, and from the late 1970s into the 1990s many Cuban and Haitian refugees arrived, taxing the city's facilities. Today over half of the population is Hispanic, and the Cuban influence has put a distinctive stamp on the city. Miami has also become a major center of trade and finance with Latin America. The city is the site of the Orange Bowl and has a major international airport.

Miami Beach, city (1990 pop. 92,639), SE Fla., on an island between Biscayne Bay and the Atlantic Ocean; inc. 1915. It is connected with MIAMI by causeways. A world-famous resort with over 350 hotels and motels along its "gold coast," including many notable ART

DECO buildings, it relies on tourism and convention business. The city was built (beginning largely in the 1920s) in an area that was mangrove swamp.

mica, general term for a large group of hydrous aluminum and potassium silicate minerals, usually occurring in scales and sheets. The most important commercial micas are muscovite and phlogopite. Muscovite, the commoner variety, is usually colorless but may be red, yellow, green, brown, or gray; it is found most often in pegmatite dikes. Phlogopite ranges in color from yellow to brown and occurs in crystalline limestones, dolomites, and serpentines. Sheet mica is used as an insulating material and in certain acoustic devices. Scrap and ground mica is used in wallpaper, fancy paint, ornamental tile, roofing, and lubricating oil.

Micah or **Micheas,** book of the OLD TESTAMENT, 33d in the Authorized Version, sixth of the Minor Prophets; it contains the prophecy of Micah, a contemporary of ISAIAH (fl. 730 B.C.), on the doom and redemption of JUDAH and ISRAEL.

Michael, archangel prominent in Jewish, Christian, and Muslim traditions. In the BIBLE he is mentioned as the guardian angel of Israel. In Christian tradition he is the conqueror of SATAN. His feast (jointly with the other archangels) is Michaelmas, Sept. 29.

Michael, Byzantine emperors. **Michael I** (Rhangabe), d. c.845 (r.811–13), was the son-in-law of NICEPHORUS I. Orthodox in religion, he restored the monastic reformer St. Theodore of Studium. He was deposed after a defeat by the BULGARS. **Michael II** (the Stammerer), d. 829 (r.820–29), helped LEO V to succeed Michael I, and himself succeeded after Leo's murder. Tolerant in religion, he himself favored ICONOCLASM. He lost (825) Crete to the Arabs. **Michael III** (the Drunkard), 836–67 (r.842–67), was the grandson of Michael II. Early in his reign iconoclasm was punished and the heretic Paulicians persecuted. The administration of government by the debauched Michael's uncle, Bardas, was marked by the missions of Saints CYRIL AND METHODIUS. Michael's favorite, Basil, ordered the murders of Bardas (866) and Michael (867), and succeeded as BASIL I. **Michael VIII,** c.1225–82 (r.1261–82), was the first of the Palaeologus dynasty. He became emperor of Nicaea (1259) by usurping the throne of JOHN IV after blinding him. In 1261 he recovered Constantinople from the Latin emperor Baldwin II and was crowned Byzantine emperor by the patriarch. For the rest of his reign he struggled with CHARLES I of Naples and with the despotate of Epirus, which Charles invaded. Michael negotiated with Pope Gregory X for a union of Eastern and Western churches (see COUNCIL, ECUMENICAL), but failed. To defeat Charles he financed the SICILIAN VESPERS (1282).

Michael, 1921–, last king of ROMANIA (1927–30, 1940–47). He became king under a regency after his father, CAROL II, was forced to renounce the throne. In 1930, however, Carol dethroned Michael. Carol was forced to abdicate by ANTONESCU in 1940, and Michael again became king. In 1947 the Communist-dominated government forced him to abdicate, and he went into exile.

Michael the Brave, d. 1601, Romanian national hero, prince of Walachia (1593–1601), of Transylvania (1599–1600), and of Moldavia (1600). Through his military victories and massacre of Turkish officials he was able to force the Turks to grant him virtual independence (1596) and his Romanian principalities. His dealings with Holy Roman Emperor RUDOLF II, however, resulted in his assassination. After his death WALACHIA and Moldavia reverted to Turkey, and TRANSYLVANIA came under Austrian domination.

Michel, Robert H(enry), 1923–, U.S. politician; b. Peoria, Ill. A Republican, Michel was first elected to the U.S. House of Representatives from Illinois in 1956. He was House minority whip (1975–81) before he became minority leader in 1981.

Michelangelo Buonarroti, 1475–1564, Italian sculptor, painter, poet. He was a towering figure of RENAISSANCE, mannerist, and baroque art. From 1490 to 1492 he lived in Lorenzo de' MEDICI's house, where he was influenced by Neoplatonic thought. His early drawings show the influence of GIOTTO and MASACCIO, whereas the marble reliefs of the *Madonna of the Stairs* and *Battle of the Centaurs* (both: Casa Buonarroti, Florence) show the influence of DONATELLO and Roman sarcophagi. In 1494 he executed statuettes for San Petronio (Bologna), and here the monk SAVONAROLA impressed him with his apocalyptic vision, which would later fuse with the artist's own tragic sense of human destiny. Between 1496 and 1501, Michelangelo worked in Rome, doing the marble *Bacchus* (Bargello, Florence) and the exquisitely balanced *Pietà* (St. Peter's, Rome). He returned to Florence in 1501, where he was commissioned to do the magnificent *David* (Academy, Florence). From these years date the *Bruges Madonna* (Notre Dame, Bruges) and the painted tondo of the *Holy Family* (Uffizi). In 1505 he was ordered back to Rome by Pope JULIUS II to do his sepulchral monument. This was the most frustrating project of his life. Michelangelo spent a year on the gigantic bronze, which was melted for cannon shortly after its completion. Shortly after awarding the contract for the tomb, Julius commissioned the decoration of the ceiling of the SISTINE CHAPEL, which Michelangelo worked on from 1508 to 1512. The ceiling is divided into three zones, the highest showing scenes from Genesis. Below are prophets and sibyls. In the lunettes and spandrels are figures identified as ancestors of Jesus or the Virgin, which seem to suggest a vision of primordial humanity. After the death of Julius II, his heirs again contracted for the execution of his monument and 30 years of litigation ensued. Michelangelo had to abandon his plan for a vast mausoleum for Julius II in St. Peter's. His colossal *Moses* (San Pietro in Vincoli, Rome) and the statues known as *Slaves* (Academy, Florence; Louvre) were to have been included. From 1520 to 1534 he worked on the Medici Chapel (San Lorenzo, Florence) and designed the elegant, mannerist Laurentian Library of this church. A forceful contrast between contemplation and action is seen in his statues of Giuliano and Lorenzo de' Medici, and his allegorical figures of *Dawn, Evening, Night,* and *Day.* In 1529 he assisted as engineer in the defense of Florence. After working on the *Last Judgment* of the Sistine Chapel and the *Conversion of Paul* and *Martyrdom of Peter* in the Pauline Chapel (Vatican), he devoted himself to architecture as chief architect of ST. PETER'S CHURCH. In his last years Michelangelo's work shows a more spiritualized and abstract form, e.g., two unfinished *Pietà* groups and the Rondanini *Pietà* (Castello Sforzesco, Milan). He thought of himself primarily as a sculptor, and a feeling for the expressive potentialities of sculptural form manifests itself in all his work. Many of his designs have survived only through his drawings, which used vigorous cross-hatching. Great collections of his drawings are in the Louvre and Uffizi.

Michelet, Jules [mēshəlā'], 1798–1874, French writer, the greatest historian of the romantic school. His *History of France* (1833–67) is a masterpiece of French literature, in terms of its style, its emotional strength, and its powerful evocation. His writing, however, is marred by emotional bias against the clergy, the nobility, and the monarchy.

Michelozzo Michelozzi, 1396–1472, Italian sculptor and architect. He shared leadership with BRUNELLESCHI and ALBERTI in establishing the Renaissance style. His best work includes the Medici-Riccardi palace at Florence, one of the finest city houses ever built, and the Medici villa at Fiesole (1458–61), noted for its terraced gardens.

Michelson, Albert Abraham, 1852–1931, American physicist; b. Prussia. He was head (1892–1931) of the physics department at the Univ. of Chicago. He designed the modern interferometer, with which he measured the speed of light to an unequaled degree of accuracy. His measurement of the length of the standard meter in Paris in terms of the wavelength of the red line of the cadmium spectrum, using the interferometer method, provided an absolute and exactly reproducible standard of length. With Edward Morley he conducted the Michelson-Morley experiment, which led to the refutation of the ETHER hypothesis and was eventually explained by Einstein's theory of RELATIVITY. Michelson became (1907) the first American to win the Nobel Prize in physics.

Michigan, upper midwestern state of the U.S., consisting of two peninsulas thrusting into the GREAT LAKES and having borders with Ohio and Indiana (S), Wisconsin (NW), and the Canadian province of Ontario (E).

Area, 58,216 sq mi (150,779 sq km). *Pop.* (1990) 9,295,297, a 0.4% increase over 1980 pop. *Capital,* Lansing. *Statehood,* Jan. 26, 1837 (26th state). *Highest pt.,* Mt. Curwood, 1,980 ft (604 m); *lowest pt.,* Lake Erie, 572 ft (174 m). *Nickname,* Wolverine State. *Motto, Si Quaeris Peninsulam Amoenam Circumspice* [If You Seek a Pleasant Peninsula, Look about You]. *State bird,* robin. *State flower,* apple blossom. *State tree,* white pine. *Abbr.,* Mich.; MI.

Land and People. The mitten-shaped Lower Peninsula is bordered by Lake MICHIGAN on the west and Lakes HURON and ERIE on the east. The sparsely populated Upper Peninsula is bounded on the south by Lake Michigan and on the north by Lake SUPERIOR, where Isle Royale National Park (see NATIONAL PARKS, table) is located. 70% of the population lives in urban areas. DETROIT, the country's seventh largest city, is by far Michigan's largest and most important city. GRAND RAPIDS, FLINT, LANSING, and ANN ARBOR are other major cities. In 1990 the population was 83% white and 14% African American.

Economy. Michigan is a heavily industrialized state. Detroit and the surrounding cities are the center of the U.S. automobile industry. Nonelectrical machinery and fabricated metals follow transportation equipment in terms of revenue. Dairy products and cattle are the leading sources of agricultural income; corn, winter wheat, soybeans, dry beans, oats, and hay are the most important crops. Michigan is a leading producer of calcium chloride, gypsum, magnesium, peat, and iron ore. With an abundance of natural beauty, Michigan is also a popular tourist destination. Lumbering and fishing supplement the economy.

Government. The constitution (adopted 1963) provides for a governor elected to a four-year term. The legislature consists of a senate whose 38 members serve four-year terms and a house with 110 members elected to two-year terms. Michigan sends 2 senators and 16 representatives to the U.S. Congress and has 18 electoral votes.

History. The region was inhabited principally by the OJIBWA, OTTAWA, and Potawatomi when the French explorer Étienne Brulé landed (1618) at Sault Sainte Marie. After the British assumed control (1763), war with Native Americans—PONTIAC'S REBELLION—erupted (1763). Michigan passed to the U.S. in 1796, although the British held it during the WAR OF 1812. Settlement was encouraged by the opening (1825) of the ERIE CANAL. During the second half of the 19th cent. a lumber boom decimated the state's huge forests. Henry FORD founded the Ford Motor Co. in 1903 and introduced the automated assembly line, thus establishing the state's modern industrial base. Lack of diversity has made Michigan particularly subject to economic problems. The auto industry suffered a serious decline during the late 1970s and early 80s and, after a brief recovery, was hit by national recession and continuing foreign competition in the late 1980s and early 90s.

Michigan, Lake, third largest (22,178 sq mi/57,441 sq km) of the GREAT LAKES, fifth largest lake in the world, and largest freshwater lake entirely within the U.S. It is 307 mi (494 km) long and 30–120 mi (48–193 km) wide, with a surface elevation of 581 ft (177 m) and a maximum depth of 923 ft (281 m), and it is joined to Lake Huron by the Straits of Mackinac. Chicago and Milwaukee are major lakeshore cities, and Indiana Dunes National Lakeshore (est. 1966) borders the southern shore. Discovered in 1634 by the French explorer Jean Nicolet, the lake passed to England in 1763 and to the U.S. as part of the NORTHWEST TERRITORY in 1796.

Mickiewicz, Adam [mētskyĕ'vĭch], 1798–1855, Polish poet. In 1823 he was arrested for nationalist activities and deported to Russia. After 1829 he lived in W Europe but devoted himself to the cause of Polish independence. His masterpiece is the epic poem *Pan Tadeusz* (1834), depicting the life of the Polish gentry.

Micmac, indigenous people largely of Canada's Maritime Provinces, with an Algonquian language of the Algonquian-Wakashan stock (see NATIVE AMERICAN LANGUAGES). Of Eastern Woodlands culture (see NORTH AMERICA, INDIGENOUS PEOPLES OF), they are expert canoeists, and although once hunters and fishermen, they now derive income from agriculture. In 1990 there were 2,765 Micmacs in the U.S.

microcomputer: see COMPUTER.

microeconomics: see under ECONOMICS.

microelectronics, branch of ELECTRONICS devoted to the design and development of extremely small electronic devices that consume very little electric power. The simplest, but least effective, approach used is to make circuit elements, such as RESISTORS, CAPACITORS, and SEMICONDUCTOR devices, extremely small but discrete. In another approach, circuit elements fabricated as thin films of conductive, semiconductive, and insulating materials are deposited in sandwich form on an insulating substrate. The most advanced method is to form circuits, called INTEGRATED CIRCUITS, within and upon single semiconductor crystals. See also TRANSISTOR.

microfiber: see SYNTHETIC TEXTILE FIBERS.

microfiche, sheet of film containing numerous pages of printed or graphic material that have been greatly reduced by microphotography. Unlike microfilm, in which individual frames are reproduced consecutively on a roll of film, a single 4 × 6-in. (10 × 15-cm) microfiche card may contain hundreds of pages, providing faster access to a desired item. The image is magnified to approximately full size by a viewing machine or reader. Microfiche is increasingly used by libraries and businesses.

micromechanics, the combination of minuscule electrical and mechanical components in a single tiny device less than 1 mm across, such as a valve or a motor. Although micromechanical production processes and applications are still in the developmental stage, efforts have begun to develop machines 1000 times smaller. **Nanotechnology** is concerned with atomic- and molecular-scale devices. Such devices can be constructed using a SCANNING TUNNELING MICROSCOPE. A single atom has been used as an electric switch, and an individual molecule used to convert alternating current into direct current. Cluster chemistry has produced small balls and tubes (see FULLERENE) containing between 10 and 1000 atoms that may be useful in forming nano-thin wires and TRANSISTORS that operate on just a few electrons. A third nanotechnological approach is to grow such devices from proteins, DNA, or synthesized organic molecules. Nanotechnologies are still in the laboratory stage, and practical applications are only envisioned.

micrometer, instrument used for measuring extremely small distances. In the micrometer caliper, the object to be measured is held between the two jaws of the instrument; the distance between the jaws is measured on a scale calibrated to the rotation of the finely threaded screw that moves one of the jaws. In astronomical and microscopic micrometers, the distance that a filament moves from one end to the other of the image of an object is read on a calibrated scale.

Micronesia, one of the three main divisions of OCEANIA, in the W Pacific Ocean, N of the equator. The principal island groups include the Caroline Islands (see PALAU and MICRONESIA, FEDERATED STATES OF), NAURU, the Gilbert Islands (see KIRIBATI), the NORTHERN MARIANA ISLANDS, and the MARSHALL ISLANDS. The inhabitants are of Australoid and Polynesian stock and speak Malayo-Polynesian languages.

Micronesia, Federated States of, independent island group (1992 est. pop. 115,000), c.271 sq mi (702 sq km), in the W Pacific Ocean; formerly part of the U.S. Trust Territory of the PACIFIC ISLANDS. The U.S. is responsible for its defense. It comprises four states—Kosrae, Pohnpei (formerly Ponape), Chuuk (formerly Truk), and Yap—and the capital, Kolonia, is on the island of Pohnpei. U.S. aid ($1 billion pledged for the 1990s) is the primary source of income. Other economic mainstays are subsistence farming, fishing, and tourism. The population is predominantly Micronesian and Christian. English is the official language, but the indigenous languages are Austronesian and Polynesian tongues. Germany purchased the islands from Spain in 1898. They were occupied (1914) by Japan, which received them (1920) as a League of Nations mandate. During WORLD WAR II U.S. forces captured the islands and in 1947 they became part of the U.S. trust territory. In 1979 they became self-governing as the Federated States of Micronesia. In 1986, they assumed free-association status with the U.S. See PACIFIC OCEAN map.

microphone, device (invented c.1877) used in broadcasting, recording, and sound-amplifying systems to convert sound into electrical energy. Its basic component is a flexible diaphragm that responds to the pressure or particle velocity of sound waves. In an electrostatic, or condenser, microphone, two parallel metal plates (electrodes) are given opposite electrical charges. One of the plates is attached to the diaphragm and moves in response to its vibrations, generating a varying voltage. An electret microphone, the most widely used type, has a permanently charged dielectic (electret) between the two electrodes. See also TELEPHONE.

microprocessor, INTEGRATED CIRCUIT containing the arithmetic, logic, and control circuitry required to interpret and execute instructions from a COMPUTER PROGRAM. When combined with other integrated circuits that provide storage for data and programs, often on a single SEMICONDUCTOR base to form a chip, the microprocessor becomes the heart of a small COMPUTER, or microcomputer. Developed during the 1970s, the microprocessor has made possible the inexpensive hand-held electronic CALCULATOR, the digital wristwatch, and the ELECTRONIC GAME. Microprocessors are also used to control consumer appliances, to regulate gasoline consumption in automobiles, and to monitor alarm systems.

microscope, optical instrument used to increase the apparent size of an object. A magnifying glass, an ordinary double convex LENS having a short focal length, is a simple microscope. When an object is placed nearer such a lens than its principal focus, i.e., within its focal length, an image is produced that is erect and larger than the object. The compound microscope, invented in the early 17th cent., consists of two or more such lenses fixed in the two extremities of a hollow metal cylinder. This cylinder is mounted upright on a screw device, which permits it to be raised or lowered above the object until a clear image is formed. The lower lens (nearer to the object) is called the objective; the upper lens (nearer to the eye of the observer), the eyepiece. When an object is in focus, a real, inverted image is formed by the lower lens at a point inside the principal focus of the upper lens. This image serves as an "object" for the upper lens, which produces another image larger still (but virtual) and visible to the eye of the observer. The compound microscope is widely used in bacteriology, biology, and medicine in the examination of such extremely minute objects as bacteria, other unicellular organisms, and plant and animal cells and tissue. Technical advances making use of different forms of light and other forms of radiation (see, e.g., ELECTRON MICROSCOPE) have increased enormously the magnification and resolution of microscopes.

Microspora, phylum of intracellular parasitic PROTOZOANS that live in almost all groups of animals. Phylum members are of economic concern because they are parasites of bees and silkworms.

microwave, ELECTROMAGNETIC RADIATION having a frequency range from 1,000 to 300,000 megahertz, corresponding to a wavelength range from 300 to 1 mm (about 12 to about 0.04 in.). Microwaves are used in MICROWAVE OVENS, RADAR, and communications links spanning moderate distances, such as CELLULAR TELEPHONE systems.

microwave oven, cooking device that uses MICROWAVES to penetrate foods and rapidly cook them. The microwaves cause water molecules in the food to vibrate, thus producing heat. Once used almost exclusively in fast-food restaurants, microwave ovens have become increasingly popular in home kitchens. Significant microwave radiation leakage occurred with some early ovens, but safeguards have eliminated the problem.

Midas, in Greek mythology, king of Phrygia. Because he befriended SILENUS, DIONYSUS granted him the power to turn everything he touched into gold. When even his food became gold, he washed away his power in the Pactolus River.

Middle Ages, period in W European history roughly from the fall of the West Roman Empire in the 5th cent. to the 15th cent., once called the Dark Ages. Christianity became the unifying force of culture. FEUDALISM and the MANORIAL SYSTEM, the HOLY ROMAN EMPIRE, the CRUSADES, and CHIVALRY fused Christian ideals with economic, political, and military institutions. Guilds in rising towns maintained the Christian spirit in economic life. Universities developed under the auspices of the church. The philosophy of SCHOLASTICISM, expounded by St. THOMAS AQUINAS, combined new learning with Christian faith. GOTHIC ARCHITECTURE and the writings of DANTE and CHAUCER show the vitality and spirit of the age. Transition to the modern age came with a money economy, political centralization, exploration, secularization, and the humanism of the RENAISSANCE. Finally, the Protestant REFORMATION shattered the medieval unity of Christianity.

Middle America, indigenous peoples of, aboriginal peoples of the area between the present-day U.S. and South America. The MAYA of the YUCATÁN, with their advanced culture, had links with the Chorotega of Nicaragua and Honduras, and these in turn had contacts with the Chibcha of Colombia. High civilizations flourished in Mexico after the domestication of corn, e.g., beside the Maya, the OLMEC, TOLTEC, MIXTEC, ZAPOTEC, and AZTEC. They developed architecture, agriculture, and stonework and metalwork to a remarkable degree. Following the Spanish conquest (16th cent.), Mexico's indigenous population was used as laborers, first under the EN COMIENDA system of tributory labor, then under peonage. Native artisans, however, continued to make contributions to painting and architecture. Not until the Mexican revolution of 1910 and the *indianismo* movement of ZAPATA were efforts made to advance Mexico's indigenous peoples socially and economically. Today descendants of the Mexican civilizations, along with Huastecs, TARASCANS, Yaquis, Tarahumaras, and other groups, constitute a major element of the population of Middle America. Both people of indigenous and mixed descent (mestizos) are found in all levels of society, and millions still speak NATIVE AMERICAN LANGUAGES.

Middle East, term applied to a region that includes SW Asia and part of NE Africa, lying W of Afghanistan, Pakistan, and India. It includes the Asian part of TURKEY; SYRIA; ISRAEL; JORDAN; IRAQ; IRAN; LEBANON; the countries of the Arabian peninsula, that is, SAUDI ARABIA, YEMEN, OMAN, UNITED ARAB EMIRATES, QATAR, BAHRAIN, KUWAIT; EGYPT; and LIBYA. The region was the site of great ancient civilizations, e.g., MESOPOTAMIA and Egypt, and it was the birthplace of JUDAISM, CHRISTIANITY, and ISLAM. It contains much of the world's oil reserves and has many strategic trade routes, e.g., the SUEZ CANAL. In the 20th cent. the area has been the scene of political turmoil and major warfare, e.g., in WORLD WAR I, WORLD WAR II, the ARAB-ISRAELI WARS, the IRAN-IRAQ WAR, and the PERSIAN GULF WAR. The term *Middle East* is also sometimes used in a cultural sense for that part of the world predominantly Islamic in culture, in which case Afghanistan, Pakistan, and the remaining countries of North Africa are included.

Middleton, Thomas, 1580–1627, English dramatist. He collaborated with DEKKER, DRAYTON, and others, and wrote (1604–11) realistic, satiric comedies, including *Michaelmas Term, A Trick to Catch the Old One,* and *A Mad World, My Masters.* Later (1621–27) he wrote two powerful tragedies, *The Changeling* (with William Rowley) and *Women Beware Women.*

Middle West or **Midwest,** U.S. region usually defined as including the N central states of OHIO, INDIANA, ILLINOIS, MICHIGAN, WISCONSIN, MINNESOTA, IOWA, MISSOURI, KANSAS, and NEBRASKA. It is a rich farm area, noted for its corn and hogs, as well as an important industrial region, home of the nation's automobile and rubber industries.

midget: see DWARFISM.

MIDI [*M*usical *I*nstrument *D*igital *I*nterface], a protocol for sending digital information between electronic music instruments and equipment, including COMPUTERS and signal processors (devices that modify sounds by adding reverberation, modifying pitch, and other means). The basic protocol addresses common functions, such as notes, timing, pitch, and pedal information. MIDI keyboards, guitars, violins, and drums have become as common as the synthesizer in ELECTRONIC MUSIC.

Midian [mĭd'ēən] or **Midianites** [–īts], in the BIBLE, a nomadic Bedouin people of N Arabia and of the lands E of Palestine. They were closely associated with the Israelites and were among the first to use the camel. MOSES married the daughter of their priest Jethro.

midnight sun, phenomenon in which the sun remains visible in the sky continuously for 24 hr or longer. It occurs in the polar regions because of the tilt of the equatorial plane to the plane of the ecliptic (the sun's apparent path through the sky). It occurs at the polar circles only at the SOLSTICE (summer for Arctic, winter for Antarctic), but as one approaches the pole it increases in occurrence up to a continuous six months (from vernal to autumnal equinox for the North Pole; the reverse for the South Pole).

mid-ocean ridge: see OCEAN; PLATE TECTONICS.

Midrash, verse-by-verse interpretation of Hebrew Scriptures, consisting of homily and exegesis, by Jewish teachers since c.400 B.C. The *Midrash Rabbah* is the most authoritative of the collections of commentaries on the TORAH and the Five Scrolls (the books Song of Solomon, Ruth, Lamentations, Ecclesiastes, and Esther in the Hebrew Bible).

midsummer day and midsummer night, feast of the nativity of St. JOHN THE BAPTIST (June 24) and the preceding night (June 23). Close to the summer SOLSTICE, midsummer has been associated with solar ceremonies since before Christianity. Supernatural beings were thought to roam on midsummer night.

Midway, island group (2 sq mi/5.2 sq km), central Pacific, c.1,150 mi (1,850 km) NW of Honolulu. Annexed by the U.S. in 1867, it is a naval base with no indigenous population. On June 3–6, 1942, the Japanese navy was crippled in the battle of Midway, fought nearby with carrier-based aircraft.

midwifery, art of assisting at childbirth. The term *midwife* for centuries referred to a woman who was an overseer during the process of delivery. Professional schools of midwifery were established in Europe in the 16th cent. Midwives are still used widely in Europe and have experienced an upsurge of popularity in the U.S. Most modern American midwives are registered nurses who have completed additional specialized training.

Mielziner, Jo [mēlzē'nər], 1900–1976, American theatrical designer; b. France. He designed sets for more than 200 productions, including *Strange Interlude* (1928), *A Streetcar Named Desire* (1947), and *Death of a Salesman* (1949).

Miës van der Rohe, Ludwig [mē'ĕs vän dĕr rō'ə], 1886–1969, German-American architect, a founder of MODERN ARCHITECTURE. In Germany, he was appointed (1930) director of the BAUHAUS. But in 1937 he left Germany to teach at the Armour Inst., Chicago (now Illinois Inst. of Technology), where he also planned a new campus. His combination of the glass skyscraper concept with surface expression of structural members is seen in the Seagram Building, New York City (1956–58; with Philip JOHNSON).

Mifflin, Thomas, 1744–1800, American Revolutionary quartermaster general (1775–78) and statesman; b. Philadelphia. He was president of the CONTINENTAL CONGRESS (1783–84), a delegate to the FEDERAL CONSTITUTIONAL CONVENTION (1787), and governor of Pennsylvania (1790–99).

Mifune Toshiro [mĭfōō'nē], 1920–, Japanese actor; b. China. A versatile actor, he appeared in many films directed by KUROSAWA AKIRA, e.g., *Rashomon* (1950), *Throne of Blood* (1957), *Yojimbo* (1960). Mifune has also performed in some U.S. films.

migraine, headache characterized by recurrent attacks of severe pain, usually on one side of the head. The pain is believed to be associated with intense vasoconstriction, followed by prolonged dilation of blood vessels leading to and within the brain. Attacks vary in duration and frequency. In classic migraines the pain is preceded by visual disturbances, sensitivity to light, nausea, and dizziness. ERGOT derivatives and sumatriptan, a serotonin agonist, can alleviate the headache; the BETA BLOCKER propranolol may prevent the condition.

Milan, Ital. *Milano,* city (1990 pop. 1,449,403), capital of LOMBARDY, N Italy, in the Po basin. It is the economic and financial heart of modern Italy, with such manufactures as textiles, machinery, chemicals, and motor vehicles. Capital of Rome's Western Empire and a Christian center, it was damaged by barbarian invasions. It became a free commune (12th cent.) and rose to leadership in Lombardy. Losing its republican liberties, it was ruled by the VISCONTIS (1277–1447) and the SFORZAS (1447–1535). Later it passed to Spain, Austria, and Napoleon I before union (1861) with Italy. Milan was severely damaged in World War II. Dominated by its white marble cathedral (1386–1813), it is also known for the renowned opera house Teatro alla Scala, the Church of Santa Maria delle Grazie (housing LEONARDO's *Last Supper*), the Brera Palace, and the Ambrosian Library.

mildew, name for certain organisms and the plant diseases they cause, and for the discoloration and disintegration of materials (e.g., leather, fabrics, and paper) caused by related fungi. The powdery mildews (Fungi division Ascomycota; see FUNGUS) form a gray-white coating on plant tissues. The downy mildews (PROTIST division Oomycota) form white, purplish, or gray patches; a downy mildew caused the potato BLIGHT and famine in Ireland (1845–49) and more recently threatened the French wine industry.

Miletus [mīlē'təs], ancient seaport of W ASIA MINOR, in Caria, near Sámos. Occupied by the Greeks (c.1000 B.C.), it became a leading IONIAN city. It led the revolt (499 B.C.) against the Persians, who sacked the city (494).

Milhaud, Darius [mēyō'], 1892–1974, French composer. His music incorporates polytonality, JAZZ, and Brazilian elements. One of the Parisian group "les SIX," he is noted for his operas *Le Pauvre Matelot* (1927; libretto by COCTEAU) and *Christophe Colombe* (1930; libretto by CLAUDEL) and for his ballets, e.g., *The Creation of the World.* (1923).

military-industrial complex, in the U.S., the link between the Defense Dept. and a permanent peacetime arms industry that enables those groups to wield extraordinary political and economic power. The term was coined by Pres. EISENHOWER in his farewell address (1961), when he warned of the threat it posed to democracy. The end of the COLD WAR has largely ended the peacetime arms buildup in the U.S. and has caused the contraction of the nation's arms industry, diminishing the power of the military-industrial complex.

military science, study and application of the rules and principles of warfare, designed to achieve success in military operations. It comprises military strategy and tactics, as adapted to utilize the latest developments in weapons and communications technology. Strategy and tactics are relative terms referring, respectively, to large-scale and small-scale military operations. Strategy may be defined as the general scheme of the conduct of a war, often referred to as "grand strategy." On the highest level it has come to mean national strategy, involving complex assessments of technological resources, national priorities, and geopolitical factors. Tactics, on the other hand, refers to the planning and execution of means to achieve strategic objectives.

militia, military organization composed of citizens enrolled by enlistment or CONSCRIPTION and trained for service in times of national emergency. When the emergency is over, militia members traditionally resume civilian status. An early prototype of the militia was developed by PHILIP II of Macedon, and the concept persisted in Europe until the rise of standing national armies in the 17th and 18th cent. The Military Company of Massachusetts, the first American militia, was followed by similar groups in other colonies; during the 19th cent. various U.S. states had their own militia, which served in all the nation's wars. After World War I these military units were established as the NATIONAL GUARD.

Milk, Harvey, 1931–78, U.S. politician and gay rights activist. In 1977 he was elected to the San Francisco Board of Supervisors, becoming first acknowledged homosexual in the U.S. to win high local office. Former city supervisor Dan White assassinated Milk and Mayor George Moscone in 1978.

milk, liquid secreted by the mammary glands of female mammals to feed their young. Cow's milk is most widely used by humans, but milk of such animals as the mare, goat, ewe, buffalo, camel, and yak is also consumed. An almost complete food, milk contains fats; proteins (mainly casein); salts; sugar (lactose); vitamins A, C, and D; some B vitamins; and minerals, chiefly calcium and phosphorus. The composition of milk varies with the species, breed, feed, and condition of the animal. Commercially produced milk commonly undergoes PASTEURIZATION to check bacterial growth and homogenization for uniformity. Dried (powdered) milk and concentrated milk have been in use since the mid-19th cent. Concentrated milk may be condensed (sweetened) or evaporated (unsweetened). Skim milk, valuable in fat-free diets, is low in vitamin A. See BUTTER; CHEESE; DAIRYING; FERMENTED MILK.

Milken, Michael R., 1946–, American financial executive; b. Calif. An executive at Drexel Burnham Lambert Inc., he transformed corporate takeovers by the use of high-yield JUNK BONDS, becoming enormously wealthy in the process. In 1989, a federal grand jury handed down a 98-count indictment against Milken for violations of federal securities and racketeering laws. He pled guilty to securities fraud and related charges in 1990, and the government dropped the more serious charges of INSIDER TRADING and racketeering.

milk of magnesia, common name for the chemical compound magnesium hydroxide $Mg(OH)_2$. The viscous, white, mildly alkaline mixture used as a medicinal antacid and laxative is a suspension of about 8% magnesium hydroxide in water.

Milky Way, large spiral GALAXY containing about 100 billion stars, including the sun. It is characterized by a central nucleus of closely packed stars, lying in the direction of the constellation Sagittarius, and a flat disk marked by spiral arms. Seen edgewise as a broad band of light arching across the night sky from horizon to horizon, the Milky Way passes through the constellations Sagittarius, Aquila, Cygnus, Perseus, Auriga, Orion, and Crux. The disk is c.100,000 LIGHT-YEARS in diameter and on the average 10,000 light-years thick (increasing up to 30,000 light-years at the nucleus). A thin halo of STAR CLUSTERS surround the galaxy, extending to about 130,000 light-years. The sun is c.28,000 light-years from the nucleus and takes 200 million years to revolve once around the galaxy.

Mill, John Stuart, 1806–73, British philosopher and economist. He received a rigorous education under his father, James Mill (1773–1836), and Jeremy BENTHAM (1748–1832), who were close friends and together had founded UTILITARIANISM. John Stuart Mill's own philosophy, influenced by his wife, Harriet Taylor, developed into a more humanitarian doctrine than that of utilitarianism's founders: he was sympathetic to socialism, and was a strong advocate of women's rights and such political and social reforms as proportional representation, labor unions, and farm cooperatives. In logic he formulated rules for the process of induction, and he stressed the method of EMPIRICISM as the source of all knowledge. *On Liberty* (1859) is probably his most famous work. Among his other books are *Principles of Political Economy* (1848), *Utilitarianism* (1863), and his celebrated *Autobiography* (1873). One of the most important liberal thinkers of the 19th cent., Mill strongly influenced modern economics, politics, and philosophy.

Millais, Sir John Everett [mĭlā'], 1829–96, English painter. He was a founder of the PRE-RAPHAELITE movement. His early work shows a painstaking rendering of detail, e.g., *Christ in the Carpenter's Shop* (1850; Tate Gall., London). A friend of RUSKIN, he was (1896) president of the Royal Academy.

Millay, Edna St. Vincent, 1892–1950, American poet; b. Rockland, Me. Known as much for her bohemian life-style as for her verse, she won fame with the lyric *Renascence* (1917) and *The Harp Weaver* (1923; Pulitzer). Later volumes include the sonnet cycle *Fatal Interview* (1931). She also wrote several verse dramas, e.g., *Aria da Capo* (1920).

Miller, Arthur, 1915–, American dramatist; b. N.Y.C. His masterpiece, *Death of a Salesman* (1949), is the story of an ordinary American destroyed by hollow values. Miller's other works, all dealing with political or moral issues, include *All My Sons* (1947), *The Crucible* (1953), *A View from the Bridge* (1955), *After the Fall* (1964), *The Price* (1968), *Playing for Time* (1980, a television adaptation), and *The Ride down Mount Morgan* (1991). His autobiography was published in 1987.

Miller, Cincinnatus Heine or **Cincinnatus Hiner:** see MILLER, JOAQUIN.

Miller, Henry, 1891–1980, American author; b. N.Y.C. He lived in Paris in the 1930s and later settled in Big Sur, Calif. His controversial novels, mixing frank sexual description, autobiographical incident, and speculation on philosophy, literature, and society, include *Tropic of Cancer* (1934) and *Tropic of Capricorn* (1939), both banned in the U.S. until 1961, and the trilogy *The Rosy Crucifixion* (1949–60). He also wrote a fine travel book, *The Colossus of Maroussi* (1941); essays; and the autobiography *My Life and Times* (1972).

Miller, Jonathan (Wolfe), 1934–, English director, actor, and writer. He was coauthor of and actor in the zany satirical revue *Beyond the Fringe* (London, 1961; N.Y.C., 1962). A physician, Miller has also directed plays for the National Theatre and television, e.g., *The Shakespeare Plays,* and operas, and has written the television series, *The Body in Question* (1978) and *Madness* (1991).

Millerand, Alexandre [mĕlräN'], 1859–1943, president of France (1920–24). Expelled from the Socialist party, he moved to the right politically and was minister of war (1912–13, 1914–15). In 1920 he was premier before becoming president.

Millet, Jean François [mĕlā'], 1814–75, French painter. He studied with Hippolyte Delaroche and was associated with the BARBIZON SCHOOL. Considered a social realist, he produced works noted for their power and simplicity, e.g., *The Gleaners* (1857; Louvre) and *The Angelus* (1859; Louvre).

millet, common name for several plants of the GRASS family cultivated mainly for cereals in the Old World and forage and hay in North America. The main varieties are foxtail, pearl, barnyard, and proso millets. Proso millet is the chief cereal in parts of Africa and Asia; the chief millet in the U.S. is foxtail millet.

Millikan, Robert Andrews, 1868–1953, American physicist and educator; b. Morrison, Ill. He taught (1896–1921) physics at the Univ. of Chicago and later (1921–45) was chairman of the executive council of the California Institute of Technology and director of the Norman Bridge Laboratory there. He received the 1923 Nobel Prize in physics for his measurement of the ELECTRON's charge and his work on the PHOTOELECTRIC EFFECT. He also studied COSMIC RAYS (which he named), X rays, and physical and electric constants.

millipede, wormlike segmented ARTHROPOD with two pairs of legs on each body segment except the first few and last. Most temperate species are small and dull in appearance, but tropical millipedes are often brightly colored. In contrast to the carnivorous CENTIPEDES, which they resemble, millipedes feed mostly on decaying vegetation.

Mills, C. Wright, 1916–62, American sociologist; b. Waco, Tex. A controversial figure, he advocated a comparative world sociology and criticized intellectuals for not using their freedom responsibly by working for social change. In *The Power Elite* (1956), he explained the power structure of postwar American society in terms of an oligarchy.

Mills, Robert, 1781–1855, American architect of the CLASSIC REVIVAL; b. Charleston, S.C. In 1836 Pres. JACKSON appointed him architect of public buildings in Washington, D.C. His major works there include the Treasury Building (1836), the Patent Office and Old Post Office (both begun 1839), and the WASHINGTON MONUMENT (designed 1833, built 1848–84, without the base he intended for it). He also designed the Bunker Hill monument and other public projects in various cities.

Milne, A(lan) A(lexander), 1882–1956, English author. He is known for his verse collections for children, *When We Were Very Young* (1924) and *Now We Are Six* (1927), and for the classic children's stories *Winnie-the-Pooh* (1926) and *The House at Pooh Corner* (1928).

Milo: see MILOS.

Miloš or **Milosh** (Milos Obrenović), 1780–1860, prince of Serbia (1817–39, 1858–60), founder of the OBRENOVIĆ dynasty and of modern SERBIA. In 1815 he led a rebellion against the Turks and, after presumably killing his rival, KARAGEORGE, was named (1817) prince of Serbia under the suzerainty of the sultan. He abdicated in favor of his sons, Milan and Peter, but was recalled in 1858.

Milošević, Slobodan, 1941–, Yugoslav-Serbian political leader. He held posts in the Communist party and state enterprises from the early 1960s, becoming party leader in Belgrade in 1984 and Serbia by 1987. Initially opposed to liberalization, he was elected (1989) president of Serbia and transformed the Serbian party into the nationalistic Socialist party. He called for the inclusion of Serbian areas of other republics in a "greater Serbia" as the price for YUGOSLAVIA's dissolution and supported Serbian militias in CROATIA and BOSNIA AND HERCEGOVINA. In 1992 he was reelected amid accusations of fraud.

Miłosz, Czesław [mē'wäsh], 1911–, Polish poet, novelist, and essayist; b. Lithuania. He has lived in the U.S. since 1960. The main source of his early poetry was the Lithuanian countryside of his youth, which also figures prominently in his autobiographical novel, *The Issa Valley* (tr. 1981). His classically styled verse appears in English translation in *Selected Poems* (tr. 1973), *Provinces* (1991), and other volumes. He is also well known for the sociopolitical essays in *The Captive Mind* (1953) and for the novel *The Seizure of Power* (1955). He was awarded the 1980 Nobel Prize in literature.

Miltiades [mĭltī'ədēz], d. 489 B.C., Athenian general in the PERSIAN WARS. In 490 B.C. he defeated the Persians at MARATHON and then marched his exhausted army 20 mi (32 km) to Athens, which he defended from the Persian fleet.

Milton, John, 1608–74, English poet. As a Cambridge undergraduate he wrote poems in Latin and English, including "Ode on the Morning of Christ's Nativity" (1629). "L'Allegro" and "Il Penseroso" were probably written soon after. Continuing his studies at home, he produced the MASQUE *Comus* (1634) and the great ELEGY "Lycidas" (1638). After a year in Italy, Milton supported the Presbyterian struggle to reform the Church of England with pamphlets attacking the episcopal form of church government. *Areopagitica* (1644), an argument for freedom of the press, grew out of dissatisfaction with

Parliament's strict censorship. Milton gradually broke with the Presbyterians and in 1649 wrote *The Tenure of Kings and Magistrates,* supporting the Independents, who had imprisoned Charles I, and arguing that subjects may depose and put to death an unworthy king. The pamphlet earned him a Latin secretaryship in CROMWELL's Commonwealth government. During this period Milton went blind and had to work through secretaries, one of them MARVELL. He had long planned to write an epic, and in retirement after the RESTORATION (1660), he worked on *Paradise Lost.* It appeared in 1667 and again, reorganized, in 1674. The story of Satan's rebellion against God and of the expulsion of Adam and Eve from the Garden of Eden, it is generally considered the greatest epic in the English language. *Paradise Regained* (1671) tells how Jesus overcame Satan's temptations. *Samson Agonistes* (also 1671) is a poetic drama modeled on Greek tragedy but with biblical subject matter. During his life Milton also wrote 18 English and five Italian SONNETS, accepted as among the best ever written.

Milwaukee, city (1990 pop. 628,088; met. area 1,432,149), seat of Milwaukee co., SE Wis., on Lake Michigan; inc. as a city 1848. The largest city in the state, it is a major GREAT LAKES port, shipping cargo from the Midwest to world ports via the SAINT LAWRENCE SEAWAY. Heavy machinery and electrical equipment, diesel and gasoline engines, and tractors are produced; the city's beer industry is famous. MARQUETTE visited the site, then a Native American trading center, in 1673. Throughout the early 19th cent. it grew as a fur-trading and shipping site. Heavy 19th-cent. immigration, especially from Germany, made it a great industrial city. The Socialist leader Victor BERGER dominated its strong labor movement. Points of interest include Marquette Univ., the Milwaukee Art Center, and a church designed by Frank Lloyd WRIGHT.

Mimas, in astronomy, natural satellite of SATURN.

mime: see PANTOMIME.

mimicry, in biology, the advantageous resemblance of one species to another, often unrelated species or to a feature of its own habitat (see PROTECTIVE COLORATION). Mimicry serves to protect the mimic from predators or to deceive its prey (e.g., ant-eating spiders that themselves resemble ants). Although most common among insects, mimicry occurs in both plants and animals.

mimic thrush, name for exclusively American BIRDS of the family Mimidae, allied to the WRENS and THRUSHES and including the mockingbird, catbird, and thrashers. Mimic thrushes are most numerous in Mexico. They are slim, robin-sized birds with slender, downcurved bills, long tails, and strong legs suited to scratching through dead leaves for insects; they also eat berries and fruit. All are famous for their imitative vocal powers; the mockingbird, the preeminent North American songbird, may mimic some 30 calls in succession.

mimosa, tree, shrub, or herb (genus *Mimosa*) of the PULSE family, found mainly in the tropics. Mimosas usually have feathery foliage and rounded clusters of fragrant pink flowers atop the branches; they are grown as ornamentals. Best known is the sensitive plant (*M. pudica*), whose leaves fold up and collapse under stimuli such as touch, darkness, or drought. The similar and related yellow-flowered ACACIA is often sold as mimosa.

minaret, in Islamic architecture, tower, from which the faithful are called to prayer by a muezzin. Most MOSQUES have one or more minarets, usually at the corners. The earliest minarets were at the Mosque of Amr (A.D. 673) in Egypt. At first, minarets were generally square; free-standing conical minarets, probably derived from Babylonian ZIGGURATS, appeared in the 9th cent. The mosque of El-Azhar (15th cent.) in Cairo is an example of the octagonal Egyptian style.

Mindanao, island (1987 est. pop. 13,093,000), Philippines, southernmost and second largest (c.36,540 sq mi/94,640 sq km) of the main Philippine islands. Davao and Zamboanga are the principal cities. The terrain is generally mountainous and heavily forested, with a high point of 9,690 ft (2,954 m) at Mt. Apo. Pineapples, mangoes, bananas, and rice are grown. Heavy industry includes steel, chemical, and fertilizer plants powered by hydroelectricity from the Maria Christina Falls, on the Agus R. The population is largely Roman Catholic but about one third is Muslim, mostly concentrated in the west; small minorities that adhere to traditional beliefs survive in isolated areas. Muslim demands for autonomy have led to guerrilla warfare.

Mindszenty, Jozsef [mĭnd'sĕntē], 1892–1975, Hungarian primate, Roman Catholic cardinal. An opponent of Communism, Mindszenty was arrested (1948) by the Hungarian government and at his trial pleaded guilty to most of the charges. It was widely believed that he had been drugged to obtain a confession. Sentenced to life imprisonment, he found refuge in the U.S. legation during the Hungarian uprising of 1956. In 1971 the Vatican arranged his departure from Hungary, and in 1974 he was removed as primate.

mine, in warfare, a bomb placed in a fixed position, to be detonated by contact, magnetic proximity, or electrical impulse. Land mines, both antitank and antipersonnel, came into wide use in World War II; they were normally equipped with pressure sensors placed slightly above or below ground. Naval mines, known since the 16th cent., were first widely employed in World War I. The modern naval mine is often equipped with sonar or magnetic sensors and is laid on or anchored just below the surface of the sea.

mineral, natural inorganic substance having a characteristic and homogeneous chemical composition, definite physical properties, and, usually, a definite crystalline form. A few (e.g., carbon, gold, iron, and silver) are elements, but most are chemical compounds. ROCKS are combinations of minerals. Important physical properties of minerals include hardness, specific gravity, cleavage, fracture, luster, color, transparency, heat conductivity, feel, magnetism, and electrical properties. Minerals originate by precipitation from solution, by the cooling and hardening of magmas, by the condensation of gases or gaseous action on rock, and by METAMORPHISM. They are of great economic importance in manufacturing; many are valued as gems.

mineral, dietary, inorganic element found in the earth's crust that is an essential nutrient, vital to normal body function. Minerals are those elements for which the body's requirement is at least 100 mg per day. Trace minerals are those that are needed in smaller amounts. Major dietary minerals include calcium and phosphorus (for bones and teeth), magnesium (for cellular metabolism), sodium (for fluid balance and muscle function), potassium (for fluid-electrolyte and acid-base balance), chloride (for water balance and digestion), and sulfur (for protein structure and enzyme activity). Other essential nutrients include dietary FATS, PROTEINS, CARBOHYDRATES, and VITAMINS.

Minerva, in Roman mythology, goddess of handicrafts and the arts; identified with the Olympian ATHENA.

Ming, dynasty: see CHINA.

Mingus, Charles, 1922–79, American jazz musician; b. Nogales, Ariz. One of the most important 20th-cent. jazz composers, he was also a bassist, pianist, bandleader, and vocalist. In the 1950s and 60s he led groups noted for their energetic improvisations and loose rhythms.

miniature schnauzer: see SCHNAUZER.

minicomputer: see COMPUTER.

minimalism, movement in American painting and sculpture that originated in New York City in the early 1960s. A reaction against the subjectivity and romanticism of ABSTRACT EXPRESSIONISM, minimalism stressed impersonality and anonymity in precise, often monumental, geometric forms and pure colors intended to have no references beyond the works themselves. Minimalist art is typified by the primary structures of such sculptors as Carl ANDRE, Donald JUDD, and Tony SMITH, and by the hard-edge paintings of such artists as Ellsworth KELLY, Kenneth Noland, and Frank STELLA.

minimalist music, style of music that developed in the 1960s in the U.S. As MINIMALISM reacted against the excesses of ABSTRACT EXPRESSIONISM, minimalist music rejected many of modern music's complexities. Generally, minimalist compositions emphasize simplicity in melodic line and harmonic progression, stress repetition and rhythm, and reduce historical or expressive reference. The use of electronic instruments is common, as are influences from Asia and Africa. Minimalist composers include Philip GLASS, Steven Reich, Terry Riley, and John Adams.

minimum wage, lowest wage legally permitted in an industry, organization, or the like. Minimum wages are aimed at assuring workers a standard of living above the lowest permitted by health and decency. The minimum has been set by labor unions (through

COLLECTIVE BARGAINING), through arbitration, and by legislation. Introduced (1894) in New Zealand, it rapidly was adopted by nearly all countries. In the U.S. a campaign by organized labor culminated in the passage (1938) of the Fair Labor Standards Act (see WAGES AND HOURS ACT), which set minimum wages for nonfarm workers in interstate commerce. The U.S. minimum wage has risen steadily over the years, reaching $4.25 per hour in 1991, and coverage has been extended to more types of workers, among them state and local government employees. A family of four with a single breadwinner working at the minimum wage, however, will have an income significantly below the official U.S. poverty level.

mining, extraction of solid MINERAL resources from the earth, including ORES (which contain commercially valuable amounts of METALS), precious stones, building stones, and solid fuels. Surface mining, open-pit, or open-cut, mining, STRIP MINING, and QUARRYING are the most common mining methods that start from the earth's surface and maintain exposure to it. Under certain circumstances surface mining can become prohibitive, and underground mining is then considered. The objective of underground mining is to extract the ore below the surface of the earth safely and economically. Entry is through a tunnel or shaft, and the ore is mined in stopes, or rooms. Material left in place to support the ceiling is called a pillar and can sometimes be recovered afterward. A modern underground mine is a highly mechanized operation, using vehicles, rail haulage, and multiple drill units. To protect miners and their equipment, much attention is paid to mine safety, including proper ventilation and roof support. There are a number of other mining methods, including *solution mining,* in which the ore is brought into a liquid solution by a chemical or bacteria and pumped to the surface; *gopher mining,* an old-fashioned method in which small, narrow holes are driven to extract the ore; and *placer mining,* in which gravel, sand, or talus is removed from deposits by hand, hydraulic nozzles, or dredging.

mink, semiaquatic carnivorous MAMMAL (genus *Mustela*), related to the WEASEL and highly prized for its thick, lustrous, rich brown fur. Found in Europe and North America, it has a slender, arched body about 20 in. (51 cm) long and a bushy tail. Minks live near water, where they feed on MUSKRATS, fishes, frogs, and birds. The mink is widely bred on farms for the fur trade.

Minkowski, Hermann [mĭnkôf'skē], 1864–1909, Russian mathematician. He evolved a four-dimensional geometry of space and time that influenced the formulation of the general theory of relativity.

Minneapolis, city (1990 pop. 368,383), seat of Hennepin co., E Minn., at the head of navigation on the Mississippi R., at St. Anthony Falls; inc. 1856. Minneapolis and adjacent SAINT PAUL are called the Twin Cities and form the heart of a major metropolitan area (1990 pop. 2,464,124). The largest city in the state and a major port, it is a financial, industrial, and rail center. Flour milling and computer and electronic industries are particularly important. In the 19th cent. it was the nation's leading lumber center. Minneapolis is noted for such cultural institutions as the Univ. of Minn., Walker Art Center, and Guthrie Theater. It has wide streets, and many lakes and parks. Extensive redevelopment was begun in the central city during the 1960s and continued into the 1980s.

Minnesota, upper midwestern state of the U.S.; bordered by Lake Superior and Wisconsin (E), Iowa (S), South Dakota and North Dakota (W), and the Canadian provinces of Manitoba and Ontario (N).

Area, 84,068 sq mi (217,736 sq km). *Pop.* (1990) 4,375,099, a 7.3% increase over 1980 pop. *Capital,* St. Paul. *Statehood,* May 11, 1858 (32d state). *Highest pt.,* Eagle Mt., 2,310 ft (702 m); *lowest pt.,* Lake Superior, 602 ft (184 m). *Nickname,* North Star State. *Motto, L'Etoile du Nord* [The Star of the North]. *State bird,* common loon. *State flower,* showy lady's slipper or pink and white lady's slipper. *State tree,* red pine. *Abbr.,* Minn.; MN.

Land and People. Iron-rich mountains, including the Vermilion and Mesabi ranges, are located in the east. In the north glaciers have left many lakes, including those in Voyageurs National Park (see NATIONAL PARKS, table), and boulder-strewn hills that give way to broad prairies in the south. The MISSISSIPPI R. originates in N Minnesota and flows northeast through the state. Winter locks the land in snow, and spring is brief; summer is hot. Nearly 70% of the population lives in urban areas. MINNEAPOLIS is the largest city, followed by its twin city, ST. PAUL, and DULUTH, the country's leading GREAT LAKES port. In 1990 over 94% of the population was white.

Economy. Agribusiness, particularly dairying, along with manufacturing, dominated by the production of processed foods and nonelectrical machinery, are leading sources of income. Other key industries produce chemicals, paper, and electronic equipment. In agricultural output beef cattle are important, as are corn, soybeans, wheat, and sugar beets. Forest products also constitute an important sector of the economy. Minnesota leads the country in iron mining.

Government. The 1858 constitution provides for a governor serving a four-year term. The legislature consists of a senate whose 67 members serve four-year terms and a house whose 134 members are elected at two-year intervals. Minnesota is represented in the U.S. Congress by two senators and eight representatives and has 10 electoral votes.

History. The region was inhabited mostly by OJIBWAS, in the east, and SIOUX, in the west, when French explorers and fur traders arrived in the mid-17th cent. By the LOUISIANA PURCHASE (1803) the U.S. acquired all of present-day Minnesota. Settlement began during the 1820s; the many Scandinavians who shaped much of the life of the state arrived later in the century. With a large rural population, Minnesota was fertile ground for the reform movements of the late 19th cent.: the National Grange (see GRANGER MOVEMENT) was founded (1867) by a Minnesotan, and later the POPULIST PARTY and the FARMER-LABOR PARTY received wide support in Minnesota. The Farmer-Labor party merged (1944) with the Democratic party, producing such national leaders as Hubert HUMPHREY and Walter MONDALE. While falling farm prices adversely affected the state in the early 1980s, Minnesota was scarcely impacted by the national recession of the late 1980s and early 90s.

minnow, any of a large family (Cyprinidae) of freshwater FISH that includes CARP, bream, chub, dace, shiners, and GOLDFISH. Most minnows are small and drab, but a few species are brightly colored. Minnows are important in freshwater aquatic life, feeding on insects, larvae, and CRUSTACEANS and in turn serving as food for larger fishes. Superior hearing has given minnows the nickname "hearing aid" fish and accounts for their characteristic wariness.

Minoan civilization [mĭnō'ən], a Bronze Age AEGEAN CIVILIZATION that flourished in CRETE. It is divided into three periods. The early Minoan period (c.3000–2200 B.C.) saw the rise of the culture from a neolithic state, with the tentative use of bronze and the appearance of hieroglyphic writing. The Middle Minoan period (c.2200–1500 B.C.) was the high point: the great palaces appeared at KNOSSOS and Phaestus, culture thrived, and linear writing was used. The Late Minoan period (c.1500–1000 B.C.) faded out in poverty, and the cultural center passed to the Greek mainland.

Minorca: see BALEARIC ISLANDS.

minor planet: see ASTEROID.

Minos [mī'nŏs, –nəs], in Greek mythology, king of CRETE, son of ZEUS and Europa. The wealthiest ruler in the Mediterranean area, he was presumably an actual ancient Cretan king for whom the MINOAN CIVILIZATION is named. In legend, he was the husband of Pasiphaë and the father of Androgeus, Glaucus, ARIADNE, and PHAEDRA.

Minotaur, in Greek mythology, monster with a bull's head and man's body. When King MINOS of CRETE failed to sacrifice a bull to POSEIDON, the god caused Queen Pasiphaë to lust after the animal. By it, she conceived the Minotaur, which was confined in the labyrinth built by DAEDALUS. There it devoured human beings until it was killed by THESEUS.

minstrel show, stage entertainment by white performers made up in blackface, popular in the 19th cent. Jokes between an "interlocutor" and gaudily dressed members of the company caricatured African Americans, creating stereotypes that lasted for decades. VAUDEVILLE or olio (medley) acts and burlesques on plays or operas were also featured.

mint, place where legal coinage is manufactured. The name is derived from the temple of Juno Moneta [Latin, = *mint*] in Rome, where silver coins were made as early as 269 B.C. Mints existed earlier elsewhere, as in Lydia and Greece. The first U.S. mint was established in Philadelphia in 1792. The U.S. Bureau of the Mint now maintains mints in that city, and in Denver and San Francisco. See also COIN.

mint, in botany, common name for the Labiatae, or the Lamiaceae, a large family of chiefly annual or perennial herbs, distributed worldwide but most common in the Mediterranean region. The family is typified by square stems, paired opposite leaves, and white, red, blue, or purple flowers. The aromatic ESSENTIAL OILS in the plants' foliage are used in perfumes, flavorings, and medicines. The true mints (genus *Mentha*), SAGE, lavender, and ROSEMARY are important sources of essential oils; these and BASIL, THYME, MARJORAM, and OREGANO are common kitchen herbs. Other well-known members of the family are CATNIP and HOREHOUND. The most commercially important true mints are peppermint (*M. piperita*), a source of menthol, and the milder spearmint (*M. spicata*).

Mint: Spearmint, Mentha spicata, a plant of the mint family

Minton, English family of potters. **Thomas Minton,** 1765–1836, founded a pottery firm at Stoke-on-Trent and created the famous willow-pattern ware. His son **Herbert Minton,** 1793–1858, developed the firm and made it famous.

minuet, French dance from Poitou, introduced at Louis XIV's court in 1650. In 3/4 meter and moderate tempo, it was danced by open couples with graceful, gliding steps. Many composers, e.g., HAYDN and W.A. MOZART, used its musical form in sonatas and symphonies.

Minuit, Peter [mĭn'yōōĭt], c.1580–1638, first director general of New Netherland. Sent to America by the Dutch West India Company, he purchased (1626) Manhattan from Native Americans for trinkets valued at $24. He later headed the group that established (1638) NEW SWEDEN.

Miocene epoch: see GEOLOGIC ERA (table).

mir, Russian peasant community. Among free peasants the mir owned the land; among SERFS it allocated land reserved for serf use. When serfdom ended (1861; see EMANCIPATION, EDICT OF) land was allotted to the mir rather than to individuals, but this proved impractical. The 1908 reforms of STOLYPIN broke many mirs into individual holdings. After the RUSSIAN REVOLUTION of 1917 the COLLECTIVE FARM replaced the mir.

Mirabeau, Honoré Gabriel Riquetti or **Riqueti, comte de** [mērābō'], 1749–91, politician of the FRENCH REVOLUTION. After a life of wild excess and repeated imprisonment, he was elected (1789) to the STATES-GENERAL. With his fiery eloquence, he became the spokesman of the third estate and tried to create a constitutional monarchy that would permit him to become prime minister. As a member of the Constituent Assembly, however, he was thwarted when the Assembly barred its members from the cabinet. Mirabeau then began secret dealings with the king and queen, but the couple did not heed his advice. He died just before his dealings with the court were discovered.

miracle play or **mystery play,** form of medieval drama, developed (10th–16th cent.) by the addition of dialogue and dramatic action to the Roman Catholic liturgy. Originally performed in Latin, miracle plays were later given in the vernacular. Based on the Scriptures and on the lives of the saints, they were given in churchyards and marketplaces on church festival days and lasted from sunrise to sunset. Principal English examples are the York Plays (1430–40), the Towneley or Wakefield Plays (c.1450), the Coventry Plays (1468), and the Chester Plays (1475–1500).

mirage, atmospheric optical illusion in which an observer sees a nonexistent body of water or an image of some object. Examples of mirages are pools of water seen over hot desert sands or hot pavement and, at sea, an inverted image of a ship seen in the sky. These phenomena can be explained by the facts (1) that light rays undergo refraction, i.e., are bent, in passing between media of differing densities, and (2) that the boundary between two such media acts as a mirror for rays of light coming in at certain angles. Mirages can be photographed.

Miranda, Francisco de [mērän'dä], 1750–1816, Venezuelan revolutionary. A Spanish army officer, he fought in both the American Revolution and the French Revolutionary Wars, was in the service of Catherine the Great, then joined (1810) the revolution against Spanish rule in VENEZUELA. He commanded rebel forces and served briefly as dictator, but military reverses forced his surrender (1812) and imprisonment. He is known as the Precursor, to distinguish him from Simon BOLÍVAR, who completed the task of liberation.

Miranda, in astronomy, natural satellite of URANUS.

Miranda v. Arizona, case decided in 1966 by the U.S. SUPREME COURT, reversing an Arizona conviction. Miranda had been questioned and had confessed without being told of his right to a lawyer. Chief Justice WARREN ruled that EVIDENCE such as Miranda's confession could not be introduced unless the defendant had, before questioning, been told of his rights through what came to be called "Miranda warnings."

Miró, Joan [mērō'], 1893–1983, Spanish surrealist painter. His work is characterized as psychic automatism, an expression of the subconscious in free form. By 1930 he had developed a lyrical style distinguished by the use of brilliant color and the playful juxtaposition of delicate lines with abstract, often amoebic shapes, e.g., *Dog Barking at the Moon* (1926; Philadelphia Mus. of Art). In some of Miró's work there is an undertone of nightmare and horror (see SURREALISM).

mirror, in OPTICS, a reflecting surface that forms an image of an object when light rays coming from that object fall upon it (see REFLECTION). A plane mirror, which has a flat reflecting surface, reflects a beam of light without changing its character. In a convex spherical mirror, the vertex, or midpoint, of the mirror is nearer to the object than the edges, and parallel rays from a light source diverge after reflection. In a concave mirror, the vertex is farther away from the object than the edges, and rays parallel to the principal axis are reflected to a single point, or principal focus. A concave parabolic mirror is the principal element of a reflecting TELESCOPE.

MIRV: see MISSILE, GUIDED.

miscarriage: see ABORTION; PREGNANCY.

misdemeanor, in law, a criminal offense, less grave than a FELONY. By federal and state laws it is usually punishable by fine or by imprisonment for less than one year.

Mishima Yukio, 1925–70, Japanese author; b. Kimitake Hiraoka. His novels are noted for their use of paradox and their exquisitely detailed characterization. They include the tetralogy *The Sea of Fertility* (tr. 1972–74), *The Sound of Waves* (1954), and *The Temple of the Golden Pavilion* (1956). Mishima committed ritual suicide after haranguing Japan's army for its powerlessness under the constitution.

Mishna, collection of interpretations of the legal portions of the TORAH and a codification of traditional Jewish practice. The Mishna and the Gemara, a commentary on the Mishna, constitute the TALMUD. Next to the Scriptures, the Mishna is the basic textbook of Jewish life and thought, covering, e.g., agriculture, Sabbath and festivals, marriage and divorce, and civil and criminal matters. The final compilation of the Mishna was made under the direction of JUDAH HA-NASI from the work of the Tannaim, a group of sages of the 1st and 2d cent. A.D., including AKIBA BEN JOSEPH. The Mishna has been widely translated and has had a considerable influence beyond the confines of Judaism.

Miskolc [mĭsh'kôlts], city (1990 pop. 196,449), NE Hungary, on the Sajó R. Hungary's second largest city, it is an industrial center producing iron and steel, cement, processed food, and other manufactures. Frequent invasions, e.g., by the Mongols (13th cent.), have marked its history. Landmarks include the Avas Reformed Church (15th cent.).

missile, guided, self-propelled, unmanned space or air vehicle carrying a high-explosive warhead (short-range missiles) or a nuclear warhead (long-range missiles). Its path can be adjusted during flight, either by automatic self-contained controls or by distant human control. Guided missiles are powered either by ROCKET engines or by JET PROPULSION. They were first developed in modern form by the Germans, who in WORLD WAR II employed V-1 and V-2 guided missiles against Great Britain and the Low Countries. Missiles may be aerodynamic, i.e., controlled by aerodynamic surfaces and following a straight-line trajectory to the target, or ballistic, i.e., powered during flight and following a parabolic trajectory. Aerodynamic missiles are of four types. Air-to-air missiles are fired by aircraft at enemy aircraft and are often guided by self-contained controls that detect and target the missile toward heat sources. Air-to-surface missiles, launched by aircraft against ground positions, are generally radio-controlled. Surface-to-air missiles, such as the U.S. Patriot missile, operate against aircraft or other missiles. Surface-to-surface missiles include antitank and naval missiles. Longer-range surface-to-surface missiles, such as the Iraqi Scud, are in fact short-range ballistic missiles. The intermediate-range ballistic missile (IRBM) can reach targets up to 1,500 nautical miles (2,400 km) away. The intercontinental ballistic missile (ICBM), first deployed by the USSR in 1958, and the submarine-launched ballistic missile (SLBM) have ranges of many thousands of miles. A multiple independently targeted reentry vehicle (MIRV) permits one booster to carry several warheads, each guided to a separate target. An antiballistic missile (ABM) is designed to detect and intercept enemy missiles. Space-, air-, sea-, and mobile land-based ABMs are barred by the 1972 ABM treaty. A cruise missile is launched like a missile but uses flipout wings and a turbofan engine to fly like an airplane to its target at altitudes of about 50 ft (15 m). A land-attack cruise missile employs internally stored computerized maps of its route to follow the contour of the terrain, making it very accurate and relatively impervious to defense systems. Cruise missiles can be launched from aircraft, surface ships, submarines, or (banned by a U.S.-Russia treaty) the ground. Guided missiles with nuclear warheads have become the key strategic weapon of modern warfare.

Missionary Ridge: see CHATTANOOGA CAMPAIGN.

missions, name of organizations that extend religious teaching and of efforts to disseminate the Christian religion. CHRISTIANITY was spread through the Roman Empire by missions, and in later centuries it was extended by missionary labors in Ireland, Germany, and Scandinavia. In the 16th cent. missions were formed in the New World, especially by the FRANCISCANS and the Jesuits (see JESUS, SOCIETY OF). In Colonial America, Roger WILLIAMS and John ELIOT did notable work among Native Americans, as did the Moravian Church. Mission activity became intense in Africa and Asia in the 19th and 20th cent. and was greatly furthered by the work of David LIVINGSTONE and Albert SCHWEITZER.

Mississippi, U.S. state in the Deep South; bordered by Alabama (E), the Gulf of Mexico (S), Arkansas and Louisiana, with most of the border formed by the Mississippi R. (W), and Tennessee (N).

Area, 47,716 sq mi (123,584 sq km). *Pop.* (1990) 2,573,216, a 2.1% increase over 1980 pop. *Capital,* Jackson. *Statehood,* Dec. 10, 1817 (20th state). *Highest pt.,* Woodall Mt., 806 ft (246 m); *lowest pt.,* sea level. *Nickname,* Magnolia State. *Motto, Virtute et Armis* [By Valor and Arms]. *State bird,* mockingbird. *State flower,* magnolia. *State tree,* magnolia. *Abbr.,* Miss.; MS.

Land and People. W Mississippi is covered by the Delta, a flat alluvial plain that gives way to hilly land in the northeast, and the Piney Woods, which extend south almost all the way to the Gulf coastal plain. The climate is subtropical in the south and temperate in the north. Mississippi is a heavily rural state, with about 47% of its residents living in urban areas. JACKSON is the largest city, followed by BILOXI and MERIDIAN. In 1990 the African-American population accounted for 35.6% of the total—the highest percentage of any state.

Economy. Only since 1965 has manufacturing surpassed agriculture in terms of revenue. The leading industries produce apparel, processed foods, furniture, transportation equipment, electrical machinery, and lumber products. Cotton, soybeans, catfish, cattle, broiler chickens, rice, and hay are important agricultural products. Oil and natural gas deposits are located under one third of the land, and their extraction is a major industry. Other industries include fishing off the coast and forestry. Despite substantial modernization efforts, Mississippi has the lowest per capita income in the U.S.

Government. The constitution of 1890 provides for a governor serving a four-year term. The legislature consists of a 52-seat senate and 122-seat house, with members of both bodies elected to four-year terms. Mississippi is represented in the U.S. Congress by two senators and five representatives and has seven electoral votes.

History. Hernando DE SOTO's expedition passed (1540–42) through the region, then inhabited by the CHOCTAW, CHICKASAW, and Natchez, but the first permanent European settlement was made (1699) by the French on Biloxi Bay. The area was taken (1779) by the Spanish, and the newly independent U.S. acquired it only after a boundary dispute with West Florida was settled (1795). New settlers arrived via the NATCHEZ TRACE, lured in part by the cotton boom. Mississippi seceded (1861) from the Union, and Jefferson DAVIS, a Mississippian, was president of the CONFEDERACY during the CIVIL WAR. The state was readmitted to the Union in 1870, but it effectively disenfranchised African Americans and instituted (1904) segregationist "Jim Crow" laws. After the disastrous Mississippi R. flood of 1927, the federal government began a huge flood-control program. During the 1960s Mississippi was a center of the CIVIL-RIGHTS movement and attracted national attention when Gov. Ross Barnett tried unsuccessfully (1962) to block the admission of an African-American student to the Univ. of Mississippi. After passage of the Federal Voting Rights Act of 1965, significant numbers of African Americans voted and many African-American state officials have been elected. Largely unable to shift from manufacturing to a service-centered economy in the face of industrial decline, Mississippi has struggled with a troubled economy into the 1990s.

Mississippi, principal river of the U.S. and of North America, flowing generally south c.2,350 mi (3,780 km) from Lake Itasca (alt. 1,463 ft/446 m) in N Minnesota to enter the Gulf of Mexico through a vast, birdsfoot-type delta in Louisiana. It forms, with the MISSOURI R., its chief tributary, the world's third longest (c.3,740 mi/6,020 km) river system. The Mississippi is navigable by ocean-going vessels to Baton Rouge, La., and by barges and towboats through a 9-ft (2.7-m) channel as far as Minneapolis, Minn., with canals circumventing rapids near Rock Island, Ill., and Keokuk, Iowa. There are over 40 dams above St. Louis, Mo., and c.1,600 mi (2,580 km) of levees below Cape Girardeau, Mo., to regulate and restrain the river's flow. Normally, the Mississippi is c.3,500 ft (1,070 m) wide near St. Louis and c.4,500 ft (1,370 m) wide at Cairo, Ill., but it reached a width of 80 mi (129 km) in places during a disastrous flood in 1927 and inundated large areas during the rainy spring of 1973 and rainy summer of 1993. In 1988 drought sent water levels to the lowest ever recorded and halted most river traffic. Seen by DE SOTO in 1541, the river was claimed by France after LA SALLE descended it to reach the Gulf of Mexico in 1682. It was ceded to Spain in 1763 and was regained by France in 1800, before it passed to the U.S. in 1803 as part of the LOUISIANA PURCHASE. Mark TWAIN's *Life on the Mississippi* (1883) describes vividly the end of the river's steamboat era, which began in 1811.

Missouri, one of the midwestern states of the central U.S.; bordered by Illinois, Kentucky, and Tennessee (E), Arkansas (S), Oklahoma, Kansas, and Nebraska (W), and Iowa (N).

Area, 69,686 sq mi (180,487 sq km). *Pop.* (1990) 5,117,073, a 4.1% increase over 1980 pop. *Capital,* Jefferson City. *Statehood,*

Aug. 10, 1821 (24th state). *Highest pt.,* Taum Sauk Mt., 1,772 ft (540 m); *lowest pt.,* St. Francis R., 230 ft (70 m). *Nickname,* Show Me State. *Motto, Salus Populi Suprema Lex Esto* [The Welfare of the People Shall Be the Supreme Law]. *State bird,* bluebird. *State flower,* hawthorn. *State tree,* dogwood. *Abbr.,* Mo.; MO.

Land and People. Two great rivers have shaped the state: the MISSISSIPPI, which forms its eastern border, and the MISSOURI, which flows west to east across the state to join the Mississippi just above St. Louis. Most of the land north of the Missouri consists of plains, while south of the river the elevations increase, especially in the Ozark Plateau. More than 68% of the population lives in urban areas. The largest city is KANSAS CITY, followed by SAINT LOUIS, a great inland port, and SPRINGFIELD. The state's population was 88% white and 11% African American in 1990.

Economy. Missouri is a heavily industrialized state, with transportation (particularly aerospace) equipment, processed foods (especially beer, flour, and beef), electrical and electronic equipment, and chemicals the leading products. The most valuable farm products in the thriving agricultural sector are cattle, hogs, soybeans, dairy foods, corn, wheat, and hay. Missouri has long led the country in the production of lead, and it also extracts barite, lime, zinc, coal, and iron. Tourism is especially important in the OZARKS.

Government. The constitution of 1945 provides for a governor elected to a four-year term. The general assembly consists of a senate whose 34 members serve four-year terms and a house whose 163 members are elected to two-year terms. Missouri is represented in the U.S. Congress by two senators and nine representatives and has 11 electoral votes.

History. When Robert Cavalier, sieur de LA SALLE, claimed the area for France in 1682, it was inhabited by Native American peoples, including the OSAGE and Missouri. In 1803 the land passed to the U.S. as part of the LOUISIANA PURCHASE, and soon St. Louis became the gateway to the West, especially after the advent of steamboat traffic on the Missouri and Mississippi rivers in the 1820s. The question of admitting the Missouri Territory into the Union became a burning national issue because it involved the question of extending slavery; the dispute was ended by the MISSOURI COMPROMISE (1821), which admitted Missouri as a slave state. INDEPENDENCE, St. Joseph, and other cities became the starting points for wagon trains traveling west, and the state's own population grew, especially with the arrival of railroads and, subsequently, of thousands of German immigrants during the 1840s and 50s. Missouri remained loyal to the Union in the CIVIL WAR and was the scene of guerrilla activities, which gave rise to postwar lawlessness on the part of Jesse JAMES and other outlaws. Industry gradually surpassed agriculture in importance, especially after World War II, when Missouri became the country's second largest manufacturer of automobiles (after Michigan). Although faced with high unemployment, the state continued to attract varied industrial and commercial enterprises in the 1980s. In 1993 record rains led to widespread flooding in the state, particularly along the Missouri and Mississippi rivers.

Missouri, longest river of the U.S., flowing c.2,565 mi (4,130 km) from its source in the Rocky Mts. to join the MISSISSIPPI R. 17 mi (27 km) N of St. Louis, Mo., forming the world's third longest (c.3,740 mi/6,020 km) river system. Its principal headwaters are the Jefferson, Madison, and Gallatin rivers, which unite to form the main stream at Three Forks, Mont. The river is navigable for 760 mi (1,223 km) to Sioux City, Iowa, by barges and towboats. Above Sioux City, its fluctuating flow is regulated by seven major dams—Gavins Point, Fort Randall, Big Bend, Oahe, Garrison, Fort Peck, and Canyon Ferry—that are part of the coordinated Missouri River Basin Project authorized by the U.S. Congress in 1944. During the rainy summer of 1993 the lower Missouri reached record levels, flooding many areas. MARQUETTE and JOLLIET passed the mouth of the river in 1673, and VÉRENDRYE explored its upper reaches in 1738. Other early explorers were David Thompson (1797), and Meriwether Lewis and William Clark (see LEWIS AND CLARK EXPEDITION) on their journey (1803–6) to the Pacific Ocean. River traffic, begun when the first steamboat reached Fort Benton in 1819, declined with the loss of freight to the railroads after the Civil War but was revitalized in the early 20th cent. through navigational improvements below Sioux City.

Missouri Compromise, 1820–21, measures passed by the U.S. Congress to end the first crisis concerning the extension of SLAVERY. Maine was admitted as a free state and Missouri as a slave state, and slavery was prohibited from the Louisiana Purchase north of 36°30′. This proviso held until 1854, when the KANSAS-NEBRASKA ACT repealed the Missouri Compromise.

mistletoe, common name for the Loranthaceae, a family of chiefly tropical parasitic herbs and shrubs with leathery leaves and waxy white berries. Mistletoes, aerial hemiparasites with green leaves that carry out PHOTOSYNTHESIS, attach themselves to their hosts by modified roots called haustoria. They are widely associated with folklore and are used as Christmas decorations. The mistletoe commonly sold in the U.S. is *Phoradendron flavescens;* most popular in Europe is the "true" mistletoe (*Viscum album*).

Mistral, Frédéric [mēsträl′], 1830–1914, French Provençal poet. He led the Félibrige movement to promote Provençal as a literary language and was its greatest poet. His best-known work is the verse romance *Mirèio* (1859). He shared the 1904 Nobel Prize in literature with José ECHEGARAY.

Mistral, Gabriela, pseud. of **Lucila Godoy Alcayaga,** 1889–1957, Chilean poet. An educator and diplomat, she was the first Latin American to receive the Nobel Prize in literature (1945). Her lyric works include *Sonnets of Death* (1914), *Desolación* (1922), *Tala* (1938), and *Lagar* (1954).

Mitchell, George J(ohn), 1933–, American politician; b. Waterville, Me. An attorney in government and private practice for most of the 1960s and 1970s, he was serving (1979–80) as a U.S. district judge when he was appointed (1980) U.S. Senator from Maine. In 1988 he succeeded Robert BYRD as Democratic (majority) leader in the Senate.

Mitchell, John Newton, 1913–88, U.S. attorney general (1969–72); b. Detroit. A law partner of Richard M. NIXON, he managed Nixon's 1968 presidential campaign. In March 1972 he became head of the president's reelection committee, but he resigned in June, at the beginning of the WATERGATE AFFAIR. Subsequent investigations led to Mitchell's indictment, trial, and conviction (Jan. 1, 1975) on charges of conspiracy, obstruction of justice, and perjury. He served 19 months in prison and was released in 1979.

Mitchell, Margaret, 1900–49, American novelist; b. Atlanta, Ga. Her one novel, *Gone with the Wind* (1936; Pulitzer), is set in Georgia during the CIVIL WAR and RECONSTRUCTION. It and the film adaptation (1939) were enormously successful.

Mitchell, Maria, 1818–89, American astronomer; b. Nantucket, Mass. The first woman to be elected to the American Academy of Arts and Sciences, she studied sunspots, nebulae, and satellites, and discovered (1847) a comet. After 1865 she was professor of astronomy at Vassar College.

Mitchell, Silas Weir, 1829–1914, American physician and author; b. Philadelphia. A pioneer in applying psychology to medicine, he was noted for his treatment of nervous disorders and for his study of the nervous system. His medical works include *Injuries of Nerves and Their Consequences* (1872) and *Fat and Blood* (1877), which summarized his well-known rest cure. His novels include historical romances and psychological studies.

Mitchell, Wesley Clair, 1874–1948, American economist; b. Rushville, Ill. He held teaching posts at several institutions, including the Univ. of California and Columbia, and helped found the National Bureau of Economic Research. One of the most eminent U.S. economists, he focused much of his research on statistical investigation of the business cycle. His major work is *Business Cycles* (1913; 2d ed. 1927).

Mitchell, William ("Billy"), 1879–1936, American general, commander of the American expeditionary air force in World War I; b. France. He advocated a large, independent air force, but his public criticism of the military for neglecting air power led to his court martial (1925) and resignation in 1926.

mite, small, often microscopic ARACHNID. Mites are often parasites of animals and plants and infest stored foodstuffs. Some burrow into the skin of mammals, causing MANGE and scabies. Chiggers, which are the larvae of harvest mites, transmit the organism that causes scrub typhus. The larger **tick,** which is related to the mite, is usually a parasite of birds and mammals, embedding its entire head under the skin and sucking the host's blood. Ticks transmit many diseases, including LYME DISEASE and ROCKY MOUNTAIN SPOTTED FEVER.

Mitford, Nancy, 1904–73, English writer. She satirized the aristocracy she was born into in novels like *The Pursuit of Love* (1945) and *Love in a Cold Climate* (1949). Her sister **Jessica Mitford,** 1917–, is a writer best known for her exposé of the funeral business, *The American Way of Death* (1963), and an autobiography, *Daughters and Rebels* (1960).

Mithra, god of ancient Persia and India. In the 5th cent. B.C. he appears as the principal Persian deity, god of light and wisdom. His cult expanded to become a worldwide religion, called **Mithraism.** In the 2d cent. A.D. it was more general in the Roman Empire than Christianity, to which it bore many similarities. Mithraism taught the dualistic struggle between the forces of good and evil and offered hope of immortality through the practice of rites and a system of rigorous ethics. It declined rapidly in the late 3d cent. A.D.

Mithridates VI, c.131–63 B.C., king of ancient PONTUS, called Mithridates the Great. The extension of his empire brought him into war with Rome. In the First Mithridatic War (88–84 B.C.) he conquered (88 B.C.) most of Asia Minor, but in 85 B.C. he was defeated there and in Greece. The Second Mithridatic War (83–81 B.C.) ended in a Roman defeat. In the Third Mithridatic War (76–63 B.C.) LUCULLUS defeated Mithridates, and POMPEY drove the king into the Crimea, where he had himself killed by a slave.

mitosis, process of nuclear division in a living cell by which the hereditary material, or CHROMOSOMES, is exactly replicated, the two parts being distributed to identical daughter nuclei. In mitosis each cell formed receives chromosomes that are alike in composition and equal in number to the chromosomes of the parent cell. Mitotic division occurs in somatic (body) cells; in germ cells (OVUM and SPERM) MEIOSIS (halving of the number of chromosomes) also takes place.

Mitterrand, François Maurice [mētəräN′], 1916–, French political leader, president of France (1981–). He fought in the Resistance during World War II and later served in the national assembly (1946–58) and senate (1959–62). In the 1950s he held several cabinet posts. He first ran for the presidency in 1965, losing to Charles DE GAULLE. In 1971 he joined and became first secretary of the Socialist party and led it to increasing success at the polls. Mitterrand lost the presidential race to Valéry GISCARD D'ESTAING in 1974 but defeated him in 1981, becoming the first Socialist president of the Fifth Republic. In his first term the Socialists nationalized banks and introduced other traditional socialist policies but later reversed those policies and instituted austerity measures when the economy faltered. He won reelection in 1988 and is the longest-serving president in the history of France. Internationally, Mitterrand has sought to strengthen the European Community and pursue an independent foreign policy in the Middle East and Africa.

Mixtec, indigenous people of SW Mexico (see MIDDLE AMERICA, INDIGENOUS PEOPLES OF) who speak a language of the Otomian stock (see NATIVE AMERICAN LANGUAGES). Important from ancient times, the Mixtec seem to have had an advanced culture before the coming of the TOLTEC. They began spreading southward about 900 and by the 14th cent. overshadowed their rivals the ZAPOTEC. Excelling in stonework and metalwork, wood carving, and pottery decoration, the Mixtec strongly influenced other Mexican cultures. They resisted the Spanish in the 16th cent., but were subjugated with the aid of the Zapotec. There are about 300,000 Mixtec-speaking people in Mexico today.

mixture: see COMPOUND.

Miyazawa Kiichi, 1919–, prime minister of Japan (1991–93). Miyazawa served (1942–52) in the finance ministry before his election to parliament in 1953. He held ministerial posts in several Liberal Democratic party (LDP) governments, including minister of foreign affairs (1974–76) and of finance (1986–88). Implicated in a bribery and corruption scandal in 1988, he resigned as finance minister. In 1991 he became prime minister. His failure (1993) to win passage of political reforms led to a split in the LDP and the loss of its parliamentary majority, and he resigned.

mks system: see METRIC SYSTEM.

Mn, chemical symbol of the element MANGANESE.

Mnemosyne: see MUSES.

Mnesicles [nĕs′ĭklēz], Greek architect, 5th cent. B.C. He designed the Propylaea, and the ERECHTHEUM is sometimes ascribed to him. Both are on the Acropolis, Athens.

Mo, chemical symbol of the element MOLYBDENUM.

Moab, ancient nation in the uplands E of the Dead Sea, now part of Jordan. The Moabites were close kin to the Hebrews, and the language of the Moabite stone (dating to 850 B.C.) is practically the same as biblical Hebrew. Moab is continually mentioned in the Bible. Its people were later absorbed by the Nabataeans.

Mobile, city (1990 pop. 196,278), seat of Mobile co., SW Ala., at the head of Mobile Bay and the mouth of the Mobile R.; inc. 1814. It is a major port and historically important shipbuilding center, with oil refineries and paper, textile, aluminum, and chemical industries. It was founded in 1710 and was the capital of French Louisiana from 1710 to 1719. Held by Britain and then Spain, it was taken by the U.S. in 1813. The city is noted for its beautiful antebellum houses, and for its annual Mardi Gras (est. early 18th cent.) and Azalea Trail Festival (est. 1929).

mobile, type of moving sculpture developed by Alexander CALDER in 1932 and named by Marcel DUCHAMP. Often constructed of colored metal pieces connected by wires, mobiles have moving parts that are sensitive to a breeze or light touch.

mobile telephone: see CELLULAR TELEPHONE.

Mobutu Sese Seko, 1930–, president of ZAÏRE (1967–); b. Joseph Désiré Mobutu. He became prime minister of the former Belgian Congo in 1966 after staging a coup that toppled the government of Joseph KASAVUBU. In 1967 he established a presidential form of government headed by himself, and in 1971 he changed the Congo's name to Zaïre. As head of a one-party state, he suppressed tribal conflicts and encouraged a sense of nationhood. At the same time he amassed a huge personal fortune, and corruption became widespread in the country. In 1991 continuing economic deterioration and unrest led him to agree to share power with opposition leaders, but he subsequently used the army to thwart change.

mockingbird: see MIMIC THRUSH.

mock orange: see SAXIFRAGE.

Model Parliament: see PARLIAMENT.

modem [*mo*dulator/*dem*odulator], device used to transmit and receive digital data over normally analog communications lines, usually as an audio signal on telephone circuits. A modem attached to a computer performs a DIGITAL-TO-ANALOG CONVERSION of data and transmits them to another modem which performs a analog-to-digital conversion that permits its attached computer to use the data. The rate of data transfer can be increased using data compression. Wireless modems send or receive data as a radio signal. A **fax modem** enables a computer to send and receive transmissions to and from a FACSIMILE MACHINE.

modern architecture, essentially homogeneous architectural style appearing in most Western countries after World War I and continuing to develop through the mid-20th cent. It possesses no appellation more precise than modern, although other labels, e.g., INTERNATIONAL STYLE and functionalism, have also been applied. A conscious attempt to assimilate modern technology is one characteristic. Technical progress in the development of materials was evident in the construction of the CRYSTAL PALACE in 1851. In the ensuing years iron, steel, and glass determined the form of many buildings, but irrelevant ornament persisted. As late as 1889 the EIFFEL TOWER found a public not yet ready to accept pure structure as beautiful. The use of a steel skeleton for a tall building began with the first SKYSCRAPER, by William Jenney, in Chicago (1883). Industrial architecture in Europe was pioneered by Peter BEHRENS, Auguste PERRET, and others. At the end of the 19th cent. a revolution occurred in the buildings and writings of Louis H. SULLIVAN and Frank Lloyd WRIGHT. Wright in the U.S. and the exponents of ART NOUVEAU in Europe introduced the concept of rhythmic flow of interior space, eliminating rigid room divisions. Conversely, the architects of de STIJL returned to more disciplined structural form. By 1920 the interrelation of building type with materials and function was widely accepted. The concept of buildings as volumes enclosed by massive materials had given way to a concentration on space supported or enclosed by light, thin materials. The idea of enclosure was de-emphasized, so that structural elements themselves came into focus. Major exponents of this view were LE CORBUSIER and Walter GROPIUS. Abstract painting and sculpture were looked to for new ideas and did much to condition the public to recognize abstract structural beauty, free from past associations. By mid-century, modern architecture and city planning, influenced by new technology and mass production, were dealing with increasingly complex social needs. Important characteristics of modern architectural works are expanses of glass and the use of reinforced concrete. Advances in elevator technology, air conditioning, and electric illumination have all had important effects. The use of an unvarying module, or basic dimensional unit, characteristic of the works of Buckminster FULLER and Moshe Safdie, among others, echoes machine-tool precision. Pioneers of the 1920s were MIËS VAN DER ROHE and Gropius. Important contributors to modern design include Marcel BREUER, Richard NEUTRA, and I.M. PEI. Criticism in the 1950s attacking modern architecture's "sterility" and "institutional" anonymity produced a tendency toward individual expression typified by Louis KAHN, E.D. STONE, Philip JOHNSON, and the architects of the "new brutalism" movement in England and the U.S. A dynamic sculptural unity characterizes the work of Le Corbusier and Eero SAARINEN. Other major modern architects include Alvar AALTO, P.L. NERVI, Paolo SOLERI, and Oscar NIEMEYER. In the 1960s, a more critical reaction to modern architecture, first enunciated in the writings of Robert VENTURI, culminated in many forms of architectural POSTMODERNISM, a movement that remained prominent into the early 1990s.

modern art: see ABSTRACT EXPRESSIONISM; BLAUE REITER, DER; BRÜCKE, DIE; CONSTRUCTIVISM; CUBISM; DADA; EIGHT, THE; EXPRESSIONISM; FAUVISM; FUTURISM; IMPRESSIONISM; MINIMALISM; NABIS; NAZARENES; PHOTOREALISM; POSTIMPRESSIONISM; POSTMODERNISM; STIJL, DE; SUPREMATISM; SURREALISM.

modern dance, theatrical dance forms that are distinct from BALLET and from show dancing of the musical comedy or variety stage. Developed in the 20th cent., primarily in the U.S., it resembles modern art and music in being experimental and iconoclastic. It began with the work of Isadora DUNCAN, Loie Fuller, and Ruth ST. DENIS in the early 20th cent. Duncan idealized emotion and emphasized freedom of movement. Fuller sought to imitate and illustrate natural phenomena, creating illusionistic effects with lighting, as did Alwin NIKOLAIS later. St. Denis, improvising on Asian sources, with elaborate costumes, evoked a sense of mystery. With her husband, Ted Shawn, she increased the popularity of modern dance in the U.S. through their influential Denishawn company and schools. The second generation of modern-dance innovators, led by Martha GRAHAM, Doris HUMPHREY, and Charles WEIDMAN, rebelled against the ART NOUVEAU exoticism and commercialism of Denishawn. They launched their own companies, Graham and Humphrey stressing stark, intellectual, dramatic movement, Weidman concentrating on comic satire. These companies dominated modern dance until the late 1940s, when more surreal, abstract forms were developed by a new group of choreographers led by Merce CUNNINGHAM. Paul TAYLOR created works to the sound of heartbeats and telephone signals, and Twyla THARP eliminated sound accompaniment entirely. Yvonne Rainier pioneered the use of nondance movement (acrobatics, marching), a development carried even further by Steve Paxton. Other influential contemporary dancer-choreographers include Meredith Monk, Bill T. Jones, and Trisha Brown. Many choreographers, e.g., Agnes DE MILLE and Alvin AILEY, have also broken down the distinctions between modern dance, ballet, and show dancing.

modernism, in religion, movement to reconcile developments of 19th- and 20th-cent. science and philosophy with historical Christianity. It arose from the application of modern critical methods to the study of the Bible and the history of dogma and stressed the humanistic aspects of religion. Its ideas permeated many Protestant churches and called forth a reaction in FUNDAMENTALISM. A similar movement in Roman Catholicism was condemned (1907) as heretical.

modernismo, movement in Spanish literature, c.1890–1920. It arose in Latin America, derived in part from the French SYMBOLISTS and PARNASSIANS. *Azul* blue (1888), by the Nicaraguan poet Rubén DARÍO, typified the new aesthetic, with its elegant form, exotic images, and subtle word music. Other major Latin American *modernistas* were José Santos Chocano, Herrera y Reissig, LUGONES, Amado Nervo, José Enrique Rodó, and SILVA. *Modernismo* spread to Spain, influencing JIMÉNEZ, UNAMUNO, and VALLE INCLÁN. After World War I, a new generation of writers rejected the mannerism and hollow elegance of *modernismo*.

Modesto, city (1990 pop. 164,730), seat of Stanislaus co., central Calif., near the northern end of the SAN JOAQUIN valley; inc. 1884. One of the nation's leading agricultural cities, it has huge facilities for food processing and winemaking.

Modigliani, Amedeo [mōdēlyä'nē], 1884–1920, Italian painter. He lived in Paris after 1906. His first work was influenced by CUBISM and AFRICAN ART, but he soon developed a unique style characterized by an elongation of form, a purity of line, and a languorous atmosphere reminiscent of Florentine MANNERISM. His short life was one of poverty and disease. Only after his death was his work prized.

Modoc, indigenous people of Northwest Coast culture (see NORTH AMERICA, INDIGENOUS PEOPLES OF), with a Sahaptin-Chinook language of the Penutian stock (see NATIVE AMERICAN LANGUAGES). They lived in SW Oregon and N California, clashing violently with the early white settlers. They were moved to a reservation in 1864, but their chief, Captain Jack, led a rebel group back to California, precipitating the Modoc War (1872–73), which ultimately divided the tribe. The Modoc now live mostly in Oregon with other groups.

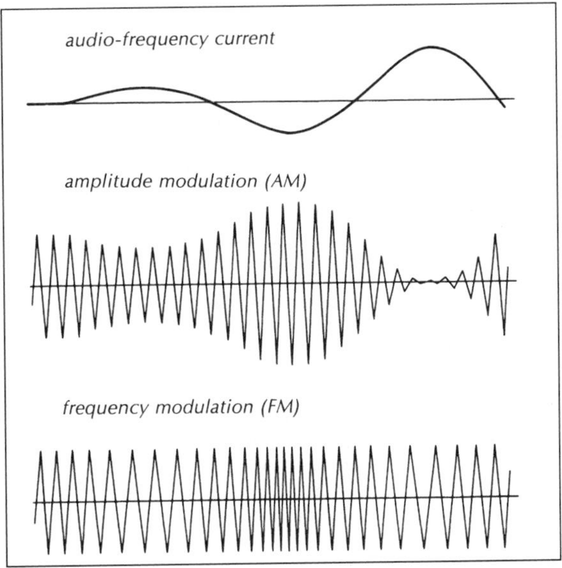

Modulation

modulation, in communications, process in which some characteristic of a WAVE (the carrier wave) is made to vary in accordance with an information-bearing signal wave (the modulating wave); demodulation is the process by which the original signal is recovered from the wave produced by modulation. In modulation the carrier wave is generated or processed so that its amplitude, frequency, or some other property varies. Amplitude modulation (AM), widely used in radio, is constant in frequency and varies the intensity, or amplitude, of the carrier wave in accordance with the modulating signal. Frequency modulation (FM) is constant in amplitude and varies the frequency of the carrier wave in such a way that the change in frequency at any instant is proportional to another time-varying signal. The principal application of FM is also in radio, where it offers increased noise immunity and greater sound fidelity at the expense of greatly increased bandwidth. In pulse modulation the carrier wave is a series of pulses that are all of the same amplitude and width and are all equally spaced. By controlling one of these three variables, a modulating wave may impress its information on the pulses. In pulse code modulation (PCM) it is the presence or absence of particular pulses in the carrier stream that constitutes the modulation.

modulation, in music, shift in the KEY center of a composition, a means of achieving variety in use since the late 15th cent. In modulating from one key to another, a chord common to both keys is used as a pivot chord. If no chord is common to the two keys, the passage may move through several keys before the desired modulation is effected.

Moerae: see FATES.

Mofaddaliyat: see MUFADDALIYAT.

Mogul or **Mughal,** Muslim empire of India (1526–1857). It was founded by BABUR and flourished until the 18th cent., when the SIKHS and MAHRATTAS triumphed over it. The British kept a puppet Mogul emperor on the throne until 1857. The flowering of Muslim art and architecture was the most lasting achievement of the Moguls.

Mogul art and architecture. A characteristic Indo-Islamic art style, evolved from PERSIAN ART AND ARCHITECTURE, evolved in India under the Mogul emperors. The school of Mogul painting began in 1549 when Emperor Humayun invited two Persian painters to direct the illustration of the *Amir Hamza,* a fantastic narrative of which some 1,400 large paintings were executed on cloth. The first Mogul monument was the mausoleum to Humayun erected by AKBAR (1556–1605), who went on to build an entire city, FATEHPUR SIKRI, making use of the low arches and bulbous DOMES that characterize the Mogul style. Modeling and perspective were also adapted from Western painting. Emperor Jahangir (1605–27) encouraged portraiture and scientific studies of birds, flowers, and animals, which were collected in albums. SHAH JAHAN (1628–58) perfected Mogul architecture and erected at Agra the tomb of his favorite wife, the TAJ MAHAL, with its symmetrical Persian plan. This period saw the amalgamation of influences into a true Mogul style. Portraiture was most highly developed and ink drawings were of high quality at the court of Shah Jahan. Under the puritanical Emperor AURANGZEB (1658–1710) the decline of the arts began, although the ornate Pearl Mosque (1662) at Delhi is worth mention. During his reign the Mogul academy was dispersed, and the artists joined Rajput courts.

mohair: see FIBER.

Mohawk: see IROQUOIS CONFEDERACY.

Mohegans, indigenous people of the Eastern Woodlands (see NORTH AMERICA, INDIGENOUS PEOPLES OF), with an Algonquian language of the Algonquian-Wakashan stock (see NATIVE AMERICAN LANGUAGES). Sometimes called Mohicans, they were a branch of the MAHICANS, occupying SW Connecticut. United with the PEQUOT in the early 1630s, they became a distinct tribe under UNCAS, who later reunited both groups into a powerful force that had British support. Sale of their land to the whites led to decline. They are known through J.F. COOPER's *The Last of the Mohicans.* In 1993 there were several hundred Mohegans in SE Connecticut.

Mohicans: see MAHICANS; MOHEGANS.

Moholy-Nagy, László [mô'hôlē-nŏ'dyə], 1895–1946, Hungarian painter, designer, and experimental photographer. A founder of CONSTRUCTIVISM, and a professor at the BAUHAUS (1923–28), he directed the Bauhaus School of Design, Chicago, until 1938, and then opened and headed the Chicago Institute of Design. His teaching influenced American commercial and industrial design, and he wrote *The New Vision* (tr. 1928) and *Vision in Motion* (1947).

Mohorovičić discontinuity or **Moho,** boundary layer between the crust and the mantle of the EARTH. It is marked by a sharp alteration in the velocity of earthquakes passing through that region.

Moi, Daniel arap, 1924–, president of Kenya (1978–). He was vice president (1967–78) under Jomo KENYATTA and succeeded to the presidency in 1978. In 1982 he made Kenya a one-party state, and his government subsequently became increasingly dictatorial and corrupt. Internal opposition and pressure from Kenya's foreign-aid donors led Moi to end one-party rule in 1991. He was reelected in 1992 in a multiparty election widely regarded as flawed.

Moirai: see FATES.

Mojave Desert or **Mohave Desert,** arid area, SE California, part of the Sonoran section of the Basin and Range physiographic division of the western U.S. It is warm throughout the year, but with marked diurnal temperature changes, and receives an average annual rainfall of 5 in. (12.7 cm), mostly in winter. **Joshua Tree National Monument** preserves the region's unique ecosystem.

molasses: see SUCROSE.

mold, multicellular FUNGUS typified by a body composed of a network of cottony filaments. The colors of molds are due to spores borne on the filaments. Most molds are SAPROPHYTES. Some species (e.g., *Penicillium*) are used in making cheese and ANTIBIOTICS. Some organisms traditionally thought to be mold (e.g., SLIME MOLD) are now considered protists.

Moldavia, historic province (c.14,700 sq mi/38,100 sq km), E Romania, separated in the east from MOLDOVA by the Prut R. and in the west from Transylvania by the Carpathian Mts. Suceava and IAŞI, its historic capitals, and Galaţi, its port on the Danube R., are its chief cities. Moldavia is a fertile plain on which grains, fruits, and other crops are grown. Lumbering and oil-drilling are the major industries. Part of the Roman province of Dacia, the area became (14th cent.) a principality under native rulers, notably Stephen the Great (r.1457–1504). It came under Turkish suzerainty in the 16th cent. and later lost Bukovina (1775) to Austria and Bessarabia (1812) to Russia. In 1856 Moldavia and WALACHIA became independent under nominal Turkish suzerainty. The accession (1859) of Alexander John CUZA as prince of both areas began the history of modern ROMANIA.

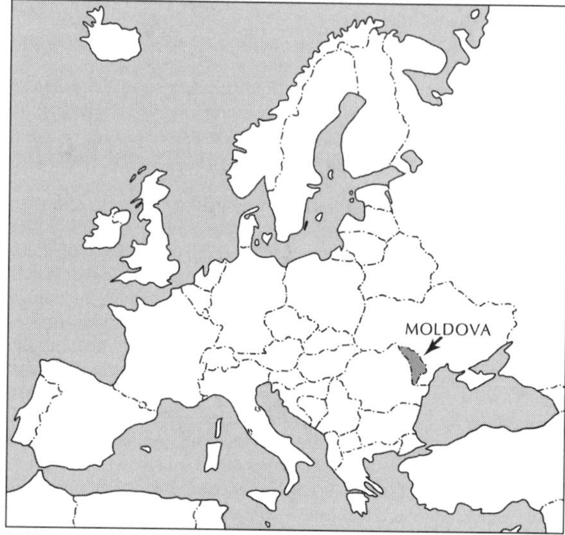

Moldova or **Moldavia,** officially Republic of Moldova, republic (1992 est. pop. 4,458,000), c.13,000 sq mi (33,670 sq km), E central Europe, formerly a constituent republic of the USSR. It borders on Romania (W) and Ukraine (E, N, and S). The capital is CHIŞINĂU. A hilly plain, Moldova produces beef and dairy cattle, honey, and such crops as grains and fruits. Major industries are food and tobacco processing, winemaking, metallurgy, and the manufacture of textiles and chemicals. About 65% of the population are Romanian-speaking Moldovans; Ukrainians and Russians make up more than a quarter of the people, and there are several smaller minorities, including the Turkish-speaking Gagauz in the south. Orthodox Christianity is the predominant religion. The official language is Moldovan (Romanian).

History. An independent principality in the 14th cent., the region fell to the Ottoman Turks in the 16th cent. Some portions passed to Russia between 1791 and 1812. Moldova was first established (1924) as the Moldavian Autonomous Soviet Socialist Republic within Ukraine. In 1940 the USSR forcibly annexed Bessarabia from Romania (which had seized the region from Russia in 1918), and it and ethnically non-Ukrainian parts of the Moldavian ASSR became the Moldavian SSR, a constituent republic of the Soviet Union. In 1991, following the failed coup against Gorbachev, the republic declared itself independent as Moldova. It joined the COMMONWEALTH OF INDEPENDENT STATES (CIS), but in 1993 the parliament failed to ratify the CIS treaty. The largely Ukrainian and Russian slice of E Moldova between the Dniester and Ukraine sought autonomy as the "Trans-Dniester Republic," and fighting erupted between Moldovan and separatist forces in 1992. A truce left the separatists in control of the area. The Gagauz have also sought autonomy.

mole, any of the small, burrowing, insectivorous MAMMALS of the family Talpidae of the Northern Hemisphere. About 6 in. (15.2 cm) long, moles have pointed muzzles and powerful, clawed front feet for tunneling. Their eyes are covered with skin or buried in fur and they have no external ears, but their senses of hearing, smell, and touch are acute. They eat half their weight daily in worms, insects, and small animals. Moles are trapped as pests and for their fur.

mole, in chemistry, a quantity of particles of any type equal to Avogadro's number (6.02252×10^{23}). One gram-atomic weight (or one gram-molecular weight)—the amount of an atomic (or molecular) substance whose weight in grams is numerically equal to the ATOMIC WEIGHT (or MOLECULAR WEIGHT) of that substance—contains exactly one mole of atoms (or molecules). For example, one mole, or 12.011 grams, of carbon contains 6.02252×10^{23} carbon atoms, and one mole, or 180.16 grams, of glucose ($C_6H_{12}O_6$) contains the same number of glucose molecules.

Molech [mō'lĕk] or **Moloch** [mō'lŏk], Canaanite god of fire to whom children were offered in sacrifice. He is also known as an Assyrian god. His worship was contrary to Hebrew law, and the prophets strongly condemned it.

molecular biology, scientific study of the molecular basis of life processes, including cellular respiration, excretion, and reproduction. One focus of molecular biology is the study of genetic material (DNA, RNA, and the nucleotides of which they are made). GENETIC ENGINEERING has used the insights of molecular biology to manipulate plant and animal genes.

molecular modeling, the computer simulation, by various means, of chemical structures or processes. Special computer-graphics programs can display three-dimensional images of molecular structures and chemical processes, showing the distances and angles of chemical bonds and the modifications that result when atoms or groups of atoms are introduced or substituted. In computer-assisted organic synthesis, the molecular structure of a compound is analyzed to discover how it might be synthesized; special databases can be searched for all occurrences of a particular molecular substructure and for ways to achieve a particular molecular transformation. Calculation-based modeling uses theoretical chemistry and complex mathematical equations to optimize chemical reactions by predicting such things as the energy required or released by reaction between two molecules. Molecular modeling has altered the way research is conducted. When results can be predicted before experiments are performed, experiments that have the highest probability of success can be chosen, potentially reducing the cost of research.

molecular weight, weight of a MOLECULE of a substance expressed in atomic mass units (see ATOMIC WEIGHT). The molecular weight is the sum of the atomic weights of the atoms making up the molecule.

molecule, smallest particle of a COMPOUND that has all the chemical properties of that compound. Molecules are made up of two or more ATOMS, either of the same ELEMENT or of two or more different elements. Ionic compounds, such as common salt, are made up not of molecules but of ions arranged in a crystalline structure (see CRYSTAL). Unlike ions, molecules carry no electrical charge. Molecules differ in size and MOLECULAR WEIGHT as well as in structure (see ISOMER).

Molière, Jean Baptiste Poquelin [môlyĕr'], 1622–73, French playwright and actor, the creator of high French COMEDY; b. Jean Baptiste Poquelin. The son of a merchant, Molière early joined the Béjart troupe of actors. After touring the provinces for 13 years, the company, now headed by Molière, returned to Paris under the patronage of Louis XIV. It performed with continuous success at the Palais Royal and was the forerunner of the Comédie Française. At once actor, director, stage manager, and writer, Molière produced farces, comedies, masques, and ballets for the entertainment of the court. Best known are the comedies of character that ridicule a vice or a type of excess by caricaturing a person who incarnates it. Among these satires are *Tartuffe* (1664)—the religious hypocrite; *Le Misanthrope* (1666)—the antisocial man; *The Miser* (1668); *The Would-be Gentleman* (1670)—the parvenu; *The Learned Women* (1672)—affected intellectuals; *The Imaginary Invalid* (1673)—the hypochondriac. Molière's genius is equally apparent in his broad farces: *The Doctor in Spite of Himself* (1666), *George Dandin* (1668), and *Scapin, the Trickster* (1671). Other works include the poetic *Amphitryon* (1668), after PLAUTUS, and *The Forced Marriage* (1664).

mollusk, animal in the phylum Mollusca, the second largest invertebrate phylum. Mostly aquatic, mollusks have usually soft, unsegmented bodies enclosed in a shell; in some forms the shell is internal, and in a few it is absent. An organ called the mantle secretes the substance that forms the shell. A muscular foot under the body is used for locomotion. Certain mollusks, such as CLAMS, OYSTERS, and SCALLOPS, are important food sources, and mollusk shells are highly valued by collectors. Mollusks include GASTROPODS, or univalves, BIVALVES, CEPHALOPODS (OCTOPUSES and SQUIDS), and CHITONS.

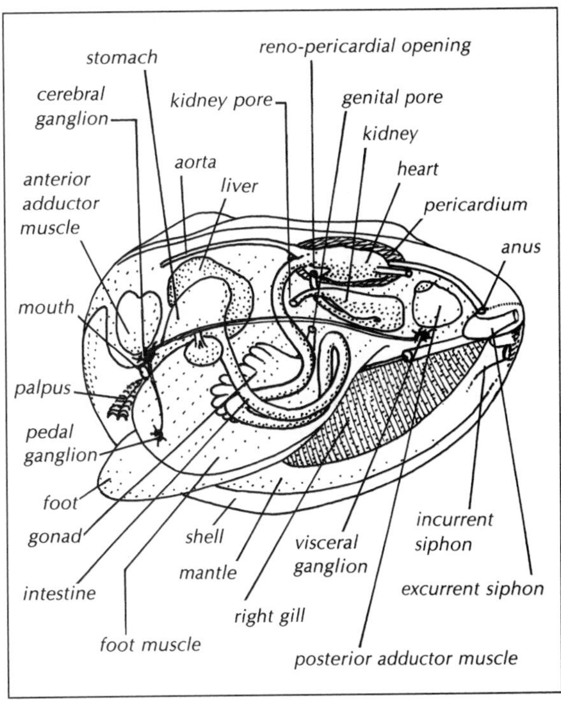

Mollusk: Internal anatomy of a clam, a mollusk of the class Pelecypoda

Molly Maguires, secret organization of Irish-Americans in the coal districts of Scranton, Pa. (c.1865–1875). Organized to combat oppressive mining conditions, the Mollies often resorted to murdering or intimidating the owner-controlled police. They called a strike in 1875, but the organization was finally broken by Pinkerton detectives hired by management. Twenty Molly Maguires were hanged.

Molnár, Ferenc [môl'när], 1878–1952, Hungarian dramatist and novelist. His best-known plays are *Liliom* (1909), made into the musical *Carousel; The Guardsman* (1910); and *The Swan* (1920). His novels include *The Paul Street Boys* (1907).

Moloch: see MOLECH.

Molokai [mō'lōkī'], island (1985 est. pop. 7,000), 261 sq mi (676 sq km), Hawaii. Molokai is generally mountainous; Mt. Kamakou (4,970 ft/1,515 m) is the highest peak. There are many cattle ranches and pineapple plantations. A leper colony (est. 1860) is on the N coast.

Molotov, Vyacheslav Mikhailovich [mô'lətəf], 1890–1986, Soviet leader. Rising rapidly through the Communist party, he became premier of the USSR in 1930. In 1941 STALIN assumed the post and Molotov became vice premier. As commissar of foreign affairs (a title later changed to foreign minister) he negotiated the 1939

Russo-German nonaggression pact. After the 1941 German invasion he worked to strengthen ties with the West, later sharing in the founding of the UN. In 1949 Vishinsky became foreign minister; Molotov remained vice premier. After Stalin's death he was again foreign minister (1953–56). Expelled from the central committee of the party for opposing KHRUSHCHEV in 1957, he was expelled from the party in 1964 and later reinstated into it in 1984.

Moltke, Helmuth Karl Bernard, Graf von, 1800–91, Prussian field marshal. Moltke was made chief of the general staff in 1858 and molded the Prussian army into a formidable war machine. His strategy was responsible for the Prussian triumphs in the Danish War (1864), the AUSTRO-PRUSSIAN WAR (1866), and the FRANCO-PRUSSIAN WAR (1870–71). He was named count (Graf) after the Prussian victory at Metz (1870).

Moluccas or **Spice Islands,** island group and province (1990 pop. 1,856,075), c.32,300 sq mi (83,660 sq km), E Indonesia, between Celebes and New Guinea. The capital is Ambon. Of volcanic origin, the Moluccas are mountainous, fertile, and humid. They are the original home of nutmeg and cloves; other spices and copra are produced. Explored by MAGELLAN (1511–12), the islands were taken by the Dutch, who secured a monopoly in the clove trade, in the 17th cent.

molybdenum (Mo), metallic element, recognized as a distinct element by Karl SCHEELE in 1778. Hard, malleable, ductile, silver-white, and high-melting, it is used in X-ray and electronic tubes, electric furnaces, and certain rocket and missile parts. It is a hardening agent in STEEL alloys. Molybdenum disulfide is used as a lubricant in spacecraft and automobiles. See ELEMENT (table); PERIODIC TABLE.

Mombasa, city (1990 est. pop. 537,000), SE Kenya, on the Indian Ocean. It is Kenya's chief port and a major commercial and industrial center. Manufactures include processed food, refined oil, cement, and glass. Most of the city is on an island connected with the mainland by a causeway. From the 8th to 16th cent. Mombasa was a center of Arab trade in ivory and slaves. Later held by the Portuguese, the Arabs, and Zanzibar, the city passed (1887) to the British, who made it the capital of their East Africa protectorate. It is the ocean terminus of the railway to Uganda.

momentum, in mechanics, the quantity of MOTION of a body. The linear momentum of a body is the product of its mass and velocity. The angular momentum of a body rotating about a point is equal to the product of its mass, its angular velocity, and the square of the distance from the axis of rotation. Both linear and angular momentum of a body or system of bodies are conserved (see CONSERVATION LAWS, in physics) if no external force acts on it or them.

Mommsen, Theodor [môm'sən], 1817–1903, German historian. His *History of Rome* (1854–56, 1885) is an unmatched recreation of Roman society and culture based on his study of ancient coins, inscriptions, and literature. It is his greatest work, although his liberal politics prejudiced his view of the ancient world. He won the 1902 Nobel Prize in literature.

Monaco, Lorenzo: see LORENZO MONACO.

Monaco, officially Principality of Monaco, independent principality (1990 pop. 29,876), c.370 acres (150 hectares), on the Mediterranean Sea, an enclave in SE France, near the Italian border. Monaco-Ville is the capital. Its beautiful location, natural harbor, mild climate, and world-famous gambling casino at Monte Carlo make Monaco a leading tourist resort. Shipping; pharmaceutical, precision instrument, and perfume manufacturing; and food processing also contribute to the economy. Monaco has no income or corporation taxes; disagreement with the French government in the 1960s led to the severe curtailment of the use of Monaco as a tax haven by French citizens. About 50% of the population is French; 16% are Monegasque, and a similar number are Italian. French is the official language, but English, Italian, and Monegasque are also spoken. The vast majority of the people are Roman Catholic. Under the 1962 constitution Monaco is governed by the ruling prince (currently RAINIER III), assisted by a minister of state, a cabinet, and an elected national council.

History. Monaco was ruled by the Genovese Grimaldi family from the 13th cent. In 1731 the French Goyon-Matignon family succeeded to the principality by marriage and assumed the name Grimaldi. Monaco passed under the protection of Spain (1542),

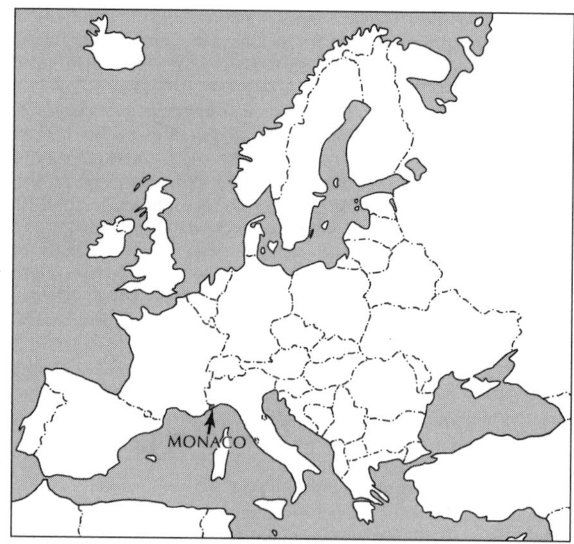

France (1641), and Sardinia (1815), returning to French protection in 1861. Until Monaco's first constitution in 1911, the prince was an absolute ruler. A treaty of 1918 provides that succession to the throne must be approved by the French government.

monarchy, form of government in which sovereignty is vested in a single person whose right to rule is generally hereditary and lifelong. In ancient societies divine descent of the monarch was often claimed. Medieval Christian monarchs were considered the appointed agents of divine will and as such were crowned by the church; their power, however, was often dependent on the nobles. Later monarchs, e.g., HENRY VIII of England and LOUIS XIV of France, became increasingly absolute and developed (16th–17th cent.) the theory of **divine right,** which claimed that the monarch was responsible not to the governed but to God alone. The GLORIOUS REVOLUTION (1688) in England and the FRENCH REVOLUTION weakened the European monarchies, and while monarchs remained symbols of national unity, real power gradually passed to constitutional assemblies, as in Great Britain and Sweden. Saudi Arabia is among the few remaining functional monarchies.

monasticism, organized life in common in a retreat from worldly life, for religious purposes. Men who belong to such communities are monks and their houses are monasteries; communities of women are commonly called convents, and their inhabitants are nuns. Vows of poverty, chastity, and obedience are typical of monastic life, which is known to most great religions—Buddhism, Jainism, Islam, and Christianity. In Christianity monasticism arose from the movement toward the extreme asceticism of a hermit's life. In the Orthodox Eastern Church monks still lead a hermitlike life, but live in common, usually following the rules prescribed by St. Basil the Great. Western monasticism was shaped by St. BENEDICT. The Benedictine abbeys under his rule preserved Roman civilization and became centers of learning in the Middle Ages. There are many Roman Catholic monastic orders, including the FRANCISCANS, the DOMINICANS, and the CARMELITES. Some orders are entirely secluded (enclosed), but most are devoted to teaching, charity, or missionary work. Generally Protestantism has not adopted monasticism.

monazite, phosphate mineral [$(Ce,La,Y,Th)PO_4$], found in the form of sand in the U.S., Madagascar, Brazil, India, Sri Lanka, and Australia. Monazite is an important source of CERIUM, THORIUM, and other RARE-EARTH METALS.

Monck, Charles Stanley, 4th **Viscount,** 1819–94, 1st governor-general of the Dominion of CANADA (1867–68). As governor-general of British North America (1861–67) he worked for confederation and formation (1867) of the dominion.

Monck or **Monk, George,** 1st **duke of Albemarle,** 1608–70, English soldier and politician. Under Oliver CROMWELL, he served in Scotland and in the first DUTCH WAR. In 1659, when the Protectorate of Richard Cromwell fell, Monck marched on London, called for a new Parliament, and declared openly for the RESTORATION of CHARLES II. Charles later heaped honors upon him. Monck also served in the Second Dutch war.

Moncton, city (1991 pop. 57,010), SE New Brunswick, E Canada, on a great bend of the Petitcodiac R. It is a major rail center for the east, with manufactures of textiles and wood and metal products. The city is named for the British general Robert Monckton (the *k* was dropped), whose capture of nearby Fort Beauséjour in 1755 ended French rule of ACADIA. Unusual features of the city are the twice-daily tidal bore that rushes up the Petitcodiac from the Bay of FUNDY and Magnetic Hill, an optical illusion.

Mondale, Walter F(rederick) "Fritz," 1928–, vice president of the U.S. (1977–81); b. Ceylon, Minn. A liberal Democrat, he was a protégé of Hubert HUMPHREY, succeeding him as U.S. senator from Minnesota (1964–77). In 1976 he was chosen by Jimmy CARTER as his running mate and was elected vice president. Carter and Mondale ran for reelection in 1980 but lost to Republicans Ronald REAGAN and George BUSH. Mondale won the 1984 Democratic presidential nomination and became the first major-party candidate to choose a woman, Geraldine FERRARO, as a running mate, but Reagan defeated him in the general election. In 1993 he was appointed U.S. ambassador to Japan.

Monday: see WEEK.

Mondrian, Piet [môn'drēän], 1872–1944, Dutch painter. Influenced by CUBISM, he developed a geometric, nonobjective style that he called neoplasticism. Cofounder of the STIJL group and the magazine *De Stijl,* he published (1920) a book on his theories called *Le Neo-Plasticisme* (French) or *Neue Gestaltung* (German). His theories influenced the BAUHAUS and MODERN ARCHITECTURE. Typical of his work are compositions using only vertical and horizontal lines at 90° angles in primary colors and sometimes black or grays against a white background.

moneran, member of the taxonomic kingdom Monera, which consists of organisms that lack cell nuclei, such as BACTERIA and BLUE-GREEN ALGAE.

Monet, Claude [mônā'], 1840–1926, French landscape painter. A founder of IMPRESSIONISM, he is considered one of the foremost figures in the history of landscape painting. He always worked outside, learning from the landscape itself. Typical of his early period is *Terrace at Le Havre* (1866; Metropolitan Mus.). He later devoted himself to painting the changes in light and atmosphere caused by changes in the hour and season, using his own observation and the laws of optics. He eliminated black and gray from his palette, breaking down light into its color components as a prism does, and repeatedly painted such subjects as haystacks, Rouen Cathedral, and the great lyrical series of water lilies (1899, 1904–25) in his own garden at Giverny (one version, c.1920, Mus. Mod. Art, N.Y.C.).

monetarism, economic theory that monetary policy, or control of the money supply, is the primary if not sole determinant of a nation's economy. Monetarists believe that management of the money supply to produce credit ease or restraint is the chief factor influencing inflation or deflation, recession or growth; they dismiss fiscal policy (government spending and taxation) as ineffective in regulating economic performance. Milton FRIEDMAN has been the leading modern spokesman for monetarism.

monetary system, international: see INTERNATIONAL MONETARY SYSTEM.

money, abstract unit of account in terms of which the value of goods, services, and obligations can be measured. By extension, the term may designate anything that is generally accepted as a means of payment. Almost all economic activity is concerned with the making and spending of money incomes. Historically, a great variety of objects have served as money, among them stones, shells, ivory, wampum beads, tobacco, furs, and dried fish, but from the earliest times precious metals have been favored because of ease of handling, durability, divisibility, and high intrinsic value. Money does not, however, depend on its value as a commodity. Paper currency, first issued about 300 years ago, was usually backed by some standard commodity of intrinsic value into which it could be freely converted on demand. By contrast, fiat money is inconvertible money made legal tender by the decree of the government. The world's first durable plastic currency was introduced by Australia in a special issue in 1988 and in a regular issue in 1992. Plastic bills are more resistant to counterfeiting than paper. The U.S. monetary system was based on BIMETALLISM during most of the 19th cent., but a full gold standard was in effect in the early 20th cent. It provided for free coinage of gold and full convertibility of currency into gold coin. The Gold Reserve Act of 1934 and later measures reduced the U.S. dollar's dependence on gold, and in 1971 the U.S. abandoned gold convertibility altogether. For years international payments were settled by CENTRAL BANK gold movements, but a new system was adopted in the 1970s (see INTERNATIONAL MONETARY SYSTEM). Most U.S. currency in circulation today consists of Federal Reserve notes, but currency and coin are less widely used as a means of payment than checks and electronic transfers, and since the mid-1980s DEBIT CARDS have become increasingly common. In the U.S. the money supply, or total amount of money in the economy, is measured in different ways: M1 includes cash plus checking-account deposits; the broader measures, M2 and M3, add MONEY-MARKET FUNDS, savings, time deposits, and other items. The money supply, a key economic barometer, is influenced by the actions of the FEDERAL RESERVE SYSTEM.

money-market fund, type of MUTUAL FUND that invests in high-yielding, short-term money-market instruments, such as U.S. government securities, COMMERCIAL PAPER, and certificates of deposit. Returns of money-market funds usually parallel the movement of short-term interest rates. Some funds buy only U.S. government securities, such as Treasury bills, while general-purpose funds invest in various types of short-term paper. They became enormously popular with investors in the early 1980s because of their high yields, relative safety, and high liquidity. Much of the money-market growth came at the expense of banks and thrift institutions. With the drop in interest rates in the late 1980s, many investors moved from money-market funds to stock mutual funds and other investments.

money supply: see MONEY.

Monge, Gaspard, comte de Péluse [môNzh], 1746–1818, French mathematician, physicist, and public official; a founder of the École polytechnique. He laid the foundations of descriptive geometry, a field essential to mechanical drawing and architectural drawing, and made important contributions to differential geometry.

Mongolia, Asian region (c.906,000 sq mi/2,346,540 sq km), bordered by Chinese territory on three sides and by Siberian Russia (N). It comprises the Republic of MONGOLIA (Outer Mongolia) and the INNER MONGOLIAN AUTONOMOUS REGION of China. A region of desert and of steppe plateau from 3,000 to 5,000 ft (910–1,510 m) high, it has a cold, dry climate and is sparsely populated. The GOBI desert is in the central section. Mongolia has traditionally been a land of pastoral nomadism; livestock raising and the processing of animal products are the main industries. Irrigation has made some cultivation possible, and there is some mining and oil drilling. In history, great hordes of horsemen repeatedly swept down from Mongolia into N China. JENGHIZ KHAN united (c.1205) Mongolia and led the MONGOLS in creating one of the greatest empires of all time. China extended its rule over the entire region by the late 17th cent., but later vied with Russia for control. Outer Mongolia broke away from China in 1911 but was later reoccupied; with the help of the Red Army, the Chinese were ousted in 1921 and the Mongolian People's Republic (renamed the Republic of Mongolia in 1991) was founded. Inner Mongolia remained under Chinese control.

Mongolia, officially State of Mongolia, republic (1992 est. pop. 2,306,000), 604,247 sq mi (1,565,000 sq km), N central Asia; also called Outer Mongolia. Bordered by Russia (N) and China (S), it occupies more than half of the region historically known as MONGOLIA. The capital is ULAN BATOR. The average elevation exceeds 5,100 ft (1,554 m); mountain ranges and high plateaus cover most of the northwest and the central south, and the GOBI desert lies in the south and east. Wide seasonal variations in temperature, rugged terrain, and an arid climate limit agriculture; nomadic year-round grazing of sheep, goats, cattle, horses, yaks, and camels has been the major occupation for centuries. A small industrial sector is based primarily on livestock processing and the manufacture of textiles and consumer goods. Some timber is cut in the north, and

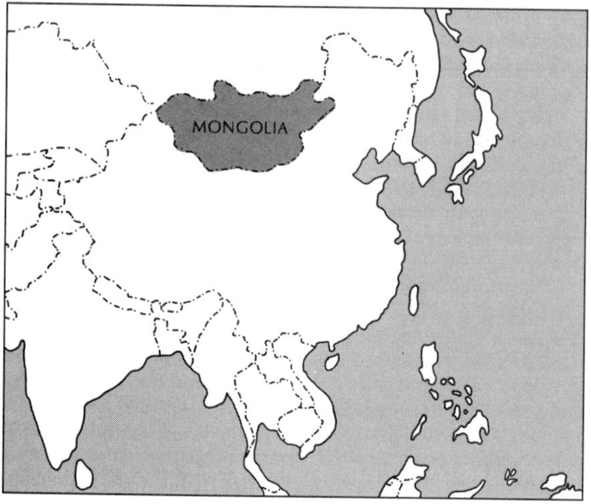

coal, copper, molybdenum, tin, tungsten, and gold are mined and processed. The population is composed primarily of Khalkha Mongols, who speak Khalkha Mongolian; there are also minorities of Oirat Mongols, Kazakhs, Chinese, and Russians. Lamaist Buddhism, discouraged by the former Communist government, has undergone a revival.

History. Mongolia's early history is that of the MONGOLS. It was under Chinese suzerainty from 1691 until the collapse of the Ch'ing dynasty in 1911, when a group of Mongol princes proclaimed an autonomous republic under Jebtsun Damba Khutukhtu (the Living Buddha of Urga). The new state was reoccupied by the Chinese in 1919, taken by the White Russians in 1921, and occupied the same year by Mongolian Communists and the Red Army. Mongolia was proclaimed an independent state, and remained a monarchy until 1924, when the Soviet-dominated Mongolian People's Republic was established. Rural collectivization and the persecution of Lama priests led to a mass exodus (1932) of people with their livestock into China's Inner Mongolia. For many years, Mongolia sided with the USSR in its dispute with China, but it later signed boundary (1983) and consular (1986) agreements with China. In 1990 a reformist Communist government, headed by Punsalmaagiyn Ochirbat, came to power. Increased political, economic, and religious freedom resulted, and many abandoned monasteries were reoccupied by Lamaist monks. The country was renamed the Republic of Mongolia in 1991. In 1992 Mongolia opened its first stock exchange and adopted a new democratic constitution. Ochirbat, running as a noncommunist, won Mongolia's first free presidential election in 1993.

Mongolian languages, group of languages forming a subdivision of the Altaic subfamily of the URALIC AND ALTAIC family of languages. See LANGUAGE (table).

Mongoloid: see RACE.

Mongols, Asian people, numbering nearly 3 million, who live in the Republic of Mongolia (formerly Outer Mongolia), Inner Mongolia (part of China), and Russia. A nomadic pastoral people, they merged their traditional shamanism with Buddhism in the 16th cent., creating Lamaism (see TIBETAN BUDDHISM). Early in the 13th cent. JENGHIZ KHAN united the feuding Mongol tribes into a powerful nation. From their capital at KARAKORUM the Mongols swept into Europe and China, by 1260 ruling a huge empire: the Great Khanate (see KUBLAI KHAN), comprising all of China; the Jagatai khanate, in Turkistan; the Kipchak khanate, in Russia (see GOLDEN HORDE, EMPIRE OF THE); and a khanate in Persia. The Mongol hordes with prominent Turkic elements came to be called TATARS. TIMUR, who founded a new empire in the 14th cent., claimed descent from Jenghiz Khan, as did BABUR, founder of the MOGUL empire. After their expulsion from China in 1382, the Mongols declined.

mongoose, small, carnivorous MAMMAL of the civet family, found in S Asia and Africa, with one species extending into S Spain. Typical mongooses (genus *Herpestes*) are weasellike in appearance, with long, slender bodies and pointed faces. They range in length from 1½ to 3½ ft (45 to 106 cm). The Indian gray mongoose (*H. edwardsi*) is known for its ability to kill snakes, including COBRAS. Mongooses are fierce hunters, and because of their destructiveness it is illegal to import them into the U.S., even for zoos.

monism, in METAPHYSICS, term applied from the 18th cent. to any theory that explains phenomena by one unifying principle or as the manifestation of a single substance, variously identified as spirit or mind (e.g., HEGEL), energy, or an all-pervasive deity (e.g., SPINOZA). The opposites of monism are pluralism, the explanation of the universe in terms of many principles or substances, and DUALISM.

monitor, any of various dragonlike, mostly tropical LIZARDS (genus *Varanus*), found in the Eastern Hemisphere. The carnivorous monitor lizard has a long head and neck, long tail, and strong legs with sharp claws. Monitors range in size from the 8-in. (20-cm) species of W Australia to the 10-ft, 300-lb (3-m, 136-kg) Komodo dragon, the giant of living lizards, which lives only on Komodo, a small Indonesian island.

Monitor and Merrimack, American ships that fought the first battle between ironclads, in the CIVIL WAR. On Mar. 9, 1862, the Confederate frigate *Merrimack,* converted into an ironclad and renamed the *Virginia,* engaged in battle at HAMPTON ROADS with the Union ironclad *Monitor.* The combat, which ended in a draw, revolutionized naval warfare.

Monk, George: see MONCK, GEORGE, 1ST DUKE OF ALBEMARLE.

Monk, Thelonious (Sphere), 1917–82, African-American pianist and composer; b. Rocky Mount, N.C. Considered one of the most important, and eccentric, modern JAZZ figures, Monk played in a dissonant, often humorous style characterized by subtle rhythmic irregularities. His many compositions include " 'Round Midnight" and "Straight No Chaser."

Thelonious Monk

monkey, PRIMATE, belonging to either of the two superfamilies Cercopithecoidea (Old World) and Ceboidea (New World). Monkeys are excellent climbers, and most are primarily arboreal. Unlike APES, they cannot swing arm-over-arm but run on branches on all fours. Nearly all live in tropical or subtropical climates. Monkeys have flat, rather human faces and highly developed hands and feet, with opposable big toes and, where present, thumbs. Old World monkeys, more closely related to apes and humans than New World monkeys, include the macaque, the BABOON, and the MANDRILL; New World monkeys include the marmoset, tamarin, and capuchin.

monkey-puzzle tree, evergreen tree (*Araucaria araucana*) native to Chile, widely cultivated as an ornamental. The symmetrical branches have an unusual angularity and are completely covered by stiff, overlapping leaves. The monkey-puzzle tree and the related Norfolk Island pine (*A. excelsa*) and bunya-bunya (*A. bidwillii*) are good timber trees. Species of *Araucaria* form the dominant vegetation of the coniferous forests of Chile and S Brazil.

Mon-Khmer languages [mōn-kəmâr'], group of languages frequently considered as a subfamily of the Southeast Asian family of languages. Included in the subfamily are Cambodian (or Khmer); Mon (or Talaing), spoken in Myanmar; and a number of other languages, such as Cham of Cambodia and southern Vietnam, and Khasi of Assam, in India. See LANGUAGE (table).

Monmouth, James Scott, duke of, 1649–85, pretender to the English throne, illegitimate son of CHARLES II. Supporters of a Protestant succession championed Monmouth as heir to Charles II. After the accession (1685) of the Roman Catholic JAMES II, Monmouth landed in Dorset and was proclaimed king, but forces loyal to James soon routed his army. Monmouth was captured and beheaded.

Monmouth, battle of, in the AMERICAN REVOLUTION, fought June 28, 1778, near Monmouth Courthouse, N.J. During an attack on the British, Gen. Charles LEE suddenly ordered a retreat. Only the arrival of Gen. WASHINGTON and Baron von STEUBEN prevented an American rout, and the British escaped.

Monnet, Jean [mônā'], 1888–1979, French economist and public official, leading proponent of European unity after World War II. He served (1919–23) as deputy general of the LEAGUE OF NATIONS. In 1947 he authored the Monnet Plan for French economic revival, which led to French participation in the MARSHALL PLAN. Following a proposal by Robert SCHUMAN, he drafted the Schuman Plan, which established (1952) the European Coal and Steel Community (ECSC). Monnet, its first president (1952–55), conceived the ECSC as the initial step toward European economic and political integration. His ideas also contributed to the development of the Common Market. See EUROPEAN UNION.

monoclonal antibody, an antibody mass-produced in the laboratory from a single clone. Monoclonal antibodies are typically made by fusing a normally short-lived, antibody-producing B cell (see IMMUNITY) to a fast-growing cell, such as a cancer cell. The resulting hybrid cell, or hybridoma, multiplies rapidly, producing large quantities of the antibody. Monoclonal antibodies are used in laboratory research and in medical tests, but their effectiveness in disease treatment has been limited. Experimental cancer therapies have used drugs or radioactive materials attached to monoclonal antibodies that, when injected into patients, home in on antigens that grow only on the surface of cancer cells.

monocotyledon: see ANGIOSPERM.

Monod, Jacques [mônō'], 1910–76, French biologist and author. He and François JACOB proposed (1961) the concepts of messenger RNA (see NUCLEIC ACID) and the operon. For their work they shared with André LWOFF the 1965 Nobel Prize in physiology or medicine. In *Chance and Necessity* (1970) Monod argued that humans are products of chance genetic mutations.

mononucleosis, infectious, acute infectious disease of older children and young adults, occurring sporadically or in epidemic form. An airborne herpes virus, known as Epstein-Barr virus, is believed to be the cause. Symptoms include fever, enlarged spleen (in about half the cases), sore throat, and extreme fatigue. HEPATITIS is common. Therapy includes bed rest and the treatment of symptoms.

Monophysitism [Gr., = belief in one nature], a heresy of the 5th and 6th cent., a reaction against NESTORIANISM. It challenged the orthodox creed of the Council of Chalcedon (451) by saying Jesus had only a divine nature. For invalidating Chalcedon, the East was put under excommunication by the pope until 519. In Syria, Egypt, and Armenia, monophysitism dominated, and a permanent schism set in by 600, resulting in the creation of the Jacobite, Coptic, and Armenian churches.

monopoly, market condition in which there is only one seller of a commodity. By virtue of control over supply, the seller exerts nearly total control over prices. By adopting laws excluding competition from an industry, governments have created public service monopolies. These may be public monopolies (e.g., the U.S. Postal Service) or publicly regulated private monopolies (e.g., power and light companies). Control of a supply by a few producers, who often act to restrain price competition, is known as an oligopoly. In the U.S., most forms of monopoly and, to a lesser extent, oligopoly are illegal under ANTITRUST LAWS. The government grants monopolies in the form of patents and copyrights to encourage the arts and sciences.

monorail, railway system whose cars run on a single rail, either above it or suspended beneath it. Driving power is transmitted from the cars to the track by means of wheels that rotate horizontally, making contact with the rail between its upper and lower flanges. Short-run monorails have been built in Houston and Seattle and at Disneyland, in Anaheim, Calif., and Walt Disney World, near Orlando, Fla. Maglev trains use a monorail-like guideway (see MAGNETIC LEVITATION).

monosodium glutamate (MSG), sodium salt of the amino acid glutamic acid, commonly used as a flavor enhancer in foods. Often found in Chinese food, it sometimes causes sensitive individuals to experience adverse physical reactions such as dizziness and flushing, known as the "Chinese Restaurant Syndrome."

monotheism, in religion, belief in one GOD. The term is applied particularly to JUDAISM, CHRISTIANITY, and ISLAM, but early ZOROASTRIANISM and Greek religion in its later stages were monotheistic as well. See also POLYTHEISM.

Monotheletism or **Monothelitism** [Gr., = one will], 7th-cent. heresy condemned by the Third Council of Constantinople (680). First proposed in 622, it said that Jesus had two natures, but operated with one will. It was adopted by Emperor HERACLIUS I as a compromise between MONOPHYSITISM and orthodoxy and was vehemently opposed by Rome.

monotreme, member of the primitive mammalian order Monotremata (sometimes considered a subclass, Prototheria), found in Australia, Tasmania, and New Guinea. The only members are the PLATYPUS and several species of ECHIDNA. They are unique among MAMMALS in laying eggs instead of bearing live young. Certain skeletal features resemble those of REPTILES, from which the monotremes evolved. Adults are toothless; males have spurs connected to poison glands on their hind feet.

Monotype: see PRINTING.

Monroe, James, 1758–1831, 5th president of the U.S. (1817–25); b. Westmoreland co., Va. He fought in several campaigns in the AMERICAN REVOLUTION and was wounded at Trenton. He studied law with Thomas JEFFERSON (1780–83) and served in the Virginia legislature (1782) and the Continental Congress (1783–86), where he opposed the Constitution for creating an overly centralized government. In the U.S. Senate (1790–94), he was a staunch Jeffersonian and a violent opponent of the FEDERALIST PARTY. Governor of VIRGINIA from 1799 to 1802, and again in 1811, he undertook diplomatic missions to England, Spain, and France, and helped negotiate (1803) the LOUISIANA PURCHASE. He served as James MADISON's secretary of state (1811–17), doubling briefly as secretary of war (1814–15). Monroe was easily elected president in 1816 and again in 1820. His administration was characterized as an "era of good feeling." He signed the MISSOURI COMPROMISE, settled boundaries with Canada, and acquired Florida (1819). In 1923 he issued the MONROE DOCTRINE, one of the most important principles of U.S. foreign policy. At the end of his term he retired to his estate, Oak Hill, near Leesburg, Va.

Monroe, Marilyn, 1926–62, American film actress; b. Los Angeles as Norma Jean Baker. A famed sex symbol, she showed real acting talent in such films as *Bus Stop* (1956), *Some Like It Hot* (1959), and *The Misfits* (1960).

Monroe Doctrine, dual principle of U.S. foreign policy enunciated Dec. 2, 1823, in Pres. MONROE's message to Congress. Formulated with the help of Madison's secretary of state, John Quincy ADAMS, it stated that the American continents were no longer open for colonization by European powers and that the U.S. would view with displeasure any European intervention in the Americas. Although never formally recognized in international law, the doctrine was invoked successfully several times and became important in U.S. foreign policy. As imperialistic tendencies grew, the Monroe Doctrine was viewed with suspicion by Latin American countries, who associated it with the possible extension of U.S. hegemony. Pres. Theodore ROOSEVELT's corollary stated (1904) that a disturbance in Latin America might force the U.S. to intervene to prevent European intervention. This interpretation was invoked extensively by presidents Taft and Wilson to justify U.S. intervention in the Caribbean. By the end of the 1920s the doctrine had become less important, and under Pres. F.D. ROOSEVELT the emphasis was on Pan-Americanism. Despite the reemergence of the specter of unilateral intervention in Latin America in the 1950s and 60s, for the most part the U.S. has continued to support hemispheric cooperation within the framework of the ORGANIZATION OF AMERICAN STATES.

Monrovia, city (1991 est. pop. 500,000), capital of Liberia, on the Atlantic Ocean at the mouth of the St. Paul R. Monrovia is Liberia's largest city and its administrative and commercial center. The city's economy revolves around its harbor, which was improved by U.S. forces under LEND-LEASE during World War II. It is a free port, and some 150 shipping companies are registered there under the Liberian flag. Manufactures include cement and refined petroleum. Monrovia was founded in 1822 as a haven for freed American slaves and was named for U.S. Pres. James MONROE. Monrovia was severely damaged during the 1990 Liberian civil war and has yet to recover.

monsoon, wind that changes direction with the seasons. Monsoons are the result of differing air pressures caused by the varied heating and cooling rates of continental landmasses and oceans. Winter monsoons associated with India and Southeast Asia are generally dry; summer monsoons in those regions are extremely wet.

montage, the art and technique of motion-picture editing in which contrasting shots or sequences are used impressionistically to affect emotional or intellectual responses. It was developed creatively after 1925 by Sergei EISENSTEIN.

Montagnais and Naskapi, Labrador peoples with almost identical languages and customs, and a Northern caribou culture (see NORTH AMERICA, INDIGENOUS PEOPLES OF). The Montagnais subsisted on moose, fish, and seals; the Naskapi on caribou, fish, and small game. Both declined rapidly after contact with whites. Some 7,000 now live as hunters and trappers in Quebec and Labrador.

Montagnards: see MOUNTAIN, THE.

Montagu, John: see SANDWICH, JOHN MONTAGU, 4TH EARL OF.

Montagu, Lady Mary Wortley, 1689–1762, English author, noted primarily for her highly descriptive letters, published in 1763. *Town Eclogues* (1747) gives an entertaining picture of contemporary manners. Her quarrel with POPE and his attack on her in his poetry are well known.

Montaigne, Michel Eyquem, seigneur de [môNtĕn'yə], 1533–92, French essayist. Initiator and greatest master of the ESSAY as a modern literary form, he was a magistrate (1557–70) and mayor of Bordeaux (1581–85). He produced his first two books of *Essays* while living in retirement between 1571 and 1580, and the third after 1586. The essays show the development of Montaigne's thinking, from a study of himself into a more general study of humanity and nature. The early works reflect his concern with pain and death. A middle period is characterized by his skepticism regarding all knowledge. Montaigne's last essays reflect his acceptance of life as good and his conviction that people must discover their own nature in order to live in peace and dignity. The *Essays,* models of the familiar, digressive style, treat a wide variety of subjects of universal concern and have greatly influenced both later French writing and English literature.

Montale, Eugenio, 1896–1981, Italian poet and critic. His poetry, complex and often pessimistic, has appeared in such volumes as *Cuttlefish Bones* (1925) and *The Four-year Notebook* (1977). Prose collections include *The Butterfly of Dinard* (1956) and *On Poetry* (1976). Montale was awarded the 1975 Nobel Prize in literature.

Montana, Joe (Joseph Clifford Montana), 1956–, American football player, b. New Eagle, Pa. One of the finest quarterbacks in the game's history, he played (1979–93) for the San Francisco 49ers, leading them to four Super Bowl championships. He was twice the NFL's player of the year (1989, 1990). His records include the highest percentage of completed passes (63.7%), most consecutive games with 300 or more yards passing (5), and most consecutive passes completed (22). He joined the Kansas City Chiefs in 1993.

Montana, Rocky Mt. state in NW U.S.; bounded by North Dakota and South Dakota (E), Wyoming (S), Idaho (W), and the Canadian provinces of British Columbia, Alberta, and Saskatchewan (N).

Area, 147,138 sq mi (381,087 sq km). *Pop.* (1990), 799,065, a 1.6% increase over 1980 pop. *Capital,* Helena. *Statehood,* Nov. 8, 1889 (41st state). *Highest pt.,* Granite Peak, 12,799 ft (3,904 m); *lowest pt.,* Kootenai R., 1,800 ft (549 m). *Nickname,* Treasure State. *Motto, Oro y Plata* [Gold and Silver]. *State bird,* Western meadowlark. *State flower,* bitterroot. *State tree,* Ponderosa pine. *Abbr.,* Mont.; MT.

Land and People. E Montana is part of the GREAT PLAINS region; W Montana is marked by the lofty peaks of the Bitterroot Range—part of the Rockies—the site of Glacier National Park. A section of Yellowstone National Park is also in the state. (See NATIONAL PARKS, table). The generally cold continental climate features heavy winter snows in the west and hot, dry summers in the east. About 52% of the population of this sparsely populated state lives in urban areas. BILLINGS is the largest city, followed by GREAT FALLS In 1990 the population was about 93% white and 6% Native American.

Economy. Montana's economy is dominated by mineral, timber, and agricultural production. Oil, coal, copper, antimony, vermiculite, and many other minerals are extracted. The state has been the site of many large water projects, and varied crops are grown on its irrigated farmland. The fertile grazing lands of the east support cattle, the most profitable agricultural product, followed by wheat, dairy products, barley, and sugar beets. Most industries are based on Montana's raw materials; among them are lumber milling and the manufacture of paper goods, processed food, and refined oil. Tourism is of growing importance.

Government. The 1973 constitution provides for a governor elected to a four-year term. The legislature consists of a senate with 50 members elected to four-year terms and a house with 100 members elected for two years. Montana sends two senators and one representative to the U.S. Congress and has three electoral votes.

History. Montana's plains were the home of the buffalo and the Native Americans they supported, including the BLACKFOOT, SIOUX, Shoshone, ARAPAHO, CHEYENNE, and SALISH, many of whose descendants continue to live in Montana on reservations. The U.S. gained possession of the region through the LOUISIANA PURCHASE (1803), and it attracted mainly trappers, the so-called MOUNTAIN MEN, until the fur supply diminished during the 1840s. The first large-scale influx of settlers came after gold was discovered (1858) and after ranching began (1860s). The indigenous tribes resisted encroachment on their lands, notably at LITTLE BIG HORN, where Gen. George CUSTER's forces were annihilated (1876), but they were soon subdued by government troops. Fierce competition erupted between cattle- and sheep-ranchers over grazing rights, and the discovery of copper (c.1880) at Butte ushered in a period of struggle among copper companies for control of the mines. From 1909 to 1918 the open range was fenced in, as homesteaders began to farm. Both farmers and miners were affected by the GREAT DEPRESSION, but the economy showed great gains during and after World War II. The national energy crisis of the 1970s resulted in a boom in Montana's energy industries, especially coal mining. Despite substantial exploitation of its natural resources, by the last years of the 20th cent. Montana was still largely made up of vast undeveloped and unpopulated places, many of great scenic beauty.

Mont Blanc, highest peak (15,771 ft/4,807 m) in Europe outside the CAUCASUS, located in the Alps near Chamonix, SE France. It was first climbed in 1786.

Montcalm, Louis Joseph de [mŏntkäm', Fr. môNkälm], 1712–59, French general. During the FRENCH AND INDIAN WARS he captured (1756–57) Fort Ontario and Fort Henry, and beat off (1758) a British attack on Fort TICONDEROGA. He defended Quebec against Gen. WOLFE's army until he lost (1759) the open battle on the Plains of Abraham, in which both Montcalm and Wolfe were killed; as a result, Quebec fell to the British.

Monte Carlo: see MONACO.

Montego Bay, city (1991 pop. 83,446), NW Jamaica. A port, railroad terminus, and commercial center, it is one of the most popular resorts in the Caribbean. There is an active trade in sugar, bananas, coffee, and rum and some light industries.

Montenegro, Serbo-Croatian *Crna Gora,* constituent republic of Yugoslavia (1991 pop. 615,000), 5,332 sq mi (13,810 sq km), SW Yugoslavia. Podgorica (renamed Titograd, 1946–92) is the capital. Only 6% of the largely mountainous region is cultivated. Tourism, shipping, aluminum production, stock raising, and mining have been economically important, but the economy has been hurt by the UN embargo against Yugoslavia. Montenegrins, the vast majority of the population, are closely related to the Serbs but form a distinct ethnic group. Most adhere to the Orthodox faith. There are Muslim, Albanian, and Serb minorities. Montenegro, a principality in the Serbian empire, continued to resist the Turks after SERBIA's defeat (1389) at Kosovo Field (see under KOSOVO). By 1499, however, most of the present-day republic was held by the Turks; Venice held the port city of Kotor. Montenegro's independence was granted in 1799. Its last monarch, NICHOLAS I, was deposed in 1918, and Montenegro was united with Serbia. In 1946 it became a Yugoslav republic; it sided with Serbia during the Yugoslav breakup and subsequent fighting.

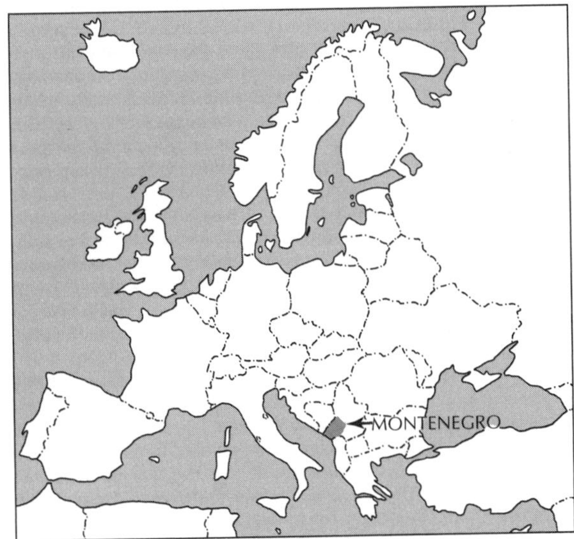

Monterey, city (1990 pop. 31,954), W Calif, on the northern side of the Monterey Peninsula, on Monterey Bay; inc. 1850. A famous resort, it is one of the oldest cities in the state and is rich in history. A presidio was built in 1770, and Monterey was capital of the Spanish territory of Alta California for much of the period 1775–1846. The U.S. Navy took the city in 1846; California's constitution was written there (1849). It became a fishing and whaling center. Numerous historical buildings stand, including a customs house (1827), California's first theater (1844), and a jail (1854).

Monterrey, city (1990 pop. 1,064,197), NE Mexico, capital of Nuevo León state, c.150 mi (240 km) S of Laredo, Texas. Mexico's second-ranking industrial center, Monterrey has the country's largest iron and steel foundries; chemicals, cement, glass, and beer are also produced. It is in a mountain valley where a moderate, dry climate and hot springs have made it a popular resort. Founded in 1579, it was captured (1846) by U.S. forces during the MEXICAN WAR.

Montespan, Françoise Athénaïs, marquise de [môNtəspäN], 1641–1707, mistress of LOUIS XIV of France. She replaced (c.1667) Mlle de La Vallière as the king's mistress and bore him several children. She was supplanted by Mme de MAINTENON.

Montesquieu, Charles Louis de Secondat, baron de la Brède et de, 1689–1755, French jurist and political philosopher. His satire on French institutions, *Persian Letters* (1721), brought him fame. *The Spirit of Laws* (1748), his greatest work, compares the republican, despotic, and monarchical forms of government, revealing the influence of John LOCKE. Montesquieu advocated the separation and balance of powers within government as a means of guaranteeing the freedom of the individual; this doctrine helped form the philosophical basis for the U.S. CONSTITUTION.

Montessori, Maria, 1870–1952, Italian educator and physician. She was the originator of the **Montessori method** of educating small children and the first woman to receive (1894) a medical degree in Italy. At the Orthophrenic School in Rome she worked as a psychiatrist with retarded children, using an environment rich in manipulative materials. In 1907 she started her first DAY-CARE CENTER, utilizing the same methods with normal preschoolers on the theory that a child will learn naturally if placed in an environment consisting of "learning games" suited to the child's abilities and interests. Relying on self-motivation and auto-education, the teacher intervenes only when a child needs help. Montessori also developed child-sized furniture. Her writings include *The Montessori Method* (1912) and *The Secret of Childhood* (1936).

Monteverdi, Claudio, 1567–1643, Italian composer, the first great figure in the history of OPERA. His first opera, *Orfeo* (1607), was revolutionary in its combination of dramatic power and orchestral expressiveness. After settling in Venice (1613) he wrote mostly church music, but continued to produce operas and MADRIGALS. He set the style for Venetian opera. His late works include *The Coronation of Poppaea* (1642).

Montevideo, city (1985 pop. 1,247,920), S Uruguay, capital of Uruguay, on the Río de la Plata. One of the continent's major ports, it is Uruguay's only large city, with nearly half its population; handles virtually all its foreign trade; has diverse manufactures; and is the base for much of the South Atlantic fishing fleet. It is a spacious, attractive city with outstanding architecture and popular beaches. Settled by the Spanish after 1724, it became Uruguay's capital in 1828.

Montez, Lola, 1818?–1861, Irish dancer who became the mistress of King Louis I of Bavaria. He made her a countess, and her influence over Bavarian political affairs was considerable. For that reason she was one of the causes of the Revolution of 1848. She was banished and eventually settled in the U.S., where she died in poverty.

Montezuma or **Moctezuma,** 1480?–1520, AZTEC emperor (c.1502–20), sometimes called Montezuma II. Warlike and despotic, he caused grave unrest among subject peoples. Believing the Spanish conquerors to be descendants of the god QUETZALCOATL, he gave them gifts to persuade them to leave, but Hernán CORTÉS captured him and attempted to govern through him. Montezuma was killed either by the Spanish or by his own rebelling people. His name is linked with fabulous treasures that the Spanish took and presumably lost at sea.

Montfort, Simon de, earl of Leicester, 1208?–1265, leader of the baronial revolt against HENRY III of England. Simon was active in forcing Henry to accept (1258) the PROVISIONS OF OXFORD. After the king's annulment (1261) of the provisions, Simon became a leader in the BARONS' WAR, and won a great victory over the king at Lewes (1264). He was then master of England. His famous Parliament of 1265, to which he summoned not only knights from each shire but also, for the first time, representatives from the boroughs, was an attempt to gain national support. Opposition to Montfort grew and was rallied in the Welsh Marches by the king's son Edward (later EDWARD I). The war was resumed, and Montfort was defeated and killed at Evesham.

Montgolfier, Joseph Michel [môNgôlfyā'], 1740–1810, and **Jacques Étienne Montgolfier,** 1745–99, French brothers, inventors of the first practical BALLOON. On June 5, 1783, they sent up near Lyons a large linen bag inflated with hot air; later that year a Montgolfier balloon sailed over Paris in the first manned free balloon flight.

Montgomery, Bernard Law, 1st **Viscount Montgomery of Alamein,** 1887–1976, British field marshal. In WORLD WAR II, he became the idol of the British public after his victory (1942) at El ALAMEIN (see NORTH AFRICA, CAMPAIGNS IN), and served in Sicily and Italy until Dec. 1943. In Normandy he was field commander of all ground forces until Aug. 1944, then led the 21st Army Group across N Germany to the Baltic. He headed (1945–46) British occupation forces in Germany and served (1951–58) as deputy commander of the Allied powers in Europe.

Montgomery, city (1990 pop. 187,106), state capital and seat of Montgomery co., E central Ala., on the Alabama R.; inc. 1819. A major agricultural market center, it is in the cotton-rich Black Belt. Fertilizer and furniture are among its important manufactures. Named state capital in 1847, it boomed as a port and cotton market. The Confederate States of America were formed (Feb. 1861) in the old capitol (built 1857), where Jefferson DAVIS was inaugurated, and Montgomery served as Confederate capital through 1861. The city is often called the "Cradle of the CONFEDERACY."

month, time required for the MOON to orbit once around the earth. The *sidereal month,* or time needed for the moon to return to the same position relative to a fixed star, averages 27 days 7 hr 43 min 12 sec; the *synodic month,* or time needed for the moon to go through its complete cycle of PHASES, averages 29 days 12 hr 44 min 3 sec. For the month's harmony with the solar calendar, see CALENDAR. Since ancient times certain lucky stones or birthstones have been connected with the months; they are often given as follows: *January* [from the god JANUS]: GARNET; *February* [from Lat., = expiatory, because of ancient rites]: AMETHYST; *March* [from the god MARS]: BLOODSTONE or AQUAMARINE; *April:* DIAMOND or SAPPHIRE; *May:* AGATE or EMERALD; *June* [from the gens *Junius*]: PEARL; *July* [from Julius CAESAR]: RUBY or ONYX; *August* [from AUGUSTUS]: carnelian or peridot; *September* [from Lat., = seven; formerly the 7th month]: chrysolite or sapphire; *October* [eight]: BERYL, TOURMALINE, or OPAL; *November* [nine]: TOPAZ; *December* [ten]: ruby, TURQUOISE, or zircon. See also WEEK; YEAR.

Montherlant, Henri de [môNtĕrläN′], 1896–1972, French author. Such novels as *The Bullfighters* (1926) and *The Bachelors* (1934), decadent and egotistical, glorify force and masculinity. His plays, all very successful, include *The Master of Santiago* (1947), *Port-Royal* (1954), and *Don Juan* (1958).

Monticello, estate near Charlottesville, Va., home and burial place of Thomas JEFFERSON, who designed it. Begun in 1770, the mansion is one of the earliest examples of the American CLASSIC REVIVAL. Today it is a national shrine.

Montpelier, city (1990 pop. 8,247), state capital (since 1805) and seat of Washington co., central Vt., on the Winooski and North Branch rivers; inc. 1855. State government and insurance offices are the chief employers; lumber and granite are produced in the area. A tourist center, the city is surrounded by the Green Mountains.

Montpensier, Anne Marie Louise d'Orléans, duchesse de [mŏNpäsyā′], 1627–93, French princess, called La Grande Mademoiselle, daughter of Gaston d'Orléans. A rebel leader in the FRONDE, she relieved (1652) Orléans with her troops and opened the gates of Paris to the prince of CONDÉ's army.

Montreal, officially **Montréal,** city (1991 pop. 1,017,666), S Quebec, E Canada, part of Montreal metropolitan area (1991 pop. 1,775,871), on Montréal Island, in the St. Lawrence R. at the entrance to the SAINT LAWRENCE SEAWAY. One of Canada's largest cities, it is second only to Paris as the largest primarily French-speaking city in the world (although it has a large English-speaking minority). It is also the nation's chief east-coast seaport and rivals TORONTO as the principal industrial, financial, and commercial center. Landmarks include 764-ft (233-m) Mt. Royal, the hill for which the city is named; historic Old Montreal (*Vieux Montréal*), along the waterfront; Place Ville Marie (built 1960s), first of several underground urban complexes that have transformed life downtown; a modern subway (opened 1966); and *Man and His World,* a permanent mini-version of the international exposition EXPO '67, on an island in the St. Lawrence. Montreal was founded in 1642 by French settlers as Ville Marie de Montréal, on the site of the Native American village of Hochelaga. Vaudreuil de Cavagnal surrendered the city to the British in 1760, and Americans under Richard Montgomery briefly held it (1775–76) during the AMERICAN REVOLUTION. Montreal's importance as a transshipment port for Great Lakes-Atlantic commerce increased rapidly after construction of the Lachine Canal (1825), which allowed ships to bypass the Lachine Rapids, and its volume of trade took another leap forward after the opening (1957) of the St. Lawrence Seaway.

Monts, Pierre du Gua, sieur de [mōn], c.1560–c.1630, French colonizer in Canada. After he and Samuel de CHAMPLAIN explored (1604–5) the coasts of New Brunswick and New England, he founded (1605) the first French colony in Canada at Port Royal (see ANNAPOLIS ROYAL).

Mont-Saint-Michel, rocky isle (1982 est. pop. 75), in the Gulf of St.-Malo, NW France. Access to this major tourist attraction is by causeway or by land at low tide. The Benedictine abbey was founded (708) by Saint Aubert. Three-story buildings and the rock summit provide a base for the abbey church, a superb achievement of Gothic architecture.

Montserrat, island (1992 est. pop. 12,600), 39.5 sq mi (102 sq km), British dependency, West Indies, one of the Leeward Islands. Plymouth is the capital. It was discovered (1493) by Columbus and colonized (1632) by the English. After years of Anglo-French rivalry it became a British possession in 1783. It has had internal self-government since 1960.

Moody, Dwight Lyman, 1837–99, American evangelist; b. Northfield, Mass. In 1870 he met Ira Sankey, who became associated with him in evangelistic campaigns in the U.S. and in Britain. In Massachusetts, Moody founded Northfield Seminary (1879) and Mt. Hermon School (1881), which were merged (1971) as the Northfield Mt. Hermon School. He also opened (1889) a Bible institute (now the Moody Bible Inst.) in Chicago.

Moody, Helen Wills: see WILLS, HELEN NEWINGTON.

Moon, Sun Myung, 1920–, South Korean religious leader. He was an engineering student and dock worker before founding (1954) the Unification Church with a doctrine loosely based on Christianity as interpreted by Moon, who is regarded by his followers as God's messenger. In the early 1990s the church reported 40,000 U.S. followers (3 million worldwide). Moon and his followers have been accused of brainwashing converts and of various illegal activities, and he was convicted (1982) in the U.S. of conspiracy to evade taxes.

moon, the single natural SATELLITE of the earth. The lunar orbit is elliptical, and the average distance of the moon from the earth is about 240,000 mi (385,000 km). The moon's orbital period around the earth, and also its rotation period, is 27.322 days. The true angular size of the moon's diameter is about ½°, which also happens to be the sun's apparent diameter. This coincidence makes possible total solar ECLIPSES. The moon's diameter is about 2,160 mi (3,476 km); it has about 1/81 the mass of the earth and is 3/5 as dense. The moon completely lacks both water and atmosphere. It has a rigid crust about 45 mi (70 km) thick, making the moon a rigid solid to a greater depth than the earth. The inner core has a radius of 600 mi (1,000 km), about 2/3 of the moon's radius. The lunar surface is divided into the densely cratered, mountainous highlands and the large, roughly circular, smooth-floored plains called maria. See also SPACE EXPLORATION; SPACE PROBE.

moonstone, type of FELDSPAR, found in Sri Lanka, Myanmar, and Madagascar, used as a gem. The refraction of light by its thin, paired internal layers causes its milky, bluish sheen.

Moor, Antonis: see MORO, ANTONIO.

Moore, Clement Clarke, 1779–1863, American poet; b. N.Y.C. A biblical scholar and educator, he is chiefly remembered for his poem "A Visit from St. Nicholas" (1823).

Moore, Douglas Stuart, 1893–1969, American composer and teacher; b. Cutchogue, N.Y. His major works, noted for their theatricality and use of the American vernacular, include *Moby Dick* (1928) for orchestra; the children's opera *The Headless Horseman* (1937); and the opera *Giants in the Earth* (1951).

Moore, George, 1852–1933, English author; b. Ireland. He introduced NATURALISM into the Victorian novel with *A Mummer's Wife* (1885). *Esther Waters* (1894) is his best-known novel. His association with the Irish literary renaissance is described in *Hail and Farewell* (3 vol., 1911–14), an autobiography.

Moore, G(eorge) E(dward), 1873–1958, English philosopher. He taught (1898–1939) at Cambridge Univ. and edited (1921–47) the journal *Mind.* First influenced by F.H. BRADLEY and KANT, Moore became more interested in critical EPISTEMOLOGY, and particularly in distinguishing between acts of consciousness and their possible objects. He also became concerned (along with Bertrand RUSSELL and WITTGENSTEIN) with the philosophical implications of linguistic analysis and questioned the definition of "reality." Although Moore provided no systematic set of philosophical doctrines, he influenced contemporary British and American philosophy, especially through his work on commonsense beliefs; his interest in the use of signs (see SEMIOTICS); his representation of REALISM; and his works on ETHICS, *Principia Ethica* (1903) and *Ethics* (1912).

Moore, Henry, 1898–1986, English sculptor. His early sculpture was rough and angular, influenced by PRE-COLUMBIAN ART. Around 1928 he developed a more personal style that gained him international repute. His works in wood, stone, and cement (done without clay models) are characterized by smooth organic shapes that include empty hollows. His favorite subjects were mother and child and the reclining figure. His works include a monument for the Univ. of Chicago.

Henry Moore sculpture Recumbent Figures

Moore, Marianne, 1887–1972, American poet; b. St. Louis. Her poetry is witty, crisp, intellectual, and often satirical. Volumes of her verse include *Poems* (1921), *Collected Poems* (1951; Pulitzer), and *Complete Poems* (1967). Among her other works are translations and essays.

Moore, Thomas, 1779–1852, Irish poet. His *Irish Melodies* (1808–34) include "Believe Me If All Those Endearing Young Charms" and "The Harp that Once through Tara's Halls." *Lalla Rookh* (1817), a long poem on Asian themes, was very popular. Moore was a friend and biographer of BYRON.

Moors, nomadic people of N Africa, originally inhabitants of Mauretania. They became Muslims in the 8th cent. and went to Spain (711), where they overran the Visigoths. They spread northward across the Pyrenees into France but were turned back by CHARLES MARTEL in 732. In S Spain, however, they established the Umayyad emirate (later caliphate) at Córdoba. The court grew in wealth, splendor, and culture. Other centers of Moorish culture were Toledo, Granada, and Seville. The Moors never established a stable central government. In the 11th cent. the caliphate fell, and Moorish Spain was captured by the ALMORAVIDS, who were supplanted in 1174 by the ALMOHADS. During this period, Christian rulers continued efforts in N Spain to recapture the south. In 1085 ALFONSO VI of León and Castile recovered Toledo. Córdoba fell in 1236, and one by one the Moorish strongholds surrendered. The last Moorish city, Granada, fell to FERDINAND V and ISABELLA I in 1492. Most of the Moors were driven from Spain, but two groups, the Mudejares and MORISCOS, remained.

moose, largest member (genus *Alces*) of the DEER family, found in N Eurasia and N North America. The Eurasian species (*A. alces*) is known in Europe as the ELK. The larger American moose is sometimes classed as a separate species (*A. americana*); it has a heavy, brown body with humped shoulders, long, lighter-colored legs, a thick, almost trunklike muzzle, and broad, flattened antlers in the male. Moose hunting is strictly regulated.

Mor, Antonis: see MORO, ANTONIO.

moraine, rock and soil debris carried and finally deposited by a GLACIER. A lateral moraine is the material that falls onto a glacier's edges from valley cliffs. A ground moraine is the debris deposited by a melting glacier. A terminal moraine is the debris left at the edge of a glacier's extreme forward movement. The great ice sheets of the Pleistocene epoch left terminal moraines stretching across North America and Europe. See also DRIFT.

Moral Majority, U.S. political action group composed of conservative, fundamentalist Christians. Founded (1979) and led (1979–87) by evangelist Rev. Jerry Falwell, the group played a significant role in the 1980 elections by its strong support of conservative candidates. It lobbied for prayer and the teaching of CREATIONISM in public schools, while opposing the Equal Rights Amendment (see FEMINISM), homosexual rights, abortion, and the U.S.-Soviet SALT treaties. It dissolved in 1989.

Moral Re-Armament: see BUCHMAN, FRANK NATHAN DANIEL.

Moravia, Alberto, 1907–90, Italian novelist; b. Alberto Pincherle. His first novel, *Time of Indifference* (1929), is a powerful study of spiritual ennui. Other novels include *The Woman of Rome* (1947), *Two Women* (1957), *The Empty Canvas* (1960), and *Time of Desecration* (tr. 1980). He also wrote short stories and essays.

Moravia, historic region, E Czech Republic, bordered by BOHEMIA (W), Slovakia (E), Czech SILESIA (N), and Austria (S). BRNO is the chief city and the former Moravian capital. Moravia consists of a fertile agricultural central valley with mountains in the east, north, and west. It is also highly industrialized, with such manufactures as steel, textiles, and shoes, and has lignite, coal, and other resources. In the 9th cent. Moravia became a great empire, ruling Bohemia, Silesia, Slovakia, and S Poland. From the early 11th cent. it was in effect a crown land of BOHEMIA, with which it passed (1526) to the HAPSBURGS of Austria. Moravia, however, retained its own diet and suffered less than Bohemia in the civil and religious strife of the 16th cent. It became an Austrian crown land in 1849. After WORLD WAR I Moravia was incorporated into the new nation of CZECHOSLOVAKIA. The MUNICH PACT (1938) transferred NW and S Moravia to Germany, which occupied (1939–45) all of Moravia during WORLD WAR II. Since 1960 the region has comprised two administrative regions, North and South Moravia. With the dissolution of Czechoslovakia (1993), Moravia became part of the Czech Republic.

Moravian Church, Renewed Church of the Brethren, or **Unitas Fratrum,** an evangelical Christian communion. It originated in Bohemia among some of John HUSS's followers, who broke with Rome in 1467. Persecution reduced their numbers, but a renewal took place after 1722 at Herrnhut, on the Saxon estate of Graf von ZINZENDORF. In America the sect founded (c.1740) Bethlehem, Pa., which has remained the center of the Moravians in the U.S. They take Scripture as the rule of faith and morals and have a simple liturgy and a modified episcopacy. Moravians number about 55,000 in the U.S.

Moray. For Scottish names spelled thus, see MURRAY.

Mordecai: see ESTHER.

More, Sir Anthony: see MORO, ANTONIO.

More, Sir Thomas (Saint Thomas More) 1478–1535, English statesman, author of *Utopia,* and martyr of the Roman Catholic Church. He received a Latin education and became a humanist through contact with John Colet, John LYLY, and ERASMUS. As a lawyer he attracted the attention of HENRY VIII, whom he served as a diplomat; More was lord chancellor (1529–32). His refused to subscribe to the Act of Supremacy, was imprisoned, and executed. He wrote works in Latin (*Utopia,* 1516) and in English, including devotions, tracts, poems, prayers, and meditations. His English works were published in 1557.

Moreau, Jeanne, 1928–, French film actress. In *Jules and Jim* (1961) she etched an ambiguous portrait of a delightful heroine capable of destroying the men who love her. Her other films include *The Lovers* (1959), *Les Liaisons dangereuses* (1960), *The Bride Wore Black* (1967), *Going Places* (1974), and *The Summer House* (1993). She has also directed films.

Morelos y Pavón, José María [mōrā'lōs ē pävōn'], 1765–1815, Mexican revolutionary leader. A liberal priest, he led (1810–13) rebel forces to initial victories over the Spanish army, becoming generalissimo. But he was defeated (1813) by Gen. ITURBIDE at Valladolid and later captured, defrocked, and executed.

Moreno Valley, city (1990 pop. 118,779), Riverside co., S Calif.; inc. 1984. It is California's fastest-growing city, having increased its population by over 300% in the 1980s. Among its industries are electronics, steel, home construction and improvement enterprises, and engineering. March Air Force Base employs many city residents.

Moreto y Cabaña, Augustin [mōrā'tō ē käbä'nyä], 1618–69, Spanish dramatist of the GOLDEN AGE. His greatest play, of more than 100, is *Disdain for Disdain.*

Morgan, American family of financiers and philanthropists. **Junius Spencer Morgan,** 1813–90, b. West Springfield, Mass., prospered at investment banking. In 1864 he assumed control of a London firm that became J.S. Morgan & Co., which handled most British investments in the U.S. His son, **John Pierpont Morgan,** 1837–1913, b. Hartford, Conn., built the family fortunes into a colossal financial and industrial empire. In 1871 he helped form Drexel, Morgan & Co. (later J.P. Morgan & Co.). His ascent to power was accompanied by dramatic financial battles, notably over railroads, against Jay GOULD, James FISK, E.H. HARRIMAN, and others. Morgan formed (1901) the U.S. Steel Corp., the first billion-dollar corporation in the world. He financed manufacturing and mining, and controlled banks, insurance companies, shipping lines, and communications systems. A popular symbol of the "money trust," he came under public criticism for many of his dealings. His numerous philanthropies included donation of part of his renowned art collection to the METROPOLITAN MUSEUM OF ART. His son, **John Pierpont Morgan,** 1867–1943, b. Irvington, N.Y., headed the house of Morgan after his father died and helped finance the Allied effort during World War I. He endowed the Pierpont Morgan Library, N.Y.C. (see under LIBRARY, table).

Morgan, John Hunt, 1825–64, Confederate general in the U.S. CIVIL WAR, famed for his daring cavalry raids behind Union lines; b. Huntsville, Ala. A raid through Kentucky, Indiana, and Ohio in 1863 was his most outstanding feat.

Morgan, Lewis Henry, 1818–81, American anthropologist; b. Aurora, N.Y. Derived from his unexcelled studies of the SENECA, *Systems of Consanguinity and Affinity of the Human Family* (1870) describes his theory correlating KINSHIP terminology with forms of marriage and rules of descent. *Ancient Society* (1877), which classifies world cultures by progressive stages of savagery, barbarism, or civilization, influenced MARX and ENGELS, who interpreted its evolutionary doctrine as support for their theory of history.

Morgan, Thomas Hunt, 1866–1945, American zoologist and pioneering geneticist, b. Lexington, Ky. Professor of experimental zoology at Columbia Univ. (1904–28) and director of the biological sciences laboratory at the California Institute of Technology (1928–45), Morgan demonstrated the physical basis of heredity and the importance of the GENE, using the fruit fly *Drosophila.* He also described the phenomena of linkage and crossing over and used them to map the arrangement of genes along the CHROMOSOME. His influential books include *The Theory of the Gene* (rev. ed., 1928). Morgan received the 1933 Nobel Prize in physiology or medicine for his work on genetics.

Morgenthau, Hans Joachim, 1904–80, German-American political scientist; b. Germany. He came to the U.S. in 1937 and taught chiefly at the Univ. of Chicago. He emphasized the role of "realism" and "national interest" in international affairs. Among his works are *Politics Among Nations* (1948, rev. ed. 1973) and *Politics in the 20th Century* (1962).

Morgenthau, Henry, Jr., 1891–1967, U.S. secretary of the treasury (1934–45); b. N.Y.C. During World War II he supervised huge sales of government bonds and advocated international monetary stabilization. He helped establish (1945) the International Monetary Fund and the World Bank.

Mörike, Eduard [mö'rikə], 1804–75, German poet and clergyman. Many of his rich lyrics were set to music by Hugo WOLF. He also wrote a novel, *Maler Nolten* (1832), and a novella, *Mozart's Journey from Vienna to Prague* (1856).

Moriscos [môrĭs'kōz], MOORS converted to Christianity after the Christian reconquest (11th–15th cent.) of Spain. The religion and customs of Muslims in the Christian parts of Spain were generally respected until the fall of Granada (1492), after which Moors who refused conversion were coerced. They rebelled (1500–1502) unsuccessfully. Although most Moors accepted conversion, others were persecuted by the INQUISITION. The Moriscos rose in a bloody rebellion (1568–71), which was put down by PHILIP II. They prospered in spite of persecution, but Philip decreed (1609) their expulsion for both religious and political reasons.

Morison, Samuel Eliot, 1887–1976, American historian; b. Boston. He taught at Harvard (1915–55). In 1926 he was appointed the official historian of Harvard and wrote the *Tercentennial History of Harvard College and University* (3 vol., 1936). Commissioned by Pres F.D. ROOSEVELT, he wrote a *History of Naval Operations in World War II* (15 vol., 1947–62). His other works include *Admiral of the Ocean Sea* (1942; Pulitzer), a biography of COLUMBUS; *John Paul Jones* (1959; Pulitzer); and *The European Discovery of America* (2 vol., 1971–74).

Morisot, Berthe [môrēzō'], 1841–95, French impressionist painter. She was a close friend and sister-in-law of MANET. Her work inclined toward pure IMPRESSIONISM, e.g., *La Toilette* (Art Inst., Chicago).

Morita Akio, 1921–, Japanese business executive. He joined with another engineer to found (1946) the Tokyo Telecommunications Co. Renamed (1958) Sony, the company developed the transitor radio and other innovative electronic products and flourished. By the early 1990s Sony had purchased CBS records and Columbia Pictures and was one of the world's largest corporations, and Morita had become one of the world's richest persons.

Morley, Sylvanus Griswold, 1883–1948, American archaeologist; b. Chester, Pa. He directed (1924–40) the Carnegie Institution expeditions at CHICHÉN ITZÁ and published an introduction to Mayan hieroglyphs (1915) and studies of the inscriptions at Copán (1920) and Petén (5 vol., 1938).

Morley, Thomas, c.1577–1603, English composer, pupil of William BYRD. His works include MOTETS, music for Anglican services, and charming MADRIGALS, as well as a guide to 16th-cent. English music practice.

Mormons, name commonly used for the members of the Church of Jesus Christ of Latter-Day Saints. The religion was founded by Joseph SMITH after he claimed that golden tablets containing the Book of Mormon were revealed to him at Palmyra, N.Y. He and his followers established (1831) a headquarters at Kirtland, Ohio. The group grew rapidly, and Smith planned to make W Missouri its permanent home until conflict with neighbors caused their expulsion (1838–39). They then moved to Nauvoo, Ill., but again hostility arose with neighbors and culminated in the mob murder of Smith and his brother Hyrum in 1844. The Mormons moved west and founded (1847) SALT LAKE CITY in Utah, where, under Brigham YOUNG, they weathered hardships and built a communal economy. Plural marriages within the group prevented Utah's admission to the Union until 1896, but in 1890 the church withdrew its sanction of polygamy. The church is led by a 3-member First Presidency and by the Council of Twelve (the Apostles). In 1990 it reported a U.S. membership of 4,267,000. Mormonism is marked by the importance of revelation, by stress on the interdependence of spiritual and temporal life, and by vigorous proselytizing. Mormon beliefs are based on the Bible, the Book of Mormon, revelations to Smith (*Doctrine and Covenants*), and *The Pearl of Great Price* (sayings attributed to Moses and Abraham). A separatist group, the Reorganized Church of Jesus Christ of Latter-Day Saints, was organized in 1852. Its headquarters are in Independence, Mo.

morning glory, common name for the family Convolvulaceae, herbs, shrubs, and small trees (many of them climbing forms) of warm regions. The tropical morning glory genus (*Ipomoea*), which includes the SWEET POTATO, and the temperate bindweed genus (*Convolvulus*) are chiefly herbaceous vines of prolific growth with colorful funnel-shaped blossoms that often open only in the morning.

Moro, Aldo, 1916–78, Italian politician. A Christian Democrat, he was minister of justice (1955–57), prime minister (1963–68, 1974–76), and foreign minister (1970–72). In 1978 he was kidnapped and murdered by the terrorist Red Brigades.

Moro, Antonio, c.1519–c.1575, Flemish portrait painter, known as Antonis Mor or Moor and Sir Anthony More. Court painter to the house of Hapsburg, he was influenced by TITIAN. His portraits, e.g.,

Mary Tudor (1554; Prado) and Alessandro Farnese (1557; Parma), influenced international court portraiture.

Morocco, officially Kingdom of Morocco, kingdom (1992 est. pop. 26,709,000), 171,834 sq mi (445,050 sq km), NW Africa, bordered by the Mediterranean Sea (N), the Atlantic Ocean (W), Mauritania (which lies beyond the disputed territory of Western Sahara, S), and Algeria (E). Principal cities include RABAT (the capital), CASABLANCA, MARRAKESH, and FEZ. The ATLAS Mts., rising to 13,671 ft (4,167 m) in Jebel Toubkal in the southwest, dominate most of the country. In the south lie the sandy wastes of the SAHARA desert, but in the north is a fertile coastal plain, home of most of the population. Agriculture and mining are the mainstays of the economy. Morocco is the world's leading producer and exporter of phosphates; other important minerals include iron ore, copper, lead, zinc, cobalt, molybdenum, and coal. Food processing and the manufacture of leather goods are also important. Half the labor force is employed in agriculture, growing cereals, citrus fruits, and vegetables. Tourism and fishing also contribute to the economy. Most Moroccans are of mixed Arab-Berber descent and are Muslim; Islam is the state religion. There are small Christian and Jewish minorities. Arabic is the official language; Berber dialects, French (a main language of commerce), and Spanish are also spoken.

History. Originally inhabited by Berbers, Morocco became a province of the Roman Empire in the 1st cent. A.D. After successive invasions by barbarian tribes, Islam was brought by the Arabs in c.685. An independent Moroccan kingdom was established in 788; its dissolution in the 10th cent. began a period of political anarchy. The country was finally united in the 11th cent. by the ALMORAVIDS, a Berber-Muslim dynasty, who established a kingdom reaching from Spain to Senegal. Unity was never complete, however, and conflict between Arabs and Berbers was incessant. European encroachment began in 1415, when Portugal captured Ceuta, and ended with the Portuguese defeat at the battle of Alcazarquivir in 1578. In the 19th and early 20th cent. the strategic importance and economic potential of Morocco once again excited the European powers, sparking an intense, often violent, rivalry among France, Spain, and Germany. Finally, in 1912, most of Morocco became a French protectorate; a small area became a Spanish protectorate. Nationalist feelings began to surface in the 1930s, becoming more militant after World War II, and in 1956 Morocco gained its independence. In 1957 the sultan became King Muhammad V. He was succeeded in 1961 by his son, HASSAN II, whose early reign, plagued by internal unrest, coups, and assassination attempts, was repressive. Hassan's position was strengthened in 1976, when Spain relinquished the Spanish Sahara to joint Moroccan-Mauritanian control. Challenged by the Polisario Front, a guerrilla movement backed by Algeria and seeking independence for the area (which they named WESTERN SAHARA), Mauritania withdrew in 1979, but Morocco continued battling there and claimed the entire territory.

Moroni, city (1990 est. pop. 23,000), capital of COMOROS.

Moronobu (Hishikawa Moronobu), c.1618–c.1694, Japanese painter and color-print designer of the *ukiyo-e* school (see JAPANESE ART). One of his few surviving works is a screen painting in the Museum of Fine Arts, Boston.

morphine, highly addictive NARCOTIC derivative of OPIUM used for the relief of pain. Morphine suppresses anxiety and alters the perception of pain, thereby producing euphoria. It also impairs mental and physical performance, reduces sex and hunger drives, and induces apathy. Its use is strictly regulated (see DRUG ADDICTION AND DRUG ABUSE).

Morrice, James Wilson, 1865–1924, Canadian painter; b. Montreal. Traveling widely, he painted subtly colored, delicately rendered landscapes, e.g. *Venice: Night* (National Gall., Ottawa).

Morris, Gouverneur, 1752–1816, American statesman; b. Morrisania, N.Y. An early supporter of the AMERICAN REVOLUTION, he helped handle the finances of the new government (1781–85) and was active in the writing of the Constitution.

Morris, Mark 1956–, American dancer and choreographer; b. Seattle. He danced for Eliot Feld and Twyla THARP before establishing his own company (1980). His dances are noted for their ingenuity and amalgamation of high and low culture.

Morris, Richard Brandon, 1904–89, American historian; b. N.Y.C. An authority on early American legal and diplomatic history, he was Gouverneur Morris Professor of History at Columbia (1959–73). His works include *Government and Labor in Early America* (1946) and *The Peacemakers* (1967). He was also editor of the papers of John Jay and was president of the American Historical Association.

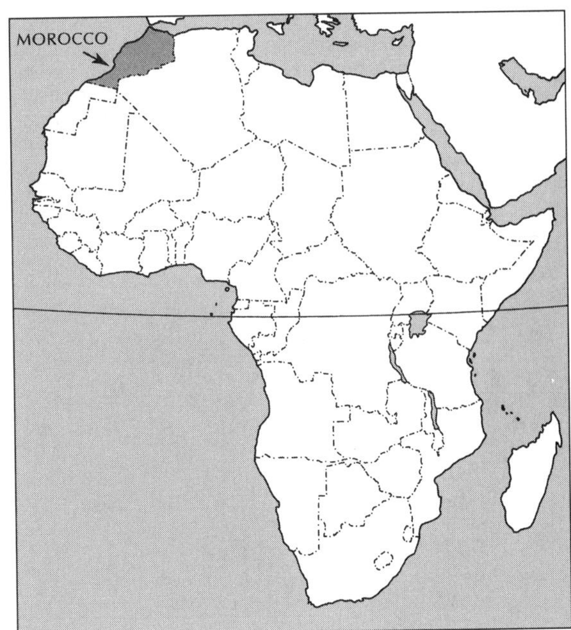

Morris, Robert, 1734–1806, American merchant, signer of the DECLARATION OF INDEPENDENCE; b. England. His role in raising money for George WASHINGTON's army earned him the title "financier of the Revolution."

Morris, William, 1834–96, English poet, artist, craftsman, designer, social reformer, and printer, considered one of the great Victorians. Influenced by RUSKIN and BURNE-JONES, he became interested in the MIDDLE AGES. He then was attached to the PRE-RAPHAELITES, and, encouraged by D.G. ROSSETTI, began to paint and write poetry, e.g., *The Earthly Paradise* (3 vol., 1868–70). In reaction to industrialism, he started (1861) the decorating firm of Morris and Co. to revitalize the splendor of medieval decorative arts (see ARTS AND CRAFTS). He made carvings, STAINED GLASS, TAPESTRIES, chintzes, and furniture. He became interested in politics and reform, forming (1884) the Socialist League, and writing *News from Nowhere* (1891), in which he states that art is the expression of joy in labor rather than a luxury. His most important venture was the Kelmscott Press (1890, Hammersmith), where he designed type, page borders, and bindings of fine books.

Morris, Wright, 1910–, American writer; b. Central City, Nev. His novels, which treat various aspects of the American experience, include *Love among the Cannibals* (1957), *Fire Sermon* (1971), and *Plains Song* (1980).

Morrison, Toni, 1931–, African-American novelist; b. Lorain, Ohio, as Chloe Anthony Wofford. She is noted for her spare but poetic language, emotional intensity, and sensitive observation of African-American life. Her novels include *The Bluest Eye* (1970), *Song of Solomon* (1977), *Tar Baby* (1981), *Beloved* (1987; Pulitzer), and *Jazz* (1992). She was awarded the Nobel Prize for literature in 1993.

Morse, Samuel Finley Breese, 1791–1872, American inventor and noted portraitist; b. Charlestown, Mass. After spending 12 years perfecting his own version of André AMPÈRE's idea for an electric TELEGRAPH, Morse demonstrated (1844) the practicability of his device to Congress and subsequently won world fame. Because many phases of the invention had been anticipated by others, his originality as the inventor of telegraphy has been questioned. Morse later experimented with submarine cable telegraphy.

Morse code [for Samuel MORSE], set of signals used on the TELE-

GRAPH and in some radio transmissions, or with a flash lamp for visible signaling. The unit of the code is the *dot,* representing a very brief depression of the telegraph key. The *dash* represents a depression three times as long as the dot. Different combinations of dots and dashes are used to code the alphabet, the numerals 1 to 9 and zero, the period, and the comma. American Morse differs considerably from International Morse. Morse code is now mainly used by amateur (ham) radio operators.

MORSE CODE

A	·—	J	·———	S	···
B	—···	K	—·—	T	—
C	—·—·	L	·—··	U	··—
D	—··	M	——	V	···—
E	·	N	—·	W	·——
F	··—·	O	———	X	—··—
G	——·	P	·——·	Y	—·——
H	····	Q	——·—	Z	——··
I	··	R	·—·		
1	·————	5	·····	9	————·
2	··———	6	—····	0	—————
3	···——	7	——···	Period	·—·—·—
4	····—	8	———··	Comma	——··——

mortar, in warfare, a short-range weapon that fires a shell on a high trajectory. The name once applied to a heavy ARTILLERY piece but lately has designated a much lighter, muzzle-loaded, smooth-bore infantry weapon—consisting principally of a tube and a supporting bipod—that fires a fairly heavy projectile in a high arc.

mortgage, in law, a pledge of property as security for payment of a debt. If the borrower (the mortgagor) fails to pay the debt, the lender (the mortgagee) has the right to seek foreclosure, a procedure through which the property is sold to satisfy the lender's claims. Almost any kind of property may be mortgaged; the most familiar mortgage is that on a home.

Mortimer, Roger de, 1st **earl of March,** 1287?–1330, English nobleman. He opposed EDWARD II in the wars of 1321–22 and escaped to France, where Edward's queen, ISABELLA, became his lover. They invaded (1326) England, deposed and murdered Edward, and had young EDWARD III crowned. Mortimer, with Isabella, then virtually ruled England until 1330, when Edward III had him tried and executed.

mosaic, art of producing surface design by closely inlaying colored pieces of marble, glass, tile, or semiprecious stone. In the Roman Empire, floors were decorated with mosaics made up of large marble slabs in contrasting colors or of small marble cubes (tesserae). Tessera floors varied from black-and-white geometrical patterns to large pictorial scenes. Glass mosaics were used in early Christian basilicas. The craft reached its height in the 6th cent. at Byzantium (later Constantinople), where the HAGIA SOPHIA was decorated with gold mosaics. The use of gold and of colors produced by metallic oxides later reached the West. In the 5th and 6th cent. RAVENNA became the center of Western mosaic art. A revival in Italy (11th–13th cent.) produced such mosaics as those in St. Mark's Church, Venice. Mosaic was also used in Russia, particularly in Kiev. The advent of FRESCO decoration in 14th-cent. Italy caused mosaic art to decline. In the 19th cent., the Gothic revival produced modern attempts at mosaics, e.g., those in WESTMINSTER ABBEY. Mosaics are important in 20th-cent. Mexico, where they continue a pre-Columbian tradition. Contemporary examples are also found in Europe, South America, and Israel.

Moscow, Rus. *Moskva,* city (1991 est. pop. 8,802,000), capital of RUSSIA and former capital of the UNION OF SOVIET SOCIALIST REPUBLICS, W central European Russia, on the Moskva R. The largest city in Russia, Moscow is the hub of its rail network, an inland port, and the site of civil and military airports. Its many manufactures include machinery and machine tools, automobiles, chemicals, and textiles. First mentioned by chroniclers in 1147, it became (c.1271) the seat of the grand dukes of Vladimir-Suzdal and (by the 15th cent.) capital of the Russian state. From the 14th cent. it was the seat of the metropolitan (later patriarch) of the Russian Orthodox Church. The capital was transferred (1712) to the new city of SAINT PETERSBURG. Built largely of wood until the 19th cent., Moscow burned many times, notably after NAPOLEON's invasion (1812). In the 19th and early 20th cent. it was the focus in Russia of social democracy and other political movements. After the RUSSIAN REVOLUTION, it was (1918–91) the capital of the USSR. Economic growth doubled the population between 1926 and 1939. In WORLD WAR II the German offensive against Moscow (1941) was stopped about 20 mi (32 km) from the city's center, but damage was minimal. Its major sections form concentric circles around the KREMLIN. Red Square, the Lenin Mausoleum, and St. Basil's Cathedral are major landmarks. Among Moscow's cultural institutions are the Univ. of Moscow (est. 1755), Russian State Library (formerly Lenin Library), Tretyakov Gallery, and Bolshoi Theater.

Moseley, Henry Gwyn Jeffreys, 1887–1915, English physicist. Studying the relations among bright-line spectra of different elements, he derived the ATOMIC NUMBERS from the frequencies of vibration of X rays emitted by each element. Moseley concluded that the atomic number is equal to the charge on the nucleus. This work explained discrepancies in the Mendeleev system (see PERIODIC TABLE).

Moses, Hebrew lawgiver; b. probably Egypt. The prototype of the prophets, in the 13th cent. B.C. he led his people out of bondage in Egypt to the edge of Canaan. According to the Bible (EXODUS; LEVITICUS; NUMBERS; DEUTERONOMY), he lived in constant touch with God, who promulgated the Law (often called Mosaic law) through Moses' mouth. Moses never entered the Promised Land but only saw it from Mt. Pisgah before he died. Authorship of the first five books of the Bible—the Pentateuch or TORAH—has traditionally been ascribed to him; hence they are called the Books of Moses.

Moses, Grandma (Anna Mary Robertson Moses), 1860–1961, American painter; b. Washington co., N.Y. A farm wife, untrained in art, she began painting in her 70s. Her popular American primitive paintings are colorful, simple, and carefree scenes of rural life.

Moslem, form of Muslim: see ISLAM.

mosque, Muslim worship building. ISLAM is little dependent on ritual, and the house and courtyard of MUHAMMAD at Medina were the first worship site. As Islam spread, almost any edifice was used, including Christian and Zoroastrian temples. The mosque's basic elements are space to assemble and some orientation so that the faithful may pray toward MECCA. This direction is marked by a *mihrab,* usually a decorated niche. The elaborate mihrabs of later mosques are covered with intricate woodwork, carved marble, or tiles. A mosque may also contain a pulpit; a *maqsura,* or enclosed space around the *mihrab,* often with lacy screen work; MINARETS; a courtyard surrounded by colonnaded or arcaded porticos with wells or fountains for ablutions; and space for a school. Early Egyptian and Syrian mosques adhered to the primitive pattern. The mosque of Omar (A.D. 691) at Jerusalem, called the Dome of the Rock, follows an octagonal Byzantine plan and has a wooden dome, but domed mosques were not common for another six centuries. In the 14th cent. a cruciform mosque with pointed vaults around a central court appeared; the arm toward Mecca was wider and deeper. The finest example of the cruciform mosque is the great mosque of Sultan Hasan (1356) at Cairo. Mosques of N Africa and Spain tended to be simple, but that at Córdoba (begun A.D. 780) was larger than any Christian church. It became the Cathedral of Córdoba in 1238. In the 15th and 16th cent., colonnaded halls were replaced by large, square, domed interiors, as in the Blue Mosque of Tabriz (1437–68) and the imperial mosque at Isfahan (1585–1612). After 1453, the converted HAGIA SOPHIA became a model for Islamic religious structures. The pointed, bulbous domes and polychrome tile decoration of Persian mosques are distinctive. Indian mosques, following the Persian style, employed stone and marble exteriors that gave them a more solid monumentality.

mosquito, small, long-legged, winged INSECT (order Diptera), related to the FLY. Most females have piercing, sucking mouthparts and feed on the blood of mammals; males feed on plant juices. Eggs are usually laid in stagnant water and the larvae are aquatic.

Many diseases, including MALARIA, YELLOW FEVER, and human ENCEPHALITIS, are transmitted by certain species of mosquitoes.

moss, small primitive plant typified by tufted growth that is usually vertical; alternately considered a member of the class Bryopsida or division Bryophyta (see BRYOPHYTE). Although limited to moist habitats because they require water for FERTILIZATION and lack a vascular system for absorbing water, mosses are extremely hardy and grow nearly everywhere. The green moss plant visible to the naked eye, seldom over 6 in. (15.2 cm) in height, is the GAMETOPHYTE generation, which gives rise to the sporophyte generation. Mosses have some importance in soil formation and provide food for certain animals. SPHAGNUM, or peat moss, is commercially valuable as the main constituent of PEAT. CLUB MOSS and SPANISH MOSS are unrelated to true moss.

most-favored-nation clause, provision in trade agreements between nations that extends to the signatories the automatic right to any tariff reduction or other trade advantage negotiated with a third country. Nations belonging to the General Agreement on Tariffs and Trade (see UNITED NATIONS) accept this principle, which is intended to promote free trade. Today there are efforts to relax this principle to accommodate developing countries seeking preferential treatment for their exports. Regional trading groups such as the European Community (see EUROPEAN UNION), which abolish tariffs within the group while maintaining them for trade with nonmembers, pose another challenge to the principle.

Mosul, city (1985 est. pop. 571,000), N Iraq, on the Tigris R. Trade in agricultural goods and exploitation of oil are the two main occupations of the inhabitants, who are mostly Arabs. The surrounding area, however, is peopled by Kurds. Mosul was devastated (13th cent.) by the MONGOLS and was part (1534–1918) of the OTTOMAN EMPIRE. Its possession by Iraq was disputed (1923–25) by Turkey but was confirmed (1926) by the League of Nations.

motet, a type of musical composition outstanding in the 13th cent., and a different type in the Renaissance. The 13th-cent. motet, originating in Paris, was a polyphonic piece for three voices: a tenor (a fragment of PLAINSONG or other melody arranged in a pattern) and two accompanying voices, sometimes based on secular French songs. The Renaissance motet, originating in Flanders, was polyphonic and unaccompanied, with a single Latin text for four to six voices. JOSQUIN DESPREZ, LASSO, PALESTRINA, TALLIS, and BYRD were important motet composers. Since BACH's time the term has referred to various kinds of sacred choral POLYPHONY.

moth, any of a large group of INSECTS that, with the BUTTERFLIES, constitutes the order Lepidoptera. Moths have two pairs of wings that function as a single pair and are covered with dustlike scales. Wingspreads range from ⅙ in. (2 mm) to 10 in. (25 cm). Many moths have PROTECTIVE COLORATION matching their background. They are distinguished from butterflies by their stouter, usually hairy bodies and feathery antennae. Most moths are nocturnal and rest with wings outspread; butterflies usually fly by day and rest with wings upraised. Moths undergo a complete METAMORPHOSIS, feeding on leaves or other plant material.

Mother Lode, belt of gold-bearing quartz veins in central California, along the western foothills of the Sierra Nevada. The discovery (1848) of alluvial gold on the South Fork of the American R. led to the California gold rush. Mark TWAIN and Bret HARTE helped make the Mother Lode famous.

mother-of-pearl or **nacre,** iridescent substance that lines the shells of some mollusks, notably the pearl OYSTER, pearl MUSSEL, and ABALONE. Valued for its delicate beauty, it is used for buttons, knife handles, and inlay work.

Motherwell, Robert, 1915–91, American painter and writer; b. Aberdeen, Wash. A painter, teacher, and theoretician of ABSTRACT EXPRESSIONISM, he painted canvases characterized by large, amorphous shapes of strong, austere colors, e.g., his best-known series, *Elegies to the Spanish Republic* (1975).

motion, in MECHANICS, the change in position of one body with respect to another. The study of the motion of bodies is called DYNAMICS. The time rate of linear motion in a given direction by a body is its *velocity;* this rate is called the *speed* if the direction is unspecified. If during a time t a body travels over a distance s, then the *average speed* of that body is s/t. The change in velocity (in magnitude and/or direction) of a body with respect to time is its acceleration. The relationship between FORCE and motion was expressed by Isaac NEWTON in his three laws of motion: (1) a body at rest tends to remain at rest, or a body in motion tends to remain in motion at a constant speed in a straight line, unless acted on by an outside force; (2) the acceleration a of a mass m by a force F is directly proportional to the force and inversely proportional to the mass, or $a = F/m$; (3) for every action there is an equal and opposite reaction. The third law implies that the total MOMENTUM of a system of bodies not acted on by an external force remains constant (see CONSERVATION LAWS, in physics). Motion at speeds approaching that of light must be described by the theory of RELATIVITY, and the motions of extremely small objects (atoms and elementary particles) are described by QUANTUM MECHANICS.

motion pictures, movie-making as an art and an industry, including its production techniques, its creative artists, and the distribution and displaying of its products (see MOTION-PICTURE PHOTOGRAPHY and CAMERA). Experiments in photographing movement were made in the U.S. and Europe well before 1900. The first motion pictures made with a single camera were by E.J. Marey, a French physician, in the 1880s. In 1889 Thomas EDISON developed the kinetograph, using rolls of coated celluloid film, and the Kinetoscope, for peep-show viewing. The LUMIÈRE brothers, in France, created the Cinématographe (1895). Projection machines were developed in the U.S. and first used in New York City in 1896. The first movie theater, a "nickelodeon," was built in Pittsburgh in 1905. Movies developed simultaneously as an art form and an industry. They had enormous immediate appeal, and were established as a medium for chronicling contemporary attitudes, fashions, and events. The camera was first used in a stationary position, then panned from side to side and moved close to or away from the subject. With the evolution of sound films in the late 1920s, language barriers forced national film industries to develop independently. In the U.S. a separation of motion-picture crafts had developed by 1908, and actors, producers, cinematographers, writers, editors, designers, and technicians worked interdependently, overseen and coordinated by a director. Hollywood, Calif., became the American movie capital after 1913. Films were at first sold outright to exhibitors and later distributed on a rental basis. By 1910 the "star system" had come into being. Directors became known for the individual character of their films and were as famous as their stars. During World War I the U.S. became dominant in the industry. In 1927 dialogue was successfully introduced in *The Jazz Singer.* Early color experiments were achieved by hand-tinting each frame. In 1932 Technicolor, a three-color process, was developed. The film industry in its heyday (1930–49) was managed by a number of omnipotent studios producing endless cycles of films in imitation of a few successful original types. In those great years Hollywood gave employment to a host of talented actors, e.g., Ingrid BERGMAN, Humphrey BOGART, Joan CRAWFORD, Bette DAVIS, Cary GRANT, Katharine HEPBURN, Spencer TRACY, and John WAYNE. In the 1950s the overwhelming popularity of TELEVISION began to erode studio profits, necessitating technological innovations such as wide-screen processes, stereophonic sound systems, and three-dimensional cinematography (3-D). By 1956 studios were compelled to produce movies made expressly for television reruns. In the 1960s many filmmakers began to work independently of the studio system, producing low-budget films that departed from the glamorous, celebrity-packed works of earlier years. Costly and elaborate science fiction productions and horror films attained unprecedented popularity in the late 1970s and 80s. During the same period movies on videotape, either purchased or rented for home viewing on a VIDEOCASSETTE RECORDER, also became important. By the early 1990s computer technology permitted "interactive" films, in which the audience controls some aspects of the plot. Among the great motion-picture directors are D.W. GRIFFITH, Mack SENNETT, John FORD, and Alfred HITCHCOCK in the U.S.; Jean RENOIR, Jean-Luc GODARD, and François TRUFFAUT in France; Ingmar BERGMAN in Sweden; F.W. MURNAU and Rainer Werner FASSBINDER in Germany; Lucino VISCONTI, Michelangelo ANTONIONI, and Federico FELLINI in Italy; Sergei EISENSTEIN and Aleksandr DOVZHENKO in the USSR; Satyajit RAY in India; and KUROSAWA AKIRA in Japan.

motor, electric, machine that converts electrical energy into mechanical energy. One type of electric motor consists of a conducting loop mounted on a nonconducting shaft. Current fed to carbon brushes enters the loop through two slip rings. A magnetic field around the loop, supplied by an iron-core field magnet, causes the loop to turn when current flows through it. In an alternating-current (AC) motor, the current flowing in the loop is synchronized to reverse direction at the moment when the plane of the loop is perpendicular to the magnetic field and there is no magnetic force exerted on the loop. Because the momentum of the loop carries it around until the current is again supplied, continuous motion results. In AC induction motors, the current passing through the loop does not come from external sources but is induced as the loop passes through a magnetic field. In direct-current (DC) motors, a split-ring commutator switches the direction of the current each half rotation to maintain the shaft's direction of motion. In a brushless DC motor, the rotating portion contains a permanent magnet and the conducting coil of wire is stationary. In any motor, the stationary parts constitute the stator, and the assembly that turns is called the rotor, or armature.

Mott, Lucretia Coffin, 1793–1880, American feminist and reformer; b. Nantucket, Mass. A Quaker lecturer for temperance, peace, labor rights, and abolition, she aided fugitive slaves and helped form the Philadelphia Female Anti-Slavery Society. When the World Anti-Slavery Convention in London (1840) refused to recognize women delegates, she joined Elizabeth Cady STANTON in organizing (1848) the first women's rights convention, in Seneca Falls, N.Y.

mound builders, in archaeology, peoples who built mounds in E central North America, concentrating in the Mississippi and Ohio river valleys, from the early 6th cent. to historic times. Probably ancestors of Native Americans found in that region by Europeans, they were politically diverse and developed distinct cultures. Artifacts indicate fine stone carving, pottery making, and weaving, as well as widespread trade in copper, mica, and obsidian. The mounds vary in size (1–100 acres/0.4–40 hectares), shape (geometric or animal effigy, e.g., Serpent Mound in Ohio), and purpose (burial, fortress, or TOTEM).

Mount, William Sidney, 1807–68, American painter; b. Setauket, N.Y. At first a portraitist, in 1836 he turned to the lively genre subjects for which he is noted, such as horse trading, country dances, and farm scenes. Mount was the first important painter to portray African Americans, and his portrayals, while stereotypical, are sympathetic.

Mountain, the, in the FRENCH REVOLUTION, nickname for the deputies of the extreme left who occupied the raised seats in the National Convention. The Montagnards [men of the Mountain] included the JACOBINS and the CORDELIERS; they ruled France in the REIGN OF TERROR (1793–94). See also PLAIN, THE.

mountain, high land mass projecting above its surroundings, usually of limited width at its summit. Some are isolated, but they usually occur in ranges. A group of ranges closely related in form, origin, and alignment is a mountain system; an elongated group of systems is a chain; and a complex of ranges, systems, and chains continental in extent is a cordillera, zone, or belt. Some mountains are remains of PLATEAUS dissected by erosion (see BUTTE; MESA). Others are cones of VOLCANOES or intrusions of igneous rock that form domes. Fault-block mountains occur where huge blocks of the earth's surface are raised relative to neighboring blocks. All the great mountain chains are either FOLD mountains or complex structures in which folding, faulting, and igneous activity have taken part. The ultimate cause of mountain building has been a source of controversy. The concept of PLATE TECTONICS, however, is the first reasonable unifying theory, hypothesizing that the earth's crust is broken into several plates that sideswipe each other or collide. Where they collide (see CONTINENTAL DRIFT), compressional stresses are generated along the margin of the plate containing a continent, causing deformation and uplift of the continental shelf and continental rise, where accumulated sediments become complex folded and faulted mountain chains. Mountains have important effects on the climate, population, economics, and civilization of the regions where they occur. Major mountain ranges include the ALPS, the ANDES, the CAUCASUS, the HIMALAYAS, the PYRENEES, and the ROCKY MOUNTAINS. The highest elevation on earth above sea level is the peak of Mt. EVEREST.

mountain climbing, the practice of climbing to elevated points for sport, pleasure, or research. It is also called mountaineering. The three principal types are (1) trail climbing, or hiking through forest trails to the top of small mountains; (2) rock climbing, the ascent of steeper mountains requiring the use of rope and steel spikes (pitons) that are driven into the rock; and (3) ice climbing, on very high mountains with peaks above the timber line. The "golden age" of mountain climbing began in the 1850s and ended with the conquest (1865) of the last of the great Alpine peaks, the Matterhorn. Mt. Everest, the world's tallest mountain, was first climbed (1953) by Edmund HILLARY and Tenzing Norkay.

mountain laurel, evergreen shrub (*Kalmia latifolia*) of the HEATH family, native to E North America. Poisonous to livestock, mountain laurel has leathery leaves and large clusters of spring-blooming pink or white flowers borne at the ends of the branches. It is the state flower of Connecticut and Pennsylvania. True LAUREL is in a separate family.

mountain lion: see PUMA.

mountain men, trappers and traders in the 1820s and 30s who opened the Rocky Mountain region. They lived in the wilderness, gathering furs, and guided the first wagon trains to OREGON. The arrival of settlers and the waning popularity of the beaver hat ended their activities by the early 1840s.

Mountbatten, Louis Francis Albert Victor Nicholas, 1st **Earl Mountbatten of Burma,** 1900–1979, British admiral; great-grandson of Queen VICTORIA. In WORLD WAR II he directed commando raids in Europe and commanded Allied operations in Burma (now Myanmar) from 1943. As viceroy of India (1947) Mountbatten concluded the negotiations for the independence of India and Pakistan. He was (1959–65) chief of the British defense staff. In 1979 he was killed when a bomb planted by Irish Republican Army members exploded aboard his fishing boat off the Irish coast.

Mountbatten, Philip: see EDINBURGH, PHILIP MOUNTBATTEN, DUKE OF.

Mount Holyoke College, at South Hadley, Mass.; founded 1837. The oldest institution of higher education for women in the U.S., it was established (as Mt. Holyoke Female Seminary) through the efforts of Mary Lyon, its first principal. It offers a broad liberal arts curriculum and grants graduate degrees through a consortium of schools.

Mounties: see ROYAL CANADIAN MOUNTED POLICE.

Mount of Olives: see OLIVES, MOUNT OF.

Mount Rainier National Park: see NATIONAL PARKS (table).

Mount Rushmore National Memorial, near Keystone, S.D., with the monumental heads of four U.S. presidents—Washington, Jefferson, Lincoln, and Theodore Roosevelt—carved on the face of a mountain. Visible for 60 mi (97 km), the heads were sculpted (1927–41) by Gutzon BORGLUM with the help of his son.

Mount Stephen, George Stephen, 1st **Baron,** 1829–1921, Canadian financier. After serving as president (1876–81) of the Bank of Montreal, he helped to finance construction (1880–85) of the Canadian Pacific Railway and was its president (1881–88).

Mount Vernon, NE Virginia, overlooking the Potomac R. near Alexandria, S of Washington, D.C.; home of George WASHINGTON from 1747 until his death in 1799. The land was patented in 1674, and the house was built (1743) by his half brother Lawrence Washington. George Washington inherited it in 1754. A wooden structure of Georgian design, the mansion has wide lawns, fine gardens, and subsidiary structures, all restored with attention to Washington's detailed notes.

mouse, any of numerous species of small RODENTS. The house mouse (*Mus musculus*), found worldwide, usually measures about 6 in. (15 cm) and weighs under 1 oz (28 grams). It has gray to brown fur, large, rounded ears, and a naked, scaly tail. It causes great destruction and contamination of food supplies, and may carry human diseases, e.g., typhoid. House mice are used in scientific experiments and sometimes kept as pets. The Old World field mouse (genus *Apodemus*) is closely related to the house mouse. In North America the name *field mouse* is applied to the VOLE.

Moussorgsky or **Mussorgsky, Modest Petrovich** [mo͞osôrg′ skē], 1839–91, Russian composer. A member of the FIVE, he was one of the first to promote a national Russian style. His finest work is the opera *Boris Godunov* (produced 1874). Other major pieces include the piano SUITE *Pictures at an Exhibition* (1874), later orchestrated by RAVEL; and *A Night on Bald Mountain* (1860–66), for orchestra. Moussorgsky made much use of folk songs. His rejection of European traditions influenced other Russian composers and also Debussy.

Moynihan, Daniel Patrick, 1927–, American sociologist and public official; b. Tulsa, Okla. He was a professor at Harvard Univ. and became an advisor to presidents KENNEDY, JOHNSON, and NIXON. Moynihan later served as ambassador to India (1973–75) and U.S. representative to the UN (1975–76). A Democratic U.S. senator from New York state since 1977, he became chairman of the Senate finance committee in 1993. He has written many books, including *Beyond the Melting Pot* (1963), with Nathan Glazer.

Mozambique, officially Republic of Mozambique, republic (1992 est. pop. 15,469,000), 302,328 sq mi (783,030 sq km), SE Africa, bordered by the Indian Ocean (E), South Africa and Swaziland (S), Zimbabwe, Zambia, and Malawi (W), and Tanzania (N). Major cities include MAPUTO (the capital) and Beira. The Mozambique Channel, an arm of the Indian Ocean, separates the country from Madagascar. The c.1,600-mi (2,575-km) coastline is indented by numerous rivers, notably the ZAMBEZI, which is navigable for c.290 mi (465 km) within the country. Africa's largest hydroelectric dam is at Cabora Bassa on the Zambezi. The northern and central interior is mountainous, rising to a high point at Monte Binga (7,992 ft/2,436 m). About one third of Lake MALAWI (Nyasa) falls within Mozambique's borders. Much of the country is covered with savanna, and there are extensive hardwood forests. Mozambique's economy is heavily based on agriculture, but fishing and some industry are being developed. The main export is shrimp. The main cash crops are cotton, cashew nuts, sugarcane, tea, and sisal. Coal, diamonds, and bauxite are mined on a small scale, but extensive mineral reserves remain unexploited. Industry is limited to the processing of raw materials (notably food and cotton) and the manufacture of fertilizers and cement. More than 95% of the people are Bantu-speaking Africans, most of whom follow traditional beliefs. There are large Christian and Muslim minorities. Most Mozambicans speak various Bantu languages, but Portuguese is the official language.

History. From the first visit of the Portuguese explorer Vasco da GAMA in 1498 until independence in 1975, the history of the region has been one of suppression and exploitation of African peoples by a European colonial power. The first traders were intent on gold and ivory shipped from the coast, but attempts to penetrate the interior met strong resistance. By the late 16th cent. Africans were forced to work on large feudal estates operated by private Portuguese adventurers with little government control, and an extensive slave trade developed in the mid-18th cent. In the 1890s Portugal launched a military campaign to crush African resistance, and after 1926 it assumed direct control of the economic exploitation of the country. The Mozambique Liberation Front (Frelimo) opened guerrilla warfare against white rule in 1964 and, after heavy fighting against a Portuguese army of about 60,000, controlled much of the country by the early 1970s. Following the 1974 military coup in Portugal a cease-fire was arranged, and Mozambique gained independence in 1975. Samora MACHEL, leader of Frelimo, became president of a Marxist regime that nationalized the land. Most of the country's 220,000 whites fled, and its relations with Portugal and the U.S. became strained. Since 1976 Mozambique has been devastated by war between the government and the Mozambique National Resistance (Renamo). Supported by right-wing elements in South Africa and the U.S., Renamo waged a brutal war, killing thousands, uprooting more, and bringing economic life to a halt. Machel was killed in a plane crash in 1986 and was succeeded as president by Joaquim Alberto Chissano. In the late 1980s Frelimo moved to end one-party rule and relax state control of the economy. Frelimo and Renamo signed an accord ending the civil war in 1992; free elections are scheduled for 1994.

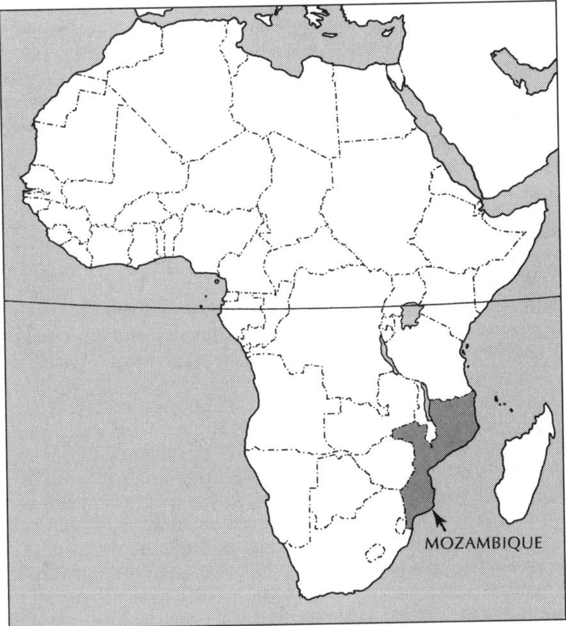

Mozart, Wolfgang Amadeus [mōt'särt], 1756–91, Austrian composer whose oeuvre represents one of the great peaks of musical history. His works, written in every genre, combine beauty of sound with classical grace and technical perfection. He learned to play harpsichord, violin, and organ from his father, **Leopold Mozart,** 1719–87, a composer and violinist. A remarkable prodigy, the young Mozart was composing by age five, presenting concerts throughout Europe as a child, and by age 13 had written concertos, sonatas, symphonies, and operettas. In Italy (1768–71) he absorbed Italian style, and in 1771 he was appointed concertmaster to the archbishop of Salzburg, a position in which he was restless. *Idomeneo* (1781), one of the best examples of 18th-cent. OPERA *seria*, was the first opera of his maturity. He moved to Vienna (1781), married, and met HAYDN, to whom he dedicated six string quartets (1782–85), testimony to the two composers' influence on each other. *The Abduction from the Seraglio* (1782), a *singspiel* combining songs and German dialogue, brought some success. He turned to the Italian *opera buffa,* creating the comic masterpiece *The Marriage of Figaro* (1786). *Don Giovanni,* considered "difficult" in its day but now recognized as one of the most brilliant operas ever written, followed in 1787. In the same year Mozart succeeded GLUCK as court composer to Joseph II; *Eine kleine Nachtmusik* (1787) is an example of the elegant occasional music he wrote in this role. In 1788 he wrote his last three symphonies, Nos. 39–41, which display his complete mastery of classical symphonic form and intense personal emotion. In Vienna he produced his last *opera buffa, Cosi fan tutte* (1790). In *The Magic Flute* (1791) he returned to the *singspiel,* bringing the form to a lyrical height. He then worked feverishly on a requiem commissioned by a nobleman; it proved to be Mozart's own, and the work was completed by his pupil Franz Süssmayr. The composer died at 35 in poverty and was buried in a pauper's grave. A catalogue of Mozart's works was made in 1862 by Ludwig von Köchel; they are usually identified accordingly, e.g., the Piano Concerto in B Flat, K. 595.

MRI: see magnetic resonance imaging under MAGNETIC RESONANCE.

MSG: see MONOSODIUM GLUTAMATE.

Mt, chemical symbol of the element MEITNERIUM.

Muallaqat [mo͝oäl"äkät'], Arabic anthology consisting of 7 (in some versions, 9 or 10) odes by 6th- or early-7th-cent. poets. Esteemed as the finest Arabic odes, they present an unsurpassed picture of pre-Islamic Bedouin life.

Mubarak, Muhammad Hosni, 1928–, president of Egypt (1981–). Air force commander (1972–75) and vice president (1975–81), he was chosen to succeed Pres. SADAT after the latter was assassinated. Mubarak continued many of Sadat's policies, particularly the CAMP DAVID ACCORDS with Israel. He also moved to mend Egypt's strained relations with other Arab states and to control the growing influence of Islamic fundamentalists in Egypt. He was reelected in 1987 and 1993.

Mucha, Alphonse [mo͝okh'ä], 1860–1939, Czech artist. His ART NOUVEAU style, characterized by twisting, swirling, flower and hair motifs, is best seen in his posters for Sarah BERNHARDT. His paintings glorify the Slavic peoples.

muckrakers, name applied to American journalists, novelists, and critics in the first decade of the 20th cent. who tried to expose the abuses of business and corruption in politics. They included Lincoln STEFFENS, Ida TARBELL, and Upton SINCLAIR. The word derives from the term *muckrake* (derived from John BUNYAN's *Pilgrim's Progress*), used by Pres. Theodore ROOSEVELT in a 1906 speech in which he agreed with some of the muckrakers' aims but said that their methods were sensational and irresponsible.

Mufaddaliyat [mo͞ofä"dälēät'] or **Mofaddaliyat** [mō–], great anthology of Arabic poetry by authors from the Golden Age of Arabic poetry (500–650), compiled by the philologist Al Mufaddal ad-Dabbi. It is also a valuable source of information on pre-Islamic Arab life.

Mugabe, Robert Gabriel [mo͞ogä'bā], 1924–, president of ZIMBABWE (1987–). He was a founder of the Zimbabwe African National Union (ZANU) in 1963 and, after imprisonment (1964–74) by the white Rhodesian government, became (1976) co-leader, with Joshua Nkomo, of the Patriotic Front. A Marxist, Mugabe led ZANU guerrilla forces until independence, and following elections in 1980 became Zimbabwe's prime minister. In 1987 he was elected president under a revised constitution.

mugwumps, in U.S. history, slang term for the Republicans who, in 1884, deserted their party nominee, James G. BLAINE, to vote for the Democratic candidate, Grover CLEVELAND.

Muhammad [Arab., = praised], 570?–632, the Prophet of ISLAM, one of the great figures of history; b. Mecca, of the tribe of Kuraish, which ruled Mecca. His daughter Fatima (see FATIMID) was his only child to have issue. When he was 40 Muhammad felt himself selected by God to be the Arab prophet of true religion. His revelations and teachings, forming the basis of Islam, are recorded in the KORAN. In his first years Muhammad made few converts and many enemies. In 622 a plan was made at Mecca to murder him, but he escaped to Yathrib. From this event, the flight, or HEGIRA, of the Prophet (622), Islam counts its dates. Muhammad spent the rest of his life at Yathrib, henceforth called Medina, the City of the Prophet, where he built his model theocratic state and from which he ruled his rapidly growing empire. By 630 he had won all Arabia. Muhammad seemed at first to have expected that the Jews and Christians would welcome him, but he was disappointed. Islam has enshrouded Muhammad's life in a mass of legends and traditions (contained in the *Hadith*). His name appears in various forms, among them Mohammed and Mahomet.

Muhammad, sultans of the OTTOMAN EMPIRE (Turkey). **Muhammad I,** 1389?–1421 (r.1413–21), was the son of BEYAZID I. He renewed Ottoman power by defeating his brothers and reuniting most of his father's empire. **Muhammad II** (the Conqueror), 1429–81 (r.1451–81), is considered the true founder of the Ottoman Empire. He destroyed the remains of the Byzantine Empire by capturing (1453) Constantinople, which he made his capital. He conquered the Balkan Peninsula, including Greece, Bosnia, and several Aegean islands, and annexed the Crimea, Trebizond, and Karamania. The reign of **Muhammad IV,** 1641–92 (r.1648–87), was marked by disorder and corruption, although Grand Vizier KÖPRÜLÜ restored (1656) some order. Muhammad suffered military defeats and was deposed. **Muhammad V,** 1844–1918, sultan (1909–18), succeeded to the throne after the Young Turks had toppled his brother, ABD AL-HAMID II. He exercised no power, the government being dominated by Enver Pasha, and during his reign Turkey lost most of its remaining European possessions in the BALKAN WARS (1912–13); it also lost Tripoli to Italy (1911–12). Germany was the dominant influence in his reign, and he sided with the Central Powers in World War I. He was succeeded by his brother, **Muhammad VI,** 1861–1926, the last sultan (r.1918–22). He was under the control of the victorious Allies and was forced to submit to a harsh peace treaty. Meanwhile, Kemal ATATÜRK established a rival government, declared the sultanate abolished (1922), and proclaimed Turkey a republic. Muhammad VI fled and died in exile.

Muhammad V, 1910–61, king of Morocco (1957–61). He became sultan in 1927. An ardent nationalist, he was deposed and exiled (1953–55) by the French, but they were forced to recall him. He obtained (1956) full sovereignty from France and Spain, and took (1957) the title of king of Morocco.

Muhammad, Elijah, 1897–1975, African-American religous and political leader; b. Elijah Poole, near Sandersville, Ga. On the disappearance of Wali Farad in 1934, he assumed leadership of the Temple of Islam in Detroit, the sect that became the BLACK MUSLIMS. Preaching black separatism, Muhammad called himself "the messenger of Allah" and exercised autocratic control over his followers through a moralistic doctrine of social reform. On his death his son **Wallace D. Muhammad,** 1933–, b. Detroit, became the movement's leader. He has moved the sect closer to orthodox Islam and lifted restrictions on political activity and military service.

Muhammad Ali, 1769?–1849, pasha of Egypt (after 1805). He was a common soldier who rose through the ranks. As pasha he was virtually independent of his nominal overlord, the Ottoman sultan. In 1811 he exterminated the MAMLUKS, who had ruled Egypt for c.700 years. He won great victories for the Turks in Arabia and the Sudan. He fought the rebels in Greece, but his fleet was destroyed (1827) at Navarino by the British, French, and Russians. In the 1830s he turned against the sultan and made inroads in Syria and Asia Minor but was forced to give up his gains by the European powers.

Muhammad Reza Shah Pahlevi, 1919–80, shah of IRAN (1941–79). He ascended the throne after the British and Russians deposed his father, REZA SHAH PAHLEVI, suspecting him of German sympathies. He fled the country briefly in 1953 during an uprising led by Muhammad MUSSADEGH but was reinstated, due in part to the support of the U.S. Iran's great petroleum wealth allowed the shah to institute far-reaching economic and social reforms. He was bitterly opposed, however, by orthodox Muslims, who resented his modernizing policies, and by liberals and leftists, who accused him of maintaining a brutal police state. Revolution broke out in the fall of 1978, and on Jan. 5, 1979, the shah fled the country. He died in exile in Egypt.

Mühlenberg, Heinrich Melchior, 1711–87, American Lutheran clergyman, patriarch of Lutheranism in America; b. Germany. He came (1742) to Pennsylvania and soon became the leader of all the Lutheran groups in the colonies. He organized (1748) the first Lutheran synod in America. His son **John Peter Gabriel Muhlenberg,** 1746–1807, b. Trappe, Pa., became an Episcopal clergyman in Woodstock, Va. He led a regiment in the American Revolution and was later a congressman from Pennsylvania. Another son of Heinrich, **Frederick Augustus Conrad Muhlenberg,** 1750–1801, b. Trappe, Pa., served as a pastor in Pennsylvania and was pastor (1773–76) at Christ (Lutheran) Church in New York City. During the Revolution he returned to Pennsylvania and was a delegate (1779–80) to the Continental Congress. He was later a congressman (1789–97) and served twice as Speaker of the House. Heinrich's great-grandson, **William Augustus Muhlenberg,** 1796–1877, b. Philadelphia, joined the Episcopal church and held pastorates in Pennsylvania. In New York City, he became (1846) rector of the Church of the Holy Communion and helped to found (1858) St. Luke's Hospital.

Muir, John, 1838–1914, American naturalist; b. Scotland. He emigrated to the U.S. in 1849 and settled in California in 1868. Muir was a conservationist and a crusader for national parks and reservations. Muir Woods National Monument in California was named for him, as was Alaska's Muir Glacier, which he discovered.

Mukden: see SHENYANG.

mulberry, common name for the Moraceae, a family of deciduous or evergreen trees and shrubs, often climbing, mostly of pantropical distribution and typified by milky sap. Several genera bear edible fruit, e.g., *Morus* (mulberries), *Ficus* (FIGS), and *Artocarpus,* which includes the breadfruit. Both the white (*M. alba*) and the red (*M. rubra*) mulberries are cultivated in North America. Mulberry fruits are tender and juicy and resemble blackberries; the fruit of *M. rubra* is used to make wine. SILKWORMS feed on mulberry leaves. The Osage orange (*Maclura pomifera*) is a hardy tree native to the south central U.S. and is a source of a durable wood and a dye. The breadfruit (*A. ultilis*) is a cultivated, staple food plant in the Pacific tropics and West Indies; its wood, fiber, and latex are also utilized.

mule, sterile, hybrid offspring of a male donkey (see ASS) and a female HORSE, bred as a work animal. It has long ears, slender legs, small hooves, and a loud bray. Cautious and temperamental, mules are slower but more surefooted than horses and have great powers of endurance. They have been used as pack and draft animals since prehistoric times.

mule, in manufacturing: see SPINNING.

Müller, Friedrich Maximilian: see MÜLLER, MAX.

Muller, Hermann Joseph, 1890–1967, American geneticist and educator; b. N.Y.C. He was awarded the 1946 Nobel Prize in physiology or medicine for discovering a technique of artificially inducing MUTATIONS by means of X rays. He also proposed and developed the theory that genes, because of their unique ability to self-replicate themselves and any alterations arising in them, are the basis of life.

Müller, Max (Friedrich Maximilian Müller), 1823–1900, German philologist and Orientalist. An authority on Sanskrit and Eastern religions, he taught at Oxford. He did more than any other scholar to popularize philology and mythology, e.g., his lectures *Science of Language* (1861, 1863).

Mulroney, Brian, 1939–, Canadian politician, prime minister of Canada (1984–93). Raised in Quebec, he was the first Canadian prime minister from the working class. After an unsuccessful bid (1976) to lead the Progressive Conservatives, he became party leader in 1983 and led the party to a landslide victory in 1984. A second electoral win (1988) assured passage of the U.S.–Canada Free Trade Agreement, and he later (1992) signed the NORTH AMERICAN FREE TRADE AGREEMENT with Mexico and the U.S. Mulroney twice failed (1990, 1992) to win approval of constitutional changes that would have given French QUEBEC special status within Canada, and he lost popularity when he proved unable to alleviate the effects of a prolonged recession in the early 1990s. He resigned as prime minister in 1993.

Multan, city (1981 pop. 696,316), E central Pakistan, in the Punjab. It is the commercial center of a farming region and has such industries as metalworking, food processing, and textile and chemical manfacturing. One of the Indian subcontinent's oldest cities, it fell to such conquerors as Alexander the Great (326 B.C.), the Arabs (8th cent.), Timur (1398), and the Sikhs (1818). The British ruled it from 1848 to 1947.

Multilateral Investment Guarantee Agency: see UNITED NATIONS (table 3).

multimedia, in personal computing, software and applications that combine text, high quality sound, graphics, and animation or video. In order to work with multimedia, a personal computer typically requires a more powerful microprocessor, increased memory and storage capabilities, a high quality monitor and a video accelerator, external loudspeakers or headphones and a sound card (or sound board) for improved sound generation, and a CD-ROM drive (see COMPACT DISC), as well as special software to utilize many of these devices. A multimedia computer may also use other devices, such as a microphone or keyboard for audio input and a videocassette recorder or camcorder for video input or output. Multimedia software is used for electronic publishing and electronic games and in employee training programs. The term *multimedia* is also used to describe home entertainment systems and other electronic products and services, particularly interactive ones, that combine text, sound, video, and the like.

multiple sclerosis, chronic degenerative disease of the central NERVOUS SYSTEM in which patches of the myelin sheath around nerve fibers are lost. The cause is unknown. Symptoms include disturbances in vision, speech, balance, and coordination, as well as numbness and tremors. The onset of the disease generally occurs between ages 20 and 40. Although it may result in severe disability, its course varies widely, with symptoms appearing at irregular intervals for years. There is no curative treatment, although drugs can sometimes reduce the severity of the symptoms.

Mumford, Lewis, 1895–90, American social philosopher and educator; b. Flushing, N.Y. A critic of architecture and city planning, Mumford argued that people must turn from dehumanizing technology back to human feelings and moral values. His books include *The Culture of Cities* (1938), *The Condition of Man* (1944), and *The City in History* (1961).

mummy, human or animal body preserved by embalming or by natural conditions. The word refers primarily to ancient burials found in Egypt. Mummies, embalmed and tightly wrapped, were preserved for over 5,000 years in the dry air of Upper Egypt, making it possible to determine fairly accurately how the great pharaohs appeared in life. Mummification seems to have been performed to prepare the body for reunification with the soul in an afterlife; royal figures, their retinue, and even food were preserved. Similar practices occurred in other parts of the world, e.g., among the INCAS. Natural mummification, caused by certain soil and climatic conditions, is seen in bodies found in Danish peat bogs dating from 300 B.C. to A.D. 300.

mumps or **epidemic parotitis,** acute contagious viral disease whose symptoms include pain and swelling of the salivary glands, pain on swallowing, and fever. Mumps usually affects children between ages five and fifteen and rarely lasts more than three days. In adults it is often more severe and may cause swelling of the meninges covering the brain and, in males, pain and swelling of the testes and, infrequently, sterility. VACCINATION can prevent the disease in individuals over 15 months old.

Munch, Edvard [mo͝ongk], 1863–1944, Norwegian painter and graphic artist. His exciting, violent, and emotionally charged style expressed his sense of isolation in themes of fear, death, and anxiety. Among his strongest and best-known works are *The Shriek* (1893), *Vampire* (1894), and *The Kiss* (1895). Munch's work was of primary importance in the birth of German EXPRESSIONISM. He also made powerful and shocking WOODCUTS.

Munda languages [mo͝on'də], group of languages spoken in parts of N and central India, and generally regarded as a subfamily of the Southeast Asian family of languages. See LANGUAGE (table).

Munich, Ger. *München,* city (1989 est. pop. 1,212,000), capital of Bavaria, S Germany, on the Isar R. It is an industrial center with such manufactures as processed food and beer and precision instruments. Founded in 1158 by HENRY THE LION, it became (1255) the residence of the WITTELSBACH family. It was the capital of the kingdom of BAVARIA after 1806 and became a cultural center in the 19th cent. NATIONAL SOCIALISM (Nazism) was founded in Munich and had its party headquarters there. The MUNICH PACT (1938) was signed in the city. Badly damaged during WORLD WAR II, it was rebuilt after 1945. Its many points of interest include the 15th-cent. Frauenkirche and the Old Pinakothek museum.

Munich Pact, 1938, agreement signed at Munich, Germany, by Germany, Great Britain, France, and Italy, which surrendered the Sudetenland, Czechoslovakia, to Germany. CZECHOSLOVAKIA, not invited to the talks, was forced to give in to the pact's terms, and President BENEŠ, realizing that he had been abandoned by his allies, resigned. British Prime Min. Neville CHAMBERLAIN, upon his return to London, announced that he had achieved "peace in our time," but the pact was widely regarded as an abject surrender to HITLER. The Munich Pact became a symbol of appeasement, and WORLD WAR II began about one year after its signing.

Muñoz Rivera, Luis [mo͞onyōs' rēvä'rä], 1859–1916, Puerto Rican journalist and nationalist. A leader of PUERTO RICO's independence movement, he headed (1901) the first cabinet under U.S. occupation. He published the *Puerto Rico Herald* in New York City, and he obtained American citizenship for Puerto Ricans.

Munro, Alice, 1931–, Canadian writer. She is known for short stories dealing with growing up in rural Ontario. Her collections include *Something I've Been Meaning to Tell You* (1974), *The Progress of Love* (1986), and *Friend of My Youth* (1990).

Munro, Hector Hugh, pseud. **Saki,** 1870–1916, English author; b. Myanmar. He is known for his witty, often bizarre stories, collected in *Reginald* (1904), *The Chronicles of Clovis* (1911), and other volumes. He also wrote novels.

Münzer, Thomas [mün'tsər], c.1489–1525, German Protestant reformer, generally linked with the ANABAPTISTS, although he rejected baptism altogether. He was an associate of LUTHER in 1519, but his position soon diverged from Luther's as he became increasingly iconoclastic in theology and radical in political and social beliefs. During the Peasants' War (1524–26) he set up a communistic theocracy at Mühlhausen. He was later overthrown and beheaded.

muon: see ELEMENTARY PARTICLES.

Murad, sultans of the OTTOMAN EMPIRE (Turkey). **Murad I,** 1326?–89 (r.1362?–89), widened Ottoman holdings by conquering Macedonia and Serbia, forced the Byzantine emperor to pay him tribute, and founded the JANISSARIES. He was assassinated. **Murad II,** 1403–51 (r.1421–51), put down Mustafa, a pretender, and established Ottoman naval power by seizing (1430) Salonica from the Venetians. In 1444 he won a great victory over the crusading LADISLAUS IV of Poland and Hungary. **Murad IV,** 1612?–1640 (r.1623–40), the last of the warrior-sultans recovered Baghdad. **Murad V,** 1840–1904 (r.1876), was declared insane and was succeeded by his brother ABD AL-HAMID II.

Murasaki Shikibu, pseud., c.978–1031, Japanese writer and court figure. She wrote the celebrated romantic *Tale of Genji*. One of the first great Japanese works of fiction, it traces the lives of Prince Genji, his wives, and their children, and subtly delineates a complex society.

Murat, Joachim [mürä'], 1767–1815, marshal of France, king of Naples (1808–15). A brilliant cavalry leader, he served in many of NAPOLEON I's campaigns, helped him to overthrow (1799) the DIRECTORY, married (1800) Napoleon's sister Caroline Bonaparte, and succeeded (1808) Joseph Bonaparte (see BONAPARTE, family) as king of Naples. He reached an agreement (1814) with Austria to keep his throne, but turned against Austria during the HUNDRED DAYS and met defeat. He was executed after trying to regain Naples.

murder: see HOMICIDE.

Murdoch, (Jean) Iris, 1919–, English novelist and philosopher. Her novels, subtle, witty, and convoluted, have elicited varying critical reaction. They include *The Flight from the Enchanter* (1956), *A Severed Head* (1961), *An Accidental Man* (1972), *Nuns and Soldiers* (1980), *The Good Apprentice* (1985), and *The Message to the Planet* (1990).

Murdoch, (Keith) Rupert, 1931–, Australian-American publishing magnate. Combining sensationalist journalism with aggressive promotion, he established a worldwide communications empire with powerful holdings in Australia; several of Britain's largest newspapers, including the prestigious *Times,* and book publisher HarperCollins; and, in the U.S., the New York *Post,* Boston *Herald, Village Voice, New York* magazine, and *TV Guide.* He also acquired 20th Century Fox film studios and established television networks in the U.S., Britain, and Asia.

Murfreesboro, city (1990 pop. 44,922), seat of Rutherford co., central Tenn., on the Stones R.; inc. 1817. The processing center of a dairy, livestock, and farm area, it produces textiles, lumber, and other products. It was the state capital (1819–26) and, in the CIVIL WAR, it was the scene of a bloody Union victory at the Battle of Murfreesboro (or Stones River), Dec. 31, 1862–Jan. 2, 1863. The city has a national battlefield and cemetery.

Murillo, Bartolomé Estéban [mo͝orē'lyō], 1617?–1682, Spanish religious and portrait painter. His early works, e.g., *Birth of the Virgin* (Louvre), show the influence of ZURBARÁN in the dramatic use of light and shadow. He was instrumental in founding (1660) the Seville Academy. From 1670 to 1682 he painted many of his major religious works, such as those for the Charity Hospital and Capuchin convent (Seville Mus.). While working on the *Marriage of St. Catherine* (1682) for the Capuchin church, Cádiz, Murillo fell from the scaffold and died. His greatest works are considered his portraits, e.g., *Knight of the Collar* (Prado) and his naturalistic genre works, e.g., *Girl and Her Duenna* (National Gall., Wash., D.C.).

Murmansk, city (1989 pop. 468,000), NW European Russia, on the Kola Gulf of the Barents Sea. The terminus of the NORTHEAST PASSAGE, it is a major ice-free port, a base for naval and fishing vessels, and the world's largest city N of the Arctic Circle. Industries include fish canneries, shipyards, and sawmills. It was a village before World War I. The port and the rail line from Saint Petersburg were built in 1915–16. Allied forces occupied Murmansk in 1918–20. In World War II it was a major supply base and port for Anglo-American convoys.

Murnau, F(riedrich) W(ilhelm) [mo͝or'nou], 1889–1931, German film director. His films, including *Nosferatu* (1922), *The Last Laugh* (1924), and *Sunrise* (1927), are noted for the use of a constantly moving camera to depict states of mind.

Murray, James, 1721?–94, British general, first civil governor of CANADA (1764–68). After his distinguished service in the FRENCH AND INDIAN WAR, he was named governor. His protection of French Canadians led to charges that he had betrayed England, but he was exonerated (1766).

Murray, Sir James Augustus Henry, 1837–1915, English lexicographer. From 1879 he was editor of the *New English Dictionary* (the *Oxford English Dictionary*), the major work of his career; it was published in 1928.

Murray, Philip, 1886–1952, American labor leader; b. Scotland. Coming to the U.S. in 1902 and working in the Pennsylvania coal mines, he rose to the vice presidency of the United Mine Workers of America (UMW) in 1920. After the formation (1935) of the CIO (see AMERICAN FEDERATION OF LABOR AND CONGRESS OF INDUSTRIAL ORGANIZATIONS), he headed its successful steelworkers' organizing campaign. When John L. LEWIS resigned as CIO president in 1940 after opposing the reelection of Pres. F.D. Roosevelt, Murray, who had split with Lewis on this issue, succeeded him. From 1942 until his death, Murray headed both the CIO and the United Steelworkers of America.

Murray, chief river of Australia, 1,609 mi (2,589 km) long. It rises in SE New South Wales, flows westward to form the NEW SOUTH WALES–VICTORIA boundary, and empties into the INDIAN OCEAN in SOUTH AUSTRALIA. Its waters, combined with those of the DARLING and MURRUMBIDGEE rivers, are used for irrigation and hydroelectricity.

Murrow, Edward R(oscoe), 1908–65, American newscaster; b. Greensboro, N.C. He was noted for his dramatic and accurate broadcasts from London during World War II. He later produced the popular television programs *See It Now* and *Person to Person.*

Murrumbidgee, river, SE Australia, flowing generally westward c.1,050 mi (1,690 km) through New South Wales to join the MURRAY R. on the Victoria border. Its irrigated valley is Australia's most productive farming area.

Muscat or **Maskat,** city (1993 pop. 329,842), capital of Oman, SE Arabia, on the Gulf of Oman. It has a fine harbor, dominated by two 15th–16th-cent. Portuguese forts, and exports dates, fish, and mother-of-pearl. Portugal held it from 1508 to 1648, and Persian princes until 1741, when it became Oman's capital.

muscle, contractile TISSUE that effects the movement of the body. Muscle tissue is classified according to its structure and function. Striated, or skeletal, muscle is under conscious control, effecting purposeful movements of limbs and other body parts. It is called striated because microscopic examination reveals alternating bands of light and dark. Smooth muscle, which lines most hollow organs, is involuntary, i.e., regulated by the autonomic nervous system. It produces movement within internal organs such as those of the DIGESTIVE SYSTEM. Cardiac muscle is striated like skeletal muscle but, like smooth muscle, is controlled involuntarily. It is found only in the HEART, where it forms that organ's thick walls. Contraction, thought to be a similar process in all types of muscle, involves the proteins actin and myosin and their arrangement within the muscle tissue.

muscovite: see MICA.

Muscovy Company or **Russia Company,** first major English joint-stock trading company; chartered in 1555. It financed trading expeditions to Russia and Asia. In 1698 its monopoly was lost, but the company continued to exist until 1917.

muscular dystrophy, any of several inherited diseases characterized by progressive wasting of the skeletal muscles. The most common form, Duchenne, is caused by an abnormal sex-linked gene located on the X chromosome and affects only boys. It begins with leg weakness before age 3 and progresses rapidly, with death often occurring before age 30. Treatment by inserting healthy cells into the muscle to produce the protein (dystrophin) that the abnormal gene should have made, has shown some success. Another form involves primarily facial and shoulder muscles and affects both sexes, usually from adolescence, and progresses more slowly.

Muses, in Greek mythology, the nine patron goddesses of the arts; daughters of ZEUS and Mnemosyne, a TITAN who personified memory. They were: Calliope (epic poetry and eloquence), Euterpe (music and lyric poetry), Erato (love poetry), Polyhymnia (oratory or sacred poetry), Clio (history), Melpomene (tragedy), Thalia (comedy), Terpsichore (choral song and dance), and Urania (astronomy).

Museum of Fine Arts, Boston; inc. 1870; opened 1876. Originally a pooling of the collections of the Boston Atheneum, Harvard Univ., and the Massachusetts Institute of Technology, the museum is privately endowed. Its collections of Eastern art, particularly from India, China, and Japan, are outstanding, as is its collection of ancient Egyptian art. It is extremely rich in 18th-cent. American paintings, especially those by J.S. COPLEY and Gilbert STUART, and has a fine collection of the works of John Singer SARGENT and the silver of Paul REVERE. The museum's West Wing, designed by I.M. PEI, opened in 1981.

Museum of Modern Art, New York City; incorporated in 1929 and privately supported. In addition to one of the world's finest collections of modern art, the museum has outstanding photography and film departments. Its first building was opened in 1939; a new wing designed by Philip JOHNSON followed (1964) and the structure was renovated and expanded in 1984.

Museum of the American Indian, Heye Foundation: see SMITHSONIAN INSTITUTION.

mushroom, fungus characterized by spore-bearing gills on the underside of an umbrella- or cone-shaped cap. The term *mushroom* is properly restricted to the plant's above-ground portion, which is the reproductive organ. Once a delicacy for the elite, edible mushrooms are now grown commercially, especially strains of the meadow mushroom (*Agaricus campestris*). Although mushrooms contain some protein and minerals, they are largely water and hence of limited nutritive value. Inedible, or poisonous, species are often popularly referred to as toadstools; one of the best-known poisonous mushrooms is the death angel (genus *Amanita*).

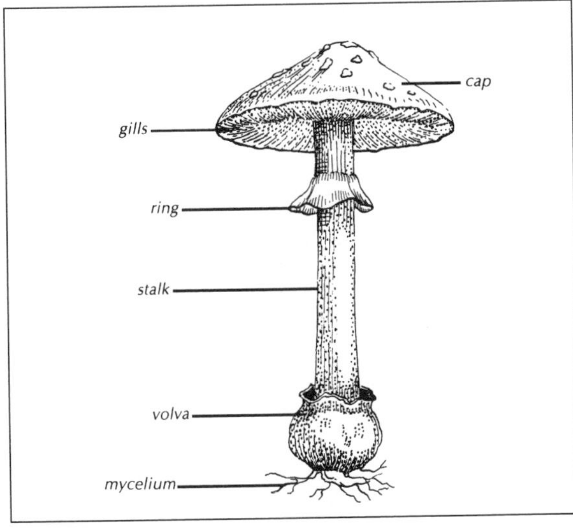

The poisonous mushroom Amanita

Musial, Stan(ley Frank), 1920–, American baseball player; b. Donora, Pa. An outfielder and first baseman for the St. Louis Cardinals (1941–63), "Stan the Man" ranks as one of the great hitters in baseball history. He won the National League batting title seven times and the most valuable player award three times. Musial compiled a lifetime batting average of .331 and hit 475 home runs. His league record of 3,630 career hits was broken by Pete ROSE in 1981.

musical comedy: see MUSICALS.

musical notation, symbols used to make a written record of musical sounds. BOETHIUS applied the first 15 letters of the alphabet to notes in use at the end of the Roman period. By the 6th cent. notation of Gregorian chant was by means of neumes, thought to derive from Greek symbols for pitch (see PLAINSONG); they indicated groupings of sounds to remind a singer of a melody already learned by ear. By the end of the 12th cent. the Benedictine monk Guido d'Arezzo had perfected the staff, placing letters on certain lines to indicate their pitch. These letters evolved into the clef signs used today. In the 15th cent. the shape of notes became round, and time signatures replaced coloration to indicate note value. The key signature developed early, although sharps were not used until the 17th cent. The five-line staff (with ledger lines used to extend the range) became standard in the 16th cent. Expression signs and Italian phrases to indicate tempo and dynamics came into use in the 17th cent. Notation for ELECTRONIC MUSIC is still not standardized but generally combines traditional symbols with specially adapted rhythm and pitch notation.

musicals, form of stage entertainment originating in late-19th-cent. England as musical comedy. Incorporating music, chorus dancing, and topical numbers, it has flourished primarily in the U.S. Important early stars were George M. COHAN and Lillian RUSSELL. The best-known composers of musicals include Irving BERLIN, Jerome KERN, Cole PORTER, Noel COWARD, George GERSHWIN, Richard RODGERS, Lorenz HART, Oscar HAMMERSTEIN 2D, Stephen SONDHEIM, and Andrew LLOYD WEBBER. Innovations came with Rodgers and Hammerstein's *Oklahoma!* (1943), which integrated music, song, and dance with a detailed plot, and *West Side Story* (1957), which introduced serious themes, causing the genre to be called simply "musicals." In the 1960s the "rock musical" (see ROCK MUSIC) came into prominence with the production of *Hair* (1967). Film musicals attained their greatest popularity in the 1930s, 40s, and 50s.

music-hall, in England, a form of entertainment featuring song, dance, acrobatics, PANTOMIME, and comic sketches, catering to the lower and middle classes. Originally offered in inns and taverns, the music-hall as a separate establishment first appeared in the mid-1800s. Following a rapid rise, the music-hall went into a decline with the coming of radio and motion pictures.

music video, performance on videotape of a recorded song, often accompanied by dance, and using quick cuts, stylization, fanciful imagery, and sometimes computer graphics. Originally promotional vehicles, most videos are in the rock idiom and are directed at a teenage audience. Although some are notable for artistic innovation, many feature the macho stars and scantily clad dancers that have become cultural clichés. Music videos were popularized by the MTV cable network (est. 1981) and have influenced advertising, television, and film.

Musil, Robert [mōō'zĭl], 1880–1942, Austrian novelist. Subtle psychological analysis marks his novels *Young Törless* (1906) and *The Man without Qualities* (3 vol., 1930–42). His style has been compared to that of PROUST.

musk, odorous substance secreted by an abdominal gland in the male musk DEER, used in PERFUME as a scent and fixative. Its odor comes from an organic compound called muscone. Musklike substances are also obtained from the MUSKRAT and the civet; some plants yield oils that resemble musk.

muskellunge: see PIKE.

musket: see SMALL ARMS.

Muskie, Edmund Sixtus, 1914–, U.S. senator from Maine (1959–80); b. Rumford, Me. He was governor of Maine (1955–57), the 1968 Democratic vice-presidential nominee, and a contender for the presidential nomination in 1972. He was Pres. CARTER's secretary of state (1980–81).

muskmelon: see MELON.

Muskogean [məskō'gēən], branch of NATIVE AMERICAN LANGUAGES belonging to the Hokan-Siouan family of North America. See NATIVE AMERICAN LANGUAGES (table).

musk ox, hoofed animal (*Ovibus moschatus*) of the CATTLE family, found in arctic North America and Greenland. The musk ox is covered with shaggy fur and has a musky odor. It has splayed hooves and broad, flat horns that downcurve along the sides of the head. Hunted to near extinction in the 19th cent., it is now restored.

muskrat, aquatic RODENT. The common muskrats (genus *Ondatra*) are found in marshes, quiet streams, and ponds in most of North America north of Mexico. They have partially webbed feet, a long tail, and shiny brown outer fur (much used commercially) with a dense undercoat. Muskrats are 10 to 14 in. (25 to 36 cm) and weigh 2 to 3 lb (0.9 to 1.4 kg). Muskrats are closely related to VOLES.

Muslim: see ISLAM.

Muslim art and architecture: see ISLAMIC ART AND ARCHITECTURE; MOGUL ART AND ARCHITECTURE.

Muslim Brotherhood, Islamic organization founded (1928) in Egypt by Hasan al-Banna and long opposed to the increasing secularization of many Islamic nations. Egypt banned the organization in 1954 when its growing influence threatened the government. Now clandestine, the group has adherents in Egypt, Syria, Sudan, and other Arab countries and has resorted to acts of political violence.

Muslim League, political organization of the Muslims of the Indian subcontinent. Founded (1906) by AGA KHAN III, it grew into an independent party under Muhammad IQBAL and, later, Muhammad Ali JINNAH. In 1947 it became the ruling party of newly formed Pakistan. It split into several factions by 1953 and declined thereafter.

Mussadegh, Muhammad [mo͞o'sädāg], 1880–1967, Iranian political leader, prime minister (1951–53). He led the militant nationalists who succeeded in nationalizing (1951) the British-owned oil industry. The shah openly opposed him and, after trying (1952) to oust Mussadegh, was forced into temporary exile. Upon the shah's return to power (1953), Mussadegh was imprisoned until 1956; after that he lived under house arrest.

mussel, edible BIVALVE mollusk, abundant in cooler seas. Mussels form extensive, crowded beds, anchoring themselves to pilings or rocks by a secretion of strong threads known as the byssus. The dark-shelled burrowing freshwater mussel is a source of PEARLS and MOTHER-OF-PEARL.

Musset, (Louis Charles) Alfred de [müsā'], 1810–57, French romantic poet. In his exquisite love lyrics, e.g., *Les Nuits* (1835–37), and his narrative poems, e.g., *Rolla* (1833), he combined classic clarity with the passionate subjectivity of ROMANTICISM. He also wrote short novels and plays, including *Lorenzaccio* (1834). An autobiographical novel, *Confession of a Child of the Century* (1836), gives an account of his unhappy love affair with George SAND.

Mussolini, Benito, 1883–1945, Italian Fascist leader and dictator. He edited Socialist newspapers but broke with the Socialists to support Italy's entry into World War I. In 1919 he organized his staunchly nationalistic followers, who wore black shirts as uniforms and practiced terrorism in armed groups. In 1921 he was elected to Parliament and founded the National Fascist party (see FASCISM). His Fascists marched (Oct. 1922) on Rome, and King VICTOR EMMANUEL III called on Mussolini to form a government. Called *Duce* leader, he gradually created a dictatorship and ended parliamentary government (1928). In 1929 he concluded the LATERAN TREATY with the Vatican. His imperialistic designs led to the conquest of Ethiopia (1935–36) and the occupation of Albania (1939). He signed (1939) an alliance with Nazi Germany, but Italy's involvement in WORLD WAR II was a military failure in Greece and N Africa. The imminent Allied invasion of the Italian mainland led to a rebellion within the Fascist party. The king dismissed Mussolini and had him imprisoned, but the Germans made him a puppet ruler in N Italy. On the German collapse (1945) Mussolini was captured by Italian partisans, summarily tried, and executed.

Mussorgsky, Modest Petrovich: see MOUSSORGSKY.

mustard, common name for the Cruciferae, a large family chiefly of herbs of north temperate regions, typified by flowers with four petals arranged diagonally ("cruciform") and alternating with the four sepals. The Cruciferae, often rich in SULFUR compounds and VITAMIN C, include many important food and condiment plants, e.g., rape, rutabaga, TURNIP, mustard, numerous CABBAGE varieties, WATERCRESS, HORSERADISH, and RADISH. The herbs called mustard are species of *Brassica* native to Europe and W Asia. Black (*B. nigra*) and white (*B. alba*) mustard are cultivated for their seeds, which are ground and used as a condiment, usually mixed to a paste with vinegar or oil. Mustards are also grown as salad plants and for greens.

mustard gas: see POISON GAS.

Mutanabbi, al-, 915–65, Arab poet, considered the greatest classical Arabic poet; b. Iraq. His early involvement with a religious cult earned him the sobriquet "the would-be prophet." He was part of the brilliant court of the Hamdanid ruler Sayf al-Dawlah in Aleppo, where he wrote many of his elaborate panegyrics.

mutation, in biology, a sudden change in a GENE, or unit of hereditary material, that results in a new inheritable characteristic. In higher animals and many higher plants a mutation may be transmitted to future generations only if it occurs in germ, or sex cell, tissue; body cell mutations cannot be inherited. Changes within the chemical structure of single genes (see NUCLEIC ACID) may be induced by exposure to radiation, temperature extremes, and certain chemicals. The term *mutation* may also be used to include losses or rearrangements of segments of CHROMOSOMES, the long strands of genes. Drugs such as colchicine double the normal number of chromosomes in a cell by interfering with cell division (see MITOSIS). Most mutations are not beneficial, however, as the environment changes, mutations may prove advantageous and contribute to evolutionary changes in a species.

Muti, Riccardo, 1941–, Italian conductor. Principal conductor (1969–81) of the Orchestra Maggio Musicale, in Florence, and (1973–82) the Philharmonia Orchestra, in London, he succeeded Eugene ORMANDY as musical director (1980–92) of the Philadelphia Orchestra (see ORCHESTRA, table). In 1986 he became musical director of Milan's La Scala opera house.

Mutsuhito: see MEIJI.

mutual assured destruction (MAD), theory of nuclear deterrence in which each side has an assured means of retaliation (second-strike capability) in the event of an enemy attack. Also known as the "balance of terror," it depends on both sides having a balance of defensive and offensive forces. Defined by Defense Secy. Robert MCNAMARA in the mid-1960s, MAD resulted in an emphasis on the production of offensive weapons and provided the theoretical foundation for arms control between the U.S. and USSR, because limits could be established on how much offensive power was necessary to assure deterrence. Each actual or potential technological advance by either side, however, destabilized the balance, and the doctrine became obsolete by the 1980s.

mutual fund, in finance, investment company or trust that has a very fluid capital stock. It is unique in that at any time it can sell, or redeem, any of its outstanding shares at net asset value (i.e., total assets minus liabilities, divided by the total number of shares). A mutual fund, also called an open-end investment company, may own the shares or bonds of several corporations (sometimes of a specified nation or industry), government securities, precious metals, or other assets. A closed-end investment company differs from an open-end company in that the number of shares sold to investors is limited and the price of the shares may fluctuate above and below the net asset value. Mutual funds are designed to provide skilled management and diversification, thereby lessening risk. Earnings are distributed to shareholders in the form of income and capital-gains dividends. See also MONEY-MARKET FUND.

Muybridge, Eadweard [mī'brĭj], 1830–1904, English photographer. A specialist in animal locomotion, he recorded motion with sequential still cameras. He invented (1881) the zoöpraxiscope to project animated images. Much of his work appeared in *Animals in Motion* (1899).

Myanmar, Myanma, or **Burma,** officially Union of Myanmar, republic (1992 est. pop. 42,642,000), 261,789 sq mi (678,033 sq km), SE Asia, bordered by India, Bangladesh, and the Bay of Bengal (W), China (N and NE), Laos and Thailand (E), and the Andaman Sea (S). Principal cities include YANGON (Rangoon), the capital, and MANDALAY. Except for the centrally located IRRAWADDY valley and delta, where most of the people live, the terrain is mountainous. The climate is mostly tropical monsoonal. About 65% of the labor force is employed in agriculture (mostly rice cultivation) and forestry (especially teak and rubber production). Rich mineral resources, not fully exploited, include petroleum, tin, copper, zinc, and coal. The nationalized industrial sector is small but expanding. Myanmar's developing economy, depressed by past political turmoil, began to recover in the 1980s. Burmans constitute about 70% of the predominantly rural population; minorities include the Shans, Karens, Kachins, Chins, Indians, and Chinese. The predominant religion is Theravada Buddhism. The official language is Burmese, but more than 100 distinct languages are spoken.

History. The Burmans established a kingdom in upper Myanmar in the 9th cent. Under King Anawrahta, who introduced Hinayana Buddhism, they gained (11th cent.) supremacy over the rival Mon kingdom and the Irrawaddy delta. The Burmese capital, Pagan, fell (1287) to the Mongols, and the area was then divided among local rulers. The Burmese Toungoo dynasty united the area in the 16th cent. A resurgence (18th cent.) of Mon rule was checked (1758) by

Alaungapaya, who extended Burmese influence. During three Anglo-Burmese Wars (1824–26, 1852, 1885) the region was annexed piecemeal to British India and did not receive limited self-government until 1937. Occupied by Japan in World War II, Myanmar, then known as Burma, achieved complete independence in 1948, with U NU as prime minister. Economic chaos and persistent opposition by insurgent minorities plagued the new government, and in 1958 leadership passed to Gen. NE WIN who restored order. U Nu was returned to power in 1960, but conditions continued to deteriorate, and in 1962 Ne Win staged a successful military coup. A new constitution, making the nation a one-party socialist republic, was adopted in 1974. Under Ne Win, Myanmar was reduced from one of the most prosperous to one of the poorest countries in SE Asia. Ne Win resigned as president in 1981 and party leader in 1988. In Sept. 1988 the military brutally crushed prodemocracy demonstrations and took direct control of the government, but later promised national elections. The antigovernment National League for Democracy, whose leader, AUNG SAN SUU KYI, was under house arrest, won the 1990 parliamentary elections, but the military refused to surrender power and continued to suppress opposition. Gen. Than Shwe became head of the junta in 1992. State control of the economy has eased in recent years, and the junta has signed cease-fires with most of the insurgent ethnic minorities.

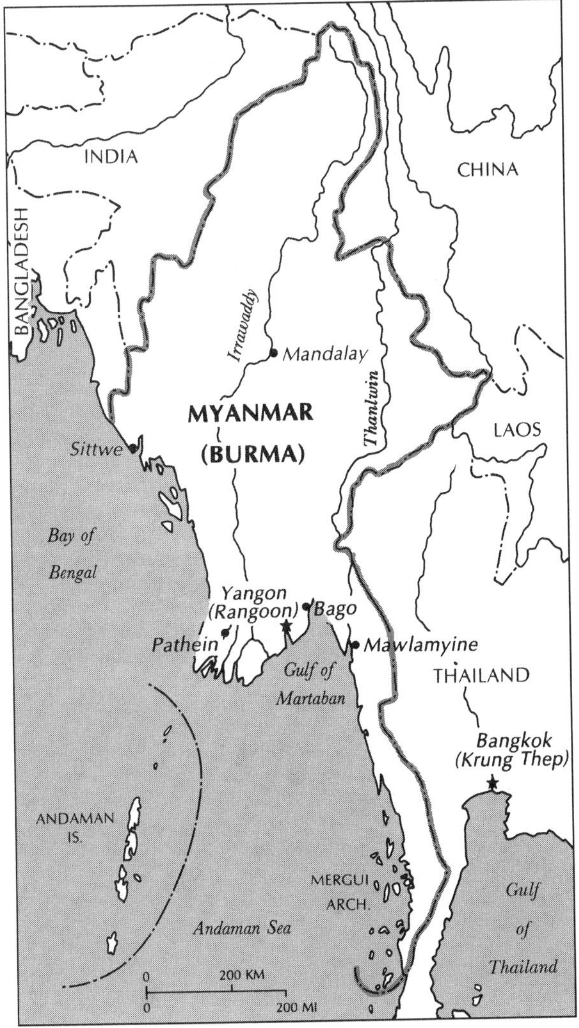

myasthenia gravis, chronic disorder of the muscles, characterized by weakness and a tendency to tire easily. Most commonly found in young adults, the disease occurs when the nerve impulses are prevented from reaching the muscles, blocking muscle contraction. It is an AUTOIMMUNE DISEASE caused by a faulty antibody that destroys ACETYLCHOLINE receptors on the muscle cells. The muscles of the head and neck are most frequently involved, those of the trunk and extremities less frequently. Symptoms typically advance irregularly, with varying intensity and severity, but there is a gradual worsening over a period of years, with the major danger resulting from respiratory paralysis or infection. Treatment can include IMMUNOSUPPRESSIVE DRUGS, drugs that increase the amount of acetylcholine available to the muscle, and PLASMAPHERESIS.

Mycenaean civilization [mīsēnē'ən], an ancient AEGEAN CIVILIZATION known from excavations at Mycenae. Undertaken by Heinrich SCHLIEMANN and others after 1876, they helped revise early Greek history. The Mycenaeans were Indo-European, Greek-speaking people who entered GREECE from the north c.2000 B.C., bringing with them advanced techniques in art and architecture. Mercantile contact with the Minoans on Crete advanced their culture, and by 1600 B.C. Mycenae had become a major center of the ancient world, competing with CRETE for maritime control of the Mediterranean. After the destruction of KNOSSOS (c.1400 B.C.) Mycenae achieved supremacy, and much of the Minoan cultural tradition was transferred to the mainland. The invasion by the Dorians (c.1100 B.C.) ushered in a period of decline, and by 900 B.C. the centers of culture and wealth had shifted elsewhere.

My Lai incident [mē lī], massacre of civilians in the VIETNAM WAR. On Mar. 16, 1968, U.S. soldiers, led by Lt. William L. Calley, invaded the South Vietnamese hamlet of My Lai, an alleged Viet Cong stronghold, and shot to death 347 unarmed civilians, including women and children. The incident was not made public until 1969. Special army and congressional investigations followed. Five soldiers were court-martialed, and one, Lt. Calley, was convicted (Mar. 29, 1971) and sentenced to life imprisonment. In Sept. 1974 a federal court overturned the conviction, and Calley was released.

myna or **mynah,** Asian STARLING, a bird found chiefly in India and Sri Lanka and known for its power of mimicry. The hill myna (*Gracula religiosa*), 12–15 in. (30–38 cm), is the best known. Glossy black with yellow head wattles, it is a forest dweller and lives mostly on fruit. When trained, it is a better mimic than the PARROT.

myopia: see NEARSIGHTEDNESS.

Myrdal, Gunnar [mēr'däl], 1898–1987, Swedish economist, sociologist, and public official. Winner, with F.A. von Hayek, of the 1974 Nobel Prize in economics, Myrdal taught at the Univ. of Stockholm (1933–50, 1960–67), held several government posts, and was executive secretary (1947–57) of the UN Economic Commission for Europe. As head of a Carnegie Corp. study (1938–42) of African Americans, he collaborated on *An American Dilemma* (1944; new ed. 1962), maintaining that the U.S. racial problem was inextricably entwined with the democratic functioning of American society. Other works include *Crisis in the Population Question* (1934), written with his wife, and *Challenge of World Poverty* (1970). His wife, **Alva Myrdal,** 1902–86, Swedish sociologist and diplomat, was Sweden's ambassador to India (1956–61) and minister for disarmament (1966–72). For her work in the area of nuclear disarmament she was awarded (1982) the Nobel Peace Price.

myrrh: see INCENSE-TREE.

myrtle, common name for the family Myrtaceae, trees and shrubs mostly native to tropical regions, especially in America and Australia. The family is characterized by usually evergreen leaves containing aromatic volatile oils; many have showy blossoms. Myrtles are of economic importance for their timber, gums and resins, oils, spices, and edible fruits. The true myrtle genus (*Myrtus*) is chiefly of the American tropics, but the classical myrtle (*M. communis*) is native to the Mediterranean area. Its glossy leaves were made into wreaths for victors in the ancient OLYMPIC GAMES. Other trees in the myrtle family include the CLOVE, EUCALYPTUS, GUAVA, and PIMENTO, or allspice.

mysteries, important secret cults in Greek and Roman religion. Possibly based on primitive fertility rites, their elaborate, mystic ritual appealed to individuals who had tired of the formalistic, state-centered rites of traditional Greek and Roman religion, and who sought a promise of personal salvation and immortality. Some mysteries were survivals of indigenous rites, while others (e.g., the cult of CYBELE) were of foreign origin. Especially important in Greece were the Eleusinian and ORPHIC MYSTERIES.

mystery story: see DETECTIVE STORY.

mysticism [Gr., = the practice of those who are initiated into the mysteries], the practice of putting oneself into direct relation with GOD, the Absolute, or any unifying principle of life. There are two general tendencies in the speculation of mystics—to regard God as outside the soul, which rises to God by successive stages, or to regard God as dwelling within the soul, to be found by delving deeper into one's own reality. The contemplative path to union conventionally requires a series of steps involving purgation, illumination, and increase of spiritual love. Various rituals may assist the process. The language of mysticism is difficult and usually symbolic; biographies and autobiographies of mystics are the major sources for direct study (for example, those of such mystics as St. THERESA of Ávila; St. JOHN OF THE CROSS; Jakob BOEHME; and Aurobindo GHOSE). Although mysticism is inseparably linked with religion, the term itself is used very broadly in English, being extended to magic, occultism, or the esoteric. Mysticism is encountered in Greek NEOPLATONISM, CHRISTIANITY, JUDAISM, BUDDHISM, HINDUISM, ISLAM, and TAOISM.

mythology, collective myths of a people and scientific study of such myths. Myths are traditional stories occurring in a timeless past and involving supernatural elements. Products of prerational cultures, myths express and explain such serious concerns as the creation of the universe and of humanity, the evolution of society, and the cycle of agricultural fertility. Myths are differentiated from folktales (e.g., Cinderella and tales from *The Arabian Nights*) by being more serious, less entertaining, more supernatural, and less rational and logical. Legends and sagas, by contrast with myths, are historical or quasi-historical in nature. Many theories have been advanced to explain myths. The Greeks' explanation of their own mythology was most fully developed in STOICISM, which reduced the gods to moral principles and natural elements. Such allegorical interpretations continued into the 18th cent. Theologians have tended to view myths (e.g., the blood myth or the myth of a golden age) as foreshadowings or corruptions of Scripture. Modern investigations of mythology began with the 19th-cent. philologist Max MÜLLER, who saw myths as having evolved from linguistic corruptions. Anthropological explanations have also abounded. Sir James FRAZER in his *Golden Bough* (1890) proposed that all myths were originally connected with the idea of fertility in nature, with the birth, death, and resurrection of vegetation as a constantly recurring motif. Bronislaw MALINOWSKI considered myths to be validations of established social patterns. Among influential psychologists, Sigmund FREUD related the unconscious myth and dream, while Carl JUNG believed that all peoples unconsciously formed the same mythic symbols. In the 20th cent. Mircea Eliade believes that myths serve to return their adherents to the time of the original creative act, and Claude LÉVI-STRAUSS contends that myths should be interpreted structurally. Important mythologies include the Greek, largely codified and preserved in the works of HOMER and HESIOD; the Roman, primarily derived from the Greek, and, with it, the best-known; the Norse, which is less anthropomorphic; the Indian (Vedic), which tends to be abstract and otherworldly; the Egyptian, which is closely related to religious ritual; and the Mesopotamian, which exhibits a strong concern with the relationship between life and death. Mythology has enriched literature since the time of AESCHYLUS and has been used by some of the major English poets, e.g., MILTON, SHELLEY, KEATS. Some great literary figures, e.g., William BLAKE, James JOYCE, Franz KAFKA, W.B. YEATS, T.S. ELIOT, and Wallace STEVENS, have constructed symbolic personal myths by reshaping old mythological materials.

N

N, chemical symbol of the element NITROGEN.

Na, chemical symbol of the element SODIUM.

NAACP: see NATIONAL ASSOCIATION FOR THE ADVANCEMENT OF COLORED PEOPLE.

Nabis [näbē'] [from Heb., = prophets], a group of artists in France active in the 1890s. The principal theorists were Paul Sérusier and Maurice DENIS, and the members included VUILLARD, BONNARD, MAILLOL, and Félix Valloton. Influenced by GAUGUIN, they developed a style characterized by flat areas of bold color and heavily outlined surface patterns. They were unified by their dislike of IMPRESSIONISM.

Nablus, city (1989 est. pop. 98,000), in the Israeli-occupied WEST BANK. It is the market center for a region where wheat and olives are grown and sheep and goats are grazed. Nablus has remains dating from c.2000 B.C. The Samaritans (see SAMARIA) made it their capital, and under Rome it was named Neapolis, from which the present name derives. The city came under Israeli occupation after the 1967 ARAB-ISRAELI WAR.

Nabokov, Vladimir [näbô'kŏf], 1899–1977, Russian-American novelist; b. St. Petersburg; one of the most original masters of 20th-cent. fiction. After the Russian Revolution of 1917 he lived in England and Germany, came to the U.S. (1940), taught at Cornell (1948–59), and settled in Switzerland (1959). Nabokov's novels are frequently experimental and obscure but are always erudite, witty, and intriguing. His early fiction, in Russian, includes *Despair* (1936) and *Invitation to a Beheading* (1938). His most famous work in English, *Lolita* (1958), the story of a middle-aged European intellectual's infatuation with a 12-year-old American "nymphet," brought him overnight fame and became a modern classic. Among his other novels are *Pnin* (1957), *Pale Fire* (1962), and *Ada* (1969). Nabokov also wrote poetry, criticism, stories, and autobiographies, and was an internationally recognized lepidopterist.

Nacogdoches [năk"ədō'chĭs], city (1990 pop. 30,872), seat of Nacogdoches co., E Tex.; settled 1779, inc. 1929. The city is located in a pine and hardwood forest. Lumbering, feed and fertilizer production, and tourism are important. Historically prominent, Nacogdoches was a Spanish bastion against French Louisiana. Settlement (1820) by Americans led to the Fredonian Rebellion (1826), a premature attempt to make Texas independent of Mexico. The city was active in the Texas Revolution (1835–36).

Nadelman, Elie, 1882–1946, Polish-American sculptor; b. Poland. He settled in the U.S. in 1914. His wood or metal sculptures have a smooth simplicity, e.g., his jaunty, urbane bronze *Man in the Open Air* (c.1915; Mus. Mod. Art, N.Y.C.).

Nader, Ralph, 1934–, U.S. consumer advocate; b. Winsted, Conn. Since his book *Unsafe at Any Speed* (1965) influenced Congress to bring automobile design under federal control, Nader has been the most prominent leader of the U.S. CONSUMER PROTECTION movement. He founded the Center for the Study of Responsive Law, the Center for Auto Safety, and the Public Interest Research Group.

Nadir Shah or **Nader Shah,** 1688–1747, shah of IRAN (1736–47), founder of the Afshar dynasty. After victories over the Afghans and the Turks, he became shah by deposing (1736) the last of the Safavid dynasty. He successfully invaded India in 1739; the great treasures he carried off included the Peacock Throne and the Koh-i-noor diamond. He greatly extended Iran's territory.

NAFTA: see NORTH AMERICAN FREE TRADE AGREEMENT.

Nagano, city (1990 pop. 347,036), central Honshu, Japan, on the Tenryu R. It produces processed food, automobile parts, and textiles. Nagano is also a religious center; Zenkoji, a 7th-cent. Buddhist temple, is there. It will be the site of the 1998 winter Olympic games.

Nagasaki, city (1990 pop. 444,616), capital of Nagasaki prefecture, W Kyushu, Japan. Nagasaki's port was the first to receive (16th cent.) Western trade, and remains one of Japan's leading ports. Shipbuilding is the chief industry. During World War II, Nagasaki was the target of the second ATOMIC BOMB ever detonated (Aug. 9, 1945) on a populated area. About 75,000 people were killed or wounded, and more than one third of the city was devastated.

Nag Hammadi, town in Egypt where 53 gnostic texts in the Coptic language and dating from the 4th cent. A.D. were discovered in 1945. The texts, which shed new light on Christian gnosticism, include gospels, apocalypses, sayings of the resurrected Jesus, and theological treatises.

Nagorno-Karabakh [nəgôr'nə-kərəbäkh], autonomous region (1990 est. pop. 192,000), 1,699 sq mi (4,400 sq km), SE Azerbaijan. Stepanakert is the capital. The mountainous region's residents are mainly Armenian. Farming and grazing are important. There are some light industries, and marble and limestone are quarried. Won by Armenia in the 1st cent. A.D., the area passed through Arab and Persian hands before being ceded to Russia (1805). In the late 1980s Armenian residents began demanding the region's inclusion in Armenia, leading to an Armenian-Azerbaijani war for control of Nagorno-Karabakh. By the end of 1993, Armenians had won control of most of the region.

Nagoya, city (1990 pop. 2,154,664), capital of Aichi prefecture, central Honshu, Japan. It is a major port, transportation hub, and industrial center producing steel, textiles, aircraft, and automobiles. The city has many universities, of which Nagoya Imperial Univ. is the best known, and two famous shrines, the Atsuta (founded 2d cent.), where the sacred imperial sword is housed, and the Higashi Honganji, which was built in 1692.

Nagy, Imre [nôj, nŏd'yə], 1895?–1958, Hungarian Communist leader. As premier (1953–55), he loosened government controls and was critical of Soviet influence. Denounced and removed from office, he was recalled as premier shortly before the 1956 uprising (see HUNGARY). After the revolt was crushed, he was tried and executed by KÁDÁR's regime.

Nahuatlan [nä'wŏt"lən], group of languages of the Uto-Aztecan branch of the Aztec-Tanoan linguistic stock of North America and Mexico. See NATIVE AMERICAN LANGUAGES (table).

Nahum, book of the OLD TESTAMENT, 34th in the Authorized Version, seventh of the Minor PROPHETS, a prophecy of doom against NINEVEH, the Assyrian capital, by Nahum the Elkoshite, who is otherwise unknown.

naiads, in Greek mythology: see NYMPH.

Naipaul, V(idiadhar) S(urajprasad) [nī'pôl], 1932–, English author; b. Trinidad. He has lived in England since 1950. Of Indian parentage, he is known for his elegant prose style, penetrating analyses of alienation, and ironic, increasingly pessimistic vision of the THIRD WORLD. He has written serious travel literature, *The Middle Passage* (1962) and *India: A Million Mutinies Now* (1990); novels, *A House for Mr. Biswas* (1961) and *Guerrillas* (1975); political essays; and an analysis of modern ISLAM, *Among the Believers* (1981).

Nairobi, city (1990 est. pop. 1,505,000), capital of Kenya, in the E African highlands. A modern metropolis with broad boulevards, it is Kenya's largest city; its administrative, communications, and economic center; and the distribution center for such agricultural products as coffee and cattle. Manufactures include automobiles, food products, chemicals, and textiles. Nairobi is linked by rail with the port of MOMBASA. Nairobi National Park, a large wildlife park nearby, attracts many tourists. Founded in 1899, Nairobi became (1905) the capital of a British protectorate (later Kenya Colony).

Naismith, James: see BASKETBALL.

Nakasone Yasuhiro, 1918–, Japanese political leader and prime minister (1982–89). He served in the Diet after 1946. A political ally of TANAKA KAKUEI, Nakasone succeeded SUZUKI ZENKO as prime minister. He increased Japan's military strength and established closer ties with the U.S. and with China. He resigned in 1989.

naked mole rat, name applied to a species (*Heterocephalus glaber*) of small RODENTS found in E Africa, whose members—the only hairless rodents—live entirely in underground colonies with a structure resembling that of insect colonies. Each colony has a queen, a breeding male, soldiers, and workers. Colony members are closely related and seem to work for the success of the whole community rather than individual survival.

Nakhichevan, autonomous republic (1990 est. pop. 310,000), 2,124 sq mi (5,501 sq km), an exclave of Azerbaijan bordered by Iran and Turkey (S) and separated from Azerbaijan by Armenia (N). Nakhichevan is the capital. Agricultural products include cotton, tobacco, rice, wine, and silk. There are salt, molybdenum, lead, and zinc deposits and various light industries. The population is mainly Azeri.

Namath, Joe (Joseph William Namath), 1943–, American football player; b. Beaver Falls, Pa. A star quarterback at the Univ. of Alabama, he received a lucrative contract from the New York Jets, sparking a bidding war for players between the National and American leagues that ultimately produced a merger. "Broadway Joe," who led the Jets to an upset victory in the 1969 Super Bowl, was known for his free life-style.

Namibia [nämĭb'ēə], officially Republic of Namibia, formerly South West Africa, republic (1992 est. pop. 1,575,000), c.318,000 sq mi (823,620 sq km), SW Africa, bordered by Angola (N), Zambia (NE), Botswana (E), South Africa (SE), and the Atlantic Ocean (W). Namibia also includes the CAPRIVI STRIP in the northeast and the former South African enclave of WALVIS BAY, which was relinquished to Namibia in 1994. WINDHOEK is the capital. The country consists of four main geographical regions: the barren Namib Desert, along the entire Atlantic coast; a large central plateau that rises to 8,402 ft (2,561 m) at Brandberg Mt.; the western edge of the KALAHARI desert; and an alluvial plain in the north. The agricultural sector of the economy is based on stock raising (cattle, goats, and sheep), with income derived mainly from Karakul pelts, meat and livestock, and dairy goods. Namibia has rich deposits of diamonds, copper, lead, uranium, manganese, zinc, tin, silver, vanadium, and tungsten; its extensive mining industry is run chiefly by foreign companies. Fishing fleets operate in the Atlantic. Meat and fish processing are important, and manufacturing is pursued on a small scale. The population includes Bantu-speaking ethnic groups and whites of South African, German, and British descent. English is

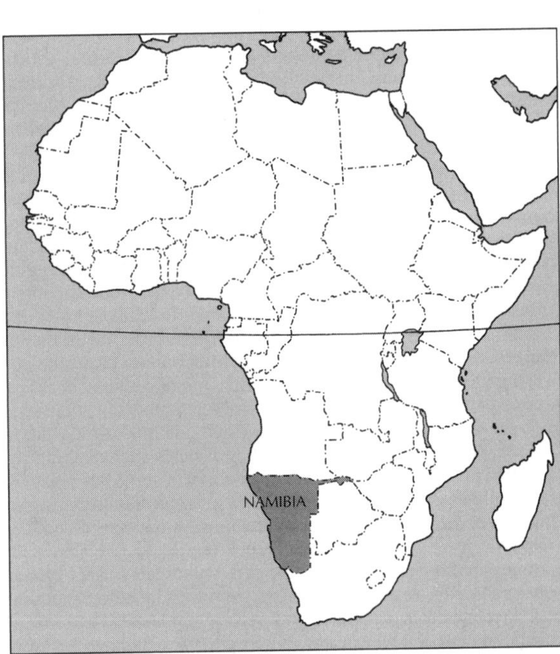

the official languages; Afrikaans is widely spoken. About half the people are Christian; the rest follow traditional beliefs.

History. The coastal regions of Namibia were explored by the Portuguese and Dutch in the early 15th cent., by English missionaries in the 18th cent., and by German missionaries in the 1840s. The German government proclaimed (1884) a protectorate over what is now Lüderitz and soon extended it to all of South West Africa. German forces crushed (1908) a revolt of the Nama and the Herero, resulting in the deaths of some 84,000 Africans. In World War I the country was occupied by SOUTH AFRICA, which afterward administered it under a League of Nations mandate. In 1945 South Africa refused to surrender its mandate and place South West Africa under the UN trusteeship system, and rejected demands by the UN General Assembly, backed (1971) by the International Court of Justice, that it withdraw. The UN adopted the name Namibia. In the 1970s South Africa proceeded with plans for independence on its own terms, holding elections and forming (1979) a national assembly, while a nationalist group, the South West Africa People's Organization (SWAPO), based largely in Angola, waged guerrilla warfare. In 1988 South Africa agreed to a UN-supervised transition to independence, and in 1990 Namibia became independent under Pres. Sam Nujoma, leader of SWAPO's guerrilla army, after SWAPO won 57% of the vote. Namibia remains dependent on South Africa as a source for needed imports and for shipment of its exports and as a market for them.

Nanchang, city (1990 est. pop. 1,350,000), capital of Jiangxi prov., China, on the Gan R. Noted for the porcelain produced in the nearby town of Jingdezhen, it is an important industrial city with products that include electronic equipment, machinery, textiles, and tractors. An old walled city, it dates from the Sung dynasty (12th cent.). Important in the Chinese revolution, it was the site of the Nanchang Uprising (1927), led by ZHOU ENLAI and ZHU DE.

Nanjing or **Nanking** [Chin. = southern capital], city (1990 est. pop. 2,500,000), capital of Jiangsu prov., E central China, on the CHANG (Yangtze) R. One of China's largest cities, it is dominated by the Chang River bridge, a crucial link in China's transport network. Nanjing's products include iron and steel, refined oil, processed food, chemicals, textiles, machinery, and motor vehicles. It served (3d–6th cent.; 14th–15th cent.; 1928–37) as capital of China and insurgents held the city (1853–64) during the TAIPING REBELLION (1850–64), the second SINO-JAPANESE WAR (1937–45), and the Chinese revolution. A celebrated literary center, it is known for its educational institutions, its large library, and its astronomical observatory.

nanotechnology: see MICROMECHANICS.

Nansen, Fridtjof, 1861–1930, Norwegian arctic explorer, statesman, scientist, and humanitarian. From 1893 to 1896 he tried to reach the NORTH POLE by drifting in ice across the polar basin in a special crush-resistant ship. Though he failed, his information on oceanography, meteorology, and diet laid the basis for future arctic work. He was professor of zoology and oceanography at the University of Christiana (now Oslo); Norway's first minister to England (1906–8); and the LEAGUE OF NATIONS high commissioner for refugees, for which he received the 1922 Nobel Peace Prize.

Nantes [näNt], city (1990 pop. 244,995), capital of Loire-Atlantique dept., W France. It is a major ocean port with such manufactures as food products and naval and farm equipment. A Roman administrative center, it was held by Norsemen (843–936) and Breton dukes (10th cent.) before union with France (1524). It has a 10th-cent. castle and a 15th-cent. cathedral.

Nantes, Edict of, 1598, decree issued at Nantes by HENRY IV of France at the end of the Wars of Religion (see RELIGION, WARS OF); the edict defined the rights of French Protestants (see HUGUENOTS). These included liberty of conscience and public worship wherever it had been previously granted, full civil rights including the right to hold public office, and Protestant control of some 200 cities. The last condition gave French Protestants a virtual state within a state and was incompatible with the centralizing policies of RICHELIEU and MAZARIN, and of LOUIS XIV. The Peace of Alais (1629) ended Protestant political privileges and persecution began after 1665 under Louis XIV. Finally, in 1685, Louis revoked the edict. Thousands of Protestants fled abroad, and several provinces were virtually depopulated. The edict's revocation greatly weakened the French economy by driving out a skilled and industrious segment of the nation.

Nantucket, island (1990 pop. 6,012), SE Massachusetts, 25 mi (40 km) S of CAPE COD. First settled in 1659, it was a major whaling center until the mid-19th cent. and is now one of the most popular summer resorts in the U.S. It is c.14 mi (23 km) long.

Naomi: see RUTH.

napalm, incendiary material used in bombs and flame throwers. Developed during World War II, napalm is a mixture of gasoline (sometimes mixed with other petroleum fuels) and a thickening agent. The thickener turns the mixture into a dense jelly that flows under pressure, as when shot from a flame thrower, and sticks to a target as it burns. Earlier SOAP thickeners have been replaced by polystyrene and similar polymers.

Naphtali: see ISRAEL, TRIBES OF.

Napier, John, 1550–1617, Scottish mathematician, the inventor of LOGARITHMS. He also introduced the decimal point in writing numbers. His *Rabdologiae* (1617) gives various methods for abbreviating arithmetical calculations, including a method of multiplication using a system of numbered rods called Napier's rods, or Napier's bones. Napier was also known as an outspoken exponent of the Protestant cause.

Naples, Ital. *Napoli,* city (1990 pop. 1,204,149), capital of Campania, S central Italy, on the Bay of Naples. A crowded, noisy city, it is a major seaport, and a commercial and industrial center. Naples has long been known for its music. A Greek colony, it was taken by Rome (4th cent. B.C.) and the Byzantines (6th cent. A.D.). It was an independent duchy from the 8th cent., later becoming (1139) part of the kingdom of Sicily. From 1282 it was the capital of the kingdom of Naples (see separate article). It fell (1860) to GARIBALDI and joined united Italy. Historic buildings include the Cathedral of St. Januarius (14th cent. and later), the Castel Nuovo (1282), and the Royal Palace (17th cent.).

Naples, kingdom of, former state in S Italy, with Naples as its capital. In the 11th and 12th cent. the Normans under ROBERT GUISCARD and his successors conquered S Italy from the Byzantines. The pope invested (1139) Roger II, Guiscard's nephew, with the kingdom of Sicily, which included lands in S Italy. The kingdom passed to the house of HOHENSTAUFEN and was ruled successively by FREDERICK II, CONRAD IV, MANFRED, and Conradin. Under them S Italy flowered. In 1266 CHARLES I (Charles of Anjou), founder of the Angevin dynasty, became king. He lost Sicily because of an armed revolt (1282) but retained his mainland possessions, which became known as the kingdom of Naples. The Angevins fought the house of Aragón for Sicily until 1373. After 1380 a struggle for succession in Naples began between Charles of Durazzo (see CHARLES III of Naples) and Louis of Anjou (later Louis I of Naples). In 1442 Naples was seized by ALFONSO V of Aragón. Meanwhile, the Angevin claims had passed to the French crown, and CHARLES VIII of France briefly seized Naples in 1495, thus starting the ITALIAN WARS. The Treaties of Blois (1504–5) gave Naples and Sicily to Spain, and heavy Spanish taxes impoverished the land. In the War of the SPANISH SUCCESSION the kingdom was seized (1707) by Austria, but it was returned (1738) to Spain and ruled by a cadet line of the Spanish BOURBONS. In 1806 the French took Naples, and Joseph Bonaparte (see BONAPARTE, family) was made king. He was succeeded (1808) by Joachim MURAT. In 1815 the Bourbons were restored, and Naples became (1816) part of the kingdom of the TWO SICILIES.

Napoleon I, 1769–1821, emperor of the French; b. Ajaccio, Corsica, son of Carlo and Letizia Bonaparte. This article covers the life of Napoleon, his part in the FRENCH REVOLUTIONARY WARS, and the major events of the **Napoleonic Wars.** Young Napoleon was sent to military schools in France and received a commission in the French artillery in 1785. After the start of the FRENCH REVOLUTION, he took part in the Corsican rebellion against Pasquale PAOLI and was forced to leave the island. Returning to France, Bonaparte was associated with the JACOBINS and gained notice by dislodging (1793) the British from Toulon. He was briefly imprisoned in 1794, but his career was reopened when the Convention was assailed (Oct. 1795) by a Parisian mob, and Napoleon was called on to disperse it. Made commander of the army in Italy, Bonaparte conducted the brilliant Italian campaign (1796–97) against Austria and

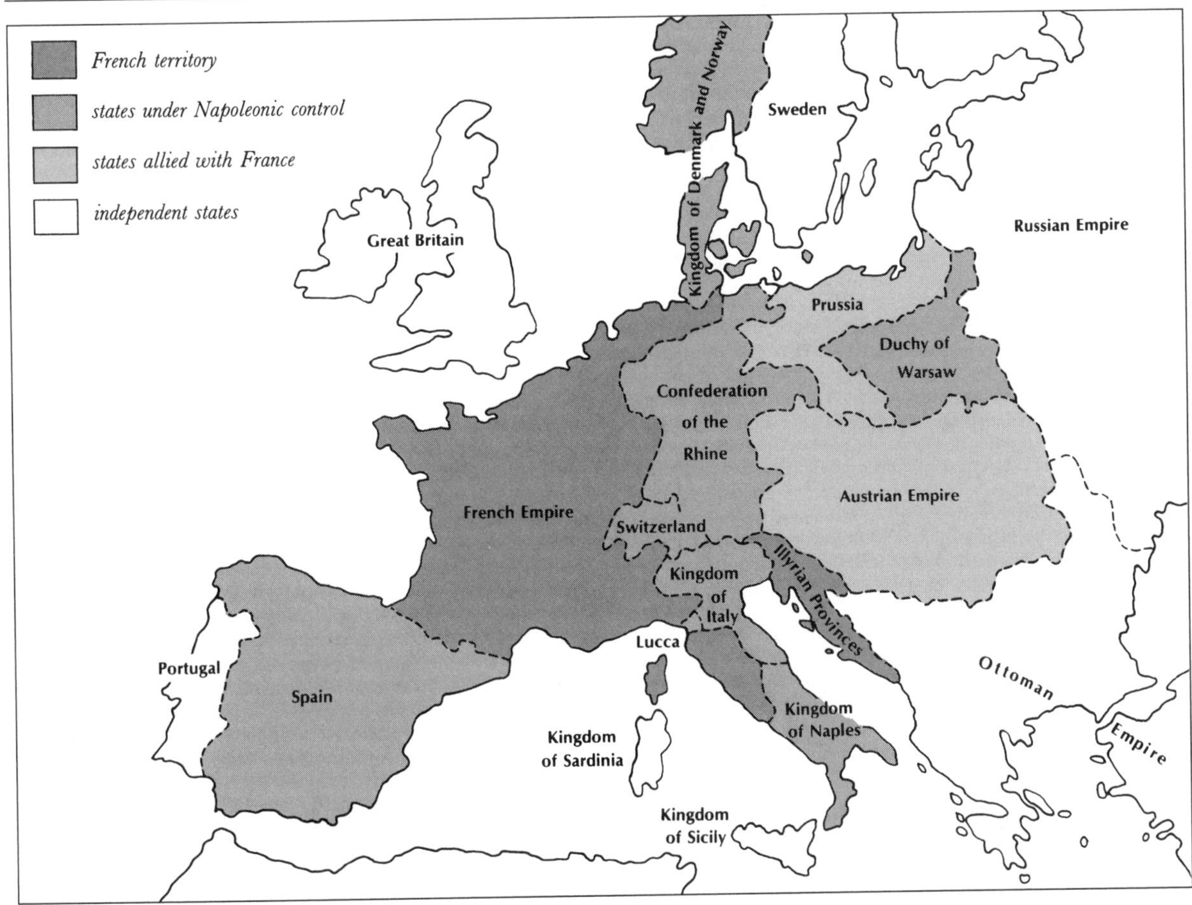

Napoleonic Europe (1821)

concluded it with the favorable Treaty of Campo Formio. Bonaparte then drew up a plan to strike at Britain's colonial empire by attacking Egypt. His victory over the Mamluks in the battle of the Pyramids (July 1798) was made useless when the French fleet was destroyed in Aboukir Bay (Aug. 1–2) by British Adm. NELSON. Leaving a hopeless situation in Egypt, Bonaparte returned to France and joined a conspiracy already hatched by Emmanuel SIEYÈS.

The Consulate. The French DIRECTORY was overthrown by the coup of 18 Brumaire (Nov. 9–10, 1799), and the Consulate was set up with Bonaparte as first consul, or dictator. He centralized the administration, stabilized the currency, and reformed the tax system. He also made peace with the Roman Catholic Church by the CONCORDAT OF 1801 and reformed the legal system with the Code Napoléon. In 1800 Napoleon defeated the Austrians at Marengo, Italy (June 14), and the treaties of Lunéville (1801) and Amiens (1802) made peace with Austria and Britain respectively. This phase is generally considered to divide the French Revolutionary Wars from the Napoleonic Wars. In 1802 Napoleon became first consul for life, and in 1803 Britain again declared war on France.

The Empire. Napoleon had himself crowned emperor in 1804 and proclaimed king of Italy in 1805. The Third Coalition was formed (1805) against him by Britain, Austria, Russia, and Sweden, but Napoleon crushed the Austrians at Ulm, and won (Dec. 2, 1805) his most brilliant victory at Austerlitz, over the Austrians and Russians. Prussia, which joined the coalition in 1806, was defeated at Jena (Oct. 14). British sea power, however, grew stronger with Nelson's victory at TRAFALGAR. Napoleon then instituted the Continental System to try to halt British trade with France and her allies. On land, war with Russia continued. The indecisive battle of Eylau (Feb. 8, 1807) was made good by Napoleon at Friedland (June 14). The treaties of Tilsit (July 1807) with Russia and Prussia left Napoleon master of the Continent. The whole map of Europe was rearranged. The HOLY ROMAN EMPIRE was dissolved (1806), and the kingdoms of Holland and Westphalia were created, with Napoleon's brothers Louis and Jérôme Bonaparte (see BONAPARTE, family) as kings. A third brother, Joseph, became (1806) king of Naples and was made (1808) king of Spain. In 1809 Austria's attempt to reopen warfare was squelched at Wagram (July 6), and Napoleon annexed the Papal States to France despite the objections of Pope PIUS VII. In 1809 Napoleon also had his marriage to the Empress JOSEPHINE, whom he had married in 1796, annulled. He then married (1810) MARIE LOUISE of Austria, who bore him a son (see NAPOLEON II).

Decline and Fall. Britain remained an opponent, and the Continental System proved difficult to enforce. Napoleon's first weakness had appeared in the PENINSULAR WAR (1808–14), and his alliance with Russia was tenuous. When Czar ALEXANDER I rejected the Continental System, Napoleon invaded (1812) Russia with the 500,000-strong *Grande Armée.* After the indecisive battle of Borodino (Sept. 7), Napoleon entered Moscow, but the winter and lack of supplies forced him to begin a disastrous retreat that became a rout after his troops crossed the Berezina R. in late November. Napoleon left his army and hastened to Paris to prepare French defenses. Prussia quickly turned against France and was joined in a coalition by Britain, Sweden, and Austria. The allies defeated the emperor at Leipzig (Oct. 1813), pursued him into France, and took Paris (Mar. 1814). Napoleon abdicated (Apr. 11, 1814) and was exiled to the island of Elba, which the allies gave him as a sovereign principality. His victors were still deliberating at the Congress of VIENNA when Napoleon landed at Cannes and marched on Paris. King LOUIS XVIII fled, and Napoleon ruled during the HUNDRED DAYS. He was defeated, however, in the WATERLOO CAMPAIGN (June 12–18, 1815) and abdicated again. Sent as a prisoner of war to the lonely British island of SAINT HELENA, he died there of cancer on May 5, 1821. His remains were returned to Paris in 1840. Estimates of Napoleon's place in history differ widely.

Beyond doubt one of the greatest conquerors of all time, he also promoted the growth of liberalism through his lasting administrative and legal reforms.

Napoleon II, 1811–32, son of NAPOLEON I and MARIE LOUISE; known as the king of Rome (1811–14), as the prince of Parma (1814–18), and after that as the duke of Reichstadt. Although Napoleon I abdicated (1815) in his favor, he never ruled. After 1815 he was a virtual prisoner in Austria.

Napoleon III (Louis Napoleon Bonaparte), 1808–73, emperor of the French (1852–70); son of Louis BONAPARTE, king of Holland; and nephew of NAPOLEON I. He spent his youth in exile and attempted (1836, 1840) two coups against the French government. Sentenced to life imprisonment, he escaped (1846) to England, returning to France after the FEBRUARY REVOLUTION of 1848. Elected to the National Assembly, he defeated (Dec. 1848) Gen. L.E. Cavaignac in the presidential election by a wide margin. Louis Napoleon's success was due largely to his name, which evoked French nostalgia for past Napoleonic glory. As president of the Second Republic, he consolidated powerful conservative support and instigated the coup of Dec. 3, 1851; the legislative assembly was dissolved, and an attempted workers' uprising was brutally suppressed. Louis Napoleon gained dictatorial powers in the new constitution of Jan. 1852, and in November a plebiscite overwhelmingly approved the establishment of the Second Empire. He became emperor as Napoleon III. For eight years he exercised dictatorial rule, tempered by material progress. Railway building was encouraged, and cities were rebuilt. The CRIMEAN WAR (1854–56) and the Congress of PARIS restored French leadership on the Continent. A supporter of Italian nationalism, Napoleon III met with Sardinian premier Camillo CAVOUR and planned a joint campaign with Sardinia to expel Austria from Italy (see RISORGIMENTO). After his costly victory at Solferino (1859), however, Napoleon III made a separate peace with Austria. Having lost popularity, the emperor began a more liberal domestic policy. This "Liberal Empire" (1860–70) enabled opposition leaders such as Jules Favre and Adolphe THIERS to become prominent. Cochin China was acquired, and Napoleon supported the building of the SUEZ CANAL. Less fortunate was his intervention (1861–67) in Mexico; U.S. opposition forced a French withdrawal. The FRANCO-PRUSSIAN WAR (1870–71) brought about his downfall. Napoleon took the field himself and was captured at Sedan. He was deposed (Sept. 4, 1870) by a bloodless revolution in Paris. After peace was restored, he lived in exile in England with his wife, EUGÉNIE. His only son was killed while serving in the British army.

Napoleonic Wars: see NAPOLEON I.

naproxen or **naproxen sodium,** a NONSTEROIDAL ANTI-INFLAMMATORY ANALGESIC DRUG used to alleviate the minor pain of arthritis, menstruation, headaches, and the like, and to reduce fever. Side effects include gastrointestinal distress and dizziness. It was approved for over-the-counter sale in the U.S. in 1994.

Nara, city (1990 pop. 349,356), capital of Nara prefecture, S Honshu, Japan. An ancient cultural and religious center, it was founded in 706 by imperial decree. Nara was (710–84) the first permanent capital of Japan. Nara is a tourist center. Nara Park, Japan's largest (1,250 acres/506 hectares) city park, includes the celebrated Imperial Museum. The East Great Temple of Nara is supposedly the largest wooden structure in the world. Near the city is wooded Mt. Kasuga, the traditional home of the gods; its trees are never cut.

Narayan, R(asipuram) K(rishnaswamy), 1906–, Indian novelist. He writes in English. His witty, perceptive depictions of Indian life include *The Financial Expert* (1952) and *Malgudi Days* (1982), a collection of short stories.

Narcissus, in Greek mythology, beautiful youth who refused all love, including ECHO's. As punishment for his indifference, he was made to fall in love with his own image in a pool, whereupon he pined away, and turned into a flower.

narcissus, showy-blossomed plant (genus *Narcissus*) of the AMARYLLIS family, native chiefly to Asia and the Mediterranean region but now widely distributed. The genus includes the yellow daffodil (*N. pseudo-narcissus*), with a long, trumpet-shaped central corona; the yellow jonquil (*N. jonquilla*), with a short corona; and the narcissus, any of several usually white-flowered species, e.g., the poet's narcissus (*N. poetica*), with a red rim on the corona. The biblical ROSE OF SHARON may have been a narcissus.

narcotic, group of drugs with potent analgesic effects, associated with alteration of mood and behavior. The chief narcotic drugs are OPIUM, CODEINE, MORPHINE, and the morphine derivative HEROIN. Narcotics are thought to act by mimicking and/or enhancing the activity of ENDORPHINS, proteins produced by the brain and believed to modulate pain and other nervous system functions. Narcotics are valuable in numbing the senses, alleviating pain, inducing sleep, and relieving diarrhea. Common side effects include nausea, vomiting, and allergic reactions. In large doses, narcotics can cause respiratory depression, COMA, and death. All narcotics are addictive; synthetic narcotics such as meperidine and METHADONE tend to be less addicting and possess fewer side effects, but they are also less potent. (See DRUG ADDICTION AND DRUG ABUSE).

Narragansett, indigenous people of the Eastern Woodlands (see NORTH AMERICA, INDIGENOUS PEOPLES OF), with an Algonquian language of the Algonquian-Wakashan stock (see NATIVE AMERICAN LANGUAGES). They occupied most of Rhode Island. Survivors of the plague of 1617 in other peoples joined the Narragansett, making them powerful. Their chief Canonicus sold land (1636) to Roger WILLIAMS and supported the colonists in the PEQUOT War. They numbered 5,000 in 1674, but KING PHILIP'S WAR destroyed Native American power in the region. In 1990 there were 2,456 Narragansetts in the U.S.

Narses, c.478–c.573, Roman general under JUSTINIAN I, rival and successor of BELISARIUS in Italy. After defeating TOTILA (552) and an army of Franks and Alemanni (554) he became exarch of Italy, but his administration was unpopular.

Naruhito, 1960–, Japanese crown prince, son of AKIHITO. He was officially invested as crown prince in 1991. In 1993 he married Owada Masako, a commoner.

Narváez, Pánfilo de [närvä'ĕth], c.1470–1528, Spanish CONQUISTADOR. In CUBA he served Diego de VELÁZQUEZ, who in 1520 sent him to MEXICO to recall CORTÉS; he failed. Commissioned to conquer FLORIDA, he arrived there in 1528, sent his ships to Mexico, and led his force inland in search of gold. Disappointed and harassed by the indigenous people, they returned to the coast, built crude vessels, and set sail for Mexico. All save CABEZA DE VACA and three others were lost.

NASA: see NATIONAL AERONAUTICS AND SPACE ADMINISTRATION.

Nash, John, 1752–1835, English architect, best known for his town plans, as in the Marylebone section of London, including Regent's Park (1818). He initiated the REGENCY STYLE and the extensive use of stucco for city building facades.

Nash, Ogden, 1902–71, American poet; b. Rye, N.Y. His humorous verses with their cleverly outrageous rhymes appeared in such volumes as *I'm a Stranger Here Myself* (1938), *You Can't Get There from Here* (1957), and *Bed Riddance* (1970).

Nashe or **Nash, Thomas,** 1567–1601, English satirist. An ardent anti-Puritan, he was involved in the pamphlet battles of the MARPRELATE CONTROVERSY. *The Unfortunate Traveller* (1594) was a forerunner of the picaresque adventure NOVEL. His plays include *Summer's Last Will and Testament* (1592), a satirical MASQUE, and *The Isle of Dogs,* a lost comedy written with Ben JONSON (1597).

Nashoba, former community, SW Tenn., near Memphis. It was established (1825) by Frances WRIGHT and others, influenced by the model of NEW HARMONY, to educate specially purchased slaves for freedom. Poor management and disease led to its collapse (1829). In 1830 the slaves were taken to Haiti.

Nashua, city (1990 pop. 79,662), seat of Hillsborough co., S N.H., on the Merrimack and Nashua rivers, near the Mass. line; settled c.1655, inc. as a city 1853. Its water power made it an early textile mill town. Manufactures include office equipment, paper, shoes, plastics, and chemicals.

Nashville, city (1990 pop. 488,374), state capital, central Tenn.; inc. as a city 1806, merged with Davidson co. 1963. A Cumberland R. port, cotton center, and railroad hub, it developed from a 1779 settlement. It was named state capital in 1843 and became (1862) an important Union base during the CIVIL WAR. A major agricultural market and important regional commercial center, it has diversified industries, including insurance, publishing, and various manufactures. Nashville is famous as a country-music center and is the site of the "Opryland" entertainment complex. Vanderbilt and Fisk universities are among its numerous educational institutions. The city has many notable buildings of classical design, including a replica (1897) of the PARTHENON.

Naskapi: see MONTAGNAIS AND NASKAPI.

Nassau, former duchy, central Germany. Most of it is now included in the state of HESSE; a smaller part is in the state of Rhineland-Palatinate. Wiesbaden was the capital. In 1255 the ruling dynasty split into two main lines. Under the Walramian line Nassau became (1806) a duchy and was absorbed (1866) by PRUSSIA. The Walramians succeeded (1890) to the grand duchy of LUXEMBOURG. The Ottonian line of Nassau settled in the Netherlands and became prominent with WILLIAM THE SILENT. Members of the Dutch line, called the house of Orange, became rulers of the Netherlands.

Nassau, city (1985 est. pop. 135,000), capital of the BAHAMAS. A port on New Providence island, it is the cultural, commercial, and financial heart of the Bahamas and is a famous winter resort. First known as Charles Towne, it was renamed in 1695. Nassau was a rendezvous for pirates in the 18th cent. and was held briefly by American revolutionaries in 1776. It has three old forts.

Nasser, Gamal Abdal, 1918–70, Egyptian army officer and political leader, first president of the republic of Egypt (1956–70). In 1952 he led the coup that deposed King FAROUK. He became premier (1954) and president (1956). He nationalized the Suez Canal in 1956, precipitating the short-lived invasion by Britain, France, and Israel. Nasser suffered a disastrous defeat in the 1967 Six-Day War (see ARAB-ISRAELI WARS), but his political support remained strong. He instituted far-reaching land reforms and economic and social development programs, the most spectacular being the building of the Aswan Dam. A pan-Arabist, he was president (1958–61) of the United Arab Republic, a short-lived merger of Egypt and Syria.

Nast, Thomas, 1840–1902, American cartoonist and painter; b. Germany. He is best known for his forceful political CARTOONS, which were instrumental in defeating Boss TWEED in New York City. Nast created the tiger, elephant, and donkey as symbols of Tammany Hall, the Republican party, and the Democratic party.

$
Th: Nast
THE "BRAINS"
THAT ACHIEVED THE TAMMANY VICTORY AT THE ROCHESTER DEMOCRATIC CONVENTION.

Thomas Nast cartoon of Tammany figure, 1871

nasturtium, herb (genus *Tropaeolum*) native to mountainous areas of the American tropics. The common nasturtiums (*T. majus* and *T. minus*) are cultivated in the U.S. for their red or yellow flowers. The plants are also used for food, e.g., the seeds are pickled as capers and the leaves and flowers are used in salads. *Nasturtium* is also the botanical name for the genus that includes the unrelated WATERCRESSES of the MUSTARD family.

Natchez, city (1990 pop. 19,460), seat of Adams co., SW Miss., on bluffs above the Mississippi R.; founded 1716, inc. 1803. The area was held by England (1763), Spain (1779), and the U.S. (1798), and was capital of the Mississippi Territory (1798–1802) and state capital (1817–21). A great river port and the cultural center of antebellum planter aristocracy, Natchez retains much of its historical character, with many fine homes. The city was taken by Union forces in 1863. It was the southern end of the NATCHEZ TRACE.

Natchez Trace, historic route, 449 mi (723 km) between NATCHEZ, Miss., and NASHVILLE, Tenn. It grew from a series of old Native American trails and was of great military and commercial importance from the 1780s to the 1830s. The Natchez Trace Parkway (est. 1938) generally follows the old route.

Natchitoches [năk'ĭtŏsh], city (1990 pop. 16,609), seat of Natchitoches parish, NW La.; inc. 1819. Its industry centers on processing agricultural products. The first permanent settlement in the LOUISIANA PURCHASE, it was founded c.1714 by the French, on the boundary between French and Spanish territory. It figured in the MEXICAN WAR and the CIVIL WAR.

Nathan, prophet in the time of DAVID and SOLOMON. With his parable of the ewe lamb, he denounced David for his abduction of BATHSHEBA. Later his advice saved the kingdom for Solomon.

Nathan, George Jean, 1882–1958, American editor and drama critic; b. Fort Wayne, Ind. He joined H.L. MENCKEN in editing *Smart Set* (1914–23) and in founding (1924) the *American Mercury,* a magazine that was the arbiter of American literary taste for a decade. Primarily a drama critic, Nathan was famous for his erudite and cynical reviews.

Nathanael, disciple mentioned only in the Gospel of St. JOHN, plausibly identified with St. BARTHOLOMEW.

Nation, Carry (Moore), 1846–1911, American temperance advocate; b. Garrard co., Ky. Convinced of her divine appointment, she gained fame in 1900 by destroying saloon liquor and property with a hatchet. Arrested 30 times, she focused public attention on the cause of PROHIBITION and helped create a mood favorable to passage of the 18th constitutional amendment.

National Academy of Sciences, private organization, est. 1863 by act of Congress, devoted to the furtherance and public uses of science. Members and nonvoting foreign associates are elected in recognition of their distinguished and continuing achievements in original research. The Academy acts as an official adviser to the federal government on matters of science and technology.

National Aeronautics and Space Administration (NASA), U.S. federal civilian agency with the mission of conducting research and developing operational programs in the areas of manned spaceflight (see SPACE EXPLORATION); lunar, planetary, and interplanetary SPACE PROBES; artificial earth-orbital SATELLITES; rocketry; and aeronautics. Its creation on Oct. 1, 1958, was spurred by American unpreparedness at the time the USSR launched (Oct. 4, 1957) *Sputnik 1,* the first artificial satellite. NASA's major installations include the Kennedy Space Center, on Merritt Island, north of Cape Canaveral, Fla., where most launchings occur; the Johnson Space Center, Houston, Tex., where U.S. manned spaceflights are controlled; and the Jet Propulsion Laboratory (operated under contract by the California Institute of Technology), Pasadena, Calif., where the U.S. Viking and Voyager deep-space probes are controlled. NASA superseded the National Advisory Committee on Aeronautics (NACA).

National Archives, official repository for records of the U.S. federal government, established in 1934 by an act of Congress. Located in Washington, D.C., and College Park, Md., it is run by the U.S. archivist.

National Association for the Advancement of Colored People (NAACP), organization of African Americans, with many white members, dedicated to ending racial inequality and segregation; est. 1910 with the merging of the Niagara Movement of W.E.B. DU BOIS and a group of concerned whites. The organization grew quickly, at first directing its efforts to eradicating lynching; by the 1950s this goal was achieved. The 1954 Supreme Court school-desegregation decision (see INTEGRATION) followed a long effort by the independent NAACP Legal Defense and Education Fund. A consistent advocate of nonviolent protest, the NAACP has at times been accused of passivity by more militant groups. In 1991 it had a membership of 345,000.

National Ballet of Canada, the leading Canadian ballet company. Based in Toronto, it was founded (1951) by Celia Franca and modeled on Sadler's Wells (now the ROYAL BALLET). Its repertoire is grounded on classics in the tradition of DIAGHILEV.

National Bureau of Standards: see NATIONAL INSTITUTE OF STANDARDS AND TECHNOLOGY.

National Council of the Churches of Christ in the United States of America, agency of 32 Protestant and Orthodox Eastern denominations, formed in 1950. Not a governing body, it promotes interchurch cooperation and is the chief instrument of the ECUMENICAL MOVEMENT in the U.S.

national debt: see DEBT, PUBLIC.

National Gallery, London, one of the permanent national art collections of Great Britain. Its Greek-style building, designed (1832–38) by William Wilkins and shared for 30 years with the Royal Academy of Arts, has been enlarged several times, most recently with the addition (1991) of the Sainsbury wing. The nucleus of the collection was 38 pictures from the Angerstein collection. It has fine collections of 15th- and 16th-cent. Italian paintings, and French, Flemish, and Dutch masters. The National Portrait Gallery was adjoined in 1896.

National Gallery of Art, Washington, D.C., a branch of the SMITHSONIAN INSTITUTION, est. by act of Congress, 1937; opened 1941. Its building and a collection of American portraits were donated by Andrew W. MELLON. The gallery received many bequests. Its outstanding collections include Italian masterpieces, American naive paintings, French art, prints and drawings, and the Index of American Design. Its East Building, designed by I.M. PEI, opened in 1978.

National Guard, U.S. militia authorized by the Constitution. During peacetime it operates under state jurisdiction and can be used by governors to quell local disturbances, as in Newark and Detroit riots in 1967. In times of war and other emergencies, it is absorbed into the standing army and is under the command of the president. It was partially mobilized during the Korean War (1951–53) and the BERLIN crisis of 1961, and some units were mobilized for the Persian Gulf War (1991–92). Enlistment is voluntary.

national health insurance: see HEALTH INSURANCE.

National Institute of Standards and Technology, U.S. government agency, est. 1901 within the Dept. of Commerce as the National Bureau of Standards, with the mission to advance the application of science and technology for the public benefit; it was renamed in 1988. Its headquarters is in Gaithersburg, Md.; additional facilities are at Boulder, Colo. Its research provides a basis for the nation's physical measurement system. The institute also investigates the properties of materials, facilitates the use of available technology, and promotes innovation.

National Institutes of Health (NIH), U.S. agency that conducts and supports biomedical research into the causes, cure, and prevention of disease. NIH maintains its own laboratories, and awards grants and contracts to universities and other private research facilities. Separate national institutes function in specific areas such as cancer; heart, lung, and blood diseases; dental research; child health; allergy and infectious diseases; aging; and mental health.

nationalism, political philosophy holding that the welfare of the nation-state is paramount, an attitude often strengthened when people share a common history, religion, language, or ethnic background. The term also refers to a group state of mind in which patriotism, or loyalty to one's country, is regarded as an individual's principal duty. Nationalism, which in its modern sense can be traced to the time of the FRENCH REVOLUTION, has played an important part in supplementing the formal institutions of society, providing much of the cohesiveness necessary for the orderly conduct of affairs in modern nations. Although it has contributed to excesses of militarism and IMPERIALISM, as in Europe under NAPOLEON I or under German Nazism (see NATIONAL SOCIALISM), it has also inspired movements against such abuses. It remains a powerful force in world politics despite the spread of trade and communications and the growing interdependence of nations, and the end of Soviet hegemony in E Europe and N Asia has led to the rise of many nationalist movements there.

nationalization, acquisition and operation by a country of businesses owned and operated by private individuals or corporations. It is usually done in the name of social and economic equality, often as part of Communist or socialist doctrine. Nationalization of foreign-owned property, e.g., the Suez Canal by Egypt (1958) and the copper-mining industry by Chile (1971), typically attempts to end foreign control of an industry or the economy and poses complex problems for INTERNATIONAL LAW. After World War II, Communist Eastern Europe nationalized all industry and most agriculture, and Western European nations nationalized some key industries, such as transportation. By the 1990s the trend in many former and current Communist countries and Western nations was toward PRIVATIZATION, mainly because political pressures have usually led governments to operate businesses very inefficiently.

National Labor Relations Board (NLRB), independent agency of the U.S. government created under the National Labor Relations Act of 1935 (Wagner Act), which affirmed labor's right to organize and engage in COLLECTIVE BARGAINING, or to refrain from such activities. The Wagner Act was later amended by the Taft-Hartley Labor Act (1947), the Landrum-Griffin Act of 1959, and the Health Care Amendments (1974). The NLRB determines proper bargaining units, conducts elections for union representation, and prevents and remedies unfair labor practices.

National Museum of Anthropology, Mexico City; present building opened 1964. The museum houses an extensive collection of artifacts from pre-Columbian Mexico, notably works of the MAYA and AZTEC civilizations. Exhibitions include studies of the peoples and animals of Mexico.

National Organization for Women (NOW), group est. 1966 to support full equality for women in America; its founder and first president was Betty FRIEDAN. Through legislative lobbying, litigation, and demonstrations it seeks to end discrimination against women. The largest U.S. women's rights group, NOW has some 250,000 members, both women and men. See also FEMINISM.

national parks. Congress laid the foundation of the U.S. National Park System in 1872 by establishing Yellowstone National Park. In 1916 the National Park Service, a bureau of the U.S. Dept. of the INTERIOR, was set up to administer 37 national parks and monuments. The National Park System now comprises more than 350 areas totaling 80,115,984 acres (32,446,973 hectares). The National Park Service directs a wide program of construction and of educational and protective work. In addition to national parks, the system includes national monuments, historic sites, historical parks, memorials, military parks, battlefields, cemeteries, preserves, recreational areas, lakeshores, seashores, parkways, scenic and historic trails, and rivers. See accompanying table.

National Radio Astronomy Observatory (NRAO), federal observatory (founded 1956) for radio astronomy, operated by Associated Universities Inc. under contract with the U.S. National Science Foundation. Its headquarters are at Charlottesville, Va. The principal instrument at its Green Bank, W.Va., facility a paraboloid transit antenna 300 ft (91 m) in diameter, collapsed in 1988; a replacement is expected to be completed in 1995. There are also six smaller antennas at Green Bank and an antenna at Kitt Peak, Ariz. Near Socorro, N.Mex., the NRAO operates the Very Large Array, a collection of 27 mobile antennas placed in a Y-shaped arrangement in order to obtain maps of celestial radio sources. The observatory also operates the Very Long Baseline Array, 10 widely separated antennas that function as a single radio telescope. The antenna sites are located in New Hampshire, Iowa, Saint Croix, Texas, New Mexico (two antennas), Arizona, California, Washington, and Hawaii; the headquarters is located at Socorro.

National Recovery Administration (NRA), 1933–36, U.S. administrative bureau established under the National Industrial Recovery Act to encourage industrial recovery and combat unemployment. Headed by Hugh S. Johnson and symbolized by the Blue Eagle, the NRA drew up over 500 industrial fair practice codes. The Supreme Court decision (May 1935) invalidating the codes crippled the NRA, but many of the NRA labor provisions were reenacted in later legislation (see NATIONAL LABOR RELATIONS BOARD; WAGES AND HOURS ACT).

National Republican party, a short-lived U.S. political party formed to oppose Andrew JACKSON in the 1832 presidential elec-

NATIONAL PARKS

Park	*Special Characteristics*
Acadia (1916)* Location: SE Me. Area: 41,888 acres (16,951 hectares)	Comprising areas on Mount Desert Island, Isle au Haut, and other smaller islands, plus the tip of the Schoodic Peninsula, the park features a scenic, wave-eroded coastline, maritime landscapes, and a rugged, glacier-scoured interior. Designated a national park in 1919.
American Samoa (1988) Location: American Samoa Area: 7,000 acres (3,645 hectares)	Comprising areas on the South Pacific islands of Ofu, Ta'u, and Tutuila, the park features the only paleotropical rain forest in the U.S. national park system, and a coral reef.
Arches (1929)* Location: E Utah Area: 73,379 acres (29,695 hectares)	Located in red-rock country overlooking the gorge of the Colorado R., the park includes an extraordinary variety of erosional features in the form of graceful arches, windows, spires, and pinnacles that change color constantly in the sunlight. Designated a national park in 1971.
Badlands (1929)* Location: SW S.D. Area: 243,508 acres (98,548 hectares)	Located in the badlands of South Dakota, with their countless gullies, steep ridges, and other erosional landforms, the park is famous for its scenery, its fossils of prehistoric animals, and its varied wildlife, including bison, bighorn sheep, deer, antelope, and prairie dogs. Designated a national park in 1978.
Big Bend (1935)* Location: W Tex. Area: 801,163 acres (324,219 hectares)	It is a triangle formed by a great bend in the Rio Grande. The park includes deep canyons, e.g., the Santa Elena Canyon. The river, desert, and Chisos mts. offer sharp contrasts in wilderness scenery. Established as a national park in 1944.
Biscayne (1968)* Location: SE Fla. Area: 173,467 acres (70,200 hectares)	Located between Biscayne Bay (W) and the Atlantic Ocean (E), the park is mostly underwater, with excellent snorkeling and scuba-diving around a living coral reef. About 25 small coral islands, or keys, form a chain across the park. Designated a national park in 1980.
Bryce Canyon (1923)* Location: SW Utah Area: 35,835 acres (14,502 hectares)	The park contains giant, horseshoe-shaped amphitheaters lined with innumerable, delicate-looking spires, pinnacles, and other erosional features carved out from layers of multicolored rocks. Authorized as a national park in 1924 and given the present name in 1928.
Canyonlands (1964)* Location: SE Utah Area: 337,570 acres (136,610 hectares)	Located in a desert region, the park contains a maze of deep canyons; many spires, pinnacles, arches, and other geological features carved by wind and water; petroglyphs drawn on rocks c.1,000 years ago; and mesas rising to more than 7,800 ft (2,377 m).
Capitol Reef (1937)* Location: S Utah Area: 241,904 acres (97,895 hectares)	The park features a dome-shaped white rock, said to resemble the U.S. Capitol Building, and a maze of deep canyons, arches, and monoliths cut through a 100-mi (160-km) uplift, known as the Waterpocket Fold, that geologists consider unique because of its size. Designated a national park in 1971.
Carlsbad Caverns (1923)* Location: SE N.Mex. Area: 46,755 acres (18,921 hectares)	These limestone caves, with remarkable stalactite and stalagmite formations and huge chambers, began forming 60 million years ago. The caverns, among the largest in the world, are inhabited by countless bats and have still not been completely explored. Designated a national park in 1930.
Channel Islands (1938)* Location: S Calif. Area: 249,354 acres (100,910 hectares)	The park, which includes Anacapa, Santa Barbara, San Miguel, Santa Cruz (the largest), and Santa Rosa islands, is known for its large rookeries of sea lions, sports fishing, and variety of nesting sea birds. Designated a national park in 1980.
Crater Lake (1902)* Location: SW Oreg. Area: 133,224 acres (74,148 hectares)	Located in the CASCADE RANGE, the park features Crater Lake (20 sq mi/52 sq km), a deep-blue lake with no outlet, in the caldera of Mt. Mazama, an ancient volcanic peak. With a maximum depth of 1,932 ft (589 m), it is the second-deepest lake in North America.
Denali (1917)* Location: S Alaska Area: 4,716,726 acres (1,908,791 hectares)	The park, which is dominated by Mt. MCKINLEY (20,320 ft/6,194 m), the highest mountain in North America, includes glaciers, caribou, sheep, moose, and grizzly bears. Originally established as Mt. McKinley National Park, it was expanded to include adjacent Denali National Monument and was renamed in 1980.
Everglades (1934)* Location: S Fla. Area: 1,506,500 acres (609,659 hectares)	A slow-moving, subtropical, marshy wilderness draining into Florida Bay and covered in places by tall prairie grasses and mangrove forests, the park is known for its rich and varied wildlife, including crocodiles, alligators, manatees, ospreys, bald eagles, and herons. Dedicated in 1947.
Gates of the Arctic (1978)* Location: N Alaska Area: 7,523,888 acres (3,044,809 hectares)	Located N of the Arctic Circle, the park (together with an adjacent preserve of 900,000 acres/364,217 hectares) is a tundra wilderness of broad valleys and razorlike peaks of the Brooks Range, known for its abundance of Arctic caribou, grizzly bears, moose, and wolves. Designated a national park in 1980.

*Date authorized

NATIONAL PARKS	
Park	*Special Characteristics*
Glacier (1910)* Location: NW Mont. Area: 1,013,595 acres (410,188 hectares)	Straddling the CONTINENTAL DIVIDE, the park contains some of the most spectacular scenery in the Rocky Mts., including glaciers, high peaks, numerous lakes and streams, and a great variety of wildlife. Adjacent to the park is Canada's Waterton Lakes National Park.
Glacier Bay (1925)* Location: SE Alaska Area: 3,225,284 acres (1,305,226 hectares)	Glaciers descending to the bay from towering, snow-covered mountains create one of the world's most spectacular displays of ice. Muir Glacier, c.265 ft (80 m) high, is the park's most famous. Wildlife includes whales, seals, eagles, and bears. Designated a national park in 1980.
Grand Canyon (1908)* Location: NW Ariz. Area: 1,218,375 acres (493,059 hectares)	The park includes the most spectacular part of the GRAND CANYON of the Colorado R. Along the forested north rim and the more accessible south rim are numerous lookouts; trails wind to the canyon floor. Designated a national park in 1919 and expanded in 1975.
Grand Teton (1929)* Location: NW Wyo. Area: 310,443 acres (125,636 hectares)	Dominated by Grand Teton (13,766 ft/4,169 m), which towers 7,000 ft (2,100 m) above the valley floor, the park embraces the most scenic portion of the glaciated, snow-covered Teton Range and was expanded in 1950 to include part of Jackson Hole. Wildlife includes moose, elk, and trumpeter swans.
Great Basin (1986)* Location: E Nevada Area: 77,100 acres (31,201 hectares)	Located in the South Snake Range, the park has exceptional scenic, biologic, and geologic attractions, including Lehman Caves, Wheeler Peak (the highest point in the park), and Nevada's only glacier. Great Basin also contains groves of bristlecone pines, the oldest living trees.
Great Smoky Mountains (1926)* Location: N.C.-Tenn. Area: 520,269 acres (210,550 hectares)	Reaching a high point of 6,642 ft (2,024 m) at Clingmans Dome, the park straddles the crest of the Great Smokies for 71 mi (114 km) and contains part of the APPALACHIAN TRAIL. The park supports luxuriant and diversified plant life. Established as a national park in 1930.
Guadalupe Mountains (1966)* Location: W Tex. Area: 86,416 acres (34,971 hectares)	The park, which features Guadalupe Peak (8,751 ft/2,667 m), rugged canyons, and unusual flora and fauna, is of special geologic interest for its exposures of one of the world's largest and most significant Permian fossil reefs. Established as a national park in 1972.
Haleakala (1916)* Location: Hawaii Area: 28,655 acres (11,596 hectares)	The park, on Maui island, extends from the summit of the dormant volcano Mt. Haleakala (10,023 ft/3,055 m) down to rainforests and rugged cliffs along the coast. Haleakala Crater, 2,720 ft (829 m) deep, is a major feature. Originally part of Hawaii National Park, it gained separate park status in 1961.
Hawaii Volcanoes (1916)* Location: Hawaii Area: 229,177 acres (92,745 hectares)	The park, on Hawaii island, contains two of the most active volcanoes in the world—Kilauea, with its fire pit, called Halemaumau, and Mauna Loa, with the active Mokuaweoweo Crater on its summit. Originally Hawaii National Park, its name was changed in 1961.
Hot Springs (1832)* Location: Central Ark. Area: 5,839 acres (2,363 hectares)	The park features 47 hot springs of reputed medicinal and healing value. The water of two springs can be seen emerging naturally; that of the other springs is piped to central reservoirs for bathhouse and therapy use. Designated a national park in 1921.
Isle Royale (1931)* Location: NW Mich. Area: 571,796 acres (231,398 hectares)	Comprising Isle Royale, the largest island in Lake Superior, and c.200 other islands, the park remains a roadless, forested wilderness. It is known for abundant wildlife, and exhibits evidence of copper mining by prehistoric Indians. Designated a national park in 1940.
Katmai (1918)* Location: SW Alaska Area: 3,716,000 acres (1,503,812 hectares)	A vast wilderness area, the park preserves volcanic features resulting from the eruption (1912) of Novarupta volcano, which caused the collapse of Mt. Katmai. For many years hot gases rose from the Valley of Ten Thousand Smokes, but the area is no longer very active. Designated a national park in 1980.
Kenai Fjords (1978)* Location: S Alaska Area: 670,000 acres (271,139 hectares)	The park features the great Harding Icefield and its radiating glaciers, many of which descend to tidewater, and a magnificent series of fjords along the coast of the Kenai Peninsula, with rain forests, sea lions, sea otters, seals, and a varied bird life. Designated a national park in 1980.
Kings Canyon (1940)* Location: E Calif. Area: 461,901 acres (186,925 hectares)	Largely wilderness, the park features summit peaks of the High Sierras and two enormous canyons on the Kings R. General Grant Grove, with giant sequoias, is a detached section of the park and was formerly the General Grant National Park (est. 1890). King Canyon adjoins Sequoia National Park.
*Date authorized	

NATIONAL PARKS

Park	*Special Characteristics*
Kobuk Valley (1978)* Location: N Alaska Area: 1,750,421 acres (708,370 hectares)	Located in rugged terrain N of the Arctic Circle, the park embraces the central valley of the Kobuk R., a centuries-old transportation route with many archaeological sites. Other features include caribou migrating routes and the Great Kobuk Sand Dunes. Designated a national park in 1980.
Lake Clark (1978)* Location: S Alaska Area: 1,750,421 acres (708,370 hectares)	Located across Cook Inlet from Anchorage, the park (and adjacent preserve of 1,214,000 acres/ 491,289 hectares) features jagged peaks of the Chigmit Mts.; lakes Clark, Fishtrap, and Iliamna; volcanoes, glaciers; and abundant wildlife. Designated a national park in 1980.
Lassen Volcanic (1907)* Location: N Calif. Area: 106,372 acres (43,047 hectares)	At the southern tip of the CASCADE RANGE, the park is dominated by the volcanic Lassen Peak (10,457 ft/3,187 m), which erupted intermittently from 1914 to 1921, and preserves lava flows, hot springs, sulfurous vents, and other evidences of volcanism. Designated a national park in 1916.
Mammoth Cave (1926)* Location: central Ky. Area: 52,419 acres (21,213 hectares)	The chief feature of the park is Mammoth Cave, one of the largest known caves in the world, with more than 190 mi (305 km) of known passageways; arrays of stalactites, stalagmites, and columns; and an underground river. Fully established as a national park in 1941.
Mesa Verde (1906)* Location: SW Colo. Area: 52,122 acres (21,093 hectares)	Set amid forested canyons and flat mesas, the park features some of the most notable and best preserved pre-Columbian cliff dwellings and related works of early man in the U.S. The dwellings cover four archaeological periods from the 1st cent. A.D. to the late 13th cent., when they were abandoned.
Mount Rainier (1899)* Location: SW Wash. Area: 235,613 acres (95,349 hectares)	Located in the CASCADE RANGE, the park is dominated by snow-crowned Mt. Rainier, 14,410 ft (4,392 m) high, a volcano dormant since 1870, from the summit of which radiate 26 glaciers, which form the greatest single-peak glacial system in the U.S. Forests and alpine meadows clothe the lower slopes.
North Cascades (1968)* Location: N Wash. Area: 504,781 acres (204,277 hectares)	Located in the CASCADE RANGE, the park has outstanding alpine scenery, including high jagged peaks, glaciers, icefalls, hanging valleys, and mountain lakes in high glacial cirques. Western slopes are rainy, with rain forests and other luxuriant vegetation; eastern slopes are drier.
Olympic (1909)* Location: NW Wash. Area: 922,654 acres (373,385 hectares)	Located in the highest part of the COAST RANGE, the park features Mt. Olympus (7,965 ft/2,427 m), coniferous rain forests, glaciers, lakes, rare elk, and some 50 mi (80 km) of shoreline along the Pacific coast. Established as a national park in 1938.
Petrified Forest (1906)* Location: E Ariz. Area: 93,533 acres (37,851 hectares)	A part of the Painted Desert, the park features the world's largest display of petrified wood and forests. The trees, dating from the Triassic period, were turned to stone when they were buried under volcanic debris and minerals replaced the original wood cells. Designated a national park in 1962.
Redwood (1968)* Location: NW Calif. Area: 110,132 acres (44,569 hectares)	Magnificent stands of virgin redwood forest are the main attraction, with many of the trees more than 2,000 years old. Other features include the world's tallest tree, 367 ft (112 m) high, 40 mi (64 km) of unspoiled Pacific coastline, and seals, sea lions, and birds living offshore.
Rocky Mountain (1915)* Location: central Colo. Area: 262,191 acres (106,109 hectares)	Straddling the CONTINENTAL DIVIDE in the Front Range of the Rocky Mts., the park features more than 100 peaks towering over 11,000 ft (3,353 m). The highest is Longs Peak (14,255 ft/4,345 m). The park also contains many lakes and waterfalls.
Sequoia (1890)* Location: E Calif. Area: 402,488 acres (162,885 hectares)	Thirty-five groves of giant SEQUOIAS, the largest living things in the world, are the main attraction. Other features include MT. WHITNEY (14,494 ft/4,418 m), highest mountain in the U.S. outside Alaska, and other jagged summits of the High Sierras. Adjoins Kings Canyon National Park.
Shenandoah (1926)* Location: N Va. Area: 196,039 acres (79,334 hectares)	Extending 80 mi (129 km) along the crest of the Blue Ridge in the APPALACHIAN MOUNTAINS, the park features views from the APPALACHIAN TRAIL and Skyline Drive of the Shenandoah valley and the surrounding mountains. Heavily forested, the area was fully established as a national park in 1935.
Theodore Roosevelt (1947)* Location: W N.D. Area: 70,447 acres (28,509 hectares)	The park features scenic badlands along the Little Missouri R., part of Roosevelt's Elkhorn Ranch, prairie land, and a burning coal vein. Designated a national park in 1978.

*Date authorized

NATIONAL PARKS

Park	*Special Characteristics*
Virgin Islands (1956)* Location: Virgin Islands Area: 14,689 acres (5,944 hectares)	Occupying about two thirds of the Caribbean island of St. John, the park features quiet headlands, coves, extensive offshore areas including reefs and underwater marine gardens, palm-fringed white sandy beaches, early Carib Indian relics, and remains of Danish colonial sugar plantations.
Voyageurs (1971)* Location: N Minn. Area: 218,035 acres (88,236 hectares)	The park contains forested lake country that is noted for its sports fishing and glacial features. In the 18th cent. the region was a trade route for French-Canadian voyageurs (fur traders). Fully established as a national park in 1975.
Wind Cave (1903)* Location: SW S.D. Area: 28,295 acres (11,451 hectares)	Located in the BLACK HILLS, the park features Wind Cave, a limestone cavern containing unusual calcite crystal and boxwork formations; strong air currents blow into or out of it, depending on local atmospheric conditions. Herds of elk and bison and colonies of prairie dogs are other attractions.
Wrangell-St. Elias (1978)* Location: SE Alaska Area: 8,331,604 acres (3,371,680 hectares)	The park contains Mt. Saint Elias (18,008 ft/5,489 m) and the nation's greatest collection of glaciers and mountain peaks above 16,000 ft (4,879 m). Wildlife include Dall sheep, migrating caribou, and wolves. Designated a national park in 1980.
Yellowstone (1872)* Location: Idaho, Mont., Wyo. Area: 2,219,791 acres (898,317 hectares)	The world's greatest geyser area, the park features Old Faithful, which erupts at regular intervals, c.200 other geysers, c.10,000 hot springs, high Rocky Mt. peaks, waterfalls, lakes, the Grand Canyon of the Yellowstone R., and grizzly bears, moose, and bison. It is the oldest national park in the U.S.
Yosemite (1890)* Location: E central Calif. Area: 761,170 acres (308,035 hectares)	Located in a glacier-scoured area of great beauty in the Sierra Nevada, the park centers on famed Yosemite Valley, surrounded by cliffs and pinnacles such as El Capitan (7,564 ft/2,300 m); and Yosemite Falls, the highest in North America, with a total drop of 2,425 ft (739 m) in two stages.
Zion (1909)* Location: SW Utah Area: 146,598 acres (59,326 hectares)	The main attractions of this park, noted for its vividly colored cliffs and rock formations, are Zion Canyon, nearly half a mile deep, cut by the north fork of the Virgin R., and the box-shaped Kolob Canyons, with sheer 1,500-ft (457-m) walls. Established as a national park in 1919.

*Date authorized

tion. Favoring high tariffs and a national bank, the party nominated Henry CLAY. Clay was badly defeated, and by 1836 the National Republicans had joined with other anti-Jackson forces to form the WHIG PARTY.

National Rifle Association of America (NRA), group founded (1871) to promote shooting, hunting, firearm safety, and wildlife conservation. It has approximately 3 million members. The NRA has vigorously opposed any form of GUN CONTROL.

National Road, U.S. highway built in the early 19th cent. Begun in 1815 and completed in 1833, it was the most ambitious U.S. road-building project undertaken up to that time. When completed, it extended from Cumberland, Md., to St. Louis, and was the great highway of Western migration. The present U.S. Highway 40 follows its route closely.

National Science Foundation (NSF), independent agency (est. 1950) of the executive branch of the U.S. government, concerned with promoting a national science policy by supporting basic research and education. The NSF does not conduct its own research but provides grants and fellowships to qualified scientists and institutions. It supports the development of improved science curriculum materials and fosters the interchange of scientific ideas nationally and internationally. Among the facilities it supports are the NATIONAL RADIO ASTRONOMY OBSERVATORY, the National Center for Atmospheric Research (Boulder, Colo.), and KITT PEAK NATIONAL OBSERVATORY (Tucson, Ariz.).

National Security Agency (NSA), independent agency within the U.S. Dept. of Defense. Founded in 1952, its primary function is to encode and decode communications intelligence, and it maintains listening posts in many nations. It was long one of the most secret U.S. agencies. It is now also responsible for computer security.

National Security Council (NSC), U.S. federal executive council established (1947) to coordinate the defense and foreign policy of the U.S. Its members are the president, vice president, and secretaries of state and defense. Their statutory advisers are the chairman of the Joint Chiefs of Staff (part of the DEFENSE Dept.) and the director of the CENTRAL INTELLIGENCE AGENCY. The national security adviser (the Assistant to the President for National Security Affairs) heads the council's staff.

National Socialism or **Nazism,** doctrines and policies of the National Socialist German Workers' party, which ruled Germany under Adolf HITLER from 1933 until Germany's defeat (1945) in WORLD WAR II, at which time it was outlawed. Members were first called Nazis as a derisive abbreviation. National Socialism appealed to the masses through nationalism—especially by playing on the humiliation suffered by Germany after its defeat in WORLD WAR I—and by a particularly virulent anti-Semitism. It attracted the bankers and industrialists by its anti-Communism and by its promise to rebuild the German economy. The party began in 1920 with GOERING, GOEBBELS, and HIMMLER among Hitler's followers. Its bible was Hitler's *Mein Kampf* (1923), and its official philosopher was Alfred ROSENBERG. Among the principles of the party were the superiority of the Aryan "master race" led by an infallible Führer (leader); the establishment of a pan-Germanic "Third Reich," which would last a thousand years; and the annihilation of Germany's "greatest enemies," the Jews and Communists. After Hitler took power, the Nazis became the sole legal party. Its policy was enforced by the Gestapo (secret police), the SS (storm troops), and the SA (the Führer's elite bodyguard). During World War II, the Germans imposed their system and dogma on Europe by force. Millions of Jews, Poles, Russians, and others were interned in CONCENTRATION CAMPS and later executed. Millions more were used for forced labor. Nazism represented a barbarity unprecedented in history.

Native American art, the diverse traditional arts of the indigenous peoples of North America (see NORTH AMERICA, INDIGENOUS PEOPLES OF). These arts were a significant part of the everyday lives of their creators. In each region at least one art form was developed in response to the environment, the ideology and way of life, and the availability of materials. In all regions animal skins were worked. The cultures of the Eastern woodlands, e.g., the tribes of the IROQUOIS CONFEDERACY, made pottery, baskets, quillwork, and beadwork as well as carved wooden masks. The Plains tribes, e.g., the SIOUX, used beads and quills to paint or decorate their hides, which

MAJOR NATIVE AMERICAN LANGUAGES *(*Asterisk indicates a dead language)*

Algonquian-Wakashan Languages *(spoken in North America)*	
ALGONQUIAN	Algonquin, Arapaho, Blackfoot, Cheyenne, Cree, Delaware, Illinois, Kickapoo, Mahican, Miami, Micmac, Mohegan, Narragansett, Nootka, Ojibwa, Ottawa, Penobscot, Pequot, Sac and Fox, Shawnee, Yurok
SALISHAN	Bella Coola, Clallam, Coeur d'Alene, Colville, Nisqualli, Okanogan, Pend d'Oreille, Puyallup, Salish, Shuswap, Spokan, Tillamook
WAKASHAN	Bella Bella, Kitamat, Kwakiutl, Makah, Nootka, Nitinat
Andean-Equatorial Languages *(spoken mainly in South America)*	
ANDEAN	
Araucanian	Huilliche (or Kunko), Mapuche, Picunche
Aymara	Cana, Caranga, Lupaca, Pacasa, Ubina
Quechua (or Kechua or Quichua)	Ayachucho, Chinchaya, Cuzquẽno, Quechua, Quiteno, Tucumano
EQUATORIAL	
Arawakan	Taino* (was spoken in the Caribbean area)
Tuṕi-Guarańi	
Tupian	Tuṕi
Guaranian	Guarańi
Jívaroan	Aguaruna, Cofan, Jivaro, Palta, Yaruro
Aztec-Tanoan Languages *(spoken in W North America and Mexico)*	
UTO-AZTECAN	
Nahuatlan	Aztec,* Chichimec,* Nahuatl (or Aztec), Nahuatlato,* Pipil, Pochutla, Toltec*
Pima-Sonoran	Huichol, Pima, Tarahumare, Tohono O'Odham, Yaqui
Shoshonean	Comanche, Hopi, Paiute, Shoshone, Ute
TANOAN	Jemez, Kiowa, Taos, Tiwa, Zuñi
Eskimo-Aleut Languages *(spoken in Alaska, Canada, Greenland, and Siberia, and on the Aleutian Islands)*	
	Aleut, Eskimo
Ge-Pano-Carib Languages *(spoken in the Carribean region and South America)*	
	Bororo, Carib, Cacibo, Ge
Hokan-Siouan Languges *(spoken in North America)*	
CADDOAN	Arikara, Caddo, Pawnee, Wichita
COAHUILTECAN	Comecrudan*
HOKAN	Pomo, Seri, Shasta, Washo, Yana*
IROQUOIAN	Cayuga, Cherokee, Mohawk, Oneida, Onondaga, Seneca, Tuscarora, Wyandot (Huron)
JICAQUE	Jicaque
MUSKOGEAN	Chickasaw, Choctaw, Creek Seminole
SIOUAN	Assiniboin, Catawba, Crow, Dakota, Hidatsa, Omaha, Osage, Sioux, Winnebago
YUMAN	Cocopa, Kamia, Maricopa, Mohave, Yavapai, Yuma
Macro-Chibchan Languages *(spoken in Central and South America)*	
CHIBCHAN	Chibcha,* Paez, San Blas
Macro-Otomanguean Languages *(spoken in Mexico and Central America)*	
	Mixtecan, Otomi, Zapotecan
Nadene Languages *(spoken in W North America)*	
ATHABASCAN	Apache, Carrier, Chasta-Costa, Chipewayan, Hoopa (or Hupa), Kutchin, Navaho, Sarsi
EYAK	Eyak
HAIDA	Haida
TLINGIT	Tlingit
Penutian Languages *(spoken in W North America and Central America)*	
HUAVE	Huave
MAIDU	Maidu
MAYAN	Huastec, Maya, Quicȟe
MIXE-ZOQUE	Mixe, Zoque
SAHAPTIN-CHINOOK	Cayuse, Chinook, Modoc, Nez Percé
TOTONACAN	Totonac
TSIMSHIAN	Tsimshian
WINTUN	Nomlaki, Patwin, Wintu
YOKUT	Chauchila, Chukchansi

were used for clothing, containers, and teepees. Using stone, ivory, and bones, the ESKIMO of the Arctic carved fine sculptures of animal life. The peoples of the Northwest Coast, e.g., the KWAKIUTL, used elaborate wood-carving techniques to fabricate houses, huge canoes, and TOTEM poles. In this work human and animal figures were stylized to abstraction. The Southwest tribes had a highly developed art whose tradition went back to pre-Columbian times. An art of strong, graphic, geometric design developed for pottery decoration. The NAVAHO developed sophisticated silver-working techniques, used largely for jewelry. In recent years, works of the ever-diminishing number of North American Indian artisans have come into vogue, e.g., jewelry, ESKIMO ART, textiles, and KACHINA dolls. Museums with major collections of Native American art include the American Museum of Natural History, N.Y.C.; Field Museum of Natural Museum, Chicago; National Museum of the American Indian, Smithsonian Inst., Washington, D.C., and N.Y.C.; and National Museum of Canada, Ottawa. See also PRE-COLUMBIAN ART AND ARCHITECTURE.

Native American Church, religious cult of NAVAHO and others, blending Christian fundamentalism with peyotism, a Native American religion that began (c.1890) among KIOWA and honored PEYOTE as a sacramental food. Peyotists of many tribes founded the Native American Church in 1918. The Navaho Tribal Council banned it in 1940 as a threat to both native Navaho culture and Christianized Navahos, but the cult flourished covertly until the council relented in 1967. Up to 80% of the Navahos in the SW are now practicing members. By the 1970s some states had changed their laws to allow the religious use of peyote.

Native American languages, languages of the native peoples of the Western Hemisphere and their descendants. The classification "Native American languages" is geographical rather than linguistic, since these languages do not belong to a single linguistic family, or stock, such as the Indo-European language family. The Native American languages cannot be differentiated as a linguistic unit from other languages of the world, but are grouped into a number of separate linguistic stocks having significantly different phonetics, vocabulary, and grammars. There is no part of the world with as many distinctly different native languages as the Western Hemisphere. For a detailed categorization of Native American languages, in alphabetical order and with geographical location indicated, see the table accompanying this article.

Native Americans: see NORTH AMERICA, INDIGENOUS PEOPLES OF; MIDDLE AMERICA, INDIGENOUS PEOPLES OF; SOUTH AMERICA, INDIGENOUS PEOPLES OF; and individual peoples.

NATO: see NORTH ATLANTIC TREATY ORGANIZATION.

natural childbirth: see under PREGNANCY AND BIRTH.

natural gas, natural mixture of flammable gases found issuing from the ground or obtained from specially driven wells. Largely a mixture of HYDROCARBONS, natural gas is usually 80 to 95% METHANE. The composition varies in different localities, and minor components may include carbon dioxide, nitrogen, hydrogen, carbon monoxide, and helium. Often found with PETROLEUM, natural gas also occurs apart from it in sand, sandstone, and limestone deposits. Natural gas began to be used as an illuminant and a fuel on a large scale in the late 19th cent., when pipelines were built to provide it to large industrial cities. It has also been used on a small scale in recent years as an alternative fuel for automobiles and other vehicles. **Liquified natural gas** (LNG) is natural gas that has been cooled and pressurized to liquify it for convenience in shipping and storage.

naturalism, in literature, an approach to reality grounded in a belief in the determining power of natural forces like heredity and environment. Émile ZOLA, the founder and chief exemplar of the school, theorized in *The Experimental Novel* (1880) that the novelist should observe and record dispassionately, like the scientist. Besides Zola and Guy de MAUPASSANT in France, naturalism included the American novelists Stephen CRANE, Theodore DREISER, and James T. FARRELL, and such modern dramatists as Henrik IBSEN, Gerhart HAUPTMANN, and Maxim GORKY.

naturalism, in philosophy, a position that attempts to explain all phenomena by means of strictly natural (as opposed to supernatural) categories. Generally considered the opposite of IDEALISM, naturalism looks for causes and takes little account of reasons. It is often equated with MATERIALISM, POSITIVISM, and EMPIRICISM. Some naturalists (e.g., COMTE, NIETZSCHE, and MARX) have professed ATHEISM, while others (e.g., ARISTOTLE, SPINOZA, and William JAMES) have accepted some form of a deity. Later thinkers such as WHITEHEAD have sought to unify the scientific viewpoint with the concept of an all-encompassing reality.

natural law, theory that some laws are fundamental to human nature and discoverable by human reason without reference to specific legislative acts or judicial decisions. It is opposed so-called positive law, which is customary or legislated and is conditioned by history and subject to continuous change. ROMAN LAW, drawing on theories of Greek STOICISM, recognized a common cause regulating human conduct; this was the basis for the later development by GROTIUS of the theory of international law. St. THOMAS AQUINAS, SPINOZA, and LEIBNIZ all interpreted natural law as the basis of ethics and morality. J.J. ROUSSEAU regarded it as the basis of democratic principles. The influence of natural law declined greatly in the 19th cent. under the impact of POSITIVISM, EMPIRICISM, and MATERIALISM, but regained importance in the 20th cent. as a corrective to totalitarian theory.

natural selection, important mechanism in Charles DARWIN's theory of EVOLUTION. As a result of various factors in the environment (e.g., temperature and the quantity of food and water available) and the geometrically increasing overproduction of plants and animals that results from the process of reproduction, a struggle for existence arises. In this struggle, according to Darwin, those organisms better adapted to the environment (that is, those having favorable differences or variations) survive and reproduce, while those least fitted do not. Favorable variations among members of the same species are thus transmitted to the survivors' offspring and spread to the entire species over successive generations. Natural selection suggests that the origin and diversification of species results from the gradual accumulation of individual modifications. Artificial selection, the selection by humans of individuals best suited for a specific purpose, is common in plant and animal breeding.

Nature Conservancy, nonprofit organization established in 1951 to preserve or aid in the preservation of natural environments. It protects wilderness areas in the U.S. and Canada and is affiliated with similar groups in Latin America and the Caribbean. It maintains the world's largest private system of nature sanctuaries.

Nauru, officially Republic of Nauru, independent nation (1992 est. pop. 9,500), c.8 sq mi (20 sq km), atoll in the Pacific Ocean near the equator. One of the world's smallest nations, it has an economy almost entirely dependent on phosphate mining, but the deposits are expected to be exhausted by the year 2000. The government has attempted to develop airline and shipping businesses, and mining income has been invested overseas with some success. Nauruans (nearly 60% of the population) are predominantly Polynesian with a mix of Micronesian and Melanesian strains. There is a large Pacific Islander minority and smaller groups of Chinese and Europeans. Nearly all the inhabitants are Christians. The official language is Nauruan, but English is commonly used in government and commerce. Nauru was discovered and named Pleasant Island by the British in 1798. It was annexed by Germany in 1888 and returned to its original name of Nauru. Occupied by Australia in World War I, it was administered by Australia until granted independence in 1968. In 1993 Australia agreed to pay Nauru $73 million for environmental damage caused by mining before independence. Nauru is a parliamentary republic with a president elected by the legislature. See PACIFIC OCEAN map.

nautilus, mollusk with a spirally coiled shell consisting of a series of chambers; as the nautilus grows, it builds larger chambers, sealing off the old ones. A CEPHALOPOD, the animal lives in the largest and newest chamber, breathing by means of gills and feeding on crabs and other animals it catches with long, slender tentacles. Nautiluses are found in deep waters of the S Pacific and Indian oceans. The PAPER NAUTILUS, which is not a true nautilus, is related to the OCTOPUS.

Navaho or **Navajo** [nä'vəhō], indigenous people of the Southwest (see NORTH AMERICA, INDIGENOUS PEOPLES OF) with an Athabascan language of the Nadene stock (see NATIVE AMERICAN LANGUAGES). Thought to have migrated from the north, the nomadic Navaho assimilated with the Shoshone and Yuma, but remained a distinct social group with over 50 clans. They farmed, hunted, and gathered plants, but became primarily pastoral after sheep were introduced in the 17th cent. Matrilineal, they have elaborate ceremonies and myths; many practice peyotism (see NATIVE AMERICAN CHURCH). Navaho metalworking, as in silver jewelry, and weaving are famous. The Navaho raided the PUEBLO and Spanish settlements in New Mexico until Kit CARSON subdued them (1863–64) by killing their sheep. In 1868, c.9,000 Navaho were given a reservation that has since grown to 16 million acres in Arizona, New Mexico, and Utah, today sustaining such enterprises as lumber, mining, and farming. Navaho-owned enterprises are growing, including the largest Native American newspaper in the U.S. and Navaho Community College, the first Native American–operated college. With a population of 219,198 in 1990, the Navaho constitute the second largest tribe in the U.S.

Navaho or **Navajo,** language belonging to the Athabascan branch of the Nadene linguistic family of North America. See NATIVE AMERICAN LANGUAGES (table).

naval conferences, series of international assemblies that met to consider the limitation of naval armaments, the rules of naval war, and other matters relating to peace. **1 London Naval Conference** (1908–9), see LONDON, DECLARATION OF. **2 Washington Conference** (1921–22), called by Pres. HARDING after WORLD WAR I, resulted in several treaties. The Five-Power Treaty (U.S., Great Britain, France, Italy, Japan) called for the scrapping of a number of ships so that an agreed-upon ratio could be reached. With the Four-Power Treaty (U.S., France, Japan, Great Britain) the signatories agreed to respect each others' possessions in the Pacific. Another treaty outlawed the use of poison gas in warfare. **3 Geneva Conference** (1927) failed to reach agreement on more comprehensive limitations on warships. **4 London Conference** (1930) saw Japan succeed in raising its ratios of warships, although France and Italy objected. Also agreed upon was an escalator clause allowing the powers to raise the number of their ships where national security was threatened. **5 London Conference** (1935) was called after Japan announced (1934) that it was withdrawing from the Washington Conference treaties. Despite this, the other powers continued to limit their warships until the outbreak of WORLD WAR II in 1939.

Navarino, battle of, Sept. 1827, naval engagement in the Greek War of Independence. It resulted from the refusal of the OTTOMAN EMPIRE (Turkey) to accept the armistice demanded by the European powers (Britain, France, and Russia). Turkey's ally Egypt had a fleet anchored at Plyos (then Navarino); it was destroyed by the fleet of the European powers. The defeat led Egypt to leave (1828) the war.

Navarre, Span. *Navarra,* autonomous region and province (1989 est. pop. 524,000), N Spain, bordered by France, between the W Pyrenees and the Ebro R. Pamplona is the capital. Navarre's mountain slopes provide cattle pastures and yield hardwoods, and its fertile valleys produce sugar beets, grains, vegetables, and grapes. Manufactures include processed food and metal products. The population is mainly of BASQUE stock. The kingdom of Navarre reached its zenith under Sancho III (r.1000–1035), who ruled most of Christian Spain. Much reduced in area, it came under French rule (1305–28) and regained importance in the HUNDRED YEARS WAR under CHARLES II (r.1349–87). Most of Navarre was annexed (1515) by Spanish king FERDINAND V. Lower Navarre, N of the Pyrenees, remained an independent kingdom until annexed (1589) by France.

navigation, science and technology of finding the position, and directing the course, of vessels and aircraft. In ancient times navigation was based on observing landmarks along the coast and the positions of the sun and the stars. A tremendous advance took place with the introduction (c.12th cent.) of the COMPASS into Europe. Instruments used to find latitude in medieval times included the ASTROLABE, the cross-staff, and the quadrant. The problem of finding the longitude, however, was not satisfactorily solved until the 18th-cent. inventions of the CHRONOMETER and the SEXTANT and the appearance (1765) of the British *Nautical Almanac.* The next great revolution in navigation occurred in the 20th cent., when radio signals came into wide use. The development of RADAR, LORAN, and radio direction-finding during World War II and, subsequently, of NAVIGATION SATELLITES caused fundamental changes in navigational practice. Inertial guidance systems, used in submarines, aircraft, and spacecraft, do not require contact with a ground base. A computer navigates the vehicle, using a gyroscope to indicate direction and an accelerometer to measure changes in speed and direction. See AIR NAVIGATION.

Navigation Acts, in English history, name given to the British Acts of Trade. An outgrowth of MERCANTILISM, the acts were designed to expand the English carrying trade, to provide England with raw materials, and to develop colonial markets for English manufactures. The threat to English shipping posed by the Dutch led to the Navigation Act of 1651. This legislation was substantially reenacted in the First Navigation Act of 1660, which gave England monopolies of certain colonial produce. In 1663 shipment from English ports was required of all foreign goods bound for the American colonies. The Molasses Act of 1733 forced colonists to buy more expensive British West Indian sugar and led to an increase in smuggling. The acts also caused colonial unrest prior to the AMERICAN REVOLUTION. Their adverse effects were felt in Ireland, in Scotland (before 1707), and in the Channel Islands, which did not share England's favored position. The acts were repealed in 1849.

navigation satellite, artificial SATELLITE designed expressly to aid navigation at sea, in the air, and on land. Two major navigational satellite systems have been launched into orbit, both by the U.S. In the Transit system (first launch, 1960), a navigator determines a ship's position by measuring the Doppler shift (see DOPPLER EFFECT) in radio signals from a Transit satellite passing overhead. In the NAVSTAR Global Positioning System (GPS), which had its first launch in 1989 and replaces the Transit system, each satellite broadcasts time and position messages continuously. A total of 24 NAVSTAR satellites are used. Precise to within a few feet for military uses and about 300 ft (90 m) for non-military uses, the GPS can also be used for non-navigation purposes, such as surveying, tracking migrating animals, and plotting the crop yields of small sections of farmland.

Navratilova, Martina, 1956–, Czech-American tennis player; b. Prague. After holding the Czech singles title (1972–74), she defected (1975) to the U.S. Known for her aggressive style, Navratilova has won more professional tennis titles (165) than any other player. From 1978 to 1987 she won the Wimbledon tournament eight times, the U.S. Open four times, the Australian Open three times, and the French Open twice; she also dominated women's doubles competition. In 1990 she won Wimbledon for the ninth time, a record.

Nazarenes, group of early 19th-cent. German artists who attempted to revive Christian art. Known as the Brotherhood of St. Luke, they worked in an unused monastery in Rome. They used early Italian and medieval German pictures as models, working within the limits of religious dogma. They influenced German art and the PRE-RAPHAELITES in England.

Nazareth, town (1989 est. pop. 51,000), N Israel, in Galilee, the home of JESUS. It is a place of pilgrimage and the trade center of a farming area. Although first mentioned in the New Testament, it predates historic times. Part of the Ottoman Empire (1517–1918), and of Britain's Palestine mandate (1922–48), Nazareth has been held by Israel since 1948.

Nazarite or **Nazirite,** in the OLD TESTAMENT, a man dedicated to God. After taking a special vow, he abstained from intoxicating beverages, never cut his hair, and avoided corpses. SAMUEL, the prophet, and SAMSON were Nazarites.

Nazca or **Nasca,** ancient indigenous culture of S Peru, fl. before A.D. 1000. The Nazca are known for their polychrome pottery and skillful weaving and dyeing. Aerial exploration of the arid tableland surrounding their valley has revealed a network of lines interspersed with giant animal forms—probably related to Nazca astronomy and religion.

Nazi, term for member of the National Socialist German Workers' party. Led by Adolf HITLER after 1920, the Nazis advocated rabid NATIONALISM, ANTI-SEMITISM, and anti-Communism. Their rule (1933–45) in GERMANY ended in defeat during WORLD WAR II. See NATIONAL SOCIALISM; see also CONCENTRATION CAMP; WAR CRIMES.

Nazianzen: see GREGORY NAZIANZEN, SAINT.

Nazimova, Alla [nəzĭ'məvə], 1879–1945, Russian-American actress. A student of STANISLAVSKY, she emigrated to the U.S. (1905), becoming its foremost IBSEN interpreter.

Nb, chemical symbol of the element NIOBIUM.

Nd, chemical symbol of the element NEODYMIUM.

Ndebele or **Matabele,** Bantu-speaking people inhabiting North and South Matabeleland, W Zimbabwe. The Ndebele originated as a tribal following in 1823 when Mzilikazi, a general under the ZULU King Shaka, fled with a number of warriors into the Transvaal; they were driven north into their present homeland by the BOERS and the Zulu. After the British suppressed an 1896 revolt, the Ndebele abandoned warfare, becoming herders and farmers. They number about 2 million.

Ndjamena [ənjä'mānä], city (1988 est. pop. 595,000), capital of Chad, on the Chari R. The city is a central African transportation hub, Chad's main administrative center, and a market for livestock, salt, dates, and grains. Founded by the French as Fort-Lamy in 1900, it was renamed in 1973.

Ndola, city (1988 est. pop. 418,000), N central Zambia, near Zaïre. It is a commercial, manufacturing, and mining center located in the rich Copperbelt, where copper was mined long before the coming of the Europeans (c.1900). Industries include cement, footwear, soap, and motor vehicle assembly.

Ne, chemical symbol of the element NEON.

Neanderthal man or **Neandertal man,** type of early human, existing 125,000–35,000 years ago and generally considered a subspecies of *Homo sapiens* (see HUMAN EVOLUTION), whose fossil remains were first found (1856) in Neanderthal, W Germany. The Neanderthals' middle Paleolithic culture (see STONE AGE) included stone tools, fire, burial, and cave shelters. The so-called classic Neanderthals were robust and had a large, thick skull, a sloping forehead, a chinless jaw, and a brain somewhat larger than that of modern humans; they stood slightly over 5 ft (152 cm). It is unclear whether Neanderthals were replaced by *Homo sapiens sapiens* or interbred with other early humans.

nearsightedness or **myopia,** defect of vision in which far objects appear blurred, but near objects are seen clearly. Because the eyeball is too long or the eye's refractive power too strong, the image is focused in front of the retina of the EYE rather than upon it. Eyeglasses with concave lenses can compensate for the refractive error (see LENS). Radial keratotomy, a surgical procedure, can repair the defect by flattening the eye, but it weakens the cornea.

Nebraska, midwestern state of the U.S.; bordered by Iowa and Missouri, across the Missouri R. (E), Kansas (S), Colorado (SW), Wyoming (NW), and South Dakota (N).

Area, 77,227 sq mi (200,018 sq km). *Pop.* (1990) 1,578,385, a 0.5% increase over 1980 pop. *Capital,* Lincoln. *Statehood,* Mar. 1, 1867 (37th state). *Highest pt.,* 5,426 ft (1,655 m), Kimball Co.; *lowest pt.,* 840 ft (256 m), SE corner of state. *Nickname,* Cornhusker State. *Motto,* Equality before the Law. *State bird,* Western meadowlark. *State flower,* goldenrod. *State tree,* cottonwood. *Abbr.,* Nebr.; NE.

Land and People. The land gradually rises east to west from the fertile, loess-covered GREAT PLAINS to the sand hills and then to the foothills of the ROCKY MOUNTAINS. The great, shallow Platte R. originates in Nebraska and flows west to east across the state to join the MISSOURI R. The continental climate is marked by intensely hot summers and severely cold winters. Over 65% of the population lives in metropolitan areas. OMAHA is the largest city, followed by LINCOLN and Grand Island. In 1990 the state was 94% white and 4% African American.

Economy. Agriculture is by far the chief source of income. The leading products are cattle, corn, hogs, soybeans, wheat, hay, and sorghum. The major industry, food processing, utilizes the state's farm output. It is followed in terms of revenue by the manufacturing of nonelectrical machinery and electrical equipment. Mining is dominated by petroleum and natural-gas extraction. Both Omaha and Lincoln are centers of the insurance industry.

Government. The state constitution (adopted 1875) provides for a governor elected to a four-year term. Nebraska is the only state with a unicameral legislature; 49 nonpartisan members are elected every four years. Nebraska is represented in the U.S. Congress by two senators and three representatives and has five electoral votes.

History. The PAWNEE, CHEYENNE, ARAPAHO, and SIOUX were among the Native American peoples that lived by hunting buffalo when the area was visited (1541) by the Spanish explorer Francisco Vásquez de CORONADO. The fur trade had been established by the French by the time the U.S. acquired the region by the LOUISIANA PURCHASE (1803). During the mid-19th cent. thousands of wagon trains passed through Nebraska on their way farther west, and the famous landmarks of Chimney Rock and Scotts Bluff are now both preserved as parts of the U.S. National Parks system. The HOMESTEAD ACT (1862) and the arrival (1867) of the railroad resulted in a land rush as settlers occupied the free land. Nebraska farmers were active in the POPULIST PARTY of the 1890s, and William Jennings BRYAN, a Nebraskan, became the national leader of both Populists and Democrats. Nebraska farmers were severely affected by drought during the GREAT DEPRESSION. Since World War II, such huge federal projects as the Missouri R. basin project have helped to make the best use of the state's water resources, particularly for crop irrigation. The state's economy remained strong, with relatively low unemployment, during the national economic difficulties of the late 1980s and early 90s. Nebraska has successfully diversified its economy by encouraging the growth of the service sector, particularly in its largest cities.

Nebuchadnezzar [nĕb"əkədnĕz'ər], d. 562 B.C., king of BABYLONIA (c.605–562 B.C.). In 597 B.C. he quelled a revolt by Judaea and set ZEDEKIAH on the throne. Putting down a new revolt, he destroyed Jerusalem (586 B.C.) and took the king and many nobles captive, thus beginning the BABYLONIAN CAPTIVITY. Under Nebuchadnezzar Babylonia flourished, and BABYLON became magnificent. His palace and temples have been excavated. The Old Testament book of Daniel depicts Nebuchadnezzar as a conceited and domineering king, and tells of his going mad and eating grass.

nebula, immense body of highly rarified gas and dust in the interstellar spaces of galaxies. A diffuse nebula, such as the CRAB NEBULA, is irregular in shape and ranges up to 100 light-years in diameter. A bright emission nebula, composed primarily of hydrogen gas ionized by nearby hot blue-white stars, radiates its own light; a bright reflection nebula, located near cooler stars, reflects the starlight. A dark nebula, which neither emits nor reflects light because it is too distant from any star, appears as an empty patch in a field of stars or as a dark cloud obscuring part of a bright nebula in the background. A planetary nebula consists of a well-defined shell of gaseous material that glows from the radiation emitted by the central hot star it surrounds. The shell, measuring about 20,000 ASTRONOMICAL UNITS in diameter, is slowly expanding, indicating that it was expelled in a nova or SUPERNOVA explosion.

Necho [nē'kō], pharaoh (609–593 B.C.) of EGYPT, of the XXVI dynasty. In the first part of his reign he invaded PALESTINE and SYRIA; his aim was to aid the Assyrians, who were besieged by NEBUCHADNEZZAR and the Babylonians. Defeated on the Euphrates in 605, he returned to Egypt. He later tried to reexcavate the Nile–Red Sea canal and sent Phoenicians on an expedition that may have circumnavigated Africa.

Necker, Jacques [nĕkĕr'], 1732–1804, French financier and statesman; b. Switzerland. In 1750 he went to Paris and became a banker. He opposed the free trade policies of A.R.J. TURGOT, was named director of the treasury (1776) by LOUIS XVI, and later became director general of finances (1777). By reform and retrenchment measures, and by borrowing at high interest to finance French involvement in the AMERICAN REVOLUTION, he sought to restore the nation's finances. In 1781 he demanded greater reform powers, but opposition from the comte de Maurepas caused Necker to resign. Louis XVI recalled him (1788) as director general of finances and minister of state. Acclaimed by the populace, he supported the summoning of the STATES-GENERAL to effect reforms. His dismissal (1789) led to the storming of the BASTILLE. Necker was once more recalled to office, but he resigned in 1790.

nectarine, name for a tree (*Prunus persica nectarina*) of the ROSE family and for its fruit, a smooth-skinned variety of the PEACH. In appearance, culture, and care the nectarine tree is almost identical to the peach tree. Occasionally a nectarine tree will produce peaches and a peach tree nectarines.

Nefertiti [nĕf"ərtē'tē] or **Nefretete** [nĕf"rĕtē'tē], fl. c.1372–1350 B.C., queen of EGYPT; wife of IKHNATON and aunt of TUTANKHAMEN. The famous and exquisite limestone bust of Nefertiti is in the Berlin Museum.

Negev or **Negeb,** hilly desert region of S Israel, c.5,140 sq mi (13,310 sq km), bordered by the Judaean Hills, the Wadi Arabah, the Sinai peninsula, and the narrow Mediterranean coastal plain; it comprises more than one half of Israel's land area. In the NW Negev, irrigation by the Israelis has reclaimed some fertile land. The region also yields copper, phosphates, and natural gas. BEERSHEBA, Arad, and ELAT are the Negev's principal cities. Israel's nuclear research center is at Dimona.

negligence, failure to act with the care required by law to protect the rights and property of others. Unless more specifically defined by the terms of a CONTRACT, "care" is the behavior of a "reasonable, prudent" person. Negligence takes innumerable forms, and negligence claims, many involving vehicular accidents, are the chief sources of current civil litigation in the U.S. See also TORT.

negotiable instrument, bill of exchange, check, promissory note, or other written CONTRACT for payment that may serve as a substitute for money. Transfer of negotiable instruments is easily accomplished and gives the holder of the contract the right to enforce fulfillment. Like COMMERCIAL PAPER, they were developed to meet the needs of trade.

Negro: see RACE.

Negroid: see RACE.

Nehemiah, book of the Bible: see EZRA.

Nehru, Jawaharlal, 1889–1964, Indian statesman, first prime minister of INDIA (1947–64). He was educated at Harrow and Cambridge, and practiced law. After the British massacre of Indian nationalists at Amritsar (1919) he became a nationalist. He was a leader of the INDIAN NATIONAL CONGRESS and an associate of GANDHI, although unlike Gandhi he favored industrialization and socialism. He participated in the negotiations that created an independent India in 1947 and served as its prime minister until his death. Although an advocate of nonviolence and neutralism in foreign affairs, he did not hesitate to employ force in opposing Pakistan in Kashmir, in seizing (1961) Goa from the Portuguese, and in resisting (1962) Chinese border incursions. He was the father of Indira GANDHI.

Nelson, Horatio Nelson, Viscount, 1758–1805, English naval hero of the FRENCH REVOLUTIONARY WARS. His destruction of the French fleet at Aboukir crippled NAPOLEON I's Egyptian expedition. Later stationed at Naples, Nelson fell in love with Lady HAMILTON, who became his mistress; he was suspected of prolonging his stay on her account. In 1801, Nelson defeated the Danes at Copenhagen. In 1805 he achieved his greatest victory, defeating the combined fleets of France and Spain at TRAFALGAR, but was mortally wounded.

nematode, member of a phylum (Nematoda) that comprises the roundworms. Nematodes live in the water or soil. Many species, such as pinworms and HOOKWORMS, are parasites of plants and animals, including humans. Some parasitic nematodes are used as biological pesticides to control insect pests.

Nemerov, Howard, 1920–91, American writer; b. N.Y.C. His poetry ranges from light to philosophical in such works as *Image and the Law* (1947) and *Collected Poems* (1977; Pulitzer). Nemerov also wrote fiction and criticism.

Nemesis, in Greek religion, the avenger; personification of the gods' retribution for violation of sacred law.

Nemirovich-Danchenko, Vladimir [nāmērō'vĭch-dän' chĕngkō], 1859–1943, Russian stage director. With STANISLAVSKY he founded (1897) the Moscow Art Theatre (see THEATER, table).

neoclassicism: see CLASSICISM.

neodymium (Nd), metallic element, discovered in 1885 by C.A. von Welsbach. A lustrous, silver-yellow RARE-EARTH METAL in the LANTHANIDE SERIES, it is present in MONAZITE and bastnasite. Neodymium is used in the manufacture of certain lasers. Its oxide is used in coloring eyeglasses and in an alloy in cigarette-lighter flints. See ELEMENT (table); PERIODIC TABLE.

neoexpressionism, international art movement that originated in the late 1970s and early 80s. Drawing on the traditions of 20th-cent. EXPRESSIONISM and rejecting a sleek modernism and the depersonalization of such movements as MINIMALISM, neoexpressionism is characterized by violent and often erotic subject matter, an ironic use of kitsch imagery, drawing that is often crude and childlike, and a vigorous painting style. Among the many artists in this varied and individualistic movement are: in the U.S., Julian Schnabel and David Salle; in Italy, Francesco Clemente and Sandro Chia; and in Germany, A.R. Penck and Georg Baselitz.

neo-impressionism: see POSTIMPRESSIONISM.

Neolithic period: see under STONE AGE.

neon (Ne), gaseous element, discovered in 1898 by William RAMSAY and M.W. Travers. A colorless, odorless, and tasteless INERT GAS, it emits a bright-red glow when conducting electricity in a tube. Neon is used in advertising signs, LASERS, Geiger counters, PARTICLE DETECTORS, and high-intensity beacons. Liquid neon is a cryogenic refrigerant. See ELEMENT (table); PERIODIC TABLE.

Neopaganism, polytheistic religious movement, practiced in small groups by partisans of pre-Christian religious traditions, e.g., Egyptian, Greek, Norse, Celtic. Neopagans are either nature-oriented or magical, and often incorporate elaborate, arcane rituals into their practices. See also WITCHCRAFT.

Neoplatonism, ancient mystical philosophy based on the later doctrines of PLATO, especially those in the *Timaeus.* Considered the last of the great pagan philosophies, it was developed in the 3d cent. A.D. by PLOTINUS. Rejecting DUALISM, he saw reality as one vast hierarchical order containing all the various levels and kinds of existence. At the center is the One, an incomprehensible, all-sufficient unity that flows out in a radiating process called emanation, giving rise to the Divine Mind, or Logos. The Logos contains all intelligent forms of all individuals. This in turn generates the World Soul, which links the intellectual and material worlds. Despite his mysticism, Plotinus' method was thoroughly rational, based on the logical traditions of the Greeks. Later Neoplatonists grafted onto its body such disparate elements as Eastern mysticism, divination, demonology, and astrology. Neoplatonism, widespread until the 7th cent., was an influence on early Christian thinkers (e.g., ORIGEN) and medieval Jewish and Arab philosophers. It was firmly joined with Christianity by St. AUGUSTINE, who was a Neoplatonist before his conversion. Neoplatonism has had a lasting influence on Western metaphysics and MYSTICISM. Philosophers whose works contain elements of Neoplatonism include St. THOMAS AQUINAS, BOETHIUS, and HEGEL.

NEP: see NEW ECONOMIC POLICY.

Nepal, officially Kingdom of Nepal, independent kingdom (1992 est. pop. 20,086,000), c.54,000 sq mi (139,860 sq km), central Asia, bordered by China (N) and India (W, S, E). Nepal comprises three major areas: forests and cultivatable land in the south; the towering HIMALAYAS, including Mt. EVEREST, in the north; and moderately high mountains in the central region, which contains the Katmandu valley and most of the population. The capital is KATMANDU. The economy is predominantly agricultural. Rice, corn, wheat, millet, jute, timber, and potatoes are the principal products. Livestock raising is also important, and manufactures include textiles and processed foods. Tourism is a major source of foreign income. The population is a mixture of Indo-Aryan, Tibetan, and other peoples; about 90% of the total are Hindus. Nepali, an Indo-European tongue, is the official language, but there are some 20 Nepalese languages.

History. A Hindu-Buddhist culture flourished in the Katmandu valley by the 4th cent. A.D. In the Middle Ages many small principalities were established. One of these, the GURKHAS, became dominant in 1768. In 1816, after a war with the British, Nepal adopted a policy of seclusion from foreign contacts. Internal power struggles led in 1846 to the dominance of the Rana family, which controlled the country until 1951. Under the Ranas, Nepal was isolated from foreign influence, and there was little economic modernization. Nepal was granted independence in 1923, and a limited constitutional monarchy was established in 1951. After a brief period of democracy (1959–60), political activity was banned. A form of partyless government, the panchayat system, was set up (1962), with executive power resting in the king. This system was narrowly approved (1980) in a national referendum. In 1990 protests led to the abolition of the panchayat system and the reestablishment of democracy and a constitutional monarchy. In the sub-

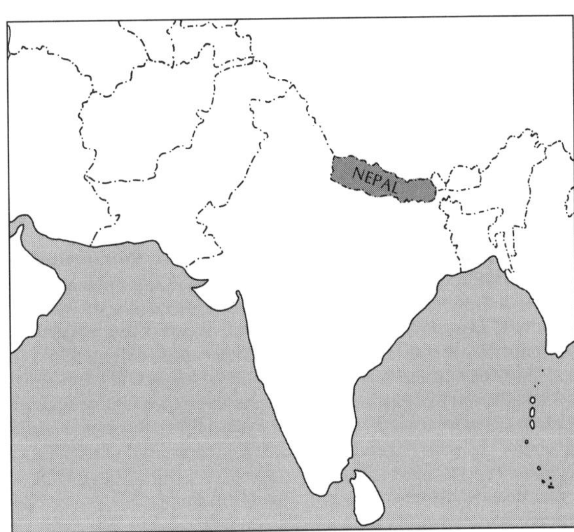

sequent elections (1991) the centrist Nepali Congress party won a slim majority in the new parliament, and Girija Prasad Koirala became prime minister. Long influenced by India, Nepal has recently developed closer ties with China.

nephrite: see JADE.

nephritis: see under KIDNEY.

nephrosis: see KIDNEY.

Neptune, in astronomy, 8th PLANET from the sun, at a mean distance of 2.7941 billion mi (4.4966 billion km); PLUTO is closer to the sun from 1978 to 2000, however, due to its highly elliptical orbit. It has an equatorial diameter of c.30,700 mi (49,400 km), a solid core, and a thick atmosphere composed of hydrogen, helium, methane, and ammonia. Its atmosphere has zones like Jupiter's and a giant storm (the Great Dark Spot). Neptune was the first planet to be discovered on the basis of theoretical calculations; such calculations, based on the observed irregularities in the motion of the planet URANUS, were made independently by John Couch ADAMS and Urbain LEVERRIER. The German astronomer Johann Galle discovered Neptune on Sept. 23, 1846, within 1° of the position predicted and sent to him by Leverrier. Neptune had two known natural satellites prior to 1989: **Triton** (discovered 1846) has a diameter of 1,700 mi (2,700 km), travels in an unusual retrograde orbit, and has several active "geysers" of nitrogen ice and gas; **Nereid** (discovered 1949) has an estimated diameter of 145 to 290 mi (235 to 470 km). The *Voyager 2* SPACE PROBE encountered Neptune in 1989, discovering six smaller, dark moons (Naiad, Thalassa, Despina, Galatea, Larissa, and Proteus) and confirming the existence of a ring system with three major bands.

Neptune, in Roman mythology, god of water. Probably an indigenous fertility god, he was later identified with POSEIDON, the Greek god of the sea.

neptunium (Np), radioactive element, discovered in 1940 by E.M. McMillan and P.H. Abelson by neutron bombardment of uranium. It is a silvery metal in the ACTINIDE SERIES and is the first TRANSURANIUM ELEMENT. Neptunium is found in very small quantities in nature in association with uranium ores. The neptunium-237 isotope has a half-life of 2 million years. See ELEMENT (table); PERIODIC TABLE.

Nereid, in astronomy, natural satellite of NEPTUNE.

nereids: see NYMPH.

Nero (Nero Claudius Caesar), A.D. 37–68, Roman emperor (A.D. 54–68), the son of Lucius Domitius Ahenobarbus and Agrippina II, who was the great-grandaughter of AUGUSTUS. Agrippina married (A.D. 49) CLAUDIUS I and persuaded him to adopt Nero. In A.D. 55, Agrippina saw that she was losing control of Nero and intrigued in favor of Claudius' son, Britannicus, but Nero poisoned the boy. Poppaea Sabina became Nero's mistress, and according to rumor she was to blame for the worst of his behavior. In A.D. 59 he murdered his mother and in A.D. 62 his wife Octavia; he later married Poppaea. When half of Rome was burned in a fire (A.D. 64), Nero accused the Christians of starting it and began the first Roman persecution. In A.D. 65 there was a plot to make Caius Calpurnius Piso emperor. The detection of this plot began a string of violent deaths, e.g., of Seneca, Lucan, and Thrasea Paetus. Nero had ambitions to be a poet and artist. Revolts in A.D. 68 caused him to commit suicide. Among his last words were, "What an artist the world is losing in me!"

Neruda, Jan [nĕ'ro͝odä], 1834–91, Czech poet. His *Stories from Malá Strana* (1878) typify early Czech realism. His lyrical poetry, resembling that of HEINE, is contained in *Ballads and Romances* and *Plain Themes* (both: 1883).

Neruda, Pablo [närō͞o'thä], 1904–73, pseud. of **Neftalí Ricardo Reyes Basualto,** Chilean poet, diplomat, and Communist leader. From the publication of the early *Twenty Love Poems and One Song of Despair* (1924) his highly personal poetry brought him enormous acclaim. His evocative poems, filled with grief and despair, proclaim the dramatic Chilean landscape and rage against the exploitation of its indigenous people. Subsequent volumes include the surrealistic *Residence on Earth* (1933), the famous *Canto general* (1950) celebrating all of Latin America, and *A New Decade: 1958–1967* (tr. 1969). Neruda received the 1971 Nobel Prize for literature while serving as ambassador to France.

nerve: see NERVOUS SYSTEM.

nerve gas: see POISON GAS.

Nervi, Pier Luigi, 1891–1979, Italian architectural engineer. In the mid-1940s he developed *ferro-cemento,* a strong, light material consisting of steel mesh and concrete that enabled him to achieve complicated building units for vast, complex structures. His innovations made possible such intricate, beautiful buildings as the exposition halls in Turin (1949–50) and the Olympic buildings in Rome (1956–59).

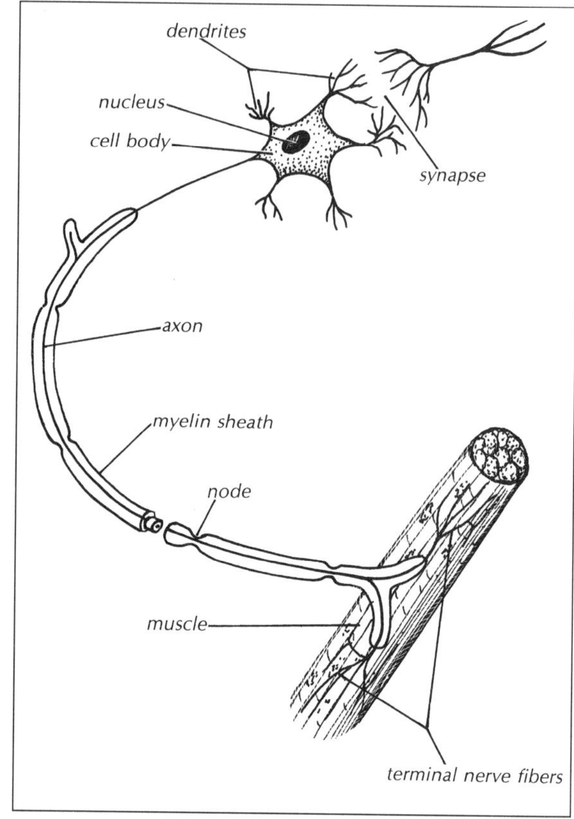

Nerve cell (neuron)

nervous system, network of specialized tissue that controls actions and reactions of the body, enabling it to adjust to its environment. The system functions by receiving signals from all parts of the body, relaying them to the BRAIN and SPINAL CORD, and then sending appropriate return signals to muscles and body organs. Virtually all multicellular animals have at least a rudimentary nervous system; in vertebrates the system is most complex. The basic unit of the nervous system is the nerve cell (neuron). Of the billions of neurons in humans, half are in the brain. The neuron consists of a cell body, containing the cell nucleus; dendrites, branchlike extensions that receive incoming signals; and the axon, the long cell extension that carries signals long distances. A neuron works by receiving chemical signals—some excitatory, some inhibitory—through its dendrites and sending electrical impulses along its axon. Chemicals (NEUROTRANSMITTERS) released at the terminal fibers of the axon diffuse across a junction called the synapse and bind to dendrites of recipient neurons. Dendrites and axons are called nerve fibers; a nerve is a bundle of nerve fibers. The nervous system has two divisions: the central nervous system and peripheral nervous system. The central nervous system, consisting of the brain and spinal cord, receives impulses from receptors in the skin and organs via sensory (afferent) nerve fibers; it returns impulses via motor (efferent) fibers to terminals in muscles and glands. Peripheral nerves mediate these pathways. The peripheral nervous system comprises cranial nerves, controlling face and neck; spinal nerves, radiating to other parts of the body; and autonomic nerves, which form a subsidiary system regulating the iris of the eye and muscles of heart, glands, lungs, stomach, and other visceral organs. The autonomic nervous system, in turn, comprises the sympathetic nervous system, which functions in response to short-term stress (e.g., increasing heart rate), and the parasympathetic nervous system, which acts in opposition to the sympathetic (e.g., lowering heart rate).

Ness, Loch, lake, 22 mi (35 km) long, N central Scotland, part of the Caledonian Canal. Ice-free all year and more than 700 ft (213 m) deep, it was first reported to be inhabited by a "monster," 40–50 ft (12–15 m) long, in newspaper accounts of 1868. Several alleged sightings have occurred since then.

Nestorianism, 5th-cent. heresy advanced by Nestorius (d. 451?), patriarch of Constantinople. It declared that Jesus was two distinct persons, one human, one divine. Nestorius opposed the title of Mother of God for the Virgin, contending that she bore Jesus only as a man. The councils of Ephesus (431) and Chalcedon (451) clarified the orthodox Catholic view that Jesus' two natures are inseparably joined in one person and partake of the one divine substance. The Nestorian Church that was formed in Persia has few connections today with Nestorianism.

Netanyahu, Benjamin, 1949–, Israeli diplomat and politician. A member of the Likud party, he served as Israel's UN representative (1984–88), deputy foreign minister (1988–91), and deputy prime minister (1991–92). In 1993 he was elected leader of the Likud party.

Netherlands, Dutch *Nederland,* officially Kingdom of the Netherlands, constitutional monarchy (1992 est. pop. 15,112,000), 15,963 sq mi (41,344 sq km), NW Europe, popularly known as Holland; bordered by the North Sea (N and W), Belgium (S), and Germany (E). Major cities include AMSTERDAM, the capital; The HAGUE, the seat of government; and ROTTERDAM. About 40% of the land is situated below sea level and is guarded by dunes and dikes. The country is crossed by drainage canals, and the main rivers are interconnected with artificial waterways. Some 27% of its land has been reclaimed from the sea over the past 1,000 years. Faced with widespread species depletion and pollution from fertilizers, the Dutch began (1990) returning 600,000 acres (almost 10% of its farmland) to natural forests, wetlands, and lakes. Despite one of the world's highest population densities, the Netherlands maintains a high standard of living. Industry provides 40% of national income, primarily from textiles, machinery, electrical equipment, iron and steel, refined petroleum, processed foods, ships, and chemicals. Agricultural commodities include dairy products (especially cheese), poultry, tobacco, and horticultural goods (especially bulbs). Foreign trade, the financial industry, and tourism are very important. Large natural gas reserves supply over half of the country's energy needs; natural gas is a major export. The population has nearly equal numbers of Protestants (mostly Calvinists) and Roman Catholics. Dutch is the almost universal language.

History. Settled in Roman times by Germanic tribes, the Low Countries (the Netherlands, Belgium, Luxembourg) passed successively to the Franks (4th–8th cent.), the Holy Roman Empire (10th cent.), and the dukes of Burgundy (14th–15th cent.); they came under Hapsburg rule after 1477 (see NETHERLANDS, AUSTRIAN AND SPANISH). In 1579 the northern provinces under WILLIAM THE SILENT broke away from Spain and formed the Union of Utrecht. Independence was declared in 1581, but the new nation—the United Provinces—was not formally recognized until 1648, after the THIRTY YEARS WAR. The 17th cent., the Netherlands' golden age, was a time of commercial prosperity, colonial expansion, religious tolerance, and cultural achievement (see DUTCH WARS; DUTCH WEST INDIA COMPANY; EAST INDIA COMPANY, DUTCH; REMBRANDT; SPINOZA; VERMEER). In the 18th cent. this supremacy was lost to England and France. Conquered by the French during the FRENCH REVOLUTIONARY WARS, the United Provinces were reconstituted (1795) as the BATAVIAN REPUBLIC; transformed (1806) by NAPOLEON I into the kingdom of Holland under Louis Bonaparte (see BONAPARTE, family); and finally, at the Congress of VIENNA (1814–15), united with present-day Belgium as the kingdom of the Netherlands. Belgium seceded in 1830. Neutral in World War I, the Netherlands suffered severely during the German occupation (1940–45) in WORLD WAR II. Postwar recovery was rapid, despite the loss of its eastern colonies (the

Netherlands gave INDONESIA independence in 1949 and relinquished Netherlands NEW GUINEA in 1962) and disastrous floods in 1953. Under a series of coalition governments, the Dutch economy (especially the industrial sector) expanded greatly and the country took a leading role in Western European integration. Queen BEATRIX ascended the nation's throne in 1980. Ruud Lubbers, a Christian Democrat, has been prime minister since 1982.

Netherlands, Austrian and Spanish, that part of the Low countries controlled from 1482 to 1794 by the HAPSBURG dynasty. The harsh rule of the Spanish Hapsburgs led to a revolt (16th–17th cent.) by which the northern provinces gained independence as the United Provinces of the NETHERLANDS. The Peace of Utrecht transferred (1714) the remaining Spanish lands to the Austrian branch of the Hapsburgs. French armies seized the area in 1794. For its later history, see BELGIUM and LUXEMBOURG.

Netherlands Antilles, islands (1992 est. pop. 184,000), 371 sq mi (961 sq km), West Indies, an autonomous part of the Netherlands. They are in two groups. The Leewards—Bonaire and CURAÇAO—lie off Venezuela. The Windwards—Saba, St. Eustatius, and SAINT MARTIN—are east of Puerto Rico. Tourism, oil refining, and offshore banking are the economic mainstays. Autonomy was granted in 1954; ARUBA was separated from the Netherland Antilles in 1986.

nettle, common name for the family Urticaceae, fibrous herbs, small shrubs, and trees found chiefly in the tropics and subtropics. Several species are covered with small stinging hairs that on contact emit formic acid, a skin irritant. Stinging nettles in the U.S. include species of *Urtica,* widely distributed, and *Laportea canadensis,* a characteristic plant of eastern forests.

network, in computing, two or more computers connected for the purposed of exchanging messages and sharing data and system resources. A LOCAL AREA NETWORK (LAN) connects personal computers and workstations (each called a node) over dedicated, private communications links. A wide area network (WAN) connects large numbers of nodes over long-distance communications links, such as common carrier telephone lines. An internet is a connection between networks. The **Internet** is a WAN that connects thousands of disparate networks in the U.S., Canada, Europe, and Asia, providing global communication between nodes on government, educational, and industrial networks.

Netzahualcóyotl [nätsäwälkō'yō təl], city (1990 pop. 1,259,543), S central Mexico. A communications center and residential area, it is one of Mexico City's largest and poorest suburban municipalities.

Neumann, Saint John Nepomucene, 1811–60, American Roman

Catholic bishop, the first American male to be canonized (1977); b. Bohemia. After studying at Prague he settled (1836) in the U.S., where he later entered the Redemptorist order. He was appointed bishop of Philadelphia in 1852. Neumann was responsible for building 80 churches and nearly 100 parochial schools. Feast: Jan. 5.

neuralgia, acute, throbbing pain along a peripheral sensory nerve, commonly in the area of the facial, or trigeminal, nerve. Its causes include SHINGLES, infections, and extreme cold. Unlike NEURITIS, neuralgia does not involve degeneration of the nerve tissue.

neural network, COMPUTER architecture modeled upon the BRAIN's interconnected system of neurons. Most neural networks are software simulations run on conventional computers. In neural computers, TRANSISTOR circuits serve as the neurons and variable RESISTORS act as the interconnecting axons and dendrites. A neural network on an INTEGRATED CIRCUIT, with 1024 silicon "neurons," has also been developed. Neural networks imitate the brain's ability to sort out patterns and learn from trial and error, discerning and extracting the relationships that underlie the data with which it is presented. They are well suited for pattern recognition, foreign language translation, process control, medical data interpretation, and PARALLEL PROCESSING implementations of conventional processing tasks.

neuritis, inflammation of a peripheral nerve, often accompanied by degenerative changes in nerve tissue. Sensory nerve involvement causes a tingling sensation or loss of sensation, while symptoms of motor nerve involvement range from slight loss of muscle tone to paralysis. Neuritis commonly occurs in DIABETES, SHINGLES, rheumatoid ARTHRITIS, and other disorders. Treatment varies, depending on the cause.

neurosis, a broad category of psychological disturbance, encompassing various mild forms of mental disorder. Until fairly recently, the term was broadly employed in contrast with PSYCHOSIS, which denoted much more severe, debilitating mental disturbances. Those disorders classified as neuroses have varied with time and with different schools of psychiatry, but they traditionally include Sigmund FREUD'S subtypes: ANXIETY, PHOBIAS, OBSESSIVE-COMPULSIVE NEUROSIS, and HYSTERIA. Refinement in diagnostic criteria led, in the 1980s, to the abandonment of the term *neurosis* in psychiatry in favor of more precise nomenclature.

neurotransmitter, chemical that transmits information across the junction (synapse) that separates one nerve cell (neuron) from another nerve cell or a muscle. Neurotransmitters are stored in the nerve cell's bulbous end (axon). When an electrical impulse traveling along the nerve reaches the axon, the neurotransmitter is released and travels across the synapse, either prompting or inhibiting continued impulses. There are more than 300 known neurotransmitters, including the ENDORPHINS and ACETYLCHOLINE.

Neutra, Richard Joseph, 1892–1970, American architect; b. Vienna. In Los Angeles after 1926, he adhered to a functionalist approach (see MODERN ARCHITECTURE), e.g., his Lovell "Heath House" (1929) and Northridge Medical Arts Building (1968).

Neutrality Act, 1935, law designed to keep the U.S. out of a possible European war by banning shipment of war matériel to belligerents and forbidding U.S. citizens to travel on belligerent vessels. Later revisions and the LEND-LEASE Act of 1941 made the law practically inoperable even before American neutrality ended with PEARL HARBOR.

neutralization: see ACIDS AND BASES; TITRATION.

neutrino, ELEMENTARY PARTICLE emitted during the decay of certain other particles. It was first postulated in 1930 by Wolfgang PAULI in order to maintain the law of conservation of energy during beta decay (see BETA PARTICLE; RADIOACTIVITY). Further studies showed that the neutrino was also necessary to maintain the conservation laws of momentum and spin. The neutrino was not detected directly until 1956. The neutrinos associated with the electron and other particles are distinct; each has its own antiparticle. Neutrinos are stable; they are created and destroyed only by particle decays involving the WEAK INTERACTION. Neutrinos appear to have little or no mass, although some experiments have suggested otherwise.

neutrino astronomy, study of stars by means of their emission of NEUTRINOS, ELEMENTARY PARTICLES that result from nuclear reactions in the stellar core and are emitted by stars along with light. Because neutrinos do not interact with matter very readily, they are very difficult to detect. Neutrino "observatories" are located in deep mines, where hundreds of feet of rock shield out COSMIC RAYS that would mask the fragile effects due to neutrinos. The sun is the most intense source of neutrinos (due to its closeness) and was the first object studied. Neutrinos have also been detected from SUPERNOVA 1987A in the Large Magellanic Cloud.

neutron, uncharged subatomic particle, discovered by James CHADWICK in 1932, of slightly greater mass than the PROTON. The stable isotopes of all elements except hydrogen and helium contain within the nucleus a number of neutrons equal to or greater than the number of protons. The preponderance of neutrons becomes more marked for very heavy nuclei. A neutron bound within the nucleus may be stable. A nucleus with an excess of neutrons, however, is radioactive; the extra neutrons (as well as any free neutrons not bound within a nucleus) convert by beta decay (see RADIOACTIVITY) into a proton, an electron, and an antineutrino. The antineutron, the neutron's antiparticle (see ANTIMATTER), was discovered in 1956. The neutron is made up of still smaller particles called QUARKS. See ELEMENTARY PARTICLES.

neutron bomb: see HYDROGEN BOMB.

neutron star, extremely small, extremely dense star roughly double the sun in mass but only a few miles in radius. According to current theories, the core of a neutron star is composed of ELEMENTARY PARTICLES and is surrounded by a fluid composed primarily of NEUTRONS squeezed in close contact. The fluid in turn is encased in a rigid, extremely dense crust a few hundred miles thick. Evidence of the existence of neutron stars is provided by PULSARS, radio sources that fluctuate in intensity in a manner that indicates that they may be rotating neutron stars. Neutron stars are believed to be the dead stellar corpses remaining after the SUPERNOVA explosion of an intermediate-mass star. See GRAVITATIONAL COLLAPSE; STELLAR EVOLUTION.

Nevada, far western state of the U.S.; bordered by Utah and Arizona (E), California (SW, W), and Oregon and Idaho (N).

Area, 110,540 sq mi (286,299 sq km). *Pop.* (1990) 1,201,833, a 50.4% increase over 1980 pop. *Capital,* Carson City. *Statehood,* Oct. 31, 1864 (36th state). *Highest pt.,* Boundary Peak, 13,143 ft (4,009 m); *lowest pt.,* Colorado R., 470 ft (143 m). *Nickname,* Silver State. *Motto,* All for Our Country. *State bird,* mountain bluebird. *State flower,* sagebrush. *State tree,* single-leaf piñon. *Abbr.* Nev.; NV.

Land and People. Nevada lies mostly within the GREAT BASIN, its mountain ranges and high plateaus alternating with valleys running north to east. The COLORADO R., which flows along the state's southwestern border, is dammed by HOOVER DAM to create Lake MEAD, the largest of many water projects in this arid state. Winters are extremely cold in the north and west; summers in the south approach ovenlike heat. Over 80% of Nevada's land is controlled by the federal government, the highest percentage in the U.S. During the 1970s and 1980s Nevada experienced the fastest rate of population increase of any state, more than doubling in size. Most new residents have settled in the two rapidly growing major cities, LAS VEGAS and RENO; over 88% of the population lives in urban areas. In 1990 Nevada was 84% white, 7% African American, and 3% Asian American.

Economy. Because of the state's legalized gambling, tourism is the largest source of income, with Las Vegas, also known for its nightlife, the most popular destination. Natural landmarks, including Lake TAHOE, on the California border, are also popular. Traditionally, mining formed the backbone of the economy; today Nevada leads the country in the extraction of gold, silver, mercury, and barite, and also produces fluorspar, pumice, tungsten, and sand and gravel. Industry is dominated by the manufacture of gaming devices, chemicals, and aerospace products. Agriculture is not highly developed because of the arid climate and rough terrain, but cattle, dairy products, hay, and potatoes are produced.

Government. The constitution (adopted 1864) provides for a governor elected to a four-year term. The legislature consists of a senate whose 20 members serve four-year terms and an assembly with 42 members elected to two-year terms. Nevada is represented in the U.S. Congress by two senators and two representatives and has four electoral votes.

History. The American explorer Jedediah S. Smith passed through Nevada in 1827, and it was subsequently explored (1843–46) by John C. FRÉMONT. Mexico ceded (1846) the area to the U.S., and MORMONS established (1858) the first permanent settlement. Real population growth, however, came after the discovery (1858) of the silver-rich COMSTOCK LODE, at Virginia City, now a restored mining town. Nevada's economic fortunes have tended to fluctuate with the unstable prices of its minerals, and its residents supported the FREE SILVER movement of the 1890s. During the 20th cent. the federal government has played an active role in the state, building huge water projects and military installations. During the 1970s opposition to federal control of land resources resulted in the so-called Sagebrush Rebellion, in which the state was authorized to sue for possession of federal lands. Nonetheless, in 1990 the U.S. owned over 85% of Nevada's land. A huge expansion of high-technology industries during the 1970s and 80s helped to make Nevada one of the fastest growing states in the SUNBELT.

Nevelson, Louise, 1900–88, American sculptor; b. Russia. Using pieces of wood, found objects, cast metal, and other materials, she constructed huge walls or enclosed boxes of complex rhythmic abstract shapes. Painted black, white, or gold, her works have a sense of structural importance and an air of mystery. They are included in such collections as the Whitney Museum and Museum of Modern Art, N.Y.C.

Nevins, Allan, 1890–1971, American historian; b. Camp Point, Ill. A prolific writer in many areas of history, he taught at Columbia Univ. (1928–58). His masterful biographies include *Grover Cleveland* (1932; Pulitzer) and *Hamilton Fish* (1936; Pulitzer). *The Ordeal of the Union* (6 vol., 1947–60) is a comprehensive history of the CIVIL WAR era. Nevins established the nation's first oral-history program at Columbia.

New Age, term popularized in the 1980s to describe a wide-ranging set of beliefs and practices. Growing from 1960s and 70s U.S. counterculture, the New Age movement maintains that a spiritual era is dawning in which individuals and society will be transformed. New Age beliefs and practices include the realization of one's spiritual self, HOLISTIC MEDICINE (including the use of crystals for healing), reincarnation, and ASTROLOGY. In music, the term refers to meditative, relaxing, usually instrumental styles.

Newark, city (1990 pop. 275,221; met. area 1,824,321), seat of Essex co., NE N.J., on the Passaic R. and Newark Bay; settled 1666, inc. as a city 1836. Only 8 mi (13 km) from New York City, it is the largest city in New Jersey, and a major port. Among its diversified industries, leather, jewelry manufacture, and insurance have long histories. Newark is also a financial center and has many state-government offices. The city has lost industry since the 1930s, and its population has declined since the 1950s, dropping by 28% from 1970 to 1990. It has a high minority population, about 58% African American and nearly 19% Hispanic. Newark's landmarks include Trinity Cathedral (1810), the Newark Museum (1909), and Cass GILBERT's courthouse (1906) with BORGLUM's statue of Lincoln. Aaron BURR and Stephen CRANE were born in the city.

New Bedford, city (1990 pop. 99,922), seat of Bristol co., SE Mass., at the mouth of the Acushnet R., on Buzzards Bay; settled 1640, inc. as a city 1847. During the AMERICAN REVOLUTION it sheltered American privateers and was burned by the British in 1778. Once one of the world's leading whaling ports, later (1840s–1920s) a cotton textile center, it has diversified industries, including fishing, and electrical and electronic manufactures. It has a substantial Portuguese-speaking population.

New Brunswick, province (1991 pop. 723,900), 28,354 sq mi (73,436 sq km), E Canada, bounded by Quebec prov. (N), the Gulf of St. Lawrence and Nova Scotia (E), the Bay of Fundy (S), and Maine (W). One of the Maritime Provinces, New Brunswick has a rolling countryside, traversed by rivers that include the St. John and the Miramichi. Its irregular coastline supports an extensive fishing industry. Lumbering and the production of pulp and paper are the major industries, and agriculture is also important. Since World War II, manufacturing and mining (chiefly zinc, silver, lead, and copper) have expanded. Tourist attractions include the spectacular FUNDY tides—the highest in the world—and the "reversing falls" at SAINT JOHN, New Brunswick's principal city. Other major cities are MONCTON and FREDERICTON, the capital.

History. The first white settlement was made in 1604 at the mouth of the St. Croix River by the French under CHAMPLAIN and sieur de MONTS. Together, Nova Scotia and the New Brunswick coast became known to the French as ACADIA. The British gained control of the area in 1713, and many of the French Acadians were later expelled (1755, 1758). Thousands of UNITED EMPIRE LOYALISTS settled in New Brunswick after the American Revolution, and a separate colony was organized (1784). Responsible (cabinet) government was achieved in 1849, and in 1867 New Brunswick joined with other colonies to form the Dominion of Canada. At present about half of the population lives in urban areas. The Progressive Conservatives controlled provincial government from 1970 to 1987, when the Liberals swept the election. New Brunswick sends 10 senators (appointed) and 10 representatives (elected) to the national parliament.

New Caledonia, French overseas territory (1992 est. pop. 175,000), land area 7,082 sq mi (18,342 sq km), in the South Pacific. It comprises New Caledonia, the Isle of Pines, the Loyalty Islands, and smaller islands; Nouméa is the capital. Industries include iron and nickel mining, and coffee and copra production. About 42% of the people are Melanesian and 37% European. Captain COOK sighted (1774) the main island; France annexed it in 1853. In the 1980s Melanesians campaigned, sometimes violently, for independence, but the population voted to remain a French territory. Under a 1988 accord New Caledonia was granted substantial autonomy.

Newcastle, city (1991 urban agglomeration pop. 432,600), New South Wales, SE Australia, on the Pacific Ocean. It is a major port and the center of the country's largest coal-mining area. Manufactures include steel, chemicals, and ships. The city was settled in 1804.

New Church: see NEW JERUSALEM, CHURCH OF THE.

Newcomen, Thomas, 1663–1729, English inventor of an early atmospheric STEAM ENGINE (c.1711) used to pump water. It was an improvement over Thomas Savery's engine (patented 1698).

New Deal, in U.S. history, term for the domestic reform program of Pres. Franklin Delano ROOSEVELT. It had two phases. The first (1933–34) attempted to provide recovery and relief from the GREAT DEPRESSION through programs of agricultural and business regulation, inflation, price stabilization, and public works; numerous emergency organizations, e.g., the NATIONAL RECOVERY ADMINISTRATION, were established. The second (1935–41) provided for social and economic legislation, e.g., SOCIAL SECURITY, to benefit the mass of working people. A number of New Deal measures were invalidated by the SUPREME COURT, and the program, which had been enthusiastically endorsed by agrarian, liberal, and labor groups, was increasingly criticized. Nonetheless, at the end of World War II most New Deal legislation was still intact.

New Delhi [dĕl'ē], city (1991 pop. 294,000), capital of India, Delhi union territory, N central India. Built (1912–29) to replace CALCUTTA as the capital, it was inaugurated in 1931. Planned by Edward LUTYENS, New Delhi's broad streets provide vistas of historic monuments and magnificent government buildings.

New Democratic party (NDP), Canadian political party, founded (1961) when the Cooperative Commonwealth Federation (CCF) reorganized and became associated with Canadian labor unions. The NDP adopted much of the CCF's democratic-socialist agenda, but broadened its appeal by putting less emphasis on specific socialist proposals. Led since 1989 by Audrey McLaughlin, the first woman to head a Canadian national party, the NDP is strongest in W Canada.

New Economic Policy (NEP), official economic program of the USSR, 1921–28. Initiated by LENIN, the NEP replaced the "war Communism" of the 1918–21 civil war period, which had caused scarcity and popular unrest. Under the NEP peasants could sell some of their produce for a profit and small businesses could operate privately. The first Five-Year Plan supplanted the NEP.

New England, region of the NE U.S., comprising MAINE, NEW HAMPSHIRE, VERMONT, MASSACHUSETTS, RHODE ISLAND, and CONNECTICUT. Agriculture was never important due to the poor, rocky soil, but excellent harbors and fisheries made it a commercial center. Manufacturing grew rapidly in the 19th cent. and has since dominated the economy. Traditional industries, e.g., shoe and textile, have largely been superseded by electronics and tourism. New England was the center of many of the historical events that led to the AMERICAN REVOLUTION.

New England Confederation or **United Colonies of New England,** 1643–1684, union for "mutual safety and welfare" formed by the British colonies of Massachusetts Bay, Plymouth, Connecticut, and New Haven. It was weakened by rivalry among the colonies and its inability to do more than advise. Its most important action was to break the power of Native Americans in KING PHILIP'S WAR.

New England Primer, American school book, first published before 1690; compiled by Benjamin Harris in Boston. It featured moralizing couplets and woodblock illustrations. About 2 million copies were sold during the 18th cent.

Newfoundland, province (1991 pop. 568,474), E Canada, consisting of the island of Newfoundland, 43,359 sq mi (112,299 sq km), and the mainland area of Labrador, 112,825 sq mi (292,218 sq km). Newfoundland island lies at the mouth of the Gulf of St. Lawrence and is bounded by the Atlantic Ocean (N, E, S). Labrador, northwest of the island, is bordered by the Atlantic Ocean (E) and by Quebec prov. (S, W). Newfoundland has a rocky, irregular coast and a generally cool and moist climate. The cod-fishing area of the GRAND BANKS, southeast of the island, is probably the best in the world and cod, lobster, herring, and salmon are caught in the coastal waters. In Labrador, cold temperatures and lack of transportation have retarded economic development. Labrador, however, is rich in mineral resources (iron, zinc, copper, asbestos, lead, oil, natural gas), and mining is the main industry. The lake district in the southwest is particularly rich in iron deposits. Timber and water power are also plentiful, and pulp and paper are important provincial products. SAINT JOHN'S, the capital, and Corner Brook, both on Newfoundland, are the province's chief cities.

History. VIKINGS visited the area (c.1000) and briefly established a settlement on Newfoundland. Sir Humphrey GILBERT claimed the island for England in 1583, but France contested English claims and the island changed hands several times. In 1763 the treaty of Paris definitely awarded Newfoundland and Labrador to Britain. Representative government was introduced in 1832 and parliamentary government in 1855. Voters rejected union with Canada in 1869, and further negotiations for union, begun in 1895, were unsuccessful. Possession of Labrador was disputed between Newfoundland and Quebec until 1927, when Newfoundland's claims were upheld by the British Privy Council. During the depression of the 1930s Britain suspended Newfoundland's self-government, and actual authority was exercised by a joint commission of Newfoundlanders and British. In 1949 Newfoundland became Canada's 10th province. The iron-centered economy suffered in the recession of the 1980s and fishing declined dramatically in the early 1990s, but offshore oil deposits show promise. Newfoundland sends six senators (appointed) and seven representatives (elected) to the national parliament.

New Granada, former Spanish colony, N South America, that included at its greatest extent modern Colombia, Ecuador, Panama, and Venezuela. Colonized by Spain in the 16th cent., the area was called "the new realm of Granada" by the explorer JIMÉNEZ DE QUESADA. Civil government was established in 1549 and the area was made a viceroyalty in 1717. After independence (1819) it became the state of Greater Colombia, but by 1830 Ecuador and Venezuela had seceded. The remainder (Colombia and Panama) became the Republic of New Granada and later (1886) the Republic of Colombia, from which Panama seceded in 1903.

New Guinea, world's second largest island (after Greenland), c.342,000 sq mi (885,780 sq km), in the SW Pacific Ocean N of Australia. It is c.1,500 mi (2,410 km) long and c.400 mi (640 km) wide. Djaja Peak (16,503 ft/5,030 m) is the highest point in the mountainous interior. The island is politically divided between Indonesia (W) and Papua New Guinea (E). Headhunting and cannibalism are still practiced in some inaccessible regions. The inhabitants include Melanesians, Papuans, and Negritos. New Guinea is the most linguistically diverse region in the world, with about 1,000 separate languages.

New Hampshire, one of the New England states of the NE U.S.; bordered by Massachusetts (S), Vermont, with the Connecticut R. forming the boundary (W), the Canadian province of Quebec (NW), and Maine and a short strip of the Atlantic Ocean (E).

Area, 9,304 sq mi (24,097 sq km). *Pop.* (1990) 1,109,252, a 20.5% increase over 1980 pop. *Capital,* Concord. *Statehood,* June 21, 1788 (9th of the original 13 states to ratify the Constitution). *Highest pt.,* Mt. Washington, 6,288 ft (1,918 m); *lowest pt.,* sea level. *Nickname,* Granite State. *Motto,* Live Free or Die. *State bird,* purple finch. *State flower,* purple lilac. *State tree,* white birch. *Abbr.,* N.H.; NH.

Land and People. Most of New Hampshire is hilly or mountainous, with the highest peaks in the White Mts., part of the APPALACHIAN system. Winters are severe, with heavy snows in the mountains; summers are relatively cool. The mountains give way to the Connecticut R. valley in the west and a coastal plain in the east. New Hampshire has had the most rapid population growth in New England, with most of the increase occurring in the south, which is part of the BOSTON metropolitan area, and over 50% of the population now lives in urban areas. MANCHESTER is the largest city, followed by NASHUA and CONCORD. In 1990 the state was 98% white.

Economy. Year-round tourism is now New Hampshire's major source of income, with visitors attracted to the state's beaches, mountains, and lakes. Manufacturing, which dominated the state's economy from the late 19th to late 20th cent., today produces such goods as nonelectrical machinery, electrical and electronic products, fabricated metals, paper, leather goods, and textiles. Intensive agriculture is hampered by stony soil and rugged terrain, but dairy products, eggs, greenhouse products, hay, vegetables, fruit, and maple syrup are key farm products. Forestry is also important.

Government. The constitution of 1784 provides for a governor serving a two-year term. The general court, the largest legislature in the country, consists of a 24-seat senate and a 400-seat assembly, with members of both bodies elected to two-year terms. New Hampshire is represented in the U.S. Congress by two senators and two representatives and has four electoral votes.

History. Puritans (see PURITANISM) from Massachusetts began settling New Hampshire during the 1620s and 30s, and it became a separate colony in 1741. New Hampshire was the first colony to declare (1776) its independence from Great Britain and to establish its own government. In the early 1800s water-powered textile manufacturing began to replace shipping (at Portsmouth), agriculture, and lumbering in economic importance. Textile manufacturing seriously declined during the GREAT DEPRESSION, and efforts were made to broaden the state's economic activities. The establishment of new industries, including electronics in S New Hampshire, successfully counterbalanced the departure of older industries to other states until the national recession of the late 1980s and early 90s caused widespread unemployment.

New Harmony, town (1990 pop. 846), SW Ind., on the Wabash R.; founded 1814 by the Harmony Society under George Rapp. In 1825 Robert OWEN established a communistic colony that became a cultural and scientific center. The nation's first kindergarten, first free public school, and first free library were established there. Some 25 Rappite buildings remain.

New Haven, city (1990 pop. 130,474), S Conn., a port where the Quinnipiac and other rivers enter Long Island Sound; inc. 1784. An educational center, the city is the seat of Yale Univ. (chartered 1701, moved to New Haven 1716) and other institutions. Its manufactures include firearms, timepieces, rubber and paper goods, and textiles. Founded (1637–38) by Puritans as a theocratic community, it was united with the Connecticut Colony in 1665.

New Hebrides: see VANUATU.

Newhouse, Samuel Irving, 1895–1979, American newspaper and magazine publisher. From 1922 to the 1970s, he acquired 31 dailies in 22 cities, including the Newark *Star Ledger*. He also controlled such magazines as *Vogue, House and Garden,* and *Mademoiselle,* and several radio stations and cable-television systems.

Ne Win, U [o͞o nä wĭn], 1911–, Burmese general and political leader; b. Shu Muang. He became prime minister by twice deposing (1958, 1962) U NU in military coups. Ne Win's "Burmese Way to Socialism" made Myanmar a police state and failed to improve the economy. In 1974 he became president under a new constitution. He resigned the presidency in 1981, and in 1988, in the face of widespread antigovernment demonstrations, he resigned the chairmanship of Myanmar's ruling party.

New Jersey, mid-Atlantic state of the U.S.; bordered by the Atlantic

Ocean (E), Delaware, across Delaware Bay (S), Pennsylvania, across the Delaware R. (W), and New York State (N).

Area, 7,836 sq mi (20,295 sq km). *Pop.* (1990) 7,730,188, a 5% increase over 1980 pop. *Capital,* Trenton. *Statehood* Dec. 18, 1787 (3d of original 13 states to ratify the Constitution). *Highest pt.,* High Point Mt., 1,803 ft (550 m); *lowest pt.,* sea level. *Nickname,* Garden State. *Motto,* Liberty and Prosperity. *State bird,* Eastern goldfinch. *State flower,* purple violet. *State tree,* red oak. *Abbr.,* N.J.; NJ.

Land and People. More than half the state is covered by coastal plains that give way to the Piedmont plains inland and to the ridges of the APPALACHIAN highlands in the northwest. One of the smallest states in area, New Jersey is the ninth most populous, the most densely settled (987 per sq mi/381 per sq km), and the most highly urbanized state, with nearly 90% of the population living in urban areas. The largest city is NEWARK; other important cities are JERSEY CITY, PATERSON, and TRENTON. Many communities are suburbs of NEW YORK CITY and PHILADELPHIA. In 1990 the state was 80% white, 13% African American, and 4% Asian American.

Economy. Service industries now provide New Jersey's largest source of income, with huge commercial expansion taking over much of its farmland. Manufacturing produces chemicals and pharmaceuticals, electronic and electrical equipment, nonelectrical machinery, fabricated metals, processed foods, and many other products. Tourism is also important, with the Atlantic shore the most popular destination. New Jersey's farms producing hay, corn, soybeans, tomatoes, blueberries, peaches, cranberries, dairy products, and other crops. The state's well-developed transportation and shipping network includes part of the Port of New York–New Jersey.

Government. The constitution (adopted 1947) provides for a governor serving a four-year term. The legislature consists of a senate whose 40 members serve four-year terms and a house of assembly with 80 members elected to two-year terms. New Jersey is represented in the U.S. Congress by 2 senators and 13 representatives and has 15 electoral votes.

History. The region was the home of the DELAWARE when Europeans, including Henry HUDSON, explored it during the early 17th cent. Although the Dutch were the first to establish a permanent settlement (1660), the area was seized by the British (1664), who held it until New Jersey became one of the Thirteen Colonies to declare (1776) its independence. Many important Revolutionary War battles were fought there, including those at Trenton, PRINCETON, and MONMOUTH (see AMERICAN REVOLUTION). Following the Revolution, a period of enormous economic expansion occurred, and industry, making use of water power for textile mills, was established. Economic growth was accompanied by political corruption, which continued until Gov. Woodrow WILSON sponsored (1910–12) a reform movement. The state's highly industrial economy expanded significantly during and after World War II. In 1976 New Jersey voters approved casino gambling in ATLANTIC CITY, which revitalized that aging seaside resort and the state's tourist trade. Visitors have also been attracted by the multi-stadium Meadowlands Sports Complex (built 1976–81), in East Rutherford. New Jersey was hard hit by recession in the early 1990s as economic growth slowed and the state suffered the effects of overdevelopment.

New Jerusalem, Church of the, or **New Church,** religious body instituted by followers of Emanuel SWEDENBORG, who are generally called Swedenborgians. It was first organized (1787) in London. In the U.S. Swedenborg's teachings had been introduced by James Glen in 1784. A New Church society was formed (1792) in Baltimore, and the church held a general convention in 1817. Its polity is modified episcopacy, with each society enjoying great freedom. A separatist group, the General Church of the New Jerusalem, was formed in the 1890s.

Newlands, John Alexander Reina, 1838–98, British chemist. He prepared the first PERIODIC TABLE of the elements arranged in the order of atomic weights. His observation that every eighth element has similar properties (the "Law of Octaves") was accepted only after Dmitri MENDELEEV's work five years later.

New Laws: see LAS CASAS, BARTOLOMÉ DE.

Newman, Barnett, 1905–71, American artist; b. N.Y.C. Forming a link between ABSTRACT EXPRESSIONISM and COLOR FIELD PAINTING, his influential canvases are frequently monumental planes of flat color cut by slender vertical bands.

Newman, John Henry, 1801–90, English churchman, Roman Catholic cardinal, a founder of the OXFORD MOVEMENT. Ordained (1824) in the Church of England, he began (1833) his series *Tracts for the Times* and helped guide the Oxford Movement. *Tract 90* (1841), which demonstrated that the Thirty-nine Articles (see CREED) were consistent with Catholicism, outraged Anglicans, and Newman converted to Catholicism in 1845. He was one of the most influential English Catholics of all time, and his *Apologia pro vita sua* (1864) is a masterpiece of religious autobiography. Newman, unlike H.E. MANNING, disapproved of the enunciation of papal infallibility in 1870; though he did not oppose the dogma itself, he lost favor with the papacy until 1879, when he was made a cardinal.

New Mexico, state in the SW U.S. At its northwestern corner are the so-called Four Corners, where Colorado, New Mexico, Arizona, and Utah meet at right angles; New Mexico is also bordered by Oklahoma (NE), Texas (E, S), and Mexico (S).

Area, 121,666 sq mi (315,115 sq km). *Pop.* (1990) 1,515,069, a 16.5% increase over 1980 pop. *Capital,* Santa Fe. *Statehood,* Jan. 6, 1912 (47th state). *Highest pt.,* Wheeler Peak, 13,161 ft (4,014 m); *lowest pt.,* Red Bluff Reservoir, 2,817 ft (859 m). *Nickname,* Land of Enchantment. *Motto, Crescit Eundo* [It Grows as It Goes], *State bird,* chaparral ("roadrunner"). *State flower,* yucca. *State tree,* piñon. *Abbr.,* N. Mex.; NM.

Land and People. New Mexico is roughly bisected by the RIO GRANDE, its principal river. Much of the topography consists of broken mesas and the high peaks of the ROCKY MOUNTAINS, which run north to south through the state. Broad, semiarid plains cover S New Mexico. Summer days of ovenlike heat are followed by cool nights, while winter brings below-freezing temperatures in most areas and heavy snowfall in the high ranges. Federally controlled land—33.2% of the total—includes Carlsbad Caverns National Park (see NATIONAL PARKS, table) and many national monuments, such as WHITE SANDS, Chaco Canyon, and Bandelier. About 73% of the population lives in urban areas. ALBUQUERQUE is the largest city, followed by Las Cruces and SANTA FE. In 1990 more than 38% of the population was Hispanic—the highest percentage in the country—9% was Native American and 76% white. The NAVAHO reservation (in New Mexico and Arizona) is the country's largest; other tribes in the state include the APACHE, PUEBLO, and UTE.

Economy. Because opportunities for irrigation are few, most farmland is used for the grazing of cattle and sheep. Hay, onions, wheat, pecans, corn, cotton, and sorghum are the principal crops. New Mexico derives much of its wealth from mining. It leads the states in production of uranium, potash, and perlite; is a large producer of natural gas; and has significant deposits of coal, oil, and other minerals. Manufacturing is dominated by the production of processed food, machinery, apparel, chemicals, and electrical equipment. About a quarter of the land is forested, and lumbering is an important activity. Tourism is a major source of income.

Government. The constitution of 1912 provides for a governor serving a four-year term. The legislature consists of a senate of 42 members elected to four-year terms and a house of 70 members serving two-year terms. New Mexico elects two U.S. senators and three representatives and has five electoral votes.

History. Prehistoric cultures long preceded the civilization of the Pueblos encountered in the 16th cent. by the Spanish, who established missions and ranches in the area despite fierce resistance by the indigenous people. With Mexico's independence (1821), the area became one of its provinces, although U.S. settlers began arriving (1822) via the SANTA FE TRAIL. At the end of the MEXICAN WAR, New Mexico was ceded (1848) to the U.S. Native American resistance finally ended with the defeat of GERONIMO, chief of the Apache, in 1886. By then a ranching boom had begun, accelerated by the arrival (1879) of the railroad. In 1943 the U.S. government built LOS ALAMOS as a center for atomic research, and the continued growth of military installations has greatly contributed to the state's economic and population growth. Service2Dsector employment is growing and is projected to constitute almost one third of the state's jobs by the year 2000.

New Netherland, American territory granted by Holland to the DUTCH WEST INDIA COMPANY in 1621. The first permanent settlement was at Fort Orange (now Albany, N.Y.), in 1624. New Amsterdam (later New York City) was bought from Native Americans in 1626. In 1664 the territory was taken by the English, who divided it into the colonies of New York and New Jersey.

New Orleans, city (1990 pop. 496,938; met. area 1,238,816), coextensive with Orleans parish, SE La., between the Mississippi R. and Lake Pontchartrain, 107 mi (172 km) from the river mouth; founded 1718, inc. 1805. Built on a bend in the river (hence called the Crescent City), it is protected by levees. A major international port and a center of business and banking, it is one of the largest and most important cities in the South. Its imports include coffee, and bananas; its exports, oil, chemicals, cotton, and grains. Coastwise traffic is heavy. Food processing is a major enterprise, and the area has oil, aerospace, and chemical industries; shipyards; and diverse manufacturing plants. The capital (from 1722) of the French colony, it became a cosmopolitan city; French influence (Creole culture) and the city's reputation for glamour and gaiety have lasted to the present. The French Quarter (Vieux Carrée), around Jackson Square, retains much of its early elegance. Contemporary landmarks include the Superdome (1975) and the Hibernia Tower. Two manifestations of the city's heterogeneous culture are its famous MARDI GRAS festival and the development of JAZZ. The city was the site of the 1984 World's Fair, and gambling was legalized in 1992, with the first casino opening on a riverboat in 1993.

Newport, city (1990 pop. 28,227), seat of Newport co., SE R.I., on Aquidneck (or Rhode) Island; settled 1639, inc. 1784. The U.S. naval base in Newport closed in 1974, causing much unemployment. A refuge for Quakers, Jews, and other religious groups in its early history, the city became in the 19th cent. one of the world's most famous resorts. Its palatial mansions are now a tourist attraction. Newport is also noted for yachting (the America's Cup races were held there for many years). Its many points of interest include the old colony house (1739), the Newport Tower (17th cent.), and the Touro Synagogue (1763), the oldest in the U.S.

Newport News, city (1990 pop. 170,045), SE Va., on the Virginia peninsula, at the mouth of the James R., off HAMPTON ROADS; inc. 1896. It is one of the world's major shipbuilding and repair centers, and a port handling raw materials in great volume. Settled c.1620, it did not grow appreciably until 1880, when the railroad arrived. In 1862 the MONITOR AND MERRIMACK fought offshore.

New South Wales, state (1992 est. pop. 5,962,000), 309,443 sq mi (801,457 sq km), SE Australia, bounded by the Pacific Ocean (E). The capital is SYDNEY; NEWCASTLE and WOLLONGONG are among the other urban centers. New South Wales produces most of Australia's steel; other manufactures include machinery, electrical products, clothing, textiles, and chemicals. The state mines about two thirds of Australia's coal and has one of the world's richest silver and zinc deposits, at BROKEN HILL. Agricultural products include beef, wool, dairy products, wheat, sugar, and fruits. New South Wales was settled in 1788 as a penal colony and until 1825 included all of Australia east of long. 135°E. It became a British colony in 1846 and was federated as a state of Australia in 1901. The AUSTRALIAN CAPITAL TERRITORY, site of CANBERRA, Australia's capital, was ceded (1911, 1915) by New South Wales to the federal government.

New Stone Age: see under STONE AGE.

New Style dates: see CALENDAR.

New Sweden, Swedish colony on the Delaware R., in parts of present-day Pennsylvania, New Jersey, and Delaware. It was founded in 1638 by the New Sweden Company, led by Peter MINUIT, with the capital at Tinicum Island. It was captured by the Dutch under Peter STUYVESANT in 1655.

newt: see SALAMANDER.

New Testament, the distinctively Christian portion of the BIBLE, 27 books dating from the earliest Christian period, transmitted in *koiné*, a popular form of Greek spoken in the biblical regions from the 4th cent. B.C. The conventional order is: four biographies of JESUS, namely the GOSPELS, Matthew, Mark, Luke, and John; a history of missionary activity, the ACTS OF THE APOSTLES; 21 letters written in apostolic times, called epistles, named (first 14) for their addressees or (last 7) for their supposed author—ROMANS, First and Second CORINTHIANS, GALATIANS, EPHESIANS, PHILIPPIANS, COLOSSIANS, First and Second THESSALONIANS, First and Second TIMOTHY, TITUS, PHILEMON, HEBREWS, JAMES, First and Second PETER, First, Second, and Third JOHN, and JUDE; and finally a prophecy, the REVELATION or Apocalypse. There are many more than these 27 early Christian works. Selection of New Testament books as canonical was slow, the present canon appearing for the first time in the Festal Epistle of St. Athanasius (A.D. 367). All major Christian churches use the same canon.

Newton, Sir Isaac, 1642–1727, English mathematician and natural philosopher (physicist); considered by many the greatest scientist of all time. He was Lucasian professor of mathematics (1669–1701) at Cambridge Univ. Between 1664 and 1666 he discovered the law of universal GRAVITATION, began to develop the CALCULUS, and discovered that white light is composed of every color in the SPECTRUM. In his monumental *Philosophiae naturalis principia mathematica* [Mathematical Principles of Natural Philosophy] (1687), he showed how his principle of universal gravitation explained both the motions of heavenly bodies and the falling of bodies on earth. The *Principia* covers DYNAMICS (including Newton's three laws of MOTION), FLUID MECHANICS, the motions of the planets and their satellites, the motions of the comets, and the phenomena of TIDES. Newton's theory that LIGHT is composed of particles—elaborated in his *Opticks* (1704)—dominated optics until the 19th cent., when it was replaced by the wave theory of light; the two theories were combined in modern QUANTUM MECHANICS. Newton also built (1668) the first reflecting TELESCOPE, anticipated the calculus of variations, and devoted much energy towards alchemy, theology, and history. He was president of the Royal Society from 1703 until his death.

newton: see FORCE.

New Year's Day, the first day of the year. Christians usually celebrated New Year's Day on Mar. 25 until the Gregorian CALENDAR (1582) moved it to Jan. 1. The Jewish New Year (1 Tishri) falls sometime in September or early October. The Chinese New Year falls between Jan. 10 and Feb. 19.

New York, mid-Atlantic state of the U.S.; bordered by Vermont, Massachusetts, Connecticut, and the Atlantic Ocean (E), New Jersey and Pennsylvania (S), Lakes Erie and Ontario and the Canadian province of Ontario (NW), and the province of Quebec (N).

Area, 49,576 sq mi (128,402 sq km). *Pop.* (1990) 17,990,455, a 2.5% increase over 1980 pop. *Capital,* Albany. *Statehood,* July 26, 1788 (11th of original 13 states to ratify the Constitution). *Highest pt.,* Mt. Marcy, 5,344 ft (1,630 m); *lowest pt.,* sea level. *Nickname,* Empire State. *Motto, Excelsior* [Ever Upward]. *State bird,* bluebird. *State flower,* rose. *State tree,* sugar maple. *Abbr.,* N.Y.; NY.

Land and People. A great valley, formed by Lakes CHAMPLAIN and George and the Hudson R., traverses the state north to south. To the west of the lakes are the wild and rugged ADIRONDACK MOUNTAINS. Most of the southern part of the state is part of the Allegheny plateau, which rises in the southwest to the Catskill Mts. Winters may vary from cold, with heavy snow, along Lakes Erie and Ontario, to mild or moderate in the southeastern coastal area; summers are generally hot, except in the Adirondacks. Nearly 85% of the population lives in metropolitan areas. NEW YORK CITY is the largest city in the U.S. and is the nation's leading financial and cultural center. Other major cities include BUFFALO, ROCHESTER, SYRACUSE, and ALBANY. New York, which ranks second only to California in population, was 74% white and 16% African American in 1990. The state also had the third largest Hispanic-American population (2,214,026), after California and Texas, and the second largest Asian-American population (693,760), after California.

Economy. New York follows first-ranked California in value of industrial output. The leading industries are printing and publishing, and the production of apparel, pharmaceuticals, instruments, nonelectrical machinery, toys and sporting goods, electronic equipment, and processed foods. The service sector is an important part of the economy and now employs the largest percent of the state's workers. New York is a fertile agricultural state: it ranks second in the country in output of apples; is among the largest producers of dairy cows and products; and grows grapes for its wine industry, vegetables, greenhouse products, hay, and many other crops. Mineral resources include crushed stone, cement, salt, and zinc. Year-round tourism is a major industry, with New York City, the Adirondacks and Catskills, and NIAGARA FALLS popular destinations.

Government. The constitution (adopted 1894) provides for a governor serving a four-year term. The legislature consists of a 60-seat senate and 150-seat legislature, with members of both bodies serving two-year terms. New York is represented in the U.S. Congress by 2 senators and 31 representatives and has 33 electoral votes.

History. Present-day New York was inhabited by Native Americans, including the MOHEGANS and the Iroquois (see IROQUOIS CONFEDERACY). Early explorers included Giovanni da VERRAZANO (1524) and Henry HUDSON (1609). The Dutch founded New Amsterdam on the lower tip of Manhattan Island in 1624. The British took the region in the Second Dutch War (1664–67) and held New York, with its busy shipping and fishing fleets and expanding farms, until the colony declared (1776) its independence. About one third of the engagements of the AMERICAN REVOLUTION took place in the state, including the key defeat of the British in the SARATOGA CAMPAIGN (1777). From the 1780s commerce increased, aided by the opening (1825) of the ERIE CANAL. Industries, beginning with textiles, also expanded. This commercial and economic growth marked the turn away from the old, primarily agricultural economy. New York was a center of numerous 19th-cent. reform movements, including Abolitionism (see ABOLITIONISTS) and WOMAN SUFFRAGE. The 1840s marked the beginning of the huge waves of European immigration that continued throughout the century, with many immigrants settling in New York City. The state's governorship has been a fertile proving ground for many 20th-cent. leaders of national prominence, including Alfred E. SMITH, Franklin D. ROOSEVELT, Thomas E. DEWEY, and Nelson A. ROCKEFELLER. New York's post–World War II shift in population from the cities to the suburbs was accompanied by the departure of many businesses to outlying areas, a trend that continued into the 1990s.

New York, City University of, at New York City; founded 1847 as the Free Academy, reorganized 1929 as the College of the City of New York, expanded and renamed 1961 as a result of legislation. It includes a graduate division, 11 four-year colleges, and several two-year community colleges in the various city boroughs. It is city- and state-supported. With an enrollment of over 180,000, it is one of the nation's largest universities.

New York, State University of, est. 1948 by the amalgamation under one board of trustees of 29 educational institutions. It now comprises all of New York's state-supported institutions of higher learning, except the colleges of the City University of New York. There are over 70 units throughout the state (including medical centers, agricultural and technical colleges, and community colleges), with a total enrollment of over 400,000, the largest in the U.S. Major university centers are in Albany, Binghamton, Stony Brook, and Buffalo (formerly the Univ. of Buffalo). Graduate degrees are offered at more than a score of campuses, and university-wide research is conducted at the Atmospheric Sciences Research Center (with headquarters at Albany), the Center for Immunology (Buffalo), the Institute for Theoretical Physics (Stony Brook), and several other facilities.

New York City (N.Y.C.), city (1990 pop. 7,322,564; met. area 8,546,846; 1992 greater met. area est. 19,600,000), SE N.Y., on New York Bay, at the mouth of the Hudson R.; chartered 1898. Each of its five boroughs is a county: Manhattan (New York co.), an island; the Bronx (Bronx co.), on the mainland, NE of Manhattan across the Harlem River; Queens (Queens co.), on Long Island, E of Manhattan across the East River; BROOKLYN (Kings co.), also on Long Island, on the East River adjoining Queens and on New York Bay; and Staten Island (Richmond co.), an island SW of Manhattan across the Upper Bay. The nation's largest city, New York is a major U.S. port, the country's trade center, and, with its banks and stock exchanges, the financial center of the world. Manufacturing accounts for a large but declining proportion of employment; clothing, chemicals, and processed foods are major products. Publishing, television and radio, advertising, and tourism are major industries. Theaters, nightclubs, shops, and restaurants draw millions of visitors.

History. Giovanni da VERRAZANO may have been the first European to explore the region, and Henry HUDSON visited it, but Dutch settlements truly began the city. In 1624 the town of New Amsterdam was established on lower Manhattan; Peter MINUIT supposedly bought the island from its Native American inhabitants for about $24 worth of trinkets. In 1664 the English seized the colony and renamed it; during the AMERICAN REVOLUTION they held it from 1776 to 1781. New York was briefly (1789–90) the U.S. capital and was state capital until 1797. By 1790 it was the largest U.S. city, and the opening (1825) of the ERIE CANAL, linking New York with the GREAT LAKES, led to even greater expansion. In 1898 a new charter was adopted, making the city Greater New York, a metropolis of five boroughs. Massive immigration, mainly from Europe, swelled the city's population in the late 19th and early 20th cent. The Flatiron building (1902) ushered in the SKYSCRAPER era that brought New York its famous skyline, and the city's first subway opened in 1904. After World War II, many African Americans from the South, Puerto Ricans, and Latin Americans migrated to the city in search of jobs. In the 1970s the city narrowly avoided bankruptcy. Its increasingly services-oriented economy boomed in the 1980s, until the stock market crashed (Oct. 1987). In the early 1990s the city again faced fiscal crisis. David DINKINS became the city's first African-American mayor in 1990, but he lost to Rudy GIULIANI in 1993. Staten Island residents voted to secede from the city in 1993, but such a move would require state approval.

Points of Interest. Noted sights include the EMPIRE STATE BUILDING, the WORLD TRADE CENTER, ST. PATRICK'S CATHEDRAL, the Cathedral of SAINT JOHN THE DIVINE, the Statue of LIBERTY, BROADWAY and Fifth Avenue, GREENWICH VILLAGE, and Central Park. Among New York's bridges are the BROOKLYN BRIDGE (opened 1883), the George Washington Bridge (1931), and the VERRAZANO-NARROWS BRIDGE (1964). ELLIS ISLAND and Castle Garden (at the Battery) were entry points for many immigrants. The UNITED NATIONS has its headquarters in New York. Cultural institutions include LINCOLN CENTER FOR THE PERFORMING ARTS and Carnegie Hall; the METROPOLITAN MUSEUM OF ART, MUSEUM OF MODERN ART, WHITNEY MUSEUM OF AMERICAN ART, and many other museums; and the New York Public Library (see library, table) and other research facilities. Among the numerous educational institutions are the City Univ. of New York, Columbia Univ., and New York Univ.

New York City Ballet, a foremost American dance company of the 20th cent. It was founded (1946) by George BALANCHINE and Lincoln Kirstein. In 1964 it moved from City Center to Lincoln Center for the Performing Arts. Under Balanchine's direction, it developed an American style that combined European tradition, austere emotion, and musicality. The company's dancers have included Jacques d'AMBOISE, Suzanne FARRELL, Melissa Hayden, Peter MARTINS (the company's present director), Maria Tallchief, and Edward VILLELLA.

New York Public Library: see LIBRARY (table).

New York Shakespeare Festival: see PAPP, JOSEPH.

New York Stock Exchange: see STOCK EXCHANGE.

New York Times Company v. Sullivan, case decided in 1964 by the U.S. SUPREME COURT. In overturning a LIBEL judgment against the *Times,* the Court held that debate on public issues would be inhibited if public officials could recover damages for honest error that produced false statements. It limited the right of recovery to cases in which actual malice (knowing publication of falsehood, or reckless disregard of the truth) could be proved.

New Zealand, island country (1991 pop. 3,434,950), 103,736 sq mi (268,676 sq km), in the South Pacific Ocean, 1,000 mi (1,600 km) SE of Australia. The major cities are WELLINGTON (the capital), AUCKLAND, and CHRISTCHURCH. New Zealand comprises two main islands, North Island and South Island, separated by Cook Strait; Stewart Island; the Chatham Islands; and several small outlying islands, of which only Raoul, in the Kermadec group, and Campbell Island are inhabited. Also part of New Zealand are the Ross Dependency, in Antarctica, and the TOKELAU ISLANDS. Residents of the self-governing COOK ISLANDS and NIUE share New Zealand citizenship. North Island, with its active volcanoes and hot springs around Lake Taupo, is subtropical in the north and temperate in the south. It contains New Zealand's major river, the Waikato. On South Island are the massive Southern Alps, with many peaks over 10,000 ft (3,048 m) high; the productive Canterbury Plains, the country's chief lowland area; acres of virgin forest; and many fjords. Among the unusual animals native to New Zealand are the ALBATROSS and KIWI. Sheep and cattle, the mainstays of the economy, provide New Zealand with exports of frozen meat (especially lamb), dairy products (especially butter), and wool. Food processing dominates the industrial sector, which also produces wood, paper products, and textiles. Tourism is of increasing importance. Most of the people are of British descent. The MAORI, native New Zealanders of Polynesian descent, numbered about 300,000 in the early 1990s; most live on North Island. English is the official language; Maori is spoken by many of the indigenous people. More than 80% of the population is Christian.

History. The Maori are thought to have migrated to the islands prior to A.D. 1400. Abel TASMAN was the first European to visit (1642) the islands, which were named for the Dutch province of Zeeland, but they attracted little interest until described in detail by Capt. James COOK, who visited them four times between 1769 and 1777. Whalers, missionaries, and traders followed, and in 1840 the first permanent European settlement was established at Wellington by E.G. WAKEFIELD. The same year the Maori signed the Treaty of Waitangi, by which they recognized British sovereignty in exchange for guaranteed possession of their land. Nevertheless, wars over land between the Maori and white settlers were waged until 1870. Originally part of the Australian colony of New South Wales, New Zealand became a separate colony in 1841 and was made self-governing in 1852. Dominion status was attained in 1907, and full independence was conferred by the Statute of Westminster (1931), which was confirmed by New Zealand in 1947. New Zealand was a leader in passing social legislation, e.g., woman suffrage (1893) and social security (1898), and it aided Britain in both world wars. Since 1983 the country has moved toward closer cooperation with Australia on economic matters. Legislative power rests with a unicameral parliament; executive power is vested in a governor general, representing the crown, and a cabinet and prime minister. The chief political parties are the National and the Labor. In 1993 the National party, in power since 1990 and led by Prime Min. James Brendan Bolger, was narrowly returned to office.

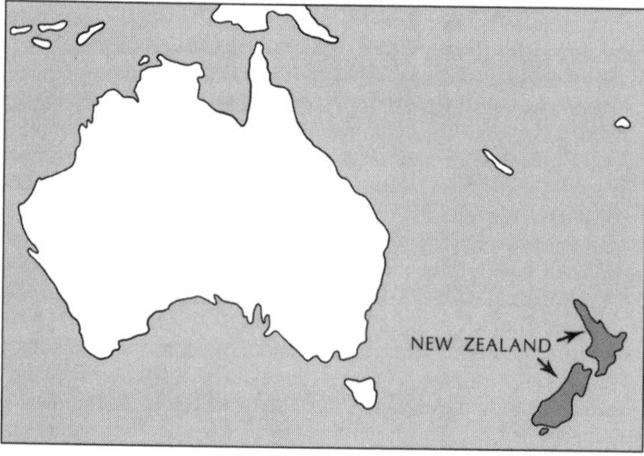

Nexø, Martin Andersen: see ANDERSEN NEXØ, MARTIN.

Ney, Michel [nā'], 1769–1815, marshal of France. Called "the bravest of the brave" by NAPOLEON I, he rose to glory rapidly in the FRENCH REVOLUTIONARY WARS. He gave decisive aid to Napoleon at Friedland (1807) and brilliantly defended the rear during Napoleon's retreat (1812) from Moscow. After Napoleon's abdication (1814) he was raised to the peerage by LOUIS XVIII, but he rejoined Napoleon for the HUNDRED DAYS and fought in the WATERLOO CAMPAIGN (1815). After Napoleon's defeat, Ney was condemned for treason by the house of peers and was shot.

Nez Percé, indigenous people of the Plateau (see NORTH AMERICA, INDIGENOUS PEOPLES OF), with a Sahaptin-Chinook language of the Penutian stock (see NATIVE AMERICAN LANGUAGES). They lived in W Idaho, NE Oregon, and SE Washington, subsisting typically on salmon and plant roots. After acquiring the horse, they became noted horse breeders and adopted other Plains traits, including the buffalo hunt. A fraudulent land cession extracted from them (1863) during the gold rush led to an uprising (1877) under Chief JOSEPH. Today those living on the Idaho reservation are mostly farmers. In 1990 there were 4,113 Nez Percé in the U.S.

Ngugi wa Thiong'o, 1938–, Kenyan writer, also known as James Ngugi. His novels include *Weep Not, Child* (1964) and *A Grain of Wheat* (1967), both about the MAU MAU uprising, and the politically controversial *Petals of Blood* (1977). A popular 1977 play written in Kikuyu was banned and led to his imprisonment (1978–79), which is described in *Detained: A Writer's Prison Diary* (1981).

Ni, chemical symbol of the element NICKEL.

niacin: see COENZYME; VITAMIN (table).

Niagara Falls, city (1990 pop. 61,840), W N.Y., at the great falls of the Niagara R.; inc. 1892. Tourism is one of its oldest industries; there are many state parks and a Native American museum. Industries include mechanical and electrochemical products. The effects of chemical dumping at the city's Love Canal drew national attention in 1978.

Niagara Falls, internationally famous waterfall, on the U.S.–Canada border between Niagara Falls, N.Y., and Niagara Falls, Ont., formed where the Niagara R. drops from Lake ERIE to Lake ONTARIO. Goat Island splits the cataract into the American Falls (167 ft/51 m high; 1,060 ft/323 m wide) and the Horseshoe, or Canadian, Falls (158 ft/48 m high; 2,600 ft/792 m wide), and overlooks the Niagara Gorge (c.7 mi/11 km long) with its Whirlpool Rapids and Whirlpool. Under terms of the Niagara Diversion Treaty (1950), water is diverted in New York to power the 13 generators of the Robert Moses Niagara Power Plant (1,950,000-kw capacity; opened 1961) and in Ontario into the Sir Adam Beck Generating Stations (1,775,000 kw; opened 1954). The falls were formed c.10,000 years ago and are retreating upstream faster in the Horseshoe Falls because of the greater volume of water there.

Niagara-on-the-Lake, town (1991 pop. 12,945), S Ontario, Canada, part of the regional municipality of Niagara (1991 pop. 393,936), on Lake ONTARIO. Located near NIAGARA FALLS, it is a popular tourist center known for its 19th-cent. atmosphere and architecture and for the annual Shaw Festival, held during the summer. Niagara-on-the-Lake was originally settled as Butlersburg in 1784. Renamed Newark, it served (1792–96) as the first capital of Upper Canada (now Ontario). The city was destroyed, along with Fort George (built 1796–99 to defend it), by the Americans in the WAR OF 1812. Subsequently rebuilt, it took its present name in 1906.

Niamey [nyämā'], largest city (1988 pop. 398,265) and capital of Niger, SW Niger, a port on the Niger R. At the crossroads of two main highways, the city handles trade for an agricultural region specializing in peanuts. Manufactures include bricks, food products, and cement. A small town when the French colonized the area (late 19th cent.), Niamey grew after it became the capital of Niger in 1926.

Nibelungen [nē'bəlo͝ong"ən] or **Nibelungs,** in Germanic myth, an evil family possessing a magic hoard of gold. The *Nibelungenlied* [–lēt"] is a Middle High German epic by a south German poet of the early 13th cent., recounting the story of Siegfried, who wins the hoard, marries Kriemhild, and captures Queen Brunhild for Kriemhild's brother Gunther. Brunhild contrives Siegfried's death, and Kriemhild wreaks vengeance on Gunther's court. *The Ring of the Nibelungs* is an operatic tetralogy by Richard WAGNER, comprising *Das Rheingold, Die Walküre, Siegfried,* and *Götterdämmerung*.

Nicaea, Councils of, two ecumenical councils of the Christian Church. The first council (325), convened by the Emperor CONSTANTINE I, rejected ARIANISM and established the divinity and equality of the Son in the Trinity. The second council (787), called to refute ICONOCLASM, declared that religious images ought to be venerated (but not worshiped).

Nicaea, empire of, 1204–61, one of the Greek states that arose after the Fourth CRUSADE set up the Latin empire of Constantinople. Founded by Theodore I, Nicaea continued the institutions of Byzantium, including emperors and patriarchs. Theodore and his successors became supreme in Asia Minor. The Nicaean emperor MICHAEL VIII captured Constantinople (1261) and restored the Byzantine Empire.

Nicaragua, officially Republic of Nicaragua, republic (1992 est. pop. 3,878,000), 49,579 sq mi (128,410 sq km), Central America; bordered by Honduras (N), the Caribbean Sea (E), Costa Rica (S), and the Pacific Ocean (SW). The capital is MANAGUA. Mountainous in the northeast, Nicaragua is the least densely populated Central American nation; the people live mainly on a narrow, volcanic belt between the Pacific and Lakes Managua and Nicaragua. The country is subject to destructive earthquakes. There are gold and tungsten mines, timbering, and some manufacturing, but the country is primarily agricultural, exporting coffee, cotton, sugarcane, bananas, seafood, and meat. The population is mainly Spanish-speaking, Roman Catholic, and predominantly mestizo. There is an English-speaking minority on the Altantic coast.

History. The first Spanish colonial cities in the area, LEÓN and Granada, were founded in 1524. Ruled as part of GUATEMALA, Nicaragua achieved independence in 1821. After brief periods as part of the Mexican Empire and the Central American Federation, Nicaragua became a separate republic in 1838. Marked by extreme liberal-conservative antagonism, the country has had an unusually violent history. Foreign interference was frequent, especially by the U.S., which from the early 19th cent. expressed interest in a possible inter-ocean waterway in Nicaragua. U.S. marines intervened in a civil war in 1912, remaining in the country until 1933. In 1937 Anastasio SOMOZA became president. The nation was ruled dictatorially by members of the Somoza family until 1979, when their regime was overthrown, after bloody fighting, by the SANDINISTAS. The Sandinistas formed a government that at first included moderate conservatives, but moved rapidly to the political left in the early 1980s. In 1984, a Sandinista leader, Daniel Ortega Saavedra, was elected president. The effects of land redistribution, literacy programs, and other reforms were nullified by costly warfare between the Sandinistas and the contras, right-wing guerrillas based outside the country and supported by the U.S. In 1990 a presidential election resulted in the unexpected defeat of Ortega by opposition candidate Violeta Barrios de Chamorro, and the Sandinista government and the contras agreed to a cease-fire. Under Chamorro, the army and police continued to be led by Sandinistas, but economic reforms were instituted and inflation reduced. The economy remained stagnant and unemployment high, however, and tense relations between the Sandinistas and their opponents threatened to undermine Chamorro's government.

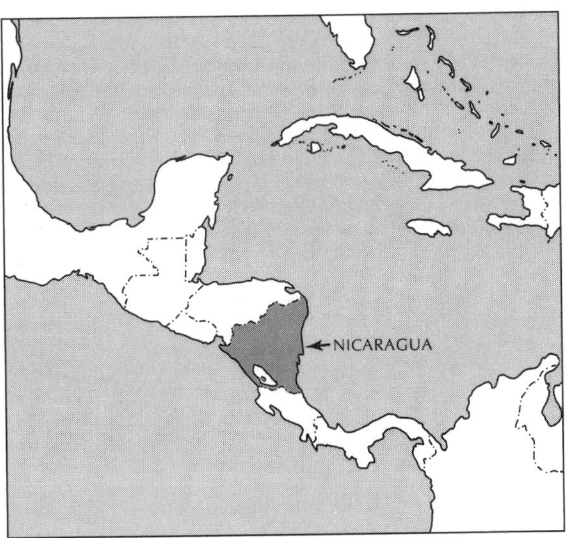

Nice [nēs], city (1990 pop. 342,439), capital of Alpes-Maritimes dept., SE France, on the Mediterranean Sea. This famous French Riviera resort relies mostly on tourists, but electronics and other manufactures are important. Nice probably originated as a Greek colony in the 5th cent. B.C. Sardinia held it from 1814 to 1860, when a plebiscite gave it to France.

Nicephorus [nīcĕf'ərəs], Byzantine emperors. **Nicephorus I,** d. 811 (r.802–811), deposed Empress IRENE. He reformed the treasury and taxation, and asserted the supremacy of emperor over church, a doctrine opposed by the monastic reformer St. Theodore of Studium. **Nicephorus II** (Phocas), c.912–969, a general under ROMANUS II, married the emperor's widow and usurped the throne (963–69). Disliked for taking land from monasteries and imposing heavy taxes to finance his wars, he was murdered by his wife's lover, who succeeded to the throne as JOHN I.

Nicholas, Saint, patron of children and sailors, of Greece, Sicily, and Russia, and of many other persons and places. Traditionally he is identified with a 4th-cent. bishop of Myra in Asia Minor. In the Netherlands and elsewhere his feast (Dec. 6) is a children's holiday. The English in New York adopted him from the Dutch, calling him Santa Claus.

Nicholas I, Saint (Nicholas the Great), c.825–867, pope (858–67), a Roman. He established the right of a bishop to appeal to Rome against his superior and blocked the divorce of LOTHAIR of Lotharingia. He supported St. IGNATIUS OF CONSTANTINOPLE over PHOTIUS as patriarch of Constantinople and sought Roman ecclesiastical jurisdiction over Bulgaria. Feast: Nov. 13.

Nicholas, czars of Russia. **Nicholas I,** 1796–1855 (r.1825–55), was the third son of PAUL I. On his first day as czar he crushed the uprising of the DECEMBRISTS. During his reign laws were codified, the first Russian railroad was completed and the condition of SERFS belonging to the state somewhat improved, but political progress was stifled and minorities were persecuted under the slogan "autocracy, orthodoxy, and nationality." Intellectual ferment generated the SLAVOPHILES AND WESTERNIZERS, and GOGOL, LERMONTOV, and PUSHKIN began a golden age in literature. Nicholas brutally suppressed the uprising in POLAND (1830–31) and in 1849 helped Austria crush the revolution in HUNGARY. He died during the disastrous CRIMEAN WAR and was succeeded by his son ALEXANDER II. **Nicholas II,** 1868–1918 (r.1894–1917), was the son of ALEXANDER III. As a youth he received little training in affairs of state. His reign continued the suppression of political opposition and persecution of minorities. Revolutionary groups proliferated, while liberals demanded constitutional government. An aggressive policy in E Asia led to defeat in the RUSSO-JAPANESE WAR (1904–5). In Jan. 1905 a peaceful crowd of petitioners was fired upon in front of the Winter Palace; this "bloody Sunday" began the 1905 Revolution. In October Count WITTE induced Nicholas to sign a manifesto promising constitutional government and basic civil liberties, but the czar dissolved the DUMA shortly after it began to sit, and Witte was replaced as premier by STOLYPIN in 1906. WORLD WAR I began in 1914; in 1915 Nicholas took command of the army, leaving Czarina ALEXANDRA FEODOROVNA and her adviser, RASPUTIN, in control of the government. Discontent spread, the army tired of war, food shortages worsened, the government tottered, and in March 1917 Nicholas was forced to abdicate (see RUSSIAN REVOLUTION). He and his family were shot in Yekaterinburg on July 16, 1918.

Nicholas of Cusa, 1401–64, German theologian and philosopher. He was a legal adviser to Church officials and a papal representative on several embassies before becoming (1440) a Cardinal. His writings, which emphasize the limits of rational investigation, are associated with NEOPLATONISM.

Nicholson, Ben, 1894–1982, English painter. Developing the purism of de STIJL with great elegance, he produced geometric abstractions of landscapes and still lifes, e.g., *Relief* (Mus. Mod. Art, N.Y.C.).

Nicholson, Jack, 1937–, American film actor. His first success was *Easy Rider* (1969), and he won Academy awards for *One Flew over the Cuckoo's Nest* (1975) and *Terms of Endearment* (1983). His other films include *Chinatown* (1974), *Prizzi's Honor* (1985), and *Batman* (1989).

Nicias [nĭsh'ēəs], d. 413 B.C., Athenian statesman and general. An opponent of CLEON and his war party, he favored peace with SPARTA during the PELOPONNESIAN WAR, and in 421 B.C. he arranged the truce known as the Peace of Nicias. Although he had opposed the project, he was placed in command of an expedition to SYRACUSE. His vacillation led to an Athenian defeat; Nicias was captured and executed.

nickel (Ni), metallic element, discovered in 1751 by A.F. Cronstedt. It is a silver-white, hard, malleable, ductile, and lustrous metal whose chief use is in the preparation of alloys, to which it brings strength, ductility, and resistance to corrosion and heat. Many stainless STEELS contain nickel. It is also used in storage batteries. Nickel's chief ores are garnierite, pentlandite and pyrrhotite. Nickel is present in most METEORITES. Trace amounts are found in plants and animals. See ELEMENT (table); PERIODIC TABLE.

Nicklaus, Jack (William), 1940–, American golfer; b. Columbus, Ohio. Considered the greatest golfer of all time, he mastered every shot. Nicknamed the "Golden Bear," he won two national amateur titles (1959, 1961) while a student at Ohio State Univ. By winning the Masters title in 1986, he raised his total of major championships to 18, far more than any other player. These included the Masters (six), the PGA (five), the U.S. Open (four), and the British Open (three).

Nicolson, Sir Harold, 1886–1968, English biographer and historian, a diplomat and a member of Parliament; b. Iran. His biographies include those on Swinburne (1926) and GEORGE V (1953). Among his other works are *Diplomacy* (1939), *The Congress of Vienna* (1946), and *The Age of Reason* (1961). He was married to V. SACKVILLE-WEST.

Nicomedia, ancient city (modern Izmit, Turkey), NW Asia Minor. It was the residence of the kings of BITHYNIA from 264 B.C. Diocletian chose it as the eastern imperial capital, but it was soon superseded by Byzantium.

Nicosia, city (1989 est. pop. 169,000), capital of Cyprus. An agricultural trade center, it manufactures textiles, leather, plastics, and other goods. It was the residence of the Lusignan kings of CYPRUS from 1192 and a Venetian possession (15th cent.) before it fell (1571) to the Turks. From Cypriot independence (1960) to the Turkish invasion (1974), it was the scene of conflict between Greeks and Turks. Its museums house notable antiquities.

Niebuhr, Barthold Georg [nē'bo͝or], 1776–1831, German historian; b. Denmark. His history of Rome (3 vol., 1811–32) may be said to have inaugurated modern scientific historical method. In it he related individual events to the political and social institutions of ancient Rome.

Niebuhr, Reinhold, 1892–1971, American religious and social thinker; b. Wright City, Mo. He taught (1928–60) at Union Theological Seminary, New York City, and became interested in social problems. In the early 1930s he shed his liberal Protestant hopes for the church's moral rule of society and became a political activist and a socialist. His writings include *Moral Man and Immoral Society* (1932), *Christianity and Power Politics* (1940), and *The Nature and Destiny of Man* (2 vol., 1941–43). His brother, **Helmut Richard Niebuhr,** 1894–1962, joined the faculty of Yale Divinity School in 1931. His thought was early influenced by KIERKEGAARD and BARTH; later, however, he turned his attention to the personal nature of humanity's relationship to God and advocated a reworking of Christianity in light of the developments of the 20th cent.

nielsbohrium (Ns), artificial radioactive TRANSURANIUM ELEMENT. Claims for its production have been made by a Soviet group at Dubna, who in 1976 bombarded bismuth with chromium ions to obtain, apparently, the Ns^{261} isotope, and by a West German group at Darmstadt, who in 1981 bombarded bismuth with chromium ions to obtain the Ns^{262} isotope. It is also called unnilseptium (Uns). See ELEMENT (table); PERIODIC TABLE.

Niemeyer (Soares), Oscar, 1907–, Brazilian architect. Influenced by LE CORBUSIER, he is noted for projects like the Ministry of Education, Rio de Janeiro (1937–43), and, especially, for his direction of the creation of the Brazilian federal capital, Brasília (1950–60).

Niemoeller or **Niemöller, Martin** [nē'mölər], 1892–1984, German Protestant churchman. A submarine commander in World War I, he later led the CONFESSING CHURCH and opposed the religious policies of HITLER's regime. He was imprisoned from 1938 to 1945. He later became (1947) president of the Evangelical Church in Hesse-Nassau and was also president (1961–68) of the World Council of Churches.

Niepce, Joseph Nicéphore [nyĕps], 1765–1833, French chemist. He originated a process of photography (see PHOTOGRAPHY, STILL) that was later perfected by Louis Daguerre. A nephew, **Claude Félix Abel Niepce de Saint-Victor,** 1805–70, also a chemist, introduced the use of albumen in photography and produced photographic engravings on steel.

Nietzsche, Friedrich Wilhelm, 1844–1900, German philosopher. An individualistic moralist rather than a systematic philosopher, influenced by SCHOPENHAUER and by his early friendship with Richard WAGNER, he passionately rejected the "slave morality" of Christianity for a new, heroic morality that would affirm life. Leading this new society would be a breed of supermen whose "will to power" would set them off from the "herd" of inferior humanity. His writings, e.g., *Thus Spake Zarathustra* (1883–91) and *Beyond Good and Evil* (1886), were later used as a philosophical justification for NAZI doctrines of racial and national superiority; most scholars, however, regard this as a perversion of Nietzsche's thought.

Niger, officially Republic of Niger, republic (1992 est. pop. 8,053,000), 489,189 sq mi (1,267,000 sq km), W Africa, bordered by Burkina Faso and Mali (W), Algeria and Libya (N), Chad (E), Nigeria and Benin (S). NIAMEY is the capital. The landlocked country is largely semidesert or part of the SAHARA, except along the NIGER R. and near the southern border. The Aïr mts., in N central Niger, rise to c.5,900 ft (1,800 m). The economy is increasingly supported by high-grade uranium ore deposits, which have been worked since the early 1970s; Niger is one of the world's leading producers. Other minerals extracted include cassiterite (tin ore), phosphates, and coal. About 90% of the work force is engaged in farming, largely of a subsistence type; major crops include millet, sorghum, cassava, and peanuts. Stock raising (cattle, sheep, goats) is also important. Manufacturing is limited mainly to basic consumer goods. There is some fishing along the Niger R. and on Lake Chad. The main ethnic groups are the Hausa (56%) and Djerma (22%). The nomadic Tuareg live in N Niger and, along with others from MALI, fought for greater autonomy in the early 1990s. About 80% of the people are Muslim; most of the rest follow traditional beliefs. French is the official language, but Hausa and Djerma are widely spoken.

History. About 1300 the TUAREG established a state centered at Agadès (Agadez), situated on a major trans-Saharan caravan route, and in the 14th cent. the Hausa founded several city-states in S Niger. Parts of the region came under the SONGHAI empire in the early 16th cent., the state of Bornu in the late 16th cent., and the Fulani people in the early 19th cent. After the Conference of BERLIN (1884–85) placed the territory of Niger within the French sphere of influence, France established military posts in the south but for a time met concerted Tuareg resistance. In 1922 Niger became a separate colony within FRENCH WEST AFRICA. Nationalist political activity, which began in 1946, was led at first by the Niger Progressive party (PPN) and in the mid-1950s by a leftist party (later called Sawaba). The PPN, which favored autonomy within the FRENCH COMMUNITY, regained power in 1958, when a referendum supported that course. Niger became fully independent in 1960, with PPN leader Hamani Diori as president (he was reelected in 1965 and 1970). Niger enjoyed political stability and maintained close ties with France. The severe Sahelian drought (1968–75) caused economic disruption and civil unrest, however, leading to an army coup (1974), suspension of the constitution, and military rule under a regime led by Lt. Col. Seyni Kountché. The new gov-

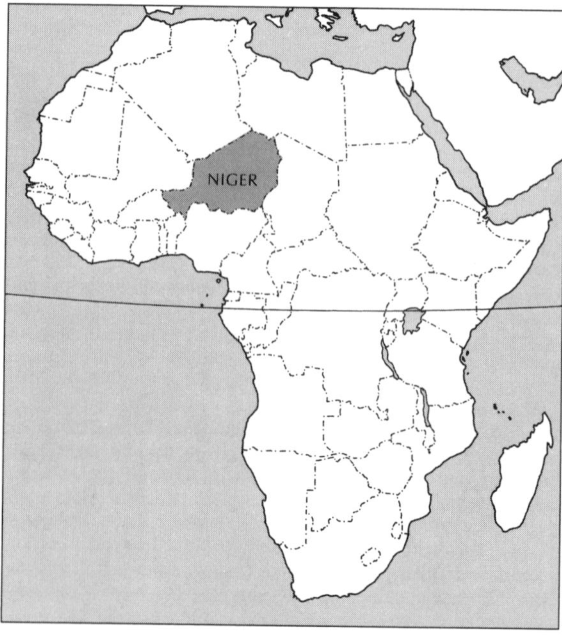

ernment curtailed French influence in the rich uranium industry, concluded a more favorable economic agreement with France, and later brought civilians into the administration. On Kountché's death (1987), Brig. Gen. Ali Saïbou became president, and he continued Niger's slow return to democracy. In 1991 a national political conference stripped Saïbou of power and installed a transitional civilian government. In free elections in 1993, Mahamane Ousmane won the presidency.

Niger, chief river of W Africa, flowing c.2,600 mi (4,180 km) in a circuitous, generally eastward course from SW Guinea to a vast delta on the Gulf of Guinea, in Nigeria. An inland delta in central Mali is irrigated by a large dam at Sansanding. The chief tributary of the Niger is the Benue R.

Nigeria, officially Federal Republic of Nigeria, republic (1991 pop. 88,514,501), 356,667 sq mi (923,768 sq km), W Africa, bordered by the Gulf of Guinea (S), Benin (W), Niger (NW and N), Chad (NE), and Cameroon (E). Nigeria is the most populous country on the continent. The nation is divided into 30 states and a federal capital territory. Major cities include LAGOS, IBADAN, OGBOMOSHO, and KANO; in 1991 the nation's capital was moved from Lagos to ABUJA. Nigeria's main geographical regions include a 500-mi (800-km) coastline of sandy beaches, behind which lies a belt of mangrove swamps and lagoons; a broad, hilly region north of the coastal lowlands, with rain forests in the south and savanna in the north; and the great plateau, a region of plains covered largely with savanna. The highest point (c.6,700 ft/2,040 m) is in the Adamawa Massif, in the east. Most of the country is drained by the NIGER R. and its tributaries. Petroleum production, which began in the late 1950s, is the mainstay of the economy; by 1987 petroleum accounted for 95% of exports. The decline in petroleum prices in the 1980s depressed economic growth and led to greatly increased international debt, and corruption has also hurt the economy. Other minerals include tin, coal, columbite, iron ore, lead, zinc, and uranium. Agriculture employs about 70% of the work force. The chief crops grown in the north include sorghum, millet, soybeans, peanuts, and cotton; those in the south include corn, rice, palm products, cacao, and rubber. Livestock raising, forestry, and fishing are also important. Growth in the manufacturing sector slowed in the 1980s; major industries include oil refining, food processing, brewing, and production of cement, aluminum, motor vehicles, and textiles. The inhabitants of Nigeria are divided into about 250 ethnic groups, but the Hausa, Yoruba, Ibo, and Fulani together make up two thirds of the population. About half the people are Muslim, living mostly in the north, and some 40% are Christian, almost all in the south; the rest follow traditional beliefs. English is the official language, but Hausa, Yoruba, Ibo, and a number of other indigenous tongues are regionally importan

History. Before the coming of the British in the late 19th cent., a series of states and city-states were established by various ethnic groups. These included the state of Kanem-Bornu, which expanded into present-day Nigeria in the 11th cent., followed by seven independent Hausa city-states (11th cent.), the Yoruba states of Oyo and BENIN (14th cent.), and the SONGHAI Empire (16th cent.). Portuguese navigators, arriving in the late 15th cent. were joined by British, French, and Dutch traders, and a lucrative slave trade developed that continued until about 1875. In the 19th cent. Muslim culture flourished in the Fulani empire, while both Bornu and the Oyo Empire were rent by civil wars. Sir George Goldie's commercial activities in the region enabled Britain to claim S Nigeria at the Conference of BERLIN (1884–85). By 1906 Britain controlled all of Nigeria and had established a protectorate over it. Under British rule, the economy grew and the country became more urbanized. In the 1950s new constitutions led to the emergence of political parties and elected representation, and Nigeria was divided (1954) into three regions: Eastern, Western, and Northern, plus Lagos. By 1959 the regions had gained internal autonomy; in 1960 Nigeria attained full independence. It became a republic in 1963, with B.N. Azikiwe as president. Severe conflicts within and between regions marked the early years of independence, climaxed by an Ibo-led coup in 1966 that resulted in the deaths of Prime Minister A.T. Balewa and two regional prime ministers, and ended civil government. A second coup that year by Hausa army officers installed a new military regime headed by Lt. Col. Yakuba Gowon. The Ibos of the Eastern Region proclaimed the independent republic of BIAFRA in 1967, precipitating a disastrous civil war that continued until Biafra's surrender in 1970. Gowon was overthrown in a military coup in 1975, but the new regime restored civilian rule in 1979, when a democratic constitution took effect and Alhaji Shehu SHAGARI became president in free elections. However, four years later a coup deposed Shagari and reestablished military rule. Maj. Gen. Ibrahim Babangida became president (1985) after another coup and later announced plans to restore civilian rule. A new constitution (1990) set national elections for 1992, but Babangida annulled the presidential results, claiming fraud. Moshood Abiola apparently won (1993) a new election, but Babangida again charged fraud. Unrest led to Babangida's resignation. Ernest Shonekan, a civilian appointed as interim leader, was forced out after three months by Gen. Sani Abacha, who became president and banned all political institutions.

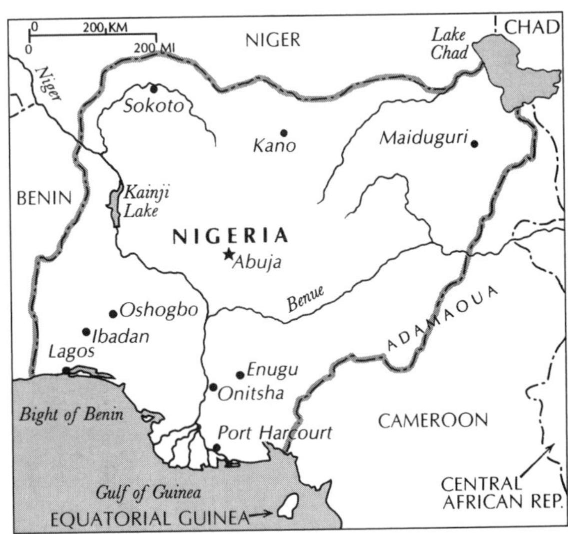

Nightingale, Florence, 1820–1910, English nurse, the founder of modern NURSING; b. Italy. Her life was dedicated to the care of the sick and war-wounded. She organized (1854) a unit of 38 women nurses for the Crimean War, and by war's end she had become a legend. In 1860 Nightingale established a nursing school at St. Thomas's Hospital, London. In 1907 she became the first woman to be given the British Order of Merit.

nightingale, migratory Old World BIRD of the THRUSH family, celebrated for the song the male sings during the breeding season. The common nightingale of England and W Europe (*Luscinia megarhynchos*), reddish-brown above and grayish-white below, winters in Africa.

nightshade, common name for the family Solanaceae, herbs, shrubs, and trees of warm regions. Many are climbing or creeping types. Rank-smelling foliage typifies many species; the odor is due to the presence of various ALKALOIDS, e.g., scopolamine, nicotine, and atropine. The chief drug plants of the family are BELLADONNA, MANDRAKE, Jimson weed, and TOBACCO. The family also includes important food plants, e.g., POTATO, TOMATO, red PEPPER, and EGGPLANT, and ornamentals, e.g., PETUNIA. The name *nightshade* is commonly restricted to members of the genus *Solanum,* typified by white or purplish star-shaped flowers and orange berries. Among the better-known species are Jerusalem cherry (*S. pseudocapsicum*), a house plant popular for its scarlet berries, and the BITTERSWEET, or woody nightshade.

Niigata, city (1990 pop. 486,087), capital of Niigata prefecture, N Honshu, Japan, on the Sea of Japan. It is the main port for W Honshu, and exports oil, machinery, and textiles. Niigata has an important chemical industry based on the area's coal and natural gas deposits and is also the site of one of the largest flower farms in E Asia.

Nijinsky, Vaslav [nyĭzhēn'skē], 1890–1950, Russian ballet dancer and choreographer. He made his debut (1907) in St. Petersburg, and later became premier danseur with DIAGHILEV. He initiated many of ballet's greatest roles, including ones in *Petrouchka, Afternoon of a Faun,* and *Sacre du Printemps*. He is considered the greatest 20th-cent. male dancer. His career was cut short (1919) by insanity.

Nike [nī'kē], in Greek myth, goddess of victory. The daughter of Pallas and Styx, she presided over all contests. Representations of her winged form include the *Victory (Nike) of Samothrace* (LOUVRE), one of the greatest Greek sculptures.

Nikko, town (1990 pop. 20,128), central Honshu, Japan, in Nikko National Park. It is a tourist resort and religious center famous for its ornate temples and shrines dating from the Edo period (1600–1868); particularly noteworthy is the great shrine housing the tomb of IEYASU.

Nikolais, Alwin, 1910–93, American dancer and choreographer; b. Southington, Conn. He formed (1949) his own company in New York City; he merged it with Murray Louis's company in 1989. His abstract, exhilarating works include *Imago* (1963), *Gallery* (1978) and *Crucible* (1985).

Nile, great river of Africa. The longest river in the world, it flows generally north c.4,160 mi (6,695 km) from its remotest headstream, the Luvironza R. (in Burundi), to enter the Mediterranean Sea through a vast, triangular delta in N Egypt. Its trunk stream is formed at Khartoum (Sudan) by the convergence of the Blue Nile (c.1,000 mi/1,610 km) and the White Nile (c.2,300 mi/3,700 km). The Blue Nile, rising in Lake Tana in a region of summer rains, was the source of Egypt's soil-replenishing annual floods prior to construction of the ASWAN HIGH DAM. The White Nile, rising in Lake VICTORIA, has a more nearly constant flow. Waters from the Nile, which nourished the most long-lived of the great ancient civilizations (see EGYPT), now supply hydroelectricity and support irrigated agriculture in Egypt and in the Sudan's Gezira.

Nilotes, people of E Africa, including the Nuer and Masai, who speak Nilotic languages. Originally from E Sudan, they now inhabit S SUDAN, N UGANDA, and N KENYA. Noted for their tall stature, they are primarily pastoralists.

Nilsson, Birgit, 1918–, Swedish soprano. Possessed of a powerful voice, she is noted for her Wagnerian roles (see WAGNER, Richard). She won international notice in Munich (1955–56) and made her U.S. debut in 1959.

Nimeiry, Muhammad Gaafur al- [nĭmĕr'ē], 1930–, Sudanese army officer and political leader. In 1969 he led the leftist military coup that toppled the civilian government. He was elected (1971) president and became (1972) prime minister. His imposition of Islamic law over both the north and non-Islamic south of Sudan in 1983 eventually led to his overthrow (1985).

Nimitz, Chester William, 1885–1966, American admiral; b. Fredericksburg, Tex. He commanded the U.S. Pacific Fleet throughout WORLD WAR II, becoming admiral of the fleet (five-star admiral) in 1944. He later served as chief of naval operations (1945–47).

Nin, Anaïs [nēn], 1903–77, American writer; b. Paris. Although she wrote several novels, including *A Spy in the House of Love* (1954), Nin is best known for six volumes of diaries (1966–76; unexpurgated ed., 1986–), recording her psychological and artistic development. She also wrote criticism and essays.

Nineveh [nĭn'əvə], ancient city, capital of the Assyrian empire, on the Tigris R. opposite modern Mosul, Iraq. Nineveh reached its full glory under SENNACHERIB and ASSURBANIPAL. Excavations have revealed palaces and a CUNEIFORM library. The city fell in 612 B.C. to a coalition of Babylonians, Medes, and Scythians. It is mentioned often in the Bible.

niobium (Nb), metallic element, discovered in 1801 by Charles Hatchett. Called columbium by metallurgists, it is a rare, soft, malleable, ductile, gray-white metal that is used in high-temperature-resistant alloys and special stainless steels. See ELEMENT (table); PERIODIC TABLE.

nirvana, in BUDDHISM, JAINISM, and HINDUISM, a state of supreme bliss; liberation from suffering and from *samsara,* one's bondage to the repeating cycle of death and rebirth, which is brought about by desire. Nirvana is attainable in life through moral discipline and the practice of YOGA, leading to the extinction of all attachment and ignorance. See also KARMA.

nitric acid, chemical compound (HNO_3), colorless, highly corrosive, poisonous liquid that gives off choking fumes in moist air. It is miscible with water in all proportions. Commercially, it is usually available in solutions of 52% to 68% nitric acid in water. Solutions containing over 86% nitric acid are commonly called fuming nitric acid. Nitric acid is a strong oxidizing agent. It reacts with metals, oxides, and hydroxides, forming nitrate salts. See also AQUA REGIA; Wilhelm OSTWALD.

nitric oxide (NO), colorless, poisonous gas formed by the combustion of nitrogen and oxygen. In the environment, it is a precursor of SMOG and ACID RAIN. In the body, it serves as a chemical messenger with a wide range of functions. It acts as a NEUROTRANSMITTER and is necessary for penile erection. It affects blood pressure and is produced by the immune system to help defend against infection and cancer. Despite its usefulness, nitric oxide can have a toxic effect on body cells and has been implicated in HUNTINGTON'S DISEASE, ALZHEIMER'S DISEASE, and arthritis.

nitrogen (N), gaseous element, discovered by Daniel Rutherford in 1772. Nitrogen is a colorless, odorless, tasteless, diatomic gas that is relatively inactive chemically; it occupies about 78% (by volume) of dry air. Its chief importance lies in its compounds, which include NITROUS OXIDE, NITRIC ACID, AMMONIA, many EXPLOSIVES, CYANIDES, FERTILIZERS, and PROTEINS. Nitrogen is present in the PROTOPLASM of all living matter; it and its compounds are necessary for the continuation of life (see NITROGEN CYCLE). See ELEMENT (table); PERIODIC TABLE.

nitrogen cycle, the continuous flow of nitrogen through the BIOSPHERE by the processes of nitrogen fixation, ammonification (decay), nitrification, and denitrification. Nitrogen is an essential constituent of all protoplasm. To enter living systems, however, it must first be "fixed" (combined with oxygen or hydrogen) into compounds that plants can utilize, such as nitrates or ammonia. Most fixation is performed by certain bacteria living in the soil or in nodules in the roots of leguminous plants (see PULSE, in botany). Plants elaborate the fixed nitrogen into plant protein; then animals consume the plants and convert plant protein into animal protein. Organic nitrogen is returned to the soil as ammonia when animal remains and wastes decay. Then nitrifying bacteria oxidize the ammonia to nitrites and the nitrites to nitrates, which can, like ammonia, be taken up by plants. Still other soil microorganisms can reduce ammonia nitrates to molecular nitrogen. See also ECOLOGY.

nitroglycerin ($C_3H_5N_3O_9$), colorless, oily, liquid EXPLOSIVE. An unstable compound that decomposes violently when heated or jarred, nitroglycerin is made less sensitive to shock when mixed with an absorbent material to form DYNAMITE. Nitroglycerin is also a component of smokeless powder and is used in medicine for relief from the symptoms of angina pectoris. It was first produced commercially by Alfred NOBEL.

nitrous oxide, chemical compound (N_2O), colorless gas with a sweetish taste and odor. Although it does not burn, it supports combustion because it decomposes into oxygen and nitrogen when heated. A major use is in dental anesthesia. It is often called laughing gas because it produces euphoria and mirth when inhaled in small amounts. It is also used in making certain canned pressurized foods, e.g., instant whipped cream.

Niue, self-governing coral island (1992 est. pop. 1,800), 100 sq mi (260 sq km), in the South Pacific Ocean, freely associated with New Zealand. Alofi is the chief town. Niue has fertile soil and exports copra, honey, and fruit. The inhabitants are mainly Polynesian.

Nixon, Richard Milhous, 1913–94, 37th president of the U.S. (1969–74); b. Yorba Linda, Calif. As a Republican U.S. representative from California (1947–51) he gained national prominence for his investigation of Alger HISS. In the Senate (1951–53), he attacked the Democratic administration as favorable to Socialism. He was elected to the vice presidency on the Republican ticket with Dwight D. EISENHOWER in 1952; they were reelected in 1956. Kept closely informed, Nixon played an important role in government affairs. He ran for president in 1960 but was defeated by John F. KENNEDY, and in 1962 he was defeated in the race for governor of California. In

1968 he again won the Republican presidential nomination and, with his running mate, Spiro T. AGNEW, defeated Hubert H. HUMPHREY and George C. WALLACE. As president, Nixon achieved a cease-fire in the VIETNAM WAR, but only after he had ordered invasions of Cambodia (1970) and Laos (1971) and the saturation bombing of North Vietnam. In other areas of foreign affairs, he initiated strategic arms limitation talks with the Soviet Union (1959) and visited (1972) the People's Republic of China. At home, he reversed many of the social and economic welfare programs of Pres. JOHNSON's administration and, hoping to woo the South into the Republican party, weakened the federal government's commitment to racial equality. His administration was plagued by economic woes that led to the imposition (1971) of wage and price controls. Despite these problems, he and Agnew were easily re-elected in 1972, winning a landslide victory over George S. MCGOVERN. (Agnew was forced to resign in 1973 and was replaced by Gerald R. Ford.) Investigations into the WATERGATE AFFAIR and studies by the Internal Revenue Service revealed pervasive corruption in Nixon's administration, and in 1974 the U.S. House of Representatives began impeachment proceedings. After completing its investigations, the House Judiciary Committee recommended (July 27–30) three articles of impeachment: obstruction of justice, abuse of power, and failure to comply with congressional subpoenas. On Aug. 5 Nixon admitted that he had ordered the FBI to stop investigating the Watergate burglary. On Aug. 9 he became the first president to resign. His successor, Gerald R. FORD, granted him a full pardon, quashing the possibility of criminal proceedings.

Nizhny Novgorod, city (1990 est. pop. 1,440,000), E European Russia, on the Volga and Oka rivers. A major river port, it has one of the largest automobile plants in Russia, as well as steel-making and other industries. Founded in 1221, it was a center of trade with the East. From 1932 to 1990 it was named Gorky for Maxim GORKY, who was born there.

Nkrumah, Kwame [nkro͞o'mä], 1909–72, prime minister (1957–60) and president (1960–66) of GHANA. He was a leader in the struggle to gain independence for the British Gold Coast (now Ghana). His leadership of the new nation grew increasingly dictatorial and autocratic, and he was ousted in 1966.

NKVD: see CHEKA; KGB.

No, chemical symbol of the element NOBELIUM.

Noah [nō'ə] or **Noe** [nō'ē], in the BIBLE, the builder of the ARK, at divine direction, that saved human and animal life from the deluge. After the flood God established a covenant with Noah. Noah's sons, Shem, Ham, and Japheth, are eponymous ancestors of races, as humanity is divided in the Bible.

Nobel, Alfred Bernhard, 1833–96, Swedish chemist and inventor. He was involved, with his family, in the development and manufacture of explosives, and his invention of DYNAMITE, a mixture of nitroglycerine and inert filler, greatly improved the safety of explosives. Inclined toward pacifism and concerned about the potential uses of the explosives he had invented, he established a fund to provide annual awards, called NOBEL PRIZES, in the sciences, literature, and the promotion of international peace.

nobelium (No), radioactive element, first produced artificially in 1958 by A. Ghiorso, T. Sikkeland, J.R. Walton, and Glenn T. SEABORG by carbon-ion bombardment of curium. It is a TRANSURANIUM ELEMENT in the ACTINIDE SERIES. Seven isotopes are known. See ELEMENT (table); PERIODIC TABLE.

Nobel Memorial Prize in Economic Science: see under NOBEL PRIZE.

Nobel Prize, award, est. and endowed by the will of Alfred NOBEL, given annually for outstanding achievement in one of five fields. By the terms of Nobel's will, the physics and chemistry prizes are judged by the Royal Swedish Academy of Sciences; the physiology or medicine prize, by Sweden's Royal Caroline Medico-Chirurgical Institute; the literature prize, by the Swedish Academy; and the peace prize, by a committee of the Norwegian parliament. Each recipient is presented with a gold medal and a monetary award (or a share of it) worth about $825,000 in 1993. The five awards were first given in 1901. The prizes are not always awarded every year, and from 1940 to 1942 no awards were made. A sixth, related award, the **Nobel Memorial Prize in Economic Science,** was established and endowed in 1968 by Sveriges Riksbank, the Swedish national bank. First awarded in 1969, it is judged by the Royal Swedish Academy of Sciences.

NOBEL MEMORIAL PRIZE IN ECONOMIC SCIENCE			
1969	Ragnar Frisch and Jan Tinbergen	1980	Lawrence R. Klein
1970	Paul A. Samuelson	1981	James Tobin
1971	Simon Kuznets	1982	George J. Stigler
1972	Sir John R. Hicks Kenneth J. Arrow	1983	Gerard Debreu
1973	Wassily Leontief	1984	Richard Stone
1974	Gunnar Myrdal Friedrich A. von Hayek	1985	Franco Modigliani
1975	Leonid V. Kantorovich Tjalling C. Koopmans	1986	James M. Buchanan
1976	Milton Friedman	1987	Robert M. Solow
1977	James E. Meade	1988	Maurice Allais
	Bertil Ohlin	1989	Trygve Haavelmo
1978	Herbert A. Simon	1990	Harry M. Markowitz, William F. Sharpe, and Merton H. Miller
1979	Sir Arthur Lewis Theodore W. Schultz	1991	Ronald H. Coase
		1992	Gary S. Becker
		1993	Robert W. Fogel and Douglass C. North

noble gas: see INERT GAS.

node, either of two points at which the ORBIT of a celestial body crosses a reference plane. The south-to-north crossing occurs at the ascending node; the north-to-south crossing at the descending node. Perturbations due to other bodies cause the nodes to move along the reference plane. See also ECLIPSE.

Nō drama: see *Japanese drama* under ASIAN DRAMA.

Noel-Baker, Philip John Noel-Baker, Baron, 1889–1982, British statesman. After helping to draft (1919) the Covenant of the LEAGUE OF NATIONS, he served (1929–31, 1936–70) as a Labour member of Parliament. After World War II he helped draft the UNITED NATIONS Charter and worked actively for world disarmament. He was awarded the Nobel Peace Prize in 1959.

Noether, (Amalie) Emmy [nö'tər], 1882–1935, German mathematician. She made important contributions to the development of abstract algebra, which studies the formal properties, e.g., ASSOCIATIVE LAW, COMMUTATIVE LAW, and DISTRIBUTIVE LAW, of algebraic operations. After finally gaining an official appointment at Göttingen Univ. in 1919, she developed the theories of ideals and of noncommutative algebras. After the Nazis dismissed her and other Jewish professors in 1933, she worked in the U.S. at Bryn Mawr College and at the Institute for Advanced Study, Princeton.

no-fault insurance: see INSURANCE.

Noguchi, Hideyo [nōgo͞o'chē], 1876–1928, Japanese bacteriologist; came to U.S., 1900. He made important studies of snake venoms and of smallpox and yellow-fever vaccines. In 1913 Noguchi isolated the *Treponema pallidum* from a syphilis patient, proving that this spirochete was the cause of syphilis; he also developed a skin test for this disease.

Noguchi, Isamu, 1904–88, American sculptor; b. Los Angeles. Noguchi, who studied under BORGLUM and BRANCUSI, is best known for his abstract sculptures designed as adjuncts to architecture. He has also designed many playgrounds and stone sculpture gardens, e.g., the UNESCO garden in Paris.

Noguchi Yone(jiro), 1875–1947, Japanese poet and critic. Writing in both English and Japanese, he helped stimulate Western interest in many Japanese artists. His works include *Japan and America* (1921) and *Selected Poems* (written in English, 1921).

Noh drama: see *Japanese drama* under ASIAN DRAMA.

noise pollution, sounds produced by human commercial and in-

NOBEL PRIZES

Year	Peace	Chemistry	Physics	Physiology or Medicine	Literature
1901	J. H. Dunant Frédéric Passy	J. H. van't Hoff	W. C. Roentgen	E. A. von Behring	R. F. A. Sully-Prudhomme
1902	Elie Ducommun C. A. Gobat	Emil Fischer	H. A. Lorentz Pieter Zeeman	Sir Ronald Ross	Theodor Mommsen
1903	Sir William R. Cremer	S. A. Arrhenius	A. H. Becquerel Marie S. Curie Pierre Curie	N. R. Finsen	Bjørnstjerne Bjørnson
1904	Institute of International Law	Sir William Ramsay	J. W. S. Rayleigh	Ivan P. Pavlov	Frédéric Mistral José Echegaray
1905	Baroness Bertha von Suttner	Adolf von Baeyer	Philipp Lenard	Robert Koch	Henryk Sienkiewicz
1906	Theodore Roosevelt	Henri Moissan	Sir Joseph Thomson	Camillo Golgi S. Ramón y Cajal	Giosuè Carducci
1907	E. T. Moneta Louis Renault	Eduard Buchner	A. A. Michelson	C. L. A. Laveran	Rudyard Kipling
1908	K. P. Arnoldson Fredrik Bajer	Sir Ernest Rutherford	Gabriel Lippman	Paul Ehrlich Élie Metchnikoff	R. C. Eucken
1909	Auguste Beernaert P. H. B. Estournelles de Constant	Wilhelm Ostwald	Guglielmo Marconi C. F. Braun	Emil T. Kocher	Selma Lagerlöf
1910	International Peace Bureau	Otto Wallach	J. D. van der Waals	Albrecht Kossel	Paul Heyse
1911	T. M. C. Asser A. H. Fried	Marie S. Curie	Wilhelm Wien	Allvar Gullstrand	Maurice Maeterlinck
1912	Elihu Root	Victor Grignard Paul Sabatier	N. G. Dalen	Alexis Carrel	Gerhart Hauptmann
1913	Henri La Fontaine	Alfred Werner	Heike Kamerlingh Onnes	C. R. Richet	Sir Rabindranath Tagore
1914		T. W. Richards	Max von Laue	Robert Barany	
1915		Richard Willstätter	Sir William H. Bragg Sir William L. Bragg		Romain Rolland
1916					Verner von Heidenstam
1917	International Red Cross		C. G. Barkla		K. A. Gjellerup Henrik Pontoppidan
1918		Fritz Haber	Max Planck		
1919	Woodrow Wilson		Johannes Stark	Jules Bordet	C. F. G. Spitteler
1920	Léon Bourgeois	Walther Nernst	C. E. Guillaume	S. A. S. Krogh	Knut Hamsun
1921	Hjalmar Branting C. L. Lange	Frederick Soddy	Albert Einstein		Anatole France
1922	Fridtjof Nansen	F. W. Aston	N. H. D. Bohr	A. V. Hill Otto Meyerhof	Jacinto Benavente y Martínez
1923		Fritz Pregl	Robert A. Millikan	Sir Frederick G. Banting J. J. R. Macleod	W. B. Yeats
1924			K. M. G. Siegbahn	Willem Einthoven	W. S. Reymont

NOBEL PRIZES *(Continued)*

Year	*Peace*	*Chemistry*	*Physics*	*Physiology or Medicine*	*Literature*
1925	Sir Austen Chamberlain Charles G. Dawes	Richard Zsigmondy	James Franck Gustav Hertz		G. B. Shaw
1926	Aristide Briand Gustav Stresemann	Theodor Svedberg	J. B. Perrin	Johannes Fibiger	Grazia Deledda
1927	F. É Buisson Ludwig Quidde	Heinrich Wieland	A. H. Compton C. T. R. Wilson	Julius Wagner-Jauregg	Henri Bergson
1928		Adolf Windaus	Sir Owen W. Richardson	C. J. H. Nicolle	Sigrid Undset
1929	Frank B. Kellogg	Sir Arthur Harden Hans von Euler-Chelpin	L. V. de Broglie	Christian Eijkman Sir Frederick G. Hopkins	Thomas Mann
1930	Nathan Soderblom	Hans Fischer	Sir Chandrasekhara V. Raman	Karl Landsteiner	Sinclair Lewis
1931	Jane Addams Nicholas Murray Butler	Carl Bosch Friedrich Bergius		Otto H. Warburg	E. A. Karlfeldt
1932		Irving Langmuir	Werner Heisenberg	E. D. Adrian Sir Charles Sherrington	John Galsworthy
1933	Sir Norman Angell		P. A. M. Dirac Erwin Schrödinger	Thomas H. Morgan	I. A. Bunin
1934	Arthur Henderson	Harold C. Urey		G. H. Whipple G. R. Minot W. P. Murphy	Luigi Pirandello
1935	Carl von Ossietzky	Frédéric Joliot-Curie Irène Joliot-Curie	Sir James Chadwick	Hans Spemann	
1936	Carlos Saavedra Lamas	P. J. W. Debye	C. D. Anderson V. F. Hess	Sir Henry H. Dale Otto Loewi	Eugene O'Neiil
1937	E. A. R. Cecil, Viscount Cecil of Chelwood	Sir Walter N. Haworth Paul Karrer	C. J. Davisson Sir George P. Thomson	Albert von Szent-Gyorgyi	Roger Martin du Gard
1938	Nansen International Office for Refugees		Enrico Fermi	Corneille Heymans	Pearl S. Buck
1939		Adolf Butenandt Leopold Ruzicka	E. O. Lawrence	Gerhard Domagk	F. E. Sillanpää
1940–1942	No prizes awarded.				
1943		Georg von Hevesy	Otto Stern	E. A. Doisy Henrik Dam	
1944	International Red Cross	Otto Hahn	I. I. Rabi	Joseph Erlanger H. S. Gasser	J. V. Jensen
1945	Cordell Hull	A. I. Virtanen	Wolfgang Pauli	Sir Alexander Fleming E. B. Chain Sir Howard W. Florey	Gabriela Mistral
1946	J. R. Mott Emily G. Balch	J. B. Sumner J. H. Northrop W. M. Stanley	P. W. Bridgman	H. J. Muller	Hermann Hesse

NOBEL PRIZES *(Continued)*

Year	*Peace*	*Chemistry*	*Physics*	*Physiology or Medicine*	*Literature*
1947	American Friends Service Committee and Friends Service Council	Sir Robert Robinson	Sir Edward V. Appleton	C. F. Cori Gerty T. Cori B. A. Houssay	André Gide
1948		Arne Tiselius	P. M. S. Blackett	Paul H. Mueller	T. S. Eliot
1949	John Boyd Orr, Baron Boyd-Orr	W. F. Giauque	Yukawa Hideki	W. R. Hess Egas Moniz	William Faulkner
1950	Ralph J. Bunche	Otto Diels Kurt Alder	C. F. Powell	Philip S. Hench Edward C. Kendall Tadeus Reichstein	Bertrand Russell, Earl Russell
1951	Léon Jouhaux	Edwin M. McMillan Glenn T. Seaborg	Sir John D. Cockcroft Ernest T. S. Walton	Max Theiler	Pär F. Lagerkvist
1952	Albert Schweitzer	A. J. P. Martin R. L. M. Synge	Felix Bloch E. M. Purcell	S. A. Waksman	François Mauriac
1953	George C. Marshall	Hermann Staudinger	Frits Zernike	F. A. Lipmann Sir Hans A. Krebs	Sir Winston L. S. Churchill
1954	Office of the United Nations High Commissioner for Refugees	Linus C. Pauling	Max Born Walther Bothe	J. F. Enders F. C. Robbins T. H. Weller	Ernest Hemingway
1955		Vincent du Vigneaud	Willis E. Lamb, Jr. Polykarp Kusch	A. H. T. Theorell	Halldór K. Laxness
1956		Sir Cyril N. Hinshelwood Nikolai N. Semenov	W. B. Shockley W. H. Brattain John Bardeen	D. W. Richards, Jr. A. F. Cournand Werner Forssmann	Juan Ramón Jiménez
1957	Lester B. Pearson	Sir Alexander R. Todd	Tsung-Dao Lee Chen Ning Yang	Daniel Bovet	Albert Camus
1958	Georges Henri Pire	Frederick Sanger	P. A. Cherenkov Igor Y. Tamm Ilya M. Frank	Joshua Lederberg G. W. Beadle E. L. Tatum	Boris L. Pasternak
1959	Philip J. Noel-Baker	Jaroslav Heyrovsky	Emilio Segrè Owen Chamberlain	Severo Ochoa Arthur Kornberg	Salvatore Quasimodo
1960	Albert J. Luthuli	W. F. Libby	D. A. Glaser	Sir Macfarlane Burnet P. B. Medawar	Alexis St.-L. Léger
1961	Dag Hammarskjöld	Melvin Calvin	Robert Hofstadter R. L. Moessbauer	Georg von Bekesy	Ivo Andrić
1962	Linus C. Pauling	M. F. Perutz J. C. Kendrew	L. D. Landau	J. D. Watson F. H. C. Crick M. H. F. Wilkins	John Steinbeck
1963	International Committee of the Red Cross League of Red Cross Societies	Giulio Natta Karl Ziegler	Eugene Paul Wigner Maria Goeppert Mayer J. Hans D. Jensen	Sir John Carew Eccles Alan Lloyd Hodgkin Andrew Fielding Huxley	George Seferis
1964	Martin Luther King, Jr.	Dorothy Mary Crowfoot Hodgkin	Charles Hard Townes Nikolai Gennadiyevich Basov Alexander Mikhailovich Prokhorov	Konrad E. Bloch Feodor Lynen	Jean-Paul Sartre

NOBEL PRIZES *(Continued)*

Year	*Peace*	*Chemistry*	*Physics*	*Physiology or Medicine*	*Literature*
1965	United Nations International Children's Emergency Fund	Robert Burns Woodward	Richard Phillips Feynman Tomonaga Shinichiro Julian Seymour Schwinger	François Jacob André Lwoff Jacques Monod	M. A. Sholokhov
1966		Robert S. Milliken	Alfred Kastler	Francis Peyton Rous Charles Brenton Huggins	S. Y. Agnon Nelly Sachs
1967		Manfred Eigen Ronald George Wreyford Norrish George Porter	Hans Albrecht Bethe	Ragnar Granit Haldan Keffer Hartline George Wald	Miguel Angel Asturias
1968	René Cassin	Lars Onsager	Luis W. Alvarez	Robert W. Holley H. Gobind Khorana Marshall W. Nirenberg	Kawabata Yasunari
1969	International Labor Organization	Derek H. R. Barton Odd Hassel	Murray Gell-Mann	Max Delbrück Alfred D. Hershey Salvador E. Luria	Samuel Beckett
1970	Norman E. Borlaug	Luis Federico Leloir	Louis Eugène Néel Hans Olof Alfven	Julius Axelrod Bernard Katz Ulf von Euler	Alexandr I. Solzhenitsyn
1971	Willy Brandt	Gerhard Herzberg	Dennis Gabor	Earl W. Sutherland	Pablo Neruda
1972		Stanford Moore William Howard Stein Christian B. Anfinsen	John Bardeen Leon N. Cooper John Robert Schreiffer	Gerald M. Edelman Rodney R. Porter	Heinrich Böll
1973	Henry A. Kissinger Le Duc Tho	Ernst Otto Fischer Geoffrey Wilkinson	Leo Esaki Ivar Giaever Brian D. Josephson	Konrad Lorenz Nikolaas Tinbergen Karl von Frisch	Patrick White
1974	Sean MacBride Sato Eisaku	Paul J. Flory	Martin Ryle Antony Hewish	Albert Claude George Emil Palade Christian de Duve	Eyvind Johnson Harry Martinson
1975	Andrei D. Sakharov	John Warcup Cornforth Vladimir Prelog	Aage N. Bohr Ben Roy Mottelson James Rainwater	David Baltimore Renato Dulbecco Howard M. Temin	Eugenio Montale
1976	Mairead Corrigan Betty Williams	William Nunn Lip- scomb	Burton Richter Samuel Chao Chung Ting	Baruch Samuel Blumberg Daniel Carleton Gajdusek	Saul Bellow
1977	Amnesty International	Ilya Prigogine	Philip W. Anderson Sir Nevill F. Mott John H. Van Vleck	Rosalyn S. Yalow Roger C. L. Guillemin Andrew V. Schally	Vicente Aleixandre
1978	Menachem Begin Anwar al-Sadat	Peter Mitchell	Peter Kapitza Arno A. Penzias Robert W. Wilson	Werner Arber Daniel Nathans Hamilton O. Smith	Isaac Bashevis Singer
1979	Mother Teresa	Herbert C. Brown Georg Wittig	Steven Weinberg Sheldon L. Glashow Abdus Salam	Allan MacLeod Cormack Godfrey Newbold Hounsfield	Odysseus Elytis
1980	Adolfo Pérez Esquivel	Paul Berg Walter Gilbert Frederick Sanger	James W. Cronin Val L. Fitch	Baruj Benacerraf George D. Snell Jean Dausset	Czesław Miłosz

NOBEL PRIZES *(Continued)*

Year	*Peace*	*Chemistry*	*Physics*	*Physiology or Medicine*	*Literature*
1981	Office of the United Nations High Commissioner for Refugees	Kenichi Fukui Roald Hoffman	Nicolaas Bloembergen Arthur Schawlow Kai M. Siegbahn	Roger W. Sperry David H. Hubel Torsten N. Wiesel	Elias Canetti
1982	Alfonso García Robles Alva Myrdal	Aaron Klug	Kenneth G. Wilson	Sune K. Bergström Bengt I. Samuelsson John R. Vane	Gabriel García Márquez
1983	Lech Walesa	Henry Taube	Subrahmanyan Chandrasekhar William A. Fowler	Barbara McClintock	William Golding
1984	Desmond Tutu	R. Bruce Merrifield	Carlo Rubbia Simon van der Meere	Cesar Milstein Georges J. F. Khler Niels K. Jerne	Jaroslav Siefert
1985	International Physicians for the Prevention of Nuclear War	Herbert A. Hauptman Jerome Karle	Klaus von Klitzing	Michael S. Brown Joseph L. Goldstein	Claude Simon
1986	Elie Wiesel	Dudley R. Herschbach Yuan T. Lee John C. Polanyi	Ernest Ruska Gerd Binnig Heinrich Rohrer	Rita Levi-Montalcini Stanley Cohen	Wole Soyinka
1987	Oscar Arias Sanchez	Donald J. Cram Charles J. Pedersen Jean-Marie Lehn	K. Alex Müller J. Georg Bednorz	Susumu Tonegawa	Joseph Brodsky
1988	UN Peacekeeping Forces	Johann Deisenhofer Robert Huber Hartmut Michel	Leon M. Lederman Melvin Schwartz Jack Steinberger	Gertrude B. Elion George H. Hitchings James Black	Naguib Mahfouz
1989	Dalai Lama	Thomas R. Cech Sidney Altman	Norman F. Ramsey Hans G. Dehmelt Wolfgang Paul	J. Michael Bishop Harold E. Varmus	Camilio José Cela
1990	Mikhail S. Gorbachev	Elias James Corey	Richard E. Taylor Jerome I. Friedman Henry W. Kendall	Joseph E. Murray E. Donnall Thomas	Octavio Paz
1991	Aung San Suu Kyi	Richard R. Ernst	Pièrre-Gilles de Gennes	Erwin Neher Bert Sakmann	Nadine Gordimer
1992	Rigobertu Menchú	Rudolph A. Marcus	Georges Charpak	Edmond H. Fischer Edwin G. Krebs	Derek Walcott
1993	F. W. de Klerk Nelson Mandela	Kary B. Mullis Michael Smith	Russell A. Hulse Joseph H. Taylor, Jr.	Richard J. Roberts Phillip A. Sharp	Toni Morrison

dustrial activities at levels and/or frequencies harmful to health or welfare. Transportation vehicles (e.g., trains) and construction equipment (e.g., pneumatic drills) are particular offenders in this regard. Federal estimates indicate that more than one in three Americans is affected by noise pollution. Apart from hearing loss, excessive noise can cause lack of sleep, irritability, heartburn, indigestion, ulcers, and high blood pressure. Noise-induced stress can create severe tension in daily living and may contribute to mental illness. The Noise Control Act of 1972 empowers the ENVIRONMENTAL PROTECTION AGENCY to determine the noise limits required to protect health and to set noise emission standards (see ENVIRONMENTALISM).

Noland, Kenneth, 1924–, American painter; b. Asheville, N.C. Associated with COLOR FIELD PAINTING, Noland is best known for stained canvases in target or chevron designs.

Nolde, Emil, 1867–1956, German expressionist painter and graphic artist; b. Emil Hansen. He was a member of the BRÜCKE group. His bold, arresting landscapes, and violent, clashing colors, combined with distortions of shape, caused bitter controversy. Among his best-known works are the woodcut *The Prophet* (1912, National Gall., Wash., D.C.) and *Christ among the Children* (Mus. Mod. Art, N.Y.C.).

nominalism, in philosophy, theory holding that universal words (*nomina*) or concepts have no objective reality outside the mind, and that only individual things and events exist objectively. The theory, contrasted to Platonic IDEALISM and, in the Middle Ages, to REALISM, is appropriate to MATERIALISM and EMPIRICISM.

Nonaligned Movement, organized movement of nations that attempted to form a third world force through a policy of nonalignment with the U.S. and the USSR. Its members, mainly from Asia, Africa, and Latin America and representing more than half the world's people, include true neutrals and many nations that were in fact aligned with one of the superpowers during the COLD WAR. Yugoslavia, India, and Indonesia were instrumental in founding (1961) the movement, which meets regularly to discuss the common interests of its members. By the early 1990s it had 111 members and, in light of the Cold War's end, was reassessing its role and redefining its identity.

nonbank, financial organization that handles public and private funds and offers some of the services, such as demand deposits or loans, that banks and savings institutions offer. Nonbanks either take deposits or make commercial loans but cannot legally do both. Nonbanks include MONEY-MARKET FUNDS and other investment companies and finance companies, and play an important role in the U.S. economy. See BANKING.

nonconformists, in religion, those who refuse to conform to the requirements (in doctrine or discipline) of an established church. The term is especially applied to Protestant dissenters from the Church of England, who arose soon after the REFORMATION. The Act of Uniformity (1662) made episcopal ordination compulsory and a distinct split unavoidable.

non-Euclidean geometry, branch of GEOMETRY in which the fifth postulate of EUCLIDEAN GEOMETRY is replaced by one of two alternative postulates. EUCLID's fifth postulate states that one and only one line parallel to a given line can be drawn through a point external to the line. The first alternative, which allows two parallels through any external point, leads to the hyperbolic geometry developed independently by Nikolai LOBACHEVSKY (1826) and János Bolyai (1832). The second, which allows no parallels through any external point, leads to the elliptic geometry developed by G.F.B. RIEMANN (1854). The results of these two types of non-Euclidean geometry are identical with those of Euclidean geometry in every respect except for the propositions involving parallel lines, either explicitly or implicitly.

Nonintercourse Act: see EMBARGO ACT OF 1807.

nonlinear dynamics, popularly called **chaos theory**, interdisciplinary science that attempts to reveal structure in seemingly unpredictable dynamic systems. In a linear system a small change produces a small and easily quantifiable systematic change, but a nonlinear system exhibits a sensitive dependence on initial conditions: small or virtually unmeasurable differences in initial conditions can lead to wildly differing results. (This is sometimes called the "butterfly effect," in reference to a 1979 address by meteorologist E.M. Lorenz entitled "Predictability: Does the Flap of a Butterfly's Wings in Brazil Set Off a Tornado in Texas?") The evolution of nonlinear dynamics was made possible by the application of high-speed computers, particularly in the area of computer graphics, to innovative mathematical theories developed during the first half of the 20th cent. Three branches of study are recognized: classical systems in which friction and other dissipative forces are paramount, such as turbulent flow in a liquid or gas; classical systems in which dissipative forces can be neglected, such as charged particles in a PARTICLE ACCELERATOR; and quantum systems, such as molecules in a strong electromagnetic field. Nonlinear dynamics has been applied to the study of diverse phenomena, such as dripping faucets, population growth, the beating heart, and the economy, to better understand the complex relationships among the various elements involved.

nonsporting dog, class of dogs formerly bred to hunt or work but now raised chiefly as pets. See individual breeds, e.g., BOSTON TERRIER, BULLDOG, CHOW CHOW, DALMATIAN, POODLE.

nonsteroidal anti-inflammatory drug (NSAID), a drug, such as IBUPROFEN, that relieves pain and suppresses inflammation in a manner similar to STEROIDS, but without the side effects of steroids. NSAIDs are commonly used to treat arthritis, gout, bursitis, and painful menstruation.

Nordhoff, Charles [nôrd'hŏf], 1830–1901, American journalist and author; b. Germany. A leading political writer and Washington correspondent, he also wrote books and articles about the sea and ships. His grandson, **Charles Bernard Nordhoff** (1887–1947), b. London, was co-author with James Norman Hall of *Mutiny on the Bounty* (1932) and other works (see BOUNTY).

norepinephrine or **noradrenaline,** the NEUROTRANSMITTER that mediates chemical communication in the sympathetic NERVOUS SYSTEM. Like other neurotransmitters, it is released at synaptic nerve endings to transmit the signal from a nerve cell to other cells. It is almost identical in structure to EPINEPHRINE. The sympathetic nervous system functions in response to short-term stress (the fight or flight response); hence norepinephrine and epinephrine increase the heart rate as well as blood pressure, increase the rate of glycogen conversion for energy, and relax bronchial smooth muscle to assist breathing.

Norfolk, city (1990 pop. 261,229), SE Va., on the Elizabeth R. and the southern side of HAMPTON ROADS; founded 1682, inc. as a city 1845. The U.S.'s largest naval base is located in its port. Virginia's largest city, Norfolk is also a major coal and grain exporter. Shipbuilding is the leading industry. The city was the object of fighting in the AMERICAN REVOLUTION and in the CIVIL WAR. Landmarks include St. Paul's Church (1738) and Fort Norfolk (1794).

Norfolk Island, external territory of Australia (1992 est. pop. 2,600), 13 sq mi (34 sq km), c.1,035 mi (1,670 km) NE of Sydney. Now a resort, the island was discovered by Capt. James COOK in 1774 and served as a convict settlement (1788–1813, 1826–55). In 1856, 194 descendants of the *Bounty* mutineers were transferred there from PITCAIRN ISLAND. Limited self-rule was granted in 1979.

Noriega, Manuel Antonio, 1938–, Panamanian general. As commander of the National Defense Forces (1982–89), he ousted the civilian president (1985) and became the de facto leader of Panama. After he was implicated in drug trafficking, the sale of U.S. secrets to Cuba and the USSR (he was also in the pay of the U.S. Army and CIA from 1955 to 1986), and other illegal activities, U.S. officials urged him to step down (Jan. 1988). A U.S. indictment on drug charges and subsequent economic sanctions proved ineffective. In Dec. 1989 the U.S. invaded Panama, captured Noriega, and brought him to Miami, where he was convicted (1992) on racketeering and conspiracy charges relating to drug trafficking.

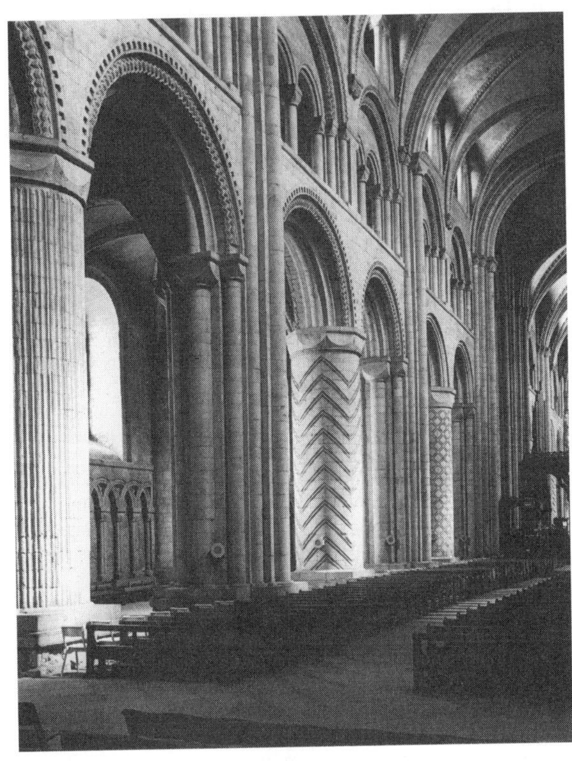

Round Norman arches of Durham Cathedral

Norman architecture, term applied to buildings erected in lands conquered by the Normans: N France, England, S Italy, and Sicily. In France and England, Norman buildings were based on the ROMANESQUE ARCHITECTURE of Lombardy. Churches, abbeys, and castles were massive and sparsely decorated, and featured round arches. The style was developed from 1066 to 1154. The great French works include the beginnings of MONT-SAINT MICHEL and two abbeys at Caen. In England the Normans began nearly all the great cathedrals, including Westminster Abbey, where only foundations remain. The only intact design is the small St. John's Chapel (c.1087) at the TOWER OF LONDON. English and French churches were cruciform and square-towered. Blind arcades, carved moldings, and grotesque sculptured animal forms were common. The ribbed vault at Durham Cathedral (begun 1093) indicated a shift from Norman to GOTHIC ARCHITECTURE. In Italy and Sicily, Byzantine and Arabic elements modified the massive Norman style.

Norman Conquest, period in English history following the defeat (1066) of King HAROLD of England by William, duke of Normandy (see WILLIAM I). The conquest was formerly thought to have brought about broad changes in English life. More recently historians have stressed the continuity of English law, institutions, and customs, but the subject remains controversial. The initial military conquest was quick and brutal. By 1070 most of the Anglo-Saxon nobles were dead or had been deprived of their land, and a Norman aristocracy was superimposed on the English. William used the existing Anglo-Saxon administrative system, and the English church gained closer ties with Europe. Norman French was spoken at the court and had a great impact on the English language. NORMAN ARCHITECTURE was also introduced into England.

Normandy, region and former province, NW France, bordering on the English Channel. Its economy is based on cattle, fishing, and tourism. Rouen, Le Havre, and Cherbourg have heavy industry. Conquered by the Romans and later (5th cent.) by the FRANKS, the area was repeatedly raided (9th cent.) by the NORSEMEN, or Normans, for whom the region is named. Normandy was ceded (991) by CHARLES III of France to their chief, Rollo, the 1st duke of Normandy. In 1066 Duke William invaded England, where he became king as WILLIAM I. During the HUNDRED YEARS WAR Normandy was permanently restored (1450) to France. The region was the scene of an Allied invasion (1944) during WORLD WAR II.

Normandy campaign: see WORLD WAR II.

Norns, Norse FATES, who spun and wove the web of life. They were usually three: Urth (Wyrd), past; Verthandi, present; and Skuld, future. The three weird sisters in Shakespeare's *Macbeth* are probably Scottish equivalents of the Norns.

Norodom Sihanouk [nōrōdŭm′ sĭhənŭk′], 1922–, king (1941–55, 1993–) of CAMBODIA. In 1955 he abdicated in favor of his father and became premier. After his father's death (1960) he again became head of state, but not king. He was deposed (1970) by LON NOL. When the KHMER ROUGE won control of Cambodia, Sihanouk returned as head of state (1975–76) but was subsequently placed under house arrest. In 1981–82, Sihanouk, in exile, forged a coalition with the Khmer Rouge and others to oppose the Vietnamese-imposed Cambodian government. After the signing of the UN-sponsored peace treaty (1991), Sihanouk returned to Cambodia, now allied with Prime Min. Hun Sen and opposed to the Khmer Rouge. He became head of state (1991) and, under a new constitution, king (1993).

Norris, Frank (Benjamin Franklin Norris), 1870–1902, American novelist; b. Chicago. Influenced by the NATURALISM of ZOLA, he wrote the novel *McTeague* (1899), on greed, and two powerful novels attacking the American railroad and wheat industries, *The Octopus* (1901) and *The Pit* (1903).

Norris, George William, 1861–1944, U.S. representative (1903–13) and senator (1914–43) from Nebraska; b. Sandusky co., Ohio. A liberal Republican, he worked to reform the rules of the House. In the Senate he voted against U.S. participation in World War I, wrote (1932) the 20th amendment to the Constitution, cosponsored (1932) the Norris-LaGuardia labor law, and fathered the bills creating (1933) the TENNESSEE VALLEY AUTHORITY.

Norse, another name for the North Germanic, or Scandinavian, group of the Germanic subfamily of the Indo-European family of languages. Norse is the language of Norway and Iceland at any period. Old Norse was the language of the EDDAS and SAGAS. See LANGUAGE (table).

Norsemen, Scandinavian VIKINGS who raided and settled on the coasts of NW Germany, the Low Countries, France, and Spain in the 9th and 10th cent. Among the causes of the influx were the desire for wealth, power, and adventure and the attempt of HAROLD I of Norway to subjugate the independent Norwegian nobles, forcing them to look to foreign conquests. The Norsemen's impact was especially lasting in N France, where they began (c.843) to sail up the French rivers, attacking, looting, and burning such cities as Rouen and Paris and ruining commerce and navigation. In 911 one of their leaders, Rollo, was given the duchy of NORMANDY by CHARLES III. Rollo's successors expanded their lands and were only nominal vassals of the French kings. The Norsemen accepted Christianity, adopted French law and speech, and continued in history as Normans.

North, Frederick, 2d **earl of Guilford,** 1732–92, British statesman, known as Lord North. As prime minister (1770–82) under GEORGE III, he pursued awkward colonial policies that led to the AMERICAN REVOLUTION. North later formed (1783) a coalition ministry with Charles James FOX.

North Africa, campaigns in, fighting in WORLD WAR II for control of the southern coast of the Mediterranean. It began in September 1940, after the swift Italian conquest of British Somaliland. The Italian army in Libya was routed, but the German Afrika Korps, commanded by Gen. ROMMEL, came to their aid. In May 1941 Rommel drove the British back to the Egyptian border, but the British mounted (Nov. 1941) a successful counterattack. On May 26, 1942, the British suffered a major defeat but dug in around ALAMEIN. Commanded by Gen. MONTGOMERY, they withstood German attacks until reinforcements arrived. Montgomery's thrust began on Oct. 23, 1942, and was a brilliant success. The Germans were forced to retreat all the way to Tunisia, where they were bottled up. Meanwhile, U.S. and British troops were occupying territories west of Rommel—Algiers, Oran, and Casablanca. In May 1943, Rommel's troops were attacked from the west by U.S. troops under Gen. EISENHOWER, from the south by Montgomery's troops, and from the southwest by a Free French army. On May 12 about 250,000 Axis soldiers capitulated. Earlier, the British had reconquered most of East Africa.

North America, third largest continent, c.9,400,000 sq mi (24,346,000 sq km), usually considered to include all the lands and adjacent islands in the Western Hemisphere located N of the Isthmus of Panama (which connects it with South America). The countries of the continent are the U.S. and Canada, known as Anglo-America; Mexico; the nations S of Mexico, known as CENTRAL AMERICA; and the island countries of the WEST INDIES (the many islands located in and around the CARIBBEAN SEA off the SE mainland coast). GREENLAND and the French islands of ST. PIERRE AND MIQUELON are also part of North America. The principal topographic feature is the North American Cordillera, a complex mountain region in the west that includes the ROCKY MTS. Mt. MCKINLEY (20,320 ft/6,194 m), in Alaska, is the highest point; the lowest point is 282 ft (86 m) below sea level, in Death Valley (see DEATH VALLEY NATIONAL MONUMENT). The climate ranges from polar to tropical, with arid and semiarid conditions predominating over much of the interior.

North America, indigenous peoples of. This article deals with the peoples who inhabited North America before the arrival of the Europeans. Now often called Native Americans, they have long been called Indians because it was initially believed that COLUMBUS had reached the East Indies. Migrating in waves from Asia (see AMERICAS, PREHISTORY OF THE), these peoples spoke widely varying NATIVE AMERICAN LANGUAGES, but all had straight black hair, dark eyes, and yellow- to red-brown skin. In 1492 they numbered 1 to 2 million N of Mexico, in six major cultural areas: Northwest Coast, Plains, Plateau, Eastern Woodlands, Northern, and Southwest.

Northwest Coast. Peoples of the Northwest Coast (e.g., KWAKIUTL, HAIDA, MODOC, TSIMSHIAN) lived along the Pacific from S Alaska to N California and spoke Nadene, Wakashan, and Tsimshian languages. They subsisted chiefly on salmon, sea and land mammals, and wild fruits, and built wooden houses and boats. Their arts included weaving, basketry, masks, and TOTEM poles. Their generally stratified societies, whose ceremonial displays of wealth included the POTLATCH, were not affected by whites until the late 18th cent.

Plains. Plains peoples lived in the grasslands from the Mississippi R. to the Rocky Mts. and from S Canada to Texas, speaking mainly Algonquian-Wakashan, Aztec-Tanoan, and Hokan-Siouan languages. Sedentary tribes (e.g., OMAHA, MANDAN, PAWNEE) farmed the river valleys and lived in walled villages of domed earth lodges. The nomadic tribes (e.g., BLACKFOOT, CHEYENNE, COMANCHE) hunted buffalo—on foot until they acquired horses in the 18th cent.—for food, clothing, and TEPEES. Their culture was characterized by warrior clans, the coup (a war honor awarded for striking an enemy with conspicuous bravery), the SUN DANCE, and bead-and-feather artwork. A mutually intelligible sign language developed among

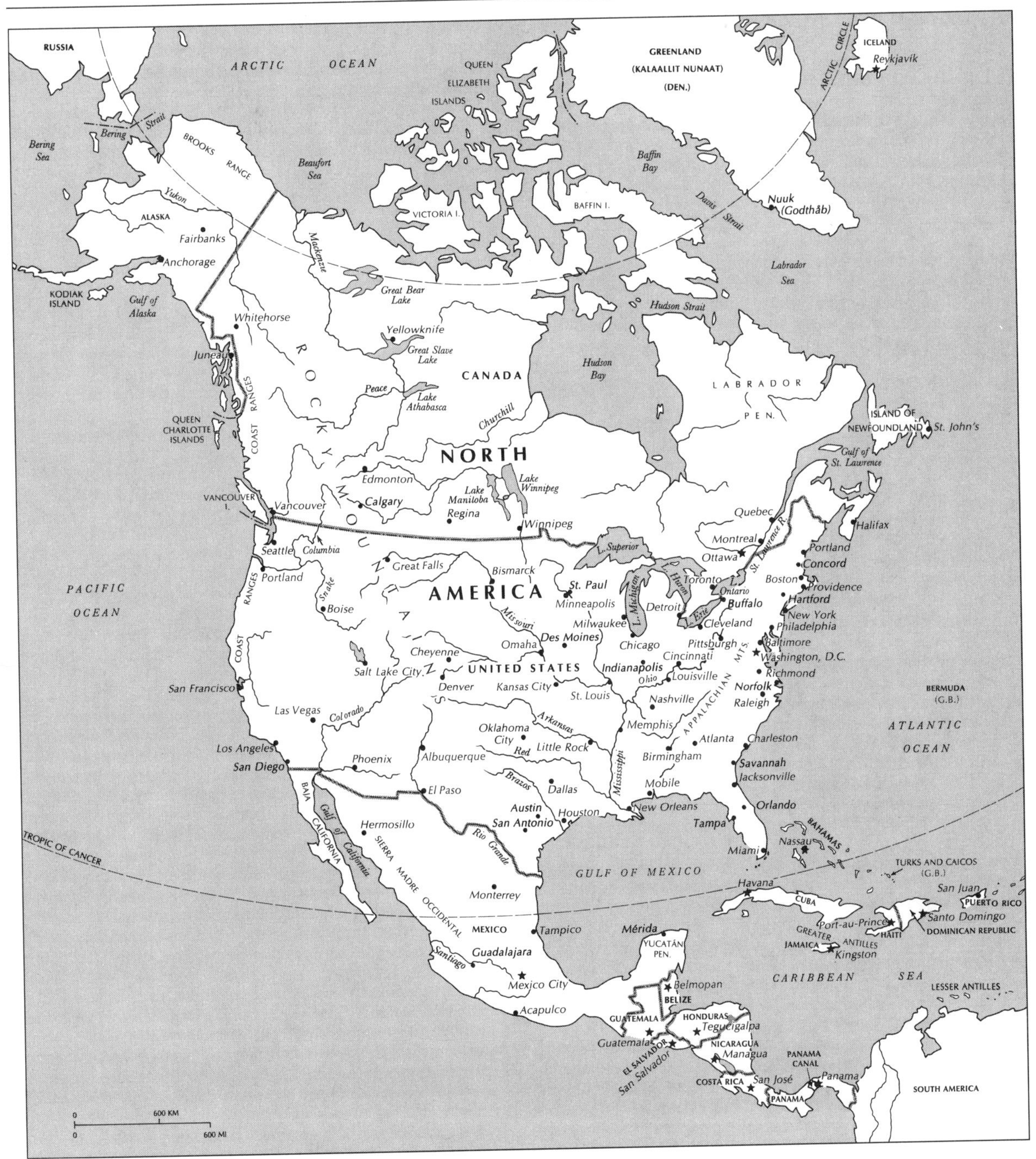

the nomadic Plains tribes, who were the last to submit to white encroachments.

Plateau. Peoples of the Plateau (e.g., Kootenai, NEZ PERCÉ, PAIUTE), from S Canada to California and the Southwest, were diverse in language and culture. Sedentary California Native Americans, living in brush shelters or lean-tos, gathered edible plants, made acorn bread, and hunted small game. Their basketry was highly developed. The harsh environment between the Cascades and the Rockies demanded a simple social, religious, and political life; Native Americans there lived in partly buried lodges and hunted small game, fished with nets and spears, and gathered insects. The adoption (c.1730) from the Plains tribes of the horse and tepee changed the plateau culture markedly.

Eastern Woodlands. In the Eastern Woodlands, Algonquian-Wakashan and Hokan-Siouan speakers predominated. Peoples from the Atlantic to the Mississippi (e.g., DELAWARE, HURON, IROQUOIS CONFEDERACY, MOHEGANS) were deer hunters; the women also grew corn, squash, and beans. Their houses included the dome-shaped wigwam and the longhouse; they used the birchbark canoe. Males wore deerskin clothing, face and body paint, and scalp locks. Peoples in the area from the Ohio R. to the Gulf of Mexico (e.g., CHEROKEE, CHOCTAW, Natchez, SEMINOLE) developed a farming and trading economy featuring a high technology and excellent pottery. A stratified society observed elaborate rites including sun worship; burial mounds (see MOUND BUILDERS) were unique to these groups.

Northern Tribes. In the semiarctic Northern area, covering most of Canada, Algonquian-Wakashan and Nadene tongues predominated. Nomadic hunters (e.g., Kutchin, MONTAGNAIS AND NASKAPI) followed caribou migrations for food, clothing, and shelter; the snowshoe was important to their material culture. Their religion centered on the SHAMAN.

Southwest. Peoples of the Southwest (e.g., APACHE, NAVAHO, PUEBLO) spoke mainly Aztec-Tanoan languages and reflected the advanced culture of the AZTECS to the south. By 700 B.C. the basketmakers had mastered intensive agriculture and pottery making. The CLIFF DWELLERS later built terraced community houses and ceremonial KIVAS on cliff ledges. The Pueblo tribes further developed farming, pottery, textiles, and a complex mythology and religion.

Contemporary Native American Life. After the long struggle (see INDIAN WARS) between whites and Native Americans came to an end in the 1890s, Native Americans settled into a life dominated by poverty, poor education, unemployment, and gradual dispersal. U.S. government policy, administered by the Bureau of INDIAN AFFAIRS, encouraged converting tribal lands into individual holdings, many of which were sold to whites. The Indian Reorganization Act of 1934 aimed at revitalization of Native American economic life, but also at assimilation into white society; the policy of the 1950s to terminate tribes aggravated the situation. In the 1970s the AMERICAN INDIAN MOVEMENT was organized, and various tribes filed suits to reclaim formerly seized lands from the U.S. Government. Beginning in the late 1970s some tribes opened high-stakes bingo halls to generate income, and the 1988 Indian Gaming Regulatory Act has led to the widespread establishment of gambling casinos by Native Americans. Of approximately 1.9 million Native Americans in the U.S. today, most live in the Southwest and mountain states. Survivors of many Eastern tribes live among whites in OKLAHOMA, while unassimilated native culture is strongest among the Pueblos of Arizona and New Mexico and among some tribes of the Pacific Northwest. See also articles on individual tribes.

North American Free Trade Agreement (NAFTA), accord establishing a free-trade zone in North America; it was signed in 1992 by Canada, Mexico, and the U.S and took effect Jan. 1, 1994. NAFTA will eliminate tariffs on goods produced by the signatory nations by 2005 and remove most barriers to cross-border investment and to the movement of goods and services. The pact contains provisions for the inclusion of additional member nations.

North Atlantic Drift, warm ocean current in the N Atlantic Ocean. It is a continuation of the GULF STREAM, the merging point being at lat. 40°N and long. 60°W. Off the British Isles, it splits into two branches, one north and one south. It is responsible for the warm climate of W Europe.

North Atlantic Treaty Organization (NATO), military alliance established (1949) by Belgium, Canada, Denmark, France, Great Britain, Iceland, Italy, Luxembourg, the Netherlands, Norway, Portugal, and the U.S., and later joined by Greece and Turkey (1952), West Germany (1955; now Germany), and Spain (1982). Its aim is to safeguard member nations from attack, originally from the threat of Soviet aggression. With the end of the COLD WAR, NATO members agreed to the use of its forces as peacekeepers in countries outside the alliance. NATO's policies are determined and coordinated by the North Atlantic Council, which has headquarters in Brussels, Belgium, and is under the chairmanship of NATO's secretary general. The Military Committee, located in Washington, D.C., includes representatives of all members except France, which ended the military integration of its forces with NATO in 1966. In the early 1990s many East European nations sought NATO membership as a counterbalance to Russian power, but they were offered more limited "partnerships" that do not require NATO members to defend them from attack.

North Carolina, state in the SE U.S.; bordered by the Atlantic Ocean (E), South Carolina and Georgia (S), Tennessee (W), and Virginia (N).

Area, 52,586 sq mi (136,198 sq km). *Pop.* (1990) 6,628,637, a 12.8% increase over 1980 pop. *Capital,* Raleigh. *Statehood,* Nov. 21, 1789 (12th of original 13 states to ratify the Constitution). *Highest pt.,* Mt. Mitchell, 6,684 ft (2,039 m); *lowest pt.,* sea level. *Nickname,* Tar Heel State. *Motto, Esse Quam Videri* [To Be Rather than to Seem]. *State bird,* cardinal. *State flower,* dogwood. *State tree,* pine. *Abbr.,* N.C.; NC.

Land and People. The low-lying coastal tidewater country, marked by Capes HATTERAS, Lookout, and Fear, gives way inland to the FALL LINE and then to the rolling hills of the Piedmont plateau, where most of the population lives. In the west the land rises to the BLUE RIDGE and GREAT SMOKY MOUNTAINS, where a NATIONAL PARK (see table) runs along part of the Tennessee border. Both ranges are part of the APPALACHIAN system. The warm, temperate climate is generally uniform throughout the state, and rainfall is abundant. A little more than 50% of the population lives in urban areas, mostly in and around CHARLOTTE, the largest city, which is followed in size by RALEIGH, GREENSBORO, and WINSTON-SALEM. In 1990 the state was 76% white and 22% African American. The state also has the largest Native American population, mainly CHEROKEE, in the SE U.S.

Economy. North Carolina leads the country in the production of tobacco and is a major producer of textiles and furniture. Electrical and electronic equipment, chemicals, and machinery are among its other leading manufactured goods. Tobacco is supplemented by the production of cattle, broiler chickens, hogs, turkeys, dairy items, soybeans, corn, and peanuts. The state is a major source of feldspar, mica, lithium, phosphate, and other minerals. The abundant forests support lumbering and allied industries, and fishing is important along the coast. Mountain and coastal resorts attract many visitors.

Government. The constitution (adopted 1970) provides for a governor elected to a four-year term. The general assembly consists of a 50-seat senate and 120-seat house, with members of both bodies serving two-year terms. The state is represented in the U.S. Congress by 2 senators and 12 representatives and has 14 electoral votes.

History. Giovanni da VERRAZANO explored the coast in 1524, and during the 1580s Sir Walter RALEIGH tried unsuccessfully to create the first British settlement in the New World, on ROANOKE ISLAND. Small farms were gradually established by c.1635 but political strife between settlers and the proprietors of the colony (who were from Virginia), as well as conflicts with the indigenous tribes, slowed settlement. North Carolina promulgated (1775) the MECKLENBURG DECLARATION OF INDEPENDENCE. After the American Revolution, however, the state, which opposed a strong central government, did not ratify the U.S. Constitution until Nov. 1789. By 1835 the final forced removal of the Cherokees began, further encouraging westward expansion. Despite considerable antislavery sentiment, the state fought on the Confederate side in the CIVIL WAR. RECONSTRUCTION saw the beginning of the modern era, with tremendous growth of industry in the Piedmont and replacement of the old plantation system by farm tenancy, which still exists. During the 1950s the value of manufactured goods surpassed that of agriculture, and industrialization continued in the 1970s and early 80s at a rate unsurpassed by any other southern state. Relatively untouched by the national recession of the early 1990s, the state has successfully shifted from traditional low-skill manufactures to high-technology industries.

North Cascades National Park: see NATIONAL PARKS (table).

Northcliffe, Alfred Charles William Harmsworth, Viscount, 1865–1922, English journalist, one of the most spectacular of popular journalists and publishers in the history of the British press; b. Ireland; brother of Harold, Viscount ROTHERMERE. He launched *Answers to Correspondents,* a weekly, in 1888 and in five years increased circulation to more than a million copies. In 1894 he bought the London *Evening News,* later founding the *Daily Mail* (1896) and the *Daily Mirror* (1903). Gaining control of the dying *Times* (1908), he put it back on its feet. His newspaper campaigns in WORLD WAR I influenced England's conduct of the war.

North Dakota, state in the N central U.S.; bordered by Minnesota (E), South Dakota (S), Montana (W), and the Canadian provinces of Saskatchewan and Manitoba (N).

Area, 70,665 sq mi (183,022 sq km). *Pop.* (1990) 638,800, a 2.2% decrease from 1980 pop. *Capital,* Bismarck. *Statehood,* Nov. 2, 1889 (39th state). *Highest pt.,* White Butte, 3,506 ft (1,069 m); *lowest pt.,* Red R., 750 ft (229 m). *Nicknames,* Sioux State; Flickertail State. *Motto,* Liberty and Union, Now and Forever, One and Inseparable. *State bird,* Western meadowlark. *State flower,* wild prairie rose. *State tree,* American elm. *Abbr.,* N.D.; ND.

Land and People. Low-lying plains in the east give way to the rolling hills of the drift prairie. In the west, across the MISSOURI R., lies an irregular plateau. In its southwestern portion, wind and rain erosion have shaped the terrain into the unusual clay and sand formations of the Badlands, part of Theodore Roosevelt National Park (see NATIONAL PARKS, table). The west is semiarid, but the east has an average annual rainfall of 22 in. (55 cm) which falls mostly in the crop-growing months. North Dakota is one of the most sparsely populated states. The population is roughly divided between urban and rural areas; the largest city is FARGO, with 74,111 residents (1990). In 1990 the population was almost 95% white, with the remainder largely Native American.

Economy. North Dakota's rich chernozem soils and fertile grasslands make agriculture the leading source of income. The most profitable farm product is wheat, followed by cattle; barley, flax, rye, and oats are also important. North Dakota possesses abundant mineral resources, especially oil, which is refined in the state; natural gas; and the country's largest reserves of lignite. Most industries are based on the processing of the state's agricultural and mineral commodities.

Government. The constitution of 1889 provides for a governor elected to a four-year term. The legislature consists of 53 senators elected to four-year terms and 106 representatives serving two-year terms. The state has two U.S. senators and one representative, and it casts three electoral votes.

History. The French explorer Pierre de la VÉRENDRYE visited the area in 1738, and he was followed by the LEWIS AND CLARK EXPEDITION (1804–5). The U.S. obtained the northwestern portion of the state by the LOUISIANA PURCHASE (1803) and the southeastern half from the British (1818). The first Europeans arrived (1812) as part of the short-lived Red River settlement, but the first permanent farming community was not established until 1851. The Dakota Territory was organized in 1861, although settlement was hampered until the indigenous tribes had been defeated militarily during the 1860s. Thousands of European immigrants subsequently arrived in the 1870s and 1880s. Growing agrarian discontent resulted in the growth of the POPULIST party, and many statewide reforms were enacted (1919). Oil was discovered in the northwest in 1951, and the national energy crisis of the 1970s spurred further exploitation of the state's energy resources. Dependence on wheat and oil, however, has made North Dakota extremely vulnerable to price fluctuations in these commodities.

Northeast Passage, water route along the northern coast of Europe and Asia, between the Atlantic and Pacific oceans. The British, seeking an all-water route to India, made (1550s) the first attempts to find the passage. The Dutch explorers Willem BARENTZ and Henry HUDSON continued the search, as did the Russians. In 1878–79 N.A.E. Nordenskjöld of Sweden first traversed the passage. Russian icebreakers now keep the route open from June to October.

Northern Indians: see NORTH AMERICA, INDIGENOUS PEOPLES OF.

northern lights: see AURORA.

Northern Mariana Islands, commonwealth of the U.S. (1992 est. pop. 47,000), c.185 sq mi (479 sq km), comprising 16 islands (6 inhabited) of the Marianas (all except GUAM), in the W Pacific Ocean; formerly part of the U.S. Trust Territory of the PACIFIC ISLANDS. The three main islands are SAIPAN, the capital of the Northern Marianas and administrative center of the trust territory; Rota; and Tinian. U.S. aid, tourism, garment making, construction, and the production of small amounts of copra, beef, and sugar are mainstays of the economy. Most of the people are Chamorros (i.e., of mixed Spanish, Filipino, and Micronesian descent). The islands were discovered (1521) and named the Ladrones (Thieves) Islands by MAGELLAN, and renamed (1668) by Spanish Jesuits. Germany purchased them from Spain in 1899. In 1914 they were captured by Japan and were made a Japanese mandate by the League of Nations in 1920. U.S. forces occupied the Marianas in 1944 during WORLD WAR II, and in 1947 they became part of the U.S. trust territory. Voters approved separate status for the islands as a U.S. commonwealth in 1975; they became internally self-governing in 1978.

Northern Territory, territory (1992 est. pop. 169,000), 520,280 sq mi (1,347,525 sq km), N central Australia. DARWIN is the capital, largest city, and chief port. Australian aborigines, nearly one fourth of the population, live on 15 reservations totaling 94,000 sq mi (243,460 sq km). Mining is the principal industry; uranium, bauxite, manganese, and copper are the most valuable mineral resources. Beef cattle, grazed in the hot, semiarid plains of the interior, are the leading agricultural product. The Northern Territory was transferred to direct rule by the commonwealth in 1911 after being part of NEW SOUTH WALES (1825–63) and SOUTH AUSTRALIA (1863–1911). It became self-governing in 1978, in preparation for eventual statehood.

Northern War, 1700–21, European conflict, the main purpose of which was to break the power of the Swedish empire, then a great world power. Sweden's chief antagonists were Russia, under PETER I, and Poland, with Denmark and England early allies of Russia. Russia was also anxious to seize some of Sweden's territories. CHARLES XII, the young Swedish king, met with initial success. After forcing Denmark out of the war he turned eastward, where he defeated a superior Russian force at Narva (1700). He invaded Poland, took Warsaw and Cracow (1702), and forced the election of STANISLAUS I as king of Poland. He was less successful in Russia. After invading Ukraine (1707) with the help of MAZEPA, he was cut off and utterly defeated by Peter at Poltava (1709). Forced into exile in Bessarabia, he induced the sultan to declare war on Russia (see RUSSO-TURKISH WARS). Meanwhile, the Swedish possessions in the north were being taken over by Russia and its allies: Denmark and Poland (which had expelled Stanislaus and again switched sides), Saxony, Hanover, and Prussia. Charles returned north in 1714 but was killed (1718) while fighting in Norway. His successors sued for peace. The war marked the end of Swedish power and the emergence of Russia as a great European power.

North Pole, northern end of the earth's axis, lat. 90°N, long. 0°, distinguished from the north MAGNETIC POLE. It was reportedly first reached by Robert E. PEARY in 1909.

North Sea, arm of the Atlantic Ocean, c.222,000 sq mi (574,980 sq km), NW Europe, separating Great Britain from Norway and central Europe. Long known for its rich cod and herring fisheries, it is now more important for the substantial oil and gas deposits discovered (1970) under its floor.

Northumbria, kingdom of, one of the Anglo-Saxon kingdoms in England. It was formed by the union (early 7th cent.) of the kingdoms of Bernicia and Deria, which had been settled (c.500) by invading Angles. At the Synod of Whitby (663) King Osiu established the Roman Church over the Celtic Church. The late 7th and 8th cent. were Northumbria's cultural golden age. In the 9th cent. much of the kingdom fell to invading Danes, but in 920 all Northumbria recognized Edward the Elder of WESSEX as overlord.

Northwest Coast Indians: see NORTH AMERICA, INDIGENOUS PEOPLES OF.

North West Company, fur-trading organization (1784–1821) which explored western Canada. Organized by Montreal trading companies, it established new trading routes and posts in the Pacific Northwest. "Northwesters" included the noted explorers Sir Alexander MACKENZIE, David Thompson, and Alexander Henry. The company's aggressive rivalry with the HUDSON'S BAY COMPANY led to ruinous warfare over the RED RIVER SETTLEMENT and to amalgamation of the two companies in 1821.

Northwest Ordinance: see ORDINANCE OF 1787.

Northwest Passage, water routes along the northern coast of North America, between the Atlantic and Pacific oceans. The idea of a short route to India and China prompted many expeditions to find the passage. The English explorer Sir Martin FROBISHER explored (1576–78) the eastern approaches to the passage. Subsequent explorations were made by John Davis, Henry HUDSON, William BAFFIN, and Sir John FRANKLIN, whose mission ended in tragedy. The expedition (1850–54) of Robert J. Le M. MCCLURE proved the passage existed, but it was not traversed until 1903–6, when Roald AMUNDSEN of Norway first accomplished the feat. In the 1960s the discovery of oil on Alaska's North Slope (see PRUDHOE BAY) renewed commercial interest in the route.

Northwest Territories, territory (1991 pop. 57,649), 1,304,896 sq mi (3,379,684 sq km), NW Canada, W of Hudson Bay, N of lat. 60°N, and E of the Yukon. It also includes the islands in Hudson and James bays and in Hudson Strait. The area is divided into three administrative districts: Keewatin, W of Hudson Bay; Mackenzie, E of the Yukon; and Franklin, in the north, including the Arctic Archipelago. Geographically the area is divided by the tree line that runs northwest to southeast from the MACKENZIE R. delta to the

Churchill area, on HUDSON BAY. TUNDRA, inhabited by Eskimos and Native Americans, extends over much of the north and east. Much development has taken place in the Mackenzie district, which is heavily forested and rich in minerals. The district contains the large Great Bear and GREAT SLAVE lakes. Mining is the major industry, and deposits of lead, zinc, oil, gold, and copper have been exploited. Trapping, the region's oldest industry, ranks second in economic importance. Great Slave Lake has a thriving fishing industry. Highways and railways are limited, and air transportation remains important. YELLOWKNIFE is the territorial capital.

History. Henry HUDSON discovered Hudson Bay in 1610, and for several decades the HUDSON'S BAY COMPANY sent explorers and traders into the area. In 1870 the company sold the region to the Canadian confederation, and the Territories' present boundaries were set in 1912. In 1992 voters in the Territories approved the division of the territory and the creation of NUNAVUT, an Eskimo-dominated territory, in the eastern half. In the western part, where the division was largely opposed, Native American and Métis (mixed race) residents are negotiating for the creation of a territory to be called Denendeh. The Northwest Territories are presently governed by a commissioner and a 24-member council and send one senator (appointed) and two representatives (elected) to the national parliament.

Northwest Territory, first national territory of the U.S., including present-day Ohio, Indiana, Illinois, Michigan, Wisconsin, and part of Minnesota. Explored by the French in the 1600s, it was ceded to Britain (1763) after the FRENCH AND INDIAN WARS, and to the U.S. (1783) after the AMERICAN REVOLUTION. The ORDINANCE OF 1787 set up the machinery for organization of the territory. British-American rivalry for control of the area continued, however, until the Treaty of GHENT (1814), ending the WAR OF 1812, gave the region irrevocably to the U.S.

Norway, Nor. *Norge,* officially Kingdom of Norway, constitutional monarchy (1992 est. pop. 4,295,000), 125,181 sq mi (324,219 sq km), N Europe, on the W Scandinavian peninsula; bordered by the North Sea (SW), the Skagerrak (S), Sweden (E), Finland and Russia (NE), the Barents Sea (N), and the Atlantic Ocean (W). Major cities include OSLO (the capital), BERGEN, and Trondheim. Norway is a rugged, mountainous country. Its 1,700-mi (2,740-km) coastline is fringed with islands and deeply indented by fjords; from the coast the land rises precipitously to high plateaus, reaching 8,098 ft (2,468 m) in the Jotunheimen range and including Jostedalsbreen, the largest glacier field in Europe. Norway's economy was transformed in the late 1960s by the discovery of large oil and gas reserves in the NORTH SEA; petroleum and gas account for over 40% of export earnings. Manufacturing, food processing, shipbuilding, forestry, fishing, the shipping and trading carried on by Norway's great merchant fleet, and the production of aluminum, pulp and paper, and electrochemicals are also important. Less than 4% of the land is cultivated; cattle, sheep, and reindeer are raised on the mountain pastures. The many rapid rivers furnish hydroelectric power, allowing most of the petroleum to be exported. The majority of the people are of Scandinavian stock, but there are many Lapps and Finns in the north. Two forms of Norwegian, Bokml and Nynorsk, are official languages. The Lutheran Church is established.

History. In the 9th cent. Norway was still divided into numerous petty kingdoms. The move toward political unity began c.900 under its first king, HAROLD I, and Christianity was established by OLAF II (r.1015–28). Dynastic feuds wracked the country until the 12th cent., when King Sverre consolidated royal power, and Norway enjoyed peace and prosperity under HAAKON IV and MAGNUS VI in the 13th cent. In 1397 the Kalmar Union united Norway, Denmark, and Sweden; Sweden broke away in 1523, but Norway was ruled by Danish governors until 1814, when Denmark ceded it to Sweden. In the 19th cent. Norwegian nationalism emerged as a potent force, and in 1905 the union with Sweden was dissolved and Norway became an independent constitutional monarchy under HAAKON VII. Norway was neutral in World War I but was occupied (1940–45) by German forces in WORLD WAR II; the Norwegian merchant fleet, however, was placed in Allied service. Postwar recovery was rapid. Economic policy included a degree of socialization under the Labor party, which dominated the government until 1965. Norway broke from its traditional neutrality by joining NATO in 1949. King Haakon, who had reigned for 52 years, died in 1957 and was succeeded by OLAF V. He died in 1991 and was succeeded by HAROLD V. Gro Harlem Brundtland, Norway's current (and first woman) prime minister, has led Labor governments in 1981, from 1986 to 1989, and since 1990.

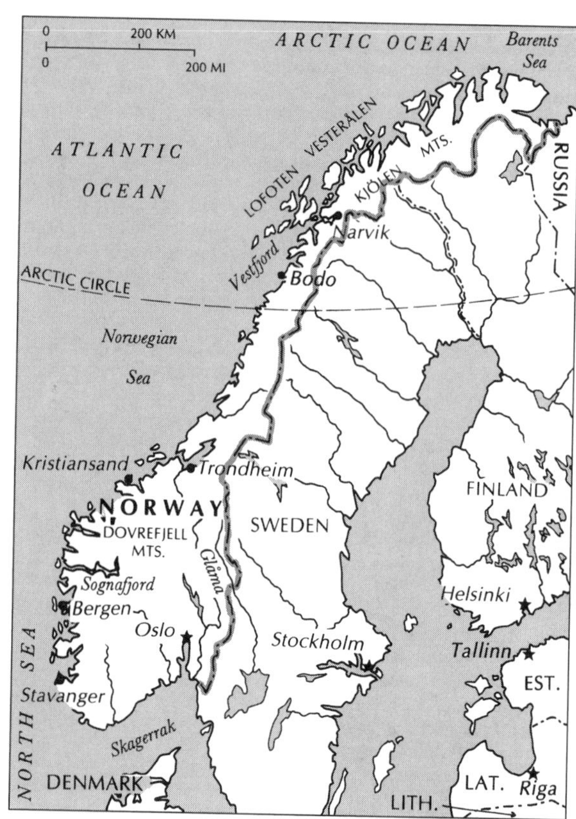

Norwegian language, member of the North Germanic, or Scandinavian, group of the Germanic subfamily of the Indo-European family of languages. Today there are two official forms of Norwegian: *bokmål* [book language] (also called *riksmål* [national language] and Dano-Norwegian), which is the language of the cities, the official and professional classes, and literature; and *nynorsk* [new Norwegian] (also called *landsmål* [country language]), which is a standardization of rural dialects and is spoken primarily in rural areas. See LANGUAGE (table).

nose, organ of breathing and smell. The external nose consists of bone and cartilage. The hollow internal nose, above the roof of the mouth, is divided by the septum (wall) into two nasal cavities extending from the nostrils to the PHARYNX. The cavities are lined with a mucous membrane, which is covered with fine hairs that help to filter dust and impurities from the air before it reaches the lungs; the air is also moistened and warmed in its passage. High in each nasal cavity is a small tract of mucous membrane containing olfactory cells. Hairlike fibers in these nerve cells, responding to various odors, send impulses along the olfactory nerve to the brain and thus produce the sense of smell.

Notre-Dame de Paris, cathedral of Paris, a major achievement of early GOTHIC ARCHITECTURE, on the Île de la Cité, in the Seine R. The cornerstone was laid in 1163, the high altar consecrated in 1183, and the nave completed except for roofing in 1196. In 1230 the nave was reconstructed and flying BUTTRESSES added. Chapels were soon added between the buttresses, altering the building's plan and aesthetic. The cathedral was not completed until the 14th cent. Its majestic west front is famous for its portals, sculptures, and huge ROSE WINDOW.

Nouakchott [nwäkshôt'], city (1987 est. pop. 285,000), capital of

Mauritania, on the Atlantic Ocean. A small village in 1957, when it became Mauritania's capital, Nouakchott has grown into the country's largest city. Its ocean port, c.4 mi (6.4 km) from the city proper, has modern storage facilities, especially for petroleum, and a deepwater harbor was built in the 1980s. The city is situated on a major highway and has an international airport.

nova: see VARIABLE STAR; SUPERNOVA.

Novalis [nōvä'lĭs], pseud. of **Friedrich von Hardenberg,** 1772–1801, German poet. Influenced by FICHTE, he was one of the great German romantics. His major work, the novel *Heinrich von Ofterdingen* (1802), describes symbolically the artist's romantic search for a "blue flower." *Hymns to the Night* (1800) is a collection of deeply religious lyrics composed after the death of his young love, Sophie von Kühn.

Nova Scotia, province (1991 pop. 899,942), 21,425 sq mi (55,491 sq km), E Canada, bordered by the Gulf of St. Lawrence (N), the Atlantic Ocean (E, S), and New Brunswick and the Bay of Fundy (E). It comprises a mainland peninsula and the adjacent CAPE BRETON ISLAND. One of the Maritime Provinces, Nova Scotia has a moderate climate and abundant rainfall. The rocky east coast has numerous bays and coves. Considerable mining (coal, gypsum, barite, salt) occurs in Nova Scotia and fishing (for cod, lobster, haddock) is next in importance. In the northwest are dairies and orchards. The province also contains a variety of manufacturing industries, including fish and food processing. Lumbering is prevalent inland, and the pulp and paper industry is significant. HALIFAX, the capital, and Sydney are among the important cities.

History. Port Royal (now ANNAPOLIS ROYAL) was settled by the French in 1605. For over 150 years the English and French bitterly contested the area, which was called ACADIA and which also included NEW BRUNSWICK and PRINCE EDWARD ISLAND. From 1713 Britain controlled the Nova Scotian peninsula, but the French retained Cape Breton Island, with its fortress of Louisbourg (see LOUISBURG). During the French and Indian War (1754–63) the British expelled (1755, 1758) most of the French Acadians and seized Louisbourg. Many UNITED EMPIRE LOYALISTS settled in Nova Scotia after the American Revolution, and Cape Breton was made (1784) a separate colony. It rejoined Nova Scotia in 1820. In 1848 Nova Scotia became the first colony to achieve responsible (cabinet) government. It joined the Canadian confederation in 1867. In recent years it has struggled to stabilize its shaky economy. The province sends 10 senators (appointed) and 11 representatives (elected) to the national parliament.

novel, sustained work of prose fiction, as distinguished from the SHORT STORY. The term derives from the Italian Renaissance *novella,* a compact, realistic tale exemplified in BOCCACCIO's *Decameron* (14th cent.). The novel also descended from the often supernatural medieval romance. A realistic precursor of the novel is PETRONIUS' *Satyricon* (1st cent.); the *Metamorphoses* (2d cent.) of APULEIUS is a fantastic prototype. The two strains converge in CERVANTES's *Don Quixote* (17th cent.). The novel established itself in England in the 18th cent. through the realistic works of Daniel DEFOE, Samuel RICHARDSON, and Henry FIELDING. During the 19th cent. it became the dominant form of literature, and many nations produced great novelists: England, Jane AUSTEN, W.M. THACKERAY, Charles DICKENS, George ELIOT, and Thomas HARDY; France, Victor HUGO, Honoré de BALZAC, and Gustave FLAUBERT; Russia, Leo TOLSTOY and Fyodor DOSTOYEVSKY; and the U.S., Nathaniel HAWTHORNE, Herman MELVILLE, Mark TWAIN, and Henry JAMES. In the 20th cent. novelists strove for greater freedom of form and expression. In superbly associative psychological novels James JOYCE, Marcel PROUST, Virginia WOOLF, and William FAULKNER represented their characters' thoughts and feelings. Thomas Mann (see MANN, family) wrote philosophical novels; Franz KAFKA produced influential symbolic novels treating the anxiety-ridden condition of modern humanity; Edith WHARTON, John O'HARA, and John UPDIKE explored complex social interactions; and Kurt VONNEGUT and Thomas BERGER created surreal fantasies on late-20th-cent. American life.

novella: see NOVEL.

November: see MONTH.

Novgorod, city (1989 pop. 229,000), NW European Russia, on the Volkhov R. Its products include chemicals, fertilizer, and furniture; tourism is also important. Among the old Russian cities, it was a medieval center of trade and culture, and the capital of the Russian state founded by Rurik (A.D. 862). Although KIEV became the capital in 886, Novgorod remained the center of foreign trade. In 1136 it became the capital of an independent republic comprising all of N Russia to the Urals. One of the four chief trade centers of the HANSEATIC LEAGUE, Novgorod levied tribute, founded colonies, and repulsed Teutonic, Livonian, and Swedish invasions. In 1478 it came under the control of MOSCOW. Its commercial importance waned after Saint Petersburg was built (1703). Many of its medieval architectural treasures were damaged during the German occupation (1941–44) in World War II.

Novosibirsk, city (1991 est. pop. 1,444,000), S Siberian Russia, on the Ob R. and the Trans-Siberian RR. A hub of river, rail, and air transport, it is SIBERIA's major industrial center producing heavy machinery, textiles, chemicals, and metals. Founded as Novonikolayevsk in 1893, during construction of the railroad, it grew as a trade center and was renamed in 1925.

Novotný, Antonín, 1904–75, Czechoslovakian Communist leader. He participated in the Communist coup of 1948 and after 1953 headed both the government and the party. His regime was characterized by repression and economic stagnation. In 1968 he was removed from power by a liberal majority headed by DUBČEK.

NOW: see NATIONAL ORGANIZATION FOR WOMEN.

Noyes, John Humphrey, 1811–86, American reformer; b. Brattleboro, Vt. Advancing a "perfectionist" doctrine that man's innate sinlessness could be regained by communion with Jesus, he developed religious and social experiments in communal living. After an earlier attempt, he founded (1848) the Oneida Community. When it failed in 1879, he moved to Canada.

Np, chemical symbol of the element NEPTUNIUM.

Ns, chemical symbol of the element NIELSBOHRIUM.

NSAID: see NONSTEROIDAL ANTI-INFLAMMATORY DRUG.

Nu, U [o͞o no͞o], 1907–, premier of MYANMAR (1948–56, 1957–58, 1960–62). He helped to secure (1948) Myanmar's independence from Britain and was its first premier. In 1962 he was deposed in a military coup led by NE WIN.

Nubia [no͞o'bēə], ancient state of NE Africa, which extended from Khartoum in the Sudan almost to Aswan in Egypt. In the 8th and 7th cent. B.C., Egypt was ruled by a Nubian dynasty. Later, in the 3d cent. A.D., an African people, the Nobatae, settled in Nubia and formed a powerful kingdom. Converted to Christianity in the 6th cent., it succumbed to the Muslims in 1366. MUHAMMAD ALI of Egypt conquered the area in the 19th cent.

nuclear disarmament: see DISARMAMENT, NUCLEAR.

nuclear energy, the energy stored in the nucleus of an ATOM and released through fission, fusion, or RADIOACTIVITY. In these processes a small amount of mass, equal to the difference in mass before and after the reaction, is converted to energy according to the relationship $E = mc^2$, where E is energy, m mass, and c the speed of light (see RELATIVITY). In fission processes, a fissionable nucleus absorbs a neutron, becomes unstable, and splits into two nearly equal nuclei. In fusion processes, two nuclei combine to form a single, heavier nucleus. Fission occurs for very heavy nuclei, while fusion occurs for the lightest nuclei. Nuclear fission was discovered in 1938 by Otto HAHN and Fritz Strassman, and was explained in 1939 by Lise MEITNER and Otto Frisch. Fission energy can be obtained by bombarding the fissionable isotope URANIUM-235 with slow neutrons in order to split it. Because this reaction releases an average of 2.5 neutrons, a chain reaction is possible, provided at least one neutron per fission is captured by another nucleus and causes a second fission. In an ATOMIC BOMB the number of neutrons producing additional fission is greater than 1, and the reaction increases rapidly to an explosion. In a NUCLEAR REACTOR, where the chain reaction is controlled, the number must be exactly 1 in order to maintain a steady reaction rate. Uranium-233 and PLUTONIUM-239 can also be used but must be produced artificially. Moreover, the fuel for fusion reactors, deuterium, is readily available in large amounts. Temperatures greater than 1,000,000°C are required to initiate a fusion, or thermonuclear, reaction. In the HYDROGEN BOMB such temperatures are provided by the detonation of a fission bomb. Sustained, controlled fusion reactions, however, require the containment of the nuclear fuel at extremely high temperatures long enough to allow the reactions to take place. At these temperatures the fuel is a PLASMA, and magnetic fields have been used in attempts to contain this plasma. To produce fusion energy, scientists have also used high-powered laser beams aimed at tiny pellets of fission fuel. In 1993 U.S. researchers achieved a fusion reaction that lasted a few seconds and generated about 6.4 million watts, using deuterium and tritium in a magnetically confined plasma. The use of tritium lowers the temperature required and increases the rate of the reaction, but it also increases the release of radioactive NEUTRONS.

nuclear magnetic resonance (NMR): see MAGNETIC RESONANCE.

nuclear physics, study of the components, structure, and behavior of the nucleus of the ATOM. It is especially concerned with the nature of matter and with NUCLEAR ENERGY. The subject is commonly divided into three fields: low-energy nuclear physics, the study of RADIOACTIVITY; medium-energy nuclear physics, the study of the force between nuclear particles; and high-energy, or particle, physics, the study of the transformations among subatomic particles in reactions produced in a PARTICLE ACCELERATOR. See ELEMENTARY PARTICLES.

nuclear reactor, device for producing nuclear energy by controlled nuclear reactions. It can be used for either research or power production. The reactor is so constructed that the fission of atomic nuclei produces a self-sustaining nuclear chain reaction, in which the produced neutrons are able to split other nuclei. A fission reactor consists basically of (1) a fuel, usually uranium or plutonium, enclosed in shielding; (2) a moderator—a substance such as graphite, beryllium, or heavy water—that slows down the neutrons so that they may be more easily captured by the fissionable atoms; and (3) a cooling system that extracts the heat energy produced. The fuel is sometimes enriched—i.e., its concentration of fissionable isotopes is artificially increased—to increase the frequency of neutron capture. The breeder reactor is a special type of reactor that produces more fissionable atoms than it consumes by using surplus neutrons to transmute certain nonfissionable atoms into fissionable atoms. The design of fusion reactors is still in an experimental stage because of the problems involved in containing the PLASMA fuel and attaining the high temperatures needed to initiate the reaction. The best fusion results (see NUCLEAR ENERGY) have been obtained (1993) using deuterium-tritium fuel (see HYDROGEN) in a tokamak reactor, which uses a powerful magnetic field to confine the plasma in a doughnut-shaped chamber.

Nuclear Regulatory Commission (NRC), independent U.S. agency (est. 1975) responsible for licensing and regulating the civilian use of nuclear energy, including setting safety standards for and overseeing the building of nuclear plants. It took over the functions of the former Atomic Energy Commission, established in 1946 to regulate the development and operation of the U.S. atomic energy program.

nuclear waste disposal: see WASTE DISPOSAL.

nuclear winter, a controversial predicted effect of a nuclear war. The theory holds that the dust and particles thrown into the atmosphere by a massive exchange of nuclear weapons would block a large percentage of sunlight, resulting in global cooling and severe, winterlike weather that would kill crops and other plants.

nucleic acid, organic substance, found in all living cells, in which the hereditary information is stored and from which it can be transferred. Nucleic acid molecules are long chains that generally occur in combination with proteins. The two chief types are DNA (deoxyribonucleic acid), the main constituent of GENES, and RNA (ribonucleic acid), which is involved in protein synthesis and transmission of DNA's genetic information. Each nucleic acid chain is composed of subunits called nucleotides, each containing a sugar, a phosphate group, and one of four bases: adenine (symbolized A), guanine (G), cytosine (C), and thymine (T). RNA contains the sugar ribose instead of the deoxyribose of DNA and the base uracil (U) instead of thymine. The specific sequences of nucleotides determine the cell's genetic information: each three-nucleotide DNA sequence specifies one particular amino acid. The long sequences of DNA nucleotides thus correspond to the sequences of amino acids in the cell's proteins. In order to be expressed as protein, the genetic information is carried to the protein-synthesizing machinery of the cell, usually in the cell cytoplasm. Forms of RNA mediate this process. DNA not only provides information but also acts as a blueprint for its own exact replication: The cell replicates its DNA by making a complementary copy of its exact nucleotide sequence: T for every A, C for every G, G for every C, A for every T. Although the triplet nucleotide code seems to be universal, the actual sequences of the nucleotides vary according to the species and individual. See also GENE; GENETIC ENGINEERING; MUTATION.

nucleus: **1** in biology, see CELL. **2** in physics, see ATOM; NUCLEAR PHYSICS.

Nuevo Laredo, city (1990 pop. 217,912), NE Mexico, across the Río Grande from Laredo, Texas. Founded in 1755, it is a major trade and transportation hub and the chief point of entry for U.S. tourists driving into Mexico. Plants that assemble goods for export to the U.S. are important to its economy.

Nuffield Radio Astronomy Laboratories, radio-astronomy observatory (founded 1945) located at Jodrell Bank, Macclesfield, Cheshire, England, and administered by the Univ. of Manchester. Its principal antenna is a fully steerable, parabolic dish 250 ft (76 m) in diameter.

nuisance, in law, an act that without legal justification interferes with safety, comfort, or use of property. A nuisance may be private (affecting only a few persons) or public (affecting many persons). Nuisances, usually treated as TORTS, may be restrained by INJUNCTION or remedied by the award of damages. Public nuisances, injurious to the community, may be prosecuted as crimes.

Nukualofa, town (1986 pop. 21,300), capital and chief port of TONGA, in the S Pacific Ocean.

nullification, in U.S. history, an extremist doctrine of STATES' RIGHTS holding that a state can declare null and void any federal law it deems unconstitutional. The KENTUCKY AND VIRGINIA RESOLUTIONS (1799) were the first notable expressions of the doctrine. The principle was invoked by SOUTH CAROLINA in 1832, at the instigation of Sen. John C. CALHOUN, to protest federal tariffs favoring Northern interests. Some senators proposed to use force against the nullifiers, but Pres. Andrew JACKSON, believing the South had a real grievance, agreed to the compromise tariff bill of 1833. South Carolina then rescinded its ordinance nullifying the tariff acts. Nullification was a forerunner of the doctrine of secession that brought about the CIVIL WAR.

number, entity describing the magnitude or position of a mathematical object or extensions of these concepts. Cardinal numbers describe the size of a collection of objects; ordinal numbers refer to position relative to an ordering, such as first, second, third, etc. Both types can be generalized to infinite collections (see INFINITY). The finite cardinal and ordinal numbers, represented by the numerals 1, 2, 3, . . . , are called the *natural numbers.* The *integers* are the natural numbers with their negatives and zero. The ratios a/b, where a and b are integers and $b \neq 0$, constitute the *rational numbers,* which may be also be represented by repeating decimals (see DECIMAL SYSTEM), e.g., $\frac{1}{2} = 0.500 \ldots$, $\frac{2}{3} = 0.666 \ldots$. The *real numbers* are all numbers representable by an infinite decimal expansion, which may be repeating or nonrepeating; they are in a one-to-one correspondence with the points on a straight line. Real numbers that have nonrepeating decimal expansions, i.e., that cannot be represented by any ratio of integers, are called *irrational.* The Pythagoreans knew in the 6th cent. B.C. that $\sqrt{2}$ was irrational. The number $\sqrt{2}$ is also an example of an algebraic number, i.e., it is the root of a POLYNOMIAL equation, in this case $x^2 - 2 = 0$. Numbers that are not algebraic are called *transcendental; e* (see separate article) and π (PI) are examples. The *imaginary numbers* were invented to deal with equations, such as $x^2 + 2 = 0$, that have no real roots. The basic imaginary unit is $i = \sqrt{-1}$. Imaginary numbers take the form yi, where y is a real number, e.g., $\sqrt{-2} = (\sqrt{2})i$. Numbers of the form $x + yi$, where x and y are real (e.g., $8 + 7i$), are called *complex numbers.* The complex numbers are in a one-to-one correspondence with the points on a plane, with one axis defining the real parts of the numbers and another axis defining the imaginary parts.

Numbers, book of the OLD TESTAMENT, fourth of the five books of the PENTATEUCH ascribed by tradition to MOSES. It continues the narrative of EXODUS, beginning at Sinai and ending at Moab on the eve of the entry into Palestine. Bare in geographical detail, it includes accounts of the curse of Balaam and other events.

number theory, branch of mathematics concerned with the properties of the integers (the NUMBERS 0, 1, −1, 2, −2, . . .). Modern number theory made its first great advances through the work of Leonhard EULER, Carl GAUSS, and Pierre de FERMAT. Much of the focus is on the analysis of prime numbers, i.e., those integers *p* greater than 1 that are divisible only by 1 and *p;* the first few primes are 2, 3, 5, 7, 11, 13, 17, and 19. The fundamental theorem of arithmetic asserts that any positive integer *a* is a product of primes that are unique except for the order in which they are listed. For example, the number 20 is uniquely the product $2 \times 2 \times 5$. This theorem was known to the Greek mathematician EUCLID, who also proved that there are an infinite number of primes.

numeration, in mathematics, process of designating NUMBERS according to a particular system. In any system of numeration a base number is specified, and groupings are then made by powers of the base number. The most widely used system of numeration is the DECIMAL SYSTEM, which uses base 10. In the decimal system the numeral 302 means $(3 \times 10^2) + (0 \times 10^1) + (2 \times 10^0)$, or $300 + 0 + 2$. The binary system, used in most computers, has a base of 2 and only two digits, 0 and 1. The binary numeral 101 means $(1 \times 2^2) + (0 \times 2^1) + (1 \times 2^0)$, i.e., $4 + 0 + 1$, or 5 in the decimal system. The decimal numeral 5 and the binary numeral 101 thus represent the same number. The ancient Babylonians used a system of base 60, which survives in our smaller divisions of time and angle, i.e., minutes and seconds.

Numidia [no͞omĭd'ēə], ancient country of NW Africa, roughly modern Algeria. In the PUNIC WARS, its king MASINISSA sided with Rome and won freedom from CARTHAGE. Jugurtha fought a fatal war with Rome, but Juba II was restored as a prince subject to Rome (1st cent. A.D.). Numidia declined after the Arabs came (8th cent.).

nun: see MONASTICISM.

Nunavut [Inuktituk, = our land], proposed Inuit (ESKIMO) territory in N Canada, embracing c.770,000 sq mi (1,994,000 sq km) of the eastern NORTHWEST TERRITORIES (approx. 60% of the entire N.W.T.). The area has a population of about 20,000, over 85% of which is Inuit. An agreement signed (1991) by Canadian and Inuit leaders provides for the transfer of 135,000 sq mi (349,650 sq km) of land to the Inuit and a cash settlement, paid over 14 years, amounting to $1.4 billion, but many specifics, such as those relating to the powers of the territorial government, remain to be settled. In 1992 residents of the Northwest Territories voted to approve the creation of Nunavut.

Nunn, Sam(uel Augustus, Jr.), 1938–, U.S. politician, b. Perry, Georgia. A lawyer, he was a member of the Georgia House of Representatives (1968–72) and became a U.S. senator in 1972. A conservative Democrat, he is one of the Senate's most powerful leaders, particularly in his role as chairman (1987–) of the Armed Services Committee.

Nuremberg, city (1989 est. pop. 480,000), Bavaria, S Germany, on the Pegnitz R. It is an industrial center with such manufactures as electrical and optical equipment and machinery. Founded by 1050 and chartered in 1219, it became a free imperial city and a trade center on the route from Italy. Humanism, science, and art flourished there during the German RENAISSANCE (15th–16th cent.), with such artists as DÜRER in residence. The city declined after the THIRTY YEARS WAR but became a center of industry during the 19th cent. A shrine of NATIONAL SOCIALISM (Nazism) and a site of armaments factories, Nuremberg was heavily bombed during WORLD WAR II; it was rebuilt after 1945. Its historic structures include the city walls (14th–17th cent.) and the Church of St. Sebald (13th cent.). Nuremberg was the site (1945–56) of a WAR CRIMES tribunal.

Nuremberg Trials: see WAR CRIMES.

Nureyev, Rudolf [no͝orě'yěf], 1938–93, Russian ballet dancer. A soloist with the KIROV BALLET from 1958, he defected (1961) while on tour in Paris. Considered the leading classical ballet dancer of his generation, he was known for his stage presence, athletic skill, and fiery grace. He had a much acclaimed partnership with Margot FONTEYN at the ROYAL BALLET. He revised and staged numerous works, and from 1983 to 1989 he was the director of the Paris Opéra Ballet.

nursery school, educational institution for children aged two to four. Chiefly private, philanthropic, or cooperative, it serves primarily to promote social and educational adjustment rather than to provide daytime child care (see DAY-CARE CENTER). The first nursery

Rudolf Nureyev and Dame Margot Fonteyn

schools were opened in London in 1907; pioneers in the U.S. include Teachers College, Columbia Univ.

nursing, profession dealing with prevention of illness and the care and rehabilitation of the sick, encompassing the physical and emotional well-being of the patient as a whole. Nursing includes individualized care on a continuing basis, the carrying out of medical regimens, coordination of necessary interdisciplinary services, and health counseling. Until the middle of the 19th cent. nurses were trained in hospitals to provide bedside care. The first school designed primarily to train nurses—rather than provide nursing service for the hospital—was established (1860) in London by Florence NIGHTINGALE. The specialty of nursing anesthesia originated at the turn of the century, and the profession in recent years has expanded to include nurse practitioners, nurse midwives (see MIDWIFERY), and nurse clinicians. Although traditionally most nurses have been women, the number of males in the profession has increased. Training includes classroom and clinical experience, as well as knowledge of automated equipment, artificial organs, and computers.

nut, in botany, a dry, one-seeded, usually oily FRUIT. True nuts include the acorn, chestnut, and hazelnut. The term *nut* also refers to any seed or fruit with a hard, brittle covering around an edible kernel, e.g., the peanut pod (a LEGUME) and almond (a drupe fruit). Others that are not true nuts are the CASHEW, COCONUT, LITCHI, PISTACHIO, and WALNUT. Nuts are a valuable food and are often cultivated in nut orchards.

nutation, slight wobbling motion of the earth's axis, superimposed on that which produces the PRECESSION OF THE EQUINOXES. Caused by the difference in gravitational attraction exerted by the sun and the moon, it has an 18.6-yr period.

nutmeg, evergreen tree (*Myristica fragrans*) native to the Moluccas. Its fruit is the source of two spices: whole or ground nutmeg, from the seed; and mace, from the fibrous seed covering that separates the seed from the husk.

nutria or **coypu,** aquatic, plant-eating RODENT, *Myocastor coypus,* of South America, resembling a small beaver with a ratlike tail. The nutria is up to 25 in. (64 cm) long, excluding the 15-in. (38-cm) sparsely haired, round tail. It has long, coarse, brown outer fur; its soft, gray undercoat is valued commercially. Descendants of nutrias escaped from fur farms are found in wetlands in the S U.S., where they are destructive pests.

Nyasa, Lake: see MALAWI, LAKE.

Nyerere, Julius Kambarage [nīˈərāˈrä], 1922–, Tanzanian politician. He was the leading nationalist of Tanganyika and became prime minister upon independence (1961) and president (1962). He was the architect of the union (1964) of Tanganyika and Zanzibar as the republic of TANZANIA and served as president (1964–85). In 1990 he stepped down as chairman of the country's single, ruling party.

nylon: see SYNTHETIC TEXTILE FIBERS.

nymph, in Greek mythology, female divinity, immortal or long-lived, associated with various natural objects or places. Some represented specific localities, e.g., the acheloids of the River Achelous; others were identified with more general physiographic features, e.g., oreads with mountains, naiads with bodies of fresh water, nereids with the Mediterranean, oceanids with the ocean, dryads with trees; and some were associated with a function of nature, e.g., hamadryads, who lived and died with a particular tree. Nymphs were regarded as young, beautiful, musical, and amorous.

O

O, chemical symbol of the element OXYGEN.

Oahu [ōäˈho͞o], island (1990 est. pop. 850,000), 593 sq mi (1,536 sq km), third largest and chief island of Hawaii. Oahu consists of two parallel mountain ranges separated by a rolling plain. Mt. Kaala (4,040 ft/1,231 m) is its highest peak. Oahu has many extinct volcanos, notably DIAMOND HEAD. HONOLULU, Hawaii's capital, and PEARL HARBOR are on the urbanized S coast. There are many fine beaches, including Waikiki. Fishing and pineapple, sugarcane, and dairy farms are important, but tourism is the economic mainstay.

oak, tree or shrub (genus *Quercus*) of the BEECH family, found in north temperate zones and POLYNESIA; the more southerly species are usually evergreen. Oaks are cultivated for ornament and are a major source of hardwood lumber. Their durable, attractively grained WOOD is valued for shipbuilding, construction, flooring, furniture, barrels, and veneer. The black oaks (e.g., scarlet, pin, willow, live, and shingle oaks) are typified by leaves with sharp-tipped lobes and by acorns that mature in two years. White oaks (e.g., the white, post, cork, and holly oaks) have smooth-lobed leaves and acorns that mature in one year. *Q. alba,* the white oak, is the most valuable timber tree of the genus; the cork oak (*Q. suber*) supplies CORK. Acorns, the fruit of oak trees, are a source of food, tannin, oil, and hog feed. Poison oak (see POISON IVY) belongs to the SUMAC family.

Oakland, city (1990 pop. 372,242; met. area 2,082,914), seat of Alameda co., W Calif., on the eastern side of San Francisco Bay; inc. 1852. It is a leading container port and railhead with shipyards, chemical plants, glassworks, and food-processing plants. It is connected by the Bay Bridge (1936), tunnels, and the Bay Area Rapid Transit system with SAN FRANCISCO and other nearby cities. There are major military supply facilities in Oakland, and it is the site of a large urban renewal project. Parts of the city were severely damaged by an earthquake in 1989, and a wind-driven fire devastated the city's northeastern section in 1991.

Oakley, Annie, 1860–1926, American markswoman; b. Darke co., Ohio, as Phoebe Anne Oakley Mozee. She was a star attraction (1885–1902) of BUFFALO BILL's Wild West Show.

Oak Ridge, city (1990 pop. 27,310), E Tenn., on the Clinch R.; founded 1942 by the U.S. government, inc. 1959. The site during World War II of development of nuclear bomb materials, Oak Ridge continues to be a major nuclear physics center, with ties to a consortium of Southern universities.

OAS: see ORGANIZATION OF AMERICAN STATES.

Oates, Joyce Carol, 1938–, American writer; b. Lockport, N.Y. In realistic novels, tinged with surrealism, she has often explored the connection between violence and love in American life. Extraordinarily prolific, she has written such novels as *A Garden of Earthly Delights* (1967), *Childwold* (1976), *Bellefleur* (1980), *Solstice* (1985), *Because It Is Bitter, and Because It Is My Heart* (1990), and *Foxfire* (1993), as well as stories, poems, criticism, and a book on boxing.

Oates, Titus, 1649–1705, English conspirator. He invented (1678) the story of the Popish Plot, describing it as a Jesuit plan to assassinate CHARLES II. In the ensuing frenzy many innocent Roman Catholics were persecuted and killed.

oats, cereal plants (genus *Avena*) of the GRASS family. Most species are annuals growing in moist temperate regions. Oats are valued chiefly as a pasturage and hay crop and for crop rotation; less than 5% of the oats grown in the U.S. is for human consumption. The common cultivated species, *A. sativa,* is native to Eurasia.

OAU: see ORGANIZATION OF AFRICAN UNITY.

Oaxaca [wähäˈkä], city (1990 pop. 212,943), S Mexico, capital of Oaxaca state. A commercial and tourist center famed for its gardens and colonial churches, it is the chief city of S Mexico and one of the nation's most historic cities. It was founded (c.1500) by the AZTECS and was taken (1522) by the Spaniards. Benito JUÁREZ and Porfirio DÍAZ were born there.

Ob, one of the great rivers of Siberia, Russia, flowing generally north c.2,300 mi (3,700 km) into an estuary on the ARCTIC OCEAN. With its chief tributary, the IRTYSH R., it forms the world's fourth-longest river (c.3,460 mi/5,600 km). Although frozen for almost half the year and subject to flooding in its middle course, the Ob is a major trade and transportation route. NOVOSIBIRSK and Barnaul are the chief ports.

Obadiah or **Abdias,** book of the OLD TESTAMENT, 31st in the Authorized Version, fourth and shortest of the Minor PROPHETS, with 21 verses. Dated from the 8th to 6th cent. B.C., it calls down doom on Edom and says Israel will triumph.

obbligato [Ital., = obligatory], in music, originally a term by which a composer indicated that a certain part was indispensable to the music. Misunderstanding of the term, however, resulted in a reversal of its meaning, so that if a part added to a song is today designated "obbligato," the part may be omitted if desired.

obelisk, slender, four-sided, tapering monument, usually a monolith, terminating in a pointed or pyramidal top. The ancient Egyptians dedicated them to the sun god and placed them in pairs at the sides of temple portals. A line of incised hieroglyphs, giving the names and titles of the pharaoh, commonly ran down each of their sides. Many obelisks were taken from Egypt, notably those called CLEOPATRA'S NEEDLES in New York City (Central Park) and London (Thames embankment). A familiar American obelisk is the WASHINGTON MONUMENT.

Oberon, in astronomy, natural satellite of URANUS.

Oberth, Hermann Julius, 1894–1989, German astronautical pioneer; b. Romania. Beginning his studies in astronautics before World War I, he proposed a liquid-propellant ROCKET in 1917 and in 1923 published his unsuccessful Ph.D. dissertation, *The Rocket into Interplanetary Space,* which discussed many aspects of rocket travel. He expanded this small pamphlet into a larger work, *The Road to Space Travel* (1929), which won wide recognition.

object-oriented programming, a modular approach to COMPUTER PROGRAM (software) design. Each module, or object, combines data and procedures (sequences of instructions) that act on the data; in traditional, or procedural, programming the data are separated from the instructions. A group of objects that have properties, operations, and behaviors in common is called a class. By reusing classes developed for previous applications, new applications can be developed faster with improved reliability and consistency of design.

oboe or **hautboy:** see WIND INSTRUMENT.

Obote, (Apollo) Milton, 1925–, president of UGANDA (1966–71, 1980–85). He became (1962) prime minister after Uganda's independence and staged (1965) a revolution to make himself president. He was overthrown (1971) by Idi AMIN, returned to power after Amin's downfall (1979), and later deposed for corrupt activities.

Obregón, Álvaro, 1880–1928, president of MEXICO (1920–24). A successful general in the Mexican revolution (1910–17), he rose (1920) against Pres. CARRANZA and became president. His administration enacted agrarian, labor, and educational reforms. Chosen president again in 1928, the anticlerical Obregón was assassinated by a fanatical Roman Catholic before he could take office.

Obrenović or **Obrenovich,** Serbian dynasty founded by Miloš Obrenović that ruled 1817–42 and 1858–1903. Its longtime rival was the KARADJORDJEVIĆ dynasty. King ALEXANDER of Serbia was the last Obrenović ruler.

O'Brien, Flann, pseud. of Brian O Nuallain, 1911–66, Irish author. O'Brien's wildly comic sense, brilliant word play, and absurdist vision are exhibited in such novels as *At Swim-Two Birds* (1939) and *The Dalkey Archive* (1964). A career civil servant, he also wrote a long-running, bitingly satirical political column for *The Irish Times* under the pseudonym Myles na Gopaleen.

observatory, astronomical, scientific facility especially equipped to detect and record astronomical phenomena. Early civilizations established primitive observatories to regulate the calendar and predict the changes of season. Later observatories were established to compile accurate star charts and an annual ephemeris that would be of use to navigators in determining longitude at sea. Early instruments used included the armillary sphere, the ASTROLABE, the quadrant, and the SEXTANT. The 17th-cent. invention of the TELESCOPE permitted not only more accurate measurement of the positions and motions of celestial bodes, but also analysis of the physical nature of the bodies. The 19th-cent. development of dry-plate photography, which permitted long exposure times, offered a much more sensitive method of recording images than the drawings made from visual observations by earlier observers. The spectroscopic study of starlight by various instruments has provided information on the temperature and chemical composition of stars, stellar motions, and magnetic fields. Optical observatories are generally located at high altitudes in sparsely populated areas to minimize adverse seeing conditions caused by weather disturbances, air turbulence, air glow, or any source of extraneous illumination. Since the mid-20th cent., astronomical observations have been extended to wavelengths outside the visible spectrum and to the neutrino (see GAMMA-RAY ASTRONOMY, INFRARED ASTRONOMY, NEUTRINO ASTRONOMY, RADIO ASTRONOMY, ULTRAVIOLET ASTRONOMY, and X-RAY ASTRONOMY) by, among other means, the use of artificial satellites equipped with telescopes (see OBSERVATORY, ORBITING).

observatory, orbiting, research SATELLITE designed to study solar radiation, ELECTROMAGNETIC RADIATION from distant stars, the earth's atmosphere, or the like. The Orbiting Solar Observatory program comprised seven satellites, launched between 1962 and 1971, to study the sun's atmosphere and the sunspot cycle. The Orbiting Geophysical Observatory program consisted of six satellites, launched between 1964 and 1969, that provided data on the earth's ATMOSPHERE, ionosphere, and magnetosphere and on the SOLAR WIND. The Orbiting Astronomical Observatory program comprised four satellites, launched between 1966 and 1972, to study astronomical phenomena at ultraviolet and X-ray wavelengths inaccessible to earthbound equipment. Because the atmosphere interferes with astronomical observations from the ground, the past two decades have seen increasing emphasis on space-based observatories. The largest such observatory is the HUBBLE SPACE TELESCOPE, launched in 1990. Other observatories include the Gamma-Ray Observatory and proposed Advanced X-Ray Astrophysics Facility. ROSAT [*RO*entgen *SAT*ellite], a joint German-U.S.-British project launched in 1990, studies both X rays and ultraviolet wavelengths never before imaged from space. It has detected a new class of bright stars that shine only in the ultraviolet part of the spectrum. The Cosmic Background Explorer (1989–93) studied microwave background radiation that no star or other known object could emit—it is believed to have come from the creation of the universe (see COSMOLOGY). See also SPACE PROBE; SPACE STATION.

obsessive-compulsive disorder, type of psychological disturbance marked by persistent unwanted patterns of thought (obsession) coupled with repetitive, ritualistic behavior designed to alleviate discomfort or dread (compulsion). The individual recognizes the thoughts and rituals as unrealistic or even repugnant, but is still unable to control them, as in the case of a person who has such recurring fears about germs that he must wash his hands excessively throughout the day. **Obsessive-compulsive personality disorder** is a separate disorder characterized by perfectionism and inflexibility that interfere with a person's ability to finish a task.

obsidian, volcanic glass, commonly black, but also red or brown, formed by LAVA that has cooled too quickly for crystals to form. Chemically it is rich in silica and similar to GRANITE. Obsidian was used extensively by primitive peoples to make knives, arrowheads, and other weapons and tools.

obstetrics: see under GYNECOLOGY.

O'Casey, Sean, 1884–1964, Irish dramatist, important in the Irish literary renaissance. His great early plays, *The Shadow of a Gunman* (1923), *Juno and the Paycock* (1924), and *The Plough and the Stars* (1926), are grim, satirical, and not always kind to the Irish people. After the last one set off a riot in the Abbey Theatre, he moved to England. His later plays, e.g., *The Silver Tassie* (1929), are more experimental. *Mirror in My House* (1956) is a collection of his six earlier autobiographical volumes.

occupational disease, illness resulting from the conditions or environment of employment. Some time usually elapses between exposure to the cause and development of the symptoms of an occupational disease. Among the causes of such diseases are toxic chemicals, such as benzene and dioxin. RADIATION SICKNESS can result from unprotected workplace exposure to radioactivity from X-ray machines and nuclear power facilities. Among the dust-related disorders are brown lung disease caused by cotton dust inhaled by textile workers, and the lung diseases caused by SILICA, ASBESTOS, iron ore, and other metals to which miners and others are exposed (see PNEUMOCONIOSIS). Health care workers have to use special care to avoid infection with infectious agents including the AIDS virus, and those who work at computers are prone to REPETITIVE STRESS INJURY. In the U.S. the OCCUPATIONAL SAFETY AND HEALTH ADMINISTRATION and the ENVIRONMENTAL PROTECTION AGENCY are charged with assuring workplace health and safety.

Occupational Safety and Health Administration (OSHA), U.S. agency established (1970) in the Dept. of Labor to develop and enforce regulations for the safety and health of workers engaged in interstate commerce. OSHA conducts inspections of workplaces, issuing citations and penalties for noncompliance, and has sought to limit the exposure of workers to hazardous substances such as lead and toxic chemicals.

ocean, interconnected mass of water covering about 71% of the surface of the earth. It is subdivided into the PACIFIC, INDIAN, ATLANTIC, and ARCTIC OCEANS. The world ocean has an area of about 139,400,000 sq mi (361,000,000 sq km), an average depth of about 12,230 ft (3,730 m), and a total volume of about 322,280,000 cu mi (1,347,000,000 cu km). Its salinity averages about 3.5% by weight. The best-known regions of the oceans, where virtually all petroleum and fishery reserves are found, are the relatively shallow waters above the continental shelves surrounding the CONTINENTS. The deep ocean floor consists mainly of vast abyssal plains. A significant feature of the ocean basins is the mid-ocean ridge system, where new oceanic crust has been forming continuously for at least 200 million years in a process of volcanic activity called seafloor spreading (see CONTINENTAL DRIFT; PLATE TECTONICS). Current theory holds that ocean water also originated through this activity. The ocean's deepest parts are the trenches, located near the margins of continents. Ocean water retains heat, and ocean currents, vitally important in dispersing heat energy, are intimately tied to planetary wind systems. The marine environment of the ocean is divided into two major realms, the benthic (ocean floor) and the pelagic (all waters above the benthic). See also DEEP SEA DRILLING PROJECT; OCEAN DRILLING PROGRAM; OCEANOGRAPHY.

Ocean Drilling Program, international project to drill and study cores of the earth's crust from beneath the oceans; it is the successor to the DEEP SEA DRILLING PROJECT. Begun in 1984 and supported by a U.S.-led international consortium of 19 nations, the program employs the drillship *JOIDES Resolution* and is administered by the National Science Foundation.

Oceania or **Oceanica,** collective name for the approximately 25,000 small islands scattered across the Pacific Ocean away from the Asian mainland. It is generally considered synonymous with the term South Seas and is divided ethnologically into MELANESIA, MICRONESIA, and POLYNESIA. Only a few thousand of the islands are inhabited, and many of these are little more than coral atolls.

Oceanian languages, aboriginal languages spoken in the region known as OCEANIA. If Oceania is restricted to the Melanesian, Micronesian, and Polynesian islands, the indigenous tongues spoken on these islands belong for the most part to the Malayo-Polynesian family of languages. If it is extended to include Australia and Malaysia, the indigenous languages of the Australian group spoken in Australia may be added as tongues of this region. In fact, the term "Oceanian languages" amounts to a geographical rather than a linguistic classification. See LANGUAGE (table).

Oceanic art, works produced by the island peoples of the S and NW Pacific, including MELANESIA (New Guinea and the islands to its north and east), MICRONESIA (the Marianas, Caroline, Marshall, and Gilbert islands), and POLYNESIA (Hawaii, New Zealand, the Marquesas, and Easter Island). Melanesian artifacts—woodcarvings and ritual masks—are often brilliantly colored and dramatically sexual in nature. They were decorated with reference to a complex mythology and influenced 20th-cent. European artists, e.g., Henry MOORE. Micronesian art objects are functional, streamlined, and highly finished, e.g. graceful canoes. Rows of figures placed on Mortlock Atoll illustrate mythological events and were thought to protect the islanders from typhoons. Very little Polynesian art survived the influx of Western missionaries, who, regarding it as idolatrous and pornographic, destroyed it. The greenish pottery of Fiji and examples of Hawaiian featherwork remain. The Marquesa islanders developed the tattoo into a fine art. On EASTER ISLAND, the abundant reddish stone, tufa, was carved into gargantuan human figures weighing as much as 20 tons. The ritual significance of most Polynesian art has been lost.

oceanids: see NYMPH.

oceanography, study of the sea integrating marine applications of geography, geology, physics, chemistry, marine biology, and meteorology. Comprehensive study of the sea dates from the 1872–76 Challenger expedition. Today there are about 250 oceanographic institutions, notably the Scripps Institution of Oceanography in California, the Woods Hole Oceanographic Institution in Massachusetts, and the Lamont-Doherty Geological Observatory of Columbia Univ. Oceanography is important to shipping, fisheries, the laying of telegraph cables, and climatological studies.

Oceanside, city (1990 pop. 128,398), San Diego co., S Calif., on the Gulf of Santa Catalina; inc. 1888. A rapidly growing residential city, it is also a commercial and trading center for a farm area. It manufactures rubber goods and has a large nursery industry; deep-sea fishing and tourism are also important. The Camp Pendleton marine base is nearby.

ocelot, medium-sized CAT (*Felis pardalis*) of Central and South America, sometimes found as far north as Texas. About 30 in. (76 cm) long, excluding the tail, and weighing up to 35 lb (18 kg), it has a yellow-brown coat with black spots, rings, and stripes. Ocelots live in forests, preying on small animals. They are hunted for their fur.

Ochoa, Severo [ōchō'ä], 1905–93, Spanish-American biochemist. He came to U.S. in 1940. For his synthesis of ribonucleic acid (RNA; see NUCLEIC ACID) Ochoa shared with Arthur KORNBERG the 1959 Nobel Prize in physiology or medicine.

Ochs, Adolph S. [ŏks], 1858–1935, American newspaper publisher; b. Cincinnati. In 1896 he acquired the failing New York *Times* and made it one of the greatest newspapers in the world. Unlike the sensationalist journalists of his day, Ochs stressed nonpartisan, almost clinical, news reporting.

O'Connell, Daniel, 1775–1847, Irish political leader. He founded (1823) the Catholic Association, whose pressure led to the CATHOLIC EMANCIPATION Act of 1829. In the British Parliament, he worked for repeal of the union of Great Britain and Ireland, for the reform of the government of Ireland, for the disestablishment of the Church of Ireland, and for a solution to the IRISH LAND QUESTION.

O'Connor, John, 1920–, American Roman Catholic cardinal, b. Philadelphia. A military chaplain for 27 years, he was ordained a bishop (1979) and became (1983) bishop of Scranton, Pa. In 1984 he was appointed archbishop of the New York archdiocese. Elevated to cardinal (1985), he has been an outspoken conservative on church doctrine and many social issues.

O'Connor, (Mary) Flannery, 1925–64, American author; b. Savannah, Ga. In the novels *Wise Blood* (1952) and *The Violent Bear It Away* (1960), and the short stories in *A Good Man Is Hard to Find* (1955) and *Everything That Rises Must Converge* (1965), she portrays contemporary Southern life as a grotesque and gothic combination of brutal comedy and violent tragedy.

O'Connor, Sandra Day: see SUPREME COURT, UNITED STATES (table 1).

octane number, a quality rating for GASOLINE indicating the ability of the fuel to resist premature detonation and to burn evenly when exposed to heat and pressure in an INTERNAL COMBUSTION ENGINE. Premature detonation, indicated by knocking and pinging noises, wastes fuel and may cause engine damage. The octane number can be increased by varying the relative amounts of the different HYDROCARBONS that make up the gasoline or by additives, e.g., tetraethyl lead. Federal regulations in the U.S. require commercial gasoline pumps to indicate the octane number, which is usually 87 or 89 for regular grade gasoline and 93 for premium grade. Since the early 1970s most AUTOMOBILES have been built to operate on low octane gasoline with little or no lead added.

Octavia, Roman matrons. **1** d. 11 B.C., sister of Emperor AUGUSTUS and wife of Marc ANTONY. She helped to maintain peace between her brother and her husband until Antony deserted her for CLEOPATRA. **2** A.D. 42–62, daughter of Emperor CLAUDIUS I and MESSALINA, and wife of NERO, who deserted her for Poppaea. She was falsely accused of adultery, banished, and put to death.

Octavian or **Octavius:** see AUGUSTUS.

October: see MONTH.

October Revolution, in Russian history: see RUSSIAN REVOLUTION.

octopus, marine mollusk, with a pouch-shaped body and eight muscular arms or tentacles; a CEPHALOPOD. It seizes its prey with the sucker-bearing arms and paralyzes it with a poisonous secretion. Octopus species range in size from only 2 in. (5 cm) in the North Atlantic to 30 ft (9 m) in the Pacific. Octopuses can change color, from pinkish to brown, and eject a dark "ink" from a special sac when disturbed. They are used for food in many parts of the world.

ode, elaborate and stately poem of some length, dating back to Greek choral songs. PINDAR's odes were poems of praise or glorification in stanzas patterned in sets of three—strophe, antistrophe, and the differently structured epode. The odes of HORACE and CATULLUS used a simpler LYRIC form. Later Europeans wrote in both Pindaric and Horatian form. Pierre de RONSARD in France and Ben JONSON, Robert HERRICK, and Andrew MARVELL in England were major RENAISSANCE odists. In general, the odes of such 19th-cent. poets as KEATS, P.B. SHELLEY, SWINBURNE, G.M. HOPKINS, and others tended to be freer in form and subject matter than the classical ode.

Oder, river, 562 mi (904 km) long, the second longest river of Poland. It rises in the NE Czech Republic and flows generally NW through Poland, then N along the Polish-German border to the Baltic Sea. Navigable from Racibórz, Poland, the Oder connects the industrial region of SILESIA with the sea. WROCŁAW, FRANKFURT-AN-DER-ODER, and SZCZECIN are the chief cities on the river.

Oder-Neisse line, post–World War II frontier between Germany and Poland along the Oder and W Neisse rivers from the Baltic Sea to the Czechoslovak (now the Czech Republic) border, proposed (1945) by the Allies at the Yalta and Potsdam conferences. The border was recognized as permanent by East Germany and Poland in 1950, but not accepted by West Germany until 1971. In 1990 a treaty between Poland and a reunified Germany reaffirmed the border.

Odessa or **Odesa,** city (1989 pop. 1,115,000), S UKRAINE, a port on the Odessa Bay of the Black Sea. It is a rail junction, the major Ukrainian port, a naval base, and the home port of fishing fleets. Shipbuilding and oil refining are among its industries. Nearby are health resorts. The city supposedly occupies the site of an ancient Miletian Greek colony. Between the 14th and 18th cent. it was held by the Lithuanians, Crimean Tatars, and Turks; in 1792 it passed to Russia. In the 19th and early 20th cent. Odessa was a center of Ukrainian and Jewish culture and of various political movements. It was the scene of a 1905 revolt led by sailors from the battleship *Potemkin.* Contested by opposing forces in the Russian civil war, it fell to the Red Army in 1920. During WORLD WAR II it was held by the Romanians and Germans (1941–44), who killed or deported c.280,000 civilians, mostly Jews.

Odets, Clifford, 1906–63, American dramatist; b. Philadelphia. Regarded as the most gifted of the American social-protest playwrights of the 1930s, he is known for such works as *Waiting for Lefty* (1935); *Awake and Sing* (1935), considered his finest play; and *Golden Boy* (1937). His later plays include *Clash by Night* (1942) and *The Country Girl* (1950).

Odin, Norse god: see WODEN.

Odoacer [ōdōā'sər] or **Odovacar,** c.435–493, Germanic chieftain. He and his soldiers were mercenaries for Rome when, in 476, the Heruli, a Germanic tribe, revolted and named Odoacer king. He seized RAVENNA and deposed ROMULUS AUGUSTULUS, last Roman emperor of the West, signifying the end of the West Roman Empire. Odoacer's authority was recognized by ZENO, emperor of the East, but in 488 Zeno sent THEODORIC THE GREAT to expel Odoacer, and Theodoric treacherously assassinated Odoacer.

Odysseus [ōdĭs'ēəs], Lat. *Ulysses,* in Greek myth, king of Ithaca; husband of PENELOPE. A Greek leader in the TROJAN WAR, HOMER depicted him as wise and cunning. In later legends he is wily, lying, and evil. His wanderings have figured prominently in world literature, notably in the *Odyssey.*

Odyssey: see HOMER.

Oedipus [ĕd'ĭpəs, ē'dĭ–], in Greek mythology, son of King Laius of THEBES and Queen Jocasta. Warned by an oracle that Oedipus would kill his father and marry his mother, his parents left the baby on a mountainside. However, he was adopted by the king of CORINTH. When grown, Oedipus heard the prophecy and, ignorant of his real parentage, fled to Thebes. On the way he met, quarreled with, and killed Laius. At Thebes he solved the SPHINX's riddle and married Jocasta. After many years he learned the truth and, in horror, blinded himself. Jocasta committed suicide. Oedipus was exiled, and Jocasta's brother, Creon, became king. Later, Oedipus' sons battled for the throne (see SEVEN AGAINST THEBES). The story of Oedipus is brilliantly dramatized in SOPHOCLES' *Oedipus Rex;* his later life is described in the same playwright's *Oedipus at Colonus.*

Oedipus complex: see COMPLEX.

Oersted, Hans Christian [ör'stĭth], 1777–1851, Danish physicist and chemist. His discovery that a magnetic needle is deflected by a conductor carrying an electric current showed a relation between ELECTRICITY and MAGNETISM and initiated the study of electromagnetism. The unit of magnetic field strength, the oersted, is named for him. Oersted was the first to isolate ALUMINUM.

O'Faoláin, Seán [ōfā'lən], 1900–91, Irish writer, b. John Francis Whelan. He is best known for his short stories about the Irish and Ireland, collected in *Midsummer Night Madness* (1932), *The Heat of the Sun* (1966), *The Talking Trees* (1971), and other volumes. He also wrote novels and biographies of DE VALERA (1932) and O'CONNELL (1938).

Offa, d. 796, king of MERCIA (757–96). Gradually he extended Mercian power to most of S England and gained the rulers of WESSEX and NORTHUMBRIA as sons-in-law. In 796 he and CHARLEMAGNE signed the first recorded English commercial treaty. He also built the entrenchment called Offa's Dyke.

Offenbach, Jacques Levy, 1819–80, French composer; b. Germany. He is famous for his OPERETTAS, of which he wrote over 100. His masterpiece was the opera *Tales of Hoffmann* (1881), after E.T.A. HOFFMANN.

offset printing: see PRINTING.

O'Flaherty, Liam, 1897–1984, Irish novelist. He wrote realistic stories about the common people, including *The Informer* (1925) and *The Assassin* (1928). *Famine* (1937) and *Land* (1946) are among his novels of 19th-cent. Ireland.

Ogaden [ōgä'dän], region, Harar prov., SE Ethiopia, bordering Somalia. It is an arid region inhabited mainly by Somali pastoral nomads. Since the 1960s it has been the focus of a secessionist movement by Somali nationalists demanding union of the Ogaden with Somalia. Somali troops invaded the region in 1977 but were repulsed a year later by Ethiopian forces with Soviet support. Warfare continued intermittently until 1988.

Ogbomosho, city (1987 pop. 582,900), SW Nigeria. It is the trade center for an agricultural region, and cotton textiles are woven. Founded in the 17th cent., the city resisted invasions by the Fulani people in the early 19th cent. and grew by absorbing refugees from Fulani attacks.

Ogden, city (1990 pop. 63,909), seat of Weber co., N Utah, at the confluence of the Ogden and Weber rivers; inc. 1851. Settled by MORMONS in the 1840s, it is surrounded by mountains, and many resorts are nearby. Aerospace and defense industries provide much employment.

Oglethorpe, James Edward, 1696–1785, English general and philanthropist. In 1733 he founded the American colony of GEORGIA as an asylum for debtors. He assured the colony's survival by defeating a Spanish force in 1742.

OGPU: see CHEKA; KGB.

O'Hara, Frank, 1926–66, American poet; b. Baltimore. O'Hara was a founder of the Poet's Theatre and later the center of the New York School of Poets. His writings include *Collected Poems* (1971).

O'Hara, John, 1905–70, American writer; b. Pottsville, Pa. An extremely popular author, he proved an acid observer of American life and diction in such novels as *Appointment in Samarra* (1934), *A Rage to Live* (1949), and *From the Terrace* (1958). His short stories, sometimes regarded as his finest works, are in such collections as *Hellbox* (1947) and *The Cape Cod Lighter* (1962).

O. Henry, pseud. of **William Sydney Porter,** 1862–1910, American short-story writer; b. Greensboro, N.C. Convicted of embezzlement and sent to prison, O. Henry later won fame and success as a writer. His short, simple stories are noted for their careful plotting, ironic coincidences, and surprise endings. Over 300 of them are collected in *Cabbages and Kings* (1904), *The Four Million* (1906), and other volumes.

O'Higgins, Bernardo, 1778–1842, South American revolutionary ruler (1817–23) of Chile. The illegitimate son of Ambrosio O'Higgins, governor of Chile (1789–96), he and SAN MARTÍN liberated (1817) Chile from Spanish rule. He became supreme director, but his reforms aroused so much opposition that he was deposed (1823).

Ohio, midwestern state of the U.S.; bordered by Pennsylvania and West Virginia (E), Kentucky (SW), Indiana (W), and Michigan and Lake Erie (N).

Area, 41,222 sq mi (106,765 sq km). *Pop.* (1990) 10,847,115, a 0.5% increase over 1980 pop. *Capital,* Columbus. *Statehood,* Mar. 1, 1803 (17th state). *Highest pt.,* Campbell Hill, 1,550 ft (473 m); *lowest pt.,* Ohio R., 433 ft (132 m). *Nickname,* Buckeye State. *Motto,* With God, All Things Are Possible. *State bird,* cardinal. *State flower,* scarlet carnation. *State tree,* buckeye. *Abbr.,* OH.

Land and People. Except for a hilly area near West Virginia, most of Ohio's land is relatively flat. Its principal river is the OHIO, which flows along the southern border. The continental climate is humid, with large variations in seasonal temperatures. About 74% of the population lives in urban areas, notably COLUMBUS (the largest city), which is followed in size by CLEVELAND, CINCINNATI, TOLEDO, and AKRON. In 1990 the state was 88% white and 11% African American.

Economy. Even though economic downturns beginning in the 1970s and lasting into the 1990s adversely affected Ohio's manufacturing sector, it is one of the nation's leading industrial states. Its leading industries produce such goods as transportation equipment, nonelectrical machinery, primary and fabricated metals, and rubber. Rich farmlands produce corn, dairy products, cattle, hay, wheat, and soybeans. Ohio's mineral output includes lime, stone and clay, and coal. Much of the state's prosperity is based on its superb transportation network, including the Lake ERIE ports of Toledo and Cleveland, which benefited from the opening (1959) of the SAINT LAWRENCE SEAWAY.

Government. The constitution of 1851 provides for a governor serving a four-year term. The general assembly consists of a senate whose 33 members serve four-year terms and a house whose 99 members are elected every two years. Ohio is represented in the U.S. Congress by 2 senators and 19 representatives and has 21 electoral votes.

History. The remains of Ohio's early inhabitants, the MOUND BUILDERS, are preserved at Mound City Group National Monument. The area was the home of the Erie, MIAMI, SHAWNEE, and OTTAWA when Robert Cavalier, sieur de LA SALLE, explored (1669) the Ohio R. valley and claimed it for France. Rivalry with England over control of the region resulted in the outbreak (1763) of the last of the FRENCH AND INDIAN WARS. Britain emerged victorious, but hostilities with Native Americans continued until their defeat at Fallen Timbers (1794). Ohio was part of the NORTHWEST TERRITORY, established by Congress in 1787. During the WAR OF 1812 considerable fighting took place on Ohio soil. After the Civil War, industrial development, aided by previous construction of canals and railroads, increased rapidly. The petroleum industry developed around Cleveland. Flooding by the Ohio and its tributaries had long been a serious problem, and a devastating flood in 1913 resulted in the construction of many state and federal water-control projects. Ohio's farmers and factory workers were hard hit by the GREAT DEPRESSION. World War II brought prosperity that continued until the late 1970s and early 80s, when the state's heavy industries were affected by the nationwide economic slowdown. The coal industry boomed, however, as a result of the national energy crisis. Weakness in the manufacturing sector triggered a new emphasis on service industries, which by the early 1990s employed over a quarter of the state's population.

Ohio, major U.S. river, flowing 981 mi (1,579 km) from the confluence of the Allegheny and Monongahela rivers at Pittsburgh, Pa., W to the Mississippi R. at Cairo, Ill. It is regulated by a modern system of locks and dams, built since 1955 to replace older structures, and is navigable by barges and pleasure craft for its entire length. Reportedly seen by LA SALLE in 1669, the river passed to British control in 1763 and to the U.S. in 1783. From then until the opening of the ERIE CANAL (1825), it was the principal route to the West.

Ohio Company, organization formed (1747) by American land speculators to settle 200,000 acres (80,940 hectares) at the forks of the Ohio R. Its activities challenged the French in the region and helped to bring on the final FRENCH AND INDIAN WAR (1754–63).

Ohio Company of Associates, in U.S. history, organization (1786–96) that bought 1,780,000 acres (720,349 hectares), at the confluence of the Ohio and Muskingum rivers, from the federal government for $1 million. The purchase hastened congressional passage of the Northwest ORDINANCE OF 1787. The first settlement, under Gen. Rufus Putnam (see under PUTNAM, ISRAEL), was at Marietta, Ohio, in 1788.

Ohlin, Bertil [o͞o'lĭn], 1889–1979, Swedish economist and political leader. He taught (1924–29) at the Univ. of Copenhagen and later at the Stockholm School of Economics. Ohlin also led Sweden's Liberal party (1944–67) and was minister of commerce (1944–45). He shared the 1977 Nobel Prize in economics for his pioneering studies of international trade.

ohm, symbol Ω, unit of electrical RESISTANCE, defined as the resistance to the flow of a steady electric current offered by a column of mercury 14.4521 grams in mass with a length of 1.06300 m and with an invariant cross-sectional area, when at a temperature of 0°C.

ohmmeter, instrument used to measure, in OHMS, the electric RESISTANCE of a conductor. It is usually included in a single package with a VOLTMETER and often an AMMETER. In normal usage, the ohmmeter operates by using the voltmeter to measure a voltage drop, then converting this reading into a corresponding resistance reading through OHM'S LAW.

Ohm's law, law stating that the electric current i flowing through a given RESISTANCE r is equal to the applied voltage v divided by the resistance, or $i = v/r$. In alternating-current (AC) circuits, where INDUCTANCES and CAPACITANCES may also be present, the law must be amended to $i = v/z$, where z is the IMPEDANCE. The law was formulated by the German physicist **Georg Simon Ohm,** 1787–1854.

oils: see ESSENTIAL OILS; FATS AND OILS; PETROLEUM.

Oisin: see OSSIAN.

Ojibwa or **Chippewa,** indigenous people of the Eastern Woodlands and Plains (see NORTH AMERICA, INDIGENOUS PEOPLES OF), with an Algonquian language of the Algonquian-Wakashan stock (see NATIVE AMERICAN LANGUAGES). In the 17th cent. they occupied the shores of Lake Superior, and drove the SIOUX across the Mississippi R. in a contest for the wild rice lands of their region. Some Ojibwa continued west to North Dakota and became the Plains Ojibwa. The sedentary Woodlands Ojibwa subsisted on fish, deer, corn, squash, and wild rice. One of the largest Native American peoples north of Mexico—over 100,000 in the U.S. alone—the Ojibwa pursue various occupations in Canada and in Michigan, Minnesota, Wisconsin, and other states.

okapi, nocturnal, ruminant MAMMAL (*Okapi johnstoni*) of the rain forests of the upper Congo R., unknown to zoologists until the early 20th cent. In shape it resembles the related GIRAFFE, but is smaller and has a shorter neck. It is red-brown with zebra-striped hindquarters.

Okeechobee, Lake, freshwater lake, SE Florida, N of the EVERGLADES, into which some of its waters drain. Though nowhere more than 15 ft. (4.6 m) deep, its c.700-sq-mi (1,800-sq-km) area makes it the fourth largest lake wholly within the U.S. There are canals (part of the Okeechobee Waterway) and extensive flood-control levees in the south.

O'Keeffe, Georgia, 1887–1986, American painter; b. Sun Prairie, Wis. Her works are marked by organic abstract forms painted in clear, strong colors. They are often strongly sexual in their symbolism, particularly her flower paintings. O'Keeffe lived much of her life in New Mexico and frequently employed Southwestern motifs in her works, e.g., *Cow's Skull, Red, White, and Blue* (1931; Metropolitan Mus.). She was married (1924–46) to Alfred STIEGLITZ, in whose gallery her work was first exhibited.

Okefenokee Swamp, large (c.600 sq mi/1,550 sq km) swamp, SE Georgia, extending into N Florida, noted for its varied and abundant wildlife. It is a saucer-shaped depression, with small islands rising above the water and its thick cover of vegetation. In Georgia, part of the swamp makes up most of the Okefenokee National Wildlife Refuge.

Okhotsk, Sea of, c.590,000 sq mi (1,528,100 sq km), NW arm of the Pacific Ocean, between the KAMCHATKA Peninsula and the KURIL ISLANDS, Russia. Ice-bound from Nov. to June and subject to heavy fogs, it connects with the Sea of Japan through the Tatar and La Pérouse straits. Magadan and Korsakov are the chief ports.

Okinawa, island (1990 pop. 1,222,458), 454 sq mi (1,176 sq km), W Pacific Ocean, SW of Kyushu; part of Okinawa prefecture, Japan. Okinawa is the largest of the RYUKYU ISLANDS. Naha is the largest city, chief port, and the site of some light industry. Sugarcane and rice are grown, and fishing is important. In a bloody campaign during WORLD WAR II, U.S. forces seized (Apr.–June 1945) the island from Japan. The Japanese lost 103,000 troops; U.S. casualties were 48,000. Okinawa was returned to Japan in 1972, but the U.S. retained its military bases.

Oklahoma, state in SW U.S.; bordered by Missouri and Arkansas (E), Texas (S, W), New Mexico, across the narrow edge of the Oklahoma panhandle (W), and Colorado and Kansas (N).

Area, 69,919 sq mi (181,090 sq km). *Pop.* (1990) 3,145,585, a 4% increase over 1980 pop. *Capital,* Oklahoma City. *Statehood,* Nov. 16, 1907 (46th state). *Highest pt.,* Black Mesa, 4,973 ft (1,517 m); *lowest pt.,* Little R., 287 ft (88 m). *Nickname,* Sooner State. *Motto, Labor Omnia Vincit* [Labor Conquers All Things]. *State bird,* scissor-tailed flycatcher. *State flower,* mistletoe. *State tree,* redbud. *Abbr.,* Okla.; OK.

Land and People. The high prairies of the west are part of the GREAT PLAINS and thus are frozen by winter winds and baked by summer heat. Elevations decline toward the east, except for the highland areas of the OZARK plateau and the Ouachita Mts. More than 67% of the population lives in urban areas, principally OKLAHOMA CITY, the largest urban center, and TULSA. Oklahoma has the largest Native American population (252,420 in 1990) of any state.

In 1990 the state was 82% white, 8% Native American, and 7% African American.

Economy. Mining, one of the principal sources of income, forms the base of the industrial sector. Oklahoma remains one of the country's largest producers of natural gas and oil, although by the early 1990s production was declining. The leading industries produce nonelectrical machinery, fabricated metals, and refined oil. Most farm income is derived from cattle, wheat, hay, cotton, dairy products, and peanuts.

Government. The constitution of 1907 provides for a governor elected to a four-year term. The legislature consists of a senate whose 48 members serve four-year terms and a house with 101 members elected for two years. Oklahoma is represented in the U.S. Congress by two senators and six representatives and has eight electoral votes.

History. The area was the home of Plains tribes, including the OSAGE, KIOWA, COMANCHE, and APACHE, when it came under U.S. control through the LOUISIANA PURCHASE (1803). Soon the federal government forced the so-called FIVE CIVILIZED TRIBES of the E U.S.—the CHEROKEE, CHOCTAW, CHICKASAW, CREEK, and SEMINOLE—to settle there, in what was to become the INDIAN TERRITORY. After the Civil War the government began assigning some of the tribes' lands to other, more recently displaced, Native Americans. With the opening of such cattle routes through the territory as the CHISHOLM TRAIL, white settlers pressed for the right to move there. A strip was opened for settlement in 1889, precipitating a huge land rush as settlers competed to claim the best lands. Later, the remaining lands of the Indian Territory were made available (1906) to white settlers. By the 1890s Oklahoma had become a major oil-producing state. During the GREAT DEPRESSION, NW Oklahoma was part of the DUST BOWL, and thousands of farmers were forced to leave their lands to become migrant laborers. The economy was revitalized during World War II, and for decades energy-related industries maintained Oklahoma's position as one of the fastest-growing SUNBELT states. Beginning in the mid-1980s, however, the state's economy was hurt (as it had been in the 1930s) by its dependence on the oil industry.

Oklahoma City (1990 pop. 444,719), state capital and seat of Oklahoma co., central Okla., on the North Canadian R.; inc. 1890. Settled overnight (1889) in a land rush, it became state capital in 1910. Oil, cattle, grain, and cotton were the major industries in its development. Today it has diversified manufactures and is the commercial center of the region. Vast in area, the city has many parks and tourist attractions.

okra: see MALLOW.

Olaf or **Olav,** kings of Norway. **Olaf I** (Olaf Tryggvason), c.963–1000 (r.995–1000), was the great-grandson of HAROLD I. A Christian convert, he overthrew Haakon (995) and undertook the conversion of Norway. After his death in battle, SWEYN of Denmark and Olaf of Sweden divided Norway. His nephew **Olaf II** (Saint Olaf), c.995–1030 (r.1015–28), continued to Christianize Norway. An uprising of nobles (1028) supporting CANUTE of England and Denmark forced him to flee. In 1030 he tried to wrest the crown from Canute's son Sweyn but died in battle. His son MAGNUS I later ruled Norway. **Olaf V,** 1903–91 (r.1957–91), was the son of HAAKON VII. After the Germans invaded Norway (1940), he led the Norwegian struggle for liberation. An extremely popular figure, he was succeeded by his son, HAROLD V.

Olbers, Heinrich Wilhelm Matthäus, 1758–1840, German physician and astronomer. Inventor (1797) of the first successful method for calculating the orbits of comets, he discovered the comet of 1815, now known as Olbers's comet, and two asteroids, Pallas (1802) and Vesta (1807).

Old Catholics, Christian denomination, established by German clergy and laymen who separated from the Roman Catholic Church when they rejected the dogma of papal infallibility issued (1870) by the First VATICAN COUNCIL. By 1874 a new church had been established with a bishop consecrated by a Dutch Jansenist bishop. It retained Roman ritual (in the vernacular), allowed priests to marry, and made confession optional.

Old Church Slavonic: see CHURCH SLAVONIC.

Oldenbarneveldt, Johan van, 1547–1619, Dutch statesman. He aided WILLIAM THE SILENT and MAURICE OF NASSAU in the struggle for independence from Spain. With Oldenbarneveldt as permanent advocate of Holland (from 1586) commerce expanded greatly and the Dutch EAST INDIA COMPANY was formed. His negotiation (1609) of a 12-year truce with Spain gave the Dutch virtual independence. As leader of those favoring control of state affairs by the States-General he clashed with the party of the nobles and the house of Orange, which used his affiliation with the Remonstrants, a sect at odds with the strict Calvinists, as a pretext for his execution.

Old English: see ENGLISH LANGUAGE.

old English sheepdog, large WORKING DOG; shoulder height, 21–25 in. (53.3–63.5 cm); weight, 55–65 lb (24.9–29.5 kg). It has a profuse double coat of gray, grizzle, blue, or blue-merle, with or without white. The breed was raised in W England in the 19th cent. as a sheep and cattle drover.

Old Stone Age: see under STONE AGE.

Old Testament, Christian name for the Hebrew Scriptures, which forms the first portion of the Christian Bible (see NEW TESTAMENT). It consists of a varying number of books, in varying order. The canon of the JEWS, adopted A.D. c.100, is drawn from one Hebrew source, the Masora, whose origin is unknown. The contemporary Jewish reckoning of the Old Testament is as follows: (1) the five books of the Law (TORAH or PENTATEUCH), i.e., GENESIS, EXODUS, LEVITICUS, NUMBERS, and DEUTERONOMY; (2) the Prophets (e.g., JOSHUA, ISAIAH) and the twelve Minor Prophets; (3) the Writings (Hagiographa), including such books as PSALMS and JOB; the Scrolls (*Megillot*), e.g., SONG OF SOLOMON and RUTH; and others. The Old Testament long used in the Christian church was based on a different text, the Septuagint, a Hellenistic Jewish translation into Greek about the 3d cent. B.C. The Latin Bible's official form was the VULGATE of St. JEROME, close to the Septuagint; the Vulgate's list and order were the canon of the Western Church. At the REFORMATION, the English Protestants considered only those books appearing in the Masora canonical; the others, regarded as suitable for instruction but not necessarily inspired, were placed by translators of the Authorized Version (AV) in an appendix to the Old Testament, the APOCRYPHA (see BIBLE). Thus the Reformed canon became the Masoretic text, but in Western order. The AV compares with the Douay Version (published by Roman Catholic scholars in France in 1610), representing the Western canon, as follows, the names in parentheses being the usual Douay names when different from AV, those in italics not appearing in AV: Genesis, Exodus, Leviticus, Numbers, Deuteronomy, Joshua (Josue), Judges, Ruth, First and Second Samuel (First and Second Kings), First and Second Kings (Third and Fourth Kings), First and Second Chronicles (First and Second Paralipomenon), Ezra (First Esdras), Nehemiah (Second Esdras), *Tobias, Judith,* Esther, Job, Psalms, Proverbs, Ecclesiastes, Song of Solomon (Canticle of Canticles), *Wisdom, Ecclesiasticus,* Isaiah (Isaias), Jeremiah (Jeremias), Lamentations, *Baruch,* Ezekiel (Ezechiel), Daniel, Hosea (Osee), Joel, Amos, Obadiah (Abdias), Jonah (Jonas), Micah (Micheas), Nahum, Habakkuk (Habacuc), Zephaniah (Sophonias), Haggai (Aggeus), Zechariah (Zacharias), Malachi (Malachias), *First* and *Second Maccabees.* Dating of the Bible is difficult; before 1000 B.C. there are few outside sources against which to check. From the time of DAVID, a chronology with checks is possible; no single system, however, is widely accepted. Authorship is known from tradition or internal evidence. Scholarship of the 19th cent. assaulted traditions about the Bible, particularly in regard to the "historical" books; but 20th-cent. archaeology has tended to support, rather than contradict, the narratives. Generally modern critics hold that in the 10th cent. B.C. the first of a series of editors began to collect folkloric and historical material. Two dominant early compilations can be traced. These were combined by in the southern kingdom of Judah some time after the fall of the northern kingdom (Israel) and form much of the Old Testament through First and Second Samuel. Other important sources of the non-prophetic books are an author or authors associated with the temple priests and the author of Deuteronomy.

Olduvai Gorge, ravine, c.295 ft (90 m) deep, in N Tanzania, at the E edge of the GREAT RIFT VALLEY. Famous hominid fossils found there by the anthropologists Louis S.B. and Mary LEAKEY and others indicate that human ancestors lived in the area as many as 1.8 million years ago.

Oligocene epoch: see GEOLOGIC ERA (table).

olive, common name for the family Oleaceae, trees and shrubs of warm, temperate climates and the Old World tropics, and for the true olive tree (*Olea europaea*), the most important member of the family commercially. Native to Asia Minor, the true olive is a small evergreen that bears a fruit (also called olive), which is pressed to obtain olive oil or is eaten. Green olives for eating are picked when full grown but unripe; purplish-black olives are usually ripe and richer in oil. The Mediterranean region is the chief area of olive production. Olive wood and ASH, also of the olive family, are hardwoods used in furniture. Popular ornamentals in the family include the LILAC, true JASMINE, and FORSYTHIA. The olive branch has been a symbol of peace since ancient times.

Oliver, Joseph "King," 1885–1938, American jazz musician; b. Abend, La. After playing in New Orleans and establishing himself as a master cornetist, he moved (1918) to Chicago. He led (1920–23) the Creole Jazz Band, which became the greatest exponent of the Dixieland JAZZ idiom. His style was exuberant and had great range. He strongly influenced Louis ARMSTRONG.

Olives, Mount of, or **Olivet,** ridge E of Jerusalem. In the OLD TESTAMENT it is associated with DAVID, Ezekiel, and Zechariah. According to the NEW TESTAMENT, it was a frequent resort of JESUS and the scene of his Ascension.

Olivier, Laurence Kerr (Baron Olivier of Brighton), 1907–89, English actor, director, and producer, often called the greatest actor of the 20th cent. Olivier was successful both in the classics, e.g., as Oedipus Rex, Richard III, and Othello, and in modern dramas, e.g., John OSBORNE's *The Entertainer* (1957) and Eugene O'NEILL's *Long Day's Journey into Night* (1971). He made several outstanding films, including *Wuthering Heights* (1939), *Henry V* (1944), and *Hamlet* (1948; Academy Award). After appearing with the Old Vic, he was director (1962–73) of the National Theatre of Great Britain (see THEATER, table). Knighted in 1947, he was the first actor to be created (1970) a life peer.

Olmec, culture of ancient peoples (1300–400 B.C.) of the E Mexico lowlands (see MIDDLE AMERICA, INDIGENOUS PEOPLES OF). A highly developed agricultural society, they left sculptured stone heads weighing over 20 tons. Earthen platforms and pyramidal mounds were common features of their major settlements. The Olmec are often regarded as the mother culture of later Middle American civilizations. The epi-Olmec, the peoples who subsequently inhabited the same lands and were probably descended at least in part from the Olmec, seem to have been the earliest users (from 31 B.C.) of the bar and dot system of recording time. Both the Olmec and epi-Olmec had hieroglyphic writing systems.

Olmsted or **Olmstead, Frederick Law,** 1822–1903, American landscape architect and writer; b. Hartford, Conn. In the 1850s he attained fame for his travel books, which describe slaveholding society in the South. When Central Park, N.Y.C., was projected (1856), he and Calvert Vaux prepared the plan that was accepted, and he supervised its execution. This was the first of many parks he designed; others are in Brooklyn (Prospect Park), Chicago, Montreal, Buffalo, and Boston. He laid out the grounds for the 1893 Columbian Exposition, Chicago (now Jackson Park).

Olympia, city (1990 pop. 33,840), state capital and seat of Thurston co., W Wash., a port at the southern tip of Puget Sound; inc. 1859. State government, lumber products, brewing, and oyster fishing are important. Olympia was settled in 1846 and became (1853) the capital of the Washington Territory. Mt. Rainier and the Olympic Mts. are in view of the city.

Olympia, ancient Greek sanctuary in the W PELOPONNESUS, near the Alpheus River. It was an important center of the worship of ZEUS and the site of the OLYMPIC GAMES. Excavation revealed the great temple, one of the SEVEN WONDERS OF THE WORLD, which housed a gold-adorned statue of Zeus by PHIDIAS.

Olympian, in Greek myth, one of the 12 gods who ruled the universe from their home on Mt. Olympus. Led by ZEUS, they were: HERA, his sister and wife; POSEIDON and PLUTO (HADES), his brothers; HESTIA, his sister; and his children, ARES, HERMES, APOLLO, HEPHAESTUS, ATHENA, APHRODITE, and ARTEMIS. Similar to humans in appearance and character, the Olympians are known to us mainly from the works of HOMER and HESIOD.

Olympias, d. 316 B.C., wife of PHILIP II of Macedon and mother of ALEXANDER THE GREAT. She reputedly had great influence in molding her son. After his death she tried to seize power, but CASSANDER had her executed.

Olympic games, series of international amateur sports contests that originated in ancient Greece. The Greek games were held once every four years, beginning (according to tradition) in 776 B.C. The games reached their height in the 5th and 4th cent. B.C., later fell into disfavor because of professionalism, and were discontinued at the end of the 4th cent. A.D. The first Olympics were confined to running, but many events were added. The modern revival of the games began in Athens in 1896. They have since been staged at four-year intervals (except during the world wars) in cities around the world. The number of entrants, of competing nations, and of sports and athletic events has steadily increased. The modern games were originally only open to amateur male athletes. Women first competed in 1912, a separate series of winter games was begun in 1924, and professional athletes began competing in some sports in 1988. After 1992 the winter games were rescheduled so that they would alternate, at two-year intervals, with the summer games. The International Olympic Committee is the governing body of the games.

OLYMPIC GAMES, 1896–1984

Summer Games

Year	*Site*		
1896	Athens, Greece	1960	Rome, Italy
1900	Paris, France	1964	Tokyo, Japan
1904	St. Louis, Mo.	1968	Mexico City, Mexico
1908	London, England	1972	Munich, West Germany
1912	Stockholm, Sweden		
1920	Antwerp, Belgium	1976	Montreal, Canada
1924	Paris, France	1980	Moscow, USSR (now Russia)
1928	Amsterdam, The Netherlands	1984	Los Angeles, Calif.
1932	Los Angeles, Calif.	1988	Seoul, South Korea
1936	Berlin, Germany	1992	Barcelona, Spain
1948	London, England	1996	Atlanta, Ga.
1952	Helsinki, Finland	2000	Sydney, Australia
1956	Melbourne, Australia		

Winter Games

1924	Chamonix, France	1960	Squaw Valley, Calif.
1928	St. Moritz, Switzerland	1964	Innsbruck, Austria
		1968	Grenoble, France
1932	Lake Placid, N.Y.	1972	Sapporo, Japan
1936	Garmisch-Partenkirchen, Germany	1976	Innsbruck, Austria
		1980	Lake Placid, N.Y.
		1984	Sarajevo, Yugoslavia
1948	St. Moritz, Switzerland	1988	Calgary, Alberta
		1992	Albertville, France
1952	Oslo, Norway	1994	Lillehammer, Norway
1956	Cortina, Italy	1998	Nagano, Japan

Olympic National Park: see NATIONAL PARKS (table).

Olympus, mountain range, c.25 mi (40 km) long, N Greece. It rises to c.9,570 ft (2,920 m) at Mount Olympus, described in Greek mythology as the home of the OLYMPIAN gods.

Olynthus [ōlĭn'thəs], ancient city of GREECE, on the Chalcidice peninsula. It headed the Chalcidian League, and opposed ATHENS and SPARTA. Originally allied with PHILIP II of Macedon against Athens, it later sought Athens' aid against Philip. DEMOSTHENES' *Olynthiac* orations urged Athens to help. Athens complied, but Philip razed the city (348 B.C.).

Omaha, indigenous people of the Plains (see NORTH AMERICA, INDIGENOUS PEOPLES OF), with a Siouan language of the Hokan-Souian stock (see NATIVE AMERICAN LANGUAGES). They migrated west from the Ohio valley to Iowa and then to NE Nebraska. In the mid-19th cent. they sold much of their land to the U.S., and after 1882 they began to own land individually. In 1990 there were 4,143 Omahas in the U.S.

Omaha, city (1990 pop. 335.795), seat of Douglas co., E Nebr., on the Missouri R.; inc. 1857. Settled in 1854, it grew as a supply point for westward migration. The largest city in the state, located in the heart of the country's farm region, it is a busy port and one of the world's great livestock markets and meat-processing centers. The city has diversified manufactures, and insurance, banking, and medical treatment and research are major enterprises. Offutt Air Force Base, headquarters of the Strategic Command (formerly the Strategic Air Command), is south of the city.

Oman, officially Sultanate of Oman, formerly Muscat and Oman, independent sultanate (1993 pop. 2,017,591), c.82,000 sq mi (212,380 sq km), SE Arabian peninsula, bounded by the Gulf of Oman (E), the Arabian Sea (S), Yemen and Saudi Arabia (W), and the United Arab Emirates (N), which separate the main portion of the country from an exclave that juts into the Strait of HORMUZ. The capital is MUSCAT. Oman comprises a coastal plain and an interior region of hills and desert. Dates, limes, nuts, and vegetables are cultivated in the north and livestock are raised in the southwest, but the major product is oil. Natural gas production and copper mining were developed in the early 1980s to diversify the economy. The population is predominantly Muslim Arab, with Pakistani, Indian, and Zanzibari minorities.

History. Occupied by Portugal in 1508 and Turkey in 1659, Oman came under Ahmad ibn Said of Yemen, founder of the present royal line, in 1741. It has had close ties with Britain since the 19th cent. In 1970 Qabus bin Said overthrew the strict regime of his father, Sultan Said bin Timur, and instituted a program of liberalization and modernization and put down (1975) leftist guerrilla forces operating in Dhofar prov., in the south. In 1980 the U.S. obtained the use of ports and airfields in Oman in exchange for economic and military aid. In 1981 Oman joined other Arab Persian Gulf nations in founding the Gulf Cooperation Council.

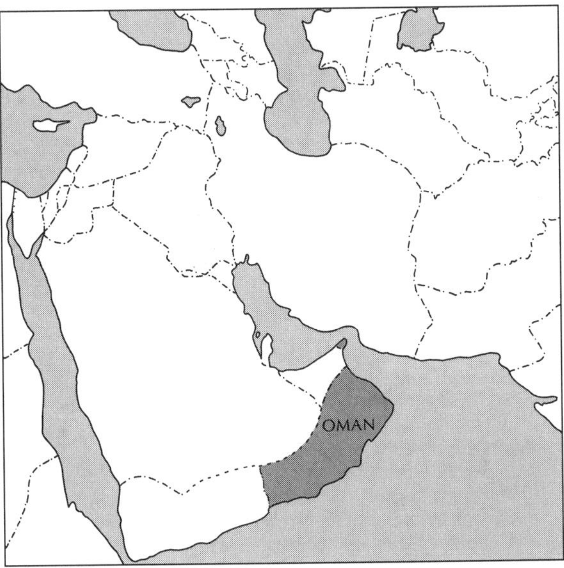

Omar Khayyam [kīäm'], fl. 11th cent., Persian poet and mathematician. He wrote mathematical studies and participated in a calendar reform, but he is best known for his *Rubaiyat* (epigrammatic quatrains), which express a hedonistic philosophy. A paraphrased English translation (1859) by Edward FITZGERALD popularized his work in the West.

ombudsman, independent official appointed to investigate citizen complaints against abuses by government officials and agencies. The ombudsman makes recommendations and in some cases has the power to make binding decisions. The office, which originated (1809) in Sweden, has been adopted by many countries and U.S. states and localities. Businesses, universities, and other private organizations also employ ombudsmen to investigate complaints.

Omdurman, city (1983 pop. 526,287), central Sudan, on the White Nile opposite KHARTOUM. It is the country's chief commercial center and part of a tri-city metropolitan area (with Khartoum and Khartoum North). The MAHDI, who is buried in the city, based his forces here for the attack on Khartoum (1885), and his successor, Khalifa Addallah, made it his capital. The battle of Karari (1898), near Omdurman, marked the defeat of the Mahdist state by an Anglo-Egyptian army under Lord KITCHENER.

Omsk, city (1989 pop. 1,148,000), SW Siberian Russia, at the confluence of the Irtysh and Om rivers, and on the Trans-Siberian RR. It is a major river port and has oil refineries and plants producing railroad equipment, farm machinery, and clothing. Founded in 1716 as a fortress, it became a transportation and administrative center in the 19th cent.

Onassis, Aristotle Socrates, 1906?–1975, Greek shipowner and financier; b. Turkey. After reviving the family tobacco business in Argentina, he received (1925) Argentinian and Greek citizenship. He bought his first ships in the early 1930s and later entered the tanker business. He was related by marriage to the Greek shipowners Stavros Livanos and Stavros Niarchos; together they formed the most powerful shipping clan in the world. He also founded (1957) Olympic Airways of Greece. In 1968 Onassis married Jacqueline Bouvier Kennedy, widow of U.S. Pres. J.F. KENNEDY.

Onassis, Jacqueline Bouvier, 1929–, American first lady; b. Southampton, N.Y. She married John Fitzgerald KENNEDY in 1953. While he was U.S. president, she supervised the restoration of the WHITE HOUSE. After her husband's assassination, she returned to private life and later married (1968) Aristotle ONASSIS.

oncology: see CANCER.

Oneida: see IROQUOIS CONFEDERACY.

O'Neill, Eugene (Gladstone), 1888–1953, widely acknowledged as America's foremost playwright; b. N.Y.C. The son of an actor, he was a prospector, seaman, derelict, and newspaper reporter—experiences he used in his plays. He created many one-act plays before writing *Beyond the Horizon* (1920; Pulitzer), the first of his full-length plays to be performed. The dramas that followed included *The Emperor Jones* (1920); *Anna Christie* (1921; Pulitzer); *The Hairy Ape* (1922); *Desire under the Elms* (1924), considered his first great play; *Strange Interlude* (1928; Pulitzer); the mighty trilogy *Mourning Becomes Electra* (1931); *Ah, Wilderness!* (1933), his only comedy; *The Iceman Cometh* (1946), often regarded as his finest work; and *A Moon for the Misbegotten* (1947). His last years were filled with family tragedy and ill health. At his death he left several important plays in manuscript, including the autobiographical masterpiece *Long Day's Journey into Night* (produced 1956; Pulitzer). Although uneven and often clumsily experimental, O'Neill's powerful work is filled with poetry and genius. He was awarded the Nobel Prize in literature in 1936.

O'Neill, Tip (Thomas Philip O'Neill, Jr.), 1912–94, American politician, Speaker of the U.S. House of Representatives (1977–87); b. Cambridge, Mass. He entered the House in 1953 as a Democrat from Massachusetts. A skillful strategist, he became majority whip in 1971 and majority leader in 1973 and was Speaker of the House from 1977 to 1987.

onion, plant (genus *Allium*) of the LILY family, of the same genus as the chive (*A. schoenoprasum*), garlic (*A. sativum*), leek (*A. porrum*), and shallot (*A. ascalonium*). Believed native to SW Asia, these plants are typified by an edible bulb composed of sugar-rich food-storage leaves that are also the source of a pungent oil. Their long, tubular, above-ground leaves are also eaten. The onion (*A. cepa*) is a cultivated biennial with many varieties; it is no longer found in the wild form. Common varieties include the red onion, the yellow onion, the white onion, and the large, delicately-flavored Bermuda and Spanish onions. The more pungent garlic, a perennial, has a bulb consisting of small bulbils called cloves. The perennial shallot has clusters of small, onionlike bulbs; the biennial leek has a single small bulb. The chive, found wild in Italy and Greece, is a perennial whose leaves are the desirable portion. *Scallion* is a popular term for any edible *Allium* species with a reduced bulb, especially the leek and shallot.

Onondaga: see IROQUOIS CONFEDERACY.

Ono no Komachi [ō'nō nō kō'mä'chē], fl. c.833–857, Japanese poet. Celebrated for her beauty and erotically charged poetry, she was among the most prominent poets of her day, displaying skill in the elegant waka form. Many legends have arisen about her love affairs and bitter end as a wandering hag.

Ontario, province (1991 pop. 10,084,885), 412,580 sq mi (1,068,582 sq km), east-central Canada. It is bordered by Hudson and James bays (N); Quebec (E); the St. Lawrence River, Lakes Ontario, Erie, Huron, and Superior, and the U.S. (S); and Manitoba (W). The most populous and third largest province, Ontario has three main geographic regions: the mineral-rich CANADIAN SHIELD area, in the west and central part of the province; the HUDSON BAY Lowlands, in the north; and the GREAT LAKES–SAINT LAWRENCE lowlands, in the south, where 90% of the population lives and where industry and agriculture are concentrated. The Toronto-Hamilton area is the most highly industrialized. Major industrial products include transportation equipment, foods, metals, electrical goods, machinery, and chemicals. Agriculture is also important, with cattle, dairy products, and hogs producing the most income; other crops are corn, wheat, and potatoes. Mining is important in the Canadian Shield area, where iron ore, copper, zinc, gold, silver, and uranium are found. The SUDBURY area is especially rich in copper and nickel. Ontario also produces lumber, and the pulp and paper industry is important. Major cities include TORONTO, the provincial capital, OTTAWA, the national capital, HAMILTON, WINDSOR, LONDON, and THUNDER BAY.

History. Ontario was explored by the French in the early 17th cent., but settlement was slow. The British, who had established (late 17th cent.) trading posts on Hudson Bay, gained control of Ontario and all of French Canada by the Treaty of Paris (1763). Many UNITED EMPIRE LOYALISTS migrated to Ontario after the American Revolution, and in 1791 it was split from Quebec and called Upper Canada. The area was a major battleground in the WAR OF 1812. In 1841 Upper Canada and Lower Canada (Quebec) were merged into a united province, but it proved unworkable because of conflict between English and French residents. In 1867 Ontario and Quebec entered the Canadian confederation as separate provinces. During the 20th cent. the mineral wealth of the Canadian Shield was exploited and the province's economy expanded enormously. Ontario's main political parties are the Liberals (most powerful in the late 19th cent.), the Conservatives (who governed from 1905 to 1985 with three Liberal interludes), and the New Democrats (who won a substantial majority in 1990). The province sends 24 senators (appointed) and 99 representatives (elected) to the national parliament.

Ontario, city (1990 pop. 133,179), San Bernardino co., SE Calif., near Los Angeles; inc. 1891. A fast-growing city, it has benefited from the success of its high-technology firms. Other industries produce aircraft and aircraft parts, wine, tile, electrical equipment, and plastics. Ontario is the site of a speedway and an international airport.

Ontario, Lake, smallest (7,540 sq mi/19,529 sq km), lowest (elevation 246 ft/75 m), and easternmost of the GREAT LAKES, between the U.S. and Canada. It is 193 mi (311 km) long and up to 53 mi (85 km) wide and 778 ft (237 m) deep. The lake is part of the St. Lawrence & Great Lakes Waterway and opens to the SAINT LAWRENCE SEAWAY and W to Lake Erie via the WELLAND SHIP CANAL. Toronto is the principal port.

onychophoran, onychophore, or **velvet worm,** wormlike animal with unsegmented, stumpy legs and velvety skin; member of the phylum Onychophora. Because onychophorans possess characteristics of both ANNELID WORMS and ARTHROPODS, they have been considered to be the "missing links" between the two groups, but DNA testing suggests that they are arthropods most closely related to spiders and scorpions.

onyx, variety of CHALCEDONY, similar to AGATE but with parallel, regular bands. Black-and-white specimens are used for cameos. Sardonyx has alternate layers of onyx and carnelian, or sard.

oolite, sedimentary rock composed of small concretions, usually of calcium carbonate, containing a nucleus and clearly defined concentric shells. In Britain, oolitic LIMESTONE is characteristic of the Jurassic geologic period.

Oort, Jan Hendrik, 1900–92, Dutch astronomer. He confirmed (1927) Bertil Lindblad's theory of the Milky Way galaxy's rotation. In the 1950s he and his colleagues used radio astronomical means to map the spiral-arm structure of the galaxy. Oort proposed (1950) that COMETS originate in a spherical cloud of material orbiting the sun at great distance (now called the Oort cloud) and that they are occasionally deflected into the inner solar system by gravitational perturbation from the passing of nearby stars.

opal, hydrous silica mineral ($SiO_2 \cdot nH_2O$), formed at low temperatures from silica-bearing water, that can occur in cavities and fissures of any rock type. Gem opal has rich iridescence and a remarkable play of colors, usually in red, green, and blue. Most precious opals come from South Australia; the opal is Australia's national gemstone. Other sources include Mexico (fire opal) and parts of the U.S.

op art, movement in the U.S. and Europe in the mid-1960s that sought to produce a purely optical art stripped of perceptual associations. Vibrating colors and pulsating moiré patterns characterized op works by such practitioners as Victor Vasarely, Richard Anuszkiewicz, and Bridget Riley.

OPEC: see ORGANIZATION OF PETROLEUM EXPORTING COUNTRIES.

open cluster: see STAR CLUSTER.

Open Door, maintenance in a certain territory of equal commercial and industrial rights for all countries. It is associated with CHINA, which in the 19th cent. was divided into spheres of influence by the major world powers. The U.S., as a lesser power, feared that an actual partition of China would damage American trade and sought to preserve equal privileges. U.S. Secy. of State John HAY advanced the Open Door policy in two notes (1899, 1900), asking the major powers to uphold the free use by all nations of the treaty ports within their spheres of influence and to respect Chinese territorial and administrative integrity. Disregard for the Open Door policy, especially by Japan (see TWENTY-ONE DEMANDS), led to the Nine-Power treaty (1922), which reaffirmed the policy but failed to stop Japanese aggression. After World War II China's full sovereignty was recognized, and the Open Door policy ceased to exist.

open-end investment company: see MUTUAL FUND.

open-hearth process, method of producing STEEL from varying proportions of limestone, scrap metal, and PIG IRON. Known in Europe as the Siemens-Martin process, it is characterized by a hearth open directly to the flames that melt the raw materials. Although the open-hearth process takes longer to refine a batch of steel, it superseded the BESSEMER PROCESS because it could use up to 100% scrap metal, could refine pig iron that had a high phosphorus content, and could produce less brittle steels. It has now largely been replaced by the BASIC OXYGEN PROCESS and ELECTRIC ARC PROCESS.

open shop: see UNION, LABOR.

opera, drama set to music. There may be spoken dialogue, but more often the music is continuous, with set pieces (solos, duets, etc.) designed to dramatize the action and display the vocal skills of the singers. Opera began in Florence, Italy, where a group of scholars and musicians promoted the principle of simple melodic declamation, emulating ancient Greek drama. Jacopo Peri's *Euridice* (1600) is generally considered the first opera. BAROQUE opera developed in Rome and Venice, reaching its peak with the work of Claudio MONTEVERDI. In 1637 the first public opera house in the world opened in Venice. The *opera seria* of the 17th and 18th cent. featured mythological themes and great pageantry. In the mid-17th cent. an international style emerged, emphasizing individual virtuosity, and interest in antiquities was superseded by a trend toward comedy. French opera from 1669 was led by J.B. LULLY and J.P. RAMEAU. The Neapolitans favored the *opera seria* of Alessandro SCARLATTI, but now added *opera buffa,* or comic opera, as in the works of Giovanni PERGOLESI. After the death of Henry PURCELL, opera in England was dominated by the Italian style championed by G.F. HANDEL. By the 18th cent. German opera had developed the *singspiel,* comic opera with spoken dialogue, which reached its culmination in the works of W.A. MOZART. Yet Italian *opera seria* dominated through the 18th cent., until the compositions of C.W. von GLUCK served to emphasize the dramatic over the musical aspects of opera. Romantic elements entered 19th cent. opera, as in Ludwig van BEETHOVEN's *Fidelio* (1805) and Carl Maria von WEBER's *Der Freischütz* (1821). These paved the way for the grandiose music dramas of Richard WAGNER. Spectacular opera became popular in France and Italy after the French Revolution, and grand opera was founded in Paris, exemplified by the works of Giacomo MEYERBEER, featuring historical themes and violent passions. Opera with spoken dialogue, or *opéra comique,* led toward OPERETTA, but also toward the serious, lyrical works of Georges BIZET and Charles GOUNOD. The works of G.A. ROSSINI, Gaetano DONIZETTI, and Vincenzo BELLINI continued to feature melody and voice, and the lyric-dramatic Italian style was exemplified by Giuseppe VERDI and, later, Giacomo PUCCINI. The 19th cent. also saw the birth of Russian opera (P.I. TCHAIKOVSKY, Modest MOUSSORGSKY, Nicolai RIMSKY-KORSAKOV). Foremost in the early 20th cent. were the romantic, dissonant works of Richard STRAUSS and the atonal operas of Alban BERG and Arnold SCHOENBERG. Contemporary operas are typically either traditional in idiom, as the works of Benjamin BRITTEN, Gian-Carlo MENOTTI, and Samuel BARBER; or avant garde, often atonal and experimental, as the compositions of H.W. HENZE, Philip GLASS, and Werner Egk.

operetta, type of light OPERA with a frivolous, sentimental story, often employing parody and satire, and containing spoken dialogue and much light, pleasant music. It developed from 19th-cent. *opéra comique.* Noted operetta composers include OFFENBACH, J. STRAUSS the younger, LEHÁR, A. SULLIVAN (with librettist W.S. GILBERT), and Victor HERBERT.

Ophir [ō'fər], seaport or region, mentioned in the BIBLE, from which the ships of SOLOMON brought great treasures, including gold, jewels, and ivory. The location of Ophir is unknown, although it has been variously identified.

ophthalmology, branch of medicine specializing in the function and diseases of the eye. It is concerned with prevention of BLINDNESS; treatment of disorders, e.g., GLAUCOMA; and surgery, including CATARACT removal and corneal TRANSPLANTATION. **Optometry** is concerned with correcting visual abnormalities (e.g., NEARSIGHTEDNESS) and the prescription of corrective lenses, including CONTACT LENSES.

Opitz, Martin [ō'pĭts], 1597–1639, leader of the Silesian school of German poetry. He was influential as a poet, critic, and metrical reformer. *Book on German Poetry* (1624) was his greatest literary contribution.

opium, dried milky juice of unripe seedpods of the opium poppy (*Papavera somniferum*). The chief constituents of opium are the alkaloids CODEINE, papaverine, noscapine, and MORPHINE, from which HEROIN is synthesized. Opium is grown worldwide; despite international laws and agreements to control its use, an illicit opium traffic persists. See NARCOTIC.

Opium War, 1839–42, conflict between Great Britain and China. Britain, seeking to end restrictions made by China on foreign trade, found a pretext for war when China prohibited the import of opium and British opium was destroyed at Guangzhou. The British were easy victors, and by the Treaty of Nanking (1842) China ceded Hong Kong to Britain and opened five ports to British trade. A second war (1856–58) ended with the treaties of Tientsin (1858), to which France, Russia, and the U.S. were party. These treaties opened 11 more ports.

Oporto, Port. *Pôrto,* city (1987 est. pop. 350,000), capital of Pôrto dist., NW Portugal, near the mouth of the Douro R. Portugal's second largest city and an Atlantic port, it is known for the wine (port) it exports, which is named for the city. Textiles and wood and leather goods are produced. The ancient settlement, probably of pre-Roman origin, became known as Portus Cale (the source of the name Portugal). It was held (716–1092) by the MOORS and was later and for some time the chief city of Portugal. Its landmarks include the Dom Luis bridge (1881–87) and the Torre dos Clérigos, a baroque tower.

opossum, name for several MARSUPIALS of the family Didelphidae, native to Central and South America, with one species in the U.S. Mostly arboreal and nocturnal animals, opossums have long noses, naked ears, prehensile tails, and black-and-white fur. They eat small animals, eggs, insects, and fruit. When frightened they collapse as if dead. Opossums are hunted as pests as well as for food and sport.

Oppenheimer, J. Robert, 1904–67, American physicist; b. N.Y.C. He taught at the Univ. of California and the California Institute of Technology and was from 1947 director of the Institute for Advanced Study at Princeton. Director (1942–45) of the laboratory at Los Alamos, N.Mex., that designed and built the first ATOMIC BOMBS (see MANHATTAN PROJECT), Oppenheimer later became a main proponent of the civilian and international control of atomic energy. He was chairman (1946–52) of the general advisory committee of the U.S. Atomic Energy Commission, but in 1953 the AEC suspended him as an alleged security risk. Oppenheimer strongly opposed (1949), on both technical and moral grounds, the development of the HYDROGEN BOMB.

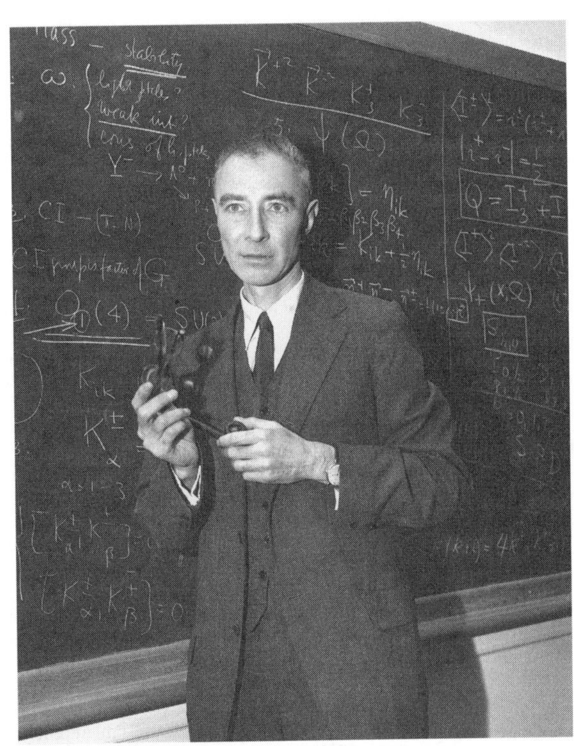

J. Robert Oppenheimer

opposition, in astronomy: see SYZYGY.

optical activity, ability of asymmetrical compounds to rotate the plane of polarized light. Optical activity is measured using right- and left-hand polarized light: the amount of optical rotation is a measure of a compound's effect on the light's velocity; the amount of circular dichroism is a measure of the absorption of the light. Compounds that rotate polarized light are called enantiomers, or optical ISOMERS. Molecular groups that possess high optical activity due to mobile electrons that interact with light are called chromophores; they are responsible for the color of certain objects (e.g., the CHLOROPHYLL chromophore in plant leaves). See also POLARIZATION OF LIGHT.

optical character recognition (OCR), method for the machine-reading of typeset, typed, and, in some cases, hand-printed letters, numbers, and symbols using OPTICAL SCANNING and a computer. The light reflected by a printed text is recorded as patterns of light and dark areas by an array of PHOTOELECTRIC CELLS in a optical scanner. A computer program analyzes the patterns and identifies the characters they represent, with some tolerance for less than perfect and uniform text. See also COMPUTER GRAPHICS.

optical disk, any of a variety of information storage disks that are played or read using a LASER. Optical disks include COMPACT DISCS (CDs and CD-ROMs) and laser discs (see VIDEO DISC). WORM [*W*rite *O*nce/*R*ead *M*any] disks can be used to record data, but once data is recorded it cannot be altered except by obliterating the old version and storing the new version on a previously unused portion of the disk. **Magneto-optical disks,** such as the rewritable optical disk and the recordable disk used with the Mini Disc player, have a special layer, as of barium ferrite, that can be magnetically polarized by a recording head when heated with a laser. Data or sound may be recorded to and erased from any portion of a magneto-optical disk multiple times.

optical sensing, in general, any method of detecting light and translating it into electric signals. This is usually accomplished by the use of various photoelectric devices, such as a PHOTOELECTRIC CELL. Optical sensing typically involves recording variations in intensity or another property of light as the light is transmitted or reflected. Optical sensing is used in various pattern-recognition systems, e.g., in BAR-CODE scanners, OPTICAL CHARACTER RECOGNITION, military reconnaissance, and astronomical observation, and in photographic development, to enhance detail and contrast.

optics, scientific study of LIGHT. Physical optics is concerned with the genesis, nature, and properties of light; physiological optics with the part light plays in vision (see EYE); and geometrical optics with the geometry involved in the REFLECTION and REFRACTION of light as encountered in the study of the MIRROR and the LENS.

optometry: see under OPHTHALMOLOGY.

oracle, in Greek religion, priest or priestess who imparted a god's response to a human questioner; also the response itself and the shrine. Methods of divination included interpretation of dreams, observation of signs, and interpretation of the actions of entranced persons. Among the famous oracles were those of ZEUS at Dodona and of APOLLO at DELPHI.

oral contraceptive or **the pill,** method of BIRTH CONTROL, usually consisting of an estrogen and a progestin (a PROGESTERONE-like substance) in pill form. Taken cyclically for 21 days each month, it elevates levels of these hormones in the blood, suppressing production of the pituitary hormones that would normally cause a woman to ovulate. Side effects include nausea, weight gain, and increased blood-clotting tendency. The use of oral contraceptives may increase the risk of cervical cancer but decrease the risk of cancer of the ovaries and endometrium, benign breast cysts, premenstrual syndrome, and iron-deficiency anemia.

Oran, city (1987 pop. 628,558), NW Algeria, on the Gulf of Oran of the Mediterranean Sea. Algeria's second largest city, Oran is a major port exporting wheat, wine, and other goods, and a commercial, industrial, and financial center. Nearby are important petrochemical installations. The site of modern Oran has been inhabited since prehistoric times, but the city's founding (10th cent.) is generally attributed to Moorish traders from Andalusia. Held alternately (1509–1791) by the Spanish and the Ottoman Turks, Oran fell to the French in 1831 and was developed as a naval base. During WORLD WAR II the city was held (1940–42) by Vichy forces. It played an important role in the Algerian independence struggle (1954–62).

Orange, city (1990 pop. 110,658), Orange co., S Calif.; inc. 1888. A citrus and nut packing, processing, and shipping center, the city grew rapidly in the 1980s. Rubber products, electronic components, and industrial furnaces are manufactured. Orange is the seat of Chapman College.

Orange, major river of S Africa, flowing generally west c.1,300 mi (2,090 km) from Lesotho through parts of the Namib and KALAHARI deserts to the Atlantic Ocean. Much of its water is diverted through two long tunnels to provide hydroelectricity and irrigation in South Africa.

orange, tree (genus *Citrus*) of the RUE family, native to China and Indochina, and its fruit. A CITRUS FRUIT, the orange is rich in VITAMIN C. Among the commercially important species are the sweet, or common, orange (*C. sinensis*), which furnishes varieties such as the navel and Valencia; the sour, or Seville, orange (*C. aurantium*), used as an understock on which to bud sweet orange varieties and in marmalade; and *C. reticulata,* which includes the mandarin orange, the tangerine, and the hardy Satsuma varieties. Oranges hybridize readily. The citrange is a cross between two varieties of orange; the tangelo is produced by crossing a tangerine and a grapefruit. Oranges may be artificially colored before marketing. They are eaten fresh, made into juice, or used in preserves and confections. Essential oils from orange rind, flowers, and leaves are used in perfumes. The orange blossom is Florida's state flower.

Orangemen, members of the Loyal Orange Institution, a society in Northern Ireland, est. 1795 to maintain Protestant ascendancy. Its name was taken from the family name of WILLIAM III of England, who defeated (1690) the Catholic JAMES II.

orangutan, APE (*Pongo pygmaeus*) found in swampy coastal forests of Borneo and Sumatra. With their extremely long arms and short, bowed legs, orangutans are highly specialized for arboreal life and rarely descend to the ground. An adult male is about 4½ ft (1.4 m) tall and weighs about 150 lb (68 kg); the body is covered with reddish fur.

oratorio, musical composition employing chorus, orchestra, and soloists and usually, but not necessarily, a setting of a sacred libretto without stage action or scenery; originally performed in an oratory of the Church of St. Philip Neri at Rome. Outstanding oratorios are by METASTASIO, SCHÜTZ, J.S. BACH, HANDEL, F.J. HAYDN, and MENDELSSOHN.

orbit, path in space described by a smaller body revolving around a second, larger body where the motion of the orbiting body is dominated by their mutual gravitational attraction (see CELESTIAL MECHANICS; GRAVITATION; KEPLER'S LAWS). The size and shape of an orbit are specified by (1) the semimajor axis (the average distance of the smaller body from the larger body) and (2) the eccentricity (the distance of the larger body from the center of the orbit divided by the length of the orbit's semimajor axis). The position of the orbit in space is determined by three factors: (3) the inclination, or tilt, of the orbital plane to the reference plane (the ECLIPTIC for sun-orbiting bodies; a planet's EQUATOR for natural and artificial satellites); (4) the longitude of the ascending NODE (measured from the vernal EQUINOX to the point where the smaller body cuts the reference plane moving south to north); and (5) the argument of pericenter (measured from the ascending node in the direction of motion to the point at which the two bodies are closest). These five quantities, plus the time of pericenter passage, are called orbital elements. The gravitational attractions of bodies other than the larger body causes perturbations in the smaller body's motions that can make the orbit shift, or precess, in space or cause the smaller body to wobble slightly.

Orcagna or **Arcagnolo,** c.1308–1368, Florentine painter, sculptor, and architect; b. Andrea di Cione. The figures in his famous altarpiece *Christ in Glory with Saints Thomas and Peter* (Santa Maria Novella, Florence) are Byzantine types. He was chief architect of the cathedral at Orvieto.

orchestra and orchestration. An orchestra is a musical ensemble, under the direction of a conductor, employing four classes of instruments: the STRINGED INSTRUMENTS, which convey the melody and the expressive qualities of the music; the woodwinds, adding color and, in some passages, the melody; the brass, adding dynamic sound (see WIND INSTRUMENTS); and the PERCUSSION INSTRUMENTS, those used to emphasize rhythm. The strings, except the harp, have several players for each part, the others usually only one. The orchestra in the modern sense did not exist before the 17th cent. Earlier instrumental music was chamber music, and parts were not assigned to specific instruments. The first known example of specific orchestration occurs in the *Sacrae symphoniae* (1597) of Giovanni Gabrieli (see under GABRIELI, ANDREA). MONTEVERDI's *Orfeo* (1607), one of the first OPERAS, demands a large, varied group of instruments. Throughout the BAROQUE period, orchestras were small, and the basso continuo was an integral part of the scoring, requiring that a harpsichord or other chord-playing instrument fill in the harmonies above the FIGURED BASS. In the latter half of the 18th cent. the continuo fell out of use, and by the late works of F.J. HAYDN and W.A. MOZART the classical orchestra was standardized. The 19th cent. saw major mechanical improvements in instruments, and the size of the orchestra expanded. Composers of the 20th cent. have generally preferred a moderate-sized orchestra and have been interested in diverse instrumental combinations (often stressing percussion) and the original exploitation of the instruments' capabilities. For a list of selected American symphony orchestras, see table.

orchid, name for the Orchidaceae, a large family of perennial herbs distributed worldwide, but most abundant in tropical and subtropical forests. The family includes many EPIPHYTES and SAPROPHYTES. Orchid flowers have three petals and three sepals, the central one modified and specialized to secrete insect-attracting nectar. The diverse flower forms are apparently complicated adaptations for

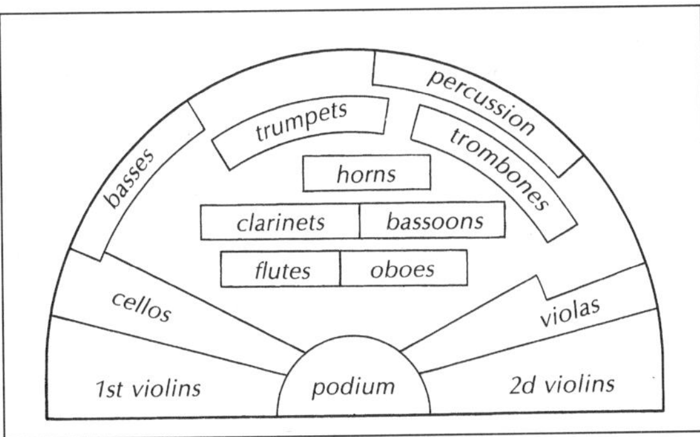

Typical seating plan of a symphony orchestra

POLLINATION by specific insects. Orchids are highly prized ornamentals. Many are native to North America, and most are bog plants or flowers of moist woodlands and meadows, e.g., the pink-blossomed lady's-slipper, or moccasin flower (*Cypripedium acaule*). A species of the tropical American genus *Vanilla* is the source of natural VANILLA flavoring.

orders of architecture. In classical styles of architecture, columnar types fall in general into five so-called classical orders: Doric, Ionic, Corinthian, Composite, and Tuscan. Each comprises the column and the entablature, and each has a distinctive character as to proportions and detail. The Roman writer Vitruvius attempted to formulate the proportioning of the three Greek orders. Doric, the earliest, was used for the PARTHENON and most Greek temples. The Doric column, thought to have developed from earlier wood construction, was massive, fluted, without a base, and topped with a simple capital; the entablature was also fairly plain. The Ionic order, largely Asiatic in origin, had a scroll-shaped capital above a more slender, fluted column; the entablature was more intricate than that of the Doric. In Greece, the only major example of the Ionic is the ERECHTHEUM. The third Greek order, the Corinthian, was little used until the Romans adopted it. It was the latest (fully developed in the 4th cent. B.C.) and the most ornate. The delicate, foliated details of the capital are its distinctive feature. The Romans used it widely in monumental architecture and developed a variant, or Composite, order that combined the Corinthian foliate pattern with a molding similar to the Ionic. The 16th-cent. Italians established a simplified form of Doric, or Tuscan, order, with unfluted columns and unadorned capital and entablature. The Renaissance saw variations of the orders, but during the CLASSIC REVIVAL strict adherence to the Greek and Roman originals was the rule.

Ordinance of 1787, in U.S. history, adopted by the Congress of Confederation to create and govern the NORTHWEST TERRITORY. It marked the beginning of Western expansion in the U.S. and set the form by which territories became states. It provided for an elected legislature when the population totaled 5,000 voting citizens, and for statehood when the population reached 60,000.

Ordovician period: see GEOLOGIC ERA (table).

ore, metal-bearing MINERAL mass that can be profitably mined. Nearly all rocks contain some metallic minerals, but often the concentration of metal is too low to justify MINING. Ores often occur in veins in rock, varying in thickness from fractions of an inch to several hundred feet. Minerals with no commercial value, called gangue minerals, are usually found mixed with the ore in the vein. Recovering minerals from their ores is one area in the field of METALLURGY.

oregano, name for several herbs used in cooking. Plants of the genus *origanum,* of the MINT family, are the usual sources of the spice sold as oregano in the U.S. and Mediterranean countries. The flavor is similar to that of MARJORAM but slightly less sweet. A related herb, *Coleus amboinicius,* is known as oregano in Mexico and the Philippines.

Oregon, one of the northwestern states of the U.S.; bordered by Washington across the Columbia R. (N), Idaho (E), Nevada and California (S), and the Pacific Ocean (W).

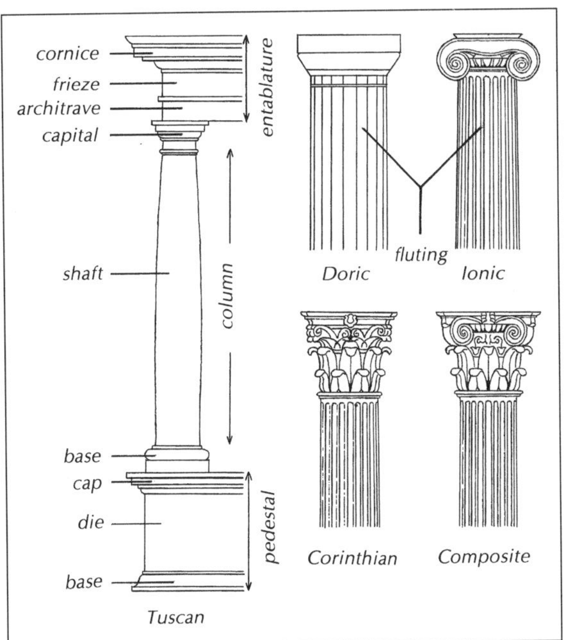

Orders of architecture

Area, 96,981 sq mi (251,181 sq km). *Pop.* (1990) 2,842,321, an 8% increase over 1980 pop. *Capital,* Salem. *Statehood,* Feb. 14, 1859 (33d state). *Highest pt.,* Mt. Hood, 11,239 ft (3,428 m); *lowest pt.,* sea level. *Nickname,* Beaver State. *Motto,* The Union. *State bird,* Western meadowlark. *State flower,* Oregon grape. *State tree,* Douglas fir. *Abbr.,* Oreg.; OR.

Land and People. Much of Oregon is covered by highlands, including the COAST RANGES, located inland from the Pacific; the CASCADE RANGE, which runs north to south through the state farther east; and the COLUMBIA PLATEAU, in the northeast. The most extensive lowlands are the river valleys of the COLUMBIA and its major tributary, the Willamette. Almost 50% of the land is controlled by the federal government. Rainfall is frequent in the west, while dry air and continental climate prevail in the east. About 70% of the population lives in urban areas, principally PORTLAND, the largest city; EUGENE; and SALEM. In 1990 the state's population was about 93% white.

Economy. Oregon's farms are famous for their apples and other fruits; greenhouse products, hay, wheat, cattle, dairy products, potatoes, and peppermint are also valuable agricultural products. Lumbering is the state's leading industry, and wood products its major manufacture. About half of the land is covered by pine forests, and Oregon has been the country's foremost lumbering state since 1950. Food processing, printing and publishing, and the manufacture of machinery, fabricated metals, and paper are also important. Oregon's salmon-fishing industry is one of the world's largest; other principal catches are tuna and crabs. Oregon's beaches, lakes, mountains, and scenic sites such as Crater Lake National Park (see NATIONAL PARKS, table) attract tourists year-round.

Government. The constitution (adopted 1857) provides for a governor serving a four-year term. The legislature consists of a senate whose 30 members are elected to four-year terms and a house with 60 members elected for two-year terms. Oregon is represented in the U.S. Congress by two senators and five representatives and has seven electoral votes.

History. Native American tribes living in the area when Capt. James COOK explored (1778) the coast in search of the NORTHWEST PASSAGE included the Bannock, Chinook, Klamath, and NEZ PERCÉ. The region became the center of an active fur trade, and representatives of John Jacob ASTOR'S AMERICAN FUR COMPANY established (1811) Astoria, the first permanent settlement. New settlers began arriving over the OREGON TRAIL in 1842–43. The region, which had been controlled jointly by the U.S. and Great Britain, became the center of the "Oregon controversy," which was resolved (1846) with the fixing of the Canadian-U.S. boundary at the 49th parallel. The arrival of the railroads (1880s) facilitated marketing of the state's lumber and wheat. Post–World War II industrial expansion has been closely tied to the construction of huge power projects, such as Bonneville Dam (completed 1943), on the Columbia, which provide abundant hydroelectricity. Because of Oregon's heavy reliance on lumbering, its economy has been severely affected by cyclical downturns in the nation's building industry. Oregon has been a leader in programs to protect the state's environment, but some environmental issues have divided its citizens, as in the 1980s and early 90s when protection of the endangered spotted owl caused a halt to some logging activities. High-technology firms migrated from California to Oregon during the late 1980s and early 90s.

Oregon Trail, route used (1840s to 70s) by Western settlers in the U.S. to reach the Oregon Territory. Their wagon trains generally started at Independence or Westport, Mo., traveled NW along the Platte and N Platte rivers to Fort Laramie, Wyo., and crossed the Rocky Mts. by the South Pass to the Colorado R. basin. The Oregon Trail continued SW to Fort Bridger, where the Mormon Trail diverged to the southwest, and then ran NW, via the Snake R., Blue Mts., and Columbia R., to the Willamette valley. It totaled c.2,000 mi (3,200 km) in length and required about six months for the average wagon train to traverse it. In 1978 it was made a national historical trail.

Orestes, in Greek mythology, son of AGAMEMNON and CLYTEMNESTRA, brother of ELECTRA and IPHIGENIA. The young Orestes was exiled after the slaying of Agamemnon by Clytemnestra and AEGISTHUS. Later he returned and, helped by Electra, killed his mother and her lover. He was pursued by the FURIES until he reached Athens, where he was tried and acquitted by the prime council, the Areopagus. To complete his purification, he took the image of ARTEMIS from Taurus (where he was reunited with Iphigenia) to Greece. His vengeance and expiation are dramatized in AESCHYLUS' *Oresteia.* SOPHOCLES and EURIPIDES also used the story.

Orff, Carl, 1895–1982, German composer and educator. His best-known work is *Carmina Burana* (1937), a secular ORATORIO derived from medieval German and Latin poems. His system for teaching music to children, based on rhythmic and verbal patterns and the pentatonic scale, is widely used.

organ, musical wind instrument in which sound is produced by one or more sets of pipes, each producing a single pitch by means of a mechanically or electrically controlled wind supply. Several keyboards (manuals) are played with the hands. Projecting knobs (stops) to the sides of the keyboard operate wooden sliders that pass under the mouths of a rank of pipes to "stop" a particular rank. The pedals of the organ are like another keyboard, played with the feet. The prevailing organ for several centuries from the 3d cent. B.C. was the Greek *hydraulos.* Organs in the Middle Ages already had several ranks of *diapason* pipes, their timbre characteristic only of the organ. The 15th cent. added stops, including those imitative of other instruments, e.g., flute. Organ building reached a peak in the German BAROQUE, then declined. The 19th cent. obscured diapason tone by adding stops imitative of orchestral sound and by the use of crescendo. While the early 20th cent. developed electrification of the mechanical parts of the organ, Albert SCHWEITZER and others led a movement back to baroque ideals.

organic chemistry, branch of CHEMISTRY dealing with CARBON compounds. Of all the elements, carbon forms the greatest number of different compounds; moreover, compounds that contain carbon are about 100 times more numerous than those that do not. Compounds containing only carbon and HYDROGEN are called HYDROCARBONS. Organic compounds containing NITROGEN are of great importance to BIOCHEMISTRY. Organic chemistry is of importance to the petrochemical, pharmaceutical, and textile industries; in textiles a prime concern is the synthesis of new organic molecules and POLYMERS.

organic farming, farming practices that exclude or avoid synthetic PESTICIDES, FERTILIZERS, growth regulators, and feed additives. Organic farmers prefer biological pest control, manure, and practices such as rotation of crops to supply plant nutrients and control pests. Interest in organic farming has been fostered by awareness of the dangers caused by INSECTICIDES and the excessive use of chemical fertilizers. See also ENVIRONMENTALISM.

Organization for Economic Cooperation and Development (OECD), international organization, formed in 1961, superseding the Organization for European Economic Cooperation. The organization has 24 full members, including Australia, Britain, Canada, France, Germany, Japan, and the U.S. Members pledge to work to promote economic growth, aid developing nations, and expand world trade. The headquarters are in Paris.

Organization of African Unity (OAU), organization (est. 1963) to promote unity, development, and defense of African states; eradicate colonialism; and coordinate economic, health, and other policies. There are 52 members.

Organization of American States (OAS), regional agency (est. 1948) to promote peace and development in the Americas. It succeeded the Pan-American Union, which became the secretariat of the OAS. The inter-American program of economic assistance called the Alliance for Progress, proposed by Pres. John KENNEDY, was created within the OAS framework in 1961. The OAS has sought to settle disputes between member nations and has discouraged foreign intervention in their internal affairs, but in the early 1990s it began to actively oppose the overthrow of democratic governments, calling for an embargo on trade with HAITI after an army coup. The OAS has 35 members, but Cuba has been excluded from participation since 1962.

Organization of Petroleum Exporting Countries (OPEC), organization (est. 1960) coordinating petroleum policies of most of the major THIRD WORLD oil-producing nations. Its members are Algeria, Gabon, Indonesia, Iran, Iraq, Kuwait, Libya, Nigeria, Qatar, Saudi Arabia, United Arab Emirates, and Venezuela. During the 1970s its members, acting as a cartel, raised oil prices sharply, causing shortages, inflation, and other problems in the oil-importing nations. Since then, however, OPEC's ability to affect oil prices has diminished.

organized crime, nationally (sometimes internationally) coordinated criminal activities. In the U.S., the term was first applied during PROHIBITION to the operations of local gang leaders, such as Al CAPONE in Chicago, who built criminal organizations on the profits of bootlegging. Organized crime has since moved into gambling, narcotics trafficking, labor racketeering, and many other activities. Under Lucky Luciano, an interstate "Syndicate" with strong political connections was put together in the 1930s. Murder, Inc., a band of professional killers, served as its enforcement arm until a legal crackdown occurred (1940–41). Despite Sen. Estes KEFAUVER's investigations (1950–51) and later law-enforcement efforts, organized crime continues to flourish, often hiding or supplementing its profits through legal "front" operations. The MAFIA, of Sicilian origin, has played an important role in the evolution of U.S. organized crime. Criminal organizations have also flourished in other countries, e.g., the yakuza of Japan and the cocaine "cartels" of Colombia.

organometallic chemistry, branch of CHEMISTRY concerned with substances that contain an organic compound or fragment bound to a metal atom or ion by a metal-carbon bond; by tradition compounds containing a metal-hydrogen bond are also included. Because organometallic compounds exhibit unique properties, organometallic chemistry is differentiated from both ORGANIC CHEMISTRY and INORGANIC CHEMISTRY. Organometallic chemistry, especially that employing organomagnesium compounds, is used to synthesize many organic compounds and has been important in the development of silicone polymers, polyvinyl chloride, and polyethylene. Many organometallic compounds, such as tetraethyl lead, formerly used in GASOLINE, and the alkyls produced by fish that have consumed mercury, are highly toxic, primarily because of the metal they contain.

Origen (Origines Adamantius), 185?–254?, Christian philosopher; b. Egypt. Origen taught in Alexandria for 28 years and became famed for his profound interpretations of the Scriptures. He attempted to synthesize the principles of Greek philosophy, particularly NEOPLATONISM and STOICISM, with those of Christianity. The most influential theologian of the early church, he is said to have written 800 works, of which few survive. His system of philosophy is contained in *On First Principles.*

Orinoco, river, Venezuela, flowing south c.1,600 mi (2,600 km) from Mt. Délgado Chalbaud, in the Guiana Highlands, to a very large, marshy delta in the northeast. The volume of flow varies markedly with the seasons. Ciudad Bolívar is the principal city on the river, which is connected to the AMAZON R. system by the Casiquiare, a natural canal.

oriole, name for various perching BIRDS of the Old World (family Oriolidae) and New World (family Icteridae). The European oriole is allied to the CROW, while the small American oriole is related to the BLACKBIRD and MEADOWLARK. Swift fliers with clear calls, orioles feed on fruit, mainly berries, or insects. Both Old World and New World orioles have orange and black (or brown) markings.

Orion [ōrī'ən], in Greek mythology, Boeotian hunter. While drunk he raped his betrothed, Merope, and was then blinded by her father. His vision was restored by the rays of the sun. At his death ARTEMIS turned him into a constellation.

Oriya [ôrē'yə], language belonging to the Indic group of the Indo-Iranian subfamily of the Indo-European family of languages. See LANGUAGE (table).

Orizaba: see CITLALTÉPETL.

Orkney Islands (1991 pop. 19,450), 376 sq mi (974 sq km), N Scotland, an archipelago of about 70 islands in the Atlantic Ocean and the North Sea. Less than half of the islands are inhabited. Fishing, farming, and the exploitation and processing of nearby North Sea oil deposits are the principal industries. Ruled by Viking, then Scottish, earls, the Orkneys passed to the Scottish crown in 1472.

Orlando, Vittorio Emanuele, 1860–1952, Italian statesman. As Italian premier (1917–19), he was one of the "Big Four" leaders at the Paris Peace Conference (1919), where he demanded territorial compensation for Italy in Dalmatia. Meeting stiff opposition from U.S. Pres. WILSON, he temporarily left the conference. When his demand was still not met, he resigned as premier. Opposed to Fascism, he gave up (1925) his seat in the Italian parliament. After World War II he served as a senator (1948–52).

Orlando, city (1990 pop. 164,693; met. area 1,072,748), seat of Orange co., central Fla.; inc. 1875. It is a resort city, and the trade and shipping center for a citrus fruit and farm area. Aerospace and electronic industries and naval facilities provide employment. The Universal Studios theme park is in Orlando; Sea World and Walt Disney World, including Epcot (Experimental Prototype Community Of Tomorrow) Center and Disney-MGM Studios Theme Park, are a short distance SW of the city.

Orléans, family name of two branches of the French royal line. The house of Valois-Orléans was founded by **Louis, duc d'Orléans,** 1372–1407, brother of CHARLES VI of France. Louis's assassination, ordered by JOHN THE FEARLESS, duke of Burgundy, caused a civil war between the Orléanists, or Armagnacs, and the Burgundians. Louis's son **Charles, duc d'Orléans,** 1391–1465, became the titular head of the Armagnacs. He was captured (1415) by the English at Agincourt and remained a captive until 1440. Charles's son ascended the French throne (1498) as LOUIS XII, but he died without a male heir. The modern house of Bourbon-Orléans (see BOURBON) was founded by **Philippe I, duc d'Orléans,** 1640–1701, a brother of LOUIS XIV. A notorious libertine, he was excluded from state affairs. His son, **Philippe II, duc d'Orléans,** 1674–1723, regent of France (1715–23) in the minority of LOUIS XV, distinguished himself in the wars of the GRAND ALLIANCE and the SPANISH SUCCESSION. To solve the financial crisis, Orléans called on John LAW, but Law's schemes collapsed in 1720. Social life during his regency reached an apex of licentiousness. The ambitions of the regent and of his descendants brought the house of Orléans into open opposition to the ruling house. The regent's great-grandson, **Louis Philippe Joseph, duc d'Orléans,** 1747–93, known as **Philippe Égalité,** supported the FRENCH REVOLUTION, voted to execute Louis XVI, and was himself guillotined during the REIGN OF TERROR. His adherents, the Orleanists, who sought a compromise between monarchical and revolutionary principles, came to power in the JULY REVOLUTION of 1830 and put Philippe Égalité's son LOUIS PHILIPPE on the French throne. After his fall (1848), they continued to support the claims of his descendants, the Orleanist pretenders. Their prospects, high under the presidency of Marshal MACMAHON, dwindled steadily, especially after the Third Republic exiled all pretenders in 1886. Louis Philippe's grandson **Louis Philippe Albert d'Orléans, comte de Paris,** 1838–94, fought on the Union side in the U.S. Civil War. He relinquished his claims to the legitimist pretender, Henri de Chambord (1873), but on Chambord's death (1883) he became head of the entire house of Bourbon. His son **Louis Philippe Robert, duc d'Orléans,** 1869–1926, succeeded his father as pretender in 1894. Born in England, he served briefly in the Indian army and traveled widely. He died childless, and his pretensions to the French throne passed to a cousin and his heirs.

Orléans, city (1990 pop. 105,111), capital of Loiret dept., N central France, an industrial and transportation center. First inhabited by the Celtic Carnutes, the city revolted against Julius CAESAR (52 B.C.) and was burned. It repelled (451) Attila but fell (498) to CLOVIS I. In the 10th cent. it became an important part of the royal domain. In 1429, during the HUNDRED YEARS WAR, JOAN OF ARC lifted the English siege of Orléans. Many historic buildings were destroyed in World War II, and the city has been extensively rebuilt, utilizing traditional architectural styles.

Orlon: see SYNTHETIC TEXTILE FIBERS.

Ormandy, Eugene, 1899–1985, American conductor; b. Hungary. He came to the U.S. in 1921, joined the Philadelphia Orchestra in 1936, and became its music director (1938–80). Ormandy is noted for his romantic interpretations.

Oromo or **Galla,** Hamitic pastoral people of W and S Ethiopia and Kenya, numbering about 20 million. They are largely Muslim. They have inhabited the Ethiopian highlands since the 16th cent., having come there from Somalia. The Oromo have historically maintained small-group autonomy from the Ethiopian government.

Orozco, José Clemente [ōrō'skō], 1883–1949, Mexican painter, one of the leaders of the Mexican renaissance. His boldly painted works often deal with social themes. He was noted for his FRESCOES, e.g., the mural *Mankind's Struggle* (1930; New School for Social Research, N.Y.C.).

orphan drug, drug developed under the U.S. Orphan Drug Act (1983) to treat a disease that affects a relatively small number of people. The terms of the orphan drug law offer tax breaks and a seven-year monopoly on drug sales to induce companies to undertake development and manufacturing of such drugs, which otherwise might not be profitable. The law has led to the introduction of valuable new drugs for the treatment of rare diseases, but some drug companies have been accused of abusing the law's provisions by making inordinately high profits on orphan drugs under monopoly.

Orpheus [ôr'fēəs, ôr'fyo͞os], in Greek mythology, Thracian musician; son of the MUSE Calliope by APOLLO or by Oeagrus, a king of Thrace. He is said to have played the lyre so beautifully that he charmed the beasts, trees, and rivers. He married the nymph Eurydice, and when she died he descended to HADES to search for her. He was allowed to return with her on condition that he not look back at her, but he disobeyed and lost her forever. Grief-stricken, he wandered for years. In one legend, he worshiped Apollo above DIONYSUS, who caused the Thracians to tear him to pieces. Orpheus was celebrated in the ORPHIC MYSTERIES.

Orphic Mysteries or **Orphism,** religious cult of ancient Greece, ascribed to Orpheus. The Orphics affirmed the divine origin of the soul, but also the dual aspect of human nature as good and evil. They believed that through initiation into the Orphic MYSTERIES and through the process of transmigration, the soul could be liberated from its inheritance of evil and achieve eternal blessedness. Orphism followed a strict ethical and moral code and adopted practices such as VEGETARIANISM for purification.

Orr, Bobby (Robert Orr), 1948–, Canadian hockey player. He ranked as the National Hockey League's finest defenseman while with the Boston Bruins (1967–76). Three times the league's most valuable player, he was the first defenseman to score 100 points in a season, and his 102 assists (1970–71) set a record. Orr played for the Chicago Blackhawks from 1976 to 1979.

Ørsted, Hans Christian: see OERSTED, HANS CHRISTIAN.

Ortega y Gasset, José [ôrtā'gä ē gäsĕt'], 1883–1955, Spanish essayist and philosopher. A professor of metaphysics at the Univ. of Madrid, he sought to establish the ultimate reality in which all else was rooted. He gained world fame with *The Revolt of the Masses*

Bobby Orr

(1929), which contends that the masses must be directed by an intellectual minority, or chaos will result.

orthodontics: see DENTISTRY.

Orthodox Eastern Church, community of Christian churches, independent but mutually recognized, originating in E Europe and SW Asia through a split with the Western church. They agree in accepting the decrees of the first seven ecumenical councils and in rejecting the jurisdiction of the pope. Orthodox and Roman Catholics view each other as schismatic, but consider the Nestorian, Coptic, and Jacobite churches heretical. The split between East and West began in the 5th cent. and became definite only with the condemnation of the patriarch of Constantinople by Pope LEO IX (1054). The CRUSADES embittered feelings, and many attempts at reunion since have failed. Eastern church liturgy is always sung and is not usually celebrated daily as in the West, and communion is given in a spoon. Parish priests may marry; bishops and monks may not. The term *Greek Church* may be used very loosely and is best confined to the patriarchate of Constantinople, the Church of Greece, and churches using the Byzantine rite (liturgy in Greek). Among the national churches, the most ancient is the Church of Cyprus, and the most important is the Russian Orthodox Church. The latter was first under Constantinople, but a patriarchate was set up in Moscow in 1589. The rite is in Old Church Slavonic. After the Russian Revolution the church suffered greatly and went into an eclipse, but a new patriarch was elected in 1943. After World War II, Communist influence greatly weakened the Orthodox churches in Bulgaria, Yugoslavia, Romania, and Poland. With the collapse of Communist rule in the countries of E Europe during the late 1980s and early 1990s, many Orthodox churches revived and gained new members. The U.S. has several Orthodox churches with ties to Old World churches. Several observers from Orthodox churches attended the Second VATICAN COUNCIL in 1962, and afterward most agreed to open a dialogue with Rome as equals.

Orthodox Judaism: see JUDAISM.

orthopedics, medical specialty concerned with deformities, injuries, and diseases of the BONES, joints, ligaments, tendons, and MUSCLES. It includes surgical treatment for fractures, bone grafting, joint and limb replacement, and the fitting of braces or other appliances.

Orton, Joe, 1933–67, British playwright. His plays, which are often farces, are characterized by violence, decadence, and attacks on establishment values, but are written in a smooth, sophisticated, powerful prose. They include *Entertaining Mr. Sloane* (1964), *Loot* (1966), and *What the Butler Saw* (1969). He was killed during a lover's quarrel.

Orwell, George, pseud. of **Eric Arthur Blair,** 1903–50, English writer. Many of his works, like *Down and Out in Paris and London* (1933), *The Road to Wigan Pier* (1937), and *Homage to Catalonia* (1938), are autobiographical and sociopolitical. *Animal Farm* (1946) is a fable about the failure of communism, and his prophetic novel *Nineteen Eighty-Four* (1949) depicts a totalitarian world. His literary essays are highly regarded.

oryx: see ANTELOPE.

Os, chemical symbol of the element OSMIUM.

Osage, indigenous people of North America (see NORTH AMERICA, INDIGENOUS PEOPLES OF) with a Siouan language of the Hokan-Siouan stock (see NATIVE AMERICAN LANGUAGES). They migrated from their prehistoric home in the Ohio valley to the Osage R. region in Missouri, where they had a typical Plains culture except that half the tribe were vegetarians. In 1810 the 5,500 Osage began to cede their lands to the U.S. and moved to a reservation in Oklahoma. They now own land individually, and the discovery of oil on the reservation has made them one of the wealthiest tribes in the U.S. In 1990 there were 9,527 Osage in the U.S.

Osaka, city (1990 pop. 2,623,831), capital of Osaka prefecture, S Honshu, Japan. The third largest city in Japan and a major port, Osaka is the focal point of a chain of industrial cities (called the *Hanshin* or *Kinki*), with machinery, electrical equipment, metals, textiles, and chemicals among the chief industries. Osaka is known for its puppet and other theaters and for its universities. Landmarks include the Buddhist temple of Shitennoji, founded 593; Temmangu, a Shinto shrine founded in 949; and HIDEYOSHI's castle (reconstructed 1931).

Osborne, John (James), 1929–, English dramatist. His *Look Back in Anger* (1956), about a restless young working-class man at war with himself and society, became the seminal work of the so-called angry young men, a group of rebellious English writers of the 1950s. Later plays include *The Entertainer* (1957), *Inadmissable Evidence* (1964), *Time Present* (1968), *Watch It Come Down* (1976), and *Déjà vu* (1991). He has also written screenplays, e.g., *Tom Jones* (1963; Academy award).

Oscan [ŏs'kən], extinct language belonging to the Italic subfamily of the Indo-European family of languages. See LANGUAGE (table).

Osceola, c.1800–1838, leader of the SEMINOLE who denounced 1832 and 1833 treaties requiring Native Americans to move west. After his warriors killed (1835) an Indian agent, Wiley Thompson, U.S. troops under Gen. Jesup drove Osceola's band southward to the Everglades. In response to peace overtures he went (1837) under a flag of truce to meet Jesup, who had him seized and imprisoned at Fort Moultrie, S.C., where he died.

oscilloscope, device based on a CATHODE-RAY TUBE used to produce a visual display of electrical signals. Typically the horizontal position of the illuminated point is controlled by the value of the independent variable (often time), while the vertical position is controlled by the dependent variable. A third signal is often used to control the brightness of the point.

Osee: see HOSEA.

Oshawa [ŏsh'əwə], city (1991 pop. 129,344), SE Ontario, on Lake Ontario, part of the regional municipality of Durham (1991 pop. 409,070). The production of automobiles, begun by the McLaughlin family in 1907 and taken over by General Motors in 1918, dominates the local economy. Oshawa was founded (1795) at the site of a French fur-trading post.

Osiris, in EGYPTIAN RELIGION, legendary ruler of predynastic Egypt and god of the underworld. Osiris symbolized the creative forces of nature and the imperishability of life. Called the great benefactor of humanity, he brought to the people knowledge of agriculture and civilization. In a famous myth he was slain by his evil brother Set, but his death was avenged by his son HORUS. The worship of Osiris, one of the great cults of ancient Egypt, gradually spread throughout the Mediterranean world and, with that of ISIS and Horus, was especially vital during the Roman Empire.

Oslo, city (1990 pop. 458,456), capital of Norway, SE Norway, at the head of a fjord of the Skagerrak. It is Norway's largest city; main port; and chief commercial, industrial, and transportation center. Founded c.1050 by HAROLD III, it became the national capital in 1299. It was rebuilt after being razed by fire in 1624. It came under HANSEATIC LEAGUE domination in the 14th cent. Oslo's modern growth dates from the 19th cent. During WORLD WAR II it was occupied (1940–45) by Germany. In the modern city, government-sponsored modern art shares attention with the medieval Akerskirke and Akershus fortress and the royal palace (1848). The city was the site of the 1952 Olympic winter games.

osmium (Os), metallic element, discovered by Smithson Tennant in 1804. It is a very hard and dense, brittle, lustrous, bluish-white metal found in platinum ores. Its tetroxide is used as a stain in microscopy, in fingerprint detection, and as a catalyst. Osmium alloys are used in fountain-pen points and instrument bearings. See ELEMENT (table); PERIODIC TABLE.

osmosis, spontaneous transfer of a liquid solvent through a semipermeable membrane that does not allow dissolved solids (solutes) to pass. Osmosis refers only to the transfer of solvent; transfer of solute is called DIALYSIS. In either case, the direction of transfer is from the area of higher CONCENTRATION of the material transferred to the area of lower concentration. If a vessel is separated into two compartments by a semipermeable membrane, if both compartments are filled to the same level with a solvent, and if solute is added to one side, then osmosis will occur, and the level of the liquid on the side containing the solute will rise. If an external pressure is exerted on the side containing the solute, the transfer of solvent can be stopped. The minimum pressure to stop solvent transfer is called the osmotic pressure. Osmosis plays an important role in the control of the flow of liquids in and out of a living CELL.

osprey, BIRD of prey related to the HAWK and the New World VULTURE, found near water in much of the world. The American osprey, or fish hawk (*Pandion haliaetus*) has a wingspan of 5 to 6 ft (152 to 183 cm) and feeds solely on live fish.

Ossian [ŏsh'ən] or **Oisin** [əshēn'], legendary Gaelic poet, supposed son of FINN MAC CUMHAIL. One cycle of Ossianic poetry treats Finn and his 3d-cent. exploits, a second tells of the hero Cuchulain. In the 1760s the Scottish poet James MACPHERSON represented his own work as Ossian's.

Ossietzky, Carl von, 1889–1938, German pacifist. Arrested (1932) for exposing the secret rearmament of Germany in his antimilitarist weekly, *Weltbühne,* he was moved to a concentration camp after Hitler's rise to power in 1933. When he was awarded the 1935 Nobel Peace Prize, the German government protested and barred all Germans from future acceptance of any Nobel Prize. Ossietzky died in prison.

Ostade, Adriaen van [vän ô'städə], 1610–85, Dutch genre painter. Trained in Frans HALS's studio, he created good-humored depictions of village and peasant life. Later, influenced by REMBRANDT, he used a warmer palette and deeper high contrast effects. Among his many works is *The Old Fiddler* (Metropolitan Mus.). He did over 1,000 oils, and about 50 graphic works. His brother and pupil, **Isaak van Ostade,** 1621–49, created many fine winter landscapes and pastoral scenes.

Ostend Manifesto, document drawn up (1854) by three U.S. ministers at Ostend, Belgium, suggesting that the U.S. should take Cuba by force if Spain refused to sell it. The three Americans—James BUCHANAN, John Y. Mason, and Pierre SOULÉ—were proslavery Democrats acting at the behest of Secy. of State William I. Marcy. When the secret manifesto was made public and denounced in the press as a plot to extend slavery, Marcy repudiated it for the U.S. government.

osteomyelitis, acute or chronic infection of the bone and bone marrow characterized by pain, high fever, and an ABSCESS at the site of infection. The infection, which may be caused by a variety of microorganisms, reaches the bone through an open wound or fracture or through the bloodstream. Treatment includes ANTIBIOTICS and sometimes surgery.

osteopathy, practice of therapy based on manipulation of bones and muscles. Osteopaths maintain that the normal body produces forces necessary to fight disease and that most ailments are due to the misalignment of bones and other faulty conditions of the muscle tissue and cartilage. Osteopathy was founded in the U.S. in 1874 by Andrew Taylor Still.

osteoporosis, disorder in which the normal replenishment of old bone tissue is disrupted, as it usually is throughout life, resulting in weakened bones and increased risk of fracture. It is most common in white women after MENOPAUSE, although it can also occur in younger women and men. It is aggravated by a variety of factors, including smoking, excessive alcohol consumption, and a sedentary lifestyle. Lost bone cannot be replaced, but treatment, including calcium supplements, exercise, and (after MENOPAUSE) ESTROGEN replacement, can prevent further bone loss.

Ostia, ancient city of Italy, at the mouth of the Tiber. Founded (4th cent. B.C.) as a protection for Rome, it became a Roman port. From the 3d cent. A.D. it declined.

Ostrava, city (1990 est. pop. 331,000), NE Czech Republic, near the junction of the Oder and Ostravice rivers. In the heart of the Czech Republic's major industrial area, Ostrava produces coal, iron, steel, railroad cars, and automobiles. It is the site of several hydroelectric stations.

ostrich, large, flightless BIRD (*Struthio camelus*) of Africa and parts of SW Asia, related to the RHEA and EMU; the largest living bird. Some males reach 8 ft (244 cm) in height and weigh from 200 to 300 lb (90 to 135 kg). The male is black, with long white plumes on wings and tail; the female is grayish brown. Ostriches can run at great speeds. They are raised commercially for skins, meat, and feathers.

Ostrogoths or **East Goths,** a division of the Goths, one of the chief groups of ancient GERMANS. In the 3d cent. the Goths split into VISIGOTHS, or West Goths, and Ostrogoths, who were subjects of the HUNS until 453. The Ostrogoths then settled in Pannonia (modern Hungary) as allies of the Byzantine Empire. Their ruler, Theodoric the Great, defeated ODOACER (493) and set up the Ostrogothic kingdom of Italy. After the murder (535) of Theodoric's daughter, Amalasuntha, who as regent for her son was under Byzantine protection, JUSTINIAN I reconquered Italy through his generals BELISARIUS and NARSES. When Narses defeated (552) an Ostrogothic revolt under TOTILA, the Ostrogothic kingdom was crushed.

Ostrovsky, Aleksandr Nikolayevich [əstrôf'skē], 1823–86, Russian dramatist. Most of his plays depict patriarchal family life; all but eight are in blank verse. His masterpiece is the tragedy *The Storm* (1860). The composers JANÁČEK, RIMSKY-KORSAKOV, and TCHAIKOVSKY drew upon his work.

Ostwald, Wilhelm [ôst'vält], 1853–1932, German physical chemist and natural philosopher; b. Latvia. He won the 1909 Nobel Prize in chemistry for his work on catalysis, equilibrium, and rates of reaction. He also studied color and originated the **Ostwald process** for preparing nitric acid. In this process, ammonia mixed with air is heated and led over a catalyst (platinum). It reacts with oxygen to form nitric oxide, which is then oxidized to nitrogen dioxide; this in turn reacts with water to form nitric acid.

Otis, Elisha Graves, 1811–61, American inventor; b. Halifax, Vt. From his invention (1852) of an automatic safety device to prevent the fall of hoisting machinery he developed the first passenger ELEVATOR (1857), a basic step in the development of the SKYSCRAPER.

Otis, James, 1725–83, American colonial political leader; b. Barnstable co., Mass. As leader of the radical wing of the American opposition to Britain, he defended colonial rights. Otis helped Samuel ADAMS draft the circular letter to other colonies denouncing the TOWNSHEND ACTS (1767).

Otomí [ōtōmē'], a Macro-Otomanguean language spoken by an indigenous people of Mexico. See NATIVE AMERICAN LANGUAGES (table).

Ottawa, indigenous people of the Eastern Woodlands (see NORTH AMERICA, INDIGENOUS PEOPLES OF), with an Algonquian language of the Algonquian-Wakashan stock (see NATIVE AMERICAN LANGUAGES). From their traditional home N of the Great Lakes they migrated to the Georgian Bay region, and in the 17th cent. controlled trade with the French on the Ottawa R. Driven away by the Iroquois and SIOUX (see IROQUOIS CONFEDERACY), they dispersed over a wide area. Under PONTIAC they rebelled with other peoples (1763–66) against British rule. The Ottawas remain scattered today. In 1990 there were 7,522 Ottawas in the U.S.

Ottawa, city (1991 pop. 313,987), capital of Canada, SE Ontario, part of the regional municipality of Ottawa-Carleton (1991 pop. 678,147), at the confluence of the Ottawa and Rideau rivers. It functions primarily as a government center but has some industry. Of special interest are the Parliament Buildings, on Parliament Hill; the National Gallery; and the National Arts Center. Ottawa was founded as Bytown in 1825 and acquired its present name in 1854. The city was selected by Queen Victoria in 1858 as the capital of the newly formed United Provinces of Canada, and began to function as such in 1865. It became the capital of modern Canada in 1867.

otter, several aquatic, carnivorous MAMMALS of the WEASEL family, found on all continents except Australia. Common river otters of Eurasia and the Americas (genus *Lutra*) are slender, streamlined, and agile, with thick, brown fur. Otters are social and playful, sliding down mudbanks and snowbanks. The South American giant otter and the sea otter of the Pacific, hunted to near extinction, are now protected.

Otto, rulers of the HOLY ROMAN EMPIRE. **Otto I** or **Otto the Great,** 912–73, emperor (962–73) and German king (936–73), son and successor of Henry I of Germany, is often regarded as the founder of the Holy Roman Empire. He brought Italy, BURGUNDY, and LOTHARINGIA under German control and broke the independence of the duchies. He married Adelaide, the widowed Italian queen, and crowned himself king of the LOMBARDS. Pope JOHN XII, who crowned Otto emperor in 962, soon found Otto too powerful and allied himself with Otto's enemies; he was unsuccessful but established the long tradition of enmity between pope and emperor. **Otto II,** 955–83, emperor (973–83) and German king (961–83), was forced to defend the great empire left him by his father. He put down a revolt by his cousin, the duke of Bavaria; repulsed Danish attacks from the north; and resisted French efforts to annex Lorraine. He was defeated by the Arabs in S Italy, and his failure to expel them greatly diminished the prestige of his empire. His son, **Otto III,** 980–1002, emperor (996–1002) and German king (983–1002), was elected king shortly before his father's death; his mother and then his grandmother acted as regent for him. He installed (996) his cousin as Pope Gregory V, and later made his tutor pope (999) as SYLVESTER II. He attempted to establish his imperial headquarters in Rome, but a Roman mob forced him to flee (1001). He died while trying to regain the city. **Otto IV,** 1175?–1218, emperor (1209–15) and German king, was the son of HENRY THE LION, duke of Saxony. His uncle, RICHARD I of England, had him named antiking to Philip of Swabia in 1178. Philip's murder (1208) was not of Otto's doing, but it revived his cause. He won over the princes and was elected emperor. He had made important concessions to the papacy regarding its Italian territories, but he quickly reverted to the HOHENSTAUFEN policy of dominance. He seized church lands and invaded Sicily, whereupon Pope INNOCENT III excommunicated him (1210). With the help of France and some German nobles, the pope succeeded in deposing him in 1215.

Otto, German kings: see OTTO, rulers of the Holy Roman Empire.

Otto I, 1815–67, first king (1833–62) of the Hellenes (Greece). The second son of Louis I of Bavaria, he was chosen by the European powers to rule over newly independent Greece. Highly unpopular, he was finally forced (1862) to abdicate.

Otto, Nikolaus August, 1832–91, German engineer. Coinventor (1867) of an INTERNAL-COMBUSTION ENGINE, he developed (1876) the four-stroke Otto cycle, widely used for automobile, airplane, and other motors.

Ottoman Empire, vast state founded in the 13th cent. by the Ottoman or Osmani TURKS and ruled by the descendants of Osman I, the empire's first sultan, until its dissolution after world War I. It was the largest of the modern states, extending into Asia, Europe, and Africa; modern TURKEY formed only a part of the empire, but the terms "Turkey" and "Ottoman Empire" are often used interchangeably. The Ottoman state began as one of the many small Turkish states that emerged in Asia Minor as the power of the Seljuk Turks declined. The Ottomans began absorbing those small states as later (14th cent.) they absorbed territory belonging to the BYZANTINE EMPIRE. The great Balkan conquests of the late 14th cent. awoke Europe to the Ottoman threat. In spite of opposition from TIMUR, the Turks, under MUHAMMAD II, conquered Constantinople in 1453 and established it as the Ottoman capital. The Ottoman Empire reached its height in the 16th cent. under SELIM I, who assumed the CALIPHATE after his victories in Syria and Egypt (1516–17), and under SULAYMAN I (the Magnificent), who brought much of the Balkan peninsula, Hungary, Persia, and Arabia under Turkish rule. The Turkish fleet, under BARBAROSSA, became the scourge of the Mediterranean. Despite Sulayman's reforms, Turkey remained a medieval state, and decline set in at his death. The Turkish fleet was destroyed (1571) at Lepanto, and other military defeats followed. Succession to the throne was a continuing problem; fratricide was common within the royal family, and later heirs were protected in luxurious isolation until they assumed the throne. Actual rule fell to the grand viziers, often hereditary, like the KÖPRÜLÜ family, and to the elite JANISSARIES. Corruption and bribery were rampant. Serious disintegration began in the 18th cent. with the RUSSO-TURKISH WARS and continued with the loss of Greece and Egypt in the early 19th cent., when Turkey became known as the Sick Man of Europe. The Western powers feared Russian expansion (see EASTERN QUESTION) and loss of their commercial arrangements. Those arrangements had, in fact, gradually caused the Ottoman Empire to lose its economic independence and to rely almost wholly on foreign capital and loans. An attempt to reform the Turkish government was made with a new constitution in 1876, but this failed when the sultan abolished the constitution. After 1908 the Young Turks, a reformist and nationalist group, were increasingly important. Turkey lost most of its remaining European territories in the BALKAN WARS (1912–13), and World War I confirmed its disintegration. Turkey sided with the losing Central Powers, and in 1918 the peace treaties ending the war formally dissolved the Ottoman Empire. In 1922 Kemal ATATÜRK overthrew the last sultan, and the history of modern Turkey began.

Otto the Great: see Otto I under OTTO, rulers of the Holy Roman Empire.

Ouagadougou or **Wagadugu** [both: wägədōō'gōō], city (1985 pop. 442,223), capital of Burkina Faso. It is a communications and economic center, as well as the market for an agricultural region. The city has rail connections with Côte d'Ivoire and road links with Niger. Founded in the late 11th cent. as the capital of the Mossi empire, it was a center of Mossi power until captured (1896) by the French.

Oudh, historic region of India: see INDIAN MUTINY.

Ouida [wē'də], pseud. of **Louise de la Ramée,** 1839–1908, English novelist. Her many sentimental romances include *Under Two Flags* (1867) and, for children, *A Dog of Flanders* (1872).

Ouwe, Hartmann von: see HARTMANN VON AUE.

ovary: see REPRODUCTIVE SYSTEM.

Overland Park, city (1990 pop. 111,790), Johnson co., NE Kansas, a residential suburb of Kansas City; inc. 1960. A rapidly growing city, it has profited from the regional growth and development in the Kansas City metropolitan area.

over-the-counter, method of buying and selling securities outside the standard STOCK EXCHANGE. The over-the-counter (OTC) market is composed of thousands of far-flung stock and bond dealers and brokers who negotiate most transactions by computer or telephone. For the most part, dealers purchase securities for their own accounts and sell them at a markup. Prices of many U.S. OTC issues are quoted on NASDAQ (National Association of Securities Dealers Automated Quotations), a computerized system.

over-the-counter drugs: see PATENT MEDICINE.

overture, instrumental musical composition written as an introduction to an OPERA, BALLET, ORATORIO, MUSICAL, or play. Early examples were simply symphonic pieces, but by C.W. von GLUCK's time it began to foreshadow what was to come in the opera. In many 19th-cent. operas and 20th-cent. musicals, the overture is a potpourri of the work's music. The concert overture is a composition in one movement.

Ovid (Publius Ovidius Naso) [ŏv'ĭd], 43 B.C.–A.D. 18, Latin poet. His highly perfected elegiacs fall into three groups—erotic poems, mythological poems, and, after he was banished to the Black Sea for unknown reasons in A.D. 8, poems of exile. The love poems include *Amores, Letters from Heroines,* and *The Art of Love.* His masterpiece *Metamorphoses,* in hexameters, is his major mythological work. *Fasti* is on myths connected with days of the year; *Tristia* is on the sorrows of exile. Ovid was a major source of inspiration for the RENAISSANCE.

ovum, in biology, specialized female plant or animal sex cell, also called the egg. In higher animals the ovum differs from the SPERM (male sex cell) in that it is larger and nonmotile. Its nucleus contains the CHROMOSOMES, which bear the hereditary material of the parent. Ova are produced in the ovary of the female; they undergo a maturation process that includes MEIOSIS, by which the number of their chromosomes is reduced by half. The union of mature sperm and ovum (see FERTILIZATION), with each bearing half the normal number of chromosomes, results in a single cell (the zygote) with a full number of chromosomes. The zygote eventually becomes a mature individual. The pattern is similar in plants that reproduce sexually. The term *egg* also refers to a complex structure, such as a bird's egg, in which the ovum is swollen with yolk (food material) and the rest of the egg is secreted around the ovum. Development from an unfertilized ovum is called PARTHENOGENESIS. See also REPRODUCTION; REPRODUCTIVE SYSTEM.

Owen, Robert, 1771–1858, British social reformer, a pioneer in the cooperative movement. In 1800 he began to convert old mills in New Lanark, Scotland, into a model industrial town, instigating reforms later reflected in the Factory Act of 1819. Believing that individual character is molded by environment and can be improved in a society based on cooperation, he founded several self-sufficient cooperative agricultural-industrial communities, including, in the U.S., NEW HARMONY, Ind. (1825). His son, **Robert Dale Owen,** 1801–77, b. Scotland, became an American social reformer, the first who publicly advocated BIRTH CONTROL (1830). He was a member of Congress (1843–47) and, in Indiana, secured (1850) extension of property rights for married women and state provision for public schools. After serving (1853–58) as U.S. minister to Naples, he became an active ABOLITIONIST.

Owen, Wilfred, 1893–1918, English poet. Owen, who died on the French front in World War I, wrote of the horror and pity of war in verse that transfigured traditional meter and diction. Siegfried SASSOON published 24 of Owen's poems posthumously (1920).

Owen Glendower, 1359?–1416?, Welsh leader. In 1400 he revolted against HENRY IV of England. Allying himself with the Percy family and with France, he had some military success and summoned (1405) his own parliament, but by 1409 the English had rendered him powerless.

Owens, Jesse, 1913–81, African-American track star; b. Alabama. While at Ohio State Univ. he broke (1935–36) several world records. At the 1936 Olympics in Berlin, Owens upset Hitler's "Aryan" theories by setting world records in the broad jump and the 200-meter race and equaling the record in the 100-meter race. His fourth gold medal came in the 400-meter relays.

owl, nocturnal BIRD of prey found worldwide, belonging to the families Tytonidae and Strigidae. Owls resemble short-necked HAWKS, except that their eyes are directed forward and surrounded by disks of radiating feathers. Their eyes are specially adapted to seeing in partial darkness, and most sleep during the day. Owls' soft, fluffy plumage makes them almost noiseless in flight. They feed on rodents, frogs, insects and small birds. Many usurp the deserted nests of other birds; others live in burrows.

ox: see CATTLE.

oxalis or **wood sorrel,** plant (genus *Oxalis*), usually with cloverlike leaves that respond to darkness by folding back their leaflets. Most cultivated forms are tropical herbs. Wild North American species include the white wood sorrel (*O. acetosella*), a plant identified as the SHAMROCK. True sorrel is a plant of the BUCKWHEAT family.

Oxenstierna, Count Axel Gustaffson, 1583–1654, Swedish statesman. Named chancellor in 1612, he was Sweden's real administrator because GUSTAVUS II was occupied with foreign wars. Oxenstierna tried to keep Sweden out of the THIRTY YEARS WAR. After Gustavus II died in battle (1632) he unified the German Protestant princes and secured France's entry into the war. As leader of the council of regency (1632–44) in the minority of CHRISTINA, Gustavus's daughter, he was virtual ruler of Sweden. He wrote the constitution of 1634, centralizing administration, and directed the war with Denmark (1643–45), in which Sweden gained several Danish provinces. Clashes with Christina diminished his power. After her abdication (1654), which he had opposed, he served her successor, CHARLES X.

Oxford, Edward de Vere, 17th **earl of,** 1550–1604, English poet. An actor, producer, and court writer, he is believed by some to have written SHAKESPEARE's plays.

Oxford, city (1991 pop. 110,103), Oxfordshire, S central England. It is famous as the seat of Oxford Univ. (est. 12th cent.). In its suburbs automobiles and steel products are manufactured. During the civil wars (17th cent.) Oxford was the royalist headquarters. It has many historic buildings, including the Ashmolean Museum and the Bodleian Library (see LIBRARY, table).

Oxford, Provisions of: see PROVISIONS OF OXFORD.

Oxford and Asquith, Herbert Henry Asquith, 1st **earl of,** 1852–1928, British statesman. Entering Parliament as a Liberal in 1886, he supported (1899) the South African War and became prime minister (1908–16). His government put through a social welfare program, including old age pensions (1908) and unemployment insurance (1911), and began a naval buildup. Asquith also secured passage of the Parliamentary Reform Act of 1911, which stripped the House of Lords of its veto power. Dissatisfaction with his leadership in World War I led to his resignation. His second wife, **Margot (Tennant) Asquith,** 1864–1945, was a prominent socialite whose frank autobiography (1920–22) created a sensation.

Oxford Group: see BUCHMAN, FRANK NATHAN DANIEL.

Oxford movement, religious movement begun in 1833 by Anglican clergy at Oxford Univ. to revitalize the Church of England by reviving certain Roman Catholic doctrines and rituals. Among its leaders were J.H. NEWMAN, John KEBLE, and R.H. Froude. Under Newman a series of pamphlets, *Tracts for the Times* (1833–41), were issued that preached Anglicanism as a via media between Catholicism and evangelicalism. The group then became known as Tractarians. Newman's *Tract 90* on the Thirty-nine Articles aroused a storm of controversy and brought the series to an end. The movement began to lose valuable supporters to Roman Catholicism, including Newman and H.E. MANNING. Its leadership passed to E.B. PUSEY, and opponents dubbed the movement "Puseyism." Its clergy, known as Anglo-Catholics, adopted innovations, such as chanting prayers, wearing vestments, and using elaborate ritual within the services. For these actions they were often labeled ritualists. This revival of ceremonial customs caused much public agitation, but the movement exerted a great influence on doctrine, spirituality, and liturgy in the ANGLICAN COMMUNION. It was responsible for the revival of Anglican religious communities and, through an emphasis on social concern, was an antecedent of CHRISTIAN SOCIALISM.

Oxford University, at Oxford, England. One of the world's most prestigious universities, it had its beginnings in the early 12th cent. Its system of residential colleges dates from the mid-13th cent., when University, Balliol, and Merton colleges were founded. Oxford was a leading center of learning in the Middle Ages. There are 35 colleges. Its Ashmolean Museum and Bodleian Library (see LIBRARY, table) are renowned. Oxford's Rhodes scholarships for foreign students were initially financed by a gift from Cecil RHODES.

oxidation and reduction, complementary chemical reactions characterized by the loss or gain, respectively, of one or more electrons by an atom or molecule. When an atom or a molecule combines, or forms a chemical bond, with oxygen, it tends to give up electrons to the oxygen. Similarly, when it loses oxygen, it tends to gain electrons. Oxidation is defined as any reaction involving a loss of electrons, and reduction as any reaction involving the gain of electrons. The two processes, oxidation and reduction, occur simultaneously and in chemically equivalent quantities; the number of electrons lost by one substance is equaled by the number of electrons gained by another substance. The substance losing electrons (undergoing oxidation) is said to be an electron donor, or a reductant. Conversely, the substance gaining electrons (undergoing reduction) is said to be an electron acceptor, or an oxidant. Common reductants (substances readily oxidized) are the active METALS, CARBON, CARBON MONOXIDE, HYDROGEN, hydrogen sulfide, and sulfurous acid. Common oxidants (substances readily reduced) include the HALOGENS, NITRIC ACID, OXYGEN, OZONE, potassium permanganate, potassium dichromate, and concentrated SULFURIC ACID. See also ANTIOXIDANT.

Oxnard, city (1990 pop. 142,216), S Calif., on the Pacific coast; inc. 1903. Its economy, formerly based on agriculture, mining, and military bases, is growing increasingly industrial and commercial. A navy missile range is nearby. Oxnard is the gateway to an island and forest resort area.

oxygen (O), gaseous element, first isolated (c.1773–74) independently by Joseph PRIESTLEY and Karl SCHEELE. A colorless, odorless, tasteless gas, it is the most abundant element on earth, constituting about half of the surface material. It makes up about 90% of water, two-thirds of the human body, and 20% by volume of air. Normal atmospheric oxygen is a diatomic gas (O_2). OZONE is a highly reactive triatomic (O_3) allotrope of oxygen (see ALLOTROPY). Oxygen forms compounds with almost all of the elements except the inert gases. The common reaction in which it unites with another substance is called oxidation (see OXIDATION AND REDUCTION). The burning of substances in air is rapid oxidation, or combustion. The RESPIRATION of plants and animals is a form of oxidation essential to the liberation of the energy stored in such food materials as carbohydrates and fats. Chief industrial uses are in STEEL production (e.g., in the BESSEMER PROCESS) and the oxyacetylene torch (see ACETYLENE); in medicine it is used to treat respiratory diseases. Liquid oxygen is used in rocket fuel systems. See ELEMENT (table); PERIODIC TABLE.

Oxyrhyncus, excavation site in Upper Egypt, now Behnesa. Important papyrus finds there (1896–97, 1906–7) retrieved lost Greek literary classics, chiefly in Roman and Byzantine scrolls dating from the 1st cent. B.C. to the 10th cent. A.D.

oyster, BIVALVE mollusk found in beds in the shallow, warm waters of all oceans. Except in the free-swimming larval stage, oysters spend their lives attached to substrates of rocks, shells, or roots by means of a cementlike secretion. The pearl oyster, from which the PEARL is obtained, is a large (12-in./30.5-cm) tropical species. The edible American, or common, oyster is harvested commercially in artificial beds on the U.S. coast.

Oz, Amos, 1939–, Israeli novelist. Richly atmospheric and often incorporating elements of fantasy, his novels usually treat the conflicts and tensions in Israeli life. They include *Elsewhere Perhaps* (1966), *My Michael* (1968), *Touch the Water, Touch the Wind* (1973), *A Perfect Peace* (1985), *Black Box* (1988), and *To Know a Woman* (1989).

Ozarks, the, or **Ozark Plateau,** forested upland region, c.50,000 sq mi (129,500 sq km), mostly in Missouri and Arkansas. Referred to locally as mountains, the Ozarks rise prominently from surrounding plains to more than 2,000 ft (600 m) in the rugged Boston Mts. The economy is based on agriculture, lead and zinc mining, and tourism, with subsistence farming and household crafts remaining as features of life in the more isolated areas.

Ozawa, Seiji, 1935–, Japanese conductor, the first prominent in the West. He led the Toronto Symphony (1965–70) and the San Francisco Symphony (1970–76), and was named music director of the Boston Symphony in 1973.

ozone, triatomic OXYGEN (O_3). Pure ozone is an unstable, faintly bluish gas with a characteristic fresh, penetrating odor. It is the most chemically active form of oxygen. Ozone is formed in the OZONE LAYER of the stratosphere (see ATMOSPHERE) by the action of solar ultraviolet light on oxygen; this layer plays an important role in preventing most ultraviolet and other high-energy radiation, which is harmful to life, from penetrating to the earth's surface. Ozone in the lower atmosphere is a pollutant that can damage lung tissue. It is produced by chemical or electrical processes, as when an electric discharge, such as lightning or from electric motors, passes through the air. Commercially, ozone is used as a disinfectant and decontaminant for air and water, as a bleaching agent, and in the production of azelaic acid (used in making plastics). Ozone is manufactured by passing dry air between two electrodes connected to an alternating high voltage.

ozone layer or **ozonosphere,** region of the stratosphere (see ATMOSPHERE) containing relatively high concentrations of OZONE, located at altitudes of 12–30 mi (19–48 km) above the earth's surface. The ozone layer prevents most ultraviolet (UV) and other high-energy radiation from penetrating to the earth's surface but allows sufficient UV to support the activation of vitamin D in humans to reach the earth. The full radiation, if unhindered by this filtering effect, would destroy animal tissue. Ozone in the ozone layer is formed by the action of solar ultraviolet light on oxygen. In 1974 scientists warned that certain industrial chemicals, e.g., CHLOROFLUOROCARBONS (CFCs), HALONS, and carbon tetrachloride, could migrate to the stratosphere where sunlight could free their chlorine atoms to form chlorine monoxide, which would deplete upper-atmospheric ozone. A seasonal decrease, or "hole," discovered in 1985 in the ozone layer above Antarctica was the first confirmation of a thinning of the layer; by 1993 the region of diminished ozone was nearly the size of North America and reached to S South America and S Australia. Less dramatic decreases have been found above other areas of the world, including the U.S. In 1987 an international agreement was reached on reducing the production of ozone-depleting compounds. Revisions in 1992 called for an end to the production of most of such compounds by 1996, and CFC emissions had dropped dramatically by 1993. Recovery of the ozone layer, however, is expected to take 50 to 100 years. Damage to the ozone layer can also be caused by sulfuric acid droplets produced by volcanic eruptions.

P

P, chemical symbol of the element PHOSPHORUS.

Pa, chemical symbol of the element PROTACTINIUM.

Pabst, G(eorg) W(ilhelm), 1885–1967, German film director; b. Austria. He used MONTAGE in such works of social realism as *The Joyless Street* (1925), *Pandora's Box* (1929), *Westfront 1918* (1930), and *The Threepenny Opera* (1931).

PAC: see POLITICAL ACTION COMMITTEE.

pacemaker, artificial, device used to stimulate a rhythmic heartbeat by means of electrical impulses. Implanted in the body when the heart's own electrical conduction system does not function normally, the battery-powered device emits impulses that trigger heart-muscle contraction at a rate preset or controlled by an external remote switch.

Pacific, War of the, 1879–84, fought between CHILE and the allied nations of PERU and BOLIVIA. It began when Bolivia rescinded (1879) a contract with a Chilean company to mine nitrates in its territory and Chile, in reprisal, seized the Bolivian port of Antofagasta. Peru was drawn into the war by a defensive alliance with Bolivia. Chilean forces conquered (1879) a Peruvian border province, gained control of the sea, and entered (1881) Lima in triumph. The treaty of Ancón (1883) assigned Bolivia's only coastal territory, Atacama (now Antofagasta), to Chile. By the truce at VALPARAISO (1884) Peru ceded Tarapacá and control of Tacna and Arica provinces to Chile; eventually, Chile returned (1929) Tacna to Peru.

Pacific Islands, Trust Territory of the, former trust territory administered by the U.S., consisting of c.2,180 islands and islets spread out over the W Pacific Ocean in the area generally known as MICRONESIA. The islands were seized by Japan from Germany in 1914, occupied by the U.S. in 1944 during WORLD WAR II, and made a trusteeship in 1947. As the result of negotiations for termination of the trusteeship, the NORTHERN MARIANAS gained U.S. commonwealth status in 1978, and three other self-governing units, under the military protection of the U.S., were established: PALAU, the Federated States of MICRONESIA, and the MARSHALL ISLANDS. The trusteeship was dissolved in 1990, but Palau remained a trust territory pending resolution of a disagreement with the U.S. over a nuclear-free provision in its proposed constitution.

Pacific Ocean, world's largest ocean, c.70,000,000 sq mi (181,300,000 sq km), occupying about one third of the earth's surface between the west coasts of North and South America and the east coasts of Australia and Asia. It has a maximum length of c.9,000 mi (14,500 km), a maximum width of c.11,000 mi (17,700 km), and a maximum depth of 36,198 ft (11,033 m) in the Challenger Deep, in the Marianas Trench c.250 mi (400 km) SW of Guam. A series of volcanoes, the so-called Ring of Fire, rims the ocean. Along the eastern shore there is a narrow continental shelf, and high mountains rise abruptly from a deep sea floor. The Asian coast is low and fringed with islands rising from a wide continental shelf.

Pacific Rim, nations bordering the Pacific Ocean, and the island countries situated in it. Asian Pacific Rim countries grew significantly in economic and political importance during the 1980s and 90s. Many Pacific Rim nations, including the U.S., are members of the Asia-Pacific Economic Cooperation (est. 1989).

Pacific scandal, 1873, charges that Canadian Prime Min. John MACDONALD had received campaign funds by promising a railroad contract to Sir Hugh Allan's syndicate. Although MacDonald denied the charges, his government resigned, and the Conservative party lost the 1873 election.

pacifism, opposition to war through individual or collective action. Motivated by religious or humanitarian impulses, pacifism is often connected with international cooperation toward the goal of disarmament. Local peace societies were founded in the U.S. (1815) and Britain (1816), and the first international peace congress met (1843) in London. The movement was advanced during the late 1800s by the work of the Frenchman Frédéric PASSY and others and was publicized through the establishment (1901) of the NOBEL PRIZE for peace. The horrors of World War I gave it new vigor after 1920, when it was influenced by both the LEAGUE OF NATIONS and GANDHI's effective practice of nonviolent (or passive) resistance. The number of British and American CONSCIENTIOUS OBJECTORS grew in World War II. In the 1960s and 70s, U.S. pacifists were in the forefront of the opposition to the VIETNAM WAR.

Paderewski, Ignace Jan [pădˈˈərĕfˈskē], 1860–1941, Polish pianist, composer, and statesman. His playing won him a reputation exceeding that of any performer since LISZT. An ardent patriot, he headed Polish governments in 1919 and 1940–41 (in exile). He died in the U.S. pleading Poland's cause. The Minuet in G for piano is his best-known work.

Padua, city (1990 pop. 220,358), in Venetia, NE Italy. A major Roman city, it was an important free commune (12th–14th cent.), then passed to the Carrara family (1318) and to Venice (1405). Its Capella degli Scrovegni has magnificent frescoes (1304–6) by GIOTTO. Among its other treasures are sculptures by DONATELLO and paintings by MANTEGNA, who was born there.

Páez, José Antonio [päˈās], 1790–1873, first president of VENEZUELA (1831–35, 1839–43). He led (1810–19) a guerrilla band and drove the Spanish from their Venezuelan stronghold. A leader of separatism from Colombia, he headed the new state of Venezuela, but he was exiled (1850–58), served as dictator (1861–63), and was exiled again.

Paganini, Niccolò, 1782–1840, Italian violin virtuoso. He extended the violin's compass by employing harmonics, perfected the use of double and triple stops, and revived *scordatura*, diverse tuning of strings. His 24 caprices for violin were adapted for piano by SCHUMANN and LISZT.

Page, Thomas Nelson, 1853–1922, American author; b. Hanover co., Va. His fictional idealizations of the Old South include the stories in *In Ole Virginia* (1887) and the novel *Red Rock* (1898). Page was ambassador to Italy (1913–19).

Pagnol, Marcel [pänyôlˈ], 1895–1974, French dramatist and film director. His is best known for his popular trilogy about Marseilles, *Marius* (1929), *Fanny* (1931), and *César* (1936). He wrote the screenplays for all three and directed *César*.

pagoda, name given in the East to a variety of buildings in tower form, usually part of a temple or monastery, and serving as shrines. The Indian masonry STUPA, chiefly pyramidal, is elaborately decorated with carvings or sculpture. The Chinese pagoda, of Indian origin, is hexagonal, octagonal, or square in plan. It is built in as many as 15 superimposed stories. From each story an upward-curving tile roof projects. Brick, faced with tiles, is the most common material. Japanese pagodas, usually square and five-storied, are made of wood and exhibit superb carpentry craftsmanship. See also CHINESE ARCHITECTURE; JAPANESE ARCHITECTURE.

Pago Pago town, (1990 pop. 10,640), capital of AMERICAN SAMOA.

Pahari [pəhäˈrē], languages or dialects of the Indic group of the Indo-Iranian subfamily of the Indo-European family of languages. See LANGUAGE (table).

Pahlavi language [päˈləvēˈ] or **Pehlevi language** [pāˈ–], member of the Iranian group of the Indo-Iranian subfamily of the Indo-European family of languages. It is also called Middle Persian. See LANGUAGE (table).

Paige, (Leroy) "Satchel," 1906?–1982, African-American baseball player; b. Mobile, Ala. Celebrated for his wit and extraordinary pitching ability, he became legendary while barnstorming in the Negro baseball leagues prior to the integration (1947) of the major

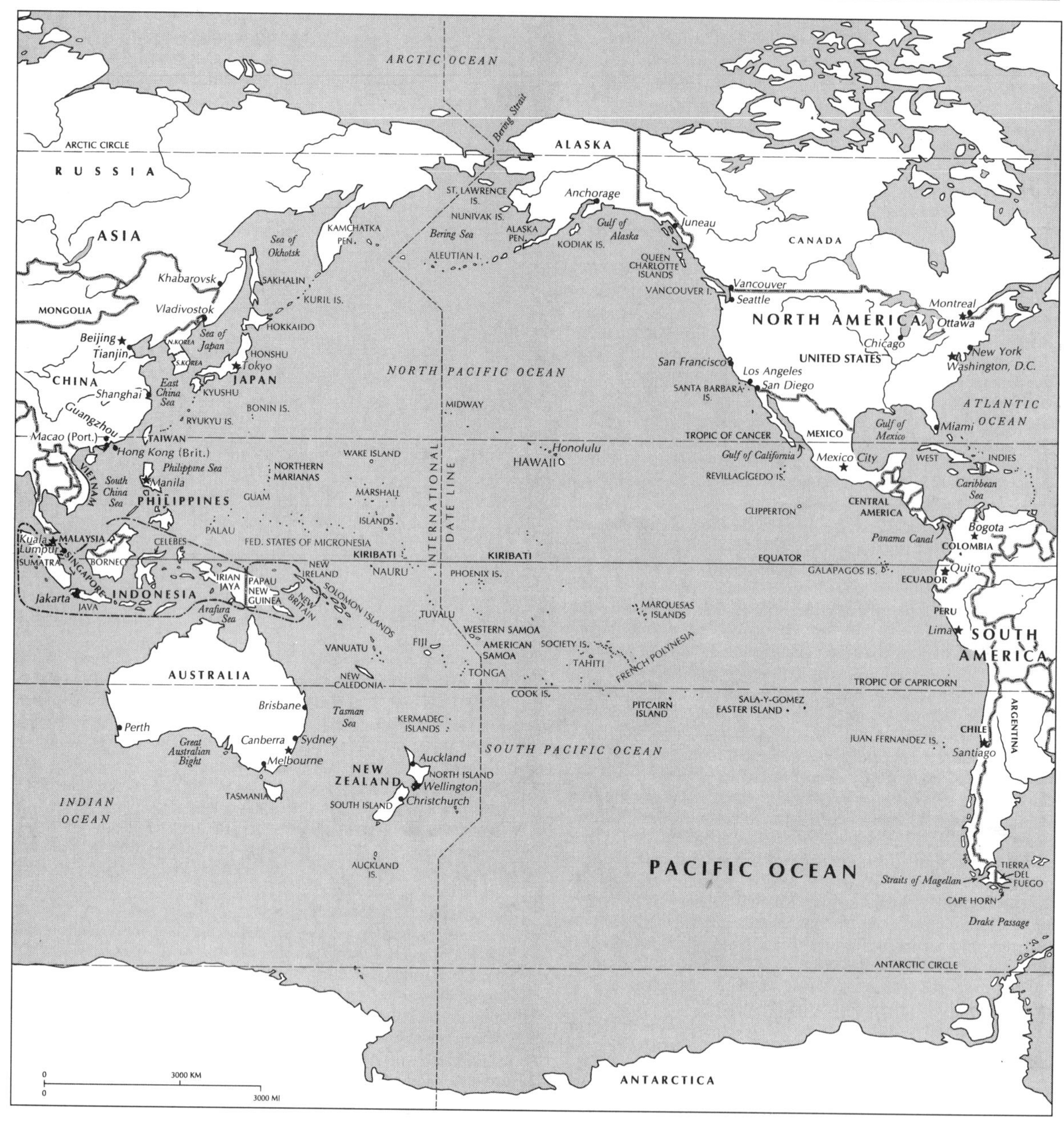

leagues, playing in as many as 2,500 games and being credited with more than 50 no-hitters. In 1948, when he was over 40, he joined the Cleveland Indians of the American League. He pitched for six seasons in the majors and was the first star of the Negro leagues to be inducted (1971) into the Baseball Hall of Fame.

Paine, Thomas, 1737–1809, Anglo-American political theorist and writer; b. England. In 1774 he emigrated to America, where he wrote (1776) the successful pamphlet *Common Sense.* During the AMERICAN REVOLUTION he began a series of 16 pamphlets (1776–83), *The Crisis.* In *The Rights of Man* (two parts, 1791, 1792), written in England, he defended the French Revolution in reply to Edmund BURKE, arguing that only democratic institutions can guarantee natural rights. To escape prosecution for treason in England, he fled to Paris, where he became a member of the National Convention and was imprisoned (1793–94) during the Reign of Terror. He wrote his deistic work *The Age of Reason* (2 parts, 1794, 1795) at this time. He returned to the U.S. in 1802.

Paiute, indigenous people of the Plateau (see NORTH AMERICA, INDIGENOUS PEOPLES OF), with a Uto-Aztecan language of the Aztec-Tanoan stock (see NATIVE AMERICAN LANGUAGES). The warlike Northern Paiute ranged over parts of California, Nevada, and Oregon; they fought miners and settlers in the 1860s. To the south lived the Southern Paiute, sometimes called Digger Indians because they lived on roots. In general, the Paiute subsisted by hunting, fishing, and root digging, and lived in wickiups (see TEPEE). The GHOST DANCE originated (c.1870) with them, and the prophet WOVOKA was a Paiute. Today many northern and southern Paiutes remain on reservations, living chiefly on agriculture and the sale of crafts. In 1990 there were 11,142 Paiutes in the U.S.

Pakistan, officially Islamic Republic of Pakistan, republic (1993 est. pop. 120,800,000), 310,403 sq mi (803,944 sq km), S Asia, on the NW corner of the Indian subcontinent, bordered by India (E), the Arabian Sea (S), Iran (SW), and Afghanistan (W and N). The capital is ISLAMABAD; other important cities are KARACHI, LAHORE, and RAWALPINDI. Pakistan may be divided into four geographic regions: an arid plateau in the west; alluvial plains in the east; hills and fertile valleys in the northwest; and high mountains of the HINDU KUSH, HIMALAYA, and Karakorum ranges in the north. The INDUS R. runs

the length of the country. Agriculture is the mainstay of the economy, with wheat, rice, cotton, and sugarcane the principal crops. Vast irrigation projects and the use of fertilizers have increased output, and the country is now self-sufficient agriculturally. The production of textiles, consumer goods, cement, and fertilizers, as well as oil refining and metal processing, are important components of Pakistan's expanding industrial base. The people are a mixture of many ethnic groups, with the Punjabis the most numerous; Pathan tribes in the northwest and Baluchis in the west have pressed for autonomous states. Islam is by far the dominant religion. Urdu is the official language, but English and Punjab, Pashto, Baluchi, and other ethnic languages are spoken.

History. The area that is now Pakistan was the site of the INDUS VALLEY CIVILIZATION, the earliest known culture on the Indian subcontinent. The territory's location placed it on the historic route from central Asia to India, and for thousands of years invaders, including Aryans, Persians, Alexander the Great, Seleucids, and Parthians, swept down on the settlements there. Muslim Arabs established themselves in S. India in A.D. 712. They were followed by Turks, who gained control of N India in the 12th and 13th cent. What is now Pakistan was part of the MOGUL empire, but at the end of the 18th cent., the Punjab region came under control of the SIKHS. The region was under British control from 1830 to 1850. The MUSLIM LEAGUE, founded in 1906 and led by Muhammad Ali JINNAH from 1916, demanded establishment of a separate Muslim state. Finally, in 1947, under the provisions of the Indian Independence Act, Pakistan—consisting of East Bengal (renamed East Pakistan in 1955) and West Pakistan, separated by 1,000 mi of Indian territory—became a separate, independent dominion, with Jinnah as governor-general. The new state faced precarious economic conditions. In addition, dissension with India, particularly over KASHMIR, was immediate and violent (see INDIA-PAKISTAN WARS), and strife between Hindus and Muslims was widespread. In 1956 Pakistan formally became a republic, but in 1958 the constitution was abrogated and martial law imposed under Gen. Muhammad AYUB KHAN, who was elected president in 1960. Under his dictatorship, a vigorous land reform and economic development program was begun, but after disastrous riots in 1968 and 1969 he resigned in favor of Gen. Agha Muhammad YAHYA KHAN. Almost from its inception, Pakistan was plagued by tension between East Pakistan, which had the majority of the population, and West Pakistan, which dominated the army and federal government. In May 1971, after the government's refusal to recognize the election victory of Sheikh Mujibur Rahman's Awami League, which advocated autonomy for East Pakistan, East Pakistan declared independence as BANGLADESH. In the ensuing civil war, West Pakistan was quickly defeated with the aid of Indian troops. Political turmoil continued in Pakistan (the former West Pakistan), and opposition to Zulfikar Ali BHUTTO, who had become president after the war, became intense. In 1977 an army coup placed Gen. Muhammad ZIA UL-HAQ in the office of president; Bhutto was arrested and later (1979) hanged. Zia died in a suspicious plane crash in 1988. A few months later the opposition Pakistan People's party won a parliamentary majority, and its leader, Benazir BHUTTO, daughter of Zulfikar Ali Bhutto, became prime minister and the first female leader of a Muslim country. In 1990 Pres. Ghulam Ishaq Khan dismissed Bhutto, charging corruption and mismanagement. In new elections her party lost its majority, and Nawaz Sharif became head of a coalition government. When he moved to reduce presidential power, he was dismissed (1993) by Ishaq Khan, precipitating a crisis that led to the resignations of both Sharif and Ishaq Khan. Bhutto's party won the most seats in new elections, and she became prime minister of a coalition government. Farooq Leghari, a Bhutto ally, was elected president.

palaeo-. For words beginning thus, see also PALEO-.

Palaeologus, ruling Greek dynasty of the Byzantine Empire, 1261–1453. Its emperors included MICHAEL VIII, Andronicus II, JOHN V, JOHN VII, JOHN VIII, and CONSTANTINE XI. Noted for learning, the family helped the Greeks to retain their culture under Turkish rule.

Palatinate [pəlăt'ĭnāt"], two regions of Germany. The Rhenish or Lower Palatinate is a district of the state of Rhineland-Palatinate. The Upper Palatinate is a district in NE Bavaria. Holy Roman Emperor FREDERICK I bestowed (1156) the title count palatine on his half-brother Conrad, who held lands E and W of the Rhine. In 1214 the Palatine passed to the Bavarian WITTELSBACH dynasty, whose holdings near Bohemia were constituted as the Upper Palatinate. In 1356 the counts palatine were confirmed as electors. The Rhenish Palatine became a center of the German REFORMATION, and the choice of Elector Frederick V (see FREDERICK THE WINTER KING) as king of Bohemia precipitated the THIRTY YEARS WAR. Both the Rhenish Palatinate and the Upper Palatinate eventually became parts of Bavaria. In 1946 the Rhenish Palatinate became part of the new state of Rhineland-Palatinate.

Palau or **Belau,** officially Republic of Belau, self-governing Micronesian island group (1992 est. pop. 15,800), c.192 sq mi (497 sq km), in the W Pacific Ocean at the extreme western end of the Caroline Islands, until 1990 part of the U.S. Trust Territory of the PACIFIC ISLANDS. It consists of c.200 small islands (8 are inhabited), of which Babelthuap (the largest and future site of the capital) and Koror (the capital) are the most important. Subsistence farming is the basis of the economy; there is some commercial fishing. Most of the population is Micronesian. Palauan is the official language, but English is also spoken. Roman Catholicism and Protestantism are the predominant religions.

History. Spain held the islands for about 300 years and sold them to Germany in 1899. Japan seized them in WORLD WAR I, administered them as a mandate for the League of Nations, and in WORLD WAR II used them as a major naval base. U.S. forces captured the islands in 1944, and in 1947 they became part of the trust territory. Voters approved (1979) a local constitution, and the islands became (1981) self-governing. Palau is the last UN trust territory because voters had not approved a compact of free association with the U.S. by the necessary 75% majority, but in a new plebiscite (1993) that required only a majority vote, the compact was approved. Kuniwo Nakamura became president of Palau in 1993. See PACIFIC OCEAN map.

Palembang, city (1990 pop. 1,141,036), capital of South Sumatra prov., on SE Sumatra, Indonesia. A deepwater port, it is one of the island's largest cities, and the trade and shipping center for the S SUMATRA oil fields. There are large oil refineries, textile mills, fertilizer factories, and food-processing plants. The Dutch began trading there in 1617, and abolished its sultanate in 1825.

Paleocene epoch: see GEOLOGIC ERA (table).

Paleolithic art, art of the most recent ice age. Knowledge of this art is largely confined to works discovered at 150 sites in W Europe, particularly to the magnificent cave paintings in N Spain and the Dordogne R. valley of SW France. Most of these works were produced during two overlapping periods. The Aurignacio-Perigordian (c.14,000–c.13,500 B.C.) includes the Lascaux cave paintings, the outdoor sculpture at Laussel, and several small, abnormally voluptuous female figures called Venuses, e.g., the Venus of Willendorf, Austria. The Solutreo-Magdalenian (c.14,000–c.9500 B.C.) includes the murals at Rouffignac and Niaux, and the ceiling of the cave at Altamira, Spain. The painting styles ascribed to CRO-MAGNON MAN embrace a variety of techniques, which include painting with fingers, sticks, pads of fur or moss; daubing; dotting; sketching with colored material and charcoal; and spray-painting through a hollow bone or by mouth. In most paleolithic caves animal figures predominate, suggesting ritual significance. Drawn with the vitality and elegance of great simplicity, they are the masterpieces of prehistoric art. See also ROCK CARVINGS AND PAINTINGS.

Paleolithic period: see under STONE AGE.

paleontology: see FOSSIL.

Paleozoic era: see GEOLOGIC ERA (table).

Palermo, city (1990 pop. 731,418), capital, largest city, and chief port of Sicily, Italy. Manufactures include textiles, processed food, and ships. A Phoenician town founded between the 8th and 6th cent. B.C., and a Carthaginian base, it was taken by Rome (153 B.C.). Later rulers included Byzantines (535–831), Arabs (831–1072), and Normans (1072–1194), whose legacies are visible in its art and architecture.

Palestine, historic region on the eastern shore of the Mediterranean Sea, comprising parts of modern Israel, Jordan, and Egypt; also known as the Holy Land. This article discusses the physical geography and history of Palestine until the UN took up the Palestine problem in 1947; for the economy and later history, see GAZA STRIP, ISRAEL, JORDAN, and WEST BANK. Palestine is the Holy Land of the Jews, promised to them by God according to the Bible; of the Christians because it was the scene of Jesus' life; and of the Muslims because Jerusalem is the traditional site of Muhammad's ascent to heaven. Palestine comprises three geographic zones: a part of the GREAT RIFT VALLEY, a ridge, and a coastal plain. The earliest known settlements in Palestine, e.g., JERICHO, may date from c.8000 B.C. An independent Hebrew kingdom was established c.1000 B.C. After c.950 B.C. this kingdom broke up into two states, Israel and Judah. Assyrians, Babylonians, Persians, Greeks, and Romans in turn conquered Palestine, which fell to the Muslim Arabs by A.D. 640. The area was the focus of the CRUSADES and was conquered by the Ottoman Turks in 1516. By the late 19th cent., ZIONISM arose with the aim of establishing a Jewish homeland in Palestine, and during World War I the British, who captured the area, appeared to support this goal. After the League of Nations approved (1922) the British mandate of Palestine, Jews immigrated there in large numbers despite Arab opposition. There was tension and violence between Jews and Arabs, and the British, unable to resolve the problem, turned (1947) the Palestine question over to the UN. See also ARAB-ISRAELI WARS; PALESTINE LIBERATION ORGANIZATION.

Palestine Liberation Organization (PLO), coordinating council for PALESTINE refugee groups, recognized (1974) by the UN and the Arab states as the government of the Palestinians. Founded in 1964, it has been dominated by the Al Fatah guerrilla group of Yasir ARAFAT. The PLO regarded ISRAEL as an illegal country and committed itself to establishing a Palestinian state, using guerrilla and terrorist attacks to achieve its goal. In 1982 the PLO was weakened when, after the Israeli siege of BEIRUT, Lebanon (see ARAB-ISRAELI WARS), PLO guerrillas in West Beirut were dispersed to other Arab countries. In 1988 the PLO responded to the Palestinian uprising, or *intifada*, in the WEST BANK and GAZA STRIP by proclaiming the establishment of an independent Palestinian state. The PLO also equivocally recognized Israel's right to exist and renounced terrorism. After Iraq's invasion of Kuwait in 1990, the PLO sided with Iraq, alienating the Saudis and Persian Gulf states that had long funded it. In 1991, with PLO agreement, Palestinians participated in peace talks with Israel. Secret negotiations between the PLO and Israel led (1993) to mutual recognition and an accord that called for limited Palestinian self-rule in Jericho and the Gaza Strip.

Palestrina, Giovanni Pierluigi da, c.1525–1594, Italian composer. He was undisputed master of the MASS, of which he wrote 105, for four, five, six, and eight parts. His other works included MOTETS, MADRIGALS, magnificats, offertories, litanies, and settings of the Song of Songs.

Pali [pä'lē], language belonging to the Indic group of the Indo-Iranian subfamily of the Indo-European family of languages. See LANGUAGE (table).

Palissy, Bernard [pälēsē'], c.1510–c.1589, French potter. Palissy created a widely imitated pottery, admired for smooth glazes in richly colored enamels. He is noted for pieces reproducing scriptural and mythological subjects and for rustic pieces with forms copied from nature.

Palladio, Andrea [päl-lä'dēō], 1508–80, Italian Renaissance architect. His measured drawings of ROMAN ARCHITECTURE, with plans of his own and a treatise based on Vitruvius, the Roman writer, were published in *The Four Books of Architecture* (1570). Palladio's formally classic buildings were mainly palaces and villas in or near Vicenza. The country houses displayed a classic temple front, and the ground plan had a central hall surrounded by rooms in absolute symmetry. Noted examples (1550s–60s) are the Villa Rotunda, Chiericati Palace, and Villa Barbaro. At Venice, Palladio adapted the classical motif to three famous church facades—San Francesco della Vigna, San Giorgio Maggiore, and Il Redentore. Palladio's works greatly influenced English architecture, through Inigo JONES and others. In the U.S., this influence can be seen in the manor houses of southern plantations, e.g., Thomas Jefferson's MONTICELLO.

palladium (Pd), metallic element, discovered in 1803 by William WOLLASTON. It is a lustrous, corrosion-resistant, silver-white metal with a great ability to absorb hydrogen. Major uses are in alloys used in low-current electrical contacts, jewelry, and dentistry and in automobile catalytic converters. See ELEMENT (table); PERIODIC TABLE.

palm, common name for the Palmae, or the Arecaceae, a large family of chiefly tropical trees, shrubs, and vines. Most species are trees, typified by a crown of compound leaves (fronds) terminating a tall, woody, unbranched stem. The fruits, covered with a tough, fleshy, fibrous, or leathery outer layer, usually contain a large amount of stored food. Important economically, especially in the tropics, palms, e.g., COCONUT and DATE palms, provide food and other products. Important palm fibers are raffia and RATTAN. **Palm oil** is fat pressed from the fruit, principally that of the coconut palm, African oil palm (genus *Elaeis*), and some other species. The oils are widely used in soap, candles, lubricants, margarine, fuel, and other products.

Palma: see MAJORCA.

Palme, Olof [päl'mə], 1927–86, Swedish political leader, prime minister (1969–76, 1982–1986). Head of the Socialist Social Democratic party, he led Sweden's rejection (1971) of European Community membership and was critical of U.S. policy in Vietnam. In 1982 Palme again became prime minister after his party won the parliamentary elections. Four years later he was assassinated by an unknown gunman.

Palmer, Arnold, 1929–, American golfer; b. Latrobe, Pa. Winner of seven major championships, he popularized golf with his victories in the 1960s. Cheered on by "Arnie's army," as his fans were known, he was the first golfer to win four Masters titles (1958, 1960, 1962, 1964). He also captured the U.S. Open (1960) and British Open (1961–62) and became the first golfer to reach $1 million in earnings.

Palmerston, Henry John Temple, 3d **Viscount,** 1784–1865, British statesman. As foreign secretary (1830–34, 1835–41, 1846–51), he supported liberal constitutionalism at home and abroad. Twice prime minister (1855–58, 1859–65), he vigorously prosecuted the CRIMEAN WAR, facilitated the unification of Italy, and suppressed the INDIAN MUTINY. His diplomacy, though reckless, advanced British prestige.

Palm Springs, city (1990 pop. 40,181), S Calif.; founded 1876, inc. 1938. It is a desert oasis and fashionable resort. The Spanish knew it as Agua Caliente (because of its hot springs) as early as 1774.

Palm Sunday: see LENT.

Palmyra, ancient city of central Syria, NE of Damascus, traditionally founded by SOLOMON. A trade center, it gradually expanded and became a powerful state after the Romans established control (A.D. c.30). Its ambitious queen, Zenobia, provoked a Roman expedition (A.D. 272), which partly destroyed Palmyra. The city declined, and after being sacked by TIMUR, it fell into ruins.

Palomar Observatory, astronomical observatory located at an altitude of 5,500 ft (1,680 m) on Palomar Mt., NE of San Diego, Calif., and operated by the California Institute of Technology. Its primary instrument is the 200-in. (500-cm) Hale reflector, which was the largest in the world at the time of its completion (1948). Its 48-in. (120-cm) Schmidt camera telescope was used to prepare a monumental photographic atlas of about three fourths of the entire sky.

pampas, c.300,000 sq mi (777,000 sq km), grassy plains of temperate S South America, extending from the **Pampa** (c.250,000 sq mi/647,500 sq km) of central and N Argentina into Uruguay. Livestock and wheat are produced in the drier west, while corn and more intensive forms of agriculture predominate in the more populous and humid east. BUENOS AIRES is the main shipping point. The Pampa is associated with the gaucho, the Argentine cowboy.

Pan, in Greek mythology, pastoral god of fertility; worshiped principally in ARCADIA. He was depicted as a merry, ugly man with a goat's horns, ears, and legs. All his myths deal with his amorous affairs. He came to be associated with the Greek DIONYSUS and the Roman FAUNUS, both fertility gods.

Panama, Span. *Panamá,* officially Republic of Panama, republic (1992 est. pop. 2,530,000), 29,209 sq mi (75,650 sq km), on the Isthmus of Panama, which connects Central and South America; bordered by Costa Rica (E), the Caribbean Sea (N), Colombia (W), and the Pacific Ocean (S). The capital is PANAMA City; other large cities are Colón and David. There are mountains in the east and west, and lowlands along both coasts. The PANAMA CANAL, which cuts through low hills in the central area, bisects the country. The nation has varied industries and promising mineral deposits, but its exports (bananas, shrimp and fish products, sugar, and coffee) lag far behind its imports. The canal provides 25% of national income and much employment. The country has become a link in the illegal Colombian drug trade and a center for drug-related financial transactions. Panama is a Spanish-speaking, Roman Catholic country; the population is of diverse descent, with a mestizo majority.

History. Spaniards founded settlements on the north coast before 1513, when Vasco Núñez de BALBOA crossed the isthmus and discovered the Pacific. This discovery—the short distance from sea to sea—has dominated Panama's history ever since. Soon the isthmus became the route by which gold from PERU reached the Atlantic in colonial times; later it was crossed by U.S. gold prospectors traveling to California after 1849. Long a part of COLOMBIA, in 1903 Panama—supported by the U.S., which wanted to build a canal across the isthmus—revolted and became a separate republic. The Panama Canal was completed in 1914. Internal politics have been stormy, with many changes of administration. In 1969 a left-leaning regime was established, dominated until his death in 1981 by Gen. Omar TORRIJOS HERRERA. After much agitation and prolonged negotiations, the U.S. turned over the Canal Zone to Panama in 1979 and agreed to eventual (1999) Panamanian control of the canal itself. When U.S. grand juries indicted Gen. Manuel NORIEGA, the de facto ruler of Panama, for narcotics smuggling, tensions increased between the two nations. The U.S. invaded Panama in Dec. 1989, captured Noriega, and brought him to Florida for trial. Guillermo Endara Galimany, who had been defrauded of victory (May 1989) in the presidential election, became president with U.S. support.

Panama, city (1990 pop. 411,549), central Panama, capital of Panama, on the Gulf of Panama, at the Pacific entrance to the PANAMA CANAL. Panama's largest city, a financial center, and industrial hub, in Spanish colonial days it was the Pacific port for transshipment of Andean gold. The city prospered with the building of the canal (1904–14) and grew rapidly after World War II.

Panama Canal, waterway across the Isthmus of Panama, connecting the Atlantic (by way of the CARIBBEAN SEA) and Pacific oceans. It was built by U.S. military engineers in 1904–14 across land leased from the Republic of PANAMA. The eradication of malaria and yellow fever in the area was a vital accomplishment. The canal is 51 mi (82 km) long, has six locks, and traverses two natural lakes, one of which is 85 ft (26 m) above sea level. With the development after 1950 of supertankers and other ships too large to navigate the canal, it lost some of its earlier strategic importance. The **Panama Canal Zone** (553 sq mi/1,432 sq km) extended 5 mi (8 km) on either side of the canal and was administered by the U.S. until 1979, when it was turned over to Panama under the terms of two U.S.-Panamanian treaties narrowly ratified (1978) by the U.S. Senate. At the end of 1999 control of the canal itself is to pass to

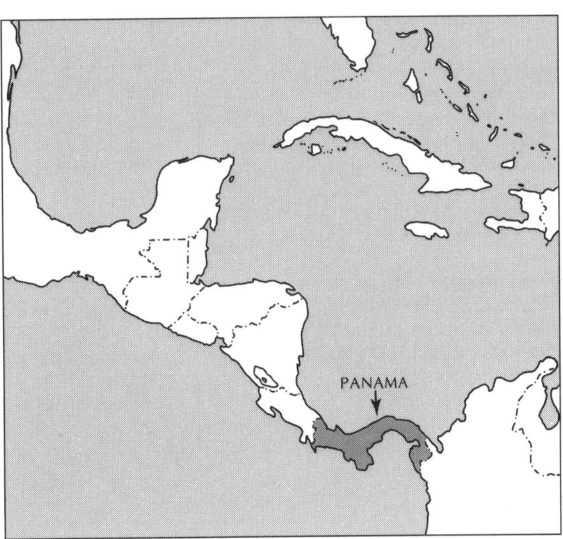

Panama, with that nation guaranteeing the neutral operation of the canal.

Pan-American Union: see ORGANIZATION OF AMERICAN STATES.

Panathenaea: see ATHENA.

Panchatantra, anonymous collection of Sanskrit animal fables, probably compiled before A.D. 500. Derived from Buddhist sources and intended for the instruction of sons of royalty, the prose fables are interspersed with aphoristic verse.

pancreas, glandular organ of the DIGESTIVE SYSTEM that secretes digestive ENZYMES and HORMONES. In humans, the pancreas is a yellowish organ that lies crosswise beneath the stomach and is connected to the small intestine at the duodenum. It produces trypsin, amylase, and lipase—enzymes essential to the digestion of proteins, carbohydrates, and fats, respectively. Small groups of cells in the pancreas, called islets of Langerhans, contain several types of specialized cells: alpha-2 cells, which produce the hormone GLUCAGON; beta cells, which produce the hormone INSULIN; and alpha-1 cells, which produce somatostatin, all of which regulate blood-sugar levels.

panda, two nocturnal Asian MAMMALS, the red panda (*Ailurus fulgens*) and giant panda (*Ailuropoda melanoleuca*). The red panda, or lesser panda, resembles a RACCOON and is found in the Himalayas and the mountains of W China and N Myanmar. The giant panda resembles a BEAR, although it is anatomically more like a raccoon; it lives in the high bamboo forests of central China. Its body is mostly white, with black limbs, ears, and eye patches; adults weight from 200 to 300 lb (90 to 140 kg). Low reproduction rates and human encroachment on its habitat have seriously endangered the giant panda.

Pandora, in Greek mythology, first woman on earth. ZEUS ordered her creation as vengeance on man and his benefactor, PROMETHEUS, to whose brother Epimetheus he sent her. Zeus gave her a box that he forbade her to open. She disobeyed and let out all the world's evils. Only hope remained in the box.

Pangaea: see CONTINENTAL DRIFT; PLATE TECTONICS.

panic, financial and economic crisis, marked by public loss of confidence in the financial structure. Panics are characterized by runs on banks and a rapid fall of the securities market, and bank failures and bankruptcies typically ensue. Perhaps the earliest panic of modern capitalism occurred in France and England in 1720, touched off by wild speculation in the stock of John LAW's colonizing company. The first real panic in the U.S. came in 1819. Others were to occur in 1837, 1857, 1869 (see BLACK FRIDAY), 1873, 1907, 1929 (when the stock-market crash precipitated a worldwide financial crisis and led to the GREAT DEPRESSION), and 1987 (see BLACK MONDAY). Banking instability, historically a major contributor to panics, became less of a threat in the U.S. with the founding of the FEDERAL DEPOSIT INSURANCE CORPORATION (FDIC) in 1933.

Panizzi, Sir Anthony [pänēt'sē], 1797–1879, English librarian; b.

Italy. He was chief librarian at the BRITISH MUSEUM (1856–67). His 91 rules (1839) became the basis of the museum's catalog. Panizzi enforced the act requiring deposition at the museum of all books copyrighted in Great Britain.

Pankhurst, Emmeline Goulden, 1858–1928, English woman suffragist. She founded (1903) the Women's Social and Political Union and urged extreme militancy in the furtherance of women's rights. In 1912–13 she was repeatedly arrested and imprisoned. During World War I she turned her energies from the women's movement to the war effort. She was nationally revered at the time of her death.

Panmunjom, village, in the demilitarized zone between North and South Korea. In the KOREAN WAR negotiations were moved to Panmunjom in Oct. 1951 and the truce was signed on July 27, 1953.

Panofsky, Erwin, 1892–1968, one of the most important American art historians of the 20th cent.; b. Germany. Particularly interested in iconography, he wrote classic studies of medieval, Renaissance, mannerist, and baroque art. His many books include *Studies in Iconology* (1939), *Albrecht Dürer* (1943), and *Early Netherlandish Painting* (1953).

pansy: see VIOLET.

Pantanal, lowland region of SW Brazil. The world's largest wetland, the Pantanal is part of the floodplain of the Paraguay R. and its tributaries. Swampy during the rainy season, it has lush grasslands during the six months it is dry.

pantheism [Gr. *pan* = all, *theos* = God], any system of belief or speculation that identifies the universe with GOD. Some pantheists view God as primary and the universe as a finite and temporal emanation from God; others see nature as the great, inclusive unity. The various types of pantheism have religious, philosophical, scientific, and poetic bases. HINDUISM is a noteworthy form of religious pantheism; philosophical pantheism is most completely represented in the monistic system of SPINOZA.

pantheon, term applied originally to a temple to all the gods. The **Pantheon,** Rome (built 27 B.C., destroyed, and rebuilt in the 2d cent. A.D. by HADRIAN), is of brick with a great hemispherical dome. In 609 it became a Christian church. The term is now applied to a monument in which the illustrious dead are buried. The Panthéon, Paris, designed by J.G. Soufflot, was built between 1764 and 1781. Several times secularized and reconsecrated, it became a national mausoleum.

panther, name commonly applied to black LEOPARDS, a color variant of the leopard, not a distinct species. The generic name *Panthera* refers to all big roaring cats.

pantomime or **mime,** silent drama using movement, gesture, and facial expression to develop a story. Although pantomime dates from ancient times, its traditional characters (e.g., Columbine and Harlequin) have their origin in the 16th-cent. Italian COMMEDIA DELL'ARTE. Popular modern pantomimists include Charlie CHAPLIN and Marcel MARCEAU.

Paoli, Pasquale [päˈōlē], 1725–1807, Corsican patriot. In 1755 he led a revolt against Genoese rule and was chosen president of CORSICA under a republican constitution. Genoa sold its rights to Corsica to the French, who defeated Paoli in 1769. He then fled to England. During the FRENCH REVOLUTION he was named (1791) governor of Corsica, but he opposed the radical turn of the revolution and with British aid drove (1794) the French from the island. A British protectorate was proclaimed, but Paoli was disappointed in his hope of becoming viceroy. In 1795 he went to England, where he died. The Corsicans, with help from the French, expelled the British in 1796.

papacy, office of the pope, head of the ROMAN CATHOLIC CHURCH. The pope is bishop of Rome and thus, according to Roman Catholic belief, the successor of St. PETER, the first bishop of the see of Rome (the Holy See). The pope claims to be head of all Christianity and the representative of Jesus Christ, a claim not accepted by the ORTHODOX EASTERN CHURCH and Protestant churches. Roman Catholics believe in papal INFALLIBILITY. On the death of a pope, a new pope is elected by the college of CARDINALS in a secret conclave. Election requires a two-thirds vote plus one. Early popes, such as CLEMENT I, asserted their right to guide the church, and with the decline of the Roman Empire in the West, the pope became an important political leader. With the founding (756) of the Papal States, the pope became a secular ruler as well. The papacy was surrounded by corruption in the 10th cent., but after the reforms of GREGORY VII in the 11th cent., the popes had great prestige. By the end of the 12th cent. INNOCENT III attempted with some success to assert his claims as arbiter of all lay affairs. In the 14th cent. the papal see was moved by CLEMENT V to Avignon and came under French control (the Babylonian captivity) from 1309 to 1378. The papacy's return to Rome was followed by the Great SCHISM (1378–1417), in which there were two or three rival popes at one time, a contest ended by the Council of CONSTANCE. In the 15th cent. the popes were characterized by worldly rule in Italy, patronizing Renaissance art, and forwarding family fortunes. This spiritual apathy led to the Protestant REFORMATION. Reform within the church followed the election of PAUL III (see REFORMATION, CATHOLIC). The loss (1870) of the Papal States proved in the end to be a boon (see LATERAN TREATY) since it made the pope perforce a purely ecclesiastic ruler with great spiritual and moral influence. He now governs only the tiny state of VATICAN CITY. The election of JOHN PAUL II of Poland in 1978 broke the long line of Italian popes that dated from the 16th cent.

Papadopoulos, George, 1919–, Greek colonel and political leader. He headed the military junta that overthrew the government in 1967. He became premier and ruled over an authoritarian government. In 1973 he abolished the monarchy and became president. He was overthrown by another military junta later that year.

Papago: see TOHONO O'ODHAM.

Papal States, from 754 to 1870 the territory under temporal rule of the popes. In 1859 the area included c.16,000 sq mi (41,440 sq km). In 754 the papacy received extensive lands in central Italy, including RAVENNA, from PEPIN THE SHORT. Papal rule in these areas was often negligible, but in the 16th cent. Pope JULIUS II consolidated papal power. NAPOLEON I conquered the Papal States in 1796, but they were restored to the pope in 1815. During the RISORGIMENTO most of the Papal States joined (1860) Sardinia and became part of the new kingdom of Italy. The rest of the area came under French protection. The fall of NAPOLEON III in France allowed Italy to seize (1870) the remaining territory, including Rome. The status of Rome was not settled until the LATERAN TREATY (1929) created VATICAN CITY.

Papandreou, George, 1888–1968, Greek political leader, premier (1964–65). In 1961 he formed the Center Union party and in 1964 he became premier. The next year he was removed from office by King CONSTANTINE II, thereby setting off the chain of events that resulted in the so-called colonels' coup (1967) and the abolition (1973) of the monarchy. His son, **Andreas Papandreou,** 1919–, held U.S. citizenship for a time (1944–64) but gave it up to serve in the Greek parliament and as an aide to his father. He was imprisoned after the 1967 coup and later exiled. In exile he formed what later became the Panhellenic Socialist Movement (Pasok). He returned to Greece after the fall (1974) of the junta and later served as Greece's first socialist premier (1981–89). After leaving office he was tried and acquitted on charges of instigating the loss of government funds and accepting bribes. He became premier again in 1993.

Papen, Franz von, 1879–1969, German diplomat and politician. In 1932 he was named chancellor, but he was unable to assemble enough support, and Kurt von Schleicher quickly succeeded him. His manipulations behind the scenes brought HITLER to power (1933). He served briefly as vice chancellor in Hitler's cabinet and as his ambassador to Turkey (1939–44). In 1946 the Nuremberg tribunal acquitted him of war crimes; he was convicted (1947) by a German "denazification court," although the sentence was later rescinded.

paper, thin, flat sheet usually made from plant fiber. It was probably invented c.105 in China, where it was made from a mixture of bark and hemp. The Moors introduced the papermaking process into Spain c.1150, and by the 15th cent., when PRINTING developed in Europe, paper mills had spread throughout the Continent. The basic papermaking process exploits the ability of plant cell fibers to bond together when a pulp made from the fibers is spread on a screen and dried. Today, paper is made principally from wood pulp combined with pulps from waste paper or, for fine grades of paper, with fibers from cotton rags. For newsprint, tissue, and

CHRONOLOGY OF POPES

In the following list the date of election, rather than of consecration, is given. Before St. Victor I (189), dates may err by one year. Antipopes—i.e., those whose elections have been declared uncanonical—are indicated.

St. Peter, d. 64? or 67?
St. Linus, 67?-76?
St. Cletus, or Anacletus, 76?-88?
St. Clement I, 88?-97?
St. Evaristus, 97?-105?
St. Alexander I, 105?-115?
St. Sixtus I, 115?-125?
St. Telesphorus, 125?-136?
St. Hyginus, 136?-140?
St. Pius I, 140?-155?
St. Anicetus, 155?-166?
St. Soter, 166?-175?
St. Eleutherius, 175?-189?
St. Victor I, 189-99
St. Zephyrinus, 199-217
St. Calixtus I, 217-22
antipope: St. Hippolytus, 217-35
St. Urban I, 222-30
St. Pontian, 230-35
St. Anterus, 235-36
St. Fabian, 236-50
St. Cornelius, 251-53
antipope: Novatian, 251
St. Lucius I, 253-54
St. Stephen I, 254-57
St. Sixtus II, 257-58
St. Dionysius, 259-68
St. Felix I, 269-74
St. Eutychian, 275-83
St. Caius, 283-96
St. Marcellinus, 296-304
St. Marcellus I, c.308-309
St. Eusebius, 309-c.310
St. Miltiades, or Melchiades, 311-14
St. Sylvester I, 314-35
St. Marcus, 336
St. Julius I, 337-52
Liberius, 352-66
antipope: Felix, 355-65
St. Damasus I, 366-84
antipope: Ursinus, 366-67
St. Siricius, 384-99
St. Anastasius I, 399-401
St. Innocent I, 401-17
St. Zosimus, 417-18
St. Boniface I, 418-22
antipope: Eulalius, 418-19
St. Celestine I, 422-32
St. Sixtus III, 432-40
St. Leo I, 440-61
St. Hilary, 461-68
St. Simplicius, 468-83
St. Felix III (or II), 483-92
St. Gelasius I, 492-96
Anastasius II, 496-98
St. Symmachus, 498-514
antipope: Lawrence, 498-505
St. Hormisdas, 514-23
St. John I, 523-26
St. Felix IV (or III), 526-30
Boniface II, 530-32
pope or antipope: Dioscurus, 530
John II, 533-35
St. Agapetus I, 535-36
St. Silverius. 536-37
Vigilius, 537-55
Pelagius I, 556-61
John III, 561-74
Benedict I, 575-79
Pelagius II, 579-90
St. Gregory I, 590-604
Sabinian, 604-6
Boniface III, 607
St. Boniface IV, 608-15
St. Deusdedit, or Adeodatus I, 615-18
Boniface V, 619-25
Honorius I, 625-38
Severinus, 640
John IV, 640-42
Theodore I, 642-49
St. Martin I, 649-55
St. Eugene I, 654-57
St. Vitalian, 657-72
Adeodatus II, 672-76
Donus, 676-78
St. Agatho, 678-81
St. Leo II, 682-83
St. Benedict II, 684-85
John V, 685-86
Conon, 686-87
antipope: Theodore, 687
antipope: Paschal, 687
St. Sergius I, 687-701
John VI, 701-5
John VII, 705-7
Sisinnius, 708
Constantine, 708-15
St. Gregory II, 715-31
St. Gregory III, 731-41
St. Zacharias, 741 -52
Stephen II, 752 (never consecrated)
Stephen II (or III), 752-57
St. Paul I, 757-67
antipope: Constantine, 767-69
antipope: Philip, 768
Stephen III (or IV), 768-72
Adrian I, 772-95
St. Leo III, 795-816
Stephen IV (or V), 816-17
St. Paschal I, 812-24
Eugene II, 824-27
Valentine, 827
Gregory IV, 827-44
antipope: John, 844
Sergius II, 844-47
St. Leo IV, 847-55
Benedict III, 855-58
antipope: Anastasius, 855
St. Nicholas I, 858-67
Adrian II, 867-72
John VIII, 872-82
Marinus I, 882-84
St. Adrian III, 884-85
Stephen V (or VI), 885-91
Formosus, 891-96
Boniface VI, 896
Stephen VI (or VII), 896-97
Romanus, 897
Theodore II, 897
John IX, 898-900
Benedict IV, 900-903
Leo V, 903
antipope: Christopher 903-4
Sergius III, 904-11
Anastasius III, 911-13
Lando, 913-14
John X, 914-28
Leo VI, 928
Stephen VII (or VIII), 928-31
John XI, 931-35
Leo VII, 936-39
Stephen VIII (or IX), 939-42
Marinus II, 942-46
Agapetus II, 946-55
John XII, 955-64
Leo VIII, 963-65, or Benedict V, 964-66, *(one of these was an antipope)*
John XIII, 965-72
Benedict VI, 973-74
antipope: Boniface VII, 974, 984-85
Benedict VII, 974-83
John XIV, 983-84
John XV, 985-96
Gregory V, 996-99
antipope: John XVI, 997-98
Sylvester II, 999-1003
John XVII, 1003
John XVIII, 1004-9
Sergius IV, 1009-12
Benedict VIII, 1012-24
antipope: Gregory, 1012
John XIX, 1024-32
Benedict IX, 1032-44
Sylvester III, 1045
Benedict IX, 1045
Gregory VI, 1045-46
Clement II, 1046-47
Benedict IX, 1047-48
Damasus II, 1048
St. Leo IX, 1049-54
Victor II, 1055-57
Stephen IX (or X), 1057-58
antipope: Benedict X, 1058-59
Nicholas II, 1059-61
Alexander II, 1061-73
antipope: Honorius II, 1061-72
St. Gregory VII, 1073-85
antipope: Clement III, 1080-1100
Victor III, 1086-87
Urban II, 1088-99
Paschal II, 1099-1118
antipope: Theodoric, 1100
antipope: Albert, 1102
antipope: Sylvester IV, 1105-11
Gelasius II, 1118-19
antipope: Gregory VIII, 1118-21
Calixtus II, 1119-24
Honorius II, 1124-30
antipope: Celestine II, 1124
Innocent II, 1130-43
antipope: Anacletus II, 1130-38
antipope: Victor IV, 1138
Celestine II, 1143-44
Lucius II, 1144-45
Eugene III, 1145-53
Anastasius IV, 1153-54
Adrian IV, 1154-59
Alexander III, 1159-81
antipope: Victor IV, 1159-64
antipope: Paschal III, 1164-68
antipope: Calixtus III, 1168-78
antipope: Innocent III, 1179-80
Lucius III, 1181-85
Urban III, 1185-87

CHRONOLOGY OF POPES *(Continued)*

Gregory VIII, 1187 Clement III, 1187-91 Celestine III, 1191-98 Innocent III, 1198-1216 Honorius III, 1216-27 Gregory IX, 1227-41 Celestine IV, 1241 Innocent IV, 1243-54 Alexander IV, 1254-61 Urban IV, 1261-64 Clement IV, 1265-68 Gregory X, 1271-76 Innocent V, 1276 Adrian V, 1276 John XXI, 1276-77 Nicholas III, 1277-80 Martin IV, 1281-85 Honorius IV, 1285-87 Nicholas IV, 1288-92 St. Celestine V, 1294 Boniface VIII, 1294-1303 Benedict XI, 1303-4 Clement V, 1304-14 John XXII, 1316-34 *antipope:* Nicholas V, 1328-30 Benedict XII, 1334-42 Clement VI, 1342-52 Innocent VI, 1352-62 Urban V, 1362-70 Gregory XI, 1370-78 THE GREAT SCHISM, 1378-1417 Roman Line Urban VI, 1378-89	Boniface IX, 1389-1404 Innocent VII, 1404-6 Gregory XII, 1406-15 Avignon Line *antipope:* Clement VII, 1378-94 *antipope:* Benedict XIII, 1394-1423 *antipope:* Clement VII, 1423-29 *antipope:* Benedict XIV, 1425-30 Pisan Line *antipope:* Alexander V, 1409-10 *antipope:* John XXIII, 1410-15 Martin V, 1417-31 Eugene IV, 1431-47 *antipope:* Felix V, 1439-49 Nicholas V, 1447-55 Calixtus III, 1455-58 Pius II, 1458-64 Paul II, 1464-71 Sixtus IV, 1471-84 Innocent VIII, 1484-92 Alexander VI, 1492-1503 Pius III, 1503 Julius II, 1503-13 Leo X, 1513-21 Adrian VI, 1522-23 Clement VII, 1523-34 Paul III, 1534-49 Julius III, 1550-55 Marcellus II, 1555 Paul IV, 1555-59 Pius IV, 1559-65 St. Pius V, 1566-72 Gregory XIII, 1572-85 Sixtus V, 1585-90 Urban VII, 1590 Gregory XIV, 1590-91	Innocent IX, 1591 Clement VIII, 1592-1605 Leo XI, 1605 Paul V, 1605-21 Gregory XV, 1621-23 Urban VIII, 1623-44 Innocent X, 1644-55 Alexander VII, 1655-67 Clement IX, 1667-69 Clement X, 1670-76 Innocent XI, 1676-89 Alexander VIII, 1689-91 Innocent XII, 1691-1700 Clement XI, 1700-1721 Innocent XIII, 1721-24 Benedict XIII, 1724-30 Clement XII, 1730-40 Benedict XIV, 1740-58 Clement XIII, 1758-69 Clement XIV, 1769-74 Pius VI, 1775-99 Pius VII, 1800-1823 Leo XII, 1823-29 Pius VIII, 1829-30 Gregory XVI, 1831-46 Pius IX, 1846-78 Leo XIII, 1878-1903 St. Pius X, 1903-14 Benedict XV, 1914-22 Pius XI, 1922-39 Pius XII, 1939-58 John XXIII, 1958-63 Paul VI, 1963-78 John Paul I, 1978 John Paul II, 1978-

other inexpensive papers, the pulp is prepared mechanically, by grinding the wood. Chemical pulp is made by boiling a mixture of wood chips with either soda, sulfite, or sulfate, a process that removes lignin. The pulp is poured onto a wire screen, where the water drains away and the fibers begin to mat. The paper layer then passes through a series of rollers that dry, press, and smooth it, and add various finishes. Writing papers contain a water-resistant substance such as rosin to prevent the spreading of ink. Kraft paper, made chemically with sulfate, is used for bags and wrapping papers because of its strength.

paper nautilus, mollusk, closely related to the octopus, with a rounded body, eight tentacles, and no fins. It is named for the delicate, papery shell, actually an egg case, that surrounds the egg-brooding female. A CEPHALOPOD found in most warm waters, it is not a true NAUTILUS.

Papineau, Louis Joseph [päpēnō'], 1786–1871, French Canadian insurgent leader. As speaker (1815–37) of Lower CANADA's assembly, he headed the Reform party. Although he was not active in the revolt of 1837, he fled to the U.S. after the rebellion was put down. He later returned (1845) to Canada and served again (1848–54) in the assembly.

Papinian (Aemilius Papinianus) [pəpĭn'ēən], d. 212, Roman jurist. A stern moralist, he became known through his writings, chiefly *Quaestiones* (37 books) and *Responsa* (19 books), as the preeminent figure in ROMAN LAW.

Papp, Joseph, 1921–91, American director and producer; b. Brooklyn, N.Y., as Yosl Papirofsky. A theatrical innovator, he made fine plays available to large and varied audiences through his New York Shakespeare Festival and the Public Theater (since 1992, Joseph Papp Public Theater) in New York City, using income from commercial successes, such as *A Chorus Line* (1975; Tony Award), to support the production of works by lesser-known playwrights. Other major productions included *Hair* (1967), *Sticks and Bones* (1971; Tony Award), and *The Pirates of Penzance* (1980; Tony Award).

paprika: see PEPPER.

Papua New Guinea, officially Independent State of Papua New Guinea, independent Commonwealth nation (1992 est. pop. 4,007,000), 183,540 sq mi (475,369 sq km), SW Pacific Ocean, north of Australia. It includes the eastern half of the mountainous island of NEW GUINEA; the Bismarck Archipelago, including New Britain and New Ireland; Bougainville and Buka, which are part of the Solomon Islands group; and other adjacent islands. PORT MORESBY is the capital and chief port. The climate is monsoonal. Mainstays of Papua New Guinea's developing economy include copper, silver, and gold mining; timber and plywood; and the cultivation of cocoa, coffee, and copra. There is also petroleum; production began in 1992. The native population is largely Melanesian and Papuan but is divided into many distinct cultures. Some 700 languages are spoken, but pidgin English is the *lingua franca.* About half the population is Christian, with Roman Catholics and Lutherans the largest sects; the rest follow traditional beliefs. The nation has a parliamentary government with a governor general, representing the British crown; a prime minister and cabinet; and a unicameral, popularly elected parliament.

History. Papua, the southern region of the country, became a British protectorate in 1884 and in 1905 passed to Australian control as the Territory of Papua. In 1884 Germany took possession of the northern region as Kaiser-Wilhelmsland; the area fell to Australia in World War I and was mandated to that nation in 1920 as the Territory of New Guinea. The two territories were combined in 1949 as the Territory of Papua and New Guinea, and became self-governing in 1973 and independent in 1975. Since 1989 Bougainville has been the scene of fighting between government and secessionist forces. Paias Wingti has been prime minister since 1992.

papyrus, plant (*Cyperus papyrus*) of the SEDGE family, now almost extinct in Egypt but universally used there in antiquity. The roots were used as fuel; the pith was eaten. The stem was used for sandals, boats, twine, mats, and cloth, and, most notably, in a paperlike writing material.

parable, in the BIBLE, term used in the GOSPELS for short illustrative narratives and figurative statements. OLD TESTAMENT parables include the unproductive vineyard (Isa. 5.1–7). Among well-known parables of JESUS are the Good Samaritan (Luke 10.29–37); the hidden treasure (Mat. 13.44); the prodigal son (Luke 15.11–32); the rich man and LAZARUS (Luke 16.19–31); the tares (Mat. 13.24–30, 36–43); and the laborers in the vineyard (Mat. 20.1–16). Parables are also common in the TALMUD.

parabola: see CONIC SECTION.

Paracas, ancient culture of Peru, probably influenced by the earlier culture of CHAVÍN DE HUÁNTAR. The Paracas are known for resin-painted pottery and textiles.

Paracel Islands, S China, group of low coral islands and reefs in the potentially oil-rich SOUTH CHINA SEA, c.175 mi (280 km) SE of Hainan Island. Also claimed by Vietnam and Taiwan, the islands were part of French INDOCHINA prior to WORLD WAR II, when they were occupied by the Japanese. They passed to China in 1945 and are the site of a Chinese airfield.

Paracelsus, Philippus Aureolus, 1493?–1541, Swiss physician and alchemist, originally named Theophrastus Bombastus von Hohenheim. Learned in alchemy, chemistry, and metallurgy, he gained wide popularity, although his contemporaries often opposed him. His work was colored by the fantastic philosophies of the time, but he rejected GALEN's humoral theory of disease; advocated the use of specific remedies for specific diseases (introducing many chemicals, e.g., laudanum, mercury, sulfur, iron, and arsenic); and noted relationships such as the hereditary pattern in syphilis, and the association of cretinism with endemic goiter and of paralysis with head injuries.

parachute, device designed to retard the descent of a falling body by creating drag as it passes through air. A parachute is usually constructed from a flexible material, such as silk, nylon, or Kevlar. A traditional parachute, when extended, has an umbrellalike form, with a series of cords converging down to a harness strapped to the user. A modern parachute is wing-shaped and has control cords that the parachutist can use to turn or even hover. Both can be folded into a small package and thus can be easily carried aboard an aircraft or strapped onto a person's body. The rate of descent for a human-carrying parachute is about 18 ft/sec (5.5 m/sec). The first successful parachute descent from a great height was made in 1797 by the French aeronaut Jacques Garnerin, who dropped 3,000 ft (920 m) from a balloon. Parachutes are used as escape systems for persons aboard aircraft unable to land safely, as braking devices for rockets, space vehicles, airplanes, and high speed surface vehicles, and as a means to land airborne military units and their equipment from transport planes. Parachute jumping for sport is known as skydiving.

paraffin, white, semitranslucent, odorless, tasteless, water insoluble, waxy solid. Though relatively inert, it burns readily in air. A mixture of HYDROCARBONS obtained from PETROLEUM during refining, paraffin is used in candles and for coating paper.

Paraguay [pâr'əgwā, –gwī], officially Republic of Paraguay, republic (1992 est. pop. 4,929,000), 157,047 sq mi (406,752 sq km), S central South America, one of two landlocked nations on the continent, enclosed by Bolivia (N, E), Brazil (W), and Argentina (S, E). The most populous region, between the Paraguay and PARANÁ rivers, is a lowland, rising to a plateau region in the east and north. To the west is a dry plain, part of the GRAN CHACO. Important cities include ASUNCIÓN (the capital), Villarrica, and Concepción. Agriculture and forestry occupy more than half of the labor force. Meat-packing, processing forest products, textile manufacturing, and brewing are the main industries. The population is largely mestizo, a mixture of Spanish and GUARANÍ strains. Spanish is the official language, but Guaraní is widely spoken. Roman Catholicism is the established religion.

History. European influence in Paraguay was introduced with the early explorations of the Río de la PLATA, beginning with Juan Diaz de Solís (1516). A colony founded at Asunción (1536 or 1537) became the center of the La Plata region. The strong rule of Hernando Arias de Saavedra, in the early 1600s, established Paraguay's virtual independence from Spanish administrators in Buenos Aires and Peru; it was also during his tenure that the Jesuit missions, so important in 16th- to 18th-cent. Paraguayan culture, were founded. Full independence from Spain came in 1811, when Paraguay's colonial officials were quietly overthrown. Then followed three great dictators who molded the future of the country: José Gaspar Rodriguez Francia, incorruptible, harsh, autocratic, known as *El Supremo,* kept Paraguay in the palm of his hand from 1814 to 1840; Carlos Antonio López held absolute power from 1844 to 1862; and his son, Francisco Solano LÓPEZ, who ruled from 1862 to 1870, involved Paraguay in a disastrous war (1865–70) with Brazil, Argentina, and Uruguay (see TRIPLE ALLIANCE, WAR OF THE) that cost the nation more than half its population. Recovery was slow, and just as conditions were beginning to improve, Paraguay was plunged into another major war—the Chaco War (1932–35) with Bolivia—from which it emerged victorious but exhausted. A rapid succession of governments followed, ending with the oppressive dictatorship (1940–48) of Higinio Morínigo, finally overthrown in 1948. After another round of short-lived regimes, Gen. Alfredo STROESSNER came to power in 1954. By suppressing opposition, he ruled until 1989, when he was overthrown by a military coup, and Gen. Andrés Rodríguez became president. Rodríguez has slowly permitted the country to move away from its authoritarian past. A promised free presidential election (1993), which Juan Carlos Wasmosy won, was marred by fraud and sabotage.

Paraguay, river, South America, chief tributary of the PARANÁ R. It flows generally south c.1,300 mi (2,090 km) from central Brazil along parts of the Brazil, Paraguay, and Argentine borders. It is a major artery in the Río de la PLATA system and is navigable for most of its length. ASUNCIÓN, Paraguay, is the chief port.

parakeet or **parrakeet,** name for a widespread group of small PARROTS, with generally green plumage, native to the Indo-Malayan region and popular as cage birds. The budgerigar, also called the shell, zebra, or grass, parakeet (*Melopsittacus undulatus*), is the best known of the true parakeets. The extinct Carolina parakeet was the only parrot native to the U.S.

Paralipomenon: see CHRONICLES.

parallax, any alteration in the relative apparent positions of objects produced by a shift in the position of the observer. Stellar parallax is the apparent displacement of a nearby star against the background of more distant stars resulting from the motion of the earth

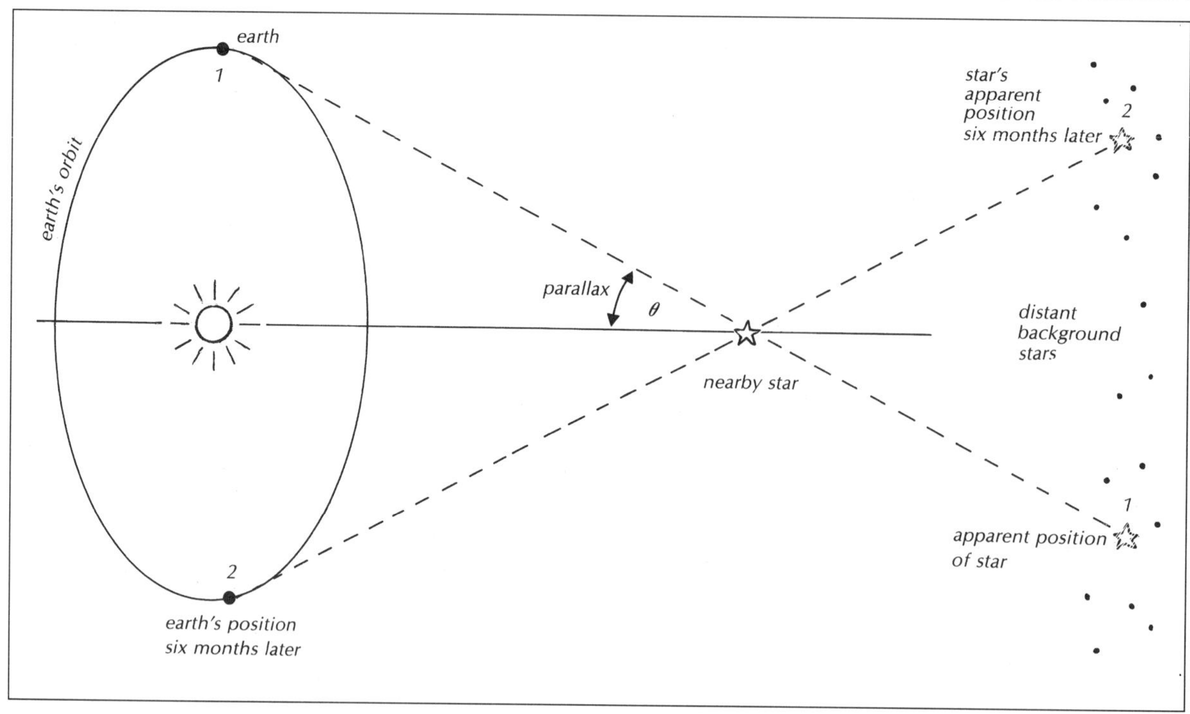

Parallax: A star's trigonometric parallax is a measure of its apparent motion against the background of more distant stars, a motion resulting from the earth's orbit around the sun. To obtain the maximum apparent motion of the star, measurements are made at two points six months apart.

in its orbit around the sun; formally, the parallax of a star is the angle at the star that is subtended by the mean distance (1 ASTRONOMICAL UNIT) between the earth and the sun. A star's distance *d* in PARSECS is thus the reciprocal of its parallax *p* in seconds of arc (or $d = 1/p$). Friedrich BESSEL measured (1838) the first stellar parallax (0.3 seconds of arc for the star 61 Cygni). Geocentric parallax, used to determine the distances of solar system objects, is measured similarly; the diameter of the earth, rather than that of its orbit, however, is used as the baseline.

parallel processing, the concurrent or simultaneous execution of two or more parts of a single COMPUTER PROGRAM, at speeds far exceeding those of a conventional COMPUTER. Parallel processing requires two or more interconnected processors, each of which executes a portion of the task; some supercomputer parallel-processing systems have as many as 256,000 MICROPROCESSORS. The processors access data through shared memory. The efficiency of parallel processing is dependent upon the development of COMPUTER LANGUAGES that optimize the division of the tasks among the processors.

Paramaribo, city (1988 est. pop. 241,000), capital of Suriname, on the Suriname R., 17 mi (27 km) from the Atlantic Ocean. It exports bauxite and agricultural products and produces cement, paint, and beer. Settled in the 1630s by British from Barbados, Paramaribo came under Dutch rule in 1815. Canals give the modern city a Dutch aspect.

paramecium, microscopic, one-celled, slipper-shaped PROTOZOAN. Paramecia are among the most complex single-celled organisms. Found in fresh water, they swim rapidly, usually in a corkscrew fashion, by means of coordinated, wavelike beats of their many short, hairlike projections, called cilia. Paramecia feed on smaller organisms, such as bacteria.

Paraná, river, SE South America. Formed by the confluence of the Paranaíba and Rio Grande rivers in SE Brazil, it flows generally south-southwest c.2,000 mi (3,200 km) to meet the Uruguay R. at the head of the Río de la PLATA estuary, in Argentina. Its major tributary is the PARAGUAY R. It is a major transport artery and has the continent's second largest drainage system.

paranoia, term denoting persistent and logically reasoned false beliefs, or delusions, often of persecution or grandeur (e.g., the belief that one has an important mission). A person with *paranoid disorder,* often known as delusional disorder, may lead a relatively normal life, since most aspects of general behavior are unaffected by the delusional beliefs. In paranoid SCHIZOPHRENIA delusions are sometimes bizarre and are accompanied by hallucinations in the form of voices that make continual remarks on a single theme. Paranoid features also figure in the nondelusional *paranoid personality disorder,* which is marked by unwarranted jealousy, mistrust, and the misconstruing of innocent remarks and gestures as demeaning or threatening.

parapsychology, study of paranormal or psychic phenomena not explainable by accepted principles of science. Scientific methodology in this field dates from the foundation (1882) in London of the Society for Psychical Research, which sought to distinguish psychic phenomena from SPIRITISM and to investigate mediums and their activities. The society studied automatic writing, levitation, and reports of ectoplasmic and poltergeist activity. Modern experiments, notably at Duke Univ. under Joseph Banks Rhine and in Britain and the USSR, have concentrated principally on EXTRASENSORY PERCEPTION (ESP) and psychokinesis (mental influence on physical objects). Scientists differ as to the validity of the results.

Pará rubber tree, large tree (*Hevea brasiliensis*) of the SPURGE family, native to tropical South America and the source of the greatest amount and finest quality of natural RUBBER. The yellow or white latex from which rubber is made occurs in vessels in the bark layers. Trees, which may grow over 100 ft (30 m) high, are tapped for the latex.

parasite, organism that obtains nourishment from another living organism (the host). The host, which may or may not be harmed, never benefits from the parasite. Many parasites have more than one host and most cannot survive apart from their host. Parasites include bacteria (e.g., those causing TUBERCULOSIS), invertebrates such as worms (e.g., TAPEWORM), and vertebrates (e.g., the CUCKOO, which lays its eggs in the nests of other birds).

parathyroid glands, four small endocrine bodies (see ENDOCRINE SYSTEM) behind the THYROID GLAND that govern calcium and phosphorus metabolism. A low calcium ion concentration in the blood causes these glands to produce parathyroid hormone, which increases calcium absorption in the intestines and kidneys and takes calcium salts from the bones. The hormone also decreases the concentration of phosphate ions, which form a relatively insoluble salt with calcium. High parathyroid hormone levels can lead to bone degeneration; low levels lead to calcium deficiency (typified by muscle spasms and, eventually, by convulsions and psychiatric symptoms).

Parcae: see FATES.

parchment, untanned animal skins, especially of sheep, calf, or goat, prepared for use as a writing material. The skins were soaked, scraped, and stretched, then rubbed with chalk and pumice. More durable than the PAPYRUS used in ancient times, parchment was the chief writing material in Europe until the advent of printing brought PAPER into wide use. Vellum is a fine grade of parchment.

Pardo Bazán, Emilia, condesa de [pär'tho bäthän'], 1852–1921, Spanish novelist and critic. In such novels as *The Mayor of Ulloa* (1886) and *Mother Nature* (1887) she introduced NATURALISM into Spanish literature.

Paris, Matthew: see MATTHEW OF PARIS.

Paris, city (1990 pop. 2,152,423; met. area 9,060,257), N central France, the French capital. It is the commercial, financial, and industrial focus of France, a major transportation hub, and a cultural and intellectual center of international renown. A beautiful city in which tourism is the main industry, Paris is cut by the Seine River. On its stately, formal right (northern) bank are many of the most fashionable streets and shops, and such landmarks as the ARC DE TRIOMPHE, Place de la Concorde, LOUVRE, and Sacré Coeur. The left bank houses governmental offices and is the site of much of the city's intellectual life. It is known for its old Latin Quarter and for such landmarks as the Sorbonne, the Luxembourg Palace, the Panthéon, and the modern Pompidou Center. The historic core of Paris is the Île de la Cité, a small island occupied in part by the Palais de Justice and the Cathedral of NOTRE DAME DE PARIS. Above the city rises the EIFFEL TOWER. Paris is divided into 20 *arrondissements* (boroughs) and governed by a mayor. A fishing village when it was conquered (52 B.C.) by CAESAR, it became an important Roman town. It was a Merovingian capital in the 5th cent. and became the national capital with the accession (987) of Hugh Capet, count of Paris. It flowered as the center of medieval commerce and SCHOLASTICISM but suffered severely during the HUNDRED YEARS WAR. Paris consistently displayed a rebellious and independent spirit, as in its resistance to Henry IV (1589–93); the first FRONDE (1648–49); the revolutions of 1789, 1830, and 1848; and the COMMUNE OF PARIS (1871). During WORLD WAR II it was occupied (1940–44) by the Germans, but was relatively undamaged.

Paris or **Alexander,** in Greek mythology, son of Priam and HECUBA. Because of a prophecy that he would destroy Troy, he was abandoned on Mt. Ida, but shepherds rescued him. Later he returned to Troy and was chosen as judge in a dispute among HERA, ATHENA, and APHRODITE. Spurning Hera, who offered him greatness, and Athena, who promised success in war, he awarded the golden apple of discord to Aphrodite, who offered the most beautiful woman in the world. His abduction of that woman, HELEN, caused the TROJAN WAR.

Paris, Congress of, 1856, conference held by Great Britain, France, the Ottoman Empire (Turkey), Sardinia, Russia, Austria, and Prussia to negotiate the peace after the CRIMEAN WAR. In the Treaty of Paris that resulted, Russia was forced back to its prewar borders and was made to accept the neutralization of the Black Sea and the placing of the lower Danube R. under international control. Moldavia and Walachia (later Romania) were given quasi-independence under the suzerainty of Turkey. Turkish integrity was guaranteed, and in return the sultan promised to improve the status of his Christian subjects. The congress also adopted the **Declaration of Paris,** which was the first major effort to codify the international law of the sea. Privateering was banned, contraband was defined and codified, and a blockade was to be legal only when it prevented access to the enemy's coastline. The U.S., which at first rejected the provisions of the declaration, finally accepted them during the Civil War. Technological advances in the 20th cent. (e.g., submarine warfare) made many of the provisions inapplicable.

Paris, Treaty of, any of several important treaties signed at or near Paris, France. **1** The Treaty of 1763 was signed by Great Britain, France, and Spain. Together with the Treaty of Hubertusburg it ended the SEVEN YEARS WAR. France lost Canada to Britain, Cuba and the Philippines were restored to Spain, and India in effect passed to Britain. From this treaty dated the colonial and maritime supremacy of Britain. **2** In the Treaty of 1783 Great Britain formally acknowledged the independence of the Thirteen Colonies as the U.S. The treaty also fixed the boundaries of the new nation. In addition, the warring European powers—Britain against France and Spain, with the Dutch as armed neutrals—effected a large-scale peace settlement. Spain reacquired the Floridas and Minorca from Britain, and Britain relinquished its restrictions on the French port of DUNKIRK. Otherwise, the territorial dispositions of the 1763 Treaty of Paris were reaffirmed. **3** The Treaty of 1814 was concluded between France on the one hand and Britain, Russia, Austria, and Prussia on the other after the first abdication of NAPOLEON I. Its provisions never went into effect owing to the return of Napoleon from Elba and the resumption of the war. **4** The Treaty of 1815 was signed after Napoleon's final surrender. Many provisions of the treaty of 1814 and the Final Act of the Congress of VIENNA remained binding. France was reduced to its 1790 borders and was forced to pay 700 million francs in reparations plus the costs of an army of occupation for five years. **5** For the Treaty of 1856, see PARIS, CONGRESS OF. **6** For the Treaty of 1898, see SPANISH-AMERICAN WAR. After WORLD WAR I several treaties were signed (1919–20) in or near Paris, the most important of which was the Treaty of VERSAILLES. After WORLD WAR II separate treaties were signed (1947) by the Allies at or near Paris with Italy, Romania, Hungary, Bulgaria, and Finland.

Paris, University of, at Paris, France; founded 12th cent. Its first endowed college, opened in 1253 and later called the **Sorbonne,** gained academic and theological distinction during the late Middle Ages and early modern times, the name Sorbonne often being used to designate the university itself. The university was suppressed during the French Revolution and replaced (1808) by a school of the centralized Univ. of France. Reestablished as the Univ. of Paris in 1890, it was divided (1970) into 13 separate, state-supported universities, each with academic autonomy.

Paris Pacts, 1954, four international agreements that recognized the full sovereignty of the Federal Republic of GERMANY (West Germany) and brought to an official end the post-WORLD WAR II occupation of that country. Participants were the former Western Allies. West Germany was permitted to rearm within certain limitations and was accepted into the NORTH ATLANTIC TREATY ORGANIZATION; it also became a member of the newly created WESTERN EUROPEAN UNION. A bilateral agreement between France and West Germany giving "European status" to the SAARLAND was later rejected by the Saarlanders.

Paris Peace Conference, 1919: see VERSAILLES, TREATY OF.

Park Chung Hee, 1917–79, president (1963–79) of South KOREA. Park took part in the military coup of 1961 and was three times elected president. His rule became increasingly dictatorial, and in 1972 he declared martial law. He was assassinated (1979) by Kim Jae Kyu, head of the Korean Central Intelligence Agency.

Parker, Charlie "Bird" (Charles Christopher Parker, Jr.), 1920–55, African-American musician and composer; b. Kansas City, Kans. A brilliant improvising saxophonist, he was, with Dizzy GILLESPIE, a leader of the bop movement in JAZZ.

Parker, Dorothy (Rothschild), 1893–1967, American writer and wit; b. West End, N.J. Her light, ironic verse is contained in such volumes as *Enough Rope* (1926) and *Death and Taxes* (1931). She also wrote satirical, often poignant short stories, e.g., "Big Blonde," collected in *Laments for the Living* (1930) and *Here Lies* (1939).

Parker, Matthew, 1504–75, English prelate, archbishop of Canterbury (1559–75). He was called by Elizabeth I to the see of Canterbury and maintained a distinctly Anglican position between Roman Catholicism and extreme Protestantism. In 1562 he revised the Thirty-nine Articles and later supervised (1563–68) the preparation of the Bishops' Bible.

Parkinson's disease or **Parkinsonism,** degenerative brain disorder initially characterized by trembling lips and hands and muscular rigidity, later producing body tremors, a shuffling gait, and eventually possible incapacity. Emotions may be affected and mental capacity impaired, but assessment of these is difficult because depression often accompanies the disease. The disease occurs when the brain cells that produce dopamine die. In cases where there is no known cause (the majority), it usually appears after age 40 and is referred to as Parkinson's disease. Parkinsonism usually refers to similar symptoms resulting from certain antipsychotic drugs, reserpine (a blood pressure drug), carbon monoxide or manganese poisoning, or MPTP (a heroin byproduct). Symptoms are treated with the drugs deprenyl (selegiline), L-DOPA (given with carbidopa to reduce side effects) and amantadine. Parkinsonism is named for English surgeon James Parkinson, who first described it in 1817.

Parkman, Francis, 1823–93, American historian; b. Boston. He overcame nervous affliction and near-blindness to become a great historian. His *Oregon Trail* (1849) is a popular account of his journey west in 1846. Parkman's many works on the history of Canada and the Northwest are marked by historical accuracy and felicity of expression. They include *Pioneers of France in the New World* (1865), *The Old Régime in Canada* (1874), and *A Half-Century of Conflict* (1892). Parkman was also an accomplished horticulturalist.

Parks, Rosa Lee 1913–, American civil-rights activist; b. Tuskegee, Ala. Her refusal to give up her seat to a white man on a bus in Montgomery, Ala., in 1955, led to a local bus boycott that inspired CIVIL-RIGHTS activists nationwide.

parlement, chief judicial body in France until 1789. The Parlement of Paris grew out of the Curia Regis king's court in the reign (1226–70) of LOUIS IX, and provincial parlements were established from the 15th cent. onward. At first strictly judicial, the parlement gradually gained political power by its function of registering royal edicts before they became law. The parlements joined in the FRONDE (1648–53), an abortive aristocratic revolt against Cardinal MAZARIN. LOUIS XV abolished (1771) them to centralize his political control, but after his death (1774) LOUIS XVI restored the parlements to pacify the privileged classes. In 1787–88 they successfully opposed fiscal reforms and forced Louis XVI to summon the STATES-GENERAL to consider the reforms. As bastions of reaction and privilege, the parlements were abolished early in the FRENCH REVOLUTION.

Parliament, legislative assembly of GREAT BRITAIN. It has evolved into the nation's sovereign power, while the monarchy remains sovereign in name only. Technically, it consists of the monarch, the House of Commons, and the House of Lords, but the term usually refers only to Commons, a democratically elected body of 651 members. The House of Lords is composed of peers and Anglican prelates. Since 1911 its powers have been negligible. The House of Commons is presided over by a nonpartisan speaker elected by Commons, which also elects the PRIME MINISTER; the executive head of government, by modern tradition, must be a member of Commons. The rest of the government's ministers, the CABINET, may be selected from either house. Thus, the executive branch is, in effect, a committee of the legislature. Elections must be held every five years; the prime minister may call elections earlier, although no more frequently than once a year. If the party in power fails to obtain a parliamentary majority on an important issue, it must call a general election. The major parties in Parliament are Conservative, Labour, and the coalition of Social Democrats and Liberals. The origins of Parliament go back to the medieval Curia Regis, or great council, a body of noble and ecclesiastical advisers to the monarch that evolved into the House of Lords. Quasi-legislative, it was primarily a judicial and executive body. In the 13th cent. representatives of the knights and burgesses were also assembled to approve royal acts. Parliamentary power grew slowly in relation to that of the monarchy. During the ENGLISH CIVIL WAR (1642–48) and its aftermath Parliament gained legislative supremacy over taxation and expenditures. Parliamentary sovereignty was permanently affirmed by the GLORIOUS REVOLUTION (1688). Demands for representation by the new classes created by the INDUSTRIAL REVOLUTION led in the 19th cent. to passage of REFORM BILLS that greatly extended male suffrage; universal male and female suffrage was granted in the 20th cent. (see REPRESENTATION OF THE PEOPLE ACTS; WOMAN SUFFRAGE).

Parmenides, b. c.515 B.C., pre-Socratic Greek philosopher. The founder of the Eleatic school, he held that unchanging being is the material substance of which the universe is composed, and that generation, change, destruction, and motion are all illusions of the senses. His major contribution to philosophy was the method of reasoned proof for assertions.

Parmigiano [pärmējä'nō] or **Parmigianino** [–jänē'nō], 1503–40, Italian painter and etcher; b. Francesco Mazzola. A mannerist (see MANNERISM) he became noted for the grace and sensuality of his style and for his elongated figures. Representative paintings are the *Vision of St. Jerome* (National Gall., London) and *The Marriage of St. Catherine* (Parma Gall.). An unusual work is a self-portrait seen in a convex mirror (Vienna). He was among the first to use ETCHING.

Parnassians [pärnăs'ēənz], group of 19th-cent. French poets, named for their journal the *Parnasse contemporain* (1866–76). It included LECONTE DE LISLE, SULLY-PRUDHOMME, VERLAINE, and HEREDIA. Influenced by GAUTIER and reacting against ROMANTICISM, they strove for faultless workmanship, precise form, and emotional detachment.

Parnassós or **Parnassus,** mountain, c.8,060 ft (2,430 m) high, Phocis, central Greece. In ancient Greece it was believed sacred to APOLLO and DIONYSUS, and to the MUSES.

Parnell, Charles Stewart, 1846–91, Irish nationalist leader. The son of a Protestant landowner, he attached himself to the HOME RULE movement and in 1875 entered the British Parliament. He used filibusters to stress the gravity of Irish problems, and his agitation on the IRISH LAND QUESTION led to violence against landlords. Imprisoned (1881–82), he was released after he promised to help check the violence. In 1886 he formed an alliance with William GLADSTONE, who attempted unsuccessfully to pass the first Home Rule Bill. One of Ireland's most effective and popular leaders, Parnell lost his political influence after being named (1889) a corespondent in a divorce suit, and died a broken man.

Parr, Catherine, 1512–48, sixth queen consort of HENRY VIII of England. She married Henry in 1543 and had a beneficent influence on the aging king. After his death, she wed (1547) Thomas SEYMOUR, but died in childbirth.

Parrish, Maxfield, 1870–1966, American artist; b. Philadelphia. Using glowing colors, he created original and highly decorative posters, magazine covers, murals, and book illustrations, e.g., *Arabian Nights*.

parrot, common name for brilliantly colored BIRDS of the pantropical order Psittaciformes. Parrots have large heads, short necks, and strong feet with two front and two back toes (for climbing and grasping). Parrots range from the 3½-in. (8.7-cm) pygmy parrot of the South Pacific to the 40-in. (100-cm) Amazon parrot of South America. Species include the PARAKEETS, cockatoos, cockateels, and macaws. Parrots are long-lived, and many are popular as cage birds; some species can learn to mimic speech.

Parry, Sir William Edward, 1790–1855, British arctic explorer and rear admiral. In 1818 he accompanied Sir John ROSS on an expedition to find the NORTHWEST PASSAGE, and later he led other attempts (1819–20, 1821–23, 1824–25). The Parry Islands bear his name.

parsec, unit of length equal to the distance (206,265 ASTRONOMICAL UNITS; 3.26 LIGHT-YEARS; 1.917×10^{13} mi; or 3.086×10^{13} km) at which a hypothetical star's PARALLAX would be one second of arc. The distance in parsecs of an object from the earth is thus the reciprocal of the parallax in seconds of the object.

Parsifal or **Sir Percivale:** see ARTHURIAN LEGEND.

Parsis or **Parsees,** religious community of India, numbering over 200,000 followers of ZOROASTRIANISM, whose ancestors migrated from Iran in the 8th cent. to escape Muslim persecution. They revere fire and other aspects of nature as manifestations of Ahura Mazdah, the divinity. To avoid contaminating fire, earth, or water, they dispose of their dead by exposing the bodies in circular towers, where vultures devour them. The Parsis are a united community, well educated and, although small, economically important.

parsley, Mediterranean aromatic herb (*Petroselinum crispum*) of the CARROT family. It has been cultivated since Roman antiquity for its foliage, used as a seasoning and garnish.

parsnip, garden plant (*Pastinaca sativa*) of the CARROT family native to the Old World and cultivated since ancient times for its long, fleshy, edible root.

Parsons, Sir Charles Algernon, 1854–1931, English engineer and inventor of a revolutionary steam TURBINE. His first turbines drove electric generators. In 1897 he constructed the *Turbinia,* the first turbine-propelled vessel; its amazing speed led to the construction of many turbine-powered warships for the British navy.

Parsons, Talcott, 1902–79, American sociologist; b. Colorado Springs, Colo. A professor at Harvard Univ. (1927–74), he is noted for his structural-functional theory, an attempt to construct one framework for classifying general and specific characteristics of societies. Parsons's books include *The Social System* (1951) and *Politics and Social Structure* (1969).

Parsons, William: see ROSSE, WILLIAM PARSONS, 3D EARL OF.

Partch, Harry, 1901–74, American composer; b. Oakland, Calif. He developed a theory of "corporeal" music based on "harmonized spoken words," writing pieces on verbal recollections and street cries. He also invented a 43-note scale.

parthenogenesis, in zoology, reproduction in which an unfertilized egg develops into a new individual. It is common in lower animals, especially insects, e.g., the APHID. In many social insects, e.g., the honeybee, unfertilized eggs produce male drones and fertilized eggs produce female workers and queens. Artificial parthenogenesis has been achieved by scientists for most major groups of animals, although it usually results in abnormal development. In plants, the phenomenon (called parthenocarpy) is rare.

Parthenon [Gr., = the virgin's place], temple to ATHENA on the Acropolis, Athens, built 447–432 B.C., the masterpiece of Greek architecture. ICTINUS and CALLICRATES were the architects; PHIDIAS supervised the sculpture. Surrounded by 46 Doric columns, the temple stands on a three-step stylobate. The body comprised a main hall, with an inner chamber (the Parthenon proper) behind it. Within the hall a Doric colonnade divided the space into a broad nave and side aisles. Toward the west end stood the colossal gold and ivory *Athena Parthenos* of Phidias, destroyed in antiquity. Sculpture groups on the east and west pediments depicted the birth of Athena and her contest with POSEIDON. Of 525 ft (160 m) of sculpture on the interior frieze, 335 ft (102 m) still exist, the western portion in place and most of the rest in the British Museum (see ELGIN MARBLES). In the 6th cent. the temple became a Christian church and later a MOSQUE (with the addition of a MINARET). Used for storing gunpowder in 1687, the center section was destroyed by an explosion, but has been reconstructed.

The Parthenon

Parthia, ancient country of Asia, SE of the Caspian Sea. It was included in the Assyrian and Persian empires, the Macedonian empire of Alexander the Great, and the Syrian empire. In 250 B.C. the Parthians, led by ARSACES, founded the Parthian empire. They defeated the Romans in 53 B.C. but were in turned vanquished by them in 39–38 B.C. The empire declined and in A.D. 226 was conquered by ARDASHIR I, the founder of the Persian Sassanid dynasty. The chief Parthian cities were Ecbatana, Seleucia, Ctesiphon, and Hecatompylos.

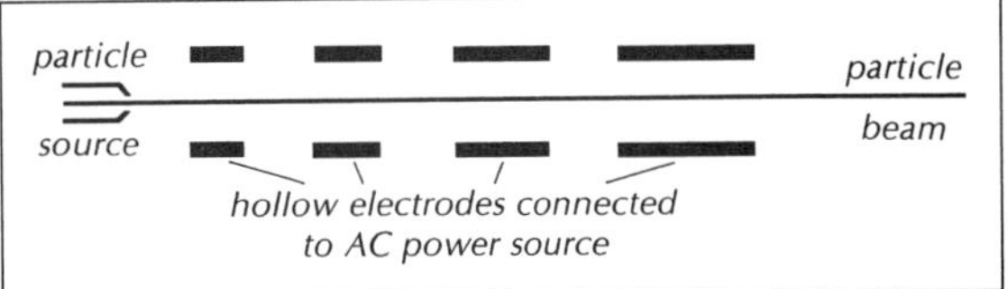

Particle accelerator: In a cyclotron, as the charged particles move faster, they spiral out of the edge of the D-shaped sections (Ds).

particle accelerator, device used to produce beams of energetic charged particles (see ELEMENTARY PARTICLES) and to direct them against various targets for studies of the structure and components of the atomic nucleus (see ATOM) and of the forces holding it together. Accelerators also have applications in medicine and industry, most notably in the production of radioisotopes. The first stage of any accelerator is an ION source to produce the charged particles from a neutral gas. The charged particles are accelerated by electric fields. In linear accelerators, which are the most powerful and efficient electron accelerators, the particle path is a straight line. The early linear accelerators used large static electric charges, which produced an electric field along the length of an evacuated tube to accelerate the particles. Present linear accelerators use electromagnetic waves to accomplish the acceleration. To reach high energies without prohibitively long paths, E.O. LAWRENCE designed the cyclotron, in which a cylindrical magnet bends the particle beam into a circular path in a hollow circular metal box that is split in half to form two *D*-shaped sections. A radio-frequency electric field is applied across the gap, accelerating the particle each time it crosses the gap. In the synchrocyclotron, used to accelerate protons, the frequency of the accelerating electric field steadily decreases to match the decreasing angular velocity of the proton caused by the increase of its mass at relativistic velocities, i.e., those close to the speed of light. In the synchrotron, a ring of magnets surrounding a doughnut-shaped vacuum tank produces a magnetic field that rises in step with the proton velocities, thus keeping the radius of their paths constant; this design eliminates the need for a center section of the magnet, allowing construction of rings with diameters measured in miles. The Superconducting Supercollider (SSC), which began construction in 1989, was to be the world's largest proton accelerator, encircling Waxahachie, Tex. (30 mi/48 km S of Dallas), with its 54-mi (87-km) oval main ring. The U.S. Congress killed the project in 1993. A smaller proton collider is under construction at CERN, outside Geneva, Switzerland.

particle detector, in physics, one of several devices for detecting, measuring, and analyzing particles and other forms of radiation entering it. For example, in the ionization chamber (consisting basically of a sealed chamber containing a gas and two electrodes between which a voltage is maintained by an external circuit) and the Geiger counter (consisting commonly of a gas-filled metal cylinder that acts as one electrode, and a needle or thin, taut wire along the axis of the cylinder that acts as the other electrode), the ionizing radiation is measured by changes in the external circuit; these changes are caused by a current resulting from the increase in charges. In other devices, ionization (see ION) is used to make visible the track of the charged particle causing the ionization: the bubble chamber is filled with liquid hydrogen or some other liquefied gas; the cloud chamber is filled with a supersaturated vapor; and the spark chamber contains a high-pressure gas that fills the gaps between a stack of metal plates or wire grids that are maintained with high voltage between alternate layers. In the scintillation counter, radiation is detected and measured by means of tiny, visible flashes produced by the radiation when it strikes a sensitive substance known as a phosphor (see PHOSPHORESCENCE).

particle physics: see ELEMENTARY PARTICLES; NUCLEAR PHYSICS.

Parti Québecois [pärtē kēbĕkwä'], Canadian provincial political party that advocates the independence of Quebec. Founded in 1968, it was long led by René LÉVESQUE. It won control of the provincial assembly in 1976 and made French Quebec's official language and passed diverse social legislation. Weakened after a 1980 provincial referendum rejected further negotiation for Quebec's independence, the party lost to the Liberals in the 1985 elections.

partridge, name for henlike BIRDS of various families. The true partridges of the Old World belong to the PHEASANT family. The gray partridge (*Perdix perdix*) of Europe, about 1 ft (30 cm) long, has been successfully introduced in parts of the U.S. The name *partridge* is also applied to the ruffed GROUSE, the BOBWHITE, and the plumed QUAIL.

parvovirus any of several small DNA viruses that cause several diseases in animals, including humans. In humans, parvoviruses cause fifth disease, or erythema infectiosum, an acute disease usually affecting young children. Symptoms include a rash that spreads from the cheeks to the extremities, low fever, fatigue, and, in adults, mild to severe joint pain and swelling. Dogs, wolves and coyotes can become infected with canine parvovirus. Puppies are most susceptible to the virus, which causes diarrhea, vomiting, and fever. Feline distemper, an often fatal disease of cats, raccoons, and minks, is characterized by fever, dehydration, loss of appetite, and a reduction in white blood cells.

Pasadena. **1** City (1990 pop. 131,591), S Calif., at the base of the San Gabriel Mts.; inc. 1866. Its manufactures include electronic and aerospace components; the California Inst. of Technology, with its NASA Jet Propulsion Laboratory, is in the city. It is the scene of the annual Tournament of Roses parade and the postseason college football game in the Rose Bowl. **2** City (1990 pop. 119,363), S Tex., on the Houston ship channel, an industrial suburb of HOUSTON; inc. 1929. The port of Houston, and oil and related industries provide much employment. NASA's manned space center (on Clear Lake) and the San Jacinto battlefield (1836) are nearby.

Pascal, Blaise, 1623–62, French scientist and religious philosopher. A mathematical prodigy, Pascal founded the modern theory of probability, discovered the properties of the cycloid, and contributed to the advance of differential calculus. In physics his experiments in the equilibrium of fluids led to the invention of the hydraulic press (see HYDRAULIC MACHINERY). As a young man Pascal came under Jansenist influence (see under JANSEN, CORNELIS), and after a profound religious experience in 1654 he entered the convent at Port-Royal, thereafter devoting his attention primarily to religious writing. His best-known works are *Provincial Letters* (1656), a defense of the Jansenists; and the posthumously published *Pensées* (1670), which preach the necessity of mystic faith in understanding the universe.

PASCAL: see PROGRAMMING LANGUAGE.

Pascal's law: see HYDRAULIC MACHINERY.

Paschal II or **Pascal II,** d. 1118, pope (1099–1118), an Italian named Ranieri. A Cluniac monk, he succeeded URBAN II. During his reign, PHILIP I of France was reconciled with the church, St. ANSELM triumphed in England, and the first Crusade was successful. In 1110 Holy Roman Emperor HENRY V invaded Italy and forced Paschal to surrender the papal position on INVESTITURE. Paschal later repudiated this surrender.

Pashto: see PUSHTU.

Pasiphaë, in Greek mythology, wife of King MINOS.

Pasolini, Pier Paolo, 1922–75, Italian writer and film director. A Marxist, he brought to his novels, poetry, and films a combination of religious and social consciousness. His films include *The Gospel According to St. Matthew* (1964), *Medea* (1969), and *Salò or The 120 Days of Sodom* (1975).

Passion play, surviving genre of the medieval MIRACLE PLAY. First given in Latin, then evolving into German by the 15th cent., it has as its subject the suffering, death, and resurrection of JESUS. The Passion play given every 10 years at Oberammergau, Bavaria, dates from 1633.

Passover: see under JEWISH HOLIDAYS.

Passy, Frédéric [päsē'], 1822–1912, French economist who shared with J.H. DUNANT the first Nobel Peace Prize (1901). He founded the International League for Permanent Peace (1867) and, with Sir William R. Cremer, the Inter-Parliamentary Union of Arbitration (1889).

pasta or **macaroni,** shaped and dried dough prepared from semolina or farina wheat flour and water, associated especially with Italian cuisine. Often mixed with eggs or egg solids, the dough is cut into many shapes. Long known in Asia, similar flour and rice pastes are believed to have been introduced into Europe during the 13th-cent. Mongol invasions.

pastel, artists' medium of chalk and pigment, tempered with gum water and usually molded into sticks; also, a work in the medium. Pastel has been very popular in France, where it was introduced in the 18th cent. It was used by such 19th-cent. masters as DEGAS, TOULOUSE-LAUTREC, WHISTLER, and CASSATT. In the 20th cent. MATISSE created superb pastels.

Pasternak, Boris Leonidovich [păs'tərnăk"], 1890–1960, Russian poet, novelist, and translator. His first book of poems was *The Twin in the Clouds* (1914). *Over the Barriers* (1916) and *My Sister, Life* (1922) established him as a major poet with a fresh, lyrical, passionate voice. In the repressive intellectual climate of the 1930s he ceased publishing his own work, devoting himself to translating works of SHAKESPEARE, GOETHE, and other major Western poets. Two World War II collections brought only censure. His masterpiece, the novel *Doctor Zhivago,* an epic treatment of the tragic upheavals of 20th-cent. Russia, was finished by 1955. Denied publication in the USSR, it was first published (1957) in Italy, and soon acclaimed worldwide. Though Pasternak was awarded the 1958 Nobel Prize in literature, official Soviet pressure compelled him to refuse it. He spent his last years at an artists' colony near Moscow, where he remained an international symbol of artistic incorruptibility.

Pasteur, Louis [păstŭr'], 1822–95, French chemist. Noted for his studies of fermentation and BACTERIA, he disproved the theory of spontaneous generation and advanced the germ theory of infection. Of great economic importance are the process of PASTEURIZATION, which he developed; his studies of silkworm disease and chicken cholera; and his discovery of ANTHRAX and RABIES vaccines. In 1888 the Pasteur Inst. was founded in Paris, with Pasteur as director, to provide a teaching and research center on virulent and contagious diseases.

pasteurization, treatment of food with heat to destroy disease-causing and other undesirable organisms. The process was developed by Louis PASTEUR in the 1860s. Modern pasteurization standards for milk require temperatures of about 145°F (63°C) for 30 min followed by rapid cooling. The harmless lactic acid bacteria that cause milk to sour survive pasteurization but are destroyed when milk is heated to ultrahigh temperatures, a process called ultrapasteurization.

pastoral, literary work based on a conventionalized portrait of shepherd or rural life, whose purity and simplicity are contrasted with the corruption and artificiality of court and city. The pastoral, found in poetry, drama, and fiction, may embrace love, death, religion, and politics as themes. The idylls of THEOCRITUS (3d cent. B.C.) introduced Daphnis, Amaryllis, and other figures who became standard fixtures of the genre. VERGIL's *Bucolics,* or eclogues, describe an imaginary Arcadia yet glorify Rome. *Daphnis and Chloë,* by LONGUS (3d cent. A.D.), was the first pastoral romance. The pastoral revived during the RENAISSANCE in the work of DANTE, PETRARCH, BOCCACCIO, and Angelo Poliziano, and it has enriched English literature from Edmund SPENSER, Sir Philip SIDNEY, and SHAKESPEARE to John MILTON's "Lycidas," P.B. SHELLEY's "onais," and Matthew ARNOLD's "Thyrsis." Its conventions had faded by the 20th cent.

Patagonia, semiarid, windswept plateau, c.300,000 sq mi (777,000 sq km), S Argentina. The sparsely populated plateau has large coal, oil, and iron ore deposits, and vast untapped mineral wealth. The origins of Patagonia's original inhabitants, such as the Tehuelches ("Patagonian giants"), and of its unusual wildlife have greatly interested paleontologists and zoologists.

Patchen, Kenneth, 1911–72, American author; b. Niles, Ohio. His poetry, diverse in genre and free in form, ranges from *Before the Brave* (1936) to *Hallelujah Anyway* (1967). His novels include *Memoirs of a Shy Pornographer* (1945).

Patenier, Joachim de: see PATINIR, JOACHIM DE.

patent, in law, governmental grant of the exclusive privilege of making, using, and selling and authorizing others to make, use, and sell an invention. The term derives from the medieval letters patent, public letters granting monopolistic control of useful goods to an individual. The first U.S. patent legislation was enacted in 1790, and the U.S. Patent Office was created in 1836. U.S. law allows the patenting of any original and useful device or process; the patent is valid for 17 years. Although there have been many independent inventors in the U.S., most important patents today are the property of large corporations.

patent medicine or **proprietary medicine,** packaged DRUGS that can be obtained without a prescription; also called **over-the-counter drugs.** Sale of patent medicines is regulated by the FOOD AND DRUG ADMINISTRATION, which evaluates their safety and effectiveness. ANALGESICS, antiseptics, some sedatives, laxatives, antacids, some cough medicines, and some skin preparations are examples of patent medicines.

Pater, Walter Horatio, 1839–94, British essayist and critic. He believed that the ideal life consisted of cultivating an appreciation for the beautiful and profound. *Studies in the History of the Renaissance* (1873), *Marius the Epicurean* (1885), *Imaginary Portraits* (1887), and other works exhibit his precise, subtle, and refined style.

Paterson, city (1990 pop. 140,891), seat of Passaic co., NE N.J., at the falls of the Passaic R.; inc. 1851. Founded (1791) by Alexander HAMILTON and others to promote industry in the newly-formed U.S., it became known as the "Silk City of the World," and in the 19th cent. was noted also as a producer of COLT revolvers and locomotives. Modern Paterson is a leading producer of textiles, clothing, electronic equipment, and plastics. The city's Great Falls Historic District contains a remarkable display of American industrial history.

Pathé, Charles [pätā'], 1863–1957, French film mogul. Pathé Frères dominated (c.1901–14) world production, world distribution, and European manufacture of film stock and equipment. The *Pathé Gazette* newsreel was among the firm's many films.

pathology, study of the cause of disease and the changes in structure and function produced in any cell, organ, or part of the body by disease. A pathologist, in modern terms, is a physician with special training in examining body tissues and excretions (including sputum, BLOOD, URINE, tissue BIOPSIES, and excised organs) for visible and microscopic changes indicative of disease. Diagnostic techniques include laboratory tests, microscopic examination, and electron microscopy which allows examination on a molecular level.

Patinir, Patenier, or **Patiner, Joachim de** [all: də pätĭnĭr'], d. 1524, Flemish landscape and religious painter. He was the first Flemish painter to regard himself primarily as a landscape painter. The small figures in his vistas were sometimes painted by other artists. A characteristic painting is *Flight into Egypt* (Antwerp).

Paton, Alan, 1903–88, South African novelist. His fiction, written with simplicity and compassion, reflects the deep conflicts that exist in South Africa. Among his novels are *Cry, the Beloved Country* (1948), *Too Late the Phalarope* (1953), and *Ah, But Your Land Is Beautiful* (1982).

patriarchy: see MATRIARCHY.

patriation bill: see CONSTITUTION ACT, 1982.

patrician [Lat., = of the fathers], member of the privileged class of ancient Rome. From the 6th cent. B.C. the PLEBS struggled constantly for political equality with the patricians. The patricians wore a distinctive tunic and shoe. Later the term became a title of honor.

Patrick, Saint, c.385–461, Christian missionary, the Apostle of Ireland. His life is largely obscured by legend. He is said to have been born in Roman Britain and enslaved by the Irish until he escaped to Gaul. He studied at Auxerre and later returned as a missionary to Ireland, where he made many converts. In 444 or 445 he established his archiepiscopal see at Armagh with the approval of Pope LEO I. By his death, Ireland was Christianized. The prime source of his life is the *Confessions,* written during his last years. Feast: Mar. 17.

Patroclus, in Greek mythology, friend of ACHILLES.

Patrons of Husbandry: see GRANGER MOVEMENT.

Patterson, P(ercival) J(ames), 1935–, Jamaican political leader. A member of the People's National party, he held ministerial posts (1972–80, 1989–92) and was deputy prime minister (1989–92) under Michael MANLEY. He succeeded (1992) Manley as prime minister when the latter resigned.

Patti, Adelina, 1843–1919, coloratura soprano; b. Spain, of Italian parents. She made her debut in New York City in 1859 and became the most popular singer of her day.

Patton, George Smith, Jr., 1885–1945, American general; b. San Gabriel, Calif. During WORLD WAR II he commanded the 3d Army, which spearheaded the liberation of France (1944) and the defeat of Germany (1945). A notorious incident (1943) in which the hot-tempered general slapped a soldier suffering from battle fatigue detracted from his brilliant military record.

Paul, Saint, d. A.D. 64? or 67?, the apostle to the Gentiles; b. Saul of Tarsus, Asia Minor. A Jew, son of a Roman citizen, he was a tentmaker. Educated in Jerusalem, he became a zealous nationalist and probably a Pharisee. Sources for his life are the ACTS OF THE APOSTLES and the Pauline Epistles. Of the epistles, ROMANS, CORINTHIANS, GALATIANS, PHILIPPIANS, COLOSSIANS, First THESSALONIANS, and PHILEMON are undoubted as Paul's work. EPHESIANS and Second Thessalonians are generally accepted. First and Second TIMOTHY and TITUS are thought in their present form to be later; HEBREWS was not written by Paul himself. Paul apparently approved of the martyrdom of St. Stephen and shortly thereafter was commissioned by the chief priest to help suppress Christianity in Damascus (A.D. 33). On his way there a light blinded him, and he heard Jesus asking, "Why persecutest thou me?" In Damascus he was found by the disciple Ananias. On regaining his sight he was baptized and began preaching. He spent 13 years, some of them in the Arabian desert, learning the faith. In A.D. 47 Paul set out with St. BARNABAS and St. MARK on his first missionary journey, establishing churches in Cyprus and Asia Minor. About A.D. 50 he was at the council of the apostles in Jerusalem, opposing the Judaistic group's support for circumcision, which would have made Christianity a Jewish sect. On his second mission (A.D. 50–53) Paul was accompanied by Silas and visited Galatia, Troas, Philippi, Salonica, Athens, and Corinth, where he remained for some time. On his third journey (A.D. 53–57) he remained two and a half years in Ephesus. On what proved to be his last visit to the Holy Land (A.D. 57–59), he was arrested in Jerusalem for provoking a riot; after two years of imprisonment and hearings, he claimed his Roman citizen's right and was taken to Rome, where he was imprisoned (A.D. 60) but allowed to conduct his ministry among his visitors. His final fate is uncertain. His tomb and shrine are at the basilica of St. Paul's Without the Walls, Rome. St. Paul dominated the apostolic age. The first Christian theological writing is found in his epistles, and he became a fountainhead of Christian doctrine.

Paul III, 1468–1549, pope (1534–49), a Roman named Alessandro Farnese. An astute diplomat, he favored reform and began the Catholic Reformation (see REFORMATION, CATHOLIC). To achieve Catholic reform, he convened (1545) the Council of TRENT and supported the newly founded Jesuits (see JESUS, SOCIETY OF). A patron of the arts, he had Michelangelo continue to decorate the SISTINE CHAPEL, and he founded the Farnese Palace.

Paul VI, 1897–1978, pope (1963–78), an Italian named Giovanni Battista Montini. He reconvened the Second VATICAN COUNCIL, which had been called (1962) by his predecessor, JOHN XXIII, and carried out many of its reforms, such as vernacularization and reform of the liturgy. Rules of fasting and abstinence were relaxed, and some restrictions on intermarriage were lifted. In 1964, Paul undertook a pilgrimage to the Holy Land and became the first pope to leave Italy in over 150 years. That journey was followed by trips to India (1964), the U.S. (1965), Africa (1969), and Southeast Asia (1970). Paul brought a new ecumenism to the church; limited doctrinal agreements were reached with the Anglicans and the Lutherans. A strong defender of papal primacy and infallibility, Paul sparked dissent from liberal church factions with his encyclical *Humanae Vitae* (1968), which reaffirmed the church's long-standing ban on contraception. He also faced challenges from Catholic traditionalists, who wished to return to the old liturgy. Although criticized, Paul was universally respected for his intellect and spirituality, his humility and compassion.

Paul I, 1754–1801, czar of Russia (1796–1801); son of CATHERINE II. Reversing his mother's policies, he limited the power of the nobility and did not continue her expansionism. He briefly joined (1798) the second coalition against France and, with Denmark, Sweden, and Prussia, formed an armed league to counter English interference in neutral shipping. He prohibited foreign travel and importation of Western books and music. A conspiracy of nobles and officers led to Paul's murder and the accession of his son, ALEXANDER I.

Paul, 1901–64, king (1947–64) of the Hellenes (Greece), brother and successor of GEORGE II. His reign was pro-Western, and he was succeeded by his son, CONSTANTINE II.

Paul, Alice, 1885–1977, American feminist; b. Moorestown, N.J. She helped found the Congressional Union for Woman Suffrage (1913), which became the National Woman's party (1917). After the passage of the Nineteenth Amendment to the U.S. CONSTITUTION, she worked for passage of an equal rights amendment.

Paul, Jean: see RICHTER, JOHANN PAUL FRIEDRICH.

Paulding, James Kirke, 1778–1860, American author, secretary of the navy under Pres. Van Buren; b. near Millbrook, N.Y. He collaborated with Washington IRVING on the periodical *Salmagundi,* and wrote satires, tales, and novels.

Pauli, Wolfgang, 1900–1958, Austro-American physicist; b. Vienna. A professor at the Federal Institute of Technology, Zürich, and a member (1935–36, 1940–46) of the Institute for Advanced Study, Princeton, N.J., he won the 1945 Nobel Prize in physics for his exclusion principle, according to which no two electrons in an atom may be in the same quantum state (see QUANTUM MECHANICS). He also posited the existence of the NEUTRINO before it was observed.

Pauling, Linus Carl, 1901–, American chemist. One of the few recipients of two Nobel prizes, he won the chemistry award in 1954 and the peace prize in 1962. His long career at the California Inst. of Technology began in 1931. He wrote a classic study of the chemical bond, and did important work in molecular biology. He is noted as an active proponent of disarmament, and as a champion of the use of large doses of vitamin C for treating the common cold and of the use of chemotherapy for mental diseases.

Pavarotti, Luciano, 1935–, Italian tenor. He made his debut in Italy in 1961, in London in 1963, and in the U.S. in 1965. Since 1968 he has appeared regularly at the METROPOLITAN OPERA, New York City. A great popular favorite, Pavarotti is noted for his brilliance and style, notably in works by BELLINI, DONIZETTI, PUCCINI, and VERDI.

Pavese, Cesare [pävĕ'sā], 1908–50, Italian poet, novelist, and translator. He translated many American works into Italian and was himself influenced by MELVILLE. His major novels include *The Comrade* (1947), *The House on the Hill* (1949), and *The Moon and the Bonfire* (1950); they all treat man's search for stability and release from isolation.

Pavlov, Ivan Petrovich, 1849–1936, Russian physiologist and experimental psychologist. Using dogs as experimental animals, he obtained secretions of the salivary glands, pancreas, and liver without disturbing the nerve and blood supply; for this work on the physiology of the DIGESTIVE SYSTEM he received the 1904 Nobel Prize in physiology or medicine. He also experimented on nervous stimulation of gastric secretions and thus discovered the conditioned reflex, a physiological reaction to environmental stimuli, which influenced the development or BEHAVIORISM. His chief work was *Conditioned Reflexes* (1926).

Pavlova, Anna Matveyevna [pävlu'və, Rus. päv'ləvə], 1881–1931, Russian ballerina. She made her debut (1899) in St. Petersburg and danced with DIAGHILEV's Ballets Russes. She was considered the greatest ballerina of her time and was noted for her classical technique. Her most famous role was *The Dying Swan*.

Pawnee, indigenous people of North America with a Caddoan language of the Hokan-Siouan stock (see NATIVE AMERICAN LANGUAGES). Their material culture was typical of the Plains (see NORTH AMERICA, INDIGENOUS PEOPLES OF), but they had elaborate myths and rituals, including a supreme god and, until the 18th cent., the custom of human sacrifice to their god of vegetation. In 1541 the Pawnee were living in S Nebraska. By the early 18th cent. they numbered 10,000, but epidemics and wars with the SIOUX greatly reduced their numbers. Fierce fighters, they never warred against the U.S., but instead provided protection in the INDIAN WARS. In 1876 they moved to a reservation in Oklahoma. In 1990 they numbered 2,892, but few were still living on the reservation.

Payne-Aldrich Tariff Act (1909), a compromise law that lowered some tariffs but increased others, contrary to the anti-protectionist plank of the 1908 Republican platform. Sponsored by Rep. Sereno E. Payne and Sen. Nelson W. ALDRICH, it was the chief issue during Pres. William H. TAFT's term.

Payton, Walter (Jerry), 1954–, American football player; b. Columbia, Miss. Playing 13 seasons (1975–87) as a running back for the Chicago Bears of the National Football League, Payton set career records in rushing yards (16,726), in total yards (21,803), and in touchdowns scored rushing (110). He rushed for over 1,000 yards in a season ten times and set a single-game record of 275 yards in 1977.

Paz, Octavio [päs], 1914–, Mexican poet and critic, distinguished for his insight, elegance, and erudition. His poetry includes *The Violent Season* (1958) and *Configurations* (1971). Among his prose works are *The Labyrinth of Solitude* (1950), *The Bow and the Lyre* (1956), *Children of the Mire: Modern Poetry from Romanticism to the Avant-Garde* (1974), and *The Monkey Grammarian* (1981). He was awarded the 1990 Nobel Prize for literature.

Paz Estenssoro, Victor [päs āstānsō' rō], 1907–, president of BOLIVIA (1952–56, 1960–64, 1985–89). He founded (1941) and helped to bring the National Revolutionary Movement (NRM) to power (1943). Elected (1951) president while in exile, he took office by means of an NRM-led revolt and instituted social reforms. He amended the constitution to permit himself a third term, and though reelected, he was ousted (1964) by a military coup. After returning to Bolivia and serving as a governmental adviser (1971), he lost two more presidential elections before he was elected to the position by the Bolivian congress (1985). In last term he reduced the government's role in the economy and controlled inflation, but with enormous social costs.

Pb, chemical symbol of the element LEAD.

PBB or **polybrominated biphenyl,** compound used as a fire retardant. In 1973 several thousand pounds of PBB were accidentally mixed with livestock feed that was later distributed to farms in west-central Michigan. Some 1.5 million chickens, 30,000 cattle, 5,900 swine, and 1,470 sheep that became contaminated with PBB before the mistake was discovered had to be destroyed. Later studies indicated that PBB had spread through the food chain; in one test of a sample of Michigan's residents, 97% of those tested had traces of PBB in fat tissue. Affected cattle suffered loss of appetite and weight loss (often leading to death), decreased milk production, and increased miscarriages. Laboratory studies have linked PBB with liver cancer in rats and with low birth weight, liver damage, and weakened resistance to disease in human beings.

PCB or **polychlorinated biphenyl,** any of a group of organic compounds that were once widely used as liquid coolants and insulators in industrial equipment, e.g., power transformers. They were later found to be dangerous environmental pollutants, however, and U.S. manufacture of PCBs ended in 1977. Research indicates that the chemical is toxic to a wide variety of animals, especially fish, and may also affect animal reproduction. As the result of a PCB leak in Japan in 1968 that contaminated rice oil, 1,000 people developed a skin disease, and babies showed signs of poisoning.

Pd, chemical symbol of the element PALLADIUM.

pea, hardy, annual, climbing plant (*Pisum sativum*) of the PULSE family, long grown for food and no longer found in the wild form. The round seeds, borne in a pod, are highly nutritious, having a high PROTEIN content. Split peas are obtained from the field pea (var. *arvense*), grown also for forage and as a green manure. The pods of sugar, or snow, peas are also eaten. The CHICKPEA and SWEET PEA belong to different genera.

Peace, river, W central Canada, flowing 945 mi (1,521 km) N and E from the confluence of the Finlay and Parsnip rivers at Williston Lake to join the Slave R. at Lake Athabasca. Its fertile middle valley in N Alberta, settled since 1900, is an important Canadian agricultural region. Sir Alexander MACKENZIE explored (1792–93) the river.

Peace Corps, U.S. agency established (1961) to assist developing countries to train manpower for their needs. The program now also sends volunteers to the former Soviet bloc nations and tries to attract people with technical training or special skills, particularly in agriculture. Volunteers serve two-year tours in foreign countries.

peach, tree *(Prunus persica)* of the ROSE family having decorative pink blossoms and a juicy, sweet, drupe fruit. Peach fruits have a characteristically fuzzy skin; the NECTARINE is the smooth-skinned variety. The numerous kinds of peaches are generally distinguished as clingstone (in which the fruit's ripe flesh does not readily separate from the seed) and freestone (flesh readily separates from the seed). Purple-leaved and double-flowering peach trees are often cultivated as ornamentals.

Peacock, Thomas Love, 1785–1866, English novelist and poet. His satires on the intellectual modes of the day include *Headlong Hall* (1816) and *Crotchet Castle* (1831). His best poems are interspersed in the novels.

peacock or **peafowl,** large BIRD of the PHEASANT family, native to E Asia. During courtship, the crested male common peacock (*Pavo cristatus*) displays his magnificent green-and-gold upper tail coverts before the drabber peahen. When the term *peafowl* is used, *peacock* refers to the male and *peahen* to the female.

Peale, Charles Willson, 1741–1827, American painter, naturalist, and inventor; b. Queen Annes co., Md. Peale studied under J.S. COPLEY and Benjamin WEST and later served as a captain in the American Revolution. Succeeding Copley as the most popular U.S. portraitist, he painted such figures as Franklin, Jefferson, Hamilton, and John Adams. His many paintings of George Washington include the earliest-known portrait (1772; Washington and Lee Univ.). Peale's scientific pursuits included paleontology, taxidermy, and such inventions as a velocipede, false teeth, and (with Thomas Jefferson) the polygraph. His brother **James Peale,** 1749–1831, b. Chestertown, Md., painted portraits, particularly miniatures, e.g., a painting of Washington (N.Y. Historical Soc.). Of Charles Willson Peale's 17 children, 4 became painters—**Titian Peale,** 1799–1885, animal painter, b. Philadelphia; **Rubens Peale,** 1784–1865, still-life painter, b. Bucks co., Pa.; **Raphaelle Peale,** 1774–1825, still-life and portrait painter, b. Annapolis, Md.; and **Rembrandt Peale,** 1778–1860, portrait and historical painter, b. Bucks co., Pa. Rembrandt Peale was a student of Benjamin West. His portraits of Washington and other contemporary figures are in Independence Hall, Philadelphia; the Metropolitan Museum; and the Museum of Fine Arts, Boston.

peanut, low plant (*Arachis hypogaea*) of the PULSE family, and its protein-rich, edible seeds. Native to South America, it is now widely cultivated. The seeds (peanuts) are eaten fresh or roasted and used in cooking and confection. They are ground to make peanut butter and yield an oil used for margarine, cooking oil, soap manufacture, and industrial purposes. The peanut plant is unusual for its geocarpy: when the pod begins to form, it is pushed into the ground by elongation of the stalk and matures underground.

pear, name for a tree (genus *Pyrus*) of the ROSE family and for its fruit. Most of the pear strains grown for fruit are varieties of the common pear *(P. communis)* or of its hybrids. The sweet and juicy fruit, broad at the base, generally narrows toward the stem; common varieties include the Bartlett, Anjou, Bosc, Comice, and Seckel. Pears are sold fresh, canned, or dried. Several pear species are cultivated as ornamentals for their blossoms, particularly the Callery, or Bradford, pear (*P. calleryana*), which is valued as a street tree, and pear wood is used in cabinetmaking. The pear is closely related to the APPLE.

pearl, hard, rounded gem formed by certain BIVALVE mollusks, particularly the pearl OYSTER and the freshwater pearl MUSSEL. In response to an irritation caused by a foreign object such as a parasite or a grain of sand within the shell, the mantle (specialized layer of tissue between the shell and body mass) secretes layers of calcium carbonate, identical in composition to MOTHER-OF-PEARL, around the object. In several years, a pearl is formed. Pearls vary in shape (from round to irregular) and color (white to black). Cultured pearls, mainly from Japan, are produced by placing a small bead in the mantle of an oyster.

Pearl, The, one of four Middle English alliterative poems, presumably by the same author, in a manuscript of c.1400. An allegorical vision of singular beauty, it is generally explained as an elegy for the poet's daughter. Two of the other poems are the homiletic *Cleanness* (or *Purity*) and *Patience.* The fourth, *Sir Gawain and the Green Knight,* is perhaps the most brilliantly conceived of all Arthurian romances (see ARTHURIAN LEGEND).

Pearl Harbor, nearly landlocked harbor on Oahu island, Hawaii, site of important U.S. military installations. It is best known as the scene of the devastating Japanese surprise air attack on Dec. 7, 1941, which catapulted the U.S. into WORLD WAR II. It is now a national historic landmark.

Pearson, Lester Bowles, 1897–1972, prime minister of CANADA (1963–68). He helped to found (1944) the UNITED NATIONS and became (1947) chairman of the UN political and security committee. As Liberal minister of Canada's external affairs (1948–57), he helped to form NATO and mediated the 1956 ARAB-ISRAELI WAR, for which he received the 1957 Nobel Peace Prize. He led the Liberal party to victory in the 1963 elections and took office as prime minister.

Peary, Robert Edwin, 1856–1920, American arctic explorer, traditionally acknowledged as the discoverer of the NORTH POLE; b. Cresson, Pa. He made several expeditions to the arctic, including GREENLAND and Peary Land, which bears his name. He claimed to reach the North Pole on April 6, 1909. Although challenged by the prior claim of Frederick Albert Cook, his accomplishment was recognized by the U.S. Congress in 1911. Recent scholarship has reopened the question.

peat, soil material consisting of partially decomposed organic matter, formed by the slow decay of aquatic and semiaquatic plants in SWAMPS and bogs. Principal types include moss peat, derived chiefly from SPHAGNUM and used as mulch and stable litter, and fuel peat, used where wood and coal are scarce. Peat is the first stage of transition from compressed plant growth to the formation of COAL.

peat moss: see SPHAGNUM.

pecan: see HICKORY.

pediatrics, branch of medicine specializing in the care of children and the treatment of childhood diseases. It includes treatment of such diseases as MEASLES, CHICKEN POX, and MUMPS; immunization against serious childhood infections such as DIPHTHERIA and WHOOPING COUGH; and recognition and treatment of disorders due to MALNUTRITION, poor hygiene, and child abuse. Other specialties include pediatric SURGERY and perinatology (the care of the fetus and newborn, and the study of diseases of infancy and SUDDEN INFANT DEATH SYNDROME).

Pedro: for Spanish and Portuguese rulers thus named, see PETER.

Pedro [pā'drō], emperors of BRAZIL. **Pedro I,** 1798–1834 (r.1822–31), fled as a child with the Portuguese royal family to Brazil and became regent of Brazil (1821) when his father, JOHN VI, returned to Portugal. Heeding his Brazilian advisers, he declared Brazil a separate empire (1822) and granted its first constitution (1824). Upon his father's death (1826), he conceded the Portuguese crown to his daughter, MARIA II. His inability to cope with Brazil's problems led him to abdicate (1831) in favor of his son, **Pedro II,** 1825–91 (r.1831–89). Pedro II was extremely popular, and his long reign was marked by internal peace and great material progress. Opposition to a law freeing the slaves brought about his downfall, however, and he was deposed in 1889.

Peel, Sir Robert, 1788–1850, British statesman, prime minister (1834–35, 1841–46). As home secretary in 1829, he secured passage of the CATHOLIC EMANCIPATION bill (which he had once opposed), and established the London police force, whose members were called Bobbies after him. Important in the emerging CONSERVATIVE PARTY, he hoped it would favor general reforms. The abandonment of custom duties and repeal (1846) of the CORN LAWS during his second prime ministry, however, split the party, forcing his resignation.

Pegasus, in Greek mythology, winged horse that sprang from the neck of the dying GORGON Medusa. Associated with the arts, he was captured by the hero BELLEROPHON, who rode him.

pegmatite: see GRANITE.

Pehlevi language: see PAHLAVI LANGUAGE.

Pei, I(eoh) M(ing) [pā], 1917–, Chinese-American architect; b. China. His designs integrate structure and environment. Among his works are Place Ville Marie, in Montreal; Government Center, in Boston; the East Wing of the National Gallery of Art, in Washington,

D.C. (1978); the West Wing of the Museum of Fine Arts, in Boston (1981); and a new, subterranean entrance complex for the Louvre, in Paris (1985), that is crowned by a glass pyramid.

Glass pyramid at the Louvre, designed by I.M. Pei

Peirce, Charles Sanders, 1838–1914, American philosopher; b. Cambridge, Mass. Viewing logic as the beginning of all philosophic study, he held that the meaning of an idea was to be found in an examination of the consequences to which the idea would lead; he coined the term PRAGMATISM to describe this principle. His followers included William JAMES and John DEWEY. Peirce was also a modern founder of SEMIOTICS. He was virtually unknown during his lifetime; his major essays appeared posthumously as *Chance, Love, and Logic* (1923), and his collected papers were published between 1931 and 1958.

Peisistratus: see PISISTRATUS.

Peking: see BEIJING.

Pekingese, TOY DOG; shoulder height, 6–9 in. (15.3–22.9 cm); weight, 6–14 lb (2.7–6.4 kg). Its long, soft coat, which may be any color, forms a ruff around the neck. As early as the 8th cent. it was kept by Chinese emperors. After a British raid on Beijing (then known as Peking) in 1860, it was brought to the West.

Peking man: see HOMO ERECTUS.

Pelé [pālā′], 1940–, Brazilian soccer player; b. Edson Arantes do Nascimento. Perhaps the greatest soccer player ever, he joined the Santos team at 16 and led Brazil's national team to world titles in 1958, 1962, and 1970. Pelé scored 1,281 career goals, and in international matches he averaged one goal per game. From 1975 to 1977 he played with the New York Cosmos, popularizing the sport in the U.S.

Pelée [pəlā′], volcano, 4,583 ft (1,397 m), on N Martinique, in the West Indies. Its great eruption of 1902 caused the death of more than 30,000 people and engulfed Saint-Pierre, the city at its base.

Peleus, in Greek mythology, father of ACHILLES.

pelican, large aquatic BIRD of warm regions, related to the CORMORANTS and gannets. Pelicans are long-necked birds with large, flat bills; they store fish in a deep, expandable pouch below the lower mandible. The white pelican (*Pelecanus onocrotalus*) of North America ranges from the NW U.S. to the Gulf and Florida coasts. It is about 5 ft (152.5 cm) long with a wingspread of 8 to 10 ft (244 to 300.5 cm).

pellagra, deficiency disease due to a lack of niacin, a component of vitamin B complex. See VITAMIN (table).

Peloponnesian League: see SPARTA.

Peloponnesian War [pĕl′əpənē′zhən], 431–404 B.C., a struggle in ancient GREECE between ATHENS and SPARTA, long-standing rivals. The war began after a contest between Athens and Corinth (Sparta's ally) over dependencies. The first important action was the invasion of Attica by a Spartan army in 431 B.C. The Athenians retired behind the walls of their city, and the Athenian fleet began raids, winning victories off Naupactus (429). A plague (430–428) wiped out a quarter of Athens' population. After PERICLES died, his successor, CLEON, won a great victory at Sphacteria (425) and rejected a Spartan bid for peace. The tide began to turn, and the Spartan leader Brasidas surprised Athens with a campaign in NE Greece that ended in a decisive Spartan victory at Amphipolas (422), in which both Brasidas and Cleon were killed. The new Athenian leader, NICIAS, arranged a peace (421), but his rival ALCIBIADES persuaded the Athenians to invade SYRACUSE. Alcibiades was accused of sacrilege, and the expedition, led by Nicias, ended in disaster (413). Alcibiades, who had fled to Sparta, sailed the Spartan fleet across the Aegean, inciting revolt in Athens' colonies. Recalled to Athens (410), he destroyed the Spartan fleet at Cyzicus, but Sparta, with a new fleet led by LYSANDER, defeated the Athenians at Notium (407), and Alcibiades was driven from Athens for good. After a last Athenian victory at Arginusae (406), Lysander crushed the Athenian navy at Aegospotamos (405) and sailed to Piraeus. Athens, besieged by land and sea, capitulated in 404. It never again regained its former importance, and for about 30 years afterward Sparta was the main power in Greece.

Peloponnesus or **Pelopónnisos,** formerly Morea, peninsula, S Greece, linked to the northern mainland by the Isthmus of Corinth. It is mainly mountainous, with fertile coastal strips in the north and west. Among its ancient Greek cities were SPARTA, CORINTH, Argos, and Megalopolis.

Pelops, in Greek mythology, son of TANTALUS. Murdered by his father, he was served at a banquet for the gods, who realized the trick, punished Tantalus, and restored Pelops, giving him an ivory shoulder for the one DEMETER had eaten. To win his wife, Hippodamia, he cheated in a chariot race and killed the charioteer Myrtilus, who cursed him before dying. Thus Pelops caused the many misfortunes visited upon his sons, ATREUS and Thyestes. The PELOPONNESUS was named for Pelops.

Pemba: see ZANZIBAR.

penance, SACRAMENT of the Roman Catholic and Orthodox Eastern churches in which a penitent confesses his or her SINS to a priest. A penance, usually of prayers, is then fixed by the priest. Roman Catholics are required to confess their serious sins before receiving communion and at least once a year. The penitent must have contrition for sin and make restitution for injuries to others.

pen-based computer, COMPUTER that uses pattern-recognition software to enable it to accept handwriting as a form of input. A stylus, which may contain special electronic circuity, is used to write on the computer display or on a separate tablet. The earliest devices were limited to recognizing geometric shapes for COMPUTER GRAPHICS applications and neatly printed alphabetic characters. Pattern recognition has improved to the level where cursive input is now acceptable, especially in PERSONAL DIGITAL ASSISTANTS.

Penderecki, Krzysztof [pändĕrĕts′kē], 1933–, Polish composer. He devised his own system of MUSICAL NOTATION to convey the effects of his unusual sonorities. His works include the *St. Luke Passion* (1963–66), a concerto for five-stringed violin (1967–68), symphonies, and several operas. He was rector (1972–87) of the Kraków conservatory.

Pendragon, Uther: see ARTHURIAN LEGEND.

pendulum, a mass suspended from a fixed point so that it can swing in an arc. The length of a pendulum is the distance from the point of suspension to the center of gravity of the mass. The period *T*, or time for one complete swing, depends on the length *l* of the pendulum and on the acceleration *g* of gravity at the pendulum's location, according to a formula derived by Christiaan HUYGENS: $T = 2\pi\sqrt{l/g}$. Huygens introduced (1673) the use of the pendulum to regulate the speed of clocks. See also HARMONIC MOTION.

Penelope, in Greek mythology, wife of ODYSSEUS, mother of Telemachus; in HOMER's *Odyssey*, a model of fidelity. Pursued by suitors during Odysseus' absence, she agreed to marry after weaving her father-in-law's shroud but unraveled her work each night. She finally promised to marry the man who could bend Odysseus' bow, but none could. Odysseus returned disguised as a beggar, bent the bow, and slew the suitors.

penguin, originally the common name for the extinct great AUK and now used, starting in the 19th cent., for unrelated Antarctic diving birds. Penguins swim by means of their flipperlike wings, using their webbed feet as rudders; they waddle awkwardly on land. Species range from the largest, the emperor (3–4 ft/91.5–122 cm in height), to the smallest, the blue. Penguins are highly gregarious and nest in colonies of up to half a million birds in 500 acres.

penicillin, any of a group of ANTIBIOTICS obtained from the molds of the genera *Aspergillis* and *Penicillium* and the first to be used successfully to treat bacterial infections in humans. Penicillin acts to inhibit cell wall formation in many gram-positive bacteria (see GRAM'S STAIN), including those that cause syphilis, pneumococcal pneumonia, and some staphylococcal and streptococcal infections. Although not active against most gram-negative bacteria, the tubercle bacillus, protozoans, fungi, or viruses, penicillin remains important in antibiotic therapy. Use of penicillin is limited by its tendency to induce allergic reactions (see ALLERGY) and because of the development of microorganisms that are resistant to its actions. Synthetic derivatives of penicillin include ampicillin, methicillin, and oxacillin. Erythromycin and other antibiotics have become important in treating infections that are resistant to penicillin.

Peninsular campaign, in the American CIVIL WAR, failed attempt (April–July 1862) by the Union army to capture RICHMOND by invading the Virginia peninsula between the York and James rivers. A Union force of 100,000 under Gen. George B. MCCLELLAN invaded the tip of the peninsula by sea and forced Confederate Gen. Joseph E. JOHNSTON to evacuate Yorktown and abandon Norfolk. The Union army drew near Richmond and beat off a Confederate attack at Fair Oaks, where Gen. Johnston was wounded. He was succeeded by Gen. Robert E. LEE, who withdrew the Confederate army to Richmond and subsequently forced McClellan to retreat from the peninsula by a brilliant counteroffensive in the SEVEN DAYS BATTLES.

Peninsular War, 1808–14, conflict between France and Great Britain on the Iberian Peninsula, growing out of the efforts of NAPOLEON I to control Spain and Portugal. When a palace revolt in Madrid (Mar. 1808) deposed the pro-French CHARLES IV, Napoleon invaded Spain and made his brother Joseph Bonaparte (see BONAPARTE, family) king of Spain (June). Both Spain and Portugal then revolted, and the British sent a force, under the future duke of WELLINGTON, to aid the rebels. Portugal was quickly won, but the fighting in Spain went on for years. By the time Napoleon abdicated, however, the British had won all of the peninsula and had penetrated France as far as Toulouse.

penis: see REPRODUCTIVE SYSTEM.

penitential psalms: see PSALMS.

Penn, William, 1644–1718, English Quaker leader and founder (1681) of PENNSYLVANIA colony as a religious and political haven for Quakers (see FRIENDS, RELIGIOUS SOCIETY OF). During his first visit there (1682–84), Penn drew up a liberal Frame of Government and established friendly relations with the indigenous tribes. He returned only once (1699–1701).

Pennell, Joseph, 1857–1926, American graphic artist and illustrator; b. Philadelphia. Influenced by WHISTLER, he is noted chiefly for his landscapes and architectural views, and his art is distinguished for its simplicity and technical perfection. Etchings, drawings, and lithographs of Pennell are in the Library of Congress (Wash., D.C.), Carnegie Institute (Pittsburgh), and Brooklyn Museum (N.Y.C.).

Pennsylvania, mid-Atlantic state of the U.S.; bordered by the Delaware River, across which lies New Jersey (E), Delaware and Maryland (S), West Virginia (SW), Ohio (W), and Lake Erie and New York (N).

Area, 45,333 sq mi (117,412 sq km). *Pop.* (1990) 11,881,643, a 0.1% increase over 1980 pop. *Capital,* Harrisburg. *Statehood,* Dec. 12, 1787 (second of original 13 states to ratify the Constitution). *Highest pt.,* Mt. Davis, 3,213 ft (980 m); *lowest pt.,* sea level. *Nickname,* Keystone State. *Motto,* Virtue, Liberty, and Independence. *State bird,* ruffed grouse. *State flower,* mountain laurel. *State tree,* hemlock. *Abbr.,* Pa.; PA.

Land and People. Coastal plains are found in the northwest and southeast. Most of Pennsylvania's terrain consists of mountains extending diagonally across the state. Ridges and valleys dominate the west; the Allegheny plateau covers the northern half of the state. Almost 70% of the population lives in metropolitan areas. PHILADELPHIA, the country's fifth largest city and a major port, is followed in size by PITTSBURGH, a major steel center; ERIE; and ALLENTOWN. In 1990 the state was 88% white and 9% African American.

Economy. Pennsylvania produces about 15% of the country's steel, and primary metals are the most profitable manufacture, followed by processed foods, fabricated metal products, and nonelectrical machinery. The state has extensive farmlands producing dairy items, cattle, corn, hay, eggs, mushrooms, and apples. Pennsylvania has long been one of the country's leading coal producers, and it is also an important source of cement, lime, and crushed stone.

Government. The constitution of 1873 provides for a governor elected to a four-year term. The general assembly consists of a senate of 50 members elected to four-year terms and a house of 203 members elected to two-year terms. Pennsylvania is represented in the U.S. Congress by 2 senators and 21 representatives and has 23 electoral votes.

History. Pennsylvania was inhabited by Native American tribes, including the DELAWARE, SHAWNEE, and Susquehanna, when the Swedes established a settlement in 1643. Control subsequently passed to the Dutch (1655) and the British (1664), who granted proprietary rights to the Quaker William PENN. He viewed his colony as a haven for persecuted religious groups; early settlers included the "Pennsylvania Dutch," who settled in the fertile Great Valley, where they are still heavily concentrated. The western frontier of Pennsylvania was the site of much fighting during the FRENCH AND INDIAN WARS. Pennsylvanians such as Benjamin FRANKLIN became leaders of the independence movement, often centered in Philadelphia, which was the premier city of the THIRTEEN COLONIES. As the geographical keystone of the colonies, Pennsylvania saw considerable fighting during the AMERICAN REVOLUTION. Iron-smelting began during the late 18th cent., and further economic growth was encouraged by the construction of canals (1820s) and railroads. Pennsylvania was the site of fighting during the CIVIL WAR, particularly in the GETTYSBURG CAMPAIGN of 1863. With the close of the war came the rapid emergence of the state as a mighty industrial commonwealth dominated by oil drilling, coal mining, and steel production. Huge industrial combines, including the U.S. Steel Co., emerged, and their plants were the scenes of violent strikes that produced a strengthened labor movement. Although Pennsylvania remains a major industrial state, its heavy industries were hurt by the national economic slowdown of the early 1980s, and the recession of the late 1980s and early 90s precipitated the loss of many manufacturing jobs. There was, however, increased demand for Pennsylvania coal, growth in the service sector, and expansion in the biotechnology and drug industries.

Pennsylvania, University of, in Philadelphia. Opened as an academy in 1751, largely through Benjamin FRANKLIN'S efforts, it was chartered (1755) as a college. By establishing (1765) the first school of medicine in what is now the U.S., it became the country's first true university, acquiring that title in 1779. Its Wharton School of Finance and Commerce (est. 1881) was the first of its kind, and its Wistar Institute of Anatomy and Biology (1892) is notable.

Pensacola, city (1990 pop. 58,165), seat of Escambia co., NW Fla., on Pensacola Bay; inc. 1822. On the site of early Spanish settlements (1559–61, 1698), it belonged to several nations before becoming (1821) part of the U.S. purchase of Florida. Fishing, shipping, and manufacturing are important. Much of the city's economic and community life centers around military air bases.

pension, periodic payments to employees who retire because of age or disability. In the 19th cent., France and Great Britain provided government pensions to civil servants. In the U.S., government pensions have been given to all war veterans since the Revolution and to federal employees since 1920. Today private pension plans (organized by municipalities, labor unions, corporations, professional associations, and others) supplement SOCIAL SECURITY, which was instituted in 1935. The federal Pension Benefit Guaranty Corp. insures the pension plans of participating U.S. companies.

Pentagon, the, structure housing the U.S. Dept. of DEFENSE, in Arlington, Va. Completed in 1943, it comprises five concentric buildings, connected by corridors, and covers an area of 34 acres (13.8 hectares).

Pentagon Papers, government study of U.S. involvement in Southeast Asia from World War II to May 1968. Commissioned by Secretary of Defense Robert S. MCNAMARA, the top secret study, completed in Jan. 1969, revealed a considerable degree of miscalculation, bureaucratic arrogance, and deception by U.S. policymakers. In particular, it found that the U.S. government had continually resisted full disclosure of its military involvement in

Southeast Asia. On June 13, 1971, the New York *Times* began a series of articles based on the study. The Justice Department obtained a court injunction against further publication on national security grounds, but the Supreme Court ruled (June 30) that constitutional guarantees of a free press overrode other considerations, and allowed further publication. The government indicted (1971) Daniel Ellsberg, a former government employee who made the Pentagon Papers available to the New York *Times*, on charges of espionage, theft, and conspiracy. On May 11, 1973, a Federal judge dismissed all charges due to improper government conduct.

pentameter [Gr., = measure of five feet], in versification, a line to be scanned in five feet, as in Thomas NASHE's "Cold doth/not sting,/ the pret/ty birds/do sing." Iambic pentameter, with short-long feet, is the most common English meter, appearing first in CHAUCER's poetry. In the *Canterbury Tales* he used rhymed pentameter couplets; since he pronounced a final *e*, the lines often had eleven syllables. Later, with the final *e* dropped, this form became the heroic couplet, used notably by John DRYDEN and Alexander POPE. Blank verse, a succession of unrhymed iambic pentameters, is primarily an English form; it has been used in the loftiest epic and dramatic verse from SHAKESPEARE and John MILTON to the present. The SONNET is one of the most successful uses of iambic pentameter in English poetry.

Pentateuch [pĕn'tətyo͞ok] [Gr., = five books], first five books of the OLD TESTAMENT, the TORAH of MOSES.

pentathlon, composite athletic event. In ancient Greece it comprised leaping, foot racing, wrestling, discus, and javelin. The modern pentathlon, an Olympic event since 1912, involves a cross-country horseback ride, a cross-country run, swimming, épée fencing, and pistol shooting.

Pentecost [Gr., = fiftieth], important Jewish and Christian feasts. In Judaism it is called *Shavuot* and marks the end of the Palestinian spring grain harvest (see JEWISH HOLIDAYS). In Christianity it commemorates the coming of the HOLY GHOST to the disciples of Jesus, 50 days after the Passover in which Jesus died. In England it is called Whitsunday.

Pentecostalism, fundamentalist Protestant religious movement that grew out of the holiness movement in the U.S. in the early 20th cent. Pentecostalists believe in baptism with the Holy Ghost, "Speaking in tongues," faith healing, and the impending second coming of Jesus. Of the many Pentecostalist churches, the Church of God in Christ and the Assemblies of God are the largest.

penumbra: see ECLIPSE; SUNSPOTS.

Penutian [pəno͞o'shən], linguistic family of indigenous peoples of North and Central America. See NATIVE AMERICAN LANGUAGES (table).

Penzias, Arno Allan, 1933–, American astrophysicist, b. Munich. He and Robert Wilson won a Nobel Prize in physics in 1978 for their study of cosmic microwave radiation. They analyzed radio emissions from a ring of gas encircling the MILKY WAY. Their work lent support to the big bang theory (see COSMOLOGY) of creation. In 1981 Penzias became vice president of research at Bell Laboratories.

peony, popular flowering plant (genus *Paeonia*) of the buttercup family. Herbaceous peonies (most varieties of *P. lactiflora*) are hardy, bushy perennials that die back each year. The large, usually spring-blooming, single or double flowers are generally shades of red, pink, or white. Tree peonies (*P. suffroticosa*) have a somewhat woody base and are usually taller, with more abundant and larger blossoms.

People's party: see POPULIST PARTY.

Peoria, city (1990 pop. 113,504), seat of Peoria co., central Ill., on the Illinois R.; inc. as a city 1845. A busy port, it is the trade and transportation hub for a region producing grain, livestock, and coal. Although it has distilleries and factories producing heavy and light industrial goods, Peoria is known for its scenic beauty. La Salle established a fort in the region in 1680. The first permanent American settlement was in 1819.

Pepin [pĕ'pĭn], rulers of the FRANKS. **Pepin of Landan** (Pepin I), d. 639?, mayor of the palace of the Frankish kingdom of Austrasia, forced the succession (629) of Dagobert I as king and established the foundation for the CAROLINGIAN dynasty. His grandson, **Pepin of Heristal** (Pepin II), d. 714, mayor of the palace (680–714) of Austrasia and Neustria, established Carolingian power over the MEROVINGIAN kings by making himself the actual ruler of the Franks. He was the father of CHARLES MARTEL and the grandfather of **Pepin the Short** (Pepin III), c.714–768, the first Carolingian king of the Franks (751–68). He overthrew the Merovingian dynasty and had himself crowned king with the support of Pope Zacharias. Pepin defended papal interests and in 754 turned over to the pope what became the foundation of the PAPAL STATES. He was the father of CHARLEMAGNE.

pepper, name for the fruits of several plants used as condiments or in medicine. **Black pepper** (*Piper nigrum*), the true pepper, is economically the most important species of the pantropical pepper family (Piperaceae). A perennial climbing shrub native to Java, it bears pea-sized berries, the "peppercorns" of commerce. Black pepper, sold whole or ground, is the whole fruit; white pepper, made by removing the dark, outer hull, has a milder, less pungent flavor. Other *Piper* species of value include the betel pepper (*P. betle*), whose leaves are a principal ingredient in BETEL. The **red peppers,** native to warm temperate and tropical regions of the Americas, are various species of *Capsicum* (of the NIGHTSHADE family). The hot varieties include cayenne pepper, whose dried, ground fruit is sold as a spice, and chili pepper, sold similarly as a powder or in a chili sauce. Paprika (the Hungarian word for red pepper) is a ground spice from a less pungent variety. The pimiento, or Spanish pepper, is a mild type; its small fruit is used as a condiment and for stuffing olives. The common garden, or bell, pepper has larger, also mild fruits; they are used as vegetables and in salads. Bell peppers are also known as green peppers because they are most often marketed while still unripe.

peppermint: see MINT.

pepsin, digestive enzyme in the STOMACH that degrades protein. Most active in the acidic medium normally present in the stomach, pepsin breaks down proteins into their readily absorbed components, i.e., PEPTIDES and AMINO ACIDS.

peptic ulcer: see under ULCER.

peptide or **polypeptide,** biochemical formed by the linkage of up to about 50 AMINO ACIDS to form an unbranched chain. Longer chains are called PROTEINS. The amino acids are coupled by a peptide bond, a special linkage in which the amide group of one amino acid binds to the carboxyl group of another. Many peptides, such as the hormones vasopressin and ACTH, have physiological or antibacterial activity.

Pepys, Samuel [pēps], 1633–1703, English public official and author of the most famous English DIARY. He was an admiralty official, sat in Parliament (1679), and in 1684 was named president of the ROYAL SOCIETY. Forced into retirement on the accession of William III, he wrote *Memoirs . . . of the Royal Navy* (1690). Pepys's diary, in cipher, was partially deciphered and published in 1825, and almost all the text appeared from 1893 to 1899. An intimate record of his private life from Jan. 1, 1660, to May 31, 1669, the diary gives a vivid picture of social life and conditions in the early RESTORATION period.

Pequot, indigenous people of the Eastern Woodlands (see NORTH AMERICA, INDIGENOUS PEOPLES OF), with an Algonquian language of the Algonquian-Wakashan stock (see NATIVE AMERICAN LANGUAGES). By 1630 their territory extended to the Connecticut R., where they fought the Pequot War (1637) against settlers. Most were killed or enslaved. Today a few hundred live on two reservations in Ledyard, Connecticut, where the Mashantucket Pequot have established one of the largest gambling casinos in the world.

perch, symmetrical freshwater FISHES of the family Percidae, related to sunfishes and sea BASSES. The yellow perch, *Perca flavescens,* is a popular game and food fish, abundant in lakes and streams, where it feeds on insects, CRAYFISH, and small fish, and grows to an average length of 1 ft (30 cm) and weight of 1 lb (.5 kg). The family includes the walleye or walleyed pike (*Stizostedion vitreum*), the sauger or sand pike (*S. canadense*), and the brilliantly colored American darters, found E of the Rockies.

percussion instrument, any instrument that produces a musical sound when struck with an implement such as a mallet, a stick, a disk, or with the hand. They are used in ORCHESTRAS and bands most often to emphasize rhythm. The most common type is the DRUM, technically known as a membranophone, which consists of a membrane stretched over a frame to be struck with sticks or with the hand. Idiophones are percussion instruments in which the vibrating agent is the solid substance of the instrument itself. These include the triangle, a steel rod bent into an angle and struck with a straight rod; sticks clicked against each other; castanets, commonly consisting of two joined pieces of wood or ivory snapped together between the palm and the fingers; cymbals, a pair of concave metal plates that are struck together; the gong, a disk struck with a mallet or drumstick; the celesta, a high-pitched instrument consisting of steel bars fastened over wood resonators and struck by hammers operated from a keyboard; the glockenspiel, a curved frame enclosing metal bars that are struck with a hammer; the xylophone, an instrument with gradated wooden slats that are struck with small mallets, and sometimes equipped with tubular resonators (in which case it is called a marimba); and the bell.

Percy, Sir Henry, 1366–1403, English nobleman, called Hotspur; son of Henry Percy, 1st earl of Northumberland. He fought against the Scots at Otterburn (1388) and Homildon (1402). Although he had earlier supported the Lancastrian cause, in 1403 Hotspur and his father planned with Thomas Percy, OWEN GLENDOWER, and Sir Edmund de Mortimer to dethrone HENRY IV. Henry triumphed at Shrewsbury, and Hotspur was slain.

Percy, Walker, 1916–90, American novelist; b. Birmingham, Ala. In such novels as *The Moviegoer* (1961), *Love in the Ruins* (1971), and *The Second Coming* (1980), Percy dealt with alienation and redemption as they impinge on Southern Christian gentlemen coping with change.

Pereira, I(rene) Rice [pərā'rə], 1907–71, American painter; b. Chelsea, Mass. Her paintings are characterized by open, framelike forms juxtaposed against bands in mazelike patterns, e.g., *Oblique Progression* (Whitney Mus., N.Y.C.).

Perelman, S(idney) J(oseph), 1904–79, American comic writer; b. Brooklyn, N.Y. The titles of some of his best-known books suggest his screwball type of humor—*Strictly from Hunger* (1937), *The Road to Miltown; or, Under the Spreading Atrophy* (1957), and *The Rising Gorge* (1961). Perelman wrote the scripts for several MARX BROTHERS films.

S.J. Perelman

Peres, Shimon, 1923–, Israeli politician. Born in Poland, he emigrated (1934) to Palestine. He held (1948–65) various posts in Israel's defense ministry and was minister of defense (1974–77). A member of the Labor party from 1968, he became its leader in 1977. He was prime minister (1984–86) and vice premier and foreign minister (1986–90) in a national unity government. Unseated (1992) as party leader by Yitzhak RABIN, Peres became foreign minister under Rabin later that year.

perestroika: see GORBACHEV, MIKHAIL SERGEYEVICH; UNION OF SOVIET SOCIALIST REPUBLICS.

Peretz or **Perez, Isaac Loeb,** 1852–1915, Polish Jewish poet, novelist, playwright, and lawyer. A voice of the renaissance of progressive culture among the Jews (*Haskalah*), he wrote in Hebrew and Yiddish of the material poverty and spiritual riches of European Jews. His finest work is contained in his Hasidic sketches, e.g., *Stories and Pictures* (1900–1901).

Pérez de Ayala, Ramón [pā'rāth dā äyä'lä], 1880?–1962 Spanish writer. His work includes such novels of ideas as *Belarmino and Apolonio* (1921), *Tiger Juan* (1926), and *The Healer of His Honor* (1926); essays; and poetry.

Pérez de Cuéllar, Javier, 1920–, Peruvian diplomat, secretary general of the UNITED NATIONS (1982–91). He entered the Peruvian foreign service in 1940 and served in several posts, including ambassador to the USSR (1969–71) and to the UN (1971–75). He represented the UN on the CYPRUS problem (1975–78) and in 1982 succeeded Kurt Waldheim as secretary general. Serving two terms, he restored the prestige of the UN and, aided in part by the end of the COLD WAR, helped to end the IRAN-IRAQ WAR and the Cambodian civil war and secure the withdrawal of Soviet troops from Afghanistan. Under his leadership UN negotiators obtained the release of the Americans held hostage by Shiites in Lebanon, and he personally negotiated a peace pact between the government and rebels in El Salvador.

Pérez Galdós, Benito [pā'rĕth gäldōs'], 1843–1920, Spanish novelist and dramatist. For his panoramic and psychologically acute treatment of Spanish society he has been called the greatest Spanish novelist since CERVANTES. His works include a cycle of 46 historical novels, *Episodios nacionales,* covering 1805 to 1874; 21 *novelas españolas contemporáneas,* including *Fortunata and Jacinta* (1886–87); and 6 *novelas españolas de la primera época,* notably *Doña Perfecta* (1876) and *La familia de Léon Roch* (1878). His plays include dramatizations of some of his novels.

performance art, art form in which live performance is the essential feature of the artwork. With roots in DADA, it originated in the "happenings" of the 1960s. Performance art incorporates elements from the visual arts, dance, music, pantomime, drama, and other forms; stresses spontaneity, evanescence, and originality; and often exhibits a keen sense of absurdity, humor, or pathos. Performance artists are varied in background and style, and include such figures as Laurie Anderson, Eric Bogosian, Bill Irwin, Reno, the Blue Man Group, and John Kelly.

perfume, aroma produced by essential oils of plants and by synthetic aromatics. The burning of incense in religious rites of ancient China, Palestine, and Egypt led gradually to the personal use of perfume, widespread in ancient Greece and Rome. During the Middle Ages Crusaders brought knowledge of perfumery to Europe from the East. After 1500 Paris was the major center of perfumemaking. Since the early 19th cent. chemists have produced thousands of synthetic scents. In the 20th cent. perfumes for men and women, most a blend of natural and synthetic scents, were produced by prominent fashion designers (see FASHION, table).

Pergamum, ancient city of Asia Minor on the Caicus R., now in Turkey. An independent kingdom, it flourished as a brilliant center of Hellenistic culture in the 3d and 2d cent. B.C. It was particularly notable for its sculptures and for a large library of books on PARCHMENT (which takes its name from the city). King Attalus III (d. 133 B.C.) bequeathed Pergamum to Rome.

Pergolesi, Giovanni Battista, 1710–36, Italian composer. He wrote two masterpieces, the short comic opera *The Maid as Mistress* (1733) and a *Stabat Mater* for treble voices and strings, as well as two operas.

Pericles, c.495–429 B.C., Athenian statesman. In 461 B.C. he secured the exile of Cimon, whom he replaced as leader of ATHENS. Under his tutelage Athens reached its zenith. The DELIAN LEAGUE was powerful, a truce was arranged (445) with Sparta that brought 14 years of peace, and democratic reforms were introduced. Pericles became a great patron of the arts, encouraging music and drama, and was responsible for the building of such great monuments as the PARTHENON and Propylaea on the Acropolis. In 430

PERIODIC TABLE

KEY

atomic number	89
atomic symbol	**Ac**
name of element	*Actinium*
atomic weight (parentheses indicate most stable isotope)	(227)
electronic configuration	2 · 8 · 18 · 32 · 18 · 9 · 2

GROUP Ia	IIa	IIIb	IVb	Vb	VIb	VIIb	VIII	VIII	VIII	Ib	IIb	IIIa	IVa	Va	VIa	VIIa	VIIIa
1 **H** *Hydro-gen* 1.00797 1																	2 **He** *Helium* 4.0026 2
3 **Li** *Lithium* 6.941 2 · 1	4 **Be** *Beryl-lium* 9.0122 2 · 2											5 **B** *Boron* 10.811 2 · 3	6 **C** *Carbon* 12.011 2 · 4	7 **N** *Nitrogen* 14.0067 2 · 5	8 **O** *Oxygen* 15.9994 2 · 6	9 **F** *Fluorine* 18.998 2 · 7	10 **Ne** *Neon* 20.183 2 · 8
11 **Na** *Sodium* 22.9898 2 · 8 · 1	12 **Mg** *Magne-sium* 24.312 2 · 8 · 2											13 **Al** *Alumi-num* 26.9815 2 · 8 · 3	14 **Si** *Silicon* 28.086 2 · 8 · 4	15 **P** *Phos-phorus* 30.9738 2 · 8 · 5	16 **S** *Sulfur* 32.064 2 · 8 · 6	17 **Cl** *Chlorine* 35.453 2 · 8 · 7	18 **Ar** *Argon* 39.948 2 · 8 · 8
19 **K** *Potas-sium* 39.102 2 · 8 · 8 · 1	20 **Ca** *Calcium* 40.08 2 · 8 · 8 · 2	21 **Sc** *Scan-dium* 44.956 2 · 8 · 9 · 2	22 **Ti** *Titanium* 47.90 2 · 8 · 10 · 2	23 **V** *Vana-dium* 50.942 2 · 8 · 11 · 2	24 **Cr** *Chro-mium* 51.996 2 · 8 · 13 · 1	25 **Mn** *Manga-nese* 54.9380 2 · 8 · 13 · 2	26 **Fe** *Iron* 55.847 2 · 8 · 14 · 2	27 **Co** *Cobalt* 58.9332 2 · 8 · 15 · 2	28 **Ni** *Nickel* 58.71 2 · 8 · 16 · 2	29 **Cu** *Copper* 63.546 2 · 8 · 18 · 1	30 **Zn** *Zinc* 65.37 2 · 8 · 18 · 2	31 **Ga** *Gallium* 69.72 2 · 8 · 18 · 3	32 **Ge** *Germa-nium* 72.59 2 · 8 · 18 · 4	33 **As** *Arsenic* 74.9216 2 · 8 · 18 · 5	34 **Se** *Sele-nium* 78.96 2 · 8 · 18 · 6	35 **Br** *Bromine* 79.904 2 · 8 · 18 · 7	36 **Kr** *Krypton* 83.80 2 · 8 · 18 · 8
37 **Rb** *Rubid-ium* 85.47 2 · 8 · 18 · 8 · 1	38 **Sr** *Stron-tium* 87.62 2 · 8 · 18 · 8 · 2	39 **Y** *Yttri-um* 88.905 2 · 8 · 18 · 9 · 2	40 **Zr** *Zirco-nium* 91.22 2 · 8 · 18 · 10 · 2	41 **Nb** *Nio-bium* 92.906 2 · 8 · 18 · 12 · 1	42 **Mo** *Molyb-denum* 95.94 2 · 8 · 18 · 13 · 1	43 **Tc** *Techne-tium* (97) 2 · 8 · 18 · 13 · 2	44 **Ru** *Ruthe-nium* 101.07 2 · 8 · 18 · 15 · 1	45 **Rh** *Rho-dium* 102.905 2 · 8 · 18 · 16 · 1	46 **Pd** *Palla-dium* 106.4 2 · 8 · 18 · 18 · 0	47 **Ag** *Silver* 107.868 2 · 8 · 18 · 18 · 1	48 **Cd** *Cadmi-um* 112.40 2 · 8 · 18 · 18 · 2	49 **In** *Indium* 114.82 2 · 8 · 18 · 18 · 3	50 **Sn** *Tin* 118.69 2 · 8 · 18 · 18 · 4	51 **Sb** *Anti-mony* 121.75 2 · 8 · 18 · 18 · 5	52 **Te** *Tellu-rium* 127.60 2 · 8 · 18 · 18 · 6	53 **I** *Iodine* 126.9045 2 · 8 · 18 · 18 · 7	54 **Xe** *Xenon* 131.30 2 · 8 · 18 · 18 · 8
55 **Cs** *Cesium* 132.905 2 · 8 · 18 · 18 · 8 · 1	56 **Ba** *Barium* 137.34 2 · 8 · 18 · 18 · 8 · 2	57–71 *Lantha-nide Series**	72 **Hf** *Hafnium* 178.49 2 · 8 · 18 · 32 · 10 · 2	73 **Ta** *Tanta-lum* 180.948 2 · 8 · 18 · 32 · 11 · 2	74 **W** *Tungsten* 183.85 2 · 8 · 18 · 32 · 12 · 2	75 **Re** *Rhenium* 186.2 2 · 8 · 18 · 32 · 13 · 2	76 **Os** *Osmium* 190.2 2 · 8 · 18 · 32 · 14 · 2	77 **Ir** *Iridium* 192.2 2 · 8 · 18 · 32 · 15 · 2	78 **Pt** *Plati-num* 195.09 2 · 8 · 18 · 32 · 16 · 2	79 **Au** *Gold* 196.967 2 · 8 · 18 · 32 · 18 · 1	80 **Hg** *Mer-cury* 200.59 2 · 8 · 18 · 32 · 18 · 2	81 **Tl** *Thal-lium* 204.37 2 · 8 · 18 · 32 · 18 · 3	82 **Pb** *Lead* 207.19 2 · 8 · 18 · 32 · 18 · 4	83 **Bi** *Bismuth* 208.9806 2 · 8 · 18 · 32 · 18 · 5	84 **Po** *Polo-nium* (209) 2 · 8 · 18 · 32 · 18 · 6	85 **At** *Astatine* (210) 2 · 8 · 18 · 32 · 18 · 7	86 **Rn** *Radon* (222) 2 · 8 · 18 · 32 · 18 · 8
87 **Fr** *Fran-cium* (223) 2 · 8 · 18 · 32 · 18 · 8 · 1	88 **Ra** *Radium* (226) 2 · 8 · 18 · 32 · 18 · 8 · 2	89–103 *Actinide Series†*	104 **Rf‡** *Ruther-fordium* (261) 2 · 8 · 18 · 32 · 32 · 10 · 2	105 **Ha‡** *Hahnium* (262) 2 · 8 · 18 · 32 · 32 · 11 · 2	106 **Unh** *Unnil-hexium* (263) 2 · 8 · 18 · 32 · 32 · 12 · 2	107 **Ns‡** *Nielsbo-hrium* (262) 2 · 8 · 18 · 32 · 32 · 13 · 2	108 **Hs‡** *Hassium* (265) 2 · 8 · 18 · 32 · 32 · 14 · 2	109 **Mt‡** *Meitne-rium* (266) 2 · 8 · 18 · 32 · 32 · 15 · 2									

*LANTHANIDE SERIES (*Rare Earth Elements*)	Symbol	Name	Atomic weight	Electron configuration
57	La	*Lanthanum*	138.91	2 · 8 · 18 18 · 9 · 2
58	Ce	*Cerium*	140.12	2 · 8 · 18 20 · 8 · 2
59	Pr	*Praseodymium*	140.907	2 · 8 · 18 21 · 8 · 2
60	Nd	*Neodymium*	144.24	2 · 8 · 18 22 · 8 · 2
61	Pm	*Promethium*	(145)	2 · 8 · 18 23 · 8 · 2
62	Sm	*Samarium*	150.35	2 · 8 · 18 24 · 8 · 2
63	Eu	*Europium*	151.96	2 · 8 · 18 25 · 8 · 2
64	Gd	*Gadolinium*	157.25	2 · 8 · 18 25 · 9 · 2
65	Tb	*Terbium*	158.9254	2 · 8 · 18 27 · 8 · 2
66	Dy	*Dysprosium*	162.50	2 · 8 · 18 28 · 8 · 2
67	Ho	*Holmium*	164.930	2 · 8 · 18 29 · 8 · 2
68	Er	*Erbium*	167.26	2 · 8 · 18 30 · 8 · 2
69	Tm	*Thulium*	168.934	2 · 8 · 18 31 · 8 · 2
70	Yb	*Ytterbium*	173.04	2 · 8 · 18 32 · 8 · 2
71	Lu	*Lutetium*	174.97	2 · 8 · 18 32 · 9 · 2

†ACTINIDE SERIES (*Radioactive Rare Earth Elements*)	Symbol	Name	Atomic weight	Electron configuration
89	Ac	*Actinium*	(227)	2 · 8 · 18 32 · 18 9 · 2
90	Th	*Thorium*	232.038	2 · 8 · 18 32 · 18 10 · 2
91	Pa	*Protactinium*	231.0359	2 · 8 · 18 32 · 20 9 · 2
92	U	*Uranium*	238.03	2 · 8 · 18 32 · 21 9 · 2
93	Np	*Neptunium*	237.0482	2 · 8 · 18 32 · 22 9 · 2
94	Pu	*Plutonium*	(244)	2 · 8 · 18 32 · 24 8 · 2
95	Am	*Americium*	(243)	2 · 8 · 18 32 · 25 8 · 2
96	Cm	*Curium*	(247)	2 · 8 · 18 32 · 25 9 · 2
97	Bk	*Berkelium*	(247)	2 · 8 · 18 32 · 27 8 · 2
98	Cf	*Californium*	(251)	2 · 8 · 18 32 · 28 8 · 2
99	Es	*Einsteinium*	(254)	2 · 8 · 18 32 · 29 8 · 2
100	Fm	*Fermium*	(257)	2 · 8 · 18 32 · 30 8 · 2
101	Md	*Mendelevium*	(256)	2 · 8 · 18 32 · 31 8 · 2
102	No	*Nobelium*	(254)	2 · 8 · 18 32 · 32 8 · 2
103	Lr	*Lawrencium*	(256)	2 · 8 · 18 32 · 32 9 · 2

‡Also called kurchatovium and unnilquadium (104); unnilpentium (105); unnilseptium (107); unniloctium (108); unnilennium (109).

B.C., during the PELOPONNESIAN WAR, he made a strong appeal to the pride and patriotism of the Athenians but was driven from office. Reinstated (429), he died six months later.

perigee and **perihelion:** see APSIS.

perinatology: see PEDIATRICS.

period, in physics: see HARMONIC MOTION; WAVE.

periodic table, chart that reflects the periodic recurrence of chemical and physical properties of the ELEMENTS when the elements are arranged in order of increasing ATOMIC NUMBER. The periodic table was devised by Dmitri MENDELEEV and revised by Henry MOSELEY. It is divided into vertical columns, or groups, numbered from I to VIII, with a final column numbered 0. Each group is divided into two categories, or families, one called the a series (the representative, or main group, elements) the other the b series (the TRANSITION ELEMENTS, or subgroup elements). All the elements in a group have the same number of VALENCE electrons and have similar chemical properties. The horizontal rows of the table are called periods. The elements of a particular period have the same number of electron shells; the number of electrons in these shells, which equals the element's atomic number, increases from left to right within each period. In each period the lighter METALS appear on the left, the heavier metals in the center, and the nonmetals on the right. Elements on the borderline between metals and nonmetals are called metalloids. Elements in group Ia are called the ALKALI METALS; in group IIa, the ALKALINE-EARTH METALS; in group VIIa, the HALOGENS; and in group 0, the INERT GASES.

periodontitis or **pyorrhea,** inflammation and degeneration of the gums and other tissues surrounding the teeth. Symptoms are bleeding gums, followed by the receding of gums from the TEETH, loosening of the teeth, and resorption of the bone supporting the teeth. Causes include poor nutrition, plaque, and poor oral hygiene.

peritoneum: see ABDOMEN.

peritonitis, acute or chronic inflammation of the peritoneum, the membrane lining the abdomen and surrounding internal organs. It is caused by invasion of bacteria or foreign matter following rupture of an internal organ, by infection from elsewhere in the body, by penetrating injury to the abdominal wall, or by accidental contamination during surgery. Treatment includes ANTIBIOTIC therapy.

periwinkle, mollusk with a conical spiral shell, a variety of SNAIL. Periwinkles are marine GASTROPODS that feed on algae and seaweed and are found at the water's edge.

Perkins, Frances, 1882–1965, U.S. secretary of labor (1933–45); b. Boston. The first woman appointed to the cabinet, she promoted and administered liberal labor legislation during Pres. F.D. ROOSEVELT'S NEW DEAL administration.

Perlman, Itzhak, 1945–, Israeli violinist. Although a victim of polio at age four, he gave a solo violin recital at ten and appeared on American television in 1958. He studied at the Juilliard School, in New York City, and has since the early 1960s appeared widely in concert. He is noted for his warmth and brilliant technique.

Perm [pyĕrm], city (1990 est. pop. 1,090,000), E European Russia, on the Kama R. A transfer center for rail and river cargo, it is a major producer of machinery in the Urals industrial and mining region and has oil refineries and chemical plants. Founded in 1780, it was named Molotov from 1940 to 1958.

Permian period: see GEOLOGIC ERA (table).

permutations and combinations, the study of techniques for counting arrangements and choices of objects; such techniques are often used in PROBABILITY problems. A permutation of a set is a way in which the elements of the set can be arranged or ordered. In general, the number of permutations of n things taken r at a time is given by $P(n,r) = n!/(n - r)!$, where the symbol $n!$, denoting the product of the integers from 1 to n, is called the n factorial. A combination is a choice of different elements from a larger set, without regard to order. In general, the number of combinations of n things taken r at a time is $C(n,r) = n!/r!(n - r)!$

Perón, Juan Domingo [pĕrōn′], 1895–1974, president of Argentina (1946–55, 1973–74). An army officer, he rose to prominence when Ramón Castillo was overthrown in 1943. He developed a following among workers, churchmen, landowners, and industrialists. In 1946 he was elected president by a huge majority. He set up a dictatorship and instituted a program of revolutionary, nationalistic measures (known as *peronismo*) which were supposed to lead to economic self-sufficiency. By the early 1950s, however, the economy had deteriorated and Perón had broken with the church. After the death in 1952 of his enormously popular wife, Eva, his support weakened, and in 1955 he was overthrown by a military coup. *Peronismo* nevertheless remained a potent political force and contributed to governmental chaos. In 1971 Perón returned to Argentina, and in 1973 he was elected president. His wife, María Estela (Isabel) Martínez de Perón (see below), was elected vice president, and she succeeded to the presidency when he died in 1974. Perón's second wife, **Eva Duarte de Perón** [dōōär'tā], 1919–52, was a minor actress before her marriage to Perón in 1945. After he became president, she virtually ran the ministries of health and labor, and she commanded a huge political following. She died of cancer at the age of 33. Perón's third wife, **María Estela (Isabel) Martínez de Perón,** 1931–, was a dancer before she married the exiled Perón in 1961. Upon her husband's death in 1974 she became president of Argentina, but in 1976 she was deposed in a military coup and placed under house arrest. Freed in 1981, she went into exile in Spain.

Perot, H(enry) Ross, 1930–, American business executive; b. Texarkana, Tex. After working for IBM, he founded (1962) Electronic Data Systems (EDS), a computer services company. During the Iranian hostage crisis (1979), he funded a successful operation to rescue two of his employees from an Iranian prison. He sold EDS to General Motors in 1984, diversified into real estate, gas, and oil, and later started a new computer services company. He ran unsuccessfully for U.S. president as an independent in 1992 and fought U.S. ratification of the NORTH AMERICAN FREE TRADE AGREEMENT.

peroxide, chemical compound containing two oxygen atoms, each of which is bonded to the other and to a radical or some element other than oxygen; e.g., in hydrogen peroxide (H_2O_2) the atoms are joined together in the chainlike structure H—O—O—H. Peroxides are unstable, releasing oxygen when heated, and are powerful oxidizing agents. Peroxides may be formed directly by the reaction of an element or compound with oxygen.

perpetual-motion machine, a machine, considered impossible to build, that would be able to operate continuously and supply useful work without needing a continuous supply of heat or fuel. A perpetual-motion machine of the first kind, which would produce more ENERGY in the form of work than is supplied to it in the form of heat, violates the first law of THERMODYNAMICS. A perpetual-motion machine of the second kind, which would continuously supply work without a flow of heat from a warmer body to a cooler body, violates the second law of thermodynamics.

Perrault, Charles [pĕrō'], 1628–1703, French poet famed for his *Mother Goose Tales* (1697) for children. One of his poems (1687) set off the celebrated "quarrel of the ancients and the moderns"; BOILEAU-DESPRÉAUX, the chief defender of the ancients, bandied insults with Perrault until 1694.

Perret, Auguste [pĕrā'], 1874–1954, French architect. He was a pioneer in the use of reinforced concrete, notably in the church of Le Raincy, near Paris (1922–23). He built warehouses, factories, residences, and theaters in this material.

Perrot, Jules, 1810–92, French dancer and choreographer. He worked (1848–59) at the Imperial Theatre in St. Petersburg. His ballets include *Esmeralda, Ondine,* and part of the original *Giselle* (1841).

Perry, Matthew Calbraith, 1794–1858, U.S. naval officer; b. South Kingstown, R.I. Commodore Perry opened up isolationist JAPAN to Western trade and influence. In 1853 he anchored his squadron of four U.S. navy ships in lower Tokyo Bay. A skilled diplomat, Perry negotiated a treaty (1854) with Tokugawa shogunate officials that permitted American ships to use two Japanese ports. His brother, **Oliver Hazard Perry,** 1785–1819, was also a U.S. naval officer. He commanded the U.S. fleet that defeated a British force in the Battle of Lake Erie (1813) during the WAR OF 1812. His report of the battle—"We have met the enemy and they are ours"—has become famous.

Perry, William James, 1927–, U.S. government official; b. Vandergrift, Pa. A former engineering professor and founder of a military electronics firm, he served as a defense undersecretary (1977–81) in the Carter administration. Appointed deputy defense secretary by Pres. Clinton in 1993, he became defense secretary in 1994.

Perse, Saint-John, pseud. of **Alexis Saint-Léger Léger,** 1887–1975, French poet and diplomat; b. Guadeloupe. He was the permanent head of the foreign affairs ministry from 1933 to 1940. His reputation as a poet of great lyric power grew after his self-imposed exile to the U.S. in 1940. His works include *Éloges* (1911), *Anabasis* (1924), *Exile* (1942), and *Seamarks* (1957). He received the 1960 Nobel Prize in literature.

Persephone [pərsĕf'ənē] or **Proserpine** [prōsûr'pənē], in Greek and Roman mythology, goddess of fertility, queen of the underworld; daughter of ZEUS and DEMETER. She was abducted by PLUTO, who held her captive in HADES. Demeter persuaded the gods to let her return to earth for eight months a year. Her story, celebrated in the ELEUSINIAN MYSTERIES, symbolized the vegetative cycle. When she left the earth, life withered; when she returned, it blossomed anew.

Persepolis [pərsĕp'əlĭs], ancient city of Persia, NE of present-day Shiraz. It was the ceremonial (but not administrative) capital of the Persian empire under DARIUS I and his successors. The ruins contain several palaces as well as a citadel.

Perseus, c.212–166 B.C., last king of MACEDON (179–168 B.C.), son and successor of PHILIP V. His anti-Roman policy caused the Third Macedonian War (171–168); he was defeated (168) by the Romans at Pydna and died in captivity.

Perseus, in Greek mythology, son of ZEUS and Danaë. Told by an oracle that Perseus would kill him, his grandfather Acrisius set him and Danaë afloat in a chest, from which they were rescued by King Polydectes. Later, seeing Perseus as an obstacle to his love for Danaë, the king sent him to fetch the head of the GORGON Medusa. The gods aided Perseus, and he slew Medusa. Fleeing from the other Gorgons, Perseus was refused aid by ATLAS, who was turned into a stone mountain by Medusa's head. On his way home, Perseus rescued ANDROMEDA and married her. Later, while competing in a discus contest, Perseus accidentally killed Acrisius, thus fulfilling the prophecy. Benvenuto CELLINI's famous statue of Perseus is in FLORENCE, Italy.

Pershing, John Joseph, 1860–1948, U.S. army officer; b. Linn co., Mo. After commanding army units during the SPANISH-AMERICAN WAR (1898) and in the Philippines (1906–13), Gen. Pershing commanded the American Expeditionary Force (1917–18) in WORLD WAR I. He was expert at molding hastily trained American troops into skilled combat units.

Persia, old name for the Asian country of IRAN, in which the ancient Persian empire had its core. The early Persians were presumably a nomadic tribe that filtered through the Caucasus to the Iranian plateau. By the 7th cent. B.C. they were established in the present region of Fars, which then belonged to the Assyrian empire. Persian rulers were early associated with the Medes, who created a strong state in the 7th cent. B.C. CYRUS THE GREAT, the first of the ACHAEMENIDS, made himself ruler of MEDIA in the mid-6th cent. B.C. and by rapid conquest established the great Persian empire. From the beginning the Persians built on the foundations of earlier states, borrowing the political structure of Assyria and the arts of Babylonia and Egypt. The country was beset by dynastic troubles, concerning first the claims of Cambyses and later those of DARIUS I. Darius organized a highly efficient centralized system of administration and extended Persian rule east into modern Afghanistan and NW India and as far north as the Danube. The Greeks revolted successfully in the PERSIAN WARS, and after the mid-5th cent. B.C. Persia was weakened by dynastic troubles, e.g., the rebellion of CYRUS THE YOUNGER against ARTAXERXES II and the successful revolt of Egypt. Finally, ALEXANDER THE GREAT destroyed the Achaemenid empire. After Alexander's death most of Persia fell to the Seleucids, who, though they introduced a fruitful Hellenistic culture, were unable to maintain control. PARTHIA, which broke away in the mid-3d cent. B.C., became a kind of successor to the old Persian empire and came to rival Rome. Its decline was followed by the establishment of a new Persian empire in A.D. c.226 under the Sassanids. This state flourished until A.D. 637, when invading Arabs took the capital, Ctesiphon. Islam replaced ZOROASTRIANISM, and the caliphate made Persia part of a larger pattern, from which modern Iran eventually emerged.

Persian art and architecture. The first finds of artistic importance are the superb ceramics of Susa and Persepolis (c.3500 B.C.). On goblets and bowls are stylized abstractions of birds and animals. Much Iranian art of the 4th, 3d, and 2d millennia is strongly influenced by that of MESOPOTAMIA. The treasure of Ziwiye (Sakiz), a hoard containing ivory, gold, and silver objects, also contained controversial Luristan bronze objects that provide a definite link with the art of the Scythians. The Ziwiye Treasure (700 B.C.) is divided into four styles: Assyrian, Scythian, proto-Achaemenid (with Greek influence), and native, or provincial. A unified style emerges in the Achaemenid period (c.550–330 B.C.) using monumental relief sculpture as an adjunct to massive architectural complexes, such as the famous *Frieze of the Archers*, from the palace of DARIUS I at Susa (Louvre). After the death of ALEXANDER THE GREAT (323 B.C.) there was internal turmoil until the rise of the Parthians (c.250 B.C.), whose art synthesized Hellenistic motifs with Iranian forms. Of greater artistic importance was the work of the SASSANIDS (A.D. 226–7th cent.). Their architecture is decorated with carved stone and stucco reliefs, and makes use of colorful stone MOSAICS. Beautiful gold and silver dishes are decorated with hunting scenes and animals in high relief. Little remains of the early centuries of Islam in Iran, but a significant innovation by the Persians was the raising of a DOME over a square hall by means of squinches. During this early period ceramics became an art form. Under the Seljuk Turks in the 11th and 12th cent., luster and "minai" ceramics with intricate scenes of court life were produced. The most famous work of the Mongol school of the 14th cent. is an illustrated book, the Demotte *Shah Namah* (The History of Kings), which is free and lively in execution. Chinese influence is seen in 15th-cent. Timurid painting. Under the Safavids illustration became decoratively patterned, as in the 16th-cent. *Shah Namah* of Shah Tamasp, which incorporates the great developments in painting of the period; it was published in facsimile as *The King's Book of Kings* in 1972. In the 17th cent. Persian art fell under the influence of Europe and India, and it rapidly degenerated.

Persian cat: see under CAT.

Persian Gulf, called the Arabian Gulf by Arabs, arm of the ARABIAN SEA, extending c.600 mi (970 km) from the mouth of the SHATT AL ARAB (N) to the Strait of HORMUZ (S), through which it connects with the Gulf of Oman. It is of great strategic importance as the chief maritime outlet for the bordering oil-rich states of Saudi Arabia, Bahrain, the United Arab Emirates, Kuwait, Iran, and Iraq. During the IRAN-IRAQ WAR the gulf was heavily mined by both sides and suffered ecologically from massive oil spills, which also occurred during the PERSIAN GULF WAR.

Persian Gulf War or **Gulf War,** Jan.–Feb. 1991, armed conflict resulting from IRAQ's invasion of KUWAIT. In Aug. 1990 Iraq invaded and annexed Kuwait, which it had long claimed. The UN Security Council called for Iraq to withdraw and subsequently embargoed most trade with Iraq. On Jan. 17, 1991, a U.S.-led coalition that included Britain, Egypt, France, Saudi Arabia, and other nations began a massive air war to destroy Iraq's forces and military and civil infrastructure. Iraq called for terrorist attacks against the coalition and launched missiles at Israel (in an unsuccessful attempt to widen the war and break up the coalition) and at Saudi Arabia. The main coalition forces invaded Kuwait and S Iraq on Feb. 24 and, over the next four days, encircled and defeated the Iraqis and liberated Kuwait. Kuwait and Iraq suffered enormous property damage, and the war led to unrest among Kurds and Shiites in Iraq. Iraq agreed to coalition peace terms but subsequently sought to frustrate the carrying out of the terms, particularly UN weapons inspections. In 1993 the U.S., France, and Britain launched several air strikes and a cruise missile strike at Iraq in response to provocations, including a planned assassination attempt on former U.S. Pres. Bush. See also IRAN-IRAQ WAR.

Persian language, member of the Iranian group of the Indo-Iranian subfamily of the Indo-European family of languages. See LANGUAGE (table).

Persian literature. The oldest extant Persian writing is found in ancient inscriptions, but it is only of historical interest. The first major literary works are the scriptures of ZOROASTRIANISM and the Pahlavi writing of SASSANID Persia. The Arab invasion (7th cent. A.D.) made Arabic the literary language and ISLAM the dominant literary theme. Many notable works of Arabic literature are by Persians. Persian reemerged as the literary language in the 9th cent., and in the following centuries classical Persian literature flowered. The great poet FIRDAUSI (10th cent.) wrote the *Book of Kings*, the national epic, and OMAR KHAYYAM (11th cent.) crafted his well-known *Rubaiyat*. Also among the great writers are the poets of SUFISM. FARID AD-DIN ATTAR, Jalal ed-Din RUMI, and SADI (12th–13th cent.) all wrote mystical poetry of the highest order, full of finely wrought symbols. In the 14th cent. HAFIZ was the author of a number of exquisite lyrics. Prose—tales, fables, allegories, and philosophical and scientific works—also flourished. The most outstanding prose works were the histories; many of these surpassed their Arabic models. After the 15th cent. Persian literature went into a decline that lasted until the rise of BABISM and BAHA'ISM in the 19th cent. brought about a religious literary revival. In the 20th cent. Western influence and the struggle for independence and social justice in Iran made political and social themes paramount, and literary language became simple and direct. Modern poets include Iradj, Abid e-Pishawari, Parwin, and Nima; S. Hedayet and M.M. Hejazi are celebrated novelists.

Persian Wars, 500–449 B.C., conflict between the Greek city-states and the Persian Empire. It began in 500 B.C., when the Ionian Greek cities, aided by ATHENS and Eretria, revolted against the despotic rule of DARIUS I. They were subdued by the Persians (494), and Darius decided to punish Athens and Eretria, and annex all of Greece. His first expedition (492) ended when his fleet was crippled by a storm. A second expedition destroyed (490) Eretria and then proceeded against Athens, which, under MILTIADES, expelled the invaders at MARATHON. (The Spartans, whose aid had been sought, arrived the day after the battle.) A third expedition, under preparation when Darius died (486), was completed by his son Xerxes I, who reached Greece in 480. His huge land force was delayed at the narrow pass of THERMOPYLAE by a small but gallant force of Spartans, who fought until they all had died. The Athenians, under THEMISTOCLES, put trust in their navy and made little effort to defend their city, which was taken (480) by the Persians. Shortly afterward the Persian fleet was crushed off Salamis by the Greeks. Xerxes returned to Persia, leaving behind a military force, which was defeated (479) at Plataea by a Greek force under the Spartan Pausanius. The Greeks also won a naval victory at Mycale. Although the wars dragged on for many years, these two victories marked the end of the Persian threat to Europe and the beginning of the period of Greek greatness.

persimmon: see EBONY.

Persius or **Aulus Persius Flaccus,** A.D. 34–62, Roman satirical poet. He wrote in the manner of HORACE and Lucilius, preaching Stoic moral doctrine (see STOICISM). He was harsh in exposing the corruption and folly of contemporary Rome.

personal computer (PC), small but powerful COMPUTER primarily used in an office or home without the need to be connected to a larger computer. PCs evolved after the development of the MICROPROCESSOR made possible the hobby-computer movement of the late 1970s, when some computers were built from components or kits. In the early 1980s the first low-cost, fully assembled units were mass-marketed. The typical configuration consists of a video display, keyboard, mouse, logic unit and memory, storage device and, often, a MODEM. Further decreases in component size have made it possible to build portable PCs, or laptops, the size of a ream of paper and smaller. Most current PCs have more computing power, memory, and storage than the large mainframe computers of the 1950s and early 60s. PCs equipped with networking and communications hardware are often used as COMPUTER TERMINALS. See also NETWORK; PERSONAL DIGITAL ASSISTANT.

personal digital assistant (PDA), lightweight, hand-held COMPUTER designed for use as a personal organizer with communications capabilities. A typical PDA has no keyboard, relying instead on recognition of handwritten input, through the use of special hardware and PEN-BASED COMPUTER software, on the surface of LIQUID CRYSTAL display screen. In addition to including such applications as a word processor, spreadsheet, calendar, and address book, PDAs are envisioned as notepads, appointment schedulers, and wireless communicators for sending and receiving data, faxes, and electronic-mail messages.

Perth, city (1991 pop. 1,143,265), capital of Western Australia, SW Australia, on the Swan R. The suburbs of Kwinana, Welshpool, and Fremantle, a port, have heavy industry. Perth is a very isolated city; ADELAIDE, the nearest large city, is c.1,400 mi (2,250 km) away. Settled in 1829, Perth received about 10,000 convict laborers in the 1850s. The Coolgardie gold rush of the 1890s brought an influx of settlers. The Univ. of Western Australia and Murdoch Univ., as well as the Art Gallery of Western Australia, are in the city, and the Kings Park botanical gardens are nearby.

Perth, town (1981 pop. 41,998), Tayside, central Scotland, on the Tay R. It is famous for its dye works and cattle markets, and has textile factories and distilleries. The capital of Scotland (11th–15th cent.), it played a role in the civil wars and in the JACOBITE rebellions.

perturbation: see CELESTIAL MECHANICS.

pertussis: see WHOOPING COUGH.

Peru [pəroo'], Span. *Perú,* officially Republic of Peru, republic (1993 pop. 22,128,466), 496,220 sq mi (1,285,210 sq km), W South America, bordered by the Pacific Ocean (W), Ecuador and Colombia (N), Brazil and Bolivia (E), and Chile (S). Major cities include LIMA (the capital), AREQUIPA, CALLAO, and Trujillo. Peru has three main geographical regions. A narrow strip along the coast is mostly desert, but fertile where irrigated by streams flowing from the mountains; Peru's leading ports, as well as the centers of its commercial agriculture, are located here. A central region, with 60% of the population, consists of three ranges of the ANDES Mts., with Huascarán as the highest peak (22,205 ft/6,768 m). The largest region, in the east, is composed of forested mountains and low-lying tropical plains drained by the AMAZON R. system. The coast and mountain regions are frequently shaken by severe earthquakes; the last major earthquake, in 1970, killed 50,000 people. Peru ranks among the world leaders in copper and silver production, and it became a petroleum exporter in 1985. Chief commercial crops are sugarcane and cotton; illegally cultivated coca, from which cocaine is made, is also important. Fishing is important. Manufactures include textiles, consumer goods, processed food, cement, refined minerals, fish meal, and fertilizer. The population is chiefly indigenous (50%), mestizo (37%), and white (13%). Spanish and Quechua are the official languages, and most of the whites and mestizos are Roman Catholic.

History. Inhabited since at least the 9th millennium B.C., Peru was later the center of several advanced indigenous cultures. The Spanish conquest of the area began in 1532, when Francisco PIZARRO and a small band of adventurers overthrew the great INCA empire, capturing and treacherously executing its ruler, Atahualpa. Lima (founded 1535) became the center of Spanish rule in South America, and the viceroyalty of Peru eventually included all Spanish-ruled lands on the continent except Venezuela. Independence, proclaimed in 1821, was achieved through the efforts of José de SAN MARTÍN and Simón BOLÍVAR and assured by the defeat (1824) of Spain at the battles of Junín and AYACUCHO. Following independence, Peruvian society remained sharply divided between the wealthy oligarchy (mostly Creoles) and the poverty-ridden majority (mostly of indigenous descent). Political life alternated between revolts and dictatorships. A disastrous war with Chile (see PACIFIC, WAR OF THE) in 1879 further slowed progress. The early 20th cent. was dominated by Pres. Augusto B. LEGUÍA (1908–12, 1919–30), a virtual dictator who promoted economic development in the interest of the wealthy minority. A radical reform party, founded in 1924 and dedicated to improving the conditions of the indigenous peoples, gained influence in the 1940s. Fernando BELAÚNDE TERRY, a moderate reformer, won election as president in 1963, but was deposed (1968) by a military junta which assumed dictatorial powers, instituted a program of social reform, and seized U.S.-owned companies. Constitutional government resumed in 1980 with elections that returned Belaúnde to the presidency. He was succeeded in 1985 by Alan García Perez. The 1980s was a decade of economic collapse, with inflation nearly 8000% in 1990. SHINING PATH guerrillas became increasingly powerful in rural and urban areas, and fighting continued into the 1990s. Alberto K. Fujimori was elected president in 1990. He reduced inflation and moved to free the economy from government control, but Peru's economic recession deepened. In 1992 Fujimori suspended the constitution, saying emergency action was needed to fight the guerrillas, drug traffickers, and corruption. His supporters won (1992) a majority in legislative elections that were boycotted by major opposition parties. Peru began to privatize most state-owned businesses in 1993, and voters narrowly approved a new constitution the same year.

Perugino [pārōōjē'nō], c.1445–1523?, Umbrian painter; b. near Perugia as Pietro di Cristoforo Vannucci. A student, with LEONARDO DA VINCI, of VERROCCHIO, and later the teacher of RAPHAEL, he helped decorate the SISTINE CHAPEL. Some of his work there was later destroyed, but the remaining *Christ Giving the Keys to St. Peter* is famous. Thereafter he worked mainly in Florence and Perugia. His tender color and simple style later became sentimental, e.g., in his *Triumph of Chastity* (Louvre) and *The Adoration of the Shepherds* (National Gall., London), his last work.

Pescadores, group of 64 small islands, c.50 sq mi (130 sq km), in Taiwan Strait, part of TAIWAN. The islands, which were ceded to Japan by China in 1895 and returned after WORLD WAR II, came under Chinese Nationalist rule after the Communist takeover of mainland China in 1949.

Pessoa, Fernando, 1888–1935, Portuguese poet. The four distinct poetic personas he claimed for himself, the messianic, the rationalist, the stoic, and the Nietzschean, reflect his disbelief in the idea of an integrated personality. His highly original verse collections include *Sonnets* (1918), *Mensagem* (1934), and *English Poems* (1922).

Pestalozzi, Johann Heinrich [pĕ"stälôt'sē], 1746–1827, Swiss educational reformer. His theories laid the foundation of modern elementary education. He was director (from 1805) of an experimental institute established at Yverdon on his principle that choice of pedagogical method should be based on the individual's development and concrete experience. He opposed memorization learning and strict discipline, and pioneered in the use of tactile objects in the teaching of natural science. He also promoted broad liberal education followed by professional training for teachers. His works include *Leonard and Gertrude* (1781–87) and *How Gertrude Teaches Her Children* (1801).

pesticide, biological, physical, or chemical agent used to kill plants or animals considered harmful to human beings; see FUNGICIDE; HERBICIDE; INSECTICIDE.

Pétain, Henri Philippe [pātăN'], 1856–1951, marshal of France, head of the VICHY government (1940–44). In WORLD WAR I he halted the Germans at Verdun (1916) and became (1917) French commander in chief. Named ambassador to Spain (1939), he succeeded (June 1940) Paul Reynaud as premier when France was on the brink of collapse in WORLD WAR II. He soon arranged an armistice with Germany. On July 10 the French constitution was suspended, and Pétain became "chief of state" at Vichy. Pétain's fascistic government collaborated with Nazi Germany and grew unpopular as it yielded to harsh German demands. In 1942 Pierre LAVAL took power, and Pétain remained chiefly a figurehead. After the Allied victory, he was convicted of treason (1945) and was sentenced to death; the sentence was commuted by Charles DE GAULLE to life imprisonment.

Peter, Saint, d. A.D. 64?, most prominent of the Twelve APOSTLES, traditionally the first bishop of Rome. His name was Simon, but Jesus called him Cephas [Aramaic, = rock], or, in Greek, Petros. A native of Bethsaida in Galilee, he was the brother of St. ANDREW. Fishermen, they were called by Jesus at the same time as James (James the Greater) and John. Peter appears in the gospels as leader and spokesman of the disciples, and Jesus most often addressed him when speaking to them. When Peter confessed Jesus to be the Christ, he was told, "Upon this rock I will build my church." With James and John, he was chosen to see the Transfiguration and after the Last Supper witnessed the agony at Gethsemane. When Jesus was betrayed, Peter denied him, as Jesus had predicted he would. After the Resurrection Jesus appeared and charged Peter to "feed my sheep." The ACTS OF THE APOSTLES describes Peter's role as leader in the early apostolic period. According to 2d-cent. sources, he apparently left Antioch for Rome A.D. c.55 and there died as head of the local church—a martyr under NERO—traditionally crucified on the Vatican Hill. Over his supposed burial place stands ST. PETER'S CHURCH, the principal shrine of Europe. Peter is said to have helped St. MARK write his gospel, but the epistles of PETER are regarded as mistakenly attributed. His successors as bishop of Rome came to be leaders of the church (see PAPACY).

Peter, czars of Russia. **Peter I** or **Peter the Great,** 1672–1725 (r.1682–1725), was the youngest child of Czar Alexis by his second wife, Natalya Naryshkin. Alexis was succeeded by Feodor III, a son by his first wife, Maria Miloslavsky. On Feodor's death a bloody struggle erupted between the Naryshkins and Miloslavskys. Peter was made joint czar with IVAN V, Feodor's feebleminded brother, under the regency of Sophia Alekseyevna, Feodor's sister. In 1689 Sophia Alekseyevna attempted a coup against Peter; she was overthrown, and for some years the Naryshkins ruled, until Peter took personal control. In 1697–98 he toured Europe, where he tried but failed to form an alliance against Turkey; laid the basis for a coalition against Sweden; studied industrial techniques; and hired craftsmen to work in Russia. He returned on news of an attempt to restore Sophia Alekseyevna; he forced her into a nunnery and took brutal revenge on her followers. The ruthless reforms that marked his reign began on the day after his return, when he personally cut off the beards of his nobles and ordered them to wear Western dress henceforth. To pursue his almost continuous wars, particularly the NORTHERN WAR (1700–1721) with Sweden under CHARLES XII, he introduced territorial conscription, enlarged and modernized the army, founded a navy, and set up military-technical schools. Financing was provided by state monopolies, poll taxes, and levies on many items. Private industry was subsidized, and state mines and factories were established to supply war materials. Peter increased the number of nobles owing service to the state; forced nobles' sons to attend military-technical schools; and created a bureaucratic hierarchy in which promotion depended on merit rather than birth. The serfs, who paid the bulk of taxes and comprised most of the soldiery, were bound more securely to their masters and to the land. The Academy of Sciences was founded, the calendar reformed, and the alphabet simplified. On the swamps of Ingermanland (ceded by Sweden in 1721) Peter had St. Petersburg built to replace the capital at Moscow. The discontented looked to his son, Alexis, who was tried for treason and tortured to death in 1718. Peter proclaimed himself "emperor of all Russia" in 1721. His second wife, crowned as CATHERINE I in 1724, succeeded him. **Peter II,** 1715–30 (r.1727–30), was the grandson of Peter I. He succeeded Catherine I under a regency. During his reign his grandfather's great minister MENSHIKOV fell from power. He was succeeded by his cousin ANNA. **Peter III,** 1728–62 (r.1762), was the son of Charles Frederick, dispossessed duke of Holstein-Gottorp, and of Anna Petrovna, daughter of Peter the Great. He succeeded his aunt, Czarina ELIZABETH. One of his first acts was to withdraw Russia from the SEVEN YEARS WAR and make an alliance with FREDERICK II of Prussia. His domestic policy included the abolition of the secret police and the extension of religious freedom. Forced to abdicate in favor of his wife, CATHERINE II, he was later murdered.

Peter, kings of ARAGÓN. **Peter III** (the Great), 1239?–85 (r.1276–85), was also king of Sicily (1282–85). He obtained from his marriage (1262) to Constance, daughter of MANFRED of SICILY, claims to the island, which he seized in 1282. Pope Martin IV excommunicated him and organized with the French a crusade against Catalonia, but Peter repulsed the French invasion. He left Aragón to his eldest son, ALFONSO III, and Sicily to his second son, James II. **Peter IV** (the Ceremonious), 1319?–87 (r.1336–87), recovered Majorca for Aragón and fought an indecisive naval war against Genoa and Pisa over SARDINIA. Although he was forced to confirm privileges granted earlier to the nobles, he defeated (1348) them in battle and withdrew their charter. He was succeeded by his son, John I.

Peter, kings of Portugal. **Peter I,** 1320–67 (r.1357–67), was the son of ALFONSO IV. Although married (1336) to Constance Manuel, he fell in love with Inés de CASTRO. When his father allowed Inés to be murdered (1355), Peter led a rebellion against him. Although peace was made and Peter formally pardoned the murderers, he had two of them executed after he became king. This act and his concern for legal reform earned him the names Peter the Severe and Peter the Justiciar. **Peter II,** 1648–1706 (r.1683–1706), ruled Portugal from 1667 as regent for his incompetent brother, ALFONSO VI. His reign was one of prosperity and peace until 1703, when he was reluctantly drawn into the War of the SPANISH SUCCESSION. **Peter III,** 1717–86, married his niece, MARIA I and was joint ruler with her from 1777 until his death.

Peter, rulers of Serbia and Yugoslavia. **Peter I,** 1844–1921, king of Serbia (1903–18) and king of the Serbs, Croats, and Slovenes (1918–21), was a member of the KARADJORDJEVIĆ dynasty and in exile while the OBRENOVIĆS were in power. The assassination (1903) of King ALEXANDER of Serbia brought him to the throne. He proved a forward-looking ruler and succeeded in unifying what later became Yugoslavia. **Peter II,** 1923–70, king of Yugoslavia (1934–45), served under a regency until 1941. His personal rule coincided with the German occupation of Yugoslavia, and he spent World War II in exile in England. In 1945 the Communist government of Marshal TITO forced his abdication.

Peter, two EPISTLES of the NEW TESTAMENT, the 21st and 22d books in the usual order, among the Catholic, or General, Epistles. Both state that they are by the apostle St. PETER. First Peter, addressed from Rome to the Christians of Asia Minor, stresses the duties of Christians and offers them consolation under persecution. Second Peter, one of the last books accepted in the New Testament canon, urges virtue and warns against false teachers.

Peter Damian, Saint, 1007?–1072, Italian reformer, Doctor of the Church. A Camaldolese monk, he was strong in the reform party of Hildebrand (later Pope GREGORY VII). In 1057 he was made cardinal. His *Gomorrhianus* is a violent denunciation of clerical abuses. Feast: Feb. 21.

Peter Lombard, c.1100–c.1160, Italian theologian, archbishop of Paris. His *Sentences,* a compilation of the often conflicting opinions of theologians, is among the most celebrated of theological works. His doctrine of the SACRAMENTS was made official by the Council of TRENT.

Petersburg, city (1990 pop. 38,386), SE Va., on the Appomattox R.; inc. as a city 1850. Located on the site of a Native American village and Fort Henry (1646), it is a port of entry and a tobacco market, and produces cigarettes, luggage, and other manufactures. The city was the object of fighting during the AMERICAN REVOLUTION and at the end of the CIVIL WAR, when it was (1864–65) the site of fierce struggles between the armies of R.E. LEE and U.S. GRANT that ended in Lee's surrender at APPOMATTOX. Its national battlefield (est. 1926) is much visited.

Peter the Cruel, 1334–69, Spanish king of CASTILE and LEÓN (1350–69). His desertion of his wife, Blanche of Bourbon, for María Padilla and his favors to the Padilla family offended the nobles and caused rebellions fomented by his half brother, later Henry II. With the help of ARAGÓN and France, Henry conquered Castile and was crowned king in 1366. Peter retaliated by defeating Henry's army with the help of England in 1367. But Henry raised a new army, which was victorious at Montiel (1369), and he killed Peter in a duel after the battle. Despite his reputation for cruelty, Peter is regarded by many historians as a defender of the rights of the commoners against the nobles.

Peter the Great: see Peter I under PETER, czars of Russia.

Pétion, Alexandre [pātyôN'], 1770–1818, Haitian revolutionary leader. After fighting to liberate HAITI from the English and French, he established (1806) a mulatto-controlled republic in S Haiti. As its president, he instituted land reform and political freedom.

Petipa, Marius, 1822?–1910, French dancer and choreographer. He was the principal creator of modern classical ballet. He brought European technique to the Imperial Theater, St. Petersburg, and expanded the male role in dance. His major works include *La Bayadère* (1875) and *Sleeping Beauty* (1890).

Petit, Roland, 1924–, French dancer and choreographer. He founded (1948) the Ballets de Paris de Roland Petit. His best known work is *Carmen* (1949), set to music from Georges BIZET's opera. He has been director of the Ballets de Marseilles since 1972.

Petition of Right, 1628, statement sent by the English PARLIAMENT to CHARLES I. It laid down four principles: no taxes without the consent of Parliament; no imprisonment without cause; no quartering of soldiers on the citizenry; and no martial law in peacetime. Charles soon violated its spirit.

őofi, sándor

Petőfi, Sándor [pĕ'töfē], 1822–49, Hungarian poet. His epic *Janos the Hero* (1845) relates the fantastic adventures of a peasant-soldier. "Rise, Magyar" (1848) voices the ideals of the Hungarian revolution, in which Petőfi died.

Petra, ancient city, in SW Jordan. The capital of the Nabataeans from the 4th cent. B.C. to the Roman occupation in A.D. 106, it remained a religious center of Arabia. An early seat of Christianity, the Muslims (see ISLAM) conquered it in the 7th cent. and the Crusaders (see CRUSADES) built a citadel there in the 12th cent.

Petrarch [pē'trärk] or **Francesco Petrarca,** 1304–74, Italian poet and humanist, a RENAISSANCE literary figure of extreme influence. At Avignon in 1327 he first saw Laura, who was to inspire his great vernacular love lyrics. He was crowned laureate at Rome in 1341, and from 1348 he worked for Italian reunification. Among the first to realize that Platonic thought and Greek studies provided a new cultural framework, he helped spread HUMANISM through his criticism of SCHOLASTICISM. Petrarch's poetry, ignoring medieval conventions, defined true emotions. His perfection of the SONNET form makes him perhaps the first modern poet. Though he valued his Latin works above those in Italian, he reached heights in both tongues.

Petrie, Sir William Matthew Flinders, 1853–1942, English archaeologist and Egyptologist. He is best known for excavations at Memphis and Thebes. He also founded (1894) the British School of Archaeology in Egypt and discovered ruins of 10 cities at Tel-el-Hesy (S of Jerusalem). His works include *Methods and Aims in Archaeology* (1904) and *Seventy Years in Archaeology* (1931).

Petrified Forest National Park: see NATIONAL PARKS (table).

petrol: see GASOLINE.

petroleum or **crude oil,** oily, flammable liquid that occurs naturally in deposits, usually beneath the surface of the earth. The exact composition varies according to locality, but it is chiefly a mixture of HYDROCARBONS. Petroleum is a fossil fuel thought to have been formed over millions of years from incompletely decayed plant and animal remains buried under thick layers of rock. Drilling for oil is a complex, often risky process. Scientific methods are used to locate promising sites for wells, some of which must be dug several miles deep to reach the deposit. Many wells are now drilled offshore from platforms standing on the ocean bed. Usually the crude oil in a new well comes to the surface under its own pressure. Later it has to be pumped or forced up with injected water, gas, or air. Pipelines or tankers transport it to refineries, where it is separated into fractions, i.e., the portions of the crude oil that vaporize between certain defined limits of temperature. Fractions are obtained by a refining process called fractional DISTILLATION, in which crude oil is heated and sent into a tower. The vapors of the different fractions condense on collectors at different heights in the tower. The separated fractions are then drawn from the collectors and further processed into various petroleum products. Generally the fractions are vaporized in the following order: dissolved NATURAL GAS, GASOLINE, naphtha, KEROSENE, diesel fuel, heating oils, and finally tars (see TAR AND PITCH). Lighter fractions, especially gasoline, are in greatest demand and their yield can be increased by breaking down heavier hydrocarbons in a process called cracking. The leading producers of petroleum are Russia, the U.S., Saudi Arabia, Iran, Iraq, China, Mexico, the United Arab Emirates, Venezuela, Nigeria, Kuwait, and Norway. The largest reserves are in the Middle East. Modern industrial civilization depends heavily on petroleum for motive power, fuel, lubrication, and a variety of synthetic products, e.g., DYES, drugs, and PLASTICS. The widespread burning of petroleum products as fuels has resulted in serious problems of air POLLUTION, and oil spilled from tankers and offshore wells has damaged ocean and coastline environments. The environmentally disruptive effects of oil wells have sometimes led to strong opposition to new drilling, as in wilderness areas of N Alaska. See also ENERGY, SOURCES OF.

petrology, branch of GEOLOGY concerned with the origin, composition, structure, and properties of ROCKS, as well as the laboratory simulation of rock-forming processes.

Petronius, d. A.D. c.66, Roman satirist, known as Petronius Arbiter because he is identified with Gaius Petronius, whom TACITUS calls the *arbiter elegantiae* in NERO's court. He is remembered as a profligate lover of luxury. Arrested in an intrigue, he slashed his veins and died in a leisurely fashion, attended by his friends. He is credited with the *Petronii arbitri satyricon,* a prose and verse romance that preserves, in colloquial language, a study of the life and manners of his time.

Petrov, Yevgeny Petrovich, pseud. of **Yevgeny Petrovich Katayev,** 1903–42, Russian writer. With Ilya Arnoldovich ILF he wrote satirical novels. After Ilf's death, Petrov became a war correspondent and was killed in battle. He was the brother of Valentin KATAYEV.

PET scan or **positron emission tomography,** medical imaging technique that measures cellular activity in the brain and other organs by tracking the movement and concentration of a radioactive tracer. The technique requires special computerized imaging equipment and uses rings of detectors around the patient to record the GAMMA RADIATION produced when the positrons emitted by the injected or inhaled tracer are annihilated in collisions with electrons. The tracer is taken up by living tissue and enables a PET scanner to measure blood flow, metabolic reaction rate, and biochemical synthesis. PET scans are being studied to determine their usefulness in detecting brain tumors and for investigating such psychological disorders as SCHIZOPHRENIA and MANIC-DEPRESSION.

Petty, Richard, 1937–, American auto racing driver; b. Level Cross, N.C. In his 35-year career (1958–92) in stock-car racing, Petty won a record 200 National Association for Stock Car Auto Racing (NASCAR) races, including a record seven Daytona 500 races. He also won a record seven NASCAR championships.

petunia, annual or perennial herb (genus *Petunia*) of the NIGHTSHADE family, native to the Americas. Valued as garden ornamentals, petunias have a straggling habit and produce an abundance of large, colorful, funnel-shaped blossoms.

Pevsner, Antoine, 1886–1962, Russian sculptor and painter. He and his brother Naum GABO worked together in 1920 on the manifesto of CONSTRUCTIVISM. Pevsner created constructivist works in bronze and other materials, e.g., his portrait of Marcel DUCHAMP (1926; Yale Univ., New Haven, Conn.).

pewter, ductile, silver-white alloy consisting mainly of tin. The addition of lead imparts a bluish tinge and increased malleability. Other metals such as antimony, copper, bismuth, and zinc may also be added. Pewter is shaped by casting, hammering, or lathe spinning on a mold. Ornamentation is usually simple. Pewter was early used in E Asia, and Roman pieces are extant. In England during the Middle Ages, pewter was the chief tableware, later being supplanted by china. It was made in America from c.1700. The craft had virtually died out by 1850 but was revived in the 20th cent. in reproductions and pieces of modern design.

peyote, spineless cactus (*Lophophora williamsii*) indigenous to the SW U.S. and Mexico. Peyote produces a drug, also called peyote, whose active substance is mescaline, a nonaddictive HALLUCINOGENIC DRUG that produces visions and changes in perception, time sense, and mood. Peyote-eating rituals are important in the NATIVE AMERICAN CHURCH.

peyotism: see NATIVE AMERICAN CHURCH.

***p*H,** range of numbers expressing the relative acidity or alkalinity of a solution. The *p*H value is the negative common LOGARITHM of the hydrogen-ion CONCENTRATION in a solution, expressed in MOLES per liter of solution. A neutral solution, i.e., one that is neither acidic nor alkaline, such as pure water, has a concentration of 10^{-7} moles per liter; its *p*H is thus 7. Acidic solutions have *p*H values ranging with decreasing acidity from 0 to nearly 7; alkaline or basic solutions have a *p*H ranging with increasing alkalinity from just beyond 7 to 14. See also ACIDS AND BASES.

Phaedra [fē'drə], in Greek mythology, daughter of MINOS and Pasiphaë, wife of THESEUS. When her stepson, Hippolytus, rejected her love, she accused him of rape, then hanged herself. The legend was dramatized by EURIPIDES, SENECA, and RACINE.

phaeophyte, member of a division (Phaeophyta) of the PLANT kingdom consisting of brown ALGAE; almost all are SEAWEEDS growing in colder parts of the world. They get their color from *a* and *c* chlorophylls and xanthophylls in the cell chloropasts. Brown algae are now usually considered PROTISTS.

Phaëthon [fā'əthən] or **Phaëton** [fā'ətən], in Greek myth, son of HELIOS. He lost control of his father's golden chariot, which in falling dried the Libyan Desert. ZEUS avoided the universe's destruction only by killing Phaëthon.

pharaoh [fâr'ō], title of the kings of ancient EGYPT. Many scholars believe that Seti I oppressed the Jews, and that his son RAMSES II was pharaoh during the Hebrew Exodus.

pharmacology, study of the changes produced in living animals by DRUGS, chemical substances used to treat and diagnose disease. It is closely related to other scientific disciplines, particularly BIOCHEMISTRY and PHYSIOLOGY. Areas of pharmacologic research include mechanisms of drug action, the use of drugs in treating disease, and drug-induced side effects. See also PHARMACY.

pharmacy, science of compounding and dispensing medication; also, an establishment used for such purposes. Modern pharmaceutical practice includes the dispensing, identification, selection, and analysis of DRUGS. Pharmacy began to develop as a profession separate from medicine in the 18th cent., and in 1821 the first U.S. school of pharmacy was established in Philadelphia. See also PHARMACOLOGY.

pharming, the use of genetically altered livestock, such as cows, goats, and pigs, to produce pharmaceutical drugs. Researchers employing GENETIC ENGINEERING techniques have introduced hybrid genes into animal embryos, creating "transgenic" animals that secrete human hormones or proteins in their milk or blood. The secreted substance is extracted from the milk or blood and purified. Still in the experimental stage as a manufacturing process, pharming is regarded as a more efficient alternative to the "bioreactor" technique of using genetically altered bacteria or specially cultured animal cells to produce drugs (see BIOTECHNOLOGY). Transgenic animals are also being studied as possible source of organs for medical TRANSPLANTATION.

pharynx, section of the DIGESTIVE SYSTEM between the mouth and esophagus. In humans the pharynx is a cone-shaped tube, continuous with both the mouth and nasal passages at its upper end and esophagus at its lower end. It connects with the EARS via the eustachian tubes and with the LARYNX by an opening covered by the epiglottis during swallowing.

phase, in astronomy, the measure of how much of the illuminated surface of a planet or natural satellite can be seen from a point at a distance from that body. The phase depends on the overlap of the half of the surface that is seen by the observer and the half that is illuminated by the sun. An inferior planet, whose orbit lies inside the earth's, shows all the phases that the moon shows; a superior planet, whose orbit lies outside earth's, is always gibbous or full.

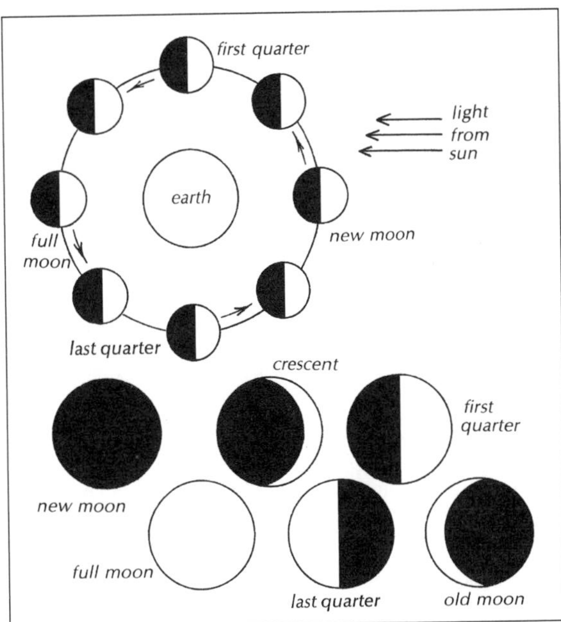

Phases of the moon as seen from the earth

phases of matter: see STATES OF MATTER.

pheasant, name for some henlike birds of the family Phasianidae, related to the GROUSE and including the Old World PARTRIDGES, the PEACOCK, some domestic and jungle fowl, and the true pheasants (genus *Phasianus*). Pheasants are typified by wattled heads and long tails, and by the brilliant plumage and elaborate courtship displays of the male. All are indigenous to Asia. The hybrid ring-necked pheasant, *P. colchicus,* is a common game bird in the U.S., where the ruffed grouse is also called *pheasant.*

Pheidias: see PHIDIAS.

phenomenology, modern school of philosophy founded by Edmund HUSSERL, who attempted to develop a philosophical method devoid of presuppositions by focusing purely on phenomena and elucidating their meaning through intuition. Anything that cannot be perceived, and thus is not immediately given to the consciousness, is excluded. The influence of phenomenology was strong, especially on EXISTENTIALISM.

pheresis: see APHERESIS; PLASMAPHERESIS.

pheromone, any chemical substance secreted by members of an animal species that alters the behavior of other members of the same species. Sex-attractant pheromones are widespread, particularly among insects. Other pheromones act as signals for alarm and defense, territory and trail-marking, and social regulation and recognition. Pheromones are now being used in insect control, e.g., as bait to attract males to field traps or, in very high concentrations, to disorient insects and prevent mating.

Phi Beta Kappa: see under FRATERNITY AND SORORITY.

Phidias or **Pheidias** [both: fĭd'ēəs], c.500–c.432 B.C., one of the greatest ancient Greek sculptors. Though numerous Roman copies of his works exist, no originals can be definitely attributed to him. His fame rests on the descriptions and estimates of ancient writers. His greatest works were the colossal chryselephantine (ivory and gold) *Athena Parthenos* at Athens (destroyed in ancient times) and *Zeus,* one of the SEVEN WONDERS OF THE WORLD. He is said to have been in charge of the PARTHENON and ACROPOLIS sculptures.

Philadelphia, name of several ancient cities. One was in Lydia, W Asia Minor, near modern Alasehir, Turkey. It was founded in the 2d cent. B.C. by Attalus II Philadelphus of Pergamum. AMMAN (capital of present-day Jordan) was renamed Philadelphia by PTOLEMY II in the 3d cent. B.C.

Philadelphia, city (1990 pop. 1,585,577; met. area 4,856,881), SE Pa., on the Delaware and Schuylkill rivers; chartered 1701.

Founded in 1681 on the site of earlier settlements by William PENN as a Quaker colony, the city has played a prominent role in American history. By 1774 it was second only to London as the largest English-speaking city in the world. The CONTINENTAL CONGRESS met there, and it was the national capital during most of the period 1777–1800. The DECLARATION OF INDEPENDENCE was signed in Independence Hall. Benjamin FRANKLIN is one of the most famous of Philadelphia residents. A commercial, banking, insurance, and transportation center, Philadelphia is the fifth largest U.S. city. It has one of the world's largest freshwater ports and is a major oil-refining center. Leading manufactures include chemicals, electrical appliances and machinery, and scientific instruments. A cultural nucleus since colonial times, the city is home to many artistic, dramatic, musical, and scientific societies, and has over 30 universities and institutions of higher learning, including the Univ. of Pennsylvania, Temple Univ., and Drexel Univ. Cultural institutions include the Pennsylvania Academy of the Fine Arts, the Philadelphia Museum of Art, and an outstanding symphony orchestra. Veterans' Stadium and Fairmount Park are major sports and recreation centers. Among the city's sights are the Liberty Bell, INDEPENDENCE HALL, Carpenters' Hall, the Betsy ROSS House, and the redeveloped Society Hill and Penn's Landing sections.

Philadelphia Museum of Art, est. 1875; present building opened 1928; owned by the city. Its outstanding collection is the John G. Johnson Collection of European old masters. Its holdings also include other European art, modern art, and works from Persia and China. The museum houses particularly fine groups of paintings by EAKINS and works by Marcel DUCHAMP.

Philemon, epistle of the NEW TESTAMENT, 18th book in the usual order, written by St. PAUL (probably A.D. c.60) to a Colossian named Philemon, asking him to forgive his fugitive slave Onesimus, who was carrying the epistle to him.

Philip, Saint, one of the Twelve APOSTLES, from Bethsaida in Galilee. He is said to have been martyred in Phrygia.

Philip, kings of France. **Philip I,** 1052–1108 (r.1060–1108), enlarged his small royal domain and quarreled with the papacy over his marriages. He was succeeded by his son, LOUIS VI. **Philip II** or **Philip Augustus,** 1165–1223 (r.1180–1223), succeeded his father, LOUIS VII. During his reign the royal domains were more than doubled, and royal power was consolidated. He seized territory from the count of Flanders and from HENRY I of England. In 1190 he left on the Third CRUSADE with Henry's successor, RICHARD I of England, but they soon quarreled, and Philip returned (1191) to France. He forced Richard's successor, King JOHN of England, to cede (1204) Normandy, Brittany, Anjou, Maine, and Touraine. In 1214, at Bouvines, he defeated the combined forces of John, Holy Roman Emperor Otto IV, and the count of Flanders. Philip condoned the crusade against the ALBIGENSES, which paved the way to the eventual annexation of S France by King LOUIS IX. The latter's son, **Philip III** (the Bold), 1245–85 (r.1270–85), took peaceful possession of Poitou, Auvergne, and Toulouse by a small cession (1279) to England. He died during an unsuccessful invasion of Aragón. His son, **Philip IV** (the Fair), 1268–1314 (r.1285–1314), arrested (1301) Bishop Saisset and caused a quarrel with Pope BONIFACE VIII, who denounced the king. Philip retaliated by convoking the first STATES-GENERAL (1302–3) to hear a justification of his actions. Threatened with excommunication, Philip had Boniface seized and later gained control of the PAPACY with the election of CLEMENT V, who transferred (1309) the papacy to Avignon. Beginning in 1294, Philip tried to conquer Guienne from EDWARD I of England, but was forced to concede (1303) the duchy to Edward. His attempts to subdue the Flemish led to the disastrous French defeat (1302) at Courtrai. His son, LOUIS X, succeeded him. **Philip V** (the Tall), c.1294–1322 (r.1317–22), was regent for his infant nephew, JOHN I. When John died (1316), Philip had himself crowned despite the claims of John's sister. This helped to establish the Salic Law in France, which excluded females from the royal succession. Philip made notable administrative, judiciary, and military reforms and was succeeded by his brother CHARLES IV. Charles IV's successor, **Philip VI,** 1293–1350 (r.1328–50), grandson of Philip III, invoked the Salic Law to set aside the claims of Charles's daughter and Charles's nephew, Edward III of England. He was the first VALOIS king of France. After 1337 his reign was dominated by the HUNDRED YEARS WAR. In 1340 the French fleet was destroyed at Sluis, and in 1346 Edward III defeated Philip at Crécy. Philip was succeeded by his son, JOHN II.

Philip, kings of Macedon. **Philip II,** 382–336 B.C. (r.359–336), was the son of Amyntas II. He seized the throne while serving as regent for his nephew Amyntas. He reorganized the army and followed a policy of expansion, annexing Amphipolis (357), the gold mines of THRACE (356), and the Chalcidice (348). When his continued threats roused ATHENS and THEBES to war against him, he crushed them at Chaeronea (338) and became master of GREECE. He was preparing an attack on Persia when he was killed. His wife, OLYMPIAS, was accused, probably falsely, of the murder. Philip's consolidation of his kingdom and creation of a powerful army paved the way for the campaigns of his son, ALEXANDER THE GREAT. **Philip V,** 238–179 B.C. (r.221–179), was the son of Demetrius II. Successful in a war in Greece (220–217), he tried to take the Roman holdings in Illyria, precipitating the First Macedonian War with Rome (215–205). It ended favorably for Philip, but in the Second Macedonian War he was decisively defeated at Cynoscephalae (197). He was succeeded by his son PERSEUS.

Philip, Spanish kings. **Philip I** (the Handsome), 1478–1506, king of CASTILE (1506), was the son of Holy Roman Emperor MAXIMILIAN I and MARY OF BURGUNDY. He inherited Burgundy and the Low Countries from his mother and was titular joint ruler of Castile with his wife, JOANNA. But her father ruled these lands as his regent, so he contested (1504) Ferdinand's regency and assumed (1506) joint rule of Castile with his wife. Philip's early death, however, and his wife's deteriorating mental condition allowed Ferdinand to resume joint control of Castile. The Low Countries passed to Philip's son, who later became Holy Roman Emperor CHARLES V. **Philip II,** 1527–98, king of Spain (1556–98), king of NAPLES and SICILY (1554–98) and, as Philip I, king of Portugal (1580–98), centralized authority under his absolute monarchy and extended Spanish colonization to the present S United States and the Philippines (which were named after him). From his father, Holy Roman Emperor Charles V, he inherited NAPLES, SICILY, the Low Countries, and other territories. After the death of his first wife, Maria of Portugal, he married (1554) Queen MARY I of England and drew that nation into his father's war with France. Following Mary's death (1558), he married Elizabeth of Valois and concluded the war with France in 1559. Philip used the INQUISITION to repress the MORISCOS and assure Spanish religious unity. He dealt with the Dutch revolt in his Low Countries domain by reconquering the southern half of the country. English support of the rebels and their persistent attacks on Spanish ships led him to plan an invasion of England by the Spanish ARMADA (1588), which was ignominiously defeated. Earlier, he succeeded in conquering Portugal (1580). Despite his conquests and the influx of gold from America, the cumulative effects of depopulation, colonial overexpansion, and burdensome taxation debilitated Spain by the end of his reign (1598). Philip was a hardworking bureaucrat with a capacity for infinite detail, and though his administration was generally just, his bureaucratic absolutism inevitably created discontent. His court was at the ESCORIAL. **Philip III,** 1578–1621, king of Spain, Naples, and Sicily, and, as Philip II, king of Portugal (1598–1621), lacked the intelligence and capacity for work of his father, Philip II, and left the actual government to the duque de Lerma. Shortly before his reign began, Spain had ended the war with France (1598) and then made peace with England (1604) and the Netherlands (1609). But the nation fought in Italy (1615–17) and entered the THIRTY YEARS WAR. Although the church prospered and the grandees accumulated vast estates, the Spanish economy declined, partly as a result of Philip's expulsion (1609–14) of the Moriscos. During Philip's reign, Spanish culture flourished and gave to the world great artists such as the author CERVANTES and the painter El GRECO. **Philip IV,** 1605–65, king of Spain, Naples, and Sicily (1621–65) and, as Philip III, king of Portugal (1621–40), intelligent but lacking energy, was unable to prevent Spain's political and economic decline. The Thirty Years War continued until 1648, and the war with France (1621–59) ended with Spain's humiliation. Portugal revolted (1640), Catalonia was occupied by the French, and Spain had to recognize the independence of the Netherlands (1648). Philip was a patron of the arts and, thanks to VELÁZQUEZ, was perhaps the most frequently portrayed king in history. The accession of **Philip V,** 1683–1746, the first Bourbon king of Spain (1700–46), precipitated the War of the SPANISH SUCCESSION (1701–14) because his grandfather, LOUIS XIV of France, had accepted the Spanish throne for Philip. By the Peace of Utrecht, Spain lost much territory, including the Spanish Netherlands, Naples, and Sicily. Philip was forced to introduce the Salic law of succession, which forbade female monarchs and thus precluded the crown's personal union with France. The indolent and melancholy Philip was dominated by women, particularly after his marriage (1714) to Elizabeth Farnese (see FARNESE, family). Under her influence, he attempted to reconquer the Italian territories, causing the formation of the QUADRUPLE ALLIANCE of 1718, to which Spain had to submit. The latter years of his reign were plagued by wars. Under Philip, however, Spain began to recover from economic stagnation.

Philip, Prince: see EDINBURGH, PHILIP MOUNTBATTEN, DUKE OF.

Philip Augustus: see Philip II under PHILIP, kings of France.

Philip of Hesse, 1504–67, German ruler, landgrave of Hesse (1509–67), champion of the REFORMATION. He was converted to Lutheranism in 1524 and founded (1531) the Schmalkaldic League to uphold Protestantism against Holy Roman Emperor CHARLES V. In 1547 Charles crushed the league and imprisoned Philip. At his death his lands were divided among his four sons (see HESSE).

Philip of Swabia, 1176?–1208, German king (1198–1208), son of Holy Roman Emperor FREDERICK I and brother of Emperor Henry VI. When he was elected king in 1198, a minority faction chose OTTO IV as antiking. The resulting war ended in 1206 in Philip's favor, but his murder by a personal enemy eventually placed Otto on the throne. Philip's role in diverting the Fourth CRUSADE (1202–4) to Constantinople for dynastic reasons has long been disputed.

Philippe Égalité: see Louis Philippe Joseph, duc D'Orléans, under ORLÉANS, family.

Philippians, EPISTLE of the NEW TESTAMENT, 11th book in the usual order, written (A.D. c.60) by St. PAUL to the Christians of Philippi (MACEDONIA), the first European city he evangelized. The book is noted for its intimate tone and its eloquence.

Philippics, series of three denunciations of PHILIP II of Macedon by DEMOSTHENES. CICERO's polemics against Marc ANTONY are also called philippics.

Philippines, the, officially Republic of the Philippines, republic (1992 est. pop. 67,114,000), 115,830 sq mi (300,000 sq km), SW Pacific Ocean, off the mainland of Southeast Asia, comprising over 7,000 tropical islands; the two largest are LUZON and MINDANAO. The capital is MANILA, on Luzon. The islands are mountainous and volcanic; earthquakes are common. Half of the working population is engaged in agriculture; rice, corn, and coconuts are the principal crops. Among the mineral resources are nickel, zinc, copper, cobalt, gold, silver, iron, and chromite. Manufactures include processed foods, clothing and textiles, electronic equipment, chemicals, refined metals, and electronics. The islands have one of the world's greatest stands of commercial timber, a major export. The great majority of the population are ethnic Malays (known as Filipinos), but there are groups of Negritos (negroid PYGMIES), Dumagats (similar to the Papuans of New Guinea), and Chinese. Roman Catholicism is the predominant religion, with Aglipayan (a Catholic offshoot), Protestant, and, in the south, Muslim minorities. Pilipino, based on Tagalog, is the national language, but English, Spanish, and some 70 native tongues are also spoken.

History. Europeans, led by Ferdinand MAGELLAN, first visited the islands, which were named for the future Philip II of Spain, in 1521. Manila, founded in 1571, became a leading commercial center of E Asia. Spanish control of the region remained secure until the 19th cent., when resentment against Spanish injustices brought about a movement for independence, which was inspired by the writings of José RIZAL and led by Emilio AGUINALDO. The SPANISH-AMERICAN WAR (1898) ended Spanish rule, but, to the nationalists' bitter disappointment, control of the islands was transferred to the U.S. An armed revolt (1899–1901) against U.S. rule was effectively crushed, but the question of Philippine independence remained a burning issue until 1934, when the internally self-governing Commonwealth of the Philippines was established. Preparations for full independence, led by the first president, Manuel L. QUEZON, were interrupted by WORLD WAR II, in which, after bitter fighting, the Philippines were occupied by Japan. Liberated (1944–45) by U.S. forces under Gen. Douglas MACARTHUR, the Philippines gained full independence in 1946. The combined tasks of reconstructing the war-torn country and building the new republic were complicated by the activities of Communist-led Hukbalahap (Huk) guerrillas, tensions over U.S. military installations, inflation, the need for land reform, and government corruption. A succession of presidents did little to help the peasant majority or to curb political violence. Ferdinand E. MARCOS, elected president (1965, 1969), reacted to increasing civil disorder by declaring martial law in 1972; a new constitution (1973) gave Marcos near-dictatorial powers. Although martial law was nominally lifted in 1981, critics accused Marcos, who was again elected president under a revised constitution, of retaining most of his former powers. Marcos fled the Philippines in 1986 after massive protests against alleged election frauds, and his opponent, Corazon AQUINO, became president. Despite great inital popularity, a new constitution, and promised land reforms, Aquino disappointed the hopes she had raised. Inherited debt, a continuing communist insurgency, natural disasters, and a number of attempted coups kept her from fulfilling many economic promises, and the country entered a prolonged recession in 1989. Fidel RAMOS succeeded (1992) her as president, winning election with less than 24% of the vote.

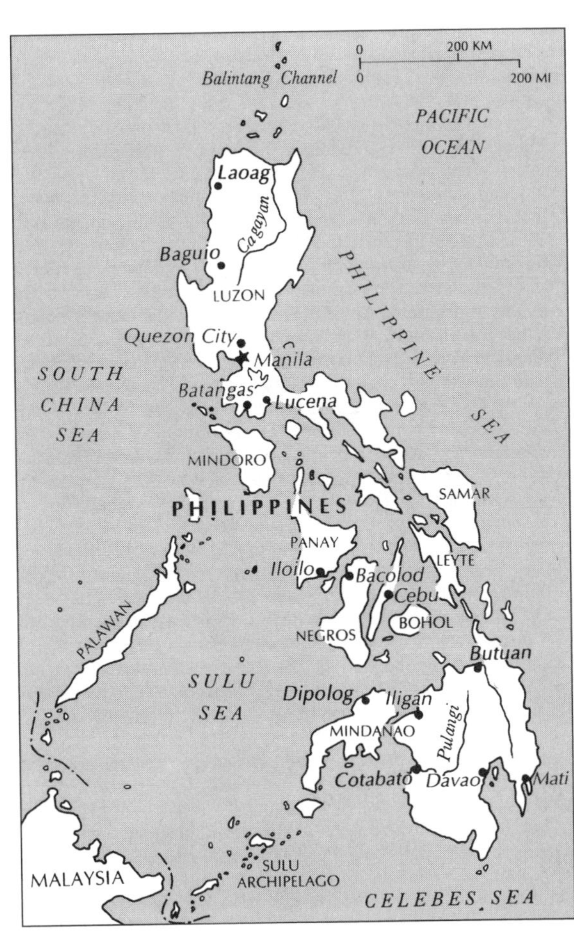

Philip the Bold, king of France: see Philip III under PHILIP, kings of France.

Philip the Bold, 1342–1404, duke of Burgundy (1363–1404); a younger son of JOHN II of France. In 1382 he helped defeat Flemish rebels, and he inherited Flanders in 1384. During the minority (1380–88) of CHARLES VI, Philip was virtual ruler of France. When the king became insane (1392), Philip fought with the king's brother, Louis d'ORLÉANS, for power. His son, JOHN THE FEARLESS, carried on the quarrel.

Philip the Fair: see Philip IV under PHILIP, kings of France.

Philip the Good, 1396–1467, duke of Burgundy (1419–67), son of JOHN THE FEARLESS. By the Treaty of Troyes (1420) he supported the English cause in France until he made peace with CHARLES VII by the Treaty of Arras (1435). He later supported (1440) the Praguerie, a revolt against Charles, and gave asylum to the rebellious DAUPHIN (later LOUIS XI). By various means, Philip acquired Hainaut, Holland, Zeeland, and other possessions. He was succeeded by his son, CHARLES THE BOLD.

Philip the Tall: see Philip V under PHILIP, kings of France.

Phillips, Wendell, 1811–84, American reformer; b. Boston. Ranked with Edward Everett and Daniel Webster as an orator, Phillips was a delegate to the World Anti-Slavery Convention in London (1840), opposed the Mexican War and annexation of Texas, advocated dissolution of the Union, and vehemently denounced slaveholding. He held that the government owed African-American slaves not only freedom but land, education, and full civil rights. After the 15th amendment to the U.S. CONSTITUTION enfranchised African Americans, Phillips continued his agitation for social reforms, including PROHIBITION, WOMAN SUFFRAGE, abolition of capital punishment, currency reform, and labor rights.

Philo Judaeus, c.20 B.C.–C.A.D. 50, Greek philosopher. A Hellenistic Jew, he attempted to synthesize revealed Greek philosophical reason and Jewish faith, often by interpreting the Bible in an allegorical way. His efforts set a precedent for future Jewish and Christian theologians.

philosophy [Gk., = love of wisdom], study of the ultimate reality, causes, and principles underlying being and thinking. Western philosophy, dating from c.600 B.C., when the Greeks established inquiry independent of theological creeds, is traditionally divided into five major branches. METAPHYSICS inquires into the nature and ultimate significance of the universe, holding reality to subsist in thought (IDEALISM), in matter (MATERIALISM), or in both (DUALISM). LOGIC is concerned with the laws of valid reasoning. EPISTEMOLOGY investigates the nature of knowledge and the process of knowing. ETHICS deals with the problems of right conduct. AESTHETICS attempts to determine the nature of beauty and the criteria of artistic judgment. Historically, philosophy falls into three major periods. Classical (Greek and Roman) philosophy emphasized a concern with the ultimate nature of reality and the problem of virtue in a political context; in fact, virtually all of the problems of philosophy were defined by the Greeks. SOCRATES, PLATO, and ARISTOTLE were the towering figures of classical philosophy. Medieval philosophy in the West was virtually inseparable from Christian thought. SCHOLASTICISM, the high achievement of medieval philosophy, was based on Aristotelian principles as preserved by Arab philosophers, notably AVICENNA and AVERROËS. St. THOMAS AQUINAS was the most prominent of the scholastics. The main concern of modern philosophy, beginning with the Renaissance, has been epistemology. DESCARTES, SPINOZA, LEIBNIZ, and other great rationalists of the 17th cent. attempted to give the new science a philosophical basis and thus paved the way for EMPIRICISM. (See articles on HOBBES; HUME; LOCKE.) KANT, representing a bridge between empirical and rationalist views, influenced the idealism of FICHTE, SCHELLING, and HEGEL. MARX, drawing from Hegel's system, developed DIALECTICAL MATERIALISM. Late in the 19th cent. philosophy and religious thinking diverged. In Europe PHENOMENOLOGY and EXISTENTIALISM, and later STRUCTURALISM and DECONSTRUCTION, developed, while Britain and the U.S. focused on the philosophy of science, epistemology, and logic, and more recently on ethics and political philosophy, as in John RAWLS' theory of justice. The many rigorous systems of Eastern philosophy are founded in religion (see BUDDHISM; CONFUCIANISM; HINDUISM; ISLAM; JAINISM; SHINTO; TAOISM; VEDANTA). See also names of individual philosophers, e.g., NIETZSCHE, Friedrich; SCHOPENHAUER, Arthur; TEILHARD DE CHARDIN, Pierre.

phlebitis, inflammation of a vein, often accompanied by a blood clot, or THROMBUS, in the affected vein. When a blood clot is present, the condition is known as **thrombophlebitis.** Blood clot formation may follow injury, surgery, childbirth, or prolonged bedrest, or may be associated with infection. The chief danger is that the clot may dislodge and travel to a vital organ, causing serious damage. Phlebitis is treated with ANTICOAGULANTS.

phloem: see BARK; STEM.

phlogiston theory, hypothesis regarding combustion. The theory, advanced by Johann Becher late in the 17th cent., postulates the presence in all flammable material of phlogiston, a substance that is without color, odor, taste, or weight and that is given off in burning. The ash of the burned material is held to be the true material. The theory was popular until the late 18th cent., when it was refuted by the work of Antoine LAVOISIER.

phlogopite: see MICA.

phlox, name for plants (genus *Phlox*) and the family Polemoniaceae, consisting of herbs, shrubs, and vines. Found chiefly in the W U.S., the family includes many popular wild and garden flowers, especially the genera *Phlox, Polemonium* (called Jacob's ladder), and *Gilia.* Most phlox are perennial, but some common garden varieties are annual hybrids.

Phnom Penh, capital of Cambodia (1990 est. pop. 800,000), at the confluence of the MEKONG and Tônlé Sap rivers, S Cambodia. The country's chief port and commercial center, it became (c.1432) the capital of the KHMER EMPIRE and (1867) of Cambodia. The city was captured (1975) when Cambodia fell to the Communist KHMER ROUGE, and most of its population (then estimated at over 700,000) was evacuated to work in the countryside. Since 1979, when the Khmer Rouge were ousted by Vietnamese forces, the city has gradually revived.

phobia, persistent, illogical, or intense fear of a specific thing or situation, recognized by the phobic person as irrational. There are many types, e.g., fear of enclosed spaces (claustrophobia), of public places from which escape might be difficult (agoraphobia), of water (hydrophobia), and of public humiliation (social phobia). Phobias are usually treated through psychotherapy, especially BEHAVIOR THERAPY.

Phobos, in astronomy, natural satellite of MARS.

Phoebe, in astronomy, natural satellite of SATURN.

Phoebus or **Phoebus Apollo:** see APOLLO.

Phoenicia [fĭnē'shə], ancient territory occupied by Phoenicians. The name Phoenicia usually refers to the heart of the territory where the great Phoenician cities, notably TYRE and SIDON, stood (corresponding roughly to the coast of present-day Lebanon). By 1250 B.C. the Phoenicians, a Semitic people, were well established as navigators and traders. Organized into city-states, they later established outposts, notably UTICA and CARTHAGE, and traveled to the edges of the known world. The Phoenicians were also fine artisans, but their greatest contribution was the ALPHABET, an idea adopted by the Greeks; the use of symbols for sounds in place of clumsier CUNEIFORM and HIEROGLYPHIC was a tremendous advance. The rise of the Greeks in the 5th cent. B.C. challenged Phoenician maritime power, and Hellenistic culture gradually absorbed the last traces of Phoenician civilization.

Phoenician art. The Phoenician region was a major trade center of the ancient world, and its art reflects the influences of Egypt, Syria, and Greece. Phoenician metalcraft and ivory work were copied in many neighboring regions, and Phoenician works in glass, jewelry, clay, alabaster, faience, and wood are found in all Mediterranean countries and Asia Minor. A well-known example of Phoenician art is a glass- and gem-inlaid ivory from Nimrud showing a lion attacking a man (British Mus.).

Phoenix, city (1990 pop. 983,403; met. area 2,122,101), state capital and seat of Maricopa co., S Ariz, on the Salt R.; inc. 1881. The largest city in Arizona and the ninth largest in the U.S., it produces electronic, computer, and aerospace equipment, as well as citrus and other food products. Phoenix boomed after World War II. The dry, sunny climate makes it a popular resort center. In the area are Native American and pioneer remains, and numerous parks.

phoenix, fabulous bird of ancient legend. When it reached 500 years of age it burned itself on a pyre from whose ashes another phoenix arose. It commonly appears in literature as a symbol of death and resurrection.

phonograph: see RECORD PLAYER.

phosphorescence, LUMINESCENCE produced by certain substances after absorbing radiant energy or other types of energy. Phosphorescence is distinguished from FLUORESCENCE in that it continues even after the radiation causing it has ceased. The luminescence is caused by electrons that are excited by the radiation and trapped in potential energy troughs, from which they are freed by the thermal motion within the crystal. As they fall back to a lower energy level, they emit energy in the form of light.

phosphorus (P), nonmetallic element, discovered c.1674 by Hennig Brand. It is an extremely poisonous, yellow to white, waxy, solid substance. Because phosphorus ignites spontaneously when exposed to air, it is stored underwater. Its major source is the mineral APATITE, found in phosphate rocks. The principal use of phosphorus is in compounds in fertilizers, detergents, insecticides, soft drinks, toxic nerve gases, pharmaceuticals, and dentifrices. Phosphorus compounds are essential in the diet. Phosphorus is a component of ADENOSINE TRIPHOSPHATE (ATP), a fundamental energy source in living things, and of calcium phosphate, the principal material in bones and teeth. See ELEMENT (table); PERIODIC TABLE.

Photius, c.820–892?, Greek churchman and theologian, patriarch of CONSTANTINOPLE. In favor of treating repentant iconoclasts leniently (see ICONOCLASM), he replaced (858) St. Ignatius of Constantinople as patriarch, but Pope St. NICHOLAS I refused to recognize him. When Photius called (867) a synod that challenged the pope, he was replaced as patriarch and condemned. Photius was again patriarch (877–86) and was recognized by Pope JOHN VIII, but he died in exile. The schism of Photius pointed out the growing differences between East and West.

photocell: see PHOTOELECTRIC CELL.

photocopying, processes that use chemical, electrical, or photographic techniques to copy printed or pictorial matter. Most familiar is *xerography,* an electrostatic process that utilizes the attractive force of electric charges to transfer an image to a charged plate. Light, reflecting off the white areas of the object to be copied, erases the charge on the corresponding areas of the plate. A plastic ink powder, called toner, sticks to the charged areas of the plate and transfers an image of the original to paper. *Thermography* uses infrared rays on heat-sensitive paper to transfer an image. Several processes use cameras to make copies of an original. The *photostat* can reduce or enlarge copied material photographically. *Microfilming* generates copies from 1/12 to 1/100 the size of the original, and advances in microphotography allow even greater miniaturization in the *microfiche,* where extremely small microphotographs are printed side by side on a card made of film. In the *transfer process,* chemically coated paper is placed in contact with the original, exposed to light, and developed. The blueprint and the whiteprint, used to reproduce the drawings of architects and engineers, are examples of transfer processes.

photoelectric cell or **photocell,** device whose electrical characteristics (e.g., current, voltage, or resistance) vary when light is incident upon it. Common photoelectric cells consist of two electrodes separated by a light-sensitive SEMICONDUCTOR material. A battery or other voltage source connected to the two electrodes sets up a current even in the absence of light; when light strikes the semiconductor section of the photocell, the current increases in proportion to the light intensity. Photocells can be used to operate switches, RELAYS, door openers, and intrusion alarms. See also PHOTOVOLTAIC CELL.

photoelectric effect, the emission of electrons by substances, especially metals, when light falls on their surfaces. The effect was discovered by Heinrich HERTZ in 1887 and explained by Albert EINSTEIN in 1905. According to Einstein's theory, light is composed of discrete particles of energy, or quanta, called PHOTONS. When the photons with enough energy strike the material, they liberate electrons that have a maximal kinetic energy equal to the energy of the photons less the work function (the energy required to free the electrons from a particular material). See also PHOTOELECTRIC CELL; QUANTUM MECHANICS.

photography, still, science and art of making permanent images on light-sensitive materials. Photography's basic principles, processes, and materials were discovered independently and virtually simultaneously by a diverse group of individuals early in the 19th cent. Johann Heinrich Schulze had discovered in 1727 that silver nitrate darkens upon exposure to light. Using Schulze's research, Thomas Wedgwood and Sir Humphry DAVY created the first photogram. The French physicist Joseph Nicéphore Niépce made the first paper negative (1816) and the first known photograph, on metal (1827). He formed a partnership with a painter, Louis Jacques DAGUERRE, who in 1839 announced his method for making a direct positive image on a silver plate—the daguerreotype. The English scientist William Henry Fox TALBOT developed a paper negative (the calotype) from which an infinite number of paper positives could be printed. Sir John Herschel (see HERSCHEL, family) discovered (1819) a suitable photographic fixing agent for paper images and is credited with giving the new medium its name. In 1851 Frederick Scott Archer developed the collodion process, or "set plate" technique, which resulted in a negative image with the fine detail of the daguerreotype and was infinitely reproducible. Soon the photograph was considered incontestable proof of an event, experience, or state of being. Among the chief photographers of the 19th cent. were the explorer W.H. JACKSON; Roger Fenton, who documented the Crimean War; Mathew B. BRADY and his photographic corps, who photographed the American Civil War; the painter Thomas EAKINS; and Eadweard MUYBRIDGE, who devised a means of making stop-action photographs. As accessory lenses were perfected, the moon and the microcosm became accessible. The development of the halftone process (see PRINTING) in 1881 made photographic reproduction possible in books and newspapers. In 1888 George EASTMAN introduced roll film and the simple Kodak box CAMERA, and photography became available to all. The medium's legitimacy as an art form was challenged by artists and critics and upheld by Alfred STIEGLITZ, founder of the Photo-Secession movement. Initially photography imitated painting, but soon a "straight" aesthetic was widely adopted whereby the image was left free of manipulation. In the early 20th cent. the documentary power of photography was exemplified in the works of Jacob RIIS. Paul STRAND combined documentary concerns with a lean, modernist vision. Eugène ATGET and Henri CARTIER-BRESSON developed intensely personal styles. Technical advances, including smaller cameras, faster films, and portable lighting, granted photojournalists unprecedented versatility, and the popular picture magazines (e.g., *Life*) provided a vast audience for documentary work. The Great Depression and World War II were major sources of important documentary photography, as evidenced in the work of Margaret BOURKE-WHITE, Walker EVANS, Dorothea LANGE, and W. Eugene SMITH. Color photography also emerged as an important force, as in the nature photographs of Eliot Porter and the microphotographs of Roman VISHNIAC. Also significant was the development of the one-step Polaroid camera, first demonstrated (1947) in black and white by Edwin LAND and later (1963) available for color images. Although many photographers have adhered to the straight aesthetic, e.g., Ansel ADAMS, Diane Arbus, and Edward WESTON, younger photographers have felt little inhibition against manipulation of the image. As photography has become a more dominant artistic medium, many painters and printmakers, e.g., Andy WARHOL, Robert RAUSCHENBERG, and David HOCKNEY, have blended photography with a variety of other techniques such as handwork, collage, and multiple images. The late 20th cent. has seen the development of a number of important technologies, among them the three-dimensional images of HOLOGRAPHY, photography from space and sensitive astronomical photography that can register even a single PHOTON, and digital imaging and processing and other COMPUTER-based techniques for recording and editing photographic images. See also HOLOGRAPHY.

photolithography: see LITHOGRAPHY.

photometry, branch of physics dealing with the measurement of the intensity of light sources. Instruments used for such measurements are called photometers; most types are based on the comparison of the light source to be measured with a light source of known intensity. The modern unit, adopted in 1948, for the measurement of light intensity is the candela (cd); it is equal to 1/60 of the intensity of one square centimeter of a BLACKBODY radiator at the temperature at which platinum solidifies (2046K).

photon or **light quantum,** the particle composing light and other forms of electromagnetic radiation. The PHOTOELECTRIC EFFECT and BLACKBODY radiation can be explained only by assuming that light energy is transferred in discrete packets, or photons, and that the energy of each photon is equal to the frequency of the light multiplied by Planck's constant *h.* Light imparts energy to a charged particle when one of its photons collides with the particle. See also QUANTUM MECHANICS.

photonics, the science and technology based on and concerned with the controlled flow of PHOTONS, or light particles. It is the optical equivalent of ELECTRONICS, and the two technologies coexist in such innovations as optoelectronic integrated circuits. Photonic applications include data storage (using OPTICAL DISKS and holograms), data transmission (see FIBER OPTICS), experimental optical computers, optical switches and light modulators (for signal processing and interconnection), and a photonic gyroscope used in commercial aircraft that has no moving parts.

photorealism, international art movement of the late 1960s and 70s that stressed the precise rendering of subject matter, often taken from actual photographs or painted with the aid of slides. Also known as superrealism, the style stressed objectivity and technical proficiency in producing images of photographic clarity, often street scenes or portraits. Well-known American photorealists include the painters Chuck CLOSE and Richard ESTES and the sculptor Duane HANSON.

photosphere: see SUN.

photosynthesis, process in which green plants use the energy of sunlight to manufacture carbohydrates from carbon dioxide and water in the presence of CHLOROPHYLL. The chlorophyll molecule is uniquely capable of converting active light energy into a latent form (glucose) that is stored in food. The initial phase of the process requires direct light; water (H_2O) is broken down into oxygen (which is released as a gas) and hydrogen. Hydrogen and the carbon and oxygen of carbon dioxide (CO_2) are then converted into a series of increasingly complex compounds that result finally in a stable organic compound, glucose ($C_6H_{12}O_6$), and water. The simplified equation for the overall reaction is $6CO_2 + 12H_2O + \text{energy} \rightarrow C_6H_{12}O_6 + 6O_2 + 6H_2O$. The oxygen released as a by-product is atmospheric oxygen, vital to respiration in plants and animals. Photosynthesis, in general, is the reverse of RESPIRATION, in which carbohydrates are broken down to release energy.

photovoltaic cell or **solar cell,** SEMICONDUCTOR diode that converts light to electric current. When light strikes the exposed active surface, it knocks electrons loose from their sites in the crystal. Some of the electrons have sufficient energy to cross the DIODE junction and pass through an external circuit. Because the current and voltage obtained from these devices are small, they are usually connected in large series-parallel arrays. Practical photovoltaic cells are currently about 10 to 15% efficient. Although cells constructed from indium phosphide and gallium arsenide are, in principle, more efficient, silicon-based cells are generally less costly. Solar cells have long been used to provide electric power for spacecraft. As costs have decreased, they have seen greater use as energy sources for irrigation pumps in remote areas, oil drilling platforms, and mountaintop microwave relay stations, and for small devices such as hand-held CALCULATORS.

Phrygia, ancient region, central Asia Minor (now central Turkey). The Phrygians, apparently Indo-Europeans, entered (c.1200 B.C.) the area from the Balkans. The kingdom of Phrygia (fl. 8th–6th cent. B.C.) is associated in Greek legend with MIDAS and GORDIUS. Phrygia was later dominated in turn by Lydia, the Gauls, Pergamum, and Rome.

Phrynichus [frĭn'ĭkəs], c.512–476 B.C., Athenian tragedian. Called by PLATO the founder of TRAGEDY, he was noted for his choreography and for introducing female characters. His *Taking of Miletus* moved the audience to tears.

Phyfe, Duncan, c.1768–1854, American cabinetmaker; b. Scotland. In the early 1790s in his New York City shop he made chairs, settees, tables, and sideboards of mahogany, satinwood, maple, and rosewood. After 1820 the excellent proportions, graceful curves, and simple decoration of his work gave way to heaviness and overornamentation.

physical chemistry, branch of science that combines the principles and methods of PHYSICS and CHEMISTRY. It provides a fundamental theoretical and experimental basis for all of chemistry, including organic, inorganic, and analytical chemistry. Important topics are chemical equilibrium, ELECTROCHEMISTRY, molecular structure, MOLECULAR WEIGHTS, reaction rates, SOLUTIONS, and STATES OF MATTER.

physical therapy or **physiotherapy,** treatment of disorders of the MUSCLES, BONES, or JOINTS resulting from injury or disease of the muscles or nerves. Treatment, by a trained physiotherapist, includes the use of such agents as water (e.g., whirlpool baths), manual and electrically-stimulated massage, heat, and exercise to stimulate nerves, prevent muscular atrophy, and train other muscles to compensate for damaged ones. See also SPORTS MEDICINE.

physician's assistant (PA), health care professional who provides patient services ranging from physical examinations to surgical procedures, under the supervision of a physician. PAs receive two years of post-college training and are licensed by the states.

physics, branch of science traditionally defined as the study of MATTER, ENERGY, and the relation between them. Physics today may be loosely divided into classical physics and modern physics. Classical physics includes the traditional branches that were recognized and fairly well developed before the beginning of the 20th cent.: MECHANICS (the study of MOTION and the FORCES that cause it), ACOUSTICS (the study of SOUND), OPTICS (the study of LIGHT), THERMODYNAMICS (the study of the relationships between HEAT and other forms of energy), and ELECTRICITY and MAGNETISM. Most of classical physics is concerned with matter and energy on the normal scale of observation. By contrast, much of modern physics is concerned with the behavior of matter and energy under extreme conditions (see, e.g., LOW-TEMPERATURE PHYSICS) or on the very small scale (see ATOM; ELEMENTARY PARTICLES; NUCLEAR PHYSICS; PARTICLE ACCELERATOR). On the very small scale, and for rapidly-moving objects, ordinary, commonsense notions of space, time, matter, and energy are no longer valid, and two chief theories of modern physics present a different picture of these concepts from that presented by classical physics. QUANTUM MECHANICS is concerned with the discrete, rather than the continuous, nature of many phenomena at the atomic and subatomic level, and with the complementary aspects of particles and waves in the description of such phenomena. The theory of RELATIVITY is concerned with the description of phenomena that take place in a frame of reference that is in motion with respect to an observer. See also ASTRONOMY; SOLID-STATE PHYSICS.

physiocrats, school of 18th-cent. French thinkers who evolved the first complete system of ECONOMICS. Physiocracy's founder, François QUESNAY, argued that the source of all wealth was the land and that only the abundance and high prices of agricultural goods could create prosperity. His followers stressed that absolute freedom of trade was essential to guarantee the most beneficial operation of "economic law," which they considered immutable. The physiocrats influenced later advocates of LAISSEZ FAIRE and contributed to the economic thinking of Adam SMITH.

physiology, study of the normal functioning of animals and plants, and of activities that maintain and transmit life. It is usually accompanied by the study of structure (see ANATOMY), the two being intimately related. Physiology considers basic activities such as METABOLISM and special functions within cells, tissues, and organs.

pi, in mathematics, the ratio of the circumference of a CIRCLE to its diameter; its symbol is π. The ratio is the same for all circles and is approximately 3.1416. The NUMBER π is irrational and transcendental. An early value was the Greek approximation $3\frac{1}{7}$; by the mid-20th cent. a computer had calculated π to 100,000 decimal places.

Piaf, Edith, 1915–63, French cabaret singer; b. Edith Giovanna Gassion. She began singing in cafes and in the streets at 15, and went on to fame in cabaret, concert, and movie appearances with her powerful, emotional style.

Piaget, Jean [pyä'jā], 1896–1980, Swiss psychologist. He is known for his contributions to child psychology, especially for his theory of cognitive and intellectual development, according to which development proceeds in genetically determined stages that always follow the same sequential order. Piaget showed that young children reason differently from adults and are often incapable of understanding logical reasoning. He wrote on the applications of dialectics and STRUCTURALISM in the behavioral sciences and attempted a synthesis of physics, biology, psychology, and epistemology. His writings include *The Child's Conception of the World* (tr. 1929) and *Genetic Epistemology* (tr. 1970).

piano or **pianoforte,** musical STRINGED INSTRUMENT whose sound is produced by vibrating strings struck by felt hammers that are controlled from a keyboard. Its earliest predecessor was the medieval dulcimer. The 14th to 16th cent. saw the rise of the harpsichord, a keyboard instrument whose strings were plucked by quills or jacks. The square harpsichord, often called the spinet, was common by the 16th cent. In c.1709 Bartolomeo Cristofori (1655–1731), a Florentine maker of harpsichords, constructed the first piano. It differed from the harpsichord in that by varying the touch one could vary the volume and duration of tone. This expressive quality was shared to some extent by the clavichord, a delicate instrument important in the 16th to 18th cent., but musical taste gradually favored the piano's greater volume and expressiveness, and it largely supplanted both the harpsichord and clavichord by 1800. C.P.E. BACH, MOZART, and HAYDN were the first major composers to write for the piano. The main body of its literature is from the 19th cent., including the works of BEETHOVEN, SCHUBERT, CHOPIN, Robert SCHUMANN, MENDELSSOHN, BRAHMS, FRANCK, LISZT, DEBUSSY, and RAVEL. The piano was originally built in the shape of a harpsichord, and this style (the grand piano) has always been the standard form. Innovations in the 19th cent. included an iron framework, a double-action striking mechanism permitting rapid repetition of tone, the upright piano (in which the strings are perpendicular to, rather than parallel to, the keys), and the player piano, which incorporates a mechanical system that automatically plays the encoded contents of a perforated paper strip. An electric piano has also been developed.

Piast, 1st dynasty of Polish dukes and kings. Duke Mieszko I (r.962–92) founded the dynasty and introduced Christianity to Poland. His son, BOLESLAUS I, was crowned king in 1025; not all of his successors, however, styled themselves king. During the reign (1079–1102) of BOLESLAUS III, four hereditary duchies were created for his four sons; a fifth son, CASIMIR II (probably a posthumous child), carved out a fifth duchy for himself and secured the hereditary right to the kingship for his descendants. Dynastic struggles continued, however, until the dynasty ended with the death (1370) of CASIMIR III. The Jagiello dynasty followed.

Picabia, Francis, 1878–1953, French painter. He was associated with IMPRESSIONISM, CUBISM, and SURREALISM, and was one of the first exponents of DADA in Europe. His works include *Physical Culture* (1913; Philadelphia Mus. Art).

Picard, Jean, 1620–82, French astronomer. His measurements led to a much improved determination of the length of a degree of meridian and consequently of the circumference of the earth. Sir Isaac NEWTON used Picard's figures to verify the accuracy of his principle of gravitation.

Picasso, Pablo (Pablo Ruiz y Picasso), 1881–1973, Spanish painter, sculptor, graphic artist, and ceramicist who worked in France; the foremost figure in 20th-cent. art. Leader of the SCHOOL OF PARIS, he was remarkable for his technical virtuosity, incredible originality, and prolificacy. Admitted to the Royal Academy of Barcelona at 15, he later moved to Paris, where he remained until 1947, then moving to the South of France. His early works, e.g., *Old Woman* (1901; Philadelphia Mus. Art), show the influence of TOULOUSE-LAUTREC. His production is usually described in series of overlapping periods. In his melancholy "blue period" such works as *The Old Guitarist* (1903; Art Inst., Chicago) depicted, in blue tones, the world of the poor. His "rose period" is characterized by a lighter palette and subjects from the circus. In 1907, Picasso painted *Les Demoiselles d'Avignon* (Mus. Mod. Art, N.Y.C.), the most significant work in the development of CUBISM and abstraction, and a herald of analytic cubism. In the synthetic phase of cubism (after 1912), his forms became larger and more representational, e.g., *The Three Musicians* (1921; Mus. Mod. Art, N.Y.C.). In the 1920s he also introduced COLLAGE. His second landmark work was *Guernica* (Reina Sofía, Madrid), an impassioned condemnation of war and fascism. In his later years, Picasso turned to creations of fantasy and comic invention. Working consistently in sculpture, ceramics, and the graphic arts, he continued to explore his personal vision until his death at 91.

Piccard, Auguste [pēkär'], 1884–1962, Belgian physicist, known for his balloon ascents into the stratosphere; b. Switzerland. In 1932 he reached an altitude of 55,500 ft (16,900 m). After 1946 he made ocean dives in a bathyscaphe of his own design. In 1960 his son, **Jacques Piccard,** 1922–, and Lt. Don Walsh of the U.S. Navy reached a depth of 35,800 ft (10,920 m) in the MARIANAS TRENCH.

piccolo: see WIND INSTRUMENT.

Piccolomini, Enea Silvio de': see PIUS II.

pickerel: see PIKE.

Pickett, George Edward, 1825–75, Confederate general in the American CIVIL WAR. He is best remembered for "Pickett's charge," the unsuccessful assault (1863) on the Union center during the GETTYSBURG CAMPAIGN that virtually annihilated his division.

Pickford, Mary, 1893–1979, American film actress; b. Canada as Gladys Smith. Called "America's Sweetheart," she played plucky heroines in such films as *The Poor Little Rich Girl* (1917) and *Tess of the Storm Country* (1922).

Mary Pickford

Picts, ancient inhabitants of N and central SCOTLAND. First mentioned in A.D. 297, the Picts formed a unified kingdom by the 7th cent. The union (c.843) of the Picts and the Scottish kingdom of Dalriada became the kingdom of Scotland.

pidgin, a lingua franca that is not the mother tongue of anyone using it and that has a simplified grammar and restricted, often polyglot, vocabulary. An example is the pidgin English used in E Asian ports, principally for trading between the English and Chinese. The majority of the vocabulary and grammar are of English origin, but there are also Malay, Chinese, and Portuguese elements. Pidgins are important national languages in Papua New Guinea and some Pacific island countries.

Piedmont, region (1990 pop. 4,357,559), 9,807 sq mi (25,400 sq km), NW Italy. The Piedmont is mostly mountainous, with the ALPS in the north and west, and the APENNINES in the south. TURIN, the capital, is a major industrial center. Wheat, corn, rice, and grapes are grown in the upper Po valley. From the 11th cent. the counts (later dukes) of SAVOY were powerful in the area. They became kings of SARDINIA in 1720 and had acquired all of modern Piedmont by 1748. France greatly influenced Piedmontese culture and ruled the area from 1798 to 1814. The region was the center of the RISORGIMENTO, and Turin was the first capital of the kingdom of Italy.

Pied Piper of Hamelin, legendary 13th-cent. figure who rid Hamelin, Germany, of its rats by charming them away with his flute playing. When he was refused payment, he charmed away the town's children in revenge. Among those who retold the tale are GOETHE and Robert BROWNING.

Pierce, Franklin, 1804–69, 14th president of the U.S. (1853–57); b. Hillsboro, N.H. He served in the New Hampshire legislature (1829–33) and in the U.S. Congress (1833–42), resigning from the Senate to practice law in Concord, N.H. In 1852, as the compromise "dark horse" presidential candidate of the badly divided Democratic party, he defeated the Whig candidate, Gen. Winfield SCOTT. Pierce's failures to unite the Democrats and to implement his expansionist foreign policy made him appear a weak, vacillating president. His one solid achievement in foreign affairs was the GADSDEN PURCHASE from Spain. Although he had favored the COMPROMISE OF 1850 on the slavery issue, he backed the KANSAS-NEBRASKA ACT of 1850 that precipitated virtual civil war between the pro- and antislavery forces in Kansas. The act enraged many Northerners and caused Pierce to be so unpopular that the Democrats passed him over for renomination; James BUCHANAN succeeded him as president. Pierce's opposition to the CIVIL WAR made him more than ever disliked in the North, where he died in obscurity.

Piero della Francesca or **Piero de' Franceschi,** c.1420–1492, major Italian RENAISSANCE painter. Early contact with the art of Florence gave him the basics of perspective, to which he added his own acute perception of nature, e.g., in the *Baptism of Christ* (National Gall., London). He delighted in the play of mathematical ratios and painted *The Flagellation of Christ* (Urbino) in a perfect, geometric framework. His most famous cycle, *The Story of the True Cross* (1452–66; Church of San Francesco, Arezzo), depicts scenes from the *Golden Legend*. He also painted court portraits, e.g., of the Duke and Duchess of Urbino (Uffizi).

Pierre, city (1990 pop. 12,906), state capital (since 1889) and seat of Hughes co., central S.Dak., on the Missouri R.; inc. 1883. Its economy is centered on agriculture (grains and cattle), tourism, and state government. Located on the site of an Arikara settlement, it was a river trade center from c.1822. The huge Oahe Dam and Lake Oahe are nearby.

Piers Plowman: see LANGLAND, WILLIAM.

piezoelectric effect, voltage (see POTENTIAL, ELECTRIC) produced between surfaces of a solid DIELECTRIC when a mechanical stress is applied to it. This effect is exhibited by certain crystals, e.g., quartz and Rochelle salt, and ceramic materials. When a voltage is applied across certain surfaces of a solid exhibiting the piezoelectric effect, the solid undergoes a mechanical distortion. Piezoelectric materials are used in TRANSDUCERS, e.g., phonograph cartridges, microphones, and strain gauges, which produce an electrical output from a mechanical input, and in earphones and ultrasonic radiators, which produce a mechanical output from an electrical input.

pig: see SWINE.

pigeon, land BIRD of the family Columbidae, cosmopolitan in temperate and tropical regions, characterized by a stout body, small head, and thick plumage. The names *dove* and *pigeon* are interchangeable, although the former generally refers to smaller birds. The rock dove (*Columba livia*) of temperate W Eurasia is the wild progenitor of the common street and domestic pigeons. The most common American wild pigeon is the small, brown mourning dove, or turtledove (*Zenaidura carolinensis*), similar to the once-abundant passenger pigeon, which became extinct in 1914.

pigeon English: see PIDGIN.

pig iron, IRON refined in a blast furnace, containing about 4% carbon and small amounts of manganese, silicon, phosphorus, and sulfur. About 95% of it is processed to make STEEL, and the balance is cast in sand molds into blocks called pigs and further processed in foundries (see CASTING).

Pike, Zebulon Montgomery, 1779–1813, American explorer; b. Lamberton, N.J. As an army lieutenant he led an expedition (1806–7) to Spanish NEW MEXICO, discovering the Colorado peak that is named after him. Promoted to brigadier general during the WAR OF 1812, he was killed in the successful assault on York (now Toronto).

pike, freshwater FISHES of the family Esocidae, found in Europe, Asia, and North America. The pike, muskellunge, and pickerel are long, thin fishes with spineless dorsal fins, large anal fins, and long, narrow jaws with formidable teeth. The muskellunge is the largest of the genus *Esox*, from 2 to 7 ft long (61 to 213.5 cm) and weighing 10 to 20 lb (4.5 to 9 kg). Carnivorous and solitary except while spawning, it eats fish, frogs, snakes, young aquatic mammals, and water fowl. The great northern pike (*E. lucius*), called jackfish in Canada, is thought to consume one fifth its weight (10–35 lb/4.5–16 kg) daily. The pickerels are smaller members of the family. Pikes are strong fighters and valued as game and food. The walleyed pike is a PERCH.

Pikes Peak, mountain, 14,110 ft (4,301 m) high, central Colo. in the Front Range of the ROCKY MOUNTAINS, at the end of the GREAT PLAINS. Colorado Springs is at its eastern base. The mountain was discovered (1806) by U.S. explorer Zebulon Pike. Its summit is accessible by highway or cog railroad.

Pilate: see PONTIUS PILATE.

Pilgrims, the 102 English Puritan separatists and others who founded the PLYMOUTH COLONY. While crossing the Atlantic Ocean on the *Mayflower*, they signed the MAYFLOWER COMPACT providing for majority rule. The Pilgrims landed at Plymouth in Dec. 1620.

pill, the: see ORAL CONTRACEPTIVE.

Pilnyak, Boris [pēlnyäk'], pseud. of **Boris Andreyevich Vogau,** 1894–1941, Russian novelist and short-story writer. He first attracted attention with his novel *The Naked Year* (1921), depicting the chaos of the revolutionary period. *The Volga Falls to the Caspian Sea* (1930) was denounced by the Soviet regime. Arrested in 1937, Pilnyak either died in prison or was executed.

Pilobolus Dance Theater, innovative dance company founded (1971) at Dartmouth College by Moses Pendleton, Jonathan Wolken, Alison Chase, and others. Its dances, which are developed collectively, typically involve gymnastics, group "structures," and overt and implied humor. Later dances have often echoed literary works. In 1980 Pendleton and Chase established Momix, an offshoot group.

pilot fish: see POMPANO.

Piłsudski, Joseph, 1867–1935, Polish general and politician. Originally a Socialist, he was repeatedly exiled and imprisoned by Russian authorities in the early part of the century. He commanded the Polish Legions that fought for the Central Powers in WORLD WAR I. In 1918 he proclaimed an independent Polish republic, with himself as chief of state and (after 1919) PADEREWSKI as premier. In 1921 he extended Poland's eastern boundary with the Treaty of Riga. He surrendered his powers and retired in 1922, but in 1926 he reassumed power by a coup. Thereafter he headed a military dictatorship with fascist overtones.

Piltdown man, name given to fossil remains found (1908) at Piltdown, England, thought to be human and 200,000 to 1 million years old. In 1950, fluorine tests and X-ray analysis proved that Piltdown man was a forgery.

Pima or **Akimel O'Odham,** indigenous North American people of the Southwest, with a Uto-Aztecan language of the Aztec-Tanoan stock (see NATIVE AMERICAN LANGUAGES). They are closely related to the TOHONO O'ODHAM. Descendants of the Hohokam, who built a network of irrigation canals, the Pima were sedentary farmers, noted for fine basketry. Warlike toward the APACHES, they befriended both Spaniards and American pioneers. The Maricopa joined them in the 19th cent. Today, in central Arizona, they live on income from agriculture, crafts, and leasing land for mineral development. In 1990 there were 14,431 Pimas in the U.S.

pimento or **allspice,** tree (*Pimenta officinalis*) of the MYRTLE family. Its dried, unripe berries are used medicinally and as a spice. The spice supposedly combines the flavors of several other spices; it is used in pickles and relishes. Pimento (more correctly, *pimiento*) is also the name of a large, sweet Spanish PEPPER.

pimpernel: see PRIMROSE.

Pinatubo, Mount, active volcano, 5771 ft (1699 m), central Luzon island, the Philippines, c.55 mi (90 km) NW of Manila. Dormant for 600 years, it began erupting on Apr. 2, 1991. Most residents had evacuated nearby areas when Pinatubo erupted catastrophically (June 15, 1991), killing over 500 people and burying over 310 sq mi (800 sq km) under volcanic ash. Landslides of rain-soaked volcanic ash caused further destruction in 1991 and 1992.

Pinchot, Gifford [pĭn'shō], 1865–1946, U.S. conservationist; b. Simsbury, Conn. He served in the U.S. Forest Service (1898–1910) until dismissed by Pres. TAFT and later joined (1912) Theodore ROOSEVELT in forming the PROGRESSIVE PARTY. A founder of the Yale school of forestry, he was professor there (1903–36). He was twice governor of Pennsylvania (1923–29, 1931–35).

Pinckney, Charles, 1757–1824, American statesman; b. Charleston, S.C. A delegate to the FEDERAL CONSTITUTIONAL CONVENTION of 1787, he was also a U.S. senator (1798–1801), minister to Spain (1801–5), and governor of SOUTH CAROLINA (1789–91, 1796–98, 1806–8). His cousin **Charles Cotesworth Pinckney,** 1746–1825, also a del egate to the Constitutional Convention, served as an envoy to France (1797) and refused to pay bribes to French officials in the XYZ AFFAIR. His brother, **Thomas Pinckney,** 1750–1828, was governor of South Carolina (1787–89) and as envoy to Spain negotiated the treaty (1795) establishing U.S. commercial relations with Spain.

Pindar, 518?–c.438 B.C., generally regarded as the greatest Greek LYRIC poet. He wrote choral lyrics and established a standard for the triumphal or epinician ode. Celebrating an athletic victory, each ode contains a narrative myth, connected with the winner, that sets an elevated moral and religious tone. Pindar's diction and complex word order do not translate easily. The 17th–18th cent. **Pindaric ode** of Abraham COWLEY, John DRYDEN, and Thomas GRAY is based loosely on Pindar's form.

Pindling, Sir Lynden O(scar), 1930–, prime minister of the Bahamas (1967–92). Leader of the Progressive Liberal party, he was (1967) the first person of African descent to become prime minister of the Bahamas, and in 1973 he led the country to independence. Pindling spurred the development of international banking and investment management as a major industry. In the 1980s he was accused of corruption and accepting bribes from drug traffickers. Those charges and a depressed economy contributed to his party's defeat in 1992.

pine, common name for the family Pinaceae, resinous woody trees chiefly of north temperate regions, with needlelike, usually evergreen leaves. The Pinaceae reproduce by means of cones rather than flowers, and have winged seeds suitable for wind distribution. The family is the largest and most important of the CONIFERS, providing naval stores (pitch, turpentine, and rosin), paper pulp, and more lumber than any other family. The family's genera include the FIR, LARCH, SPRUCE, HEMLOCK, CEDAR, DOUGLAS FIR, and true pines. True pines (genus *Pinus*) can be identified by the leaf arrangement: in each species a specific number of needles (one to five) is contained in a sheath. The ponderosa, or Western yellow, pine (*P. ponderosa*) is second only to the Douglas fir as a commercial timber tree in North America; the Scotch pine (*P. sylvestris*), ranging from Scotland to Siberia, is one of the most valuable European timber trees. The white pine (*P. strobus*) of E North America has straight-grained softwood with little resin; it is used for interior trim and cabinetwork. A major source of naval stores is the longleaf, or Southern yellow, pine (*P. palustris*); its highly resinous wood is also used for heavy construction and paper pulp. Several Mediterranean and American pines yield edible seeds, called pine nuts.

pineal body or **pineal gland,** pea-sized organ situated in the BRAIN. Generally regarded as an endocrine gland (see ENDOCRINE SYSTEM) even though no pineal HORMONE has been isolated in humans, it may exert some influence on sexual development by secreting a substance called melatonin.

pineapple, fruit of a spiny herbaceous plant (*Ananas comosus*) of the BROMELIAD family. Native to South America, the pineapple plant is widely cultivated in tropical regions; Thailand supplies the major portion of the world's canned pineapple. The fruit, whose spiny skin is yellowish brown when ripe, is sweet and juicy; it is topped by a distinctive rosette of green leaves.

Pine Bluff, city (1990 pop. 57,140), seat of Jefferson co., S central Ark., on the Arkansas R.; inc. 1839. A port and the trade center for a lumber and farm area, it has industries making electrical goods and wood and paper products. The huge Pine Bluff Arsenal, north of the city, is the U.S. Army's chief chemical and biological research center.

Pinero, Sir Arthur Wing, 1855–1934, English dramatist. His early successes were farces and sentimental comedies, but plays like *The Profligate* (1889) and *The Second Mrs. Tanqueray* (1893) brought him fame as a serious social dramatist.

Pines, Isle of: see YOUTH, ISLE OF.

Ping-Pong: see TABLE TENNIS.

pink, common name for some members of Caryophyllaceae, a family of small herbs chiefly of north temperate zones, typified by swollen stem nodes and notched, or "pinked," petals ranging in color from white to red and purple. The family includes several ornamentals and many wildflowers and weeds. Ornamental pinks include the fragrant flowers of the genus *Dianthus,* among which are the many varieties of carnation and sweet William. Baby's breath (*Gypsophila paniculata*) is an unusual pink in being a bushy plant; it is often used by florists as a bouquet filler.

Pinkerton, Allan, 1819–84, American detective; b. Scotland. In Chicago he founded (1850) what became the Pinkerton National Detective Agency. During the Civil War he directed an espionage system behind the Confederate lines. His agency, which solved numerous railroad robberies, also gathered the evidence that broke up the MOLLY MAGUIRES in the 1870s. It subsequently became notorious as a private police force for hire to management as strikebreakers.

pinkeye: see CONJUNCTIVITIS.

Pinochet Ugarte, Augusto [pēnōchā' o͞ogär' tā], 1915–, president of Chile (1973–90). An army general, he led the coup that overthrew Pres. Salvador ALLENDE. He instituted conservative economic measures and harshly suppressed political dissent. His bid to remain president for another eight years was rejected in a national plebiscite in 1988, and the following year Patricio Aylwin was elected president. Pinochet, however, remained commander of the army.

pinochle, card game played by two to four players, with a deck of 48 cards made up of two each of nine through ace in all four suits, developed in the U.S. in the 19th cent. Auction pinochle, probably the most popular form of the game, is based on a complicated system of bidding. Four-hand, or partnership, pinochle, and bottom card–trump opening pinochle are popular. In all of these, an arbitrary point goal, not simply game, is often set.

pinophyte, member of a division (Pinophyta) of the plant kingdom consisting of the GYMNOSPERMS. In some classifications, the term refers only to the CONIFERS.

Pinter, Harold, 1930–, English dramatist. In his "comedies of menace," the commonplace is invested with tension and mystery, often through the use of silence. *The Dumbwaiter* (1957), *The Birthday Party* (1958), *The Caretaker* (1960), *The Homecoming* (1965), *Betrayal* (1978), and *Moonlight* (1993) are among his best-known plays. His screenplays include *The Servant* (1963) and *The French Lieutenant's Woman* (1981).

pinyin [Chin. *pinyin zimu* = phonetic alphabet], system of romanization of Chinese written characters, approved in 1958 by the government of the People's Republic and officially adopted by it in 1979. Its use replaces that of the more complex Wade-Giles system (1859; modified 1912), among others. Objectives of pinyin include promoting a national language, establishing a means for writing non-Chinese (minority) languages in China, and encouraging foreigners to learn Chinese. Pinyin is not used in Taiwan or in Hong Kong.

Pinza, Ezio, 1895–1957, Italian-American basso; b. Italy. He achieved success at the METROPOLITAN OPERA (N.Y.C.) and appeared on Broadway in *South Pacific* (1949).

Pinzón, Martín Alonzo [pēnthōn'], d. 1493, Spanish navigator. Commander of the *Pinta* on COLUMBUS's first voyage (1492), he deserted Columbus in the Antilles for six weeks and upon his return was censured for treasonable conduct. His younger brother, **Francisco Martín Pinzón,** fl. 1492, was master of the *Pinta.* Another brother, **Vicente Yáñez Pinzón,** fl. 1492–1509, commanded the *Niña.* When the *Santa María* was wrecked, he took Columbus aboard. He explored the mouth of the AMAZON (1500), was governor of PUERTO RICO from 1505, and explored the coasts of YUCATÁN, HONDURAS, and VENEZUELA (1508–9).

pion: see ELEMENTARY PARTICLES.

Pioneer, in space exploration: see SPACE PROBE, table.

Pippin: for Frankish rulers thus named, see PEPIN.

Piraiévs or **Piraeus,** city (1981 pop. 196,389), E central Greece, on the Saronic Gulf. Part of Greater Athens, it is the chief port of Greece and a commercial center. It was built in 450 B.C. and was connected to Athens by the famed Long Walls, which were destroyed (404 B.C.) by Sparta.

Pirandello, Luigi, 1867–1936, Italian author; b. Sicily. A major figure in 20th-cent. theater, he was awarded the 1934 Nobel Prize in literature. In the 1890s he began to write poetry and short stories, then produced seven novels, including *The Late Mattia Pascal* (1904). His fame, however, rests on his grimly humorous plays dealing with illusion and reality, which he began writing during World War I. They include *Right You Are If You Think You Are*

(1917), *Six Characters in Search of an Author* (1921), *Henry IV* (1922), and *Tonight We Improvise* (1930).

Piranesi, Giovanni Battista, 1720–78, Italian engraver and architect. In Rome he made engravings, notable for their accuracy and grandeur, of the city's buildings and monuments. Some digressed from documentary into fanciful reconstruction.

piranha or **caribe,** predatory freshwater FISH of the family Characidae, found in E and central South America, especially in the AMAZON. The piranha (genus *Serrasalmus*) has powerful jaws and razor-sharp triangular teeth and is capable of killing cattle and human beings. The largest piranha is c.2 ft (60 cm) long.

Pirenne, Henri [pērĕn'], 1862–1935, Belgian historian. In *Mohammed and Charlemagne* (1935), he attributed the collapse of Western civilization to the spread of Islam, a thesis that aroused much controversy. He also wrote a *History of Belgium* (7 vol., 1899–1932) and *Medieval Cities* (1927).

Pisa, city (1990 pop. 102,150), in TUSCANY, N central Italy, on the Arno R. It is a center of commerce and industry, producing vehicle parts, glass, and drugs. An Etruscan town, it prospered under Rome. It was a strong maritime republic from the 9th to 11th cent. A Ghibelline center (13th–14th cent.), Pisa fell to FLORENCE in 1406. GALILEO was born and taught there. The school of sculpture founded by Nicola PISANO flourished in the city. Its Romanesque cathedral and Leaning Tower are famous.

Cathedral and Leaning Tower at Pisa

Pisa, Council of: see SCHISM, GREAT.

Pisanello [pēzänĕl'lō], c.1395–1455?, Italian RENAISSANCE medalist, painter, and draftsman; b. Antonio Pisano, called Vittore Pisano. His only surviving FRESCOES are the *Annunciation* (San Fermo, Verona) and *St. George and the Princess* (Sant' Anastasia, Verona). He was the first Renaissance artist to revive the antique medal form of portraiture, and his medals, valued for their historic as well as their artistic merit, include a portrait of Francesco Sforza (Victoria and Albert Mus., London). He was also a superb draftsman.

Pisano, Andrea [pēzä'nō], c.1290–c.1348, Italian sculptor, also called Andrea da Pontedera. His most important work is the first bronze doors for the baptistery in Florence, depicting the life of John the Baptist. He was influenced by GIOTTO, whom he succeeded as head of the work on the Florence cathedral.

Pisano, Nicola, b. c.1220, d. between 1278 and 1284, major Italian sculptor. He founded a new school of sculpture in Italy, imbued with the classical spirit. His first great work was the hexagonal pulpit consisting of scenes from the life of Jesus for the baptistery in Pisa. He later concentrated on the human figure, recreating a style of monumental dignity. For the fountain at Perugia he and his son designed 24 statues and twice that many reliefs (1278). His son, **Giovanni Pisano,** b. 1250, d. after 1314, was a sculptor and architect. He helped his father and also did independent works, e.g., the pulpit for the cathedral at Pisa.

Pisano, Vittore: see PISANELLO.

Piscator, Erwin, 1893–1966, German theatrical director and producer. With Bertolt BRECHT he was the chief exponent of epic theater, in which narrative, montage, self-contained scenes, and rational argument were used to create a shock of recognition in the spectator. His experimental productions in Berlin and New York City greatly influenced Western theater methods.

Pisistratus or **Peisistratus** [pīsĭs'trətəs], 605?–527 B.C., tyrant of ATHENS. Having achieved popularity with liberal land laws, he seized power c.560 B.C. Under his rule Athens won SALAMIS and established hegemony in the Dardanelles. Exiled twice by his rivals, he nevertheless ruled until his death, and was succeeded by his sons Hippias and Hipparchus.

Pissarro, Camille [pēsärō'], 1830–1903, French impressionist painter; b. Virgin Islands. Allied with the impressionists (see IMPRESSIONISM), he experimented with SEURAT's color theories before developing a freer, more vital interpretation of nature, as seen in *Bather in the Woods* (Metropolitan Mus.). He was the teacher and friend of GAUGUIN, CÉZANNE, and CASSATT.

pistachio, tree or shrub (genus *Pistacia*) of the SUMAC family. The pistachio nut of commerce is obtained from *P. vera,* native to Turkey, Syria, and Palestine; the trade supply comes primarily from Iran, Syria, Turkey, Greece, Italy, and, in the U.S., California. The nut is a greenish seed that is eaten salted or used in confections.

pistil: see FLOWER.

pistol: see SMALL ARMS.

Piston, Walter, 1894–1976, American composer and teacher; b. Rockland, Me. A neoclassicist, he composed in traditional forms, e.g., SYMPHONIES, CONCERTOS, and string quartets, and wrote studies of HARMONY, COUNTERPOINT, and orchestration.

Pitcairn Island, volcanic island (1992 pop. 52), 2.5 sq mi (6.5 sq km), South Pacific, near the Tropic of Capricorn. The only inhabited island in the Pitcairn Islands group, it was discovered (1767) by the British and colonized (1790) by mutineers from the British naval vessel BOUNTY and Tahitian women. Their descendents, who speak a dialect of English, still inhabit the island; they are all Seventh-Day Adventists. It has been a British possession since 1839.

pitch, in music, the position of a tone in the musical scale, today designated by a letter name and determined by the frequency of vibration of the source of the tone. An international conference held in 1939 set a standard for A above middle C of 440 cycles per second.

pitch: see TAR AND PITCH.

pitchblende, dark, lustrous, massive variety (largely UO_2) of the mineral uraninite, a source of RADIUM and URANIUM. Pitchblende and uraninite occur as primary constituents of quartz veins and with other metals, chiefly in the Great Lakes region in Canada, the Colorado Plateau in the U.S., Australia, the Czech Republic, South Africa, and Zaïre.

Pitcher, Molly (Mary Ludwig Hays or Heis), 1744–1832, American Revolutionary heroine; b. near Trenton, N.J. She earned her nickname by carrying water for her husband, John, and other soldiers in the battle of MONMOUTH (1778).

pitcher plant, any of several insectivorous plants with leaves adapted as "pitchers" for trapping insects. Lured by nectar and the plant's coloration, the insects drown in the rainwater solution contained in the pitcher and are digested by plant ENZYMES and, perhaps, BACTERIA. There are three families: the American family, Sarraceniaceae, including the common pitcher plant (*Sarracenia purpurea*), found in the bogs of E North America; the Old World tropical family, consisting of the genus *Nepenthes,* found chiefly in BORNEO; and the Australian pitcher plant (*Cephalotus follicularis*), the only species in its family.

Pithecanthropus: see HOMO ERECTUS.

Pitt, William, 1st **earl of Chatham,** 1708–78, British statesman. His criticism of the War of the AUSTRIAN SUCCESSION led to the downfall (1742) of Robert WALPOLE. By denouncing government policy in the SEVEN YEARS WAR, Pitt became head of a coalition government in 1757; his shrewd policy led to the defeat of the French in India and Canada. He formed another ministry in 1766, but mental illness forced him to retire (1768). During the AMERICAN REVOLUTION he urged conciliation, and then, breaking with the WHIGS, favored any settlement short of independence. He was known as the Great Commoner for his insistence on constitutional rights. His son, **William Pitt,** 1759–1806, entered Parliament in 1781 and became prime minister in 1783 at age 24. He pursued liberal policies, including new taxes to cut the national debt, reforms in India and Canada, and parliamentary reform. His liberal policies ended with the FRENCH REVOLUTIONARY WARS. His military coalitions against France failed to achieve victory on land, and financial support for Britain's allies caused a monetary crisis. Pitt obtained (1800) the union of Great Britain and Ireland by bribery, but failed to win CATHOLIC EMANCIPATION and resigned in 1801. Recalled to office in 1804, he died soon after hearing of Napoleon's victory at AUSTERLITZ.

Pittsburgh, city (1990 pop. 369,879; met. area 2,056,705), seat of Allegheny co., SW Pa., at the meeting of the Allegheny and Monongahela rivers, which there form the Ohio R.; settled 1760, inc. 1816. One of the world's largest inland ports, it is a center for corporate headquarters, research, and commerce. Steel manufacturing is its major heavy industry; glass, machinery, chemicals, and petroleum products are also produced. Located on the site of the 18th-cent. Fort Duquesne (later Fort Pitt), the city is hilly, with diverse industrial and residential neighborhoods. Pittsburgh's huge and innovative urban renewal program, which produced the Gateway Center and other projects, began in 1950 and produced a construction boom in the 1980s. The city's educational and cultural institutions include the Univ. of Pittsburgh and the Carnegie Institute.

pituitary gland, small, oval endocrine gland (see ENDOCRINE SYSTEM) that lies at the base of the BRAIN. It is called the master gland because the other endocrine glands depend on its secretions for stimulation. The pituitary has two distinct lobes, anterior and posterior. The anterior lobe secretes at least six hormones: HUMAN GROWTH HORMONE, which stimulates overall body growth; ACTH (adrenocorticotropic hormone), which controls steroid hormone secretion by the adrenal cortex (see ADRENAL GLAND); thyrotropic hormone, which stimulates the activity of the THYROID GLAND; and three gonadotropic hormones, which control growth and reproductive activity of the gonads (ovaries and testes). The posterior lobe secretes antidiuretic hormone, which causes water retention by the kidneys, and oxytocin, which stimulates the MAMMARY GLANDS to release milk and also causes uterine contractions. An overactive pituitary during childhood can cause gigantism; during adulthood, it can cause acromegaly. DWARFISM results from pituitary deficiency in childhood.

pit viper, poisonous SNAKE of the family Crotalidae. Like the Old World true VIPERS, pit vipers have long, hollow, erectile fangs. In addition, they have special heat-receiving organs, or pits, that help them sense warm-blooded animals, an ability especially useful at night, when many of them hunt. Pit vipers include the RATTLESNAKE, COPPERHEAD, and WATER MOCCASIN.

Pius II, 1405–64, pope (1458–64), an Italian named Enea Silvio de' Piccolomini. He became (1439) secretary to Antipope Felix V (Amadeus VII of Savoy) and gained a reputation as a humanist scholar. He became a priest in 1446. As pope he issued (1460) a bull condemning the doctrine that ultimate authority in the church rested in the general councils rather than with the pope. He tried in vain to unite Christian rulers in Europe against the Turks and quarreled with LOUIS XI of France and the Bohemian king George of Podebrad. Among his literary works is an autobiography.

Pius V, Saint, 1504–72, pope (1566–72), an Italian named Michele Ghislieri, a Dominican. A leading figure in the Catholic Reformation (see REFORMATION, CATHOLIC), he put the decrees of the Council of TRENT into vigorous effect. He excommunicated Elizabeth I of England and united Spain and Venice against the Turks, thus helping to bring about the Christian victory at the battle of LEPANTO. Feast: Apr. 30.

Pius VII, 1740–1823, pope (1800–23), an Italian named Barnaba Chiaramonti. He and NAPOLEON I signed the CONCORDAT of 1801, but much of it was vitiated by Napoleon's Organic Articles, which Pius would not accept. In 1804, Napoleon made Pius come to Paris to consecrate him as emperor, and the French took Rome (1808) and the Papal States (1809). When Pius excommunicated the assailants of the Holy See, he was taken to France as a prisoner and forced to sign a new concordat. This humiliation Pius bore with stolid dignity. After Napoleon's downfall, Pius disavowed the enforced contract, recovered the Papal States at the Congress of VIENNA, and set about restoring the church. He reconstituted the JESUITS in 1814.

Pius IX, 1792–1878, pope (1846–78), an Italian named Giovanni M. Mastai-Ferretti. Driven from Rome by revolution in 1848, he returned (1850) and ruled with the aid of NAPOLEON III's troops. Opposed to the unification of Italy, he refused to deal with the Italians after they seized (1870) Rome. The resulting Roman Question was not resolved until the LATERAN TREATY of 1929. Pius also had difficulties in Germany with the Kulturkampf. In 1869 he convened the first VATICAN COUNCIL, which enunciated the doctrine of papal infallibility. His pontificate of 32 years was the longest in history.

Pius X, Saint, 1835–1914, pope (1903–14), an Italian named Guiseppe Sarto. In the decree *Lamentabili* (1907) and the encyclical *Pascendi* (1907), Pius condemned religious MODERNISM. He opposed anticlerical laws in France, set up commissions to recodify canon law and translate the Bible anew, and encouraged the use of PLAINSONG. Concerned with the poor, he was widely venerated during his life and afterward (1954) was canonized by Pius XII. Feast: Aug. 21.

Pius XI, 1857–1939, pope (1922–39), an Italian named Achille Ratti. Before his election he was a papal nuncio to Poland and archbishop of Milan. His papacy was marked by great diplomatic activity and many important statements. The LATERAN TREATY (1929) ended the quarrel between the church and the Italian state, but Pius expressed his strong disapproval of Fascist methods in a letter, *Non abbiamo bisogno* (1931). A concordat with Germany (1933) was flouted by the Nazis, and the pope in a powerful encyclical (*Mit brennender Sorge,* 1937) denounced the Nazi government. He also issued the statement *On Atheistic Communism.* He opposed nationalism, racism, and anti-Semitism. He criticized laissez-faire capitalism in the encyclical *Quadragesimo anno* (1931) and renewed the plea for social reform made 40 years before by Leo XIII. Pius called for greater lay participation in all things religious—this he called Catholic Action. He was also concerned with the rights of Eastern Catholics and native cultures. One of his chief assistants was Eugenio Pacelli (later PIUS XII).

Pius XII, 1876–1958, pope (1939–58), an Italian named Eugenio Pacelli. Appointed papal secretary of state in 1930 by PIUS XI, he gained great diplomatic experience and negotiated (1933) the concordat with Nazi Germany. As pope during World War II, he believed that the Vatican could best work to achieve peace by maintaining formal relations with all the belligerents. He tried to alleviate the suffering of prisoners of war and displaced persons, but was later much criticized for not speaking out against Nazi persecution of the Jews and for not doing enough to protect them in Italy. After the war, Pius asked Catholics to oppose communism and excommunicated (1949) Italian Catholics who joined the Communist party. In the papal bull *Munificentissimus Deus* (1950), he defined the dogma of the Assumption of the Virgin Mary. He also reformed (1956) the Holy Week liturgy, relaxed the rules for fasting, permitted evening Mass, and favored the appointment of native hierarchies in overseas dioceses.

Pizarro, Francisco, c.1476–1541, Spanish CONQUISTADOR, conqueror of PERU. The illegitimate son of a gentleman, he accompanied Ojeda to COLOMBIA in 1510 and was with BALBOA when he discovered the PACIFIC. In 1524, with Diego de Almagro, he began searching the coasts of Ecuador and Peru for the fabled INCA empire. In 1532 he met the Inca emperor Atahualpa. Professing friendship, he took the emperor prisoner, exacted ransom, and executed him. The conquest of Peru was complete with the capture of CUZCO, later successfully defended in a counterattack by MANCO CAPAC, the new Inca emperor. Pizarro founded Lima as Peru's capital. He sent Almagro to conquer CHILE, but cheated him of promised territory. Almagro rebelled, seized Cuzco, but was defeated and executed. Pizarro was later assassinated by Almagro's followers. Francisco's greed and ambition, extreme even in a conquistador, had offset his resourcefulness, courage, and cunning. His brother **Gonzalo Pizarro,** 1506–1548, was a lieutenant in the conquest. He aided in the defense of Cuzco (1536–37), conquered Bolivia, and fought against Almagro. Governor of Quito from 1539, he led a revolt against the liberalized laws of the Spanish viceroy and was executed. A half-brother, **Hernando Pizarro,** fl. 1530–60, fought in the conquest and defended Cuzco. He defeated and executed Almagro in 1538. Because of his standing at the Spanish court, he was sent to Spain to argue the Pizarros' cause, but was lightly imprisoned for 20 years. Another brother, **Juan Pizarro,** d. 1536, aided Francisco in the conquest of Peru. He fought in the defense of Cuzco against the forces of Manco Capac in 1536 and was killed leading an attack against the Inca fortress Sacsahuamán.

placebo, inert chemical substance used instead of a DRUG. Placebos contain no medicine, but many patients show medical improvement when given a placebo or an ineffective treatment, a result known as the *placebo effect.* Because of this, placebos are used as controls in drug testing to assure unbiased, reliable results. In double-blind studies, both patient and doctor do not know whether a placebo or drug is administered. A traditional placebo's lack of side effects, however, often identifies it, so an older drug is sometimes used in drug tests instead of or in addition to a placebo.

plague, a general term used for any contagious epidemic disease, but usually used to refer specifically to bubonic plague, or the Black Death, an acute infectious disease caused by the bacterium *Pasteurella pestis* (*Yersinia pestis*), transmitted to humans by fleas from infected rats. Symptoms include high fever; chills; prostration; enlarged, painful lymph nodes (buboes), particularly in the groin; and, in its black form, hemorrhages that turn black. Invasion of the lungs by the bacterium causes a rapidly fatal form of the disease (pneumonic plague), which can be transmitted from one person to another via droplets. Epidemics have occurred throughout history, the best known being the Black Death that swept Europe and parts of Asia in the 14th cent., killing as much as three quarters of the population in less than 20 years. The disease is still prevalent in some areas of the world, but such ANTIBIOTICS as tetracycline and streptomycin have greatly reduced the mortality rate.

Plain, the, in the FRENCH REVOLUTION, the independent members of the National Convention. The name was applied because they sat on the lower benches in contrast to the raised seats of the radical MOUNTAIN. The Plain was a leaderless mass, but it aided in the overthrow (1794) of Maximilien ROBESPIERRE.

Plains Indians: see NORTH AMERICA, INDIGENOUS PEOPLES OF.

plainsong or **plainchant,** all early unharmonized melody in free rhythm, but usually synonymous with Gregorian chant, the liturgical music of the ROMAN CATHOLIC CHURCH. Texts are taken from the MASS, the BIBLE, and hymns. Four main dialects of plainsong developed in the Western church: Ambrosian, Roman, Mozarabic, and Gallican. Gregorian chant derives originally from Jewish and Greek music, but is named after Pope GREGORY I, under whose reign church music was codified. In the Middle Ages polyphony largely supplanted plainsong, and distortions crept into its performance. In the 19th cent., the Benedictine monks of Solesmes, France, through years of research established the original form and rhythm of the chant. The tonality of Gregorian chant is based on the system of eight MODES; the system of neumes developed for chant notation (see MUSICAL NOTATION) is still used.

planarian, any of several groups of turbellarians—free-living, primarily carnivorous FLATWORMS—with a three-branched digestive cavity. Most are freshwater forms, but marine and terrestrial planarians exist. White, gray, brown, black, or sometimes transparent, planarians range in size from ⅛ to 1 in. (0.32 to 2.54 cm), although some tropical forms are as big as 2 ft (60 cm). Some species can regenerate severed parts of the body, in some cases even producing entire individuals from small pieces.

Planck, Max, 1858–1947, German physicist. From his hypothesis (1900) that atoms emit and absorb energy only in discrete bundles (quanta) instead of continuously, as assumed in classical physics, QUANTUM MECHANICS was developed. Planck received the 1918 Nobel Prize in physics for his work on BLACKBODY radiation. He was professor (1889–1928) at the Univ. of Berlin and president (1930–35) of the Kaiser Wilhelm Society for the Advancement of Science, Berlin. Planck's constant (see QUANTUM MECHANICS) is named for him.

plane, in mathematics, flat surface of infinite extent but no thickness. A plane is determined by (1) three points not in a straight line; (2) a straight line and a point not on the line; (3) two intersecting lines; or (4) two parallel lines.

planet, any of the nine relatively large, nonluminous bodies—MERCURY, VENUS, EARTH, MARS, JUPITER, SATURN, URANUS, NEPTUNE, and PLUTO—that revolve around the sun (see SOLAR SYSTEM). By extension, any similar body discovered revolving around another star would also be called a planet. The ASTEROIDS are sometimes called minor planets. The major planets are classified either as inferior, with an orbit between the sun and the orbit of the earth (Mercury and Venus), or as superior, with an orbit beyond that of the earth (Mars, Jupiter, Saturn, Uranus, Neptune, and Pluto). The terrestrial planets—Mercury, Venus, Earth, and Mars—resemble the earth in size, chemical composition, and density. The Jovian planets—Jupiter, Saturn, Uranus, and Neptune—are much larger in size and have thick, gaseous atmospheres (much thicker in the cases of Jupiter and Saturn) and lower densities. Pluto is unclassified. The rapid rotation of the latter planets results in polar flattening of 2–10%, giving them an elliptical appearance. In 1992 radio astronomers reported evidence that strongly suggested the existence of two to three planets orbiting a PULSAR in the Milky Way about 1300 light-years from earth.

planetarium, optical device used to project a representation of the heavens onto a domed ceiling; the term also designates the building that houses such a device. As the axis of the device moves, beams of light are emitted through lenses and travel in predetermined paths on the ceiling. The juxtaposition of lights reproduces a panorama of the sky at a particular time as it might be seen under optimum conditions. The motions of the celestial bodies—typically the fixed stars, the sun, moon, and planets, and various nebulae—are accurately represented, although they can be compressed into much shorter time periods.

planetoid: see ASTEROID.

plane tree, sycamore, or **buttonwood,** deciduous tree (genus *Platanus*) indigenous to northern temperate regions. The dry, seedlike fruits are compressed into a hard, brown ball, which, when ripe, separates into windborne, downy tufts. The genus includes the American sycamore (*P. occidentalis*) and the Oriental plane (*P. orientalis*), both used for their wood. The London plane (*P. acerifolia*) is much used as an ornamental shade tree in cities.

plankton, very small to microscopic plants and animals that have little or no power of locomotion and drift or float in surface waters. Plankton is found worldwide in fresh and salt water. The plant forms include DIATOMS and dinoflagellates (see PYRROPHYTE); planktonic animals include PROTOZOANS, small CRUSTACEANS, JELLYFISH, COMB JELLIES, and FISH eggs and larvae. In the ocean, plankton is the source of food, either directly or indirectly through the food chain, for all marine animals.

Plano, city (1990 pop. 128,713), Collin co., N Texas, c.20 mi (32 km) NE of Dallas; inc. 1873. Spurred by the burgeoning Dallas–Fort Worth area, it is a booming financial and commercial center with many office complexes and housing developments. Manufactures include compact discs, plastics, metal products, and satellite communications equipment.

plant, an organism of the plant kingdom (Plantae). Plants comprise the three divisions of bryophytes (mosses, liverworts, and hornworts) and nine divisions of vascular plants (horsetails, ferns, conifers, flowering plants, etc.). All plants are multicellular and have cells with cell walls, nuclei, and vacuoles. They are usually anchored in one place and grow continually, having no maximum size. They manufacture their own food and give off oxygen in the process of PHOTOSYNTHESIS, thus representing the primary source of food for animals and providing oxygen for the earth's atmosphere. Although traditionally contrasted with animals, plants are now usually considered to be one of at least five kingdoms of living things (see CLASSIFICATION).The scientific study of plants is BOTANY.

plantain, annual or perennial weed (genus *Plantago*), of wide distribution. Many species are lawn pests, and the pollen is often a hay fever irritant. *P. psyllium,* or fleawort, is cultivated in Spain and France for its mucilaginous seed coats, which are used as a laxative. A tropical plant related to the BANANA is also called plantain.

plant louse: see APHID.

Planudes Maximus or **Maximus Planudes,** c.1260–c.1330, Byzantine monk and classical scholar whose edition of the GREEK ANTHOLOGY was standard until the 17th cent. His prose version of AESOP's fables is outstanding.

plasma, in physics, a fully ionized gas containing approximately equal numbers of positive and negative IONS. A plasma is an elec-

MAJOR PLANETS OF THE SOLAR SYSTEM

Planet	*Distance from the sun (AU)**	*Period of revolution*	*Period of rotation*	*Mass (earth = 1)*	*Diameter (earth = 1)*	*Known satellite*
Mercury	0.39	88 days	59 days	0.06	0.38	0
Venus	0.72	225 days	243 days	0.82	0.95	0
Earth	1	365 days	24 hours	1	1	1
Mars	1.52	687 days	25 hours	0.11	0.53	2
Jupiter	5.20	12 years	10 hours	317.89	11.19	16
Saturn	9.54	29 years	10 hours	95.15	9.44	18
Uranus	19.18	84 years	16 hours	14.54	4.10	15
Neptune	30.06	165 years	18 hours	17.23	3.88	8
Pluto	39.44	248 years	6.4 days	0.002?	0.18	1

* AU = Astronomical Unit (Earth = 1)

tric conductor and is affected by magnetic fields. The study of plasmas, called plasma physics, is important in efforts to produce a controlled fusion reaction (see NUCLEAR ENERGY; NUCLEAR REACTOR). In nature, plasmas are thought to occur in the interior of stars and in interstellar gas, making plasma a form of matter in the universe (see STATES OF MATTER).

plasmapheresis, procedure in which plasma (the liquid portion of the blood) is separated from donated blood, the blood cells being returned to the donor. In some diseases, such as MYASTHENIA GRAVIS, plasmapheresis is used to attempt to remove the disease-causing substances from the blood.

plaster of Paris: see GYPSUM.

plastic, any synthetic organic material that can be molded under heat and pressure into a shape that is retained after the heat and pressures are removed. There are two basic types of plastic: THERMOSET, which cannot be resoftened after being subjected to heat and pressures; and THERMOPLASTIC, which can be repeatedly softened and reshaped by heat and pressure. Plastics are made up chiefly of a binder consisting of long chainlike molecules called POLYMERS. Binders can be natural materials, e.g., CELLULOSE, or (more commonly) synthetic RESINS, e.g., BAKELITE. The permanence of thermosetting plastics is due to the heat- and pressure-induced cross-linking reactions the polymers undergo. Thermoplastics can be reshaped because their linear or branched polymers can slide past one another when heat and pressure are applied. Adding plasticizers and fillers to the binder improves a wide range of properties, e.g., hardness, elasticity, and resistance to heat, cold, or acid. Adding pigments imparts color. Plastic products are commonly made from plastic powders. In compression molding, heat and pressure are applied directly to the powder in the mold cavity. Alternatively, the powder can be plasticized by outside heating and then poured into molds to harden (transfer molding); be dissolved in a heating chamber and then forced by a plunger into cold molds to set (injection molding); or be extruded through a die in continuous form to be cut into lengths or coiled (extrusion molding). The first important plastic, CELLULOID, has been largely replaced by a wide variety of plastics known by such trade names as Plexiglas, Lucite, Polaroid, and CELLOPHANE. New uses continue to be found and include contact lenses, machine gears, nonmoving engine parts, and artificial body parts. The widespread use of plastics has led to environmental problems. Because plastic products do not decay, large amounts accumulate as waste. Disposal is difficult because they melt when burned, clogging incinerators and often emitting harmful fumes, e.g., the hydrogen chloride gas given off by POLYVINYL CHLORIDE, and because many products into which they are made, such as plastic bottles, do not compact as readily in landfills. However, recycling is increasingly emerging as an alternative to disposal, particularly in communities with limited landfill capacity. See also POLYPROPYLENE; POLYURETHANES; TEFLON.

plastic surgery, surgical repair of congenital or acquired deformities and reconstruction of tissue disfigured by accidents such as severe burns or by removal of extensive cancers. It is also used to restore vital movement and function of destroyed tissues. The technique was first developed after World War I and is now also used for cosmetic purposes, e.g., to reshape a nose or remove sagging skin from around the eyes. Techniques include skin grafts, transplantation of bone or ligament from other parts of the body, and implants of various kinds. Modern plastic surgeons often employ CAT SCANS to produce computer-generated images that are used to plan or simulate complex reconstructive surgeries.

Plata, Río de la, estuary, c.170 mi (270 km) long and up to 120 mi (190 km) wide, in SE South America, between Uruguay and Argentina. It is formed by the PARANÁ and Uruguay rivers and is part of a major system of inland navigation. Two national capitals, BUENOS AIRES and MONTEVIDEO, are on the estuary.

plateau, elevated, more or less level portion of the earth's surface bounded on at least one side by steep slopes. Plateaus are formed by successive lava flows, upward-folding earth movements, or the erosion of adjacent lands. Notable plateaus include the COLORADO and COLUMBIA PLATEAUS in the U.S. and the DECCAN in India.

Plateau Indians: see NORTH AMERICA, INDIGENOUS PEOPLES OF.

plate tectonics, modern theory of CONTINENTAL DRIFT that has revolutionized geologists' understanding of EARTH history. It holds that the earth's crust is divided into contiguous, moving plates that carry the embedded CONTINENTS. Plate boundaries are marked by lines of EARTHQUAKE and volcanic activity (see VOLCANO). One kind of boundary is at the mid-ocean ridges, where tensional forces open rifts, allowing new crustal material to well up from the earth's mantle and become welded to the trailing edges of the plates (see OCEAN). When a continent straddles such a rift it is split apart, forming a new ocean area (e.g., the RED SEA and the Gulf of California). The ocean trenches mark subduction zones, where plate edges dive steeply into the mantle and are reabsorbed. A third boundary type occurs where two plates slide past each other in a shearing manner along great transform FAULTS (e.g., the SAN ANDREAS FAULT in California). MOUNTAIN ranges form where two plates carrying continents collide (e.g., the HIMALAYAS), or where ocean crust is subducted along a continental margin (e.g., the ANDES). Geologists believe that c.200 million years ago there was a supercontinent, Pangaea, which subsequent plate movements have split and resplit into the continents and islands we recognize today.

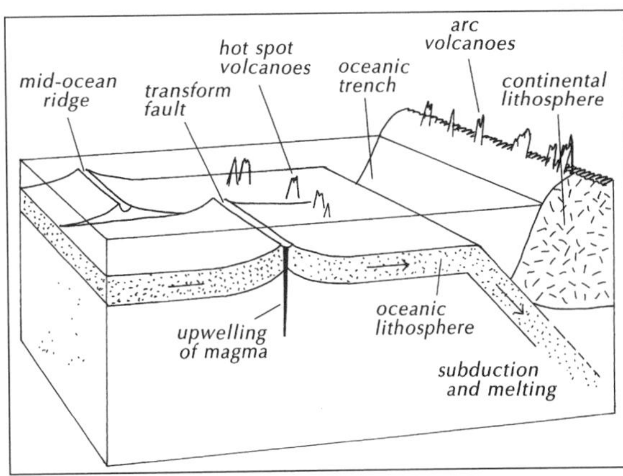

Plate tectonics: Schematic model of the oceanic crust, showing the three types of plat boundaries

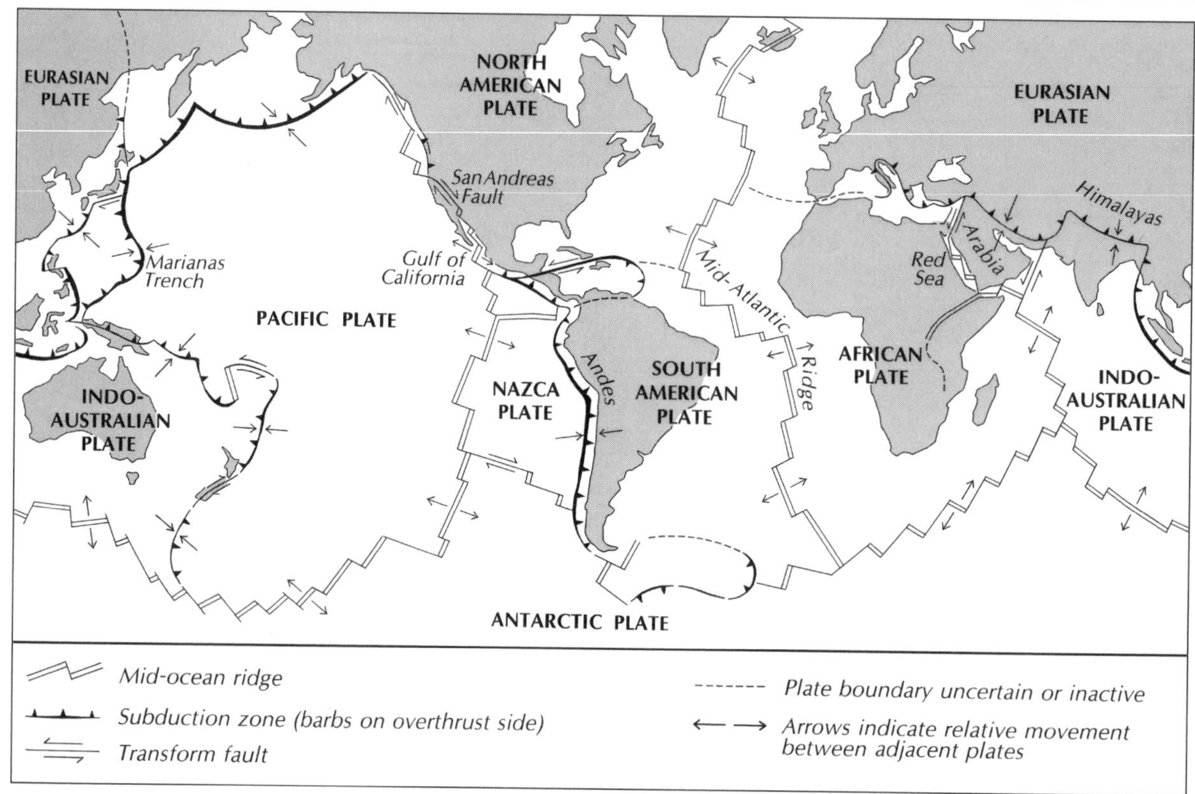

Plate tectonics: Map of the world showing major plates and plate boundaries

Radar mapping of Venus has revealed some apparent effects of subduction on that planet's surface.

Plath, Sylvia, 1932–63, American poet; b. Boston. Her finely crafted, intensely personal poems, known for their sharp, often violent imagery, appear in such volumes as *The Colossus* (1960), *Ariel* (1965), and *Collected Poems* (1981). She also wrote an autobiographical novel, *The Bell Jar* (1962, England; 1971, U.S.). Plath committed suicide in London.

platinum (Pt), metallic element, known in natural alloy form since antiquity. It is a malleable, ductile, lustrous, silver-white, chemically inactive metal. Platinum and its alloys are used in surgical tools, laboratory utensils, electrical-resistance wires, contact points, standard masses, jewelry, dentistry, and very powerful magnets. Platinum is used as a CATALYST in automobile catalytic converters and in many commercial processes. See ELEMENT (table); PERIODIC TABLE.

Plato, 427?–347 B.C., Greek philosopher. In 407 B.C. he became a pupil and friend of SOCRATES. After living for a time at the Syracuse court, Plato founded (c.387 B.C.) near Athens the most influential school of the ancient world, the Academy, where he taught until his death. His most famous pupil there was ARISTOTLE. Plato's extant work is in the form of epistles and dialogues, divided according to the probable order of composition. The early, or Socratic, dialogues, e.g., the *Apology, Meno,* and *Gorgias,* present Socrates in conversations that illustrate his major ideas—the unity of virtue and knowledge and of virtue and happiness. They also contain Plato's moving account of the last days and death of Socrates. Plato's goal in dialogues of the middle years, e.g., the *Republic, Phaedo, Symposium,* and *Timaeus,* was to show the rational relationship between the soul, the state, and the cosmos. The later dialogues, e.g., the *Laws* and *Parmenides,* contain treatises on law, mathematics, technical philosophic problems, and natural science. Plato regarded the rational soul as immortal, and he believed in a world soul and a Demiurge, the creator of the physical world. He argued for the independent reality of Ideas, or Forms, as the immutable archetypes of all temporal phenomena and as the only guarantee of ethical standards and of objective scientific knowledge. Virtue consists in the harmony of the human soul with the universe of Ideas, which assure order, intelligence, and pattern to a world in constant flux. Supreme among them is the Idea of the Good, analogous to the sun in the physical world. Only the philosopher, who understands the harmony of all parts of the universe with the Idea of the Good, is capable of ruling the just state. In Plato's various dialogues he touched upon virtually every problem that has occupied subsequent philosophers; his teachings have been among the most influential in the history of Western civilization, and his works are counted among the world's finest literature. See also NEOPLATONISM.

Platt Amendment, a rider attached to the Army Appropriations bill of 1901. It stipulated the conditions for U.S. intervention in CUBA that virtually made the island a U.S. protectorate. Proposed by Sen. Orville H. Platt of Connecticut, it was part of a Cuban-U.S. treaty until abrogated in 1934. Under its terms the U.S. established—and has retained—a naval base on Guantánamo Bay.

Plattdeutsch [plät'doich], Low German, spoken mainly in N Germany, a region of lowlands. See LANGUAGE (table).

platypus, semiaquatic egg-laying MAMMAL, or MONOTREME (*Ornithorhynchus anatinus*), of TASMANIA and E Australia. Also called duckbill, it has a rubbery, duckbill-shaped muzzle, no teeth, and no external ears. Its head, body, and tail are broad, flat, and covered with dark-brown fur; its feet are webbed. The adult male is about 2 ft (60 cm) long. The platypus eats small freshwater animals, which it hunts with the aid of electroreceptors on its bill, and lives in burrows along stream banks.

Plautus (Titus Maccius Plautus), c.254–184 B.C., Roman comic poet. His plays, adapted from Greek New COMEDY, are popular and vigorous representations of middle-class and lower-class life. Writing in idiomatic Latin and with a genius for situation and coarse humor, Plautus is famous for his stock comic figures, e.g., the knavish, resourceful slave or the braggart soldier. His works were freely adapted by JONSON, SHAKESPEARE, MOLIÈRE, and others.

player piano: see PIANO.

Plaza Lasso, Galo [plä'sä lä'sō], 1906–87, president of ECUADOR (1948–52). An experienced diplomat and liberal democrat, he permitted unprecedented political freedoms and brought a measure of economic prosperity to the country. He later served as a UN mediator.

plebeians: see PLEBS.

plebs or **plebeians** [Lat., *plebs* = people], general body of Roman citizens, as distinct from the PATRICIAN class. They lacked, at first, most of the patrician rights, but gradually achieved political equality by 300 B.C.

Pleiad [from Pleiades], group of seven tragic poets of ALEXANDRIA who flourished c.280 B.C. Only the work of Lycophron survives. A group of seven 16th-cent. French poets took the name **Pléiade.** They included Pierre de RONSARD (the leader) and Joachim DU BELLAY. Their purpose was to encourage the writing of French as against Latin so as to establish a vigorous literary language. They cultivated the use of classical and Italian forms, e.g., the SONNET.

Pleiades, a galactic cluster (see STAR CLUSTER) in the constellation Taurus.

Pleiades, in Greek mythology, seven daughters of ATLAS, attendants of ARTEMIS. Pursued by ORION, they were turned into stars.

Pleistocene epoch: see GEOLOGIC ERA (table).

Plekhanov, Georgi Valentinovich, 1857–1918, Russian revolutionary and social philosopher, often called the father of Russian Marxism. Opposed to political terror, he broke (1879) with the populist movement and left Russia (1880). Turning to MARXISM, he helped to found the group that became the Russian Social Democratic Labor party and with V.I. LENIN, published the newspaper *Iskra* [spark]. His view that socialist revolution could not occur in Russia until CAPITALISM and industrialization developed further became the basis for the anti-Leninist Menshevik position after the party split (1903) into BOLSHEVISM AND MENSHEVISM. After the Feb. 1917 RUSSIAN REVOLUTION he returned from exile and opposed the Bolsheviks; after their victory he retired from political life. Among his works are *Socialism and Anarchism* (tr. 1895) and *Fundamental Problems of Marxism* (tr. 1929).

Plessy v. Ferguson, case decided in 1896 by the U.S. SUPREME COURT, upholding Louisiana's right to segregate racially "separate but equal" railway carriages. The Court held that the 14th amendment to the U.S. CONSTITUTION mandated political but not social equality. The decision led to comprehensive Southern segregation laws, maintained until BROWN V. BOARD OF EDUCATION (1954).

pleurisy, inflammation of the pleura, the membrane that covers the LUNGS and lines the chest cavity. It is sometimes accompanied by fluid (effusion) that fills the chest cavity; when the fluid is infected, the condition is known as empyema. Dry pleurisy usually occurs with bacterial infections, whereas pleurisy with effusion is associated with chronic lung conditions, such as TUBERCULOSIS. Treatment is directed at the underlying cause.

Pliny the Elder, A.D. c.23–A.D. 79, Roman naturalist; b. Cisalpine Gaul. His one surviving work, *Historia naturalis,* consists of 37 books that deal with the nature of the physical universe, geography, anthropology, zoology, botany, and mineralogy. Although impressive in scope, this encyclopedic work, mostly secondhand information, is useless as science. His nephew, **Pliny the Younger,** 62?–c.113, was an orator and statesman who is remembered for his letters, which are an excellent mirror of Roman life.

Pliocene epoch: see GEOLOGIC ERA (table).

PLO: see PALESTINE LIBERATION ORGANIZATION.

PL/1: see PROGRAMMING LANGUAGE.

Plotinus, 205–270, Hellenistic philosopher, founder of NEOPLATONISM; b. Egypt. He went to Alexandria c.232 to devote himself to philosophy. After 244 he lived in Rome, where his school gained a wide following. In addition to Plato, Plotinus drew on other Greek philosophers, and on Zoroastrianism and possibly Hinduism. He explained the deity by developing the idea of emanation, and his teachings are infused with MYSTICISM. Although he rejected Christianity, Plotinus' influence on the early Christian thinkers, particularly St. AUGUSTINE, was profound. Plotinus' writings were collected by his pupil Porphyry under the title *The Enneads.*

Plovdiv, city (1989 est. pop. 375,000), S central Bulgaria, on the Maritsa R. Bulgaria's second largest city, it is the chief market for a fertile area and has such industries as lead and zinc smelting, textiles, and food processing. Built by the Thracians, it was held (4th cent. B.C.–8th cent. A.D.) by Macedon, Rome, and Byzantium. It fell to Turkey c.1360 and passed to Russia in 1877. In 1885 it became part of Bulgaria. It has several Bulgarian Orthodox churches and Turkish mosques.

plover, common name for some shore BIRDS of the family Charadriidae, small to medium in size, found worldwide in ice-free lands. Plovers are wading birds with markings of black or brown above and white below. The best-known plovers in America are the noisy killdeer (*Charadrius vociferus*), found in pasturelands, the black-bellied (*Squatarola squatarola*) and golden (*Pluvialis dominica*) plovers, which migrate as far as 2,000 mi (3,220 km) annually, and the piping plover (*Charadrius melodus*), which is endangered along the Atlantic coast.

plum, name for many species of trees (genus *Prunus*) of the ROSE family, and their fruits. Numerous varieties and hybrids exist. The name *damson* is applied to several varieties of the common garden plum (*P. domestica*) having small leaves and small, oval, usually tart fruits. Greengage and prune plums are also varieties of *P. domestica.* Many varieties are used as ornamentals; these usually have red or purple foliage and double pink, white, or lilac flowers. Prunes are dried plums.

plumbago: see GRAPHITE.

Plutarch, A.D. 46?–c.120, Greek essayist and biographer. After traveling widely, he settled as a priest in his native BOEOTIA. His great work is *The Parallel Lives,* paired biographies of Greeks and Romans. Sir Thomas North's translation (1579) profoundly affected English literature, e.g., supplying the material for Shakespeare's *Julius Caesar* and *Antony and Cleopatra.* Plutarch's pride in Greece does not prejudice his treatment of Roman subjects. Concerned primarily with character and morality, he employed anecdotal material.

Pluto, in astronomy, 9th and usually most distant PLANET from the sun, at a mean distance of 3.67 billion mi (5.90 billion km). Because of the high eccentricity (0.250) of its elliptical orbit, Pluto occasionally (e.g., between 1978 and 2000) comes closer than the planet NEPTUNE to the sun. Discovered in 1930 by Clyde Tombaugh, Pluto has a diameter of c.1,400 mi (2,300 km). Its surface consists largely of frozen nitrogen. It is thought to have a rocky, silicate core; its thin atmosphere contains methane. Pluto forms a double planet system with its one known satellite, **Charon,** which has a diameter about half of Pluto's. Charon was discovered by James Christy in 1978.

Pluto, in Greek religion, god of the underworld, son of CRONUS and RHEA; also called HADES and, by the Romans, Dis. He ruled Hades with his wife, PERSEPHONE.

plutonium (Pu), radioactive element, first produced artificially by Glenn SEABORG and colleagues in 1940 by deuteron bombardment of uranium oxide. It is a silver-gray TRANSURANIUM ELEMENT in the ACTINIDE SERIES and is found in very small quantities in nature in association with uranium ores. Plutonium is a fission fuel for NUCLEAR REACTORS and weapons (see ATOMIC BOMB; NUCLEAR ENERGY). It is an extremely dangerous poison, collecting in bones and altering the production of white blood cells. See ELEMENT (table); PERIODIC TABLE.

Plymouth, city (1991 pop. 243,373), Devon, SW England, on Plymouth Sound. The Three Towns that Plymouth has comprised since 1914 are Plymouth, Stonehouse, and Devonport. Plymouth is an important port and naval base. It was the last port touched by the MAYFLOWER before its voyage to America in 1620.

Plymouth, town (1990 pop. 45,608), seat of Plymouth co., SE Mass., on Plymouth Bay; founded 1620. Plymouth is the oldest settlement in New England and a major tourist attraction. It has light industries but is primarily known for its historical sights, including Plymouth Rock, near which is moored the replica *Mayflower II;* several 17th-cent. houses; and the Plimoth Plantation re-creation of the settlement.

Plymouth Colony, settled by the PILGRIMS in MASSACHUSETTS in 1620. The settlers had difficulty surviving early hardships, although a treaty with neighboring tribes assured peace for 50 years. Under the MAYFLOWER COMPACT the colony developed into a quasi-theocracy, ruled by a governor (see BRADFORD, WILLIAM) and a council; a representative body, the General Court, was introduced in 1638. The colony expanded to include 10 towns and in 1643 joined the New England Confederation, which gave it critical aid during KING PHILIP'S WAR (1675–76). Plymouth Colony was incorporated into the royal colony of Massachusetts in 1691.

Pm, chemical symbol of the element PROMETHIUM.

pneumoconiosis, any of a group of chronic LUNG diseases caused by the inhalation of dust particles. Commonly known as black lung and primarily found among coal miners, sandblasters, and metal grinders, it may be caused by the inhalation of SILICA (silicosis), ASBESTOS (asbestosis), IRON filings (siderosis), COAL dust, or other mineral or metal dust. Particles collect in the lungs and become sites for the development of fibrous tissue that replaces elastic lung tissue, often resulting in decreased lung function. Symptoms include shortness of breath, wheezing, cough, and susceptibility to PNEUMONIA, TUBERCULOSIS, and other respiratory infections. See also OCCUPATIONAL DISEASE.

pneumonia, acute infection of one or both lungs that can be caused by a bacterium, usually the pneumococcus bacterium, virus, fungus, or other organism. Symptoms include high fever, pain in the chest, difficulty in breathing, coughing, and sputum. Viral pneumonia is generally milder than the bacterial form. *Pneumocystis carinii* pneumonia, which is caused by a parasitic protozoan, generally only occurs in patients whose immune system is suppressed, as in AIDS or LEUKEMIA. ANTIBIOTICS are used to treat bacterial pneumonia and have greatly reduced the mortality rate of the disease.

Po, chemical symbol of the element POLONIUM.

Pocahontas, c.1595–1617, daughter of Chief Powhatan of the POWHATAN CONFEDERACY of Virginia. She is said to have saved the life of Capt. John SMITH as Powhatan was about to execute him. Later, held hostage at Jamestown for the return of her father's English prisoners, she became a Christian and married (1614) a settler, John ROLFE. The union brought peace for eight years. Rolfe took her to England (1616), where she was received as a princess. She died during the trip home and was buried at Gravesend, England.

Pocatello, city (1990 pop. 46,080), seat of Bannock co., SE Idaho, on Portneuf R. near its junction with the Snake R.; inc. 1889. A railroad center since 1882, it is a shipping and processing point for a livestock and farm area; it has phosphate mining and other industries, and a sizable tourist trade. Idaho State Univ. is located there.

Po Chü-i [bô jü-ē], 772–846, Chinese poet. A prolific author, he wrote in simple, clear language. "Everlasting Wrong" (806), his most noted poem, recounts the sufferings of Emperor Ming Huang (685–762) and Yang Kuei-fei, his ill-fated concubine.

pocket gopher: see GOPHER.

Podgorny, Nikolai Viktorovich, 1903–83, Soviet political leader. He was chairman of the Ukrainian Communist party (1957–63) and became (1960) a full member of the Presidium. Although he was elected chairman (1965–77) of the Presidium after KHRUSHCHEV'S fall, he was later removed from the the body and demoted (1977) to deputy of the Supreme Soviet.

Podhoretz, Norman, 1930–, American editor and essayist; b. Brooklyn, N.Y. As chief editor (1960–) of *Commentary,* he turned the Jewish monthly into an influential forum of social criticism. He has written two memoirs, *Making It* (1967), which traces his rise to power among New York intellectuals, and *Breaking Ranks* (1979), which explains his switch from liberalism to neoconservatism.

podiatry, science concerned with disorders, diseases, and deformities of the feet. Podiatrists treat such common conditions as bunions, corns and calluses, and ingrown toenails; perform minor surgery; and prescribe medicines and orthopedic devices. A practitioner in the U.S. must be licensed; training is similar to that for medicine in most respects, except that it is largely limited to a single area of the body.

Poe, Edgar Allan, 1809–49, one of the most brilliant and original writers in American literature; b. Boston. Orphaned in 1811, he was raised by Mr. and Mrs. John Allan of Richmond, Va. He attended the Univ. of Virginia and West Point briefly but was forced to leave both because of infractions. After publishing three volumes of poems (1827, 1829, 1831) Poe was an editor, critic, and short-story writer for magazines and newspapers in Richmond, Philadelphia, and New York City. His compelling short stories, such as "The Masque of the Red Death" and "The Fall of the House of Usher," create a universe that is beautiful and grotesque, real and fantastic. Poe is also considered the father of the modern detective story, e.g., "The Murders in the Rue Morgue" (1841). His poems (including "The Bells," "The Raven," and "Annabel Lee") are rich with musical phrases and sensuous images. Poe was an intelligent and witty critic who often theorized about the art of writing, as in his essay "The Poetic Principle." His most important works include *The Narrative of Arthur Gordon Pym* (1838), *Tales of the Grotesque and Arabesque* (1840), and *The Raven and Other Poems* (1845). A complex, tormented figure, Poe died of alcoholism.

poet laureate, British title conferred by the crown on a poet whose duty it is to write commemorative verse. It is an outgrowth of medieval custom and later royal patronage of poets; the modern laureateship is usually a lifetime appointment. Ben JONSON had what amounted to a laureateship, but DRYDEN, in 1670, was the first given the title. Among later laureates have been WORDSWORTH (1843–50), TENNYSON (1850–92), John MASEFIELD (1930–67), John BETJEMAN (1972–84), and Ted HUGHES (1984–). In 1985 the U.S. Congress established an American poet laureateship, elevating what had previously been the position of poetry consultant to the Library of Congress. The U.S. post is awarded yearly by the librarian of Congress, but a poet may hold it for a series of years. The American poet laureate is not obligated to write any verse. The first U.S. poet laureate was Robert Penn WARREN (1986–87); Mona Van Duyn, the current U.S. poet laureate, was appointed in 1992.

poetry. For LYRIC poetry, see BALLAD; ELEGY; ODE; PASTORAL; SONNET. For narrative poetry, see EPIC; ROMANCE. Dramatic poetry is treated incidentally in the article TRAGEDY. See also technical discussions of FREE VERSE; PENTAMETER; RHYME.

Poggio Bracciolini, Gian Francesco [pôd'jō brät"chōlē'nē], 1380–1459, Italian humanist. Chancellor and historiographer of the republic of Florence, he rediscovered many classical works, e.g., LUCRETIUS' *On the Nature of Things.* His *Facetiae* (1474) is a collection of earthy fables and anticlerical satires.

pogrom, violent government-condoned attacks perpetrated against Russian Jews between 1881 and the RUSSIAN REVOLUTION. Backed by official ANTI-SEMITISM, they stimulated large-scale Jewish emigration to the U.S. Pogroms also existed in Germany and Poland under HITLER.

Poincaré, (Jules) Henri [pwăNkärā'], 1854–1912, French mathematician, physicist, and author; cousin of Raymond POINCARÉ. One of the greatest mathematicians of his age, Poincaré, by research in the theory of functions, enlarged the field of mathematical physics. He also did notable work in differential equations and celestial mechanics and wrote extensively on the philosophy of science.

Poincaré, Raymond, 1860–1934, French statesman; cousin of Jules POINCARÉ. He served as president (1913–20) and premier (1912–13, 1922–23, 1926–29). A conservative and a nationalist, he called for harsh punishment of Germany after World War I and sent (1923) French troops into the RUHR to force Germany to pay reparations. In 1928 he stabilized the franc.

poinsettia: see SPURGE.

Pointe-Noire [pwăNt-nwär], city (1984 pop. 294,203), chief seaport of Congo, on the Atlantic Ocean. Oil refining and offshore oil drilling are major industries; processed food and wood and aluminum products are manufactured. The city is also a sport-fishing center. Founded in 1883, Pointe-Noire became important after construction of the harbor and completion (1948) of the railroad to BRAZZAVILLE. It was (1950–58) the capital of the French Congo.

pointer, large SPORTING DOG; shoulder height, 23–26 in. (58.4–66.4 cm); weight, 50–60 lb (22.7–27.2 kg). Its short coat is usually white, with liver, black, yellow, or orange markings. Developed in England over 300 years ago, it hunts game birds by scent. It stands rigidly poised with its nose facing the game, directing the hunter to it.

pointillism: see POSTIMPRESSIONISM.

poison, any chemical that produces a harmful effect on a living organism. Almost any substance can act as a poison if it enters the body in sufficiently large quantities or in an abnormal way; e.g., water inhaled into the lungs becomes an asphyxial poison. The severity of a poison is determined by the nature of the poison itself, the concentration and amount ingested, the route of entry, the length of exposure, and the age, size, and health of the victim. Common poisonous substances include ARSENIC, CYANIDE, STRYCHNINE, LEAD, MERCURY, acids, venoms, HERBICIDES, and CURARE and other drugs.

poison gas, any of various gases sometimes used in CHEMICAL WARFARE or riot control because of their poisonous or corrosive nature. These gases may be roughly grouped according to the portal of entry into the body and their physiological effects. Vesicants (blister gases, e.g., mustard gas and lewisite) produce blisters on all body surfaces; lacrimators (tear gas) cause severe eye irritation; sternutators (vomiting gases) cause nausea; nerve gases inhibit proper nerve function; and lung irritants cause pulmonary edema. World War I marked the first effective use of poison gas and the introduction of gas masks. The use of poison gas has been limited since World War I by fear of retribution, although the military powers have continued to develop new gases.

poison hemlock, lethally poisonous herb (*Conium maculatum*) of the CARROT family, native to the Old World but now naturalized in parts of the U.S. It has clusters of small white flowers and a purple-mottled stem. The poisonous principle (the ALKALOID coniine) causes paralysis, convulsions, and eventual death. The plant was used in ancient Greece to execute criminals; a famous example was SOCRATES.

poison sumac: see POISON IVY.

Poitier, Sidney, 1927–, African-American film actor and director; b. Miami, Fla. He has starred in such films as *The Defiant Ones* (1958); *Lilies of the Field* (1963; Academy Award); *In the Heat of the Night* (1967); *A Patch of Blue* (1973) and *A Piece of the Action* (1977), both of which he directed; and, for television, *Separate but Equal* (1992).

Poitiers, Diane de: see DIANE DE POITIERS.

Poitiers [pwätyā′], city (1990 pop. 82,507), capital of Vienne dept., W Central France. It is an industrial, agricultural, and communications center. Before Roman rule it was the capital of the Pictons, a Gallic people. Later, its Christian orthodoxy and its monasteries made it a religious center. The Visigoths, Franks, Muslims, Normans, and English held it or sacked it in turn. In 1356 EDWARD THE BLACK PRINCE defeated JOHN II of France there. Historic architecture includes Roman amphitheaters and churches, and homes dating from the 4th cent. to the Renaissance.

poker, card game, traditionally a cutthroat gambling game, now an internationally popular social game. It remains basically a gambling game played for either money or chips. During betting intervals, each player must fold (leave the game), call (equal the bet made), or raise (increase the bet made). All bets are placed together to form a pot. The game's object is to win the pot either by holding the best hand or by bluffing (inducing opponents to drop). The two basic forms are draw poker, in which all cards remain hidden, and stud poker, in which some are dealt face-up.

Poland, Pol. *Polska,* officially Republic of Poland, republic (1992 est. pop. 38,386,000), 120,725 sq mi (312,677 sq km), central Europe; bordered by Germany (W), the Baltic Sea and the Kaliningrad oblast of Russia (N), Lithuania (NE), Belarus and Ukraine (E), and the Czech Republic and Slovakia (S). Major cities include WARSAW (the capital), ŁÓDŹ, KRAKÓW, WROCŁAW, POZNAŃ, and GDAŃSK. The country is generally low-lying, except in the south, where the Sudeten and CARPATHIAN mountains form a natural barrier between Poland and the Czech Republic and Slovakia. Poland's main rivers, including the Vistula and the Oder, are important routes to the BALTIC SEA. Industry, which has expanded rapidly since World War II, contributes more than half of the gross domestic product. Leading manufactures include machinery, iron and steel, chemicals, textiles, and processed food. Agricultural products include rye, potatoes, sugar beets, and wheat. Poland is an important producer of coal, sulfur, and copper. Industry was largely controlled by the state, but steps toward privatization have been taken; most farms are privately run. Nearly all of the population is Polish, and Roman Catholicism is the dominant religion.

History. The Slavic groups that occupied the area of present-day Poland were first united under the Piast dynasty and Christianized in the 10th cent. The crown eventually passed to the Jagiello dynasty (r.1386–1572), under whom Poland enjoyed its golden age.

The arts and sciences flourished, and a Polish-Lithuanian state, created in 1569, maintained an empire that reached from the Baltic to the Black Sea. In the 16th and 17th cent. much territory was lost to Sweden and Russia, and with the accession (1697) of the electors of Saxony as kings of Poland, national independence was virtually lost (see NORTHERN WAR; POLISH SUCCESSION, WAR OF THE). Three successive partitions (1772, 1793, 1795) among Prussia, Austria, and Russia resulted in the disappearance of Poland from the map of Europe. Polish nationalism persisted, and in 1918, following World War I, an independent Poland was proclaimed, with Joseph PILSUDSKI as chief of state. The Treaty of VERSAILLES (1919) redrew Poland's boundaries, but a dispute over the eastern border led to war with Russia (1920–21); the Treaty of Riga awarded Poland parts of its claims. A republican constitution was adopted in 1921, but in 1926 Pilsudski assumed dictatorial power, which passed to a military junta after his death (1935). On Sept. 1, 1939, citing as cause Poland's refusal to surrender the port of Gdańsk (Danzig), Germany invaded Poland, thus precipitating WORLD WAR II. On Sept. 17 Russia (then allied with Germany) invaded from the east, and the country was divided between Germany and Russia. When Germany attacked the USSR in 1941, all of Poland came under German rule. Massacres, starvation, and CONCENTRATION CAMPS such as that at Óswięcim (Auschwitz) decimated the population; about 6 million Poles, including some 3 million Jews, were killed. The Germans were expelled from Poland in 1945, and a provisional government was set up under Soviet auspices. Government-controlled elections in 1947 gave the Communists full control, and in 1952 Poland became a people's republic on the Soviet model. In 1956 widespread riots against Soviet control brought to power "rightist deviationist" Władysław Gomułka. A period of increased freedom followed, but by the 1960s Gomułka had reverted to the more rigid policies of his predecessors. Rapidly increasing food prices led to riots in 1970, and Gomułka was replaced by Edward Gierek, who instituted many reforms and controlled inflation. Poland's gravest postwar crisis began in 1980 (and removed Gierek from power), when strikes by factory workers, miners, and farmers spread throughout the country. An independent labor union, known as SOLIDARITY and led by Lech WALESA, demanded greater worker control in industry. The nation's economy deteriorated, bringing severe shortages of food and other goods. In 1981 Gen. Wojciech JARUZELSKI became premier. He imposed martial law, and Solidarity leaders were arrested. In 1982 Solidarity itself was banned. Martial law was ended in 1984, and all imprisoned Solidarity members released by 1986. In 1985 Jaruzelski became president. In 1989 the government agreed to legalize the union and reorganize the parliament and presidency. In limited free elections, Solidarity-supported candidates won (1989) nearly all the seats they contested. The parliament narrowly reelected Jaruzelski president, and he offered the premiership to Tadeusz Mazowiecki of Solidarity. Mazowiecki initiated a transition to a free-market economy, which brought economic hardship and disruption. In 1990 Walesa became president, defeating Mazowiecki in a free election. In 1991 parliamentary elections gave 29 parties seats. Hanna Suchocka became Poland's first woman premier in 1992, but she lost a no-confidence vote the next year. In new elections the Democratic Left Alliance (former Communists) and Polish Peasant party (PPP) together won a majority, and Waldemar Pawlak, of the PPP, became (1993) premier.

Poland, Partitions of, three successive efforts (1772, 1793, 1795) by Austria, Russia, and Prussia to remove Poland from the map by dividing its territories among themselves. In 1772 large parts of the country were divided among FREDERICK II of Prussia, CATHERINE II of Russia, and MARIA THERESA of Austria. In 1793, after it had become apparent that the remaining portion of independent Poland was showing signs of regeneration, Russia and Prussia invaded the country and took more land. Only the central section of Poland remained independent, and the three powers took that in 1795. Poland's partition was confirmed by the Congress of VIENNA (1814–15), but Russia received a much larger share.

Polaris or **North Star,** star nearest the north celestial pole (see ASTRONOMICAL COORDINATE SYSTEMS). It is in the Little Dipper portion of the constellation Ursa Minor (see URSA MAJOR). Polaris's location less than 1° from the pole makes it a very important navigational star; it always marks due north from an observer. See PRECESSION OF THE EQUINOXES.

polarized light, light in which the vibration of the electric or magnetic field is confined to one plane. Ordinary light consists of a mixture of waves vibrating in all directions perpendicular to its line of propagation. Polarized light can be obtained to a varying extent (depending on the angle of incidence) by reflection. It can also be obtained by double refraction in certain crystals, such as calcite. These crystals have the property of refracting unpolarized light in two different directions, the ordinary ray and the extraordinary ray; both are polarized in directions perpendicular to each other.

Polaroid camera: see LAND, EDWIN HERBERT.

pole, magnetic: see MAGNETIC POLE.

police dog: see GERMAN SHEPHERD.

poliomyelitis or **polio,** acute viral infection that, in its severe form, invades the nervous system and causes paralysis. In its mild form the disease produces mild symptoms (e.g., low-grade fever, malaise), or none. Also known as infantile paralysis, it is found worldwide, occurring mainly in children. The SALK vaccine (injected killed-virus vaccine) and the SABIN vaccine (oral live-virus vaccine) have greatly reduced the incidence of polio, nearly eradicating it from developed nations. In 1985 the World Health Organization began an effort to eradicate polio worldwide by 2000. The last reported case of polio in the Americas was in 1991.

Polish Corridor, strip of German territory awarded to newly independent Poland by the Treaty of VERSAILLES in 1919, providing access to the Baltic Sea. Free German transit was permitted across the area, which separated EAST PRUSSIA from the rest of Germany. Disputes over the corridor and the adjacent free city of Danzig (see GDAŃSK) later led to the German invasion of Poland (1939) and WORLD WAR II.

Polish language, member of the West Slavic group of the Slavic subfamily of the Indo-European family of languages. See LANGUAGE (table).

Polish Succession, War of the, 1733–35, European conflict arising out of rival claims to the Polish throne. France supported STANISLAUS I, while the Holy Roman emperor and Russia supported AUGUSTUS III. In 1734 Stanislaus was forced to flee to France, but the war continued along the Rhine and in Italy. There Spain and Sardinia allied themselves with France, hoping to regain Italian territories then in the control of the emperor. The Treaty of Vienna (1735) called for a complicated dynastic reshuffling. Stanislaus (and France) got the duchies of Lorraine and Bar; Spain got Naples and Sicily; and the emperor retained Parma.

politburo, the central policy-making and governing body of the Communist party of the Soviet Union (1917–91) and of other Communist parties. The politburo of the USSR was ostensibly elected by the party's central committee to direct party affairs between central committee plenary sessions; in reality, it governed the country. Although its size varied, it consisted of 15 voting members and 5 to 8 nonvoting members. It was called the presidium from 1952 to 1966.

political action committee (PAC), American organization formed by a corporation, labor union, or association to raise money for political activity. Funds can be gathered by voluntary contributions from members, employees, or shareholders. Since the election reform of 1974, which limited individual campaign contributions and set guidelines for PACs, their number has grown to over 4,000. Many represent special interest groups, e.g., the National Rifle Association or United Auto Workers; others are large conservative or liberal coalitions. Most PACs have directed their contributions toward congressional elections, in which they can contribute $5,000 to a candidate for each campaign (primary, runoff, and general election). Some, however, have conducted independent negative campaigns against candidates they oppose.

political science, study of the processes, institutions, and activities of government. Although the study of politics dates back to ARISTOTLE and PLATO, political science only emerged as a separate discipline toward the end of the 19th cent. It includes the fields of political theory, national government, comparative government, and international relations.

Polk, James Knox, 1795–1849, 11th president of the U.S. (1845–49); b. Mecklenburg co., N.C. He practiced law in Columbia, Tenn., before serving in the state legislature (1823–25) and the U.S. House of Representatives (1825–39), where he was Speaker (from 1835) and a leading Jacksonian Democrat. He was elected (1839) governor of TENNESSEE but was defeated for reelection by the Whig candidate. When the 1844 Democratic convention became deadlocked, Polk, a "dark horse," was advanced as a compromise candidate for president and won nomination. He narrowly defeated Henry CLAY in the 1844 election. As president, Polk proved to be his own man, even ignoring former Pres. Andrew JACKSON's wishes on several matters. His promises to achieve "four great measures"—reduction of the tariff, reestablishment of an independent treasury, settlement of the Oregon boundary dispute, and acquisition of California—were kept. Despite the aggressive Democratic slogan of FIFTY-FOUR FORTY OR FIGHT, Polk resolved the dispute with Britain over OREGON by adopting the 49th parallel as the territory's northern boundary. His ordering U.S. troops to the Rio Grande brought about the MEXICAN WAR, which resulted in U.S. acquisition not only of California but of the entire Southwest. Few presidents have equaled Polk's record of attaining his stated aims. Hard work undermined his health, however, and he died a few months after leaving office.

poll, technique for determining popular attitudes or opinions on given questions. Preelection polling by U.S. newspapers dates from 1824, and polling at voting places to report election returns dates from 1883; magazines conducted national polls in the early 20th cent. A scientific method called sampling was developed in the 1930s. Using a small percentage of voters, a pollster could predict election outcomes more accurately than with the old straw-ballot technique. George GALLUP's correct prediction in the 1936 presidential election brought wide recognition of the sampling method. Polling technique has grown increasingly sophisticated and is an important part of social science methodology; it is also widely used in market research and in advertising. Poll results also now influence decisions by government officials. The creation of opinion by polling itself, the so-called bandwagon effect, has drawn criticism. Politicians and special-interest groups have sometimes attempted to use this effect to political advantage by asking deliberately slanted questions under the guise of a poll.

Pollaiuolo [pōl-läyo͞o-ô'lō], family of Florentine artists. **Jacopo Pollaiuolo** was a noted 15th-cent. goldsmith. His son and pupil, **Antonio Pollaiuolo,** 1429?–1498, goldsmith, painter, sculptor, and engraver, headed one of Florence's foremost workshops. He is said to have been the first artist to study anatomy by dissection. His mastery of figures in action can be seen in the painting *Dancing Nudes* (Arcetri, Italy) and in a painting and a bronze statuette of *Hercules and Antaeus* (both: Uffizi). In Rome he executed the bronze tomb of Sixtus IV. His brother, **Piero Pollaiuolo,** 1443–96, was associated with him. Piero is generally considered an inferior artist, as seen in his independent works, e.g., the *Virtues* (Uffizi). Their nephew **Simone del Pollaiuolo,** 1457–1508, nicknamed Il Cronaca, was an architect, responsible for the noble Strozzi palace. He also worked on the Great Hall of the Palazzo Vecchio (1495) and the Church of San Salvatore al Monte (1504).

pollen, minute, usually yellow grains, borne on the anther sac at the tip of the stamen (the male reproductive organ of the FLOWER) or in the male cone of a CONIFER. Pollen grains are the male GAMETOPHYTE generation of seed plants. They are formed by the division, or MEIOSIS, of pollen mother cells and contain half the number of chromosomes of the parent plant. See also POLLINATION.

pollination, transfer of POLLEN from the male reproductive organ (the stamen of a FLOWER or staminate cone of a CONIFER) to the female reproductive organ (pistil or pistillate cone) of the same or another flower or cone. The most common agents of pollination are flying insects (for most flowering plants) and wind (for most trees and all GRASSES and conifers). The devices that operate to ensure cross-pollination and prevent self-pollination are highly varied and intricate. They include different maturation times for the pollen and eggs of the same plant; separate staminate and pistillate flowers on the same or separate plants; chemical properties that make the pollen and eggs of the same plant sterile to each other; and special mechanisms and arrangements that prevent the pollinating agent from transferring a flower's pollen to its stigma. Pollination should not be confused with FERTILIZATION, which it may precede by some time—a full season in some conifers.

polliwog: see TADPOLE.

Pollock, Jackson, 1912–56, American painter, pioneer of ABSTRACT EXPRESSIONISM; b. Cody, Wyo. Influenced by PICASSO and also by SURREALISM in his attempt to express, rather than illustrate, feeling, Pollock developed an abstract art in which he vigorously drew or "dripped" complicated linear rhythms onto enormous canvases. His attack on the canvas and his devotion to the act of painting led to the term "action painting." His work is in important collections throughout the U.S.

poll tax, uniform tax levied on every adult in the community. Poll taxes are traceable to ancient tax systems and have long been criticized as an unfair burden on the poor. Historically, in the U.S., they were enacted in the South as a prerequisite for voting, disfranchising many African Americans and poor whites. The 24th amendment to the U.S. CONSTITUTION (1964) forbids a poll tax as a prerequisite for voting in federal elections, and in 1966 the Supreme Court extended the ruling to all elections.

pollution, contamination of the environment as a result of human activities. During the 20th cent. pollution problems have arisen in all industrialized areas as well as in various inland and coastal waters and stretches of ocean. The capacity of the BIOSPHERE to disperse, degrade, and assimilate human wastes is in question (see ECOLOGY). An early sign of environmental limits was the air pollution of the INDUSTRIAL REVOLUTION, brought on by the burning of coal to run mills and machinery. It was not until after World War II, however, that pollution came to be viewed by many as a threat to the health of the planet. By the 1960s, population increases, industrial expansion, and burgeoning truck and automobile use were producing wastes in such quantity that natural dispersing and recycling processes could not always keep pace. Exacerbating the problem was the appearance of synthetic substances that degrade extremely slowly or not at all: plastics, fibers, organic pesticides such as DDT, industrial chemicals such as PCBS (polychlorinated biphenyls), and the wastes from their manufacture. Thus, garbage and toxic chemicals polluted the land and infiltrated ground and surface waters. Pesticides have poisoned wildlife, and industrial waste products have contaminated drinking water and, in more severe cases, caused evacuation of homes (e.g., Love Canal area, Niagara Falls, N.Y., 1978). Effects of industrial wastes have spread over larger areas as well, e.g., when toxic MERCURY reached high concentrations in widely distributed species of food fish in the early 1970s. Airborne industrial wastes created ACID RAIN and, with automobile emissions, produced severe air-pollution problems, including SMOG, in many urban and suburban communities. The contribution of pollutants to global environmental problems, such as GLOBAL WARMING and depletion of the earth's OZONE LAYER, has prompted international meetings and agreements. Radioactive materials from the nuclear reactor accident at CHERNOBYL spread through E Europe and Scandinavia; lack of appropriate disposal facilities has led some countries to dump radioactive wastes in the oceans. Current evidence strongly implicates various pollutants in numerous human health problems, such as CANCER; BIRTH DEFECTS; genetic changes; chronic headaches, fatigue, and irritability; and digestive disorders. By the 1970s many organizations and governments were seeking means of controlling pollution (see ENVIRONMENTALISM). In the U.S., Congress established the Environmental Protection Agency and passed numerous laws for pollution control. WASTE DISPOSAL, long considered routine, has also become an increasingly complex science and a major industrial challenge. Waste disposal specialists seek solutions to the safe disposal of many hazardous substances, including highly toxic radioactive wastes. See also NOISE POLLUTION.

pollution allowance, government-issued permit to emit a certain amount of a pollutant; the holder of the permit may use it to pollute legally or may sell the permit for a profit. The allowance issued to a polluter is reduced over time as permitted levels of a pollutant are cut. By specifying reductions in emissions but leaving the polluter to decide how to cut them, the system is intended to provide incentives to lessen both pollution and compliance costs. A company that cuts its pollution below its permitted level may sell the surplus allowance; a company that exceeds its limits without purchasing an extra allowance is fined. Under the 1990 Clean Air Act, federal allowances for sulfur dioxide emissions are issued to polluters; additional allowances are auctioned.

Pollux, Greek hero: see CASTOR AND POLLUX.

Polo, Marco, 1254?–1324?, Venetian traveler in CHINA. He left Venice in 1271 with his father and uncle, who had previously journeyed as far east as Kaifeng, in China (1266). The party reached the court of KUBLAI KHAN, in Cambuluc (present-day BEIJING), in 1275. Marco Polo became the khan's favorite and served him in China, India, and SE Asia. He returned to Venice in 1295. His account of his travels has been of great value to historians.

polo, ball and goal game played on horseback. Outdoor polo is played by two teams of four on a grass field with goalposts at either end. An indoor match is played with teams of three. In both versions, play is directed toward striking a ball (wooden in outdoor polo, rubber in indoor) with a long, flexible mallet into the goal. Because of the frequent collisions between horses (called polo ponies), each player must change mounts several times during a match. The origin of polo is uncertain, but it was played by British officers in India in the 19th cent. and then spread to England and the U.S.

polonium (Po), radioactive element, discovered in PITCHBLENDE by Marie CURIE in 1898. Extremely rare, it has 34 isotopes, more than any other element. Polonium has found use in small, portable radiation sources and in the control of static electricity. See ELEMENT (table); PERIODIC TABLE.

Pol Pot, 1928?–, Cambodian Communist leader; b. Saloth Sar. After the KHMER ROUGE victory in Cambodia in 1975, he became (1976) prime minister. Under his regime, widespread executions, forced labor, and famine killed an estimated 3 million Cambodians. In 1979 Vietnam invaded and ousted the Khmer Rouge from Phnom Penh, establishing a government led by Heng Samrin, but Pol Pot remained head of the Khmer Rouge, which retained control of large areas of Cambodia. In late 1979 he was replaced as prime minister by Khieu Samphan and named Khmer Rouge army chief. He officially retired in 1985, but he is believed still to head the Khmer Rouge.

Polybius [pōlĭ'bēəs], 203? B.C.–120 B.C., Greek historian; b. Megalopolis. In Rome, under the patronage of the Scipio family, he wrote a great universal history. Of the 40 books written, only the first five survive intact. Polybius tried to explain the sudden rise of Rome; his history covers the Mediterranean world from before c.220 to 146 B.C.

Polydorus, Greek sculptor: see LAOCOÖN.

polyester: see SYNTHETIC TEXTILE FIBERS.

polygamy: see MARRIAGE.

polygon, closed plane figure bounded by straight-line segments (sides) intersecting at points called vertices. Polygons of 3, 4, 5, 6,

7, 8, 10, and 12 sides are called, respectively, triangles, quadrilaterals, pentagons, hexagons, heptagons, octagons, decagons, and dodecagons. In a regular polygon, e.g., an *equilateral triangle* or a *square* (four sides), the sides are of equal length and meet at equal angles. A triangle is *isosceles* if two sides are equal and *scalene* if all sides differ in length; a *right triangle* has one right angle (90°). A quadrilateral is a *rhombus* if its four sides are equal, a *trapezoid* if it has one pair of parallel sides, and a *parallelogram* if it has two pairs of parallel sides. A *rectangle* is a parallelogram with four right angles.

polyhedron, closed solid bounded by plane faces, each of which is a POLYGON. There are only five possible regular polyhedrons, having congruent faces, each a regular polygon and meeting at equal angles. These are the Platonic solids: the tetrahedron (bounded by four equilateral triangles); the hexahedron, or cube (six squares); the octahedron (eight equilateral triangles); the dodecahedron (12 regular pentagons); and the icosahedron (20 equilateral triangles).

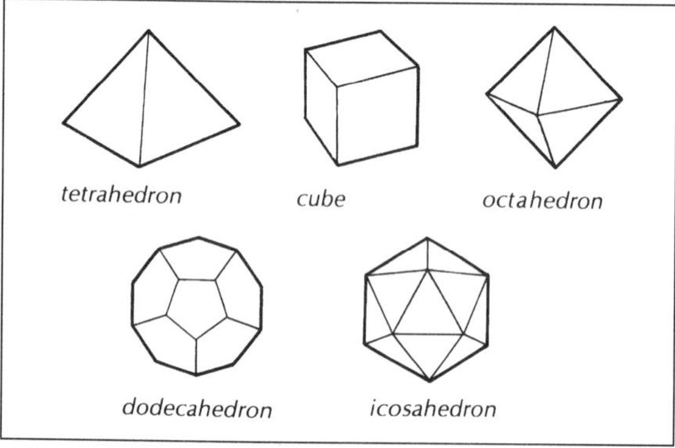

The five regular polyhedrons

Polyhymnia: see MUSES.

Polykleitos, Polycletus, or **Polyclitus** [pŏlĭklī'təs, –klē'–, –klī'–], two Greek sculptors of the school of Argos. **Polykleitos,** the elder, fl. c.450–c.420 B.C., made many bronze statues of athletes. His ideal of physical perfection, the "canon of Polykleitos," became the standard for sculptors. It is seen in his statues the *Doryphorus,* or *Spear-Bearer* (Naples), the *Diadumenus* (National Mus., Athens), and an *Amazon,* all known through copies. **Polykleitos,** the younger, fl. 4th cent. B.C., a sculptor and architect, designed the great theater at EPIDAURUS.

polymer, chemical compound with high molecular weight consisting of a number of structural units linked together by covalent bonds. The simple molecules that may become structural units are themselves called monomers. A structural unit is a group having two or more bonding sites. In a linear polymer, the monomers are connected in a chain arrangement and thus need only have two bonding sites. When the monomers have three bonding sites, a nonlinear, or branched, polymer results. Naturally occurring polymers include CELLULOSE, PROTEINS, natural RUBBER, and SILK; those synthesized in the laboratory have led to such commercially important products as PLASTICS, synthetic fibers, and synthetic rubber.

polymerase chain reaction (PCR), laboratory process in which a particular DNA segment from a mixture of DNA chains is rapidly replicated, producing a large, readily analyzed sample of a piece of DNA. In PCR, DNA is immersed in a solution containing the ENZYME DNA polymerase, unattached nucleotide bases (the subunits that DNA is composed of), and "primers," short sequences of nucleotides designed to bind with an end of the desired DNA segment. Two primers are used: one primer binds at one end of the desired segment on one of the two paired DNA strands, and the other primer binds at the other end but on the other strand. The solution is heated to break the bonds between the strands of the DNA. When the solution cools, the primers bind to the separated strands, and DNA polymerase quickly builds a new strand by joining the free nucleotide bases to the primers. When this process is repeated, a strand that was formed with one primer binds to the other primer, resulting in a new strand that is restricted solely to the desired segment. Thus, the region of DNA between the primers is selectively replicated. Further repetitions of the process can produce billions of copies of a small piece of DNA in several hours. PCR was developed in 1985 by Kary B. Mullis, who was awarded the 1993 Nobel Prize in chemistry for his work. It is used in DNA FINGERPRINTING and in medical tests to identify diseases from the infectious agent's DNA. See also NUCLEIC ACID.

Polynesia, one of the three main divisions of Oceania, in the central and S Pacific Ocean. The principal island groups include the Hawaiian islands (see HAWAII), TONGA, Samoa (see AMERICAN SAMOA; WESTERN SAMOA), and the islands of FRENCH POLYNESIA. Languages spoken are of Malayo-Polynesian origin.

Polynesian languages: see MALAYO-POLYNESIAN LANGUAGES.

Polynices: see SEVEN AGAINST THEBES.

polynomial, mathematical expression containing terms of one or more variables or constants that are connected by addition or subtraction. No variable can appear as a divisor or have fractional exponents. In one unknown, the general form of a polynomial is $a_0x^n + a_1x^{n-1} + a_2x^{n-2} + \ldots + a_{n-1}x + a_n$ where n is a positive integer and $a_0, a_1, a_2, \ldots, a_n$ are any numbers. The *degree* of a polynomial in one variable is the highest power of the variable. A polynomial of degree 2, i.e., $ax^2 + bx + c$ (where *a, b,* and *c* are any numbers), is called a *quadratic.*

polyp and medusa, names for the two body forms of animals (COELENTERATES) of the phylum Cnidaria—one, the polyp or hydroid, is stationary; the other, the medusa, is free-swimming. Both consist of a cylindrical body with a mouth surrounded by stinging tentacles at one end. The polyp is elongated and attaches to the ocean bottom with the mouth and tentacles pointing upward; the medusa is rounded and swims with the mouth down and tentacles dangling. Some cnidarians are always polyps, some are always medusae, and some take both medusa and polyp forms during their life cycles. Common polyps are the SEA ANEMONE and HYDRA; a common medusa is the JELLYFISH. In many species, such as CORAL, the polyps form colonies. The Portuguese man-of-war is an elaborate floating colony of polyplike and medusalike individuals.

polypeptide: see PEPTIDE.

Polyphemus [pŏlĭfē'məs], in Greek mythology, a CYCLOPS. In the *Odyssey,* ODYSSEUS and his men were imprisoned in his cave, but they escaped by making him drunk and blinding him.

polyphony, music whose texture is formed by the harmonic interweaving of several independent melodic lines through the use of COUNTERPOINT. Contrasting terms are *homophony,* wherein one part dominates while the others form a chordal accompaniment; and *monophony,* wherein there is a single melodic line (as in PLAINSONG). Polyphony developed by the late 9th cent. and culminated in the great age of polyphony in the 15th and 16th cent. Although polyphony was overshadowed by HARMONY in the BAROQUE period and by homophony in the classical and romantic periods, in the 20th cent. there has been renewed interest in polyphonic aspects of musical texture and structure.

polypodiophyte, member of a division (Polypodiophyta, sometimes called Pterophyta or Filicophyta) of the plant kingdom consisting of the FERNS.

polypropylene, lightweight PLASTIC, a POLYMER of propylene. It is less dense than water and resists moisture, oils, and solvents. It is used to make packaging material, textiles, luggage, ropes that float, and, because of its high melting point (250°F/121°C), objects that must be sterilized.

polytheism, belief in a plurality of gods, not necessarily equal in importance, each of which is distinguished by a special function. The Indian VEDAS, for example, feature Agni the fire god, Vayu the wind god, and Indra the storm god. Dynastic Egypt had hundreds of deities, but worship (as in Greek Olympianism) was city-centered. The gods of polytheistic systems are organized into a cosmic family, featured in legend and myth and expressing beliefs about the individual's relationship to the universe. The lesser deities of polytheism tend to diminish with time until the religion exhibits monotheistic tendencies. Thus the Olympian sky god ZEUS became the head of all Olympian deities; the Egyptian RA became the supreme god; and the several thousand Vedic gods were gradually displaced by the trinity of VISHNU, SHIVA, and BRAHMA. See MONOTHEISM.

polyurethanes, large group of PLASTICS that occur in a wide variety of forms. As a flexible foam, it is used for cushions and carpet backings. As a rigid foam, it can be molded into furniture or used as insulation. Some polyurethanes are highly elastic, e.g., Lycra, a fiber used in stretch clothing; others form hard protective coatings.

polyvinyl chloride (PVC), thermoplastic that is a POLYMER of vinyl chloride. By adding plasticizers, hard PVC RESINS can be made into a flexible, elastic PLASTIC, used as an electrical insulator and as a coating for paper and cloth in making fabric for upholstery and raincoats.

Pombal, Sebastião José de Carvalho e Melo, marquês de [pŏŏmbäl′], 1699–1782, Portuguese chief minister (1756–77) under King Joseph. An anticlerical absolutist, he curbed the INQUISITION and expelled the Jesuits from PORTUGAL. He built up Brazil and strengthened commerce. Pombal ruthlessly put down all opposition, imprisoning thousands. He was deposed after Joseph's death (1777) and was banished.

pomegranate, deciduous, thorny shrub or small tree (*Punica granatum*) native to semitropical Asia and grown in the Mediterranean region. It has long been cultivated as an ornamental and for its fruit. The roughly apple-sized fruit contains many seeds, each within a fleshy red seed coat, enclosed in a tough yellowish-to-deep-red rind. It is eaten fresh or used for grenadine syrup.

Pomerania, largely lowland region in Poland and Germany, bordering the Baltic Sea. W Pomerania became (1181) a duchy of the HOLY ROMAN EMPIRE, while E Pomerania, or Pomerelia, came (1466) under Polish rule and passed (1772) to PRUSSIA, becoming known as West Prussia. Parts of W Pomerania were ruled (1648–1814) by Sweden, and from 1815 to 1919 all of Pomerania was held by Prussia. From 1919 to 1939 Pomerania was divided among Germany, Poland, and the free city of Danzig (GDAŃSK). During WORLD WAR II Germany held (1939–40) all of Pomerania. In 1945 Poland was awarded most of the region; the rest was part of East Germany until German reunification.

Pomeranian, sturdy TOY DOG; shoulder height, c.6 in. (15.3 cm); weight, 3–7 lb (1.4–3.2 kg). Its abundant double coat forms a ruff on the neck. Descended from the larger sledge dogs of Iceland and Lapland, it became popular when Queen Victoria obtained one in the late 19th cent.

Pomona, city (1990 pop. 131,723), Los Angeles co., S Calif. at the foot of the San Gabriel Mts.; inc. 1888. It is a rapidly growing residential, industrial, and commercial suburb of Los Angeles. Manufactures include canned fruits and vegetables, building materials, paper products, and military equipment. It is the seat of California State Polytechnic Univ.

Pompadour, Jeanne Antoinette Poisson Le Normant d'Étioles, marquise de [pŏm′pədôr], 1721–64, mistress of LOUIS XV of France for about five years after 1745. She was his confidante until her death. She urged the appointment of certain ministers and fostered French ties with Austria, but her influence on state policy has been exaggerated.

pompano, marine FISH of the family Carangidae, mackerel like fishes abundant in warm seas around the world. Swift swimmers with deeply forked tails, most are valued as food fish. The family includes the amberfishes, leather jacks, cavallas or jacks, moonfishes, casabes, and pompanos. The best-known leather jack is the pilot fish (*Naucrates ductor*), which follows ships and sharks, feeding on discarded scraps. The amberfishes (genus *Seriola*) include the California yellowtail, weighing up to 40 lb (18 kg), and the amberjack, common off the Florida coast and weighing up to 100 lb (45 kg). The warm-water common pompano, found from the Carolinas to Texas, reaches 18 in. (45 cm) in length and is considered among the most delicious of food fish.

Pompeii, ancient city of S Italy, a port near Naples and at the foot of Mt. Vesuvius. It was a Samnite city before it became Roman (1st cent. B.C.). Pompeii was a flourishing port and a prosperous resort. An earthquake in A.D. 63 damaged the city, and the eruption of Mt. VESUVIUS in A.D. 79 buried Pompeii and the nearby city of Herculaneum under cinders and ashes that preserved their ruins. Pompeii was rediscovered in 1748, and excavations have revealed in great detail the habits and manners of life in Roman times.

Pompeius Magnus: see POMPEY.

Pompey (Cneius Pompeius Magnus) [pŏm′pē], 106–48 B.C., Roman general, the rival of Julius CAESAR. Sometimes called Pompey the Great, he fought for SULLA successfully and forwarded Roman conquests in Spain. He helped to end the slave revolt of SPARTACUS (72 B.C.) and was elected (70 B.C.) consul. Soon afterward he destroyed the pirates infesting the Mediterranean and vanquished (65 B.C.) MITHRIDATES VI of Pontus. Back in Rome, he met senatorial opposition and was driven into alliance with the senate's enemy, Caesar. The First Triumvirate was established (60 B.C.), and Caesar, Marcus Licinius CRASSUS, and Pompey became rulers of Rome. Pompey's wife, JULIA, who was Caesar's daughter, kept peace between her husband and father, but after her death (54 B.C.) Pompey became Caesar's jealous enemy. He went over to the senate and became consul (52 B.C.). Breaking with the senate, Caesar crossed (49 B.C.) the RUBICON, and the civil war began. Pompey was defeated at Pharsala (48 B.C.) and fled to Egypt, where he was killed.

Pompidou, Georges [pôNpēdōō′], 1911–74, president of France (1969–74). From 1944 he was an aide to Charles DE GAULLE, who named him premier in 1962. Elected president after De Gaulle resigned, Pompidou worked to improve France's economy and foreign relations. He died in office.

Pompidou, Centre National d'Art et de Culture Georges: see BEAUBOURG.

Ponce [pōn′sā], city (1990 pop. 159,151), S Puerto Rico. It is an industrial center and the island's chief Caribbean port. Tourism, sugar refining, and distilling are important. Founded in the early 16th cent., it is one of the oldest cities in the Americas.

Ponce de León, Juan [pŏns də lē′ŏn], c.1460–1521, Spanish explorer and European discoverer of FLORIDA. He conquered PUERTO RICO in 1508 and was governor (1509–12). In 1513 he landed in Florida. According to legend, he was seeking a "fountain of youth." He returned in 1521 to settle near Tampa Bay but was mortally wounded in a Native American attack.

Ponchielli, Amilcare [pōngkyĕl′lē], 1834–86, Italian composer of *La Gioconda* (1876) and several other operas.

pond lily: see WATER LILY.

Pons, Lily, 1904–76, French-American coloratura soprano. After 1931 she sang with the METROPOLITAN OPERA (N.Y.C.). She was particularly noted for her performances in DELIBES's *Lakmé* and DONIZETTI's *Daughter of the Regiment*.

Ponselle, Rosa, 1897–1981, American operatic soprano; b. Meriden, Conn. She made her debut in New York City in 1918. Ponselle was noted for her power and expressiveness.

Pontiac, fl. 1760–66, chief of the OTTAWA. He encouraged opposition to the British and participated in PONTIAC'S REBELLION, but his exact role initiating that uprising is uncertain. When the uprising failed (1766), he is said to have gone west and been murdered by ILLINOIS, but this account is not generally accepted.

Pontiac, industrial city (1990 pop. 71,166), seat of Oakland co., SE Mich., on the Clinton R.; founded 1818, inc. as a city 1861. Its early trades, notably carriage making, paved the way for automobile manufacturing, its leading industry. The OTTAWA chief PONTIAC is said to be buried nearby; the area has many parks and lakes.

Pontiac's Rebellion or **Pontiac's Conspiracy,** 1763–66, Native American uprising against the British at the end of the FRENCH AND INDIAN WARS, so called after one of its leaders, PONTIAC, chief of the OTTAWA. Angry at the British for fortifying and settling Native American lands, the Ottawa and allied tribes terrorized white settlers in western Pennsylvania, Maryland, and Virginia but failed to seize British forts at Detroit and Fort Pitt (now Pittsburgh). After some of his strongest allies sued for peace, Pontiac signed a peace treaty and was pardoned.

Pontius Pilate [pŏn′shəs pī′lət], fl. A.D. 26, Roman procurator of JUDAEA. He was supposedly a ruthless governor. His attempt to evade responsibility in the trial of JESUS was caused by his fear of the high priests' power and his difficult responsibility for the peace of Palestine. Tradition says he committed suicide at Rome.

Pontoppidan, Henrik [pôntô′pĭdän], 1857–1943, Danish novelist. His major work, *Lucky Peter* (5 vol., 1898–1904), attacks bourgeois life in Copenhagen. He shared the 1917 Nobel Prize in literature with K.A. GJELLERUP.

Pontormo, Jacopo da, 1494–1556, Florentine painter; b. Jacopo Carrucci. One of the creators of MANNERISM, he painted in a nervous, contorted style. His *Visitation* (the Annunziata, Florence) is famous. He also painted many excellent portraits, including one of Cosimo the Elder (Uffizi).

Pontus, ancient country, NE Asia Minor (now Turkey), on the Black Sea coast. Pontus flourished from the 4th cent. B.C. In the 1st cent. B.C. King MITHRIDATES VI conquered Asia Minor and the Crimea and threatened Greece, but the Romans under POMPEY defeated him in 65 B.C. Rome later joined Pontus to the province of Galatia-Cappadocia.

pony express, horseback relay mail service (1860–61) from Saint Joseph, Mo., to Sacramento, Calif., extending c.2,000 mi (3,200 km). Relay riders traveled the distance in about eight days. After a transcontinental telegraph line was completed in Oct. 1861, the pony express was ended. The **Pony Express National Historic Trail** was established in 1992 to preserve the trail and commemorate those who rode it.

poodle, popular dog, divided into three types, which differ in size: the standard, a NONSPORTING DOG, shoulder height, over 15 in. (38.1 cm), weight, 40–55 lb (18.1–24.9 kg); the miniature, also a nonsporting dog, shoulder height, 10–15 in. (25.4–38.1 cm), weight, 14–16 lb (6.4–7.3 kg); and the toy, a TOY DOG, shoulder height, up to 10 in. (25.4 cm), weight, c.6 lb (2.7 kg). The dense coat, of any solid color, is usually clipped in a variety of styles. The breed probably originated in Germany, but is associated with France, where it was used as a waterfowl retriever.

pool: see BILLIARDS.

poor law: see SOCIAL WELFARE.

pop art, movement that emerged at the end of the 1950s as a reaction against the seriousness of ABSTRACT EXPRESSIONISM. Pop artists used the imagery of comic strips, soup cans, soda pop bottles, and other common images to express abstract formal relationships. Artists such as Roy LICHTENSTEIN and Andy WARHOL attempted to fuse elements of popular and high culture and to erase the boundaries between the two.

Pope, Alexander, 1688–1744, English poet. He suffered physical disabilities and was largely self-taught. By age 17 he was regarded as a prodigy. Known for his literary quarrels, Pope nevertheless had many close friends. His interest in Tory politics was strengthened by friendship with SWIFT and by involvement in the SCRIBLERUS CLUB. Pope's poetry falls into three periods. In the first he wrote descriptive poetry e.g., the *Pastorals* (1709) and *Windsor Forest* (1713); the famous *Essay on Criticism* (1711), defining the doctrine of CLASSICISM; the mock-heroic *Rape of the Lock* (1714), ridiculing fashionable life; and two poems on love, "Elegy to the Memory of an Unfortunate Lady" and "Eloise to Abelard." After 1717, during the second period, his translations of the *Iliad* (1720) and *Odyssey* (1725–26), and his edition of Shakespeare (1725), made him rich. In the last period, living outside London at Twickenham, he wrote moral poems and SATIRES, including *The Dunciad* (1728–43), a mock epic attacking hack writers; *Imitations of Horace* (1733–38), including the "Epistle to Arbuthnot" (1735), his personal apologia; and the famous *Essay on Man* (1734), summarizing current philosophical speculation. A master craftsman, Pope is now generally regarded as the leading 18th-cent. English poet and as the greatest of all English verse satirists.

Popish Plot: see OATES, TITUS.

poplar: see WILLOW.

Popocatépetl [pōpəkăt'əpĕtəl, pōpō"kätā'pətəl], [Aztec, = smoking mountain], snow-capped volcano, 17,887 ft (5,452 m) high, second highest peak in Mexico. Quiescent since colonial times, the volcano occasionally emits vast clouds of smoke and sulfur fumes.

Popper, Sir Karl Raimund, 1902–, Anglo-Austrian philosopher; b. Vienna. A professor (1949–69) at the London School of Economics, Popper viewed knowledge as an individual, unpredictable act of genius not limited to verifiable statements (as the proponents of LOGICAL POSITIVISM held). His studies of the philosophical and political consequences of work in the sciences and what he called the pseudo-sciences (e.g., psychology) and his attacks on historicism (the view that there are historical laws) as a tool of totalitarian thought are presented in *The Logic of Scientific Discovery* (1931) and *The Open Society and Its Enemies* (1945). His later works include *Objective Knowledge* (1972) and *The Self and Its Brain* (with J.C. Eccles; 1977).

poppy, name for some members of Papaveraceae, a family composed chiefly of herbs of the Northern Hemisphere, typified by a milky or colored sap. Many are cultivated for their brilliantly colored but short-lived blossoms. The true poppy genus, *Papaver,* includes the Oriental poppy (*P. orientale*), bearing a large scarlet flower with a purplish-black base; the corn poppy (*P. rhoeas*); and the Iceland poppy (*P. nudicaule*). The opium poppy (*P. somniferum*) is the most important species economically. The sap of its unripe seed pods is the source of the narcotics OPIUM, MORPHINE, CODEINE, and HEROIN. Its seed (poppyseed) is not narcotic and is used as birdseed and in baking; oil from the seed is also used in cooking and for paints, soaps, and varnishes. Other genera in the family are also called poppies, e.g., the celandine poppy (*Stylophorum diphyllum*) and the California poppy (*Eschscholtzia californica*), the state flower of California.

popular music: see COUNTRY AND WESTERN MUSIC; FOLK SONG; JAZZ; REGGAE; ROCK MUSIC; SALSA.

popular sovereignty: see SQUATTER SOVEREIGNTY.

populations, stellar: see STELLAR POPULATIONS.

Populist party, American political party expressing the agrarian protest of the late 19th cent., when farmers suffered from declining agricultural prices. Many believed that the federal government's currency policy favored Eastern banks and industrialists at the expense of farmers and workers. Delegates from farm and labor groups met at Omaha in 1892 and formed the Populist party. Its platform called for the free coinage of silver and plenty of paper money, among other popular reforms. The Populist presidential candidate, James B. WEAVER, won more than 1 million votes in the 1892 election. But after the Democrats adopted free coinage of silver and ran William J. BRYAN for president in 1896, and agrarian insurgency had declined, in part as the result of rising farm prices, the Populist party dissolved. In some states the party was known as the People's party.

porcelain, white, hard, nonporous, translucent pottery. First made by the Chinese during the T'ang period (618–906) to withstand the great heat of their kilns, traditional porcelain was hard paste (a combination of kaolin, a white clay that melts at high temperature; and petuntse, a feldspar mineral that forms a glassy cement to bind the vessel permanently). It was exported to the Islamic world and highly prized. During the Yüan period (1280–1368) blue-and-white ware was produced with cobalt blue from the Middle East, and from the 14th to 17th cent. other colors were used as well. Most European porcelain is soft paste (clay combined with an artificial compound, e.g., ground glass) and is not as strong as Chinese porcelain. In Europe, porcelain was first commercially produced (1710) in Meissen, Germany. The English have strengthened porcelain with bone ash since 1750.

porcupine, member of either of two RODENT families, characterized by having some of its hairs modified as bristles, spines, or quills. Loosely attached, the quills pull out easily, remaining embedded in predators that come in contact with them. The North American, or Canadian, tree porcupine (*Erethizon dorsatum*) is found in wooded areas over most of North America, excluding the SE U.S. It forages in trees at night. Members of most species weigh 50 to 60 lb (23 to 27 kg).

porphyry, igneous ROCK of large crystals (phenocrysts) embedded in a groundmass. The term refers only to the rock's texture, not to its chemical or mineral composition.

porpoise, small WHALE of the family Phocaenidae, distinguished from the DOLPHIN by its smaller size (4–6 ft/120–180 cm) and rounded, beakless head. Black above and white below, porpoises are found in all oceans and prey on fish. In North America dolphins are often called porpoises.

port: see WINE.

Port-au-Prince, city (1987 est. pop. 800,000), SW Haiti, capital of Haiti. The country's largest city, commercial center, and chief seaport, it is laid out like an amphitheater around a bay. Founded in 1749 by French sugar planters, it became the colonial capital in 1770, replacing Cap-Haïtien. Although it has some manufactures, e.g., cement, food processing, and textiles, it has remained economically backward and has suffered frequent damage from earthquakes, fires, and civil warfare.

Porter, Cole, 1891–1964, American composer and lyricist; b. Peru, Ind. He is noted for his witty, sophisticated lyrics and affecting melodies. His MUSICALS include *Kiss Me, Kate* (1948) and *Can-Can* (1953). "Night and Day," "Begin the Beguine" and "Let's Do It" are among his best-known songs.

Porter, Katherine Anne, 1890–1980, American author; b. Indian Creek, Tex. Her masterful short stories, accomplished in style, form, and language, are included in such volumes as *Flowering Judas* (1930), *Pale Horse, Pale Rider* (1939), and her collected short stories (1965; Pulitzer). Her one novel, *Ship of Fools* (1962), is a moral allegory set aboard a German ship in 1931.

Porter, William Sydney: see O. HENRY.

porter: see BEER.

Portinari, Candido, 1903–62, one of Brazil's best-known modern painters. He was noted for his scenes of Brazilian life, and his mature style was fluid, expressionistic, and somewhat surrealistic. Portinari is known for his murals, e.g., *War* and *Peace* (1955; UN General Assembly Building, N.Y.C.).

Portland. **1** City (1990 pop. 64,358), seat of Cumberland co., SW Maine, on Casco Bay and including five islands in the bay; settled c.1632, inc. 1786. Maine's largest city and commercial center, it has a deepwater harbor, and imports oil and other goods destined for Montreal. It is the shipping and processing point for a vast farming, lumbering, and resort area, and has shipyards, canneries, and foundries. Portland was state capital from 1820 to 1832. The LONGFELLOW house and Portland Head Lighthouse (est. 1791) are noteworthy. **2** City (1990 pop. 437,319; met. area 1,239,842), seat of Multnomah co., NW Oreg., on the Willamette R.; inc. 1851. Founded in 1845, it grew rapidly as a supply point for western gold fields. The largest city in Oregon and the leading exporting port on the West Coast, it manufactures paper and wood products, electronic instruments, and machinery. The city grew rapidly after 1850, serving as a supply point for the California and Alaska gold fields. Its varied architecture includes a neoclassical city hall and the postmodernist Portland Building designed by Michael Graves. The Univ. of Portland, Reed College, and museums of science and advertising are among the many institutions in the area. The region is noted for its dramatic scenery; Mt. Hood is nearby.

Port Louis, city (1987 est. pop. 140,000), capital of Mauritius, on the Indian Ocean. It is the country's largest city and its economic center. Its economy is based on its well-sheltered port, which handles the country's international trade. Sugar is the leading export, and manufactures include cigarettes and rum. Founded by the French in 1735, Port Louis became an important naval base. It is largely populated by descendants of laborers who came from India in the 19th cent. Points of interest include the hilltop Citadel (1838).

Port Moresby, town (1990 pop. 193,242), capital of Papua New Guinea, on the SE coast of the island of NEW GUINEA. The nation's largest city and chief port, it was founded by Capt. John Moresby, who landed there in 1873. It was the chief Allied base on New Guinea during WORLD WAR II. A new capital is being built in suburban Waigani.

Pôrto Alegre, city (1990 est. pop. 1,387,000), SE Brazil, capital of Rio Grande do Sul state, at the mouth of the Guaíba R. A major commercial center and the nation's chief river port, it exports agricultural products and has a shipyard and processing industries. It is noted as a cultural and literary center. Founded c.1742, it is a handsome, modern city, with many colonial and baroque buildings preserved.

Port of Spain, city (1990 pop. 50,878), capital of Trinidad and Tobago, on the island of Trinidad. The nation's industrial hub and one of the major shipping centers in the Caribbean, it also has fine botanical gardens. It was the capital (1958–62) of the Federation of the WEST INDIES.

Portolá, Gaspar de [pôrtōlä'], fl. 1734–84, Spanish explorer in the Far West. He was sent in 1767 to be governor of the Californias and to expel the Jesuits (see JESUS, SOCIETY OF). He founded SAN DIEGO in 1769 and the mission of San Carlos, in Monterey Bay, in 1770. He was governor of Puebla, Mexico, from 1776 to 1784.

Porto-Novo, city (1984 est. pop. 164,000), capital of Benin, a port on the Gulf of Guinea. It is the shipping center for an agricultural region whose chief product is palm oil (the leading export). The capital of a small African kingdom in the 16th cent., Porto-Novo became (17th cent.) a Portuguese trading post and a center of slave trafficking to the Americas. It was taken by the French in 1883 and became the capital of Dahomey (now BENIN) in 1900.

Portsmouth, city (1990 pop. 103,907), SE Va., on the Elizabeth R. and HAMPTON ROADS, adjacent to NORFOLK; est. 1752, inc. 1858. Forming with Norfolk a major naval operations center, Portsmouth has a huge naval hospital and the largest concentration of drydocks in the nation. From the 18th cent. many U.S. warships were built there, including the CHESAPEAKE, the ironclad *Virginia* (see MONITOR AND MERRIMACK), and the first battleship and aircraft carrier. The city is also a busy commercial seaport.

Portugal, officially Portuguese Republic, republic (1992 est. pop. 10,449,000), 35,553 sq mi (92,082 sq km), SW Europe, on the W Iberian Peninsula; bordered by Spain (E and N) and the Atlantic Ocean (W and S). It includes the MADEIRA ISLANDS and the AZORES in the Atlantic Ocean. MACAO, Portugal's last overseas territory, will revert to China in 1999. Principal cities are LISBON (the capital), OPORTO, Coimbra, and Setúbal. Northern Portugal is dominated by mountains and high plateaus, while the south is mostly rolling countryside and plains. The country is crossed by the Tagus and Douro rivers. Portuguese agriculture, although noted for its vineyards, olive groves, and almond trees, is hampered by antiquated techniques, and food must be imported. Fishing (tuna and sardines) is important, as are food processing and the manufacture of textiles and clothing, chemicals, and cement. There are large forests, and Portugal supplies a major portion of the world's cork. The great majority of the largely homogeneous population are Roman Catholic, and Portuguese is the official language.

History. The area that is now Portugal (see LUSITANIA) was conquered (A.D. c.5) by the Romans, overrun (from the 5th cent.) by Germanic tribes, and taken (711) by the MOORS. Portugal became

an independent kingdom in 1139 under ALFONSO I, and with the conquest of Algarve in 1249 by ALFONSO III the Moors were driven out and the kingdom consolidated. The reign of JOHN I (r.1385–1433), founder of the Aviz dynasty, introduced Portugal's glorious period of colonial and maritime expansion; by the 15th cent. the Portuguese empire extended to Asia, Africa, and America. But decline was rapid. In 1580 PHILIP II of Spain seized Portugal, which remained under Spanish rule until a revolt in 1640 established the Braganzas, Portugal's last royal line. In the Napoleonic Wars, French forces occupied (1807–11) Portugal (see PENINSULAR WAR) and the royal family fled to the Portuguese colony of BRAZIL. In 1822 Brazil became independent. JOHN VI was forced to accept a liberal constitution in the same year, but opposition to the monarchy remained strong. In 1910 a revolution overthrew Manuel II and established a Portuguese republic. A period of great instability ensued. In 1926 a military coup overthrew the government, and in 1932 Antonio de Oliveira SALAZAR became prime minister and virtual dictator of a right-wing corporative state, a position he held until ill health forced his replacement by Marcello Caetano in 1968. In 1974, a bloodless coup brought a moderate form of democracy. Almost all Portuguese overseas territories subsequently gained independence, GUINEA-BISSAU in 1974, and ANGOLA, CAPE VERDE, MOZAMBIQUE, and SÃO TOMÉ AND PRINCIPE in 1975. In the years since, Portugal has seen increasing stability. Aníbal Cavaço Silva, of the center-right Social Democratic party, has been premier since 1985.

Portuguese language, member of the Romance group of the Italic subfamily of the Indo-European family of languages. See LANGUAGE (table).

portulaca: see PURSLANE.

Posada, José Guadalupe [pōsä'thä], 1852–1913, Mexican artist. An enormously popular artist, he strongly influenced the generation of OROZCO and RIVERA. Posada's work is characterized by violent imagery, distortion, caricature, and vigorous lines and contrasts. An ardent opponent of the Porfirio DÍAZ dictatorship, he produced thousands of prints attacking it, which were sold cheaply to the masses.

Poseidon [pōsī'dən], in Greek religion, god of the sea, protector of all waters. Powerful, violent, and vengeful, he carried the trident, with which he caused earthquakes. He was the husband of Amphitrite and the father of many sons, most either brutal men (e.g., ORION) or monsters (e.g., POLYPHEMUS). He was also important as Hippios, god of horses, and was the father of PEGASUS. The Romans identified him with NEPTUNE.

positivism, in philosophy, a system of thought opposed to METAPHYSICS and maintaining that the goal of knowledge is simply to describe the phenomena experienced. Its basic tenets are contained in the works of Francis BACON, George BERKELEY, and HUME. The term itself was coined by COMTE, whose doctrines influenced the development of much of 19th- and 20th-cent. thinking, especially that of LOGICAL POSITIVISM.

positron: see ANTIMATTER; ELECTRON.

positron emission tomography: see PET SCAN.

Postal Service, United States, independent U.S. agency reorganized (1971) from the former Post Office Dept. to provide mail processing and delivery services within the U.S. It also protects the mails from loss or theft and is empowered to change postal rates and to ban from the mails what it considers to be seditious, fraudulent, or obscene. It is governed by an 11-member board and headed by the postmaster general.

postimpressionism, term coined by Roger FRY, referring to the work of some late 19th-cent. painters who, although they developed their varied styles quite independently, were united in their rejection of IMPRESSIONISM. They include CÉZANNE, VAN GOGH, GAUGUIN, MATISSE, PICASSO, and BRAQUE. The term embraces a far wider school of thought than the neo-impressionism of SEURAT and SIGNAC, whose more systematic approach (called divisionism or pointillism) used dabs of pure color that were supposed to be mixed by the viewer's eye to produce intense color effects.

postmodernism, in architecture, international movement that emerged in the 1960s and became prominent in the late 1970s and 80s. A reaction to the orthodoxy and austerity of the INTERNATIONAL STYLE, it is characterized by the incorporation of historical details, use of decorative structural elements, a more personal and exaggerated style, and some reference to popular modes of building. Postmodernism was greatly affected by the writings of Robert VENTURI. The style is evident in his buildings and in those of such architects as Michael GRAVES, Denise Scott Brown, and Robert Stern, and in the later work of Philip JOHNSON.

post-traumatic stress disorder (PTSD), mental disorder that follows an occurrence of extreme psychological stress, such as that encountered in war or resulting from violence, childhood abuse, or serious accident. Symptoms include emotional numbness, nightmares or "flashbacks," insomnia, heightened sensitivity to sudden noises, and outbursts of violent behavior.

postulate: see AXIOM.

potassium (K), metallic element, discovered in 1807 by Sir Humphry DAVY, who decomposed potash with an electric current. It is a soft, silver-white, extremely reactive ALKALI METAL. Potassium is the seventh most abundant element in the earth's crust and the sixth most abundant of the elements in solution in the oceans. It is an essential nutrient for plants and animals. Potassium compounds are used in fertilizers, soaps, explosives, glass, baking powder, tanning, and water purification. See ELEMENT (table); PERIODIC TABLE.

potassium hydroxide: see ALKALI.

potassium nitrate: see SALTPETER.

potato or **white potato,** perennial plant (*Solanum tuberosum*) of the NIGHTSHADE family, and its swollen underground stem (tuber), a widely used vegetable. Probably native to the Andes, the potato was introduced (via Europe) into North America c.1600. With its high carbohydrate content, it is a primary food for Western peoples; it is also a source of STARCH, flour, ALCOHOL, dextrin, and fodder. Potatoes are usually propagated by planting pieces of the tubers that bear two or three "eyes," the buds of the underground stems or by planting seed potatoes or mini-tubers. The SWEET POTATO is unrelated.

potato blight: see BLIGHT; MILDEW.

Potemkin, Grigori Aleksandrovich, 1729–91, Russian field marshal and favorite of CATHERINE II. He took part in the coup that made Catherine czarina (1762) and was created count for serving in her first war with Turkey (1768–74). Her lover for a time, he remained one of her chief advisers, encouraging her in an unsuccessful plan to break up the OTTOMAN EMPIRE and reestablish a Christian empire in the conquered region. For his part in annexing the Crimea (1783) he was created prince and appointed governor of the new province, which he administered ably.

potential, electric, work per unit electric charge expended in moving a charged body from a reference point to any given point in an electric field. The potential at the reference point is considered to be zero, while the reference point itself is usually chosen to be at infinity. The change in potential associated with moving a charged body is independent of the actual path taken and depends only on the initial and final points. Potential is measured in VOLTS and is sometimes called voltage. See also ELECTRIC CIRCUIT; ELECTROMOTIVE FORCE.

potential energy: see ENERGY.

potentiometer or **voltage divider,** manually adjustable variable electrical resistor that has a RESISTANCE element attached to an ELECTRIC CIRCUIT by three contacts, or terminals. The ends of the resistance element are attached to the two input voltage conductors of the circuit, and the third contact, attached to the output of the circuit, is usually a movable terminal that slides across the resistance element, dividing it into two resistors. Because the position of the movable terminal determines what percentage of the input voltage (see POTENTIAL, ELECTRIC) is applied to the circuit, a potentiometer can be used to vary the magnitude of the voltage, e.g., in radio volume and television brightness controls.

Potiphar: see JOSEPH.

potlatch, lavish ceremonial feast among Northwest Coast tribes (see NORTH AMERICA, INDIGENOUS PEOPLES OF), at which the host distributed valuable gifts to guests to earn prestige. Recipients were obliged to reciprocate with more lavish gifts at a future potlatch. In its modern form, at the end of the 19th cent., the potlatch was used to bankrupt an enemy.

Potomac, scenic river of the E U.S., flowing 285 mi (459 km) SE from the vicinity of Cumberland, Md., to the Chesapeake Bay.

Washington, D.C., just below the Great Falls, is the head of navigation.

Potosí, city (1985 est. pop. 113,000), capital of Potosí dept., S Bolivia. Built at an altitude of c.13,780 ft (4,200 m) in the ANDES Mts., it is one of the highest cities in the world. It was founded in 1545 at the foot of one of the richest ore mountains ever discovered. Its silver mines were eclipsed by more accessible ones in Peru and Mexico after 1600, but modern technology has again made the area a source of silver, as well as of tin, lead, zinc, and copper.

Potsdam, city (1989 est. pop. 143,000), capital of BRANDENBURG, E Germany. A rail junction and industrial center, it produces processed foods, textiles, boats, and other goods. It was the chief residence of FREDERICK II of Prussia, who built (1745–47) the palace and park of Sans Souci. The city was badly damaged in WORLD WAR II. The Potsdam Conference (1945) was held there by the Allies.

Potsdam Conference, meeting (July 17–Aug. 2, 1945), of the principal Allies of WORLD WAR II (the U.S., the USSR, Great Britain) to clarify and implement agreements previously reached at the YALTA CONFERENCE. The chief participants were Pres. TRUMAN, Premier STALIN, and Prime Min. CHURCHILL (who was replaced by ATTLEE after Churchill's Conservative party lost the British election). The resulting Potsdam Agreement established four-power (American, British, Russian, French) occupation zones for postwar Germany. A comprehensive reordering of the German economy and German institutions was part of the agreement. The Council of Foreign Ministers was established to consider peace settlements. The conference issued an ultimatum to Japan either to surrender or risk total destruction. The rift between the Soviet Union and the Western Allies caused the Potsdam Agreement to be consistently breached, which was an early manifestation of the COLD WAR.

Potter, Beatrix, 1866–1943, English author and illustrator. Her unsentimental, humorous animal stories, with her own drawings and watercolors, number 25 and include *The Tale of Peter Rabbit* (1902) and *The Tailor of Gloucester* (1903).

Poulenc, Francis [po͞olăNk'], 1899–1963, French composer and pianist, one of "les SIX." His lyrical, spontaneous works include piano pieces, e.g., *Mouvements perpetuels* (1918); songs; the ballet *Les Biches* (1924); chamber music; the Mass in G (1937); and operas, e.g., *Dialogue of the Carmelites* (1957).

Pound, Ezra Loomis, 1885–1972, one of the most influential and controversial figures in 20th-cent. poetry; b. Hailey, Idaho. In 1907 he left the U.S. for Europe, eventually settling in England. There he led the IMAGISTS before founding VORTICISM, and there he encouraged and influenced other writers such as T.S. ELIOT and James JOYCE. In 1920 he moved to Paris; by 1925 he was settled in Italy, where he developed many of the economic theories that led him to broadcast Fascist propaganda during World War II. Indicted for treason after the war, he was confined to a U.S. mental hospital (1946–58). On his release he returned to Italy. Pound's major poems are "Homage to Sextus Propertius" (1918); *Hugh Selwyn Mauberley* (1920); and the *Cantos* (1925–60), a brilliant, often obscure, epic that weaves together many diversified cultural threads in an attempt to reconstruct the history of civilization. He is also noted for his translations from many languages.

Pound, Roscoe, 1870–1964, American jurist; b. Lincoln, Nebr. He was dean of Harvard law school (1916–36). In influential works on jurisprudence, like *Spirit of the Common Law* (1921), Pound argued for greater recognition of social interests in legal thinking.

pound: see ENGLISH UNITS OF MEASUREMENT; WEIGHTS AND MEASURES, table.

pound-foot: see TORQUE.

Poussin, Nicolas [po͞osăN'], 1594–1665, French painter. Although he spent most of his life in Italy, his painting became the standard for French classical art. He studied MANNERISM in France and antique monuments in Rome. The BAROQUE styles of Pietro da CORTONA and Giovanni Lanfranco can be seen in several of Poussin's works, e.g., *Martyrdom of St. Erasmus* (1629; Vatican). The works of TITIAN and VERONESE influenced his choice of mythological and elegiac subjects whereas his preoccupation with the works of antiquity and of RAPHAEL resulted in a new clarity of composition, e.g., *Adoration of the Magi* (1633; Dresden). He was also interested in the philosophical possibilities of painting, and this intellectualization influenced painting far into the 19th cent. As first painter to LOUIS XIII, he administered the decoration of the Great Gallery of the LOUVRE. His later works emphasized the contemplative aspects of his subject. In such works as the *Death of Phocion* (1648) he constructed a classical landscape ordered with mathematical precision. Of his last works, the four paintings in the series *The Four Seasons* (1660–64; Louvre) are the most imposing.

Powell, Adam Clayton, Jr., 1908–72, African-American politician and clergyman; b. New Haven, Conn. As pastor (from 1937) of New York City's Abyssinian Baptist Church, he became known as a militant African-American leader and flamboyant U.S. congressman (1945–70). He was expelled (1967) by the House of Representatives for misusing public funds and unbecoming conduct, but the U.S. Supreme Court overturned (1969) his expulsion.

Powell, Anthony, 1905–, English novelist. In his 12-volume series *A Dance to the Music of Time,* which begins with *A Question of Upbringing* (1951) and ends with *Hearing Secret Harmonies* (1976), he provides a panoramic look at English upper- and middle-class life over a 60-year period.

Powell, Colin (Luther), 1937–, African-American U.S. army general, the highest ranking African-American officer in U.S. history and chairman (1989–93) of the Joint Chiefs of Staff; b. N.Y.C. He served two tours of duty (1962–63, 1968–69) during the Vietnam War and later served in both command (commander, 2d Brigade, 101st Airborne Division, 1976–77; commander, V Corps, Europe, 1986) and political (military assistant to the Deputy Defense Secy., 1979–81, and to the Defense Secy., 1983–86) positions. From 1987 to 1989 he was Pres. Reagan's national security adviser. In 1989 he was made a four-star general and was appointed chairman of the Joint Chiefs of Staff. Powell played an influential role in the planning of U.S. strategy during the PERSIAN GULF WAR.

Powell, John Wesley, 1834–1902, American geologist and ethnologist; b. Mt. Morris (now part of New York City). Noted for his explorations of the western U.S., he made a survey of the Colorado R. in 1869, passing through the Grand Canyon by boat, a hazardous feat described in his *Explorations of the Colorado River* (1875). His efforts helped establish the U.S. Geological Survey, which he headed from 1881 to 1894.

Powell, Lewis Franklin, Jr., 1907–, associate justice of the U.S. SUPREME COURT (1971–87); b. Suffolk, Va.; grad. Washington and Lee Law School (1931) and Harvard Law School (1932). He was a practicing lawyer and president (1964–65) of the American Bar Association prior to his appointment to the Supreme Court by Pres. Nixon. Powell tended to take conservative positions on the Court, especially in criminal justice cases, but he sometimes voted with the Court's liberals on social issues, such as abortion.

power, in physics, the time rate of doing WORK or of producing or expending ENERGY. The unit of power in the METRIC SYSTEM is the watt, which equals 1 joule per second. It is also the amount of power that is delivered to a component of an electric circuit when a current of 1 ampere flows through the component and a voltage of 1 volt exists across it. The ENGLISH UNIT OF MEASUREMENT is the horsepower, which equals 550 foot-pounds per second or 746 watts.

power, electric, is the rate per unit of time at which electric ENERGY is consumed or produced. Electric POWER is usually measured in watts or kilowatts (1,000 watts). The energy supplied by a current to an appliance enables it to work or to provide other forms of energy such as light or heat. The amount of electric energy an appliance uses is found by multiplying its power rating by the operating time. Units of electric energy are usually watt-seconds (joules), watt-hours, or kilowatt-hours (the choice for commercial applications). Generally, practical electric-power-generating systems convert mechanical energy into electric energy (see GENERATOR). Whereas some electric plants obtain mechanical energy from moving water (water power or hydroelectric power), the vast majority derive it from heat engines in which the working substance is steam generated by heat from combustion of fossil fuels or nuclear reactions (see NUCLEAR ENERGY; NUCLEAR REACTOR). Although the conversion of mechanical energy to electric energy may approach 100% efficiency, the conversion of heat to mechanical energy is about 41% efficient for a fossil-fuel plant and about 30% for a nuclear plant. It is thought that a magnetohydrodynamic generator, which operates by using directly the kinetic energy of gases produced by combustion, would have an efficiency of about 50%. Although FUEL CELLS develop electricity by direct conversion of hydrogen, hydrocarbons, alcohol, or other fuels, with an efficiency of 50 to 60%, their high cost has restricted their use to space programs. SOLAR ENERGY has been recognized as a feasible power source. It can be exploited through wind TURBINES, PHOTOVOLTAIC CELLS, and heat engines, as well as through both conventional and low-head hydroelectric power plants. Research and development is bringing down the costs. An important problem in utilizing solar energy is related to the variable nature of sunlight and wind. To minimize energy losses from heating of conductors and to economize on the material needed for conductors, electricity is usually transmitted at the highest voltages possible. As modern TRANSFORMERS are virtually loss free, the necessary steps upward or downward in voltage are easily accomplished. Electric utilities producing power are tied together by transmission lines into large systems called power grids. They are thus able to exchange power, so that a utility with low power demand can assist another with a high demand. See also ENERGY, SOURCES OF.

Powhatan Confederacy, a group of 30 Native American tribes of the Eastern Woodlands (see NORTH AMERICA, INDIGENOUS PEOPLES OF), of the Algonquian branch of the Algonquian-Wakashan linguistic stock (see NATIVE AMERICAN LANGUAGES). The Powhatan lived in 200 palisaded settlements along coastal Virginia and Chesapeake Bay, hunting, fishing, and raising corn. Chief Powhatan, or Wahunsonacock, was head of the confederacy when JAMESTOWN was settled in 1607. The English seized his best land, but secured peace through John ROLFE's marriage (1614) to Powhatan's daughter POCAHONTAS. In 1622 Powhatan's successor, Opechancanough, attacked the English, killing 350; he was murdered after leading a last uprising (1644). After 1722 the tribes mixed with the settlers, and the confederacy disappeared. Their descendants include the Chickahominy and other small tribes of the Virginia and Chesapeake area.

Poznań [pôz'nänyə], Ger. *Posen,* city (1989 est. pop. 586,000), W central Poland, on the Warta R. It is a port and producer of machinery, metals, and chemicals. Founded by the 10th cent., it passed to Prussia (1793, 1815) before reverting (1919) to Poland. In 1956 labor unrest in Poznań spread to other cities, leading to major political changes in Poland. The city possesses a Gothic cathedral and a 16th-cent. city hall.

Pr, chemical symbol of the element PRASEODYMIUM.

Prado, Madrid, national Spanish museum of painting and sculpture, one of the finest in Europe. Situated on the Paseo del Prado, it was begun by the architect Juan de Villanueva in 1785 for Charles III, as a museum of natural history, and finished under Ferdinand VII. It was maintained by the royal family and called the Royal Museum until 1868, when it became national property. The Prado has priceless masterpieces from the Spanish, Flemish, and Venetian schools, e.g., works by El GRECO, GOYA, RUBENS, and TITIAN.

praetor or **pretor,** in ancient Rome, a magistrate. In 242 B.C. two praetors were appointed; the urban praetor decided cases in which citizens were parties, and the peregrine praetor decided cases between foreigners.

Praetorians, bodyguard of the ancient Roman emperors, formally organized in the time of AUGUSTUS from the troop that had guarded the general commanding in Rome. They attended the emperor wherever he went, had special privileges, and in times of trouble chose many of the emperors. CONSTANTINE I disbanded them in 312.

pragmatic sanction, decision of state dealing with a matter of great importance. The **Pragmatic Sanction of Bourges,** issued by CHARLES VII of France in 1438, sharply limited papal power over the church in France. It began a long period of tense relations between church and state in France. There have been many pragmatic sanctions, but, when used alone, the term always refers to the **Pragmatic Sanction,** 1713, issued by Holy Roman Emperor CHARLES VI, whereby all the HAPSBURG lands would be inherited by his daughter, MARIA THERESA (but not the imperial dignity, which was elective). Owing to a long campaign by the emperor, most of the European powers accepted the sanction; the major exception was the Bavarian elector (later Emperor CHARLES VII), who was married to one of the Hapsburg princesses passed over in favor of Maria Theresa. In spite of the guarantees her father had obtained, when Maria Theresa acceded to the Hapsburg succession in 1740, she had to defend her rights in a long and bitter struggle, the war of the AUSTRIAN SUCCESSION. (1740–48). The treaty of Aix-la-Chapelle (1748) confirmed the Pragmatic Sanction.

pragmatism, method of philosophy in which the truth of a proposition is measured by its correspondence with experimental results and by its practical outcome. Thus pragmatists hold that truth is modified as discoveries are made and that it is relative to time and place and purpose of inquiry. C.S. PEIRCE and William JAMES were the originators of the system, which influenced John DEWEY.

Prague [präg], Czech *Praha,* city (1990 pop. 1,214,772), capital and largest city of the Czech Republic, on both banks of the Vltava R. It is a port, an industrial center producing automobiles, machinery, and other manufactures, and one of Europe's great historic cities. A trading center by the 10th cent., it became the capital of BOHEMIA and was later (14th–17th cent.) one of the residences of the emperors of the HOLY ROMAN EMPIRE. The religious reformer John HUSS taught at its university (est. 1348). HAPSBURG rule began in 1526. Prague figured prominently in the THIRTY YEARS WAR (1618–48), the War of the AUSTRIAN SUCCESSION (1740–48), the SEVEN YEARS WAR (1756–63), and the REVOLUTIONS OF 1848. In 1918 it became the capital of the new Czechoslovak republic. It was occupied (1939–45) by the Germans during World War II. In 1968 Prague was the center of Czech resistance to the Soviet invasion. With the dissolution of Czechoslovakia in 1993, Prague became the capital of the Czech Republic. The old section is an architectural treasure, the site of such buildings as Hradčany Castle (14th cent.) and the Gothic Cathedral of St. Vitus. The city's cultural tradition is typified by such figures as KEPLER, SMETANA, DVOŘÁK, KAFKA, and ČAPEK.

Praia, city (1980 pop. 37,676), capital of CAPE VERDE.

prairie dog, short-tailed, ground-living, herbivorous RODENT (genus *Cynomys*) of the SQUIRREL family, found in the W U.S. and N Mexico and related to ground squirrels, CHIPMUNKS, and marmots. Prairie dogs, named for their barking cries, are 12 to 15 in. (30 to 36 cm) long with short, buff-colored fur. Black-tailed prairie dogs live in colonies of connected burrows; these may extend many miles and include thousands of individuals.

prairies, generally level, originally grass-covered and treeless plains of North America, stretching from Ohio to the Great Plains. They correspond to the PAMPAS and LLANOS of South America, the STEPPE of Eurasia, and the high VELD of South Africa. Often called the vanishing grasslands, prairies are among the most productive agricultural regions.

Prakrit [prä'krĭt], any number of languages belonging to the Indic group of the Indo-Iranian subfamily of the Indo-European family of languages. See LANGUAGE (table).

praseodymium (Pr), metallic element, discovered in 1855 by C.A. von Welsbach. It is a soft, malleable, ductile, silver-yellow RARE-EARTH METAL in the LANTHANIDE SERIES. Its compounds are used in carbon electrodes for arc lighting and to color enamel and glass. See ELEMENT (table); PERIODIC TABLE.

Praxiteles [prăksĭt'əlēz], fl. c.370–330 B.C., famous Attic sculptor. His *Hermes with the Infant Dionysus* is the only undisputed extant original by any of the ancient masters. Copies of his most renowned statues, e.g., the *Aphrodite of Cnidus* (Vatican), *Apollo Sauroctonus* (Vatican), and *Apollino* (Florence), illustrate his choice of youthful gods and other beings in which joy of life finds expression. In its delicate, perfect modeling and strength of conception, his treatment of marble is unsurpassed.

praying mantis, large, slender, slow-moving winged INSECT, so called because of its habit of standing on its hind legs, with the forelegs raised as if in prayer. Mantises range in length from 1 to 5 in. (2.5 to 12.5 cm). Their typically green or brown PROTECTIVE COLORATION camouflages them among leaves and twigs. Voracious predators, they feed on insects and other invertebrates; the female often eats the male after mating.

Precambrian time or **Precambrian era:** see GEOLOGIC ERA (table).

precession of the equinoxes, westward motion of the EQUINOXES along the ECLIPTIC. The precession, first noted (c.120 B.C.) by HIPPARCHUS and explained (1687) by Isaac NEWTON, is primarily due to the gravitational attraction of the moon and sun on the earth's equatorial bulge, which causes the earth's axis to describe a cone in somewhat the same fashion as a spinning top. As a result, the equinoxes, which lie at the intersections of the celestial equator and the ecliptic, move on the celestial sphere (see ASTRONOMICAL COORDINATE SYSTEMS). Similarly, the celestial poles move in circles on the celestial sphere, so that at various times different stars occupy positions at or near one of these poles (see POLARIS). After about 26,000 years the equinoxes and poles lie again at nearly the same points on the celestial sphere. The gravitational influences of the other planets cause a much smaller amount of precession.

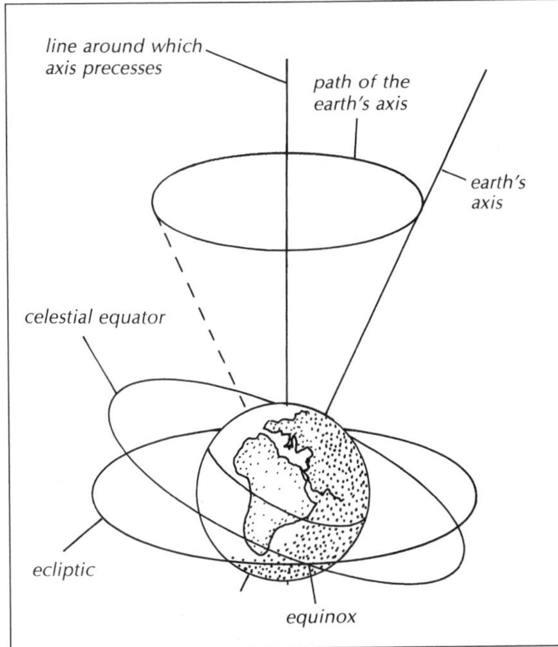

Precession of the equinoxes (the points at which the earth's celestial equator intersects its ecliptic) is due to the slow rotation of the earth's axis around a perpendicular to the ecliptic.

precipitate, a solid obtained by precipitation, i.e., the separation of a substance from a SUSPENSION, sol (see COLLOID), or SOLUTION. In a suspension, such as sand in water, the solid spontaneously precipitates (settles out) on standing. In a sol the particles are precipitated by coagulation. A solute may be precipitated by evaporation or by the addition of a compound that reacts with the solute to form an insoluble precipitate. In each case, the precipitate formed may settle out spontaneously or may be collected by filtration or centrifugation.

pre-Columbian art and architecture. Long before Europeans arrived in the Western Hemisphere, Mexico, Central America, and the Andean region of South America were the site of indigenous civilizations whose remains reveal exceptional artistic achievement. The MAYA of Yucatán and adjacent areas of Central America developed (300 B.C.–A.D. 300) an elaborate calendar, monumental palaces and pyramids, polychrome pottery, stone stelae, and stylized wall paintings and bas-reliefs. Their diverse architectural styles are seen at Tikal, Piedras Negras, Palenque, and UXMAL. The OLMEC civilization, to the west, is noted for its stone carvings: small, detailed jade objects and colossal, realistic basalt heads. The finest Olmec period, 800–400 B.C., is typified by objects found at La Venta. To the west of the Olmec and Maya regions was TEOTIHUACÁN, an extraordinary urban center of pyramids, temples, and royal processional roads dating from the 1st cent. A.D. to 700. To the south are the ruins of Copán and Quiriguá, with their huge, elaborately carved stelae. More delicate forms are seen in the stucco sculptures of Palenque. After Teotihuacán was destroyed (c.700) by invaders, much of north and central Mexico was dominated by the TOLTEC, who invaded such Maya areas as CHICHÉN ITZÁ (c.987) and influenced local styles. The last native conquerors were the AZTEC, whose civilization fell to the Spanish in 1519. By 1344 the Aztec had founded a magnificent capital, Tenochtitlán, on the site of present-day MEXICO CITY. Its eclectic style drew on traditions of conquered areas and reflected the harsh Aztec religion in carved depictions of human sacrifice. Craftsmen of subjugated groups, especially the MIXTEC, created magnificent works in jade, gold, feathers, pottery, and textiles. The Mixtec and ZAPOTEC built superb architectural and decorative structures in OAXACA, at Monte Albán and Mitla, until A.D. c.900. Ceramic figurines of early date (c.500 B.C.) have been found at Tlatilco, in the Valley of Mexico. Fanciful, often grotesque terra-cotta figurines were created (A.D. c.300–900) in the western Mexican states of Nayarit, Jalisco, and Colima. In Peru, pre-Inca cultures produced such splendid works as the Cupisnique pottery of the north coast, the pottery and textiles of Paracas, and the pottery of the NAZCA and Mochica civilizations. The painted portrait heads of the Mochica are the high point of realism in pre-Columbian art. Their Pyramid of the Sun, the largest in South America, attests to their gifts as builders. Other pre-Inca cultures include the TIAHUANACO and the CHIMU. The Chimu capital, CHAN CHAN, was a great center until the INCA conquered the Chimu in the 15th cent. The cities of CUZCO and MACHU PICCHU and the fortresses of Sacsacsahuamán and Ollantaytambo show the unsurpassed engineering skill of the Inca. Their stone carving and metalwork is of the highest quality in the world. The Inca civilization was conquered by the Spanish in 1538.

predestination, in theology, doctrine that asserts that God predestines from eternity the salvation of certain souls. So-called double predestination, as in Calvinism, is the added assertion that God also foreordains certain souls to damnation. Based on the omniscience and omnipotence of God, predestination is closely related to the doctrines of divine providence and grace. The Roman Catholic Church teaches that predestination is consistent with FREE WILL since God moves the soul according to its nature. Calvinism rejects the role of free will, maintaining that grace is irresistible.

preeclampsia: see TOXEMIA.

pregnancy and birth. *Pregnancy,* the process in which the female mammal carries and nurtures within it the developing young, is the period between fertilization of an egg (conception) and expulsion of a developed fetus (birth). Once fertilized, an egg divides into a tiny ball of cells and embeds itself in the wall of the uterus, a muscular, expandable organ. At this early stage of development, the growing organism is called the embryo. Some cells of the embryo develop into the placenta (a disk of tissue that brings nourishment from the mother and accepts waste substances from the fetus); the umbilical cord (the cord between embryo and placenta, carrying nutrients and waste); and the protective amniotic sac and fluid surrounding the embryo. During the course of human pregnancy, changes take place in the mother's body to meet the fetal demands on it: The uterus and breasts enlarge, and blood composition and volume change. It takes about 280 days for the embryo (in later stages called the fetus) to develop the structures and organs of a fully formed human. *Birth* is the process by which the fetus is expelled from the uterus. Rhythmic contractions of the uterus, called labor, dilate the neck (cervix) of the uterus and expel the baby and later the placenta. *Natural childbirth* is birth with little or no use of painkilling drugs. In the Lamaze method, prospective parents are taught physical and mental techniques for reducing pain and discomfort and participating more fully in the birth process. Birth by the "Leboyer method" emphasizes extremely gentle handling of the newborn. CESAREAN SECTION is delivery of an infant by removing it from the uterus surgically. See also AMNIOCENTESIS; CHORIONIC VILLUS SAMPLING; GYNECOLOGY; MIDWIFERY.

prehistoric man: see HUMAN EVOLUTION.

premenstrual syndrome (PMS), any of various symptoms experienced by women of childbearing age in the days immediately preceding MENSTRUATION. The symptoms include behavioral changes, emotional upsets, swelling and soreness of the breasts, and headaches. Some 70–90% of menstruating women are said to have PMS on a cyclical basis. The exact cause is unknown, but it may be due to various hormonal imbalances.

premier: see PRIME MINISTER.

Prendergast, Maurice Brazil, 1859–1924, American painter; b. St. John's, N.F., Canada. A member of the EIGHT, Prendergast traveled to Europe many times and evolved a style akin to POST-IMPRESSIONISM but executed with freer brush strokes. His landscapes and figure compositions evoke the quality of a lively tapestry, e.g., *Promenade, Gloucester* (Whitney Mus., N.Y.C.).

Pre-Raphaelites, brotherhood of English painters and poets, formed in 1848 to protest low standards in British art. The principal founders were D.G. ROSSETTI, W. Holman HUNT, and John MILLAIS. They turned from the materialism of industrialized England, seeking refuge through literary symbolism and imagery in the beauty and simplicity of the medieval world. Influenced by the NAZARENES, they imitated the innocence of style of Italian painters prior to RAPHAEL. They attracted numerous followers, e.g., Edward BURNE-JONES and William MORRIS, before the movement disbanded after 1853. Their works are nostalgic in tone, and brightly colored, with meticulous detail and mannered style.

Presbyterianism, form of Christian church organization based upon administration by a hierarchy of courts composed of clerical and lay presbyters. In polity it stands between episcopacy and CONGREGATIONALISM. Presbyters (or elders) manage the spiritual conduct of the church; deacons and trustees may handle temporal affairs. The church courts, from lowest to highest, are the court of the congregation or session; the presbytery or colloquy; the synod; and the general assembly, presided over by a moderator. Presbyterianism is the main branch of the Reformed churches and embodies the principles of CALVINISM. It holds the Bible as the sole rule of faith and has two sacraments, baptism and the Lord's Supper. Calvinism first influenced the churches of Geneva and of the HUGUENOTS, and John KNOX founded (1557) a Presbyterian church in Scotland. Francis MAKEMIE, an Irish missionary, set up the first presbytery in America at Philadelphia in 1706. In 1983 the United Presbyterian Church in the United States of America and the Presbyterian Church in the United States merged to form the Presbyterian Church (USA). It has about 2.9 million members. In Europe the Church of Scotland, the Calvinistic Methodist Church in Wales, the Presbyterian Church of England, and the Presbyterian Church of Ireland are major Presbyterian bodies.

preschool education: see HEAD START; KINDERGARTEN; NURSERY SCHOOL.

Prescott, William Hickling, 1796–1859, American historian; b. Salem, Mass. He is famous for two colorful, vivid accounts of the exploits of the CONQUISTADORS, *History of the Conquest of Mexico* (1843) and *The Conquest of Peru* (1847).

preserving: see CANNING.

president, head of state and often head of government in modern REPUBLICS. Presidential powers vary widely. In parliamentary republics, such as India and Italy, the office is largely ceremonial, with executive power exercised by the PRIME MINISTER or premier. In France and Russia the president has considerable power but shares some executive functions with the premier. In the U.S. the president is the head of state and commander in chief of the armed forces, as well as the chief executive officer, responsible for carrying out the law. A U.S. citizen must be at least 35 years old and native-born to be president, and can serve only two four-year terms. In some countries presidents have assumed dictatorial powers, occasionally installing themselves as "president for life."

presidium: see POLITBURO.

Presley, Elvis, 1935–77, American singer; b. Tupelo, Miss. Influenced by rhythm and blues and COUNTRY AND WESTERN MUSIC, he played guitar and rose to stardom in 1956, dominating ROCK MUSIC until 1963. In performance he had a pleasant baritone voice and an aggressive, sexual delivery. His hits include "Heartbreak Hotel" and "Don't Be Cruel."

press, freedom of the, liberty to print information and opinions without prior government restraint. The publisher is legally responsible for what is printed and can be sued for LIBEL and other infringements of the law. The struggle against CENSORSHIP began in England in the 16th–17th cent. In the American colonies it began in 1734, when the John Peter ZENGER case established the precedent that criticism that is true is not libelous. Freedom of the press, guaranteed by the federal government under the 1st amendment to the U.S. CONSTITUTION, is guaranteed by the states under the 14th amendment. Restrictions have occurred, however. During WORLD WAR I the Espionage (1917) and Sedition (1918) acts censored pro-German publications. Justice Oliver Wendell HOLMES set down (1919) a criterion of "clear and present danger," still a guideline for Congress and the courts. In WORLD WAR II the Office of Censorship obtained general voluntary compliance. Censorship for national security reasons was carefully limited by the Supreme Court in the "Pentagon Papers" case (1971), in which the *New York Times* was allowed to print secret government documents concerning the Vietnam War. Freedom of the press may also be limited by restricted access to government information; this concerned was addressed by the FREEDOM OF INFORMATION ACT. The extension of freedom of the press to the electronic media is complicated by the fact that radio and television airwaves are public property, and that broadcasters operate under licensing agreements.

pressure, ratio of the force acting on a surface to the area of the surface. A fluid (liquid or gas) exerts a pressure on all bodies immersed in it. For a fluid at rest, the difference in pressure between two points in it depends upon only the density of the fluid and the difference in depth or altitude between the two points. Atmospheric pressure is measured with a BAROMETER. Other instruments for measuring pressure are commonly termed pressure gauges; they include the Bourdon gauge and the manometer. See also ARCHIMEDES' PRINCIPLE; GAS LAWS; HYDRAULIC MACHINERY.

Prester John, legendary Christian priest and king who ruled over a vast, wealthy empire in either Asia or Africa. Dating from the 12th cent., his legend was fueled in the Middle Ages by widely circulated letters purporting to be his.

pretor: see PRAETOR.

Pretoria, city (1985 pop. 443,059), administrative capital of South Africa and of TRANSVAAL prov. The city has important industries, especially iron and steel, as well as automobile assembly plants, railroad and machine shops, and flour mills. Founded in 1855, it became the capital of the South African Republic (the Transvaal) in 1860.

Pretorius, Andries Wilhelmus Jacobus, 1799–1853, Boer leader. His defeat (1838) of the ZULUS led to the founding of the Boer Republic of Natal. In 1848 he created the nucleus of what became the TRANSVAAL. The city of PRETORIA is named for him. His son, **Martinus Wessel Pretorius,** 1818?–1901, became the first president (1857–77) of the Transvaal; concurrently he was president (1859–63) of the Orange Free State. After Britain annexed the Transvaal in 1877, he served with Paul KRUGER in a government opposed to British rule. See also SOUTH AFRICA.

preventive medicine, medical practice that focuses on preventing physical or mental illness in the individual or the community. It encompasses such activities as VACCINATION, diet and health counseling, various diagnostic procedures, public hygiene, and educational campaigns. Modern dentistry has made extensive use of preventive techniques in reducing tooth and gum disease.

Previn, André, 1929–, American conductor, composer, and pianist; b. Germany, as Andreas Ludwig Priwin. He has recorded classical music since 1946, and in the 1950s he made a number of highly successful JAZZ piano albums. He has also composed film scores. Previn conducted the London Symphony (1968–79) and Royal Philharmonic (1987–92) and served as musical director of the Pittsburgh Symphony (1976–1984), Los Angeles Philharmonic (1984–89), and Royal Philharmonic (1985–86).

Prevost, Sir George [pre'vō], 1767–1816, British soldier and governor in chief (1811–15) of CANADA. As commander of British forces in the WAR OF 1812 he was publicly humiliated for a British retreat (1813) and defeat (1814) at Plattsburg.

Prévost d'Exiles, Antoine François [prāvō'dāgzēl'], known as **Abbé Prévost,** 1697–1763, French author. He entered a Benedictine abbey (1720), but fled (1728) to lead an adventurous life in England, Holland, and Germany. Returning to France, he was named head of a priory (1754) by the pope. Of his writings, only the brilliant psychological novel *Manon Lescaut* is still widely read.

Priam, in Greek mythology, king of Troy, husband of HECUBA.

priapulid, member of a small phylum (Priapulida) of predatory unsegmented marine worms that live in the sand and mud at the sea bottom. The largest are 4–6 in. (10–17 cm) long, but most species are less than .05 in. (.2 cm) in size. They have a spiny body with an anterior that can be everted or inverted into the trunk for locomotion or feeding.

Price, (Mary) Leontyne, 1927–, African-American soprano; b. Laurel, Miss. She has sung at the METROPOLITAN OPERA (N.Y.C.) since 1961, and is known for the range and power of her voice, e.g., in the title roles of VERDI's *Aïda* and PUCCINI's *Madame Butterfly*.

Pride, Thomas, d. 1658, parliamentary soldier in the ENGLISH CIVIL WAR. Acting on orders of the army council, he undertook (Dec. 1648) **Pride's Purge,** expelling 143 members (mostly Presbyterians) from Parliament on grounds they were royalists.

Priestley, J(ohn) B(oynton), 1894–1984, English writer. His works include criticism, e.g., *The English Novel* (1927); novels such as *Bright Day* (1946); social and experimental drama, e.g., *The Glass Cage* (1957); history; mysteries; and social criticism.

Priestley, Joseph, 1733–1804, English theologian and scientist. Trained for the Presbyterian ministry, he later adopted Unitarian views and wrote widely on theological and philosophical issues. His improved techniques for studying gases led to his discovery of sulfur dioxide, ammonia, and what he called "dephlogisticated air," the gas that Antoine LAVOISIER named OXYGEN. He was an opponent of orthodox doctrines, England's colonial policy, and the slave trade. Due to his sympathy with the aims of the French Revolution, his house was wrecked and his library and laboratory were destroyed. In 1794 he emigrated to the U.S.

primate, member of the mammalian order Primates, which includes human beings, APES (e.g., GIBBONS, ORANGUTANS, CHIMPANZEES, and GORILLAS), MONKEYS (e.g., BABOONS and MANDRILLS), and prosimians, or lower primates (e.g., TREE SHREWS, LEMURS). Nearly all inhabit warm climates and are arboreal, although a few are terrestrial. Unspecialized anatomically, primates are distinguished by social organization and evolutionary trends within the order tending toward increased dexterity and intelligence.

Primaticcio, Francesco [prēmätēt'chō], 1504–70, Italian painter, called Le Primatice by the French. He was influenced by GIULIO ROMANO's methods of illusionism. Invited (1532) by FRANCIS I of France to help decorate the castle at Fontainebleau, he became director of the project in 1540. Only a few of his works there survive. He decorated other châteaus, designed tomb monuments for Francis I and Henry II, and extended the influence of Italian art in France.

prime meridian, meridian designated 0° LONGITUDE, from which all other longitudes are measured. By international convention, it passes through the original site of the Royal Observatory in GREENWICH, England. For this reason it is often called the Greenwich meridian.

prime minister or **premier,** in parliamentary systems, the head of government, but not of state, and chief member of the CABINET. Under the procedure evolved in Great Britain and followed by most parliamentary systems, the officeholder is the leader of the party with a majority of members in the legislature and is himself or herself a member of that body. If support is lost in the legislature, the prime minister is expected to resign. In France and Russia the premier, appointed by the president, has fewer powers than the premiers of many other countries.

prime number: see NUMBER THEORY.

prime rate: see INTEREST.

primitivism, in art, fresh and fanciful style of works by untrained artists such as Henri ROUSSEAU and Grandma MOSES; also, the style of early American naïve painters such as Edward HICKS and various European schools prior to c.1450.

Primo de Rivera, Miguel [prē'mō t͟hā rēvä'rä], 1870–1930, Spanish dictator (1923–30). Seizing power in a coup (1923), he dissolved the CORTES and established a military directory. Although his military government was replaced (1925) by a civil one, he continued to rule with an iron hand. After a liberal uprising failed (1929), he was forced to resign (1930) because of his government's economic failures.

primrose, name for the genus *Primula* of the family Primulaceae, low perennial herbs found on all continents. The family includes the primroses, cyclamens (genus *Cyclamen*), and pimpernels (genus *Anagallis*). Species of all these genera are cultivated as rock-garden, border, and pot plants. The primrose is a common and favored wildflower of England, and several species are indigenous to North America. The EVENING PRIMROSE is not a true primrose. Cyclamens are chiefly native to the Alps; *C. indicum* is a common florists' pot plant in the U.S. The scarlet pimpernel (*A. arvensis*), native to Eurasia but naturalized in the U.S., has flowers that close on the approach of bad weather.

Prince Edward Island, province (1991 pop. 129,765), 2,184 sq mi (5,657 sq km), E Canada. Canada's smallest and least populous province, it is separated from New Brunswick and Nova Scotia by the Northumberland Strait. CHARLOTTETOWN is the capital. One of the Maritime Provinces, Prince Edward Island has generally low, level land and is c.140 mi (225 km) long and up to 35 mi (56 km) wide. White sandy beaches line the deeply indented north shore, where Prince Edward Island National Park attracts many tourists. Much of its economy depends on government (federal and provincial) spending and employment. Fishing is an important industry, and livestock, fruits, vegetables, and potatoes are also produced. Manufacturing is largely limited to food processing. Jacques CARTIER landed on the island in 1534, and CHAMPLAIN named it Île St. Jean in 1603. The French made the first permanent settlement in 1719, and the British gained permanent control of the island in 1763. That year the island was annexed to Nova Scotia, but it became a separate colony in 1769. In 1799 it was renamed in honor of Edward, duke of Kent. Lord SELKIRK established (1803) a colony of Scots there, and their descendants still form a large part of the population. Responsible (cabinet) government was achieved in 1851. In 1864 delegates from the Maritime Provinces met at Charlottetown to discuss union, the first step toward Canadian confederation, achieved in 1867. Prince Edward Island did not join the confederation until 1873. Catherine Callbeck became Canada's first female provincial premier in 1993 when she led the Liberals to a sweep. The province sends four senators (appointed) and four representatives (elected) to the national parliament.

Princeton, borough (1990 pop. 12,016) and adjacent township (1990 pop. 13,198), W N.J.; settled late 1600s, borough inc. 1813. It is the seat of Princeton Univ., the Inst. for Advanced Study, other educational institutions, and many corporate headquarters and research centers. Princeton was the scene of a Revolutionary War victory by WASHINGTON's army (Jan. 3, 1777), and the university's administration building, Nassau Hall, was the seat of the CONTINENTAL CONGRESS from June to Nov. 1783. Princeton was the birthplace of Paul ROBESON and the home of Albert EINSTEIN.

Princeton University, at Princeton, N.J. Founded in 1746 as the College of New Jersey, at Elizabeth, N.J., by evangelical Presbyterians, it was moved in 1756 to Princeton, where it was to become one of the nation's leading institutions of higher education. It gained university status in 1896 and, under Woodrow WILSON, introduced (1905) the preceptorial system, which led to a greater degree of individualized instruction. In addition to its college and graduate school, Princeton is noted for its school of public and international affairs and for plasma physics, aerospace, and population research.

printed circuit, ELECTRIC CIRCUIT in which the metallic conducting paths connecting circuit components are affixed to a flat, insulating base board typically composed of plastic, glass, ceramic, or some other DIELECTRIC. Conducting paths may be placed on the base by etching, die stamping, or spraying the pattern through a stencil or mask. The circuit components, such as RESISTORS and CAPACITORS, are not usually produced by these processes but rather are mounted afterward on the base.

printer, COMPUTER output device that records data as a sequence of discrete alphanumeric or graphic characters on paper or another medium. *Impact printers* use a mechanical hammering device to produce each character. A formed character printer forces metal or plastic characters against an inked ribbon to produce a sharp image on paper; the characters may be on a moving bar, a rapidly rotating chain, a rotatable ball, or wheel spokes. A *dot matrix printer* uses a matrix of tiny pegs that, when hit from behind against a ribbon, impart a set of dots to form a character on the paper; a wide variety of characters and graphics are created using different dot combinations. Non-impact printers use thermal and electrostatic, rather than mechanical, techniques. *Bubble-jet printers* (or *ink-jet printers*) squirt heated ink through a matrix of holes to form characters. *Laser printers* form an image of the output on a selenium-coated drum using laser light that is turned on and off by data from the computer and then transfer the output from the drum using PHOTOCOPYING techniques. *Thermal-wax-transfer printers* and *dye-sublimation printers* use heat to transfer color pigment from a ribbon to a special paper to produce photographic-quality color images.

printing, the reproduction of lettered or illustrated matter through the use of mechanical, photographic, or electrostatic devices. In addition to the letters themselves, the elements involved in printing include the press and various methods for setting type and for making the reproducing printing surface, or plate. The press used by Johannes GUTENBERG in 15th-cent. Germany was a hand press, in which ink was rolled over the raised surfaces of hand-set letters held within a form and the form was then pressed against a sheet of paper. The hand press remained in use for all forms of printing until the early 19th cent. A steam-powered press with a flat type-bed was used by *The Times* of London beginning in 1814. In 1847 the American Richard Hoe developed a high-speed rotary press in which the printing surface was wrapped around a cylinder. Later presses used continuous rolls of PAPER and incorporated folding, cutting, and paper-moving devices that vastly increased printing speed. The first mechanical typesetter, the Linotype machine, was invented by Ottmar Mergenthaler in 1884. Operated by a typewriter-keyboard, it assembles brass matrices into a line and casts the line as a single metal slug. Other machine-set type systems were developed, notably the Monotype (first used in 1897), which casts individual characters from a punched tape produced by a keyboard operator. The development of photocomposed "cold type" (as distinguished from "hot," or cast-metal, type) has further increased typesetting speeds. Computerized phototypesetters project the digitized images of type onto a film that is then used to make a plate. **Letterpress** is printing from a raised, inked surface. Various inventions have improved the letterpress printing surface, especially the stereotype, which can produce a large metal plate of a newspaper page from a mold made of pulp; and the later electrotype, which uses an electrolytic process to create a curved metal plate. In **intaglio,** the design to be produced is cut below the surface of the plate, and the incised lines are filled with ink that is then transferred to paper (see ENGRAVING; ETCHING). Photogravure is an intaglio process in which the plate is produced photographically. **Offset,** or **planographic, printing,** derived from LITHOGRAPHY, uses a plate treated so that ink will adhere only to the areas that will print the design. The plate transfers its ink to a rubber cylinder, which in turn offsets it onto paper. Color printing is achieved by photographically separating four basic colors (black, magenta, yellow, and cyan, a blue-green) from the original picture, making a plate for each color, then using the plates to print the colors consecutively over one another. See also PHOTOCOPYING.

prion, unidentified infectious agent thought to cause a group of human and animal diseases (Creutzfeldt-Jacob disease, kuru, scrapie, bovine spongiform encephalitis) known as **prion diseases.** The diseases slowly attack brain tissue, often leaving microscopic spongelike holes, and are characterized by accumulations of abnormal forms of a protein, called *prion protein,* that occurs naturally in brain tissue. Prion dieases have both hereditary and infectious components; some scientists believe the abnormal prion protein is the infectious agent. There is no effective treatment. See also SLOW VIRUS.

Priscian (Priscianus Caesariensis) [prĭsh'ən], fl. 500, Latin grammarian who taught at Constantinople. His *Commentarii grammatici,* in 18 books, long a standard text, was the basis of work by Rabanus Maurus in the Middle Ages.

prism, in optics, a piece of translucent glass or crystal with a triangular cross section, used to form a SPECTRUM of light by separating it according to colors. Prisms are also used in optical instruments, such as binoculars, for changing the direction of light rays by total internal reflection.

prison, place of confinement for the punishment and rehabilitation of criminals. By the late 18th cent. in Europe, when imprisonment punished all but capital crimes, Cesare BECCARIA and John Howard began urging reform of inhumane conditions, efforts continued in the 19th cent. by Elizabeth FRY and, in the U.S., by Dorothea DIX. Irish influences led to the practice of parole. In the U.S., 20th-cent. reforms, aimed primarily at rehabilitation, include psychiatric aid, vocational training, and work-release programs, although the notorious chain gangs, in which chained convicts are forced to do heavy labor, and corporal punishment have not entirely disappeared. U.S. prisons range from local jails to state and federal penitentiaries, with special facilities for juveniles, the sick, and the criminally insane. Overcrowding, tense race relations, and insufficiently professional correctional staffs contributed to major riots in U.S. prisons in recent decades, and rates of recidivism (return to crime) among prisoners have remained high. Since 1982 many states have used prison "boot camps" with military-like regimens in an attempt to shock first offenders and bolster their self-esteem, as well as lower the long-term costs of crime and imprisonment, but the results of such programs are unclear.

Pritchett, V(ictor) S(awdon), 1905–, English writer. A craftsman who has contributed to several genres, he is best known for his short stories, collected in many volumes, e.g., *Complete Collected Stories* (1991). Other works include *A Cab at the Door* (1968) and *Midnight Oil* (1972), memoirs; and *The Tale Bearers* (1980), literary essays.

privacy, right of, the right to be protected from unwarranted intrusion by the government, media, or other institutions or individuals. The U.S Supreme Court decision in GRISWOLD V. CONNECTICUT (1965) banned intrusion into marital privacy as a violation of constitutional rights, and sexual privacy was a main foundation of the court's ROE V. WADE decision (1973) overturning state ABORTION statutes. The Privacy Act of 1974 provides for disclosure of, and personal access to, all federal records containing personal information, regulates their transfer to others, and allows for legal remedies in cases of their misuse under the law. The Right to Financial Privacy Act (1978) limits federal access to financial records but places few restrictions on access by states, businesses, and others. The privacy of most other information is not guaranteed. Computer and telecommunications advances have made credit, medical, and other data a readily available, highly marketable commodity, raising many concerns about individuals' privacy.

privatization, return of businesses to private ownership after they have been the property of the state. It is the reverse of NATIONALIZATION. With the collapse of the Soviet empire and its Communist economies, the trend toward privatization has been particularly strong in the nations of the former USSR and Eastern Europe. Privatization has also increased in Western Europe, e.g., Great Britain and France, and in many underdeveloped nations as socialism has lost credibility. In the U.S., the term has often been broadly applied to the contracting out of the management of public schools, prisons, airports, sanitation services, and a variety of other government-owned institutions, especially at the state and local levels.

probability, branch of MATHEMATICS that measures the likelihood that an event will occur. The theory of probability was first developed by Blaise PASCAL in the 17th cent. as a means of solving gambling problems; it was advanced by Pierre de LAPLACE in the early 19th cent. Given an experiment (e.g., tossing a coin), each possible outcome is assigned a number, called a probability measure, that corresponds to its chance of occurring. Probabilities must be between 0 and 1 inclusive (0 corresponding to impossibility, 1 to certainty), and the sum of all probabilities of simple outcomes of an experiment must be 1. For example, if a symmetrical coin is to be tossed, both possible outcomes, heads and tails, have probabilities of ½, because they have equal chances of occurring. Probabilities are often assigned on the basis of relative frequency of occurrence. For example, if weather records for 40 years show that the sun shone 32 times on July 1, then one would assign a probability of 32/40, or 4/5, to the event that the sun will shine on July 1. Similar probability computations are used in insurance calculations. By adding or multiplying the probabilities of simple events, one can determine the probabilities of compound events, e.g., the probability that a husband and wife will both live to be 70. Sometimes sophisticated counting techniques, such as PERMUTATIONS AND COMBINATIONS, must be used. The application of probability to data collected from samples is the province of STATISTICS.

Procopius [prōkō'pēəs], d. 565?, Byzantine historian. His high connections and public offices give his histories great value as first-hand accounts. His chief works are *Procopius's History of His Own Time* and the largely scandalous and often scurrilous court chronicle *Secret History of Procopius.*

prodigal son, parable of JESUS about a young man who leaves home and becomes a wastrel; repentant, he returns and is received with joyful welcome.

productivity, in economics, the output of any aspect of production per unit of input. It is a measure of the output of a worker, machine, or an entire national economy in the creation of goods and services to produce wealth. Output can be measured in output per acre for land, per hour for labor, or as a yearly percentage for capital. A high national productivity typically indicates efficient production of goods and services and a competitive economy.

profit, in economics, the amount of money remaining from a business enterprise after all expenses, including taxes, have been paid. It is also called return on capital, or earnings. The various kinds of profit include that of the entrepreneur, as payment for management or risk-taking; that of the capitalist, in the form of interest; and that of the landlord, in the form of rent. Profit is the major incentive for production in a capitalist country, but with the rise of a salaried managerial class it has become less personal and more institutional in character.

progeria, syndrome of unknown etiology causing premature aging in children; also known as Hutchinson-Gilford syndrome. Affected children appear normal up to the first year of life. Gradually, characteristics of the disorder become apparent—retarded growth and physical development, loss of body fat, absence of body hair, and baldness. Eventually the child develops dry, wrinkled skin, ARTERIOSCLEROSIS, and other conditions associated with old age. There is no treatment, and death occurs by the second decade.

progesterone, female sex hormone that induces changes in the lining of the uterus essential for implantation of a fertilized egg (see MENSTRUATION). In a pregnant woman, progesterone prevents spontaneous abortion (miscarriage) and prepares the MAMMARY GLANDS for milk production.

programming language, syntax, grammar, and symbols or words used to give instructions to a COMPUTER. Because computers work with binary numbers (see NUMERATION), first-generation languages, called machine languages, required the writing of long strings of binary numbers to represent such operations as add, subtract, and compare. Later improvements allowed octal, decimal, or hexadecimal representation of binary strings. It is difficult to write error-free programs in machine language; many languages have been created to make programming easier and faster. Symbolic, or assembly, languages—second-generation languages—were introduced in the early 1950s. They use simple mnemonics such as "A" for add or "M" for multiply, which are translated into machine language by a COMPUTER PROGRAM called an assembler. An extension of such a language is the macro instruction, a mnemonic (such as "READ") for which the assembler substitutes a series of simpler mnemonics. In the mid-1950s, a third generation of languages came into use. Called high-level languages because they are largely independent of the hardware, these algorithmic, or procedural, languages are designed for solving a particular type of problem. Unlike machine or symbolic languages, they vary little between computers. They must be translated into machine code by a program called a *compiler* or *interpreter.* The first such language was FORTRAN (*FOR*mula *TRAN*slation), developed about 1956 and best used for scientific calculation. The first commercial language, COBOL (*CO*mmon *B*usiness *O*riented *L*anguage), was developed about 1959. ALGOL (*ALGO*rithmic *L*anguage), developed in Europe about 1958, is used primarily in mathematics and science, as is APL (*A P*rogramming *L*anguage), published in 1962. PL/1 (*P*rogramming *L*anguage *1*), developed in the late 1960s, and ADA (for Ada Augusta, countess of Lovelace, biographer of Charles BABBAGE), developed in 1981, are designed for both business and scientific use. For PERSONAL COMPUTERS the most popular languages are BASIC (*B*eginners *A*ll-purpose *S*ymbolic *I*nstruction *C*ode), developed in 1967 and similar to FORTRAN, and Pascal (for Blaise PASCAL, who built the first successful mechanical calculator), introduced in 1971 as a teaching language. Modula 2, a Pascal-like language for commercial and mathematical applications, was introduced in 1982. The C language, introduced (1972) to implement the Unix operating system, has been extended to C++ to deal with the rigors of OBJECT-ORIENTED PROGRAMMING. Fourth-generation languages are nonprocedural—they specify what is to be accomplished without describing how. The first one, FORTH, developed in 1970, is used in scientific and industrial control applications. Most fourth-generation languages are written for specific purposes. Fifth-generation languages, which are still in infancy, are an outgrowth of ARTIFICIAL INTELLIGENCE research. PROLOG (*PRO*gramming *LOG*ic) is useful for programming logical processes and making deductions automatically. Many other languages have been designed to meet specialized needs. GPSS (*G*eneral *P*urpose *S*ystem *S*imulator) is used for modeling physical and environmental events, and SNOBOL (*S*tring-*O*riented *S*ymbolic *L*anguage) and LISP (*LIS*t *P*rocessing) are designed for pattern matching and list processing. LOGO, a version of LISP, was developed in the 1960s to help children learn about computers. PILOT (*P*rogrammed *I*nstruction *L*earning, *O*r *T*esting) is used in writing instructional software, and Occam is a nonsequential language that optimizes the execution of a program's instructions in PARALLEL-PROCESSING systems.

program trading, form of computerized securities trading, also known as **index arbitrage.** Program traders exploit price differences between stock-index futures and the stocks represented by such futures using sophisticated computer programs, simultaneously monitoring and making trades in the commodity and stock markets. Program trading was widely blamed for the stock market crash on Oct. 19, 1987 (see BLACK MONDAY). Restrictions on, and the opposition of businesses to, such trades have since led most brokerage firms to abandon the practice.

progression, in mathematics, SEQUENCE of quantities, called terms, with a fixed relationship between consecutive terms. In an *arithmetic progression* each term is derived from the preceding one by adding a given number d, called the common difference. An example is 3, 7, 11, 15, . . . , where $d = 4$. The nth, or general, term is $a + (n - 1)d$, where a is the first term. In a *geometric progression* each term is derived by multiplying the preceding term by a given number r, called the common ratio. In the sequence 1, 3, 9, 27, . . . , for example, $r = 3$. The nth term is ar^{n-1}. In a *harmonic progression* the terms are the reciprocals of the terms of an arithmetic progression, e.g., $\frac{1}{3}$, $\frac{1}{7}$, $\frac{1}{11}$, $\frac{1}{15}$, ...

Progressive Conservative party, Canadian political party formed (1942) by the merger of the Conservative party and elements of the Progressive party. The Conservative party, which advocated strong ties to Britain and national economic development, dominated post-confederation (1867) Canadian politics. After the 19th cent., it was in relative decline. The 1942 merger led the party to advocate a more reform-minded program, and John DIEFENBAKER, prime minister from 1957 to 1963, forged a new party base in the W provinces. The issue of autonomy for Quebec, however, contributed to the two decades of mostly Liberal rule that followed. Progressive Conservative leader Brian MULRONEY was prime minister from 1986 to 1993, when the unpopularity of his economic policies led him to resign. Kim CAMPBELL, the party's and Canada's first female leader, briefly governed and led the party (1993) before she and all but two of the party's parliamentary candidates were rejected at the polls. She was succeeded as party leader by Jean Charest.

progressive education, movement in American education. Between the late-19th and mid-20th cent. many educational programs grew out of the American reform effort called the progressive movement and its sources in the philosophies of Jean Jacques ROUSSEAU, Johann PESTALOZZI, and Friedrich FROEBEL. A pluralistic phenomenon, it embraced industrial training, agricultural and social education, and educational theorists' new instructional techniques. The progressives insisted that education be a continuous reconstruction of living experience, with the child the center of concern. John DEWEY maintained that schools should reflect society. His Laboratory School in Chicago (1896–1904), the public schools of Gary, Ind., and Winnetka, Ill., and such independent schools as the Dalton School and the Lincoln School of Teachers College, Columbia Univ. (both N.Y.C.), were notable progressive institutions. Progressive education gained wide acceptance in American schools in the first half of the 20th cent., and by the

1950s, after its alleged collapse, the progressive movement had effected a permanent transformation in the character of the American school. Other reform movements in education similar to, or affected by, progressive education include the open classroom and the reforms of Maria MONTESSORI.

Progressive party, three separate political organizations that were active in the presidential elections of 1912, 1924, and 1948. The first Progressive party (the Bull Moose party) was formed by dissident Republicans who supported former Pres. Theodore ROOSEVELT against Pres. William H. TAFT. Its platform called for the direct election of U.S. senators, WOMAN SUFFRAGE, and many social reforms. The party drew over 4 million votes, more than Taft received, and resulted in the election of the Democratic candidate, Woodrow WILSON. The second Progressive party nominated Sen. Robert M. LA FOLLETTE for president and advocated public control of natural resources and recognition of labor unions, among other reforms. La Follette polled nearly 5 million votes in 1924 but carried only his home state of Wisconsin. The party remained active in the state until 1946. The third Progressive party accused Pres. Harry S TRUMAN of fomenting the COLD WAR and ran the former vice president Henry A. WALLACE against him in 1948. Wallace polled only slightly more than 1 million votes as Truman won reelection.

prohibition, laws outlawing the manufacture and distribution of alcoholic beverages. In the 19th cent., U.S. TEMPERANCE MOVEMENTS urged prohibition, and the Prohibition party made it (1869) a national issue. It gained impetus in World War I, when conservation policies limited liquor output. In 1919 the 18th amendment to the CONSTITUTION established prohibition, but enforcement, through the VOLSTEAD ACT, failed to abolish bootlegging and the widespread lawbreaking associated with it. The 21st amendment repealed (1933) prohibition.

Prokofiev, Sergei Sergeyevich [prōkôf'ēĕf], 1891–1953, Russian composer. A student of GLIÈRE and RIMSKY-KORSAKOV, he toured the world as a pianist and conductor until 1938, when he returned to the USSR. His early works are often harsh and strident; later pieces are lyrical, simplified, and popular in style. Prokofiev's important works include seven symphonies, e.g., the *Classical Symphony* (1916–17); concertos; chamber music; operas, e.g., *The Love for Three Oranges* (1921); ballets, including *Romeo and Juliet* (1935–36; 1940); the symphonic fairy tale *Peter and the Wolf* (1936); and orchestral suites, e.g., *Lieutenant Kije* (1934).

proletariat, in Marxist theory, the class of workers who depend for their means of existence on the sale of their labor for purposes of industrial production. Karl MARX believed that this class, formed by the rise of CAPITALISM, would become the overwhelming majority, revolt against their exploitation, seize power from the BOURGEOISIE, or capitalist class, and create a classless society.

Prometheus, in Greek mythology, TITAN benefactor of man, whom, in one legend, he created. He stole fire from the gods, gave it to man, and taught him many arts and sciences. In retaliation, ZEUS plagued man with PANDORA and her box of evils, and chained Prometheus to a mountain, where an eagle preyed on his liver. In some myths HERCULES released him. Prometheus is the subject of many literary works, including AESCHYLUS' *Prometheus Bound* and SHELLEY's *Prometheus Unbound*.

promethium (Pm), artificially produced radioactive element, first identified definitely by J.A. Marinsky and colleagues in 1945 by ion-exchange chromatography. It is a RARE-EARTH METAL in the LANTHANIDE SERIES. The promethium-147 isotope is used in the making of phosphorescent materials, in nuclear-powered batteries for spacecraft, and as a radioactive tracer. See ELEMENT (table); PERIODIC TABLE.

pronghorn or **prongbuck,** hoofed herbivorous MAMMAL (*Antilocapra americana*) of the W U.S. and N Mexico. Related to the ANTELOPES, it is the size of a goat, with a light brown coat and pronged horns. It lives in small bands on open plains, browsing on shrubs and grasses. The pronghorn is the swiftest of North American mammals. Nearly exterminated by hunting, it is now protected.

propane ($CH_3CH_2CH_3$), colorless gaseous HYDROCARBON that occurs in NATURAL GAS and PETROLEUM. Propane is sold compressed in cylinders, often mixed with other hydrocarbons, and is used as fuel in lamps, gas grills, certain home and portable stoves, and certain cigarette lighters.

proper motion (μ), apparent angular motion of a star on the celestial sphere, usually measured in seconds of arc per year. A star's transverse velocity v_T, i.e., its motion across the line of sight to the star (as opposed to its RADIAL VELOCITY, or line-of-sight velocity), is calculated in kilometers per second from the equation $v_T = 4.74 \mu/p$, where p is the star's PARALLAX, expressed in seconds of arc.

Propertius, Sextus, c.50 B.C.–c.16 B.C., Roman elegiac poet, a member of the circle of MAECENAS. A master of the Latin ELEGY, he wrote with vigor and passion.

property, in law, the right of ownership, i.e., the exclusive right to possess, enjoy, and dispose of an object of value; also, the object of value possessed, enjoyed, and disposed of by right of ownership. Modern Anglo-American property law provides for the ownership of nearly all things of economic value; there are exceptions, such as the high seas or outer space, which are not subject to ownership. The law divides property into realty (real property) and personalty (personal property). Realty is chiefly land and improvements built thereon; personalty is chiefly movable objects whose distribution the owner can determine by sale, WILL, or gift. Realty, in medieval times, was the basis of wealth and the keystone of the social structure; its ownership was controlled to protect society. The ownership of personalty, being of minor importance, was almost unfettered. With the rise of commerce and a large landless middle class, personalty became the dominant form of property, and the law of realty gradually became assimilated in most respects into that of personalty. For special types of property, see COPYRIGHT, PATENT.

prophet, in the BIBLE, religious leader of Israel, especially in the period of the kingdoms and the Babylonian captivity. In Israel the prophet was believed to have been inspired by God to guide the chosen people. The Major Prophets are ISAIAH, JEREMIAH, EZEKIEL, and DANIEL. The Minor Prophets are HOSEA, JOEL, AMOS, OBADIAH, JONAH, MICAH, NAHUM, HABAKKUK, ZEPHANIAH, HAGGAI, ZECHARIAH, and MALACHI. The title is also given to others, e.g., MOSES and ELIJAH. A Christian belief is that the HOLY GHOST "spoke through the prophets" (Nicene CREED), who foretold the life and passion of Jesus. Some varieties of Protestantism (e.g., ANABAPTISTS) have emphasized "inspired" utterance or behavior. Islam recognizes MUHAMMAD as the last and greatest of the prophets.

proportion, in mathematics, the equality of two RATIOS. Two pairs of quantities a, b and c, d are in proportion if $a/b = c/d$. For example, the lengths of two sides of any triangle and the lengths of the corresponding two sides of any similar (same-shaped) triangle are in proportion.

proprietary medicine: see PATENT MEDICINE.

Proserpine: see PERSEPHONE.

prosimian: see PRIMATE.

prostate gland, gland in the male REPRODUCTIVE SYSTEM situated below the neck of the bladder, encircling the urethra. The prostate produces a thin, milky, alkaline fluid that is secreted into the urethra at the time of emission of semen, providing an added medium for the life and motility of sperm. Prostatic enlargement, common in men over 50, can interfere with urination; it is treated by surgically removing the prostate or by giving finasteride (Proscar), a drug that shrinks the enlarged gland.

prosthesis, an artificial replacement for a missing body part, or a device designed to improve a specific body function. Prostheses include artificial limbs, false teeth, hearing aids, artificial kidneys, and implanted pacemakers. Recent improvements have included lighter materials, more realistic appearance, and greater flexibility, which allow a more normal continuation of daily activities, including participation in such sports as skiing, basketball, and running.

prostitution, granting of sexual access for payment. An epidemic of SEXUALLY TRANSMITTED DISEASE in 16th-cent. Europe led to the first serious efforts to control prostitution, and public health considerations motivated much subsequent regulatory legislation. International cooperation to control the traffic in prostitutes began in 1899. In the U.S. James Robert Mann's White Slave Traffic Act (1910) forbade interstate and international transportation of women for immoral purposes. Today houses of prostitution are illegal in all states but Nevada. In Britain a parliamentary act of 1959 forbids open solicitation but permits the practice of prostitution at home. Some European nations regulate prostitution as a public health measure.

protactinium (Pa), radioactive element, discovered as a decay product of uranium-238 by K. Fajans and O. Göhring in 1913. A shiny silver-gray metal with 14 isotopes, it is found in uranium ores. Alpha decay of protactinium leads to formation of ACTINIUM. See ELEMENT (table); PERIODIC TABLE.

Protagoras, c.490–421 B.C., Greek philosopher. One of the leading SOPHISTS, he is most famous for the saying "Man is the measure of all things." He held that all truth is relative to the individual who holds it. Protagoras denied the possibility of objective knowledge and refused to differentiate between sense and reason. None of his works has survived, but his views are presented in the Platonic dialogue that bears his name.

protective coloration, in animals, coloration or color pattern that facilitates escape from observation by predators or prey or serves as a warning device to predators or others of the same species. The most widespread form of protective coloration is called cryptic resemblance, in which the coloration and patterns on the skin of the animal enable it to blend in with the coloration of its habitat. In some animals (e.g., the CHAMELEON), the pigmentation changes to resemble the surrounding environment. Some animals undergo a seasonal variation (e.g., the WEASEL, which is usually brown with white underparts, but in snowy regions acquires a white coat in winter and is known as an ERMINE).

protectorate, in international law, state which, while retaining nominal independence, surrenders part of its sovereignty, such as control over foreign affairs, in return for protection by a stronger state. (The relationship between the two states may also be termed a *protectorate.*) The territory of the protected state remains distinct from, and its nationals are not citizens of, the protecting state. Protectorates appear in ancient Greek and Roman history; in modern times, European colonies were often governed as protectorates, but this form of political relationship is disappearing from today's world. See also TRUSTEESHIP, TERRITORIAL.

protein, any of the group of highly complex organic compounds found in all living cells. Protein is the most abundant class of all biological molecules, comprising about 50% of cellular dry weight. Classified by biological function, proteins include the ENZYMES, which catalyze cellular reactions; collagen, keratin, and elastin, which are structural, or support, proteins; HEMOGLOBIN and other transport proteins; casein, ovalbumin, and other nutrient proteins; antibodies, which are necessary for IMMUNITY; protein HORMONES, which regulate METABOLISM; and proteins such as actin and myosin, the contractile muscle proteins, that perform mechanical work. Structurally, proteins are large molecules composed of one or more chains of varying amounts of the same 22 AMINO ACIDS, which are linked by PEPTIDE bonds. Each protein is characterized by a unique and invariant amino acid sequence. Protein chains may contain hundreds of amino acids; some proteins also incorporate phosphorus or such metals as iron, zinc, and copper. The amino acid sequence also determines the molecule's three-dimensional structure; this so-called native state is required for proper biological function. The information for the syntheses of the specific amino acid sequences from free amino acids is carried by the cell's NUCLEIC ACIDS. Dietary protein is food that contains the amino acids necessary to construct the proteins described above. Complete proteins, generally of animal origin, contain all the amino acids necessary for human growth and maintenance; incomplete proteins, from plant sources such as grains, legumes, and nuts, lack sufficient amounts of one or more essential amino acid. See also RNA.

Protestantism, form of Christian faith and practice that originated with the principles of the REFORMATION. The term, used in many senses, applies to Christians not belonging to the Roman Catholic Church or to an Orthodox Eastern church. Two distinct branches of Protestantism grew out of the Reformation. The evangelical churches of Scandinavia and Germany were followers of Martin LUTHER, and the reformed churches in other countries were followers of John CALVIN and Huldreich ZWINGLI. A third major branch, episcopacy, developed in England, but since the OXFORD MOVEMENT in the 19th cent. many Anglicans reject the term because they tend to agree with Roman Catholics on most doctrinal points except the primacy of the pope.

Protestant Union, 1608–21, also known as the Evangelical League, an alliance of German Protestant rulers of cities and states for the avowed purpose of a mutual defense of their lands, persons, and rights. It was formed to block attempts by the Holy Roman emperor and the Catholic princes of Germany to restore all church lands that had been appropriated by the Protestant princes. Never very effective, the union went out of existence three years after the outbreak of the THIRTY YEARS WAR.

protist, member of the taxonomic kingdom Protista (or Protoctista), which consists of one-celled organisms that live freely or in small colonies, such as PROTOZOANS and ALGAE. Most protists were formerly classified as either animals or plants.

Protogenes [prōtŏj'ənēz], fl. c.300 B.C., Greek painter, considered second only to APELLES by the ancients. His best-known work, the *Ialysus,* was removed by VESPASIAN to Rome, where it perished in the burning of the Temple of Peace.

proton, subatomic particle having a single positive electrical charge and constituting the nucleus of the ordinary hydrogen ATOM. Every atomic nucleus contains one or more protons. The mass of the proton is about 1,840 times the mass of the ELECTRON and slightly less than the mass of the neutron. Protons are made of still smaller particles called QUARKS. In 1919 Ernest RUTHERFORD discovered the proton as a product of the disintegration of the atomic nucleus. The antiproton, the proton's antiparticle (see ANTIMATTER), was discovered in 1955. Research into the possibility that the proton may decay has been inconclusive but suggests that its lifetime is at least 10^{31} years. See ELEMENTARY PARTICLES.

protoplasm, term once used for the fundamental material of which all living things were thought to be composed. It is still accepted that all living organisms are made largely of the same classes of substances (e.g., salts and organic molecules), that some of these are organized into structures large enough to be seen in the microscope, and that water almost always is the most abundant material. The term is rarely used anymore in a strictly scientific sense. The unity of living matter is now described in terms of the CELL as the unit of all living organisms and of molecules such as PROTEINS and NUCLEIC ACIDS.

protozoan, member of an informal grouping (sometimes considered a subkingdom) of microscopic one-celled PROTISTS. Most are solitary, but a few live in simple colonies. The majority are aquatic, living in fresh or salt water; some live in soil. Despite their small size and lack of multicellular organization, protozoans carry on all the metabolic functions of higher animals: digestion, excretion, respiration, and coordination of movement. Some species can photosynthesize, and many are parasitic (see MICROSPORA and APICOCOMPLEXA), often causing diseases in humans and other animals.

Proudhon, Pierre Joseph [pro͞odhôN'], 1809–65, French social theorist. He achieved notice with his anarchist pamphlet *What Is Property?* (1840). After the REVOLUTION OF 1848 he became a member of the constituent assembly. He advocated "mutualism," in which small groups would interact economically and politically within the framework of agreement on basic principles. Opposed to force, he believed that ethical progress would make government superfluous. His works include *System of Economic Contradictions; or, The Philosophy of Poverty* (1846).

Proust, Joseph Louis [pro͞ost], 1754–1826, French chemist. He discovered grape sugar and established the law of definite proportions (also known as Proust's law), which states that elements in a compound are present in a fixed proportion by weight.

Proust, Marcel, 1871–1922, French novelist. He was one of the great literary figures of modern times. As a youth, he mingled ambitiously in Parisian society, but later he became increasingly withdrawn. After 1907, he lived mainly in a cork-lined room, working at night on his monumental cyclic novel, *Remembrance of Things Past* (1913–27; tr. 1922–32, in 7 vol.). Discursive, but alive with brilliant metaphor and sense imagery, the work is rich in psychological, philosophical, and sociological understanding, a vital theme being the link between external and internal reality found in time and memory. In Proust's scheme, the individual is isolated, society is false and ruled by snobbery, and artistic endeavor is raised to a religion.

Provençal [prôväNsäl'], member of the Romance group of the Italic subfamily of the Indo-European family of languages. Although spoken by several million people in France, it has no official status in that country. Also called LANGUE D'OC, Provençal became important in the Middle Ages as the medium of the great literature of the TROUBADOURS. See LANGUAGE (table).

Provence [prôväNs'], region and former province, SE France. NICE and MARSEILLES are the chief cities. Fruits, vegetables, and cattle are economic mainstays. The coast was settled (c.600 B.C.) by the Greeks and later colonized (2d cent. B.C.) by the Romans. Christianity was implanted early. In 933 Provence became part of the kingdom of ARLES. It later passed to the Angevin dynasty of Naples (1246) and to France (1486).

Proverbs, book of the OLD TESTAMENT, 20th in the Authorized Version, a collection of moral and other maxims. The practical teachings are individual and universal rather than nationalistic. Ascribed to SOLOMON, the book probably dates from the 9th to the 2d cent. B.C.

Providence, city (1990 pop. 160,728), state capital and seat of Providence co., NE R.I., a port on Providence Bay; founded 1636 by Roger WILLIAMS, inc. as a city 1832. The largest city in the state, it is a major shipping center famous for its silverware and jewelry industries. Other manufactures include textiles and electronic equipment. An early refuge for religious dissenters, Providence industrialized after the Revolution. Points of interest include Brown Univ.; the Rhode Island School of Design; the old statehouse; and the capitol, designed by McKim, Mead, and White.

Provincetown, resort town (1990 pop. 3,561), SE Mass., on the tip of CAPE COD; founded c.1700, inc. 1727. The PILGRIMS landed there (1620) before proceeding to PLYMOUTH. Once a whaling and smuggling center, Provincetown in the 20th cent. gained fame as an artists' colony and well-preserved colonial settlement. Fishing and tourism are its main industries. The Cape Cod National Seashore is adjacent to the town.

Provisions of Oxford, 1258, a scheme of governmental reform forced upon HENRY III of England by his barons. Drawn up by Simon de MONTFORT, it provided for an advisory council and tried to limit the king's power to tax. Henry's repudiation (1261) of the agreement led to the BARONS' WAR (1263–67), in which the king triumphed.

Provo, city (1990 pop. 86,835), seat of Utah co., N central Utah, on the Provo R., near Utah Lake; inc. 1851. Settled by MORMONS in 1849, it grew as a shipping point for the region's mines. Fruit, iron and steel manufactures, and textiles are its leading products. Brigham Young Univ. is located in the city. The Wasatch Range is nearby.

Prudhoe Bay, inlet of the Arctic Ocean, N Alaska. Oil from large deposits (the first discovered in 1968) is transported S to the port of Valdez via the Alaskan Pipeline (completed in 1977). Prudhoe Bay oil makes Alaska the leading petroleum-producing state in the U.S.

Prud'hon, Pierre Paul [prüdôN], 1758–1823, French painter. Noted for his subtle use of light and shadow, he gained recognition with *Truth Descending from the Heavens Led by Wisdom* (1796; Louvre). His portrait of Empress Josephine is in the Louvre.

prune: see PLUM.

Prussia, former kingdom, and largest and most important of the German states. BERLIN was the capital. Originally, Prussia was the name only of the area later called EAST PRUSSIA. In 1618, by then a duchy, it passed to the elector of BRANDENBURG. In 1660 full independence from Polish suzerainty was obtained by FREDERICK WILLIAM, the Great Elector. The electors of Brandenburg gradually acquired other lands, and in 1701 Elector Frederick III had himself crowned "king in Prussia" as Frederick I. He remained a prince of the Holy Roman Empire as elector of Brandenburg, but not as king of Prussia, which lay outside imperial boundaries. This gave the kings of Prussia some independence from the emperor. King FREDERICK WILLIAM I (r.1713–40) worked to unify the state and built an efficient army. His son FREDERICK II (r.1740–86) won most of SILESIA from Austria in the War of the AUSTRIAN SUCCESSION and entered the SEVEN YEARS WAR. Prussia gained further territory in the partitions of POLAND (1772–95). The kingdom was eclipsed by the rise of France under NAPOLEON I but had a major part in the defeat (1813–15) of the French. In 1862 Otto von BISMARCK became Prussian premier; he sought to unify Germany under Prussian leadership. After territorial gains in the AUSTRO-PRUSSIAN WAR and the FRANCO-PRUSSIAN WAR, the Prussian king was proclaimed (1871) emperor of Germany as WILLIAM I. Thereafter, the history of Prussia is essentially that of GERMANY. Prussia remained a kingdom in the German Empire until Germany became a republic in 1918. Prussia was abolished as a state in 1947 and divided among West Germany, East Germany, the Russian Republic of the USSR (now Russia), and Poland.

Pryor, Richard, 1940–, African-American comedian; b. Peoria, Ill. His wildly inventive comic style is seen in such films as *Silver Streak* (1976), *Richard Pryor Live in Concert* (1979), *Stir Crazy* (1980), and *Jo Jo Dancer Your Life Is Calling* (1986).

Richard Pryor

Psalms or **Psalter,** book of the OLD TESTAMENT, 19th in the Authorized Version, a collection of 150 poetic pieces, since the last centuries B.C. the chief hymnal of the Jews and subsequently of Christians. Many are attributed to DAVID, SOLOMON, and others. Most took their present form between c.537 B.C. and c.100 B.C. Bible versions vary in dividing them, and numbering is therefore confusing. According to the text, the psalms are in five groups (numbering according to the Authorized Version): 1–41; 42–72; 73–89; 90–106; 107–150. They vary in tone and subject. Psalms of contrition, or penitential psalms, include 6, 32, 38, 51 (Miserere), and 130 (De profundis). Some are imprecatory, e.g., 52, 64, 137. Some, e.g., 78, 105–107, emphasize Israel's history. Didactic psalms include 37, 49, and 50. Some seem especially adapted to public worship, e.g., 95 (Venite). Others have been regarded as Messianic, e.g., 2, 8, 16. There are psalms elsewhere in the BIBLE, e.g., 1 Sam. 2.1–10. The history of translation of the psalms is more extensive than that of any other part of the Old Testament.

Psalter: see PSALMS.

psaltery: see STRINGED INSTRUMENT.

psilotophyte, member of a division (Psilotophyta) of vascular plants characterized by the lack of roots; one species also lacks leaves. The green stem carries out PHOTOSYNTHESIS, and the life cycle is very much like that of FERNS.

Psyche [sī'kē], in Greek mythology, personification of the human soul. Loved by EROS, she was forbidden to look at him. When she disobeyed he left her, but after a series of trials she became immortal and was reunited with him forever.

psychedelic drug: see HALLUCINOGENIC DRUG.

psychiatry, branch of medicine concerned with the diagnosis and treatment of mental disorders. Psychiatrists are licensed physicians who complete a three-year residency in psychiatry after their medical training. Modern techniques such as PSYCHOTHERAPY and PSYCHOANALYSIS can be traced to the pioneering work of Sigmund FREUD, who turned to the behavior and emotional history of the patient for clues to his or her psychological disorder. Research has discovered that biological, genetic, psychological, and social components contribute to many types of mental illness. This causal diversity is reflected in treatment, which may include the use of drugs that influence NEUROTRANSMITTER functions in the brain, ELECTROCONVULSIVE THERAPY (ECT), PSYCHOTHERAPY, and BEHAVIOR THERAPY.

psychoanalysis, system of PSYCHOTHERAPY. The origins of psychoanalysis can be traced to Sigmund FREUD's observation that the physical symptoms of patients suffering from HYSTERIA tended to disappear after apparently forgotten material was made conscious. From this he developed the basic postulate of psychoanalysis: the existence of a dynamic UNCONSCIOUS that influences every action but operates with material that is not subject to recall by normal processes. This "forgetting" he termed repression (see DEFENSE MECHANISM), and he made the conscious recognition of repressed experiences the keystone of psychoanalytic therapy. After experimenting with HYPNOTISM to probe the unconscious, Freud introduced two techniques—free association, whereby patients voice their thoughts exactly as they arise, and DREAM interpretation; these are still the main therapeutic tools of psychoanalysis. In addition, Freud and his followers developed a vast theory of the human psyche that stresses the role of two instincts—the sexual instinct and the death instinct. According to the theory, these two drives balance one another in the well-adjusted individual; if dammed up, they produce NEUROSIS. Freud also developed a theory of the human personality, dividing it into three parts: the id (reservoir of unconscious instinctual drives, dominated by the pleasure principle and desirous of instant gratification); the superego (internal censor, or conscience); and the ego (mediator between the id, the superego, and the demands of society or reality). Other significant figures in the field of psychoanalysis include C.G. JUNG, Alfred ADLER, Otto RANK, Karen HORNEY, Erich FROMM, Harry Stack SULLIVAN, and Carl ROGERS. Although traditional psychoanalysis has been criticized for its rigidity, costliness, and failure to consider biological causes, psychoanalytic theory has greatly influenced child rearing, social-work practice, education, the social sciences, medicine, and the arts.

psychobiology, study of anatomical and biochemical structures and processes and their effect on behavior. It is closely related to physiological psychology. Areas of investigation include hormonal and biochemical changes in nerves, glands, and muscles, and how these changes influence development, emotions, and learning.

psycholinguistics, study of the psychological states and mental activity associated with language usage. An important focus is the largely unconscious application of grammatical rules that enables the production and comprehension of sentences. Psycholinguists investigate the relationship between language and thought and often study linguistic performance and language acquisition, especially in children. The work of Noam CHOMSKY and other proponents of TRANSFORMATIONAL-GENERATIVE GRAMMAR have greatly influenced the field.

psychological warfare, a number of propaganda techniques designed to weaken the enemy's morale and to discredit the government of the opposition. Among those used are propaganda broadcasts intended for enemy troops and civilians and the forced political indoctrination of prisoners of war under stressed conditions, popularly known as brainwashing.

psychology, science or study of the thought processes and behavior of humans and other animals in their interaction with their environment. Psychologists study sensory perception, emotion and motivation, problem solving, use of language and other mental tasks, group interaction, adjustment to social and physical environment, and the normal and abnormal development of these processes. Psychology encompasses a very broad range of specialties and approaches including BEHAVIORISM; GESTALT; neuropsychology, which studies the interaction of brain function and behavior; and clinical psychology, which focuses on the diagnosis and treatment of psychological problems.

psychosis, broad category of psychological disturbance, encompassing the most serious emotional disturbances, often rendering the individual incapable of staying in contact with reality. Until fairly recently, the term was broadly employed in contrast with NEUROSIS, which denoted milder mental disturbances. Psychoses have traditionally included such symptoms as hallucinations and delusions, and such disorders as PARANOIA and SCHIZOPHRENIA. The symptoms can be classified as organic, i.e., those associated with actual damage to the brain caused by advanced syphilis, senility, and drug abuse; or functional, i.e., those in which there is no brain damage. ELECTROCONVULSIVE THERAPY and drug therapy are used to treat people with serious psychological disorders. Refinement in diagnostic criteria led, in the 1980s, to the abandonment of the term *psychosis* in psychiatry, in favor of more precise nomenclature.

psychosomatic disorder, emotional disturbance that is manifested as a physical disorder, such as childhood ASTHMA, ULCERS, HYPERTENSION, endocrine disturbances, and possibly even HEART DISEASE. In most cases the illness occurs only when there is both a physiological predisposition and psychological stress. Treatment may involve a medical regimen or techniques such as BIOFEEDBACK as well as PSYCHOTHERAPY. Psychosomatic medicine is now subsumed under the broader field of **behavioral medicine**, which includes the study of a wider range of physical ailments. Studies suggesting that a large percentage of deaths are rooted in behavior have underlined the importance of the discipline.

psychotherapy, treatment of mental disorders using psychological methods. Psychotherapy does not include physiological interventions, such as drug therapy or ELECTROCONVULSIVE THERAPY. Psychotherapy usually stresses helping patients to examine their own ideas about themselves and their lives; it may involve treatment of an individual, a family, or a group. Sigmund FREUD developed the original form of psychotherapy, PSYCHOANALYSIS. BEHAVIOR MODIFICATION aims to eliminate undesirable habits or irrational fears using the principles of conditioning. Cognitive therapies try to show the client that certain, usually negative, thoughts are irrational, the goal being to restructure such thoughts into positive, constructive ideas. GROUP PSYCHOTHERAPY allows clients to observe the effects of behaviors on others in a controlled setting.

psychotomimetic drug: see HALLUCINOGENIC DRUG.

Pt, chemical symbol of the element PLATINUM.

pterosaur, any member of an order (Pterosauria) of extinct flying reptiles that lived 210 million to 135 million years ago. They had an elongated fourth finger that formed the leading edge of their two membranous, featherless wings. Some were as small as sparrows, but some pterodactyls had wingspans of 40 ft. (12 m). Pterosaurs lived near water and ate insects and other animals.

Ptolemaic system, historically the most influential of the geocentric cosmological theories, i.e., theories that placed the earth motionless at the center of the universe with all celestial bodies revolving around it. The system is named for the astronomer PTOLEMY (Claudius Ptolemaeus), who in the 2d cent. A.D. combined simple circular motions to explain the complicated wanderings of the planets. Ptolemy explained RETROGRADE MOTION by assuming that each planet moved in a circle called an epicycle, whose center was in turn carried around the earth in a circular orbit called a deferent. The Ptolemaic system dominated astronomy until the advent of the heliocentric COPERNICAN SYSTEM in the 16th cent.

Ptolemy [tŏl'əmē], rulers of the Macedonian dynasty of EGYPT (323 B.C.–30 B.C.). **Ptolemy I,** d. 284 B.C., a leading general of ALEXANDER THE GREAT, became one of the DIADOCHI. After Alexander's death he received Egypt, declared himself king (305 B.C.), and laid the basis for Ptolemaic administration. He sought to make ALEXANDRIA the cultural center of the Greek world, especially by founding its library. His son, **Ptolemy II,** c.308–246 B.C. (r.285–246), continued his father's work, completing the Pharos (see SEVEN WONDERS OF THE WORLD). He encouraged the translation of the PENTATEUCH into the Greek Septuagint and had a canal built from the Nile to the Red Sea. Ptolemy ended the war with Syria and increased his prestige by siding with Rome in the first PUNIC WAR. His son, **Ptolemy III,** d. 221 B.C. (r.246–221), renewed war with

Syria. During his reign Egyptian fleets controlled most of the coast of Asia Minor, and the kingdom was enlarged. **Ptolemy V,** d. 180 B.C. (r.205–180), came to the throne as a small boy. Civil war characterized his reign; Syrian and Macedonian invasions cost Egypt all of Palestine and much of Asia Minor. **Ptolemy VI,** d. 145 B.C. (r.180–145), became king as an infant; the Syrians forced him to share the throne with his brother (later Ptolemy VII). Trouble between the brothers brought about intervention by Rome. Ptolemy VI was killed while fighting over the Syrian throne. **Ptolemy VII,** d. 116 B.C. (r.145–116), put his brother's young son to death and succeeded to the throne. He survived a revolt (130–127) by his brother's widow, Cleopatra, and ruled peacefully though despotically. He drove the scholars from Alexandria, causing the spread of Alexandrian culture. **Ptolemy XI,** d. 51 B.C. (r.80–58, 55–51), was unseated by the Alexandrians because of his misrule but was restored with the aid of POMPEY. He made the Roman senate executor of his will and named Pompey guardian of his son, Ptolemy XII. **Ptolemy XII,** 61?–47 B.C. (r.51–47), was from the start overshadowed by his sister, CLEOPATRA, who became his wife and ruled with him. She revolted (48) against the power of his advisers. At this juncture the defeated Pompey arrived in Egypt and was killed by Ptolemy's adviser Pothinus. Julius CAESAR followed immediately, fell under Cleopatra's influence, and forced Ptolemy to share the throne again.

Ptolemy (Claudius Ptolemaeus), fl. 2d cent. A.D., Greco-Egyptian mathematician and geographer, the last great astronomer of ancient times. He systematized and recorded the knowledge of Alexandrian men of science. In his famous treatise, the 13-volume *Almagest,* which remained influential until the time of COPERNICUS, he presented the geocentric cosmological theory known as the PTOLEMAIC SYSTEM; the treatise also contained a catalog of more than 1,020 stars, as well as a table of chords and other mathematical information. His *Geography,* despite its many errors, remained in use until the 16th cent. Ptolemy discovered the irregularity in the moon's motion known as the evection and wrote the *Tetrabiblos,* a study of astrology.

Pu, chemical symbol of the element PLUTONIUM.

public access television, in the U.S., noncommercial cable television channels set aside for nonprofit organizations and private citizens. The purpose is to avoid monopolization of cable TV by a few sources and to ensure programming of local community interest. The 1984 Cable Act allows municipalities to require cable franchise holders to provide a public access channel and make available equipment, studio space, and technical assistance.

public debt: see DEBT, PUBLIC.

public relations, activities and policies used to create public interest in a person, idea, product, institution, or business establishment. The field began in the early 20th cent., when American businesses responded to attacks by social reformers. Public relations serves particular interests by presenting them to the public in the most favorable light. Toward this end, many research techniques and communications media are used. Public relations differs from propaganda, which is generally government supported, international in scope, and political in nature. The earliest form of public relations and still the most widely practiced is publicity, whose principal instrument is the press release.

public television, noncommercial television with largely educational programming. In the U.S., it began as National Educational Television (NET), but was reorganized in 1968 as government-financed public TV under the Corporation for Public Broadcasting. Public TV avoids the limits on content that result from the pressures of advertisers. Despite severe cuts in government funding, public TV, through viewer subscriptions and corporate underwriting, continues to produce shows that would not be seen on commercial TV, particularly children's programming and documentaries. Shows are selected and distributed by the Public Broadcasting System, an association of public TV stations.

Public Works Administration (PWA), federal agency established (1933) by the NEW DEAL administration of Pres. Franklin D. ROOSEVELT to promote employment and increase public purchasing power. It administered the construction of many public buildings, bridges, dams, and other similar projects. The PWA became a division of the Federal Works Agency in 1939 and was liquidated in the 1940s.

Puccini, Giacomo [po͞ot-chē′nē], 1858–1924, Italian composer. One of the pre-eminent composers of Italian opera, he is noted for his lyric style, masterful orchestration, and his sometimes sentimental effects, as in *Manon Lescaut* (1893), *La Bohème* (1896), *La Tosca* (1900), *Madame Butterfly* (1904), and *Turandot* (produced, 1926).

Pudovkin, Vsevolod Ilarionovich [po͝odôf′kĭn], 1893–1953, Russian film director. Ranked with EISENSTEIN and DOVZHENKO, he used MONTAGE in such films as *Mother* (1926), *The End of St. Petersburg* (1927), and *Heir to Genghis Khan* (1928).

Puebla, city (1990 pop. 1,054,921), E central Mexico, capital of Puebla state. It is a major agricultural and industrial center and a tourist resort noted for the colored tiles that decorate its buildings. It has one of the finest cathedrals in Mexico. Founded in the mid-16th cent., it long was a vital link between Mexico City and the coast.

Pueblo, Spanish name for the indigenous people who occupied stone or adobe community houses in more than 80 villages (pueblos) in the Southwestern culture area (see NORTH AMERICA, INDIGENOUS PEOPLES OF). They are the descendants of the prehistoric Anasazi culture (see CLIFF DWELLERS) of Utah, Colorado, Arizona, New Mexico, and N Mexico. By 2000 B.C. the earliest agriculturalists, known as the Cochise culture, were raising corn. The Mogollon people, with the first bows and arrows and true pottery in North America, built the first village settlements in the 1st cent. A.D., while their contemporaries, the basket makers, were living in caves. Irrigation and surface houses with KIVAS developed between 400 and 700, but multistoried cliff houses on MESAS marked the Great Pueblo Period, from 1050 to the end of the 13th cent. By 1630, 90 years after CORONADO had explored the Pueblo villages, Spanish missionaries had converted 60,000 Pueblos to Christianity. In 1680 Popé led the pueblos in a revolt that drove the Spanish out for 12 years; those in New Mexico were recaptured in 1692, but the Western Pueblos remained free. The contemporary Pueblos are quite diverse linguistically (see NATIVE AMERICAN LANGUAGES) and culturally. Their culture is the oldest N of Mexico, dating back 700 years for the still-occupied HOPI, ZUÑI, and ACOMA pueblos. Several of the two dozen surviving pueblos have retained pre-Spanish social systems and community organization to a surprising degree. They are sedentary farmers; men are weavers and women potters. The position of women remains high, and the KACHINA cult and other secret societies continue to enjoy major emphasis. In 1990 there were over 50,000 Pueblos in the U.S.

Pueblo, city (1990 pop. 98,640), seat of Pueblo co., S central Colo., on the Arkansas R., in the foothills of the Rockies; inc. 1885. It is the trade and shipping center for a timber, coal, and farm area. Its steel industry is huge; wire, concrete, and lumber are also produced. The city was laid out (1860) on the site of a trading post (1842).

Puente, Tito (Ernesto Antonio Puente, Jr.), 1923–, American musician and bandleader; b. N.Y.C. A popularizer in the 1950s of such Latin American musical forms as the cha-cha and mambo, he was instrumental in the development of the SALSA in the 1970s.

Puerto Rico [Span., = rich port], officially Commonwealth of Puerto Rico, island (1990 pop. 3,522,037), 3,425 sq mi (8,871 sq km), West Indies, c.1,000 m (1,610 km) SE of Miami. It is a self-governing entity in association with the U.S. The capital is SAN JUAN; other urban centers include BAYAMÓN, PONCE, Carolina, and Caguas. Easternmost of the Greater Antilles, it is bounded by the Atlantic (N), the Caribbean (S), the Dominican Republic (W), and the Virgin Islands (E). Puerto Rico is crossed by mountain ranges, notably the Cordillera Central, which rises to 4,389 ft (1,388 m). The climate is tropical. Sugarcane was long the chief product, but it has been superseded by livestock and dairy production. Coffee, tobacco, and fruits are other leading crops. The dense population, however, depends chiefly on industrial employment; the manufacture of machinery, chemicals, pharmaceuticals, textiles, electronic equipment, and plastics, as well as oil refining, are important. Tourism is also a major source of revenue. Population growth and social problems have led to much emigration, and one third of all Puerto Ricans live in the U.S. Puerto Ricans share the rights and duties of U.S. citizens, except that they do not pay federal income taxes and do not vote in national elections (unless living on the mainland). The Puerto Ricans are descended from Spanish colonists, with admixed aboriginal native and African strains. Spanish and English are the official languages, but Spanish is predominant. Roman Catholicism is the main religion.

History. When COLUMBUS arrived in 1493, Arawaks lived on Puerto Rico, which they called Boriquén or Borinquén. PONCE DE LEÓN began the conquest in 1508. Sugar culture was introduced, strategic San Juan was fortified, and African slaves replaced the annihilated Arawaks as workers in a growing plantation culture. In the 19th cent. popular unrest led finally to Spain's granting of some autonomy in 1898. After the SPANISH-AMERICAN WAR, Puerto Rico was ceded (1898) to the U.S., which set up (1900) an administration under an American governor. Meanwhile an independence movement grew. In 1917 Puerto Ricans were granted U.S. citizenship. As U.S. holdings in the one-crop sugar economy increased, large corporations encroached on land that had been used to grow subsistence food, and the subsequent economic distress was not relieved until World War II. After the war, "Operation Bootstrap," encouraging American industrial investment with tax incentives, began to change the nature of the economy. In 1952 the Commonwealth of Puerto Rico was proclaimed. Nationalist agitation continued, however. By the 1960s statehood advocates and supporters of continued commonwealth status held power alternately, while advocates of independence eschewed the electoral process. In 1992 Pedro Rosello, a statehood advocate, was elected governor, but voters chose commonwealth status by a narrow margin in a 1993 referendum.

Puerto Vallarta [väyär'tä], city (1990 pop. 111,175), Jalisco state, W Mexico. Since the 16th cent. it has been a stopover for ships sailing along the coast. Today it is one of Mexico's largest resorts, known for its sports fishing and luxurious facilities.

Pueyrredón, Juan Martín de [pwāīrādōn'], 1776–1850, Argentine general, supreme director of the United Provinces of La Plata (1816–19). He resisted the invasion of Buenos Aires by the British (1806). He held several posts in the revolutionary government, including that of commander of the patriot Army of the North (1811–12).

puffin, migratory diving BIRD of the AUK family. Puffins have dumpy bodies, short legs set far back, small wings, and a large, brilliantly colored bill adapted for carrying several fish at once. Clumsy on land and in flight, they are expert swimmers. Puffins nest in colonies in burrows or rock cavities on northern islands.

Pugachev, Emelian Ivanovich [po͞ogəchôf'], d. 1775, leader of the 1773–74 Russian peasant uprising. A Don COSSACK, he claimed to be PETER III, announced the end of serfdom, and gathered an army of Cossacks, serfs, and TATARS. After seizing towns in the Volga and Ural regions he was caught and executed. The revolt led CATHERINE II to strengthen serfdom.

Puget Sound, island-studded inlet of the Pacific Ocean, NW Washington, extending S c.100 mi (160 km) to Olympia and navigable by large ships. Seattle and Tacoma are important shoreline cities. Discovered in 1787, the sound was explored and named in 1792 by Capt. George Vancouver for his aide, Peter Puget.

Puig, Manuel, 1932–90, Argentine novelist. One of Latin America's most creative writers, he explored the myths and realities of contemporary Argentine life. He is best known for the novel *Kiss of the Spider Woman* (1976), which was made into a film (1985) and Broadway musical (1993). Other novels include *Betrayed by Rita Hayworth* (1968) and *Blood of Requited Love* (1982).

Pulaski, Casimir [pəlăs'kē], c.1748–1779, Polish patriot and soldier. After fighting against Russian domination of Poland, he commanded (1777–79) patriot troops in the AMERICAN REVOLUTION. He was killed while leading his own cavalry unit, the Pulaski Legion, in the attack on SAVANNAH.

Pulitzer, Joseph, 1847–1911, American newspaper publisher; b. Hungary. As owner and publisher after 1878, he made the St. Louis *Post-Dispatch* a success; in 1883 he bought the New York *World.* His aggressive methods of building up this paper; its Sunday issue; and the use of illustrations, news stunts, crusades against corruption, cartoons, and bold news coverage helped his paper compete with HEARST's *Journal* in sensationalism and in circulation. Later his *World* became the outstanding Democratic organ in the U.S. After 1890 partial blindness kept him from political activity, but he directed his papers no less closely than before. He left funds to endow what is now the graduate school of journalism at Columbia Univ., and he endowed the PULITZER PRIZES.

Pulitzer Prizes, annual awards for achievements in American journalism, letters, and music. The prizes are paid from the income of a fund left by Joseph PULITZER to the trustees of Columbia Univ. They have been awarded by the trustees each May since 1917, on the recommendation of an advisory board, with American themes preferred. Fourteen prizes are given in journalism. The prizes in letters are for fiction, drama, poetry, history, biography or autobiography, and general nonfiction, and the music prize was added in 1943. Each is accompanied by $3,000 award.

pulley: see MACHINE.

pulsar, in astronomy, a celestial object that emits brief, sharp pulses of radio waves. The pulses recur at precise intervals; the time between pulses ranges from 1.5 msec to 4 sec. Pulsars are believed to be rotating NEUTRON STARS that emit radio waves in a narrow beam. Because of the rotation of the star, the beam will sweep across the line of sight, causing the observed pulses.

pulse, in botany, common name for Leguminosae or Fabaceae, a large family of herbs, shrubs, and trees, also called the pea, or legume, family. The family is typified by usually compound leaves, a fruit that is a LEGUME (a type of pod), and FLOWERS with an irregular butterflylike shape. Many species have thorny branches. The seeds of the family are rich in PROTEIN; in many areas where meat is scarce, legumes, e.g., BEANS, PEAS, LENTILS, PEANUTS, SOYBEANS, and CAROB, are staples. Some species are fodder and forage plants, e.g., CLOVER, ALFALFA, soybeans, and vetch. The root nodules of these food and forage plants have BACTERIA that fix NITROGEN (see NITROGEN CYCLE), making them valuable as cover crops and green manure (see FERTILIZER). The family also provides gums and RESINS, dyes and tannins, timber, medications, oils, flavorings, fibers, and insecticides, and some legumes are ornamentals, e.g., ACACIAS, LOCUSTS, MIMOSAS, and WISTERIAS.

pulse, in physiology, alternate expansion and contraction of artery walls as HEART action varies blood volume within them. Artery walls are elastic and become distended by the increase in blood volume when the heart contracts. When the heart relaxes, this volume decreases and the walls contract, propelling the blood through the arteries. The result is a pressure wave, with a pulsation for each heartbeat. See also BLOOD PRESSURE.

puma or **cougar,** New World member (*Felis concolor*) of the CAT family. Also called mountain lion, catamount, and panther, it ranges from S British Columbia to southernmost South America. Pumas vary in size (up to 7 ft/2.1 m) and color according to locale and live in many kinds of country, preying on animals as large as deer.

pumice, volcanic glass formed by the solidification of LAVA permeated with gas bubbles. It has the chemical composition of GRANITE, but is of low enough density to float on water. Pumice is used primarily as an ABRASIVE.

pump, device to lift, transfer, or increase the pressure of a fluid (liquid or gas) or to create a VACUUM. In a simple *reciprocating pump* used to lift water, a piston moves back and forth in a cylinder equipped with intake and outflow valves. On the piston's upstroke, atmospheric pressure forces water into the empty space beneath the piston. On the downstroke, the water in the cylinder is forced to flow above the piston. Reversing direction, the piston moves up, allowing more water to come up under it into the cylinder and lifting the water held above it to an outlet pipe. The *rotary pump* is like the reciprocating pump in that it allows a fluid to fill a space that then decreases in volume. The rotary pump, however, has no valves and uses rotating components in place of a piston. A *jet pump* (e.g., a perfume atomizer) uses a fast-moving stream of liquid or air as the moving force. COMPRESSORS are used to force air or other gases into a closed container.

pumpkin, common name for the genus *Cucurbita* of the GOURD family, including the pumpkins and squashes. Although the names are often used interchangeably, pumpkin, in the U.S., usually refers to *C. pepo* and its varieties (which also include the summer squashes). The most popular of these is a vine bearing orange fruits, or pumpkins, used as pie filling and also carved into jack-o'-lanterns at Halloween. Squash usually refers to *C. maxima,* which includes the winter squashes (e.g., Hubbard), or *C. moschata,* which includes the cushaws.

Punch and Judy, traditional English puppet play, deriving from COMMEDIA DELL'ARTE. Punch is cruel and boastful; his wife, Judy, whom he beats, is a loud, faithless nag.

Punic Wars, three distinct conflicts between Carthage and Rome. When they began, Rome had nearly completed the conquest of Italy, while CARTHAGE controlled NW Africa and the islands and the commerce of the W Mediterranean. When they ended, Carthage was ruined, and Rome was the greatest power W of China. The **First Punic War,** 264–241 B.C., grew immediately out of a quarrel between the Sicilian cities of Messana (now Messina) and Syracuse that involved Rome and Carthage. The Romans won naval victories at Mylae (260) and Cape Ecnomus (256), but a Roman excursion to Africa failed (255). Although HAMILCAR BARCA blocked the Romans in Sicily, a Roman victory at sea off the Aegadian Isles (241) caused Carthage to sue for peace. The treaty gave Sicily to Rome, but the Romans, contrary to the treaty, invaded Sardinia and Corsica. When the Carthaginians under HANNIBAL took (219) the Spanish city of Saguntum (present-day Sagunto), a Roman ally, Rome declared war. This **Second Punic War,** or Hannibalic War, 218–201 B.C., was one of the titanic struggles of history. It was marked by Hannibal's invasion of Italy and his initial victory there, but Hannibal's ultimate failure came at the battle of ZAMA (202) in Africa. Carthage surrendered its Spanish province and its war fleet to Rome and never recovered. The **Third Punic War,** 149–146 B.C., originated when Rome charged Carthage with a breach of treaty. Rome declared war, blockaded the city, and razed it.

Punjab [Sanskrit, = five rivers], historic region, bounded by the Indus R. (W) and Jumna R. (E), in Pakistan and NW India. A center of the ancient INDUS VALLEY CIVILIZATION, it is a semiarid but productive wheat-growing region, irrigated by the Jhelum, Chenab, Ravi, Sutlej, and Beas rivers, which unite to form the Panjnad R. and join the INDUS R. The Punjab was a province of British India from 1849 until 1947, when it was partitioned. The western areas (c.58,000 sq mi/150,220 sq km) became the province of West Punjab (now Punjab) in Pakistan, and the eastern areas (c.91,000 sq mi/235,690 sq km) became part of India, where they now form, after several reorganizations, the states of Haryana, Punjab, and part of Himachal Pradesh. Over 60% of the people of Punjab are SIKHS, and Sikh separatists have sought an independent nation since 1947.

Punjabi [pŭnjä'bē], language belonging to the Indic group of the Indo-Iranian subfamily of the Indo-European family of languages. See LANGUAGE (table).

punk rock: see ROCK MUSIC.

Purcell, Henry [pûr'səl], c.1659–1695, considered England's finest native composer. He was the organist at Westminster Abbey (1679–95). Combining lyrical melody, harmonic invention, and mastery of COUNTERPOINT to create an English BAROQUE style, he wrote the opera *Dido and Aeneas* (1689); *The Fairy Queen* (1692), a MASQUE; songs for public occasions, e.g., odes for St. Cecilia's Day; instrumental works; and church music.

purgatory, in the teaching of the Roman Catholic Church, the state after death in which the soul destined for heaven is purged of all unpunished or unrepented minor SINS. Souls in purgatory may be aided by the prayers of the living. The Orthodox have not adopted the Western terms for the concept of purgatory, and Protestants have generally abandoned it.

Purim: see under JEWISH HOLIDAYS.

purine, type of organic compound found in the NUCLEIC ACIDS of plant and animal tissue. The two major purines distributed almost universally in living systems are the bases adenine and guanine, present in DNA and RNA.

Puritanism, in the 16th and 17th cent., a movement for reform in the Church of England that had a profound influence on the social, political, ethical, and theological ideas in England and America. Originating in the reign of ELIZABETH I, the movement opposed the ecclesiastical establishment and aimed at purifying the church—hence the name Puritan. Many Puritans sided with the parliamentary party in the ENGLISH CIVIL WAR and held great power between 1640 and 1660. They were cast out of the Church of England after the RESTORATION. In America the early New England settlements were Puritan in origin and theocratic in nature. The spirit of Puritanism long persisted there, and the idea of congregational democratic government was carried into the political life of the state as one source of modern democracy.

purslane, common name for some plants of Portulaceae, a family of chiefly New World herbs and shrubs. The true purslanes, or portulacas (genus *Portulaca*), include many species indigenous to the U.S. The pussley, or common purslane (*P. oleracea*), is a common trailing weed in America; it and the European variety are used as potherbs and greens. Some species, e.g., the showy-blossomed rose moss, or garden purslane (*P. grandiflora*), are cultivated in gardens. Many wildflowers are members of the family, including the bitterroot (*Lewisia rediviva*), the state flower of Montana.

Pusan, city (1985 pop. 3,514,798), extreme SE South Korea. It is the nation's second largest city and largest port, with an excellent natural harbor. It has served as a main southern gateway to Korea from Japan and is also the southern terminus of the main railroad line from SEOUL. A leading industrial, commercial, and shipbuilding center, Pusan is also a popular resort city. During the KOREAN WAR it was (Aug.–Sept. 1950) the site of a UN beachhead. Historic landmarks include several medieval palaces.

Pusey, Edward Bouverie [pyo͞o'zē], 1800–82, English clergyman, leader in the OXFORD MOVEMENT. In 1828 he was made regius professor of Hebrew at Oxford and canon of Christ Church. He formally aligned himself with the Oxford movement in late 1833 and wrote the tracts on fasting (1834) and baptism (1836) in the series *Tracts for the Times.* When John Henry NEWMAN withdrew from the Oxford movement in 1841, Pusey became its leader. He strongly defended High Church views and advocated the doctrine of the Real Presence, holding that the body and blood of Jesus Christ were actually present in the Eucharist. He assisted (1845) in the establishment of the first Anglican sisterhood, and his sermon "The Entire Absolution of the Penitent" (1846) established the Anglican practice of private confession. In 1851 he preached "The Rule of Faith," which is credited with checking secessions to Roman Catholicism.

Pushkin, Aleksandr Sergeyevich [po͝osh'kĭn], 1799–1837, Russian poet and prose writer. Born to a noble family, he published his first major poem, *Russlan and Ludmilla,* in 1820. In that year both his "Ode to Liberty" and some satirical verses offended the court, and he was exiled to S Russia. There he composed such Byronic poems as *The Prisoner of the Caucasus* (1821). He was ordered to his family's estate in 1824 but was pardoned in 1826, settling first in Moscow and then in St. Petersburg. He died of wounds received in a duel. The first to use the vernacular and to draw heavily on Russian history and folklore, Pushkin is revered as the founder of modern Russian poetry. His masterpiece is the verse-novel *Eugene Onegin* (1825–31), adapted as an opera by TCHAIKOVSKY. Among his other works are the verse-drama *Boris Godunov* (1831), the basis of a MOUSSORGSKY opera; the historical poem *The Bronze Horseman* (1833); the story "The Queen of Spades" (1834), also adapted by Tchaikovsky; *The Captain's Daughter* (1836), a short novel of the 1773–75 PUGACHEV uprising; and *The Negro of Peter the Great* (1837), an unfinished novel about Pushkin's maternal great-grandfather.

Pushtu [pŭsh'to͞o], language belonging to the Iranian group of the Indo-Iranian subfamily of the Indo-European family of languages. It is also called Pashto and Afghan. See LANGUAGE (table).

pussy willow: see WILLOW.

Putnam, Israel, 1718–90, American Revolutionary general; b. Salem (now Danvers), Mass. A farmer, he joined the Continental army and was prominent at the battle of BUNKER HILL. He commanded the disastrous battle of Long Island (1776). His cousin, **Rufus Putnam,** 1738–1824, b. Sutton, Mass., was also an American Revolutionary general. A founder of the OHIO COMPANY OF ASSOCIATES, he supervised (1788) the building of Marietta, Ohio.

puts and calls, in securities trading, contracts allowing the holder to buy (a call) or sell (a put) a given stock at a specific price in a designated period of time. Both are options that add flexibility to the securities market and permit investors to diminish their risks. In return for a put or call, an investor pays a fee to the seller of the option, who pays a commission to the broker who brought the parties together. Calls are generally used by investors seeking to profit from a rise in stock prices while avoiding sharp losses; puts are used to profit from a fall in stock prices. Both are generally written for one to six months.

Puvis de Chavannes, Pierre [püvē′ də shävän′], 1824–98, French mural painter. After studying with DELACROIX, he secured his reputation with the painting *War* (Amiens). His chaste murals with allegorical figures are in the Sorbonne and the Boston Public Library.

Pu Yi, Henry, 1906–67, last emperor (1908–12) of China, under the name Hsuan T'ung. In 1934 he became Emperor K'ang Te of the Japanese puppet state of Manchukuo, or Manchuria. Captured (1945) by the Russians, he was returned (1950) to China and imprisoned until 1959.

PVC: see POLYVINYL CHLORIDE.

Pygmalion, in Greek mythology, king of Cyprus, sculptor of a beautiful statue of a woman. When he prayed to APHRODITE for a wife like it, she brought the statue (Galatea) to life, and Pygmalion married her.

Pygmies or **Pigmies,** nomadic hunting and gathering peoples of equatorial Africa (sometimes called Negrillos) whose adult males average under 5 ft (1.5 m) in height. They were probably the sole inhabitants of the Congo valley before farming was developed. Numbering c.150,000, they live in small bands, dependent largely on the forest for their food, although they trade with the settled agriculturalists around them. Pygmy groups include the Akkas, in the upper Nile R. valley; the Batwas, in the great bend of the Congo R.; and the Mbuti, in the Ituri forest of NE Zaïre.

Pyle, Ernie (Ernest Taylor Pyle), 1900–45, American journalist; b. Dana, Ind. In 1935 he began writing a syndicated column about the lives of typical Americans. During WORLD WAR II he wrote about the experiences of ordinary soldiers and sailors, and became one of the most popular war correspondents. Awarded the Pulitzer Prize for distinguished correspondence in 1944, he was killed by Japanese fire.

Pyle, Howard, 1853–1911, American illustrator and writer; b. Wilmington, Del. Pyle specialized in writing and illustrating tales of chivalry and adventure for young people, e.g., *The Merry Adventures of Robin Hood* (1883), reconstructing the past with engaging simplicity and penetrating realism.

Pylos [pī′lŏs], harbor of ancient MESSENIA, Greece, site of a 13th-cent.-B.C. Mycenaean palace, possible dwelling of King Nestor, in Greek mythology. The Bay of Pylos was the scene of an Athenian victory over SPARTA (425 B.C.) and, in modern times, of the battle of Navarino (1827) in the Greek war of independence.

Pym, Barbara (Mary Crampton), 1913–80, English writer. After success with such novels as *Excellent Women* (1952) and *A Glass of Blessings* (1958), her works went out of print. In 1977, after publishing *Quartet in Autumn*, she was praised by several British critics. Her books are quiet comedies, often dealing with older, usually frustrated, and isolated characters.

Pym, John, 1583?–1643, English statesman. He was a leading Puritan opponent of the royalist party of CHARLES I in both the Short and Long Parliaments. Charles tried to remove him from the Commons by military arrest. After the outbreak of the ENGLISH CIVIL WAR Pym arranged an alliance (1643) with Scotland based on English acceptance of the Solemn League and Covenant (see COVENANTERS).

Pynchon, Thomas, 1937–, American novelist; b. Glen Cove, N.Y. Considered a major writer, he is noted for his extravagant sense of humor and imagination. He creates a wild, dark, and labyrinthine world in novels that include *V.* (1963), *The Crying of Lot 49* (1966), *Gravity's Rainbow* (1973), *Slow Learner* (1984), and *Vineland* (1990).

Pyongyang [pyŭng′yäng′], city (1986 est. pop. 2,000,000), capital of North Korea, NW Korea. Near large iron and coal deposits, it is a major industrial center, producing steel, machinery, and armaments. Korea's oldest city, Pyongyang was founded, according to legend, in 1122 B.C. and served as the capital of several Korean kingdoms. It became the capital of North Korea in 1948 and was captured (1950) by UN forces during the KOREAN WAR. The city was later retaken by the North Koreans and rebuilt along modern lines. Only six gates remain of Pyongyang's great walls. Other landmarks include tombs (1st cent. B.C.) with notable murals.

pyorrhea: see PERIODONTITIS.

pyramid. The true pyramid exists only in Egypt. Usually of stone, it is square in plan, with triangular sides facing the compass points, sloping at an angle of about 50° and meeting at an apex. The oldest Egyptian tombs are MASTABAS. The true pyramid evolved about the IV dynasty (2680–2565 B.C.) and was favored through the VI dynasty (2420–2258 B.C.). Later pyramid tombs were archaisms. Each monarch built his own pyramid, in which his mummified body might be preserved for eternity. Entrance was through an opening in the north wall. A small passage, traversing lesser chambers, led to the sepulchral chamber, excavated from the bedrock deep beneath the immense pile. Usually of stone blocks laid in horizontal courses, pyramids were sometimes of mud brick with stone casing. Most notable are the three pyramids of Gizeh (IV dynasty). The Great Pyramid of Khufu or Cheops (2680 B.C.), one of the SEVEN WONDERS OF THE WORLD, is the largest ever built—13 acres (5.3 hectares) in area and 482 ft (147 m) high. Pyramidal structures are found also in Mesopotamia (the ZIGGURAT) and in Central America and Mexico. The Mayan pyramids, built in steep, receding blocks, were topped by ritual chambers. Some had interior tomb crypts.

Pyramus and Thisbe [pĭr′əməs, thĭz′bē], in classical myth, Babylonian lovers. Arriving at their trysting place, Thisbe fled a lion and dropped her mantle. Pyramus found the garment bloodied and, thinking Thisbe dead, killed himself. On returning, Thisbe killed herself. The white fruit of the mulberry tree that stood on the spot, was bloodied and remained red.

Pyrenees, mountain range, SW Europe, separating Spain from France. Rich in timber, pasturage, and hydroelectric power resources, the range extends 270 mi (435 km) from east to west and reaches a high point of 11,168 ft (3,404 m) in the Pico de Aneto in Spain. Along the steep slopes on the French side are many resorts and the noted place of pilgrimage, LOURDES.

pyrimidine, type of organic compound based on a six-membered carbon-nitrogen ring. Virtually all animal and plant tissue contains the pyrimidines thymine, cytosine, and uracil as part of certain COENZYMES and in the NUCLEIC ACIDS.

pyrite or **iron pyrites,** the most common sulfide mineral (FeS_2), brass yellow in color, found in crystals and massive, granular, and stalactite forms. In spite of its nickname, "fool's gold," it is often associated with gold. Pyrite, widely distributed in rocks of all ages, is used chiefly as a source of SULFUR for sulfuric acid.

pyroxene, name for a group of widespread magnesium, iron, and calcium silicate minerals. They are commonly white, black, and brown, but other varieties occur. Found chiefly in igneous and metamorphic rocks, they are abundant in lunar rocks.

Pyrrhus [pĭr′əs], c.318–272 B.C., king of EPIRUS. He invaded MACEDON (291) but was driven out (c.286). To aid the Tarentines, he went to Italy (280), where he defeated the Romans at Heraclea and Asculum, but with such heavy losses that he said: "One more such victory and I am lost"; thus the term "Pyrrhic victory." Defeated by the Romans at Beneventum (275), he turned again to Macedon, defeating Antigonus II (273). He was later killed in Argos. His sole accomplishment was the ruin of Epirus.

pyrrophyte, member of a division (Pyrrophyta) of the PROTIST kingdom consisting of mostly single-celled and photosynthetic organisms (dinoflagellates) that move using long, whiplike flagella. Traditionally considered PLANTS, pyrrophytes are extremely abundant in tropical oceans, where they are important in the food chain and largely responsible for the phosphorescence visible at night.

Pythagoras, c.582–c.507 B.C., pre-Socratic Greek philosopher. We know little of his life and nothing of his writings; all of our knowledge comes from his followers, the **Pythagoreans,** a mystical brotherhood he founded at Crotona. Members of the order regarded Pythagoras as a demigod and attributed all their doctrines to him. They believed in the transmigration of souls, and followed moral and dietary practices in order to purify the soul for its next embodiment. Skilled mathematicians, they influenced early Euclidian geometry, e.g., through the Pythagorean theorem (which states that the square of the length of the hypotenuse of a right triangle equals the sum of the squares of the lengths of the other two sides). They were also among the first to teach that the earth is a spherical planet revolving about a fixed point. Beginning with the discovery of numerical relations between musical notes, they taught that the essence of all things was number and that all relationships—even abstract concepts like justice—could be expressed numerically.

Pythian games, in ancient GREECE, games held at DELPHI every four years to honor APOLLO. They included musical, literary, and athletic contests.

Pythias: see DAMON AND PYTHIAS.

python, nonvenomous constrictor SNAKE of the BOA family, found in tropical regions of the Old World and the South Pacific islands. It kills its prey by squeezing them in its coils. The reticulated, or royal, python (*Python reticulatus*), one of the largest snakes in the world, may reach a length of 30 ft (9 m) or more.

Q

Qaddafi, Muammar al- [käddä′fē], 1942–, Libyan army officer and head of state (1969–). He led the 1969 army coup that deposed King Idris I. As head of state he has blended Arab nationalism, revolutionary socialism, and Islamic orthodoxy into a stridently anti-Western and anti-Israeli dictatorship, financed by LIBYA's vast oil resources. In 1986 Qaddafi survived a U.S. air raid launched in response to Libya's support of TERRORISM, but several of his children were hurt or killed.

Qatar [kä′tär], officially State of Qatar, independent emirate (1992 est. pop. 484,000), c.4,400 sq mi (11,400 sq km), on a largely barren peninsula in the PERSIAN GULF, bordering Saudi Arabia and the United Arab Emirates (S). The capital is DOHA. The economy of Qatar is dominated by oil, which accounts for over 90% of exports and government income. Oil revenues have been used to diversify the economy, including the development of natural gas fields, chemicals, iron and steel, cement, and fertilizer industries and banking. A minority (25%) of the population are Qataris (Arabs of the WAHHABI sect of Islam); the rest are largely Pakistanis, Indians, other Arabs, and Iranians. Arabic is the official language, but English is also widely spoken. The country is an absolute monarchy. Qatar was ruled by BAHRAIN from the 1700s until the mid-1800s, when Great Britain and the Ottoman Empire began vying for control of the peninsula. It was a British protectorate from 1916 until 1971, when it became independent. The present emir, Sheikh Khalifa ibn Hamad al-Thani, came to power in 1972 after ousting his cousin.

Qingdao or **Tsingtao** [both: chĭng-dow], city (1990 est. pop. 2,060,000), SE Shandong prov., E China, on the YELLOW SEA. Famous for its beaches, Qingdao is one of China's tourist centers and the leading industrial city in Shandong province. It makes textiles, machinery, railroad equipment, and processed food and tobacco. Leased to Germany (1898–1919), the city retains German influences in architecture and in the beer from its well-known brewery, established by the Germans. It was the site of a U.S. naval base from 1945 to 1949.

Qiqihar or **Tsitsihar** [both: chē-chē-här], city (1990 est. pop. 1,380,000), S central Heilongjiang prov., NE China. It is an industrial city producing locomotives, machine tools, and other heavy industrial goods. One of the oldest Chinese communities in NE China, it is in winter one of the coldest of all Chinese urban areas.

Qom or **Qum** [both: kôm], city (1986 pop. 543,139), W central Iran. Located in a semiarid region, it is an industrial and transportation center. Important to Shiite Muslims since early Islamic times, Qom contains the lavish tomb of Fatima al-Masuma (d. 816) and became a place of pilgrimage in the 17th cent. After 1979 the city was the home of Ayatollah KHOMEINI.

quadrature, in astronomy: see ELONGATION; SYZYGY.

Quadruple Alliance, one of three European alliances. **1** The Quadruple Alliance of 1718 was formed by Great Britain, France, the Holy Roman emperor, and the Netherlands, in opposition to PHILIP V of Spain and his efforts to nullify the results of the War of the SPANISH SUCCESSION by taking over Sicily. It was generally successful. **2** The Quadruple Alliance of 1814 consisted of Great Britain, Austria, Prussia, and Russia and aimed at strengthening the coalition against NAPOLEON I. It is sometimes confused with the HOLY ALLIANCE (to which Britain did not belong). **3** The Quadruple Alliance of 1834 consisted of Great Britain, France, Spain, and Portugal. Its purpose was to strengthen the government of ISABELLA II of Spain against the pretensions of the CARLISTS. The alliance broke up after the Spanish marriages (of Isabella and her sister) in 1846, which Britain opposed.

quail, name for small, extremely popular game BIRDS of the PHEASANT family, including the New World quails, the Old World quails and PARTRIDGES, and the true pheasants. In parts of the U.S. the BOBWHITE is called quail. The California quail (*Lophortyx californicus*), grayish with black and white markings and a forward-curving head plume, can be found in city parks. Quails have great reproductive potential, laying 12 to 15 eggs per clutch. They eat harmful insects and seeds and travel in flocks called coveys.

Quakers: see FRIENDS, RELIGIOUS SOCIETY OF.

Quantrill, William Clarke, 1837–65, Confederate guerrilla leader in the American CIVIL WAR; b. Dover, Ohio. His band of irregulars fought and pillaged in Missouri and Kansas, and sacked (1863) LAWRENCE, Kans., killing 150 civilians. Quantrill was killed by Union troops.

quantum chromodynamics (QCD), quantum field theory that describes the properties of the STRONG INTERACTIONS between QUARKS

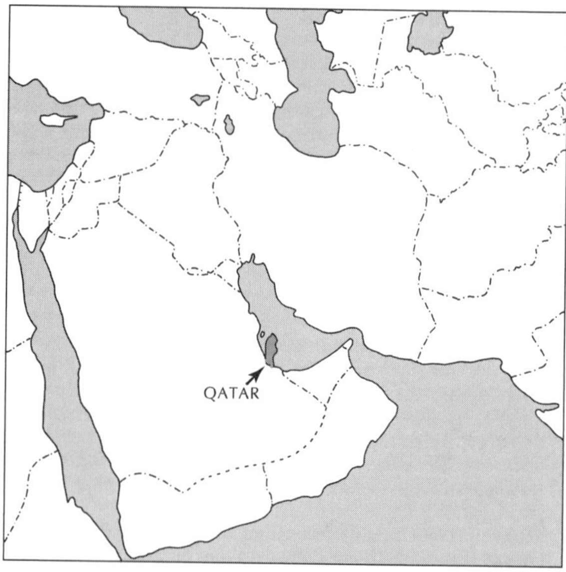

and between PROTONS and NEUTRONS in the framework of QUANTUM MECHANICS. Quarks possess a distinctive property called color that governs their binding together to form other ELEMENTARY PARTICLES. Analogous to electric charge in charged particles, color is of three varieties, arbitrarily designated as red, blue, and yellow. Quarks interact by emitting and absorbing gluons. Eight kinds of gluons are required to transmit the strong force between quarks, e.g., a blue quark might interact with a yellow quark by exchanging a blue-antiyellow gluon. See also QUANTUM ELECTRODYNAMICS.

quantum electrodynamics (QED), quantum field theory that describes the properties of ELECTROMAGNETIC RADIATION and its interaction with electrically charged matter in the framework of QUANTUM MECHANICS. The fundamental equations of QED apply to the emission and absorption of light by atoms and the basic interactions of light with ELECTRONS and other ELEMENTARY PARTICLES. Charged particles interact by emitting and absorbing PHOTONS, the particles of light that transmit electromagnetic forces. For this reason, QED is also known as the quantum theory of light. See also QUANTUM CHROMODYNAMICS.

quantum mechanics or **quantum theory,** branch of mathematical physics that deals with the emission and absorption of energy by matter and with the motion of material particles. Because it holds that energy and matter exist in tiny, discrete amounts, quantum mechanics is particularly applicable to ELEMENTARY PARTICLES and the interactions between them. According to the older theories of classical physics, energy is treated solely as a continuous phenomenon (i.e., WAVES), and matter is assumed to occupy a very specific region of space and to move in a continuous manner. According to the quantum theory, energy is emitted and absorbed in a small packet, called a quantum (pl. quanta), which in some situations behaves as particles of matter do; particles exhibit certain wavelike properties when in motion and are no longer viewed as localized in a given region but as spread out to some degree. The quantum theory thus proposes a dual nature for both waves and particles, with one aspect predominating in some situations and the other predominating in other situations. Quantum mechanics is needed to explain many properties of matter, such as the temperature dependence of the SPECIFIC HEAT of solids, as well as when very small quantities of matter or energy are involved, as in the interaction of elementary particles and fields, but the theory of RELATIVITY assumes importance in the special situation where very large speeds are involved. Together they form the theoretical basis of modern physics. (The results of classical physics approximate those of quantum mechanics for large scale events and those of relativity when ordinary speeds are involved.) Quantum theory was developed principally over a period of thirty years. The first contribution was the explanation of BLACKBODY radiation in 1900 by Max PLANCK, who proposed that the energies of any harmonic oscillator, such as the atoms of a blackbody radiator, are restricted to certain values, each of which is an integral (whole number) multiple of a basic minimum value. The energy E of this basic quantum is directly proportional to the frequency ν of the oscillator, or $E = h\nu$, where h is a constant, now called Planck's constant, having the value 6.63×10^{-34} joule-second. In 1905 Albert EINSTEIN proposed that the radiation itself is also quantized according to this same formula, and he used the new theory to explain the PHOTOELECTRIC EFFECT. Niels BOHR used the quantum theory in 1913 to explain both atomic structure and atomic spectra, showing the connection between the energy levels of an atom's electrons and the frequencies of light given off and absorbed by the atom. Quantum mechanics, the final mathematical formulation of the quantum theory, was developed during the 1920s. In 1924 Louis de BROGLIE proposed that particles exhibit wavelike properties. This hypothesis was confirmed experimentally in 1927 by Clinton J. Davisson and Lester H. Germer, who observed DIFFRACTION of a beam of electrons. Two different formulations of quantum mechanics were presented following de Broglie's suggestion. The wave mechanics of Erwin SCHRÖDINGER (1926) involves the use of a mathematical entity, the wave function, which is related to the probability of finding a particle at a given point in space. The matrix mechanics of Werner HEISENBERG (1925) makes no mention of wave functions or similar concepts but was shown to be mathematically equivalent to Schrödinger's theory. Quantum mechanics was combined with the theory of relativity in the formulation of P.A.M. DIRAC (1928), which also predicted the existence of ANTIPARTICLES. A particularly important discovery of the quantum theory is the uncertainty principle, enunciated by Heisenberg in 1927, which places an absolute theoretical limit on the accuracy of certain measurements; as a result, the assumption by earlier scientists that the physical state of a system could be measured exactly and used to predict future states had to be abandoned. Other developments of the theory include quantum statistics, presented in one form by Einstein and S.N. Bose (Bose-Einstein statistics, which apply to BOSONS) and in another by Dirac and Enrico FERMI (Fermi-Dirac statistics, which apply to FERMIONS); quantum electronics, which deals with interactions involving quantum energy levels and resonance, as in LASERS; quantum gravitation, the quantum theory of gravitational fields; and **quantum field theory.** In quantum field theory, interactions between particles result from the exchange of quanta: electromagnetic forces arise from the exchange of PHOTONS, weak nuclear forces (see WEAK INTERACTION) from the exchange of W AND Z PARTICLES, strong nuclear forces (see STRONG INTERACTION) from the exchange of gluons, and GRAVITATION from the exchange of gravitons. See also QUANTUM ELECTRODYNAMICS; QUANTUM CHROMODYNAMICS.

quark, any of a group of ELEMENTARY PARTICLES that are the basic constituents of all hadrons. Quarks have fractional charges of ⅓ or ⅔ of the basic charge of the electron or proton. There is evidence for five kinds, or flavors, of quarks: up, down, strange, charm, and bottom; a sixth, labeled top, has yet to be discovered. Each flavor of quark is believed to come in three varieties, differing in a property called color. The baryons, a subgroup of the hadrons that includes the proton and neutron, consist of three quarks. A proton consists of two up quarks and a down quark, and a neutron of two down quarks and an up quark. Three antiquarks make up the antibaryons. Mesons, the other subgroup, consist of a quark-antiquark pair.

quarrying, open, or surface, excavation of rock used for various purposes, including construction, ornamentation, and road building. The methods depend on the desired shape of the stone and its physical characteristics. Sometimes the rock is shattered by the use of explosives (e.g., for roadbeds). For building stones, a process called broaching, or channeling, is used, whereby holes are drilled and wedges inserted and hammered until the stone splits off. This method was probably used by the ancient Egyptians and the Incas.

quartz, one of the commonest rock-forming minerals (SiO_2), and one of the most important constituents of the earth's crust. It occurs in crystals, often distorted and commonly twinned. Varieties are classified as crystalline (e.g., AMETHYST) and cryptocrystalline (having crystals of microscopic size, e.g., CHALCEDONY and CHERT). SAND and SANDSTONE are clastic quartzes.

quartzite, ROCK composed of firmly cemented QUARTZ grains, commonly resulting from the METAMORPHISM of sandstone and distinguished from the latter by fracturing across, rather than along, the line of cementing material between its constituent grains of sand.

quasar, one of a class of faint blue celestial objects, starlike in appearance, that are currently believed to be the most distant and most luminous objects in the universe. The spectral lines of quasars have enormous RED SHIFTS that seem to imply that they are receding from our galaxy with speeds as great as 95% of the speed of light. If HUBBLE'S LAW for the expansion of the universe is extrapolated to include quasars, they may be as far as 12 billion LIGHT-YEARS away and consequently as intrinsically luminous as 1,000 galaxies combined.

quasicrystal or **quasiperiodic solid,** solid body that exhibits such crystalline features as symmetry and repeating patterns of unit cells (regular arrangements of atoms, molecules, or ions) but—unlike a CRYSTAL—requires more than one type of unit cell to achieve large-scale order. Quasicrystals exhibit symmetries (e.g., icosahedral and decagonal) not seen in crystals. Quasicrystals are usually metallic alloys and have stronger magnetic properties and exhibit greater elasticity at higher temperatures than crystals.

Quasimodo, Salvatore, 1901–68, Italian poet and translator; b. Sicily. Five volumes of verse (1930–38) established him as a leader of Italy's "hermetic" poets, whose verbal complexity was derived from the French SYMBOLISTS. His later, more humanistic poetry includes *Day after Day* (1947) and *To Give and To Have* (1966). Quasimodo was awarded the 1959 Nobel Prize in literature.

Quayle, J(ames) Danforth, 1947–, vice president of the U.S. (1989–93); b. Indianapolis. A conservative Indiana Republican, he served in the U.S. House of Representatives (1977–81) and Senate (1981–89). In 1988 he was elected vice president on the ticket headed by George BUSH. Quayle led the Bush administration's efforts to reduce government regulations, particularly environmental ones, that affected businesses.

Quebec, Fr. *Québec,* province (1991 pop. 6,895,963), 594,855 sq mi (1,540,680 sq km), E Canada, bounded by Hudson Strait (N), Labrador and the Gulf of St. Lawrence (E), New Brunswick and the U.S (S), Hudson Bay and Ontario (W). Quebec is the largest and second most populous of the provinces. It is the center of French Canadian culture, French-speaking people making up c.80% of the population. The chief cities include MONTREAL, the largest city; QUEBEC city, the capital; LAVAL; and TROIS RIVIÈRES. The CANADIAN SHIELD covers the northern nine tenths of the province. To the south lies the great SAINT LAWRENCE R., along whose banks are the lowlands that are the centers of agriculture and industry. In the southeast, south of the St. Lawrence, are the APPALACHIAN Highlands and the GASPÉ PENINSULA. The forests of the north yield valuable timber, and throughout the north copper, iron, zinc, silver, and gold are mined. Asbestos is found in the Appalachian Highlands. The rivers have been, and are being, extensively developed for hydroelectric power. The small farms of the lowlands produce dairy products, sugar beets, and tobacco. Quebec's main manufactures are refined petroleum, food products, motor vehicles, clothing, furniture, iron and steel, chemicals, and metal and paper products.

History. Jacques CARTIER explored (1534–35) the St. Lawrence region, and in 1608 CHAMPLAIN built a trading post on the site of Quebec city. French explorers, traders, and missionaries then penetrated the continent, and in 1663 the area, known as New France, became a royal colony. After the FRENCH AND INDIAN WAR of 1754–63 the colony came under British rule. To conciliate the French inhabitants the British passed (1774) the QUEBEC ACT, by which the area retained its French language and institutions. After the American Revolution, many British UNITED EMPIRE LOYALISTS came to Quebec, and in 1791 Upper Canada (now ONTARIO) was separated from Quebec (Lower Canada). French Canadian resentment against the British led to an unsuccessful revolt (1837) sparked by Louis PAPINEAU. Upper and Lower Canada were united in 1841, but in 1867 Quebec and Ontario joined the Canadian confederation as separate provinces. In the 20th cent. Quebec sought to broaden its provincial rights in Canada. In 1976 the separatist Parti Québécois won a large majority in the provincial assembly and passed laws to discourage the use of English, but Quebec voters rejected the party's "sovereignty-association" plan in a 1980 referendum. Since 1985 the Liberal party, led by Robert Bourassa and, since 1994, by Daniel Johnson, has controlled the assembly. Separatism revived in 1990 when the 1987 Meech Lake accord, which recognized Quebec as a "distinct society," failed to be ratified by all the provinces. Quebec sends 24 senators (appointed) and 75 representatives (elected) to the national parliament.

Quebec, Fr. *Québec,* city (1991 pop. 167,517), provincial capital of Quebec, part of the Québec urban community (1991 pop. 490,271), on the St. Lawrence R. The population is largely French-speaking, and the city is a focus of French Canadian nationalism. The chief industries are shipbuilding and tourism. Features of special interest include the historic Old Lower Town, centered in restored Place Royale at river level; the old Upper Town, dominated by the huge Chateau Frontenac hotel (1892), at the top of Cape Diamond, a 300-ft-high (90-m) bluff; the Citadel fortress (1832); and the Parliament Building or National Assembly (1877–86). Quebec was founded by CHAMPLAIN in 1608 and, after a brief period of English rule (1629–32), was made the capital of New France in 1663. In 1759 English forces under James Wolfe defeated the French under Gen. MONTCALM on the Plains of Abraham and captured the city. It became the capital of Lower Canada (now Quebec province) in 1791 and was twice the capital of the United Provinces of Canada (1851–55, 1859–65).

Quebec Act, 1774, creation of a permanent British government in CANADA, which also granted religious freedom to Roman Catholics. The THIRTEEN COLONIES considered it one of the INTOLERABLE ACTS because it nullified many of their claims to Western lands; thus it helped to start the AMERICAN REVOLUTION.

Quechua, Kechua [both: kĕch'o͞oə, –wä], or **Quichua** [kēch'wä], linguistic family belonging to the Andean branch of the Andean-Equatorial stock of Native American languages. See NATIVE AMERICAN LANGUAGES (table).

Queen Anne's lace or **wild carrot,** herb (*Daucus carota*) of the CARROT family, native to the Old World but naturalized in North America. Similar in appearance to the cultivated carrot (which is believed to be derived from this plant), it has feathery foliage but a woody root. The tiny white flowers bloom in a lacy, flat-topped cluster or umbel.

Queen Anne's War: see FRENCH AND INDIAN WARS.

Queensberry, John Sholto Douglas, 8th **marquess of:** see BOXING.

Queensland, state (1992 est. pop. 3,022,000), 667,000 sq mi (1,727,530 sq km), NE Australia. Almost half of Queensland's residents live in metropolitan BRISBANE, the capital. Sugar is the main export crop; cotton and wheat are also important. Tropical fruits are grown in the half of the state located in the tropics. Beef cattle and sheep predominate in drier areas W of the EASTERN HIGHLANDS, where the Great Artesian Basin (376,000 sq mi/973,840 sq km) is a valuable water source. Queensland has deposits of bauxite (near Weipa); copper, silver-lead, zinc, and phosphate (near Mt. Isa); nickel (near Townsville); and coal, oil, and natural gas. Tourism and manufacturing have grown in importance since the 1960s. Originally settled as a penal colony (1824–43, at Moreton Bay), Queensland became a separate colony in 1859 and a federated state of Australia in 1901.

Quemoy: see MATSU AND QUEMOY.

Quental, Antero de [kĕntäl'], 1842–91, Portuguese poet. The author of *Odes modernas* (1865), *Sonetos* (1881), and other volumes, he also helped organize the Portuguese Socialist party. Ill health led to his suicide. He is considered a principal modern Portuguese poet.

Quesnay, François [kĕnā'], 1694–1774, French economist, founder of the physiocratic school. A physician to Louis XV, he began his economic studies in 1756, when he wrote for the *Encyclopédie.* His chief work is *The Economical Table* (1758), which he and his followers believed summed up the natural law of economy. Quesnay and other PHYSIOCRATS greatly influenced the thought of Adam SMITH.

Quetzalcoatl [Nahuatl, = feathered serpent], ancient deity and legendary ruler of the TOLTEC in Mexico. An early Toltec ruler credited with the discovery of corn, the arts, and science is also called Quetzalcoatl. As god of civilization, identified with the wind and the planet Venus, Quetzalcoatl represented the forces of good and light. The name was adopted by the AZTEC and linked to their chief god; their emperor MONTEZUMA mistook the invading Spanish for the hosts of Quetzalcoatl returning (as promised in legend) from travels over the sea. The MAYA Kulkulcán, also represented by a feathered serpent, probably derived from the same historical figure as Quetzalcoatl.

Quevedo y Villegas, Francisco Gómez de [kāvā'*th*ō ē vēlyā'gäs], 1580–1645, Spanish writer. A major figure of the GOLDEN AGE, he wrote brilliant moral satires such as *Visions* (1627); the picaresque novel *The Life of Buscón* (1626); much verse; and political and religious works.

Quezon, Manuel Luis [kā'sōn], 1878–1944, first president (1935–44) of the Commonwealth of the PHILIPPINES. He crusaded tirelessly for Philippine independence from the U.S. During WORLD WAR II he led a government-in-exile in the U.S.

Quezon City, city (1990 pop. 1,667,000), central Luzon, Philippines, adjacent to MANILA. Although it is the nation's largest city, it is usually considered a Manila suburb. It was the Philippine capital from 1948 to 1976, when Manila replaced it. It is the seat of the Univ. of the Philippines.

quicklime: see CALCIUM OXIDE.

quicksilver: see MERCURY.

Quidor, John [kĭdôr'], 1801–81, American painter; b. Tappan, N.Y. Best known for scenes inspired by the writings of Washington IRV-

ING, Quidor often mingled the macabre with humor in scenes placed in mysterious romantic settings.

quilting, form of needlework in which two layers of fabric separated by an interlining are sewn together, usually in a pattern of back or running stitches. A traditional means of adding warmth to fabric in Europe and Asia, it has been used in America since colonial times to make bed covers (quilts). Until c.1750 quilts were of the pieced, or patchwork, type; later, appliqué and trapunto (padding or cording) also became popular. Old quilts are prized by collectors. The art survives in rural Southern areas and in traditional communities, such as the Amish, and has also been revived by textile artists.

quince, shrub or small tree (genera *Chaenomeles* and *Cydonia*) of the ROSE family. The common quince (*Cydonia oblonga*) is a spineless tree. Its edible fruit is similar to the related APPLE and PEAR but is very astringent and is used mainly in preserves; marmalade is said to have first been made from quince. Flowering quinces (genus *Chaenomeles*) are cultivated for their profuse, usually thorny branches and scarlet, pink, or white flowers.

Quine, Willard Van Orman, 1908–, American philosopher and mathematical logician; b. Akron, Ohio. He studied under WHITEHEAD and CARNAP and taught (1936–78) at Harvard Univ. Much of his work deals with the implications of viewing language as a logical system. He disputed KANT's distinction between analytic and synthetic statements, arguing that any statement can be held to be true once a language's system of reference is adjusted. In the field of logic he made important contributions to SET theory. His works include *A System of Logic* (1934), *Word and Object* (1938), *Philosophy of Logic* (1969), and *Methods of Logic* (3d ed., 1972).

quinine, ALKALOID isolated from the bark of several species of *Cinchona* trees. Prior to the development of synthetic agents, quinine was the specific drug treatment for MALARIA. It is used in a soft drink known as tonic, which is often mixed with alcoholic beverages. Excessive use may cause cinchonism, a condition characterized by ringing of the ears, dizziness, and headache.

Quintilian (Marcus Fabius Quintilianus), A.D. c.35–c.95, Roman rhetorician and teacher. His influential *Institutio oratoria,* a survey of education, literature, the principles of rhetoric, and the life and training of the orator, demonstrates the necessity of moderation and good taste.

Quiroga, Juan Facundo, 1790–1835, Argentine leader. As overlord of the Andean provinces he was a zealous and ruthless advocate of federalism. He rejected the unitarian constitution of 1826 and participated in the civil strife that followed. He was later assassinated, probably at ROSAS's instigation.

Quisling, Vidkun, 1887–1945, Norwegian fascist leader. Minister of defense (1931–33), he founded the fascist Nasjonal Samling national unity party. He helped the Germans prepare the conquest of Norway (1940), and they installed him as premier (1942–45). After the war he was tried for high treason and shot. From his name came the word *quisling* [traitor].

Quito [kē'tō], city (1990 pop. 1,387,887), N central Ecuador, capital of Ecuador and of Pichincha prov. Though unimportant economically, it is Ecuador's political and cultural center and second largest city. It is famous for its splendid setting, lying at an elevation of 9,350 ft (2,850 m) in a fertile Andean valley at the foot of a volcano. The colonial city was built at the site of the capital of the INCA kingdom of Quito, captured for Spain in 1534. In 1822 it was liberated from Spain by Antonio José de SUCRE. Although the city has often been damaged by earthquakes, many fine examples of Spanish colonial architecture remain, including the great Church of San Francisco.

Quivira [kēvē'rä], land explored by CORONADO (1541) and other Spanish explorers. The exact site is unknown, but it is generally identified with Wichita villages in Kansas.

Qum: see QOM.

Qumran [ko͞omrän'], ancient village on the northwest shore of the Dead Sea, in the Israeli-occupied WEST BANK. It is famous for the nearby caves in which the DEAD SEA SCROLLS were found. The first archaeologists to excavate the ruins at Qumran identified them with an ascetic community that produced the scroll known as the *Manual of Discipline,* but recent interpretations by other archaeologists have suggested the inhabitants of the ruins lived in relative luxury.

R

Ra or **Re,** in EGYPTIAN RELIGION, sun god, one of the most important gods of ancient Egypt. Called the creator and father of all things, he was chief of the cosmic deities. Early Egyptian kings alleged descent from him. Various other Egyptian gods, e.g., AMON, were identified with him. His symbol is the PYRAMID.

Ra, chemical symbol of the element RADIUM.

Rabat, city (1990 est. pop. 1,472,000), capital of Morocco, on the Atlantic Ocean at the mouth of the Bou Regreg estuary. The city is a minor port and has textile industries. There have been settlements there since ancient times. It became a Muslim fortress A.D. c.700 and was a stronghold of corsairs in the 17th and 18th cent. Prior to independence (1956), Rabat was the capital of the French protectorate of Morocco. Landmarks include the old city walls and the ruins of the Tour Hassan (12th cent.), a large, unfinished mosque.

rabbi [Heb., = my teacher], the title of a Jewish religious leader. The term first came into common use among Palestinian Jews in the late 1st cent. A.D. During the Middle Ages the rabbi, in addition to being a legal scholar, began to assume the roles of teacher, preacher, and communal leader. In the 1970s the Reform and Conservative rabbinical seminaries began to admit female students, and the acceptance of women rabbis has made slow but steady progress. Orthodox Judaism has maintained its traditional position against women rabbis.

rabbit, MAMMAL of the family Leporidae, which includes the HARE. Rabbits and hares have large front teeth, short tails, and hind legs and feet adapted for running and jumping. The term *rabbit* generally refers to small, running animals that give birth to blind, naked young; *hare* refers to larger, hopping forms with longer ears and legs whose young are born furred and open-eyed. Wild rabbits are up to 16 in. (41 cm) long and have grayish-brown fur. The European common rabbit (*Oryctolagus cuniculus*), native to S Europe and Africa, is now found worldwide. It lives in elaborate, adjoining warrens and is chiefly nocturnal, feeding on vegetation. All domestic rabbits belong to this species.

Rabelais, François [räblā'], c.1490–1553, French humanist, one of the great comic geniuses of literature. Joining the Franciscan order, Rabelais studied Greek and Latin as well as science, law, philology, and letters. He later left the Franciscans to become a Benedictine monk. He received (1530) a degree in medicine from the Univ. of Montpellier, where he later taught (1537–38). He went to Lyons (1532) to practice medicine, and it was there that his satirical masterpiece, *Gargantua and Pantagruel* (1532–62), was published. The work, in five books, is as gigantic in scope as the physical size of its heroes. Beneath its broad, often ribald humor are serious discussions of education, politics, philosophy, and religion. The breadth of Rabelais's learning and his zest for life are evident. The work was condemned by the Sorbonne, however, and Rabelais was saved from persecution for heresy only by the protection of his friend, Cardinal Jean du Bellay. He spent his last years as curate at Meudon (1550–52).

Rabi, Isidor Isaac [rŏb'ē], 1898–1988, American physicist; b. Austria. He taught physics at Columbia from 1929 and was chairman (1952–56) of the general advisory committee to the U.S. Atomic Energy Commission. Rabi is known for his work on magnetism, molecular beams, and quantum mechanics. He won the 1944 Nobel Prize in physics for his discovery and measurement of the radio-frequency spectra of atomic nuclei whose magnetic spin has been disturbed.

rabies or **hydrophobia,** acute, often fatal disease of mammals, caused by a virus transmitted from an animal to another animal or to humans through infected saliva, usually through a bite. After a variable incubation period, rabies produces fever, headache, nausea, and pain at the site of the bite, followed by convulsions, inability to drink fluids (hence hydrophobia), apathy, and death. An antirabies vaccine is administered to the bite victim to prevent the disease from developing, and vaccine-laced bait can control the disease in wild animals.

Rabin, Yitzhak, 1922–, Israeli general and political leader, first native-born prime minister of Israel (1974–77, 1992–). A brigade commander in the 1948 ARAB-ISRAELI WAR, Rabin rose to chief of staff by 1964 and was credited with Israel's victory in the Six-Day War (1967). After serving (1968–73) as ambassador to the U.S., he was elected to parliament as a Labor party deputy. He served (Mar.–May 1974) as labor minister before becoming prime minister. As defense minister (1984–90) in the Labor-Likud coalition government, he ordered a harsh crackdown on the Arab uprising in the WEST BANK in the late 1980s. Rabin ousted Shimon PERES as Labor party leader in 1992 and led Labor to victory in the national elections, becoming prime minister and defense minister. In 1993 he agreed to a peace accord with the PLO that called for limited Palestinian self-rule in Jericho and the Gaza Strip.

Rabinowitz, Shalom: see SHOLOM ALEICHEM.

raccoon, nocturnal New World MAMMAL (genus *Procyon*) with a heavily furred body, pointed face, and handlike forepaws. It has mixed gray, brown, and black hair, a black face mask, and black rings on the tail. The common raccoon of North America (*Procyon lotor*) is found from S Canada to South America, except in parts of the Rocky Mts. and in deserts. Highly omnivorous, it is adaptable to civilization and will feed on garbage. Its fur is commercially valuable.

race, one of the group of populations constituting humanity. Genetically, a race may be defined as a group with gene frequencies differing from those of the other groups in the human species (see GENETICS), although the genes in question make up a tiny percentage of the total human genome. The term *race* is inappropriate when applied to national, religious, or cultural groups, nor can the biological criteria of race be equated with mental characteristics (intelligence, personality, character). Races arose in response to MUTATION, selection, geographic adaptation, and genetic drift; racial differentiation occurred relatively late in history. In the 19th and early 20th cent., Joseph Arthur Gobineau and Houston Stewart Chamberlain attributed cultural and psychological values to race, proposing theories of racial superiority, an approach that culminated in the vicious racial doctrines of Nazi Germany. By limiting the criteria to certain physical characteristics, anthropologists at one time agreed on the existence of three relatively distinct groups of people, namely, Caucasoid, Mongoloid, and Negroid, distinguished by such traits as skin color, hair type and color, shape of body, head, and facial features, and blood traits. Today, however, anthropologists stress the heterogeneity of world population, and many reject the concept of race outright.

Rachel, wife of JACOB and mother of JOSEPH and Benjamin. She is one of the four Jewish matriarchs.

Rachel [räshĕl'], 1828–58, French actress; b. Switzerland as Elisa Félix. The great tragic actress of her day, she excelled in the works of RACINE (*Phèdre*) and CORNEILLE.

Rachmaninoff, Sergei Vasilyevich [räkhmä'nēnôf], 1873–1943, Russian composer, conductor, and pianist. His romantic, dramatic music was strongly influenced by his friend TCHAIKOVSKY. His notable works include four piano CONCERTOS, Prelude in C Sharp Minor (1892), Rhapsody on a Theme by Paganini (1934), three SYMPHONIES, and many songs.

Racine, Jean [räsēn'], 1639–99, French dramatist. He is the prime exemplar of French CLASSICISM. His third play, *Andromaque* (1667), established him as France's leading tragic dramatist, displacing CORNEILLE and earning him the patronage of Louis XIV as well as the enmity of Corneille's friends (including MOLIÈRE). His next six tragedies were all masterpieces, unsurpassed in nobility of verse, simplicity of diction, psychological realism, and dramatic construction: *Britannicus* (1669), *Bérénice* (1670), *Bajazet* (1672), *Mithridate* (1673), *Iphigénie en Aulide* (1674), and *Phèdre* (1677). His only comedy was *The Litigants* (1668), satirizing the law courts. A concerted attack on *Phèdre* led Racine to give up the theater, but Mme de MAINTENON persuaded him to write *Esther* (1689) and *Athalie* (1691) for performance at her school in Saint-Cyr. These differ from the earlier plays in their biblical subjects and use of a chorus.

Racine, industrial city (1990 pop. 84,298), seat of Racine co., SE Wis., on Lake Michigan, at the mouth of the Root R.; inc. 1848. It is a port with diversified manufactures, including floor wax and farm and electrical machinery. Three buildings in Racine were designed by Frank Lloyd WRIGHT.

Rackham, Arthur, 1867–1939, English illustrator and watercolorist. He is best known for his delicately colored, imaginative children's book illustrations, e.g., for *Peter Pan* (1906) and *Alice in Wonderland* (1907).

racquetball, sport played indoors by two or four players, combining elements of handball and such racket games as SQUASH. It is played on a standard handball court 40 ft (12.2 m) long, 20 ft (6.1 m) wide, and 20 ft high, with a back wall at least 12 ft (3.6 m) high. The fiber-strung racket is attached to the player's wrist with a thong, and the ball is slightly larger and lighter than that used in handball. Racquetball was developed in the early 1950s and enjoyed a boom in popularity throughout the U.S. in the 1970s.

radar [*ra*dio *d*etection *a*nd *r*anging], system or technique for detecting the position, motion, and nature of a remote object by means of radio waves reflected from its surface. Pulse radar systems use a single directional ANTENNA to transmit and receive the waves. They transmit pulses of electromagnetic waves (usually MICROWAVES), some of which are reflected by objects in the path of the beam. Reflections are received by the radar unit, processed electronically, and converted into images on a CATHODE-RAY TUBE. The antenna must be connected only to the transmitter when sending and only to the receiver while receiving; this is accomplished by switching from one to the other and back again in the fraction of a microsecond between pulses. The distance of the object from the radar source is determined by measuring the time required for the radar signal to reach the target and return. The direction of the object with respect to the radar unit is determined from the direction in which the pulses were transmitted. In most units, the beam of pulses is continuously rotated at a constant speed, or it is scanned (swung back and forth) over a sector at a constant rate. Pulse radar is used primarily for aircraft and naval navigation and for military applications. In **Doppler radar,** or continuous-wave radar, two antennas are used—one to transmit and the other to receive. Because the time a continuous-wave signal takes to reach the target and return cannot be measured, Doppler radar cannot determine distance. The velocity of the object is determined using the DOPPLER EFFECT. If the object is approaching the radar unit, the frequency of the returned signal is greater than the frequency of the transmitted signal; if the object is receding, the returned frequency is less; and if the object is not moving relative to the radar unit, the frequency of the returned signal is the same as the frequency of the transmitted signal. Doppler radar can measure wind rotation inside a thunderstorm and is used to identify possible tornados. See also STEALTH TECHNOLOGY.

Radcliffe, Ann (Ward), 1764–1823, English novelist. Her *Romance of the Forest* (1791), *Mysteries of Udolpho* (1794), and *The Italian* (1797), characterized by brooding landscapes, terror, and suspense, were among the first gothic romances.

Radcliffe-Brown, Alfred Reginald, 1881–1955, English anthropologist. He viewed social relations and institutions as interdependent parts of a social system, analyzing them in relation to the whole. His structural-functional analyses greatly advanced social anthropology as a science. He also contributed to the study of KINSHIP.

Radcliffe College: see HARVARD UNIVERSITY.

radial velocity, the speed with which a star moves toward or away from the sun. It is measured from the RED SHIFT or blue shift in the star's spectrum. See also PROPER MOTION.

radiation, the emission or transmission of energy in the form of WAVES through space or through a material medium; the term also applies to the radiated energy itself. The term includes electromagnetic, acoustic, and particle radiation, and all forms of ionizing radiation. According to QUANTUM MECHANICS, ELECTROMAGNETIC RADIATION may be viewed as made up of PHOTONS. Acoustic radiation is propagated as sound waves. Examples of particle radiation are alpha and beta rays in RADIOACTIVITY, and COSMIC RAYS.

radiation sickness, illness caused by the effects of radiation on body tissues. It may be acute, delayed, or chronic and may occur as a result of cumulative exposure to small doses of radiation (as in a plant, a laboratory, or the environment); or exposure to radiation from a nuclear explosion or accident. Symptoms may be mild and transitory, or severe, depending on the type of radiation, the dose, and the rate at which exposure is experienced. They include weakness, loss of appetite, vomiting, diarrhea, a tendency to bleed, increased susceptibility to infection, and—in severe cases—brain damage and death. Mild radiation sickness is a common side effect of radiation therapy for CANCER. Exposure to radiation is of concern even in small doses because of possible long-term genetic effects and increased cancer rates in exposed people.

radio, transmission or reception of ELECTROMAGNETIC RADIATION in the radio frequency range from one place to another without wires. For the propagation and interception of radio waves, a transmitter and receiver are employed. A radio wave carries information-bearing signals; the information may be encoded directly on the wave by periodically interrupting its transmission (see TELEGRAPH) or impressed on the carrier frequency by a process called MODULATION, e.g., amplitude modulation (AM) or frequency modulation (FM). In its most common form, radio transmits sounds (voice and music) and pictures (TELEVISION). The sounds (or images) are converted into electrical signals by a MICROPHONE (or camera tube), amplified (see AMPLIFIER), and used to modulate a carrier wave that has been generated by a transmitter. The modulated carrier is also amplified, then applied to an ANTENNA that converts the electrical signals to electromagnetic waves that radiate into space at the speed of light. Receiving antennas intercept part of this radiation, convert it back into electrical signals, and feed it to a receiver. Once the basic signals have been separated from the carrier wave, they are fed to a LOUDSPEAKER or CATHODE-RAY TUBE, where they are converted into sound and visual images, respectively. Some celestial bodies and interstellar gases emit relatively strong radio waves that are observed with radio telescopes composed of very sensitive receivers and large directional antennas (see RADIO ASTRONOMY). Long-range radio signals enable communications between astronauts and ground-based controllers and carry information from SPACE PROBES as they travel to and encounter distant planets. The invention of the TRANSISTOR and other microelectronic devices (see MICROELECTRONICS) led to the development of portable transmitters and receivers. Military applications of radio include the proximity fuse and various types of RECONNAISSANCE SATELLITES. Radio signals sent by NAVIGATION SATELLITES can be used by special receivers to determine one's position. Citizens band (CB) radios, operating at frequencies near 27 megahertz, are used in vehicles for communication while traveling. See also BROADCASTING; COMMUNICATIONS SATELLITES; RADAR.

radioactive dating: see DATING.

radioactive nuclear waste: see WASTE DISPOSAL.

radioactivity, spontaneous disintegration or decay of the nucleus of an atom by emission of particles, usually accompanied by ELECTROMAGNETIC RADIATION. Natural radioactivity is exhibited by several elements, including RADIUM and URANIUM. The radiation produced is of three types: the *alpha particle,* which is a nucleus (two protons and two neutrons) of an ordinary helium atom; the *beta particle,* which is a high-speed electron or, in some cases, a positron (the electron's antiparticle); and GAMMA RADIATION, which is a type of electromagnetic radiation with very short wavelengths. The rate of disintegration of a radioactive substance is commonly designated by its half-life, which is the time required for one half of a given quantity of the substance to decay. Radioactivity may be induced in stable elements by bombardment with particles of high energy. See also DATING; ISOTOPE.

radio astronomy, study of celestial bodies by means of the radio waves they emit and absorb naturally. These waves are received by specially constructed antennas called radio telescopes. The most common design consists of a parabolic "dish" of open metal latticework that focuses the radio waves into a concentrated signal that is filtered, amplified, and, finally, analyzed using a computer. Groups of antennas can also be linked by computer to form a single radio telescope, such as the Very Large Array and Very Long Baseline Array of the NATIONAL RADIO ASTRONOMY OBSERVATORY. The radio signals received from outer space are extremely weak, and long observing times are required to collect a useful amount of energy. There are several basic types of galactic radio emissions. The type first discovered, accidentally in 1931 by Karl JANSKY, is spread over a wide band of radio frequencies. It is produced when free electrons are scattered by collisions with heavier ions in the ionized interstellar gases surrounding hot, bright STARS. A second type, called synchrotron radiation, is emitted by energetic electrons as they rapidly spiral within the strong magnetic fields existing in the vicinity of SUPERNOVA remnants. A third type, originating in INTERSTELLAR MATTER, radiates at discrete frequencies characteristic of the quantum jumps (see QUANTUM MECHANICS) made by electrons in the atoms and molecules, e.g., atomic hydrogen and formaldehyde, in the interstellar medium. PULSARS, stellar radio sources that regularly radiate periodic bursts of energy, were discovered in 1968. Radio waves also come from outside our Milky Way galaxy. Some extragalactic sources are detected only by their radio emission, but others have been identified with optically observed GALAXIES and QUASARS. In addition to localized radio sources, there is uniform low-level radio noise from every direction in the sky. This cosmic background radiation is believed to be an indication that the universe began with an explosive "big bang" rather than having always existed in an unchanging steady state (see COSMOLOGY).

Radio Free Europe, broadcasting organization headquartered in Munich, Germany, that provides daily programs to the peoples of Poland, the Czech Republic, Slovakia, Romania, Bulgaria, the Baltic states, and the former Yugoslav republics in their own languages; broadcasts to Hungary ended in 1993. Founded in 1950, it is privately operated, although mainly financed by the U.S. government. Its broadcasts include news and political commentaries, music, sports, and other entertainment. In 1976 Radio Free Europe was merged with **Radio Liberty,** which broadcasts to the former republics of the USSR and was founded in 1951.

radioimmunoassay (RIA), highly sensitive laboratory technique used to measure minute amounts of substances including antigens, hormones, and drugs present in the body. The substance or antigen (a foreign substance in the body that causes antibody production) to be measured is injected into an animal, causing it to produce antibodies. Serum containing the antibodies is withdrawn and treated with a radioactive antigen and later with a nonradioactive antigen. Measurements of the amount of radioactivity are then used to determine the amount of antigen present. The technique was developed by Solomon Berson and Rosalyn Yalow. Yalow was awarded the 1977 Nobel Prize in physiology or medicine for her work.

radioisotope: see ISOTOPE.

radiometer, instrument for the detection or measurement of ELECTROMAGNETIC RADIATION, particularly INFRARED RADIATION. Radiometers that function by increasing the temperature of the device are called thermal detectors; examples include the bolometer and the THERMOCOUPLE.

radiosonde, group of instruments for simultaneous measurement and radio transmission of meteorological data. The instrument package is usually carried into the atmosphere by a WEATHER BALLOON; it may, however, also be carried by a rocket (rocketsonde) or dropped by parachute (dropsonde).

radio telescope: see RADIO ASTRONOMY.

radish, herb (*Raphanus sativus*) of the MUSTARD family, with an edible, pungent root used as a relish. There are many varieties, with red, white, or black roots of different shapes and sizes, some quite large. HORSERADISH is not a radish but a related plant of the mustard family.

Radisson, Pierre Esprit [rädēsōN′], c.1632–1710, French explorer. His accounts of his travels are questioned in part, but he is said to have been with the first explorers to enter MINNESOTA. He transferred his allegiance to the English, made trips to HUDSON BAY (1668, 1670), and was influential in the formation of the HUDSON'S BAY COMPANY.

radium (Ra), radioactive metallic element, discovered in PITCHBLENDE in 1898 by Pierre and Marie CURIE. It is a rare, lustrous, white ALKALINE-EARTH METAL that resembles barium in its chemical properties. Radium compounds are found in uranium ores. The RADIOACTIVITY of radium and its compounds is used in the treatment of cancer. Radium compounds are mixed with a phosphor in luminous paints. In its radioactive decay, radium emits alpha, beta, and gamma rays and produces heat. See ELEMENT (table); PERIODIC TABLE.

radon (Rn), gaseous radioactive element, discovered by Ernest RUTHERFORD in 1899. A colorless, chemically unreactive INERT GAS, it is the densest gas known. Highly radioactive (emitting alpha rays), it is used chiefly in the treatment of cancer by radiotherapy. In homes and other buildings in some areas of the U.S., radon produced by the radioactive decay of uranium-238 present in soil and rock can reach levels regarded as dangerous, but the seriousness of the problem is unclear. See ELEMENT (table); PERIODIC TABLE.

Raeburn, Sir Henry, 1756–1823, Scottish portrait painter. He was influenced by Sir Joshua REYNOLDS. His forceful work displays his virtuoso brush technique. He painted over 700 portraits, mostly of notable Scots; many are in the National Gallery of Scotland, Edinburgh.

Raffles, Sir Thomas Stamford Bingley, 1781–1826, British East Indian administrator. As lieutenant governor of Java (1811–15) and of Bencooleen, in SUMATRA (1818–23), he launched many reforms. In 1819 he secured the transfer of SINGAPORE to the British EAST INDIA COMPANY.

Rafsanjani, (Ali Akbar) Hashemi, 1934–, Iranian religious and political leader, president of Iran (1989–). A Shiite cleric and supporter of Ayatollah KHOMEINI, Rafsanjani was imprisoned several times during the 1960s and 70s. After the Shah's ouster (see MUHAMMAD REZA SHAH PAHLEVI), he helped found the Islamic Republican party and became parliament speaker (1980–89). From 1988 to 1989 he was also acting commander in chief of the armed forces. In 1989 Rafsanjani was elected president. He has sought to revive Iran's economy and has moved to improve relations with the West and reestablish Iran as a regional power. He was reelected in 1993.

Ragnarok [räg′nərŏk″], in Norse mythology, doomsday, on which the gods of ASGARD, led by Odin (see WODEN), would fight the forces of evil, led by LOKI. After the battle, the universe would be destroyed by fire and a new golden age would appear.

ragtime: see JAZZ.

ragweed, weedy herb (genus *Ambrosia*) of the COMPOSITE family, mostly native to America. They have greenish flowers and subdivided leaves. Their POLLEN is one of the primary hay fever irritants, especially that of the common ragweed (*A. artemisiifolia*) and great ragweed (*A. trifida*).

rail, name for some marsh BIRDS of the family Rallidae, cosmopolitan in distribution, except in polar regions. Their extremely slender bodies are protectively colored in drab browns and reds. There are two major types: the long-billed rails, which include the king and water rails; and those with short, conical bills, including the black rails. Rails, including the gallinule and coot, are probably the most widely distributed bird family.

railroad or **railway,** form of transportation most commonly consisting of steel rails, called tracks, on which freight cars, passenger cars, and other rolling stock are drawn by one or more powered LOCOMOTIVES. Other types of railroads include single, self-propelled cars; cable-drawn units, used on steep grades; and monorails, whose cars travel along a single rail. Crude railways pulled by horses along wooden rails were used for mining purposes as early as the 16th cent., but the modern railroad began with the steam locomotives pioneered by the Englishmen Richard Trevithick and George STEPHENSON in the early 1800s. Steam-powered freight and passenger services were first provided by the Stockton and Darlington Railway in England in 1825. In the U.S., the Baltimore & Ohio RR began operation in 1828 with horse-drawn cars, but after the successful run (1830) of the *Tom Thumb,* a locomotive built by Peter COOPER, steam power was used. Many short-run railroads began to appear in the U.S. in the 1840s. Early improvements in railroading included sleeping cars, patented (1856) by G.M. Pullman; the first all-steel car (1859); and the use of steel rather than wrought iron rails (by 1863). U.S. railroad building reached a historic climax with the completion of the first transcontinental railway. The Union Pacific, building westward from Nebraska, and the Central Pacific, building eastward from California, met at Promontory Point, Utah, on May 10, 1869. Railroad tracks, which had varied in width for many years (preventing cars from passing from one line to another), were standardized in the mid-1880s at 4 ft 8½ in. (1.44 m). After the CIVIL WAR, which gave tremendous impetus to railroads, the great battles of the railway financiers began, involving such people as Cornelius VANDERBILT, Jay GOULD, James FISK, J.J. Hill, and E.H. HARRIMAN. Competition from other sources led to the decline of U.S. railroads beginning in the 1920s. After World War II railroad companies claimed annual deficits in passenger service. Their plight was dramatized when the Penn Central filed for bankruptcy in 1970. In that year Congress acted to create Amtrak, a quasipublic agency that took over all intercity passenger service in the U.S., and in 1976 the federal government set up the ConRail system to operate six bankrupt railroads in the northeast.

Henry Raeburn portrait of the Rt. Hon. Francis Hastings

ConRail was privatized in 1987. Despite sharp cutbacks in service and track mileage, both systems suffered persisting financial problems. In most countries other than the U.S. railroads have long been nationalized or heavily subsidized by government. High-speed passenger trains, such as the "bullet" and TGV trains, have been developed in Japan, France, and Germany, and maglev trains (see MAGNETIC LEVITATION) have been run experimentally on short tracks in several countries. See also MONORAIL.

rain, liquid form of precipitation. It consists of drops of water falling from CLOUDS; if the drops are very small, they are collectively termed *drizzle.* Clouds contain huge amounts of tiny water droplets. Raindrops are formed as additional water vapor from the air condenses on the droplets. When the raindrops become too heavy to be supported by the air currents in the cloud, they slowly fall. Collisions with other raindrops continue to increase their size until they hit the ground. Under warm, dry conditions, raindrops can evaporate completely before they land; such raindrops are called *virga.* Rainfall is one of the primary factors of climate. Average annual rainfall can vary from less than 1 in. (2.5 cm) in an arid DESERT to over 400 in. (1,000 cm) in some rainforests. Factors that control rainfall include the belts of converging-ascending air flow (see DOLDRUMS), air temperature, moisture-bearing winds, ocean currents, location and elevation of mountains, and the proximity of large bodies of water. See also HAIL; SLEET; SNOW.

rainbow, arc showing the colors of the spectrum, which appears when sunlight shines through water droplets. It often appears after a brief shower late in the afternoon. The sun, the observer's eye, and the center of the arc must be aligned—the rainbow appears in the part of the sky opposite the sun. It is caused by the refraction and reflection of light rays from the sun: a ray is refracted as it enters the raindrop, reflected from the drop's opposite side, and refracted again as it leaves the drop and passes to the observer.

Rainey, Joseph Hayne, 1832–87, first African-American elected to the U.S. House of Representatives; b. Georgetown, S.C. The son of a free man, he fled to the West Indies during the Civil War. Returning to South Carolina, he served (1867–70) as a Republican in the state senate. In the U.S. House of Representatives (1870–79) he was a leader in the fight to secure civil rights for the newly freed slaves.

rain forest, type of forest found in areas of high precipitation and typically containing a vast array of plant and animal life. The best known and most ecologically diverse are the tropical rain forests of South America and Asia, but there are important temperate rain forests, such as those in the NW U.S. and New Zealand. In the late 20th cent. the clearing of these areas for logging, agriculture, and other purposes has precipitated erosion and species loss and perhaps accelerated GLOBAL WARMING.

Rainier III [rĕnyā'], 1923–, prince of MONACO (1949–). He succeeded his grandfather, Louis II, as prince and married (1956) American film actress Grace Kelly (see GRACE, princess of Monaco).

raisin: see GRAPE.

Rajputs, dominant people of Rajputana, an historic region of NW India coextensive with present-day Rajasthan. Mainly Hindus of the warrior CASTE, but including some Muslims, their many clans claim divine origin. They were powerful in the 7th cent., but by 1616 had submitted to the MOGULS. In the 18th cent. they expanded their territory, but they were driven back by the British in the 19th cent. Many Rajput princes maintained states under the British, but they gradually lost power after India gained independence (1947).

Rákóczy [rä'kôtsĭ], noble Hungarian family. **Sigismund Rákóczy,** 1544–1608, was elected (1607) prince of Transylvania to succeed Stephen BOCSKAY. His son, **George I Rákóczy,** 1591–1648, became prince of Transylvania in 1630. In 1644 he attacked Holy Roman Emperor FERDINAND III, overran Hungary, and obtained (1645) religious freedom for Hungarians. He was succeeded as prince by his son, **George II Rákóczy,** 1621–60, who was deposed in 1657 and died in a Turkish invasion of Transylvania. His grandson, **Francis II Rákóczy,** 1676–1735, led a Hungarian uprising (1703) against Austrian rule. He was elected (1704) "ruling prince" by the diet, and the Hungarian nobles proclaimed (1707) the HAPSBURG dynasty deposed in Hungary. Rákóczy, however, suffered severe defeats (1708, 1710), and the Austrians and Hungarians negotiated a peace at Szatmar in 1711. Rákóczy refused to accept it and thereafter lived in exile. He is a national hero in Hungary.

Raleigh or **Ralegh, Sir Walter,** 1554?–1618, English soldier, explorer, courtier, and man of letters. A favorite of ELIZABETH I, and a rival of Robert Devereux, earl of ESSEX, Raleigh was given position and vast estates in Ireland. He conceived and organized the colonizing expeditions to America that ended tragically with the "lost colony" on ROANOKE ISLAND, Va. With Christopher MARLOWE and George CHAPMAN, he was associated with the poetic group known as the "school of night," which won a reputation for atheism. In 1595 he embarked on an expedition up the Orinoco R. in Guiana in search of EL DORADO. His fortunes fell with the accession of JAMES I, who was convinced of his enmity. He was convicted of treason and imprisoned in the tower. Released in 1616, he made another expedition to the Orinoco in search of gold. It failed, and he returned to England where he was executed under the original sentence of treason. Raleigh wrote poetry, political essays, and philosophical treatises.

Raleigh, city (1990 pop. 207,951), state capital and seat of Wake co., central N.C. The state's second largest city, it is a government, cultural, trade, and industrial center, manufacturing food, pharmaceutical, and electrical products. It is also an airline hub. With Durham and Chapel Hill, it is part of North Carolina's Research Triangle complex. Selected as the capital in 1788, it was laid out and incorporated in 1792. Points of interest include the birthplace of Andrew JOHNSON and several 18th-cent. houses.

Rallis, George John, 1918–, Greek political leader. He served in the legislature from 1950 and held cabinet posts before being imprisoned and exiled (1967–68) by the military regime then in power. Named foreign minister in 1978, Rallis became prime minister in 1980 but lost the 1981 election to Andreas Papandreou (see under PAPANDREOU, GEORGE).

Rama or **Ram,** Hindu hero and god: see RAMAYANA.

Ramadan, in ISLAM, the ninth month of the Muslim year, during which all Muslims must fast during daylight hours. Indulgence of any sort, e.g., food, drink, or sexual activity, is forbidden during the fast; a few, e.g., soldiers and the sick, are excused. Ramadan, which commemorates the first revelation of the KORAN to MUHAMMAD, falls in different seasons because of the lunar calendar.

Ramakrishna or **Sri Ramakrishna Paramahansa,** 1836–86, Hindu mystic. He became a devotee of the goddess KALI c.1855 and lived for the rest of his life at her temple in Dakshineswar, outside Calcutta. He taught that all religions are valid means of approaching God. His saintliness attracted a large following, and after his death his teachings were spread by disciples, in the West notably by Swami Vivekananda, a major exponent of VEDANTA philosophy.

Ramanujan, Srinivasa [rämä'nŏŏjən], 1889–1920, Indian mathematician. A self-taught genius in pure mathematics, he made original contributions to function theory, power series, and number theory.

Ramapithecus: see HUMAN EVOLUTION.

Ramayana, story of Rama, classical Sanskrit epic of India, probably composed in the 3d cent. B.C. Based on legend, it is traditionally the work of Valmiki, a minor character. The *Ramayana* relates the adventures of Rama, who is deprived of his throne by guile and exiled with his wife, Sita. When Sita is abducted by a demon king, he allies himself with Sugriva, the monkey king, and Hanuman, a monkey general. After a great battle in Lanka (Sri Lanka), Rama frees Sita and regains his kingdom. In contemporary Hinduism, Rama, who is also called Ram, is often worshipped as a god.

Rameau, Jean Philippe [rämō'], 1683–1764, French composer and theorist. His two treatises on HARMONY introduced the important theory of chord inversion. He wrote elegant harpsichord and chamber works, and more than 30 stage works, e.g., the opera *Castor et Pollux* (1737).

Rameses or **Ramesses:** see RAMSES.

Ramos, Fidel Valdez, 1928–, Philippine general and politician, president of the Philippines (1992–). A career army officer, he became deputy chief of staff of the armed forces in 1981 and chief of staff in 1986. When AQUINO challenged MARCOS's "victory" in the 1986 presidential election, Ramos supported her. He served (1988–92) as Aquino's defense secretary, and he won the 1992 presidential election with her backing.

Rampal, Jean-Pierre, 1922–, French virtuoso flutist. He has played in several chamber groups and is most celebrated as a soloist of great brilliance.

Ramsay, Allan, 1685?–1758, Scottish poet. A pastoral comedy, *The Gentle Shepherd* (1725), is his most famous work. Ramsay compiled several collections of Scottish poems and songs, contributing greatly to the vernacular revival climaxed by Robert BURNS.

Ramsay, Sir William, 1852–1916, Scottish chemist. He synthesized (1876) pyridine from acetylene and prussic acid. Ramsay discovered helium and was codiscoverer (with Lord RAYLEIGH) of argon and (with Morris Travers) of krypton, neon, and xenon. Knighted in 1902, he won the 1904 Nobel Prize in chemistry for his work on gases.

Ramses [răm'sēz], **Rameses,** or **Ramesses** [both: răm'əsēz"], Egyptian kings of the XIX and XX dynasties. **Ramses I,** d. c.1314 B.C., succeeded Horemheb, the founder of the XIX dynasty, ruled one year, and was succeeded by his son Seti I. Seti's son, **Ramses II,** d. 1225 B.C. (r.1292–1225 B.C.), usurped the throne from his brother. Under him EGYPT acquired unprecedented splendor, the empire extending from S Syria to the fourth cataract of the Nile. War with the HITTITES continued until he concluded a treaty (1280) and married (1267) a Hittite princess. He left monuments throughout Egypt, notably at KARNAK, LUXOR, and THEBES, and the great rock temple at ABU SIMBEL. The period was characterized by great luxury, increased slavery, and the growth of a mercenary army, all contributors to Egypt's eventual decline. Ramses II was probably the pharaoh of exile in the OLD TESTAMENT. **Ramses III,** d. 1167 B.C. (r. c.1198–1167), second king of the XX dynasty, fought off invasions by the Libyans and by Mediterranean sea peoples. He was the last Egyptian king to hold part of PALESTINE. Under him the accumulation of slaves and riches weakened the social structure. His wife, TIY, plotted against him. The XX dynasty was to be ruled by eight other kings named Ramses until it ended in 1090 B.C.

Rancho Cucamonga, city (1990 pop. 101,409), S Calif. Situated in a vast suburban corridor, it is part of San Bernadino's metropolitan area. A rapidly growing residential area, it almost doubled in population between 1980 and 1990. It is the site of the restored 19th-cent. Casa de Rancho Cucamonga.

Rand, Ayn, 1905–82, Russian-American novelist; b. Saint Petersburg, Russia. After coming (1926) to the U.S., she worked as a screenwriter. Her novels espouse a philosophy of rational self-interest that opposes the altruistic tendencies of the modern welfare state. Her best-known novels include *The Fountainhead* (1943) and *Atlas Shrugged* (1957).

Rand, the: see WITWATERSRAND.

Randolph, A(sa) Philip, 1889–1979, African-American labor leader; b. Crescent City, Fla. In 1925 he founded the Brotherhood of Sleeping Car Porters, then an African-American union, and was president until 1968. An untiring fighter for CIVIL RIGHTS, he is credited with helping to establish the Fair Employment Practices Committee in World War II. He was a leading opponent of segregation in the armed forces and of racial discrimination in organized labor. He was appointed (1955) a vice president of the AMERICAN FEDERATION OF LABOR AND CONGRESS OF INDUSTRIAL ORGANIZATIONS and directed (1963) the massive March on Washington for Jobs and Freedom.

Randolph, Edmund, 1753–1813, American statesman; b. Williamsburg, Va. A founding father of the United States, he proposed (1787) the Virginia plan, which considerably influenced the CONSTITUTION OF THE UNITED STATES; the plan called for a bicameral legislature with a lower house elected according to population and an upper house elected by the lower. He was the nation's first attorney general (1789–93) and its second secretary of state (1794–95). His cousin, **John Randolph,** 1773–1833, b. Prince George co., Va., served five terms (between 1799 and 1829) in the U.S. Congress and vigorously opposed FEDERALIST PARTY policies. Edmund Randolph's uncle, **Peyton Randolph,** c.1721–1775, b. Williamsburg, was president (1775) of the first CONTINENTAL CONGRESS.

Ranger, in space exploration: see SPACE PROBE, table.

Rangoon: see YANGON.

Rank, Otto, 1884–1937, Austrian psychoanalyst. As one of Sigmund FREUD's first and most valued pupils, Rank analyzed the underlying significance of myths. In his later work, he diverged from Freud and emphasized the birth trauma as the central cause of NEUROSIS.

Ranke, Leopold von [räng'kə], 1795–1886, German historian, generally recognized as the father of the modern objective historical school. An outstanding teacher, he inaugurated at the Univ. of Berlin the seminar system of teaching history. His *Universal History* (9 vol., 1881–88) and his studies of aspects of the 16th, 17th, and 18th cent. demonstrate his aim to reconstruct unique periods of the past as they actually were and to avoid injecting the history of former times with the spirit of the present.

Ransom, John Crowe, 1888–1974, American poet and critic; b. Pulaski, Tenn. A great stylist, he wrote elegant, impersonal verse in such collections as *Poems about God* (1919) and *Two Gentlemen in Bonds* (1926). He taught at Vanderbilt Univ. (1914–37), where he was a founder of the *Fugitive* (1922–25), and at Kenyon College (1937–58), where he founded the influential *Kenyon Review.* A "new critic," he voiced his literary theories in such works as *The World's Body* (1938) and *The New Criticism* (1941).

Rao, P(amulaparti) V(enkata) Narasimha, 1921–, Indian politician, prime minister of India (1991–). A member of the Congress-I party (see INDIAN NATIONAL CONGRESS), Rao held (1980–89) various ministerial posts in the governments of Indira and Rajiv GANDHI. After Rajiv Gandhi's assassination, Rao was chosen to lead the Congress party and became prime minister upon winning (1991) a plurality of seats in parliament. He moved decisively to reduce the government's economic role and encourage foreign investment, but was confronted with religious unrest incited by the Hindu religious parties.

Rao, Raja [rou], 1909–, Indian novelist. Among his works, written in English, are the novels *Kanthapura* (1938), *The Serpent and the Rope* (1960), and *Comrade Kirillov* (1976), and *The Cow of the Barricades and Other Stories* (1947). From 1965 to 1980 he was professor of philosophy at the Univ. of Texas.

rape, in law, the crime of performing sexual intercourse without the subject's consent. The victim may be deemed legally incapable of consent if incapacitated (e.g., drugged or intoxicated) or below an age specified by statute (statutory rape). In recent years statutory definitions of rape have been in flux. For example, by some definitions the rapist may be of either sex; in actuality, however, almost all instances of prosecuted rape involve an assault by a man on a woman. In some countries, and in several U.S. states, a wife may charge her husband with rape.

Raphael Santi or **Raphael Sanzio,** 1483–1520, major Italian RENAISSANCE painter; b. Urbino. Raphael's work is the clearest expression of the harmony and balance of High Renaissance composition. His father, Giovanni Santi, court poet and painter to the duke of Urbino, taught him the elements of art. After his father's death, Raphael entered the workshop of PERUGINO, whose influence is seen in *The Crucifixion* and *The Knight's Dream* (both: National Gall., London). The Colonna Altarpiece (Metropolitan Mus.) marks the end of Raphael's Perugian period. The five predella scenes, including *Agony in the Garden* (Metropolitan Mus.) and *Pietà* (Gardner Mus., Boston), show the influences of MICHELANGELO, MASACCIO, LEONARDO, and Fra Bartolomeo. In these scenes he achieved a freer, more able, deeper interpretation than in his earlier work. In Florence (1504–8) he produced his self-portrait (Uffizi) and the numerous Madonnas renowned for their sweetness of expression. At Rome, his style matured, benefiting from Michelangelo's influence. He was wholly responsible for the Stanza della Segnatura in the Vatican (see VATICAN CITY), the two largest walls representing the *School of Athens* and the *Triumph of Religion.* In the Stanza d'Eliodoro he painted, among others, *The Miracle of Bolsena* and *The Deliverance of St. Peter.* The *Sistine Madonna* (Dresden) is from his Roman period. In 1514 he succeeded BRAMANTE as chief architect of the Vatican, and he designed ten tapestries for the SISTINE CHAPEL. Raphael was deeply indebted to the sculpture of antiquity, and he achieved a harmony and monumentality of interpretation that were emulated far into the 19th cent.

rap music or **hip-hop,** influential genre of popular music that originated in the mid-1970s among African-American and Hispanic performers in New York City. Rap generally consists of chanted, often improvised, street poetry usually accompanied by disco or funk music. Detractors have criticized many performer's boastful promotion of violence and misogyny; others admire rap's inventiveness and sociopolitical awareness. Rap performers of the late 1980s and early 90s included Public Enemy, NWA (Ice Cube), and Queen Latifah.

rare-earth metals, group of chemical elements including those in the LANTHANIDE SERIES, usually YTTRIUM, sometimes SCANDIUM and THORIUM, and rarely ZIRCONIUM. Promethium, which is not found in nature, is not usually considered a rare-earth metal. The metals occur together in minerals as their oxides (RARE EARTHS) and are difficult to separate because of their chemical similarity. The cerium metals are a subgroup, consisting of the elements with atomic numbers between 57 and 63 and ytterbium.

rare earths, oxides of the RARE-EARTH METALS. The name of an earth is formed from the name of its element by replacing *-um* with *-a*. Once thought to be very scarce, they are widely distributed and fairly abundant in the earth's crust. Rare-earth minerals include bastnasite, cerite, euxenite, gadolinite, MONAZITE, and samarskite. Mixed rare earths are used in glassmaking, ceramic glazes, and glass-polishing abrasives, and as catalysts for petroleum refining. Individual purified rare earths are used in lasers and as color-television picture-tube phosphors.

Rasmussen, Knud Johan Victor, 1879–1933, Danish explorer and ethnologist; b. Greenland. Of Eskimo ancestry through his mother, he began in 1902 a lifelong study of the ESKIMO and in 1910 established Thule station as a base for exploration. Seeking proof that the Eskimo originated in Asia, he was the first to traverse (1921–24) the NORTHWEST PASSAGE. His translated works include *Across Arctic America* (1927).

raspberry, name for several thorny shrubs (genus *Rubus*) of the ROSE family and for their fruit (see BRAMBLE).

Rasputin, Grigori Yefimovich [răspyōō′tĭn], 1872–1916, Russian holy man and courtier. A semiliterate peasant, he mixed religious fervor with sexual indulgence. His ability to check the bleeding of the czarevich, a hemophiliac, gave him power over Czarina ALEXANDRA FEODOROVNA and, through her, over Czar NICHOLAS II. In 1911 Rasputin's unscrupulous appointees began to fill high posts. After 1915, with the czar at the front in WORLD WAR I, the government was increasingly undermined. Amid suspicions that Rasputin and the czarina were plotting to make peace with Germany, a group of nobles murdered him.

Rastafarianism, religious-cultural movement that began (1930s) in Jamaica. Rastafarians believe that HAILE SELASSIE, also named Ras Tafari, the last emperor of Ethiopia, is the messiah. REGGAE music is heavily influenced by Rastafarianism. There are some 180,000 Rastafarians worldwide.

rat, any of various stout-bodied RODENTS, usually having a pointed muzzle and long, scaly tail. The name refers particularly to the two species of house rat, the brown, or Norway, rat (*Rattus norvegicus*) and the black, or Alexandrine, rat (*R. rattus*). The brown rat is the larger of the two, growing up to 10 in. (25 cm) long, excluding the tail, and sometimes weighing more than a pound (.5 kg). Rats spread human diseases and destroy food supplies; efforts to exterminate them have been relatively unsuccessful. Many other rodents are also called rats, e.g., the MUSKRAT.

ratio, the quotient of two numbers, often used for comparison. For example, in a school with 500 children and 25 teachers, the teacher-pupil ratio is 25/500 = 1/20.

rational number: see NUMBER.

rattan, climbing PALM (genera *Calamus* and *Daemonorops*) of tropical Asia. Rattan leaves, unlike those of most palms, are not clustered in a crown, and they have long barbed tips by which the plant climbs to treetops. Commercial rattan, a tough, flexible CANE of uniform diameter used for wickerwork, is obtained from the plant's long stem.

rattlesnake, poisonous New World SNAKE of the PIT VIPER family, distinguished by a rattle at the end of the tail. The rattle, a series of dried, hollow segments of skin, makes a whirring sound when shaken, serving to warn attackers. Most species are classified in the genus *Crotalus,* including the largest and deadliest, the eastern diamondback rattlesnake, *C. adamanteus,* of the S and SE U.S. The SIDEWINDER is a North American desert species.

Ratzel, Friedrich, 1844–1904, German geographer. A major influence on other geographers, he pioneered in developing anthropogeography and helped found modern political geography. In *Anthropogeography* (2 vol., 1882–91) and *Political Geography* (1897), he emphasized the importance of *Lebensraum*—the physical space occupied by a population—as a factor determining human activity.

Rauschenberg, Robert [rou′shənbûrg], 1925–, American artist; b. Port Arthur, Tex. Executed with great spontaneity, his paintings use images and objects from everyday life. *Gloria* (1956) is typical of his collages known as "combines."

Ravel, Maurice [răvĕl′], 1875–1937, French composer. With DEBUSSY he became a leading exponent of IMPRESSIONISM, composing highly original, fluid music within classical forms. His works for the piano include *Valses Nobles et Sentimentales* (1911) and *Le Tombeau de Couperin* (1917). Among his orchestral works are *Rhapsodie Espagnole* (1908) and *Bolero* (1928).

raven, the largest member of the CROW family, found in arctic and temperate regions of the Northern Hemisphere. The raven (*Corvus corax*) is a glossy, black scavenging bird about 26 in. (66 cm) long with a call resembling a guttural croak; it can be taught to mimic human speech.

Ravenna, city (1990 pop. 136,166), in Emilia-Romagna, N central Italy, connected to the Adriatic by a canal. It is a farm-market and industrial center. A Roman naval port, it was the capital of the Western Empire (402–76), of the Ostrogoths (5th–6th cent.), and of the Byzantine exarchs (6th cent.–751). PEPIN THE SHORT took it from the LOMBARDS and gave it to the pope (754). Ruled by the Da Polenta family (13th–15th cent.), it returned to papal control in 1509. Ravenna is famous for its 5th- and 6th-cent. mosaics, as in the Church of San Vitale (547), and for its Roman and Byzantine buildings.

Rawalpindi, city (1981 pop. 457,091), NE Pakistan. It is an industrial center producing refined oil and gas, steel, chemicals, and other manufactures. Sikhs settled the area in 1765. When the British occupied the PUNJAB in 1849, Rawalpindi became a major military outpost; it remains the Pakistani army's headquarters. It was Pakistan's interim capital from 1959 to 1970.

Rawlings, Jerry, 1947–, Ghanaian military and political leader. He led a coup that ousted the military junta in 1979, but stepped aside to allow a civilian president, Hilla Limann, to govern. In Dec. 1981, Rawlings deposed Limann and suspended the constitution, banning all political parties, and later introduced (1983) economic reforms that helped revive the economy. Rawlings won a free presidential election in 1992.

Rawlinson, Sir Henry Creswicke, 1810–95, English Orientalist and administrator. The results of his deciphering of the CUNEIFORM of the Behistun inscriptions of Darius I were published in 1846. He also helped prepare *The Cuneiform Inscriptions of Western Asia* (5 vol., 1861–64).

Rawls, John, 1921–, American philosopher; b. Baltimore. His *A Theory of Justice* (1971) greatly influenced liberal thinking. It gives a systematic account of justice as fairness, outlines the proper reach of (and limitations on) individual liberty, and distinguishes acceptable from unacceptable forms of social inequality.

Ray or **Wray, John,** 1627–1705, English naturalist. He was extremely influential in laying the foundations of systematic biology. Together with his pupil Francis Willughby, he planned a complete classification of the animal and vegetable kingdoms. His work—the botanical part of the project—includes the important *Historia plantarum* (3 vol., 1686–1704). Ray was the first to name and make the distinction between monocotyledons and dicotyledons and the first to define and explain the term *species* in its modern sense.

Ray, Man, 1890–1976, American artist; b. Philadelphia. A founder of the DADA movement in Paris and New York, Ray was celebrated for his surrealist paintings, photographs, and films. He invented the rayograph, a photograph made by direct application of objects to a light-sensitive plate.

Ray, Satyajit, 1912–92, Indian film director; b. Bengal. His trilogy *The Song of the Road* (1955), *The Unvanquished* (1957), and *The World of Apu* (1958) brought Indian film to world attention. His other work includes *Two Daughters* (1961), *Distant Thunder* (1973), *The Middleman* (1975), and *The Stranger* (1991). In 1992

Scene from The World of Apu, *directed by Satyajit Ray, 1958*

he was awarded a special Academy Award for lifetime achievement.

ray, flat-bodied cartilaginous marine FISH (order Batoidea), related to the SHARK. Most rays have broad, flat, winglike pectoral fins along the sides of the head, whiplike tails, eyes and spiracles on top of the head, and mouth and GILL slits underneath. Many rays, such as the skates, lie on the seafloor and feed on smaller animals, e.g., snails. Fertilization is internal, and most bear live young. The largest rays are the top-swimming mantas, which may be up to 22 ft (7 m) wide and weigh up to 3,000 lb (1,360 kg). Rays also include stingrays and sawfishes.

Rayburn, Sam, 1882–1961, U.S. legislator; b. Rome co., Tenn. A Democratic U.S. representative from Texas (1913–61), he helped to pass NEW DEAL legislation. Rayburn served a record 17 years (1940–61, except for two terms) as Speaker of the House. One of his protégés was Lyndon B. JOHNSON.

Rayleigh, John William Strutt, 3d **Baron,** 1842–1919, English physicist. He was professor (1887–1905) at the Royal Institution, London. For discovering argon (with Sir William RAMSAY) he won the 1904 Nobel Prize in physics. He is known for his research in sound and light, his study of Boyle's law (see GAS LAWS) applied to low-pressure gases, and his determination of electrical units.

rayon, synthetic fiber made from CELLULOSE, or textiles woven from such fiber. Silklike rayon, the first SYNTHETIC TEXTILE FIBER, was produced in 1884 by a French scientist, Hilaire de Chardonnet. In rayon manufacturing, cellulose, chiefly from wood pulp, is dissolved by chemicals and forced under pressure through minute holes in a metal spinneret, emerging as filaments. The filaments are doubled and twisted into silky yarns or cut into staple lengths and spun. Spun rayon can be treated to simulate wool, linen, or cotton.

Rb, chemical symbol of the element RUBIDIUM.

Re, chemical symbol of the element RHENIUM.

reactance: see IMPEDANCE.

reactor, nuclear: see NUCLEAR REACTOR.

Reading, city (1990 pop. 78,380), seat of Berks co., SE Pa., on the Schuylkill R.; founded 1748, inc. as a city 1847. An early iron-producing town, it was an ordnance center during the Civil War. Today it is best known for its factory outlets, especially in clothing, and has diverse manufactures. The birthplace of Daniel BOONE is nearby.

Reagan, Ronald Wilson, 1911–, 40th president of the U.S. (1981–88); b. Tampico, Ill. A film actor who was president of the Screen Actors Guild, he was a supporter of the NEW DEAL long before he joined the Republican party in 1962 and began to champion right-wing causes. As governor of California for two terms (1967–75), he cut state welfare and medical services and education funds. After leaving office, he campaigned for the 1976 Republican presidential nomination but lost narrowly to Pres. Gerald FORD. Four years later he won the nomination and, with his running mate, George BUSH, resoundingly defeated Pres. Jimmy CARTER. His presidency had barely begun when he was shot by a would-be assassin, John Hinckley, Jr., on Mar. 30, 1981; he recovered quickly. Advocating a balanced budget to combat inflation, he reversed long-standing political trends by obtaining Congressional passage of large income-tax cuts, decreased social-program spending, and increased defense spending (for both conventional weapons and such programs as the STRATEGIC DEFENSE INITIATIVE). He was reelected in 1985, defeating Democratic candidate Walter MONDALE. Reagan adopted a firm stance in relations with the USSR and against possible Communist expansion, especially in Central America (see IRAN-CONTRA AFFAIR). Nonetheless, he made important steps in U.S./Soviet nuclear disarmament negotiations, signing the INF treaty with the USSR (see DISARMAMENT, NUCLEAR). His tax and spending policies, however, led to enormous peacetime budget deficits, greatly increasing the national debt.

realism, in art, broadly, an unembellished rendering of natural forms. Specifically, the term refers to the mid-19th-cent. movement against French academicism. Realist painters portrayed ugly or commonplace subjects without idealization. Major realists include COURBET, J.F. MILLET, and DAUMIER. See also PHOTOREALISM.

realism, in literature, an attempt to describe life without idealization or romantic subjectivity. Although not limited to any one century or school, it is most often identified with the 19th-cent. French writers Gustave FLAUBERT and Honoré de BALZAC. George ELIOT introduced it in England, W.D. HOWELLS in the U.S. Realism has been chiefly concerned with the commonplaces of middle-class life. In drama it is most often associated with Henrik IBSEN. A reaction against its emphasis on externals led to the psychological realism of Henry JAMES and others. See also NATURALISM.

realism, in philosophy. **1** In medieval philosophy, realism was the position that universals or general concepts have existence independent of both the human mind and individual objects. It is a position directly opposite to NOMINALISM. **2** In EPISTEMOLOGY, realism represents the theory that individual things exist independently of the mind's perception of them, as opposed to IDEALISM, which holds that reality exists only in the mind.

real number: see NUMBER.

Réaumur, René Antoine Ferchault de [rā'əmyoor], 1683–1757, French physicist and naturalist. He invented an alcohol thermometer and the Réaumur temperature scale. He studied the composition of Chinese porcelain, which led him to develop an opaque glass, and the composition and manufacture of iron and steel, and published (1734–42) an exhaustive study of insects.

Rebecca or **Rebekah,** in the BIBLE, wife of ISAAC and mother of JACOB and ESAU. Jacob was his mother's favorite, and for him she devised their deception of the blind Isaac. She is one of the four Jewish matriarchs.

recall: see INITIATIVE, REFERENDUM, AND RECALL.

recession: see under DEPRESSION.

Recife, chief city (1990 est. pop. 1,375,000) of NE Brazil, a port on the Atlantic Ocean; also known as Pernambuco. Cut by many waterways, it lies partly on the mainland and partly on an island and is often called the Brazilian Venice. It is an important transportation center; its economy is based on the processing and export of cotton, sugar, and coffee. Industrial products include glass, ceramics, pharmaceuticals, and synthetic rubber. Founded (1548) by the Portuguese, Recife was briefly held by the British (1595) and the Dutch (1630–54).

recitative, musical declamation for solo voice, used in OPERA and ORATORIO for dialogue and narration. Its development at the end of the 16th cent., enabling words to be clearly understood and natural speech rhythms to be followed, made possible the rise of opera. In the 17th cent., the rapid patter of *recitative secco,* punctuated by occasional accompanying chords, served only to advance the action; by the 18th cent., more strict measure and full orchestral accompaniment helped to highlight recitative passages of dramatic interest. In Wagner's *Sprechgesang,* the melody is completely molded to the text.

recombinant DNA: see GENETIC ENGINEERING.

reconnaissance satellite, artificial SATELLITE launched by a country to provide intelligence information on the military activities of foreign countries. There are four major types. *Early-warning satellites* detect enemy missile launchings. *Nuclear-explosion detection satellites* are designed to detect and identify nuclear explosions in space. *Photo-surveillance satellites* provide photographs of enemy military activities, e.g., the deployment of intercontinental ballistic missiles (ICBMs). There are two subtypes: close-look satellites provide high-resolution photographs that are returned to earth via a reentry capsule, whereas area-survey satellites provide lower-resolution photographs that are transmitted to earth via radio. Later satellites have combined these two functions. Other satellites use radar to provide images of enemy activity when there is cloud cover or it is dark. *Electronic-reconnaissance (ferret) satellites* pickup and record radio and radar transmissions while passing over a foreign country. The U.S. and Russia (before 1991, the USSR) have launched numerous reconnaissance satellites since 1960.

Reconstruction, in U.S. history, period (1865–77) of readjustment following the CIVIL WAR. When the war ended the defeated South was a ruined land, and its old social and economic order had collapsed. Pres. Andrew JOHNSON tried to shift political control in the South from the old planter aristocracy to small farmers and artisans by disenfranchising all former Confederate officers and making certain property liable to confiscation. Under the provisional governors he appointed, most Southern states abolished slavery and ratified the Thirteenth Amendment (1865), guaranteeing freedom for African Americans. However, they also enacted laws severely limiting the civil rights of African Americans (the "Black Codes") and elected disenfranchised Confederate leaders to state and federal offices. Radical Republicans in Congress, led by Thaddeus STEVENS, refused to seat Southern representatives and passed various Reconstruction acts, which were designed to protect African Americans, over the president's vetoes. African-American civil rights were incorporated in the Fourteenth Amendment (1868). Radical congressmen enacted the Reconstruction Act of 1867 that set up five military districts in the South and made army authority supreme. When Johnson continued to oppose the radical leaders and defied the Tenure of Office Act, Congress impeached him; he was not convicted, but his program was scuttled. After the Fifteenth Amendment (1870) had guaranteed African Americans the right to vote, terrorist groups such as the KU KLUX KLAN kept them from voting. Eventually, radical Republican governments were overthrown and white rule was restored. Reconstruction officially ended in 1877, when all federal troops were withdrawn from the South. Its legacy was the one-party "solid South" and a lasting racial bitterness.

Reconstruction Finance Corporation (RFC), U.S. government agency (1932–57) created during the GREAT DEPRESSION to stimulate the economy by lending money to financial, industrial, and agricultural institutions. During the NEW DEAL its operations were broadened to finance war plants, loan money to foreign governments, and pay for disaster damages. RFC loans totaled about $50 billion.

Reconstructionist Judaism: see JUDAISM.

recorder: see WIND INSTRUMENT.

record player or **phonograph,** device for reproducing sound that has been recorded as a spiral, undulating groove on a disk; it was superseded by the COMPACT DISC player in the 1980s. The disk, or phonograph record, is placed on the record player's motor-driven turntable, which rotates the record at a constant speed. A tone arm, containing a pickup at one end, is placed on the record and touches the groove with a stylus, or needle, that vibrates as the record revolves. The TRANSDUCER, also part of the pickup, converts these vibrations into corresponding electrical signals, which are increased in size by an AMPLIFIER and then passed to a LOUDSPEAKER that converts them into sound. The turntable, amplifier, and loudspeaker are typically separate components in modern sound-reproducing systems. The first phonograph was built by Thomas EDISON in 1877. See also STEREOPHONIC SOUND.

rectifier, component of an ELECTRIC CIRCUIT that changes alternating current to direct current. Rectifiers operate on the principle that current passes through them freely in one direction, but only slightly or not at all in the opposite direction. See also DIODE; ELECTRON TUBE.

recycling: see WASTE DISPOSAL.

redbird: see CARDINAL.

red cedar: see ARBORVITAE; JUNIPER.

Red Cloud, 1822–1909, chief of the Oglala SIOUX. He led opposition to the BOZEMAN TRAIL through Native American lands in Colorado and Montana. The Fetterman Massacre (1866) and Red Cloud's raids finally led to the trail's abandonment (1868). Red Cloud later lived at peace with whites, but he was deposed as chief (1881) and retired to the Pine Ridge Reservation, S.D.

Red Cross, international organization concerned with alleviating suffering and promoting public health; formed (1863) at the urging of Jean Henry DUNANT, a Swiss citizen who had witnessed the suffering at the battle of Solferino (1859). The GENEVA CONVENTION of 1864 adopted the red cross as a symbol of neutral aid. Most governments have signed later treaties and conventions. Today there are over 150 national societies, and two international bodies based in Geneva; the blanket agency for all Red Cross groups is the International Movement of the Red Cross and Red Crescent. The work of the Red Cross has grown to include aid to refugees, e.g., Arab refugees in the Middle East; exchanges of sick and wounded soldiers, initiated during the Korean War; and disaster relief. The American Red Cross (founded 1881 by Clara BARTON) also conducts a blood-supply program.

red giant: see STELLAR EVOLUTION.

Redgrave, family of English actors. **Sir Michael Redgrave,** 1908–85, was the star of many plays, e.g., *Hamlet, Macbeth, Uncle Vanya,* and *The Family Reunion* (1939), and several films, e.g., *The Lady Vanishes* (1939) and *The Browning Version* (1951). His elder daughter, **Vanessa Redgrave,** 1937–, starred in the London production of *The Prime of Miss Jean Brodie* (1966) and has appeared in such films as *Blow-Up* (1967), *Isadora* (1968), *Julia* (1976), *The Ballad of the Sad Cafe* (1991), and, for television, *Playing for Time* (1980). Her outspoken support for left-wing causes has made her a controversial figure. Her sister, **Lynn Redgrave,** 1943–, best known for her role in the film *Georgy Girl* (1966), has also appeared on the stage, e.g., *Saint Joan* (1977), and on television.

Red Guards, in Chinese history, politically active students of the CULTURAL REVOLUTION (1966–69), who organized units to carry out MAO ZEDONG's aim of rerevolutionizing Chinese society. As their numbers grew, the units engaged in factional struggles, and in 1968 Mao suppressed the movement.

Redon, Odilon [rədôN′], 1840–1916, French painter and lithographer. An artist of lyrical and mystical vision, he created translucent flower pieces and often depicted literary subjects, symbolically conceived and related to the work of writers such as POE and BAUDELAIRE. *Silence* (Mus. Mod. Art, N.Y.C.), is a representative work. He was a precursor of SURREALISM.

red pepper: see PEPPER.

Red River, flowing 1,222 mi (1,967 km) from two branches in the Texas Panhandle to join the Mississippi R. in Louisiana. Blocked until the mid-1800s by the Great Raft, a 160-mi (257-km), centuries-old logjam, the river is now navigable to Shreveport, La. During the Civil War, Union forces were defeated there at Sabine Crossroads.

Red River Rebellion: see RIEL, LOUIS.

Red River Settlement, pioneer colony, largely in MANITOBA, Canada, founded by the HUDSON'S BAY COMPANY and settled (1812–15) by impoverished Scottish and Irish immigrants. Fur traders and métis (half-breeds), goaded by the rival NORTH WEST COMPANY, opposed the colony violently; 22 persons were killed in the 1816 massacre of Seven Oaks. The violence ended (1821) with union of the two companies, and the Red River settlements flourished.

Red Sea, narrow sea, c.1,450 mi (2,330 km) long and up to 225 mi (362 km) wide, separating NE Africa and the Arabian Peninsula. It connects with the Gulf of ADEN (S) through the narrow BAB EL MANDEB and divides in the north to form the Gulfs of Suez and Aqaba. The sea, which has a high salt content and is dotted with small islands and dangerous coral reefs, forms an important link in the MEDITERRANEAN SEA–SUEZ CANAL–INDIAN OCEAN sea lane.

red shift, the systematic increase in the wavelength of all light received from a celestial object; it is observed in the shifting of individual lines in the SPECTRUM of the object toward the red, or longer-wavelength, end of the visible spectrum. Most observed red shifts are the result of the DOPPLER EFFECT; they are also produced by gravitation in dense, compact stars in accordance with the general theory of RELATIVITY. See also HUBBLE'S LAW; QUASAR.

reduction, in chemistry: see OXIDATION AND REDUCTION.

redwood: see SEQUOIA.

Redwood National Park: see NATIONAL PARKS (table).

Reed, Sir Carol, 1906–76, English film director. Among his films are *The Stars Look Down* (1939), *Odd Man Out* (1946), *The Fallen Idol* (1948), *The Third Man* (1949), *Outcast of the Islands* (1941), *Our Man in Havana* (1960), and *Oliver!* (1968; Academy Award).

Reed, John, 1887–1920, American journalist; b. Portland, Ore. His *Ten Days That Shook the World* (1919) is considered the best eyewitness account of the 1917 RUSSIAN REVOLUTION. Reed helped found the Communist Labor party in the U.S. He died of typhus in Moscow and is buried at the Kremlin.

Reed, Thomas Brackett, 1839–1902, American legislator; b. Portland, Me. A Republican congressman (1876–99) and Speaker of the House (1889–91, 1895–99), "Czar" Reed used the office to facilitate orthodox Republican legislation.

Reed, Walter, 1851–1902, American army surgeon; b. Gloucester Co., Va. In 1900 he headed a commission to investigate a YELLOW-FEVER outbreak among U.S. soldiers in Cuba. Using volunteers, the commission proved Carlos Juan FINLAY'S theory that the disease was transmitted by a mosquito and not by direct contact. In 1901 it published its findings.

reed, name for several plants of the GRASS family. The common American reed (*Phragmites communis*) is a tall perennial widely distributed in wet places. It has stout, creeping rootstalks and a large, plumelike panicle. The giant reed (*Arundo donax*), similar in appearance but native to the Mediterranean region, has long been used to make reed instruments, e.g., the panpipe of PAN.

reef: see CORAL REEFS.

referendum: see INITIATIVE, REFERENDUM, AND RECALL.

reflection, return of a wave, such as light, from a surface it strikes into the medium through which it has traveled. The law of reflection states that the angle of reflection (the angle between the reflected ray and the normal, or line perpendicular, to the surface at the point of reflection) is equal to the angle of incidence (the angle between the incident ray and the normal). See ECHO; MIRROR; REFRACTION.

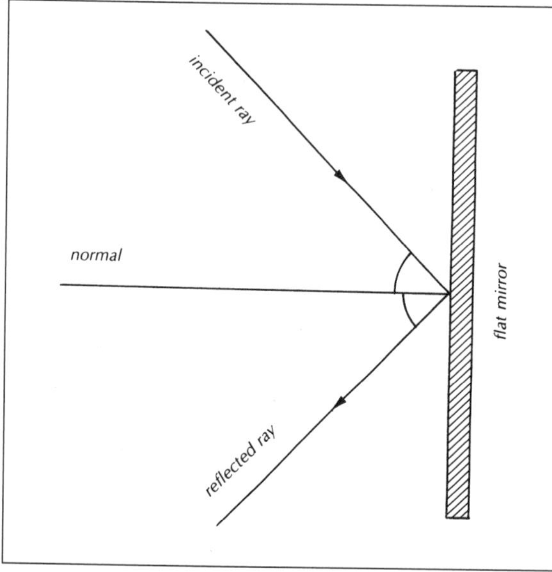

Reflection from a flat mirror

Reformation, religious revolution in Western Europe in the 16th cent. Beginning as a reform movement within the Roman Catholic Church, the Reformation ultimately led to freedom of dissent. The preparation for the movement was long and there had been earlier calls for reform, e.g., by John WYCLIF and John HUSS. Desire for change within the church was increased by the RENAISSANCE, with its study of ancient texts and emphasis on the individual. Other factors that aided the movement were the invention of printing, the rise of commerce and a middle class, and political conflicts between German princes and the Holy Roman emperor. The Reformation began suddenly when Martin LUTHER posted 95 theses on the church door at Wittenberg on October 31, 1517. Open attack on the doctrines and authority of the church followed and led to Luther's breach with the church (1520), which the Diet of Worms (1521) failed to heal. His doctrine was of justification by faith alone instead of by sacraments, good works, and meditation, and it placed a person in direct communication with God. Luther's insistence on reading the Bible placed on the individual a greater responsibility for his own salvation. The new church spread in Germany and Scandinavia, especially among princes and people who hoped for a greater degree of freedom. The conflict between the Lutherans and the Catholic Emperor CHARLES V was long and bitter. A temporary settlement was reached at the Peace of Augsburg (1555), but continued discord contributed later to the THIRTY YEARS WAR. Outside Germany, a different type of dissent developed under Huldreich ZWINGLI in Zürich, and within Protestantism differences arose, such as doctrinal arguments on the Lord's Supper. These were debated, inconclusively, at the Colloquy of Marburg (1529) by Luther and Philip MELANCHTHON on one side and Zwingli and Johannes Oecolampadius on the other. More radical ideas were spread, particularly among the lower classes, by such leaders as CARLSTADT, Thomas MÜNZER, and JOHN OF LEIDEN. In 1536 Geneva became the center for the teachings of John CALVIN, perhaps the greatest theologian of Protestantism. In France the HUGUENOTS, fired by Calvin's doctrine, resisted the Catholic majority in the Wars of RELIGION (1562–98). Calvinism superseded Lutheranism in the Netherlands, and it spread to Scotland through the efforts of John KNOX. In England the Reformation took its own course. HENRY VIII issued the Act of Supremacy (1534), which rejected papal control and created a national church (see ENGLAND, CHURCH OF). Calvinistic thought was, however, strong in England, and it influenced later reforms. On the Continent, divisions within the Protestant churches served to forward the Counter Reformation (see REFORMATION, CATHOLIC), which rewon some territory for Catholicism. The end (1648) of the Thirty Years War brought some stabilization, but the force of the Reformation did not end. The movement, and its fruit, Protestantism, has continued to exert influence to the present day, with its emphasis on personal responsibility and individual freedom, its refusal to take authority for granted, and its influence in breaking the hold of the church upon life and the consequent secularization of life and attitudes.

Reformation, Catholic, 16th-cent. reform of the Roman Catholic Church, largely in response to the Protestant Reformation; popularly called the Counter Reformation. Since the time of St. Catherine of Siena (14th cent.) there had been a growing demand in the church for reform, but it was hampered by church quarrels, notably the Great SCHISM. Consequently the church became home to many ills such as SIMONY, worldliness, and corruption among the higher clergy, ignorance in the priesthood, and general spiritual apathy. It was not until 1543, when PAUL III became pope and St. IGNATIUS OF LOYOLA founded the Jesuits (see JESUS, SOCIETY OF) that major reform began. Paul summoned the Council of TRENT, which was the central feature of the Catholic Reformation; the Jesuits became the reform's crusaders. The council uprooted simony, standardized worship, reorganized church administration, set educational requirements for priests, and scrutinized the morals of the clergy. A new spirit entered the church, as seen in the work of Saints Charles Borromeo, THERESA of Ávila, and VINCENT DE PAUL, and Catholicism reclaimed its initiative in Europe.

Reform Bills, in British history, name given to three major measures in the 19th cent. that liberalized representation in Parliament. Despite population shifts and the rise of new social classes during the INDUSTRIAL REVOLUTION, representation in Parliament had not altered much since the 17th cent. The **Reform Bill of 1832,** passed by Charles GREY'S Whig ministry, redistributed the seats in the interest of larger cities and gave the vote to middle-class men. Benjamin DISRAELI and the Conservatives passed the **Reform Bill of 1867,** enfranchising working men in the towns and more than doubling the electorate. The **Reform Bill of 1884,** under William GLADSTONE, reduced rural qualifications and added 2 million voters. It was not, however, until the passage of the REPRESENTATION OF THE PEOPLE ACTS in the 20th cent. that Britain adopted universal male and female suffrage.

Reformed Church in America, Protestant denomination founded in colonial times by Dutch settlers and formerly known as the Dutch Reformed Church. In Holland the Reformed Church grew in the 16th cent. from the Calvinist Reformation. In 1571 the synod at Emden adopted presbyterian polity and formulated a liturgical form of worship. The Belgic Confession of Faith (1561) and the Heidelberg Catechism (1563) formed the basis of faith. In America a congregation was formed in New Amsterdam in 1628. In 1754 an assembly declared itself independent of the classis (i.e., governing body) of Amsterdam, and in 1792 a constitution was adopted. The present name became official in 1867. In 1990 the church reported a membership of 326,850.

Reform Judaism: see JUDAISM.

refraction, the deflection of a wave on passing obliquely from one transparent medium into a second medium in which its speed is different, as the passage of a light ray from air into glass. The index of refraction of a transparent medium is equal to the ratio of the speed of light in a vacuum to the speed of light in the medium. Snell's law states that the ratio of the sine of the angle i of incidence (angle between the incident ray and the normal, or line perpendicular to the boundary between the two mediums at the point of refraction) to the sine of the angle r of refraction (angle between the refracted ray and the normal) is equal to the ratio of the refracting medium's index of refraction n_r to the original medium's index of refraction n_i.

refrigeration, process for drawing heat from substances to lower their temperature, often for purposes of preservation. Mechanical refrigeration systems (first patented in 1834) are based on the principle that absorption of heat by a fluid (refrigerant) as it changes from a liquid to a gas lowers the temperature of the objects around it. In the compression system, employed in electric home refrigerators, a COMPRESSOR, controlled by a thermostat, exerts pressure on a refrigerant gas (usually FREON or AMMONIA, but a hydrochlorofluorocarbon is expected to replace freon in the mid-1990s), forcing it to pass through a condenser, where it loses heat and liquefies. When the liquid is circulated through refrigeration coils, it vaporizes, drawing heat from the air surrounding the coils. The refrigerant gas then returns to the compressor, and the cycle is repeated. In the absorption system, widely used in commercial installations, ammonia is used to cool brine, which is then piped into the refrigerated space. See also AIR CONDITIONING; HEAT PUMP.

Regency style, in English architecture, flourished during the regency and reign of GEORGE IV (1811–30). The major architect was John NASH, who built the Royal Pavilion, Brighton (1815–22), an example of diversity of style with its Indian exterior and exotic Asian furnishings. The main trend, however, was neoclassical, as seen in the work of John Soane and in Nash's Regent's Park, London. Bay windows, balconies, and eclectic furniture design were characteristic.

Regensburg, city (1989 est. pop. 119,000), Bavaria, S Germany, a port at the confluence of the Danube and Regen rivers. It is an industrial center with such manufactures as electronic equipment and motor vehicles. Founded by the Romans, it was a medieval trade center, a free imperial city, and the home (16th–19th cent.) of the imperial diet. In 1810 it passed to BAVARIA. An airplane-manufacturing center during WORLD WAR II, it was heavily bombed. Its historic buildings include a Gothic cathedral (13th–16th cent.).

Reger, Max [rā'gər], 1873–1916, German composer, pianist, and conductor. He was highly esteemed for such complex organ music as *Fantasy and Fugue in C Minor* and *Fantasy and Fugue on Bach.* His many other works include compositions for orchestra and for piano and over 300 songs.

reggae, Jamaican popular music that developed in the 1960s among Kingston's poor blacks, drawing on American "soul" music. Many of its highly political songs proclaim the tenets of the Rastafarian religious movement. Springy, offbeat rhythm characterizes its sound. Bob Marley (1945–81) and his group, the Wailers, and Toots and the Maytals are among the best-known performers.

Regina, city (1991 pop. 179,178), provincial capital, S Saskatchewan, W Canada, on Wascana Creek and Lake. Oil refining and the processing of agricultural products are major industries. Regina (named in honor of Queen Victoria) was founded in 1882 and was the capital (1883–1905) of the Northwest Territories before becoming (1905) the capital of newly created Saskatchewan.

Regulator movement, organized efforts by backcountry settlers in North and South Carolina to restore law and order in the 1760s. In SOUTH CAROLINA, planters and small farmers created an association to try criminals and resolve legal disputes. In NORTH CAROLINA the Regulators protested actions of corrupt officials with acts of violence. When law and order were restored by 1771, the Regulators disbanded.

Rehnquist, William Hubbs: see SUPREME COURT, UNITED STATES (table 1).

Rehoboam [rē"əbō'əm], Hebrew king, son of SOLOMON. After Solomon's death (c.922 B.C.) the northern tribes revolted against Rehoboam and set up the kingdom of Israel with JEROBOAM I as their king. Rehoboam continued to rule the southern kingdom of Judah.

Reich, Wilhelm, 1897–1957, Austrian psychiatrist and biophysicist. He broke with FREUD, fled Nazi Germany, and later settled in New York City. He emphasized the importance of sexual fulfillment for personal well-being. Later, he argued that sexual success depended partly on orgone energy. The orgone box, a device he invented to restore energy, was declared a fraud by the Food and Drug Administration. He died in prison while serving a two-year sentence for contempt of court and violation of the Food and Drug Act. He became a hero of student radicals of the 1960s, with their motto "make love, not war."

Reichstadt, Napoleon, duke of: see NAPOLEON II.

Reichstag, German imperial parliament; name for the Diet of the Holy Roman Empire, for the lower chamber of the federal parliament of the North German Confederation, and for the lower chamber of the federal parliament of Germany (1871–1945). Under the German empire, the Reichstag had little real power and was mainly a deliberative body. In the republic established in 1919, it became the supreme legislative body; it represented the people directly, and the upper chamber, the Reichsrat, represented the various German states. Shortly after HITLER took power (1933), he dissolved the Reichstag and called for new elections. A violent campaign ensued, and on Feb. 27, 1933, a fire destroyed part of the Reichstag building. Hitler used the fire, which was later known to have been set by a lone arsonist, to blame the Communists and whip up public furor. As a result, the Nazis won a slight majority in the elections. In March the Reichstag voted Hitler dictatorial powers. Thereafter, it was summoned to meet only sporadically and to approve important government measures. After WORLD WAR II, the Reichstag and Reichsrat were replaced by other legislative bodies.

Reign of Terror, 1793–94, period of the FRENCH REVOLUTION. It was essentially a war dictatorship to preserve the republic during the FRENCH REVOLUTIONARY WARS. The Committee of Public Safety was created (Apr. 6, 1793) to rule the nation and included Maximilien ROBESPIERRE, the dominant member, and Lazare CARNOT. It aimed to root out counterrevolutionaries, raise new armies, and regulate the economy. The Law of Suspects (Sept. 1793) defined those who could be arrested for treason and was enforced by the Committee of General Security and the Revolutionary Tribunal; several thousand were guillotined. The government was centralized, and the nation was mobilized militarily. Price and wage ceilings were set. In June 1794 the Revolutionary Tribunal was strengthened, and executions increased. However, popular discontent grew, and the Reign of Terror was ended by the overthrow (July 1794) of Robespierre.

reindeer, ruminant MAMMAL (genus *Rangifer*) of the DEER family, found in arctic and subarctic regions of Eurasia and North America. The Eurasian reindeer (*R. tarandus*) stands about 4 ft (120 cm) at the shoulder and weighs about 250 lb (113 kg); its long fur is light brown in summer and whitish in winter. Domesticated for centuries in Lapland and S Siberia, they provide meat, milk, clothing, and transportation. A reindeer can travel 40 mi (64 km) a day, pulling twice its own weight. The wild reindeer of North America are called CARIBOU.

Reiner, Fritz, 1888–1963, American conductor; b. Budapest. After serving as conductor of the People's Opera in Budapest (1911–14) and the Court Opera in Dresden (1914–21), he came (1922) to the U.S. as conductor of the Cincinnati Symphony (1922–31). He was later musical director of the Pittsburgh Symphony (1938–48), the Metropolitan Opera (1948–53), and the Chicago Symphony (1953–62). He was known for his ruthless insistence on precision and clarity.

Reinhardt, Max, 1873–1943, Austrian theatrical director; b. Max Goldmann. A great innovator and a master of spectacle, he staged gigantic productions, full of pageantry and color, at his theaters in Berlin. His world-famous productions included *The Lower Depths, Oedipus Rex,* and *The Miracle.* He founded the Salzburg Festival in 1920. He fled NAZI Germany in 1933, becoming a U.S. citizen in 1940.

relativity, physical theory, introduced by Albert EINSTEIN, that discards the concept of absolute motion and instead treats only relative motion between two systems or frames of reference. Space and time are no longer viewed as separate, independent entities but rather as forming a four-dimensional continuum called SPACE-TIME. In 1905 Einstein enunciated the special relativity theory, in which the hypothesis that the laws of nature are the same in different moving systems also applies to the propagation of light, so that the measured speed of light is constant for all observers regardless of the motion of the observer or of the source of light. From these hypotheses Einstein reformulated the mathematical equations of physics. In most phenomena of ordinary experience the results from the special theory approximate those based on Newtonian dynamics, but the results deviate greatly for phenomena occurring at velocities approaching the speed of light. Among the assertions and consequences of the special theory are the propositions that the maximum velocity attainable in the universe is that of light; that mass increases with velocity; that mass and energy are equivalent; that objects appear to contract in the direction of motion; that the rate of a moving clock seems to decrease as its velocity increases; that events that appear simultaneous to an observer in one system may not appear simultaneous to an observer in another system. The special theory became the foundation of the study of ELEMENTARY PARTICLE and of QUANTUM MECHANICS. Einstein expanded the special theory of relativity, which is principally concerned with submicroscopic physics, into a general theory (completed in 1915) that is principally concerned with the large-scale effects of GRAVITATION (see also COSMOLOGY). The general theory recognizes the equivalence of gravitational and inertial mass, and asserts that material bodies produce the curvature of the space-time continuum and that the path of a body is determined by this curvature. The theory predicts that a ray of light is deflected by a gravitational field; observations of starlight passing near the sun, first made by Arthur EDDINGTON and colleagues during a 1919 eclipse of the sun, confirmed this. The theory also predicts a RED SHIFT of spectral lines of substances in a gravitational field, a result confirmed by observation of light from white dwarf stars. Finally, the theory also accounts for the entire observed perihelion motion of the planet Mercury, only part of which could be explained by Newtonian CELESTIAL MECHANICS. Reconciling the theory with QUANTUM MECHANICS in a UNIFIED FIELD THEORY has proven difficult. Superstring theory (see STRING THEORY) may be able to link quantum gravitation (the study of quantum fields in a curved space-time) with the other quantum theories. See also MOTION.

relay, electromechanical switch in which the variation of current in one ELECTRIC CIRCUIT controls the flow of electricity in another circuit. A relay consists of a movable contact connected to an ELECTROMAGNET by a spring. When the electromagnet is energized by the controlling current, it exerts a force on the contact that overcomes the pull of the spring and moves the contact so as to either complete or break a circuit. When the electromagnet is de-energized, the contact returns to its original position.

religion, a system of thought, feeling, and action shared by a group that gives members an object of devotion; a code of ethics governing personal and social conduct; and a frame of reference relating individuals to their group and the universe. Usually, religion concerns itself with what transcends the known, the natural, or the expected; it is an acknowledgment of the extraordinary, the mysterious, and the supernatural. The evolution of religion cannot be precisely determined. In addition to the more elementary forms of belief and practice, such as ANIMISM, ancestor worship, totemism, and SPIRITISM, there are the commonly termed higher religions, which embody a principle of transcendence. These include POLYTHEISM, in which there are many gods; DUALISM, which posits equally powerful deities of good and evil; MONOTHEISM, in which there is a single god; supratheism, in which the devotee participates in the religion through a mystical union with the godhead; and PANTHEISM, in which the universe is identified with God. Religions are also classifed as revealed (i.e., by divine agency) or nonrevealed (i.e., the result of human inquiry). JUDAISM, CHRISTIANITY, and ISLAM are revealed religions, and BUDDHISM, HINDUISM, and TAOISM are largely nonrevealed religions.

Religion, Wars of, 1562–98, series of civil wars in France, also called the HUGUENOT Wars. The successive Protestant leaders were Louis I de CONDÉ, Gaspard de COLIGNY, and Henry of Navarre (later HENRY IV). The Catholic party was headed by the house of GUISE. CATHERINE DE' MEDICI and her sons, CHARLES IX and HENRY III, vainly tried to straddle the issue. The wars were marked by cruelty on both sides. The first three wars (1562–63, 1567–68, 1568–70) ended favorably for the Protestants. The massacre of SAINT BARTHOLOMEW'S DAY began the fourth war (1572–73). The fifth and sixth wars (1574–76, 1577) granted religious freedom; the Catholic LEAGUE was formed in retaliation. The seventh war (1580) was inconsequential. In 1585 Henry of Navarre was named heir presumptive to Henry III, and that precipitated the War of the Three Henrys (the third was Henri, 3d duc de Guise). After Henry IV's accession (1589) he was forced to fight the League and its ally, Spain; he defeated them in 1594. The Treaty of Vervins and the Edict of NANTES restored peace and temporarily established religious toleration.

relocation center, in U.S. history, camp in which Japanese and Japanese-Americans were interned during World War II. Fearing a Japanese invasion, the army, under the War Relocation Authority, forcibly moved approximately 120,000 people, most of whom were American citizens, from the West Coast. Although some who proved their loyalty were released after July 1943, most were detained until Dec. 1944; the last center closed in Mar. 1946. The internees suffered property losses estimated at $400 million. In 1988 the government agreed to give $20,000 and an apology to each of the surviving internees.

Remarque, Erich Maria [rəmärk'], 1897–1970, German-American novelist. His first novel and masterpiece is *All Quiet on the Western Front* (1929), a bitter antiwar story based on his experiences in World War I. His later works deal with the postwar situation in Germany. After 1939, Remarque lived in the U.S.

Rembrandt Harmenszoon van Rijn or **Ryn** [rĕm'brănt], 1606–69, Dutch painter, etcher, and draftsman, the greatest master of the Dutch school. He got his most valuable training in the Amsterdam studio of Pieter Lastman, who influenced his sense of composition and frequent choice of religious and historical themes. Rembrandt's works sometimes reflected the dramatic use of light and shadow of CARAVAGGIO, e.g., *The Money Changer* (Berlin). The more detailed, delicate manner of ELSHEIMER is seen in *The Tribute Money* (London). Rembrandt returned to Leiden, his birthplace, in 1625. There he began to teach and started the series of nearly 100 self-portraits that reveal his continued stylistic growth and profound self-awareness. In 1632 he moved to Amsterdam where he became established as a portrait painter with his group portrait *Anatomy Lesson of Dr. Tulp* (1632; The Hague), a traditional subject to which he gave radical treatment. His joyous marriage to Saskia van Ulyenburgh, a burgomaster's daughter, brought him wealth and social position. During this period his work acquired a new richness of color and plasticity of form, best seen in *The Sacrifice of Abraham* (Saint Petersburg). In 1642 Saskia died giving birth to Titus, their only son, who was later to become Rembrandt's favorite subject. During that same year he completed his most famous group portrait, *The Shooting Company of Capt. Frans Banning Cocq* (Rijks Mus., Amsterdam), called *The Night Watch* before cleaning (1946–47) revealed it to be a daytime scene. In the last 20 years of his life, after his financial ruin, he withdrew from society and created many of his masterpieces, e.g., *Aristotle Contemplating the Bust of Homer* (1653; Metropolitan Mus.), and *The Polish*

Rider (Frick Coll., N.Y.C.). To the late 1660s belong *The Family Group* (Brunswick) and *The Jewish Bride* (Rijks Mus.), both loosely structured, flamelike in color, and psychologically penetrating. *The Syndics of the Cloth Guild* (1662; Rijks Mus.) has been described as the culmination of Dutch portrait painting. Rembrandt's prodigious output included 600 paintings, 300 etchings, and nearly 2,000 drawings. The universal appeal of his art lies in its profound humanity.

Remington, Frederic, 1861–1909, American artist; b. Canton, N.Y. Drawing his inspiration from the American West, he portrayed cowboys, Native Americans, soldiers, and horses in spirited action in his popular bronzes, paintings, and illustrations. Western themes also mark his books, e.g., *Pony Tracks* (1895).

remora, warm-water FISHES of the family Echeneidae, with an oval sucking disk on top of the head. The remora uses this disk to attach itself to large fish, whales, sea turtles, and small boats, thus traveling without effort and eating scraps of the host's prey. The sharksucker species may reach 3 ft (90 cm) in length.

Remus: see ROMULUS.

Renaissance [Fr., = rebirth], term used to describe the rich development of Western civilization that marked the transition from the MIDDLE AGES to modern times. In Italy the Renaissance emerged by the 14th cent. and reached its height in the 15th and 16th cent.; elsewhere in Europe it may be dated from the 15th to the mid-17th cent. In outlook the Renaissance brought new importance to individual expression, self-consciousness, and worldly experience; culturally it was a time of brilliant accomplishments in scholarship, literature, science, and the arts (see RENAISSANCE ART AND ARCHITECTURE). More generally, it was an era of emerging nation-states and exploration, and the beginning of a revolution in commerce. The Renaissance first appeared in Italy, where relative political stability, economic expansion, wide contact with other cultures, and a flourishing urban civilization provided the background for a new view of the world. Fine libraries and learned academies and universities flourished. Scholars, poets, craftsmen, and artists were supported by such great patrons as the MEDICI family of Florence, Popes JULIUS II and LEO X, the doges of Venice, and the SFORZA family of Milan. The increased interest in and knowledge of the classical age was reflected in the works of PETRARCH, and the intellectual orientation was toward a secular HUMANISM, exemplified by the works of Lorenzo VALLA. In literature, the romance of the Renaissance was expressed by BOCCACCIO; MACHIAVELLI provided its most telling political commentary. The humanist emphasis on the individual was typified in the ideal of the Renaissance man, the man of universal genius, best exemplified by LEONARDO DA VINCI. This ideal also led to the courtier, the ideal gentleman whose behavior was codified by CASTIGLIONE. Humanism in art found expression in a more realistic view of nature, seen in the works of Leonardo, MICHELANGELO, and RAPHAEL, while Renaissance architects such as ALBERTI, BRUNELLESCHI, BRAMANTE, and Michelangelo utilized classical forms. In France, classicism in literature was displayed by Pierre de RONSARD and Joachim DU BELLAY; RABELAIS expressed the Renaissance's sensual vitality. In Germany, the Renaissance interacted closely with the Protestant REFORMATION and was somewhat more somber. The Netherlands produced ERASMUS, the most notable of all the humanists, and Germany gave birth to Albrecht DÜRER and the younger Hans HOLBEIN. England was represented in learning and literature by Sir Thomas MORE, Francis BACON, and William SHAKESPEARE. In Spain, Cervantes wrote his masterpiece, *Don Quixote,* and in Sweden, Queen CHRISTINA, patron of DESCARTES, encouraged scholarship, literature, and the arts at court. The Renaissance intellectual outlook and its concomitant cultural manifestations were gradually replaced by those of the ENLIGHTENMENT. The term *renaissance* is now often used to designate the flowering of various civilizations and eras.

Renaissance art and architecture. A radical break with medieval methods of representing the visible world occurred in Italy during the second half of the 13th cent. The sculptor Nicola PISANO evoked interest in the sculptural forms of classical antiquity. In painting, GIOTTO led the way in restoring monumentality and dignity to the human figure and working toward a more realistic depiction of space. After the Black Death in 1348 came a marked decline in artistic activity until the second decade of the 15th cent., when FLORENCE became the center of art and art theory. Together with the early humanists (see HUMANISM), artists shared a growing esteem and enthusiasm for physical nature, the individual, and classical antiquity. The architects BRUNELLESCHI and ALBERTI, along with the sculptor DONATELLO, were the first to visit Rome to study the ancient ruins and incorporate classical principles into their work; they were also intensely preoccupied with representing the dimensions of nature on a flat surface. With MASACCIO and UCCELLO, they pioneered the system of perspective, while Fra ANGELICO and Fra Filippo LIPPI developed a unifying color scheme. Antonio POLLAIUOLO, CASTAGNO, and above all LEONARDO DA VINCI devoted themselves to the study of human anatomy. During the 15th cent. artists came to be supported not only by churchmen but also by private patrons, who demanded pictures of secular subjects, including themselves, and thus the art of portraiture flourished. The MEDICI circle of Neoplatonic thought profoundly influenced BOTTICELLI and MICHELANGELO. In the early 16th cent. the artistic center shifted from Florence to Rome. The works of Leonardo, Michelangelo, and RAPHAEL can be said to have brought to a culmination all the heroic proportions, unequaled harmony, and noble ideals for which the High Renaissance (c.1490–1520) is known. MANNERISM followed. Meanwhile, by the beginning of the 16th cent. Venetian art had come into its full glory with the great Venetian colorists Bellini (see BELLINI, family), GIORGIONE, TITIAN, VERONESE, and TINTORETTO. Their superb achievements came as the effects of the golden age of painting in the Low Countries were felt across Europe. In the 1420s, the van EYCKS developed oil painting and, with it, the ability to achieve subtle variations in light and color. They did not practice geometric perspective, but created the appearance of reality with minutely detailed observations of daily life. Robert CAMPIN, Roger van der WEYDEN, and Hugo van der GOES of the 15th cent. were followed in the 16th cent. by such masters as BOSCH and Pieter Bruegel (see BRUEGEL, family). In Germany, SCHONGAUER and DÜRER made the first and greatest contributions in woodcuts and engraving. FRANCIS I brought Italian architects and painters, such as Leonardo, to France, and in the 1530s the influence of mannerism began to be felt at Fontainebleau. The art of England and Spain was influenced by Netherlandish painting until the 16th cent., when the Italian Renaissance began to permeate Europe. The rebirth of classical architecture that took place in Italy in the 15th cent. and spread in the following century through Europe terminated the supremacy of the Gothic style. The ORDERS OF ARCHITECTURE and the structural elements of Rome—ARCHES, VAULTS, DOMES, and decorative forms—served as a treasury for 15th-cent. designers. Brunelleschi, the earliest great architect of the Renaissance, produced the churches of San Lorenzo and Santo Spirito, and the revolutionary plan for the dome of the Cathedral of Florence. Alberti, the first major theoretical architect of the Renaissance, was influenced by the Roman Vitruvius, and he in turn influenced later architects. Several architects, including Leonardo, designed such variations on the centralized structure as the polygonal and Greek-cross plans, and BRAMANTE's circular Tempietto (c.1502) in Rome. Other great Italian architects were PALLADIO and VIGNOLA. In France, Francis I built many châteaus where Renaissance details were grafted onto Gothic structures. The LOUVRE (begun 1546) usually serves as the start of the classical period in France. The move by Inigo JONES (1619) toward pure classical style decisively established Palladian design in England. In Germany in the mid-16th cent. the medieval love for picturesque forms still dominated, although transferred to classical motifs. Resembling Elizabethan work in England, this German style lacked truly great architects and was never fully developed as in France and England. Nuremberg and Rothenburg ob der Tauber are rich in works of the period. In Spain, Gothic and Moorish forms mingled with the new classical forms; the palace of Charles V at Granada (1527) is a superb building of the period.

René, 1409–80, titular king of Naples (1435–80), rival claimant of ALFONSO V of Aragón and Ferdinand I of Naples. The second son of Louis II of Naples, he inherited through marriage Bar (1430) and Lorraine (1431). On the death (1434) of his brother, Louis III of Naples, he inherited Anjou, Provence, and a claim to the throne of Naples. He was adopted as heir by Queen Joanna II of Naples (d. 1435) but was defeated (1442) by Alfonso V and retired to France. On René's death Anjou passed to the French crown. His titles to

Provence and Naples passed to his nephew Charles, count of Maine (d. 1481), and then to the French crown. His daughter, MARGARET OF ANJOU, married Henry VI of England.

Reno, Janet, 1938–, attorney general of the United States (1993–), the first woman to hold the office; b. Miami, Fla. A graduate of Harvard Law School (1963), she was assistant state's attorney (1973–76) and state's attorney (1978–93) for Dade co., Fla. Known for her attention to child abuse and children's rights cases, juvenile justice reform, and drug abuse cases, she was appointed U.S. attorney general by Pres. CLINTON in 1993.

Reno, city (1990 pop. 133,850), seat of Washoe co., W Nev., on the Truckee R.; inc. 1903. Tourism—spurred by a crisp climate, legalized gambling, resort facilities, a busy entertainment industry, and quick divorce laws—made Reno famous. Mining and agriculture are also important to its economy. Settled at a river ford on the Donner Pass route to California, the city was laid out when the railroad arrived.

Renoir, Jean [rənwär'], 1894–1979, French film director; son of Pierre Auguste RENOIR. Such films as *Le Crime de Monsieur Lange* (1935), *La Grande Illusion* (1937), and *Le Règle du jeu* (1939) exemplify his humanism and cinematic mastery.

Renoir, Pierre Auguste, 1841–1919, French impressionist painter and sculptor; father of Jean RENOIR. At 13 he was a decorator of factory-made porcelain. Later he was a friend of Bazille, MONET, and SISLEY. In the 1870s he began to earn his living with portraiture, e.g., *Madame Charpentier and her Children* (1876; Metropolitan Mus.). Simultaneously he developed the ability to paint joyous, shimmering color and flickering light in outdoor scenes such as the festive *Moulin de la Galette* (1876; Louvre). His ecstatic sensuality, opalescent colors, and admiration of the Italian masters carried him beyond IMPRESSIONISM. His most celebrated paintings include *Luncheon of the Boating Party* (1881; Phillips Coll., Wash., D.C.).

repetitive stress injury (RSI), injury caused by repeated movement of a particular part of the body. Often seen in workers whose physical routine is unvaried, RSI has become epidemic since computers have entered the workplace. Constant computer typing can cause one form of RSI, carpal tunnel syndrome, a sometimes disabling pain and tingling in the thumb and first two fingers, caused by swelling and pressure on the median nerve as it passes through the wrist. To avoid the high costs of RSI, some businesses have introduced ergonomic workstations and enforced rest periods.

Repin, Ilya Yefimovich, 1844–1930, Russian painter and sculptor. A realist who studied at the St. Petersburg Academy, Repin was influenced by IMPRESSIONISM while visiting Paris (1873–74). He believed that art served a social purpose. In paintings such as *The Arrest of a Political Offender*, he was critical of the political regime.

Representation of the People Acts, laws passed by the British Parliament to continue the franchise reform begun by the REFORM BILLS. The Representation of the People Act of 1918 gave the vote to most women over 30 and to most men over 21. The act of 1928 enfranchised women on the same terms as men. The act of 1949 codified electoral practices, and the act of 1969 lowered the voting age to 18.

Representatives, United States House of: see CONGRESS OF THE UNITED STATES.

reproduction, the ability of living systems to give rise to new systems similar to themselves. The term may refer to self-duplication of a single cell, of a group of cells and organs, or of a complete organism. Reproductive processes vary tremendously, but two fundamental types may be distinguished: asexual reproduction, in which a single organism separates into two or more parts, each genetically identical to the parent; and sexual reproduction, in which a pair of specialized reproductive (sex) cells fuse, creating an individual that combines two sets of genetic characteristics. Asexual reproduction is found in all plants and in some one-celled and invertebrate animals. In one-celled organisms it takes the form of MITOSIS, the division of one individual into two new, identical individuals. Primitive filamentous organisms, such as FLATWORMS, reproduce by fragmentation, in which a piece of the parent breaks off and develops into a new individual. Most fungi, many PROTOZOANS, and some plants reproduce by means of SPORES. In budding, the means by which YEASTS and animals such as the HYDRA reproduce, a small protuberance (bud) on the parent increases in size until a wall forms to separate the new individual. Sexual reproduction occurs in many one-celled organisms and in all multicellular plants and animals; it involves the FERTILIZATION of one sex cell (gamete) by another, producing a new cell (zygote), which develops into a new organism. In higher plants and animals two clearly different kinds of sex cells (distinguished as OVUM and SPERM) fuse. Multicellular plants alternate reproducing sexually and asexually (see GAMETOPHYTE). Although asexual reproduction ensures that beneficial combinations of characteristics will be passed on unchanged, sexual reproduction permits the offspring to inherit endlessly varied combinations of characteristics (because of the fusion of two different parental nuclei), providing for new variations that may improve a species and further enhance its chances of survival.

reproductive system, in animals, the organs concerned with production of offspring. In humans and other mammals the female reproductive system produces the female reproductive cells (eggs, or ova) and includes an organ (uterus) in which the fetus develops.

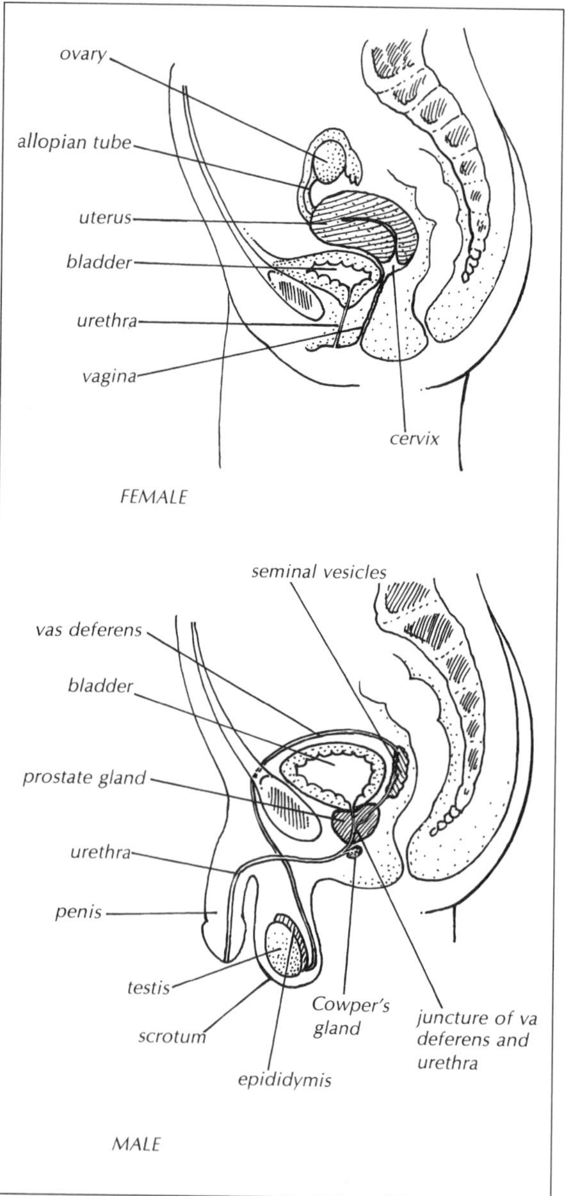

Reproductive system

The male reproductive system produces the male reproductive cells (sperm) and includes an organ (penis) that deposits the sperm within the female. In the female, the mature egg, or OVUM, passes from the ovary into the fallopian tube, where fertilization occurs if sperm are present. From the fallopian tube the ovum passes into the uterus, or womb. If the egg has not been fertilized, the endometrium (lining of the uterus) degenerates and sloughs off, and MENSTRUATION occurs. If the egg has been fertilized, it becomes embedded in the lining of the uterus about one week after fertilization (see PREGNANCY). The lower end of the uterus, called the cervix, is connected to the vagina, a passage joining the uterus with the external genitals. The vagina receives sperm during sexual intercourse and is the passageway through which menstrual blood is eliminated and birth takes place. In the male reproductive system, SPERM are produced in the testes, two organs contained in the scrotum, an external sac in the groin. The testes also produce the hormone TESTOSTERONE and a portion of the seminal fluid, the liquid in which the sperm are carried. From each testis the sperm move into a passage (epididymis) and then into a long duct (vas deferens); fluids from the PROSTATE GLAND and seminal vesicles also enter this duct. Just before ejaculation, contractions along the ducts mix the sperm with the seminal and prostatic fluids to form semen. During ejaculation semen is propelled into the urethra (the canal through the penis) and discharged. See also BIRTH CONTROL; FERTILITY DRUG; FERTILIZATION; STERILITY.

reptile, dry-skinned, usually scaly, cold-blooded VERTEBRATE of the class Reptilia. Reptiles are found in a variety of habitats in warm and temperate zones and range in size from 2-in. (5-cm) long lizards to 30-ft (9-m) long snakes. Typically they have low-slung bodies with long tails, supported by four short legs; snakes are limbless. They are mostly terrestrial, although a few are aquatic; all breathe air through lungs and have thick, waterproof skins. Unlike AMPHIBIANS, they do not possess GILLS at any stage of their development. Nearly all lay porous, shelled eggs or bear their young on land. The living orders of reptiles are the TURTLES; ALLIGATORS, caimans, CROCODILES, and gavials; LIZARDS and SNAKES; and the TUATARAS. Reptiles evolved from amphibians and were the dominant fauna in the Mesozoic era, often called the Age of Reptiles.

republic, sovereign nation whose chief of state is not a monarch, usually governed by representatives of a widely based electorate. The U.S. is a federal republic, while France is a centralized republic. Technically, Great Britain is a constitutional MONARCHY, not a republic. The USSR, in theory a group of federated and even autonomous regions, was in fact a centralized republic until shortly before its collapse (1991).

Republican party, major American political party, the other being the DEMOCRATIC PARTY. It was founded (1854) by opponents of the extension of slavery into the territories. The election of the Republican presidential candidate, Abraham LINCOLN, in 1860 precipitated the secession of the Southern states and the CIVIL WAR. Lincoln's RECONSTRUCTION policies were opposed by radical Republicans such as Charles SUMNER and Edwin Stanton, whose candidate, Ulysses S. GRANT, was elected in 1868 and 1872. With the election of Rutherford B. HAYES (1876), Republican domination of the South ended. In the period that followed, the Democratic and Republican parties differed little in their policies. Theodore ROOSEVELT succeeded the assassinated William MCKINLEY in 1901 and was reelected in 1904. His policies combined "trust busting" and other domestic reforms with an imperialist foreign policy. The Republicans, under Herbert HOOVER, were blamed for the GREAT DEPRESSION, and the party lost every presidential election between 1932 and 1952, when Dwight D. EISENHOWER became president. The WATERGATE AFFAIR during the administration of Richard M. NIXON damaged the party's prestige. In 1980 a Republican, Ronald REAGAN, was elected president. He was succceeded in 1988 by his vice president, George BUSH, but a recession and anemic recovery led to Bush's defeat (1992) by Democrat Bill CLINTON.

requiem, proper MASS for the souls of the dead, performed on All Souls Day, at funerals, and on request. Since the Second VATICAN COUNCIL, the traditional requiem has been modified: black vestments are no longer required, and the famous *Dies irae* sequence describing the Judgment and asking Jesus for mercy is now optional. Requiem music has a traditional Gregorian setting; other requiem music has been composed, e.g., by Mozart and Verdi.

resin, any of a class of amorphous solids or semisolids. Natural resins occur as plant exudations (e.g., of pines and firs), and are also obtained from certain scale insects. They are typically yellow to brown in color, tasteless, and translucent or transparent. Oleoresins contain ESSENTIAL OILS and are often sticky or plastic; other resins are exceedingly hard, brittle, and resistant to most solvents. Resins are used in VARNISH, SHELLAC, and lacquer and in medicine. Synthetic resins, e.g., BAKELITE, are widely used in making PLASTICS. See also AMBER; TURPENTINE.

resistance, property of an electric conductor by which it opposes flow of electricity and dissipates electrical energy away from the ELECTRIC CIRCUIT, usually as heat. Resistance is basically the same for alternating- and direct-current circuits. A high-frequency alternating current, however, tends to travel near the surface of a conductor. Because such a current uses less of the available cross section of the conductor, it meets with more resistance than direct current. The unit of resistance is the OHM. See also CONDUCTION; IMPEDANCE; OHM'S LAW; SUPERCONDUCTIVITY.

resistor, two-terminal ELECTRIC CIRCUIT component that generates heat by offering opposition to an electric current. The most common forms of resistors are made from fine wires of special alloys wound onto cylindrical forms or from a molded composition material containing carbon and other substances in varying amounts. Resistors are rated for the maximum amount of power that they can safely handle.

Respighi, Ottorino [rāspē'gē], 1879–1936, Italian composer. He is best known for his romantic SYMPHONIC POEMS, *The Fountains of Rome* (1917), *The Pines of Rome* (1924), and *Roman Festivals* (1929). He also wrote other orchestral works, chamber music, piano pieces, and operas.

respiration, process by which an organism exchanges gases with its environment. The term commonly refers to the overall process by which oxygen is taken from the air and transported to the cells for the OXIDATION of organic molecules, while the products of oxidation, carbon dioxide and water, are returned to the environment. In single-celled organisms, gas exchange occurs directly. The cells lose their high concentration of carbon dioxide to the environment by simple diffusion, while the environment provides its higher concentration of oxygen to the cells, also by diffusion. In complex animals, where internal cells are distant from the external environment, respiratory systems facilitate the passage of gases to and from internal tissues. In lower animals such as FLATWORMS, exchange occurs through a moist surface membrane. In FISH, blood vessels in the gills are exposed for direct exchange with the external (aquatic) environment. In plants, gas exchange occurs in the stomates, respiratory organs found mostly in leaves. In human beings and other vertebrates, gas exchange takes place in the LUNGS. In breathing—the mechanical procedure for getting air to and from the lungs—muscles enlarge the chest cavity to force air in and reduce it to expel air. Actual gas exchange in the lungs occurs in cup-shaped air sacs called alveoli. Organisms that utilize respiration to obtain energy are aerobic, or oxygen-dependent. Organisms able to live in the absence of oxygen are called anaerobic; they obtain energy from fuel molecules solely by FERMENTATION or GLYCOLYSIS. In biochemistry, *respiration* refers to the series of biochemical oxidations in which organic molecules—such as carbohydrates, amino acids, and fatty acids—are converted to carbon dioxide and water. The chemical energy thus obtained is trapped and stored for later use by the cells in ADENOSINE TRIPHOSPHATE (ATP).

Restoration, in English history, the reestablishment of the monarchy on the accession (1660) of CHARLES II. The term often refers to the whole period from 1660 to the fall of JAMES II in 1688. After the death of Oliver CROMWELL, reaction against Puritan and military control favored recall of the exiled king. Upon his return to power, Charles, guided by Edward Hyde, 1st earl of CLARENDON, and others, restored militant Anglicanism and tried to assert the old Stuart absolutism. The unwillingness of both Charles and his brother and successor, James II, to accept their financial dependence on Parliament was one cause of James's deposition in the GLORIOUS REVOLUTION (1688). The period was marked by an advance in colonization and trade, the DUTCH WARS, the birth of the WHIG and TORY

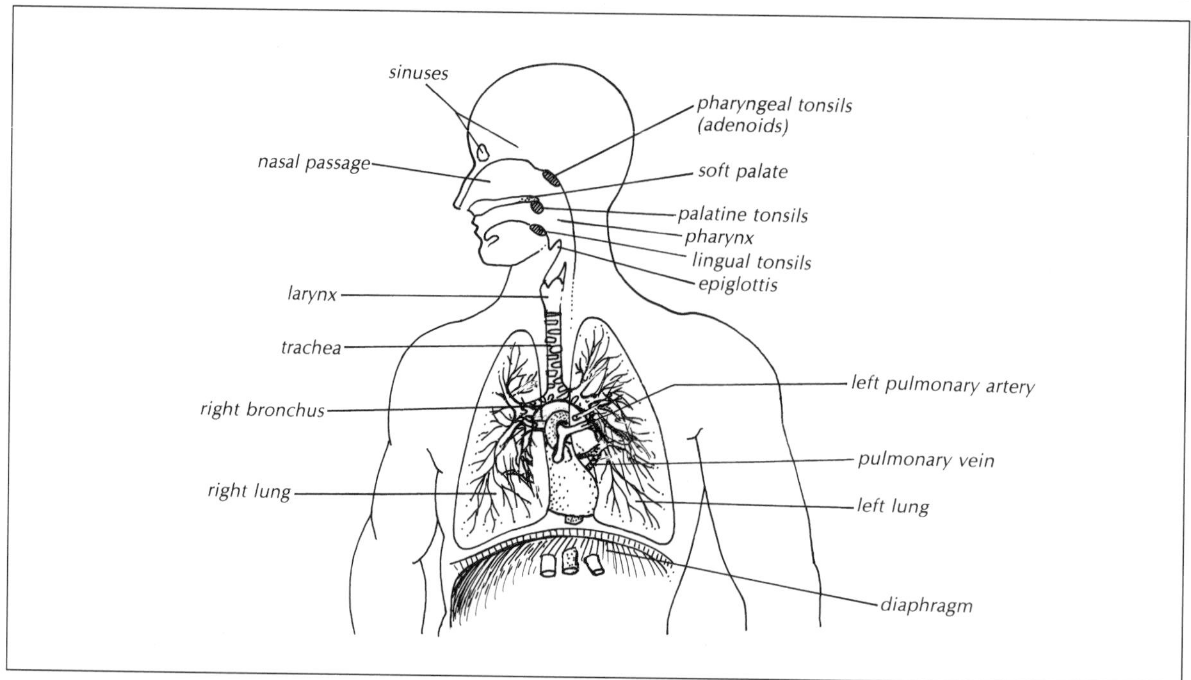

Respiratory system

parties, opposition to Roman Catholicism, and the revival of drama and poetry.

resurrection, arising again from death to life. The resurrection of Jesus is the cornerstone of Christianity. It guaranteed his mission and promised the resurrection of all people. Christian belief is that on Judgment Day people's souls will be reunited with their risen (but glorified and immortal) bodies.

retriever: see SPORTING DOG.

retrograde motion, in astronomy, real or apparent movement of a planet, satellite, asteroid, or comet from east to west relative to the fixed stars. The most common direction of motion in the solar system, for both orbital revolution and axial rotation, is from west to east. Bodies in the solar system with real retrograde orbits include four satellites of Jupiter, one of Saturn, one of Neptune, and some asteroids and comets. All the planets exhibit apparent retrograde motion when they are nearest the earth (at inferior conjunction for the inferior planets and at opposition for the superior planets; see SYZYGY) because of the relative speeds of the planets in their orbits about the sun.

retrovirus, type of RNA VIRUS that, unlike other RNA viruses, reproduces by transcribing itself into DNA. An enzyme called reverse transcriptase allows a retrovirus's RNA to act as the template for this RNA to DNA transcription. The resultant DNA inserts itself into a cell's DNA and is reproduced along with the cell and its daughters. Retroviruses sometimes destroy the cells whose DNA they alter, as in AIDS, and sometimes cause them to become cancerous, as in certain LEUKEMIAS.

Reuben [ro͞o'bən], in the BIBLE, JACOB's eldest son and ancestor of one of the 12 tribes (see ISRAEL, TRIBES OF). At the occupation of Palestine his tribe, with that of Gad, was allotted pastureland E of the Jordan.

Réunion, overseas department of France (1992 est. pop. 626,000), c.970 sq mi (2,510 sq km), one of the Mascarene Islands, in the Indian Ocean c.430 mi (690 km) E of Madagascar. Saint-Denis, the capital, and Le Port, the main port, are the chief cities. Réunion is a mountainous island of volcanic origin, and the population is concentrated in the coastal lowlands. Sugar, from sugarcane, is the chief product and export; molasses, bananas, and rum are also important. The islanders are the mixed descendants of French colonists and their East African, Indian, and Indochinese slaves and laborers. Most of the inhabitants are Roman Catholic. French, the official language, and a creole patois are spoken. The island was known to the Arabs and visited by the Portuguese in the 1500s but remained uninhabited until settled by the French (c.1642) as a penal colony. In 1665 it became a French East India Company outpost, exporting coffee in the 18th cent. and sugar after 1815. In 1947 Réunion was made a French overseas department.

Reuther, Walter Philip, 1907–70, American labor leader; b. Wheeling, W.Va. After working in a Detroit automobile plant, he became an organizer for the United Automobile Workers (UAW) and rose to the presidency in 1946. He was severely wounded by an unknown assailant in 1948, as was his brother Victor (also a union leader) in 1949. Elected president of the CIO in 1952, he helped engineer (1955) the merger of his organization with the AFL (see AMERICAN FEDERATION OF LABOR AND CONGRESS OF INDUSTRIAL ORGANIZATIONS). Reuther, a liberal, clashed repeatedly with the more conservative George MEANY, president of the AFL-CIO, and in 1968 he led the UAW out of the federation. Reuther died in a plane crash.

Revelation or **Apocalypse,** 27th and last book of the NEW TESTAMENT, written A.D. c.95 on Patmos by one John; whether he was the disciple St. JOHN is disputed. This book is a mysterious prophetic work, consisting mainly of visions showing the overcoming of evil and persecution and the triumph of God and the martyrs. The careful plan depends heavily on patterns of sevens, e.g., letters to seven churches in Asia Minor and the opening of the seven seals on the scroll in the hand of God. The style is majestic, with constant allusion to OLD TESTAMENT prophecies, especially those of EZEKIEL, DANIEL, and ISAIAH. New interpretations of the book have appeared in every period of Christian history.

Revere, Paul, 1735–1818, American Revolutionary leader; b. Boston. A silversmith and soldier, he joined the SONS OF LIBERTY and was a courier (1774) for the rebels. He was immortalized in LONGFELLOW's poem for his "midnight ride" of April 18, 1775, to warn the Massachusetts minutemen about British troop movements at the start of the AMERICAN REVOLUTION (see LEXINGTON AND CONCORD).

revolutions of 1848, series of revolutionary explosions in Europe. Major causes were the crop failures of 1846–47, widespread political repression, and the emergence of NATIONALISM. The most successful was the FEBRUARY REVOLUTION, in France, which overthrew LOUIS PHILIPPE and established the Third Republic. In the German states the liberal revolutions resulted in the FRANKFURT PARLIAMENT, which favored German unification. In the HAPSBURG empire the revolutionists demanded more autonomy; in Italy, however, the RISORGIMENTO sought to expel the Hapsburgs. Despite their early successes, the revolutions generally failed as the old order reestablished control. In some cases the revolutions were put down by force; in others they were taken over by middle-class moderates.

revolver: see SMALL ARMS.

Rex cat: see under CAT.

Rexroth, Kenneth, 1905–82, American poet; b. South Bend, Ind. A leader of the San Francisco literary revival and briefly associated with the BEAT GENERATION, he is best known for his poetry, e.g., *In What Hour* (1940), *In Defense of the Earth* (1956), and *New Poems* (1974). He also wrote many critical essays and translated Asian poetry.

Reye's syndrome, a combination of acute encephalopathy and fatty infiltration of internal organs, especially the liver. Its cause is unknown, but it usually occurs in children following an acute viral infection (particularly influenza and chicken pox), especially when they have been given aspirin or other salicylates while ill. The symptoms, which occur about a week after the virus, are vomiting and disorientation and may be followed by seizures, coma, and respiratory arrest. There is no specific treatment.

Reykjavik, [rā'kyävēk], city (1989 pop. 96,737), SW Iceland, capital of Iceland. It is the country's chief port and center of its cod fishing industry. Founded in 874 A.D., it is the home of the *Althing*, or Icelandic parliament, the oldest in Europe. The city's heating system uses nearby hot springs. Reykjavik was the site of 1986 disarmament talks between the U.S. and USSR.

Reymont, Władysław Stanisław [rā'mônt], 1867–1925, Polish novelist and short-story writer. His novels include *The Promised Land* (1899), attacking modern industrial society, and *The Peasants* (4 vol., 1904–9), the great prose epic of Polish village life. He was awarded the 1924 Nobel Prize in literature.

Reynolds, Albert, 1935–, Irish politician, prime minister of the Republic of Ireland (1992–). A successful business executive, Reynolds won (1977) a seat in the Irish parliament as a member of the FIANNA FÁIL party. Reynolds was minister of posts and telegraphs and of transport (1979–81), of energy (1982), and of industry and commerce (1987–88) under Prime Min. HAUGHEY. In 1988 he became finance minister, but he resigned in 1991 after he challenged Haughey for the party leadership and lost. When Haughey later resigned (1992), Reynolds succeeded him.

Reynolds, Sir Joshua, 1723–92, English portrait painter. Considered historically the most important English painter, he raised the artist to a position of respect in England. After studying first in London, then in Italy, Reynolds used his wit and charm to take London by storm. He was besieged with portrait commissions, ran his own gallery, and was elected president of the Royal Academy when it was founded in 1768. His annual discourses for the Academy were a significant exposition of academic style, propounding eclectic generalization over direct observation, and allusion to the classical past over the present. The Grand Style, thus propounded, greatly influenced English portraiture. Reynolds painted more than 2,000 portraits and historical paintings depicting almost every notable person of his time, including Dr. Johnson, Mrs. Siddons, and Edmund Burke.

Reza Shah Pahlevi, 1877–1944, shah of IRAN (1925–41). An army officer, he led a coup in 1921 and became premier in 1923. In 1925 he deposed the last of the Kajar dynasty, proclaimed himself shah, and proceeded to modernize Iran. In 1941 he was deposed by British and Russian forces because of his German sympathies. He was succeeded by his son, MUHAMMAD REZA SHAH PAHLEVI.

Rf, chemical symbol of the element RUTHERFORDIUM.

Rh, chemical symbol of the element RHODIUM.

Rhaeto-Romanic [rē'tō-rōmăn'ĭk], generic name for several related dialects of the Romance group of the Italic subfamily of the Indo-European family of languages. They include Romansh, an official Swiss language; Ladin; and Friulian. See LANGUAGE (table).

rhea, South American flightless BIRD (order Rheiformes), superficially resembling the OSTRICH. Weighing from 44 to 55 lb (20 to 25 kg) and standing up to 60 in. (152 cm) tall, rheas lack the ostrich's plumelike tail feathers. A herbivore, the rhea inhabits the PAMPAS and SAVANNAS, often feeding with cattle.

Rhea, in astronomy, natural satellite of SATURN.

Rhea, in Greek mythology, a TITAN; wife and sister of CRONUS; mother of ZEUS, POSEIDON, PLUTO, HESTIA, HERA, and DEMETER. She aided Zeus in the overthrow of Cronus. Associated with fertility, her worship was prominent in CRETE. In Rome Rhea was worshiped as Magna Mater and identified with Ops.

Rhee, Syngman, 1875–1965, 1st president (1948–60) of the Republic of KOREA. Educated in the U.S., he became a leader in South Korea during the U.S. occupation following WORLD WAR II. His rule grew autocratic, and in May 1960, after riots, he was forced out of office and into exile in Hawaii.

Rheims [rēmz], Fr. *Reims*, city (1990 pop. 180,620), NE France. It is a center of the CHAMPAGNE industry. A Roman city, it has been an archiepiscopal see since the 8th cent. It is the traditional coronation place of French kings: Clovis I (496) and Charles VII (1429, with JOAN OF ARC at his side) were crowned there. Its Gothic cathedral, heavily damaged in World War I, has been restored. In 1945, at the end of World War II, Germany signed the surrender agreement in Rheims.

rhenium (Re), metallic element, discovered in 1925 by Walter Nodack and colleagues. It is a very dense, high-melting, silver-white metal occurring in platinum and molybdenum ores, and in many minerals. It gives improved ductility and high-temperature strength to its alloys, which are used in electrical contacts, electronic filaments, thermocouples, and photographic flash lamps. See ELEMENT (table); PERIODIC TABLE.

rheumatic fever, serious inflammatory disease occurring as a complication of infection by streptococcal bacteria. Appearing chiefly in children, the disease is characterized by fever, painless nodules under the skin on the elbows or knees, rash, involuntary jerking movements, and inflammation of connective tissue in the joints and in the HEART. When severe, the disease can produce permanent heart damage. The course of the disease and its effects on the heart vary greatly. ANTIBIOTICS, ASPIRIN, CORTISONE, and rest are the usual treatments.

Rh factor, protein substance present on the surface of the red blood cells of most (85% or more) people and capable of inducing an intense antigen-antibody reaction (see IMMUNITY). When Rh-positive blood is given to an Rh-negative person or when fetal Rh-positive blood (inherited from the father) is mixed with maternal Rh-negative blood during pregnancy, the Rh-negative person develops antibodies to the foreign Rh factor. A serious or even fatal reaction may occur in subsequent mixing of two blood types, as in repeat transfusions or other pregnancies involving an Rh-positive fetus. In the latter case, the possibility of a fetal or newborn reaction (called erythroblastosis fetalis) can be prevented by the administration to the Rh-negative mother of a special immune globulin that suppresses antibody formation. In other cases, when the immune globulin is not given, the reaction must be treated by total blood exchange shortly before or after birth. See also BLOOD GROUPS.

Rhine, (Ger. *Rhein*, Fr. *Rhin*, Du. *Rijn*), principal river of W Europe, rising in the Rheinwaldhorn Glacier of Switzerland and flowing generally north c.820 mi (1,320 km), passing through or bordering on Liechtenstein, Austria, Germany, France, and the Netherlands. It flows through a broad-floored rift valley from Basel to Bingen and a scenic gorge from Bingen to Bonn before forming a vast delta near Emmerich and dividing into the Lek, Waal, and other distributaries that enter the North Sea through several mouths near Rotterdam. The river is navigable by ocean vessels to Cologne and by barges to Basel. The Rhine-Main-Danube Canal links the Rhine with the DANUBE.

Rhineland, region of W Germany, along the Rhine R. The Allies occupied most of the region after WORLD WAR I, until 1930. The Treaty of VERSAILLES (1919) had prohibited German fortifications in the region, but in 1936 the Germans began building the Siegfried Line, an extensive system of defenses that the Allies in WORLD WAR II penetrated with difficulty.

rhinoceros, massive, hoofed MAMMAL of Africa, India, and SE Asia, characterized by one or two horns on the snout made of congealed hair. A thick-skinned vegetarian, it has poor vision but excellent senses of smell and hearing. Solitary and unpredictable, the rhinoceros feeds at night and rests in the shade in the daytime. It has been hunted for its horns, sold powdered as an aphrodisiac and for use in folk medicines, and three of the five species are near extinction.

rhizome or **rootstock,** fleshy, creeping, underground STEM by means of which some plants propagate themselves. Buds that form at the joints produce new shoots. If a rhizome is split, it does not die (unlike a ROOT) but becomes several plants instead of one. Common rhizome-producing plants are ginger and iris.

Rhode Island, smallest state in the U.S., located in New England; bounded by Massachusetts (N and E), the Atlantic Ocean (S), and Connecticut (W).

Area, 1,214 sq mi (3,144 sq km). *Pop.* (1990) 1,003,464, a 5.9% increase over 1980 pop. *Capital,* Providence. *Statehood,* May 29, 1790 (13th of the original 13 states to ratify the Constitution). *Highest pt.,* Jerimoth Hill, 812 ft (248 m); *lowest pt.,* sea level. *Nickname,* Little Rhody. *Motto,* Hope. *State bird,* Rhode Island red. *State flower,* violet. *State tree,* red maple. *Abbr.,* R.I.; RI.

Land and People. Narragansett Bay cuts inland c.30 mi (50 km) into Rhode Island to Providence and contains several large islands. Coastal lowlands give way to higher terrain and steep, glaciated hills in the west. Rhode Island is the second most densely populated state in the U.S. (after New Jersey); 86% of the population lives in urban areas. PROVIDENCE, the largest city and capital, dominates the state and is followed in size by Warwick, Cranston, and Pawtucket. In 1990 the population was 91% white and 4% African American.

Economy. The state's small agricultural sector is best known for its Rhode Island Red chickens; it also produces greenhouse and dairy products, potatoes, eggs, and other farm products. Rhode Island is intensively industrialized, and the jewelry business in Providence is one of the largest in the world. Other products include toys, machinery, textiles, silverware, and primary and fabricated metals. Narragansett Bay, which abounds in shellfish and flounder, supports a thriving fishing industry. Tourists are attracted to Rhode Island's beaches, the famous mansions of NEWPORT, and Block Island.

Government. The constitution (adopted 1842) provides for a governor elected to a two-year term. The general assembly consists of a 50-seat senate and 100-seat house, with members of both bodies elected for two years. The state is represented in the U.S. Congress by two senators and two representatives and has four electoral votes.

History. After the Puritan Roger WILLIAMS was banished (1635) from the Massachusetts Bay Colony, he purchased land from the NARRAGANSETT and founded a settlement on the site of present-day Providence. New settlers were attracted to the colony by the promise of religious freedom, and a commercial shipping economy flourished. In 1776 Rhode Island became one of the Thirteen Colonies to renounce its allegiance to Great Britain. After the American Revolution, shipping declined, but Samuel Slater built (1790) the first successful cotton-textile mill in the U.S., and an abundance of water power led to the rapid development of manufacturing. Rhode Island's political and economic life was dominated by mill owners until well into the 20th cent., when competition from the South resulted in a continuing decline in the state's textile industry. The growth of new high-technology industries such as electronics and the growth of the service sector, now the chief employer in the state, have helped to revitalize the economy.

Rhodes, Cecil John, 1853–1902, British imperialist and business magnate. After making a fortune (1870s) in the Kimberly diamond fields of South Africa, he entered (1881) the Parliament of the Cape Colony and was (1890–96) prime minister and virtual dictator. He persuaded Britain to annex Bechuanaland in 1884 and conspired to topple the Boer government of the Transvaal. Forced to resign (1896) after he was implicated in Sir Leander Starr JAMESON's raid into the TRANSVAAL, he devoted himself to the development of the country that was called Rhodesia in his honor (now ZIMBABWE). He also founded the Rhodes scholarships.

Rhodes or **Ródhos,** island (1981 pop. 40,392), c.540 sq mi (1,400 sq km), Greece, in the Aegean Sea, near Turkey; largest of the DODECANESE island group. Its fertile coastal areas produce wheat, tobacco, cotton, and olives. Tourism and fishing are important. Colonized by DORIANS before 1000 B.C., it reached its height as a commercial and cultural center in the 4th–3d cent. B.C. Julius CAESAR studied at its renowned school of rhetoric. After its decline, Rhodes was an ally of Rome. Captured (1204) from the Byzantine Empire during the Crusades, it was held by the KNIGHTS HOSPITALERS (1282–1522) and the Ottoman Turks before it was taken by Italy in 1912. In 1947 it was ceded to Greece. The famed Colossus of Rhodes (see under COLOSSUS), a statue erected (292–280 B.C.) by the citizens of the ancient capital city of Rhodes, was destroyed by an earthquake in 224 B.C.

Rhodesia: see ZIMBABWE.

rhodium (Rh), metallic element, discovered in 1804 by William WOLLASTON. A silver-white, lustrous, brilliant, tarnish-resistant, and chemically-resistant metal, rhodium is used to plate jewelry and searchlight reflectors. Its major use is in platinum and iridium alloys, to which it gives improved strength and the ability to withstand higher temperatures. See ELEMENT (table); PERIODIC TABLE.

rhododendron, shrub (genus *Rhododendron*) of the HEATH family, found chiefly in mountainous areas of the arctic and north temperate zones. They typically have large, shiny, leathery evergreen leaves and clusters of large pink, white, or purplish flowers. North American species include the great laurel, or rose bay (*R. maximum*), West Virginia's state flower; and the Western rhododendron (*R. californicum*), Washington's state flower. AZALEAS are in the same genus.

rhodophyte, member of a division (Rhodophyta) of the multicellular PROTISTS consisting of red ALGAE. Considered PLANTS in some classification systems, rhodophytes are found primarily in warm and temperate marine waters and have a characteristic red or purplish color.

Rhône, major river of France, its lower course forming the cradle of Provençal culture. It rises in the Swiss Alps, flows west through Lake Geneva, and southwest and south (from Lyon) across France before dividing near Arles to form the Grand Rhône and Petit Rhône, which enter the Mediterranean Sea near Marseilles. Major tributaries are the Isère, Saône, and Durance.

rhubarb: see BUCKWHEAT.

rhyme or **rime,** literary artifice used in versification. It appears in Asian poetry but was almost unknown in Greece and Rome. When accentual meters replaced classical quantitative meters, rhyme developed, especially in Latin Christian poetry. In medieval vernacular verse, end rhyme (at a line end), assonance (repeated similar vowel sounds), and alliteration (repeated consonants, especially at word beginnings) were common. From 1300 until the 16th-cent. rise of blank verse (see PENTAMETER) rhyme was the outstanding verse device. Many modern poets use imperfect or approximate rhymes (e.g., *groaned* and *ground*). Single, or masculine, rhyme dominates in English, double, or feminine, rhyme in Spanish and Italian; German and French use both. Triple rhymes are uncommon in serious verse. Words spelled but not sounded alike are sometimes called eye rhymes. Set patterns of rhyme form such verse structures as the SONNET and heroic couplet.

rhythm, basic element of music concerned with the duration of tones and the stresses or accents placed upon them. The formulation in the 12th cent. of basic rhythmic patterns (modes) led to the development of meter, the division of a composition into units of equal time value. The rhythmic characteristics are a major factor in the analysis of the style of a composer or period.

Ribbentrop, Joachim von, 1893–1946, German foreign minister under HITLER (1938–45). He was influential in forming the Rome-Berlin Axis (1936) and the German-Soviet pact (1939). He was hanged as a war criminal.

ribbon worm, carnivorous, elongated, often flattened marine worm (phylum Nemertinea) characterized by a distinctive proboscis—sometimes tipped with a sharp spike and secreting a toxic mucus—used for food-capture, defense, and burrowing. Ribbon worms range in size from a fraction of an inch to 90 ft (27 m).

Ribera, Jusepe, José, or **Giuseppe** [rēbä'rä], c.1590–1652, Spanish BAROQUE painter. He was court painter to the Spanish viceroy in Naples. Greatly influenced by CARAVAGGIO, he combined Caravaggesque naturalism with a Spanish feeling of mysticism. His early works, e.g., *Drunken Silenus* (1626; Naples) are sombre in tone, but after c.1635 his work shows freer brushwork and brighter colors with a silvery effect, e.g., *Trinity* (1636–37; Prado).

Ricardo, David, 1772–1823, British economist; of Dutch-Jewish parentage. After amassing a fortune at an early age, he turned to science and later, influenced by Adam SMITH, to political economy. His major work, *The Principles of Political Economy and Taxation* (1817), containing his important theories on the determination of wages and value, holds that wages tend to stabilize around the subsistence level and that the value of almost any good is a function of the labor needed to produce it. His thinking greatly influenced the development of classical economics.

Ricci, Matteo [rēt'chē], 1552–1610, Italian missionary to China. A JESUIT, he was sent to China in 1582. He made few converts, but brought Christianity into good repute. Ricci sent back to Europe a detailed report on China.

Rice, Elmer, 1892–1967, American dramatist; b. N.Y.C. He is noted for such plays as *The Adding Machine* (1923), a satirical, expressionistic drama; *Street Scene* (1929; Pulitzer; operatic version by Kurt WEILL, 1947), a realistic play about tenement life; and *Dream Girl* (1945), a romantic comedy.

rice, cereal GRAIN (*Oryza sativa*) of the GRASS family, probably native to the Ganges, Tigris, Chang (Yangtze), and Euphrates river deltas. Requiring warmth and abundant moisture, the plant is an annual, from 2 to 6 ft (61 to 183 cm) tall, with a round, jointed stem, long, pointed leaves, and seeds borne in a dense head on separate stalks. Thousands of rice strains are now known, both cultivated and wild. Estimates are that half the world's population subsists wholly or partially on rice. The largest producers are China, India, Indonesia, Bangladesh, and Thailand; most is consumed domestically. Brown rice has greater food value than white, since the outer coatings, which are polished away to yield white rice, contain protein and minerals, while the white endosperm is chiefly carbohydrate. As a food, rice is low in fat and (compared to other grains) protein. The beverage SAKE is brewed from rice.

Rich, Adrienne, 1929–, American poet; b. Baltimore. Her mature poetry, concerned largely with feminist issues and the need for communication, includes *Diving into the Wreck* (1973), *The Dream of a Common Language* (1978), *Time's Power* (1989). *Of Woman Born* (1976) is a prose investigation of motherhood.

Richard, kings of England. **Richard I, Richard Cœur de Lion** [kör də lyôN'], or **Richard Lion-Heart,** 1157–99 (r.1189–99), was duke of Aquitaine from 1172 and fought against his father, HENRY II, and later against his brothers. As king, he set out (1190) on the Third CRUSADE with PHILIP II of France and stormed the city of Acre. Richard concluded a treaty with SALADIN permitting Christians to visit the holy places of Jerusalem. On his return, he was captured (1192) and became the prisoner of Holy Roman Emperor HENRY VI. Henry exacted from Richard a huge ransom and recognition of England's status as a fief of the Empire. Released in 1194, Richard returned briefly to England. He was killed in a minor battle in France. Although he was seldom in England, Richard's military prowess made him a central figure in English romance. **Richard II,** 1367–1400 (r.1377–99), was the son of EDWARD THE BLACK PRINCE. He succeeded his grandfather EDWARD III. His minority was dominated by rival nobles, notably his uncle JOHN OF GAUNT. Richard quelled (1381) the Peasants' Revolt of Wat TYLER and after 1382 began to assert his rule, but met with opposition from the nobles. In 1388 his uncle Thomas of Woodstock, duke of Gloucester, the duke of Hereford, and others forced Richard to dismiss his favorites, but the king soon reasserted his authority. He had Gloucester murdered (1397), but Hereford, banished in 1398, returned (1399), forced Richard to abdicate, and was crowned HENRY IV. Richard died a prisoner at Pontefract Castle, probably violently. **Richard III,** 1452–85 (r.1483–85), was a younger brother of EDWARD IV. He gained control of his 12-year-old nephew EDWARD V, and had himself proclaimed king. Young Edward and his brother were imprisoned and murdered, probably on Richard's orders. In 1485 Henry Tudor, a claimant to the English throne, landed in Wales, defeated and killed Richard at the battle of Bosworth Field, and ascended the throne as HENRY VII. Richard was the last of the Yorkist kings, and his death ended the Wars of the ROSES.

Richard, Maurice [rēshärd'], 1921–, Canadian hockey player. His entire career (1942–60) was spent with the Montreal Canadians. "The Rocket," who set many National Hockey League scoring records, was the first to score 50 goals in a regular season (then 50 games). His career total was 544 goals.

Richard Cœur de Lion: see Richard I under RICHARD, kings of England.

Richard Lion-Heart: see Richard I under RICHARD, kings of England.

Richards, Ann Willis, 1933–, U.S. politician; b. Waco, Tex. A Democrat, she served (1977–82) as county commissioner in Travis co., Tex., before she was elected (1982) to the first of two terms as Texas state treasurer. She was elected governor of Texas in 1990.

Richardson, Elliot Lee, 1920–, U.S. government official; b. Boston. After serving (1965–69) as Republican lieutenant governor and attorney general of Massachusetts, he served (1970–73) in Pres. NIXON's cabinet as secretary of health, education, and welfare; secretary of defense; and attorney general. He resigned in Oct. 1973 rather than carry out Nixon's order to fire the special prosecutor in the WATERGATE AFFAIR. He was U.S. ambassador to Great Britain (1975–76) and ambassador-at-large (1977–80).

Richardson, Henry Hobson, 1838–86, American architect; b. St. James Parish, La. He was noted for his revival of Romanesque design. Trinity Church, Boston (1872–77), his first and finest monumental work, is a superb example of the highly popular "Richardson Romanesque" style. His many other buildings include the Marshall Field wholesale store, Chicago. Richardson also elevated the position of the decorative crafts.

Richardson, John, 1796–1852, first Canadian novelist to write in English. His works include the frontier romances *Wacousta* (1832) and *The Canadian Brothers* (1840).

Richardson, Samuel, 1689–1761, English novelist. A prosperous printer, he was asked to compose a guide to letter writing. Working around a central theme, he wrote instead a moral NOVEL in letter form—*Pamela; or, Virtue Rewarded* (1740). He later wrote two more epistolary novels, *Clarissa Harlowe* (1747–48) and *The History of Sir Charles Grandison* (1753–54). Verbose and sentimental, all were very popular and are today valued for their drama, detail, and insight into women.

Richelieu, Armand Jean du Plessis, cardinal and **duc de** [rēshəlyö'], 1585–1642, chief minister of LOUIS XIII of France. He gained the favor of the king's mother, MARIE DE' MEDICI, and was made secretary of state (1616), cardinal (1622), and chief minister (1624). In 1630 Marie conspired against Richelieu, but the king had her exiled. Richelieu then enjoyed full control of the government until his death. Domestically, he centralized royal authority by destroying the political power of the HUGUENOTS with the capture of La Rochelle (1628) and the Peace of Alais (1629). Conspiracies by the nobles were rigorously suppressed. In foreign affairs, he rejected Marie de' Medici's pro-HAPSBURG policy, and in 1635 France openly entered the THIRTY YEARS WAR against the Hapsburgs. In France the war led to heavy taxation and caused dissatisfaction with his rule. Richelieu encouraged trade and the arts; he was the founder of the learned society known as the French Academy.

Richler, Mordecai, 1931–, Canadian novelist. His comic novels reflect his Jewish upbringing in Montreal. Best known is *The Apprenticeship of Duddy Kravitz* (1959). Others include *St. Urban's Horseman* (1971) and *Solomon Gursky Was Here* (1989).

Richmond, city (1990 pop. 203,056), state capital, E Va., on the James R.; settled 1637, inc. as a city 1782. A deepwater port and financial and commercial center, it is a major tobacco market and manufacturer of tobacco products. Its industries produce chemicals, textiles, and other goods. Laid out in 1737, Richmond became capital of Virginia in 1779. During the CIVIL WAR, it was capital of the CONFEDERACY and the constant object of Union forces. Threatened in the PENINSULAR CAMPAIGN (1862) and WILDERNESS CAMPAIGN (1864), it fell to Gen. GRANT and was burned in April 1865. Richmond National Battlefield Park contains several battle sites. Places of interest include the capitol (1785), designed by Thomas JEFFERSON; the White House of the Confederacy, now a museum; and Hollywood Cemetery, with the graves of James Monroe, John Tyler, Jefferson Davis, and some 18,000 Confederate soldiers.

Richter, Johann Paul Friedrich, pseud. **Jean Paul,** 1763–1825, German novelist. His works combine the idealism of FICHTE with the sentimentality of STURM UND DRANG. *Quintus Fixlein* (1796), *Siebenkäs* (1796–97), *Titan* (1800–1803), and other novels, all popular in his lifetime, are warm, humorous portrayals of simple life.

Richter scale: see EARTHQUAKE.

Ricimer, d. 472, Roman general of the Germanic Suebi tribe. After defeating the Vandals (a Germanic tribe), he deposed (456) West Roman Emperor Avitus. Thereafter he ruled Italy through his puppet emperors, the most able of whom was MAJORIAN.

Rickenbacker, Edward Vernon, 1890–1973, American war hero and airline executive; b. Columbus, Ohio. Driving racing cars at 16, he set several speed records. In WORLD WAR I he became the leading U.S. air ace by destroying 26 enemy aircraft. As president (1938–53) and chairman (1954–63) he built Eastern Airlines into a major passenger and transport system.

rickets, bone disease caused by a deficiency of vitamin D, often resulting in knock-knees, bowlegs, and deformities of the chest and pelvis. See VITAMIN (table).

Rickover, Hyman George, 1900–86, U.S. admiral; b. Russia. He directed construction of the first atomic-powered submarine, *Nautilus* (launched 1954), and other nuclear ships. Later he became chief of the Naval Reactors Branch of the Atomic Energy Commission. A controversial figure because of his outspoken opinions, he was promoted to full admiral at the age of 73. He was on active duty until 1981; in 1982 he retired.

Ride, Sally K., 1951–, American astrophysicist and astronaut; b. Encino, Calif. With a Ph.D. in physics from Stanford Univ., she joined NASA in 1978, where she was an astronaut (1979–87) and helped design the robot arm for the space shuttle. In 1983 she became the first American woman in space. She also served (1986) on the Presidential commission investigating the CHALLENGER disaster. In 1989 she became professor of physics and director of the California Space Institute at the Univ. of Calif., San Diego.

Sally Ride

Ridgway, Matthew Bunker, 1895–1993, U.S. general; b. Fort Monroe, Va. He led (1942–44) the 82d Airborne Division in the Allied invasion of Europe during WORLD WAR II and replaced (1951) Gen. MACARTHUR as commander of UN forces in the KOREAN WAR. He served as supreme commander (1951–53) of NATO forces in Europe and as army chief of staff (1953–55).

Ridley, Nicholas, c.1500–1555, English prelate, reformer, and Protestant martyr. As bishop of Rochester (1547) he strengthened the Reformed teachings at Cambridge and in 1548 under EDWARD VI took part in compiling the Book of Common Prayer. He became bishop of London in 1550. After the accession of the Roman Catholic MARY I, he was imprisoned (1553) and took part (1554) in the Oxford disputations along with Thomas CRANMER and Hugh LATIMER. Ridley refused to recant his Protestantism and was burned as a heretic with Latimer at Oxford.

Riel, Louis [rēĕl'], 1844–85, Canadian insurgent leader. He led Native Americans and métis (half-breeds) in the RED RIVER SETTLEMENTS of MANITOBA to rebel (1869–70) when their land was transferred from the HUDSON'S BAY COMPANY to the Canadian government, but the rebellion collapsed, and Riel fled. Returning to Canada (1884), he led rebels attempting to secure land titles in SASKATCHEWAN. In an engagement (1885) at Batoche, Riel was captured, tried, and hanged.

Riemann, (Georg Friedrich) Bernhard [rē'män], 1826–66, German mathematician. His great contributions to mathematics include his work on the theory of the functions of complex variables and his method of representing such functions on coincident planes or sheets (Riemann surfaces). He laid the foundations of a NON-EUCLIDEAN GEOMETRY representing elliptic space and generalized to *n* dimensions the work of Carl GAUSS in differential geometry, thus creating the basic tools for the mathematical expression of the general theory of relativity. Riemann was also interested in mathematical physics, particularly in optics and electromagnetic theory.

Riemenschneider, Tilman [rē'mənshni"dər], c.1460–1531, German RENAISSANCE sculptor. He created slender figures with delicately carved, expressive faces in ordered compositions. His works include the stone *Adam and Eve* (Würzburg Mus.) and the wooden altar in Rothenburg ob der Tauber.

Rienzi [rēĕn'tsē] or **Rienzo, Cola di,** 1313?–1354, Roman popular leader. Pope CLEMENT VI made him a papal notary, and Rienzi went to Rome, where he received (May 1347) wide dictatorial powers, which he claimed to hold under the pope's sovereignty. He sought to rally other cities and dreamed of a popular Italian empire. Clement, aroused at his actions, incited the barons against him, and Rienzi was defeated (1347) and fled. Clement's successor, Innocent VI, sent him (1352) to Italy with Cardinal Albornoz, who made him a senator. Rienzi reentered Rome in triumph, but his violent and arbitrary rule soon led to a popular uprising and his subsequent murder.

Riesener, Jean Henri, 1734–1806, French cabinetmaker. With J.F. Oeben, whom he later succeeded as director of the Arsenal workshop in Paris, he created Louis XV's writing desk. His work is in the Louvre and other collections.

Rietveld, Gerrit Thomas [rēt'fĕlt], 1888–1965, Dutch architect and designer. He created (c.1917) a chair that introduced into furniture

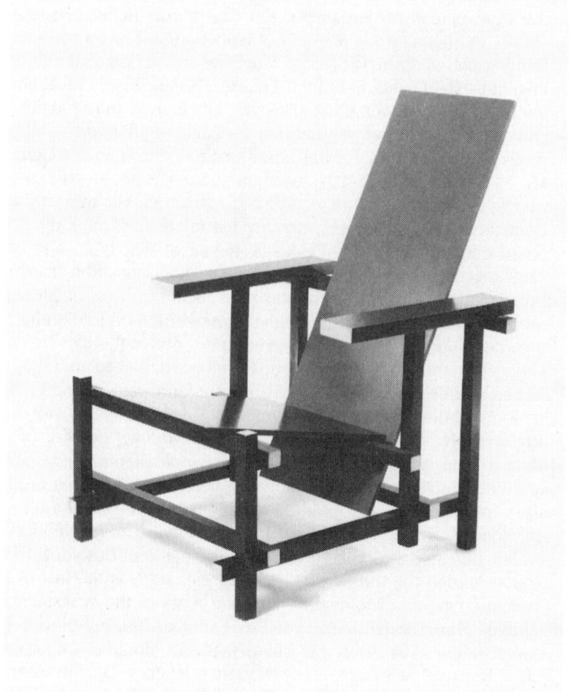

Chair designed by Gerrit Rietveld

design a light, dematerialized effect. A member of the STIJL, he designed buildings that in their weightlessness and equilibrium are related to MONDRIAN's paintings.

rifle: see SMALL ARMS.

Riga [rēʹgə], city (1989 pop. 915,000), capital of LATVIA, north-central Europe, on the Daugava R. near its entry into the Gulf of Riga. It is a major Baltic port, rail junction, military base, and leading industrial center. Among its manufactures are machines, ships, and diesel engines. Long settled by Baltic tribes, Riga became (1201) the seat of the Livonian Brothers of the Sword, a German military order dedicated to Christianizing the Baltic region. Riga joined the HANSEATIC LEAGUE in 1282. After the Livonian Order was dissolved (1561) the city passed to Poland (1581), Sweden (1621), and Russia (1721). It became the capital of independent Latvia in 1920 and was the capital of the Latvian SSR (1940–91) while the country was forcibly annexed by the USSR. During World War II Riga was occupied (1941–44) by Germany.

Right, Petition of: see PETITION OF RIGHT.

right ascension: see ASTRONOMICAL COORDINATE SYSTEMS.

rigor mortis: see DEATH.

Riis, Jacob August [rēs], 1849–1914, Danish-American journalist; b. Denmark. After emigrating to the U.S. in 1870, he became a reporter for the New York *Tribune* and *Evening Sun.* His stories about slum dwellings and abuses in lower-class urban life were collected as *How the Other Half Lives* (1890). He founded a pioneer settlement house in New York City (named for him in 1901) and aided public park and playground movements.

Riley, James Whitcomb, 1849–1916, American poet; b. Greenfield, Ind. Known as the Hoosier poet, he wrote popular verse noted for its humor, pathos, and sentimentality, e.g., "Little Orphant Annie," "The Raggedy Man." Collections of his poems include *Rhymes of Childhood* (1890) and *Knee Deep in June* (1912).

Rilke, Rainer Maria [rĭlʹkə], 1875–1926, German poet; b. Prague. The greatest lyric poet of modern Germany, sensitive and introspective, he was greatly influenced by his extensive travels. Rilke developed a rich poetic style characterized by striking visual imagery and by symbolism. Although his first book of poetry appeared in 1894, his mature mysticism first found expression 10 years later with *Stories of God* (1904). He achieved fame with *Poems from the Book of Hours* (1905). Well known are the two-volume *New Poems* (1907–8) and Rilke's own favorite verse, his *Duinese Elegies* (1923), which contain his highest praise of human existence. Rilke's reputation has grown enormously since his death.

Rimbaud, Arthur [răNbōʹ], 1854–91, French poet whose hallucinatory and dreamlike verse anticipated the SYMBOLISTS. Works include *The Drunken Boat; Illuminations,* prose poems; and a confessional autobiography, *Season in Hell.* After a close and violent relationship with VERLAINE (1872–73), Rimbaud stopped writing poetry at age 19 and thereafter wandered through Europe and Africa.

Rimmer, William, 1816–79, American sculptor; b. England. He was a doctor whose knowledge of anatomy is apparent in the few works of stone sculpture that survive, e.g., *Falling Gladiator* (Metropolitan Mus.). Rimmer was also an influential art teacher and the author of texts on drawing.

Rimsky-Korsakov, Nicolai Andreyevich, 1844–1908, Russian composer. One of The FIVE, he used Russian history and legend as a source for most of his operas, e.g., *The Snow Maiden* (1881), *The Maid of Pskov* (1873, rev. 1892), *Le Coq d'Or* (1909). His best-known orchestral work, *Scheherezade* (1888), exemplifies his romantic exoticism and mastery of orchestral color. Among his students was Igor STRAVINSKY.

rings, planetary: see JUPITER; SATURN; URANUS.

ringworm or **tinea,** any of several FUNGAL INFECTIONS of the skin characterized by dry, scaly patches or blisterlike elevations, which usually burn or itch. The most common sites of infection include the scalp, groin (a condition called jock itch), and the feet (a condition called athlete's foot). Ringworm is treated with oral griseofulvin or topical antifungals.

Rio de Janeiro, city (1990 est. pop. 6,042,000), SE Brazil, capital of Rio de Janeiro state, former capital of Brazil, on Guanabara Bay of the Atlantic Ocean. Brazil's second largest city and principal port, Rio (as it is popularly called) has diverse manufactures and handles much of the nation's foreign trade. It is predominantly a modern city, with a new airport and subway system. A cosmopolitan city, long the cultural center of Brazil, it is also its greatest tourist attraction. Rio is celebrated for its pre-Lenten carnival and for its beautiful natural setting within an amphitheater of low mountains. Noted landmarks are Sugar Loaf Mt., which dominates the harbor, and Corcovado peak, with its colossal statue of Jesus. Founded by French HUGUENOTS in 1555, the city was taken by Portugal in the 1560s. It replaced Bahia (now SALVADOR) as Brazil's capital in 1763 and was supplanted by BRASILIA in 1960.

Rio Grande, major North American river, flowing c.1,885 mi (3,000 km) S and SE from the San Juan Mts. (SW Colorado) to the Gulf of Mexico. It forms the U.S.-Mexico boundary between the twin cities of El Paso, Tex., and Juárez, Mex., and Brownsville, Tex., and Matamoros, Mex. The river, known in Mexico as the Río Bravo del Norte, is unnavigable, but is an important source of internationally regulated irrigation.

Riordan, Richard J., 1930–, U.S. business executive and politician; b. Flushing, N.Y. He parlayed an inheritance into a fortune through venture capitalism, real estate, and LEVERAGED BUYOUTS. In 1993 he was elected mayor of Los Angeles, becoming the first Republican to win in 32 years.

RISC processor [*R*educed *I*nstruction *S*et *C*omputer], COMPUTER arithmetic-logic unit that uses a minimal instruction set, emphasizing the instructions used most often and optimizing them for the fastest possible execution. Software for RISC processors must handle more operations than traditional CISC [*C*omplex *I*nstruction *S*et *C*omputer] processors, but RISC processors have advantages in applications that benefit from faster instruction execution, such as engineering and graphics workstations and PARALLEL-PROCESSING systems.

Risorgimento, period of cultural nationalism and political activism in the 19th cent. that led to the unification of Italy. Italy was fragmented in the Middle Ages, and from the 16th to 18th cent. foreign influence was virtually complete. After the Napoleonic wars, revolutionary groups such as the Carbonari emerged. The literature of Alessandro MANZONI, Ugo FOSCOLO, and others stimulated nationalism. Political activity was carried on by three groups. Giuseppe MAZZINI led the radicals, who were republican and anticlerical. The conservative and clerical faction generally advocated a federation headed by the pope. The moderates favored unification under the house of SAVOY, which ruled Sardinia. Sardinia assumed leadership of the Risorgimento in 1848 when revolts broke out across Italy. King Charles Albert of Sardinia tried to drive the Austrians out of N Italy but was defeated at Custoza (1848) and Novara (1849), and abdicated. Revolutions elsewhere were suppressed, including one at Rome, where Mazzini had formed a short-lived republic. The liberal movement, however, gradually coalesced around Charles Albert's son and successor, VICTOR EMMANUEL II, and his minister, the conte di CAVOUR. Cavour sought and received French aid against Austria, but the battles (1859) of Magenta and Solferino were so costly that the French signed a separate armistice. Austria retained Venetia, and Sardinia gained only Lombardy. In 1860 Tuscany, Modena, Parma, Bologna, and the Romagna voted for union with Sardinia. GARIBALDI's spectacular conquest (1860) of the kingdom of the TWO SICILIES was followed by Sardinia's annexation of Umbria and the Marches. The kingdom of Italy was proclaimed in 1861. Italy received Venetia for its role in the AUSTRO-PRUSSIAN WAR of 1866 and seized Rome from the pope in 1870. Unsatisfied Italian nationalism continued in the form of IRREDENTISM.

Ritsos, Yannis, 1909–90, Greek poet. One of modern Greece's best known poets, he moved from classical themes to a deeply personal lyricism. His verse reflects both his own life experience, including his opposition to the Greek junta, which resulted in exile and house arrest.

river, stream of water larger than a brook or creek. Runoff after precipitation flows downward by the shortest and steepest course. Runoffs of sufficient volume and velocity join to form a stream that, by the EROSION of underlying earth and rock, deepens its bed. It becomes perennial when it cuts deeply enough to be fed by groundwater or when it has an unlimited source (e.g., the SAINT LAWRENCE flowing from the Great Lakes). Sea level is the ultimate base level for a river, but the floor of a lake or basin into which a river flows may become a local and temporary base level. Rivers modify topography by both erosion and deposition (see e.g., DELTA). Young streams have steep-sided valleys, steep gradients, and irregularities in the bed. Mature rivers have valleys with wide floors and a more smoothly graded bed. Old rivers have courses graded to base level and run through broad, flat areas. See also articles on individual rivers, e.g., AMAZON; NILE.

Rivera, Diego, 1886–1957, one of modern Mexico's foremost painters. Inspired by native Mexican art and by his experiences in Europe (1907–9, 1912–21), he painted large murals dealing with Mexican life, history, and social problems, e.g., in the Palace of Fine Arts (Mexico City). Murals in the Detroit Institute of Arts typify his interpretation of industrial America. He was married to Frida KAHLO.

Rivera, Primo de: see PRIMO DE RIVERA, MIGUEL.

river blindness or **onchocerciasis,** disease caused by the parasitic worm, *Onchocerca volvulus.* It is transmitted by blackflies, and results in severe itching, disfiguring lesions, and lesions of the eye that can lead to blindness. It occurs primarily in Africa, Central and South America, and Yemen. The new drugs ivermectin and amocarzine have begun to help control the disease.

Rivers, William Halse Rivers, 1864–1922, English anthropologist, pioneer in the study of mental functions among preliterate peoples. He introduced the genealogical method into sociological research in his classic study *The Todas* (1906). An expedition to Melanesia produced his monumental *History of Melanesian Society* (1914). In *Instinct and the Unconscious* (1920) and *Medicine, Magic, and Religion* (1924) he was among the first to fuse ethnology with psychoanalytic theory.

Riverside, city (1990 pop. 226,505), seat of Riverside co., S Calif.; inc. 1883. It is famous for its orange industry; the forerunner of the California Fruit Growers' Exchange was begun there in 1892. Located in a rapidly growing metropolitan area (1990 pop. 2,588,793) that includes San Bernardino and Ontario, the city now has companies that manufacture electronic and aerospace equipment, aluminum, and other products.

Riviera, fashionable Mediterranean resort area in SE France and N Italy, famed for its scenery, warm climate, and excellent beaches. Major resorts include Nice, Cannes, and Saint-Tropez along the French Côte d'Azure, Monte Carlo in MONACO, and Rapallo, Portofino, and San Remo in Italy.

Riyadh [rēäd'], city (1988 est. pop. 2,150,000), capital of Saudi Arabia. It is situated in an oasis in the central part of the country. The nation's main commercial and transportation center, it has industries including oil refining and cement manufacturing. Its architecture formerly represented the classical Arabic style, but many large modern structures have been built since the 1970s. The city suffered light damage from Iraqi missiles during the PERSIAN GULF WAR.

Rizal, José [rēsäl'], 1861–96, Philippine patriot, author, and physician. His novel *The Lost Eden* (1886) attacked the Spanish regime in the PHILIPPINES, and he was exiled in 1887. After his return (1893), he was arrested and executed for alleged revolutionary activities. His death sparked a revolt.

Rizzio, David [rĭt'sēō], 1533?–1566, favorite of MARY QUEEN OF SCOTS. An Italian musician, he became Mary's secretary. Jealous nobles persuaded Lord DARNLEY, Mary's husband, that Rizzio was her lover, and with Darnley's aid they murdered him in Mary's presence in Holyrood Palace.

Rn, chemical symbol of the element RADON.

RNA or **ribonucleic acid,** NUCLEIC ACID, found mostly in the cytoplasm of CELLS, that is important in the synthesis of proteins. The amount of RNA varies from cell to cell. RNA, like the structurally similar DNA, is a chain made up of subunits called nucleotides; unlike DNA, RNA contains ribose as its sugar and uracil as one of its bases instead of thymine. In protein synthesis, messenger RNA (mRNA) replicates the DNA code for a protein and moves to organelles (specialized cell structures) called ribosomes, which are themselves composed of protein and a type of RNA called ribosomal RNA (rRNA). At the ribosomes, transfer RNA (tRNA) assembles AMINO ACIDS to form the protein specified by the messenger RNA.

roach: see COCKROACH.

road runner: see CUCKOO.

Roanoke, city (1990 pop. 96,397), SW Va., on the Roanoke R.; settled c.1740, inc. 1882. Situated between the Blue Ridge and Allegheny Mts., it is the gateway to the SHENANDOAH VALLEY. It is the region's commercial center, and has railroad shops and industries making a variety of products, including furniture, textile goods, chemicals, and electrical equipment.

Roanoke Island, 12 mi (19 km) long and 3 mi (4.8 km) wide, off the NE coast of North Carolina between Albemarle and Pimlico sounds, site of the earliest English colony in North America. The first colonists, sent out by Sir Walter RALEIGH, landed in Aug. 1585 but returned to England in 1586. A second group, arriving in 1587, disappeared by the time additional supplies were brought from England in 1591. Artifacts from the "lost colony" are displayed in Fort Raleigh National Historic Site on the island.

Robbe-Grillet, Alain [rôb-grēyā'], 1922–, French novelist. He is considered the originator of the French "new novel" in which story is subordinated to structure and the significance of external reality is stressed above psychological motivation or plot development. His works include the novels *Jealousy* (1957), *Topology of a Phantom City* (1975), *Djinn* (tr. 1982), and *Recollections of the Golden Triangle* (tr. 1986); *Last Year at Marienbad* (1961), a screenplay; and *Ghosts in the Mirror* (1984), a memoir.

robbery: see LARCENY.

Robbia: see DELLA ROBBIA.

Robbins, Jerome, 1918–, American dancer and choreographer; b. N.Y.C. He danced in MUSICALS and joined the AMERICAN BALLET THEATRE (1940) and, as associate artistic director, the NEW YORK CITY BALLET (1949). He is noted for his exuberant choreography for musicals, e.g., *West Side Story* (1957), and ballets, e.g., *Fancy Free* (1944) and *Dances at a Gathering* (1969). He succeeded (1969) BALANCHINE as ballet master at the City Ballet and was (1983–90) co–ballet master in chief.

Robert, kings of France. **Robert I,** c.865–923 (r.922–23), revolted (922) against CHARLES III (the Simple) and was crowned king, but was soon killed in battle. His son-in-law, Raoul of Burgundy, succeeded him. **Robert II** (the Pious), 970–1031 (r.966–1031), was the son of HUGH CAPET. Pious and learned, he tried to strengthen royal power and acquired the duchy of BURGUNDY for the crown.

Robert, kings of Scotland. **Robert I** or **Robert the Bruce,** 1274–1329 (r.1306–29), was a skillful and courageous leader who freed Scotland of English control. After he defied EDWARD I of England by being crowned (1306) at Scone, Robert was defeated (1306) at Methven and fled to the island of Rathlin, off the Irish coast. Returning to Scotland in 1307, he defeated EDWARD II at Bannockburn in 1314 and captured Berwick in 1318. He was recognized as king by the English in the Treaty of Northampton (1328). **Robert II,** 1316–90 (r.1371–90), was the founder of the STUART dynasty. During most of his reign his sons directed the government, repelling English invasions and winning a great victory at Otterburn in 1388. Robert's eldest son, **Robert III,** 1340?–1406 (r.1390–1406), was crippled by a horse; thereafter, real power was held by his brother, Robert Stuart, duke of Albany, 1340?–1420.

Robert, dukes of Normandy. **Robert I** (the Magnificent), d. 1035, duke (1027–35), made his illegitimate son William (later WILLIAM I of England) his heir and died on a pilgrimage to Jerusalem. **Robert II** (Robert Curthose), c.1054–1134, duke (1087–1106), succeeded his father, William I of England, in Normandy. He fought against his brothers, WILLIAM II and HENRY I of England. In 1106 he was defeated and imprisoned by Henry.

Robert Curthose: see Robert II under ROBERT, dukes of Normandy.

Robert Grosseteste: see GROSSETESTE, ROBERT.

Robert Guiscard [gēskär'], c.1015–1085, Norman conqueror of S Italy. Robert joined (c.1046) his brothers in S Italy and fought to expel the Byzantines. In 1059 Pope Nicholas II invested him with Apulia, Calabria, and Sicily. Sicily was wrested (1061–91) from the Arabs by Robert's brother Roger, and the Normans gained Calabria (by 1060), Bari (1071), Salerno (1076), and eventually most of Benevento. In 1081 Robert assaulted the Byzantine empire, conquered Corfu, and defeated (1082) Emperor ALEXIUS I. In 1084 he aided Pope GREGORY VII against Holy Roman Emperor HENRY IV. Robert then resumed his eastern wars but died of fever at Cephalonia. He was succeeded in Apulia by his youngest son, Roger.

Robert Joffrey Ballet, a major American dance company. It was founded (1954) in New York City by the dancer-choreographer Robert Joffrey. Its modern repertory includes works choreographed by George BALANCHINE, Antony TUDOR, and Alvin AILEY.

Robert of Courtenay, d. 1225, Latin emperor of CONSTANTINOPLE (1218–28). He was defeated (1224) by Nicaea and Epirus, and his realm was reduced to the city of Constantinople.

Roberts, Kenneth Lewis, 1885–1957, American author; b. Kennebunk, Me. He is known for his series of American historical novels *Chronicles of Arundel* (1930–34). His later novels include *Northwest Passage* (1937) and *Lydia Bailey* (1946).

Robertson, Ethel Richardson: see RICHARDSON, HENRY HANDEL.

Robertson, Oscar, 1938–, American basketball player; b. Charlotte, Tenn. After starring at the Univ. of Cincinnati, Robertson, known as "the Big O," became one of professional basketball's greatest players in his career with the Cincinnati Royals (1960–70) and Milwaukee Bucks (1970–74). Only 6 ft 4 in. (193 cm) in height, he was a superb playmaker (with a record 9,887 lifetime assists) as well as a leading scorer. Robertson's career total of 26,710 points (25.7 per game average) is among the highest achieved.

Robertson, Pat (Marion Gordon Robertson), 1930–, American evangelist and politician, b. Lexington, Va. A Baptist minister, he founded (1960) the Christian Broadcasting Network. As host of a television talk show that blends evangelical religion with conservative politics, he has attained a large following. Robertson campaigned unsuccessfully for the 1988 Republican presidential nomination.

Robert the Bruce: see Robert I under ROBERT, kings of Scotland.

Robeson, Paul, 1898–1976, African-American actor and bass singer; b. Princeton, N.J. He was noted for his roles in Eugene O'NEILL's *Emperor Jones* (1925; film, 1933) and Jerome KERN's *Show Boat* (1928; film, 1936) and for his interpretations of SPIRITUALS. His espousal of leftist causes made him a controversial figure.

Robespierre, Maximilien Marie Isidore [rôbespyĕr'], 1758–94, leader in the FRENCH REVOLUTION, called the Incorruptible. A lawyer, he became attached to the democratic and deistic theories of J.J. ROUSSEAU. He was elected to the STATES-GENERAL (1789) and the National Convention (1792), and became leader of the JACOBINS in their struggle with the GIRONDISTS. In 1793 he was elected to the Committee of Public Safety, which he dominated throughout the REIGN OF TERROR. Robespierre overthrew both the extreme left and the moderates in the Convention and also instituted a new civic religion. Robespierre's position, however, became precarious as the Convention began to feel threatened by the emergency measures of the Terror. On July 27, 1794, rightists joined the PLAIN in a rising in the Convention, and Robespierre was arrested, tried, and guillotined (July 28).

robin or **robin redbreast,** common name for a migratory BIRD of the THRUSH family.

Robin Hood, legendary 12th-cent. English hero who robbed the rich to help the poor. With his band of outlaws he lived in Sherwood Forest. He figures in LANGLAND's *Piers Plowman* and many Middle English ballads.

Robinson, Edward G., 1893–1973, American film actor; b. Romania as Emmanuel Goldenberg. He often played tough guys, e.g., in *Little Caesar* (1930) and *Key Largo* (1948), and character parts, e.g., in *Double Indemnity* (1944).

Robinson, Edwin Arlington, 1869–1935, American poet; b. Head Tide, Me. His most lasting work is his early verse, mainly austere and probing portraits of residents of a small New England town, such as "Miniver Cheevy" and "Richard Cory." His later poems include long psychological narratives, e.g., *Avon's Harvest* (1921), *The Man Who Died Twice* (1924; Pulitzer), and Arthurian romances. Volumes of his collected poems were published in 1921 (Pulitzer) and 1937.

Robinson, Frank, 1935–, African-American baseball player and manager; b. Beaumont, Tex. The only player ever to be voted the Most Valuable Player in both major leagues, he became the first African-American manager in major league history, with the Cleveland Indians (1975–77). He also managed the San Francisco Giants (1981–84) and Baltimore Orioles (1988–91).

Robinson, Jackie (Jack Roosevelt Robinson), 1919–72, African-American baseball player; b. near Cairo, Ga. He was the first African American to play in the major leagues; Robinson excelled in four sports at the Univ. of California, Los Angeles, and in 1945 he was signed by Branch Rickey of the Brooklyn Dodgers. He joined (1946) the Dodgers' farm team in Montreal, where he starred at second base and led the league in batting. In 1947 major-league precedent was shattered when he was brought up to Brooklyn. A fierce competitor, daring base runner, and solid hitter, Robinson led the Dodgers to 6 World Series appearances in his 10 years (1947–56) with the team. He was the first African American to be inducted into (1962) the National Baseball Hall of Fame.

Robinson, Sugar Ray, 1920–89, American boxer; b. Detroit, as Walker Smith. After winning (1946) the welterweight championship, he gained the middleweight title an unprecedented five times between 1951 (knocking out Jake La Motta) and 1958 (defeating Carmen Basilio). Of 202 professional bouts he lost only 19, most of them late in his career. He was rated the best boxer of his time.

Robinson-Patman Act: see under ANTITRUST LAWS.

robotics, the design and construction of self-controlled machines (robots) that sense (by means of vision systems or some other type of sensor) aspects of their environment and that are capable physically (e.g., by means of a mechanical arm) of acting upon it. The Czech dramatist Karel ČAPEK coined the word *robot* (from the Czech *robota,* drudgery) in his 1921 satirical play *R.U.R.,* and robots, or automatons, have long played a role in fantastic literature. Present-day robots, which bear little resemblance to the often humanoid figures of SCIENCE FICTION, are essentially computer-controlled machine tools that can be programmed to perform any of a number of functions, such as welding an automobile chassis or assisting a surgeon in performing delicate operations. Robots can perform dangerous, uncomfortable, tiring, or monotonous tasks, and do them with greater speed and accuracy than can human beings. Robots play an increasingly significant role in the movement toward industrial AUTOMATION and COMPUTER-ASSISTED MANUFACTURING. Robots for use in services, such as delivering meals and supplies in a hospital, have been slower to develop because of the greater complexity of the environment in which they must interact.

Rob Roy [Scottish Gaelic, = red Rob], 1671–1734, Scottish outlaw; b. Robert MacGregor. Deprived of their estates, he and his highland clan lived largely by stealing cattle and selling protection against thieves. Sentenced (1727) to be transported, he was later pardoned. He is remembered chiefly as he figures in Sir Walter SCOTT's novel *Rob Roy* (1818).

Robusti, Jacopo: see TINTORETTO.

Rocard, Michel (Louis Léon), 1930–, French politician. He supported (1974) François MITTERRAND for the presidency and merged his party with the new Socialist party, but later became Mitterrand's rival. He held several ministerial posts from 1981 to 1985. He became premier in 1988 but was replaced by Edith CRESSON in 1991. After the electoral rout of the Socialists in 1993, Rocard became party leader, vowing to broaden and revive the party.

Rochambeau, Jean Baptiste Donatien de Vimeur, comte de [rôshaNbō'], 1725–1807, marshal of France. During the AMERICAN REVOLUTION he landed (1780) at Newport, R.I., with a French army of 6,000, and with Gen. WASHINGTON planned the victorious YORKTOWN CAMPAIGN (1781). In the FRENCH REVOLUTION he commanded the Northern Army, but resigned (1792) and was imprisoned in the REIGN OF TERROR. Napoleon restored his rank.

Rochester, John Wilmot, 2d **earl of,** 1647–80, English poet and courtier. A notorious Restoration rake, he is best known for the witty and polished *Satyr against Mankind* (1675).

Rochester, city (1990 pop. 231,636; met. area 1,002,410), seat of Monroe co., W N.Y., on the Genesee R. and Lake ONTARIO; inc. 1817. It is a leading producer of optical and photographic equipment, and many other manufactures. Rochester developed as an ERIE CANAL town; its many parks and nurseries earned it the name the "Flower City." The Univ. of Rochester and the Eastman School of Music are among the city's many noted institutions.

rock, aggregate of solid matter composed of one or more of the MINERALS forming the earth's crust. Rocks are commonly divided into three major classes depending on their origin. *Igneous rocks* (e.g., BASALT, GRANITE, OBSIDIAN, PORPHYRY, PUMICE) result from the cooling and solidification of molten matter from the earth's interior. If formed below the surface, such rock is said to be intrusive (as in a BATHOLITH). If formed at the surface, it is extrusive. *Sedi-*

mentary rocks (e.g., CHALK, CLAY, COAL, LIMESTONE, SAND, SANDSTONE, SHALE) originate from the consolidation of sediments deposited chiefly through the action of EROSION on older rocks of all kinds. The characteristic feature of sedimentary rocks is their stratification. *Metamorphic rocks* (e.g., GNEISS, MARBLE, QUARTZITE, SCHIST, SLATE) originate from the alteration of the texture and mineral constituents of existing rocks of any type under extreme heat and pressure within the earth (see METAMORPHISM). See also PETROLOGY.

rock carvings and paintings, designs on rock surfaces attributed to primitive humans; they appear on every continent. The PALEOLITHIC ART of W Europe reached great aesthetic heights in naturalistic cave drawings of animals, hunting scenes, rites, and daily activities; in Australia and the Americas designs were more symbolic and geometric. Stenciled human hands appeared in many places. Petroglyphs were incised with a stone; polychrome pictographs were made with charcoal and earth pigments mixed with grease, gum, or water.

Rockefeller, family of American industrialists, bankers, and philanthropists. **John Davison Rockefeller,** 1839–1937, b. Richford, N.Y., established an oil refinery with partners in 1863, and in 1870 he organized the Standard Oil Co. of Ohio. By strict economy, mergers with competitors, and ruthless elimination of opponents he soon dominated the U.S. oil-refining industry. His numerous companies were consolidated (1899) under the Standard Oil Co. of New Jersey, but the U.S. Supreme Court ordered (1911) this holding company dissolved on antitrust grounds, and the subsidiaries became independent corporations. Rockefeller retired in 1911 with a fabulous fortune. His philanthropies, amounting to some $500 million, included the Rockefeller Institute for Medical Research (1901; now Rockefeller Univ.) and the Rockefeller Foundation (1913); he also founded (1892) the Univ. of Chicago. His brother, **William Rockefeller,** 1841–1922, b. Tioga co., N.Y., was associated with the Standard Oil Co. His vast resources built up the National City Bank of New York. John D. Rockefeller's son, **John Davison Rockefeller, Jr.,** 1874–1960, b. Cleveland, managed his father's interests from 1911. His most notable philanthropies included the restoration of colonial WILLIAMSBURG, Va., and donation of the site of UN headquarters, N.Y.C. He founded (1931) Rockefeller Center and funded Riverside Church (both: N.Y.C.). His five sons all became famous in various fields. **John Davison Rockefeller, 3d,** 1906–78, b. N.Y.C., helped manage the family interests and was active in creating Lincoln Center for the Performing Arts (N.Y.C.) and the United Negro College Fund. **Nelson Aldrich Rockefeller** became vice president of the U.S. (see separate article). **Laurance S. Rockefeller,** 1910–, b. N.Y.C., is noted for his interest in conservation and wildlife protection. **Winthrop Rockefeller,** 1912–73, b. N.Y.C., served (1967–71) as Republican governor of Arkansas. **David Rockefeller,** 1915–, b. N.Y.C., became a leading international banker during his career (1948–81) with the Chase Manhattan Bank, which he headed from 1961. **John Davison Rockefeller, 4th,** 1937–, b. N.Y.C., son of John Davison Rockefeller, 3d, was elected governor of West Virginia on the Democratic ticket in 1977 and 1980 and was elected to the U.S. Senate in 1985.

Rockefeller, Nelson Aldrich, 1908–79, vice president of the U.S. (1974–77); b. Bar Harbor, Me. The second son of John D. Rockefeller, Jr. (see ROCKEFELLER, family), he held several federal posts and was governor of New York for four terms (1966–73). A liberal Republican, he unsuccessfully sought the presidential nomination three times in the 1960s. He was named vice president under the 25th amendment of the CONSTITUTION by Gerald FORD, who had become president upon Richard NIXON's resignation.

Rockefeller Center, building complex in New York City, between 48th and 51st St. and Fifth and Sixth Ave., built between 1931 and 1939. Radio City Music Hall and the central fountain with Paul MANSHIP's statue of Prometheus are well known.

Rockefeller Foundation: see FOUNDATION.

rocket, any vehicle propelled by ejection of the gases produced by combustion of self-contained propellants. Tremendous pressure is exerted on the walls of the combustion chamber, except where the gas exits at the rear; the resulting unbalanced force, or thrust, on the front interior wall of the chamber pushes the rocket forward. The most vital component of any rocket is the propellant, which accounts for 90 to 95% of the rocket's total weight. A propellant consists of two elements, a fuel and an oxidant; engines that are based on the action-reaction principle and that use air instead of carrying their own oxidant are properly called jets (see JET PROPULSION). Liquefied gases, e.g., hydrogen as fuel and oxygen as oxidant, are more powerful propellants, whereas solid explosives, e.g., NITROGLYCERIN as oxidant and nitrocellulose as fuel, are more reliable. The chemical energy of the propellants is released in the form of heat in the combustion chamber. The rocket's exit nozzle usually converges to a narrow throat, then diverges to obtain maximum energy from the exhaust gases moving through it. No currently practical single-stage rocket can reach orbital velocity (5 mi/sec, or 8 km/sec) or the earth's ESCAPE VELOCITY (7 mi/sec, or 11 km/sec). Hence SPACE EXPLORATION requires multistage rockets; two or more rockets are assembled in tandem and ignited in turn; as their fuel is used up, each of the lower stages detaches and falls back to earth. When extremely large thrust is required, several rockets may be clustered and operated simultaneously. Rocket NAVIGATION is usually based on inertial guidance; internal GYROSCOPES are used to detect changes in the position and direction of the rocket.

Rockford, city (1990 pop. 139,426), seat of Winnebago co., N Ill., on the Rock R.; inc. 1839. The state's second largest city, it is in the heart of the Corn Belt and is a hub for regional agriculture. Rockford is also a manufacturing center producing machine tools, screws, fasteners, farm implements, and automobile parts. The city was founded (1834) on the site of a battle in the BLACK HAWK WAR.

rock music, hybrid of African-American and white American musical forms: blues (see JAZZ), rhythm and blues, GOSPEL MUSIC, COUNTRY AND WESTERN MUSIC, and harmony group music. In 1955 Bill Haley's song "Rock Around the Clock" set off a rock 'n' roll craze because of its exciting, heavy beat and the urgent call to dance and action of its lyrics. With songs on adolescent concerns like school, cars, and young love, African-American artists like Chuck Berry vied for popularity with whites like Buddy Holly. Most successful was Elvis PRESLEY. In the 1960s Detroit produced Motown, an African-American style with lead story lines sung over tight harmony by such groups as the Temptations and the Supremes. Rock surged after 1962 as the BEATLES, the ROLLING STONES, and other English groups introduced a sophisticated lyricism. In 1965 the folk singer Bob DYLAN began a folk-rock synthesis. Rock also turned to social protest and rebellion as groups like the Jefferson Airplane spoke to youth seeking new experience through drugs (acid rock). A large-scale production trend brought rock MUSICALS, e.g., *Hair* (1968), and opera, e.g., *Tommy*, by the Who (1969). By the end of the 1960s, rock was heard largely in concert and such festivals as Woodstock, held near Bethel, N.Y., in Aug. 1969. In the 1970s country rock, a fusion of country and western and rock 'n' roll, grew popular, as did disco, a repetitive dance music. English influence returned later in the decade with punk rock, expressing the discontent of working-class youth. Punk's stripped-down form and aggressiveness were echoed in the less political and more art-conscious American new wave. During the 1980s the MUSIC VIDEO became important. By the early 1990s, the pounding rhythms and strong, sometimes shocking spoken lyrics of RAP MUSIC had achieved broad popularity.

Rockne, Knute (Kenneth), 1888–1931, American football coach; b. Norway. He played football at the Univ. of Notre Dame, where, with Gus Dorais, he led an upset (1913) of a heavily favored Army team by using the forward pass, a legal but unused tactic. As head coach (1918–31) he established Notre Dame's great football tradition by winning 105 games against 12 losses and 5 ties. He died in a plane crash.

rock 'n' roll: see ROCK MUSIC.

Rockwell, Norman, 1894–1978, American illustrator; b. N.Y.C. Enormously popular, he is best known for his *Saturday Evening Post* covers. Rockwell specialized in finely drawn, richly anecdotal scenes of everyday small-town life.

Rocky Mountain goat, hoofed, ruminant MAMMAL (*Oreamnos americanus*) of the mountains of NW North America. Not a true GOAT, it has a bearded chin; sharp, black horns; and a long, thick, white coat. It is extremely surefooted, and lives on steep cliffs in small herds, feeding on vegetation.

Rocky Mountain National Park: see NATIONAL PARKS (table).

Rocky Mountain sheep: see BIGHORN.

Rocky Mountains, major mountain system of W North America, forming the CONTINENTAL DIVIDE and extending more than 3,000 mi (4,800 km) from New Mexico to Alaska. Mt. Elbert (14,431 ft/4,399 m) is the highest point. The mountains are topographically divided into the Southern, Central, and Northern Rockies (all in the U.S.), the Canadian Rockies (Canada), and the Brooks Range (Alaska). They are rich in minerals and lumber and are the site of several NATIONAL PARKS (see table). These include Rocky Mountain, Yellowstone, Grand Teton, and Glacier national parks in the U.S. and Jasper, Banff, Glacier, Yoho, Kootenay, and Mt. Revelstoke national parks in Canada. The Rockies were long a major barrier to transcontinental travel. The principal U.S. pass, South Pass (SW Wyoming), was crossed by the OREGON TRAIL.

Rocky Mountain spotted fever, infectious disease caused by a rickettsia harbored by wild rodents and other animals and carried by infected ticks that attach themselves to humans. Symptoms include chills, high fever, and a rose-colored skin rash, appearing first on the wrists and ankles and spreading to the trunk, with spots turning deep red and running together. The disease, most prevalent in the NW U.S., is treated effectively with the ANTIBIOTIC tetracycline.

rococo, style in architecture, especially in interiors and the decorative arts, which originated in France and spread throughout 18th-cent. Europe. In contrast with heavy BAROQUE grandiloquence, rococo was an art of exquisite refinement and linearity. The engravers J.A. Meissonier and Nicholas Pineau helped to spread the style through Europe. Parisian tapestry weavers, cabinetmakers, and bronze workers followed the trend. Motifs such as shells, scrolls, branches, and flowers appeared in delicate and ingenious compositions; the style also incorporated chinoiserie motifs. The major French exponents were the painters WATTEAU, BOUCHER, and FRAGONARD, and the architect GABRIEL. In Germany and Austria, CUVILLIÈS was the pioneer. The brilliantly decorated Italian rococo, especially important in Venice, was epitomized by TIEPOLO. In England the furniture of CHIPPENDALE was especially notable.

rodent, member of the largest mammalian order, Rodentia, characterized by front teeth adapted for gnawing and cheek teeth adapted for chewing. The approximately 1,800 species of Rodentia are worldwide in distribution and are divided into three suborders. The Sciuromorpha, or squirrellike rodents, include SQUIRRELS, CHIPMUNKS, and BEAVERS. The Myomorpha, or mouselike rodents, include a variety of MOUSE and RAT species, as well as species of HAMSTER, LEMMING, and GERBIL. The Hystricomorpha, or porcupinelike rodents, include the PORCUPINE, GUINEA PIG, and CHINCHILLA.

rodeo, form of entertainment based on the riding and roping skills of the Western cowboy. It is also an organized sport in which professional rodeo cowboys compete for millions of dollars in prizes. Staged in outdoor arenas, the modern rodeo comprises five classes: bareback bronc-riding, saddle bronc-riding, bull riding, calf roping, and steer wrestling (bulldogging). The first formal rodeo was held (1888) in Prescott, Ariz. Rodeos have gained popularity in many parts of the U.S. and Canada.

Roderick, d. 711?, last Visigothic king in Spain (710–711?). Although little is known about his reign, colorful legends about this "last of the Goths" are included in Spanish and English literature. He was overthrown in 711 by the invading Moors.

Rodgers, Bill (William Henry Rodgers), 1947–, American distance runner; b. Hartford, Conn. He helped to popularize distance running in the U.S. He won the Boston Marathon and the New York City Marathon four times each between 1975 and 1980.

Rodgers, Richard (Charles), 1902–79, American composer; b. N.Y.C. With Lorenz HART, he wrote such MUSICALS as *The Girl Friend* (1926), *Babes in Arms* (1937), and *Pal Joey* (1940). With Oscar HAMMERSTEIN, 2d, he composed such musicals as *Oklahoma!* (1943; Pulitzer), *Carousel* (1945), and *The King and I* (1951).

Rodilla, Simon: see WATTS TOWERS.

Rodin, Auguste [rōdăN'], 1840–1917, French sculptor. In the Salon of 1877 he exhibited a male nude, *The Age of Bronze* (1876; Paris), which was both praised and condemned. His critics unjustly accused him of casting it from life, but the furor gained him the patronage of the undersecretary of fine arts, and the government gave him a studio in Paris. From 1880 Rodin worked on studies for the *Gate of Hell,* two great bronze doors that were never finished; among the 186 figures intended for them are *Adam and Eve* (1881; Metropolitan Mus.) and *The Thinker* (1879–1900; Paris). These, together with his group *The Burghers of Calais* (completed in 1894) are among his most famous works. Rodin's work is realistic, but imbued with a profound, romantic poetry. He is also known for his drawings, portrait busts, and marble groups, e.g., *Ugolino* (1882), *The Kiss* (1886), and *The Hand of God* (1897–98; all Rodin Mus., Paris).

Roebling, John Augustus, 1806–69, American engineer; b. Prussia. After coming to the U.S. in 1831, he demonstrated the practicability of steel cable and began manufacturing it at Trenton, N.J. A pioneer in the building of suspension BRIDGES, Roebling designed, beginning in 1844, suspension bridges of increasing size at Pittsburgh; Niagara Falls, N.Y.; Wheeling, W.Va.; and Cincinnati. Shortly after beginning his most ambitious project, the BROOKLYN BRIDGE, he died from a tetanus infection following an accident at the site. His son **Washington Augustus Roebling,** 1837–1926, b. Saxonburg, Pa., completed (1883) the bridge and took over (1888) the Trenton plant.

Roemer, Olaus or **Ole,** 1644–1710, Danish astronomer. Through observations of the eclipses of Jupiter's satellites, he discovered that light travels through space at a finite, noninstantaneous velocity; his measurement of this velocity was a reasonable first approximation of the currently accepted value. Roemer made the first practical transit instrument (1690) and the earliest transit circle (1704).

Roentgen or **Röntgen, Wilhelm Conrad** [both: rĕnt'gĭn, rŭnt'–], 1845–1923, German physicist. For his discovery of a short-wave ray—the Roentgen ray, or X RAY—he received (1901) the first Nobel Prize in physics.

Roethke, Theodore, 1908–63, American poet; b. Saginaw, Mich. He combined a love of the land of the Midwest with a vision of individual development, and his tone ranged from acid wit to simple feeling. His volumes include *Open House* (1941), *The Waking* (1953; Pulitzer), and *The Far Field* (1964).

Roe v. Wade, case decided in 1973, with a companion case, *Doe v. Bolton,* by the U.S. SUPREME COURT. Justice Blackmun, for the Court, ruled that states may not ban abortions in the first six months of pregnancy; that a fetus is not a "person" protected by the 14th amendment to the U.S. CONSTITUTION; and that the amendment protects a woman from state intrusion into her decision as to whether or not to bear a child. Blackmun asserted, however, that the right to an abortion is not absolute: After the first trimester the state may regulate that right for health reasons; after six months it may ban abortions except in cases in which the woman's health is in danger. The Court, in later decisions, limited the scope of *Roe* (see ABORTION).

Rogers, Carl R(ansom), 1902–87, American psychologist; b. Oak Park, Ill. He introduced what he called a nondirective approach to the treatment of psychological problems. In *Client-Centered Therapy* (1951), he explained that by neutrally reflecting clients' feelings, the therapist can create an empathetic and accepting environment in which patients regulate the direction and speed of their own growth. Rogers's method greatly influenced the course of PSYCHOTHERAPY. His works include *On Becoming a Person* (1966) and *On Personal Power* (1977).

Rogers, John, 1829–1904, American sculptor; b. Salem, Mass. His anecdotal clay sculptures ("Rogers groups") attained great popularity, and thousands of copies were made by machine of such subjects as *Going to the Minister* and *The Wounded Scout.*

Rogers, Robert, 1731–95, American colonial soldier; b. Methuen, Mass. During the last FRENCH AND INDIAN WAR, Major Rogers commanded (1758–63) British rangers in daring expeditions against French outposts and helped to defend Fort DETROIT. He fell into disgrace for trading illicitly with Native Americans but was acquitted of treasonable dealings with the French. He fought for the Loyalists in the Revolution.

Rogers, Will(iam Penn Adair), 1879–1935, American humorist, the "cowboy philosopher"; b. Oolagah, Indian Territory (now Okla.). Through movies, books, radio, and newspaper columns, his salty political and social comments gained him wide popularity.

Roger van der Weyden: see WEYDEN, ROGER VAN DER.

Roget, Peter Mark [rōzhā'], 1779–1869, English physician and lexicographer. His *Thesaurus of English Words and Phrases* (1852), later edited by his son and by his grandson, is a standard reference work.

Rohmer, Eric, 1920–, French film director and writer; b. Jean Marie Maurice Schérer. His studies of relationships between men and women include *My Night at Maude's* (1968), *Claire's Knee* (1970), *Chloe in the Afternoon* (1972), *The Marquise of O.* (1976), *Le Beau Mariage* (1982), *Summer* (1986), and *My Girlfriend's Boyfriend* (1988).

Rojas, Fernando de [rō'häs], 1465?–1541?, Spanish novelist. His dramatic novel of passion, *La Celestina* (1499), is considered a masterpiece of Spanish literature.

Rojas Zorrilla, Francisco de [thôrē'lyä], 1607–48, Spanish dramatist of the GOLDEN AGE. Of his many plays, the best known is *None Beneath the King* (1650), a drama of honor. His plots were borrowed by others, including CORNEILLE.

Roland, French hero of the medieval epic *Song of Roland* (11th or 12th cent.). Historically, Roland was one of Charlemagne's commanders, killed when the rear guard of the Frankish army, returning from Spain, was ambushed by the Basques in the Pyrenees in 778. Legend makes Roland one of Charlemagne's peers and his nephew, transforms the Basques into Saracens, and locates the pass at Roncesvalles. The poem is marked by its unified conception, its vivid and direct narrative, and its predominantly warlike spirit. Roland is also the hero of other CHANSONS DE GESTE.

Rolfe, John, 1585–1622, English colonist in Virginia. He immigrated (1610) to JAMESTOWN and introduced tobacco cultivation. Rolfe married (1614) POCAHONTAS, daughter of a Powhatan chief, who went (1616) with him to England. After her death, he returned to Virginia and remarried.

Rolland, Romain [rôläN'], 1866–1944, French author and pacifist. He wrote biographies of Beethoven (1903), Michelangelo (1908), Tolstoy (1911), and Mahatma Gandhi (1924). His major fictional work is *Jean-Christophe* (1906–12), a 10-volume study of a German-born musician and of contemporary European civilization. His best-known play is *The Wolves* (1898). He received the 1915 Nobel Prize in literature.

Rolling Stones, English ROCK MUSIC group that rose to prominence in the mid-1960s and continues to exert great influence. Members have included singer Mick Jagger (1943–); guitarists Brian Jones (1944–69), Keith Richards (1943–), and Ron Wood (1941–); bassist Bill Wyman (1941–), who left the band in 1993; and drummer Charlie Watts (1941–). The group's songs, written mostly by Jagger and Richards, include "Satisfaction," "Sympathy for the Devil," and "Paint It Black." They have appeared widely in concert and in films, e.g., *Gimme Shelter* (1970).

Rølvaag, Ole Edvart [röl'vôkh], 1876–1931, Norwegian-American novelist; b. Norway; came to U.S. in 1896. He is famous for the trilogy *Giants in the Earth* (1927), *Peder Victorius* (1929), and *Their Father's God* (1931), powerful novels treating the struggles of Norwegian pioneers in America.

Roman architecture. Early Roman architects were inspired by post-and-lintel and more refined Greek forms, and drew on Etruscan and Asian models for the semicircular arch, VAULT, and DOME. To these elements they added the use of concrete, leading, after the 2d cent. B.C., to revolutionary structural forms. Of early Rome and the republic (c.500 B.C.–27 B.C.), the aqueducts outside the city of Rome are the most impressive remains. The principal Roman works belong to the period 100 B.C.–A.D. 300. The reign of AUGUSTUS initiated centuries of vast building enterprises. The special feature of Roman design was the combined use of ARCHES (eventually the main structural element) and columns, which served as buttresses or decoration. Concrete replaced cut-stone construction after the 2d cent. B.C. Brick was used in all periods, especially baked brick for facing during the Empire. Stucco, porphyry, alabaster, and marble were also used to finish buildings. Brick vaults were developed fully, their buttresses integrated into the interior. Immense unencumbered vaults, e.g., those of the PANTHEON, created pure spatial effects. Splendor and utility were the Roman ideals, as opposed to the subtle refinement of the Greeks. Urban planning was extensive. Towns were laid out according to a logical plan, focusing on a forum, with colonnades and principal buildings surrounding it. In Rome itself successive forums were built by the emperors. Temples, conforming to the Etruscan type, were elevated on high bases. Facing the forum, they were without side porticos. The type is seen at the Maison Carrée, Nîmes, France. Circular temples included that of Vesta at Tivoli (1st cent. B.C.). The Romans developed the BASILICA, baths, AMPHITHEATER, and triumphal arch. Roman theaters combined stage and auditorium in a unified structure. Baths, probably derived from Greek gymnasia, were built on a totally unprecedented scale, in luxurious detail. Houses typically had an atrium with a roof opening, and the Greek peristyle was used. Four- or five-story urban houses suggested the modern tenement. A third house type was the luxurious country villa.

Roman art. From the 7th to the 3rd cent. B.C., ETRUSCAN ART flourished in central Italy, including Latium and Rome. After 400 B.C., the imitation of Greek models, combined with a trend toward naturalism, e.g., *Mars of Todi* (Vatican), produced the establishment of Hellenistic realism by the beginning of the Roman Empire, e.g., *Orator* (Museo Archeologico, Florence). After the Roman conquest of Greece (c.146 B.C.), Greek artists came to Rome and found a ready market for works done in the classical manner or as copies of Greek originals. Their influence was important and indicates the eclecticism of Roman taste. Roman portraits, however, had a very remote and Italianate origin—the custom of having death masks taken and preserved with busts copied from them. By the time of the Empire, art had become allied with the ideal of service to the state. It led to a distinctly Roman style of portrait bust, concerned with pictorial refinement and psychological penetration. The magnificent reliefs from the Arch of Titus, Rome, commemorating the conquest of Jerusalem in A.D. 70, mark the climax of illusionism in historical relief sculpture. From the time of TRAJAN (A.D. 98–117), the art of the Eastern provinces began to have greater influence. The spiral band of low reliefs on Trajan's Column (Rome) suggests the Middle Eastern or Egyptian illustrative tradition. After a brief return to the classical style under HADRIAN and the Antonines, e.g., the equestrian statue of Marcus Aurelius (Rome), a tendency toward abstraction became more apparent. It later developed into the stiff, iconographic forms of the early Christian and Byzantine eras. The last example of Roman monumental sculpture is in the reliefs of the Arch of Constantine, Rome (c.315). Roman painting was also influenced by Greece; unfortunately, much of it has perished. What remains suggests that the art was mainly one of interior decoration. The largest group of paintings exists in POMPEII. Many paintings, e.g., the *Aldobrandini Wedding* and the *Odyssey Landscapes* (Vatican), are thought to be Roman copies of Greek originals. These three-dimensional techniques were duplicated in MOSAICS, extensively produced throughout the empire. The famous pottery of Arretium (now Arezzo) was mass-produced and widely exported. Early pots had a black finish, and later examples had a red glaze with low-relief decorative figures. Roman minor arts emphasized sumptuous materials. CAMEOS and gold jewelry were extensively produced. During the 1st cent. A.D., new processes were invented for making glass and imitating precious stones, which made possible the production of fine murrhine vases.

Roman Catholic Church, Christian church headed by the pope, the bishop of Rome. "Roman Catholic" is a 19th-cent. British coinage, but is now in common use among English-speaking people. Roman Catholics are spread worldwide and probably number in the hundreds of millions, although no census has been made. The vast majority belong to the Roman rite. Even in the West, however, there are variant rites such as the Ambrosian, the Dominican, and the Mozarabic. In the East there are groups in communion with the pope that also have other rites—Byzantine, Antiochene, Chaldean, Alexandrian, and Armenian. All members of the church accept the gospel of Jesus as handed down by the church, the teachings of the Bible, and the church's interpretations of those teachings. They also believe that God conveys His grace directly to humanity through the SACRAMENTS. The Eucharist (see MASS) is the center of Catholic worship. The clergy, except for parish priests of the Eastern rites, do not marry, and the church structure, from the parish priests through the bishops to the pope, is administered in the papal court at Rome. Outside the secular organization of the church are the orders of regular priests, monks, and nuns (see MONASTICISM). In the early centuries of CHRISTIANITY, the pope came to command great authority in Western Europe. The contest between the PAPACY and lay rulers over ecclesiastic and lay power was very important in the Middle Ages. The pope was under French domination at Avignon (1309–78), and the church was later rocked by the Great SCHISM. The Protestant REFORMATION in the 16th cent. split the church, and the Counter Reformation (see REFORMATION, CATHOLIC) corrected many abuses. In the 19th cent. Pope PIUS IX proclaimed the doctrine of papal INFALLIBILITY, and in the 19th and 20th cent. the church moved to adjust to modern political and social conditions. Since the Second VATICAN COUNCIL (1962–65) more simplicity and flexibility have been introduced. The first U.S. diocese was formed in 1790, and the U.S. church grew steadily as waves of Roman Catholic immigrants arrived in the 19th and 20th cent. In 1990 there were 58,568,015 Roman Catholics in the U.S.

romance [O.Fr., = something written in the popular language, i.e., a Romance language]. The *roman* of the Middle Ages in Europe was a chivalric and romantic narrative (see CHIVALRY). It was lengthened into the *roman d'aventure*, or romance of love and adventure, from which the modern romance derives (see NOVEL).

Romance languages, group of languages belonging to the Italic subfamily of the Indo-European family of languages. See LANGUAGE (table).

Roman Empire: see BYZANTINE EMPIRE; HOLY ROMAN EMPIRE; ROME.

Romanesque architecture and art prevailed throughout Europe from the mid-11th to the mid-12th cent. ROMAN ARCHITECTURE was the main inspiration, but Byzantine and Eastern components were incorporated. Certain characteristics—the massive west facades crowned by a tower or twin towers, the complex eastern parts housing the sanctuary, the rhythmic alternation of piers and columns in the nave—represent advanced stages of a long evolution. The development of Romanesque architecture owes much to the primacy accorded to vaulting. Early Christian architecture had confined masonry vaulting (see VAULT) to small structures. Larger basilican buildings had wood roofs. Romanesque churches sustained massive barrel vaults, which required the reinforcement of load-bearing walls. The presence of galleries above the aisles and the few wall openings are doubtless due originally to structural considerations. They, in turn, created a somberly impressive atmosphere. Monastic communities were centers of development: Cluniac churches at Tours, Toulouse, and Compostela, connected with the great pilgrimages, featured large ambulatories with radiating chapels, designed to facilitate access to the relics. Noted Romanesque buildings include: France—the abbey church of St. Madeleine Vezelay (c.1090–1130); Germany—the cathedral of Speyer (1060; reconstructed after 1082); Italy—the cathedral (1063–92) and baptistery (1153) in Pisa, and the church of San Miniato al Monte, Florence (c.1070). In the late 12th cent. developments in N France and in England pointed towards the Gothic (see NORMAN ARCHITECTURE). Romanesque art was marked by the revival of monumental forms, notably sculpture and fresco painting, developed in close association with architecture. An element of realism, paralleling the first flowering of vernacular literature, came to the fore in direct and naïve observation of details from daily life and a heightened emphasis on emotion and fantasy. The pilgrimages and crusades contributed to a broadened formal vocabulary. Ornamental complexity, ecstatic expression, and a profusion of zoomorphic, vegetal, and abstract motifs abounded. In France, themes portrayed on the tympanums of such churches as Moissac and Autun emphasized the majesty of Jesus and the terrors of hell. Metalwork was an important art, and crucifixes and other church objects were highly refined. Limoges became a major metal and enamelwork center. The large walls of the churches encouraged fresco painting, and manuscript illumination, with a greatly expanded fund of pictorial imagery, also flourished.

Romania or **Rumania,** republic (1992 est. pop. 23,170,000), 91,699 sq mi (237,500 sq km), SE Europe; bordered by Hungary (NW), Yugoslavia (SW), Bulgaria (S), the Black Sea (SE), and Ukraine and Moldova (E and N). Major cities include BUCHAREST (the capital), CLUJ-NAPOCA, Timişoara, and IAŞI. The CARPATHIAN Mts., which include the Transylvanian ALPS, cut through Romania from north to southwest; the highest peak is at Moldoveanu (8,343 ft/2,543 m). The principal rivers are the DANUBE and its tributary, the Prut. Traditionally an agricultural country, Romania greatly expanded its industrial base after World War II, and by 1980 industry contributed over 65% of national income. Leading manufactures include iron and steel, machinery, transport vehicles, and chemicals. The chief farm products are corn and other grains, sugar beets, potatoes, and fruits (notably grapes for wine). Romania is a major producer of petroleum and natural gas, but oil reserves are being depleted and some fuel must be imported. Coal, copper, and iron ore are mined. Romanian is the official language. The vast majority of the people are Romanian, but there are Hungarian, Gypsy, German, and other minorities. Gypsies have faced increasing public violence since the end of Communist rule. By far the largest religious body is the Romanian Orthodox Church.

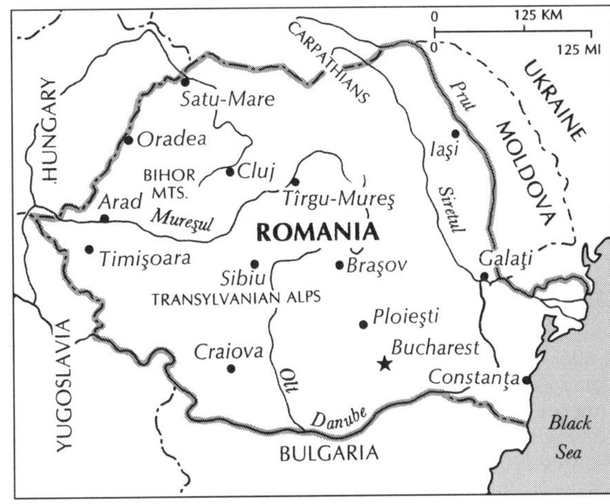

History. Present-day Romania corresponds roughly to the ancient province of DACIA, which, after Romanization (2d–3d cent.), was overrun successively by the Goths, Huns, Avars, Bulgars, Magyars, and Mongols. After the 13th cent. two Romanian principalities, Moldavia and WALACHIA, were formed. They became vassal states of the OTTOMAN EMPIRE and, later, Russian protectorates. In 1861 the two principalities were united as Romania, which obtained full independence in 1878 and was proclaimed a kingdom in 1881. Romania won S Dobruja in the second BALKAN WAR (1913) and joined (1916) the Allies in WORLD WAR I, after which it was awarded Bukovina, TRANSYLVANIA, part of the Banat, and Crişana-Maramureş. Romanian politics in the years that followed were marked by violence, turmoil, and corruption; assassination as a political instrument was not unusual. In the 1930s violence increased with the rise of the fascist IRON GUARD, and in 1940 Ion ANTONESCU overthrew King CAROL II and established a dictatorship. Romania joined Germany in the war against the USSR in 1941. After Soviet troops entered the country in 1944, Romania surrendered and Antonescu's regime was overthrown. In 1947 a Communist-led government came to power, forced King MICHAEL to abdicate, and established a republic. Nationalization of industry and agriculture was completed by 1948. From 1965 to 1989, Romania was ruled by Nicolae CEAUSESCU, who pursued a foreign policy independent of the Soviet Union that won him favor in the West. At home, however, he reduced the country to poverty to pay for a radical program of modernization. In Dec. 1989 antigovernment violence broke out in Timişoara and spread to other cities. Army units joined the uprising and Ceausescu fled, but he was captured, tried, and executed. The National Salvation Front, headed by Ion Iliescu, subsequently won (1990) a national election marred by violence, and Iliescu became president. Iliescu was reelected in 1992. Iliescu's government has failed to reorganize state-run industries, creating an economic crisis.

Romanian language, member of the Romance group of the Italic subfamily of the Indo-European family of languages. See LANGUAGE (table).

Romanic: see ROMANCE LANGUAGES.

Roman law, system of law of the Romans, from the founding of ROME (753 B.C.) to the fall of the Eastern Empire (A.D. 1453); it is the basis of modern CIVIL LAW. First codified in 450 B.C. in the Twelve Tables (tablets on which the laws were inscribed), early Roman law was highly formalistic. Procedural knowledge was restricted to a body of patrician priests, but as a result of plebeian pressure this material was reduced to writing (c.250 B.C.), thus broadening the law's social base. By the late 3d cent. B.C. Roman law comprised the *jus civile*, governing relations among Romans, and the *jus gentium*, governing dealings with foreigners; the latter, more flexible, eventually became universal. After c.100 B.C. new principles, notably the *jus honorarium*, a body of magisterial law to supplement, aid, and correct existing law, were vigorously developed. With the establishment (27 B.C.) of the Roman Empire, the development of law passed into the hands of the emperors, and imperial enactments were abundant. The growing complexity of the law gave birth to a class of trained jurists, most prominent of whom was PAPINIAN (d. A.D. 212), and by the early 4th cent. most branches of Roman law were fully developed. Codification was completed (535) during the reign of JUSTINIAN I in the *Corpus Juris Civilis*, the culminating work of Roman legal scholarship and the model for most of the legal systems in continental Europe. After the fall of the Western Empire, Roman law persisted as part of GERMANIC LAW and CANON LAW, and in the Eastern (Byzantine) Empire. Revival of classical studies during the Renaissance led to the resurrection of Roman law as the basis for the civil law that developed in a large part of the world. Even COMMON LAW countries, such as England, have felt the influence of Roman law, particularly in commercial law and the rules of EQUITY.

Romano, Giulio: see GIULIO ROMANO.

Romanov [rō'mənŏf, Rus. rəmä'nəf], ruling dynasty of Russia, 1613–1917. The first wife of Czar IVAN IV was Anastasia Romanov, whose grand-nephew Michael was chosen czar in 1613. In the following list of Michael's successors, the names of rulers not descended from him are in brackets: Alexis, 1645–76; Feodor III, 1676–82; Ivan V, 1682–89; PETER I, 1682–1725 (ruled jointly with Ivan V until 1689); [CATHERINE I, 1725–27]; Peter II, 1727–30; Anna, 1730–40; IVAN VI, 1740–41; ELIZABETH, 1741–62; PETER III, 1762; [CATHERINE II, 1762–96]; PAUL I, 1796–1801; ALEXANDER I, 1801–25; NICHOLAS I, 1825–55; ALEXANDER II, 1855–81; ALEXANDER III, 1881–94; NICHOLAS II, 1894–1917. After the murder of Nicholas II and his immediate family in 1918, the surviving Romanovs fled abroad.

Roman Question: see LATERAN TREATY.

Roman religion. The indigenous ancient Italic religion was essentially animistic, holding that spirits (numina) dwelling in natural objects controlled human destiny. The earliest unit for their worship was the family and household. When the early agricultural communities coalesced into the Roman state, the family ritual formed the basis for state ritual, ruled by the king as chief priest. The supreme triad of deities was that of JUPITER, MARS, and Quirinus. Many foreign gods were adopted from the 7th cent., and from the 3d cent. B.C. the old Roman deities were equated with the Greek gods whose attributes they took on. The influence of EPICURUS and STOICISM were also felt. In the last two centuries of the republic the people, grown distant from the formalistic state religion, sought salvation and a promise of afterlife in the Greek MYSTERIES and various Middle Eastern cults, e.g., those of the GREAT MOTHER OF THE GODS, ISIS and OSIRIS, and MITHRA, creating a religious climate in which Christianity would flourish and eventually triumph.

Romans, EPISTLE of the NEW TESTAMENT, sixth book in the usual order, by St. PAUL, probably written A.D. c.58. It is addressed by Paul to the Christian church at Rome, apparently to introduce himself and his teaching before his visit. Its subject, the achieving of salvation through faith, is central in Paul's teaching and is the theme also of GALATIANS. In Romans, Paul argues that reliance on the Mosaic Law is not enough, and that God has not broken His promise to His chosen people but is working toward universal redemption. The epistle is claimed as an authority by many divergent theologies, e.g., by both Lutherans and Roman Catholics.

Romansh: see RHAETO-ROMANIC.

romanticism, term applied to literary and artistic movements of the late 18th and 19th cent., in revolt against CLASSICISM and against philosophical rationalism, with its emphasis on reason. Spurred in part by the libertarian and egalitarian ideals of the FRENCH REVOLUTION, the romantics are associated with belief in a return to nature and in the innate goodness of humans, as expressed by Jean Jacques ROUSSEAU; admiration for the heroic and for the individuality and imagination of the artist; exaltation of the senses and emotions over reason and intellect; and interest in the medieval, exotic, primitive, and nationalistic. Critics date English literary romanticism from the publication of William WORDSWORTH and S.T. COLERIDGE's *Lyrical Ballads* (1798), though William BLAKE's mysticism foreshadowed the movement. Romantic poets like Lord BYRON, John KEATS, and P.B. SHELLEY focused on the individual's highly personal response to life, as did Thomas DE QUINCEY and William HAZLITT in prose. The gothic romance and the historical novels of Sir Walter SCOTT witnessed the cult of medievalism. German romanticism flourished in the STURM UND DRANG drama of GOETHE and SCHILLER, the lyric poetry of NOVALIS and HEINE, and the philological and folk researches of HERDER and the brothers GRIMM. Romanticism was exemplified in France by CHATEAUBRIAND, Victor HUGO, DUMAS PÈRE, LAMARTINE, Alfred de MUSSET, and George SAND. The movement's influence, however, was worldwide, as evidenced by the works of the Russian Aleksandr PUSHKIN; the Italian Giacomo LEOPARDI; and the Americans J.F. COOPER, E.A. POE, and the transcendentalists (see TRANSCENDENTALISM). In the visual arts, romantics rejected classical formalism while remaining outside the 19th-cent. realist mainstream, as with DELACROIX and J.M.W. TURNER. Romanticism in music, stressing emotion and freedom of form, reached its zenith in the work of BERLIOZ, MENDELSSOHN, SCHUMANN, CHOPIN, LISZT, and WAGNER, who attempted in his operas a synthesis of all the arts.

Romanus, Byzantine emperors. **Romanus I,** d. 948 (r.914–44), deposed the young CONSTANTINE VII. Romanus defended CONSTANTINOPLE against the BULGARS. His two sons overthrew him. **Romanus II,** 939–63 (r.959–63), was the profligate son of Constantine VII. Romanus's wife, Theophano, was the actual ruler. His reign saw the victories of NICEPHORUS II over the Arabs. When Romanus died, Nicephorus married Theophano and became emperor. **Romanus III,** c.968–1034 (r.1028–34), succeeded Constantine VIII by marrying his daughter, ZOË. He depleted the treasury and abolished needed taxes. His general George Meniaces took Edessa from the Saracens (1032). **Romanus IV,** d. 1072 (r.1067–71), succeeded Constantine X by marrying his widow. He was routed by the Seljuk Turks at Manzikert. His stepson deposed and blinded him, succeeding as Michael VII.

Romany [rŏm'ənē, rō-'], language belonging to the Dardic group of the Indo-Iranian subfamily of the Indo-European family of languages. Romany is the mother tongue of the GYPSIES. See LANGUAGE (table).

Romberg, Sigmund, 1887–1951, Hungarian-American composer. He wrote over 70 romantic OPERETTAS, including *The Student Prince* (1924), *The Desert Song* (1926), and *The New Moon* (1928).

Rome, Ital. *Roma,* city (1990 pop. 2,803,931), capital of Italy and see of the pope, whose residence, VATICAN CITY, is a sovereign state within the city of Rome. Rome is also the capital of Latium, a region of central Italy, and of Rome prov. It lies on both banks of the Tiber R. Called the Eternal City, it is one of the world's richest cities in history and art, and one of its great cultural, religious, and intellectual centers. Modern Rome retains many of the great monuments of its rich past. Among them are the Forum and the COLOSSEUM, the LATERAN, SAINT PETER'S CHURCH and other great churches (e.g., St. Mary Major, St. Lawrence without the Walls, St. Paul's without the Walls, St. Peter in Chains), and graceful palaces and villas (e.g., Farnese Palace, Farnesina, Borghese Villa). The immense riches of art and its religious importance make Rome one of the most visited cities of the world. It is also a great center of commerce with varied industries, e.g., printing, publishing, manufacturing, and motion pictures. The remainder of this article treats the history of Rome and of the **Roman Empire.**

Rome before Augustus. Ancient Rome was built on the east, or left, bank of the Tiber. The seven hills of the ancient city are the

RULERS OF THE ROMAN EMPIRE *(including dates of reign)*

Augustus, grandnephew of Julius Caesar, 27 B.C.–A.D. 14
Tiberius, stepson of Augustus, A.D. 14–A.D. 37
Caligula, grandnephew of Tiberius, 37–41
Claudius, uncle of Caligula, 41–54
Nero, stepson of Claudius, 54–68
Galba, proclaimed emperor by his soldiers, 68–69
Otho, military commander, 69
Vespasian, military commander, 69–79
Vitellius, military commander, 69
Titus, son of Vespasian, 79–81
Domitian, son of Vespasian, 81–96
Nerva, elected interim ruler, 96–98
Trajan, adopted son of Nerva, 98–117
Hadrian, ward of Trajan, 117–38
Antoninus Pius, adopted by Hadrian, 138–61
Marcus Aurelius, adopted by Antonius Pius, 161–80
Lucius Verus adopted by Antonius Pius; ruled jointly with Marcus Aurelius, 161–69
Commodus, son of Marcus Aurelius, 180–92
Pertinax, proclaimed emperor by the Praetorian Guard, 193
Didius Julianus, bought office from the Praetorian Guard, 193
Severus, proclaimed emperor, 193–211
Caracalla, son of Severus, 211–17
Geta, son of Severus, ruled jointly with Caracalla, 211–12
Macrinus, proclaimed emperor by his soldiers, 217–18
Heliogabalus, cousin of Caracalla, 218–22
Alexander Severus, cousin of Heliogabalus, 222–35
Maximin, proclaimed emperor by soldiers, 235–38
Gordian I, made emperor by the senate, 238
Gordian II, son of Gordian I, ruled jointly with his father, 238
Balbinus, elected joint emperor by the Senate, 238
Pupienus Maximus, elected joint emperor with Balbinus by the senate, 238
Gordian III, son of Gordian II, 238–44
Philip (the Arabian), assassin of Gordian III, 244–49
Decius, proclaimed emperor by the soldiers, 249–51
Hostilianus, son of Decius, colleague of Gallus, 251
Gallus, military commander, 251–53
Aemilianus, military commander, 253
Valerian, military commander, 253–60
Gallienus, son of Valerian, coemperor with his father and later sole emperor, 253–68
Claudius II, military commander, 268–70
Aurelian, chosen by Claudius II as successor, 270–75
Tacitus, chosen by the senate, 275–76
Florianus, half brother of Tacitus, 276
Probus, military commander, 276–82
Carus, proclaimed by the Praetorian Guard, 282–83
Carinus, son of Carus, 283–85
Numerianus, son of Carus, joint emperor with Carius, 283–84
Diocletian, militiary commander, divided the empire; ruled jointly with Maximian and Constantius I, 284–305
Maximian, appointed joint emperor by Diocletian, 286–305
Constantius I, joint emperor and successor of Diocletian, 305–6
Galerius, joint emperor with Constantius I, 305–10
Maximin, nephew of Galerius, 308–13
Licinius, appointed emperor in the West by Galerius; later emperor in the East, 308–24
Maxentius, son of Maximian 306–12
Constantine I (the Great), son of Constantius I, 306–37
Constantine II, son of Constantine I, 337–40
Constans, son of Constantine I, 337–50
Constantius II, son of Constantine I, 337–61
Magnentius, usurped Constans' throne, 350–53
Julian (the Apostate), nephew of Constantine I, 361–63
Jovian, elected by the army, 363–64
Valentinian I, proclaimed by the army; ruled in the West, 364–75
Valens, brother of Valentinian I; ruled in the East, 364–78
Gratian, son of Valentinian I; coruler in the West with Valentinian II, 375–83
Maximus, usurper in the West, 383–88
Valentinian II, son of Valentinian I, ruler of the West, 375–92
Eugenius, usurper in the West, 392–94
Theodosius I (the Great), appointed ruler of the East by Gratian, later sole emperor; last ruler of united empire, 375–95

Emperors in the East

Arcadius, son of Theodosius I, 395–408
Theodosius II, son of Arcadius, 408–50
Marcian, brother-in-law of Theodosius II, 450–57
Leo I, chosen by the senate, 457–74
Leo II, grandson of Leo I, 474

Emperors in the West

Honorius, son of Theodosius I, 395–423
Maximus, usurper in Spain, 409–11
Constantius III, named joint emperor by Honorius, 421
Valentian III, nephew of Honorius and son of Constantius III, 425–55
Petronius Maximus, bought office by bribery, 455
Avitus, placed in office by Goths, 455–56
Majorian, puppet emperor of Ricimer, 457–61
Libius Severus, puppet emperor of Ricimer, 461–65
Anthemius, appointed by Ricimer and Leo I, 467–72
Olybrius, appointed by Ricimer, 472
Glycerius, appointed by Leo I, 473–74
Julius Nepos, appointed by Leo I, 474–75
Romulus Augustulus, put in office by Orestes, his father, 475–76

Palatine, Capitoline, Quirinal, Viminal, Esquiline, Caelian, and Aventine. Tradition tells of the founding of Rome by ROMULUS in 753 B.C. and of rule by the TARQUIN family, the Etruscan royal house (see ETRUSCAN CIVILIZATION). The young city was probably under Etruscan rule until c.500 B.C., when the Romans overthrew the monarchy and established the Roman republic. The PATRICIAN class controlled the government, but the majority PLEBS in time gained much power and privilege. In 390 B.C. Rome was sacked by the Gauls, but during the 4th and 3d cent. B.C. it extended its influence over W Latium and S Etruria, conquered the Samnites, and became master of central and S Italy. Rome also came in full contact with Greek culture, which modified Roman life tremendously. Rome's rapid conquests met the like ambitions of CARTHAGE, which ruled the W Mediterranean. In a titanic struggle called the PUNIC WARS, Rome utterly destroyed Carthage. The Roman Republic then turned its attention eastward and rapidly expanded Roman dominion. At home, however, class dissension produced slave uprisings, e.g., that of SPARTACUS, and attempts were made at reform (see GRACCHI, family). Rome was forced by the Social War (90–88 B.C.) to extend citizenship widely in Italy, but the republic was nevertheless doomed. The struggle between Marius and SULLA led to a civil war. POMPEY emerged as a popular champion and found an ally in Julius CAESAR, a popular democratic leader. With Marcus Licinius Crassus (see CRASSUS, family), Pompey and Caesar formed the First Triumvirate (60 B.C.). Caesar then left Rome and acquired fame in the GALLIC WARS. Within ten years Pompey and Caesar fell out, and by his victory at Pharsala (48 B.C.) Caesar became master of Rome. The rule of Caesar completed the destruction of the republic and laid the foundations of the empire.

The Roman Empire. After Caesar's assassination (44 B.C.) the Second Triumvirate was formed by Caesar's grandnephew, Octavian (later AUGUSTUS), ANTONY, and Marcus Aemilius Lepidus (see LEPIDUS, family). This alliance dissolved as well, and in 31 B.C. Octavian's forces defeated Antony and CLEOPATRA at Actium. Octavian emerged supreme and is usually considered the first Roman emperor. He organized provincial government and the army, rebuilt Rome, and patronized the arts and letters. His rule began a long period (200 years) of peace called the *Pax Romana* in which the empire prospered. An extensive system of Roman roads made transportation easier, and commerce and industry were developed. Literary and artistic interests were important, although they nearly always tended to imitate Greek and Eastern styles. Augustus died in A.D. 14 and was succeeded in turn by his stepson TIBERIUS; by CALIGULA, a cruel tyrant; and by CLAUDIUS I, who conquered half of Britain. The emperor NERO (r.A.D. 54–68), an unparalleled tyrant, began the persecution of CHRISTIANITY, which was spreading throughout the empire. Under TRAJAN (r.A.D. 98–117) the empire's eastern boundaries were pushed past Armenia and Mesopotamia. Marcus Aurelius (r.161–180) ruled in what is commonly called the Golden Age of the empire, but the 3d cent. was a time of turmoil. In 284 DIOCLETIAN was made emperor by the army. He reformed the government and divided the empire into four regions, two in the East and two in the West. CONSTANTINE I (r.306–37) moved the capital from Rome to Byzantium, renamed Constantinople, and granted religious toleration to Christians. After the death (395) of THEODOSIUS I, the empire was permanently divided into E and W sections, and Rome rapidly lost its political importance. The West sank into anarchy, and Italy was ravaged by invaders. Rome was taken by ALARIC I (410) and by Gaiseric (455), and Pope LEO I is said to have kept ATTILA from sacking it. In 476 the last emperor of the West, Romulus Augustulus, was deposed by the Goths under ODOACER; this date is commonly accepted as the end of the W Roman Empire. The Eastern or BYZANTINE EMPIRE continued until the 15th cent. The so-called Dark Ages that followed in Western Europe could not eradicate the profound imprint left by Roman civilization. Italy itself, however, did not recover from the fall of Rome until the 19th cent.

Later History. The history of Rome in the Middle Ages is essentially that of two institutions, the PAPACY and the commune of Rome. Rome was ruled by the Goths in the 5th cent. and fell under Byzantine rule from the 6th to the 8th cent. With the emergence (8th cent.) of the PAPAL STATES, Rome, their capital, once again rose to importance. CHARLEMAGNE and later Holy Roman emperors visited the city to be crowned by the popes. Papal authority was challenged unsuccessfully in the 12th cent. by the communal movement led by Arnold of Brescia, and civil strife arose between GUELPHS AND GHIBELLINES. During the "Babylonian captivity" of the popes at AVIGNON (1309–78), conditions in Rome were in constant turmoil, but in the 15th cent. the city became a center of the RENAISSANCE. Countless artists and architects served the papal court, and Rome, as it is today, is largely a product of their work. Noble and baroque monuments were erected in the 17th and early 18th cent. In 1809 Rome and the Papal States were annexed to France by NAPOLEON I, but papal rule was restored in 1814. After a republic was declared (1849) in Rome, French troops intervened to restore the pope. When the kingdom of Italy was proclaimed (1861), it included most of the Papal States, but not Rome, which remained a virtual French protectorate under NAPOLEON III. After Napoleon III's fall, Rome became (1871) the Italian capital, but the conflict between the pope and Italy was not solved until the LATERAN TREATY (1929), which gave the pope sovereignty over Vatican City. In WORLD WAR II Rome fell to Allied forces on June 4, 1944.

Rømer, Olaus: see ROEMER, OLAUS.

Rommel, Erwin, 1891–1944, German field marshal, known as the "desert fox" and regarded as one of the most brilliant generals of WORLD WAR II. He commanded the Afrika Korps in the North African campaigns (1941–43). His string of victories was broken by the British at EL ALAMEIN (1942). In 1944 he took part in the attempt on Hitler's life and was forced to take poison when the plot failed.

Romney, George, 1734–1802, English portrait painter. After studying in Italy, he rivaled Sir Joshua REYNOLDS in popularity. His portraits of women are facile and charming, e.g., his many portraits of Lady Emma HAMILTON, and those of men are studied and impressive, e.g., *Self-portrait* (1782; National Portrait Gall., London). In his last years, he turned to literary subjects such as *Milton and his Daughters.*

Romulus, in Roman legend, founder of Rome. He and his twin, Remus, were sons of MARS and Rhea Silvia, daughter of Numitor, king of Alba Longa. Amulius, usurper of Numitor's throne, threw them in the Tiber, but they floated ashore. They were suckled by a she-wolf and reared by a shepherd. When grown, they slew Amulius and made Numitor king. They then founded a city (traditionally 753 B.C.) on the spot where they were rescued from the Tiber. They later quarreled, and Romulus killed Remus. Romulus populated Rome with fugitives from other countries and gave them wives abducted from the SABINE tribe. After a long reign Romulus vanished in a thunderstorm; he was thereafter worshiped as the god Quirinus.

Romulus Augustulus, d. after 476, last West Roman emperor (475–76). His father, Orestes, ruled for him. He was deposed by ODOACER and sent away with a pension.

Ronsard, Pierre de [rôNsär'], 1524?–1585, French Renaissance poet, leader of the Pléiade (see under PLEIAD). Named poet royal, he wrote prolifically, producing poems on many themes, especially patriotism, love, and death. His best-known love poems appear in *Sonnets pour Hélène* (1578). *La Franciade* (1572), an unfinished epic, was his most ambitious effort. He was one of France's greatest poets.

Röntgen, Wilhelm Conrad: see ROENTGEN.

Roosevelt, Eleanor, 1884–1962, b. N.Y.C. She was a niece of Theodore ROOSEVELT and a distant cousin of Franklin ROOSEVELT, whom she married. She worked for social betterment as a lecturer, newspaper columnist, and world traveler. A U.S. delegate to the UN, she was made chairman of the Commission for Human Rights in 1946. In the 1950s she led the liberal wing of the Democratic party.

Roosevelt, Franklin Delano, 1882–1945, 32d president of the U.S. (1933–45); b. Hyde Park, N.Y. The scion of an old, wealthy New York family, he earned (1905) a law degree at Columbia Univ. and entered politics by winning election (1910) to the state senate. As leader of the anti-Tammany Democratic reformers, he campaigned for Woodrow WILSON in the 1912 election. He served as assistant secretary of the navy (1913–20) and ran as vice presidential candidate with James Cox on the losing Democratic ticket in 1920. The next year he was stricken with poliomyelitis; though crippled for life, he eventually regained partial use of his legs. He supported Gov. Al SMITH's presidential candidacy and, at Smith's urging, ran successfully for governor in 1928. Reelected in 1930, Gov. Roosevelt learned to deal with the problems of the GREAT DEPRESSION. Nominated by the Democrats in 1932, he defeated Pres. HOOVER. The new president, taking office at the height of the economic crisis, assured troubled Americans that "the only thing we have to fear is fear itself." He acted quickly during the so-called Hundred Days (Mar.–Jan. 1933) to rush through Congress a flood of fiscal and social reform measures aimed at reviving the economy by a vast expenditure of public funds. He set up many new agencies, including the NATIONAL RECOVERY ADMINISTRATION and the PUBLIC WORKS ADMINISTRATION, to reorganize industry and agriculture under government regulation. These programs and social reforms, such as SOCIAL SECURITY, became known as the NEW DEAL. He was aided by a BRAIN TRUST of advisers, including Raymond Moley and Rex Tugwell, cabinet officers Henry WALLACE and Harold ICKES, and special counselor Harry HOPKINS. Roosevelt was the first president to

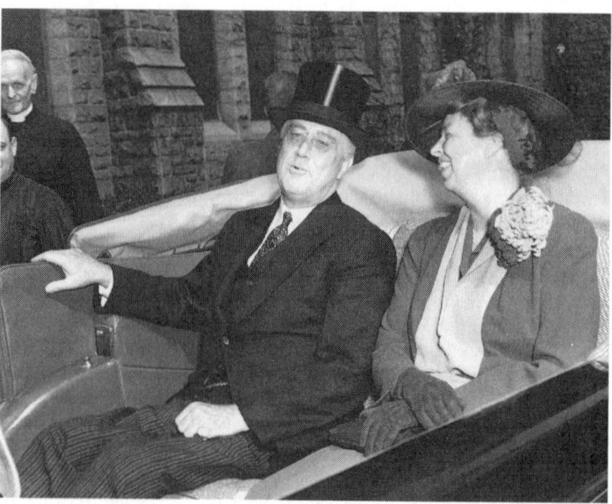

Franklin Delano Roosevelt and Eleanor Roosevelt

broadcast over the radio; his "fireside chats" explained issues and policies to the people. He easily won reelection in 1936. But the U.S. SUPREME COURT declared a number of New Deal measures unconstitutional, and he failed (1937) in an attempt to reorganize the Court. In foreign affairs his administration recognized (1933) the Soviet Union and initiated a "good neighbor" policy toward Latin America. With the outbreak (1939) of World War II, Roosevelt extended aid to Britain and began LEND LEASE, while building up U.S. armed forces by the first peacetime SELECTIVE SERVICE (1940). He broke precedent by seeking and winning (1940) a third presidential term and, later (1944), a fourth. After the Japanese attack on PEARL HARBOR, Roosevelt, as commander in chief, directed the nation's immense war effort, held conferences with Winston CHURCHILL and other Allied leaders, and worked to establish the UN. On April 12, 1945, he died suddenly from a cerebral hemorrhage.

Roosevelt, Theodore, 1858–1919, 26th president of the U.S. (1901–9); b. N.Y.C. The delicate son of a distinguished family, he made determined efforts to overcome the frail health that would markedly affect his character. After graduating (1880) from Harvard, he served (1882–84) as a Republican state legislator. Bereaved by the deaths (1884) of his mother and his wife, Alice Hathaway Lee, he retired to his ranch in the Dakota Territory. Returning to New York in 1886, he married Edith Kermit Carow and served on the Civil Service Commission, as head (1895–97) of the New York City police board, and as assistant secretary (1897–98) of the navy. In 1898 he formed, with Leonard WOOD, the ROUGH RIDERS regiment that fought in Cuba during the SPANISH-AMERICAN WAR; he came home a hero. He was elected (1900) vice president under William MCKINLEY, and upon McKinley's assassination in Sept. 1901 became president at the age of 42. An activist and an innovative leader, he set about "trust busting" by initiating some 40 lawsuits against the big trusts. He also fathered important conservation legislation. His championship of the rights of the "little man" captured the people's imagination, and he was reelected (1904) by a landslide. His second administration secured passage of the Pure Food and Drug Act of 1906. His progressive reforms aimed at regulation, not abolition, of big business. Roosevelt decisively increased the power of the president, particularly in foreign affairs. Claiming that the U.S. had the right to impose order in Latin America, he intervened (1903) in a civil war in Panama to foster construction of the PANAMA CANAL. He mediated (1904) the end of the RUSSO-JAPANESE WAR, for which he won the 1906 Nobel Peace Prize. Although he had hand-picked William Howard TAFT to succeed him, he became angry at Taft's apparent lack of progressive principles and split the Republican party in 1912 by running for president as the third-party PROGRESSIVE, or Bull Moose, candidate. He outpolled Taft but lost the election. During his busy career he found time for big game hunting and for writing many books.

Root, Elihu, 1845–1937, American public official; b. Clinton, N.Y. A successful corporation lawyer, he served (1899–1904) as U.S. secretary of war and was responsible for the PLATT AMENDMENT, permitting U.S. intervention in Cuba. As secretary of state (1905–9) under Theodore ROOSEVELT, he concluded (1908) an agreement with Japan to keep peace in the Pacific. He received the 1912 Nobel Peace Prize.

root, in botany, the descending axis of a plant (as contrasted with the STEM), usually growing underground but also growing in air (see EPIPHYTE) and water. Roots serve to absorb and conduct water and dissolved minerals (see SAP); to anchor the plant; and, often, to store food. Some plants have a main root (tap root) that is larger than the branching roots; others have many slender root branches. Roots grow primarily in length, with growth occurring at the tip, which is protected by a cap of cells (root cap) that break off and are replaced as the root probes through the soil. Root hairs, tiny cellular projections from the surface of the growing portion, absorb water and minerals from the soil. Root systems help prevent soil EROSION.

rootstock: see RHIZOME.

Rorem, Ned, 1923–, American composer and author; b. Richmond, Ind. Although he has written a wide range of compositions, he is best known for his vocal works, e.g., *Air Music* (1975; Pulitzer) and *5 Prayers for the Young* (1977). He has also published a series of deftly written journals.

Rosa, Salvator, 1615–73, Italian BAROQUE painter, etcher, and satiric poet of the Neapolitan school. He established his reputation with *Prometheus* (Corsini Palace, Rome). Rosa worked in Florence and Rome. He is best known for his spirited battle pieces, for his marines, and especially for his tempestuous landscapes.

Rosario, city (1991 pop. 1,095,301), E central Argentina, on the Paraná R. It is a railroad hub with fine port facilities and is an export center for the central and northern provinces. Settled in the 17th cent., it grew after 1870 with the development of the PAMPA, which extends to the west.

Rosas, Juan Manuel de, 1793–1877, Argentine dictator, governor of Buenos Aires prov. (1829–32, 1835–52). He led his gaucho (cowboy) troops in support of the conservatives and federalism in 1820. He became governor of Buenos Aires (1829) and temporarily destroyed the unitarian cause. Returned to office in 1835, he assumed dictatorship over most of Argentina and instituted a regime of terror. In 1852, because of foreign difficulties and an economic crisis, a revolt led by Urquiza and backed by Brazil and Uruguay succeeded, and Rosas fled to England.

Rose, Pete(r Edward), 1941–, American baseball player; b. Cincinnati. A switch-hitter who played outfield and infield positions, he played for the Cincinnati Reds (1963–78, 1984–87), Philadelphia Phillies (1979–83), and Montreal Expos (1984). Nicknamed "Charlie Hustle," he won three National League batting titles (1968, 1969, 1973), set (1978) a modern league record by hitting safely in 44 straight games, and broke (1985) Ty COBB's record of 4,191 hits. Rose's 4,256 hits and his 10 seasons with over 200 hits are both records. He also managed the Reds from 1984 to 1989. For betting on baseball games, Rose received a lifetime suspension from baseball in 1989 and was later denied admission to the Hall of Fame while the suspension was in effect. In 1990 he pled guilty to federal income tax evasion.

rose, common name for some members of the family Rosaceae, herbs, shrubs, and trees distributed over most of the earth. Roses are often thorny, and many typically have a fleshy fruit, such as a rose hip or an apple. The largest genera are *Rubus,* including the blackberry, raspberry, loganberry, and other BRAMBLES; *Rosa,* the true roses; and *Prunus,* including the ALMOND, APRICOT, CHERRY, NECTARINE, PEACH, and PLUM. Other members of the family, also of economic importance, are the APPLE, PEAR, QUINCE, and STRAWBERRY. The true roses, the most popular ornamentals of the family, are esteemed as cultivated plants and as cut flowers for their often fragrant, showy blossoms. Attar of rose, a PERFUME oil, is obtained from the damask rose, and the rose hips of *R. rugosa* are a source of VITAMIN C. Favorite flowers in many lands since prehistoric times, roses have been used medicinally and eaten in preserves and salads. New York, North Dakota, Iowa, and the District of Columbia have adopted different species of rose as their emblems.

Roseau, town and seaport (1991 pop. 20,755), capital of DOMINICA.

rose hip: see ROSE.

rosemary, evergreen, shrubby perennial (*Rosmarinus officinalis*) of the MINT family, native to the Mediterranean region. It has small blue flowers and aromatic leaves; the latter are used for seasoning. An extract of the flowers is used in perfumes and medicines.

Rosenberg, Alfred, 1893–1946, German NAZI leader. His book *The Myth of the 20th Century* (1930) supplied HITLER with the spurious philosophical and scientific basis for the Nazi racist doctrines. As minister to the occupied E European countries after 1941, he was responsible for the Nazi atrocities there. He was hanged as a war criminal.

Rosenberg Case, in U.S. history, an espionage case in which Julius Rosenberg (1918–53), an electrical engineer who had worked for the army signal corps, and his wife, Ethel (1916–53), were found guilty of transmitting top-secret data on nuclear weapons to the USSR. Much of the evidence against the Rosenbergs came from Mrs. Rosenberg's brother, David Greenglass. Despite many appeals for clemency, the Rosenbergs were executed on June 19, 1953. The case aroused great controversy; many claimed that the COLD WAR political climate made a fair trial impossible and that the evidence against the Rosenbergs came from a confessed spy; others questioned the value of the material they had allegedly passed to the USSR and argued that the death penalty was too severe.

Rosenfeld, Morris, 1862–1923, American Yiddish poet; b. Russian Poland as Moshe Jacob Alter. He worked as a tailor by day and a poet by night, writing of the hell of the sweatshops. He also edited several Yiddish periodicals. *Songs of the Ghetto* (1897) is well known.

rose of Sharon, name for several plants, especially *Hibiscus syriacus,* of the MALLOW family. The rose of Sharon of the Bible is thought to be either a NARCISSUS or the MEADOW SAFFRON.

Roses, Wars of the, name given to the struggle (1455–85) for the throne of England between the houses of LANCASTER (whose badge was a red rose) and YORK (whose badge was a white rose). In the mid-15th cent. the weak Lancastrian king HENRY VI was controlled by a faction including William de la Pole, duke of Suffolk, Edward Beaufort, duke of Somerset, and MARGARET OF ANJOU, Henry's queen. They were opposed by Richard, duke of York, who gained support from the popular unrest caused by the reverses of the HUNDRED YEARS WAR and by the corruption at court. York was appointed protector during the king's insanity (1453–54), but was excluded from the royal council when the king recovered. He then resorted to arms. The factions met at St. Albans (1455), the Yorkists won, and York again became protector (1455–56). The wars, however, continued. In 1460 the Yorkists captured the king at Northampton and struck a compromise whereby Henry remained king and York was named his successor. Queen Margaret, whose son was thus disinherited, raised an army and defeated the Yorkists at Wakefield in 1460. Here York was killed, and his son Edward assumed his claim. Margaret's army rescued the king at the second battle of St. Albans (1461), but Edward meanwhile was victorious at Mortimer's Cross and assumed the throne as EDWARD IV. Henry was recaptured (1465) and the Yorkists seemed to be in command. A quarrel then developed over the king's marriage, and Richard Neville, earl of Warwick, and the king's brother George, duke of Clarence, deserted Edward. They allied (1470) with Queen Margaret, drove Edward into exile, and restored Henry VI. Edward soon returned and triumphed at Barnet and Tewkesbury in 1471. Margaret was imprisoned and Henry VI died, probably slain on Edward's orders. After 12 years of peace, Edward was succeeded (1483) by his 12-year-old son EDWARD V, but the boy's uncle Richard, duke of Gloucester, usurped the throne as RICHARD III. Opposition to Richard advanced the fortunes of Henry Tudor, now the Lancastrian claimant, and he defeated and killed Richard at Bosworth Field in 1485. Henry seized the throne as HENRY VII, and his marriage to Edward IV's daughter Elizabeth united the houses of Lancaster and York. It is generally said that the wars ended feudalism in England, because the nobles who participated in them suffered a great loss of life and property, and were, as a class, unable to contest the strong Tudor monarchy.

Rosetta Stone, basalt slab inscribed by priests of PTOLEMY V in hieroglyphic, demotic, and Greek. Found (1799) by troops of NAPOLEON I near the city of Rosetta, N Egypt, it is now in the British Museum. The stone provided J.F. CHAMPOLLION and other scholars with the key to translating Egyptian hieroglyphics.

rose window, large, stone-traceried, circular window of medieval churches. It developed from the Romanesque wheel window. In Gothic CATHEDRALS it appears over the west front or on a transept end. Early examples, e.g., at CHARTRES, were filled with plate tracery. The typical rose, as at Rheims, was filled with radiating and intermediate bars. In the final, flamboyant period, wavy curves and more intricate patterns suggest an open rose.

Rosh Hashanah: see under JEWISH HOLIDAYS.

Ross, Betsy, 1752–1836, American seamstress; b. Philadelphia as Elizabeth Griscom Ross. Although she did make flags during the AMERICAN REVOLUTION, the legend that she designed and made the first American national flag is generally discredited.

Ross, Sir James Clark, 1800–1862, British explorer and naval officer. He studied Eskimo life on several voyages. On an expedition with his uncle, John ROSS, he located the north magnetic pole. Studying earth magnetism in Antarctica (1839–43), he discovered Ross Sea and followed the Ross ice shelf for hundreds of miles. He also found Victoria Land and much of Graham Land.

Ross, Sir John, 1777–1856, British explorer. Searching (1818) for the NORTHWEST PASSAGE, he explored BAFFIN BAY. In 1829–33 he discovered the Gulf of Boothia (named for his patron, Sir Felix Booth) and King William Island. He wrote two books about his search for the Northwest Passage.

Rose window (Cathedral of Notre-Dame, Paris)

Ross, John, or **Kooweskoowe,** 1790–1866, CHEROKEE chief; b. Tennessee, of Scottish and Cherokee parents. He resisted removal of his people from ancestral Tennessee lands, but a Cherokee minority ceded (1835) the area to Georgia. In 1838–39 he led his people on an arduous journey to Oklahoma (known as the "trail of tears") and became chief of the united Cherokee nation.

Rossellini, Roberto [rōs-sĕl-lē'nē], 1906–77, Italian film director. His *Open City* (1945), and *Paisan* (1946) were key neorealist films; his other works include *General Della Rovere* (1959), *The Rise of Louis XIV* (1966), and *Socrates* (1970).

Rossetti, Dante Gabriel, 1828–82, English poet and artist. In 1848, with the painters W. Holman Hunt and John Everett MILLAIS, he founded the brotherhood of PRE-RAPHAELITES. John RUSKIN championed the group and bought many of Rossetti's paintings. Rossetti's poetry, like his paintings, is noted for its pictorial effects and atmosphere of luxurious beauty. His early poem "The Blessed Damozel" and the sonnet sequence "The House of Life" are his finest works. The first edition of his collected poems appeared in 1870. His sister, **Christina (Georgina) Rossetti,** 1830–94, was also a poet. Deeply religious, she lived a reclusive life. Much of her poetry is melancholy or religious; "Uphill" and "When I Am Dead, My Dearest" concern death. Her best work is in *Goblin Market and Other Poems* (1862).

Rossini, Gioacchino Antonio, 1792–1868, Italian composer. Of his many lively operas, *The Barber of Seville* (1816) is his comic masterpiece. After composing the opera *William Tell* (1829), he wrote only songs, piano pieces, and the *Stabat Mater* (1842).

Rosso, Il, 1495–1540, Italian painter. A founder of MANNERISM, he was known for his distorted treatment of space, e.g., *Daughters of Jethro* (Uffizi). As court painter to FRANCIS I of France, he worked on the palace at Fontainebleau.

Ross Sea, arm of the Pacific Ocean between Victoria Land and Marie Byrd Land in ANTARCTICA, discovered in 1841 by Sir James Clark ROSS. Its southern extension is the Ross Ice Shelf, a great frozen area which is the source of huge ICEBERGS. McMurdo Sound, on its western side, has been the most important staging point for exploration and scientific investigation of Antarctica.

Rostand, Edmond [rôstäN'], 1868–1918, French poet and dramatist. He is best known for *Cyrano de Bergerac* (1897), a tour de force of dramatic poetry. Other plays include *L'Aiglon* (1900) and the barnyard fable *Chantecler* (1910).

Rostenkowski, Dan(iel David), 1928–, U.S. politician; b. Chicago.

A Democrat, he was elected as a U.S. representative from Illinois in 1958. Rostenkowski became chairman of the House Ways and Means Committee in 1981. He helped secure (1983) legislation to keep the SOCIAL SECURITY system solvent and played a major role in the passage (1986) of a new federal tax code.

Rostock or **Rostock-Warnemünde,** city (1989 est. pop. 254,000), Mecklenburg–West Pomerania, N Germany, on the Baltic Sea. It is an industrial center and major seaport. Manufactures include ships, machinery, and chemicals; the fishing industry is also important. Chartered in the 13th cent., Rostock became a leading member of the HANSEATIC LEAGUE. It was heavily damaged in WORLD WAR II.

Rostropovich, Mstislav, 1927–, Russian cellist, pianist, and conductor. He made his cello debut in 1940, toured with the Moscow Philharmonic, and taught at the Moscow Conservatory until his friendship with Aleksandr SOLZHENITSYN and his support for Soviet dissidents brought him into official disfavor in the early 1970s. Since 1977 he has been musical director of the National Symphony Orchestra, Washington, D.C. His wife is the soprano Galina Vishnevskaya.

Roszak, Theodore [rô'shäk], 1907–81, American sculptor; b. Poland. His abstract metal sculptures are irregular and explosive in form, symbolic and fantastic in content. *Thorn Blossom* (Whitney Mus., N.Y.C.) is representative.

Roth, Philip, 1933–, American novelist; b. Newark, N.J. His witty, ironic fiction, dealing chiefly with middle-class Jewish life, includes his comic masterpiece, *Portnoy's Complaint* (1969), as well as the more sober novels *My Life as a Man* (1974), *Zuckerman Unbound* (1981), *Zuckerman Bound* (1985), *The Counterlife* (1987), and *Operation Shylock* (1993). The short stories in *Goodbye Columbus* (1959) gained Roth his initial recognition. He also wrote the autobiographical *Patrimony: A True Story* (1991), which deals with the death of his father.

Rothermere, Harold Sidney Harmsworth, 1st **Viscount** [rŏth'ərmēr], 1868–1940, English publisher. He was the financial wizard of the publishing firm headed by his brother Alfred, Viscount NORTHCLIFFE, and headed the vast newspaper empire after his brother's death.

Rothko, Mark, 1903–70, American painter; b. Russia; emigrated to the U.S. in 1913. He was a leading exponent of ABSTRACT EXPRESSIONISM, and his mature works are often huge canvases with floating rectangles of luminous color. An example is *No. 10* (1950; Mus. Mod. Art, N.Y.C.).

Rothschild, prominent family of European bankers. **Mayer Amschel Rothschild,** 1743–1812, son of a money-changer in the Jewish ghetto in Frankfurt, laid the foundations of the family fortune as the financial agent for the landgrave of Hesse-Kassel. Of his five sons, the oldest continued the business in Frankfurt, while the other four established branches in Vienna, London, Naples, and Paris. All five were created barons (1822) by Francis I of Austria, a title that continues in the family. The ablest of the brothers was **Nathan Meyer Rothschild,** 1777–1836, who opened the London branch in 1805. As an agent of the British government in the Napoleonic Wars, he was instrumental in the ultimate defeat of NAPOLEON I. Under his guidance and that of his son, **Baron Lionel Nathan de Rothschild,** 1808–79, the family gained immense power by floating large international loans (e.g., the Irish famine loan, 1847; the Crimean War loan, 1856), but its virtual monopoly was broken as state financing improved. Lionel became (1858) the first Jewish member of Parliament, and many members of the family were prominent philanthropists, patrons of the arts, sportsmen, writers, or physicians.

rotifer, microscopic aquatic or semiterrestrial tubelike worm (phylum Rotifera). As a rule, only female rotifers are seen; in some species the male has never been observed. Eggs usually develop parthenogenetically, i.e., without fertilization, to produce only females.

rotor: see GENERATOR; MOTOR, ELECTRIC.

Rotterdam, city (1991 est. pop. 583,000), W Netherlands, on the Nieuwe Maas R. near the North Sea. One of the world's largest, most modern ports, it has a huge transit trade and such industries as shipyards, oil refineries, and petrochemical plants. The city was chartered in 1328. It grew rapidly after construction (1866–90) of the New Waterway gave ocean vessels access to the port. During World War II the city's center was destroyed by German bombs.

Rouault, Georges [ro͞o-ō'], 1871–1958, French expressionist artist. His thickly encrusted, powerfully colored images, outlined in black, are suggestive of icons and STAINED GLASS. He painted sorrowful clowns, corrupt judges, and prostitutes, but the sufferings of Jesus was his favorite subject. His best-known works include the series of 60 prints called *Miserere,* and the paintings *Three Judges* and *Christ Mocked by Soldiers* (both: Mus. Mod. Art, N.Y.C.).

roughage: see FIBER, DIETARY.

Rough Riders, popular name for the 1st Regiment of U.S. Cavalry Volunteers in the SPANISH-AMERICAN WAR (1898), organized largely by Theodore ROOSEVELT. Commanded by Leonard WOOD, it fought chiefly in Cuba, and its exploits, especially at San Juan Hill, were highly publicized.

Roundheads, derisive name for the supporters of Parliament in the ENGLISH CIVIL WAR (1642–48). The name referred to the short haircuts worn by some Puritans in contrast to the wigs worn by the king's supporters, called Cavaliers.

roundworm: see NEMATODE.

Rousseau, Henri [ro͞osō'], 1884–1910, French primitive painter. Self-taught, he is best known for his fantastic landscapes, e.g., *The Snake Charmer* (1907; Louvre), and his haunting *Sleeping Gypsy* (1897; Mus. Mod. Art, N.Y.C.).

Rousseau, Jean Jacques, 1712–78, Swiss-French philosopher and political theorist; b. Geneva. A member of DIDEROT's circle, he was one of the great figures of the French ENLIGHTENMENT and probably the most significant of those who shaped 19th-cent. ROMANTICISM, influencing such figures as KANT, GOETHE, ROBESPIERRE, TOLSTOY, and the French revolutionists. Rousseau's most celebrated theory was that of the "natural man." In his *Discourse on the Inequalities of Men* (1754) and *Social Contract* (1762) he maintained that human beings were essentially good and equal in the state of nature but were corrupted by the introduction of property, agriculture, science, and commerce. People entered into a SOCIAL CONTRACT among themselves, establishing governments and educational systems to correct the inequalities brought about by the rise of civilization. *Émile* (1762), a didactic novel, expounds Rousseau's theory that education is not the imparting of knowledge but the drawing out of what is already in the child. From the 1760s Rousseau was tormented by persecution mania, and he lived his later years in seclusion. His *Confessions* (1781) created a new, intensely personal style of autobiography.

Rousseau, Théodore, 1812–67, French landscape painter, leader of the BARBIZON SCHOOL. His landscapes are grave and full of a deep love of solitude.

Roussel, Albert [ro͞osĕl'], 1869–1937, French composer. His early works are influenced by IMPRESSIONISM and 18th-cent. music; he later experimented with Eastern techniques. His late works, e.g., his Second Symphony (1920), feature subtle melodic inflections and sharp dissonances.

Rowe, Nicholas, 1674–1718, English dramatist. His best plays, *The Fair Penitent* (1703) and *Jane Shore* (1714), stories of men's cruelty to women, prefigure later 18th-cent. domestic tragedies. His edition of SHAKESPEARE (1709) was the first to divide the plays into acts and scenes.

rowing, the art of propelling a boat by means of oars operated by hand. In racing, each member of the rowing team, or crew, uses both hands to pull one oar through the water. The boat, or shell, is sometimes steered by a coxswain, who also directs the speed and rhythm of the crew's strokes. Sculling is a variant of rowing in which each oarsman controls two oars, one in each hand. Rowing crews have two, four, or eight members, with or without a coxswain; sculling teams consist of one, two, or four members. The most famous annual rowing event is the Oxford-Cambridge race, in England, held since 1829.

Rowlandson, Thomas, 1756–1827, English caricaturist. As a humorous and critical commentator on the social scene, he quickly gained celebrity for his drawings such as *Vauxhall Gardens* (1784), and his famous *Tour of Dr. Syntax* with text by William Combe. The fluidity of his line is likened to French ROCOCO, but his spirited, and sometimes coarse, humor is in the English style.

Roxana or **Roxane,** d. 311 B.C., wife of ALEXANDER THE GREAT. She and Alexander's posthumous son, Alexander IV, were embroiled in the wars of the DIADOCHI and were imprisoned by CASSANDER. They were later killed.

Roxas, Manuel [rō'häs], 1894–1948, Philippine statesman. In WORLD WAR II he joined the Japanese puppet government, but secretly aided the Philippine underground. In 1946 he became the first president of the Republic of the PHILIPPINES.

Royal Ballet, the principal British ballet company, based at the Royal Opera House, Covent Garden, London. It was formed from Sadler's Wells Ballet and Sadler's Wells Theatre Ballet. Its prima ballerinas have included Alicia MARKOVA and Margot FONTEYN. Choreographers have included Frederick ASHTON and Antony TUDOR. Its performances are noted for lavish classic drama.

Royal Canadian Mounted Police, constabulary organized (1873) as the Northwest Mounted Police to bring law and order to the Canadian west and to prevent tribal disorders. The present name was adopted in 1920. The corps' daring exploits in pursuit of criminals earned it a romantic reputation and the popular name Mounties. It now numbers more than 19,000 and includes the police forces of all provinces but Ontario and Quebec.

Royal Danish Ballet, one of the oldest major ballet companies. It was established (1748) at the opening of Denmark's Royal Theater in Copenhagen and was developed by Vincenzo Galeotti, Auguste BOURNONVILLE, and Harold Lander. Its style is noted for light, precise footwork. Star dancers have included Erik BRUHN and Peter MARTINS.

Royal Highlanders: see BLACK WATCH.

Royal Society, organization est. 1660 in London by a group of learned men to promote scientific discussion. It stimulates scientific research and publishes its *Proceedings* and *Philosophical Transactions.* Granted a royal charter in 1662, the Royal Society advises the British government (from which it receives subsidies) on scientific matters.

royalties: see COPYRIGHT.

Rozelle, Pete (Alvin Rozelle), 1926–, American football executive, b. South Gate, Calif. Commissioner of the National Football League (1960–89), he guided the NFL through its merger with the American Football League and its expansion from 12 to 28 teams, and negotiated lucrative television contracts.

Ru, chemical symbol of the element RUTHENIUM.

Ruanda-Urundi, former colonial territory in central Africa, now divided between the independent states of RWANDA and BURUNDI.

rubber, any solid substance, usually elastic, that can be vulcanized to improve its elasticity and add strength; the term includes natural rubber, or caoutchouc, and a wide variety of synthetic rubbers, which have similar properties. Rubbers are composed chiefly of CARBON and HYDROGEN, but some synthetics also have other elements, e.g., chlorine, fluorine, nitrogen, or silicon. All are compounds of high molecular weight; each consists of a series of one kind of molecule (e.g., isoprene in natural rubber) hooked together in a long chain to form a very flexible, larger molecule, the POLYMER. Natural rubber is obtained as latex, a milky suspension of rubber globules found in a large variety of plants, chiefly tropical and subtropical. An important source is the PARÁ RUBBER TREE. Latex can be shipped for processing either as a liquid or coagulated by acid and rolled into sheets. For most purposes rubber is ground, dissolved in a solvent, and compounded with other ingredients, e.g., fillers, pigments, and plasticizers. Known in pre-Columbian times by the indigenous peoples of South and Central America, rubber first attracted interest in Europe in the 18th cent. Vulcanization, a process invented (1839) by Charles GOODYEAR, revolutionized the rubber industry. It usually involves heating raw or compounded rubber with SULFUR, causing sulfur bridges to form between molecules. The product is nonsticky, elastic, and resistant to heat and cold. Natural rubber is used chiefly to make tires and inner tubes because it is cheaper than synthetic rubber and has greater resistance to tearing when hot. Natural rubber can be treated to make foam rubber and sponge rubber. The first synthetic rubber was made in Germany in World War I. Today synthetics, e.g., Buna S, neoprene, butyl, and nitrile, account for most of the world's rubber production. Made from COAL, PETROLEUM, NATURAL GAS, and ACETYLENE, synthetic rubbers are resilient over a wider temperature range than natural rubber and are more resistant to aging, weathering, and attack by certain substances, notably, oil, solvents, oxygen, and ozone. SILICONE rubbers are used in insulation. POLYURETHANES are used in tires, in shoes, and as foams. Neoprene is used for making hose and tank linings. Butyl rubber is used in inner tubes and as insulation.

rubber plant, name for several plants, e.g., PARÁ RUBBER TREE, Castilla tree, Ceará tree, and guayule, all of which are sources of the milky fluid, called latex, used to make RUBBER. The India-rubber tree (*Ficus elastica*), a common houseplant, is an Asian FIG.

Rubbia, Carlo, 1934–, Italian physicist. He shared the 1984 Nobel Prize in physics with Simon VAN DER MEER for their discovery of the W AND Z PARTICLES, which convey the WEAK INTERACTION, one of the four fundamental forces of nature. Rubbia also led a team at CERN that produced theoretical evidence for the sixth QUARK.

rubella or **German measles,** acute infectious viral disease, causing a rash and fever. It is mild and uncomplicated unless contracted during the first three months of pregnancy, when it can cause serious damage to the fetus (see BIRTH DEFECTS). VACCINATION against rubella is given to children and advised for young women who have not had the disease.

Rubens, Peter Paul, 1577–1640, foremost Flemish painter of the 17th cent.; b. Siegen, Westphalia. He served (1600–1608) as court painter to the duke of MANTUA, who sent him to Spain where he painted the magnificent equestrian portrait of the duke of Lerma (Conde Valdelagrana Coll., Madrid). In 1608 he returned to Antwerp, where within five years he became known as the greatest painter of his country. He organized an enormous workshop of skilled apprentices and associates, among them VAN DYCK and JORDAENS. *Raising of the Cross* and *Descent from the Cross* (1610 and 1611; cathedral, Antwerp) date from this period. He also executed a series of large allegorical paintings of the life of Marie de' Medici (Louvre). His associates did much of the work on them, but Rubens designed them and added the finishing touches. In this way, his workshop produced numerous monumental works. In 1626 Rubens entered the diplomatic service. In Spain on a diplomatic mission (1628), he became acquainted with Velázquez, and painted the royal family. While in England, he painted *Allegory of War and Peace* (National Gall., London), and was knighted for his peacemaking efforts. During the last 10 years of his life, he did his most joyous and finest pictures. *The Judgement of Paris* and *Three Graces* (Prado) and *Venus and Adonis* (Metropolitan Mus.) belong to this period. The volume of his work is enormous; more than 2,000 paintings have been attributed to his studio, and each shows the mark of his genius. The influence of the Italians is clear in his monumental compositions, but his color, technique, and lusty spirit are Flemish. Despite his superb religious painting, a pagan joy of life is his most characteristic quality. He explored all fields of painting, and some of his small works, e.g., *Peasant Dance* (Prado) are among his masterpieces.

rubeola: see MEASLES.

Rubicon, stream that in the days of early Rome divided GAUL from Italy. In 49 B.C. Julius CAESAR led his army across it, defying the Roman senate and commencing civil war. He reportedly said, "The die is cast." Thus, to cross the Rubicon is to take an irrevocable step.

rubidium (Rb), metallic element, discovered spectroscopically by Robert BUNSEN and Gustav KIRCHHOFF in 1861. A very soft, silver-white ALKALI METAL, it is extremely reactive, and must be kept out of contact with air and water. It has few commercial uses. See ELEMENT (table); PERIODIC TABLE.

Rubinstein, Anton Grigoryevich, 1829–94, Russian virtuoso pianist, composer, and educator. He founded the St. Petersburg Conservatory in 1862 and was its director. His brother, **Nicholas Grigoryevich Rubinstein,** 1835–81, also a pianist and teacher, founded (1864) and headed the Moscow Conservatory.

Rubinstein, Arthur, 1887–1982, Polish-American pianist; b. Poland. He was particularly known for his lyric interpretations of CHOPIN and for his championing of Spanish works.

ruby, gem, transparent red variety of CORUNDUM, found chiefly in Myanmar, Thailand, and Sri Lanka. Star rubies (showing an internal star when cut with a rounded top) are rare. Synthetic rubies are produced by fusing aluminum oxide; chromium oxide is added to provide the appropriate color.

rudder, in aviation: see AIRPLANE.

Rudolf, rulers of the HOLY ROMAN EMPIRE. **Rudolf I** or **Rudolf of Hapsburg,** 1218–91, German king (1273–91), first ruler of the HAPSBURG dynasty, was elected king after an interregnum of 20 years in which there was no accepted German king or emperor. His defeat of Ottocar II of Bohemia greatly added to the Hapsburg lands. **Rudolf II,** 1552–1612, emperor (1576–1612), was mentally unbalanced and delegated imperial power to his brother Matthias. Rudolf's reign was turbulent and a prelude to the THIRTY YEARS WAR.

Rudolf, 1858–89, Austrian archduke, only son of Emperor FRANCIS JOSEPH. Rudolf's mysterious death (officially ruled a double suicide with his mistress, Baroness Mary Vetsera), at Mayerling left his cousin, FRANCIS FERDINAND, heir to the Austro-Hungarian throne. The "Mayerling tragedy" has been the subject of novels, plays, and films.

Rudolf of Hapsburg: see Rudolf I under RUDOLF, rulers of the Holy Roman Empire.

rue, common name for various members of the family Rutaceae, mostly woody shrubs or small trees, often evergreen and spiny, of temperate and tropical regions. They are typified by glands that produce an essential oil widely utilized for flavorings, perfume oils, and drugs; the foliage, fruits, and flowers are noticeably fragrant. Chief in importance are the CITRUS FRUITS. Several species of the family yield lumber used in cabinetmaking, e.g., the ORANGE and the species called satinwood. More specifically, the name *rue* refers to the shrubby herbs of the genus *Ruta,* found from the Mediterranean to E Siberia. The common rue (*R. graveolans*) has greenish-yellow flowers, blue-green leaves, and a strong odor. Its leaves are sometimes used in flavorings, beverages, and cosmetics.

Rufinus, d. 395, Roman statesman, minister to THEODOSIUS I and virtual ruler for ARCADIUS. He was assassinated by Gothic mercenaries, perhaps by order of STILICHO.

Rugby, town (1986 est. pop. 84,900), Warwickshire, central England. Rugby is known chiefly as the seat of one of the great English public schools, Rugby School (est. 1567). RUGBY football originated at the school in 1823.

rugby, game that originated (1823) on the playing fields of Rugby School, in England. It is similar in some respects to SOCCER and American FOOTBALL. The amateur version is played by two teams of 15 players on a field about 160 yd (146 m) long and 75 yd (69 m) wide, with goal lines 110 yd (101 m) apart and two in-goals (corresponding to football's end zones). The ball may be kicked, carried, or passed (to the sides or rear); tackling is permitted, but blocking is forbidden. Scoring is by carrying the ball into the in-goal or by kicking it between the goal posts. Professional rugby, known as Rugby league, is played by 13-player teams under somewhat different rules.

Ruhr, region, NW Germany, located along and N of the Ruhr R. and E of the Rhine R. Its concentration of industries, begun in the 19th cent. when the KRUPP and Thyssen concerns built large coal and steel empires, made it one of the world's greatest industrial complexes. In the 1980s the coal and steel industries declined; by the 1990s more than half the workforce was employed in services. Among the principal cities are ESSEN, DUISBURG, Bottrop, Gelsenkirchen, Bochum, and DORTMUND.

Ruisdael or **Ruysdael, Jacob van** [both: rois'däl], c.1628–1682, Dutch painter and etcher, the most celebrated of the Dutch landscape painters. His work shows northern nature in a somber mood. Overcast skies throw restless light on gnarled oak and beech trees. His later work emphasizes humanity's insignificance amid the splendor of nature. Important works include *Jewish Cemetery* (Detroit Inst. of Art) and *Wheatfields* (Metropolitan Mus.). He also produced some very fine etchings. He influenced French and English landscapists for 200 years.

Ruiz, Juan [ro͞oēth'], 1283?–1350?, Spanish poet and archpriest of Hita. For his *Book of Good Love* (c.1330), a satirical panorama of medieval society, he has been called the Spanish CHAUCER.

rum, fermented, distilled, and aged spirituous liquor made from the molasses and foam that rise to the top of boiled sugarcane juice. Naturally colorless, it becomes brown when caramel is added and the liquor is stored in casks. The best-known producer is Jamaica, but rum is also made in Cuba, Brazil, Trinidad, Puerto Rico, and the U.S.

Rumania: see ROMANIA.

Rumelia or **Roumelia** [both: ro͞omē'lēə], region of S Bulgaria, between the Balkan and Rhodope mountains. Historically, Rumelia denoted the Ottoman Empire's Balkan possessions; the Ottoman province of Rumelia included much of present-day Yugoslavia, Bosnia and Hercegovina, Bulgaria, European Turkey, N Greece, Macedonia, and part of Albania. **Eastern Rumelia,** in present-day S Bulgaria, was created in 1878 (see BERLIN, CONGRESS OF) and was annexed by Bulgaria in 1885.

Rumford, Benjamin Thompson, Count, 1753–1814, American-British scientist and administrator; b. Woburn, Mass. After leaving America (1776), he served as the British undersecretary of the colonies (1780–81). In contrast to the prevalent belief that HEAT was a substance, he stated that it was produced by the motion of particles. Rumford made valuable experiments with gunpowder, introduced improved methods of heating and cooking, and founded the Royal Institution in England.

Rumi, Jalal ed-Din or **Jalal ud-Din** [ro͞o'mē], 1207–73, Persian poet, one of the greatest Sufi poets. Rumi's lyrics express mystic thought in finely wrought symbols. His main work is *Mathnawi,* a poetic exposition of SUFISM in eight books.

ruminant, any of a group of even-toed mammals that chew their cud, i.e., regurgitate and rechew already swallowed food. Ruminants have three- or four-chambered stomachs. In the first chamber (the rumen), food is mixed with fluid to form a soft mass (the cud or bolus), which, after regurgitation and rechewing, passes through the rumen into the other stomach chambers for digestion. Goats, sheep, cows, camels, and antelope are ruminants.

rummy, card game played by two to six players with a standard deck. Seven cards are dealt to each player; remaining cards are left in a stock pile. Drawing and discarding, a player's objective is to meld (put down three or four cards of the same rank or sequence in the same suit); the first player to meld all his cards wins. Variants are gin rummy and canasta.

Runcie, Robert Alexander Kennedy, 1921–, archbishop of Canterbury (1980–91). Bishop of St. Albans from 1970 to 1980, he was enthroned as the 102d archbishop of Canterbury in 1980, succeeding Donald Coggan. He is noted for developing links with the Orthodox Eastern Church and for his work on behalf of the Anglican ministry in Africa.

runes, ancient characters used in Teutonic, Anglo-Saxon, and Scandinavian inscriptions, probably first used c.300 by the OSTROGOTHS, who may have derived them from Hellenic-Italian writing. Adapted to carving, they consisted of perpendicular, oblique, and a few curved lines. They were used extensively in N Europe, Iceland, and the British Isles before Christianity, persisting in Scandinavia into the Middle Ages.

Runnymede or **Runnimede,** historic meadow, near Egham, Surrey, S England, on the south bank of the Thames R., W of London. Either on this meadow or on nearby Magna Carta Island, King JOHN accepted the MAGNA CARTA (1215).

Runyon, (Alfred) Damon, 1884–1946, American writer and journalist; b. Manhattan, Kans. He is best known for his humorous stories, written in the slangy idiom of New York City's Broadway and underworld characters, e.g., *Guys and Dolls* (1931).

Rupert, Prince, 1619–82, count palatine of the Rhine; b. Prague. He was the son of FREDERICK THE WINTER KING and grandson of James I of England. He served the Dutch in the THIRTY YEARS WAR and was an outstanding royalist general during the ENGLISH CIVIL WAR. After the English RESTORATION he was a privy councillor to Charles II and, as an admiral, played an important part in the Dutch Wars. He was one of the founders of the HUDSON'S BAY COMPANY.

Rupert's Land, Canadian territory held (1670–1870) by the HUDSON'S BAY COMPANY. The area, named for Prince RUPERT, the first governor of the company, comprised the drainage basin of HUDSON BAY. In 1869–70 the company transferred Rupert's Land to Canada for £300,000 but retained certain blocks of land for trading and other purposes.

Rupp, George Erik, 1942–, American educator, president of Columbia Univ. (1993–); b. Summit, N.J. A Presbyterian minister, he was on the faculty of the Harvard Divinity School from 1974 to 1977 and was later dean (1979–85) of the school. President of Rice Univ. from 1985, he was named president of Columbia in 1993.

Rush, Benjamin, 1745?–1813, American physician; b. Byberry (now in Philadelphia), Pa. He was the first professor of chemistry in the colonies, at the College of Philadelphia. He signed the Declaration of Independence and was a member (1776–77) of the Continental Congress. He established (1786) in Philadelphia the first free dispensary in the U.S. and became (1792) professor of medicine at the Univ. of Pennsylvania. His bleeding and purging of patients aroused controversy. A pioneer in psychiatry and a prolific writer, he also founded the first American antislavery society and served (1797–1813) as treasurer of the U.S. mint in Philadelphia.

rush, any plant of the family Juncaceae; more loosely, a tall, grasslike, often hollow-stemmed plant of various families. The common, or bog, rush (*Juncus effusus*) is widely distributed in swamps and moist places of the Northern Hemisphere; the slender rush (*J. tenuis*) is found in drier surroundings. Some wood rushes (genus *Luzula*), which grow on dry ground, are relished by livestock. Rushes are used for basketwork, mats, and chair seats, and as wicks. The scouring rush is a HORSETAIL.

Rush-Bagot Convention, 1817, agreement between the U.S. and Great Britain concerning the Canadian border. It consisted of an exchange of notes by Acting U.S. Secy. of State Richard Rush and Charles Bagot, British minister in Washington, and provided for disarmament of the U.S.-Canadian frontier. The convention set a precedent for the amicable settlement of Anglo-American difficulties, and inaugurated a policy of peace between the U.S. and Canada.

Rushdie, Salman, 1947–, British author; b. Bombay. His first novels, including *Shame* (1983) and *Midnight's Children* (1981), are examples of magical realism. His allegorical novel *The Satanic Verses* (1988) enraged many Muslims, including the Ayatollah KHOMEINI, who sentenced Rushdie to death, and Rushdie went into hiding. *Haroun and the Sea of Stories,* a novel, was published in 1990.

Rusk, (David) Dean, 1909–, U.S. secretary of state (1961–69). After serving in the State Dept. (1946–51) and as president of the Rockefeller Foundation (1952–61), he became secretary of state in Pres. John F. KENNEDY's cabinet and continued to hold the post under Pres. Lyndon B. JOHNSON. A firm believer in the use of military force to prevent Communist expansion, he strongly defended the VIETNAM WAR.

Ruskin, John, 1819–1900, English critic and social theorist. His first work, *Modern Painters* (5 vol., 1843–60), begun as a defense of J.M.W. TURNER, held that art is a "universal language" based on national and individual integrity and morality. *The Seven Lamps of Architecture* (1849) and *The Stones of Venice* (1851–53) applied this idea to architecture. Ruskin began to address social and political questions c.1857; in *Unto This Last* (1860) and *Munera Pulveris* (1862–63) he attacked the ugliness and waste of modern industrial England. *Sesame and Lilies* (1865) and other works proposed social reforms, some of which—old-age pensions, nationalization of education, organization of labor—are now widely accepted. In 1870 Ruskin was appointed Slade Professor at Oxford, the first professor of art in England.

Russell, Bertrand Arthur William Russell, 3d **Earl,** 1872–1970, British philosopher, mathematician, and social reformer; b. Wales. The grandson of Lord John Russell, the 1st Earl Russell, he succeeded to the earldom in 1931. While teaching at Cambridge Univ. Russell produced his most important works, *Principles of Mathematics* (1903) and, with Alfred North WHITEHEAD, *Principia Mathematica* (3 vol., 1910–13), in which he attempted to show how the laws of mathematics could be deduced from the basic axioms of logic. His work influenced 20th-cent. symbolic logic (see LOGIC), SET theory in mathematics, and LOGICAL POSITIVISM, especially in the work of his student Ludwig WITTGENSTEIN. An undogmatic but zealous rationalist, Russell was deeply convinced of the logical independence of individual facts and the dependence of knowledge on the data of original experience. Well known for his social views, he was an active pacifist during World War I. In 1927 he and his wife founded the highly experimental Beacon Hill School. His liberal views on marriage, sex, adultery, and homosexuality made him controversial during most of the 1930s. He abandoned pacifism during World War II in the face of the Nazi threat, but reverted to it after the war, becoming a leader in the "ban the bomb" movement to halt the manufacture of nuclear weapons. In the 1960s he and Jean-Paul SARTRE organized European opposition to U.S. involvement in the Vietnam War. Russell's radicalism kept him from a traditional academic career, and he supported himself chiefly by his writings, many of them widely read, e.g., *Marriage and Morals* (1929), *A History of Western Philosophy* (1945), and his autobiography (3 vol., 1967–69). In 1950 he was awarded the Nobel Prize in literature.

Russell, Bill (William Felton Russell), 1934–, African-American basketball player; b. Monroe, La. Named All-American while on the Univ. of San Francisco team, he played on the gold-medal-winning U.S. team at the 1956 Olympics. That year he joined the Boston Celtics; in his 13 seasons with the team he won the most valuable player award five times. Since leaving the Celtics in 1969, he has been a television sports announcer and a coach (1973–77) for the Seattle SuperSonics. His biography, *Second Wind,* appeared in 1979.

Russell, George William, pseud. **A.E.,** 1867–1935, Irish author. An Irish nationalist, editor, reformer, and painter, he was a major figure in the Irish literary renaissance. His poems and plays, mystical and melodious, include *Homeward: Songs by the Way* (1894) and *The Candle of Vision* (1918).

Russell, Henry Norris, 1877–1957, American astronomer; b. Oyster Bay, N.Y. At Princeton Univ. he taught (1905–47) astronomy and directed (1912–47) its observatory. Russell showed that a study of the motion of the periastron of the orbit of eclipsing variable stars could provide information on the internal structure of the component stars. He developed a theory of STELLAR EVOLUTION that led him to construct, independently of Ejnar Hertzsprung, the HERTZSPRUNG-RUSSELL DIAGRAM, and he determined the abundance of various chemical elements in the solar atmosphere. He also analyzed the spectra of several chemical elements.

Russell, Lillian, 1861–1922, American singer and actress; b. Clinton, Iowa, as Helen Louise Leonard. Beautiful and flamboyant, she excelled in light opera.

Russia or **Russian Federation,** Rus. *Rossiya,* republic (1992 est. pop. 149,527,000), 6,591,100 sq mi (17,070,949 sq km), occupying most of E Europe and N Asia, extending c.5,000 mi (8,000 km) from the Baltic Sea to the Pacific Ocean. It is bounded by Ukraine, Belarus, Latvia, Estonia, the Gulf of Finland, Finland, and Norway (W); the Barents, Kara, Laptev, East Siberian, and Chukchi seas—arms of the Arctic Ocean (N); the Bering Sea, Sea of Okhotsk, and Sea of Japan—arms of the Pacific Ocean (E); China, Mongolia, Kazakhstan, the Caspian Sea, Azerbaijan, Georgia, and the Black Sea (S). The Kaliningrad oblast is a Russian exclave on the Baltic, bordered by Lithuania and Poland. The capital and largest city is MOSCOW. From 1922 to 1991 Russia, as the Russian Soviet Federative Socialist Republic, was the largest and most important constituent republic of the UNION OF SOVIET SOCIALIST REPUBLICS and, in most respects, it is the USSR's successor. The term *Russia* also designates the area inhabited by the Russian people as distinguished from other East Slavs and from non-Slavic peoples, and is often loosely applied to the entire former Soviet Union.

Geography. Covering more than a tenth of the earth's land area, Russia is the world's largest nation and ranks sixth in population. The climate, generally continental, varies from extreme cold in N Russia and Siberia (where Verkhoyansk, the world's coldest settled place, is located), to subtropical along the Black Sea. Most of European Russia is flatland, except for the URALS, the CAUCASUS (the site of Mt. Elbrus, 18,481 ft/5,633 m, Russia's highest peak), and scattered highlands; it includes TAIGA, TUNDRA, and the largest lakes in Europe, Ladoga and Onega. The fertile Russian Plain is drained by such rivers as the DNEIPER, DON, and VOLGA. The vast majority of the population lives in European Russia. In the central European region Moscow and NIZHNY NOVOGOROD (Gorky) are among the major cities; SAINT PETERSBURG (Leningrad), the second largest city, is in NW European Russia. KAZAN, SAMARA, and VOLGOGRAD are the major cities in the Volga region, and YEKATERINBURG (Sverdlovsk) is in the Urals. Asian Russia is divided into SIBERIA, occupying the vast central region of the country, and the RUSSIAN FAR EAST, bordering on the Pacific.

Economy. Despite the end of Communist rule and the disintegration of the USSR, Russian industry and agriculture remain largely owned and managed by the remnants of the bureaucratic state. Collapse of Communist rule has brought severe disruptions to the economy, with increased shortages of food and consumer goods and high inflation. Laws have been passed that permit private and foreign purchase of state enterprises, and many barriers to private ownership of agricultural land were removed by decree in 1993. The government has also ended most price controls in an effort to stimulate the economy and begin a transition to capitalism. In 1992 the sale, through a voucher system, of state enterprises to Russian citizens began, about half the state-owned businesses were privatized by the end of 1993. Farmland is divided into state farms, COLLECTIVE FARMS, and privately held plots; land reform is expected to lead to the breakup of many state and collective farms. Major crops are rye, wheat, and other grains, potatoes, sugar beets, and flax. Other important farm products include dairy products, meat, and furs. Russia is the world's major producer of timber and a leading fishing nation. It has substantial mineral resources, including major deposits of coal, iron, petroleum and natural gas, bauxite, asbestos, copper, and gold. Among its other energy resources are hydropower and nuclear energy. The nation's vast industries produce a wide range of both capital and consumer goods. Russian ports include KALININGRAD, Saint Petersburg, and VLADIVOSTOK.

People. Russians make up 83% of the country's population; there are Ukrainian and non-Slavic minorities. Russian is the official language. Although religious practice was long suppressed or discouraged under Soviet rule, many people worship in the Russian Orthodox Church (see ORTHODOX EASTERN CHURCH); other religions include Roman Catholicism, Protestantism, Judaism, Islam, and Buddhism.

Government. The Russian government is headed by a popularly elected executive president (established 1991). Under the constitution approved in 1993, the Federal Assembly consists of two chambers, the 178-member indirectly elected Federation Council (the upper house) and the 450-member popularly elected State Duma (the lower house). Ethnically non-Russian areas are constituted as 21 republics (formerly autonomous republics), 1 autonomous oblast (region), and 10 autonomous okrugs (national areas); there are 49 Russian oblasts (the cities of Moscow and St. Petersburg also have oblast status) and 6 Russian krays (territories). Oblasts and krays are roughly equivalent to provinces.

History. Russia was inhabited in the Paleolithic period. By the 7th cent. B.C. the Scythians (see SCYTHIA) controlled the north shore of the BLACK SEA and the CRIMEA. The KHAZARS built (7th–10th cent. A.D.) a powerful state in S Russia, and by the 9th cent. the East SLAVS had settled in the N UKRAINE and nearby regions. The Russian state is said to have been established by Rurik, leader of a band of Scandinavian traders and warriors (the Varangians), who founded (862) a dynasty at NOVGOROD. His successor, Oleg, made (882) KIEV the capital of KIEVAN RUSSIA, and Christianity became the official religion under VLADIMIR I, who adopted (988–89) the Greek rite. Kievan Russia broke up into principalities in 1054 and was destroyed (1237–40) by invading Mongols (see TATARS) who established the empire of the GOLDEN HORDE.

Imperial Russia. In the 15th cent. IVAN III, grand duke of MOSCOW, ceased to pay tribute to the Tatars and expanded his territory of conquest. IVAN IV further extended Russian rule and took the title "czar of all Russia" in 1547. The death of Czar Boris GODUNOV in 1605 was followed by the "Time of Troubles," a period marked by the appearance of pretenders (see DMITRI) and an invasion (1609) by SIGISMUND III of Poland. The Poles were expelled in 1612 and in 1613 Michael ROMANOV was made czar, thus beginning a dynasty that ruled Russia until 1917. PETER I (r.1689–1725) undertook the Westernization of Russia and enacted many administrative reforms, but he also increased autocracy and enserfment (see SERF). In 1703 Peter founded SAINT PETERSBURG, the new capital, on land won in the NORTHERN WAR. He also began the RUSSO-TURKISH WARS. Under CATHERINE II (r.1762–96), Russia became a great power, expanding its borders in the west and south (see POLAND, PARTITIONS OF). The suppression of the PUGACHEV revolt (1773–75) strengthened the privileged classes. During the reign of ALEXANDER I, the French under NAPOLEON I took (1812) Moscow; but after Napoleon's defeat and the peace arranged at the Congress of VIENNA, Russia and Austria emerged as the chief powers on the Continent (see HOLY ALLIANCE). Liberalism in the Russian upper classes led to an unsuccessful revolt (1825) by the DECEMBRISTS. Under the reactionary rule of NICHOLAS I, Russia crushed an uprising (1830–31) in Poland and helped Austria subdue a revolt (1848–49) in Hungary. Its attempts to dominate the Turks led to the CRIMEAN WAR (1854–56). ALEXANDER II freed the serfs in 1861 (see EMANCIPATION, EDICT OF), but grew increasingly conservative. Meanwhile, Russia's expansion continued into the CAUCASUS, Turkistan, and E Asia (see RUSSIAN FAR EAST). Alexander II's assassination (1881) was followed by a period of reaction under ALEXANDER III and NICHOLAS II, the last Russian czar. The disastrous RUSSO-JAPANESE WAR (1904–5) led to the Revolution of 1905; Nicholas was forced to grant a constitution and a parliament (see DUMA). Repression continued, however, under Nicholas's premier, P.A. STOLYPIN. Leftist militancy (see BOLSHEVISM AND MENSHEVISM) and WORLD WAR I completed Russia's collapse. During the RUSSIAN REVOLUTIONS of 1917, Nicholas II was forced to abdicate; the Bolsheviks, led by LENIN, took power. Russia withdrew from the war by the Treaty of BREST-LITOVSK, but civil war ensued and lasted until the Soviet regime emerged victorious in 1920. In 1917 Russia was proclaimed the Russian SFSR and in 1922 it became part of the USSR. For the history of Russia as part of the USSR (1922–91), see UNION OF SOVIET SOCIALIST REPUBLICS.

Post-Soviet Russia. Under Soviet Pres. GORBACHEV, the end of repressive political controls permitted nationalist movements to arise in the constituent republics of the USSR. In 1990 Boris YELTSIN and other nationalists and reformers were elected to the Russian parliament; Yeltsin was subsequently chosen Russian president. Under Yeltsin, Russia declared its sovereignty (but not its independence) and began to challenge the central government's authority. In 1991 Yeltsin was reelected in the first popular election for president in the history of the Russian Republic. He and the leaders of eight other republics reached a power-sharing agreement with Gorbachev, but its imminent signing provoked a coup attempt (Aug. 1991) by Soviet hard-liners. In the aftermath, the USSR disintegrated. With Ukraine and Belarus, Russia established the COMMONWEALTH OF INDEPENDENT STATES. When Gorbachev resigned (Dec. 1991), Yeltsin had already taken control of most of the central government, and Russia assumed the USSR's UN seat. Yeltsin also moved rapidly to end or reduce state control of the economy, but control of parliament by former Communists led to conflicts and power struggles. In Sept. 1993 Yeltsin suspended the parliament and called for new elections. Parliament retaliated by naming Vice Pres. RUTSKOI acting president, and attempted an armed uprising, which was crushed by the army. Rutskoi and others were jailed, and the parliament dissolved. In Dec. 1993 voters approved a new constitution that strengthened presidential power, but they also supported many of Yeltsin's opponents, such as ultranationalist Vladimir ZHIRINOVSKY, in the legislative elections. The Russian Federation has had to confront movements for autonomy or independence in several ethnically based regions and republics, such as Tatarstan (see TATARS) and Chechenya (a republic in the N Caucasus), and there have been violent conflicts between ethnic groups, particularly in the Caucasus.

RUSSIAN AND SOVIET RULERS FROM 1462
(including dates of reign or in power)

House of Rurik
Ivan III (the Great), 1462–1505
Vasily III, 1505–33
Ivan IV (the Terrible), 1533–84
Feodor I, 1584–98
House of Godunov
Boris Godunov, 1598–1605
Feodor II, 1605
Usurpers
Dmitri, 1605–6
Vasily IV, 1606–10
Interregnum, 1610–13
House of Romanov
Michael, 1613–45
Alexis, 1645–76
Feodor III, 1676–82
Ivan V and Peter I (the Great), 1682–96
Peter I (the Great), 1696–1725
Catherine I, 1725–27
Peter II, 1727–30
Anna, 1730–40
Ivan VI, 1740–41
Elizabeth, 1741–62
Peter III, 1762
Catherine II (the Great), 1762–96
Paul I, 1796–1801
Alexander I, 1801–25
Nicholas I, 1825–55
Alexander II, 1855–81
Alexander III, 1881–94
Nicholas II, 1894–1917
Provisional Government
Prince Georgi Lvov, Mar.–July 1917
Aleksandr Kerensky, July–Nov. 1917
Soviet Russia and the USSR
Vladimir Lenin, 1917–24
Joseph Stalin, Lev Kamenev, and Grigori Zinoviev, 1924–26
Joseph Stalin, 1926–53
Nikita Khrushchev and Georgi Malenkov, 1953–55
Nikita Khrushchev and Nikolai Bulganin, 1955–58
Nikita Khrushchev, 1958–64
Leonid Brezhnev, 1964–82
Yuri Andropov, 1982–84
Konstantin Chernenko, 1984–85
Mikhail Gorbachev, 1985–91
Russian Federation
Boris Yeltsin, 1991–

Russia Company: see MUSCOVY COMPANY.

Russian Blue cat: see under CAT.

Russian Far East, formerly the Soviet Far East, region (1989 est. pop. 7,941,000), c.2,400,000 sq mi (6,216,000 sq km), E Russia, comprising the entire NE coast of Asia. Often considered part of SIBERIA, the area was treated separately in Soviet regional schemes. It borders Sakha (formerly Yakutia, NW); the East Siberian Sea (N); Bering Sea (NE); Sea of Japan (SE); China (S); and Yablonovy Mts. (SW). The region includes mountains, TAIGA, and TUNDRA. It is virtually self-sufficient economically. VLADIVOSTOK and other cities produce iron, steel, petroleum, lumber, and other products. Resources include coal, oil, and gold. Farming, fishing, and hunting are major occupations. Over 25 ethnic groups inhabit the region. Russian colonization began in the late 16th cent. From the mid-19th to early 20th cent. various parts of the region were acquired from China and Japan, and it was incorporated into the USSR in 1922. In the 1960s and 70s there were Sino-Soviet border clashes along the AMUR and USSURI rivers.

Russian Federation: see RUSSIA.

Russian language, member of the East Slavic group of the Slavic subfamily of the Indo-European family of languages. See LANGUAGE (table).

Russian Revolution, violent upheavals in Russia ending in the overthrow of the czarist government in 1917. By 1905 discontent permeated all classes: the peasants, workers, army, intelligentsia, national and religious minorities, and segments of the bourgeoisie and aristocracy. The RUSSO-JAPANESE WAR (1904–5) revealed the corruption and incompetence of the regime of NICHOLAS II. The Revolution of 1905 began in January, when troops fired on a peaceful crowd of workers who, led by a priest, were marching to the Winter Palace in St. Petersburg to petition the czar. This "bloody Sunday" was followed by months of disorders throughout Russia. In October the czar granted basic civil liberties and a parliament, or DUMA, but the first and second dumas were soon dissolved and the revolutionary movement was ruthlessly suppressed. WORLD WAR I, which began in 1914, brought the situation to a head. By March 1917 (February in the Old Style calendar), military defeats, acute civilian suffering, and government ineptness had led to food riots and strikes in Petrograd (the capital's new, less Germanic name) and Moscow. Many soldiers refused to help put down the disorders. In mid-March the czar tried unsuccessfully to dissolve the fourth duma. The insurgents seized Petrograd, the duma appointed a provisional government under Prince LVOV, and Nicholas was forced to abdicate. Most welcomed the end of autocracy, but the new government had little support, and its power was limited by the Petrograd workers' and soldiers' council, or SOVIET, which controlled troops, communications, and transport. The government called for a general amnesty, civil liberties, and a constituent assembly elected by universal suffrage, but said nothing about the war or about redistribution of land. The soviet demanded peace, and demonstrations forced the foreign minister to resign in May. In April, LENIN had returned to Russia to lead the small Bolshevik party (see BOLSHEVISM AND MENSHEVISM) under the slogans "end the war," "all land to the peasants," and "all power to the soviets." KERENSKY replaced Lvov as head of the government in July. Those who wanted to limit the soviet's power rallied around General Z.G. Kornilov, whose attempt in September (October, Old Style) to seize Petrograd was put down with the help of the Bolsheviks and other socialists. Lenin urged the soviet, in which the Bolsheviks now had a majority, to take power. On the night of Nov. 6 (Oct. 24, Old Style) Bolshevik workers and sailors captured the government buildings and the Winter Palace. The Second All-Russian Congress of Soviets approved the coup, after the Menshevik and SOCIALIST REVOLUTIONARY PARTY delegates had left the meeting. A cabinet (the Council of People's Commissars) was set up with Lenin as chairman. The Congress of Soviets called for an end to the war and gave private and church lands to the village soviets. Bolsheviks soon took Moscow and other cities. Workers' control was established in factories, banks were nationalized, and an economic council was formed. The constituent assembly met in Jan. 1918, but was disbanded by Bolshevik troops. The Cheka (political police) was set up to eliminate the opposition. In March, Russia made peace (see BREST-LITOVSK, TREATY OF). Civil war between Bolshevik (Red) and anti-Bolshevik (White) forces raged until 1920, centering in S Russia, Ukraine, and Siberia. It was accompanied by the intervention of British, American, French, and other armies, allegedly to protect Allied supplies. The Bolsheviks' military victory, due partly to the lack of cooperation among their opponents and partly to the reorganization of the Red Army by TROTSKY, was won at the cost of vast devastation.

Russian Soviet Federative Socialist Republic (RSFSR), former constituent republic of the UNION OF SOVIET SOCIALIST REPUBLICS, since 1991 the independent nation of RUSSIA.

Russian wolfhound: see BORZOI.

Russo-Japanese War, 1904–5, imperialistic conflict growing out of rival designs on MANCHURIA and Korea. Russia had penetrated those territories and refused (1904) to negotiate with Japan over spheres of influence there. Japan then bottled up the Russian fleet at Port Arthur (now Lüshun, China), defeated a Russian army at Mukden (now Shenyang), and destroyed the Russian fleet off the Tsushima islands. Peace was brought about by U.S. Pres. Theodore ROOSEVELT. Japan emerged as a world power. Russia's defeat contributed to the 1905 RUSSIAN REVOLUTION.

Russo-Turkish Wars, 1697–1878, series of campaigns in which Russia expanded at the expense of the OTTOMAN EMPIRE (Turkey). In 1696 PETER I won the first Russian victory by capturing the fortress at Azov; it was recaptured (1711) by AHMED III. In 1736 war broke out again, with Austria as a Russian ally. The Russians recaptured Azov and won a spectacular battle at Jassy, Moldavia (1739), but the treaty forced on Russia by Austria erased most of Russia's gains. The first major Russo-Turkish War (1768–74) began when Sultan Mustafa III, encouraged by France, declared war on CATHERINE II of Russia. The Russians conquered the Crimea, installed a pro-Russian khan there, and overran Moldavia and Walachia. The treaty ending the war solidified Russia's Crimea gains (Catherine annexed it outright in 1783), gave Russia a voice in Turkish domestic matters, and allowed it navigation rights on the Black Sea. These developments alarmed the Western powers, exacerbating what became known as the EASTERN QUESTION. Catherine's second war (1787–92) gave Russia the SW UKRAINE, with Odessa. The war of 1806–12 gave it Bessarabia. The war of 1828–29, linked with the Greek War of Independence, completed the conquest of the Caucasus and brought Russian power to its zenith. But in 1853 Turkey had the backing of Great Britain and France in the CRIMEAN WAR; the Congress of PARIS (1856) ending that war was a significant setback for Russian influence in the Middle East. The last Russo-Turkish War resulted from an anti-Turkish uprising (1875) in Bosnia and Hercegovina. Serbia and Montenegro joined in, and Russia openly entered the war in 1877. The Treaty of San Stefano (1878) ended the war on terms so beneficial to Russia that the Western powers, in alarm, revised the terms at the Congress of BERLIN.

rust, in chemistry, the result of the corrosion of iron, by way of OXIDATION, in the presence of water. The combination of iron with oxygen results in the deterioration of the surface of the metal. Rust is brittle and easily flakes off the metal.

rust, in plant pathology, name for a FUNGUS of the order Uredinales and for the plant diseases such fungi cause. Rusts form reddish patches of spores on their hosts. Some species grow entirely on one host; others need host plants of two separate species to complete their life cycles (e.g., the cedar rust, which grows on CEDAR and APPLE trees). Rusts attack GRAIN crops and many fruits, vegetables, ornamentals and trees.

Rust Belt, economic region in the NE U.S., centered on Illinois, Indiana, Michigan, Ohio, and Pennsylvania. The term gained currency in the 1970s as this formerly dominant industrial area suffered from factory abandonment and manufacturing shifts to SUNBELT cities and Mexico, unemployment, outmigration, loss of electoral votes, and overall decline. The states began to recover, however, in the early 1990s.

rutabaga: see TURNIP.

Ruth, Babe (George Herman Ruth), 1895–1948, American baseball player; b. Baltimore. He was the most famous player in the game's history. Signed at 19 by the minor-league Baltimore Orioles, he was sold to the Boston Red Sox, for whom he became an outstanding pitcher (1914–19), winning 87 games and losing 44. After being moved to the outfield because of his hitting prowess, he was sold (1920) to the New York Yankees, where he became a baseball legend. As a Yankee he led the league in home runs for 10 seasons, setting (1927) the existing record of 60 home runs in one season. (Roger MARIS hit 61 in a longer schedule.) "The Bambino" hit 714 home runs in his career, a record finally broken (1974) by Henry AARON. He led the Yankees to seven pennants, and Yankee Stadium, built in 1923, came to be known as "the house that Ruth built." He played briefly for the Boston Braves in 1935.

Ruth, book of the OLD TESTAMENT, eighth in the Authorized Version, tells the story of the fidelity of a Moabite widow (Ruth) to her widowed mother-in-law (Naomi). Ruth returns with Naomi to Bethlehem from Moab and there marries Naomi's kinsman Boaz. Ruth and Boaz were ancestors of DAVID. The story probably dates in final form from 450 to 250 B.C.

Ruthenia, Latinized form of *Russia.* The term was applied to Ukraine when the medieval princes of Galich took the title kings of Ruthenia. Later, in Austria-Hungary, *Ruthenians* denoted the Ukranian population of W Ukraine. After 1918 *Ruthenia* referred only to the easternmost province of Czechoslovakia, also known as the Carpathian, or Transcarpathian, Ukraine; it became part of the Soviet Ukraine in 1945.

ruthenium (Ru), metallic element, discovered in 1827 by G.W. Osann in crude platinum ore. It is a hard, lustrous, silver-gray metal that is usually alloyed with other metals to provide hardness and corrosion resistance. Its compounds are used to color ceramics and glass. See ELEMENT (table); PERIODIC TABLE.

Rutherford, Ernest Rutherford, 1st **Baron,** 1871–1937, English physicist; b. New Zealand. He taught at McGill Univ., Montreal (1898–1907) and the Univ. of Manchester (1907–19) and was director from 1919 of the Cavendish Laboratory, Cambridge. Rutherford discovered and named alpha and beta radiation (see RADIOACTIVITY) and helped propose a theory of radioactive transformation of atoms for which he received the 1908 Nobel Prize in chemistry. On the basis of experiments carried out under his direction, he concluded (1911) that the ATOM is a small, heavy nucleus surrounded by orbital electrons. Rutherford was the first to split atomic nuclei artificially.

rutherfordium (Rf), artificial radioactive TRANSURANIUM ELEMENT. Claims for its production have been made by a Soviet group in Dubna who, in 1964, bombarded plutonium with neon ions to obtain, apparently, the Rf^{260} isotope, and by an American group at the Univ. of California, Berkeley who, in 1969, bombarded californium with carbon nuclei to obtain the Rf^{257} and Rf^{259}, and possibly the Rf^{258}, isotopes. It is also called kurchatovium (Ku) and unnilquadium (Unq). See ELEMENT (table); PERIODIC TABLE.

rutile, mineral, one of three forms of titanium dioxide (TiO_2). It occurs in crystals, often in twins or rosettes, and is typically brownish red, although there are black varieties. Rutile is found in igneous and metamorphic rocks, chiefly in Switzerland, Norway, Brazil, and parts of the U.S.

Rutland, city (1990 pop. 18,230), seat of Rutland co., W Vt., on the Otter and East creeks; settled c.1770, inc. as a city 1892. It has diverse small industries, and marble quarrying, begun c.1845, still flourishes nearby. Headquarters for the Green Mountain National Forest, Rutland is a tourist center located near many lakes and ski areas.

Rutledge, Ann, 1813?–1835, American innkeeper's daughter, linked in romantic speculation to Abraham LINCOLN; lived in New Salem, Ill. Her death grieved Lincoln deeply, and from this one fact, W.H. Herndon wove the story (denied by Mrs. Lincoln and found unconvincing by historians) of Lincoln's love for her. Actually, Ann was engaged to Lincoln's friend John McNamar.

Rutledge, John, 1739–1800, American statesman and jurist; b. Charleston, S.C. A political force in South Carolina, where he served as president (1776–78) and governor (1779–82), he was twice a delegate (1774–76, 1782–83) to the CONTINENTAL CONGRESS and was a delegate to the 1787 FEDERAL CONSTITUTIONAL CONVENTION. He served as associate justice of the U.S. SUPREME COURT (1789–91) and was named second chief justice in 1795, but the Senate rejected the nomination and he sat for only five months.

Rutskoi or **Rutskoy, Aleksandr Vladimirovich,** 1947–, Russian politician; b. Ukraine. A Russian nationalist and former air force officer who fought in AFGHANISTAN, he was YELTSIN's vice presidential running mate in 1991. As vice president, Rutskoi supported Yeltsin during the coup attempt against GORBACHEV, but he later became Yeltsin's critic and rival. In 1993, after Yeltsin suspended the parliament, its deputies named Rutskoi acting president. Rutskoi called for an armed uprising to oust Yeltsin, but it was crushed by the army and he was jailed.

Ruysdael, Jacob van: see RUISDAEL, JACOB VAN.

Rwanda [ro͝oän′dä], officially Republic of Rwanda, republic (1992 est. pop. 8,206,000), 10,169 sq mi (26,338 sq km), E central Africa, bordered by Zäire (W), Uganda (N), Tanzania (E), and Burundi (S). KIGALI is the capital. Most of the country, consisting of steep mountains and deep valleys, is situated at 5,000 ft (1,520 m) or higher. The Virunga mountain range N of Lake Kivu rises to 14,787 ft (4,507 m) at Mount Karisimbi. The economy is overwhelmingly agricultural, largely of the subsistence type. The major cash crops are coffee, tea, and pyrethrum; plaintains, cassava, sweet potatoes, pulses, and sorghum are among the food crops. Tin ore, wolframite, beryl, and colombo-tantalite are mined in large quantities. Manufacturing is limited to basic consumer goods, textiles, and chemicals. Economic development is impeded by a large population and lack of easy access to the sea. About 90% of the population are Hutu, 9% are Tutsi, and 1% are Twa (PYGMIES). About half follow traditional beliefs. Most of the rest are Roman Catholic; there are some Muslim Tutsi. Kinyarwanda and French are the official languages, but Swahili is widely used.

History. The early history of Rwanda is similar to that of BURUNDI. By the late 18th cent. a single Tutsi-ruled state, headed by a *mwami* (king), occupied much of Rwanda and dominated the Hutu, the vast majority of the population. In 1890 Rwanda accepted German overrule without resistance and became part of German East Africa. Belgian forces occupied the country in WORLD WAR I, and in 1919 it became part of the Belgian mandate of RUANDI-URUNDI (a UN trust territory in 1946). In 1957 the Hutu demanded a greater voice in the country's affairs, and on the accession (1959) of Kigeri V fighting erupted between them and the Tutsi. The victorious Hutu gained control of the country, and some 100,000 Tutsi fled to nearby states. Rwanda became independent in 1962, with Grégoire Kayibanda as president. In 1973 a coup installed Maj. Gen. Juvénal Habyarimana as head of a military regime. Civilian rule was restored under a new constitution that established (1978) a one-party state, but Habyarimana remained president. In 1990 Rwanda was invaded by forces composed largely of Tutsi exiles. Intermittent warfare continued into 1993, when a peace accord was signed. The treaty calls for power-sharing and the repatriation of Tutsi exiles.

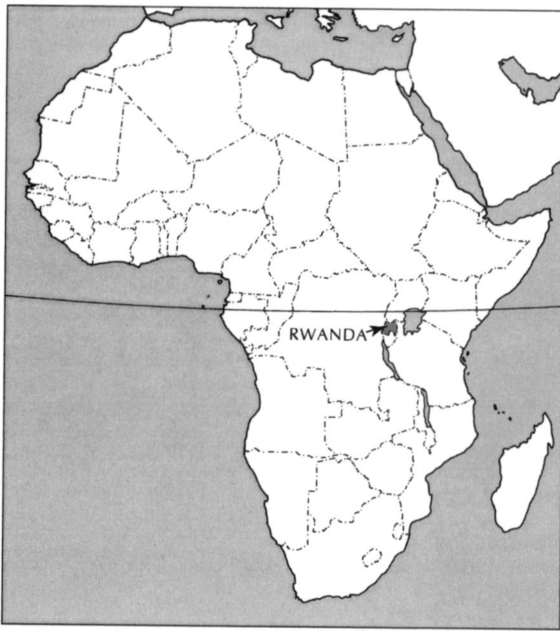

Ryan, Nolan 1947–, American baseball pitcher; b. Refugio, Texas. A right-hander with a blazing fastball, he played with the New York Mets, California Angels, Houston Astros, and Texas Rangers while in the major leagues (1967–93). He had 324 career wins, including a record seven no-hitters, and set records for career (5714) and single-season (383) strikeouts.

Ryder, Albert Pinkham, 1847–1917, American painter; b. New Bedford, Mass. He produced only about 160 canvases, now considered among the finest in American art. Small in size, they are grand in design and feeling, luminous and subtle in color. Moonlight and the sea predominate in paintings that evoke a lonely, poetic mood. Ryder's paintings are in most major American museums, e.g., *Death on a Pale Horse* (Cleveland Mus.) and *The Flying Dutchman* (National Gall., Wash., D.C.).

rye, cereal plant (*Secale cereale*) of the GRASS family, important chiefly in central and N Europe. The GRAIN, or seed, is used for pumpernickel and the lighter-colored rye bread (made from a mixture of rye and wheat flour), as a stock feed, and in the distillation of whiskey and gin. The plant, which grows well in areas where the soil is too poor and the climate too cool for wheat, is also grown for hay and pasturage and as green manure and a cover crop.

Russia leads in world production. ERGOT, a fungous infection, is poisonous and can make rye unsafe for use.

Rye House Plot, conspiracy (1683) to assassinate CHARLES II of England and his brother (later JAMES II) at Rumbold's Rye House in Hertfordshire. The plot miscarried, and its discovery led to the executions of the great Whig leaders Lord John Russell and Algernon Sidney on flimsy evidence.

Ryukyu Islands, archipelago (1990 est. pop. 1,500,000), SW Japan, c.1,850 sq mi (4,790 sq km), extending c.650 mi (1,050 km) SW from Kyushu, between the East China and Philippine seas. The Ryukyus consist of three principal groups: the Amami Islands (N); Okinawa Islands, including OKINAWA; and Sakishima Islands (S). The climate is subtropical, with heavy rains and frequent typhoons. The entire archipelago was incorporated into the Japanese empire in 1879 and passed to the U.S. in 1945. The Amami group was returned to Japan in 1953, the rest of the archipelago in 1972.

S

S, chemical symbol of the element SULFUR.

Sá, Mem de [sä], d. 1572, Portuguese governor general of Brazil (1557?–1572). He founded the city of RIO DE JANEIRO.

Saadi: see SADI.

Saadia ben Joseph al-Fayumi, 882–942, Jewish scholar, known as Saadia Gaon; b. Egypt. Under his leadership the great Jewish Academy at Sura, Babylonia, became the highest seat of Jewish learning. He compiled a prayer book, or *siddur;* translated the Bible into Arabic; and wrote on Hebrew grammar, on philosophy, and on religion.

Saarinen, Eero [sä'rĭnĕn], 1910–61, Finnish-American architect. He established a reputation with the General Motors Technical Center, Warren, Mich. (1951–55). An innovator, he is famous for the circular chapel and concrete-dome auditorium (1955) at the Massachusetts Institute of Technology, and for the Trans World Airlines terminal, N.Y.C. His Dulles International Airport, Chantilly, Va., was finished posthumously. His father, **Eliel Saarinen,** 1873–1950, was an architect and city planner. He built the Helsinki railway station, and many buildings in the U.S.

Saarland, state (1990 est. pop. 1,065,000), 991 sq mi (2,567 sq km), SW Germany. The area was formerly called the Saar or the Saar Territory. Saarland is highly industrialized, with iron and steel manufacturing based on vast coal fields. Saarbrücken is the capital. The autonomous Saar Territory was created by the Treaty of VERSAILLES. In 1935 a plebiscite reunited it with Germany. After WORLD WAR II it was again made autonomous, but French economic influence there caused friction between France and West Germany. From 1957 until German reunification in 1990, Saarland was a state in West Germany.

Sabah, self-governing E Malaysian state (1990 est. pop. 1,470,000), 29,545 sq mi (76,522 sq km), on the South China and Sulu seas, bordered by Kalimantan (Indonesian Borneo, S) and Brunei and Sarawak (W). The capital is Kota Kinabalu. Mountainous and densely forested, it exports oil, timber, rubber, and copra. It constituted the British protectorate of North Borneo from 1882 until it joined the Federation of Malaysia in 1963.

Sabbatai Zevi [säbätī' tzvē'], 1626–76, Jewish mystic and pseudo-Messiah; b. Turkey. A student of the CABALA, in 1648 he proclaimed himself the Messiah, named 1666 as the millennium, and gathered a host of followers. He attempted to land in Constantinople in 1666, was captured, and, to escape death, embraced Islam. The Sabbatean movement was revived in the 18th cent. by Jacob FRANK.

Sabbath [Heb., = repose], last day of the week (Saturday), observed as a holy day of rest by the Jews. Early Christians observed the first day of the week in commemoration of the Resurrection; hence Sunday became the Christian Sabbath.

Sabin, Albert Bruce, 1906–93, American physician and microbiologist; b. Belostok, Russia (now Białystok, Poland); came to U.S., 1921. In 1939 he began teaching research pediatrics at the Univ. of Cincinnati. A researcher on viral and other infectious diseases, he developed (c.1959) a live-virus vaccine for immunization against POLIOMYELITIS.

Sabines, ancient people of central Italy, in the Sabine Hills, NE of Rome. From the earliest days there was a Sabine element in Rome. The Sabines warred with Rome, but by the 3d cent. B.C., they were completely amalgamated.

Sacajawea, Sacagawea, or **Sakakawea,** sometimes called **Bird Woman,** 1784–1884?, Shoshone woman, sole woman and guide on the LEWIS AND CLARK EXPEDITION. She had been captured and sold to a Mandan, then traded to Toussaint Charbonneau, interpreter for the expedition. When the expedition reached her native upper Missouri R. region, she proved invaluable as a guide and interpreter. On the return journey, she and Charbonneau remained with the Mandan. Some historians believe that she died c.1812.

Sac and Fox, closely related Native American tribes with an Eastern Woodlands culture and some Plains traits (see NORTH AMERICA, INDIGENOUS PEOPLES OF), belonging to the Algonquian branch of the Algonquian-Wakashan language stock (see NATIVE AMERICAN LANGUAGES). In the 17th cent. about 6,500 Sac and Fox lived by farming and hunting in NE Wisconsin. The Fox, fierce warriors, fought the French, who by 1730 had all but exterminated the tribe. Survivors joined the Sac (or Sauk) and went to Illinois. A fraudulent treaty forced them to move (1831) to Iowa, but they returned (1832) and fought the BLACKHAWK WAR against U.S. troops. In 1990 there were 4,517 Sac and Fox in the U.S.

Sacco-Vanzetti Case. In Apr. 1920, Nicola Sacco and Bartolomeo Vanzetti were arrested for the murder of a paymaster and his guard in South Braintree, Mass. Both men were anarchists (see ANARCHISM) and feared deportation; they gave false statements and were armed. Despite contradictory evidence, both were found guilty in July 1921 and sentenced to death. Many believed that the trial had been unfair and that the two men's political beliefs had convicted them. By 1927, when the Massachusetts supreme court and a governor's commission upheld the proceedings, the case had become a cause célèbre. The execution of Sacco and Vanzetti on Aug. 22, 1927, was preceded by worldwide sympathy demonstrations, and debate on the case continued in later years.

Sachs, Hans [zäks], 1494–1576, German poet, leading MEISTERSINGER of the Nuremberg school. A shoemaker, he wrote many songs, tales in verse (*Schwänke*), and Shrovetide plays. "The Nightingale of Wittenberg" is a poem in LUTHER's honor. Sachs is a key figure in Richard WAGNER's *Die Meistersinger.*

Sachs, Nelly, 1891–1970, German poet and translator. After 1940 she lived in Sweden. Her poetry describes the suffering of the European Jews, e.g., *O the Chimneys* (1967). She shared the 1966 Nobel Prize in literature with S.Y. AGNON.

Sackville-West, V(ictoria Mary), 1892–1962, English writer; wife of Sir Harold NICOLSON. A member of the BLOOMSBURY GROUP, she published poetry, e.g., *The Land* (1926), but is better known for her novels *The Edwardians* (1930) and *All Passion Spent* (1931).

sacrament, an outward sign of something sacred. Christians generally believe sacraments were instituted by Jesus and are visible signs of invisible GRACE. Traditionally, the Orthodox, Roman Catholics, and certain Anglicans believe in seven sacraments—Eucharist (see COMMUNION), BAPTISM, CONFIRMATION, PENANCE, ANOINTING THE SICK, matrimony (see MARRIAGE), and HOLY ORDERS—which, they hold, bestow grace. Most Protestant denominations recognize two sacraments, baptism and communion, and hold that faith, rather than the sacraments, provides grace.

Sacramento, city (1990 pop. 369,365; met. area 1,481,102), state capital and seat of Sacramento co., central Calif., on the Sacramento R. at its confluence with the American R.; settled 1839, inc. 1850. A deepwater port, it is the shipping and processing center for a rich fruit-growing and truck-farming area, and important in electronics and missile manufacture. Government and the military are major employers. Points of interest include Fort Sutter, the capitol building (1860), and the Crocker Art Gallery. The city grew after gold was discovered (1848) at nearby Sutter's Mill, and it became state capital in 1854.

Sacramento, longest river in California, flowing c.380 mi (610 km) SW from near Mt. Shasta to join the San Joaquin R. in a wide delta at San Francisco Bay. Navigable c.260 mi (420 km) to Red Bluff by small vessels, the Sacramento contributes irrigation water to arid S California as part of the Central Valley Project. Keswick and Shasta are the chief dams.

Sadat, Anwar al-, 1918–81, Egyptian president (1970–81). He succeeded NASSER as president. In 1973 he led Egypt into war with Israel (see ARAB-ISRAELI WARS), but later he joined (1978) with Israeli premier Menachem BEGIN in negotiating the CAMP DAVID ACCORDS. He and Begin shared the 1978 Nobel Peace Prize. He was assassinated by Muslim zealots.

Sade, Donatien Alphonse François, comte de [säd], 1740–1814, French author, known as the **marquis de Sade.** Charged with numerous sexual offenses, he spent 27 years in prisons or asylums, writing obscene romances, including *Justine* (1791). His theory that since sexual deviation and criminal acts exist in nature, they are natural, foreshadowed modern psychological thought. *Sadism,* the infliction of pain to attain sexual pleasure, is named for him.

Sadi or **Saadi,** 1184–1291, Persian poet, one of the finest Sufi writers (see SUFISM). His masterpiece is *Garden of Roses* (1258), a miscellany of prose and poetry suffused with warmth of feeling and lofty religious thought.

Safdie, Moshe, 1938–, Israeli-Canadian architect. He was the designer of "Habitat," a system of prefabricated housing modules originally built for Montreal's Expo '67. His more recent work includes the Museum of Civilization, Quebec (1984) and the National Gallery of Canada, Ottawa (1984).

safflower, Eurasian thistlelike herb (*Carthamus tinctorius*) of the COMPOSITE family; also called false saffron. It has long been cultivated in S Asia and Egypt for food and medicine, and as a substitute for true SAFFRON dye; in the U.S. it is important as the source of safflower oil, used in cooking.

saffron, fall-flowering plant (*Crocus sativus*) of the IRIS family, and the yellow dye obtained from it. Native to Asia Minor, it has long been cultivated for the orange-yellow stigmas of its pistils (see FLOWER), which yield saffron powder, the source of the dye. The powder is used in perfumes and medicines and for flavoring. One ounce of saffron powder requires stigmas from about 4,000 flowers.

Safire, William L., 1929–, American journalist and speechwriter; b. N.Y.C. Since 1973, his editorial columns in the New York *Times* have provided a consistent conservative editorial voice. His *On Language* column decries abuses of language. From 1969 to 1973 he was a speechwriter for Pres. NIXON.

saga, in Old Norse Literature, a narrative in prose or verse centering on a legendary or historical figure or family. Sagas were composed from the 11th to the mid-14th cent. and first written down c.1200. Exemplary are the *Sturlungasaga* (a history saga), *Njala* (a family saga), and *Volsungasaga* (a mythical heroic saga), in all of which the epic element is strong and the depiction of heroic society vivid. Other noted sagas are the *Heimskringla* of SNORRI STURLUSON, the *Laxdœla,* the *Grettla,* the *Frithjof,* and *Gisli.*

Sagan, Carl (Edward), 1934–, American astronomer and popularizer of science; b. N.Y.C. Sagan is known for his research on the possibilities of extraterrestrial life (see EXOBIOLOGY), including the experimental production of amino acids from basic chemicals by radiation, and has been involved with several NASA space probes. His books include *The Dragons of Eden* (1977; Pulitzer), *A Path Where No Man Thought* (1990), with Richard Turco, on NUCLEAR WINTER, and *Shadows of Forgotten Ancestors* (1992), with Ann Druyan. He created and hosted the television science series *Cosmos* (1980).

Sagan, Françoise, pseudonym of **Françoise Quoirez,** 1935–, French novelist. She became famous with her precocious first work, *Bonjour tristesse* (1954), acclaimed for its portrayal of a sophisticated, disillusioned French society. Her many other novels include *Un Certain Sourire* (1956) and *Aimez-vous Brahms?* (1959).

sage, aromatic herb or shrub (genus *Salvia*) of the MINT family. The common sage of herb gardens (*S. officinalis*), native from S Europe to Asia Minor, is a strongly-scented shrubby perennial; its dried leaves are used as a seasoning and in a tea. Ornamental sages, popularly called salvia, include the scarlet sage (*S. solendens*), noted for its neat spikes of usually red flowers.

sagebrush, name for several species of the genus *Artemesia,* deciduous shrubs of the COMPOSITE family, especially abundant in arid regions of W North America. The common sagebrush (*A. tridentata*) is a silvery-gray, low shrub with a pungent odor of sage, although it is unrelated to true SAGE. Common in the West, sagebrush is an important forage plant. It is the state flower of Nevada.

Saginaw, city (1990 pop. 69,512), seat of Saginaw co., S Mich., on the Saginaw R., 15 mi (24 km) from Lake Huron; inc. 1857. Located in an agricultural area long inhabited by Native Americans, it was a 19th-cent. fur and lumber center, and is now an industrial city producing diverse manufactures. Salt, coal, and oil deposits are nearby.

Sahara, world's largest desert, c.3,500,000 sq mi (9,065,000 sq km), extending c.3,000 mi (4,830 km) east to west and c.1,200 mi (1,930 km) north to south across N Africa; it is bordered on the south by the SAHEL. Rainfall ranges from less than 5 in. (12.7 cm) to 10 in. (25 cm), with dry periods occasionally lasting for years. Nighttime temperatures often drop below freezing, and daytime temperatures have been recorded at over 135°F (57°C) in the shade. The surface of the desert ranges from sand dunes (erg), covering about 15%, to stone plateaus (hammada) and gravel surfaces (reg), covering about 70%, to several deeply dissected mountain massifs (Ahaggar, Tibesti, and Aïr), infamous in the past for the shelter they provided to marauders preying on desert travelers. Vast underground aquifers, filled with water thought to date from the Pleistocene epoch, when the Sahara was wetter, underlie much of the region, and there are important deposits of iron ore, phosphates, oil, and natural gas.

Sahel, semiarid region extending across N central Africa from Senegal (W) to Ethiopia (E). It has more rainfall (8–16 in./20–40 cm) and better grazing lands than the SAHARA desert, to the north, but it is periodically afflicted by droughts that reduce its normally meager water supply and shatter its grazing and agricultural economy. The drought of 1967–74 was particularly devastating, causing mass migration and contributing to the starvation of hundreds of thousands of people.

Saida: see SIDON.

Saigon: see HO CHI MINH CITY.

sailfish, marine game and food FISH of the family Istiophoridae, related to the SWORDFISH and MARLIN. Its high, wide dorsal fin, or sail, is deep blue with black spots. The average length of a sailfish is 6 ft (180 cm). The Atlantic species (*Istiophorus americanus*), found as far north as Cape Cod in summer, averages 60 lb (27 kg). The Pacific *I. orientalis* grows to 100 lb (45 kg).

sailing, as a sport, the art of navigating a sailboat for recreational or competitive purposes. In racing, competition is generally restricted to boats of the same class. Boats are classified according to their sails and masts. The most common types are the sloop (one mast, two sails), schooner (usually two masts and five sails), yawl (two masts, four sails), and ketch (two masts, five sails). Sloops, from 10 to 70 ft (3.05–21.34 m) are generally used for racing, and the other types, usually more than 20 ft (6.1 m) long, for recreational cruising. Especially popular today are the 16 to 23 ft (4.88–7.01 m) one-design boats, such as the Star (designed 1911), Snipe, Comet, Mercury, and Lightning. Although sailing is popular throughout the world, international competition since World War II has been dominated by the U.S., Great Britain, Australia, and the USSR (now Russia). The oldest and most prestigious event in international racing is the *America's* Cup series for large sloops, begun in 1851 and won by the U.S. until 1983, when it was taken by the Australians. In 1987 the U.S. regained the cup. The results of the 1988 race, in which New Zealand unsuccessfully challenged the U.S. and nonstandard boats were used, were disputed in court but upheld on appeal. Since 1992, larger, faster boats have been used in the cup races. Other important sailboat events include the Admiral's Cup, the Bermuda Race, the Trans-Pacific Race, and the Whitbread Round the World Race. Sailing competition has been part of the Olympics since 1900.

sailplane: see GLIDER.

Saint. For canonized and uncanonized saints, see under the proper name, e.g., THOMAS AQUINAS, SAINT. For surnames and place names beginning thus, see in alphabetical position here: thus, SAINT EXUPÉRY, ANTOINE DE; SAINT LOUIS.

saint, in Christian theology, a person who shares in the holiness of God. To New Testament authors, the church was the community of saints, but the word came to be used for those who live in heaven. The Virgin MARY is the chief saint, and the ANGELS are counted as saints. The Roman Catholic and Orthodox LITURGIES commemorate the saints with special feast days. In East and West criteria for recognition of sainthood are martyrdom, holiness of life, miracles in life and after death, and a popular cult. The addition of a name to the official list of saints is called canonization. In 1969 the Roman Catholic Church dropped certain saints, including St. Christopher, from its liturgical calendar because of doubts about their historicity.

Saint Augustine, city (1990 pop. 11,692), seat of St. Johns co., NE Fla.; founded 1565, inc. 1824. The oldest city in the U.S., it is a port and tourist and fishing center with some light industry. Famous sights include two Spanish structures that are now national monuments, the Castillo de San Marcos (1672–96) and Fort Matanzas (1742). The city's strategic importance made it the object of fighting on many occasions from 1586, when it was attacked by Sir Francis DRAKE, through the CIVIL WAR, when it was occupied by Union forces.

Saint Bartholomew's Day, massacre of, murder of French Protestants, or HUGUENOTS, by Roman Catholics, beginning on Aug. 24, 1572. The presence of many Huguenots in Paris for the wedding of Henry of Navarre (later HENRY IV) gave CATHERINE DE' MEDICI and the reluctant King CHARLES IX a chance to plan a general massacre. Admiral COLIGNY was the first victim. The massacre spread to other parts of France and caused the resumption of the WARS OF RELIGION (1562–98).

Saint Bernard, massive WORKING DOG; shoulder height, 25–29 in. (64–74 cm); weight, 140–170 lb (64–77 kg). There is a smooth-coated and a rough-coated variety, both in mixtures of white, red, and brindle. Bred (18th cent.) by monks of the Hospice of the St. Bernard Pass, in the Swiss Alps, for rescue and guide work, the breed was perfected in 19th-cent. England.

Saint Catharines, city (1991 pop. 129,300), SE Ontario, Canada, part of the regional municipality of Niagara (1991 pop. 393,936). It is an industrial city located on the WELLAND SHIP CANAL. Manufactures include canned fruit, wine, automobile parts, and electrical equipment. The city was founded in 1790. Port Dalhousie, site of the annual Royal Henley Regatta, became part of St. Catharines in 1961.

Saint Christopher and Nevis: see SAINT KITTS-NEVIS.

St. Clair, Arthur, 1743–1818, American general; b. Scotland. During the AMERICAN REVOLUTION, he abandoned Fort TICONDEROGA without a fight (1777) but was exonerated by a court-martial (1778). He was the first governor of the NORTHWEST TERRITORY (1787–1802), and was defeated by Native American forces there in 1792.

Saint Clair, Lake, on the U.S.-Canada border, NE of Detroit, Mich. Part of the St. Lawrence & Great Lakes Waterway, it is connected with Lake Huron to the north by the St. Clair R. and with Lake Erie to the south by the Detroit R. Its area is c.490 sq mi (1,270 sq km).

Saint Croix [sānt kroi], largest of the U.S. VIRGIN ISLANDS.

St. Denis, Ruth [dĕn'ĭs], 1877?–1968, American dancer; b. Newark, N.J., as Ruth Dennis. She is known for "Oriental" dances that had widespread influence on MODERN DANCE. With her husband Ted Shawn, she founded the Denishawn schools in Los Angeles and New York City (1920). Works include *Radha* (1906) and *The Nautch* (1908).

Sainte-Beuve, Charles Augustin [săNt-böv], 1804–69, French literary critic and historian. Much of his vast critical output was collected as *Monday Chats* (1851–62). His great work was *Port-Royal* (1840–59), a six-volume history of 17th-cent. French culture. Though his work reveals his taste, learning, and passion for truth, his biographical approach to literature has been largely abandoned.

Saint Exupéry, Antoine de [săNtĕgzüpārē'], 1900–44, French author and aviator, lost in action in World War II. His writings, e.g., *Night Flight* (1931), reflect his feeling for the open skies and his love of freedom of action. His fable *The Little Prince* (1943) is beloved by adults and children alike.

Saint Gall, Ger. *Sankt Gallen,* city (1990 pop. 73,191), capital of Saint Gall canton, NE Switzerland, on the Lake of Constance. The textile center of E Switzerland, it grew around the hermitage of St. Gall and joined the Swiss Confederation in 1454. Its library of medieval manuscripts is world famous.

Saint-Gaudens, Augustus [sānt-gôd'ənz], 1848–1907, foremost American sculptor of his time; b. Ireland. He is best known for his heroic public monuments, such as the figures of Abraham Lincoln (Lincoln Park, Chicago) and Gen. Sherman (Central Park, N.Y.C.). He also did portrait tablets, plaques, and low reliefs.

Saint George's, city (1989 est. pop. 7,800), capital of GRENADA.

Saint Gotthard, mountain massif in the Swiss ALPS, rising to 10,472 ft (3,192 m). It is crossed by the Saint Gotthard Pass (6,935 ft/2,114 m) and by the Saint Gotthard Tunnel (9¼ mi/15 km long), one of the world's longest rail tunnels. A second, 31-mi (50-km) tunnel is planned; it would be completed in 2010.

Saint Helena, island (1992 est. pop. 6,700), 47 sq mi (122 sq km) in the S Atlantic, 1,200 mi (1,931 km) W of Africa. With ASCENSION and TRISTAN DA CUNHA, it comprises the British dependency of St. Helena. Discovered uninhabited by the Portuguese in 1502, it became a crown colony in 1834. It is best known as the place of exile (1815–21) of NAPOLEON I.

Saint Helens, Mount, active volcano, 8,365 ft (2,551 m; 9,677 ft/2,950 m before its 1980 eruption), SW Washington, in the Cascade Range. Dormant for 120 years, it erupted violently on May 18, 1980, following a series of earth tremors beginning Mar. 20. The eruption killed some 65 persons, sent a volcanic plume 60,000 ft (18,300 m) into the air, triggered fires and mudslides, and blanketed a large area with volcanic ash. Less violent eruptions followed, notably in Apr. 1982. The volcano and surrounding area are now a national monument.

Saint John, city (1991 pop. 74,969), S New Brunswick, E Canada, at the mouth of the Saint John R. on the Bay of Fundy. It has an excellent, ice-free harbor and is the commercial, industrial, and transportation center of New Brunswick. There are pulp and paper mills, oil refineries, large shipyards, and food-processing plants. The city was established (1631–35) as a French trading post and passed several times between France and England before coming under permanent English rule in 1758. Its most rapid growth began with the arrival in 1783 of a large party of UNITED EMPIRE LOYALISTS from the newly independent U.S. Then known as Paar Town, the city became St. John in 1785. The "reversing falls" of the St. John R., caused by the exceptionally high Fundy tides, are famous.

Saint John: see VIRGIN ISLANDS.

Saint John's, city (1986 est. pop. 36,000), capital of ANTIGUA AND BARBUDA.

Saint John's, city (1991 pop. 95,770), provincial capital, SE Newfoundland, E Canada, overlooking a fine harbor. Its major industries include fish processing and the manufacture and repair of fishing equipment, boats, and marine engines. One of the oldest settlements in North America, its site was discovered and named by John CABOT in 1497 and thought to have been settled shortly thereafter. It was formally occupied by England in 1583 and taken several times by the French before coming under permanent English rule in 1762.

Saint John the Divine, Cathedral of, New York City. Chartered by the Episcopal diocese in 1873 and begun in 1892, it is still under construction. In 1911 the original Romanesque design was altered to the Gothic style design of Ralph Adams CRAM. The nave was built (1916–43), but other construction was interrupted by World War II. In 1979 work on the cathedral was resumed.

Saint Kitts-Nevis, officially Federation of Saint Kitts and Nevis, island nation (1992 est. pop. 40,100), 101 sq mi (262 sq km), West Indies, in the Leeward Islands. The capital is Basseterre, on St. Kitts. Nevis, the smaller island, has its own assembly and a large degree of political autonomy with respect to its own internal affairs. Agriculture dominates economy, with sugar growing and refining providing the largest share of the islands' export income. In recent years tourism has grown in importance, and the government has encouraged diversification of the agricultural sector and development of manufacturing. The vast majority of the population are descendants of Africans originally brought to the islands as slaves. English is the official language. The Anglican and other Protestant churches are the predominant faiths. The islands were visited (1493) by Columbus but not settled until 1623 (by the British) and 1625 (by the French). They were awarded (1783) to Britain. In 1967, together with ANGUILLA, which returned to British rule in 1971, they became autonomous in internal affairs, and achieved full independence in 1983. Since 1980 the government has been led by Prime Min. Kennedy Simmonds of the People's Action Movement.

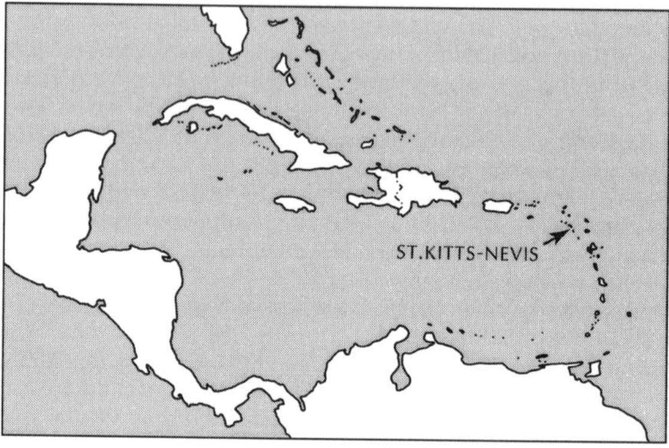

St. Laurent, Louis Stephen [săN lōräN′], 1882–1973, prime minister of CANADA (1948–57). He was minister of internal affairs (1946–48) in Mackenzie KING's government, and succeeded him as Liberal party leader and prime minister.

Saint Lawrence, major North American river, flowing 744 mi (1,197 km) NE from Lake Ontario to the Gulf of St. Lawrence and forming 120 mi (193 km) of the U.S.-Canada border. Although closed by ice from mid-December to mid-April, the river is the chief outlet for shipping on the Great Lakes, having been canalized as part of the SAINT LAWRENCE SEAWAY.

Saint Lawrence Seaway, international waterway, E North America, built by the U.S. and Canada and opened in 1959, that allows oceangoing vessels access to Lake Ontario through a 27-ft (8-m) channel on the SAINT LAWRENCE R. Principal locks on the seaway are St. Lambert (18 ft/5.5 m lift); Côte Ste Catherine (30 ft/9.1 m), bypassing Lachine Rapids; Lower and Upper Beauharnois (82 ft/25 m, including the Beauharnois Canal, built 1932); Bertrand H. Snell (45 ft/13.7 m); Dwight D. Eisenhower (38 ft/11.6 m); and the Iroquois Guard Lock (3 ft/91 cm). Hydroelectric facilities are operated along the seaway, which, together with improved channels between the GREAT LAKES, forms the St. Lawrence & Great Lakes Waterway, linking all of the lakes with the Atlantic Ocean.

St. Leger, Barry, 1737–89, British officer in the AMERICAN REVOLUTION. During the SARATOGA CAMPAIGN (1777) he laid siege to Fort Stanwix. He was forced to retreat to Canada when his frightened troops, mostly Native Americans, deserted.

Saint Louis, city (1990 pop. 396,685; met. area 2,444,099), E Mo., on the Mississippi R., below the mouth of the Missouri; settled 1764, inc. as a city 1822. The second largest city in the state, it is a major river port, rail hub, financial center, and market. Its manufactures include chemicals, transportation equipment, electronic components, textiles, and beer. Originally a fur-trading post, it was held by the French and the Spanish and passed to the U.S. by the LOUISIANA PURCHASE. The gateway to the Missouri R. and the West, St. Louis grew rapidly after the War of 1812. Eero SAARINEN's Gateway Arch, 630 ft (192 m) high, is its best-known landmark. Washington Univ. and the St. Louis Symphony Orchestra are two of the city's many well-known institutions.

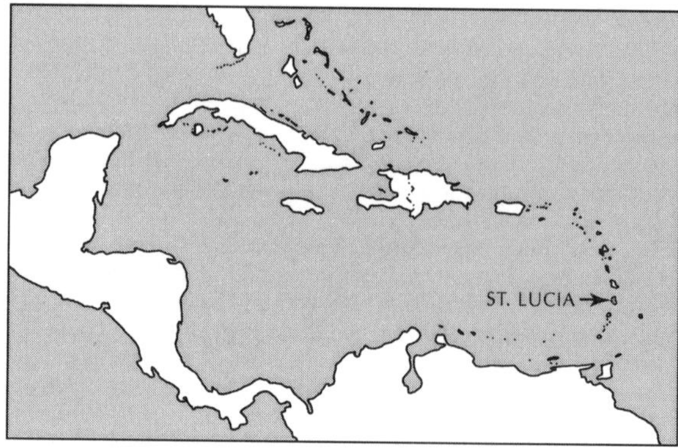

Saint Lucia [sānt lo͞o′shə], island nation (1992 est. pop. 152,000), 238 sq mi (616 sq km), West Indies, one of the Windward Islands. The capital is Castries. A lush volcanic island with mountains rising abruptly from the sea, St. Lucia is much favored by vacationers. It also earns foreign exchange from traditional exports—bananas, cocoa beans, coconut oil, and copra—and its oil refinery and oil transshipment facilities. The population is largely of African descent. English is the official language, but a French patois is widely spoken. Roman Catholicism is the predominant religion. COLUMBUS probably sighted St. Lucia in 1502, but hostile Caribs prevented early colonization attempts. The first successful settlement was by the French in the late 1600s, but Britain gained control in 1803. A member of the short-lived WEST INDIES Federation (1958–62), St. Lucia gained self-government in 1967 and independence in 1979. The conservative United Workers' party, with John Compton as prime minister, has been in power since 1982.

Saint Mark's Church, Venice, named after the city's tutelary saint. The reconstruction of the original Romanesque basilical church was completed c.1071. From the 12th cent. on, it became through alterations and adornments a splendid Byzantine monument, reflecting Venice's prominence in trade with the East. In the 14th cent. the facade received Gothic additions. The plan is a Greek cross, with a central dome and a dome over each arm. The west front's five portals open on the Piazza San Marco. The facade is encrusted with marble and mosaics; the lower interior walls are sheathed in marble; and the vaults and domes are covered with mosaics set against a gold background. The bronze Four Horses of Saint Mark's, probably from a Roman triumphal arch, stand on the gallery over the main entrance.

Saint Martin, island, 37 sq mi (96 sq km), in the Leeward Islands, West Indies. Since occupation (1648) by the Dutch and French, it has been divided. The northern part (1990 pop. 28,518; capital, Marigot) is in GUADELOUPE. The southern part (1989 est. pop. 29,500; chief town, Philipsburg) is in the NETHERLANDS ANTILLES. It is a tourist resort.

Saint Moritz, Ger. *Sankt Moritz,* town (1990 est. pop. 5,300), Grisons canton, SE Switzerland, in the Upper Engadine. It is a famous winter sports center and year-round resort with mineral springs. The winter Olympic games were held there in 1928 and 1948.

Saint Patrick's Cathedral, New York City, largest Roman Catholic cathedral in the U.S., on Fifth Ave. between 50th and 51st St. Planned by James Renwick, the cathedral was built between 1858 and 1879. It has 12 side chapels. The Lady Chapel behind the high altar was added later.

Saint Paul, city (1990 pop. 272,235), state capital and seat of Ramsay co., E Minn., a port at the head of navigation on the Mississippi R., next to MINNEAPOLIS, with which it forms the Twin Cities; inc. 1854. The industrial, commercial, and cultural center of a vast fertile region, it is also a railroad hub. Computers, electronic equipment, petroleum products, automobiles, appliances, and abrasives are major manufactures. The area was settled in the early 1800s, and the site was an important river landing by 1823. St. Paul, mapped out along the river in 1846, became territorial capital in 1849 and state capital in 1858. The railroad arrived in 1862 and the city subsequently became the center of a railroad empire. St. Paul is noted for its parks; for over 900 lakes in the vicinity; for its capitol (1904) designed by Cass GILBERT, with its huge marble dome; and for its annual Winter Carnival.

Saint Paul's Cathedral, London, masterpiece of Sir Christopher WREN and of the English BAROQUE, on Ludgate Hill. A Saxon cathedral there burned in 1087 and was replaced by a Norman structure (13th cent.). In 1561 St. Paul's burned again. Inigo JONES appended a classical facade after 1628, but the great fire of London (1666) almost destroyed the church. In 1668 Wren was given permission to demolish the church and build a new one. His Greek cross design was modified to include a long nave and choir. Construction of the cathedral took place between 1675 and 1710. The three-aisled nave and choir extend east and west from a central crossing, over which rises a huge DOME, pierced at the crown to allow a view of the lantern. The exterior dome rises above a colonnaded drum and supports the lantern and cross. St. Paul's was damaged by bombs in World War II and was not completely reconstructed until 1962.

Saint Petersburg, formerly **Leningrad,** city (1990 est. pop. 5,036,000), NW European Russia, at the head of the Gulf of Finland on both banks of the Neva R. and on the islands of its delta. The second largest Russian city, it is a major sea and river port and rail junction. Principal industries include the production of electric equipment, machinery, chemicals, drugs, ships, and refined oil. The city is also a center for education and scientific research. Construction of Saint Petersburg began (1703) under PETER I, who employed Italian and French architects. The city's landmarks include the Winter Palace, HERMITAGE museum, Alexander Nevsky monastery, the Cathedral of St. Isaac, and a university. From 1712 to 1918 it replaced MOSCOW as the capital. A brilliant cultural center, the city was immortalized by such writers as PUSHKIN and TOLSTOY. In 1914 it was renamed Petrograd. The city was in the forefront of the RUSSIAN REVOLUTION. On LENIN's death in 1924, it was renamed Leningrad. Many thousands of its citizens died during WORLD WAR II when the people heroically withstood the prolonged German siege (1941–44). The city's original name was restored in 1991.

Saint Petersburg, city (1990 pop. 238,629), W Fla., a port of entry on Tampa Bay and the Gulf of Mexico, at the southern end of the Pinellas peninsula; inc. 1892. It is a winter resort and residential community, with an annual average of 360 sunny days. Citrus fruit, fishing, and recreational and electronic equipment industries are important. Its huge yacht basin and two bridges crossing the bay to Tampa are notable.

Saint Peter's Church, Rome, principal church of Roman Catholicism and one of the largest churches in world, built mainly between 1506 and 1626 on the site of earlier churches. Appointed by Pope Julius II in 1506, BRAMANTE, the first architect, seems to have planned a Greek cross. He was succeeded by RAPHAEL (1514), Antonio da San Gallo (1520), and MICHELANGELO (1547), who completed the structure up to the drum of the great DOME. Giacomo della Porta modified the design and finished the dome. In the 16th cent. there was controversy over whether the church would be built in the form of a Greek or a Latin cross. The problem was resolved in favor of the Latin cross when Carlo Maderno added the nave and facade (1607–14). Urban VIII dedicated the church in 1626. BERNINI completed (1629–62) the great design, creating a forecourt with an elliptical piazza bounded by quadruple colonnades. The Dome of St. Peter's stands 404 ft (123 m) from the pavement and has an interior diameter of 137 ft (42 m).

Saint Pierre and Miquelon, French territorial collectivity (1990 pop. 6,392), 93 sq mi (241 sq km), nine largely barren islands S of Newfoundland, Canada, in the Gulf of St. Lawrence. St. Pierre, on the like-named island, is the capital. Fishing is the main occupation; the Grand Banks are nearby. The islands were colonized (1604) by France, taken by the British three times, and restored to France in 1814. They became a French overseas department in 1976 and a territorial collectivity in 1985.

Saint-Saëns, (Charles) Camille [săN-säNs], 1835–1921, French composer. His many works are brilliantly crafted and orchestrated, but often lack imaginative force. Best known for the opera *Samson et Dalila* (1877), he also wrote symphonies, concertos, and SYMPHONIC POEMS.

Saint-Simon, Claude Henri de Rouvroy, comte de [săN-sēmôN'], 1760–1825, French social philosopher. He advocated a society led by scientists and industrialists and based on a scientific division of labor resulting in spontaneous social harmony. His works, among them *The New Christianity* (1825), influenced later socialist thought.

Saint-Simon, Louis de Rouvroy, duc de, 1675–1755, French courtier, author of voluminous memoirs (pub. 1788) of the court of LOUIS XIV. Remarkable for their psychological observation and brilliant sketches, the memoirs, despite a disregard for literary technique, are a monument of French literature. Based on his own notes and on contemporary journals covering the years 1691–1751, Saint-Simon's account is intensely personal and emotional, reflecting his inability to accept the rise of the bourgeoisie and his resentment against Louis XIV. Though full of errors, the memoirs are an indispensable historical source.

Saint Thomas: see VIRGIN ISLANDS.

Saint Valentine's Day (Feb. 14). Originally the Roman feast of Lupercalia, it was Christianized in memory of the martyr **St. Valentine** (d. A.D. 270). In the Middle Ages, Valentine became associated with the union of lovers under conditions of duress. Today the holiday is celebrated with the exchange of romantic or comic messages called "valentines."

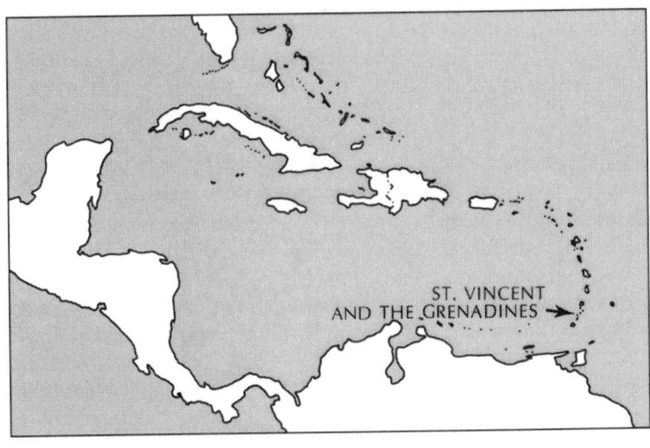

Saint Vincent and the Grenadines, independent Commonwealth nation (1992 est. pop. 115,000), 150 sq mi (388 sq km), West Indies, in the Windward Islands, comprising the island of St. Vincent (140 sq mi/363 sq km) and the northern islets of the Grenadines, an archipelago that extends southward from the main island. The capital is Kingstown. St. Vincent is mountainous and forested, with mild climate. SOUFRIÈRE volcano, 4,048 ft (1,234 m) high, dominates St. Vincent; it erupted in 1902 and 1979. Exports include bananas, arrowroot, and copra, and tourism is important, but per capita income remains very low. The people are mainly descendants of Africans who were brought as slaves during the colonial period; English is spoken. The main religions are Methodism, Anglicanism, and Roman Catholicism. St. Vincent was visited by COLUMBUS in 1498 and colonized by the British in the late 1700s. Attempts to subdue the hostile Caribs failed, and the British deported most of them in 1797. Self-government was granted in 1969, full independence in 1979. Since 1984 the islands have been governed by the centrist New Democratic party under Prime Min. James Mitchell.

St. Vitus's dance: see under CHOREA.

Saipan, island (1990 pop. 38,896), capital of the NORTHERN MARIANA ISLANDS.

sake, Japanese fermented liquor, from 12% to 16% alcohol. Made from rice, it is yellowish and sherrylike in flavor.

Sakhalin, formerly Saghalien, island, c.29,500 sq mi (76,400 sq km), E Russia, off the mainland in the Sea of Okhotsk, N of Hokkaido, Japan. With the KURIL ISLANDS to the east, it forms Sakhalin oblast. Cold and damp, with heavily forested mountain ranges, Sakhalin is important to the economy of the RUSSIAN FAR EAST for its coal, iron, oil, and offshore gas deposits. Japan ceded Sakhalin to Russia in 1875 in exchange for the Kuril Islands, regained control (1905) of areas south of lat. 50°N (called Karafuto), and, in 1951, renounced all claims to Sakhalin, though not to the Kuriles, which Soviet forces had occupied in 1945.

Sakharov, Andrei Dmitriyevich, 1921–89, Soviet nuclear physicist and human-rights advocate; first Soviet citizen to receive the Nobel Peace Prize (1975). From 1948 to 1956 he helped develop the USSR's hydrogen bomb. In the 1960s he became a critic of the arms race and of Soviet repression. His internal exile to the city of Gorky (now Nizhny Novgorod) in 1980 inspired worldwide protest; it was lifted by Gorbachev in 1986. In 1989 he was elected to the Soviet parliament.

Saki: see MUNRO, HECTOR HUGH.

Saladin, 1137?–1193, Muslim warrior and sultan of Egypt, the great opponent of the Crusaders; b. Mesopotamia, of Kurdish descent. He used his position as vizier to overthrow the Fatimid dynasty and establish himself (1171) as the first Ayyubid sultan. He greatly expanded his territories, thereby clashing with the Crusaders (see CRUSADES). With a large force of Muslims (called Saracens by the Christians) he won the battle of Hattin (1187), which led to his capture of Jerusalem. The Third Crusade (1189) was gathered to regain Jerusalem. During this Crusade Saladin and King RICHARD I of England met in the conflict celebrated in chivalric romance. Saladin triumphed over the Crusaders and left the Latin Kingdom of Jerusalem with only a thin strip of coastline. Saladin was a learned man and a great patron of the arts.

Salamanca, city (1988 est. pop. 159,000), capital of Salamanca prov., W central Spain, in León, on the Tormes R. Food processing and tourism are important industries. Taken by Hannibal (220 B.C.), the city was held by the Romans, Visigoths, and Moors (8th–11th cent.). Its university (founded early 13th cent.) was world famous. Among the city's landmarks are the colonnaded Plaza Mayor, a Roman bridge, and a 12th-cent. cathedral.

salamander, AMPHIBIAN (order Urodela) having a tail and small, weak limbs that can regenerate. Found in damp regions of the northern temperate zone, they are abundant in North America. Most are under 6 in. (15 cm) long, although the giant salamander of Japan may reach 5 ft (1.5 m). Usually nocturnal and feeding on small animals such as insects and worms, salamanders are mostly terrestrial as adults, although some are aquatic and a few arboreal. **Newts** are a large, widely distributed family of salamanders.

Salamis, island, E Greece, in the Saronic Gulf. Off its shore, during the PERSIAN WARS, the Greek fleet, led by THEMISTOCLES, decisively defeated the Persians (480 B.C.).

Salazar, António de Oliveira [sələzär'], 1889–1970, dictator of PORTUGAL (1932–68). A professor of political economy, he became finance minister (1926, 1928) and stabilized the nation's finances. As premier he established (1933) a corporate state and suppressed the opposition. Although he supported FRANCO, he allowed the Allies to use the Azores as a military base in World War II. Later he encouraged Portugal's economic development and tried to suppress revolts in its African colonies. After suffering a stroke in 1968, he was replaced as premier by Marcello CAETANO.

Salem. 1 City (1990 pop. 38,091), seat of Essex co., NE Mass., on an inlet of Massachusetts Bay; inc. 1629. Once a world-famous port and center of the China trade, it is now a tourist center with light industries. Salem was the scene (1692) of infamous witchcraft trials. The birthplace of Nathaniel HAWTHORNE is preserved, along with the House of Seven Gables (1668). Pioneer Village is a reproduction of a 1630 settlement. **2** City (1990 pop. 107,786), state capital and seat of Marion co., NW Oreg., on the Willamette R.; inc. 1857. A major food-processing center, it has wood product, paper, and electronics industries, in addition to state government offices. Founded 1840–41 by Methodist missionaries, it became capital of Oregon Territory in 1851 and remained so with statehood (1859).

sales tax: see TAXATION.

Salic law, rule of succession in some noble families of Europe forbidding the succession by females or those descended in the female line to titles or offices. It was mistakenly thought to be part of the *Lex Salica* (see GERMANIC LAWS), which concerned only succession to property. The VALOIS and BOURBON families in France maintained it, notably in the successions of PHILIP V and PHILIP VI. In Spain the Salic law was rescinded in favor of ISABELLA II. It prevented the succession in Hanover of Queen VICTORIA of England.

Salinas, city (1990 pop. 108,777), seat of Monterey co., W Calif.; inc. 1874. It is the shipping and processing center for a valley famous for its lettuce. Fruits, artichokes, and dairy goods are also produced, and rubber is manufactured. The home of John STEINBECK, a Salinas native, is open to visitors.

Salinas de Gortari, Carlos, 1948–, Mexican economist and government official, president of Mexico (1988–). A member of the Institutional Revolutionary party (PRI) since 1966, he held a series of finance ministry posts (1971–79) before serving (1979–81) in the ministry of planning and budget under Miguel DE LA MADRID HURTADO. After de la Madrid became president, Salinas became (1982) his minister of planning and budget. In 1987 de la Madrid supported Salinas for the presidency, and as the PRI candidate he subsequently won (1988) an election marred by allegations of fraud. Salinas worked to revive Mexico's economy by curbing inflation and reducing government involvement. He also improved political and economic relations with the U.S., signing the NORTH AMERICAN FREE TRADE AGREEMENT in 1992.

Salinger, J(erome) D(avid), 1919–, American author; b. N.Y.C. With pathos and humor he depicts the individual caught in a banal, restricting world. His only novel, *The Catcher in the Rye* (1951), quickly became a classic; also popular are his short stories, e.g., *Nine Stories* (1953), *Franny and Zooey* (1961).

Salisbury, Robert Arthur Talbot Gascoyne-Cecil, 3d **marquess of,** 1830–1903, British statesman. The Conservative foreign minister under Benjamin DISRAELI, he attended the Congress of Berlin (1878). As prime minister (1885–86, 1886–92, 1895–1902), he avoided alignments in European affairs and dealt with the SOUTH AFRICAN WAR. His governments provided for free public education (1891) and workers' compensation (1897).

Salisbury, Robert Cecil, 1st **earl of,** 1563–1612, English statesman, son of William Cecil, Baron BURGHLEY. He succeeded his father as principal secretary to ELIZABETH I in 1598 and arranged the peaceful accession (1603) of JAMES I. Under James, he directed virtually the entire government, reduced the king's debts, and tried to curb James's extravagance.

Salisbury or **New Sarum,** city (1991 pop. 105,318), Wiltshire, S England. It was founded in 1220, when the bishopric was moved there from Old Sarum. Its great cathedral (1220–60) is a splendid example of Early English architecture and has the highest spire (404 ft/123 m) in England.

Salisbury, Zimbabwe: see HARARE.

Salish or **Flathead,** indigenous people of W Montana who spoke a Salishan language of the Algonquian-Wakashan stock (see NATIVE AMERICAN LANGUAGES). They were called "flatheads" by neighboring Columbia R. peoples who shaped the front of the head to a point. After acquiring horses, the Salish adopted the buffalo and TEPEE culture of the Plains (see NORTH AMERICA, INDIGENOUS PEOPLES OF) and struggled with the BLACKFOOT for hunting lands. Most now live on a Montana reservation that they share with a small band of Kootenai. In 1990 there were over 5,000 Salish in the U.S.

Salishan [sā'lĭshən, săl'–], branch of the Algonquian-Wakashan linguistic family of North America; spoken by Native Americans of the NW United States and Canada. See NATIVE AMERICAN LANGUAGES (table).

Salk, Jonas Edward, 1914–, American physician and microbiologist; b. N.Y.C. He taught at the universities of Michigan and Pittsburgh and was director (1963–75) of the Salk Inst. for Biological Studies at the Univ. of California, San Diego. While at Pittsburgh he developed a killed-virus vaccine against POLIOMYELITIS.

Sallust (Caius Sallustius Crispus) [săl'əst], 86 B.C.–c.34 B.C., Roman historian. His major work is *War of Catiline,* or *Catiline,* an account of the conspiracy of CATILINE.

salmon, marine FISH of the family Salmonidae that spawn in fresh water, including salmon, trout, and char. The herring like Salmonidae are characterized by soft, rayless, adipose fins and live in cold, oxygen-rich waters. They are generally a uniform silver in color. The Atlantic salmon (genus *Salmo*), once abundant, is threatened by pollution, damming, and overfishing. It feeds on CRUSTACEANS at sea and small fish while spawning and reaches 15 lb (6.8 kg). The Pacific salmon (genus *Oncorhynchus*), comprising five species, is commercially the most important. The largest, the chinook, may reach 100 lb (45 kg); the blueback forms the bulk of canned salmon. Pacific salmon are famed for their grueling journeys of hundreds of miles to their headwater breeding grounds. The genus *Salvelinus* includes the European chars and the North American brook trout.

salmonellosis, infection caused by intestinal bacteria of the genus *Salmonella.* The most common form is gastroenteritis, an intestinal disease usually resulting from contaminated food. Symptoms include nausea, abdominal pains, diarrhea, and fever; it can lead to death, especially in people with impaired immune systems. Treatment includes rest, replacement of lost body fluids, and ANTIBIOTICS. The generalized form is often called paratyphoid fever because it resembles TYPHOID FEVER. Milk, especially unpasteurized (raw) milk, undercooked chicken and eggs, and food prepared in an unsanitary manner are major sources of the disease; it is also contracted through exposure to infected pets, such as turtles and iguanas. Increased rates of salmonellosis have led to recommendations to keep foods refrigerated, cook them thoroughly, and wash cooking surfaces, utensils, and hands immediately after preparing foods.

Salome [səlō'mē], daughter of Herod Philip and Herodias. She is generally supposed to be the daughter who danced to obtain the head of JOHN THE BAPTIST.

Salonica: see THESSALONIKI.

salsa, American popular music, developed largely in New York City in the 1970s. It blends the rhumba and other dance forms; Cuban, Puerto Rican, Dominican, and other Latin American strains; ROCK MUSIC; and JAZZ. Salsa is chiefly performed, and often danced simultaneously, by singers; percussionists; and brass, guitar, and keyboard players. Artists include Machito, Eddie Palmieri, Tito PUENTE, and Rubén BLADES.

SALT (Strategic Arms Limitation Talks): see DISARMAMENT, NUCLEAR.

salt, chemical compound (other than water) formed by a chemical reaction between ACIDS AND BASES; by direct combination of metal with nonmetal, e.g., SODIUM CHLORIDE (common table salt); by reaction of a metal with a dilute acid; by reaction of a metal oxide with acid; by reaction of a nonmetallic oxide with a base; or by reaction of two salts with each other to form two new salts. Most salts are ionic compounds. The chemical formula indicates the proportion of atoms of the elements making up the salt. A salt is classified as acidic, basic, or normal if it has, respectively, hydrogen (H), hydroxyl (OH), or neither in its formula. A salt undergoes dissociation when dissolved in a polar solvent, e.g., water (see HYDROLYSIS).

salt, common: see SODIUM CHLORIDE.

Salt Lake City, city (1990 pop. 159,936; met. area 1,072,227), state capital and seat of Salt Lake co., N central Utah, on the Jordan R., near the GREAT SALT LAKE, at the foot of the Wasatch Range; inc. 1851. Food-processing, oil-refining, smelting, computer and electronics, and warehousing industries are important. Founded (1847) by Brigham YOUNG as the capital of the MORMON community, it has become a major religious center. The gigantic Temple (1853–93) is at the city's heart. Other points of interest include the state capitol (1914), and the Brigham Young home (1877) and Memorial (1897).

saltpeter or **potassium nitrate,** chemical compound (KNO_3), occurring as colorless prismatic crystals or as a white powder. When heated, it decomposes to release oxygen. Saltpeter has been used in gunpowder manufacture since about the 12th cent.; it is also used in explosives, fireworks, matches, and fertilizers, and as a food preservative.

Salvador or **Bahia,** city (1990 est. pop. 2,050,000), capital of Bahia state, E Brazil. An Atlantic port, it processes and ships cacao, tobacco, sugar, and other products of a fertile crescent, the Recôncavo. The city was found in 1549, flourished with the rise of sugar plantations, and was the leading center of colonial Brazil and the capital of Portugal's possessions in America until 1763. An influx of plantation slaves was the source of its African heritage. It is now a tourist center noted for its 16th-cent. cathedral.

Salvation Army, Protestant denomination and international nonsectarian Christian organization for evangelical and philanthropic work. Begun (1865) in England as the East London Revival Society by William BOOTH, with his wife, Catherine, it was designated the Salvation Army in 1878. It was organized along military lines and sought to minister to physical as well as spiritual needs. In the U.S. work began in 1880 with a branch in Pennsylvania. The beliefs of the group generally agree with those of most Protestant evangelicals, but SACRAMENTS are not practiced. The Salvation Army is distinguished by its work with the armed services and by its aid to the victims of disasters all over the world.

salvia: see SAGE.

Salween, river, c.1,750 mi (2,820 km) long, Southeast Asia. It rises in Tibet and flows through SW China and Myanmar to enter the Gulf of Martaban, in E Myanmar, near Moulmein. Flowing through gorges for much of its length, the river is navigable for only c.75 mi (120 km). It varies up to 65 ft (20 m) in depth between wet and dry seasons.

Salyut: see SPACE EXPLORATION, table.

Salzburg, city (1991 pop. 143,971), capital of Salzburg prov., W central Austria. It is an industrial, tourist, and transportation center. Settled by the Celts and later a Roman trading center, it was long the residence of powerful archbishops. The city was secularized in 1802 and passed to Bavaria (1809), but was returned (1815) to Austria by the Congress of VIENNA. Salzburg's superb landmarks include a 7th-cent. Benedictine abbey and a monument to PARACELSUS. MOZART was born in Salzburg and is honored with an annual music festival; HOFMANNSTHAL's morality play *Everyman* is performed annually in the cathedral square.

Samara, city (1990 est. pop. 1,256,000), E central European Russia, on the left bank of the Volga and at the mouth of the Samara R.; called **Kuybyshev** from 1935 to 1991. A port and rail center, located near a hydroelectric plant, it manufactures automobiles, aircraft, and other industrial products. Grain and livestock are the chief exports. Founded in 1586, Samara was the Volga's grain center. Industry grew as railroads to Siberia and central Asia were built (early 20th cent.). During World War II the USSR's central government was moved (1941–43) from Moscow to the city.

Samaras, Lucas [sämär'əs], 1936–, American sculptor; b. Greece. Using unusual materials such as colored string, plastics, chicken wire, and feathers, he has created variations on everyday forms like boxes, scissors, and chairs. He is known for his reclusiveness.

Samaria, ancient city, central Palestine, NW of Nablus (Shechem), Jordan. Samaria was built by King Omri as the capital of the northern kingdom of Israel in the early 9th cent. B.C. It fell in 721 B.C. to Assyria. Destroyed in 120 B.C. by John Hyrcanus (see MACCABEES), it was rebuilt by HEROD the Great. It is the traditional burial place of JOHN THE BAPTIST. The city gave its name to the **Samaritans,** a sect recognizing only the Pentateuch of the Bible. In Jesus' time a great enmity existed between them and the Jews since each claimed to be the only true inheritors of Abraham and Moses. A small group of Samaritans still live at Nablus. The Samaritan language is a type of Aramaic.

samarium (Sm), metallic element, discovered in 1879 by P.E. Lecoq de Boisbaudran. It is a lustrous, silver-white RARE-EARTH METAL of the LANTHANIDE SERIES. Uses include pyrophoric alloys in cigarette-lighter flints, magnets in computer memories, and nuclear-reactor control rods. See ELEMENT (table); PERIODIC TABLE.

Samarkand or **Samarqand,** city (1987 est. pop. 388,000), UZBEKISTAN, on the Trans-Caspian RR. A major cotton and silk center, it also produces wine, tea, and such industrial goods as vehicle parts. The oldest central Asian city—and one of the world's oldest cities—Samarkand was on the ancient trade route between the Middle East and China. It was conquered (329 B.C.) by ALEXANDER THE GREAT, fell (8th cent. A.D.) to the Arabs, and became (9th cent.) a center of Islamic culture. Sacked (1220) by JENGHIZ KHAN, it revived as the capital of TIMUR's empire (14th–15th cent.). Samarkand fell to the Uzbeks c.1500 and to Russia in 1868. The city's old quarter contains Timur's mausoleum and many ancient mosques.

Samoa: see AMERICAN SAMOA; WESTERN SAMOA.

Sámos, island (1991 pop. 41,850), c.181 sq mi (469 sq km), SE Greece, in the Aegean Sea, near Turkey; one of the Sporades island group. Its economy is based on agriculture, wine-making, tobacco processing, and shipbuilding. A cultural and maritime center in ancient times, it was the home of AESOP and the birthplace of PYTHAGORAS.

Samoyed, muscular WORKING DOG; shoulder height, 19–23.5 in. (48.3–59.7 cm); weight, 35–65 lb (15.9–29.5 kg). Its weather-resistant double coat may be white, biscuit, or cream. Raised by the Samoyed people of N Siberia thousands of years ago, it was used to herd reindeer and haul sledges.

Sampras, Pete, 1971–, American tennis player; b. Washington, D.C. The youngest man ever to win the U.S. Open (1990), he is known for his powerful serve and well-placed shots. In 1993–94 he won Wimbledon and the U.S. and Australian open titles, becoming the first man to win three majors in a row since the mid-1960s.

Samson, in the BIBLE, judge of Israel whose strength lay in his long hair. The Philistines accomplished his destruction through the woman Delilah, who cut off his hair. Captured and blinded, Samson regained his strength as his hair grew long again. He then pulled down the Philistine temple, killing both himself and his captors.

Samuel, two books of the OLD TESTAMENT, 9th and 10th in the Authorized Version, a narrative of events in Hebrew history, covering the careers of Samuel, SAUL, and DAVID (roughly the 11th cent. B.C.). Scholars detect at least two main strands, based on divergent attitudes toward the establishment of the monarchy. One section (2 Sam. 9–20) is apparently the oldest piece of narrative in the Bible. The prophet Samuel (fl. 1050 B.C.) was the last judge of Israel.

Samuelson, Paul A., 1915–, American economist; b. Gary, Ind. Winner of the 1970 Nobel Prize in economics, he has been on the faculty of the Massachusetts Institute of Technology since 1941 and has held a variety of government posts. As adviser to Presidents KENNEDY and JOHNSON, he helped shape the tax legislation and antipoverty efforts of the 1960s. A supporter of Keynesian economics (see KEYNES), he is known for his work *Economics* (1948; 12th ed. 1985), a standard textbook for many years.

samurai, knights of feudal Japan, retainers of the daimyo, or barons. This aristocratic class arose in the 12th cent. and was consolidated in the TOKUGAWA period. Samurai followed a code of honor called the bushido. The class was abolished after the MEIJI restoration (1868).

San, African people who live largely in the Kalahari and surrounding areas of Namibia and Botswana. They number about 85,000. Traditionally, the San were nomadic hunters and food-gatherers who traveled in groups of 25–60 and had no social classes and few private possessions. Many, however, now live in settlements and work on cattle ranches or farms. Their languages include clicking sounds that are rarely found in other languages. They were called Bushmen by whites, but that term is now considered derogatory.

Sana, San'a, or **Sanaa,** city (1986 pop. 427,150), capital of Yemen. The largest city in S ARABIA, it lies inland on a high plain and is linked to the Red Sea port of Hodeida by road. An Islamic cultural center, it is also a trade center for grapes and other crops grown nearby. A pre-Islamic settlement, it was held by Ethiopia in the 6th cent. and by the Ottoman Turks in the 17th cent. and from 1872 to 1918, when Yemen became independent. In 1990, when Yemen and Southern Yemen merged, it became the unified nation's capital.

San Andreas fault, the principal FAULT in a network of faults extending more than 600 mi (965 km) from NW California to the Gulf of California. It marks the boundary of two crustal plates (see PLATE TECTONICS) moving in relation to each other, causing horizontal displacement along the fault. Total displacement has been estimated at c.350 mi (560 km) since the fault's formation over 30 million years ago. Such movement causes EARTHQUAKES, thousands of which, mostly of low magnitude, occur annually.

San Antonio, city (1990 pop. 935,935; met. area 1,302,099), seat of Bexar co., S central Tex., at the source of the San Antonio R.; inc. 1837. The third largest city in Texas and the tenth largest in the U.S., it is the site of a military training and medical complex, and the industrial, trade, and financial center of an agricultural region. Manufactures include processed foods, aircraft, and chemicals. The Spanish visited the area long before they established (1718–31) a series of missions. San Antonio was the leading Texas settlement in the Spanish and Mexican days. In the Texas Revolution, Texans captured it (1835) and Mexicans attacked its ALAMO. The Mexican flavor remains today, and the city has a large Spanish-speaking population. It is known for its artists' colonies and museums, its many educational institutions, and numerous historical sites.

San Bernardino, city (1990 pop. 164,164), seat of San Bernardino co., S Calif., at the foot of the San Bernardino Mts.; inc. 1854. Its manufactures include steel, aerospace, and electronics products. San Bernardino is in a growing metropolitan area that includes the cities of Ontario and Riverside. Explored (1772) and settled by the Spanish, the city was laid out by MORMONS in the 1850s.

Sánchez Ferlosio, Rafael [sän'chĕth fărlō'syō], 1927–, Spanish novelist; b. Italy. A master of the Spanish language, he has written such novels as *The Labors and Fortunes of Alfanhuí* (1951) and *The One Day of the Week* (1956).

Sand, George [säN], pseud. of **Amandine Aurore Lucie Dupin, baronne Dudevant,** 1804–76, French novelist. Her unconventional life was symbolized by the male attire she adopted to protest the unequal treatment accorded to women, and by her open and notorious liaisons with the writer Jules Sandeau, with Alfred de MUSSET, and with CHOPIN. After her divorce from Baron Dudevant (1836), she supported herself and her two children chiefly by her writing. Of her 80-odd novels, *The Haunted Pool* (1846) and *Fanchon the Cricket* (1850) are masterpieces. Notable also are *Indiana* (1832) and *Lélia* (1833), espressing her feminist beliefs. All her works are distinguished by a romantic love of nature and an extravagant moral idealism. Much of her work was autobiographical, notably *She and He* (1859), which concerns her life with Musset, and *A Winter on Majorca* (1841), about her life with Chopin.

sand, rock material occurring in the form of loose, rounded or angular grains, varying in size from 0.06 to 2 mm in diameter. It is formed by the WEATHERING and decomposition of all types of ROCK, its most abundant mineral constituent being QUARTZ. Sand has numerous uses, particularly in the manufacture of bricks, cement, glass, concrete, explosives, and abrasives. See also DESERT; QUARTZITE; SANDSTONE.

sandalwood, name for several fragrant tropical woods, especially that of *Santalum album*, a partially parasitic evergreen tree native to India. Oil distilled from the wood is much used as a perfume and in medicine. Red sandalwood, obtained from *Pterocarpus santalinus*, is used in dyes.

Sandburg, Carl, 1878–1967, major American poet; b. Galesburg, Ill. His experiences as a laborer, soldier, socialist political worker, and journalist informed his poetry. Drawing his inspiration from America's past and present, influenced by Walt WHITMAN, Sandburg wrote vigorous, impressionistic free verse that celebrated ordinary people and things. Collections of his poems include *Chicago Poems* (1916), *Cornhuskers* (1918; Pulitzer), *The People, Yes* (1936), *Complete Poems* (1950; Pulitzer), and *Harvest Poems, 1910–1960* (1960). Sandburg also collected folk ballads and songs in *The American Songbag* (1927) and wrote an epic biography of Lincoln (6 vol., 1926–39; vol. 3–6, Pulitzer); children's books, e.g., *Rootabaga Stories* (1922); and the autobiographical *Always the Young Strangers* (1953).

sand dollar, marine invertebrate animal (an ECHINODERM), related to the STARFISH. The sand dollar has a rigid, flattened, circular shell consisting of numerous small skeletal plates. Small spines enable the animal to burrow under the surface of the sand. Tube feet on the underside of the body are used for locomotion and to convey food particles to the mouth.

San Diego, city (1990 pop. 1,110,549; met. area 2,498,016), seat of San Diego co., S Calif., on San Diego Bay. The city is the second largest in California and the sixth largest in the U.S. Its excellent natural harbor has made it a fishing and shipping port, and a major naval center. Aerospace, electronics, shipbuilding, biotechnology, and other industries are important. Tourism and convention business are large factors in the economy. Explored and claimed by Spain in 1542, it was the site of the first of Fr. Junípero SERRA's missions and a historic fort, the Presidio (both 1769). The area has many other historic sites, including the Cabrillo National Monument. San Diego is also a cultural, medical, oceanographic, and research center, and its aquatic park and enormous zoo are well known. Since 1988 the *America*'s Cup sailing races have been held at San Diego.

Sandinistas, members of a left-wing Nicaraguan political group, the Sandinist National Liberation Front (FSLN). The group, named for Augusto Cesar SANDINO, a former insurgent leader, was formed in 1962 to oppose the regime of Anastasio SOMOZA-DEBAYLE. In 1979 they launched an offensive from Costa Rica and Honduras that toppled Somoza. The Sandinistas established a ruling junta that nationalized such industries as banking and mining, postponed elections, and moved steadily to the left, eventually espousing Marxist-Leninist positions. They were opposed by U.S.-supported guerrillas known as contras (see NICARAGUA). In 1984, Sandinista Daniel Ortega Saavedra became president in a national election that was boycotted by some opposition groups. In 1990 the opposition candidate, Violeta Barrios de Chamorro, defeated Ortega, but the Sandinistas continued to dominate the police and army.

Sandino, Augusto Cesar, 1893–1934, Nicaraguan patriot. He waged a successful guerrilla resistance against the U.S. Marine occupation of Nicaragua (1927–33). When he came out of hiding for peace talks, he was murdered by National Guardsmen led by Anastasio SOMOZA.

sandpiper, name for some shore BIRDS of the family Scolopacidae, including the SNIPE and CURLEW. Sandpipers are small wading birds with long, slender bills for probing in sand or mud for small invertebrates. Their plumage is usually brown or gray streaked above and buff with streaks or spots below. Most are found in flocks on seacoasts throughout the Northern Hemisphere.

sandstone, sedimentary ROCK formed by the cementing together of SAND grains. The hardness varies depending on the cementing material. Sandstone is widely used in construction and industry. It can also be crushed and used like sand.

Sandwich, John Montagu, 4th **earl of,** 1718–92, British politician. He was secretary of state (1763–65, 1770–71) and first lord of the admiralty (1748–51, 1763, 1771–82). He was unpopular for charges (1763) of obscenity against John WILKES and was later blamed for British defeats in the American Revolution. He supposedly invented the sandwich.

San Francisco, city (1990 pop. 723,959; met. area 1,603,678), W Calif., on a peninsula between the Pacific and San Francisco Bay, which are connected by the strait called the Golden Gate; inc. 1850. It is an industrial nucleus, a market for mine and farm products, a transportation hub, and a financial and insurance center. With the Bay area it forms one of the nation's largest ports and a major center of trade with E Asia, Hawaii, and Alaska. Its industries are increasingly white-collar but processed food and clothing are produced; tourism is an economic mainstay. The city is also one of the nation's cultural centers. Founded by the Spanish (1776) as Yerba Buena, it was taken and renamed by the Americans in 1846. The California gold rush (1848) led to great growth; with the arrival of newcomers from all over the world in the late 19th cent. the city took on a cosmopolitan air. The earthquake and fire of April 18–20, 1906, devastated the city, but it was quickly rebuilt. The opening of the Panama Canal and San Francisco's role as a supply and embarkation point in World War II increased the city's importance. On Oct. 17, 1989, another earthquake damaged the city, especially its Marina district. A gracious, picturesque city with a mild climate, it is famous for its individuality. Points of interest include its cable cars, which carry passengers on its steep hills; the San Francisco–Oakland Bay Bridge (opened 1936) and Golden Gate Bridge (opened 1937); Chinatown; Fisherman's Wharf; Telegraph Hill; the mansions of Nob Hill; the opera house; symphony hall (1980); and numerous institutions of learning.

Sanger, Frederick, 1918–, British biochemist. One of the few recipients of two Nobel prizes, he won the chemistry award in 1958 for identifying the amino-acid sequence of insulin and shared the 1980 award in chemistry for developing a method, important in recombinant DNA research, for rapidly determining the chemical structure of pieces of DNA.

Sanger, Margaret (Higgins), 1883–1966, American leader in the BIRTH-CONTROL movement; b. Corning, N.Y. Personal experience and work as a nurse convinced her that family limitation, especially where poverty was a factor, was a necessary step in social progress. Her promotion of birth control brought indictment and arrests, but public and court support gradually grew. She organized the first American (1923) and international (1925) birth-control conferences, formed (1923) a committee to lobby for birth-control laws, and helped establish clinics around the world.

Sanhedrin, ancient Jewish legal and religious institution in Jerusalem. There probably were two Sanhedrins: one, like a legal court, political and civil; the other, the Great Sanhedrin, purely religious. The political Sanhedrin perished after the destruction of the Temple in A.D. 70, but the religious Sanhedrin continued as the rabbinic patriarchate until about A.D. 425.

San Joaquin, river, central California, flowing c.320 mi (510 km) N from the Sierra Nevada to join the Sacramento R. in a vast delta on an inlet of San Francisco Bay. It is navigable by oceangoing vessels c.40 mi (60 km) to Stockton. Its valley, now irrigated by water from the Central Valley Project, is one of the state's chief agricultural areas.

San José, city (1989 pop. 287,535), central Costa Rica, capital of Costa Rica. It is the country's largest city and its economic, political, and social center, dominating the central plateau. It is also the distribution point for imports. A modern city with many parks, it has a mixture of Spanish and North American architecture. The city was founded c.1738 and has two universities.

San Jose, city (1990 pop. 782,248; met. area 1,497,557), seat of Santa Clara co., W Calif.; founded 1777, inc. 1850. In a rich wine- and fruit-producing area, San Jose is a fast-growing industrial city in SILICON VALLEY. Manufactures include aerospace, computer, and other high-technology products. At the southern end of San Francisco Bay, San Jose was the capital of California from 1849 to 1851. The city was damaged by an earthquake in 1989.

San Juan, city (1990 pop. 426,832), capital, chief port, and commercial center of PUERTO RICO, on the NE coast. Sugar, tobacco, coffee, fruit, and other agricultural products are exported. Tourism is a major industry. Sugar refining, rum distilling, metalworking, clothing, publishing, and various light manufactures are also important. Its bay was named Puerto Rico [rich port] by PONCE DE LEÓN, who began a settlement at nearby Caparra in 1508. It has one of the finest harbors in the WEST INDIES and fine beaches. The old city (founded 1521) is noted for its colonial atmosphere; El Morro castle (begun 1539) is the most famous of its buildings.

San Marino, officially Republic of San Marino, republic (1992 est. pop. 23,400), 24 sq mi (62 sq km), in the APENNINES, SW of Rimini, Italy. San Marino (1988 est. pop. 4,140) is the capital; Serravalle is

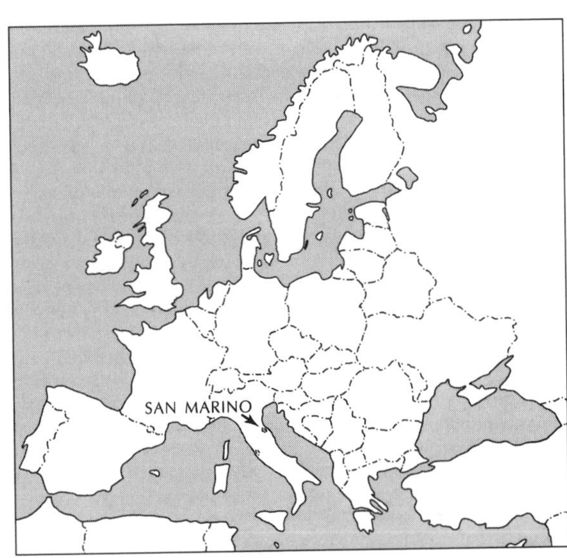

the only other town. Tourism, light industries, farming, and the sale of postage stamps and duty-free consumer goods are the chief sources of income. Major products include building materials, textiles, ceramics, and wine. The Italian-speaking Sanmarinese are largely Roman Catholic.

History. San Marino claims to be Europe's oldest existing state. According to tradition, in the 4th cent. A.D. Marino, a Christian stonecutter, took refuge on Mt. Titano, the chief geographical feature of San Marino. A community was formed by the mid-5th cent. and its independence recognized by the papacy in 1631. San Marino volunteers served with the Italians in both world wars, and Allied aircraft bombed the tiny republic in 1944. Following a period (1947–57) of Communist-led coalition governments, a series of coalitions headed by Christian Democrats held sway until 1978, when a Communist-led coalition again came to power. A coalition of Communists (renamed Progressive Democrats in 1990) and Christian Democrats governed the country from 1986 to 1992, when the Christian Democrats formed a coalition with the Socialists.

San Martín, José de [sän märtēn′], 1778–1850, South American revolutionary leader. A professional soldier, he joined (1812) the revolution against Spain in his native ARGENTINA and commanded patriot forces in Upper Peru. In 1817 he invaded CHILE by a daring march across the Andes and defeated the Spanish at Chacabuco with the aid of Bernardo O'HIGGINS; they soon completed (1818) the liberation of Chile. San Martín seized (1821) Lima and became protector of Peru, but he resigned (1822) the post and permitted Simón BOLÍVAR to liberate the country.

San Pedro Sula, city (1988 pop. 460,600), NW Honduras. A Caribbean port serving the banana and sugar plantations of the north, it has an increasing number of light industries.

San Salvador, city (1990 est. pop. 485,000), central El Salvador, the country's capital and largest city and a trade and communications center. Situated on a volcanic slope, it is subject to severe earthquakes and has been rebuilt often. It was founded in the early 1600s and was (1831–38) the capital of the Central American Federation. It is a modern city with broad avenues and many parks.

Sanskrit [săn′skrĭt], language belonging to the Indic group of the Indo-Iranian subfamily of the Indo-European family of languages. Sanskrit was the classical standard language of ancient India, and some of the oldest surviving Indo-European documents are written in Sanskrit. The oldest known stage of Sanskrit is Vedic or Vedic Sanskrit, so called because it was the language of the VEDA, the most ancient extant scriptures of HINDUISM. See LANGUAGE (table).

Sanskrit literature, main body of the classical literature of India. The literature is divided into two main groups and periods—the Vedic (c.1500–c.200 B.C.), when the Vedic form of Sanskrit prevailed, and the Sanskrit (c.200 B.C.–A.D. c.1100), when classical Sanskrit (a development of Vedic) predominated. Early Sanskrit literature, however, overlapped the Vedic. The early Vedic period (c.1500–c.800 B.C.), that of the VEDA, was a poetic and creative age. Subsequently (c.800–c.500 B.C.), the priestly class concerned itself more with ritual and wrote the *Brahmanas,* prose commentaries explaining the Vedas' relation to ritual. Later portions of the *Brahmanas* are theosophical treatises; these include the philosophical *Upanishads* (see VEDANTA). In the final stage of the Vedic period (c.500–c.200 B.C.) the *Sutras,* which deal with Vedic ritual and customary law, were written. A sutra well known in the West is the *Kamasutra* of Vatsyayana, concerning the art and practice of love. In the middle of the sutra period, the grammar of Panini (c.350 B.C.) formalized classical Sanskrit. Nearly all Sanskrit literature, except for works on grammar and philososphy, is in verse. The early Sanskrit period (c.500–c.50 B.C.) is one of epics; the greatest of these are the MAHABHARATA, which includes the BHAGAVAD-GITA, and the RAMAYANA. Sanskrit lyric poetry is artificial in technique and mainly stanzaic. Many lyrics are gemlike miniatures, portraying emotion and nature, and most are erotic. Nonetheless, there are many lyrics that are ethical in tone. Sanskrit drama probably derived from dance and religious ritual (see ASIAN DRAMA). In its fables and fairy tales (A.D. c.400–1100) the didactic quality of Sanskrit literature is most pronounced, and often the characters in a tale themselves tell stories until there are many levels to the narrative. The PANCHATANTRA is the most important work in this style. Sanskrit today is chiefly used in academic exercises. Modern INDIAN LITERATURE is mostly written in vernacular languages and English.

Santa Ana, city (1990 pop. 293,742), seat of Orange co., S Calif., in the fertile Santa Ana valley; inc. 1886. A light industrial center, it produces such manufactures as aerospace and electronic equipment, sporting goods, and electrical connectors. The insurance industry is also economically important.

Santa Anna, Antonio López de, 1794–1876, Mexican general and dictator. A clever opportunist, he ruled MEXICO during most of the period from 1824 to 1855, his fortunes rising and falling rapidly as he shifted his allegiance from party to party. His victory (1829) over the Spanish at Tampico gained him popularity and the presidency (1833). He was defeated and captured (1836) by the Texas rebels at San Jacinto, but he quickly regained his power. He commanded the Mexican troops in the MEXICAN WAR, where his defeats forced him into exile. He returned to power (1853–55) until exiled again.

Santa Barbara, city (1990 pop. 85,571), seat of Santa Barbara co., S Calif., on the Pacific Ocean; inc. 1850. A beautiful residential and resort city, it has electronics and aerospace firms and an orchid industry. The city is known for its Spanish architecture, and its mission (est. 1786, present building 1820) is famous. Oil fields are in the area and offshore; a 1969 oil-rig leak caused great damage.

Santa Barbara Islands, eight rugged islands off the coast of S Calif., extending c.150 mi (240 km) W into the Pacific Ocean. They include Anacapa, Santa Barbara, San Miguel, Santa Cruz, and Santa Rosa islands (all now part of Channel Islands National Park), and San Nicolas, Santa Catalina (a tourist center), and San Clemente islands. They were discovered in 1542 by Juan Rodríguez Cabrillo, a Portuguese explorer.

Santa Claus: see NICHOLAS, SAINT.

Santa Fe, city (1990 pop. 55,854), state capital and seat of Santa Fe co., N N.Mex., at the foot of the Sangre de Cristo Mts. It is an administrative and tourist center. Founded c.1609 by the Spanish, it was a Spanish–Native American trade center for over 200 years. Taken by the U.S. in 1846, it has been a seat of government since its founding, the oldest capital city in the U.S. It has many historic churches and an outstanding opera company.

Santa Fe Trail, caravan route of the W U.S., extending c.780 mi (1,260 km) from INDEPENDENCE, Mo., to SANTA FE, N.Mex. Following the first party of traders, led by William Becknell in 1822, annual wagon caravans made the 40- to 60-day trip over the trail to Santa Fe, returning after a 4- to 5-week stay. In 1880 the Santa Fe RR reached Santa Fe, marking the death of the trail. It became a national historic trail in 1987.

Santander, Francisco de Paula [säntändär′], 1792–1840, Colombian revolutionary. He helped to liberate COLOMBIA from Spanish rule and served (1821–28) as vice president under BOLÍVAR, who later accused him of complicity in a plot (1828) to assassinate Bolívar and banished him. Later, he returned and was president of New Granada (Colombia and Panama).

Santa Rosa, city (1990 pop. 113,313), seat of Sonoma co., W Calif.; inc. 1868. Located in the fertile Sonoma Valley, the city is a rapidly growing industrial, retail, and financial center. Luther BURBANK lived there, and his gardens are preserved as a monument. Also notable is the Church of One Tree (1874), now housing the Ripley Memorial Museum.

Santa Sophia: see HAGIA SOPHIA.

Santayana, George, 1863–1952, American philosopher; b. Spain. He emigrated to the U.S. in 1872, graduated from Harvard Univ., and was (1889–1912) a noted teacher there. In 1912 he retired from teaching and thereafter lived in Europe. Santayana viewed the mind as being placed in and responsive to a physical, biological context; at the same time he emphasized the mind's rational and imaginative vision of physical beauty. He considered religion an imaginative creation of real value but without absolute significance. His philosophical works include *The Sense of Beauty* (1896), *The Life of Reason* (1905–6), *The Realms of Being* (4 vol., 1927–40), and *Dominations and Powers* (1951). His only novel, *The Last Puritan* (1935), had great success.

Santería, religion originating in W Africa, developed by YORUBA slaves in Cuba, and practiced by an estimated one million in the U.S. Blending African beliefs with those of Roman Catholicism, it fuses Christian saints with African deities (orishas). Rites are led by a priest or priestess, and reincarnation is a main belief. One of its most important rituals involves animal sacrifice, which was ruled a constitutional religious practice in a 1993 Supreme Court decision.

Santiago, city (1992 pop. 4,233,060), central Chile, capital of Chile and of Santiago prov., on the Mapocho R. Chile's largest city, housing a third of the country's population, it is the commercial and political heart of the republic and a manufacturing center with iron and steel foundries. The city is modern in appearance, but its ground plan is colonial. Since its founding in 1541, Santiago has survived floods, earthquakes, and an attack by the Mapuche people. In the early 1970s it was the scene of mass political demonstrations.

Santiago de Cuba, city (1989 est. pop. 405,000), SE Cuba, capital of Oriente prov. It is Cuba's second largest city and a major port, with some industrial plants. A former capital of Cuba founded by the Spanish in the 16th cent., it was the scene of heavy fighting (1898) during the SPANISH-AMERICAN WAR. Fidel CASTRO's attack on an army garrison here (July 26, 1953) launched the Cuban Revolution.

Santiago de los Caballeros, city (1981 pop. 278,638), N Dominican Republic. The second largest city in the country, it is the commercial hub of its most densely populated area, the fertile Cibao lowland. It was founded c.1495 and is one of the oldest cities in the Americas.

Santillana, Iñigo López de Mendoza, marqués de [säntēl yä'nä], 1398–1458, Spanish poet, critic, and literary patron. The chief literary figure of his day, he wrote the first literary criticism and SONNETS in Spanish, and commissioned translations of works by VERGIL, PETRARCH, and DANTE. He is best known, however, for his popular songs, or *serranillas*.

Santo Domingo, former colony of Spain, on the island of HISPANIOLA. It included what is now the DOMINICAN REPUBLIC and, in its early days, HAITI. COLUMBUS discovered the island and founded the first settlement there in 1492. Spanish colonists established an agricultural economy in the east. The west was undeveloped until settled by French planters in the 1600s; it was ceded to France in 1697. In 1795 Spain ceded the rest of the island to France, but the settlers in the east rebelled and restored (1808–9) Spanish rule. They declared independence in 1821 but were conquered by Haiti the next year. The Haitians were expelled in 1844, and the Dominican Republic was established.

Santo Domingo, city (1981 pop. 1,313,172), S Dominican Republic, capital and largest city and port of the Dominican Republic, on the Caribbean Sea. Founded Aug. 4, 1496, by Bartholomew Columbus, it may be the oldest continuously inhabited settlement in the Western Hemisphere. It was the first seat of Spanish colonial administration in the New World and was the capital of the colony of SANTO DOMINGO. Almost entirely destroyed by a hurricane in 1930, it was rebuilt and was called Ciudad Trujillo (after Rafael TRUJILLO) until 1961. Now a city of wide avenues and modern buildings, it has the oldest cathedral in the Americas (begun 1514). The world's largest lighthouse is just outside the city.

Santorini: see THERA.

Santos-Dumont, Alberto [sän'to͞ozh-dümôN'], 1873–1932, Brazilian aeronaut active in France. He was the first to construct and fly (1898) a gasoline-motored AIRSHIP. He made several pioneering lighter-than-air flights; established (1903) the first airship base, at Neuilly, France; and built (1909) a successful small monoplane.

Sanzio, Raphael: see RAPHAEL SANTI.

São Paulo, city (1990 est. pop. 11,129,000), capital of São Paulo state, SE Brazil, on the Tietê R. The largest city in South America, it is an ultramodern metropolis dominating a vast, agriculturally rich hinterland. It is Brazil's commercial, financial, and industrial center, manufacturing textiles, processed food, chemicals, and other products, and is the nation's major transportation hub, with (since 1975) its first subway system. It is also a cultural and educational center, with several symphony orchestras and art museums, and four universities. The city is the site of the Bienal, an important international art exposition. Founded by Jesuits in 1554, São Paulo was the site at which Emperor Dom PEDRO I declared Brazil's independence from Portugal in 1822. It was a minor commercial city until the start of coffee cultivation in the state in the 1880s. More recent growth owes much to hydroelectric power development.

São Tomé [souN to͞omĕ], city, (1984 pop. 34,997), capital of SÃO TOMÉ AND PRINCIPE.

São Tomé and Principe [o͞oomĕ, prēn' sēpə], officially Democratic Republic of São Tomé and Principe, island republic (1992 est. pop. 132,000), 372 sq mi (964 sq km), W Africa, in the Gulf of Guinea, c.150 mi (240 km) W of Gabon. São Tomé is the capital and chief town. The country consists of the volcanic islands of São Tomé, Principe, Pedras, Tinhosas, and Rolas, which rise to 6,640 ft (2,024 m) on São Tomé. Lying just north of the equator, the islands are covered with thick vegetation. The economy is based entirely on the export of tropical produce, notably cocoa (about 80% of export earnings), copra, coffee, bananas, and palm oil. Small processing factories are the only industry. The native inhabitants are mainly descendants of African slaves brought from the mainland. The official language is Portuguese, and Roman Catholicism is the predominant faith.

History. The islands were discovered in 1471 by the Portuguese explorers Pedro Escobar and Jaõa Gomes; the São Tomé settlement was founded in 1483. Except for a century of Dutch rule (1641–1740), the islands were held by the Portuguese until independence was granted in 1975. The plantation economy was established in the 18th cent. Upon independence, Manuel Pinto da Costa, leader of a Gabon-based nationalist movement, became president. The first years were marked by economic hardship caused by the departure of the Portuguese and of a large number of contract and migrant workers. The government has sought to strengthen the economy through agrarian reforms and by seeking foreign investment in industry and tourism. In 1991 Pinto da Costa was succeeded by Miguel Trovoada, who won the country's first free presidential election.

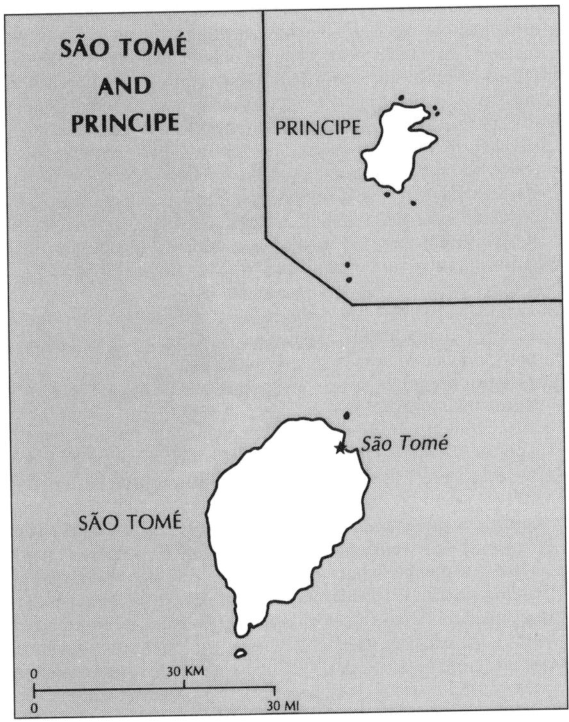

sap, plant fluid consisting of water and dissolved substances. The term is generally applied to all the fluid that moves through the xylem (see WOOD) and phloem (see BARK) of the STEMS of higher plants. Water with dissolved minerals ascends to the leaves via the xylem vessels; the solution with food produced by the leaves descends to other parts via the phloem.

Sapir, Edward [səpēr'], 1884–1939, American linguist and anthropologist; b. Germany. His studies on the ethnology and linguistics of certain Native American groups contributed greatly to the development of descriptive linguistics.

sapphire, GEM, transparent blue variety of CORUNDUM, found chiefly in Thailand, India, Sri Lanka, and Myanmar. Like rubies, some sapphires show an internal star when cut with a round top. Synthetic stones are made by fusing aluminum oxide, with titanium oxide added for color.

Sappho, fl. early 6th cent. B.C., greatest of the early Greek lyric poets; b. Lesbos. Facts on her life are scarce and only fragments of her poetry survive, the longest seven stanzas. She wrote in Aeolic dialect, in many meters, one of which (the Sapphic) is named for her. Her love lyrics, characterized by passion and simplicity, greatly influenced CATULLUS, OVID, and SWINBURNE.

Sapporo, city (1990 pop. 1,671,765), capital of Hokkaido prefecture, SW Hokkaido, Japan. One of Japan's most rapidly growing urban centers, Sapporo is famous for its annual snow festival. It was the site of the 1972 winter Olympics. Food processing, lumbering, woodworking, and printing are the major industries.

saprophyte, any plant that relies on dead organic matter for its food; most do not have CHLOROPHYLL and therefore cannot photosynthesize. Saprophytes include most fungi (see FUNGUS) and a few flowering plants, e.g., some ORCHIDS. They aid in the breakdown of dead plants and animals.

sapsucker: see WOODPECKER.

Sara or **Sarah,** wife of ABRAHAM and mother of ISAAC. She was one of the four Jewish matriarchs. After she gave birth to Isaac in her old age, she became jealous of her handmaid Hagar, Abraham's concubine, whom she drove (with Hagar's son ISHMAEL) into the desert.

Saracens, term used by Christians in the Middle Ages to designate Muslims in general, although strictly the term applied only to the people of NW Arabia. In Spain the term MOORS was used.

Sarajevo [sâr″əyā′vō], city (1987 est. pop. 341,250), capital of BOSNIA AND HERCEGOVINA, on the Bosnia R. Its traditional manufactures include metal products and textiles, and lignite and other metals were mined nearby, but economic activity has been depressed by civil war since 1992. The majority of the population is Muslim, and the city is noted for its Muslim architecture. Founded in 1263, it was held by the Turks from 1429 and passed to Austria-Hungary in 1878. The assassination (1914) of Archduke FRANCIS FERDINAND and his wife there sparked WORLD WAR I. Part of Yugoslavia after 1918, Sarajevo became the capital of independent Bosnia in 1992 and has been under Serbian siege since Apr. 1992. A NATO ultimatum led to the withdrawal or inactivation of the Serbian artillery surrounding Sarajevo in 1994. The city was the site of the 1984 winter Olympic games.

Sarasate, Pablo de [säräsä′tā], 1844–1908, Spanish violin virtuoso. He wrote many brilliant violin pieces in the Spanish idiom; his most popular work was *Zigeunerweisen.*

Saratoga campaign, in the AMERICAN REVOLUTION, a series of engagements fought (June–Oct. 1777) in NEW YORK. To split the colonies along the Hudson, the British planned a three-pronged advance on Albany—S from Canada, N from New York City, E along the Mohawk R. The northern force never arrived. The eastern force, under Barry ST. LEGER, besieged Fort Stanwix (Aug. 3) but, frightened by a rumor (Aug. 22), retreated to Canada. Coming south, John BURGOYNE captured TICONDEROGA (July 6), but was later defeated in a raid on Bennington (Aug. 14–16). Burgoyne halted near Saratoga Springs, where American forces, under Horatio GATES, prevented him from breaking through at Freeman's Farm (Sept. 19) and Bemis Heights (Oct. 7). Outnumbered and surrounded, Burgoyne surrendered (Oct. 17). This was the first great American victory, and probably the decisive battle, of the Revolution.

Saratoga Springs, resort and residential city (1990 pop. 25,001), E N.Y.; inc. as a city 1915. Skidmore College is a major employer; the city has dairy and light manufacturing industries. The scene of a battle (1777) in the Revolution, Saratoga Springs was famous in the 19th cent. for its mineral waters; it became one of the country's most fashionable resorts, with a casino, horse racing, and other attractions.

Sarawak, self-governing state (1990 est. pop. 1,669,000), 48,342 sq mi (125,206 sq km), Malaysia, in NW Borneo and on the South China Sea, bordered by Brunei and Sabah (NE) and Kalimantan or Indonesian Borneo (S, W). Kuching is the capital. Its chief products are petroleum, rice, sago, and rubber. Sarawak was ceded (1841) by the sultan of BRUNEI to James BROOKE, an Englishman, who became rajah of the independent state. A British protectorate from 1888, it remained under the rule of the Brookes until they ceded it to Britain in 1946. In 1963 it joined the Federation of Malaysia.

sarcodinian, member of a phylum (Sarcodina) of ameboid PROTOZOANS, unicellular organisms that move and capture food by means of pseudopods, flowing temporary extensions of the cytoplasm and body wall. The phylum is divided into the flagellates and the sarcodines (including the AMEBAS and foraminiferans).

sardine: see HERRING.

Sardinia, island (1990 pop. 1,657,562), 9,032 sq mi (24,092 sq km), W Italy, in the Mediterranean Sea. The capital, Cagliari, is on the south coast. It is mainly mountainous, rising to 6,016 ft (1,834 m) in Mt. Gennargentu, with sheep and goat pastures inland and some agriculture in upland valleys and southwest coastal regions. Mining (lead, zinc, antimony) and fishing are important industries. Sardinia, a source of grain and salt for ancient Rome, was for centuries under the nominal authority of outside overlords. After it was granted (1720) to VICTOR AMADEUS II of SAVOY, he and his successors, as kings of Sardinia, exercised feudal privileges until 1835. Part of the Kingdom of Italy from 1861, the Sardinians were granted limited regional autonomy in 1947.

Sardinia, Kingdom of, name given to the holdings of the house of SAVOY in 1720, when the Treaty of London awarded the island of Sardinia to Savoy to compensate for its loss of Sicily to Austria. The kingdom included Sardinia, Savoy, Piedmont, and Nice. The Congress of VIENNA (1815) added Liguria. It grew during the RISORGIMENTO, and in 1861 VICTOR EMMANUEL II of Sardinia became king of Italy.

sardonyx: see ONYX.

Sardou, Victorien [särdo͞o′], 1831–1908, French dramatist. He wrote some 70 plays, ranging from light comedy to historical melodrama. His best farce is *Divorçons!* (1880). Other works include such BERNHARDT vehicles as *Fédora* (1882) and *La Tosca* (1887), the basis of Puccini's opera.

Sargasso Sea, part of the north Atlantic Ocean between the West Indies and the Azores, at about 30°N lat. This relatively still sea is the center of a great swirl of ocean currents and is noted for the abundance of seaweed on its surface. Bermuda is in the northwestern part of the sea.

Sargent, John Singer, 1856–1925, American painter; b. Italy. In 1884 he moved to London, where he spent most of his life, painting the dashing, flattering portraits of social celebrities for which he is famous. A prolific painter of great facility, he was brilliant in his treatment of textures and a virtuoso in his handling of brush stroke. Sargent also painted many impressionistic watercolor landscapes early and late in his career. Notable portraits are Isabella Stewart GARDNER (Gardner Mus., Boston) and Mme X (Metropolitan Mus.).

Sargon I (Sargon of Akkad), c.2334–2279 B.C., Mesopotamian ruler. One of the earliest empire-builders, he founded the first Semitic dynasty, which flourished for 150 years and controlled much of southwestern Asia.

Sargon II, d. 705 B.C., king of Assyria (721–705 B.C.) and founder of the last Assyrian dynasty. He completed the conquest of Samaria begun by his predecessor Sahalmaneser V and deported the Israelites so widely throughout Assyria that they became "the lost tribes of Israel."

Sarmatia, ancient district about the Don R. occupied by the Sarmatians, 3d cent. B.C.–2d cent. A.D. They spoke an Indo-Iranian language, and were nomadic relatives of the Scythians. The term Sarmatia is also used for the land along the Danube and over the Carpathians, where the Sarmatians were later driven by the HUNS. The Sarmatians allied with Rome against the GERMANS, by whom they had been scattered by the 3d cent. A.D.

Sarney, José, 1930–, president of Brazil (1985–90). He became vice president when Brazil's military rulers voluntarily surrendered power to a conservative civilian government in 1985, and president when president-elect Tancredo Neves (Apr. 1985) died. He failed to cope with Brazil's massive foreign debt and runaway inflation.

Sarnoff, David, 1891–1971, American radio and television pioneer;

b. Russia. He worked for the Marconi Wireless Co., winning recognition as the narrator of the *Titanic* disaster (1912). After the Radio Corp. of America absorbed (1921) Marconi, Sarnoff became general manager. As president (after 1930) and chairman of the board (from 1947) of RCA, he played a major role in the development of television.

Saroyan, William, 1908–81, American author; b. Fresno, Calif. A prolific writer, he combined optimism, sentimentality, and love of country in plays, e.g., *The Time of Your Life* (1939; Pulitzer); novels, e.g., *The Human Comedy* (1942); short stories, e.g., *My Name Is Aram* (1940); and autobiographical works.

Sarraute, Nathalie [särōt′], 1900–, French novelist; b. Russia. Her experimental "anti-novels" focus upon the psychological preoccupations and passing sensations of individuals. They include *Tropisms* (1939), *The Planetarium* (1959), and *Fools Say* (1976).

sarsaparilla, name for various plants and for an extract from their roots, used in medicine and beverages. True sarsaparilla is obtained from tropical American species of the genus *Smilax* of the LILY family; these have thick rootstalks and thin roots several feet long. Wild sarsaparilla (*Aralia nudicaulis*), related to GINSENG, is used as a substitute source for the extract.

Sarto, Andrea del, 1486–1531, Florentine High RENAISSANCE painter. He was given the title "faultless painter" for his FRESCOES of St. Philip's life (Cloisters of the Annunziata, Florence). His harmonious color and consonance of figure and background are seen in *Madonna of the Harpies* (Uffizi) and *Holy Family* (Metropolitan Mus.).

Sartre, Jean-Paul [sär′trə], 1905–80, French philosopher and author, a leading exponent of EXISTENTIALISM. His writings examine the individual as a responsible but lonely being, adrift in a meaningless universe with a terrifying freedom to choose. His existentialist works include the monumental treatise *Being and Nothingness* (1943); the plays *The Flies* (1943), *No Exit* (1944), and *The Respectful Prostitute* (1947); and the novels *Nausea* (1938) and *The Age of Reason* (1945; first of a trilogy). *The Critique of Dialectical Reason* (1960) combined MARXISM and existentialism whereas *The Family Idiot* (1982) explored FLAUBERT from a Freudian viewpoint. Sartre declined the 1964 Nobel Prize in literature.

Saskatchewan, province (1991 pop. 988,928), 251,699 sq mi (651,900 sq km), W Canada, bounded by the Northwest Territories (N), Manitoba (E), North Dakota and Montana (S), and Alberta (W). Northern Saskatchewan is part of the desolate but mineral-rich CANADIAN SHIELD, and to the south is a mixed forest belt of marketable timber. The CHURCHILL and the Saskatchewan are the main rivers. Only in S Saskatchewan has there been substantial settlement or development. Except for small areas of grazing and mixed farming, this region is basically devoted to the growing of hard wheat. Oil and natural gas are the most important minerals; other minerals include uranium, copper, zinc, gold, coal, and potash. Most industries process raw materials. REGINA, the capital, and SASKATOON are the chief cities.

History. The area's first trading posts were established (c.1750) by the French, but the HUDSON'S BAY COMPANY made the first permanent settlement at Cumberland House in 1774. In 1870 the company ceded its rights to the Canadian government, and the area became part of the NORTHWEST TERRITORIES. The building of the railway (1882) attracted many settlers and opened trade through the GREAT LAKES. A rebellion (1884–85) led by Louis RIEL was suppressed, and Saskatchewan became a province in 1905. The Progressive Conservatives were in power from 1982 to 1992, when they lost to the New Democrats. Saskatchewan sends 6 senators (appointed) and 14 representatives to the national parliament.

Saskatoon, city (1991 pop. 186,058), Saskatchewan, W Canada, on the South Saskatchewan R. It is the chief center of central and N Saskatchewan, with oil refineries, grain elevators, flour mills, stockyards, and meat- and potash-processing plants. Saskatoon was settled in 1883 and grew rapidly after the coming of the railroad (1890). The Univ. of Saskatchewan is there.

sassafras: see LAUREL.

Sassanid or **Sassanian,** last dynasty of native rulers to reign (A.D. c.224–c.640) in Persia before the Arab conquest. ARDASHIR I was the first of the dynasty. They were much occupied with wars, and their enemies included the Romans, White Huns, and Armenians. They restored the ancient religion of ZOROASTRIANISM, which virtually disappeared again after the dynasty fell. The last Sassanid ruler, Yazdagird III, fled the country when it was overrun by Arab invaders.

Sassoon, Siegfried, 1886–1967, English poet and novelist. An officer in World War I, he wrote of war's brutality and wastefulness in grim, forceful verse in *The Old Huntsman* (1917), *Counter-Attack* (1918), and other collections. His novels include the semiautobiographical trilogy collected as *The Memoirs of George Sherston* (1937).

Sassou-Nguesso, Denis, 1943?–, Congolese army officer, president of Congo (1979–92). He served (1977–79) as the minister of national defense. As president he won approval for a new Marxist constitution, signed (1981) a friendship treaty with the USSR, and maintained strong economic ties with France. The increasing economic impoverishment of the Congo, however, led to a national political conference (1991) that stripped him of many powers. In 1992 he ran for reelection in a democratic contest and came in third.

Sastre, Alfonso [sä′strā], 1926–, Spanish dramatist. His controversial plays, including *Condemned Squad* (1953), *Death Thrust* (1960), and *The Gloomy Comrade* (1972), deal with injustice, alienation, and violence from a Marxist and existentialist point of view.

Satan [Heb., = adversary], in Judaism, Christianity, and Islam, the principle of evil conceived as a person; also called the Devil. In Christian tradition Satan was the leader of the angels who rebelled against God and who were cast out of heaven. He and his followers are seen as tempters of humanity and the source of evil in the world. He has numerous other names, such as Lucifer, Beelzebub, Evil One, and Prince of Darkness.

satellite, artificial, object launched by a ROCKET into orbit around the earth or, occasionally, another solar-system body (see SPACE PROBE). A satellite in circular orbit at an altitude of 22,300 mi (35,880 km) has a period of exactly 24 hr, the time it takes the earth to rotate once on its axis; such an orbit is called synchronous. If such an orbit also lies in the equatorial plane, it is called geostationary, because the satellite will remain stationary over one point on the earth's surface. The first artificial satellite, *Sputnik 1,* was launched by the USSR on Oct. 4, 1957. *Explorer 1,* the first American satellite, was launched on Jan. 31, 1958. The principal types of satellites are COMMUNICATIONS SATELLITES, NAVIGATION SATELLITES, RECONNAISSANCE SATELLITES, and WEATHER SATELLITES. Major U.S. scientific research satellites include many Explorer satellites and various orbiting OBSERVATORIES, such as the HUBBLE SPACE TELESCOPE. Major Soviet or Russian space-science satellite programs include Elektron, Proton, Prognoz, and many Cosmos satellites. The U.S. has also launched several Landsat remote-imaging satellites to survey the earth's resources by means of special television cameras and radiometric scanners. The similar French SPOT satellite provides higher-resolution photographs of the earth.

satellite, natural, celestial body orbiting a planet. The earth's only satellite is the MOON; thus satellites of other planets are often referred to as moons. The largest in the solar system is Jupiter's Ganymede, whose radius of 1,639 mi (2,638 km) is larger than that of the planet Mercury. See also PLANET (table); articles on individual planets.

Satie, Erik [sätē′], 1866–1925, French composer. He rejected ROMANTICISM and IMPRESSIONISM and developed an abstract, often witty, and deceptively simple style. Satie's harmonic innovations are evident in such early piano pieces as *Sarabandes* (1887) and *Gymnopédies* (1888), while some of his later works, e.g., *Socrate* (1918), foreshadowed the neoclassicism of STRAVINSKY. He was the center of the group of young composers known as "les SIX."

satin spar: see GYPSUM.

satire, a work of literature or art that, by inspiring laughter, contempt, or horror, seeks to correct the follies and abuses it uncovers. The Roman poets HORACE and JUVENAL became models for the two leading types of satire: Horatian satire is mild, amused, and sophisticated; Juvenalian is vitriolic and indignant. Noted satirists include VOLTAIRE, Alexander POPE, William HOGARTH, Jonathan SWIFT, Oscar WILDE, Mark TWAIN, Evelyn WAUGH, James THURBER, Kingsley AMIS, and Philip ROTH.

Sato Eisaku, 1901–75, Japanese prime minister (1964–72). A Liberal-Democrat, he signed (1969) a treaty with the U.S. that re-established (1972) Japanese sovereignty in Okinawa. Sato was awarded the 1974 Nobel Peace Prize for his efforts to halt the spread of nuclear weapons.

Saturday: see WEEK; SABBATH.

Saturn, in astronomy, 6th PLANET from the sun, at a mean distance of 886.7 million mi (1.4270 billion km). It has an equatorial diameter of 74,980 mi (120,660 km) and an atmosphere of hydrogen, helium, and traces of methane and ammonia. Like Jupiter, Saturn has counterflowing easterly and westerly winds. Saturn's most remarkable feature is its ring system, composed of billions of water-ice particles orbiting around the planet. The main rings are at distances ranging from 4,140 to 49,880 mi (6,670 to 80,270 km) above the cloud tops, and two other tenuous rings orbit much more distantly. Saturn also has at least 18 natural satellites. The largest is **Titan** (diameter: 3,200 mi/5,150 km); discovered by Christiaan HUYGENS in 1655, it is the only natural satellite in the solar system with a substantial atmosphere. Saturn has six major icy satellites. The most prominent feature of heavily cratered **Mimas,** the innermost, is a large impact crater about one third the diameter of the satellite. Certain broad regions of **Enceladus** are uncratered, indicating geological activity that has somehow resurfaced the satellite within the last 100 million years. **Tethys** also has a very large impact crater, as well as an extensive series of valleys and troughs that stretches three quarters of the way around the satellite. Both **Dione** and **Rhea** have bright, heavily cratered leading hemispheres and darker trailing hemispheres with wispy streaks thought to be produced by deposits of ice inside various surface troughs or cracks. **Iapetus,** the outermost of the large icy satellites, has a dark leading hemisphere and a bright trailing hemisphere. The remaining eleven satellites, some sharing orbits with others, are smaller in size. The two largest of these, dark-surfaced **Phoebe** and irregularly shaped **Hyperion,** orbit far from the planet. Saturn has been encountered by three SPACE PROBES: *Pioneer 11* (1979), *Voyager 1* (1980), and *Voyager 2* (1981). Photos and other data from *Voyager 2* indicate the possibility of at least five more small satellites.

Saturn, in Roman religion, god of harvests; husband of Ops; father of JUPITER, JUNO, CERES, PLUTO, and NEPTUNE; identified with CRONUS. After the TITANS' fall, he was said to have fled to Italy, settled on the CAPITOLINE HILL, civilized the people, and taught them agriculture. On his festival, the Saturnalia, work ceased, gifts were exchanged, and war was outlawed.

satyr, in Greek myth, a forest and mountain creature. Part human, with a horse's tail and ears, and a goat's horns and legs, satyrs were merry, drunken, lustful devotees of DIONYSUS.

Saudi Arabia, officially Kingdom of Saudi Arabia, kingdom (1992 prelim. pop. 16,929,294), 829,995 sq mi (2,149,690 sq km), SW Asia, occupying most of the Arabian peninsula, bounded by Jordan, Iraq, and Kuwait (N), the Persian Gulf, Qatar, and the United Arab Emirates (E), Yemen and Oman (S), and the Red Sea (W). RIYADH is the capital, JIDDA the principal port. Saudi Arabia has five major physical regions: the great Rub al-Khali, a sand desert occupying the entire south and southeast; the Nejd, a vast, barren plateau in the center; the Hejaz and Asir, along the RED SEA, with mountains rising from an arid coastal plain; and the Eastern Province, along the PERSIAN GULF, site of the country's rich oil resources. The climate is usually hot and dry, although the humidity along the coasts is high. Saudi Arabia has at least one quarter of the world's oil reserves, and the oil industry dominates the economy. Huge revenues from oil exports have been used to diversify the industrial base; metals, chemicals, plastics, cement, and fertilizer are now produced. Irrigation projects have reclaimed many acres of desert, and grains, dates, citrus fruits, and vegetables are grown. Nomadic BEDOUINS raise camels, sheep, goats, and horses. Income is also derived from Muslim pilgrims who travel from all parts of the world to the holy cities of MECCA and MEDINA. The overwhelming majority of the population are Arabs who adhere to the Wahhabi sect of Islam, but 27% of the population consists of resident foreigners. Arabic is the official language.

History. ARABIA has been inhabited for thousands of years by nomadic Semitic tribes. With the birth (A.D. 570) of MUHAMMAD, in Mecca, Arabia was briefly the center of Islam, but by the end of the 7th cent. the area was disunited. Modern Saudi Arabia owes its existence to IBN SAUD, an adherent of the puritanical WAHHABI Muslim sect. Beginning in 1902 he conquered the Nejd, Al Hasa, and Hejaz regions, and in 1932 he proclaimed himself king of a united Saudi Arabia. Oil was discovered in 1936; commercial production began in 1938. Ibn Saud died in 1953 and was succeeded by his eldest son, Saud. In 1964 Saud was deposed by FAISAL, who secured (1974) an agreement giving the Saudis a 60% majority ownership of foreign oil concessions in their country. Under both monarchs, Saudi Arabia aided (1962–67) royalist forces against Egyptian-backed republican rebels in YEMEN. In 1975 Faisal was assassinated; he was replaced by KHALID, who inaugurated a program of industrialization and social welfare. In the conflict with Israel, Saudi Arabia has generally supported the Arab states, although as a friend of the U.S. it is a somewhat moderating force. Its moderating influence has also been felt in the ORGANIZATION OF PETROLEUM EXPORTING COUNTRIES (OPEC), in which it has acted to stabilize petroleum prices. Khalid died in 1982 and was succeeded as king by FAHD. Military clashes, oil-policy disputes, and rioting Iranian pilgrims in Mecca led Saudi Arabia to sever diplomatic relations with Iran in 1989. In 1990 the kingdom joined the coalition that opposed Iraq's forcible annexation of Kuwait, and the forces of the coalition were largely based in N Saudi Arabia (see PERSIAN GULF WAR). In 1992 King Fahd decreed a new constitution; among its features were an appointed national council (est. 1993) with the right to review, but not overrule, government acts, but the royal family's power was basicly undiminished.

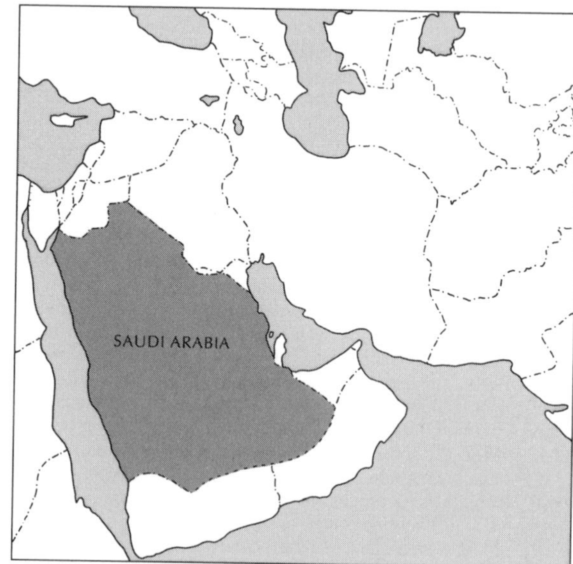

Saul, fl. 11th cent. B.C., first king of the ancient Hebrews. DAVID was first the protégé, then the rival, finally the successor, of Saul. Defeated and wounded in battle with the Philistines on Mt. Gilboa, Saul committed suicide rather than be captured. Though he was unsuccessful in defeating the Philistines, Saul paved the way for national unity under David.

Saul of Tarsus: see PAUL, SAINT.

Sault Sainte Marie Canals [so͞o sānt mərē′], popularly called the **Soo Canals,** two toll-free ship canals on the U.S.-Canada border. Bypassing rapids in the St. Marys R. between lakes Huron and Superior, they are a vital link in the St. Lawrence & Great Lakes Waterway. The deeper U.S. canal (1.6 mi/2.6 km long and 80 ft/24 m wide) accommodates larger vessels than the Canadian canal (1.4 mi/2.3 km long and 60 ft/18 m wide).

Saussure, Ferdinand de, 1857–1913, Swiss linguist. One of the founders of modern LINGUISTICS, he established the structural study of language, emphasizing the arbitrary relationship of the linguistic sign to that which it signifies. Saussure distinguished synchronic linguistics (studying language at a given moment) from diachronic linguistics (studying the changing state of a language over time); he further opposed what he named *langue* (the state of a language at a certain time) to *parole* (the speech of an individual). Saussure's most influential work is the *Course in General Linguistics* (1916), a compilation of notes on his lectures.

Savage's Station: see SEVEN DAYS BATTLES.

savanna or **savannah,** tropical or subtropical grassland lying on the margin of the trade-wind belts. Its climate is characterized by a rainy period in summer and a dry winter when the grass withers. The largest savannas are in Africa.

Savannah, city (1990 pop. 137,560), seat of Chatham co., SE Ga., near the mouth of the Savannah R.; inc. 1789. A busy commercial port, the city has chemical, plastics, lumber, paper, and other industries. The oldest city in Georgia, founded in 1733 by James OGLETHORPE, Savannah was the commercial rival of CHARLESTON. It was the object of fighting in the American Revolution and in the Civil War. Its historic district has fine old homes, churches, and shady streets.

Savimbi, Jonas, 1934–, Angolan rebel leader. In 1966 he founded the National Union for the Total Independence of Angola (UNITA), a guerrilla group opposed to Portuguese rule in Angola. When independence came (1975), UNITA was the weakest of three groups competing for power, but Savimbi benefited from support from the U.S. and South Africa, who were opposed to Angola's Marxist government, and civil war ensued. In 1991 Savimbi and the Angolan government agreed to a truce, and multiparty elections, but when Savimbi and UNITA lost (1992) in the elections they resumed fighting.

savings and loan association, also known as **building and loan association,** type of financial institution that accepts savings from the public and invests those savings primarily in home MORTGAGES. A savings and loan association (S&L) may be organized as either a mutual or capital-stock institution. Of the 4,700 associations in the U.S., 55% operate under a federal charter, the others being chartered by the states. The first U.S. S&L was founded in 1831. A period of rapid expansion came after World War II, fed by the boom in new housing. In the late 1970s, however, many S&Ls were in serious difficulty. While receiving low interest on old outstanding mortgages, the S&Ls had to pay much higher rates for new funds, because of record-high INTEREST rates. Many depositors had also switched into other investments, such as MONEY-MARKET FUNDS. In response to these problems the legal restrictions on S&Ls were eased in 1982. A new crisis arose when bad loans, poor investments, and fraud caused an increasing number of S&Ls to fail and the Federal Savings and Loan Insurance Corporation (FSLIC) became insolvent. In 1989 the FSLIC was dissolved, its insurance functions given to a new entity supervised by the FEDERAL DEPOSIT INSURANCE CORPORATION, and the Resolution Trust Corporation was established to take over failed S&Ls and dispose of their assets. The bailout of the failed S&Ls is expected to cost as much as $400–500 billion over 30 years.

savings bank: see BANKING.

Savonarola, Girolamo, 1452–98, Italian religious reformer. A DOMINICAN, he became popular in Florence for his eloquent attacks on moral laxity and for his predictions, some of them accurate. After the MEDICI were exiled (1494), he became spiritual ruler of Florence and imposed a severe regime. He supported the invasion of Italy by CHARLES VIII of France, hoping that Charles would help in forming a democratic government in Florence and reforming the scandalously corrupt court of Pope ALEXANDER VI. Excommunicated (1497) after ignoring the pope's order to stop preaching, Savonarola was finally executed as a false prophet.

Savoy, house of, dynasty that ruled Savoy and Piedmont from the 11th cent., Sicily (1713–20), Sardinia (1720–1861), and Italy (1861–1946). Its first historical member was an 11th-cent. count who held lands in Savoy and Piedmont. Through marriage and diplomacy his successors expanded their holdings in France, Switzerland, and Italy. AMADEUS VIII acquired the ducal title in 1416. By 1536 Savoy had lost its Swiss possessions, and FRANCIS I of France occupied the rest of the duchy. In 1559 EMMANUEL PHILIBERT obtained the restoration of his duchy and made Turin his capital. His grandson VICTOR AMADEUS II became (1713) king of Sicily for his role in the War of the SPANISH SUCCESSION. Sicily was exchanged (1720) with Spain for Sardinia, and the state became known as the kingdom of Sardinia. In 1831 Charles Albert, of the cadet line of Savoy-Carignano, became king. He involved Sardinia in the RISORGIMENTO, by which his son, VICTOR EMMANUEL II, became (1861) king of Italy. Victor Emmanuel II's son, Humbert I (r.1878–1900), was assassinated. Humbert's son and successor, VICTOR EMMANUEL III, abdicated after World War II. His son, Humbert II, reigned briefly (1946) before Italy became a republic.

Saxe, Maurice, comte de [säks], 1696–1750, marshal of France, an illegitimate son of AUGUSTUS II of Poland. A brilliant commander, he led the French to victory at Fontenoy (1745) and Raucoux (1746) in the War of the AUSTRIAN SUCCESSION. His *Mes Rêveries* (1757) is a remarkable work on the art of war.

saxifrage, name for some members of the Saxifragaceae, a diverse family of herbs, shrubs, and small trees of cosmopolitan distribution. The true saxifrages (primarily the genus *Saxifraga*) comprise a group of low rock plants often cultivated as rock-garden and border plants, e.g., the strawberry geranium (*S. sarmentosa*). The Eastern early saxifrage (*S. virginiensis*) and the Western umbrella plant (*S. peltata*) are American wildflowers. The arctic and alpine *S. oppositifolia* is one of the northernmost of flowering plants. The genus *Ribes*, a group of berry-bearing shrubs including the gooseberry and CURRANT, is of minor economic importance. The mock orange, or syringa (genus *Philadelphus*), has white, sometimes fragrant flowers similar to orange blossoms, and the hydrangea (genus *Hydrangea*), another member of the family, has showy flat-topped clusters of white, pink, or blue flowers.

Saxo Grammaticus, c.1150–c.1220, the first important Danish historian. The first nine books of his *Gesta Danorum* record oral tradition and legends; the remaining seven are a valuable record of contemporary events.

Saxons, Germanic people living in S Jutland in the 2d cent. In the 3d and 4th cent. they raided the coasts of the North Sea, and by the 5th cent. they had settled in N Gaul. Raiding Saxons began (c.450) to settle in Britain. By the 6th cent. they and the Angles were founding ANGLO-SAXON kingdoms, with WESSEX dominant. Continental or "Old Saxons" in 566 became tributaries of the FRANKS, and were finally conquered (804) by CHARLEMAGNE. The treaty of Verdun (843) included Saxon lands in the area that is modern Germany.

Saxony, Ger. *Sachsen,* state (1990 est. pop. 4,970,000), 6,561 sq mi (16,993 sq km), E Germany. DRESDEN is its capital; other important cities are CHEMNITZ and LEIPZIG. Saxony was originally the land of the SAXONS, which in Frankish times was in NW Germany. In the 9th cent. the first duchy of Saxony, one of the five stem duchies of medieval Germany, was created. The duchy was broken up after Holy Roman Emperor FREDERICK I ousted (1180) HENRY THE LION from the fief. In 1356 the duke of Saxe-Wittenburg was made a permanent elector of the Empire. His territory, called **Electoral Saxony,** lay east of the original stem duchy. In 1425 it passed to the WETTIN family. It was a center of the German REFORMATION in the 16th cent. In 1697 the elector of Saxony became king of Poland as AUGUSTUS II. The death (1763) of his son, AUGUSTUS III, ended the union with Poland. The period 1697 to 1763 was one of cultural and artistic flowering in Saxony and in its capital, Dresden. Saxony had retained the Polish crown in the War of the POLISH SUCCESSION (1733–35) but lost prestige in the War of the AUSTRIAN SUCCESSION (1740–48) and the SEVEN YEARS WAR (1756–63). Saxony was raised (1806) to a kingdom by NAPOLEON I in return for changing sides (1806) in the FRENCH REVOLUTIONARY WARS, but after his defeat it lost nearly half of its land to Prussia. The remaining **kingdom of Saxony** was defeated by Prussia in the AUSTRO-PRUSSIAN WAR (1866) and joined the German Empire in 1871. Under the Weimar Republic it became (1918) the state of Saxony. In 1949 it became part of East Germany. It was abolished as an administrative unit in 1952 but reconstituted upon German reunification (1990).

saxophone: see WIND INSTRUMENT.

Sayers, Dorothy Leigh, 1983–1957, English writer. Her erudite detective stories feature the nobleman-detective Lord Peter Wimsey and include *Strong Poison* (1930), *Murder Must Advertise* (1933), and *The Nine Tailors* (1934).

Sb, chemical symbol of the element ANTIMONY.

Sc, chemical symbol of the element SCANDIUM.

scabies: see MANGE.

Scalawags, derogatory term used in the South after the CIVIL WAR to describe white Southerners who joined the Republican party and aided the RECONSTRUCTION program.

scale, in music, any series of TONES arranged in a step-by-step rising or falling of PITCH. The scale most used in Western musical composition until the end of the 19th cent. was the diatonic scale, a series of seven tones. (The addition of a final top note, with a frequency twice that of the lowest note, defines this sequence as an *octave.*) The intervals of the diatonic scale were defined by PYTHAGORAS in the 6th cent. B.C. as five whole tones (t) and two semitones (s) in the order ttsttts. By the time of J.S. BACH, the chromatic scale of 12 equal semitones (as in the white and black keys of a keyboard scale) had become established, and the scales beginning on these notes remained the basis of Western TONALITY until the innovations of such modern composers as SCHOENBERG. DEBUSSY used a scale of six equal whole tones in his works. The pentatonic scale of five whole tones is prevalent in Asian music.

scale, in zoology, a flattened bony or horny outgrowth of the skin of an animal, particularly in FISHES and REPTILES, that serves primarily as protection. Fish scales, composed mostly of bone, form directly in the skin membrane; the type and number of scales figure in the identification of a species. Most reptiles have horny scales, or scutes, but some (e.g., the CROCODILE) have both horny and bony scales. In SNAKES, scales aid in movement. Birds have scales on the feet and sometimes the legs. Some mammals (e.g., the rat and the mouse) have tail scales.

Scalia, Antonin: see SUPREME COURT, UNITED STATES (table 1).

Scaliger, Joseph Justus, 1540–1609, French classical scholar. He became (1562) a Protestant and taught at Geneva (1572–74) and Leiden (from 1593). He was learned in mathematics, philosophy, and many languages, and established rules of criticism for studying texts and the classics. He surveyed known methods of measuring time and placed the study of calendars and dates on a scientific basis.

Scaliger, Julius Caesar, 1484–1558, Italian philologist and physician in France. In his *De causis linguae Latinae* (1540) he analyzed CICERO's style, criticizing the earlier studies of his humanist predecessors. He wrote commentaries on the medical and botanical works of HIPPOCRATES, Theophrastus, and ARISTOTLE, and urged an improved classification of plants. In his *Poetics* (1561), he extolled VERGIL and SENECA.

scallion: see ONION.

scallop or **pecten,** marine BIVALVE mollusk distinguished by rounded, ridged shells with radiating ribs and flared "wings" at the hinge. Scallops swim by flapping their shells with a powerful adductor muscle, the only part that is eaten as food.

Scanderbeg or **Skanderbeg,** c.1404–1468, Albanian national hero. The son of an Albanian prince, he was born George Castriota. He abjured Islam in 1443, styled himself prince of Albania, and devoted the rest of his life to defending Albania against Turkish invasion, on occasion allying himself with Venice, Naples, Hungary, and the pope. After his death Albania fell to the Turks.

Scandinavia, region of N Europe, consisting of NORWAY and SWEDEN (on the Scandinavian Peninsula), DENMARK, and usually also including FINLAND, ICELAND, and the FAEROE ISLANDS. Its people share similar histories and cultures, and most, except for the Finns and Lapps (see LAPLAND), speak closely related Germanic languages.

scandium (Sc), metallic element, discovered in 1879 by L.F. Nilson. A soft, silver-white RARE-EARTH METAL, it is in relatively greater abundance in the sun and certain stars than on earth. It is used in nickel alkaline storage batteries and as a radioactive tracer. See ELEMENT (table); PERIODIC TABLE.

scanning tunneling microscope, device for imaging and manipulating individual atoms on the surfaces of materials. The underlying principle of the microscope is the TUNNELING of electrons between a probe and the surface of the sample under study; the flow of electrons will vary as the distance between the probe and the sample changes. As the probe is moved above the surface, its height is continually adjusted, however, to keep the flow constant, and the fluctuations in height are recorded to produce a map of the surface. Microscopic manipulation of atoms is accomplished by applying a voltage pulse or a combination of electrostatic and chemical forces between the probe and the sample; a single atom can be extracted and deposited on the probe, which can then be moved and the atom redeposited on the surface. The microscope was developed in the early 1980s by Gerd Binnig and Heinrich Rohrer, who were awarded the 1986 Nobel Prize in physics for their work.

scarab beetle or **scarab,** heavy-bodied, oval, often brightly colored or iridescent BEETLE. Some, called dung beetles, feed on animal dung and are important in recycling organic matter and disposing of disease-breeding wastes. Another group, which feeds on living plants and includes the Japanese and June beetles, are major crop and garden pests. Representations of scarabs, carved in stone or other materials, were popular in ancient Egypt and Rome.

Scarlatti, Alessandro, 1660–1725, Italian composer. A leader of the Neapolitan school, he helped establish the conventions of *opera seria,* perfecting the *aria da capo* and the three-part OVERTURE. He wrote over 100 operas, church music, songs, and hundreds of CANTATAS. His son, **(Giuseppe) Domenico Scarlatti,** 1685–1757, a harpsichord virtuoso known chiefly for his over 500 harpsichord SONATAS, is considered the founder of modern keyboard technique.

scarlet fever, acute, contagious respiratory infection caused by streptococci bacteria. Symptoms include a sore throat, fever, headache, white-coated tongue with red spots (strawberry tongue), and a skin rash. The disease usually occurs before age ten and is spread by direct contact. ANTIBIOTICS are used to treat severe cases and reduce the possibility of complications.

Schacht, Hjalmar Horace Greeley, 1877–1970, German financier. He conceived the plan that stabilized the German currency in the 1920s and was president of the Reichsbank (1923–30, 1933–39). Although he supported the NAZIS, he was placed in a concentration camp for his alleged part in the plot against HITLER (1944). He was acquitted (1946) of war crimes by the Nuremberg tribunal.

Schapiro, Meyer, 1904–, American art historian; b. Lithuania. A champion of modern art in the 1930s, he has since done important studies in early Christian, medieval, and contemporary art, exploring such areas as the relationship of art to sociology and psychoanalysis. His essays include "The Nature of Abstract Art" (1937) and "Leonardo and Freud" (1956). His books include *Romanesque Art* (1977) and *Modern Art: 19th and 20th Centuries,* (2 vol., 1978–79).

Schechter, Solomon, 1847–1915, Hebrew scholar; b. Romania. Schechter's identification of the hitherto missing Hebrew version of Ecclesiasticus won him international acclaim. As president of Jewish Theological Seminary (N.Y.C.), he brought together a faculty of scholars whose work defined the Conservative movement (see JUDAISM).

Scheele, Karl Wilhelm [shā'lə], 1742–86, Swedish chemist. A pharmacist, he prepared and studied OXYGEN (c.1773), but his published account (1777) appeared after Joseph PRIESTLEY's. He discovered NITROGEN independently of Daniel Rutherford and showed it to be a constituent of air. His treatise (1774) on MANGANESE aided in the discovery of that element and also of barium and chlorine. He isolated glycerin and many acids.

Scheherazade: see THOUSAND AND ONE NIGHTS.

Schelling, Friedrich Wilhelm Joseph von, 1775–1854, German philosopher. First influenced by the IDEALISM of J.G. FICHTE, he held the concept of the Absolute to represent the ultimate unity of mind and matter. Later Schelling saw history as a series of stages progressing toward that unity, and (unlike Fichte) held that nature itself progressed toward the Absolute. His concept of art as the unity of the natural and the spiritual, a bridge between German idealism and ROMANTICISM, influenced COLERIDGE.

scherzo [Ital., = joke], term denoting various types of musical compositions, primarily lively and surprising in rhythm or melody. The term may also refer to a movement of a symphony or sonata.

Schiaparelli, Giovanni Virginio [skyäpärĕl'lē], 1835–1910, Italian astronomer. He discovered (1861) the asteroid Hesperia. While director (1862–1900) of the Brera Observatory, Milan, he observed what he called canals on the surface of the planet Mars and showed that meteor swarms move through space in cometary orbits.

Schick test, a diagnostic test (developed c.1910) to evaluate susceptibility to DIPHTHERIA. A small amount of dilute diphtheria TOXIN is injected into the skin. The appearance of redness and swelling at the infection site within a week indicates low levels of antibody (i.e., little IMMUNITY) against the toxin and thus susceptibility to the disease.

Schiele, Egon [shē'lə], 1890–1918, Austrian expressionist painter and draftsman. His taut, linear style emphasizes anatomical structure. With KOKOSCHKA, he led the Austrian expressionist movement until his death from influenza at 28.

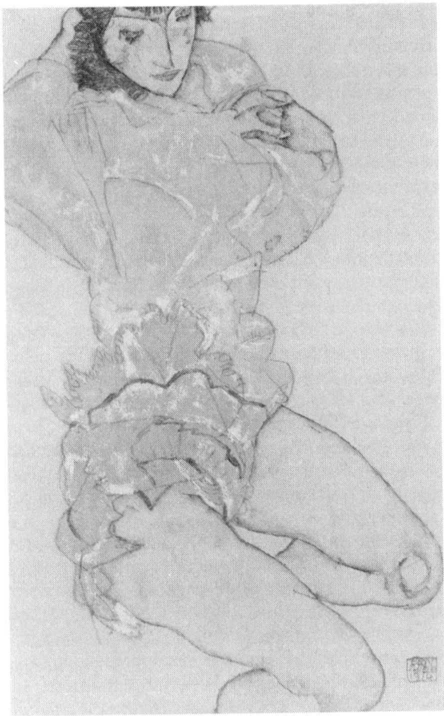

Egon Schiele's Woman in Yellow, *1914*

Schiller, Friedrich von, 1759–1805, German dramatist, poet, and historian, one of the greatest of German literary figures, second only to GOETHE. Educated at the duke of Württemberg's military academy, where he was forced to study medicine, Schiller soon turned to writing. His attack on political tyranny in *The Robbers* (1781) brought him fame, and Schiller fled his post as army surgeon to become a dramatist for the Mannheim theater. His second youthful success was *Don Carlos* (1785, performed 1787). In 1787 he settled in Weimar, where he was appointed a professor at the Univ. of Jena (1789), married (1790) the writer Charlotte von Lengefeld, and became close to Goethe, in whom his classical idealism, nobility of mind, and high ethical principles found a receptive spirit. Together they edited the literary periodicals *Horen* (1795–97) and *Musenalmanach* (1796–1800). Influenced by the philosophy of KANT, Schiller developed his aesthetic theories, stressing the sublime and the creative powers of humanity. He wrote several important treatises on aesthetics. Among his masterpieces are the dramatic trilogy *Wallenstein* (1798–99); *Mary Stuart* (1800), his most popular play; and *Wilhelm Tell* (1804), a technically masterful study of history and hero. Also noteworthy are his translations of SHAKESPEARE and RACINE, and his ballades and philosophical lyrics. His "Ode to Joy" (1785) was used by BEETHOVEN for the finale of the Ninth Symphony.

Schism, Great, or **Schism of the West,** division (1378–1417) within the Roman Catholic Church. Shortly after GREGORY XI returned the PAPACY from Avignon to Rome, he died (1378). URBAN VI was elected pope, but soon alienated those in the church. The cardinals declared his election null and elected Robert of Geneva (Antipope Clement VII). Clement set up court in Avignon, but Urban continued to reign at Rome. They and their successors formed two lines of popes. The Council of Pisa (1409) tried unsuccessfully to depose GREGORY XII of the Roman line and Benedict XIII of the Avignon line, and elected a second antipope, Alexander V, who was soon succeeded by the energetic Baldasarre COSSA as John XXIII. The schism was ended by the Council of Constance (1414–18) that accepted Gregory's resignation, deposed Benedict and John, and elected MARTIN V as pope.

schist, metamorphic ROCK (see METAMORPHISM) having a foliated (plated) structure in which the component flaky minerals are visible to the naked eye. Schists' mineral crystals are larger than those of SLATES and smaller than those of GNEISSES (the other two foliated metamorphic rocks).

schistosomiasis, bilharziasis, or **snail fever,** disease caused by a parasitic blood FLUKE of the genus *Schistosoma.* The larvae of the parasites are harbored by snails and infect humans who bathe in infested waters. In the body, the flukes settle in the blood vessels of the intestines or bladder and use the body's own immune system to trigger part of their life cycle. The disease often affects the liver. It is treated with the drug praziquantel.

schizophrenia, severe mental disorder characterized by delusions (e.g., a belief that one's thoughts are being broadcast to the world so that others can hear them), hallucinations (e.g., voices that insult, continually comment, or give commands), loosening of associations or incoherence, a flat or inappropriate facial expression, and physical rigidity or agitation. It occurs most commonly, but not always, in late adolescence or early adulthood. Possible causes under study include viral infection during pregnancy, genetic inheritance, abnormal fetal brain development, or a combination of these. In the past a high percentage of patients required long-term hospitalization, but advances in the use of antipsychotic drugs, which apparently act by blocking the NEUROTRANSMITTERS serotonin and dopamine in the brain, have made the outlook for remission of schizophrenia more hopeful.

schizophyte, member of a division of the plant kingdom consisting of the BACTERIA and BLUE-GREEN ALGAE. These organisms are now usually placed in the MONERAN kingdom.

Schlegel, Friedrich von [shlā'gəl], 1772–1829, German philosopher, critic, and writer, the most prominent founder of German ROMANTICISM. Educated in law, he turned to writing. With his brother, August Wilhelm, he published the *Athenaeum,* the principal organ of the romantic school. His lectures in Jena (1800) and in Paris (1802) on history, language, and literature had a widespread influence. His study of Sanskrit and of Indian civilization, *On the Language and Wisdom of India* (1808), was outstanding. In his early period, Schlegel held that wisdom depends on the recognition of what he called "romantic irony"—that truth changes from experience to experience. Later he joined (1808) the Roman Catholic Church, and his views became more conservative. His brother, **August Wilhelm von Schlegel,** 1767–1845, was a scholar and poet. He is most noted for his extraordinary translations of SHAKESPEARE (1797–1810).

Schleiden, Matthias Jakob, 1804–81, German botanist. With Theodor SCHWANN, he is credited with establishing the foundations of the CELL theory. An 1838 paper, though mistaken in some aspects, recognized the significance of the nucleus in cell propagation.

Schleiermacher, Friedrich Daniel Ernst [shlī'ərmäkh"ər], 1768–1834, German Protestant theologian. Originally a Moravian, he became (1794) a Reformed preacher and was a professor at Halle (1804–7) and Berlin (from 1810). His *Religion: Speeches to Its Cultured Despisers* (1799) defined religion as an absolute dependence on a monotheistic God, reached through intuition and independent of dogma, and showed both his closeness to the Romantics and his Pietist background. *The Christian Faith* (1821–22), his major work, systematically developed his earlier ideas and viewed Christianity as the highest manifestation of religion.

Schlesinger, Arthur M(eier), 1888–1965, American historian; b. Xenia, Ohio. He taught at Harvard (1924–54). His well-known works on colonial history include *The Colonial Merchants and the American Revolution* (1918). He is also known for his interest in social history, as in *The Rise of the City* (1933). In 1928 he became an editor of the *New England Quarterly.* His son, **Arthur M(eier) Schlesinger, Jr.,** 1917–, b. Columbus, Ohio, is also a historian. His brilliant *Age of Jackson* (1945; Pulitzer) stimulated a reconsideration of the Jacksonian period. *The Age of Roosevelt* (3 vol., 1957–60) is a sweeping analysis of the NEW DEAL period. Schlesinger was an aide to Pres. KENNEDY and wrote a study of Kennedy's White House years, *A Thousand Days* (1965; Pulitzer); he also wrote a biography of the president's brother, *Robert Kennedy and His Times* (1978).

Schleswig-Holstein, state (1990 est. pop. 2,595,000), c.6,050 sq mi (15,670 sq km), N Germany. Kiel is the capital and chief port. Flanked on the W by the North Sea and on the E by the Baltic, Schleswig-Holstein occupies the base of the Jutland Peninsula and extends from the Elbe R. north to the Danish border. Farming, fishing, and manufacturing are important occupations; tourism is also a mainstay. The duchy of Schleswig, created in 1115, was a hereditary fief held from the kings of Denmark. The duchy of Holstein was part of the HOLY ROMAN EMPIRE after 1111. Both were inherited (1460) by CHRISTIAN I of Denmark. In the 19th cent., disputes over their status led to conflict between Denmark and the GERMAN CONFEDERATION. In 1864 Austria and Prussia declared war on Denmark, which was easily defeated. In 1866, after the AUSTRO-PRUSSIAN WAR, Schleswig and Holstein were annexed by Prussia. Schleswig-Holstein was a West German state from 1946 until German reunification in 1990.

Schliemann, Heinrich, 1822–90, German archaeologist who discovered the ruins of TROY. A student of HOMER from childhood, he amassed a fortune in business and retired at 41 to search for Homeric sites. Relying on details from Homer's poems, he began (1871) excavations at Hissarlik, now accepted as the site of Troy, and uncovered four superimposed towns. His other notable discoveries, described in his vast writings, were at Mycenae (1876–78), ITHACA (1878), and Tiryns (1884–85).

Schlüter, Andreas [shlü'tər], 1664–1714, German sculptor. He was the most important German exponent of the BAROQUE style. His works include the statue of King Frederick I in front of Königsberg castle, and the *Great Elector*, an equestrian group on the Long Bridge, Berlin.

Schmidt, Helmut, 1918–, German political leader, chancellor of West Germany (1974–82). A member of the Social Democratic party, he was minister of defense (1969–72) and of finance (1972–74) in the cabinet of Willy BRANDT. He became chancellor upon Brandt's resignation. Schmidt's aims were to improve relations with East Germany and the USSR, and to maintain the prosperous West German economy. In 1982 he lost a confidence vote in the lower house of the German parliament to Helmut KOHL of the Christian Democratic party.

Schmidt-Rottluff, Karl, 1884–1976, German painter and woodcut artist. He cofounded and named the BRÜCKE, and is known for his WOODCUTS.

schnauzer, sturdy, wirehaired dog. Developed in S Germany, it is divided into three breeds. The standard—shoulder height, 17–20 in. (43.1–50.8 cm); weight, 27–37 lb (12.3–16.8 kg)—is a WORKING DOG that dates to the 15th cent., when it was used as a ratter, farm dog, and guardian. The giant—shoulder height, 21½–25½ in. (54.6–64.8 cm); weight, 65–78 lb (29.5–35.4 kg)—and the miniature, a TERRIER—shoulder height, 12–14 in. (30.5–35.6 cm); weight, 13–15 lb (5.9–6.8 kg)—were both developed at the end of the 19th cent. All three breeds may be pepper and salt, silver, or black in color.

Schneiderman, Rose, 1884–1972, American labor leader; b. Poland. After emigrating to the U.S. in 1890, she was for many years active in the Women's Trade Union League, becoming national president in 1928. Probably the best-known woman trade unionist in the U.S., she was also an official of the NATIONAL RECOVERY ADMINISTRATION, secretary of the New York state department of labor (1937–44), and a member of Pres. F.D. Roosevelt's BRAIN TRUST.

Schnitzler, Arthur [shnĭts'lər], 1862–1931, Austrian dramatist and novelist. His works are known for their sparkling wit and brilliant style, unique mixture of melancholy and cheerfulness, and clinical observations of the pathological. Dramas such as *Anatol* (1893) and *The Reckoning* (1895) are studies of the problems of love and sexual faithfulness.

Schoenberg, Arnold, 1874–1951, Austrian composer. He became a U.S. citizen in 1941. Schoenberg revolutionized modern music by establishing the 12-tone technique of SERIAL MUSIC as an important organizational device. His early works, e.g., *Verklärte Nacht* (1899), expanded WAGNER's and MAHLER's use of the chromatic scale. His later works are highly contrapuntal (see COUNTERPOINT). In 1908 he completely abandoned TONALITY (see ATONALITY) in a set of piano pieces and a song cycle. He first employed the 12-tone technique in a work in his Suite for Piano (1924). Schoenberg's other compositions include two chamber SYMPHONIES (1906; 1906–40), a piano CONCERTO (1942), various chamber works, and an unfinished opera, *Moses und Aron* (1932–51), considered his masterpiece. He was also a teacher; his students included Alban BERG and Anton von WEBERN.

scholasticism, philosophy and theology of Western Christendom in the Middle Ages. Basic to scholastic thought is the use of reason to deepen the understanding of what is believed on faith, and ultimately to give a rational content to faith. Its formal beginnings are identified with St. ANSELM (late 11th cent.), who tried to prove the existence of God by purely rational means. ABELARD stressed the rational approach in considering the most important philosophical question of the 12th cent., the question of universals (see NOMINALISM; REALISM). The early church fathers, notably St. AUGUSTINE, incorporated PLATO's doctrines and NEOPLATONIC thought into Christian theology. The 13th cent., the golden age of medieval philosophy, was marked by two important developments: the growth of universities (especially at Paris and Oxford); and the availability in Latin translation of the works of ARISTOTLE and the commentaries of AVICENNA and AVERROËS. The closely wrought, rational system of St. THOMAS AQUINAS is regarded as the greatest achievement of the scholastic age and the ultimate triumph of the effort to "Christianize Aristotle." Later opponents of Aquinas, e.g., St. BONAVENTURE, DUNS SCOTUS, and WILLIAM OF OCCAM, broke the synthesis of faith and reason. The secular currents of the Renaissance and the growth of the natural sciences brought on the decline of scholastic metaphysics, although its approach continued to be followed in politics and law. In 1879 Pope LEO XIII proclaimed the system of Aquinas to be the official Catholic philosophy.

Scholem, Gershom Gerhard, 1897–1982, Jewish scholar; b. Berlin. His work made the study of the history of CABALA and Jewish mysticism an important scholarly discipline. A professor at the Hebrew Univ., Jerusalem, he wrote over 500 articles and books, including *Major Trends in Jewish Mysticism* (1941) and *Kabbalah* (1974).

Schongauer, Martin [shōn'gou-ər], 1430–91, German engraver and painter. He is known for his ENGRAVINGS of religious subjects, e.g., *The Wise and Foolish Virgins.* He was one of the earliest engravers to use copper plates, and his 115 engravings, signed M+S and executed with amazing virtuosity, were important to the development of German art.

Schoolcraft, Henry Rowe, 1793–1864, American ethnologist; b. near Albany, N.Y.; foremost pioneer in Native American studies. As an Indian agent (1822–41) in the Great Lakes region he conducted ethnological research among the OJIBWA, and after 1841 he continued his studies in the East. His chief work is *Historical and Statistical Information Respecting . . . the Indian Tribes of the United States* (6 vol., 1851–57).

school of Paris. The center of international art until after World War II, Paris was a mecca for artists. The school of Paris includes many styles and movements. The practitioners and adherents of FAUVISM, CUBISM, and ORPHISM all belonged to the school of Paris, as did many others whose styles fit no one category. After the war, New York City challenged Paris's preeminence, though the school of Paris continued to produce major figures, e.g., Jean DUBUFFET.

Schopenhauer, Arthur, 1788–1860, German philosopher. A solitary figure who failed to rival HEGEL as a lecturer in Berlin, he considered himself the successor of KANT, but equated Kant's "thing-in-itself" with a blind, impelling force manifesting itself in individuals as the will to live. Schopenhauer saw the world as a constant conflict of individual wills resulting in frustration and pain. Pleasure is simply the absence of pain and can be achieved only through the renunciation of desire (a concept that reflects Schopenhauer's studies of Hindu scripture). His most important work is *The World as Will and Representation* (1818). His doctrine of the primacy of the will influenced NIETZSCHE and FREUD.

Schreiner, Olive, pseud. **Ralph Iron,** 1855–1920, South African writer and feminist. Her best-known work is the autobiographical novel *The Story of an African Farm* (1883).

Schröder, Friedrich Ludwig, 1744–1816, German actor, manager, and dramatist. The most celebrated German actor of his day, he introduced SHAKESPEARE to Germany, raised theatrical standards, and furthered the STURM UND DRANG movement.

Schrödinger, Erwin, 1887–1961, Austrian theoretical physicist. For his mathematical development (1926) of wave mechanics, a form of QUANTUM MECHANICS, and his formulation of the wave equation that bears his name, he shared with Paul DIRAC the 1933 Nobel Prize in physics.

Schubert, Franz (Peter), 1797–1828, Austrian composer, one of the foremost exponents of ROMANTICISM. German LIEDER reached their finest expression in his lyrical songs, especially in the great cycles *Die schöne Müllerin* [fair maid of the mill] (1823) and *Die Winterreise* [the winter's journey] (1827). His SYMPHONIES are the final extension of the classical SONATA forms, and the Fifth (1816), Eighth (the *Unfinished,* 1822), and Ninth (1828) rank with the finest orchestral music. Well known for such chamber works as the Quartet in D Minor (*Death and the Maiden,* 1824) and the Quintet in A Major (*The Trout,* 1819), Schubert also wrote stage music, choral music, MASSES, and much piano music.

Schulberg, Budd, 1914-, American novelist and screenwriter; b. N.Y.C. Tending to deal with characters from a sociological perspective, his works include novels, e.g., *What Makes Sammy Run?* (1941) and *The Disenchanted* (1950), and screenplays, e.g., the Oscar-winning *On the Waterfront* (1954) and *A Face in the Crowd* (1957)

Schuller, Robert, 1926–, American Protestant minister, b. Alton, Iowa. His Reformed Church in America is housed in a multimillion-dollar "Crystal Cathedral" in Garden Grove, Calif. Since 1970 his evangelical television program has become one of the top religious broadcasts in the U.S.

Schultz, Theodore W., 1902–, American economist; b. Arlington, S.D. He taught at Iowa State College (1930–43) and the Univ. of Chicago (1943–61). A specialist in agricultural economics and the economic problems of underdeveloped countries, he shared the 1979 Nobel Prize in economics. His books include *Economic Growth and Agriculture* (1968).

Schulz, Charles M., 1920–, American cartoonist; b. Minneapolis. Creator of the COMIC STRIP *Peanuts,* he expresses a droll philosophy through the children and animals that populate his cartoon world, including the puzzled and victimized Charlie Brown, his bossy friend Lucy, and Snoopy, a romantic, self-deluded beagle.

Schuman, Robert, 1886–1963, French statesman. He was finance minister (1946, 1947), premier (1947–48), and foreign minister (1948–53) in the Fourth Republic. The Schuman Plan led to the formation (1952) of the European Coal and Steel Community, the first step in the creation of the EUROPEAN UNION.

Schuman, William (Howard), 1910–92, American composer; b. N.Y.C. He was head of the Juilliard School of Music (1945–62) and president of Lincoln Center (1962–69). Among his works are symphonies, an opera, a ballet, the American Festival Overture (1939), concertos, and chamber works. His CANTATA *A Free Song* (1943) won the first PULITZER PRIZE in music.

Schumann, Robert (Alexander), 1810–56, German composer, a leader of the romantic movement. His brilliant piano music (e.g., *Carnaval, Kinderszenen*) occupied him until 1840, when he began to write orchestral music and songs, in which he achieved a superb fusion of vocal melody and piano accompaniment. His orchestral works (e.g., Piano Concerto in A Minor, 1841–45; *Rhenish* Symphony, 1850) infuse classical forms with an emotional intensity that foreshadowed his later nervous breakdown. An articulate critic, he championed younger composers such as CHOPIN and BRAHMS. His wife, **Clara Josephine (Wieck) Schumann,** 1819–96, was an outstanding concert pianist.

Schumpeter, Joseph Alois [shŏŏm'pā"tər], 1883–1950, Austrian-American economist. After practicing law and teaching at the Univ. of Graz and at Bonn, he emigrated (1932) to the U.S. and later became a professor at Harvard. His major contributions to economics were the theory of the entrepreneur as the dynamic factor in the business cycle and the theory of the economic development of CAPITALISM.

Schurz, Carl [shŏŏrts], 1829–1906, American political leader; b. Germany. As U.S. senator from Missouri (1869–75), he helped form the LIBERAL REPUBLICAN PARTY (1872). Later he was secretary of the interior (1877–81). In 1884 he led the MUGWUMPS against James G. BLAINE (1884). Schurz supported William MCKINLEY for president in 1896 (for his currency views) and William J. Bryan in 1900 (for his anti-imperialism). An active editor and writer, he gained broad influence through honesty and fearlessness.

Schuschnigg, Kurt von [shŏŏsh'nĭk], 1897–1977, Austrian chancellor. He became chancellor after the assassination (1934) of Engelbert DOLLFUSS. In 1936 he forced E.R. von Starhemberg to resign as vice chancellor and became sole head of the semi-Fascist Austrian government. He prevented Austria's annexation to Germany until he lost (1937) the support of MUSSOLINI. German troops occupied Austria in 1938, and Schuschnigg was held prisoner until 1945. He later settled in the U.S.

Schütz, Heinrich, 1585–1672, German composer. His *Dafne* (1627; now lost) has been called the first German OPERA. The outstanding master of 17th-cent. church music, he wrote ORATORIOS and settings of the Passion that combined the Venetian style of alternating choirs and the dramatic declamation of Florentine monody with German POLYPHONY. This choral style influenced German music through the time of HANDEL and BACH.

Schuyler, Philip John [skī'lər], 1733–1804, American Revolutionary general; b. Albany, N.Y. He was accused of negligence and replaced by Horatio GATES as commander of the SARATOGA CAMPAIGN when TICONDEROGA was abandoned without a shot (1777). He was later acquitted by a court-martial.

Schwann, Theodor, 1810–82, German physiologist and histologist. Originator with Matthias SCHLEIDEN of the cell theory, he demonstrated that the cell is the basis of animal as well as plant tissue. He also demonstrated the living nature of yeasts and described the nerve sheath known by his name.

Schwartz, Delmore, 1913–66, American poet; b. Brooklyn, N.Y. His extremely intellectual poetry is in such books as *In Dreams Begin Responsibilities* (1938) and *Summer Knowledge* (1959). He also wrote short stories and a verse play, *Shenandoah* (1941).

Schwarzkopf, Elisabeth, 1915–, German lyric soprano. She gained an international reputation for subtlety and versatility in recitals, ORATORIOS, and opera. She is particularly renowned for her LIEDER interpretations.

Schwarzkopf, H. Norman, 1934–, American general, b. Trenton, N.J. He served two tours of duty during the VIETNAM WAR, the first (1965–66) as an adviser and the second (1969–70) in command of an infantry battalion. In 1983 he was deputy commander of U.S. forces in the invasion of Grenada. As commander in chief (1988–91) of the U.S. Central Command (responsible for the Middle East and Africa), he led U.S. and Western forces in the PERSIAN GULF WAR.

Schweitzer, Albert, 1875–1965, Alsatian theologian, musician, and medical missionary. A doctor, he established (1913) a hospital at Lambaréné, Gabon, which received broad international support and at which he lived most of his life. An organist and expert on the music of BACH, He wrote a biography of the composer (1905) and coedited his music (1912–14). Schweitzer's ethical philosophy, developed in his *Philosophy of Civilization* (1923), rests on his concept of "reverence for life." As a theologian, in works such as *The Quest of the Historical Jesus* (1906, tr. 1910), he rejected the historical infallibility of Jesus while following him spiritually. Honored for his many accomplishments, Schweitzer was awarded the 1952 Nobel Peace Prize.

Schwenkfeld, Kaspar von [shvĕngk'fĕlt], 1490–1561, German religious reformer. After meeting Thomas MÜNZER and CARLSTADT at Wittenberg, he devoted himself to the reform movement in Silesia. Martin LUTHER opposed his supposed Anabaptist learnings, and after Lutheranism became dominant in Silesia, Schwenkfeld was forced to move to Strasbourg and then to Ulm. An anathema was proclaimed against him by the Lutherans, and his books were banned. He offered (1540) a full statement of faith, which enunciated the distinction between the outward and transitory word of God as given in the Scriptures and an inward spirit, which was divine, eternal, and necessary for salvation. His followers, known as **Schwenkfeldians** or **Schwenkfelders,** were persecuted and

Albert Schweitzer

fled in the 18th cent. to America and other parts of Europe. The sect still exists in Pennsylvania.

Schwitters, Kurt [shvĭt'ərs], 1887–1948, German artist. He invented *Merz* (trash) constructions. His COLLAGES are among the outstanding creations in this medium.

science fiction, literary genre to which a background of science or pseudoscience is integral. Although fantastic, it contains elements within the realm of future possibility. Science fiction began with the late-19th-cent. work of Jules VERNE and H.G. WELLS. The appearance of the magazines *Amazing Stories* (1926) and *Astounding Science Fiction* (1937) encouraged good writing in the field, which was further spurred by post–World War II technological developments. Contemporary writers of science fiction include Robert HEINLEIN, Isaac ASIMOV, A.E. van Voght, Alfred Bester, Arthur C. CLARKE, Frederik Pohl, Stanisław LEM, William Gibson, Doris LESSING, and Ursula K. LeGuin. The genre's effectiveness as an instrument for social criticism can be seen in such works as Aldous HUXLEY's *Brave New World* (1932), Ray BRADBURY's *Fahrenheit 451* (1953), and Kurt VONNEGUT's *Cat's Cradle* (1963).

scientific notation, means of expressing very large or very small numbers in a compact form, to simplify computation. In this notation any number is expressed as a number between 1 and 10 multiplied by the appropriate power of 10 (see DECIMAL SYSTEM; EXPONENT). For example, 32,000,000 in scientific notation is 3.2×10^7, and 0.00526 is 5.26×10^{-3}.

Scientology, Church of, quasireligious sect founded (1954) by science fiction writer L. Ron Hubbard (1911–86) and largely based on his book *Dianetics* (1950). The church believes that the soul can be cleared of its negative energy through "processing." Often viewed as a cult, Scientology's tenets have been widely challenged and its practices subject to various governmental investigations. Membership figures are unavailable, but by 1987 there were over 450 church facilities worldwide.

scintillation counter: see PARTICLE DETECTOR.

scion, in horticulture: see GRAFTING.

Scipio, ancient Roman patrician family of the Cornelian gens. During the 3d and 2d cent. B.C. they were distinguished by their love of Greek culture and learning. Their wealth and extravagance were detested by the family of CATO the Elder, who worked hard to ruin them. **Scipio Africanus Major** (Publius Cornelius Scipio Africanus) 234?–183 B.C., a Roman general, was the conqueror of HANNIBAL in the PUNIC WARS. In the Second Punic War, Scipio conquered Spain and ended the war by defeating Hannibal at Zama (202) in Africa. He returned home in triumph and retired from public life; he was named Africanus after the country he conquered. **Scipio Africanus Minor,** c.185–129 B.C., Roman general, was the destroyer of CARTHAGE. He was adopted by the eldest son of Scipio Africanus Major and earned a great reputation as a patron of Greek literature and of Roman writers, notably TERENCE and Laelius, and he was the lifelong friend of POLYBIUS, his protégé. As consul (147) he went to Africa and terminated the Third Punic War with the capture and destruction of Carthage. On his return to Rome he attempted to destroy the Gracchan reforms (see GRACCHI). A great public quarrel arose, and Scipio was found dead in his bed. No inquiry was made, and it was generally said that he was murdered by someone of the Gracchan party.

Scofield, Paul, 1922–, English actor. He gained international renown for his portrayal of Sir Thomas MORE in *A Man for All Seasons* (stage, 1961; film, 1966). He has also starred in *King Lear* (film, 1971), *A Delicate Balance* (film, 1973), and *Volpone* (1977).

Scopas, Greek sculptor, fl. 4th cent. B.C. He was the first to express violent feeling in marble faces. His style is seen in fragments from the Temple of Athena Alea, Tegea, and in Roman copies of his work, e.g., *Ludovisi Ares* (Rome).

Scopes trial, July 1925, the trial of public school teacher John T. Scopes, in Dayton, Tenn., for teaching Charles DARWIN's theory of EVOLUTION, the teaching of which was against state law. C.S. DARROW was defense attorney, and W.J. BRYAN aided the prosecutor. Scopes was convicted but released on a technicality. The law was repealed in 1967.

Scoresby, William, 1789–1857, English explorer. On yearly voyages (1803–22) to Greenland, he mapped, made soundings, and noted the flora and fauna. He studied terrestrial magnetism there and in Australia (1856). His books helped to lay the foundations of arctic geography.

scorpion, invertebrate animal (order Scorpionida) with a pair of powerful, pincerlike claws and a hollow, poisonous stinger at the tip of the tail; an ARACHNID. Most are 1–3 in. (2.5–7.6 cm) long, but some measure as much as 6 in. They seize and crush prey with their large claws, immobilizing it by stinging if necessary. With the exception of the fatal stings of *Androctonus australis* of the Sahara and several Mexican species, scorpion stings, although painful, are not usually dangerous to humans.

Scotch: see WHISKEY.

Scotland, political division of the United Kingdom of Great Britain and Ireland (1991 pop. 4,962,152), 30,414 sq mi (78,772 sq km), comprising the northern portion of the island of Great Britain and many surrounding islands, including the ORKNEYS, SHETLANDS, and HEBRIDES. It is bounded by England (S), the Atlantic Ocean (N and W), and the North Sea (E). It has 2,300 mi (3,700 km) of deeply indented coastline. Scotland may be divided into three main geographical regions: the southern uplands, the central lowlands, and the HIGHLANDS of the north, location of Great Britain's highest peak, Ben Nevis (4,406 ft/1,343 m). EDINBURGH is the capital and GLASGOW the largest city and chief port. Principal rivers are the Clyde, Forth, Dee, Tay, and Tweed. In 1707 Scotland was united with ENGLAND and WALES as the United Kingdom of GREAT BRITAIN. They share one PARLIAMENT, but Scotland retains its own systems of law (based on Roman law) and education. The Church of Scotland, which is Presbyterian, is legally established. English is the predominant language, although some 60,000 Scots also speak Gaelic; few speak only Gaelic.

History. The Picts, in Scotland from prehistoric times, along with Gaels or Celts from Ireland, prevented the Romans from penetrating far into Scotland, although the Romans did succeed in introducing Christianity before they left in the 5th cent. After the Roman evacuation, four Scottish kingdoms emerged. In the mid-9th cent. KENNETH I united and established the nucleus of the kingdom of Scotland, and by the 11th cent. his descendants ruled most of present-day Scotland. The following centuries were marked by dissension and turbulence among the nobles and struggle for independence from England, especially under Robert the Bruce (later

ROBERT I). A brief respite of internal peace during the reign of James IV was followed by the turmoil of the REFORMATION, brought to Scotland primarily by John KNOX. By the time MARY QUEEN OF SCOTS arrived (1561) in Scotland, Catholicism had almost disappeared from the Lowlands. Mary's struggle against Protestantism ended in her loss (1567) of the throne and her subsequent execution (1587). Mary's son, James VI of Scotland, succeeded (1603) ELIZABETH I on the English throne as JAMES I, thus uniting the two crowns. In 1707 the Act of Union formally united the governments of the two kingdoms. Union eventually proved economically favorable for Scotland, and its textile and metallurgical industries flourished in the 18th and 19th cent. The concentration of heavy industry made Scotland an important arsenal in both world wars, and in the 1970s Aberdeen became the center of North Sea oil development. Scotland's limited home rule was extended in 1978. However, there remains a persistent nationalist movement for greater autonomy.

Scotland, Church of, the established national church of Scotland. Under John KNOX Scotland came under the influence of Calvinism. Parliament abolished the jurisdiction of the Roman Catholic Church in 1560 and established (1592) PRESBYTERIANISM. However, James VI (JAMES I of England) and later Stuart monarchs attempted to restore episcopacy, and much confusion and unrest resulted (see COVENANTERS). A Presbyterian church was finally ensured by the Act of Settlement (1690) and the union (1707) of England and Scotland. In a dispute over patronage and state interference, Thomas Chalmers led a secession (1843) and formed the Free Church of Scotland. This church merged (1900) with the United Presbyterian Church to form the United Free Church of Scotland. In 1929 most of this body rejoined the Church of Scotland.

Scotland Yard, headquarters of the Criminal Investigation Department (CID) of the London Metropolitan Police. Named after a street in London, it became police headquarters in 1829. Other CID headquarters, New Scotland Yard, were built along the Thames embankment in 1890. Scotland Yard moved to new premises in 1967 but retains its name.

Scott, Sir George Gilbert, 1811–78, English architect. He was prominent in the GOTHIC REVIVAL as a designer and as a restorer of Gothic edifices, notably Ely Cathedral (1847) and WESTMINSTER ABBEY. He also designed (1860–70) the buildings for the home office and foreign office, the Albert Memorial, and St. Pancras Station, London. His grandson, **Sir Giles Gilbert Scott,** 1880–1960, also an architect, designed ecclesiastical buildings, including the Liverpool Cathedral (1904–27).

Scott, Robert Falcon, 1868–1912, British naval officer who commanded two antarctic expeditions. On the first (1901–4), in the *Discovery,* he discovered Edward VII Peninsula, surveyed the coast of Victoria Land, and explored the continent itself. On a second voyage, launched in 1910, he left his base on the Ross Sea and headed for the SOUTH POLE. Pulling sledges by hand, the party of five arrived there on Jan. 18, 1912, only to find that Roald AMUNDSEN had preceded them by a month. On their return, beset by illness, hunger, and blizzards, they all died.

Scott, Sir Walter, 1771–1832, Scottish novelist and poet. After translating Goethe's *Götz von Berlichingen* in 1799, Scott published *Minstrelsy of the Scottish Border* (2 vol., 1802; enl. ed., 3 vol., 1803), a collection of old ballads. *The Lay of the Last Minstrel* (1805), his first major poem, was followed by *Marmion* (1808) and *The Lady of the Lake* (1810). *Waverley* (1814) was a great success, becoming the first of the "Waverley Novels," romances of Scottish life that reveal Scott's gift for storytelling and vivid characterization. The series included *Guy Mannering* (1815), *Old Mortality* (1816), *Rob Roy* (1818), *The Heart of Midlothian* (1818), and *The Bride of Lammermoor* (1819). In 1820, at the height of his fame, Scott was made a baronet. *Ivanhoe* (1820) was his first historical romance in prose. Most of the novels that followed were in the historical style; they include *Kenilworth* (1821), *Quentin Durward* (1823), and *The Talisman* (1825). In 1825 Scott faced financial catastrophe. He had assumed responsibility for a printing firm, Ballantyne's, in 1813 and had been meeting its expenses out of advances from his publishers, Constable and Co. When a depression ruined both firms in 1825, Scott, instead of declaring bankruptcy, set out to pay both his debt and much of Constable's; in the process his health was destroyed. After his death the rest of the debt was paid from the earnings of his books.

Scott, Winfield, 1786–1866, American general; b. near Petersburg, Va. A hero of the WAR OF 1812, he also served the U.S. as a peacemaker in the CAROLINE AFFAIR and the AROOSTOOK WAR. Appointed supreme commander of the U.S. army (1841–61), in the MEXICAN WAR he led the southern expedition in a triumphant campaign from Veracruz to Mexico City (1847), which confirmed him as a daring strategist and bold fighter. Now very much a national hero, he ran (1852) for president as the Whig candidate but was defeated by Franklin PIERCE. Scott was vain and pompous—his nickname was "Old Fuss and Feathers"—but he was also generous and fair. He is generally considered the greatest American general between G. WASHINGTON and R.E. LEE.

Scottish terrier, short-legged TERRIER; shoulder height, c.10 in. (25 cm); weight, 18–22 lb (8.2–10 kg). Its wiry coat may be gray, brindle, grizzle, black, sandy, or wheaten. Perfected in Scotland in the mid-19th cent., the scottie was used to hunt small game, particularly badgers.

Scotto, Renata, 1934–, Italian soprano. She made her debut at La Scala, in Milan, in 1953 and at the METROPOLITAN OPERA, in New York City, in 1965. Noted for her versatility and dramatic intensity, she excels in the Italian repertory, e.g., BELLINI's *Norma* and PUCCINI's *Madame Butterfly*.

Scottsboro Case. In 1931 nine African-American youths were tried in Scottsboro, Ala., on charges of having raped two white women in a freight car passing through Alabama. The nine were sentenced to death or to 75 to 99 years in prison. The U.S. SUPREME COURT twice reversed the convictions on procedural grounds. At the second trial one of the women recanted her testimony. In 1937 charges against five were dropped. Three others were freed in the 1940s, and the last escaped in 1948 to Michigan, which refused to return him to Alabama. The last known surviving "Scottsboro boy" was pardoned by Alabama's parole board and governor in 1976.

Scottsdale, city (1990 pop. 130,069), Maricopa co., central Ariz., a suburb of Phoenix; settled 1895, inc. 1951. It is a resort and retirement center in a rapidly expanding metropolitan area. Electronic equipment is an important manufacture. Taliesin West, an architectural community and school founded by Frank Lloyd WRIGHT, is N of the city.

Scotus: see DUNS SCOTUS.

scouring rush: see HORSETAIL.

Scranton, city (1990 pop. 81,805), seat of Lackawanna co., NE Pa., in a mountain region on the Lackawanna R.; inc. 1866. It is the commercial and industrial center of Pennsylvania's anthracite region. Iron was first forged there in 1797. When mining decreased after World War II, a successful citizens' plan brought about diversified industry, much of it textile. The city is in a popular recreational area.

Scribe, Augustin Eugène [skrēb], 1791–1861, French dramatist. He wrote over 300 plays and many librettos for composers such as MEYERBEER and VERDI. Among the best of his well-structured comedies is *The Ladies' Battle* (1851).

Scriblerus Club, English literary group (c.1713–14), formed to satirize "false tastes in learning." ARBUTHNOT, GAY, POPE, and SWIFT were members. *Memoirs of . . . Martinus Scriblerus* (1741) was primarily Arbuthnot's work.

Scripps, Edward Wyllis, 1854–1926, American newspaper publisher; b. Rushville, Ill. He started the Cleveland *Penny Press* (later the *Press*) in 1878. Having purchased additional papers, he set up the Scripps-McRae League (1895), the first chain of newspapers in the U.S. It developed its own news service, and in 1907 Scripps set up the United Press Association. He also organized the Newspaper Enterprise Association to furnish his papers with features and illustrations.

scuba: see DIVING, DEEP-SEA.

sculling: see ROWING.

scurvy, deficiency disorder caused by a lack of vitamin C (ascorbic acid) in the diet. See VITAMIN (table).

scutage, feudal payment, usually cash, by a vassal to his lord, especially to a king, instead of military service. Its incidence increased in the 12th cent. with the rise of professional military knights. Kings of England financed wars for their French lands by scutage. In the MAGNA CARTA (1215), King JOHN of England pledged not to impose scutage without the consent of his barons. The growth of taxes after the reign of EDWARD III displaced scutage in England.

Scylla and Charybdis [sĭl'ə, kərĭb'dĭs], in Greek mythology, sea monsters. They lived on either side of the Strait of Messina. Scylla seized sailors and devoured them, and Charybdis, the whirlpool, created shipwrecks. ODYSSEUS passed safely between them, as did JASON and the Argonauts.

Scythia, ancient region from the Danube to the borders of China, occupied by the Scythians, warlike mounted nomads who came from Russia in the 1st millennium B.C. Before the 9th cent. B.C. they formed a kingdom in the E Crimea. In the 7th cent. B.C. they invaded Mesopotamia, Syria, and the Balkans. Surviving attacks by DARIUS I of Persia (512 B.C.) and ALEXANDER THE GREAT (c.325 B.C.), they were driven back to S Russia after 300 B.C. but were displaced there (2d or 1st cent. B.C.) by the related Sarmatians (see SARMATIA).

SDI: see STRATEGIC DEFENSE INITIATIVE.

Se, chemical symbol of the element SELENIUM.

sea, law of the, international agreement regulating the use and exploitation of the world's oceans. The UN-sponsored Law of the Sea Treaty (1982) calls for limited, and strictly controlled, mining of the seabed; establishes in general the 12-mile limit for territorial waters; gives all nations' ships the right of "innocent passage" through crucial straits; and sets up international antipollution regulations. Most of the industrial nations opposed the restrictions on seabed mining, but Third World nations, the chief beneficiaries of the agreement, favored the treaty and created the majority that passed it. The U.S., Britain, and Germany have not signed the treaty, and the U.S. and other nations have sought to renegotiate the provisions on seabed mining. The treaty will officially come into force when it is ratified by 60 nations, but many provisions are already internationally accepted.

sea anemone, predominantly solitary marine polyp (see POLYP AND MEDUSA), usually attached to submerged objects. Many of these animals are beautifully colored and look like flowers when their tentacle-encircled feeding end is open. They are mostly 1–4 in. (2.5–10 cm) long; a few are 3 ft (90 cm) in diameter. Most sea anemones are predators, immobilizing their prey with stingers located in the tentacles.

Seaborg, Glenn Theodore, 1912–, American chemist. Professor and later chancellor at the Univ. of California, Berkeley, he worked at the Univ. of Chicago during World War II on the development of the atomic bomb and later was chairman (1961–71) of the U.S. Atomic Energy Commission. He shared with Edwin M. McMillan the 1951 Nobel Prize in chemistry for work on transuranium elements. Seaborg is codiscoverer of the elements PLUTONIUM, AMERICIUM, CURIUM, BERKELIUM, CALIFORNIUM, EINSTEINIUM, FERMIUM, MENDELEVIUM, and NOBELIUM.

Seabury, Samuel, 1729–96, American clergyman, first bishop of the Protestant EPISCOPAL CHURCH; b. Connecticut. Although a Loyalist during the American Revolution, he was chosen (1783) to be bishop of Connecticut and was consecrated (1784) by bishops of the Scottish Episcopal Church at Aberdeen.

sea cow: see SIRENIAN.

sea cucumber, flexible, elongated invertebrate animal with a cucumber-shaped, leathery body; an ECHINODERM. Most are under 1 ft (30.5 cm). Many sea cucumbers eject most of their internal organs when sufficiently irritated, later regenerating a new set.

seafloor spreading: see OCEAN; PLATE TECTONICS.

sea gooseberry: see COMB JELLY.

seahorse, small, bony-plated FISH of the family Syngnathidae, usually found in warm waters. Its elongated head and snout, flexed at right angles to its body, suggest those of a horse. Members of different species range from 2 to 8 in. (5 to 20 cm). Weak swimmers, they anchor themselves by curling their thin, prehensile tails around seaweed. While mating, the female seahorse injects eggs into a pouch on the underside of the male, where they are fertilized and then develop until the young are expelled. The related pipefish look more fishlike.

Sea Islands, chain of more than 100 low, sandy barrier islands, off the Atlantic coast of South Carolina, Georgia, and N Florida. First settled by the Spanish in the 16th cent., they became the earliest important cotton-growing area in the U.S., specializing in the production of long-staple (or sea island) cotton. Now a popular resort area, they include unspoiled Cumberland Island National Seashore (Ga.); forts Sumter and Moultrie (S.C.); Hilton Head (S.C.), and the ruins of Fort Frederica, on St. Simons Island (Ga.), built (1736–48) by James OGLETHORPE to secure the region against the Spanish.

seal, fin-footed MAMMAL (pinniped) of the family Phocidae, usually marine, with front and hind feet modified as flippers. Seals have streamlined bodies with a thick, subcutaneous layer of fat, and most inhabit cold or temperate regions. All species leave the water at least once a year to breed; some species migrate. Seals live on fish and shellfish; many dive deep to feed, navigating by means of echolocation. True seals lack external ears. They are polygamous and gregarious, and most live in one of three geographical regions: northern, antarctic, and the warm waters of the Mediterranean, Caribbean, and Hawaiian seas. Seals are extensively hunted for food, fur, hides, and oil.

sea lily: see CRINOID.

sea lion, fin-footed marine MAMMAL (pinniped) of the eared seal family. The sea lion has external ears (unlike the true SEAL), a long, flexible neck, supple forelimbs, and hind flippers. Males may reach 8 ft (2.4 m) in length. Sea lions live close to shore in the oceans of the Southern Hemisphere and in the N Pacific, feeding on fish and SQUID. To breed they gather in colonies, where the males assemble harems. Most species are protected.

seaplane, airplane designed to take off from and alight on water. The two most common types are the floatplane, whose fuselage is supported by struts attached to two or more pontoon floats, and the flying boat, whose boat-hull fuselage is constructed with the buoyancy and strength necessary to alight and float on water. First built and flown in 1911 by Glenn CURTISS, the seaplane developed rapidly in the 1920s and 30s and for a time was the largest and fastest aircraft in the world.

search warrant, in U.S. law, written order by a court directing an officer to search in a specified place for specified objects and to seize them if found. The objects sought may be stolen goods or contraband or physical evidence of the commission of a crime. The Fourth Amendment of the U.S. CONSTITUTION provides, in effect, that a search warrant may be issued only on oath or affirmation that a crime was probably committed and that the items sought are probably in the place sought to be searched. Courts generally exclude from evidence in a trial information obtained by tapping telephone conversations without a court order or objects obtained by illegal search. See also MAPP V. OHIO.

Sears Tower, Chicago, the world's tallest building. Constructed (1970–74) for Sears, Roebuck and Co., it rises 110 stories to a height of 1,454 ft (443 m), 104 ft (32 m) taller than New York City's WORLD TRADE CENTER. Designed by the firm of Skidmore, Owings and Merrill, the Sears Tower is supported structurally by square tubes of welded steel. It has an exterior of black aluminum and bronze-toned glass cut by black bands and topped by a 20-story tower.

sea slug, usually brightly colored marine GASTROPOD mollusk that lacks a shell as an adult. Most sea slugs, or nudibranchs, creep along the sea bottom or cling to vegetation below the tide line; a few swim in the open ocean. Most are under 1 in. (2.5 cm) long.

seasonal affective disorder (SAD), recurrent fall or winter depression characterized by excessive sleeping, social withdrawal, overeating, and weight gain. Thought to be due in part to decreased sensitivity of the eye's retina, SAD is treated with regular exposure to bright light.

sea spider, long-legged, spiderlike marine invertebrate animal with at least four pairs of walking legs; an ARTHROPOD. Most sea spiders are tiny and live near the shore, crawling around on the surface of animal colonies or seaweeds.

sea squirt: see TUNICATE.

sea star: see STARFISH.

Seattle, city (1990 pop. 516,259; met. area 1,972,961), seat of King co., W Wash., built on hills between Puget Sound and Lake Washington; settled 1851–52, inc. 1869. The largest city in the Pacific Northwest, it is the region's cultural, financial, commercial, transportation, and industrial hub. Aircraft, forest products, and chemicals are the most important of its many manufactures. Seattle's enormous port is the main link with oil-rich Alaska and is important in trade with Asia. The city is close to scenic mountain and coastal recreational areas. It is also an educational and cultural center, with many museums, theaters, and musical groups. Seattle's distinctive skyline landmark is the 600-ft (183-m) Space Needle, built for the 1962 World's Fair. Seattle prospered with the coming of the railroad in 1884 and became a boom town with the 1897 Alaska gold rush. Long a center of radical labor activity, it was the scene of a major general strike in 1919.

sea urchin, sphere-shaped marine invertebrate animal (an ECHINODERM) with a rigid body wall and long, sharp, movable, sometimes poisonous spines used for protection and locomotion. Sea urchins prefer shallow waters and rocky bottoms. The roe of some species is considered a delicacy.

seaweed, multicellular marine ALGAE. Most have a stemlike basal disk (holdfast) and a leaflike frond of varying length and shape. The simplest seaweeds are green algae and occur in shallow waters as threadlike filaments, irregular sheets, or branching fronds. Brown algae, which are the largest and most numerous of the seaweeds, grow at depths of 50–75 ft (15–23 m), and include the large kelps—sources of iodine and potassium salts, potash, fertilizer, and medicines. Red algae, some of which are fernlike, are found at the greatest depths (100–200 ft/30–61 m); commercial AGAR is obtained from a red alga. Seaweeds provide food and habitat for many marine organisms and are indispensable to the marine food web. Seaweed, especially species of red algae, is an important part of the human diet in some regions.

Sebastian, 1554–78, king of Portugal (1557–78). Sickly, headstrong, and devoutly religious, he determined to win glory by fighting the Muslims in N Africa. In 1578 he invaded MOROCCO with a large force of mercenaries, but his lack of military experience contributed to his crushing defeat at Alcazarquivir, where he was killed.

Sebastiano del Piombo [pyôm'bō], c.1485–1547, Italian painter; b. Sebastiano Luciani. He was influenced by MICHELANGELO, e.g., *Raising of Lazarus* (National Gall., London). In 1531 he was appointed *piombo* (keeper of the papal seals). His portraits include one of Christopher Columbus (Metropolitan Mus.).

Secession, War of: see CIVIL WAR.

second (sec or s), fundamental unit of time in all systems of measurement. In practical terms, the second is 1/60 of a minute and 1/3,600 of an hour. Since 1967 it has been calculated by atomic standards to be 9,192,631,770 periods of vibration of the radiation emitted at a specific wavelength by a cesium-133 atom.

secret police, secret, often terroristic, police agency operating for its government's political purposes. In democratic societies secret or quasi-secret police are usually limited to investigation, and suspects usually have the right to an open trial. Elsewhere, where they are accountable only to the executive branch of government, secret police often investigate, apprehend, judge, and punish in secrecy. The USSR's secret police (see KGB) was most active and feared during STALIN's purges (1934–39); it also operated the nation's forced-labor camp system. Under NATIONAL SOCIALISM, Germany's Gestapo and SS (headed by Heinrich HIMMLER) had vast powers of summary arrest, internment and execution. They controlled the CONCENTRATION CAMPS, carrying out atrocities throughout occupied Europe during World War II.

Secret Service, United States, law enforcement division of the U.S. Dept. of the TREASURY, created (1865) to investigate and prevent counterfeiting of currency. After the assassination of Pres. William MCKINLEY (1901), the Secret Service was also charged with protecting the president. This protection has since been extended to the vice president, president-elect, vice president-elect, major presidential candidates, former presidents, and certain members of their families.

Secretariat: see UNITED NATIONS (table 2).

Securities and Exchange Commission (SEC), U.S. government agency created by the Securities Exchange Act (1934) and charged with overseeing the public issuance and sale of corporate securities. It requires companies to submit full public-disclosure statements before issuing securities on the open market. It also regulates stock exchanges, brokers, and dealers in securities, and sets margin requirements for bank credit in security trading. The five commissioners are appointed by the president.

Security Council: see UNITED NATIONS (table 2).

sedge, common name for the Cyperaceae, a family of grasslike and rushlike herbs found worldwide but especially in subarctic and temperate marshes. More specifically, the name *sedge* is used for the genus *Carex* of this family. Sedges differ from true GRASSES in having solid, usually triangular stems. Most are perennial, reproducing by RHIZOMES. Bulrushes are sedges of the genus *Scirpus;* some species are grown as ornamentals. Other members of the family include PAPYRUS and the Asian water chestnut (*Eleocharis tuberosa*), valued by the Chinese for its edible TUBERS. Some sedges are woven into mats and chair seats; a few provide coarse hay.

sedimentary rock: see ROCK.

sedition, in law, acts or words tending to excite disaffection against governmental authority. The scope of the offense was broad in early COMMON LAW, even permitting prosecution for insults to the king. In the U.S., although sedition statutes have been enacted, constitutional protection of speech and press has confined enforcement to times of war and great stress. See ALIEN AND SEDITION ACTS.

seed, ripened ovule of the pistil of a FLOWER, consisting of the plant embryo, stored food material (endosperm), and a protective coat. True seeds vary in size from dustlike (as in some orchids) to very large (the coconut seed). Seeds undergo a period of dormancy before GERMINATION. Many seeds are frequently confused with the FRUIT enclosing them, as in the GRAINS and NUTS. The seed-bearing plants (ANGIOSPERMS and GYMNOSPERMS) are the highest plants in the evolutionary scale; lower plants (MOSSES and FERNS) propagate by means of SPORES.

Seferis, George [sĕfĕr'ēs], pseud. of **Giorgos Seferiadis,** 1900–1971, Greek poet, critic, and diplomat. His highly symbolic poetry invokes classical themes and the theme of exile. Volumes include *Turning Point* (1931), *The Cistern* (1932), and *Collected Poems, 1924–1955* (tr. 1969). He was awarded the 1963 Nobel Prize in literature.

Segal, George, 1924–, American sculptor; b. N.Y.C. Connected with the POP ART movement, he is known for his life-sized white plaster human figures in everyday situations.

segmented worm: see ANNELID WORM.

Segovia, Andrés, 1893–1987, Spanish guitarist. Famous for his transcriptions, concerts, and recordings, he was largely responsible for contemporary interest in the guitar. Such composers as FALLA, ROUSSEL, and VILLA-LOBOS wrote music for him.

seignorial system: see MANORIAL SYSTEM.

Seine, river, N France flowing generally NW c.480 mi (770 km) into an estuary on the English Channel near Le Havre. Chief cities on its route are Paris, where many bridges span the river, and Rouen, which is accessible to oceangoing vessels.

seismology, study of EARTHQUAKES and related phenomena using instruments called seismographs. In general, a recording device is connected to a heavy mass that, when earth tremors occur, remains still due to inertia. The relative motion between the EARTH and the instrument is magnified and recorded on a rotating drum by a stylus. Through the use of three such instruments the location and severity of earthquakes can be detected. Seismology is also used to locate oil (by analyzing waves from detonated explosions), to detect underground nuclear tests, and to determine the configuration and depth of the ocean floor.

Selden, John, 1584–1654, English jurist and scholar. From 1623 Selden was active in Parliament's struggle to assert its rights against the Crown. A man of great erudition, he was a legal antiquarian (*England's Epinomus,* 1610), an Orientalist (*De Diis Syris,* 1617), and a student of the origins of English law. He is popularly known through *Table Talk* (1689), a record of his conversations kept by his secretary.

selective service, in U.S. history, term for CONSCRIPTION, or mandatory service in the armed forces. It was first introduced (1863) during the Civil War, although those who were able could buy their way out of service. The Selective Service Act of 1917 required all men between the ages of 21 and 30 to register, and by the end of World War I, 2.8 million men had been inducted into military service. Peacetime conscription, initiated in 1940, was greatly expanded after the U.S. entered World War II; between 1940 and 1947, 10 million men were inducted. Retained after the war, selective service was the basis for recruitment during the Korean and Vietnam wars. It was abolished in favor of an all-volunteer military establishment in 1973. Draft registration for 18-year-old men was reinstituted in 1980.

selenium (Se), nonmetallic element, discovered by Jöns Jakob BERZELIUS in 1817. Selenium is used in pigments, photographic exposure meters, electronics, and xerography. See ELEMENT (table); PERIODIC TABLE.

Seles, Monica, 1973–, Yugoslav tennis player. She won her first major tournament, the French Open, in 1990 at the age of 16 and since 1991 has dominated professional women's tennis. Her major tournament victories include three Australian (1991–93), three French (1990–92), and two U.S. (1991–92) opens. In 1993 she was stabbed while playing in a tournament in Hamburg, Germany.

self-help group, nonprofessional organization formed by people with a common problem or situation, for the purpose of pooling resources, gathering information, and offering mutual support, services, or care. Self-help groups began to spread in the U.S. following World War II and proliferated rapidly in the 1960s and 70s. Among these groups are such organizations as ALCOHOLICS ANONYMOUS and those for the victims and families of victims of specific diseases, child abuse, suicide, and crime. Groups concerned with a shared situation include those for the elderly, single parents, and homosexuals. The definition of such groups sometimes includes social-advocacy organizations and halfway services (e.g., drug rehabilitation centers). Although self-help groups may draw on, or offer a bridge to, professional assistance, free services are usually provided by the members themselves through meetings, publications, and individual contacts.

Selim, sultans of the OTTOMAN EMPIRE (Turkey). **Selim I** (the Grim), 1467–1520 (r.1512–20), deposed his father and killed his brothers. His defeat (1514) of the Persians added territory to the empire but began the long rivalry between Persia and Turkey. By assuming the CALIPHATE, he made himself and his successors spiritual as well as temporal rulers. Although bloodthirsty and inflexible, he was an able organizer and reformer. **Selim II** (the Drunkard), c.1524–1574 (r.1566–74), suffered the Turkish naval defeat at Lepanto (1571), the first severe setback at the hands of the Christians. **Selim III,** 1761–1808 (r.1789–1807), suffered defeats (but no great loss of territory) in the second of the RUSSO-TURKISH WARS. He forced Napoleon's troops out of Egypt (1801), which was restored to him. However, Egypt, Albania, and Serbia all became virtually independent during his reign. He was strangled at the order of Mustafa IV, who had succeeded him.

Seljuks: see TURKS.

Selkirk, Alexander, 1676–1721, Scottish sailor whose adventures suggested to DEFOE the story of *Robinson Crusoe.* Put ashore at his own request in the Juan Fernández Islands, Selkirk remained there for over four years before his rescue (Feb. 1709).

Selkirk, Thomas Douglas, 5th **earl of,** 1771–1820, Scottish philanthropist. Emigration to America seemed to him the best solution for the poverty of his countrymen, so he acquired and successfully settled (1803) a large tract on Prince Edward Island. A later attempt—the RED RIVER SETTLEMENT (1812–16) in what is now S Manitoba and N North Dakota and Minnesota—led to violence between rival settlers and litigation that cost Selkirk most of his fortune.

Selma, city (1990 pop. 23,755), seat of Dallas co., S central Ala., on the Alabama R., in a fertile farm area; inc. 1820. A market center, its light industries make farm implements and other products. It was ravaged in 1865, but antebellum houses remain. In 1965 Selma was a focus of world attention during a voter registration drive led by Dr. Martin Luther KING, Jr.

Selznick, David O., 1902–65, American film producer; b. Pittsburgh. After founding Selznick International Pictures in 1936, he made such films as *Gone with the Wind* (1939), *Rebecca* (1940), and *The Third Man* (1949).

semantics [Gr., = significant], in general, the study of the relationships between words and meanings. The empirical study of word meanings in existing languages is a branch of linguistics; the abstract study of meaning in relation to language or symbolic logic systems is a branch of philosophy. Both are called semantics. The field has three basic concerns: the relations of words to the objects denoted by them; the relations of words to the interpreters of them; and, in symbolic logic, the formal relations of signs to one another (syntax). Among the major linguistic semanticists is Noam CHOMSKY. A related theoretical orientation has been developed by such anthropologists as LÉVI-STRAUSS. Philosophical semanticists have included FREGE, Bertrand RUSSELL, and WITTGENSTEIN. A related field, general semantics, studies the ways in which the meanings of words influence human behavior.

Semarang, city (1990 pop. 1,250,971), capital of Central Java prov., N Java, Indonesia, at the mouth of the Semarang R. An important port, it is one of Java's major commercial centers. There are textile and shipbuilding industries, and tobacco, sugar, rubber, coffee, and kapok are exported.

semiconductor, solid material (see SOLID-STATE PHYSICS) whose electrical conductivity at room temperature lies between that of a conductor and that of an insulator (see CONDUCTION; INSULATION). At high temperatures its conductivity approaches that of a metal, and at low temperatures it acts as an insulator. In a semiconductor there is a limited movement of electrons, depending upon the crystal structure of the material used. Incorporation of certain impurities in a semiconductor enhances its conductive properties. The impurities either add free electrons or create holes (electron deficiencies) in the crystal structures of the host substances by attracting electrons. Thus there are two semiconductor types: the *n*-type (negative), in which the current carriers (electrons) are negative, and the *p*-type (positive), in which the positively charged holes move and carry the current. The elements germanium and silicon and the compounds indium antimonide, gallium arsenide, and aluminum phosphide are semiconductors. Semiconductors are used in electronic devices such as COMPUTERS, PHOTOELECTRIC CELLS, RECTIFIERS, and TRANSISTORS.

Seminole, indigenous people of the Eastern Woodlands (see NORTH AMERICA, INDIGENOUS PEOPLES OF), with a Muskogean language of the Hokan-Siouan stock (see NATIVE AMERICAN LANGUAGES). They separated from the CREEK in the 18th cent. To escape white encroachment they fled to Florida, where they absorbed remnants of the Apalachee tribe and runaway slaves. They fought Andrew JACKSON (1817–18) and, led by OSCEOLA, again battled U.S. forces in the Seminole War (1835–42), after which most of them moved to Oklahoma, becoming one of the FIVE CIVILIZED TRIBES. In 1990 there were 13,797 Seminoles in the U.S.

semiotics or **semiology,** the study of an aspect of a culture as a formal system of signs; it is founded on the work of the American logician C.S. PEIRCE and French linguist Ferdinand de Saussure. Saussure's recognition that the relation of words to things is not natural but arbitrary and that a language is essentially a self-contained system of signs, wherein each element is meaningless by itself and meaningful only by its differentiation from the other elements, was key to the development of modern semiotics. His linguistic model influenced literary criticism, contributing to a move away from the study of an author's biography or a work's social setting and toward the internal structure of the text and the text's relationship to other texts. Semiotics is not limited to language, however, as virtually any aspect of a culture (e.g., gesture, clothing, and toys) can function and be analyzed as a sign; see STRUCTURALISM.

Semiramis, mythical Assyrian queen, said to have founded BABYLON. After a long reign she vanished in the form of a dove; she was thereafter worshiped as a deity. Her legend is probably based on Sammuramat, regent of ASSYRIA (810–805 B.C.).

Semites, term originally designating the descendants of Shem, son of NOAH. It was later applied to speakers of related languages presumed to derive from a common tongue, Semitic, including the Arabs, Akkadians, Assyrians, Canaanites, and Hebrews. By 2500 B.C. the pastoral nomadic Semites, who had originated in the Arabian peninsula, began migrating north and west to MESOPOTAMIA, the Mediterranean coast, and the Nile R. delta. In Mesopotamia they became dominant (see ASSYRIA; BABYLONIA). In Phoenicia they were the first great seafaring people. The Hebrews, who, with other

Semites, settled in Palestine, became leaders of a new nation and religion (see JEWS; JUDAISM).

Semitic languages, subfamily of the Hamito-Semitic family of languages. See LANGUAGE (table).

Senate, United States: see CONGRESS OF THE UNITED STATES.

senate, Roman, governing council of the Roman republic. An outgrowth of the royal privy council, it gained immense power as Rome expanded in the 3d and 2d cent. B.C., sending out armies, making treaties, and organizing the new domain. Membership was limited to ex-magistrates, who belonged almost entirely to old families. Its tone tended to be reactionary, yet there was no real challenge to its authority until the agitation of the GRACCHI. This failed, but a popular party grew up to oppose the conservatives. Although it was thoroughly defeated by SULLA, the struggle was resumed later, with Julius CAESAR heading the popular group and POMPEY heading the senatorial party. Caesar triumphed (48 B.C.), and though he was assassinated, the senate was proscribed (43 B.C.) and did not regain power. Docile under AUGUSTUS, it became a mere cipher in the later empire.

Sendak, Maurice Bernard, 1928–, American writer and illustrator of children's books; b. N.Y.C. His wild, fantastic illustrations appear in over thirty children's books, including his own *Where the Wild Things Are* (1963), *In the Night Kitchen* (1970), *Outside over There* (1981), and *We Are All in the Dumps with Jack and Guy* (1993).

Sender, Ramón José [sāndĕr'], 1902–82, Spanish novelist. A Loyalist in the SPANISH CIVIL WAR, he left Spain in 1939 and became a U.S. citizen in 1946. His novels, dealing with social injustice, include *Imán* (1929), *The King and the Queen* (1949), and *Requiem for a Spanish Peasant* (1960). He also wrote plays, stories, poetry, and literary criticism.

Seneca (Lucius Annaeus Seneca), c.3 B.C.–A.D. c.65, Roman philosopher, dramatist, and statesman. A noted orator, he tutored NERO and was virtual ruler in the first years of the emperor's reign. His suicide after accusations of conspiracy was considered remarkably noble by the Romans. A Stoic, he wrote moral and philosophical essays, but he is best known for his tragedies, written apparently for recitation. These, including *Hercules Furens* and *Medea,* profoundly affected Renaissance TRAGEDY with their gloomy atmosphere, bombastic rhetoric, and STOICISM.

Seneca: see IROQUOIS CONFEDERACY.

Senefelder, Aloys, 1771–1834, German lithographer; b. Bohemia. He invented LITHOGRAPHY in Munich c.1796. He published an account of the history of the invention in 1818.

Senegal, officially Republic of Senegal, republic (1992 est. pop. 8,205,000), 76,124 sq mi (197,161 sq km), W Africa, bordered by the Atlantic Ocean (W), Mauritania (N), Mali (E) and Guinea and Guinea-Bissau (S). The nation of GAMBIA is an enclave in the southwest. Major cities include DAKAR (the capital), Thiès, and Kaolack. Most of the country is low-lying and covered with savanna, which becomes semidesert in the SAHEL region of the north. The 250-mi (400-km) coastline is sandy north of Dakar and swampy or muddy to the south. Senegal is primarily agricultural, but industry is expanding. By far the most important cash crop is peanuts, which supplies 75% of farm exports; groundnut processing (oil and oilcake) is the largest industry. The main food crops are millet, sugarcane, rice, and corn. Large numbers of cattle, sheep, and goats are raised. Manufactures include cement, chemicals, textiles, fertilizers, and the processing of fish taken by the sizable coastal fleet. The principal minerals extracted are phosphate rock, limestone, and iron ore; deposits of petroleum and natural gas have been found offshore. The chief ethnic groups are the Wolof, Fulani, Serer, Tukolor, Soninke, Malinke, and Diola. About 90% of the people are Muslim, about 5% are Christian, and the rest follow traditional beliefs. French is the official language.

History. In the middle of the 1st millennium A.D. the region was settled by migrating Wolof and Serer peoples, followed (9th cent.) by the Tukolor, whose state of Tekrur dominated the Senegal R. valley until the 14th cent. The Portuguese arrived (1444–45) and established trading stations; they were displaced by the Dutch and French in the 17th cent. French influence was extended into the interior after 1697, but control of bases in Senegal alternated between France and Britain from the SEVEN YEARS WAR (1756–63) until 1815, when they were finally returned to France. Senegal became a French colony in 1895, remaining part of FRENCH WEST AFRICA until it was made an autonomous republic within the FRENCH COMMUNITY in 1958. Full independence was achieved in 1960, with Léopold SENGHOR as president. By the mid-1960s Senghor had consolidated his power by removing Prime Minister Mamadou Dia and creating a one-party state. A period of civil unrest followed, marked by demonstrations, strikes, and a worsening economic situation resulting from the drought in the Sahel region. In 1978 Senegal again held multiparty elections, which were won by Senghor's Senegalese Socialist party. After his retirement (1980), Senghor was succeeded (1981) as president by Prime Min. Abdou Diouf, who was reelected in 1988 and 1993 amid allegations of fraud. Since the early 1980s there has been sporadic fighting with separatists in the southern province of Casamance, which is largely separated from Senegal by Gambia. In 1981 Senegal joined GAMBIA in a confederation known as Senegambia, but Senegal ended (1989) the association when Gambia refused to move toward closer union. The nation's relations with neighboring Mauritania deteriorated during the late 1980s over the treatment the citizens of each received in the other country; tensions were aggravated by Senegalese opposition to Mauritania's oppression of its black minority.

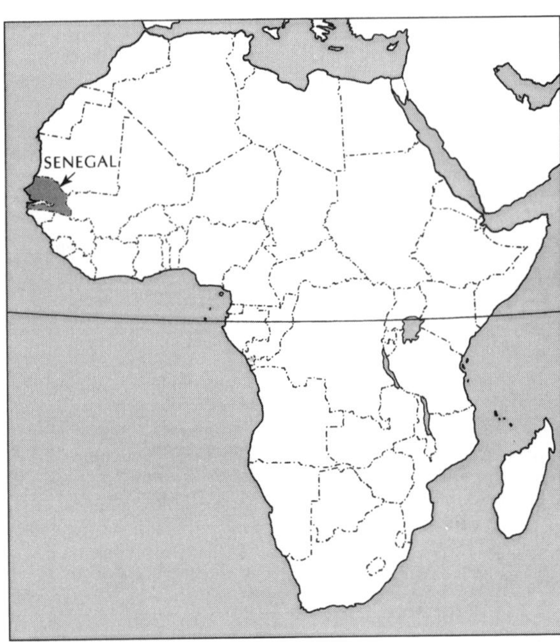

Senegambia: see GAMBIA; SENEGAL.

Senghor, Léopold Sédar [säNgôr'], 1906–, African statesman and poet, president (1960–80) of SENEGAL. He was a leader of the pan-African movement and became president of the new republic of Senegal in 1960. He was one of the formulators of the concept of *négritude,* which rejected the French policy of assimilation and affirmed the African heritage. He retired voluntarily in 1980, and in 1984, became the first black member of the French Academy.

Sennacherib [sĕnăk'ərĭb] or **Senherib I,** d. 681 B.C., king of Assyria (705–681 B.C.). The son of Sargon, he spent his reign trying to maintain the empire. He defeated the Egyptians (701 B.C.) and prepared to take Jerusalem, but instead exacted only tribute. He fought successfully in Babylonia and destroyed Babylon (c.689 B.C.). At NINEVEH he built a magnificent palace. He was murdered, possibly by his sons.

Sennett, Mack, 1880–1960, American film director and producer; b. Canada. His Keystone studios (1912–35) made thousands of short and full-length slapstick comedies. Charlie CHAPLIN, Buster KEATON, and others began their film work at Keystone.

sense, faculty by which external or internal stimuli are conveyed to the brain. The special senses (sight, hearing, smell, and taste) convey external stimuli via receptors in the EYE, EAR, NOSE, and taste buds (see TONGUE). Most somatic sensations, such as touch, heat, cold, and pain, originate with receptors in the skin; a few, such as hunger, result from internal stimuli.

Seoul or **Kyongsong,** city (1985 pop. 9,639,077), capital of South Korea, NW South Korea. The political, commercial, industrial, and cultural center of the nation, Seoul is also a highway and railroad hub. It is linked by rail with its port, INCHON. Before Korea's partition in 1945, Seoul's easy access to industrial raw materials stimulated the establishment of iron, steel, and other primary industries. With most of the raw materials now in North Korea, the city has emphasized textile manufacturing and consumer industries. Founded in 1392, Seoul served as capital of the Yi dynasty until 1910. Heavily damaged during the KOREAN WAR, the city has been extensively rebuilt along modern lines. Seoul retains three gates of its ancient wall and three imperial palaces. The city was the site of the 1988 summer Olympic games.

separation: see DIVORCE.

separation of powers, political doctrine that provides for the splitting of governmental functions into separate but equally important legislative, executive, and judicial areas. Largely modeled on the philosophy of MONTESQUIEU, it aims to prevent tyranny and promote individual freedom by relying on a system of checks and balances. In the U.S., separation of powers is outlined in Articles I–III of the Constitution. The system has been somewhat weakened by the growing strength of the presidency.

separatists, in religion, Christian groups, e.g., Pilgrims and Quakers, who withdrew from the Church of England. They desired freedom from church and civil authority, control of each congregation by its membership, and changes in ritual. They became known as Independents in the 17th cent.

Sephardim, one of the major divisions of JEWS, comprising those who in the Middle Ages resided in the Iberian Peninsula, and their descendants. With the migration of the Iberian Jews, particularly after their expulsion from Spain in 1492, Sephardic traditions were transferred to North Africa and the Middle East and adopted by local Jews; today the term *Sephardim* covers all Jews historically native to the Middle East. Sephardic ritual and liturgy follow the Babylonian tradition (the Ashkenazim, Jews from Germany and their descendants, follow Palestinian tradition). Sephardic Jews spoke a dialect called Ladino (Judeo-Spanish or Spanioli), a blend of medieval Castilian and Hebrew, Turkish, Arabic, and other elements. The Sephardim who were forced to convert to Christianity between 1391 and 1497 were given the pejorative name *Marranos* [pigs] by Christians. As they moved to more tolerant lands, the Marranos openly returned to Judaism. They and their descendants founded the Jewish communities of Hamburg, Amsterdam, London, and New Amsterdam (N.Y.C.).

sepiolite: see MEERSCHAUM.

Sepoy Rebellion: see INDIAN MUTINY.

September: see MONTH.

septicemia, invasion of the bloodstream by bacteria, a grave condition commonly known as blood poisoning. Primary causes include local infections that the body's defenses are unable to contain and progressing tissue infections. Symptoms are fever, chills, prostration, and skin eruption. The condition is treated with massive doses of ANTIBIOTICS.

sequence, in mathematics, ordered set of mathematical quantities, called *terms*. A sequence can be finite, like 1, 2, 3, . . . , 50, which has 50 terms, or infinite, like 1, 2, 3, . . . , which has no final term. An infinite sequence may or may not have a limit. Frequently there is a rule for determining the terms in the sequence, as in the FIBONACCI sequence and in various types of PROGRESSIONS. See also SERIES.

sequoia, name for the redwood (*Sequoia sempervirens*) and for the big tree, or giant sequoia (*Sequoiadendron giganteum*), both huge, evergreen CONIFERS of the BALD CYPRESS family, and for extinct related species. The redwood, which grows to 385 ft (117 m) in height, is probably the world's tallest tree; it is found along the central Pacific coast of the U.S. Its trunk is 10 to 25 ft (3 to 7.6 m) in diameter. The giant sequoia, which grows to 325 ft (99 m) in height, with a trunk of 10 to 30 ft (3 to 9.1 m), is found in California on the western slopes of the Sierra Nevadas; some are believed to be 3,000 to 4,000 years old. The reddish, decay-resistant heartwood of both species is valued for outdoor construction. Sequoias are now protected in parks.

Sequoia National Park: see NATIONAL PARKS (table).

Sequoyah, c.1766–1843, CHEROKEE leader; b. Tennessee. He created a written Cherokee language, a syllabary in which 85 English letters and variations were used as symbols for Cherokee sounds. A newspaper and parts of the Bible were printed in Cherokee. From 1822 he taught thousands of Native Americans to read and write, helping to unite the Cherokee and make them leaders among the tribes. The giant SEQUOIA tree is named for him.

Serbia, Serbo-Croatian *Srbija,* constituent republic of Yugoslavia (1988 est. pop. 9,762,000), 34,107 sq mi (88,337 sq km), E Yugoslavia, the larger of the two remaining republics (the other is MONTENEGRO) of Yugoslavia. It is bounded by Croatia (NW), Hungary (N), Romania (NE), Bulgaria (E), Macedonia (S), and Albania, Montenegro, and Bosnia and Hercegovina (W). BELGRADE is the capital. The west and south are largely mountainous; NE Serbia, part of the Danubian plain, provides most of Yugoslavia's foodstuffs. Grains, hemp, sugar beets, flax, grapes, and plums are among the chief crops. Manufactures include iron and steel, tranport vehicles, and plastics; mining is also important. Serbs make up the vast majority of the population; they belong largely to the ORTHODOX EASTERN CHURCH and use the Cyrillic alphabet. Mostly Muslim Albanians predominate in KOSOVO in the southwest, and there is a smaller Hungarian minority in Vojvodina prov. in the north.

History. Serbs settled (6th–7th cent.) in the Balkans and were Christianized in the 9th cent. A Serbian kingdom emerged (13th cent.) and under STEPHEN DUŠAN (r.1331–55) became the most powerful Balkan state. Defeat (1389) at Kosovo Field (see under KOSOVO) brought Serbia under Turkish domination from the 14th to 19th cent. In 1829 the Turks granted the Serbs autonomy under a hereditary prince, and a lengthy feud between the KARADJORDJEVIĆ and OBRENOVIĆ families ensued. Proclaimed (1882) a kingdom, Serbia emerged from the BALKAN WARS (1912–13) as a major Balkan power. When a Serbian nationalist assassinated (1914) Austrian Archduke FRANCIS FERDINAND, Austria declared war on Serbia, thus precipitating WORLD WAR I. In 1918 the country was included in the Kingdom of the Serbs, Croats, and Slovenes (later YUGOSLAVIA), with PETER I of Serbia as king. A puppet government was set up in Serbia by the Germans during World War II, and in 1946 Serbia became a republic within Yugoslavia. In the early 1990s, as CROATIA and SLOVENIA sought greater autonomy, Serbia, led by Slobodan MILOŠEVIĆ, insisted first on preserving a Serb-dominated Yugoslavia and then on a "greater Serbia" that would include Serbian areas in other republics. War erupted in Croatia and BOSNIA AND HERCEGOVINA, and UN-sponsored economic sanctions severely disrupted the Serbian economy.

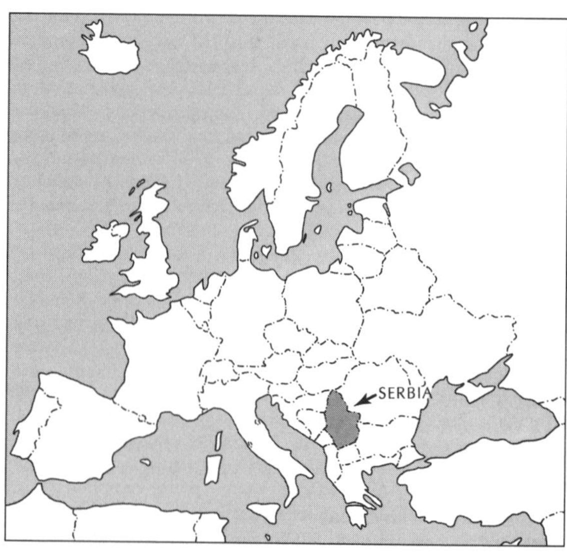

Serbo-Croatian [sûr'bō-krōā'shən], language belonging to the South Slavic group of the Slavic subfamily of the Indo-European family of languages. Although it is actually one language, Serbo-Croatian is designated as Serbian when spoken by Serbs and written in a form of the Cyrillic alphabet, but as Croatian when spoken by Croats and written in a modified version of the Roman alphabet. See LANGUAGE (table).

Serengeti plain in NE Tanzania, SE of Lake Victoria near Kenya. Part of Tanzania's central plateau, it is the site of **Serengeti National Park**, c.5,700 sq mi (14,800 sq km), est. 1941. There the world's largest concentrations of wildebeest and gazelle are found, as well as zebras, lions, hippopotamuses, giraffes, and hyenas. Poaching has decimated the park's elephants and rhinoceroses.

serf, under FEUDALISM and the MANORIAL SYSTEM, a half-free peasant attached to the land held under the lord of the manor, for whom he performed servile labor. Serfs traditionally had certain inviolable rights, and their labor service was governed by custom. In the MIDDLE AGES serfdom developed in France, Spain, and Italy, then spread to Germany and Slavic lands. In England after the Norman Conquest, most free VILLEINS became serfs. In the Hapsburg monarchy serfdom was ended (1781) by JOSEPH II, in France by the French Revolution (1789), and in Russia by ALEXANDER II (1861).

sergeanty: see SERJEANTY.

serial music, those compositions based on an arrangement (called a series or row) of patterns of pitch, rhythm, or dynamics. The term is often used synonymously with TWELVE-TONE MUSIC, which is a kind of serial music. Important composers of this music include Igor STRAVINSKY and Walter PISTON.

series, in mathematics, the indicated sum of a SEQUENCE. A series may be finite or infinite, depending on the number of terms in the sequence. As one takes sums of progressively more terms in an infinite series, these partial sums form a new sequence of values that may or may not approach a certain value, called the limit of the series. If they do, the series is said to converge to that limit; if not, the series diverges.

serigraphy: see SILK-SCREEN PRINTING.

serjeanty or **sergeanty,** a type of land tenure in English FEUDALISM in return for personal, often menial, service. Ceremonial relics of it survive at royal coronations.

Serkin, Rudolf, 1903–91, Austrian-American pianist; b. Bohemia. Serkin was an outstanding interpreter of the music of Mozart and Beethoven. He made his U.S. debut in 1933. His son **Peter Serkin,** 1947–, b. N.Y.C., is also a pianist.

serotonin, biochemical first recognized as a powerful vasoconstrictor occurring in blood serum and other tissues, and subsequently found in wasp and scorpion venom and in various fruits and nuts. One role of the compound is as a NEUROTRANSMITTER that may participate in such diverse functions as learning, sleep, and control of mood. Its structural similarity to certain mind-altering drugs, such as LSD, has prompted speculation that serotonin may have a role in mental disorders, such as schizophrenia.

serpentine, widely distributed hydrous magnesium silicate mineral ($3MgO{\cdot}2SiO_2{\cdot}2H_2O$), formed by the alteration of other minerals or rocks containing magnesium. Usually green, it may also be reddish, yellowish, black, or nearly white. It is sometimes used as a gem; massive varieties are used like marble for decoration, although they are too easily damaged by exposure to be used for exteriors. Fibrous serpentine is chrysotile, a commercial ASBESTOS.

Serra, Junípero, 1713–84, Spanish Franciscan missionary in North America. He directed the founding of nine FRANCISCAN missions in California between 1769 and 1782.

Servetus, Michael [sərvē'təs], 1511–53, Spanish theologian and physician. He early came in contact with reformers in Germany and Switzerland, but his views, particularly about the TRINITY, were condemned by both Roman Catholics and Protestants. He fled to France, where he gained fame in medicine. After he had a work on theology secretly printed (1553), the INQUISITION moved against him. He escaped from prison, but he was seized in Geneva, on John CALVIN's order, and tried and burned there.

Servile Wars, in Roman history, three uprisings of slaves (134?–132? B.C., 104?–101? B.C., 73–71 B.C.). The first two took place in Sicily. The third was the uprising by SPARTACUS in S Italy that was eventually put down with great cruelty by Marcus Licinius Crassus (see CRASSUS, family) and POMPEY.

sesame, herb (*Sesamum indicum*) of the family Pedaliaceae cultivated for its seeds since ancient times, found chiefly in the Old World tropics. Sesame seeds, or bennes, are black or white and yield an oil that resists turning rancid. The oil is used extensively in India for cooking, soap manufacture, food, and medicine, and as an adulterant in OLIVE oil. The seeds are used in baking and confectionery.

Sessions, Roger, 1896–1985, American composer and teacher; b. Brooklyn, N.Y. His early music is romantic and harmonic; later it became austere and complex. His works include music for ANDREYEV's *Black Maskers* (1923), eight SYMPHONIES (1927–68), and the *Concerto for Orchestra* (1982; Pulitzer).

set, in mathematics, collection of entities, called the elements or members of the set, that may be material objects or conceptual entities. Braces, { }, are commonly used to enclose the listed elements of a set, e.g., if A is the set of even numbers between 1 and 9, then $A = \{2,4,6,8\}$. The elements may also be described within braces, e.g., the set B of real numbers that are solutions to the equation $x^2 = 9$ can be written as $B = \{x{:}x^2 = 9\}$, which is read "the set of all x such that $x^2 = 9$." In fact, $B = \{3,-3\}$. There are three basic set operations: intersection, union, and complementation. The intersection of two sets, denoted by the symbol $\cap$, is the set containing the elements common to both. The union of two sets, denoted by $\cup$, is the set of all elements belonging to at least one of the original sets. Thus, if $C = \{1,2,3,4\}$ and $D = \{3,4,5\}$, then $C \cap D = \{3,4\}$ and $C \cup D = \{1,2,3,4,5\}$. In any discussion the set of all elements under consideration is the universal set U; the complement of A, written A', is the set of all elements of the universal set that are not in A; if $U = \{1,2,3,4,5\}$ and $A = \{1,2,3\}$, then $A' = \{4,5\}$. A set with no elements, e.g., the set of all foreign-born U.S. presidents, is called the null, or empty, set and is symbolized by $\varnothing$. Membership in a set is indicated by the symbol $\in$; thus, $x \in A$ means that x is a member of the set A. If the set B contains at least all the elements of the set A, then A is a subset of B, written $A \subset B$. Set theory is involved in many areas of mathematics and has important applications in such other fields as computer technology and atomic and nuclear physics.

SETI [*S*earch for *E*xtra*T*errestrial *I*ntelligence], name given to a series of independent programs to detect radio signals from civilizations beyond the solar system. In 1960 Project Ozma, the first such program, focused on the nearby stars Epsilon Eridani and Tau Ceti. Since then some 50 searches, mostly of limited duration and concentrating on stars similar to the sun, have been conducted without success. In 1992 the High Resolution Microwave Survey (HRMS) was initiated. Using radio telescopes around the world in a planned ten-year search, HRMS envisioned a two-pronged approach. One group is focusing on more than 800 solar-type stars within 100 LIGHT-YEARS of Earth; the other was to conduct an all-sky survey, but this was halted by a funding cutback in 1993. HRMS will monitor only microwave frequencies because there are few natural sources of emissions in that range and researchers hope that extraterrestrials would recognize that range as a quiet region of the electromagnetic spectrum suited to sending a message.

Seton, Saint Elizabeth Ann, 1774–1821, American Roman Catholic leader, also called Mother Seton; b. Elizabeth Ann Bayley, N.Y.C. Soon after she was widowed, she became (1805) a Roman Catholic. In 1808 she opened a school in Baltimore at the invitation of Bishop Carroll and later moved to Emmitsburg, Md., where she opened the first Catholic free school. She formed the first American congregation of the Daughters of Charity (Sisters of Charity) and served as its superior. Canonized in 1975, she was the first native-born U.S. saint. Feast: Jan. 4.

Seton, Ernest Thompson, 1860–1946, American writer and artist; b. England. He interpreted nature for children, as in *Wild Animals I Have Known* (1898, new ed. 1942), and organized the Woodcraft Indians, a precursor of the BOY SCOUTS.

setter: see SPORTING DOG.

Settlement, Act of, 1701, passed by the English Parliament to provide that if WILLIAM III and Princess (later Queen) ANNE died without heirs, succession should pass to Sophia, electress of Hanover, granddaughter of JAMES I, and to her Protestant heirs. Fear of the

JACOBITES partially prompted the measure, which also limited the power of the crown. The house of HANOVER, which became the British royal house in 1714, owed its claim to this act.

Seurat, Georges [sörä'], 1859–91, French neo-impressionist painter. He devised the pointillist technique of painting with tiny dots of pure color (see POSTIMPRESSIONISM). His works include *A Sunday Afternoon on the Island of La Grande Jatte* (Art Inst., Chicago).

Seuss, Dr., pseud. of **Theodor Seuss Geisel,** 1904–91, American author and illustrator of children's books; b. Springfield, Mass. His books blend whimsy, zany humor, catchy verse, and outlandish illustrations. His style is evidenced in *Horton Hears a Who* (1954), *The Cat in the Hat* (1957), *How the Grinch Stole Christmas* (1957), and *Green Eggs and Ham* (1960).

Sevan [syĭvän'], lake, c.540 sq mi (1,400 sq km), in Armenia, at an altitude of 6,280 ft (1,914 m), the largest lake of the Caucasus. The Razdan R. is its only outlet. An extensive hydroelectric system has been developed in the area.

Sevastopol, city (1989 pop. 355,000), S UKRAINE, on the Crimean peninsula and the Bay of Sevastopol, a BLACK SEA inlet. It is a port and major naval base. Among its industries are shipbuilding and lumber milling. It stands near the site of Chersonesus, a Greek colony founded in 421 B.C., which became part of the empire of ROME (1st cent. B.C.) and of the BYZANTINE EMPIRE (4th cent. A.D.). A medieval trade center, it was destroyed by the TATARS in 1399. When Russia annexed (1783) the CRIMEA, Sevastopol was refounded as the chief base of its Black Sea fleet. In the CRIMEAN WAR it was besieged for 349 days (1854–55). In WORLD WAR II it was virtually destroyed during an eight-month siege (1941–42) by German and Romanian forces, who occupied it until 1944. Control of the Black Sea fleet has become an important issue since Ukrainian independence (1991).

Seven against Thebes, in Greek legend, seven heroes. They made war on Eteocles when he refused to share the Theban throne with his brother Polynices, as agreed after the exile of their father, OEDIPUS. The brothers killed each other, and, of the Seven, only Adrastus survived. Their sons, the Epigoni, conquered Thebes 10 years later and gave the kingdom to Thersander, son of Polynices. AESCHYLUS and EURIPIDES dramatized the legend.

Seven Days battles, in the U.S. CIVIL WAR, the Confederate counteroffensive (June 26–July 2, 1862) that ended the Union drive to capture Richmond, Va., in the PENINSULAR CAMPAIGN. After the battle of Fair Oaks, Confederate Gen. R.E. LEE moved to cut off Union forces under G.B. MCCLELLAN from their base at White House Landing. The Confederates attacked the Union advance force under Fitz-John Porter at Mechanicsville but were repulsed (June 26). Porter fell back to Gaine's Mill, where his outnumbered corps was defeated (June 27). When McClellan tried to move his base to the James R. to add naval protection, Lee failed to stop him at Savage's Station (June 29) and Frayser's Farm (June 30). McClellan stood (July 1) at Malvern Hill and repeatedly repulsed Confederate attacks. But he declined to take the offensive and withdrew to the James R., allowing Lee, who suffered heavy losses, to save RICHMOND.

Seventh-Day Adventists: see ADVENTISTS.

Seven Weeks War: see AUSTRO-PRUSSIAN WAR.

Seven Wonders of the World, in ancient classifications, were the Great PYRAMID of Khufu, or all the pyramids, with or without the SPHINX; the Hanging Gardens of Babylon, with or without the walls; the mausoleum at Halicarnassus; the Artemision at EPHESUS; the COLOSSUS of Rhodes; the Olympian ZEUS statue by PHIDIAS; and the Pharos lighthouse at Alexandria, or, instead, the walls of Babylon.

Seven Years War, 1756–63, worldwide conflict fought in Europe, North America, and India between France, Austria, Russia, Saxony, Sweden, and (after 1762) Spain, on one side, and Great Britain, Prussia, and Hanover on the other. Two main issues were involved: French and English colonial rivalries in North America and India, and the struggle for supremacy in Europe of MARIA THERESA of Austria and FREDERICK II of Prussia. In the aftermath of the War of the AUSTRIAN SUCCESSION (1740–48) the European powers began maneuvering for alliances preparatory to a new show of strength. Hostilities began when Prussia invaded Saxony (1756) and BOHEMIA (1757). Despite Frederick's brilliant early victories at Rossbach (1757), Leuthen (1757), and Zorndorf (1758), by 1759 his situation had become nearly hopeless. In 1760 the Russians occupied Berlin briefly, but Frederick expelled them and went on to defeat the Austrians at Torgau. His final victory came only after the accession of PETER III of Russia, who made (1762) a separate peace with him. Sweden also left the war. Now fighting alone in the east, Frederick defeated the Austrians at Burkersdorf (1762). Meanwhile, England, after an inauspicious start, won victories at Krefeld (1758) and Minden (1759), in N Germany, and soundly defeated the French at Louisburg (1758) and Quebec (1759), in North America, and at Plassey (1757) and Pondichery (1761), in India. After protracted negotiations, peace was made at Hubertusburg and at Paris (see PARIS, TREATY OF, 1763). The war confirmed Prussia's new rank as a leading European power and made Britain the world's chief colonial power. France lost most of its overseas possessions.

Severus or **Septimius Severus** (Lucius Septimius Severus), 146–211, Roman emperor (193–211); b. Africa. He took the imperial throne by force, put down opponents, and pacified the empire in Mesopotamia, GAUL, and Britain. He died at York. Severus left the empire to his sons, but one son, CARACALLA, took power.

Sevier, John [səvēr'], 1745–1815, American political leader; b. near New Market, Va. A prominent frontiersman in the AMERICAN REVOLUTION, he was governor of the state of FRANKLIN (1785–88) and of TENNESSEE (1796–1801, 1803–9).

Seville, Span. *Sevilla,* city (1988 est. pop. 663,000), capital of Seville prov. and chief city of ANDALUSIA, SW Spain, on the Guadalquivir R. Seville is a major port connected with the Atlantic by a river and canal. Among its manufactures are tobacco products, armaments, and perfume. Important from Phoenician times, Seville fell to the MOORS in A.D. 712 and was the seat (1023–1091) of an independent emirate under the Abbadids. Taken (1248) by FERDINAND III of Castile, it later was a center for New World trade. One of the world's most beautiful cities, Seville contains many landmarks, e.g., the Moorish alcazar and the Gothic cathedral (1401–1519). The city was the site of the 1992 world's fair.

Sewall, Samuel, 1652–1730, American colonial jurist; b. England. He was one of the judges who tried the Salem witchcraft cases (1692) and shared responsibility for condemning 19 persons to death. He later (1697) publicly confessed the error of these convictions and thereafter observed an annual day of repentance.

Seward, William Henry, 1801–72, American statesman; b. Orange co., N.Y. As senator from New York (1849–61), he was an antislavery advocate. He became secretary of state (1861) in Pres. LINCOLN's cabinet, where his efforts to dominate were overcome only by Lincoln's ingenuity. He was an able statesman, adept in handling diplomatic matters such as the TRENT AFFAIR. He continued in his post under Pres. Andrew JOHNSON and supported the RECONSTRUCTION policy. His most notable act was the farsighted purchase of ALASKA (1867), denounced at the time as "Seward's folly."

Sewell, Anna, 1820–78, English writer. Her only work, *Black Beauty* (1877), a novel about a horse, is a children's classic.

sewing machine, device that stitches cloth and other materials. The machine's invention is attributed primarily to Elias HOWE (1846) and Isaac M. SINGER (1850). In the typical home sewing machine, an eye-pointed needle, raised and lowered at great speed, pierces cloth lying on a steel plate, casting a loop of thread on the underside of the seam. A second thread, fed from a shuttle under the plate, passes through the loop and is interlocked with the upper thread as it is drawn up by the rising needle. Modern electric-powered machines, some controlled electronically, are capable of producing many types of stitches, and specialized machines have been devised for sewing particular items.

sextant, instrument (invented 1731) for measuring the altitude of a celestial body. The image of the body is reflected from the index mirror to the mirror half of the horizon glass and then into the telescope. If the movable index (or image) arm, to which the index mirror is attached, is then adjusted so that the horizon is seen (through the transparent half of the horizon glass) with the reflected image of the body lined up with it, the body's altitude can be read from the index-arm position on the graduated arc.

sex therapy, treatment of sexual disorders and dysfunction, including IMPOTENCE, orgasmic dysfunction, premature ejaculation, and lack of sexual responsiveness. Pioneered by MASTERS AND JOHNSON

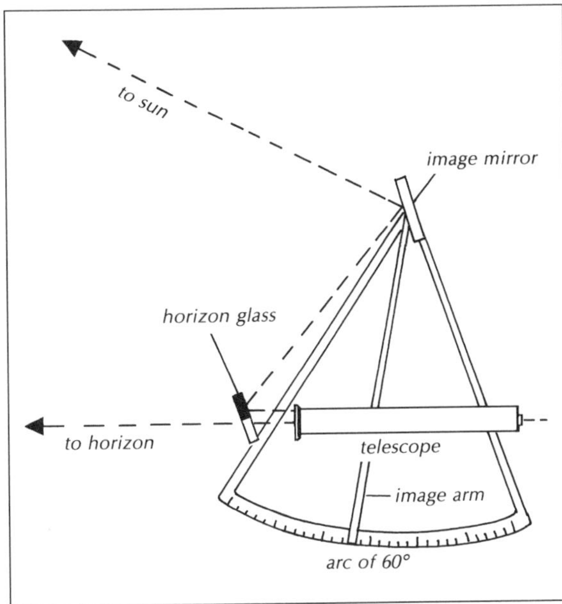

Sextant

in the early 1970s, sex therapy is based on the premise that sexual behavior is learned and that problems can be alleviated through sex education, sensitization exercises, and improved communication between sexual partners. Treatment is generally short-term and focused on the sexual problem and is most successful when it includes the patient's sexual partner.

Sexton, Anne (Harvey), 1928–74, American poet; b. Newton, Mass. Collections of her lyrical, ironic, and confessional poetry include *To Bedlam and Part Way Back* (1960), *Live or Die* (1966; Pulitzer), and *The Complete Poems* (1981). She committed suicide at 46.

sexual harassment, sexual or sexist behavior that creates a hostile or offensive situation or environment. Sexual harassment can be verbal or physical in nature and ranges from sexist or sexually suggestive remarks and actions to pressure from an employer for a sexual relationship and sexual assault. Sexual harassment has been regarded as sex discrimination by federal courts since 1977 and by the Supreme Court since 1986. In 1991 it became a prominent political issue when, during hearings on Clarence Thomas's appointment to the Supreme Court, Anita Hill accused him of having sexually harassed her when she was his aide.

sexually transmitted disease (STD) or **venereal disease,** any of several infectious diseases almost always transmitted through sexual contact. These diseases include GONORRHEA, SYPHILIS, AIDS, CHLAMYDIA, HUMAN PAPILLOMAVIRUS, TRICHOMONIASIS, and genital HERPES SIMPLEX. The incidence of STDs has risen in recent years despite advances in diagnosis and treatment, possibly because of changes in sexual behavior (the SEXUAL REVOLUTION), the emergence of drug-resistant strains, symptomless carriers, lack of public education, and taboos that make patients reluctant to seek treatment.

sexual revolution, term denoting the sweeping changes in sexual mores in Western societies in the latter half of the 20th cent. It ranges from growing social tolerance of divorce, birth control, abortion, and premarital and extramarital sex, to movements for women's liberation and gay rights, to changing perceptions of men's and women's roles in the home and the workplace.

Seychelles [sāshĕlz′], officially Republic of Seychelles, republic (1992 est. pop. 69,500), 175 sq mi (453 sq km), comprising about 100 islands in the Indian Ocean, c.1,000 mi (1,600 km) E of Kenya. The capital and only urban center and port is Victoria, located on the largest island, Mahé (c.55 sq mi/140 sq km), where about 90% of the population lives. The other principal islands are Praslin, La Digue, Silhouette, and Curieuse. Most farming is of the subsistence type; copra, coconuts, and cinnamon are the principal export crops. Fishing is important—fish products are the largest export—but tourism is the principal economic activity. The people are mainly of European and African descent. Most are Roman Catholic and speak a creole patois, but English and French are the official languages.

History. The Seychelles were explored by Vasco da GAMA in 1502, but colonization, by French planters and their slaves, did not begin until 1768. Britain took possession of the islands in 1794 and administered them as part of MAURITIUS until they became a crown colony in 1903. After the first legislative elections (1948), gradual progress was made toward self-government, and Seychelles became independent in 1976. The coalition government was headed by a pro-Western president, James Mancham, and a leftist prime minister, France Albert René. In 1977 René assumed power in a bloodless coup and suspended the constitution. A presidential government and one-party state headed by René was established in 1979; he was reelected in 1984 and 1988. A 1981 attempt by a group of South African mercenaries to overthrow René failed. A multiparty democracy was reestablished in 1993, and René, running against Mancham, won reelection.

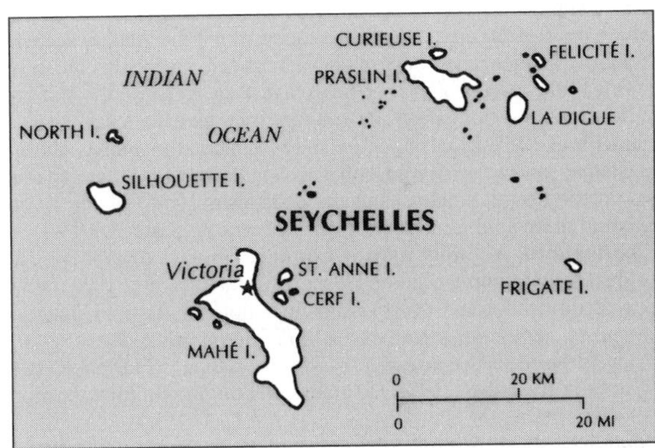

Seymour, Jane, 1509?–1537, third queen consort of HENRY VIII of England. Henry's resolve to marry Jane led to the trial and execution for treason of his second wife, Anne BOLEYN. Soon after, Jane and Henry were married (1536), and in 1537 their son, EDWARD VI, was born. Jane died 12 days later.

Seymour, Thomas, Baron Seymour of Sudeley, 1508?–49, lord high admiral of England; uncle of EDWARD VI. He married (1547) the dowager queen, Catherine PARR; tried to oust his brother, the duke of Somerset, as Edward's guardian; and tried to marry the future ELIZABETH I. He was convicted of treason and executed.

Sforza [sfôr′tsä], Italian family that ruled MILAN from 1450 to 1535. The first prominent member was **Muzio Attendolo Sforza,** 1369–1424, who became a noted condottiere leader of mercenary soldiers and took the surname Sforza [the forcer]. His illegitimate son, **Francesco I Sforza,** 1401–66, was also a famous soldier. He married (1441) Bianca Maria, the illegitimate daughter of Filippo Maria Visconti (see VISCONTI, family), duke of Milan, after whose death Francesco made himself duke (1450). His eldest son, **Galeazzo Maria Sforza,** 1444–76, duke 1466–76, was a patron of the arts but a dissolute and cruel ruler. He was assassinated by republicans. His son, **Gian Galeazzo Sforza,** 1469–94, became duke on his father's death. He was deprived (1480) of the duchy by his uncle, **Ludovico Sforza,** who held him prisoner until his death. Ludovico, 1451?–1508, duke 1494–99, was called *Il Moro* [the Moor] because of his swarthy complexion. His alliance with France helped start (1494) the ITALIAN WARS, but in 1495 he turned against the French. In 1499 LOUIS XII of France expelled him from Milan. Ludovico's attempt to retake the city failed (1500) at Novara, where he was captured, and he died in prison. He is especially remembered as a patron of LEONARDO DA VINCI and BRAMANTE. His son, **Massimiliano Sforza,** 1493–1530, recovered (1512) Milan with help from the HOLY LEAGUE, but surrendered it again to the French in 1515. His brother, **Francesco II Sforza,** 1495–1535, regained the duchy with aid from Holy Roman Emperor CHARLES V. He had no heirs, and Milan passed to Spain in 1559.

Shaba, formerly **Katanga,** region and province, (1984 pop. 3,874,019), c.200,000 sq mi (518,000 sq km), SE Zaïre. The capital is LUBUMBASHI. Eastern Shaba is an enormously rich mining area and supplies most of the world's cobalt as well as extensive quantities of copper and other minerals. Upon Zaïrian independence in 1960, the region seceded and proclaimed itself a republic; a civil war ensued that was ended in 1963 with the use of UN troops. The Belgian firm that controlled Shaba's mining interests was nationalized in 1966.

Shackleton, Sir Ernest Henry, 1874–1922, British explorer. After experience gained (1901–3) in the Robert F. SCOTT expedition, he commanded a south polar expedition (1907–9) during which Mt. Erebus was climbed, the south magnetic pole was located, and the plateau was crossed to within 100 mi (160 km) of the SOUTH POLE. Commanding a transantarctic expedition (1915), he led his party 180 mi (290 km) to safety on floes to Elephant Island after ice crushed his ship. From there he and a few others sailed c.800 mi (1,290 km) on wild seas, crossed South Georgia Island to a whaling station, and rescued the Elephant Island party and others. He died on a fourth voyage and was buried on South Georgia Island in the S Atlantic.

shad, FISH of the HERRING family, found along the Atlantic coast of North America and successfully introduced on the Pacific coast. One of the largest of the herring (6 lb/2.7 kg average), the shad has delicious but bony flesh. Its roe is valued as a delicacy.

Shafi'i, al-, 767–820, Islamic jurist. He founded the Shafi'i school of Islamic law, which gives equal weight to the traditions (hadith) and the Koran, emphasizing the consensus (ijma) of the Islamic community as the most important secondary source of law.

Shaftesbury, Anthony Ashley Cooper, 7th **earl of,** 1801–85, English social reformer. In the House of Commons after 1826, he was a leading advocate of government action to alleviate injustices caused by the INDUSTRIAL REVOLUTION. He introduced laws providing for care of the insane (1845) and limiting child labor (1842) and the work day (1847). He also promoted the building of model tenements.

Shagari, Alhaji Shehu, 1925–, president of Nigeria (1979–83). In 1978 he helped form the National party, and his subsequent election as president marked the end of 13 years of military rule in Nigeria. Continued economic problems and government corruption eventually led to his overthrow (1983).

Shah Jahan or **Shah Jehan,** 1592–1666, Mogul emperor of INDIA (1628–58). During his reign MOGUL ART AND ARCHITECTURE reached their height; the TAJ MAHAL is a leading example. He was deposed (1658) and imprisoned by his son AURANGZEB.

Shahn, Ben, 1898–1969, American painter and graphic artist; b. Lithuania; emigrated to the U.S. in 1906. Shahn frequently used powerful realism or lyrical abstraction to express social and political themes, e.g., his paintings on the SACCO-VANZETTI CASE. Shahn also painted important murals, worked in photography, and created striking posters.

Shaka, c.1787–1828, founder of the Zulu empire. He became (1816) chief of the Zulu clan. After strengthening the army and turning the Zulus into a powerful military nation, he was feared throughout SE Africa. His half-brothers, claiming that he was insane, murdered him.

Shakers, popular name for members of the United Society of Believers in Christ's Second Appearing. Their name derives from the trembling produced by religious emotions. Originating (1747) in England as Shaking Quakers, they grew under the leadership of Ann LEE (d. 1784). She and eight followers moved (1774) to New York. By 1826, 18 communities had been founded in the U.S. Shakers practiced celibacy, lived communally, and believed in a deity with male and female natures. The movement is all but extinct. Shaker furniture and handicrafts are noted for their fine design.

Shakespeare, William, 1564–1616, English dramatist and poet, considered the greatest of all playwrights; b. Stratford-upon-Avon. He was the son of a Stratford businessman and probably attended the local grammar school, acquiring a grounding in the classics. In 1582 he married Anne Hathaway. They had three children. Little else is known of his life before 1592, when he appeared as a playwright in London. He may have been a member of a traveling theater group, and some evidence in his early style suggests he may have been a schoolmaster. In 1594 he became an actor and playwright for the Lord Chamberlain's Men (the King's Men under James I). It is thought that he played supporting roles, e.g., the Ghost in *Hamlet.* In 1599 he became a part owner of the Globe Theatre, and in 1608 of the Blackfriars Theatre. He retired to Stratford in 1613.

The Plays. The chronology of the plays is uncertain, but style and content analysis give a reasonable approximation of their order (see table). They fall roughly into three periods. In the first are history plays, beginning with the three parts of *Henry VI,* and comedies. At this stage Shakespeare's historical tragedies (*Titus Andronicus*) lack depth of characterization and are somewhat bombastic. The comedies are essentially classical imitations, with strong elements of FARCE (*The Comedy of Errors*). The last play in this first period, *Romeo and Juliet* (c.1594), evidences Shakespeare's maturing talent. The versification is more complex, and rhythms reflect the speaker's state of mind, a technique he developed with increasing subtlety. In the second period, from *Richard II* (c.1595) through *Twelfth Night* (c.1599), Shakespeare produced histories and tragedies in which characterization and practical elements are successfully blended. In the COMEDIES of this period he moved away from farce toward idyllic ROMANCE (*As You Like It*). The third period, from 1600, saw the appearance of Shakespeare's major TRAGEDIES, beginning with *Hamlet,* and "problem plays." The tragedies, after *Othello,* present clear oppositions of order to chaos, and good to evil, on all levels. The style becomes increasingly compressed and symbolic. *Pericles, Cymbeline, The Winter's Tale,* and *The Tempest* are tragicomedies, with full tragic potential but a harmonious resolution through grace, a term with divine as well as artistic implications. Shakespeare has been criticized for failing to propound a philosophy, but the enduring appeal of his plays lies in his human vision, which recognizes the complexity of moral questions, and in the unparalleled richness of his language.

Sources and Editions. Eighteen of the plays appeared in print during Shakespeare's life, but the source for all except *Pericles* and *Two Noble Kinsmen* (of dubious authorship) is the First Folio of 1623. The plays were first published with act and scene divisions and stage directions by Nicholas ROWE (1709). Two major sources used by Shakespeare were Raphael HOLINSHED's *Chronicles of England, Scotland, and Ireland* (1577) for the English historical plays, and Sir Thomas North's translation (1579) of PLUTARCH's *Lives.* He altered many other source materials to suit his purposes.

The Poetry. Shakespeare would be well known for his poetry alone. His first published works were the narratives *Venus and Adonis* (1593) and *The Rape of Lucrece* (1594). The love poem *The Phoenix and the Turtle* appeared in 1601. But his major achievement is the *Sonnets* (1609, written in the 1590s). In them Shakespeare exercises his talent for compressing meaning, fully realized in his later work. Addressed (numbers 1–126) to the unidentified "W.H." and (numbers 127–152) to the mysterious "dark lady," the SONNETS treat the themes of time, mutability, and death, and their transcendence through love and art.

shale, sedimentary ROCK formed by the consolidation of mud or CLAY, having the property of splitting into thin layers parallel to its bedding planes. Shales comprise an estimated 55% of all sedimentary rocks and often contain large numbers of fossils. Oil shales are widely distributed in the W U.S. and may be a future source of petroleum.

Shalikashvili, John Malchase David [shälē"käshvē'lē], 1936–, U.S. army officer; b. Poland. Drafted into the army, he became a commissioned officer in 1959, served in Vietnam (1968–69) as an adviser, and rose (1989) to lieutenant general. He led the 9th Infantry (1987–89) and was deputy commander in chief of the U.S. Army in Europe (1989–91) and commander of NATO forces (1992–93). In 1993 he became the first foreign-born chairman of the Joint Chiefs of Staff.

shallot: see ONION.

Shalmaneser [shălmənē'zər], kings of Assyria. **Shalmaneser I,** d. 1290 B.C., moved the capital from Assur to Calah and established a royal residence at Nineveh. **Shalmaneser III** (r.859–824 B.C.) won an indecisive victory over Benhadad of Damascus and AHAB of Israel at Karkar, on the Orontes R. In Calah he built an enormous ziggurat. **Shalmaneser V,** d. 722 B.C., attacked Hosea of Israel, but died in the siege of SAMARIA.

shaman, among tribal peoples, a magician, medium, or healer who owes his powers to mystical communion with the spirit world. Shamanism is based on ANIMISM; the shaman shields humans from destructive spirits by rendering the spirits harmless. He receives his power from a spirit who selects him and whom he cannot refuse. Characteristically, he goes into auto-hypnotic trances, during which he is said to be in contact with spirits. He occupies a position of great power and prestige in his tribe. Noted especially among Siberians, shamans are also found among the Eskimos, some Native American tribes, in SE Asia, and in Oceania.

Shamir, Yitzhak, 1915–, Israeli politician. Born in Poland, he emigrated (1935) to Palestine, where he joined the Zionist movement. Arrested (1946) by the British, he escaped to France. Returning to Palestine in 1948, he served in the Israeli secret service. He helped to found (1973) the conservative Likud party, becoming its leader and prime minister upon the retirement of Menachem BEGIN in 1983. In 1984 and 1988, Likud and Labor formed a government of national unity in which Shamir served as foreign minister (1984–86) and prime minister (1986–90). From 1990 to 1992 Shamir was prime minister of a Likud-led right-wing government.

Shammai, c.50 B.C.–A.D. c.30, Palestinian rabbi. A leader of the SANHEDRIN, Shammai adopted a rigorous style of interpretation of HALAKAH that opposed the teachings of HILLEL.

shamrock, plant with leaves composed of three leaflets. According to legend, it was used by St. PATRICK to explain the Trinity. The identity of the true shamrock has long been debated, but the plants most often designated as shamrocks are the white CLOVER, *Trifolium repens;* the small hop clover, *T. procumbens;* and the wood sorrel, *Oxalis acetosella* (see OXALIS). The shamrock is the emblem of Ireland.

Shang or **Yin,** dynasty: see CHINA.

Shanghai, city (1990 est. pop. 7,830,000), in, but independent of, Jiangsu prov., E China, on the Huangpu R. Administered directly by the central government, Shanghai is one of the world's great seaports, the largest city of China, and the country's most important foreign trade center. Shanghai is the leading industrial city of China, with steelworks, textile mills, shipyards, and oil refineries. Its factories produce various heavy and light industrial goods, such as machinery, chemicals, electronic equipment, aircraft, and precision tools. Since Shanghai was declared (1990) a special economic zone, the government has spent billions of dollares to modernize the city's transportation and other facilities. Shanghai comprises a commercial center (the former International Settlement), which is Western in appearance; an older quarter with crowded streets and wooden buildings; and industrial and residential sections ringing the city. Shanghai became a treaty port in the 19th cent. and there were extraterritorially administered British, American, and French concessions until World War II. The Chinese Communist party's first Congress was held there in 1921.

Shankara: see VEDANTA.

shape memory, property possessed by certain ALLOYS that allows them to return, when heated, to their original shape after having been deformed. This effect results because, as the alloy is deformed, it undergoes a martensitic (or athermal) transformation—a solid-state transition that rapidly changes the crystalline structure of the alloy without thermal activation—that is readily reversed once an appropriate amount of heat is applied. Among the alloys are copper-aluminum-nickel, copper-zinc-aluminum, nickel-titanium, and iron-manganese-silicon. Applications of shape memory include heat-activated fasteners, switches, eyeglass frames, orthopedic devices, teeth braces, and blood clot filters.

Shapiro, Karl, 1913–, American poet; b. Baltimore. As a soldier he wrote such volumes as *V-Letter and Other Poems* (1944; Pulitzer). Later books include *Poems of a Jew* (1958) and *Collected Poems* (1978). His critical essays appear in such collections as *Beyond Criticism* (1953) and *The Poetry Wreck* (1975).

Shapley, Harlow, 1885–1972, American astronomer; b. Nashville, Mo. He was a staff astronomer (1914–21) at Mt. Wilson Observatory and later director (1921–52) of Harvard Observatory. He established that CEPHEID VARIABLES are pulsating stars rather than eclipsing binaries. Through his study of Cepheids in globular STAR CLUSTERS he determined the size of the MILKY WAY galaxy as well as the position of its center and of the sun within the galaxy.

sharecropping, farm tenancy system once common in parts of the U.S. that arose from the cotton plantation system after the CIVIL WAR. Landlords provided land, seed, and credit; croppers—initially former slaves—contributed labor and received a share of the crop's value, minus their debt to the landlord. The system's abuses included emphasis on single cash crops, high interest charges, and cropper irresponsibility. Farm mechanization and reduced cotton acreage have virtually ended sharecropping.

shark, predatory cartilaginous FISH (order Selachii), found in all seas but most abundant in warm waters. About 250 species exist, ranging from the 2-ft (60-cm) pygmy shark to the 50-ft (15-m) whale shark. Sharks have pointed snouts and crescent-shaped mouths with several rows of sharp, triangular teeth. The most feared is the white shark, or man-eater (*Carcharodon carcharias*), reaching 20 ft (6 m) in length, which feeds on large fish and other animals and is known to attack swimmers and boats without provocation. Unlike other sharks, the whale shark and basking shark are harmless plankton feeders. Shark meat is nutritious, and shark oils are used in industry. Tanned sharkskin is a durable LEATHER.

Sharon, Ariel, 1928–, Israeli soldier and politician. A brilliant military strategist, he took part in all of the ARAB-ISRAELI WARS. He served (1973–74, 1977–) in the Israeli parliament, helped to found the Likud coalition, and was minister of agriculture (1977–81) and of defense (1981–83). He was the chief architect of the 1982 Israeli invasion of Lebanon and was criticized for allowing Lebanese Christian forces into Palestinian refugee camps in West BEIRUT and the massacre of civilians that resulted. He also was minister of trade and industry (1984–90) and minister of housing (1990–92); in the latter post he worked to increase Jewish settlement in the occupied territories.

Shastri, Shri Lal Bahadur, 1904–66, Indian prime minister (1964–66). He held several governmental posts before succeeding Jawaharlal NEHRU.

Shatt al Arab, tidal river, 120 mi (193 km) long, formed by the confluence of the TIGRIS and EUPHRATES rivers in SE Iraq and flowing southeast along part of the Iran-Iraq border to the PERSIAN GULF. Iraq and Iran have disputed navigation rights on the Shatt al Arab since 1935, when an international commission awarded the rights to Iraq, leaving Iran with control of only the approaches to its ports of Abadan and Khorramshahr. The issue contributed to the outbreak of the IRAN-IRAQ WAR in 1980.

Shavuot: see under JEWISH HOLIDAYS.

Shaw, George Bernard, 1856–1950, Irish playwright and critic. His dramas of ideas revolutionized the Victorian stage, and his criticism is considered superb. In 1925 he was awarded the Nobel Prize in literature. A Fabian socialist, Shaw was a popular speaker and wrote five novels before becoming a music critic for London newspapers in 1888. After 1895, as drama critic for the *Saturday Review,* he won readers to IBSEN. His early plays were collected in

George Bernard Shaw

Plays Pleasant and Unpleasant (1898). Among the "unpleasant" plays was *Mrs. Warren's Profession* (1893), a jibe at Victorian attitudes on prostitution. The "pleasant" plays included *Arms and the Man* (1894), satirizing romantic attitudes toward love and war, and *Candida* (1893). In 1897 *The Devil's Disciple,* on the American Revolution, was a success in New York City. It was published along with *Caesar and Cleopatra* (1899) and *Captain Brassbound's Conversion* (1900). Shaw's major plays came in the next 15 years: *Man and Superman* (1905), on men, women, and marriage; *Major Barbara* (1905), arguing poverty as the root of all evil; and *Androcles and the Lion* (1912), satirizing Christianity. *Pygmalion* (1913) was his most successful play. A satire on English class attitudes, it was the basis for the 1956 musical *My Fair Lady.* Of Shaw's later plays, *Saint Joan* (1923), a dramatic consideration of JOAN OF ARC, is best known. His most notable nonfiction work is probably *The Intelligent Woman's Guide to Socialism and Capitalism* (1928).

Shaw, Henry Wheeler: see BILLINGS, JOSH.

Shawnee or **Shawano,** indigenous people of the Eastern Woodlands (see NORTH AMERICA, INDIGENOUS PEOPLES OF), with an Algonquian language of the Algonquian-Wakashan stock (see NATIVE AMERICAN LANGUAGES). By the mid-18th cent. they were concentrated in Ohio, where they fought in most wars of the Old Northwest. In 1795 they were forced to move into Indiana. There TECUMSEH and his brother Tenskwatawa, the Shawnee Prophet, established the tribe in a village on the Tippecanoe R., which William Henry HARRISON destroyed (1811). The Shawnee were then moved farther west, eventually to Oklahoma. In 1990 there were 6,179 Shawnees in the U.S.

Shays, Daniel [shāz], c.1747–1825, American soldier; b. probably Hopkinton, Mass. After fighting in the AMERICAN REVOLUTION, he led **Shays's Rebellion** (1786–87), an armed revolt in W Massachusetts. Economically depressed farmers demanding relief prevented the courts from sitting and attacked the Springfield arsenal. They were dispersed by state troops. Shays escaped and was pardoned in 1788.

shear: see STRENGTH OF MATERIALS.

Sheba, biblical name of a region of S Arabia, including Yemen and the Hadhramaut; it was also called Saba. Its inhabitants, Sabaeans or Sabeans, established an ancient culture there, as shown by inscriptions in a Semitic language. The biblical queen of Sheba (called Balkis in the Muslim tradition) visited Solomon in the 10th cent. B.C. With the rise of Islam (7th cent. A.D.), Sheba came under Muslim control.

Sheeler, Charles, 1883–1965, American painter; b. Philadelphia. His characteristic style is a cool simplification in planes and volumes of industrial forms and rural buildings, e.g., *Midwest, 1954* (Walker Art Center, Minneapolis). His photographs reflect a similar simplification and impersonality.

sheep, wild and domesticated ruminant MAMMALS (genus *Ovis*). Wild sheep, which include the BIGHORN, are agile rock climbers with large, spiraling horns. Present-day domesticated sheep are thought to be derived chiefly from the mouflon of SARDINIA and CORSICA and the urial of Asia. An adult male is called a ram; a female, a ewe; an infant, a lamb. Sheep are bred for their WOOL, meat (mutton or lamb, according to age), skins, and MILK (from which CHEESE is made). Important breeds include the Cotswold, Hampshire, Leicester, Lincoln, Merino, Rambouillet, and Suffolk.

sheepdog: see WORKING DOG.

Sheffield, city (1991 pop. 501,202), South Yorkshire, N England. One of the leading industrial cities of England, it is famous for its cutlery, especially the fused copper and silver metalware known as Sheffield plate.

Sheherazade: see THOUSAND AND ONE NIGHTS.

shellac, solution of lac, a RESIN exuded by a scale insect, in alcohol or acetone. The color ranges from light yellow to orange; the darker shellacs are the less pure. When bleached it is known as white shellac. Applied to surfaces, e.g., wood, shellac forms a hard coating when the solvent evaporates. Shellac is used as a spirit VARNISH, as a protective covering for drawings and plaster casts, for stiffening felt hats, and in electrical insulation.

Shelley, Percy Bysshe, 1792–1822, English poet. In 1810 he entered Oxford, where he read the philosophical writings of William GODWIN and others. In 1811 he and a friend published a pamphlet, *On the Necessity of Atheism,* and were expelled. Later that year he married Harriet Westbrook. His first major poem, *Queen Mab,* privately printed in 1813, advocated social and political reform through the abolition of various established institutions. In 1814 he went to France with Godwin's daughter, Mary. In 1816, after Harriet's suicide, he and Mary were married. *Alastor, or The Spirit of Solitude,* appeared in 1816; *The Revolt of Islam* in 1818. In that year the Shelleys settled in Italy, where his mature works were written, among them the poetic dramas *The Cenci* (1819) and *Prometheus Unbound* (1820); *Adonais* (1821), an elegy to John KEATS; and the lyrics "Ode to the West Wind" (1819) and "To a Skylark" (1820). In 1821 Shelley wrote "A Defence of Poetry," his most important prose work. He was drowned while sailing in 1822. Shelley's poetry reveals his belief in reason and the perfectability of humanity. His lyric poems are superb in their beauty and grandeur. His wife, **Mary Wollstonecraft Shelley,** 1797–1851, was the daughter of William Godwin and Mary WOLLSTONECRAFT. Her fame rests on the science-fiction novel *Frankenstein* (1818). Among her other novels is *The Last Man* (1826).

Shem: see NOAH.

Shenandoah National Park: see NATIONAL PARKS (table).

Shenandoah valley, scenic depression in the APPALACHIAN MTS., c.150 mi (240 km) long, between the Blue Ridge and Allegheny mountains, in N Va., occupied in part by the Shenandoah R. and by Shenandoah National Park (see NATIONAL PARKS, table). It was an important corridor in the early westward movement of pioneers and figured prominently in the "valley campaign" of Stonewall JACKSON (1862) and other events of the Civil War.

Shenchen: see SHENZHEN.

Shenyang, formerly Mukden, city (1990 est. pop. 4,540,000), capital of Liaoning prov., NE China, on the Hun R. It is one of China's leading industrial cities and the economic center of NE China. Industries include machinery, machine tools, metals, tractors, transformers, and chemicals. An important historical site, Shenyang was the capital of the MANCHUS in China and the site of the Japanese invasion of MANCHURIA in 1931 (the "Mukden Incident").

Shenzhen [shĕn'jŭn'], city (1991 est. pop. 2,385,000), S Guangdong prov., SE China, on the South China Sea, just N of Hong Kong. One of China's first designated special economic zones (1979), Shenzhen has experienced enormous economic growth. Manufactures include electronic and computer equipment, chemicals, processed foods, textiles, construction materials, and pharmaceuticals.

Shepard, Alan Bartlett, Jr., 1923–, American astronaut; b. East Derry, N.H. He was the first American to be launched into space. On May 5, 1961, Shepard in *Freedom 7* (*Mercury-Redstone 3*) made a 15-min suborbital flight down the Atlantic missile range. While commanding the *Apollo 14* lunar-landing mission (Jan. 31–Feb. 9, 1971), he became the fifth person to walk on the moon. He retired (1974) from NASA and the U.S. navy (as a rear admiral).

Shepard, Sam, 1943–, American playwright and actor; b. Fort Sheridan, Ill., as Samuel Shepard Rogers III. A product of the 1960s counterculture, Shepard combines wild humor, grotesque satire, myth, and haunting language evocative of Western movies to create a subversive POP-ART vision of America. His plays include *Curse of the Starving Class* (1977), *Buried Child* (1978; Pulitzer), *True West* (1980), and *States of Shock* (1991). He wrote the screenplay for and acted in *The Right Stuff* (1983), which made him a movie star.

Sheraton, Thomas, 1751–1806, English furniture designer. A Baptist preacher and writer, he published his designs in manuals such as the *Cabinet-Maker and Upholsterer's Drawing-Book* (1791–94). His style is marked by delicacy, simplicity, straight lines, classical motifs, and inlay decoration.

Sheridan, Philip Henry, 1831–88, Union general and outstanding cavalry officer in the U.S. CIVIL WAR; b. Albany, N.Y. His charge over Missionary Ridge (Nov. 1863) in the CHATTANOOGA CAMPAIGN contributed largely to the Union victory. In 1864, while leading the Army of the Shenandoah, he defeated the Confederates and laid waste the countryside. Surprised by a counterattack at Cedar Creek, Sheridan made a famous ride to the battlefield and turned a near defeat into a decisive victory. In April 1865 he cut off the Confederate retreat at APPOMATTOX and forced Gen. LEE to surrender.

Sheridan, Richard Brinsley, 1751–1816, English dramatist and

Sam Shepard

politician; b. Dublin. His masterpieces, *The Rivals* (1775) and *School for Scandal* (1777), COMEDIES of manners blending RESTORATION wit and 18th-cent. sensibility, are affectionate satires on fashionable society. Other works include *The Critic* (1779), a dramatic burlesque; *The Duenna* (1775), a comic opera; and *A Trip to Scarborough* (1777). He entered Parliament in 1780.

Sherman, William Tecumseh, 1820–91, Union general in the U.S. CIVIL WAR; b. Lancaster, Ohio. He distinguished himself in the VICKSBURG and CHATTANOOGA campaigns (1863). Appointed commander in the West (Mar. 1864), he embarked on the ATLANTA CAMPAIGN and took the city (Sept. 2). He burned Atlanta (Nov. 15) and set off, with a force of 60,000, on his famous march to the sea, devastating the country. After capturing Savannah (Dec. 21), he turned north through South Carolina, again wreaking havoc, and received the surrender of Gen. J.E. JOHNSTON (Apr. 26, 1865). Sherman, whose famous statement that "war is hell" expressed his belief in the need for ruthlessness in modern warfare, is considered one of the greatest Civil War generals. His brother, **John Sherman,** 1823–1900, was secretary of the treasury (1877–81) and secretary of state (1897–98). As a U.S. senator from Ohio (1861–77, 1881–97), he was associated with passage (1890) of the Sherman Antitrust Act and the SHERMAN SILVER PURCHASE ACT.

Sherman Antitrust Act: see under ANTITRUST LAWS.

Sherman Silver Purchase Act, 1890, passed by the U.S. Congress to supplant the BLAND-ALLISON ACT OF 1878. It required the U.S. government to double its purchase of silver and to increase money in circulation. When put into operation, it threatened to undermine the U.S. Treasury's gold reserves, and it was repealed in 1893.

Sherrington, Sir Charles Scott, 1857–1952, English neurophysiologist. He introduced the term and concept of synapse, described the motor functions of the spinal cord, and demonstrated that when one set of muscles is stimulated, an opposing set is simultaneously inhibited. His work on reflex integration was synthesized in his classic *The Integrative Action of the Nervous System* (1906). For his isolation and functional analysis of the neuron, he shared with Edgar Adrian the 1932 Nobel Prize in physiology or medicine.

sherry, naturally dry, fortified wine containing 15% to 23% alcohol; originally made from grapes of the Jérez de la Frontera region in Spain. The term now includes wines of S Spain, the U.S., Latin America, and South Africa. After fermentation, sherry is fortified with BRANDY and aged. Blending and, in some cases, sweetening produce a wide variety of sherries.

Sherwood, Robert Emmet, 1896–1955, American dramatist; b. New Rochelle, N.Y. His plays range from comedy—*Reunion in Vienna* (1931), to melodrama—*The Petrified Forest* (1935), to biography—*Abe Lincoln in Illinois* (1938; Pulitzer). He also wrote a memoir of his years in the F.D. ROOSEVELT administration, *Roosevelt and Hopkins* (1948; Pulitzer).

Shetland Islands, archipelago, 552 sq mi (1,427 sq km), off N Scotland. They consist of c.100 islands c.70 mi (110 km) long, about a fourth of which are inhabited. The largest are Mainland (where Lerwick, the main town, is located), Yell, Unst, Fetlar, Whalsey, and Bressay. Oil, produced offshore in the North Sea since the 1970s, supplements income from traditional sheep, cattle, and knitware industries. Tourism is also important. The hardy Shetland pony and the SHETLAND SHEEPDOG originated there. Occupied by Norsemen by the 9th cent., the islands were annexed to Scotland in 1472.

Shetland sheepdog, agile WORKING DOG; shoulder height, 13–16 in. (33–40.6 cm); weight, c.15 lb (7 kg). Its dense double coat is usually a mixture of black, blue, and sable, with white and tan markings. The sheltie was developed (19th cent.) to tend the small sheep of the Shetland Islands.

Shevardnadze, Eduard A(mvrosiyevich), 1927–, Soviet-Georgian political leader and diplomat, president of GEORGIA (1992–). Head of the Georgian Communist party (1972–85), he became (1985) Soviet foreign minister under GORBACHEV. He sought improved relations with the West and the end of the COLD WAR. During his tenure the USSR withdrew from Afghanistan, signed new arms-control agreements, and supported the U.S.-led coalition in the PERSIAN GULF WAR. In 1990 he resigned, warning of approaching dictatorship. He joined Boris YELTSIN in opposing the attempted coup (1991) against Gorbachev and again served as foreign minister (Nov.–Dec. 1991) as the USSR disintegrated. In 1992, after Georgian Pres. Zviad Gamsakhurdia's ouster, he became president of Georgia.

Shevchenko, Taras [shĭvchĕn'kō], 1814–61, Ukrainian poet and artist. Born a serf, he became a noted realist painter and published Ukrainian ballads in Russian. For opposing serfdom and autocracy in *The Heretic* (1845), he was sentenced to military service in Central Asia (1847–57), but he continued to produce lyric poetry and novels in exile. He died a week before the abolition of serfdom was proclaimed.

Shih Tzu, active TOY DOG; shoulder height, 8–11 in. (20.3–27.9 cm); weight, 9–18 lb (4.1–8.2 kg). Its long, soft double coat may be any color. Probably descended from the LHASA APSO, it originated in Tibet and was sent as a gift by Dalai Lamas to Chinese emperors as early as the 16th cent.

Shiites [Arab., = sectarians], members of one of the two great divisions of ISLAM, the other, much more numerous, being the SUNNI. There are important Shiite communities in Iran (where they predominate), Iraq, Yemen, Pakistan, Lebanon, and Oman. The schism arose over MUHAMMAD's successor, or caliph. The Shiites supported Ali, Muhammad's son-in-law. They believe that the divine line of descent from Muhammad will culminate in the twelfth IMAM, hidden from the usurpers, who will appear on the Last Day as the MAHDI. The Shiites also differ from the Sunni in matters of law and ceremony.

Shikoku, island (1990 pop. 4,240,265), Japan. The smallest (7,247 sq mi/18,770 sq km) of Japan's major islands, it is located in the south, separated from HONSHU and KYUSHU by the Inland Sea. The island is mostly mountainous, with little land suitable for farming, and has a warm, mild climate. Population is concentrated in the industrial belt along the northern coast, where Takamatsu and Matsuyama are the largest cities.

Shiloh [shī'lō], in the BIBLE, town, now Khirbet Seilun in the Israeli-occupied WEST BANK, NNE of Jerusalem. It was the home of the prophets Eli and Ahijah and the place where the ARK of the Covenant rested after the conquest of Judah.

Shiloh, battle of, Apr. 6–7, 1862, in the U.S. CIVIL WAR. On Apr. 6, the Confederates routed Union troops under U.S. GRANT in a surprise attack at Shiloh Church meetinghouse, Tenn. The next day Grant, with reinforcements from the Army of the Ohio, counterattacked, and the Confederates withdrew to Corinth, Miss. The battle, one of the war's bloodiest, with losses of over 10,000 on each side, set the stage for later Union victories in the West.

shingles or **herpes zoster,** infection of a ganglion, or nerve center, with severe pain and a blisterlike eruption in the area of the nerve distribution, due to the same virus that causes CHICKEN POX. Most common in people past age 50, it often involves the area of the upper abdomen and lower chest, but may appear along other nerve pathways.

Shining Path, Span. *Sendero Luminoso,* Peruvian Communist guerrilla force, officially the Communist party of Peru. Founded (1970) by Abimael Guzmán Reynoso as an orthodox Marxist-Leninist offshoot of the Peruvian Communist party, the Shining Path turned to TERRORISM in 1980. By the mid-1980s it had several thousand guerrillas, largely in rural Peru; it began urban terrorism in the late 1980s. In 1992 Pres. Fujimori instituted martial law, and the subsequent capture of Guzmán set the guerrillas back.

Shinn, Everett, 1876–1953, American painter; b. Woodstown, N.J. The youngest member of the EIGHT, he is best known for his street and theater scenes, e.g., *Revue* (Whitney Mus., N.Y.C.). He was also an outstanding illustrator and muralist.

Shinto, ancient native religion of Japan still practiced in a form modified by the influence of Buddhism and Confucianism. In its present form it is characterized less by religious doctrine or belief than by the observance of traditional rituals and customs involving reverence of ancestors, the celebration of popular festivals, and pilgrimages to shrines believed to house a great host of mostly beneficent supernatural beings or deities called *kami.* Shinto beliefs and rituals were transmitted orally long before the introduction (5th cent.) of Chinese writing into Japan; much of the ancient belief is gathered in three later compilations of records, rituals, and prayers—the *Kojiki* (completed A.D. 712), the *Nihongi* (completed A.D. 720), and the *Yengishiki* (10th cent.). These accounts describe the development of early Japanese religion from the worship of the forces and forms of nature to a stage of polytheism in which spiritual conceptions had only a small place. The most exalted among the deities was the sun goddess, Amaterasu-o-mi-kami, held to be the ancestor of the line of emperors of Japan, each of whom was chief priest by divine right. In 1882 all Shinto organizations were divided into two groups, government-supervised state shrines and sectarian churches. A powerful tool in the hands of the militarists, state Shinto collapsed with the defeat of Japan in World War II and the disavowal (1946) by Emperor HIROHITO of his divinity. Sectarian Shinto still thrives; there is no dogmatic system and no formulated code of morals, but some newer sects stress world peace and brotherhood.

ship, large craft in which persons and goods can be conveyed on water. The term *boat* properly applies only to smaller craft, but some vessels may be called by either name. Ancient ships were propelled by oars, sails, or both; the trireme used by the Greeks and the Romans was the most famous warship of ancient times. In the Middle Ages, VIKING ships, propelled by both oars and sails, carried LEIF ERICSSON to America. The introduction of the mariner's COMPASS and the transoceanic voyages of the Portuguese and of COLUMBUS and other explorers of the New World gave impetus to the building and navigation of ships. With differences in the number and positions of masts, and sails either square-rigged or fore-and-aft, a number of different types of ships appeared. Building wooden ships became an important industry, especially in Britain and the U.S. Later, the STEAMSHIP replaced the sailing ship and steel replaced wood, making possible the construction of much larger ships. The steam engine was followed by the steam TURBINE and, early in the 20th cent., by the DIESEL ENGINE. In the 1950s nuclear marine engines were introduced. Today, some freight ships are equipped with cargo-handling machines that rival the power of any on the docks, and the latest generation of mammoth oil-carriers (supertankers) includes the largest ships that ever put to sea. Although the airplane has led to the virtual demise of the great ocean liner, luxurious cruise ships continue to be built. The pivotal vessels of modern warfare are the AIRCRAFT CARRIER and the SUBMARINE, but any sizable navy still includes destroyers, cruisers, and frigates.

shipworm or **teredo,** wormlike marine BIVALVE mollusk that bores in wood. It is a greatly elongated CLAM, with two ridged shells that function as boring tools enclosing only the front of the body. Shipworms burrow in submerged wood, feeding on wood particles and minute organisms; they do enormous damage to piers and ships.

Shirley, James, 1596–1666, English dramatist. His plays include *The Lady of Pleasure* (1635), a comedy realistically portraying London society; *The Traitor* (1631), a tragedy; and *The Triumph of Peace* (1633), a MASQUE.

Shiva, one of the major gods of HINDUISM; in the Hindu trinity he represents the force of destruction and cosmic dissolution (see also BRAHMA; VISHNU).

shock, condition in which the cardiovascular system is unable to provide adequate BLOOD circulation to body tissues. It may be due to inadequate pumping by the HEART (heart failure), hemorrhage, extensive BURNS, or low BLOOD PRESSURE. Symptoms include weakness, pallor, cold and moist skin, thirst, nausea, and, in severe cases, unconsciousness. Because shock can be fatal, emergency treatment, such as BLOOD TRANSFUSIONS and administration of fluids and oxygen, should be given while the cause is being diagnosed.

Shockley, William Bradford, 1910–89, American physicist; b. London. At Bell Laboratories, he, John Bardeen, and Walter H. Brattain produced (1947) the first TRANSISTOR, for which they shared the 1956 Nobel Prize in physics. Shockley later aroused controversy with his theory of black intellectual inferiority, which was rejected by most social scientists.

shock wave, wave formed of a zone of extremely high pressure within a fluid (see FLUID MECHANICS), especially one such as the atmosphere, that propagates through the fluid at supersonic speed, i.e., faster than the speed of SOUND. Shock waves are caused by the sudden, violent disturbance of a fluid, such as that created by a powerful explosion or by the supersonic flow of a fluid over a solid object (see SONIC BOOM).

Shoemaker, Bill (William Lee Shoemaker), 1931–, American jockey; b. Fabens, Tex. The most successful jockey in history, he won his first race at 18. By the time he retired in 1990 he had won 8,833 races, including four Kentucky Derbies, five Belmont Stakes, and three Preakness Stakes. He was the first jockey to win over $100 million.

shogun, title of the feudal military dictators who from the 12th to the 19th cent. were the actual rulers of Japan. The title dates back to 794 and originally meant commander of the imperial armies. It was established as a system of military government by Yoritomo after 1185. The shogunate was held in turn by the Minamoto family and their successors, with their capital at Kamakura (1192–1333); the Ashikaga, with their capital at Kyoto (1338–1597); and the TOKUGAWA, with their capital at Edo (Tokyo) after 1603. The overthrow (1867) of the Tokugawa shogunate in the MEIJI restoration marked the beginning of modern Japan.

Sholokhov, Mikhail Aleksandrovich [shô'ləkhŏf], 1905–84, Russian novelist. His most famous work, *And Quiet Flows the Don* (1928–40), depicts the effects of World War I, the RUSSIAN REVOLUTION (1917), and the civil war on COSSACK life. *Virgin Soil Upturned* (1932–60) deals with agricultural collectivization. Sholokhov was awarded the 1965 Nobel Prize in literature.

Sholom Aleichem [shō'ləm älā'khəm] [Heb., = Peace be unto you], pseud. of **Shalom Rabinowitz,** 1859–1916, Russian Yiddish writer. Perhaps best known for his humorous novels and stories of life among poor and oppressed Russian Jews, Sholom Aleichem was influential in establishing Yiddish as a literary language. The sketches collected in *Tevye's Daughters* (1894) formed the basis for the successful Broadway musical *Fiddler on the Roof* (1964).

shooting, firing with rifle, shotgun, pistol, or revolver at fixed or moving targets. In the sport of small-bore rifle shooting, the targets range in distance from 50 ft to 200 yd (15.24–182.88 m); in pistol and revolver, from 50 ft to 50 yd (15.24–45.72 m); and in long-range rifle, from 200 to 1,000 yd (182.88–914.4 m). Competitors shoot from four positions with the rifle—prone, sitting, kneeling, and standing. In skeet or trapshooting marksmen fire shotguns at small disks ("clay pigeons") hurled into the air by a mechanical device (the trap). Major U.S. tournaments are sponsored by the National Rifle Association (formed 1871).

shorthand, any brief, rapid system of writing used in transcribing the spoken word. Such systems date from ancient times. Modern systems began with Timothy Bright's 500 symbols (1588). Many others followed. The phonetic system of Isaac Pitman (1837) is, with improvements, still used in English-speaking countries. Employing geometric outlines with variations in shading, slope, and position to denote variations in meaning, it is difficult to learn but permits great speed. The business shorthand system of John Robert Gregg, published in 1888, is popular. Its curved outlines resemble ordinary script; the pen is rarely lifted, and variations in length indicate variations in meaning. Some systems, such as Speedwriting, employ shortened forms of longhand. Keyboard machines are also used to write shorthand, especially in law courts.

short story, brief prose fiction. The term embraces a variety of narratives, from stories focusing on events to character studies, from "short short" stories to long, complex narratives (sometimes called novellas) like Thomas Mann's (see MANN, family) *Death in Venice* (1912). Most often the short story concentrates on creating a single dynamic effect, and is limited in character and situation. Precursors of the short story can be found in the BIBLE, the medieval GESTA ROMANORUM, and the works of BOCCACCIO and CHAUCER. The modern short story dates from the 19th-cent. works of Nathaniel HAWTHORNE, E.A. POE, Herman MELVILLE, Nikolai GOGOL, Guy de MAUPASSANT, and Anton CHEKHOV. Twentieth-cent. masters of the form include Henry JAMES, Sherwood ANDERSON, Katherine MANSFIELD, Ernest HEMINGWAY, Katherine Anne PORTER, Flannery O'CONNOR, John CHEEVER, J.D. SALINGER, Donald BARTHELME, and Raymond CARVER.

short takeoff and landing aircraft (STOL), heavier-than-air craft capable of taking off or landing with only a short length of runway (1,000 ft/305 m), but incapable of taking off vertically (see VERTICAL TAKEOFF AND LANDING AIRCRAFT). STOL aircraft have large wings that are equipped with special aerodynamic devices, such as slotted flaps, drooped leading edges, and auxiliary spoilers that augment lift, increase stability, and improve the effect of control surfaces.

Shostakovich, Dmitri, 1906–75, Soviet composer. He scored his first successes with his First Symphony (1925), the opera *The Nose* (1930), and the ballet *The Golden Age* (1930). He sought official approval and survived the changing tides of opinion. His outstanding works include a piano concerto (1933), the Piano Quintet (1940), the Second String Quartet (1944), and the Ninth Symphony (1945).

Shreveport, city (1990 pop. 198,525), seat of Caddo parish, NW La., on the Red R. near the Ark. and Tex. lines; inc. 1839. It is an oil and natural gas center. Cotton and lumber are important products and its manufactures include machinery and chemicals. Oil was discovered in 1906, spurring the city's growth.

shrew, small, insectivorous MAMMAL of the family Soricidae, of Eurasia and the Americas. Related to MOLES, they include the smallest mammals (under 2 in./5.1 cm). Light-boned and fragile, with mouselike bodies, shrews are terrestrial and nocturnal and can produce a protective musky odor. They have the highest known metabolic rate of any animal and must eat incessantly to survive.

shrimp, small CRUSTACEAN with 10 jointed legs and a nearly cylindrical, translucent body. Unlike the closely related LOBSTERS and CRABS, which are crawlers, shrimp are primarily swimmers. Shrimp are widely distributed in temperate and tropical salt and fresh waters. Some grow to 9 in. (23 cm) long, but most are smaller. One of the most popular crustacean foods, shrimp are fished throughout the world.

shrub, any woody, perennial, bushy plant that branches into several stems or trunks at the base and is smaller than a TREE. Tree species may grow as shrubs under unfavorable conditions. In regions of extreme climatic conditions, e.g., the Arctic, where trees do not thrive, shrubs provide valuable food and wood. Common shrubs include the LILAC, mock orange, viburnum, FORSYTHIA, and AZALEA.

shuffleboard, sport in which players use cue sticks to push disks onto a triangular scoring diagram at either end of a concrete or terrazzo court (52 ft/15.85 m long and 6 ft/1.83 m wide). Each diagram is divided into 7-, 8-, and 10-point sections, and there is a penalty area of minus 10 points. Shuffleboard probably originated in 13th-cent. England. It has long been a popular recreation for the elderly.

Shula, Don(ald Francis), 1930–, American football coach, b. Grand River, Ohio. A college and National Football League (NFL) back, he began coaching (1959) at the Univ. of Virginia. After seasons with the Detroit Lions (1960–62) and Baltimore Colts (1963–69), he joined (1970) the Miami Dolphins and transformed the floundering team. Shula holds the NFL record for most wins as a coach.

Shultz, George Pratt, 1920-, U.S. public official; b. N.Y.C. An economist and educator, he was Pres. NIXON's secretary of labor (1969–70), director of the Office of Management and Budget (1970–72), and secretary of the treasury (1972–74). As Pres. REAGAN's secretary of state (1982–89), he was known for his ability to effect compromises. He was criticized for failing to oppose more strongly the operations that led to the IRAN-CONTRA AFFAIR.

Si, chemical symbol of the element SILICON.

Siamese cat: see under CAT.

Siamese language: see THAI LANGUAGE.

Siamese twins, congenitally united organisms that are complete or nearly complete individuals, developing from a single fertilized ovum that has divided imperfectly. Siamese twins are attached at the abdomen, chest, back, or top of the head, depending on where division of the fertilized ovum failed, and can often be separated surgically after birth.

Sian: see XI'AN.

Sibelius, Jean (Julius Christian) [sĭbā'lyo͞os], 1865–1957, Finnish composer. A highly personal, romantic composer, he represents the culmination of nationalism in Finnish music. He is best known for orchestral works such as SYMPHONIC POEMS, e.g., *Finlandia* (1900), *Valse triste* (1903); a violin concerto (1903); and seven symphonies.

Siberia, vast geographical region with no precise boundaries, c.2.9 million sq mi (7.5 million sq km), mostly in Russia. As generally delineated, it extends east across N Asia from the URALS to the Pacific coast region known as the RUSSIAN FAR EAST, and south from the TUNDRA regions along the ARCTIC OCEAN margins, through the great TAIGA forest zone, to the STEPPES of Central Asia and Mongolia. Most of Siberia is sparsely populated, with NOVOSIBIRSK, OMSK, Tomsk, Novokuznetsk, and Irkutsk the principal cities. Russians and Ukrainians, migrating east from European Russia since the 13th cent., are now more numerous than indigenous ethnic groups. Transportation facilities are limited, the LENA, OB, and YENISEI rivers (and their tributaries) serving as the principal north-south routes and the Trans-Siberian RR (completed 1905) as the chief east-west route. Extreme cold in the north and scanty, irregular precipitation in the south limit the region's agricultural potential, and most development is based on Siberia's rich oil, natural gas, coal, iron ore, gold, timber, and other resources. Russia's conquest of Siberia was completed in 1598. From the early 17th cent. it has been notorious as the site of penal colonies and as a place of exile for political prisoners.

Siberian husky, muscular WORKING DOG; shoulder height, 20–23½ in. (50.8–59.7 cm); weight, 35–60 lb (15.9–27.2 kg). Its weather-resistant, dense coat is usually black, white, tan, gray, or combinations of these colors. Its origins date back thousands of years in N Siberia, where it was raised by the Chukchi people to pull sleds. The term *husky* is often used to designate any mixed-breed arctic sled dog.

sibyl, in classical mythology, a prophetess. There were said to be as many as 10 sibyls. The most famous was the Cumaean Sibyl, who sold TARQUIN the Sibylline Books, prophecies about Rome's destiny that were burned in 83 B.C.

Sicilian Vespers, 1282, a rebellion of the Sicilians against CHARLES I of Naples that broke out at the start of VESPERS on Easter Monday. Byzantine Emperor MICHAEL VIII and PETER III of Aragón were involved in the plot, and Peter accepted the crown of SICILY. A 20-year war between Aragón and Naples ensued. Sicily remained independent of Naples until 1442, when ALFONSO V of Aragón reunited the two areas.

Sicily, island (1990 pop. 5,172,785), S Italy, in the Mediterranean Sea, separated from the mainland by the Strait of Messina. Sicily gained limited autonomy in 1947 as part of the Sicilian region (9,925 sq mi/25,706 sq km), which also includes several smaller islands. PALERMO is the regional capital. Mainly mountainous, it reaches a high point of 10,700 ft (3,261 m) in volcanic Mt. ETNA. Though it has fertile soils and a mild climate, it has suffered chronic poverty, causing many Sicilians to emigrate. Wheat, olives, citrus, nuts, and wine are leading agricultural products, and there are oil and natural gas, textile, and chemical industries. Sicily passed from Byzantine to Arab control in the 9th cent. It was conquered by Normans (1060–91) and came under Spanish rule following the SICILIAN VESPERS revolt (1282). In 1860 GARIBALDI conquered the island, which then voted to become part of the Kingdom of Sardinia and ultimately of a unified Italy.

Sickert, Walter Richard, 1860–1942, English painter. Apprenticed to WHISTLER and later working with DEGAS, he was a link between French and English turn-of-the-century painting. His preferred subjects were music halls and London demimonde scenes.

sickle-cell anemia, inherited disorder occurring mainly among Africans and people of African descent but also among people from the Mediterranean and India, in which the red blood cells (erythrocytes) assume distorted, sicklelike shapes. Because of a genetically transmitted chemical abnormality in the HEMOGLOBIN molecule, the red blood cells are fragile and subject to rupture, causing chronic ANEMIA, fever, abdominal and joint pains, and JAUNDICE. There is no cure, and many patients die young from complications.

Siddons, Sarah Kemble, 1755–1831, English actress, best-known member of the KEMBLE family. Famed for such Shakespearean roles as Desdemona in *Othello* and Volumnia in *Coriolanus,* she was unequaled as Lady Macbeth.

sidereal period: see SYNODIC PERIOD.

sidereal time, time measured relative to the fixed stars. The *sidereal day* is the period during which the earth completes one rotation on its axis, so that some chosen star reappears on the observer's celestial meridian; it is 4 min shorter than the solar day (see SOLAR TIME) because the earth moves in its orbit about the sun.

sidewinder, desert RATTLESNAKE (*Crotalus cerastes*) of the SW U.S. This 2-ft (60-cm) pale yellow and pink snake is named for its method of locomotion: It throws out successive loops at oblique angles so that it appears to move sideways. This form of movement allows it to traverse sand, which has little traction.

Sidney or **Sydney, Sir Philip,** 1554–86, English author. A diplomat and courtier at Queen ELIZABETH I's court, he was a model of Renaissance chivalry. As patron, critic, and exemplar he influenced English poetry. His works include the verse idylls of *Arcadia* (1590), the first renowned PASTORAL in English; his prose criticism known as *The Defense of Poesie,* or *An Apology for Poetry* (1595); and *Astrophel and Stella* (1591), one of the great SONNET sequences.

Sidon or **Saida,** city (1988 est. pop. 38,000), SW Lebanon, on the Mediterranean Sea. An ancient seaport of PHOENICIA, it remained important through Roman times and was famous for its purple dyes and glassware. Glassblowing is said to have begun at Sidon. During the 1982 Israeli invasion of S Lebanon, the city was captured from the PALESTINE LIBERATION ORGANIZATION by Israeli forces after heavy fighting (see ARAB-ISRAELI WARS).

Siegfried [sēg'frēd] or **Sigurd** [sĭg'ərd], folk hero of early and medieval Germanic mythology. His legend, important in several epics, recounts his killing of the dragon Fafnir, his marriage to GUDRUN (or Kriemhild), his love and betrayal of BRUNHILD, and his death. See VOLSUNGASAGA; NIBELUNGEN.

Siemens, Sir William, 1823–83, English electrical engineer; b. Germany. He went to Britain to introduce his and his brother Ernst's electroplating device and became a British citizen in 1859. He was head of the English branch of the Siemens firm, which made electrical apparatus. Siemens invented (1851) a water meter and developed, with his brother Frederick, a regenerative furnace that was the prototype for the open-hearth steelmaking process.

Siena, city (1990 pop. 58,278), in TUSCANY, central Italy. It is a tourist center and is known for its wine and marble. Of ancient origin, it was a free commune by the 12th cent. and grew into a wealthy republic. It fell to Emperor CHARLES V in 1555 and then passed to the MEDICI. Siena's artistic fame is tied to the work of the Sienese school (13th–14th cent.), represented by such painters as DUCCIO, Simone MARTINI, and the LORENZETTI brothers. Siena is noted for its medieval town square, the Piazza del Campo, and such buildings as the Gothic Palazzo Pubblico, the Mangia tower, and the Gothic cathedral.

Sienkiewicz, Henryk [shĕnkyĕ'vēch], 1846–1916, Polish novelist and short-story writer. His best-known historical novel, *Quo Vadis?,* concerns Christianity in NERO's time. His trilogy *With Fire and Sword* (1883), *The Deluge* (1886), and *Pan Michael* (1887–88) deals with the fight for Polish independence. He was awarded the 1905 Nobel Prize in literature.

Sierra Leone, officially Republic of Sierra Leone, republic (1992 est. pop. 4,457,000), 27,699 sq mi (71,740 sq km), W Africa, bordered by the Atlantic Ocean (W), Guinea (N and E), and Liberia (S). FREETOWN is the capital. The 350-mi (560-km) Atlantic coastline is made up of a belt of low-lying mangrove swamps, except for the mountainous Sierra Leone Peninsula (site of Freetown), and has some wide, sandy beaches. The eastern half of the country is mostly mountainous, rising to 6,390 ft (1,948 m). Sierra Leone's economy is predominantly agricultural; two thirds of the people are engaged in mostly subsistence farming. Palm kernels, cacao, ginger, and coffee are the leading cash crops, and large numbers of livestock and poultry are raised. Minerals are the main source of income; diamonds (which account for about half of export earnings), iron ore, gold, bauxite, and rutile are the most important. Manufactures are limited mainly to refined petroleum, agricultural processing, and consumer goods. The two main ethnic groups are the Mende and the Temne. Most people follow traditional beliefs; there are Muslim and Christian minorities. English is the official language, and Krio, a mixture of English and several indigenous languages, is the lingua franca.

History. The Temne were living along the coast when the Portuguese landed in 1460 on the Sierra Leone Peninsula, which, after c.1500, was the scene of European trading in ivory, timber, and small numbers of slaves. Mande-speaking people from present-day Liberia moved into the region in the mid–16th cent. and later established four Mende states. An attempt to resettle freed slaves on the peninsula failed in 1787, but in 1792 about 1,100 freed slaves from Nova Scotia founded Freetown. The new colony was controlled by a private company and had little contact with the interior. Britain took over Freetown in 1808, and during the next 50 years about 50,000 liberated slaves were settled there. To forestall French ambitions in the region, the British established a protectorate over the interior in 1896. After World War II, the African population was given some political power, but the Creoles, who were descendants of freed slaves living in Freetown, were largely excluded from the government. Independence came in 1961, with Milton Margai (a Mende) as prime minister. Siaka Stevens, leader of a Temne-based party, took office in 1967 but was immediately ousted in a military coup. He returned to power in 1968, after another army revolt. In 1971 Sierra Leone became a republic, with Stevens as president. The early 1970s were marked by considerable unrest,

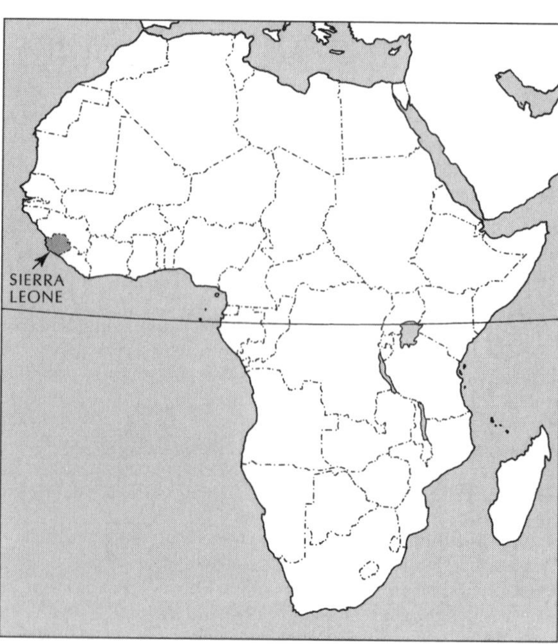

and troops from Guinea were brought in to support the regime. Stevens succeeded in creating a one-party state under a new 1978 constitution, but student and labor protests continued into the 1980s. In 1985 Maj. Gen. Joseph Saidu Momoh, running unopposed, was elected president. Momoh was overthrown in 1992, and a junta established military rule; Capt. Valentine Strasser later became president.

Sierra Madre, rugged mountain system of Mexico, mostly between 6,000 and 12,000 ft (1,829 to 3,658 m) and rising to a high point of 18,700 ft (5,700 m) at the inactive volcano ORIZABA. The system includes the Sierra Madre Oriental (E), the Sierra Madre Occidental (W), and the Sierra Madre del Sur (S), which together form the dissected edges of the central Mexican plateau. The mountains are rich in silver, gold, and other minerals.

Sierra Nevada, mountain range, c.400 mi (640 km) long and up to 80 mi (130 km) wide, mostly in E California. It is known for its spectacular scenery, especially in the High Sierras and in Yosemite, Sequoia, and Kings Canyon NATIONAL PARKS (see table). The range reaches its highest point (14,491 ft/4,417 m) at Mt. WHITNEY.

Sieyès, Emmanuel Joseph [syāĕs′], 1748–1836, French statesman. Before the FRENCH REVOLUTION he was a clergyman known as Abbé Sieyès. Elected (1789) to the STATES-GENERAL, he helped to write the Declaration of the Rights of Man and Citizen and the constitution of 1791. By prudent silence, he lived through the REIGN OF TERROR, and in 1799 he entered the DIRECTORY, which he helped NAPOLEON to topple later that year. After the Bourbon restoration, he lived in exile (1816–30) in Brussels.

Sigismund, 1368–1437, Holy Roman emperor (1433–37), German king (1410–37), king of Hungary (1387–1437) and of Bohemia (1419–37). His election as German king was initially contested by his half brother, the former German king, WENCESLAUS. Sigismund backed Baldassarre COSSA (John XXIII), the strongest of the schismatic popes, in the Council of Constance that ended (1417) the Great SCHISM. After the conference, Sigismund secured the condemnation and burning of John HUSS, despite his promise to Huss of a safe conduct. As a result, his assuming the Bohemian crown in 1419 set off the Hussite Wars (see HUSSITES). His reign was one of constant turmoil, including recurring attacks by the Turks in Hungary. He was the last emperor of the LUXEMBOURG dynasty.

Sigismund, Polish kings. **Sigismund I,** 1467–1548, king of POLAND (1506–48), was the son of CASIMIR IV. He established a regular army and allied himself with Holy Roman Emperor MAXIMILIAN I as protection against Russia. By the double marriage of the children of his brother, Uladislaus II of Bohemia and Hungary, with the grandchildren of Maximilian, Bohemia and Hungary later passed (1526) to the Hapsburgs. His son, **Sigismund II** or **Sigismund Augustus,** 1520–72, king of Poland (1548–72), created (1569) a unified kingdom out of his Polish and Lithuanian fiefs, and acquired Courland and parts of Livonia. He halted the spread of Protestantism by peaceful means and by encouraging Catholic reform. **Sigismund III,** 1566–1632, king of Poland (1587–1632) and king of Sweden (1592–99), was the son of John III of Sweden and Catherine, sister of Sigismund II of Poland. A Roman Catholic, he was resented by the Protestant Swedes and was deposed by his uncle, who ruled as CHARLES IX. Between 1600 and 1629 Sigismund attempted to reclaim his Swedish claims. He intervened in Russia by supporting the pretender DMITRI, but his army was expelled from Russia in 1612.

Signac, Paul [sēnyäk′], 1863–1935, French painter. Associated with the divisionist technique, he painted with broader strokes than did SEURAT (see POSTIMPRESSIONISM). His works include *Port of St. Tropez* (1916; Brooklyn Mus., N.Y.C.).

sign language, substitute for speech, derived from gestures and facial expressions that accompany speech. It is used, e.g., where silence is a rule, as among Trappist monks; or to overcome language barriers, as among Plains tribes. Sign language for the deaf was systematized in 18th-cent. France and brought to the U.S. by T.H. GALLAUDET; it is usually taught along with the manual alphabet and lip reading.

Signorelli, Luca, 1441?–1523, Italian painter of the Umbrian school. MICHELANGELO was influenced by his powerful treatment of anatomy and his dramatic realism. His apocalyptic series decorating the Cappella Nuova in the Orvieto Cathedral includes *Story of the Anti-Christ, End of the World, Paradise,* and *Inferno.* The infernal scenes are remarkable for their evocation of fiends and the tortures of Hell.

Sigurd: see SIEGFRIED.

Sihanouk, Norodom: see NORODOM SIHANOUK.

Sikhs, religious community of some 16 million worldwide, centered on N India, mainly in the Punjab. Its founder, the mystic guru teacher Nanak (c.1469–c.1539), taught monotheism and opposed idolatry and the CASTE system. He believed in the fundamental identity of all religions and stressed religious exercises and MEDITATION. Gradually becoming united and developing military power under a series of gurus, the Sikhs were militarized to oppose Islam by Govind Singh (1666–1708), the tenth and last guru, who created a warrior fraternity and introduced the Sikh practices of wearing a turban and never cutting the hair. In the late 19th cent. conflict with the British led to the subjugation of the Sikh state in the Punjab (established earlier by Ranjit Singh). Following the partition (1947) of British India, the Sikhs fought the Muslims of the Punjab in a fierce holy war, after which some 2.5 million Sikhs moved from W Punjab (now part of Pakistan) to E Punjab, in India. In the early 1980s Indian Sikhs demanding an independent state resorted to terrorism, leading to turmoil in Punjab. In 1984 the Indian army stormed the Sikhs' Golden Temple, at Amritsar, which had been occupied by Sikh militants. Prime Min. Indira Gandhi was assassinated by her Sikh bodyguards in retaliation, after which mobs attacked Sikhs throughout India. Unrest in Punjab continued into the early 1990s.

Sikh Wars (1845–49), two conflicts preceding the British annexation of the PUNJAB. In 1845, fearing British intentions, the SIKHS crossed the Sutlej R. and attacked British troops south of the Punjab. They were defeated by the British and forced to cede KASHMIR, pay a large indemnity, and accept a British protectorate. In 1848, a Sikh uprising resulted in another full-scale war; at its end the victorious British annexed all Sikh territory.

Sikkim, state (1991 pop. 403,612), 2,745 sq mi (7,110 sq km), NE India, bordered by Nepal (W), Tibet (N), and Bhutan (E). The capital and only town is Gangtok. Located in the E HIMALAYAS, most of Sikkim is mountainous. Subsistence agriculture dominates the economy, rice, corn, and millet being the principal crops. Copper is mined, and cotton weaving is an important local craft. The people are predominantly of Nepalese extraction; Buddhism was the state religion, but the majority of the population is Hindu. Tibetans began to settle in Sikkim in the 16th cent., and in 1642 a Tibetan king started a hereditary line of Sikkimese rulers that lasted until 1975. The territory was a British protectorate from 1890 to 1947. In 1950 India assumed responsibility for Sikkim's defense, foreign relations, and communications, and Indian-built roads ended Sikkim's isolation from the outside world. In 1975 the Sikkimese voted to abolish the monarchy and became the 22d state of India.

Sikorsky, Igor Ivanovich, 1889–1972, American aeronautical engineer; b. Russia. He built and flew the first multimotored airplane (1913), but is best known for his work on the development of HELICOPTERS. In 1941 he established an endurance record for sustained flight in a helicopter of his own design.

silenus, in Greek mythology, part bestial, part human creature of forests and mountains. Followers of DIONYSUS, the sileni are usually represented as aged SATYRS. In some legends Silenus is the oldest satyr, the son of HERMES or PAN, and the companion, adviser, or tutor of Dionysus.

Silesia, region of E central Europe, extending along both banks of the Oder R. and bounded in the south by the Sudetes Mts. Most of Silesia is in Poland, a much smaller part in the Czech Republic, and a tiny area in Germany. WROCŁAW is among the chief cities. Silesia is largely agricultural and forested. The most important part is Upper Silesia, in Poland, one of the largest industrial concentrations in Europe, with extensive deposits of coal, lignite, and other resources. Austria ceded (1742) most of Silesia to Prussia during the war of the AUSTRIAN SUCCESSION. After WORLD WAR I the region was partitioned among Germany, Poland, and Czechoslovakia. The MUNICH PACT (1938) divided most of Czechoslovak Silesia between Germany and Poland, and during WORLD WAR II Germany occupied (1939–45) Polish

Silesia. After the war Poland annexed most of German Silesia and expelled the German residents.

silhouette, outline image, especially a solidly filled-in profile drawing or cutout pasted against a lighter background. Silhouette drawings were very popular in late-18th-cent. Europe, replacing miniatures at French and German courts. Profile portraits and silhouette illustrations abounded in 19th-cent. England and America. Silhouette drawings decreased in popularity after the invention of the daguerreotype (see DAGUERRE).

German silhouette of Napoleon, 19th cent.

silica or **silicon dioxide,** chemical compound (SiO_2). It is widely and abundantly distributed throughout the earth, both in the pure state (colorless to white) and in silicates (e.g., QUARTZ, OPAL, SAND, SANDSTONE, CLAY, GRANITE); in skeletal parts of various plants and animals, such as certain protozoa and DIATOMS; and in the stems and other tissue of higher plants. Because silica has a low thermal coefficient of expansion, it is used in objects subjected to wide ranges of heat and cold. It is the principal ingredient of common GLASS. **Silica gel** is a porous, colloidal form of silica that is used as a drying agent and as a catalyst and catalyst carrier.

silicon (Si), nonmetallic element, discovered by Jöns Jakob BERZELIUS in 1824. Silicon has brown amorphous and dark crystalline allotropic forms. The second most abundant element (28% by weight) of the earth's crust, it occurs in compound form as SILICA, SILICON CARBIDE, and silicates. Silicon adds strength to alloys, and is used in integrated circuits and other semiconductor devices. It is found in many plants and animals. See ELEMENT (table); PERIODIC TABLE.

silicon carbide, chemical compound (SiC) occurring as hard, dark iridescent crystals that are heat resistant, and insoluble in water and other common solvents. It is used as an ABRASIVE, in refractory materials, and in special parts for nuclear reactors. Silicon carbide fibers impart increased strength and stiffness to plastics and light metals.

silicon dioxide: see SILICA.

silicone, POLYMER in which atoms of SILICON and OXYGEN alternate in a chain; bound to the silicon atoms are various organic groups, e.g., the methyl group (CH_3). Silicones may be liquids, RUBBERS, RESINS, or greases. Water repellent, chemically inert, and stable at extreme temperatures, silicones are used as protective coatings and electrical insulators and in caulk. Implants consisting of silicone gel surrounded by hard silicone were used in reconstructive and cosmetic breast surgery. Questions about the long-term safety of the implants ended their use in 1992.

Silicon Valley, an industrial region, approximately 20 mi (32 km) long, between Palo Alto and San Jose in California, where many microchip manufacturing and design companies are located. The name derives from high purity silicon used in making these electronic devices.

silk, fiber produced by the SILKWORM in making its cocoon, or textiles woven from such fiber. Legend has it that sericulture (the raising of silkworms) began in China in 2640 B.C. Raw silk was exported, but the export of silkworm eggs was punishable by death. Silkworm eggs and seeds of the mulberry tree, on which the worm feeds, were supposedly smuggled to Constantinople in A.D. c.550; thereafter Byzantium was famed for its silk textiles. In the 8th cent. the Moors brought sericulture and silk weaving to Spain and Sicily, where exquisite silk fabrics were being woven by the 12th cent. Italy developed great silk-weaving centers—Lucca, Florence, and Venice—in the 13th and 14th cent. The French city of Lyons became a weaving center in the 15th cent. In 1685 HUGUENOTS fleeing France after the revocation of the Edict of Nantes brought the art to England, where it became centered at Spitalfields, in London. In the American colonies, attempts to establish sericulture ultimately failed. The Asian *Bombyx mori,* which feeds on mulberry leaves, produces the finest silk and is thus the most widely raised silkworm. Wild silk is made by the tussah worm of India and China, which feeds on oak leaves. Silk manufacture begins with the reeling (unwinding) of the silk from the cocoons. In throwing, the raw silk is twisted and doubled to achieve various strengths and thicknesses. The silk is boiled in soap to remove the natural gum, then bleached or dyed. It is woven on delicate specialized looms to produce a wide variety of fabrics, e.g., taffeta, faille, velvet, crepe. Modern silk production is highly mechanized, but the finest fabrics are still handwoven.

silk-screen printing, multiple PRINTING technique, also called serigraphy, involving the use of stencils. Paint is applied to a fabric screen, penetrating areas not blocked by a stencil. Several stencils are used to produce a multicolored print. As a commercial medium, silk-screen printing has been used by such modern artists as Andy WARHOL.

silkworm, name for the larva of various species of MOTHS, indigenous to Asia and Africa but now domesticated and raised for SILK production throughout most of the temperate zone. After hatching, the larvae feed voraciously on MULBERRY leaves. When they mature, they attach themselves to a twig and spin a thick, strong cocoon from a single continuous filament of pale yellow silk about a half-mile long. After about a week, the cocoon is unwound, and the silk processed. Only enough cocoons to ensure adequate reproduction are allowed to hatch. The most widely raised silkworm is the larva of *Bombyx mori.*

Sillanpää, Frans Eemil [sĭl'länpă"], 1888–1964, Finnish novelist, the foremost Finnish writer of his time. His works include *Meek Heritage* (1919), about the Finnish civil war, and *The Maid Silja* (1931), about the collapse of old values. He received the 1939 Nobel Prize in literature.

Sills, Beverly, 1929–, American operatic soprano; b. Brooklyn, N.Y., as Belle Silverman. She is famous for her light coloratura voice and her acting ability. After she retired from singing she was general director of the New York City Opera (1979–89) and chairwoman of Lincoln Center (1994–).

Silone, Ignazio [sēlō'nā], 1900–1978, Italian novelist and journalist; b. Secondo Tranquilli. An anti-Fascist, he lived in exile from 1931 to 1944 and devoted his writings to promoting socialism without sacrificing human or literary values. His novels include *Fontamara* (1933), *Bread and Wine* (1937), and *A Handful of Blackberries* (1952).

silt, mostly QUARTZ mineral particles that are between SAND and CLAY in size and are formed by WEATHERING and decomposition of pre-existing rock. Hardened silt becomes a sedimentary rock called siltstone.

Silurian period: see GEOLOGIC ERA (table).

Silva, José Asunción [sĭl'vä], 1865–96, Colombian poet. One of the creators of MODERNISMO, he committed suicide at 31, despondent over his debts, the death of a sister, and the loss of a manuscript at sea just before its publication. His poems, collected after his death, include "Nocturne III," an elegy for his sister, and "Twilight."

silver (Ag), metallic element, one of the first metals used by humans. Pure silver is nearly white, lustrous, soft, very ductile, malleable, and an excellent conductor of heat and electricity. It is used in mirrors, coins, utensils, antiseptics, jewelry, and for electrolytic plating of tableware (see SILVERWORK). Silver nitrate is its most important compound. Silver reacts with hydrogen sulfide in air to form silver sulfide (tarnish). Photographic emulsions contain silver halides, which are sensitive to light. Silver alloys are used in dentistry and electrical contacts. Sterling silver contains 92.5% silver and 7.5% copper. Silver is obtained from the ores argentite, cerargyrite, pyrargyrite, stephanite, and proustite. See ELEMENT (table); PERIODIC TABLE.

silverfish, primitive wingless INSECT about ½ in. (1.27 cm) long, named for the tiny silvery scales on its body. Common indoors in cool, damp places, silverfish eat starch from bookbindings, wallpaper, and clothing.

silversides, small shore FISH (family Antherinidae) named for the silvery stripe on either side of its body, abundant in warmer waters of the Atlantic and Pacific. Related to mullets, silversides, also known as whitebait, feed on small CRUSTACEANS and insects. Included in the family are the top and jack smelts and the California grunion (5–8 in./12.5–20 cm), which rides in on high tides to lay its eggs in the sand and is often found beached.

silverwork, term encompassing ecclesiastical and domestic utensils, jewelry, buttons, weapons, horse trappings, boxes, and other articles. It involves embellishments such as chasing, repoussé, filigree, and inlaying. The art was highly developed in ancient times, as shown by Asian, Egyptian, Phoenician, Roman, and Byzantine examples. Much early Italian and French silverwork was melted down for reuse and thus lost. German, Swiss, Italian, Spanish, and English silverwork reached heights of ornamentation between the 15th and 18th cent. Much N European ecclesiastical silver work was destroyed during the Reformation, and little early English silver survived the Wars of the Roses. Sheffield plate, an innovation of the mid-18th cent., led to important silver plate industries in England and, later, the U.S. In colonial America silversmithing was an important trade, attracting several hundred silverworkers from Europe. Colonial silver was simple in design and is prized by collectors. Silverwork is a traditional art of the indigenous peoples of the Americas and is still practiced by them today.

Silvester: see SYLVESTER.

Simcoe, John Graves, 1752–1806, first British governor (1792–96) of Upper Canada (ONTARIO). To make the province a strong colony, he encouraged immigration of American Loyalists and fostered agricultural development.

Simenon, Georges, 1903–89, Belgian author. An extremely prolific writer, he is best known for his 84 detective novels featuring Inspector Maigret. He also wrote more than 100 psychological novels, including *The Stain on the Snow* (1938) and *The Cat* (1976), as well as many articles, short stories, and novellas.

Simeon I, c.863–927, ruler (893–927) and first czar (925–27) of Bulgaria. During his rule the first Bulgarian empire attained its greatest power. He ravaged the Byzantine Empire and conquered most of Serbia. He was a patron of culture.

Simeon: see ISRAEL, TRIBES OF.

Simi Valley city (1990 pop. 100,217), Ventura co., SW Calif.; laid out 1887, inc. 1969. A rapidly growing and highly residential Los Angeles suburb, it has many light manufactures, e.g., plastics, apparel, sewage units, and liquid oxygen. The Reagan Presidential Library is W of the city. The city achieved notoriety in 1992 when a jury there acquitted the police officers accused in the beating of Rodney King.

Simnel, Lambert, c.1475–1525, impostor and pretender to the English throne. In 1486, claiming to be Edward, earl of Warwick (who was then imprisoned in the TOWER OF LONDON), he rallied Yorkist support in Ireland and invaded England. He was defeated and captured at the battle of Stoke (1487) by the forces of HENRY VII. Simnel was later pardoned.

Simon, Saint, one of the Twelve APOSTLES. In the Gospels he is called the Canaanite or Cananaean or Zelotes, terms that may refer to an association with the zealots, a devout and strongly anti-heathen Jewish sect.

Simon, in the BIBLE. **1** One of the MACCABEES. **2** Or Simon Peter: see PETER, SAINT. **3** Simon of Cyrene, bystander made to carry Jesus' cross. He was probably an African Jew. **4** Simon Magus, Samaritan sorcerer who attempted to buy spiritual power from the apostles. From this comes the term SIMONY.

Simon, Herbert Alexander, 1916–, American social scientist; b. Milwaukee, Wis. A professor at Carnegie-Mellon Univ., Simon was an early authority on uses of computers in business management. For his theories on decision making he won the 1978 Nobel Prize in economics. His *Scientific Discovery* was published in 1987.

Simon, (Marvin) Neil, 1927–, American playwright; b. N.Y.C. His popular comedies of middle-class life include *Barefoot in the Park* (1963), *The Odd Couple* (1965), and his autobiographical trilogy: *Brighton Beach Memoirs* (1984), *Biloxi Blues* (1985), and *Broadway Bound* (1986). *Lost in Yonkers* (1991; Pulitzer Prize) is distinguished from his other works by its more serious, sometimes anguished tone. He has also written screenplays.

Simone Martini: see MARTINI, SIMONE.

Simonides of Ceos, c.556–468? B.C., Greek lyric poet. After the PERSIAN WARS he was a rival of PINDAR at the court of Syracuse. He wrote epigrammatic verse of many kinds. Two of his finest epitaphs are on the fallen at MARATHON and THERMOPYLAE.

Simons, Menno: see MENNO SIMONS.

simony, in CANON LAW, buying or selling of any spiritual benefit for a temporal consideration. Because of the frequency of simony at times in the history of the Roman Catholic Church, the church now has strict laws against it; e.g., simony in a papal election invalidates the election, no priest may ask for a baptismal fee, and the sale of INDULGENCES is prohibited.

simple harmonic motion: see HARMONIC MOTION.

Simplon, pass, 6,590 ft (2,009 m) high, in the Swiss Alps near Brig, at the Swiss-Italian border. Its 12.3-mi (19.8-km) railroad tunnel system is Europe's longest.

Simpson, Sir George, 1792?–1860, governor of the HUDSON'S BAY COMPANY in CANADA (1821–56). He encouraged the company's expansion and the exploration of its vast territory. In 1841–42 he traveled overland around the world.

Simpson, George Gaylord, 1902–84, American paleontologist and zoologist; b. Chicago. His deductions, from studies of fossil material, that species reach adaptive peaks and suffer accidental dispersion contributed greatly to the study of evolution. He held several paleontology positions at the American Museum of Natural History (1927–59) and also taught at Columbia (1945–59) and Harvard (1959–70).

Simpson, Louis, 1923–, American poet; b. Jamaica. His finely crafted, witty poems are in *At the End of the Open Road* (1963; Pulitzer) and *People Live Here: Selected Poems 1949–1983* (1984).

Simpson, O(renthal) J(ames), 1947–, American football player; b. San Francisco. As a running back for the Univ. of Southern California, he won the 1968 Heisman Trophy as the best college player of the year. He played with the Buffalo Bills (1969–77) and San Francisco 49ers (1978–79) and gained 11,236 yards rushing during his career. Simpson set season records (now broken) for most yards gained (2,003; 1973) and most touchdowns (23; 1975) and still holds the season record for yards rushing per game (143; 1973). He later became a sportscaster and movie actor.

sin, in religion, unethical act in disobedience to a personal God. In ancient Israel, there were personal sin and national sin—usually idolatry. Some Christians hold that all acts are good, indifferent, or sinful; others that there are no indifferent acts. Roman Catholics are required to confess mortal sins, i.e., those committed with knowing and deliberate intent in a serious matter (see PENANCE); other sins are venial. The seven deadly sins are pride, covetousness, lust, anger, gluttony, envy, and sloth.

Sinai, triangular peninsula, c.23,000 sq mi (59,570 sq km), NE Egypt, between the SUEZ CANAL and Gulf of Suez (W) and the Gulf of AQABA and Strait of Tiran (W). The peninsula, which has a very hot and dry climate, rises to over 8,500 ft (2,590 m) in the south, where Moses is said to have received the Ten Commandments, and is level and sandy in the north. Israeli troops occupied the Sinai briefly in 1956 and again from 1967 to 1980–82, when they withdrew over two years under the terms of the CAMP DAVID ACCORDS (1978) and Egyptian-Israeli peace treaty (1979).

Sinanthropus: see HOMO ERECTUS.

Sinatra, Frank (Francis Albert Sinatra), 1915–, American singer and actor; b. Hoboken, N.J. He gained great popularity in the late 1930s with his romantic, casual renditions of songs such as "I'll Never Smile Again." He has appeared in many films, e.g., *From Here to Eternity* (1953).

Sinclair, Upton, 1878–1968, American novelist; b. Baltimore. An ardent Socialist, he was deeply involved in politics, and his interest in social and industrial reform underlies most of his over 80 books. Sinclair's novels include *The Jungle* (1906), a brutally graphic account of the Chicago stockyards; *King Coal* (1917); *Oil!* (1927); and *Little Steel* (1938). He also wrote a cycle of 11 novels dealing with world events from 1914 that feature Lanny Budd as hero; the third of these, *Dragon's Teeth* (1942), won the Pulitzer Prize.

Sindhi [sĭn'dē], language belonging to the Indic group of the Indo-Iranian subfamily of the Indo-European family of languages. See LANGUAGE (table).

Singapore, officially Republic of Singapore, republic (1992 est. pop. 2,792,000), c.240 sq mi (620 sq km), SE Asia, S of the Malay Peninsula, comprising Singapore Island and about 60 islets. There is no administrative distinction between the country and Singapore city, where the government and port is located. Singapore Island is largely low-lying and has a tropical climate. It is almost entirely urbanized and densely populated; there is a remnant rain forest in the Bukit Timah reserve. Singapore is one of the world's great commercial centers, and its citizens enjoy one of the highest standards of living in Asia. Its port, at Keppel Harbor, is one of the world's largest and busiest. The economy is supported primarily by manufacturing, service industries, and trade; shipbuilding is also important. Agriculture plays a minor role, and the country imports most of its food. The population is mainly Chinese; Malays and Indians constitute large minorities. Buddhism, Islam, Hinduism, and Christianity are the major religions. Malay, Chinese, Tamil, and English are the official languages.

History. Singapore was a sparsely populated island when the British East India Company purchased it in 1819 through the efforts of Sir T.S. RAFFLES. Ceded to Britain in 1824, it became (1826) part of the STRAITS SETTLEMENTS colony. After occupation by the Japanese in WORLD WAR II, Singapore became a British crown colony in 1946 and a self-governing state in 1959. Under Lee Kuan Yew, the first prime minister, Singapore underwent economic development and modernization. It joined Malaya, SARAWAK, and SABAH in the Federation of MALAYSIA in 1963 but withdrew in 1965. Continuing economic growth assured the political dominance of Lee and the People's Action party, despite growing opposition and governmental restrictions on personal and political freedoms. In 1990 Goh Chok Tong became prime minister, but Lee retained considerable governmental influence and remained party leader.

Singer, Isaac Bashevis, 1904–91, American Yiddish author; b. Poland. He came to the U.S. in 1935. Perhaps the greatest of the Yiddish writers based in New York City, he frequently treated the loneliness of old age and the Jewish sense of alienation. His characters are often tormented by demons, as in the novel *Satan in Goray* (1955). Singer wrote many novels, short stories, e.g., *The Collected Stories of Isaac Bashevis Singer* (1981), plays and children's books. He was awarded the 1978 Nobel Prize in literature. His brother, **Israel Joshua Singer,** 1893–1944, b. Poland, emigrated to the U.S. in 1934. He also wrote in Yiddish. His epic novel, *The Brothers Ashkenazi* (1936), is about Jewish industrialism.

Singer, Isaac Merritt, 1811–75, American inventor; b. Rensselaer co., N.Y. He patented a practical SEWING MACHINE (1851) that could do continuous stitching, and made 20 subsequent improvements (1851–65). Although he lost an infringement suit to Elias HOWE, his company was so well established that it took the lead in a subsequent combination of manufactures and pooling of patents.

Singhalese [sĭng'gəlēz], language belonging to the Indic group of the Indo-Iranian subfamily of the Indo-European family of languages. See LANGUAGE (table).

Sinkiang: see XINJIANG.

Sinn Féin [shĭn fān] [Irish, = we ourselves], Irish nationalistic movement that triumphed in the establishment of the Irish Free State (see IRELAND). Organized (1905) by Arthur GRIFFITH, an advocate of an economically and politically self-sufficient Ireland, it adopted passive resistance to the British, but gained little support before World War I. The British suppression of the Easter Rebellion (1916) greatly stimulated Sinn Féin's growth, and it was reorganized in 1917 under the leadership of Eamon DE VALERA. It set up an Irish assembly called the Dáil Éireann that declared Irish independence. The resulting disorders were countered violently by British military irregulars known as Black and Tans, but continued resistance led ultimately to the establishment (1922) of the Irish Free State. Sinn Féin virtually came to an end after De Valera withdrew (1927) and entered the Irish Dáil with the new FIANNA FÁIL party. A few intransigents merged with the IRISH REPUBLICAN ARMY, whose political arm is still known as the Sinn Féin. Gerry Adams has headed the latter group since 1983.

Sino-Japanese War, Second, 1937–45. Japan used the Manchurian Incident—the bombing (1931) of a Japanese railway in Manchuria—as a pretext for occupying Manchuria and establishing the puppet state of Manchukuo. In 1933 and 1935 the Japanese won further concessions, and full war erupted after a clash (July 1937) between Japanese and Chinese forces in Beijing. The Japanese soon occupied Beijing and Tianjin and, after a protracted struggle, took Shanghai and the national capital, Nanjing. In late 1938 Hankou and Guangzhou fell. The Nationalist government was driven back to a temporary capital at Chongqing, and despite vast and bloody fighting its cause continued to decline. The Japanese attack (1941) on PEARL HARBOR merged the Sino-Japanese War with WORLD WAR II. Allied aid and advisers provided some relief, but China's military position deteriorated until Apr. 1945. After Japan's capitulation, Japanese troops in China formally surrendered (Sept. 9, 1945). Manchuria was restored to China, as were Taiwan and the Pescadores, which Japan had received after the First Sino-Japanese War (1894–95).

Sino-Tibetan languages, family of languages spoken in central and SE Asia. See LANGUAGE (table).

sintering, process of forming objects by heating a metal powder. When the metal powder is chemically or mechanically produced, compacted into the desired shape, and heated, the powder particles join together to form a solid object.

sinus, cavity or hollow space in the body, usually filled with air or blood. In humans, the paranasal sinuses, mucous-lined cavities in the bones of the face, are connected by passageways to the nose and probably help to warm and moisten inhaled air. In invertebrates, spaces through which blood returns to the heart are also called sinuses.

Sion: see ZION.

Siouan [so͞o'ən], branch of Native American languages belonging to the Hokan-Siouan linguistic family of North and Central America (including Mexico). See NATIVE AMERICAN LANGUAGES (table).

Sioux or **Dakota,** confederation of seven Native American tribes, the dominant group of the Hokan-Siouan stock (see NATIVE AMERICAN LANGUAGES). They had a typical Plains culture (see NORTH AMERICA, INDIGENOUS PEOPLES OF), including buffalo hunts and the SUN DANCE. In the mid-18th cent. the Sioux inhabited the N Great Plains and the western prairies. Of 30,000 Sioux, some 15,000 were Teton, of whom 3,000 were Oglala. The Sioux sided with the British in the AMERICAN REVOLUTION and the WAR OF 1812. They later made treaties with the U.S., but some Sioux revolted (1862) and killed more than 800 settlers and soldiers. By a treaty of 1867 the Sioux agreed to retire to a Dakota reservation. When gold was found in the BLACK HILLS, an influx of prospectors precipitated Sioux resistance under such chiefs as SITTING BULL, RED CLOUD, and CRAZY HORSE. Gen. George CUSTER was defeated (1876) and his troops annihilated at the Battle of the LITTLE BIGHORN. In 1890, 200 Sioux were killed at WOUNDED KNEE. Sioux and other supporters of the AMERICAN INDIAN MOVEMENT occupied Wounded Knee in 1973 to protest U.S. neglect of Native American civil rights. In 1979 the Sioux were awarded $105 million for the taking of their lands, resolving a legal action begun in 1923. Now mostly farmers and ranchers, the Sioux numbered over 100,000 in 1990; over 40% live in South Dakota.

Sioux Falls, city (1990 pop. 100,814), seat of Minnehaha co., SE S.Dak., on the Big Sioux R.; settled 1856, inc. as a city 1883. The largest city in the state, it has huge stockyards and meat-packing plants, diversified manufactures, and commercial and financial institutions. The falls provide hydroelectric power; sandstone is quarried nearby.

Siqueiros, David Alfaro [sēkä'rōs], 1896–1974, eminent Mexican painter. His art was generally related to his socialist revolutionary activities. Siqueiros's paintings convey violent social protest through dynamic brushwork, dramatic contrasts in light and shade, and heroic themes. Among his best-known works are murals at the National Preparatory School (1922–24) and at the Polytechnic Institute (1952), both in Mexico City.

Siren, in Greek myth, one of three sea nymphs, whose song lured sailors to shipwreck on the rocky coast where they lived. ODYSSEUS escaped them by tying himself to a mast and stopping his men's ears; the Argonauts were saved by ORPHEUS' music.

sirenian or **sea cow,** large, aquatic MAMMAL of the order Sirenia. Living sirenians are the dugong and the manatee, both found in warm, sheltered waters, where they feed exclusively on sea vegetation. Their heavy, fishlike bodies end in a horizontally flattened fin; their skin is gray and virtually hairless. Sluggish and shy, they spend their entire lives in the water. Sirenians may reach 12 ft (3.6 m) in length and 600 lb (270 kg) in weight. The Florida manatee (*Trichechus manatus*) is protected.

sisal hemp, important cordage fiber obtained from the leaves of several species of agave, of the AMARYLLIS family, and from related genera. The fiber, used especially for twine and considered second in strength to MANILA HEMP, is obtained chiefly from the true sisal (*Agave sisalana*) and henequen (*A. fourcroydes*).

Sisley, Alfred, 1839–99, impressionist landscape painter; b. Paris, of British parents. He was influenced by MONET, but his use of the "rainbow palette" was less bold. His works include *Street in Moret* (Art Inst., Chicago).

Sistine Chapel [for Sixtus IV], private chapel of the popes in the VATICAN. Built (1473) for Pope SIXTUS IV, it is world famous for its decorations. Frescoes by PERUGINO, BOTTICELLI, GHIRLANDAIO, and others are on the side walls. The best known, however, are MICHELANGELO's paintings on the ceiling of scenes from the Bible. Below these are his figures of the prophets and sibyls, all prefiguring the salvation of Christianity. His awesome *Last Judgment* is on the altar wall. The chapel also has a notable collection of illuminated music manuscripts. Cleaning and restoration of the frescoes began in 1980 and was completed in 1994.

Sisyphus [sĭs'ĭfəs], in Greek mythology, founder and king of CORINTH. Angered by his disrespect, ZEUS condemned him to push a heavy rock up a steep hill eternally.

Sitka, city (1990 pop. 8,588), SE Alaska, in the Alexander Archipelago, on Baranof Island; inc. 1971. Fishing, canning, lumbering, and pulp-processing are its industries. Sitka was founded (1799) by Aleksander BARANOF; after 1802 it became the capital of Russian America. A decisive battle between the Russians and the TLINGIT occurred there in 1804, commemorated in the Sitka National Historical Park. In the city in 1867 the U.S. officially took possession of Alaska, and it remained the Alaskan capital until 1900.

Sitting Bull, c.1831–90, SIOUX chief and victor in the battle of LITTLE BIGHORN (1876) against George Armstrong CUSTER. He and his followers fled to Canada, were promised a pardon, and returned (1881) to settle on a reservation. He appeared (1885) in BUFFALO BILL's Wild West Show but encouraged the Sioux to refuse to sell their land and advocated the Ghost Dance religion (see PAIUTE). He was killed while allegedly resisting arrest.

Sitwell, Dame Edith, 1887–1964, English poet and critic, **Sir Osbert Sitwell,** 1892–1969, English author, and **Sir Sacheverell Sitwell,** 1897–1988, English art critic. The Sitwells are probably the most famous English literary family of the 20th cent. All three were interested in contemporary movements in the arts and were noted for frivolity and precocity, although a somber note underlies their work. Edith Sitwell, a noted eccentric and wit, wrote critical essays, biographies, and poetry influenced by the French SYMBOLISTS, which appeared in many volumes, including *Collected Poems* (1954). Her *Façade,* an entertainment in abstract, rhythmic verse, with music by William WALTON, was first read in 1922. Osbert Sitwell wrote light satiric verse, novels, stories, and memoirs. His five-volume family reminiscence (1944–50) is a rich source of Edwardiana. Sacheverell Sitwell is known for his art studies, biographies, e.g., *Mozart* (1932), and travel books.

Sivaji, 1627–80, Indian ruler, leader of the MAHRATTAS. He spent his entire life fighting the MOGUL rulers and succeeded in carving out a considerable domain. In 1674 he crowned himself king of the Mahratta empire.

six, les, a group of young French composers—HONEGGER, MILHAUD, POULENC, Georges Auric, Louis Durey, and Germaine Tailleferre—who in 1918–19 joined Erik SATIE in reacting against the impressionism of DEBUSSY and RAVEL. They collaborated with Jean COCTEAU, their literary prophet.

Six-Day War: see ARAB-ISRAELI WARS.

Six Nations: see IROQUOIS CONFEDERACY.

Sixtus IV, 1414–84, pope (1471–84), an Italian named Francesco della Rovere, a Franciscan. He struggled with LOUIS XI of France over control of the French church and Louis's attempt to interfere in Naples. A quarrel with the MEDICI family of Florence became critical after Sixtus's nephew conspired to overthrow the Medici in the so-called Pazzi Conspiracy (1478). Sixtus waged war on Florence thereafter. Although a nepotist, he was a good administrator. He consented to the Spanish INQUISITION but welcomed Jews expelled from Spain. He founded the SISTINE CHAPEL.

Sixtus V, 1521–90, pope (1585–90), an Italian named Felice Peretti, a Franciscan. Sent (1565) to Spain to look into the alleged heresy of the Archbishop of Toledo, he fell out with his companion, the future GREGORY XIII, and they became lifelong enemies. As pope he lavished money on rebuilding Rome and left a huge surplus in the treasury, but in so doing he nearly ruined commerce in the Papal States. He set the maximum number of cardinals at 70 and authorized PHILIP II of Spain to send the Spanish ARMADA against England.

Skagerrak, strait, c.150 mi (240 km) long and 85 mi (140 km) wide, separating Denmark and Norway. It is one of the straits linking the North Sea and the Baltic Sea.

Skanderbeg: see SCANDERBEG.

skate: see RAY.

skating, gliding along an ice surface on keellike runners called ice skates. Originally a means of travel, skating became a well-established sport by the 17th cent. and has since developed into speed skating, figure skating, and ice dancing. Competition in these has become an important part of the Olympic winter games. Figure skating, one of the most beautiful and graceful events in all sport, was invented by an American, Jackson Haines, in the 1860s.

In the Olympics it is divided (since July 1990) into original program and free skating sections. Ice dancing, which increased in popularity during the 1980s, combines aspects of pair figure skating and ballroom dancing. The ice carnival, made popular by Sonja HENIE and other Olympic champions, has become a favorite American amusement. Skating is also integral part of ice HOCKEY. **Roller skating,** gliding over a smooth surface on skates with rollers or wheels, gained a large following after dance movements were adopted from ice skating. The development of skates suitable for use outside a rink, as well as of roller blades (skates with the wheels arranged in a single line), resulted in the growth of roller skating in the 1980s and 90s.

Skeat, Walter William, 1835–1912, English philologist. A professor of Anglo-Saxon at Cambridge (1878–1912), he translated many early English works and wrote *An Etymological Dictionary of the English Language* (1882), a standard reference work.

skeleton, stiff supportive framework of the body. The two basic types are the exoskeleton and the endoskeleton. The shell of the clam is an exoskeleton that provides formidable protection but is bulky and severely restricts movement. The firm, flexible insect skeleton combines protective armor and a framework for attachment of muscles used in rapid movement. Such exoskeletons must be shed periodically to allow for growth (all exoskeletons are nonliving) and thus tend to limit size. The endoskeleton, a framework of living material enclosed within the body of vertebrates, permits larger size and freedom of movement. The general arrangement of skeletal parts into skull, spinal column, and ribs is the same in all vertebrates. The human skeleton consists of 206 bones, held together by flexible tissue consisting of cartilage and ligaments. In addition to its supportive function, the skeleton provides sites for the attachment of MUSCLES and protects vital organs, such as the BRAIN, SPINAL CORD, HEART, and LUNGS.

Skelton, John, 1460–1529, English poet and humanist. Tutor to Prince Henry (later HENRY VIII), he is best remembered for his scathing SATIRES on the court and clergy—*The Bowge of Court* (1499), *Speke, Parrot* (1521), *Colin Clout* (1522)—and for the mock dirge *Phillip Sparrow*. His short lines, insistent rhymes, and alliteration are highly individual.

skepticism, philosophic position holding that the possibility of knowledge is limited, because of either the limitations of the mind or the inaccessibility of its object. The term is used more loosely to denote any questioning attitude. The earliest skeptics included the Greek Sophists (5th cent. B.C.) and PROTAGORAS. HUME is famous for his theoretical skepticism, but more closely linked to skepticism was the AGNOSTICISM of KANT, who demonstrated that certain problems are insoluble by reason. DESCARTES used skepticism as a methodology. The scientific method, which demands that all assumptions be questioned, is skeptical to a degree, although the POSITIVISM of scientists assumes that material effect is impossible without material cause.

skiing, sport of sliding over snow on skis—long, narrow, flexible runners made of highly polished wood, metal, plastic, or other materials. Other equipment includes heavy boots, attached to the skis with safety-release bindings, and a pair of poles to aid in accelerating, turning, and balancing. Originally a vital means of travel, skiing began as an organized sport in Norway in the 19th cent. Since the 1930s the sport (mainly downhill) has enjoyed a tremendous boom, spurred by the development of ski tows and ski lifts, and the use of artificial snow. Traditional competitive skiing comprises four events: (1) downhill, a steep descent in a race against time; (2) slalom, raced on a sharply twisting course marked off by flags; (3) the ski jump, from specially prepared slopes and scored on distance and form; and (4) cross-country, a stamina test over a long course, ranging from 10 to 50 km (6 to 31 mi) in the Olympic games. The first two are known as Alpine events, the last two as Nordic events. Alpine competition now also includes giant slalom and supergiant slalom, which resemble the slalom but use longer, less twisted courses that permit faster speeds; speed skiing, raced on a straight, specially prepared, downhill track that permits speeds in excess of 125 mph (200 kph); and the freestyle events of mogul skiing (emphasizing jumps and turns), ballet skiing (somewhat like figure skating), and aerials (acrobatic twists, flips, and the like performed in the air). The

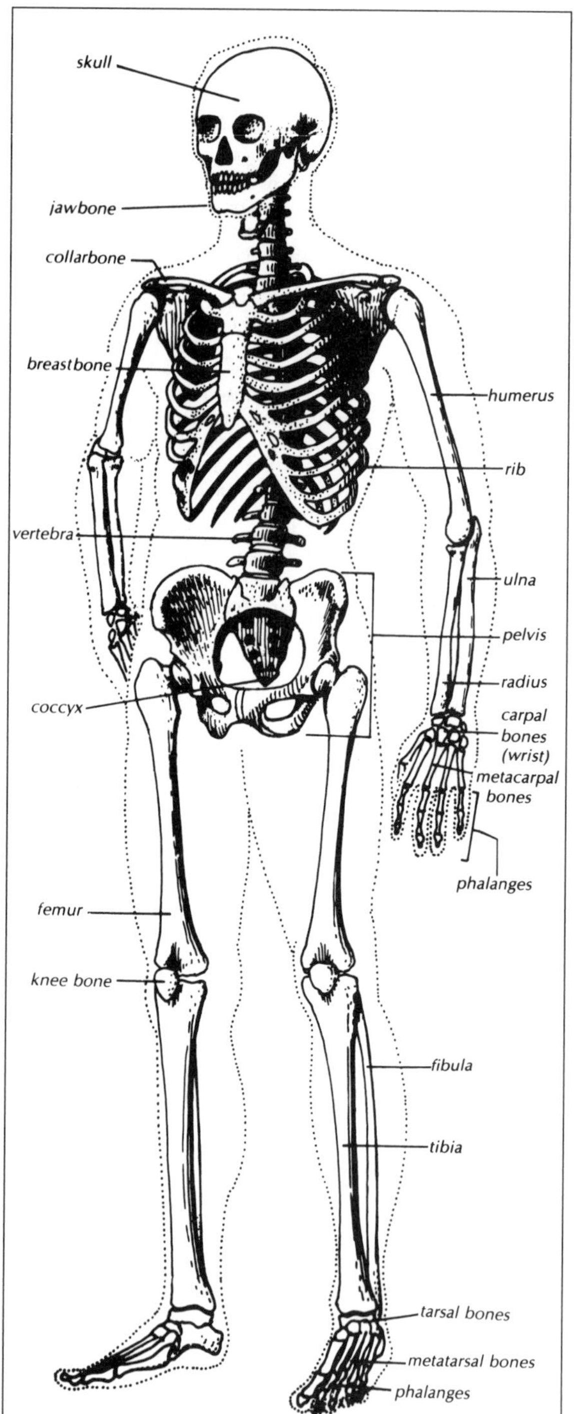

Human skeleton

Nordic biathlon combines cross-country skiing with target shooting. **Snowboarding** is a form of skiing that uses a single wide ski (snowboard) and no poles. It has similarities to surfing and skateboarding and originated in the 1970s.

skin, flexible tissue enclosing the body of a VERTEBRATE. In mammals, the skin is a complex organ of numerous structures serving vital protective and metabolic functions. It consists of two main cell layers: a thin outer layer (epidermis) and a thicker inner layer (dermis). The epidermis contains melanin, the pigment that gives the skin color. Evolutionary adaptations of epidermis include

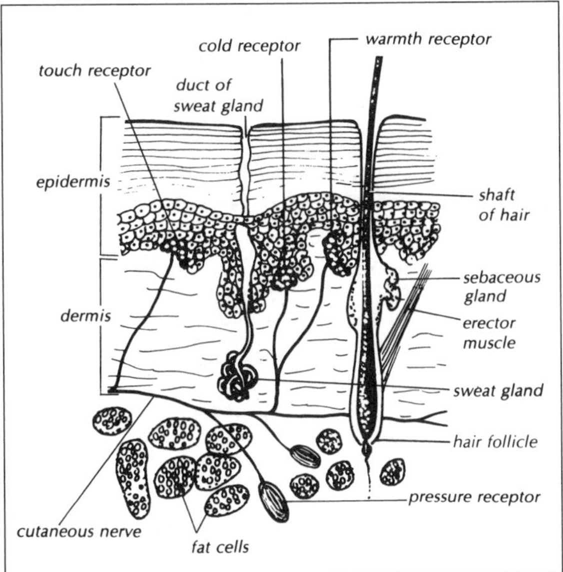

Cross-section of skin

horns, hooves, HAIR, FEATHERS, and SCALES. The dermis consists of CONNECTIVE TISSUE containing BLOOD vessels, lymph channels, nerve endings, sweat glands, sebaceous glands, fat cells, hair follicles, and MUSCLES. The nerve endings, called receptors, perform an important sensory function, responding to various stimuli, including light touch, pressure, pain, heat, and cold. The skin provides a barrier against invasion from outside organisms and protects underlying tissues and organs from abrasion and other injury. Its pigment shields the body from dangerous ultraviolet rays in sunlight. Skin prevents excessive loss of bodily moisture and in humans also performs functions that help maintain normal body temperature.

skin diving: see DIVING, DEEP-SEA.

Skinner, B(urrhus) F(rederic), 1904–90, American psychologist; b. Susquehanna, Pa. A Harvard professor, Skinner was the leading exponent of BEHAVIORISM, a school of psychology that rejects the unobservable and focuses on patterns of responses to external rewards and stimuli. Skinner did extensive research with animals, using the reward technique, which he also applied to human learning in the teaching machine he invented. Such machines and accompanying programmed instruction have profoundly affected educational theories and methods in the U.S. Skinner's well-known works include *The Behavior of Organisms* (1938), *Walden Two* (1961), and *About Behaviorism* (1974).

Skinner, Otis, 1858–1942, American actor; b. Cambridge, Mass. He won lasting fame in *Kismet* (1911). His daughter, **Cornelia Otis Skinner,** 1901–79, American actress and author, b. Chicago, was noted for her original monologues.

skin patch, transdermal patch, or **transdermal delivery system,** adhesive patch used to deliver a controlled dose of a drug through the skin over a period of time. A skin patch uses a special membrane to control the rate at which the liquid drug contained in the reservoir within the patch can pass through the skin and into the bloodstream. Some drugs must be combined with substances, such as alcohol, that increase their ability to penetrate the skin in order to be used in a skin patch. Drugs administered through skin patches include scopolamine (for motion sickness), nicotine (for quitting smoking), estrogen (for MENOPAUSE and to prevent osteoporosis after menopause), and nitroglycerin (for angina).

Skopje [skôp'yə] or **Skoplje** [skôp'əlyə], city (1987 est. pop. 445,000), capital of MACEDONIA, on the Vardar R. in the northern part of the country. A transport and trade center, it produces chemicals, cement, and machinery. Dating from Roman times, it fell to Serbia (1282) and to the Turks (1392). Part of Yugoslavia after 1918, it became (1946) the capital of the new constituent republic of Macedonia, which gained independence in 1992. The city, which contains a Turkish citadel and two 15th-cent. mosques, was badly damaged (1963) by an earthquake.

skunk, several related New World MAMMALS of the WEASEL family, characterized by their striking black-and-white-striped fur and the strong, offensive odor they spray for defense. When severely provoked, the skunk squirts a mist from glands under the tail that causes choking and tearing of the eyes. Skunks are generally avoided by predators. They feed on rodents, insects, eggs, carrion, and vegetation, and live in one or more families in rock piles and abandoned burrows. Hunted for their fur, skunks range in size from 9 to 18 in. (23 to 46 cm), excluding the tail.

sky diving: see PARACHUTE.

Skye, island, 670 sq mi (1,735 sq km), largest of the Inner HEBRIDES, off W Scotland. Tourism, fishing, and farming are important; cattle and sheep are raised. "Bonny Prince Charlie" (see Charles Edward Stuart, under STUART, JAMES FRANCIS EDWARD) took refuge there in 1746.

Skylab: see SPACE EXPLORATION, table.

skylark: see LARK.

skyscraper, modern building of great height, constructed on a steel skeleton. The form originated in the U.S., and many late-19th-cent. technological developments contributed to its evolution. In 1887 the first elevator was installed, and with the eventual perfecting of high-speed electric elevators skyscrapers were free to attain any height. The early tall masonry buildings required very thick walls in the lower stories, which limited floor space. The use of cast iron to permit thinner walls was followed by cage construction, in which iron frames supported the floors, while the walls were self-supporting. The first fully steel-frame building was the Home Insurance Building in Chicago (1883), designed by William Jenney. Chicago subsequently became the center of skyscraper development. Early New York City examples include the Flatiron Building (1902) and Cass GILBERT's Woolworth Building (1913), which epitomized, with its Gothic ornamentation, the adaptation of earlier styles to modern construction. Louis SULLIVAN gave impetus to a new aesthetic, emphasizing underlying structure and fenestration, e.g., the Carson Pirie Scott Building (1899–1904), in Chicago. In 1916, New York established legal control over the height and plan of buildings; regulations regarding setting back walls above a determined height gave rise to the characteristic stepped profile. Skyscraper placement and design are a major concern of city planning. The tallest skyscraper is the SEARS TOWER, Chicago, 110 stories, 1454 ft (473 m). Major New York City skyscrapers are the twin towers of the WORLD TRADE CENTER, 110 stories, 1350 ft (442 m); the EMPIRE STATE BUILDING, 102 stories, 1250 ft (412 m); and the Chrysler Building, 77 stories, 1046 ft (349 m).

slander: see LIBEL AND SLANDER.

slate, fine-grained, characteristically gray-blue ROCK formed by the METAMORPHISM of SHALE. It splits into perfectly cleaved, broad, thin layers; this property is known as slaty cleavage. Better grades of slate are used for roofing.

Slatkin, Leonard, 1944–, American conductor; b. Los Angeles. Noted for his interpretations of 20-cent. American music, he has led the New Orleans Philharmonic (1977–79) and St. Louis Symphony Orchestra (1979–).

Slaughterhouse Cases, cases decided by the U.S. Supreme Court in 1873. In 1869 the Louisiana legislature granted a monopoly to a specific slaughterhouse to protect the people's health. Other operators claimed a violation of their rights under the 14th amendment. The Court decided against the operators, holding that their claims were beyond the scope of the amendment, whose original purpose was to guarantee the freedom of former slaves. Since then, the courts have expanded the interpretation of other guarantees in the amendment.

slavery, institution whereby one person owns another and can exact from that person labor or other services, found among both primitive and advanced peoples. Greek slaves had some legal protection, but in the Roman Empire agricultural (estate) slavery gave landowners nearly absolute power over slaves, though manumission (emancipation) gave freedmen status in Rome's social system. Early Christians did not oppose slavery, but economic changes replaced the agricultural slave with the semifree SERF in the Middle Ages. Islam also accepted slavery: eunuch slaves guarded the harem. In the 15th and 16th cent., European exploration of the African coasts led to a lucrative, brutal slave trade carried out by the British, French, Dutch, Spanish, and Portuguese. African slaves, in demand in the Americas, were brought to Virginia in 1619. The slave trade developed a triangular pattern: goods were transported from British ports to the west coast of Africa, where they were exchanged for slaves, who were taken to the New World and traded for agricultural staples for the return to England. The movement to abolish slavery for economic and humanitarian reasons began in the 18th cent. Britain outlawed (1807) the slave trade and abolished (1833) slavery in the British Empire. In the U.S., slavery had disappeared in the North by the early 19th cent. but had become integral to the South's plantation system; the ABOLITIONISTS regarded it as an unmitigated evil. Attempts to compromise on permitting slavery in the western territories—the MISSOURI COMPROMISE, the COMPROMISE OF 1850, and the KANSAS-NEBRASKA ACT—failed to resolve the issue. Sectional opposition over STATES' RIGHTS and the FUGITIVE SLAVE LAWS, the UNDERGROUND RAILROAD, the DRED SCOTT CASE, the WILMOT PROVISO, and John BROWN's raid on Harpers Ferry, Va., heightened tensions. The formation of the Republican party with its antislavery platform and the election of Abraham LINCOLN (1860) led to the secession of Southern states and the CIVIL WAR. Northern victory ended U.S. slavery, and Lincoln's EMANCIPATION PROCLAMATION (1863) freeing the slaves in secessionist states was followed by the 13th amendment to the CONSTITUTION. In the late 19th cent. international action against the remaining slave trade (especially that of Muslim powers) began. The LEAGUE OF NATIONS and later the UNITED NATIONS have continued efforts to abolish slavery and similar systems of forced labor, but millions still live or work in such conditions worldwide.

Slavic languages, also called Slavonic, a subfamily of the Indo-European family of languages. See LANGUAGE (table).

Slavic religion, pre-Christian religious practices among the Slavs of Eastern Europe. Information about the myths and legends of the early pagan Slavs is fragmentary, but certain beliefs were common. Earliest rites were based on the principle that the natural world is inhabited and directed by beneficial and harmful spirits of nature. Later, these mysterious forces were anthropomorphized into divinities with special powers and functions. The supreme god of the East and South Slavs was Perun, god of lightning and thunder, who controlled the elements of nature. Svarog, known to most Slavs, was regarded as the father of the deities. Byelobog [the White God] and Chernobog [the Black God], representing the forces of good and evil, reflected the Slavic belief in the dualistic nature of the universe. The Baltic Slavs had a particularly rich tradition and many cults, including the powerful one of Radogost-Svarazic. With the coming of Christianity, the great divinities of the Slavs vanished in name, but many elements of pagan belief survived in popular tradition and in Christian Slavic religious ceremonies.

Slavonic: see SLAVIC LANGUAGES.

Slavs, Europe's largest ethnic and linguistic group, speakers of related Indo-European languages. They are divided into West Slavs (Poles, Czechs, Slovaks), South Slavs (Serbs, Croats, Slovenes, Macedonians, Bulgars), and East Slavs (Russians, Ukrainians, Belarussians). Religiously and culturally, the Slavs may be divided into two groups: those who are of the Eastern Orthodox faith and use the Cyrillic alphabet, and those who have been historically affiliated with the Roman Catholic Church and use the Roman alphabet. Slavs are believed to be descendants of Neolithic tribes of GALICIA; over the centuries they have intermixed with Turko-Tatars, Germans, Mongols, Greeks, and Illyrians. A sedentary agricultural people, they were probably dominated by the conquering Scythians, Sarmatians, Goths, Huns, and Avars. By the 6th cent. Slavs were in E Germany, and in 576 and 746 they invaded the BYZANTINE EMPIRE. The westernmost tribes adopted Christianity in the 9th cent. In the 12th cent. German expansion eastward pushed the Slavs east of the Elbe R. Most powerful of the early Slavic states was KIEVAN RUSSIA, which was destroyed by the MONGOLS in the 13th cent. From the 18th cent. through WORLD WAR I the West and South Slavs struggled for liberation from Turkish, German, and Magyar domination. Pan-Slavism was continually hampered by conflicting national aspirations, e.g., Polish vs. Russian, Croatian vs. Serbian.

sleep, resting state in which an individual becomes relatively quiescent and unaware of the environment. During sleep, most physiological functions, such as body temperature, blood pressure, and breathing rate, decrease. It is also a time of repair and growth, when some tissues proliferate more rapidly, and appears linked to the immune system. In healthy people, for example, lack of sleep causes an immune response resembling that to an infection. Humans cycle repeatedly through four stages of sleep, each 1½–2 hours long. Rapid eye movement (REM) sleep, associated with dreaming, occurs during Stage 1 sleep at the end of each cycle. It has been hypothesized that while deeper (non-REM) stages of sleep are physically restorative, REM sleep is psychically restorative. It is also believed to integrate new information into the brain (see also DREAMS). Dream or sleep deprivation results in changes in personality and in impairment of physical, perceptual, and intellectual processes.

sleeping pill, a pill containing medication that induces sleep. BENZODIAZEPINES such as temazepam (Restoril) and triazolam (Halcion) have for the most part replaced BARBITURATES as drugs of choice for insomnia.

sleeping sickness: see ENCEPHALITIS.

sleet, precipitation of small, partially melted grains of ice. As raindrops or melted snowflakes fall, they pass through layers of air having different temperatures. If they pass through a layer with a temperature below the freezing point, they become sleet. Sleet occurs only during the winter, whereas HAIL may fall at any time of the year.

Slick, Sam: see HALIBURTON, THOMAS CHANDLER.

Slidell, John [slīdĕl', slī'dəl], 1793–1871, American politician and diplomat; b. N.Y.C. A U.S. senator from Louisiana (1853–61), he joined the Confederacy in 1861 and was Confederate commissioner to France, where he became one of the principals in the TRENT AFFAIR.

slime mold or **slime fungus,** organism usually classified with the PROTOZOANS but showing equal affinity to the fungi (see FUNGUS). Slime molds have complex life cycles with an animallike motile phase, in which feeding and growth occur, and a plantlike immotile reproductive phase. The motile phase, commonly found under rotting logs and damp leaves, consists of either solitary amebalike cells or a brightly colored multinucleate mass of protoplasm called a plasmodium, which creeps about and feeds by ameboid movement (see AMEBA). In the reproductive phase, slime molds are transformed into one or more reproductive structures, each consisting of a stalk topped by a spore-producing capsule. When the spores germinate they release amebalike cells; in plasmodium-forming species, the cells grow and the nucleus subdivides to form a plasmodium.

Sloan, Alfred Pritchard, 1875–1966, American businessman and philanthropist; b. New Haven, Conn. A draftsman for the Hyatt Roller Bearing Co., he rose to president (1901) before selling the company to General Motors (GM) in 1916. As president (1923–37) and chairman (1937–56) of GM, he helped lead the corporation to dominance in the U.S. auto industry. His philanthropic interests included the Sloan-Kettering Institute for Cancer Research (N.Y.C.).

Sloan, John, 1871–1951, American painter; b. Lock Haven, Pa. A member of the EIGHT, he is known for his nudes and city scenes painted with a directness that sometimes verges on satire. Characteristic paintings are *McSorley's Bar* (Detroit Inst. of Arts) and *Wake of the Ferry* (Phillips Coll., Wash., D.C.). Sloan was also a gifted illustrator and etcher.

sloth, tailless, arboreal MAMMAL found in tropical forests of Central and South America. The three-toed sloth (genus *Bradypus*), with three-toed front feet and five-toed hind feet, has a dense, gray-brown furry coat and is about the size of a house cat. Clinging to branches with powerful, curved claws, sloths eat, sleep, and travel upside down. Although sluggish, they can strike swiftly if attacked.

Slovakia, Slovak *Slovensko*, republic (1993 est. pop. 5,300,000), 18,917 sq mi (48,995 sq km), central Europe, formerly a constituent republic of Czechoslovakia. Slovakia is bordered by the Czech Republic (W), Austria (SW), Hungary (S), Ukraine (E), and Poland (N). The capital, BRATISLAVA, is a port on the Danube R., which forms part of Slovakia's southern borders. Other important cities include Košice, Trnava, Nitra, Komarno, and Nové Zámky. Most of Slovakia is traversed by the Carpathian Mts., with their vast forests,

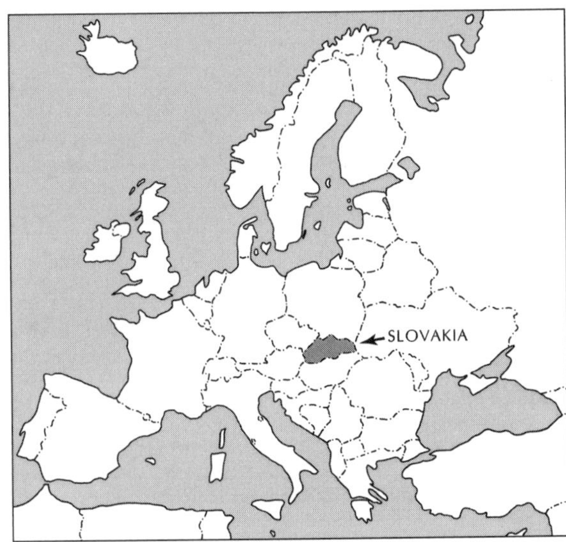

sheep pastures, and rich mineral resources, including iron, copper, and coal. The valleys are drained by the Váh R. and other Danube tributaries. Several rivers have been dammed for hydroelectric power, including the Danube at Cunovo in 1992. Much industrialization occurred under the Communists, including weapons manufacturing, shipbuilding, and metal processing; these state-owned enterprises contracted severely during the move toward a free market after 1990. S Slovakia is chiefly agricultural; crops include wheat, barley, and sugar beets. The majority of the people are Slovaks, who are ethnically and linguistically related to the Czechs; there are Hungarian, Gypsy, and other minorities. Roman Catholicism is the predominant faith, but there are also sizable Protestant (notably Lutheran), Eastern Orthodox, and Uniate groups.

History. The area, part of the 9th-cent. empire of MORAVIA, was primarily under Hungarian rule from the 10th cent. In 1526 Slovakia and W Hungary passed to the Hapsburgs after Louis II of Hungary was defeated by the Ottomans. In the 19th cent. there was a Slovak national revival, in part in reaction to the Germanization of Slovakia in the previous century. After WORLD WAR I, Slovakia became (1918) part of the new nation of CZECHOSLOVAKIA. The minority Slovaks, however, campaigned for greater autonomy from the Czech-dominated, centralized state. In 1938 Slovakia was made an autonomous unit by the MUNICH PACT and later (1939–45) was a German puppet state. The Czechoslovak state was reestablished in 1945, and after 1948 the Communist government curtailed Slovak autonomy until 1969, when Slovakia was granted autonomy over local affairs. With the end (1990) of Communist rule, Slovakia gained greater control over its affairs and budget, as well as some power-sharing with the national government. Discontent with depressed economic conditions resulting from free-market reforms brought nationalists led by Slovak Prime Min. Vladimír Mečiar to power in 1992, and Czech and Slovak leaders agreed to Slovakian independence and the dissolution of Czechoslovakia (Jan. 1, 1993). Slovakia's ethnic Hungarians, worried by Slovak nationalism, have sought special cultural protections in the new republic.

Slovenia, Slovenian *Slovenija,* officially Republic of Slovenia, republic (1992 est. pop. 1,963,000), 7,817 sq mi (20,246 sq km), S central Europe, formerly a constituent republic of Yugoslavia. Bordered by Croatia (S), the Gulf of Trieste and Italy (W), Austria (N), and Hungary (E), Slovenia is largely situated in the Karst plateau and Julian Alps. LJUBLJANA is the capital; other large cities are Maribor and Kranj. Slovenia was the wealthiest and most industrialized Yugoslav republic. Manufactures include steel, machinery, motor vehicles, electrical equipment, textiles and clothing, and pharmaceuticals, and mineral resources include oil, coal, and mercury. Farming and stock-raising are important occupations; grains, potatoes, and fruit are the major crops, and wine is produced. The vast majority of the population are Slovenes; there are Italian, Hungarian, Croatian, Serb, and Bosnian Muslim minorities. Slovenian, a South Slavic tongue, is the official language. Roman Catholicism is the predominant religion.

History. Ruled by Rome from the 1st cent. B.C., the region was settled by the South Slavs (6th cent. A.D.) and passed to the FRANKS (788), the dukes of BAVARIA (843), and the HAPSBURGS (1335), becoming part of Austria. In 1918 Slovenia was incorporated into YUGOSLAVIA. During WORLD WAR II it was divided (1941–45) among Germany, Italy, and Hungary. After the war a small part of Italy's Venezia Giulia region was added to Slovenia. In 1991 the republic proclaimed its independence after Serbia refused to agree to a looser Yugoslav confederation. Fighting broke out briefly when the Yugoslav army attempted to retake border posts seized by Slovenia, but a cease-fire led to the withdrawal of Yugoslav forces. Milan Kučan, first elected in 1990, is president of Slovenia.

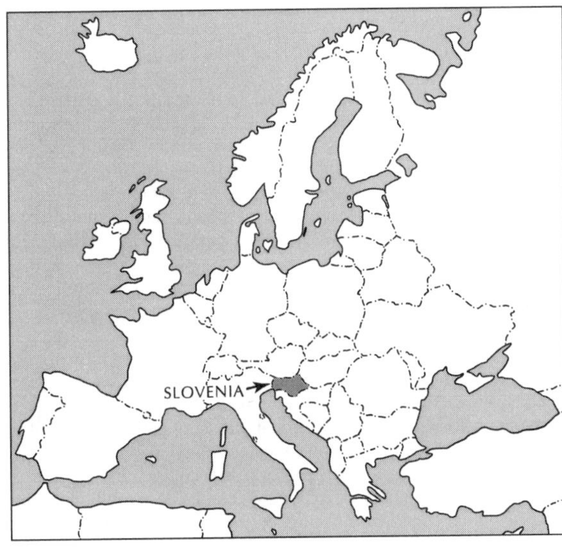

slow virus, virus, such as a lentivirus, that causes symptoms in an infected host long after the original infection. Slow viruses are believed by some to cause a group of slowly developing diseases that includes Creutzfeld-Jacob disease and scrapie. See also PRION.

slug, terrestrial GASTROPOD mollusk, a form of SNAIL, with a rudimentary shell and a lung for breathing air. Feeding at night, slugs devour both the roots and aerial portions of plants; some species are serious garden pests.

Sm, chemical symbol of the element SAMARIUM.

small arms, firearms designed primarily to be carried and fired by one person, as distinguished from heavy arms, or ARTILLERY, from which such weapons developed in the late 1300s. At first, small arms were nothing more than small, hand-held cannon fired by placing a small flame at the touchhole. In the matchlock—the first real handgun—a trigger moved the flame to the touchhole; in its successors, the wheel lock and flintlock, a spark-producing mechanism ignited the GUNPOWDER. Among early weapons of this kind were the musket, fired from the shoulder, and the pistol, held and fired with one hand. The rifle, invented in the 15th cent., is a firearm with a rifled bore (that is, with spiral grooves that impart a spinning motion to the bullet, giving it greater accuracy). Rifles first came into widespread use in the American colonies. Two major innovations of the early 19th cent. were the percussion cap, a small capsule filled with fulminate of mercury that exploded when struck and fired the gun instantly; and the gas-expanding bullet, which, after being dropped down the barrel of a rifle, would expand when fired to fit the barrel's rifling. Both sides in the U.S. CIVIL WAR used a rifled musket. Thereafter, all guns became rifled with the exception of the shotgun, a smooth-bored, short-range gun firing a single slug or several small shot. Practical breech-loading, or rear-loading, firearms came into general use about 1870; by the 1880s magazine loading, smokeless powder, and bolt action had been introduced. Although a crude "revolving pistol" existed in the late 16th cent., the modern revolver was introduced c.1835 by Samuel COLT. Colt's revolving cylinder permitted his gun to be fired six times without reloading. The revolver and the magazine-loading rifle were the standard small arms of the later 19th cent., but around 1900 a host of new automatic weapons were developed. The heavy Gatling gun, used in the U.S. Civil War, was the forerunner of the modern, rapid-firing machine gun, which achieved its full potential during the trench warfare of World War I and remains an important military firearm. The 1920s saw the development of submachine guns, notably the Thompson submachine gun (or "tommy gun"), an easily portable automatic weapon that fired 450–600 cartridges per minute. During World War II the bolt-action rifle was supplanted by the semiautomatic Garand rifle—a lightweight, self-loading, clip-fed shoulder weapon; it was used by U.S. forces through the KOREAN WAR. The American M-16 rifle, still widely used, can fire accurately up to 500 yd (460 m) when hand-held and up to 800 yd (730 m) when mounted. Other effective weapons include the Russian AK-47 Kalashnikov automatic rifle and the Israeli Uzi submachine gun.

smallpox, acute, highly contagious, sometimes fatal, disease causing a high fever and successive stages of severe skin eruptions. Caused by a virus that may be airborne or spread by direct contact, smallpox has occurred in epidemics throughout history. Edward JENNER, at the end of the 18th cent., demonstrated that cowpox virus was an effective vaccine against the disease. By the end of the 1970s, VACCINATION programs, such as those by the World Health Organization, had eliminated the disease worldwide.

smart card, small device that resembles a credit card but contains electronic circuitry that stores encoded information. The card and the computerized system with which it is used are designed to provide and record information about the user or the user's account. A smart card may be used to authorize payments or purchases without the need for telephone links to the card-issuer or to maintain computerized individual medical records without the need for a centralized database or computer system.

smart weapon, missile or steerable bomb equipped with a LASER or TELEVISION guidance system. In the case of a smart bomb with a laser guidance system, an aircraft pilot aims a laser beam at the target, a COMPUTER keeps the beam locked on the target, and the bomb has a sensor programmed to find the reflection of the laser's light. A guidance computer adjusts the path of the bomb after it is released, using movable fins to steer. A television guidance system uses a television camera in the nose of the weapon to lock onto the image of the target identified by the pilot.

smell: see NOSE.

smelt, small, slender FISH of the family Osmeridae, allied to the grayling of the SALMON family. Most species are marine, but some spawn in fresh water and some are landlocked in lakes. The American smelt, or icefish (*Osmerus mordax*), averages 10 in. (25 cm) in length and is valued as a food fish.

smelting, any process of melting or fusion, especially to extract a metal from its ORE. Processes vary depending on the ore and metal involved, but they are typified by the use of the BLAST FURNACE and the reverberatory furnace.

Smetana, Bedřich [smĕ'tänä], 1824–84, Czech composer. The creator of a national style in Czech music, he is best known for the opera *The Bartered Bride* (1866). Almost all his music is programmatic, including the SYMPHONIC POEM *My Fatherland* (1879) with its famous section, *The Moldau,* and his two string quartets, *From My Life* (1876, 1882).

Smith, Adam, 1723–90, Scottish economist, founder of the classical school of ECONOMICS. While professor of moral philosophy at the Univ. of Glasgow, he wrote his *Theory of Moral Sentiments* (1759), which attracted international interest. In the 1760s he traveled in France, met some of the PHYSIOCRATS, and started to write his masterpiece, *An Inquiry into the Nature and Causes of the Wealth of Nations,* published in 1776. Smith postulated the theory of the division of labor and emphasized that value arises from the labor used in production. He believed that in a LAISSEZ FAIRE economy the impulse of self-interest would bring about the public welfare. Although opposed to monopoly and the concepts of MERCANTILISM, he admitted that restrictions on free trade (such as the NAVIGATION ACTS) were sometimes necessary. Although some of Smith's theories were voided by the experience of the INDUSTRIAL REVOLUTION, his influence on later economists has never been surpassed.

Smith, Alfred Emanuel, 1873–1944, American politician; b. N.Y.C. As four-time governor of New York (1919–20, 1923–28), he was forceful and well-liked, and he achieved many reforms. In 1928 he ran on the Democratic ticket as the first Roman Catholic candidate for president, but he was defeated by Herbert HOOVER.

Smith, Bessie, 1898?–1937, African-American singer; b. Chattanooga, Tenn. In the 1920s she became the favorite singer of the JAZZ public. The power and beauty of her voice earned her the title "Empress of the Blues."

Smith, David, 1906–65, American sculptor; b. Decatur, Ind. His mature works, in wrought iron and cut steel, exhibit totemlike forms and a use of space that recalls CONSTRUCTIVISM, e.g., *Hudson River Landscape* (Ogunquit Mus., Maine).

Smith, Donald Alexander: see STRATHCONA AND MOUNT ROYAL, DONALD ALEXANDER SMITH, 1ST BARON.

Smith, Ian Douglas, 1919–, Rhodesian politician. As a member of the white supremacist Rhodesian Front party, he became (1964) prime minister and in 1965 unilaterally declared Rhodesia independent from Britain. He maintained minority white rule until the election of a black prime minister, Abel Muzorewa, in 1979. He continued to lead the white minority in parliament after the country was proclaimed the Republic of ZIMBABWE and after the election of Robert MUGABI as prime minister (1980). In 1987, however, he was suspended from his position due to conflict with Mugabi.

Smith, Jedediah Strong, 1799–1831, American explorer and one of the greatest MOUNTAIN MEN; b. near Binghamton, N.Y. His western travels opened the rich fur-trapping country and showed the way for pioneers who came later. Arriving in St. Louis (1822), he joined William Ashley's expedition. In 1824 he helped lead a party through South Pass, in Wyoming, beginning use of that route. In 1826–27 he traveled southwest from Great Salt Lake, crossed the Colorado R. and the Mojave Desert, arrived at the San Gabriel (Calif.) mission, and then with two men made the first recorded crossing of the Sierra Nevada and the Great Salt Desert from west to east. Smith later traveled from California to Ft. Vancouver, surviving Native American attacks that killed 26 of his party, but he himself was killed along the Cimarron R. by Comanches.

Smith, John, c.1580–1631, English colonist in America. A member of the JAMESTOWN council, the resourceful and tactful Smith carried the colony through periods of hardship (1607–9). The celebrated story of his capture by Powhatan (see POWHATAN CONFEDERACY) and rescue by POCAHONTAS is probably true.

Smith, John, 1938–, British Labour politician. A Scottish lawyer, he was first elected to Parliament in 1970 and held several junior ministerial posts (1974–78) before serving as secretary of state for trade (1978–79). He succeeded Neil KINNOCK as party leader in 1992. A member of Labour's right wing, Smith has played a major role in moderating the party's leftist policies and reducing union influence.

Smith, Joseph, 1805–44, American MORMON leader, founder of the Church of Jesus Christ of Latter-Day Saints; b. Sharon, Vt. After moving to Palmyra, N.Y., he claimed that visions revealed (1823) to him the existence of secret records, which he said he had unearthed in 1827 in the form of golden tablets and translated as the Book of Mormon. As prophet and seer, he founded (1830) a church in Fayette, N.Y. The hostility of neighbors led him to move to Kirtland, Ohio, to Missouri, and finally to Nauvoo, Ill. Disaffection grew within the sect, and more trouble with non-Mormons led to his arrest, along with that of his brother Hyrum, on charges of treason. On June 27, 1844, both brothers were murdered by a mob at Carthage, Ill. Smith's revelations, including one on plural marriage (made public eight years after his death), were accepted as doctrine by the Mormons, who increased greatly after his death.

Smith, Sydney, 1771–1845, English clergyman and writer. A founder of the *Edinburgh Review* (1802), he championed the rights of the oppressed, as in the "Peter Plymley" letters (1807–8) urging CATHOLIC EMANCIPATION.

Smith, Tony, 1912–80, American sculptor; b. South Orange, N.J. Also an architect, Smith was allied with the MINIMALISM art movement. He is known for monumental modular sculptures that employ geometric forms in monochromatic plywood or metal.

Smith, W. Eugene, 1918–78, American photojournalist; b. Wichita, Kans. Among the foremost modern documentarians, Smith recorded World War II in the Pacific and produced a wide range of powerful photo-essays, including "Country Doctor" (1948), "Pittsburgh" (1956), and *Minamata* (1975).

Smithsonian Institution, research and educational center, largely in Washington, D.C.; est. 1846 under terms of the will of James Smithson, of London, who in 1829 bequeathed his fortune to the U.S. Today, it is a vast complex that includes the National Air and Space Museum, the National Gallery of Art, the National Museum of American History, the National Museum of Natural History, the National Portrait Gallery, the Joseph H. Hirshhorn Museum and Sculpture Garden, the National Postal Museum, the National Zoological Park, museums of African and Asian art, and other institutions. The John F. Kennedy Center for the Performing Arts is an independent bureau within the institution. The National Museum of the American Indian, containing the collections of the former Museum of the American Indian, Heye Foundation (N.Y.C.), includes the George Gustav Heye Center in New York City and a planned main museum in Washington, D.C. The Cooper-Hewitt Museum of Decorative Arts and Design, in New York City, is also part of the Smithsonian.

smog, dense, visible air POLLUTION, commonly of two types. The gray smog of older industrial cities like London and New York comes from the massive combustion of coal and fuel oil in or near the city, releasing ashes, soot, and sulfur compounds into the air. The brown smog characteristic of Los Angeles and Denver is caused by automobile emissions. Smog, which usually results in reduced visibility and can irritate the eyes and respiratory system, may be dangerous to people with respiratory ailments. It can also damage metal, rubber, and other materials.

Smollett, Tobias George, 1721–71, Scottish novelist. A ship's surgeon and later an editor, he wrote *Roderick Random* (1748), *Peregrine Pickle* (1751), *Ferdinand Count Fathom* (1753), and *Humphrey Clinker* (1771), his major success, all adventure novels drawn largely from experience. Rich in character, plots, and satire, they influenced many, including DICKENS.

Smoot, Reed, 1862–1941, U.S. senator from Utah (1903–33); b. Salt Lake City. The first Mormon elected to the U.S. Senate, he helped write the HAWLEY-SMOOT TARIFF ACT (1930).

smut, name for plant diseases caused by a FUNGUS of the order Ustilaginales. Smut produces sootlike masses of spores on the host, lowers its vitality, and often causes deformities. Serious threats to grain crops, smuts do not alternate hosts as do the RUSTS. Severe annual crop losses are caused by the corn smut, oat smut, and loose smut of wheat. Bunt, the most serious smut, attacks young wheat seedlings and destroys the GRAIN.

Smuts, Jan Christiaan, 1870–1950, South African statesman and soldier. Of Boer stock, he fought against the British in the SOUTH AFRICAN WAR. After concluding that British-Boer cooperation was essential in South Africa, he was instrumental in the creation (1910) of the Union of South Africa. Smuts held office continuously (1910–19) in Louis BOTHA's cabinet and was a signer of the treaty of VERSAILLES. He was prime minister (1919–24, 1939–48). During WORLD WAR II Smuts was made a field marshal and held a high place on British war councils. He was active in organizing the UN.

Smyrna, Turkey: see İZMIR.

Sn, chemical symbol of the element TIN.

snail, GASTROPOD mollusk with a spirally coiled shell; there are thousands of species on land and in water. In aquatic species, respiration is carried on by gills; terrestrial forms often have lungs. Snails secrete a slimy substance over which they move by contractions of their muscular foot. Many species are eaten.

Snake, river, NW U.S., flowing c.1,038 mi (1,670 km) from Yellowstone National Park (NW Wyoming) to become the chief tributary of the Columbia R., which it joins near Pasco, Wash. A scenic river with spectacular gorges, notably Hell's Canyon (c.125 mi/200 km long and up to 7,900 ft/2,400 m deep), it is also an important source of hydroelectricity and irrigation.

snake, limbless REPTILE of the order Squamata, which also includes the LIZARDS. The snake's extremely long, narrow body has many vertebrae, and paired internal organs are arranged linearly rather than side by side; all snakes are deaf. Some snakes—constrictors—crush their prey by wrapping their bodies around it and squeezing; others—venomous snakes—inject a toxic substance into their victims. The approximately 2,700 snake species, of which about four fifths are nonvenomous, are distributed throughout most temperate and tropical zones of the world. About two thirds of all species, most of them nonvenomous, belong to the family Colubridae, including garter and grass snakes. Most poisonous New World snakes belong to the PIT VIPER family, while venomous Old World snakes are the true VIPERS. The family Boidea includes the largest snakes, e.g., BOAS and PYTHONS, and the family Elapidae (snakes with inflatable neck hoods) includes the COBRA.

snapdragon, cultivated garden and greenhouse plant (*Antirrhinum majus*) of the figwort family, native to the Mediterranean area. Its showy blossoms, resembling a dragon's snout, display a wide range of colors and varieties.

snapper, carnivorous, spiny-finned FISH of the family Lutianidae, chiefly of tropical coastal waters. Snappers are active and voracious, with large mouths and sharp teeth. Best known is the red snapper, an important food fish. Found from the Gulf of Mexico N to LONG ISLAND, it grows up to 3 ft (90 cm) long and weighs up to 35 lb (16 kg).

snare drum: see DRUM.

Snead, Sam(uel Jackson), 1912–, American golfer; b. Hot Springs, Va. He won his first major title, the Professional Golfers' Association (PGA) championship, in 1942 and again in 1949 and 1951. He also captured the Masters three times (1949, 1952, 1954) and the British Open once (1946). A master of long-iron play, "Slamming Sammy" won over 80 PGA tournaments, far more than any other golfer in history.

Snell's law: see REFRACTION.

snipe, shore BIRD of the SANDPIPER family, native to the Old and New World. The common, or Wilson's, snipe (*Capella gallinago*) is a game bird of marshes and meadows. The mud snipe, or woodcock (*Scolopax rusticola*), is a nocturnal woodland bird.

SNOBOL: see PROGRAMMING LANGUAGE.

Snorri Sturluson [snôr'rē stür'lüsôn] or **Sturleson** [–lĕsôn], 1178–1241, Icelandic chieftain and historian, the leading figure in medieval Norse literature. He is the author of the *Prose Edda* (see EDDA) and of the *Heimskringla,* a SAGA of great literary merit that recounts Norwegian history to 1177. One of the most influential people of his day, he became involved in political intrigues and was assassinated.

Snow, C(harles) P(ercy) (Baron Snow of Leicester), 1905–80, English author. A physicist, he also held important positions in the British government. His 11-volume novel series, *Strangers and Brothers* (1940–70), which analyzes power and the relation between science and the community, also delineates the changes in English life in the 20th cent.

snow, precipitation formed by the sublimation of water vapor into solid crystals at temperatures below freezing. A snowflake, like a raindrop (see RAIN), forms around a dust particle. Snowflakes form symmetrical (hexagonal) crystals, sometimes matted together if they fall through air warmer than that of the cloud in which they originated. Apparently, no two snow crystals are alike; they differ from each other in size, lacy structure, and surface markings. Snowfall has been produced artificially by introducing dry-ice pellets into clouds that contain unfrozen water droplets at temperatures below the freezing point. Melted, 10 in. (25 cm) of snow is approximately equal to 1 in. (2.5 cm) of rainfall. See also GLACIER.

snowboarding: see SKIING.

snow plant: see INDIAN PIPE.

Snyder, Gary, 1930–, American poet; b. San Francisco. Associated with the BEAT GENERATION of the 1950s, he lived in Japan from 1956 to 1968. His poetry, influenced by ZEN BUDDHISM and Native American culture, celebrates the peace found in nature and decries its destruction; volumes include *Myths and Texts* (1960) and *Turtle Island* (1974; Pulitzer).

Snyders, Frans, 1579–1657, most celebrated Flemish still-life and animal painter. Influenced by RUBENS, he often collaborated with Rubens and JORDAENS, sometimes painting the animals in their pictures. He is best known for his spirited scenes of the hunt and of animal struggles, e.g., *Stag Hunt* (The Hague) and *Lions Chasing a Deer* (Metropolitan Mus.).

soap, any of a group of organic compounds that are metallic salts of fatty acids. A soap of tallow and wood ashes was used as early as the 1st cent. A.D. by Germanic tribes. In the American colonies it was made from waste fats and lye, which is a strong alkali leached from wood ashes. The resulting chemical reaction, called saponification, remains the basis of soap manufacture today. FATS AND OILS are heated with an alkali, e.g., sodium hydroxide (which gives hard soaps) or potassium hydroxide (which gives soft soaps). Sodium or potassium may be replaced in the alkali by other metals, e.g., aluminum, calcium, or magnesium, to make soaps used in industry as paint driers, ointments, and lubricating greases, and in waterproofing. After the alkali and fats have reacted, salt is added to form a curd of the soap. Glycerol (glycerin), a valuable by-product used as a solvent and sweetener, can then be removed by DISTILLATION. Varying the composition or method of processing affects the lathering, cleansing, and water-softening properties. Soap can be formed as bars, chips, flakes, beads, or powders and may contain perfumes, dyes, germicides, or so-called builders, which assist in rough cleaning. Like modern soapless detergents (usually sulfonated alcohols), soaps cleanse by lowering the surface tension of water, by emulsifying grease, and by absorbing dirt into the foam. Soap is less effective than detergent in hard water because the salts that make the water hard react with the soap to form insoluble curds (e.g., the "ring" left in bathtubs).

soapstone or **steatite,** metamorphic ROCK (see METAMORPHISM) in which the characteristic mineral is TALC. It is gray to green, has a soapy feel, and resists acids and heat. Soft and easily carved, it is a popular sculpture medium. Soapstone is also used to make sinks and laundry tubs. The chief deposits are in the U.S., Canada, and Norway.

soccer, ball and goal game usually played outdoors, also called association football or simply football. Played in more than 140 countries, it is by far the most popular international sport. Two opposing teams of 11 players each compete on a field preferably measuring 120 yd by 75 yd (110 m by 70 m). A goal 8 yd (7.3 m) wide and 8 ft (2.4 m) high, backed with netting, is centered on each end line. The object of the game is to advance an inflated leather ball into the opponent's goal (worth one point). The ball is kicked (often dribbled with short kicks) or advanced by the head or other parts of the body, but only the goalkeeper may use the hands. Rules infractions result in free kicks for the opposing team. The first recorded soccer (football) game took place in England in 217 A.D., and by the 12th cent. the annual Shrove Tuesday contest was a regular event. In the 19th cent. the game was refined to emphasize only the kicking aspects. It gained tremendous popularity after spreading from Britain to the Continent. The highlight of international play is the quadrennial World Cup competition; soccer has been an Olympic sport since 1900. In the U.S., where soccer has been overshadowed by American FOOTBALL, the game was a fast-growing sport in the 1970s and 80s at many levels, from little league to collegiate. Professional American soccer leagues, however, have not succeeded. The North American Soccer League, formed in 1968, folded in 1985.

social contract, agreement by which human beings are said to have abandoned the "state of nature" in order to form the society in which they now live. HOBBES, LOCKE, and J.J. ROUSSEAU each developed differing versions of the social contract, but all agreed that certain freedoms had been surrendered for society's protection and that the government has definite responsibilities to its citizens. Similar ideas were used in the 18th cent. as justification for both the American and the French revolutions. The concept has generally been discarded as a theoretical basis of political life but was revived in the 20th cent. by U.S. philosopher John Rawls.

Social Credit, economic plan in Canada. It was based on the theories of Clifford Hugh Douglas, who held that the basic cause of economic depression was unequal distribution resulting from lack of purchasing power, and proposed issuing "social dividends" to every citizen. This scheme proved unworkable, and other measures were blocked by the federal government and the courts. The Social Credit party has held power in ALBERTA (1935–71) and British Columbia (1952–72, 1975–91).

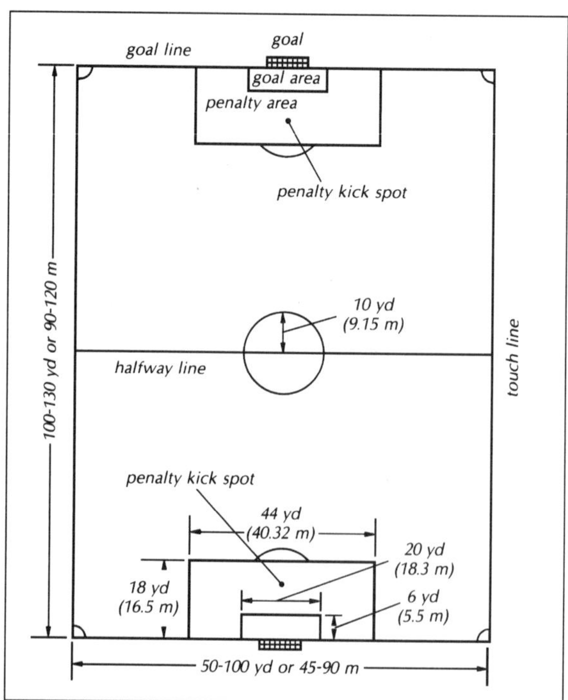

A soccer (association football) field. The opening of the goal is 24 ft (7.3 m) wide and 8 ft (2.44 m) high.

Social Darwinism, belief that societies and individual human beings develop in a manner consistent with the principles of biological EVOLUTION proposed by Charles DARWIN, i.e., that "survival of the fittest" enables only superior people to gain wealth and power. Social Darwinism has been used to justify IMPERIALISM, and although popular in the late 19th cent., it has been widely attacked in modern times.

Social Democratic party (SDP), British political party founded (1981) to offer a centrist alternative to the more extreme positions of the ruling Conservatives on the right and Labour on the left. The SDP began with the defection of 12 Labour members of Parliament who opposed their party's leftward drift. The party joined with the LIBERAL PARTY in 1982 in a statement of common principles and merged with the Liberals in 1988. Some members re-formed the SDP in 1988, but they disbanded in 1990.

Social Gospel, liberal movement within American Protestantism that attempted to apply biblical teachings to problems associated with industrialization. It grew in the late 19th cent. under the leadership of Washington Gladden and Walter Rauschenbusch, who believed in social progress and the essential goodness of human beings. New Deal legislation in the 1930s embodied many Social Gospel ideals.

socialism, general term for the political and economic theory that advocates collective or government ownership and management of the means of production and distribution of goods. It arose in the late 18th and early 19th cent. as a reaction to the hardships caused by CAPITALISM and the INDUSTRIAL REVOLUTION. F.N. BABEUF, the first theorist who may properly be called socialist, propounded the doctrine of class war later seen in MARXISM. Utopian socialists such as Charles FOURIER, Robert OWEN, and the comte de SAINT-SIMON rejected the notion of class struggle. Louis BLANC and P.J. PROUDHON were among other leading socialists. The *Communist Manifesto* (1848), by Karl MARX and Friedrich ENGELS, argued the inevitability of a proletarian-led international revolution. Ferdinand LASSALLE founded (1863) the first workers' party in Germany, and by the 1870s there were socialist parties in most European countries. Doctrinal disputes between gradualists and revolutionists culminated in the split of Russian socialism into BOLSHEVISM AND MENSHEVISM. After the 1917 RUSSIAN REVOLUTION international socialism and COMMUNISM split irrevocably. Present-day socialist parties play an important role in Western European electoral politics. Usually called democratic socialist parties, they have favored a variable economic mix of capitalism and state control. In the THIRD WORLD, socialist programs have stressed land reform and centralized economic planning, often through a one-party state, but since the 1980s there has been a movement toward reduced state control of the economy.

Socialist Labor party, in the U.S., formed in 1877 by New York City socialists. In the 1880s it concentrated unsuccessfully on electoral politics; in the 1890s, led by Daniel De Leon, it shifted its emphasis to militant labor activities. It declined when De Leon's opponents withdrew (1899) to join the less militant Socialist Democratic party.

socialist realism, Soviet artistic and literary doctrine prescribing the optimistic depiction of socialist society in conventionally realistic terms. Proclaimed by the Union of Soviet Writers as compulsory practice in 1932, the doctrine was less stringently enforced after STALIN's death, although it remained official policy in the USSR until the country's demise. It has remained a dominant, state-sponsored mode of art and literature in China.

Socialist Revolutionary party, Russian populist party founded 1901. It called for an end to autocracy, a classless society, distribution of land to peasants, and self-determination of minorities. The party carried out political assassinations. It participated in the 1917 RUSSIAN REVOLUTION but by 1922 was suppressed by the Soviet government.

social security, public program providing for economic security and welfare. While programs vary from one country to another, all provide some cash payment to defray income loss or deficiency due to sickness, old age, or unemployment. (In socialist nations the insured person makes no direct contribution toward the coverage.) Germany adopted a social security program in the 1880s and Great Britain's program, begun in 1911, was expanded after World War II. The U.S. Social Security Act (1935) established unemployment compensation, retirement insurance, and federal assistance for state welfare programs. The HEALTH INSURANCE plans Medicare and Medicaid and supplemental security income (SSI) for the disabled were added later. Administered principally by the Social Security Administration of the Dept. of HEALTH AND HUMAN SERVICES, the U.S. system is threatened by economic factors and by changing patterns in DEMOGRAPHY—most significantly, the increasing number of older persons receiving benefits as compared to those persons working and contributing to the program through taxes. Most developed countries face similar problems in funding their social security systems.

social welfare or **public charity,** organized assistance to the needy. England's poor law (1601) was the first extensive state effort to aid the needy; it required work of the able-bodied and provided apprenticeships for children. Modern SOCIAL SECURITY programs for broad groups of people, not just the poor, began in Germany in the 1880s with health insurance for workers; they were instituted in Britain in 1911 and the U.S. in 1935 (see SOCIAL SECURITY). Great Britain and the Scandinavian countries, often termed "welfare states," have wide-ranging social welfare programs, including comprehensive HEALTH INSURANCE providing free or low-cost medical services for all. In the U.S. the term "welfare" is usually limited to the Aid to Families with Dependent Children (AFDC) program, which has its origins in the NEW DEAL. Proposals for changes to or elimination of AFDC have been a fixture of U.S. politics since the late 1960s. Private charities, international relief bodies (e.g., the RED CROSS), and UN agencies (e.g., UNICEF) also provide various social services.

social work, organized efforts to help individuals and families adjust to the community and to adapt the community to their needs. Early charitable activities were aimed at alleviating maladjustments piecemeal. The French sociologist and economist P.G.F. Le Play was the first to apply (1850s) scientific methods to the solution of the problem of poverty. Later in the 1800s, the English investigator Charles Booth developed the social survey method, providing a basis for determining the extent of social maladjustment. In the 1930s, to deal with economic DEPRESSION, the U.S. government joined private, state, and local social work efforts. Modern methods of social work include casework (helping individuals and families with physical, mental, and such social problems as child neglect, alcoholism, drug abuse), group work (e.g., social settlement), and community organization (coordinating community efforts and funding). Social work has been steadily professionalized, and special graduate schools have been established to train social workers.

Society of Friends: see FRIENDS, RELIGIOUS SOCIETY OF.

sociobiology, study of the effect of biological processes on animal and human behavior. Sociobiologists hold that behavior patterns are genetically determined and are governed by the process of natural selection. The theory has contributed to the understanding of certain evolutionary traits in the animal world, such as how the helpfulness of nonreproducing animals in a group is determined in part by the need to insure survival of the group's offspring. It is controversial, however, when applied to human behavior in such areas as aggressiveness, sex differences, mate selection, and parenting behavior. Edward O. WILSON's *Sociobiology* (1975) was instrumental in defining the field.

sociolinguistics, study of language as it affects and is affected by social relations. It encompasses such concerns as bilingualism, lingua franca, and other ways that language use is influenced by contact among people of different language communities. Sociolinguists also examine dialects, accents, and diction as they affect varying social contexts and distinctions, status within a society, and such areas as class, ethnic, and regional differences.

sociology, the scientific study of collective human behavior. The term was coined (1838) by Auguste COMTE, who attempted to identify the unifying principles of society at different stages of human social development. Major contributions to 19th-cent. sociology were made by Karl MARX, who emphasized the economic basis of the organization of society and saw in class struggle the main agent of social progress, and by Herbert SPENCER, who applied Darwinian principles to the study of human society. The founders of modern sociology are Émile DURKHEIM, who pioneered the scientific use of comparative empirical evidence and statistical data, and Max WEBER, who developed historical and theoretical models as a tool of sociological analysis. Theorists in the 20th cent. have focused on conflict (drawing on Marx's work), structural-functionalism (developed by Talcott PARSONS and advanced by Robert K. MERTON), and symbolic interaction (developed by George Herbert Mead and Herbert Blumer).

Socotra, mountainous island (1,383 sq mi/3,582 sq km) of Yemen, at the mouth of the Gulf of ADEN, c.150 mi (250 km) E of the African mainland. The islanders fish, farm, and herd; the main exports are dried fish and pearls. Under British control from 1834, Socotra was a refueling station before being ceded (1967) to Southern Yemen, which merged with Yemen in 1990.

Socrates, 469–399 B.C., Greek philosopher of Athens, generally regarded as one of the wisest people of all time. It is not known who his teachers were, but he seems to have been acquainted with the doctrines of PARMENIDES, HERACLITUS, and ANAXAGORAS. Socrates himself left no writings, and most of our knowledge of him and his teachings comes from the dialogues of his most famous pupil, PLATO, and from the memoirs of XENOPHON. Socrates is described as having neglected his own affairs, instead spending his time discussing virtue, justice, and piety wherever his fellow citizens congregated, seeking wisdom about right conduct so that he might guide the moral and intellectual improvement of Athens. Using a method now known as the Socratic dialogue, or dialectic, he drew forth knowledge from his students by pursuing a series of questions and examining the implications of their answers. Socrates equated virtue with the knowledge of one's true self, holding that no one knowingly does wrong. He looked upon the soul as the seat of both waking consciousness and moral character, and held the universe to be purposively mind-ordered. His criticism of the Sophists and of Athenian political and religious institutions made him many enemies, and his position was burlesqued by ARISTOPHANES. In 399 B.C. Socrates was tried for corrupting the morals of Athenian youth and for religious heresies; it is now believed that his arrest stemmed in particular from his influence on Alcibiades and Critias, who had betrayed Athens. He was convicted and, resisting all efforts to save his life, willingly drank the cup of poison hemlock given him. The trial and death of Socrates are described by Plato in the *Apology, Crito,* and *Phaedo.*

sodium (Na), metallic element, discovered in 1807 by Sir Humphry DAVY; its compounds have been known since antiquity. A silver-white, very reactive ALKALI METAL, it must be stored out of contact with air and water. The metal is used in arc-lamp lighting and as a heat-transfer liquid in nuclear reactors. Widely used compounds include SODIUM CHLORIDE (common salt), SODIUM BICARBONATE (baking soda), SODIUM CARBONATE (soda ash), hydroxide (lye), nitrate, phosphates, and BORAX. SOAP is made with sodium hydroxide. Sodium compounds are widely distributed in rocks, soil, oceans, salt lakes, mineral waters, and salt deposits, and are found in the tissues of plants and animals. Sodium is an essential element of the diet. See ELEMENT (table); PERIODIC TABLE.

sodium bicarbonate or **sodium hydrogen carbonate,** chemical compound ($NaHCO_3$), a white crystalline or granular powder, commonly known as bicarbonate of soda or baking soda. It is soluble in water and very slightly soluble in alcohol. Because it evolves carbon dioxide gas when heated above 50°C (122°F), it is used in baking powder. It is sometimes used medically to correct excess stomach acidity.

sodium carbonate, chemical compound (Na_2CO_3) soluble in water and very slightly soluble in alcohol. Pure sodium carbonate is a white, odorless powder that absorbs moisture from the air and forms a strongly alkaline water solution. One of the most basic industrial chemicals, it is usually produced by the Solvay process. The chief uses of sodium carbonate are in glassmaking and the production of chemicals.

sodium chloride (NaCl), common salt. It is a chemical compound containing equal numbers of positively charged sodium and negatively charged chlorine IONS. The colorless-to-white crystals have no odor but a characteristic taste. When dissolved in water, the ions move about freely and conduct electricity (see ELECTROLYSIS). Salt is essential in the diet of humans and animals, and is a part of blood, sweat, and tears. Salt is widely used for the seasoning, curing, and preserving of foods. Its major use is in the production of CHLORINE, SODIUM, and sodium hydroxide. Salt makes up nearly 80% of the dissolved material in seawater and is also widely distributed in solid deposits. Manufacture and use of salt is one of the oldest chemical industries.

sodium hydroxide: see ALKALI.

Sodom and Gomorrah [gəmŏr'ə], in the BIBLE, two of the Cities of the Plain (the others being Admah, Zeboiim, and Zoar, which was spared) destroyed by fire from heaven because of their unnatural carnal wickedness. They were probably located near the southern end of the Dead Sea and may have been destroyed by an earthquake c.1900 B.C.

Soeharto: see SUHARTO.

Sofia [sōfē'ə], city (1990 est. pop. 1,221,000), capital of Bulgaria, W central Bulgaria, on a high plain surrounded by the Balkan Mts. It is Bulgaria's industrial center, with such manufactures as machinery, metal products, foodstuffs, and textiles. Settled by the Thracians, it was held (1st–14th cent.) by Rome, Byzantium, and the first and second Bulgarian kingdoms. It passed to Turkey in 1382 and to Russia in 1878. After 1879 it was the capital of independent Bulgaria. During World War II the Germans occupied Sofia until 1944, when it fell to Soviet forces. Landmarks include many old churches, mosques, and synagogues, the parliament building, and the former royal palace.

softball, a variant of baseball, played with a larger ball on a smaller field. The ball is about 12 in. (30 cm) in circumference, about 3 in (8 cm) larger than a baseball; the infield is 60 sq ft (5.6 sq m), about 30 sq ft (2.8 sq m) smaller than a baseball infield. Two teams of nine players each compete (until 1946, 10 players). Major differences from baseball are that the ball must be pitched underhand and a regulation game is seven innings. The game, invented in Chicago in 1888, is played by both men's and women's teams in the U.S., with annual sectional and world series championships. An international federation regulates the game.

software: see COMPUTER PROGRAM.

soil, surface layer of earth containing organic matter and capable of supporting vegetation. A few inches to several feet thick, soil consists of fine rock material, HUMUS, air, and water. The arrangement of soil particles—soil structure—together with organic matter (including microorganisms and living roots) determines the soil's capacity to retain gases, water, and plant nutrients. Soil varies with the type of vegetation, climate, and parent rock material. Soil fertility—determined in part by texture, chemical composition, water supply, and temperature—can be maintained or improved by FERTILIZERS or by cultivation practices.

Soka Gakkai [sō'kä gäk'kī] [Value Creation Society], Japan-based lay Buddhist group, founded (1930) by Makiguchi Tsunesaburo. Soka Gakkai seeks to apply the teachings of Nichiren, a 13th-cent. Japanese Buddhist who emphasized the importance of the *Lotus Sutra,* to the modern world and particularly stresses the need for world peace. An evangelistic movement, it flourished in the post-war years and now has members worldwide. In 1964 Soka Gakkai leaders founded the Komeito, or Clean Government, political party in Japan.

Sokolova, Lydia [sukəlu'və], 1896–1974, English ballerina; b. as Hilda Munnings. She joined (1913) DIAGHILEV's Ballets Russes and was the principal character dancer until it disbanded in 1929. She retired to teach and coach in England.

solar cell: see PHOTOVOLTAIC CELL.

solar energy, any form of ENERGY radiated by the SUN, including light, radio waves, and X rays. Solar energy is needed by green plants for the process of PHOTOSYNTHESIS, which is the ultimate source of all food. The energy in fossil fuels (e.g., COAL and PETROLEUM) and other organic fuels (e.g., WOOD) is derived from solar energy. Difficulties with these fuels have led to the invention of devices that directly convert solar energy into usable forms of energy, such as electricity. Solar batteries, which operate on the principle that light falling on photosensitive substances causes a flow of electricity, play an important part in astronautics but are presently too expensive to be in common use on the earth (see PHOTOVOLTAIC CELL). Thermoelectric generators convert the heat generated by solar energy directly into electricity. Heat from the sun is used in air-drying a variety of materials and in producing salt by the evaporation of sea water (see DESALINATION). Experimental solar heating systems can supply heat and hot water for domestic use; heat collected in special plates on the roof of a house is stored in rocks or water held in a large container. Such systems, however, usually require a conventional heater to supplement them. Solar stoves, which focus the sun's heat directly, are employed in regions where there is perennial sunlight.

solar system, the SUN and the family of PLANETS, natural SATELLITES, ASTEROIDS, METEORS, and COMETS that are its captives. The principal members of the sun's retinue are the nine major planets; in order of increasing distance from the sun, they are MERCURY, VENUS, EARTH, MARS, JUPITER, SATURN, URANUS, NEPTUNE, and PLUTO. All the planets orbit the sun in approximately the same plane (that of the ECLIPTIC) and move in the same direction (from west to east). Current theories suggest that the solar system was formed from a NEBULA consisting of a dense nucleus, or protosun, surrounded by a thin shell of gaseous matter extending to the present edges of the solar sytem. Because of gravitational instabilities, the nebula eventually broke up into whirlpools of gas, called protoplanets, within the rotating mass. In time the protoplanets condensed to form the planets.

solar time, time defined by the position of the sun. The observer's **local solar time** is 0 hr (noon) when the center of the sun is on the observer's meridian. The *solar day* is the time it takes for the sun to return to the same meridian in the sky. The length of the solar day varies throughout the year because the earth moves with varying speed in its orbit and because the equatorial plane is inclined to the orbital plane. It is thus more convenient to define time in terms of the **mean solar time,** or average of local solar time; hence every mean solar day is of equal length. The *equation of time* is the difference between the local solar time and the mean solar time at a given location. **Civil time** is mean solar time plus 12 hr; the civil day begins at midnight, whereas the mean solar day begins at noon. **Greenwich mean time** (GMT) is the local civil time at the former site of the Royal Observatory in Greenwich, England, which is located on the PRIME MERIDIAN (0° longitude). **Standard time** is the civil time within one of the 24 time zones into which the earth's surface is divided. Within a zone all locations keep the same time, namely, the mean solar time of the central meridian (except when DAYLIGHT SAVING TIME is in effect).

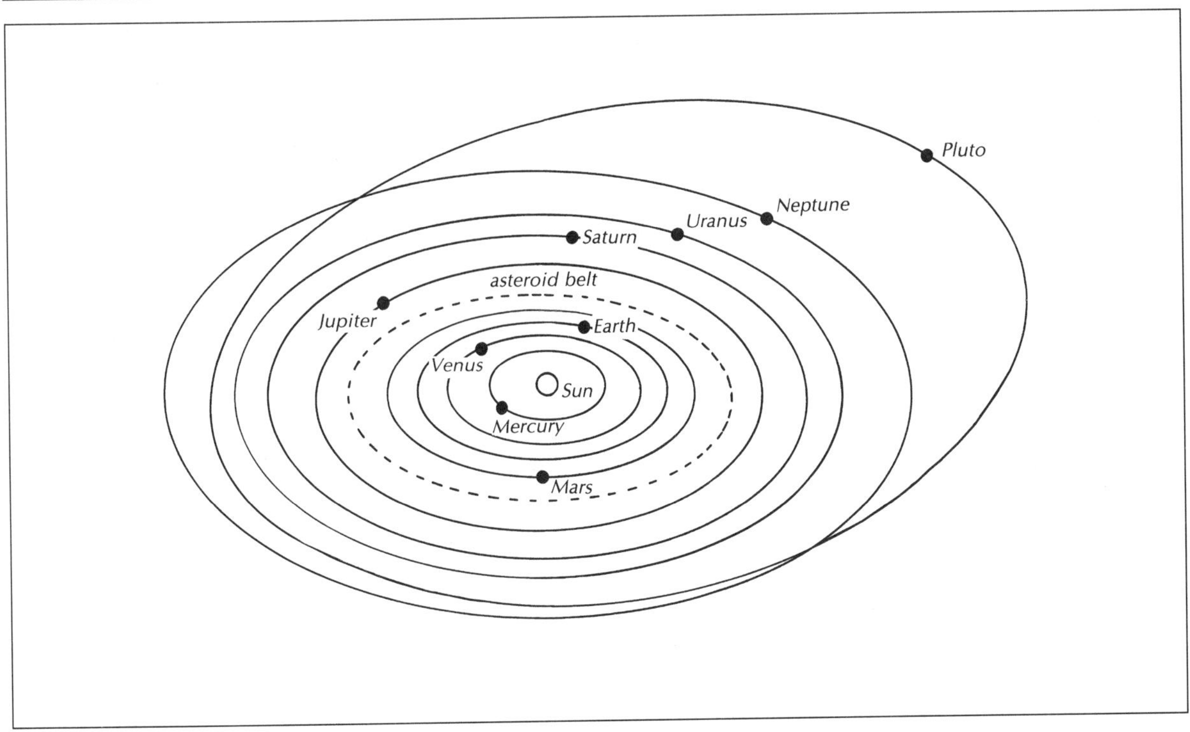

Solar system

Zone times generally differ by a whole number of hours from GMT. See also SIDEREAL TIME.

solar wind, stream of ionized hydrogen and helium that radiates outward from the sun, carrying away about 1 million tons of gas per sec. Near the earth the solar wind normally has a velocity of 450 mi/sec (700 km/sec). The wind is believed to extend to between 100 and 200 ASTRONOMICAL UNITS from the sun. COMET tails always point away from the sun because of the pressure exerted by the solar wind. The interaction of the solar wind with the earth's magnetic field is also responsible in part for such phenomena as the AURORAS and geomagnetic storms.

solder, metal ALLOY used in the molten state as a metallic binder. The type of solder to be used is determined by the metals to be united. Soft solders are commonly composed of lead and tin and have low melting points. Hard solders (i.e., silver solders) have high melting points. When brass is used in the solder or when brass surfaces are to be joined, the process is known as brazing, although the name is sometimes applied also to other hard soldering.

sole: see FLATFISH.

solenoid, device made of a long wire wound many times into a tightly packed cylindrical coil. If current is sent through a solenoid made of insulated wire and having a length much greater than its diameter, a uniform magnetic field will be created inside the solenoid. The magnetic field can be intensified by inserting a ferromagnetic core into the solenoid.

Soleri, Paolo, 1919–, Italian-American architect. His functional, organic style is seen in his designs for self-sufficient desert communities, which he terms arcalogies, notably one at Arcosanti, near Scottsdale, Ariz.

solfeggio, in music, systems of vocal exercises employing a series of syllables originally devised by the Benedictine monk Guido d'Arezzo (c.990–1080) for the purpose of vocalization and for practice in sightsinging. These "solmization" syllables are now commonly known in the form *do, re, mi, fa, sol, la, si* (or *ti*), *do.*

solid: see STATES OF MATTER.

Solidarity, Polish trade union federation formed in September 1980. Led by Lech WALESA, it grew rapidly in size and political power and soon posed a threat to Poland's Communist government by its sponsorship of labor strikes and other forms of public protest. On Dec. 13, 1981, however, the Polish government launched a crackdown by declaring martial law, suspending Solidarity, and imprisoning most of its leaders. Despite these actions, and the formal abolition of the union in 1982, demonstrations in support of Solidarity continued in Poland. In 1989 Solidarity was reinstated, limited free elections were held, and candidates supported by the union won a resounding victory. In 1990 Walesa became president of Poland and resigned his union post. Solidarity has since placed greater emphasis on traditional trade union matters.

solid-state physics, the study of properties exhibited by atoms because of their association and regular, periodic arrangement in CRYSTALS. Besides mechanical and thermal properties, electric conductivity (see CONDUCTION) is one of the most important properties of solids. METALS are highly conductive and offer little resistance to electric currents. Most solid nonmetals are insulators; they offer virtually infinite resistance to electric currents. SEMICONDUCTORS, which possess electrical conductivity that is neither very high nor very low, are used in TRANSISTORS.

solid waste: see WASTE DISPOSAL.

Soliman. For Ottoman sultans thus named, see SULAYMAN.

Solomon, d. 922 B.C., king of the ancient Hebrews, son and successor of DAVID. His mother was BATH-SHEBA. The reign of Solomon was eminently peaceful, marked by foreign alliances, notably with Egypt and with Phoenicia (he was on especially good terms with Hiram of Tyre). He developed trade and commerce. As he grew older, his despotism became worse and finally led to the revolt of JEROBOAM I. Solomon's wisdom is proverbial. He built the first Hebrew temple at Jerusalem. PROVERBS and ECCLESIASTES were ascribed to him, and the SONG OF SOLOMON bears his name.

Solomon Islands, independent Commonwealth nation (1992 est. pop. 360,000), land area c.11,600 sq mi (29,785 sq km), comprising GUADALCANAL and other islands and atolls stretching in a 900-mi (1,450-km) chain across the SW Pacific Ocean E of New Guinea; the extreme northwestern islands in the chain, Bougainville and Buka, are part of PAPUA NEW GUINEA. The capital is Honiara, on Guadalcanal. The mountainous islands are sparsely populated and largely covered with rain forest. Subsistence farming and fishing are mainstays of the economy, with small exports of timber, fish, copra, cocoa, and palm oil. The inhabitants are largely Melanesians; there are Polynesians on some outlying atolls. Over a hundred languages are spoken, and a Melanesian pidgin is the lingua franca. Most Solomon Islanders are Christian.

History. Visited in 1568 by the Spaniard Álvaro de Mendeña de Neira, the Solomons were colonized by Europeans and missionaries in the 18th and 19th cent. Germany took possession of the N Solomons in 1885 but relinquished (1900) all except Buka and Bougainville to Britain, which had created (1893) a protectorate in the S Solomons. During WORLD WAR II the islands were invaded (1942) by Japan and liberated (1943–44) by U.S. forces after heavy fighting. They became self-governing in 1976 and independent in 1978. Support by Solomon Islanders for secessionists on Bougainville has strained relations with Papua New Guinea. Francis Billy Hilly became prime minister in 1993. See PACIFIC OCEAN map.

Solomon R. Guggenheim Museum, N.Y.C.; founded 1939. A major gallery of modern art, it is known for its circular building designed by Frank Lloyd WRIGHT (completed 1959); a 10-story addition was completed in 1992. Its collection includes works by BRANCUSI and KANDINSKY. The museum is part of the Solomon R. Guggenheim Foundation, which also operates the Peggy Guggenheim Collection in Venice, Italy.

Solon [sō'lən], c.639–c.559 B.C., Athenian statesman. Elected leader in 594, he instituted sweeping economic and social reforms, and made important constitutional changes. Although bitterly opposed at first, Solon's reforms became the basis of the Athenian state. He also introduced a more humane law code to replace the code of DRACO.

solstice, either of two points on the ECLIPTIC where the sun's apparent position on the celestial sphere (see ASTRONOMICAL COORDINATE SYSTEMS) reaches the greatest angular distance (about 23½°) above or below the celestial equator. At the time of the summer solstice, about June 22, the sun is directly overhead at the TROPIC OF CANCER; at the time of the winter solstice, about December 22, it is directly overhead at noon at the TROPIC OF CAPRICORN. In the Northern Hemisphere these dates mark the beginnings of summer and winter and the days of the longest and shortest hours of daylight.

Solti, Sir Georg [shôl'tē], 1912–, English conductor; b. Hungary. He made his conducting debut in Budapest in 1933 and subsequently led orchestras in Switzerland, Germany, and France. Solti was music director (1969–91) of the Chicago Symphony Orchestra and principal conductor and artistic director (1979–83) of the London Philharmonic.

solution, in chemistry, homogeneous mixture of two or more substances. The dissolving medium is called the solvent, and the dissolved material is called the solute. In most common solutions, the solvent is a liquid, often water, and the solute may be a solid, gas, or liquid. Syrups are solutions of sugar, a solid, dissolved in water. Household AMMONIA is a solution of ammonia gas in water, and VINEGAR is a solution of acetic acid, a liquid, in water. Some ALLOYS are solutions of one solid in another. A solution is said to be saturated when it contains the maximum amount of solute that can be dissolved. See also COLLOID; COMPOUND; CONCENTRATION; ELECTROLYSIS; SUSPENSION.

Solyman. For Ottoman sultans thus named, see SULAYMAN.

Solzhenitsyn, Aleksandr Isayevich [sôl″zhənēt'sĭn], 1918–, Russian writer. After army service in World War II, he was imprisoned (1945–53) and exiled in Siberia (1953–56). His novel *One Day in the Life of Ivan Denisovich* (1962), based on his labor-camp experiences, was published with KHRUSHCHEV's help, but a 1966 story was his last work published in the USSR. His novels *The First Circle* and *Cancer Ward,* both highly critical studies of life under STALIN, were published abroad in 1968. In 1970 he was awarded the Nobel Prize in literature. *August 1914* (1971), a novel, and *The Gulag Archipelago* (1973–75), a documentary study, were also published abroad. In 1974 Solzhenitsyn was arrested and deported to West Germany. He settled in Switzerland and after 1976 lived in the U.S. Also a critic of Western democracy, he has called for a paternal, autocratic government for Russia that would be rooted in the Orthodox Church and Russian nationalism.

Somalia, country (1992 est. pop. 7,235,000), 246,200 sq mi (637,657 sq km), E Africa, directly south of the Arabian Peninsula across the Gulf of Aden, also bordered by Ethiopia and Kenya (W), Djibouti (NW), and the Indian Ocean (E). MOGADISHU is the capital; other

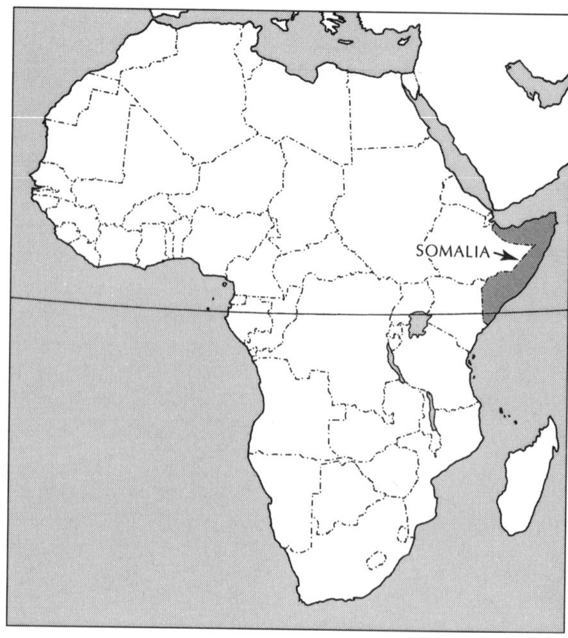

large cities are Harghessa, Berbera, and Kismayu. The country is arid and semidesert, with a barren coastal lowland rising to the great interior plateau (generally c.3,000 ft/910 m high), which stretches to the northern and western highlands. Pastoralism is the dominant mode of life, and herding (both nomadic and sedentary) of camel, sheep, goats, and cattle is the principal occupation. Live animals, hides, skins, and clarified butter (ghee) make up the majority of exports. The major cash crops are bananas, citrus fruits, and sugarcane; subsistence crops include sorghum and corn. Processing of raw materials constitutes the bulk of the small but growing industry. The most valuable mineral resource is uranium; many other minerals are largely unexploited. Petroleum deposits have been found, and a refinery was built in 1979. The Somali, who are the vast majority of the population, are divided into many clans and subclans. There are Italian, Indian, and Pakistani minorities. Islam is the state religion. Somali is the official language, but Arabic, English, and Italian are in wide use.

History. Muslim Arabs and Persians established trading posts along Somalia's coasts from the 7th to 10th cent., and Somali warriors joined Muslim sultanates in their battles with Christian Ethiopia in the 15th and 16th cent. Britain, France and Italy began to dominate the region in the 19th cent. Britain established a protectorate in 1887 and concluded an agreement with France in 1888 defining their Somali possessions. Italy created a small protectorate in 1889, added territory in the south, and in 1925 detached Jubaland from KENYA. Somali-speaking districts of ETHIOPIA were combined with Italian Somaliland in 1936 to form ITALIAN EAST AFRICA. Britain conquered Italian Somaliland in WORLD WAR II, and the former colony, renamed Somalia, gained internal autonomy in 1956 and independence in 1960. The presence of some 350,000 Somalis in neighboring countries stirred demands for a "Greater Somalia," and fighting erupted with Ethiopia in 1964 over the OGADEN region, which Somalia claims. In 1969 a coup led by Maj. Gen. Muhammad Siyad Barre resulted in a socialist state. In 1977 the corrupt and repressive regime broke with the USSR over Soviet aid to Ethiopia and received aid during the 1980s from the U.S. The Somali army invaded the Ogaden region in 1978 but was defeated (1979) by Ethiopian forces; skirmishes continued into the early 1980s. Barre was ousted (1991) by rebels after intense and bloody fighting. The Somali National Movement gained control of the north, the old British Somaliland, and proclaimed it the Somaliland Republic. In Mogadishu and most of the south the United Somali Congress achieved control, but savage warfare erupted between rival subclans. Almost a quarter of the population faced starvation because of the fighting. Troops from the U.S. and other nations entered Somalia in late 1992 to assure distribution of food aid; control of the operation passed to the UN in 1993. A national cease-fire was signed, but no central government was formed. Fighting again erupted (1993) in Mogadishu as the UN unsuccessfully attempted to arrest Gen. Mohammed Farah Aidid, and clan-based fighting increased in 1994 as the U.S. and other nations began withdrawing their troops.

somatotropin: see HUMAN GROWTH HORMONE.

Somerset, Edward Seymour, duke of, 1506?–1552, protector of England; brother of Jane SEYMOUR. He gained custody of his nephew, the young EDWARD VI, after the death (1537) of HENRY VIII, and was named protector. He wielded almost royal authority in effecting Protestant reforms and with Thomas CRANMER introduced (1549) the first Book of Common Prayer. Somerset defeated the Scots at Pinkie (1547), but his failure to halt INCLOSURE caused unrest. After the execution of his brother Thomas SEYMOUR, Somerset was deprived of the protectorate (1549) by John Dudley (later duke of Northumberland) and was beheaded.

Somoza, Anastasio [sōmō'sä], 1896–1956, president of NICARAGUA (1937–47, 1950–56). As head of the national guard, he seized power by a coup (1937) and ruled as dictator for nearly 20 years. He was assassinated. His older son, **Luis Somoza Debayle,** 1922–67, succeeded him as president (1957–63) and somewhat liberalized the regime. His younger brother, **Anastasio Somoza Debayle,** 1925–80, also ruled as dictator and president (1967–72, 1974–79) until his regime was overthrown (1979) by the SANDINISTAS. He fled to Paraguay, where he was assassinated.

sonar, device for the location of submerged objects and for submarine detection and communication at sea. Capable of rotation, it can scan a surrounding area. The device projects subsurface sound waves and, as a HYDROPHONE, listens for returning echoes, determining the range and bearing of submerged targets. Returning signals may be audibly sounded through a loudspeaker and/or visually displayed by a CATHODE-RAY TUBE. Simpler sonar devices are used as depth finders and to locate schools of fish.

sonata, in music, type of instrumental composition that arose in Italy in the 17th cent., at first merely designating an instrumental piece as contrasted to a piece with voice, called a CANTATA. The BAROQUE sonata, later called trio sonata, most commonly featured two melody instruments, usually violins or flutes, with a bass instrument and a keyboard instrument playing the thorough bass (see FIGURED BASS). In the later 18th cent. sonatas for groups of instruments were designated as string quartets or SYMPHONIES, and the term *sonata* was limited to pieces for one keyboard instrument or for one solo instrument (e.g., violin) with keyboard accompaniment. The keyboard sonata, developed by such composers as G.B. Sammartini and featuring one outstanding melodic line with harmony provided by a bass instrument, influenced the classical sonata perfected by HAYDN, MOZART, and BEETHOVEN. The first movement of the classical sonata (and sometimes other movements as well) observes a pattern called **sonata form,** consisting of two parts, a musical statement of several contrasting themes, followed by the development of those themes and a recapitulation of the original statement. This form is employed in string quartets, symphonies, and concertos as well. After the classical era LISZT developed the use of one thematic idea in all movements.

Sondheim, Stephen, 1930–, American composer and lyricist; b. N.Y.C. He wrote lyrics for Leonard BERNSTEIN's *West Side Story* (1957) and Jule Styne's *Gypsy* (1959) and to his own music in such MUSICALS as *Company* (1970), *A Little Night Music* (1973), *Sweeney Todd* (1979), *Sunday in the Park with George* (1984; Pulitzer), and *Into the Woods* (1987). He is noted for his sophisticated, cynical lyrics and his ability to make his songs further plot development.

Songhai or **Songhay,** largest ancient empire of W Africa, in the region that is now MALI. It was founded c.700 by Berbers, and its rulers accepted Islam c.1000. Gao was its capital. Its greatest rulers were Sonni Ali (1464–92), who took TIMBUKTU, the former capital of the MALI empire; and Askia Muhammad I (c.1493–1528), whose death began the empire's decline, accelerated by a Moroccan invasion (1590).

Song of Solomon, Song of Songs, or **Canticles,** book of the OLD TESTAMENT, 22nd in the Authorized Version, traditionally ascribed to King SOLOMON, but possibly as late as the 3d cent. B.C. It is a collection of love poems, generally accepted as an allegory or PARABLE of God's love for Israel.

Song Qingling: see under SOONG, family.

sonic boom, SHOCK WAVE produced by an object moving through the air at supersonic speed, i.e., faster than the speed of sound. An object, such as an airplane, moving through the air generates sound. When the speed of the object exceeds the speed of sound, the object forces the sound ahead of itself faster than the speed at which the sound would ordinarily travel. The piled-up sound takes the form of a violent shock wave propagating behind the object.

sonnet, poem of 14 lines, usually in iambic PENTAMETER, restricted to a definite rhyme scheme. There are two prominent types: the Petrarchan, composed of an octave and a sestet (rhyming *abbaabba cdecde*); and the Shakespearean, consisting of three quatrains and a couplet (rhyming *abab cdcd efef gg*). Sonnets were highly popular in RENAISSANCE Italy, and thereafter in Spain, Portugal, France, and England. German and English romantics (see ROMANTICISM) revived the form, which remains popular. Notable sonneteers include, besides PETRARCH and SHAKESPEARE, DANTE, Edmund SPENSER, Philip SIDNEY, John KEATS, Elizabeth Barrett BROWNING, George MEREDITH, Edna St. Vincent MILLAY, and W.H. AUDEN.

sonography: see ULTRASOUND.

Sons of Liberty, secret organizations formed in the American colonies to protest the STAMP ACT (1765). They were organized by merchants, businessmen, lawyers, journalists, and others most affected by the act.

Sontag, Susan, 1933–, American writer; b. N.Y.C. A brilliant and original thinker, she is known for her analyses of contemporary culture. Her essay collections include *Against Interpretation* (1966), *About Photography* (1977), *Illness as Metaphor* (1978), and *Under the Sign of Saturn* (1980). Sontag has also written short stories and novels, including *The Volcano Lover: A Romance* (1992), and written and directed films.

Soong [so͝ong], Chinese family, prominent in public affairs. **Soong Yao-ju,** or **Charles Jones Soong,** 1866–1918, graduated from Vanderbilt Univ. and was a Methodist missionary in Shanghai. His son **T.V. Soong,** 1894–1971, served in the KUOMINTANG government as finance minister (1928–31, 1932–33), foreign minister (1942–45), and president of the Executive Yuan (1945–47). After 1949 he lived in the U.S. Among his sisters, **Soong Ch'ing-ling** or **Song Qingling,** 1892–1981, married (1914) SUN YAT-SEN. Following his death (1925) she broke with the Kuomintang after its expulsion (1927) of the Communists. She was reconciled (1937) with the Kuomintang but again left in 1946 and after 1949 served as vice chairman of the government of the People's Republic of China. Another sister, **Soong Mei-ling,** c.1897–, married (1927) Chiang Kai-Shek and campaigned to enlist U.S. support for the Nationalist Chinese struggle against the Communists. After the Nationalists lost, she joined (1950) her husband in Taiwan. In 1978 their son, Chiang Ching-Kuo, (see under CHIANG KAI-SHEK) became president of Nationalist China (Taiwan).

Sophia, 1630–1714, electress of Hanover, daughter of FREDERICK THE WINTER KING and granddaughter of JAMES I of England. In 1701 the British Parliament settled on Sophia, a Protestant, and her issue the succession to the British crown. Thus her son GEORGE I became (1714) the first English king of the Hanoverian dynasty.

Sophists, originally, itinerant teachers in 5th-cent. Greece who received fees for their lectures. PROTAGORAS was an early, respected Sophist. Others who followed him, less interested in the pursuit of truth than in the political use of rhetoric, were burlesqued by ARISTOPHANES and criticized by PLATO and ARISTOTLE, judgments that gave the term its present, derogatory meaning.

Sophocles, c.496–406 B.C., Greek tragic poet, younger contemporary of AESCHYLUS and older contemporary of EURIPIDES. A respected public figure, a general and a priest, he won many dramatic prizes from 468 on, composing in all about 123 dramas. An innovator, he added a third actor, increased the size of the CHORUS, abandoned the trilogy for the self-contained tragedy, and introduced scene painting. Seven complete plays and over 1,000 fragments survive. His best-known works are *Antigone* (c.441); *Oedipus Rex* or *Oedipus Tyrannus* (c.429), the apex of Greek dramatic irony; *Electra; Trachiniae; Philoctetes* (409); and *Oedipus at Colonus* (401).

Sophocles' characters are dramatically interesting in that their fates are determined more by their own faults than by the Aeschylean gods; as such they have profoundly influenced Western TRAGEDY.

Sophonias: see ZEPHANIAH.

soprano: see VOICE.

Sorbonne: see PARIS, UNIVERSITY OF.

Sorel, Agnès [sôrĕl], c.1422–1450, mistress (1444–50) of CHARLES VII of France. She was the first officially recognized royal mistress in France and wielded much influence. The financier Jacques CŒUR was rumored to have had her poisoned.

sorghum, tall, coarse annual (*Sorghum vulgare*) of the GRASS family, similar in appearance to CORN and probably indigenous to Africa. Valued for their drought resistance, its varieties include the sweet sorghums, which yield molasses from the cane juice; the broomcorns, which yield a fiber used for brooms; the grass sorghums, used for pasture and hay; and the grain sorghums, used primarily for stock and poultry feed and, in the Old World, for human food.

sorority: see FRATERNITY AND SORORITY.

sorrel, name for several plants, particularly species of dock (see BUCKWHEAT) and OXALIS.

Soto, Hernando de: see DE SOTO, HERNANDO.

Soufrière, volcano, 4,048 ft (1,234 m) high, on the island of St. Vincent, West Indies. Its great eruption of 1902 killed more than 1,000 people and devastated a third of the island.

soul, the vital, immaterial life principle, generally conceived as existing within human beings and sometimes within all living things, inanimate objects, and the universe as a whole. In more primitive religions (forms of ANIMISM and SPIRITISM), the soul is thought to control both motor and mental processes; death, the cessation of these processes, is thus viewed as caused by the departure of the soul. PANTHEISM denies the individuation of human souls, and MATERIALISM declares the soul nonexistent. A widespread concept in religion is that of immortality, which usually postulates the existence of a soul that lives apart from the body after death. Dualistic concepts posit a God-given soul distinct from, and antagonistic to, an inferior, earth-bound body. For many Western philosophers the term *soul* is indefinable. Others consider *soul* synonymous with *mind.*

sound, pressure WAVES that propagate through air or other media. Sounds are generally audible to the human ear if their frequency lies between 20 and 20,000 vibrations per second. Sound waves with frequencies below the audible range are called subsonic, and those with frequencies higher than the audible range are called ultrasonic (see ULTRASONICS). When a body, such as a violin string, vibrates, or moves back and forth, its movement in one direction pushes the molecules of the air before it, crowding them together. When it moves back again past its original position and on to the other side, it leaves behind it a nearly empty space. Alternately the body thus causes in a given space a crowding together of the air molecules (a condensation) and a thinning out of the molecules (a rarefaction). The condensation and rarefaction make up a sound wave; such a wave is called longitudinal, or compressional, because the vibratory motion is forward and backward along the direction that the wave is following. Because such a wave consists of a disturbance of particles of a material medium, sound waves cannot travel through a vacuum. The velocity of sound in air at 32°F (0°C) is 1,089 ft/sec (331.9 m/sec), but at 68°F (20°C) it is increased to about 1,130 ft/sec (344.4 m/sec). Sound travels more slowly in gases than in liquids, and more slowly in liquids than in solids. The pitch of a sound depends upon the frequency of vibration; the higher the frequency, the higher the pitch. Loudness, or intensity of sound, is measured in units called DECIBELS. See also ACOUSTICS; DOPPLER EFFECT; ECHO; INTERFERENCE.

sound barrier: see AERODYNAMICS.

sour gum: see BLACK GUM.

Sousa, John Philip [sōō'zə], 1854–1932, American bandmaster and composer; b. Washington, D.C. He improved the instrumentation and quality of band music. From 1880 to 1892 he led the U.S. Marine Band and in 1892 formed his own band and successfully toured the world. He wrote some 100 marches, many immensely popular, e.g., "Semper fidelis" (1888) and "The Stars and Stripes Forever" (1897).

Souter, David Hackett: see SUPREME COURT, UNITED STATES (table 1).

South, the, region of the U.S., variously defined but including at most 14 states—MARYLAND, VIRGINIA, NORTH CAROLINA, SOUTH CAROLINA, GEORGIA, FLORIDA, KENTUCKY, TENNESSEE, ALABAMA, MISSISSIPPI, ARKANSAS, LOUISIANA, OKLAHOMA, and TEXAS. The basic agricultural economy of the Old South, determined by the warm climate and fertile soil, led to the development of twin institutions—the plantation system and SLAVERY—that made the South a section apart. Its doctrine of STATES' RIGHTS brought on secession, the CIVIL WAR, and, ultimately, the death of the Old South during RECONSTRUCTION. After World War II the South experienced profound economic, social, and political changes—including the development of diversified industry, the emergence of a genuine two-party system, and INTEGRATION—that brought the region closer to the rest of the nation.

South Africa, Afrik. *Suid-Afrika,* officially Republic of South Africa, republic (1992 est. pop. 41,688,000), 471,442 sq mi (1,221,037 sq km), S Africa, bordered by the Atlantic Ocean (W), Namibia (NW), Botswana and Zimbabwe (N), Mozambique and Swaziland (NE), and the Indian Ocean (E and S). LESOTHO is an independent enclave in E South Africa. PRETORIA is the administrative capital, CAPE TOWN the legislative capital, and BLOEMFONTEIN the judicial capital. Other major cities include JOHANNESBURG and DURBAN. Under the policy of racial separation called apartheid about 14% of the land was set aside for black South Africans in ten "homelands" (originally called BANTUSTANS). Four such territories (TRANSKEI, BOPHUTHATSWANA, VENDA, and CISKEI) were declared independent, but no other nation recognized them. The homelands were reabsorbed into South Africa under the new constitution. The economy of South Africa—almost entirely white-controlled but with a work force that is largely nonwhite (over 75%)—is highly advanced and diversified. Mining, the foundation of the country's wealth, has been surpassed by industry as the chief economic sector. Manufactures include processed food, beverages (including wine), textiles, clothing, forest products, chemicals, iron and steel, metal products, machinery, and motor vehicles. Gold, the chief mineral extracted, accounts for two thirds of mining revenue. South Africa also ranks as a leading producer of diamonds, chrome, platinum, vanadium, manganese, and fluorspar, and there are large deposits of copper, coal, uranium, antimony, iron ore, and other minerals. Agriculture, stock-raising, forestry, fishing, and tourism are also important. Crops include corn and other grains, vegetables, peanuts, deciduous and citrus fruit, cotton, tobacco, and sugarcane. The population consists of black South Africans (about 74% of the total); whites, mostly Afrikaners (Boers) and those of English descent (14%); persons of mixed descent (9%); and Asians, largely of Indian descent (3%). English and Afrikaans are the official languages, but there are 10 main African languages, including Zulu and Xhosa, and a lingua franca called Fangalo that was developed in the mines. Most South Africans are Christian (Dutch Reformed, independent black Christian, Anglican, Methodist, Roman Catholic, and Lutheran); there are also Hindus, Muslims, traditional Africans, and Jews.

History. Bantu-speaking peoples moved into the region from E central Africa about 1500. The first permanent European settlement, a Dutch EAST INDIA COMPANY station, was set up in 1652. By 1707 there were about 1,780 freeholders of European descent in South Africa, with about 1,100 slaves. The first of a long series of wars broke out (1779) between the Xhosa people and white farmers, known as Boers, who had moved inland. Britain replaced the Dutch at the Cape in 1795 and was awarded the territory by the Congress of VIENNA in 1814. Disturbed by British rule, which accorded legal rights to free blacks and Coloureds and abolished slavery, some 12,000 Boers left the Cape in what is known as the Great TREK (1835–43) into the interior and Natal. Britain annexed Natal (1843), but the Boer republics of Orange Free State and the Transvaal were established (1850s). The discovery of diamonds (1867) and especially of gold (1886) spurred great economic development. Following increasing tension between the non-Afrikaner whites (Uitlanders) and the dominant Afrikaners, the two Boer republics declared war on Britain. The SOUTH AFRICAN WAR (Boer War; 1899–1902) was won by the British, who established

(1910) the Union of South Africa, with dominion status. South Africa joined the Allies in World War I and afterward received a mandate over South West Africa (Namibia). Under Prime Minister J.B.M. HERTZOG (1924–39) South Africa gained final British recognition of independence (1931), prospered economically, and further suppressed nonwhites. J.C. SMUTS brought South Africa into World War II on the Allied side. Through the policy of APARTHEID (complete segregation), white supremacy was strengthened during the regimes of H.F. VERWOERD (1958–66), B.J. Vorster (1966–78), and P.W. BOTHA (1978–89), leaders of the National party, which ruled from 1948 to 1993. F.W. DE KLERK, who became president in 1989, removed the ban on the AFRICAN NATIONAL CONGRESS (ANC) and other antiapartheid parties and released Nelson MANDELA and other political prisoners. All remaining apartheid laws were repealed (1991), and an interim constitution ending white rule was completed in 1993. A multiparty transitional government council was formed, and the first elections open to all races were held in April 1994. The ANC won over 60% of the vote, and Mandela was elected president.

South African War or **Boer War,** 1899–1902, war of the South African Republic (Transvaal) and the Orange Free State against Great Britain. Beginning with the acquisition (1814) of the Cape of Good Hope, the British had gradually increased their territorial possessions in South Africa. The Boers (Dutch) already settled in some of these areas resented the British advance; their hostility was inflamed after the discovery (1886) of gold brought an influx of British prospectors into the Transvaal. The Boers denied these newcomers citizenship and taxed them heavily, despite British protests. The situation was aggravated in 1895 by the Jameson raid (see JAMESON, SIR LEANDER STARR), which was interpreted as a British plot to seize the Transvaal. A military alliance (1896) of the TRANSVAAL and the Orange Free State followed. The British dispatched troops to defend what they considered their commercial rights, and the Boer states declared war (Oct. 12, 1899). The large and well-equipped Boer forces won early victories, capturing Mafeking (now MAFIKENG) and besieging Kimberley and Ladysmith. But the tide turned in 1900 with the landing of heavy British reinforcements. Under the leadership of F.S. Roberts and Lord KITCHENER, the British occupied all the major cities and formally annexed the Boer states; Kitchener remained only for mopping up. The Boers, however, began guerrilla attacks, led by such people as Louis BOTHA and J.C. SMUTS. Kitchener gained victory by interning Boer women and children and by building blockhouses to cut off large areas. His troops then combed the country, section by section. The Treaty of Vereeniging (May 31, 1902) ended hostilities. The Boers accepted the British sovereign in return for a promise of responsible government in the near future; amnesty was granted to all who had not broken the rules of war. Bitterness caused by the war continued to affect political life in South Africa.

South America, fourth largest continent, c.6,880,000 sq mi (17,819,000 sq km), extending c.4,750 mi (7,640 km) north to south and up to 3,300 mi (5,300 km) east to west. It is connected with North America by the Isthmus of Panama. The great chain of the ANDES Mts., running nearly the length of the continent and reaching a high point of 22,835 ft (6,960 m) in Mt. ACONCAGUA (in Argentina), is the dominant landform. Major lowlands include the LLANOS, along the ORINOCO R.; the basin of the AMAZON R., containing the world's largest rain forest; the GRAN CHACO; and the PAMPAS. South America is rich in iron ore, copper, tin, and hydroelectric potential, and has significant oil deposits. The countries of South America are Argentina, Bolivia, Brazil, Chile, Colombia, Ecuador, Guyana, Paraguay, Peru, Suriname, Uruguay, and Venezuela; the French overseas department of French Guiana is also on the continent (see separate articles). The fast-growing population, approaching 300 million in the early 1990s, is becoming increasingly urbanized. Half of it is concentrated in the nation of Brazil, which occupies more than a third of the continental landmass.

South America, indigenous peoples of, aboriginal peoples of South America, from the Isthmus of Panama to Tierra del Fuego. An estimated 30 million people were living there when Europeans arrived. In the Andean region extensive remains show developed cultures at CHAVÍN DE HUÁNTAR and among the PARACAS in Peru. The Mochica, CHIMU, and NAZCA in Peru, the Chibcha and AYMARA of the Andes, and the ARAUCANIANS of Chile had socially complex pre-Columbian cultures (see PRE-COLUMBIAN ART AND ARCHITECTURE), surpassed only by the INCA. Descendants of these peoples live in Ecuador, Peru, Bolivia, NW Argentina, and Chile. QUECHUA, the Inca language, is the most widespread linguistic stock (see NATIVE AMERICAN LANGUAGES). Since the Spanish conquest indigenous peoples have been used as laborers, poorly paid and lacking political representation; these conditions of semiservitude are changing slowly. Some, notably the Inca, play a significant role in the national culture; but many live in small, peripheral groups. A few descendants of the Arawaks and Caribs live in Venezuela, the Guianas, and N Brazil. The GUARANÍ in Brazil are few and scattered, but in Paraguay their language is widely spoken and they form a significant element. Among tropical forest groups are the JÍVARO of Ecuador. The Colorados of W Ecuador and the Puelches and Tehuelches, hunters of Patagonia, are virtually extinct. A dwindling number of Fuegians, so called for their campsites at Tierra del Fuego, live by hunting and fishing. In general the indigenous peoples of South America continue to be assimilated into white-dominated national cultures as their traditional ways of life and homelands are encroached on by population growth and industrial development.

Southampton, Henry Wriothesley, 3d **earl of,** 1573–1624, English nobleman and patron of letters. Best known as a patron of SHAKESPEARE, some thought the sonnets were dedicated to him. He took part in the rebellion (1601) of the earl of Essex and was sentenced to life imprisonment. JAMES I restored him to favor and he became (1619) a privy councilor. He died of fever while leading an expedition against the Spanish in the Netherlands.

South Australia, state (1992 est. pop. 1,458,000), 380,070 sq mi (984,381 sq km), S central Australia. Most people live in metropolitan ADELAIDE, the capital. Grains, meat, and wine grapes are important agricultural products, with farming largely confined to the irrigated MURRAY R. valley. Much of the land is desert and other areas unsuitable for agriculture. Iron ore, mined at Whyalla, is the chief mineral. Metals, vehicles, and electrical equipment are among the manufactures. South Australia was settled in 1836 as a free (i.e., nonpenal) colony. It became a federated state of Australia in 1901 and transferred its northern areas, now known as the NORTHERN TERRITORY, to the federal government in 1911.

South Bend, city (1990 pop. 105,511), seat of St. Joseph co., N Ind., on the St. Joseph R.; inc. as a city 1865. An industrial city in a farming region, it produces paint, machinery, plastics, and other manufactures. The Studebaker corporation was founded there in 1852. The city was settled c.1820 as a fur-trading post. The Univ. of Notre Dame is nearby.

South Carolina, state of the SE U.S.; bordered by North Carolina (N), the Atlantic Ocean (E), and Georgia (SW).

Area, 31,055 sq mi (80,432 sq km). *Pop.* (1990) 3,486,703, an 11.8% increase over 1980 pop. *Capital,* Columbia. *Statehood,* May 23, 1788 (8th of original 13 states to ratify the Constitution). *Highest pt.,* Sassafras Mt., 3,560 ft (1,086 m); *lowest pt.,* sea level. *Nickname,* Palmetto State. *Mottos, Dum Spiro Spero* [While I Breathe, I Hope] and *Animis Opibusque Parati* [Prepared in Mind and Resources]. *State bird,* Carolina wren. *State flower,* Carolina jessamine. *State tree,* palmetto. *Abbr.,* S.C.; SC.

Land and People. The partly marshy coast gives way to a plain, separated from the rolling hills of the Piedmont plateau by the FALL LINE. The BLUE RIDGE Mts. are in the extreme northwest. The coastal climate is humid and subtropical; inland temperatures become cooler as the altitude increases. Almost 55% of the population lives in urban areas, principally in COLUMBIA, the largest city, the port city of CHARLESTON, and GREENVILLE. In 1990 the state was 69% white and 30% African American.

Economy. The major agricultural products are soybeans, tobacco, cattle, eggs, corn, peaches, and cotton (which formerly dominated the entire economy). The 12.2 million acres (5 million hectares) of woods support a valuable forestry industry. Manufacturing—the sector that employs the highest percentage of South Carolinians—is heavily based on the state's primary commodities. Textiles, chemicals, nonelectrical machinery, apparel, and paper and pulp are the most important products. Commercial fishing is important offshore. Tourism is now a leading industry, with many visitors attracted to the SEA ISLANDS, Myrtle Beach, and Charleston.

Government. The constitution (adopted 1895) provides for a governor elected to a four-year term. The general assembly consists of a senate whose 46 members serve four-year terms and a house of 124 members elected for two years. South Carolina is represented in the U.S. Congress by two senators and six representatives and has eight electoral votes.

History. When explorers for Spain and France penetrated the area during the 16th cent., the principal Native American peoples inhabiting the region were the CHEROKEE, Catawba, and Yamasee. England subsequently claimed the region and sent (1670) the first Europeans to establish a permanent settlement at Albemarle Point (near present-day Charleston). The cultivation of rice and indigo on large plantations using slave labor was the basis of a prosperous economy. In 1776 South Carolina became one of the 13 colonies to declare its independence from Great Britain. After the American Revolution, cotton began to dominate the economy. South Carolina was already a prominent proponent of STATES' RIGHTS when it became the first state to secede from the Union in 1860. The firing on FORT SUMTER by Confederate troops (April 12, 1861) precipitated the CIVIL WAR. After the RECONSTRUCTION era the vast majority of African Americans lost the right to vote, and in 1895 segregationist "Jim Crow" laws were enacted. It was not until 1947 that African Americans were permitted to vote in Democratic primaries and not until 1970 that they were elected to the state legislature. Cotton farming declined during the 1920s because of destruction of crops by the boll weevil and erosion of the land, and industry has since dominated the economy.

South China Sea, western arm of the Pacific Ocean, c.1,000,000 sq mi (2,590,000 sq km), bordering S China, Vietnam, Malaysia, the Philippines, and Taiwan. It covers the shallow Sunda Platform (less than 200 ft/61 m deep) in the southwest and depths of up to c.18,000 ft (5,490 m) in the northeast. The Gulfs of Tonkin (N) and Siam (S) are its chief embayments. Many islands dot the sea, which is subject to violent typhoons.

South Dakota, state in N central U.S.; bordered by North Dakota (N), Minnesota and Iowa (E), Nebraska (S), and Wyoming and Montana (W).

Area, 77,047 sq mi (199,552 sq km). *Pop.* (1990) 696,004, a 0.8% increase over 1980 pop. *Capital,* Pierre. *Statehood,* Nov. 2, 1889 (40th state). *Highest pt.,* Harney Peak, 7,242 ft (2,209 m); *lowest pt.,* Big Stone Lake, 962 ft (293 m). *Nickname,* Coyote State. *Motto,* Under God the People Rule. *State bird,* ring-necked pheasant. *State flower,* pasque flower. *State tree,* Black Hills spruce. *Abbr.,* S.D.; SD.

Land and People. The MISSOURI R. cuts a wide path southward through the center of the state, dividing it into two regions. The

east consists of broad prairies of fertile chernozem soils. The rough, high terrain of the west includes the mineral-rich BLACK HILLS and the Badlands, an area of startling, eroded sand-and-clay formations. The usually dry climate is marked by hot summer days and winter blizzards. The population is evenly divided between rural and urban areas. The leading cities, in order of size, are SIOUX FALLS, Rapid City, and Aberdeen. In 1990 over 91% of the population was white and over 7% were Native Americans.

Economy. Primary industries, including agriculture, are very important. The arid west is the site of many cattle and sheep ranches. Principal crops, mostly from irrigated land in the east, include corn, oats, wheat, sunflowers, soybeans, and sorghum. The largest U.S. gold mine is in the Black Hills. The leading manufactures are processed foods, nonelectrical machinery, electrical and electronic equipment, and lumber. Both service and tourist sectors have been growing rapidly. Mount Rushmore, as well as Badlands and Wind Cave national parks (see NATIONAL PARKS, table), and gambling (legalized in 1989) draw many visitors to the state.

Government. The constitution of 1889 provides for a governor elected to a four-year term. The legislature consists of 35 senators and 70 representatives who serve for two years. South Dakota sends two senators and one representative to the U.S. Congress and has three electoral votes.

History. When the region was explored (1742–43) by the sons of the Pierre Galtier, sieur de la VÉRENDRYE, it was inhabited by the sedentary Arikara and nomadic SIOUX, who lived by hunting the abundant buffalo. The U.S. acquired (1803) the area as part of the LOUISIANA PURCHASE. Although fur-traders were subsequently active, little settlement took place until Gen. George CUSTER confirmed (1874) that there was gold in the Black Hills. A huge influx of prospectors occurred. The Sioux, who had been granted the land in 1868 and refused to sell it, were gradually and brutally subdued, infamously in the massacre at WOUNDED KNEE (1890). The arrival of railroads stimulated both ranching and farming, despite recurrent droughts. South Dakota was a center (c.1900) of the POPULIST party. Four dams in the Missouri basin were constructed after World War II to control flood waters. Many Indians on South Dakota's reservations were leaders of the activist Native American movement in the 1970s and early 80s. During the 1980s the state became a center of U.S. credit card operations, as service, finance, and trade industries assumed added importance in its economy.

Southeast Asia, region (1990 est. pop. 442,500,000), c.1,740,000 sq mi (4,506,600 sq km). As usually defined, it includes BRUNEI, CAMBODIA, INDONESIA, LAOS, MALAYSIA, MYANMAR, the PHILIPPINES, SINGAPORE, THAILAND, and VIETNAM. A tropical rainy climate with seasonal monsoon winds predominates over most of the area. The chief crop is rice. Population is unevenly distributed, with very high densities in many lowland areas, and there is great diversity of culture, history, ethnic composition, language, and religion. Southeast Asia was once the site of several great Eastern civilizations, notably that of the KHMER EMPIRE, in what is now Cambodia and Laos. In the 16th cent. Europeans began the conquest of the entire area, with the exception of Thailand (Siam). Southeast Asia was the scene of heavy fighting during WORLD WAR II. After the war most of the countries achieved independence.

Southeast Asian languages, family of languages, sometimes called Austroasiatic, spoken in SE Asia. According to one school of thought, it has three subfamilies: the MON-KHMER LANGUAGES, the MUNDA LANGUAGES, and the Annamese-Muong subfamily. There is considerable evidence, but no definite proof, that all these groups are derived from a single ancestor. See LANGUAGE (table).

Southeast Asia Treaty Organization (SEATO), formed (1954) by Australia, France, Great Britain, New Zealand, Pakistan, the Philippines, Thailand, and the U.S. in response to the French defeat in Indochina. Designed to oppose Communist advances in that area, SEATO lacked substantial support and was dissolved in 1977.

Southern Christian Leadership Conference (SCLC), civil-rights organization founded in 1957 by Martin Luther KING, Jr., and headed by him until his assassination in 1968. Composed largely of African-American clergymen from the South, it advocated nonviolent passive resistance as the means of securing equality for African Americans. It sponsored the massive march on Washington in 1963. Ralph Abernathy headed (1968–77) the SCLC after King's death, but its influence has declined.

southern lights: see AURORA.

Southey, Robert, 1774–1843, English writer. A poet, historian, biographer, and translator, he became poet laureate in 1813. He is remembered for his friendships with COLERIDGE and WORDSWORTH; his epic poem *A Vision of Judgment* (1821); and such short poems as "The Battle of Blenheim."

South India, Church of, merger of six major Protestant denominations in India. It was formed (1947) from Anglican, Methodist, Presbyterian, Reformed, Congregational, and Lutheran bodies. The union, especially in its reconciliation of the Anglican view of apostolic succession with the views of the other groups, is cited as a landmark in the ECUMENICAL MOVEMENT.

South Pole, southern end of the earth's axis, lat. 90°S and long. 0°, distinguished from the south MAGNETIC POLE. It was first reached by Roald AMUNDSEN in 1911.

South Sea Bubble, popular name in England for speculation in the South Sea Co. formed (1711) by Robert Harley. The company assumed the national debt in return for an annual payment by the government plus a monopoly of British trade with the islands of the South Seas and South America. Fraudulent schemes resulted and the bubble burst (1720). Robert WALPOLE was made first lord of the treasury and chancellor of the exchequer and moved to restore the company's credit.

Southwestern Indians: see NORTH AMERICA, INDIGENOUS PEOPLES OF.

Soutine, Chaïm, 1894–1943, French expressionist painter; b. Lithuania. In 1913 he joined the bohemian society of the SCHOOL OF PARIS. His turbulent, visceral works often depict human corrosion and depravity. Characteristic is his *Page Boy at Maxim's* (Albright-Knox Gall., Buffalo).

Sovern, Michael Ira, 1931–, American lawyer and educator, president of Columbia Univ. (1980–93); b. N.Y.C. He graduated from the Columbia Univ. Law School in 1955 and after 1957 he was on its faculty. Dean of the law school from 1970 to 1979, he was named president of Columbia in 1980.

soviet [Rus., = council], primary unit in the political organization of the Soviet Union. The first soviets were revolutionary committees organized by socialists among striking workers during the 1905 RUSSIAN REVOLUTION. When the 1917 Revolution broke out, workers', peasants', and soldiers' soviets were formed throughout Russia. Their central executive committees included adherents of BOLSHEVISM AND MENSHEVISM, and members of the SOCIALIST REVOLUTIONARY PARTY. When the Bolsheviks under V.I. LENIN took control of the soviets in Petrograd and other cities, their success was assured. Soviets (1918–20) in Bavaria, Hungary (see KUN, BÉLA), and the Baltic republics, however, were short-lived. The soviets, elected by universal suffrage, became the basic political unit in the USSR, forming a hierarchy culminating in the Supreme Soviet. In reality, they were dominated by the Communist party and the POLITBURO. In Russia the soviets survived the disintegration (1991) of the USSR, but in 1993 YELTSIN called for them to dissolve and reorganize as smaller *dumas* [assemblies]. Although some resisted, many complied.

Soviet Far East: see RUSSIAN FAR EAST.

Soweto, collective name for a group of townships inhabited by Africans, located 10 mi (16 km) SW of JOHANNESBURG, South Africa. In 1976 Soweto was the scene of severe violence that began as a African student protest against the use of the Afrikaans language in schools. The rioting spread to other black urban centers, and more than 600 people were killed when the army quashed the riots.

soybean, soya bean, or **soy pea,** plant (*Glycine max*) of the PULSE family, native to tropical and warm temperate regions of E Asia, where it has been a principal crop for at least 5,000 years. There are over 2,500 varieties in cultivation, producing high-PROTEIN beans of many sizes, shapes, and colors. Soybeans are used in many forms, e.g., oil, soybean meal, soy sauce, soy milk, and bean curd, and as a COFFEE substitute. Soybean oil is also valuable for its use in the manufacture of other products, e.g., glycerin, soaps, and plastics. The green crop is used for forage and hay.

Soyer, three brothers, American painters; b. Russia; emigrated to the U.S. in 1912. **Raphael Soyer,** 1899–1987, and **Moses Soyer,** 1899–1974, twins. They used New York City residents as their main subjects. Raphael's subdued, realistic style expresses an intimate sympathy with people, as in *Office Workers* (Whitney Mus., N.Y.C.). Moses' figures are usually in higher-keyed colors or sharper black-and-white contrasts, as in *Old Worker* (Phillips Coll., Wash., D.C.). **Isaac Soyer,** 1907–81, also specialized in scenes of everyday life, e.g., *Employment Agency* (Whitney Mus., N.Y.C.).

Soyinka, Wole, 1934–, Nigerian playwright, poet, and novelist; b. Akinwande Oluwole Soyinka. Written in English, his works fuse Western and YORUBA traditions. His play *The Invention* (1955) brought him notice in London. Other works include the plays *A Dance of the Forests* (1962) and *A Play of Giants* (1984); the novel *The Interpreters* (1965); and the autobiography *Aké: Years of Childhood* (1982). A champion of Nigerian democracy, Soyinka has been jailed and exiled at various times. In 1986 he was awarded the Nobel Prize for literature.

Soyuz: see SPACE EXPLORATION, table.

Spaak, Paul Henri, 1899–1972, Belgian statesman and Socialist leader. He was Belgium's foreign minister almost continuously from 1938 to 1966, premier (1938–39, 1946, 1947–49), first president of the UN General Assembly (1946), chairman of the Council for Economic Recovery (1948–49), secretary general of NATO

MANNED SPACE PROGRAMS

Program	*Country*	*Years of Launchings*	*Number of Crew*	*Missions and Major Accomplishments*
Apollo: Command and Service Modules	U.S.	1968–73	3	First manned flight to moon (Frank Borman, James Lovell, and William Anders, *Apollo 8*; Dec. 21–27, 1968); used to take Lunar Excursion Module to lunar orbit (*Apollos 10–17; 1969–72*); ferried astronauts to *Skylab*.
Apollo: Lunar Excursion Module (LEM)	U.S.	1969–72	2	First manned lunar landing (Neil Armstrong and Buzz Aldrin in *Apollo 11*, July 20, 1969); five other successful manned lunar landings (*Apollos 12* and *14–17*; 1969–72).
Apollo: Lunar Rover	U.S.	1971–72	2	Motorized lunar surface rover used on *Apollos 15-17*.
Apollo-Soyuz Test Project (ASTP)	U.S., USSR	1975	3 (Apollo) 2 (Soyuz)	First international docking in space (Thomas Stafford, Deke Slayton, and Vance Brand in *Apollo 18*; Aleksei Leonov and Valery Kubasov in *Soyuz 19* ; July 16–18, 1975).
Gemini	U.S.	1965–66	2	First U.S. extravehicular activity (Edward White in *Gemini 4*; June 3,1965); first close rendezvous of two spacecraft (Walter Schirra and Thomas Stafford in *Gemini 6* with *Gemini 7*; Dec. 15, 1965); first manned docking of two spacecraft (Neil Armstrong and David Scott in *Gemini 8* with an Agena rocket stage; Mar. 16, 1966).
Mercury	U.S.	1961–63	1	First U.S. manned (suborbital) flight (Alan Shepard, *Mercury-Redstone 3* or *Liberty Bell 7*; May 5, 1961); first U.S. manned orbital flight (John Glenn, *Mercury-Atlas 6* or *Friendship 7*; Feb. 20, 1962).
Mir	USSR/Russia	1986	2+	Earth-orbit space station; enlarged using Kvant science modules. Space endurance record of nearly 366 days (Vladimir Titov and Musa Maranov, Dec. 21, 1987–Dec. 21, 1988).
Salyut	USSR	1971–86	2+	Earth-orbit space stations (seven launched). Mir is improved version.
Skylab	U.S.	1973–74	3	Earth-orbit space station; three 3-person crews visited for 28, 59, and 84 days, the last a U.S. space-endurance record.
Soyuz	USSR	1967–81	1,2, or 3	First extravehicular transfer of crew members from one spacecraft to another (Yevgeny Khrunov and Aleksei Yeliseyev from *Soyuz 5* to *Soyuz 4*; Jan. 16, 1969); ferried cosmonauts to Salyut.
Soyuz T	USSR	1979–86	2 or 3	Improved version of Soyuz; ferried cosmonauts to Salyut.
Soyuz TM	USSR/Russia	1987–	2 or 3	Improved version of Soyuz T; used to ferry cosmonauts to Mir.
Spacelab	European Space Agency		2 payload specialists	Orbital workshop (with open pallets for scientific instruments) to be carried into space by space shuttle.
Space Shuttle	U.S.	1981–	2–7	First reusable space vehicle (see article).
Voskhod	USSR	1964–65	2 or 3	First extravehicular activity (Aleksei Leonov in *Voskhod 2*; Mar. 18, 1965).
Vostok	USSR	1961–63	1	First manned spaceflight (Yuri Gargarin in *Vostok 1*; Apr. 12, 1961); first simultaneous spaceflights (Andrian Nikolayev in *Vostok 3* and Pavel Popovich in *Vostok 4*; Aug. 1962); first woman in space (Valentina Tereshkova in *Vostok 6*; June 16–19, 1963).

(1957–61), and a founder of the Common Market (see EUROPEAN UNION).

space exploration, the investigation of physical conditions in space and on stars, planets, and natural satellites through the use of artificial SATELLITES, SPACE PROBES, and manned spacecraft. Although studies from earth using optical and radio TELESCOPES had accumulated much data on the nature of celestial bodies, it was not until after World War II that the development of powerful ROCKETS made direct space exploration a technological possibility. Manned spaceflight progressed from the simple to the complex, starting with suborbital and orbital flights by a single ASTRONAUT or cosmonaut (Mercury and Vostok); subsequent highlights include the launching of several crew members in a single capsule (beginning with Gemini and Voskhod), rendezvous and docking of two spacecraft (beginning with Gemini and performed internationally in the *Apollo-Soyuz Test Program*), lunar orbit and landing (Apollo), the launching of space stations (Salyut, Skylab, and Mir), and the launching of a reusable space vehicle, the SPACE SHUTTLE. In 1992 the U.S. and Russia agreed to cooperate on space exploration projects.

Spacelab: see SPACE EXPLORATION, table.

space law, principles of law governing the exploration and use of outer space. The 1967 Outer Space Treaty, signed by most nations, states that INTERNATIONAL LAW applies to outer space and that while

SPACE PROBE PROGRAMS

Program	*Country*	*Years of Launchings*	*Missions and Major Accomplishments*
Galileo	U.S.	1989	Orbiter/probe mission to Jupiter; returned images of Antarctica (1991), first close photographs of asteroids (Gaspra, 1991; Ida, 1993).
Giotto	European Space Agency	1985	Flyby mission to Halley's comet. (Japan and the USSR conducted similar missions.)
Helios	U.S.; West Germany	1974, 1976	Two probes passed within 30 million mi (48 million km) of sun; studied solar wind and surface, interplanetary magnetic field, and cosmic rays.
Luna	USSR	1959, 1963–66, 1968–76	First probes to enter solar orbit, impact the moon, and photograph far side of moon (*Lunas 1, 2,* and *3;* all 1959); first probes to achieve soft lunar landing and lunar orbit (*Lunas 9* and *10;* both 1966); first automated lunar-soil sample return and lunar-surface rover (*Lunas 16* and *17;* both 1970).
Lunar Orbiter	U.S.	1966–67	Five spacecraft inserted into lunar orbit photographed 95% of lunar surface, focusing particularly on potential Apollo landing sites.
Magellan	U.S.	1989	Radar map of Venus's surface (1990–92); measurements of Venus's gravity (1993–).
Mariner	U.S.	1962, 1964, 1967, 1969, 1971, 1973	First successful flybys of Venus (*Mariner 2;* 1962) and Mars (*Mariner 4;* 1964); first probe (*Mariner 9;* 1971) to orbit another planet (Mars); first flyby of Mercury and first dual planet probe (*Mariner 10;* 1973).
Mars	USSR	1960, 1962, 1969, 1971, 1973	First probe to enter Martian atmosphere (*Mars 6;* 1973).
Pioneer	U.S.	1958–60, 1965–69, 1972–73, 1978	First deep-space probe (*Pioneer 5;* 1960); first successful flybys of Jupiter (*Pioneer 10;* 1973) and Saturn (*Pioneer 11;* 1979); first radar probe of cloud-covered surface of Venus (*Pioneer-Venus 1;* 1978). Early missions (*Pioneers 1* to *4;* 1958–59) were unsuccessful lunar-orbit or -flyby attempts.
Ranger	U.S.	1961–62, 1964–65	First probe to return thousands of high-resolution pictures before lunar impact (*Ranger 7;* 1964).
Surveyor	U.S.	1966–68	First probe to return thousands of pictures from lunar surface (*Surveyor 1;* 1966); first chemical analysis of lunar soil (*Surveyor 5;* 1967).
Ulysses	U.S., European Space Agency	1990	Study of sun from polar orbit planned in 1994 and 1995. Examined Jupiter's magnetic field in flyby (Feb. 1992).
Venera	USSR	1961–62, 1965, 1967, 1969–70, 1972, 1975, 1978, 1981	First successful Venus atmospheric entry (*Venera 4,* 1967); first probe to survive to Venusian surface (*Venera 7,* 1970); first probe to return television pictures from Venusian surface (*Venera 9,* 1975).
Viking	U.S.	1975	First successful Mars landers (*Vikings 1* and *2,* 1976), which conducted search-for-life experiments and returned first television pictures from Martian surface; surface also photographed extensively by orbiters.
Voyager	U.S.	1977	Jupiter, and Saturn, Uranus, and Neptune flybys discovered Jupiter's rings, volcanoes on Jovian Satellite Io, new satellites of Jupiter, Saturn, Uranus, and Neptune, and complex structure of Saturn's ring system (*Voyagers 1* and *2,* 1981–89).
Zond	USSR	1964–65, 1967–70	First probe to achieve circumlunar flyby and return to earth (*Zond 5,* 1968).

all states may freely explore and use outer space, territorial claims in space are prohibited. Other treaties dealing with rescue and return of astronauts, liability for damage caused by space objects, and registration of space objects became effective, respectively, in 1968, 1972, and 1976. A treaty on the potential use of the moon's resources, drafted by the UN in 1979, has been signed by several nations; the U.S. has not yet signed it.

space medicine, study of the medical and biological effects of space travel on living organisms. The principal aim is to discover how well and for how long humans can withstand conditions encountered in space and to study their ability to readapt to the earth's environment after travel in space. Medically significant aspects of space travel include WEIGHTLESSNESS, inertial forces experienced during liftoff, radiation exposure, the absence of day-night cycle (see BIORHYTHM), and heat produced within the spacecraft. Participants in SPACE EXPLORATION initially suffered from symptoms such as nausea, sensory disorientation, and poor muscular coordination. Longer flights, having longer periods of weightlessness, have shown that physical adaptations specifically developed in gravity-bound earth organisms (e.g., weight-bearing muscles, gravity-sensing portions of the inner ear, and BLOOD PRESSURE) are especially affected. Shielding and protective clothing prevent exposure to radiation from space and from nuclear reactors on board and regular schedules help mimic day-night cycles.

space probe, unmanned space vehicle, usually carrying sophisticated instrumentation, designed to explore various aspects of the

RULERS OF SPAIN SINCE 1474 *(including dates of reign)*

Union of Castile and Aragón

Isabella I (of Castile), ruled jointly with Ferdinand II (of Aragón), 1474–1504
Ferdinand II, ruled jointly with Isabella I as Ferdinand V of Castile, 1474–1504; ruled Aragón only, 1504–16; ruled Castile as regent, 1506–16

Hapsburg Dynasty

Joanna (the Mad), daughter of Ferdinand and Isabella, ruled Castile only (jointly with Philip I in 1506), 1504–6
Philip I (the Handsome), son of Holy Roman Emperor Maximilian I; ruled Castile jointly with Joanna, 1506
Charles I (Holy Roman Emperor Charles V), son of Joanna and Philip, 1516–56
Philip II, son of Charles I, 1556–98
Philip III, son of Philip II, 1598–1621
Philip IV, son of Philip III, 1621–65
Charles II, son of Philip IV, 1665–1770

Bourbon Dynasty

Philip V, great-grandson of Philip IV, 1700–1746
Ferdinand VI, son of Philip V, 1746–59
Charles III, younger son of Philip V, 1759–88
Charles IV, second son of Charles III, 1788–1808
Ferdinand VII, son of Charles IV, 1808

French Intrusion

Joseph Bonaparte, 1808–13

Bourbon Restoration

Ferdinand VII, restored, 1813–33
Isabella II, daughter of Ferdinand VII, 1833–68

Elective Monarchy

Francisco Serrano y Domínguez, regent, 1869–70
Amadeus, elected by a constituent assembly, 1870–73

First Republic

Estanislao Figueras, president, 1873
Francisco Pi y Margall, president, 1873
Nicholás Salmerón y Alonso, president, 1873
Emilio Castelar y Ripoll, prime minister, 1873–74

Bourbon Restoration

Alfonso XII, son of Isabella II, 1874–85
Alfonso XIII, son of Alfonso XII, 1886–1931

Second Republic

Niceta Alcalá Zamora, president, 1931–36
Manuel Azaña, president, 1936–39

Nationalist Government

Francisco Franco, chief of state, 1939–75

Constitutional Monarchy

Juan Carlos I, grandson of Alfonso XIII, 1975–

SOLAR SYSTEM. Unlike an artificial SATELLITE, which is placed in more or less permanent orbit around the earth, a space probe is launched with enough energy to escape the gravitational field of the earth (see ESCAPE VELOCITY) and navigate between planets. Radio contact between the control station on earth and the space probe provides a channel for transmitting data recorded by on-board instruments back to earth. A probe may be directed to orbit a planet, to soft-land instrument packages on a planetary surface, or to fly by one or more planets and/or natural satellites, approaching within a few thousand miles. See table of space probe programs.

space shuttle, reusable U.S. space vehicle. It consists of a winged orbiter, two solid-rocket boosters, and an external tank. Lift-off thrust is derived from the orbiter's three main liquid-propellant engines and the boosters. After 2 min the latter use up their fuel, are separated from the spacecraft, and—after deployment of parachutes—are recovered following splashdown. After about 8 min of flight, the orbiter main engines shut down; the external tank is then jettisoned and burns up as it reenters the atmosphere. The orbiter meanwhile enters orbit after a short burn of its two small Orbiting Maneuvering System (OMS) engines. To return to earth, the orbiter turns around, fires its OMS engines to reduce speed, and, after descending through the atmosphere, lands like an airplane. Following four orbital test flights (1981–82) of the space shuttle *Columbia,* operational flights began in Nov. 1982. The 25th shuttle flight ended in disaster on Jan. 28, 1986, when *Challenger*, on its 10th flight, exploded shortly after liftoff, killing all seven crew members. Shuttle flights were suspended until Sept. 1988 and then resumed on a more conservative schedule. The shuttle program has resulted in several notable achievements, including the rescue and repair of disabled satellites (including the HUBBLE SPACE TELESCOPE) and the first three-person spacewalk (1992). It has also conducted experiments designed to test the ability of astronauts to assemble and maintain a SPACE STATION. NASA was forced, however, to reemphasize expendable rockets to reduce the cost of placing payloads in space.

space station or **space platform,** artificial earth satellite, usually manned, that is placed in a fixed orbit and can serve as a base for astronomical observations, zero-gravity materials processing, satellite repair, or (possibly) weapons, or as a staging area for constructing large communications satellites to be placed in geosynchronous orbit. Early examples of space stations are the American *Skylab* and the Soviet Salyut and Russian Mir spacecraft (see SPACE EXPLORATION, table). NASA, in conjunction with Japan, Canada, and the European Space Agency, is developing a space station that would be assembled in space beginning in the late 1990s. Russia joined the project in 1993. The American physicist Gerard O'Neill proposed the construction of space colonies—very large space stations built from lunar or asteroidal material and inhabited by several thousand people.

space telescope: see HUBBLE SPACE TELESCOPE.

space-time, central concept in the theory of RELATIVITY that replaces the earlier concepts of space and time as separate absolute entities. In space-time, events in the universe are described in terms of a four-dimensional continuum in which each observer locates an event by three spacelike coordinates and a timelike coordinate. The choice of the last is not unique; hence, time is not absolute but is relative to the observer.

Spahn, Warren Edward, 1921–, American baseball player; b. Buffalo. He pitched for the Boston (later, Milwaukee) Braves from 1942 to 1964. Before retiring at age 44, he won 363 games, a record for left-handers and the fifth best ever.

Spain, Span. *España,* officially Kingdom of Spain, country (1992 est. pop. 39,118,000), 194,884 sq mi (504,750 sq km), SW Europe, on the IBERIAN PENINSULA and including the BALEARIC ISLANDS, CANARY ISLANDS, and five enclaves in Morocco. Spain is bordered by the Bay of Biscay and France (N), the Mediterranean Sea (E and SE), and Portugal and the Atlantic Ocean (W). The small principality of ANDORRA is wedged between Spain and France in the PYRENEES. The Strait of Gibraltar separates Spain from North Africa. (GIBRALTAR itself is a British possession.) Spain has 17 geographic and historic regions, now constituted as autonomous communities (regions), that generally correspond to the old Christian and Moorish kingdoms. MADRID is the capital; other major cities include BARCELONA, VALENCIA, and SEVILLE. The center of Spain forms a vast plateau extending from the Cantabrian Mts. in the north to the Sierra Morena in the south, and from the Portuguese border in the west to low ranges in the east. The plateau is generally arid and thinly populated. It is cut from west to east by mountain chains and the valleys of the Douro (Duero), Tagus, and Guadiana rivers. To the northeast of the plateau is the broad valley of the Ebro R. The southernmost section, ANDALUSIA, is crossed by the fertile valley of the Guadalquivir R. The highest peak in continental Spain is Mulhacén (11,411 ft/3,478 m), in the Sierra Nevada.

People. The Spanish people display great regional diversity; a desire for political independence remains particularly strong among the Catalans and the BASQUES. The Castilian dialect is the standard language, but Catalan, Galician, and Basque are spoken. Roman Catholicism is the predominant religion.

Economy. Spain is primarily an agricultural country, with wheat, olive oil, potatoes, sugar beets, and citrus fruits among the leading crops. It is also a leading producer of cork and wine. Spanish industry produces textiles, iron and steel products, ships, automobiles, processed foods, chemicals, and various consumer goods. Rich deposits of iron, coal, and zinc are mined in the Cantabrian Mts.; petroleum and copper are also produced. Tourism and fishing are important sources of income.

Government. Spain is a constitutional monarchy. Since 1975 the reigning monarch has been King JUAN CARLOS I. The parliament (CORTES) consists of a chamber of deputies, with 350 members, and senate, with 208 members. The leading political groups are the Socialist party and the conservative People's party. A new constitution was approved by national referendum in 1978.

Early History. Spain was known to early Mediterranean peoples as far back as the Stone Age. The Phoenicians established colonies c.1100 B.C. and were followed by the Carthaginians and the Greeks. The Romans conquered Spain in the 2d cent. B.C. and made the region a colony. Christianity was introduced in the 1st cent. A.D. In 409 Spain was overrun by Germanic invaders, and in 419 a Visigothic kingdom was set up. After Spain was invaded (711) from N Africa by Muslim BERBERS, the last Visigothic kingdom collapsed. The MOORS, as the Muslim invaders were known, soon conquered the entire peninsula except for ASTURIAS and the Basque country. Under the Moors, Spanish cities, industry, and agriculture prospered and a distinctive architecture (exemplified by the Alhambra in GRANADA) flourished. But the Moors never controlled N Spain, and over the centuries the northern Christian kingdoms expanded (see ARAGÓN and CASTILE) while the Moors became divided. The fall of Granada (1492) made the Spanish monarchs FERDINAND V and ISABELLA I rulers of all Spain. Catholic leaders expelled the Jews in 1492 and attempted to convert the Muslims by force. America was discovered (1492) by Columbus, and the beginnings of a huge colonial empire in the New World were established.

The Golden Age and Decline. Gold and silver from the Americas flowed into Spain in great quantities, and by the 16th cent. Spain was the most powerful country in the world. Under its first HAPSBURG king, Charles I (r.1516–56; Holy Roman emperor after 1519 as CHARLES V), Spain entered its Golden Age, when a brilliant artistic, cultural, and intellectual life flourished. During this period the church's dominance grew, reaching its peak in the INQUISITION. But Spanish power in Europe began its long decline during the reign of Charles's son, PHILIP II (r.1556–98). The Spanish ARMADA was defeated (1588) by England, and continuous wars in Europe sapped the country's strength. The accession (1700) of the BOURBON dynasty in Spain provoked the War of the SPANISH SUCCESSION. Drawn into the Napoleonic Wars, Spain was occupied by French troops and given (1808) a French king, Joseph Bonaparte (see BONAPARTE, family), but by 1814 Spanish resistance forces and the British had expelled the French (see PENINSULAR WAR). In the mid-19th cent. Spain was torn by internal struggles (see CARLISTS). On the abdication (1868) of ISABELLA II, a constitutional monarchy was established, followed by a short-lived republic (1873–74). The last remnant of Spain's colonial empire in America was lost (1898) during the SPANISH-AMERICAN WAR.

Modern Spain. In 1923 a military dictatorship was established under PRIMO DE RIVERA. King ALFONSO XIII was deposed (1931) and a second republic was created. But opposition from both the left and the right, as well as from Catalan separatists, eventually undermined the republic. The election of a leftist coalition in 1936 precipitated the SPANISH CIVIL WAR (1936–39). The Insurgents, under Francisco FRANCO, embraced most conservative groups, notably monarchists, the army, the church, and the fascists. After a savage conflict the pro-republican forces (Loyalists) were defeated and a dictatorship under Franco was set up. During WORLD WAR II Spain aided the AXIS but did not enter the war. The 1950s and 60s were marked by growing prosperity and by agitation for political freedom. In 1969 Franco appointed Prince Juan Carlos, grandson of Alfonso XIII, as his successor. Following Franco's death in 1975, King JUAN CARLOS and his premier, Adolfo SUÁREZ GONZÁLEZ, steered Spain toward parliamentary democracy. With all political parties, including the Communists, legalized by 1977, the first parliamentary election was held that year, and Suárez's Democratic Center received a plurality. In 1981 Leopoldo CALVO SOTELO became premier following Suárez's resignation. The following year the Socialist party won a sweeping victory in nationwide elections, bringing into power the first left-wing government since before the civil war, with Socialist leader Felipe GONZÁLEZ MÁRQUEZ as premier. Violence associated with Basque and Catalan separatism remained a problem in the 1980s. Rightist civil guards seeking greater centralization seized the Spanish parliament in 1981. Lacking support, however, the coup was quickly put down. Spain joined the European Community in 1986, and despite widespread opposition to Spain's membership in NATO, Spaniards voted (1987) to remain in the alliance. Voters returned the Socialists to office in 1986, 1989, and, as a minority government, 1993. In the early 1990s the country slipped into a deep recession.

spaniel: see SPORTING DOG.

Spanish-American War, 1898, conflict between Spain and the U.S. Demands by Cuban patriots for independence from Spain were supported by large numbers of Americans. Pro-rebel sentiment was inflamed by the biased reporting of the U.S. "yellow press," heavy losses of American investment caused by guerrilla warfare, and an appreciation of Cuba's strategic importance to a projected Central American canal. The publication of a Spanish letter disparaging Pres. MCKINLEY, and the sinking (Feb. 15) of the U.S. battleship MAINE in Havana harbor, intensified U.S. feeling against Spain. The U.S. demanded Spanish withdrawal from Cuba. On Apr. 24 Spain declared war on the U.S. On May 1 a U.S. naval squadron under George DEWEY thoroughly defeated the Spanish fleet in Manila harbor, in the Philippines. On May 28 the U.S. established a blockade of Santiago de Cuba; when the Spanish fleet attempted to escape (June 1), it was destroyed. Meanwhile, U.S. troops, including the famed ROUGH RIDERS, engaged in some heavy fighting (July 1) at El Canay and San Juan Hill. On July 17 Santiago was captured, effectively ending the war. An armistice was signed Aug. 12, and peace was arranged by the Treaty of Paris (Dec. 10). The Spanish empire was practically dissolved; Cuba was freed, but under U.S. tutelage; Puerto Rico and Guam were ceded to the U.S.; and the Philippines were surrendered to the U.S. for $20 million. The U.S. emerged from the war with new international power.

Spanish civil war, 1936–39, conflict in which conservative forces in Spain overthrew the second Spanish republic. The war pitted the Nationalists, led by the landed aristocracy, Roman Catholic Church, military leaders, and the fascist FALANGE party, against the Loyalists, consisting of liberals, anarchists, socialists, and Communists. In July 1936, Gen. FRANCO led an army revolt in Morocco and invaded Spain to support right-wing rebels. The Nationalist army overran conservative areas in N Spain, while the Loyalists remained strong in CATALONIA and the BASQUE PROVINCES. Volunteers abroad formed International Brigades to fight for the Loyalists, who received supplies from the Soviet Union. Fascist Italy and Nazi Germany aided the Nationalists with modern arms and some 60,000 troops. The Loyalist side was riven by factional strife that was exacerbated by the Communists' suppression of anarchists and Trotskyites. Nationalist forces, unified under Franco, gradually wore down republican strength, conquering Barcelona and Madrid in early 1939. For Italy and Germany the war was a testing ground for modern armaments and techniques to be used in WORLD WAR II. For the youth of the 1930s, saving the Spanish republic was the idealistic cause of the era. But the civil war's huge death toll, human suffering, and material devastation were unparalleled in Spanish history. The war also ushered in a long era of right-wing dictatorship, that ended only with Franco's death in 1975.

Spanish colonial art and architecture, fl. 16th–early 19th cent. The art of the Spanish colonies followed the development of styles in Spain, but had original features in different regions, with the main centers in Peru and Mexico. The earliest colonial buildings have disappeared, but by the end of the 16th cent. a durable monumental architecture had been achieved. Intricate ornamentation was often used, as in the plateresque decorations on the earliest cathedral in the New World, in Santo Domingo, Dominican Republic (1512–41). However, most of the buildings of the colonial period are massive and simple, e.g., the Spanish missions of California. In 16th-cent. Mexico the great builders were the Augustinian, Franciscan, and Dominican orders, which introduced the open chapel. During most of the 17th and 18th cent. the baroque style held sway, but contrasts between plain and decorated surfaces were maintained. A more conservative trend was manifested in the simple, severe buildings of Colombia. The colonial ultrabaroque reached a climax in the cathedral in Mexico City, with its strong light-and-shade patterns, rich carvings, and violent alternations of curves and angles. Central American buildings were generally provincial versions of the Mexican. Meanwhile, Peru evolved a rich architecture, more massive than the Mexican, with wall surfaces divided into large compartments rather than covered with shallow carving as in Mexico. A fine example of Peruvian architecture is the Church of San Agustín in Lima (1720). The great days of Spanish colonial architecture ended with the rise of neoclassicism in the late 18th cent. The fine artists of the Spanish colonies, many of them indigenous people who gave colonial art its unique flavor, mainly portrayed religious subjects from the New Testament. Indigenous sculptors, notably in Mexico, Guatemala, Paraguay, and Peru, developed a powerful folk art, employing polychrome wood, terra cotta, and architectural bas-reliefs. In painting, the conceptions were frequently original and charged with remarkable intensity and piety. Native strains were also noticeable in the broadsides of so-called folk-lithography, often political in nature, common in 18th- and 19th-cent. Mexico and Venezuela. See also MEXICAN ART AND ARCHITECTURE.

Spanish language, member of the Romance group of the Italic subfamily of the Indo-European family of languages. See LANGUAGE (table).

Spanish Main, the coast of NW South America, particularly the section between Panama and the ORINOCO R., from which Spanish treasure fleets carried gold back to Spain in colonial times. Buccaneers preying on the vessels as they passed through the CARIBBEAN SEA made the term a symbol of piratical romance.

Spanish moss, fibrous grayish-green EPIPHYTE (*Tillandsia usneoides*) of the BROMELIAD family, found in tropical America and the Southern U.S. Spanish moss, also called Florida, long, or southern moss, grows hanging from trees and has inconspicuous flowers. It is not a true MOSS.

Spanish Succession, War of the, 1701–14, general European war fought for the succession to the Spanish empire. CHARLES II, the Hapsburg king of Spain, was childless, and negotiations over his eventual successor began long before his death. The chief claimants were Philip, son of Louis XIV of France; Archduke Charles (later Holy Roman Emperor CHARLES VI), son of Emperor Leopold I; and Joseph Ferdinand, electoral prince of Bavaria. England and Holland, opposed to the extension of either French Bourbon or Austrian Hapsburg power into Spain, favored Joseph Ferdinand. In 1698 all the powers agreed to the complicated First Partition Treaty. By its terms, Joseph Ferdinand was to get the crown; in return, Spanish territories were to go to Austria and France. Joseph Ferdinand died before Charles, however, and the treaty went into jeopardy. In 1700 the duke of Anjou, grandson of Louis, named by the dying Charles as his successor, ascended the throne as PHILIP V. England, Holland, Austria, and most of the German states then went to war against France. Bavaria sided with France, as did Portugal and Savoy until 1703, when they switched sides. Military operations began in the Low Countries and became general in 1703. The great allied commanders, the English duke of MARLBOROUGH and the imperial general Prince EUGENE OF SAVOY, won such major victories as Blenheim and Gibraltar (1704), Ramillies (1706), Oudenarde (1708), and Malplaquet (1709). The campaigns in Spain were indecisive, however, and in 1711 England quit the war. Charles VI had become emperor, and he represented as great a threat to the English as did the Bourbons. In 1713 England, Holland, and France signed the Peace of Utrecht. Charles continued the war until 1714. Although Philip remained on the Spanish throne, the principle of BALANCE OF POWER had been established in European dynastic affairs.

Spark, Muriel, 1918–, Scottish novelist. Her witty novels expose both the petty foibles of her characters and the dark side of human experience. They include *Memento Mori* (1958), *The Girls of Slender Means* (1963), and *Loitering with Intent* (1981). *The Prime of Miss Jean Brodie* (1961) became an acclaimed stage, film, and television production.

spark chamber: see PARTICLE DETECTOR.

sparrow, small, perching, New World BIRD (genus *Passer*) of the FINCH family. Field and hedge birds inconspicuously colored in dull grays and browns, sparrows have stout, conical beaks adapted to seed eating, and are valuable to farmers in destroying weed seeds.

Sparta, city of ancient Greece, capital of Laconia, on the Eurotas R. in the S PELOPONNESUS. The CITY-STATE of Sparta was founded by Dorian Greeks who conquered Laconia and Messenia (c.735–715 B.C.). It was a center of wealth and culture. However, after 600 B.C. Sparta cultivated only the military arts, and the city became an armed camp. The ruling class, the Spartiates, gave themselves wholly to war. Only Spartiates were citizens with legal and civil rights. Below this warrior class were the perioeci (freemen permitted to carry on commerce and handicrafts) and helots (serfs bound to the land). The Spartan government was headed by two hereditary kings, and there were a council of elders and a general assembly of citizens. But the real rulers were the board of five ephors (overseers), elected annually, who conducted the business of the state secretly. By the 6th cent. B.C. Sparta was the strongest city in Greece. In the PERSIAN WARS Sparta fought beside Athens at THERMOPYLAE and Salamis (480), and at Platea (479). Afterward, Sparta's rivalry with Athens intensified, leading to the PELOPONNESIAN WAR (431–404), which wrecked the Athenian empire. Sparta emerged triumphant but was decisively defeated by Thebes at Leuctra (371). Sparta subsequently fell an easy prey to Macedon and declined. It prospered under the Romans but was devastated by the Goths in A.D. 395.

Spartacus, d. 71 B.C., Roman gladiator, leader of a slave revolt that was the last and most important of the SERVILE WARS. He escaped from the gladiators' school at Capua, gathered many runaway slaves about him, and in 72 B.C. dominated much of S Italy. He was killed in battle when Marcus Licinius Crassus (see CRASSUS, family) and POMPEY put down the revolt. They crucified some 6,000 captured slaves.

Spartacus party or **Spartacists,** German radical socialist party, the precursor of the German Communist party. Among its founders in 1916 were Karl Liebknecht (1871–1919) and Rosa Luxemburg. In

Jan. 1919 the Spartacists, newly transformed as the German Communist party, led a general strike and revolt in Berlin that was put down by the army within a week. Liebknecht and Luxemburg were brutally murdered by the soldiers.

spearmint: see MINT.

Special Drawing Rights (SDRs), type of international monetary reserves established (1968) by the International Monetary Fund (IMF). Created in response to concern over the limitations of gold and dollars as the sole means of settling international accounts, SDRs were designed to augment international liquidity. Also known as "paper gold," SDRs are assigned to the accounts of IMF members in proportion to their contributions to the fund. Each member agrees to accept them as exchangeable for gold or reserve currencies, and deficit countries can use them to purchase stronger currencies. In 1976 the IMF increased the share of the less-developed countries and moved to make SDRs the primary reserve asset of the INTERNATIONAL MONETARY SYSTEM, supplanting gold and dollars.

special prosecutor: see INDEPENDENT COUNSEL.

species: see CLASSIFICATION.

specific gravity, the ratio of the WEIGHT of a given volume of a substance to the weight of an equal volume of a reference substance, usually water. See DENSITY.

specific heat, ratio of the HEAT CAPACITY of a substance to the heat capacity of a reference substance, usually water. Because the heat capacity of water is 1 Btu/lb per degree Fahrenheit or 1 cal/g per degree Celsius, the specific heat of a substance relative to water will be numerically equal to its heat capacity.

spectral class, a classification of stars by their SPECTRUM and LUMINOSITY. The stars were originally divided into seven main classes designated by the letters O, B, A, F, G, K, and M; since 1924 four other classes (R, N, S, and W) have been added. R, N, and S are similar to the K and M types but have somewhat different characteristics; W indicates a Wolf-Rayet star, the hottest type of star that shines with a steady light. Each of the letter classes has subdivisions indicated by the numerals 0 through 9; 0 signifies the hottest type and 9 the coolest within a class. A Roman numeral—ranging from I (supergiant) to V (normal dwarf or main sequence)—is added to the spectral class to specify the luminosity, or intrinsic intensity, of a star.

SPECTRAL CLASSES: CHARACTERISTICS

Type	*Color*	*Temperature*	*Strong Lines*
O	blue-white	35,000°C	ionized helium
B	blue-white	21,000°C	helium
A	white	10,000°C	hydrogen
F	creamy	7,000°C	ionized calcium
G	yellow	6,000°C	calcium
K	orange	4,500°C	titanium oxide
M	red	3,000°C	titanium oxide

spectroscope, optical instrument for producing spectral lines and measuring their wavelengths and intensities, used in spectral analysis (see SPECTRUM). In the simple prism spectroscope, a collimator, with a slit at the outer end and a lens at the inner end, transforms the light entering the slit into a beam of parallel rays. A prism or diffraction grating disperses the light coming from the collimator, and the spectrum formed is observed with a small telescope. A **spectrograph** uses a camera or a photomultiplier tube instead of a telescope; the photomultiplier tube allows real-time spectrographic analysis and greater accuracy. Such analysis (spectroscopy) is used to analyze the composition of unknown materials in many disparate fields.

speech: see LANGUAGE.

speed: see MOTION.

Speer, Albert [shpār], 1905–81, German architect and NAZI leader. He was HITLER'S official architect and was Nazi minister of armaments (1942–45). He served 20 years in prison after being sentenced as a war criminal (1946) by the Nuremberg tribunal. His memoirs, *Inside the Third Reich* (tr. 1972), were widely read.

Speke, John Hanning [spēk], 1827–64, English explorer in Africa. In 1858 he and Sir Richard BURTON discovered Lake TANGANYIKA. Speke also discovered Lake VICTORIA. In 1862 he proved that the Victoria NILE R. issues from the north end over Ripon Falls.

speleology, systematic exploration of CAVES, popularly called spelunking. It includes the measuring and mapping of caves and reporting on the flora and fauna found in them.

Spencer, Herbert, 1820–1903, English philosopher. Together with Charles DARWIN and Thomas Henry HUXLEY he was responsible for the acceptance of the theory of evolution, and he coined the phrase "survival of the fittest," later attributed to Darwin. He projected a vast work, *Synthetic Philosophy,* that would apply the principle of evolutionary progress to all branches of knowledge; the numerous volumes published between 1855 and 1893 covered such subjects as biology, psychology, sociology, and ethics. He is credited with the establishment of sociology as a discipline in the U.S.

Spender, Stephen, 1909–, English poet and critic. In the 1930s he was an associate of AUDEN and MACNEICE; his autobiography, *World within World* (1951), records the period. His poems are collected in many volumes, e.g., *The Still Centre* (1939) and *Generous Days* (1971), and he has written social and literary criticism and fiction.

Spener, Phillip Jakob [shpā'nər], 1635–1705, German theologian, founder of the devotional movement in LUTHERANISM known as Pietism. As a Lutheran pastor in Frankfurt, he instituted (1670) meetings for fellowship and Bible study to counteract the barren intellectualism in the church. These *Collegia Pietatis* led to a religious revival in Germany and in other parts of Europe despite the opposition of the orthodox clergy. He helped found (1694) the Univ. of Halle.

Spengler, Oswald, 1880–1936, German historian and philosopher. His major work, *The Decline of the West* (2 vol., 1918–22), reflects his view that every culture passes through a life cycle from youth through maturity and old age to death, and that Western culture had entered the period of decline.

Spenser, Edmund, 1552?–1599, English poet. A friend of many eminent court and literary figures, he was appointed to a secretaryship in Ireland in 1580, and lived in County Cork thereafter. Patterning his literary career on VERGIL, he first published 12 pastoral eclogues of *The Shepheardes Calendar* (1579). *Complaints* and the elegy *Daphnaida* appeared in 1591. In 1595 *Colin Clouts Come Home Againe,* a PASTORAL allegory dealing with a journey to London and the vices of court life, appeared, as did the ELEGY *Astrophel,* the SONNET sequence *Amoretti,* and the complex wedding poem *Epithalamion* in honor of his marriage. *Fowre Hymnes,* explaining his Platonic and Christian views on love and beauty, and *Prothalamion* came in 1596. In the same year the second three books of his unfinished masterpiece, *The Faerie Queene,* were published (the first three had been published in 1590). The poem is an EPIC that treats moral virtues allegorically. Its excellence lies in the depth of Spenser's moral vision, and in the Spenserian nine-line stanza he invented for it. Spenser was recognized by contemporaries as the foremost poet of the time.

sperm or **spermatozoon,** specialized male sex cell. It is smaller than the female sex cell (OVUM) and has a flagellum, which provides motility. The formation of sperm, like that of the ovum, requires MEIOSIS, which reduces the chromosome number by half. An ovum fertilized by a sperm (called a zygote) has the full number of chromosomes restored to it. See also REPRODUCTION; REPRODUCTIVE SYSTEM.

sphagnum or **peat moss,** economically valuable MOSS (genus *Sphagnum*) typically growing as a floating mat in freshwater bogs. Sphagnums are the principal constituent of PEAT. They are highly absorbent and are commercially important as packing material and absorbent dressings.

sphalerite, zinc sulfide mineral (ZnS), occurring worldwide, sometimes in crystals but more often in massive form, in a variety of colors. Often found in association with GALENA, it is the most important source of ZINC.

sphere, in geometry, a solid whose surface consists of points all at the same distance r (the radius) from a certain fixed point (the center). The term *sphere* refers both to the surface and to the space it encloses. The area of the surface of a sphere is given by the formula $S = 4\pi r^2$ and the volume of a sphere is given by $V = \frac{4}{3}\pi r^3$.

sphinx, mythical beast of ancient Egypt, usually represented in art as having a human head and the body of a lion. It frequently symbolized the pharaoh as an incarnation of the sun god RA. The most famous one is the Great Sphinx, a colossal stone figure at Al Jizah. Sphinxes were also depicted throughout the ancient Middle East and Greece.

spider, mostly terrestrial ARACHNID, with a two-part body, four pairs of legs, and four pairs of eyes. Spinnerets (specialized organs under the abdomen) produce silk thread for binding prey or making webs, cocoons, and lines for floating. Spiders live chiefly on insects and other arthropods; some large species prey on small snakes, mammals, and birds. All spiders paralyze their prey with venom produced in poison glands under the head; several species, such as the BLACK WIDOW, have bites that are painful or even dangerous to humans. See also TARANTULA.

Spielberg, Steven, 1946–, American film director; b. Cincinnati. His technically polished films include *Jaws* (1975), *Close Encounters of the Third Kind* (1977), *Raiders of the Lost Ark* (1981), *E.T.: The Extra-Terrestrial* (1982), *The Color Purple* (1985), *Jurassic Park* (1993), and *Schindler's List* (1993).

spinach, annual plant (*Spinacia oleracea*) of the goosefoot family, probably Persian in origin. The leaves are high in VITAMINS and iron, and numerous varieties are cultivated.

spinal cord, length of nerve-fiber bundles carrying information (electrical and chemical signals) through the NERVOUS SYSTEM. The spinal cord carries sensory impulses from the trunk and limbs to the brain; it returns commands from the brain to the muscles and glands. Anatomically, the spinal cord runs nearly the length of the trunk and merges with the brainstem. The spinal cord is housed within the **spinal column,** a bony column that also forms the main structural support of the SKELETON. The spinal column consists of segments (vertebrae) linked by flexible joints and held together by gelatinous disks of cartilage and by ligaments. Each vertebra has a roughly cylindrical body, winglike projections, and a bony arch. The arches, positioned next to one another, create the tunnellike space that houses the spinal cord.

spinal meningitis: see MENINGITIS.

spindle: see SPINNING.

spinet: see PIANO.

Spingarn, Joel Elias, 1875–1939, American educator and critic; b. N.Y.C. A professor of literature at Columbia (1899–1911), he wrote such studies as *A History of Literary Criticism in the Renaissance* (1899) and *The New Criticism* (1911). Spingarn was also a prominent officer of the NAACP.

spinning, the drawing out, twisting, and winding of FIBERS into a continuous thread or yarn. From antiquity until the INDUSTRIAL REVOLUTION, spinning was a household industry. The earliest tools were the distaff, a hand-held stick on which the cotton, flax, or wool fiber was wrapped; and the spindle, a shorter stick, held in the other hand, notched at one end and weighted at the other. The twirling of the spindle twisted the fiber into thread. In Europe from the 14th to 16th cent. the distaff and spindle were replaced by the spinning wheel, a spindle set in a frame and turned by a belt passing over a wheel. The great wheel, also called the wool or walking wheel, was turned by hand; the more elaborate flax, or Saxony, wheel was operated by a foot treadle. In 18th-cent. England, improvements in the loom, increasing the demand for yarn, stimulated such inventions as James HARGREAVES's spinning jenny (c.1765), which spun 8 to 11 threads at once; Richard ARKWRIGHT's spinning frame (1769), which made more tightly twisted, stronger threads; and Samuel CROMPTON's mule spinning frame (1779), which combined the best features of the two earlier machines. Using water power and, later, steam, spinning became a factory enterprise.

Spinoza, Baruch or **Benedict,** 1632–77, Dutch philosopher. A member of the Sephardic Jewish community of Amsterdam, Spinoza received a thorough education in the tradition of medieval philosophical texts as well as in the works of DESCARTES, HOBBES, and other writers of the period. After charges of heretical thought and practice led to his excommunication from the Jewish community in Amsterdam in 1656, he Latinized his name to Benedict. He was by trade a lens grinder, modestly rejecting offers of an academic career, but he nevertheless became celebrated in his own day and was regularly visited by other philosophers. Spinoza's system is monist, deductive, and rationalistic. Politically he posited the idea of the SOCIAL CONTRACT, but unlike Hobbes he visualized a community in which human beings derive most advantage from the rational renunciation of personal desire. He rejected the concept of FREE WILL, holding human action to be motivated by one's conception of self-preservation. A powerful, or virtuous, person acts out of understanding; thus freedom consists in being guided by the law of one's own nature, and evil is the result of inadequate understanding. He saw the supreme ambition of the virtuous person as the "intellectual love of God." Spinoza shared with Descartes an intensely mathematical appreciation of the universe: truth, like geometry, follows from first principles, and is accessible to the logical mind. Unlike Descartes, however, he regarded mind and body (or ideas and the physical universe) as merely different aspects of a single substance, which he called alternately God and Nature, God being Nature in its fullness. This pantheism was considered blasphemous by the religious and political authorities of his day. Of his works, only *A Treatise on Religious and Political Philosophy* (1670) was published during his lifetime. His *Ethics, Political Treatise,* and *Hebrew Grammar* are included in his posthumous works (1677).

spiritism or **spiritualism,** belief that the human personality survives death and can communicate with the living through a medium sensitive to its vibrations. The communication may be psychic, as in clairvoyance or trance speaking, or physical, as in automatic writing or ectoplasmic materializations. Modern U.S. spiritism dates from the activities (1848) of medium Margaret Fox and her sisters, later admitted to be fraudulent. Spiritualistic phenomena are now under scientific investigation (see PARAPSYCHOLOGY).

spiritual, a deeply emotional, often profoundly melancholy, religious FOLK SONG, characterized by syncopation, polyrhythmic structure, and the pentatonic scale of five whole tones. The text is often biblical. Spirituals were long thought to be the spontaneous creation of African-American slaves and the only original folk music of the U.S. In the 1920s G.P. Jackson proposed the theory that these spirituals were in fact adapted from or inspired by 19th-cent. camp-meeting revival songs of the Southern white population. Spirituals are now considered to be an amalgamation of African musical traditions and religious songs of the 19th-cent. white South, which produced a form of folk music distinctly African-American in character. Spirituals are related to the sorrow songs that are the source of the blues (see JAZZ).

Spitsbergen, formerly **Vestspitsbergen,** largest island (15,075 sq mi/39,044 sq km) of SVALBARD, a Norwegian possession in the Arctic Ocean. Coal mining is a major industry.

Spitz, Mark Andrew, 1950–, American swimmer; b. Modesto, Calif. Known as a great freestyle swimmer, he won four individual events in the 1972 Olympics, setting world records in the 100- and 200-meter freestyle races. He also won two gold medals in 1968 and three in 1972 for team relays.

spleen, soft, purplish-red organ that lies on the left side of the abdominal cavity, under the diaphragm. The spleen filters foreign organisms and old red blood cells from the bloodstream by means of phagocytic cells that engulf and destroy them. Certain white blood cells are formed in the spleen. The spleen also manufactures red blood cells in the fetus toward the end of pregnancy and takes over again after birth if the bone marrow fails to perform that function.

Spock, Benjamin McLane, 1903–, American author and pediatrician; b. New Haven, Conn. His *Common Sense Book of Baby and Child Care* (1946; later *Baby and Child Care*) has sold more copies than almost any other book published in the U.S. He wrote widely on child-rearing, and became (1955) professor of child development at Western Reserve Univ. In 1967 he resigned to devote his full time to the peace and antinuclear movements. He was the 1972 presidential candidate for the People's party.

Spode, English family of potters. **Josiah Spode I,** 1733–97, founded a pottery firm in 1770 at Stoke-on-Trent. He developed a transparent but durable bone china that is still made. After 1797, under his son **Josiah Spode II,** 1754–1827, the firm was known for blue-and-white ware with novel designs, such as hunting scenes.

spoils system, in U.S. history, the practice of giving appointive offices to loyal members of the party in power. Used by the earliest presidents, particularly Thomas JEFFERSON, the spoils system became extensive during the administration of Andrew JACKSON. The corruption and inefficiency bred by the system reached staggering proportions under U.S. GRANT; reaction led to the creation of the CIVIL SERVICE Commission in 1871. The spoils system has, however, continued for some federal and many state offices.

Spokane, city (1990 pop. 177,196), seat of Spokane co., E Wash., at the falls of the Spokane R.; inc. 1881. It is a port of entry, and the commercial, transportation, and industrial center of the "Inland Empire," a productive grain, fruit, and livestock region. Its manufactures are diversified. Spokane's business and cultural life were reinvigorated by development for the fair "Expo '74." A cultural and educational center, the city has a noted museum of Native American culture.

sponge, aquatic invertebrate animal of the phylum Porifera. All but one family are marine. Colonies of adult sponges, often brilliantly colored, live attached to rocks, corals, or shells, exhibiting so little movement that 18th-cent. naturalists considered them plants. The sponge's body is like a sac. Water is drawn into a central cavity through many tiny holes in the body wall and expelled through a large opening at the top. Hard materials embedded in the body wall form a skeleton. The dried skeletons of colonial sponges have been used to hold liquid since ancient times. Natural sponges are light gray or brown when dried and irregular in shape.

spontaneous combustion, phenomenon in which a substance unexpectedly bursts into flame without apparent cause. Spontaneous combustion occurs when a substance undergoes a slow oxidation that releases heat in such a way that it cannot escape the substance; the temperature of the substance consequently rises until ignition takes place.

spore, term applied both to a resistant or resting stage occurring among unicellular organisms such as bacteria and to an asexual reproductive cell of multicellular plants that gives rise to a new organism without FERTILIZATION. A spore is typically a cell surrounded by a cell wall that may be tough and waterproof, permitting the cell to survive unfavorable circumstances.

sporophyte: see GAMETOPHYTE.

sporozoan: see APICOCOMPLEXA.

sporting dog, class of dogs bred for pointing, flushing, and retrieving game. They hunt by air scent (as opposed to most HOUNDS, which are ground scenters), and their quarry is mainly game birds. Pointers stand rigidly, with nose and body pointing at their quarry, directing hunters to its location. Setters, originally trained to crouch in front of game, were later taught to point. Retrievers find and return killed game to the hunter. See individual breeds, e.g., COCKER SPANIEL, ENGLISH SPRINGER SPANIEL, GOLDEN RETRIEVER, IRISH SETTER, LABRADOR RETRIEVER, POINTER, WEIMARANER.

sports medicine, branch of medicine concerned with prevention, treatment, and study of injuries received during participation in sports. "Tennis elbow"; shoulder, knee, back, and leg injuries; stiffness and pain in joints; and tendinitis are some of the conditions involved. Treatments and prevention techniques include mechanical supports, exercise programs for strengthening and improving flexibility, PHYSICAL THERAPY, and—in severe cases—surgery. Sports medicine is also concerned with the abuse of so-called performance-enhancing drugs, such as ANABOLIC STEROIDS. Sports medicine was initially practiced primarily by physicians associated with professional sports teams, but with increased interest in amateur sports and physical fitness programs in the 1970s and 80s, it grew rapidly.

Spotsylvania, rural county, NE Virginia, formerly part of the estate of Gov. Alexander Spotswood. In the CIVIL WAR it was the scene of the battles of FREDERICKSBURG and CHANCELLORSVILLE, and of the battles of the Wilderness and Spotsylvania Courthouse in the WILDERNESS CAMPAIGN.

Spratly Islands, group of low islands and coral reefs in the central SOUTH CHINA SEA, claimed by China, Taiwan, and Vietnam, and in part by Malaysia, the Philippines, and Brunei. Valued primarily for the petroleum and gas potential of the surrounding waters, various islands in the Spratlys are occupied by the claimants, except for Brunei.

spring, in geology, natural flow of water from the ground or from rocks, representing an outlet for the water that has accumulated in permeable rock strata underground. Mineral springs have a high mineral content. See also ARTESIAN WELL; GEYSER; HOT SPRING.

springer spaniel: see ENGLISH SPRINGER SPANIEL.

Springfield. **1** City (1990 pop. 105,227), state capital and seat of Sangamon co., central Ill., on the Sangamon R.; settled 1818, inc. as a city 1840. In a rich coal and farm area, it is a governmental, commercial, medical, insurance, and business center, with varied industries. Abraham LINCOLN, a longtime resident, is buried nearby, and there are numerous sites associated with him. Vachel LINDSAY's birthplace is now a museum. **2** Industrial city (1990 pop. 156,983), seat of Hampden co., SW Mass., a port on the Connecticut R.; inc. 1641. It has chemical, plastics, machinery, paper, and printing and publishing industries. Settled (1636) by Puritans, Springfield was a scene of Shays's Rebellion (1786–87; see under SHAYS, DANIEL), and a station on the UNDERGROUND RAILROAD. A U.S. armory there (1794–1966) developed the Springfield army rifles. Dr. James Naismith invented (1891) basketball at Springfield College, which houses a hall of fame for the sport. **3** City (1990 pop. 140,494), seat of Greene co., SW Mo., in a resort area of the OZARKS; inc. 1838. It is the trade and shipping center for an area producing livestock, grains, and corn. Food processing and diverse manufactures are important. A Civil War battlefield and the Mark Twain National Forest are nearby.

spruce, evergreen tree or shrub (genus *Picea*) of the PINE family, widely distributed in the Northern Hemisphere. The needles are angular in cross section, not flattened as in the related HEMLOCKS and FIRS. Spruces are a major source of pulpwood for PAPER manufacture; the light, straight-grained wood is also used in construction. Common North American spruces include the red spruce (*P. rubens*), white spruce (*P. glauca*), and black spruce (*P. mariana*) of the East; the Engelmann spruce (*P. engelmanii*) of the Rockies; and the Sitka spruce (*P. sitchensis*) of the Pacific forest belt. The Siberian spruce (*P. obovata*) grows in the huge coniferous forests (see TAIGA) of Russia.

spurge, common name for the family Euphorbiaceae, herbs, shrubs, and trees of greatly varied structure and almost cosmopolitan distribution, although most species are tropical. The spurges are of great economic importance; the sap of most species is a milky latex, and that of the PARÁ RUBBER TREE is the source of much of the world's natural RUBBER. The genus *Manihot* includes CASSAVA, the source of tapioca and the most important tropical root crop after the SWEET POTATO. The cactuslike euphorbias (genus *Euphorbia*) are among the most common Old World desert SUCCULENTS and comprise most of the species commonly called spurge. Many are cultivated for their often colorful foliage and the showy bracts enclosing their "naked flowers" (i.e., FLOWERS lacking petals and sometimes sepals). The poinsettia, native to Central America and sometimes classed in a separate genus (*Poinsettia*), is a popular Christmas plant with large rosettes of usually bright-red bracts.

Spyri, Johanna [shpē′rē], 1827–1901, Swiss author. She is best known for *Heidi* (1880) and other popular children's stories set in the Swiss Alps.

squash: see GOURD; PUMPKIN.

squash, game played on four-walled court with a small, hollow hard-rubber ball and a round-headed, gut-strung racket. A serve must hit the front wall above a service line 6½ ft (1.98 m) high, with subsequent caroms off the sidewalls permitted. The ball may be returned before it hits the floor, and a point is scored when either player fails to return the ball before it touches the floor twice. The game may be played by partners. Squash probably originated in the late 19th cent. and has become a popular game in U.S. colleges. National championships are conducted for men and women.

squatter sovereignty, in U.S. history, doctrine under which SLAVERY was permitted in territories, the final question of its legal status being left to territorial settlers when they applied for statehood.

First proposed in 1847, it was incorporated into the COMPROMISE OF 1850 and the KANSAS-NEBRASKA ACT. Its chief exponent, Stephen A. DOUGLAS, called it "popular sovereignty," but opponents of slavery contemptuously called it "squatter sovereignty."

squid, carnivorous marine mollusk with 10 sucker-bearing arms; a CEPHALOPOD. Among the most highly developed invertebrates, the squid has eyes similar to those of humans, relatively sophisticated nervous and circulatory systems, and no external shell. Squids prey on fish, which they seize in their tentacles; when in danger, they emit a cloud of ink from a special sac. Squids range in size from 2 in. (5 cm) to the 50-ft (15.2-m) giant squid, the largest of all invertebrates. Squid is a favorite food in the Mediterranean region and E Asia.

squill, low, usually spring-blooming bulbous herb (genus *Scilla*) of the LILY family. The flowers, commonly deep blue but also white, rose, or purplish, are borne along a leafless stem; the leaves are usually narrow. Species of *Scilla* are used in rock gardens and borders.

squirrel, small or medium-sized RODENT of the family Sciuridae, found worldwide except in Australia, Madagascar, and polar regions. Typical tree squirrels (genus *Sciurus*), including the Eurasian red squirrel (*S. vulgaris*) and the North American gray squirrels, are day-active animals with slender bodies, thick fur, and bushy tails. In addition to tree squirrels the family includes the CHIPMUNK, WOODCHUCK, PRAIRIE DOG, and FLYING SQUIRREL.

Sr, chemical symbol of the element STRONTIUM.

Sri Lanka [srē läng'kə], officially Democratic Socialist Republic of Sri Lanka, island republic (1992 est. pop. 17,632,000), S Asia, 25,332 sq mi (65,610 sq km), in the Indian Ocean, SE of India. The capital is COLOMBO. The island is mainly flat or gently rolling; among the mountains in the south central area is Adam's Peak (7,360 ft/2,243 m), sacred to Buddhists. Plantation crops, principally tea, rubber, and coconuts, dominate the agricultural sector of the economy and are important exports. Manufactures include textiles (the most important export), processed agricultural products, and consumer goods. Sri Lanka is also a leading producer of high-grade graphite. The population is composed mainly of Sinhalese, who are Theravada Buddhists. Hindu Tamils make up a large minority, and there are smaller Muslim, European, and Eurasian minorities. The national languages are Sinhala (the official language) and Tamil. English is also spoken.

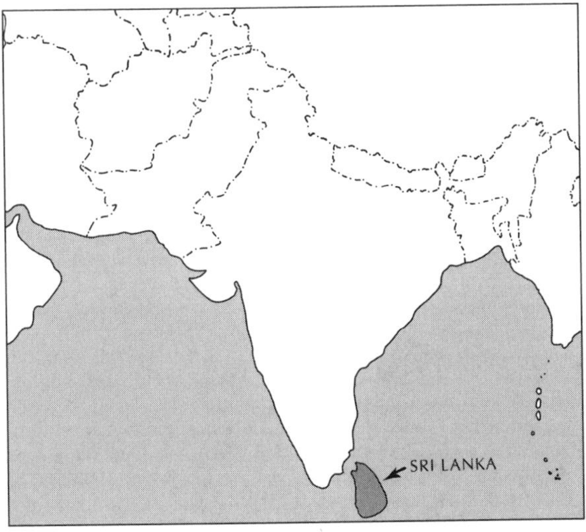

History. The aboriginal inhabitants were conquered in the 6th cent. B.C. by the Sinhalese, from N India, who established their capital at Anuradhapura. With the introduction of Buddhism in the 3d cent. B.C. the island became one of the world centers of that religion. Europeans were drawn by the spice trade, and the island came under the Portuguese (16th cent.), the Dutch (17th cent.), and the British, who made it the crown colony of Ceylon in 1798. A nationalist movement arose during World War I, and the island was granted independence in 1948. The new nation was challenged by rapid population growth, economic difficulties, and separatist demands by the Tamil minority. After the assassination of Prime Minister S.W.R.D. Bandaranaike in 1959 his widow, Sirimavo BANDARANAIKE, served as prime minister (1960–65, 1970–77), implementing such policies as nationalization of Western-owned businesses. A new constitution in 1972 adopted the Sinhalese name Sri Lanka and declared the country a republic. Economic crises and social unrest continued to plague the nation, and Mrs. Bandaranaike's party was overwhelmingly defeated by the conservatives in 1977, who consitutionally changed the government to a presidential one. Western-style capitalism was promoted by Pres. J.R. Jayewardene, who was reelected in 1982; in 1989 Ranasinghe Premadasa became president. Hostility among Sri Lanka's ethnic groups continued to be a serious problem into the 1990s. Tamil forces, allegedly supplied by the government of India, kept the nation in civil war through much of the 1980s and seized control of the Jaffna peninsula in the north. India's attempt to mediate the conflict, including stationing (1987–90) its troops in Tamil areas, was unsuccessful, and fighting resumed in 1990. In 1993 Premadasa was assassinated; he was succeeded as president by Prime Min. Dingiri Banda Wijetunga.

Ssu-ma Ch'ien [so͞o'mä chyĕn], 145?–90? B.C., Chinese historian of the Han dynasty, called the Father of Chinese history. He wrote *Shih chi* [records of the historian], a history in 130 chapters of China and all regions and peoples known at that time. It became a model for later dynastic histories.

Staël, Germaine de [stäl], 1766–1817, French-Swiss woman of letters; daughter of Suzanne and Jacques NECKER. Her Paris salon was a powerful political and cultural center until 1803, when her spirited opposition to NAPOLEON I caused her exile. She retired to her estate at Coppet, on Lake Geneva, where she again attracted a brilliant circle. Her principal work, *On Germany* (1810), with its enthusiasm for German ROMANTICISM, tremendously influenced European thought and letters. Her other works include a sociological study of literature (1800); the novels *Delphine* (1802) and *Corinne* (1807); and a memoir, *Ten Years of Exile* (1818).

Stafford, Jean, 1915–79, American writer; b. Covina, Calif. Her finely wrought, gently ironic work includes the novels *Boston Adventure* (1944) and *The Catherine Wheel* (1952), and her widely acclaimed *Collected Stories* (1969; Pulitzer).

stained glass, windows made of colored glass. An art form of great antiquity in E Asia, used by Muslim designers in their intricate windows, it became one of the most beautiful achievements of medieval art. Christian churches had colored glass windows as early as the 5th cent., but the art of stained glass reached its height in the Middle Ages, particularly 1150–1250. As the massive Romanesque wall was eliminated, the use of glass expanded. Integrated with the lofty verticals of Gothic architecture (see GOTHIC ARCHITECTURE AND ART), large windows provided greater illumination that was regarded as symbolic of divine light. Early glaziers followed a CARTOON to cut the glass and fired the painted pieces in a kiln. Metallic oxides fused with the glass in the melting pot to produce the jewel-like colors of small pieces whose irregular surfaces created scintillating refractions of light. The pieces were fitted into channeled lead strips, the leads were soldered together, and the glass was installed in an iron framework. Outstanding examples of 12th-cent. stained glass can be found in the windows of such churches as Saint-Denis, in Paris, and CANTERBURY, in England. Among the finest 13th-cent. works are the windows at CHARTRES and the SAINTE-CHAPELLE in Paris. With improved glassmaking many medieval qualities vanished, and by the 16th cent. a lesser art was produced with larger, smoother pieces and sophisticated painting techniques. In the 19th cent., ROMANTICISM and the GOTHIC REVIVAL caused renewed interest in stained glass. Important contributions to the art were made by William MORRIS, in England, and John LA FARGE and Louis Comfort TIFFANY, in the U.S. In modern art the medium has been used by ROUAULT, MATISSE, and CHAGALL.

stainless steel: see STEEL.

stalactite and stalagmite, mineral forms found in CAVES; sometimes collectively called dripstone. A stalactite is an icicle-shaped mass of CALCITE that hangs from the roof of a cave, formed by the precipitation of calcite from groundwater. A stalagmite is a cone of calcite rising from the floor of a cave, formed by the same process. Stalactites and stalagmites often meet to form solid pillars. The many colors often seen in these formations are caused by impurities.

Stalin, Joseph Vissarionovich, 1879–1953, Russian revolutionary, head of the USSR (1924–53). A Georgian cobbler's son named Dzhugashvili, he joined the Social-Democratic party while a seminarian and soon became a professional revolutionary. In the 1903 party split (see BOLSHEVISM AND MENSHEVISM) he sided with LENIN. Stalin attended party congresses abroad and worked in the Georgian party press. In 1912 he went to St. Petersburg, where he was elected to the party's central committee. About this time he took the name Stalin ("man of steel"). His sixth arrest (1913) led to four years of Siberian exile. After the RUSSIAN REVOLUTION of March 1917, he joined the editorial board of the party paper *Pravda.* When the Bolsheviks took power (Nov. 1917) he became people's commissar of nationalities. He also played an important administrative role in the civil war (1918–20). In 1922 Stalin was made general secretary of the party. Lenin, before he died in 1924, wrote a "testament" urging Stalin's removal from the post because of his arbitrary conduct; but in the struggle to succeed Lenin, Stalin was victorious. By 1927 he had discarded his erstwhile allies BUKHARIN, KAMENEV, and ZINOVIEV; in 1929 TROTSKY, his major rival for the succession, was exiled from the USSR. Forcible agricultural collectivization and breakneck industrialization began in 1928. The state, instead of "withering away," as Marx had foreseen, was glorified. Nationalism was revived as "socialism in one country." The military was reorganized along czarist lines. Conservatism permeated official policy on art, education, and the family. Political repression and terror reached a height in the 1930s. In a public trial Bukharin, Kamenev, Zinoviev, and others were charged with conspiring to overthrow the regime; they confessed and were executed. Enormous numbers of ordinary citizens also fell victim. Stalin's foreign policy in the 1930s focused on efforts to form alliances with Britain and France against NAZI Germany; the 1939 Russo-German nonaggression pact marked the failure of these efforts. In 1941 Stalin took over the premiership from MOLOTOV. The German invasion (June 22) found him unprepared; at war's end (1945) 20 million Russians were dead (see UNION OF SOVIET SOCIALIST REPUBLICS). At the TEHERAN CONFERENCE and the YALTA CONFERENCE Stalin gained Western recognition of a Soviet sphere of influence in Eastern Europe. The paranoia of his last years led to a period of terror reminiscent of the 1930s. On his death (1953) his body was placed next to Lenin's. In 1956, at the 20th Party Congress, KHRUSHCHEV denounced Stalin's tyranny, but "destalinization" has never been thoroughgoing.

Stalingrad: see VOLGOGRAD.

stamen: see FLOWER.

Stamford, city (1990 pop. 108,056), SW Conn., on Long Island Sound; settled 1641, inc. as a city 1893. It is a residential suburb of New York City, and the headquarters site for a large number of major U.S. corporations. Office equipment, bearings, and chemicals are manufactured.

Stamp Act, 1765, revenue law passed by the British Parliament requiring publications and legal documents in the American colonies to bear a tax stamp. The act was vehemently denounced, and organizations formed to resist it (see SONS OF LIBERTY). The **Stamp Act Congress,** Oct. 1765, adopted the Declaration of Rights and Grievances, which declared the tax unconstitutional because the colonists were not represented in Parliament. The Stamp Act was repealed in 1766.

standard deviation: see STATISTICS.

standard of living, level of consumption of goods and services to which an individual or group is accustomed, usually thought of in national terms. Although an evaluation of a standard of living is relative, the use of GROSS NATIONAL PRODUCT or per capita income provides a more objective yardstick for comparing the living standards of two or more countries. The elements that make up a standard of living include not only the goods consumed but also the number of dependents in a family, educational opportunities, and the amount spent for health and recreation. In the U.S. the standard of living has been climbing steadily, but in periods when prices rise faster than does per capita income, as in the late 1970s, the living standard may actually decline.

standard time: see SOLAR TIME.

Standish, Miles or **Myles,** c.1584–1650, American colonist; b. England. Accompanying the PILGRIMS to America (1620), he became the military leader of PLYMOUTH COLONY and a founder of Duxbury, Mass. He is familiar as the disappointed suitor in LONGFELLOW's poem *The Courtship of Miles Standish.*

Stanhope, Philip Dormer: see CHESTERFIELD, PHILIP DORMER STANHOPE, 4TH EARL OF.

Stanislaus, Polish kings. **Stanislaus I,** 1677–1766, king of POLAND (1704–9, 1733–35) and duke of Lorraine (1735–66), was born Stanislaus Leszczynski. Early in the NORTHERN WAR, CHARLES XII of Sweden deposed AUGUSTUS II of Poland and installed Leszczynski, a Polish nobleman. In 1709, however, Stanislaus was forced to yield the crown to Augustus and retire to France. There his daughter, Marie Leszczynska, married LOUIS XV, with whose help Stanislaus attempted (1733) to wrest the crown from Augustus, thus precipitating the War of the POLISH SUCCESSION. At its conclusion, he retained his royal title but renounced his actual rights in return for the duchy of Lorraine. **Stanislaus II,** 1732–98, was the last king of Poland (1764–95). With the support of Frederick II of Prussia and Catherine II of Russia (his former mistress), he was elected (1764) to succeed AUGUSTUS III. He was a virtual puppet of Russia, and during his reign Poland was dismembered (see POLAND, PARTITIONS OF).

Stanislavsky, Constantin, 1863–1938, Russian theatrical director, teacher, and actor, cofounder of the Moscow Art Theatre (see THEATER, table); b. Constantin Sergeyevich Alekseyev. His innovative technique for actors, emphasizing emotional truth and inner motivation and known today as the Stanislavsky Method, revolutionized modern acting. He was the first to produce many of CHEKHOV's plays.

Stanley, Sir Henry Morton, 1841–1904, British explorer and journalist. In 1871 he was sent by the New York *Herald* to find David LIVINGSTONE in Africa, where he delivered his famous greeting, "Dr. Livingstone, I presume?" On another expedition (1874–79) he explored the length of the Congo R., and on a third journey (1879–84), under Belgian auspices, he helped to organize the future Independent State of the Congo (see ZAÏRE).

Stanton, Elizabeth Cady, 1815–1902, American reformer and feminist; b. Johnstown, N.Y. With Lucretia MOTT she organized (1848) the first U.S. women's rights convention, and from 1852 she led the women's movement with Susan B. ANTHONY. An able journalist, gifted orator, and persuasive promoter of FEMINISM, Stanton was president (1869–90) of the National Woman Suffrage Association and editor (1868–70) of *Revolution,* a militant women's rights magazine.

star, hot, incandescent sphere of gas (usually more than 90% hydrogen) that is held together by its own gravitation and emits light and other forms of electromagnetic radiation whose ultimate source is nuclear energy. The universe contains billions of galaxies, and each GALAXY contains billions of stars, which are frequently bunched together in STAR CLUSTERS of as many as 100,000. The stars visible to the unaided eye are all in our own galaxy, the MILKY WAY. The visible stars are divided into six classes according to their apparent MAGNITUDE. Stars differ widely in mass, size, temperature, age (see STELLAR POPULATIONS), and LUMINOSITY. About 90% of all stars have masses between one tenth and 50 times that of the sun. The most luminous stars (excluding supernovas) are about a million times more powerful than the sun, while the least luminous are only a hundredth as powerful. VARIABLE STARS fluctuate in luminosity. Red giants, the largest stars, are hundreds of times greater in size than the sun. At the opposite extreme, WHITE DWARFS are no larger than the earth, and NEUTRON STARS are only a few kilometers in radius. The central region, or core, has a temperature of millions of degrees. At this temperature nuclear energy is released by the fusion of hydrogen to form helium. By the time nuclear energy reaches the surface of the star, it has been largely converted into visible light with a spectrum characteristic of a very hot body. The theory of STELLAR EVOLUTION states that a star must change as it consumes its hydrogen in the nuclear reactions that power it. When all its nuclear fuel is exhausted, the star dies, possibly in a SUPERNOVA explosion.

starch, white, odorless, tasteless CARBOHYDRATE powder. It plays a vital role in the BIOCHEMISTRY of both plants and animals. Made in green plants by PHOTOSYNTHESIS, it is one of the main forms in which plants store food. Animals obtain starch from plants and store it as GLYCOGEN. Both plants and animals convert starch to GLUCOSE when energy is needed. Commercially, starch is made chiefly from CORN and POTATOES. Corn syrup and corn sugar made from cornstarch are widely used to sweeten food products. Starch is also used to stiffen laundered fabrics and to size paper and textiles.

Star Chamber, ancient meeting place of the king's councilors in WESTMINSTER PALACE, London, named for the stars painted on the ceiling. From the 15th cent. the role of the council as an equity and prerogative court increased and it extended its jurisdiction over criminal matters, especially under the TUDORS. Abuses of its power under JAMES I and CHARLES I led to its abolition in 1641.

star cluster, group of neighboring stars that resemble each other in certain characteristics that suggest a common origin. Galactic, or open, clusters typically contain from a few dozen to about a thousand loosely scattered stars and exist in regions rich in gas and dust, such as the spiral arms of the galaxy. More than 1,000 galactic clusters, including the Hyades and Pleiades in the constellation Taurus, have been catalogued in the Milky Way. Globular clusters are spherical aggregates of thousands or millions of densely concentrated stars and exist in the outer halo of the galaxy. The brightest of the more than 100 globular clusters so far detected in the galaxy are Omega Centauri and 47 Tucanae, both seen with the unaided eye in the southern skies. X-ray sources have been detected in some globular clusters.

starfish or **sea star,** star-shaped carnivorous marine invertebrate animal (an ECHINODERM), found worldwide in shallow waters. The spiny body has five or more tapering arms radiating from a central area. Usually dull yellow or orange but occasionally brightly colored, starfish vary in size from under ½ in. (1.3 cm) to over 3 ft (90 cm).

Stark, John, 1728–1822, American Revolutionary soldier; b. Londonderry, N.H. As commander of the New Hampshire militia in the SARATOGA CAMPAIGN, he repulsed the British in the battle of Bennington (1777).

starling, any of a group of originally Old World BIRDS of the family Sturnidae, now distributed worldwide. The common starling (*Sturnus vulgaris*) is found throughout North America. Insect eaters, starlings have iridescent black plumage and a long bill. They mimic bird songs and other sounds, and are considered pests since they collect in large, noisy flocks and drive away smaller, more desirable birds.

Star of Bethlehem, name of the luminous celestial object in the eastern sky that, as related in the New Testament, led the Wise Men to Bethlehem. The phenomenon may have been caused by the conjunction of the planets Jupiter, Saturn, and Mars, or by the appearance of a nova or a comet.

Starr, Belle, 1848?–89, American outlaw; b. near Carthage, Mo., as Myra Belle Shirley. Her home in Oklahoma was a retreat for outlaws. Imprisoned briefly for horse theft in 1883, she was later shot to death by an unknown person.

Star-spangled Banner, The, U.S. national anthem, beginning, "O say can you see." The words were written by Francis Scott KEY, a Washington, D.C., lawyer who watched the bombardment of Fort McHenry by the British in Sept. 1814. The fort withstood the attack, and the sight of the American flag at dawn inspired Key's verses, set to a popular English tune. Its designation as national anthem by executive order in 1916 was confirmed by an act of Congress in 1931.

START (Strategic Arms Reduction Talks): see DISARMAMENT, NUCLEAR.

Star Wars: see STRATEGIC DEFENSE INITIATIVE.

State, United States Department of, federal executive department responsible for the implementation of American foreign policy. Created in 1789, it is the oldest federal department, and its head, the secretary of state, is the ranking member of the cabinet. While some of its original functions (such as supervision of the U.S. Mint) have been transferred to other departments, it has expanded with the growth of the U.S. as a world power. The Dept. of State is in charge of the Foreign Service and maintains delegations (embassies, consulates, and special missions) in other countries. Such secretaries of state as George C. MARSHALL (1947–49), John Foster DULLES (1953–59), and Henry KISSINGER (1973–76) have played important roles in making U.S. foreign policy.

States-General or **Estates-General,** French national assembly in which the three chief states (clergy, nobles, and commons) were represented as separate bodies. Like the English PARLIAMENT, it originated in the king's council, but it never gained the financial control that made the English Parliament powerful. The first States-General was summoned (1302) by PHILIP IV to obtain national approval for his anticlerical policy. Later meetings often opposed the king or even won temporary concessions, but the continuous consolidation of royal power prevented its growth. After the States-General of 1614, the estates were not convoked again until 1789. In that year LOUIS XVI assembled the estates as a last resort to solve France's financial crisis. In June 1789 the third estate (commons), joined by some of the clergy, declared itself the National Assembly, an act that began the FRENCH REVOLUTION.

states of matter, forms of matter differing in several properties because of differences in the motions of and the forces between the molecules (or atoms or ions) of which they are composed. There are three common states of matter: solid, liquid, and gas. The molecules of a solid are limited to vibrations about a fixed position, giving a solid both a definite volume and a definite shape. When heat is applied to a solid, its molecules begin to vibrate more rapidly until, at a temperature called the MELTING POINT, they break out of their fixed positions and the solid becomes a liquid. Because the molecules of a liquid are free to move throughout the liquid but are held from escaping by intermolecular forces (see ADHESION AND COHESION), a liquid has a definite volume but no definite shape. As more heat is added to the liquid, some molecules near the surface gain enough energy to evaporate, or break away completely from the liquid, and change to a gaseous state. Finally, at a temperature called the BOILING POINT, molecules throughout the liquid become energetic enough to escape, forming bubbles of vapor that rise to the surface; the liquid thus changes completely to a gas. Because its molecules are free to move in every possible way, a gas has neither a definite shape nor a definite volume but expands to fill any container in which it is placed. The reverse processes of melting and boiling are, respectively, freezing and condensation. See also CRYSTAL; GAS LAWS; KINETIC-MOLECULAR THEORY OF GASES; PLASMA.

states' rights, in U.S. history, a doctrine based on the 10th amendment to the CONSTITUTION, which states: "The powers not delegated to the United States by the Constitution, nor prohibited by it to the States, are reserved to the States respectively, or to the people." Controversy over interpretation of this clause arose immediately. The Federalists, led by Alexander HAMILTON, favored a broad interpretation. Thomas JEFFERSON and the "strict constructionists" insisted that all powers not specifically granted the federal government be reserved to the states; the KENTUCKY AND VIRGINIA RESOLUTIONS were the first formulations of this doctrine. The issue was central to the HARTFORD CONVENTION (1814–15), called by New Englanders to express officially their hostility to the federal government. The fight over the constitutionality of the Bank of the U.S. provided a major setback for states' rights; the Supreme Court's decision in MCCULLOCH V. MARYLAND (1819) greatly expanded the scope of federal power. An extreme expression of states' rights was the ordinance of NULLIFICATION, led by Sen. John C. CALHOUN and passed (1832) by South Carolina in response to the tariff acts of 1828 and 1832. Ultimately, states' rights was used by the proslavery states to justify secession. In the 20th cent., states' rights was revived by Southern opponents of the federal civil-rights program. But states' rights is not exclusive to any section or party, and the vast increase in the powers of the federal government has led to renewed interest in the doctrine.

statics, branch of MECHANICS concerned with the maintenance of equilibrium in bodies by the interaction of FORCES upon them. In a state of equilibrium the resultant of all outside forces acting on a body is zero, thus keeping the body at rest.

statistical mechanics, quantitative study of systems that consist of a large number of interacting elements, such as the molecules of a gas or the PHOTONS of visible light. The nature of an individual molecule and the interactions between any pair of molecules may be well understood, but understanding the behavior of a system consisting of a large number of molecules with many possible interactions can present an almost overwhelming challenge. Statistical mechanics provides a mathematical framework upon which an understanding of such a system can be built, usually on a microscopic or atomic scale. Modern statistical mechanics recognizes three types of systems: those that obey Maxwell-Boltzmann statistics, those that obey Bose-Einstein statistics, and those that obey Fermi-Dirac statistics. Maxwell-Boltzmann statistics apply to systems of classical particles, such as the atmosphere. The other two types deal with systems in which the effects decribed by QUANTUM MECHANICS cannot be ignored. Bose-Einstein statistics apply to systems of subatomic particles called BOSONS, and Fermi-Dirac statistics to those called FERMIONS. Statistical mechanics has yielded insights into the nature of MAGNETISM, PHASE TRANSITIONS, and SUPERCONDUCTIVITY.

statistics, branch of applied mathematics dealing with the collection and classification of data by numerical characteristics and the use of these data to make inferences and predictions in uncertain situations. Generally, measurements taken from a small group, the sample, are used to infer the behavior of a larger group, the population, as in television ratings and election predictions. The theory of PROBABILITY is necessary to determine how well the sample represents the population. The most widely used tools are the (arithmetic) mean and the median. The mean of a set of numbers is their sum divided by the number of elements in the set, e.g., for the five numbers 7, 7, 8, 10, and 11, the mean is $(7 + 7 + 8 + 10 + 11)/5 = 43/5 = 8.6$. The median of a set is the number that divides the set in half, so that as many numbers are larger than the median as are smaller. The median of 7, 7, 8, 10, and 11 is 8. (If the set has an even number of elements, the median is the number halfway between the middle pair.) Another important statistical measure is the standard deviation, which indicates how closely the data are clustered about the mean. Statistics is used in scientific and social research, insurance, and many other fields.

stator: see GENERATOR; MOTOR, ELECTRIC.

STD: see SEXUALLY TRANSMITTED DISEASE.

Stead, Christina, 1902–83, Australian novelist. She wrote unsentimentally about human obsession and the problem of evil, as in *The Man Who Loved Children* (1940), *A Little Tea, A Little Chat* (1948), and *The Little Hotel* (1975).

steady-state theory: see COSMOLOGY.

stealth technology, materials and techniques used in the construction of mobile military systems, such as aircraft, tanks, and ships, to significantly reduce their detection by an enemy, primarily by enemy radar. Among the techniques used in the U.S. F-117A fighter and B-2 bomber, for example, are a low profile with no surfaces that reflect radar directly back, the intensive substitution of radar-opaque composites for metals, and an overall coating of a radar-absorbing material.

steam engine, machine for converting heat energy into mechanical energy, using steam as the conversion medium. When water is boiled into steam its volume increases about 1,600 times, producing a force that can be used to move a piston back and forth in a cylinder. The piston is attached to a crankshaft that converts the piston's back-and-forth motion into rotary motion for driving machinery. From the Greek inventor HERO OF ALEXANDRIA to the Englishman Thomas NEWCOMEN, many persons contributed to the work of harnessing steam. However, James WATT's steam engine (patented 1769) offered the first practical solution by providing a separate chamber for condensing the steam and by using steam pressure to move the piston in both directions. These and other improvements by Watt prepared the steam engine for a major role in manufacturing and transportation during the INDUSTRIAL REVOLUTION. Today steam engines have been largely replaced by more efficient devices, e.g., the steam TURBINE, the electric MOTOR, the INTERNAL-COMBUSTION ENGINE, and the DIESEL ENGINE.

steamship, watercraft propelled by a STEAM ENGINE or a steam TURBINE. A number of experimental steam-powered vessels were built in the late 18th cent., and in 1807 Robert FULTON's *Clermont* made the 150-mi (240-km) trip from New York City to Albany in 32 hr. The *Savannah,* a full-rigged sailing ship fitted with engines and paddlewheels, made the first Atlantic Ocean crossing by a steam-propelled vessel in 1819. Two British SHIPS made the first crossing under steam power alone in 1838. By the late 1850s the screw propeller was replacing paddlewheels, and the steamship began to supplant the sailing ship. Great liners were plying the Atlantic on regular schedules by the end of the century. The sea-going leviathans of the 20th cent., such as the *Queen Mary* (1934), the *Queen Elizabeth* (1938), and the *United States* (1951), were turbine-powered steamships. Ships using fission-generated heat to produce steam proved uneconomical for commerce, but most large naval vessels use nuclear-powered steam plants. Today commercial steamships have given way to more fuel-efficient diesel-powered ships.

steatite: see SOAPSTONE.

steel, ALLOY of IRON, CARBON, and small proportions of other elements. Steelmaking involves the removal of iron's impurities and the addition of desirable alloying elements. Steel was first made by cementation, a process of heating bars of iron with charcoal so that the surface of the iron acquired a high carbon content. The bars were then fused together, yielding a metal harder and stronger than the individual bars but lacking uniformity in these properties. The crucible method, consisting of melting iron together with other substances in a crucible, is one of the costlier steelmaking processes, employed only for making special steels (e.g., the famous blades of Damascus). The OPEN-HEARTH PROCESS, BASIC OXYGEN PROCESS and ELECTRIC ARC PROCESS are the methods most commonly used in modern steelmaking; the BESSEMER PROCESS is a historically important method that has been superseded. Steel is often classified by its carbon content: a high-carbon steel is hard and brittle; low- or medium-carbon steel can be welded and tooled. Alloy steels, now the most widely used, contain one or more elements that give them special properties. Aluminum steel is smooth and has a high tensile strength. Chromium steel is used in automobile and airplane parts because of its hardness, strength, and elasticity. Nickel steel is the most widely used of the alloys; it is nonmagnetic and has the tensile properties of high-carbon steel without the brittleness. Stainless steel has a high tensile strength and resists abrasion and corrosion because of its high chromium content; it is used in kitchen utensils and plumbing fixtures. See also CASEHARDENING; GALVANIZING.

Steele, Sir Richard, 1672–1729, English essayist and playwright; b. Dublin. His first play, *The Funeral,* appeared in 1701 and was followed by three more comedies: *The Lying Lover* (1703), *The Tender Husband* (1705), and *The Conscious Lovers* (1722). Steele held various minor governmental posts before starting his periodical the *Tatler* (1709–11), on which he was soon joined by Joseph ADDISON. Their partnership led to the founding of the *Spectator* (1711–12), *Guardian* (1713), and lesser periodicals, all graced by Steele's spontaneous, witty ESSAYS. A Whig partisan and member of Parliament from 1713, Steele wrote the pamphlet *Crisis* (1713) in opposition to SWIFT. He also founded (1720) the first theatrical paper.

Steen, Jan [stān], 1626–79, Dutch genre painter. Steen's nearly 900 paintings show the influence of the major Dutch masters except REMBRANDT. His humorous and moralistic works offer a picture of life in his day. He was a superb draftsman and portraitist, and his favorite themes were revelry and feasting, e.g., *The Prince's Birthday* (Rijks Mus., Amsterdam) and *Skittle Players* (National Gall., London).

Steffens, (Joseph) Lincoln, 1866–1936, American author; b. San Francisco. A magazine editor (1902–11) and a MUCKRAKER, he wrote articles exposing municipal corruption, collected in such volumes as *The Shame of the Cities* (1904) and *Upbuilders* (1909). His famous autobiography (1931) casts light on his era.

Stegner, Wallace, 1909–93, American writer; b. Lake Mills, Iowa. He wrote perceptively of the American West in short stories, e.g.,

The Woman on the Wall (1950); novellas, e.g., *On a Darkling Plain* (1940); and novels, e.g., *The Big Rock Candy Mountain* (1943), *Angle of Repose* (1971; Pulitzer), and *Crossing to Safety* (1987).

Steichen, Edward [stī'kən], 1879–1973, American photographer; b. Luxembourg. In Paris Steichen was renowned for his painterly photographs. With Alfred STIEGLITZ he established photography as an art. He helped develop aerial photography in World War I and directed U.S. naval combat photography in World War II. As head of the Museum of Modern Art's photography department (1947–62) he organized the *Family of Man* exhibition (1955).

Stein, Gertrude, 1874–1946, American author; b. Allegheny, Pa. She went abroad in 1902 and from 1903 until her death lived mainly in Paris. During the 1920s she led a cultural salon, acting as a patron for such artists as PICASSO and MATISSE and influencing such writers as HEMINGWAY, Sherwood ANDERSON, and F. Scott FITZGERALD. Stein's own innovative writing emphasized the sounds and rhythms rather than the sense of words. Her works include short stories, e.g., *Three Lives* (1909); a long narrative, *The Making of Americans* (1925); autobiographical works, notably the *Autobiography of Alice B. Toklas* (1933); critical essays, e.g., *How to Write* (1931) and *Lectures in America* (1935); "cubist" poetry, e.g., *Tender Buttons* (1914); and operas, notably *Four Saints in Three Acts* (1934), with music by Virgil THOMSON.

Gertrude Stein

Steinbeck, John, 1902–68, American writer; b. Salinas, Calif. His works are marked by a compassionate understanding of the world's disinherited. His best-known novel, *The Grapes of Wrath* (1939; Pulitzer), treats the plight of 1930s Dust Bowl farmers turned migrant laborers while presenting a universal picture of victims of disaster. Among Steinbeck's other novels are *Tortilla Flat* (1935), *Cannery Row* (1945), *East of Eden* (1952), and *The Winter of Our Discontent* (1961). His other books include the novella *Of Mice and Men* (1937; later made into a play); short stories, notably the exquisite "The Red Pony" in *The Long Valley* (1938); nonfiction works, e.g., *A Russian Journal* (1948), *America and Americans* (1966); and screenplays. Steinbeck was awarded the 1962 Nobel Prize in literature.

Steinem, Gloria, 1934–, American journalist and feminist; b. Clarklake, Mich. A journalist during the 1960s, she became a spokeswoman for FEMINISM, helping organize (1971) the Women's Political Caucus, and was founding editor of *Ms.* magazine (1971–87). Her books include *Outrageous Acts and Everyday Rebellions* (1983) and *Revolution from Within* (1992).

Steiner, Rudolf, 1861–1925, German occultist and social philosopher. Originally an adherent of THEOSOPHY, he founded (1912) his own system, which he called anthroposophy. It attempted to explain the world in terms of human spiritual nature, or a level of thinking independent of the senses. More than 170 private schools throughout the world are based on his pedagogical and philosophic teachings.

Steinmetz, Charles Proteus, 1865–1923, American electrical engineer; b. Germany; came to U.S., 1889. He joined the General Electric Co. in 1892. His discovery of the law of hysteresis made it possible to reduce the loss of efficiency in electrical apparatus resulting from alternating magnetism. His method for calculating alternating current revolutionized electrical engineering.

stele, stone or terra-cotta slab, usually oblong, set upright. Used as votives or memorials, they were commonly carved with inscriptions and designs. Stelae were often used as commemorative stones in ancient Egypt and as boundary markers in Mesopotamia. Greek marble funerary stelae, with painted reliefs of the dead, are monuments of classical art. Ancient stelae are also found in China and in Mayan ruins.

Stella, Frank, 1936–, American painter; b. Malden, Mass. His earlier paintings are generally large, often with precise, concentric angular stripes or curved motifs that emphasize the frequently irregular shape of his canvases. In more recent work, he has favored a more improvised, dynamic idiom in mixed media.

Stella, Joseph, 1877–1946, American painter; b. Italy. He is best known for his cubist- and futurist-inspired works, done c.1920, expressing the dynamism of New York City.

stellar evolution, life history of a STAR. The initial phase of stellar evolution is contraction of the protostar from the interstellar gas (see INTERSTELLAR MATTER). In this stage, which typically lasts millions of years, half the gravitational potential energy released by the collapsing protostar is radiated away and half goes into increasing the temperature of the forming star. Eventually the temperature becomes high enough for the fusion of hydrogen to form helium. The star then enters its longest period in stellar evolution. Because most stars are in this stage and fall along a diagonal line in the HERTZSPRUNG-RUSSELL DIAGRAM, they are called main-sequence stars. As the star's helium content builds up, the core contracts and releases gravitational energy, which heats up the core and increases the rate of hydrogen consumption. The increased reaction rates cause the stellar envelope to expand and cool, and the star becomes a red giant. Eventually, the contracting stellar core will reach temperatures in excess of 100,000,000K. At this point, helium burning sets in, and the star starts shrinking in size. In the further course of evolution, the star may become unstable, possibly ejecting some of its mass and becoming an exploding nova or SUPERNOVA or a pulsating VARIABLE STAR. The end phase of a star depends on its mass. A low-mass star may become a WHITE DWARF; an intermediate-mass star may become a NEUTRON STAR; and a high-mass star may undergo complete GRAVITATIONAL COLLAPSE and become a black hole.

stellar populations, two distributions of star types. Population I stars are recently formed stars (see STELLAR EVOLUTION) that lie mostly on the main sequence of the HERTZSPRUNG-RUSSELL DIAGRAM. They are located mainly in the interstellar dust of the arms of spiral galaxies, in galactic, or open, STAR CLUSTERS, and in irregular galaxies. The older and highly evolved population II stars are formed early in the history of a galaxy from pure hydrogen with a possible admixture of primordial helium. Population II stars are found mainly in the arms, central nucleus, and halo of spiral galaxies and in elliptical galaxies.

stem, supporting structure of a plant, serving also to conduct and store food materials. Stems of herbaceous and woody plants differ: herbaceous plants usually have pliant, green stems with relatively more pith and an almost inactive CAMBIUM; woody stems are covered by BARK and increase in height and diameter because of an active cambium. Tendrils, thorns, and runners (stolons) are specialized aerial stems; BULBS, corms, RHIZOMES, and TUBERS are specialized underground stems. The stems of dicotyledons (see ANGIOSPERM) and GYMNOSPERMS consist of upward-conducting xylem (see WOOD) on the inside and downward-conducting phloem arranged on either side of the cambium. In monocotyledons, which generally lack cambium, bundles of xylem and phloem are scattered throughout the stem.

Stendhal [stăNdäl'], pseud. of **Marie Henri Beyle,** 1783–1842,

French author. He was an officer in Napoleon's army and later served as consul in Italy. His amorous involvements are reflected in *On Love* (1822), a psychological analysis of love that predates FREUD. Although largely unappreciated during his lifetime, his *The Red and the Black* (1831) and *The Charterhouse of Parma* (1839), noted for their character analysis, rank among the world's great novels. The Stendhalian hero has an egoism that derives its energy from passion, has its own moral code, and unswervingly pursues happiness in the form of love or power.

Stengel, Casey (Charles Dillon Stengel), 1891?–1975, American baseball player and manager; b. Kansas City, Mo. He played (1912–25) major-league baseball with five teams and then managed in the minor leagues. The colorful Stengel achieved greatness with the New York Yankees, managing them to 10 pennants and 7 world championships (5 in a row) in 12 seasons (1949–60). He managed the New York Mets from 1962 to 1965.

Stenmark, Ingemar, 1956–, Swedish skier. Nicknamed the "Silent Swede," he won 86 World Cup races in 16 years, including two Olympic gold medals (1980), and was World Cup champion three times (1976–78).

stenography: see SHORTHAND.

Stephen, Saint or **Stephen I,** 975–1038, duke (977–1001) and first king (1001–38) of Hungary. Because of his Christianizing and pro-German policy he had to put down revolts by pagan nobles. His crown remains a sacred symbol of Hungarian national identity. Feast: Aug. 16 (in Hungary, Aug. 20).

Stephen, 1097?–1154, king of England (1135–54); grandson of WILLIAM I. He swore fealty to HENRY I's daughter, MATILDA, but on Henry's death was proclaimed king. He constantly struggled to maintain his throne, and he quarreled repeatedly with the English clergy. Matilda, aided by her half brother Robert, earl of Gloucester, captured Stephen in 1141 and reigned briefly before Stephen was released and regained the throne. When his son Eustace died, Stephen was forced to name (1153) Matilda's son Henry, later HENRY II, as heir.

Stephen I, king of Hungary: see STEPHEN, SAINT (975–1038).

Stephen, Sir Leslie, 1832–1904, English writer and critic. He edited the *Cornhill Magazine* (1871–82) and was the first editor of *The Dictionary of National Biography* (1882–91). His books include *History of English Thought in the Eighteenth Century* (1876) and biographies of Samuel JOHNSON, POPE, SWIFT, George ELIOT, and HOBBES. Virginia WOOLF was his youngest daughter.

Stephen Báthory, 1533–86, king of POLAND (1575–86), prince of Transylvania (1571–75). Elected king, he married the daughter of SIGISMUND II, the last Jagiello king. He fought several successful campaigns against Russia, particularly for control of Livonia, but failed in efforts to crusade against the Turks and to make Russia a vassal state.

Stephen Dušan or **Dushan,** c.1308–1355, king (1331–46) and czar (1346–55) of SERBIA. After usurping his father's crown, he conquered Bulgaria, Macedonia, Thessaly, and Epirus. He brought Serbia to its greatest power, but his empire disintegrated after his death.

Stephens, Alexander Hamilton, 1812–83, American politician; b. Taliaferro co., Ga. He was U.S. congressman from Georgia (1843–59). Opposed to secession, he remained loyal to Georgia when the state seceded. Elected vice president (1861–65) of the CONFEDERACY, he consistently opposed the policies of Pres. DAVIS. After the war he was interned for several months.

Stephens, James, 1882–1950, Irish poet and fiction writer. A leading figure in the Irish literary renaissance, he is best known for his fanciful prose, e.g., in *The Crock of Gold* (1912), *The Demi-Gods* (1914), and *Deirdre* (1923).

Stephenson, George, 1781–1848, English engineer and locomotive builder. He created a traveling engine to haul coal (1814) and the first LOCOMOTIVE using the steam blast (1815). His locomotive *Rocket* won an 1829 contest and was used on the Liverpool-Manchester Railway. He became engineer for several of the new railroads. His son **Robert Stephenson,** 1803–59, and a nephew, **George Robert Stephenson,** 1819–1905, were railroad engineers and bridge designers.

steppe, temperate grassland of Eurasia, consisting of level, generally treeless plains. The term is sometimes applied to the PRAIRIES of the U.S., the PAMPAS of South America, and the high VELD of South Africa. There are three vegetation zones: the wooded steppe (having deciduous trees and the highest rainfall), the tillable steppe (consisting of productive agricultural lands), and the non-tillable steppe (a semidesert).

stereochemistry, study of the three-dimensional configuration of the atoms that make up a MOLECULE and of the ways in which this arrangement affects the physical and chemical properties of the molecule. Central to stereochemistry is the concept of isomerism. ISOMERS are sets of chemical compounds having identical atomic composition but different structural properties. Stereochemistry is particularly important in BIOCHEMISTRY and molecular biology.

stereoisomer: see ISOMER.

stereophonic sound, sound recorded simultaneously by two or more MICROPHONES placed in different positions relative to the sound source. The recorded sound is played back through LOUDSPEAKERS placed more or less as the recording microphones were placed. The voices or instruments composing the sound thus seem to be spread out as they would be naturally in the recording hall. Quadrophonic reproduction utilized four microphones and four loudspeakers to further enhance the effect, but it was not commercially successful. Surround Sound uses special encoding and processing to enhance the effect and also requires additional loudspeakers. It is used in movie theaters and more expensive home entertainment systems.

sterility, inability to reproduce (see REPRODUCTIVE SYSTEM); also called infertility. In the male, malfunctioning of the sex glands, or testes, usually results in the production of defective sperm or a decreased number of sperm, causing sterility. In the female, malfunctioning of the sex glands, or ovaries, disturbs ovulation (production of the egg cell). Structural deformity (e.g., blockage of a tube), metabolic and infectious diseases, and psychological factors may also cause sterility. Voluntary sterilization is a form of BIRTH CONTROL.

sterilization: see BIRTH CONTROL.

Sterling Heights, city (1990 pop. 117,810), SE Mich., a growing suburb of DETROIT, 19 mi (31 km) NE of the city.

Stern, Isaac, 1920–, American violinist; b. USSR. He came to the U.S. as an infant. A child prodigy and a leading contemporary virtuoso, he has made many successful world tours since 1937.

Sterne, Laurence, 1713–68, English author; b. Ireland. A country churchman, he went to London in 1760 and published the first volume of his masterpiece *Tristram Shandy.* Although Dr. JOHNSON and others denounced it on moral and literary grounds, it was a great success. Eight more volumes followed (1761–67). A mixture of character sketches, digressions, and dramatic action into which the author constantly obtrudes himself, *Tristram Shandy* is based on LOCKE's association of ideas. By recording internal impressions, Sterne greatly expanded the scope of the NOVEL. His other books are *Journal to Eliza* (1767) and *A Sentimental Journey* (1768).

steroid, any of class of LIPIDS having a molecular structure based on four joined carbon rings with hydrogen molecules attached. Steroids differ from one another only in the additional atoms attached to the central structure. Many steroids are biologically active HORMONES. The class includes the sex hormones TESTOSTERONE, ESTROGEN, and PROGESTERONE, corticosteroids such as CORTISONE, several forms of vitamin D, CHOLESTEROL, and the BILE acids. Steroids are used in oral contraceptives and in the treatment of ARTHRITIS, ADDISON'S DISEASE, and certain skin ailments. ANABOLIC STEROIDS have been abused by bodybuilders and athletes in an attempt to increase muscle mass and strength. Steroids are found in plants and invertebrates as well as in vertebrates.

Stesichorus, fl. c.600 B.C., Greek LYRIC poet. Legend says he invented the choral "heroic hymn" and added the epode to the strophe and antistrophe, much used thereafter, e.g., by the tragedians and PINDAR.

Stettin: see SZCZECIN.

Steuben, Friedrich Wilhelm, Baron von [styo͞o'bən], 1730–94, Prussian army officer, general in the AMERICAN REVOLUTION. He helped to train the Continental army and to mold it into a powerful striking force.

Stevens, John, 1749–1838, American inventor; b. N.Y.C. After serving as state treasurer (1776–77) and surveyor general (1782–83) of

New Jersey and playing a leading role in the establishment of the first U.S. patent laws, he procured patents for various steam boilers and auxiliary devices and built (1806–8) the *Phoenix,* a seagoing steamboat (see STEAMSHIP). He later pioneered in railroad development, building an early locomotive.

Stevens, John Paul: see SUPREME COURT, UNITED STATES (table 1).

Stevens, Thaddeus, 1792–1868, U.S. representative from Pennsylvania (1849–53, 1859–68); b. Danville, Vt. A leader of the radical Republicans' RECONSTRUCTION program after the Civil War, he viewed the defeated Southern states as "conquered provinces." Sincerely desiring African-American betterment but eager to maintain the Republican party in power, he proposed the Fourteenth Amendment, guaranteeing civil rights. He was a leader in the impeachment of Andrew JOHNSON.

Stevens, Wallace, 1879–1955, American poet; b. Reading, Pa. While pursuing a career as an insurance executive, Stevens wrote elegant, philosophic verse often concerned with creating order from chaos. His books of poetry include *Harmonium* (1923), *The Man with the Blue Guitar* (1937), *Transport to Summer* (1947), and *Collected Poems* (1954; Pulitzer). His ideas are elaborated in the essays of *The Necessary Angel* (1951), and the poems, plays, essays, and epigrams of *Opus Posthumous* (1957).

Stevenson, Adlai Ewing, 1835–1914, U.S. vice president (1893–97); b. Christian co., Ky. His grandson, **Adlai Ewing Stevenson** (1900–65), b. Los Angeles, was governor of Illinois (1949–53). The unsuccessful Democratic presidential candidate in 1952 and 1956, he nonetheless gained enormous respect as a spokesman for liberal reform and internationalism. His son, **Adlai Ewing Stevenson, 3d,** 1930–, b. Chicago, served as U.S. senator from Illinois (1970–81). He ran unsuccessfully for governor of Illinois in 1982 and 1986.

Stevenson, Robert Louis, 1850–94, Scottish novelist, poet, and essayist. His first books, *An Inland Voyage* (1878) and *Travels with a Donkey in the Cévennes* (1879), were accounts of his wanderings on the Continent. In 1880 he went to the U.S., where he married Frances Osbourne. Four plays written with W.E. HENLEY had little success, but the adventure novel *Treasure Island* (1883) and *A Child's Garden of Verses* (1885) were very popular. In 1886 came two of his best-known works, *Kidnapped,* an adventure tale set in Scotland, and *The Strange Case of Dr. Jekyll and Mr. Hyde,* a science fiction thriller with moral overtones. *The Master of Ballantrae* (1889) was begun at Saranac Lake, N.Y., where Stevenson, a tuberculosis sufferer, had gone in search of a congenial climate. In 1889 he settled in Samoa, where he wrote three novels with Lloyd Osbourne, his stepson. He died there, leaving *Weir of Hermiston* (1896) and *St. Ives* (1897) unfinished.

Stewart, James, 1908–, American film actor; b. Indiana, Pa. Famous for his slow drawl and homespun charm, he starred in such films as *Mr. Smith Goes to Washington* (1939), *The Philadelphia Story* (1940; Academy Award), *Harvey* (1950), and *Vertigo* (1958).

stibnite, antimony sulfide mineral (Sb_2S_3), the most important ore of ANTIMONY. It is found in many parts of the world, often in association with arsenic, calcite, gold, quartz, and silver. Silvery gray in color, stibnite was used in ancient times by women to darken eyebrows and eyelashes. It is now used in alloys, in explosives, in vulcanizing rubber, and as an emetic.

stick insect: see WALKING STICK.

Stieglitz, Alfred [stēg'lĭts], 1864–1946, American photographer, editor, and art exhibitor; b. Hoboken, N.J. In his magazines, e.g., the seminal *Camera Work* (1902–17), and his galleries, including "291" and "An American Place," he sought to establish photography as an art while promoting modern French and American painting. Chief among his photographs are the series of portraits of his wife, Georgia O'KEEFFE; and studies of New York City.

Stijl, de [də stīl] [Dutch, = the style], Dutch nonfigurative art movement (1917–1931), also called neoplasticism. Its leaders were the artists Theo van Doesburg and Piet MONDRIAN. They advocated purifying art, eliminating subject matter in favor of abstract elements and primary colors. Their austerity of expression influenced architects Gerrit RIETVELD and J.J.P. Oud.

Stiles, Ezra, 1727–95, American theologian and educator; b. North Haven, Conn. He was a pastor at Newport, R.I., and Portsmouth, N.H., before serving (1778–95) as president of Yale. At Yale he taught church history and encouraged the sciences.

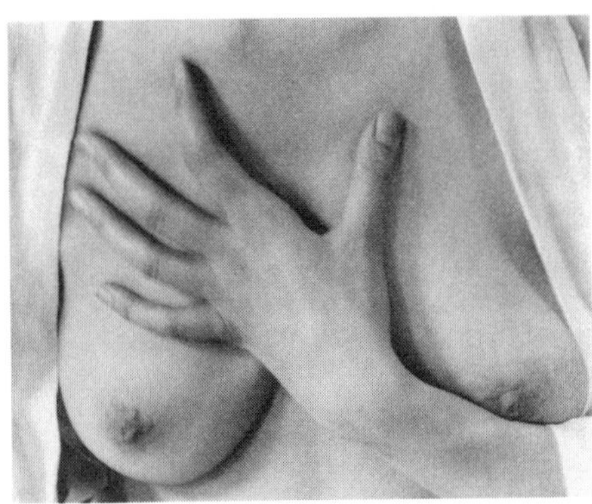

Stieglitz photo of Georgia O'Keefe, 1919

Stilicho, Flavius, d. 408, Roman statesman and general. He was the chief general of THEODOSIUS I and regent for HONORIUS in the West (395–408). His rival RUFINUS influenced ARCADIUS against him. Honorius had him arrested for high treason; although there was no evidence to support the charge, Stilicho did not resist execution.

Stilwell, Joseph Warren, 1883–1946, American general; b. Palatka, Fla. In WORLD WAR II he was commander in the China-Myanmar-India area. Defeated by the Japanese in Myanmar (1942), he retreated to India, then successfully counterattacked (1943–44) in Myanmar. An astute but frequently tactless general, he was known as "Vinegar Joe."

Stimson, Henry Lewis, 1867–1950, American statesman; b. N.Y.C. He was twice secretary of war (1911–13, 1940–45). As secretary of state (1929–33) he denounced the Japanese invasion of MANCHURIA in a declaration of policy that came to be known as the Stimson Doctrine.

stimulant: see DRUG.

stoat: see ERMINE.

Stockdale, James B(ond), 1923–, U.S. naval officer; b. Abingdon, Ill. A fighter pilot and highly decorated career naval officer (1946–79), he was the highest ranking U.S. prisoner of war (1965–73) in North Vietnam. He rose to the rank of vice admiral and was (1976–79) president of the Naval War College. Stockdale was H. Ross PEROT's vice-presidential running mate in 1992.

stock exchange, organized market for the trading of stocks and bonds. In Europe a stock exchange is called a bourse. Stock exchanges exist in all important financial centers of the world. Members of an exchange buy and sell for themselves or for others, charging commissions. A stock may be traded only if it is listed on an exchange after having met certain requirements. In the U.S., regulations are set by the governing board of each exchange and by the SECURITIES AND EXCHANGE COMMISSION. The New York Stock Exchange (founded 1790) is the largest in the U.S., handling more than 70% (in market value) of all transactions. The American Stock Exchange (Amex), also in New York City, and regional exchanges account for the remainder. Unlisted shares, often of smaller companies, are traded in the growing OVER-THE-COUNTER market. The NASDAQ (National Association of Securities Dealers Automated Quotations) system, an over-the-counter U.S. organization, accounts for the fifth largest stock trade in the world. Increasing computerization of stock trading may eventually render trading on a stock exchange floor obsolete.

Stockhausen, Karlheinz, 1928–, German composer and music theorist. He often uses TWELVE-TONE MUSIC techniques and is a major proponent of ELECTRONIC MUSIC. His compositions, e.g., *Gruppen* (1959), are characterized by complex COUNTERPOINT, free RHYTHMS, dissonance, percussive effects, and the use of improvisation by performers.

Stockholm, city (1989 pop. 671,742), capital of Sweden, E Sweden. It is the nation's largest city and its economic and administrative hub, with an important shipbuilding industry and diverse manufactures. A cultural center, the city has a noted opera house (1898), the Royal Dramatic Theatre (1908), and many museums. Founded in the mid-13th cent., it became the official capital (1634) under Queen CHRISTINA. Built on several peninsulas and islands, modern Stockholm is famed for its striking design, e.g., the new city hall (1911–1923) and the residential districts. The Great Square was the site of a massacre (1520) instigated by CHRISTIAN II of Denmark. Most of the NOBEL PRIZES are awarded in Stockholm.

Stockton, Frank R(ichard), 1834–1902, American writer; b. Philadelphia. Among his humorous novels are *Rudder Grange* (1879) and its sequels. He is also known for his short stories, e.g., *The Lady or the Tiger?* (1884), and his children's books.

Stockton, city (1990 pop. 210,943), seat of San Joaquin co., central Calif., on the San Joaquin R.; inc. 1850. Located at the head of the river's delta, its harbor can accommodate seagoing trade. Processing and distribution of the San Joaquin Valley's farm products is important. Its manufactures include farm machinery, building materials, and boats.

Stoicism, school of philosophy founded by Zeno of Citium c.300 B.C. Influenced by Socratic ideals and by the thought of HERACLITUS, ARISTOTLE, and PLATO, the Stoics held that all reality is material but is shaped by a universal working force (God) that pervades everything. Only by putting aside passion, unjust thoughts, and indulgence, and by performing one's duty with the right disposition can a person live consistently with nature and thus achieve true freedom. The school was especially well received in the Roman world; CICERO, SENECA, EPICTETUS, and MARCUS AURELIUS were all Stoics.

Stoker, Bram, 1847–1912, English novelist. He is best known for *Dracula* (1897), a horror novel about the vampire Count Dracula. He was manager to the actor Sir Henry IRVING.

Stokowski, Leopold, 1882–1977, American conductor; b. England. As the highly dramatic conductor of the Philadelphia Orchestra (1912–36), he introduced many unknown contemporary works. He later conducted other famous orchestras for brief periods, and in 1962 he founded the American Symphony Orchestra.

STOL aircraft: see SHORT TAKEOFF AND LANDING AIRCRAFT.

Stolypin, Piotr Arkadevich [stəlĭ'pĭn], 1862–1911, Russian premier and interior minister (1906–11) for NICHOLAS II. His regime of courts-martial executed hundreds for revolutionary activities (1906–7). By reforming the land distribution system created in 1861 (see EMANCIPATION, EDICT OF), which gave land to the community (Mir) rather than to individuals, he tried to create a loyal class of peasant landowners. His secret police carried out repression, but he allowed reactionary groups to go on committing anti-Jewish outrages. He was assassinated by a revolutionary who was also a police agent.

stomach, saclike organ of the DIGESTIVE SYSTEM located between the esophagus and the INTESTINES. The human stomach is a muscular, elastic, pear-shaped bag lying crosswise in the abdominal cavity, beneath the diaphragm. Food enters the stomach from the esophagus, and is converted into a semiliquid state by muscular action and by the digestive enzymes in the gastric juice secreted by the glands. The pyloric sphincter, which separates the stomach from the small intestine, remains closed until the food has been appropriately modified and is ready to be emptied into the duodenum, the first section of the small intestine.

Stone, Edward Durell, 1902–78, American architect; b. Fayetteville, Ark. With Philip L. Goodwin, he designed the Museum of Modern Art, N.Y.C. (1937–39). He won renown for his U.S. Embassy, New Delhi (1958), in which he used Muslim motifs including lacy grillwork. His later buildings include the Kennedy Center for the Performing Arts (1971), Washington, D.C.

Stone, Harlan Fiske, 1872–1946, associate justice (1925–41) and 12th chief justice (1941–46) of the U.S. SUPREME COURT; b. Chesterfield, N.H.; LL.B., Columbia Univ. (1898). As U.S. attorney general (1924–25), he helped restore faith in the Department of Justice after the TEAPOT DOME scandal. On the Court he was noted for his vigorous minority opinions, many upholding NEW DEAL legislation.

Stone, Lucy, 1818–93, American leader in the women's movement (see FEMINISM); b. near West Brookfield, Mass. In 1870 she founded the *Woman's Journal,* which became the official organ of the National American Woman Suffrage Association. After her marriage to **Henry Brown Blackwell** (1825–1909) in 1855, she called herself Mrs. Stone as a matter of principle. *Woman's Journal* was edited by Stone and Blackwell. On Stone's death, their daughter, **Alice Stone Blackwell** (1857–1950), became coeditor. The Lucy Stone League was formed in 1921 to work for women's rights.

Stone Age, period beginning with the earliest human development, c.2 million years ago. It is divided into three periods. The **Paleolithic period,** or **Old Stone Age,** was the longest phase of human history, roughly coextensive with the Pleistocene Epoch (see GEOLOGIC ERA, table). Its most outstanding feature was the development of *Homo sapiens* (see HUMAN EVOLUTION). Paleolithic peoples were generally nomadic hunters and gatherers who sheltered in caves, used fire, and fashioned stone tools. Their cultures are identified by distinctive stone-tool industries: Pre-Chellean, Abbevillian (or Chellean), and Acheulian in the Lower Paleolithic; Mousterian in the Middle Paleolithic, associated with NEANDERTHAL MAN; and Aurignacian, Solutrean, and Magdalenian in the Upper Paleolithic. By the Upper Paleolithic there is evidence of communal hunting, constructed shelters, and belief systems centering on MAGIC and the supernatural. ROCK CARVINGS AND PAINTINGS reached their peak in the Magdalenian culture of CRO-MAGNON MAN. The **Mesolithic period,** or **Middle Stone Age,** began at the end of the last glacial era, over 10,000 years ago. Cultures included gradual domestication of plants and animals, formation of settled communities, use of the bow, and development of delicate stone microliths and pottery. Notable Mesolithic cultures were the early Azilian and Tardenoisian, over most of Europe; the middle Mesolithic Maglemosian, in the Baltic and N England; the late Ertebolle, or kitchen-midden culture; and the Natufiar, in the Middle East. The time periods and cultural content of the **Neolithic period,** or **New Stone Age,** vary with geographic location. The earliest known Neolithic culture developed from the Natufian in SW Asia between 8000 and 6000 B.C. People lived in settled villages, cultivated grains and domesticated animals, developed pottery and weaving, and evolved into the urban civilizations of the BRONZE AGE. In SE Asia a distinct type of Neolithic culture cultivated rice before 2000 B.C. New World peoples independently domesticated plants and animals, and by 1500 B.C. Neolithic cultures existed in Mexico and South America that led to the AZTEC and INCA civilizations.

Stonehenge, group of standing stones on Salisbury Plain, Wiltshire, S England. Preeminent among MEGALITHIC MONUMENTS in the British Isles, Stonehenge is enclosed by a circular ditch 300 ft (91 m) in diameter. The stones are arranged in four series: the two outermost form circles; the third is a horseshoe shape; the fourth is an ovoid form. Within the ovoid lies the Altar Stone. Most archaeologists agree that Stonehenge served some sort of religious function. In 1963 the British astronomer Gerald Hawkins theorized that Stonehenge was used as a huge astronomical instrument.

Stonehenge

Stone Mountain Memorial, memorial to the CONFEDERACY carved on Stone Mt., NW Georgia, near Atlanta. It represents, in bas-relief, the equestrian figures of Robert E. Lee, Stonewall Jackson, and Jefferson Davis. Commissioned in 1916, it was begun by Gutzon

BORGLUM, the sculptor of Mt. Rushmore, but was not completed until 1969, by Walter K. Hancock.

stoneware, hard pottery made of siliceous paste fired at high temperature to make it glassy (vitrified). Stoneware is heavier and more opaque than PORCELAIN, and differs from TERRA COTTA in being nonporous. Fired stoneware is usually grayish, but colors may vary widely with the clay used. Produced in China since ancient times, it was the forerunner of Chinese porcelain. Stoneware was made in Germany in the 12th cent. and elsewhere in Europe by the 14th. The English potter Josiah WEDGWOOD developed two important types. Today stoneware remains one of the most common types of pottery.

Stoppard, Tom, 1937–, English playwright; b. Czechoslovakia. He became prominent with the comic and pathetic play *Rosencrantz and Guildenstern Are Dead* (1966), about characters in Shakespeare's *Hamlet*. In later works, e.g., *The Real Inspector Hound* (1968), *The Real Thing* (1982), and *Hapgood* (1988), he continued to find significance in wordplay and bizarre juxtapositions of language and character.

Storey, David (Malcolm), 1933–, English novelist and playwright. His northern working-class upbringing and professional rugby career contributed to his novel *This Sporting Life* (1960). Later novels include *Saville* (1976) and *Present Times* (1984). Storey is probably better known for his plays, e.g., *The Restoration of Arnold Middleton* (1967), *Home* (1970), and *The Changing Room* (1971).

stork, mute, long-legged wading BIRD of the family Ciconiidae. Found in most of the warmer parts of the world, it has long, broad, powerful wings. The American wood stork, a white bird c.4 ft (122 cm) tall with a greenish-black tail, is found in temperate and tropical regions.

Storm, Theodor [shtôrm], 1817–88, German poet and novelist. Nostalgic lyricism marks his early works, such as the story *Immensee* (1852). His later writings, notably the novel *The Rider of the White Horse* (1888), show a sense of tragedy. *Aquis Submersus* (1877) is a historical novella.

storm, disturbance of the ordinary atmospheric conditions marked by strong winds and (usually) precipitation. Types of storms include the extratropical CYCLONE, the tropical cyclone (HURRICANE), the TORNADO, and the THUNDERSTORM. The term is also applied to blizzards, dust storms, and sandstorms in which high wind is the dominant meteorological element.

Storm and Stress: see STURM UND DRANG.

Story, Joseph, 1779–1845, American jurist, associate justice of the SUPREME COURT (1811–45); b. Marblehead, Mass. His decision in *Martin v. Hunter's Lessee* (1816) established the power of the court to review constitutional issues raised in state cases. His legal writings rank among the foremost influences on American jurisprudence.

stout, alcoholic beverage: see BEER.

Stowe, Harriet Beecher, 1811–96, American writer; b. Litchfield, Conn.; daughter of Lyman BEECHER; sister of Henry Ward BEECHER. Her antislavery novel *Uncle Tom's Cabin* (1852) was very influential in spreading abolitionist sentiment, as was the dramatization of the book that followed. Notable among the 16 volumes she wrote are a second novel of slavery, *Dred* (1856), and novels of New England life, e.g., *The Minister's Wooing* (1859), *Old Town Folks* (1869). Stowe was also dedicated to such other reform movements as temperance and woman suffrage.

Strabo [strā'bō], b. c.63 B.C., d. after A.D. 21, Greek geographer, historian, and philosopher. He studied and traveled widely and wrote historical sketches (47 books), quoted by later authorities but almost all lost. His *Geographia*, based on his observations and on works of predecessors, contains historical data and descriptions of people and places; it is a rich source of ancient knowledge. Almost all extant, its 17 books include two defining the scope of geography, eight on Europe, six on Asia, and one on Africa.

Strachey, (Giles) Lytton, 1880–1932, English biographer and critic. A member of the BLOOMSBURY GROUP, he revolutionized the art of biography, writing selective, critical, witty works, e.g., *Eminent Victorians* (1918) and *Queen Victoria* (1921).

Stradivari, Antonio [strädēvä'rē] or **Antonius Stradivarius,** 1644–1737, Italian violinmaker of Cremona. Recognized in his time, Stradivari produced over 1,000 instruments; his workmanship brought the violin to perfection. Two of his sons continued the craft after his death.

Strafford, Thomas Wentworth, 1st **earl of,** 1593–1641, English statesman. As lord deputy of Ireland (1632–40), he enforced the rule of CHARLES I. After the English humiliation by the Scots in the first BISHOPS' WAR, he was recalled (1639) to become the king's adviser. Strafford led the English to disaster in the second Bishops' War, and was beheaded after Parliament accused him of plotting to use Irish troops against England.

strain: see STRENGTH OF MATERIALS.

Straits Settlements, collective name for certain former British colonies in Southeast Asia. They originally consisted (1826–58) of the British EAST INDIA COMPANY territories of Pinang, SINGAPORE, and Malacca. In 1867 they became a crown colony, to which several dependencies of Singapore were later added. The Straits Settlements crown colony was dissolved in 1946. Singapore became a separate crown colony; Labuan became part of British N Borneo (see SABAH); Pinang and Malacca were incorporated into the Malayan Union (see MALAYSIA).

Strand, Paul, 1890–1976, American photographer; b. N.Y.C. His elegant images of Manhattan life and 20th-cent. machines were promoted by STIEGLITZ. Strand also made landscape and nature photographs and documentary films.

Strasberg, Lee, 1901–82, American acting teacher and director, cofounder (1931) of the Group Theatre. An initiator of the STANISLAVSKY acting method in the U.S., he headed New York City's Actors' Studio from 1948. His first film appearance was in *The Godfather, Part II* (1974).

Strasbourg, city (1982 pop. 252,264), capital of Bas-Rhin dept., NE France. The city is a port on the RHINE. It is heavily industrialized (e.g., metal casting, machinery, oil refining), and its goose-liver pâté is famous. It became an important city in Roman times. Destroyed (5th cent.) by the HUNS and rebuilt, it became (923) part of the HOLY ROMAN EMPIRE. It emerged as a free imperial city in the 13th cent. The city and its university were Protestant centers in the 16th cent. Seized (1681) by Louis XIV, Strasbourg increasingly adopted French customs and speech. Ceded to Germany (1871), it was regained by France in 1919. Its cathedral (1015–1439) is a masterpiece of Rhenish architecture.

Strategic Arms Limitation Talks and **Strategic Arms Reduction Talks:** see DISARMAMENT, NUCLEAR.

Strategic Defense Initiative (SDI), U.S. defense program to develop a "shield" against ballistic missile attack, announced in 1983 by Pres. REAGAN. The SDI proposal envisioned developing a number of defensive weapons systems, primarily based in space, to destroy incoming nuclear missile warheads while they were still in space. A space-based SDI system was criticized as destabilizing, impractical, and a probable violation of the 1972 Antiballistic Missile Treaty. The end of the COLD WAR led to criticism that SDI was unnecessary, and in 1991 Pres. BUSH called for a more limited version using rocket-launched interceptors based on the ground at a single site; deployment of this system is scheduled for 1998. Emphasis was also placed on developing missile defenses for the battlefield. In 1993 SDI was renamed the Ballistic Missile Defense program, and it was revealed that the only successful test (1984) of a ground-launched interceptor in the 1980s had been rigged for propaganda purposes. In 1987 the USSR revealed it had a similar program.

strategy and tactics: see MILITARY SCIENCE.

Stratford-upon-Avon, town (1991 pop. 117,788), Warwickshire, central England, on the Avon R. A market town with light industries, it is famous as the birthplace of William SHAKESPEARE. Annual Shakespeare festivals are held there.

Strathclyde, one of the early Celtic or Welsh kingdoms of Britain. It was in SW Scotland, and Dumbarton was the principal town. Little is known of its history. In 945 King Edmund of Wessex defeated Strathclyde and awarded it to King Malcolm of Scotland. It was permanently absorbed by Scotland in the 11th cent.

Strathcona and Mount Royal, Donald Alexander Smith, 1st **Baron,** 1820–1914, Canadian financier. He emigrated (1838) from Scotland and worked for the HUDSON'S BAY COMPANY, of which he was governor (1889–1914). He and his associates gained control

(1878) of the Great Northern lines and completed (1885) the Canadian Pacific Railway. He was Canadian high commissioner (1896–1914) in England.

stratigraphy: see GEOLOGY.

stratosphere: see ATMOSPHERE.

Straus, family of American merchants, public officials, and philanthropists. **Isidor Straus,** 1845–1912, b. Rhenish Bavaria, emigrated to the U.S. in 1854. In New York City he and his brother Nathan became associated (1874) with R.H. Macy & Co., acquiring ownership of the firm in 1896. He served (1894–95) in the U.S. Congress. His brother **Nathan Straus,** 1848–1931, b. Rhenish Bavaria, was an outstanding philanthropist, particularly in child health, and a prominent Zionist leader. Another brother, **Oscar Solomon Straus,** 1850–1926, b. Rhenish Bavaria, was minister (1887–89, 1898–1900) and ambassador (1909–10) to Turkey, and secretary of commerce and labor (1906–9). A son of Isidor Straus, **Jesse Isidor Straus,** 1872–1936, b. N.Y.C., became president (1919) of R.H. Macy & Co. and served (1933–36) as ambassador to France. **Nathan Straus,** 1889–1961, b. N.Y.C., son of the elder Nathan Straus, served (1921–26) in the New York state legislature and headed (1937–42) the U.S. Housing Authority.

Strauss, Richard, 1864–1949, German composer and conductor. His romantic SYMPHONIC POEMS, e.g., *Death and Transfiguration* (1889), *Till Eulenspiegel's Merry Pranks* (1895), *Thus Spake Zarathustra* (1895), are evocative and richly orchestrated. His highly dramatic operas, which develop Richard WAGNER's leitmotif concept, include *Salomé* (1905) and, with librettos by HOFMANNSTHAL, *Electra* (1909), *Der Rosenkavalier* (1911), and *Ariadne auf Naxos* (1912).

Stravinsky, Igor (Fedorovich), 1882–1971, Russian-American composer, widely considered the greatest and most versatile composer of the 20th cent. In Russia he was a student of RIMSKY-KORSAKOV. His first strikingly original compositions, *The Firebird* (1910) and *Petrouchka* (1911), were written for DIAGHILEV's Ballets Russes. In the ballet *The Rite of Spring* (1913), a masterpiece of modern music, Stravinsky used radically irregular RHYTHMS and harsh dissonances. He later employed an austere, neoclassical style, as in *The Soldier's Tale* (1918) and *Oedipus Rex* (1927). After becoming a U.S. citizen (1945), he experimented with TWELVE-TONE MUSIC, e.g., *Cantata* (1952), *Septuor* (1953), and the ballet *Agon* (1957). Stravinsky's fresh, meticulously crafted, innovative music revitalized European musical expression and achieved new sonorities and orchestral colors.

strawberry, low, herbaceous perennial (genus *Fragaria*) of the ROSE family, native to temperate regions. It is grown for its edible red fruits, which are used fresh, frozen, in preserves and confectionery, and for flavoring. The common strawberry (*F. chiloensis*) is believed native to Chile and W North America; it has probably hybridized to some extent with the wild strawberry (*F. virginiana*) of E North America. Most species propagate by runners, or stolons, slender horizontal stems.

stream of consciousness, literary technique for recording the thoughts and feelings of a character without regard to their logical association or narrative sequence. The writer attempts to reflect all the forces affecting the psychology of a character at a single moment. Introduced by the French writer Edouard Dujardin in *We'll to the Woods No More* (1888), the technique was used notably by James JOYCE, Virginia WOOLF, and William FAULKNER.

Streicher, Julius, 1885–1946, German NAZI leader. An early member of the Nazi party, he published *Der Stürmer*, a periodical known for its sadistic and anti-Semitic mania. He was convicted at the Nuremberg trials and hanged as a war criminal.

strength of materials, the capacity of materials to withstand stress (the internal force exerted by one part of an elastic body upon an adjoining part) and strain (the deformation or change in dimension occasioned by stress). When a body is subjected to a pull, it is said to be under tension, or tensional stress; when it is compressed, it is under compression, or compressive stress. Shear, or shearing stress, results when a force tends to make part of a body slide past the other part. Torsion, or torsional stress, occurs when external forces tend to twist a body around an axis. The elastic limit is the maximum stress that a material can sustain and still return to its original form. The ratio of tensile stress to strain for a given material is called its Young's modulus. Hooke's law states that, within the elastic limit, strain is proportional to stress.

Stresemann, Gustav [shtrā'zəmän], 1878–1929, German statesman. A founder (1918) of the conservative German People's party, he served briefly (1923) as chancellor and then as foreign minister (1923–29). His primary aim was to reestablish Germany as a respected nation following World War I. He accepted the Dawes Plan (1924) and the Young Plan (1924) for Germany's reparations payments. He also was a principal architect of the LOCARNO PACT (1925) and signed the KELLOGG-BRIAND PACT (1928). He shared the 1926 Nobel Peace Prize with Aristide BRIAND.

stress: see STRENGTH OF MATERIALS.

stress test or **exercise electrocardiography,** in medicine, a test that evaluates the performance of the heart by subjecting it to controlled amounts of physical stress. Such tests, which include walking on a treadmill, measure the heart's reaction to an increased demand for oxygen. The test ends when the patient reaches a predetermined heart rate or experiences chest pain or fatigue.

Streuvels, Stijn [strö'vəls], pseud. of **Frank Lateur,** 1871–1969, Flemish novelist and short-story writer. Streuvels wrote moving portraits of everyday life, of which *The Flax Field* (1907) is his masterpiece.

strike, concerted work stoppage by a group of employees to achieve economic or other goals. It is the chief weapon of organized labor. Work stoppages in North America date from colonial times, but the first nationwide strike (by railroad workers) occurred in 1877. Strikes became more frequent in the late 19th cent. with the development of strong labor organizations such as the KNIGHTS OF LABOR. The use by the employer of armed guards or of police, either to harass pickets or to protect strikebreakers, often resulted in violence. The 1960s and 70s witnessed a growing number of strikes by public employees, notably teachers, municipal workers, policemen, and firemen. A suspension of work on the employer's part is called a lockout. Strikes over jurisdictional disputes, to determine which union should be the bargaining agent for employees, were outlawed in 1947. The general strike, involving workers in all industries of a locality or nation, is common in Europe.

Strindberg, (Johan) August [strĭnd'bĕr"yə], 1849–1912, Swedish author whose novels, plays, stories, histories, and poems reveal him as the greatest master of the Swedish language and an influential innovator in dramatic and literary form. His personal life was tumultuous, marked by three disastrous marriages and periods of persecution mania. Among his 70-odd plays are the naturalistic free-verse dramas *The Father* (1887), which vividly expresses his derogatory view of women, and the psychological *Miss Julie* (1888). Later plays, e.g., *A Dream Play* (1902) and *The Ghost Sonata* (1907), reflect his adoption of Swedenborgian mysticism (see SWEDENBORG) and employ experimental, expressionistic techniques that have greatly influenced modern theater. Other works include the novels *The Red Room* (1879) and *Inferno* (1897), the stories in *Married* (1884–85), and his bitter autobiography, *Son of a Servant* (1886).

stringed instrument, musical instrument whose tone is produced by vibrating strings. Those instruments played with a bow are principally of the VIOL and VIOLIN families. Those whose strings are plucked, either by finger or with a pick (plectrum), include the lyre, any of various ancient instruments with arms projecting from the sound box and having from 3 to 12 strings; the HARP; and a number of fretted instruments, in which narrow strips of wood or metal, called frets, mark the places on the keyboard where the player's fingertips should be applied to stop the strings and produce various notes. Fretted instruments include the balalaika, a Russian instrument having a triangular body, a long fretted neck, and usually three strings; the banjo, often used in COUNTRY AND WESTERN MUSIC, having four to nine strings and a round body resembling a tambourine; and the lute, popular in the Middle Ages and Renaissance, and the mandolin, both having a pear-shaped body and rounded back. Related to the lute is the guitar, which has six strings, a flat back, and a body curved inward to form a waist; it appeared in Spain as early as the 12th cent. and is used in both classical and folk music. Much smaller and more limited than the guitar, but developed from it, is the ukulele, which has four strings. The dulcimer, psaltery, and zither are stringed instruments constructed of a variable number of strings stretched over a flat sound box. The dulcimer is struck with small mallets; the psaltery and zither are plucked. The psaltery flourished in Europe from the 12th cent. until the late Middle Ages. The dulcimer, which originated in the Middle East, was adopted in Europe in the Middle Ages. The zither is derived from the psaltery and dulcimer. Stringed instruments operated by a keyboard include the PIANO and its predecessor, the clavichord, whose strings are struck by mallets or hammers. Keyboard instruments whose strings are plucked by means of quills or jacks include the spinet and virginal, small, legless instruments similar to the clavichord, and the harpsichord. See also ORCHESTRA.

string theory, theoretical description of ELEMENTARY PARTICLES that treats them as one-dimensional curves, or "strings." Traditional models of interactions between elementary particles are based on quantum field theory (see QUANTUM MECHANICS), which treats the particles as dimensionless points. Although quantum theories have been formulated for three of the four fundamental FORCES—the STRONG INTERACTION, WEAK INTERACTION, and ELECTROMAGNETISM—theoretical physicists have not developed a workable theory of GRAVITATION that is consistent with the principles of quantum mechanics. Treating elementary particles as strings, however, permits the derivation of a quantum theory that encompasses all four forces. **Superstring theory,** a combination of string theory and SUPERSYMMETRY, treats particles as very short (10^{-33} cm along its single dimension, which is 10^{20} smaller than the diameter of a proton) closed strings, or string loops. All of the masses, charges, and other properties of elementary particles result from the vibration of these superstrings at different frequencies. The complex mathematical basis of superstrings involves 10 dimensions: 9 spatial dimensions, 6 of which are hidden from view, and time. Because superstring theory provides a unified description of all elementary particles and fundamental forces, it is sometimes called "the theory of everything."

strip mining, process of extracting coal (or certain metallic ores) in which the surface material is removed to expose a coal seam or bed. The coal is then usually removed in a separate operation. The environment can be protected by respreading soil and by seeding or planting grass or trees on the fertilized, restored surface. Sometimes the terms *open-pit, open-cast,* or *surface mining* are used in the same sense as *strip mining.*

Stroessner, Alfredo [shtrös'nər], 1912–, president of PARAGUAY (1954–89). He commanded the armed forces and took power in a 1954 military coup. His totalitarian rule brought order and monetary stability. He was "reelected" to his eighth successive term as president in 1988 but was overthrown in a coup in Feb. 1989.

stroke or **cerebrovascular accident** (CVA), destruction of brain tissue due to impaired blood supply caused by intracerebral hemorrhage, THROMBOSIS (clotting), or embolism (obstruction caused by clotted blood or other foreign matter circulating in the bloodstream). It is a leading cause of death worldwide. Stroke is most common in the elderly, but may occur at any age; predisposing conditions include ARTERIOSCLEROSIS, DIABETES, and HYPERTENSION. Symptoms develop suddenly and can range from almost unnoticed clumsiness or headache to severe paralysis, speech and mental disturbances, and coma. Treatment depends on the cause of the stroke and may include ANTICOAGULANTS, surgery, and PHYSICAL THERAPY.

strong interaction or **strong nuclear force,** force responsible for the binding of the protons and neutrons in an ATOM's nucleus and of the ELEMENTARY PARTICLES called QUARKS in protons and neutrons. The strong interaction is mediated, or carried, by gluons. It is one of four fundamental FORCES of nature; the others are GRAVITATION, electromagnetism, and the WEAK INTERACTION.

strontium (Sr), metallic element, first recognized as distinct from barium by A. Crawford in 1790. A soft, silver-yellow ALKALINE-EARTH METAL, it is stored away from air and water. Strontium-90 from nuclear fallout is absorbed in plants and animals, and may induce bone cancer and leukemia. See ELEMENT (table); PERIODIC TABLE.

Strozzi, Bernardo [strôt'sē], 1581–1644, Italian painter. One of the greatest of the 17th-cent. Italian painters who made the transition from MANNERISM to the BAROQUE style, he was influenced by RUBENS. His early work, e.g., *St. Augustine Washing Christ's Feet* (Genoa), shows strong high-contrast effects, but later his palette lightened.

structuralism, general term for the analysis of aspects of culture as culturally interconnected signs that can be studied to reconstruct the underlying systems of relationships (e.g., the formal units and rules of a language, or the elements of myths and how they enable a society to frame an understanding of the world, as in the work of Claude LÉVI-STRAUSS). No single item in such a system has meaning except as an integral part of a set of structural connections. These interconnections are said to be binary in nature and are viewed as the permanent, organizational categories of experience. Structuralism's modern origins are in the semiology (see SEMIOTICS) of Ferdinand de SAUSSURE. In France after 1968 this search for the deep structure of the mind was criticized by DERRIDA and other "post-structuralists," who abandoned the goal of reconstructing reality scientifically in favor of "deconstructing" (see DECONSTRUCTION) the illusions of METAPHYSICS.

structural linguistics: see LINGUISTICS.

Strutt, John William: see RAYLEIGH.

Struve [shtrōō'və], family of astronomers. **Friedrich Georg Wilhelm von Struve,** 1793–1864, b. Germany, directed the Dorpat Observatory (1817–34) and later the Pulkovo Observatory (1834–64) near St. Petersburg. He discovered numerous previously undetected double stars and was, with Friedrich BESSEL and Thomas Henderson, one of the first to make a reliable determination of stellar parallax. His son, **Otto Wilhelm von Struve,** 1819–1905, succeeded him as director of the Pulkovo Observatory. He discovered about 500 double stars and a satellite of Uranus, and he estimated the sun's velocity. Otto Wilhelm's grandson, **Otto Struve,** 1897–1963, b. Russia, came to the U.S. in 1921. He was director of the Yerkes and McDonald observatories (1932–47), the Leuschner Observatory (1950–59) of the Univ. of California, Berkeley, and the National Radio Astronomy Observatory (1959–62). He made notable studies in stellar spectroscopy and of stellar rotation, interstellar matter, and stellar evolution.

strychnine, bitter ALKALOID drug derived from the seeds of a tree (*Strychnos nux-vomica*) native to Sri Lanka, Australia, and India. A potent stimulant, the drug has been used as a rat poison for five centuries. Strychnine poisoning is characterized by violent convulsions and is fatal unless promptly treated with barbiturate sedatives and ARTIFICIAL RESPIRATION.

Stuart or **Stewart,** royal family that ruled Scotland and England. It began (c.1160) as a family of hereditary stewards of Scotland, and gained the Scottish crown with the accession of ROBERT II in 1371. The marriage of James IV of Scotland to MARGARET TUDOR, daughter of Henry VII of England, eventually made Henry's granddaughter MARY QUEEN OF SCOTS a claimant to the English throne. This claim was recognized when her son, James VI of Scotland, became JAMES I of England in 1603. After the execution of CHARLES I and the period of the Commonwealth and the Protectorate, CHARLES II was restored to the throne. With the deposition of JAMES II, the crown passed to MARY II and her husband, WILLIAM III. ANNE, the last Stuart to rule England, saw the crowns of Scotland and England permanently joined by the Act of UNION (1707). On Anne's death (1714) the crown passed to the Hanoverian GEORGE I by the Act of Settlement. The Hanoverian claim was through a granddaughter of James I. Parliamentary rule of succession was adopted to thwart the claim (upheld by the JACOBITES) to the throne by the Roman Catholic James II and his descendants. After 1807 this claim ceased to be politically important.

Stuart or **Stewart, Alexander, duke of Albany,** 1454?–1485, second son of JAMES II of Scotland. Imprisoned (1479) by his brother JAMES III, who suspected him of plotting against the throne, he escaped to England. To gain English support, Albany agreed to rule Scotland as England's vassal. He returned (1482) to Scotland with an English army, but was reconciled briefly with his brother. Sentenced (1483) to death by the Scots, he again fled and died in exile.

Stuart or **Stewart, Arabella,** 1575–1615, cousin of JAMES I of England. Her descent from MARGARET TUDOR had placed her next after James in the succession to ELIZABETH I, and many thought her title preferable. Her marriage (1610) to William Seymour (later marquess of Hertford), who was also of royal descent, was viewed as threatening by James, who imprisoned them. They escaped, but Arabella was recaptured and died in prison.

Stuart, Gilbert, 1755–1828, foremost American portrait painter of his day; b. North Kingstown, R.I. A protégé of Benjamin WEST, he first achieved success in London. He returned to America and settled in Boston. Stuart's brilliant, elegant style of portraiture was partially modeled after REYNOLDS and GAINSBOROUGH. Among his many celebrated portraits are three famous ones of George Washington: the Vaughan type (1795), a bust; the Lansdowne type (1796), a full-length study; and the unfinished Athenaeum Head (Mus. Fine Arts, Boston), commissioned c.1796 by Martha Washington and immortalized on the U.S. one-dollar bill. There are many replicas of these works.

Stuart, Henry: see DARNLEY, HENRY STUART, LORD.

Stuart, James Ewell Brown (Jeb Stuart), 1833–64, Confederate cavalry commander in the U.S. CIVIL WAR. He was known for bold raids of reconnaissance; his circuit of Gen. MCCLELLAN's Union army (June 1862) and his foray to the rear of John Pope's forces (Aug. 1862) provided Gen. LEE with invaluable information. He fought at the battles of BULL RUN (1861) and FREDERICKSBURG (1862) and commanded at CHANCELLORSVILLE. His greatest cavalry battle was at Brandy Station (1863). He was mortally wounded (1864) at Yellow Tavern.

Stuart or **Stewart, James Francis Edward,** 1688–1766, claimant to the English throne; son of JAMES II and Mary of Modena; called the Old Pretender. After the GLORIOUS REVOLUTION (1688), he was taken to France, where he was recognized as James III of England after the death (1701) of his father. In England the Act of SETTLEMENT excluded the male STUART line from succession, and James's hopes of succeeding Queen ANNE were dashed by the peaceful succession of GEORGE I in 1714. James's supporters, called JACOBITES, hatched many unsuccessful plots to restore him as king, including the rising of the earl of Mar (1715), which brought James to Scotland. He later retired to Rome. His son **Charles Edward Stuart,** 1720–88, was known as Bonnie Prince Charlie and as the Young Pretender. He led the rising of 1745, which ended in defeat at Culloden Moor in Scotland. Charles escaped, finally settling in Rome. He is the subject of much romantic literature. His brother **Henry Benedict Maria Clement Stuart,** known as **Cardinal York,** 1725–1807, was the last of the direct male Stuart line to claim the English throne (as Henry IX). He became (1747) a Roman Catholic cardinal and at his death bequeathed to GEORGE IV (then prince of Wales) the Stuart crown jewels.

Stuart, Mary: see MARY QUEEN OF SCOTS.

Stubbs, William, 1825–1901, English historian, the bishop of Chester (from 1884). His critical studies of source materials transformed the study of medieval history. He wrote *The Constitutional History of England* (3 vol., 1874–78).

stupa [Sanskrit, = mound], Buddhist monument of tumulus, or mound, form, containing relics. The stupa is probably derived from pre-Buddhist burial mounds. The oldest known prototypes are enormous earth mounds (c.700 B.C.) at Lauriya Nandangarh, NE India. They were the burial places of royalty. At Sanchi and Bharnut are the earliest proper stupas, hemispherical earth masses faced with brick or stone. Processional paths surrounded the structures, the whole enclosed with a stone railing and topped by a balcony. Stupas are found in all countries where BUDDHISM was practiced.

sturgeon, primitive marine and freshwater FISH of N Eurasia and North America. It has reduced scalation, a mostly cartilaginous skeleton, upturned tail fins, and a toothless mouth set far back under its jaw. It sucks up its food—CRAYFISH, SNAILS, larvae, and small fish—from the water bottom. The largest is the Russian sturgeon, or beluga (*Acipenser huso*), reaching a length of 13 ft (396 cm) and a weight of 1 ton (908 kg). Smoked sturgeon and sturgeon caviar are valued as food. The North American pallid sturgeon (*Scaphirhynchus albus*) is an endangered species.

Sturluson or **Sturleson, Snorri:** see SNORRI STURLUSON.

Sturm und Drang or **Storm and Stress,** movement in German literature, fl. c.1770–84. The name derives from a play (1776) by Friedrich von Klinger. Under the influence of J.J. ROUSSEAU, HERDER, and LESSING, German authors stressed with great intensity both subjectivity and the revolt of youthful genius against accepted standards. GOETHE's *Götz von Berlichingen* (1773) and *Sorrows of Young Werther* (1774) and SCHILLER's *Robbers* (1781) are representative works.

Stuttgart, city (1989 est. pop. 563,000), capital of Baden-Württemberg, SW Germany, on the Neckar R. It is an industrial center with such manufactures as electrical and photographic equipment, textiles, and pianos, and is the home of the renowned Stuttgart Ballet. Chartered in the 13th cent., it became (15th cent.) the capital of Württemberg. The city's historic center was almost entirely destroyed during WORLD WAR II and has since been restored. Historic buildings include the 12th-cent. Stiftskirche and the rococo Solitude Palace (1763–67). The city also contains such striking modern structures as the city hall and the concert hall.

Stuttgart Ballet, the first major German ballet company. It became prominent in the 1960s under the direction of John Cranko. It focuses on full-length story productions, e.g., *Romeo and Juliet* and *Eugene Onegin*.

Stuyvesant, Peter [stī'vəsənt], c.1610–1672, Dutch director-general of the North American colony of New Netherland (1647–64). The one-legged Stuyvesant was a harsh, autocratic ruler, intolerant of religious dissenters. He expanded the colony by conquering NEW SWEDEN (1655). Overwhelmed by a surprise English attack, he surrendered (1664) New Netherland to England.

Styron, William, 1925–, American novelist; b. Newport News, Va. His powerful, deeply felt, and often poetic novels include *Lie Down in Darkness* (1951), *The Confessions of Nat Turner* (1967; Pulitzer), and *Sophie's Choice* (1979), which was made into a movie (1982). He also wrote the autobiographical *Darkness Visible* (1990).

Styx [stĭks], in Greek mythology, sacred river in HADES crossed by the souls of the dead, who were ferried by Charon.

Suárez, Francisco, 1548–1617, Spanish Jesuit theologian and philosopher. His works include a commentary on THOMAS AQUINAS's *Summa Theologica;* the metaphysical study *Disputationes Metaphysicae;* and *Tractatus de Legibus,* on international law.

Suárez Gonzáles, Adolfo, 1932–, Spanish political leader. He became secretary-general of the reformed Falange movement after FRANCO's death (1975). In 1976 King JUAN CARLOS appointed him premier, and in 1977 he led his Democratic Center Union to victory in SPAIN's first free elections in 41 years. His centrist government instituted democratic procedures, and his coalition again won the 1979 elections under the new constitution. He resigned in 1981. In 1982 he founded the Democratic and Social Center party.

subduction zone: see PLATE TECTONICS.

submarine, naval craft capable of operating underwater for an extended period of time. Cornelis DREBBEL built (c.1620) a leather-covered rowboat that could remain under water as long as 15 hr. The first submarine used in combat was invented by the American David Bushnell in 1776; many of its principles were adopted by Robert FULTON in his *Nautilus,* a submarine successfully operated (1800–1801) on the Seine R., in France. Although the Confederates used several submersible craft in the Civil War, it was the work of John Holland and Simon Lake that advanced considerably the development of the modern submarine in the U.S. A Holland submarine became the first for the U.S. navy in 1900; Lake's *Argonaut* was (1898) the first submarine to navigate extensively in the open sea. E-boats, the first U.S. diesel-engine submarines, appeared in 1912 and were the first to cross the Atlantic Ocean. Both sides used submarines extensively in WORLD WAR I, especially Germany, whose 200-ton U-boats inflicted heavy damage on Allied shipping. Larger and improved submarines played a major role in WORLD WAR II, in which the Allies and neutrals lost some 4,770 ships to these raiders. The advent of nuclear energy brought about major changes in submarine propulsion and striking power. The first nuclear submarine, the U.S.S. *Nautilus,* was completed in 1954. Nuclear submarines can remain submerged for almost unlimited periods of time and can fire cruise or ballistic missiles at enemy land targets from a submerged position. Nuclear attack submarines, for deployment against other submarines and shipping, have also been built. See also SUBMERSIBLE.

submersible, small, mobile undersea research vessel capable of functioning at great depths. Submersibles have a crew compartment within a pressure hull, life-support and power systems, sensors (cameras, sonar hydrophones, and other equipment), and usually external mechanical arms that are used to collect samples and perform other tasks. Among the better-known submersibles are the *Alvin*, which was used to explore the wreck of the *Titanic* and is capable of diving to 13,000 ft (3,960 m) with a crew of three, and the *Aluminaut*, which is constructed of high-strength aluminum alloys and is able to operate at 15,000 ft (4,570 m) with a crew of six.

succory: see CHICORY.

succulent, any fleshy plant, typically with reduced leaves and an outer surface covered with a waxy substance (cutin) that reduces evaporation from the inner, water-storing tissue. Many are indigenous to dry regions. Species of CACTUS, ALOE, and YUCCA are succulents.

Suckling, Sir John, 1609–42, English Cavalier poet, gallant at the court of CHARLES I, wit, and gamester, said by John AUBREY to have invented cribbage. *Fragmenta Aurea* (1646) collected his poems, plays, letters, and tracts. He is best known for the lyric "Why so pale and wan, fond lover?"

Sucre, Antonio José de [so͞o'krā], 1795–1830, South American revolutionary leader. He joined (1811) the revolution against Spain and became the chief lieutenant of Simón BOLÍVAR. A military genius, Sucre won victories at Pichincha (in ECUADOR; 1822) and at Junín and AYACUCHO (in PERU; 1824); the latter battle assured South America's independence. He served (1825–28) as president of the new state of BOLIVIA and repelled (1828) a Peruvian invasion of Ecuador.

Sucre, city (1985 est. pop. 86,700), S central Bolivia, capital of Chuquisaca dept. and constitutional capital of Bolivia. (The administrative capital, since 1898, has been LA PAZ, but the supreme court is in Sucre.) It was founded as La Plata in 1538 and was also called Chuquisaca and Carcas before being renamed for Antonio José de SUCRE in 1839. A major agricultural center, it supplies the mining towns of the barren ALTIPLANO. It is also the seat of the national university, San Francisco Xavier (est. c.1625).

sucrose (empirical formula: $C_{12}H_{22}O_{11}$), common table sugar, a white, crystalline solid with a sweet taste. Common names, which indicate the natural source, include cane sugar, beet sugar, and maple sugar. A disaccharide (see CARBOHYDRATE), sucrose can be hydrolized to yield invert sugar, a mixture of unequal amounts of FRUCTOSE and GLUCOSE. Sucrose is obtained from the "juice" of sugar cane or sugar beets and from the sap of the sugar maple. It is evaporated to give first a brownish liquid, called molasses; further evaporation yields a brownish sugar. The color, due to impurities, is removed by charcoal used in the refining process.

Sudan, officially Republic of Sudan, republic (1992 est. pop. 28,305,000), 967,494 sq mi (2,505,813 sq km), the largest country in Africa, bordered by Egypt (N), the Red Sea (NE), Eritrea and Ethiopia (E), Kenya, Uganda, and Zaïre (S), the Central African Republic and Chad (W), and Libya (NW). The principal cities are KHARTOUM (the capital) and OMDURMAN. The most notable geographical feature is the NILE R., which, with its tributaries, flows through eastern Sudan from south to north. Rainfall in Sudan, more plentiful in the south, diminishes as one moves north; thus the southern part of the country is characterized by swampland and rain forest, the central region by savanna and grassland, and the north by desert and semidesert. There are mountains in the northeast, south, center, and west; the highest point is Kinyetti (10,456 ft/3,187 m), in the southeast. Agriculture, mostly of a subsistence nature, dominates the economy. Long-staple cotton, the principal cash crop, is raised in the irrigated Gezira region. Other crops include sorghum, millet, peanuts, sesame, dates, and sugarcane. Cotton, gum arabic (about 80% of world production), sesame, and peanuts are exported. The small mining industry extracts chromite, copper and manganese ores, gypsum, and gold. Manufacturing is largely devoted to consumer goods. The population is divided into three main groups: northerners, who are Muslim and speak Arabic (the official language); westerners, largely Muslim and originally (20th cent.) from W Africa; and southerners, who follow traditional beliefs mostly and speak Nilotic languages. There is a Christian minority in the south.

History. Northeast Sudan, called NUBIA in ancient times, was colonized by Egypt about 2000 B.C. and was ruled by the CUSH kingdom from the 8th cent. B.C. to the 4th cent A.D. Most of Nubia was converted to Coptic Christianity in the 6th cent., but by the 15th cent. Islam prevailed. In 1821 the north was conquered by Egypt, but a revolt by the nationalist MAHDI in 1881 forced an Egyptian withdrawal. In the 1890s an Anglo-Egyptian force under Herbert KITCHENER destroyed the theocratic Mahdist state, and in 1899 most of Sudan came under the joint rule of Egypt and Britain (with Britain exercising actual control). Independence was achieved in 1956. In 1955 the animist southerners, fearing that the new nation would be dominated by the Muslim north, began a civil war that lasted 17 years. In 1972 Pres. Muhammad Gaafar al-NIMEIRY ended the war by granting the south a measure of autonomy. However, his imposition of Islamic law on the entire country in 1983 reopened the conflict. Nimeiry was deposed by a military coup in 1986. A short-lived civilian government was overthrown in 1989 by Lt. Gen. Omar Hassan al-Bashir; he officially became president in 1993. Bashir's government strictly enforced Islamic law, banned opposition parties, and jailed dissidents. In 1992 and 1994 the army mounted offensives against the rebels in S Sudan and ousted them from many areas. In recent years Sudan has supported Muslim fundamentalists internationally.

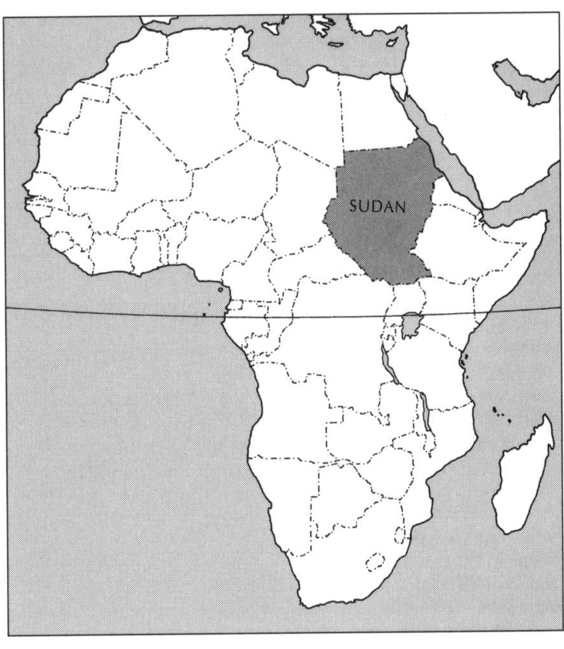

Sudbury, city (1991 pop. 92,884), central Ontario, Canada, part of the regional municipality of Sudbury (1991 pop. 161,210). Located in the CANADIAN SHIELD, it is the center for an important mining region that produces much of the Western world's nickel and large quantities of copper and other metals. Settlement began in 1887, after mineral deposits were discovered there.

sudden infant death syndrome (SIDS) or **crib death,** sudden, unexpected, and unexplained death of an apparently well infant under one year (usually between 2 weeks and 8 months). SIDS accounts for 10% of infant deaths and is the second-highest cause of death (after accidents) in infancy. The risk is higher in males, in low-birth-weight infants, in lower socioeconomic levels, during cold months, and for babies who sleep face down. Current theories suggest that the infant may have immature lungs, may have problems with brain-stem control of breathing, or may be rebreathing carbon dioxide; SIDS victims are thought to have brief episodes of apnea (breathing stoppage) before the fatal one. An alarm system that detects breathing abnormalities is sometimes used with infants suspected of being prone to SIDS.

Sudermann, Hermann [zo͞o'dərmän], 1857–1928, German dramatist and novelist. One of the early German naturalists, he wrote immensely popular works of psychological insight and social criticism, notably the novel *Dame Care* (1887); the play *Fritzchen* (1897); and the novel *The Song of Songs* (1908), which exposes the crudity and immorality of the Prussian aristocracy and the corruption of Berlin society.

Sudetenland, region, N Czech Republic, named for the Sudetes, a mountain range running along the Polish-Czech border. Traditionally part of BOHEMIA, the Sudetenland was for centuries the home of a largely German-speaking population. The area was annexed to Germany by the MUNICH PACT (1938). It was restored to Czechoslovakia in 1945, and most of its German population was expelled. With the dissolution of Czechoslovakia (1993), it became part of the Czech Republic.

Suetonius (Caius Suetonius Tranquillus), A.D. c.69–c.140, Roman biographer. His *Lives of the Caesars* survives almost in full. Filled with anecdote, Suetonius' lively work was taken as a model by later biographers.

Suez Canal, canal, Egypt. The most important constructed waterway in the Eastern Hemisphere, it is c.100 mi (160 km) long, connecting the Mediterranean Sea (N) with the Gulf of Suez and the Red Sea (S), and greatly reducing the distance by sea between Europe and S and E Asia. Built (1859–69) by the French engineer Ferdinand de LESSEPS, it was acquired by Great Britain in 1875 and nationalized by Egypt in 1956. The canal, which has no locks, was closed to Israeli shipping and cargoes from 1948 to 1975 and to all shipping from 1967 to 1975, following the ARAB-ISRAELI WAR of 1967. Cleared of mines and wreckage, it was reopened in 1975 and enlarged (1976–80).

Sufism, Muslim philosophical and literary movement. It emerged among the SHIITES in the late 10th and early 11th cent., borrowing ideas from NEOPLATONISM, BUDDHISM, and CHRISTIANITY. Some members stressed ascetic practices; others stressed quietism. All were united in emphasizing the immediate personal union of the soul with God. The movement was strongest in Persia. The greatest philosophical exponent of Sufism was al-GHAZALI, and its greatest poets were the Persians Abu Said ibn Abi al-Khair, Farad ad-Din Attar, HAFIZ, Jami, and OMAR KHAYYAM.

sugar, compound of CARBON, HYDROGEN, and OXYGEN, belonging to a class of substances called CARBOHYDRATES. Sugars fall into three groups. Monosaccharides are the simple sugars, e.g., FRUCTOSE and GLUCOSE. Disaccharides, made up of two monosaccharide units, include LACTOSE, MALTOSE, and SUCROSE. The less familiar trisaccharides, made up of three monosaccharide units, include raffinose, found in sugar BEETS.

sugarcane, tall tropical perennial (genus *Saccharum*) of the GRASS family, native to Asia. It somewhat resembles CORN and SORGHUM, with a large terminal panicle and a noded stalk. Sugarcane and the sugar BEET are the major sources of SUGAR. The cane is harvested by cutting down the stalks and pressing them to extract the juice, which is concentrated by evaporation. Refined sugar is produced by precipitating out nonsugar components; it is almost pure SUCROSE. Cuba and India together produce over one third of the world's cane sugar. Sugarcane by-products include molasses, RUM, ALCOHOL, fuel, and livestock feed.

Suharto or **Soeharto,** 1921–, president of INDONESIA (1968–). A relatively unknown general, he led (1965) the army in crushing a Communist coup and effectively replaced Pres. SUKARNO. He became acting president in 1967, was elected president in 1968, and was reelected in 1971, 1978, 1983, 1988, and 1993. Under his leadership, Indonesia achieved political stability and economic growth, but dissent was suppressed in the name of consensus and Suharto and his family used their power to enrich themselves.

Sui, dynasty: see CHINA.

suicide, the deliberate taking of one's own life. It may be dictated by social convention, as with hara-kiri, in Japan, or by custom, as in those primitive societies in which nonproductive elders were expected to end their own lives for the welfare of the group. Long condemned by Judaism, Christianity, and Islam, suicide remains a crime in some countries. Britain abolished punishment for attempted suicide in 1961, and by the early 1990s only two U.S. states still listed suicide as a crime. Eighteen states, however, have laws against helping someone to commit suicide. Suicide and attempted suicide are now more often considered the result of psychological factors, such as severe DEPRESSION, guilt, and AGGRESSION, or of chronic illness. Suicidal behavior is also viewed as a form of communication, a cry for help. In the U.S., most suicide attempts are by women, but out of 30,000 successful suicides (1989), 24,000 were by men. In recent years the suicide rate among the elderly has risen 21%; the rate for people ages 15-23 has tripled since 1950. In the 1990s a right-to-die movement has supported the principle of doctor-assisted suicide in certain cases (see EUTHANASIA).

suite, in music, instrumental form derived from dance and consisting of a series of movements usually in the same key but contrasting in rhythm and mood. As the connection with actual dancing disappeared, the BAROQUE suite evolved, establishing the basic movements as allemande, courante, sarabande, and gigue. Suites for orchestra (including the partitas of J.S. BACH) were sometimes called OVERTURES. The 19th-cent. suite became a collection of pieces from the incidental music for plays or from ballet scores (as GRIEG's *Peer Gynt Suite*).

Sukarno, 1901–70, Indonesian statesman. With Mohammad HATTA, Sukarno played a crucial role in establishing (1945) the republic of INDONESIA and became its first president. In 1959 he assumed dictatorial powers and in 1963 proclaimed himself president for life. He increased Indonesian ties with China, and in 1965 a Communist coup was put down by the military under Gen. SUHARTO, who stripped Sukarno of power. In 1966 he was removed from the presidency and remained under house arrest until his death. His daughter, **Megawati Sukarnoputri,** 1947–, became leader of the opposition Indonesia Democratic party in 1993.

Sukkoth: see under JEWISH HOLIDAYS.

Sulayman, sultans of the OTTOMAN EMPIRE (Turkey). **Sulayman I** or **Sulayman the Magnificent,** 1494–1566 (r.1520–66), son and successor of SELIM I, ruled the Ottoman Empire at its height of power and prestige. He continued his father's conquests in the Balkans and the Mediterranean, conquering (1521) Belgrade and expelling (1522) the Knights Hospitalers from Rhodes. He annexed most of Hungary and entered into an alliance with FRANCIS I of France against the Hapsburgs. His vassal BARBAROSSA made the Turkish fleet the terror of the Mediterranean. On the whole, however, Sulayman was unsuccessful in his naval warfare against Holy Roman Emperor CHARLES V and Venice. He lost (1535) Tunis to Charles and failed to take Vienna (1529) and Malta (1565). He undertook several successful campaigns against Persia and conquered the Arabian coastlands. Sulayman was distinguished for his justice; his legal, military, and educational reforms were outstanding. He lived in great pomp and splendor and was a generous patron of the arts, architecture, and literature. He had two of his sons executed for conspiracy and was succeeded by another son, SELIM II. **Sulayman II,** 1642–91 (r.1687–91), was occupied during his brief reign with the war against Austria. Mustafa KÖPRÜLÜ was his grand vizier.

sulfa drug, any of a class of synthetic chemical substances derived from sulfanilamide and used to treat bacterial infections. These drugs inhibit the action of para-aminobenzoic acid, a substance bacteria need in order to reproduce. Sulfa drugs are used to treat fungal and urinary tract infections, leprosy, and ulcerative colitis, but resistant strains of microorganisms (streptococci, meningococci, and shigella) have made the drugs less effective. ANTIBIOTICS have largely replaced sulfa drugs in the treatment of bacterial infections.

sulfur (S) or **sulphur,** nonmetallic element, known to antiquity as the biblical brimstone and recognized as an element by Antoine LAVOISIER in 1777. Solid sulfur is yellow, brittle, odorless, tasteless, and insoluble in water. Sulfur is widely distributed in minerals and ores, some volcanic regions, and large underground deposits, and often occurs with coal, natural gas, and petroleum. It is found in most proteins and protoplasm of plants and animals. Sulfur is used in GUNPOWDER, matches, RUBBER vulcanization, insecticides, and the treatment of certain skin diseases. SULFURIC ACID is its most important compound; others are used as disinfectants, refrigerants, organic solvents, and SULFA DRUGS. See ELEMENT (table); PERIODIC TABLE.

sulfuric acid, chemical compound (H_2SO_4), colorless, odorless, extremely corrosive, oily liquid. It is sometimes called oil of vitriol. Concentrated sulfuric acid is a weak acid (see ACIDS AND BASES) and a poor ELECTROLYTE because relatively little is dissociated into ions at room temperature. When cold it does not react readily with such common metals as iron or copper. When hot it is an oxidizing agent. Hot concentrated sulfuric acid reacts with most metals and with several nonmetals, e.g., sulfur and carbon. When concentrated sulfuric acid is mixed with water, large amounts of heat are released. Sulfuric acid is a strong acid and a good electrolyte when diluted. A very important industrial chemical, sulfuric acid is produced by the oxidation and dissolution in water of sulfur dioxide (SO_2).

Sulla, Lucius Cornelius, 138 B.C.–78 B.C., Roman general, leader of the conservative senatorial party. He and MARIUS both wanted the appointment as commander against MITHRIDATES VI of Pontus; Sulla got it by marching (88 B.C.) against Rome. He conquered Mithridates, sacked (86 B.C.) Athens, and returned triumphantly to Rome. In the civil war that followed, he defeated the Marians. He massacred 8,000 prisoners and declared himself dictator (82 B.C.). Sulla retired (79 B.C.) after a reign notorious for cruelty and illegality.

Sullivan, Anne: see MACY, ANNE SULLIVAN.

Sullivan, Sir Arthur (Seymour), 1842–1900, English composer and conductor. He is famous for a series of brilliant comic operas (or OPERETTAS) written with the librettist W.S. GILBERT, e.g., *Trial by Jury* (1875), *H.M.S. Pinafore* (1878), *The Mikado* (1885), and *Ruddigore* (1887). He also wrote such serious music as the oratorio *Kenilworth* (1864) and the opera *Ivanhoe* (1886).

Sullivan, Harry Stack, 1892–1949, American psychiatrist; b. Norwich, N.Y. As head of the William Alanson White Foundation (1934–43) and the Washington School of Psychiatry (1936–47), he collaborated with psychologists and sociologists to develop his belief that PSYCHOANALYSIS needed to be supplemented by a thorough study of the impact of cultural forces upon the personality. He also contributed significantly to the understanding of SCHIZOPHRENIA and obsessional states.

Sullivan, John L(awrence), 1858–1918, American boxer; b. Roxbury, Mass. A powerful right-handed puncher, he won (1882) the bare-knuckles heavyweight championship over Paddy Ryan. The "Great John L.," idol of American sports fans, won (1889) the last bare-knuckles title bout over Jake Kilrain but, using gloves, was beaten (1892) by James J. Corbett.

Sullivan, Louis Henry, 1856–1924, American architect; b. Boston. He was of great importance in the evolution of MODERN ARCHITECTURE in the U.S. His dominating principle, that outward form should express function, countered the late-19th-cent. revival of traditional classicism, and gained few adherents. Associated after 1880 with Dankmar Adler, he became prominent with functionally straightforward designs like the Wainwright Building, St. Louis (1890), and the Transportation Building at the World's Columbian Exposition, Chicago (1893). Sullivan's views were published as *Kindergarten Chats* (1918) and *The Autobiography of an Idea* (1924). Few of his buildings survive, but he influenced a generation of American architects.

Sully, Thomas, 1783–1872, American painter; b. England. Influenced by Benjamin WEST and Thomas LAWRENCE during a stay in London, he returned to America and settled in Philadelphia in 1810. An elegant and romantic portraitist, he recorded such notable subjects as Queen Victoria (Metropolitan Mus.) and Presidents Jefferson and Monroe (U.S. Military Acad., West Point, N.Y.). Sully also painted noteworthy historical compositions, e.g., *Washington's Passage of the Delaware* (Mus. Fine Arts, Boston).

Sully-Prudhomme, René François Armond [sülē'-prüdôm'], 1839–1907, French poet, one of the PARNASSIANS. His works include *Justice* (1878) and *Happiness* (1888), long philosophical poems. In 1901 he received the first Nobel Prize in literature.

sulphur: see SULFUR.

Sulzberger, Arthur Hays, 1891–1968, American newspaper publisher; b. N.Y.C. He joined the New York *Times* in 1918, succeeding his father-in-law, Adolph S. OCHS, as publisher in 1935. He retained the paper's fine news coverage and built the *Times* radio station, WQXR, into a leader in news and music. His son, **Arthur Ochs Sulzberger,** 1926–, b. N.Y.C., was president (1963–79) and publisher (1963–92) of the *Times* and became chairman of the New York Times Co. in 1979. His son, **Arthur Ochs Sulzberger, Jr.,** 1951–, b. Mt. Kisco, N.Y., became publisher of the *Times* in 1992.

sumac or **sumach,** common name for the family Anacardiaceae, trees and shrubs native chiefly to the tropics but ranging into north temperate regions and typified by resinous, often acrid sap, a source of tannin. The sap of some plants in the family, e.g., POISON IVY, also contains an ESSENTIAL OIL that is a toxic skin irritant. PISTACHIO, MANGO, and CASHEW are members of the family that provide food. The true sumacs belong to the genus *Rhus.* Most *Rhus* species contain tannin, and some are cultivated for it. Several North American species have brilliant fall foliage; the fruit of the common staghorn sumac (*R. typhira*) of the E U.S. is used to make wine and for medicinal purposes.

Sumatra, island (1990 est. pop. 36,882,000), westernmost and second largest island of Indonesia, c.183,000 sq mi (473,970 sq km). Hot and rainy, it is c.1,110 mi (1,790 km) long and up to 270 mi (435 km) wide, with swamps in the east and a densely forested, mountainous interior. Mt. Kerintji (12,467 ft/3,800 m), in the volcanic Barisan range, is the highest point. Sumatra is sparsely settled but of great economic importance for its rich deposits of oil, coal, gold, silver, and tin and bauxite (on its offshore islands) and its productive rubber, coffee, tea, and sugarcane plantations. MEDAN and PALEMBANG are the chief population centers.

Sumer and **Sumerian civilization.** A notable non-Semitic culture appeared in S Mesopotamia (Sumer) at least as early as the 5th millennium B.C. By 3000 B.C. Sumerian city-states, e.g., Erech, Kish, Lagash, and UR, developed considerable power based on irrigated agriculture. Pottery and metalwork were made into fine arts, and the Sumerians probably invented CUNEIFORM writing. The Sumerians were the rivals of Semitic cities such as AKKAD and ultimately were conquered by them. A Sumerian revival under the third dynasty of Ur (c.2060 B.C.) lasted until that dynasty fell to ELAM, and the growth of BABYLONIA ended the Sumerians as a nation.

Sumerian and Babylonian art. The artistic tradition of MESOPOTAMIA was remarkable for its antiquity, variety, and richness. The art of the Sumerian civilization (found in excavations at UR, BABYLON, Erech, Mari, Kish, and Lagash) influenced all the major cultures of ancient W. Asia. Sumerian techniques and motifs were widely available because of the invention of CUNEIFORM writing before 3000 B.C. Clay was the Sumerians' most abundant material; stone, wood, and metal had to be imported. From very early times, their workmanship was of the highest quality, e.g., an alabaster vase from Erech (c.3500 B.C.; Iraq Mus., Baghdad). A major peak of artistic achievement is represented by a marble head, *Lady of Warka,* from Erech (c.3200 B.C.; Iraq Mus.). Ur yielded much outstanding Sumerian work, e.g., a wooden harp with the head of a bull on top, showing mythological scenes in gold and mosaic inlay on the sound box (c.2650 B.C., Univ. of Penn., Philadelphia). The famous votive stone sculptures from Tell Asmar represent tall, bearded figures with huge, staring eyes and long, pleated skirts. The ZIGGURAT temple was the most striking architectural achievement of the Sumerians; a ziggurat at Erech extended over half a million square ft (46,500 sq m). Among other Sumerian arts, the cylinder seals, used to mark documents or property, were highly sophisticated. Sculpture reached new heights under Sargon, king of Akkad, and a bronze head from Nineveh (c.2300 B.C.; Iraq Mus.) is thought to be his portrait. Invasions from the east destroyed Sargon's empire, but the city of Lagash survived. It was beautified with many statues of its governor Gudea, and other works of art. The glory of Sumer was revived from 2200 to 2100 B.C. During this period the great ziggurat of the moon god at Ur was constructed. Invasions of Semitic peoples from what are now Iran and Syria ended the last Sumerian golden age. The palace at Mari reveals the brilliance of a vanished world. In the 18th cent. B.C., BABYLONIA under HAMMURABI dominated Mesopotamia. A carved diorite head showing the marks of age on a sensitive face (1792–1750 B.C.; Louvre) is thought to be his portrait. A sculpture from Mari of a fertility goddess (Aleppo Mus.), holding a vase from which water flows down her skirt, attests to the genius of Babylonian sculptors. After Hammurabi's death, Mesopotamia was torn for centuries by invasions. It was not until the reign of NEBUCHADNEZZAR (c.605–562 B.C.) that the Babylonians developed to perfection one of their most striking arts: the polychrome-glazed brick walls modeled in relief, of which the foremost example is the Ishtar gates of Babylon. These contain 575 reliefs of lions, dragons, and bulls (6th cent. B.C.; one lion is in the Metropolitan Mus.) of superb workmanship.

The king's palace, its hanging (balconied) gardens, the Ishtar gates, and the processional road made Babylon the most magnificent city of its time. Less than a century later, Babylonia fell to more invasions, with the Persians, Greeks, and Romans ruling in succession. It was not until excavations in the 19th cent. A.D. that archaeologists brought to light its history, artwork, and influence.

summer solstice: see SOLSTICE.

Sumner, Charles, 1811–74, U.S. senator from Massachusetts (1851–74); b. Boston. An aggressive abolitionist, he was physically assaulted by Rep. Preston S. Brooks after making a strong antislavery speech (May 19–20, 1856). He was a leader of the radical Republicans' RECONSTRUCTION program and was active in the impeachment of Andrew JOHNSON.

sun, intensely hot, self-luminous body of gases (mainly hydrogen and helium) at the center of the SOLAR SYSTEM. The sun is a medium-size main-sequence STAR. Its mean distance from the earth is defined as one ASTRONOMICAL UNIT. The sun is c.865,400 mi (1,392,000 km) in diameter; its volume is about 1,300,000 times, and its mass 332,000 times, that of the earth. At its center, the sun has a density over 100 times that of water, a pressure of over 1 billion atmospheres, and a temperature of about 15,000,000K. This temperature is high enough for the occurrence of nuclear reactions, which are assumed to be the source of the sun's energy. Hans BETHE proposed a cycle of nuclear reactions known as the carbon cycle, in which carbon acts much as a catalyst, while hydrogen is transformed by a series of reactions into helium and large amounts of high-energy gamma radiation are released. The so-called proton-proton process is now thought to be a more important energy source: the collision of two protons ends with the production of helium atoms and the release throughout of gamma radiation. The bright surface of the sun is called the photosphere; its temperature is about 6000K. During an ECLIPSE of the sun, the chromosphere (a layer of rarified gases above the photosphere) and the corona (a luminous envelope of extremely fine particles surrounding the sun, outside the chromosphere) are observed. See also SOLAR WIND; SUNSPOTS.

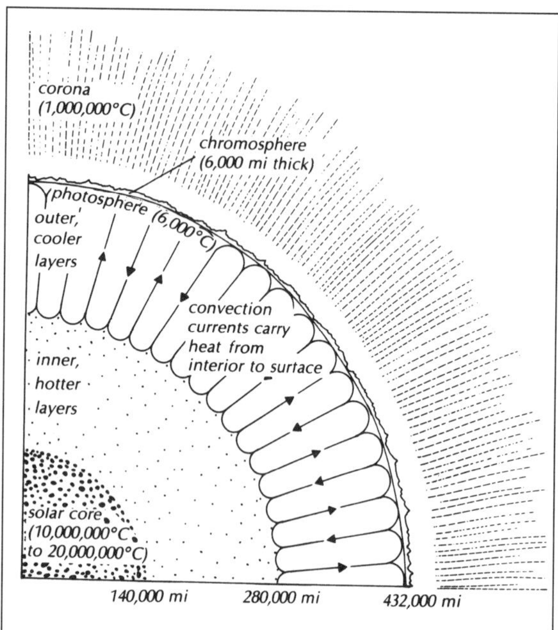

Structure of the sun

Sun Belt or **Sunbelt,** popular name for the southern tier of U.S. states. It is generally considered to focus on California, Arizona, Texas, and Florida and to extend north and east as far as Virginia. It embraces a diverse area that—because of rapid economic growth, high federal spending levels, and climatic advantages—has experienced (1960–90) rapid gains in population and political importance as a result of migration from the so-called Frost Belt states of the N U.S. east of the Rockies.

sun dance, a summer ceremony among the indigenous peoples of the Plains (see NORTH AMERICA, INDIGENOUS PEOPLES OF), consisting of usually eight days of ritual smoking, fasting, and penance through self-torture. The rites were discouraged by missionaries and the U.S. government to such an extent that they are now almost forgotten and their true meaning has been lost.

Sunday, Billy (William Ashley Sunday), 1863–1935, American evangelist; b. Ames, Iowa. A professional baseball player (1883–90), he worked (1891–95) for the YMCA and later became an evangelist (1896) and a Presbyterian minister (1903).

Sunday: see SABBATH; WEEK.

sundial, instrument that indicates the time of day by the shadow, cast on a surface marked to show hours or fractions of hours, of an object on which the sun's rays fall. The shadow-casting object is called a gnomon. Corrections must be made for the difference (which varies daily) between solar (or apparent) time and clock (or mean) time and for the difference in longitude between the position of a sundial and the standard-time meridian of a given locality.

sunfish: see BASS.

sunflower, any annual or perennial herb (genus *Helianthus*) of the COMPOSITE family, native to the New World. The flower heads are commonly bright yellow and may reach 1 ft (30 cm) in diameter. Different parts of the common sunflower (*H. annuus*) are used in many ways: the seeds as a poultry food, bread grain, and a source of oil; the flowers for the production of nectar; and the leaves for fodder. It is the state flower of Kansas. Other species are used for food (see JERUSALEM ARTICHOKE) and as garden flowers.

Sung, dynasty: see CHINA.

Sungari, chief river of NE China, c.1,150 mi (1,850 km) long, flowing generally north to join the AMUR R. on the China-Russia border. The river, which passes the industrial cities of Jilin (Kirin) and HARBIN, is navigable for most of its length and is an important trade artery. Fengman Dam, begun under Japanese occupation during World War II and completed in 1946, provides hydroelectricity for Jilin.

Sunni [Arab. *Sunna,* = tradition], adherents of the largest branch of ISLAM, usually considered traditionalist or orthodox. The Sunni comprise about 85% of all Muslims. Unlike the SHIITES, they accept the traditions (Sunna) of MUHAMMAD as authoritative and approve the historic order of Muhammad's first four successors. (The Shiites maintain that Ali, the fourth, should have been the first.) Differences in ritual and law divide the Sunni into adherents of four schools: the Hanafites, the Malikites, the Shafites, and the Hanbalites.

Sunnyvale, city (1990 pop. 117,229), W Calif., near San Francisco; settled 1849, inc. 1912. It is a residential and industrial city in the Santa Clara Valley. Little of the once rich farmland is left; today the area processes food and makes electronic equipment, paper products, and pharmaceuticals.

sunset laws, statutes that deal with the tendency of government agencies and programs to be self-perpetuating by providing for their periodic review.

sunshine laws: see FREEDOM OF INFORMATION ACT.

sunspots, dark, usually irregularly-shaped spots on the SUN's surface that are actually solar magnetic storms. The temperature of the spots is lower than that of the surrounding photosphere; thus the spots are, by contrast, darker. All but the smallest show a dark central portion (the umbra) with a lighter outer area (the penumbra). Sunspot activity reaches a maximum once every 11 years.

Sun Yat-sen, 1866–1925, Chinese revolutionary leader. Born near Guangzhou, he received (1892) a medical degree in Hong Kong and practiced in that city. Thereafter he plotted to overthrow the Ch'ing dynasty of China and to establish a republic. Influenced by Karl MARX, Sun organized (1905) in Japan a revolutionary league, the T'ung Meng Hui, and developed a political theory based on the Three People's Principles: nationalism, democracy, and the people's livelihood. After revolution erupted in China, Sun was elected (1911) provisional president of the Chinese republic. He soon resigned in favor of YÜAN SHIH-KAI, who became increasingly dictatorial. Sun became director of the KUOMINTANG party, revolted against Yüan, and became (1921) president of a self-proclaimed national government at Guangzhou. In 1924, to hasten the conquest of N China, he began cooperating with Chinese Communists and accepted aid from the USSR. After the Kuomintang-Communist split (1927), each group claimed to be his heirs. Sun's wife was Soong Ch'ing-ling (see under SOONG, family).

superconductivity, total disappearance of electrical resistance in a wire or circuit. Discovered in 1911, superconductivity only appears in a specific material below a critical temperature. The major problems confronting the possible applications of superconductivity were the extremely low temperatures initially required (only a few degrees above absolute zero) and the fact that a strong magnetic field could destroy it. In recent years much research has been done in the field of "high-temperature" superconductivity using composite substances. In 1993 scientists reported attaining superconductivity at 161K (−112°C). The highest-temperature superconductors, however, required extremely high atmospheric pressures and have mercury, a toxic metal, as a component.

superego: see PSYCHOANALYSIS.

superfluidity, the capability of liquid helium cooled below a temperature of 2.19K (the lambda point) to flow freely, even upward, with no measurable friction and viscosity. Superfluid helium flows easily through capillary tubes (see CAPILLARITY) that resist the flow of ordinary fluids, and a DEWAR FLASK filled with superfluid helium from a larger container will empty itself back into the original container because the liquid helium flows spontaneously in an invisible film over the surface of the flask.

Superior, Lake, second largest (31,820 sq mi/82,414 sq km) lake in the world, largest freshwater lake in the world, and largest, highest (surface elevation 602 ft/183 m), and deepest (up to 1,302 ft/397 m) of the GREAT LAKES, on the U.S.-Canada border. Part of the St. Lawrence & Great Lakes Waterway, it is connected with Lake Huron by the St. Marys R. and the SAULT SAINTE MARIE CANALS.

supernova, exploding star (see VARIABLE STAR) that suddenly increases its energy output as much as a billionfold and then slowly fades to less than its original brightness. At peak intensity, it can outshine the entire galaxy in which it occurs. Supernovas represent a catastrophic stage of STELLAR EVOLUTION; a sudden implosion of the core of certain massive stars (see GRAVITATIONAL COLLAPSE) produces a rapidly rotating collapsed stellar remnant (see PULSAR), the explosive ejection of the stellar envelope at great velocity, and the release of enormous quantities of energy. Over 120 extended galactic radio sources have been identified as supernova remnants. Of these, only four have been positively associated with explosions that were observed in recorded history; they occurred in 1006, 1054 (the remnant of which is now visible as the CRAB NEBULA), 1572, and 1604. In 1987 a supernova visible to the naked eye (the first since 1604) appeared in the Large MAGELLANIC CLOUD.

superrealism: see PHOTOREALISM.

supersonic speed: see SHOCK WAVE; SONIC BOOM.

supersymmetry, in physics, theory concerning the relationship of the ELEMENTARY PARTICLES called BOSONS to those known as FERMIONS, and vice versa, and linking the four fundamental FORCES. In supersymmetry every ordinary elementary particle has as its counterpart a superparticle with similar properties except for angular momentum, or "spin," which differs by a half unit. According to supersymmetry, each ordinary fermion has a superpartner that is a boson, and each ordinary boson has a superpartner that is a fermion. The superpartners of fermions are named by adding the prefix *s-* to the fermion's name, e.g., the squark is the QUARK's counterpart, and those of bosons by adding the suffix *-ino* to the root of the boson's name, e.g., the photino is the PHOTON's counterpart. Proof of the theory—discovery of the predicted particles through their creation and detection in a PARTICLE ACCELERATOR—requires extremely high energy levels that are beyond the capability of current devices. See SUPERSTRING.

supply and demand, in classical economics, factors that are said to determine price and that may be thought of as the guiding forces in an economy based on private property. Supply refers to the varying amounts of a good that producers will supply at different prices; in general, a higher price yields a greater supply. Demand refers to the quantity of a good that consumers want (and are able to buy) at any given price. According to the law of demand, demand decreases as the price rises. In a perfectly competitive market, the upward-sloping supply curve and the downward-sloping demand curve yield a supply-and-demand schedule that, where the curves intersect, reveals the equilibrium, or market, price of an item. In reality, however, monopolies, government regulation, and other factors combine to limit the effect of supply and demand.

supply-side economics, school of economic thought based on the belief that economic expansion will result from lower tax rates. The theory holds that a reduction in taxes will increase supply (see SUPPLY AND DEMAND) by encouraging production, providing greater incentives to work, and stimulating the savings and investment needed to support business growth. Greater supply would also mean a slowdown in inflation. A tax cut, according to supply-side economics, would not reduce overall tax revenues, because increased prosperity will offset the effects of lower tax rates. Grounded in the historic economic doctrine of LAISSEZ FAIRE, the philosophy found a modern champion in Arthur Laffer and provided much of the rationale for Pres. REAGAN's tax-cut program (1981). Supply-siders maintain that the tax cuts spurred economic growth, but critics argue that the program caused massive federal deficits, penalized the poor and middle class, and induced excessive speculation that damaged the U.S. economy.

suprematism, Russian nonobjective art movement founded (1913) by Casimir MALEVICH in Moscow, parallel to CONSTRUCTIVISM. Suprematism sought "to liberate art from the ballast of the representational world." Major works consisted of geometric shapes flatly painted on a pure canvas surface. Malevich's *White on White* (Mus. Mod. Art, N.Y.C.) embodies the movement's principles. Its dissemination through the BAUHAUS influenced modern art and design.

Supreme Court, United States, highest court of the U.S., established by Article 3 of the CONSTITUTION. It has ultimate jurisdiction over all cases arising under the Constitution, laws, and treaties of the U.S. Since 1869 it has comprised nine members—the chief justice and eight associate justices—named by the president, subject to Senate confirmation. Its decisions are rendered by majority vote. Cases are brought before the Court by appeal—when the ruling of the highest state court concerning the constitutionality of statutes is questioned—or by a writ of certiorari, granted at the Court's discretion, to review decisions by lower courts. As the court of last resort it has two functions: interpreting acts of Congress and determining whether federal and state statutes conform to the Constitution. Under the tenure (1801–35) of the "great chief justice," John MARSHALL, the principle of judicial review of congressional enactments was firmly established in MARBURY V. MADISON (1803). The powers of the federal government were confirmed in such cases as Gibbons v. Ogden (1824), which allowed the government to regulate interstate commerce. In contrast to such assertiveness, the Court later refused, in the DRED SCOTT CASE (1857), to take a stand against slavery. During the NEW DEAL of the 1930s, the Supreme Court struck down several major pieces of social legislation. In the 1950s, under Chief Justice Earl WARREN, it moved to protect the rights of minorities, as in BROWN V. BOARD OF EDUCATION OF TOPEKA, KANSAS (1954), outlawing public-school segregation. The judicial liberalism of the "Warren Court" receded in the 1970s with the appointment of Chief Justice Warren BURGER and others during the Nixon administration. The Court's more conservative approach (e.g., UNIVERSITY OF CALIFORNIA REGENTS V. BAKKE) was strongly reinforced by the appointments of Pres. Reagan and Pres. Bush. In 1986 William Rehnquist replaced Warren Burger as Chief Justice. Under his leadership the conservative court has taken a more active role in reversing or modifying some past Supreme Court decisions.

Supreme Soviet: see SOVIET.

Sur: see TYRE.

Surabaya, Surabaja, or **Soerabaja** [all: so͞orəbī'ə], city (1990 pop. 2,483,871), capital of East Java prov., NE Java, Indonesia, on the Kali Mas R. Surabaya is the country's second largest city and its major naval base. A commercial and industrial center, it has railroad shops, automobile assembly and oil processing plants, and manufactures textiles, glass, and fertilizer. Damaged during the Indonesian independence struggle, it has been extensively rebuilt.

surface tension, the cohesion forces (see ADHESION AND COHESION) at the surface of a liquid. The molecules within a liquid are at-

1. UNITED STATES SUPREME COURT

Rehnquist, William Hubbs, 1924–, Chief Justice; b. Milwaukee, Wisc., grad. Stanford Law School (1952). He was an assistant attorney general from 1969 until his appointment to the Supreme Court (1971) by Pres. Nixon. A conservative Republican, he became known on the Court as a staunch advocate of law-and-order. He was appointed chief justice by Pres. Reagan in 1986.

Blackmun, Harry Andrew, 1908–, b. Nashville, Ill., grad. Harvard Law School (1932). He served as judge of the U.S. Court of Appeals for the Eighth Circuit from 1959 until his appointment to the Supreme Court (1970) by Pres. Nixon. Blackmun has tended toward a liberal view on civil rights while remaining essentially conservative in other areas.

Ginsburg, Ruth (Joan) Bader, 1933–, b. Brooklyn, N.Y., grad. Columbia Law School (1959). She taught law and was a women's rights lawyer before her appointment (1980) to the U.S. Court of Appeals for the District of Columbia. Regarded as a moderate, she was appointed by Pres. Clinton in 1993.

Kennedy, Anthony M., 1936–, b. Sacramento, Calif., grad. Harvard Law School (1961). He was named to the U.S. Court of Appeals, Ninth Circuit, in 1975. He served in this position until his appointment (1988) to the Court by Pres. Reagan. The court's youngest member, he is regarded as a political and legal conservative.

O'Connor, Sandra Day, 1930–, b. El Paso, Tex., grad. Stanford Law School (1952). She served as judge of the Arizona Court of Appeals from 1979 until her appointment (1981) by Pres. Reagan as the first woman on the Supreme Court. A conservative, she has shown an interest in preserving and strengthening states' powers.

Scalia, Antonin, 1936–, b. Trenton, N.J., grad. Harvard Law School (1960). He was an assistant attorney general in the Justice Department from 1974–77 and was appointed (1982) to the U.S. Court of Appeals for the District of Columbia. Appointed (1986) to the Court by Pres. Reagan, he is conservative but has taken libertarian positions on certain issues.

Souter, David Hackett, 1939–, b. Melrose, Mass., grad. Harvard Law School (1966). He was attorney general of New Hampshire (1976–78) and served as an associate justice of the New Hampshire superior court (1978–83) and supreme court (1983–90). In 1990 he was appointed by Pres. Bush to the Supreme Court.

Stevens, John Paul, 1920–, b. Chicago, Ill., grad. Northwestern Univ. School of Law (1947). He served as judge of the U.S. Court of Appeals for the Seventh Circuit from 1970 until his appointment to the Supreme Court (1975) by Pres. Ford. Stevens is regarded as independent and moderately conservative.

Thomas, Clarence, 1948–, b. Pin Point, Ga., grad. Yale Law School (1974). He headed the Equal Employment Opportunity Commission (1982–89) prior to his appointment (1990) to the U.S. Court of Appeals for the District of Columbia. A conservative and the only African-American justice, he was appointed by Pres. Bush in 1991.

tracted equally from all sides, but those near the surface experience unequal attractions and thus are drawn toward the center of the liquid mass by this net force. A result of surface tension is the tendency of a liquid to reduce its exposed surface to the smallest possible area.

surfing, sport of gliding toward the shore on a breaking wave, done on a board from 4 to 12 ft (122 to 366 cm) long. The larger surfboards have a stabilizing fin in the rear. The surfer paddles toward the beach until an incoming wave catches the board, then stands up and glides along or just under the crest of the wave. Developed in Hawaii, surfing spread to California in the 1920s and, by the 1960s, had become popular with youth in the U.S., Australia, and other countries.

Surgeon General, United States, head of the U.S. Public Health Service, which is responsible for protecting the people's health, reporting to the public on health issues, and collaborating with other countries in health activities.

surgery, branch of medicine concerned with the diagnosis and treatment of injuries and pathological conditions requiring manual or instrumental operative procedures. Surgery has been performed since prehistoric times (bloodletting, opening of abscesses) and was practiced with great skill and cleanliness by the ancient Greeks and Romans. During the Middle Ages in Europe unskilled and uneducated barber-surgeons dominated the field, and postoperative infection and GANGRENE were common. Surgery became more professional in the 18th cent. and entered its modern phase in the 19th cent. with the introduction of antiseptic techniques, sterilization, and ANESTHESIA. More recent advances include BLOOD TRANSFUSION techniques, new diagnostic tools (X RAYS, CAT SCAN, ULTRASOUND), ANTIBIOTICS and other DRUGS, microsurgery, and organ TRANSPLANTATION. Such techniques as balloon ANGIOPLASTY and endoscopic surgery (see ENDOSCOPE), utilizing tiny instruments and miniaturized video cameras and requiring smaller incisions, are now replacing some more invasive surgery.

Suriname [so͝orĭnäm′, –năm′], officially Republic of Suriname, republic (1992 est. pop. 410,000), 63,037 sq mi (163,266 sq km), NE South America, bordered by the Atlantic Ocean (N), French Guiana (E), Brazil (S), and Guyana (W). PARAMARIBO is the capital. It is part of the Guiana region. Suriname is one of the world's great producers of bauxite, which accounts for about 70% of export earnings. Rice is the chief crop, and sugarcane, bananas, coffee, and coconuts are also grown. Timber and wood products are also important. The population is mixed, with Asian Indians, Creoles, and Indonesians the largest ethnic groups. Dutch is the official language, but most of the people speak Sranang Tongo, a native patois. Hinduism, the Roman Catholic and Moravian churches, and Islam are the predominant faiths.

History. The Dutch established a colony here in 1616, and Dutch possession was confirmed by the Congress of VIENNA in 1815. Known as Netherlands or Dutch Guiana, the colony was granted a parliament in 1866. Suriname became autonomous in 1954 and independent in 1975. Just prior to independence, some 100,000 Surinamese, mainly of Asian descent, migrated to the Netherlands.

2. SUPREME COURT JUSTICES THROUGHOUT HISTORY *(including dates on bench)*

CHIEF JUSTICES

John Jay, 1789–95	Salmon P. Chase, 1864–73	Harlan F. Stone, 1941–46
John Rutledge, 1795	Morrison R. Waite, 1874–88	Fred M. Vinson, 1946–53
Oliver Ellsworth, 1796–1800	Melville W. Fuller, 1888–1910	Earl Warren, 1953–69
John Marshall, 1801–35	Edward D. White, 1910–21	Warren E. Burger, 1969–86
Roger B. Taney, 1836–64	William H. Taft, 1921–30	William H. Rehnquist, 1986–
	Charles E. Hughes, 1930–41	

ASSOCIATE JUSTICES

John Rutledge, 1789–91	David Davis, 1862–77	Owen J. Roberts, 1930–45
William Cushing, 1789–1810	Stephen J. Field, 1863–97	Benjamin N. Cardozo, 1932–38
James Wilson, 1789–98	William Strong, 1870–80	Hugo Black, 1937–71
John Blair, 1789–96	Joseph P. Bradley, 1870–92	Stanley F. Reed, 1938–57
Robert H. Harrison, 1789–90	Ward Hunt, 1873–82	Felix Frankfurter, 1939–62
James Iredell, 1790–99	John M. Harlan, 1877–1911	William O. Douglas, 1939–75
Thomas Johnson, 1791–93	William B. Woods, 1881–87	Frank Murphy, 1940–49
William Paterson, 1793–1806	Stanley Matthews, 1881–89	James F. Byrnes, 1941–42
Samuel Chase, 1796–1811	Horace Gray, 1882–1902	Robert H. Jackson, 1941–54
Bushrod Washington, 1798–1829	Samuel Blatchford, 1882–93	Wiley B. Rutledge, 1943–49
Alfred Moore, 1799–1804	Lucius G. C. Lamar, 1888–93	Harold H. Burton, 1945–58
William Johnson, 1804–34	David J. Brewer, 1890–1910	Thomas C. Clark, 1949–67
Henry Brockholst Livingston, 1806–23	Henry B. Brown, 1891–1906	Sherman Minton, 1949–56
Thomas Todd, 1807–26	George Shiras, Jr., 1892–1903	John M. Harlan, 1955–71
Gabriel Duval, 1811–36	Howell E. Jackson, 1893–95	William J. Brennan, Jr., 1956–90
Joseph Storey, 1811–45	Edward D. White, 1894–1910	Charles E. Whittaker, 1957–62
Smith Thompson, 1823–43	Rufus W. Peckham, 1896–1909	Potter Stewart, 1958–81
Robert Trimble, 1826–28	Joseph McKenna, 1898–1925	Byron R. White, 1962–93
John McLean, 1829–61	Oliver W. Holmes, 1902–32	Arthur J. Goldberg, 1962–65
Henry Baldwin, 1830–44	William R. Day, 1903–22	Abe Fortas, 1965–69
James M. Wayne, 1835–67	William H. Moody, 1906–10	Thurgood Marshall, 1967–91
Philip P. Barbour, 1836–41	Horace H. Lurton, 1910–14	Harry A. Blackmun, 1970–
John Catron, 1837–65	Charles E. Hughes, 1910–16	Lewis F. Powell, Jr., 1971–87
John McKinley, 1837–52	Willis Van Devanter,1911–37	William H. Rehnquist, 1971–
Peter V. Daniel, 1841–60	Joseph R. Lamar, 1911–16	John Paul Stevens, 1975–
Samuel Nelson, 1845–72	Mahlon Pitney, 1912–22	Sandra Day O'Connor, 1981–
Levi Woodbury, 1845–51	James C. McReynolds, 1914–41	Antonin Scalia, 1986–
Robert C. Grier, 1846–70	Louis D. Brandeis, 1916–39	Anthony M. Kennedy, 1988–
Benjamin R. Curtis, 1851–57	John H. Clarke, 1916–22	David H. Souter, 1990–
John A. Campbell, 1853–61	George Sutherland, 1922–38	Clarence Thomas, 1991–
Nathan Clifford, 1858–81	Pierce Butler, 1923–39	Ruth Bader Ginsburg, 1993–
Noah H. Swayne, 1862–81	Edward T. Sanford, 1923–30	
Samuel F. Miller, 1862–90	Harlan F. Stone, 1925–41	

In 1980 a coup led by Sgt. Major Désiré Bouterse brought the soldiers' civilian allies to power; Bouterse assumed complete control from 1982 to 1987. In 1990 he again ousted the elected government and installed his political allies, but new elections (1991) gave his opponents control of parliament and Ronald Venetiaan became president. Bouterse resigned as army chief in 1992 amid corruption charges.

surrealism, literary and art movement influenced by Freudianism (see FREUD, SIGMUND), dedicated to expressing the imagination as revealed in DREAMS, free of the conscious control of reason and convention. Founded (1924) in Paris by André BRETON with his *Manifesto of Surrealism,* it can be traced back to French poets such as Arthur RIMBAUD, Charles BAUDELAIRE, and Guillaume APOLLINAIRE and to the Italian painter Giorgio de CHIRICO. In literature, surrealism was confined almost exclusively to France, and was based on the associations and implications of words. Its adherents included Paul Éluard and Jean COCTEAU, famous for his surrealist films. In art the movement was dominant in the 1920s and 30s. Salvador DALI and Yves TANGUY used dream-inspired symbols such as melting clocks. Max ERNST and René MAGRITTE used incongruous elements realistically painted. These "verists" differed from "absolute" surrealists, such as Joan MIRÓ, who used images from the subconscious.

Surrey, Henry Howard, earl of, 1517?–1547, English poet. He translated two books of Vergil's *Aeneid,* introducing blank verse into the English language, and with his friend Sir Thomas WYATT popularized the Petrarchan SONNET form.

surrogate mother, a woman who agrees, usually by contract and for a fee, to bear a child for a couple who are childless because the wife is infertile or physically incapable of carrying a developing fetus. Often the surrogate mother is the biological mother of the child, conceiving it by means of ARTIFICIAL INSEMINATION with sperm from the husband. In gestational surrogacy, the wife is fertile but incapable of carrying a growing fetus; the child is conceived by IN VITRO FERTILIZATION using her eggs and her husband's sperm, and the resulting embryo is implanted in the surrogate mother's uterus. Surrogate motherhood has raised complex ethical and legal issues, and lawsuits over custody after the child's birth have resulted from both types of surrogacy. In the highly publicized Baby M case (1986–88), Mary Beth Whitehead, the surrogate (and biological) mother, sued William and Elizabeth Stern, the baby's father and his wife, for custody of the child. Although the surrogate mother was not awarded custody in the Baby M case, she was granted visitation rights. A number of states have passed laws banning paid surrogacy.

surveying, accurate measurement of points and lines of direction on the earth's surface for the purpose of preparing maps or locating boundary lines. *Hydrographic surveying* records such features as bottom contours, buoys, channels, and shoals in bodies of water and along coastlines. *Land surveying* includes both *geodetic* *surveying*, used for large areas and taking into account the curvature of the earth's surface (see GEODESY); and *plane surveying*, which deals with areas sufficiently small that the earth's curvature is negligible and can be disregarded.

Surveyor, in space exploration: see SPACE PROBE, table.

Su Shih: see SU TUNG-P'O.

suspension, in chemistry, mixture of two substances, one of which is finely divided and dispersed in the other. Particles in a suspension are larger than those in COLLOIDS or SOLUTIONS, and they precipitate (see PRECIPITATE) if the suspension is allowed to stand undisturbed. Common suspensions include sand in water, dust in air, and droplets of oil in air.

Sussex, kingdom of, one of the Anglo-Saxon kingdoms of England, located south of the Weald. It was settled (late 5th cent.) by the Saxons and converted (681–86) to Christianity. Conquered (685–88) by WESSEX, Sussex later fell (by 771) to King Offa of MERCIA. In 825 Sussex submitted to King Egbert of WESSEX.

Sutherland, Graham, 1903–80, English painter. He is famous for his paintings of war devastation. *Thorns* is a series of paintings realistically executed in sharp, cruel forms and symbolic of Jesus' Passion.

Sutherland, Dame Joan, 1926–, Australian soprano. She is famed for her performance of the bel canto opera repertory (see VOICE), e.g., the title role in DONIZETTI's *Lucia de Lammermoor.*

sutra: see SANSKRIT LITERATURE.

Sutter, John Augustus, 1803–80, American pioneer; b. Germany as Johann August Suter. He established a colony in California. Gold was discovered at his mill in 1848, and the activities of the fortune-seekers who swarmed over his land ruined him. Bankrupt, he moved to Pennsylvania in 1873.

Suttner, Bertha (Gräfin Kinsky), Freifrau von, 1843–1914, Austrian novelist and pacifist. Her pacifist novel *Lay Down Your Arms* (1889) had great social impact. She was the first woman awarded the Nobel Peace Prize (1905).

Su Tung-p'o or **Su Shih,** 1036–1101, Chinese poet and official, considered the greatest poet of the Sung dynasty. His satiric verses and opposition to official policy often cost him his position. Regret for the evanescence of beauty and the short span of life are frequent themes in his work.

Suva, city (1986 pop. 71,608), capital of FIJI, on Viti Levu.

Suvorov, Aleksandr Vasilyevich [so͞ovô'rəf], 1729–1800, Russian field marshal. He fought in the RUSSO-TURKISH WARS of 1768–74 and 1787–92, and put down the PUGACHEV revolt and the 1794 Polish uprising. In the FRENCH REVOLUTIONARY WARS of 1798–99 he drove the French from N Italy and planned to march on Paris, but was ordered to join General Korsakov and Austrian Archduke Charles in Switzerland. While Suvorov's force was struggling through the St. Gotthard Pass, Charles was ordered back to the Rhine and Korsakov was defeated. Suvorov led his troops to Lindau and refused to undertake further action with the Austrians. Russia soon withdrew from the war.

Suzuki Harunobu: see HARUNOBU.

Suzuki Zenko, 1911–, Japanese politician. A founder of the ruling Liberal-Democratic party (1955), he became prime minister on the death of Ohira Masayoshi (1980). Criticism from within the party and a failure to reinvigorate the economy resulted in his resignation (1982).

Svalbard, island group (1992 est. pop. 3,000), 23,958 sq mi (62,051 sq km), in the Arctic Ocean, located c.400 mi (640 km) north of and belonging to Norway. The main islands are SPITSBERGEN, the largest, and Nordaustlandet, Edgeøya, Barentsøya, and Prins Karls Forland. Ice fields and glaciers cover more than 60% of the area. Mining, notably of coal, is the chief industry. Whaling and fur trading were important in the past. The islands were awarded to Norway by international treaty in 1920.

Svein: see SWEYN.

Sverdlovsk: see YEKATERINBURG.

Sverdrup, Otto, 1855–1930, Norwegian explorer. After participating in two arctic trips, he led an expedition (1898–1902) that sought to reach the NORTH POLE by Smith Sound but failed because of ice in Kennedy Channel. However, valuable topographical observations were made and unknown lands were found and explored.

Swabia, historic region in SW Germany. In the 9th cent. Swabia became one of the five stem duchies of medieval Germany; it included Alsace and E Switzerland. The duchy was bestowed on the HOHENSTAUFFEN dynasty in 1079 and broke up into many feudal and ecclesiastical holdings when the dynasty died out (1268). From the 14th to 16th cent. cities, nobles, knights, and prelates in the region formed Swabian leagues to protect trade and regional peace.

Swabian League, 1488–1534, association of Swabian cities and other powers in SW Germany for the protection of trade and for regional peace. It was supported by the Holy Roman emperors and comprised 26 cities. The league backed the election (1519) of Emperor CHARLES V and helped to defeat the peasants in the Peasants' War. Its dissolution was brought about through internal stresses, partly caused by the religious split brought on by the REFORMATION.

Swahili language, member of the Bantu group of African languages. See AFRICAN LANGUAGES (table); BANTU LANGUAGES.

swallow, common name for small perching BIRDS of the family Hirundinidae, of almost worldwide distribution. Swallows have long, narrow wings, forked tails, and weak feet. They are extremely graceful in flight, able to make abrupt changes in speed and direction. Their plumage is blue or black with a metallic sheen. American species include the common American barn swallow (*Hirundo rustica*) and the purple martin (*Progne subis*).

Swammerdam, Jan, 1637–80, Dutch naturalist. He was a pioneer in the use of the microscope and was probably the first to detect (1658) red blood cells. Before he turned to religious contemplation, his chief interest was the study of invertebrates; his descriptions of them, together with accurate and exquisitely executed drawings, was published posthumously in 1737–38.

swamp, shallow body of water in a low-lying, poorly drained depression, usually containing abundant plant growth. A notable example of a U.S. swamp is the EVERGLADES in S Florida. Because the bottom of a swamp is at or below the water table, swamps serve to channel runoff into the groundwater supply, thus helping to stabilize the water table. During periods of very heavy rains, a swamp can act as a natural flood-control device. The increased use of drained swampland for urban development results in greater runoff and probability of flooding as well as the destruction of wildlife habitats. The term *bog* usually refers to a swampy depression with a low level of oxygen in the water and a thick floating mat of living and dead organic matter. *Marsh* implies a large wetland where low-lying grasses, rushes, and sedges predominate.

swan, large aquatic BIRD, related to the DUCK and GOOSE, with a long, gracefully curved neck. The orange-billed white trumpeter swan (*Cygnus buccinator*), seen in parks, breeds in the wild in parts of Europe, Asia, and the U.S. The trumpeter swan of North America (*Olor buccinator*), which has a trumpetlike call during the breeding season, was once nearly extinct but is now protected.

Swann v. Charlotte-Mecklenburg County Board of Education, case decided in 1971 by the U.S. SUPREME COURT. The Court held that the constitutional mandate (see BROWN V. BOARD OF EDUCATION) to desegregate public schools did not require all schools in a district to reflect the district's racial composition, but that the existence of all-white or all-black schools must be shown not to result from segregation policies. The Court added that because bus transportation had traditionally been employed by school systems, busing could be used in efforts to correct racial imbalances.

Swaziland, officially Kingdom of Swaziland, kingdom (1992 est. pop. 913,000), 6,705 sq mi (17,366 sq km), SE Africa, bordered by South Africa (S, W, and N) and Mozambique (E). The administrative capital is MBABANE. The country is mountainous, with steplike plateaus descending from the highveld in the west and then rising to the plateau of the Lebombo Mts. The four major river systems have vast hydroelectric potential and are used for irrigation. Agriculture, including forestry and ranching, is the principal sector of the economy, and sugar, wood pulp and timber, and cattle are the leading exports. There are large mineral deposits, the most important of which are asbestos and coal. Swaziland has close economic ties with South Africa. The Swazi (a Bantu people) constitute 90% of the population; the rest are South Africans and Europeans. English and Siswati, the Swazi language, are the official languages. About half of the people practice traditional religions; most of the rest are Christian.

History. Fleeing Zulu attacks, the Swazi arrived in present-day

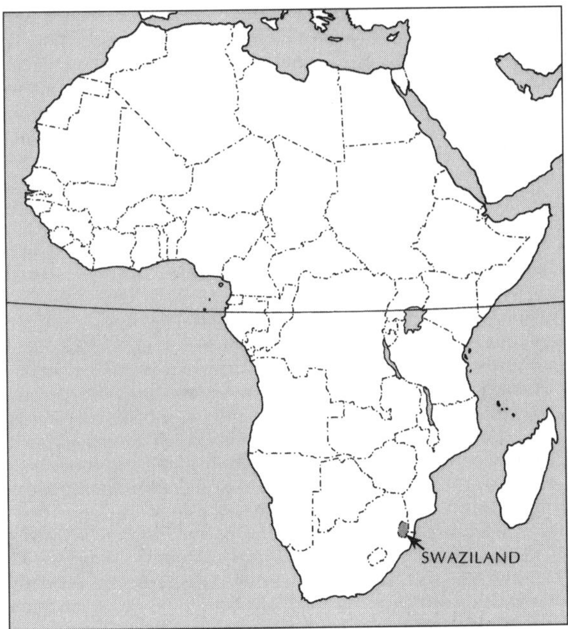

Swaziland from Mozambique in the early 19th cent. Europeans seeking concessions soon moved in, and Swaziland became a British High Commission Territory in 1903. It received limited self-government in 1963 and gained full independence in 1968, under King Sobhuza II. In 1973 he suspended the constitution, and the new constitution (1978) so diluted the vote that the king ruled nearly absolutely. Upon Sobhuza's death in 1982, crown prince Makhostine succeeded him, as Mswati III; the period of the regency (1982–85) was marked by factional politics and governmental instability. In the early 1990s there was increasing pressure in Swaziland for political democratization, and free parliamentary elections were held in 1993. The king, however, still holds most power.

Sweden, Swed. *Sverige,* officially Kingdom of Sweden, constitutional monarchy (1992 est. pop. 8,602,000), 173,648 sq mi (449,750 sq km), N Europe, on the E Scandinavian peninsula; bordered by Norway (W), Finland (NE), the Gulf of Bothnia (E), the Baltic Sea (SE), and the Skagerrak and Kattegat (SW). Major cities include STOCKHOLM (the capital), GÖTEBORG, MALMÖ, and UPPSALA. The two main geographical regions are the mountainous north, including part of LAPLAND, and the low-lying south, where most of the population lives. Rivers and over 100,000 lakes make up nearly one third of the area. Sweden is a highly industrialized nation with one of the highest living standards in the world. It is a producer of iron and other metal ores. Manufactures include high-grade steel, metal goods, machinery, transport equipment, forest products, and ships, much of which is exported. Farming produces dairy products, grain, sugar beets, potatoes, livestock, and poultry. The fur industry is also important. The people are largely ethnically homogeneous Swedish speakers; Finns and Lapps are the largest minorities. Over 90% of all Swedes belong to the Lutheran church.

History. Most Swedes are descendants of Germanic tribes that were probably settled in Scandinavia by the Neolithic period. By the 10th cent. A.D. the Swedes had extended their influence to the Black Sea. Christianity, introduced c.829, became fully established in the 12th cent. under Eric IX. Sweden and Norway were united (1319) under MAGNUS VII, and in 1397 the Kalmar Union united Denmark, Norway, and Sweden. The Danes dominated the union, however, and in 1523, stirred to resistance by a massacre (1520) of Swedish nobles at Stockholm, the Swedes rose against the Danes and established a separate state with GUSTAVUS I as king. Under GUSTAVUS II (r.1611–32), who successfully opposed the Hapsburgs in the THIRTY YEARS WAR, and CHARLES X (r.1654–60), who led successful wars against Poland and Denmark, Sweden became one of the great powers of Europe, controlling Finland, Latvia, Estonia, and other parts of the Baltic coast by the end of the 17th cent. The great period of empire came to an end, however, with the rise of a unified Russia and the defeat of Sweden in the NORTHERN WAR (1700–1721). In the Napoleonic Wars, in which Sweden fought against France, Sweden lost (1809) Finland to Russia but was awarded (1814) Norway, which remained in union with Sweden until 1905. The 19th cent. was marked by industrial progress, liberalization of government, and, because of poor economic conditions, large-scale emigration to the U.S. In the following century Sweden avoided involvement in both world wars (and preserved its neutrality during the COLD WAR) and initiated a sweeping program of economic expansion and social welfare legislation that made it one of the most prosperous and progressive nations in the world. From the mid-1960s, however, Swedish economic growth slowed, and the 1970s and 80s saw sizable increases in unemployment and the rate of inflation. Charles XVI Gustavus succeeded his grandfather, Gustavus VI, as king in 1973. Except for a short period (1976–82) of conservative control, the Social Democrats, led by Olof PALME from 1969, governed Sweden for over half a century. In 1986 Palme was assassinated and was succeeded by Ingvar Carlsson. Center-right parties won control of parliament in 1991, and Carl Bildt became prime minister. In 1992 recession and a currency crisis forced the government to pass austerity measures that raised taxes and cut services.

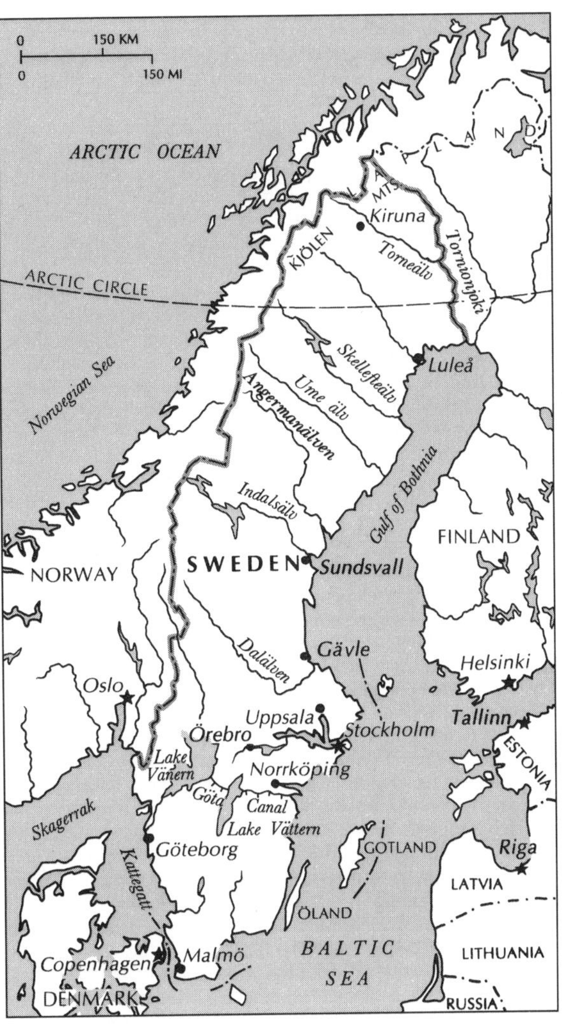

Swedenborg, Emanuel, 1688–1772, Swedish scientist, religious teacher, and mystic. His religious system is sometimes called Swedenborgianism. Appointed (1716) assessor of the Royal College of Mines, his engineering skill made him widely known; he also published many works on philosophy, humanists, the animal kingdom, the brain, and psychology before resigning in 1747. He then gave himself wholly to the contemplation of spiritual matters, believing that God had revealed the true inner doctrines of the divine word to him alone. The teachings of his New Church were set forth in 1757, when he believed the second coming of the Lord had taken place. He had not planned to found a new sect, but his disciples organized the Church of the NEW JERUSALEM after his death.

Swedish language, member of the North Germanic, or Scandinavian, group of the Germanic subfamily of the Indo-European family of languages. See LANGUAGE (table).

Sweelinck, Jan Pieterszoon, 1562–1621, Dutch organist and composer. The line of his pupils descends directly to J.S. BACH and HANDEL. His organ FUGUES give separate parts to the pedals.

sweeteners, artificial, substances used as low-calorie sugar substitutes. Saccharin, cyclamates, and aspartame have been the most commonly used artificial sweeteners. Saccharin, a coal-tar derivative three hundred times as sweet as sugar, was discovered in 1879. Cyclamates were approved for consumer use in 1951, but were banned in 1969 because of suspected carcinogenic properties. Aspartame, an amino-acid compound, was discovered in 1965.

sweet gum: see WITCH HAZEL.

sweet pea, annual climbing plant (*Lathyrus odoratus*) of the PULSE family, native to S Europe but now widely cultivated for its fragrant flowers. There are three main types: dwarf, summer flowering (garden sweet peas), and winter flowering (florists' sweet peas). The flowers may be various colors; the vines climb by tendrils and require support.

sweet potato, trailing perennial plant (*Ipomoea batatas*) of the MORNING GLORY family, native to the New World tropics. Raised mainly for human consumption, sweet potatoes are the most important tropical root crop and are grown in many varieties. Rich in VITAMIN A, they yield starch, flour, glucose, and alcohol. The sweet potato, which is unrelated to the POTATO, is often confused with the YAM, which belongs to another family.

sweet William: see PINK.

Sweyn or **Svein,** c.960–1014, king of Denmark (986–1014), son of Harold Bluetooth. He rebelled against his father, who was killed in battle, but Sweyn was expelled shortly after his accession by Eric the Victorious of Sweden. He later married Eric's widow, was restored to his throne, and joined Sweden in conquering Norway. In 1003–4 Sweyn invaded England for the second time (he had earlier exacted DANEGELD from ÆTHELRED) and established his rule there in 1013. His son CANUTE succeeded him in England (1014) and Denmark (1018).

Swift, Jonathan, 1667–1745, Anglo-Irish author and master of satire; b. Dublin. His early works were *The Battle of the Books,* upholding the superiority of the ancients to the moderns, and *Tale of a Tub,* a satire on religious excesses (both published 1704). Swift was active in Whig politics with ADDISON and STEELE, but turned against the party over its unfriendliness to the Anglican church. Pamphlets on ecclesiastical and political issues, in which he usually supported the Tories, engaged him from 1708 to 1714. In 1713 he joined the SCRIBLERUS CLUB and in 1714 was made dean of St. Patrick's Cathedral, Dublin. He became a hero to the Irish with his *Drapier's Letters* (1724) and the savage *Modest Proposal* (1729), in which he ironically advocated the breeding of Irish babies to be fed to the rich as a means of reducing Ireland's poverty. His masterpiece, *Gulliver's Travels* (1726), a ruthless SATIRE on human folly and 18th-cent. England, is unequaled in the intensity of its moralism. Ironically, it was later turned into an expurgated children's story.

swift, name for small, swallowlike BIRDS of the family Apodidae, found worldwide, chiefly in the tropics. Swifts are the most rapid flying animals known. In the U.S. the common Eastern species is the chimney swift (*Chaetura pelagica*). Western species include the black, Vaux's, and white-throated swifts. Nests of E Asian swifts, made entirely of a salivary secretion, are used in bird's-nest soup.

swimming, self-propulsion through water, usually as a competitive sport or recreation. The principal swimming strokes are the crawl, backstroke, sidestroke, breaststroke, and butterfly. The crawl, or Australian crawl, is considered the speediest. In executing it, the body is prone and alternating overarm strokes are used. The backstroke is done in a supine position with alternate over-the-head strokes. The sidestroke entails a forward underwater stroke with the body on one side. The breaststroke is accomplished in a prone position using a frog kick and movement of the arms from a point in front of the head to shoulder level. The butterfly, the most difficult and exhausting stroke, is done in a prone position with a dolphin kick and a windmill-like double arm movement. In freestyle swimming any stroke may be used, but the crawl is usually favored. Swimming became organized as an amateur sport in the late 19th cent. It is a major Olympic event for both men and women. See also DIVING, SPRINGBOARD AND PLATFORM.

Swinburne, Algernon Charles, 1837–1909, English poet and critic. His first success, the poetic drama *Atalanta in Calydon* (1865), exhibited his talent for musical, sensuous language. The poems in *Poems and Ballads* (first series, 1866) were attacked by some for their sensuality and pagan sentiments but lauded by others for their technical genius. Swinburne's enthusiasm for Italian unification found expression in *A Song of Italy* (1867) and *Songs before Sunrise* (1871). His other poetic works include a dramatic trilogy about Mary Queen of Scots (1865–81); the second series of *Poems and Ballads* (1878); and the long poem *Tristram of Lyonesse* (1882). His literary criticism was extensive, ranging from Shakespeare to Dickens. Because of his poor health, which had been weakened by epilepsy and alcoholism, he was cared for during the last 30 years of his life by Theodore Watts-Dunton.

swine, cloven-hoofed MAMMALS of the family Suidae, native to the Old World and typified by long, mobile snouts, thick, bristly hides, and small tails. Domesticated swine, commonly called hogs or pigs (the latter more correctly reserved for young swine), are probably descended chiefly from the wild swine, or wild boar (*Sus scrofa*), of Eurasia and N Africa. Hogs are bred for their fat (lard), flesh (prepared as ham, bacon, and pork), and other products (e.g., LEATHER for gloves and footballs, and bristles for brushes). Commercially raised swine are grouped as meat-type (e.g., Hereford and Berkshire), lard-type (e.g., Poland China, Duroc, and Spotted), or bacon-type (e.g., Yorkshire and American Landrace). Hogs are highly susceptible to many diseases transmissible to humans, among them TRICHINOSIS.

swine fever: see HOG CHOLERA.

swing music: see JAZZ.

Swiss Guards, Swiss mercenaries who fought in various European armies from the 15th to the 19th cent. They were put at the disposal of foreign armies by the Swiss government in diplomatic treaties known as capitulations. They were especially important in the French army of LOUIS XIV and on the side of the royalists in the BOURBON Restoration. The Swiss banned all capitulations in 1874. Today the Swiss Guard exists only as the personal guard of the pope.

Switzerland, Fr. *Suisse,* Ger. *Schweiz,* Ital. *Svizzera,* officially Swiss Confederation, federal republic (1992 est. pop. 6,828,000), 15,941 sq mi (41,287 sq km), central Europe; bordered by France (W), Germany (N), Austria and Liechtenstein (E), and Italy (S). Major cities include BERN (the capital), ZÜRICH, BASEL, and GENEVA. The Jura Mts., in the northwest, and the spectacular ALPS, in the south, occupy about 70% of the country's area. The Swiss Plateau, a narrow, hilly region between the two mountain ranges, has most of the country's population. The Rhine and Rhône rivers have their sources in Switzerland, and there are many lakes, among them Geneva and Constance. With few natural resources (waterpower is a notable exception) and a largely barren soil, Switzerland has attained prosperity through technological skill and export manufacturing. Principal products are machinery, precision instruments, chemicals, pharmaceuticals, watches, jewelry, textiles, and foodstuffs (notably cheese and chocolate). Tourism and international finance are important sources of income. German, French, Italian, and Romansh (a Rhaeto-Roman dialect) are the national languages. The population is about evenly divided between Roman Catholics and Protestants.

History. Conquered by Rome in 58 B.C., the region that is modern Switzerland fell successively to Germanic tribes (5th cent. A.D.), Swabia and Burgundy (9th cent.), and the Holy Roman Empire (1033). By the 13th cent. the HAPSBURGS controlled much of the region, and their encroachment on local privileges led to the formation of a defense league (1291), the basis of the Swiss confederation, by the cantons, or states, of Uri, Schwyz, and Unterwalden. Later, other cantons joined the league, and wars against the Hapsburgs resulted in virtual independence in 1499. The loose Swiss confederation was seriously split in the 16th cent. by the REFORMATION (see CALVIN, JOHN; ZWINGLI), and religious civil wars wracked the country for almost two centuries. However, Switzerland remained neutral in the Thirty Years War, and its independence was recognized in the Peace of Westphalia in 1648. In 1798, during the French Revolution, French armies swept into Switzerland and established the Helvetic Republic. The confederation was substantially restored in 1815 by the Congress of VIENNA, which also guaranteed Switzerland's perpetual neutrality. In 1847 a brief and almost bloodless civil war resulted in the transformation of Switzerland into a more centralized federal state. Armed neutrality was maintained throughout both world wars. Since 1959 Switzerland has been governed by a four-party liberal-conservative coalition. The Swiss maintain a permanent observer status at the UN. In 1986 Swiss voters overwhelmingly rejected consideration of UN membership, but in 1992 they voted to join the World Bank and International Monetary Fund.

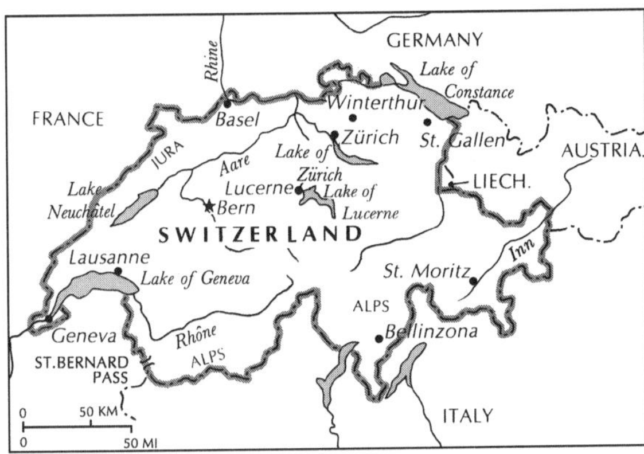

sword, weapon used in personal combat; it consists of a blade with a sharp point and one or two cutting edges, set in a hilt (handle) and usually protected by a metal case or cross guard. It developed from the dagger early in the Bronze Age. Blade materials evolved from iron to steel to finely tempered steel. Short swords with two cutting edges were used by the Greeks and Romans; very large, two-handed ones were favored by medieval knights. Well-known swords have included the curved scimitar of the Persians and Arabs and the long, single-edge Japanese SAMURAI sword set in a long hilt. Other types are the curved saber, favored by European CAVALRY, and the épée, or dueling sword, a straight, narrow, and stiff thrusting weapon without cutting edges. Obsolete as a military weapon, the sword still plays a part in military ceremonies. See FENCING.

swordfish, large food and game FISH (*Xiphias gladius*) of warmer Atlantic and Pacific waters, related to the SAILFISH and MARLIN. Its sharp, broad, elongated upper jaw is used to flail and pierce the smaller fish it eats. Swordfish, which breed as far north as Nova Scotia, may reach 15 ft (457 cm) in length and 1,000 lb (454 kg) in weight. They are commercially valuable.

sycamore: see PLANE TREE.

Sydenham, Thomas, 1624–89, English physician. A founder of modern clinical medicine and epidemiology, he conceptualized the causes and treatments of epidemics and provided classic descriptions of gout, smallpox, malaria, scarlet fever, hysteria, and chorea. He advocated observation instead of theorizing to determine the nature of disease and introduced the use of cinchona bark (containing quinine) to treat malaria and of laudanum to treat other diseases.

Sydenham's chorea: see under CHOREA.

Sydney, Sir Philip: see SIDNEY, SIR PHILIP.

Sydney, city (1991 urban agglomeration pop. 3,698,500), capital of New South Wales, SE Australia, surrounding Port Jackson inlet, on the Pacific Ocean. It is Australia's largest city, chief port, and main cultural and industrial center. Manufactures include ships, refined oil, chemicals, textiles, and automobiles. Sydney Harbour and Port Botany are the main ports. Founded as a penal colony in 1788, Sydney is Australia's oldest settlement. Its population surged during the Australian gold rushes of the 1850s. Sydney replaced MELBOURNE as the nation's largest population center after World War II. Landmarks include the Sydney Harbour Bridge (1932); the Gladesville Bridge (1964); the modernistic Sydney Opera House complex (1973); and the Centrepoint Tower (1981), Australia's tallest building. The city has several universities and museums, including the National Gallery of Art and the Australia Museum. In 1994 portions of suburban Sydney were devastated by wildfires. Sydney will be the site of the 2000 summer Olympic games.

Sylla, Lucius Cornelius: see SULLA, LUCIUS CORNELIUS.

syllogism, in logic, a mode of argument that forms the core of the body of Western logical thought, consisting of a sequence of three propositions such that the first two imply the conclusion. ARISTOTLE's formulations of syllogistic logic held sway in the Western world for over 2,000 years. The categorical syllogism comprises three categorical propositions, statements of the form *all A are B, no A are B, some A are B,* or *some A are not B.* A categorical syllogism contains precisely three terms: the major term, which is the predicate of the conclusion; the minor term, which is the subject of the conclusion; and the middle term, which appears in both premises but not in the conclusion.

Sylvester II, d. 1003, pope (999–1003), a Frenchman named Gerbert. Widely celebrated for his learning, he taught the Holy Roman Emperor OTTO III, who aided his election to the papacy. Sylvester energetically supported the Christianization of Poland and Hungary. He was the first French pope.

Sylvester, James Joseph, 1814–97, English mathematician. He taught in England and the U.S., and founded the *American Journal of Mathematics.* He is known for his work on algebraic invariants, matrices, determinants, and number theory, much of it in collaboration with Arthur CAYLEY.

symbiosis, habitual cohabitation of organisms of different species. The term usually applies to a dependent relationship that is beneficial to both members (also called mutualism). Symbiosis includes parasitism, a relationship in which the PARASITE depends on and may injure its host; COMMENSALISM, an independent and mutually beneficial relationship; and helotism, a master-slave relationship found among social animals. Symbiosis may occur between two kinds of plants (e.g., LICHEN-forming alga and fungus), two kinds of animals (e.g., herbivores and cellulose-digesting gut microorganisms), or a plant and an animal (e.g., FIG and fig wasp).

symbolic logic: see LOGIC.

symbolists, in literature, school that originated in late-19th-cent. France in opposition to NATURALISM and REALISM. Symbolism sought to convey impressions by suggestion rather than by direct statement, and it spread from poetry to the other arts. Experiments with FREE VERSE outlived symbolism itself. BAUDELAIRE was the greatest precursor of the movement, which included the poets MALLARMÉ, RIMBAUD, VERLAINE, and, later, CLAUDEL and VALÉRY; MAETERLINCK in drama; and DEBUSSY in music. Symbolism influenced the DECADENTS and IMAGISTS, as well as major 20th-cent. British and American poets like T.S. ELIOT and Wallace STEVENS.

Symonds, John Addington, 1840–93, English writer. His major work is *The Renaissance in Italy* (7 vol., 1875–86). Other writings include *Studies of Greek Poets* (1873–76), literary biographies, translations, and books of verse.

Symons, Arthur, 1865–1945, English poet and critic. A leading English SYMBOLIST, he interpreted the poetry of the French DECADENTS to the British through criticism, translations, and his own poems. *The Symbolist Movement in Literature* (1899) is his chief critical work.

symphonic poem, type of one-movement orchestral composition created by Franz LISZT; also called **tone poem.** Based on an idea or theme from a poetic, dramatic, or other nonmusical artistic source, it often "tells a story," as in Liszt's *Les Préludes;* Richard

STRAUSS's *Don Juan;* or RESPIGHI's *Pines of Rome;* or may simply be the impressionistic portrayal of the theme, as in DEBUSSY's *Afternoon of a Faun.*

symphony, a major work for orchestra with one or more movements in sonata form (see under SONATA). The Italian operatic overture, called sinfonia, was standardized by Alessandro SCARLATTI at the end of the 17th cent. into three sections (fast, slow, fast). In the 18th cent. HAYDN and MOZART synthesized all preceding techniques into the Viennese classical symphony, consisting of four movements (fast; slow; a dance, e.g., minuet; fast finale, e.g., rondo). BEETHOVEN expanded the dimensions of this form, intensifying the element of personal expression and introducing the use of a CHORUS in the symphony. The classical ideal continued in the symphonies of SCHUBERT, MENDELSSOHN, and SCHUMANN, but classical elements were sometimes overshadowed by romantic traits. Reacting against the romantic orchestral style, BRAHMS revived the classical model as defined by Beethoven. BRUCKNER combined classical form with Wagnerian harmonies and melodic structure (see WAGNER, RICHARD). Other important composers were DVOŘÁK and TCHAIKOVSKY, in the 19th cent., and MAHLER and SIBELIUS in the 20th cent. Contemporary composers such as STRAVINSKY and HINDEMITH have treated the symphony form with much freedom.

synagogue [from Gr., = assembly], place of assembly for Jewish worship. The institution probably dates from the Babylonian exile (6th cent. B.C.). By the 1st cent. A.D. it had become the center of Jewish religious, intellectual, and communal life. The destruction of the Temple in A.D. 70 and the dispersion of the Jews increased the synagogue's importance. In modern times in the West, its central role has shifted to purely religious activities, although recently that trend has been somewhat reversed. In the U.S., the Orthodox, Conservative, and Reform synagogue associations are organized in the Synagogue Council of America. See also JUDAISM.

synchrocyclotron: see PARTICLE ACCELERATOR.

synchrotron: see PARTICLE ACCELERATOR.

syncline: see FOLD.

syndicalism, economic and political doctrine that advocates control of the means of production by organized bodies of workers. Syndicalists view any form of state as an instrument of oppression and believe that the trade union should be the basic organization unit of society. They advocate direct action such as the general STRIKE and industrial sabotage. Syndicalism, especially strong in France, declined after World War I because of competition from Communist unions, government suppression, and political splits. In the U.S. it was represented chiefly by the INDUSTRIAL WORKERS OF THE WORLD.

Synge, John Millington [sĭng], 1871–1909, Irish poet and dramatist. Intense and poetic, his plays depict the harshness of rural Irish life. His one-act play *Riders to the Sea* (1904) is considered one of the finest tragedies ever written. In 1904 Synge, with W.B. YEATS and Lady GREGORY, helped found the Abbey Theatre, which presented his comedies *The Well of the Saints* (1905) and *The Playboy of the Western World* (1907).

synodic period, length of time it takes a solar-system body to return to an identical alignment (e.g., conjunction or opposition; see SYZYGY) with another body as seen from the earth. Because the earth moves in its orbit around the sun, the synodic period differs from the **sidereal period,** the length of time a body takes to complete a orbit relative to a background star.

Synoptic Gospels: see GOSPEL.

synthesizer: see ELECTRONIC MUSIC.

synthetic textile fibers, artificial FIBERS produced industrially by either synthesizing POLYMERS or altering natural fibers (see RAYON). Polyesters, e.g., Dacron, produced by the polymerization of the product of an alcohol and organic-acid reaction, are strong and wrinkle-resistant; microfiber, which was introduced in 1986, is a variety of polyester that has extremely thin filaments. Nylon, a synthetic thermoplastic material introduced in 1938, is strong, elastic, resistant to abrasion and chemicals, and low in moisture absorbency. Orlon, the trade name for a polyacrylonitrile fiber made from natural gas, oxygen, and nitrogen, combines bulk, light weight, and resistance to acids and sun. Vinyl fibers, e.g., Saran, are also widely used. See also FIBERGLASS.

syphilis, SEXUALLY TRANSMITTED DISEASE caused by the spirochete *Treponema pallidum.* Some medical historians believe that syphilis was first recorded among sailors who had returned to Spain from the New World in 1493, but others have concluded that syphilis was already present in the Old World. It is most commonly transmitted by sexual contact, although transmission can occur through infected blood or an open wound, or from mother to fetus. Primary syphilis is characterized by a chancre, a superficial skin ULCER, at the site of infection; secondary, by generalized eruption of the skin and mucous membranes and inflammation of eyes, bones, and central nervous system; tertiary, by chronic skin lesions, damage to the heart and aorta, and central nervous system degeneration sometimes leading to blindness and insanity. Syphilis is treated with PENICILLIN, usually successfully unless extensive nervous system damage has occurred. New resistant strains have complicated treatment.

Syracuse, city (1990 pop. 124,606), SE Sicily, Italy, on the Ionian Sea. It is a port and market and tourist center. Founded (734 B.C.) by Corinthian Greeks, it became the leading city of ancient Sicily under the tyrant Gelon, who defeated CARTHAGE in 480 B.C. It was a center of Greek culture (AESCHYLUS, PINDAR, THEOCRITUS, and ARCHIMEDES lived there) under several tyrants, e.g., Hiero I and II, DIONYSUS THE ELDER, DIONYSUS THE YOUNGER, and DION OF SYRACUSE, whose reigns alternated with periods of democracy. Syracuse defeated Athens (414 B.C.), reached its height, then fell to Rome (212 B.C.) and declined. It was later conquered by Arabs (9th cent.) and Normans (1085). Numerous ruins testify to its past greatness.

Syracuse, city (1990 pop. 163,860), seat of Onondaga co., central N.Y., a port on Onondaga Lake and the Barge Canal; settled c.1788, inc. as a city 1848. Its many manufactures include air conditioners, electrical and electronic equipment, and automotive parts. Settled where salt springs had been discovered in 1654, Syracuse was a salt-making center until after the Civil War. When that industry declined, the city's favorable position on the ERIE CANAL fostered its industrial growth. It is an educational and cultural center with several colleges and museums.

Syr Darya, one of the principal rivers of arid central Asia, c.1,380 mi (2,220 km) long, used extensively for irrigation. It is formed in the FERGANA VALLEY, E Uzbekistan, by the confluence of the Naryn and Kara Darya rivers (which rise in the snowy Tian Shan) and flows west through N Tajikistan, then northwest through E Uzbekistan and S Kazakhstan along the edge of the KYZYL KUM desert to the northern end of the ARAL SEA.

Syria, officially Syrian Arab Republic, republic (1992 est. pop. 13,730,000), 71,467 sq mi (185,100 sq km), SW Asia, bordered by Israel, Lebanon, and the Mediterranean Sea (W), Turkey (N), Iraq (E), and Jordan (S). Principal cities include DAMASCUS (the capital) and ALEPPO. Most of Syria is occupied by the Syrian Desert, which is crossed by the EUPHRATES R. In the west are the Anti-Lebanon

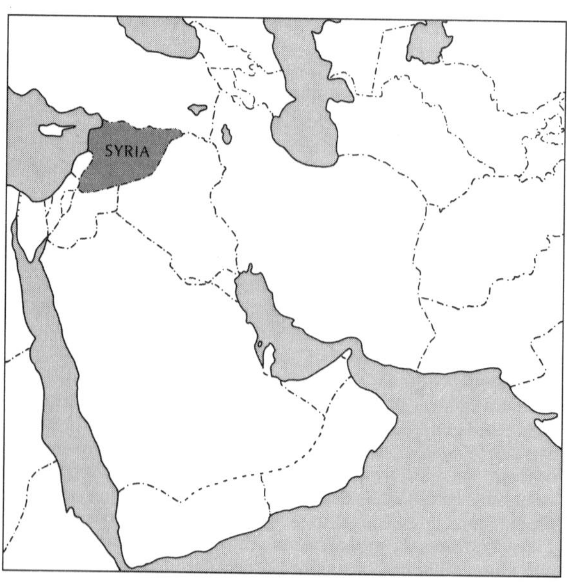

Mts., including Mt. Hermon (9,232 ft/2,814 m), Syria's highest point; in the southwest the fertile plain of Hawran extends from the Jabal al-Duruz Mts. to the Sea of Galilee. Major crops include wheat, vegetables, sugar beets, barley, cotton, and tobacco. The state plays a major role in the economy, and a large-scale industrialization program begun after World War II has diversified the formerly agricultural economy. Petroleum production, small compared to that of other Middle Eastern countries, provides the leading export. Refined petroleum, cement, textiles, processed foods, chemicals, and precision-engineered products are the chief manufactures. The Euphrates Dam supplies most of the nation's electric power. Most Syrians are Arabic-speaking Muslims, mainly Sunnite with significant Alawite and Druse minorities; there are also Kurds, Armenians, and Circassians. About 10% of the people are Christian, mainly Orthodox. Arabic is the official language.

History. Situated on trade and military routes between the Mediterranean and Mesopotamia, Syria (which historically included all of modern Syria and Lebanon, and parts of Israel, Jordan, Iraq, and Saudi Arabia) has always been an object of foreign conquest. Settled (c.2100 B.C.) by the Amorites, a Semitic people from the Arabian peninsula, it fell to the HITTITES (15th–13th cent B.C.), the Assyrians and Babylonians (11th–6th cent. B.C.), the Persians (6th–4th cent. B.C.), and the Greeks (333 B.C.). Syria was Hellenized by the Seleucids and had fallen to Rome by 63 B.C. After a period of Byzantine rule (5th–7th cent. A.D.) Syria was conquered (633–40) by Muslim Arabs. Most Syrians converted to Islam, and Damascus, as the usual capital of the Umayyad caliph (661–750), became the center of the Islamic world. The area was later ruled by the Seljuk Turks, the MONGOLS, SALADIN, and the MAMLUKS. Christians also came to Syria on the CRUSADES (11th–14th cent.). It was part of the OTTOMAN EMPIRE from 1516 until the end of WORLD WAR I, and in 1920 France received a League of Nations mandate over the Levant States (roughly modern Syria and Lebanon). During WORLD WAR II Free French forces granted (1944) independence to Syria, but French troops did not leave until 1946. Syria joined with Egypt in the United Arab Republic in 1958, but withdrew in 1961. Independent Syria has been characterized by economic growth, political instability, and uncompromising hostility toward Israel (see ARAB-ISRAELI WARS). In 1981 Israel exacerbated the situation by annexing the GOLAN HEIGHTS, captured from Syria in the Six-Day War (1967). Syrian troops entered Lebanon in 1976, ostensibly to quell civil strife. During the 1982 Israeli invasion of Lebanon they suffered severe losses in combat with Israeli forces. The ruling Ba'ath party, which came to power in a 1963 coup, maintains a policy of socialism and Arab nationalism. In the 1980s Syria experienced internal unrest, moved closer to the USSR, espoused hard-line Arab positions, and was linked to international terrorists. By 1990, however, Syria was trying to improve relations with Western nations. Syria participated in initial peace talks with Israel in 1991.

Syriac [sēr′ēăk″], late dialect of ARAMAIC, which is a Hamito-Semitic language. See LANGUAGE (table).

syzygy, alignment of three celestial bodies along a straight or nearly straight line. Viewed from one of these bodies, the other two will be either in conjunction (aligned in the same direction) or in opposition (aligned on opposite sides of the sky). An inferior planet, whose orbit lies inside the earth's, can, in reference to the sun as seen from the earth, be either in inferior conjunction (lying directly between the earth and the sun) or in superior conjunction (on the opposite side of the sun from the earth); unlike a superior planet, whose orbit lies outside the earth's, and unlike the moon, an inferior planet can never be in opposition to the sun as seen from the earth. See also ELONGATION.

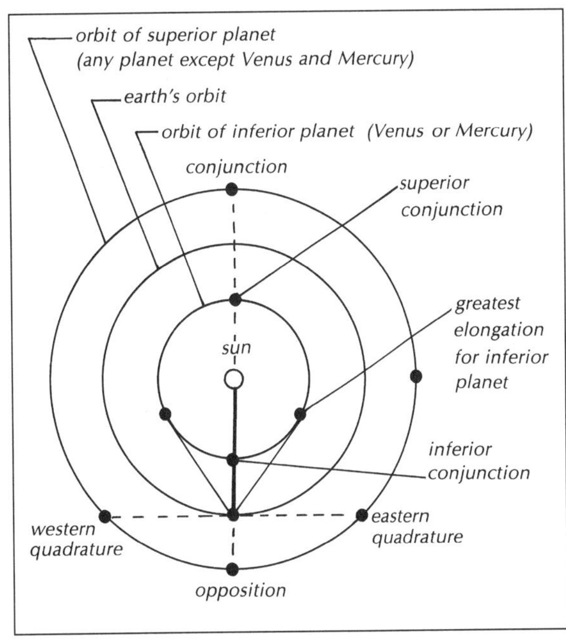

Syzygy: Alignments of celestial bodies necessary to produce syzygy (opposition, inferior conjunction, and superior conjunction) and quadrature conditions

Szatmar, Peace of: see RÁKÓCZY, FRANCIS II.

Szczecin [shchĕ′tsĕn], Ger. *Stettin,* city (1989 est. pop. 409,000), NW Poland, on the Oder R., former capital of the Prussian province of POMERANIA. It is a major Baltic port and an industrial center with shipyards, ironworks, and chemical plants. A member of the HANSEATIC LEAGUE from the 13th cent., the city was ruled (1648–1720) by Sweden and then passed to Prussia. In 1945 it was transferred from Germany to Poland, and its German population was expelled and replaced by Poles.

Szent-Gyorgyi, Albert von [sĕnt″-dyördyĭ], 1893–1986, American biochemist; b. Hungary; came to U.S., 1947. For his studies of biological oxidations and his discovery of ascorbic acid in adrenal glands, he received the 1937 Nobel Prize in physiology or medicine. He studied muscle chemistry, discovered the protein actin in muscle, and was the first to isolate vitamin C. He directed (1947–75) research at the Inst. of Muscle Research, Woods Hole, Mass.

Szilard, Leo [sĭ′lärd], 1898–1964, American nuclear physicist and biophysicist; b. Hungary. Working with Enrico FERMI at the Univ. of Chicago, he developed the first self-sustained nuclear reactor based on uranium fission. One of the first to realize that nuclear chain reactions could be used in bombs, and instrumental in urging the U.S. government to create the first atomic bomb, he later actively opposed nuclear warfare.

T

Ta, chemical symbol of the element TANTALUM.

table tennis, ball and racket game, basically a miniature form of TENNIS. It is also called Ping-Pong, a trade name. The game is played on a table that measures 9 ft by 5 ft (2.74 m by 1.52 m). A transverse net 6 in. (15.24 cm.) high divides the surface. Players use a round-bladed paddle to hit the small celluloid ball. A point is scored when a service goes foul or a player fails to return a ball properly. The game originated in the late 19th cent. and first became popular in England. It is a major competitive sport in E Asia.

taboo or **tabu,** prohibition of an act or the use of an object or word under pain of severe punishment. A Polynesian word, *taboo* can apply to something sacred or to the dangerous or unclean. The object of a taboo in Polynesia is believed to have a power, or *mana,* so strong that it may be approached only by priests; breaking the taboo may require the ritual purification, or even death, of the offender to cleanse the community. Taboos are often declared at life changes, such as birth, death, and marriage, and are commonly recorded on a clan's TOTEM.

Tabriz [täbrēz'], city (1986 pop. 971,482), NW Iran, on the Aji Chai (Talkheh) R. It is a summer resort and a commercial, industrial, and transportation center. Tabriz, then known as Tauris, was (3d cent. A.D.) the capital of Armenia under King Tiridates III. It was sacked (c.1029) by the Oghuz Turks and captured (1054) by the Seljuk Turks. The city prospered under the Mongols (13th–14th cent.), and in 1514 it was taken by the Ottoman Turks. Owing to frequent earthquakes, Tabriz has only a few historic sites, e.g., the Blue Mosque (15th cent.).

tabu: see TABOO.

Taché, Sir Étienne Paschal [täshā'], 1795–1865, Canadian statesman. He served (1848–57) in several national administrations and as joint premier (1856–57, 1864) with J.A. MACDONALD. In 1864 he presided over the Quebec conference that helped to prepare for Canada's confederation.

Tacitus (Cornelius Tacitus), A.D. c.55–A.D. c.117, Roman historian. His high moral tone and severe criticism of contemporary Rome, fallen from the virtuous vigor of the old republic, underlies his three major works: the *Germania* (an account of the German tribes); the *Histories* (of which four books and a fragment, covering Galba's reign, A.D. 68–69, and the beginning of VESPASIAN's, survive); and the *Annals* (of which 12 books, covering the reign of TIBERIUS and parts of the reigns of CLAUDIUS and NERO, survive).

Tacoma, city (1990 pop. 176,664), seat of Pierce co., W Wash., on Commencement Bay and the Puget Sound at the mouth of the Puyallup R.; inc. 1884. It is a major seaport and a rail terminus, and one of the Northwest's leading industrial cities. Wood products, boats, and chemicals are important manufactures. Beautifully situated between bay and mountains, with Mt. Rainier in sight, Tacoma has a mild climate and draws many tourists.

tadpole, larval, aquatic stage of AMPHIBIANS, also called polliwog. Hatching from the egg, the tadpole is gill-breathing and legless and propels itself by means of a tail. During METAMORPHOSIS it develops lungs, legs, and other adult organs and, in the FROG and TOAD, loses the tail.

Tadzhikistan: see TAJIKISTAN.

Taegu [tī'gōō'], city (1985 pop. 2,029,853), S South Korea. A railroad junction and marketplace for an extensive agricultural and mining region, Taegu also has important textile and machine industries. It was a major bastion for UN forces during the KOREAN WAR and served as the temporary capital of South Korea.

Taft, William Howard, 1857–1930, 27th president of the U.S. (1909–13) and 10th chief justice of the U.S. Supreme Court (1921–30); b. Cincinnati. He was secretary of war (1904–8) and a close adviser to Pres. Theodore ROOSEVELT. Running as Roosevelt's successor in 1908, he defeated William Jennings BRYAN. He continued Roosevelt's policies, i.e., "trust busting" and, in Latin America, "dollar diplomacy," but he was more conservative than Roosevelt and antagonized the progressive elements in his party. His relations with Roosevelt deteriorated, and in 1912 he found himself running for reelection against his former mentor, who had formed the PROGRESSIVE PARTY (Bull Moose party). The Republican vote was split, and the Democratic candidate, Woodrow WILSON, won. Taft was appointed (1921) chief justice by Pres. HARDING; his chief contribution to the court was his administrative efficiency. His son, **Robert Alphonso Taft,** 1889–1953, was a U.S. senator from Ohio (1938–53) and the leader of conservative Republicans. An opponent of Pres. F.D. ROOSEVELT's New Deal, he was a leading advocate of isolationism before World War II. He helped write the Taft-Hartley Labor Act (1947). He strongly opposed postwar Democratic policies, voting against ratification of NATO and condemning the Korean and China policies of the Truman administration. Known as "Mr. Republican," he was a three-time candidate (1940, 1948, 1952) for the Republican presidential nomination. He served briefly (1953) as Senate majority leader until his death.

Taft-Hartley Labor Act: see LABOR LAW.

Tagalog language: see MALAYO-POLYNESIAN LANGUAGES.

Taglioni, Maria, 1804–84, Italian ballerina; b. Stockholm. She was a great success in *La Sylphide* (1832) at the Paris Opéra. She was known for her ethereal style and high elevations, and is considered a major ballerina of the romantic period.

Tagore, Sir Rabindranath, 1861–1941, Indian writer and philosopher. Born to a wealthy Bengali family, he studied law in England. He drew on classical Indian literature for his approximately 50 dramas, 100 books of verse (much of which he set to music), 40 novels and books of short fiction, essays, and such philosophical works as *Sadhana: The Realization of Life* (1913). For the poems in *Gitanjali* (1912) and for other writings he won the 1913 Nobel Prize in literature. In 1915 he was knighted. His school, Santiniketan [abode of peace], founded at Bolpur in 1901, grew into Visva-Bharat Univ., stressing social reform and world unity.

Tahiti, island (1988 pop. 115,820), 402 sq mi (1,041 sq km), S Pacific, in the Society Islands, FRENCH POLYNESIA. The capital is Papeete. It relies on tourism and produces vanilla, fruits, and copra. Settled by Polynesians (14th cent.), it was visited in the 18th cent. by Capt. James COOK and Lt. William BLIGH. It became French in 1843. GAUGUIN painted his best-known works there.

Tahoe, Lake, scenic resort lake, between NE California and W Nevada, in the E Sierra Nevada. It lies 6,228 ft (1,898 m) above sea level, has an area of 193 sq mi (500 sq km), is up to 1,645 ft (501 m) deep, and feeds into the Truckee R.

taiga, northern coniferous-forest belt of Eurasia, bordered on the north by the treeless TUNDRA and on the south by the STEPPE, comprising about one third of the world's forestland. The climate is characterized by long, severe winters and short summers. The principal species of trees are cedar, pine, spruce, larch, birch, and aspen.

Taine, Hippolyte Adolphe [tĕn], 1828–93, French critic and historian. His deterministic theories, viewing the individual as the product of heredity and environment, became the theoretical basis of NATURALISM. His sociohistorical method of analysis influenced philosophy, aesthetics, literary criticism, and the social sciences. Works include *On Intelligence* (1870) and *The Origins of Contemporary France* (1876–93).

Taipei, city (1988 est. pop. 2,637,000), N Taiwan, capital of Taiwan and provisional capital of the Republic of China. Taiwan's largest city, it is the political, cultural, and industrial center of the island. Important manufactures include electronic and electrical goods, textiles, metals, and chemicals. Developed under Japanese rule

(1895–1945), Taipei became the headquarters of CHIANG KAI-SHEK's Nationalists when they fled the mainland of China in 1949.

Taiping Rebellion, 1850–64, revolt against the Ch'ing dynasty of China. It was led by Hung Hsiu-ch'üan, a visionary who evolved a political creed including derived elements of Protestantism. His object was to found a new dynasty, the Taiping [great peace]. In 1853 the rebels captured Nanjing and made it their capital. They were finally defeated by new provincial armies and aid from the Western powers. An army led by C.G. GORDON successfully defended Shanghai.

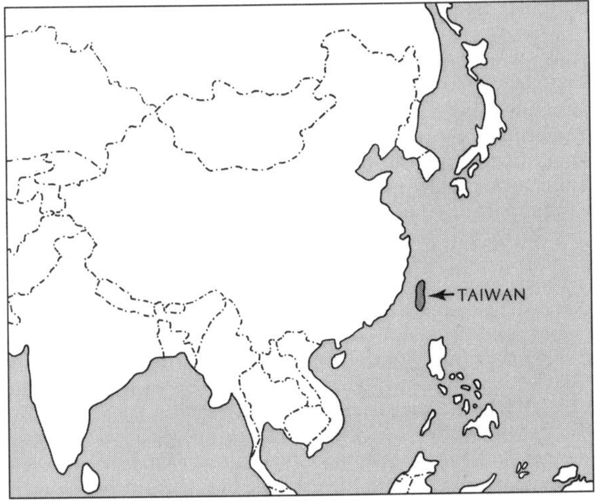

Taiwan, Portuguese *Formosa,* officially Republic of China, island (1992 est. pop. 20,879,000), 13,885 sq mi (35,961 sq km), in the Pacific Ocean, separated from the mainland of S China by the 100-mi-wide (161-km) Taiwan Strait. Together with the PESCADORES and MATSU AND QUEMOY, it is the seat of the Republic of China government, which claims the right to rule all China. The capital is TAIPEI. Other major cities include KAOHSIUNG, Tainan, Taichong, and Chilung. About one quarter of Taiwan's land area is cultivated; rice, wheat, sugarcane, and sweet potatoes are the most important crops. In the 1970s industry replaced agriculture as the major export earner. Light industry is the major manufacturing sector, with electronics predominating. Other manufactures include electrical equipment, chemicals, motor vehicles, and machinery, and service industries are increasingly important. The main natural resources are woods and other forest products. The majority of Taiwanese are ethnic (Han) Chinese who began to emigrate to Taiwan in the 15th cent.; they speak the Mandarin, Fujianese (Amoy), and Hakka dialects. There is also a small number of Kiaoshan (Malayan) aborigines. Religions include Confucianism, Taoism, Buddhism, and Christianity.

History. First settled by the Chinese in the 7th cent., the island was reached by the Portuguese in 1590. It was held by the Dutch in the 1640s, and by China's Ch'ing dynasty from 1683. Occupied by Japan after the First Sino-Japanese War (1894–95), Taiwan remained in Japanese hands until 1945. When CHIANG KAI-SHEK and the Nationalists, or Kuomintang, were ousted (1949) from mainland CHINA by the Communists, they shifted the seat of their government to Taiwan. The U.S. long supported and aided the Nationalists, but in the 1970s Taiwan's international political position had eroded. In 1971 it lost China's seat in the UN to the People's Republic of China, and in 1979 the U.S. broke diplomatic relations with the Nationalists to establish relations with the People's Republic of China, although retaining substantial economic and cultural ties. Martial law, in effect since 1949, was lifted in 1987, and many jailed political dissidents were freed. Pres. Chiang Ching-kuo died in 1988 and was succeeded by LEE TENG-HUI, a Taiwan native. In 1991 Lee ended emergency rule, which had permitted the domination of the National Assembly by aging mainland delegates elected in 1947. In elections in 1992 the Kuomintang retained control of the assembly, but the major opposition party won nearly a third of the seats.

Taiyuan [tī-yüän], city (1990 est. pop. 1,960,000), capital of Shanxi prov., N China, in one of the world's richest coal and iron areas. It is a hub of coal mining and steel production, with machine, chemical, and other industries.

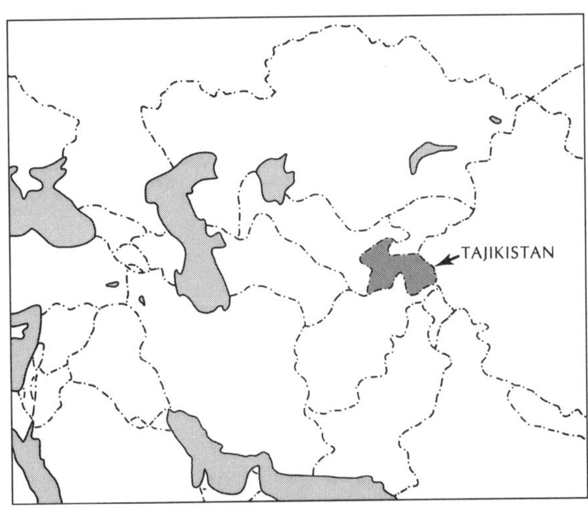

Tajikistan or **Tadzhikistan,** officially Republic of Tajikstan, republic (1992 est. pop. 5,680,000), 55,251 sq mi (143,100 sq km), central Asia, formerly a constituent republic of the USSR. It borders China (E); Afghanistan (S); Kyrgyzstan (N); and Uzbekistan (W, NW). The capital is DUSHANBE; other important cities are Khujand, Yavan, and Qŭrghonteppa (Kurgan-Tyube). The largely mountainous nation has what was the USSR's highest mountain, Communism Peak, formerly Garmo Peak (24,590 ft/7,495 m). The economy is largely agricultural, producing cotton, wheat, barley, fruit, mulberry trees (for silk), and livestock; irrigation is essential for most farming. Mineral resources include coal, antimony, gold, and salt. Manufactures are largely agriculture-related and include textiles, carpets, and leather products, canned goods, and metalworking. The majority of the population are Tajiks, a Sunni Muslim people; Uzbeks and Russians are the largest minorities. The official language is Tajik, which is closely related to Persian (Farsi).

History. Probably descended from the inhabitants of ancient Sogdiana, a Persian province between the Amu Darya and Syr Darya, the Tajiks were successful in farming, crafts, and trade by the 9th cent. Between the 13th and 19th cent. they were ruled by the Mongols, Uzbeks, and Russians. In the aftermath of the Russian Revolution (1917), the Tajiks rebelled and were not subdued by the Bolsheviks until 1921. The territory became an autonomous republic in Soviet Uzbekistan in 1924; in 1929 it became the Tadzhik SSR, a constituent republic of the USSR. Tajikistan declared (1991) its independence following the failed coup against Soviet Pres. Gorbachev. When the Tajik president sought to suspend the Communist party, the Communist majority in the parliament replaced him, which led pro-Islamic and pro-democratic opposition groups and their eastern Tajikistan allies to try to bring down the new president, former party boss Rakhman Nabiyev. In 1992 Nabiyev was ousted by opposition militias, and an ethnically based civil war erupted. Forces allied with the former Nabiyev government retook the capital, and the parliament elected Emomali Rakhmonov president. Fighting between government troops, supported by the Russian army, and pro-Islamic forces persisted along the Afghanistan border. Tajikistan is a member of the COMMONWEALTH OF INDEPENDENT STATES.

Taj Mahal, mausoleum, Agra, N India, the finest example of late Indian Muslim architecture. The Mogul emperor Shah Jahan ordered it after the death (1629) of his wife, Mumtaz Mahal. Designed by a Turkish architect, it was built (1630–48) in a walled garden with an oblong reflecting pool. The white marble exterior is inlaid with semiprecious stones, floral designs, and arabesques. The dome, 80 ft (24.4 m) high and 50 ft (15.2 m) in diameter inside, forms a bulb outside, tapering to a spire topped by a crescent. The octagonal tomb chamber is lit by light passing through intricately carved screens.

Takeshita Noboru, 1924–, Japanese politician. He won 11 terms in parliament; was chief cabinet secretary (1971–72, 1974), construction minister (1976), and finance minister (1979–80; 1982–86); and was chosen (1987) to head the ruling Liberal Democratic party (LDP). He became prime minister and led Japan's emergence as a champion of the developing nations of Asia. He resigned in 1989. The head of the largest faction in the LDP, Takeshita remains a powerful force in Japanese politics.

Talbot, William Henry Fox, 1800–77, English inventor of photographic processes. From 1841 on he patented methods of making negatives and prints. His book *The Pencil of Nature* (1844) is illustrated with photographs.

talc, hydrous magnesium silicate mineral [$Mg_3Si_4O_{10}(OH)_2$], translucent to opaque, occurring in a range of colors and having a greasy, soapy feel. It is found in thin layers and in granular and fine-grained masses. SOAPSTONE is a granular form of talc. Important sources include Austria, Canada, India, and the U.S. Talc is used in making paper (as a filler), paints, powders, soap, lubricants, linoleum, electrical insulation, and pottery.

tallage, under FEUDALISM, a tax much like AIDS. In Norman England it partly replaced the DANEGELD. Kings and lords levied it on the towns within their demesne lands, but it was resisted and disappeared (c.1340) under Edward III. In France the upper classes were exempt from tallage, called the *taille,* and the burden of it fell mainly on peasants.

Tallahassee, city (1990 pop. 124,773), state capital and seat of Leon co., NW Fla.; inc. 1825. State government and state universities are the major employers; wood products and processed food are produced. Tallahassee, in a hilly, picturesque area, was an Apalachee settlement when DE SOTO arrived in 1539. Capital of the Florida Territory from 1824, it resisted Union attacks in the CIVIL WAR. The city is noted for its old homes and antebellum charm.

Talleyrand or **Talleyrand-Périgord, Charles Maurice de** [tăl-'ērănd"], 1754–1838, French statesman and diplomat. Despite his notorious impiety, he was made (1789) bishop of Autun and represented the clergy at the STATES-GENERAL of 1789. He supported the FRENCH REVOLUTION at first, but after the fall of the monarchy fled to England (1792) and then to the U.S. (1794). Returning to France (1796), he was foreign minister under the DIRECTORY (1797–99) and NAPOLEON I (1799–1807); however, Napoleon tended to ignore Talleyrand's cautious advice. After Napoleon's defeat Talleyrand persuaded the allies to restore (1814) the Bourbon monarchy and represented France at the Congress of VIENNA (1815), where he scored his greatest diplomatic triumphs. He later served LOUIS PHILIPPE as ambassador to London. Often labeled an opportunist, Talleyrand consistently aimed at peace and stability for Europe as a whole.

Tallinn, city (1989 pop. 482,000), capital of ESTONIA, north central Europe, on the Gulf of Finland opposite HELSINKI. It is a major Baltic port with a picturesque Old Town and a center of such industries as shipbuilding and metallurgy. Known to geographers by 1154, Tallinn was destroyed in 1219 by the Danes, who built a fortress on the site. A member of the HANSEATIC LEAGUE from 1285, it passed (1346–1710) to the Livonian Knights, Sweden, and Russia. It became the capital of independent Estonia in 1919 and was the capital of the Estonian SSR while the country was forcibly annexed by the USSR (1940–91).

Tallis or **Tallys, Thomas,** c.1510–1585, English composer. Best known for his hymn tunes, services, and anthems, he also wrote MOTETS, MADRIGALS, and instrumental music.

Talmud [Aramaic from Heb., = learning], compilation of Jewish Oral Law, with rabbinical commentaries, as distinguished from the Scriptures, or Written Law. Its two divisions are the MISHNA (in Hebrew), the text of the Oral Law, and the Gemara (in Aramaic), a commentary on the Mishna, which it supplements. The Gemara developed out of the interpretations of the Mishna by the Amoraim (Jewish scholars of A.D. c.200–c.500), whose hairsplitting arguments made the work a treasury of information and comment. The legal sections of the Talmud are known as the HALAKAH; the poetical digressions—legends and anecdotes—constitute the Aggada. Both the Palestinian and Babylonian schools produced Talmuds: the Talmud Yerushalmi (Jerusalem Talmud, compiled c.5th cent.) and the Talmud Babli (Babylonian Talmud, c.6th cent.); the latter became the authoritative work. A vast literature of commentaries on the Gemara, including those of Rashi, interpreted the older rulings in the light of the new experience of life in Christian Europe in the Middle Ages. A similar process has helped to keep the tradition alive in modern times. See also JUDAISM.

Tamar: see AMNON.

tamarack: see LARCH.

Tamayo, Rufino [tämä'yō], 1899–1991, one of Mexico's leading modern painters. Influenced by CUBISM, FAUVISM, and Mexican folklore, Tamayo concentrated on the formal and decorative in painting. A characteristic example is *Women of Tehuantepec* (1939; Albright-Knox Art. Gall., Buffalo).

tambourine: see DRUM.

Tamerlane: see TIMUR.

Tamil [tăm'ĭl], Dravidian language of India. See LANGUAGE (table).

Tammany, popular name for the Democratic political machine in New York City. The Tammany Society, or Columbian Order of New York City, was formed c.1786 and incorporated in 1789. At first mostly social, by the mid-1830s it was a dominant political force, fighting for reforms for the common people but increasingly controlled by the privileged classes. With the added support of newly arrived immigrants willing to exchange votes for badly needed assistance, corrupt Tammany bosses, e.g., William M. TWEED, ruled the city for almost a century. Following the state investigations (1930–31) headed by Samuel Seabury, Tammany suffered a telling defeat in the election of 1932 and did not regain its strength in succeeding elections. It had a brief revival after World War II but passed out of existence as a political machine during the mayoralty of John V. Lindsay (1966–74).

Tampa, city (1990 pop. 280,015; met. area 2,067,959), seat of Hillsborough co., W Fla., a port on Tampa Bay; inc. 1855. A highly industrialized city, it is the center of a metropolitan area that includes Clearwater and St. Petersburg. It is a resort and processing and shipping hub for the area's products, particularly phosphates. It has a shrimp fleet, breweries, and a famous cigar industry, centered in its colorful Ybor City section. Nearby Busch Gardens, a theme park with an African zoo and tropical gardens, is a well-known tourist attraction. The Spanish explored the area in 1528, but European settlement began only in 1823. Tampa was an important military base in the SPANISH-AMERICAN WAR.

Tampico, city (1980 pop. 271,636), E Mexico, on the Pánuco R. a few miles inland from the Gulf of Mexico. It is a major port and industrial center that has burgeoned in the 20th cent. since the discovery of oil. It has fisheries, refineries, shipyards, and varied manufactures. Once a Huastec site, it was settled by the Spaniards after 1530.

Tanaka Kakuei, 1918–93, Japanese prime minister (1972–74). A Liberal Democratic party (LDP) member, he normalized (1972) diplomatic ties with the People's Republic of China. Tanaka was forced to resign (1974) because of alleged financial malfeasance. He was later tried for accepting over $2 million in bribes from Lockheed Corp. and was convicted in 1983. He remained a powerful figure in Japanese politics until 1987, when TAKESHITA NOBORU won control of the LDP faction Tanaka had led.

Tananarive: see ANTANANARIVO.

Tancred, 1076–1112, a Crusader from 1096 (see CRUSADES). He took part in the captures of Antioch (1098), Jerusalem (1099), and Haifa (1100), and was regent for his uncle, BOHEMOND I. He took Edessa (1104) and was briefly ruler of Antioch. He refused to yield his conquests to Byzantine Emperor ALEXIUS I.

Taney, Roger Brooke [tô'nē], 1777–1864, 5th chief justice of the U.S. SUPREME COURT (1836–64); b. Calvert co., Md. As U.S. attorney general (1831–33) and secretary of the treasury (1833–34) under Pres. JACKSON, he helped crush the second BANK OF THE UNITED STATES. As chief justice, one of his most notable opinions was in the Charles River Bridge Case (1837), in which he reversed the Court's nationalist trend and curbed the growth of monopolies. Under his guidance, the Court also recognized the doctrine of STATES' RIGHTS. Taney's most notorious decision was in the DRED

SCOTT CASE (1857); his ruling that slaves and their descendants had no rights as citizens and that Congress could not forbid slavery in the territories helped precipitate the CIVIL WAR, tarnished the image of the Court, and, until a recent rehabilitation, destroyed Taney's reputation as a jurist.

T'ang, dynasty: see CHINA.

Tanganyika, Lake, freshwater lake in the GREAT RIFT VALLEY of E Africa, c.420 mi (680 km) long and up to 45 mi (72 km) wide. Considered the second deepest lake in the world, it has a maximum depth of c.4,700 ft/1,400 m.

tangelo: see ORANGE.

tangerine: see ORANGE.

Tangshan, city (1990 est. pop. 1,500,000), NE Hopeh prov., China. A coal-mining center, Tangshan is also a major industrial hub producing iron and steel, machinery, motor vehicles, chemicals, and other products. Virtually destroyed in 1976 by a massive earthquake that killed over 250,000 people, it has since been rebuilt.

Tanguy, Yves [täNgē'], 1900–1955, French surrealist painter. A merchant seaman, he took up painting after seeing a work by CHIRICO. His imaginary dream landscapes are filled with amorphous floating objects and personages (see SURREALISM).

Tanizaki Junichiro, 1886–1965, Japanese writer. Often implicitly critical of adopting Western ways, he is perhaps best known for *Makioka Sisters* (1943–48), an account of a traditional, pre-World War II Osaka family. His other novels include *Some Prefer Nettles* (1928) and *The Key* (1956).

tank, military, armored vehicle that has caterpillar traction and is armed with machine guns, cannon, rockets, or flamethrowers. It was developed by the British and first used (Sept. 1916) in WORLD WAR I. In WORLD WAR II tanks and tank tactics were greatly improved. The German army, using large numbers of tanks, overran Poland in less than a month. In mass tank battles on the plains of Europe and N Africa the tide often swung toward the side with the best tanks. Since World War II the basic features of tanks and tank tactics have remained unchanged, although there have been numerous technological refinements. Tanks are vulnerable to recoilless weapons and various antitank missiles, but they remain indispensable, because of their mobility and versatile weaponry, wherever the terrain is suitable to their operation.

tannin, tannic acid, or **gallotannic acid** (approximate empirical formula: $C_{76}H_{52}O_{46}$), colorless to pale yellow, astringent, organic substance found in a wide variety of plants. Tannin can be extracted with hot water from the bark of oak, hemlock, chestnut, and mangrove; certain sumac leaves; plant gall; coffee; tea; and walnuts. In leather making, animal skin is treated with tannin to make it resist decomposition. Tannin is also used to make inks, as a mordant for DYES, and in medicine as an astringent and for treating burns.

tanning, process by which skins and hides are made into LEATHER. Vegetable tanning (shown in Egyptian tomb paintings dating from 3000 B.C.) uses tannin, is usually employed for heavy leathers, and requires more than a month to complete. Mineral tanning includes alum tanning and chrome tanning, the process most common today, requiring only a few hours. In oil tanning, or chamoising, a method used by Native Americans, the pelt is treated with fats and hung to dry; the leather is usually napped on both sides. A modern tanning process employs artificial agents (syntans).

tantalum (Ta), metallic element, discovered in 1802 by A.G. Ekeberg. A rare, hard, malleable, blue-gray metal, it is extremely ductile and highly corrosion-resistant. Uses include electrolytic capacitors, chemical equipment, wires, abrasives, and dental and surgical instruments. See ELEMENT (table); PERIODIC TABLE.

Tantalus, in Greek mythology, king of Sipylos; son of ZEUS; father of PELOPS. Angered by his abominable behavior, Zeus condemned him to TARTARUS. There he suffered thirst and hunger in the presence of water and fruit he could not reach.

Tantra, in Hinduism and Buddhism, esoteric tradition of ritual and YOGA. It is known for the use of MANTRA (mystical words); mandala (sacred diagrams); worship of Shakti (female deities); and, more so in Hindu Tantra, ritual use of wine, meat, and sexual intercourse, in order to awaken the force called *kundalini* and merge with the Godhead. In Hindu Tantra the practices may be symbolic or material. In Buddhist Tantra those rituals opposing the moral precepts of Buddhism have been dropped, but the complex MEDITATION practices have been retained.

Tanzania, officially United Republic of Tanzania, republic (1992 est. pop. 27,792,000), 364,898 sq mi (945,087 sq km), E Africa, formed in 1964 by the union of Tanganyika and ZANZIBAR, an island in the W Indian Ocean. Mainland Tanzania is bordered by Mozambique, Malawi, and Zambia (S), Zaïre, Burundi, and Rwanda (W), Uganda and Kenya (N), and the Indian Ocean (E). Part of the country's boundaries are formed by three major lakes: MALAWI (Nyasa) in the south, TANGANYIKA in the west, and VICTORIA in the north. Principal cities are DODOMA (the capital) and DAR-ES-SALAAM (the former capital). Tanzania has three geographic zones: a fertile, coastal lowland; a vast interior plateau; and several mountain regions, with the famed Mt. KILIMANJARO (19,340 ft/5,895 m), the highest point in Africa, in the northeast. Serengeti, in the Kilimanjaro region, is one of several national parks and wildlife reserves. The economy is overwhelmingly agricultural, with most of the work force employed in subsistence farming, raising cassava and corn. Sisal, cotton, coffee, cloves, and cashew nuts are the major cash crops and supply the bulk of exports. Major manufactures include processed farm goods, textiles, and consumer items; refined petroleum, aluminum goods, and cement are also produced. Tanzania mines diamonds and other gemstones, gold, and salt; large iron-ore and coal reserves are mostly unexploited. Virtually all the people are members of Bantu speaking ethnic groups, but there are Arab and Indian minorities. About a quarter of the people adhere to traditional beliefs; the rest are about equally divided between Muslim and Christian religions. Swahili and English are the official languages.

History. A fossil found in OLDUVAI GORGE in NE Tanzania has been identified as the remains of a direct ancestor of modern humans, about 1.75 million years old. The area was later the site of Paleolithic cultures. By about A.D. 900 traders from SW Asia and India had settled on the coast, and there were commercial contacts with China. A century later the migration of Bantu-speaking peoples into the interior of Tanzania was well under way. Kilwa Kisiwani (situated on an island) became a major trade center by about 1200, dealing in gold, ivory, and other goods. In 1498 the Portuguese explorer Vasco da GAMA became the first European visitor; he made Kilwa tributary in 1502, and within a few years Portugal controlled most of the coast. Following incursions by the Zimba, a warlike African people, the Portuguese were expelled in 1698. In the 18th cent. Arabs from Oman established commercial control over the region, and in 1841 the Omani capital was moved from Muscat to Zanzibar. At the same time new caravan routes, trafficking in slaves

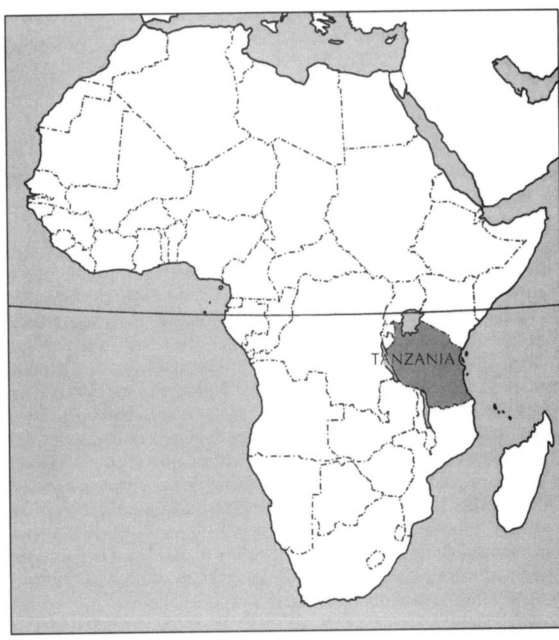

and ivory, were opened into the interior. German influence in Tanganyika grew in the 1880s, and the territory became a German protectorate in 1891. Following occupation by British and South African troops in WORLD WAR I, Tanganyika was made a British mandate. It gained independence in 1961, becoming a republic, with Julius NYERERE as president, in 1962. In 1964 it merged with newly independent Zanzibar to form the United Republic of Tanzania. President of Tanganyika 1962–64 and of Tanzania 1964–85, Nyerere instituted his own brand of "African socialism" called *ujamaa* (pulling together). Peasants were organized into village collectives; factories and plantations were nationalized; state-run corporations were established; egalitarianism was encouraged; major investments were made in primary schools; a one-party state was formed; and tribal conflicts were avoided. The steep rise in oil prices in the 1970s, however, and sharp drops in the value of Tanzania's exports—coffee and sisal hemp—reduced the country to poverty. Nyerere's successor as president, Ali Hassan Mwinyi, began an economic recovery program involving cuts in government spending, decontrol of prices, and encouragement of foreign investment, and modest growth resumed. In 1993 opposition parties were legalized and multiparty elections set for 1995.

Taoism, philosophy and religion of China. The philosophical system derives chiefly from the *Tao-te-ching,* a book traditionally ascribed to LAO-TZE but probably written in the mid-3d cent. B.C. It describes an ideal human condition of freedom from desire and of effortless simplicity, achieved by following the Tao [Chin., = path], the spontaneous, creative, effortless path taken by natural events in the universe. Quietistic in outlook, Taoists condemned as symptoms of excessive government the social virtues expounded by CONFUCIUS. Philosophical Taoism was later expounded in the brilliant satirical writings of Chuang-tze (c.369–c.286 B.C.). Later Taoism stressed the search for effects, such as immortality, supposed to flow from the Tao, and encouraged the study of ALCHEMY. By the 5th cent. A.D. Taoism had adopted many features of Mahayana BUDDHISM and offered a fully developed religious system for those who found the largely ethical system of CONFUCIANISM inadequate. In the 1950s, after the establishment of the Communist regime, Taoism was officially proscribed in China, and since the Cultural Revolution (1966–69) the religion has flourished mainly in Taiwan. Taoist ideas have enjoyed wide circulation in the West in the late 20th cent.

Taos, town (1990 pop. 4,065), seat of Taos co., N N.Mex., between the Rio Grande and the Sangre de Cristo Mts.; founded c.1615, inc. 1934. It developed (principally after 1898) as an art colony frequented by John MARIN, D.H. LAWRENCE, and others. Taos is now the site of studios, galleries, and a school of art. For years an important Spanish and Native American trading post, Taos was the center of the Pueblo Revolt (1680). Kit CARSON's house and grave are in Taos, and the Carson National Forest is nearby.

tape recorder, device for recording and replaying of sound, video, and digital information on plastic or paper tape. In an audio tape recorder, sound is picked up by a MICROPHONE and transformed into an electric current. The current is fed to a TRANSDUCER (in the tape recorder's recording head), which converts the current into corresponding magnetic flux variations that magnetize the fine particles of iron, cobalt, or chromium oxides on the tape as it passes by the head. During playback the tape passes over the playback head (often the same one used for recording) and the tape's magnetic field induces a current in the transducer. The current is then amplified and used to reproduce sound through a LOUDSPEAKER. "Tape hiss," sound composed of high frequencies picked up at random during recording, is suppressed by several systems, among them Dolby, Dolby-B, Dolby-C, and dbx. Digital audio tape (DAT) and digital compact cassette (DCC) recorders transform audio signals into digital pulses, which are then stored on the tape. Both eliminate tape hiss and reproduce sound more accurately than analog recorders. Digital tape recording devices are also used to store programs and data for COMPUTERS. See also VIDEOCASSETTE RECORDER.

tapeworm, name for parasitic flatworms in the class Cestoda, segmented worms sometimes reaching 15–20 ft (4.6–6.1 m) in length. Tapeworms attach themselves to the intestinal wall of the host, which may be VERTEBRATES or ARTHROPODS. Humans become infected with tapeworms from eating infected meat or fish. Infestation may produce no symptoms or may produce abdominal distress and weight loss. Drug treatment destroys the parasite.

tapir, nocturnal, herbivorous MAMMAL (genus *Tapirus*) of the jungles of Central and South America and SE Asia. Related to the HORSE and RHINOCEROS, it is about the size of a donkey and piglike in appearance, with a long, flexible snout and short legs. Tapirs live in forests, browsing on twigs; they swim well and can run fast when in danger. The Central American species (*T. bairdi*) is threatened by the destruction of its rain-forest habitat.

tar and pitch, viscous, dark-brown to black substances, obtained by the destructive DISTILLATION of certain organic materials, e.g., COAL, WOOD, and PETROLEUM. Although the terms *tar* and *pitch* are sometimes used interchangeably, pitch is actually a component of tar that can be isolated by heating. Tar, more or less fluid, is now used to produce BENZENE and various other substances. Tar from pine wood is used to make SOAP and medicinals. Coal tar derivatives are used to make DYES, cosmetics, and synthetic flavoring extracts. Pitch tends to be more solid than tar and is used to make roofing paper, in VARNISHES, as a coal-dust binder in making fuel briquettes, and as a lubricant. ASPHALT is a naturally occurring pitch.

tarantula, name for several species of large, hairy SPIDERS found in the Americas. The tarantula's body may measure 3 in. (7.6 cm) long and, with legs extended, up to 10 in. (25.4 cm) across. The largest may kill small vertebrates, but most feed on ARTHROPODS. Tarantula bites, although painful, are not usually dangerous to humans.

Tarascan, indigenous people of S Mexico (see MIDDLE AMERICA, INDIGENOUS PEOPLES OF), speaking a language with no known relation to other languages. Tarascan settlements date from 500 B.C. They had a well-developed civilization by the time the Spanish arrived and were subjugated by the Spanish only with difficulty. Traditionally known for weaving and hummingbird-feather mosaics, the Tarascans are still noted for their weaving, as well as for music and lacquerware. They are chiefly an agricultural people, with fewer than 100,000 inhabiting villages today in the state of Michoacán. Many Tarascans work as migrant laborers in the U.S.

Tarawa, most populous atoll (1985 pop. 24,598) of KIRIBATI, in the Pacific Ocean near the equator, site of the national capital, Bairiki. Formerly the administrative center of the British Gilbert and Ellice Islands colony, Tarawa was occupied during WORLD WAR II by Japan and fell (1943) to U.S. marines after a bloody battle.

Tarbell, Ida Minerva, 1857–1944, American author; b. Erie co., Pa. A leading MUCKRAKER, she is remembered for her investigations of industry, particularly in her *History of the Standard Oil Company* (1904). She also wrote several biographies.

tariff, tax on imported and, more rarely, exported goods. It is also called a customs duty. Tariffs, unlike other taxes, often have a broadly economic rather than narrowly financial goal, being designed less to increase a nation's revenue than to protect domestic industries from foreign competition. For that reason, protective tariffs, as they are often called, are opposed by advocates of free trade. In ancient times customs duties were assessed for the use of trade and transportation facilities, but by the 17th cent. they came to be levied only at the boundary of a country and usually only on imports. European powers established special low tariff rates for their colonies (see MERCANTILISM and NAVIGATION ACTS). Britain and France, in particular, used preferential tariffs to regulate the flow of raw materials from, and domestic manufactured goods to, their colonies. Other European nations retaliated by raising their tariffs, ushering in a period of high protective tariffs that lasted through the GREAT DEPRESSION. Since World War II the trend has been toward freer trade. Customs unions such as the Common Market (1957; see EUROPEAN UNION) have lowered or even eliminated tariffs among large groups of nations. Finally, the General Agreement on Tariffs and Trade (see UNITED NATIONS, table 3) has, since the 1950s, been responsible for generally lower tariffs around the world.

Tarkenton, Fran(cis Asbury), 1940–, American football player; b. Richmond. One of football's greatest passing quarterbacks, he established lifetime records for most completions (3,686), most yards gained passing (47,003), and most touchdown passes (342) during his career with the Minnesota Vikings (1961–66, 1972–78) and New York Giants (1967–71).

Tarkington, (Newton) Booth, 1869–1946, American author; b. Indianapolis. He is noted for novels of small-town midwestern life, e.g., *The Gentleman from Indiana* (1899), *The Magnificent Ambersons* (1918; Pulitzer), and *Alice Adams* (1921; Pulitzer). He is also known for such amusing novels of youth as *Penrod* (1914) and *Seventeen* (1916). His plays include a dramatization of his historical romance *Monsieur Beaucaire* (1901).

taro: see ARUM.

tarots, playing cards used mainly for fortune-telling, generally believed to have been introduced into Europe by gypsies in the mid-15th cent. In addition to 56 pictorial cards in four suits much like a modern 52-card deck, there are 22 additional pictorial cards, numbered 0 to 21. The pictures on the 78 cards are allegorical, representing forces of nature and the virtues and vices of humanity. Systems of interpretation vary greatly.

Tarquin, legendary Etruscan family ruling in early Rome. **Lucius Tarquinius Priscus** is said to have come to Rome on the advice of his prophetess wife, Tanaquil. There he was made king (616 B.C.). His son, **Lucius Tarqinius Superbus** (Tarquin the Proud), murdered his father-in-law, Servius Tullius, to get the throne. He ruled with despotism and cruelty. His son, **Sixtus Tarquinius,** ravaged Lucrece, the wife of his kinsman, **Tarquinius Collatinus.** The Romans drove Tarquin the Proud from the throne (510 B.C.). Lars Porsena tried to restore the family; failing, he made peace with Rome.

tarragon, perennial aromatic Old World herb (*Artemisia dracunculus*) of the COMPOSITE family. It has long been cultivated for its leaves, used for flavoring vinegar, salads, sauces, soups, and pickles.

Tartarus, in Greek mythology, lowest region of HADES, where the wicked, e.g., SISYPHUS, TANTALUS, were punished.

Tasaday, small band of supposed hunter-gatherers in a Philippine rain forest, allegedly contacted by Westerners for the first time in 1971 and reported to have lived in caves and to have used stone tools. The Philippine government has restricted scientific study, so it has been difficult to verify their status. On the basis of many kinds of evidence, it is widely believed that they are a hoax perpetrated by a former government official.

Tashkent: see TOSHKENT.

Tasman, Abel Janszoon, 1603?–59, Dutch navigator. In 1642 he discovered TASMANIA, which he named Van Diemen's Land, and NEW ZEALAND. He was the first explorer to circumnavigate AUSTRALIA, proving it to be an island continent.

Tasmania, island state (1992 est. pop. 470,000), 26,383 sq mi (68,332 sq km), SE Australia. It is separated from the mainland by Bass Strait and lies 150 mi (240 km) S of the state of Victoria. It is the smallest, wettest, and most mountainous of the Australian states. Hobart is the capital and largest city. Manufactures include metal products, textiles, and wood products. Copper, tin, lead, zinc, and iron ore are mined. Lamb, beef, veal, wool, fruits, and hops are important agricultural products. The Dutch navigator Abel TASMAN discovered the island and named it Van Diemen's Land in 1642. Capt. James COOK visited it in 1777, and in 1803 Great Britain took possession and established a penal colony at Hobart. The indigenous population was wiped out in the 19th cent., but a few thousand mixed-race descendants survive. Tasmania became a separate colony in 1825 and was federated as a Australian state in 1901.

Tasmanian devil, voracious MARSUPIAL (*Sarcophilus harrisi*) of the Dasyure family, now found only on Tasmania. Its body is about 2 ft (60 cm) long with a large head and weak hindquarters. Very strong for its size, it preys on animals larger than itself; it has been relentlessly hunted for its destruction of livestock and poultry.

Tasman Sea, arm of the South Pacific Ocean, between Australia and New Zealand. It was named for the Dutch explorer Abel TASMAN.

Tasso, Torquato, 1544–95, major Italian poet and tragic figure of the RENAISSANCE. He gained fame at 18 with the narrative *Rinaldo,* and in 1565 was invited to the court of the ESTE at Ferrara. There he wrote the PASTORAL play *Aminta* (1573) and the first version of his masterpiece, *Jerusalem Delivered* (1575), a religious EPIC about the First CRUSADE. That same year he suffered a blow to the head that left him intermittently insane. He greatly influenced MILTON, and the legend of his doomed love for Leonora d'Este was immortalized by BYRON, GOETHE, and others.

taste: see TONGUE.

Tatars or **Tartars,** Turkic-speaking peoples living mostly in Russia and Central Asia. They are largely SUNNI Muslims. Originally a nomadic tribe from E Central Asia, the Tatars intermixed with MONGOLS in the hordes of JENGHIZ KHAN, and the term Tatars came to mean invaders under Mongol leadership. When the Mongols receded eastward, the Tatars continued to dominate Russia, Ukraine, and Siberia. They adopted ISLAM in the 14th cent. In the late 15th cent. the Tatar empire (see GOLDEN HORDE, EMPIRE OF THE) broke up into separate states that fell under Russian or Ottoman Turkish rule. By the 16th cent. most Tatars were settled agriculturists. Tatar leaders, traders, and institutions had great influence on Russian history. In 1783 the last Tatar state, the Crimea, was annexed to Russia. Most Tatars live in the Volga region (where Tatarstan, the Tatar republic, is located) and the Urals, and some live in small groups in W Siberia. The Crimean Tatars were exiled to Kazakhstan and Uzbekistan in 1945 for alleged collaboration with the Germans in WORLD WAR II; in 1956 they regained their civil rights, and since the late 1980s many have returned to Crimea. Following the disintegration of the USSR, Tatarstan leaders began to press the Russian government for increased powers for the autonomous republic. In a 1992 referendum, over 61% of the voters supported a "sovereign" Tatarstan.

Tatarstan: see TATARS.

Tate, (John Orley) Allen, 1899–1979, American poet and critic; b. Winchester, Ky. A professor at several colleges, he edited the magazines *Fugitive* (1922–25) and *Sewanee Review* (1944–46). His perceptive critical writings include *On the Limits of Poetry* (1948) and *The Man of Letters in the Modern World* (1955). His skillful poetry, filled with bitter imagery, can be found in several volumes, notably *Collected Poems* (1977).

Tate, Nahum, 1652–1715, English poet and dramatist. He adapted SHAKESPEARE and with John DRYDEN wrote the second part of *Absalom and Achitophel* (1682). He was named poet laureate in 1692. POPE attacked him in the *Dunciad.*

Tate Gallery, London, originally the National Gallery of British Art. The building was given by Sir Henry Tate and opened in 1897 with 65 British paintings. It was extended by the Turner Wing (1910), three galleries for modern foreign art (1916), the John Singer Sargent Wing (1926), and the Glore Gallery (1987). Its collections of works by William BLAKE, J.M.W. TURNER, and the PRE-RAPHAELITES are particularly notable.

Tawney, Richard Henry [tô'nē], 1880–1962, English historian; b. Calcutta. A leading socialist and Labour party economist, he was an expert on early modern capitalism. He wrote *The Agrarian Problem in the 16th Century* (1912) and *Religion and the Rise of Capitalism* (1926).

taxation, system used by governments to obtain money from people and organizations. The revenue collected is used by the government to support itself and to provide public services. Although taxation is compulsory, it does not guarantee a direct relationship between the amount contributed by a citizen and the extent of services received. An enforced levy to meet an emergency is distinguished from taxation as not being part of a long-term system (e.g., capital levy, a high, one-time tax on a subject's total capital, usually imposed after a war). Fees for special services, such as postage, are not considered taxes. A government may secure its revenue without taxation, as from natural resources, manufactured products, or services, but nearly all nations today rely on taxation as their principal source of income. Ease of collection is considered a merit in a tax, and ability to pay is one test of the amount that an individual should contribute. Taxes are classified as proportional, progressive, or regressive, depending on how they relate to the ability to pay. A *proportional* tax takes the same percentage of each person's income, whether rich or poor. A *progressive* tax, such as the U.S. INCOME TAX, has a higher rate for persons with higher incomes. A general sales tax (a levy on the sale of goods and services, usually as a percentage of the selling price) is considered *regressive,* for in disregarding a person's ability to pay, it, in effect, taxes the poor more heavily than the wealthy by requiring the poor to spend a larger proportion of income on basic needs. Increases or decreases in taxes, or changes in the types of taxes levied, are often used to regulate a nation's economy. For example, the 1981 federal tax law aimed at stimulating the U.S. economy lowered individual income taxes, gave businesses faster DEPRECIATION write-offs, provided savings incentives, and allowed for indexing (see INDEX NUMBER). See also specific types of taxes, e.g., EXCESS PROFITS TAX; INHERITANCE TAX.

taxidermy, process of preserving vertebrate animals in lifelike form by mounting the cleaned skins on a manmade skeleton. Once employed chiefly to preserve hunting trophies and souvenirs, taxidermy is now used mainly by science museums.

Taylor, Edward, c.1642–1729, considered America's foremost colonial poet; b. England. He came to America in 1668. A Congregational minister and ardent Puritan, he wrote verse similar to that of England's METAPHYSICAL POETS. His poetry was first published in 1939.

Taylor, Elizabeth, 1932–, American film actress; b. England. Noted for her beauty, her films include *A Place in the Sun* (1951), *Cleopatra* (1962), *Who's Afraid of Virginia Woolf?* (1966; Academy Award), and *A Little Night Music* (1977).

Elizabeth Taylor

Taylor, Frederick Winslow, 1856–1915, American industrial engineer; b. Germantown, Pa. Taylor, called the father of scientific management, developed management methods that were successfully introduced into many industries. See also TIME AND MOTION STUDY.

Taylor, Maxwell Davenport, 1901–87, U.S. general; b. Keytesville, Mo. He commanded airborne divisions in Europe during WORLD WAR II and was superintendent of West Point (1945–49). After commanding (1953–54) U.S. forces in Korea and the Far East, he served as army chief of staff (1955–59) but resigned when Pres. EISENHOWER disregarded his argument for an expanded, flexible army capable of fighting a limited war. Pres. KENNEDY named him chairman of the joint chiefs of staff (1962–64). As ambassador to South Vietnam (1964–65) under Pres. Lyndon JOHNSON, he urged U.S. support for the VIETNAM WAR.

Taylor, Paul, 1930–, American MODERN DANCE choreographer; b. Pittsburgh, Pa. He made his debut (1953) with Merce CUNNINGHAM, danced (1955–61) with Martha GRAHAM's company, and formed (1955) his own company. His early choreography was witty and innovative; his later works, such as *Le Sacre du Printemps (The Rehearsal)* (1980) and *Company B* (1991)., have been less radical.

Taylor, Zachary, 1785–1850, 12th president of the U.S. (1849–50); b. Orange co., Va. He joined the army in 1808, winning the nickname "Old Rough and Ready" in the BLACK HAWK WAR (1832) and in campaigns against the SEMINOLE in Florida. He took command (1845) of the army in Texas and won victories in the MEXICAN WAR, concluding with the decisive battle of Buena Vista (1847) against great odds. A popular hero, he was elected president on the Whig ticket in 1848. As president, he supported the WILMOT PROVISO and favored the rapid admission of California and New Mexico to the Union. His free-soil views put him in opposition to the measures that became the COMPROMISE OF 1850. Charges of corruption were lodged against members of his cabinet, but before he could order a reorganization he died of cholera on July 9, 1850. He had been in office only one year and four months. He was succeeded by Millard FILLMORE.

Tay-Sachs disease, rare hereditary disease caused by a genetic mutation that leaves the body unable to produce an enzyme necessary for fat metabolism in nerve cells, producing central NERVOUS SYSTEM degeneration. In infants, it is characterized by progressive mental deterioration, blindness, paralysis, epileptic seizures, and death by age four. Adult-onset Tay-Sachs occurs in persons who have a genetic mutation that is similar but allows some production of the missing enzyme. The disease occurs primarily among Jews of Eastern European descent but is also found in French Canadians whose roots are in the St. Lawrence region, certain Cajuns in Louisiana, and some Amish communities. Tay-Sachs can be detected in a fetus by CHORIONIC VILLUS SAMPLING or AMNIOCENTESIS. There is no treatment for Tay-Sachs.

Tb, chemical symbol of the element TERBIUM.

TB, in medicine: see TUBERCULOSIS.

Tbilisi [tabĭl'ēsē] or **Tiflis,** city (1989 pop. 1,260,000), capital of GEORGIA, SW Asia, on the Kura R. and the Transcaucasian RR. Its industries produce machinery, woven silk, and processed foods. Tbilisi was built on a site settled in the 4th cent. B.C. It was ruled (4th–11th cent A.D.) by the Persians, Arabs, Khazars, and Turks; was the capital of an independent Georgian state (1096–1225); and was held (13th–18th cent.) by the Mongols, Iranians, and Turks. It passed to Russia in 1801. From 1918 to 1920 Tbilisi was again the capital of an independent Georgia; Georgia became independent again in 1991 when the USSR disintegrated.

Tc, chemical symbol of the element TECHNETIUM.

Tch-. For Russian names beginning thus and not listed here, see CH-; e.g., for Tchekhoff, see CHEKHOV.

Tchaikovsky, Peter Ilyich [chĭkôf'skē], 1840–93, one of the most popular and influential Russian composers. He studied at the St. Petersburg Conservatory and later taught at the Moscow Conservatory (1865–78). An annuity from a wealthy patroness, Mme von Meck, allowed him for years to devote himself to music. Richly orchestrated, his music is melodious, intensely emotional, and often melancholy. Among the most successful of his compositions are his orchestral works, notably his last three symphonies; the fantasy *Romeo and Juliet* (1869, rev. 1870, 1879); the ballets *Swan Lake* (1876), *The Sleeping Beauty* (1889), and *The Nutcracker* (1892); the Piano Concerto in B Flat Minor (1875); and the Violin Concerto in D (1878). His operas include *Eugene Onegin* (1879) and *The Queen of Spades* (1890).

Tchelitchew, Pavel [chālĕ'chĕf], 1898–1957, Russian-American painter. His compositions are complex and fantastic, using multiple images and triple perspective to recreate the motion of the body. The best known of these is *Hide and Seek* (Mus. Mod. Art, N.Y.C.).

Te, chemical symbol of the element TELLURIUM.

tea, tree or bush, its leaves, and the beverage made from the leaves. The plant (*Thea sinensis, Camellia thea,* or *C. sinensis*) is an evergreen related to the CAMELLIA and native to India and probably parts of China and Japan. In the wild it grows to about 30 ft (9.1 m) in height, but in cultivation it is pruned to 3 to 5 ft (91 to 152 cm). Tea plants require a well-drained habitat in a warm climate with ample rainfall; the leaves are prepared by drying, rolling, and firing (heating). Black teas (e.g., pekoes), unlike green teas, are fermented before firing; oolong teas are partially fermented. Tea's stimulating properties are due to CAFFEINE, and its astringency to tannin. Grown in China since prehistoric times, tea was produced on a commercial scale there by the 8th cent. It was introduced (17th cent.) into Europe by the Dutch EAST INDIA COMPANY, and its popularity helped spur the opening of E Asia to Western commerce. In colonial America a tax on tea led to the BOSTON TEA PARTY (1773). Today tea is used by more people and in greater quantity than any beverage except water.

teak, tall deciduous tree (*Tectona grandis*) of the VERVAIN family, native to India and Malaysia but now widely cultivated in tropical areas. Teakwood is moderately hard, easily worked, and very durable. The wood contains an ESSENTIAL OIL that resists the action of water and prevents the rusting of iron, and the heartwood is resistant to termites. Superior to all other woods for shipbuilding, teak is also used in furniture, flooring, and general construction.

Teamsters Union, giant U.S. labor UNION formed in 1903; its full name is the International Brotherhood of Teamsters, Chauffeurs, Warehousemen, and Helpers of America. Most members are truck drivers, but some are in agriculture, sales, optics, and other fields. The Teamsters grew steadily under the presidency (1907–52) of Daniel J. Tobin, especially after 1933, when they organized the long-distance trucking industry. During the presidency of Tobin's two immediate successors, Dave Beck and J.R. HOFFA, charges of corruption were leveled against the union. The revelations of a Senate Committee led the AFL-CIO to expel the Teamsters in 1957, and both Beck and Hoffa were later imprisoned. Subsequent presidents Frank E. Fitzsimmons (1971–81), Roy Lee Williams (1981–83, convicted of conspiring to bribe a senator), Jackie Presser (1983–88), and William J. McCarthy (1988–91) failed to improve its tarnished image. The union rejoined the AFL-CIO in 1987. In a union-wide secret ballot forced by the government in 1991, Ronald R. Carey, an insurgent candidate, was elected president. In 1990 the Teamsters had 1.7 million members.

Teapot Dome, in U.S. history, scandal that began during the administration of Pres. HARDING. In 1921, Sec. of the Interior Albert B. Fall secretly leased the naval oil reserves at Teapot Dome, Wyo., and Elk Hills, Calif., without competitive bidding. A Senate investigation (1922–23) revealed that Edward L. Doheny, who had leased the Elk Hills oil field, had "loaned" Fall large sums of money without interest, as had Harry F. Sinclair, recipient of the Teapot Dome lease. Fall was subsequently fined and sentenced to prison. Both Doheny and Sinclair were acquitted of bribery on legal technicalities, but Sinclair was later imprisoned for contempt of the Senate and attempted jury tampering. The oil fields were restored (1927) to the U.S. government by a Supreme Court decision.

tear gas: see POISON GAS.

Teasdale, Sara, 1884–1933, American poet; b. St. Louis. Her volumes of delicate, highly personal lyrics include *Love Songs* (1917; Pulitzer) and *Strange Victory* (1933). She committed suicide.

technetium (Tc), artificially produced radioactive element, discovered in a sample of deuteron-bombarded molybdenum in 1937 by C. Perrier and E.G. Segrè. The silver-gray metal is used in radioactive tracer studies. Spectra of some stars indicate the presence of the element; the naturally occurring element has not been found on earth. See ELEMENT (table); PERIODIC TABLE.

Tecumseh, 1768?–1813, chief of the SHAWNEE; b. Ohio. A noted military leader, he planned a confederacy of tribes to resist U.S. encroachment, but the defeat of his brother, the Shawnee Prophet, at Tippecanoe (1811) ended the Native American military movement. Tecumseh then fought alongside the British against the Americans in the WAR OF 1812. He died in the battle of the Thames.

teeth, hard, calcified structures embedded in the bone of the jaw that perform the function of chewing food. An adult mouth contains 32 permanent teeth. A tooth consists of the crown, the portion visible in the mouth, and one or more roots embedded in a gum socket. The gums cushion the teeth, while the jawbone firmly anchors the roots. The center of each tooth is filled with soft pulpy tissue containing blood vessels and nerves. Hard, bony dentin surrounds the pulp and makes up the bulk of the tooth. The root portion has an overlayer of cementum, and the crown has a layer of enamel, the hardest substance in the body.

Teflon, trade name for a solid, chemically inert POLYMER of tetrafluoroethylene (C_2F_4), $F_2C{=}CF_2$. Stable up to temperatures around 572°F (300°C), Teflon is used in electrical insulation, gaskets, and in making low-adhesion surfaces, e.g., for nonstick cookware.

Tegucigalpa [tāgo͞osēgäl'pä], city (1988 est. pop. 552,000), S central Honduras, capital and largest city of Honduras. Founded in 1579 in a mountain valley, it was a Spanish colonial gold and silver mining center. It vied with Comayagua, its twin city across the Choluteca R., as the republic's capital until 1880. Its older section, built on a steep slope with narrow, stair-stepped streets, is unusually picturesque.

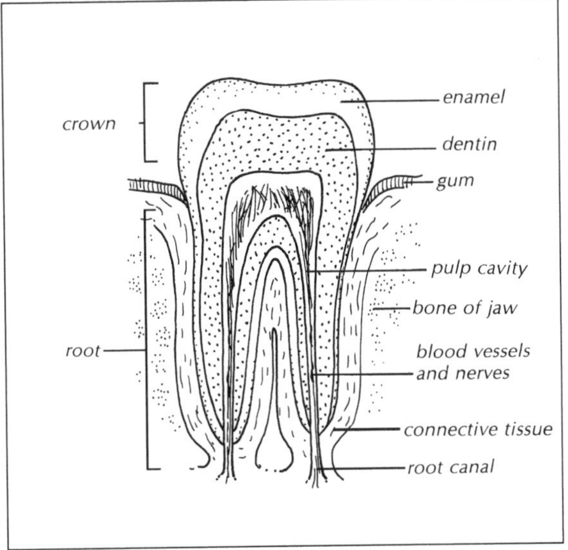

Cross-section of a tooth

Teheran or **Tehran,** city (1986 pop. 6,042,584), capital of Iran, N Iran, near Mt. Damavand. It is Iran's largest city and its administrative, industrial, and commercial hub. It is also a leading center for the sale and export of carpets. Teheran rose to importance after the nearby city of Ragy was destroyed (13th cent.) by the Mongols, and in 1788 it became the capital of Persia. During World War II it was the site of the TEHERAN CONFERENCE (1943). Under MUHAMMAD REZA SHAH PAHLEVI (r.1941–79) the city was modernized. In 1979 Iranian militants seized the U.S. embassy in Teheran and held 52 Americans hostage for 444 days (until Jan. 20, 1981).

Teheran Conference, Nov. 28–Dec. 1, 1943, meeting in Iran during WORLD WAR II of U.S. Pres. F.D. ROOSEVELT, British Prime Min. Winston CHURCHILL, and Soviet Premier Joseph STALIN. Agreement was reached on Allied plans for the war against Germany and for postwar cooperation in the UNITED NATIONS.

Teilhard de Chardin, Pierre, 1881–1955, French paleontologist and philosopher. A Jesuit, Teilhard was forced to abandon teaching in 1926 because of his attempts to reconcile original sin with his concept of evolution. Thereafter he worked (1926–46) in China as a paleontologist and was involved in the discovery of Peking man (see HOMO ERECTUS). He also wrote *The Phenomenon of Man* (published posthumously, 1955), in which he outlined his concept of cosmic evolution and his conviction that belief in evolution does not entail rejection of Christianity. He saw humankind as the axis of the cosmic flow and the key to the universe, and evolution as leading ultimately to the "Omega Point," variously interpreted as the integration of all individual consciousness and as the second coming of Jesus. His works received unusually wide popular response after their posthumous publication.

Te Kanawa, Dame Kiri, 1944–, New Zealand opera and concert singer. She has appeared with the New York Metropolitan Opera, the Munich Opera, and other major opera houses worldwide. She is noted for her performances of the role of the Countess in *The Marriage of Figaro* and Rosalinde in *Die Fledermaus.*

Tel Aviv–Jaffa, city (1989 est. pop. 330,000), W central Israel, on the Mediterranean Sea. It is Israel's second largest city, its financial and commercial center, and a major diamond-processing center. The city is also a tourist resort with wide, attractive beaches. Tel Aviv was founded (1909) by Jews from Jaffa, a major Arab population center, and its population grew dramatically after 1920. It was Israel's first capital (1948–49) and many foreign embassies are still located in the city. A cultural center, it is the site of many theaters, leading museums, and several musical organizations, in-

MAJOR REFLECTING TELESCOPES

Telescope	*Observatory*	*Aperture*	*In Operation*	*Location*	*Elevation*
W.M. Keck Telescope (Keck I)	W.M. Keck Observatory	394 in./ 1,000 cm	1993	Mauna Kea, Hawaii	13,600 ft/ 4,194 m
Bolshoi Teleskop Azimutalnyi	Special Astrophysical Observatory,	236 in./ 600 cm	1976	Zelenchukskaya, Russia	6,791 ft/ 2,070 m
George Ellery Hale Telescope	Palomar Observatory	200 in./ 508 cm	1948	Palomar Mt., California	5,597 Ft/ 1,706 m
Multiple Mirror Telescope	Mt. Hopkins Obsrvatory,	177 in./ 450 cm	1979	Mt. Hopkins, Arizona	8,530 ft/ 2,600 m
Nicholas U. Mayall Reflector	Kitt Peak National Observatory	158 in./ 400 cm	1973	Kitt Peak, Arizona	6,772 Ft/ 2,064 m
————	Cerro Tololo Inter-American Observatory	158 in./ 400 cm	1976	Cerro Tololo, Chile	7,871 ft/ 2,399 m
Anglo-Australian Telescope	Anglo-Australian Observatory	153 in./ 389.3 cm	1975	Siding Spring Mt., Australia	3,819 ft/ 1,164 m
United Kingdom Infrared Telescope	UKIRT Unit of the Royal Observatory, Edinburgh	150 in./ 380.2 cm	1979	Mauna Kea, Hawaii	13,759 ft/ 4,194 m
Canada-France-Hawaii Telescope	————	142 in./ 360 cm	1979	Mauna Kea, Hawaii	13,780 ft/ 4,200 m
E.S.O. 3.6-meter Telescope	European Southern Observatory	141 in./ 357 cm	1976	Cerro La Silla, Chile	7,874 ft/ 2,400 m

cluding the Israel Philharmonic. Tel Aviv and Jaffa were merged in 1950. During the PERSIAN GULF WAR the city was subjected to Iraqi missile attacks.

telegraph, electrically operated device or system for distant communication (the first ever invented) by means of visible or audible signals. The method used throughout most of the world, based in large part on the mid-19th-cent. work of Samuel F.B. MORSE, utilizes an ELECTRIC CIRCUIT set up customarily by using a single overhead wire and employing the earth as the other conductor to complete the circuit. In the telegraph's simplest form, an electromagnet in the receiver is activated by alternately making and breaking the circuit. Reception by sound, with the MORSE CODE signals received as audible clicks, is the basis for a low-cost, reliable method of signaling. In addition to wires and CABLES, telegraph messages are now sent by such means as RADIO waves, MICROWAVES, and COMMUNICATIONS SATELLITES. **Telex** is a telegraphy system that transmits and receives messages in printed form. Today the telegraph is less widely used, having been supplanted by TELEPHONES, FACSIMILE MACHINES, and electronic mail.

Teleki, Count Paul [tĕ'lĕkĭ], 1879–1941, Hungarian premier (1920–21, 1939–41). He signed (1940) the Berlin Pact (see AXIS). When it became evident that Germany would force Hungary to invade Yugoslavia, Teleki committed suicide.

Telemachus, in Greek mythology, son of ODYSSEUS.

Telemann, Georg Philipp, 1681–1767, German composer. Extremely prolific, and in his day more popular than J.S. BACH, he wrote over 600 overtures, 40 operas, 12 services for the year, and other works in almost every form. His style combines COUNTERPOINT and airs from Italian opera.

teleology, in philosophy, term applied to any system attempting to explain a series of events in terms of ends, goals, or purposes. It is opposed to mechanism, which holds that all events are explained by the mechanical principles of causation. Teleologists have frequently identified purpose in the universe as God's will. The teleological proof of the existence of God argues that since there is design in the world, there must be a designer (God). A more recent, evolutionary view finds purpose in the higher levels of organic life but holds that it is not necessarily based on any transcendent being.

telephone, device for transmitting and receiving sound, especially speech, usually by means of wires in ELECTRIC CIRCUITS. The telephones now in general use are developments of the device invented by Alexander Graham BELL and patented by him in 1876 and 1877. A modern telephone transmitter, which is essentially a carbon MICROPHONE, contains loosely packed carbon grains. When someone speaks into the telephone, the diaphragm vibrates, causing the carbon grains to be compressed and released. This motion varies the current flow in the associated electric circuit. The current, when transmitted to a distant identical instrument, causes the diaphragm in it to vibrate in response to the fluctuations induced by the nearby magnetic field. Telephone lines used include ordinary open-wire lines; lead-sheathed CABLES consisting of many lines; coaxial cables; and, most recently, glass fibers (see FIBER OPTICS). Coaxial cables and fiber-optic lines are placed underground, but other cables may be either overhead or underground. Long-distance transmission of telephone messages is often accomplished by means of RADIO and MICROWAVE transmissions. In some cases microwaves are sent to an orbiting COMMUNICATIONS SATELLITE, from which they are relayed back to a distant point on the earth. Sophisticated services, including automatic switching systems, automatic dialing, call forwarding, and conference calling, have been developed in recent years. Telephone systems are increasingly important to the transmission of messages and data between digital devices, such as computers. To improve accuracy and speed, analog telephone systems (in which the shape of the electrical signal is analogous to the shape of the sound wave) are being replaced by digital systems. A digital system rapidly samples the sound waves and encodes them as binary pulses that can be decoded by the receiver. Such a system can carry more messages over the same link at the same time. In addition, computers can communicate over telephone circuits without MODEMS, greatly enhancing the efficiency of NETWORKS. See also CELLULAR TELEPHONE.

telescope, system of LENSES, MIRRORS, or both used to gather light from a distant object and form a real optical image of it. In the refracting telescope, or refractor (invented early 17th cent.), light is bent, or refracted, as it passes through a convex objective lens so that it converges to a point—the focus—behind the lens. In a reflecting telescope, or reflector (invented 1672), light is reflected by a concave paraboloidal mirror and brought to a focus in front of the mirror. The image is diverted to a more convenient location by one of several means (see diagrams of the Newtonian, Cassegrain, and Coudé foci). Reflecting telescopes that are radically different from conventional ground-based systems are the multimirror telescope, which uses multiple small, less expensive mirrors to

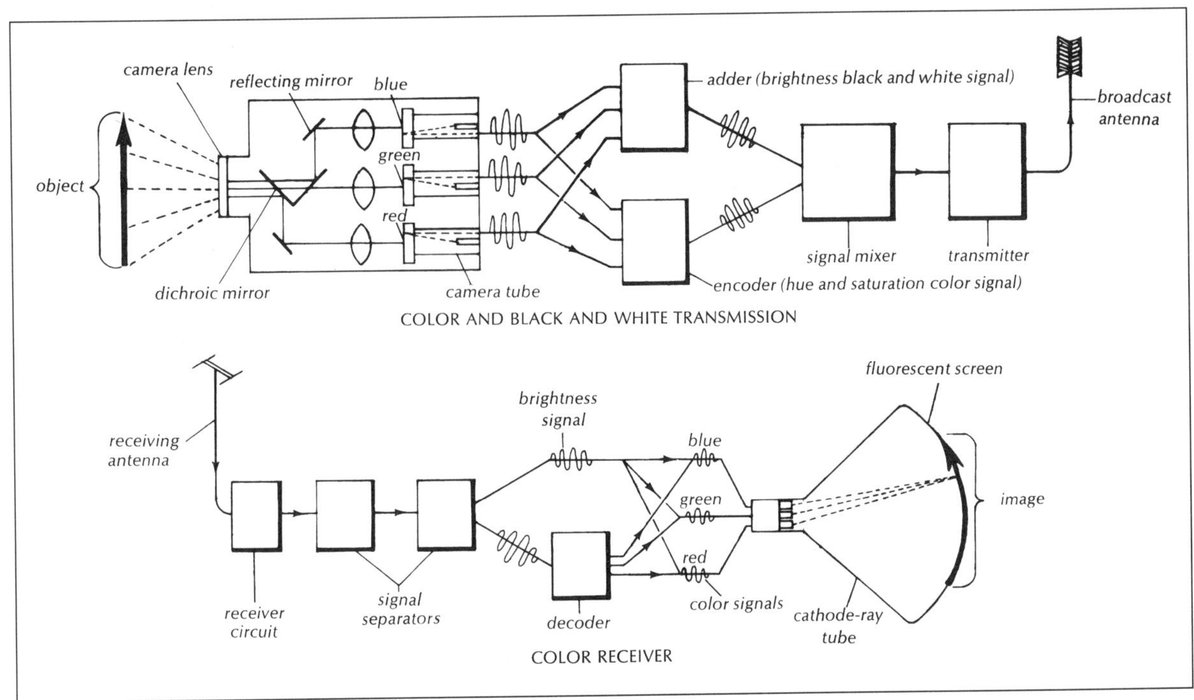

Television video transmission and reception: The camera lens focuses collected light rays into mirrors, which separate the image into its three primary color component images. Each color component is focused onto the face of a camera tube. The scanning beam of each tube converts the primary color image into a color signal. The adder combines the three color signals to make the brightness signal. The encoder combines the signals to transmit hue and saturation information. A black-and-white tlevision receiver processes only the brightness signal. A color-television receiver separates the received signal into brightness and hue and saturation components, which are recombined to produce primary color signals for the picture tube.

achieve the same light-gathering power as a very expensive large mirror; the liquid mirror telescope, which uses a rotating mirror with a liquid mercury surface; and the HUBBLE SPACE TELESCOPE. A third type of telescope, the catadioptric system, focuses light by a combination of lenses and mirrors; two examples are the Schmidt camera telescope (invented 1930), used primarily for wide-angle photography of star fields and consisting of a spherical mirror and a special correction lens used in front of the tube, and the Maksutov telescope (invented 1941), which has a spherical meniscus in place of the Schmidt's correcting plate. A recent innovation is the multitelescope array, which employs interferometry techniques, adaptive optics, and reconstructive imaging by COMPUTERS to simulate the imaging power of a large telescope. The size of the object's image is the product of its angular size in radians (1 radian ≈ 57°) as seen from the telescope and the focal length (the distance from the focus to the lens or mirror). The brightness of the image depends on the telescope's total light-gathering power and hence is proportional to the area of the objective lens or primary mirror, or to the square of its diameter. A telescope's resolving power, or smallest angular separation between two light points that can be unambiguously distinguished, is proportional to the ratio of the wavelength of light being observed to the diameter of the telescope. The magnification, or magnifying power, of a telescope is the ratio of the angular sizes of the virtual image seen by the observer and the actual angular size, or, equivalently, to the ratio of the focal lengths of the objective and the ocular, or eyepiece. The mounting of a telescope must be massive, to minimize mechanical vibration that would blur the image, and must provide rotation about two perpendicular axes, to allow the telescope to be pointed in any direction. In the altazimuth mounting, used primarily for terrestrial telescopes, one axis points to the zenith and allows rotation along the horizon, and the other allows changes in altitude. Most astronomical telescopes use the equatorial mounting, in which one axis points at the celestial pole. Rotation about this polar axis allows changes in right ascension or celestial longitude; rotation about the declination axis, at right angles to it, allows changes in declination or celestial latitude. To compensate for the earth's rotation, a clock-drive mechanism is generally provided to turn the polar axis east to west at the rate of one rotation per sidereal day. See also OBSERVATORY, ASTRONOMICAL; RADIO ASTRONOMY.

teletext: see VIDEOTEX.

television, transmission and reception of still or moving images by means of electrical signals, especially by means of ELECTROMAGNETIC RADIATION using the techniques of RADIO. One of the most widely used image pickup devices, or camera tubes, is the iconoscope (invented by Vladimir ZWORYKIN, 1923), which consists of a thin sheet of mica upon which thousands of microscopic globules of a photosensitive silver-cesium compound have been deposited. Backed with a metallic conductor, this expanse of mica becomes a mosaic of tiny PHOTOELECTRIC CELLS and CAPACITORS. The differing light intensities of various points of a scene cause the cells of the mosaic to emit varying quantities of electrons. The cells are left with positive charges in strengths proportional to the electrons lost. An electron gun, or "scanner," passes its beam across the cells. As it does so, the charge is released, causing an electrical signal to appear on the back of the mosaic, which is connected externally to an AMPLIFIER. The strength of the signal is proportional to the amount of charge released. In the Vidicon, another type of pickup tube, the photoemissive mosaic is replaced by a photoconductive layer, resulting in increased efficiency. More recently the pickup tube has been replaced by solid-state semiconductors called charged-coupled devices (CCD). When light from an image is focused on a CCD, a pattern of electrical charges, which vary in proportion to the amount of light, is created. These charges are then transmitted to an amplifier. The CCD's small size and light weight have resulted in compact, all-solid-state cameras that have revolutionized remote television broadcasting. The scanning process, which is the essence of television accomplishment, operates as the human eye does in reading a page of printed material, i.e., line by line. A complex circuit of horizontal and vertical deflection coils controls this movement and causes the electron beam to scan the back of the mosaic 30 times per second. Two principal means of recording television programs for future use are videotape recording and kinescope. Videotape recording is similar to conventional tape recording except that because of the wide frequency range—4.2 megahertz (MHz)—occupied by a video signal, the effective speed at which the tape passes the recording head is kept very high. Sound is recorded along with the video signal on the same tape. Kinescope is a method in which programs are recorded on motion-picture film. Appropriate changes in the signal-carrying circuitry allow kinescopes to be played back from a developed negative as well as from a positive. Systems for recording television programs on discs have also been developed (see VIDEODISC). When a television program is broadcast, the varying electrical signals are amplified and used to modulate a carrier wave (see MODULATION); the modulated carrier is usually fed to an ANTENNA, where it is converted to electromagnetic waves and broadcast over a large region. The waves are sensed by antennas connected to television receivers, and the image is reconstructed essentially by reversing the pickup operation. The final image is displayed on the face of a CATHODE-RAY TUBE, where an electron beam scans the fluorescent face, called the "screen," line for line with the pickup scanning. The tube's inside face glows when hit by the electrons, and the visual image is reproduced. Color television today uses an "element-sequential" system. Light from the subject is broken up into its three primary-color components (red, blue, and green), which are simultaneously scanned by three pickups. In the receiver the signals are brought together again. Each element, or dot, on the picture tube screen is subdivided into areas of red, blue, and green phosphors. Beams from three electron guns, modulated by the three color signals, scan the elements together in such a way that the beam from the gun using a given color signal strikes the phosphor of the same color. Digital television uses digital amplifier circuitry to improve sound and picture quality and also to allow the screen to be divided into windows, each displaying the image from a different transmission. High-definition television (HDTV) uses at least twice the number of scanning lines as, and a wider screen than, conventional television. These features enable HDTV to produce a picture that is sharper and more detailed, rivaling that produced by motion-picture film. Nonexperimental analog HDTV broadcasting began in Japan in 1991. Its acceptance has been slow due to the high cost of HDTV receivers and limited broadcast hours. The Federal Communications Commission is expected to approve a digital HDTV-system standard for the U.S. in 1995. See BROADCASTING; CABLE TELEVISION; VIDEOCASSETTE RECORDER.

telex: see TELEGRAPH.

Tell, William, legendary Swiss hero. A native of Uri, he refused obeisance to Gessler, the Austrian bailiff. As punishment he was forced to shoot an apple off his young son's head. In revenge, Tell killed Gessler, setting off the revolt that ousted the bailiffs on Jan. 1, 1308. The legend is a distortion of actual events that led in 1291 to the formation of the Everlasting League among the forest cantons of Uri, Schwyz, and Unterwalden. The best-known treatments of the story are SCHILLER's drama (1804) and ROSSINI's opera (1829).

Teller, Edward, 1908–, American physicist; b. Hungary. During World War II he did atom-bomb research at Columbia. He was instrumental in making possible the first successful U.S. HYDROGEN-BOMB explosion (1952) and was director (1952–60) of the Univ. of California's Livermore Radiation Laboratory. Teller also was a major proponent of Pres. Reagan's STRATEGIC DEFENSE INITIATIVE, particularly of the use of nuclear-powered X-ray lasers for missile defense, an approach that was abandoned in 1992.

tellurium (Te), semimetallic element, discovered in 1782 by Franz von Reichenstein. A silver-white, lustrous, brittle metalloid, it occurs in calaverite and sylvanite. It is used as an additive in steel to increase ductility and as a catalyst for petroleum cracking. See ELEMENT (table); PERIODIC TABLE.

Telugu [tĕl'əgōō"], Dravidian language of India. See LANGUAGE (table).

Tempe, city (1990 pop. 141,865), S Ariz., on the Salt R.; inc. 1894. A fast-growing Phoenix suburb, it is a health resort, an agricultural center, seat of Arizona State Univ., and home of the Phoenix Cardinals football team. Native American ruins are nearby.

tempera, painting method in which finely ground pigment is mixed with a base such as albumen, egg yolk, or thin glue. When used on wood panels, as it was for altarpieces and easel paintings, it was applied on a smooth, white gesso underpainting. Tempera produces clear, pure colors that resist oxidation. Known from antiquity, it was the exclusive panel medium in the Middle Ages. It was not supplanted by the more subtle oil paint until c.1400 in N Europe and c.1500 in Italy. A modern revival of tempera included the 19th-cent. Swiss artist Arnold Böcklin and the 20th-cent. Americans SHAHN and WYETH.

temperance movements, organized efforts to induce people to abstain from alcoholic beverages. In response to increasing alcoholism, local and, later, international temperance societies (e.g., the Woman's Christian Temperance Union) developed in the 19th cent. in the U.S., Great Britain, and N Europe. In the U.S. they worked for liquor laws and in 1919 secured federal PROHIBITION. Outstanding temperance workers included Susan B. ANTHONY and Carry NATION.

temperature, the measure of the relative warmth or coolness of an object. The temperature of a substance measures not its heat content but rather the average kinetic energy of its molecules. Temperature is measured by means of a THERMOMETER or other instrument having a scale calibrated in units called degrees. A temperature scale is determined by choosing two reference temperatures and dividing the temperature difference between these points into a certain number of degrees. The size of the degree depends on the particular temperature scale being used. The most common reference temperatures are the MELTING POINT of ice and the BOILING POINT of water. The Celsius (centigrade) scale takes 0°C as the melting point and 100°C as the boiling point. The Fahrenheit scale assigns 32°F to the melting point and 212°F to the boiling

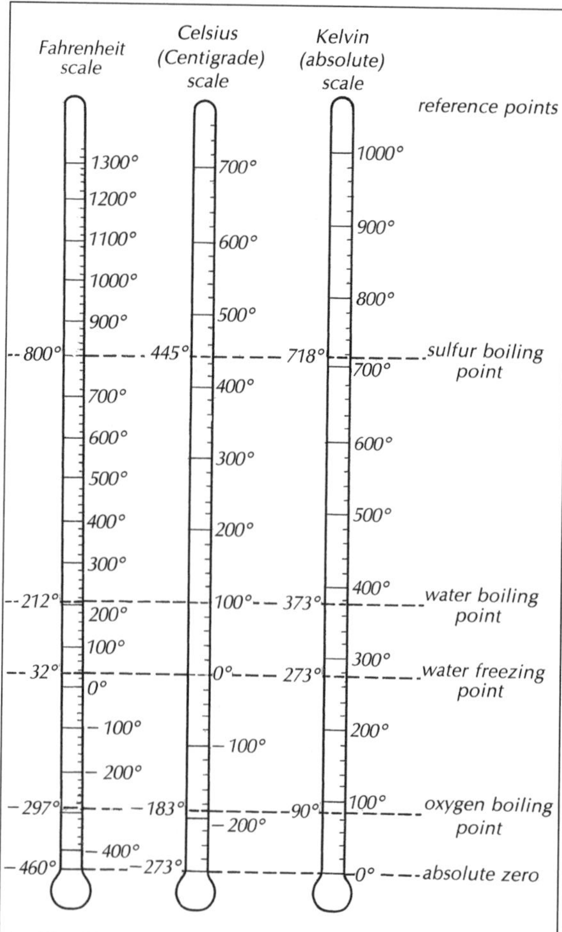

Temperature scales

point. The Réamur scale, used in some parts of Europe, sets the melting point at 0°R and the boiling point at 80°R. The Kelvin, or thermodynamic, scale is an absolute scale having degrees the same size as those on the Celsius scale, but assigning 0K to absolute zero, the theoretical lower limit of temperature (see diagram). See also ENERGY; GAS LAWS; HEAT; THERMODYNAMICS.

tempo, in music, the speed at which a composition is played. The composer's intentions as to tempo are conventionally indicated by a set of Italian terms such as *presto* (very fast), *allegro* (fast), *andante* (moderate, literally "walking"), *adagio* (slow), and *largo* (very slow); *accelerando* and *ritardando* are used to indicate a momentary increase or decrease of tempo. Although composers since Beethoven's time have given indications of speed, tempo has always remained a point of subjective interpretation.

Ten Commandments or **Decalogue,** in the Bible, the summary of divine law given by God to MOSES on Mt. Sinai. They are paramount in the ethical systems of Judaism, Christianity, and Islam. The order and division of the commandments differ somewhat in different Christian churches.

tendon, tough cord of dense connective tissue that attaches muscle to bone. If the muscle is thin and wide, the tendon may be a thin sheet. Tendons transfer muscle power over a distance, e.g., forearm muscles contract and pull on tendons that pull on finger bones to produce finger movements.

Teneriffe or **Tenerife:** see CANARY ISLANDS.

Teng Hsiao-p'ing: see DENG XIAOPING.

Tennessee, state in S central U.S.; bordered by North Carolina (E), Georgia, Alabama, and Mississippi (S), the Mississippi R., across which lie Arkansas and Missouri (W), and Kentucky and Virginia (N).

Area, 42,244 sq mi (109,412 sq km). *Pop.* (1990) 4,877,185, a 6.2% increase over 1980 pop. *Capital,* Nashville. *Statehood,* June 1, 1796 (16th state). *Highest pt.,* Clingmans Dome, 6,643 ft (2,026 m); *lowest pt.,* Mississippi R., 182 ft (56 m). *Nickname,* Volunteer State. *Motto,* Agriculture and Commerce. *State bird,* mockingbird. *State flower,* iris. *State tree,* tulip poplar. *Abbr.,* Tenn.; TN.

Land and People. In E Tennessee are ranges of the APPALACHIAN MOUNTAINS, including the GREAT SMOKY MOUNTAINS and the Cumberland Plateau. Central Tennessee has the gently rolling hills of its bluegrass country, and the west the flat Mississippi floodplain. The climate varies greatly, with severe winters in the mountainous eastern region and hot, humid summers in the western plains. More than 60% of the population lives in urban areas. MEMPHIS is the largest city, followed by NASHVILLE and KNOXVILLE. In 1990 the state was 83% white and 16% African American.

Economy. Tennessee's industrial sector, the leading source of employment, has become increasingly diversified, with chemicals, processed foods, transportation equipment, and machinery the principal products. The leading agricultural products are soybeans, cattle, dairy products, hogs, tobacco, corn, and hay. The state leads the nation in the extraction of pyrites and zinc, and produces coal, stone, and cement. The Grand Ole Opry, in Nashville, and Great Smoky Mts. National Park (see NATIONAL PARKS, table) are popular tourist destinations.

Government. The constitution of 1870 provides for a governor elected to a four-year term. The general assembly consists of a senate whose 33 members serve four-year terms and a house with 99 members elected every two years. The state is represented in the U.S. Congress by two senators and nine representatives and has 11 electoral votes.

History. The remains of the early MOUND BUILDERS can be found in Tennessee. It was the home of the CHEROKEE, CHICKASAW, and SHAWNEE when Robert Cavalier, sieur de LA SALLE, built (c.1682) a fort there. In 1756 the area was ceded to Britain. After the American Revolution, residents formed a short-lived independent government, the state of FRANKLIN (1784–88). Settlement increased, and by the late 1830s Native Americans had been forcibly removed to present-day Oklahoma. Although many residents opposed slavery, Tennessee seceded (1861) from the Union, and the state was—after Virginia—the bloodiest battlefield of the CIVIL WAR. Readmitted to the Union in 1866, Tennessee replaced the plantation system with farm tenancy, and coal mining and textile manufacturing grew in importance. The state attracted (1925) international attention with the famous SCOPES TRIAL, which tested a state law forbidding the teaching of EVOLUTION. The TENNESSEE VALLEY AUTHORITY (TVA), established (1933) by the federal government to provide cheap and abundant hydroelectric power, has been chiefly responsible for changing the basis of the state's economy from agriculture to diversified industry. From the late 1970s to early 90s, Tennessee has seen an influx of new businesses, especially from northern industrial states and Japan, and the trade and service sectors of its economy have grown.

Tennessee, river, c.650 mi (1,050 km) long, principal tributary of the Ohio R., which it joins at Paducah, Ky., after flowing N from the vicinity of Knoxville, Tenn. The once flood-prone river has been converted by the TENNESSEE VALLEY AUTHORITY into a series of lakes impounded by nine major dams. The river is linked to the Tombigbee R. and Gulf of Mexico by the Tennessee-Tombigbee Waterway.

Tennessee Valley Authority (TVA), U.S. government–owned corporation created (1933) to integrate development of the Tennessee R. basin area. Headquartered there, it undertook (1940) construction of a system of multipurpose dams and steam-generating facilities that has produced relatively cheap energy. It now also operates nuclear power plants and other energy facilities. The availability of low-cost power attracted businesses to the area and led to economic growth. TVA has also carried out land conservation, health, and education programs.

Tenniel, Sir John [tĕn'yəl], 1820–1914, English caricaturist and illustrator. Well known for his original, good-humored political cartoons in *Punch* (1851–1901), he is also famous for his illustrations of Lewis CARROLL's *Alice in Wonderland* and *Through the Looking Glass.*

tennis, indoor or outdoor game for two players (singles) or four players (doubles). Although originally lawn tennis was played only on grass courts, today the surfaces are more often of clay, asphalt, or synthetics. The court measures 78 ft by 27 ft (23.8 m by 8.2 m) for singles play; it is 4.5 ft (1.4 m) wider for doubles. A net 3 ft (91 cm) high in the middle divides the court laterally. Play is directed toward hitting the inflated, felt-covered ball (about the size of a baseball) with an oval-headed, fiber-strung racket into the opponent's court so that he or she cannot make a proper return. Points are scored in the progression 15, 30, 40, and game, with six games required to take a set. Usually, three set victories decide a match in men's play, two set victories in women's play. Modern tennis was developed in 1873 by an Englishman, Major Walter C. Wingfield, who borrowed from older forms of the game. The first "world championship," held (1877) at Wimbledon, England, became the famous tournament of that name. In the U.S., where tennis was introduced in 1874, the national men's championship has been contested since 1881, the women's since 1887. The Davis Cup international team competition (begun in 1900) focused world attention on the sport. Major tournaments, originally restricted to amateurs, have been open to professionals since 1968. Tennis has been an Olympic sport since 1988.

Tennyson, Alfred Tennyson, 1st **Baron,** 1809–92, English poet. His first book, *Poems, Chiefly Lyrical* (1830), was followed by *Poems* (1832), which included "The Lotus-Eaters" and "The Lady of Shalott." *Poems* (1842) expressed philosophic doubts in a materialistic age. "Locksley Hall," "Ulysses," "Morte d'Arthur," and other poems in the volume won acclaim. *The Princess* (1847) was followed by *In Memorian* (1850), an elegy sequence prompted by the death in 1833 of the poet's friend Arthur Henry Hallam. Tennyson became poet laureate in 1850. In 1855 *Maud* appeared. Between 1859 and 1888 he completed *Idylls of the King,* a 12-part Arthurian epic. In 1883 he was made a peer. A spokesman for the values of the Victorian age, and its most famous poet, Tennyson is today recognized for his mastery of poetic technique, superb use of sensuous language, and profundity of thought.

tenor: see VOICE.

tenpins: see BOWLING.

Ten Years War, 1868–78, fought by Cuban revolutionaries against Spanish domination of CUBA. The warfare was guerrilla fighting without major battles, but it raged furiously in the eastern provinces. Spanish forces carried out bloody reprisals against the patriots, who retaliated by attacking all Spanish supporters. The war dragged on until Gen. Arsino Martinez de Campos of Spain negotiated the Treaty of Zanjón, granting reforms and governmental representation to Cubans (promises that were not kept). The war foreshadowed the Cuban war of independence (1895–98) and the SPANISH-AMERICAN WAR.

Teotihuacán, ancient commercial and religious center, 30 mi (48 km) NE of Mexico City, of an influential civilization that flourished between A.D. 300 and 900. The largest and most impressive urban site of ancient America, it is laid out in a grid and dominated by the Pyramid of the Sun. Other notable buildings include the Pyramid of the Moon and the Temple of QUETZALCOATL. The people of Teotihuacán brought sculpture, ceramics, the carving of stylized stone masks, and mural painting to a high degree of refinement. Their designs indicate a complex religious system. At its peak the city's population was over 100,000.

tepee, wickiup, and wigwam, types of dwelling used by Native Americans of various culture areas (see NORTH AMERICA, INDIGENOUS PEOPLES OF). The tepee, or tipi, used by nomadic Plains tribes, usually consisted of buffalo hides stretched over a cone formed of tent poles; it was strong and easy to move. Tribes to the south and west used the wickiup, made of brush or mats stretched over arched poles. The wigwam of the Eastern Woodlands, a domed or conical frame covered with bark or mats, might be either a single-family or a communal dwelling.

Tepe Gawra [Kurdish, = great mound], important settlement site in MESOPOTAMIA, N Iraq. Excavations (from 1927) unearthed 24 levels, dating from the 5th to 2d millennium B.C., with more advanced civilizations at the oldest levels (5000–3000 B.C.).

terbium (Tb), metallic element, discovered in 1843 by C.G. Mosander. It is a silver-gray, soft, ductile, malleable RARE-EARTH METAL in the LANTHANIDE SERIES. Terbium is used in lasers, semiconductor devices, and phosphors for color-television picture tubes. See ELEMENT (table); PERIODIC TABLE.

Ter Borch or **Terborch, Gerard** [tər bôrkh′], 1617–81, Dutch genre and portrait painter. He portrayed the life of the wealthy Dutch burgher class in elegant and serene paintings. His most famous pictures include *The Guitar Lesson* (National Gall., London) and the celebrated group portrait *The Peace of Münster* (1648; National Gall., London).

Terbrugghen, Hendrick [tĕrbro͝og′hən], 1588–1629, Dutch painter. Influenced by CARAVAGGIO, he painted intimate, restrained genre scenes that foreshadow in coloring the work of VERMEER. Many are nighttime scenes. A characteristic work is *Old Man Writing* (Smith College Mus., Northampton, Mass.).

Terence (Publius Terentius Afer), c.185 or 195–c.159 B.C., Roman writer of COMEDY; b. Carthage. Six of his comedies survive, freely adapted from the Greek plays of MENANDER and others. Polished and urbane, they are characterized by gentle humor and realistic characterization.

Teresa, Saint: see THERESA, SAINT.

Teresa, Mother, 1910–, Roman Catholic missionary in India, winner of the 1979 Nobel Peace Prize; b. Skopje (now in Macedonia) as Agnes Gonxha Bojaxhiu. Of Albanian parentage, she went to India at 17, becoming a nun and teaching school in Calcutta. In 1948 she left the convent and founded the Missionaries of Charity, which now operates schools, hospitals, orphanages, and food centers in more than 25 countries.

Tereshkova, Valentina Vladimirovna, 1937–, Soviet cosmonaut. She was the first woman to orbit the earth, in *Vostok 6* on June 16–19, 1963. She left the Soviet space program soon after and married cosmonaut Andriyan Nikolayev.

termite or **white ant,** soft-bodied social INSECT that feeds mainly on wood. Termites live in colonies of hundreds or thousands, consisting of large numbers of nonreproductive "workers" and "soldiers" and one or a few reproductive members—"kings" and "queens." Some build huge mounds, up to 40 ft (12.2 m) high, to house their colonies. Turning wood into cellulose by means of specialized bacteria or protozoans in the digestive tract, termites do millions of dollars of damage annually.

term limits, statutory limitations placed on the number of terms officeholders may serve. The issue of term limits became important in the U.S. during the late 1980s and early 90s, and focused on members of the U.S. Congress. Proponents feel that limitation cuts down on entrenched incumbents' abuses of power and their obsession with reelection, thus making government more responsive. Many call for a constitutional amendment similar to the 22d Amendment, which limits the president's tenure, to set uniform national limits. Opponents of limits cite the benefits of seniority and experience conferred by years in office. Colorado voters passed a term limits initiative in 1990, and in 1992 voters in 14 states approved various term limits laws. State term limits on federal legislators have been challenged in the courts.

tern, sea BIRD of the Old and New World, smaller than the related GULL, with long, pointed wings and forked tails. Also called sea swallows because of their graceful flight, they plunge headlong into the water to catch small fish.

Terpsichore: see MUSES.

terra cotta [Ital. = baked earth], form of hard-baked clay widely used in the decorative arts, especially as an architectural material, either in its natural red-brown color, painted, or with a baked glaze. Its early prevalence as a medium of artistic expression is indicated by vases, figurines, and tiles from predynastic Egypt; ancient Assyria, Persia, and China; and pre-Columbian Central America. Terra cotta first gained architectural importance in Greece, where from c.7th cent. B.C. it was used for roof tiles and ornamental details. Its golden age was the RENAISSANCE, when it was widely used in the architecture of N Italy and N Germany. It was later established in Italy as a sculptural material, and reached great distinction as a decorative material in the polychrome enameled reliefs of the DELLA ROBBIA family. Terra-cotta work in building and decoration spread from Italy in the 16th cent., often through migrant Italian artisans, to France and England. In the 18th cent. sculptors such as HOUDON used the material for sketches. Widely used in the U.S. in modern times as an exterior covering for steel structural skeletons, terra cotta was employed with particular skill by Louis SULLIVAN. Notable modern sculptures in terra cotta include those by MAILLOL, EPSTEIN, and PICASSO.

terrier, class of dogs originally bred to start small game and vermin from their burrows or to go to earth and kill their prey. Today they are raised chiefly as pets. See individual breeds, e.g., AIREDALE TERRIER, CAIRN TERRIER, FOX TERRIER, SCHNAUZER, SCOTTISH TERRIER, WEST HIGHLAND WHITE TERRIER.

territorial waters: see SEA, LAW OF THE.

Terror, Reign of: see REIGN OF TERROR.

terrorism, term usually applied to organized acts or threats of violence designed to intimidate opponents or to publicize grievances. The term dates from the REIGN OF TERROR (1793–94) in the French Revolution but has taken on additional meaning in the 20th cent. Political terrorism may be part of a government campaign to eliminate the opposition, as under HITLER, MUSSOLINI, STALIN, and others, or it may be part of a revolutionary effort to overthrow a regime, a common tactic in guerrilla warfare. Terrorism by radicals (of both the left and right) and by nationalists became widespread after World War II. Contemporary revolutionary groups that engage in terrorist activity include the "provisional" wing of the IRISH REPUBLICAN ARMY; the PALESTINE LIBERATION ORGANIZATION; and the SHINING PATH, in Peru.

Terry, Dame Ellen Alicia, 1848–1928, English actress; mother of Edward Gordon Craig. As leading lady (1878–1902) to Sir Henry IRVING she was admired for her charm and grace in Shakespearean roles, especially Beatrice in *Much Ado about Nothing.*

Tertullian, c.160–c.230, Roman Christian theologian. Converted (c.197) to Christianity, he became a formidable writer in defense of the faith. Some of Tertullian's opinions, however, differed from Catholic thought, and he left the church (213) to join the schismatic Montanists. Eventually he formed his own sect, the Tertullianists.

Tesla, Nikola, 1856–1943, American electrician and inventor; b. Croatia (then in Austria-Hungary); came to U.S., 1884. A pioneer in high-tension electricity, he made many discoveries and inventions of great value to the development of radio transmission and to the field of electricity, including an arc-lighting system, the Tesla induction motor, the Tesla coil, and various generators and transformers.

Test Act, 1673, passed by the British Parliament to exclude from public office (military and civil) all those who refused to take oaths of allegiance and supremacy, to receive communion according to the Church of England, and to renounce belief in transubstantiation. It was directed mainly against Catholics. In 1678 it was extended to members of Parliament. The act was repealed (1828) at the time of CATHOLIC EMANCIPATION.

testes: see REPRODUCTIVE SYSTEM.

testosterone, principal male sex HORMONE. An ANABOLIC STEROID secreted by the testes (and synthesized in small amounts in the ovaries and placenta), it is necessary for the development of the external genitals in the male fetus, and at puberty its increased levels are responsible for male secondary sex characteristics (e.g., facial hair).

test-tube baby: see IN VITRO FERTILIZATION.

tetanus or **lockjaw,** acute infectious disease of the nervous system caused by TOXINS of the *Clostridium tetani* bacillus. Tetanus may follow the introduction of bacterial spores by any type of injury, including puncture wounds, animal bites, gunshot wounds, lacerations, and fractures. The toxin acts on the motor nerves and causes muscle spasms, most frequently in the jaw (lockjaw) and facial muscles. The disease is treated with an antitoxin or human immune globulin, but it is preferable to prevent tetanus by immunization.

Tethys, in astronomy, natural satellite of SATURN.

Tetley, Glen, 1926–, American modern dancer and choreographer; b. Cleveland, Ohio. He studied in New York City with Hanya Holm and danced with Martha GRAHAM's company. He danced (1962–65) with the Netherlands Dance Theater, becoming (1969) artistic director, and the Stuttgart Ballet (1974–76). His works include *Voluntaries* (1973) and *Greening* (1975).

Teton Range, range of the Middle Rocky Mts., in Wyoming and Idaho, part of Grand Teton National Park (see NATIONAL PARKS, table). It reaches its highest point (13,747 ft/4,190 m) at Grand Teton.

Teutones or **Teutons:** see GERMANS.

Teutonic Knights or **Teutonic Order** [to͞oton'ĭk], German military religious order founded (1190–91) in the Holy Land during the Third CRUSADE. It was made up of nobles, and its knights took monastic vows. It moved to E Europe in the early 13th cent. and in 1226 began a crusade against the heathen Prussians. Within 50 years the order established itself as the ruling government of PRUSSIA, which it Christianized by exterminating the native population and repopulating it with Germans. Its governments in East Prussia, West Prussia, and (after 1309) Pomerelia were under the protection of both pope and emperor. Despite that, Poland seized (1446) West Prussia and Pomerelia. The order's own grand master, Albert of Brandenberg, accepted (1525) the Reformation and declared Prussia a secular duchy with himself as duke, thereby stripping the Teutonic Order of all importance.

Texas, largest state in the coterminous U.S., located in the Southwest; bounded by Oklahoma (N), Arkansas and Louisiana (E), the Gulf of Mexico (SE), the Rio Grande, across which lies Mexico (S), and New Mexico (W).

Area, 267,338 sq mi (692,405 sq km). *Pop.* (1990) 16,986,510, a 19.4% increase over 1980 pop. *Capital,* Austin. *Statehood,* Dec. 29, 1845 (28th state). *Highest pt.,* Guadalupe Peak, 8,751 ft (2,667 m); *lowest pt.,* sea level. *Nickname,* Lone Star State. *Motto,* Friendship. *State bird,* mockingbird. *State flower,* bluebonnet. *State tree,* pecan. *Abbr.,* Tex., TX.

Land and People. The topography rises gradually from east to west. The Gulf coastal plain, perpetually wet with heavy rains, gives way inland to the southern extension of the Great Plains. Farther west is the semiarid tableland of the Llano Estacado and the Davis and Guadalupe mountains. About 80% of the population lives in urban areas. HOUSTON, the largest city in Texas and the fourth largest in the U.S., is followed in size by DALLAS, SAN ANTONIO, EL PASO, AUSTIN, and FORT WORTH. The state's population, the nation's third largest, is more than 25% Hispanic, and Hispanics have long had a significant influence on the state. In 1990 the state was over 75% white and 12% African American.

Economy. Texas is the nation's wealthiest mineral producer. The economy is dominated by the abundant energy resources, and the state is the leading U.S. source of natural gas and second largest U.S. oil producer. Other important minerals include helium, salt, sulfur, sodium sulfate, and clays. Industries include oil refining and the manufacture of machinery, transportation equipment, food products, and chemicals. In the 1980s and 90s research and development and manufacture of high-technology electronic equipment also became an important part of the state's economy. Only California surpasses Texas in the value of its agricultural output. Products of its farms and ranches include cattle, cotton, and cottonseed, as well as sorghum, wheat, dairy products, corn, and rice. Fishing thrives along the Gulf Coast. Tourism is important; Big Bend and Guadalupe Mts. national parks (see NATIONAL PARKS, table) and Padre Island National Seashore are popular destinations.

Government. The amended constitution of 1876 provides for a governor serving a four-year term. The legislature consists of a senate with 31 members elected to four-year terms and a house with 150 members serving two-year terms. Texas is represented in the U.S. Congress by 30 representatives and 2 senators and has 32 electoral votes.

History. The APACHE, COMANCHE, and other tribes inhabited the area when the Spanish established (1682) their first settlement on the site of present-day El Paso. Settlers from the U.S. began arriving in large numbers after Moses AUSTIN obtained (1821) a colonization grant. His son, Stephen F. AUSTIN, established the first American settlement. The Texas Revolution erupted (1835) when American settlers routed Mexican troops and declared (1836) their independence, which they were forced to defend in battles such as that at the ALAMO. The annexation of Texas by the U.S. in 1845 precipitated the MEXICAN WAR. Texas fought on the side of the CONFEDERACY during the Civil War. The discovery (1901) of the spectacular Spindletop oil field, near Beaumont, and of the E Texas oilfield in 1930 revolutionized the state's economy and resulted in prosperity. In the 1980s troubles in the oil industry, banking, and real estate ended economic growth, bringing widespread business failure and unemployment. The early 1990s, however, saw economic diversification and the beginnings of recovery.

Th, chemical symbol of the element THORIUM.

Thackeray, William Makepeace, 1811–63, English novelist and satirist. He briefly edited a magazine before going to Paris to study art in 1834. On returning to England in 1837 he did literary hack work and illustration. In 1840 his wife became insane; to pay for her care and that of their two daughters he worked continually, contributing to magazines such brilliantly satirical writings as *The Yellowplush Correspondence* (1837–38), in which a footman comments on literary and social trends; parodies of sentimental fiction; and illustrations. His *Book of Snobs* (1848) was very popular, as was the novel *Vanity Fair* (1848), a satirical panorama of upper-middle-class life, and the autobiographical novel *Pendennis* (1850). The publication of *Henry Esmond* (1852) was followed by an American tour, after which *The Newcomes* appeared (1853–55). On his second visit to the U.S. (1855–56) he gave lectures, published in 1860 as *The Four Georges.* The Esmond story continued in *The Virginian* (1857–59). In 1860 Thackeray became editor of the new *Cornhill* magazine, in which his last novels appeared.

Thaddaeus, apostle: see JUDE, SAINT.

Thailand, Thai *Prathet Thai* [land of the free], officially Kingdom of Thailand, formerly Siam, constitutional monarchy (1992 est. pop. 57,624,000), 198,455 sq mi (514,000 sq km) SE Asia, bordered by Myanmar (W, NW), Laos (N, E), Cambodia (SE), and Malaysia and the Gulf of Thailand (S). BANGKOK is the capital. A fertile, thickly populated plain, the core of the country, rises to mountains and forests in the north and the Korat plateau in the northeast and east; a narrow, mountainous peninsula extends southward into the Gulf of Thailand. The climate is tropical monsoonal. Thailand's economy is heavily agricultural. Rice is the main crop and the major factor in a normally favorable trade balance; rubber, teak, and tin are also valuable commodities. Industry is minor, and handicraft production exceeds factory output. Tourism is an important source of foreign exchange. Thais, ethnically related to the Shan of Myanmar and the Lao of Laos, constitute 75% of the population; there are large Chinese, Malay, Khmer, and Vietnamese minorities. Theravada Buddhism is the state religion. Thai is the official language.

History. The Thais migrated to the area from China in the 13th cent., establishing kingdoms at Sukhothai (1238) and Ayutthaya (c.1350) and extending their power into neighboring states. The arrival of Portuguese traders in the 16th cent. marked the beginning of Siam's relations with the West. The kingdom was threatened with colonization by the French and British in the 19th cent., but although it lost its claims to Cambodia, Laos, and other territories, adroit diplomacy enabled it to retain its independence. Although modernized under Kings Mongkut (r.1851–68) and Chulalongkorn (r.1868–1910), Siam remained an absolute monarchy until a bloodless coup in 1932 forced Prajadhikop (r.1925–35) to grant a constitution. The country was renamed Thailand in 1939. After occupation by the Japanese during WORLD WAR II, Thailand experienced internal unrest, several military coups, and periods of martial law. In the VIETNAM WAR Thailand strongly supported the U.S. and was a site of U.S. air bases. In the war's aftermath, thousands of Vietnamese and Cambodian refugees severely strained the Thai economy in the 1970s and 80s. The military remained politically powerful into the 1990s, influencing governments through parties aligned with it and ousting prime ministers it opposed, most recently in 1991. In 1992 pro-military parties won a parliamentary majority, and the supreme commander of the military claimed the prime ministership. Demonstrations against military participation in the government led to its fall. In new elections (Sept. 1992) parties opposed to the military won a majority, and Chuan Leekpai became prime minister.

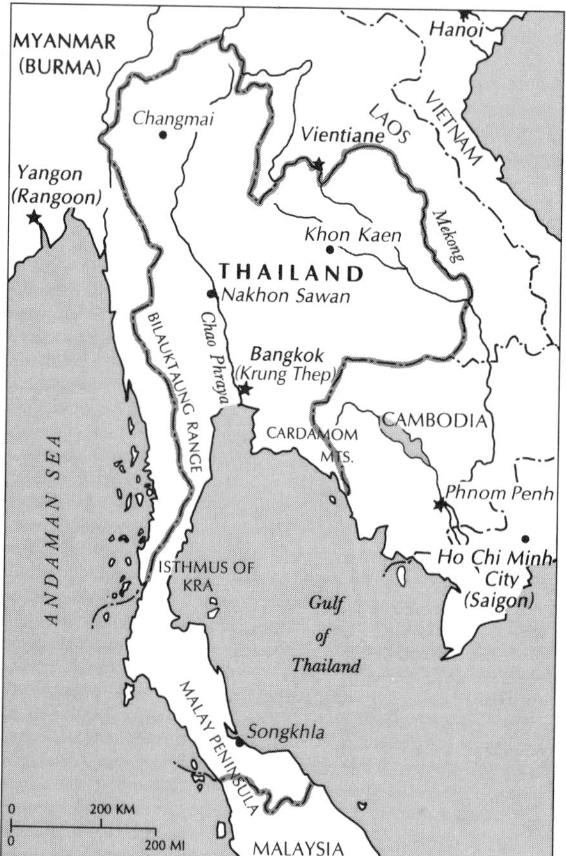

Thai language [tī], formerly Siamese, member of the Tai or Thai subfamily of the Sino-Tibetan family of languages. See LANGUAGE (table).

Thales, c.636–c.546 B.C., pre-Socratic Greek philosopher of Miletus, reputed founder of the Milesian or Ionian school of philosophy. The first recorded Western philosopher, Thales explained the physical world as deriving not from a mythological creation but from a single underlying substance, which he believed to be water. He is said to have introduced geometry into Greece and to have predicted a solar eclipse in 585 B.C. His pupils included ANAXAGORAS, ANAXIMANDER, and DIOGENES.

thalidomide, sleep-inducing drug found to produce skeletal defects in developing fetuses. It was sold without prescription in Europe from 1957 to 1961, when its use by pregnant women was correlated with a high incidence of babies born with shortened, malformed limbs (c.8,000 worldwide). This discovery stimulated the adoption of strict regulations in the testing of new drugs in the U.S.

thallium (Tl), metallic element, discovered by William Crookes in 1861. A soft, malleable, lustrous, silver-gray metal, it resembles aluminum chemically and lead physically. The metal is used in certain electronic components, and its sulfate is used as an insecticide. See ELEMENT (table); PERIODIC TABLE.

Thames, principal river of England, flowing generally east c.210 mi (340 km) from the Cotswold Hills through Oxford, Reading, and the center of London to a long estuary on the North Sea. In its upper course (near Oxford) it is often called the Isis. The Thames is spanned by more than two dozen bridges in London. The river is tidal to Teddington, and a flood-control barrier now protects London from inundation by North Sea gales.

Thanksgiving Day, national holiday in the U.S. commemorating the harvest reaped by the Plymouth Colony in 1621. The first national Thanksgiving Day was proclaimed by Pres. Washington for Nov. 26, 1789. Pres. Lincoln revived the custom in 1863. In 1941 Congress decreed that Thanksgiving should fall on the fourth Thursday of November. The customary turkey dinner is a reminder of the four wild turkeys served at the PILGRIMS' first thanksgiving feast.

Thant, U [thänt], 1909–74, Burmese diplomat, secretary general (1962–72) of the UNITED NATIONS. He became acting secretary general in 1961, on the death of Dag HAMMARSKJÖLD. Influential in settling disputes in West New Guinea (1962) and the Congo (now ZAÏRE; 1963), he played a mediating role in the CUBAN MISSILE CRISIS (1962), but was less successful in efforts to resolve the VIETNAM WAR. He retired in 1972.

Tharp, Twyla, 1941–, American dancer and choreographer; b. Portland, Ind. An eclectic, innovative choreographer and dancer, she danced (1963–65) with Paul TAYLOR. She led her own dance companies (1967–85, 1986–88) and was with the AMERICAN BALLET THEATRE as an artistic associate and resident choreographer (1988–89). Since 1989 she has choreographed dances for various groups. She has also choreographed for stage and film musicals.

Thatcher, Margaret (Hilda Roberts), 1925–, British political leader, the first woman prime minister of Great Britain (1979–90). Elected (1959) to Parliament, she replaced (1975) Edward HEATH as Conservative party leader. She became prime minister after the Conservatives won in 1979, and announced a monetarist policy designed to curtail inflation by reducing the money supply and cutting social programs. In 1982 Thatcher responded to Argentina's seizure of the FALKLAND ISLANDS by dispatching troops who, after a brief war, regained the islands. A strong advocate of the free market, she sold off many state-owned enterprises and benefited when the economy grew in the mid and late 1980s. In foreign affairs she was a staunch ally of the U.S. and a strident opponent of greater economic and political integration in the European Community (EC). Her uncompromising position on the EC and her backing of an unpopular local government tax contributed to her downfall in the Conservative party; she was succeeded by John MAJOR. She was the longest serving British prime minister in the 20th cent. In 1992 Thatcher retired from the House of Commons and was created Baroness Thatcher of Kesteven.

Thayendanegea: see BRANT, JOSEPH.

theater, building in which dramatic performances take place. Theater in ancient Greece developed from the worship of the god DIONYSUS, when religious rituals were performed in a natural AMPHITHEATER at the foot of a hill. The *orchēstra,* a level, circular space where the drama was performed, mainly by the CHORUS, was surrounded by a large, semicircular, open-air auditorium. The original religious nature of Greek drama made audiences receptive to the cosmic themes of TRAGEDY. As the religious and choral elements of drama diminished, the orchestra was reduced in size and importance, and by the Hellenistic period (2d–1st cent. B.C.) the focus of the action had shifted to a raised stage known as the *proskenion.* Roman theaters were based on Greek models but were built on a grandiose scale, being enclosed within exterior walls (although the interior was open to the air) and having elaborate stages. Roman audiences never evinced an interest in serious drama, but they accepted romantic COMEDY as long as it had elements of FARCE. Banned by the Christian church for several centuries after the fall of Rome, drama returned to the Western world in the 9th cent. in the form of liturgical plays, performed first in churches and later (by the 13th cent.) outdoors on both fixed and mobile stages, in churchyards and market squares (see MIRACLE PLAY). The development of the modern theater dates from 1618, when Gian-Battista Aleotti built the Teatro Farnese at Parma, Italy, utilizing the proscenium arch to create a picture-frame stage and a U-shaped seating area for the audience. The separation of audience from stage was further intensified in the 19th cent. by the introduction of a curtain and the use of gas lighting, which made it possible to darken the auditorium. While the proscenium arch stage continues to dominate in the commercial theater, there has been much work to restore a vital relationship between audience and stage, and alternatives to the traditional designs include both the thrust stage, a platform surrounded by the audience on three sides, and the arena (theater-in-the-round), which is completely surrounded by the audience. For descriptions of individual theaters and theater groups, see the table accompanying this article.

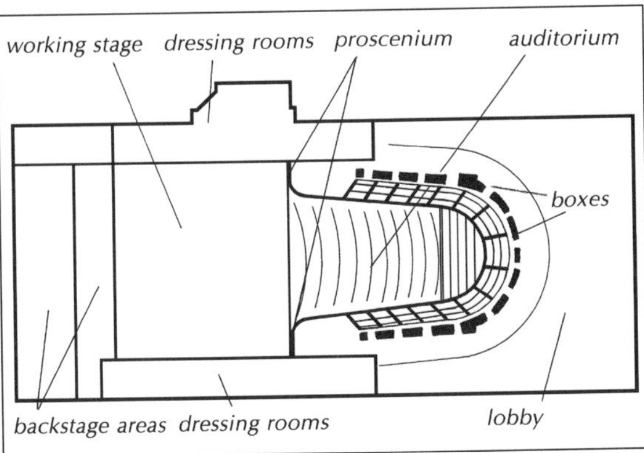

Theaters

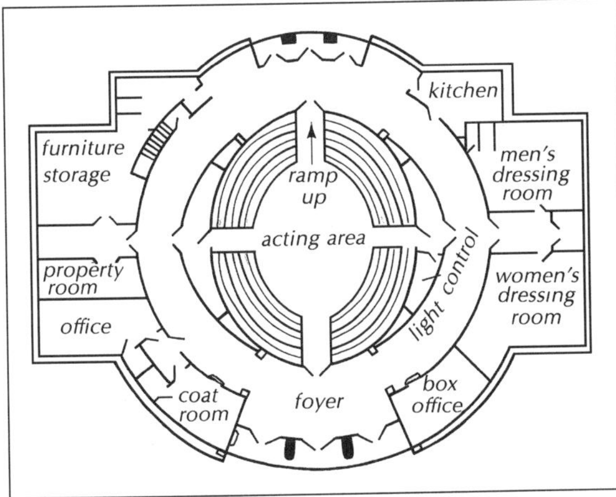

Thebes [thēbz], city of ancient S Egypt, on the NILE. In the XI dynasty (beginning c.2134 B.C.) it was a royal residence and a center of worship of the god AMON. Kings and nobles were buried in the Valley of the Tombs. Thebes declined with the empire: it was sacked by the Assyrians (661 B.C.). The surviving temples and tombs, including that of TUTANKHAMEN, are among the most splendid in the world.

Thebes, ancient city of BOEOTIA, Greece. At the end of the 6th cent. B.C. rivalry developed with ATHENS, and Thebes sided with Persia in the PERSIAN WARS. Later, Thebes joined the confederation against SPARTA in the PELOPONNESIAN WAR and ended Spartan domination with a decisive victory at Leuctra (371 B.C.). Thebes joined Athens against PHILIP II of Macedon, who defeated them at Chaeronea (338). A Theban revolt caused ALEXANDER THE GREAT to destroy the city (336). It was rebuilt by CASSANDER (c.315) but never regained its former greatness. The modern Thivai occupies the site of the Theban ACROPOLIS, part of which survives.

Themistocles [thəmĭs'təklēz], c.525–c.460 B.C., Athenian statesman. He was elected an archon (leader) in 493 B.C. In the PERSIAN WARS he persuaded the Athenians to build up their navy, and it was his strategy that brought about the decisive Athenian victory over the Persians at SALAMIS (480). He was exiled (c.471) and lived in Persia until his death.

Theocritus, fl. c.270 B.C., Hellenistic Greek poet. Inventor of the PASTORAL, he raised that form to its height. His style is finished and sometimes artificial, but the bucolic characters in his idylls seem alive. VERGIL, SPENSER, and others drew heavily on Theocritus.

theodolite, optical instrument used for a number of purposes in surveying, navigation, and meteorology. It consists of a telescope fitted with a spirit level and mounted on a tripod so that it is free to rotate about its vertical and horizontal axes. Theodolite measurements of the altitude and azimuth of a WEATHER BALLOON at precise intervals are used to compute the estimated wind velocity and direction of the portion of the atmosphere through which the balloon is passing.

Theodora, d. 548, Byzantine empress. She is alleged in the unreliable *Secret History* of PROCOPIUS to have been an actress and prostitute before her marriage (523) to JUSTINIAN I, who made her joint ruler. She helped to suppress the Nika rebellion caused by internal political strife, and she influenced Justinian's favorable policies toward MONOPHYSITISM.

Theodore Roosevelt National Park: see NATIONAL PARKS (table).

Theodoric the Great, c.454–526, king of the OSTROGOTHS and conqueror of Italy. Under Byzantine emperor ZENO he was made (484) consul and sent (488) to Italy to defeat ODOACER. He took RAVENNA in 493, and shortly after Odoacer's surrender Theodoric murdered him. His great power in Italy freed him of Byzantine supervision, and his long rule was beneficent. He respected Roman institutions and improved public works. The end of his reign was clouded by a quarrel with the pope over his ARIANISM and by his hasty execution of BOETHIUS. His tomb is one of Ravenna's finest monuments.

Theodosius, Byzantine rulers. **Theodosius I** (the Great), 346?–95, Roman emperor of the East (379–95) and emperor of the West (392–95), was the son of Theodosius, a general of Emperor Gratian, who chose him as joint ruler. He made an advantageous peace (381) with the marauding VISIGOTHS, securing Goths for his army. He overthrew the usurper Maximus, Gratian's assassin, and restored the legal successor, VALENTINIAN II. After Valentinian was killed (392) Theodosius defeated and killed (394) the usurper Arbogast and his puppet emperor, Eugenius. Baptized in 380, Theodosius rooted out ARIANISM and paganism, and called the First Council of CONSTANTINOPLE. To reverse his excommunication for massacring rebellious citizens, he did penance before AMBROSE, bishop of Milan. He divided the empire, leaving the East to his son ARCADIUS and the West to his son HONORIUS, thus making a permanent partition. **Theodosius II,** 401–50, Roman emperor of the East (408–50), was the son and successor of Arcadius. A scholar and theologian, Theodosius called the Council of Ephesus (431), which condemned NESTORIANISM, and he upheld the Robber Synod (449; see EUTYCHES). He founded (425) the Univ. of Constantinople and published (438) the Theodosian Code. During his reign ATTILA raided the empire.

Theognis, fl. 6th cent. B.C., Greek didactic poet. His passionate elegies to his young friend Cyrnus counsel moderation, faithfulness, and duty.

theology, in CHRISTIANITY, the systematic study of the nature of GOD and His relationship with humanity and with the world. (Asserting that other religions have theologies is controversial; e.g., within JUDAISM God is held to be unknowable.) The great theological problems of ancient times were the relation of JESUS to God and the relations of Jesus and God to humanity. The struggle over ARIANISM (on the nature of Jesus) is probably the most serious theological quarrel Christianity has known, and the problem of GRACE still arouses theologians. In the Middle Ages SCHOLASTICISM systematized study of revealed truths, examining and clarifying an entire theological scheme; while scholasticism attempted to combine faith and reason, it forbade rational investigation of the bases of revealed truth. In the 19th cent. a new rational theology associated with biblical "higher criticism" arose; it accepted the adequacy of reason to criticize every truth. Such 20th-cent. existentialist theologians as Paul TILLICH and Reinhold NIEBUHR stressed that people, however well endowed with reason, must ultimately rely on the goodness of God.

theorem, in mathematics and logic, statement in words or symbols that can be established by means of deductive logic; it differs from an AXIOM in that a proof is required for its acceptance. A *lemma* is a theorem that is demonstrated as an intermediate step in the proof of another, more basic theorem. A *corollary* is a theorem that follows as a direct consequence of another theorem or an axiom.

theosophy [Gr., = divine wisdom], philosophical system with affinities to MYSTICISM that claims insight into the nature of God and the world through direct knowledge, philosophical speculation, or a physical process. Theosophy deduces the essentially spiritual nature of the universe from an assumption of the absolute reality of the essence of God. Theosophists generally believe that evil exists as a product of finite human desires; individuals can overcome it by arousing their latent spiritual powers. Emphasis is given to allegorical interpretation of sacred writings and doctrines. The Renaissance philosopher PARACELSUS combined scientific ideas with theosophical speculation. More recent theosophists include Jakob BOEHME, F.W.J. SCHELLING, and Emanuel SWEDENBORG. Asian philosophy and theology, especially of India, contain a vast body of theosophical doctrine, and modern theosophy draws much of its vocabulary from Indian sources. The Theosophical Society, with which theosophy is now generally identified, was founded in 1875 by Helena Petrovna Blavatsky. See also CABALA; GNOSTICISM; NEOPLATONISM.

Theotocopoulos, Domenicos: see GRECO, EL.

Thera or **Santorini,** volcanic island (1981 pop. 11,381), c.30 sq mi (80 sq km), SE Greece, in the Aegean Sea; one of the Cyclades. It is noted for its wine. In the Bronze Age Thera came under the influence of Crete (see MINOAN CIVILIZATION), but a devastating volcanic eruption (c.1645 B.C.) buried the island's settlements and threw massive amounts of dust into the earth's atmosphere, affecting the weather worldwide. It was resettled and later occupied (9th cent. B.C.) by the DORIANS. Excavations at a Minoan site have uncovered many well-preserved frescoes. Some controversial theories have equated ancient Thera with ATLANTIS.

Theresa or **Teresa, Saint** (Theresa of Ávila), 1515–82, Spanish CARMELITE nun, Doctor of the Church, one of the great mystics, and a leading figure in the Catholic Reformation (see REFORMATION, CATHOLIC). In 1562 she founded, at Ávila, the first of many convents of the Discalced Carmelites. St. Theresa combined intense practicality with the most rarefied spirituality. An excellent and tireless manager, she was endowed with great personal charm, tact, and boundless good nature. With her associate, St. JOHN OF THE CROSS, she produced a remarkable awakening of religious fervor that spread far beyond Spain. Her writings, notably her *Life* and the *Way of Perfection,* are among the greatest in mystical literature. Feast: Oct. 15.

Theresa or **Teresa, Saint** (Theresa of Lisieux), 1873–97, French CARMELITE nun, one of the most widely loved saints of the Roman Catholic Church, also known as the Little Flower of Jesus. Born Thérèse Martin, she entered an obscure convent at Lisieux at age 15 and died of tuberculosis nine years later. She exemplified the "little way"—achieving goodness by performing the humblest tasks. Her spiritual autobiography is one of the most widely read religious autobiographies. She was canonized in 1925. Feast: Oct. 1.

thermal capacity: see HEAT CAPACITY.

thermochemistry: see CHEMISTRY.

thermocouple, a temperature-measuring device formed by joining the ends of two strips of dissimilar metals in a closed loop, with the two junctions at different temperatures. Because the voltage that arises in this circuit is proportional to the temperature difference between the junctions, the temperature at one junction can be determined if the other junction is maintained at a known temperature.

thermodynamics, branch of science concerned with the nature of HEAT and its conversion into other forms of ENERGY. Heat is a form of energy associated with the positions and motion of the molecules of a body (see KINETIC-MOLECULAR THEORY OF GASES). The total energy that a body contains as a result of the positions and the motions of its molecules is called its internal energy. The first law of thermodynamics states that in any process the change in a system's internal energy is equal to the heat absorbed from the environment minus the WORK done on the environment. This law is a general form of the law of conservation of energy (see CONSERVATION LAWS). The second law of thermodynamics states that in a system the ENTROPY cannot decrease for any spontaneous process. A consequence of this law is that an engine can deliver work only when heat is transferred from a hot reservoir to a cold reservoir or heat sink. The third law of thermodynamics states that all bodies at absolute zero would have the same entropy; this state is defined as having zero entropy.

thermometer, instrument for measuring TEMPERATURE. A clinical thermometer consists of a small vacuum tube of uniform bore, with a temperature scale etched on its front. The tube is closed at one end and connected at the other with a chamber containing mercury or another liquid. When the chamber is heated, the fluid expands and rises into the tube.

thermonuclear energy: see NUCLEAR ENERGY.

thermoplastic, a material that repeatedly softens or melts when heated and hardens when cooled. Thermoplastic polymers consist of long polymer chains that are not connected to each other, e.g., not cross-linked. Thermoplastics include polyethylene, polypropylene, polystyrene, polyester, polyvinyl chloride, acrylics, nylons, spandex-type polyurethanes, polyamides, polycarbonates, fluorocarbons, and cellulosics.

Thermopylae, pass, E central Greece, between the cliffs of Mt. Oeta and the Malic Gulf. In ancient times it was an entrance into Greece from the north. There, in 480 B.C. the Spartans lost an heroic battle against the Persians.

thermoset, a material that can not be softened on heating. In a thermosetting polymer, the long polymer chains are joined to each other, e.g., cross-linked, during fabrication through the use of chemicals, heat, or radiation; this process is called curing or vulcanization. Important thermosets include alkyds, phenolics, ureas, melamines, epoxies, polyesters, silicones, rubbers, and polyurethanes.

Theseus, in Greek mythology, Athenian hero; son of King Aegeus. Of his many adventures the most famous was the slaying of the MINOTAUR, which he accomplished with the help of ARIADNE, daughter of King MINOS of Crete. As king of Athens he instituted several reforms, notably the federalization of the Attic communities. In the land of the AMAZONS he abducted Antiope, who bore him Hippolytus. When a vengeful Amazon army invaded Athens Theseus defeated it. Antiope was killed, and Theseus later married PHAEDRA. When he and his friend Pirithoüs attempted to take PERSEPHONE from HADES, they were imprisoned there until HERCULES rescued Theseus. When Theseus returned to Athens he found it corrupt and rebellious. He sailed to Skyros, where he was murdered by King Lycomedes.

Thespis, fl. 534 B.C., Attic Greek dramatist, traditionally the inventor of TRAGEDY. He is said to have modified the DITHYRAMB by introducing an actor separate from the chorus, enabling spoken dialogue to develop.

Thessalonians, two epistles of the NEW TESTAMENT, 13th and 14th books in the usual order, by St. PAUL (A.D. c.52). First Thessalonians, after a reminiscence of the founding of the Christian church at THESSALONIKI, gives advice on moral behavior and corrects a doctrinal point regarding the general resurrection. Second Thessalonians, a shorter letter, strongly condemns notions that the Second Coming is at hand.

Thessaloníki or **Salonica,** city (1981 pop. 402,443), N Greece, in Macedonia. It is a major port and industrial center, exporting grain, tobacco, and ores. Founded in 315 B.C. by Cassander, king of Macedon, it linked BYZANTIUM with the Adriatic region in Roman times and was the Roman provincial capital of Macedon after 146

B.C. The kingdom of Thessaloníki (1204), comprising most of N and central Greece, was the largest fief of the Latin Empire of CONSTANTINOPLE. It was variously held by the Greeks, Byzantines, and Ottoman Turks before being conquered (1912) by Greece in the BALKAN WARS. Although the city was devastated by a fire in 1917 and damaged severely in World War II, it retains many ancient ruins and fine churches.

Thessaly [thĕs'əlē], ancient region of N Greece. It was settled before 1000 B.C. Its chief cities were Larissa, Crannon, and Pherae. It was powerful in the 6th cent. B.C., but internal conflicts caused its decline. United briefly (374) by Jason, the tyrant of Pherae, it again became a force in Greece, but it was subjugated (344) by PHILIP II of Macedon. A province in the late Roman Empire, it passed to the Turks (1355) and then to modern Greece (1881).

Thetis, in Greek mythology, a nymph; mother of ACHILLES.

thiamine: see COENZYME; VITAMIN (table).

Thiers, Adolphe [tyĕr], 1797–1877, French statesman and historian. As a journalist, Thiers attacked the reactionary government of CHARLES X and helped bring about the JULY REVOLUTION of 1830. He held ministerial posts under LOUIS PHILIPPE and was premier (1836, 1840, 1848). After the FEBRUARY REVOLUTION of 1848, he opposed the Second Empire of NAPOLEON III. Thiers headed the provisional government after France's defeat in the FRANCO-PRUSSIAN WAR, crushed the COMMUNE OF PARIS, and was president (1871–73) of the republic. His historical works on the French Revolution and Napoleon are today considered superficial and inaccurate.

Thieu, Nguyen Van [tē'o͞o, tyo͞o], 1923–, president (1967–75) of South VIETNAM. In 1963 he helped lead the coup that overthrew Pres. DIEM. He was elected president in 1967 and continually opposed negotiations with North Vietnam to end the VIETNAM WAR. When South Vietnam fell to the Communists (1975) Thieu fled into exile.

Thimphu or **Thimbu,** city (1990 est. pop. 27,000), capital of BHUTAN.

Third World, name applied to the technologically less-advanced, or developing, nations of Asia, Africa, and Latin America. The term was originally used to distinguish these countries from the Western nations and those that formed the Eastern bloc and usually excludes China.

Thirteen Colonies, in U.S. history, the British North American colonies that joined together in the AMERICAN REVOLUTION and became the original states of the U.S. They were: NEW HAMPSHIRE, MASSACHUSETTS, RHODE ISLAND, CONNECTICUT, NEW YORK, NEW JERSEY, PENNSYLVANIA, DELAWARE, MARYLAND, VIRGINIA, NORTH CAROLINA, SOUTH CAROLINA, and GEORGIA.

Thirty Tyrants, 404–403 B.C., oligarchy installed in ancient Athens by the Spartan commander LYSANDER after Sparta had won the PELOPONNESIAN WAR. It was overthrown at Piraeus by THRASYBULUS.

Thirty Years War, 1618–48, general European war, fought mainly in Germany. Although the war had many issues, it may be considered mainly a struggle of German Protestant princes and foreign powers (France, Sweden, Denmark, England, the United Provinces) against the unity and power of the HOLY ROMAN EMPIRE (represented by the HAPSBURGS) allied with the Catholic princes of Germany. The Hapsburg empire then included Austria, Spain, Bohemia, most of Italy, and the S Netherlands. The war began in Prague, when the Protestant Bohemian nobles deposed the Catholic King Ferdinand (later Emperor FERDINAND II) and elected the Protestant FREDERICK THE WINTER KING. The imperialist forces under TILLY and the Catholic League under Duke Maximilian I of Bavaria quickly defeated the Bohemians (1620) and other Protestant forces in the PALATINATE (1622–23). Thus ended the war's first phase. The second phase began in 1625 when CHRISTIAN IV of Denmark invaded Germany on the side of the Protestant princes, although his chief purpose was to halt Hapsburg expansion into N Germany. Defeats by WALLENSTEIN in 1626 and Tilly in 1627 forced him to withdraw. Imperialist forces promptly overran Schleswig, Holstein, and Jutland. In 1629 Christian signed a peace with the emperor, surrendering the N German bishoprics. That and the emperor's attempt to declare void Protestant titles to lands in N Germany represented a further threat to the Protestant forces. GUSTAVUS II of Sweden now entered the war. Like Christian of Denmark, he feared imperial designs in the north. He invaded Germany and enjoyed successes at Breitenfeld (1631) and Lech (1632). Gustavus was killed at Lützen (1632), although his troops were victorious. The anti-imperialist forces, including the Swedes, continued to fight. By 1634, however, Germany was in ruin, her fields devastated and blood-soaked. A general desire for peace led to the Peace of Prague (1635). It was accepted by all participants and helped to reconcile Protestants and Catholics. A general peace seemed to be forthcoming, but Cardinal RICHELIEU of France was unwilling to see the Hapsburgs retain power. He brought France openly into the war in 1635, beginning the last and bloodiest phase of the struggle. It then spread to the Low Countries, Italy, Scandinavia, and the Iberian Peninsula. The anti-imperialist commanders—Bernard of Saxe-Weimar; the Swedes Baner, Wrangel, and TORSTENSSON; and Louis II de CONDÉ and Turenne of France—were victorious. Peace talks began in 1640 but proceeded slowly, not being completed until 1648 (see WESTPHALIA, PEACE OF). The war had been devastating to the German people, and German agriculture, commerce, and industry were in ruins. Politically, the Holy Roman Empire was left a mere shell, and Hapsburg power had begun its long decline. France emerged as the chief power of Europe.

thistle, spiny, usually weedy plant, most commonly members of the COMPOSITE family that have spiny leaves and often showy heads of purple, rose, white, or yellow flowers. The Scotch thistle (usually identified as *Onopordum acanthium*), cultivated as an ornamental, is the national emblem of Scotland. The Russian thistle is a TUMBLEWEED.

Thomas, Saint, one of the Twelve APOSTLES, called Didymus. He refused to believe in the Resurrection until he saw Jesus' wounds; hence the expression "doubting Thomas."

Thomas, Clarence: see SUPREME COURT, UNITED STATES (table 1).

Thomas, Dylan, 1914–53, Welsh poet. His *Eighteen Poems* (1934) brought fame and controversy, which grew with *The Map of Love* (1939), *The World I Breathe* (1939), *Deaths and Entrances* (1946), and *In Country Sleep and Other Poems* (1952). His largely autobiographical prose, touched with fantasy, includes *Portrait of the Artist as a Young Dog* (1940), *Adventures in the Skin Trade* (1955), and *Quite Early One Morning* (1955). Thomas's mastery of sound, perhaps related to his fine voice, is evident in his radio piece *A Child's Christmas in Wales* (published 1954) and the drama *Under Milk Wood* (1954). His imagery is complex and difficult, but his humor and love of life attract immediately.

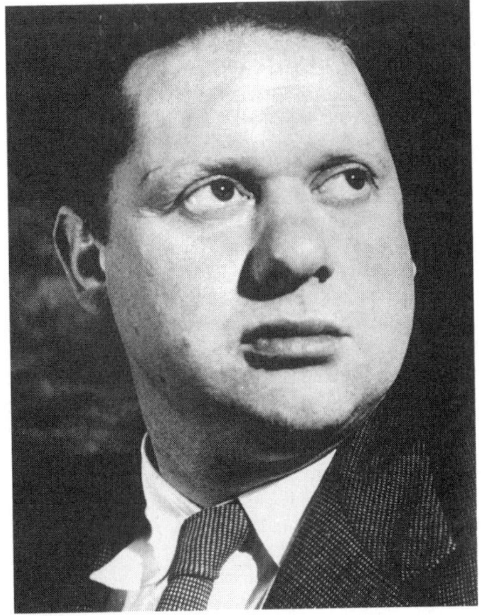

Dylan Thomas

Thomas, George Henry, 1816–70, Union general in the American CIVIL WAR; b. Southampton co., Va. He fought at the battle of SHILOH, and after his success in the CHATTANOOGA CAMPAIGN became known as the "Rock of Chickamauga." In 1864 he defeated Gen. HOOD in the battle of NASHVILLE.

Thomas, Martha Carey, 1857–1935, American educator and feminist; b. Baltimore. Appointed (1884) to organize Bryn Mawr College for women, she was dean and taught English until 1894, then was president until 1922. A leader of the WOMAN SUFFRAGE movement, she wrote *The Higher Education of Women* (1900).

Thomas, Norman Mattoon, 1884–1968, American socialist leader; b. Marion, Ohio. Originally a Presbyterian minister, Thomas became leader of the Socialist party in 1926 and was repeatedly (1928, 1932, 1936, 1940, 1944, and 1948) its candidate for the presidency.

Thomas à Becket, Saint, or **Saint Thomas Becket,** 1118–70, English martyr, archbishop of Canterbury. Of good family and well educated, he attracted the attention of HENRY II, who made him chancellor (1155). Then, in an attempt to curb the growing power of the church, the king nominated his friend as archbishop of Canterbury. Foreseeing trouble, Thomas was reluctant to accept, but in 1163 he was ordained priest and consecrated archbishop. Henry and Thomas were soon opposed, particularly over the king's efforts to gain jurisdiction over "criminous clerks," clergymen accused of crime. Thomas, refusing to accept the Constitutions of CLARENDON and opposing the growing royal power, fled to the Continent (1164). In 1170 a kind of peace was arranged, and Thomas returned to England. Meanwhile, Henry had his son crowned by the archbishop of York; the bishops who took part in this ceremony were suspended by the pope. Antipathy between the king and archbishop grew strong, and in December 1170 the king issued his fateful plea to be rid of the archbishop. On Dec. 29, 1170, Thomas was murdered in Canterbury cathedral by Henry's partisans. The Christian world was shocked by Thomas's death, and in 1174 the king was forced to do penance at the saint's tomb in Canterbury, which became the greatest of English shrines. Feast: Dec. 29.

Thomas à Kempis, b. 1379 or 1380, d. 1471, German monk. In the Netherlands, he became (c.1413) an Augustinian priest. The great devotional work *The Imitation of Christ* has been traditionally ascribed to him, although some scholars doubt his authorship.

Thomas Aquinas, Saint, 1225–74, Italian philosopher and theologian, Doctor of the Church; known as the Angelic Doctor. He is the greatest figure of SCHOLASTICISM, one of the principal saints of the Roman Catholic Church, and the founder of the system declared (1879) by Pope Leo XIII the official Catholic philosophy. His major work, the monumental *Summa Theologica* (1267–73), is a systematic exposition of Christian theology on philosophical principles. His shorter treatise, *On Being and Essence* (1256), contains his metaphysics. St. Thomas's system embraces the moderate REALISM of Aristotle and is in opposition to the Platonism and Neoplatonism that had prevailed in Catholic theology since the time of St. AUGUSTINE. Unlike the Platonists, to whom truth was a matter of faith, St. Thomas held that faith and reason constitute two harmonious realms; theology and science cannot contradict each other. Likewise, there can be no conflict between philosophy and theology. In his universe, everything is arranged in ascending order to God, the only necessary, self-sufficient being. St. Thomas succeeded in synthesizing the naturalistic philosophy of Aristotle and Christian belief, perhaps the greatest achievement of medieval philosophy. Feast: Mar. 7.

Thompson, Benjamin: see RUMFORD, BENJAMIN THOMPSON, COUNT.

Thompson, Ernest Seton: see SETON, ERNEST THOMPSON.

Thomson, James, 1700–1748, Scottish poet. His most famous poem, *The Seasons* (1726–30), contains descriptions of nature that challenged the urban, artificial school of POPE and influenced forerunners of ROMANTICISM like Thomas GRAY.

Thomson, Sir Joseph John, 1856–1940, English physicist. Cavendish professor of experimental physics (1884–1919) at Cambridge, he won the 1906 Nobel Prize in physics for his study of the conduction of electricity through gases. Thomson discovered (1897) the ELECTRON and studied its charge and mass. He developed the mathematical theory of heat and electricity and worked with "positive rays" (positive ion beams), which led to a means of separating atoms and molecules according to their atomic weights. His long tenure as director of the Cavendish Laboratory at Cambridge helped make it a leading center for atomic research.

Thomson, Virgil, 1896–1989, American composer and music critic; b. Kansas City, Mo. Until c.1926 he wrote in a dissonant, neoclassic style; later he used a simplified style influenced by SATIE. His works include the operas *Four Saints in Three Acts* (1928) and *The Mother of Us All* (1947), with librettos by Gertrude STEIN; music for films, e.g., *The River* (1937); a CANTATA on the poems of Edward LEAR (1973); and many organ, piano, and chamber works.

Thomson, William: see KELVIN, WILLIAM THOMSON, 1ST BARON.

Thon Buri: see under BANGKOK, Thailand.

Thor, Germanic **Donar,** Norse god of thunder, might, and war; also associated with marriage, the hearth, and agriculture. He was armed with a magical hammer that returned to him, iron gloves, and a belt of strength. He was identified with the Roman JUPITER, whose day became Thor's day (Thursday).

Thoreau, Henry David, 1817–62, one of the most influential figures in American thought and literature; b. Concord, Mass. An advocate of TRANSCENDENTALISM, he was a close friend of EMERSON, with whom he edited the transcendentalist magazine *The Dial.* Thoreau built a cabin at Walden Pond, near Concord, in 1845 and remained there for more than two years. There he lived out his philosophy of individualism, observing nature, reading, and expanding on his ideas and activities in a journal that he later distilled into his most famous work, *Walden* (1854). The journal was also the source of his first book, *A Week on the Concord and Merrimack Rivers* (1849), as well as of several posthumously published works, e.g., *Excursions* (1863), *Cape Cod* (1865). Thoreau was also a significant naturalist and a powerful social critic. His essay "Civil Disobedience" (1849) has had far-reaching influence on various movements and on such leaders as GANDHI and Martin Luther KING.

Thorfinn Karlsefni, fl. 1002–15, Icelandic leader of an attempt to settle NORTH AMERICA. According to Norse SAGAS, he set out c.1010 to settle in Vinland, a section of North America discovered by LEIF ERICSSON. Thorfinn returned to GREENLAND after three years. There is much disagreement on the dates of his expedition and the sites visited.

thorium (Th), radioactive element, discovered in 1828 by Jöns Jakob BERZELIUS. A soft, ductile, lustrous, silver-white metal in the ACTINIDE SERIES, it has 12 known isotopes. It is important for its potential conversion into the fissionable fuel uranium-233 for use in NUCLEAR REACTORS. See ELEMENT (table); PERIODIC TABLE.

Thorndike, Edward Lee, 1874–1949, American educator and psychologist; b. Williamsburg, Mass. His great contributions to educational psychology were the tests he devised to measure children's INTELLIGENCE and ability to learn. He also compiled dictionaries for children and young adults. His influential works include *Animal Intelligence* (1898–1901), *Mental and Social Measurements* (1904), and *The Fundamentals of Learning* (1932).

Thornton, William, 1759–1828, American architect; b. Tortola, British Virgin Islands. His plans for the CAPITOL at Washington, D.C., were approved (1793) by Pres. WASHINGTON, and he supervised the project (1794–1802). Despite later alterations, much of the facade and central portion remain his design.

Thorpe, Jim (James Thorpe), 1888–1953, American athlete; b. near Prague, Okla. He was one of the greatest all-around male athletes the U.S. has ever produced. Part Native American, he played football at the Carlisle (Pa.) Indian School and led (1911–12) his team to upsets over several highly rated colleges. In the 1912 Olympics he won events in the PENTATHLON and DECATHLON. He surrendered his medals after it was revealed that he had played semiprofessional baseball, but they were restored posthumously in 1982. He later played professional football with the Canton (Ohio) Bulldogs.

Thorvaldsen or **Thorwaldsen, Albert Bertel** [both: tôr′ välsən], 1770–1844, Danish sculptor. He was a leader of the neoclassicists, and his adherence to Greek art is seen in his *Jason* (1802–3), rendered with respect for antique prototypes. He designed (1819) the famous *Lion of Lucerne*, a memorial to the SWISS GUARD, and his historical portrait sculptures include *Conradin, Last of the Hohenstaufen* (Naples). The Thorvaldsen Museum, Copenhagen, has a large collection of his work.

Thothmes I: see THUTMOSE I.

Thousand and One Nights or **Arabian Nights,** a series of anonymous stories in Arabic, a classic of world literature. The cohesive plot device concerns the efforts of Scheherazade, or Sheherazade, to keep her husband, Schariar, legendary king of Samarkand, from killing her by entertaining him with a tale a night for 1,001 nights. The best-known stories are those of Ali Baba, Sinbad, and Aladdin. Many are set in India, but their individual origins are unknown. The present form of the collection is Muslim in spirit and is thought to be from Persia or an Arabic-speaking country.

Thousand Islands, group of islands, N New York and S Ontario, in the St. Lawrence R., E of Lake Ontario. Extending c.50 mi (80 km), they are a popular resort area. The five-span Thousand Islands Bridge (7 mi/11 km long) crosses several of the more than 1,800 islands in the group, many of which are privately owned.

Thousand Oaks, residential city (1990 pop. 104,352), Ventura co., S Calif.; inc. 1964. The rapidly growing city has light industry and manufacturing. Once known as the Conejo Valley, it became a stagecoach stop in 1874. California Lutheran College is there, and Oxnard Air Force Base is nearby.

Thrace, region of SE Europe comprising NE Greece, S Bulgaria, and European Turkey, bordered by the Black Sea in the northeast, and the Sea of Marmara and the Aegean Sea in the south. Its major cities are ISTANBUL, Edirne, and Plovdiv. Mainly an agricultural region, it produces grains, tobacco, silk, cotton, and olive oil. The ancient Thracians had a developed culture in the BRONZE AGE but were considered barbarians by the Greeks, who established colonies there by 600 B.C. to exploit the gold and silver mines. The region benefited from Roman rule (1st cent. B.C.), but from the 3rd cent. A.D. it was a battleground for competing empires, e.g., Byzantine, Bulgarian, Ottoman. The present national boundaries were established in 1923.

Thrasybulus [thrăs"əbyōō'ləs], d. c.389 B.C., Athenian statesman. Banished by the THIRTY TYRANTS installed in Athens by Sparta after the Peloponnesian War, he gathered a force of exiles in Thebes and overthrew (403) the Tyrants.

Three Emperors' League, informal alliance formed in 1872 by the emperors of Austria-Hungary, Germany, and Russia. Its aims were to preserve the social order of the conservative powers of Europe and to keep the peace between Austria-Hungary and Russia, which were traditional rivals. The league was eventually superseded by the TRIPLE ALLIANCE AND TRIPLE ENTENTE.

Three Kings: see WISE MEN OF THE EAST.

Three Mile Island, site of a nuclear power plant 10 mi (16 km) south of Harrisburg, Pa. On Mar. 28, 1979, failure of the cooling system of the No. 2 NUCLEAR REACTOR led to overheating and partial melting of its uranium core and production of hydrogen gas, which raised fears of an explosion and dispersal of radioactivity. Thousands living near the plant left the area before the 12-day crisis ended, during which time some radioactive water and gases were released. A federal investigation, assigning blame to human, mechanical, and design errors, recommended changes in reactor licensing and personnel training, as well as in the structure and function of the NUCLEAR REGULATORY COMMISSION. The accident also increased public concern over the dangers of nuclear power and slowed construction of other reactors. See also NUCLEAR ENERGY.

thrombolytic drug or **clot-dissolving drug,** substance, such as streptokinase or tissue plasminogen activator (tPA), that causes the breakdown of blood clots that obstruct the flow of blood through the vessels. Its uses include injection during or shortly after a heart attack to prevent clots from blocking blood flow to the heart muscle.

thrombosis, obstruction of an artery or vein by a blood clot, or thrombus. An arterial thrombosis is generally more serious, usually blocking the supply of oxygen and nutrients to some area of the body; a thrombus in one of the arteries leading to the heart (causing a heart attack) or to the brain (causing a STROKE) can result in death. A thrombus in the vein is known as phlebothrombosis or thrombophlebitis (see PHLEBITIS). Thrombosis is treated with ANTICOAGULANTS and THROMBOLYTIC DRUGS.

thrush, BIRD of the family Trudidae, found worldwide and noted for its beautiful song. Most thrushes are modestly colored, with spotted underparts; some have bright plumage, e.g., the red-breasted American ROBIN (*Trudus migratorius*), and the Eastern BLUEBIRD, bright blue with a red breast. Other thrushes are the hermit thrush, NIGHTINGALE, European "blackbird," and wheatear.

Thucydides [thōōsĭd'ĭdēz], c.460–c.400 B.C., Greek historian of Athens, one of the greatest of ancient historians. His one work, a history of the PELOPONNESIAN WAR to 411 B.C., is a military record, devoid of social and political references apart from those pertaining to the war. It is marked by accuracy and a studied impartiality and is noted for its eloquent speeches, particularly the funeral oration of PERICLES.

Thugs, Indian religious sect of murderers and thieves that existed from the 13th cent. to the 19th cent., when the British finally suppressed it. Members of the sect worshiped the goddess Kali and committed their murders in sacrifice to her. They were also known as the Phansigars [stranglers] because they strangled their victims, usually wealthy travelers.

Thule, name the ancients gave to the northernmost land of Europe, an island found c.310 B.C. by the Greek Pytheas and since then identified with various northern lands. "Ultima Thule" figuratively means the farthest goal of human effort.

thulium (Tm), metallic element, discovered in 1879 by P.T. Cleve. A soft, malleable, ductile, lustrous silver-white RARE-EARTH METAL in the LANTHANIDE SERIES, it forms compounds with oxygen and the halogens, most of which are light green. Thulium-170 emits X rays and is used in portable X-ray units. See ELEMENT (table); PERIODIC TABLE.

thunder, sound produced when a flash of LIGHTNING passes through air, heating the adjacent air and causing it to expand rapidly. A short flash of lightning creates a relatively short crash of thunder. Rolling thunder occurs either when there is a long flash of lightning, generating thunder over a great distance, or when obstructions such as clouds, mountains, or differing layers of air cause echoes and reverberations. See also THUNDERSTORM.

Thunder Bay, city (1991 pop. 113,946), W Ontario, on the Thunder Bay Inlet of Lake SUPERIOR. It is Canada's principal lakehead port on the GREAT LAKES and handles much of the grain shipped from Canada's prairie provinces. Other industries include oil refining and the manufacture of steel, chemicals, and transportation equipment. Thunder Bay, formed in 1970 by the amalgamation of the former twin cities of Fort William and Port Arthur, is at the former site of a 17th-cent. fur-trading post and of a fort built (1801) by the NORTH WEST COMPANY as its western headquarters.

thunderstorm, violent local atmospheric disturbance accompanied by LIGHTNING, THUNDER, and heavy RAIN, often by strong gusts of WIND, and sometimes by HAIL. The typical thunderstorm caused by convection occurs on a hot summer afternoon when the sun's warmth has heated a large body of moist air near the ground. This air rises and is cooled by expansion. The cooling condenses the water vapor in the air, forming a cumulus CLOUD. If the process continues violently, the cloud becomes immense; the summit often attains a height of 4 mi (6.5 km) above the base, and the top spreads out in the shape of an anvil as the transition to a cumulonimbus cloud occurs. The turbulent air currents within the cloud cause a continual breaking up and reuniting of the raindrops, building up strong electrical charges that result in lightning.

Thurber, James, 1894–1961, American humorist; b. Columbus, Ohio. He was a staff member (1927–33) of and principal contributor to the *New Yorker* magazine. A deep psychological insight underlies his wistful, ironic cartoons and stories. Collections of his works include *The Owl in the Attic* (1931), *The Thurber Carnival* (1945), and *Thurber Country* (1953). He collaborated with E.B. WHITE on the satire *Is Sex Necessary?* (1929) and with Elliott Nugent on the play *The Male Animal* (1940).

Thuringia [thōōrĭn'je], Ger. *Thüringen,* state (1990 est. pop. 2,684,000), c.6,000 sq mi (15,540 sq km), central Germany. WEIMAR is the capital. The area's first occupants, the ancient Germanic tribe of Thuringians, fell to the Franks in the 6th cent. A.D. and were converted to Christianity in the 8th cent. By the 11th cent. Thuringia's rulers, dominated after 1247 by the WETTIN dynasty of Saxony, had emerged as princes of the Holy Roman Empire. The division of the Wettin lands in 1485 gave the major share to the Ernestines, who split Thuringia into several duchies (e.g., Saxe-Coburg, Saxe-Gotha, Saxe-Weimar). A center of the Lutheran Reformation (16th cent.), Thuringia joined the German Confederation (1815) and the German Empire (1871). After expulsion of their rulers in 1918, the duchies merged under the Weimar Republic as the state of Thuringia. The state was reconstituted as part of East

Germany in 1946, abolished in 1952, and reconstituted again in 1990 upon German reunification.

Thursday: see WEEK.

Thutmose [thŭt'mōz, tŭt–] or **Thothmes** [thŏth'mēz, tōt'mĕs], kings of EGYPT. **Thutmose I,** d. 1495 B.C. (r. c.1525–1495 B.C.), was the third ruler of the XVIII dynasty and the successor of AMENHOTEP I. He conquered the NILE up to the Third Cataract, and reached the EUPHRATES through Syria. His son **Thutmose II** (r. c.1495–1490 B.C.) married his half-sister, Hatshepsut, who took over the real power of government. After his death she became regent for Thutmose III, his son by a minor queen, and ruled for 22 years. At her death (1468) **Thutmose III,** d. 1436 B.C., emerged as sole ruler of Egypt and as a great conqueror. He consolidated SYRIA, except PHOENICIA, and reduced every ruler N of the Euphrates to tributary status. His empire (the zenith of the New Empire) enriched Egypt with wealth and with manpower. He also built temples up and down the Nile.

Thyestes: see ATREUS.

thyme, aromatic, shrubby plant (genus *Thymus*) of the MINT family. Common thyme, used as a seasoning, is the Old World *T. vulgaris,* an erect plant with grayish branches. It is cultivated mainly in Spain and France.

thymus gland, mass of glandular tissue located in the neck or chest of most vertebrates (see ENDOCRINE SYSTEM). Found in the upper chest under the breastbone in humans, the thymus is essential to the development of the body's system of IMMUNITY beginning in fetal life. The thymus processes white blood cells known as lymphocytes (see BLOOD), which kill foreign cells and stimulate other immune cells to produce antibodies. The gland grows throughout childhood until puberty and then gradually decreases in size.

thyroid gland, endocrine gland (see ENDOCRINE SYSTEM), situated in the neck, that regulates the body's metabolic rate (see METABOLISM). It consists of two lobes connected by a narrow isthmus. Thyroid tissue is made up of millions of tiny, saclike follicles that store thyroid hormone in the form of thyroglobulin, a protein containing iodine. When secreted into the bloodstream, thyroglobulin is converted to thyroxine and small amounts of other similar hormones. Sufficient dietary iodine and stimulation by the PITUITARY GLAND are necessary for proper thyroxine production. Metabolic disorders result from oversecretion or undersecretion of the thyroid.

thyristor, semiconductor switch used chiefly in power-control applications. Also called a silicon-controlled rectifier (SCR), it is a variation of the TRANSISTOR. A thyristor is capable of producing large direct currents by rectification of alternating currents and can be automatically triggered "off" for specified periods of time. Thyristors are used in variable-speed electric motors, power supplies for electrochemical processes, lighting and heating control, and controllers for electric utility power systems.

Ti, chemical symbol of the element TITANIUM.

Tiahuanaco, ancient ruin in W Bolivia, near Lake TITICACA. Perhaps the work of the AYMARA, it was probably the center of a pre-Incan empire. Building, never completed, began before A.D. 500. Stone blocks weighing up to 100 tons were brought from several miles off, fitted, notched, and dressed with a precision unequaled even by the INCA. Tiahuanaco painted pottery is one of the great achievements of PRE-COLUMBIAN ART.

Tianjin or **Tientsin,** city (1990 est. pop. 5,770,000), NE China, on the Hai R. Located in E central Hebei prov., it is administered directly by the central government. Tianjin is one of China's largest cities, a leading international port, and a transport center for N China. It is an important manufacturing center specializing in steel, machinery, chemicals, textiles, and food processing. A 19th-cent. treaty port, it was occupied by Western powers during the BOXER UPRISING (1900) and was the site of foreign concessions until 1946.

Tiberius (Tiberius Julius Caesar Augustus), 42 B.C.–A.D. 37, Roman emperor (A.D. 14–37); son of Tiberius Claudius Nero and Livia Drusilla, later wife of AUGUSTUS. He was governor of Transalpine Gaul and campaigned in Germany and Illyricum. In A.D. 14 he succeeded Augustus as emperor and continued his policies, except that he cut luxury expenses. By doing so and by reforming taxes, he improved the government's financial state but made himself extremely unpopular. In later years he grew suspicious and ruled from Capri.

Tibet, Mandarin *Xizang,* autonomous region (1990 pop. 2,196,000), c.471,700 sq mi (1,221,700 sq km), SW China, bordered by Myanmar (SE); India, Bhutan, and Nepal (S); India and Kashmir (W); and Chinese provinces (N, E). Major cities are LHASA (the capital), Xigazê, and Gyangzê. Tibet is largely a high arid plateau surrounded by mountain ranges, including the HIMALAYAS in the south and the Kunlun in the north. The CHANG (Yangtze), MEKONG, and BRAHMAPUTRA rivers rise in Tibet. The economy is predominantly pastoral, based on raising livestock, particularly yaks; the leading crop is barley. The inhabitants are of Mongolic stock and speak a Tibeto-Burman language. They follow a form of Buddhism known as Lamaism (see TIBETAN BUDDHISM), the chief figures of which are the DALAI LAMA and the Panchen Lama; until the Chinese suppressed the monasteries in the 1960s, as much as one sixth of the male population were Lamaist monks.

History. An independent kingdom flourished in Tibet by the 7th cent. A.D. It was under Mongol influence from the 13th to the 18th cent., when it came under nominal Chinese control. With the overthrow of the Ch'ing dynasty in China in 1911, Tibet reasserted its independence, which it maintained until 1950. In that year China invaded; Tibet was made an autonomous region of China in 1951. An anti-Chinese uprising in 1959 was crushed and repressive measures introduced. The Dalai Lama and many priests fled to India; but by the 1980s some Buddhist temples had resumed operation. In the late 1980s there were violent anti-Chinese demonstrations in Tibet, and martial law was imposed (1989). Despite government repression, demonstrations against Chinese rule have continued.

Tibetan art and architecture have been almost entirely religious in character (see TIBETAN BUDDHISM). The art of Tibetan Lamaism retains strong elements drawn from HINDUISM and BUDDHISM in India, and was later influenced by the arts of Nepal and China. In architecture, the chorten, or Tibetan STUPA, was derived from Indian prototypes. Tibet is famed for its gigantic monastery-cities housing thousands of monks, such as the one in Zhaxilhünbo (15th cent.). The 17th-cent. monastery at Lhasa has a series of monastic skyscrapers that echo the forms of surrounding mountain peaks. Tibetan sculpture, often gilt bronze statuettes, consists of slim, elegant figures with heart-shaped heads, resembling the Indian Pala or Nepalese figures and frequently ornamented with elaborate jewels. Tibetan paintings appear most frequently in the form of tankas or temple banners, usually in brilliant colors on cotton or silk. The central figures of tankas may follow Nepalese or Indian types, but their decorative details are often Chinese. It is difficult to date these paintings, since the text, canons of proportion, and technical rules for making them have been almost unvaried for centuries. Although the symbolism is highly complex, there are representations of the BUDDHA in his myriad aspects.

Tibetan Buddhism, religion derived from the Indian Mahayana form of BUDDHISM and prevailing in Tibet, Bhutan, Sikkim, Mongolia, and parts of Siberia and SW China. Much of its ritual is based on TANTRA and on Bon shamanism, a primitive Tibetan religion. Tradition has it that Buddhism was introduced into Tibet in the 7th–8th cent. A.D. Buddhist texts and commentaries were later translated from the Sanskrit. Suppressed at first by the Bon shamans, the new faith was reformed in the 11th cent. by an Indian monk, Atisa, founder of the Kadampa sect. The 13th cent. brought rule by the Sas-Kya abbots, chosen by Kublai Khan. Ensuing corruption led to the much-needed reforms of the Yellow Hat sect (14th–15th cent.). In 1641 a ruling Mongol prince granted temporal and spiritual control over all Tibet to the fifth grand lama [Tibetan, = superior one], the Dalai Lama. The Dalai Lama soon became the temporal leader of Tibet, and spiritual supremacy resided with the chief abbot of the Zhaxilhünbo monastery near Xigazê, known as the Panchen Lama. Succession to either position is said to depend on direct reincarnation. Dedicated Tibetan Buddhists seek NIRVANA, but the popular religion retains shamanistic elements and includes hymns and prayers and the worship of many spirits. In 1959, following the Tibetan revolt against the Chinese, the 14th Dalai Lama went into exile in India. The Chinese installed the Panchen Lama in his place as ruler, and repressed Buddhism in Tibet. Since the 1980s, however, there has been greater tolerance of religious practice in Tibet.

Tibetan language, member of the Tibeto-Burman subfamily of the Sino-Tibetan family of languages. See LANGUAGE (table).

tick: see MITE.

Ticonderoga, resort village (1990 pop. 2,770), NE N.Y., on a neck of land between Lakes George and Champlain; settled 17th cent., inc. 1889. At Ticonderoga and nearby Crown Point, battles of the FRENCH AND INDIAN WAR and AMERICAN REVOLUTION were fought. Fort Ticonderoga (built 1755, restored 1909) is now a museum.

tidal wave: see TSUNAMI.

tide, alternate rise and fall of sea level in oceans and other large bodies of water. These changes are caused by the gravitational attraction of the moon and, to a lesser extent, of the sun for the earth. At any one time there are two high tides on the earth, the direct tide on the side facing the moon, and the indirect tide on the opposite side. It is believed that the indirect tide is caused by the moon actually pulling the earth away from the water on the far side. The average interval between high tides is about 12 hr 25 min. The typical tidal range, or difference in sea level between high and low tides, in the open ocean is about 2 ft (0.6 m), but it is much greater near the coasts. The world's widest tidal range occurs in the Bay of FUNDY in E Canada. Tides are also raised in the earth's solid crust and atmosphere.

Tieck, Ludwig [tēk], 1773–1853, German writer. He led the transition from STURM UND DRANG to ROMANTICISM. His fairy tales, e.g., *The Blond Eckbert* (1796); poetic drama, e.g., *Kaiser Octavianus* (1804); and fiction exemplify the romantic approach to these genres. Tieck translated *Don Quixote* and completed with others the translations of SHAKESPEARE begun by A.W. von Schlegel (see under SCHLEGEL, FRIEDRICH VON).

Tientsin: see TIANJIN.

Tiepolo, Giovanni Battista [tyĕ'pōlō], 1696–1770, Italian painter. He was the most important Venetian painter and decorator of the 18th cent. Having won fame for his FRESCOES in the Labia Palace and the doge's palace, he was summoned (1750) to Würzburg (Bavaria) to do frescoes illustrating the life of Emperor Frederick I. In 1752 he went to Madrid to decorate the royal palace with such frescoes as the *Apotheosis of Spain.* As pure virtuosity, Tiepolo's scintillating brushwork, superb draftsmanship, and clarity of color are unsurpassed.

Tierra del Fuego [Span., = land of fire], archipelago, 28,476 sq mi (73,753 sq km), separated from the southern tip of mainland South America by the Strait of MAGELLAN and divided between Chile and Argentina. The region is sparsely populated and subject to high winds and heavy rainfall. The economy is based on petroleum and sheep.

Tiffany, Louis Comfort, 1848–1933, American artist and designer; b. N.Y.C. After studying painting, he founded the interior-decorating firm of Tiffany Studios in New York City. It specialized in *favrile* glasswork, ranging from lamps and vases to stained-glass windows, characterized by iridescent colors and natural forms in the ART NOUVEAU style.

tiger, large carnivore (*Panthera tigris*) of the CAT family, found in the forests of Asia. Its yellow-orange coat features numerous prominent black stripes. Males may attain 10 ft (3 m) in length and 650 lb (290 kg) in weight. Tigers are solitary, mainly nocturnal hunters and are good swimmers but poor climbers. They have been extensively hunted for their pelts and for their bones (used in traditional Chinese medicines) and are a threatened species.

Tigris, major river of SW Asia, flowing c.1,150 mi (1,850 km) generally southeast from the Taurus Mts., E Turkey, across a wide floodplain in Iraq, to join the EUPHRATES at BASRA and to form the SHATT AL ARAB. It is widely used for irrigation in Iraq and increasingly in Turkey, and is navigable by shallow draft vessels upstream to Basra. Some of the great cities of ancient MESOPOTAMIA, including NINEVEH, Ctesiphon, and Seleucia, stood on the banks of the river, called the Hiddekil in the Bible.

Tijuana [tēhwä'nä], city (1990 pop. 742,686), NW Mexico, just south of the U.S. border. A growing center of light industry, it has prospered mainly as a border resort noted for its racetracks and bullfights. The border at Tijuana is crossed by some 14 million tourists a year.

Tilden, Bill (William Tatem Tilden II), 1893–1953, American tennis player; b. Philadelphia. He became one of the world's foremost tennis stars, winning the U.S. singles title seven times in the 1920s and the British singles title three times (1920–21, 1930). "Big Bill" led the U.S. to victory in Davis Cup play and later won professional titles.

Tilden, Samuel Jones, 1814–86, American political leader; b. New Lebanon, N.Y. A successful lawyer, Tilden was elected governor of New York in 1874 and was the Democratic candidate for president in 1876. He polled more popular votes than the Republican, Rutherford B. HAYES. There were disputed electoral votes in several states, however, and a congressional commission of eight Republicans and seven Democrats, voting on strict party lines, awarded all the disputed states to Hayes, making him the winner by one electoral vote.

till: see DRIFT.

Till Eulenspiegel: see EULENSPIEGEL, TILL.

Tillich, Paul Johannes [tĭl'ĭk], 1886–1965, American philosopher and theologian; b. Germany. He taught theology in Germany until his opposition to the Nazi regime caused his dismissal (1933). He then taught at Union Theological Seminary, New York City (1933–54), Harvard Univ. (1954–62), and the Univ. of Chicago (1962–65). His thought embraced the concept of the "Protestant Principle" and aimed at a correlation of the questions arising out of the human condition and the divine answers drawn from the symbolism of Christian revelation.

Tilly, Johannes Tserklaes, count of, 1559–1632, imperial general in the THIRTY YEARS WAR; b. Belgium. He commanded the army of the Catholic League and won victories in Bavaria and the Palatinate. He assumed command of the imperial army (1630) and stormed Magdeburg (1631), where his troops massacred the populace and sacked the city. He was defeated by the Swedish army of Gustavus II at Breitenfeld (1631) and on the Lech (1632), where he was mortally wounded.

timberline, elevation above which trees cannot grow. Its location is influenced by latitude, prevailing wind directions, and exposure to sunlight. The timberline is roughly marked by the 50°F (10°C) isotherm. In general, it is highest in the tropics and descends in elevation toward the poles.

Timbuktu, city (1987 pop. 31,925), central Mali, connected to the Niger R. by a canal system. Its salt trade and handicraft industries make it an important meeting-place for the nomads of the SAHARA. Founded (11th cent.) by the TUAREG, it became by the 14th cent. a major commercial and cultural center in the MALI empire and was famous for its gold trade. Under the SONGHAI empire (15th and 16th cent.) the city was a center of Muslim learning, but it declined after being sacked by the Moroccans in 1593. It fell to the French in 1894.

time and motion study, analysis of the operations required to produce a manufactured article in a factory, with the aim of increasing efficiency. Each operation is studied minutely and analyzed in order to eliminate unnecessary motions and thus reduce production time and raise output. The first effort at time study was made by F.W. TAYLOR in the 1880s. Early in the 20th cent., Frank and Lillian Gilbreth developed a more systematic and sophisticated method of time and motion study for industry, taking into account the limits of human physical and mental capacity and the importance of a good physical environment.

Times Square: see BROADWAY.

Timişoara [tēmēshwä'rä], Hung. *Temesvár,* city (1989 est. pop. 333,000), W Romania, on the Beja Canal. Its manufactures include textiles, processed food, and machinery. Annexed to Hungary in 1010, it fell to the Turks (1552) and to the HAPSBURGS (1718). In 1920 it passed to Romania. Its Roman Catholic and Orthodox cathedrals date from the 18th cent.

Timor, island (c.13,200 sq mi/34,200 sq km), Indonesia, largest and easternmost of the Lesser Sundas. It is long, narrow, and almost wholly mountainous. Rice, coconuts, and coffee are grown; stretches of grassland support cattle. The inhabitants are of Malayan and Papuan descent. Divided between the Portuguese and the Dutch by treaties in 1859 and 1914, the Dutch (western) half became part of the new nation of Indonesia in 1950. In 1975 Portuguese Timor declared its independence as East Timor, but Indonesia invaded and annexed it. Guerrillas fought the Indonesian army into the 1990s, and the army responded brutally in an attempt to crush resistance.

Timothy, two epistles of the NEW TESTAMENT, 15th and 16th books in the usual order. With TITUS they make up the Pastoral Epistles, giving advice on governing a church. First Timothy discusses public prayer and the qualifications of the clergy. Second Timothy is more personal, emphasizing courage and fidelity and warning of trials to come.

Timur or **Tamerlane,** c.1336–1405, Mongol conqueror, first of the TIMURIDS; b. Kesh, near Samarkand. From SAMARKAND, his capital, he invaded Persia, S Russia, India (where he took Delhi), and the Levant. In Asia Minor he defeated (1402) the Ottoman Turks and captured their sultan, Beyazid I. He died while planning an invasion of China. Though notorious for his acts of cruelty—he may have slaughtered 80,000 in Delhi—he was a patron of the arts.

Timurids, dynasty founded by TIMUR. At his death (1405), his empire extended from the Euphrates to the Jaxartes and Indus rivers. By 1410 the Western empire, including Baghdad, had been lost to the so-called Black-Sheep Turkoman horde. But the Eastern empire, ruled by Shah Rukh, Timur's son, flourished. His great cities, SAMARKAND and HERAT, became the center of Persian culture and commerce. His son, Ulagh Beg (r.1447–49), made Samarkand a center of Muslim civilization. After him, the Timurid empire fell to the White-Sheep Turkoman horde and the Uzbeks. BABUR is regarded as the last of the Timurids.

tin (Sn), metallic element, known and used by humans at least as early as the BRONZE AGE. It is a lustrous, silver-white, very soft, and malleable metal that can be rolled, pressed, or hammered into extremely thin sheets (tin foil). A tin coating, applied by dipping or electroplating, protects iron, steel, copper, and other metals from rust. Compounds of tin are used for mordants in dyeing, for weighting silk, and as reducing agents. Stannous fluoride, added to toothpastes and water supplies, prevents tooth decay. Toxic organic compounds are used as fungicides and catalysts. Cassiterite, or tinstone, is the chief ore. See ELEMENT (table); PERIODIC TABLE.

Tinbergen, Jan [tĭn'bĕr″gən], 1903–, Dutch economist. Professor at the Netherlands School of Economics (1933–73), he shared, with Ragnar FRISCH, the first Nobel Prize in economics (1969), for work in ECONOMETRICS.

Tinbergen, Nikolaas, 1907–88, British zoologist, b. Netherlands. For his work in reviving and developing the science of animal behavior, he shared the 1973 Nobel Prize in physiology or medicine with Karl von FRISCH and Konrad LORENZ. His studies of the display behavior of certain species revealed that such displays result from a state of conflict between opposing motivations ("fight or flee"). He also clarified the evolutionary origins of many social signals and their subsequent ritualization.

Tindal or **Tindale, William:** see TYNDALE, WILLIAM.

Tintoretto [tēntōrĕt'tō], 1518–94, Venetian painter; b. Jacopo Robusti. He was called Il Tintoretto [little dyer] from his father's trade. He supposedly studied with TITIAN, but tradition has it that his precocity made Titian jealous. His early paintings are difficult to verify because he assimilated the styles of others, e.g., Bonifazio Veronese and Paris Bordone. His *St. Mark Rescuing a Slave* (1548; Academy, Venice) shows MICHELANGELO's influence but has startling lighting effects and a dramatic rendering of the narrative. In the next decade, his work tended toward MANNERISM, with flickering light, distorted figures, and irrational spatial elements, e.g., in his *Last Judgment* (Madonna dell'Orto, Venice). His cycle of paintings for the Scuolo di San Rocco (begun 1564) includes an enormous *Crucifixion* and is remarkable for startling changes in viewpoint, frenetic movement, and mystic conception. The last phase of his art was highly visionary, with almost phosphorescent lighting effects, e.g., in his *Last Supper* and *Entombment* (San Giorgio Maggiore, Venice). His works in American collections include the *Finding of Moses* and *Miracle of the Loaves and Fishes* (both: Metropolitan Mus.) and *Baptism of Clorinda* (Art Inst., Chicago).

tipi: see TEPEE.

Tippett, Sir Michael, 1905–, English composer. He has utilized British folk and American JAZZ elements in some of his music. His works include the ORATORIO *A Child of Our Time* (1946); the operas *The Knot Garden* (1970) and *The Mask of Time* (1984); and four symphonies (1945, 1958, 1973, 1977).

Tiradentes [tērəthĕn'təs], 1748–92, Brazilian revolutionary patriot; b. José Joaquim da Silva Xavier. In the late 1780s he led an independence movement against Portuguese rule and for democratic government; the movement was betrayed and Tiradentes was executed.

Tiranë [tērä'nə] or **Tirana,** city (1990 est. pop. 210,000), capital of Albania, central Albania, on the Ishm R. The country's largest city, it is located on a fertile plain and produces textiles, metal products, and other manufactures. Lignite is mined nearby. The city, founded in the early 17th cent. by the Turks, was enlarged (1920) when it became the capital. Tiranë was held (1939–43) by Italy during World War II. Government buildings and an 18th-cent. mosque are located in Scanderbeg Square, the city's center.

Tiresias [tīrē'shəs, –sēəs], in Greek mythology, blind soothsayer who appears in many legends, e.g., OEDIPUS.

Tirso de Molina [tēr'sō dā mōlē'nä], pseud. of **Fray Gabriel Téllez,** 1584?–1648, Spanish dramatist. A major figure of the Spanish GOLDEN AGE, he wrote *The Trickster of Seville* (1630), the first literary treatment of the Don Juan legend, as well as several hundred other plays.

tissue, in biology, aggregation of similar cells. In animals, the epithelial, nerve, connective, and muscle tissues are fundamental; blood and lymph are commonly classed separately as vascular tissues. Organs usually consist of several tissues. Higher plants contain meristem tissue (cells that grow, divide, and differentiate), protective tissue like cork, storage and support tissues, and vascular tissues.

tissue culture, the growing of plant or animal CELLS outside of the body, as in a nutrient medium in a laboratory. It is used in the study of specific cells, the production of various cellular products, and the classification of tumors. Plant tissue cultures are also used to CLONE plants with desired qualities, such as a type of disease resistance or flower color.

Tisza, Count Stephen [tĭ'sŏ], 1861–1918, Hungarian premier (1903–5, 1913–17). Tisza sought to make Hungary a forceful partner in the AUSTRO-HUNGARIAN MONARCHY. He first opposed war with SERBIA in 1914 but later approved it. After taking a military command in World War I he was assassinated.

Titan, in astronomy, natural satellite of SATURN.

Titan, in Greek mythology, one of 12 primeval deities; children of URANUS and GAEA. They were CRONUS, Iapetus, Hyperion, Oceanus, Coeus, Creus, Theia, RHEA, Mnemosyne, Phoebe, Tethys, and Themis. Their descendants, e.g., PROMETHEUS, ATLAS, HECATE, HELIOS, were also called Titans. Led by Cronus, they deposed Uranus and ruled the universe. They were in turn overthrown by the OLYMPIANS, led by ZEUS, in a battle called the Titanomachy. Afterward Cronus ruled the Isle of the Blessed and Atlas held up the sky. The others, except Prometheus, who had helped Zeus, were condemned to TARTARUS.

Titania, in astronomy, natural satellite of URANUS.

Titanic, British liner that sank on the night of Apr. 14–15, 1912, after striking an iceberg in the North Atlantic. The disaster, which occurred on the ship's maiden voyage, claimed the lives of more than 1,500 of the 2,200 people aboard. Many perished because of a shortage of lifeboats. More stringent safety rules for ships and an iceberg patrol were later instituted. An expedition led by Robert G. Ballard discovered the wreck in 1987.

titanium (Ti), metallic element, discovered in 1791 by William Gregor. It is a lustrous, silver-white, and very corrosion-resistant metal that is ductile when pure and malleable when heated. The metal and its alloys, which are light in weight and have very high tensile strength, are used in aircraft, spacecraft, naval ships, guided missiles, and armor plate for tanks. Titanium dioxide is used as a gemstone (titania) and paint pigment. Widely distributed in compounds (e.g. RUTILE) in nature, titanium is present in the sun and certain other stars, in meteorites, and on the moon. See ELEMENT (table); PERIODIC TABLE.

Titian [tĭsh'ən], c.1490–1576, Venetian painter; b. Pieve di Cadore, in the Dolomites, as Tiziano Vecellio. One of the most celebrated artists of the RENAISSANCE, Titian had immense influence on succeeding generations of painters, especially in his use of color. He studied painting in the shop of Gentile and Giovanni Bellini (see BELLINI, family) and worked with GIORGIONE. After their deaths, he was considered the finest painter in Venice. In 1518 he completed the famous altarpiece of the *Assumption of the Virgin* (Church of Santa Maria Gloriosa dei Frari, Venice), and for the rest of his career he was showered with honors and commissions from the rulers of Europe. Emperor CHARLES V made him a Count Palatine, and Philip II of Spain was one of his patrons. In 1545, Titian went to Rome, where he met MICHELANGELO and did the striking (unfinished) portrait of Pope Paul III and his grandsons Ottavio (the second duke of Parma) and Cardinal Alessandro Farnese (Pinacoteca, Naples). For Cardinal Farnese he did a *Danaë* (Naples), of which he later made several versions. He painted the magnificent *La Gloria* (1554; Prado) for Charles V, and in 1553 he started a cycle of mythological paintings for Philip II, which included *Diana and Callisto* and *Diana Surprised by Acteon* (both 1559; National Gall. Edinburgh), and the *Rape of Europa* (1559; Gardner Mus., Boston). Titian's work can be divided into three phases. The first shows the influence of Bellini and Giorgione, e.g., in *Sacred and Profane Love* (c.1513; Borghese Gall., Rome). Full dramatic monumentality and great sumptuousness of color characterize the second phase, e.g., in *Christ Crowned with Thorns* (c.1542; Louvre). In his last phase, an intense mystical spirit and a new looseness of brush stroke and subtlety of color can be seen, e.g., in *Pietà* (Academy, Venice), which was intended for his own tomb and finished by Palma Giovane.

Titicaca, largest freshwater lake in South America, c.3,200 sq mi (8,290 sq km), located high in the ANDES between Bolivia and Peru, at an elevation of c.12,500 ft (3,810 m). It is by far the highest large lake in the world. The densely populated shores have been a center of civilization on the ALTIPLANO since before the time of the INCAS.

Titius-Bode law, empirical relationship between the mean distances of the planets from the sun. If each number in the series 0, 3, 6, 12, 24, . . . (where a new number is twice the previous number) is increased by 4 and then divided by 10 to form the series 0.4, 0.7, 1.0, 1.6, 2.8, 5.2, 10.0, 19.6, 38.8, 77.2, . . . , the law holds that this series gives the mean distances of the planets from the sun, expressed in ASTRONOMICAL UNITS. This relationship was discovered (1766) by Johann Titius and published (1772) by Johann Bode. It agreed well with the actual mean distances of the planets then known (and of Uranus and the asteroid belt, both discovered later), but not with those of the later-discovered planets Neptune and Pluto.

titmouse, BIRD of the family Paridae, which includes tits, titmice, and CHICKADEES. Small birds with short, pointed bills and gray and brown plumage, titmice are found chiefly in the Northern Hemisphere. They travel in flocks with other birds, e.g., nuthatches and WOODPECKERS, and can be taught tricks.

Tito, Josip Broz, 1892–1980, Communist president of Yugoslavia (1953–80). He served in the Red Army during the Russian civil war and led the partisan movement against the German occupation of Yugoslavia in WORLD WAR II. At the end of the war he firmly controlled the government and Communist party. He had his rival, Gen. MIHAJLOVIĆ, executed and forced the abdication of King PETER II. From 1945 until his death Tito ruled with virtually no opposition, partly because of his highly efficient secret police. He broke with STALIN in 1948, freed Yugoslavia from the external control of the USSR, and made it the most liberal Communist nation in Europe. He was a leader of the nonaligned nations.

titration, the determination of the CONCENTRATION of acids or bases (see ACIDS AND BASES) in SOLUTION by the gradual addition of an acidic solution of known volume and concentration to a basic solution of known volume, or vice versa, until complete neutralization (observable by the color change in an added INDICATOR, such as phenolphthalein) has occurred.

Titus (Titus Flavius Sabinus Vespasianus), A.D. 39–81, Roman emperor (A.D. 79–81). Son of Emperor VESPASIAN, he acted as coruler with his father after A.D. 71. He captured and destroyed Jerusalem in A.D. 70. On succeeding his father, he pursued a policy of conciliation, sought popular favor, and became known as a benevolent ruler. His brother DOMITIAN succeeded him. The **Arch of Titus** was erected by Domitian to commemorate Titus's conquest of Jerusalem.

Titus, EPISTLE of the NEW TESTAMENT, 17th book in the usual order. With First and Second TIMOTHY it makes up the Pastoral Epistles, purportedly by St. PAUL. Titus deals with matters of church government.

Tiy [tē], fl. 1385 B.C., queen of Egypt; wife of Amenhotep III, mother of IKHNATON. She was unusually influential in state affairs. **Tiy,** fl. 1167 B.C., wife of RAMSES III, plotted against him but failed to gain the throne for her son.

Tiziano Vecellio: see TITIAN.

Tl, chemical symbol of the element THALLIUM.

Tlingit, 14 related indigenous peoples of the Pacific Northwest (see NORTH AMERICA, INDIGENOUS PEOPLES OF), with a language of the Nadene stock (see NATIVE AMERICAN LANGUAGES). They lived on the coast of SE Alaska and nearby islands, with a typical Northwest Coast culture. After Russians built (1799) a fort near the site of SITKA, there was constant conflict with the Tlingit. In settlements of claims against the government the Alaska tribes received (1971) millions of acres of land and almost $1 billion, with which a tribal corporation was established. In 1990 there were 13,925 Tlingits in the U.S.

Tm, chemical symbol of the element THULIUM.

TNT or **trinitrotoluene,** $CH_3C_6H_2(NO_2)_3$, crystalline AROMATIC COMPOUND. Trinitrotoluene is a high EXPLOSIVE, but, unlike NITROGLYCERIN, it is unaffected by ordinary shocks and must be set off by a detonator. Because it does not react with metals, it can be used in filling metal shells. It is often mixed with other explosives, e.g., with ammonium nitrate to form amatol.

toad, certain insect-eating AMPHIBIANS of the order Anura, similar to the FROG but often more terrestrial as adults. Commonly referring to species with shorter legs, a stouter body, and thicker skin than the frog, the term *toad* is properly restricted to the so-called true toads (family Bufonidae). These are characterized by warty skins, prominent parotid glands behind the eyes, and a white, poisonous fluid exuded through the skin and from the parotid glands. Ranging from 1 to 7 in. (2.5 to 18 cm) in size, toads inhabit cool, moist places and lay their eggs in water.

toadstool: see MUSHROOM.

tobacco, plant (genus *Nicotiana*) of the NIGHTSHADE family, and the product manufactured from its leaf and used in cigars and cigarettes, snuff, and pipe and chewing tobacco. The chief commercial species, *N. tabacum,* is believed native to tropical America. The tobacco plant is a coarse, large-leaved perennial, but it is usually cultivated as an annual. Tobacco requires a warm climate and rich, well-drained soil. After being picked, the leaves are cured, fermented, and aged to develop aroma. The amount of nicotine (the ALKALOID responsible for tobacco's narcotic and soothing effect) varies, depending on tobacco strain, growing conditions, and processing. The use of tobacco originated among natives of the New World in pre-Columbian times. Introduced into Spain and Portugal in the mid-16th cent., initially as a panacea, it spread to other European countries, and by 1619 tobacco had become a leading export crop of Virginia. Since the 1950s there has been concern over the harmful effects of nicotine, the tarry compounds, and CARBON MONOXIDE in tobacco smoke; smoking has been especially linked to lung cancer and heart disease.

Tobago: see TRINIDAD AND TOBAGO.

Tobin, James, 1918–, American economist; b. Champaign, Ill. Sterling Professor of Economics at Yale, Tobin won the 1981 Nobel Prize in economics for his analyses of the impact of financial markets on spending and investment. He also served (1961–62) on the President's Council of Economic Advisers.

Tobit, biblical book included in the Western canon but not in the Hebrew Bible, and placed in the APOCRYPHA in the Authorized Version. It tells of Tobit, a devout, blind Jew in exile, and of his son Tobias. Tobias and his dog are led by the archangel Raphael to the house of Sara, who is afflicted by the demon Asmodeus. Tobias marries Sara, exorcises the demon, and cures his father's blindness. The book probably was composed before 200 B.C.

Tobruk, city (1984 pop. 75,282), NE Libya, a port on the Mediterranean Sea. During WORLD WAR II it was an objective fiercely contested (1941–42) by the British and Germans. First seized by Allied forces, Tobruk was briefly held by the Germans and then retaken by the British.

Tocqueville, Alexis de, 1805–59, French social philosopher. Prominent in French politics, he was briefly foreign minister after the REVOLUTION OF 1848. His fame rests on his classic work *Democracy in America* (2 vol., 1835), based on observations made during a trip to the U.S. A liberal, he believed that political democracy and social equality would eventually replace Europe's aristocratic institutions.

Togo, officially Togolese Republic, republic (1992 est. pop. 3,959,000), 21,622 sq mi (56,000 sq km), W Africa, bordered by the Gulf of Guinea (S), Ghana (W), Burkina Faso (N), and Benin (E). LOMÉ is the capital. Beyond a sandy strip along the coast are, successively, a region of fertile clay soils, the Mono Tableland, a mountainous area rising to c.3,940 ft (1,200 m), and, in the extreme north, the rolling sandstone Oti Plateau. The standard of living in Togo is among the highest in W Africa. Most of the labor force is engaged in agriculture, but mining is of growing importance. The principal food crops are manioc, millet, yams, and corn; the leading cash crops are coffee, cocoa, palm kernels, cotton, and peanuts. Major deposits of high-quality phosphates have been worked on a large scale since 1963; Togo is one of the world's ten largest phosphate producers. An oil refinery processes crude oil imported from Nigeria. The principal ethnic groups are the Ewe in the south and Voltaic-speaking peoples in the north. Most adhere to traditional beliefs, but there is a large Christian, and a smaller Muslim, minority. French is the official language.

History. Formerly part of the German protectorate of TOGOLAND (1886–1914), the area that is now Togo was administered by France after World War I (1922–1960). It gained independence, as the Republic of Togo, in 1960, resisting attempts by Kwame Nkrumah of Ghana (which includes the former British Togoland) to merge the two nations. The early years of the republic were characterized by political instability. In 1967 Lt. Col. Gnassingbé Eyadéma came to power in a bloodless coup and established an authoritarian, one-party state. By 1991 growing unrest led him to relinquish power to an transitional government, but the army forced partial restoration of his powers. Togolese voters approved (1992) a new constitution that reduced presidential power. In 1993 Eyadéma won reelection in a contest that was boycotted by the main opposition parties.

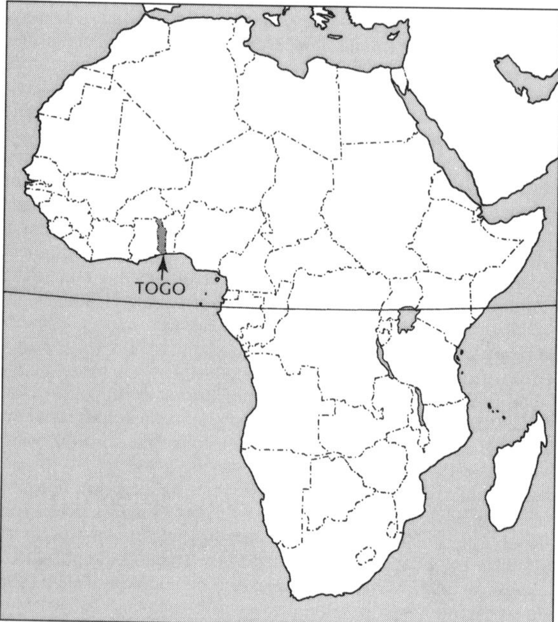

Togo Heihachiro, 1846–1934, Japanese admiral, Japan's greatest naval hero. In the RUSSO-JAPANESE WAR he defeated Russian fleets at Port Arthur (1904) and in the battle of Tsushima (1905), thus establishing Japanese naval superiority.

Togoland, historic region (c.33,500 sq mi/86,800 sq km) in W Africa. Its western part is now in GHANA, and its eastern part is the Republic of TOGO.

Tohono O'Odham or **Papago,** indigenous people of the Southwest (see NORTH AMERICA, INDIGENOUS PEOPLES OF), speaking a Uto-Aztecan language of the Aztec-Tanoan stock (see NATIVE AMERICAN LANGUAGES). Like their PIMA neighbors, they are descended from the Hohokam peoples. Farmers and cattle raisers, they were severely oppressed by the APACHES. Today most live on reservation lands near Tucson, Ariz.; income from leases of mineral-bearing lands have added to tribal resources. In 1990 there were 16,041 Tohono O'Odham in the U.S.

Tojo Hideki, 1884–1948, Japanese general and prime minister (1941–44). A militarist, he approved the attack on Pearl Harbor and other Japanese offensives in WORLD WAR II. At home his regime asserted totalitarian control. In Apr. 1945, Tojo recommended that the war be fought to a finish. After Japan's defeat, he was tried by the Allies as a war criminal and was convicted and executed.

Tokelau, formerly Union Islands, dependency of New Zealand (1992 est. pop. 1,800), c.6 sq mi (16 sq km), South Pacific Ocean, consisting of three small atolls: Atafu, Nukunonu (the largest), and Fakaofa. The Polynesian inhabitants have a subsistence economy; copra is the chief export. Tokelau was discovered in 1765 and was a British possession from 1889 to 1925, when it was mandated to New Zealand. In 1948 New Zealand acquired formal sovereignty (effective 1949).

Tokugawa [tō″ko͞ogä′wä], family that held the shogunate (see SHOGUN) and controlled Japan from 1603 to 1867. Founded by IEYASU, the Tokugawa regime was a centralized feudalism, and the Tokugawa themselves ruled directly about one fourth of the country. The daimyo, or barons, owed allegiance to the Tokugawa but were permitted to rule their own domains. Despite its efficient organization, the regime collapsed in 1867 during the MEIJI restoration.

Tokyo, city (1990 pop. 8,163,127), capital and largest city of Japan, E central Honshu, at the head of Tokyo Bay. Greater Tokyo consists of an urban area, farms and mountain villages, and the Izu Islands; with YOKOHAMA it forms the world's most populous metropolitan area (1991 est. pop. 27,245,000). Tokyo is the administrative, financial, and cultural center of Japan. It is also a major industrial and transportation hub, with the world's first public monorail line and high-speed "bullet trains" that link it with other cities. Manufactures include electronic equipment, automobiles, and a wide variety of consumer goods. It is a world economic center that rivals New York and London. Founded in the 12th cent. as Edo, it was the capital of the shogunate from 1603 to 1868, when the emperor was restored to power and made Edo the nation's capital, renaming it Tokyo. In 1923 an earthquake and fire destroyed nearly half the city. Heavy Allied bombing in World War II devastated much of Tokyo, including nearly all of its industrial plants. Left intact were the imperial palace and surrounding embassies, the diet (government) building, and many office buildings. The city's famed landmarks include the Meiji and Hie shrines, ancient temples, and the Korakuen landscape garden. The Ginza is Tokyo's shopping and entertainment center. One of the world's foremost educational cities, Tokyo has over 100 colleges and universities. Frequent rebuilding in the wake of disasters has made it one of the world's most modern cities.

Tolbert, William Richard, Jr., 1913–80, president of LIBERIA (1971–80). A protegé of William Tubman, Tolbert succeeded him as president in 1971. He was killed (1980) in a coup led by Samuel K. Doe, an army sergeant.

Toledo, Francisco de [tōlā′thō], 1515?–84, Spanish viceroy of PERU (1569–81). He consolidated the Spanish conquest of Peru by breaking the power of the great landowners. He unjustly had the Inca leader Tupac Amaru executed (1571).

Toledo [tōlā′thō], city (1988 est. pop. 59,600), capital of Toledo prov., central Spain, in New Castile, on the Tagus R. Predating Rome, to which it fell in 193 B.C., it was later (6th cent.) the capital of the Visigothic kingdom. Its archbishops have long been Spain's primates. Under the MOORS (712–1085) and the kings of CASTILE it was a center of Moorish, Spanish, and Jewish culture and was noted for its sword blades and textiles. In the 16th cent. it was the seat of the Spanish INQUISITION. Many works by El Greco (see GRECO, EL), who lived in Toledo, hang in the cathedral (begun

1226), the Hospital of San Juan Bautista (15th–16th cent.), and the Church of Santo Tomé.

Toledo, city (1990 pop. 332,943), seat of Lucas co., NW Ohio, on the Maumee R. and Lake Erie; inc. 1837. It is one of the major GREAT LAKES shipping, commercial, and industrial cities. Glass, oil products, machines, tools, and automobile parts are leading manufactures. Gen. Anthony WAYNE built Fort Industry there (1794) after the Battle of Fallen Timbers; the city was settled in 1817. The area was the object of an Ohio-Michigan border dispute (the "Toledo War," 1835–36). Toledo's Museum of Art and the Univ. of Toledo are notable institutions.

Tolkien, J(ohn) R(onald) R(euel), 1892–1973, English novelist and scholar. A medievalist at Oxford Univ., he became famous as the author of *The Hobbit* (1937) and the epic trilogy *Lord of the Rings* (1954–56), all fantasy novels about the mythological kingdom of Middle Earth; the posthumous *Silmarillion* (1977) continues the saga.

Toller, Ernst [tôl'ər], 1893–1939, German expressionist dramatist and poet (see EXPRESSIONISM). His plays of social protest include *Transfiguration* (1919), *Man and the Masses* (1920), and *The Machine-Wreckers* (1922). He left Germany in 1932. In 1939 he committed suicide in New York City.

Tolstoy, Leo, Count, Rus. *Lev Nikolayevich Tolstoy* [təlstoi'], 1828–1910, Russian novelist and philosopher. Of a noble family, he was orphaned at nine and brought up by aunts. He left the university without a degree and returned to his family estate, Yasnaya Polyana, where he tried to aid and educate the serfs. After a profligate period in Moscow and St. Petersburg, he joined his brother, an officer, in the Caucasus (1851). In 1852 he enlisted. *Childhood* (1852), part of an autobiographical trilogy that includes *Boyhood* (1854) and *Youth* (1857), was his first published work. Leaving the army in 1855, he lived alternately on his estate and in St. Petersburg. In 1862 he married Sophia Andreyevna Bers, a young, well-educated girl, who bore him 13 children. *War and Peace,* his first masterpiece, appeared in 1863–69. An epic of the Napoleonic invasion, it illustrates Tolstoy's view that history proceeds inexorably to its own ends. *Anna Karenina* (1875–77), his second masterpiece, is a tragedy of adultery with profound social and spiritual dimensions. Around 1876 Tolstoy underwent a crisis culminating in his conversion to a doctrine of Christian love, nonviolent acceptance of evil, and renunciation of wealth. He devoted the rest of his life to practicing and propagating his faith, expounded in such works as *What I Believe* (1884). He considered wrong such institutions as the government and church; he was excommunicated in 1901, but his fame protected him from serious state interference. Moral issues are central to his later works, notably "The Death of Ivan Ilyich" (1886), a story; *The Power of Darkness* (1886), a drama; and the novel *Resurrection* (1899). In the essay *What Is Art?* (1898) he argued that the artist is morally bound to create works understandable to most people, and denounced his own earlier works. In 1910 a breach with his family caused Tolstoy to leave home; he died a few days later.

Toltec [Nahuatl, = master builders], indigenous civilization of Mexico, probably with ancient links to the MIXTEC and ZAPOTEC (see MIDDLE AMERICA, INDIGENOUS PEOPLES OF). The Toltec warrior aristocracy gained ascendancy in the valley of Mexico after the fall (900) of TEOTIHUACÁN, making their own capital at Tollán (Tula). Masters of architecture and the arts, they were advanced workers of stone and smelters of metals, had a calendric system, and are said to have discovered the intoxicant pulque. Their religion, centering on the god QUETZALCOATL, incorporated human sacrifice, sun worship, and a sacred ball game. The Toltec dominated the MAYA (11th–13th cent.) until nomadic Chichimec peoples destroyed their empire, opening the way for the AZTEC.

tomato, plant (*Lycopersicon esculentum*) of the NIGHTSHADE family, and its fruit (commonly considered a vegetable because of its uses). Numerous varieties are cultivated, e.g., the small cherry tomato, the yellow pear tomato, and the large, red beefsteak tomato. Popular in salads and processed into juice, catsup, and canned goods, the tomato was recognized as a valuable food only within the last century.

Tombstone, city (1990 pop. 1,220), SE Ariz.; inc. 1881. During a silver boom (1877–90) it had a reputation as one of the West's richest and most lawless towns. That and its climate made it a popular tourist attraction. It was named a national historic landmark in 1962. Famous sights include Boot Hill cemetery; the Bird Cage Theater; and the O.K. Corral, scene of a famous 1881 gun battle.

Tom Thumb, 1838–83, American entertainer; b. Bridgeport, Conn., as Charles Sherwood Stratton. A midget whose height never exceeded 40 in. (101.5 cm), he achieved fame and fortune when the showman P.T. BARNUM arranged for his exhibition (1842–82). He later appeared with his wife, a dwarf.

tom-tom: see DRUM.

tonality, in music, quality by which all TONES of a composition are heard in relation to a central tone called the keynote, or tonic. Some relationship to a tonic is characteristic of all music except that in which it is deliberately avoided (see ATONALITY and TWELVE-TONE MUSIC). The term *tonality* is also used in contrast to *modality* (see MODE).

tone. In music, a tone is distinguished from noise by its definite PITCH, caused by the regularity of the vibrations that produce it. Any tone possesses the attributes of pitch, intensity, and quality. Pitch is determined by the frequency of the vibration, measured by cycles per second. Intensity, or loudness, is determined by the amplitude, measured in decibels. Quality is determined by the overtones (subsidiary tones), the distinctive timbre of any instrument being the result of the number and relative prominence of the over tones it produces. The term *whole tone* or *whole step* refers to the interval of a major second, as in moving from one white key to the adjoining white key on the piano. *Halftone, semitone,* or *half step* refers to the interval of a minor second, as in moving from a white key to the adjoining black key on the piano.

tone poem: see SYMPHONIC POEM.

Tonga, officially Kingdom of Tonga, independent constitutional monarchy (1992 est. pop. 103,000), 270 sq mi (699 sq km), in the S Pacific Ocean. It comprises c.170 islands, of which the three main groups are Tongatapu, Haapai, and Vavau. Nukualofa, in Tongatapu, is the capital. Tonga has a tropical climate and a mainly subsistence farming economy. Copra, bananas, and postage stamps printed for purely philatelic purposes are the chief exports. The king is the head of state and also dominates the national legislature, which consists of the king's cabinet, nine noble members, and nine commoners. The islands were discovered between 1616 and 1643 and renamed the Friendly Islands by Capt. James COOK, who visited them in 1773 and 1777. English missionaries arrived (1797) and helped to strengthen British political influence. In 1900, Tonga became a British protectorate but remained internally self-governing. A new treaty in 1968 reduced British control, and Tonga became fully independent in 1970. In the late 1980s reformers won the commoner seats in the assembly and called for increasing commoner representation, but the king opposed any change that would dilute the monarchy's power. The present ruler is King Taufa'ahau Tupou IV (1965–). See PACIFIC OCEAN map.

tongue, muscular organ on the floor of the mouth in higher animals. In humans it functions primarily in chewing, swallowing, and speaking. The human tongue is covered by a mucous membrane containing small projections, or papillae, which give it a rough surface. Tiny taste organs, or buds, are found on the papillae, with many concentrated toward the back of the tongue. Sweet, sour, salty, and bitter flavors stimulate the taste cells in these buds to send impulses along associated nerves to the brain.

Tonkin, historic region (c.40,000 sq mi/103,600 sq km), Southeast Asia, bordered by China (N), the Gulf of Tonkin (E), Annam (S), and Laos (S, W); now part of Vietnam. The capital was HANOI. Tonkin was conquered by the Chinese in 111 B.C. and became independent in A.D. 939. Governed by native dynasties until French expeditions arrived in 1873 and 1882, Tonkin was the scene of a colonial war (complicated by Chinese intervention) that ended with a French protectorate. The Japanese occupied the region during WORLD WAR II. In 1954, after an independence struggle against the French, Tonkin became part of North Vietnam. It was incorporated into united Vietnam after the VIETNAM WAR.

Tonkin Gulf resolution, in U.S. history, Congressional resolution (1964) authorizing military action in Southeast Asia. After U.S. destroyers allegedly were attacked in the Gulf of Tonkin in 1964 by North Vietnamese gunboats, Pres. Lyndon B. JOHNSON asked Congress for authority to retaliate and for a mandate for future military action. The resolution passed overwhelmingly and Johnson and his successor, Richard NIXON, regarded it as authorization to pursue the VIETNAM WAR in Southeast Asia. Congress repealed it in 1970.

tonsils, name commonly referring to the palatine tonsils, two ovoid masses of lymphoid tissue on either side of the throat, at the back of the tongue. The pharyngeal tonsils, or adenoids, are similar masses located in the space between the back of the nose and the throat. The lingual tonsils are situated on the back of the tongue. The tonsils act as filters against disease organisms.

Toomer, Jean, 1894–1967, African-American writer; b. Washington, D.C., as Nathan Eugene Toomer. A major figure of the HARLEM RENAISSANCE, he is known for one work, *Cane* (1923), a collection of stories, poems, and sketches about African-American life in rural Georgia and the urban North.

topaz, aluminum silicate mineral $[Al_2SiO_4(F,OH)_2]$, used as a gem. Commonly colorless or some shade of yellow, the stone is transparent with a vitreous luster. Topaz crystals occur in highly acidic igneous rocks and in metamorphic rocks. Important sources include Brazil, Siberia, Myanmar, and Sri Lanka.

Topeka, city (1990 pop. 119,883), state capital and seat of Shawnee co., NE Kans., on the Kansas R.; inc. 1857. It was laid out (1854) by Free Staters, and became state capital in 1861. The noted Menninger Clinic is one of its several psychiatric research and therapy institutions. Agricultural marketing and shipping are major economic activities. Known for its broad, tree-lined streets, it has a notable museum and library.

topology, branch of MATHEMATICS concerned with those properties of geometric figures that are invariant under continuous transformations. A continuous transformation is a one-to-one correspondence between the points of one figure and the points of another figure such that points that are arbitrarily close on one figure are transformed into points that are also arbitrarily close on the other figure. Two figures are topologically equivalent if one can be deformed into the other by bending, stretching, twisting, or the like, but not by tearing, cutting, or folding; thus topology is sometimes popularly called "rubber-sheet geometry." A circle and a square are topologically equivalent, as are a cylinder and a sphere, but a torus (doughnut shape) is not equivalent to a sphere, because no amount of bending or twisting will change it into a sphere. Topology may be roughly divided into *point-set topology,* which considers figures as SETS of points having such properties as being open, closed, compact, connected, and so forth; *combinatorial topology,* which considers figures as combinations (complexes) of simple figures (simplexes) joined together in a regular manner; and *algebraic topology,* which makes extensive use of algebraic methods, particularly those of group theory. There is considerable overlap among these branches.

Torah [Heb., = teachings or learning], Hebrew name for the PENTATEUCH, the first five books of the Bible. The Torah, or Written Law, which Orthodox Jews believe was revealed directly by God to MOSES on Mt. Sinai, laid down the fundamental laws of moral and physical conduct. In a wider sense the Torah comprises all teachings of JUDAISM, including the entire Hebrew Scripture, the TALMUD, and any generally accepted rabbinical interpretation.

tornado, dark, funnel-shaped cloud containing violently rotating air that develops within a heavy cumulonimbus cloud mass and extends to the earth. The diameter of a tornado varies from a few feet to a mile; the rotating winds reach velocities of 200 to 300 mph (320 to 480 km/hr), and the updraft at the center may reach 200 mph (320 km/hr). In comparison with a HURRICANE, a tornado covers a much smaller area but is much more violent and destructive. The atmospheric conditions required for the formation of a tornado include great thermal instability, high humidity, and the convergence of warm, moist air at low levels with cooler, drier air above. Tornadoes occuring over water are called waterspouts.

Toronto, city (1991 pop. 635,395), provincial capital, S Ontario, part of the municipality of metropolitan Toronto (1991 pop. 2,275,771), on Lake Ontario. Ringed by fast-growing suburbs, it is Canada's second largest city, a major commercial and financial hub, and Ontario's principal GREAT LAKES port and industrial center. The skyline of the city, which changed dramatically beginning in the 1960s, is marked by such landmarks as the CN (Canadian National) Tower, one of the world's tallest free-standing structures; the golden towers of Royal Bank Plaza; and the avant-garde architecture of Eaton Square and the O'Keefe Centre. The city occupies the site of a French fort (1749–59), in an area purchased by the British from Native Americans in 1787. Proclaimed (1793) the capital of Upper Canada (now Ontario), it was settled in part by Loyalists fleeing the American Revolution. It was twice raided by Americans and partly destroyed during the WAR OF 1812. Then known as York, it was renamed Toronto in 1834.

Toronto, University of, at Toronto, Ont., Canada; founded 1827 (as King's College); achieved university status 1849. It is the largest university in Canada. Provincially supported, it has faculties in the arts and sciences and many professional fields, as well as schools of graduate studies and physical and health education. The university also includes the Royal Conservatory of Music.

torque or **moment of force,** a quantity expressing the effectiveness of a force to change the net rate of rotation of a body. It is equal to the product of the force acting on the body and the distance from its point of application to the axis around which the body is free to rotate. Units of torque include the foot-pound (or pound-foot), the dyne-centimeter, and the newton-meter.

Torquemada, Tomás de [tôrkāmä'thä], 1420–98, Spanish churchman. A DOMINICAN, he became (1483) inquisitor general of Castile and Aragón. His reputation for cruelty derives from the harsh procedures that he devised for the Spanish INQUISITION. He was largely responsible for the expulsion (1492) of the Jews.

Torrance, city (1990. pop. 133,107), Los Angeles co., S Calif.; inc. 1921. An industrial center, it has aircraft, electronics, and oil industries, and numerous other manufactures.

Torrens, Sir Robert Richard, 1814–84, Australian statesman; b. Ireland. He secured the passage (1858) of the Torrens Act, a landholding reform which substituted public registration of title for the old conveyance system.

Torres Bodet, Jaime [tôr'rās bôdĕt'], 1902–74, Mexican writer and diplomat. Among his books of poetry are *Fervor* (1918), symbolist in tone; *Crypt* (1937); and the bilingual *Selected Poems* (1964). Such fictional works as *Margarita of the Mist* (1927) and *Birth of Venus* (1941) reveal his erudite playfulness.

Torrijos Herrera, Omar [tōrē'hōs ārā'rä], 1929–81, Panamanian military ruler. After seizing power in a military coup (1968), he curtailed civil liberties and instituted economic and social reforms. He signed (1978) the Panama-U.S. treaties that transferred the PANAMA CANAL and Panama Canal Zone to PANAMA.

torsion: see STRENGTH OF MATERIALS.

Torstensson, Lennart, 1603–51, Swedish general in the THIRTY YEARS WAR. Trained by GUSTAVUS II in the use of the new mobile field artillery, he led (1641–46) the Swedish troops to many victories. He was the military teacher of CHARLES X.

tort, in law, a civil wrong against a person or property for which damages may be claimed as compensation. A tort violates duties imposed by law on all persons, as distinguished from the duties a CONTRACT imposes on the parties making it. CRIMINAL LAW involves state action against wrongdoers, while torts give the injured parties the right to sue. A wrongful act may be both a tort and a crime; thus, the crime of BURGLARY may be actionable as the tort of trespass. Torts are classified primarily as intentional, e.g., LIBEL, ASSAULT, FRAUD, or as injury arising from NEGLIGENCE. Damages are usually awarded in tort cases. They may be nominal, symbolic recognition of the wrong done, even though substantial harm did not occur; or compensatory, to redress the plaintiff's loss or injury. Where there was fraud or intentional wrongdoing, the court may award punitive or exemplary damages to punish the defendant. In some circumstances, e.g., NUISANCE, the court may issue an INJUNCTION.

tortoise, terrestrial TURTLE, especially one of the family Testudinidae. Tortoises inhabit warm regions worldwide except in Australia. Most famous is the giant tortoise of the Galapagos Islands (*Testudo elephantopus*), which can be over 4 ft (120 cm) long and weigh over 500 lb (225 kg). Tortoises are extremely long-lived; some are known to have survived for more than 150 years.

Tory, English political party. The name was used derogatorily for supporters of the duke of York (later JAMES II). After 1688 the Tories comprised mainly country gentry who were closely identified with the Church of ENGLAND. Reaching their zenith under Queen ANNE, with Robert Harley and Henry St. John as leaders, they were discredited for JACOBITE leanings under GEORGE I. Power passed for the next 50 years to their rivals, the WHIGS. Revived (after 1783) by the younger William PITT, the Tories became reactionary after the French Revolution, and lost strength following the REFORM BILL of 1832. Remnants of the Tory party became known as the CONSERVATIVE PARTY.

Toscanini, Arturo [tōskänē'nē], 1867–1957, Italian conductor, one of the world's greatest conductors. He began his career as conductor of the Rio de Janeiro opera (1886). Returning to Italy, he conducted the premieres of LEONCAVALLO's *Pagliacci* (1892) and PUCCINI's *La Bohème* (1896), and was later musical director at La Scala, Milan. In the U.S., he conducted at the METROPOLITAN OPERA (1908–14), the New York Philharmonic (1926–36), and the NBC Symphony, which was formed for him (1937–54).

Toshkent or **Tashkent,** city (1992 est. pop. 2,133,000), capital of UZBEKISTAN, central Asia, in the foothills of the Tian Shan mts. The largest central Asian city, and among the oldest, it is the economic heart of the region, with such manufactures as textiles, farm machinery, and consumer goods. The Toshkent oasis produces cotton, fruits, and grains. First mentioned in the 1st cent. B.C., Toshkent came under Arabic rule (7th cent. A.D.) and passed to KHOREZM (12th cent.). It fell (13th–15th cent.) to JENGHIZ KHAN, TIMUR, and the Uzbeks. Under Russian rule after 1865, it was the capital of the Turkistan Autonomous SSR (1918–24) and replaced (1930) SAMARKAND as the capital of the Uzbek SSR (independent as Uzbekistan since 1991). A major earthquake in 1966 heavily damaged the city.

totem, an object, usually an animal or plant, revered by an individual or a particular social group. A group totem represents the bond of unity and is often considered the ancestor or brother of the group's members; marriage between those of one totem is often prohibited as incest. The group's symbol and protector, the totem may be pictured on the body or masks, or carved on totem poles.

Totila or **Baduila,** d. 552, last king of the OSTROGOTHS (541–52). By taking Naples (543) and Rome (546) he became master of central and S Italy. JUSTINIAN I spurned his peace offers and sent (552) an army under NARSES against him. Totila was routed and killed, leaving Italy under Byzantine control.

Tottel, Richard, 1530?–1594?, English publisher. His anthology, *The Book of Songs and Sonnets* (1557), known as Tottel's Miscellany, presented poems by Sir Thomas WYATT and other poets of the English Renaissance.

toucan, perching BIRD of the New World tropics, related to the WOODPECKERS. Toucans vary in size from the jay-sized toucanets to the 24-in. (62-cm) tocos of the Amazon basin. Their enormous, often brightly colored, canoe-shaped bills are adapted to cutting up fruits and berries.

touch-me-not, common name for any plant of the genus *Impatiens* of the JEWELWEED family.

Toulouse, city (1990 pop. 358,688), capital of Haute-Garonne dept., S France, on the Garonne R. A cultural and commercial center, it is also the center of the French aerospace industry. A part of Roman Gaul, it was (419–508) the capital of the Visigoths and (781–843) of the Carolingian kingdom of Aquitaine. Under the counts of Toulouse, who ruled most of the region of Languedoc, it was the artistic and literary center of medieval Europe. It passed to the French crown in 1271. An old quarter and many buildings are preserved, e.g., a Romanesque basilica and Gothic cathedral.

Toulouse-Lautrec, Henri de [to͞olo͞oz'-lōtrĕk'], 1864–1901, French painter and lithographer. His growth was permanently stunted, the result of a childhood accident. Influenced by DEGAS, he was inspired by sporting subjects and the life of music halls, cabarets, and circuses. His work is graphic in nature. Using garish and artificial colors, he brought new immediacy to his posters, particularly those of the Moulin Rouge. His works include *At the Moulin de la Galette* (1892; Art Inst., Chicago).

Touré, Sékou [to͞orā'], 1922–84, president of GUINEA (1958–84). A Marxist who rose through the labor movement, he became president of Guinea when it left (1958) the FRENCH COMMUNITY. Despite generally repressive rule and anti-Western policy, he later encouraged private U.S. investment to support Guinea's gradually deteriorating economy.

tourmaline, complex aluminum and boron silicate mineral $[(Na,Ca)(Al,Fe,Li,Mg)_3Al_6(BO_3)_3Si_6O_{18}(OH)_4]$, used as a gem. Colors are red, pink, blue, green, yellow, violet, and black; sometimes it is colorless. Two or more colors, arranged in zones or bands with sharp boundaries, may occur in the same stone. Tourmalines are found in pegmatite veins in granites, gneisses, schists, and crystalline limestone. Important sources include Elba, Brazil, Russia, Sri Lanka, and parts of the U.S.

tournament or **tourney,** in the Middle Ages, public contest between armed horsemen in simulation of real battle. Based on the ideas of chivalry and accompanied by much pageantry, the tourney probably originated in France in the 11th cent. The field, or lists, was enclosed by barriers and flanked by pavilions for notables. Because many knights were killed or injured, a less dangerous version known as tilting was devised.

tourney: see TOURNAMENT.

Tours, city (1990 pop. 129,509), capital of Indre-et-Loire dept., W central France. It is a wine market and tourist center. A Gallo-Roman town, it was a center of medieval Christian learning, notably under GREGORY OF TOURS and ALCUIN. There CHARLES MARTEL halted (732) the Moorish conquest of Europe. It has produced many great artists.

Toussaint L'Ouverture, François Dominique [to͞osăn' lo͞o vĕrtür'], c.1774–1803, Haitian patriot. A self-educated, freed slave, he joined the black rebellion (1791) to liberate the slaves. With Generals DESSALINES and CHRISTOPHE, he forced (1798) the British to withdraw from HAITI, quelled (1799) a mulatto uprising, and resisted a French invasion (1802). But he was treacherously seized by the French and died in a dungeon in France. His valiant life and tragic death made him a symbol of the fight for liberty.

Tower of London, ancient fortress, east of the City of London, on the N bank of the Thames. Formerly a royal residence and jail for illustrious prisoners, it is now an arsenal and museum. A dry moat and castellated walls surround the White Tower, built c.1078. Subsequent towers include the Wakefield Tower, which houses the crown jewels. The Traitors' Gate and Bloody Tower are associated with notables including Sir Thomas MORE and Anne BOLEYN. Many persons beheaded there or on neighboring Tower Hill are buried in the chapel. Yeomen of the Guard (Beefeaters) still guard the Tower.

Townes, Charles Hard, 1915–, American physicist and educator; b. Greenville, S.C. He taught (1948–59) at Columbia Univ. and was provost (1961–66) of the Massachusetts Institute of Technology. For his work on the theory and application of the MASER and for other work in quantum electronics connected with both maser and LASER devices, he shared with Nikolai Basov and Alexander Prokhorov the 1964 Nobel Prize in physics.

Townsend, Francis Everett, 1867–1960, American reformer; b. Fairbury, Ill. In 1933, at the height of the GREAT DEPRESSION, he proposed a relatively simple old-age pension plan. Although bills to enact the Townsend plan were continually defeated, its popularity contributed to passage of SOCIAL SECURITY legislation.

Townshend Acts, 1767, revenue acts passed by the English Parliament to replace the repealed STAMP ACTS. They placed duties on various items imported into the American colonies. The colonists reacted strongly, and the BOSTON MASSACRE and the BOSTON TEA PARTY were among the resulting incidents.

toxemia, disease state caused by the presence in the blood of bacterial TOXINS or other harmful substances. The effects of the bacterial endotoxins include fever, hemorrhage, and shock; exotoxins attack specific tissues, e.g., botulinus toxin affects the nervous system. The term toxemia is also used for **preeclampsia,** a condition occurring late in pregnancy that is associated with high blood pressure, protein in the urine, and edema; it was believed to be caused by toxins. If untreated it can lead to eclampsia—maternal convulsions and COMA—and renal and cardiovascular damage or death.

toxic shock syndrome, acute, sometimes fatal, disease characterized by high fever, nausea, diarrhea, lethargy, blotchy rash, and sudden drop in blood pressure. It is caused by several toxin-producing strains of bacteria, particularly streptococcal and staphylococcal bacteria. Streptococcal forms, in which the bacterium typically enters the body through a cut, are more common. Staphylococcal toxic shock is most prevalent among menstruating women using high absorbency tampons.

toxic waste: see POLLUTION; WASTE DISPOSAL.

toxin, poison produced by living organisms. **Exotoxins,** secreted by bacterial cells, have specific reaction sites in the host; e.g., the toxin associated with DIPHTHERIA affects mucous membranes and that associated with BOTULISM destroys nerve tissue. Substances such as snake venom are also considered exotoxins. The pathological effects of **endotoxins,** which are formed inside bacterial cells and freed when they die, are similar regardless of the type of bacteria (see TOXEMIA). The presence of toxins stimulates the production of antibodies, or antitoxins, one of the body's defenses against disease (see IMMUNITY).

toy dog, class of very small breeds of dogs kept as pets. Some are selectively bred small forms of larger breeds; others are naturally small. See individual breeds, e.g., CHIHUAHUA, MALTESE, PEKINGESE, POMERANIAN, SHIH TZU, toy POODLE.

Toynbee, Arnold Joseph, 1889–1975, English historian. In his major work, *A Study of History* (12 vol., 1934–61), he propounded the problems of history in terms of great cultural groups and civilizations rather than of nationalities. The main thesis of the work is that the well-being of a civilization depends on its ability to respond successfully to challenges, human and environmental. Of 26 civilizations in history, he saw only Western Latin Christendom as still alive.

toyon: see CHRISTMASBERRY.

track and field athletics, sports of foot racing, hurdling, jumping, vaulting, and weight throwing. They are usually separated into two categories—track (the running events) and field (the throwing and vaulting events). Individuals and teams compete on a field comprising an oval track and an infield for the field events. In the U.S. the most popular events include the 100-m, 200-m, 400-m, 880-m, the 1,500-m, 3,000-m (women), 5,000-m (men), and 10,000-m runs; the 100-m (women), 110-m (men), and 400-m hurdle races; the 400-m and 1,600-m relays; the long (or broad) jump; the high jump; the pole vault; the shot put; the discus throw; the javelin throw; and the hammer throw. The DECATHLON is the major composite event in Olympic track and field competition. Cross-country, distance, and walking races are usually classed with track and field athletics, as is the MARATHON RACE. The sport dominated the original OLYMPIC GAMES in ancient Greece.

Tracy, Spencer, 1900–1967, American film actor; b. Milwaukee, Wis. He won Academy Awards for his character portrayals in *Captains Courageous* (1937) and *Boys' Town* (1938). Other films include *Adam's Rib* (1949) and *The Last Hurrah* (1958).

trade union: see UNION, LABOR.

Trafalgar, battle of, Oct. 21, 1805, naval encounter of the Napoleonic Wars, fought off Cape Trafalgar, on the SW coast of Spain. The British fleet, under NELSON, won a brilliant victory over the French and Spanish navies under Pierre de Villeneuve. Nelson was fatally wounded in the encounter.

tragedy, form of drama, central to Western literature, in which a person of superior intelligence and character, a leader of the community, is overcome by the very obstacles he is struggling to remove. The earliest tragedies were part of the Attic religious festival held in honor of the god DIONYSUS (5th cent. B.C.). The most famous ancient tragedies are probably the *Oresteia* of AESCHYLUS, SOPHOCLES' *Oedipus Rex,* and EURIPIDES' *Trojan Women.* ARISTOTLE pointed out tragedy's ritual function: the spectators are purged of their own emotions of pity and fear through their vicarious participation in the drama. The dramas of the Roman tragedian SENECA were based on certain conventions—unity of time and place, violence, bombast, revenge, and the appearance of ghosts. Seneca's plays served as models for such RENAISSANCE tragedies as Christopher MARLOWE's *Tamburlaine* (1587) and Thomas KYD's *Spanish Tragedy* (1594). These in turn prefigured the towering tragedies of the period: Marlowe's *Dr. Faustus* (1588); SHAKESPEARE's *Othello, Macbeth, Hamlet* and *King Lear* (1600–1607), and John WEBSTER's *Duchess of Malfi* (1614). All of these plays dramatize the conflicts of kings, conquerors, or, at the very least, geniuses. The tradition of the tragic hero continued for the next 300 years in the work of the Spaniards LOPE DE VEGA and CALDERÓN DE LA BARCA; the Frenchmen Pierre CORNEILLE and Jean RACINE; and the Germans G.E. LESSING, GOETHE, and SCHILLER. Tragedy can reflect another vision of life, again rooted in religious drama—the mystery plays and morality plays of medieval France and England. These plays, of which EVERYMAN is the best known, emphasize the accountability and suffering of ordinary people. The tragic lot of the common people is explored in such later dramas as George Lillo's domestic tragedy *The London Merchant* (1731) and Georg BÜCHNER's political tragedy *Danton's Death* (1835). In Henrik IBSEN's *A Doll's House* (1879) and *An Enemy of the People* (1882), ordinary people behave heroically, acknowledging their faith in the validity of the tragic vision. The cataclysmic events of the 20th cent. have produced a radical diminution of that vision. In such plays as Eugene O'NEILL's *Mourning Becomes Electra* (1931), Bertolt BRECHT's *Mother Courage* (1941), Arthur MILLER's *Death of a Salesman* (1949), and Samuel BECKETT's *Waiting for Godot* (1953), life is depicted as so horrible and absurd that heroic behavior is not only impossible, it is irrelevant.

Traherne, Thomas, 1636?–1674, English METAPHYSICAL POET. His finest work, expressing an ardent, childlike love of God, appeared in the 1670s but was lost until rediscovered and published as *Poems* (1903) and *Centuries of Meditations* (1908).

trailing arbutus, Mayflower, or **ground laurel,** American wildflower (*Epigaea repens*) of the HEATH family. The plant blooms in early spring; its creeping stems bear clusters of fragrant pink or white flowers, sometimes hidden by the hairy evergreen leaves. It is the provincial flower of Nova Scotia and the state flower of Massachusetts.

Trajan (Marcus Ulpius Trajanus), A.D. c.53–117, Roman emperor (A.D. 98–117); b. Spain. The adopted son and successor of Emperor Nerva, he brought DACIA under Roman control and conquered much of PARTHIA. He did much building in Rome (including the Forum of Trajan). HADRIAN succeeded him.

tranquilizer, drug whose action on the central nervous system relieves emotional agitation. Antipsychotic drugs, or major tranquilizers, ease the symptoms of psychotic states, including agitation, delusions, and anxiety. These drugs include chlorpromazine (Thorazine), the first agent to be widely applied to mental disorders and still the standard drug. ANTIANXIETY DRUGS, or minor tranquilizers, are prescribed to relieve anxiety and tension. See also LITHIUM.

transactinide elements, chemical elements with atomic numbers greater than 103, that of lawrencium, the last member of the ACTINIDE SERIES. See TRANSURANIUM ELEMENTS.

transcendentalism, in American literature, movement that flourished in New England c.1836–60. A reaction against Calvinist orthodoxy and Unitarian rationalism, it was influenced by the German idealist philosophers, notably KANT, and by such English authors as CARLYLE, COLERIDGE, and WORDSWORTH. Its tenets included belief in God's immanence in humans and nature, and in individual intuition as the highest source of knowledge. An optimistic philosophy, it emphasized individualism, self-reliance, and rejection of traditional authority. Its ideas were most eloquently expressed in the essays of EMERSON and in *Walden* (1854) by THOREAU. Other important transcendentalists included George Ripley, Bronson ALCOTT, and Margaret FULLER. Their journal was *The Dial* (1840–44); BROOK FARM stemmed from the movement.

transcendentalism, in philosophy, term describing systems holding that there are modes of being beyond the reach of mundane experience. It is closely associated with KANT, who states that transcendental elements of thought (such as concepts of space and time and categories of judgment) cannot be perceived directly through experience; nevertheless, they add to empirical knowledge. He called these elements *noumena* (as opposed to *phenomena*).

Transcendental Meditation: see MEDITATION.

transdermal patch or **transdermal delivery system:** see SKIN PATCH.

transducer, device that accepts an input of energy in one form and produces an output of energy in some other form, with a known, fixed relationship between the input and output. One class of transducers consists of devices that produce an electrical output signal, e.g., MICROPHONES, RECORD-PLAYER cartridges, and PHOTOELECTRIC CELLS. Other transducers accept an electrical input, e.g., LOUDSPEAKERS, light bulbs, and SOLENOIDS. Transducers may be either active or passive. Active transducers require a source of energy in addition to the input signal to produce the output signal, whereas passive transducers require only an input signal.

transformational-generative grammar, linguistic theory associated with Noam CHOMSKY, particularly with his *Syntactic Structures* (1957), and with Chomsky's teacher Zellig Harris. Generative grammar attempts to define rules that can generate the infinite number of grammatical (well-formed) sentences possible in a language. It starts not from a behaviorist analysis of minimal sounds but from a rationalist assumption that a deep structure underlies a language, and that a similar deep structure underlies all languages. Transformational grammar seeks to identify rules (transformations) that govern relations between parts of a sentence, on the assumption that beneath such aspects as word order a fundamental structure exists. Transformational and generative grammar together have been the starting point for a tremendous growth in LINGUISTICS studies since the 1950s.

transformer, electrical device that transfers an alternating current or voltage (see POTENTIAL, ELECTRIC) from one ELECTRIC CIRCUIT to another using electromagnetic INDUCTION. A simple transformer consists of two coils of wire electrically insulated from each other and arranged so that a change in the current through the primary coil will produce a change in voltage across the secondary coil. The ratio of the alternating-current (AC) output voltage to the AC input voltage is approximately equal to the ratio of the number of turns in the secondary coil to the number of turns in the primary coil. This capability for transforming voltages is the basis for a great many applications. Transformers are classified according to their use; power transformers (see POWER, ELECTRIC) are used to transmit power at a constant frequency, audio transformers are designed to operate over a wide range of frequencies with a nearly constant ratio of input to output voltage, and radio-frequency transformers operate efficiently within a narrow range of high frequencies.

transform fault: see FAULT; PLATE TECTONICS.

transgenic animal: see PHARMING.

transistor, electronic device used as a voltage and current AMPLIFIER, consisting of SEMICONDUCTOR materials that share common physical boundaries. The materials most commonly used are silicon and germanium into which impurities have been introduced. In *n*-type semiconductors there is an excess of free electrons, or negative charges, whereas in *p*-type semiconductors there is a deficiency of electrons and therefore an excess of positive charges. Transistors are a key component of INTEGRATED CIRCUITS and are used in many applications, including RADIO receivers, electronic COMPUTERS, and automatic control instrumentation (e.g., in spaceflight and guided missiles). Since the invention (announced in 1948) of the transistor by the American physicists John BARDEEN, Walter H. Brattain, and William Shockley, many types have been designed. These are generally classified as bipolar or field effect. A **bipolar transistor** consists of three layers—the top and bottom layers, called the emitter and the collector, are of one conductivity type, while the middle layer, called the base, is of the other conductivity type. The dividing surfaces between the conductivity types are called *p-n* junctions. The electrons pass through the junctions from one layer to the other. The transistor action is such that if the electric POTENTIALS on the segments are properly determined, a small current between the emitter and base connections results in a large current between the emitter and collector connections, thus producing current and amplification. A **field-effect transistor** functions in a similar fashion except that the resistance to the electron flow is modulated by an external electric field. In a junction field-effect transistor (JFET), the controlling electric field is produced by a reversed bias *p-n* junction (one in which a voltage is applied so as to make the *p* side negative relative to the *n* side); in a metal oxide semiconductor field-effect transistor (MOSFET), the electric field is due to a charge on a CAPACITOR formed by a metal electrode and an insulating oxide layer that separates the electrode from the body of the semiconductor. See also MICROELECTRONICS; THYRISTOR

transit instrument or **transit,** telescope devised to observe stars as they cross the meridian of LONGITUDE and used for determining time. Its viewing tube swings on a rigid horizontal axis restricting its movements to the arc of the meridian. The meridian circle (a modern transit) is equipped with precisely graduated circles mounted on the horizontal axis and with stationary verniers, or reading microscopes, mounted on the fixed supports of the telescope that enable the observer to read the circles. By giving both the altitude and transit time, this instrument yields the right ascension and declination—the position on the celestial sphere—of the star (see ASTRONOMICAL COORDINATE SYSTEMS).

transition elements or **transition metals,** elements of group VIII and the b groups (I through VII) of the PERIODIC TABLE, characterized by the filling of an inner *d* or *f* electron orbital as atomic number increases. Many chemical and physical properties of these elements are due to their unfilled *d* or *f* orbitals. Transition elements generally have high densities and melting points, magnetic properties, and variable valence arising from the electrons in the *d* or *f* orbitals. These metals form stable coordination complexes, or complex IONS, many of which are highly colored and exhibit paramagnetism.

Transkei, black South African homeland, or BANTUSTAN (1990 est. pop. 4,500,000), 15,831 sq mi (41,002 sq km), SE South Africa, declared independent by South Africa in 1976, but not recognized as independent by any other nation. It borders on Lesotho (N) and the Indian Ocean (SE); the capital is Umtata. Most of its inhabitants are Xhosa. The first homeland to be granted independence, Transkei severed diplomatic relations with South Africa from 1978 to 1980 over territorial disputes. It was reabsorbed into South Africa in 1994.

Transleithania: see AUSTRO-HUNGARIAN MONARCHY.

transmission, in AUTOMOBILES, system for transmitting power from the engine to the wheels. The system is designed to change the high rotational speed and low torque (turning force) of the engine's crankshaft into the higher-torque rotation needed to turn the wheels over a range of speeds. A **manual transmission** consists of a system of interlocking GEAR wheels arranged so that by operating a lever the driver can choose one of several ratios of speed between an input shaft turned by the engine and an output shaft that turns the wheels. For a standing start the driver selects the first, or lowest, gear, which produces high turning power at a low output shaft speed. Higher gears produce less torque at higher output shaft speeds. To allow smooth shifting from one gear to another, a clutch mechanism disengages the engine from the transmission during gear changes. The **automatic transmission** (introduced in 1939), in which gear changes are made without driver intervention, uses a fluid device called a torque converter to connect the engine with the gearbox and to control gear changes. A **continuously variable transmission** uses a belt that connects two variable-diameter pulleys to provide an unlimited number of ratio changes and uninterrupted power to the wheels.

transpiration, in terrestrial plants, loss of water by evaporation mainly through the pores (stomata) of the LEAF but also through the plant's surface cells. The pull of transpiration on the fluid in the plant is one cause of the ascent of SAP from the ROOTS, and thus helps provide the necessary moisture for cell functions (see PHOTOSYNTHESIS). Desert plants are modified in ways that decrease transpiration (see SUCCULENT).

transplantation, medical, process by which a tissue or organ is removed and replaced by a corresponding part. Transplants usually range from those employing tissue (such as skin, bone, or cartilage) from the patient's own body (called an autograft transplant) to those involving the replacement of vital organs (such as the heart or kidney) from the body of another individual (a homograft, or allograft, transplant). Transplantation of complex organs calls for the surgical connection of the larger blood vessels of the donor organ to those of the recipient; connective tissue cells gradually link the graft and host tissues. Replacements for diseased or defective tissue (e.g., a cornea or the heart) are generally obtained from donors who have died; paired, large, or regenerating organs or tissues such as kidney, skin, bowel, bone marrow, or blood can be donated by living individuals (see BLOOD TRANSFUSION). Tissue can also come from aborted fetuses, as in FETAL TISSUE IMPLANTS. Organs such as the heart must be transplanted as soon after the donor's death as possible; skin, corneas, bone, and some blood fractions can be stored. Transplanted tissue from another individual contains antigens that stimulate an immune response by the host's lymphocytes (see BLOOD; IMMUNITY), and the main obstacle to successful transplantation is the rejection of foreign tissue by the host. To minimize rejection, an antigenic typing system (called the HLA system and similar to blood typing) is used to determine the degree of tissue compatibility between the donor and the recipient. IMMUNOSUPPRESSIVE DRUGS are also used to interfere with the production of antibodies (the body's usual response to foreign substances) in the recipient. Current research is using the increased knowledge of immune response on the molecular level to manipulate the body into accepting foreign tissue. Human tissue grafting was first performed about 100 years ago by Jacques Reverdin, a Swiss surgeon. In 1902 the French surgeon Alexis CARREL developed a method of joining blood vessels that made the transplantation of organs feasible and stimulated the use of transplantation in experimental biology. The first successful transplant of a human KIDNEY was made by Richard H. Lawler in Chicago in 1950; and the first human HEART transplant was performed by the South African surgeon Christiaan BARNARD in 1967. Since then, advances in BIOENGINEERING have also made possible the implantation of artificial body parts, such as artificial joints, and in 1982 resulted in implantation of the first permanent artificial heart (see HEART, ARTIFICIAL). Investigations continue into the development of completely artificial organs. Human transplants have also been made experimentally using organs from baboons, chimpanzees, and monkeys since 1963.

Transportation, United States Department of, federal executive department established (1967) to coordinate and administer overall transportation policy. Its divisions have jurisdiction in the areas of highway planning and construction; urban mass transit; railroads; aviation; and the safety of waterways, ports, highways, and oil and gas pipelines. It also includes the U.S. COAST GUARD.

transuranium elements, radioactive chemical elements with atomic numbers greater than 92 (URANIUM). Only NEPTUNIUM (at. no. 93) and PLUTONIUM (at. no. 94) occur in nature; they are produced in minute amounts in the radioactive decay of uranium. The transuranium elements of the ACTINIDE SERIES were discovered as synthetic radioactive isotopes. Both American and Soviet scientists claimed to have discovered independently the unstable transactinide elements 104, 105, and 106, and West German scientists reported discovering the unstable transactinide elements 107, 108, and 109.

Transvaal, province (1991 est. pop. 8,630,000), 110,450 sq mi (286,065 sq km), NE South Africa, situated at an elevation of 3,000–6,000 ft (910–1,830 m) in the VELD. It has produced much of the world's gold since deposits were discovered in the WITWATERSRAND (or Rand) in 1886. The province also mines diamonds and produces coal, uranium, platinum, and chromium. Much of South Africa's industry is concentrated along the Rand and around PRETORIA, JOHANNESBURG, and other Transvaal cities. First settled (mid-1830s) by Boer farmers, it became the first Republic of South Africa and led resistance to British rule. Under the new South African constitution of 1994 it was divided into several provinces.

Transylvania, historic region and province (21,292 sq mi/55,146 sq km), central Romania, separated in the south from Walachia by the Transylvanian Alps and in the east from Moldavia and Bukovina by the Carpathian Mts. CLUJ-NAPOCA is the chief city. Transylvania has deposits of lignite, iron, and other resources, and produces steel, chemicals, and other manufactures. Agriculture, stock raising, and wine making are also important. Part of the Roman province of Dacia, Transylvania was ruled (11th–16th cent.) by Hungary. Magyars, Germans, Romanians, and other peoples settled the area. From the 15th cent. Turkey and Austria vied for control of the region; Austrian control was established in 1711. Transylvania was part of Hungary in the Austro-Hungarian Empire (1867–1918). After WORLD WAR I the region was ceded to Romania. Hungary annexed N Transylvania in 1940; after WORLD WAR II it was returned to Romania.

Travis, William Barrett, 1809–36, hero of the Texas Revolution. He was in command of the Texas troops defending the ALAMO. After SANTA ANNA's Mexican forces stormed the fort (Mar. 1836), all the defenders, including Travis, Davy CROCKETT, and James BOWIE, were massacred.

Treasury, United States Department of the, federal executive department established (1789) to advise the president on fiscal policy and act as financial agent for the government. It receives and pays out money for the government, and through the SECRET SERVICE it is also in charge of protecting the president. Its divisions also include the U.S. Mint, the INTERNAL REVENUE SERVICE, the Office of the Comptroller of Currency, the Bureau of Engraving and Printing, the Customs Service, the U.S. Savings Bond Division, the Bureau of Alcohol, Tobacco, and Firearms, the Bureau of Public Debt, and the Office of Thrift Supervision (1989).

Treaty of Paris: see PARIS, TREATY OF.

Treaty of Versailles: see VERSAILLES, TREATY OF.

Trebizond, empire of, 1204–1461, one of the Greek states that sprang up after the overthrow (1204) of the Byzantine Empire by the army of the Fourth CRUSADE. Founded by the Comnenus brothers, David and ALEXIUS I of Trebizond, Trebizond remained independent when the Byzantine Empire was restored (1261). Although at times subject to Turks or Mongols, Trebizond grew prosperous as the trade route through Asia Minor to E Asia, and from Russia and the Middle East to Europe. In 1461 this last refuge of Hellenistic culture fell to the Ottoman Turks under MUHAMMAD II.

Tree, Ellen: see under KEAN, EDMUND.

Tree, Sir Herbert Beerbohm, 1853–1917, English actor-manager; b. Herbert Draper Beerbohm; half brother of Max BEERBOHM. As a manager he was noted for his Shakespearean productions, in which he stressed visual elements with elaborate effects. His wife and leading lady, **Helen Maud Holt,** 1863–1937, was especially adept at comedy.

tree, perennial woody plant with a single main STEM (the trunk or bole) from which branches and twigs extend to form a characteristic crown. Trees are either deciduous, i.e., having broad leaves that are shed at the end of the growing season, or evergreen (see CONIFER), having needle- or scale-like leaves that are shed at intervals of 2 to 10 years. Some broad-leafed shrubs follow the conifer pattern, and the LARCH sheds its needle-like leaves deciduously. Tree identification is through leaf shape and overall appearance. Trees are an important source of wood, food, and products such as resins, RUBBER, QUININE, turpentine, and CELLULOSE.

tree shrew, small, arboreal prosimian, or lower PRIMATE, of the family Tupaiidae, found in S Asia. Tree shrews superficially resemble squirrels and are usually brown, reddish, or olive in color, with large eyes, good vision, and flexible hands with sharp claws. They are territorial, omnivorous, and extremely active and quarrelsome.

Treitschke, Heinrich von [trīch'kə], 1834–96, German historian, professor, and Prussian state historiographer. Anti-Semitism and a fanatic nationalism distort the excellent scholarship of his works, notably his *History of Germany in the Nineteenth Century* (5 vol., 1879–94).

trek, in South African history, the great migration (1835–36) of Dutch farmers (Boers); called the Great Trek. Escaping British domination of the Cape of Good Hope, they founded the Orange Free State, the Transvaal, and Natal.

trench: see OCEAN; PLATE TECTONICS.

Trent, Council of, 1545–47, 1551–52, 1562–63, ecumenical council of the Roman Catholic Church. Convoked by Pope PAUL III to meet the crisis of the Protestant REFORMATION, it was the chief expounder of the Catholic reform (see REFORMATION, CATHOLIC). Its definitions and reform decrees treated Scripture, the sacraments, education, the Mass, the clergy, relics, feasts, and other topics. The reforms touched all aspects of religious life and set the pattern of modern Catholicism. The official *Catechism of the Council of Trent* was published in 1566.

Trent Affair, a diplomatic incident between the U.S. and Great Britain during the American CIVIL WAR. In Nov. 1861 Capt. Charles Wilkes halted the British mail packet *Trent* and removed two Confederate commissioners, J.M. Mason (see under MASON, GEORGE) and John SLIDELL, and had them interned in Boston. The British reacted sharply, and for a time it appeared they might retaliate by either recognizing the CONFEDERACY or declaring war on the U.S. The U.S. secretary of state, W.H. SEWARD, sent a note disavowing the action and released the men, thereby averting a crisis.

Trenton, city (1990 pop. 88,675), state capital (since 1790) and seat of Mercer co., W N.J., at the head of navigation on the Delaware R.; settled by Friends 1679, inc. as a city 1792. Situated between New York and Philadelphia, it is a transportation center and an important industrial city. Its pottery industry dates from colonial times. Steel cables, rubber goods, textiles, plastics, and a variety of metal products are manufactured. On Dec. 26, 1776, having crossed the Delaware unexpectedly, George WASHINGTON defeated a Hessian force at Trenton; the Americans then struck at PRINCETON. A 155-ft (47-m) granite monument commemorates the battle.

Trevelyan, Sir George Otto, 1838–1928, English historian and politician. A Whig member of the House of Commons (1865–97), he wrote the pro-American *American Revolution* (4 vol., 1899–1907) and *George the Third and Charles Fox* (1912). His works were popular in the U.S. His son, **George Macaulay Trevelyan,** 1876–1962, taught history at Cambridge and was master of Trinity College (1940–51). He was a master of the "literary" school of historical writing, and his reaction against the "scientific" school was influential. His best-known works include *History of England* (1926), *British History in the Nineteenth Century* (1922), and *England under Queen Anne* (3 vol., 1930–34).

triangle, in music: see PERCUSSION INSTRUMENT.

triangulation: see GEODESY.

Triassic period: see GEOLOGIC ERA (table).

triathlon, sports competition composed of three activities: swimming, bicycling, and running. Triathlons range in difficulty from the Ironman Triathlon (est. 1978) in Hawaii—a 2½-mile swim, 112-mile bicycle race, and 26-mile run—to much easier races like the Central Park (N.Y.C.) Triathlon—¼-mile swim, 12-mile bicycle race, and 5-mile run.

tribe, social group, usually with a distinguishing area, dialect, cultural homogeneity, and unifying social organization. It ordinarily has a leader and may have a common ancestor or patron deity. Member families or small communities are linked by economic, social, religious, or blood ties. In a narrower sense, *tribe* refers to the widest territorially defined, politically independent unit in a tribal society.

tribune, in ancient Rome, one of various officers. There were military tribunes, senior officers of the legions, elected by the people from c.508 B.C. to 367 B.C. The office of tribune of the PLEBS, designed to protect plebeian rights, especially against abuse by magistrates, was formed in 493 B.C. By 449 B.C. there were ten tribunes who were plebeians elected by an assembly of plebs. The tribune's person was inviolable. He had the right to veto a decision of a magistrate and the right to prosecute corrupt magistrates before a public body.

trichinosis or **trichiniasis,** parasitic disease caused by the roundworm *Trichinella spiralis,* following ingestion of raw or inadequately cooked meat, especially pork. The larvae mature in the intestines and are carried by the bloodstream to muscles, where they become embedded and remain. The host experiences irregular fever, profuse sweating, and muscular soreness; these symptoms usually subside soon after infestation, although vague muscle pain and fatigue may persist.

trichomoniasis, sexually transmitted disease caused by the parasitic protozoan *Trichomonas vaginalis.* In women, it can cause urinary tract infection and a painful vaginitis marked by a thin, foamy, irritating discharge. In men, it can infect the urethra and bladder. The infection is treated with metronidazole (Flagyl).

Trier [trēr], Fr. *Trèves,* city (1989 est. pop. 95,700), Rhineland-Palatinate, W Germany, on the Moselle R. It is a port, an industrial center with such manufactures as textiles and tobacco products, and the hub of the Moselle wine region. Founded c.15 B.C. by AUGUSTUS, it was a commercial and cultural center under the Romans and as part of the HOLY ROMAN EMPIRE. The city was held (19th–20th cent.) by France and by Prussia. Its historic structures include an amphitheater (c.100) and a Romanesque cathedral (11th–12th cent.). Karl MARX was born in Trier.

Trieste, city (1990 pop. 233,047), capital of Friuli-Venezia Giulia, NE Italy, at the head of the Adriatic. A major seaport, it is a commercial and industrial center. A medieval free commune menaced by Venice, it placed itself (1382) under the Austrian dukes. It became a free port in 1719. A center of IRREDENTISM, Trieste and its province were annexed (1919) by Italy. After World War II they were claimed by Yugoslavia, made (1947) a free territory under UN protection, and divided (1954) between the two countries, with Italy receiving the city. Landmarks include the Cathedral of San Giusto and Miramar castle.

triglyceride, ester formed from glycerol and three fatty acid molecules. FATS AND OILS are triglycerides. In humans, triglycerides supply fuel for energy. They are stored in adipose (fat) tissue or float in the bloodstream. Normally, triglycerides are obtained from foods, but excessive sugar and alcohol consumption can cause them to be synthesized in the body. Elevated levels of triglycerides in the blood are associated with an increased risk of heart disease.

trigonometry, the study of certain mathematical relations originally defined in terms of the angles and sides of a right triangle, i.e., one containing a right ANGLE (90°). Six basic relations, or trigonometric functions, are defined. If *A, B,* and *C* are the angles of a right triangle ($C = 90°$) and *a, b,* and *c* are the lengths of the respective sides opposite these angles, then six functions can be expressed for one of the acute angles, say *A,* as various ratios of the opposite side (*a*), the adjacent side (*b*), and the hypotenuse (*c*), as set out in the table. Although the actual lengths of the sides of a right triangle may have any values, the ratios of the lengths will be the same for all similar right triangles, large or small. It may be seen that $\sin B = \cos A$, $\cos B = \sin A$, $\tan B = \cot A$, and so forth. The values of the sine and the cosine are always between 0 and 1, the values of the secant and the cosecant are always equal to or greater than 1, and the values of the tangent and the cotangent are unbounded, increasing from 0 without limit. The values of the trigonometric functions can be found in a set of tables or on a calculator. The notion of the trigonometric functions is extended beyond 90° (the largest angle size in a right triangle) by defining the functions with respect to CARTESIAN COORDINATES; the functions then take on negative as well as positive values in a pattern that

TRIGONOMETRIC FUNCTIONS

Function (abbreviation)	Definition
sine (sin)	$\sin A = \dfrac{\text{opposite}}{\text{hypotenuse}} = \dfrac{a}{c}$
cosine (cos)	$\cos A = \dfrac{\text{adjacent}}{\text{hypotenuse}} = \dfrac{b}{c}$
tangent (tan)	$\tan A = \dfrac{\text{opposite}}{\text{adjacent}} = \dfrac{a}{b}$
cotangent (cot or ctn)	$\cot A = \dfrac{\text{adjacent}}{\text{opposite}} = \dfrac{b}{a}$
secant (sec)	$\sec A = \dfrac{\text{hypotenuse}}{\text{adjacent}} = \dfrac{c}{b}$
cosecant (csc)	$\csc A = \dfrac{\text{hypotenuse}}{\text{opposite}} = \dfrac{c}{a}$

repeats every 360°. This repeating, or periodic, nature of the trigonometric functions leads to important applications in the study of such periodic phenomena as light and electricity. A general triangle, not necessarily containing a right angle, can also be analyzed by means of trigonometry. Spherical trigonometry, the study of triangles on the surface of a sphere, is important in surveying, navigation, and astronomy.

Trilling, Lionel, 1905–75, American critic; b. N.Y.C. A professor at Columbia, he wrote essays (e.g., *The Liberal Imagination,* 1950, *The Opposing Self,* 1955) that combine social, psychological, and political insights with literary criticism and scholarship. His other works include a novel and biographies. His wife, **Diana Trilling,** 1905–, b. N.Y.C., is a literary and cultural critic. Her works include *We Must March My Darlings* (1977), a collection of essays; *Mrs. Harris* (1981), an analysis of the murder of a successful physician; and *The Beginning of the Journey* (1993), a memoir.

trillium or **wake-robin,** attractive spring wildflower (genus *Trillium*) of the LILY family, native to North America and E Asia. The single flower may be white, pink, dark red, yellow, or green, and the leaves, petals, and sepals are typically in threes.

trilobite, extinct marine invertebrate animal (an ARTHROPOD) with a flat, oval body covered by a horny shell; the name refers to a pair of furrows that divide the body lengthwise into three sections. Trilobites were abundant in Cambrian and Ordovician seas; they became extinct in the Permian period (see GEOLOGICAL ERAS, table).

Trinidad and Tobago, officially Republic of Trinidad and Tobago, republic (1992 est. pop. 1,299,000), West Indies, N of Venezuela, comprising the islands of Trinidad (1,864 sq mi/4,828 sq km) and Tobago (116 sq mi/300 sq km). The capital is PORT OF SPAIN (on Trinidad). Trinidad is predominantly flat, with low mountains in the north; Tobago is mountainous and forested. The climate of both islands is warm and humid. More industrialized than most West Indian nations, the country exports chemicals, petroleum products, bananas, cocoa, and sugar; has natural gas resources under development; and derives income from tourism. Unemployment is high, however. More than half the people are of African descent, and most of the rest Asian Indian. English (the official language) and a French patois are spoken.

History. Trinidad was visited by COLUMBUS in 1498 and was a Spanish outpost until it was taken by Britain in 1797. Tobago, which had been held by the Dutch and French, became British in 1803, and the islands were joined politically in 1888. After a brief period in the WEST INDIES Federation, they became an independent state in 1962 and a republic with a parliamentary system of government in 1976. Prime Min. Eric Williams and his People's National Movement (PNM) dominated Trinidadian politics from independence until his death in 1981. In 1987 A.N.R. Robinson, leader of the National Alliance for Reconstruction, became prime minister. He survived an attempted coup in 1990, but discontent with his economic austerity program returned the PNM to power in 1991, and Patrick Manning become prime minister.

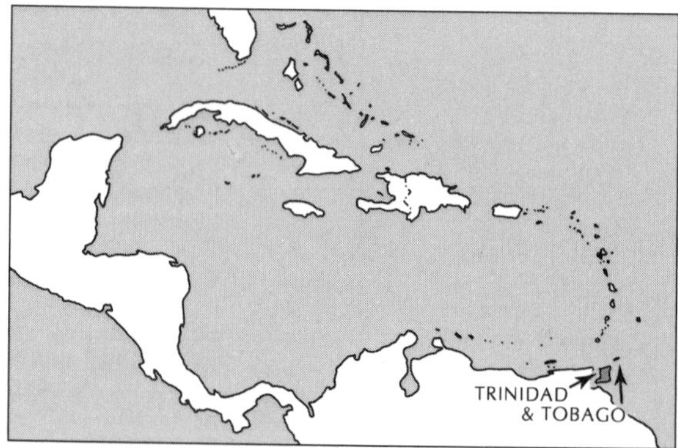

Trinity, fundamental doctrine of Christianity by which God is considered as existing in three persons—the Father, the Son (who became incarnate as JESUS), and the HOLY GHOST. The doctrine was defined very early, but received amplification at the first ecumenical councils.

Triple Alliance, War of the, 1865–70, fought by PARAGUAY against the alliance of ARGENTINA, BRAZIL, and URUGUAY. Paraguayan dictator Francisco Solano LÓPEZ imprudently declared war (1865) to revenge Brazil's military reprisals following Uruguay's civil war. Paraguay heroically defended itself against its larger, more powerful neighbors, but a large part of its male population was killed, and the country was devastated.

Triple Alliance and Triple Entente, two opposing international combinations of states that dominated Europe's history from 1882 until they came into armed conflict as the Central Powers and the Allies, respectively, in WORLD WAR I. Although there were numerous areas of contention between the two groups, the two principal problems that finally brought them to war involved rival claims in Morocco and the Balkans. The **Triple Alliance** was formed when the secret Dual Alliance of Germany and Austria-Hungary (1879) was joined by Italy in 1882. Serbia also joined in 1882, and Romania in 1883. Italy and Romania were never entirely comfortable within the alliance, however, and in fact both fought on the side of the Allies in the war. The **Triple Entente** followed the rapprochement (1890) between France and Russia and their secret Dual Alliance (openly acknowledged in 1895). In 1904, France and Britain, despite their traditional rivalry, formed the Entente Cordiale, which was brought about mainly because of their disquiet over German commercial and colonial imperialism. In 1907, Britain formally joined the Dual Entente, thereby converting it to the Triple Entente.

Tripoli, city (1984 pop. 990,697), capital of Libya, NW Libya, a port on the Mediterranean Sea. It is Libya's largest city and a commercial and industrial center. Manufactures include processed food and textiles. The city was founded (probably 7th cent. B.C.) by Phoenicians. It was captured by the Romans (1st cent. B.C.), the Vandals (5th cent. A.D.), and the Arabs (7th cent.). The Spanish took it in 1510, the Ottoman Turks in 1551. Tripoli became a major base of the Barbary pirates, whom the U.S. fought (1801–5) in the TRIPOLITAN WAR. It passed to Italy in 1911 and was taken (1943) by the British during WORLD WAR II. Some Roman monuments remain. In response to Libya's alleged support of terrorist activity, the U.S. bombed Tripoli in 1986.

Tripolitan War, 1800–1815, intermittent conflict between the U.S. and the BARBARY STATES. Piracy had long been a normal source of income in the N African Barbary States, and the U.S. adopted the practice, common to European nations, of paying tribute to buy immunity from pirate raids. When the pasha of Tripoli demanded (1800) more tribute than previously agreed upon, the U.S. refused payment and hostilities broke out. A settlement of sorts was effected in 1805, but tribute demands continued until 1815, when a squadron under DECATUR forced the dey of Algiers to sign a treaty renouncing the practice.

Tristan: see TRISTRAM AND ISOLDE.

Tristan da Cunha [trĭs'tăn də ko͞o'nə], group of volcanic islands (1991 est. pop. 300), S Atlantic, about midway between South Africa and South America. They were discovered by the Portuguese in 1506, annexed by Great Britain in 1816, and made a dependency of the British colony of SAINT HELENA in 1938. The inhabitants were evacuated to Britain following a volcanic eruption in 1961 but returned in 1963.

Tristram and Isolde, medieval romance. An Anglo-Norman version of c.1185 is the oldest extant. GOTTFRIED VON STRASSBURG wrote a German version c.1200. The story, originally independent, was later incorporated into ARTHURIAN LEGEND. The basic plot in all versions involves Tristram's journey to Ireland to bring Isolde back to Cornwall to be the bride of his uncle, King Mark. A potion the couple unknowingly swallow makes them fall in love. Modern treatments of the tale include those by SWINBURNE and Richard WAGNER.

tritium: see HYDROGEN.

Triton, in astronomy, natural satellite of NEPTUNE.

Triumvirate, in ancient Rome, ruling board or commission of three men. Triumvirates were common in the Roman republic. The **First Triumvirate** was the alliance of Julius CAESAR, POMPEY, and Marcus Licinius Crassus (see CRASSUS, family), formed in 60 B.C., but the alliance had no official sanction. The **Second Triumvirate**

was legally established by the senate in 43 B.C. and was renewed in 37 B.C. The members were Octavian (AUGUSTUS), Marc ANTONY, and Marcus Aemilius Lepidus (see LEPIDUS, family).

Trois Rivières or **Three Rivers,** city (1991 pop. 49,426), S Quebec, E Canada, at the junction of the St. Maurice and St. Lawrence rivers. It is one of Quebec's principal ports and industrial centers, with the manufacture of pulp and paper dominating the economy. Trois Rivières was founded in 1634 by CHAMPLAIN. It was a fortified port and a base for French exploration and missionary work in the interior during the 17th and 18th cent.

Trojan War, in Greek mythology, war between Greeks and Trojans. It began when PARIS abducted HELEN, wife of MENELAUS. Under AGAMEMNON, the Greeks besieged Troy for nine years. They finally won when, pretending to depart, they left a wooden horse, which the Trojans, ignoring the warnings of CASSANDRA and LAOCOÖN, took into the city. Warriors hidden in the horse opened the city gates to the Greek army, which sacked Troy. Among the Greek heroes were ACHILLES, Patroclus, ODYSSEUS, and Nestor; the Trojan heroes, led by HECTOR, included AENEAS, Memnon, and Penthesilea. The gods took a great interest in the war. HERA, POSEIDON, and ATHENA aided the Greeks, while APHRODITE and ARES favored the Trojans. The war's final year forms the main part of HOMER's *Iliad.* The Trojan War probably reflected a real war c.1200 B.C. over control of trade in the DARDANELLES.

Trollope, Anthony, 1815–82, English novelist. Although he did not publish his first novel until he was 40, he produced some 50 books, many written while he was working as a civil servant. Henry JAMES stated that Trollope's greatness lies in his "complete appreciation of the usual." His Barsetshire novels—among them *The Warden* (1855), *Barchester Towers* (1857), *The Small House at Allington* (1864), and *The Last Chronicle of Barset* (1867)—are a series of six books depicting, sometimes satirically, the lives of ordinary people in the fictional county of Barsetshire. Trollope's later novels are more concerned with politics and urban society. They include *Phineas Finn* (1869) and *The Prime Minister* (1876), two of the six Palliser novels. He also wrote travel books, and biographical and autobiographical works. His mother, **Frances Trollope,** 1780–1863, was also a novelist and travel writer.

trombone: see WIND INSTRUMENT.

Tropic of Cancer, parallel of LATITUDE at 23°27′ north of the EQUATOR. It is the northern boundary of the TROPICS and marks the farthest point north at which the sun can be seen directly overhead at noon. The sun reaches its vertical position over the Tropic of Cancer at about June 22, the summer SOLSTICE in the Northern Hemisphere.

Tropic of Capricorn, parallel of LATITUDE at 23°27′ south of the equator. It is the southern boundary of the TROPICS and marks the farthest point south that the sun can be seen directly overhead at noon. The sun reaches its vertical position over the Tropic of Capricorn at about December 22, the summer SOLSTICE for the Southern Hemisphere.

tropics, all the land and water of the earth between the TROPIC OF CANCER and the TROPIC OF CAPRICORN. The entire zone receives the sun's rays more directly than areas in higher latitudes, and therefore the average annual temperature is higher and seasonal changes in temperature are less. However, because of factors other than latitude (e.g., distance from the ocean, prevailing winds, elevation), several different climatic types are found, including rain forest, STEPPE, SAVANNA, and DESERT.

tropism, response of a plant or one of its parts, involving orientation toward (positive tropism) or away from (negative tropism) one or more external stimuli. For example, plant roots grow toward gravity and moisture and away from light. Other tropistic stimuli are heat, electricity, and chemical agents. The term *taxis* is applied to similar involuntary movements in animals and motile unicellular plants.

Trotsky, Leon [trôt′skē], 1879–1940, Russian revolutionary, a leader in the founding of the USSR; b. Lev Davidovich Bronstein. The son of a prosperous farmer, he became a Marxist in 1896. Exiled to Siberia in 1900, he escaped in 1902 with a passport bearing the name of one of his jailers, Trotsky. In London, with LENIN, he edited the Social-Democratic journal *Iskra* ("the spark"). After the 1905 RUSSIAN REVOLUTION he led the St. Petersburg SOVIET, or workers' council, but was soon arrested. In prison he formulated his theory of permanent revolution, predicting that in Russia bourgeois and socialist revolution would be combined and that worldwide proletarian revolution would follow. Escaping from Siberia again, he worked as a journalist in Vienna, Paris, and New York City. He returned to Russia in May 1917, and was a leading organizer of the Bolshevik seizure of power in Nov. 1917. In the new cabinet he was people's commissar for foreign affairs, but differences with Lenin over the Treaty of BREST-LITOVSK (1918) led him to resign. As people's commissar of war he organized the victorious Red Army in the civil war (1918–20). On Lenin's death (1924), Trotsky and STALIN were the chief rivals for succession. Stalin, general secretary of the party and a skilled infighter, opposed Trotsky's advocacy of world revolution with his plan for "socialism in one country." Trotsky was ousted as commissar of war (1925), expelled from the party (1927), and deported from the USSR (1929). Turkey granted him asylum. In 1933 he moved to France and in 1935 to Norway, which under Soviet pressure expelled him in 1936. In the Moscow treason trials (1936–38) he was accused of heading an anti-Soviet plot. Settling in Mexico City, he continued to oppose Stalinism in his writings, until his murder by Spanish-born Ramón Mercader.

troubadours, aristocratic poet-musicians (fl. late 11th–13th cent.) of S France (Provence). Their poems were sung in a dialect called *langue d'oc* and favorite subjects were courtly love, war, and nature. Many troubadours were noblemen and crusader knights; famous ones included Peire Vidal and Bertrand de Born. They declined after many were caught up in the Albigensian Crusade (see ALBIGENSES). Their counterparts in N France were called TROUVÈRES.

trout: see SALMON.

trouvères, medieval poet-musicians (fl. late 12th–13th cent.) of N and central France. The trouvères imitated the TROUBADOURS of the south. Their songs, written in a dialect called *langue d'oïl,* include love lyrics, romances, and the heroic CHANSONS DE GESTE.

Troy, ancient city of Asia Minor, also called Ilion or, in Latin, Ilium; known from Homer's account of the TROJAN WAR in the *Iliad.* Excavations by Heinrich SCHLIEMANN and others identified the site of the ancient city as the mound called Hissarlik, in Asian Turkey. It was established as a Phrygian city, with a culture dating from the BRONZE AGE.

troy weights: see ENGLISH UNITS OF MEASUREMENT; WEIGHTS AND MEASURES, table.

Trucial States: see UNITED ARAB EMIRATES.

Trudeau, Garry, 1948–, American cartoonist. Trudeau created the comic strip *Doonesbury* (1975; Pulitzer). The comic strip has addressed such controversial issues as Watergate, the drug culture, homelessness, and homosexuality, and some newspapers run *Doonesbury* on the editorial page. In 1983 he coauthored a stage version of the comic strip.

Trudeau, Pierre Elliott [tro͞odō′], 1919–, prime minister of CANADA (1968–79, 1980–84). He served (1967–68) in Lester PEARSON's ministry and succeeded him as Liberal party leader and prime minister. His government pursued a policy of independence of U.S. influence and promoted Canada's control of its economy. Trudeau sought to redefine federal-provincial relations and to contain the QUEBEC separatist movement. Briefly out of office (1979–80) after the Conservatives won the 1979 election, he returned to power in 1980. That year he proposed a new constitution for Canada, independent of the British Parliament, and on Apr. 17, 1982, Queen Elizabeth II signed the CONSTITUTION ACT, 1982, which gave Canada complete independence.

Truffaut, François, 1932–84, French film director. His engrossing, often charming, films have great visual power. They include *The 400 Blows* (1959), *Jules and Jim* (1961), *Day for Night* (1973), and *The Last Métro* (1980).

truffle, edible, subterranean FUNGUS harvested commercially chiefly in W Europe, although there are hundreds of species in N America. Truffles are small, solid, fleshy SAPROPHYTES that usually grow close to the roots of trees in woodlands. The several species range in color from gray or brown to nearly black and have a piquant, aromatic flavor. The wild truffles of the forests of Périgord, France, have long been regarded as a delicacy, and their collection is an important industry. They are hunted with dogs and hogs, which are able to scent them out underground. Truffles are cultivated in N Spain, France, and the U.S.

Trujillo Molina, Rafael Leonidas [trōōhē'yō mōlē'nä], 1891–1961, president of the DOMINICAN REPUBLIC (1930–38, 1942–52). After seizing power by an army coup (1930), he ran an efficient but ruthless dictatorship for 31 years until his assassination. He accomplished considerable material progress, but his terroristic methods led to unprecedented repression.

Truman, Harry S, 1884–1972, 33rd president of the U.S.; b. Lamar, Mo. He grew up on a farm near Independence, Mo., and served in World War I. In 1919 he married Elizabeth (Bess) Virginia Wallace; they had one daughter, Mary Margaret. After a decade in local Democratic politics, he was elected U.S. senator in 1934 and reelected in 1940. During World War II, he achieved national prominence as chairman of a committee investigating government spending. He was nominated for vice president in 1944 and elected along with Pres. Franklin D. ROOSEVELT. Roosevelt's death on Apr. 12, 1945, thrust Truman into the presidency at a crucial time—the closing days of World War II. After the war in Europe ended on May 8, Truman authorized the use of the ATOMIC BOMB against Japan at HIROSHIMA (Aug. 6) and NAGASAKI (Aug. 9). On Aug. 14, Japan surrendered. Truman's domestic program, essentially a continuation of Roosevelt's NEW DEAL, was frustrated by the resurgence of the Republicans, who won control of Congress in 1946. In foreign affairs, increasing tensions with the USSR resulted in the COLD WAR. Truman took increasingly tough stands. The Truman Doctrine (1947) was aimed at protecting Greece and Turkey from Communist domination. The MARSHALL PLAN (1947) was designed to effect the economic recovery of Western Europe. The NORTH ATLANTIC TREATY ORGANIZATION (1949) was a multinational defense plan. In the 1948 presidential election Truman won a stunning (and unexpected) victory over Thomas E. DEWEY. Foreign affairs also dominated his second term, particularly American involvement in the KOREAN WAR. Truman chose not to run for reelection in 1952 and retired to Independence. His term of office was marked by controversy from beginning to end. Among his controversial acts were his decision to use the atomic bomb, the "loss" of China to the Communists, and his firing of Gen. Douglas MACARTHUR during the Korean War. He was much respected for his plain speaking and for his ability to make hard decisions, however, and during the 1970s public opinion polls consistently showed him to be among the most admired of American presidents.

Trumbull, John, 1750–1831, American poet; b. Westbury, Conn. One of the CONNECTICUT WITS, he was the author of the satires *The Progress of Dulness* (1772–73) and *M'Fingal* (1775–82).

Trumbull, John, 1756–1843, American painter; b. Lebanon, Conn.; son of Gov. Jonathan Trumbull. He studied under Benjamin WEST in London and there began his life work, a series of historical paintings on the American Revolution. His small paintings, e.g., *Battle of Bunker's Hill* (1786), and his miniature studies for the series (the best done 1789–93) are among his finest works. Several of Trumbull's historical panoramas are in the CAPITOL rotunda.

Trump, Donald, 1946–, American businessman; b. N.Y.C. After attending the Wharton business school, he joined the family real estate business. He attracted public attention for his flamboyant dealings in real estate, casinos, sports, and transportation. Among his holdings are Trump Tower in New York City, and Trump Castle, Trump Plaza, and the Taj Mahal casino in Atlantic City.

trumpet: see WIND INSTRUMENT.

trust, corporate, in the U.S., a large-scale business combination. Typically, a corporate trust is created when stockholders in various enterprises assign control of these concerns to a single holding company and its board of trustees, thus eliminating competition. A *horizontal trust* combines corporations in the same line of business. A *vertical trust* controls all or part of a series of operations from the procurement of raw materials to the retailing of a product. By extension, the term *trust* has been applied to any very large business regarded as operating monopolistically in restraint of trade. See also ANTITRUST LAWS.

trusteeship, territorial, system (est. 1946) whereby nations administer dependent territories under the supervision of the UN Trusteeship Council. (See UNITED NATIONS, table). Its aim is to bring all territories to self-governing status. It succeeded the MANDATES system of the LEAGUE OF NATIONS. After World War II there were 11 trust territories; of these, all except Palau (administered by the U.S.) have now gained self-governing status.

Tryon, William, 1729–88, English colonial governor in North America. He was governor of North Carolina (1765–71), where he rigorously suppressed the REGULATOR MOVEMENT. He was also governor of New York (1771–78) during the AMERICAN REVOLUTION.

trypanosome, microscopic one-celled organism (PROTOZOAN) that usually lives as a parasite in the bloodstream of a vertebrate. Most undergo part of their development in the digestive tracts of insects that transmit the parasite with their bite. Some cause serious diseases in humans and animals, e.g., African sleeping sickness, caused by *Trypanosoma gambiense* and transmitted by the TSETSE FLY.

tsetse fly, any of several blood-sucking African FLIES. Several species transmit the TRYPANOSOME that causes African sleeping sickness in humans.

Tshombe, Moise Kapenda [chōm'bā], 1919–69, political leader in the Republic of the Congo (now ZAÏRE). When the Belgian Congo became independent in 1960, he became provisional president of the rich Katanga (now Shaba) province, which he proclaimed in secession from the rest of the Congo. He had strong Belgian backing, but eventually he was forced (1963) to capitulate. In 1964 he became premier of the Congo in a coalition government, but he was ousted in 1965 and went into exile. In 1967 he was kidnapped and taken to Algeria, where he died incommunicado.

Tsimshian, indigenous people of the Northwest Coast (see NORTH AMERICA, INDIGENOUS PEOPLES OF), probably with a Penutian language (see NATIVE AMERICAN LANGUAGES). They lived along the coast of British Columbia and Alaska, subsisting on codfish, halibut, and salmon, and also water and land mammals. Today the Tsimshian, on a reservation in their region, earn a living by fishing and forestry. In 1990 there were 2,432 Tsimshian in the U.S.

Tsin, dynasty: see CHINA.

Tsinan: see JINAN.

Tsingtao: see QINGDAO.

Tsiolkovsky, Konstantin Eduardovich [tsēōlkōv'skē], 1857–1935, Russian inventor and rocket expert. His most important theoretical work was concerned with the possibility of rocket flight into outer space. His *Investigation of Outer Space by Means of Reaction Apparatus* appeared in 1903. In 1929 he presented a design for a multistage rocket. He also conceived of artificial earth satellites, including manned space platforms.

Tsitsihar: see QIQIHAR.

Tsukuba Science City [tsōōkōō'bä], city (1984 est. pop. 34,000), central Honshu, Japan. Planned (1963) as a scientific research center, it was the site of a science exposition in 1985. Over 40 research facilities are there, including a high-energy physics laboratory and the Univ. of Tsukuba.

tsunami [tsōōnä'mē], **seismic sea wave,** or **tidal wave,** series of catastrophic ocean waves generated by earthquakes, volcanic eruptions, or landslides beneath the sea. In the open ocean tsunamis may have wavelengths of up to several hundred miles but heights of less than 3 ft (1 m). Because this ratio is so large, tsunamis can go undetected until they approach shallow waters along a coast. Their height as they crash upon the shore mostly depends on the geometry of the submarine topography offshore, but they can be as high as 100 ft (30 m) and cause severe damage and loss of life.

Tsushima Shuji: see DAZAI OSAMU.

Tsvetayeva or **Tsvetaeva, Marina Ivanovna,** 1892–1941, Russian poet. She was a major Russian poet, who survived the civil war, emigrated to Prague and Paris, and returned to Russia (1939). She wrote on a variety of subjects, using language and rhythms skillfully. Particularly noteworthy are her longer poems *Poem of the Mountain* (1926), *Poem of the End* (1926), and *Ratcatcher* (1925–26). Her works were not published in the USSR until 20 years after her death.

Tuareg, nomadic BERBERS of the Sahara, numbering about 800,000. Nominally Muslim, they have their own language and alphabet and have traditionally maintained a feudal society. Fiercely independent and in control of the trans-Saharan trade in slaves, gold, and ivory for hundreds of years, they resisted European conquest. During the 1970s drought, many starved or were forced to leave the desert. Groups of Tuaregs have fought for autonomy from Niger and Mali since the 1980s.

tuatara or **tuatera,** lizardlike REPTILE (*Sphenodon punctatus*), last survivor of the order Rhynchocephalia, which flourished in the early Mesozoic era before the rise of DINOSAURS. Also called sphenodon, it lives on a few islands off New Zealand, where it is protected. The olive-colored, yellow-speckled tuatara reaches 2 ft (60 cm) or more in length and has a spiny crest down its neck and back.

tuba: see WIND INSTRUMENT.

tuber, enlarged tip of a RHIZOME (underground STEM) that stores food. Tubers, although modified, contain all the usual stem parts—BARK, WOOD, pith, and nodes.

tuberculosis, contagious disease caused by the bacterium *Mycobacterium tuberculosis,* identified by Robert KOCH in 1882. Also known as TB and consumption, the disease primarily affects the lungs, although the intestines, joints, and other parts of the body may also become infected. It is spread mainly by inhalation, occasionally by ingestion through contaminated foods (e.g., unpasteurized milk) and utensils. Symptoms as the disease progresses include fever, weakness, loss of appetite, and, in the pulmonary form, cough and sputum. The incidence of tuberculosis—once affecting millions—greatly decreased in many developed countries with improved sanitation, early detection through X rays and skin tests, and antituberculosis drugs, but in the late 1980s the number of cases began to rise, particularly among AIDS patients, the poor, and immigrants from developing countries. Another troubling development was the spread of strains resistant to isoniazid, the drug most often used in treatment. A vaccine, Bacillus Calmette Guérin (BCG), that confers partial, temporary immunity is given by the World Health Organization to high-risk children.

Tubman, Harriet, c.1820–1913, African-American ABOLITIONIST; b. Dorchester co., Md. A slave, she escaped in 1849 and became one of the most successful "conductors" on the UNDERGROUND RAILROAD, leading more than 300 slaves to freedom. She was a friend of leading abolitionists and worked for Union forces during the Civil War as a laundress, nurse, and spy.

Tuchman, Barbara W(ertheim), 1912–89, American historian; b. N.Y.C. She won the Pulitzer Prize for history twice, for *The Guns of August* (1962), about the onset of WORLD WAR I, and for *Stilwell and the American Experience in China* (1971). Her other works include *The Zimmermann Telegram* (1958); *A Distant Mirror* (1978), a study of the 14th cent.; and *Practicing History* (1982), an essay collection.

Tucker, Richard, 1914–75, American tenor; b. Brooklyn, N.Y. He made his debut at the METROPOLITAN OPERA (1945) and became one of its leading lyric tenors in French and Italian operas.

Tucson, city (1990 pop. 405,390), seat of Pima co., SE Ariz.; inc. 1877. Located in a desert valley surrounded by mountains, it has a dry, sunny climate and is a tourist center. It also has electronic, optic, aerospace, and research industries, and processes and distributes the area's cotton and livestock. Copper mining is important in the area. The present city was established (1776) as a walled presidio. It was transferred to the U.S. by the GADSDEN PURCHASE (1853). Points of interest include the nearby San Xavier mission (present building 1783–97), the Arizona-Sonora Desert Museum, the Univ. of Arizona, and several military bases.

Tudor, royal family that ruled England (1485–1603). Its founder was a Welshman named Owen Tudor who married CATHERINE OF VALOIS, the widow of HENRY V. Their son Edmund married Margaret Beaufort (a descendant of JOHN OF GAUNT) and had a son Henry, who assumed the Lancastrian claims to the throne. Henry defeated RICHARD III at Bosworth Field and became (1485) king as HENRY VII. By his marriage to Elizabeth of York, Henry united the Lancastrian and Yorkist claims. Of his children, MARGARET TUDOR married JAMES IV of Scotland, Mary of England married LOUIS XII of France, and Henry succeeded him as HENRY VIII. Three of Henry VIII's children, EDWARD VI, MARY I, and ELIZABETH I, ruled England. The Tudors strengthened the English monarchy and witnessed a flowering of culture. The accession (1603) of JAMES I, a descendant of Margaret Tudor, began the STUART dynasty.

Tudor, Antony, 1909–87, English choreographer and dancer. He was influenced by expressionism and the MODERN DANCE idiom, and is known for the psychological dramas, e.g., *Romeo and Juliet* (1942), *Undertow* (1945), and *The Tiller in the Fields* (1978), he has created for the AMERICAN BALLET THEATRE (ABT) and other companies. He was ballet director at the Metropolitan Opera (1957–63) and associate director of the ABT (1974–1980).

Tudor style, phase of English architecture and decoration in the reigns (1485–1558) of Henry VII, Henry VIII, and Mary I, a transitional style between Gothic Perpendicular and Palladian. Manor houses, built for the new trading families, exhibit the style's characteristics of greater domesticity and privacy: rooms multiplied as the great hall's importance diminished; oak-paneled interiors had plaster relief ornament; furniture increased. Exteriors showed modified perpendicular features, e.g., square-headed, mullioned windows. Brickwork combined with half-timber, high pinnacled gables, and numerous chimneys to create a distinctive look. Principal Tudor examples are parts of Hampton Court Palace (begun 1515) and some colleges of Oxford and Cambridge.

Tuesday: see WEEK.

Tu Fu [do͞o fo͞o], 712–70, Chinese poet, considered the greatest Chinese poet. Pervaded by an ironic awareness of spiritual and social decay, his poetry expresses bitterness over his poverty-stricken life and laments the sufferings of the poor and the corruption and cruelty of the imperial court.

Tuileries [twē'lərēz], former palace in Paris. Planned by Catherine de' Medici and begun (1564) by Philibert DELORME, it occupied part of the present Tuileries gardens. It was rarely used until 1789, when Louis XVI was forced to move there from Versailles (see FRENCH REVOLUTION). Napoleon I made it his chief residence, as did his successors. The palace was destroyed by fire during the COMMUNE OF PARIS (1871). The formal gardens, by LENÔTRE, remain, affiliated with the LOUVRE.

tulip, hardy plant (genus *Tulipa*) of the LILY family, native from the Mediterranean to Japan and widely cultivated by the Dutch. Tulips, which are grown from BULBS, have deep, cup-shaped flowers of many rich colors. Said to have been introduced into Europe from Turkey in 1554, they were objects of wild financial speculation in 17th-cent. Holland.

tulip tree: see MAGNOLIA.

Tull, Jethro, 1674–1741, English agriculturist and inventor. He advocated the use of manures, pulverizing the soil, planting with drills, and thorough tilling of the soil during the growing period. He invented (c.1701) a mechanical drill for sowing.

Tully: see CICERO.

Tulsa, city (1990 pop. 367,302), seat of Tulsa co., NE Okla., on the Arkansas R.; inc. 1898. It is a major center of the U.S. oil industry, with refineries and business and research offices; aerospace and metal-processing industries are also important. Tulsa grew after the coming of the railroad in 1882 and boomed when oil was discovered nearby in 1901. A waterway connecting the city with the Gulf of MEXICO was opened in 1971, making the city an inland port.

tumbleweed, plant that breaks from its roots at maturity, dries into a rounded tangle of branches, and rolls long distances with the wind, scattering seeds as it goes. Tumbleweeds are especially abundant in PRAIRIE and STEPPE regions. One of the most common is the Russian thistle (*Salsola pestifer*), not a THISTLE but a member of the goosefoot family. Native to Asia, it is a pest on the prairies of the W U.S.

tumor or **neoplasm,** tissue composed of cells that grow in an abnormal way; it may be benign or malignant. Normal tissue contains feedback controls that allow for tissue repair but do not permit expansion once a certain number of cells have developed. Tumor cells, lacking such feedback controls, proliferate and monopolize body nutrients. Benign tumors, which differ from normal tissue in structure, grow excessively and, although rarely fatal, may grow large enough to interfere with normal functioning and require surgical removal. Malignant tumors (see CANCER) also grow excessively, but their cells lack the biological controls that normally keep cells specialized; these cells can infiltrate surrounding normal tissue and may later spread (metastasize) via BLOOD and the LYMPHATIC SYSTEM to other sites. Both benign and malignant tumors are classified according to the type of tissue in which they are found. For example, fibromas are neoplasms of fibrous connective tissue, and melanomas are abnormal growths of pigment (melanin) cells.

tuna or **tunny,** largest FISH of the MACKEREL family. Hunted as game and food, the family includes the little tuna (10 lb/4.5 kg) of the Atlantic, the most important commercially; the bluefin tuna (*Thunnus thynnus*), the giant of bony fishes (200–500 lb/90–225 kg); and the Pacific albacore (up to 60 lb/27 kg), marketed as "whitemeat tuna."

tundra, treeless plains to the north of the coniferous forest belt in N North America and N Eurasia. For most of the year the mean monthly temperature is below the freezing point. Winters are long and severe, and mean monthly summer temperatures rarely exceed 50°F (10°C). Precipitation is slight and evenly distributed throughout the year. The underlying subsoil (permafrost) is always frozen. Mosses, lichen, and some flowering plants grow during the brief summer, and the few large animal species include the caribou, arctic fox, and snowshoe rabbit. The tundra is a fragile, easily disturbed ecosystem.

tungsten (W) or **wolfram,** metallic element, first isolated in 1783 by the de Elhuyar brothers. It is a silver-white to steel-gray, very hard, ductile metal (one of the most dense) and has a higher melting point than any other metal. Tungsten is used for wires and for filaments for light bulbs and electronic tubes. Tungsten STEELS are hard and strong at high temperatures. Tungsten carbide is used in place of diamond for dies and as an abrasive. See ELEMENT (table); PERIODIC TABLE.

tunicate, marine CHORDATE with a resemblance in the larval stage to VERTEBRATES. Familiar tunicates are the sea squirts, or ascidians, sedentary filter-feeders with cylindrical bodies, usually found attached to rocks. The tunic, or thick vest, for which they are named, is transparent or translucent and composed of CELLULOSE, a material extremely rare in the animal kingdom. Some tunicates have gelatinous containers called houses instead of tunics.

Tunis, city (1984 pop. 596,694), capital of Tunisia, NE Tunisia, on the Lake of Tunis. Its major products include textiles, carpets, and olive oil; tourism is important economically. The city has notable mosques, the Univ. of Tunis (1960), and a national museum. The ruins of CARTHAGE are nearby. Tunis is probably pre-Carthaginian; it became the capital of Tunisia under the Hafsid dynasty (13th–16th cent.). After the Turks took the city in 1534, Tunis prospered as a center of piracy and trade. French occupation lasted from 1881 to 1956. Tunis was an important base during World War II. From 1979 to 1990 it was the headquarters of the ARAB LEAGUE.

Tunisia, Fr. *Tunisie,* officially Republic of Tunisia, republic (1992 est. pop. 8,446,000), 63,378 sq mi (164,150 sq km), NW Africa, bordered by Algeria (W), the Mediterranean Sea (N and E), and Libya (SE). TUNIS is the capital. The ATLAS MOUNTAINS in the north form a dry plateau that merges with fertile plains near the coast; in the south, below the Chott Djerid and other salt lakes, stretches the SAHARA desert. The irregular coastline has several fine harbors. Agriculture is the mainstay of the economy, but mining and tourism are important. Wheat, barley, grapes, olives, sugar beets, citrus fruits, and dates are the leading crops, and phosphates and petroleum are the principal minerals. Manufactured goods include steel, textiles, and processed food. Remittances from Tunisians working abroad, particularly in France, are an important source of foreign currency. The population is largely Berber and Arab, and Islam is the dominant religion. Arabic the official language, although French is widely spoken.

History. Settled in the 12th cent. B.C. by Phoenicians, Tunisia became (6th cent. B.C.) the center of the powerful city-state of CARTHAGE, which was destroyed by Rome in 146 B.C. Taken by the Vandals (5th cent. A.D.) and the Byzantines (6th cent.), the Arabs conquered Tunisia in the 7th cent., and the Berber population was converted to Islam. The area came under a succession of Muslim rulers, reaching its peak under the Berber Hafsid dynasty (c.1230–1574). In the late 16th cent. Tunisia was seized by the Ottoman Turks, and as one of the BARBARY STATES it became a stronghold of pirates, on whom the treasury depended for several centuries. European intervention began in the 19th cent., and in 1881 Tunisia became a French protectorate. Nationalist agitation, which first surfaced in the 1920s, became intense after World War II, and independence was achieved in 1956. In 1957 the country became a republic, with Habib BOURGUIBA as president. Under Bourguiba, who was elected president-for-life in 1975, Tunisia was a moderate Arab state, following a generally pro-Western foreign policy; support for a negotiated settlement with Israel strained the country's relations with its Arab neighbors, however. Domestically, Bourguiba emphasized modernization and planned economic growth. In 1981 he authorized the legal formation of opposition political parties, indicating a possible shift in the direction of liberal democracy. In 1987 Bourguiba was deposed, on grounds of senility, by Gen. Zine el-Abidine BEN ALI, who promised continued democratic reform, but he has ruled in an increasingly autocratic fashion and sought to crush Islamic-fundamentalist opposition to his government. In recent years relations with Libya have improved, and Tunisia joined with its North African neighbors in forming (1989) the Arab Maghreb Union (see under MAGHREB).

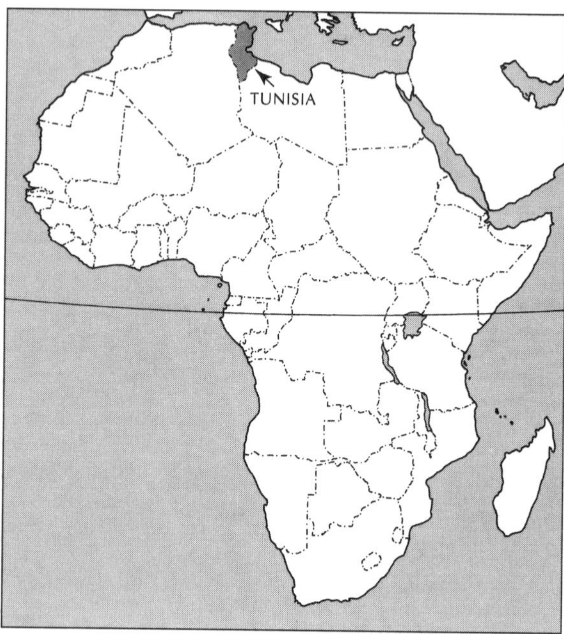

tunneling, in physics, quantum-mechanical effect by which a particle can pass through a barrier that the particle has insufficient energy to overcome, a process forbidden by ordinary classical mechanics. Tunneling results from the wavelike properties of particles; the wave associated with the particle "decays" through the barrier—the wave's amplitude decreases—but the amplitude of the wave on the other side of the barrier is large enough that there is a finite probability of finding the particle there. The tunnel DIODE was the first convincing demonstration of tunneling in solids. Tunneling between two superconducting materials is known as the Josephson effect.

Tunney, Gene (James Joseph Tunney), 1898–1978, American boxer; b. N.Y.C. He won (1922) the light-heavyweight title over Battling Levinsky, but lost it that same year (to Harry Greb) in his only defeat as a professional. In 1926 he defeated Jack DEMPSEY for the heavyweight championship and repeated his victory in 1927. He retired as champion in 1928.

Tupac Amaru [tōōpäk'ämä'rōō], 1742?–81, Spanish-American reformer and revolutionary of Inca descent. He led an unsuccessful revolt (1780) in what is now Peru against Spanish suppression of the indigenous people and was captured and executed. Many of the reforms he fought for were eventually granted.

tupelo: see BLACK GUM.

Tupí: see GUARANÍ.

turbine, rotary engine that uses a continuous stream of fluid (gas or liquid) to turn a shaft that can drive machinery. In the **hydraulic turbines** used in hydroelectric power stations, falling water strikes a series of blades or buckets attached around a shaft, causing the

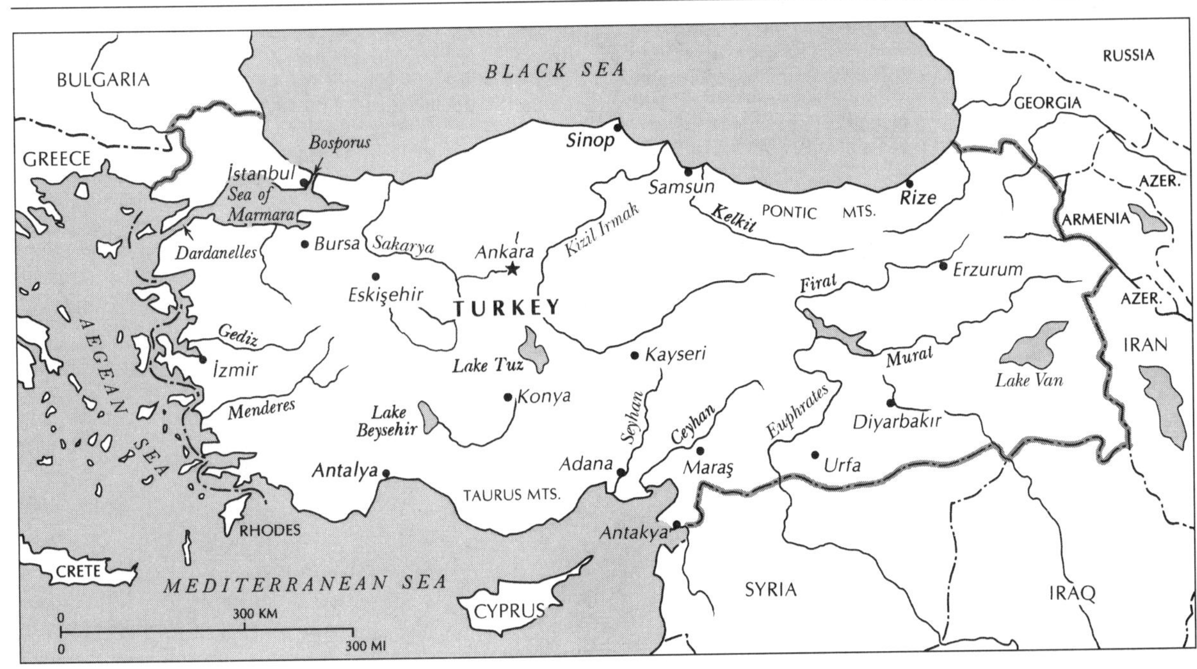

shaft to rotate, this motion in turn being used to drive the rotor of an electric GENERATOR. In a **steam turbine,** high-pressure steam forces the rotation of disks attached to a shaft. Steam turbines are used to drive most large electric generators and ship propellers. The term **gas turbine** is usually applied to a unit whose essential components are a COMPRESSOR, a combustion chamber, and a turbine. The turbine drives the compressor, which feeds high-pressure air into the combustion chamber; there it is mixed with a fuel and burned, providing high-pressure gases to drive the turbine. In a turboprop engine, the turbine is used to turn a propeller as well as the compressor. In a turbojet engine, the gases first drive the turbine and then are expelled from the engine to provide propulsion. Gas turbines are used mainly as aircraft engines (see JET PROPULSION).

turbulence, in physics, a state of constant, irregular change in the flow of a fluid. Turbulence is characteristic of systems that consist of large numbers of particles, and its unpredictability and randomness long thwarted attempts to understand it. Developments in NONLINEAR DYNAMICS have led to an understanding of the onset of turbulence, and the use of SUPERCOMPUTERS has resulted in improved modeling of turbulent states. Until the early 1970s it was held that laminar, or smooth, flow became turbulent through a gradual increase in instability until the flow became unpredictable. Experimental work, however, has shown that the onset of turbulence occurs abruptly.

Turgenev, Ivan Sergeyevich [to͝orgā'nyĭf], 1818–83, Russian novelist, short-story writer, and dramatist. Born to a landowning family, he first achieved literary success with "Khor and Kalinich" (1847), a story of peasant life included in *A Sportsman's Sketches* (1852); the book may have figured in ALEXANDER II's abolition of serfdom. In 1850 Turgenev wrote his best-known play, *A Month in the Country;* it was to influence CHEKHOV. The novels *Rudin* (1855), *A Nest of Gentlefolk* (1859), and *On the Eve* (1860) were followed by his masterpiece, *Fathers and Sons* (1861); like his other novels, it is a study of the intelligentsia. His later works include the novels *Smoke* (1867) and *Virgin Soil* (1877), and such stories as "First Love" (1870).

Turgot, Anne Robert Jacques [türgō'], 1727–81, French economist and statesman. As intendent of Limoges (1761–74) he won acclaim for his policies of encouraging new agricultural methods, free trade, and industry. In 1774 he became controller general of finances under LOUIS XVI and tried thereafter to enact stringent reforms. His six edicts (1776), which included the abolishment of guilds and the proposed taxation of all landowners, aroused the opposition of vested interests and forced his resignation (1776). Turgot was also a contributor to the ENCYCLOPÉDIE.

Turin, city (1990 pop. 1,002,863), capital of PIEDMONT, NW Italy. An industrial center and transportation hub, it produces motor vehicles, textiles, and machinery. Rome, the Lombards, and the Franks held it, and it became (12th–13th cent.) a free commune. It passed to the house of SAVOY c.1280, and became, in turn, capital of Savoy (after 1562), of the kingdom of Sardinia (1720–1861), and of the new Italian kingdom (1861–64). It suffered heavy damage in World War II; most of the important buildings that remain date from the 17th–19th cent.

Turing, Alan Mathison, 1912–54, British mathematician and computer theorist. His early work in predicate logic led to a proof (1937) that some mathematical problems are not susceptible to solution by automated computation. During World War II, he was instrumental in breaking the German Enigma cipher. After the war he helped design computers and did groundwork in the field of ARTIFICIAL INTELLIGENCE. See also TURING TEST.

Turing test, a procedure to test whether a computer is capable of humanlike thought. As proposed (1950) by British mathematician Alan TURING, a person sits with a teletype machine isolated from two correspondents—one is another person, one is a computer. By asking questions through the teletype and studying the responses, the isolated person tries to determine which correspondent is human and which the computer. If that proves impossible, the computer is credited with having passed the test.

Turkey, Turk. *Türkiye,* officially Republic of Turkey, republic (1990 pop. 56,969,109), 301,380 sq mi (780,574 sq km), SW Asia and SE Europe, bordered by Iraq, Syria, and the Mediterranean Sea (S), the Aegean Sea (W), Greece and Bulgaria (NW), the Black Sea and Georgia (N), and Armenia and Iran (E). Major cities include ANKARA (the capital), ISTANBUL, IZMIR, and ADANA. Asian Turkey, which constitutes 97% of the country, is separated from European Turkey by the BOSPORUS, the Sea of Marmara, and the DARDANELLES. European Turkey is largely rolling agricultural land, while Asian Turkey is mostly highland and mountains, with narrow lowland strips along the seacoasts. The economy is basically agricultural, but industrialization has been emphasized since the late 1940s. Chief crops include wheat and other cereals, cotton, tobacco, and fruit; livestock raising is important. Leading manufactures are textiles, processed foods, iron and steel, petroleum, cement, chemicals, and forest products. Coal and lignite, chromium, copper, iron, antimony, and mercury are mined; some petroleum is produced. Turkey is also noted for its carpets, Meerschaum pipes, and pottery.

The Turks, a highly composite ethnic mixture, mostly speak Turkish; there is a sizable Kurdish minority (see KURDISTAN). The country is almost entirely Muslim, with small groups of Orthodox Christians and other religions.

History. Anatolia, the western portion of Asian Turkey, is one of the oldest inhabited regions in the world. Turkey was part of the Hittite, Persian, Roman, Byzantine, Seljuk, and Ottoman empires. However, Turkey's history as a national state does not begin until after WORLD WAR I, when the Treaty of Sèvres (1920) reduced the once mighty OTTOMAN EMPIRE to insignificance. In 1923 the present boundaries of Turkey (except for Alexandrette, acquired in 1939) were established and Turkey was formally proclaimed a republic, with Kemal ATATÜRK as its first president. During the 15 years of his authoritarian rule, the country's political and economic structure as well as its religious and social bases were transformed. Islam ceased to be the state religion; the Latin alphabet replaced Arabic script; new industries were developed under state ownership; and women were emancipated. When Kemal died (1938), Turkey was becoming a Western-style state. Ismet İnönü, who succeeded Atatürk, kept Turkey neutral during most of WORLD WAR II; it joined the Allies only in Feb. 1945. Turkey became a member of NATO in 1952 and permitted the establishment of U.S. military bases. Political turmoil in the 1950s resulted in a military coup (1960), and a new constitution in 1961 created the second Turkish republic. Civilian rule returned in 1973. Clashes between the left and right increased during the late 1970s, and in 1980 the armed forces, led by Gen. Kenan Evren, once again seized power. A new constitution was approved by Turkish voters in 1982, and Evren was elected to a seven-year term as president. He was succeeded by Turgut Özal, a conservative politician, in 1989. Parliamentary elections in 1991 ousted Özal's Motherland party from government and shifted power to the new prime minister, Süleyman DEMIREL, of the conservative True Path party. Pres. Özal died in 1993 and was succeeded by Demirel and Tansu Çiller became prime minister, the first woman to hold that post. Tension with Greece has been a chronic problem. In 1974 a Greek-oriented coup in CYPRUS prompted Turkey to invade and occupy part of that island; war between Greece and Turkey was averted only by U.S., British, and UN intervention. Since the mid-1980s there has been fighting in SE Turkey between government forces and Kurdish guerrillas.

turkey, large, nonmigratory game and poultry bird of the family Meleagrididae, related to the GROUSE and PHEASANT. Turkeys are indigenous to the New World, where fossils date back to the Oligocene era. The domestic turkey is descended from the Mexican turkey, taken to Europe by CONQUISTADORS in the 16th cent. The wild turkey is a woodland bird, gregarious except at breeding time, and a good flier.

Turkic [tûr'kĭk], group of languages forming a subdivision of the Altaic subfamily of the URALIC AND ALTAIC family of languages. See LANGUAGE (table).

Turkish language, member of the Turkic subdivision of the Altaic subfamily of the URALIC AND ALTAIC family of languages. See LANGUAGE (table).

Turkmenistan or **Turkmenia,** republic (1992 est. pop. 3,838,000), 188,455 sq mi (488,100 sq km), central Asia, formerly a constituent republic of the USSR. It borders Afghanistan and Iran (S); Uzbekistan and Kazakhstan (E, NE); and the Caspian Sea (W). The capital is ASHGABAT (Ashkhabad); other important cities include Chardgov, Nebitdag, Dashhowuz, and Mary (Merv). The Kara Kum desert occupies 90% of the country; the Kara Kum canal provides irrigation and hydroelectricity. Turkmenistan's natural gas desposits have made it one of the wealthiest of the former Soviet states; among its other resources are oil, salt, phosphate, mirabilite, and sulfur. Karakul sheep (whose wool is made into carpets), cattle, and other livestock are raised, and silkworms are bred. Cotton is the chief crop; others include grains, sesame, and wine grapes. Industries include metalworking, oil refining, and many agriculturally related manufactures. The Turkmens (or Turkomans), a Sunni Muslim, Turkic-speaking people, comprise 60% of the population; other groups include Russians, Uzbeks, Kazakhs, and Tatars. Turkmen is the official language, and Russian is widely spoken.

History. Turkmenistan was part of the kingdom of ancient Persia and was later (8th–19th cent.) ruled by the Arabs, the Seljuk Turks (see KHOREZM), JENGHIZ KHAN, TIMUR and the TIMURIDS, and the Uzbeks. Under Russian rule from 1881, the area initially resisted the Bolsheviks but fell to the Red Army by 1920. In 1925 the Turkmen Soviet Socialist Republic was formed from Turkmenian portions of Soviet Turkistan. In 1991 the republic's parliament declared Turkmenistan independent following a referendum; after the Soviet Union collapsed, the republic joined the COMMONWEALTH OF INDEPENDENT STATES. The former Communist party has retained its hold on power in Turkmenistan, although there has been some movement toward privatizing the economy. Pres. Saparmurad Niyazov was reelected in 1992; he was the only candidate in the election.

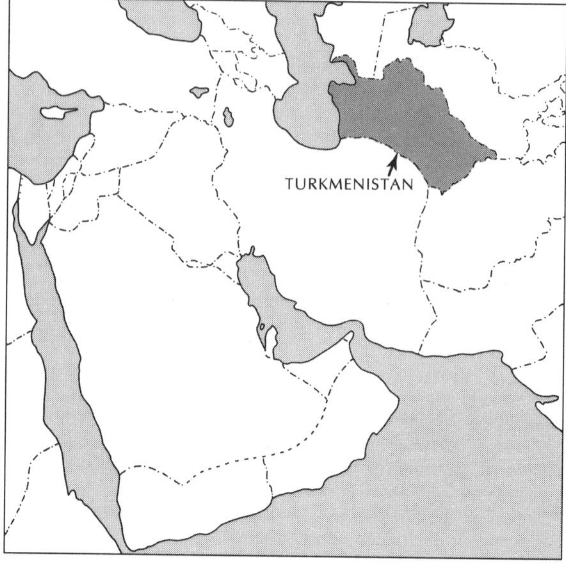

Turks, Turkic-speaking peoples found today in Turkey, the Soviet Union, Chinese Turkistan, Iran, and Afghanistan, totaling 73 million. Of widely varying histories and ethnic intermixtures, the different groups vary greatly in appearance and culture, being unified chiefly by linguistic affinity and social organization. The name Turk was first used in the 6th cent. by the Chinese for a nomadic people whose empire stretched from Mongolia to the Black Sea. Turkic peoples controlled this vast area until 924. The most important Turkic groups in the history of W Asia and Europe were the Seljuks and the Ottoman Turks. After the Turks adopted ISLAM, they began migrating in great numbers to the Middle East. By 1055 the Seljuks had conquered Iran; by 1071 they controlled Armenia, Syria, and much of Asia Minor. In the 12th cent. the Seljuk empire broke up into independent states that were overrun in the next century by JENGHIZ KHAN. After the Mongol wave receded, the Osmanli Turks completed the overthrow of the BYZANTINE EMPIRE, and in the 14th and 15th cent. they created the vast OTTOMAN EMPIRE. See also BULGARS, EASTERN; CUMANS; GOLDEN HORDE, EMPIRE OF THE; KHAZARS; TATARS; UIGURS.

Turks and Caicos Islands [kī'kōs], British dependency (1992 est. pop. 12,700), 166 sq mi (430 sq km), a group of over 30 cays and islands SE of the Bahamas. The capital, Jamestown, is on Grand Turk. Offshore banking and tourism are the economic mainstays; lobster and conch the primary exports. The population is largely of African descent.

turmeric: see GINGER.

Turner, Frederick Jackson, 1861–1932, American historian; b. Portage, Wis. He taught at the Univ. of Wisconsin (1885–1910) and Harvard (1910–24). His address "The Significance of the Frontier in American History," delivered before the American Historical Association in 1893, was an epoch-making work that opened up new and important fields for historical study. His other works include *The Rise of the New West* (1906) and *The Significance of Sections in American History* (1932).

Turner, John Napier, 1929–, prime minister of Canada (1984). A Liberal, he entered parliament in 1962 and served in various ministerial posts after 1968. When Prime Min. TRUDEAU resigned in 1984, Turner succeeded him. The Liberals were soundly defeated in elections several months later; Turner remained party leader until 1990.

Turner, Joseph Mallord William, 1775–1851, English landscape painter, the foremost English romantic painter and the most original of English landscape artists. He began exhibiting at the Royal Academy at the age of 16. He had a remarkable ability to distill the best from the tradition of landscape, and he traveled constantly, making inspirational sketches. His *Sun Rising through Vapor* (National Gall., London) shows Dutch influence, whereas *Crossing the Brook* (Tate Gall., London) shows the influence of CLAUDE LORRAIN. Despite his success, Turner lived the life of a recluse, maintaining a large gallery for exhibiting his works. His painting became increasingly abstract as he strove to portray light, space, and the elemental forces of nature. Characteristic of his later period is *Rain, Steam, and Speed* (National Gall., London). His late Venetian works, which describe atmospheric effects with brighter colors, include *The Grand Canal* (Metropolitan Mus.) and *Approach to Venice* (National Gall., Wash., D.C.). He encountered criticism as his style became increasingly free, but was defended by Sir Thomas LAWRENCE and the youthful RUSKIN. He left more than 19,000 watercolors, drawings, and oils to the nation.

Turner, Nat, 1800–1831, African-American slave and revolutionary; b. Southampton co., Va. Believing himself divinely appointed to lead his fellow slaves to freedom, he commanded about 60 followers in a revolt (1831) that killed 55 whites. Although the so-called Southampton Insurrection was quickly crushed and Turner was caught and hanged six weeks later, it was the most serious uprising in the history of U.S. slavery and virtually ended the organized abolition movement in the South.

Turner, Ted (Robert Edward Turner III), 1938–, American television broadcasting executive; b. Cincinnati. He founded (1976) a television station, WTBS, and built it into the Turner Broadcasting System, including (1980) the Cable News Network (CNN), (1988) a movie channel, and (1992) the Cartoon Network. He also owns the Atlanta Braves baseball team and Atlanta Hawks basketball team and won the 1977 *America*'s Cup yachting race. He married Jane FONDA in 1991.

turnip, garden vegetable of the same genus (*Brassica*) of the MUSTARD family as the CABBAGE, native to Europe. Grown for its edible green leaves (greens) and its nutritious rounded primary root, it is also used as stock feed. The two principal kinds are the white (*B. rapa*) and the yellow (*B. napobrassica*), also known as rutabaga or Swedish turnip.

turpentine, yellow to brown semifluid oleoresin (see RESIN) exuded from the sapwood of pines, firs, and other conifers. It consists of an ESSENTIAL OIL (oil of turpentine) and a type of resin called rosin. Commercial turpentine is oil of turpentine with the rosin removed. When pure, it is a colorless, transparent, oily liquid with a penetrating odor and characteristic taste. Turpentine is used chiefly as a solvent and drying agent in paints and VARNISHES.

turquoise, hydrous aluminum and copper phosphate mineral $[Al_2(OH)_3PO_4{\cdot}H_2O + Cu]$. Usually found in microscopic crystals, it is opaque with a waxy luster, varying in color from greenish gray to (gem-quality) sky blue. Because of their porosity, the gem varieties absorb dirt and grease, changing the color to an unattractive green; exposure to heat or sunlight can also harm the color. The finest specimens are from Iran; other sources are the Sinai peninsula and the SW U.S.

turtle, REPTILE (order Chelonia) with an armorlike shell and strong, beaked, toothless jaws. Turtles are found throughout most of the temperate and tropical world. The land-living species are commonly called TORTOISES; the name *terrapin* is generally applied to large freshwater or brackish water species. Turtles range in length from a few inches to over 7 ft (11 m); many specimens have lived over 50 years in captivity. The 200 to 300 species of turtle are classified in 12 families. The largest family of the Northern Hemisphere is the family of common freshwater turtles (Emydidae). Turtles are the oldest living group of reptiles, dating back to the time of the earliest DINOSAURS.

Tuscany region (1990 pop. 3,560,582), 8,876 sq mi (22,989 sq km), N central Italy, bordering on the Tyrrhenian Sea in the W. FLORENCE is the capital. The region is mostly hilly and mountainous. There is much industry, but farming is also important. Tuscany's Chianti wine is world famous. The region was the home of the ETRUSCAN CIVILIZATION and was conquered (mid-4th cent. B.C.) by the Romans. In the 11th and 12th cent. many cities became free communes, and some (PISA, Lucca, SIENA, and Florence) developed into strong republics. Under the MEDICI, the ruling family of Florence, Tuscany became (1569) a grand duchy. In 1860 it voted to unite with Sardinia and became (1861) part of the new kingdom of Italy. The area was a leading cultural center in the Renaissance.

Tuscarora: see IROQUOIS CONFEDERACY.

Tussaud, Marie Gresholtz [to͞osō'], Swiss modeler in wax. While imprisoned in France during the REIGN OF TERROR, she modeled heads of famous persons, using heads from decapitated bodies. In 1802 she inherited her uncle J.C. Curtius's wax museum and immigrated to London, where she established Madame Tussaud's Exhibition, a museum that remains a major tourist attraction.

Tutankhamen or **Tutenkhamon** [to͞ot"ängkä'mən, –ĕngk–], fl. c.1350 B.C., Egyptian king of the XVIII dynasty; son-in-law of IKHNATON. Ikhnaton had replaced the god AMON with Aton; under Tutankhamen this movement ended, and the capital was moved back to THEBES, sacred to Amon. Tutankhamen's tomb was found (1922) almost intact by Howard CARTER and the earl of CARNARVON, providing great impetus to Egyptology.

Gold mummy case from tomb of Tutankhamen

Tutsi or **Watutsi,** cattle-raising people of central Africa; they are also known as Watusi or Batusi. An aristocratic people, they are a minority in both RWANDA and BURUNDI, countries that are former Tutsi kingdoms. The Tutsi, who probably originated in Ethiopia, long held the peasant Hutu in feudal subjugation. In the 1970s, 80s, and 90s, despite much integration of Tutsi and Hutu culture, many members of both tribes died in bloody fighting in Burundi and Rwanda. The Tutsi are spectacularly tall, often over 7 ft (2.1 m) in height.

Tutu, Desmond Mpilo, 1931–, South African religious leader. He was the first black to be Anglican dean of Johannesburg (1975), general secretary of the South African Council of Churches (1978), bishop of Johannesburg (1984), and the archbishop of Cape Town (1986). He advocates nonviolence and interracial reconciliation in the struggle against APARTHEID and has worked in the West to encourage economic sanctions against the South African government. In 1984, he was awarded the Nobel Peace Prize.

Tutuola, Amos, 1920–, Nigerian novelist, noted for his idiosyncratic use of Yoruba legend and fantasy in tales written in a vernacular African English. His first novel, *The Palm-Wine Drunkard* (1952), is probably his best known.

Tuvalu, island nation (1992 est. pop. 9,500), 10 sq mi (26 sq km), composed of nine low coral atolls, formerly known as the Ellice (or Lagoon) Islands, scattered over the W Pacific Ocean. The capital is Fongafale, on Funafuti. Subsistence farming and fishing are mainstays of the economy, with copra the chief cash crop for export. Postage stamps and coins, however, are the largest source of foreign earnings. The population is primarily Polynesian; nearly all are members of the Protestant Church of Tuvalu.

History. The islands were discovered by Capt. John Byron in 1764 and were administered by Britain as part of a protectorate (1892–1916) and as part of the Gilbert and Ellice Islands colony (1916–74). The colony became self-governing in 1971, and in 1974 Ellice Islanders voted for separate British dependency status as Tuvalu. The islands became independent in 1978. Since 1989 Bikenibeu Paeniu has been prime minister. See PACIFIC OCEAN map.

TVA: see TENNESSEE VALLEY AUTHORITY.

Twain, Mark, pseud. of **Samuel Langhorne Clemens,** 1835–1910, one of the masters of American literature; b. Florida, Mo. After a boyhood in Hannibal, Mo., and work as a printer, he became a Mississippi River pilot (1857). In 1862 he moved west and began writing for newspapers, first in Virginia City, Nev., then in San Francisco, taking as a pseudonym a term from his river pilot days, "Mark Twain." He first won fame with his comic tale "The Celebrated Jumping Frog of Calaveras County" (1865). After a trip to Hawaii (1866), he became a successful humorous lecturer and, after a journey to the Holy Land, he published *The Innocents Abroad* (1869). In 1870 he married and settled in Hartford, Conn., where he wrote some of his best work: *The Gilded Age* (1873), a satirical novel written with Charles Dudley WARNER; *The Prince and the Pauper* (1882), a children's novel; the nonfictional *Life on the Mississippi* (1883); the satire *A Connecticut Yankee in King Arthur's Court* (1889); and the two famous evocations of his youth, *The Adventures of Tom Sawyer* (1876) and *The Adventures of Huckleberry Finn* (1884). In *Huckleberry Finn,* widely considered his masterpiece, Twain created one of the most memorable characters in American fiction, painted a realistic picture of 19th-cent. life, and revolutionized the language of fiction through his use of vernacular speech. In 1893, plunged into debt, he lectured his way around the world, recording his experiences in *Following the Equator* (1897). His later years were saddened by the deaths of two daughters and his wife, and his later works, e.g., *The Man Who Corrupted Hadleyburg* (1899), *What Is Man?* (1905), *The Mysterious Stranger* (1916), are somber, pessimistic, and misanthropic.

Tweed, William Marcy, 1823–78, American politician and Tammany leader; b. N.Y.C. "Boss Tweed" controlled nominations and patronage in New York City Democratic politics after 1857 through his control of the TAMMANY organization. He and the notorious **Tweed Ring,** which consisted of Tweed, the mayor, the city comptroller, and the city chamberlain, sold political favors and defrauded the city of at least $30 million, largely through padded construction contracts. Jay Gould and James FISK were business cronies, and after 1868 Tweed extended his influence to Albany. Reformers, notably S.J. TILDEN and Thomas NAST, effected his downfall, and he died in prison.

Tweed Ring: see under TWEED, WILLIAM MARCY.

Twelfth Night, Jan. 5, the vigil or eve of EPIPHANY, so called because it is the 12th night from Christmas.

Twelve Tables: see ROMAN LAW.

twelve-tone music, those compositions based on a particular ordering (called a series or row) of the twelve pitches that constitute the diatonic SCALE divided into equal semitones. Thus it is one type of SERIAL MUSIC. Abandoning the melodic and harmonic interweaving of lines featured in works of traditional TONALITY, the twelve-tone system evolved in the 1920s in the works of A. SCHOENBERG and his pupils A. BERG and A. von WEBERN. It has been used by such contemporary composers as Milton BABBITT and Pierre BOULEZ. See also ATONALITY.

Twenty-one Demands, 1915, ultimatum secretly presented to China by Japan during WORLD WAR I. They included control of the German leasehold in Shantung prov., rights to exploit Manchuria and Mongolia, and control of Chinese coal deposits. Other powers were to be excluded from further territorial concessions. The Japanese also sought control of China's military, commercial, and financial affairs, but this provision was dropped, partly at U.S. insistence. Chinese President YÜAN SHIH-KAI was forced to accept the remaining demands.

Two Sicilies, kingdom of the, name adopted (1816) by the kingdoms of NAPLES and Sicily when they were officially merged under King FERDINAND I. The kingdom was conquered (1860) by GARIBALDI and became part of the kingdom of Italy.

Tycho Brahe: see BRAHE, TYCHO.

Tyler, Anne, 1941–, American novelist; b. Minneapolis. Often set in the American South, her novels portray ordinary human life, particularly family relationships, with wit and great perception. Among her novels are *A Slipping Down Life* (1970), *Dinner at the Homesick Restaurant* (1982), *The Accidental Tourist* (1985), *Breathing Lessons* (1988), and *Saint Maybe* (1991).

Tyler, John, 1790–1862, 10th president of the U.S.; b. Charles City co., Va. Educated in law at the College of William and Mary, he was the son of John Tyler (1747–1813), governor of Virginia from 1808 to 1811. The younger Tyler also was governor (1825–27) of VIRGINIA and U.S. senator (1827–36). A moderate states' rights Democrat, he was a reluctant supporter of Andrew JACKSON during his two terms as president but eventually broke with the Democrats and joined the new WHIG PARTY. In 1840 he was running mate to the Whig presidential candidate, William Henry HARRISON, and they waged the victorious "Tippecanoe and Tyler too" campaign. Harrison died on Apr. 4, 1841, after only one month as president, and Tyler became the first vice president to succeed to the presidency. Tyler was never close to the Whig leaders, particularly Henry CLAY, and after he vetoed Whig measures and his cabinet had resigned, he quickly alienated most of them and found himself a president without a party. The Whigs rejected him in 1844 and nominated Clay. Tyler's chief accomplishments as president were the WEBSTER-ASHBURTON Treaty (1843) with Great Britain and the annexation of Texas as a state.

Tyler, Royall, 1757–1826, American author; b. Boston. A lawyer and law professor, he was chief justice of the Vermont supreme court (1807–13). He is remembered for his comedy *The Contrast* (1787) and for other plays, a novel, verse, and essays.

Tyler, Wat, d. 1381, English rebel, leader of the Peasants' Revolt of 1381. After the Black Death of 1348–49 had killed much of England's population, labor was scarce and wages rose. Parliament passed (1351) the Statute of Labourers to restrict wages, and nobles sought to hold their labor by enforcing old manorial rights. This bred discontent; rebellion broke out when the poll tax was increased (1380). Tyler and the rebels seized Canterbury, then marched to London, burning and plundering houses. RICHARD II came to meet Tyler and promised to abolish serfdom, feudal service, and market monopolies. A second meeting ended in a brawl in which Tyler was mortally wounded. The king's promises were forgotten, and the revolt was harshly suppressed.

Tylor, Sir Edward Burnett, 1832–1917, pioneering English anthropologist who specialized in primitive mentality and animism. His essentially modern cultural theories are expounded in *Anthropology* (1881, abr. ed. 1960).

Tyndale, Tindal, or **Tindale, William,** c.1494–1536, English biblical translator and Protestant martyr. Sympathetic with the new learning, he translated the New Testament into English. Opposed in England, he went to the Continent, where he met Martin LUTHER and began (1525) printing his New Testament. In England it was suppressed (1526), but he continued translating the Scriptures and writing tracts defending the English REFORMATION. He was seized (1535) in Antwerp, condemned for heresy, and executed. His work was the basis for the Authorized (King James) BIBLE.

Tyndall, John, 1820–93, English physicist, science lecturer, and writer; b. Ireland. He was professor (1853–87) and superintendent (1867–87) at the Royal Institution, London. He investigated light, sound, and radiant heat and studied Alpine glaciers. The scattering of light by COLLOIDS, known as the Tyndall effect, is named for him.

typewriter, instrument for producing printed letters by manual operation. The first practical commercial typewriter was invented in the U.S. in 1867 by Christopher Sholes and his colleagues, and was manufactured by the gunsmith Philo Remington in 1874. This early model had only capital letters; a shift-key model appeared in 1878. The electric typewriter came into use c.1935. In the 1960s some machine designs replaced type levers with a type-surfaced metal ball that moves rapidly across a stationary paper holder; the metal ball was later replaced by a daisy wheel. Computerized typewriters can store data and reproduce it automatically, as well as function as a personal computer printer, but in many instances typewriters have been replaced by word processors or computers using WORD PROCESSING programs.

typhoid fever, acute generalized infection caused by *Salmonella typhosa.* The main sources of infection are contaminated water or milk and food handlers who are carriers. Symptoms include high fever, rose-colored spots on the abdomen and chest, and diarrhea or constipation. Complications, especially in untreated patients, may be numerous. The disease is treated with the ANTIBIOTIC chloramphenicol; typhoid VACCINATION is a valuable preventive measure.

typhoon: see HURRICANE.

typhus, any of a group of infectious diseases caused by rickettsias, microorganisms classified between bacteria and viruses. Symptoms include fever and the early onset of rash and headache. Typhus is treated with ANTIBIOTICS and can be prevented by VACCINATION.

tyrant, in ancient history, ruler who gained power by usurping the legal authority. Greek tyranny was an outgrowth of the struggle of the rising popular classes against the aristocracy. Usually, a leader won popular support, overthrew the existing government, and seized power. Many tyrants ruled well and with benefit to their subjects. The word had no connotation of moral censure until the rise of constitutional, democratic government in Athens in the 5th cent. B.C. Greek tyrants included Periander of Corinth and PISISTRATUS of Athens.

Tyre or **Sur,** town (1988 est. pop. 14,000), SW Lebanon, on the Mediterranean Sea. Built on an island, it was an ancient seaport of PHOENICIA and had far-flung colonies by 1100 B.C. The Tyrians founded CARTHAGE in the 9th cent. B.C. Tyre was famous for its commerce and its purple Tyrian dye. Although taken by the Assyrians, Babylonians, and Persians, the city survived. It also recovered from a siege and sack by Alexander the Great, who built a mole that has since made the island a peninsula. In A.D. 64 the city became part of the Roman Empire. Later a Crusader stronghold, it was destroyed by Muslims in 1291. The city contains many Greco-Roman remains. In 1982 Tyre, a stronghold of the PALESTINE LIBERATION ORGANIZATION, fell to Israeli forces after heavy fighting during the Israeli invasion of S Lebanon (see ARAB-ISRAELI WARS).

Tyrol, prov. (1991 pop. 630,350), W Austria, in the Alps. The region attracts many tourists. Farming, forestry, and salt production are important occupations, and their are chemical industries. Conquered by Rome in 15 B.C., Tyrol was later part of the Frankish empire. It passed to Bavaria in 1805 but was returned to Austria in 1815. S Tyrol was given to Italy in 1919.

Tyrrhenian Sea, part of the Mediterranean Sea, lying between the west coast of peninsular Italy and the islands of Sardinia, Corsica, and Sicily. NAPLES and PALERMO are major ports.

Tyson, Mike G., 1966–, American boxer; b. N.Y.C. At 20, Tyson became the youngest heavyweight champion in history with a second-round knockout of Trevor Berbick in 1986. He had compiled a 37–0 record when he lost the title to James (Buster) Douglas in 1990. In 1992 he was convicted of rape and other charges in Indiana and sentenced to three concurrent 10-year terms in prison, 4 years of which were suspended.

Tyumen [tyo͞omĕn'yə], city (1989 pop. 478,000), SW Siberian Russia, on the Tura R. On the Trans-Siberian RR, Tyumen is a major transfer point for river and rail freight. It also has shipyards, and the surrounding area is rich in oil and natural gas. Founded in 1585, Tyumen is the oldest city in SIBERIA.

Tz'u Hsi [tso͞o shē], 1834–1908, dowager empress of China (1861–1908) and regent (1861–73, 1874–89, 1898–1908). Consort of Emperor Hsien Feng (d. 1861), she bore his successor, T'ung Chih, and after his death (1875) named her nephew, Kuang Hsü, to the throne. In 1898 she resumed the regency after he had tried to enact political reforms. She encouraged the BOXER UPRISING against foreigners.

U

U, chemical symbol of the element URANIUM.

Uccello, Paolo [o͞ot-chĕl'lō], c.1396–1475, Florentine painter. One of the earliest masters of perspective, he was little appreciated in his own time. Uccello's rigorous system of perspective and unsparing realism are combined in his cycle of *Noah* for Santa Maria Novella. His most famous scenes are from the *Battle of San Romano* (Uffizi; Louvre; and National Gall., London), notable for his experiments with foreshortening.

Udall, Nicholas, 1505–56, English dramatist and schoolmaster. His one extant play, *Ralph Roister Doister* (c.1553), is regarded as the first complete English COMEDY. It blends influences of TERENCE and PLAUTUS with native English humor.

Ueberroth, Peter V., 1937–, American business and sports executive, b. Evanston, Ill. President of the organizing committee for the financially successful 1984 Los Angeles Olympics, he served (1984–89) as commissioner of major league baseball. He also headed (1992–93) efforts to rebuild LOS ANGELES after the 1992 riots.

Uffizi [o͞of-fē'tsē], palace in Florence, Italy, built in the 16th cent. by VASARI for Cosimo I de' Medici as public offices. It houses the state archives of Tuscany and the **Uffizi Gallery,** one of the richest art collections in the world. The Florentine, Italian, Dutch, and Flemish schools are all well represented. Among its Greek, Roman, and Renaissance sculptures is the Venus of the Medici (Greek, 3d cent. B.C.). In 1993 a car bomb damaged or destroyed portions of the palace and some works of art.

UFO: see UNIDENTIFIED FLYING OBJECT.

Uganda [yo͞ogän'də, o͞ogän'dä], officially Republic of Uganda, republic (1992 est. pop. 19,386,000), 91,133 sq mi (236,036 sq km), E central Africa, bordered by Tanzania and Rwanda (S), Zaïre (W), Sudan (N), and Kenya (E). KAMPALA is the capital. Uganda lies astride the equator. Most of the country is a fertile plateau, in the center of which is Lake Kyoga. Around the perimeter are the lakes Albert, Edward, and Victoria; the Albert Nile R.; and several mountain ranges, with Margherita Peak (16,794 ft/5,119 m), the country's highest point, in the southwest. The economy is overwhelmingly agricultural, with cassava, sweet potatoes, plantains, millet, and sorghum the chief subsistence crops, and coffee (up to 90% of export earnings), cotton, tea, and tobacco the principal cash crops. Stock-raising, fishing, and hardwood production are also significant. Uganda's economy, especially the vital farming sector, was devastated during the Idi AMIN regime of the 1970s and subsequent civil war. Two thirds of the population belong to Bantu-speaking ethnic groups; Nilotic speakers make up most of the rest. English is the official language, but Swahili is widely spoken. Most

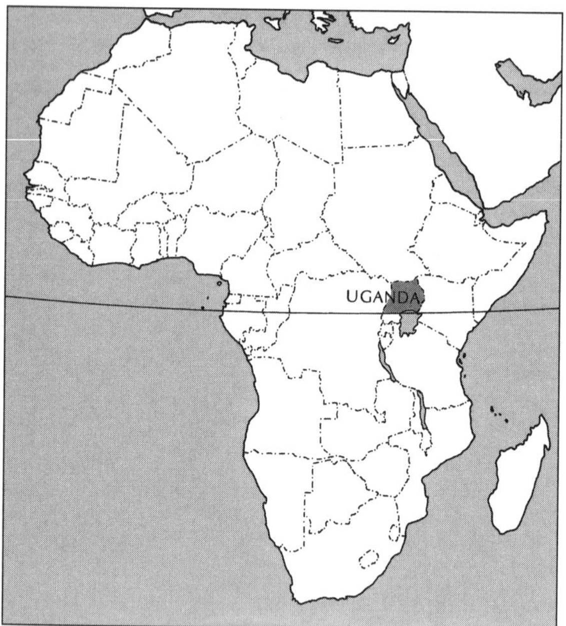

of the people are Christians, but many follow traditional beliefs as well; a small minority are Muslims.

History. Around A.D. 1100 Bantu-speaking people migrated into the area that is now Uganda, and by the 14th cent. they were organized into several independent kingdoms. The most powerful of these were Bunyoro (16th–17th cent.) and later (18th–19th cent.) Buganda. Visits by J.H. SPEKE (1862) and H.M. STANLEY (1875) opened the area to British influence, and Buganda became a British protectorate in 1894. The protectorate was subsequently extended to the rest of Uganda, but the independence of Buganda's rulers hampered the development of national unity. In 1962 Uganda gained independence under a federal constitution that gave Buganda a large measure of autonomy. However, under the leadership of A. Milton OBOTE, a new constitution was adopted in 1966, abolishing the traditional kingdoms and concentrating power in the hands of Obote, who became president. Obote was overthrown in 1971 by Maj. Gen. Idi Amin, who inaugurated a period of dictatorial rule that plunged the nation into chaos. He purged the Lango and Acholi tribes, moved against the army, and in 1972 expelled 60,000 non-citizen Asians. By 1977, it is estimated, 300,000 Ugandans had been killed in Amin's reign of terror. Finally, in 1979, an invasion by Tanzanian troops and Ugandan exiles drove out Amin's forces, and Amin fled the country. Elections in 1980 returned Obote to the presidency, but he was deposed in 1986 by the army, which was then defeated by rebel forces led by Yoweri Museveni. Museveni made progress in stabilizing the country and permitted the restoration (1993) of the traditional kingships, but Uganda has suffered from the effects of widespread AIDS.

Ugarit [o͞ogərēt'], ancient city, capital of the Ugarit kingdom, W Syria. Excavations (begun in the 1920s) have uncovered remains of the city dating from the 5th millennium B.C. Its greatest period was the 15th and 14th cent. B.C., and the city declined in the 12th cent. B.C. Ugaritic is a Semitic language related to classical Hebrew.

Ugrian [yo͞o'grēən, o͞o'–] or **Ugric** [yo͞o'grĭk, o͞o'–], subgroup of the Finno-Ugric group of languages, which is, in turn, a subdivision of the Uralic subfamily of the URALIC AND ALTAIC family of languages. See LANGUAGE (table).

Uhland, Ludwig [o͞o'länt], 1787–1862, German poet, leader of the Swabian group. His lyrics and ballads, including "The Minstrel's Curse" and "The Good Comrade," made him one of the most popular German poets of the romantic period.

Uigurs or **Uighurs,** Turkic-speaking people, numbering 4 million, living mainly in W China. They became prominent in the 7th cent. when they supported the T'ang dynasty (see CHINA). In 744 they took Mongolia. When ousted (840) by the Turkic Kyrgyz, they founded an empire in XINJIANG, China, that lasted until the MONGOL invasion (13th cent.). The Uigurs were nomads with some agriculture and trade. First converted to MANICHAEISM, they later became SUNNI Muslims. Today most people in the Xinjiang Uygur Autonomous Region are of Uigur descent.

Ukraine, Ukr. *Ukraina,* republic (1992 est. pop. 51,940,000), 232,046 sq mi (601,000 sq km), SE Europe, formerly a constituent republic of the USSR. It borders Poland (NW); Slovakia, Hungary, Romania, and Moldova (SW); the Black Sea and Sea of Azov (S); Russia (E, NE); and Belarus (N). Its capital is KIEV; the chief BLACK SEA port is ODESSA. DNIPROPETROVSK, DONETSK, and KHARKIV are major industrial centers. Long known as the "breadbasket of the Soviet Union," Ukraine has rich farmlands that produce wheat and other grains, potatoes, sugar beets, sunflowers, and flax. Grain production has fallen, however, since independence. Resources include iron, coal, manganese, zinc, mercury, petroleum, and natural gas. There is also a great concentration of heavy industry, including metallurgical, machine-building, and chemical industries. Many industries, however, are heavily subsidized, and this has contributed to Ukraine's economic collapse since independence. The population is largely Ukrainian; there are Russian and other minorities. The official language is Ukrainian, but Russian is also widely spoken. The Orthodox Eastern and West Ukrainian Catholic churches are the largest faiths.

History. The Ukrainians are descended from Neolithic pastoral tribes of the Dnieper and Dniester valleys. SCYTHIA ruled most of Ukraine (8th–1st cent. B.C.). Invasions (3rd–6th cent. A.D.) by the Goths (see OSTROGOTHS; VISIGOTHS), HUNS, and Avars were followed by KHAZAR rule (7th–9th cent.), which ended with the rise of KIEVAN RUSSIA. The region fell to the Mongols of the GOLDEN HORDE (13th cent.) and was ruled by Poland-Lithuania (14th–17th cent.) before coming under Russian control in the late 18th cent. (see COSSACKS; MAZEPA; POLAND, PARTITIONS OF). In 1918 it declared its independence, but that ended with the triumph of the Bolsheviks and the founding of the Ukrainian Soviet Socialist Republic in 1922. During World War II Ukraine was devastated by the German occupation (1941–44). Postwar treaties enlarged the republic. With the coming of *glasnost,* Ukrainian nationalist and separatist sentiments were increasingly voiced. In 1991, following the failed hard-line coup against Soviet Pres. Gorbachev, the republic declared its independence from the USSR. In a popular election, Leonid KRAVCHUK was elected as the nation's first president, and Ukraine joined Russia and Belarus in founding the COMMONWEALTH OF INDEPENDENT STATES (CIS), precipitating the total collapse of the USSR. Disagreements between the president and parliament impeded economic reform and led to the scheduling of early elections for 1994. Ukraine has been extremely wary of Russia's influence in post-Soviet interrepublican affairs and has moved to limit its economic integration with the Russian-dominated CIS. CRIMEA, with its Russian majority

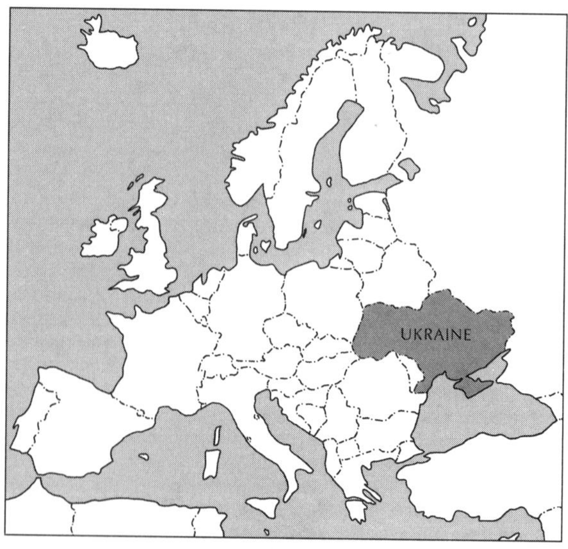

and the Russian Black Sea fleet port at SEVASTOPOL, has been a particular trouble spot.

Ukrainian language, also called Little Russian, member of the East Slavic group of the Slavic subfamily of the Indo-European family of languages. See LANGUAGE (table).

ukulele: see STRINGED INSTRUMENT.

Ulaanbaatar: see ULAN BATOR.

Uladislaus [o͞o″lä′dĭslous], Hungarian kings. **Uladislaus I:** see LADISLAUS III, king of Poland. **Uladislaus II,** c.1456–1516, king of Hungary (1490–1516) and, as Ladislaus II, king of Bohemia (1471–1516), was the son of CASIMIR IV of Poland. In 1478 MATTHIAS CORVINUS, king of Hungary, acquired Moravia, Silesia, and Lusatia from him. On Matthias's death (1490) Uladislaus was elected king of Hungary, but he proved a weak ruler. In 1515 he concluded a treaty with Holy Roman Emperor MAXIMILIAN I by which Hungary and Bohemia eventually passed to the HAPSBURG dynasty.

Ulan Bator or **Ulaanbaatar** [both: o͞olän′bä′tôr], city (1987 est. pop. 511,000), capital of Mongolia, in the E central part of the country. The political, cultural, economic, and transportation center of the country, it lies on a railroad linking (since 1955) Russia and Beijing. Manufactures include woolen textiles, clothing, soap, paper, and cast iron. Founded in 1649 as a monastery town, Ulan Bator still preserves the monastery section and is the seat of the nation's only university. It became the Mongolian capital in 1924.

Ulanova, Galina [o͞olä′nuvə], 1910–, Russian ballerina. She made her debut in 1928. She spent the first half of her career at the KIROV BALLET (1928–44) and was then the prima ballerina (1944–62) of the BOLSHOI BALLET. She was noted for her performances in *Giselle* and *Swan Lake.*

Ulbricht, Walter, 1893–1973, Communist leader (1950–71) in the German Democratic Republic (East Germany). He exiled himself (1933) to the USSR and returned to Germany with the Russian troops in 1945. A hard-line party leader, he was responsible for building (1961) the Berlin Wall.

ulcer, inflamed, open sore, usually slow to heal, on the skin or mucous membranes. It may develop as a result of injury, prolonged bed rest, vascular disease, or unknown reasons; therapy is directed at the underlying cause. **Peptic ulcers** occur in the mucous membrane of the intestinal tract in areas accessible to acid secreted by the stomach. The exact causes are unknown, but the bacterium *Helicobacter pylori* is a contributing factor in many peptic ulcers. Use of ASPIRIN and some other ANALGESICS, increased stomach acid secretion, alcoholic beverages and cigarettes, and tissue vulnerability to the acid, and emotional disturbance are also believed to play a part. Treatment includes antacids, drugs that block gastric-acid secretion, and antibiotics.

Ullmann, Liv (Johanne), 1939–, Norwegian stage and film actress; b. Japan. She is best known for her roles in films directed by Ingmar BERGMAN, e.g., *Persona* (1966), *Shame* (1968), *Cries and Whispers* (1972), and *Autumn Sonata* (1978).

Ulster, northernmost of the historic provinces of Ireland. Six of its nine counties make up Northern Ireland, often referred to as Ulster; the rest are in the Republic of Ireland.

ultrasonics, the study and application of SOUND waves with frequencies greater than 20,000 cycles per second, i.e., beyond the range of human hearing. Ultrasounds are commonly produced by piezoelectric transducers. They are used for nondestructive testing, and for the cleaning of fine machine parts and surgical instruments. In medicine, ULTRASOUND devices are used to examine internal organs without surgery. Ultrasonic whistles are audible to dogs and are used to summon them.

ultrasound, in medicine, technique that uses sound waves to study and treat hard-to-reach body areas. In scanning with ultrasound, high-frequency sound waves are transmitted to the area of interest and the returning echoes recorded. First developed in World War II to locate submerged objects, the technique is now widely used in virtually every branch of MEDICINE, e.g., in obstetrics to study the fetus, in cardiology to detect heart damage, and in ophthalmology to detect retinal problems. It is also used to heat joints, relieving arthritic joint pain, and for such procedures as lithotripsy, in which shock waves break up kidney stones, eliminating the need for surgery. Ultrasound is noninvasive, involves no radiation, and avoids the possible hazards—such as bleeding, infection, or reactions to chemicals—of other diagnostic methods.

ultraviolet astronomy, study of celestial objects by means of ULTRAVIOLET RADIATION. Because atmospheric interference makes UV radiation difficult to observe from ground-based telescopes, high-altitude balloons, sounding rockets, and orbiting OBSERVATORIES are employed. UV line spectrum measurements are used to discern the chemical composition, densities, and temperatures of interstellar gas and dust, and the temperature and composition of hot, young stars. UV observations can also provide essential information about the evolution of galaxies.

ultraviolet radiation, invisible ELECTROMAGNETIC RADIATION with frequencies (about 10^{15} to 10^{18} Hz) between that of visible violet light and X rays; it ranges in wavelength from about 400 to 4 nanometers. Ultraviolet (UV) radiation can be detected by the FLUORESCENCE it induces in certain substances and by its blackening of photographic film. Most of the UV component of sunlight is absorbed by the OZONE LAYER of the atmosphere, but UV-B radiation (280–320 nanometers) can cause sunburn and skin cancer and UV-A radiation (320–400 nanometers) can cause photosensitivity reactions and possibly skin cancer. Vitamin D is produced in humans by the action of UV radiation on ergosterol, a substance present in the skin. UV radiation can also be produced artificially in arc lamps, and black light is long wavelength UV radiation (365 nanometers).

Ulysses, Latin for ODYSSEUS.

Ulysses, in space exploration: see SPACE PROBE (table).

Umar ibn al-Khattab, c.586–644, 2d Muslim caliph. An early convert to Islam, he expanded the borders of the Muslim empire. Tradition credits him with instituting such Muslim practices as the obligatory pilgrimage (hajj) to Mecca.

umbra: see ECLIPSE; SUNSPOTS.

Umbrian [ŭm′brēən], extinct language belonging to the Italic subfamily of the Indo-European family of languages. See LANGUAGE (table).

Umbriel, in astronomy, natural satellite of URANUS.

Unamuno, Miguel de, 1864–1936, Spanish philosophical writer; of Basque descent. His major work, *The Tragic Sense of Life in Men and Nations* (1913), expresses his highly individualistic EXISTENTIALISM, a philosophy based on faith in faith itself. He also wrote poetry, essays, and novels, all expressing his impassioned concern with life and death.

Uncas, c.1588–c.1683, first chief of the MOHEGANS. An ambitious but troublesome subchief of the PEQUOT, he formed a new tribe and sided with the British in the Pequot Wars (1638). For the rest of his life he was embroiled in difficulties with other Native Americans and with the British.

uncertainty principle: see HEISENBERG, WERNER; QUANTUM MECHANICS.

Uncle Sam, name used to designate the U.S. government. The origin of the term is uncertain, but some sources attribute it to Samuel Wilson (1766–1854) of Troy, N.Y. Wilson, whose nickname was "Uncle Sam," was an inspector of army supplies in the WAR OF 1812.

unconscious, in psychology, that aspect of mental life that is separate from immediate consciousness and is not subject to recall at will. Sigmund FREUD regarded the unconscious as a vast portion of the mind, including the instinctual drives and the repressed residue of unacceptable experiences and desires. C.G. JUNG added the concept of an inherited unconscious, known as the collective unconscious, to the Freudian view. Although some psychological schools reject the idea of the unconscious, most modern psychologists accept that a person has latent, or unretrieved, memories and ideas.

Underground Railroad, in U.S. history, loosely organized system for helping fugitive slaves escape to Canada or to areas of safety in free states. Although legend has it as a highly organized group with "passengers", "conductors," and "stations," in fact it seldom operated in an organized manner, and most help to fugitives was given by individual persons.

Undset, Sigrid [o͝on′sĕt], 1882–1949, Norwegian novelist. Her masterpiece, the trilogy *Kristin Lavransdatter* (1920–22), tells of love and religion in medieval Norway. Always strongly ethical, her writing deepened in religious intensity after her conversion (1924) to Roman Catholicism. She was awarded the 1928 Nobel Prize in literature.

UNESCO, abbreviation for United Nations Educational, Scientific, and Cultural Organization. See UNITED NATIONS (table 3).

unemployment insurance, compulsory or voluntary insurance against loss of wages during involuntary unemployment. Most W European countries adopted some form of unemployment compensation early in the 20th cent. The U.S. program, introduced in 1935, covers about 85% of the work force. Each state has its own laws and operates its own program.

Ungaretti, Giuseppe, 1888–1970, Italian poet; b. Egypt. His pure style, achieved by condensation to essentials, is in the tradition of the French SYMBOLISTS. His works are collected in the 12 volumes of *Life of a Man* (1958).

Unh, chemical symbol of the element UNNILHEXIUM.

unicameral system: see LEGISLATURE.

UNICEF, the United Nations Children's Fund (originally, United Nations International Children's Emergency Fund). See UNITED NATIONS (table 4).

unicorn, fabulous equine beast with a horn in the middle of its forehead. It was once considered native to India and was reportedly seen throughout the world. Pure white, it has been used as a symbol of virginity and, in iconography, is associated with the Virgin Mary and with Jesus. Hunting the unicorn was a tapestry subject in the late Middle Ages and Renaissance.

unidentified flying object (UFO) or **flying saucer,** an object or light phenomenon reportedly seen in the sky whose appearance, trajectory, and general dynamic and luminescent behavior do not suggest a logical, conventional explanation. Although many alleged sightings have been interpreted as reflections of the sun's rays from airplanes, as weather balloons, or as various meteorological phenomena, some sightings remain unexplained by investigators in terms of known phenomena.

Unification Church: see MOON, SUN MYUNG.

unified field theories, in physics, a set of theories that seeks to relate all the known, basic forces that exist in nature. Scientists generally agree upon the existence of four basic forces. Two of these, ELECTROMAGNETISM and GRAVITATION, are long-range forces, and the other two, the WEAK INTERACTION and STRONG INTERACTION, are short-range forces, effective only at the scale of the atomic nucleus. Early field theories, such as James Clerk MAXWELL's electromagnetic theory, were extended by quantum field theory (see QUANTUM MECHANICS). The first modern theory was the ELECTROWEAK THEORY, which succeeded in unifying electromagnetism and the weak interaction. Grand unification theories (GUTs) unify the electroweak interactions with the strong interaction. No GUT has as yet been verified. A new class of unified field theories called supergravity theories propose to unify gravitation with the other basic forces; like the GUTs, these are unverified.

uniformitarianism, the doctrine that past geological changes in the earth were brought about by the same causes as those now taking place. As first advanced in 1785 by James HUTTON, it stressed the slowness and gradualness of rates of change. It was initially overshadowed by the doctrine of CATASTROPHISM and was opposed because it seemed contrary to religious beliefs. In the 19th cent. it gained support through the efforts of Sir Charles LYELL. More recent theories, which effect something of a synthesis, are based upon Lyell's conception of the slow operation of historic geological forces over the vastness of time but allow for periods when such activity was accelerated and intensified.

Union, Act of. For the union of England and Scotland (1707), see GREAT BRITAIN; for the union of Ireland with Great Britain (1800), see IRELAND.

union, labor, or **trade union,** association of workers for the purpose of improving their economic status and working conditions through COLLECTIVE BARGAINING. Historically there have been two major types of labor unions: the horizontal, or craft, union, in which all the members are skilled in a certain craft (e.g., carpenters); and the vertical, or industrial, union, composed of workers in the same industry, whatever their particular skills (e.g., automobile workers). A company union is an employee-controlled union having no affiliation with other labor organizations. The term *closed shop* refers to a company that hires only union members. In a union shop, employees are required to join a union within a specified time after being hired. An open shop does not restrict its employees to union members. Labor unions are essentially the product of the INDUSTRIAL REVOLUTION of the 19th cent. In Great Britain miners and textile workers were organized in the 1860s. Most European labor organizations today are either political parties or are affiliated with political parties, usually left-wing ones. Many union movements in the underdeveloped countries have led anti-colonial campaigns toward political independence. In the U.S. unions began developing in the 1830s. Among the important early organizations were the KNIGHTS OF LABOR and the INDUSTRIAL WORKERS OF THE WORLD. A milestone in the history of American unionism came in 1886 with the formation of a group that eventually became the AMERICAN FEDERATION OF LABOR AND CONGRESS OF INDUSTRIAL ORGANIZATIONS (AFL-CIO), an association that includes nearly all of the larger U.S. unions. The U.S. labor movement gained support from such NEW DEAL laws as the Wagner Act (1935), creating the NATIONAL LABOR RELATIONS BOARD, but later was restricted by the Taft-Hartley Act of 1947 and the Landrum-Griffin Act of 1959 (see LABOR LAW). By the late 1970s some 20 states had banned the closed shop through "right-to-work" laws. In bargaining with companies in economically troubled industries in the 1980s, U.S. unions often sought to save existing jobs through concessions ("give-backs") of earlier gains, and in 1993 unions unsuccessfully fought passage of the North American Free Trade Agreement, fearing job losses if it were ratified. U.S. union membership has steadily declined from its peak of 35.5% of the nonagricultural workforce in 1945; in 1992, when U.S. unions had 16,390,000 members, it stood at 15.8%. Internationally, world trade unionism was split after 1949 between two rival organizations: the World Federation of Trade Unions (1945) and the International Confederation of Free Trade Unions (1949). The International Labor Organization is a specialized agency of the UNITED NATIONS.

Union of Soviet Socialist Republics (USSR), Rus. *Soyuz Sovetskikh Sotsialisticheskikh Respublik,* former republic, E Europe and N Asia. Also called the Soviet Union, it was the successor to the Russian Empire and the first state based on Marxist socialism (see also MARXISM; COMMUNISM). Until 1989 the Communist party indirectly controlled all levels of government; the party's politburo effectively ruled the country, and its general secretary was the country's most powerful leader. Soviet industry was owned and managed by the state, and agricultural land was divided into state farms, COLLECTIVE FARMS, and small, privately held plots (3% of cropland). Politically the USSR was divided (from 1940 to 1991) into 15 constituent or union republics—ARMENIA, AZERBAIJAN, Belorussia (see BELARUS), ESTONIA, GEORGIA, KAZAKHSTAN, Kirghizia (see KYRGYZSTAN), LATVIA, LITHUANIA, Moldavia (see MOLDOVA), Russia, Tadzhikistan (see TAJIKISTAN), TURKMENISTAN, UKRAINE, and UZBEKISTAN—ostensibly joined in a federal union, but until the final year or so of the USSR's existence the republics had little real power. The rest of this article deals with the history of the USSR from 1920 to its collapse in 1991. For the history of the period prior to 1920 see RUSSIA; RUSSIAN REVOLUTION; and BREST-LITOVSK, TREATY OF. For events from 1991 on and for other information, see the articles on the former constituent republics and the COMMONWEALTH OF INDEPENDENT STATES.

History. In the struggle for succession after LENIN's death (1924), STALIN won out over TROTSKY. The NEW ECONOMIC POLICY (1921–28) gave way to full government control of agriculture and industry under the first Five-Year Plan (1928–32). By the late 1930s agriculture had been collectivized, largely forcibly; industrialization accelerated; and health and literacy greatly improved. State and party power over all aspects of life was enforced by the SECRET POLICE and bureaucracy; the COMINTERN guided Communist parties abroad. Stalin's purges of the 1930s claimed as victims such Soviet leaders as BUKHARIN, KAMENEV, and ZINOVIEV, and many millions of ordinary citizens. The USSR signed (1939) a nonaggression pact with Germany and, at the start of WORLD WAR II, invaded E Poland, gained a hard-earned victory in the Russo-Finnish War (1939–40), and occupied and forcibly annexed ESTONIA, LATVIA, and LITHUANIA (1940). Following their surprise attack (1941) on the USSR, the Germans overran much of the western part of the country. However, after the Russian triumph (1943) at Stalingrad (now VOLGOGRAD), the USSR began a counteroffensive that ended in Soviet victory. The war left c.20 million Soviet citizens dead. Postwar Soviet relations with the U.S. soon deteriorated into a COLD WAR, and the USSR extended its domination over much of Eastern Europe. After Stalin's death (1953) Soviet domestic and foreign policy became more flexible under Nikita KHRUSHCHEV. In the field of technology the USSR developed (1949) atomic weapons, orbited (1957) the first artificial earth satellite, and launched (1961) the first manned orbital flight. In 1956 revolts against Soviet influence were suppressed in HUNGARY and POLAND. The USSR took part in talks on nuclear DISARMAMENT, but provoked (1962) the CUBAN MISSILE CRISIS. Khrushchev was replaced in 1964, and by 1970 Leonid BREZHNEV had emerged as the most powerful Soviet leader. After Brezhnev's death in 1982, Yuri ANDROPOV and then Konstantin CHERNENKO served briefly as head of the government. Chernenko's successor was Mikhail GORBACHEV (1985). Gorbachev initiated political and economic reforms intended to liberalize and revitalize Soviet society while preserving central state and party control. The two principles of his policy were *perestroika* (restructuring) and *glasnost* (openness). Economic *perestroika*, aimed at decentralizing the command economy and providing limited opportunities for land ownership and free enterprise, produced few discernible results. Shortages of food and consumer goods became more acute than ever. Political *perestroika*, coupled with *glasnost*, had the effect of opening the system to more rapid and radical changes. The new Congress of People's Deputies and Supreme Soviet publicly debated, criticized, and investigated government policies. The end of repressive political controls permitted nationalist and separatist movements to arise in the constituent republics, and ethnic hostilities flared. In 1991 Gorbachev reached an agreement on power sharing with the leaders of nine of the republics, but the imminent signing of this agreement provoked a coup attempt (Aug. 1991) by hard-liners in the central government. Opposition to the coup, particularly by the Russian Republic government of Boris YELTSIN, led to its collapse and a rapid shift of power to reformers and the republics. Gorbachev resigned as leader of the Communist party, and the party was stripped of its property and suspended. Constituent republics declared their independence (all had already declared their sovereignty), and a new government was formed that gave far greater power to the republics. One of its first acts was to recognize the independence of Estonia, Latvia, and Lithuania. Attempts by Gorbachev to negotiate a new, permanent economic and political union to replace the USSR failed to find a formula satisfactory to the republics. On Dec. 8, 1991, Belarus, Russia, and Ukraine agreed to form the COMMONWEALTH OF INDEPENDENT STATES, rendering the Gorbachev government superfluous, and Russia began expropriating the ministries and property of the USSR by decree. A new commonwealth agreement was signed (Dec. 21) by 11 republics and replaced the old, centralized union with an association of independent nations; Gorbachev resigned four days later. Fifteen countries and the commonwealth emerged from the collapse of the USSR, but in most respects Russia is the true successor of the Soviet Union.

Unitarianism, in general, the form of Christianity that denies the doctrine of the TRINITY, believing that God exists only in one person. Modern Unitarianism originated in the Reformation period under such leaders as Michael SERVETUS and Faustus Socinus. The latter's views took root in England under John BIDDLE. In America the movement took hold in the liberal wing of Congregationalism as early as 1785, and adherents gradually formed a new denomination. Its doctrines were stated (1819) by William Ellery CHANNING, and the American Unitarian Association was formed in 1825. The sect holds no particular profession of faith, nor has a creed been adopted. Congregational polity prevails. The Association merged (1961) with the Universalist Church of America to form the Unitarian Universalist Association. In 1991 the association reported a membership of 141,315.

Unitas, John, 1933–, American football player; b. Pittsburgh. After playing at the Univ. of Louisville, he played semiprofessional ball until signed (1956) by the Baltimore Colts. One of the game's great passers, he led them to four championships (including a Super Bowl victory in 1971) in his 17 seasons. At retirement he held lifetime records for most completions (2,830) and most yards gained passing (40,239), both since broken by Fran TARKENTON.

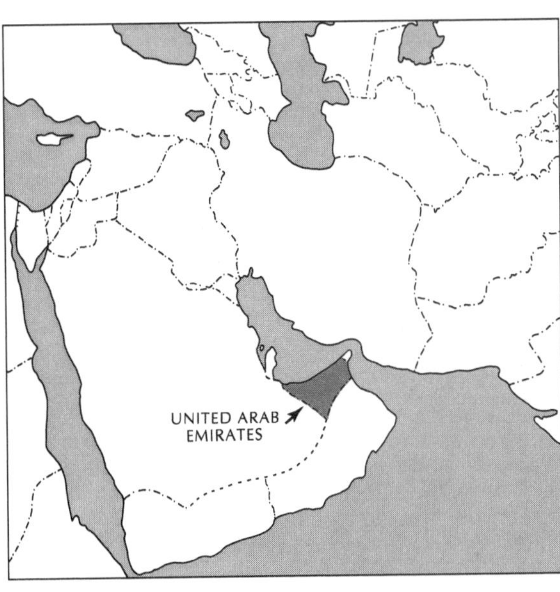

United Arab Emirates, federation of emirates (1992 est. pop. 2,522,000), c.30,000 sq mi (77,700 sq km), SW Asia, on the E Arabian Peninsula, bordered by the Persian Gulf (N), the Gulf of Oman (E), Oman (S), Saudi Arabia (S, W), and Qatar (NW). It comprises the emirates (in fact, sheikhdoms) of Abu Dhabi (with 80% of the area), Ajman, Dubai, Fujairah, Ras al-Khaimah, Sharjah, and Umm al-Qaiwain. The city of Abu Dhabi is the capital. The land is largely hot, dry desert; in the east is a portion of the Jabal al Akhdar Mts. The economy is dominated by oil, first exploited in the 1960s; oil exports rank among the world's largest, and oil revenues have made the per capita income one of the world's highest. There are also rich natural-gas deposits. Fishing and pearling are traditional occupations. The indigenous population, Sunni Muslim Arabs, is outnumbered by foreign-born workers, mostly from Asia, attracted by the petroleum boom. The official language is Arabic, but Farsi and English are widely used. Overall governmental authority is invested in the Supreme Council, which consists of the seven sheikhs; a majority of five (including both Abu Dhabi and Dubai) must agree to any action.

History. Formerly known as the Trucial States, Trucial Coast, or Trucial Oman, the seven constituent emirates were bound to Great Britain by truce (1820) and agreement (1892). After World War II Britain granted autonomy to the emirates, and in 1971 the independent federation was formed; neighboring QATAR and BAHRAIN, which originally were to be part of the federation, opted for separate statehood. Following a period of severe internal tensions in the late 1970s, there was progress toward political unity in the 1980s, but rivalry between Abu Dhabi and Dubai has hampered closer cooperation.

United Church of Christ, American Protestant denomination formed in 1957 by a merger of the General Council of Congregational Christian Churches and the Evangelical and Reformed Church. There are approximately 1.7 million members. See CONGREGATIONALISM.

United Empire Loyalists, Canadian settlers who remained loyal to the British crown and emigrated from the Thirteen Colonies during and immediately after the AMERICAN REVOLUTION. Numbering up to 50,000, they settled principally in NOVA SCOTIA and QUEBEC.

United Kingdom: see GREAT BRITAIN.

United Nations (UN), international organization established immediately after World War II to maintain international peace and security and to achieve cooperation in solving international economic, social, cultural, and humanitarian problems. It replaced the

UNITED NATIONS MEMBERS *(including year of entry)*

Afghanistan, 1946
Albania, 1955
Algeria, 1962
Andorra, 1993
Angola, 1976
Antigua and Barbuda, 1981
Argentina, 1945
Armenia, 1992
Australia, 1945
Austria, 1955
Azerbaijan, 1992
Bahamas, 1973
Bahrain, 1971
Bangladesh, 1974
Barbados, 1966
Belarus, 1945
Belgium, 1945
Belize, 1991
Benin, 1960
Bhutan, 1971
Bolivia, 1945
Bosnia and Hercegovina, 1992
Botswana, 1966
Brazil, 1945
Brunei, 1984
Bulgaria, 1955
Burkina Faso, 1960
Burundi, 1962
Cambodia, 1955
Cameroon, 1960
Canada, 1945
Cape Verde, 1975
Central African Republic, 1960
Chad, 1960
Chile, 1945
China, 1945
Colombia, 1945
Comoros, 1975
Congo, 1960
Costa Rica, 1945
Côte d'Ivoire, 1960
Croatia, 1992
Cuba, 1945
Cyprus, 1960
Czech Republic, 1993
Denmark, 1945
Djibouti, 1977
Dominica, 1978
Dominican Republic, 1945
Ecuador, 1945
Egypt, 1945
El Salvador, 1945
Equatorial Guinea, 1968
Eritrea, 1993
Estonia, 1991
Ethiopia, 1945
Fiji, 1970
Finland, 1955
France, 1945
Gabon, 1960
Gambia, 1965
Germany, 1973
Ghana, 1957
Greece, 1945
Grenada, 1974
Guatemala, 1945
Guinea, 1958
Guinea-Bissau, 1974
Guyana, 1966
Haiti, 1945
Honduras, 1945
Hungary, 1955
Iceland, 1946
India, 1945
Indonesia, 1950
Iran, 1945
Iraq, 1945
Ireland, 1955
Israel, 1949
Italy, 1955
Jamaica, 1962
Japan, 1956
Jordan, 1955
Kazakhstan, 1992
Kenya, 1963
Kuwait, 1963
Kyrgyzstan, 1992
Laos, 1955
Latvia, 1991
Lebanon, 1945
Lesotho, 1966
Liberia, 1945
Libya, 1955
Liechtenstein, 1990
Lithuania, 1991
Luxembourg, 1945
Macedonia, 1993
Madagascar, 1960
Malawi, 1964
Malaysia, 1957
Maldives, 1965
Mali, 1960
Malta, 1964
Marshall Islands, 1991
Mauritania, 1961
Mauritius, 1968
Mexico, 1945
Micronesia, Federated States of, 1991
Moldova, 1992
Monaco, 1993
Mongolia, 1961
Morocco, 1956
Mozambique, 1975
Myanmar (Burma), 1948
Namibia, 1990
Nepal, 1955
Netherlands, 1945
New Zealand, 1945
Nicaragua, 1945
Niger, 1960
Nigeria, 1960
North Korea, 1991
Norway, 1945
Oman, 1971
Pakistan, 1947
Panama, 1945
Papua New Guinea, 1975
Paraguay, 1945
Peru, 1945
Philippines, 1945
Poland, 1945
Portugal, 1955
Qatar, 1971
Romania, 1955
Russia, 1945 (as the USSR from 1945 to 1991)
Rwanda, 1962
Saint Kitts-Nevis, 1983
Saint Lucia, 1979
Saint Vincent and the Grenadines, 1980
San Marino, 1992
São Tomé and Principe, 1975
Saudi Arabia, 1945
Senegal, 1960
Seychelles, 1976
Sierra Leone, 1961
Singapore, 1965
Slovakia, 1993
Slovenia, 1992
Solomon Islands, 1978
Somalia, 1960
South Africa, 1945
South Korea, 1991
Spain, 1955
Sri Lanka, 1955
Sudan, 1956
Suriname, 1975
Swaziland, 1968
Sweden, 1946
Syria, 1945
Tajikistan, 1992
Tanzania, 1961
Thailand, 1946
Togo, 1960
Trinidad and Tobago, 1962
Tunisia, 1956
Turkey, 1945
Turkmenistan, 1992
Uganda, 1962
Ukraine, 1945
United Arab Emirates, 1971
United Kingdom, 1945
United States, 1945
Uruguay, 1945
Uzbekistan, 1992
Vanuatu, 1981
Venezuela, 1945
Vietnam, 1977
Western Samoa, 1976
Yemen, 1947
Yugoslavia, 1945
Zaïre, 1960
Zambia, 1964
Zimbabwe, 1980

LEAGUE OF NATIONS. The name was coined by Pres. F.D. ROOSEVELT in 1941 to describe the countries fighting against the Axis in WORLD WAR II. It was first used officially on Jan. 1, 1942, when 26 states joined in the Declaration by the United Nations, pledging to continue their joint war effort and not to make peace separately. The UN Charter, the organization's governing treaty, was drawn up in 1945 at a conference held in San Francisco. The principal organs, as specified in the Charter, are the General Assembly, the Security Council, the Economic and Social Council, the Trusteeship Council, the International Court of Justice, and the Secretariat (see table 2). The Secretariat, with the secretary general at its head, handles all administrative functions. Trygve LIE, the UN's first secretary general, was succeeded by Dag HAMMARSKJÖLD, U THANT, Kurt WALDHEIM, Javier PÉREZ DE CUÉLLAR, and Boutros BOUTROS-GHALI. In 1945 there were 51 members; by 1993 the number had reached 184 (see table 1). At the outset, close cooperation among the members was expected, but hopes for essential accord were soon dashed by the COLD WAR, which hampered the functioning of many UN organs. Early UN peacekeeping efforts included the establishment of armed forces to repel (1950) the North Korean attack on South Korea (see KOREAN WAR); the mobilization of troops and peacekeeping forces for the Congo (see SHABA), CYPRUS, and the Middle East (see ARAB-ISRAELI WARS). The UN has prospered as a forum for debate intended to defuse international conflict, and it has worked to aid economic and technological development in developing nations. With the end of the cold war, the UN has become increasingly important to preserving and restoring international peace, most notably in Kuwait, with the authorization of the use of force against Iraq after its invasion (see PERSIAN GULF WAR), but also in Cambodia, somewhat less succesfully in Somalia, and elsewhere. As the demand for peacekeeping forces has increased, however, the funds to pay for them have become harder to raise, and nations have not always been willing to contribute troops, particularly if the risks are high.

United Nations Children's Fund: see UNITED NATIONS (table 4).

United Nations Conference on Trade and Development: see UNITED NATIONS (table 4).

United Nations Educational, Scientific, and Cultural Organization: see UNITED NATIONS (table 3).

United Nations High Commissioner for Refugees: see UNITED NATIONS (table 4).

United Nations Industrial Development Organization: see UNITED NATIONS (table 3).

2. BODIES DESIGNATED BY THE CHARTER OF THE UNITED NATIONS

Name	*Location*	*Purpose and Function*
General Assembly	New York	Chief deliberative body of UN. All member states represented. Annual session begins Sept. Studies political, social, economic issues; makes recommendations but no advisements on issues under Security Council consideration, unless the Council so requests. Passes UN budget; sets assessments. Work conducted in part through seven main committees (on specified issues); also procedural, and ad hoc standing, committees.
Security Council	New York	Primary responsibility to preserve peace. Compact executive organ; in theory, functions continuously. Fifteen members: five permanent "big powers" (U.S., Russia, China, France, U.K.); ten chosen (five each year) for two-year terms by General Assembly. Permanent members must vote unanimously on substantive issues, but abstentions are allowed in practice. Security Council acts after complaint by member or notification by General Assembly or Secretary General, or on own volition. Makes recommendations on "disputes," takes action (economic sanctions or military action) on "threats to peace," "acts of aggression." Council not limited by bar on UN "domestic" intervention.
Economic and Social Council	New York	Members (54) elected (18 each year) for three-year terms by General Assembly. Meets at least twice yearly; investigates economic, social questions; reports to Assembly and to other organs. Coordinates specialized agencies; arranges international consultations. Functional (e.g., on the status of women; on population) and regional commissions carry out much of the work.
Secretariat	New York	Performs all UN administrative functions. Headed by Secretary General, who customarily serves five years. Authorized to bring situations to attention of various UN organs. Impartial party in effecting conciliation. Empowered to perform functions entrusted by other UN organs. Aided by large staff.
International Court of Justice	The Hague	Superseded WORLD COURT. Fifteen judges chosen by General Assembly and Security Council for nine-year terms; five reelected every three years. Nine-judge quorum. Hears disputes between member states, issues advisory opinions on matters presented by UN organs. Limited jurisdiction in disputes between states; questions of INTERNATIONAL LAW, breaches of international obligations, reparations for breaches. Judgments not appealable, binding only for case and parties (no system of precedent).
Trusteeship Council	New York	Established for UN control of non–self-governing territories, replacing League of Nations MANDATES (see TRUSTEESHIP, TERRITORIAL). Power to administer in territory essentially complete. Consists of the administering power, other permanent Security Council members, and elected members. Only territory remaining within jurisdiction is U.S.-administered PALAU.

United Nations Relief and Works Agency for Palestinian Refugees in the Near East: see UNITED NATIONS (table 4).

United Service Organizations (USO), organization that supplies social, recreational, welfare, and spiritual facilities to members of the armed forces. Associated agencies include the YMCA, YWCA, SALVATION ARMY, and many others. Organized in 1941, the USO is supported by contributions and volunteers; it conducts programs at some 175 locations.

United States, officially United States of America, republic (1990 pop. 248,709,873; 1993 est. pop. 257,908,000), 3,618,770 sq mi (9,372,143 sq km), North America. It is the world's third largest country in population and the fourth largest country in area. The U.S. consists of 50 states and a federal district—the site of the capital, WASHINGTON, D.C. It also has numerous outlying island territories and areas. The coterminous (48-state) U.S. extends across central North America from the Atlantic Ocean (E) to the Pacific Ocean (W) and from Canada (N) to Mexico and the Gulf of Mexico (S). The state of ALASKA occupies the northwestern part of the continent between the Arctic and Pacific oceans, bounded by Canada (E). The state of HAWAII, an island chain, is situated in the central Pacific, c.2,100 mi (3,400 km) SW of San Francisco. Outlying islands include, in the West Indies, PUERTO RICO (since 1952 a commonwealth associated with the U.S.) and the U.S. VIRGIN ISLANDS and, in the Pacific, AMERICAN SAMOA, GUAM, the NORTHERN MARIANAS (since 1986 a commonwealth associated with the U.S.), PALAU (a trust territory), WAKE ISLAND, and other possessions. The largest state (586,412 sq mi/1,518,807 sq km) is Alaska, and the smallest (1,214 sq mi/3,144 sq km) is RHODE ISLAND. The most populous is CALIFORNIA (1990 pop. 29,760,021). NEW YORK, LOS ANGELES, and CHICAGO are the largest U.S. cities.

Land. The coterminous U.S. is dominated by eastern and western mountain complexes, the five GREAT LAKES in the north, and a vast central plains region, nearly all of which is drained by one of the world's major river systems, the MISSISSIPPI, with its great tributaries, the MISSOURI and the OHIO. In the east the ancient, eroded APPALACHIAN MOUNTAINS, with many differentiated ranges, extend SW from Canada to Alabama. East and south of these mountains is the Atlantic–Gulf Coastal Plain. The Atlantic and Gulf coasts are essentially coastlines of submergence, with numerous estuaries, islands, and barrier beaches backed by lagoons. The Northeast has many fine natural harbors. Stretching over 1,000 mi (1,600 km) between the eastern and western mountain systems are the Interior Plains, once covered by a great inland sea. Forming the eastern portion are the fertile central lowlands, the nation's agricultural heartland; to the west are the GREAT PLAINS, a treeless, undulating plateau area that rises gradually to the foothills of the ROCKY MOUNTAINS. The lofty, geologically young Rockies extend NW from New Mexico into Canada and Alaska. Farther west are the CASCADE RANGE, with its many volcanic peaks; the SIERRA NEVADA, which includes Mt. WHITNEY (14,491 ft/4,417 m), the highest point in the coterminous U.S.; and the COAST RANGES, abutting on the narrow Pacific Coastal Plain. Between the Rockies and the ranges of the far west is the Intermontane Region, an expanse of plateaus, basins, and lower ranges through which great rivers such as the COLUMBIA and the COLORADO have cut deep gorges (see GRAND CANYON). There are several deserts in the Southwest, in one of which (DEATH VALLEY, Calif.) is found the lowest point in the U.S. (282 ft/86 m below sea level). Alaska is largely mountainous, rising to 20,320 ft (6,194 m) at Mt. MCKINLEY, the highest point in North America. Hawaii's islands are the tops of volcanoes rising from the ocean floor. The country has a wide variety of climates, ranging from the tropical (in Florida and Hawaii) to the subarctic tundra (in Alaska), and from the moderate Mediterranean (in S California) to the humid continental (in the northeastern states). Rainfall is heaviest in the Pacific Northwest, lightest in parts of the Southwest.

People. More than half the U.S. population is urban, and the great majority is of European descent. Until the immigration law of 1924, the country was a "melting pot" of nations. The original colonists on the Atlantic coast were chiefly from the British Isles. In addition, numerous African were transported as slaves to work the planta-

3. SPECIALIZED AGENCIES OF THE UNITED NATIONS

Agency	*Date Affiliated with UN;[1] Headquarters*	*Number of Members[2]*	*Purpose and Function*
Food and Agriculture Organization (FAO)	1945; Rome	169	Improve rural conditions, agricultural production and distribution; raise nutritional levels.
General Agreement on Tariffs and Trade (GATT)	1958; Geneva	114	Work to reduce tariffs and eliminate other barriers to international trade. Slated to be replaced by the World Trade Organization in 1995.
International Atomic Energy Agency (IAEA)	1957; Vienna	130	Promote peaceful uses of atomic energy. Buy and sell fuels and materials; assist in peaceful applications.
International Bank for Reconstruction and Development (IBRD)	1945; Washington	160	Further economic development through guaranteed loans, technical advice. Train member-state officials. Also called World Bank; IFC and IDA (below) affiliated.
International Civil Aviation Organization (ICAO)	1947; Montreal	173	Encourage orderly aviation growth. Improve standards for aircraft navigation, airworthiness, pilot licensing.
International Development Association, (IDA)	1960; Washington	144	Extend credit on easier terms to nations, mainly developing, that do not qualify for IBRD loans.
International Finance Corporation (IFC)	1957; Washington	148	Aid less-developed members by promoting private enterprise in their economies. Provide risk capital.
International Fund for Agricultural Development (IFAD)	1977; Rome	147	Finance agricultural projects to introduce, expand, improve food production, raise nutritional levels.
International Labor Organization (ILO)	1946; Geneva	168	Improve labor conditions, living standards; promote social justice; protect foreign workers.
International Maritime Organization (IMO)	1948; London	147	Promote cooperation on technical matters, maritime safety, navigation; encourage antipollution measures.
International Monetary Fund (IMF)	1945; Washington	178	Promote monetary cooperation, currency stabilization, trade expansion; meet balance-of-payments difficulties.
International Telecommunication Union (ITU)	1947 (1865); Geneva	172	Regulate, standardize, plan, coordinate international telecommunications; allot radio frequencies.
Multilateral Investment Guarantee Agency (MIGA)	1988; Washington	115	Encourage foreign investment in developing members by providing insurance against noncommercial losses (e.g., government action, civil unrest, warfare).
United Nations Educational, Scientific, and Cultural Organization (UNESCO)	1946; Paris	171	Reduce social tensions by encouraging interchange of ideas, cultural achievements; improve education.
United Nations Industrial Development Organization (UNIDO)	1967; Vienna	159	Promote industrial development in developing nations; help formulate industrial-development policies.
Universal Postal Union (UPU)	1947 (1875); Bern	177	Unite countries for reciprocal exchange of correspondence; aid and advise on improving postal services.
World Health Organization (WHO)	1948; Geneva	187	Promote highest health standards; set drug and vaccine standards; health and research guidelines.
World Intellectual Property Organization (WIPO)	1974; (1883); Geneva	132	Promote protection of intellectual property, inventions, copyrights, access to patented technology.
World Meteorological Organization (IWMO)	1950 (1878); Geneva	166	Promote cooperation between world meteorological stations; standardize observations; encourage research.

Key (1) Date in parentheses is date that predecessor organization began operation.
(2) In almost all cases, agencies have member states that are not members of the UN General Assembly.

tions in the South. By the mid-19th cent., as settlement of the West was accelerating, Irish and German immigrants came in great numbers, soon to be followed by Scandinavians. After the Civil War the new arrivals were mainly from E and S Europe (notably Italy, Greece, Poland, Russia, and the Balkans), and immigration from E Asia began. Despite early resentments and conflicts, the people of

4. SELECTED OTHER UNITED NATIONS AGENCIES	
Name	*Purpose and Function*
United Nations International Children's Emergency Fund (UNICEF)	Assist children and adolescents worldwide, particularly in devastated areas and developing countries, with educational services, health care. Nobel Peace Prize, 1965.
United Nations Conference on Trade and Development (UNCTAD)	Accelerate economic growth in developing countries. Review policies of these and industrialized countries influencing trade and development.
United Nations High Commissioner for Refugees (UNHCR)	Seek permanent solution to refugee problem; protect refugees under its mandate; coordinate voluntary agency efforts; assist most-needy groups. Nobel Peace Prize, 1954, 1981.
United Nations Relief and Works Agency for Palestinian Refugees in the Near East (UNRWA)	Provide food, health services, education, vocational training for approximately 1.8 million displaced by ARAB-ISRAELI WARS.

European origin have coalesced into a somewhat homogeneous group. This has been less true of arrivals from Africa, Asia, and Latin America and their descendants. African Americans are the principal non-European group; they constitute a substantial minority throughout the southern states and are a majority in many southern and some northern cities. Japanese and Chinese are numerous in Hawaii, and there are large Chinese communities in eastern and West Coast cities. Spanish-speaking peoples from Latin America (especially Mexico) have tended to congregate in urban areas. There are also Native Americans, many of whom live on reservations (see NORTH AMERICA, INDIGENOUS PEOPLES OF), Eskimos, and Aleuts. Since the 1980s the largest numbers of immigrants have come from Asia and Latin America. The people of the U.S. enjoy religious freedom. The great majority are Christian, with Protestants outnumbering Roman Catholics and the Orthodox Eastern Church having many adherents. Islam and Judaism are the faiths of two other substantial groups of Americans.

Economy. The U.S. is one of the principal industrial nations of the world and has tremendous agricultural and mineral resources. Although it has been virtually self-sufficient in the past, an enormous increase in consumption (especially of energy) in the late 20th cent. has made it increasingly dependent on certain imports. Nevertheless, it is the world's foremost producer of electrical power from all sources, as it is of natural gas, lead, aluminum, and several other minerals, and it is among the leaders in the production of crude oil, coal, copper, iron ore, silver, and zinc. In total value of manufactures, the U.S. leads all other nations by a substantial margin, being the principal producer of synthetic rubber, petrochemicals, and many other products. In the 1980s service industries (including banking and finance, information services, and others) became an increasingly important sector of the economy. Long considered the "breadbasket of the world," the U.S. has an agricultural sector of unparalleled efficiency. Although its relatively small farm population has been increasingly threatened by a cost-price squeeze, it has consistently produced surpluses of many crops (notably grains) for export. Major exports other than food products include motor vehicles and parts, aircraft and parts, chemicals, and computers and parts. Imports include ores, petroleum, machinery, transportation equipment, and paper. Canada, Japan, Mexico, Germany, and the United Kingdom are its leading trade partners. Since the 1970s the U.S. balance of trade has been generally unfavorable, but the nation still has a rising gross domestic product ($5.4 trillion in 1990). Development of the U.S. economy has been spurred by the growth of a complex network of transportation (rail, highway, air, and inland waterway) and communications (telephone, radio, television, computer, and fax machine) that has made possible the creation of one of the world's most sophisticated marketing mechanisms.

Government. The U.S. is a federal republic in which power is divided between a central governing authority and the individual states. The principal framework of government is the CONSTITUTION OF THE UNITED STATES, drawn up in 1787. The federal government consists of three branches: executive, legislative, and judicial. Executive power is vested in the PRESIDENT, who conducts the nation's administrative business with the aid of a CABINET consisting mainly of the secretaries (heads) of the various federal departments, e.g., the departments of STATE, TREASURY, DEFENSE, and AGRICULTURE. The CONGRESS OF THE UNITED STATES, the legislative branch, is bicameral, consisting of a Senate and a House of Representatives. The judicial branch is formed by the federal courts, the highest of which is the nine-member U.S. SUPREME COURT, which also functions as the court of last resort for the 50 state judiciary systems. Members of Congress and members of the ELECTORAL COLLEGE, which formally chooses the president and vice president, are elected by universal suffrage.

History. England, Spain, and France were the chief nations to establish colonies in what is now the U.S. The first permanent European settlement in the present U.S. was ST. AUGUSTINE, Fla., founded by the Spanish in 1565, and the first permanent English settlement was established at JAMESTOWN, Va., in 1607. The British eventually extended their rule over most of the Atlantic coast, and in the FRENCH AND INDIAN WARS they ousted the French from Canada and the Old Northwest. Increasing conflict between Britain and the American colonies led to the AMERICAN REVOLUTION, the DECLARATION OF INDEPENDENCE (1776), and the creation of the U.S. Governed from 1781 under the Articles of CONFEDERATION, the U.S. opted for a stronger national government in the Constitution, drawn up at the FEDERAL CONSTITUTIONAL CONVENTION (1787). George WASHINGTON served as the first president. Controversy over the division of power between the states and the federal government gave rise to the first political parties (see FEDERALIST PARTY; DEMOCRATIC PARTY). Settlement of the frontier added new states to the Union, and the LOUISIANA PURCHASE (1803) secured a vast new territory to the west. The violation of U.S. shipping by the British led ultimately to the WAR OF 1812. Andrew JACKSON, the seventh president, sometimes considered the incarnation of frontier democracy, was elected in 1828 and provided a strong executive attuned to popular support. The annexation (1845) of TEXAS precipitated the MEXICAN WAR, in which the U.S. defeated Mexico, acquiring California and most of the present Southwest. The Pacific Northwest was added by a peaceful settlement (1846) with Britain (see OREGON). Meanwhile, the South, with its doctrine of STATES' RIGHTS, was becoming estranged from the North over the issue of slavery. After the election (1860) of Abraham LINCOLN to the presidency, the South seceded from the Union and formed the CONFEDERACY. The CIVIL WAR that ensued ended in complete victory for the North. The RECONSTRUCTION period that followed was marked by bitter struggles, including the impeachment (1868) of Pres. Andrew JOHNSON. The remainder of the 19th cent. was marked by railroad building, the disappearance of the American frontier, and massive industrialization. The U.S. gained additional territory with the purchase of Alaska (1867); the annexation of Hawaii (1898); and the conquest of Spanish possessions, e.g., Puerto Rico, Guam, and the PHILIPPINES, in the SPANISH-AMERICAN WAR (1898). Despite the efforts of Pres. WILSON to keep the U.S. neutral, the nation entered WORLD WAR I on the Allied side in 1917, but after the war it settled into an isolationist policy. The GREAT DEPRESSION began in 1929 and reached worldwide proportions. To combat it, Pres. F.D. ROOSEVELT launched a sweeping reform program called the NEW DEAL. The U.S. entered WORLD WAR II on the Allied side after the Japanese attack (1941) on PEARL HARBOR. After the war the U.S. emerged as a world power, but relations with the USSR deteriorated into the COLD WAR. In the

CANADA
CAPE FLATTERY
Puget Sound
Seattle
Tacoma
Olympia
WASHINGTON
Spokane
Portland
Columbia
Salem
COAST RANGES
CASCADE RANGES
OREGON
IDAHO
Boise
Snake
ROCKY MOUNTAINS
Great Falls
Helena
MONTANA
Yellowstone
NORTH DAKOTA
Bismarck
Missouri
SOUTH DAKOTA
Pierre
Rapid City
GREAT PLAINS
WYOMING
PACIFIC OCEAN
Great Salt Lake
GREAT SALT LAKE DESERT
Ogden
Salt Lake City
Provo
Reno
Carson City
NEVADA
Sacramento
San Francisco
San Francisco Bay
San Jose
SIERRA NEVADA
Fresno
CALIFORNIA
DEATH VALLEY
Las Vegas
UTAH
Laramie
Cheyenne
North Platte
NEBRASKA
Platte
South Platte
Boulder
Denver
COLORADO
Colorado Springs
Pueblo
KANSAS
Arkansas
GRAND CANYON
Colorado
San Juan
Santa Barbara
MOJAVE DESERT
Los Angeles
San Diego
Little Colorado
ARIZONA
Sante Fe
Albuquerque
NEW MEXICO
Cimmaron
Canadian
Amarillo
Oklahoma City
OKLAH
Lawton
Phoenix
Tucson
Rio Grande
Roswell
Lubbock
Gulf of California
El Paso
Abilene
Brazos
TEXAS
San Angelo
Pecos
Austin
San Antonio
MEXICO
Neuces
Laredo
Rio Grande
RUSSIA
Barrow
ARCTIC OCEAN
BROOKS RANGE
Bering Strait
ARCTIC CIRCLE
SEWARD PENINSULA
ST. LAWRENCE ISLAND
Fairbanks
ALASKA
CANADA
Yukon
Bering Sea
ALASKA RANGE
Anchorage
Lake Iliamna
KENAI PENINSULA
Gulf of Alaska
Juneau
ALASKA PENINSULA
KODIAK ISLAND
ALEXANDER ARCHIPELAGO
ALEUTIAN IS.
PACIFIC OCEAN
600 KM
600 MI
KAUAI
Kauai Channel
OAHU
Honolulu
Kaiwi Channel
MOLOKAI
MAUI
Alenuihaha Channel
HAWAII
Hilo
HAWAII
PACIFIC OCEAN
200 KM
200 MI

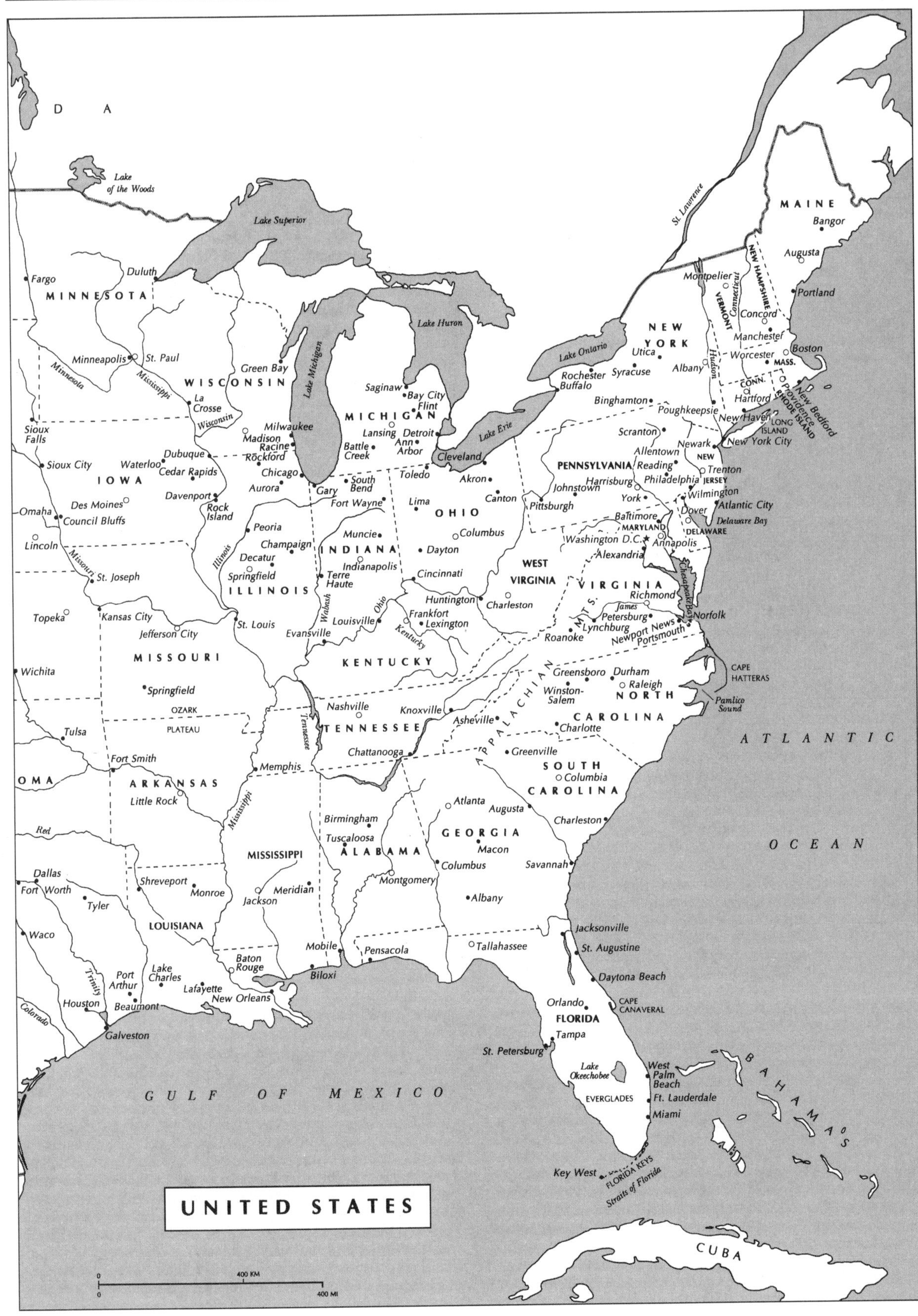

Cross-references are indicated by SMALL CAPS.

PRESIDENTS OF THE UNITED STATES *(with vice presidents, political parties, and dates in office)*

George Washington, 1789–97
John Adams

John Adams [Federalist] 1797–1801
Thomas Jefferson

Thomas Jefferson [Democratic-Republican] 1801–9
Aaron Burr, 1801–5
George Clinton, 1805–9

James Madison [Democratic-Republican] 1809–17
George Clinton, 1809–12
(no Vice President, April, 1812–March, 1813)
Elbridge Gerry, 1813–14
(no Vice President, Nov., 1814–March, 1817)

James Monroe [Democratic-Republican] 1817–25
Daniel D. Tompkins

John Quincy Adams [Democratic-Republican] 1825–29
John C. Calhoun

Andrew Jackson [Democratic] 1829–37
John C. Calhoun, 1829–32
(no Vice President, Dec., 1832–March, 1833)
Martin Van Buren, 1833–37

Martin Van Buren [Democratic] 1837–41
Richard M. Johnson

William H. Harrison [Whig] 1841
John Tyler

John Tyler [Whig] 1841–45
(no Vice President)

James Knox Polk [Democratic] 1845–49
George M. Dallas

Zachary Taylor [Whig] 1849–50
Millard Fillmore

Millard Fillmore [Whig] 1850–53
(no Vice President)

Franklin Pierce [Democratic] 1853–57
William R. King, 1853
(no Vice President, April, 1853–March, 1857)

James Buchanan [Democratic] 1857–61
John C. Breckinridge

Abraham Lincoln [Republican] 1861–65
Hannibal Hamlin, 1861–65
Andrew Johnson, 1865

Andrew Johnson [Democratic/National Union] 1865–69
(no Vice President)

Ulysses Simpson Grant [Republican] 1869–77
Schuyler Colfax, 1869–73
Henry Wilson, 1873–75
(no Vice President, Nov., 1875–March 1877)

Rutherford Birchard Hayes [Republican] 1877–81
William A. Wheeler

James Abram Garfield [Republican] 1881
Chester A. Arthur

Chester Alan Arthur [Republican] 1881–85
(no Vice President)

Grover Cleveland [Democratic] 1885–89
Thomas A. Hendricks, 1885
(no Vice President, Nov., 1885–March, 1889)

Benjamin Harrison [Republican] 1889–93
Levi P. Morton

Grover Cleveland [Democratic] 1893–97
Adlai E. Stevenson

William McKinley [Republican] 1897–1901
Garret A. Hobart, 1897–99
(no Vice President, Nov., 1899–March, 1901)
Theodore Roosevelt, 1901

Theodore Roosevelt [Republican] 1901–9
(no Vice President, Sept., 1901–March, 1905)
Charles W. Fairbanks, 1905–9

William Howard Taft [Republican] 1909–13
James S. Sherman, 1909–12
(no Vice President, Oct., 1912–March, 1913)

Woodrow Wilson [Democratic] 1913–21
Thomas R. Marshall

William Gamaliel Harding [Republican] 1921–23
Calvin Coolidge

Calvin Coolidge [Republican] 1923–29
(no Vice President, 1923–25)
Charles G. Dawes, 1925–29

Herbert Clark Hoover [Republican] 1929–33
Charles Curtis

Franklin Delano Roosevelt [Democratic] 1933–45
John N. Garner, 1933–41
Henry A. Wallace, 1941–45
Harry S Truman, 1945

Harry S Truman [Democratic] 1945–53
(no Vice President, 1945–49)
Alben W. Barkley, 1949–53

Dwight David Eisenhower [Republican] 1953–61
Richard M. Nixon

John Fitzgerald Kennedy [Democratic] 1961–63
Lyndon B. Johnson

Lyndon Baines Johnson [Democratic] 1963–69
(no Vice President, 1963–65)
Hubert H. Humphrey, 1965–69

Richard Milhous Nixon [Republican] 1969–74
Spiro T. Agnew, 1969–73
(no Vice President, Oct. 10,1973–Dec. 6, 1973)
Gerald R. Ford, 1973–74

Gerald Rudolph Ford [Republican] 1974–77
(no Vice President, Aug. 9,1974–Dec. 19, 1974)
Nelson A. Rockefeller, 1974–77

Jimmy Carter [Democratic] 1977–81
Walter F. Mondale

Ronald Wilson Reagan [Republican] 1981–89
George H. W. Bush

George H. W. Bush [Republican] 1989–93
J. Danforth Quayle

Bill Clinton [Democratic] 1993–
Al Gore, Jr.

KOREAN WAR, during the administration of Harry S TRUMAN, the U.S. took the leading role in combating the Communist invasion of South Korea. The U.S. economy boomed after World War II, and, spurred by Soviet advances in technology, the U.S. embarked on a large SPACE EXPLORATION program. In the 1960s domestic turmoil and violence erupted as African Americans became dissatisfied with the slow progress of INTEGRATION and protesters demonstrated against U.S. involvement in the VIETNAM WAR, which had escalated during the presidencies of Lyndon B. JOHNSON and Richard M. NIXON. In 1974 Nixon resigned following the WATERGATE AFFAIR, and Gerald R. FORD became president. Pres. Jimmy CARTER (1977–81) presided over a period of stagflation, a combination of economic recession and high inflation, and this, coupled with his inability to win the release of U.S. hostages held by IRAN, contributed to his defeat (1980) by Ronald REAGAN (1981–89). Reagan cut taxes, slashed social programs, and increased defense spending. The result was eight years of economic growth (from 1982) and a tripling of the national debt. Under George BUSH, elected president in 1988, the U.S. invaded (1989) Panama to depose Manuel NORIEGA and led the coalition that ousted (1991) Iraq's army from Kuwait (see PER-

SIAN GULF WAR). Internationally, the U.S. gained from the collapse of Communism in the former USSR and E Europe and from friendly relations with RUSSIA, but domestically it suffered from recession (1990–91) and from continuing high budget deficits. Anemic economic growth in the recession's wake and the strong independent candidacy of Ross PEROT enabled Bill CLINTON to defeat (1992) Bush and become the first Democratic president in 12 years. The economy gradually improved in 1993, and the budget deficit eased due to that and a tax increase and spending cuts. The NORTH AMERICAN FREE TRADE AGREEMENT, signed in 1992 with Canada and Mexico, was ratified (1993) and took effect on Jan. 1, 1994.

United States Air Force Academy, at Colorado Springs, Colo.; federal educational institution for training young men and women to be officers in the U.S. air force. The academy was authorized by Congress in 1954. Instruction began at Denver in 1955, and the Colorado Springs campus opened in 1958. To be considered for appointment, applicants must be nominated by elected (or certain appointed) U.S. officials. Cadets undertake a four-year course of instruction and receive full scholarships and monthly allotments to cover personal expenses.

United States Coast Guard Academy, at New London, Conn.; federal educational institution (created 1876) for training young men and women to be officers in the U.S. coast guard. Unlike the other military academies, it gains its candidates through a nationwide competition rather than through appointments by political officials. A cadet's four-year education consists of military and academic instruction, including professional training at sea. Cadets receive full scholarships as well as pay and allowances.

United States Merchant Marine Academy, at Kings Point, Long Island, N.Y.; federal educational institution for training young men and women to be merchant marine officers. The academy, dedicated in 1943, is maintained by the Dept. of Transportation. An applicant must be nominated by a U.S. senator or representative. The four-year course, emphasizing maritime and naval specialties, includes tours of service aboard a merchant vessel.

United States Military Academy, at West Point, N.Y.; federal educational institution for training young men and women to be officers in the U.S. army; founded 1802. To be considered for appointment, applicants must be nominated by elected (or certain appointed) U.S. officials. Cadets undertake a four-year course of instruction with summers devoted to practical military training. They receive full scholarships and monthly allotments to cover personal expenses.

United States Naval Academy, at Annapolis, Md.; federal educational institution for training young men and women to be officers of the U.S. navy and marine corps; founded 1845. To be considered for appointment, applicants must be nominated by elected (or certain appointed) U.S. officials. The academy's four-year course includes scientific and general studies as well as technical courses on naval subjects and practical work at sea. Midshipmen (trainees) receive full scholarships and monthly allotments to cover personal expenses.

univalve: see GASTROPOD.

universal gas constant: see GAS LAWS.

universalism, religious doctrine that holds that it is God's purpose to save every individual from sin through divine grace. The doctrine is old, but it did not become an organized movement until modern times. In 1779 John Murray became pastor of the first Universalist church in the U.S., and in 1790 a convention decided on a congregational polity. Initially Calvinistic, the group later moved toward UNITARIANISM. In 1961 the Universalist Church of America merged with the Unitarians to form the Unitarian Universalist Association.

Universal Postal Union: see UNITED NATIONS (table 3).

University of California Regents v. Bakke, case decided in 1978 by the U.S. SUPREME COURT, which held in a closely divided decision that race could be a factor—considered in choosing a diverse student body—in university admissions decisions. The Court also held, however, that the use of quotas in such AFFIRMATIVE-ACTION programs was not permissible; thus, the Univ. of California, Davis, medical school had, by maintaining a 16% minority quota, discriminated against Bakke, a white applicant. The legal implications of the decision were clouded by the Court's division.

Universal Product Code: see BAR CODE.

unnilennium (Une): see MEITNERIUM.

unnilhexium (Unh), artificial radioactive TRANSURANIUM ELEMENT. Claims for its production have been made by a Soviet group at Dubna, who in 1974 bombarded lead with chromium ions to obtain the Unh^{259} and Unh^{260} isotopes, and groups in California at the Lawrence Berkeley and Lawrence Livermore Laboratories, who, also in 1974, bombarded californium with oxygen ions to obtain the Unh^{263} isotope. See ELEMENT (table); PERIODIC TABLE.

unniloctium (Uno): see HASSIUM.

unnilpentium (Unp): see HAHNIUM.

unnilquadium (Unq): see RUTHERFORDIUM.

unnilseptium (Uns): see NIELSBOHRIUM.

Upanishads, speculative and mystical scriptures of HINDUISM, composed beginning c.900 B.C., forming the final section of the VEDA. A heterogeneous compilation of material from various sources that together are regarded as the wellspring of Hindu religion and philosophy, the Upanishads (112 are extant) form the basis for the later philosophical schools of VEDANTA. The principal early Upanishads expound the doctrine of BRAHMAN, the universal self or soul, and its identity with the *atman*, or individual self or soul. The scriptures also contain information on Vedic sacrifice and YOGA.

Updike, John, 1932–, American author; b. Shillington, Pa. His elegantly written fiction usually deals with the tensions and tragedies of contemporary middle-class life, as in the quartet of novels covering the life of Harry Angstrom: *Rabbit, Run* (1960), *Rabbit Redux* (1971), *Rabbit Is Rich* (1981; Pulitzer Prize), and *Rabbit at Rest* (1990; Pulitzer Prize). His other novels include *Couples* (1970), *The Witches of Eastwick* (1984), and *Memories of the Ford Administration* (1992), and he also writes short stories, literary criticism, and poetry.

Upper Volta: see BURKINA FASO.

Uppsala, city (1988 pop. 159,998), capital of Uppsala co., E Sweden. Once the coronation place of Swedish kings, it is now a cultural and industrial center producing machinery, clothing, and other manufactures. Its 13th-cent. Gothic cathedral is the burial place of GUSTAVUS I, LINNAEUS, and SWEDENBORG. Its university (est. 1477) is the oldest in Sweden.

Ur, ancient city of SUMER, S Mesopotamia, on the Euphrates. Also called Ur of the Chaldees, it was flourishing by 3500 B.C. In the Bible it is identified as the home of ABRAHAM. Captured (c.2340 B.C.) by Sargon, it later became independent. Ur, however, declined after the 6th cent. B.C. and never recovered. C. Leonard Woolley led the excavation of the city in the 1920s.

Uralic and Altaic languages [yo͝orăl'ĭk, ăltā'ĭk], two groups of related languages thought by many scholars to form a single Uralic and Altaic linguistic family. However, other authorities hold that the Uralic and Altaic groups constitute two unconnected and separate language families. Uralic includes Finnish and Hungarian; Altaic includes Turkish and Mongolian. See LANGUAGE (table).

Urals or **Ural Mountains,** mountain system extending north-south c.1,500 mi (2,400 km) across W Russia into N Kazakhstan, part of the traditional border between Europe and Asia. Naroda (6,212 ft/1,893 m), in the north, is the highest point. Except in the polar and northern sections, the mountains are densely forested, with lumbering an important industry. They are also enormously rich in minerals, including coal, iron ore, aluminum, copper, manganese, potash, and oil. Huge industrial centers, part of the Urals industrial area (c.290,000 sq mi/751,500 sq km), are located at YEKATERINBURG (Sverdlovsk), Magnitogorsk, CHELYABINSK, Nizhni Tagil, and PERM. During World War II entire industries were transferred to the Urals from the W USSR.

Urania: see MUSES.

uraninite: see PITCHBLENDE.

uranium (U), radioactive metallic element, discovered in oxide form in PITCHBLENDE by M.H. Klaproth in 1789. A silver-white, hard, dense, malleable, ductile, highly reactive metal in the ACTINIDE SERIES, it occurs naturally as a mixture of three ISOTOPES. Because of a constant decay rate, the age of uranium samples can be estimated (see DATING). The rare uranium-235 isotope is the only naturally occurring fission fuel for NUCLEAR ENERGY. Breeder reactors convert the abundant but nonfissionable uranium-238 into fissionable plutonium-239. Uranium-235 and plutonium-239 are also practicable fissionable nuclei for ATOMIC BOMBS. See ELEMENT (table); NUCLEAR REACTOR; PERIODIC TABLE; RADIOACTIVITY.

Uranus, in astronomy, 7th PLANET from the sun, at a mean distance of 1.7832 billion mi (2.8696 billion km). It has a diameter of 32,490 mi (52,290 km) and a solid core with a thick atmosphere composed mostly of hydrogen, helium, methane, and ammonia. Detected on Mar. 13, 1781, by Sir William HERSCHEL, it was the first planet discovered in modern times with the aid of a telescope. The extreme (98°) inclination of Uranus's equatorial plane with respect to its orbital plane gives the planet a retrograde rotation, i.e., a rotation opposite to the direction of revolution. Prior to 1986, Uranus was known to have five natural satellites: **Titania,** the largest, with a diameter of 650 mi (1,040 km), and **Oberon** were discovered by Herschel in 1787; **Ariel** and **Umbriel,** by William Lassell in 1851; and **Miranda,** by Gerard Kuiper in 1948. In 1977 astronomers detected a system of narrow rings of small, dark particles orbiting around the planet. When the *Voyager 2* SPACE PROBE flew by Uranus in 1986, it discovered ten more moons and confirmed the existence of ten rings.

Uranus, in Greek mythology, the heavens, first ruler of the universe; son and husband of GAEA; father of TITANS, CYCLOPS, and Hundred-handed Ones. Uranus was castrated and dethroned by CRONUS. His blood, falling onto Earth, produced the vengeful FURIES; from his discarded flesh and the sea APHRODITE arose.

Urban II, c.1042–1099, pope (1088–99), a Frenchman named Odo (or Eudes) of Lagery. A Cluniac monk, he worked closely with GREGORY VII and as pope furthered Gregory's reforms. His sermon at Clermont (1095) brought about the First CRUSADE.

Urban VI, 1318?–1389, pope (1378–89), a Neapolitan named Bartolomeo Prignano. Chosen as successor to Gregory XI, he proved violent and unruly, whereupon the cardinals went to Anagni and elected Robert of Geneva as antipope, thus beginning the Great SCHISM. Urban probably murdered five cardinals who opposed him; many believe he was insane.

urban enterprise zone: see ENTERPRISE ZONE.

Urdu [o͝or'do͞o], language belonging to the Indic group of the Indo-Iranian subfamily of the Indo-European family of languages. It is the official tongue of Pakistan. See LANGUAGE (table).

urea, organic compound, formula $CO(NH_2)_2$, that is the principal end product of nitrogen metabolism in most mammals. Most of the nitrogen in protein eventually appears in urea, which is concentrated by the KIDNEYS and excreted in urine.

ureter: see URINARY SYSTEM.

urethra: see URINARY SYSTEM.

Urey, Harold Clayton [yo͝or'ē], 1893–1981, American chemist. He taught at Johns Hopkins, Columbia, the Univ. of Chicago, and the Univ. of California. For his isolation of deuterium (heavy hydrogen) he won the 1934 Nobel Prize in chemistry; he later isolated heavy isotopes of oxygen, nitrogen, carbon, and sulfur. During World War II, in connection with the atomic bomb project, he worked on methods of separating uranium isotopes and on the production of heavy water.

urinary system, group of organs of the body concerned with excretion of urine. In humans, the urinary system includes the kidneys, ureters, bladder, and urethra. Blood containing waste products enters the KIDNEYS through the renal artery. The kidneys purify the blood by filtering out waste products, which, together with water, form URINE. From the kidneys, urine passes through thick-walled tubes called ureters into the bladder, a muscular sac that temporarily stores the urine and contracts to expel it. Urine released from the bladder flows into the urethra, the canal carrying it to the outside of the body.

urine, clear, amber-colored fluid formed by the KIDNEYS and carrying waste products of METABOLISM out of the body. Urine is 95% water, in which urea, uric acid, mineral salts, toxins, and other waste products are dissolved. It may also contain ordinary substances used by the body but excreted by the kidneys when excessive amounts are present in the bloodstream. Analysis of urine is important in detecting diseases. See also URINARY SYSTEM.

Ursa Major and **Ursa Minor** [Lat., = the great bear; the little bear], two conspicuous northern CONSTELLATIONS. In the U.S., part of Ursa Major is called the Big Dipper (or the Drinking Gourd) and part of

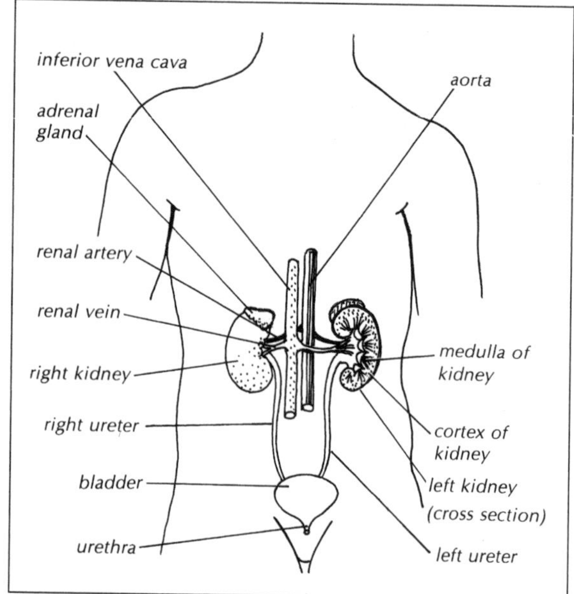

Urinary system

Ursa Minor, the Little Dipper. POLARIS is at the extreme end of the Little Dipper.

Uruguay [yo͞o'rəgwā, –gwī], officially Eastern Republic of Uruguay, republic (1992 est. pop. 3,142,000), 68,536 sq mi (177,508 sq km), SE South America, the continent's second smallest country (after Suriname); bordered by Argentina (W), Brazil (N), the Atlantic Ocean (E), and the Río de la Plata (S). The capital is MONTEVIDEO, where over 40% of the people live. An alluvial plain, known as the Banda Oriental, occupies the south, while to the north is a region of grasslands and low hills. Uruguay's economy is based on sheep and cattle. Grains for cattle and human consumption make up the bulk of the crops, and manufacturing is led by the processing of animal and agricultural products; meat, wool, hides, and skins are the leading exports. The country has abundant fisheries. Most of the population is of Spanish and Italian descent; about 10% is mestizo. Spanish is the principal language, and Roman Catholicism the chief religion.

History. The first permanent European settlement in present-day Uruguay was established in 1624 by the Spanish, who controlled the Banda Oriental until the 1800s. Uruguay declared for independence with its neighbor Argentina in 1810, but in 1814, led by José ARTIGAS, determined to fight for a separate existence. In 1820 Uruguay's other neighbor, Brazil, occupied Montevideo, and it was not until 1828, after Brazil had been defeated at Ituzaingó, that an independent Uruguay was achieved. Immediately thereafter, a civil war broke out, which, becoming entwined with an uprising in Argentina, resulted in a long siege of Montevideo and did not end until 1851. In 1864 Uruguay again became involved with her neighbors, this time in a war with Brazil and Argentina against Paraguay (see TRIPLE ALLIANCE, WAR OF THE). Revolutions and counterrevolutions followed, and it was not until the regime of José Battle y Ordóñez in the early 20th cent. that Uruguay began the social and material progress that made it one of the more stable and prosperous nations of South America. However, economic problems and social unrest in the 1960s and 1970s, heightened by the terrorism of the Tupamaros, a Marxist guerrilla group, led to the installation of a repressive military regime in 1973. The ruling generals initiated moves that gradually returned the nation to democracy and political liberty, and in 1985 Julio Sanguinetti became president. Luis Alberto Lacalle succeeded him in 1990. Lacalle has attempted to reduce state programs and the state's role in the economy but has had only modest success.

Ussher or **Usher, James** [both: ŭsh'ər], 1581–1656, Irish Protestant prelate and scholar. By 1605 he was chancellor of St. Patrick's Cathedral, Dublin, and later became bishop of Meath (1620 or

1621) and archbishop of Armagh (1625). He was greatly admired for his learning and established a chronology that set the date of creation at 4004 B.C. and was long used in some editions of the King James Version of the Bible.

Ussuri [o͞oso͞o'rē], river, c.365 mi (590 km) long, Far Eastern Russia. It flows N to the Amur R. at Khabarovsk, forming part of the China-Russia border. Border clashes between Chinese and Soviet forces occurred along the river in 1969 and 1972.

usury: see INTEREST.

Utah, state in the W U.S.; bordered by Idaho and Wyoming (N), Colorado (E), Arizona (S), and Nevada (W).

Area, 84,916 sq mi (219,932 sq km). *Pop.* (1990) 1,722,850, a 17.9% increase over 1980 pop. *Capital,* Salt Lake City. *Statehood,* Jan. 4, 1896 (45th state). *Highest pt.,* Kings Peak, 13,528 ft (4,126 m); *lowest pt.,* Beaverdam Creek, 2,000 ft (610 m). *Nickname,* Beehive State. *Motto,* Industry. *State bird,* seagull. *State flower,* sego lily. *State tree,* blue spruce. *Abbr.,* UT.

Land and People. The Wasatch Range of the ROCKY MOUNTAINS runs north to south through the center of largely arid Utah, with the COLORADO PLATEAU to the east and the GREAT BASIN to the west. GREAT SALT LAKE and Bonneville Salt Flats are the remnants of Pleistocene-era Lake Bonneville. The generally dry climate is characterized by abundant sunshine and high temperatures in the southwestern desert, in contrast to the cooler weather and lower temperatures of the high plateaus and mountains. Often spectacularly scenic, Utah is the site of Glen Canyon National Recreation Area; Bryce Canyon, Arches, Canyonlands, and Zion national parks (see NATIONAL PARKS; table); and several national monuments. Over 60% of the land is controlled by the federal government. MORMONS constitute over two thirds of the population, of which more than 85% lives in urban areas, including those of SALT LAKE CITY, Utah's largest city, PROVO, and OGDEN. In 1990 the state was 94% white.

Economy. Much of the workforce is directly or indirectly involved in mining, and Utah extracts significant quantities of copper, oil, gold, magnesium, molybdenum, beryllium, coal, asphalt, silver, lead, tin, and other minerals. The major crops, which are heavily dependent on irrigation, are hay, wheat, apples, barley, alfalfa seed, and corn, although the bulk of agricultural income is derived from cattle and dairy products. Utah is a center of aerospace and military-related industries and also produces nonelectrical machinery, processed foods, transportation equipment, and computer-related items. The tourism industry is also important.

Government. The constitution (adopted 1895) provides for a governor serving a four-year term. The legislature consists of a senate with 30 members elected for four years and a house with 75 members elected to two-year terms. Utah is represented in the U.S. Congress by three representatives and two senators and has five electoral votes.

History. The remains of cliff-dwellers are preserved at Capitol Reef National Park (see NATIONAL PARKS, table). The UTE, PAIUTE, Goshiute, and NAVAHO inhabited the region when Spanish missionaries arrived (1776). The area passed (1848) to the U.S., and wagon trains on the OREGON TRAIL began passing through. In 1847 Mormons under the leadership of Brigham YOUNG began to settle Utah. Their subsequent petitions for statehood were denied because of the Mormon practice of polygamy. This dispute escalated (1857) into the Utah War, which briefly pitted settlers against U.S. army troops. In 1890 the church repudiated polygamy, and statehood was subsequently granted. Mining accelerated after the discovery of new mineral deposits in the early 20th cent. The extension of the COLORADO R. and other water projects and the growth of defense-related and high-technology industries since World War II have gradually provided Utah with a diversified economy.

Utamaro (Kitagawa Utamaro), 1753–1806, Japanese color-print artist, the first of the great masters of the *ukiyo-e* school (see JAPANESE ART). His were the first Japanese prints to become familiar in the West. His idealized, sensuous women and his book of *Insects* (1788) reveal a keen observation of nature.

Ute, Native Americans speaking a Shoshonean language of the Uto-Aztecan branch of the Aztec-Tanoan stock (see NATIVE AMERICAN LANGUAGES) and having a culture typical of the western Plains (see NORTH AMERICA, INDIGENOUS PEOPLES OF). They were nomadic people who celebrated the SUN DANCE. Fierce warriors, they ranged southward from their homeland in W Colorado and E Utah to menace the villages of the PUEBLO, selling captives into slavery. Some Utes fought with Kit CARSON against the NAVAHO in the CIVIL WAR. In 1868 they were placed on a Colorado reservation, but in 1880 they were moved to less desirable land. Most Utes still live in Utah and Colorado, with those on reservations deriving income from oil and gas leases, farming, cattle-raising, and tourism. In 1990 there were 7,273 Utes in the U.S.

uterus: see REPRODUCTIVE SYSTEM.

Uthman ibn al-Affan, d. 656, 3d Muslim caliph. A wealthy Meccan merchant, he converted to Islam and became caliph after the death of UMAR IBN AL-KHATTAB. He pursued Umar's policy of conquest, though less successfully, and built an administrative system of fiefdoms based on nepotism and the adoption of an official version of the Koran. Factional disputes escalated after his murder, at Medina, in 656.

Utica [yo͞o'tĭkə], ancient N African city, NW of Carthage. Supposedly founded by Phoenicians from TYRE (c.1100 B.C.), it joined Rome against CARTHAGE in the Third PUNIC WAR. Later it was the capital of the Roman province of Africa. It was destroyed by the Arabs A.D. c.700.

utilitarianism, in ethics, the theory that the rightness or wrongness of an action is determined by the goodness or badness of its consequences. Jeremy BENTHAM, founder of the theory, held that the greatest happiness of the greatest number is the fundamental and self-evident principle of morality. His student John Stuart MILL used the principles of utilitarianism to advocate political and social reform, increased democracy, and the emancipation of women. Herbert SPENCER developed a utilitarian ethics based on evolutionary changes.

Uto-Aztecan [yo͞o'tō-ăztĕk'ən], branch of the Aztec-Tanoan linguistic stock. The languages belonging to this stock are spoken in North and Central America. See NATIVE AMERICAN LANGUAGES (table).

Utopia [Gr., = no place], influential book by Sir Thomas MORE (1516) depicting an ideal state that has given its name to all such visions. Utopian writers criticize present conditions and outline vast revolutionary schemes without, however, describing the concrete steps necessary to realize them. The term is applied retrospectively to PLATO's *Republic* and St. AUGUSTINE's *City of God,* as well as to the more worldly Renaissance Utopias of RABELAIS and Francis BACON. ROUSSEAU's promotion of the idea of a primitive Golden Age and of man's innate goodness in turn influenced the

Utopian socialist communities envisioned by Claude, duc de SAINT-SIMON, Charles FOURIER, P.J. PROUDHON, and others. Utopian experiments, however, generally proved short-lived. The Utopian romance became a popular form of literature in the 19th cent., e.g., Samuel BUTLER's *Erewhon* (1872) and Edward BELLAMY's *Looking Backward* (1888), as did the satiric anti-Utopian novel in the 20th cent., e.g., Aldous HUXLEY's *Brave New World* (1932) and George ORWELL's *1984* (1949).

Utrecht, city (1991 est. pop. 232,000), capital of Utrecht prov., central Netherlands. It is an industrial center, with such manufactures as machinery, cement, and food. Founded by Rome, it became (7th cent.) an episcopal see. It was a major medieval center of commerce and was ruled by bishops until ceded (1527) to Emperor Charles V. In 1713 it was the site of the signing of the Peace of Utrecht ending the war of the SPANISH SUCCESSION. It is noted for its 14th-cent. cathedral and its university (est. 1636).

Utrillo, Maurice, 1883–1955, French painter; son of the painter Suzanne Valadon. His favorite theme was street scenes of Paris. His personal style was based on a modified CUBISM and a fine sense of atmosphere and composition.

Uxmal [o͞oshmäl′], ancient city, N Yucatán peninsula, Mexico. A Late Classic period MAYA center, Uxmal flourished between 600 and 900. The site has several fine examples of Mayan architecture, including the Nunnery, with elaborate stone mosaic friezes; the Governor's Palace, with some 20,000 carved stone elements in its facade; and the Pyramid of the Magician. The Maya abandoned Uxmal shortly after 950.

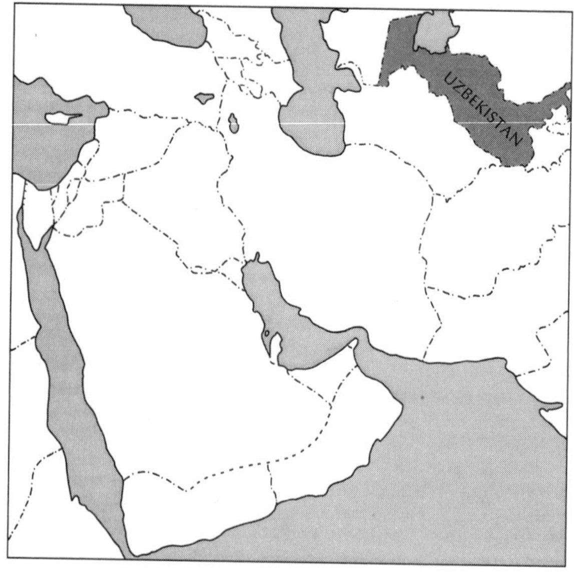

Uzbekistan, officially Republic of Uzbekistan, republic (1992 est. pop. 21,627,000), 173,552 sq mi (449,500 sq km), central Asia, formerly a constituent republic of the USSR. It borders Afghanistan (S); Turkmenistan (SW); Kazakhstan (W, N); and Kyrgyzstan and Tajikistan (E). TOSHKENT, the capital, and SAMARKAND are the chief cities. The northwest is largely part of the KYZYL KUM desert and borders the Aral Sea in the extreme north; the southeast has fertile loess soil and touches on the Tian Shan mountains. The Amu Darya and Syr Darya pass through the country, providing irrigation for its farms. Major economic activities include the growing of cotton and rice; stock-raising; and machine building, textile manufacturing, metallurgy, and food processing. Oil, natural gas, and coal are the major resources; there are also zinc, copper, tungsten, and other ores. The Uzbek, a Turkic-speaking people, make up the majority of the population; other groups include Russians, Tajiks, Kazakhs, and Tatars. Sunni Islam is the predominant religion, and the Orthodox church is the largest non-Islamic faith. Uzbek is the official language, but Russian and other ethnic languages are also spoken.

History. The ancient Persian province of Sogdiana, the region was ruled (4th–15th cent.) by ALEXANDER THE GREAT, Arabs, the Seljuk Turks of KHOREZM, JENGHIZ KHAN, TIMUR, and the TIMURIDS. The cities of Samarkand, Bukhara, and Toshkent, situated on trade routes to China, India, Persia, and Europe, were centers of prosperity, culture, and luxury. In the early 16th cent., the Uzbek invaded from the northwest. A remnant of the empire of the GOLDEN HORDE, they took their name from Uzbeg Khan (d. 1340), from whom their rulers claimed descent. Later in the 16th cent., the Uzbek domain was extended over parts of Persia, Afghanistan, and Chinese Turkistan, but the empire soon broke into separate principalities. These fell under Russian control largely between 1865 and 1873. In 1918, after a failed attempt to form a Western-style democratic republic, the region became part of the USSR; the Uzbek Soviet Socialist Republic was established in 1924. Following the failed hard-line coup against Soviet Pres. Gorbachev, Uzbekistan declared (1991) its independence from the USSR and later joined the COMMONWEALTH OF INDEPENDENT STATES. The former Communist party retained its hold on power. In 1991 Islam Karimov, in power since 1990, was elected president, but major opposition parties were not allowed to run candidates in the election. Opposition groups have since been suppressed.

V

V, chemical symbol of the element VANADIUM.

Vaca, Cabeza de: see CABEZA DE VACA, ÁLVAR NÚÑEZ.

vaccination, means of producing active IMMUNITY against disease by the introduction of weakened live or killed microorganisms that stimulate the body to produce antibodies against more dangerous forms of the microorganism. Vaccination was used in ancient times in China, India, and Persia, and was introduced in the West in the late 18th cent. by E. JENNER. Vaccination has eradicated SMALLPOX and prevents such diseases as DIPHTHERIA, POLIOMYELITIS, RABIES, and TYPHOID. Experimental vaccines are being tested for certain cancers. Vaccines also control animal pests by conferring temporary infertility.

vacuum, theoretically, space devoid of matter. A perfect vacuum has never been obtained; the best artificial vacuums contain less than 10^5 gas molecules per cc, compared with about 30×10^{18} molecules per cc for air at sea level. In intergalactic space, the regions with the highest vacuum are estimated to contain less than one molecule per cc. Several kinds of **vacuum pumps** have been devised, e.g., the ion pump, which ionizes gas molecules and draws them to a charged collector, and the cryogenic pump, which condenses gas molecules on an extremely cold surface of a container.

vagina: see REPRODUCTIVE SYSTEM.

Vaillant, George Clapp [văl′yănt], 1901–45, American archaeologist; b. Boston, known for his syntheses of early Mexican culture and AZTEC history. He worked in the Southwest, Egypt, and Central America. His works include *Indian Arts in North America* (1939).

Valdivia, Pedro de [väldē'vyä], c.1500–1554, Spanish CONQUISTADOR, conqueror of CHILE. Accompanying Francisco PIZARRO during the conquest of PERU, he received Pizarro's permission to subdue Chile in 1540. The capital, SANTIAGO, was founded in 1541, but the colony did not prosper because of the scarcity of gold and the ferocity of the ARAUCANIANS. Valdivia returned to Peru for further aid in 1547 and helped quell the rebellion of Gonzalo PIZARRO. Governor of Chile from 1549, he founded CONCEPCIÓN (1550) and Valdivia (1552). He was killed in the Araucanian rebellion of 1553.

valence or **oxidation state,** combining capacity of an ATOM expressed as the number of single bonds the atom can form or the number of electrons an ELEMENT gives up or accepts when reacting to form a compound. The valence of an atom is determined by the number of electrons in the outermost, or valence, electron shell. An atom exists in its most stable configuration when its outermost shell is completely filled; in combining with other atoms, it thus tends to gain or lose valence electrons in order to attain a stable configuration. The valence of many elements is determined from their ability to combine with hydrogen or to replace it in compounds.

Valencia, autonomous region and former kingdom (1987 est. pop. 3,754,000), E Spain, on the Mediterranean Sea. Largely mountainous, with a fertile coastal plain, Valencia is the "garden of Spain." Citrus and other fruits, rice, and wine grapes are among its crops. Manufactures include ceramics and metal products. The area was conquered (8th cent.) by the MOORS, became (1022) an independent emirate, and was ruled (1094–99) by the CID. It was conquered (1238) by ARAGÓN but preserved its political identity within Aragón and, later, in the Spanish state.

Valencia, city (1988 est. pop. 744,000), capital of Valencia prov., E Spain. A picturesque winter resort, it lies in a fertile region near its Mediterranean port, El Grao. It has shipyards and produces textiles, metal products, and chemicals. A Roman colony, it was held (8th–13th cent.) by the MOORS. Conquered by James I of Aragón (1238), it gained commercial and cultural importance; intellectual eminence followed. Landmarks include the cathedral (13th–15 cent.), 14th-cent. fortified towers built on Roman foundations, and the Gothic silk exchange.

Valens, c.328–378, Roman emperor of the East (364–78). Unlike his brother and coruler of the West, VALENTINIAN I, he embraced ARIANISM. He was killed in a disastrous defeat by the VISIGOTHS at Adrianople. THEODOSIUS I succeeded him.

Valentine, Saint, d. c.270, Roman martyr-priest. Possibly because his feast, Feb. 14, was close to a pagan love festival, Valentine became known as a patron of lovers. The lovers' greeting cards sent on this day are called valentines. His feast was dropped from the liturgical calendar in 1969.

Valentine's Day: see SAINT VALENTINE'S DAY.

Valentinian, Roman emperors of the West. **Valentinian I,** 321–75 (r.364–75), was coruler of the East with his brother VALENS. He reduced taxes and allowed religious freedom. His son, **Valentinian II,** 371?–392, (r.375–392), ruled jointly until 383 with his brother Gratian, who made THEODOSIUS I emperor of the East. He was expelled (387) from Italy by Maximus but restored (388) by Theodosius. Later he was murdered, probably by the Frankish general Arbogast. **Valentinian III,** 419–55 (r.425–55), was at first under the regency of his mother, Galla Placidia. The Vandals and HUNS invaded the empire during his reign. An ineffectual monarch, he allowed the general Aetius to rule (433–54). Valentinian murdered Aetius (454) and was himself murdered.

Valentino, Rudolph, 1895–1926, American film actor; b. Italy. He became one of the screen's first sex symbols in such silent films as *The Sheik* (1921) and *Blood and Sand* (1922).

Valera, Eamon de: see DE VALERA, EAMON.

Valéry, Paul [välārē'], 1871–1945, French poet and critic. A follower of the SYMBOLISTS, he was one of the greatest French poets of the 20th cent. His masterpiece, *The Young Fate* (1917), long and somewhat obscure, and *Graveyard by the Sea* (1920) offer the best examples of Valéry's poetics. His prose works include five collections of essays, all called *Variety* (1924–44), and four dialogues on subjects ranging from the arts to mathematics. He received many honors.

Valkyries [vălkēr'ēz], in Germanic myth, Odin's warrior maidens. They presided over battles, chose those who were to die, and bore heroes' souls to Valhalla, hall of heroes in ASGARD. Chief among them was BRUNHILD. They are prominent in Richard WAGNER's *Die Walküre.*

Valla, Lorenzo, c.1407–1457, Italian humanist. At 26 he wrote *On Pleasure,* an analysis of pleasure and a humanistic condemnation of SCHOLASTICISM. His masterpiece is *On the Elegance of the Latin Language* (1435–44), a brilliant and influential philological defense of classical Latin.

Vallandigham, Clement Laird, 1820–71, American political leader, leader of the COPPERHEADS in the CIVIL WAR; b. New Lisbon (now Lisbon), Ohio. A lawyer and former Democratic congressman (1858–63), Vallandigham was briefly imprisoned in 1863 for maintaining in a speech that the war was being fought to free African-American slaves and enslave whites. The 1864 Democratic platform reflected his pro-Southern views.

Valle Inclán, Ramón del [vä'lyā ēnklän'], 1866?–1936, Spanish writer. His most notorious works, the erotic tales in *Femeninas* (1895) and the semiautobiographical *Sonata* novels (1902–5; tr. *The Pleasant Memoirs of the Marquis de Bradomín*), show the influence of MODERNISMO, while such poetic works as *The Aroma of Legends* (1907) express a symbolist aesthetic. His originality is most marked in his *esperpentos,* grotesque caricatures of Spanish life, particularly of aristocratic and military brutality, reminiscent of the nightmare etchings of GOYA; they include the play *Bohemian Lights* (1920) and the novel *The Tyrant* (1926).

Vallejo, César [väyä'hō], 1895–1938, Peruvian poet. Of indigenous and European ancestry, he was dedicated to social justice. After 1923 he lived in Europe, where he became a Marxist and supported the Republicans in the SPANISH CIVIL WAR. His poetry includes *Black Heralds* (1918), *Human Poems* (1939), and *Spain, Let This Cup Pass from Me* (1940).

Vallejo [vaəlā'hō, –ō], city (1990 pop. 109,199), Solano co., W Calif., on San Pablo Bay at the mouth of the Napa R.; inc. 1866. A rapidly growing port city, it has numerous dry dock and shipbuilding facilities. The U.S. naval shipyard on Mare Island, west of Vallejo, was established (1854) by Adm. David Farragut. The city is also a trade and processing center for farm products. Founded (1851) to be the state capital, it was the nominal capital from 1852 to 1853.

valley fever or **coccidioidomycosis,** systemic disease endemic to the SW U.S. and other arid regions of the Americas, contracted by inhaling dust containing spores of the fungus *Coccidioides immits*. From the respiratory tract, it can spread to the skin, bones, and central nervous system. Manifestations range from complete absence of symptoms to systemic infection and death.

Valley Forge, on the Schuylkill R., NE Pa. During the AMERICAN REVOLUTION it was the encampment of the Continental Army, Dec. 1777–June 1778. The winter was severe but the suffering troops were held together by loyalty to Gen. WASHINGTON and the patriotic cause.

Valois, Dame Ninette de [văl'wä], 1898–, English BALLET dancer, choreographer, and director; b. Ireland. She was choreographic director of the Abbey (Dublin) and Old Vic (London) theaters. In 1931 she established the Sadler's Wells Ballet School, London, and later she became director of the Vic-Wells Ballet (now the ROYAL Ballet).

Valois [välwä'], royal house of France that ruled from 1328 to 1589. It succeeded the CAPETIANS when PHILIP VI, son of Charles of Valois and grandson of PHILIP III, became king. The direct Valois line ended (1498) with CHARLES VIII; the dynasty was continued by LOUIS XII (Valois-Orléans) and by FRANCIS I (Valois-Angoulême). At the death of HENRY III (1589), HENRY IV of the house of BOURBON succeeded to the throne.

Valparaiso, city (1990 est. pop. 277,000), central Chile, capital of Valparaiso dept., on a bay of the Pacific Ocean. Chile's chief port, it is a major industrial center and the terminus of a trans-Andean railroad. Its setting is a natural amphitheater. The business district, crowded onto a narrow waterfront terrace, is connected by cable railways to residential areas on the surrounding slopes. Founded in 1536, Valparaiso grew rapidly in the late 19th cent.

value-added tax, levy imposed on businesses at all levels of production of a good or service, and based on the increase in price, or value, added to the good or service by each level. Because all stages of a value-added tax are ultimately passed on to the consumer in the form of higher prices, it has been described as a hidden sales tax. Originally introduced in France (1954), it is now used by most W European countries. See also TAXATION.

vampire, in folklore, animated corpse that sucks the blood of humans, usually enslaving its victims and making them vampires. Vampires could be warded off with charms and killed by a stake driven through the heart. Literature's most famous vampire is Bram STOKER'S *Dracula* (1897).

vanadium (V), metallic element, discovered in 1801 by A.M. del Rio. It is a soft, silver-gray metal that adds strength, toughness, and heat resistance to STEEL alloys. Vanadium compounds, especially the pentoxide, are used in ceramics, glass, and dyes and are important as catalysts in the chemical industry. See ELEMENT (table); PERIODIC TABLE.

Van Allen radiation belts, two belts of RADIATION outside the earth's atmosphere, extending from c.400 to c.40,000 mi (c.650 to c.65,000 km). The region of the belts is called the magnetosphere. The high-energy protons and electrons that compose the belts circulate along the earth's magnetic lines of force. These particles are probably emitted by the sun in its periodic solar flares and, after traveling across space, are captured by the earth's magnetic field. The belts were discovered by detectors (developed by American physicist James Van Allen and colleagues) aboard *Explorer 1,* the first U.S. artificial satellite. A belt of high-energy oxygen, nitrogen, and neon ions located within the inner Van Allen radiation belt was detected in the late 1980s and identified in 1993.

Vanbrugh, Sir John, 1664–1726, English dramatist and architect. His best-known plays, *The Relapse* (1696) and *The Provoked Wife* (1697), are imbued with Restoration wit and cynicism. As his repute as an architect grew, he turned away from the stage, becoming WREN'S principal colleague. He is especially noted for Blenheim Palace (the culmination of English BAROQUE) and Castle Howard.

Van Buren, Martin, 1782–1862, 8th president of the U.S. (1837–41); b. Kinderhook, N.Y. A lawyer, he became active in New York State Democratic politics and one of the leaders of the Albany Regency. He served (1821–28) in the U.S. Senate. Elected governor of NEW YORK in 1828, he became one of Andrew Jackson's supporters and resigned (1829) to become Jackson's secretary of state (1829–31). He was Jackson's running mate in the 1832 presidential election and was elected vice president. Largely through Jackson's influence, he was the Democratic candidate for president in 1836 and won. He intended to continue Jackson's policies, but the Panic of 1837 and the hard times that followed made him very unpopular. To meet the economic crisis, he proposed (1837) the INDEPENDENT TREASURY SYSTEM. In foreign affairs, he attempted to mediate the differences with Great Britain that arose from the CAROLINE AFFAIR and the AROOSTOOK WAR. He was defeated for reelection in 1840 by William Henry HARRISON, the WHIG PARTY candidate. He remained a power in Democratic politics, but in 1848 he ran for president as the candidate of the FREE-SOIL PARTY and managed to throw the election to Zachary TAYLOR. He supported Abraham LINCOLN in the secessionist crisis.

Vancouver, George, 1757–98, English navigator and explorer. He commanded an expedition (1791–94) to take over Nootka Sound, assigned to England by the Nootka Convention, and thoroughly explored the NW coast of America. He also circumnavigated the island now called VANCOUVER ISLAND.

Vancouver, city (1991 pop. 471,844), SW British Columbia, W Canada, on Burrard Inlet of the Strait of Georgia. The city, known for its mild climate and spectacular backdrop of mountains (part of the COAST RANGE), is Canada's third largest (and largest western) city, its principal Pacific port, and the chief western terminus of the trans-Canadian railroads, highways, and airways. Oil refining, fish processing, and the manufacture of textiles dominate a diversified industrial economy. Notable attractions include Stanley Park, an anthropology museum, and aquarium. Originally called Granville, it was settled before 1875 and renamed for Capt. George VANCOUVER in 1886. It was the site of an international exposition in 1986.

Vancouver Island, island, 12,408 sq mi (32,137 sq km), SW British Columbia, Canada, separated from the mainland by Juan de Fuca, Georgia, and Queen Charlotte straits. It is c.285 mi (460 km) long and c.30–80 mi (50–130 km) wide, and reaches a high point of 7,219 ft (2,200 m) at Golden Hinde Mt. Victoria is the largest city. The island was first sighted (1774) by Juan Pérez, explored (1778) by Capt. James COOK, and circumnavigated (1792) by Capt. George VANCOUVER. It was a separate colony (1849–1866) before becoming part of British Columbia.

Vanderbilt, Cornelius, 1794–1877, American railroad magnate; b. Staten Island, N.Y. After working on ferries around New York City as a boy, he gained control of the ferry lines, expanded his shipping interests, and came to be known as Commodore Vanderbilt. During the California gold rush he opened (1851) a shipping line from the East Coast to California via Nicaragua. He entered the railroad field during the Civil War; by 1867 he had gained control of the New York Central RR and by 1873 had connected Chicago with New York City by rail. From the large fortune amassed by his railroad empire he founded Vanderbilt Univ. (Nashville, Tenn.). A son, **William Henry Vanderbilt,** 1821–85, b. New Brunswick, N.J., succeeded his father as president of the New York Central, and gave liberally to Vanderbilt Univ. and other institutions. William's son **Cornelius Vanderbilt,** 1843–99, b. Staten Island, N.Y., helped establish the Vanderbilt Clinic and the Cathedral of ST. JOHN THE DIVINE (both: N.Y.C.). Another son, **George Washington Vanderbilt,** 1862–1914, b. Staten Island, N.Y., donated land for Teachers College, Columbia Univ., and built the estate "Biltmore" near Asheville, N.C. **Harold Sterling Vanderbilt,** 1884–1970, b. Suffolk co., N.Y., grandson of William, won the America's Cup yachting races three times in the 1930s and largely developed (1925) the modern game of contract bridge.

Van der Goes, Hugo: see GOES, HUGO VAN DER.

van der Meer, Simon, 1925–, Dutch physical engineer. He worked with Carlo RUBBIA at CERN, where they discovered the W AND Z PARTICLES, the subatomic particles that convey the WEAK INTERACTION. In 1984 they were awarded the Nobel Prize in physics.

van der Waals, Johannes Diderik [van dər vals], 1837–1923, Dutch physicist. His theory of corresponding states (1880) contained an equation of state (now named for him) for homogeneous substances in terms of pressure, volume, and temperature (see GAS LAWS); unlike the ideal gas law, his equation contains constant factors (different for each real substance) to account for the fact that molecules are of finite size and experience weak forces of mutual attraction (van der Waals forces). For this work and for the discovery of the law of binary mixtures he won the 1910 Nobel Prize in physics.

van der Waals equation: see GAS LAWS.

Van der Weyden, Roger: see WEYDEN, ROGER VAN DER.

Van Diemen's Land: see TASMANIA.

Van Dyck or **Vandyke, Sir Anthony,** 1599–1641, Flemish portrait and religious painter and etcher. Born in Antwerp, Belgium, he was the assistant and collaborator of RUBENS. In 1620 he traveled to England and then to Italy, where he painted portraits of the Genoese nobility. An outstanding example is the portrait of Marchesa Elena Grimaldi (National Gall., Wash., D.C.). When he returned to Antwerp in 1627, where he rivaled Rubens in popularity, he painted a famous series of religious pictures. In his portraits, Van Dyck conferred upon his sitters elegance, dignity, and refinement, qualities pleasing to royalty and aristocracy. In 1632 he was invited to England by CHARLES I, and his portraits of Charles are in the Louvre and Buckingham Palace. He became court painter and was overwhelmed with commissions. From 1634 to 1635 he was in Antwerp, where he painted his masterly *Lamentation.* Although similar in technique to that of Rubens, his work has more restrained color and refined form. The patrician image of English aristocrats that he created greatly influenced the direction of English portraiture. Examples of his portraits include those of James Stuart and of the Marchesa Durazzo (both: Metropolitan Mus.).

Vandyke, Sir Anthony: see VAN DYCK, SIR ANTHONY.

Vane, Sir Henry, 1613–62, English statesman. A Puritan, he emigrated to America in 1635 and was elected (1636) governor of

Massachusetts. His support of Anne HUTCHINSON cost him reelection in 1637, and he returned to England. He sat in the Short and Long Parliaments and secured (1643) the Solemn League and Covenant with Scotland. He was influential under Oliver CROMWELL until the two quarreled in 1653. After the RESTORATION, Vane was executed for treason.

Van Gogh, Vincent [văn gō], 1853–90, Dutch postimpressionist painter. His works are perhaps better known generally than those of any other painter. The great majority were produced in 29 months of frenzied activity interspersed with epileptoid seizures and despair that finally ended in suicide. His early work, the Dutch period (1880–85), consists of dark, greenish-brown, heavily painted studies of peasants and miners, e.g., *The Potato Eaters* (1885; Municipal Mus., Amsterdam). After moving from the Netherlands to Paris, he met PISSARRO, who encouraged him to adopt a colorful palette, e.g., *Père Tanguy* (1887; Niarchos Coll., Paris). His work from his last months at Arles is characterized by the heavy impasto and rhythmic linear style so identified with him; it includes the incomparable series of sunflowers (1888). His last works include the swirling, climactic *Starry Night* (Mus. Mod. Art, N.Y.C.) and the ominously distressed *Wheatfield with Crows* (Van Gogh Foundation, Amsterdam).

vanilla, vine (genus *Vanilla*) of the ORCHID family, native to hot damp climates of Central America but now cultivated in other tropical regions. The fruits yield vanilla, a popular flavoring usually marketed as an alcoholic extract. The commercial plant is usually *V. fragrans;* the source of the flavor is an aromatic essence, vanillin. Vanilla flavoring, now usually artificially synthesized, is also obtained from the tonka bean, which contains coumarin, a substance with a vanilla-like aroma.

Vannucci, Pietro: see PERUGINO.

Van Ostade, Adriaen: see OSTADE, ADRIAEN VAN.

Van Rensselaer, Stephen, 1764–1839, American politician, called the Patroon; b. N.Y.C. As the largest landholder in New York, he was long involved in state affairs and served in Congress (1822–29). In the WAR OF 1812, his troops were defeated in the battle of Queenston. His vote in the House assured the 1825 election of J.Q. ADAMS as president.

van't Hoff, Jacobus Hendricus [vänt hôf], 1852–1911, Dutch physical chemist. His studies in molecular structure laid the foundation of stereochemistry. For his work in chemical dynamics and osmotic electrical conductivity he won (1901) the first Nobel Prize in chemistry.

Vanuatu, officially Republic of Vanuatu, republic (1992 est. pop. 175,000), 5,570 sq mi (14,426 sq km), comprising a 450-mi (724-km) chain of islands in the South Pacific Ocean E of Australia, formerly called the New Hebrides. Espiritu Santo and Efâte, site of Vila (the capital), are the two largest islands. The group is forested and mountainous. The chief industries are copra production, tuna fishing, manganese mining, and cattle raising. Additional revenues derive from a growing tourist industry and the development of Vila as a corporate tax haven. The population is predominantly Melanesian. English and French are the official languages, but Bislama, a pidgin, is widely spoken.

History. The islands were visited in 1606 by the Portuguese and were systematically explored in 1774 by Capt. James COOK. In 1887 they were placed under an Anglo-French naval commission, which was replaced (1906) by a condominium. In 1980 they became independent as Vanuatu, and a secession movement on Espiritu Santo was put down with aid from Papua New Guinea and Britain. A member of the Commonwealth, Vanuatu has a president, a prime minister and council, and a unicameral parliament. A coalition led by Prime Min. Maxime Carlot has governed Vanuatu since 1991. See PACIFIC OCEAN map.

Van Vechten, Carl, 1880–1964, American author; b. Cedar Rapids, Iowa. A leading music critic and distinguished photographer, he was also a novelist whose sophisticated 1920s works include *Nigger Heaven* (1926) and *Spider Boy* (1928).

vaporization: see STATES OF MATTER.

Varanasi, formerly **Benares,** city (1991 pop. 1,026,467), Uttar Pradesh state, N central India, on the Ganges R. The holiest Hindu city, it has c.1,500 temples, palaces, and shrines. Steps lead to the sacred GANGES, where Hindus bathe. About 1 million pilgrims visit the city annually. BUDDHA is said to have begun preaching nearby. The mosque of AURANGZEB, on the city's highest ground, is the most notable building of India's MOGUL period. The city is also known for its silk brocades and brassware.

Varèse, Edgard [värĕz'], 1885–1965, French-American composer. A bold innovator, he achieved dissonant effects by using extreme registers of orchestral instruments combined with ELECTRONIC MUSIC. His works include *Hyperprism* (1923), *Ionisation* (1931), and *Poème Electronique* (1958).

Vargas, Getúlio Dornelles [vär'gəs], 1883–1954, president of BRAZIL (1930–45, 1951–54). He led a revolt and established a dictatorship (1930), and introduced (1937) a corporate state. Ousted (1945) by an army coup, he was again elected president (1950); he resigned (1954) under army pressure and committed suicide.

Vargas Llosa, Mario [vär'gäs yō'sä], 1936–, Peruvian novelist. Technically innovative, his novels are penetrating studies of Peruvian life. They include *The Time of the Hero* (1962), *The Green House* (1966), *Conversations in the Cathedral* (1969), *Aunt Julia and the Scriptwriter* (tr. 1982), and *The War of the End of the World* (tr. 1984). In 1990 Vargas Llosa was an unsuccessful candidate for president of Peru.

variable star, star that varies, either periodically or irregularly, in the intensity of its light. Variable stars are grouped into three broad classes: the pulsating variables, the eruptive variables, and the eclipsing variables. In **pulsating variables,** which account for more than half of the known variable stars, slight instabilities cause the star alternatively to expand and to contract, resulting in changes in absolute luminosity and temperature. The pulsating variables can be subdivided into short-term, long-term, semiregular, and irregular variables. *Short-term variables* have periods ranging from less than one day to more than 50 days; among them are the important but rare CEPHEID VARIABLES. Commoner short-term variables are the RR Lyrae stars; about 2,500 of this type are known in our galaxy. They have periods of less than one day, and all have roughly the same intrinsic brightness, which makes them another useful distance indicator. The *long-term variables* are the most numerous of the pulsating stars. They are red giant and supergiant stars with periods ranging from 80 to 300 days. *Semiregular variables* are stars whose periodic variations are occasionally interrupted by sudden bursts of light. *Irregular variables* show no periodicity in their variations in brightness. The **eruptive variables** are highly unstable stars that suddenly and unpredictably increase in brightness. *T Tauri stars* are the least violent of these explosive stars. *Novas* are small, very hot stars that suddenly increase thousands of times in luminosity; their decline in luminosity is much slower, taking months or years. SUPERNOVAS, upon exploding, increase millions of times in brightness and are totally disrupted. **Eclipsing variables** are not true (intrinsic) variables but rather are BINARY STAR systems.

varicose vein, superficial vessel that is abnormally twisted, lengthened, or dilated, seen most often on the legs and thighs and usually attributed to inefficient valves within the vein. Conditions such as PREGNANCY or obesity, or increased pressure from prolonged standing, reduce the support of tissues surrounding the veins, causing them to dilate. Treatment includes use of support hosiery and, if necessary, surgical removal.

Varna, city (1989 est. pop. 311,000), E Bulgaria, on the Black Sea. A major port, it has shipyards, produces chemicals and other manufactures, and is a summer resort. Founded by the Greeks (580 B.C.), it was held (1st–14th cent.) by Rome, Byzantium, and the second Bulgarian kingdom. After 1391 it was ruled by the Turks. It was ceded to independent Bulgaria in 1878.

varnish, solution of gum or of natural or synthetic RESINS that dries to a thin, hard, usually glossy film; it may be transparent, translucent, or tinted. Oil varnishes are made from hard gum or resin dissolved in oil. Spirit varnishes, e.g., SHELLAC, are usually made of soft gums or resins dissolved in a volatile solvent. Enamel is varnish with added pigments. Lacquer may be either a synthetic or natural varnish. As a decorative or protective coating, varnish has been used for oil paintings, for string instruments, and, by the ancient Egyptians, for mummy cases.

Varro, Marcus Terentius, 116 B.C.–21? B.C., Roman writer. A legate and soldier, he was also known as one of the most erudite people of his day. He wrote an estimated 620 volumes in almost every field of knowledge. The only work to survive intact is *De re rustica libri III* [three books on farming], an important source for VERGIL's *Georgics.*

Vasa [vä′zə], Pol. *Waza,* royal dynasty of Sweden (1523–1654) and Poland (1587–1668). GUSTAVUS I founded the dynasty in Sweden. His grandson, the Catholic SIGISMUND III of Poland, lost the Swedish throne (1599) to his uncle CHARLES IX, and thereafter the Protestant and Catholic lines warred with each other. CHRISTINA, daughter of GUSTAVUS II, was the last of the Swedish Vasa line. Sigismund's son LADISLAUS IV was succeeded by his brother JOHN II, the last of the Polish line.

Vasari, Giorgio, 1511–74, Italian architect, writer, and painter. He is best known for his entertaining biographies of artists, *Lives of the Artists* (1550), the basic source of knowledge of Renaissance and mannerist artists. He painted portraits of the Medici and designed the UFFIZI as well as churches and palaces in Arezzo and in Pisa.

Vasco da Gama: see GAMA, VASCO DA.

vasectomy, minor surgical procedure for sterilization of the male, involving excision of the vas deferens, the thin duct that carries sperm cells away from the testicles (see REPRODUCTION). It is performed as a permanent method of BIRTH CONTROL.

vassal: see FEUDALISM.

Vatican City, officially State of the Vatican City, independent state, (1992 est. pop. 800), 108.7 acres (44 hectares), in Rome, Italy. It is the seat of the central government of the ROMAN CATHOLIC CHURCH and the pope is its absolute ruler. It includes the papal palace, SAINT PETER'S CHURCH, the SISTINE CHAPEL, many museums housing some of the world's finest art treasures, the Vatican Library (see LIBRARY, table), the Vatican Gardens, and Belvedere Park. The state, which issues its own currency and postage stamps, has its own citizenship, flag, diplomatic corps, newspaper (*L'Osservatore Romano*), railroad station, and broadcasting facility. The SWISS GUARD is the pope's personal bodyguard. The Vatican palace has been the residence of the pope since the late 14th cent., when the papal court was restored from AVIGNON, France, to Rome. The sovereignty of Vatican City was officially established in 1929 by the LATERAN TREATY between the PAPACY and the Italian government.

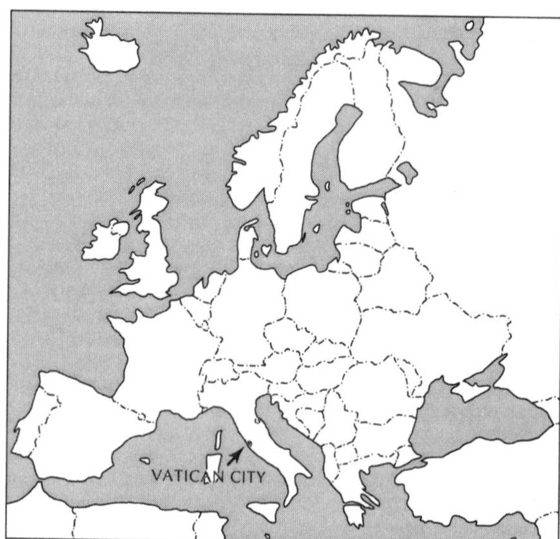

Vatican Councils, two ecumenical councils of the Roman Catholic Church. The first council (1869–70) was convened by Pope PIUS IX and enunciated the dogma of papal infallibility. It ended when Italian troops seized Rome for the new kingdom of Italy. The second council (1962–65), popularly called Vatican II, was convened by Pope JOHN XXIII and continued by PAUL VI. It sought to renew the church spiritually and to reconsider its place in the modern world. The council made wide-ranging changes in the liturgy (including vernacularization), moved toward greater lay participation, and encouraged the ECUMENICAL MOVEMENT.

vaudeville, stage entertainment consisting of unrelated songs, dances, acrobatic and magic acts, and humorous skits and sketches. From its beginnings in barrooms, vaudeville in the 1880s was an attraction in hundreds of theaters in the U.S. The rise of radio and movies brought its decline, but the vaudeville revue was revived on television. Such entertainers as George M. COHAN, Harry HOUDINI, Eddie Cantor, and W.C. FIELDS began their careers in vaudeville.

Vaudreuil-Cavagnal, Pierre de Rigaud, marquis de [vōdrö′yə-kävänyäl′], 1698–1765, last French governor of New France (1755–60). Although devoted to the interests of native-born Canadians, he failed to check government corruption and hampered Gen. MONTCALM's conduct of military operations, thus contributing to France's loss (1760) of Canada to the British.

Vaughan, Henry, 1622–95, English metaphysical poet; b. Wales. He signed himself Silurist after the ancient inhabitants of Wales. His greatest poems, in *Silex Scintillans* (1650, 1655), focus on mystical communion with nature and include "Ascension Hymn," "The World," and "The Retreat."

Vaughan Williams, Ralph, 1872–1958, English composer. He is noted for his use of English FOLK SONG, as in *Norfolk Rhapsodies* (1905–7) and arrangements of "Greensleeves." Among his compositions are nine symphonies, e.g., *A London Symphony* (1914, rev. 1920); the *Fantasia on a Theme by Thomas Tallis* (1910); operas; choral music; CONCERTOS; and songs, e.g., *Five Mystical Songs* (1911).

vault, curved ceiling over a room. It is generally composed of separate units of a material such as bricks, tiles, or blocks, so shaped that when assembled their weight can be concentrated on the proper supports. (Vaults may also be formed of homogeneous material, e.g., concrete.) These separate units exert not only the downward pressure of their weight, but also side thrusts that must be met with resistance in the form of thickened walls or of BUTTRESSES, as in Romanesque and Gothic architecture. Vaults may also be designed so that their thrusts oppose or counteract. The Egyptians used brick vaulting for drains. The Chaldeans and Assyrians appear to have made use of high domes and barrel vaults. The Greeks used no vaults. Etruscan technique was absorbed by the Romans, who, using concrete (see ROMAN ARCHITECTURE), developed a mature system. Roman vaults were perfectly rigid, devoid of external thrust, and required no buttresses. Thus they could be placed over vast spaces. Medieval systems developed from Roman vaulting. The tunnel, or barrel vault, spans two walls like a continuous arch. The cross, or groined vault, at the intersection of two barrel vaults, forms four arched openings. Ribs to strengthen the groins and sides of a vault appeared in the 11th cent., and became gradually the organic supporting skeleton of Gothic architecture. The pointed ARCH was used in vaulting oblong compartments. In England these developments culminated in the 15th cent. in the perpendicular style. Renaissance architects returned to the basic Roman forms. Modern vaulting is largely accomplished with reinforced concrete. See also GOTHIC ARCHITECTURE AND ART.

Vavilov, Nikolai Ivanovich, 1887–1943?, Russian botanist and geneticist. Trying to trace the origins of various crops by locating areas with the greatest number and diversity of their species, he reported (1936) Ethiopia and Afghanistan as the birthplaces of agriculture and hence of civilization. He divided cultivated plants into those domesticated from wild forms, e.g., oats and rye, and those known only in cultivation, e.g., corn. He reportedly died in a Soviet concentration camp after losing favor to Trofim LYSENKO, whose theories he opposed.

Veblen, Thorstein, 1857–1929, American economist and social critic; b. Cato Township, Wis., of Norwegian parents. In his writings Veblen was able to dissect American social and economic institutions and analyze their psychological bases, thus laying the foundations for the school of institutional economics. He pioneered in interpreting the role of technicians in modern society and described a basic conflict between the processes of technology (or "industry"), which tend toward maximum efficiency of production, and those of "business," which, in his view, restrict output

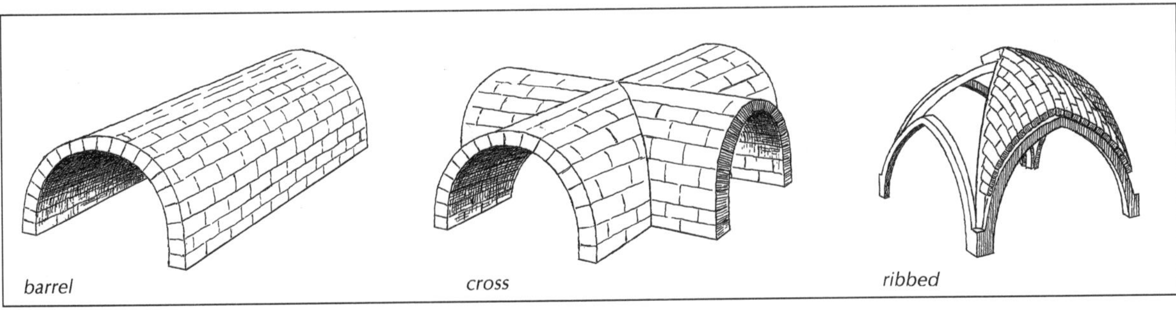

Vaults

and manipulate prices to maximize profit. His major work was *The Theory of the Leisure Class* (1899), in which he coined the famous phrase "conspicuous consumption." Other books included *The Theory of Business Enterprise* (1904) and *The Engineers and the Price System* (1921).

Vecellio: see TITIAN.

vector, quantity having both magnitude and direction. Many physical quantities are vectors, e.g., force, velocity, and momentum. The simplest representation of a vector is an arrow connecting two points: $\overrightarrow{AB}$ designates the vector represented by an arrow from point *A* to point *B*, whereas $\overrightarrow{BA}$ designates the vector of equal magnitude from *B* to *A*. In order to compare vectors and to operate on them mathematically, it is necessary to have some reference system that determines scale and direction, such as CARTESIAN COORDINATES. A vector is frequently symbolized by its components with respect to the coordinate axes. Suppose, for example, that the point *A* has coordinates (2,3) and the point *B* has coordinates (5,7). The *x*-component of $\overrightarrow{AB}$, i.e., its size with respect to the *x*-axis, is the difference between the *x*-coordinates of the points *A* and *B*, or $5 - 2 = 3$; the *y*-component is $7 - 3 = 4$. Thus $\overrightarrow{AB}$ becomes [3,4]. Knowledge of the components of a vector enables one to compute its magnitude—in this case, 5, by the Pythagorean theorem $[(3^2 + 4^2)^{1/2} = 5]$—and its direction (from TRIGONOMETRY). There are an infinite number of vectors with the components [3,4], all of which have the same magnitude and direction; they are considered equal. The concept of a vector can be extended to three or more dimensions. To add two vectors **U** and **V**, one can add their corresponding components to find the resultant vector **R**, or one can graph **U** and **V** on a set of coordinate axes and complete the parallelogram formed with **U** and **V** as adjacent sides to obtain **R** as the diagonal from the common vertex of **U** and **V**. The scalar, or dot, product of two vectors **A** and **B** is a nondirectional (scalar) quantity with a magnitude of $\mathbf{A \cdot B} = |A|\,|B| \cos \theta$, where θ is the angle between **A** and **B**. The vector, or cross, product of **A** and **B** is a vector whose magnitude $\mathbf{A \times B} = |A|\,|B| \sin \theta$ and whose direction is perpendicular to both **A** and **B** and pointing in the direction in which a right-hand screw would advance if turned from **A** to **B** through the angle θ.

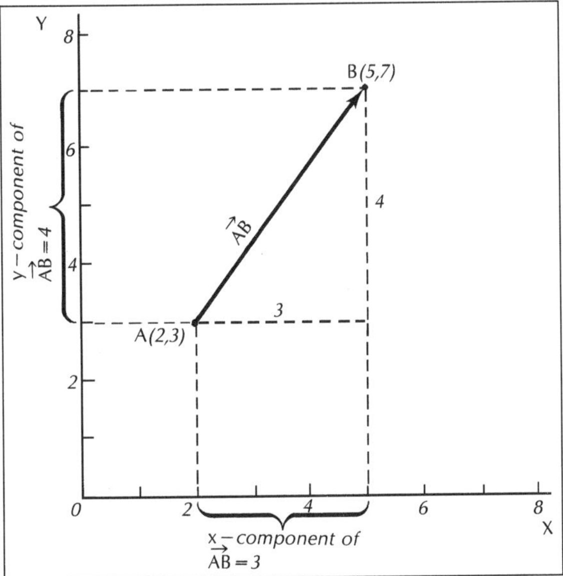

Vector: The components of the vector AB are given by its projections on each of the coordinate axes.

Veda [Skt., = knowledge], oldest scriptures of HINDUISM and the most ancient religious texts in an Indo-European language, still accepted to some extent by all Hindus as the authoritative statement of the essential truths of Hinduism. It is the literature of the Aryans who invaded NW India c.1500 B.C. Influenced by indigenous religious ideas, it was compiled from c.1000 to c.500 B.C. The Veda consists of four types of literature. The *Samhita,* the basic compilation of prayers and hymns, ascribed to inspired seer-poets, includes a threefold canonical body of hymns—the *Rig-Veda, Sama-Veda,* and *Yajur-Veda*—and the *Atharva-Veda,* a collection of magic spells. The *Brahmanas* are prose explanations of the sacrifice. The *Aranyakas* contain instructions for meditation as the mental performance of sacrifice. The UPANISHADS are works of mysticism and speculation. Vedic writings expressed the idea of a single underlying reality embodied in Brahman, the absolute Self. The Vedic sacrifice, with its invocation of any of 33 Vedic gods through MANTRAS or hymns, became increasingly elaborate with the passage of time, and the sacrifice came to be regarded as the fundamental agency of creation.

Vedanta [Skt., = the end of the Veda], one of the six classical systems of INDIAN PHILOSOPHY. The term refers to the teaching of the UPANISHADS (the last section of the VEDA) and also to the knowledge of its ultimate meaning. By extension the term refers to schools based on the Brahma Sutras of Badarayana (early centuries A.D.), which summarize Upanishadic doctrine. Most important is the nondualist (*advaita*) Vedanta of Shankara (A.D. 788–820), who taught that spiritual liberation is achieved not by ritual action but by eradication of ignorance—e.g., the belief that the illusory multiplicity of the world is real—and by attainment of the knowledge of BRAHMAN, the absolute Self. The qualified nondualist Ramanuja (1017?–1137?) advocated devotion as the means of salvation, and held that the world and souls are real but depend on God. The dualist Vedanta of Madhva (1197–1276) asserted the permanently separate reality of the world, souls, and God. Vedanta is a living tradition, with profound influence on the intellectual and religious life of India. Modern Vedantists include Swami Vivekananda, Aurobindo GHOSE, and Sarvepalli Radhakrishnan.

vegetable, popular name for many food plants and for their edible parts. No clear distinction exists between a vegetable and a FRUIT. Vegetables are valuable sources of vitamins, minerals, starches, and proteins.

vegetable sulfur: see CLUB MOSS.

vegetarianism, theory and practice of eating only fruits, vegetables, cereal grains, nuts, and seeds, and excluding meat, fish, or fowl, and often eggs and dairy products. The basis of the practice may be religious, ethical, economic, or nutritional, and its followers differ in strictness of observance. Practiced since ancient times by religious groups, vegetarianism as a separate movement developed in the mid-19th cent., particularly in England and the U.S.

Veil, Simone, 1927–, French politician. A lawyer, she served (1974–79) as minister of health under GISCARD D'ESTAING, sponsoring (1974) a liberalized abortion law. Elected to the European Parliament (see EUROPEAN UNION) in 1979, 1984, and 1989, she served (1979–82) as its president. In 1993 she became French housing and urban and social affairs minister.

Velasco, José María, 1840–1912, Mexican painter. He is noted for landscapes, employing a variety of hues and minutely observed detail, e.g., *The Bridge of Metlac* (1881). A teacher of Diego RIVERA, Velasco was rejected by Mexican academics, but his reputation was restored after his death.

Velasco, Luis de, d. 1564, Spanish viceroy (1550–64) of New Spain, now MEXICO. A humanitarian ruler, he helped the indigenous people and fostered exploration. The Univ. of Mexico was founded during his administration. His son, **Luis de Velasco,** 1534–1617, was also viceroy of New Spain (1590–95, 1607–11) and of Peru (1595–1604).

Velasco Alvarado, Juan [väläs'kō älvärä'thō], 1910–, president of PERU (1968–75). As army commander in chief, he led the junta that deposed (1968) Pres. Belaúnde Terry. He expropriated U.S.-owned oil companies, instigated land reform, and nationalized large industries. He was deposed (1975) in a bloodless coup.

Velasco Ibarra, José María [väläs'kō ēbä'rä], 1893–1979, president of ECUADOR. He served five times as president between 1934 and 1972, but was deposed by the military four times. In his last term (1968–72), he established a dictatorship to cope with political chaos and terrorism.

Velázquez, Diego de [vālä'kā], 1460–1524?, Spanish CONQUISTADOR, first governor of CUBA. He sailed on Christopher Columbus's second voyage to Hispaniola (1493) and was sent to conquer Cuba by Diego Columbus in 1511. By 1514, with the aid of Pánfilo de NARVÁEZ, the conquest was complete. He disassociated himself from Diego Columbus and declared himself governor of Cuba. In 1519 he sent Hernán CORTÉS to conquer MEXICO. Distrusting him, Velázquez sent Narváez to compel Cortés's return to Cuba, but was defeated.

Velázquez, Diego Rodríguez de Silva y, 1599–1660, the most celebrated painter of the Spanish school. Born in Seville, he was apprenticed at 11 to Francisco de Herrera and then to Francisco Pacheco. His earliest paintings, e.g., *Christ and the Pilgrims of Emmaus* (Metropolitan Mus.), show a strong naturalistic tendency. He was introduced to the court, and his equestrian portrait of PHILIP IV won him recognition. At 25 he was made court painter. During his first years there he painted the celebrated *Borrachos* [the drunkards] (Prado). During a trip to Italy (1629–31) Velázquez painted two large figure compositions, *The Forge of Vulcan* (Prado) and *Joseph's Coat* (Escorial). To his second period (1631–49) belong *Christ on the Cross,* the series of dwarfs and buffoons of the court, and the *Menippus* (all: Prado). His only nude, *Venus and Cupid,* also called the *Rokeby Venus* (1650; National Gall., London), emphasizes the vanity of the goddess. To his last period (1651–60) belong the *Coronation of the Virgin,* the famous full-length portraits of Mariana of Austria and the Infanta Margarita, and *The Maids of Honor* (all: Prado). Velázquez's development as an artist was extraordinarily steady. His first forms were monumental, and enveloped in strong chiaroscuro (high-contrast effects). He slowly evolved a subtle, intellectual art based on exquisite color values, with a consummate use of silver tones reminiscent of EL GRECO. However, in his worldliness and compassion he is far removed from El Greco. He imbued each subject, from dwarf to king, with a sense of dignity and individual worth.

veld or **veldt,** grassy, undulating PLATEAUS of South Africa and Zimbabwe, ranging in elevation from c.500 to c.6,000 ft (150 to 1,830 m). Abundant crops of potatoes and corn are grown, and large cattle herds are grazed; the area also has industrial and mining centers.

velvet worm: see ONYCHOPHORAN.

velocity: see MOTION.

Venda, former black South African homeland, or BANTUSTAN, (1990 est. pop. 600,000), 2,861 sq mi (7,410 sq km), proclaimed independent (1979) by South Africa but not recognized by other nations. It comprised connected areas in NE TRANSVAAL, near the Zimbabwe border. The capital was Thohoyandou. The population consists largely of Luvenda-speaking ethnic groups. Venda was reabsorbed into South Africa in 1994.

Venera, in space exploration: see SPACE PROBE, table.

venereal disease: see SEXUALLY TRANSMITTED DISEASE.

Veneziano, Domenico: see DOMENICO VENEZIANO.

Venezuela [vĕnəzwā'lə], officially Republic of Venezuela, republic (1992 est. pop. 20,676,000), 352,143 sq mi (912,050 sq km), N South America, bordered by Brazil (S), Colombia (W and SW), Guyana (E), and the Caribbean Sea (N). Principal cities include CARACAS (the capital) and MARACAIBO. A land of vivid contrasts, Venezuela has four major geographical regions: the oil-rich coastal lowlands; the ORINOCO R. basin, whose vast plains (LLANOS) support a great cattle industry; the Guiana Highlands, a largely unexplored wilderness occupying more than half the nation's territory and noted for scenic wonders such as ANGEL FALLS; and the densely populated Venezuelan highlands, a spur of the ANDES that rises to 16,427 ft (5,007 m) in the Sierra Nevada de Mérida and that is the nation's political and commercial hub. Venezuela enjoys the highest per capita income in Latin America because of its astonishing oil wealth, first exploited in 1918, which accounts for over 80% of its export earnings. Coffee, the mainstay of the economy before the oil boom, is still produced; other leading crops are cocoa, sugarcane, bananas, corn, sorghum, and rice. Manufactures include food products, building materials, textiles, chemicals, and automobiles. The country established a customs union with Colombia in 1991. The population is 67% mixed descent, 21% European descent, 10% African descent, and 2% indigenous peoples. The principal language is Spanish; the main religion is Roman Catholicism.

History. COLUMBUS discovered the mouths of the Orinoco in 1498, and Spanish settlements were established on the coast in the 1520s, but the major task of conquest was accomplished by German adventurers, notably Nikolaus Federmann. For a time an adjunct of NEW GRANADA, from the 16th to 18th cent. Venezuela was frequently raided by British buccaneers. The war for independence from Spain, begun in 1810 under Francisco de MIRANDA, was completed in 1821 by Simón BOLÍVAR (born in Venezuela), who made the area part of the federal republic of Greater Colombia. A separatist movement led by José Antonio PÁEZ succeeded (1830) in

making Venezuela an independent state. During much of its history the nation has been dominated by *caudillos* (military dictators) from the landholding class, notably Juan Vicente GÓMEZ, who came to power in 1908 and ruled for 27 years as an absolute tyrant until his death in 1935; he did, however, force the state (with the help of foreign oil concessions) into national solvency and material prosperity. A military junta, headed by Rómulo BETANCOURT and committed to democracy and social reform, gained power in 1945, but a coup three years later once again established a repressive military dictatorship, led from 1952 by Col. Marcos Pérez Jiménez. A popular revolt in 1958 restored democratic rule under President Betancourt, and since that time free elections have been held. In 1976, the oil industry was nationalized. Pres. Carlos Andrés Pérez (1974–79, 1989–93) survived two coup attempts in 1992, but in 1993 he was removed from office on corruption charges. Rafael Caldera Rodríguez became president in 1994; he had previously held the office from 1969 to 1974.

Venezuela Boundary Dispute, over the demarcation between VENEZUELA and British Guiana (now GUYANA), which caused tension between Great Britain and the U.S. in the 19th cent. The dispute was intensified in 1841, when gold was discovered in the border area, but the British refused arbitration. In 1887, Venezuela cut diplomatic ties with Great Britain. In 1895, Pres. CLEVELAND declared that the United States had a duty to determine the boundary and would resist British aggression beyond that line. The British recognized this broad interpretation of the MONROE DOCTRINE, and the boundary, generally favorable to Britain, was finally drawn in 1899.

Venice, Ital. *Venezia,* city (1992 est. pop. 73,000), capital of Venetia, NE Italy. Built on 118 alluvial islets within a lagoon in the Gulf of Venice, it is joined to the mainland by bridges and is politically united with the mainland city of Mestre. Canals and bridges give access among islands; gondolas and other boats are the only conveyances. There are many lanes, squares, and a few streets, and the houses are built on piles. Tourism is important. Manufactures include ships, lace, and glass. Refugees fleeing the Lombards settled (5th cent.) the islands and organized (687) under a doge. The communities formed (9th cent.) a city that came to dominate the Adriatic and became Europe's leading sea power. Marco POLO symbolized its spirit of enterprise in the 13th cent. Serving as the main link between Europe and Asia, Venice reached the height of its power in the 15th cent. and began to decline at the century's end. It fell (1797) without resistance to NAPOLEON I, who delivered it to Austrian rule. It became part of Italy in 1866. Venice reached artistic glory during the Renaissace, with TITIAN and TINTORETTO the giants of the Venetian school. It was also the most original artistic city of 18th-cent. Italy, as represented by such painters as TIEPOLO and CANALETTO. Architecturally, Venice is marked by Byzantine influences, felt most strongly in the famous SAINT MARK'S CHURCH. Later architecture is a graceful baroque style, e.g., the churches of San Giorgio Maggiore and Santa Maria della Salute. Other landmarks include the Gothic Doges' Palaces, the Grand Canal, and the Bridge of Sighs.

ventricular assist device: see HEART, ARTIFICIAL.

Ventris, Michael George Francis, 1922–56, English linguist. With John Chadwick he deciphered and published *Documents in Mycenaean Greek* (1956). His theory indicates that Linear B, a Mycenaean script found at Knossos, Pylos, and other sites, was an archaic form of the Greek language.

Venturi, Robert, 1925–, American architect; b. Philadelphia. A prominent figure in postmodernism, he advocated an unorthodox, mannered, eclectic, and humorous architecture and emphasized the validity and vitality of American roadside strip buildings and advertising. His influential books include *Complexity and Contradiction in Modern Architecture* (1966) and (with Stephen Izenour and Denise Scott-Brown) *Learning from Las Vegas* (1972). A more restrained, historical approach often characterizes his later work, as in the Sainsbury wing of the National Gallery, London, (1991) and several buildings at Princeton Univ.

Venus, in astronomy, 2d PLANET from the sun, at a mean distance of 67.2 million mi (108.2 million km). It has a diameter of 7,519 mi (12,100 km); terrains that can be subdivided into lowland plains (20%), rolling uplands (70%), and highlands (10%), and are marked by extensive volcanism and the apparent effects of subduction (see PLATE TECTONICS); and an atmosphere whose chief gas is carbon dioxide. The entire surface of Venus is opaquely covered by a dense cloud layer, a primary component of which is sulfuric acid. The atmospheric pressure at the surface of the planet is 90 times that of earth. Because its greatest ELONGATION is 47°, Venus can never be seen much longer than 3 hr after sunset or 3 hr before sunrise. It has no known satellites. SPACE PROBES that have encountered Venus include *Mariner 2, 5,* and *10* (1962, 1967, and 1974); *Pioneer-Venus 1* and *2* (1978); and numerous Soviet Venera spacecraft. The U.S. *Magellan* space probe made (1990–92) a radar survey of Venus, mapping 99% of the planet.

Venus, in Roman religion, goddess of vegetation; identified from the 3d cent. B.C. with the Greek APHRODITE, goddess of love and of beauty. In imperial times she was worshiped as Venus Genetrix, mother of AENEAS; Venus Felix, bringer of good fortune; Venus Victrix, bringer of victory; and Venus Verticordia, protector of feminine chastity. Among the famous sculptures of the goddess are the *Venus of Milo* (LOUVRE) and the *Venus of Medici* (UFFIZI, Florence).

Venus's-flytrap, insectivorous or carnivorous bog plant (*Dionaea muscipula*) native to the Carolina savannas, now widely cultivated as a novelty. The leaves, borne in a low rosette, resemble bear traps. They are hinged at the midrib, each half bearing sensitive bristles; when a bristle is touched by an insect, the halves snap shut and the marginal teeth interlock to imprison the insect until it is digested.

Veracruz, city (1990 pop. 327,522), E central Mexico, on the Gulf of Mexico. Rivaling TAMPICO as the nation's main port, it is the industrial center of a major oil region and is popular with tourists because of its scenery and beaches. Founded c.1600, it has been a frequent landing site for foreign invasions, notably by the U.S. (1847) and France (1862). A 17th–18th-cent. fortress guards the harbor.

verbena: see VERVAIN.

Vercingetorix [vûr″sĭnjĕt′ərĭks], d. 46 B.C., leader of the Gauls in a revolt against Rome that was put down by Julius CAESAR. He was captured when Caesar besieged and took the fort of Alesia (52 B.C.). After gracing Caesar's triumph, Vercingetorix was put to death.

Verdi, Giuseppe [vâr′dē], 1813–1901, foremost Italian operatic composer. He is famous for such dramatic and superbly melodic operas as *Rigoletto* (1851), *Il Trovatore* (1853), *La Traviata* (1853), *La forza del destino* (1862), and *Aïda* (1871), in which the elements of his earlier style reach maturity. Three operas are based on plays by Shakespeare: *Macbeth* (1847, rev. 1865) and the two masterpieces of his old age, *Otello* (1887) and *Falstaff* (1893). Verdi is also known for his magnificent *Requiem* (1874).

Verdun, town (1982 pop. 21,516), NE France. A transportation center with varied industry, it was a commercial center under Rome and the CAROLINGIANS (9th cent.) and a free city of the HOLY ROMAN EMPIRE until seized (1552) by HENRY II. Almost destroyed in a famous WORLD WAR I battle (Feb.–Dec. 1916), it was rebuilt. The battlefield and cemeteries form a national shrine.

Vere, Edward de: see OXFORD, EDWARD DE VERE, 17TH EARL OF.

Vérendrye, Pierre Gaultier de Varennes, sieur de la [vāräN-drē′], 1685–1749, explorer in W Canada and the U.S.; b. Quebec. After serving in the French army in Canada and then in Europe, he returned to New France. From 1731, when he obtained a monopoly on the western fur trade, to 1744, he played an important role in the extension of the western frontiers of New France. With his sons, he established trading posts and forts in what is now W Ontario and Manitoba and sought an overland passage to the Western Sea (Pacific Ocean). The various expeditions that Vérendrye either undertook or commissioned also traversed the Dakotas and may have entered Wyoming.

Verga, Giovanni, 1840–1922, Italian novelist; b. Sicily. His early novels of passion are in the style of the French realists. Later works, marked by simplicity and strict accuracy, gave rise to the term *verismo.* A novella, *Cavalleria rusticana* (1880), was the basis for MASCAGNI's 1890 opera. Major works are *The House by the Medlar Tree* (1881), *Little Novels of Sicily* (1883), and *Mastro-Don Gesualdo* (1889).

Vergennes, Charles Gravier, comte de [vĕrzhĕN], 1717–87,

French statesman. As foreign minister of LOUIS XVI, he signed (1778) France's alliance with the Americans in the AMERICAN REVOLUTION and helped negotiate the Treaty of PARIS (1783).

Vergil or **Virgil** (Publius Vergilius Maro), 70–19 B.C., greatest of Roman poets; b. near Mantua; a resident of Rome from 41 B.C. Early life on his father's farm was central to his education. The *Eclogues* or *Bucolics* (37 B.C.) idealized rural life in the manner of THEOCRITUS. Vergil then turned to realistic and didactic rural poetry in the *Georgics* (30 B.C.), seeking, like HESIOD, to convey the charm of real life and work on the farm. He spent the rest of his life working on his national epic, the *Aeneid,* one of the greatest long poems in world literature. Vergil's AENEAS is a paragon of Roman virtues—familial devotion, loyalty to the state, and piety. The 12 books follow Aeneas from TROY's fall through his affair with the Carthaginian queen, DIDO, to the founding of the Roman state. The poem, in dactylic hexameters of striking regularity, is central to all Latin literature. A favorite of AUGUSTUS, Vergil influenced poets from DANTE on.

Verhaeren, Émile [värärĕn′], 1855–1916, Belgian poet and critic who wrote in French. His passion for social reform found expression successively in works that display a disgust with humanity, pessimism over industrialization, and finally an optimistic glorification of human energy. These include *Flemish Women* (1883), *The Hallucinated Countrysides* (1893), and *The Manifold Splendor* (1906).

Veríssimo, Érico Lopes [vərēs′sēmo͝o], 1905–75, Brazilian writer. His novels include *Crossroads* (1935), *The Rest Is Silence* (1943), and the trilogy *Time and the Wind* (1949–62). His lectures in the U.S. were published as *Brazilian Literature* (1945). From 1953 to 1956 he was director of the Dept. of Cultural Affairs of the Pan American Union.

Verlaine, Paul [vĕrlĕn′], 1844–96, French poet. While still a young man, Verlaine formed a tempestuous liaison with a young poet, Arthur RIMBAUD. The relationship ended tragically when Verlaine shot and wounded Rimbaud. Imprisoned for two years, he returned to the Catholic faith, but his later life was marked by drunkenness and debauchery. His poetry, possessing a rare musicality, includes such early PARNASSIAN works as *Saturnian Poems* (1866); some noble religious verse from his prison years (in *Wisdom,* 1881); and *Romances without Words* (1874), establishing him as an early SYMBOLIST. His only important prose work is *The Accursed Poets* (1884), about his fellow symbolists.

Vermeer, Jan or **Johannes,** 1632–75, Dutch genre and landscape painter. He spent all his life in Delft. Although admitted to the painters' guild and twice its dean, he enjoyed slight recognition in his lifetime. Today he is ranked among the greatest Dutch masters and the foremost of all colorists. His most frequent subjects were intimate interiors, often with the solitary figure of a woman, exquisitely depicted with luminous blues and yellows, pearly highlights, and subtle gradations of reflected light. Only about 35 paintings can be attributed to him with certainty; they include *The Letter* (Rijks Mus., Amsterdam), *View of Delft* (The Hague), *Soldier and Laughing Girl* (Frick Coll., N.Y.C.), and *Young Woman with a Water Jug* (Metropolitan Mus.).

Vermigli, Pietro Martire [värmē′lyē], 1500–1562, Italian Protestant reformer, also known as Peter Martyr. An honored Augustinian scholar and preacher, he became a Protestant and fled to Switzerland, Strasbourg, and, at the invitation of Archbishop Cranmer, to England, where he taught at Oxford (1547–53). Under Mary I he left England and returned to Strasbourg and then went to Zürich as a professor. He had some influence on the episcopal changes in the Church of England and on the revision of the Book of Common Prayer.

Vermont, New England state of the NE U.S.; bordered by the Connecticut R., across which lies New Hampshire (E), Massachusetts (S), New York, with Lake Champlain forming almost half the border (W), and the Canadian province of Quebec (N).

Area, 9,609 sq mi (24,887 sq km). *Pop.* (1990) 562,758, a 10% increase over 1980 pop. *Capital,* Montpelier. *Statehood,* Mar. 4, 1791 (14th state). *Highest pt.,* Mt. Mansfield, 4,393 ft (1,340 m); *lowest pt.,* Lake Champlain, 95 ft (29 m). *Nickname,* Green Mountain State. *Motto,* Freedom and Unity. *State bird,* hermit thrush. *State flower,* red clover. *State tree,* sugar maple. *Abbr.,* Vt.; VT.

Land and People. The forested Green Mts., which traverse the state in a generally north-to-south direction, constitute the dominant physiographical feature. The slate- and granite-rich Taconic Mts. are located in the southwest. Vermont has a variable temperate climate with abundant rainfall. The small rural village is a more characteristic feature of the Vermont landscape than large urban areas; only 32% of the population lives in urban areas, the lowest percentage in the U.S. BURLINGTON is the largest city, followed by RUTLAND and MONTPELIER. In 1990 the state was nearly 98% white.

Economy. Manufacturing is the state's largest source of income, with machine tools, furniture, nonelectrical machinery, computer components, processed foods, and pulp and paper among the leading products. Dairy farming has long dominated the agriculture of this, the most rural U.S. state; Vermont ships milk in huge quantities to metropolitan Boston and New York. The chief crops are apples, maple syrup, silage corn, and hay. Stone, including Vermont's famous marble, granite, and slate; asbestos; talc; and sand and gravel are extracted. Year-round tourism is vital to the economy.

Government. The amended constitution of 1793 provides for a governor serving a two-year term. The general assembly consists of a 30-seat senate and 150-seat house, with members of both bodies elected for two years. Vermont is represented in the U.S. Congress by one representative and two senators and has three electoral votes.

History. Iroquois (see IROQUOIS CONFEDERACY) and ALGONQUIAN groups inhabited the area when Samuel de CHAMPLAIN explored (1609) the lake that bears his name. In 1741 the colony of New Hampshire claimed the area; a dispute later arose with New York, which also claimed it. Vermont's settlers resisted New York's claims, and Ethan ALLEN and his GREEN MOUNTAIN BOYS were active in the cause until 1775, when their armed violence was diverted to fighting the British in the AMERICAN REVOLUTION. From 1781 to 1791 Vermont functioned as a sovereign state, before joining the Union. During the 19th cent. manufacturing became more prevalent, and the rural population declined as farmers migrated west to more fertile farmlands. Rapid population growth began after World War II and continued into the 1990s, with most of the increase occurring in the southern part of the state, where new industries have arisen.

vernal equinox: see EQUINOX.

Verne, Jules [vûrn, vĕn′], 1828–1905, French novelist, father of modern SCIENCE FICTION. His enormously popular romances include the prophetic *Journey to the Center of the Earth* (1864), *Twenty Thousand Leagues Under the Sea* (1870), and *Around the World in Eighty Days* (1873).

Verner, Karl Adolf [vûr′nər], 1846–96, Danish philologist. His fame rests on **Verner's law,** a linguistic formulation showing that certain consonantal alternations in Germanic languages are the result of patterns of alternation in the position of word accent in the parent language.

Verona, city (1990 pop. 263,589), in Venetia, NE Italy. On a road to central Europe, it has had commercial and strategic importance from Roman times. A barbarian base (5th–6th cent.), it became a free commune (12th cent.) and the site (13th–14th cent.) of GUELPH AND GHIBELLINE strife. It was ruled by Venice (1404–1797) and Austria (1797–1805, 1814–66) until union with Italy. Many monuments survived damage in World War II, e.g., a large Roman amphitheater and the Gothic Scaligeri tombs.

Veronese, Paolo [vārōnā′zā], 1528–88, Italian painter of the Venetian school; b. Verona as Paolo Caliari. He was particularly influenced by TITIAN. Both his characteristic opulent use of color and many figures arranged in a sinuous spatial pattern can be seen in *Age and Youth* and *Hera Presenting Gifts to Venice* (Ducal Palace, Venice). Complex mannerist devices are evident in the Giustiniani Altarpiece (San Francesco della Vigna, Venice). Veronese is known chiefly for his religious feast scenes, which he interpreted in a notably secular manner. The *Supper at Emmaus* (Louvre) and the *Marriage at Cana* (1562; Louvre) depict fashionable courtiers, horses, dogs, apes, and lavish accessories. His *Rape of Europa* (1576; Ducal Palace, Venice), one of his most famous works, reveals his harmonious tonalities and rich textures. Veronese ranks among the greatest of Venetian decorative painters and among the best colorists.

Verrazano, Giovanni da [dä vĕr'rät'sänō], c.1480–1527, Italian navigator and explorer. Exploring the coast of NORTH AMERICA for France, he may have been the first European to enter New York Bay. He was killed by natives in the WEST INDIES.

Verrazano-Narrows Bridge, New York City, the longest vehicular suspension bridge in the U.S., spanning the Narrows at the entrance to New York harbor. Designed by O.H. Ammann and completed in 1964, it has a main span of 4,260 ft (1,298 m).

Verrocchio, Andrea del [vār-rôk'kyō], 1435–88, Florentine sculptor and painter; b. Andrea di Michele di Francesco di Cioni. He was a leading figure in the early RENAISSANCE. Many of his paintings are lost, but his hand is evident in the *Baptism of Christ* (Uffizi), assisted by LEONARDO DA VINCI. A virtuoso sculptor in metal, he was primarily concerned with spirited movement and the elaboration of detail, e.g., his graceful *Boy with Dolphin* and lithe *David* (Bargello). His awesome figure for the equestrian monument of the condottiere Bartolomeo Colleoni (Venice) was not cast until after his death.

Versailles, city (1982 pop. 95,240), capital of Yvelines dept., N central France. It is the site of the elaborate palace and gardens built (mid-17th cent.) for LOUIS XIV, which represent the height of the French classical style. The FRENCH REVOLUTION forced Louis XVI to move (1790) from there to Paris. Under Louis Philippe, Versailles became a national monument.

Versailles, Treaty of, any of several treaties signed at Versailles, France. **1** For the treaty of 1783, see PARIS, TREATY OF. **2** The Treaty of 1871, signed at the end of the Franco-Prussian War by BISMARCK for Germany and THIERS for France and ratified in the Treaty of Frankfurt (1871). France was forced to give up most of Alsace and Lorraine, pay a large indemnity, and accept a German army of occupation. **3** The Versailles Treaty of 1919 is the most famous of the treaties because it was the chief one ending World War I. The "Big Four" negotiating it were Pres. WILSON (U.S.), Premier CLEMENCEAU (France), Prime Min. LLOYD GEORGE (Britain), and Premier ORLANDO (Italy). The treaty called for the creation of the LEAGUE OF NATIONS. It forced on Germany the burden of reparations and placed limits on German armed forces. It restored Alsace and Lorraine to France, gave Prussian Poland and most of West Prussia to Poland, made Danzig a free city, put Germany's colonies under the League of Nations, placed the Saar under French administration, called for plebiscites in various territories newly freed from the Central Powers, and called for the demilitarization of the RHINELAND. American opposition to the League of Nations resulted in the refusal of the U.S. Senate to ratify the treaty. In 1935, HITLER unilaterally abrogated most of the terms of the Treaty of Versailles.

vertebrate, any animal having a backbone or spinal column. All vertebrates belong to the subphylum Vertebrata of the phylum CHORDATA. The five classes of vertebrates are FISH, AMPHIBIANS, REPTILES, BIRDS, and MAMMALS. Vertebrates are comparatively large, have a high degree of specialization of their parts, and are bilaterally symmetrical. All have an interior skeleton, a brain enclosed in a cranium, a closed circulatory system, and a heart divided into two, three, or four chambers; most have two pairs of appendages modified as fins, limbs, or wings in the different classes. Animals without backbones are called INVERTEBRATES.

vertical circle, the great circle on the celestial sphere that passes from the observer's zenith through a given celestial body or a specified celestial point. See also ASTRONOMICAL COORDINATE SYSTEMS.

vertical takeoff and landing aircraft (VTOL), craft capable of rising and descending vertically from and to the ground, thus requiring no runway. Some examples are the AIRSHIP and the BALLOON, which are very inefficient in their forward motion, and the HELICOPTER, which has very limited performance. Convertiplanes are VTOL craft that can fly horizontally with the same effectiveness as a conventional airplane. Their vertical lift during takeoff is provided by a rigid rotor that spins about a vertical axis, by tilted propellers, or, as in some jet VTOL craft, such as the British-built Harrier, by vanes that can direct the engine thrust upward or forward.

vervain, common name for some members of the family Verbenaceae, herbs, shrubs, and trees of warmer regions of the world. Well-known wild and cultivated members of the family include species of *Lantana* and *Verbena*. Many cultivated verbenas (herbs and shrubs) have fragrant blossoms and leaves that are sometimes used for distillation of oils and for tea, as are those of the similar lemon verbena (*Lippia citriodora*). Wild American species are usually called vervains. Economically, the most important member of the family is TEAK.

Verwoerd, Hendrik Frensch [fərvōōrt'], 1901–66, South African prime minister (1958–66). A harsh proponent of white supremacy, he intensified the Nationalist policy of APARTHEID. When South Africa became (1961) a republic, he severed its connections with the British Commonwealth. He was assassinated.

Vesalius, Andreas, 1514–64, Flemish anatomist. At the Univ. of Padua he produced his chief work, the notably illustrated *De humani corporis fabrica* (1543), based on studies made by dissecting human cadavers. His discoveries in anatomy overthrew many hitherto uncontested doctrines of GALEN and caused criticism to be directed against himself. He was physician to Emperor Charles V and his son Philip II.

Vespasian (Titus Flavius Vespasianus), A.D. 9–79, Roman emperor (A.D. 69–79), founder of the Flavian dynasty. Vespasian was proclaimed emperor by the soldiers and erected the Colosseum. His reign was noted for its order and prosperity. The warfare he waged against the Jewish rebels was completed by his son TITUS.

vespers, in the Christian church, principal evening office. In the Roman rite it consists of prayers, psalms, a lesson, the *Magnificat*, and an antiphon. The similar Anglican evening prayer, evensong, is often called vespers.

Vespucci, Amerigo [vāspōōt'chē], 1454–1512, Italian navigator in whose honor America is named. In 1499 he sailed to the WEST INDIES and discovered the mouth of the AMAZON. Later he sailed (1501) along the N coast of SOUTH AMERICA. Vespucci evolved a system for computing nearly exact longitude. His acceptance of South America as a separate continent altered Europeans' understanding of the world.

Vesta, in Roman religion, goddess of hearth and home; identified with the Greek HESTIA. Her priestesses, the **vestals,** were chosen in childhood from prominent Roman families. Serving for 30 years, they were sworn to chastity. Their duties included preparing sacrifices and tending the sacred fire. The vestals were very influential in Roman society.

Vestris, Gaetan [vĕs'trēs], 1729–1808, Italian-French classical dancer. He joined the Paris Opéra and became dancing master to Louis XVI of France. He was the first dancer to discard the mask and to use his face in mime. His son **Auguste Vestris,** 1760–1842?, debuted with the Paris Opéra at 12 and was its leading dancer for 36 years.

Vestris, Lucia Elizabeth (Bartolozzi), 1797–1856, English actress-manager. Known as Mme Vestris, she was the first woman to lease a theater (1831). She produced Shakespearean comedy as well as BURLESQUES and FARCES, and was known for her realistic stage settings and props.

Vesuvius, active volcano, SE Italy, overlooking the Bay of Naples. The height of the main cone changes with each eruption, varying within a few hundred feet of the 4,000-ft (1,219-m) level. Often surmounted by a faint plume of smoke, the volcano erupts frequently and is occasionally destructive. The earliest recorded eruption (A.D. 79) buried the Roman cities of POMPEII, HERCULANEUM, and Stabiae.

Veterans Administration: see VETERANS AFFAIRS, UNITED STATES DEPARTMENT OF.

Veterans Affairs, United States Department of, federal executive department established in 1989; formerly the Veterans Administration (est. 1930), an independent U.S. government agency. It provides medical and rehabilitation services, including medical centers, clinics, and nursing homes, for eligible veterans and offers pensions, educational assistance, loan guarantees, insurance, burial costs, and other benefits to qualifying veterans and their dependents. The National Cemetery System is operated by the department.

Veterans' Day (Nov. 11), U.S. holiday, formerly called Armistice Day in commemoration of the armistice ending WORLD WAR I. Since 1954 the day has honored all who have fought for the U.S.

veterinary medicine, prevention, diagnosis, and treatment of animal diseases. The first veterinary school opened in France in 1761; veterinary schools arose in the U.S. about the time of the Civil War. Veterinarians complete a four-year postgraduate program before becoming licensed. They usually specialize in either small animals such as pets, or large animals, such as horses and farm animals. Veterinary research has made important contributions to medicine in general; for example, forms of VACCINATION devised for animals were found to be effective for humans. Since World War II the development of live- and modified live-virus vaccines, ANTIBIOTICS, and sulfonamides has led to the prevention and control of once incurable animal diseases.

veto, power of the chief executive to disallow laws passed by the legislature. In the U.S. the president's veto can be overridden by a two-thirds vote of Congress. The president cannot veto only a portion of a bill, nor can he veto Constitutional amendments. The governors of the states also have veto power, and most also have a line-item veto, which enables them to veto specific items in an appropriations bill without vetoing the entire bill. In the Security Council of the UNITED NATIONS, the five permanent members have a veto power to block any action.

Viaud, Julien: see LOTI, PIERRE.

Vicente, Gil [Port. vēsĕnt'ə, Span. vēthĕn'tā], 1470?–1536?, Portuguese dramatist and poet. A major figure of the Iberian Renaissance, he is ranked second only to CAMÕES. A humanist, he created plays for court presentation varying from farcical interludes to tragicomedies. Some religious, some satirical, they attack the corrupt clergy and the superficial glory of empire belied by increasing national poverty; they also include songs of his own composition. He wrote in Portuguese, in Spanish, and in a combination of the two.

Vichy, city (1982 pop. 30,527), central France. Hot springs have made it a foremost spa. The **Vichy government** was the regime set up (1940) by Marshal PÉTAIN during WORLD WAR II, after the Franco-German armistice. It controlled unoccupied France and its colonies. A truncated parliament replaced the Third Republic with an authoritarian state. Vichy became a German tool in the hands of LAVAL, DARLAN, and others. When the Allies invaded Africa in 1942, Hitler seized all of France. The Vichy regime fled before the Allied advance and fell at war's end.

Vicksburg campaign, in the U.S. CIVIL WAR, the fighting (Nov. 1862–July 4, 1863) for control of the Mississippi R. By late 1862, the Union controlled all of the river except for the 200 miles below Vicksburg, Miss. Impregnable on its bluff overlooking the river, Vicksburg repulsed all efforts to storm it by troops under the overall command of Gen. Ulysses S. GRANT. In May 1863 Grant opened siege, and after six weeks of defense the Confederates surrendered. Vicksburg's fall completed the encirclement of the CONFEDERACY.

Vico, Giovanni Battista or **Giambattista,** 1688–1744, Italian philosopher and historian. Vico's philosophy of history, little known until the 19th cent., is regarded as the precursor of modern theories of history. For Vico, history was the account of the birth, development, and decay of human societies and institutions. He urged the study of language and mythology as a means of understanding earlier societies. He thus departed from previous systems of writing history either as the biographies of great individuals or as the unfolding of God's will. His cyclical theory of history was an important influence on the DIALECTICAL MATERIALISM of Karl MARX. Vico's major work was *New Science* (1725), which he completely revised in 1730 and 1744.

victims' rights, rights of victims to have a role in the prosecution of the perpetrators of crimes against them. Nearly all U.S. states have enacted some victims' rights legislation. Such laws typically ensure that victims receive respectful and compassionate treatment, that they are informed at critical stages of the criminal prosecution, and that their courtroom attendance and comments are invited when appropriate. Some critics have voiced the fear that such laws influence the outcome of trials by assuming the accused is guilty.

Victor Amadeus II, 1666–1732, duke of Savoy (1675–1713), king of Sicily (1713–20), and king of Sardinia (1720–30). In the War of the SPANISH SUCCESSION (1701–13), he and his cousin, EUGENE OF SAVOY, defeated the French in 1706. The Peace of Utrecht gave (1713) Victor Amadeus a kingdom in Sicily, which was seized (1718) by Spain. In 1720 he ceded his claim to Sicily in exchange for Sardinia and became its king. He abdicated in 1730.

Victor Emmanuel, Italian kings. **Victor Emmanuel I,** 1759–1824, king of Sardinia (1802–21), recovered Sardinia's mainland territories after Napoleon's fall. His reactionary rule led to an uprising, and he abdicated. **Victor Emmanuel II,** 1820–78, king of Sardinia (1849–61), was the first king of united Italy (1861–78). Aided by his minister, the conte di CAVOUR, he continued the wars of the RISORGIMENTO, and in 1861 the kingdom of Italy was proclaimed with Victor Emmanuel asking. His grandson, **Victor Emmanuel III,** 1869–1947, king of Italy (1900–46), joined (1915) the Allies in WORLD WAR I. During MUSSOLINI's Fascist regime he was king in name only, although he gained the titles emperor of Ethiopia (1936) and king of Albania (1939). He abdicated (1946) after WORLD WAR II. See also SAVOY, HOUSE OF.

Victoria, 1819–1901, queen of Great Britain and Ireland (1837–1901) and empress of India; daughter of Edward, duke of Kent (fourth son of GEORGE III), and Princess Mary Louise Victoria of Saxe-Coburg-Saalfeld. She succeeded WILLIAM IV. As a woman, she was barred from succession in Hanover, so her accession in Britain ended the connection between the British and Hanoverian thrones. In 1840 she married her first cousin Prince ALBERT, and the marriages of their nine children linked the British royal house to the royalty of Russia, Germany, Greece, Denmark, and Romania. Victoria's first prime minister, Lord MELBOURNE, became a friend, but her interest in foreign affairs caused friction with Lord PALMERSTON. In 1861, Prince Albert died; the queen's extreme grief led to her seclusion for three years. Her emergence was largely due to Benjamin DISRAELI, who with William GLADSTONE dominated politics in the latter part of her reign. Disraeli secured for her the title of empress of India. Victoria's Diamond Jubilee (1897) proved her to be enormously popular. Although not highly intelligent, she was of high moral character and extremely conscientious. Her reign, the longest in English history, saw the rise of industrialism at home and imperialism abroad.

Victoria, state (1992 est. pop. 4,452,000), 87,884 sq mi (227,620 sq km), SE Australia, on the Indian Ocean and the Tasman Sea. MELBOURNE, the capital, and GEELONG are among the major cities. The second-smallest and most densely populated Australian state, Victoria is highly industrialized. Manufactures include automobiles, pharmaceuticals, textiles, and processed food. Despite its small size, it is also one of Australia's leading agricultural states, producing wheat and other grains, dairy products, and lamb and mutton. Lignite, oil, and natural gas are important resources. The first permanent settlements were established at Portland Bay in 1834 and at Melbourne in 1835. Originally part of NEW SOUTH WALES, Victoria became a separate colony in 1851 and was federated as a state of Australia in 1901.

Victoria, city (1991 pop. 71,228), provincial capital, SW British Columbia, part of the Capital Regional District (1991 pop. 299,550), on VANCOUVER ISLAND and Juan de Fuca Strait. Known for its mild winters (freezing temperatures are rare) and many parks, it is the largest city on the island and the second largest in the province. Victoria was founded (1843) as Fort Camosun, a HUDSON'S BAY COMPANY post. The city was laid out and settled (beginning in 1851) as the capital of the crown colony of Vancouver Island. It became the capital of all of British Columbia in 1871.

Victoria, city (1985 est. pop. 23,000), capital of the SEYCHELLES.

Victoria, Lake, or **Victoria Nyanza,** lake, E Africa, c.26,830 sq mi (69,490 sq km), largest freshwater lake in Africa and second largest in the world. One of the chief sources of the NILE R., it occupies a shallow depression at an altitude of 3,725 ft (1,135 m).

Victoria and Albert Museum, South Kensington, London. It opened in 1852 as the Museum of Manufacturers, at Marlborough House. The name was soon changed to Museum of Ornamental Art, and the collection included objects of all styles and periods. The present building, designed by Sir Aston Webb, was given its name in 1899 by Queen Victoria. It opened in 1909 as purely an art museum, embracing the Royal College of Art, an art library, and the collections of the India Museum. Its paintings and sculptures, especially early Italian works, are celebrated. RAPHAEL's cartoons for the SISTINE CHAPEL tapestries are among its great treasures, which also include glass, jewelry, textiles, and medieval enamels.

Victoria Falls, famous waterfall, S central Africa, on the Zambia-Zimbabwe border. The falls are c.1 mi (1.6 km) wide, with a maximum drop of 420 ft (128 m), and are formed as the ZAMBEZI R. plummets into a narrow gorge, now partially flooded by KARIBA DAM.

Victorian style, in architecture, an eclectic fashion based on revivals of older styles. The promoter of taste in VICTORIA's reign (1837–1901) was Prince ALBERT. He sponsored the forward-looking CRYSTAL PALACE, but also a dry Tuscan Renaissance revival, e.g., at Osborne House, Isle of Wight. A romantic return to Gothic is seen in the rebuilding of WESTMINSTER PALACE (1840–60). See also GOTHIC REVIVAL.

Victory of Samothrace: see NIKE.

Vidal, Gore, 1925–, American novelist, playwright, and critic; b. West Point, N.Y. An acute and acerbic observer of the American scene, he brilliantly satirized U.S. history and life in the novels *Myra Breckinridge* (1968), *Burr* (1973), *1876* (1976), *Lincoln* (1988), and *Hollywood* (1990). His other works include the plays *Visit to a Small Planet* (1955) and *The Best Man* (1960); the historical novels *Julian* (1964) and *Creation* (1981); and the essay collections *The Second American Revolution* (1982) and *United States: Essays 1952–1992* (1993).

videocassette recorder (VCR), device that can record television programs or the images from a video camera on magnetic tape (see TAPE RECORDER); it can also play pre-recorded tapes. The VCR converts the separate audio and video portions of a television or video camera signal to magnetic flux variations to magnetize the tape. The video recording heads move in a direction almost perpendicular to the tape movement, resulting in tracks that run diagonally across the tape width and increasing tape capacity. A **camcorder** combines a video camera and VCR in a single hand-held machine.

videodisc or **videodisk,** disk used with a special player and television to reproduce both pictures and sound. A videodisc player cannot record television programs off the air for later playback, unlike a VIDEOCASSETTE RECORDER (VCR). Videodiscs, however, generally produce pictures that are clearer in detail and truer in color than those produced by VCR tapes, and they also offer better sound quality. Two quite different videodisc systems have been developed. One operates much like a PHONOGRAPH, using a mechanical stylus that senses varying patterns of electrical capacitance imprinted in grooves on the disc surface. This format has largely fallen into disuse. The other, known as a laser disc system, uses a LASER to read a track cut in a spiral pattern on the inside surface of the disc. On a laser disc, video is recorded as an analog signal and the soundtrack is either an analog or, in more recent versions, a digital signal.

video game: see ELECTRONIC GAME.

videotex, communications service that is linked to an adapted TELEVISION receiver or a PERSONAL COMPUTER by telephone lines, CABLE TELEVISION facilities, or the like, and that allows a user to retrieve and display alphanumeric and pictorial information at home. There are two forms of videotex systems. One-way *teletext* systems permit the selection and display of such general information as airline schedules, traffic conditions, and traditional newspaper content. *Viewdata* systems are more specific and provide for two-way, or interactive, communication. Specific questions may be researched by accessing the appropriate database: e.g., bank balances can be verified and bills paid, and travel and hotel reservations can be made. In Japan and Europe, government-operated videotex systems—Captain in Japan, Prestel in Britain, Bildschirmtext in Germany, and Minitel in France—are well established. In North America, systems have been developed by newspaper publishers (called electronic news) and banks. With the growing popularity of the personal computer, database services are becoming more significant; these make the home user part of an interactive NETWORK, provide electronic mail and bulletin board facilities in addition to traditional videotex services, and provide additional computing power and data-storage facilities.

Vienna, Ger. *Wien,* city and prov. (1991 pop. 1,533,176), capital of Austria, NE Austria, on the Danube R. It is a cultural, commercial, industrial, and transportation center; tourism is also economically important. Settled by Celts, Vienna became a Roman military center. It was the residence of the Holy Roman emperors and, after 1806, of the emperors of Austria. In 1529 and 1683 it was besieged by the Turks. In the 18th cent. HAYDN, MOZART, BEETHOVEN, and SCHUBERT lived there, and many magnificent buildings were erected, including the Hofburg (imperial residence), the Schönbrunn palace, and St. Peter's Church. In the late 19th cent., with BRAHMS, MAHLER, SCHOENBERG, FREUD, and SCHNITZLER in residence, the city continued to flourish, raising splendid cultural and administrative edifices around the famous boulevard the Ringstrasse. After Austria was annexed (1938) to Nazi Germany, the city's Jewish population (c.115,000) was reduced to 6,000 by the end of the war. The city itself was heavily damaged in WORLD WAR II. Captured (1945) by the Russians, it was divided into four Allied occupation zones until 1955, when Austria was reunited as a neutral state.

Vienna, Congress of, 1814–15, international conference to remake Europe after the downfall of NAPOLEON I. All the European states that had existed before the Napoleonic upheaval were represented; however, the major powers (Austria, Russia, Prussia, and Britain) made the decisions, although France quickly won an equal voice. The problems confronting the congress were extremely thorny and complex. Its main purpose was to create a balance of power that would preserve the peace. The Concert of Europe that ensued attests to the fact that it generally succeeded. The congress opened with a series of glittering balls, and then the delegates settled down to hard bargaining. The unexpected return (1815) of Napoleon from Elba shocked the congress into burying its differences long enough to reach important agreements. The Final Act of Vienna was issued only nine days before Napoleon's defeat at Waterloo. The many accomplishments of the Congress of Vienna include the following: The Confederation of the Rhine was created to replace the defunct Holy Roman Empire. Louis XVIII of France and Ferdinand VII of Spain were restored. The various Italian states went to the major powers. Britain acquired several strategic colonial territories. The Netherlands were united. Russia got Finland and effective control over the new kingdom of Poland. Prussia was given much of Saxony and important parts of Westphalia and the Rhine Province. Sweden got Norway. The peace terms for France were contained in a separate treaty (see PARIS, TREATY OF). An auxiliary accomplishment of the Congress of Vienna was the formulation of the rules of diplomacy that are still are in effect.

Vientiane, city (1985 est. pop. 377,000), administrative capital and largest city of Laos, N central Laos, on the Mekong R. The city has light industries and is a trading center for forest products, textiles, and hides. It is noted for its canals, its houses built on stilts, and its many pagodas. It was the capital of a Lao kingdom from 1707, was sacked by the Siamese in 1827, and passed to the French in 1899. The population is about half that of 1975, the result of the flight of many Laotians after a Communist takeover that year and of the government's relocation program (see LAOS).

Viet Cong, officially *Viet Nam Cong San* [Vietnamese Communists], Communist insurgents in South Vietnam. Some 10,000 Communist troops remained in hiding in South Vietnam when the Communists withdrew to North Vietnam after the 1954 GENEVA CONFERENCE. They resorted to open warfare to overthrow the U.S.-supported South Vietnamese regime (see VIETNAM WAR) and were later reinforced by North Vietnamese troops. The political organization of the Viet Cong, the National Liberation Front (NLF), was established in 1960.

Viet Minh, officially *Viet Nam Doc Lap Dong Minh* [League for the Independence of Vietnam], coalition of Communist and nationalist groups that fought the Japanese (during WORLD WAR II) and the French (see DIENBIENPHU). The Communists within the coalition became dominant and were absorbed (1951) by the Communist party of North Vietnam. See also VIETNAM WAR.

Vietnam, officially Socialist Republic of Vietnam, republic (1992 est. pop. 68,964,000), 128,401 sq mi (332,559 sq km), SE Asia, bordered by Cambodia and Laos (W), China (N), and the South China Sea (E, S). Major cities are HANOI (the capital) and HO CHI MINH CITY (formerly Saigon). The terrain is generally rugged; the two principal regions, the Red R. delta in the north and the Mekong R. delta in the south, are linked by a narrow, mountainous strip. Agriculture, primarily the growing of rice, is the basis of the economy, engaging more than 80% of the work force; Vietnam is a major rice exporter. Peanuts, corn, sweet potatoes, and beans are also grown for subsistence; cash crops include cotton, jute, coffee, and tea. Fishing is also important. Mining, particularly of coal, heavy industry, and most of the timber resources are concentrated in the north. Offshore petroleum deposits have been developed, and crude oil is exported. About 80% of the population are Vietnamese. Significant minorities include highland tribal peoples such as the Nungs and Meos and Cambodians and Thais. Large numbers of ethnic Chinese fled the country after a border clash with China in 1979. Buddhism and Roman Catholicism are practiced, but religion is discouraged by the government.

History. The area that is now Vietnam is composed of the historic regions of TONKIN, ANNAM, and COCHIN CHINA. European traders arrived in the early 16th cent. The French captured Saigon in 1859, organized the colony of Cochin China in 1867, and declared protectorates over Tonkin and Annam in 1884. The three were merged with Cambodia in 1887 to form French INDOCHINA. A nationalist movement arose in the early 20th cent., gaining momentum during the Japanese occupation in WORLD WAR II. After the Japanese withdrew in 1945 the VIET MINH, a coalition of nationalists and Communists, established a republic headed by HO CHI MINH. French attempts to reassert control and establish Bao Dai as emperor resulted in the French Indochina War (1946–54), which ended with the French defeat at DIENBIENPHU. At the Geneva Conference of 1954 Vietnam was provisionally divided, pending nationwide free elections, into Communist North Vietnam and nationalist South Vietnam. Fearing a Communist victory, the regime of Ngo Dinh DIEM refused to hold the scheduled elections and declared the south an independent republic in 1955. The VIETNAM WAR ensued, with the U.S. aiding South Vietnam. A cease-fire was signed and U.S. troops withdrawn in 1973, but the Communists overran the south in 1975, reunifying (1976) the country. The regime launched a large-scale resettlement and reeducation program to suppress continued opposition in the south. In 1978–79 it invaded Cambodia, overthrowing the regime of POL POT and provoking a brief invasion of N Vietnam by China. Continued political and social upheaval took its toll on the economy and also prompted the flight of great numbers of refugee boat people. In the late 1980s economic failure and food shortages, both exacerbated by a U.S. economic embargo, led to decentralization and limited free enterprise; the party retained tight political control. In 1994 the U.S. ended the embargo in response to Vietnam's cooperation in the search for missing American servicemen. Since 1991 the Communist party has been led by Do Muoi; Vo Van Kiet, an economic reformer, is premier.

Vietnam Veterans Memorial, war memorial in Washington, D.C., built 1982. Designed by American sculptor and architect Maya Ying Lin, it is a sloping, V-shaped, 493-ft (150-m) black granite wall that descends 10 feet (3.05 meters) below grade level at its vertex; the wall is inscribed with names of the more than 58,000 Americans killed or missing during the VIETNAM WAR. Nearby are sculptures of three soldiers by Frederick E. Hart (erected 1984) and of three nurses and a wounded soldier by Glenna Goodacre (erected 1993).

Vietnam War (1954–75), war in Southeast Asia between the government of South VIETNAM, aided by the U.S., and Communist insurgents, aided by North Vietnam. Following France's defeat in the French Indochina war (1946–54), Vietnam was divided into North and South Vietnam by the Geneva Conference (1954). War soon broke out in South Vietnam as Communist-led guerrillas (the Viet Cong) tried to overthrow the South Vietnamese government. From 1961 the U.S. supplied support troops to South Vietnam, and following the TONKIN GULF RESOLUTION (1964) the war quickly escalated (U.S. troops numbered c.550,000 by 1969). Although historians now view the Tet Offensive (1968) as a major defeat for the Viet Cong, its immediate impact in the U.S. was to increase opposition to the war. Under Pres. NIXON the U.S. began a policy of increased bombing and troop withdrawals. In 1973 a cease-fire agreement was signed at Paris that allowed U.S. troops to withdraw, but it solved few problems. The war finally ended in a Communist victory in 1975, when the North Vietnamese launched their final offensive and routed the South Vietnamese army.

viewdata: see VIDEOTEX.

Vigée-Lebrun, Élisabeth [vēzhā'-ləbröN'], 1755–1842, French portrait painter. Painter and friend to MARIE ANTOINETTE, she is known for two portraits of the Queen (Versailles) and one of Mme de STAËL (Louvre).

Vignola, Giacomo da [vēnyō'lä], 1507–73, leading late Renaissance Italian architect, papal architect (after 1550) to Julius III. He succeeded MICHELANGELO in charge of work at St. Peter's (1564). His finest productions are the Villa Caprorola, near Viterbo, and the Villa Giulia, Rome, as well as the interior for the Church of the Gesù, Rome (1568), which greatly influenced ecclesiastical architecture. He wrote (1562) a universally known treatise on the ORDERS OF ARCHITECTURE.

Vigny, Alfred Victor, comte de [vēnyē'], 1797–1863, French author. Stressing the lonely struggle of the individual in a hostile universe, he expressed the philosophy of ROMANTICISM. His best-known poems are in *Poems Ancient and Modern* (1826) and *Destinées* (1864). Prose works include the novel *The Spider and the Fly* (1826) and *Chatterton* (1835), a play.

Viking, in space exploration: see SPACE PROBE, table.

Vikings, Scandinavian warriors who raided the coasts of Europe and the British Isles from the 9th to 11th cent. The world's best shipbuilders, they were driven as far as Greenland and North America by overpopulation, internal dissension, quest for trade, and thirst for adventure. Many Vikings settled where they had raided (see NORSEMEN). The Viking Age ended with the introduction of Christianity into Scandinavia; the emergence of the kingdoms of Norway, Denmark, and Sweden; and the rise of European states strong enough to repel invasion.

Vila, town (1989 est. pop. 19,400), capital of VANUATU, on Efâte island.

Villa, Pancho (Francisco Villa) [vē'yä], c.1877–1923, Mexican revolutionary; b. Doroteo Arango. A bandit in N Mexico, he joined (1910) the rebels and fought vigorously for Pres. MADERO and later against Gen. HUERTA and Pres. CARRANZA. He and ZAPATA occupied (1914–15) Mexico City, but he was decisively defeated (1915) by Gen. OBREGÓN. After Villa's forces killed (1916) some American citizens at Columbus, N.Mex., a U.S. army expedition pursued Villa in Mexico for 11 months without success. At times a rebel against injustice, but always an undirected, destructive force, Villa became a national hero.

Villa-Lobos, Heitor [vē'lä-lô'bôs], 1887–1959, Brazilian composer. He is known for his use of Brazilian folk music, as in his series *Chôros*. His compositions include symphonies, operas, concertos, chamber music, and songs.

Villanovan culture, the culture of a people of N Italy in the early Iron Age (c.1100–700 B.C.). The Villanovans are believed to have come into Italy from Central Europe, and they lived over much of central Italy. They had a reasonably advanced IRON AGE culture.

villein, a peasant under the medieval MANORIAL SYSTEM. By the 13th cent. in England, SERFS came to be called villeins. The villein was attached to the manor and paid dues to and performed servile labor for the lord. A number of factors caused **villeinage** to disappear in England in the 14th cent. Growing towns weakened the manorial system, and money rents began to replace labor dues. Moreover, the PLAGUE of 1349, by greatly reducing the population, improved the bargaining power of labor.

Villella, Edward, 1936–, American ballet dancer; b. Long Island, N.Y. He studied with BALANCHINE and joined the NEW YORK CITY BALLET in 1957. He had a vigorous, dynamic style and a large repertoire that included *The Prodigal Son*. He served as artistic coordinator of the Eglevsky Ballet (1979–84) and director of the Oklahoma Ballet (1983–85) before founding the Miami City Ballet in 1986.

Villon, François [vēyôN'], 1431–1463?, French poet. Confessedly a vagabond and rogue from his student days, Villon was banished from Paris after killing a man in 1455. He fell in with the *coquillards*, a band of thieves, and for them he composed his ballads in thieves' jargon. Besides these, his chief works are the *Lais* or *Little Testament* (1456) and *Testament* (1461), each of which is a series of facetious bequests to family, friends, and, especially, enemies. Interspersed in the *Testament* are ballads such as "Ballade des dames du temps jadis," with the famous refrain, "But where are the snows of yesteryear?" Other poems include "Ballad of the Hanged," written during the author's anticipation of that fate. Alternately compassionate, ironic, ribald, penitent, and rebellious, Villon is one of the great medieval poets, but with an intensely personal message that ranks him with the moderns.

Villon, Jacques, 1875–1963, French painter; brother of Marcel DUCHAMP and Raymond DUCHAMP-VILLON. An exponent of CUBISM, he is known for his refinement of the cubist style.

Vilnius, city (1989 pop. 582,000), capital of LITHUANIA, N central Europe, on the Neris R. Its industries include machine building and food processing. Lithuania's capital from 1323, and the site of one of Europe's oldest universities, Vilnius declined after Lithuania and Poland were merged (16th cent.). After 1795 it was ruled by Russia (see POLAND, PARTITIONS OF). The city was disputed by Poland and Lithuania from 1918 to 1938; in 1939 it was restored to Lithuania, which was forcibly annexed by the USSR (1940–91). During WORLD WAR II Vilnius was occupied (1941–44) by the Germans, whose virtual extermination of the Jewish population ended its long tradition as a leading E European center of Jewish learning.

Viña del Mar, city (1992 est. pop. 317,000), central Chile, on the Pacific Ocean, near VALPARAISO. Founded in 1874, it is now one of the most popular resort cities in South America, with luxurious hotels, a gambling center, and fine beaches. There are also some industries and a naval base.

Vincent de Paul, Saint, 1580?–1660, French priest renowned for charitable work. His activism and holiness brought about a revival of French Catholicism. In 1625 he founded an order of secular priests (Lazarists or Vincentians); he also founded the Sisters of Charity. Feast: Sept. 27.

Vinci, Leonardo da: see LEONARDO DA VINCI.

vinegar, sour liquid consisting mainly of acetic acid and water, produced by the action of bacteria on dilute solutions of ETHANOL derived from previous yeast FERMENTATION. The alcoholic liquor used, e.g., cider or wine, determines the characteristic color and flavor. Acetic fermentation may be impeded by an excessive growth of mother of vinegar, a slimy mass of bacteria, or of the parasitic vinegar eel, a minute, threadlike worm. Vinegar is used as a salad dressing, as a preservative, as a mild disinfectant, and, in cooking, as a fiber softener.

Vinson, Frederick Moore, 1890–1953, 13th chief justice of the U.S. SUPREME COURT (1946–53); b. Louisa, Ky.; LL.B., Centre College (1911). He served in the U.S. House of Representatives (1923–29, 1931–38), on the U.S. Court of Appeals (1938–43), and as secretary of the treasury (1945–46). As chief justice, he upheld the powers of the federal government in opposition to claims of individual rights.

Vinson Massif, peak, 16,066 ft (4,897 m), highest point in Antarctica, located in the Ellsworth Mts. Named for Carl Vinson, a U.S. politician, it was first climbed in 1966 by an American expedition led by Nicholas B. Clinch.

viol, family of bowed STRINGED INSTRUMENTS, the most important ensemble instruments from the 15th to the 17th cent., when they lost their position to the VIOLIN family and became virtually extinct until the revival of interest in early music in the 20th cent. The viol, a chamber instrument with a soft, sweet tone, differs from the dynamically more brilliant violin. It usually has sloping shoulders, a flat back, and deeper ribs than the violin, is tuned in fourths rather than fifths, and usually is played upright, resting on or between the knees, the bow held with the palm upward. The viol was built in four principal sizes—treble, alto, tenor, and bass—which were used in ensemble, or "consort." The double-bass viol, or *violone*, survived all other viols to become (with some modifications) the modern double bass.

viola: see VIOLIN.

viola da gamba [Ital., = knee viol], term for the bass viol, originally the name of the whole VIOL family.

violet, common name for some members of the family Violaceae, chiefly perennial herbs (and sometimes shrubs) found on all continents. Violets (genus *Viola* and similar related species) are popular florists', garden, and wild flowers. Violets have fragrant, deep purple to yellow or white blossoms. Various species, especially the sweet, or English, violet (*V. odorata*), have been used in perfumes, dyes, and medicines, and have been candied. The common pansy was derived from the Old World *V. tricolor*. Its irregularly shaped, variously colored flowers have five velvety petals. A violet is the floral emblem of three states (New Jersey, Rhode Island, and Wisconsin). Some unrelated plants are also called violets, e.g., the AFRICAN VIOLET of the GESNERIA family.

violin, family of STRINGED INSTRUMENTS having wooden bodies whose backs and fronts are slightly convex, the fronts pierced by two *f*-shaped resonance holes. There are four strings, tuned in fifths, across which the player draws a horsehair bow; a variety of sounds may be produced by different bowing techniques. The fingers of the left hand are used to stop the strings against the fingerboard, thus changing the pitch by shortening the vibrating length of the strings. With their versatility, brilliance, and wide dynamic range, the instruments of the violin family have long dominated the ORCHESTRA. The first instrument of this type appeared about 1510 as the *viola da bracchio* (arm viol). The present-day violin was developed toward the end of the 16th cent., and the peak of violin-making was reached over the following century by such master craftsmen as the Amati, Guarneri, and STRADIVARI families of Cremona, Italy. The violin, the smallest and most agile member of the family, has from the beginning been a major solo instrument and the principal orchestral instrument. The viola is about one-seventh larger than the violin and is tuned a fifth lower. It is used mainly in the orchestra and chamber music, but recently has become more popular as a solo instrument. Both violin and viola are supported by the shoulder and held firm under the chin. The violoncello, often called cello, is about twice as wide and twice as long as the violin, and is tuned an octave lower. Because of its size, it is played between the knees, like members of the VIOL family. The double-bass violin was superseded in the 18th cent. by the double-bass viol or *violone,* which with some modifications became the modern double bass, the lowest-pitched instrument of the orchestral string section.

Viollet-le-Duc, Eugène Emmanuel [vyôlā'-lə-dük], 1814–79, French architect and writer. He was the most prominent exponent of the GOTHIC REVIVAL in France, celebrated for his restoration work. His efforts included restoration of the Sainte Chapelle and work on NÔTRE-DAME DE PARIS. His other restorations include the cathedrals of Amiens, Chartres, and Rheims; the château of Pierrefonds; and the city of Carcassonne. His writings, which he illustrated himself, emphasize the organic quality of Gothic structures.

violoncello: see VIOLIN.

viper, poisonous SNAKE of the family Viperidae, found in Eurasia and Africa. Characterized by erectile, hypodermic fangs, vipers range in size from under 1 ft (30 cm) to nearly 6 ft (2 m) and often have zigzag or diamond markings. Best known are the European asp (*Vipera aspis*), native to S Europe, and the common European viper, or adder (*V. berus*), found throughout Europe and N Asia. The PIT VIPERS of the Americas belong to a different family.

Virchow, Rudolf [fĭr'khō], 1821–1902, German pathologist. He taught at the Univ. of Würzburg and then directed the Pathological Inst. in Berlin. A founder of cellular pathology, he contributed to nearly every branch of medicine and to anthropology, and introduced sanitary reforms in Berlin. Elected a member of the Prussian lower house and later of the Reichstag, he was a leader of the liberal Progressive party opposed to BISMARCK.

Virgil: see VERGIL.

Virginia, state of the south-central U.S.; bordered by the Atlantic Ocean (E), North Carolina and Tennessee (S), Kentucky and West Virginia (W), and Maryland and the District of Columbia (N and NE).

Area, 40,817 sq mi (105,716 sq km). *Pop.* (1990) 6,187,358, an 15.7% increase over 1980 pop. *Capital,* Richmond. *Statehood,* June 25, 1788 (10th of original 13 states to ratify the Constitution). *Highest pt.,* Mt. Rogers, 5,729 ft (1,747 m); *lowest pt.,* sea level. *Nickname,* Old Dominion. *Motto, Sic Semper Tyrannis* [Thus Always to Tyrants]. *State bird,* cardinal. *State flower,* dogwood. *State tree,* dogwood. *Abbr.,* Va.; VA.

Land and People. The coastal plain, or tidewater region, is generally flat and partly swampy. At the FALL LINE it gives way to the generally rolling, fertile Piedmont Plateau. Farther west, the BLUE RIDGE Mts. are separated by the Valley of Virginia from the Allegheny Mts. The overall climate is mild; rainfall is well distributed. Almost 70% of the population lives in urban areas. VIRGINIA BEACH is the largest city. NORFOLK, the center of the huge port industry of the HAMPTON ROADS, is the second largest city, followed by RICHMOND, NEWPORT NEWS, and CHESAPEAKE. In 1990 the state was 77% white and 19% African American.

Economy. By the early 1990s service industries had displaced manufacturing as the chief source of income and employment. Manufacturing continues to be important, however, with textiles; transportation, electric, and electronic equipment; processed foods; and chemicals among the leading products. The principal agricultural commodities are dairy products, cattle, soybeans, tobacco, broiler chickens, peanuts, and corn. Coastal fisheries yield a large annual catch, especially of oysters and crabs. Tourists are attracted to the state's mountain areas, including Shenandoah National Park (see NATIONAL PARKS, table) and the Skyline Drive, and historic sites, including Colonial WILLIAMSBURG.

Government. The constitution (adopted 1970) provides for a governor elected to a four-year term. The general assembly consists of a senate with 40 members serving four-year terms and a house with 100 members elected for two years. Virginia sends 2 senators and 11 representatives to the U.S. Congress and has 13 electoral votes.

History. In 1607 JAMESTOWN, the first permanent English settlement in North America, was founded in Virginia. A prosperous economy developed, based on shipping and tobacco cultivation and utilizing slaves. Virginia was a leader in the movement culminating in the AMERICAN REVOLUTION and was the first of the Thirteen Colonies to declare its independence from Great Britain. Among Virginia's native sons were George WASHINGTON, commander of the Continental Army, and Thomas JEFFERSON, drafter of the Declaration of Independence, both of whom subsequently served as presidents of the new nation. Virginia seceded (1861) from the Union, and Richmond became the capital of the CONFEDERACY. The state was the chief battleground of the CIVIL WAR. Virginia was readmitted to the Union in 1870, and during the postwar period the economy was diversified. After the 1954 Supreme Court school desegregation decision, attempts to integrate Virginia's schools proceeded slowly, but integration had been generally accepted by 1970. The nation's energy shortage brought a sudden boom to the coal-mining industry, in the southwestern part of the state, during the late 1970s and early 1980s. From 1989 to 1993 L. Douglas WILDER served as Virginia's, and the nation's, first elected African-American governor.

Virginia, in Roman legend, daughter of the centurion Virginius, who stabbed her to save her from the lust of Appius Claudius Crassus (see CLAUDIUS, Roman gens), a decemvir. This precipitated the fall of the decemvirs.

Virginia Beach, city (1990 pop. 393,069), SE Va., on the Atlantic coast. Formed by the merger (1963) of the town of Virginia Beach and Princess Anne co., it encompasses 302 sq mi (782 sq km), reaching 28 mi (45 km) to the North Carolina border. A tourist center with miles of beautiful beaches, it also has several large military bases. In its southern section horses and dairy cows are raised. The Chesapeake Bay Bridge-Tunnel links the city with DELMARVA. The Cape Henry Cross marks the site of the first landing of colonists (1607).

Virginia City, village (1990 est. pop. 900), seat of Storey co. W Nevada; settled 1859. Now a tourist center, it was the site of the COMSTOCK LODE and a major hub for the mining of silver and gold.

Virginia Company, name of two English colonization companies chartered by King JAMES I in 1606. One founded the PLYMOUTH COLONY; the other, later known as the London Company, founded colonies in the South, notably JAMESTOWN, Va.

Virginia creeper, woody vine (*Parthenocissus quinquefolia*) of the GRAPE family, popular as a wall covering. It has blue-black berries and clings by disk-tipped tendrils, with some branches hanging free. The five-fingered leaves are sometimes confused with the three-fingered POISON IVY.

Virginia Resolutions: see KENTUCKY AND VIRGINIA RESOLUTIONS.

Virgin Islands, group of about 100 small islands, WEST INDIES, E of Puerto Rico, owned by the U.S. and Great Britain, constituting the westernmost part of the Lesser Antilles. Their tropical climate and picturesque quality, enhanced by Old World architecture, make them a popular tourist destination. However, the population, mostly of African descent, remains poor. Columbus discovered and named the islands in 1493. The **Virgin Islands of the United States** (1990 pop. 101,809), 133 sq mi (344 sq km), a U.S. territory, encompasses the southern and western islands. The capital is Charlotte Amalie on St. Thomas. The group is composed of 68 islands, but only three are important: St. Croix (1990 pop. 50,139), St. Thomas (1990 pop. 48,166), and St. John (1990 pop. 3,504). St. Thomas (32 sq mi/83 sq km) is mountainous and has fine harbors. St. Croix (80 sq mi/207 sq km) is flatter; manufacturing, tourism, and agriculture dominate its economy. Christiansted is the chief town. Much of St. John (20 sq mi/52 sq km) is occupied by the Virgin Islands National Park (see NATIONAL PARKS, table). The Danish settled St. Thomas in 1672, acquired St. John in 1683, and bought St. Croix from France in 1733. The islands were purchased from Denmark in 1917; the islanders became U.S. citizens in 1927. The Dept. of the Interior administers the islands, which have a locally elected governor and senate.

British Virgin Islands. The **British Virgin Islands,** a British dependency (1991 pop. 16,644), 59 sq mi (153 sq km), are to the northeast. Of more than 30 islands, the most important are Tortola, Anegada, and Virgin Gorda. Road Town, the capital, is on Tortola. Tourism, farming, and fishing are the chief economic activities. Britain acquired the islands from the Dutch in 1666.

Virgin Islands National Park: see NATIONAL PARKS (table).

Viriatus, d. 139 B.C., leader of the Lusitani, group of Iberian tribes. He headed a successful rebellion (147 B.C.) against Roman rule, inflicted defeats on Roman armies, and maintained an independent state until some of his followers accepted Roman bribes and killed him.

viroid, microscopic infectious agent, much smaller than a VIRUS, that infects higher plants such as potatoes, tomatoes, and cucumbers, causing stunted or distorted growth and sometimes death. It can be transmitted by pollen, seed, or farm implements. Some scientists believe viroids, which consist of a short strand of RNA, are parts of normal RNA that have gone awry.

virtual reality (VR), computer-generated environment with and within which people can interact. VR encompasses a range of interactive computer environments, from text-oriented on-line forums and multiplayer games to complex simulations that combine audio; video, animation, or three-dimensional graphics; and scent. Some of the more realistic effects are achieved using a helmetlike apparatus with tiny computer screens, one in front of each eye and each giving a slightly different view so as to mimic stereoscopic vision. Sensors attached to the participant (e.g., gloves, bodysuit, footwear) pass on his or her movements to the computer, which changes the graphics accordingly to give the participant the feeling of movement through the scene. Computer-generated physical feedback adds a "feel" to the visual illusion, and computer-controlled sounds and odors reinforce the virtual environment. Other VR systems, such as FLIGHT SIMULATORS, use larger displays and enclosed environments to create an illusion. Less complicated systems for PERSONAL COMPUTERS manipulate an image of three-dimensional space on a computer screen. VR is used in some ELECTRONIC GAMES, in amusement-park attractions, and to simulate construction designs. Experimental and envisioned uses include education, industrial design, surgical training, and art.

virus, infectious agent composed mainly of NUCLEIC ACID within a protein coat (capsid), ranging in size from 10 to 200 nanometers; they can be seen only with an electron microscope. During the stage of their life cycle in which they are free and infectious, viruses do not carry out the usual functions of living cells, such as RESPIRATION and growth; when they enter a living plant, animal, or bacterial cell, they make use of the host cell's chemical energy and protein- and nucleic-acid-synthesizing ability to replicate themselves. Some, like the BACTERIOPHAGES, have protein tails used for infecting the host. Each virus attacks a specific type of cell, for example, cold viruses attack cells of the lungs and the AIDS virus attacks T4 cells of the immune system. Viral nucleic acids are single- or double-stranded and may be DNA or RNA. After viral components are made by the infected host cell, virus particles are released. Often, the virus alters the intracellular environment enough to damage or kill the cell; if enough cells are destroyed, disease results. Some viruses do not kill cells but transform them into a cancerous state (see CANCER); some can remain latent for a long time. Viruses cause measles, mumps, yellow fever, poliomyelitis, influenza, and several costly plant diseases. Some viral infections can be treated with drugs called ANTIVIRALS, and VACCINATION is useful in effecting immunization against many viruses. See also RETROVIRUS.

virus, computer: see COMPUTER VIRUS.

Visconti [vēskôn'tē], Italian family that ruled MILAN from the 13th cent. until 1447. **Ottone Visconti,** 1207–95, archbishop of Milan, was recognized as lord of the city in 1277. **Matteo I Visconti,** 1255–1322, supported the imperial or Ghibelline faction (see GUELPHS AND GHIBELLINES) and became imperial vicar of Milan. Later Viscontis increased and consolidated Milanese territory. **Gian Galeazzo Visconti,** 1351?–1402, embarked on a systematic program of conquest, first in Venetia, then in central Italy. He bought (1395) the hereditary title of duke of Milan from Holy Roman Emperor WENCESLAUS and defeated (1401) the German king Rupert, when Rupert tried to assert his rule in Italy. Gian Galeazzo sought to establish an Italian kingdom, but he died of the plague while preparing an attack on Florence, his chief enemy. His daughter, Valentina, married Louis d'ORLÉANS; it was through her that LOUIS XII and FRANCIS I of France derived their claims to Milan in the ITALIAN WARS. The dukedom passed to Gian Galeazzo's sons, first to **Giovanni Maria Visconti,** 1389–1412, a cruel ruler who was assassinated, and then to **Filippo Maria Visconti,** 1392–1447. Filippo Maria's daughter and heir, Bianca Maria, married Francesco I SFORZA, who became duke of Milan after the fall of the short-lived Ambrosian Republic (1447–50).

Visconti, Luchino, 1906–76, Italian film and stage director. His neorealist *Ossessione* (1943) and *La terra trema* (1948) were followed by such films as *The Leopard* (1962), *Death in Venice* (1970), and *Conversation Piece* (1975).

viscosity, resistance of a fluid to flow. This resistance acts against the motion of any solid object through the fluid, and also against motion of the fluid itself past stationary obstacles. Viscosity also acts internally on the fluid between slower- and faster-moving adjacent layers. All fluids exhibit viscosity to some degree.

Vishniac, Roman [vĭsh'nēăk], 1897–1990, Russian-American biologist, photographer, linguist, art historian, and philosopher; b. Russia. From 1933 to 1939 he recorded the life of Central European Jews in photographs. He was a pioneer of time-lapse and light-interruption photography, and became renowned for his photomicroscopy of living organisms.

Vishnu, one of the great gods of HINDUISM; in the Hindu trinity he is the preserver (see also BRAHMA; SHIVA).

Visigoths or **West Goths,** a division of the Goths, one of the chief groups of ancient GERMANS. Separated from the OSTROGOTHS, or East Goths, they moved (376) into Roman territory under pressure of the HUNS. They routed the East Roman emperor VALENS at Adrianople (378), and their kings, ALARIC I and Ataulf, led them across Italy, sacking Rome in 410. The Visigoths expanded N to the Loire, made Toulouse their capital, and took Vandal lands in Spain. King Euric (r.466–c.484) brought them to their peak of power. After Alaric II lost (507) lands N of the Pyrenees to the Franks under CLOVIS, the Visigoths were essentially restricted to Spain. They became Christians and merged with the Spanish population. Anarchy followed the death (672) of King Recceswinth. Their last king, Roderick, was defeated (711) by the MOORS, who thus ended the Visigothic kingdom.

vision: see EYE.

vitamin, organic compound required in the diet of animals, including humans, for normal growth and maintenance of life. Vitamins provide the only source of certain COENZYMES necessary for METABOLISM, the biochemical processes that support life. Since vitamins differ widely in chemical structure, there is no common chemical grouping. They were originally classified as fat-soluble or water-soluble, but as more were discovered, they were also classified alphabetically. The fat-soluble vitamins are stored in body fat and may therefore accumulate in quantities that can be toxic; vitamins A, D, E, and K are fat-soluble. Most water-soluble vitamins are rapidly excreted in the urine and thus rarely cause toxicity, even when ingested in excessive amounts; the B-complex vitamins and vitamin C are water-soluble. A well-balanced diet—including sufficient amounts of fruit and vegetables as well as eggs, meat, fish, or fowl (that is, a good source of protein)—usually satisfies the minimum vitamin requirement of human beings. An inadequate vitamin intake can lead to deficiency diseases, but there is growing evidence that vitamins have roles in health beyond the prevention of deficiency diseases. Vitamins C and E act as ANTIOXIDANTS and may prevent LDL CHOLESTEROL from clogging arteries, and vitamin K inhibits loss of bone calcium in post-menopausal women. See table of vitamins accompanying this article.

Vitruvius, c.90–c.20 B.C., Roman architect. He wrote the oldest extant Western treatise on architecture, *De Architectura* or the "Ten Books." An invaluable document of Roman and Greek architectural history and building practices, its rediscovery in the early 15th cent. ushered in the revival of the classical orders in Italian Renaissance architecture.

Vivaldi, Antonio, c.1675–1741, Italian composer, the greatest master of the Italian BAROQUE. His style is characterized by driving RHYTHM, clarity, and lyrical melody. He is known chiefly for his instrumental music—SONATAS, CONCERTOS (of which he wrote 447), and concerti grossi, e.g., *The Four Seasons.* He helped standardize the three-movement concerto form and influenced J.S. BACH, who arranged 10 of his concertos.

vivisection, use of living animals for scientific research. Rats, mice, guinea pigs, and rabbits are those used most frequently. The practice of vivisection dates back to ancient times and has contributed to progress in understanding ANATOMY, PHYSIOLOGY, disease processes, and GENETICS. Antivivisectionists and animal rights activists have actively opposed vivisection, sometimes pressuring researchers with vandalism and harassment. Guidelines of the National

VITAMINS			
Vitamin	*Important Sources*	*Function*	*Deficiency Disease(s)*
A	Green leafy or yellow vegetables, fish-liver oils, egg yolk, milk, butter	Essential to skeletal growth, skin, epithelial tissue, visual process; ANTIOXIDANT	Night blindness, xerophthalmia, skin abnormalities. *Overdose* may cause skin, hair, bone abnormalities
B_1(thiamine)	Whole grains, liver, lean pork, yeast, legumes, nuts	Important in METABOLISM of CARBOHYDRATES	Beriberi (neurological, gastrointestinal disorders; heart affected in severe cases)
B_2(riboflavin)	Milk, green leafy vegetables, liver and organs, eggs	Synthesis of COENZYMES; biochemical OXIDATIONS AND OXIDATION AND REDUCTIONS	Lesions of skin, mouth, eyes
Niacin	Liver, lean meat, yeast, fish, wheat germ, peanuts	Component of coenzymes in oxidations and reductions	Pellagra (skin disease, diarrhea, dementia, ultimately death)
B_6(pyridoxine)	Lean meat, liver, seeds, milk, whole grains, egg yolk	Coenzyme in metabolism of AMINO ACIDS, PROTEINS	Decreased hemoglobin production, ANEMIA; in infants, convulsions
Biotin	Synthesized by intestinal bacteria; also found in liver, egg yolk, yeast, kidney	Coenzyme in metabolism of carbohydrates, fats, amino acids	(Deficiency produced by large doses of raw egg white and antibiotics; symptoms include dry skin, anemia)
Pantothenic acid	Liver, kidney, egg yolk, yeast	Part of coenzyme A, major metabolic agent	(Deficiency produced only in laboratory animals)
Folic acid	Green leafy vegetables, liver, yeast	Involved in synthesis of nucleic acids, rapidly synthesizing (e.g., intestinal) cells, red blood cells	Forms of anemia
B_{12}(cobalamin)	Liver, kidney, lean meat, bivalves, fish, eggs, cheese	Amino, fatty acid metabolism; production of proteins	Associated with pernicious anemia caused by lack of "intrinsic factor" that B_{12} dosage can cure
C (ascorbic acid)	Citrus fruits, tomatoes, peppers, cabbage, potatoes, berries	Important in collagen (connective tissue) synthesis, resistance to infection and stress; ANTIOXIDANT	Scurvy (weakened capillaries, internal hemorrhaging, anemia, general debility, ultimately death)
D	Exists in human skin and is activated by exposure to sunlight; also found in fish liver oils, fortified milk, yeast, egg yolk	Regulates utilization of calcium, phosphorus in bone formation	Lack of sunlight causes rickets: in children, bowlegs, knock-knees; in adults, softening of bones (osteomalacia). *Overdose* may cause kidney damage, calcium deposits
E (tocopherol)	Peanut, vegetable oils; wheat germ, fortified cereals, green leafy vegetables, eggs	ANTIOXIDANT; important in pregnancy and for newborns	Anemia in newborns
K	Liver, green leafy vegetables; also synthesized by intestinal bacteria	Essential to blood clotting; role in liver production of the protein prothrombin	Abnormally long clotting time. Deficiency not of dietary origin. K does not treat HEMOPHILIA.

Institutes of Health, the Agriculture Dept., and other public and private organizations try to ensure ethical and sensitive use of animals.

Vladimir I or **Saint Vladimir** [vlăd'əmēr], d. 1015, first Christian grand duke of Kiev (980–1015). To succeed his father, Sviatoslav, as ruler of KIEVAN RUSSIA he defeated his two brothers. In about 988 he became a Christian and married Anna, sister of Byzantine Emperor BASIL II.

Vladivostok, city (1990 est. pop. 642,000), Far Eastern Russia, on a peninsula between two bays of the Sea of Japan. It is the chief Russian port and naval base in the Pacific (kept open in winter by icebreakers), the terminus of the Trans-Siberian RR and the Northern Sea Route, and a base for fishing and whaling fleets. Its industries include shipbuilding, chemicals, and food processing. Founded in 1860, it was an outpost for Russian expansion in East Asia. It was occupied by Allied armies in 1917 after the Bolshevik Revolution; the Japanese remained until 1922. The city was a major port for World War II LEND-LEASE supplies.

Vlaminck, Maurice de [vlämăNk'], 1876–1958, French painter, writer, and printmaker. Influenced by VAN GOGH and African sculpture, he was associated with FAUVISM. He is best known for *Village in the Snow* (Philadelphia Mus. Art).

voice, in music. Singing voices are classified by ranges as soprano and contralto (or alto), the high and low female voices, with mezzo-soprano as an intermediate classification; and as tenor and bass, the high and low male voices, with baritone as intermediate classification. The sound of the castrato (a male singer with an artificially high voice, the result of castration in boyhood), for which many 17th- and 18th-cent. soprano and alto roles were intended, is approached today by the countertenor. Choral music generally requires a range of about an octave and a half for each voice; a solo singer must have at least two octaves. Over the centuries great changes have taken place in the art of singing within Western musical culture, and modern singers can only approximate the timbre of earlier eras. Gregorian chant may have been sung with a nasal timbre resembling Asian technique. Bel canto, the virtuosic art of vocal technique that flourished from the 17th to 19th cent., has been revived in the 20th cent.

Voice of America (VOA), a broadcasting service of the U.S. Information Agency, a U.S. government body. Founded in 1942, the VOA produces and broadcasts English- and foreign-language radio programs in many parts of the world to promote a favorable impression of the U.S. It features news reports and entertainment.

volcano, aperture in the crust of a planet or natural satellite through which gases, LAVA, and solid fragments are discharged. The term is also applied to the conical MOUNTAIN (cone) built up around the vent by ejected matter. Volcanoes are described as active, dormant, or extinct. On earth about 500 are known to be active. Belts of volcanoes are found along the crest of the mid-ocean ridge system under the OCEAN and at converging crustal plate boundaries (see PLATE TECTONICS). There are also isolated volcanoes not associated with crustal movements (e.g., the Hawaiian Islands; see HAWAII), which may form from rising magma regions called hot spots. Eruptions range from the quiet type (Hawaiian) to the violently explosive (e.g., PELÉE and KRAKATOA). In 1971 the *Mariner 9* SPACE PROBE revealed that the planet MARS also has volcanoes, including the largest in the solar system, Olympus Mons. *Voyager 1* photographed (1979) at least eight active volcanoes on Io, a satellite of JUPITER, and *Magellan* provided (1991) evidence of widespread volcanism on VENUS.

Volcker, Paul, 1927–, American economist; b. Cape May, N.J. After working as an undersecretary in the Treasury Department (1969–74) and president of the New York Federal Reserve Bank (1975–79), he was head of the FEDERAL RESERVE SYSTEM (1979–87). He pursued a restrictive monetary policy to combat inflation, but was forced by a stagnant economy and high unemployment to support increased monetary growth during the mid-1980s.

vole, mouselike RODENT (called field or meadow mouse in North America) related to the LEMMING. Found in Eurasia, N Africa, and North America, most voles are from 3½ to 7 in. (9 to 18 cm) long and have gray or brown coats and short tails. They eat mainly grasses but also feed on seeds and insects; they nest in dense growth or shallow burrows.

Volga, river, c.2,300 mi (3,700 km) long, W Russia, longest river in Europe (as the continent is traditionally defined). It rises at an elevation of only 742 ft (226 m) in the Valday Hills near Moscow and winds east past Nizhny Novgorod and Kazan, then south past Samara and Volgograd to enter the CASPIAN SEA below sea level in a wide delta near Astrakhan. Canals connect the river with the Baltic Sea (N), with Moscow, and with the Don R. and the Black Sea (S). The Volga carries about half of all river freight in Russia. Numerous dams (bypassed by locks) provide hydroelectricity along much of its course and water for irrigation of the southern STEPPES. The river, known in Russian folklore as "Mother Volga," has played an incalculable part in the life of the Russian people.

Volgograd, formerly **Stalingrad,** city (1990 est. pop. 1,006,000), SE European Russia, a port on the Volga R. and the eastern terminus of the Volga-Don Canal. Its industries include shipyards, oil refineries, and steel and aluminum mills. Nearby is one of the world's largest hydroelectric power dams. Founded in 1569 as Tsaritsyn, the city fell to the Cossack rebel armies of Stenka Razin (1670) and PUGACHEV (1774). It was renamed Stalingrad in 1925. In WORLD WAR II it was virtually destroyed and thousands were killed (Sept. 1942–Feb. 1943) before German forces surrendered. After the turning point at Stalingrad, Soviet forces took the offensive on the eastern front. The city was renamed Volgograd in 1961.

volleyball, indoor or outdoor game in which opposing teams of six players bat a large, inflated ball back and forth across a net. The court, 60 ft (18.29 m) by 30 ft (9.14 m), is divided by a net 8 ft (2.44 m) high at the top. Any part of the body may be used to bat the ball. Points are scored by the serving team when its opponent allows the ball to touch the ground. Volleyball originated (1895) in Holyoke, Mass., and became an Olympic event in 1964.

Volsted Act, in U.S. history, the law passed in 1919 to enforce the Eighteenth Amendment, which prohibited the sale, manufacture, and transportation of all alcoholic beverages. The law was sponsored by Rep. Andrew Volsted of Minnesota. It became void after the repeal of the amendment in 1933.

Volsungasaga [vŏl'sŏŏng-gəsä'gə] [Icelandic, = saga of the Volsungs], Icelandic prose SAGA based on earlier poetic materials and probably assembled late in the 13th cent. (Its German counterpart is the Nibelungenlied: see under NIBELUNGEN.) Its heroine, GUDRUN, accomplishes the ruin of the Volsungs, who are led by Sigurd (see SIEGFRIED). Brynhild (see BRUNHILD) is Sigurd's beloved, whom he betrays.

volt (V), unit of voltage or, more technically, of electric POTENTIAL and ELECTROMOTIVE FORCE. It is defined as the difference of electric potential existing across the ends of a conductor having a resistance of 1 OHM when the conductor is carrying a current of 1 AMPERE.

Volta, Alessandro, Conte, 1745–1827, Italian physicist. He invented the so-called Volta's pile (or voltaic pile), the electrophorus (a device to generate static electric charges), and the voltaic CELL. The VOLT, a unit of electrical measurement, is named for him.

Volta, river of Ghana, W Africa, flowing south to the Gulf of Guinea at Ada. Akosombo Dam (completed 1965), c.60 mi (97 km) from the river's mouth, impounds Lake Volta, one of the world's largest artificial lakes (c.3,275 sq mi/8,480 sq km). The lake now extends more than 250 mi (400 km) upstream into N Ghana, beyond the point at which the Volta is formed by the confluence of the White Volta and Black Volta rivers.

voltage: see ELECTROMOTIVE FORCE; POTENTIAL, ELECTRIC.

voltage divider: see POTENTIOMETER.

Voltaire, François Marie Arouet de [vôltĕr'], 1694–1778, French philosopher and author; b. François Marie Arouet. He was a leading figure of the ENLIGHTENMENT. Twice unjustly imprisoned (1717–18, 1726) and then banished to England (1726–29), he developed a hatred of judicial arbitrariness coupled with an admiration of English liberalism. Returning to France, he resided at Cirey, in Lorraine, with Mme Du Châtelet, who exerted an important intellectual influence on him. Upon her death in 1749, he went to live at the court of Prussia, but his relationship with FREDERICK II was stormy, and Voltaire left in 1753. He settled on an estate near Geneva. His triumphal return to Paris in 1778 proved too much for him, and he died soon after. Voltaire's work is immense; and his influence, enormous. His *Letters concerning the English Nation* (1733) initiated the vogue for English philosophy and science (especially for Locke and Newton) that characterized the French Enlightenment. The *Philosophical Dictionary* (1764) distilled his political and religious biases. He wrote many tragedies, among them *Brutus* (1730) and *Zaïre* (1732). His great historical works—*The Age of Louis XIV* (1751) and the *Essay on Manners* (1756)—pioneered a new approach, emphasizing culture and commerce as much as politics and war. Most widely read today is his satirical masterpiece, *Candide* (1759).

voltmeter, instrument used to measure, in VOLTS, differences in electric POTENTIAL, or voltage, between two points in a circuit. Most voltmeters are based on the d'Arsonval GALVANOMETER and are of the analog type, i.e., they give voltage readings that can vary over a continuous range, as indicated by a scale and pointer. Digital voltmeters, which provide voltage readings represented by groups of digits, are, however, becoming increasingly common. A voltmeter is often combined with an AMMETER and an OHMMETER in a multipurpose instrument.

Von. For some German names beginning thus, see under the proper name; e.g., for Von Bismarck, see BISMARCK, OTTO VON.

von Braun, Wernher [vôn broun], 1912–77, German-American ROCKET engineer. He was technical director (1937–45) of the German rocket research center at Peenemünde, where the V-2 rocket and other weapons were developed. In 1945, von Braun and many members of his team were brought to the U.S., where he worked on guided missiles for the army and later, as director of NASA's Marshall Space Flight Center, led the development of the Saturn rockets used in the Apollo manned lunar-landing missions. He became (1970) deputy associate administrator of NASA.

Vondel, Joost van den, 1587–1679, Dutch poet and dramatist; b. Germany. Considered the greatest Dutch writer, he produced verse that is melodious, sonorous, and seemingly effortless. Of his highly baroque Christian dramas, the most famous are *Gysbrecht van Aemstel* (1637) and *Lucifer* (1654).

Vonnegut, Kurt, Jr., 1922–, American novelist; b. Indianapolis, Ind. With wry charm, dark humor, and plots that sometimes resemble science fiction he protests the horrors of the 20th cent. Vonnegut's novels include *Player Piano* (1951), *Slaughterhouse Five* (1969), *Deadeye Dick* (1982), and *Hocus Pocus* (1990).

von Neumann, John [noi'män], 1903–57, American mathematician; b. Hungary; came to U.S., 1930. He was associated with the Inst. for Advanced Study after 1933 and was appointed (1954) a member of the U.S. Atomic Energy Commission. A founder of the theory of games (see GAMES, THEORY OF), he also made fundamental contributions to quantum theory and to the development of the atomic bomb. Von Neumann was a leader in the design and development of high-speed electronic computers.

Von Sternberg, Josef, 1894–1969, American film director; b. Austria as Jo Sternberg. His visually striking films include *The Blue Angel* (1930), *Morocco* (1930), *Shanghai Express* (1932), and *The Scarlet Empress* (1934), all of which star Marlene DIETRICH.

voodoo, religious beliefs and practices, W African in origin but with Roman Catholic and West Indian accretions, found in the New World, principally in Haiti. Voodooistic ritual is characterized by ecstatic trances and magical practices. Despite opposition, voodoo continues to flourish.

Voroshilov, Kliment Yefremovich [vərəshē'ləf], 1881–1969, Soviet military leader and public official. He was a Red Army commander in the civil war (1918–20), commissar for defense (1925–40), and commander in WORLD WAR II. A member of the Supreme Soviet from 1937, he became president of the USSR when STALIN died (1953). Ousted by KHRUSHCHEV in 1960, he was reelected to the party central committee in 1966.

Vörösmarty, Mihály [vö'röshmŏr"tē], 1800–1855, Hungarian poet, the leading figure of Hungarian ROMANTICISM. He is best known for his patriotic lyrics, e.g., *The Call* (1837), and his splendid national epics, e.g., *Zolan's Flight* (1825).

Vorster, Balthazar Johannes [fôr'stər], 1915–83, South African political leader. Elected to parliament in 1953 as a member of the Nationalist party, he later served as minister of justice (1961–66), repressing opponents of APARTHEID. After the assassination of Hendrik VERWOERD in 1966 he became prime minister. He pursued a somewhat conciliatory foreign policy while maintaining apartheid at home. He resigned for reasons of health in 1978 but served in the ceremonial position of president until a financial scandal forced his resignation in 1979.

vorticism, short-lived 20th-cent. art movement related to FUTURISM. Its members sought to simplify forms into machinelike angularity. Its major exponent was GAUDIER-BRZESKA, a French sculptor, and its largest following was in England, where Ezra POUND and Wyndham LEWIS wrote about it.

Voskhod: see SPACE EXPLORATION, table.

Vostok: see SPACE EXPLORATION, table.

Voyager, in space exploration: see SPACE PROBE, table.

Voyageurs National Park: see NATIONAL PARKS (table).

Voznesensky, Andrei Andreyevich [vəznyəsyān'skē], 1933–, Russian poet. Trained as an architect, he first published his poems, e.g., "Fire in the Architectural Institute," in 1958. He became popular and gave readings in the USSR and abroad. English translations of his work by AUDEN and other poets appear in such collections as *Antiworlds* (1967).

Vries, Hugo de: see DE VRIES, HUGO.

VTOL aircraft: see VERTICAL TAKEOFF AND LANDING AIRCRAFT.

Vuillard, Édouard [vüēyär'], 1868–1940, French painter and lithographer. A member of the NABIS, he is known for his scenes of Montmartre and especially for his canvases that evoke the intimacy of home life.

Vulcan, in Roman religion, fire god. Originally a god of volcanoes, he was later identified with the Greek HEPHAESTUS.

vulcanization: see RUBBER; THERMOSET.

Vulgate: see BIBLE.

vulture, large BIRD of prey of temperate and tropical regions, also called BUZZARD. Old World vultures, of the family Accipitridae, are allied to HAWKS and EAGLES; the American vultures and CONDORS belong to the family Cathartidae. American vultures have no syrinx and are thus voiceless, emitting only weak hisses. They feed mainly on carrion. Most have dark plumage and small, naked heads. Normally solitary, they gather in crowds to feed.

W

W, chemical symbol of the element TUNGSTEN.

Waals, Johannes Diderik van der: see VAN DER WAALS.

WAC: see WOMEN'S ARMY CORPS.

Waco, city (1990 pop. 103,590), seat of McLennan co., east-central Tex., on the Brazos R.; inc. 1856. Located in the rich blacklands prairie area, it is an agricultural and shipping center. Diversified manufactures include tires, glass, machinery, and clothing. Baylor Univ. is in Waco. In 1993 a deadly shootout near Waco between federal officers and a religious cult headed by David Koresh led to a 51-day siege that ended in a blaze that killed 83 people.

Wade, Benjamin Franklin, 1800–78, U.S. senator from Ohio (1851–69); b. near Springfield, Mass. One of the radical Republicans, Wade was instrumental in forming the RECONSTRUCTION policies after the Civil War. As president pro tempore of the Senate, he would have become president if Andrew JOHNSON had been convicted of impeachment charges.

Wafd, Egyptian political party founded in 1919 and dominant from 1924 to 1952. It called for independence and extensive reforms, and was frequently at odds with the monarch. The party was dissolved after NASSER set up a one-party system in 1956. It reemerged in 1983 as the New Wafd party, becoming one of the larger permitted opposition parties.

Wages and Hours Act, legislation passed by the U.S. Congress (1938) to establish employment standards for workers engaged directly or indirectly in interstate commerce; also called Fair Labor Standards Act. The measure initially provided for a MINIMUM WAGE of 25¢ per hour and a maximum work week of 44 hours, and the Wage and Labor Division was created in the Dept. of Labor to oversee its enforcement. Since that time, coverage under the law has been extended to additional categories of workers. Congress has also periodically raised the minimum wage, which by 1991 had reached $4.25 per hour.

Wagner, Honus (John Peter Wagner), 1874–1955, American baseball player; b. Mansfield (now Carnegie), Pa. He began (1897) his major-league career with Louisville and joined Pittsburgh in 1900. Hans, as he was also known, subsequently starred at shortstop for the Pirates until retiring in 1917. He led the league in batting eight times, compiled a lifetime average of .329, and had 3,430 hits.

Wagner, Richard, 1813–83, German composer. His OPERAS represent the fullest musical and theatrical expression of German ROMANTICISM and exerted a profound influence on later composers. He used a continuous flow of melody instead of sharply differentiated RECITATIVE and ARIA, and called his operas "music-dramas" to signify their fusion of text and music. Wagner achieved remarkable dramatic unity in his works, due in part to his development of the leitmotif, a brief passage of music used to characterize an episode, person, or idea. His librettos, which he wrote himself, are drawn chiefly from German mythology. His operas include *Rienzi* (1838–40), *The Flying Dutchman* (1841), *Tannhäuser* (1843–44), and *Lohengrin* (1846–48), which brought the German romantic opera to its culmination. Wagner participated in the REVOLUTION OF 1848 and was forced to flee Dresden, where he had held a conducting post. Aided by LISZT, he escaped to Switzerland, staying there 10 years and writing essays, notably *Oper und Drama* (1851), that define his aesthetics. Wagner's *Der Ring des Nibelungen* (1853–74), a tetralogy that embodies most completely his aesthetic principles, comprises *Das Rheingold* (1853–54), *Die Walküre* (1854–56), *Siegfried* (1856–69), and *Götterdämmerung* (1874). In 1872 Wagner moved to Bayreuth, Bavaria, where he completed the Ring cycle and built a theater, the Festspielhaus, adequate for the performance of his works; the complete *Ring* was presented there in 1876. Wagner's other later compositions are *Tristan und Isolde* (1857–59); *Die Meistersinger von Nürnberg* (1862–67), his only comic opera; and his last work, *Parsifal* (1877–82), a sacred festival drama. His second wife, **Cosima Wagner,** 1837–1930, the daughter of Liszt, was closely involved with his work. After his death, she was largely responsible for the continuing fame of the Bayreuth festivals.

Richard Wagner

Wagner, Robert Ferdinand, 1877–1953, American legislator; b. Germany. A longtime Democratic senator (1927–49) from New York, he was one of F.D. ROOSEVELT's most effective allies in Congress during the early NEW DEAL days. The National Labor Relations Act (1935) is known as the Wagner Act. His son, **Robert Ferdinand Wagner, Jr.,** 1910–91, b. N.Y.C., was mayor of New York City from 1954 to 1966.

Wagram, town, NE Austria. NAPOLEON I forced (1809) Archduke Charles of Austria to concede defeat at Wagram, under the heaviest artillery attack recorded as of that time.

Wahhabi or **Wahabi,** reform movement in ISLAM; the ruling family of SAUDI ARABIA are among its adherents. It was founded in Arabia by Muhammad ibn Abd al-Wahhab (c.1703–1791), who converted the Saud tribe. He taught that all accretions to Islam after the 3d cent. of the Muslim era—i.e., after c.950—were spurious and must be expunged. This view involved essentially a purification of the SUNNI sect. The Wahhabis advocated austerity in worship and in living, but their code is less strict today. The movement, although centered in Arabia, has also spread eastward to India and Sumatra and westward to North Africa and the Sudan.

Wainwright, Jonathan Mayhew, 1883–1953, American general; b. Walla Walla, Wash. In WORLD WAR II, Wainwright assumed command in the Philippines (1942) and led the gallant but hopeless fight (Mar.–May 1942) that ended with the surrender of Bataan and Corregidor. He was a prisoner of the Japanese until 1945.

Waite, Morrison Remick, 1816–88, 7th chief justice of the U.S. SUPREME COURT (1874–88); b. Lyme, Conn. He gained prominence as counsel for the U.S. in the ALABAMA CLAIMS. As chief justice, his most influential rulings concerned STATES' RIGHTS and the due process clause of the 14th amendment to the CONSTITUTION.

Waite, Terry (Terence Waite), 1939–, British church official. An adviser to Robert RUNCIE, the Archbishop of Canterbury, he successfully negotiated the release of British hostages in Iran (1981) and Libya (1985). His later efforts to free U.S. hostages in Beirut were unsuccessful and were compromised by his association with Lt. Col. Oliver North (see IRAN-CONTRA AFFAIR), and he was kidnapped (Jan. 1987) by Shiite Muslims during talks there. Waite was released in Nov. 1991.

Wajda, Andrzej [vī'dä], 1926–, Polish film director. His films are often studies of Poland's history and contemporary politics. They include *Canal* (1956), *Ashes and Diamonds* (1958), *Man of Marble* (1977), *Man of Iron* (1981), *Danton* (1982), and *Korczak* (1990).

Wakashan [wäkăsh'ən], branch of the Algonquian-Wakashan linguistic family of North America. See NATIVE AMERICAN LANGUAGES (table).

Wakefield, Edward Gibbon, 1796–1862, British colonial statesman. His influential ideas led to the founding (1836) of a colony of free settlers (instead of convicts) in South Australia and to the colonization of New Zealand.

Wake Island, atoll with three islets (Wake, Wilkes, and Peale), 3 sq mi (7.8 sq km), central Pacific, between Hawaii and Guam. There is no indigenous population; it is a U.S. military and commercial base. Wake Island, which is administered by the U.S. Air Force, was annexed from the Spanish in 1898 and held by the Japanese, 1941–45.

wake-robin: see TRILLIUM.

Waksman, Selman Abraham, 1888–1973, American microbiologist; b. Russia; came to U.S., 1910. As a microbiologist (1918–54) at the New Jersey Agricultural Experiment station, he studied with his colleagues the role of microorganisms in the decomposition of organic matter, the origin and nature of humus, and the production of substances detrimental to some bacteria. For his discovery of streptomycin and of its value in treating tuberculosis he won the 1952 Nobel Prize in physiology or medicine.

Walachia or **Wallachia,** historic region (29,568 sq mi/76,581 sq km), S Romania, separated from Transylvania and the Banat region by the Transylvanian Alps (NW); from Yugoslavia (W) and Bulgaria (S) by the Danube R.; and adjoining Moldavia (NE). BUCHAREST, Romania's capital, is the chief city. Walachia contains the rich Ploeşti oil fields and is Romania's main industrial area, producing chemicals, heavy machinery, and other manufactures. It is also a rich agricultural region. Part of the Roman province of Dacia, it became a principality c.1290 and came under Turkish suzerainty in the 14th cent. Prince MICHAEL THE BRAVE (r.1593–1601) ended foreign domination, but on his death Walachia again fell to the Turks. In the 19th cent. Russia occupied the area repeatedly; in 1856 Walachia and Moldavia became virtually independent. The accession (1859) of Prince Alexander John CUZA in both principalities began the history of modern ROMANIA.

Walcott, Derek, 1930–, West Indian poet; b. Saint Lucia. His poetry eloquently explores the richness and contradictions of the mixed racial and cultural heritage of the West Indies. His volumes include *In a Green Night* (1962), the autobiographical *Another Life* (1973), and *Omeros* (1990), which echoes the *Iliad* and *Odyssey* as it examines the past and present of Saint Lucia and the Caribbean. He has also written plays based on West Indian folk traditions, including *Dream on Monkey Mountain* (1970). Walcott was awarded the Nobel Prize for literature in 1992.

Waldemar, kings of Denmark. **Waldemar I** (the Great), 1131–82 (r.1157–82), gained his domain in wars with CANUTE and Sweyn III. He increased his prestige by marrying his daughters to the sons of FREDERICK I, PHILIP II of France, and Eric X of Sweden. His son, Canute VI, succeeded him. **Waldemar II,** 1170–1241 (r.1202–41), was the second son of Waldemar I. He conquered much of Estonia but lost Schwerin, in Germany. His son, Eric IV, succeeded him.

Waldemar IV (Valdemar Atterdag), c.1320–1375 (r.1340–75), by 1361 had united Denmark, which foreign rulers had dismembered. He defeated (1362) the HANSEATIC LEAGUE but was forced (1370) to grant it free trade in Denmark. He was succeeded by Olaf, son of his daughter, MARGARET I, and Haakon VI of Norway.

Waldenses or **Waldensians,** Protestant religious sect of medieval origin. They originated in the late 12th cent. as the Poor Men of Lyons, a band organized by Peter Waldo. As lay preachers, they stressed poverty and proclaimed the Bible as the sole rule of faith and life. The group was declared heretical in 1184 and 1215, and persecution persisted until the 18th cent. After the REFORMATION they adapted their views to those of the Reformed Church. A group of Waldensians settled in the U.S. at Valdese, N.C.

Waldheim, Kurt, 1918–, Austrian diplomat, secretary general (1972–81) of the UNITED NATIONS and president of Austria (1986–92). When Austria entered the UN (1958), Waldheim joined its delegation and served (1965–68) as its permanent representative. After failing (1971) to win the Austrian presidency, he returned to the UN and was elected secretary general. In 1986, he was elected president of Austria despite reports of his activities as a German intelligence officer during World War II.

Waldstein, Albrecht von: see WALLENSTEIN.

Wales, Welsh *Cymru,* political division (principality) of the United Kingdom of Great Britain and Northern Ireland (1991 pop. 2,811,865), 8,016 sq mi (20,761 sq km), on the western peninsula of the island of Great Britain; bordered by the Irish Sea (N), the Bristol Channel (S), England (E), and Cardigan Bay and St. George's Channel (W). Physically, it is dominated by the Cambrian Mts., which rise to 3,500 ft (1,085 m) at Mt. Snowdon. Principal cities are CARDIFF, the capital and largest city, and Swansea. Rivers include the Severn, Wye, Teifi, and Dee. The great coalfields and major industries are concentrated in the south, as is most of the population. About one quarter of the population speaks Welsh. Wales united politically with England in 1536.

History. Celtic-speaking Welsh clans, in Wales since prehistory, were little affected by either the Roman or the Anglo-Saxon occupations of Great Britain, although they were converted to Christianity by Celtic monks. The disparate clans gradually coalesced, and border wars with England were constant. In the 11th cent. WILLIAM I of England set up earldoms along the Welsh border, but for 200 years Welsh soldiers resisted the English threat to their independence. Following a brief relaxation of English pressure in the 12th cent., during which Welsh medieval culture flowered, English conquest of Wales was finally accomplished in 1282 by EDWARD I, who, to placate Welsh sentiment, initiated the English custom of entitling the king's eldest son prince of Wales. Welsh antagonism toward the English overlords persisted, and in the 15th cent. OWEN GLENDOWER led a brief revolt. In 1485 a Welshman became the first Tudor king of England, Henry VII. The process of administrative assimilation of Wales begun during his reign was completed under HENRY VIII, who signed the Act of Union (1536); Welsh representatives entered the English parliament, Welsh law was abolished, and English was established as the official language of legal proceedings. Welsh political history became that of GREAT BRITAIN. The Industrial Revolution tapped the mineral wealth of Wales, and S Wales was soon the chief coal-exporting region of the world. Industrialization brought poverty and unemployment, however, especially in the 1920s and 30s. Following the boom of World War II, the government undertook a full-scale program of industrial redevelopment, including nationalization of the mines. Political nationalism survives as an issue; in 1979 Welsh voters decisively defeated a British proposal for limited home rule.

Walesa, Lech [väwĕnz'ə], 1943?–, Polish labor and politcal leader, president of POLAND (1990–). In 1980 he assumed leadership of the independent trade union SOLIDARITY. A moderate, he gained numerous concessions from the authorities before his arrest and internment in the military crackdown of 1981. Released in Nov. 1982, he was awarded the 1983 Nobel Peace Prize. A leader in Poland's peaceful change from Communist rule to pluralistic democracy in 1989, Walesa became increasingly critical of the Solidarity-led government of Premier Tadeusz Mazowiecki. In 1990 Walesa was elected president of Poland, defeating Mazowiecki, and resigned his Solidarity post.

Walker, Alice, 1944–, African-American novelist and poet; b. Eatonton, Ga. She brings her travel experience in Africa and memories of the CIVIL-RIGHTS movement to an examination of the experiences of African Americans in the South. Among her books are *Revolutionary Petunias and Other Poems* (1973), *The Color Purple* (1982; Pulitzer), and *Possessing the Secret of Joy* (1992).

Walker, James John, 1881–1946, American politician; b. N.Y.C. A TAMMANY Democrat, Jimmy Walker was mayor of New York (1925–32). He was immensely popular until evidence of corruption forced his resignation.

walking stick or **stick insect,** extremely long-bodied, slow-moving, herbivorous INSECT, principally Asian and tropical in distribution. Walking sticks have green, gray, or brown bodies that closely resemble twigs or grass stems, camouflaging them against predators. Most are wingless and have long antennae. Some species, the longest insects in the world, achieve a length of over 1 ft (33 cm).

wallaby: see KANGAROO.

Wallace, Alfred Russel, 1823–1913, English naturalist. From his study of comparative biology in Brazil and the East Indies, he evolved a concept of EVOLUTION similar to that of Charles DARWIN. His special contribution to the evidence for evolution was in biogeography; he systematized the science and wrote *The Geographical Distribution of Animals* (2 vol., 1876) and a supplement, *Island Life* (1881).

Wallace, George Corley, 1919–, U.S. public official, governor of Alabama (1963–67, 1971–79, 1983–87); b. Clio, Ala. An avowed segregationist, he led an unsuccessful attempt to block integration of the Alabama public schools in the early 1960s. Prevented by law from succeeding himself as governor, he had his wife, **Lurleen Burns Wallace** (1926–68), run (1966) successfully in his place. Wallace ran unsuccessfully for president as a third-party candidate in 1968. In 1972, while campaigning for the Democratic presidential nomination, he was shot and paralyzed by a would-be assassin. In 1982 he was again elected governor, this time with the support of Alabama's African Americans. He retired in 1986.

Wallace, Henry Agard, 1888–1960, vice president of the U.S. (1941–45); b. Adair co., Iowa. As Pres. F.D. ROOSEVELT's secretary of agriculture (1933–41) he administered the NEW DEAL agricultural programs. He was Roosevelt's third-term vice president but in 1944 was replaced on the ticket by Harry S TRUMAN. An opponent of U.S. COLD WAR policies, he ran against Truman in 1948 on the Progressive party ticket but won no electoral votes. His father, **Henry Cantwell Wallace,** 1866–1924, was a founder of the journal *Wallaces' Farmer* and served (1921–24) as secretary of agriculture in the administrations of Presidents HARDING and COOLIDGE.

Wallace, Lew(is), 1827–1905, American novelist; b. Brook-ville, Ind. A lawyer, territorial governor, and diplomat, he is remembered as author of the novel *Ben Hur* (1880).

Wallenberg, Raoul, 1912–47, Swedish diplomat. Assigned to Budapest during World War II, he is credited with saving as many as 20,000 Hungarian Jews from being deported to NAZI death camps, e.g., by supplying them with Swedish passports. He was arrested when the Soviet army entered Budapest. His death in prison was reported (1957) by Soviet authorities but there were recurring stories that he had been seen alive. In 1991 Soviet authorities released KGB records that, although they did not contain proof that Wallenberg was dead, appeared to confirm that he had died in 1947.

Wallenstein or **Waldstein, Albrecht Wenzel Eusebius von** [wäl'ənstīn], 1583–1634, Bohemian general in the THIRTY YEARS WAR. The owner of vast estates in Bohemia, he raised an army (1625) for Emperor FERDINAND II and became chief imperial general. He won important victories, but the enmity of the German princes led to his dismissal in 1630. Although he was recalled in 1632, Wallenstein conducted (1634) secret peace negotiations, which led to charges of treason, and he was murdered, probably at the emperor's instigation.

Waller, Edmund, 1606–87, English poet and member of Parliament. "Waller's Plot" (1643) attempted to secure the city of London for CHARLES I. His polished verse, including "Go, lovely rose" (pub. 1645), is important for its contribution to the development of the heroic couplet.

Waller, Fats (Thomas Wright Waller), 1904–43, African-American pianist, singer, and composer; b. N.Y.C. His songs and humor made him popular, and his piano style influenced many. "Ain't Misbehavin' " and "Honeysuckle Rose" are among his best-known songs.

walleye or **walleyed pike:** see PERCH.

Wallis and Futuna Islands, French overseas territory (1992 est. pop. 17,000), South Pacific, consisting of two small groups of volcanic islands. Matautu is the chief town. Timber is exported. Under French control from 1842, they became a territory in 1961.

Wall Street, lower Manhattan, N.Y.C., center of the city's great financial district. The area is the site of major U.S. stock exchanges and other important institutions. By extension, the term "Wall Street" has come to designate U.S. financial interests.

walnut, common name for some members of the family Juglandaceae, chiefly deciduous trees of the north temperate zone, typified by large, aromatic compound leaves. Several species are commercially important for their lumber and edible nuts (usually encased in leathery or woody hulls). The family includes the HICKORY and pecan, and the walnuts (genus *Juglans*). The dark-colored wood of the black walnut (*J. nigra*) of E North America, and the English, or Persian, walnut (*J. regia*), native to W Asia, is unusually hard and durable; it is valued for furniture, paneling, musical instruments, and other uses. The nut of the English walnut is usually the walnut sold commercially. The butternut, or white walnut (*J. cinerea*), also of E North America, is valued for its timber; its sweet, oily nut is not commercially important.

Walpole, Horace or **Horatio,** 4th **earl of Orford,** 1717–97, English author; son of Sir Robert WALPOLE. An admirer of the medieval, he built a pseudo-Gothic showplace castle at Strawberry Hill, near Twickenham, and in 1757 started a press there, publishing Thomas GRAY's Pindaric odes and his own works. His reputation rests on more than 3,000 letters (1732–97) that give an invaluable picture of Georgian England. His gothic romance, *The Castle of Otranto* (1765), anticipated ROMANTICISM.

Walpole, Sir Hugh (Seymour), 1884–1941, English novelist; b. New Zealand. He gained fame with *Fortitude* (1913) and wrote historical novels like *Rogue Herries* (1930), autobiographical fiction, stories, biographies, and plays.

Walpole, Robert, 1st **earl of Orford,** 1676–1745, English statesman. His successful handling of the financial wreckage of the SOUTH SEA BUBBLE led to his appointment (1721) as first lord of the treasury and chancellor of the exchequer. A WHIG, he shared power with Viscount TOWNSHEND until 1730, but thereafter his ascendancy was complete until 1742. He enjoyed the confidence of GEORGE I and GEORGE II, promoted trade, and mollified the largely Tory gentry by reducing the land tax. In foreign affairs he favored friendship with France, but was drawn into a war with Spain. Military reverses then enabled a growing opposition to force his resignation (1742). He is usually described as the first prime minister.

walrus, marine MAMMAL (*Odobenus rosmarus*) found in arctic seas. Largest of the fin-footed mammals, it has long tusks, light-brown wrinkled hide, and bristly cheek pads; an adult male may weigh up to 3,000 lb (1,400 kg). Walruses live on beaches near shallow water in herds of about a hundred animals and eat mainly shellfish. Hunted for blubber, hides, and ivory, they are now endangered.

Walter, Bruno, 1876–1962, German-American conductor; b. Bruno Walter Schlesinger. He was a conductor in Germany and Austria until the NAZIS forced him to leave. In the U.S. he led the Metropolitan Opera, NBC Symphony, and New York Philharmonic.

Walter, Thomas Ustick, 1804–87, American architect; b. Philadelphia. His main building of Girard College, Philadelphia (1833–47), was one of the most ambitious works of the CLASSIC REVIVAL. In 1851 he was hired to design extensions of the CAPITOL. He added the Senate and House wings as well as the cast iron dome, and rebuilt the west front.

Walton, Izaak, 1593–1683, English writer. His *Compleat Angler; or, the Contemplative Man's Recreation* (1653), a treatise on fishing and a picture of peace and simple virtue, is one of the most famous books in English. He also wrote biographies of his friends John DONNE (1640) and George HERBERT (1670).

Walton, Sam(uel Moore), 1918–92, American retailing executive, b. Kingfisher, Okla. After 17 years of operating franchise retail stores, he opened the first Wal-Mart Discount City in 1962. The company flourished, went public (1970), and became (1991) America's largest retailer—a multibillion dollar business that made him one of the world's richest people.

Walton, Sir William Turner, 1902–83, English composer. His works include *Façade* (1923), settings of poems by Edith SITWELL; *Portsmouth Point* (1925), an overture; two symphonies (1935, 1961); *Belshazzar's Feast* (1931), an ORATORIO; *Troilus and Cressida* (1954), an opera; concertos; chamber works; and scores for films, e.g., *Hamlet* (1947).

waltz, romantic dance in triple time. It evolved from the German *Ländler* and became popular in the 18th cent. The Viennese waltz was made famous by the two Johann STRAUSSES. The waltz was introduced into the U.S. in the 19th cent.

Walvis Bay, city (1985 pop. 9,687), W central Namibia, on an arm of the Atlantic Ocean. The chief port for Namibia, it is a railway center and has a fishing fleet. It was annexed by Britain and incorporated into the Cape Colony in 1878. The Walvis Bay exclave (c.430 sq mi/1,110 sq km) was retained by South Africa at Namibia's independence (1990) but was relinquished in 1994.

wampum, beads or disks made by Native Americans from mollusk shells, used for money, ornaments, or ceremonial exchange during treaties. Wampum is Algonquian for "white string of beads," but there is also a more valuable purple variety. It was especially prized in the Eastern Woodlands and Plains areas, reaching inland tribes through trade. Wampum belts often had pictographic designs.

Wandering Jew, legendary Jew who mocked or mistreated Jesus on his way to the cross and who was condemned to wander on earth until Judgment Day. Common in Western European literature, the story first appeared in 13th-cent. chronicles, but the wanderer was not identified as a Jew until the 17th cent.

W and Z particles, ELEMENTARY PARTICLES that mediate, or carry, the fundamental force associated with WEAK INTERACTIONS. Their discovery, at CERN in Geneva, Switzerland, in the early 1980s, was an important confirmation of the ELECTROWEAK THEORY, which unified the electromagnetic and weak forces and predicted the existence of the particles. Quite massive for elementary particles, the *W* and *Z* particles have roughly 100 times the mass of the proton. *W* particles have a charge of 1 or −1; *Z* particles have a charge of 0.

Wang Ching-wei [wäng jĭng-wā], 1883–1944, Chinese political leader. A disciple of SUN YAT-SEN, he led the left wing of the KUOMINTANG party. In the Second SINO-JAPANESE WAR he left (1938) the Kuomintang and became (1940) premier of the Japanese puppet government at Nanjing.

Wankel engine: see INTERNAL-COMBUSTION ENGINE.

wapiti, large North American DEER (*Cervus canadensis*), called ELK in America. Males stand up to 5 ft (150 cm) at the shoulder and weigh up to 1,000 lb (450 kg). The coat is grayish brown, with a chestnut mane and a yellowish rump. Once abundant, the wapiti now lives in small numbers under protection in NATIONAL PARKS and refuges.

Warbeck, Perkin, 1474?–1499, pretender to the English throne. Persuaded by Yorkist adherents to impersonate the son of EDWARD IV, he landed (1497) in Cornwall and proclaimed himself Richard IV. Captured by HENRY VII, he was hanged.

warbler, name applied in the New World to BIRDS of the wood warbler family (Parulidae) and in the Old World to a family (Sylviidae) of small songsters. American warbler species are brightly plumed in the spring, usually yellow marked with black, gray, olive green, or white. Some crawl on trees and are called creepers. Best known are the yellow warbler, which often nests in gardens, and the redstart. Warblers are of great value as destroyers of insects that damage forest trees.

war crimes, violations of the laws of war. After WORLD WAR II three classes of offenses were recognized as war crimes: crimes against peace, e.g., planning or waging a war of aggression; conventional war crimes, or violations of the accepted laws or customs of warfare; and crimes against humanity, including extermination, enslavement, deportation, and other inhumane acts. From Nov. 1945 to Oct. 1946 a tribunal at Nuremberg, Germany, established by Britain, France, the USSR, and the U.S., tried Nazi leaders for war crimes (see CONCENTRATION CAMP; HOLOCAUST) and sentenced some of them to death. Another war tribunal, conducted (1946–47) in Tokyo by 11 nations, tried and sentenced alleged Japanese war criminals. Critics questioned the legal basis of some of the charges at these trials, and some view such trials as violations of sovereignty and as acts of vengeance by the victors. In the early 1990s, in reaction to war crimes committed by various parties during the breakup of YUGOSLAVIA, the UN established a war crimes commission and attempted to gather evidence for prosecutions. See also INTERNATIONAL LAW; MY LAI INCIDENT.

Ward, Artemus, pseud. of **Charles Farrar Browne,** 1834–67, American humorist; b. Waterford, Me. He began in 1858 a famous series of "Artemus Ward's Letters," supposedly written by a carnival manager who commented on current events in a New England dialect. He wrote for the *Cleveland Plain Dealer* and *Vanity Fair.*

Ward, Mrs. Humphry, 1851–1920, English novelist and social worker; b. Mary Augusta Arnold; granddaughter of English educator Thomas Arnold. *Robert Elsemere* (1888) and other novels dramatize her views on the social application of religion.

Ward, Lester Frank, 1841–1913, paleontologist and a founder of American SOCIOLOGY; b. Joliet, Ill. In *Dynamic Sociology* (1883), *Applied Sociology* (1906), and other works he developed the theory of telesis, or planned social evolution.

War Department, United States, former federal executive department organized (1789) to administer the military establishment. During the 19th cent. it also had many quasi-military functions, such as supervising RECONSTRUCTION in the South. With the creation (1947) of the National Military Establishment, which later became (1949) the Dept. of DEFENSE, it was reconstituted as the Dept. of the Army, a division within the Dept. of Defense.

Ware, Henry, 1764–1845, American clergyman, instrumental in the founding of UNITARIANISM in the U.S.; b. Sherborn, Mass. His appointment (1805) as Hollis professor of divinity at Harvard aroused opposition and hastened the separation of the Unitarians from the Congregationalists. His son **Henry Ware,** 1794–1843, b. Hingham, Mass., was also a clergyman and a Harvard professor. He edited (1819–22) the first Unitarian organ, the *Christian Disciple.*

warfare: see FORTIFICATION; MILITARY SCIENCE; PSYCHOLOGICAL WARFARE.

Warhol, Andy, 1930?–87, American artist; b. Philadelphia? A leading figure in the POP ART movement, he is known for multi-image silk-screen paintings that make use of monotony and repetition. His imagery often comes from commonplace objects such as dollar bills and soup cans. Warhol made a number of idiosyncratic films, e.g., *The Chelsea Girls* (1966).

Andy Warhol's Campbell's Soup, *1962*

Warner, Charles Dudley, 1829–1900, American editor and author; b. Plainfield, Mass. Publisher of the Hartford *Courant* and editor of two major literary series, he collaborated with Mark TWAIN on the novel *The Gilded Age* (1873).

Warner, Seth, 1743–84, hero of the AMERICAN REVOLUTION; b. Roxbury, Conn. He was one of the leaders of the GREEN MOUNTAIN BOYS, and in 1775 he captured Crown Point, N.Y. He shared with John STARK the victory at Bennington in 1777.

Warner, William Lloyd, 1898–1970, U.S. social anthropologist. After studying the Australian aborigines, he applied the research methods of cultural anthropology to class structure and status in contemporary American society. His works include *A Black Civilization* (1937), *Social Class in America* (1949), and with others, the Yankee City series (1941–59).

War of 1812, armed conflict between the U.S. and Great Britain, 1812–15. It was partly occasioned by U.S. insistence on neutral shipping rights during the Franco-British hostilities of the FRENCH REVOLUTIONARY WARS and the wars of NAPOLEON I. British impressment of sailors and confiscation of U.S. ships were causes of strong anti-British sentiment. The outbreak of hostilities stemmed from clashes in the West between American frontiersmen and the British and their indigenous allies over American encroachment onto land claimed by the British. The battle of Tippecanoe (Nov. 7, 1811) was an outstanding example. The "war hawks" in the U.S. Congress prevailed, and war was declared on June 18, 1812. The early land confrontations—at Detroit, on the Niagara R., and in Queenston Heights—proved how ill-prepared the U.S. forces were. The small American navy fared better; the early victories of Isaac Hull, commanding the *Constitution,* and Stephen DECATUR were notable. In 1813, however, British naval superiority prevailed until the victory of Capt. Oliver Perry (see under PERRY, M.C.) on Lake Erie in September. The low point of the war for the U.S. was the British capture of Washington, D.C., in Aug. 1814. But the Americans were successful at the battle of the Thames, Plattsburgh, and FORT MCHENRY, and the British entered into serious negotiations to end the hostilities. The Treaty of GHENT (signed Dec. 24, 1814) brought the war to an indecisive end. But the Americans had a final triumph. On Jan. 14, 1815, after the treaty had been signed, Andrew JACKSON's troops defeated the British decisively at the battle of NEW ORLEANS. The war ushered in a period of great American nationalism and increasing isolation from European affairs.

Warren, Earl, 1891–1974, 14th chief justice of the U.S. SUPREME COURT (1953–69); b. Los Angeles; B.L., Univ. of California (1912). He was attorney general (1939–43) and governor (1943–53) of California, and an unsuccessful vice-presidential candidate in 1948. One of the most dynamic chief justices, Warren guided the Court in a number of landmark civil-rights and individual-liberties decisions. Most notable was BROWN V. BOARD OF EDUCATION (1954), in which public-school segregation was ruled unconstitutional (see INTEGRATION). While chief justice, Warren headed the commission that investigated the assassination of Pres. KENNEDY (see WARREN COMMISSION).

Warren, Mercy Otis, 1728–1814, American writer; b. Barnstable, Mass. A patriot, she wrote two satirical plays against the Tories, *The Adulateur* (1773) and *The Group* (1775), and later composed a history of the AMERICAN REVOLUTION (3 vol., 1805).

Warren, Robert Penn, 1905–89, American man of letters; b. Guthrie, Ky. One of the Southern agrarian poets associated with the *Fugitive* magazine (1922–25), he won early acclaim for verse that was influenced by the METAPHYSICAL POETS. His later poems were simpler and more regional. Volumes of his poetry include *Brother to Dragons* (1953), *Promises* (1957; Pulitzer), and *Now and Then* (1979; Pulitzer). Also an important novelist concerned with the moral dilemmas of the modern world, he wrote *All the King's Men* (1946; Pulitzer), about a political demagogue resembling Huey LONG; and *Wilderness* (1961). With Cleanth Brooks he compiled the textbooks *Understanding Poetry* (1938) and *Modern Rhetoric* (1949). In 1986 he was named the first official U.S. POET-LAUREATE.

Warren, city (1990 pop. 144,864), SE Mich., a suburb of DETROIT; est. 1837, inc. as a city 1957. It manufactures tools and dies, automobile parts, and processed steel. A General Motors technical center is located there, and the Detroit Arsenal makes military vehicles.

Warren Commission, official inquiry into the assassination of U.S.

Pres. John F. KENNEDY. Established by Pres. Lyndon JOHNSON on Nov. 29, 1963, it was headed by Chief Justice Earl WARREN. After holding exhaustive private hearings and conducting its own investigations, the commission issued its report on Sept. 24, 1964. It found no evidence of a conspiracy and concluded that Lee Harvey Oswald, acting alone, had killed Kennedy; it also found that Jack Ruby, the Dallas restaurant owner who shot and killed Oswald, had also acted alone. In ensuing years, the report was subjected to close examination and widespread criticism. In 1979 a congressional committee concluded, on the basis of acoustical evidence, that two people had shot at Kennedy, but that interpretation was later criticized as flawed. Sealed government files containing the evidence reviewed by the commission were opened to the public in 1993. The details of the assassination and the commission's report continue to spark often contentious debate.

Warsaw, city (1989 est. pop. 1,651,000), capital of Poland, central Poland, on both banks of the Vistula R. It is an industrial center with manufactures such as machinery, automobiles, and chemicals. Warsaw is one of Europe's great historic cities. Settled by the 11th cent., it became Poland's capital (1596); passed (1795) to Prussia; was the capital of the grand duchy of Warsaw (see POLAND); and later, under Russian rule, was the scene of nationalist uprisings (1830, 1863). In 1918 the city became the capital of the restored Polish state. During the German occupation (1939–45) in WORLD WAR II, a Jewish ghetto was isolated that contained (1942) c.500,000 persons; virtually all perished, either in CONCENTRATION CAMPS or after the armed Jewish uprising (Feb. 1943). In 1944 Polish nationalists tried unsuccessfully to oust the Germans while the Soviet army remained inactive across the Vistula. After 1945 large-scale reconstruction began that included the medieval Stare Miasto [old town], with its marketplace and 14th-cent. cathedral.

Warsaw Pact: see WARSAW TREATY ORGANIZATION.

Warsaw Treaty Organization or **Warsaw Pact,** former mutual defense alliance among Albania, Bulgaria, Czechoslovakia, East Germany, Hungary, Poland, Romania, and the USSR during the COLD WAR. Established in 1955, it was Communist Eastern Europe's equivalent of the NORTH ATLANTIC TREATY ORGANIZATION. Its unified command had headquarters in Moscow, and its forces were used to suppress democratic movements, e.g., in 1968 in Czechoslovakia. Albania withdrew in 1968, and East Germany ceased to be a member prior to German reunification (1990). The alliance was dissolved in 1991.

wart, circumscribed outgrowth of the skin caused by a virus, usually a papillomavirus. Warts may appear anywhere on the skin but are most common on the hands. The sexually transmitted HUMAN PAPILLOMAVIRUS produces warts in the genital area, certain types of which may develop into cancer. Some warts disappear spontaneously; others persist for many years.

Washington, Booker T(aliaferro), 1856–1915, African-American educator; b. Franklin co., Va. The son of a slave, he worked in salt furnaces and coal mines after the Civil War, until he entered the Hampton Institute (Va.). He became (1879) an instructor there and developed the night school. In 1881 he was chosen to organize a normal and industrial school for African Americans at Tuskegee, Ala., and under his direction Tuskegee Institute became one of the leading African-American educational institutions, emphasizing industrial training as a means to self-respect and economic independence. He was an able orator but drew opposition from many African-American leaders, including W.E.B. DU BOIS, for maintaining that it was pointless for African Americans to demand social equality before attaining economic independence. His many published works include his autobiography, *Up from Slavery* (1901).

Washington, George, 1732–99, 1st president of the U.S., commander in chief of the Continental Army in the AMERICAN REVOLUTION, called the "Father of his Country"; b. Feb. 22, 1732 (Feb. 11, 1731, O.S.), Westmoreland co., Va., into a wealthy family. He became a surveyor as a young man and was one of the principals of the OHIO COMPANY, whose purpose was the exploitation of Western lands. An officer in the militia, he fought in the last of the FRENCH AND INDIAN WARS and was named (1755) commander in chief of the Virginia militia with the rank of colonel. He resigned in 1759, married, and turned his attention to his plantation, MOUNT VERNON. He was a delegate (1774–75) to the CONTINENTAL CONGRESS, which named him commander of the Continental forces after the outbreak of hostilities with the British. He assumed command (July 3, 1775) in Cambridge, Mass., and succeeded in capturing Boston from the British (Mar. 17, 1776). Unable to defend New York City (see LONG ISLAND, BATTLE OF), he was forced to retreat successively to Westchester co., New Jersey, and Pennsylvania. He developed his military skill by trial and error as he went along. On Christmas night, 1776, with morale at its lowest ebb, he and his troops crossed the Delaware R. and defeated the British at Trenton and Princeton, N.J. Less successful in his attempts to defend Philadelphia at BRANDYWINE and Germantown, he spent the winter of 1777–78 at VALLEY FORGE in great misery and deprivation. But he emerged with increased powers from Congress and a well-trained, totally loyal army. After the battle of MONMOUTH (June 28, 1778), his fortunes improved and subsequent victories preceded the surrender of Gen. Cornwallis on Oct. 19, 1781 (see YORKTOWN CAMPAIGN). Washington retired to Mount Vernon, but his dissatisfaction with the new government (see CONFEDERATION, ARTICLES OF) led him back into public life. He presided over the second FEDERAL CONSTITUTIONAL CONVENTION (1787), where his prestige and reputation were incalculable in the adoption of the CONSTITUTION OF THE UNITED STATES. He was chosen unanimously as the first president and took office on Apr. 30, 1789. His efforts to remain aloof from partisan politics were unsuccessful, and the influence of Alexander HAMILTON moved him increasingly toward conservatism. His second term, openly Federalist, was bitterly criticized by the Jeffersonians. Sickened by the partisan struggles, he refused a third term and retired for the last time to Mount Vernon in 1797. He died two years later, universally regarded as the one without whom the American Revolution and the new republic could not have succeeded. His wife, **Martha Washington,** 1731–1802, was born Martha Dandridge in New Kent co., Va. Her first husband, by whom she had two children, was Daniel Parke Custis, who died in 1757, leaving her one of the wealthiest women in Virginia. She and Washington had no children.

Washington, one of the U.S. states of the Pacific Northwest; bordered by Idaho (E), Oregon (S), the Pacific Ocean (W), and the Canadian province of British Columbia (N).

Area, 68,192 sq mi (176,617 sq km). *Pop.* (1990) 4,866,692, an 17.8% increase over 1980 pop. *Capital,* Olympia. *Statehood,* Nov. 11, 1889 (42d state). *Highest pt.,* Mt. Rainier, 14,410 ft (4,395 m); *lowest pt.,* sea level. *Nickname,* Evergreen State. *Motto, Alki* [By and By]. *State bird,* willow goldfinch. *State flower,* Western rhododendron. *State tree,* Western hemlock. *Abbr.,* Wash., WA.

Land and People. PUGET SOUND, in the northwest, separates the bulk of the state from the Olympic Peninsula, which receives the highest average rainfall of any region in the U.S. Farther inland, the CASCADE RANGE runs north to south across the state, and east of it the land is largely dry. Temperatures are generally moderate. One of the peaks in the Cascades, Mount SAINT HELENS, an active volcano, erupted in a violent, destructive explosion in 1980. The ROCKY MOUNTAINS traverse the northwest, and the COLUMBIA PLATEAU is located in the south. The principal river is the COLUMBIA, one of the world's greatest sources of hydroelectric power. Over 76% of the population lives in urban areas. SEATTLE is the largest city, followed by SPOKANE and TACOMA. In 1990 the state was over 88% white, with the minority population about equally divided among African Americans, Asian Americans, and Hispanics.

Economy. Washington is the country's leading manufacturer of jet aircraft and also produces missiles and spacecraft. Other leading industries are lumbering; the production of pulp and paper, chemicals, and primary metals; and the processing of agricultural goods. The major farm products are cattle, dairy commodities, hops, spearmint oil, wine grapes, wheat, raspberries, and apples (Washington is the leading U.S. producer). The state's chief minerals are sand and gravel, cement, stone, and diatomite. Fishing, especially for salmon, is important. Tourists are attracted year-round to such scenic areas as Olympic, North Cascades, and Mt. Rainier national parks (see NATIONAL PARKS, table) and the Coulee Dam National Recreation Area.

Government. According to the constitution of 1889, the governor is elected to a four-year term. The legislature consists of a senate with 49 members serving four-year terms and a house of 98 members elected for two years. Washington is represented in the U.S. Congress by two senators and nine representatives and has 11 electoral votes.

History. Washington was the home of the Chinook, NEZ PERCÉ, Yakima, and other tribes when Capt. James COOK explored (1778) the area and the British explorer George VANCOUVER sailed (1792) into Puget Sound. Britain and the United States subsequently contested the region, and "Fifty-four forty or fight"—referring to a proposed U.S. northern boundary set at lat. 54°40′N—became a slogan of the 1844 presidential campaign; war was finally averted by setting the boundary at lat. 49°N in 1846. The first great influx of settlers came in the 1880s, when rail transport became possible. During the early 20th cent. Washington was a center of radical labor activity, including that of the INDUSTRIAL WORKERS OF THE WORLD, which often resulted in violent strikes. Aircraft manufacturing boomed during World War II and has continued to provide the state's industrial base. In addition, Washington has recently attracted many firms moving from California.

Washington, D.C., capital of the U.S. (1990 pop. 606,900; met. area 3,923,574), coextensive with the District of Columbia, on the Potomac R.; inc. 1802. The legislative, administrative, and judicial center of the U.S., it has little industry; federal employees dominate the labor force. The city is a center of business and finance, and houses many professional and trade associations. It is also a major tourist attraction. Its location (1790) was a compromise between northern and southern interests. George WASHINGTON selected the exact site, and the "Federal City" was designed by L'ENFANT. Congress first met there in 1800. The British sacked the city during the WAR OF 1812. It developed slowly, assuming its present gracious aspect, with wide avenues and many parks, only in the 20th cent. Its many imposing government buildings are built of white or gray stone in the classical style. The CAPITOL, WHITE HOUSE, Supreme Court Building, National Archives, Constitution Hall, and Library of Congress (see LIBRARY, table) are well known. Ford's Theater, where Pres. LINCOLN was shot, is a museum. Best known of the city's monuments are the WASHINGTON MONUMENT, LINCOLN MEMORIAL, JEFFERSON MEMORIAL, and VIETNAM VETERANS MEMORIAL. Its academic institutions include American Univ., the Catholic Univ. of America, Georgetown Univ., George Washington Univ., and Howard Univ. Cultural attractions include the NATIONAL GALLERY OF ART, the SMITHSONIAN INSTITUTION, and the John F. Kennedy Center for the Performing Arts. The Walter Reed Army Medical Center is one of many medical and research facilities. The city's downtown area has undergone substantial urban redevelopment. Washington has through its history been a focus of national political activity, e.g., the Bonus Marchers of 1932 and civil-rights and antiwar demonstrations of the 1960s and 70s. For the city's political status, see DISTRICT OF COLUMBIA.

Washington, Treaty of, May 1871, between the U.S. and Great Britain. It settled the ALABAMA CLAIMS, which had arisen during the U.S. CIVIL WAR, and provided for arbitration of Canadian-American boundary and fisheries disputes.

Washington Monument, white marble obelisk in Washington, D.C., honoring George WASHINGTON. Completed in 1884 and opened to the public in 1888, it is 555 ft 5⅛ in. (169.3 m) high.

wasp, winged INSECT of the same order (Hymenoptera) as the ANT and BEE. Wasps have biting mouthparts and a thin stalk attaching the thorax to the abdomen ("wasp waist"); females have a sting, which they can use repeatedly, for paralyzing prey. Most species are solitary, but paper wasps, hornets, and yellow jackets are social. Social wasps usually are divided into three castes: egg-laying queens, workers (sexually undeveloped females), and drones (males). They build papery nests consisting of either a single comb (paper wasps) or a large group of combs inside a papery sheath (hornets and yellow jackets). The nest may be underground. In all solitary wasps the female seals a single egg in a nest with paralyzed prey for food; potter, or mason, wasps and mud-dauber wasps are solitary wasps that build nests of mud.

Wassermann, August von, 1866–1925, German physician and bacteriologist. He directed experimental therapy and serum research (1906–13) at the Koch Inst. and experimental therapy (from 1913) at the Kaiser Wilhelm Inst. He developed inoculations against cholera, typhoid, and tetanus, and devised (1906) the **Wassermann test** for diagnosing syphilis. Positive reaction when blood or spinal fluid is tested indicates the presence of antibodies formed as a result of syphilis infection.

waste disposal, generally, the disposal of waste products resulting from human activity. Once a routine concern, the disposal of waste has become a pressing problem in the 20th cent. because of the growth of population and industry and the toxicity of many new industrial byproducts. Traditionally, waste was often dumped into nearby streams. Sewer systems, which date back at least to the 6th cent. B.C. in Rome, were widely introduced in U.S. cities in the mid-19th cent. In the absence of sewerage, waste has often been stored in underground cesspools, which leach liquids into the soil but retain solids, or in simple sewage tanks, e.g., septic tanks, in which organic matter disintegrates. Raw sewage is now commonly treated before being discharged as effluent, usually by reducing solid components to a semiliquid sludge. Although sludge can be processed, e.g., as fertilizer, it has often been buried or dumped at sea, a practice outlawed in the U.S. since 1992. Some recent systems have employed artificial wetlands to treat waste water. Most *solid waste* in the U.S., such as municipal refuse, is deposited in open dumps. More sophisticated methods of disposal include the sanitary landfill, where waste is spread thin and separated by layers of tamped earth, and special incinerators that burn combustible waste while generating steam (for heating) and/or gases (to run turbines). The recycling of noncombustible products such as glass and metals, e.g., aluminum cans, is growing and offers long-range hope for disposal. *Toxic wastes* include many chemicals, some generated in substantial quantities as common industrial byproducts, e.g., heavy metals (notably mercury, lead, and cadmium), certain hydrocarbons, and some poisonous organic solvents. Although detoxification using bacteria, irradiation, and chemical systems is now being performed with more frequency, such substances have traditionally been sealed in metal drums and deposited underground or in the ocean. The containers have often corroded and leaked their contents, polluting the land and water supply (see POLLUTION) and prompting the U.S. Congress to pass the 1980 "Superfund" act, which assigned broad financial responsibility for toxic waste cleanup. One of the greatest modern hazards is *radioactive waste,* produced in increasing amounts as byproducts of research, nuclear weaponry, and nuclear-power generation and particularly dangerous because many kinds remain lethal for thousands of years. In the U.S., these materials are now stored in temporary sites; permanent storage solutions have encountered many technical difficulties and public objections to specific sites. A process to solidify nuclear waste and reduce its potential danger as a contaminant is one option. Highly radioactive waste is expected to be stored permanently underground at Yucca Mt., Nev., but the site will not be ready until 2010. See also ECOLOGY; ENVIRONMENTALISM.

Watauga Association, government (1772–75) of settlers along the Watauga R., E Tenn. It joined NORTH CAROLINA in 1775, tried to form another independent state (see FRANKLIN, STATE OF) in 1784, and became part of TENNESSEE in 1796.

water, odorless, tasteless, transparent liquid that is colorless in small amounts but exhibits a bluish tinge in large quantities. It is the most abundant liquid on earth. In solid form (ice) and liquid form it covers about 70% of the earth's surface. Chemically, water is a compound of hydrogen and oxygen whose formula is H_2O. The two H—O bonds form an angle of about 105°—an arrangement that results in a polar molecule, because there is a net negative charge toward the oxygen end (the apex) of the V-shaped molecule and a net positive charge at the hydrogen ends. Consequently, each oxygen atom is able to attract two nearby hydrogen atoms of two other water molecules. These hydrogen bondings keep water liquid at ordinary temperatures. Because water is a polar compound, it is a good solvent. Because of the hydrogen bondings between molecules, the latent heats of fusion and of evaporation and the HEAT CAPACITY of water are all unusually high. For these reasons water serves both as a heat-transfer medium (e.g., ice for cooling and steam for heating) and as a temperature regulator (the water in lakes and oceans helps regulate the climate). Water is chemically active, reacting with certain metals and metal oxides to form bases, and with certain oxides of nonmetals to form acids.

Although completely pure water is a poor conductor of electricity, it is a much better conductor than most pure liquids because of its self-ionization, i.e., the ability of two water molecules to react to form a hydroxyl ion (OH^-) and a hydronium ion (H_3O^+).

water buffalo: see BUFFALO.

water bug, air-breathing aquatic BUG, with a sharp sucking beak. Waterbugs are usually found on or below the surface of quiet streams and ponds. Giant water bugs are the largest bugs and among the largest insects; one South American form attains a length of over 4 in. (10 cm). Other water bugs include the water boatmen, backswimmers, water scorpions, and water striders.

Waterbury, city (1990 pop. 108,961), W Conn., on the Naugatuck R.; settled 1674, inc. 1853. Its brass industry began in the 18th cent.; clocks and watches, tools, precision instruments, and plastics are important industries.

water chestnut: see SEDGE.

watercolor painting, in its wider sense, all pigments mixed with water rather than oil, including FRESCO and TEMPERA as well as aquarelle (the process now commonly called watercolor). Gouache and distemper are also watercolors, but prepared with gluey bases. The earliest existing paintings, found in Egypt, are watercolors. Gouache was used by Byzantine and Romanesque artists, and the illuminated manuscripts of the Middle Ages were produced with watercolor. The medium was used during and after the RENAISSANCE by DÜRER, REMBRANDT, VAN DYCK, and others to tint and shade drawings and woodcuts. In the 18th cent. the modern aquarelle grew into a complete painting technique. Quick and easy to apply, the aquarelle's colors are at once brilliant, transparent, and delicate. The medium was popular in England, where its masters were CONSTABLE and J.M.W. TURNER. Many 19th-cent. painters used watercolor extensively, largely for landscapes. In France they included DAUMIER, DELACROIX, and GÉRICAULT, and later, CÉZANNE and DUFY. Among notable American watercolorists are J.S. SARGENT, Winslow HOMER, PRENDERGAST, MARIN, and SHEELER.

watercress, hardy perennial European herb (*Nasturtium officinale*) of the MUSTARD family, widely naturalized in North America, found in or around water. It is cultivated commercially for its small, pungent leaflets, used as a peppery salad green or garnish. The ornamental plant whose common name is NASTURTIUM is unrelated.

waterfall, sudden drop in a stream formed where it passes over a layer of harder rock to an area of softer, more easily eroded rock. As a stream grows older, the waterfall, by undercutting and erosion, normally moves upstream and loses height until it becomes a series of rapids and finally disappears. Because of the waterpower that waterfalls can provide, many cities are located near them. Notable examples are NIAGARA FALLS and VICTORIA FALLS.

water gas, colorless, poisonous gas that burns with an intensely hot, bluish flame. It is mainly a mixture of carbon monoxide and hydrogen and is almost entirely combustible. The gas is made by treating white-hot, hard coal or coke with a blast of steam, forming carbon monoxide and hydrogen. It is important in the preparation of hydrogen, as a fuel in the making of steel, and in other industrial processes, e.g., the FISCHER-TROPSCH PROCESS.

Watergate affair, in U.S. history, series of scandals involving Pres. Richard NIXON. In July 1972 agents of Nixon's reelection committee were arrested in Democratic party headquarters, in the Watergate apartment building in Washington, D.C., after an attempt to tap telephones there. They were tried and convicted in 1973, but District Court Judge John Sirica suspected a high-echelon conspiracy, and when one of the convicted burglars, James McCord, wrote a letter to Sirica charging a massive cover-up, the affair erupted into a national scandal. A special Senate committee, headed by Sen. Sam ERVIN, held televised hearings (1973) in which John Dean, the former White House counsel, stated that members of the Nixon administration, notably Attorney General John MITCHELL, had known of the Watergate burglary. The hearings also revealed that Nixon had taped conversations in the Oval Office, and when the special prosecutor appointed to investigate the affair, Archibald Cox, requested these tapes, Nixon fired him. Cox had begun to uncover widespread evidence of political espionage by the Nixon reelection committee, illegal wiretapping of citizens by the administration, and corporate contributions to the Republican party in return for political favors. His successor as special prosecutor, Leon Jaworski, succeeded in getting the tapes and subsequently obtained indictments and convictions of several high-ranking administration officials, including Mitchell and Dean. Public confidence in the president waned. In July 1974 the House Judiciary Committee adopted three articles of impeachment against him, the first for obstruction of justice. On Aug. 9, 1974, Nixon became the first U.S. president to resign from office. One month later his successor, Gerald FORD, pardoned him.

water lily, common name for some members of the family Nymphaeaceae, freshwater perennials found throughout most of the world. Often having large shield-shaped leaves and showy blossoms of various colors, the family includes water lilies, lotuses, and pond lilies (genera *Nymphaea, Nelumbo,* and *Nuphar,* respectively). Well-known species include the blue or white Egyptian lotus of the genus *Nymphaea,* the national emblem of Egypt, and the Indian lotus of the genus *Nelumbo,* sacred to several Asian religions. Many members of the family have edible seeds or TUBERS.

Waterloo campaign, June 1815, last action of the Napoleonic Wars, ending with the battle of Waterloo (June 18), fought near Brussels, Belgium. NAPOLEON I, returned from exile, faced the allied armies of Britain, Prussia, Austria, and Russia. He defeated a Prussian force at Ligny, then turned his attention to the British, under WELLINGTON. The British took up a strong position S of Waterloo; resisted successfully; and, after being joined by BLÜCHER's Prussian forces, routed the French. Napoleon abdicated on June 22. Wellington's victory was a triumph, but the campaign itself was marked by confusion and miscalculation on both sides.

watermelon, plant (*Citrullis vulgaris*) of the GOURD family, native to Africa. The fleshy, juicy fruit, which can be red to pink, yellow, or white, is eaten fresh; the rind is pickled; and the seeds are also eaten. One white-fleshed variety, the citron melon, is used like citron in preserving. There are also hybrid seedless varieties.

water moccasin or **cottonmouth,** venomous SNAKE (*Ancistrodon piscivorus*) of the swamps and bayous of the S U.S. A PIT VIPER, it has a heat-sensitive organ for detecting warm-blooded prey. The average length is 3 to 4 ft (90 to 120 cm). If startled it raises its head and shows the white interior of its mouth—hence the name *cottonmouth.*

water pollution: see POLLUTION.

water polo, swimming game played in a pool by teams of seven players each, including a goalie. The object is to maneuver—by head, feet, or one hand—a large leather ball into net-enclosed goals at opposite ends of the pool. Rough defensive techniques are permitted, including ducking (holding a player under water). The game, played by club and college teams, was developed in England in the 1870s and later became popular in the U.S. It has been an Olympic event since 1900.

waters, territorial: see SEA, LAW OF THE.

watershed, elevation or divide separating the CATCHMENT AREA, or drainage basin, of one river system from another. The Rocky Mts. and the Andes form a watershed between westward-flowing and eastward-flowing streams. The term is also often synonymous with drainage basin.

water skiing, sport of riding on skis along the water's surface while being towed by a motorboat. Competitive water skiing consists of the slalom, in which skiers maneuver around a series of buoys; jumping, from an inclined ramp 6 ft (1.8 m) high; and trick riding, involving intricate routines. The sport probably originated on the French Riviera in the early 1920s.

waterspout: see TORNADO.

water table, the top zone of soil and rock that is saturated with water. Its level varies with topography and rainfall. Natural springs are formed when the water table meets the ground's surface, and water wells operate by penetrating into the water table.

water wheel, ancient device for utilizing the power of flowing or falling water. The oldest known wheel, probably first used in the Middle East, was essentially a grindstone mounted atop a vertical shaft whose vaned or paddled lower end dipped into a swift stream. In the 1st cent. B.C. a horizontal shaft came into use; the wheel attached to it had radial vanes around its edge. Today the water wheel has been largely replaced by the TURBINE.

Watson, James Dewey, 1928–, American biologist and educator; b. Chicago. For their work in establishing the molecular structure of

DNA, he and Francis CRICK shared the 1962 Nobel Prize in physiology or medicine with Maurice Wilkins. Watson's *Double Helix* (1968) is an account of their work. He was head of the U.S. human genome research program from 1989 to 1992.

Watson, John Broadus, 1878–1958, American psychologist; b. Greenville, S.C. He originated the school of psychology called BEHAVIORISM, in which behavior is described in terms of physiological responses to stimuli; the concept of conscious or unconscious mental activity is rejected. His best-known books are *Psychology from the Standpoint of a Behaviorist* (1919) and *Behaviorism* (1925).

Watson, Thomas John, 1874–1956, American industrialist and philanthropist; b. Campbell, N.Y. After rising from clerk to sales executive in the National Cash Register Co., he became (1914) president of the Computing-Tabulating-Recording Co., renamed International Business Machines Corp. (IBM) in 1924. He became chairman in 1949. Pushed by his son (see below), he widened IBM's line in the 1950s to include electronic COMPUTERS, and at his death IBM had assets of over $600 million and a world market of 82 countries. His son, **Thomas John Watson, Jr.,** 1914–93, b. Dayton, Ohio, was president of IBM (1952–61), chairman (1961–71), and chairman of the executive board (1972–79). He early recognized the importance of computers and maintained IBM's dominance in that and other advanced technologies. He was (1979–81) U.S. ambassador to the USSR.

Watson, Tom (Thomas Sturges Watson), 1949–, American golfer; b. Kansas City, Mo. Considered the successor to Jack NICKLAUS as the game's foremost player during the late 1970s and early 80s, Watson won the British Open in 1975, 1977, 1980, and 1982–83, the Masters in 1977 and 1981, and the U.S. Open in 1982.

Watt, James, 1736–1819, Scottish inventor. Repairing a Newcomen STEAM ENGINE, he devised improvements that resulted in a new type of engine (patented 1769) with a separate condensing chamber, an air pump to bring steam into the chamber, and insulated engine parts. He also perfected a rotary engine. Watt coined the term *horsepower*.

watt: see POWER.

Watteau, Jean-Antoine [wätō], 1684–1721, French painter of Flemish descent. He studied (1704–8) in the studio of Claude Gillot, a painter of theatrical life, which later became the subject of some of Watteau's finest paintings, e.g., *Love in the French Theatre* (Berlin). One of the great colorists of all time, Watteau executed gay and sensuous scenes in shimmering pastel tones, influencing fashion and garden design in the 18th cent. *The Embarkation for Cythera* (1717; Louvre) is a characteristic work.

Watts Towers, group of towers built (1921–54) by Simon Rodilla (or Rodia), 1879–1965, in Watts, Los Angeles. Unique, fanciful structures reminiscent of GAUDÍ's work, they incorporate stone, steel, cement, and discarded elements, e.g., bottle caps.

Watutsi: see TUTSI.

Waugh, Evelyn (Arthur St. John), 1903–66, English novelist. The foremost social satirist of his generation, he gained fame with *Decline and Fall* (1928) and *Vile Bodies* (1930). In *Black Mischief* (1932) and *Scoop* (1938), he satirized Ethiopia; and in *The Loved One* (1948), Hollywood mortuary customs. A conservative moralist, he is best known for *Brideshead Revisited* (1945), about the spiritual regeneration of an aristocratic Catholic family. Equally serious is his World War II trilogy (1952–61).

wave, in physics, the transfer of ENERGY by some form of regular vibration, or oscillatory motion, either of some material medium (see SOUND) or by the variation of intensity of the field vectors of an electromagnetic field (see ELECTROMAGNETIC RADIATION). In longitudinal, or compressional, waves the vibration is in the same direction as the transfer of energy; in transverse waves the vibration is at right angles to the transfer of energy. The amplitude of a wave is its maximum displacement. The distance between successive crests or successive troughs is the wavelength $\lambda$of a wave. One full wavelength of a wave represents one complete cycle, that is, one complete vibration in each direction. All waves are referenced to an imaginary synchronous motion in a circle; thus one complete cycle is divided into 360 degrees. The phase is that part of the cycle, expressed in degrees, that is completed at a certain time. The various phase relationships (see diagram) between combining waves determine the type of interference that takes place. The frequency ν of a wave is equal to the number of crests (or troughs) that pass a given fixed point per unit of time. The period T of a wave is the time lapse between the passage of successive crests (or troughs). The speed υ of a wave is determined by its wavelength and its frequency according to the equation $\upsilon = \lambda\nu$. Because the frequency is inversely related to the period T, this equation also takes the form $\upsilon = \lambda/T$.

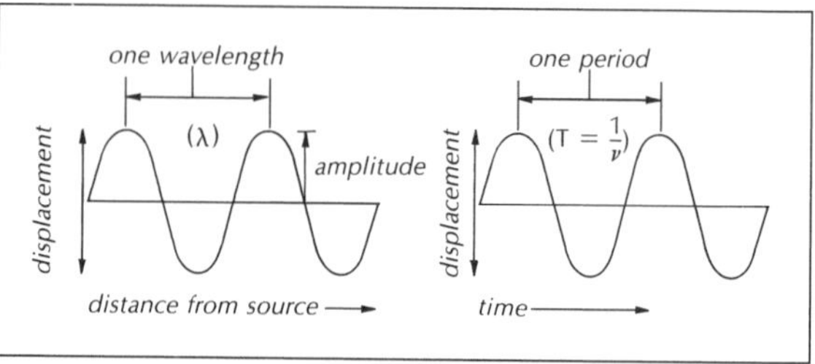

Wave diagrams showing the displacement of a wave plotted against distance from source and atainst time. A wave travels one wavelength during one period.

Wavell, Archibald Percival Wavell, 1st **Earl,** 1883–1950, British field marshal and viceroy of India (1943–47). In WORLD WAR II he routed (1940–41) Italian forces in N Africa, but was forced back by the Germans. He then held command in India. As viceroy, he tried to prepare India for self-rule.

wax, substance secreted by glands on the abdomen of the bee and known commonly as beeswax; also various substances resembling beeswax. Chemically, waxes are complex mixtures of esters, fatty acids, free alcohols, and higher hydrocarbons. They are usually harder and less greasy than fats, but like fats they are less dense than water and insoluble in it. Waxes can be obtained from plants (e.g., carnauba wax from palm leaves) or animals (e.g., lanolin from wool fibers and spermaceti from sperm whales). PARAFFIN and ozocerite are mineral waxes composed of hydrocarbons. Japan wax and Bayberry wax are composed chiefly of fats.

wax painting: see ENCAUSTIC.

waxwing, any of three species (genus *Bombycilla*) of perching songbirds of the Northern Hemisphere. Waxwings have crests (raised only in alarm) and brownish-gray plumage with flecks of red pigment resembling sealing wax on the wings. The species are the cedar waxwing; the Bohemian, or greater, waxwing; and the Japanese waxwing, found only in NE Asia.

Wayne, Anthony, 1745–96, American general; b. Chester co., Pa. He is most famous for the capture (1779) of Stony Point, N.Y., during the AMERICAN REVOLUTION. After the war, he fought in the INDIAN WARS in the West and won a notable victory at the battle of Fallen Timbers (1794). He was known as "mad Anthony Wayne."

Wayne, John, 1906–79, American film actor; b. Winterset, Iowa, as Marion Michael Morrison. Extremely popular, he often played tough heroes. His films include *Stagecoach* (1939), *The Quiet Man* (1952), and *True Grit* (1969; Academy Award).

weak interaction or **weak nuclear force,** force that is associated with radioactivity and particle decay and is mediated, or carried, by the W AND Z PARTICLES. The weak interaction is one of four fundamental forces of nature; the others are GRAVITATION, electromagnetism, and STRONG INTERACTION.

weasel, small, lithe, carnivorous MAMMAL of the family Mustelidae, which also includes the MINK, FERRET, WOLVERINE, SKUNK, BADGER, and OTTER. All members of the family have scent glands, used chiefly for territorial marking but sometimes for defense. Found in Eurasia, N Africa, and the Americas, weasels are characterized by long bodies and necks, short legs, small ears, and dense, lustrous fur (usually brown with white underparts). They hunt small animals at night, often killing more than they can eat.

weather, state of the atmosphere at a given time and place with regard to temperature, air pressure, humidity, wind, cloudiness, and precipitation. The term *weather* is restricted to conditions over short periods of time; conditions over long periods are referred to as climate. The study of weather and its forecasting is called METEOROLOGY.

weather balloon, BALLOON, usually helium-inflated, used in the measurement and evaluation of atmospheric conditions. Atmospheric-pressure and other meteorological information may be sent by radio from the balloon (see RADIOSONDE); monitoring of its movement (see THEODOLITE) provides information about winds at its flight level.

weathering, term for the processes by which ROCK at the surface of the earth is disintegrated and decomposed by the action of atmospheric agents, water, and living things. Some of the processes are mechanical, e.g., the impact of running water. Others are chemical, e.g., oxidation, hydration, or carbonization. Weathering aids in the formation of soil and prepares materials for EROSION.

weather satellite, artificial SATELLITE used to gather data on a global basis for improvement of weather forecasting. Information is provided about cloud cover, storm location, temperature, and heat balance in the earth's atmosphere. Satellite instruments may also be used to locate sea- and aircraft and track the movement of marine life and pollution. The first experimental weather satellite was *Tiros 1,* launched by the U.S. in 1960. The U.S. National Operational Meterological System consists of both polar-orbiting and geostationary satellites. The U.S. Dept. of Defense also operates sun-synchronous polar-orbiting satellites that provide global meteorological data for military purposes. Russia, India, Japan, and the European Space Agency also operate weather satellites.

Weaver, James Baird, 1833–1912, American politician; b. Dayton, Ohio. He was a U.S. representative from Iowa (1879–81, 1885–89). A free-silver advocate, he was the presidential candidate of the GREENBACK PARTY in 1880 and of the POPULIST PARTY in 1892.

Weaver, Robert Clifton, 1907–, U.S. secretary of housing and urban development (1966–68); b. Washington, D.C. Pres. Lyndon B. JOHNSON named him to head the newly created housing department in 1966, making Weaver the first African American to serve in a presidential cabinet.

Webb, Beatrice Potter, 1858–1943, English socialist economist. In 1892 she married **Sidney James Webb,** 1859–1947, and they worked together as leaders of the FABIAN SOCIETY, in the building of the LABOUR PARTY, and in the creation (1895) of the London School of Economics. In 1913 they founded the *New Statesman.* Sidney Webb was elected to Parliament in 1922 and became Baron Passfield in 1929. Co-authors of *The History of Trade Unionism* (1894), *Industrial Democracy* (1897), *Soviet Communism* (2 vol., 1935), and other works, the Webbs made major contributions to most of the political and social reforms of their time.

Webb, Philip Speakman, 1831–1915, English architect. He was influential in the mid-19th-cent. revival of residential architecture based on Queen Anne and GEORGIAN STYLES. A friend and supporter of William MORRIS, he built for him (1859) the Red House, Bexley Heath, and collaborated with him afterwards. He also designed furniture, tiles, and stained glass.

Webb, Sidney James: see under WEBB, BEATRICE POTTER.

Webber, Andrew Lloyd: see LLOYD WEBBER, ANDREW.

Weber, Carl Maria Friedrich Ernst von [fən vā'bər], 1786–1826, German composer. Considered the founder of German romantic OPERA, he wrote 10 operas, including *Der Freischütz* [the marksman] (1821) and *Oberon* (1826). Among his instrumental works is the popular *Invitation to the Dance* (1819).

Weber, Max, 1864–1920, German sociologist and political economist who greatly influenced sociological theory. His concept of "ideal types," or generalized models of real situations, provided a basis for comparing societies. Opposing the Marxian view of the preeminence of economic causation, he emphasized the role of religious values, ideologies, and charismatic leaders in shaping societies. His famous *Protestant Ethic and the Spirit of Capitalism* (1904–5) related Calvinist ideals to the rise of capitalism.

Weber, Max, 1881–1961, American painter; b. Russia; emigrated to the U.S. at age 10. His early work was influenced by CUBISM, e.g., *Chinese Restaurant* (Whitney Mus., N.Y.C.). He explored Jewish subject matter, beginning c.1917, and in the 1930s he handled social themes. Energetic in line, Weber's later paintings were increasingly abstract.

Webern, Anton von [fən vā'bərn], 1883–1945, Austrian composer. A pupil of Arnold SCHOENBERG, he wrote TWELVE-TONE MUSIC. His music is characterized by unusual combinations of instruments, a broken melodic line, and extreme brevity. Written mainly for small orchestral groups or voice, his compositions include *Six Bagatelles* (1913) and *Variations* (1940).

Webster, Daniel, 1782–1852, American politician; b. Salisbury (now in Franklin), N.H. A lawyer famous for his oratory, Webster won national recognition in the Dartmouth College case and MCCULLOCH V. MARYLAND (both 1819). A Federalist, he represented New Hampshire in the House of Representatives (1813–17). After moving to Boston, he again served in the House (1823–27) and was senator from Massachusetts (1827–41, 1845–50). A leader in the new WHIG PARTY, he was the presidential candidate of one of its factions in 1836. As secretary of state (1841–43) under Pres. W.H. HARRISON, he was responsible for the WEBSTER-ASHBURTON TREATY. Reelected to the Senate, he placed the union above all other issues, and his support of the COMPROMISE OF 1850 greatly diminished his political influence. He was again secretary of state (1850–52) in Pres. Millard FILLMORE's administration.

Webster, John, 1580?–1634, English dramatist. His reputation rests on two tragedies, *The White Devil* (c.1608) and *The Duchess of Malfi* (c.1614), somber revenge dramas that reveal a profound understanding of human suffering.

Webster, Margaret, 1905–72, American actress, producer, and director; b. N.Y.C. With Eva LE GALLIENNE she founded (1946) and managed the American Repertory Theatre. From 1948 to 1951 she directed the Margaret Webster Shakespeare Company.

Webster, Noah, 1758–1843, American lexicographer and philologist; b. West Hartford, Conn. A graduate of Yale, he fought in the American Revolution and then practiced law in Hartford. His *Grammatical Institute of the English Language,* in three parts—speller, grammar, and reader (1783–85)—was the first of the books that made him for many years the chief American authority on English. The first part, the *Elementary Spelling Book,* helped standardize American spelling. It was a basic text in schools, and frontier children learned to read from it. By 1850, when the population was under 23 million, about 1 million copies of the book were sold annually. Webster's efforts contributed to passage of a national copyright law (1790). A Federalist, he proposed the adoption of a constitution in *Sketches of American Policy* (1785). In 1793 he began the *American Minerva* newspaper in New York City. Later he was among the first trustees of Amherst College. His *Compendious Dictionary* (1806) was followed by his greatest work, *The American Dictionary of the English Language* (1812); 12,000 of its 70,000 words had not appeared in such a work before. He completed the 1840 revision; through many revisions since then the dictionary has retained its popularity.

Webster-Ashburton Treaty, 1842, between the U.S., represented by Secy. of State Daniel WEBSTER, and Great Britain, represented by Lord Ashburton. It settled various boundary disputes between Canada and the U.S., including those in the Northeast that had led to the AROOSTOOK WAR and others in the GREAT LAKES area, and served as an important precedent for future peaceful settlements of disputes between Canada and the U.S.

Weddell Sea, arm of the Atlantic Ocean, bordered by the Antarctic Peninsula and Coats Land; named for James Weddell, who claimed to have discovered it in 1823. The vast Ronne and Filchner ice shelves are at the head of the sea.

Wedekind, Frank [vā'dəkĭnt], 1864–1918, German dramatist. A forerunner of EXPRESSIONISM, he stressed man's primal instincts, as in *The Awakening of Spring* (1909). His plays *Earth Spirit* (1895) and *Pandora's Box* (1903) were the source for the libretto of Alban BERG's opera *Lulu.*

Wedgwood, Josiah, 1730–95, English potter. He built a factory and model village near Stoke-on-Trent in 1769, eventually transforming pottery from a minor industry to one of great importance. He developed a cream-colored earthenware, a veined ware resembling granite, and a black ware called Egyptian stoneware. For his jasper ware, in blue or other colors with white Greek figures in cameolike relief, he used designs by artists such as John FLAXMAN. Wedgwood also helped improve roads, schools, and living conditions for his workers.

Wednesday: see WEEK.

COMMON WEIGHTS AND MEASURES

American and British units	*Metric system*	*Conversion factors*
LENGTH		
1 inch (in.) = 1/36 yard = 1/12 foot 1 foot (ft) = ⅓ yard 1 yard (yd; basic unit of length) 1 rod (rd) = 5½ yards 1 furlong (fur.) = 220 yards = ⅛ mile 1 mile (mi) = 1,760 yards = 5,280 feet 1 fathom (fath) = 6 feet 1 nautical mile = 6,076.1 feet	1 millimeter (mm) = 1/1,000 meter 1 centimeter (cm) = 1/100 meter 1 decimeter (dm) = 1/10 meter 1 meter (m; basic unit of length) 1 dekameter (dkm) = 10 meters 1 kilometer (km) = 1,000 meters	1 inch = 2.54 centimeters 1 foot = 0.305 meter 1 yard = 0.914 meter 1 mile = 1.609 kilometers 1 nautical mile = 1.852 kilometers 1 centimeter = 0.39 inch 1 meter = 39.37 inches = 3.28 feet = 1.094 yards 1 kilometer = 0.62 mile
AREA		
American and British units	*Metric System*	*Conversion factors*
1 square inch (sq in.) = 1/1,296 square yard = 1/144 square foot 1 square foot (sq ft) = 1/9 square yard = 144 square inches 1 square yard (sq yd; basic unit of area) = 9 square feet 1 square rod (sq rd) = 30¼ square yards 1 acre = 4,840 square yards = 160 square rods 1 square mile (sq mi) = 3,097,600 square yards = 640 acres	1 square centimeter (sq cm) = 1/10,000 square meter 1 square decimeter (sq dm) = 1/100 square meter 1 square meter (sq m; basic unit of area) 1 are (a) = 100 square meters 1 hectare (ha) = 10,000 square meters = 100 ares 1 square kilometer (sq km) = 1,000,000 square meters	1 square inch = 6.45 square centimeters 1 square foot = 0.093 square meter 1 square yard = 0.84 square meter 1 acre = 0.405 hectare 1 square mile = 2.59 square kilometers 1 square centimeter = 0.155 square inch 1 square meter = 1.2 square yards = 10.8 square feet 1 hectare = 2.47 acres 1 square kilometer = 0.386 square mile
VOLUME AND CAPACITY *(liquid and dry)*		
American and British units	*Metric system*	*Conversion factors*
1 cubic inch (cu in.) = 1/46,656 cubic yard = 1/1,728 cubic foot 1 cubic foot (cu ft) = 1/27 cubic yard = 1,728 cubic inches 1 cubic yard (cu yd; basic unit of volume) = 27 cubic feet 1 U.S. fluid ounce (fl oz) = 1/128 U.S. gallon = 1/16 U.S. pint 1 gill (gi) = 1/32 gallon = 4 fluid ounces 1 cup = ¼ quart = ½ pint = 8 fluid ounces 1 pint (pt) = ⅛ gallon = ½ quart = 16 fluid ounces 1 quart (qt) = ¼ gallon = 32 fluid ounces 1 U.S. gallon (gal; basic unit of liquid capacity in the U.S.) = 231 cu in. 1 dry pint (dry pt) = 1/64 bushel = ½ dry quart 1 peck (pk) = ¼ bushel 1 U.S. bushel (bu; basic unit of dry capacity in the U.S.) = 2,150.4 cubic inches 1 British imperial fluid ounce (fl oz) = 1/160 imperial gallon 1 imperial gallon (gal; basic unit of liquid capacity in some Commonwealth nations) = 277.4 cubic inches 1 imperial bushel (bu; basic unit of dry capacity in some Commonwealth nations) = 2,219.4 cubic inches	1 cubic centimeter (cc) = 1/1,000,000 cubic meter 1 cubic decimeter (cu dm) = 1/1,000 cubic meter = 1,000 cubic centimeters 1 cubic meter (cu m) = 1 stere (s; basic unit of volume) 1 milliliter (ml) = 1/1,000 liter = 1 cubic centimeter 1 centiliter (cl) = 1/100 liter = 10 milliliters 1 deciliter (dl) = 1/10 liter 1 liter = 1 cubic decimeter (basic unit of capacity) 1 dekaliter (dkl) = 10 liters 1 hectoliter (hl) = 100 liters = 1/10 cubic meter 1 kiloliter (kl) = 1,000 liters	1 cubic inch = 16.4 cubic centimeters 1 cubic foot = 0.0283 cubic meter 1 cubic yard = 0.765 cubic meter 1 fluid ounce = 29.6 milliliters 1 U.S. pint = 0.473 liter 1 U.S. quart = 0.946 liter 1 U.S. gallon = 3.8 liters 1 imperial gallon = 1.2 U.S. gallons = 4.5 liters 1 dry pint = 0.55 liter 1 dry quart = 1.1 liters 1 U.S. bushel = 0.97 imperial bushel = 35.24 liters 1 imperial bushel = 1.03 U.S. bushels = 36.37 liters 1 cubic centimeter = 0.06 cubic inch 1 cubic meter = 1.3 cubic yards 1 milliliter = 0.034 fluid ounce 1 liter = 1.06 U.S.quarts 1 dry liter = 0.9 dry quart 1 dekaliter = 0.28 U.S. bushel

week, period of time shorter than the month, commonly seven days. The seven-day week is said to have originated in ancient times in W Asia, probably in Mesopotamia. It is thought to have been a planetary week predicated on the concept of the influence of the planets: the sun, the moon, and five bodies recognized today as PLANETS—Mars, Mercury, Jupiter, Venus, and Saturn. The Hebrew week is based chiefly on the SABBATH, which comes every seventh day. In the Roman Empire the planetary week was at first preeminent, and the use of planetary names, based on the names of pagan deities, continued even after CONSTANTINE I made (c.321) the Christian week, beginning on Sunday, official. The Roman names for the days pervaded Europe; in most languages the forms are translations from Latin or attempts to assign corresponding names of divinities. The Latin names, their translations, the English equiv-

COMMON WEIGHTS AND MEASURES *(Continued)*

WEIGHT OR MASS

American and British units: avoirdupois	*Metric system*	*Conversion factors*
1 grain= 1/7,000 pound = 1/437.5 ounce 1 dram (dr) = 1/256 pound = 1/16 ounce 1 ounce (oz) = 1/16 pound 1 pound (lb; basic unit of weight or mass) 1 short hundredweight =100 pounds 1 long hundredweight = 112 pounds 1 short ton = 2,000 pounds 1 long ton = 2,240 pounds *American and British units: troy and apothecaries'* 1 grain = 1/7,000 avoirdupois pound = 1/480 troy ounce 1 pennyweight (dwt) = 24 grains = 1/20 troy ounce 1 apothecaries' dram (dr ap) = 60 grains = 1/8 apothecaries' ounce 1 troy or apothecaries' ounce (oz t or oz ap) = 480 grains = 1/12 troy or apothecaries' pound 1 troy or apothecaries' pound (lb t or lb ap) = 5,760 grains= 12 troy or apothecaries' ounces	1 milligram (mg) = 1/1,000,000 kilogram = 1/1,000 gram 1 centigram (cg) = 1/100,000 kilogram = 1/100 gram 1 decigram (dg) = 1/10,000 kilogram = 1/10 gram 1 gram (g) = 1/1,000 kilogram 1 dekagram (dkg) = 1/100 kilogram = 10 grams 1 hectogram (hg) = 1/10 kilogram = 100 grams 1 kilogram (kg; basic unit of weight or mass) 1 metric ton (t) = 1,000 kilograms	1 grain = 64 milligrams 1 avoirdupois ounce = 28.35 grams 1 troy or avoirdupois' pound = 0.82 avoirdupois pound = 0.37 kilogram 1 avoirdupois pound = 1.2 troy or apothercaries' pounds = 0.45 kilogram 1 short ton = 0.9 metric ton 1 milligram = 0.015 grain 1 gram = 0.035 avoirdupois ounce 1 kilogram = 2.205 avoirdupois pounds 1 metric ton = 1.1 short tons

alents, and their derivations follow: *dies solis* [sun's day], Sunday; *dies lunae* [moon's day], Monday; *dies Martis* [MARS' day], Tuesday [Tiw's day]; *dies Mercurii* [MERCURY's day], Wednesday [Woden's day]; *dies Jovis* [Jove's or JUPITER's day], Thursday [THOR's day]; *dies Veneris* [VENUS' day], Friday [Frigg's day]; and *dies Saturni* [SATURN's day], Saturday.

Weems, Mason Locke, 1759–1825, American author; b. Anne Arundel co., Md. An Anglican preacher and traveling bookseller, Parson Weems is chiefly remembered for his biography (c.1800) of George WASHINGTON, which contains the apocryphal story of the cherry tree.

Wegener, Alfred Lothar, 1880–1930, German geologist, meteorologist, and arctic explorer. He is known for his theory of CONTINENTAL DRIFT, set forth in his *The Origin of Continents and Oceans* (1915), and for his expeditions to Greenland, where he eventually lost his life.

Weidman, Charles, 1901–75, American modern dancer and choreographer; b. Lincoln, Neb. He danced (1920–27) with the Denishawn companies, before forming (1927) a company with Doris HUMPHREY. His MODERN DANCES combined abstract movement with gestures based on his own mime technique. In 1945 he founded his own company and school. In 1960 he established the Expression of the Two Arts Theater (N.Y.C.).

Weierstrass, Karl Wilhelm Theodor [vī'ərshträs], 1815–97, German mathematician. He developed the modern theory of functions. An advocate of the modern, rigorous approach to analysis and number theory, he did much to clarify the foundations of these subjects.

weight, measure, expressed in pounds or grams, of the force of gravity on a body (see GRAVITATION). Because the weights of different bodies at the same location are proportional to their masses, weight is often used as a measure of MASS. Unlike the mass, the weight of a body depends on its location in the gravitational field of the earth or of some other astronomical body.

weightlessness, the absence of any observable effects of GRAVITATION. Apparent weightlessness is encountered by astronauts in a spacecraft orbiting the earth. The gravitational force acting on the astronauts and other objects in the spacecraft is exactly canceled by the centrifugal force arising from the common accelerated motion of the spacecraft, astronauts, and spacecraft objects.

weight lifting, competitive sport and training technique for athletes. Meets are conducted according to weight classes, ranging from flyweight to super heavyweight. The contestant raising the greatest total of weights in three standard lifts—two-hand or military press, clean-and-jerk, and snatch—is declared the winner. Weight lifting has long been popular in Europe, Egypt, Turkey, and Japan. The E European nations have excelled in Olympic competition.

weights and measures, units and standards for expressing the amount of some quantity, such as length, capacity, or weight; the science of measurement standards and methods is known as metrology. Crude systems of weights and measures probably date from prehistoric times. Early units were commonly based on body measurements and on plant seeds or other agricultural objects. As civilization progressed, technological and commercial requirements led to increased standardization. Units were usually fixed by edict of local or national rulers and were subdivided and multiplied or otherwise arranged into systems of measurement. Today the chief systems are the ENGLISH UNITS OF MEASUREMENT and the METRIC SYSTEM. The United States is one of the few countries still using the former system.

Weil, Simone [vāy], 1909–43, French philosopher and mystic. Intellectually outstanding from childhood, she became a secondary-school teacher, wrote for socialist and Communist journals, and worked in Spain during the Civil War. After an intense mystical experience in 1938 she became a practicing Roman Catholic, subordinating all activity to an inward spiritual attendance upon a God whose presence is absolute but not manifest. Her spiritual and social-philosophic writings were collected posthumously, notably in *Waiting for God* (1951) and *The Need for Roots* (1952).

Weill, Kurt [vīl], 1900–50, German-American composer. In Europe he was best known for the satirical operas *The Threepenny Opera* (1928) and *The Rise and Fall of the City of Mahagonny* (1927, rev. 1930), both with librettos by BRECHT. Condemned as decadent by the NAZIS, he came to the U.S. in 1935. There he wrote such sophisticated MUSICALS as *Knickerbocker Holiday* (1938, with Maxwell ANDERSON) and *Lady in the Dark* (1941). Among his last, more serious works is *Street Scene* (1947). He was married to Lotte LENYA.

Weimar [vī'mär], city (1989 est. pop. 63,400), capital of THURINGIA, central Germany, on the Ilm R. It is a cultural and industrial center with such manufactures as farm machinery and chemicals. Known in the 10th cent., it became (16th cent.) the capital of the duchy of

Saxe-Weimar. The presence (18th–19th cent.) of GOETHE and SCHILLER made Weimar the literary center of Europe; later LISZT and NIETZSCHE lived there. In 1919 the city was the scene of the national assembly that established the republican government known as the "Weimar Republic." Landmarks include the parish church, which has an altarpiece by CRANACH, and the Goethe National Museum. The CONCENTRATION CAMP Buchenwald was located (1937–45) near the city.

Weimaraner, large, muscular SPORTING DOG; shoulder height, 23–27 in. (58.4–68.6 cm); weight, 55–85 lb (25–38.6 kg). Its short, smooth coat is gray; its tail is docked. Developed in Germany in the early 19th cent., it was first bred to hunt large game and later used for upland bird hunting.

Weinberg, Steven, 1933–, American nuclear physicist; b. N.Y.C. He helped develop the ELECTROWEAK THEORY, which unified ELECTROMAGNETISM and the WEAK INTERACTION. The theory was verified when the W AND Z PARTICLES were discovered by RUBBIA and VAN DER MEER. In 1979 he shared the Nobel Prize in physics with Abdus Salam and Lee Glashow. His writings include *Dreams of a Final Theory* (1992).

Weir, Julian Alden [wēr], 1852–1919, American painter; b. West Point, N.Y.; son of Robert Walter Weir, a HUDSON RIVER SCHOOL painter. Connected with early American IMPRESSIONISM, he used subtle gradations of light and tone in his works, e.g., *Autumn* (Corcoran Gall., Wash., D.C.).

Weir, Peter, 1944–, Australian film director. His work, which helped to bring Australian film to world attention, includes *Picnic at Hanging Rock* (1975), *Gallipoli* (1981), and *The Year of Living Dangerously* (1983).

Weismann, August, 1834–1914, German biologist. A professor at the Univ. of Freiburg (1866–1912), he originated the germ-plasm theory of heredity, which stresses the unbroken continuity of the germ plasm and the nonheritability of ACQUIRED CHARACTERISTICS.

Weiss, Peter, 1916–82, German-Swedish writer, film director, and painter. His philosophical drama on the nature of revolution, *The Persecution and Assassination of Jean Paul Marat as Performed by the Inmates of the Asylum of Charenton Under the Direction of the Marquis de Sade* (1964), and his play *The Investigation* (1965) were international successes. He was a Marxist from the mid-1960s; his social and political views are expressed in the dramas *Vietnam Discourse* (1968), *Trotsky in Exile* (1970), and *Hölderlin* (1971).

Weizmann, Chaim, 1874–1952, scientist and Zionist leader, first president (1948–52) of ISRAEL; b. Russia. A British subject from 1910, he combined a life of science with efforts toward the creation of a Jewish state. During World War I he developed a synthetic acetone for the production of explosives. In 1917 he helped procure from the British government the pro-Zionist Balfour Declaration (see BALFOUR, ARTHUR JAMES). A longtime leader of the World Zionist Organization, he was named president of Israel in 1948. His nephew, **Ezer Weizman,** 1924–, helped found and served (1948–66) in the Israeli air force, rising to the rank of general and commanding officer before entering politics. He was minister of transport (1969–70), defense (1977–80), communications (1984–88), and science (1988–92). He was elected president of Israel in 1993.

Weld, Theodore Dwight, 1803–95, American abolitionist; b. Hampton, Conn. A disciple of the evangelist Charles G. Finney, Weld trained other Finney converts at Lane Seminary, in Cincinnati, and helped select (1834) the "Seventy"—agents for the American Anti-Slavery Society who spread the ABOLITIONIST gospel throughout the North. Weld married (1838) the abolitionist Angelina GRIMKÉ and was an editor of the *Emancipator.* His *American Slavery as It Is* (1839) was a source for Harriet Beecher STOWE's *Uncle Tom's Cabin* and was considered second only to Stowe's book in its influence on the antislavery movement.

welding, process for joining separate pieces of metal in a continuous metallic bond. In cold-pressure welding, high pressure is applied at room temperature. Forge welding (or forging) is done by means of hammering, with the addition of heat. In most processes, the points to be joined are melted, additional molten metal is added as a filler, and the bond is allowed to cool. In the Thomson process, melting is caused by resistance to an applied electric current. Another process is that of the atomic hydrogen flame, in which hydrogen molecules passing through an electric arc are broken into atoms by absorbing energy. Outside the arc the molecules reunite, yielding heat to weld the material in the process.

welfare: see SOCIAL WELFARE.

Welland Ship Canal, canal, SE Ont., Canada, W of Buffalo, N.Y., linking lakes Erie and Ontario. It is 27.6 mi (44.4 km) long, with a minimum depth of 30 ft (9 m), and forms a vital part of the St. Lawrence & Great Lakes Waterway. Eight locks (each 859 ft/262 m long, 80 ft/24 m wide, and 30 ft/9 m deep) overcome the 326-ft (99-m) difference in elevation between the lakes and bypass NIAGARA FALLS. The canal was built (1914–32) to replace a canal opened in 1829, and was modernized and enlarged in 1972.

Welles, Gideon, 1802–78, American politician; b. Glastonbury, Conn. A Jacksonian Democrat, he left the party over the slavery issue and helped found (1856) the REPUBLICAN PARTY. A staunch supporter of Abraham LINCOLN, he was secretary of the navy during the CIVIL WAR and later supported Pres. Johnson's RECONSTRUCTION policy.

Welles, Orson, 1915–85, American film director and actor; b. Kenosha, Wis. *Citizen Kane* (1940), considered his masterpiece, is noted for its technical brilliance and structural complexity. His other films include *The Lady from Shanghai* (1947) and *Touch of Evil* (1962).

Scene from Citizen Kane, *directed by Orson Welles, 1940*

Wellesley, Richard Colley Wellesley, Marquess, 1760–1842, British colonial administrator. As governor general of India (1797–1805), he extended British influence, wiped out French power, and, aided by his brother Arthur (later duke of WELLINGTON), checked the power of the native rulers. He was foreign secretary (1810–12), lord lieutenant of Ireland (1821–28; 1833–34), and a supporter of CATHOLIC EMANCIPATION.

Wellington, Arthur Wellesley, 1st **duke of,** 1769–1852, British soldier and statesman. Stationed in India (1796–1805), he assisted his brother Richard WELLESLEY by defeating the MAHRATTA chiefs. He brilliantly directed (1809–13) the PENINSULAR WAR that drove the French out of Spain and defeated (1815) NAPOLEON I in the WATERLOO CAMPAIGN. As prime minister (1828–30) he secured passage of the CATHOLIC EMANCIPATION bill (which he had previously opposed). Wellington later served as foreign secretary (1834–35) and minister without portfolio (1841–46) under Sir Robert PEEL.

Wellington, city (1991 pop. 150,301), capital of New Zealand, at the southern tip of North Island, on an inlet of Cook Strait. It is New Zealand's second largest city, its chief administrative and transportation center, and a major port. Manufactures include clothing, transportation equipment, processed food, and textiles. Founded in 1840, it became the capital in 1865. It has a symphony orchestra, ballet and opera companies, and several museums.

Wells, H(erbert) G(eorge), 1866–1946, English author and social thinker. Having taught biology, he wrote fantastic and pseudoscientific novels like *The Time Machine* (1895) and *The War of the Worlds* (1898). He turned to realism in *Kipps* (1905) and *Tono-*

Bungay (1909), and finally to increasing pessimism in *The Shape of Things to Come* (1933). He also wrote the famous *Outline of History* (1920).

Welsh language, member of the Brythonic group of the Celtic subfamily of the Indo-European family of languages. See LANGUAGE (table).

Welty, Eudora, 1909–, American author; b. Jackson, Miss. A regional writer with a gift for dialect, she peoples her fiction with the eccentric, comic, but vital inhabitants of rural Mississippi. Her novels include *The Ponder Heart* (1954), *Losing Battles* (1970), and *The Optimist's Daughter* (1972; Pulitzer). Her collected stories were published in 1980, and she also published the autobiographical *One Writer's Beginnings* in 1984.

Wenceslaus, Saint, d. 929, duke of Bohemia. A pious Christian, he made peace with HENRY I (Henry the Fowler) of Germany. He engendered enmity among the nobles and was assassinated by his brother Boleslav I, who succeeded him. The patron saint of Bohemia, he is the "good King Wenceslaus" of the English Christmas carol. Feast: Sept. 28.

Wenceslaus, 1361–1419, Holy Roman emperor (uncrowned) and German king (1378–1400), king of Bohemia (1378–1419) as Wenceslaus IV, elector of Brandenburg (1373–76); son and successor of Emperor CHARLES IV. His main interest was always Bohemia, and he was ultimately deposed (1400) as German king by the ELECTORS. He never accepted his successor, Rupert, but in 1411 he agreed to the election of his half brother, SIGISMUND, as emperor. Wenceslaus was popular with the common people of Bohemia, but quarreled with the nobles and clergy. He supported John HUSS and tried to prevent his burning, which was carried out at the instigation of Sigismund. Wenceslaus's death and the succession of Sigismund as king of Bohemia led to the Hussite Wars (see HUSSITES).

Wenceslaus IV, king of Bohemia: see WENCESLAUS, Holy Roman emperor.

werewolf: see LYCANTHROPY.

Werfel, Franz [vĕr′fəl], 1890–1945, Austrian writer; b. Prague. His belief in human brotherhood is expressed in his lyric verse, in expressionist and conventional plays, and in such internationally known novels as *The Forty Days of Musa Dagh* (1933), *The Song of Bernadette* (1941), and the comedy *Jacobowsky and the Colonel* (1944). In 1938, Werfel fled Nazi-occupied Austria, later settling in the U.S.

Wergeland, Henrik [vĕr′gəlän], 1808–45, Norwegian poet and patriot, the leading Norwegian literary figure of his era. His greatest work was the verse drama *Creation, Man, and Messiah* (1830). He worked zealously for the causes of liberty, democracy, tolerance, and international cooperation; and his *English Pilot* (1844) voiced his ultimate goal: the liberation of the human mind.

Werner, Abraham Gottlob, 1750–1815, German geologist. He was the first to classify minerals systematically. Although his theory of neptunism (that the earth's lands precipitated out of an original world ocean) is now rejected, geology is indebted to him for applying chronology to rock formations and for his precise definitions.

Wertheimer, Max: see GESTALT.

Wertmuller, Lina, 1926?–, Italian film director; b. Archangela Felice Assunta Wertmüller von Elgg Spanol von Braucich. Her surreal comedies include *The Seduction of Mimi* (1972), *Love and Anarchy* (1973), *Swept Away* (1974), and *Seven Beauties* (1976).

Wesley, John, 1703–91, English evangelical preacher and founder of METHODISM, was ordained (1728) a priest in the Church of England and led a group of students at Oxford, including his brother Charles and George WHITEFIELD. They were derisively called "methodists" for their methodical devotion to study and religious duties. In 1735 the Wesleys accompanied James OGLETHORPE to Georgia, where John was deeply influenced by Moravian missionaries. On May 24, 1738, at a religious meeting in London, he experienced an assurance of salvation through faith in Jesus alone, which was his message for the rest of his life. In his evangelistic work, he is said to have preached 40,000 sermons and, on the advice of Whitefield, he preached in the open air. Because of his Arminianism and belief in Christian perfection, he repudiated (c.1740) the Calvinist doctrine of election, which led to a break with Whitefield. In 1784 he established the legal status of Methodist societies, and although he did not form a separate church, he did make plans for the societies to continue after his death. His brother, **Charles Wesley,** 1707–88, was also a priest of the Church of England and a Methodist evangelical preacher. He wrote some 6,500 hymns, including "Hark! The Herald Angels Sing" and "Jesus, Lover of My Soul."

Wessex, one of the Anglo-Saxon kingdoms of England. It may have been settled as early as 495 by the Saxons. King Ceawlin (560–93) consolidated the area between the upper Thames R. valley and the lower Severn, but until the end of the 8th cent. Wessex was overshadowed successively by KENT, NORTHUMBRIA, and MERCIA. EGBERT (802–39) became overlord of all England, but the kingdom then declined in the face of Danish invasions. The Danes were halted by ALFRED (r.871–99), and thereafter the history of Wessex becomes that of England. After a period of Danish rule (1016–42), EDWARD THE CONFESSOR (1042–66), last of the Wessex line of Alfred, succeeded to the English throne.

West, Benjamin, 1738–1820, American painter; b. Springfield, Pa. In 1760 he went to live in Europe, where he settled in London, espoused neoclassicism, and was appointed historical painter to GEORGE III in 1772. West executed more than 400 canvases, chiefly historical, mythological, and religious subjects on a heroic scale. He had many students, particularly American painters studying abroad, such as ALLSTON, S.F.B. MORSE, Gilbert STUART, and J.S. COPLEY. Among his best-known works are *Death of General Wolfe* (Grosvenor Gall., London) and *Penn's Treaty with the Indians* (Pennsylvania Acad. Fine Arts, Philadelphia).

West, Nathanael, 1903–40, American novelist; b. N.Y.C. as Nathan Weinstein. An innovative and original writer, he revealed the sterility and grotesqueness underlying the American dream. His bitter and influential novels are: *The Dream Life of Balso Snell* (1931), *A Cool Million* (1934), and *The Day of the Locust* (1939).

West, Dame Rebecca, 1892–1983, English writer; b. Ireland, as Cicily Fairfield. The author of such psychological novels as *The Return of the Soldier* (1918) and *Birds Fall Down* (1966), she is best known for a historical study of Yugoslavia, *Black Lamb and Grey Falcon* (1942), and an insightful look at traitors and spies, *The New Meaning of Treason* (1964).

West Bank, territory between Israel and Jordan, located W of the Jordan R. and the Dead Sea (1992 est. pop. 1,362,000), c.2,165 sq mi (5,607 sq km), occupied by Israel since the ARAB-ISRAELI WAR of 1967. Many Israelis refer to it as JUDAEA and SAMARIA. It includes the cities of HEBRON, JERICHO, and NABLUS, and the Old City of JERUSALEM. The north is fertile; the south largely barren. Olives, fruit, and citrus products are produced; small-scale industries manufacture goods such as cement and textiles. The inhabitants are mostly Muslim Arab Palestinians; there are about 120,000 Israeli Jewish settlers. After the partition of PALESTINE and the formation (1948) of Israel, the territory was annexed (1950) by Jordan. Following the 1967 war, the UN Security Council called for Israel's withdrawal from the West Bank. The CAMP DAVID ACCORDS (1978) incorporated plans for Arab self-rule in the region. A peaceful resolution, however, was impeded by the establishment of Israeli settlements in the area and by Israeli-PLO hostility (Arab states, including Jordan, recognized the PALESTINE LIBERATION ORGANIZATION [PLO] as the sole representative of the West Bank Arabs in 1974). A 1993 accord between Israel and the PLO called for limited Palestinian self-rule in Jericho and the GAZA STRIP by mid-1994.

Western Australia, state (1992 est. pop. 1,658,000), 975,290 sq mi (2,527,633 sq km). It is the largest state in Australia, comprising the entire western part of the continent. Only the southwest corner is fertile. Half of the population lives in metropolitan PERTH, the capital. Wheat, wool, and meat are the chief agricultural products. The inland and northern areas are rich in minerals, notably iron ore, nickel, and gold. Principal manufactures are industrial metals, machinery, and transportation equipment. A penal colony was established at Albany in 1826, and a colony of free settlers arrived in the Perth-Fremantle area in 1829. Governed at first by NEW SOUTH WALES, Western Australia received its own governor in 1831. It became a separate colony in 1890 and a federated state of Australia in 1901.

Western European Union (WEU), organization founded (1955) for defensive, economic, social, and cultural purposes by Belgium, France, West Germany (now Germany), Great Britain, Italy, Luxembourg, and the Netherlands. Portugal and Spain (1988) and Greece (1992) later joined. Initially its primary function proved to be the supervision of German rearmament under the PARIS PACTS; since 1960 it has been concerned mainly with military affairs. Under the Maastricht treaty (1992), the WEU is envisioned as the future military arm of the EUROPEAN UNION. In 1993 the WEU established the Eurocorps, a joint force drawn from some of its members.

Western Reserve, region in NE Ohio. Territory retained (1786) by Connecticut when that state ceded claims to other western lands, much of it was given to those of its citizens whose property was burned in the American Revolution. It became part of the NORTHWEST TERRITORY in 1800.

Western Sahara, formerly **Spanish Sahara,** territory (1992 est. pop. 201,000), 102,703 sq mi (266,000 sq km), occupied by Morocco, NW Africa, bordered by the Atlantic Ocean (W), Morocco (N), Algeria (NE), and Mauritania (E and S). Part of the SAHARA Desert, the land is extremely arid and is covered with stones and sand. The main towns are El Aaiún (or Laayoun; the former capital), Dakhlah (formerly Villa Cisneros), and Semara. The traditional economy is based on the raising of goats, camels, and sheep and the cultivation of date palms. There is some fishing. Rich deposits of phosphates were first exploited in the 1970s; potash and iron have also been found. The people are Arabs and Berbers, most of whom are Sunni Muslim. Arabic is the chief language.

History. Although visited by the Portuguese in 1434, the area that is now Western Sahara had little contact with Europeans until the 19th cent. In 1884 Spain proclaimed a protectorate over the coast, and a Spanish province, known as Spanish Sahara, was established in 1958. In 1976 Spain transferred the territory to Morocco and Mauritania, but following guerrilla action by the Polisario Front, a nationalist group based in Algeria and seeking self-government for the Saharans, Mauritania withdrew in 1979. Morocco then occupied the Mauritanian portion. The guerrillas continued attempts to liberate Western Sahara, renaming it the Saharan Arab Democratic Republic. A temporary truce signed in 1990 was made permanent (1991), but a referendum on the area's status has been delayed by disputes over who could vote.

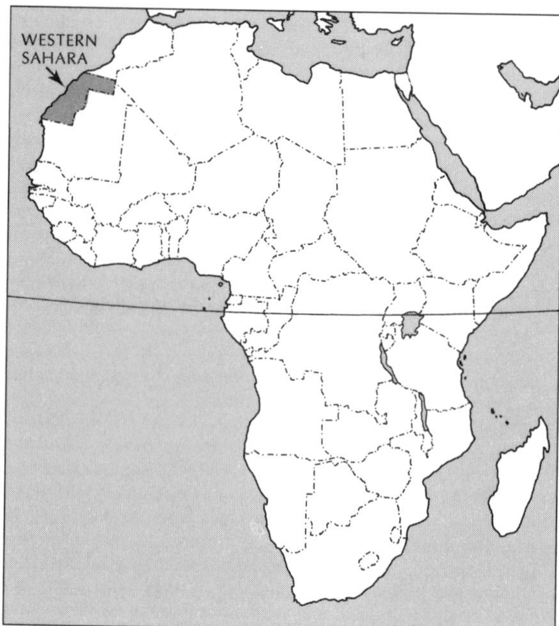

Western Samoa, officially Independent State of Western Samoa, constitutional monarchy (1992 est. pop. 195,000), 1,133 sq mi (2,934 sq km), comprising nine islands in the SW Pacific Ocean, of which the largest are Savai'i and Upolu. Most of the population live on Upolu, where Apia, the capital, is located. The main islands are crossed by extinct volcanic ranges and have a tropical climate. Subsistence farming and fishing are mainstays of the economy, with tourism contributing significantly to local prosperity. Some timber is exported. The predominantly Polynesian population is almost entirely Christian, mainly Protestant. Samoan and English are the official languages.

History. Samoa was visited by the Dutch in 1722. It granted trading privileges to the U.S. in 1878 and to Germany and Britain in 1879. In 1899, the U.S. annexed eastern Samoa (see AMERICAN SAMOA) and the western islands passed to German control. New Zealand occupied the German islands in 1914 during World War I and subsequently administered them as a League of Nations mandate and a UN Trust Territory. They gained independence as Western Samoa in 1962. Executive power rests in a chief of state, chosen by the legislative assembly from among the royal families, and the vast majority of the members of the legislature are chosen by the Samoan clan chiefs. Chief Susuga Malietoa Tanumafili II has been chief of state since 1962. See PACIFIC OCEAN map.

West Germany: see GERMANY.

West Highland white terrier, sturdy, compact TERRIER; shoulder height, c.11 in. (27.9 cm); weight, 13–20 lb (5.9–9.1 kg). It has a dense, white, water-resistant double coat. It was developed in Scotland in the early 19th cent. to hunt small game both on land and in the water.

West Indies, archipelago, sometimes called the Antilles, extending c.2,500 mi (4,020 km) in a wide arc E and S from Florida to Venezuela, and separating the Atlantic Ocean from the Gulf of Mexico and the CARIBBEAN SEA. The four main island groups are the BAHAMAS; the Greater Antilles (CUBA, JAMAICA, HISPANIOLA, PUERTO RICO); the Lesser Antilles (the Leeward and Windward islands, BARBADOS, and TRINIDAD AND TOBAGO); and the Dutch West Indies, or Netherlands Antilles (ARUBA, CURAÇAO, Bonaire). The warm climate and clear tropical seas of the islands support a large tourist industry, and there are some exports, notably bauxite and sugar. People of African descent predominate. The **West Indies Federation,** established (1959) by ten former British possessions, broke up in 1962 because of economic disparities between its members. Some of the participants later formed (1967) the **West Indies Associated States,** a British-sponsored confederation, but they left it one by one as they achieved full independence during the 1970s and early 80s.

Westinghouse, George, 1846–1914, American inventor and manufacturer; b. Central Bridge, N.Y. His railroad inventions included the air BRAKE (1868) and automatic signal devices. He formed companies in 1869 and 1882 to manufacture them. He also pioneered in introducing into the U.S. the high-tension alternating-current system for transmission of electricity. Over 400 patents were credited to Westinghouse.

Westminster Abbey, originally the abbey church of a Benedictine monastery in London. A major English Gothic structure, it is a national shrine. In 1245 Henry III demolished a Norman church and began a new eastern portion, inaugurating centuries of development. The chapter house was built in 1250, the cloisters and main monastic buildings in the 14th cent. The nave was completed in the 16th cent., as was Henry VIII's Lady Chapel with its noted fan vaulting. Christopher WREN and Nicholas HAWKSMOOR built (1722–40) the western towers. French influence is seen in the nave, the highest in England, and in the flying buttresses. Almost all English monarchs since William I have been crowned in the Abbey, and noted English subjects are buried there, e.g., Chaucer and Robert Browning in the Poets' Corner.

Westminster Palace or **Houses of Parliament,** in London. The present Gothic structure was built (1840–60) by Sir Charles Barry to replace ancient buildings largely destroyed by fire in 1834. Edward the Confessor built the original palace, a royal abode until the 16th cent., when it became the meeting place for Parliament. The Great Hall (late 11th cent.), the finest example of medieval open-timber work, was destroyed by fire bombs in 1941. Westminster Hall, the only original portion intact, serves as an entrance hall.

Westmoreland, William Childs, 1914–, U.S. general; b. Spartanburg co., S.C. A career army officer, he commanded (1964–68) U.S. troops in the VIETNAM WAR.

Weston, Edward, 1886–1958, American photographer; b. Highland

Park, Ill. Famed for stark, superbly printed images of Western landscapes, nudes, and natural formations, Weston greatly influenced photographic art.

Westphalia, Peace of, 1648, general settlement of the THIRTY YEARS WAR. It marked the end of the HOLY ROMAN EMPIRE as an effective institution and inaugurated the modern European state system. It also marked the end of the era of religious warfare, with a genuine effort being made toward religious toleration. The chief participants were France and Sweden on one side and Spain and the Holy Roman Empire on the other. Although he had died before it met, the Peace of Westphalia represents a triumph of the policies of the duc de RICHELIEU. The sovereignty of the German states was recognized, as was that of the Netherlands and the Swiss Confederation. The empire was continued in name only. Sweden and France won important territories, and France emerged as the dominant European power.

West Point, U.S. military post on the Hudson R. N of New York City. An important fort during the AMERICAN REVOLUTION, since 1802 it has been the site of the UNITED STATES MILITARY ACADEMY.

West Virginia, E central state of the U.S.; bordered by Pennsylvania and Maryland (N), Virginia (E), and Kentucky and Ohio, which lies across the Ohio R. (W).

Area, 24,181 sq mi (62,629 sq km). *Pop.* (1990) 1,793,477, an 8% decrease from 1980 pop. *Capital,* Charleston. *Statehood,* June 20, 1863 (35th state). *Highest pt.,* Spruce Knob, 4,863 ft (1,483 m); *lowest pt.,* Potomac R., 240 ft (73 m). *Nickname,* Mountain State. *Motto, Montani Semper Liberi* [Mountaineers Are Always Free]. *State bird,* cardinal. *State flower, Rhododendron maximum,* or "Big Laurel." *State tree,* sugar maple. *Abbr.,* W.Va.; WV.

Land and People. West Virginia is very hilly and rugged. Nearly the entire state is in the Allegheny Plateau, except for the eastern panhandle, which is part of the Appalachian Plateau. The climate is generally humid, with hot summers (except in the high mountains) and cool-to-cold winters. Only about 36% of the population lives in urban areas, making West Virginia the nation's second most rural state (after Vermont). CHARLESTON is the largest city, followed by HUNTINGTON and WHEELING. In 1990 the state was over 96% white.

Economy. Because of the rugged terrain, farming is not extensive in most of the state. The leading agricultural commodities are cattle, dairy products, apples, turkeys, peaches, hay, and tobacco. The state has extensive mineral resources—only Kentucky produces more coal—and is the leading extractor of natural gas E of the Mississippi. These mineral resources are utilized by the state's industries, which manufacture machinery, chemicals, primary and fabricated metals (especially steel), and stone, clay, plastic, and glass products. About 65% of West Virginia is forested in valuable hardwoods, which support a major lumber industry. Tourism is growing, and White Sulphur Springs is a particularly popular destination.

Government. The constitution of 1872 provides for a governor elected to a four-year term. The legislature consists of a senate with 34 members elected to four-year terms and a house with 100 members elected for two years. The state is represented in the U.S. Congress by two senators and three representatives and has five electoral votes.

History. Among the remains of early MOUND BUILDERS, West Virginia's earliest inhabitants, are those preserved at Moundsville. Explorers and fur traders reached the area in the 1670s, and German families established (c.1730) the first European settlement. As additional settlers crossed the mountains to live in the area they eventually came into conflict with the French, a struggle which resulted in the last FRENCH AND INDIAN WAR (1754–63). Industrial development during the early 19th cent. was spurred by river traffic on the MISSISSIPPI and OHIO and by completion of the NATIONAL ROAD at Wheeling. Largely opposed to slavery, the residents of this portion of Virginia established (1863) a separate state after Virginia had seceded from the Union. During the early 20th cent. West Virginia experienced considerable industrial expansion, but also serious labor strife, especially in the coal mines. The economy declined severely by the 1960s. By the late 1970s West Virginia's mining sector boomed with the increased demand for coal, but during the 1980s energy prices and mine employment plummeted. The state saw a modest recovery by the early 1990s, however, as foreign investment, tourism, and the service sector grew.

wetlands, ecosystems in which the WATER TABLE is at or near the surface. They are divided into estuarine and freshwater systems and subdivided into bogs, SWAMPS, and marshes. Their sluggish water often creates a rich habitat for plants and wildlife, and they are spawning and feeding grounds for numerous animal species. Many wetlands were destroyed by urban growth and farming before their value was recognized, but environmental regulations and groups now attempt to protect or restore them.

Wettin [vĕt'ĭn], [German dynasty], the various branches of which ruled in Saxony, Thuringia, Poland, Great Britain, Belgium, and Bulgaria. The Wettins were margraves of Meissen from c.1100 and soon expanded into Saxony and Thuringia. In 1485 the dynasty split into the Albertine and Ernestine lines, various branches of which ruled until the 20th cent. From one of the Ernestine branches (Saxe-Coburg-Gotha) are descended the royal houses of Great Britain (through Prince Albert) and Belgium (through Leopold I).

Weyden, Roger van der [vī'dən], c.1400–1464, early Flemish master, known also as Roger de la Pasture. Believed to have studied with Robert CAMPIN, he was also influenced by Jan van EYCK. His portrayal of piety and of intangible emotions, e.g., in his *Descent from the Cross* (c.1435; Prado), is unsurpassed. His sculptural treatment of figures in the *Entombment* (Uffizi) and *Virgin and Child with Saints* (Frankfurt) bears a strong resemblance to Italian religious art of the time. His religious paintings and his portraits, e.g., of Francesco d'Este (Metropolitan Mus.), have simplicity and psychological penetration blended with the monumental. He had a highly individual style. His tradition was carried on by such painters as Dierick Bouts and Hans MEMLING.

whale, aquatic MAMMAL of the order Cetacea, found in oceans worldwide. Adapted to an entirely aquatic life, they have a fishlike shape, nearly hairless skin, an insulating layer of blubber, and flipperlike forelimbs; the tail is flattened horizontally and used for propulsion. Surfacing to breathe, whales expel air through a dorsal blowhole. They have good vision and excellent hearing, and many species use echolocation for underwater navigation. Most whales travel in schools, often migrating thousands of miles. There are two major groups of whales, the toothed, including the sperm whale (which DNA studies suggest is more closely related to baleen whales), killer whale, beluga (or white whale), and narwhal; and the toothless, or baleen, including the blue, finback, gray, right, humpback, and minke whales. Species vary greatly in size and include the largest animal that has ever lived, the blue whale, up to 100 ft (30 m) long and 150 tons. Commercial whaling has reduced all large species to endangered status. The intelligence and communication systems of the whale are subjects of scientific investigation.

whale shark: see SHARK; FISH.

Wharton, Edith (Newbold Jones), 1862–1937, American author; b. N.Y.C.; settled in France, 1913. Her works range widely, but she is particularly known for her subtle, ironic, and superbly crafted fictional studies of turn-of-the-century New York society, as in her best and most characteristic novels, *The House of Mirth* (1905) and *The Age of Innocence* (1920; Pulitzer). Wharton's many other novels include *The Valley of Decision* (1902), *The Custom of the Country* (1913), and *Hudson River Bracketed* (1929). Least characteristic, but most successful, of her works is the starkly tragic novella of New England, *Ethan Frome* (1911). Among Wharton's short-story collections are *Crucial Instances* (1901), *Certain People* (1930), and *Ghosts* (1937). She also wrote travel books, literary criticism, and poetry.

wheat, cereal plant (genus *Triticum*) of the GRASS family, a major food and an important commodity of the world GRAIN market. The plant is an annual (probably derived from a perennial) that grows best where the weather is cool during its early growth. Modern wheat varieties are usually classified as winter wheats (fall-planted and unusually winter-hardy) and spring wheats (spring-planted). Hard-kerneled varieties (hard wheats) yield flour with a high gluten content, used to make breads; soft-kerneled ones (soft wheats) are starchier, and their flour is used to make cakes and biscuits. Durum wheat is a very hard-kerneled wheat used in PASTA products. Wheat is also used in the manufacture of BEER and WHISKEY, and the grain, the BRAN (the residue from milling), and the rest of the plant are valuable livestock feed. Wheat was one of the first grains to be cultivated: bread wheat was grown in the Nile R. valley by 5000 B.C. Major modern wheat-producing areas include the U.S., Canada, China, W Europe, Ukraine, Kazakhstan, Russia, India, Pakistan, and Australia.

Wheatley, Phillis, 1753?–84, American poet; brought from Africa, 1761. The first important African-American writer in America, she was the slave of a Boston merchant, who educated her. Her work includes *Poems on Various Subjects* (1773).

Wheatstone, Sir Charles, 1802–75, English physicist and inventor. He was coinventor of an electric telegraph and also invented an automatic transmitter, an electric recording device, and an automatic telegraph. Wheatstone is credited with inventing the concertina, improving the stereoscope and dynamo, and popularizing a method for the measurement of electric resistance using a network now known as the Wheatstone bridge.

wheel and axle: see MACHINE.

Wheeling, city (1990 pop. 34,882), seat of Ohio co., W.Va., in the Northern Panhandle, on the Ohio R.; settled 1769, inc. as a city 1836. It is a manufacturing and commercial center in a coal and natural-gas area. Industrial products include steel, chemicals, ceramics, glass, and textiles. Located on the site of a 1774 fort, Wheeling became the western terminus of the NATIONAL ROAD in 1818. It was the scene of the Wheeling Conventions (1861–62), which led to the creation of the state of West Virginia.

whelk, large marine SNAIL having a thick-lipped spiral shell with many protuberances, found in temperate waters. Whelks are scavengers and carnivores, feeding on crabs, lobsters, and other shellfish. The largest species, the knobbed whelk, grows up to 16 in. (40.6 cm).

Whig, English political party. The name was probably derived from *whiggamor* [cattle driver], a 17th-cent. term of abuse for Scottish Presbyterians. The party upheld the power of Parliament against the crown and was supported by the landed gentry and merchants against the aristocratic TORY group. The accession (1714) of GEORGE I began a long period of Whig control. The dominant figure until 1742 was Sir Robert WALPOLE, who gave the party political power and shaped modern British cabinet government. After the accession (1760) of GEORGE III, the Whigs were largely in opposition, and under the leadership of Charles James FOX became identified with dissent, industry, and social and parliamentary reform. Whig ministries under the 2d Earl GREY and Lord MELBOURNE were in power from 1830 to 1841 and passed the REFORM BILL of 1832. Thereafter the Whigs became part of the Liberal party.

Whig party, one of the two dominant political parties in the U.S. in the second quarter of the 19th cent. It grew out of the NATIONAL REPUBLICAN PARTY and several smaller groups, notably the ANTI-MASONIC PARTY. Created primarily to oppose Andrew Jackson's DEMOCRATIC PARTY, it was beset by factions from the beginning and was never able to forge a unified, positive party position. Daniel WEBSTER and Henry CLAY were its great leaders, representing, respectively, the "Northern Whigs" and the Southern "Cotton Whigs." In 1840 they were able to unify behind a popular military hero, W.H. HARRISON, as a presidential candidate. He was elected but died after only a month in office. His successor, John TYLER, quickly alienated the Whig leaders in Congress and was read out of the party. In 1848 the Whigs elected another military hero, Zachary TAYLOR. He too died in office but his successor, Millard FILLMORE, remained a loyal party man. The party was already disintegrating, however, chiefly over the SLAVERY issue. The FREE-SOIL PARTY and its successor, the REPUBLICAN PARTY, absorbed most of the Northern Whigs. The Cotton Whigs went into the Democratic party. In 1852 Gen. Winfield SCOTT was the last Whig presidential candidate.

whippet, small, slender HOUND; shoulder height, 18–22 in. (45.7–55.8 cm); weight, c.20 lb (9 kg). Its smooth coat is usually white, tan, or gray. It was developed in England in the mid-18th cent. and used for coursing hares in an enclosed area. Today it is a race dog and a pet.

whippoorwill: see GOATSUCKER.

whiskey, spirituous liquor distilled from a fermented mash of grains, usually rye, barley, oats, wheat, or corn, and matured in wood casks, usually for three or more years. Inferior grades are made from potatoes, beets, or other roots. Scotch whisky, usually a blend, takes its dry, somewhat smoky flavor from the barley malt, cured with peat, used in its preparation. The somewhat similar Irish whiskey, for which no peat is used, has a full, sweet taste. American whiskeys, classified as rye or as bourbon (a corn liquor), are higher in flavor and deeper in color than Scotch or Irish whiskeys. Canadian whiskey, characteristically light, is produced from cereal grain only. First distilled in monasteries in 11th-cent. England, whiskey has been manufactured commercially since the 16th cent.

Whiskey Rebellion, 1794, uprising by settlers W of the Alleghenies who opposed Alexander HAMILTON's excise tax of 1791. The settlers regarded the tax as discriminatory and rioted against the tax collectors. Pres. WASHINGTON sent troops; they put down the rebellion easily and many arrests were made. Two rebels were convicted of treason, but the president pardoned them. The government's power to enforce its laws had been proved, but the FEDERALIST PARTY suffered politically.

Whiskey Ring, group of distillers and public officials who defrauded the U.S. government of liquor taxes. Soon after the Civil War, large distillers bribed government officials in order to retain tax proceeds. Only after the ring became a public scandal did the Treasury Dept. act. The distilleries were seized (May 1875), over $3 million in taxes was recovered, and eventually 110 persons were convicted. Pres. GRANT intervened to gain the acquittal of his personal secretary, O.E. Babcock.

Whistler, James Abbott McNeill, 1834–1903, American painter; b. Lowell, Mass. In 1855 he went to Paris, where he acquired an appreciation of works by VELÁZQUEZ and Japanese prints, both of which influenced the color and design of much of his work. He settled in London in 1859 and became known as an etcher, wit, and dandy. To publicize his credo of art for art's sake, he resorted to elaborate exhibits, polemics, and lawsuits. Toward the end of his life, he won recognition for his admirable draftsmanship, exquisite color, and great technical proficiency. In order to de-emphasize the subjective content of his paintings, he called them by abstract titles, e.g., *Arrangement in Gray and Black* (the famed portrait of his mother, 1872; Louvre). A superb etcher, Whistler also excelled in lithography, watercolor, and pastel. In addition, he wrote brilliant critical essays and influenced art theory in works like *Ten O'Clock* (1888). The most representative collection of his work is in the Freer Gallery of Art (Wash., D.C.), which contains his "Peacock Room."

James Whistler's Arrangement in Gray and Black, *1872*

Whitby, Synod of: see CELTIC CHURCH.

White, Andrew Dickson, 1832–1918, American educator and diplomat; b. Homer, N.Y. As chairman (1864–67) of the New York state senate education committee, he founded, with Ezra CORNELL, Cornell Univ., devoted to practical higher education, including agriculture and the mechanical arts. Desiring an institution free of attachments to all sects and parties, White endorsed a system of free elective studies at Cornell. His writings include *History of the Warfare of Science with Theology in Christendom* (1896).

White, Edward Douglass, 1845–1921, associate justice (1894–1910) and 9th chief justice (1910–21) of the U.S. SUPREME COURT; b. Lafourche parish, La. He was judge of the Louisiana supreme court (1879–80) and a U.S. senator (1891–94). On the U.S. Supreme Court he was generally conservative in his decisions, and he is best known for his "rule of reason" opinions in the antitrust cases against the Standard Oil and American Tobacco companies in 1911.

White, Edward Higgins, II, 1930–67, American astronaut; b. San Antonio. While serving as pilot of *Gemini 4* (June 3–7, 1965), he became the first American to perform extravehicular activity. He had been selected to be command-module pilot for the first manned Apollo flight, but was killed with crewmates Virgil Grissom and Roger Chaffee on Jan. 27, 1967, when a fire occurred in the spacecraft during a preflight ground test.

White, E(lywn) B(rooks), 1899–1985, American writer; b. Mt. Vernon, N.Y. A witty, satiric observer of contemporary society, he wrote for the *New Yorker.* In addition to light, humorous verse, his works include *Is Sex Necessary?* (with James THURBER, 1929), *One Man's Meat* (1942), and *Here Is New York* (1949). Among White's children's books are *Stuart Little* (1945) and *Charlotte's Web* (1952).

White, Patrick, 1912–90, Australian novelist; b. London. He spent a life farming in the Australian outback and writing in a hypnotically descriptive style about the suffering of extraordinary people. His novels include *The Happy Valley* (1939), *Voss* (1957), *The Eye of the Storm* (1974), *A Fringe of Leaves* (1977), and *The Twyborn Affair* (1980). He was awarded the 1973 Nobel Prize in literature.

White, Stanford, 1853–1906, American architect; b. N.Y.C. In 1879 he entered with C.F. MCKIM and William R. Mead into a partnership that influenced architecture over a long period. White's special talent was in interior design and furnishing, and the decorative aspects of a building. His two surviving New York City works, the Washington Arch and the Century Club, reveal his interest in Renaissance ornament. White was shot and killed in Madison Square Garden by Harry K. Thaw because of his affair with Thaw's wife, Evelyn Nesbit Thaw.

White, T(erence) H(anbury), 1906–64, English author; b. India. His tetralogy *The Once and Future King* (1939–58) is a dramatic, idiosyncratic retelling of the ARTHURIAN LEGEND. He also wrote *The Goshawk* (1951) and *A Book of Beasts* (1954).

White, William Allen, 1868–1944, American author; b. Emporia, Kans. As editor of the Emporia *Gazette* (1895–1944) he was a spokesman for grass-roots liberal Republicanism. White also wrote fiction, biographies of Woodrow WILSON and Calvin COOLIDGE, and an autobiography (1946).

white dwarf, in astronomy, star that is abnormally faint for its white-hot temperature. It has the mass of the sun, the radius of the earth, and a central density about one million times that of water. White dwarfs have exhausted their nuclear fuel and represent one of the final stages of STELLAR EVOLUTION (see also GRAVITATIONAL COLLAPSE).

Whitefield, George, 1714–70, English evangelistic preacher, leader of the Calvinistic Methodist church. At Oxford he joined the Methodist group led by John and Charles WESLEY. Beginning in 1738 he made seven trips to America, where he was influential in the GREAT AWAKENING. After becoming an Anglican priest, he adopted (c.1741) Calvinistic views, especially concerning predestination. He broke with the Wesleys and led the Calvinistic Methodists, who were numerous in Wales. Whitefield continued to draw great throngs on his evangelistic tours. He died in Newburyport, Mass.

Whitehead, Alfred North, 1861–1947, English mathematician and philosopher. He taught mathematics at the Univ. of London (1911–24) and philosophy at Harvard Univ. (after 1924). *Principia Mathematica* (3 vol., 1910–13), which he wrote with Bertrand Russell, is a landmark in the study of logic. His inquiries into the structure of science provided the background for his metaphysical work. His "philosophy of organism" (for which he developed a special vocabulary) viewed the universe as consisting of processes of becoming, and God as interdependent with the world and developing from it. His many works include *Science and the Modern World* (1925) and *Process and Reality* (1929).

Whitehorse, city (1991 pop. 17,925), capital of Yukon Territory, NW Canada, on the Yukon R. Developed as an important supply center during the KLONDIKE gold rush (1897–98), it is now chiefly an administrative and tourist center for surrounding mining, fur-trading, and hunting areas. Whitehorse replaced DAWSON as the territorial capital in 1952.

White House, official name of the mansion of the president of the U.S., on Pennsylvania Ave., Washington, D.C. It was designed by James HOBAN on a site chosen by George WASHINGTON and begun in 1792. John ADAMS was the first president to live there. After it was burned (1814) by the British, it was restored and painted white. It had, however, been called the "White House" earlier. Theodore Roosevelt made the name official. Of Virginia freestone, it is simple and stately, four stories high and about 170 ft (52 m) long by 85 ft (26 m) wide. On the north front, forming the main entrance, is a portico of Ionic columns reaching from ground to roof pediment. It is balanced by a semicircular colonnaded balcony on the south. The east and west terraces, executive office (1902), and east wing (1942) have been added. Large receptions are usually held in the East Room. The elliptical Blue Room is the scene of many social and official receptions. The grounds cover about 18 acres (7 hectares).

Whiteman, Paul, 1891–1967, American conductor; b. Denver. In 1924 he inaugurated "symphonic jazz" by introducing GERSHWIN'S *Rhapsody in Blue.* He also encouraged the writing of concert JAZZ.

White Russia: see BELARUS.

White Sands, desert area, S central N.Mex., site of a major U.S. missile-testing range. On July 16, 1945, the first atomic bomb was exploded there at Holloman Air Force (formerly Alamogordo Air) Base. The area includes a national monument and a wildlife refuge.

white shark: see SHARK.

Whitlam, (Edward) Gough, 1916–, Australian prime minister (1972–75). His Labor government was plagued by economic problems and in 1975, during a budget crisis, he was dismissed by Governor General Sir John Kerr. Defeated (1975, 1977) at the polls, he retired from politics in 1978.

Whitman, Marcus, 1802–47, American Protestant missionary in the Oregon country; b. Federal Hollow (later Rushville), N.Y. A physician, he founded (1836) a mission at Waiilaptu. He returned East but in 1843 was part of the "great emigration" over the OREGON TRAIL. He was killed by the Cayuse.

Whitman, Walt(er), 1819–92, one of the greatest American poets; b. West Hills, N.Y. Early in his life he worked as a printer, teacher, newspaper editor, and carpenter. In 1855 he published the volume that was to make his reputation, *Leaves of Grass* (containing the emblematic "Song of Myself"), which the poet continued to enlarge and revise through a number of editions until his death. Innovative in its use of rhythmical free verse and its celebration of sexuality, the book in time proved the single most influential volume of poems in American literary history. In its own day, however, only a few, notably EMERSON, recognized its genius. Whitman worked as a Civil War nurse (1862–65), publishing war poetry in *Drum-Taps* (1865) and *Sequel to Drum-Taps* (1865–66). His later works include the prose collections *Democratic Vistas* (1871). A semi-invalid after a stroke in 1873, he lived in Camden, N.J. Whitman, who inspired later poets to experimentation in both prosody and subject matter, was the preeminent celebrator of individual freedom and dignity, democracy, and human brotherhood.

Whitney, Eli, 1765–1825, American inventor of the COTTON GIN; b. Westboro, Mass. He completed (1793) a model gin that rapidly separated the fiber of short-staple cotton from the seed. Whitney was unable to meet the demand for the machine, and his 1794 patent received legal protection only from 1807 to 1812. Thus the invention, which created great wealth for others who copied his model, gained him little. In 1798 he began producing the first firearms with standardized, interchangeable parts.

Whitney, Mount, second highest peak in the U.S. (after Mt. McKinley, Alaska), in the Sierra Nevada, central Calif. It is 14,491 ft (4,417 m) high and was named for the U.S. geologist Josiah D. Whitney, who surveyed it in 1864.

Whitney Museum of American Art, N.Y.C., founded 1930 by Gertrude Vanderbilt Whitney; opened 1931. The museum actively supports American art through the purchase and exhibition of work by living artists. Its extensive collection is housed in a building designed by Marcel BREUER and opened in 1966.

The Whitney Museum of American Art

Whittier, John Greenleaf, 1807–92, American poet; b. near Haverhill, Mass. A Quaker, he was a vigorous and politically powerful abolitionist editor and writer, especially from 1833 to 1840. After the Civil War he devoted himself completely to poetry. Although he often celebrated the common people, as in *Songs of Labor* (1850), his best work, e.g., *Moll Pitcher* (1832), *Snow-bound* (1866), and *Maud Muller* (1867), pictures the life, history, and legends of New England. Such poems as "Barbara Frietchie," "Marguerite," and "The Barefoot Boy," as well as his nearly 100 hymns, made Whittier one of the most popular poets of his time.

Whittington, Richard, 1358–1423, English merchant and three-time lord mayor of London. He made his fortune as a mercer and supplied large loans to HENRY IV and HENRY V. A legend later arose that Whittington gained his fortune when his cat was sold to the ruler of Morocco.

whooping cough or **pertussis,** highly communicable, infectious disease, predominantly of childhood. The early stage is manifested by symptoms of an upper respiratory infection; after about two weeks, a series of paroxysmal coughs are followed by a characteristic high-pitched "whoop" as a breath is taken. A serious disease, whooping cough may give rise to such complications as PNEUMONIA, convulsions, and brain damage; infants should be immunized against the disease as early as possible.

Whorf, Benjamin Lee, 1897–1941, American linguist and anthropologist; b. Winthrop, Mass. A significant figure in Mayan and Aztec LINGUISTICS, he also collaborated with Edward SAPIR to develop the Sapir-Whorf hypothesis, or linguistic relativity principle. It posits language as an array of formal categories that group experiences into usable classes, vary across cultures, and influence thought.

Wichita, indigenous people of the Plains (see NORTH AMERICA, INDIGENOUS PEOPLES OF), with a Caddoan language of the Hokan-Siouan stock (see NATIVE AMERICAN LANGUAGES). They once lived in Kansas, ranging into Oklahoma and Texas. Distinctive features of their culture were conical grass houses and a horn dance for land fertility. By 1765 they had been forced into Oklahoma by hostile tribes; later, reduced by smallpox to 2,500, they occupied the site of Wichita, Kansas. After ceding their lands to the U.S. (1872), they were settled on an Oklahoma reservation. In 1990 there were 1,275 Wichitas in the U.S.

Wichita, city (1990 pop. 304,011), seat of Sedgwick co., south-central Kans., on the Arkansas and Little Arkansas rivers; inc. 1870. The largest city in the state, it is the commercial and industrial center of S Kansas. Besides its huge aircraft industry, it has railroad shops, flour mills, meat-packing houses, and various manufactures. Founded (1868) on the site of a WICHITA village, it boomed as a cow town in the 1870s; oil was discovered nearby in 1915.

wickiup: see TEPEE, WICKIUP, AND WIGWAM.

Wickliffe, John: see WYCLIF, JOHN.

Wiclif, John: see WYCLIF, JOHN.

Wieland, Christoph Martin [vē'länt], 1733–1813, German poet and novelist. In an elegant rococo style, he treated themes from antiquity and fairy tales, e.g., *Oberon* (1780). His political satires include *The Golden Mirror* (1772) and *The Republic of Fools* (1774). Wieland also edited the influential literary journal *Teutsche Merkur* (1773–1810) and translated SHAKESPEARE.

Wiener, Norbert, 1894–1964, American mathematician and educator; b. Columbia, Mo. Known for his theory of CYBERNETICS and his contributions to the development of computers and calculators, Wiener also did research in probability theory and the foundations of mathematics.

Wiesel, Elie, 1928–, Romanian-American writer; b. Sighet, Romania. At 16 he was imprisoned in Nazi concentration camps at Auschwitz and Buchenwald, where his family perished. After the war, he studied at the Sorbonne. In the 1950s he was a correspondent for Israeli, American, and French newspapers. He became a U.S. citizen in 1963. The autobiographical novel *Night* (1958) recounts the horrors he witnessed as a death camp inmate. His novels, plays, retellings of biblical stories, and collections of Hasidic tales have focused on the importance of remembering the Holocaust. He was awarded the Nobel Peace Prize in 1986.

Wiggin, Kate Douglas (Smith), 1856–1923, American author; b. Philadelphia. An organizer of the kindergarten movement, she wrote such popular children's books as *Timothy's Quest* (1890) and *Rebecca of Sunnybrook Farm* (1903).

Wigglesworth, Michael, 1631–1705, American poet; b. England; came to New England, 1638. A Puritan clergyman, he wrote didactic verse, e.g., *Day of Doom* (1662), that reflects his dedication to his austere faith.

Wight, Isle of [wīt], island county (1991 pop. 126,600), 147 sq mi (381 sq km), S England. The island, which is a popular summer resort, is 23 mi (37 km) long and 13 mi (21 km) wide. The chief towns are Newport, the capital, and Cowes, a famous yachting center. Conquered (A.D. 43) by the Romans, it was (10th cent.) the Danish headquarters, and was taken by the English crown in 1293.

wigwam: see TEPEE, WICKIUP, AND WIGWAM.

Wilberforce, William, 1759–1833, British statesman and humanitarian. A friend of the younger William PITT, he secured passage (1807) of a bill abolishing the slave trade, and worked to suppress slavery in the British Empire. His son, **Samuel Wilberforce,** 1805–73, was bishop of Oxford from 1845 and of Winchester from 1869. He was influential in restoring ecclesiastical authority to English church conventions.

Wilbur, Richard, 1921–, American poet; b. N.Y.C. His skillfully crafted, original, and often wittily intellectual verse is collected in such volumes as *Things of This World* (1956; Pulitzer) and *The Mind-Reader* (1976).

wild carrot: see QUEEN ANNE'S LACE.

Wilde, Oscar (Oscar Fingall O'Flahertie Wills Wilde), 1854–1900, Irish writer. A follower of PATER and RUSKIN, he glorified beauty for itself alone. His genius was best expressed in his superbly witty plays, particularly *The Importance of Being Earnest* (1895). In his only novel, *The Picture of Dorian Gray* (1891), a young man is corrupted by sensual indulgence and moral indifference. Wilde's poems *The Ballad of Reading Gaol* (1898) and *De Profundis* (1905) were inspired by the prison term (1895–97) he served because of his homosexuality. He also wrote short stories, fairy tales, and essays.

wildebeest: see GNU.

Wilder, Billy, 1906–, American film director, producer, and writer;

b. Austria. He won Academy Awards for *The Lost Weekend* (1945), *Sunset Boulevard* (1950), and *The Apartment* (1960). Among his other films are *Stalag 17* (1953), *Some Like It Hot* (1959), and *Fedora* (1979).

Wilder, L(awrence) Douglas, 1931–, African-American political leader; b. Richmond, Va. In 1969 he won election (as a state senator) to the Virginia legislature, the first African American to do so since RECONSTRUCTION. He later served as Virginia's lieutenant governor (1986–90) and governor (1990–94); in the latter post he became the first elected African-American governor in the U.S.

Wilder, Thornton (Niven), 1897–1975, American author; b. Madison, Wis. His plays and novels maintain that true meaning and beauty are found in ordinary experience. His first important work was the novel *The Bridge of San Luis Rey* (1927; Pulitzer). Among his other novels are *The Cabala* (1926), *The Woman of Andros* (1930), and *Theophilus North* (1973). A serious and original dramatist who often used nonrealistic theatrical techniques, Wilder achieved critical recognition with the classic play *Our Town* (1938; Pulitzer). His other plays include *The Skin of Our Teeth* (1942; Pulitzer) and *The Matchmaker* (1954).

Wilderness campaign, in the U.S. CIVIL WAR, a series of engagements (May–June 1864) fought in the Wilderness region W of Fredericksburg, Va. Union Gen. U.S. GRANT attempted to clear the wild woodland prior to his planned attack on the main Confederate army of Gen. R.E. LEE. But Lee attacked first and a series of bloody encounters resulted, especially at Spotsylvania Courthouse (May 8–19). Grant then assaulted a strongly entrenched Confederate force at Cold Harbor and was repulsed with horrible slaughter. After losing 60,000 soldiers, Grant withdrew and moved against Petersburg.

Wilderness Road, principal route of westward U.S. migration, c.1790–1840. Running from Virginia through the CUMBERLAND GAP to the OHIO R., it was blazed in 1775 by Daniel BOONE. Abandoned after the building of the NATIONAL ROAD, its route is traced by part of U.S. 25, the Dixie Highway.

wildlife refuge, haven or sanctuary for animals in an area of land or land and water set aside and maintained for their preservation and protection. In the U.S. game laws were passed in various states as early as the late 17th cent. Modern wildlife-conservation policy began with a conference called by Pres. Theodore ROOSEVELT in 1908 to inventory the nation's natural resources. Recent legislation includes the Endangered Species Acts of 1966, 1969, and 1973. Today the U.S. Wildlife Refuge System, administered by the Fish and Wildlife Service, comprises 503 areas nationwide to protect big game (e.g., bison, bighorn sheep, and elk); small game; waterfowl; and colonial nongame birds such as pelicans, terns, and gulls. Most numerous are waterfowl refuges, which supply areas for breeding, wintering, resting, and feeding along major flyways during MIGRATION. Refuges have also been established by private individuals and societies such as the Nature Conservancy and National Audubon Society. Other countries also maintain parks, refuges, and game preserves. See also INTERNATIONAL UNION FOR THE CONSERVATION OF NATURE AND NATURAL RESOURCES.

wild rice, tall aquatic plant (*Zizania aquatica*) of the GRASS family, of a genus separate from common RICE (*Oryza*). Wild rice is a hardy annual with broad blades, reedy stems, and large terminal panicles. It grows in shallow water along the margins of ponds and lakes in the N U.S. and S Canada; certain varieties also grow in the South. The seed was long harvested from the wild by primitive methods, but newer strains have permitted cultivation. It was an important food of some Native Americans, especially in the Great Lakes region.

Wilhelmina, 1880–1962, queen of the NETHERLANDS (1890–1948), daughter of WILLIAM III. Her mother, Emma of Waldeck-Pyrmont, was regent until 1898. Wilhelmina married (1901) Prince Henry of Mecklenburg-Schwerin (d. 1934). When the Germans invaded the Netherlands (1940) in World War II she and her government fled to England. She returned in 1945, later abdicating in favor of her daughter, JULIANA.

Wilkes, Charles, 1798–1877, American naval officer and explorer; b. N.Y.C. In command of a government exploring expedition, he circled the globe (1838–42) with a group of scientists. They did research in the S PACIFIC and explored the Antarctic. As commander of the *San Jacinto* during the CIVIL WAR, he removed two Confederate officials from the British ship *Trent*, which almost caused the U.S. and Britain to go to war (see TRENT AFFAIR).

Wilkes, John, 1727–97, English politician and journalist. Entering Parliament in 1757, Wilkes attacked GEORGE III in his periodical the *North Briton*, and was expelled (1764) and imprisoned. Although repeatedly reelected, he was not allowed to take his seat until 1774. He then defended the liberties of the American colonies. Although a demagogue, Wilkes is remembered as a champion of freedom.

Wilkins, Sir George Hubert, 1888–1958, British explorer; b. Australia. After several arctic expeditions, he was the first to explore the region by air (1928), traveling from ALASKA to Spitsbergen. He was knighted that same year. In 1931 he headed an arctic submarine expedition.

Wilkins, Roy, 1901–81, African-American social reformer and civil-rights leader; b. St. Louis, Mo. As leader (1931–77) of the NATIONAL ASSOCIATION FOR THE ADVANCEMENT OF COLORED PEOPLE, Wilkins tirelessly advanced the cause of racial equality achieved through constitutional means, opposing both white supremacy and African-American separatism. He is credited by many as the principal architect of school desegregation and the 1964 Civil Rights Act.

Wilkinson, James, 1757–1825, American general; b. Calvert co., Md. He served in the AMERICAN REVOLUTION and was implicated in the Conway Cabal to remove WASHINGTON as commander in chief. Later he was a key figure in the conspiracy to split off the Southwest as a separate republic allied to Spain. Although in the pay of Spain himself, he was the chief government witness (1807) at the treason trial of Aaron BURR, and narrowly missed indictment.

will, in philosophy and psychology, term used to describe the faculty of mind that is alleged to stimulate motivation of purposeful activity. The concept has been variously interpreted by philosophers, some accepting will as a personal faculty or function (e.g., PLATO, ARISTOTLE, THOMAS AQUINAS, DESCARTES, and KANT) and others seeing it as the externalized result of the interaction of conflicting elements (e.g., SPINOZA, LEIBNIZ, and HUME). Still others describe will as the manifestation of personality (e.g., HOBBES, SCHOPENHAUER, and NIETZSCHE). The reality of individual will is denied altogether by the theological doctrine of determinism (see FREE WILL). Modern psychology considers the concept unscientific and has looked to other factors, such as unconscious motivation or physiological influence, to explain human actions.

Willard, Emma, 1787–1870, American educator, pioneer in women's education; b. Emma Hart, in Berlin, Conn. She founded (1821) Troy Female Seminary to offer collegiate education to women and new opportunity to women teachers. She published history textbooks and worked to improve common schools and women's education.

Willard, Frances, 1838–1898, American educator and temperance leader; b. Churchville, N.Y. She believed women could gain political power through the temperance crusade. As president of the Women's Christian Temperance Union, she supported women's suffrage. She helped found the Prohibition party (1882) and wrote *Women and Temperance* (1883).

William, emperors of Germany. **William I,** 1797–1888, emperor of Germany (1871–88) and king of Prussia (1861–88), was an essentially conservative ruler. Upon assuming the crown he set about reorganizing the army. When this met with opposition from parliament, he appointed (1862) Otto von BISMARCK prime minister, and was thereafter guided almost completely by Bismarck, who suppressed all opposition to the king and himself. Prussia began its series of military triumphs: the Danish war over SCHLESWIG-HOLSTEIN (1864), the Austro-Prussian War (1866), and the Franco-Prussian War (1870–71). Upon the surrender of NAPOLEON III, Bismarck had William crowned emperor of a unified Germany. William's rule was crucial in modern history, for it saw the rise of Germany as a great European power. **William II,** 1859–1941, emperor of Germany and king of Prussia (1888–1918), son and successor of Frederick III (r. March–June 1888), was the grandson of William I of Germany and Queen Victoria of England. His overbearing character soon clashed with that of Bismarck, whom he dismissed in 1890. Thereafter he was the dominant force in German affairs. His naval, colonial, and commercial aspirations antagonized Great Britain, France, Russia, and the United States, however, and his support of Austria's Balkan policy was a direct cause of WORLD WAR I. The Allies insisted on his abdication (1918) after the defeat of Germany. He lived in exile in the Netherlands.

William, kings of England. **William I** or **William the Conqueror,** 1027?–1087 (r.1066–1087), was the illegitimate son of Robert I, duke of Normandy, and succeeded to the dukedom in 1035. While visiting (1051) England, he was probably named by his cousin EDWARD THE CONFESSOR as successor to the throne, and in 1064 he extracted a promise of support from HAROLD, then earl of WESSEX. In 1066, hearing that Harold had been crowned king of England, William raised an army and crossed the Channel. He defeated and slew Harold at HASTINGS and was crowned king. William immediately built castles and harshly put down the rebellions that broke out; by 1072 the military part of the NORMAN CONQUEST was virtually complete. He substituted foreign prelates for many English bishops, and land titles were redistributed on a feudal basis (see FEUDALISM) to his Norman followers. After 1075 he dealt frequently with continental quarrels. William ordered a survey (1085–86) of England, the results of which were compiled as the DOOMSDAY BOOK. He was one of the greatest English monarchs and a pivotal figure in European history. His son Robert II succeeded him in Normandy, while another son, **William II** or **William Rufus,** d. 1100 (r.1087–1100), succeeded him in England. William II had utter contempt for the English church and extorted large sums of money from it. He occupied Normandy when Robert II left on a crusade, and gained control (1097) of the Scottish throne. He was killed while hunting, and his death may not have been an accident. His brother HENRY I succeeded him. **William III,** 1650–1702, king of England, Scotland, and Ireland (1689–1702), was the son of William II, prince of Orange. He became stadtholder of the Netherlands in 1672 and fought in the DUTCH WAR of 1672–78. In 1674 he made peace with England and married (1677) Mary, the Protestant daughter of James, duke of York (later JAMES II of England). After James's accession, William kept in contact with the king's opponents and in 1688 was invited by them to England. He landed with an army and brought about the GLORIOUS REVOLUTION. James was allowed to escape, and William accepted (1689) the offer of Parliament and reigned jointly with his wife, MARY II. William also accepted the BILL OF RIGHTS (1689), which greatly reduced royal power. He defeated (1690) the exiled James at the battle of the Boyne in Ireland and was involved in continental wars until LOUIS XIV recognized him as king in 1697. In England he relied increasingly on WHIG ministers, who were responsible for the establishment (1694) of the Bank of England and the policy of a national debt. William's popularity was diminished after the death (1694) of his childless wife and by the War of the SPANISH SUCCESSION. He was succeeded by Queen ANNE. **William IV,** 1765–1837, king of Great Britain and Ireland (1830–37), was the third son of GEORGE III. Generally passive in politics, he reluctantly gave his promise to the 2d Earl GREY to create, if necessary, enough peers to pass the REFORM BILL of 1832. Political leadership was left to the duke of WELLINGTON, Earl Grey, Viscount MELBOURNE, and Sir Robert PEEL. Good-natured but eccentric, William was only moderately popular. He was succeeded by his niece VICTORIA.

William, kings of the Netherlands and grand dukes of Luxembourg. **William I,** 1772–1843 (r.1815–40), was the son of Prince William V of Orange. He led the Dutch army (1793–95) in the FRENCH REVOLUTIONARY WARS. In 1815 the Congress of VIENNA made him first king of the NETHERLANDS; his domain included BELGIUM and LUXEMBOURG. Belgium rebelled in 1830 (see LONDON CONFERENCE). Forced to liberalize the Dutch constitution, he abdicated. **William II,** 1792–1849 (r.1840–49), was the son of William I. He led (1830) the Dutch army against the Belgians. As king he was compelled to grant (1848) further constitutional reforms. **William III,** 1817–90 (r.1849–90), was the son of William II. He ruled as a constitutional monarch in cooperation with the States-General. On his death his daughter, WILHELMINA, became queen of the Netherlands, and Luxembourg passed to Duke Adolf of Nassau.

William, king of Scotland: see WILLIAM THE LION.

William I, prince of Orange: see WILLIAM THE SILENT.

William of Occam or **Ockham,** c.1285–1349, English philosopher. An exponent of SCHOLASTICISM, he was charged (1324) with heresy by Pope John XXII and fled (1328) to the protection of the pope's great enemy, Holy Roman Emperor Louis IV; his political writings thereafter supported the temporal power of the emperor over that of the pope. Occam's teachings mark an important break with previous medieval philosophy. Adhering to the position of NOMINALISM, he rejected the Aristotelian REALISM of St. Thomas Aquinas, specifically denying the existence of universals except in people's minds and language. He disputed the self-evidence of the Aristotelian final cause and of the existence of God, denying the competence of reason in matters of faith. This led him to hold that logic can be studied outside the province of metaphysics, a position that proved important in the development of scientific enquiry. In logic, Occam is remembered for his use of the principle of parsimony, formulated as "Occam's razor," which enjoined economy in explanation with the axiom "It is vain to do with more what can be done with less."

William of Orange. For William I, prince of Orange, see WILLIAM THE SILENT; for William III, king of England, see under WILLIAM, kings of England.

Williams, Eric, 1911–81, Trinidadian scholar and politician. Having received his doctorate from Oxford (1938), he left a teaching post at Howard Univ. to foster Caribbean nationalism. He founded the People's National Movement (1956) and served as prime minister of Trinidad and Tobago from independence (1962) until his death.

Williams, Hank, 1923–53, American country singer and songwriter; b. near Georgiana, Ala. He is one of the most important figures in country music's history. His melancholy voice and powerful, simply written songs continue to attract fans.

Williams, Roger, c.1603–1683, American colonial clergyman, advocate of religious freedom, founder of RHODE ISLAND; b. England. Banished by the Puritans from Massachusetts, he established PROVIDENCE in 1636 and welcomed religious dissenters there. In 1654 he became president of the combined colonies of Providence, Newport, Narragansett, and Warwick. He was a trusted friend of the indigenous tribes.

Williams, Ted (Theodore Samuel Williams), 1918–, American baseball player; b. San Diego. One of the finest natural hitters the game has ever known, he played (1939–60) with the Boston Red Sox

Ted Williams

continuously, except for military service in World War II and Korea. The tall, left-handed-hitting outfielder, known as the "Splendid Splinter," led the American League in batting six times and in home runs four times. He was the last player to bat over .400 (.406 in 1941). His career totals included a batting average of .344 and 521 home runs. Williams managed the Washington Senators (later, Texas Rangers) from 1969 to 1972.

Williams, Tennessee (Thomas Lanier Williams), 1914–83, one of America's foremost playwrights; b. Columbus, Miss. His poetic dramas, filled with tension and brilliant dialogue, explore society's passions and frustrations. He scored his first successes with *The Glass Menagerie* (1945) and *A Streetcar Named Desire* (1947; Pulitzer). His other plays include *Cat on a Hot Tin Roof* (1955; Pulitzer), *Sweet Bird of Youth* (1959), *The Night of the Iguana* (1961), and *Small Craft Warnings* (1972). Williams also wrote short stories, two novels, verse, and his *Memoirs* (1975).

Williams, William Carlos, 1883–1963, one of the most important modern American poets; b. Rutherford, N.J. A practicing physician, Williams was an acute observer of American life. In his mature verse he developed a lucid, vital style reflecting idiomatic speech and faithful to ordinary things seen and heard. His books of poetry include *Collected Poems* (1934), *Pictures from Brueghel* (1963; Pulitzer), and his major work, the five-volume philosophical poem *Paterson* (1946–58). Williams also wrote critical essays, e.g., *In the American Grain* (1925); short stories; plays; and novels.

Williamsburg, city (1990 pop. 11,530), SE Va., on a peninsula between the James and York rivers; settled 1632 as Middle Plantation, laid out and renamed 1699, inc. 1722. It is a great tourist attraction. Capital of Virginia from 1699 to 1779, it later declined, but in 1926 large-scale restoration began: hundreds of buildings were removed, renovated, or rebuilt, and today Williamsburg retains its colonial appearance. William and Mary College (founded 1693) is located there.

William the Lion, 1143–1214, king of Scotland (1165–1214). William aided the rebellion in England of HENRY II's sons, but was captured by Henry and forced to sign (1174) the treaty of Falaise, which made Scotland a feudal possession of England. In 1189 he bought an annulment of the treaty from RICHARD I. His alliance (1168) with LOUIS VII of France started the long French-Scottish friendship.

William the Silent or **William of Orange** (William I, prince of Orange), 1533–84, principal founder of Dutch independence. A member of the house of NASSAU, he inherited (1544) the principality of Orange, in S France, and was made (1555) stadtholder of Holland, Zeeland, and Utrecht. He opposed repression of the NETHERLANDS by PHILIP II of Spain and helped form the GUEUX party (1566). The duke of ALBA was sent to put down the rebellion (1567), while William, in exile, raised an army to drive the Spanish out. In 1576 the provinces of the Netherlands united under William, but in 1580 he was forced to seek the aid of FRANCIS, duke of Alençon and Anjou. Philip put a price on William's head in 1581, and at a critical stage of the independence struggle he was assassinated.

Willkie, Wendell Lewis, 1892–1944, American political leader; b. Elwood, Ind. A lawyer and head of a giant utility company, he became the unexpected Republican candidate for president in 1940. An opponent of isolationism, he supported F.D. ROOSEVELT's foreign policy but attacked NEW DEAL domestic programs. He attempted to liberalize the REPUBLICAN PARTY.

willow, common name for some members of the family Salicaceae, deciduous trees or shrubs of worldwide distribution. The family comprises the willows and poplars and is typified by male and female flowers borne in catkins on separate plants. The narrower-leaved willows (genus *Salix*) flourish in cold, wet ground. The weeping willow (*S. babylonica*), native to China, and the North American pussy willow (*S. discolor*), with silky catkins, are cultivated as ornamentals. The poplars (genus *Populus*), including the cottonwoods and aspens, usually have heart-shaped or ovate leaves. The white, or silver, poplar (*P. alba*), a popular ornamental native to Eurasia, is now naturalized in North America. The cottonwoods, also called poplars, typically have seeds covered with fibrous coats, which when released at maturity clump together in cottony balls. The quaking aspen (*P. termuloides*), of the mountains of the W U.S., has leaves that quiver in the slightest breeze. Large stands of aspen trees often consist of one or two clones connected at the roots. The yellow poplar, or tulip tree, is an unrelated plant of the MAGNOLIA family.

Wills, Helen Newington, 1906–, American tennis player; b. Alameda co., Calif. Generally considered to have been the foremost woman tennis player of her era, she won the U.S. singles title seven times between 1923 and 1931 and the British singles title eight times between 1927 and 1938.

Wilmington, city (1990 pop. 71,529), seat of New Castle co., NE Del., on the Delaware R. and the Christina and Brandywine streams; settled 1638, inc. as a city 1832. E.I. DU PONT's first powder mill was established on the Brandywine in 1802, and the city grew into a great chemical center. Delaware's largest city and a thriving port, it has many company headquarters and diverse industries and is also a financial center. The city has been Swedish (1638), Dutch (1655), and British (1664). Old Swedes Church (1698) and the nearby Hagley and Winterthur museums and Longwood Gardens are of particular interest.

Wilmot, John: see ROCHESTER, JOHN WILMOT, 2D EARL OF.

Wilmot Proviso, 1846, amendment to a bill put before the U.S. House of Representatives during the MEXICAN WAR. The bill provided a $2 million appropriation for the settlement of border disputes with Mexico. The proviso, sponsored by Rep. David Wilmot of Pennsylvania, would have prohibited SLAVERY in any territory acquired in the Mexican War. The amendment failed in the Senate and never became law, but it created great bitterness and helped crystallize the conflict between North and South.

Wilson, Sir Angus, 1913–91, British writer; b. South Africa. His novels depict a society corrupt in both its public and private aspects. They include *Anglo-Saxon Attitudes* (1956), *No Laughing Matter* (1967), and *Setting the World on Fire* (1980). Wilson has also published collections of short stories.

Wilson, August, 1945–, African-American playwright; b. Pittsburgh, Pa. His emotionally powerful plays are concerned with the experiences of African Americans during the 20th cent. Wilson's plays include *Ma Rainey's Black Bottom* (1984), *Fences* (1987; Pulitzer), *The Piano Lesson* (1990; Pulitzer), and *Two Trains Running* (1992).

Wilson, Charles Thomson Rees, 1869–1959, Scottish physicist. He was Jacksonian professor of natural philosophy at Cambridge. Noted for his studies of atmospheric electricity, he devised a method for protecting barrage balloons from lightning during World War II. For his invention of the Wilson cloud chamber (see PARTICLE DETECTOR) for studying the activity of ionized particles, he shared with Arthur COMPTON the 1927 Nobel Prize in physics.

Wilson, Edmund, 1895–1972, probably the foremost American social and literary critic of the 20th cent; b. Red Bank, N.J. In the 1920s he was an editor of *Vanity Fair* and the *New Republic.* As a critic, he explored the social, psychological, and political conditions that shape literary ideas, a task facilitated by his knowledge of Marxian and Freudian theory. Among his major works are *Axel's Castle* (1931), a study of symbolism; *The Wound and the Bow* (1941); *The Shores of Light* (1952); and *Patriotic Gore* (1962). His social studies include *To the Finland Station* (1940), on the European revolutionary tradition; and *The American Earthquake* (1958), on the Great Depression. Versatile, with wide-ranging interests, he also wrote novels, short stories, plays, and memoirs.

Wilson, Edmund Beecher, 1856–1939, American zoologist; b. Geneva, Ill. He taught at Columbia Univ. (1891–1928), where he initiated genetic research. His main work was on the function of the cell in heredity and on the role of the chromosomes (including the significance of the sex chromosome). His major writing was *The Cell in Development and Inheritance* (1896).

Wilson, Edward O(sborne), 1929–, American biologist and leading proponent of SOCIOBIOLOGY; b. Birmingham, Ala. Educated at the Univ. of Alabama and at Harvard, he joined the Harvard faculty in 1956 and later became professor of zoology. His exhaustive study of ants and other social insects (on which he is the world's chief authority) led to publication of *Sociobiology* (1975), a controversial work on the genetic factors in human behavior; *On Human Nature* (1978; Pulitzer); and, with Bert Hölldobler, *The Ants* (1990; Pulitzer).

Wilson, (James) Harold, 1916–, British prime minister (1964–70, 1974–76). An economist, Wilson was elected to Parliament in 1945 as a Labour party member. He became a spokesman for the party's left wing and in 1963 was elected party leader. As prime minister Wilson worked for closer ties to Europe and to bolster the sagging British economy. His efforts to solve the problem of Rhodesia (see ZIMBABWE) failed. In 1976 he unexpectedly announced his retirement as prime minister and was later knighted. He retained his seat in the House of Commons until created Baron Wilson of Rievaulx (1983).

Wilson, Lanford, 1937–, American playwright; b. Lebanon, Mo. He is a master of realistic dialogue in which monologue, conversation, and direct address overlap. His favorite themes are decay, dissolution, and loss. Among his plays are *The Hot l Baltimore* (1973), *The Fifth of July* (1977), *Talley's Folly* (1979; Pulitzer), *Burn This* (1987), and *Redwood Curtain* (1993).

Wilson, Pete(r Barton), 1933–, U.S. politician; b. Lake Forest, Ill. A lawyer and moderate Republican, he served in the state assembly (1967–72) and as mayor of San Diego (1972–83) before he was elected (1982, 1986) to the U.S. Senate from California. Wilson became governor of California in 1991.

Wilson, (Thomas) Woodrow, 1856–1924, 28th president of the U.S. (1913–21); b. Staunton, Va. He was educated in law at Princeton Univ., the Univ. of Virginia, and Johns Hopkins Univ. (Ph.D., 1886). A noted scholar, he taught at Bryn Mawr College and Wesleyan Univ. before becoming (1890) professor of jurisprudence and political economy at Princeton. In 1902 he became president of Princeton. In 1910 he was elected governor of New Jersey on a reform Democratic ticket. As governor (1911–13) he accomplished various important reforms. At the 1912 Democratic convention he was nominated for president on the 46th ballot, largely through the efforts of W.J. BRYAN and E.M. House. He was elected president when the Republican vote was split between W.H. TAFT and Theodore ROOSEVELT. Wilson's domestic program, known as the "New Freedom," was generally progressive; among its accomplishments were the FEDERAL RESERVE SYSTEM (1913), the FEDERAL TRADE COMMISSION (1914), and the Clayton Antitrust Act (1914). In foreign affairs, the early difficulties with Mexico (see HUERTA, VICTORIANO; VILLA, FRANCISCO) were soon overshadowed by the outbreak of WORLD WAR I in Europe. Wilson's early efforts to maintain U.S. neutrality were shaken by the sinking (1915) of the LUSITANIA and other German aggressions. Nevertheless, he ran for reelection in 1916 on the boast of having "kept us out of war," and narrowly defeated Charles Evans HUGHES, the Republican candidate. Relations with Germany continued to deteriorate and war was declared on Apr. 6, 1917. Wilson viewed the war as necessary to make the world "safe for democracy" and quickly put the nation on a war footing. Looking forward to peace, he enunciated his plans for its implementation with his FOURTEEN POINTS. When the war ended, he sailed (Dec., 1918) for Europe to take part in the peace talks. Wilson's idealism was widely admired in Europe, and he was looked upon as the best hope for a just peace. Despite his disappointment with the eventual treaty (see VERSAILLES, TREATY OF), he pinned his great hopes on the LEAGUE OF NATIONS. At home, however, isolationism had reasserted itself, particularly among the Republicans in Congress. Wilson's last efforts as president were spent in a futile attempt to win U.S. ratification of (and thus membership in) the League. Exhausted from his labors, he suffered a stroke in Sept. 1919 and never fully recovered. He was awarded the 1919 Nobel Peace Prize.

Wilson, William Bauchop, 1862–1934, American labor leader; b. Scotland. He worked in Pennsylvania coal mines as a child and in 1890 helped organize the United Mine Workers of America. A Democratic congressman (1907–13), he headed a committee that drafted the bill creating the U.S. Dept. of LABOR and served (1913–21) as the first secretary of labor.

Winchester, town (1991 pop. 96,386), Hampshire, S England. It was the capital of the Anglo-Saxon kingdom of WESSEX. Even after the NORMAN CONQUEST, when LONDON gained political ascendancy, Winchester remained England's center of learning. It is the site of Winchester College (est. 1382), one of the country's great public schools. The city also exerted great ecclesiastical influence, as reflected in its magnificent cathedral (11th–14th cent.)

Winckler, Hugo, 1863–1913, German Orientalist. A professor at the Univ. of Berlin, he helped excavate the Phoenician city of Sidon. During excavations at BOĞAZKÖY (1906–7) he discovered CUNEIFORM tablets in Hittite.

wind, flow of air parallel to the earth's surface. The direction of wind is indicated by a weather vane. A wind is named according to the direction from which it is blowing, e.g., a wind blowing from the north is a north wind. Wind velocity is measured by means of a cup anemometer, an instrument with three or four small hollow metal hemispheres set so that they catch the wind and revolve about a vertical rod; an electrical device records the revolutions of the cups and thus the wind velocity. Winds are caused by the unequal heating of the earth's surface by the sun. Warmer air expands, becomes lighter, and rises. Cooler air rushes in from surrounding areas to fill the empty space. This process continues, creating a steady flow of air called a convection current. This, along with the rotation of the earth (see CORIOLIS EFFECT) and other secondary factors, causes the basic planetary wind systems that circle the earth, bringing constant changes in the weather.

Windaus, Adolf [vĭn'dous], 1876–1959, German chemist. A professor of chemistry and director of the chemistry laboratories at the Univ. of Göttingen, he won the 1928 Nobel Prize in chemistry for his work on sterols, especially in relation to vitamins. He discovered and synthesized vitamin D_3, the component of vitamin D most important in preventing rickets.

Wind Cave National Park: see NATIONAL PARKS (table).

windflower: see ANEMONE.

Windhoek [vĭnt'ho͝ok], largest city (1988 est. pop. 115,000) and capital of Namibia. A communications and economic center, it is linked with South Africa's railroad network and conducts a large trade in Karakul sheep skins. In 1892 the city became the capital of the German colony of South West Africa; it was captured by South African troops in World War I. Windhoek still retains a German flavor.

wind instrument, any musical instrument whose tone is produced by a vibrating column of air. In the pipe ORGAN the column of air is set into motion by mechanical means. Other wind instruments are blown by the player and are divided into two groups, the woodwinds and the brass winds or brasses. The woodwinds include the instruments in the flute, clarinet, and oboe families. The brasses include the French horn, bugle, cornet, trombone, trumpet, and tuba. The wind passage of an instrument, called its bore, may be either cylindrical (as in the clarinet, trumpet, trombone, and most flutes) or conical (as in the oboe, French horn, and tuba). The length of the bore (the longer the bore, the lower the pitch) and the kind of mouthpiece (which affects the timbre) are more important than the material (metal or wood) and the shape (straight or round).

Woodwinds. The tone of woodwind instruments is produced by an airstream directed against an edge, either by blowing across or into a mouth hole (as in the flutes), or by forcing air against one or two thin strips of cane, wood, or metal set into the mouthpiece (as in the reed instruments). The foremost type of flute between the 16th and early 18th cent. was the recorder, an instrument with a soft tone, played vertically. It has enjoyed renewed popularity in the 20th cent., and is now available in plastic as well as wood. The transverse flute, with its greater volume and range of pitches, became the principal orchestral flute in the mid-18th cent. Transverse flutes were originally made of wood, but are now often made of silver. The fife, a small transverse flute used for military music, has been largely replaced by the stronger piccolo. The clarinet family includes all single-reed instruments. Clarinets are played vertically and are made in a variety of keys. B-flat and A clarinets are standard orchestral instruments; the higher E-flat clarinet, usually a band instrument, is occasionally used in the orchestra. The saxophone, although a member of the clarinet family and thus considered a woodwind, has a conical bore and is made of brass. Alto, tenor, and baritone saxophones are most frequently used, especially in bands. Members of the oboe family are those with double-reed mouthpieces. The family includes the English horn, an alto oboe used in opera and orchestral music; the bassoon, which plays in the tenor and bass registers; and the contrabassoon or double bassoon, the lowest voice of the family, consisting of a tube over 16 ft (5 m) long, doubled upon itself four times.

Brasses. The brasses, in which the lips of the player perform the function of reeds, include the bugle, cornet, trombone, trumpet, and tuba, all of which have cup-shaped mouthpieces, and the French horn, with a funnel-shaped mouthpiece. The bugle, a conical tube coiled once upon itself, is used principally for military and naval bugle calls. Common to orchestras and bands, the trumpet has a cylindrical bore in the shape of a flattened loop, and three valves to regulate pitch. The cornet, with its more conical bore, has greater agility than the trumpet but a less brilliant tone. The trombone, having a cylindrical bore twice bent on itself, has a sliding section that regulates pitch as it lengthens or shortens the instrument. "Tuba" is a general term for a group of low-pitched, valved brass wind instruments, including the familiar contrabass tuba and the sousaphone.

windmill, mechanical device that harnesses wind power in order to pump water, grind grain, power a sawmill, or drive an electrical generator. Windmills were probably not known in Europe before the 12th cent., but thereafter they became the chief source of power until the advent of the STEAM ENGINE during the Industrial Revolution. The operational apparatus of the typical Dutch windmill is a four-to-six-armed structure that carries sails made of light wood or canvas. Revolving in the wind, the sail mechanism turns a shaft that operates the pump, millstone, or saw. Modern windmills are made of various lightweight materials. New types, such as the wind turbine used to generate electricity, are designed to turn even in light winds. Their output—depending on their size and on wind speeds—can vary from 1 kw to the 2,500 kw produced by the newest experimental model.

wind shear, change in the direction or speed of the wind over a comparatively short distance. Shear is usually horizontal in direction, but under certain conditions it may be vertical. Microburst wind shear is an extremely violent downward blast of air that hits the earth and radiates outward. With its sharp shifts in wind direction and relative wind speed it can cause an aircraft to lose lift and crash, especially during takeoff or landing.

Windsor, family name of the royal house of Great Britain. The name Wettin, family name of Prince ALBERT, consort of Queen VICTORIA, was changed to Windsor by GEORGE V in 1917. ELIZABETH II decreed that she and her descendants bearing the title of prince or princess would retain the name Windsor.

Windsor, Edward, duke of: see Edward VIII under EDWARD, kings of England.

Windsor, Wallis Warfield, duchess of, 1896–1986, American-born wife of Edward, duke of Windsor, who as EDWARD VIII abdicated (1936) the British throne in order to marry her. She obtained a divorce from her second husband, E.A. Simpson, in Apr. 1937 and married Edward in June. Special letters patent denied her a share in his royal rank of duke.

Windsor, city (1991 pop. 191,435), SE Ontario, on the Detroit R., opposite DETROIT, Mich. It is a port of entry and a major Canadian industrial center, with automobiles, industrial machinery, and processed food among its principal manufactures. The area was first settled (1749) by French colonists and in the 1790s attracted many Loyalists fleeing the American Revolution. Several towns were combined in 1935 to create the modern city of Windsor.

Windsor, town (1986 est. pop. 132,000), Berkshire, S central England, on the Thames R. The importance of the town derives from **Windsor Castle,** the chief residence of English rulers since WILLIAM I. The castle was improved and rebuilt by several sovereigns. Part of the castle was severely damaged by fire in 1992.

wind tunnel, device for studying the interaction between a solid body and an airstream. A wind tunnel simulates the conditions of an aircraft in flight by causing a high-speed stream of air to flow past a model of the aircraft (or part of an aircraft) being tested. The model is mounted on wires so that lift and drag forces on it can be determined by measuring the tension in the wires. Pressures on the model surface are measured through small flush openings on the surface. Wind tunnels are also used to study the effect of wind on other objects, such as automobiles, buildings, and bridges. See AERODYNAMICS.

Windward Islands: see WEST INDIES.

wine, alcoholic beverage made by FERMENTATION of the juice of the grape. Wines are distinguished by color, flavor, bouquet (aroma), and alcoholic content. They may be red (when whole crushed red or black grapes are used), white (using green grapes or the juice of other grapes only), or rosé (when the skins of red or black grapes are removed after fermentation has begun). Wines are also classified as dry (when grape sugar ferments completely) or sweet (when some sugar remains). There are three main types of wine: natural (still), fortified, and sparkling. The alcoholic content of natural wine comes from fermentation. Fortified wine (e.g., SHERRY, port, Madeira) has brandy or other spirits added to it. Sparkling wine (CHAMPAGNE is the best known) is fermented a second time after bottling. Wine is differentiated by the variety of grape, climate, location and soil of the vineyard, and treatment of the grapes before and during wine making. Fermentation starts when wine yeasts on the skins of ripe grapes come in contact with the grape juice (called must). Run off into casks, the new wine then undergoes a series of chemical processes, including oxidation, precipitation of proteins, and fermentation of chemical compounds, that create characteristic bouquet. After periodic clarification and aging in casks, the wine is ready to be bottled. The world's leading wine producer is France, with outstanding products from Bordeaux and Burgundy, the Loire and Rhone valleys, and Alsace. Other major producers are Italy, Spain, Germany, Chile, Argentina, South Africa, Australia, and the U.S. In the U.S., California is the leading wine-producing region, making European-type wines from grapes of the Old World species. The term *wine* is also applied to beverages made from other plants, e.g., dandelion and elderberry.

Winged Victory: see NIKE.

Winnebago, indigenous North American people with a Siouan language of the Hokan-Siouan stock (see NATIVE AMERICAN LANGUAGES). They lived in Wisconsin and had an Eastern Woodlands culture with some Plains traits (see NORTH AMERICA, INDIGENOUS PEOPLES OF), observing many elaborate ceremonies such as the buffalo dance and the winter feast. They sided with the British in the AMERICAN REVOLUTION and the WAR OF 1812 and secretly joined (1832) the SAC AND FOX in the BLACK HAWK WAR against U.S. troops. Much reduced in population, the Winnebago settled on reservations in Nebraska and Wisconsin. In 1990 there were 6,920 Winnebagos in the U.S.

Winnipeg, city (1991 pop. 616,790), provincial capital, Manitoba, W Canada, at the confluence of the Red and Assiniboine rivers. Long the largest city of the Canadian prairies, it remains one of the world's great wheat-marketing centers. The city is on the site of the French-built Fort Rouge (1738) and the North West Company's Fort Gibraltar, later renamed Fort Garry, then Fort Winnipeg. It began its modern development as an outlet for produce of the prairies when it was first reached by rail in 1881.

Winston-Salem, city (1990 pop. 143,485), seat of Forsyth co., central N.C., in the Piedmont. It is the nation's chief tobacco manufacturer, with extensive storage and auction facilities. Brewing, textiles, and electrical-equipment manufacturing are also important. The city is the financial and shipping center for NW North Carolina. Salem originated (1766) as a MORAVIAN settlement, and many early buildings remain. Winston was established in 1849, and the two communities merged in 1913. Wake Forest Univ. is in the city.

wintergreen or **checkerberry,** low evergreen plant (*Gaultheria procumbens*) of the HEATH family, native to sandy and acid woods of E North America and often cultivated. It has a creeping stem, erect branches, glossy, oval leaves, and small, waxy, white flowers followed by crimson fruits. The aromatic leaves are a source of wintergreen oil (now mostly obtained from the sweet birch or made synthetically), used in medicine and as a flavoring.

Winters, Yvor, 1900–1968, American poet and critic; b. Chicago. A professor at Stanford Univ. (1928–68), he wrote controversial criticism that emphasized the moral content of art. His major critical work is *In Defense of Reason* (1947). His poetry, e.g., *Collected Poems* (1952), ranges from austere to lyrical.

winter solstice: see SOLSTICE.

Winthrop, John, 1588–1649, governor of the Massachusetts Bay Colony; b. England. A member of the MASSACHUSETTS BAY COMPANY, he headed (1629) the group that founded Boston colony. As a distinguished member of the colony—he was elected governor 12 times—he helped shape its theocratic policies. A conservative, he opposed all efforts to liberalize religious or governmental policies. His son **John Winthrop,** 1606–76, b. England, became a lawyer and emigrated to Massachusetts Bay in 1631. In 1633 he was commissioned governor of the new colony at Saybrook (now Deep River), Conn., and in 1646 he founded New London. He was governor (1657, 1659–76) of Connecticut and accomplished (1664) the union of the Connecticut and New Haven colonies. His son **John Winthrop** (Fitz-John Winthrop), 1638–1707, b. Ipswich, Mass., also served as colonial governor of Connecticut. He went to England to serve in Oliver CROMWELL's army, but returned to America (1663) and fought in King Philip's War (1675–76). Elected governor in 1698, he ably served until his death.

Wirt, William, 1772–1834, U.S. attorney general (1817–29); b. Bladensburg, Md. Wirt was the prosecutor of Aaron BURR in 1807, and in 1832 ran for president on the ANTI-MASONIC PARTY ticket. He also wrote sketches in the style of Joseph ADDISON.

Wisconsin, upper midwestern state of the U.S.; bounded by Lake Superior and the Upper Peninsula of Michigan (N), Lake Michigan (E), Illinois (S), and Iowa and Minnesota (W), with the Mississippi R. forming much of that border.

Area, 56,154 sq mi (145,439 sq km). *Pop.* (1990) 4,891,769, a 4% increase over 1980 pop. *Capital,* Madison. *Statehood,* May 29, 1848 (30th state). *Highest pt.,* Timms Hill, 1,952 ft (595 m); *lowest pt.,* Lake Michigan, 581 ft (177 m). *Nickname,* Badger State. *Motto,* Forward. *State bird,* robin. *State flower,* wood violet. *State tree,* sugar maple. *Abbr.,* Wis.; WI.

Land and People. Wisconsin's most notable physical feature is its profusion of lakes: over 8,500, including Lake Winnebago (the largest). Much of the state consists of gently rolling uplands giving way to prairies in the south. Summers are pleasantly cool, except in the south, where temperatures are warm. Winters are often severely cold in the north. Over 65% of the population lives in urban areas. The largest city is MILWAUKEE, followed by MADISON and the port city of GREEN BAY. In 1990 the state was almost 92% white and 5% African American.

Economy. The state's principal manufactured products include industrial machinery, processed foods (especially cheese, butter, meat, and beer), fabricated metals, pulp and paper, and transportation and farm equipment. The chief source of farm income is dairy products (Wisconsin is the second largest U.S. producer), followed by cattle, corn, and hogs. The principal minerals extracted are sand and gravel, stone, lime, zinc, and copper. About 45% of the land is forested, and there is a vigorous lumbering industry.

Government. The amended constitution of 1848 provides for a governor serving a four-year term. The legislature consists of a senate with 33 members elected to four-year terms and a house with 99 members serving for two years. Wisconsin is represented in the U.S. Congress by two senators and nine representatives and has 11 electoral votes.

History. When the Frenchman Jean Nicolet arrived at the site of Green Bay in 1634 in search of furs and the NORTHWEST PASSAGE, the region was the home of the WINNEBAGO, KICKAPOO, and other tribes. Many of them were subsequently displaced by the OTTAWA and HURON, who were forced into the area by white settlement farther east. Great Britain obtained control of the area in 1763, and it formally passed to the U.S. in 1783, becoming part of the NORTHWEST TERRITORY. Wisconsin again fell into British hands temporarily during the WAR OF 1812. Large-scale settlement began in the 1820s, with settlers arriving via the ERIE CANAL and GREAT LAKES. Conflicts with Native Americans culminated in the BLACK HAWK WAR (1832), in which the tribes were brutally crushed. During the mid-19th cent. huge numbers of German immigrants arrived. In the 1870s the great pine forests of N Wisconsin were drastically reduced by a great lumber boom. Early in the 20th cent. Robert M. LA FOLLETTE gained national prominence as the leader of the Progressive movement, which had widespread support in Wisconsin resulting in much social legislation later adopted by other states and the federal government. Since World War II the state's industrial sector has undergone considerable expansion, and in the late 1980s and early 90s its economy weathered the national recession.

Wisdom, biblical book included in the Western canon and the Septuagint, but not in the Hebrew Bible, and placed in the APOCRYPHA in the Authorized Version. Traditionally called the Wisdom of Solomon, the book includes an exhortation to seek wisdom and a history of God's care of the Jews. It is a supreme example of wisdom literature (pre-Christian Jewish philosophical writings).

Wise, John, 1652–1725, American clergyman, exponent of the democratic principles of modern CONGREGATIONALISM; b. Roxbury, Mass. Pastor at Ipswich, Mass., from 1680, he opposed Increase and Cotton Mather (see under MATHER, RICHARD) by resisting the plan to place individual churches under the jurisdiction of associations of ministers.

Wise Men of the East, Magi, or **Three Kings,** men who came, bearing gifts of gold, frankincense, and myrrh, to adore the newborn JESUS. They were guided by the Star of Bethlehem. Christian tradition has set their number as three, called them kings, and named them Caspar or Gaspar, Melchior, and Balthazar. The EPIPHANY commemorates their visit.

Wissler, Clark, 1870–1947, American anthropologist; b. Wayne, Ind. A student of Franz BOAS, he originated the influential "culture area" concept for interpreting ethnographic data. In 1931 he became the first professor of anthropology at Yale Univ. His works include *Relation of Nature to Man in Aboriginal America* (1926) and *Indians of the United States* (1949).

wisteria or **wistaria,** woody, twining vine (genus *Wistaria*) of the PULSE family, cultivated and highly esteemed for the beautiful pendant clusters of lilac, white, or pink flowers. Two species are native to the U.S., but the showier Asian species are commonly cultivated.

witchcraft, exercise of supernatural powers through occult arts such as MAGIC, sorcery, and satanism. Its origins lie in the belief in separate powers of good and evil in ancient pagan cults and in religions including GNOSTICISM and ZOROASTRIANISM. The Christian church persecuted witches from the 14th to the 18th cent.: under the Spanish Inquisition, up to 100 alleged witches were burned in a day; in 1692, 20 persons were executed as witches in Salem, Mass. In the 20th cent. there has been a revival of witchcraft known as Wicca and based on a reverence for nature, the worship of a fertility goddess, a restrained hedonism, and group magic aimed at healing. See also SHAMAN.

witch hazel, common name for some members of the family Hamamelidaceae, trees and shrubs found mostly in Asia. The family includes the winter hazels (genus *Corylopsis*), the witch hazels (genus *Hamamelis*), the sweet gums (genus *Liquidambar*), and the witch elders (genus *Fothergilla*). The American witch hazel (*H. virginiana*), whose leaves resemble those of the HAZEL, is a fall-blooming shrub or small tree found E of the Rockies. The name *witch hazel* is also applied to an astringent liniment obtained from the leaves and bark of the plant. Sweet gums are characterized by their star-shaped leaves, their brilliant fall coloring, and their round fruits with hornlike projections. Their hard wood is used for cabinetmaking.

witenagemot [wĭt″ənəgĭmōt′] [Old Eng., = meeting of counselors], a session of counselors (the witan) of a king in Anglo-Saxon England. Such a body existed in each Anglo-Saxon kingdom. Composed of nobles and churchmen appointed by the king, the witan advised him on important matters. It probably had the power (especially in WESSEX) to elect a king.

Wither, George, 1588–1667, English poet. He was imprisoned for the satire *Abuses Stript and Whipt* (1613). There he wrote five pastorals, *The Shepherd's Hunting* (1615). His later works include *Fidelia* (1617) and *Fair Virtue* (1622).

Witherspoon, John, 1723–94, American clergyman, signer of the DECLARATION OF INDEPENDENCE; b. Scotland. A Presbyterian minister, he emigrated (1768) to America to become president of what is now Princeton Univ. He represented New Jersey at the CONTINENTAL CONGRESS.

Witt, Jan de [vĭt], 1625–72, Dutch statesman. As leader of the republican party he was elected (1653) grand pensionary, with control of state affairs and commerce. He negotiated an end to the first and second DUTCH WARS (1652–67) and the War of DEVOLUTION (1667–68). He sought to end the power of the house of Orange, but at the outset of the third Dutch war (1672–78) William of Orange (later WILLIAM III of England) was made stadtholder by popular acclaim, and de Witt resigned. He and his brother, Cornelius, a naval officer, although cleared of treason charges, were killed by a mob.

Witte, Count Sergei Yulyevich [vĭt'ə], 1849–1915, Russian statesman. He encouraged the development of industry with the help of foreign capital and Siberian colonization as finance minister (1892–1903) for NICHOLAS II, negotiated peace after the RUSSO-JAPANESE WAR (1904–5), and was premier from Oct. 1905 to April 1906.

Wittelsbach, German dynasty. It ruled BAVARIA from 1182, when Count Otto of Wittelsbach was given the duchy of Bavaria by Holy Roman Emperor Frederick I and ruled as Otto I. His son, Otto II, added the Rhenish Palatinate to the family's domains. In the following centuries the two domains were sometimes ruled together and sometimes separately by different branches of the Wittelsbachs. The dynasty's high point was reached in 1742, when Elector Charles Albert became Holy Roman Emperor CHARLES VII. In 1799 all family lands were united under a single ruler, Maximilian I, who in 1806 became king of a much-enlarged Bavaria. The dynasty ended when Louis III was deposed in 1918.

Wittenberg, city (1989 est. pop. 53,400), Saxony-Anhalt, E Germany, on the Elbe R. Today an industrial and mining center, it was first mentioned in the 12th cent. Martin LUTHER and Philip MELANCHTHON taught at its university, which became (16th cent.) the focus of the Protestant REFORMATION. Lucas CRANACH the elder founded a school of painting there. The 15th-cent. Schlosskirche, where LUTHER nailed his 95 theses, still stands.

Wittgenstein, Ludwig Josef Johan, 1889–1951, Austrian philosopher. He studied (1912–13) at Cambridge Univ. under Bertrand RUSSELL. In Vienna in the 1920s he came in contact with adherents of LOGICAL POSITIVISM; they were profoundly influenced by his first major work, the *Tractatus Logico-philosophicus* (1921), which posits a close, formal relationship between language, thought, and the world. Language and thought work literally like a picture of the real world, and to understand any sentence one must grasp the reference of its constituents, both to each other and to the real. Language, however, can indicate an area beyond itself; unsayable things (e.g., things not demonstrable) do exist, and sentences whose structure of meaning amounts to nonsense can result in philosophical insight. Thus Wittgenstein, unlike the logical positivists, allowed for the possibility of a metaphysics. He returned to Cambridge in 1929, and his philosophy entered a second phase, represented by *Philosophical Investigations* (1953). Revising his earlier analysis of language, he now saw language as a response to, as well as a reproduction of, the real. His work greatly influenced what has come to be called ordinary-language philosophy, which maintains that all philosophical problems arise from the illusions created by the ambiguities of language.

Witwatersrand or **the Rand,** rich gold-mining area and chief industrial region of South Africa, in the TRANSVAAL, between the Vaal and Olifants rivers. It includes SOWETO township and the cities of JOHANNESBURG, Benoni, Boksburg, Springs, and Germiston. The Rand produces about one third of the world's total gold output annually. Other major industries include steel milling, machine building, diamond cutting, and the manufacture of textiles and furniture.

Wladislaw, Wladyslaw, or **Wladislas,** Polish rulers: see LADISLAUS.

Wobblies: see INDUSTRIAL WORKERS OF THE WORLD.

Wodehouse, (Sir) P(elham) G(renville), 1881–1975, English novelist and humorist. He is famous for his comic stories of a forever-Edwardian England, featuring Bertie Wooster and his unflappable valet, Jeeves, e.g., *The Inimitable Jeeves* (1924).

Woden, Norse **Odin,** in GERMANIC RELIGION, the supreme God. He established the laws that governed the universe, created the first man and woman, and controlled human destiny. His wife was FRIGG, and his children included Thor, Balder, and Tiw.

Wöhler, Friedrich [vö'lər], 1800–1882, German chemist. Professor at the Univ. of Göttingen, he devised a method for isolating ALUMINUM that he also used to isolate BERYLLIUM and YTTRIUM. Wöhler's synthesis of urea opened a new era in organic chemistry and contributed to the theory of isomerism. He also contributed to the chemistry of metabolism.

Wolf, Hugo [vôlf], 1860–1903, Austrian composer. One of the supreme masters of the German art song, he wrote over 300 LIEDER, in which he adapted WAGNER's musical conceptions. He also wrote an opera, choral works, and chamber music.

wolf, carnivorous MAMMAL related to the JACKAL and DOG. Three wolf species are generally recognized: the gray wolf (*Canis lupus*), the red wolf (*C. rufus*), and the prairie wolf, or COYOTE. The gray wolf, also called timber wolf in North America, resembles a GERMAN SHEPHERD, with a shaggy coat, erect ears, and a bushy tail; the male is usually about 3 ft (90 cm) high at the shoulder and weighs about 100 lb (45 kg). Ruthless hunting nearly exterminated the gray wolf in the 48 states. The red wolf is smaller, 16 in. (41 cm) high at the shoulder and about 60 lb (27 kg), and ranges in color from reddish to nearly black. It is now mainly found in SE Texas and SW Louisiana but has been reintroduced in North Carolina and Tennessee.

Wolfe, James, 1727–59, British soldier. He captured LOUISBURG (1758) and defeated (1759) Gen. MONTCALM on the Plains of Abraham, causing Canada to fall to the British. Both Wolfe and Montcalm were killed in the battle.

Wolfe, Thomas (Clayton), 1900–1938, major 20th-cent. American novelist; b. Asheville, N.C. His four mammoth, highly autobiographical novels, *Look Homeward, Angel* (1929), *Of Time and the River* (1935), *The Web and the Rock* (1939), and *You Can't Go Home Again* (1940), follow a young man from his boyhood in the rural South to his career as a teacher and writer in New York City. The last two books were organized by his editor, Maxwell Perkins, from the material left after Wolfe's premature death. Characterized by lyrical and dramatic intensity and by an obsessive sense of memory, time, and place, the novels present a sweeping picture of American life. Wolfe's other writings include short stories and a writer's journal.

Wölfflin, Heinrich [völf'lĭn], 1864–1945, Swiss art historian. His theory of form greatly influenced art criticism. His works include *Classic Art* (1899).

wolfram: see TUNGSTEN.

Wolfram von Eschenbach [ĕsh'ənbäkh], c.1170–c.1220, German poet. One of the greatest German minnesingers (poets and singers of courtly love), he led a restless, roving life. His only complete work is the famous chivalric poem *Parzival,* noted for its lyricism, humor, and depth of conception. It is the source for the libretto of Richard WAGNER's music drama *Parsifal.*

Wollaston, William Hyde, 1766–1828, English scientist. His achievements include the discovery (1802) of the dark lines (Fraunhofer lines) in the solar spectrum; the invention of the reflecting goniometer and the camera lucida; the discovery of the elements PALLADIUM and RHODIUM; and the establishment of the equivalence of galvanic and frictional electricity. He endowed the Wollaston science medal, awarded annually by the Geological Society, London.

Wollongong, city (1991 pop. 239,900), New South Wales, SE Australia. It is a major iron and steel center; other manufactures include refined copper, chemicals, and textiles. Port Kembla, an important port and the site of one of the world's largest integrated steelworks, was merged with Wollongong in 1947.

Wollstonecraft, Mary, 1759–97, English author and feminist. After publishing *Vindication of the Rights of Woman* (1792), the first great document of FEMINISM, she lived in Paris and befriended leaders of the French Revolution. She married (1797) William GODWIN, but died giving birth to a daughter who became the noted writer Mary Wollstonecraft SHELLEY.

Wolsey, Thomas, 1473?–1530, English statesman and prelate, cardinal of the Roman Catholic Church. He rose rapidly in the service of the young HENRY VIII and by 1514 virtually controlled English domestic and foreign policy. Becoming cardinal and lord chancellor in 1515, he tried unsuccessfully to make England the mediator between France and the Holy Roman Empire. He was twice a candidate for the papacy. His enormous wealth and lavish living caused considerable resentment, and his enemies at court used Henry's divorce from KATHARINE OF ARAGÓN as a means for his ruin. Wolsey incurred the king's anger by failing to secure a quick and favorable decision on the divorce from the church. In Oct. 1529 he lost the chancellorship and all honors except the archbishopric of York. In Nov. 1530 he was arrested on false charges of treason; he died on his way to London.

wolverine or **glutton,** heavy, short-legged, bearlike MAMMAL (*Gulo gulo*) related to the WEASEL, c.3–3½ ft (91–106 cm) long. It inhabits the mountains of North America and Eurasia near the timberline, feeding on many different animals. Its long, dark-brown, frost-proof fur is prized by Eskimos as trim for hoods and cuffs.

woman suffrage, the right of women to vote. First proposed in the U.S. in 1848, the struggle for suffrage was led by Elizabeth Cady STANTON, Lucretia MOTT, Susan B. ANTHONY, Lucy STONE, and other feminists working on both the state and federal levels. The 19th amendment to the Constitution (1920) granted nationwide woman suffrage. In Great Britain John Stuart MILL argued (1869) eloquently for the right of women to vote. More effective was the militant movement that emerged (1903) under Emmeline PANKHURST. In 1928 equal voting rights for all women replaced the limited woman suffrage granted in 1918. Today women are enfranchised in all but a few nations.

wombat, shy, nocturnal MARSUPIAL of Australia and Tasmania, related to the KOALA. Thick-set, with a large head, short legs, a short tail, and a shuffling gait, it is about 3 ft (91.5 cm) long. Wombats live in burrows in forests and grasslands and eat grass, roots, and bark.

Women's Army Corps (WAC), U.S. army organization that enlisted women for noncombatant military duty. Created as an auxiliary corps in 1942, after U.S. entry into World War II, it was formally established within the regular army in 1948. It reached a peak enlistment of nearly 100,000 in 1945. The WAC was dissolved in 1978.

women's movement: see FEMINISM; WOMAN SUFFRAGE.

Wood, Grant, 1891–1942, American painter; b. Anamosa, Iowa. Influenced by German and Flemish primitive painting, he is noted for his paintings of the 1930s, in which stern people and stylized landscapes offer rigid, decorative images of the rural Midwest. Perhaps the best-known of these is *American Gothic* (1930; Art Inst., Chicago).

Wood, Leonard, 1860–1927, U.S. general; b. Winchester, N.H. He commanded the ROUGH RIDERS in the SPANISH-AMERICAN WAR. As governor general of the Philippines (1921–27), he pursued a harsh, unpopular policy.

wood, in botany, tissue (xylem) forming the bulk of the STEM of a woody plant. Xylem conducts the SAP upward from the ROOT system to the LEAF, stores food, and provides support; it is composed of various cell types specialized for each function. Xylem is formed in the growing season by the CAMBIUM. In temperate regions, cells formed in the spring or wet season are larger and thinner-walled than those formed in the summer or dry season; this results in conspicuous ANNUAL RINGS. Conifer wood (softwood) has a uniform, nonporous appearance; deciduous trees have a vessel-permeated xylem with a complex appearance, often called hardwood. Freshly cut wood contains much moisture and is dried (seasoned) in the sun or in kilns before use.

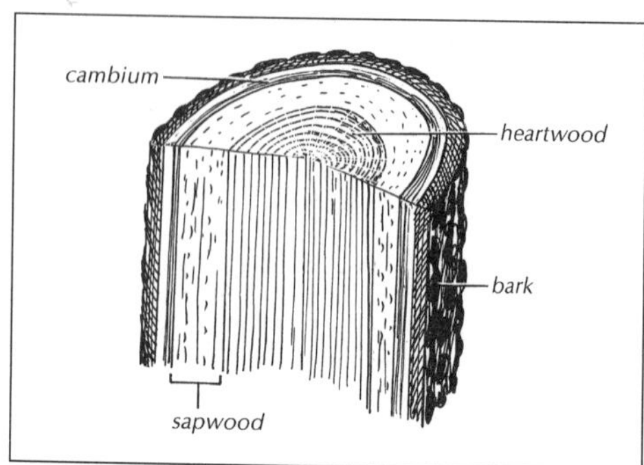

Wood: cross-section fo a woody stem

woodchuck or **groundhog,** species of marmot. This large RODENT, found throughout most of Canada and the NE U.S., has a heavyset body (about 2 ft/60 cm long, excluding the tail) and is covered with coarse, brownish hair. According to superstition the groundhog leaves its burrow on Feb. 2, Groundhog Day, and returns underground for six weeks if it sees its shadow, indicating six more weeks of winter.

Woodcock, Leonard Freel, 1911–, American labor leader and diplomat; b. Providence, R.I. A machine assembler in Detroit, he became active in the United Auto Workers (UAW) and succeeded (1970) Walter REUTHER as its president. In 1977 he was named head of the U.S. liaison mission in Beijing, People's Republic of China. After full diplomatic relations were established in 1979, he served (1979–81) as ambassador.

woodcut and wood engraving, prints made from designs cut in relief (where material is cut away to leave the design that is printed) on wood, in contrast to INTAGLIO methods (where the lines that are incised are printed) such as ENGRAVING and ETCHING. Woodcutting, the oldest form of printmaking, is done by cutting soft wood with a knife along the grain. Woodcuts appeared in Europe at the beginning of the 15th cent. At that time the same artist designed and carved the block. Later the cutting was often performed by specialists. Used for the block books that preceded printing, woodcuts were often employed as book illustrations after the invention of the printing press. During the RENAISSANCE the most eminent woodcut designers were DÜRER and Hans Holbein, the Younger (see under Hans HOLBEIN, the Elder). With the increasing popularity of engraving on metal, interest in woodcuts declined. It was not revived until the 1890s, with the prints of such artists as GAUGUIN and MUNCH. Many artists of the 20th cent. have used the woodcut; they include DERAIN, DUFY, MAILLOL, and BASKIN. The **wood engraving** is made on hard, end-grained wood carved with a graver or burin. The medium, in which lines usually print white on a black background, was popularized in 18th-cent. England by Thomas Bewick, who produced illustrations for a number of books, including John GAY's *Fables* (1779). Wood engraving was very popular in the 19th cent., in France (where its master was DORÉ), in England, and in the U.S.

Woodhull, Victoria (Claflin), 1838–1927, and **Tennessee Claflin,** 1846–1923, American journalists; b. Ohio. From childhood to early adulthood they were traveling spiritualists. In 1870 they began *Woodhull and Claflin's Weekly,* a sensational journal that supported such controversial goals as woman suffrage, free love, and socialism; in 1872 it published the first English translation of *The Communist Manifesto.* That same year Victoria Woodhull became the first woman candidate for president, running on the People's party ticket with Frederick DOUGLASS. The sisters moved to England in 1877.

woodpecker, name for some members of the family Picidae, climbing BIRDS found in much of the world. Woodpeckers typically have sharp, chisellike bills for pecking holes in trees, where they find insects. Among the North American species are the sociable downy woodpecker (*Picus pubescens*); the hairy woodpecker (*P. villosus*); and the red-crested or pileated woodpecker (*Hylotomus pileatus*). The flickers (genus *Melanerpes*), the only brown-backed woodpeckers, sometimes capture insects in the ground. The sapsuckers, which drink sap through small holes, can damage trees.

Woodson, Carter Goodwin, 1875–1950, African-American educator; b. New Canton, Va. Retiring from teaching (1922), he helped organize (1915) and devoted his time to the Association for the Study of Negro Life and History. He founded and edited the group's publication, the *Journal of Negro History.*

wood sorrel: see OXALIS.

Woodstock, town (1990 pop. 6,290), SE N.Y., in the foothills of the Catskill Mts. In the area are an artists' colony and a summer art school. The town gave its name to the most famous of the music festivals of the 1960s and 70s, held (Aug. 1969) near Bethel, N.Y., c.45 mi (70 km) to the SW.

Woodville, Elizabeth, 1437–92, queen consort of EDWARD IV. She married (1464) Edward in secret and provoked the anger of the powerful Richard Neville, earl of Warwick, but after the marriage became public she obtained many favors for her family. When Edward died (1483), their son EDWARD V became king, but was seized by his uncle, who usurped the throne as RICHARD III. Richard voided Elizabeth's marriage and Edward V and his younger brother were declared illegitimate and imprisoned. After HENRY VII seized the throne, he married (1486) Elizabeth's daughter Elizabeth.

Woodward, Robert Burns, 1917–79, American chemist. A professor at Harvard Univ., he was one of the first to determine the structure of such organic compounds as penicillin, strychnine, terramycin, and aureomycin. For his synthesis of organic compounds (e.g., quinine, patulin, cholesterol, cortisone, strychnine, lysergic acid, lanosterol, reserpine, chlorophyll, and tetracycline) he won the 1965 Nobel Prize in chemistry.

wool, fiber from the fleece of the domestic SHEEP. Wool is warm, absorbent, elastic, strong, and crease-resistant. It was probably the first FIBER to be made into cloth, since herding flocks was the first step in the change from primitive culture and wool is found only on domesticated sheep. Egyptian, Babylonian, and Peruvian archaeological remains have yielded fragments of woolen fabrics. England, with a heritage of sheep raising and weaving from its early history and from Roman influence, became Europe's great wool-producing country, and wool was the staple of British industry until the 18th cent., when COTTON began to supplant it. In the American colonies sheep raising began at JAMESTOWN, and SPINNING and weaving were important domestic industries. The first factory in America using water power to weave wool was opened at Hartford, Conn., in 1788. The U.S. now produces a substantial amount of the world's wool; other major producers include Australia, Great Britain, Russia, and Kazakhstan. In wool making, sheep are sheared with mechanical clippers. The wool is then sorted according to fineness, crimp, length of fiber, and felting qualities, and dirt and lanolin are removed. Wool may be bleached or dyed as fleece, yarn, or cloth. Woolen cloth is woven from short-staple fibers spun into soft yarn. Worsted yarn produces cloth with a hard, smooth texture, e.g., gabardine, serge.

Woolf, Virginia (Stephen), 1882–1941, English novelist. She was an innovative influence on the 20th-cent. novel. With her husband, Leonard Woolf, she set up the Hogarth Press in 1917. Their home was the center for the BLOOMSBURY GROUP. In her writing she concentrated on the flow of ordinary experience through the STREAM OF CONSCIOUSNESS technique. Her prose is poetic, symbolic, and visual. Woolf's novels include *Mrs. Dalloway* (1925), *To the Lighthouse* (1927), *Orlando* (1928), *The Waves* (1931), and *Between the Acts* (1941). Her criticism is contained in *The Common Reader* (1925) and volumes of essays, letters, and diaries. She also wrote two feminist tracts, *A Room of One's Own* (1929) and *Three Guineas* (1938).

Woollcott, Alexander, 1887–1943, American author; b. Phalanx, N.J. Known for his flamboyance and sardonic wit, he was a well-known drama critic (1914–28) for major New York City dailies. His gossipy essays are collected in *While Rome Burns* (1934) and *Long Long Ago* (1943).

Woolworth, Frank Winfield, 1852–1919, American merchant; b. Rodman, N.Y. Starting (1879) with a five-and-ten-cent store in Lancaster, Pa., he extended his business throughout the U.S. and to other countries. In 1911 the F.W. Woolworth Co. was incorporated, with ownership of over 1,000 five-and-dimes, and he became director of various financial firms. In 1913 he built the Woolworth Building (N.Y.C.), then the world's tallest building (792 ft/241.4 m).

Worcester, city (1990 pop. 169,759), seat of Worcester co., central Mass., on the Blackstone R.; inc. 1722. The river's canalization (1822) brought rapid industrialization. Manufactures include machinery, metal goods, chemicals, plastics, and pharmaceuticals. Settled in 1673, the city was the scene of Native American attacks (1675, 1683) and fighting in Shays's Rebellion (1786; see under SHAYS, DANIEL). It is the site of Clark Univ. and the College of the Holy Cross.

word processing, use of a computer program or a dedicated hardware and software package to write, edit, and print a document. Text is entered using a keyboard similar to a typewriter's. Most word processors have various functions that allow a person to revise text without retyping an entire document, and a document's format—type size, line spacing, margins, page length, and the like—usually can be readily altered. Documents are stored on magnetic disk or tape for later retrieval and use.

Wordsworth, William, 1770–1850, English poet. After graduating from Cambridge in 1791, Wordsworth went abroad. In 1792, a Frenchwoman, Annette Vallon, bore him a daughter, but they never married. He returned to England imbued with the spirit of the FRENCH REVOLUTION. In 1793 *An Evening Walk* and *Descriptive Sketches* were published. Prevented by the REIGN OF TERROR from returning to France, Wordsworth settled in Dorsetshire with his sister Dorothy, 1771–1855, who throughout his life shared his poetic vision; her journals were published after her death. With his close friend Samuel Taylor COLERIDGE, Wordsworth wrote *Lyrical Ballads* (1798), an attempt to use the language of ordinary speech in poetry. This famous book, which included his "Tintern Abbey," introduced ROMANTICISM into England. A second edition (1800) contained an essay outlining Wordsworth's poetic principles. In 1799 Wordsworth and his sister moved to Grasmere, in the Lake District, where they lived thereafter. He married Mary Hutchinson in 1802. The second version of *The Prelude,* a long autobiographical poem, was completed in 1805 but not published until after his death (the other versions are 1799 and 1850). *Poems in Two Volumes* (1807) included "Ode: Intimations of Immortality." Few notable works were written thereafter, apart from *The Excursion* (1814), "Laodamia" (1815), and *Memorials of a Tour of the Continent, 1820* (1822). In 1843, having long since put aside radicalism, Wordsworth was named poet laureate. Today he is recognized for his profundity of thought, love of nature, and innovative use of language.

work, in physics, transfer of ENERGY by a force acting against a resistance or a body and resulting in displacement. Work W has a magnitude equal to the scalar product (see VECTOR) of the force F and the distance d of the resulting movement; thus $W = Fd$ cos , where is the angle between the directions of the force and the movement. The foot-pound (ENGLISH UNITS OF MEASUREMENT), the erg (cgs system), and the joule (mks system) are the units of work or energy expended, respectively, by a 1-lb force acting through a distance of 1 ft, by a 1-dyne force through 1 cm, and by a 1-newton force through 1 m. One foot-pound equals 1.356 joules; 1 erg equals 10^{-7} joules.

workers' compensation or **workmen's compensation,** payment by employers for the cost of injuries, or some occupational diseases, received by employees in the course of their work. Benefits usually cover medical expenses, payments for incapacity to work, and, increasingly, vocational rehabilitation. Workers' compensation legislation was first passed in Germany, Austria, and Great Britain in the late 1800s, and by 1920 all but six states in the U.S. had passed some form of it. U.S. state legislation covers over 85% of all workers.

working dog, class of dogs raised either to herd cattle and sheep, as draft animals, as wartime message carriers, in police and rescue work, as guardians, or as guide dogs. See individual breeds, e.g., BOXER, COLLIE, DOBERMAN PINSCHER, GERMAN SHEPHERD, GREAT DANE, OLD ENGLISH SHEEPDOG, ST. BERNARD.

Work Projects Administration (WPA), 1935–43, U.S. government agency during the NEW DEAL. It was established as the Works Progress Administration, and its name was changed in 1939. The WPA undertook extensive building and improvement projects to provide work for the unemployed. It constructed 116,000 buildings, 78,000 bridges, and 651,000 mi (1,047,000 km) of public roads. Also included under the WPA were the Federal Arts Project, Federal Theatre Project, Federal Writers' Project, and National Youth Administration.

World Bank: see INTERNATIONAL BANK FOR RECONSTRUCTION AND DEVELOPMENT.

World Council of Churches, international, interdenominational organization of Protestant and Orthodox churches, begun at Amsterdam in 1948. The council has no power over the 335 member churches, but provides an opportunity for cooperation in matters of common concern. The headquarters are at Geneva, Switzerland.

World Court, popular name of the Permanent Court of International Justice, established (1920) by the LEAGUE OF NATIONS. Headquartered at The HAGUE, it comprised 15 judges empowered to render judgments in international disputes brought before them. The U.S. never joined the court, but an American jurist always sat on its bench. Dissolved in 1945, the court was supplanted by the UN International Court of Justice (see UNITED NATIONS, table).

World Health Organization: see UNITED NATIONS (table 3).

World Intellectual Property Organization: see UNITED NATIONS (table 3).

World Meteorological Organization: see UNITED NATIONS (table 3).

World Trade Center, building complex in lower Manhattan, N.Y.C., consisting of seven buildings and a shopping concourse. Most prominent are the 110-story, rectangular twin towers rising to 1,350 ft (411 m), second in height only to Chicago's SEARS TOWER. Designed by Minoru YAMASAKI and Emery Roth, the towers and concourse portion of the center was completed in 1973 at a cost of $750 million. A massive bomb explosion damaged portions of the complex in 1993.

World War I, 1914–18, also called the Great War, conflict, chiefly in Europe, among most of the world's great powers. On one side were the Allies (chiefly France, Britain, Russia, and the U.S.); on the other were the Central Powers (Germany, Austria-Hungary, and Turkey). Prominent among the war's causes were the imperialist, territorial, and economic rivalries of the great powers. The German empire in particular was determined to establish itself as the preeminent power on the Continent. The Germans were also intent on challenging the naval superiority of Britain. However, it was rampant nationalism—especially evident in the Austro-Hungarian empire—that furnished the immediate cause of hostilities. On June 28, 1914, Archduke FRANCIS FERDINAND, heir apparent to the Austro-Hungarian throne, was assassinated at Sarajevo by a Serbian nationalist. One month later, after its humiliating demands were refused, Austria-Hungary declared war on Serbia. Other declarations of war followed quickly, and soon every major power in Europe was in the war. On the Western Front, the Germans smashed through Belgium, advanced on Paris, and approached the English Channel. After the first battles of the MARNE and YPRES, however, the Germans became stalled. Grueling trench warfare and the use of poison gas began all along the front, and for the next three years the battle lines remained virtually stationary despite huge casualties at VERDUN and in the Somme offensive during 1916. On the Eastern Front, the Central Powers were more successful. The Germans defeated (Aug.–Sept. 1914) the Russians at Tannenberg and the Masurian Lakes. Serbia and Montenegro fell by the end of 1915. In the south, the Italian campaigns were inconclusive, though they benefited the Allied cause by keeping large numbers of Austrian troops tied down there. In Turkey, the Allies' ambitious Gallipolli Campaign (1915), an attempt to force Turkey out of the war, was a costly failure. In the Middle East, T.E. LAWRENCE stirred Arab revolt against Turkey. U.S. neutrality had been threatened since 1915, when the British ship LUSITANIA was sunk. By 1917 unrestricted German submarine warfare had caused the U.S. to enter the war on the side of the Allies. An American Expeditionary Force, commanded by Gen. PERSHING, landed in France and saw its first action at Château-Thierry (June 1917). In Mar. 1918 the new Soviet government signed the Treaty of BREST-LITOVSK with the Central Powers. The Germans were stopped just short of Paris in the second battle of the Marne, and an Allied counteroffensive was successful. The Turkish and Austro-Hungarian empires, disintegrating from within, surrendered to the Allies, as did Bulgaria. After revolution erupted in Germany, the armistice was signed on Nov. 11, 1918. The Treaty of VERSAILLES and the other treaties that ended the war changed the face of Europe and the Middle East. Four great empires—Germany, Austria-Hungary, Russia, and Turkey—had disappeared by the end of the war. Replacing them were governments ranging from monarchies and sheikhdoms through constitutional republics to the Marxist socialist state of the USSR. The war itself had been one of the bloodiest in history, without a single decisive battle. A total of 65 million men and women had served in the armies and navies; an estimated 10 million persons had been killed and double that number wounded. Such statistics contributed to a general revulsion against war, leading many to put their trust in multinational disarmament pacts and in the newly formed LEAGUE OF NATIONS.

World War II, 1939–45, conflict involving every major power in the world. On one side were the Allies (chiefly Great Britain, the U.S., and the Soviet Union) and on the other side the Axis powers (Germany, Japan, and Italy). The conflict resulted from the rise of totalitarian, militaristic regimes in Germany, Japan, and Italy after WORLD WAR I. Partly responsible also were the humiliating peace treaties forced on Germany after that war and the worldwide economic disorders brought on by the GREAT DEPRESSION of the 1930s. In Asia the second SINO-JAPANESE WAR (1931) was followed by continuing Japanese aggression. In 1936 Benito MUSSOLINI conquered Ethiopia for Italy, thereby dramatizing the ineffectuality of the LEAGUE OF NATIONS. French and British appeasement of Adolf HITLER's Nazi regime in Germany culminated in the MUNICH PACT (1938), which sacrificed much of Czechoslovakia to Germany. France and Britain, nevertheless, began to rearm and to offer guarantees to other potential victims of German aggression, notably Poland. In Aug. 1939 Germany and the Soviet Union, previously bitter enemies, concluded a nonaggression pact, thus freeing Hitler to invade Poland (Sept. 1). France and Britain immediately declared war on Germany, officially beginning World War II. The Germans won a quick victory in Poland, and went on to occupy Norway and Denmark in 1940. In May they overran the Low Countries, broke into France, and swept to the English Channel. On June 22 France surrendered (although a Free French force continued to fight). Britain, under Prime Min. Winston CHURCHILL, was left to fight alone. The Battle of Britain (Aug.–Oct. 1940), Germany's attempt to bomb Britain into submission, was the only German failure of the war's early years. Axis land operations continued in N Africa and in the Balkans, where Greece and Yugoslavia were occupied. On June 22, 1941, Germany invaded the Soviet Union, bringing that nation, under Premier Joseph STALIN, into the war. Meanwhile, the U.S., under Pres. F.D. ROOSEVELT, was drawing closer to the Allies. On Dec. 7, 1941, Japan attacked PEARL HARBOR, bringing the U.S. into the war. But Axis successes continued. By 1942 Japan had conquered the Philippines, many other Pacific islands, and all of Southeast Asia; German forces in the Soviet Union reached Stalingrad and the Caucasus; ROMMEL seemed about to take Cairo; and German submarines were threatening to wipe out Allied shipping. Late in 1942, however, the Allies began to rally. In N Africa, British Gen. MONTGOMERY's rout of Rommel at Alamein (Oct. 1942; see NORTH AFRICA, CAMPAIGNS IN), and the landing of U.S. troops in Algeria, resulted in Allied victory in Africa. The Allies conquered Sicily and S Italy, and Italy surrendered (Sept. 1943). In the Pacific, U.S. forces won (1942) the naval battles of the Coral Sea and Midway, landed on GUADALCANAL, and began the island-hopping strategy that by 1945 had won back the Philippines and brought a striking force to Japan's doorstep at IWO JIMA and OKINAWA. The German surrender at Stalingrad (1943; see VOLGOGRAD) was followed by a Soviet offensive that by 1944 had taken Russian troops deep into Poland, Hungary, and the Balkans. In the battle of the Atlantic, the German submarine fleet was virtually destroyed. German resistance in N Italy was stubborn, however, especially at Cassino and Anzio. On June 6, 1944 (known thereafter as D Day), the final Allied campaign began with the landing of troops in Normandy. In August a second force landed in S France. By late 1944 Belgium and France were liberated, and the war had been carried into the Netherlands and Germany. Allied bombing, meanwhile, was destroying German industrial centers. In Dec. 1944 the Germans staged a last-ditch counterattack in the Ardennes. By Jan. 1945, however, the Allies were continuing their drive into Germany. The Russians had conquered E Germany to the Oder. On March 7 the Western Allies broke through the Siegfried Line, crossed the Rhine, and overran W Germany. In Apr. 1945, after Hitler's suicide, German resistance collapsed, and on May 7, 1945, Germany surrendered unconditionally. The Allies now turned their attention to the Pacific. The Soviet Union declared war on Japan and occupied Manchuria. In Aug. 1945, while U.S. troops were preparing to invade Japan's home islands, Pres. TRUMAN ordered the dropping of the ATOMIC BOMB on HIROSHIMA and NAGASAKI. Japan announced its surrender on Aug. 14, 1945, thereby bringing to an end the costliest war in history.

World Wildlife Fund (WWF), international organization formed to raise money for conservation projects, est. 1961. The international organization became (1986) the **Worldwide Fund for Nature,** but the affiliated group in the U.S. retained its original name. It has been responsible for international agreements on conservation and has supported research on ENDANGERED SPECIES, including the giant PANDA, its symbol.

worm, term for various unrelated invertebrates with soft, often long and slender bodies. The most primitive are the FLATWORMS, including the PLANARIANS, FLUKES, and TAPEWORMS. RIBBON WORMS are colorful marine carnivores, and several loosely related groups of tube-like worms (e.g., horsehair worms, NEMATODES, and ROTIFERS). The segmented or ANNELID WORMS include the EARTHWORMS and LEECHES. Although it has no taxonomic validity, the term *worm* is also used for the SHIPWORM (a type of CLAM), some insect larvae (e.g., the armyworm and inchworm), and the acorn worm.

Worms, Diet of, 1521, most famous of the imperial diets held at Worms, Germany. Called by Holy Roman Emperor CHARLES V, it took up, among other business, the matter of Martin LUTHER. Luther appeared under a safe-conduct and refused to yield his position, traditionally ending his defense with: "Here I stand. I cannot do otherwise. God help me. Amen." The Edict of Worms, issued May 25, declared him an outlaw, thus hardening the lines of the REFORMATION.

Wounded Knee, creek and village (1990 pop. 18) in South Dakota, site of the last major battle of the INDIAN WARS (Dec. 29, 1890), in which U.S. troops killed almost 200 Sioux, including women and children. In 1973, 200 members of the AMERICAN INDIAN MOVEMENT occupied the village of Wounded Knee for 69 days, demanding a Senate investigation into the condition of Native Americans.

Wovoka, c.1858–1932, prophet of the messianic GHOST-DANCE religion, a PAIUTE. He taught that pacifism and the sacred dance would cause the whites to disappear and would free all Native Americans from death, disease, and misery. After his supernatural "bullet-proof" ghost shirts failed tragically at WOUNDED KNEE, the appeal of his religion waned.

WPA: see WORKS PROJECTS ADMINISTRATION.

Wrangell–St. Elias National Park: see NATIONAL PARKS (table).

Wren, Sir Christopher, 1632–1723, English architect, astronomer, and mathematician. After the great fire of 1666, he produced a masterly plan for the rebuilding of London, never executed. He designed, however, many new buildings, most notably ST. PAUL'S CATHEDRAL. From 1670 to 1711 he executed 52 London churches, noted for their varied and original designs and fine spires, e.g., St.-Mary-le-Bow. Among his secular works were the Sheldonian Theatre, Oxford; Trinity College Library, Cambridge; Chelsea Hospital, London; and others. His buildings exhibit great elegance, clarity, and dignity.

wren, small, plump, perching songbird of the primarily New World family Troglodytidae. Its plumage is usually brown or reddish above and white, gray, or buff below. Among the best singers are the canyon, Carolina, and winter wrens. Wrens are valuable insect destroyers.

wrestling, sport in which two unarmed opponents grapple with one another. The object is to secure a fall, i.e., to pin the opponent's shoulders to the floor. Two distinctly different styles exist today. Greco-Roman wrestling, popular in continental Europe, permits no holds below the waist and takes place mostly on the ground. Free-style wrestling, favored in the U.S., Britain, and elsewhere, permits tackling, tripping, and other rough features. In amateur wrestling, contestants are classified by weight. One of the earliest sports known, wrestling was extremely popular among the ancient Greeks. Competition in both styles is part of the modern Olympic program. Jujitsu (see MARTIAL ARTS) and sumo are forms of wrestling practiced in Japan. Professional wrestling, popular in the U.S., is less a competitive sport than a staged entertainment.

Wright, Frances (Fanny), 1795–1852, Scottish-American reformer, later known as Mme Darusmont. She founded (1825) NASHOBA, a colony for freed slaves near Memphis, Tenn., and after its failure worked for women's rights, universal education, abolition of slavery, and birth control. Wright also edited, with Robert Dale OWEN, the *Free Enquirer*.

Wright, Frank Lloyd, 1869–1959, American architect; b. Richland Center, Wis. He worked with Louis SULLIVAN. Beginning in 1893 he built a series of homes in and around Chicago with low horizontal lines echoing the landscape—his "prairie style," e.g., the Robie House, Chicago (1909). From the beginning he practiced radical innovation in both structures and aesthetics. He did pioneer work in integrating machine methods and materials into a true architectural expression. Many of his innovations, e.g., open planning—eliminating traditional room division to achieve fluid inner space—set standards. The Larkin Building, Buffalo, N.Y. (1904, destroyed 1950), and Oak Park Unity Temple, near Chicago (1906), were highly influential early designs. The Imperial Hotel, Tokyo (1916–23, demolished 1968), and Wright's home, "Taliesin," Spring Green, Wis. (1911, twice rebuilt), were especially famous. Later designs included the Kaufmann house, "Falling Water," Bear Run, Pa. (1936–37), cantilevered over a waterfall; and the Guggenheim Museum, N.Y.C. (1946–59), with its spiral ramp.

Wright, Jim (James Claud Wright, Jr.), 1922–, U.S. politician, speaker of the U.S. House of Representatives (1987–89); b. Fort Worth, Tex. A Texas state representative (1947–49) and mayor (1950–54) of Weatherford, Tex., he was elected as a U.S. representative from Texas in 1954. A moderate Democrat, he became House majority leader in 1976. In 1987 he became House speaker, but he resigned two years later amid charges of unethical conduct.

Wright, Orville, 1871–1948, b. Dayton, Ohio, and **Wilbur Wright,** 1867–1912, b. near New Castle, Ind., American airplane inventors. Influenced by Otto LILIENTHAL's glider flights, the Wright brothers used their Dayton bicycle shop to construct their early aircraft. Their use of movable wing assembly parts to direct the craft was an important advance. With an engine Orville designed, they made on Dec. 17, 1903, near Kitty Hawk, N.C., the first four controlled, sustained flights in a power-driven AIRPLANE.

Wright, Patience Lovell, 1725–86, American sculptor; b. Bordentown, N.J. Her wax portraits were the earliest recorded sculptures made in the American colonies. Wright lived in England from 1772, where she modeled likenesses of the king, the queen, and other notables. A son, **Joseph Wright,** 1756–93, was a portrait painter. A characteristic example of his work is a portrait of John Jay (N.Y. Historical Soc.).

Wright, Richard, 1908–60, African-American author; b. near Natchez, Miss. Wright wrote powerfully of the plight of African Americans in America. His major works are the novel *Native Son* (1940, unexpurgated ed. 1991) and the autobiography *Black Boy* (1945). He also wrote other novels, short stories, and nonfiction.

Wrocław [vrôts'läf], Ger. *Breslau,* city (1989 est. pop. 636,000), SW Poland, on the Oder (Odra) R. It is a port and an industrial center with such manufactures as heavy machinery and computers. Settled before the 11th cent., it became (1163) the capital of SILESIA and passed to BOHEMIA (1335), the HAPSBURGS (1526), and PRUSSIA (1742). In 1945 it was given to Poland, and its German residents were expelled. Historic buildings include a 13th-cent. cathedral and a Gothic town hall.

wrought iron, commercially purified IRON. In the Aston process, pig iron is refined in a Bessemer converter and then poured into molten iron-silicate slag. The resulting semisolid mass is passed between rollers that squeeze out most of the slag. Wrought iron is tough, malleable, ductile, and corrosion-resistant, and melts only at high temperature. It is used to make ornamental ironwork, rivets, bolts, pipes, chains, and anchors.

Wuhan, city (1990 est. pop. 3,750,000), capital of Hubei prov., central China, at the junction of the Han and Chang (Yangtze) rivers. The great industrial, commercial and transportation hub of central China, Wuhan comprises the former cities of Hankou, Hanyang, and Wuchang. Wuhan is a center of Chinese iron and steel production and an inland port that can handle oceangoing vessels, even though it is 600 mi (970 km) from the sea.

Wuhsi: see WUXI.

Wundt, Wilhelm Max [vo͝ont], 1832–1920, German physiologist and psychologist. In 1878 he founded at Leipzig the first laboratory for experimental psychology. His experimental method remains a permanent contribution to psychology.

Wu P'ei-fu [wo͞o pā-fo͞o], 1874–1939, Chinese general. After military service under the Ch'ing dynasty, he supported YÜAN SHIH-KAI as president of China. After 1916 Wu warred with other leaders for control of N China. He was defeated (1926) by CHIANG KAI-SHEK's Northern Expedition.

Württemberg [vur'təmbĕrk"], former state, SW Germany. STUTTGART was the capital. It included the Swabian Jura in the south and part of the Black Forest in the west, and was divided between the medieval duchies of FRANCONIA and SWABIA. Under the HOLY ROMAN EMPIRE, the counts of Württemberg expanded (after the 11th cent.) their territory and were raised to ducal rank in 1495. Under Duke Frederick II (later King Frederick I), Württemberg, through its alliance with NAPOLEON I, acquired additional territory and became an electorate (1803) and a kingdom (1806). It supported Prussia in the AUSTRO-PRUSSIAN WAR (1866) and the FRANCO-PRUSSIAN WAR (1870–71) and joined (1871) the German empire. The monarchy was abolished in 1918, and in 1919 Württemberg joined the Weimar Republic. Temporarily partitioned after WORLD WAR II, it was incorporated (1952) into the new West German (since 1990, German) state of Baden-Württemberg.

Wuxi or **Wuhsi** [both: wōō-shē], city (1987 est. pop. 860,000), S Jiangsu prov., China, on the GRAND CANAL. Long famous for its silks and scenery, Wuxi remains a center of the silk industry and an important tourist attraction. It is also well-known for high-technology and light-industrial products.

Wyandot: see HURON.

Wyatt, Sir Thomas, 1503–42, English poet and statesman. Wyatt served Henry VIII and is thought to have been Anne BOLEYN's lover before her marriage. Influenced heavily by the Italian love poets, he wrote the first SONNETS in English. He also wrote lyrics, rondeaus, satires, and psalms.

Wyatt, Sir Thomas, d. 1554, English rebel. Objecting to MARY I's planned marriage to PHILIP II of Spain, he raised an army in Kent and marched (1554) on London. He failed to capture Mary or take the city, and was hanged for treason.

Wycherley, William [wĭch'ərlē], 1640?–1716, English dramatist. His comedies include *Love in a Wood* (1671), *The Gentleman Dancing-Master* (1672), *The Country Wife* (1674), and *The Plain Dealer* (1676). Although his plays are the most vicious and licentious of RESTORATION comic dramas, he earned a prominent place in English stage history with his brilliant wit and satire.

Wyclif, Wycliffe, Wickliffe, or **Wiclif, John** [all: wĭk'lĭf], c.1328–1384, English reformer. He believed that Jesus is humanity's overlord and championed the people against the abuses of the church. Wyclif attacked orthodox church doctrine, especially that of transubstantiation, and held that the Scriptures are the supreme authority. Condemned (1380, 1382) as a heretic, he was left undisturbed in his retirement. His teachings were spread by "poor priests" (see LOLLARDRY) and influenced John HUSS. Wyclif brought about the Wyclif Bible, the first English translation of the Latin Bible.

Wyeth, Andrew Newell [wī'əth], 1917–, American painter; b. Chadds Ford, Pa.; son of the illustrator N.C. Wyeth. One of the most popular contemporary American painters, Wyeth portrays the people and places of rural Pennsylvania and Maine in a meticulous, naturalistic style that is so intense and immediate as to appear surreal. His best-known painting is *Christina's World* (1948; Mus. Mod. Art, N.Y.C.). His son **James Browning Wyeth,** 1946–, b. Wilmington, Del., is also an artist.

Wylie, Elinor (Hoyt), 1885–1928, American author; b. Somerville, N.J. Her highly polished, melodious, and deeply emotional poetry is included in such collections as *Nets to Catch the Wind* (1921) and *Angels and Earthly Creatures* (1929). Among her delicately wrought novels, filled with ironic fancy, are *Jennifer Lorn* (1923), *The Orphan Angel* (1926), and *Mr. Hodge and Mr. Hazard* (1928).

Wyoming, state of the W U.S.; bordered by South Dakota and Nebraska (E), Colorado and Utah (S), Idaho (W), and Montana (N).

Area, 97,914 sq mi (253,597 sq km). *Pop.* (1990) 453,588, an 3.7% decrease from 1980 pop. *Capital,* Cheyenne. *Statehood,* July 10, 1890 (44th state). *Highest pt.,* Gannett Peak, 13,804 ft (4,210 m); *lowest pt.,* Belle Fourche R., 3,100 ft (946 m). *Nickname,* Equality State. *Motto,* Equal Rights. *State bird,* meadowlark. *State flower,* Indian paintbrush. *State tree,* cottonwood. *Abbr.,* Wyo.; WY.

Land and People. E Wyoming is part of the GREAT PLAINS, except in the northeast, where the BLACK HILLS are located. Farther west, the ranges of the ROCKY MOUNTAINS, which include the dramatic Wind River and TETON ranges, cut across the state diagonally. The cool, dry climate brings mild summers and severe winters to most of the state. Almost 50% of the land is controlled by the federal government. Sparsely populated Wyoming has the smallest population of any state, and almost two thirds of the residents live in urban areas. The largest city is CHEYENNE, followed by CASPER. In 1990 the state was over 94% white.

Economy. Wyoming's economy is almost entirely dominated by primary production. Mining is the leading source of income; the state is one of the leading U.S. producers of coal, oil, and natural gas, uranium, and sodium carbonate. Portland cement and crushed stone are also important. Agriculture is dominated by cattle and sheep ranching. The principal dry farm crops are wheat, beans, barley, and oats; the leading irrigated crop is sugar beets. Tourism is the second largest source of income. Visitors are attracted by rodeos, excellent hunting and fishing, and two spectacular NATIONAL PARKS (see table), Yellowstone and Grand Teton. The small industrial sector is dominated by oil refining, food processing, and the manufacture of clay, glass, and wood products.

Government. The state constitution of 1890 provides for a governor serving a four-year term. The legislature consists of a senate with 30 members serving four-year terms and a house with 64 members elected for two-year terms. Wyoming is represented in the U.S. Congress by two senators and one representative and has three electoral votes.

History. Present-day Wyoming was the home of many Native American tribes, including the CROW, Shoshone, CHEYENNE, ARAPAHO, and SIOUX, who lived by hunting buffalo. During the early 19th cent. the so-called MOUNTAIN MEN trapped furs in the area. With the decline of the fur trade during the 1840s, the few settlers began to supply wagon trains crossing the area on the OREGON TRAIL, and later the BOZEMAN and Overland trails, which cut through the South Pass on their way west. The arrival (1868) of the Union Pacific RR was a great stimulus to settlement. The Native Americans were conquered by the late 1870s, and large-scale ranching began. The activities of cattle rustlers and vigilante groups reached a climax in the cattle war of Johnson County (1892), which was followed by conflicts between sheep- and cattle-ranchers. Petroleum production began in the 1880s. In the 1920s the state's TEAPOT DOME oil deposits became the symbol of corruption in the administration of Pres. Warren G. HARDING. The national energy crisis of the 1970s brought a dramatic boom to Wyoming's energy industries, especially coal mining. By the mid-1980s, however, the state's economy had declined due to a fall in energy prices and a lack of diversity, and environmental problems precipitated by the energy industry had become a concern.

Wyspiański, Stanisław [vĭspyä'nyəskē], 1869–1907, Polish dramatist, painter, and poet. With such plays as *The Legion* (1900) he founded modern Polish drama. His artistic work includes murals, stained-glass windows, and costumes.

Wyss, Johann David [vēs], 1743–1818, Swiss author. He wrote the children's classic *The Swiss Family Robinson* (1813), based on Daniel DEFOE's *Robinson Crusoe.* His son, **Johann R. Wyss,** 1781–1830, was professor of philosophy at Berne and wrote the Swiss national anthem.

Wyszynski, Stefan Cardinal, [vĭzĭn'skē], 1901–81, Roman Catholic primate of POLAND (1949–81). He was imprisoned (1953–56) by the Communist authorities. After his release, however, he achieved a degree of church autonomy unequaled in any other Communist country.

X

Xe, chemical symbol of the element XENON.

xenon (Xe), gaseous element, discovered spectroscopically in 1898 by William RAMSAY and M.W. Travers. It is a rare, colorless, odorless, tasteless INERT GAS used in certain photographic-flash lamps, in high-intensity arc lamps for motion-picture projection and for arena and stadium lighting, in high-pressure arc lamps to produce ultraviolet light, and in numerous radiation-detection instruments. See ELEMENT (table); PERIODIC TABLE.

Xenophon [zĕn'əfən], c.430 B.C.–c.355 B.C., Greek historian. A well-to-do young disciple of SOCRATES, he joined the Greek force (the Ten Thousand) that supported CYRUS THE YOUNGER of Persia. They fought well, but after the disastrous battle of Cunaxa (401 B.C.), they were left to fight their way home through unknown and hostile land. He was chosen a leader and told the story of this heroic retreat in his most famous work, the *Anabasis.* His other works include the *Hellenica* and the *Memorabilia.* He lived and wrote in exile in Sparta.

xerography: see PHOTOCOPYING.

Xerxes, c.519–465 B.C., king of Persia, son of DARIUS I. He continued his father's campaign against Greece for its role in the Ionian revolt by establishing alliances with Carthage and other Greek city-states and mounting (480) a military expedition. His armies scored a devastating victory at Thermopylae and destroyed Attica. His navy's limited success at Artemisium was reversed by the triumph of the Greek fleet at Salamis. After his defeat, he retired to his court at Susa, where he was murdered.

Xhosa, Bantu-speaking people of S Africa, formerly called Kafirs or Kaffirs by European colonialists. Farmers and cattle raisers, the Xhosa, who inhabited their lands for centuries before European settlement, lived traditionally in patrilineal clans governed by an elected chief and council. Today they predominate in the BANTUSTAN of Transkei, but many live in other parts of South Africa.

Xiamen [shēä-mŭn] or **Amoy** [əmoi'], city (1986 est. pop. 344,000), S Fujian prov., China, on Xiamen island at the mouth of the Jiulong R. Fishing, shipbuilding, and food processing are the major industries. The city was one of the earliest seats of European commerce in China. Xiamen is a special economic zone (authorized 1980).

Xi'an or **Sian** [both: shē-än], city (1990 est. pop. 2,760,000), capital of Shaanxi prov., N central China, in the Wei R. valley. Located on the main east-west RR and the primary transport center for central China, Xi'an is one of China's industrial and commercial hubs. It produces steel, machinery, textiles, and light industrial products and is an important cultural center. The tomb of Shih Huang-Ti, who unified China in 221 B.C., was discovered in Xi'an in 1974. Filled with thousands of full-sized terra cotta horses and soldiers, it is one of China's most important archeological sites and tourist attractions.

Xinjiang [shĭn'jēäng] or **Sinkiang** [sĭn'kyăng], officially Xinjiang Uygur Autonomous Region, autonomous region (1990 pop. 15,156,000), c.660,000 sq mi (1,709,400 sq km), NW China, bordered by Russia (N), Kazakhstan, Kyrgyzstan, Tajikistan, and Afghanistan (W), Kashmir and Tibet (S), and Qinghai and Gansu provs. and the Republic of Mongolia (E). The capital is Ürümqi. Agriculture and stock raising are important, and there are extensive mineral deposits. Manufactures include chemicals, farm machinery, and oil. China's nuclear arms program is centered at Lop Nur in W Xinjiang. The UIGURS, a Turkic people, are the largest ethnic group, and 12 other minority nationalities, many of them also Turkic, also live in the region; ethnic Chinese, however, are approaching numerical parity with the Uigurs. Islam is widely practiced. Also known as Chinese, or Eastern, Turkistan, Xinjiang first passed to China in the 1st cent. B.C. It was subsequently occupied by the Uzbeks (7th cent.), Tibetans (8th cent.), Uigurs, Arabs (10th cent.), Mongols (13th cent.), and Manchus (18th cent.). It became a Chinese province in 1881; in the 1960s and 70s it was the site of Sino-Soviet border clashes. In the early 1990s there was increasing discontent with Chinese rule among the Turkic peoples of Xinjiang.

X ray, invisible, highly penetrating ELECTROMAGNETIC RADIATION of much shorter wavelength (higher frequency) than visible light. The wavelength range for X rays is from about 10^{-8} m to about 10^{-11} m. Hard X rays have higher frequencies and are more penetrating; soft X rays have lower frequencies and are less penetrating. Discovered in 1895 by Wilhelm ROENTGEN, X rays are produced by the impact of high-energy electrons (of several thousands of eV) on a metal anode in a highly evacuated glass bulb. Among other applications, X rays are used in diagnostic medicine and in the study of crystal structure (see X-RAY CRYSTALLOGRAPHY). X rays provide a image of the body's interior when they pass through it and strike a photographic plate or fluorescent screen; denser materials absorb more X rays and appear brighter. Several techniques, known as X-ray microscopy or microradiography, can provide enlarged images of the structure of an opaque object.

X-ray astronomy, study of celestial objects by means of the X RAYS they emit. The sun was the first celestial body found to emit X rays. Since then many X-ray sources—such as centers of GALAXIES, clouds of extremely hot gas between galaxies, and double stars in which one star is a NEUTRON STAR—have been discovered. Because X rays are difficult to observe from the ground due to atmospheric interference, high-altitude balloons, sounding ROCKETS, and orbiting OBSERVATORIES must be used. The High Energy Astrophysical Observatory II, or Einstein Observatory, detected several thousand new X-ray sources in our galaxy and beyond. See also GAMMA-RAY ASTRONOMY.

X-ray crystallography, study of the molecular structure of crystalline compounds through X-ray DIFFRACTION techniques. When an X-ray beam bombards a crystal, the atomic structure of the crystal causes the beam to scatter in a specific pattern. This phenomenon, known as X-ray diffraction, occurs when the wavelength of the X rays and the distances between atoms in the crystal are of similar magnitude. X-ray crystallography provides information on the positions of individual atoms in the crystal, the distances between atoms, the angles of the atomic bonds, and other features of molecular geometry. The technique is also used to determine the structure of proteins, nucleic acids, and other substances.

xylem: see STEM; WOOD.

xylophone: see PERCUSSION INSTRUMENT.

XYZ Affair, name usually given to an incident (1797–98) in Franco-American diplomatic relations. In 1797 Pres. John Adams named a three-member commission—John MARSHALL, Elbridge GERRY, and C.C. Pinckney—to resolve Franco-American disputes. It was hinted to them through Mme de Villette that the French foreign minister, Charles Maurice de TALLEYRAND, would require bribes and loans totaling $250,000 before talks could begin. The commissioners held secret negotiations concerning the money with X (Jean Conrad Hottinguer), Y (an American banker in Hamburg named Bellamy), and Z (Lucien Hauteval). When news of the talks became public and created an uproar in the U.S., the whole mission collapsed. Franco-American differences were finally settled by the Convention of 1800.

Y

Y, chemical symbol of the element YTTRIUM.

Yahweh: see GOD.

Yahya Khan, Agha Muhammad, 1917–80, Pakistani general and president (1969–71). He was commander in chief of the army (1966–69) and succeeded Gen. AYUB KHAN as president. The defeat (1971) of Pakistan's army and the secession of Bangladesh from Pakistan forced his resignation. He was placed under house arrest for five years.

yak, bovine MAMMAL (*Bos grunniens*) of TIBET and adjacent regions. Oxlike in build, with humped shoulders, a long, thick coat, and large, upcurved horns, it has been hunted to near extinction. The wild yak may reach 65 in. (165 cm) at the shoulder. Yaks live in isolated herds at elevations above 14,000 ft (4,300 m). Long domesticated, they are a source of milk, meat, and leather, and are used as draft animals.

Yale University, at New Haven, Conn.; founded 1701, the third-oldest institution of higher learning in the U.S. First called the Collegiate School, it opened at what is now Clinton, Conn., later moving to Old Saybrook and (1716) to New Haven, where it was renamed in honor of a benefactor, Elihu Yale. It achieved a substantial scholastic reputation as a college before expanding (19th cent.) into one of the premier American universities. The first Ph.D. degree in the U.S. was bestowed there in 1861. The Peabody Museum of Natural History and the Yale Art Gallery are renowned, and the university library is one of the nation's largest.

Yalow, Rosalyn Sussman, 1921–, American medical physicist; b. N.Y.C. She did research on the medical use of radioisotopes, radioimmunoassay, and radiation chemistry. In 1977, she was awarded the Nobel Prize in medicine or physiology for research on the role of hormones in the chemistry of the body.

Yalta Conference, 1945, meeting at Yalta (Crimea, USSR; now in Ukraine), of British Prime Min. CHURCHILL, U.S. Pres. F.D. ROOSEVELT, and Soviet Premier STALIN. Among the chief decisions agreed upon by the "Big Three" were these: (1) a four-power occupation of Germany (with France being the fourth power); (2) a founding conference for the UN to be held later that year; (3) the Soviet Union's agreement to enter the war against Japan after Germany's defeat; receiving occupation areas in the East in return; and (4) a guarantee of representative government in Poland. Because of the secrecy of its agreements and what were considered by some to be undue concessions to the Soviet Union, the Yalta Conference has long been the subject of heated controversy.

Churchill, Roosevelt, and Stalin at the Yalta Conference, 1945

Yalu, river, c.500 mi (800 km) long, flowing generally southwest to the Bay of Korea at Dandong and forming part of the China-North Korea border. The river generates hydroelectricity at the Supung Dam above Sinuiju, North Korea, and is used to float timber to sawmills. China's involvement in the KOREAN WAR began (1950) when its troops crossed the Yalu.

yam, common name for some members of the family Dioscoreaceae, tropical and subtropical climbing herbs and shrubs with starchy RHIZOMES often cultivated for food. The thick rhizomes, especially of the genus *Dioscorea,* often weigh up to 30 lb (13.6 kg) and are an important food source for humans and livestock. The SWEET POTATO, erroneously called yam, belongs to the MORNING GLORY family.

Yamasaki, Minoru, 1912–86, American architect; b. Seattle. His designs are seen in airport buildings in St. Louis (1951) and Boston (1968); at the U.S. Consulate General, Kobe, Japan; at the U.S. science pavilion for the Seattle Exposition (1962); and at the WORLD TRADE CENTER complex, N.Y.C.

Yamoussoukro, city (1990 est. pop. 100,000), capital of Côte d'Ivoire. Located in the central part of the country, it is the birthplace of Pres. HOUPHOUËT-BOIGNY. The government began transferring here in 1983, but most government offices and foreign embassies remain in the former capital, ABIDJAN. The world's largest Christian church, the Basilica of Our Lady of Peace, is in Yamoussoukro.

Yan'an or **Yenan** [both: yĕn-än], city (1986 est. pop. 87,000), N Shaanxi prov., China. It is a regional market center. Famed as the terminus of the LONG MARCH (1934–35) and capital of the Chinese Communist base areas (1936–47), the city and its monuments attracted millions of visitors in the 1960s and 70s. Since 1978 and the de-emphasis of MAO ZEDONG's leadership, far fewer visitors have gone to Yan'an.

Yangon [yäng′gōn] or **Rangoon,** largest city (1983 pop. 2,458,712) and capital of Myanmar, near the mouth of the Yangon R. A major port, it is the country's foremost industrial, commercial, and transportation center. Its products include rice, teak, oil, and steel. Dominated by the ancient golden-spired Shwe Dagon Pagoda, it was a fishing village until it was made the capital (1753) by Alaungpaya, founder of the last line of Burman kings. Modernized under British colonial rule (1852–1937), it was severely damaged by an earthquake (1930) and by bombing in World War II.

Yangtze or **Yangzi:** see CHANG.

Yaoundé, city (1990 est. pop. 750,000), capital of Cameroon. It is the country's administrative, financial, and communications center, and a regional trade center for coffee, cocoa, copra, sugarcane, and rubber. Founded (1888) by German ivory-traders, it was (1919–40, 1946–60) the capital of the French CAMEROONS and became (1960) the capital of Cameroon.

yard: see ENGLISH UNITS OF MEASUREMENT; WEIGHTS AND MEASURES, table.

Yaroslav, 978–1054, grand duke of Kiev (1019–54); son of VLADIMIR I. Designated by his father to rule Novgorod, he wrested Kiev from his brother. He consolidated Kiev's power, but civil war among his sons followed his death.

Yb, chemical symbol of the element YTTERBIUM.

Yeager, Chuck (Charles Elwood Yeager), 1923–, American aviator. A fighter pilot during World War II, he was a test pilot during the early postwar years. Among other records, he was the first person to fly faster than the speed of sound (1947) and set a world speed record of 1,650 miles per hour (1953). His obvious bravery, technical skill, and unaffected manner have to a large public made him the quintessential American hero. He wrote (with Leo Janos) *Yeager* (1985).

year, time required for the earth to complete one orbit about the sun. The **tropical,** or **solar, year** measured relative to the sun is the time (365 days, 5 hr, 48 min, 46 sec of mean SOLAR TIME) between successive vernal EQUINOXES. The **sidereal year** is the time (365 days, 6 hr, 9 min, 9.5 sec of mean solar time) required for the earth to complete an orbit of the sun relative to the stars; it is longer than the tropical year because of the PRECESSION OF THE EQUINOXES. The **anomalistic year** is the time (365 days, 6 hr, 13 min, 53.0 sec of mean solar time) required for the earth to go from its perihelion point once around the sun and back to this point; its greater length is due to the slow rotation of the earth's orbit as a whole.

yeast, name for certain microscopic, unicellular fungi (see FUNGUS), and for commercial products consisting of masses of yeast cells. Yeasts consist of oval or round cells that reproduce mainly by budding (a small outgrowth on the cell's surface increases in size until a wall forms to separate the new individual, or bud) but also by means of SPORES. They are used in alcoholic FERMENTATION and to leaven bread. Brewer's yeast is high in B-complex vitamins and is used as a dietary supplement. Certain other fungi are also sometimes called yeasts.

Yeats, William Butler, 1865–1939, Irish poet and playwright. The son of an artist, he studied painting and lived in London and in Sligo, where many of his poems are set. Fascinated by Irish legend and the occult, he soon became a leader of the Irish literary renaissance. His first work, the drama *Mosada* (1886), reflects these concerns, but the long poems in *The Wanderings of Oisin* (1889) show an intense nationalism, a feeling strengthened by his hopeless passion for the Irish patriot Maud Gonne. Yeats's poetry before 1900 reveals his debt to SPENSER, SHELLEY, and the PRE-RAPHAELITES. Verses from this period include "The Lake Isle of Innisfree" and "When You Are Old." In 1898 he helped found the Irish Literary Theatre, where his *The Countess Cathleen* (1899) and *Cathleen ni Houlihan* (1902) were performed. *The Hour Glass* (1904), *The Land of Heart's Desire* (1904), and *Deirdre* (1907) appeared at the Abbey Theatre. His prose tales were collected in *The Celtic Twilight* (1893) and the symbolic *Secret Rose* (1897). As he grew older, Yeats's poetry moved from transcendentalism to a more physical realism. Polarities between the physical and the spiritual were central in poems like "Sailing to Byzantium" and "The Second Coming." Some of his best work came late, in *The Tower* (1928) and *Last Poems* (1940). The prose work *A Vision,* an occult view of history written after 1917 with his wife, Georgie Hyde-Lees, was a source for much of his later work. Yeats received the Nobel Prize in literature in 1923.

Yekaterinburg or **Ekaterinburg,** formerly **Sverdlovsk,** city (1990 est. pop. 1,370,000), E European Russia, in the eastern foothills of the central URALS, on the Iset R. Among the region's largest cities, it is a western terminus of the Trans-Siberian RR and a major producer of turbines, ball bearings, and other manufactures. Nearby are gold and copper mines. It was founded in 1721 and named for CATHERINE I. In 1918, NICHOLAS II and his family were shot in Yekaterinburg. It was renamed Sverdlovsk in 1924. During World War II much industry was moved to the region from the European USSR. In 1991 the original name of the city was restored.

yellow daisy: see BLACK-EYED SUSAN.

yellow fever, acute infectious disease caused by a virus transmitted by the bite of the female *Aedes aegypti* mosquito. It causes fever, chills, prostration, JAUNDICE, and, in severe cases, internal hemorrhage, COMA, and death. Endemic to many tropical and subtropical areas, the disease was once prevalent in the Caribbean. In 1900 a team headed by Walter REED proved the mosquito-transmission theory of the Cuban physician C.J. FINLAY, and U.S. Surgeon General W.C. Gorgas led mosquito-eradication and sanitation procedures to control the disease before construction of the Panama Canal could begin. The disease now occurs in sporadic outbreaks, and immunization is an effective preventive measure.

Yellowknife, town (1991 pop. 15,179), capital of the Northwest Territories, NW Canada, on Great Slave Lake and the Yellowknife R. It was founded in 1935, moved to a new site in 1945, and became the territorial capital in 1967. Gold mining is the principal industry.

Yellow River: see HUANG HE.

Yellow Sea or **Huang Hai,** western arm of the Pacific Ocean, between China's east coast and Korea. The shallow sea, which has a maximum depth of c.500 ft (150 m), is underlaid by potentially rich oil deposits. Bo Hai, in the northwest, is the largest inlet. South of Korea it becomes the EAST CHINA SEA. Colored silt, deposited by feeder rivers, gives the Yellow Sea its name.

Yellowstone National Park: see NATIONAL PARKS (table).

Yeltsin, Boris Nikolayevich, 1931–, Soviet and Russian political leader, president of RUSSIA (1991–). Appointed Moscow Communist party boss by Mikhail GORBACHEV in 1985, he was ousted (1987) after clashing with conservatives and criticizing Gorbachev's reforms as inadequate. In 1987 he won election to the USSR's Supreme Soviet as an opposition member. In 1990 he was elected to the Russian Republic's Supreme Soviet, was elected Russian president by the Supreme Soviet, and resigned from the Communist party. He retained (1991) the presidency in a popular election. A populist and Russian nationalist, he became Gorbachev's chief liberal opponent. His opposition to the attempted coup against Gorbachev (Aug. 1991) shifted power to the reformers and republics, and he helped to found (Dec. 8, 1991) the COMMONWEALTH OF INDEPENDENT STATES, ending attempts to preserve the USSR. As president of an independent Russia, he moved to end state control of the economy and privatize most enterprises. Economic difficulties and political opposition, particularly from the Supreme Soviet (parliament), slowed his program and forced compromises. In Sept. 1993 Yeltsin suspended parliament and called for new elections. When parliament's supporters resorted to arms, they were crushed by the army and jailed. Although he won approval of his proposed constitution in the Dec. 1993 voting, many of his opponents won seats in the new legislature. In foreign affairs, Yeltsin greatly improved relations with the West and signed (1993) the START II nuclear DISARMAMENT treaty with the U.S. He failed, however, to secure more than a limited amount of economic aid.

Yemen, officially Republic of Yemen, republic (1992 est. pop. 10,395,000), 207,000 sq mi (536,000 sq km), SW Asia, on the S Arabian peninsula, bordered by Saudia Arabia (N), Oman (E), the Gulf of Aden (S), and the Red Sea (W); formed in 1990 by the union of Yemen Arab Republic (Yemen or Northern Yemen) and the People's Democratic Republic of Yemen (Southern Yemen). The capital is SANA; the port of ADEN is the commercial capital. A narrow coastal plain rises to interior highlands and the Rub al Khali desert. The country includes several islands, e.g., Perim and SOCOTRA. Yemen is very poor, with a per capita income that is among the lowest in the world. Most of the population is engaged in growing grains, vegetables, fruits, cotton, coffee, and khat (a narcotic shrub), and raising sheep, goats, and camels. There are oil reserves, and imported oil is processed into petroleum products for export. Other manufacturing, largely based on agricultural products, provides little revenue. Salt is the only commercially exploitable mineral. Handicrafts are important in the economy, as are remittances sent home by Yemenis working abroad. The great majority of the inhabitants are Arabs, about two thirds of which are Sunni Muslims and the rest Shiite Muslims. Arabic is the official language.

History. Once part of the ancient Sabaean kingdom (fl. c.750 B.C.–115 B.C.), Yemen was later ruled by the Himyarites, Romans, Ethiopians, and Persians. It was conquered by Muslim Arabs in the

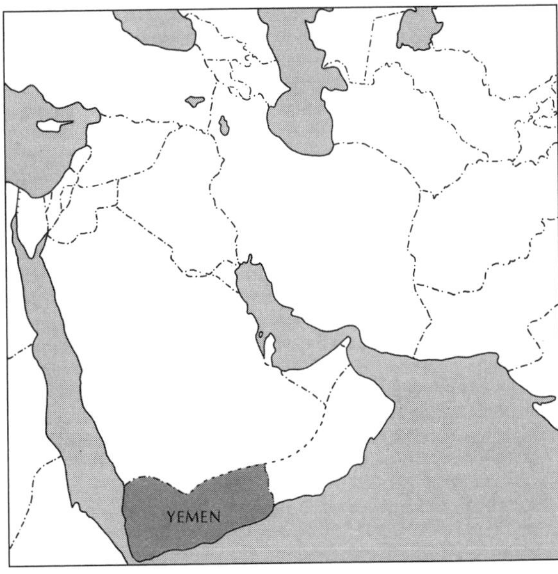

7th cent. A.D., and in the 16th cent. it became part of the OTTOMAN EMPIRE. The northwestern portion bordering on the Red Sea was established in 1918 as an independent kingdom (known as Yemen or Northern Yemen) ruled by the Rassite dynasty, imams of the Zaidi Shiite sect of Islam. In 1962 an army coup led to the proclamation of a republic. Civil war followed, with Egypt supporting the republicans and Saudi Arabia and Jordan backing the royalists; it ended in 1970 with a republic in place. The southern portion bordering on the Gulf of Aden was penetrated in the 19th cent. by the British, who conquered ADEN in 1839 and between 1886 and 1914 signed a number of protectorate treaties with local rulers. Aden was made a crown colony in 1935 and the area to its east became the Aden Protectorate in 1937. In the 1960s, nationalist groups demanding independence began a terrorist campaign against the British, and independence was granted to Southern Yemen in 1967. The National Liberation Front gained control of the government and established a Marxist regime in 1971. Unity agreements between the two Yemens in 1971 and 1981 were not implemented because of recurrent warfare, but a merger negotiated in 1989 resulted in formal unification in 1990. Pres. Ali Abdullah Saleh of Northern Yemen became president.

Yenan: see YAN'AN.

Yenisei, great river of SIBERIA, c.2,500 mi (4,020 km) long. It is formed by the confluence of the Bolshoi Yenisei and Maly Yenisei rivers near the Mongolian border and flows west, then generally north, to enter the Arctic Ocean through the Kara Sea. The river is frozen during the winter; the ice of its upper course melts earlier in the spring than that of its lower course, causing extensive flooding. Part of the Yenisei's great hydroelectric potential is harnessed at Krasnoyarsk and Sayan.

yeoman, class in English society. It generally means a free landowner of a rank lower than the gentry. Certain retainers in noble and royal households were also called yeomen. The Yeomen of the Guard, often called Beefeaters, became the bodyguard of the English monarch. The more modern military use of the term dates from the 18th cent., when volunteer cavalry units called yeomanry were used to suppress riots.

yerba maté: see MATÉ.

Yerevan, city (1990 est. pop. 1,200,000), capital of ARMENIA, SW Asia, on the Razdan R. The city's industries produce metals, machine tools, electrical equipment, and chemicals. Archaeological evidence indicates that the fortress of Yerbuni stood on the city's site in the 8th cent. B.C. Known in the 7th cent. A.D., Yerevan was the capital of the kingdom of Armenia under Persian rule and later (14th–19th cent.) part of the empires of TIMUR, Persia, Turkey, and Russia. In 1920 it became the capital of the Armenian Soviet Socialist Republic, which became independent in 1991 when the USSR disintegrated.

yeti: see ABOMINABLE SNOWMAN.

Yevtushenko, Yevgeny Aleksandrovich [yĕv'tōōshĕng'-kō], 1933–, Russian poet. With VOZNESENSKY and others he helped revive Russian lyric poetry. In works such as "Babi Yar" (1961) and "The Heirs of Stalin" (1962) he exposed serious defects in Soviet society. His long poems include *The Bratsk Station* (1964–65) and *Kazan University* (1970). He wrote the novel *Wild Berries* (tr. 1984).

yew, evergreen tree or shrub (genus *Taxus*) of the family Taxaceae, somewhat similar to HEMLOCK but bearing red berrylike fruits instead of true cones. Of somber appearance, with dark green leaves, yews have been associated with death and funeral rites since antiquity. The wood of the English yew (*T. baccata*) was used for the longbows of English archers, and the wood of several species is still so used. The Pacific, or Western, yew (*T. brevifolia*), native to the NW U.S. and British Columbia, is valued for its bark, which is processed to yield paclitaxel (Taxol), a drug used to treat ovarian cancer.

Yiddish language, member of the West Germanic group of the Germanic subfamily of the Indo-European family of languages. Although it is not a national language, Yiddish is spoken by about 4 million Jews all over the world, especially in Argentina, Canada, France, Israel, Mexico, Romania, and the U.S. Before the annihilation of 6 million Jews by the Nazis, Yiddish was the tongue of more than 11 million people. See LANGUAGE (table).

YMCA: see YOUNG MEN'S CHRISTIAN ASSOCIATION.

YMHA and YM-YWHA: see YOUNG MEN'S AND YOUNG WOMEN'S HEBREW ASSOCIATION.

yoga [Skt., = union], general term for spiritual disciplines, followed for centuries by devotees of both HINDUISM and BUDDHISM, to attain higher consciousness and liberation from ignorance, suffering, and rebirth. It is also the name of one of the six orthodox systems of INDIAN PHILOSOPHY. *Raja yoga* royal yoga was expounded by Patanjali (2d cent. B.C.), who divided the practice into eight stages, the highest of which is samadhi, or identification of the individual consciousness with the Godhead. Hindu tradition in general recognizes three main types of yoga: *jnana yoga,* the path of wisdom and discrimination; *bhakti yoga,* the path of love and devotion to a personal God; and *karma yoga,* the path of selfless action. *Hatha yoga,* widely practiced in the West, emphasizes physical control and postures. *Kundalini yoga,* associated with TANTRA, is based on the physiology of the "subtle body." It attempts to open centers of psychic energy called *chakras,* said to be located along the spinal column, and to activate the *kundalini,* a force located at the base of the spine. Yoga is usually practiced under the guidance of a guru, or spiritual teacher. Contemporary systems of yoga stress attaining spiritual realization without withdrawing from the world, as the older traditions taught.

yogurt: see FERMENTED MILK.

Yokohama, city (1990 pop. 3,220,350), capital of Kanagawa prefecture, SE Honshu, Japan. The second largest city in Japan and a leading seaport, it is part of the extensive urban-industrial belt around Tokyo. When U.S. Commodore Matthew C. PERRY first visited Yokohama in 1853, it was a small fishing village. Among its present industries are shipyards, steel mills, oil refineries, chemical plants, and many types of factories. Yokohama has a variety of Christian churches, Shinto shrines and temples, and many parks and gardens.

Yom Kippur: see under JEWISH HOLIDAYS.

Yom Kippur War: see ARAB-ISRAELI WARS.

Yonkers, city (1990 pop. 188,082), SE N.Y., on the Hudson R. just N of the Bronx (N.Y.C.); inc. 1855. Its famous elevator works date from 1852. Other manufactures include chemicals, electronic equipment, and clothing. Yonkers was a trade center in colonial days.

York, Alvin Cullum, 1887–1964, American soldier known as Sergeant York; b. Fentress co., Tenn. For his heroic actions in the Argonne forest (Oct. 8, 1918), York received the highest decorations of the French and American governments. He was the greatest popular hero of WORLD WAR I.

York, city (1991 pop. 98,745), N Yorkshire, N England. Its manufactures include chocolate and precision instruments, and it is a great rail center. A major Roman military post, it was later important in the Kingdom of NORTHUMBRIA. An archbishopric since the 7th cent., it is the ecclesiastical center of N England and the site of the Norman Cathedral of St. Peter (York Minster). York was the Viking city of Jorvik from 867–1067.

York, house of, royal house of England, dating from the creation (1385) of Edmund of Langley, fifth son of EDWARD III, as duke of York. The claims to the throne of his grandson, Richard, duke of York, in opposition to HENRY VI, head of the house of LANCASTER, resulted in the Wars of the ROSES. The royal members of the house of York were EDWARD IV, EDWARD V, and RICHARD III. The houses of York and Lancaster were united by the marriage (1486) of the Lancastrian HENRY VII to Elizabeth, daughter of Edward IV.

Yorkshire terrier, spirited TOY DOG; shoulder height, c.9 in. (22.8 cm); weight, 4–7 lb (1.8–3.2 kg). Its long, fine coat is steel-blue and tan. It was developed by cross-breeding in England, in the mid-19th cent.

Yorktown campaign, 1781, the closing military operations of the AMERICAN REVOLUTION. After his unsuccessful Carolina campaign (1780–81), Gen. CORNWALLIS retreated into Virginia, fortified Yorktown, and awaited reinforcements from Sir Henry CLINTON in New York. Clinton delayed, however, and the French fleet under Adm. de GRASSE blockaded Chesapeake Bay. Generals Washington and ROCHAMBEAU rushed south with French troops, while STEUBEN and LAFAYETTE maintained a brilliant holding action. Unable to escape, Cornwallis surrendered on Oct. 17, 1781, thereby bringing victory to the rebellious Colonies.

Yoruba, people of SW Nigeria, numbering about 13 million. They are unusual among Africans in their tendency to form urban communities. Today many of the largest cities of Nigeria, e.g., LAGOS and IBADAN, are in Yorubaland. The old Yoruba kingdom of Oyo dominated both Benin (see BENIN, former kingdom) and Dahomey (see BENIN, republic), but after 1700 its power waned. In the early 19th cent. the Yoruba were divided among several smaller states.

Yosemite National Park: see NATIONAL PARKS (table).

Yoshida Shigeru [yō'shēdä], 1878–1967, Japanese statesman. He led the Liberal party after 1945 and was prime minister five times between 1946 and 1954. During his administration a new constitution was promulgated, land reforms instituted, and the postwar U.S. occupation ended.

Young, Andrew Jackson, Jr., 1932–, African-American civil-rights leader, clergyman, and public official; b. New Orleans. He was a leading civil-rights activist in the 1960s and, as a Democrat from Georgia, served (1973–77) in the U.S. House of Representatives. Under Pres. CARTER, Young was permanent representative to the UN (1977–79) and was noted for his outspokenness. He served as mayor of Atlanta (1982–89) and ran for, but failed to win, the Democratic nomination for governor of Georgia in 1990.

Young, Brigham, 1801–77, American MORMON, leader of the Church of Jesus Christ of Latter-Day Saints; b. Whitingham, Vt. He was perhaps a greater molder of Mormonism than its founder, Joseph SMITH. Young led a group to the Mormon community at Kirtland, Ohio, and became (1835) one of the Council of Twelve. He became prominent after the persecutions of Mormons in Missouri and was a leader in the move to Nauvoo, Ill. After Smith's assassination (1844), he was the chief figure in maintaining church unity and was henceforth the dominant person in Mormonism. Young led (1846–47) the great migration west and directed the settlement at Salt Lake City. In Utah he exercised supreme control, and the Mormon cooperative theocracy prospered. He headed the church, and after the creation of the U.S. provisional government, he became territorial governor. Trouble between the U.S. and the Mormons over polygamy and church power led to the U.S. military expedition of 1857–58, but Young avoided an open break with the government, although he lost his post as governor. He probably had 27 wives, and unjustified charges of sensuality were often leveled against him. He was, in reality, a stern moralist, as well as a brilliant leader.

Young, Cy (Denton T. Young), 1867–1955, American baseball player; b. Gilmore, Ohio. In 22 seasons (1890–1911) as a pitcher for the Cleveland Indians, St. Louis Cardinals, Boston Red Sox, and Boston Braves, he won 511 games, more than any other pitcher in history. He pitched 76 shutouts and 3 no-hit games, one of which was a perfect game.

Young, Edward, 1683–1765, English poet and dramatist, famous for his long didactic poem *The Complaint, or Night Thoughts on Life, Death, and Immortality* (1742–45), an influence on ROMANTICISM. He also wrote a series of satires, *The Universal Passion* (1725–28).

Young, Lester, 1909–59, African-American musician; b. Woodville, Miss. Young was, with Coleman HAWKINS, a major influence on tenor saxophone style; his work greatly influenced the modern JAZZ of the 1950s. Billie HOLIDAY gave him the nickname "President," which later became "Prez."

Young, Thomas, 1773–1829, English physicist, physician, and Egyptologist. He was professor of natural philosophy (1801–3) at the Royal Institution, where he presented the modern physical concept of energy, and was elected (1811) a staff member of St. George's Hospital, London. He stated (1807) a theory of color vision known as the Young-Helmholtz theory and described the vision defect called ASTIGMATISM. Reviving the wave theory of LIGHT, Young applied it to refraction and dispersion phenomena. He also established a coefficient of elasticity (Young's modulus; see STRENGTH OF MATERIALS) and helped to decipher the ROSETTA STONE.

Young, Whitney Moore, Jr., 1921–71, African-American civil-rights leader; b. Lincoln Ridge, Ky. A social worker by profession, he joined the National Urban League in 1947 as director of industrial relations for St. Paul, Minn. He headed the League from 1961 until his death and was one of the leading CIVIL-RIGHTS activists of the 1960s.

Younger, Cole (Thomas Coleman Younger), 1844–1916, American outlaw; b. Jackson co., Mo. He and his two brothers joined the outlaw band of Jesse JAMES and were captured (1876) during an attempted bank robbery at Northfield, Minn. Cole Younger was paroled in 1901 and lived peacefully thereafter.

Young Men's and Young Women's Hebrew Associations (YMHA, YWHA), organizations that promote health, social activities, recreation, and Jewish culture among Jews of all ages. The first YMHA was founded in Baltimore in 1854. A YWHA was organized as an auxiliary of the New York City YMHA in 1888, and the first independent YWHA was formed in 1902. The organizations have since merged under the name **Jewish Community Centers,** although many retain the designation YM-YWHA.

Young Men's Christian Association (YMCA), organization originally concerned with the spiritual and social well-being and the physical and intellectual development of young men. Begun (1844) in London, it took root in the U.S. in 1851 and now has branches on all continents. Membership, which is not limited to men or Christians, is 12.7 million.

Young Pretender: see under STUART, JAMES FRANCIS EDWARD.

Young's modulus: see STRENGTH OF MATERIALS.

Youngstown, city (1990 pop. 95,732), seat of Mahoning co., NE Ohio, in a coal and iron region near the Pa. line; founded 1797, inc. 1849. The first iron furnace was built in 1803, and Youngstown became one of the country's largest iron and steel centers until the 1970s; some steel is still produced. Rubber goods, electric lamps, and a variety of other products are also manufactured there.

Young Turks: see OTTOMAN EMPIRE.

Young Women's Christian Association (YWCA), organization devoted to promoting the welfare of women and girls through opportunities for spiritual, social, intellectual, and physical development. The nondenominational movement grew out of mid-19th cent. British homes and prayer unions for young women. The first official American YWCA was in New York (1858). The world organization, based in Geneva, was established in 1894. There are some 2 million members; men may join as associate members.

Yourcenar, Marguerite, 1903–87, French novelist; b. Belgium, as Marguerite de Crayencour. She has lived in the U.S. since 1939. She is noted for her reconstructions of historical eras and people, as in *Memoirs of Hadrian* (1951), about the Roman emperor, and *The Abyss* (1968), set in N Europe in the 16th cent. In 1980 she became the first woman to be admitted to the French Academy.

Youskevitch, Igor [yo͝oskē'vĭch], 1912–, Russian ballet dancer. He joined (1938) the Ballet Russe de Monte Carlo, danced (1946–55) with the Ballet Theater (N.Y.C.), and returned to the Ballet Russe. He is famed for his classic style, e.g., *Afternoon of a Faun.*

Youth, Isle of, formerly **Isle of Pines,** island, 1,180 sq mi (3,056 sq km), off the coast of SW Cuba. It was discovered by COLUMBUS in 1494 and passed to U.S. control in 1898, after the SPANISH-AMERICAN WAR. Because its name was omitted from the PLATT AMENDMENT, defining Cuba's boundaries, it was claimed by both the U.S. and Cuba until a treaty signed in 1925 confirmed Cuba's possession. Near Nueva Gerona, the capital, is a prison in which political dissidents have been detained by several regimes.

Ypres, battles of, three major battles of WORLD WAR I fought at Ypres, in SW Belgium. In the first (Oct.–Nov. 1914) the British, at great cost, stopped the German "race to the sea." In the second (Apr.–May 1915) the Germans unsuccessfully assaulted the British salient. Poison gas was used for the first time. In the third (Oct.–Nov. 1917), also known as Passchendaele, the British attacked the German line but advanced only 5 mi (8 km) at a cost of 300,000 lives.

Ypsilanti or **Hypsilanti,** prominent Greek family of Phanariots. **Alexander Ypsilanti,** c.1725–c.1807, was dragoman (minister) of the Ottoman emperor and hospodar (governor) of Walachia (1774–82, 1796–97) and of Moldavia (1768–88). He was executed by the sultan for conspiracy. His son, **Constantine Ypsilanti,** 1760–1816, was hospodar of Moldavia (1799–1801) and of Walachia (1802–6). He was deposed for being pro-Russian and was reinstated in 1807 by the Russians. He encouraged the Serbian revolt against Turkey. His elder son, **Alexander Ypsilanti,** 1792–1828, was a leader in the Greek War of Independence and led unsuccessful uprisings in Moldavia and Walachia. After being defeated by the Turks, he was imprisoned in Austria, where he died. His younger brother, **Demetrios Ypsilanti,** 1793–1832, also played a prominent part in the Greek revolt. In 1821 he captured Trípolis, Turkey's chief fort on the Peloponnesus. In 1828 he became commander of the Greek forces in E Greece. He resigned in 1830 after differences with other Greek leaders.

ytterbium (Tb), metallic element, discovered by J.C.G. de Marignac in 1878. A soft, malleable, ductile, lustrous, silver-white RARE-EARTH METAL in the LANTHANIDE SERIES, it forms many compounds. It is widely distributed in a number of minerals, but has no commercial uses. See ELEMENT (table); PERIODIC TABLE.

yttrium (Y), metallic element, first isolated by Friedrich WÖHLER in 1828. Yttrium is an iron-gray RARE-EARTH METAL. Its oxide is used in making red phosphors for color-television picture tubes. See ELEMENT (table); PERIODIC TABLE.

Yüan, dynasty: see CHINA.

Yüan Shih-kai [yüan shŭr-kī], 1859–1916, president of China (1912–16). He was entrusted with defending the Ch'ing empire against the revolution of 1911, but on his advice the Emperor Hsuan T'ung (Henry PU YI) resigned. Soon after, SUN YAT-SEN, who had been elected the first president of China, resigned in Yüan's favor. Yüan's rule proved dictatorial, and in 1916 he briefly assumed the title of emperor.

Yucatán, peninsula, c.70,000 sq mi (181,000 sq km), extending from SE Mexico into Belize and Guatemala. It is a low, flat limestone tableland rising to c.500 ft (150 m) in the south. Its northern continuation is the oil-rich Campeche bank, under Campeche Bay and the Gulf of Mexico. The climate is hot and dry in the north, hot and humid in the south. Centuries before the Spanish arrived (early 16th cent.), Yucatán was the seat of the great civilization of the MAYA, whose descendants predominate in today's population. The developing economy is based on tourism, the production of oil and lumber, and light industry and assembly plants.

yucca, stiff-leaved, stemless or treelike SUCCULENT (genus *Yucca*) of the LILY family, native mainly to Mexico and the SW U.S. Yuccas produce a large stalk of white or purplish blossoms. They are pollinated by the yucca moth, and in its absence they rarely produce FRUIT. Species include the Adam's-needle (*Y. filamentosa* and others), the Joshua tree (*Y. brevifolia*), and the Spanish dagger (*Y. gloriosa*). Roots of some species are used for soap.

Yugoslavia, Serbo-Croatian *Jugoslavija,* officially Federal Republic of Yugoslavia, federal republic (1992 est. pop. 10,642,000), 39,439 sq mi (102,147 sq km), SE Europe, on the Balkan Peninsula; bordered by the Adriatic Sea, Bosnia and Hercegovina, and Croatia (W), Hungary (N), Romania and Bulgaria (E), and Macedonia and Albania (S). It is (since 1992) a federation of two republics: SERBIA and MONTENEGRO. Four other Yugoslav republics, SLOVENIA, CROATIA, BOSNIA AND HERCEGOVINA, and MACEDONIA, declared independence in 1991 and 1992. Principal cities include BELGRADE (the capital), Niš, Novi Sad, Priština, and Podgorica. About half of Yugoslavia is mountainous. Agriculture is largely concentrated in NE Serbia, along the Danubian plain. Crops include corn, wheat, sugar beets, and potatoes, and there are extensive vineyards. Yugoslavia's major industries are metal processing and the production of textiles, machinery, chemicals, and glass. Mining is also important; there are significant deposits of coal, copper, petroleum, and iron. The nation's breakup and the resulting civil war and international economic embargo have led to economic collapse and hyperinflation. The Yugoslav people consist of Serbs and Montenegrins (closely related to Serbs), who use the Cyrillic alphabet and belong to the ORTHODOX EASTERN CHURCH, and other ethnic groups, mainly Albanians (see KOSOVO) and Hungarians. Serbs and Montenegrins share the same language, Serbo-Croatian.

History. Yugoslavia's existence as a nation began after World War I. Of its component republics, only Serbia (which included the present independent republic of Macedonia) and Montenegro were independent states in 1914; Croatia, Slovenia, and Bosnia and Hercegovina belonged to the AUSTRO-HUNGARIAN MONARCHY. The movement for unification, led by Serbia, was a major cause of WORLD WAR I. In 1918 the "Kingdom of the Serbs, Croats, and Slovenes" was proclaimed. The name was changed to Yugoslavia in 1929 and a parliamentary constitution adopted in 1931. From its inception, the new country was plagued by demands for autonomy by Croatian and Macedonian nationalists, culminating in 1934 with the assassination of King ALEXANDER. Tension also arose from territorial disputes with Italy, Hungary, and Bulgaria. Yugoslavia had joined Czechoslovakia and Romania in the LITTLE ENTENTE in the 1920s, but in 1939 it drew closer to the AXIS powers. A coup in 1941 brought a neutral government to power, but soon afterwards Yugoslavia was invaded and occupied by Germany and its allies. Partisan troops, led by royalist Gen. Draza MIHAJLOVIĆ and Communist Marshal Josip TITO, battled the occupation forces until 1943, when civil war erupted between the rival leaders. Tito, supported by the USSR and Britain, was victorious. By 1944 the Germans had been driven from Yugoslavia, and in 1945 Tito became premier, deposed the king, and established a Communist state closely allied with the USSR. In 1948 Tito broke with the Soviet leadership. He developed a "national communism," abandoning farm collectivization and, to some extent, centralized government controls; intellectual freedom was restricted, however, and renewed Croatian nationalist agitation was suppressed. After Tito's death (1980), a collective presidency was established. In 1990 the Communist party relinquished its monopoly on political power. Previously contained ethnic tensions became more prominent, and Slovenia and Croatia declared (1991) independence, a move resisted by Serbia and its president, Slobodan MILOŠEVIĆ. In Croatia battling between Croatian forces and Serb militias escalated into civil war (1991–92). Bosnia and Hercegovina (1991) and Macedonia (1992) also became independent, and intense fighting erupted (1992) in Bosnia. The UN imposed economic sanctions, including a naval blockade, on Yugoslavia for supporting Serbian forces in Bosnia and withheld recognition of the new Yugoslav state established by Serbia and Montenegro.

Yukawa Hideki, 1907–81, Japanese physicist. In 1935 he predicted the existence of the pi meson (or pion; see ELEMENTARY PARTICLES), a particle that is heavier than an electron but lighter than a proton and that carries the STRONG INTERACTION between particles in the atomic nucleus. After particles corresponding to his prediction were discovered in 1947, Yukawa was awarded the 1949 Nobel Prize for physics.

Yukon, major river of NW North America, flowing c.2,000 mi (3,200 km) from Atlin Lake in BRITISH COLUMBIA, Canada, through the SW YUKON TERRITORY and across central Alaska before entering the BERING SEA through a large delta near Norton Sound. Rich in hydroelectric potential and an important salmon-fishing area, it is, for three months of the year, navigable by river boats to WHITEHORSE, in the Yukon, c.1,755 mi (2,860 km) upstream.

Yukon Territory, region (1991 pop. 27,797), 186,299 sq mi (482,515 sq km), NW Canada, bordered by the Arctic Ocean (N), the Northwest Territories (E), British Columbia and Alaska (S), and Alaska (W). WHITEHORSE is the capital (since 1952) and largest town; DAWSON is next in importance. Although most of the territory is in the YUKON R. watershed, the northern and southeastern regions drain into the MACKENZIE R. system. The extreme north is uninhabited, and throughout the Yukon winters are long and cold. Most settlements are located along riverbanks. The leading industry in the territory is mining; lead, zinc, silver, gold, and copper are the principal minerals. Manufacturing is relatively unimportant, but tourism is gaining in importance because of the Yukon's great natural beauty. The Alaska Highway and other all-weather roads have been built since World War II. Fur traders from the HUDSON'S BAY COMPANY explored the region in the 1840s and several posts were set up. After the famous gold strikes in the Klondike R. region in the 1890s, more than 30,000 people came in search of gold. The Canadian government, which acquired the Yukon from the Hudson's Bay Company in 1870, first administered it as part of the NORTHWEST TERRITORIES and made it a separate district in 1895. The Yukon became a separate territory in 1898. Native land claims and the desire for provincial status have dominated recent politics. The government consists of a federally appointed commissioner and an elected legislative council. The Yukon sends one senator (appointed) and one representative (elected) to the national parliament.

Yuman [yo͞oʹmən], branch of Native American languages belonging to the Hokan-Siouan linguistic stock of North America and Central America. See NATIVE AMERICAN LANGUAGES (table).

YWCA: see YOUNG WOMEN'S CHRISTIAN ASSOCIATION.

YWHA: see YOUNG MEN'S AND YOUNG WOMEN'S HEBREW ASSOCIATION.

Z

Zacharias or **Zachary, Saint,** pope (741–52), a Calabrian Greek. A guardian of church authority, he persuaded the Lombards to restore some towns to the papacy and favored the Frankish king PEPIN THE SHORT. His letters, notably to St. BONIFACE, are still extant. Feast: Mar. 22.

Zagreb, city (1991 est. pop. 706,800), capital of CROATIA, in the N central part of the country on the Sava R. It is Croatia's largest city and a major financial and industrial center. Manufactures include machinery and chemicals. Site of a Roman town, Zagreb was ruled by Hungary from the 13th cent. and, under the AUSTRO-HUNGARIAN MONARCHY, became (1867) the capital of an autonomous Croatia. After 1918 it was part of YUGOSLAVIA until Croatia declared its independence in 1991. A modern city, it contains the historic Kaptol district, with the Catholic cathedral (begun 1093).

Zagros, mountain system of W Iran, extending c.1,100 mi (1,770 km) southeast from the Turkish-Armenian-Azerbaijan frontier (N) to the Strait of Hormuz (S) along the western edge of the central Iranian plateau. Mt. Sabalan (15,592 ft/4,752 m) is the highest peak. The Zagros decrease in elevation and become increasingly arid toward the south. Kurds, Lurs, Bakhtiaris, Kashkais, and other minorities are the chief inhabitants. Iran's great oil fields lie along the western foothills.

Zaharias, Mildred "Babe" Didrikson: see DIDRIKSON, BABE.

Zaïre [zīʹēr, zäērʹ], officially Republic of Zaïre, formerly Republic of the Congo (1960–65) and Democratic Republic of the Congo (1965–71), republic (1992 est. pop. 39,084,000), c.905,000 sq mi (2,344,000 sq km), central Africa, bordered by Angola (SW), Congo (W), the Central African Republic and Sudan (N), Uganda, Rwanda, Burundi, and Tanzania (E), and Zambia (SE). Principal cities include KINSHASA (the capital), Kananga, and LUBUMBASHI. Virtually all of Zaïre, which lies astride the equator, is part of the vast CONGO (Zaïre) R. drainage basin. North central Zaïre is a large plateau covered with rain forest. To the east, on the Uganda border, are the Ruwenzori Mts., which rise to over 16,000 ft (4,880 m), and lakes Albert, Edward, and Tanganyika. Savanna-covered plateaus in the southeast rise to c.6,800 ft (2,070 m). Zaïre's mineral wealth is the mainstay of the economy, accounting for about 75% of export earnings. Most important are copper, diamonds (the world's leading producer), cobalt (65% of world reserves), zinc, manganese, and uranium; offshore petroleum production began in 1975. The principal food crops are cassava, yams, maize, rice, groundnuts, plantains, and pulses. The leading farm exports are palm products, coffee, and rubber; large amounts of timber (notably ebony and teak) are also produced. Manufactures include processed metals, foodstuffs, textiles, clothing, iron and steel, cement, and chemicals. Nonetheless, Zaïre has failed to harness the full potential of its vast natural resources. It experienced a severe decline in per capita income after 1973 and near total economic collapse, brought on by corruption and a governmental crisis, in the early 1990s. The population is made up of some 200 ethnic groups, the majority of which speak a Bantu language; there are also Nilotic speakers in the north, and scattered groups of PYGMIES. French is the official language, but Swahili and Lingala are widely spoken. About 50% of the people are Catholic, 20% Protestant, and 10% Muslim, but many also adhere to traditional beliefs.

History. Pygmies were probably the earliest inhabitants of the region, but by the end of the 1st millennium B.C. Bantu speakers migrated into Zaïre from the northwest. The Bantu worked the copper deposits from about 700 A.D., eventually coalescing into independent, often complex, states, including the Lunda kingdom of Mwata Yamo (est. 15th cent.), in SW Zaïre; a Luba empire (est. early 16th cent.), in central Shaba; the Kuba kingdom of the Shongo (est. early 17th cent.), in S Zaïre; and the Lunda kingdom of Mwata Kazembe (est. 18th cent.), near the present Zaïre-Zambia border. Following the visit of Diogo Cão in 1482, the Portuguese, who were active in trading, established a presence in the region. Beginning in the 1870s the territory was colonized and unified by LEOPOLD II of Belgium, who in 1885 privately founded and headed an independent state (the Congo Free State) in the Congo Basin; it was annexed by Belgium in 1908, becoming the colony of the Belgian Congo. Under Belgian rule the Congo became a rich field for European investment, especially in mining operations and plantations. Nationalist sentiment, led by Joseph KASAVUBU and Patrice LUMUMBA, reached a peak in the 1950s, and Belgium was forced to grant independence in 1960. However, the new Republic of the Congo was soon torn by ethnic and personal rivalries. Within weeks the army mutinied, and Moïse TSHOMBE declared the copper-rich province of Katanga (now SHABA), of which he was provisional president, to be independent. The ensuing civil war, which involved UN forces, Belgian troops, and U.S. and Soviet support of opposing factions, did not end until 1963, when Katanga agreed to rejoin the republic. By the end of the 1960s the country had begun to experience a degree of political stability. Col. Joseph Mobotu (later MOBUTO SESE SEKO), who took power in 1965, served as president from 1970, suppressing tribal conflicts and instilling a sense of nationhood. The U.S. supported him as a regional bulwark against communism despite his regime's corruption. A ban on opposition political parties was ended only in 1990, in response to growing political unrest. Economic deterioration, loss of Western

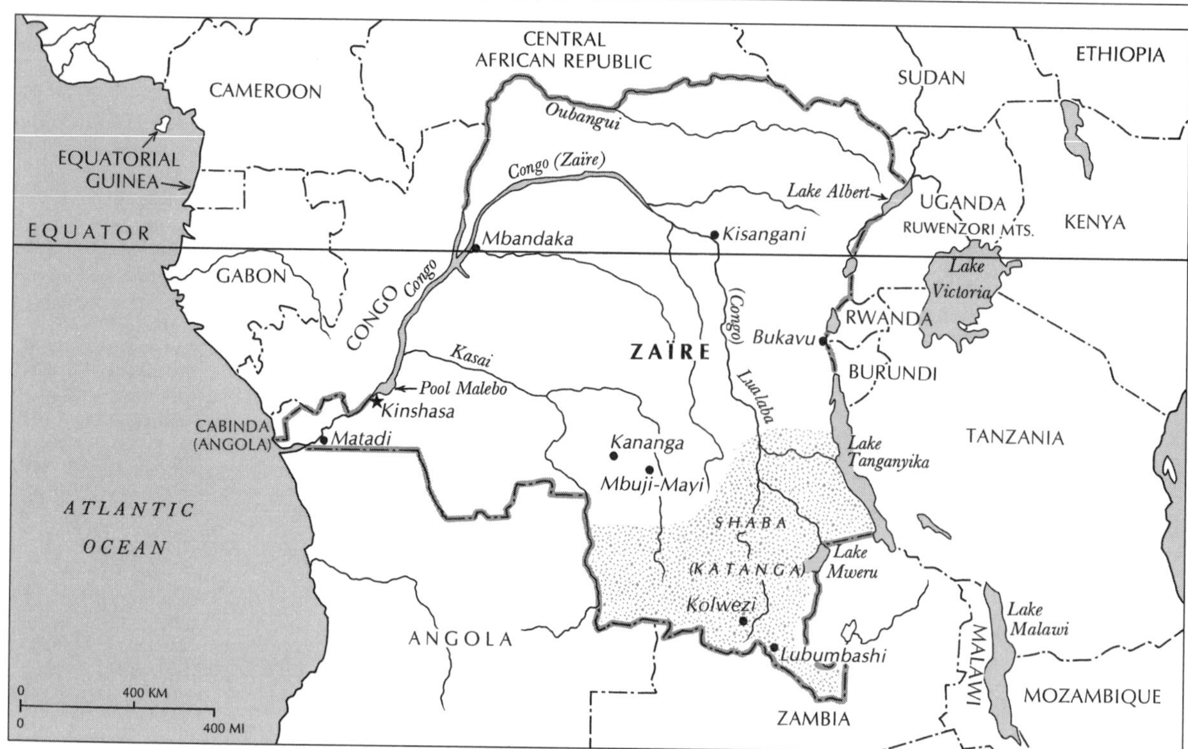

support with the end of the cold war, failure of a national political conference, and rioting begun by unpaid soldiers led Mobutu to agree to a coalition government with opposition leaders in 1991. He retained control of the army and important government ministries, however, and later replaced the prime minister. Economic collapse has continued unabated.

Zaïre, river: see CONGO.

Zama [zā'mə], ancient town near the northern coast of Africa, in present Tunisia. Scipio Africanus Major defeated HANNIBAL at or near Zama in the final battle of the Second PUNIC WAR (202 B.C.), but there were several towns named Zama.

Zambezi, river, flowing c.1,700 mi (2,740 km) through S central Africa to the Mozambique Channel. Part of its large hydroelectric potential is harnessed by KARIBA DAM (completed 1959), on the Zimbabwe-Zambia border, and Cabora Bassa Dam (completed 1975), in Mozambique. VICTORIA FALLS and many rapids restrict navigation to local traffic.

Zambia [zăm'bēə], officially Republic of Zambia, republic (1992 est. pop. 8,745,000), 290,584 sq mi (752,614 sq km), S central Africa, bordered by Zaïre (N), Tanzania (NE), Malawi and Mozambique (E), Zimbabwe, Botswana, and Namibia (S), and Angola (W). Major cities include LUSAKA (the capital), KITWE, and NDOLA. Zambia is on a highland plateau, which rises in the east; the country's highest point (c.7,120 ft/2,170 m) is on the Nyika plateau, adjacent to Malawi. VICTORIA FALLS and the huge Lake Kariba (formed by KARIBA DAM), both on the border with Zimbabwe, are part of the ZAMBEZI R., which drains the western part of the country. Zambia's economy is dependent almost entirely on its mineral wealth, notably copper, of which it is one of the world's leading producers, and cobalt; coal, zinc, lead, and manganese are also important. Manufactures include food products, textiles and clothing, and building materials. Much of the population is engaged in subsistence farming, however, growing corn and other grains, beans, peanuts, and tobacco and raising cattle. About 98% of the inhabitants are members of Bantu-speaking ethnic groups, but English is the official language. Some 70% of the population is Christian, equally divided between Roman Catholics and Protestants; the rest follow traditional beliefs.

History. Some Bantu-speaking peoples migrated into the region that is now Zambia around A.D. 1200, but the ancestors of most modern Zambians arrived from present-day Angola and Zaïre between the 16th and 18th cent. The British explorer David LIVINGSTONE first visited Zambia in 1851 and later discovered Victoria Falls. In 1890 Cecil Rhodes's British South Africa Company began to administer the area under treaties signed with African leaders; it became the protectorate of Northern Rhodesia in 1911 and passed under British administration in 1924. Massive copper deposits were discovered in N central Zambia in the late 1920s, and European colonists began to pour into the area. However, economic prosperity was not shared with the African laborers who worked in the mines, and who staged periodic strikes to protest their treatment, finally organizing a nationalist movement in 1946. In 1953, despite the protests of the black nationalists, Southern Rhodesia (now Zimbabwe), Northern Rhodesia, and Nyasaland (now Malawi) were brought together by Britain in the Federation of Rhodesia and Nyasaland. The federation was dissolved in 1963, when Nyasaland and Northern Rhodesia withdrew, and the Republic of Zambia was proclaimed independent in 1964, with Kenneth KAUNDA as president. Kaunda ended European economic domination and in 1972 created a one-party state. In the 1970s Zambia suffered severe economic hardship as a result of its opposition to the white regime in Southern Rhodesia and a drop in copper prices. Demonstrations in 1990 led Kaunda to legalize opposition parties. Multiparty presidential and parliamentary elections were held in 1991, and Kaunda was overwhelmingly defeated by Frederick Chiluba, whose party also won control of parliament.

Zampieri, Domenico: see DOMENICHINO.

Zangwill, Israel, 1864–1926, English author. A journalist, he also wrote *Children of the Ghetto* (1892), *Dreamers of the Ghetto* (1898), and *The Melting Pot* (1914).

Zanzibar, region (1988 pop. 375,539), 950 sq mi (2,461 sq km), Tanzania, E Africa, consisting chiefly of the islands of Zanzibar and Tumbatu, in the Indian Ocean. The major city is also named Zanzibar. The economy of the region is almost entirely agricultural, and Zanzibar and the nearby island of Pemba produce a large portion of the world's cloves. The Portuguese gained control in 1503, using the island as a base for territorial expansion on the African coast and for the slave trade. In 1698 Zanzibar and Pemba fell to the rulers of Oman. Under the Omani sultanate of Zanzibar (est. 1840), Muslim traders pushed deep into Africa in search of

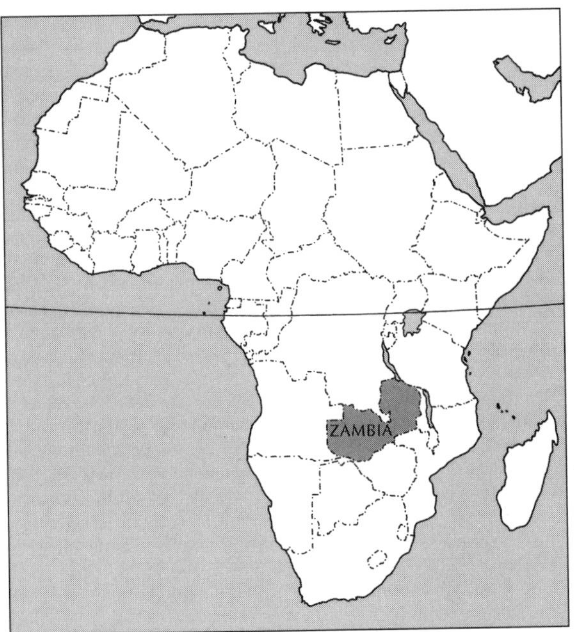

slaves and ivory. The islands became a British protectorate in 1890 and an independent nation in 1963. In 1964 leftists deposed the sultan, and the two islands merged with Tanganyika to form TANZANIA. Zanzibar retains control of its internal affairs.

Zapata, Emiliano, c.1879–1919, Mexican revolutionary. A tenant farmer of indigenous descent, he tried to recover (1908) expropriated village lands, and he led (1910–19) an army of indigenous people in the Mexican revolution with the goal of regaining the land. In defense of this program, he fought federal governments and largely controlled S Mexico. His army occupied Mexico City three times (1914–15), but he finally retired to Morelos, where he was treacherously killed by a government emissary. Zapata is still revered by Mexicans of indigenous descent.

Zápolya, John: see JOHN I, king of Hungary.

Zápolya, John Sigismund: see JOHN II, king of Hungary.

Zápolya, Stephen [zä'pôlyŏ], d. 1499, palatine (regent) of Hungary (1492–99). He fought (1479–81) against the Turks and conquered (1481–85) the archduchy of Austria for King MATTHIAS CORVINUS. His son became King JOHN I of Hungary.

Zapotec, indigenous people of S Mexico (see MIDDLE AMERICA, INDIGENOUS PEOPLES OF), whose language is often placed in the Macro-Otomanguean division (see NATIVE AMERICAN LANGUAGES). They had no traditions or migration legends, but believed themselves born directly from rocks, trees, and jaguars. The early Zapotec were agricultural city-dwellers whose religion involved ancestor worship and a cult of the dead. A high civilization flourished some 2,000 years ago at their religious center at Mitla and city of Monte Albán. Their arts, architecture, writing, mathematics, and calendar suggest links with the OLMEC, MAYA, and TOLTEC. About 1300 the MIXTEC took their cities, but the Zapotec remained autonomous until the arrival of the Spanish by allying with the AZTEC. The Zapotec number c.300,000; their culture blends native and Spanish elements.

Zaragoza [thärägō'thä] or **Saragossa,** city (1988 est. pop. 582,000), capital of Zaragoza prov. and chief city of Aragón, NE Spain, on the Ebro R. It is the center of a fertile agricultural region; its manufactures include vehicles and wood products. Held by the Romans, Goths, and MOORS (from the 8th cent.), it was taken (1118) by ALFONSO I of Aragón. In the PENINSULAR WAR the city yielded to a French siege (1808–9) only after some 50,000 defenders had died. Zaragoza is rich in art and contains two cathedrals.

Zea, Francisco Antonio [sā'ä], 1770–1822, Colombian revolutionary. After being imprisoned in Spain for revolutionary activities, he helped Simón BOLÍVAR liberate South America and was vice president (1819) of Venezuela and of Greater Colombia.

zebra, herbivorous, hoofed African MAMMAL (genus *Equus*), distinguished from other HORSES by its striking pattern of alternating white and dark brown (or black) stripes. Standing about 4 ft (120 cm) high, the zebra has a heavy head, a stout body, and a short, thick mane. It inhabits open plains or brush country in herds of up to 1,000, often mixing with other grazing animals, e.g., ANTELOPE, and can run at speeds of up to 40 mi (60 km) per hr.

zebu, domestic MAMMAL of the CATTLE family, *Bos indicus*, found in E Asia, India, and Africa. It has a large, fatty hump and is fawn, gray, black, or bay. The zebu has great endurance and is used in India for riding and draft purposes. In the U.S. zebus are called Brahman cattle.

Zebulun: see ISRAEL, TRIBES OF.

Zechariah [zĕk"ərī'ə] or **Zacharias** [zăk"ərī'əs], book of the OLD TESTAMENT, 38th in the Authorized Version, 11th of the Minor PROPHETS, dated 519 and 517 B.C. It contains a section with eight visions of restitution for JERUSALEM; another, perhaps later, section prophesies troubles and ultimate redemption.

Zedekiah [zĕd"əkī'ə], last king of Judah (c.597–586 B.C.). He was set on the throne as the puppet of NEBUCHADNEZZAR, but he allied himself with the Egyptians. The Babylonians then destroyed the kingdom of Judah and carried Zedekiah with his people into captivity in Babylonia.

Zelaya, José Santos [sālä'yä], 1853–1919, president of NICARAGUA (1894–1909). Zelaya ruled as dictator and developed transportation, coffee growing, and education while draining the country's resources for his own profit. His attempt to foment revolutions in neighboring states alarmed the U.S., which helped rebel forces to overthrow him.

zemstvo [zĕmst'vō] [Rus., from *zemlya* = land], local assembly in Russia, 1864–1917. Begun under ALEXANDER II, the zemstvo handled education, health, and other district matters, and chose delegates to the provincial assembly. In 1917 (see RUSSIAN REVOLUTION) the SOVIET replaced the zemstvo.

Zen Buddhism, Buddhist sect of Japan and China, based on the practice of MEDITATION rather than on adherence to a particular scriptural doctrine. Its founder in China was the legendary Bodhidharma (5th cent. A.D.), who taught "wall-gazing" and followed the Yogacara or Consciousness School of BUDDHISM, which held consciousness as real, but not its objects. The characteristic Zen teaching of sudden enlightment, or *satori*, goes back to Hui-neng, an illiterate master of the 7th cent. who defined enlightenment as the direct seeing of one's own "original nature" (i.e., Buddha). The golden age of Zen (8th–9th cent.) developed a unique style of oral instruction, including nonrational elements such as the *koan*, a subject given for meditation, usually in the form of a paradoxical saying, to test the enlightenment of students of Zen. After the persecution of Buddhism in 845, Zen emerged as the dominant Chinese sect. Two main schools, the *Lin-chi* (Jap. *Rinzai*), emphasizing the *koan* and *satori*, and the *Ts'ao-tung* (Jap. *Soto*), emphasizing the practice of meditation (*zazen*), were transmitted to Japan in the 14th cent. and greatly influenced politics and culture (e.g., poetry, painting, landscape gardening, the tea ceremony, and flower arranging) before declining in the 16th and 17th cent. Revived in the 18th cent., Zen thought was made known in the West by the writings of D.T. Suzuki, and after World War II it attracted interest in the U.S.

Zenger, John Peter, 1697–1745, American journalist; b. Germany. In 1734 he was imprisoned for political articles published in his newspaper, the New York *Weekly Journal*. Andrew Hamilton (1676?–1741) secured his acquittal in 1735. The case was an important landmark in establishing freedom of the press in America.

Zeno, d. 491, Roman emperor of the East (474–91) who succeeded his son, LEO I. He made peace with the Vandal king GAISERIC and made concessions to ODOACER in Italy. He freed the East from the raids of the Ostrogoths and encouraged their king, Theodoric the Great, to invade Italy (488).

Zeno of Elea, c.490–c.430 B.C., Greek philosopher of the Eleatic school founded by PARMENIDES. Zeno's only known work, extant in fragmented form, uses a series of paradoxes to show the error of commonsense notions of time and space, thereby demonstrating Parmenides' doctrine that motion and multiplicity are logically impossible. Contemporary thinkers have shown renewed interest in the problems Zeno raised.

Zephaniah [zĕf'ənī'ə] or **Sophonias** [sōfōnī'əs], book of the OLD TESTAMENT, 36th in the Authorized Version, 9th of the Minor PROPHETS. The prophet lived in the second half of the 7th cent. B.C. The book consists of a denunciation of Judah for idolatry and wealth and a prophecy of salvation and the return from captivity of a remnant of Israel.

Zeppelin, Ferdinand, Graf von, 1838–1917, German army officer and airship inventor and builder. He invented (1900) the first rigid AIRSHIP and built (1906) one that had a speed of 30 mi (48 km) per hr.

Żeromski, Stefan [zhĕrôm'skē], 1864–1925, Polish novelist, short-story writer, and poet. In such novels as *Homeless People* (1900), *Ashes* (1904), and *Faithful River* (1912) he expressed a deep concern with freedom and social justice.

Zeus [zo͞os], in Greek religion, supreme god; son of CRONUS, whom he succeeded, and RHEA; brother and husband of HERA. After the overthrow of the TITANS, when lots were cast to divide the universe, the underworld went to HADES, the sea to POSEIDON, and the heavens and earth to Zeus. An amorous god, he loved goddesses, nymphs, and mortals, and fathered many children. Ruling from his court on Mt. Olympus, Zeus was the symbol of power, rule, and law; the rewarder of good; and the punisher of evil. Also the god of weather (his most famous weapon was the thunderbolt) and fertility, he was worshiped in connection with almost every aspect of life. The Romans equated Zeus with their own supreme god, JUPITER.

Zhangjiakou or **Changkiakow** [both: jäng-jēä-kou], city (1986 est. pop. 493,000), NW Hebei prov., China. A major trade center for N China and Mongolia, it has food-processing plants, machine shops, and tanneries. An important Ch'ing dynasty military center, it declined somewhat after the opening (1905) of the Trans-Siberian RR.

Zhao Ziyang, 1919–, premier of China (1980–87), general secretary of the Communist party (1987–89). Zhao was purged in the CULTURAL REVOLUTION, but was later rehabilitated. In 1975 he was named governor of Sichuan prov. He was elected to the politburo in 1979, later succeeded HUA GUOFENG as premier, and became party general-secretary in 1987. A proponent of economic liberalization, he supported the students in the pro-democracy demonstrations in May 1989, but was overruled by the party and subsequently removed from power.

Zhengzhou or **Chengchow** [both: jŭng-jō], city (1990 est. pop. 1,710,000), capital of Henan prov., E central China. It is one of China's textile centers and a flourishing industrial city. A major railway center linking BEIJING and GUANGZHOU on the north-south RR and XI'AN and SHANGHAI on the east-west RR, Zhengzhou was the site of major fighting during the Cultural Revolution (1966–69).

Zhirinovsky, Vladimir Volfovich, 1946–, Russian politician; b. Kazakhstan. A lawyer, he founded the Liberal Democratic party, an extreme right Russian nationalist group, in 1990 and finished (1991) a distant third behind YELTSIN in the Russian Republic's presidential election. He later defended the failed coup against GORBACHEV (1991) and was an outspoken critic of Yeltsin, but he did not join the parliament's bid to oust Yeltsin in 1993. Although he was denounced as a fascist by his opponents, his party subsequently won the largest share (23%) of the popular vote in the 1993 legislative elections.

Zhivkov, Todor, 1911–, Bulgarian Communist leader. He was a partisan leader in World War II and became (1954) Communist party first secretary. He also held important posts in the government, including premier (1962–71) and head of state (1971–89). He resigned his government and party posts in 1989 and was later expelled from the party and convicted (1992) of corruption.

Zhou Enlai or **Chou En-lai** [both: jō ĕn-lī], 1898–1976, Chinese Communist leader. He studied in Europe and there became a founder of the Chinese Communist party. He returned (1924) to China and joined SUN YAT-SEN, who was then cooperating with the Communists. In 1927 Zhou organized a general strike in Shanghai that led to the city's capture by CHIANG KAI-SHEK and the Nationalists in the Northern Expedition. After the break (1927) between Chiang and the Communists, Zhou held prominent Communist military and political posts. He participated in the LONG MARCH (1934–35) of the Communist army, and after the creation of the People's Republic of China (1949) he was foreign minister (1949–58) and premier (1949–76). He headed the Chinese delegation to the Geneva Conference of 1954 and to the Bandung Conference (1955). He is believed to have been largely responsible for China's reestablishment of contacts with the West in the 1970s.

Zhu De or **Chu Teh** [both: jo͞o dŭ], 1886–1976, Chinese Communist soldier. In 1922 he went to Europe, where he joined the Chinese Communist party. He returned to China and in 1927, when CHIANG KAI-SHEK broke with the Communists, Zhu joined MAO ZEDONG. Zhu led (1934–35) his section of the Red Army on the LONG MARCH to NW China and commanded Communist forces in the Second SINO-JAPANESE WAR. He left his military post to become deputy chairman of the People's Republic of China (1954); he became chairman of the National People's Congress in 1959.

Zhukov, Georgi Konstantinovich [zho͞o'kôf], 1896–1974, Soviet marshal. He fought in the RUSSIAN REVOLUTION (1917) and the civil war (1918–20). In WORLD WAR II he defended Moscow (1941), defeated the Germans at Stalingrad (1943), helped lift the Leningrad siege (1944), and took Berlin (1945). Defense minister after 1955, he was ousted by KHRUSHCHEV (1957); when Khrushchev fell, Zhukov appeared again in public.

Zia ul-Haq, Mohammad, 1924–88, president of Pakistan (1978–88). An army general, he headed the junta that overthrew (1977) Prime Min. Z.A. BHUTTO and imposed martial law. Zia assumed the presidency in 1978. He lifted martial law in 1985, and after the dismissal of Prime Minister Mohammed Khan Junejo, dissolved the Parliament and called a general election (1988). He was killed in a plane crash.

zidovudine: see AZT.

Ziegfeld, Florenz [zēg'fĕld], 1869–1932, American theatrical producer; b. Chicago. He is best known for the *Ziegfeld Follies,* an extraordinarily elaborate revue produced annually for 24 years, starting 1907. His other productions include *Show Boat* (1927) and *Bitter Sweet* (1929).

ziggurat, form of temple common to the Sumerians, Babylonians, and Assyrians, built from the end of the 3d millennium B.C. to the 6th cent. B.C. It was a pyramidal brick structure with receding tiers, set on a rectangular, square, or oval platform, with a shrine at the summit.

Zimbabwe [zĭmbäb'wā], officially Republic of Zimbabwe, republic (1992 est. pop. 11,033,000), 150,803 sq mi (390,580 sq km), S cen-

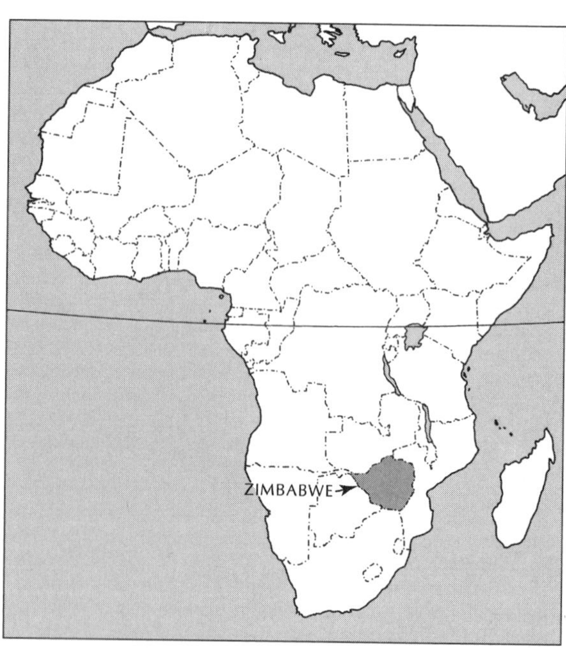

tral Africa, bordered by Zambia (N), Mozambique (NE and E), and Botswana (SW and W). Principal cities include HARARE (the capital) and BULAWAYO. Most of Zimbabwe consists of a high plateau, the highveld (above 4,000 ft/1,219 m), that crosses the country from southwest to northeast; on either side of it are the middleveld (below 4,000 ft/1,219 m) and the lowveld (below 3,000 ft/914 m). The Eastern Highlands, a narrow belt along the Mozambique border, are the site of Mt. Inyangani (8,503 ft/2,592 m), the country's highest point. The economy is supported mainly by agriculture and mining. The principal cash crops include tobacco, corn, tea, cotton, sugarcane, and peanuts. The leading mineral exports are gold and nickel. Forests in the southeast yield valuable hardwood. Among Zimbabwe's industrial products are iron and steel, cement, food products, machinery, textiles, and consumer goods. The population consists primarily of Bantu-speaking ethnic groups, mostly Shona with a large Ndebele minority. There are also about 100,000 people of European descent who remained after independence and continue to dominate Zimbabwe's economy, and small Asian and mixed race minorities. English is the official language, but the Shona and Ndebele speak their own languages. Most of the population practice traditional African religions, but 25% is Christian and the Asians are Muslim and Hindu.

History. Early Iron Age cultures in present-day Zimbabwe were supplanted by Bantu-speaking peoples who migrated into the area after the 5th cent. A.D. In the early 16th cent. the Portuguese developed trade with Shona-dominated states, which in the 1830s became subject to Ndebele invaders. In 1889 Cecil Rhodes's British South Africa Company obtained a charter to colonize the region, which they called Rhodesia. The company founded (1890) Fort Salisbury and in 1893 defeated the Ndebele and took control of the territory. In 1922 the settlers rejected incorporation into the Union of South Africa and chose to make Southern Rhodesia a self-governing British colony, a status achieved in 1923. Thereafter a series of white governments developed the economy but failed to share the benefits with the African majority. Joining Northern Rhodesia (now Zambia) and Nyasaland (now Malawi), in 1953 Southern Rhodesia became a member of the Federation of Rhodesia and Nyasaland, which disbanded in 1963, when the other members moved toward independence. Ian SMITH, a staunch conservative who became prime minister in 1964, proclaimed the colony's unilateral independence (as Rhodesia) from Britain in 1965, an act the British denounced as rebellion. In 1970 Rhodesia became a republic, with complete separation of the franchise along racial lines. UN economic sanctions were applied against the Smith regime, and two African nationalist groups, led by Joshua Nkomo and Robert MUGABE, launched guerrilla attacks against the government. Smith and three moderate black leaders agreed (1978) to set up an interim biracial government, and elections were held in 1979, but Britain and the black nationalists rejected the settlement. Finally, a London conference reached an accord on legal independence under black majority rule, and the new state of Zimbabwe came into being in 1980. The government of national unity, established upon independence, ended in 1982, when Prime Minister Mugabe ousted Nkomo from the cabinet. In 1987 the country adopted a presidential system of government, and Mugabe became president. In an attempt to end factional fighting, Mugabe and Nkomo agreed to merge their parties the same year. By 1990 the restrictions imposed by the accord of 1980, such as reserving a portion of the legislature for white representation, had been removed, and the national state of emergency, which dated to 1965, was ended.

Zimbabwe [Bantu, = stone houses], ruined city, SE Zimbabwe, found c.1870 and believed by some to be the biblical OPHIR, site of King Solomon's mines. Archaeological evidence shows that it was first occupied (3d cent.) by early IRON AGE peoples; later African cultures built the great wall (11th cent.) and richly decorated buildings.

zinc (Zn), metallic element. A lustrous, bluish-white, fairly reactive metal, zinc is ductile and malleable when heated. It is commercially important in GALVANIZING iron and in the preparation of certain alloys, e.g., BRASS and sometimes BRONZE. It is used for the negative plates in certain electric batteries, and for roofing and gutters. Zinc compounds are numerous and widely used. Zinc is essential for growth of plants and animals. See ELEMENT (table); PERIODIC TABLE.

zinnia, plant (genus *Zinnia*) of the COMPOSITE family, native chiefly to Mexico. The common garden zinnia (*Z. elegans*) is a rather coarse, easily cultivated annual, popular as a cut flower for its warm colors—ranging from white and yellow to red and purple—and for its bold, stiff aspect. The zinnia is the state flower of Indiana.

Zinoviev, Grigori Evseyevich [zēnô'vēĕf], 1883–1936, Soviet leader. He sided with LENIN in the 1903 Social-Democratic party split (see BOLSHEVISM AND MENSHEVISM). After the RUSSIAN REVOLUTION of Nov. 1917, he led the COMINTERN (1919–26) and served on the Communist party politburo (1921–26). After Lenin's death (1924) Zinoviev, KAMENEV, and STALIN shared power. In 1925 Stalin turned on Zinoviev and Kamenev, and they joined the TROTSKY faction. Zinoviev was expelled from the party in 1927 but was readmitted in 1928 with little power. In 1935 he was tried for alleged involvement in the death of Stalin's aide Sergei M. Kirov. In 1936 Zinoviev, Kamenev, and others were tried for treason and executed.

Zinzendorf, Nikolaus Ludwig, Graf von [tsĭn'tsəndôrf], 1700–1760, German churchman, patron, and bishop (from 1737) of the refounded MORAVIAN CHURCH. Reared under Pietistic influences, he established (1722) a Moravian colony called Herrnhut on his Saxony estates, but was exiled (1736) for his religious views. In America (1741–43) he helped to found Moravian congregations in E Pennsylvania. He was allowed to return to Saxony in 1747.

Zion or **Sion,** part of JERUSALEM. It is defined in the BIBLE as the City of David. There is controversy about its exact location. The name is symbolic of Jerusalem, of the Promised Land, of Israel's hope of returning to Palestine (hence the term ZIONISM), and, among Christians, of heaven.

Zionism, movement for reconstituting a Jewish state in Palestine. Dating from the Roman destruction of Jerusalem (A.D. 70) and the dispersion of the JEWS, the movement emerged in its modern form as a response to European ANTI-SEMITISM. The first World Zionist Congress was convened (1897) in Basel, Switzerland, by Theodore HERZL. The movement, under Chaim WEIZMANN, was given impetus by the Balfour Declaration (see BALFOUR, Arthur James) of 1917, which promised the Jews a national homeland in PALESTINE, then part of the OTTOMAN EMPIRE. After WORLD WAR II and the HOLOCAUST, increased Jewish settlement in the British mandate of Palestine led to armed conflict with the British and with the Arab inhabitants. Zionism was divided between followers of the militant Zionist leader Vladimir Jabotinsky (including Menachem BEGIN), who demanded unrestricted immigration throughout Palestine, and those, led by David BEN-GURION, who reluctantly accepted the UN plan for partition. After the creation of the state of ISRAEL (1948), the World Zionist Congress was separated from the Israeli government. The present-day Zionist movement facilitates immigration to Israel and supports cultural and educational activities in Israel and elsewhere.

Zion National Park: see NATIONAL PARKS (table).

zirconium (Zr), metallic element, discovered in oxide form by M.H. Klaproth in 1789. It is a very strong, malleable, ductile, lustrous, silver-gray metal that is extremely resistant to heat and corrosion. Zirconium is used in flashbulbs and to clad uranium fuel for nuclear reactors; its compounds are used as refractory material in furnaces, crucibles, and ceramic glazes. See ELEMENT (table); PERIODIC TABLE.

zither: see STRINGED INSTRUMENT.

Zn, chemical symbol of the element ZINC.

zodiac, zone of the sky that includes about 8° on either side of the ECLIPTIC. The apparent paths of the sun, the moon, and the major planets all fall within this zone. The zodiac is divided into 12 equal parts of 30° each, each part being named for a CONSTELLATION and represented by a sign (see table). Because of the PRECESSION OF THE EQUINOXES, the equinox and solstice points have each moved westward about 30° in the last 2,000 years; thus the zodiacal constellations, which were named in ancient times, no longer correspond

Aries	The Ram	♈	March 21-April 19
Taurus	The Bull	♉	April 20-May 20
Gemini	The Twins	♊	May 21-June 21
Cancer	The Crab	♋	June 22-July 22
Leo	The Lion	♌	July 23-Aug. 22
Virgo	The Virgin	♍	Aug. 23-Sept. 22
Libra	The Balance	♎	Sept. 23-Oct. 23
Scorpio	The Scorpion	♏	Oct. 24-Nov. 21
Sagittarius	The Archer	♐	Nov. 22-Dec. 21
Capricornus	The Goat	♑	Dec. 22-Jan. 19
Aquarius	The Water Bearer	♒	Jan. 20-Feb. 18
Pisces	The Fishes	♓	Feb. 19-March 20

to the segments of the zodiac represented by their signs. The zodiac is of importance in ASTROLOGY.

Zoë, d. 1050, Byzantine empress, daughter of CONSTANTINE VIII. She ruled jointly with her first husband, ROMANUS III, and, after his murder (1034), with her second husband, Michael IV, who perhaps was involved in the murder. Michael's successor and nephew, Michael V, briefly exiled Zoë in 1042, but she soon deposed and blinded him. She then ruled with her third husband, Constantine IX, and her sister, Theodora. Their reign was remarkable for intellectual brilliance and extraordinary corruption. This period saw the final schism between the Eastern and Western churches.

Zog, 1895–1961, king of Albania (1928–46). Originally named Ahmedi Zogu, he was premier (1922–24) and dictator (1925–39). In 1928 he proclaimed himself king. He abdicated after World War II, which he spent in exile.

Zola, Émile [zôlä′], 1840–1902, French novelist, the leading exemplar of NATURALISM. Influenced by TAINE, he wrote a vast series of novels depicting Second Empire French society in minute and often sordid detail. Best known are *The Dram Shop* (1877), *Nana* (1880), and *Germinal* (1885). His zeal for social reform and staunch anti-Catholicism led him to take a strong stand in the DREYFUS AFFAIR with his article "J'accuse" (1898). Prosecuted for libel, he escaped to England, remaining there until amnestied a few months later.

Zond, in space exploration: see SPACE PROBE (table).

zoological garden or **zoo,** public or private park where living animals are kept for exhibition and study. Most animals are captured in their native habitat, although some are born in captivity. Many modern zoos attempt to save species faced with extinction by breeding them in captivity, and a few species have been reintroduced into the wild. A modern trend is the exhibition of animals in enclosures simulating their natural habitats rather than in cages. The menageries and aviaries of ancient China, Egypt, and Rome were famous. Notable present-day zoos include those in the Bronx (N.Y.), San Diego, Chicago, London, Paris, and Berlin.

zoology, in biology, the study of ANIMALS. Early efforts to classify animals were based on physical resemblance, habitat, or economic use (see CLASSIFICATION). The invention of the microscope and the use of experimental techniques expanded zoology as a field and established many of its branches, e.g., CYTOLOGY, HISTOLOGY, embryology, PHYSIOLOGY, and GENETICS. Modern zoology studies cell structure and function, as well as psychological, anthropological, and ecological aspects of animals.

Zorach, William [zŏr′äk], 1887–1966, American sculptor; b. Lithuania; emigrated to the U.S. when he was four. Without formal training in sculpture, he evolved a style of monumental simplicity and solidity in his stone or wood pieces. A typical example is *Future Generation* (Whitney Mus., N.Y.C.).

Zoroaster, c.628 B.C.–c.551 B.C., religious teacher and prophet of ancient Persia, founder of ZOROASTRIANISM. Zoroaster is derived from the Greek form of Zarathushtra (or Zarathustra), his Persian name. During his lifetime the new religion he founded spread rapidly. The circumstances of Zoroaster's death are not known.

Zoroastrianism, religion founded by ZOROASTER, but with many later accretions. Its scriptures are the *Avesta* or the *Zend Avesta.* According to Zoroaster, there are good spirits, or *ahuras,* headed by Ahura Mazdah (also Ormazd or Ormuzd), opposed by evil spirits, the *daevas* or *divs,* led by Ahriman. The war between these two supernatural hosts will result in the ultimate triumph of Ahura Mazdah. The first period of Zoroastrianism was under the ACHAEMENIDS. Alexander's conquest of Persia sent Zoroastrianism into a decline. It reemerged (A.D. c.226) under Ardashir I, who established the Sassanian dynasty and tried to revive Achaemenian culture. In the mid-7th cent. Persia fell to Islam, and Zoroastrianism virtually disappeared. Aside from the PARSIS of India, fewer than 10,000 persons in Iran practice the religion today.

Zorrilla y Moral, José [thôrē′lyä ē mōräl′], 1817–93, Spanish romantic dramatist and poet. His works include the popular play *Don Juan Tenorio* (1844); *Granada* (1852), a retelling of legends in verse; and an autobiography.

Z particle: see W AND Z PARTICLES.

Zr, chemical symbol of the element ZIRCONIUM.

Zuccaro [tso͝ok′kärō], **Zuccari,** or **Zucchero,** Italian painters, two brothers who were leading late mannerists in Rome (see MANNERISM). **Taddeo Zuccaro,** 1529–66, was painter to Pope Julius III and Pope Paul IV. He and his brother painted historical and mythological scenes for Caprarola Palace, as well as frescoes in the Vatican. Taddeo's other works in Rome include the *Dead Christ* (Borghese Gall.). **Federigo Zuccaro,** 1543–1609, was associated with his brother, but traveled extensively in Europe. He painted portraits of Queen Elizabeth and Mary Stuart and did work for Philip II in the ESCORIAL in Spain. He constructed and decorated the Zuccari Palace and was one of the first to develop lectures and theoretical discussions on art.

Zuckmayer, Carl [tso͝ok′mīər], 1896–1977, German dramatist. His successful comedies include *The Merry Vineyard* (1925), *The Captain of Köpenick* (1931), and *The Devil's General* (1946); the last two were adapted as films. During World War II Zuckmayer lived in the U.S. His best-known screenplay is *The Blue Angel* (1930).

Zuider Zee, former North Sea inlet, N Netherlands. Most of it was enclosed by a dam (1932) to form the IJSSELMEER.

Zukerman, Pinchas, 1948–, Israeli violinist and conductor. A violin protégé of Isaac STERN, he came to the U.S. in 1962 and made his New York City debut in 1963. He is a noted chamber music performer and was (1980–87) musical director of the St. Paul (Minn.) Chamber Orchestra.

Zulu, African people whose historic home is Zululand, in South Africa. Traditionally, the Zulu lived as members of an extended family in a fenced compound (kraal), headed by the oldest man. Their economy often still depends on cattle raising. The prolonged absence of a majority of the men, many employed in distant cities and mines, has, however, weakened tribal society. The Zulu became historically important with the conquests of their chief Shaka (d. 1828), and they later resisted Boer settlers. In 1878, under CETEWAYO, they defeated several British forces, but Britain triumphed in 1879. Their lands were annexed by Britain in 1887 and incorporated into Natal in 1897. The Zulu-dominated Inkatha Freedom party (see BUTHELEZI, MANGOSUTHU GATSHA) initially opposed the accord between the AFRICAN NATIONAL CONGRESS and the South African government but participated in the 1994 multiracial elections.

Zuñi, pueblo (1990 pop. 7,405), W New Mexico, in the Zuñi reservation. Built c.1695, it is on the site of one of the seven original Zuñi villages attacked in 1540 by CORONADO, who was seeking the mythical gold-rich cities of Cibola. The inhabitants are PUEBLO people of the Zuñian linguistic family (see NATIVE AMERICAN LANGUAGES). Sedentary farmers, they are noted for basketry, pottery, turquoise jewelry, and weaving, and for the ceremonial dances of the traditional religion most still practice.

Zurbarán, Francisco de [tho͝orbärän′], 1598–1664, Spanish BAROQUE painter. His early paintings often suggest the austere simplicity of wood sculpture, e.g., *St. Michael* (Metropolitan Mus.). His later realistic style is seen in his famous *Apotheosis of St. Thomas Aquinas* (1631; Seville).

Zürich [tsü′rĭkh], city (1990 pop. 342,861), capital of Zürich canton and the largest Swiss city, N Switzerland, on the Lake of Zürich. The commercial and intellectual center of German-speaking Switzerland, it is a banking and publishing center; among its manufactures are machine tools. Built on a site occupied since Neolithic times, the city was conquered (58 B.C.) by the Romans and, after the 5th cent., passed to the Alemanni, the Franks, and Swabia. It was an imperial free city after 1218 and joined the Swiss Confederation in 1351. Under the influence of ZWINGLI (16th cent.) it became the leading power of the Swiss Reformation. It has the largest Swiss university and a world-famous polytechnic school (both est. 19th cent.).

Zweig, Arnold [tsvīk], 1887–1968, German novelist and dramatist. Among his best-known works is the trilogy of novels including *Education Before Verdun* (1935), *The Case of Sergeant Grischa* (1927), and *The Crowning of a King* (1937), and *The Axe of Wandsbek* (1947), a powerful study of life in Germany in 1937. A Zionist, Zweig went to Palestine during the NAZI era. After 1948 he lived in East Germany.

Zweig, Stefan [tzvīk], 1881–1942, Austrian biographer, poet, and novelist. Outstanding are his sensitive biographies, notably of Marie Antoinette (1932) and Mary Queen of Scots (1935). He went into exile (1934) during the NAZI period, eventually emigrating (1941) to Brazil, where he committed suicide.

Zwingli, Huldreich or **Ulrich** [tsvĭng'lē], 1484–1531, Swiss Protestant reformer. A Roman Catholic priest, he was considerably influenced by the humanist precepts of ERASMUS. He later accepted Martin LUTHER's doctrine of justification by faith alone, but his independent study of the Scriptures had led him after 1516 to question and finally to renounce the teaching of the Roman church. He became (1518) a vicar in Zürich and began preaching against many church practices. The beginning of the REFORMATION in Switzerland dates from his lectures (1519) on the New Testament, in which he proclaimed the Scriptures to have sole authority. In 1523, Zwingli presented his doctrines in 67 theses, which were approved by a general council in Zürich and instituted in the local churches. In 1525 the Catholic Mass was replaced by a reformed service in his church. He became embroiled in an argument with the Lutherans about the nature of the Eucharist, and Zwingli and Luther could reach no agreement at the Marburg Colloquy (1529). Zwingli was killed at Kappel in a war with the Catholic Swiss cantons. The Reformation in Switzerland passed to John CALVIN, who built his theological system on the groundwork laid by Zwingli, but he resisted Zwingli's more radical teaching on baptism and the Lord's Supper.

Zworykin, Vladimir Kosma, 1889–1982, American physicist and inventor; b. Russia. He came to the U.S. in 1919 and joined (1929) the Radio Corp. of America, becoming vice president in 1947. He and his co-workers developed the iconoscope, a scanning tube for the TELEVISION camera, and the kinescope, a cathode-ray picture tube in the television receiving apparatus.

zydeco, American musical form originating among the Cajuns and African-American Creoles of Louisiana. Drawing on elements of jazz, country and western music, and blues, it is characterized by its creole flavor and strong dance rhythms.